Model of dictionary layout

headword and pronunciation

gangrene *gang'grēn*, *n* necrosis of part of the body, with decay of body tissue, resulting from a failure in the blood supply to the part. — *adj* **gangrenous** (*gang'gri-nəs*) mortified. [Gr. *gangraina*, gangrene.]

gangster. See under **gang**[1].

reference to main entry with superscript number indicating a homograph

gangue or **gang** *gang*, *n* rock in which ores are embedded. [Fr., — Ger. *Gang*, a vein.]

gangway *gang'wā*, *n* a gangplank, usu. with sides for the protection of users, giving access on to or out of a ship; an opening in a ship's side to take a gangway; any passageway on a ship; an aisle between rows of seats; the cross-passage halfway down the House of Commons. — *interj* make way, make room to pass. [O.E. *gangan*, to go, and **way**.]

clear **definitions** separated by semi-colon (;)

ganister or **gannister** *gan'is-tər*, *n* a hard, close-grained siliceous stone, found in N. England. [Perh. from quarry at *Gannister*, Cheshire.]

headword with alternative form

ganja *gän'jə*, *n* an intoxicating preparation, the female flowering tops of Indian hemp, i.e. marijuana. [Hind. *gā̃jā*.]

gannet *gan'ət*, *n* a large white sea-bird of the family *Sulidae*, with black-tipped wings; a greedy person (*colloq*). — *n* **gann'etry** a breeding-place of gannets. [O.E. *ganot*, a sea-fowl.]

classification label (shown *after* a specific meaning where it does not apply to all)

gannister. See **ganister**.

cross-reference to main entry

ganoid *gan'oid*, *adj* (of fish scales) having a glistening outer layer over bone; (of fishes) belonging to an order that commonly have such scales. — *n* a ganoid fish. — *n* **ganoin** (*gan'ō-in*) a calcareous substance, forming an enamel-like layer on ganoid scales. [Gr. *ganos*, brightness, *eidos*, appearance.]

derivative word with grammatical label and pronunciation

gansey *gan'zi*, *n* a woollen sweater, a jersey. [From the island of *Guernsey*.]

gantry *gan'tri*, *n* a stand for barrels; the shelving, racks, etc. in which drinks are displayed in a bar; a platform or bridge for a travelling crane, railway signals, etc.; the servicing tower beside a rocket on its launching pad. — **gantry crane** a crane in bridge form with vertical members running on parallel tracks. [Perh. O.Fr. *gantier* — L. *cantērius*, a trellis — Gr. *kanthēlios*, a pack ass.]

etymology showing word origin, history and formation (the — sign indicates 'derived from')

Chambers Concise Dictionary

Chambers Concise Dictionary

Chief Editor
Catherine Schwarz

Managing Editor
Virginia Klein

Editors
George Davidson, Jock Graham
M A Ruth Martin, Fred McDonald
Fergus McGauran, Anne Seaton
Howard Sergeant

Chambers

This edition published 1991 by W & R Chambers Ltd
43-45 Annandale Street, Edinburgh EH7 4AZ

First published as *Chambers Concise 20th Century Dictionary* 1985
Published as *Chambers Concise Dictionary* 1988

We have made every effort to mark as such all words which we believe to be trademarks. We should also like to make it clear that the presence of a word in the dictionary, whether marked or unmarked, in no way affects its legal status as a trademark.

ISBN 0 550 10570 0 Standard
ISBN 0 550 10571 9 Thumb Index

A catalogue record for this book is available from the British Library

Computing services by Computing Laboratory, University of St Andrews
Typeset in Great Britain at the University Press, Cambridge
Printed in Great Britain at the Bath Press, Avon

Contents

Preface

Every good dictionary is both a product and a reflection of its times, and this new edition of *Chambers Concise Dictionary* comes with all the clarity, comprehensiveness and authority appropriate to the information technology of the 90s.

A fresh look at what the user requires of dictionaries, both as regards content and accessibility, influenced the approach of the editors throughout the years of planning and compilation of this dictionary.

Up-to-dateness and width of coverage have been high priorities of the editors. This is shown not only in the wealth of new words added to the dictionary, but also in the many new meanings of 'old' words. The vibrancy and vitality of English today is reflected in many ways. For example, words previously regarded as slang have now become accepted as colloquial and these changes in usage have been clearly indicated. Nouns may now be used as verbs, as **kebab** 'to skewer'. Adjectives may also have become nouns, as with **renewable**.

The editors have retained in the dictionary, adequately and sympathetically defined, a number of words that are no longer in the forefront of the English language of today, but which, for good historical and linguistic reasons, still merit a place in an up-to-date dictionary such as the *Concise*.

Great importance has been attached to ensuring that the dictionary should be easy to use. Chambers has a tradition of listing words under their related headwords, as for example **historical** under **history, preference** under **prefer**. Apart from being linguistically sound, this has been a space-saving feature enabling us to provide larger numbers of words in a manageable extent. Where, however, this practice has seemed to us to be less helpful to the user we have separated the words into independent entries, showing their relationships by means of the word origins.

Again with ease of use in mind, we have aimed to avoid using contractions in the definitions. For example, rather than *'pop.'*, *'iron.'*, and *'gen.'* we have *'popularly'*, *'ironic'* and *'generally'*. The text has been systematically modernised and streamlined, directness and immediateness replacing the rather formal style and language of the previous edition. We have also aimed to make as many definitions as possible 'one-stop'; that is, all information required for full understanding is given within the definition itself, so that there is no need for the user to refer to other entries. Where we felt, however, that such one-stop treatment would be cumbersome or would diminish the value of the definition, we have not followed this course.

Close co-operation between our editorial and design teams has created a dictionary which, with its clear, uncluttered, undaunting and immediately readable pages, projects an image of modern lexicography that is accessible and authoritative. We are confident that *Chambers Concise Dictionary* will be as much a pleasure to use as it has been to produce.

C S

Using the dictionary

(see also inside front cover)

Order of entries

All entries are listed alphabetically, each entry having as a basic pattern the following elements:

(1) Headword
(2) Pronunciation
(3) Part of speech label
(4) Definition(s)
(5) Etymology

Within this framework there are often subheads – words that are derived from the headword (*derivatives*), or *compounds* or *phrases* that include the headword or one of its derivatives. This grouping of related words within an entry preserves and explains their etymological 'family' link, while at the same time ensuring that space is used as effectively as possible.

Structure

The main elements of an entry are explained in greater detail below:

1. Headword

The word (in **bold** type) projecting at the head of an entry is referred to as the headword. Headwords are listed in alphabetical order.

Superscript numbers are added to headwords where necessary (see e.g. **cape**[1], **cape**[2]) to indicate homographs (words of identical spelling but of different meaning, origin, etc.).

Included in the headword list, in alphabetical order, are **cross-references**, words of which the full entry, or on which further information, is to be found elsewhere in the dictionary. Also included in the alphabetical headword sequence are **abbreviation** and **symbol** entries, which follow full-word entries of identical spelling, and which themselves are followed by **prefix, suffix** and **combining form** entries (see page x).

2. Pronunciation

(see also inside back cover)

The respelling system (detailed in the inside back cover) has been used in this dictionary. It is a method that is intelligible to a large number of people who are not familiar with phonetic symbols, and one that allows for more than one interpretation – so that each user of the dictionary may choose a pronunciation in keeping with his or her speech.

Pronunciation guidance (in *italic* type) follows the headword, and is given elsewhere in an entry in parentheses where helpful. The main, current British pronunciations are given, and also significant US etc. variants if appropriate, but the numerous possible regional variations cannot be covered individually in a dictionary of this size. See pages xi and xii for details on American English and other varieties.

Guidance on stress patterns in words of more than one syllable is given by the use of the stress mark ('), which *follows* the syllable that has the main accent, both in respelling and in bold subheads for which no full or partial respelling is required.

3. Part of speech label

Following the pronunciation at the head of an entry is a label to indicate the headword's part of speech (e.g. *adj* for adjective, *n* for noun). A further part of speech label may follow a set of definitions, to show that the preceding bold word is also used as another type of word (e.g. **gash** *vt* to cut deeply into. – *n* a deep, open cut).

Part of speech labels are given after all headwords except phrasal items, and before each direct derivative word. Compound nouns are not labelled.

Entries for prefix, suffix and combining form items treat all compound subheads as derivative items, i.e. they have individual part of speech labels.

4. Definition(s)

Definitions in the dictionary entries are ordered and grouped with a view to clarity, ease of comprehension and use. Normally the most common meanings are given first, unless an earlier, perhaps more specific, sense serves to clarify or explain its subsequent use. In general, obsolete, rare, dialect and archaic senses are omitted from this dictionary, in favour of current, modern uses, although certain items in these categories, felt to be of special help or interest to the modern reader, have been included.

Definitions are separated by semi-colons.

In abbreviation and symbol entries, definitions are listed alphabetically.

5. Etymology

The etymology is given in square brackets at the end of each entry. If no etymology is shown, this indicates that the origin and history of the headword is unknown or uncertain. The sign '—' indicates 'derived from'. A bold word given as an etymology directs the reader to that word entry as the derivation; other etymologies may direct the reader directly to another etymology. A bold prefix given as an etymology indicates that the headword is formed from that prefix plus the remaining word-item; both elements may be found at their separate dictionary entries.

For abbreviations used in etymologies and elsewhere in the dictionary, see pages xiv-xvi.

6. Subheads

Subheads are bold-print items not listed as separate entries, but listed and explained within an entry. Note the order in which subheads appear in an entry:

(a) *Direct derivatives*
These are words which are formed by adding a suffix or ending either to the headword or to the root word. They are given, alphabetically, immediately after the various meanings of the headword. Each is given a grammatical (part of speech) label. Their pronunciation basically follows that of the headword, with stress marks placed *after* the syllable with the main accent. Where necessary, fuller respelling guidance is given in parentheses. If the meaning of a regular, direct derivative is readily deducible, it may be undefined.

(b) *Compounds*
Compound words (i.e. those made up of two or more words, the first being the entry headword or one of its derivatives) follow any direct derivatives. They may be hyphenated, one-word or two-word compounds. If the compound's meaning is evident from its two parts, it may be undefined. Where no grammatical label has been given at a compound, it is to be assumed to be a noun. Those compounds which do not begin with the headword or derivative of the headword are listed under the third category, the phrases.

(c) *Phrases*
Following any direct derivatives and any compound words, all phrasal items relating to the headword are listed alphabetically. These may be phrases, phrasal verbs or idioms, or compounds which do not begin with the headword or any of its derivatives.

7. Alternative forms

Words spelt or formed in more than one way, but sharing the same meaning(s) and use, are shown in the dictionary linked by the word 'or'. Where a number of such alternatives are shown, strict alphabetical order may be waived in order to show the most commonly used form at the head of the list.

At headwords, alternative forms that have different pronunciations are each followed immediately by their appropriate pronunciation(s). If the pronunciation follows both headword forms, it applies to both forms.

In hyphenated compound words, an alternative form may be shown only by the alternative element of the compound (e.g. **hunt'ing-box, -lodge** or **-seat**).

8. Inflections

Inflected words are shown, following a colon, after the definition(s) of a word (if any). Plural forms and verb participles etc. are shown only if they are irregular in formation, or warrant special clarification. Comparative and superlative forms of adjectives are given (again only by the same criteria) *in parentheses* following the adjective or its grammatical label. Current *equivalent* feminine forms appear alongside the masculine forms, whereas distinctively or less commonly used feminine forms are shown, following a colon, after the definition(s).

9. Classification labels

A label relating to the classification (e.g. *colloq, slang, chem, electr, psychol*) of a word or meaning *precedes* the list of meanings where it applies to all of the meanings given.

Where a label applies to only one definition in a list, it immediately *follows* that definition.

A label which precedes the part of speech label at the head of an entry applies to *all* meanings of the word *and* to its derivatives and their meanings unless or until it is cancelled by a further classification label. This applies also where there is only one sense and one meaning of a word.

Classification labels are shown in italic print.

Foreign words A bracketed abbreviation in roman type (e.g. Fr., Ger.) preceding the part of speech label at the head of an entry signifies that the word is still regarded as a foreign word, rather than as a naturalised English word. German nouns have been spelt with a capital letter, as they are in their country of origin.

10. Alternative pronunciations

As for alternative word forms, alternative pronunciations are shown in the dictionary linked by the word 'or', or by a comma in a string of alternatives. The main, current British pronunciations of a word are given, and also significant and commonly-encountered US, Australian etc. variants as applicable.

Alternative pronunciations at a headword are generally given in full. Elsewhere in an entry simply the syllable or syllables of a word which may be pronounced alternatively are given.

In all alternative or partial pronunciations, that part of a word not included in the respelling is to be assumed unchanged from the main pronunciation given earlier in the entry.

11. Prefix, suffix and combining forms

These entries are treated as ordinary word entries except in the respects specified below.

In the respelling given at a prefix or similar headword, often no stress pattern is specified, as it varies according to the words formed with that element.

Entries for prefix, suffix and combining form items (as already noted in 3.) show a separate part of speech label at each compound subhead 'nested' within the entry, treating them as derivatives of the headword.

If more than one definition is given they generally follow an initial linking word and a colon (e.g. **dia-** *pfx* denoting: through; across; during; composed of).

American English

Despite increased contact and communication between Britain and America there are still major differences in the forms of English spoken and written in the two countries.

Spelling

Spelling differences in a number of individual words (e.g. *maneuver, defense,* and *practice* as a verb) have been noted in the dictionary. Groups of words in which the spelling is different are as follows:

Brit.	U.S.	
our	*or*	American spellings such as *color, humor,* have often been noted in the text.
re	*er*	*center, meter, reconnoiter, saltpeter, theater,* etc. But, to show the hard sound of *c* or *g*: *acre, lucre, massacre, ogre,* etc.
ll	*l*	Americans have single *l* in all derivatives in *-ed, -ing, -er* (or *-or*) of words ending in an *l*: *canceled, -ing, caroled, -ing, chiseled, -ing, counseled, -ing, -or, disheveled, -ing, equaled, -ing, imperiled, -ing, jeweled, -ing, -er, libeled, -ing, -er, reveled, -ing, -er, traveled, -ing, -er, victualed, -ing, -er,* etc. Also *woolen, marvelous.*
l or *ll*	*ll*	*enroll, enthrall, instill, thralldom.*
l	*ll*	In *fulfill, skillful, willful.* In nouns in *-ment*: *enrollment, enthrallment, fulfillment, installment.*
pp	*p*	*kidnaped, -ing, -er, worshiped, -ing, -er.*
tt	*t*	*carbureted, -or.*
ae, oe or *e*	*e*	The tendency to replace *ae* and *oe* in words from Greek or Latin by *e* is more strongly developed in the United States than in Britain: e.g. *etiology, hemoglobin, esophagus.*
ise or *ize*	*ize*	In verbs and their derivatives that may be spelt *-ise* or *-ize*, Americans prefer *-ize*.

Pronunciation

American pronunciation is naturally not the same in all areas and in all classes, but generally speaking it shows differences from British English pronunciation in the following respects (not specifically noted in the dictionary):

Brit.	U.S.
ä	Various shorter forms of the vowel are common in place of English *ä*.
i	Where British English has *i* in final position, as in *happy*, Americans tend to pronounce the vowel *ē*.
ö	Alternative form *ä* is common in words such as *haunt, launch, saunter, taunt, vaunt.*
o	A longer vowel than the normal British one is heard in *coffee, long, officer, soft,* etc., (mostly words in which the vowel is followed by *f, th, s, r, g, ng*); *ä* also is widely used in these words. *Block, pond, probable, top,* etc. always have *ä*.
ū	In British English this is a diphthong; in American English it often loses its diphthongal character when preceded by *t, d, n, l* or *s*, becoming *o͞o*.
-īl	In the commoner words Americans pronounce *-il*, as *agile* (*aj'il*), *fertile, fragile, futile, hostile, versatile.* In *infantile* and *juvenile,* both *-il* and *-īl* are heard; *gentile* is always pronounced *-īl*; *mercantile* is usually pronounced *-ēl*.
t	In words such as *batter, butter, writing,* the *-tt-/-t-* is pronounced with a sound similar or identical to that of the *-dd-/-d-* of *madder, shudder, riding.*

Vowels and diphthongs before *r*

Brit.	U.S.
ā	In America, this is commonly pronounced as a diphthong, the first element of which approaches a lengthened form of *e*. Sometimes the second element, ə, is not pronounced when the diphthong occurs in initial or medial position in a word; for example, the usual pronunciation of *Maryland* is *mer'i-lənd.*
a	Some Americans tend to make a sound approaching *e*, so that *marry*, for instance, approximates to *merry*.
i	The sound heard in *squirrel, stirrup,* and commonly also in *syrup,* approaches *û*.
u	In English speech, when *ur* is followed by a vowel, the sound of the *u* is not *û*, but Americans tend to pronounce the same vowel in *her* and *hurry*. Other examples are *occurring, worry,* and *courage.*
är spelt *er*	In words such as *clerk* and *Derby* where English speech preserves an older pronunciation *är*, American speech follows the spelling, pronouncing the words *klûrk, dûr'bi,* etc.
-ə-ri	Americans tend to give words in *-ary* and *-ory* a stronger secondary accent and to pronounce *-er'ē* and *-ōr'ē*. Examples are *necessary, monetary, secondary, temporary, obligatory, peremptory, respiratory.*

Some individual differences in the sounds of certain words and prefixes are noted in the dictionary, e.g. *tomato, schedule, simultaneous, anti-.*

Some variations in vocabulary and meaning between British English and American English are indicated in the dictionary, e.g. *bonnet/hood; braces/suspenders.* A few words used only in the U.S. are likewise indicated, e.g. *sidewalk.*

Some other varieties of English

British English and American English are only two of the many varieties of English which exist in the world today. Other forms of English exist elsewhere, notably in Canada, South Africa, India and Pakistan, Australia and New Zealand. These differ to a greater or lesser extent from the English of Britain and America with regard to vocabulary, grammar, pronunciation and sometimes spelling. Many words or meanings of words unique to these regional forms are noted in the dictionary, e.g. *baas, billabong, coloured, hartal, joey*. Some guidance on the pronunciation and spelling is given in the following notes. The grammatical differences are for the most part beyond the scope of a dictionary.

Canadian English

In spelling, Canadian usage stands midway between American English and British English. The usage is however far from uniform and varies from province to province and even from person to person. Hence such spellings as *color, traveler* and *center*, which reflect American usage, and *colour, traveller* and *centre*, which reflect the British, are to be found alongside each other.

In pronunciation Canadian English exhibits features found in both American and British English although it more commonly follows American English, e.g. speakers of Canadian English pronounce *tomato* with an *ā* as do speakers of American English.

Brit.	**Can.**
r	Like American English, Canadian English pronounces *r* in the word-final position and before a consonant.
t	In the pronunciation of many Canadians, words such as *matter* and *madder* rhyme, as in American English.
i	The sound heard in *squirrel*, etc. approaches *û*.
-īl	Of the words which end in *-īl* in British English, some e.g. *docile, textile, fragile*, end in *-īl* as in British English, while others such as *missile* and *fertile* end in *-il* as in American English.
ī, ow	Canadian English differs from both American and British English in its treatment of the vowels *ow* and *ī*, in that the vowels in for example *loud* and *ride* do not rhyme with those of *lout* and *write*.

English in Australia and New Zealand

Although there are differences between the English spoken in Australia and that of New Zealand, some of which will be commented on below, the two varieties are sufficiently similar to each other to be treated together here.

The spelling of Australian English traditionally follows that of British English but American spelling is now sometimes also found.

Among the features of pronunciation that can be noted are as follows:

Brit.	**Austr., N.Z.**
r	As in British English, *r* is not pronounced before a consonant or at the end of a word, except by speakers in the southern part of the South Island of New Zealand.
i	Australian and New Zealand English has *ē* in words such as *happy, very*, where British English has *i*. In closed unstressed syllables, where British English has *i*, Australian and New Zealand English have *e*, as for example in *mistake, defeat, ticket*, etc.
o͞or	The pronunciation *ŏŏə* of words like *sure, pure*, etc. has been almost entirely superseded by either *ö* or *o͞oə*.
ä	In many words in which British English has *ä*, Australian and New Zealand English have *a*. In words ending in *-ance*, New Zealand English has *ä* where Australian English has *a* or *ä*. In Australian English *lather* is pronounced with *a*, but in New Zealand with *ä*.
ō	Before *l*, this tends to be pronounced as *o*.

English in South Africa

In spelling, South Africa follows British English. In pronunciation, the following features are notable:

Brit.	**S. Africa**
r	The S. African English treatment of *r* word-finally and before consonants is the same as that of British English.
i	S. African English has *ē* where British English has *i* in *very, secretary*, etc. In other positions, *i* is pronounced more centrally than in British English, with a vowel close to *ə*.
a, e, ä etc.	There is a tendency to raise these vowels to values approaching *e, i, o/ö*, etc. so giving *de'dē* for *daddy*, *kit'l* for *kettle*, and so on.
ār	This is normally pronounced as a long *e* or *ā* sound in words like *bear, fair*, etc.

English in the Indian Subcontinent

English in India, Pakistan and Bangladesh is normally learned as a second language, and is often greatly influenced by the speaker's first language. Thus no homogeneous Indian English can be described here but only a number of features about which one may make some general remarks.

Two common features of Indian English are the use of retroflex *ṭ, ḍ*, etc. for British English *t, d*, etc., and the substitution of *p, t, d* for *f, th, dh*. Speakers whose native language is Hindi or Urdu tend to insert an *i* before the initial consonant clusters in words such as *speech, school*, because these consonant groups do not occur in initial positions in Hindi or Urdu.

Indian English pronounces word-final *r* and pre-consonantal *r*.

Vowels in unstressed syllables are often pronounced in the way they would be in stressed syllables, where British English has *ə* or *i*.

Characters used in etymologies

A brief guide to the pronunciation of some of the non-English characters which appear most frequently in etymologies is given below. The pronunciations given are necessarily approximate as it is not always possible to convey the exact phonetic values intended by means of respelling symbols or verbal explanations.

Vowels

Symbol	Sound
ā, ē, ī, ū	In etymologies, these are long vowels with the sounds (or approximately the sounds) represented by the respelling symbols *a* or *ä*, *ā* or *e*, *ē*, and *o͞o* respectively.
ō	This represents a long *o* or *ö* sound or a monophthongal pronunciation of the respelling character *ō*.
ȳ	A long *ü* sound.
ǣ	A long vowel similar in sound to the RP pronunciation of respelling symbol *a*.
a, e, etc., *ă, ĕ,* etc.	Short vowels corresponding to *ā, ē*, etc., with values, varying from language to language, similar to those of the corresponding long vowels or those of the short vowels of English.
â, ê, î ô, û	In some languages, e.g. Middle High German, these symbols are used for long vowels with the values *ä, ā, ē, ō, o͞o* respectively.
ä, ö	These have the values of respelling symbols *e/ā* and *ø/œ* respectively.
ĩ etc.	The diacritic ˜ is used, as in the respelling, to show nasalisation of vowels.

Consonants

Symbol	Sound
ḍ, ṭ, ṇ, ṣ, ẓ.	These are retroflex counterparts of *d, t,* etc.
ṛ	In Sanskrit, a vowel rather than a consonant; in Hindi, etc., a consonant formed by the tongue moving from a retroflex position to strike against the teeth-ridge.
ḥ	The normal *h*-sound of English.
ṁ	This marks nasalisation of the preceding vowel or the following consonant in Sanskrit.
ñ	A sound similar to *ny*, as in Sp. *cañon.*
ṅ	The sound written *ng* in the respelling and in English orthography.
ś	In Sanskrit, etc., a sound similar to *sh.*
c	In Sanskrit, etc., a sound midway between *k* and *ch*; in Turkish, the sound of *j* as in *judge.*
ç	In French, Arabic and Portuguese, this represents the sound *s*: in Turkish, *ch.*
ş	In Turkish, the sound *sh.*
q	A sound similar to *k* but pronounced slightly farther back in the mouth.
ğ	This marks a lengthening of the preceding vowel in Turkish.
gg	In Gothic, the sound *ng.*
'	In Russian words, this represents a 'soft sign', marking a *y*-like palatalisation of the preceding consonant: in Chinese words, it is a mark of strong aspiration; in Arabic, Hebrew and Hawaiian, a glottal stop.
ʽ	In Arabic and Hebrew, a sound like *hh* but produced rather deeper in the throat.

Abbreviations used in the dictionary

(Note that abbreviations shown in roman with stops may also occur *without stops* when printed in italic, as labels.)

abbrev.	abbreviation
abl.	ablative
accus.	accusative
A.D.	*anno domini*
adj.	adjective
adv.	adverb
Afr.	Africa(n)
A.Fr.	Anglo-French
Afrik.	Afrikaans
agri	agriculture
alg	algebra
Am.	America(n)
anat	anatomy
anthrop	anthropology
antiq	antiques, antiquity
app.	apparently
approx.	approximately
Ar.	Arabic
archaeol	archaeology
archit	architecture
arith	arithmetic
As.	Asia(n)
Assyr.	Assyrian
astrol	astrology
astron	astronomy
attrib.	attributive(ly)
augm.	augmentative
Austr.	Australia(n)
A.V.	Authorised Version
b.	born
bacteriol	bacteriology
Bav.	Bavarian
B.C.	before Christ
Beng.	Bengali
biochem	biochemistry
biol	biology
Bohem.	Bohemian
bot	botany
Br.	Britain, British
Braz.	Brazilian
c	(L. *circa*) about
Can.	Canada, Canadian
cap	capital
caps	capitals
Caribb	Caribbean
cartog	cartography
Celt.	Celtic
cent.	century
cf.	(L. *confer*) compare
Ch	Church
chem	chemical, chemistry
chem eng	chemical engineering
Chin.	Chinese
civ eng	civil engineering
cm.	centimetre(s)
C of E	Church of England
colloq.	colloquial(ly)
compar.	comparative
comput	computers, computing
conj.	conjunction
conn.	connected, connection
contr.	contracted, contraction
Copt.	Coptic
Corn.	Cornish
corres.	corresponding
crystall	crystallography
cu.	cubic
Czech.	Czechoslovakian
d.	died
Dan.	Danish
dat.	dative
demonstr.	demonstrative
deriv.	derivative, derived, derivation
derog	derogatorily
Dict., dict.	Dictionary, dictionary
dimin.	diminutive
Du.	Dutch
E.	East
EAfr	East Africa(n)
EAnglian	East Anglian
eccles	ecclesiastical
ecol	ecology
econ	economy
educ	education
e.g.	(L. *exempli gratia*) for example
Egyp.	Egyptian
electr	electrical, electricity
embryol	embryology
Eng.	England, English
eng	engineering
entom	entomology
erron.	erroneous(ly)
esp.	especially
etc.	(L. *et cetera*) and so on
ety.	etymology
euph.	euphemism, euphemistic(ally)
Eur.	Europe(an)
exc.	except
fem.	feminine
ff.	following (pages), folios
fig	figurative(ly)
Finn.	Finnish
fl.	(L. *floruit*) flourished
Flem.	Flemish
fol.	followed, following
fort	fortification
Fr.	French
Fris.	Frisian
fut.	future
Gael.	Gaelic
geog	geography
geol	geology
geom	geometry
Ger.	German(y)
Gmc.	Germanic
Goth.	Gothic
Gr.	Greek
gram	grammar
Heb.	Hebrew
Hind.	Hindustani
hist	historic, history
hort	horticulture
Hung.	Hungarian
hyperb	hyperbolically
Icel.	Icelandic (Modern)
i.e.	(L. *id est*) that is
illit	illiterate
imit.	imitative
immun	immunology
imper.	imperative
imperf.	imperfect
impers.	impersonal
incl.	including
Ind.	India(n)
indef.	indefinite
indic.	indicative
infin.	infinitive
infl.	influenced
instrum.	instrumental (case)

interj.	interjection	*npl*	noun plural	*pr t*	present tense
interrog.	interrogative	*ns*	nouns	*psychol*	psychology
intrans.	intransitive	*nsing*	noun singular	q.v., qq.v.	(L. *quod vide*) which see
Ir.	Ireland, Irish	N.T.	New Testament	R.C.	Roman Catholic (Church)
irreg.	irregular(ly)	*nuc*	nuclear	refl.	reflexive
Is.	Island(s), Isle(s)	N.Z.	New Zealand	rel.	related, relative
It.	Italian, Italy	O.	Old	*relig*	religion, religious
I.V.R.	International Vehicle Registration	obs.	obsolete	*rhet*	rhetoric
Jap.	Japanese	O.E.	Old English	Rom.	Romanian
Jav.	Javanese	O.Fr.	Old French	Rum.	Rumanian
kg.	kilogram(s)	O.Fris.	Old Frisian	Russ.	Russian
km.	kilometre(s)	O.H.G.	Old High German	R.V.	Revised Version
L.	Latin	O.Ir.	Old Irish	S.	South
lb.	(L. *libra*(*e*)) pound(s)	O.N.	Old Norse	*SAfr*	South Africa(n)
L.G.	Low German	O.N.Fr.	Old Northern French	*SAm*	South America(n)
lit.	literal(ly)	O.Sax.	Old Saxon	*SAsia*	South Asia(n)
Lith.	Lithuanian	opp.	opposed, opposite	Sax.	Saxon
L.L.	Low (or Late) Latin	*org*	organic	Scand.	Scandinavian
mach	machinery	orig.	original(ly)	Scot.	Scottish
Malay.	Malaysian	*ornithol*	ornithology	*sculp*	sculpture
masc.	masculine	O.T.	Old Testament	*SEAsia*	South East Asia(n)
math	mathematical, mathematics	p.	participle	sep.	separate
M.Du.	Middle Dutch	Pak.	Pakistan(i)	Serb.	Serbian
M.E.	Middle English	*palaeog*	palaeography	sfx.	suffix
mech	mechanical, mechanics	*palaeontol*	palaeontology	*Sing*	Singapore
Med.	Mediaeval	*pa p*	past participle	sing.	singular
med	medicine	pass.	passive	Sinh.	Sinhalese
metall	metallurgy	*pa t*	past tense	Slav.	Slavonic
metaphys	metaphysics	*pathol*	pathology	*sociol*	sociology
meteorol	meteorology	perf.	perfect	Sp.	Spanish
Mex.	Mexican	perh.	perhaps	*SpAm*	Spanish America(n)
M.Flem.	Middle Flemish	pers.	person, personal	*specif*	specifically
M.Fr.	Middle French	Pers.	Persian	sq.	square
M.H.G.	Middle High German	Peruv.	Peruvian	st.	stone
microbiol	microbiology	*petr*	petrology	subj.	subject, subjective, subjunctive
mil	military	pfx.	prefix	superl.	superlative
M.L.G.	Middle Low German	*pharm*	pharmacy	*surg*	surgery
mm.	millimetre(s)	*pharmacol*	pharmacology	s.v.	(L. *sub verba*) under the word
mod.	modern	*philat*	philately	Sw.	Swedish
mus	music	*philol*	philology	*SWEng*	South West England
N.	New, North	*philos*	philosophy	symb.	symbol
n	noun	*phon*	phonetics	t.	tense
NAm	North America(n)	*phot*	photography	*tech*	technology
nat hist	natural history	*phys*	physics	*telecomm*	telecommunications
naut	nautical	*physiol*	physiology	*teleg*	telegraphy
neg.	negative	pl.	plural	*theat*	theatre, theatrical
neut.	neuter, neutral	Pol.	Polish	*theol*	theology
N.L.	New Latin	*pol econ*	political economy	trans.	transitive, translation
no.	number	Port.	Portuguese	*trig*	trigonometry
nom.	nominative	poss.	possessive, possible, possibly	Turk.	Turkish
Norm.	Norman	prep.	preposition	*TV*	television
Norw.	Norwegian	pres.	present		
		prev.	previous(ly)		
		prob.	probably		
		pron.	pronoun		
		Prov.	Provençal		
		pr p	present participle		

U.K.	United Kingdom	usu.	usually	*vt*	verb transitive
ult.	ultimately	*v*	verb	*vulg*	vulgar(ly)
U.S.	United States (of America)	*vet*	veterinary medicine	W.	West
				WAfr	West Africa(n)
U.S.S.R.	Union of Soviet Socialist Republics	*vi*	verb intransitive	W.Ind.	West Indian, West Indies
		Viet.	Vietnamese		
		voc.	vocative	*WIndies*	West Indies

A

A or **a** *ā*, *n* the first letter in the modern English alphabet (also see **alpha**); a note, the major sixth of the scale of C (*mus*); something or someone of first class or order, or of a class arbitrarily designated A; the designation of the principal series of paper sizes, ranging from A0 (841 × 1189 mm.) to A10 (26 × 37 mm.); one of the four blood types in the ABO blood group system. — **A1** (*ā wun*) first-rate, excellent; (of a ship) in first-class condition — as originally designated in Lloyd's Register of Shipping; **A'-road** a trunk or a principal road; **A'-side** (*recorded music*) the side of a single which holds the principal track being marketed. — **from A to B** from one point or place to another; **from A to Z** from beginning to end.

A or **A.** *abbrev* for: Academician; Academy; ace (*cards*); acre(s); advanced; alto (*mus*); amateur; America; American; ammeter; ampere; answer; area; argon (now usu. **Ar**; *chem*); Associate (of a society, etc.); atomic; atomic weight; Australia; Australian; Austria (I.V.R.). — **A'-bomb** atomic bomb; **A level** advanced level, (a pass in) an examination generally taken after seven years of secondary education, esp. in England and Wales. — Also *adj* (often with *hyphen*).

Å *symbol* for Ångström or angstrom.

a *ə*, also (esp. emphatic) *ā*, *adj* the indefinite article, a broken down form of **an** used before a consonant sound. [O.E. *ān*, one.]

a or **a.** *abbrev* for: about; absent; acceleration; accepted; acre; acreage; acting; active; adjective; advance; advanced; afternoon; *anno* (L.), in the year; *annus* (L.), year; anonymous; answer; *ante* (L.), before; anterior; are (metric measure); atto-.

a-^{1} *ə-*, *pfx* a reduced form of the O.E. preposition *an*, *on*, on, in, at, as in *abroad*, *afloat*, *asleep*, *a-begging*, and occasionally used separately as a preposition, as in *once a year*.

a-^{2} *ə-*, *a-* or **an-** *ən-*, *an-*, *pfx* without, not, opposite to, as in *amoral*, *anaemia*, *anodyne*. [Gr., without, not.]

AA *abbrev* for: Alcoholics Anonymous; anti-aircraft; Architectural Association; Associate of Arts; Australian Army; Automobile Association.

a̅a̅ or **A̅A̅** *symbol* for (in prescriptions, etc.) in equal quantities, of each. [L.L. *ana* — Gr., again.]

AAA *abbrev* for: Amateur Athletic Association; American Automobile Association; Australian Automobile Association.

AAC *abbrev* for: Amateur Athletic Club; *anno ante Christum* (L.), in the year before Christ; Army Air Corps (*US*).

AAM *abbrev* for air-to-air missile.

A & M *abbrev* for (Hymns) Ancient and Modern.

A & R *abbrev* for: artists and recording; artists and repertoire.

aar *abbrev* for: against all risks (*commerce*); average annual rainfall.

aardvark *ärd'värk*, *n* the antbear, a long-nosed African edentate that feeds on termites, etc. [Du. *aarde*, earth, *vark* (now *varken*), pig.]

aardwolf *ärd'wo͝olf*, *n* a hyena-like mammal of southern Africa that feeds mainly on termites and carrion. [Du. *aarde*, earth, *wolf*, wolf.]

AB *ā-bē'*, *n* one of the four blood types in the ABO blood group system.

AB *abbrev* for: able-bodied (seaman); Advisory Board; Alberta (Canadian province); *Artium Baccalaureus* (L.), Bachelor of Arts (*US*); autobahn.

ab-^{1} *ab-*, *pfx* opposite to, from, away from, as in *abnormal*. [L. *ab*, from.]

ab-^{2} *ab-*, *pfx* used to indicate a centimetre-gram-second electromagnetic unit. [**absolute**.]

a/b *abbrev* for airborne.

abaca *ä-bä-kä'*, *n* a plantain grown in the Philippine Islands; its fibre, called Manila hemp. [Tagálog.]

abaci. See **abacus.**

aback *ə-bak'*, *adv* backwards; said of sails pressed backward against the mast by the wind (*naut*). — **taken aback** taken by surprise. [O.E. *on bæc*, on back; see **a-**^{1}.]

abacus *ab'ə-kəs*, *n* a frame used for counting, containing rods on which are moveable beads; a piece of flat stone between the capital of a column and the architrave (*archit*): — *pl* **ab'aci** (*-sī*) or **ab'acuses**. [L. *abacus* — Gr. *abax*, *-akos*.]

abaft *ə-bäft'*, (*naut*) *adv* and *prep* behind; towards the stern. [**a-**^{1} and O.E. *bæftan*, after — pfx. *be-* and *æftan*, behind.]

abalone *ab-a-lō'nā*, *n* an edible mollusc, whose shell has a pearly lining. [Am. Sp. *abulón*.]

abampere *ab-am'pār*, (*electr*) *n* a unit equivalent to 10 amperes. [**ab-**^{2} and **ampere**.]

abandon *ə-ban'dən*, *vt* to give up; to desert; to give (oneself) over without restraint; to give up all claims to. — *n* the condition of letting oneself go; careless freedom of action. — *adj* **aban'doned** completely deserted; given up, as to a vice; profligate, dissolute. — *adv* **aban'donedly**. — *n* **abandonee'** (*law*) an insurer to whom a wreck has been abandoned. — *n* **aban'donment**. [O.Fr. *abandoner*, to put at one's disposal or in one's control.]

abase *ə-bās'*, *vt* to degrade, belittle; to humble; to lower, put down. — *adj* **abased'**. — *n* **abase'ment**. [O.Fr. *abaissier* — L. *ad*, to, L.L. *bassus*, low.]

abash *ə-bash'*, *vt* to strike with shame or embarrassment; to disconcert. — *adj* **abashed'**. [O.Fr. *esbahir*, to astound.]

abate *ə-bāt'*, *vi* to grow less; to subside; to be abated (*law*). — *vt* to nullify, to bring down (*law*); to lessen, reduce; to mitigate, blunt. — *adj* **abāt'able**. — *adj* **abāt'ed** blunted; diminished; lowered; subdued. — *n* **abate'ment**. [O.Fr. *abatre*, to beat down — L. *ab*, from, and *batuĕre*, to beat.]

abattoir *ab'ə-twär*, *n* a public slaughterhouse. [Fr.; see ety. for **abate**.]

abaxial *ab-ak'si-əl*, (*bot*) *adj* away from the axis. [**ab-**^{1}.]

abbacy *ab'ə-si*, *n* the office or jurisdiction of an abbot; the time during which one is abbot. — *adj* **abbatial** (*ab-ā'shl*). [L.L. *abbātia*, abbey.]

abbé *ab'ā*, *n* a courtesy title for a French priest or cleric. [Fr., orig. abbot.]

abbess *ab'es*, *n* a woman who is head of an abbey. [L.L. *abbātissa*, fem. of *abbās*, abbot.]

abbey *ab'i*, *n* a convent under an abbot or abbess, or (*loosely*) a prior or prioress; the church now or formerly attached to such an abbey; a name often retained by an abbatial building that has become a private house: — *pl* **abb'eys**. [O.Fr. *abaïe* (Fr. *abbaye*) — L.L. *abbātia*, abbey.]

abbot *ab'ət, n* a male head of an abbey (*fem* **abb'ess**). — *n* **abb'otship**. [L.L. *abbās, abbātis* — Aramaic *abbā*.]

abbr. or **abbrev**. *abbrev* for: abbreviated; abbreviation.

abbreviate *ə-brē'vi-āt, vt* to shorten; to contract; to abridge. — *n* **abbrēviā'tion** an act of shortening; a shortened form, esp. part of a word. — *n* **abbrē'viātor**. — *adj* **abbrē'viatory** (*-ə-tər-i*). [L. *abbreviāre, -ātum* — *ab* (intensive) and *brevis*, short.]

ABC *ā-bē-sē', n* the alphabet (so-named from its first letters); the first rudiments, the basics; anything arranged alphabetically.

ABC *abbrev* for: American Broadcasting Company; Australian Broadcasting Corporation.

abd *abbrev* for: abdicated; abridged.

abdabs. See **habdabs**.

abdicate *ab'di-kāt, vt* and *vi* formally to renounce or give up (office or dignity). — *adj* **ab'dicable**. — *n* **abdicā'tion**. [L. *ab*, from or off, *dicāre, -ātum*, to proclaim.]

abdomen *ab'də-mən, n* the belly; (in mammals) the part between diaphragm and pelvis; (in arthropods) the hind-body. — *adj* **abdominal** (*ab-dom'i-nəl*). — *adv* **abdom'inally**. [L. *abdōmen, -inis*.]

abducent *ab-dū'sənt*, (*anat*) *adj* (of a muscle) drawing back. [See **abduct**.]

abduct *ab-dukt', vt* to take away by fraud or violence; to kidnap; (of a muscle) to cause abduction in (a part of the body). — *n* **abductee'** a person who is abducted. — *n* **abduction** (*-duk'shən*) the carrying away, esp. of a person by fraud or force; muscular action drawing one part of the body (such as an arm or finger) away from another or away from the median axis of the body. — *n* **abduc'tor** someone who abducts; a muscle that draws away (*anat*). [L. *abducĕre* — *ab*, from, *ducĕre, ductum*, to draw, lead.]

abeam *ə-bēm'*, (*naut*) *adv* in a line at right angles to a vessel's length, on the beam. [**a-**[1] and **beam**.]

abele *ə-bēl'* or *ā'bl, n* the white poplar-tree. [Du. *abeel*, ult. — L. *albus*, white.]

abelia *ə-bēl'i-ə, n* a plant of the *Abelia* genus of shrubs of the honeysuckle family with pink or white flowers. [Clarke *Abel*, 1780–1826, English physician and botanist.]

Aberdeen *ab-ər-dēn'* (or sometimes *ab'*), *adj* of or originating in *Aberdeen* or Aberdeenshire. — *n* (in full **Aberdeen terrier**) a coarse-haired kind of Scottish terrier. — *adj* **Aberdō'nian** of Aberdeen. — Also *n*. — **Aberdeen Angus** (*ang'gəs*) a breed of hornless, black cattle.

aberrate *ab'ər-āt, vi* to wander or deviate from the right way. — *n* **aberrance** (*-er'*) or **aberr'ancy**. — *adj* **aberr'ant** wandering, straying; having characteristics not strictly in accordance with type (*bot* and *zool*). — *n* **aberration** (*ab-ər-ā'shən*) a deviation from the usual, normal, or right course, direction or behaviour; a wandering of the intellect, mental lapse; a non-convergence of rays, owing to difference in refrangibility of different colours (**chromatic aberration**) or to difference of focus of the marginal and central parts of a lens or mirror (**spherical aberration**); an apparent displacement of a star (*astron*). [L. *aberrāre, -ātum* — *ab*, from, *errāre*, to wander.]

abet *ə-bet', vt* to incite by encouragement or aid (used chiefly in a bad sense; see also **aid and abet** under **aid**): — *pr p* **abett'ing**; *pa p* **abett'ed**. — *n* **abet'ment**. — *n* **abett'er** or (esp. *legal*) **abett'or**. [O.Fr. *abeter* — *à* (L. *ad*, to), and *beter*, to bait; see **bait**.]

abeyance *ə-bā'əns, n* a state of suspension or temporary inactivity; the state of being without a claimant (as of a peerage). — *adj* **abey'ant**. [O.Fr. *abeance* — *à* (L. *ad*, to), and *beer, baer*, to gape, open wide.]

abhor *əb-hör', vt* to shrink from with horror; to detest, loathe: — *pr p* **abhorr'ing**; *pa t* and *pa p* **abhorred'**. — *n* **abhorrence** (*əb-hor'əns*) extreme hatred; something that is abhorred. — *adj* **abhorr'ent** repugnant; strongly opposed or out of keeping; detestable; detested; detesting. — *adv* **abhorr'ently**. — *n* **abhorr'er**. [L. *abhorrēre* — *ab*, from, and *horrēre*, to bristle, shudder.]

abide *ə-bīd', vt* to endure; to tolerate; to meet, face, sustain; to wait for, bide. — *vi* to remain; to dwell or stay; to conform to, adhere to, comply with, obey (with *by*): — *pa t* and *pa p* **abōde'** or **abīd'ed**. — *n* **abīd'ance**. — *adj* **abīd'ing** continual, permanent. — *adv* **abīd'ingly**. [O.E. *ābīdan* — pfx. *ā-*, and *bīdan*, to wait.]

à bientôt *a byẽ-tō*, (Fr.) see you again soon.

ability *ə-bil'i-ti, n* the quality or fact of being able (to); power (physical and mental); strength; skill. [O.Fr. *ableté* (Fr. *habilete*), remodelled on its source, L. *habilitās, -ātis* — *habēre*, to have, hold.]

ab init. *abbrev* for **ab initio** (*ab in-ish'i-ō* or *-it'i-ō*; L.) from the beginning.

abiosis *ā-bī-ō'sis*, (*med*) *n* absence of life. — *adj* **ābiot'ic** without life; inanimate. [**a-**[2] and Gr. *biotikos* — *bios*, life.]

abject *ab'jekt, adj* mean; worthless; grovelling; base, contemptible. — *n* **abjec'tion**. — *adv* **ab'jectly**. — *n* **ab'jectness**. [L. *abjicĕre, abjectum* — *ab*, from, *jacĕre*, to throw.]

abjure *ab-jo͞or', vt* to renounce on oath or solemnly; to recant; to repudiate. — *n* **abjurā'tion**. — *n* **abjur'er**. [L. *ab*, from, *jurāre, -ātum*, to swear.]

abl. *abbrev* for ablative.

ablation *ab-lā'shən, n* removal, esp. surgical removal of an organ or body-tissue, etc.; decrease caused by melting, evaporation, weathering, or (in *aerospace*) by heat friction on re-entering the atmosphere. — *vt* **ablate** (*ab-lāt'*). — *adj* **ablative** (*ab'lə-tiv*) pertaining to ablation; in or belonging to a case which in Indo-European languages originally expressed *direction from*, or *time when*, later extended to other functions (*gram*). — *n* the ablative case; a word in the ablative. — *adj* **ablatī'val**. — *n* **ablā'tor** the heat shield of a spacecraft. — **ablative absolute** in Latin a phrase generally comprising a noun or pronoun coupled with another noun, an adjective or a participle, both in the ablative case and usu. indicating the time or cause of an event. [L. *ablātus*, past p. of *auferre*, to carry off, remove.]

ablaut *äp'lowt* or *ab'lowt*, (*philol*) *n* a variation in root vowel as in sing, sang, song, sung. [Ger., *ab*, off, *Laut*, sound.]

ablaze *ə-blāz', adv* and *adj* in a blaze, on fire; gleaming brightly. [**a-**[1] and **blaze**[1].]

able *ā'bl, adj* (*compar* **a'bler**, *superl* **a'blest**) having enough strength, power or means (to do a thing); skilful. — *adj* **a'ble-bodied** free from disability, etc.; robust. — *adv* **a'bly**. — **able seaman** or **able-bodied seaman** (abbrev. **AB**) a seaman able to perform all the duties of seamanship and having a higher rating than the ordinary sailor. — **able seawoman** or **able-bodied seawoman**. [See **ability**.]

-able *-ə-bl, adj sfx* capable of (being); able to (be); worthy of (being); likely to (be); that must (be); suitable for; in accordance with; causing. — *n sfx* **-ability**. — *adv sfx* **-ably**. — See also **-ible**. [O.Fr.]

ablution *ə-blo͞o'shən, n* (often in *pl*) the act of washing, esp. the body; ceremonial washing; (in *sing*) the wine and water used to rinse the chalice, drunk by the officiating priest (*RC relig*). — *adj* **ablu'tionary**. — *n* **ablutomane** (*ə-blo͞o'tō-mān*) a person obsessed with cleanliness. [L. *ablūtiō, -ōnis* — *ab*, away, *luĕre*, to wash.]

ABM *abbrev* for antiballistic missile.

abnegate *ab'ni-gāt, vt* to deny; to renounce. — *n* **abnegā'tion**. — *n* **ab'negātor**. [L. *ab*, away, *negāre*, to deny.]

abnormal *ab-nör'ml, adj* not normal. — *n* **abnor'malism.** — *n* **abnormality** (*ab-nör-mal'i-ti*). — *adv* **abnor'mally.** — *n* **abnor'mity.** — **abnormal load** (usu. of road transport) a larger or heavier load than is generally carried. [Fr. *anormal* — L.L. *anormalus* — Gr. *anōmalos* (see **anomaly**).]

ABO blood group system *ā'bē-ō blud grōōp sis'təm, n* (*med*) a system by which human blood is classified into four groups (O, A, B, AB) according to the antigens carried by the red blood cells.

Abo *ab'ō*, (*Austr*; *offensive*) *n* short for Aboriginal or Aborigine: — *pl* **Ab'ōs.**

aboard *ə-börd', adv* or *prep* on board; in or into a ship, railway train, etc.; alongside (*naut*). [**a-**[1] and **board.**]

abode *ə-bōd', n* a dwelling-place, home. — **of no fixed abode** (*legal*) having no regular, habitual address. [**abide.**]

abolish *ə-bol'ish, vt* to put an end to. — *adj* **abol'ishable.** — *n* **aboli'tion.** — *adj* **aboli'tional.** — *adj* **aboli'tionary.** — *n* **aboli'tionism.** — *n* **aboli'tionist** a person who seeks to abolish anything, e.g. slavery or capital punishment. [L. *abolēre*, *-itum*.]

abomasum *ab-ō-mā'səm, n* the fourth or true stomach of ruminants: — *pl* **abomā'sa.** — *adj* **abomā'sal.** [**ab-**[1] and L. *omāsum*, tripe, paunch.]

abominate *ə-bom'in-āt, vt* to abhor, detest. — *adj* **abom'inable** hateful; detestable. — *n* **abom'inableness.** — *adv* **abom'inably.** — *n* **abominā'tion** extreme aversion; a detested object, anything abominable. — *n* **abom'inator.** — **abominable snowman** a mythical hairy man-like creature supposed to live in the Himalayas (also called the **yeti**). [L. *abōminārī*, *-ātus*, to turn from as being of bad omen; see **omen.**]

ab origine *ab ō-rij'in-ē* or *-rēg'in-e*, (L.) from the very first, from the source.

aborigine *ab-ə-rij'i-nē* or *-ni, n* an original or native inhabitant of a country, esp. (now often, and in Australia always, with *cap*) Australia. — *adj* **aborig'inal** (often with *cap*) earliest, primitive, indigenous. — *n* (now often, and in Australia always, with *cap*) an aborigine; (with *cap*) an Australian Aboriginal language. — *n* **aboriginality** (*-al'i-ti*). — *adv* **aborig'inally.** [L. (pl.) *aborīginēs* — *ab*, from, *orīgō*, *-inis*, beginning.]

abort *ə-bört', vi* to miscarry in birth; to come to nothing; to fail before getting fully under way or reaching a viable stage of development. — *vt* to cause to abort; to check or call off (an attack, mission, etc.) at an early stage. — *n* an instance of abortion (esp. of a rocket launch). — *n* **abor'ticide** (*-i-sīd*) the killing of a foetus in the womb; a drug or agent causing this (also called an **abortifacient**). — *adj* **abortifacient** (*-i-fā'shənt*) causing abortion. — Also *n.* — *n* **abor'tion** the premature expulsion of an embryo or a foetus, either occurring naturally (**spontaneous abortion**) or by artificial means (**induced abortion**), esp. in the first three months of pregnancy; the procuring of an induced abortion; anything that fails in the course of coming into being. — *n* **abor'tionist** a person who procures abortion. — *adj* **abor'tive** unsuccessful; brought out or produced in an imperfect condition; checked in development. — *adv* **abort'ively.** — *n* **abort'iveness.** — **abortion pill** a drug taken orally that brings about abortion; **contagious abortion** contagious bacterial infections of cattle and of horses, causing abortion. [L. *aborīrī*, *abortus* — pfx. **ab-**[1] and *orīrī*, to rise.]

aboulia or **abulia** *a-bōō'li-ə* or *a-bū'li-ə, n* loss of willpower; inability to make decisions. [**a-**[2] and Gr. *boulē*, will.]

abound *ə-bownd', vi* to exist in great plenty; to be rich (with *in*); to be filled (with *with*). — *adj* **abound'ing.** [O.Fr. *abunder* — L. *abundāre*, to overflow.]

about *ə-bowt', prep* round on the outside of; around; here and there in; near in place, time, size, etc.; on the person of; connected with; concerning; engaged in. — *adv* around; halfway round, in the opposite direction (e.g. *to face about*); nearly; here and there; on the opposite tack; in motion or activity. — **about'-face** a complete change of opinion, attitude, etc. — Also *vi.* — Also **about'-turn.** — **about to** on the point of (doing etc.; also **just about to**); (in *neg*) not likely or keen (to do something) (*colloq*); **bring about** to cause to take place; **come about** to happen in the course of time; **go about** to prepare to do; **turn about** alternately; in rotation. [O.E. *onbūtan* — *on*, in, *būtan*, without.]

above *ə-buv', prep* over; in or to a position higher than that of; beyond in degree, amount, etc.; too magnanimous or proud for. — *adv* overhead; in a higher position, order or power; in an earlier passage (of text, etc.); in heaven. — *adj* mentioned in an earlier passage. — *adj* **above'-board** open, without deception. — *adj* **above'-mentioned.** — *adj* **above'-named.** — *adj* **above'-the-line** of or pertaining to the Government's expenditure and revenue allowed for in its original estimates and provided for by taxation; of or pertaining to the expenditure and revenue detailed in a company's profit and loss account. — **above oneself** conceited. [Late O.E. *ābufan* — O.E. *ā-*, on, *bufan*, above.]

Abp *abbrev* for Archbishop.

abr. *abbrev* for: abridged; abridgment.

abracadabra *ab-rə-kə-dab'rə, n* a magic word; a spell or conjuring word; gibberish. [Found in a 2nd-cent. poem.]

abrade *ə-brād', vt* to wear down or off. — *adj* and *n* **abrā'dant.** [L. *ab*, from, *rādĕre*, *rāsum*, to scrape.]

abranchiate *ə-brang'ki-āt*, (*zool*) *adj* without gills. [**a-**[2] and Gr. *branchia*, gills.]

abrasion *ə-brā'zhən, n* a wearing away; a worn-down or grazed place. — *adj* **abrā'sive** (*-ziv* or *-siv*) tending to abrade; harsh; (of a person) tending to irritate or annoy. — *n* a substance used to clean, smooth, etc. by scratching and grinding. [Ety. as for **abrade.**]

abreaction *ab-rē-ak'shən*, (*psychol*) *n* the resolution of a neurosis by reviving forgotten or repressed ideas of the event first causing it. — *vi* **abreact'.** [**ab-**[1] and **reaction.**]

abreast *ə-brest', adv* with fronts in line; side by side; (with *of*) keeping pace with. [**a-**[1] and **breast.**]

abridge *ə-brij', vt* to shorten; to epitomise; to curtail. — *n* **abridg'er.** — *n* **abridg'ment** (or sometimes **abridge'ment**) contraction; shortening; an epitome or synopsis. [O.Fr. *abregier* — L. *abbreviāre*.]

abroad *ə-bröd', adv* in or to another country; over a wide area; at large; out of doors; current. [**a-**[1] and **broad.**]

abrogate *ab'rō-gāt, vt* to annul, rescind. — *n* **abrogā'tion.** — *adj* **ab'rogātive.** — *n* **ab'rogātor.** [L. *ab*, away, *rogāre*, *-ātum*, to ask, or to propose a law.]

abrupt *ə-brupt', adj* broken off or as if broken off; sudden, unexpected; precipitous, steep; (of manners) short, rude. — *adv* **abrupt'ly.** — *n* **abrupt'ness.** [L. *abruptus* — *ab*, from, *rumpĕre*, *ruptum*, to break.]

ABS *abbrev* for anti-lock braking system.

abs. *abbrev* for: absence; absent; absolute; absolutely; absorbent; abstract.

abscess *ab'ses* or *-sis*, (*med*) *n* a collection of pus in a cavity, usu. causing an inflamed swelling. [L. *abscessus* — *abs*, from, *cēdĕre*, *cēssum*, to go, retreat.]

abscind *ab-sind', vt* to cut off. — *n* **abscissa** (*ab-sis'ə*) (*math*) the intercept between a fixed point and the foot of an ordinate; the *x*-co-ordinate in analytical geometry: — *pl* **abscissae** (*ab-sis'ē* or *-sis'ī*). — *n* **abscission** (*-sizh'ən*) an act of cutting off, or state of being cut off; organised shedding of a part (e.g. a leaf or fruit) (*bot*). [L. *abscindĕre*, *abscissum*, to cut off.]

abscise *ab-sīz'*, (*bot*) *vi* to fall off by abscission. — *vt* to cause to separate by abscission. — *n* **abscisin** (*-sis'in*) any of a number of plant hormones which promote abscission. [L. *abscīsus*, past p. of *abscīdere* — *abs*, away, *caedere*, to cut.]

abscissa, abscissae, abscission. See under **abscind**.

abscond *ab-skond'*, *vi* to hide, or get out of the way, esp. to escape a legal process. — *n* **abscond'ence**. — *n* **abscond'er**. [L. *abscondere* — *abs*, from, *condere*, to hide.]

abseil *ab'sāl*, *vi* to let oneself down a rock face using a double rope. — *n* **ab'seiling**. [Ger. *ab*, down, *Seil*, rope.]

absent *ab'sənt*, *adj* not present; inattentive, dreamy. — *vt* (*ab-sent'*; usu. *reflexive*) to keep away. — *n* **ab'sence** the state of being not present; want, lack; non-existence; inattention. — *n* **absentee'** a person who is absent; a person who makes a habit of living away from his or her estate or office. — *n* **absentee'ism** the practice of absenting oneself from duty. — *adv* **ab'sently**. — *adj* **absent-mind'ed** inattentive to surroundings; preoccupied. — *adv* **absent-mind'edly**. — *n* **absent-mind'edness**. [L. *absēns*, *-sentis*, pres. p. of *abesse* — *ab*, away from, *esse*, to be.]

absinth or **absinthe** *ab'sinth*, *n* a bitter, green aniseed-flavoured liqueur containing (orig. at all events) extract of wormwood; the wormwood plant. [Fr. *absinthe* — Gr. *apsinthion*.]

absolute *ab'sə-lōōt* or *-ūt*, *adj* free from limits, or conditions; certain, positive; complete; unlimited; free from mixture, pure; independent of relation to other things; peremptory, decisive; unrestricted by constitutional checks; out of ordinary syntactic relation, as the Latin *ablative absolute* (*gram*). — *n* (with *the*; often with *cap*) that which is absolute, self-existent, uncaused. — *adv* **ab'solutely** separately, by itself; unconditionally; positively; completely — an emphatic affirmative (*ab-sə-lōōt'li* or *-lūt'*). — *n* **ab'soluteness**. — *n* **absolu'tion** release from punishment or guilt; remission of sins, declared officially by a priest. — *n* **ab'solutism** government by a ruler with unrestricted power; adherence to the doctrine of the Absolute. — *n* **ab'solutist**. — Also *adj*. — *adj* **absol'utory**. — **absolute alcohol** water-free alcohol; **absolute magnitude** the magnitude that a star would have at a standard distance of 10 parsecs; **absolute majority** a majority, in an election, etc., which is greater than the total number of votes for all other candidates; **absolute pitch** perfect pitch; **absolute temperature** temperature measured on the Kelvin scale or Rankine scale; **absolute zero** the zero of the absolute scale of temperature (approx. −273°C). [L. *absolūtus*, past p. of *absolvere*; see **absolve**.]

absolve *əb-zolv'* or *əb-solv'*, *vt* to loose or set free from guilt; to pardon; to give absolution to or for; to acquit without blame. — *n* **absolv'er**. [L. *absolvere* — *ab*, from, *solvere*, to loose.]

absorb *ab-sörb'* or *əb-zörb'*, *vt* to suck in or swallow up; to take in, incorporate; to take up and transform (energy) instead of transmitting or reflecting (*phys*); to engage wholly, engross. — *n* **absorbabil'ity**. — *adj* **absorb'able**. — *adj* **absorbed'** swallowed, soaked up; entirely occupied, engrossed. — *adv* **absorb'edly**. — *n* **absorb'ency**. — *adj* **absorb'ent** able to absorb. — *n* something that absorbs. — *n* **absorb'er**. — *adj* **absorb'ing** engrossing the attention. — *adv* **absorb'ingly**. — *n* **absorp'tion** the act of absorbing; entire occupation of mind. — *adj* **absorp'tive** having power to absorb. — *n* **absorp'tiveness**. — *n* **absorptiv'ity**. — **absorption bands** or **lines** dark bands or lines interrupting a spectrum. [L. *ab*, from, *sorbēre*, *sorptum*, to suck in.]

abstain *ab-stān'*, *vi* to hold or refrain (from; *specif* from voting or from drinking alcohol). — *n* **abstain'er**. — *n* **absten'tion**. [Fr. *abstenir* — L. *abs*, from, *tenēre*, to hold.]

abstemious *ab-stē'mi-əs*, *adj* restrained in relation to food, drink, or other pleasures. — *adv* **abstē'miously**. — *n* **abstē'miousness**. [L. *abstēmius* — *abs*, from, *tēmētum*, strong wine.]

abstention. See **abstain**.

abstergent *ab-stûr'jənt*, (*med*) *adj* cleansing, purging. — *n* a cleansing agent. — *n* **abster'sion** a cleansing or purging process. — *adj* **abster'sive** having the quality of cleansing; purgative. — Also *n*. [L. *abstergēre*, *-tersum*, to wipe away.]

abstinent *ab'stin-ənt*, *adj* abstaining; temperate, self-restrained in one's appetites. — *n* **ab'stinence** an abstaining or refraining, especially from some indulgence (with *from*). — *adv* **ab'stinently**. [L. *abstinēns*, *-entis*, pres. p. of *abstinēre*; see **abstain**.]

abstract *ab-strakt'*, *vt* to form a general concept from consideration of particular instances; to separate or remove; to summarise. — *n* (*ab'strakt*) a summary or abridgment; that part or thing which represents the essence; an abstraction; an abstract painting or sculpture. — *adj* (*ab'strakt*) abstracted; existing only as a mental concept (opp. to *concrete*); theoretical; (of terms) denoting a quality of a thing apart from the thing, e.g. 'redness'; representing ideas in geometric and other designs (*visual arts*); using words primarily for their auditory and rhythmic qualities (*poetry*). — *adj* **abstract'ed** drawn off (with *from*); removed; absent-minded. — *adv* **abstract'edly**. — *n* **abstract'edness**. — *n* **abstrac'ter** or **abstrac'tor**. — *n* **abstrac'tion** the act of abstracting; the state of being abstracted; abstract quality or character; absent-mindedness; a thing existing only in idea, a theory; a term or composition that is abstract. — *adj* **abstrac'tional**. — *n* **abstrac'tionist** a person dealing in abstractions or unrealities. — *adj* and *n* **abstrac'tive**. — *adv* **ab'stractly**. — *n* **ab'stractness**. — **abstract expressionism** a development in art that began in America in the 1940s in which the expression of the artist's feelings informs his or her abstract representations. [L. *abs*, away from, *trahere*, *tractum*, to draw.]

abstruse *ab-strōōs'*, *adj* difficult to understand. — *adv* **abstruse'ly**. — *n* **abstruse'ness**. [L. *abstrūsus*, thrust away.]

absurd *ab-sûrd'*, *adj* senseless, meaningless; ridiculous. — *n* **absurd'ity** or **absurd'ness**. — *adv* **absurd'ly**. [L. *absurdus* — *ab*, from, *surdus*, deaf, indistinct.]

ABTA *ab'tə*, *abbrev* for Association of British Travel Agents.

abulia. See **aboulia**.

abundance *ə-bun'dəns*, *n* ample sufficiency; great plenty; a call of nine tricks (*solo whist*); (or **abundance ratio**) the proportion of one isotope to the total (for a specified element) (*phys*). — *n* **abun'dancy**. — *adj* **abun'dant**. — *adv* **abun'dantly**. [See ety. for **abound**.]

abuse *ə-būz'*, *vt* to make a bad use of; to take undue advantage of; to betray (e.g. a confidence); to revile, or swear at; to maltreat; to violate. — *n* **abusage** (*ə-bū'sij*) wrong use, esp. of words or grammar. — *n* **abuse** (*ə-būs'*) wrong use; an evil or corrupt practice; hurt or maltreatment; betrayal (of confidence); bad usage. — *n* **abuser** (*ə-bū'zər*). — *adj* **abū'sive** (*-siv*) containing, giving, or in the nature of, abuse; (of speech) coarse, rude, insulting. — *adv* **abū'sively**. — *n* **abū'siveness**. [L. *ab*, from, *ūti*, *ūsus*, to use.]

abut *ə-but'*, *vi* to end or lean (on, upon or against). — *vt* to border: — *pr p* **abutt'ing**; *pa t* and *pa p* **abutt'ed**. — *n* **abut'ment** an endwise meeting or junction; that part on which a limb of an arch ends or rests (*archit*); a place of abutting. — *n* **abutt'al** an abutment; (in *pl*) boundaries. — *n* **abutt'er** (*law*) a person whose property abuts. — *adj* **abutt'ing**. [O.Fr. *abouter*, to touch by an end, and O.Fr. *abuter*, to touch at the end.]

abuzz *ə-buz'*, *adv* and *adj* in a state of animated excitement; in a buzz. [a-[1] and **buzz**.]

abvolt *ab'volt*, *n* 10^{-8} volts. [**ab-**[2] and **volt**[2].]

abysmal *ə-biz'məl*, *adj* very bad (*colloq*); very deep, bottomless; unfathomable. — *adv* **abys'mally**. [O.Fr. *abisme*.]

abyss *ə-bis'*, *n* a bottomless gulf; hell; anything very deep, such as the depths of the sea. — *adj* **abyss'al**. [Gr. *abyssos*, bottomless.]

AC *abbrev* for: air-conditioned, air-conditioning; air-craft(s)man; alternating current (*electr*); *ante Christum* (L.), before Christ; appellation (d'origine) contrôlée; Companion of (the Order of) Australia.

Ac (*chem*) *symbol* for actinium.

a/c *abbrev* for: account; account current.

acacia *ə-kā'shyə* or *-shə*, *n* a wattle, any plant of the genus *Acacia*; the *false acacia* or robinia. [L. — Gr. *akakiā*.]

academe *ak-ə-dēm'*, (*formal* or *literary*) *n* the world of scholars; academic life. — *n* **acadēm'ia** academic life. [Ety. as for **academy**.]

academy *ə-kad'ə-mi*, *n* a higher or specialised school, or a university; a society for the promotion of science or art; a riding-school. — *adj* **academic** (*-dem'ik*) of an academy or university; scholarly; formal; theoretical only, of no practical importance or consequence. — *n* a person studying or teaching at a university, esp. one who has narrow scholarly tastes (sometimes *derog*). — *adj* **academ'ical**. — *n* (in *pl*) university garb. — *adv* **academ'ically**. — *n* **academician** (*ə-kad-ə-mish'ən*) a member of an academy, esp. of the French Academy or the Royal Academy of Arts (London) or the Royal Scottish Academy (Edinburgh). — *n* **academ'icism**. — *n* **acad'emist** an academic; an academician. [Gr. *Akadēmeiā*, Plato's school of philosophy, from the name of the garden, outside Athens, where Plato taught.]

Acadian *ə-kā'di-ən*, *adj* and *n* Nova Scotian. [Fr. *Acadie*, Nova Scotia — Micmac Ind. *ākăde*, abundance.]

acajou *ak'ə-zhōō* or *ak-ə-zhōō'*, *n* the cashew tree or its fruit or gum; a kind of mahogany. [See **cashew**.]

acanthus *ə-kanth'əs*, *n* any plant of the prickly-leaved genus **Acanthus**; a conventionalised representation of an acanthus leaf, in classical decorative arts, esp. on Corinthian capitals. — *adj* **acanth'ine** of, like, or ornamented with, acanthus. — *adj* **acanth'oid** like acanthus. — *adj* **acanth'ous** spiny. [Gr. *akantha*, prickle, *akanthos*, acanthus.]

a cappella *a* or *ä kap-el'ə*, *adj* and *adv* (of choral music) unaccompanied. [It., in the church style.]

acarus *ak'ə-rəs*, *n* a mite: — *pl* **ac'arī**. — *adj* **acā'rian**. — *n* **acarī'asis** disease due to or infestation by mites. — *n* **acaricide** (*a-kar'i-sīd*) a mite killer. — *n* **ac'arid** one of the **Acar'ida**, the order of Arachnida to which mites and ticks belong. — *adj* and *n* **acar'idan**. — *adj* **ac'arine**. — *adj* **ac'aroid** mite-like. — *n* **acarol'ogist**. — *n* **acarol'ogy**. [Gr. *akari*, a mite.]

ACAS *ā'kas*, *abbrev* for Advisory, Conciliation and Arbitration Service.

acatalectic *a-kat-ə-lek'tik*, (*prosody*) *adj* having the full number of syllables. — *n* an acatalectic verse or line. [Gr. *akatalēktos* — **a-**[2] and see **catalectic**.]

acc. *abbrev* for: according; account (also **acct** or **a/c**); accusative (also **accus.**).

accede *ək-sēd'*, *vi* to come to office or dignity; to join up, become a party, hence agree or assent (with *to*). — *n* **accēd'ence**. — *n* **accēd'er**. [L. *accēdĕre*, *accēssum*, to go near — *ad*, to, *cēdĕre*, to go.]

accelerando *ak-sel-ər-an'dō*, It. *ät-chel-er-än'dō*, (*mus*) *adj* and *adv* with increasing speed. [It.]

accelerate *ək-sel'ər-āt*, *vt* to increase the speed of; to hasten the progress or occurrence of. — *vi* to become faster. — *n* **accelerā'tion** increase of speed; rate of change of velocity; a cumulative advance ahead of the normal or theoretical; the power or means of accelerating. — *adj* **accel'erative** quickening. — *n* **accel'erātor** any person or thing that accelerates, esp. a substance that accelerates chemical action, a nerve or muscle that increases rate of action, an apparatus for changing the speed of a machine, or one for imparting high energies to atomic particles. — *adj* **accel'eratory**. [L. *accelerāre*, *-ātum* — *ad*, to, *celer*, swift.]

accent *ak'sənt*, *n* stress on a syllable, word or note; a mark used to direct this stress; a mark over a letter to indicate differences of stress, pitch, length, etc.; any way of pronouncing speech characteristic of a region, a class, or an individual; a distinguishing mark; a significant word, or words generally (*poetic*); a touch bringing out some particular effect (*painting*); (in *pl*) speech, language. — *vt* (*ək-sent'*) to express or mark the accent of; to utter; to accentuate. — *adj* **accent'ūal**. — *adv* **accent'ūally**. — *vt* **accent'ūate** to mark, play, or pronounce with accent; to emphasise. — *n* **accentūā'tion**. [L. *accentus* — *ad*, to, *cantus*, song.]

accept *ək-sept'*, *vt* to take (something offered); to receive; to reply to in the affirmative, say yes to; to view favourably, tolerate; to understand. — *adj* **accept'able** worth accepting; welcome, pleasing; capable of being accepted, tolerable; satisfactory, adequate. — *n* **accept'ableness**. — *adv* **accept'ably**. — *n* **acceptabil'ity**. — *n* **accept'ance** accepting; favourable reception; acceptableness; an agreeing to terms; an accepted bill; acceptation. — *n* **accept'ancy**. — *n* **accept'ant** a person who accepts. — *adj* ready to receive. — *n* **acceptā'tion** sense in which a word, etc., is understood. — *n* **accept'er**. — *n* **accept'or** someone who accepts something, esp. a bill of exchange; an impurity in semiconductor material which increases the conductivity of the material. — **accepting house** a financial institution, such as a merchant bank, which accepts bills of exchange. [L. *acceptāre* — *accipĕre*, *acceptum* — *ad*, to, *capĕre*, to take.]

access *ak'ses*, *n* approach; admittance; a way of opportunity, approach or entrance; addition or accession; onset or attack of illness; a fit (of illness or passion). — *vt* to locate or retrieve information; to retrieve information from (a computer), or from a computer in (a particular location); to gain access to, succeed in reaching. — *n* and *adj* **access'ary** accessory (esp. in legal senses). — *n* **accessibil'ity**. — *adj* **access'ible** within reach; approachable; easily comprehensible. — *adv* **access'ibly**. — *n* **accession** (*ak-sesh'ən*) the act or event of acceding; a coming, esp. to office or dignity, or as an addition; that which is added; assent. — *vt* to enter in a book as an accession to a library. — *vt* **access'orise** or **-ize** to add accessories to. — *adj* **access'ory** additional; subsidiary; aiding, or participating in, a crime (*law*) or misdeed, but not as principal. — *n* anything that is secondary, additional, or non-essential; someone who helps others commit a crime or allows them to do so. — *adj* **accessor'ial**. — *adv* **access'orily**. — **accessary before** (or **after**) **the fact** someone who helps a criminal before (or after) the committing of a crime; **access broadcasting** and **access television** radio and television programmes put out independently by groups of people who want to bring their points of view to public notice; **Access® card** a credit card issued by a group of banks; **access road** a minor road built to give access to a house, locality, motorway, etc.; **access television** see **access broadcasting**; **access time** the time needed for information stored in a computer to be retrieved. [See ety. for **accede**.]

acciaccatura *ät-chäk-a-tōō'rə*, (*mus*) *n* a short appoggiatura. [It. *acciaccare*, to crush.]

accidence *ak'sid-əns*, *n* the part of grammar that deals with inflexions of words. [L. *accidens*; see **accident**.]

accident *ak'sid-ənt*, an unforeseen or unexpected event; a chance; a mishap. — *adj* **accidental** (*-dent'*) happening by chance; not essential. — *n* a sharp, flat, or natural not in the key-signature (*mus*). — *n* **accident'alism** the state or quality of being accidental. — *n* **accidental'ity.** — *adv* **accident'ally.** — *adj* **ac'cident-prone** more than normally liable to have accidents. — **a chapter of accidents** a series of accidents. [L. *accidēns*, *-entis*, pres. p. of *accidĕre*, to happen.]

acclamation *ak-lə-mā'shən*, *n* a shout of applause or assent; enthusiastic approval or welcome. — *vt* **acclaim** (*ə-klām'*) to hail or declare by acclamation; to welcome with enthusiasm. — *adj* **acclamatory** (*ə-klam'ə-tər-i*). [L. *acclāmāre* — *ad*, to, *clāmāre*, *-ātum*, to shout; see **claim.**]

acclimatise or **-ize** *ə-klī'mə-tīz*, (also in U.S. **acclimate** *ak'lə-māt* or *ə-klī'māt*) *vt* to accustom (a person, animal or plant etc.) to a new climate or environment. — *n* **acclīmatīsā'tion** or **-z-**. [Fr. *acclimater* — *à*, to, *climat*, climate.]

acclivity *ə-kliv'i-ti*, *n* an upward slope. — *adj* **accliv'itous.** [L. *ad*, to, *clīvus*, a slope.]

accolade *ak'əl-ād* or *-ād'* or *ak-ol-äd'*, *n* the action used in conferring knighthood, formerly an embrace, a kiss, now a tap on each shoulder with the flat of a sword; high award, or praise publicly given. [Fr., — L. *ad*, to, *collum*, neck.]

accommodate *ə-kom'ə-dāt*, *vt* to adapt; to adjust; to harmonise; to provide or supply (with); to find or provide room, etc., for; to oblige. — *adj* **accomm'odable.** — *adj* **accomm'odāting** ready to make adjustment; obliging. — *n* **accommodā'tion** adaptation; adjustment, esp. of the eye to change of distance; settlement or compromise; a convenience; lodgings, living quarters; space for what is required; a loan of money. — *adj* **accomm'odātive.** — *n* **accomm'odātor.** — **accommodation address** an address to which mail may be sent but which is not that of the addressee's home or office; **accommodation ladder** a stairway outside of a ship allowing access to and from small boats, etc., alongside; **accommodation road** a road giving access to buildings, etc., off the public road. [L. *accommodāre*, *-ātum* — *ad*, to, *commodus*, fitting.]

accompany *ə-kum'pə-ni*, *vt* to go or be in company with; to attend; to go along with; to perform an accompaniment to or for (*mus*); to associate, join, or couple. — *n* **accom'panier.** — *n* **accom'paniment** that which accompanies; a subsidiary part or parts supporting a solo (*mus*). — *n* **accom'panist** a player of accompaniments. [Fr. *accompagner*; see **company.**]

accomplice *ə-kom'plis* or *-kum'*, *n* a person who helps another or others to commit a crime. [L. *complex*, *-icis*, joined; pfx. unexplained.]

accomplish *ə-kom'plish* or *-kum'*, *vt* to complete; to fulfil; to achieve. — *adj* **accom'plishable.** — *adj* **accom'plished** complete, finished; highly skilled, expert. — *n* **accom'plisher.** — *n* **accom'plishment** completion; an achievement; an acquired skill, esp. in matters of culture or social behaviour. [O.Fr. *acomplir* — L. *ad*, to, *complēre*, to fill up; see **complete.**]

accord *ə-körd'*, *vi* to agree; to correspond (with). — *vt* to give or grant (to a person). — *n* agreement; harmony. — *n* **accord'ance** agreement; conformity; a granting. — *adj* **accord'ant.** — *adv* **accord'antly.** — *n* **accord'er.** — *adj* **accord'ing** in accordance. — *adv* **accord'ingly** suitably; in agreement (with what precedes); therefore. — **according as** in proportion as; depending on whether; **according to** in accordance with, or agreeably to; as asserted by; **of one's own accord** spontaneously, voluntarily; **with one accord** with spontaneous unanimity. [O.Fr. *acorder* — L. *ad*, to, *cor*, *cordis*, the heart.]

accordion *ə-kör'di-ən*, *n* a portable musical instrument consisting of folding bellows, keyboard, and metal reeds. — *n* **accor'dionist.** [**accord.**]

accost *ə-kost'*, *vt* to approach and speak (often threateningly) to; to speak first to; to solicit as a prostitute. — *adj* **accost'able.** [O.Fr. *acoster* — L. *ad*, to, *costa*, a rib, a side.]

accouchement *a-ko͞osh'mã* or *-mənt*, *n* giving birth to a child. [Fr.]

account *ə-kownt'*, *vt* to reckon; to judge, value. — *vi* to reckon; to keep accounts; to give a reason or explanation; to give a statement of money dealings; to answer as one responsible. — *n* reckoning; a reckoning of money or other responsibilities; a statement of money owing; money deposited in a bank or building society etc.; a credit agreement between a customer and a supplier (e.g. a retail store or a financial institution) that involves the provision of goods or services in return for payment on agreed terms; the period of time (usu. a fortnight) allowed before accounts are settled (*stock exchange*); a business relationship, or a specific part of a company assigned to handle such; value; estimation; consideration; sake; a descriptive report; a performance. — *n* **accountabil'ity.** — *adj* **account'able** responsible; explicable. — *n* **account'ableness.** — *adv* **account'ably.** — *n* **account'ancy** the office, work or profession of an accountant. — *n* **account'ant** a person who keeps, or is skilled in, accounts. — *n* **account'antship.** — *n* and *adj* **account'ing.** — **account'-book** a book for keeping accounts in. — **bring** or **call to account** to demand of someone an explanation or justification of what they have done; to reprimand; **by all accounts** according to general opinion; **give a good account of oneself** to give a good performance; to do well; **hold to account** to hold responsible; **on** or **to account** as an instalment or interim payment; **on account of** because of; **on no account** not for any reason; **on one's own account** on one's own responsibility; **take into account** to take into consideration; **take no account of** to overlook or fail to take into consideration; **turn to good account** to turn to advantage. [O.Fr. *aconter* — L. *ad*, to, *computāre*, to reckon; see **compute** and **count**[2].]

accoutre *ə-ko͞o'tər*, *vt* to dress or equip (esp. a warrior). — *n* **accou'trement** (*-tər-* or *-trə-*) equipping; (usu. in *pl*) dress; military equipments. [Fr. *accoutrer*, earlier *accoustrer*.]

accredit *ə-kred'it*, *vt* to show to be true or correct; to accept as true; to provide with or send with credentials; to certify; to attribute (to); to ascribe to (*with* the thing attributed); to accept (a student) for university entrance on the basis of work done in school as opposed to an examination (*NZ*). — *n* **accreditā'tion.** — *adj* **accred'ited** provided with credentials; certified officially; (of livestock) certified free from a particular disease, e.g. brucellosis. [Fr. *accréditer* — *à*, to, *crédit*, credit.]

accrete *ə-krēt'*, *vi* to grow together; to become attached. — *vt* to unite; to form or gather round itself. — *n* **accrē'tion** continued growth; the growing together of parts that are usually separate; an extraneous addition. — *adj* **accrē'tive.** [L. *accrēscĕre*, *accrētum* — *ad*, to, *crēscĕre*, to grow.]

accrue *ə-kro͞o'*, *vi* to come as an accession, increment or product; to fall (to one) by way of advantage; to fall due. — *n* **accru'al.** [O.Fr. *acrewe*, what grows up to the profit of the owner — *acreistre* — L. *accrēscĕre*.]

acct *abbrev* for account.

acculturation *ə-kul-chər-ā'shən*, *n* the process or result of assimilating the features of another culture. — *adj* **accul'tural.** — *vt* and *vi* **accul'turate.** [L. *ad*, and **culture.**]

accumulate *ə-kūm'ūl-āt*, *vt* to heap or pile up. — *vi* to increase greatly; to go on increasing. — *adj* heaped up. — *n* **accūmūlā'tion** (or *ak-ūm'*) heaping up; a heap or mass. — *adj* **accūm'ūlātive** growing by progressive addition; cumulative. — *n* **accūm'ūlātor** a thing or person that accumulates; a means of storing energy, esp. an electric battery that can be recharged; in a computer, etc., a device that performs arithmetical operations and stores the results. — **accumulator** or **accumulator bet** a bet on four or more races, original stake and winnings from each race being laid on the next race. [L. *ad*, to, *cumulus*, a heap.]

accurate *ak'ū-rit*, *adj* exact. — *n* **acc'ūracy** (*-ə-si*) correctness; exactness. — *adv* **acc'ūrately.** — *n* **acc'ūrateness.** [L. *accūrātus*, performed with care — *ad*, to, *cūra*, care.]

accursed *ə-kûrs'əd* or *-kûrst*, *adj* cursed, doomed; worthy of a curse. [O.E. pfx. *ā-*, and *cursian*, to curse.]

accus. *abbrev* for accusative.

accuse *ə-kūz'*, *vt* to bring a charge against (with *of*). — *adj* **accūs'able.** — *n* **accūs'al** accusation. — *n* **accūsā'tion** the act of accusing; a charge brought. — *adj* **accūs'ative** accusing; in or belonging to a grammatical case which expresses the direct object of transitive verbs. — *n* a word in the accusative case. — *adj* **accūsatī'val.** — *adj* **accūsatō'rial** of an accuser; (of a trial) in which the judge is not the same person as the prosecutor. — *adj* **accūs'atory** containing accusation. — *adj* **accused'.** — *n* (*sing* or *pl*) the person or persons accused. — *n* **accūs'er.** [L. *accūsāre, -ātum* — *ad*, to, *causa*, cause, partly through O.Fr. *accuser*.]

accustom *ə-kus'təm*, *vt* to make familiar by custom (with *to*); to habituate. — *adj* **accus'tomary.** — *adj* **accus'tomed** usual; frequent; habituated; in the habit. — *n* **accus'tomedness.** [O.Fr. *acostumer* — *à*, to, *costume*, *coustume*; see ety. for **custom.**]

AC/DC *ā-sē-dē'sē*, *abbrev* for alternating current/direct current. — *adj* bisexual (*slang*).

ACE *ās*, *abbrev* for: Advisory Centre for Education; Association for the Conservation of Energy.

ace *ās*, *n* a unit; the one in dice, cards, dominoes, etc.; a single point; a hole in one (see under **hole**; *golf*); a winning serve (*tennis*); a jot; a person of distinguished achievement, an expert (*colloq*). — *adj* of highest quality; outstanding. — **an ace up one's sleeve** a decisive but hidden advantage; **play one's ace** to use one's best weapon, resource, etc.; **within an ace of** within a hair's-breadth of. [Fr. *as* — L. *as*, unity.]

acedia *ə-sē'di-ə*, *n* listlessness; torpor; sloth. [Gr. *akēdiā, akēdeia* — **a-**[1] and *kēdos*, care.]

acephalous *a-*, *ä-* or *ə-sef'ə-ləs*, *adj* headless. [Gr. *akephalos* — *a-* (privative) and *kephalē*, head.]

ACER *ā'sər*, *abbrev* for Australian Council for Educational Research.

acerbic *ə-sûr'bik*, *adj* bitter and sour. — *vt* **acerbate** (*as'ər-bāt*) to embitter; to irritate. — *n* **acer'bity.** [L. *acerbus*.]

acet- *as'it-*, *a-* or *ə-set'-* or *a-sēt'-* or **aceto-** (*-ō-*), *combining form* denoting vinegar. — *n* **ac'etal** a liquid formed by oxidation of alcohol, etc. — *n* **ac'etate** a salt of acetic acid; short for **acetate rayon,** an artificial fibre made from cellulose acetate. — *adj* **acetic** (*-sēt'* or *-set'*) of, of the nature of or producing, vinegar (**acetic acid**), the sour principle in vinegar. — *n* **acetificā'tion** (*-set*). — *vt* and *vi* **acet'ify** to turn into vinegar. — *n* **ac'etone** a ketone. — *adj* **ac'etose** acetous. — *adj* **acē'tous** like, or producing, vinegar; sour. — *n* **acetyl** (*as'i-til, -tīl* or *a-sē'til*) the radical of acetic acid (**acetyl-salicylic acid** aspirin). — *n* **acetylene** (*-set'*) a gas used in welding, synthesising acetic acid, illumination, etc. [L. *acētum*, vinegar.]

acetabulum *as-et-ab'ū-ləm* or *-ēt-*, (*zool*) *n* the hollow that receives the head of the thigh-bone; the cavity that receives a leg in the body of insects; in various animals, a sucker: — *pl* **acetab'ūla.** — *adj* **acetab'ūlar.** [L. *acētābulum*, a vinegar cup.]

acetate, acetic etc., **acetone, acetyl, acetylene.** See under **acet-**.

ACGB *abbrev* for Arts Council of Great Britain.

achatina *a-kə-tē'nə* or *-tī'nə*, *n* a giant African snail. [L. *achates*, agate and sfx. *-ina*, -ine.]

ache *āk*, *n* a continued pain. — *vi* to be in or be the site of continued pain; to long (for). — *n* **ach'ing.** — *adj* **ach'y.** [The verb was properly *ake*, the noun *ache*, as in *speak*, *speech*. — O.E. *acan* (vb.), *æce* (n.).]

achene *a-kēn'*, (*bot*) *n* a dry, one-seeded fruit, formed of one carpel, as in the buttercup. — *adj* **achē'nial.** [From Gr. *a-* (privative) and *chainein*, to gape.]

Acheron *ak'ər-on*, (*Gr mythol*) *n* one of the rivers of Hades. — *adj* **Acheron'tic.** [Gr. *Acherōn*.]

achieve *ə-chēv'*, *vt* to perform; to accomplish; to win. — *adj* **achiev'able.** — *n* **achieve'ment** achieving; something achieved; an exploit; an escutcheon or armorial shield granted in memory of some achievement (*heraldry*); escutcheon, armour, etc., hung over a tomb. [Fr. *achever*, from *à chief (venir)* — L.L. *ad caput*, to a head; see **chief.**]

Achillean *ak-il-ē'ən*, *adj* like *Achilles*, the great Greek hero in the Trojan war, invulnerable except in the heel, by which his mother held him when she dipped him in the Styx. — **Achilles' heel** a person's most vulnerable point; **Achilles' tendon** the attachment of the muscles of the calf of the leg to the heel-bone (*physiol*).

achondroplasia *ak-on-drō-plā'zhi-ə*, *n* dwarfism characterised by shortness of the arms and legs. — *adj* **achondroplastic** (*-plas'tik*). [Gr. *a-* (privative) and *chondros*, cartilage, *plassein*, to make.]

achromatic *ak-rō-mat'ik*, *adj* transmitting light without much chromatic aberration; without colour. — *n* **a'chromat** an achromatic lens. — *adv* **achromat'ically.** — *vt* **achrō'matise** or **-ize** to render achromatic. — *n* **achrō'matism** the state of being achromatic. — *n* **achromatopsia** (*ə-krō-mə-top'si-ə*; Gr. *ops*, eye) total colour blindness. [Gr. *a-* (privative) and *chrōma*, *-atos*, colour.]

acicular *as-ik'ū-lər*, *adj* needle-shaped; slender and sharp-pointed. — *adj* **acic'ulate** marked as if with needle-scratches. [L. *acicula*, dimin. of *acus*, a needle.]

acid *as'id*, *adj* sharp; sour; (of soil) having an acid reaction; biting, keen (*fig*); ill-natured, morose (*fig*); pertaining to, of the nature of or having the properties of, an acid (*chem*); relating to acid house (q.v.). — *n* a substance with a sour taste; any of a class of substances which turn vegetable blues (e.g. litmus) red, and combine with bases, certain metals, etc., to form salts (*chem*); any of a class of substances that dissolve in water with the formation of hydrogen ions (*chem*); any of a class of substances that can transfer a proton to another substance, etc. (*chem*); something harsh, biting or sarcastic (*fig*); LSD or other hallucinogenic drug (*slang*). — *adj* **acid'ic.** — *adj* **acidifī'able.** — *n* **acidificā'tion.** — *vt* **acid'ify** to make acid; to convert into an acid. — *vi* to become acid: — *pr p* **acid'ifying**; *pa t* and *pa p* **acid'ified.** — *n* **acid'ity** the quality of being acid or sour. — *n* **acidō'sis** (*med*) the presence of acids in the blood beyond normal limits. — *vt* **acid'ūlate** to make slightly acid. — *adj* **acid'ūlous** slightly sour; caustic, sharp (*fig*). — **acid drop** a sweet flavoured with tartaric acid; **Acid House** or **acid house** a fashionable craze first apparent in the late 1980s involving large crowds of young people meeting in otherwise empty buildings (e.g. a warehouse) to hold **Acid House parties,** gatherings held in a hypnotic atmosphere produced by bright flashing lights and **Acid House music,** extremely loud repetitive music produced originally by sampling existing songs and always featuring strong complex percussion patterns, such gatherings often associated with the activities of drug-pushers; **acid rain** rain, hail or snow etc. containing sulphur and nitrogen compounds and other pollutants; **acid test** a test for gold by acid; a searching test (*fig*). — **put the acid on** (*colloq*; *Austr* and *NZ*) to apply pressure (on a person). [L. *acidus*, sour — *acēre*, to be sour.]

acierate *as'i-ər-āt*, *vt* to turn into steel. — *n* **ac'ierage** the covering of a metal plate with a film of iron. [Fr. *aciérer* — *acier*, steel. — L.L. *aciārium* (*ferrum*), lit. edging (iron) — L. *aciēs*, edge.]

acinus *as'i-nəs*, *n* one of the small fruits that make up an aggregate fruit like the raspberry; an aggregate fruit; a pip: — *pl* **ac'inī**. — *adj* **acinā'ceous**. — *adj* **acin'iform**. [L. *acinus*, berry, pip.]

ack-ack *ak'-ak*, *adj* anti-aircraft. [Formerly signallers' name for the letters AA.]

acknowledge *ək-nol'ij*, *vt* to admit to be or recognise as true, or genuine, or valid, or one's own; to confess; to admit awareness of; to express gratitude for or thanks to; to intimate receipt of. — *adj* **acknowl'edgeable**. — *n* **acknowl'edgment** (sometimes **acknowl'edgement**) recognition; admission; confession; thanks; an intimation of receipt. [See **knowledge**.]

acme *ak'mi*, *n* the top or highest point; the culmination or perfection in the career of anything. [Gr. *akmē* — *akē*, a point.]

acne *ak'ni*, *n* a skin disease caused by inflammation of the sebaceous follicles, as on the chin or nose. — **acne rosacea** (*rō-zā'shi-ə*) a chronic disease of the skin of the nose, cheeks and forehead, characterised by flushing and redness of the skin, pimples and pustules. — Also **rosa'cea**. [Perh. Gr. *akmē*, a point.]

acolyte *ak'ə-līt*, *n* someone in minor orders, next below subdeacon (*RC*); an inferior church officer; an attendant or assistant; a faithful follower. [Gr. *akolouthos*, an attendant — *akoloutheein*, to follow.]

aconite *ak'ə-nīt*, *n* wolfsbane or monkshood or other plant of the genus *Aconitum*; poison obtained from it, or (*poetic*) deadly poison in general (often **aconī'tum**). — *adj* **aconit'ic**. — *n* **aconitine** (*-kon'*) a poisonous alkaloid from aconite. — **winter aconite** an early-flowering plant of the buttercup family. [L. *aconītum* — Gr. *akonīton*.]

acorn *ā'körn*, *n* the fruit of the oak. — **a'corn-cup** the woody cup-shaped part of an acorn that holds the nut. [O.E. *æcern*; form influenced by confusion with **corn**[1] and perh. **oak** (Northern *aik*, O.E. *āc*).]

acoustic *ə-kōōs'tik* or **acoustical** *-əl*, *adj* of or relating to the sense of hearing or to the theory of sound; used in hearing; operated by sound vibrations; (of musical instruments) not electric. — *n* **acous'tic** acoustic properties. — *adv* **acous'tically**. — *n* **acoustician** (*-ti'shən*) an expert in the science of acoustics; a person who makes or repairs acoustic instruments, etc. — *n* **acous'tics** (as *sing*) the science of sound; (as *pl*) acoustic properties. [Gr. *akoustikos* — *akouein*, to hear.]

acquaint *ə-kwānt'*, *vt* to let know; to inform. — *n* **acquaint'ance** knowledge, esp. if it falls short of intimacy; a person (sometimes persons) known slightly. — *n* **acquaint'anceship** slight knowledge. — *adj* **acquaint'ed** personally known; having personal knowledge of (usu. with *with*). [O.Fr. *acointer* — L. *ad*, to, *cognitus*, known.]

acquiesce *ak-wi-es'*, *vi* to rest satisfied or without making opposition; to assent (with *in*). — *n* **acquiesc'ence** quiet assent or submission. — *adj* **acquiesc'ent** acquiescing. — *n* a person who acquiesces. — *adv* **acquiesc'ently**. — *adv* **acquiesc'ingly**. [L. *acquiēscēre* — *ad*, to, *quiēs*, rest.]

acquire *ə-kwīr'*, *vt* to gain, get; to achieve. — *n* **acquīrabil'ity**. — *adj* **acquīr'able** that may be acquired. — *n* **acquīr'al**. — *adj* **acquired'**. — *n* **acquire'ment** acquisition; something learned or got by effort, not a gift of nature. — *n* **acquisition** (*ak-wi-zish'ən*) the act of acquiring; that which is acquired. — *adj* **acquisitive** (*ə-kwiz'*) desiring or eager to acquire. — *n* **acquis'itiveness**. — **acquired taste** a liking that comes after some experience; a thing so liked (often ironically); **Acquired Immune Deficiency Syndrome** see **AIDS**. [L. *acquīrěre*, *-quīsītum* — *ad*, to, *quaerěre*, to seek.]

acquit *ə-kwit'*, *vt* to free; to release; to discharge, as a debt; to discharge (oneself of a duty); hence to behave, conduct (oneself); to prove (oneself); to release from an accusation: — *pr p* **acquitt'ing**; *pa t* and *pa p* **acquitt'ed**. — *n* **acquitt'al** a judicial discharge from an accusation. — *n* **acquitt'ance** a discharge from an obligation or debt; a receipt in evidence of such a discharge. [O.Fr. *aquiter* — L. *ad*, to, *quiētāre*, to quiet, settle; see **quit**.]

acre *ā'kər*, *n* a measure of land equivalent to approx. 0.4 hectares (4840 sq. yards); (in *pl*) lands, estates; (in *pl*) a very large area or amount (*colloq*). — *n* **acreage** (*ā'kər-ij*) area in acres. [O.E. *æcer*, field.]

acrid *ak'rid*, *adj* biting; pungent. — *n* **acrid'ity**. [L. *ācer*, *ācris*, sharp, keen; n. sfx. perh. as in *acid*.]

acridine *ak'ri-dēn* or **acridin** *-din*, *n* a compound found in coal-tar, a parent substance of dyes and anti-bacterial drugs. [**acrid** and n. sfx. *-ine*.]

acriflavine *ak-ri-flā'vēn* or *-vin*, or **acriflavin** *-vin*, *n* an antiseptic. [*acridine* and *flavin*(*e*).]

Acrilan® *ak'ri-lan*, *n* a type of acrylic fibre (somewhat resembling wool).

acrimony *ak'ri-mən-i*, *n* bitterness of feeling or language. — *adj* **acrimō'nious**. — *adv* **acrimō'niously**. [L. *ācrimōnia* — *ācer*, sharp.]

acro- *ak-rō-*, *combining form* denoting tip, point, summit. [Gr. *akron*, tip, end, *akros*, highest, outermost.]

acrobat *ak'rō-bat*, *n* a person who performs balancing acts on a tightrope; a tumbler; a performer of gymnastic feats. — *adj* **acrobat'ic**. — *npl* **acrobat'ics** acrobatic performances (often *fig*). — *nsing* the art of the acrobat. [Gr. *akrobatēs*, acrobat, *akrobatos*, walking on tiptoe — *akron*, point, and the root of *bainein*, to go.]

acrogen *ak'rō-jən*, *n* a non-flowering plant with the growing-point at the tip — a fern or moss. — *adj* **acrogenous** (*ə-kroj'i-nəs*). [Gr. *akron*, point, *-genēs*, born.]

acromegaly *ak-rō-meg'ə-li*, *n* a disease characterised by overgrowth, esp. of the face, hands and feet. — *adj* **acromegal'ic**. [Gr. *akron*, point, *megas*, *megalos*, great.]

acronychal *ə-kron'ik-əl*, *adj* at nightfall (of the rising or setting of stars). — *adv* **acron'ychally**. [Gr. *akronychos*, at nightfall — *akron*, point, *nychos*, *-eos*, night.]

acronym *ak'rə-nim*, *n* a word formed from, or based on, the initial letters or syllables of other words, such as *radar*. — *n* **acronymā'nia** a craze for forming acronyms. — *adj* **acronym'ic** or **acron'ymous**. [**acro-** and Gr. *onyma*, name.]

acropetal *ə-krop'i-tl*, (*bot*) *adj* in the direction of the tip of the plant. — *adv* **acrop'etally**. [Gr. *akron*, petal, L. *petěre*, to seek.]

acrophobia *ak-rō-fō'bi-ə*, *n* fear of heights. [Gr. *akron*, tip, *akros*, highest, *phobos*, fear.]

acrosome *ak'rō-sōm*, *n* a structure containing enzymes, found at the tip of the sperm, associated with the penetration process into the egg cell. [**acro-** and **-some**[2].]

acrospire *ak'rō-spīr*, (*bot*) *n* the first leaf that sprouts from a germinating seed. [M.E. *akerspire* — O.E. *æhher*, ear, **spire**[1].]

across *ə-kros'*, *prep* from side to side of; on or to the other side of; crosswise. — Also *adv*. — *adj* **across-the-board'** of wage increases, etc., applying in all cases (**across the board** *adv*). — **come across** to find or meet by chance; to hand over information, confession, money, etc., in answer to demand or inducement (*colloq*); **get** or **come across** to take effect; **get it across** to make acceptable, to bring to a successful issue; to explain; **put it across (someone)** to deceive (someone). [**a-**[1] and **cross**.]

acrostic *ə-kros'tik*, *n* a poem or puzzle in which the first (or last) letters of each line spell a word or sentence; an acronym. [Gr. *akros*, extreme, *stichos*, a line.]

acrylic *ə-kril'ik*, *n* a synthetic fibre; acrylic resin. — Also *adj*. — **acrylic acid** a very reactive acid belonging to the series of oleic acids; **acrylic resins** thermoplastic resins derived from acrylic acid used in making paints, plastics etc. [*acro(lein)* and Gr. *hȳlē*, matter.]

ACT *abbrev* for Australian Capital Territory.

act *akt*, *vi* to produce an effect; to behave oneself; to perform, as on the stage; to feign. — *vt* to perform; to imitate or play the part of. — *n* something done or doing; the process (of doing); a decree; a legislative enactment; a distinct main section of a play; an individual performance, as in a variety show. — *n* **actabil'ity**. — *n* **act'ing** action; the act or art of performing an assumed or a dramatic part; feigning. — *adj* performing some duty temporarily, or for another. — *n* **act'or**, *fem* **act'ress** a person who acts on the stage, in films etc. — **act as** to perform the duties of; **act of God** a result of natural forces, unexpected and not preventable by human foresight; **act of grace** a favour, esp. a pardon granted by a sovereign; **act of parliament** see **parliament; act on** to exert an influence on; to act in accordance with; **act out** to play as an actor; **act up** (*colloq*) to behave badly; **act up to** to come in practice up to the standard of; to fulfil; **get in on** or **get into the act** (*colloq*) to start participating in something apparently profitable already taking place in order to share in the benefits; **get one's act together** to get oneself organised (*colloq*); **put on an act** to make a pretence; to show off. [L. *āctus*, *-ūs*, an action, doing, *āctum*, a thing done, *āctor*, a doer, actor.]

act. *abbrev* for: acting; active.

ACTH *abbrev* for **adrenocorticotropic** (*ə-dren'ō-kör-ti-kō-trop-ik*) **hormone** a hormone secreted by the pituitary gland which stimulates the adrenal cortex; also produced synthetically and used as a treatment for e.g. rheumatoid arthritis and skin diseases. [**adreno-** and **cortex**, and Gr. *trophē*, food.]

actin- *ak-tin-* or **actino-** *-o-*, *combining form* denoting ray. — *n* **actinia** (*-tin'*) a sea-anemone: — *pl* **actin'iae** or **actin'ias**. — *adj* **actin'ic** of or showing actinism. — *n* **ac'tinide** or **ac'tinoid** any element of a group from atomic number 89 (actinium) upwards. — *n* **ac'tinism** the chemical action of radiant energy. — *n* **actin'ium** a radioactive metal (atomic no. 89; symbol **Ac**) found in pitchblende. — *n* **actinom'eter** an instrument for measuring the heat-intensity or the actinic effect of light rays. — *adj* **actinomor'phic** (*biol*) radially symmetrical. — *n* **ac'tinon** actinium emanation, an isotope of radon. — **actinic glass** glass that impedes actinic rays; **actinic rays** those rays (esp. ultraviolet) that have a marked chemical action. [Gr. *aktīs*, *aktīnos*, ray.]

action *ak'shən*, *n* acting; activity; behaviour; a deed; an operation; a gesture; fighting; a battle; a lawsuit, or proceedings in a court; the movement of events in a drama, novel, etc.; the mechanism, esp. of a keyboard instrument. — *adj* **ac'tionable** giving ground for a lawsuit. — *n* **ac'tionist** an activist. — **action committee** or **group** members of an organisation who are chosen to take active measures; **action painting** an American version of tachism in which paint is dripped, spattered, smeared, etc. onto the canvas; **action replay** on television, the repeating of a piece of film, e.g. the scoring of a goal in football, usu. in slow motion; **action stations** posts to be manned during or preparatory to battle (often *fig*). [Fr., — L. *āctiō*, *-ōnis*.]

active *ak'tiv*, *adj* acting; in actual operation; given to action; brisk; busy; nimble; practical (opp. to *speculative*); effective; (of a volcano) liable to erupt, not extinct; (of bacteria, etc.) potent; radioactive; of that voice in which the subject of the verb represents the doer of the action (*gram*). — *vt* **ac'tivate** to make active; to increase the energy of; to make radioactive. — *n* **activā'tion**. — *n* **ac'tivātor**. — *adv* **ac'tively**. — *n* **ac'tiveness**. — *n* **ac'tivism** a philosophy of creative will; a policy of direct vigorous (and sometimes militant) action. — *n* **ac'tivist** a believer in activism. — *n* **activ'ity** quality, state, or fact of being active; occupation, esp. recreational pursuit; (esp. in *pl*) doings. — **active immunity** immunity due to the making of antibodies within the organism; **active list** a list of full-pay officers engaged in or available for service; **active service** service in the battle area; **activity holiday** a holiday offering participation (and usu. training or coaching) in a particular occupation, esp. sport. [L. *āctīvus*.]

actor, actress. See under **act**.

ACTT *abbrev* for Association of Cinematograph Television and Allied Technicians.

ACTU *abbrev* for Australian Council of Trade Unions.

actual *ak'tū-əl* or *ak'chōō-əl*, *adj* real; existing in fact; at the time being, current. — *vt* **ac'tualise** or **-ize** to make actual; to realise in action. — *n* **actualisā'tion** or **-z-**. — *n* **ac'tualist** a person who looks to actual facts. — *n* **actuality** (*-al'i-ti*) the fact or state of being actual; realism; a newsreel or current affairs programme (also **actualités** *ak-tü-al-ē-tā*, Fr.). — *adv* **ac'tually** as a matter of fact. [Fr. *actuel* — L.L. *āctuālis*.]

actuary *ak'tū-ər-i*, *n* a person who makes the calculations connected with insurance. — *adj* **actuarial** (*-ā'ri-əl*). — *adv* **actuā'rially**. [L. *āctuārius* (*scriba*), a clerk.]

actuate *ak'tū-āt*, *vt* to put into, or incite to, action. — *vi* to act. — *n* **actūā'tion**. — *n* **ac'tūātor**. [L. *āctus*, action; see **act**.]

acuity *ə-kū'i-ti*, *n* sharpness. [L.L. *acuitās*, *-ātis* — L. *acus*, needle.]

acumen *ə-kū'men* or *ak'ū-mən*, *n* quickness of perception. — *vt* **acū'minate** to sharpen; to give a point to. — *adj* (*bot*) tapering to a point. — *n* **acūminā'tion**. [L. *acūmen*, *-inis*, a point.]

acupuncture *ak'ū-pungk-chər*, *n* the science (orig. Chinese) of puncturing the skin with needles at specified points (**ac'upoints**) in order to cure illness, relieve symptoms, or effect anaesthesia. [L. *acus*, needle, **point, puncture**.]

acute *ə-kūt'*, *adj* sharp; sharp-pointed; keen; piercing; finely discriminating; shrewd; urgently pressing; of a disease, coming to a crisis (as opp. to *chronic*). — *n* an acute accent. — *adv* **acute'ly**. — *n* **acute'ness**. — **acute accent** a mark (´) over a letter used to indicate pronunciation; **acute angle** an angle smaller than a right angle. [L. *acūtus*, past p. of *acuĕre*, to sharpen.]

ACW *abbrev* for aircraft(s)woman.

acyclic *ā-* or *a-sī'klik*, *adj* not periodic. [**a-**[1] and Gr. *kyklos*, a wheel.]

AD or **A.D.** *abbrev* for *anno domini* (L.), in the year of the Lord, now used in numbering the years since the year when Christ was thought to have been born.

ad *ad*, (*colloq*) *n* advertisement; see **advertise**.

ad *abbrev* for: after date; *ante diem* (L.), before the day.

adage *ad'ij*, *n* an old saying; a proverb. [Fr., — L. *adagium* — *ad*, to, and root of *āiō*, I say.]

adagio *ə-dä'jō* or *-jyō*, (*mus*) *adv* slowly. — *adj* slow. — *n* a slow movement: — *pl* **ada'gios**. [It., — *ad agio*, at ease.]

Adam *ad'əm*, *n* the first man, according to the book of Genesis. — *adj* applied to a style of architecture, interior decoration and furniture, designed by Robert and James Adam in the 18th century. — *n*

Ad'amite a descendant of Adam; a person who goes about naked. — **Adam's ale** water; **Adam's apple** the projection of the thyroid cartilage in front of the throat. — **not know someone from Adam** (*colloq*) not to know someone, or who someone is. [Heb. *Adām*.]

adamant *ad'əm-ənt* or *-ant*, *adj* unyielding. — *adj* **adaman'tine.** [Gr. *adamas*, *-antos*, prob. orig. steel, also diamond.]

adapt *ə-dapt'*, *vt* to make fit or suitable; to modify; to adjust. — *n* **adaptabil'ity.** — *adj* **adapt'able.** — *n* **adaptation** (*ad-əp-tā'shən*) the fact, act, process or result of adapting. — *adj* **adapt'ative.** — *adj* **adapt'ed** modified to suit; suitable. — *n* **adapt'er** or **adapt'or** someone who, or that which, adapts; an attachment or accessory enabling a piece of apparatus to be used for a purpose, or in conditions, other than that, or those, for which it was orig. intended, esp. a device that will connect two parts of different sizes, or a device that enables one to connect two electrical devices (e.g. a plug and socket) that have incompatible terminals, or that allows more than one electrical appliance to be powered from one socket. — *n* **adap'tion** adaptation. — *adj* **adapt'ive.** — *adv* **adapt'ively.** — *n* **adapt'iveness.** [Fr. *adapter* — L. *adaptāre* — *ad*, to, and *aptāre*, to fit.]

ADAS *abbrev* for Agricultural Development and Advisory Service.

ADC *abbrev* for: aide-de-camp; analog-to-digital converter.

add *ad*, *vt* to put, join, or annex (to something else); to sum up, compute the sum of; to say further. — *vi* to make an addition; to increase (with *to*); to find the total of numbers, etc. — *n* **add'er.** — *n* **addi'tion** the act of adding; a person or thing added. — *adj* **addi'tional** added. — *adv* **addi'tionally.** — *adj* **additi'tious** increasing. — *adj* **add'itive** characterised by addition; to be added. — *n* a substance added to foodstuffs or other commodities for a special purpose e.g. as a preservative. — **adding machine** an apparatus for performing basic arithmetical calculations. — **add up** to amount on adding; to be consistent; to point to a reasonable conclusion. [L. *addĕre*, *additum* — *ad*, to, *dăre*, to put.]

addax *ad'aks*, *n* a large African antelope with long slightly twisted horns. [L., from an African word.]

addend *ad'end* or *ə-dend'*, *n* a number or quantity added. [**addendum.**]

addendum *ə-den'dəm*, *n* a thing to be added, as supplementary material to a book, etc.: — *pl* **adden'da.** [L. gerundive of *addĕre*; see **add.**]

adder[1] *ad'ər*, *n* a viper (q.v.), the only venomous snake found in Britain. — **ad'der's-wort** or **add'erwort** the bistort, or snakeweed, supposed to cure snake-bite. [O.E. *nædre* (*an adder* for *a nadder*).]

adder[2]. See **add.**

addict *ə-dikt'*, *vt* (usu. in passive) to give up (to), devote, apply habitually (to). — *n* (*ad'ikt*) a slave to a habit or vice, esp. drugs. — *adj* **addict'ed** inclined or given up (to); dependent on. — *n* **addict'edness.** — *n* **addic'tion** the state of being addicted; a habit that has become impossible to break. — *adj* **addict'ive** tending to cause addiction; habit-forming. [L. *addīcĕre*, *addictum* — *ad*, to, *dīcĕre*, to declare.]

Addison's disease *ad'i-sənz diz-ēz'*, *n* a disease characterised by wasting, weakness, low blood-pressure, and pigmentation of the skin (bronzed skin) due to failure of the adrenal glands. [Dr Thomas *Addison* (1793–1860), who investigated it.]

addition, etc., **additive.** See **add.**

addle *ad'l*, *adj* bad (as an egg); empty; muddled. — *vt* and *vi* to make or become addle. — *adj* **add'led.** — *n* **add'lement.** — *adj* **add'le-brained, add'le-headed** or **add'le-pated** muddleheaded. [O.E. *adela*, mud.]

address *ə-dres'*, *vt* to apply or devote (oneself; with *to*); to apply oneself to; to direct; to aim; to speak directly to; to send; to put an indication of destination upon. — *n* act or mode of addressing; deportment; adroitness; a formal communication in writing; a speech; a place to which letters etc. may be directed; a place where a person or organisation etc. may be found; the place where a person lives; a name, label or number that identifies the location of a stored item of data, etc. (*comput*; (in *pl*) attentions of the nature of courtship. — *adj* **addressed'** aimed; directed. — *n* **addressee'** the person to whom a communication is addressed. — *n* **address'er** or **address'or.** — *n* **Addressograph**® (*ə-dres'ō-gräf*) a machine for printing addresses automatically, on envelopes, etc. — **address book** a notebook, usu. with alphabetical thumb-index, in which names and addresses can be entered. [Fr. *adresser* — L.L. *addirectiare* — L. *ad*, to, *directum*, straight; see **dress, direct.**]

adduce *ə-dūs'*, *vt* to bring forward in discussion, to cite or quote. — *adj* **addūc'ent** drawing inward or together, as a muscle does. — *n* **addūc'er.** — *adj* **addūc'ible.** — *vt* **adduct** (*ə-dukt'*) to draw inward or together. — *n* **adduc'tion** the act of adducing or of adducting. — *adj* **adduc'tive** tending to bring forward. — *n* **adduc'tor** an adducent muscle. [L. *addūcĕre*, *adductum* — *ad*, to, and *dūcĕre*, to bring.]

à demi *a də-mē*, (Fr.) by halves, half.

aden- *ad-ən-*, *combining form* denoting gland. — *n* **adenitis** (*ad-ən-ī'tis*) inflammation of glands. — *adj* **ad'enoid** glandlike; glandular. — *n* (usu. in *pl*) enlargement of glandular tissue at the back of the nose. — *adj* **adenoid'al** of adenoids; affected by, or as if by, adenoids (e.g. of a voice). — *n* **adenō'ma** a benign tumour like, or originating in, a gland: — *pl* **adenō'mata** or **adenō'mas.** — *adj* **adenō'matous.** [Gr. *adēn*, gland.]

adept *ad'ept*, *ə-dept'* or *a-dept'*, *adj* completely skilled (at or in). — *n* an expert. — *n* **adept'ness.** [L. *adeptus* (*artem*), having attained (an art).]

adequate *ad'i-kwit* or *-kwāt*, *adj* sufficient; competent. — *adv* **ad'equately.** — *n* **ad'equateness.** — *n* **ad'equacy** (*-kwə-si*). [L. *adaequātus*, made equal — *ad*, to, and *aequus*, equal.]

à deux *a dø*, (Fr.) of two, between two, two-handed; **à deux mains** (*mɛ̃*) with both hands; for two hands.

ad fin. *abbrev* for *ad finem* (L.), at, towards, or to, the end.

adharma *ə-där'mä* or *ə-dûr'mə*, *n* unrighteousness (opp. of **dharma**). [Sans.]

adhere *əd-* or *ad-hēr'*, *vi* to stick (to); to remain fixed or attached (to); to remain faithful (as to a party, a leader, a doctrine); to agree. — *n* **adhēr'ence** state of adhering. — *adj* **adhēr'ent** sticking. — *n* a person who adheres; a follower; a partisan. — *n* **adhēr'er.** [L. *ad*, to, *haerēre*, *haesum*, to stick.]

adhesion *əd-hē'zhən*, *n* the act of adhering or sticking; strong, firm contact; reunion of separated surfaces (*surg*); abnormal union of parts that have been inflamed (*pathol*); (often in *pl*) a band of fibrous tissue joining such parts. — *adj* **adhē'sive** (*-siv* or *-ziv*) sticky; apt to adhere. — *n* a substance used for sticking things together e.g. glue. — *adv* **adhē'sively.** — *n* **adhē'siveness.** [See **adhere.**]

adhibit *əd-hib'it*, *vt* to apply; to attach; to admit; to administer. — *n* **adhibi'tion.** [L. *adhibēre*, *-itum* — *ad*, to, *habēre*, to hold.]

ad hoc *ad hok*, (L.) for this special purpose (used as *adj* and *adv*). — **ad hocery** (*hok'ə-ri*; *facetious*) the use of ad hoc measures — improvisation or pragmatism.

ad hominem *ad hom'in-em*, (L.) to the man, addressed to the feelings or prejudices of the hearer or reader; dealing with an opponent by attacking their character instead of answering their argument.

ADI *abbrev* for approved driving instructor.

adiabatic *ad-i-ə-bat'ik*, *adj* without transference of heat. — *adv* **adiabat'ically**. [**a-**[1] and Gr. *dia*, through, *batos*, passable.]

adiaphoron *ad-i-af'ə-ron*, *n* (in theology and ethics) any tenet or usage considered non-essential: — *pl* **adiaph'ora**. — *n* **adiaph'orism**. — *n* **adiaph'orist**. — *adj* **adiaph'orous**. [Gr. — *a-* (privative) and *diaphoros*, differing — *dia*, apart, *pherein*, to carry.]

adieu *ə-dū*, *interj* (I commend you) to God; farewell, good-bye. — *n* a farewell: — *pl* **adieus** or **adieux** (*ə-dūz'*). [Fr. *à Dieu*, to God.]

ad infinitum *ad in-fin-ī't'əm* or *-ēt'ŏŏm*, (L.) to infinity; for ever. — *abbrev* **ad inf.**

ad init. *abbrev* for *ad initium* (L.), at or to the beginning.

ad interim *ad in'tər-im*, (L.L.) for the meantime. — *abbrev* **ad int.**

adiós *ad-ē-os'*, *interj* good-bye. [Sp., lit. to God.]

adipocere *ad'i-pō-sēr* or *-sēr'*, *n* a fatty, waxy substance resulting from the decomposition of animal bodies in moist places or under water, but not exposed to air. [L. *adeps*, *adipis*, soft fat, and *cēra*, wax.]

adipose *ad'i-pōs*, *adj* fatty. — *n* **adiposity** (*-pos'i-ti*). — **adipose tissue** the structure in the animal body which contains the fat. [L. *adeps*, *adipis*, soft fat.]

adit *ad'it*, *n* an opening or passage, esp. into a mine. [L. *adĭtus* — *ad*, to, *ire*, *ĭtum*, to go.]

adj. *abbrev* for: adjective; adjourned; adjustment.

adjacent *ə-jā'sənt*, *adj* lying near or next (to). — *n* **adjā'cency**. — *adv* **adjā'cently**. [L. *ad*, to, *jacēns*, *-entis*, pres. p. of *jacēre*, to lie.]

adjective *aj'ik-tiv*, *n* a word added to a noun to qualify it. — *adj* added; (of dyes) requiring a mordant. — *adj* **adjectival** (*-tīv'l*), — *adv* **adjectī'vally**. — *adv* **ad'jectively**. [L. *adjectīvum* (*nōmen*), added (word) — *adjicĕre*, *-jectum*, to add.]

adjoin *ə-join'*, *vt* to join on; to lie next to. — *vi* to be in contact. — *adj* **adjoin'ing**. [L. *adjungĕre* — *ad*, to, *jungĕre*, to join.]

adjourn *ə-jûrn'*, *vt* to put off to another day; to postpone; to discontinue (a meeting) in order to reconstitute it at another time or place. — *vi* to suspend proceedings and disperse. — *n* **adjourn'ment**. [O.Fr. *ajorner* — L.L. *adiurnāre* — L. *ad-* to, *diurnus*, daily; cf. **journal**[1].]

Adjt *abbrev* for Adjutant.

Adjt-Gen. *abbrev* for Adjutant-General.

adjudge *ə-juj'*, *vt* to decide; to assign; to award. — *n* **adjudg'ment** (sometimes **adjudge'ment**). [O.Fr. *ajuger* — L. *adjūdicāre*; cf. **judge**.]

adjudicate *ə-jŏŏ'di-kāt*, *vt* to determine judicially; to pronounce; to award. — *vi* to pronounce judgment; to act as judge in a competition between amateurs in one of the arts, e.g. music. — *n* **adjudica'tion** act or process of adjudicating. — *n* **adju'dicātor**. [L. *adjūdicāre*, *-ātum*.]

adjunct *aj'ungkt* or *aj'ungt*, *adj* joined or added. — *n* a thing or person joined or added, but subordinate or not essentially a part; any word or clause enlarging the subject or predicate (*gram*). — *n* **adjunction** (*ə-jungk'shən*). — *adj* **adjunct'ive**. — *adv* **adjunct'ively**. — *adv* **adjunct'ly**. [L. *adjunctus* past p. of *adjungĕre*, to join.]

adjure *ə-jŏŏr'*, *vt* to charge on oath; to command, request solemnly. — *n* **adjurā'tion** (*aj-*). — *adj* **adjur'atory**. — *adj* **adjur'ing**. [L. *adjūrāre* — *ad*, to, *jūrāre*, *-ātum*, to swear.]

adjust *ə-just'*, *vt* to regulate; to adapt; to alter; to settle. — *vi* to adapt oneself (to). — *adj* **adjust'able**. — *n* **adjust'er** someone who or something that adjusts; see under **average** and **loss**. — *n* **adjust'ment**. — *n* **adjust'or** an organ or faculty that determines behaviour in response to stimuli. [L.L. *adjuxtāre*, to put side by side — L. *juxtā*, near; confused by association with *jūstus*, right.]

adjutant *aj'ŏŏ-tənt*, *n* an officer specially appointed to assist a commanding officer; (usu. **adjutant bird**) a large Indian stork or crane. — *n* **ad'jutancy** the office of an adjutant; assistance. — **adjutant-gen'eral** head of a department of the general staff; the executive officer of a general: — *pl* **adjutants-gen'eral**. [L. *adjūtāns*, *-antis*, pres. p. of *adjūtāre*, frequentative of *adjŭvāre* — *ad*, to, *jŭvāre*, to assist.]

adjuvant *aj'ŏŏ-vənt*, *adj* helping. — *n* a help. — *n* **ad'juvancy**. [Fr. — L. *ad*, to, *jŭvāre*, to help.]

ad-lib *ad-lib'*, *adv* spontaneously, freely. — *adj* impromptu, extemporised. — *vt* and *vi* to extemporise, to speak without preparation, esp. to fill up time. — *n* an improvised speech; a spontaneous remark (often humorous). — *n* **ad-libb'er**. — *n* **ad-libb'ing**. [L. *ad libitem*, at pleasure.]

ad loc. *abbrev* for *ad locum* (L.), at the place.

Adm. *abbrev* for Admiral.

ad-man or **adman** *ad'man*, *n* a man who works in advertising. [**ad** (for advertisement) and **man**.]

admin. See under **administer**.

administer *əd-min'is-tər*, *vt* to govern; to manage, to control as a manager, steward, substitute, or executor; to dispense (justice, rites); to supervise the swearing (of an oath); to give (medicine, treatment). — *vi* to minister. — *adj* **admin'istrable**. — *adj* and *n* **admin'istrant**. — *vt* **admin'istrate** to administer. — *n* **administrā'tion** (*colloq* shortening **ad'min**) the act of administering; management; dispensation of sacraments; the government. — *adj* **admin'istrative** concerned with administration. — *n* **admin'istrātor** a person who manages or directs; the person to whom is committed the administration or distribution of the personal estate of a deceased person, in default of an executor; a person empowered to act for someone legally incapable of acting for themselves (*Scots law*): — *fem* **admin'istrātrix**. — *n* **admin'istrātorship**. [L. *administrāre*, *-ātum* — *ad*, to, *ministrāre*, to minister.]

admirable, etc. See **admire**.

admiral *ad'mər-əl*, *n* the chief commander of a navy; a naval officer ranking with a general in the army (**admiral of the fleet** ranking with field-marshal); an admiral's flagship; the chief ship in a fleet of merchantmen or fishing boats; a butterfly of certain kinds (see **red**, **white**). — *n* **ad'miralship**. — *n* **Ad'miralty** the board administering the Royal Navy (since 1964 under the British Ministry of Defence); the building where it transacts business. [O.Fr. *a(d)miral* — Ar. *amīr-al-bahr*, a lord of the sea, confused with L. *admīrābilis*.]

admire *əd-mīr'*, *vt* to have (or express) a high opinion of. — *adj* **admirable** (*ad'mir-əb-əl*) worthy of being admired. — *n* **ad'mirableness**. — *adv* **ad'mirably**. — *n* **admirā'tion** the act of admiring; wonder, together with esteem, love, or veneration. — *adj* **ad'mirātive**. — *n* **admīr'er** a person who admires; a lover. — *adv* **admīr'ingly**. [Fr. *admirer* — L. *ad*, at, *mīrāri*, to wonder.]

admissible, etc. See **admit**.

admit *əd-mit'*, *vt* to allow to enter (with *into* or *to*); to let in; to concede; to acknowledge; to confess; to be capable of (also *vi* with *of*): — *pr p* **admitt'ing**; *pa p* **admitt'ed**. — *n* **admissibil'ity**. — *adj* **admiss'ible** that may be admitted or allowed (generally, or specially as legal proof). — *n* **admission** (*-mish'ən*) the act of admitting; anything admitted or conceded; permission to enter; the price charged for entry. — *adj* **admiss'ive**. — *adj* **admitt'able** that may be admitted. — *n* **admitt'ance** admission. — *adj* **admitt'ed** acknowledged, conceded; (of a law clerk) qualified to practise as a solicitor, having been admitted to the Law Society's roll of solicitors. — *adv* **admitt'edly**. [Partly through Fr., — L. *admittĕre*, *-missum* — *ad*, to, *mittĕre*, *missum*, to send.]

admix *ad-* or *ad-miks'*, *vt* to mix with something else. — *n* **admix'ture** the action of mixing; what is added to the chief ingredient of a mixture. [L. *ad*, to, and **mix.**]

admonish *əd-mon'ish*, *vt* to warn; to reprove mildly. — *n* **admon'ishment** admonition. [O.Fr. *amonester* — L.L. *admonestāre* — L. *admonere* — *ad*, to, *monēre*, to warn.]

admonition *ad-mon-ish'ən* or *ad-mən-ish'ən*, *n* reproof; advice; warning. — *adj* **admonitive** (*ad-mon'*) or **admon'itory** containing admonition. — *n* **admon'itor.** [L. *admonitiō*, *-ōnis*; cf. **admonish.**]

ADN *abbrev* for People's Democratic Republic of Yemen (I.V.R.).

ad nauseam *ad nö'zi-am*, (L.) to the point of producing disgust.

ado *ə-doo'*, *n* a to-do; bustle; trouble; difficulty; stir or fuss: — *pl* **ados'**. [*at do*, Northern English infin. with **at** instead of **to**, borrowed from Scand.]

adobe *ə-dō'bi*, *n* a sun-dried brick; a house made of such bricks; (also **adobe clay**) a name for any kind of mud which, when mixed with straw, can be sun-dried into bricks. — Also *adj*. [Sp., — *adobar*, to plaster.]

adolescent *ad-ə-les'ənt*, *adj* growing from childhood to maturity; between puberty and full maturity; belonging to or typical of this state; immature. — *n* a young person between childhood and adulthood. — *n* **adolesc'ence** the state or time of being adolescent. [L. *adolēscēns*, *-entis*, pres. p. of *adolēscere*, to grow up.]

Adonis *ə-dō'nis*, *n* a particularly handsome youth or young man; a beau or dandy; the young man loved by Aphrodite (*Gr mythol*). [Gr. *Adōnis* — Phoenician *adōn*, lord.]

adopt *ə-dopt'*, *vt* to take voluntarily as one's own child, with the rights of one's own child; to take into any relationship; to take as one's own; to take up; to take over; to take (a precaution, etc.); to choose formally (e.g. a candidate); to endorse or approve (e.g. a resolution, minutes). — *adj* **adopt'ed** taken by adoption. — *n* **adopt'er.** — *n* **adop'tianist** or **adop'tionist.** — *n* **adop'tion.** — *adj* **adopt'ive** that adopts or is adopted. [L. *adoptāre* — *ad*, to, *optāre*, to choose.]

adore *ə-dör'*, *vt* to worship; to love or revere intensely. — *adj* **ador'able.** — *n* **ador'ableness.** — *adv* **ador'ably.** — *n* **adorā'tion.** — *n* **ador'er.** — *adv* **ador'ingly.** [L. *ad*, to, *ōrāre*, to pray.]

adorn *ə-dörn'*, *vt* to deck or dress; to embellish. — *n* **adorn'ment** ornament; decoration. [O.Fr. *äorner*, *adorner* — L. *adōrnāre* — *ad*, to, *ōrnāre*, to furnish.]

ADP (*comput*) *abbrev* for automatic data processing.

ad referendum *ad ref-ər-en'dum* or *-doom*, (L.) to be further considered.

ad rem *ad rem* (L.) to the point; to the purpose.

adren- *ə-dren-* or *ə-drēn-*, also **adreno-** *ə-dren-ō-* or *ə-drēn-ō-*, *combining form* denoting: adrenal; adrenal glands; adrenaline. — *adj* **adrenal** (*ə-drē'nəl*) beside the kidneys; of or relating to the adrenal glands. — *n* an adrenal gland. — *n* **adrenaline** or **adrenalin** (*ə-dren'ə-lin*) a hormone secreted by the adrenal glands that causes constriction of the arteries, so increasing blood pressure and stimulating the heart muscle; also produced synthetically (as **Adrenalin®**) for this property. — **adrenocorticotropic hormone** see **ACTH**. — **adrenal glands** two small ductless glands over the kidneys which secrete adrenaline and steroids. [L. *ad*, to, *rēnēs*, kidneys.]

adrift *ə-drift'*, *adj* or *adv* drifting; loose from moorings; left to one's own resources, without help, guidance, or contacts; cut loose; off course, inaccurate (*colloq*). [**a-**[1] and **drift.**]

adroit *ə-droit'*, *adj* dexterous; skilful; ingenious. — *adv* **adroit'ly.** — *n* **adroit'ness.** [Fr. *à droit*, according to right — L. *directus*, straight; see ety. for **direct.**]

adsorb *ad-sörb'*, *vt* of a solid or a liquid, to accumulate on its surface a thin film of a gas or liquid that is in contact with it (cf. **absorb**). — *n* **adsorb'ate** the vapour or liquid adsorbed. — *n* **adsorb'ent** a solid (as charcoal) that adsorbs a gas, etc. in contact with it. — *n* **adsorp'tion.** [L. *ad*, to, *sorbēre*, to suck in.]

adsuki bean *ad-soo'ki bēn*. Same as **adzuki bean.**

ad summum *ad sum'um* or *ad soom'oom*, (L.) to the highest point.

ADT (*NAm*) *abbrev* for Atlantic Daylight Time.

aduki bean *a-doo'ki bēn*. Same as **adzuki bean.**

adulate *ad'ū-lāt*, *vt* to fawn upon, to flatter; to praise excessively. — *n* **adūlā'tion.** — *n* **ad'ūlātor.** — *adj* **ad'ūlatory.** [L. *adūlārī*, *adūlātus*, to fawn upon.]

adult *ad'ult* or *ə-dult'*, *adj* grown-up; mature; of or for adults; suitable for the mature person only, esp. of pornographic material. — *n* a grown-up person, animal or plant. — *n* **ad'ulthood.** [L. *adultus*, past p. of *adolēscere*, to grow up; see **adolescent.**]

adulterate *ə-dult'ər-āt*, *vt* to debase or falsify, by mixing with something inferior or spurious. — *adj* defiled by adultery; spurious; corrupted by base elements. — *n* **adult'erant** that with which anything is adulterated. — *n* **adulterā'tion** the act of adulterating; the state of being adulterated. — *n* **adult'erātor** a person who adulterates a commodity. [L. *adulterāre*, *-ātum*, prob. from *ad*, to, and *alter*, another.]

adulterer *ə-dult'ər-ər*, *fem* **adult'eress**, *n* a person guilty of adultery. — *adj* **adult'erous** pertaining to, of the nature of or guilty of, adultery. — *adv* **adult'erously.** — *n* **adult'ery** voluntary sexual intercourse between a married person and someone who is not their legal partner; lack of chastity generally (*Bible*); applied esp. by theologians to marriages disapproved of, expressing reproach or scorn; image-worship. [**adulterate.**]

adumbrate *ad'um-brāt*, *vt* to give a faint shadow of; to outline faintly; to foreshadow; to overshadow. — *n* **adumbrā'tion.** [L. *adumbrāre*, *-ātus* — *ad*, to, *umbra*, a shadow.]

adv. *abbrev* for: advent; adverb; *adversus* (L.), against; advisory; advocate.

ad valorem *ad val-ör'əm*, (L.) according, or in proportion, to value (*abbrev* **ad val.**).

advance *əd-väns'*, *vt* to put forward; to promote; to further; to raise in price; to supply beforehand; to pay before due time; to lend, esp. on security. — *vi* to move or go forward; to approach esp. aggressively (with *on*); to make progress; to rise in rank or in value. — *n* a forward move; progress; an increase; a rise in price, value or wages; payment beforehand; a loan; an approach, overture, move towards agreement, favour, etc. — *adj* forward (of position); made, given, etc., ahead of time. — *adj* **advanced'** at, or appropriate to, a far-on stage (of education, thought, emancipation, life, etc.). — *n* **advance'ment** promotion; furthering; payment in advance. — **advanced level** see **A level; advanced gas-cooled reactor** (*abbrev* **AGR**) a nuclear reactor in which carbon dioxide is used as a coolant; **advance factory** a factory built to encourage development, in the belief that a firm will take it over; **advance** (or **advanced**) **guard** a guard or party in front of the main body. — **in advance** beforehand; in front. [O.Fr. *avancer* — L.L. *abante* (Fr. *avant*) — L. *ab ante*, from before; the prefix refashioned later as if from *ad*.]

advantage *əd-vänt'ij*, *n* superiority over another; a favourable condition or circumstance; gain or benefit; the first point after deuce (*tennis*). — *vt* and *vi* to benefit or profit. — *adj* **advantageous** (*ad-vən-tā'jəs*) of advantage; useful (with *to* and *for*). — *adv* **advantā'geously.** — *n* **advantā'geousness.** — **advantage rule** in games, a rule under which an infringement and its penalty are overlooked when this is to the advantage of the non-offending side. —

advantage server (or **advantage striker**) the server (or the striker) has gained the first point after deuce; **have the advantage of** to recognise without being recognised; **take advantage of** to avail oneself of; to make undue use of an advantage over; **to advantage** so that the merits are readily perceived. [Fr. *avantage* — *avant*, before; see **advance**.]

advection *ad-vek'shən*, (*meteorol*) *n* movement horizontally of air or atmospheric conditions. [L. *advectio* — *ad*, to, *vehĕre*, to carry.]

advent *ad'vənt* or *-vent*, *n* a coming or arrival; (with *cap*) the first or the second coming of Christ; the period immediately before the Christian festival of the Nativity, including four Sundays. — *n* **Ad'ventist** a person who expects an imminent second coming of Christ; a millenarian who expects a golden age after the second coming of Christ. [L. *advenire*, *adventum*, to approach, happen — *ad*, to, *venire*, to come; *adventus*, arrival.]

adventitious *ad-vən-tish'əs*, *adj* accidental; additional; foreign; appearing casually; developed out of the usual order or place. — *adv* **adventi'tiously**. [L. *adventicius*, extraneous.]

adventure *əd-ven'chər*, *n* a remarkable incident; an enterprise; a commercial speculation; an exciting experience; the spirit of enterprise. — *n* **adven'turer** a person who engages in hazardous enterprises; a soldier of fortune, or speculator; someone who pushes their fortune, esp. by unscrupulous means: — *fem* **adven'turess** (chiefly in bad sense). — *adj* **adven'turesome** adventurous. — *n* **adven'turism** the practice of engaging in hazardous and ill-considered enterprises; in foreign policy, opportunism employed in the service of expansionism. — *n* and *adj* **adven'turist**. — *adj* **adventuris'tic**. — *adj* **adven'turous** enterprising; ready to incur risk. — *adv* **adven'turously**. — *n* **adven'turousness**. — **adventure playground** a playground with objects that can be used by children for building, to climb on, etc. [L. *adventūrus*, fut. p. of *advenire*, to approach, happen — *ad*, to, *venire*, to come; partly through Fr.]

adverb *ad'vûrb*, *n* a word added to a verb, adjective, or other adverb to express some modification of the meaning or an accompanying circumstance. — *adj* **adverb'ial** (*əd-*). — *adv* **adverb'ially**. [L. *adverbium* — *ad*, to, *verbum*, a word.]

ad verbum *ad vûr'bəm*, (L.) to a word; word for word.

adversarial *ad-vər-sār'i-əl*, *adj* combative; antagonistic; hostile, esp. on party lines in politics. [Ety. as for **adversary**.]

adversary *ad'vər-sər-i*, *n* an opponent. — *adj* **adversative** (*əd-vûrs'*) denoting opposition, inconsistency, or variety. — *adj* **ad'verse** (*-vûrs*) contrary (with *to*); opposed; unfavourable; facing the main axis (*bot*). — *adv* **ad'versely**. — *n* **ad'verseness**. — *n* **advers'ity** adverse circumstances; misfortune. [L. *adversus* — *ad*, to, and *vertĕre*, *versum*, to turn.]

advert[1] *ad-vûrt'*, *vi* (with *to*) to turn one's attention; to refer. — *n* **advert'ence** or **advert'ency** attention; heedfulness; regard. — *adj* **advert'ent** attentive; heedful. — *adv* **advert'ently**. [L. *advertĕre* — *ad*, to, *vertĕre*, to turn.]

advert[2]. See under **advertise**.

advertise or (esp. US) **-ize** *ad'vər-tīz* or *-tīz'*, to give notice of; to give public information about merits claimed for; to draw attention to; to offer for sale by public notice, printed or broadcast. — *vi* to issue advertisements; to ask (for) by means of public notice, e.g. in a newspaper. — *n* **advertisement** (*əd-vûr'tis-mənt*), or (esp. US) **-z-** (*-tiz-* or *ad-vûr-tīz'mənt*) the act of advertising; a public notice (*colloq abbrev* **ad** or **ad'vert**); a short performance recorded for radio, TV etc. to advertise goods or services (*colloq abbrev* **ad** or **ad'vert**); any device for obtaining public favour or notoriety. — *n* **ad'vertīser**. — *n* **ad'vertīsing**. [Fr. *avertir*, *avertiss-* — L. *advertĕre*; see **advert**[1].]

advertorial *ad-vər-tö'ri-əl* (orig. *US*) *n* an advertisement presented as if it is editorial material. — Also *adj*. [*advert*isement and edit*orial*.]

advice *əd-vīs'*, *n* counsel; information (usu. in *pl*); formal official intelligence about anything; specially skilled opinion, as of a physician or lawyer. [O.Fr. *advis* — L. *ad visum*, according to what is seen or seems best.]

advise *əd-vīz'*, *vt* to counsel; to recommend; to inform; to announce. — *vi* to consult (with). — *n* **advīsabil'ity**. — *adj* **advīs'able** to be recommended; expedient; open to advice. — *n* **advīs'ableness**. — *adv* **advīs'ably**. — *adj* **advīsed'** having duly considered; considered; deliberate; apprised; amenable to advice. — *adv* **advīs'edly** (*-id-li*) after consideration; intentionally; wisely, prudently. — *n* **advīs'edness** deliberate consideration; prudent procedure. — *n* **advīs'er** or **advīs'or** a person who advises; a teacher appointed by a British education authority to advise on the teaching and development of his or her subject. — *n* **advīs'ership**. — *n* **advīs'orate** the body of advisers appointed by an education authority. — *adj* **advīs'ory** having the attribute or function of advising. [O.Fr. *aviser*, and L.L. *advisāre*; cf. **advice**.]

advocaat *ad'vō-kät*, *n* a liqueur containing raw eggs and flavourings; a medicinal drink of eggs, rum and lemon-juice. [Du. *advokaatenborrel*, advocate's dram, as a clearer of the throat.]

advocate *ad'və-kit* or *ad'və-kāt*, *n* an intercessor or defender; a person who pleads the cause of another; a person who is qualified to plead before the higher courts of law — the ordinary name in Scotland and some other countries, corresponding to barrister in England; a person who recommends or urges something e.g. a certain reform, method, etc. — *vt* (*ad'və-kāt*) to plead in favour of; to recommend. — Also *vi* (with *for*). — *n* **ad'vocacy** (*-kə-si*) the function of an advocate; a pleading for; defence. — *n* **advocā'tion**. — *n* **ad'vocātor**. — *adj* **ad'vocātory**. — **Lord Advocate** the principal law-officer of the crown and public prosecutor of crimes for Scotland. [O.Fr. *avocat* and L. *advocātus* — *advocāre*, *-ātum*, to call in — *ad*, to, *vocāre*, to call.]

advt *abbrev* for advertisement.

adze *adz*, *n* a cutting tool with an arched blade which is set at right angles to the handle. [O.E. *adesa*.]

adzuki bean *ad-zōō'ki bēn*, *n* a type of kidney bean grown esp. in China and Japan. [Jap. *azuki*.]

ae. or **aet.** *abbrev* for *aetatis* (L.), of his or her age, aged (so many years).

AEA *abbrev* for: Air Efficiency Award; Atomic Energy Authority.

AEB *abbrev* for Associated Examining Board.

AEC (*US*) *abbrev* for Atomic Energy Commission.

aecidium *ə-sid'i-əm* or **aecium** *ē'si-əm*, (*bot*) *n* a cup-shaped fructification in rust fungi: — *pl* **aecid'ia** or **aec'ia**. — *n* **aecid'iospore** or **aec'iospore** spore produced in it. [Gr. (dimin. of) *aikiā*, injury.]

aedes *ā-ē'dēz*, *n* a member of the **Aedes** genus of mosquitoes including *Aedes aegypti*, the species that carries yellow fever and dengue fever. [Gr. *aedes*, distasteful.]

aegis *ē'jis*, *n* protection; patronage. [Gr. *aigis* (in mythology, a shield belonging to Zeus, or to Pallas).]

aegrotat *ē-grō'tat* or *ē'-grō-tat*, *n* in universities, a medical certificate of illness, or a degree granted on it. [L. *aegrōtat*, is sick, 3rd pers. sing. pres. indic. of *aegrōtāre* — *aeger*, sick.]

aeolian *ē-ō'li-ən*, *adj* pertaining to, acted on by, or due to the agency of, the wind; aerial. — **aeolian** (or **Aeolian**) **harp** a sound-box with strings tuned in unison, sounding harmonics in a current of air; **aeolian rocks** (*geol*) rocks deposited by wind, as desert sands. [L. *Aeolus* — Gr. *Aiolos*, god of the winds.]

aeolotropy *ē-əl-ot'rə-pi, n* variation in physical properties according to direction. — *adj* **aeolotrop'ic.** [Gr. *aiolos*, changeful, *tropē*, a turn.]

aeon or **eon** *ē'on, n* a vast age; eternity; the largest, or a very large division of geological time. — *adj* **aeō'nian** eternal. [L. *aeon* — Gr. *aiōn*.]

Aepyornis *ē-pi-ör'nis, n* a gigantic Recent fossil wingless bird of Madagascar. [Gr. *aipys*, tall, and *ornis*, bird.]

aerate *ā'ər-āt, vt* to put air into; to charge with air or with carbon dioxide or other gas (as in the production of **aerated waters**); to excite, perturb (*colloq*). — *n* **aerā'tion** exposure to the action of air; mixing or saturating with air or other gas; oxygenation of the blood by respiration. — *n* **ā'erātor** an apparatus for the purpose of aeration. — **aerated concrete** lightweight concrete made by a process which traps gas bubbles in the mix. [L. *āēr*, air.]

AERE *abbrev* for Atomic Energy Research Establishment.

aerial *ā'ri-əl, adj* of, in or belonging to the air; airy; unreal; lofty; atmospheric; elevated; performed high above the ground, e.g. *aerial acrobatics*; connected with aircraft, e.g. used in or against, aircraft; using aircraft (e.g. *aerial support, aerial reconnaissance, aerial warfare*); carried out from aircraft; growing in air (*biol*). — *n* a wire or rod, etc. exposed to receive or emit electromagnetic waves; an antenna. — *n* **aer'ialist** a person who performs on the high wire or trapeze. — n **aeriality** (*-al'i-ti*). — *adv* **aer'ially.** — **aerial railway** or **ropeway** such a system for overhead conveyance. [L. *āërius* — *āēr*, air.]

aerie. Same as **eyrie.**

aeriform *ā'r-i-förm, adj* gaseous; unreal. [L. *āēr*, air, and *fōrma*, form.]

aero- *ā'ər-ō-* or *ār-ō-, combining form* signifying air. — *nsing* **aerobat'ics** the art of performing stunts in the air. — *npl* aerial acrobatics. — *n* **a'erobe** an organism that requires free oxygen for respiration. — *adj* **aerobic** (*-ōb'* or *-ob'*) requiring free oxygen for respiration; effected by aerobes, as in a biochemical change; involving the activity of aerobes; of, for or relating to, aerobics. — *adv* **aerob'ically.** — *nsing* **aerob'ics** exercising by means of such rhythmic activities as walking, swimming or cycling, etc., in order to improve physical fitness through increased oxygen consumption; a system intended to increase fitness and improve body-shape, consisting of fast, repeated and strenuous gymnastic exercises (also **Aerobics®**). — *n* **aerobī'ont** an aerobe. — *n* **a'erobus** an airbus; a passenger helicopter. — *n* **a'erodrome** an area, with its buildings, etc., used for the take-off and landing of aircraft. — *adj* **aerodynam'ic** or **aerodynam'ical.** — *adv* **aerodynam'ically.** — *nsing* **aerodynam'ics** the dynamics of gases. — *n* **aeroem'bolism** an airman's condition similar to caisson disease, caused by rapid ascent to high altitudes. — *n* **a'ero-engine** an aircraft engine. — *n* **a'erofoil** a body (e.g. wing, tail plane) shaped so as to produce an aerodynamic reaction (lift) normal to its direction of motion, for a small resistance (drag) in that plane. — *n* **a'erogram, a'erogramme** or **aér'ogramme** an air letter; a sheet of thin paper, with postage stamp imprinted, to be folded and sent by airmail at a special low rate. — *n* **a'erolite** or **a'erolith** a meteoric stone or meteorite. — *adj* **aerolit'ic.** — *adj* **aerolog'ical.** — *n* **aerol'ogist.** — *n* **aerol'ogy** the branch of science that deals with the atmosphere. — *n* **a'eronaut** (Gr. *nautēs*, a sailor) a balloonist or airman. — *adj* **aeronaut'ic** or **aeronaut'ical.** — *nsing* **aeronaut'ics** the science or art of aerial navigation. — *n* **aeron'omist.** — *n* **aeron'omy** the science of the earth's atmosphere. — *adj* **aerophob'ic** (or *-fōb'*). — *n* **a'erophyte** an epiphyte (Gr. *phyton*, a plant); **a'eroplane** any heavier-than-air power-driven flying-machine, with fixed wings; a small plane for aerostatic experiments (see **plane²**). — *n* **a'erosol** a colloidal system, such as a mist or a fog, in which the dispersion medium is a gas; a liquid, e.g. insecticide, in a container under pressure; the container. — *n* **a'erospace** the earth's atmosphere together with space beyond; the branch of technology or of industry concerned with the flight of spacecraft through this. — *adj* to do with, or capable of operating in, air and/or space. [Gr. *āēr*, air.]

Aeschna *esk'nə, n* a genus of large usu. colourful dragonflies.

Aesculapian *ēs-kū-lā'pi-ən*, or *es-, adj* to do with or relating to the art of healing. [L. *Aesculāpius*, Gr. *Asklēpios*, god of healing.]

aesthesia or in U.S. **esthesia** *es-thēz'i-ə* or *ēs-*, also **aesthēsis** *es-* or *ēs-thē'sis, n* feeling; sensitivity. — *n* **aesthēs'iogen** something producing sensation, esp. a stimulus or suggestion producing a sensory effect on a subject under hypnosis. — *adj* **aesthēsiogen'ic.** [Gr. *aisthanesthai*, to feel or perceive.]

aesthete *es'thēt* or *ēs', n* a professed disciple of aestheticism; a person who affects an extravagant love of art. — *adj* **aesthetic** (*es-thet'ik, is-* or *ēs-*) orig. relating to perception by the senses; generally relating to possessing, or pretending to possess a sense of beauty; artistic or affecting to be artistic. — *adj* **aesthet'ical** to do with or relating to aesthetics. — *adv* **aesthet'ically.** — *n* **aesthetician** (*-tish'ən*) someone devoted to or versed in aesthetics; a beauty therapist (*US*). — *vt* **aesthet'icise** or **-ize** (*-sīz*) to render aesthetic. — *n* **aesthet'icism** the principles of aesthetics; the cult of the beautiful, applied esp. to a late 19th-century movement to bring art into life, which developed into affectation. — *n* **aesthet'icist.** — *nsing* **aesthet'ics** the principles of taste and art; the philosophy of the fine arts. [Gr. *aisthētikos*, perceptive — *aisthanesthai*, to feel or perceive.]

aestival or in U.S. **estival** *ēs-tī'vəl* or *es-, adj* of summer. — *vi* **aes'tivate** (*-ti-vāt*) to pass the summer, esp. (usu. of animals and insects) in a state of torpor. — *n* **aestivā'tion** a spending of the summer; manner of folding in the flower-bud (*bot*); arrangement of foliage leaves relative to one another in the bud (*bot*); dormancy during the dry season (*zool* and *bot*). [L. *aestīvus*, *aestīvālis*, relating to summer.]

aet. See **ae.**

aet *abbrev* for after extra time.

aether *ē'thər, n.* Same as **ether** (but not generally used in the chemical sense).

aetiology or in U.S. **etiology** *ē-ti-ol'ə-ji, n* the science or philosophy of causation; an inquiry into the origin or causes of anything, esp. a disease. — *adj* **aetiolog'ical.** [Gr. *aitiologiā* — *aitiā*, cause, *logos*, discourse.]

AEU *abbrev* for Amalgamated Engineering Union.

AEW *abbrev* for airborne early warning.

AF *abbrev* for: Admiral of the Fleet; Associate Fellow; audio frequency.

AFA *abbrev* for Amateur Football Association.

afar *ə-fär', adv* from a far distance (usu. *from afar*); at or to a distance (usu. *afar off*). [**of** and **on** with **far.**]

afara *ə-fär'ə, n* a type of West African tree having a light-coloured, straight-grained wood. [Yoruba.]

AFC *abbrev* for: Air Force Cross; Association Football Club.

affable *af'ə-bl, adj* easy to speak to; courteous, esp. towards inferiors; pleasant, friendly. — *n* **affabil'ity.** — *adv* **aff'ably.** [Fr., — L. *affābilis* — *affārī*, to speak.]

affair *ə-fār', n* that which is to be done; business; any matter, occurrence, etc.; a minor battle; a matter of intimate personal concern; a thing (*colloq*); a romantic intrigue, a love affair; an affaire; (in *pl*) transactions in general; (in *pl*) public concerns.

[O.Fr. *afaire* (Fr. *affaire*) — *à* and *faire* — L. *ad*, to, *facĕre*, to do; cf. **ado**.]

affaire *a-fer*, (Fr.) *n* liaison, intrigue; (usu. with name of chief person involved following or preceding) an episode or incident arousing speculation and scandal. — **affaire d'honneur** (*a-fer do-nœr*) affair of honour (a duel).

affect[1] *ə-fekt'*, *vt* to act upon; to infect or attack as a disease does; to influence; to move the feelings of; (in *passive* only) to assign, allot. — *n* (*af'ekt*) the emotion that lies behind action (*psychol*); pleasantness or unpleasantness of, or complex of ideas involved in, an emotional state (*psychol*). — *adj* **affect'ed**. — *adj* **affect'ing** having power to move the emotions. — *adv* **affect'ingly**. — *adj* **affect'ive** of, arising from, or influencing, emotion. — *adv* **affect'ively**. — *n* **affectivity** (*af-ek-tiv'i-ti*). [L. *afficĕre*, *affectum* — *ad*, to, *facĕre*, to do.]

affect[2] *ə-fekt'*, *vt* to make a show of preferring; to do, wear or inhabit, by preference; to assume; to assume the character of; to make a show or pretence of. — *vi* to incline, tend. — *n* **affectā'tion** (*af-ik-*) assumption of or striving after an appearance of what is not natural or real; pretence. — *adj* **affect'ed** full of affectation; feigned. — *adv* **affect'edly**. — *n* **affect'edness**. — *n* **affect'er**. [L. *affectāre*, *-ātum*, frequentative of *afficĕre*; see **affect**[1] above.]

affection *ə-fek'shən*, *n* the act of influencing; emotion; disposition; inclination; love; attachment; an attribute or property; a disease. — *adj* **affec'tional**. — *adj* **affec'tionate** full of affection; loving. — *adv* **affec'tionately**. — *n* **affec'tionateness**. [L. *affectiō*, *-ōnis*.]

affenpinscher *af'en-pinsh-ər*, *n* a small dog related to the Brussels griffon, having tufts of hair on the face. [Ger., — *Affe*, monkey, and *Pinscher*, terrier.]

afferent *af'ər-ənt*, (*physiol*) *adj* bringing inwards, as the nerves that convey impulses to the central nervous system. [L. *afferēns*, *-entis* — *ad*, to, and *ferre*, to carry.]

affiance *ə-fī'əns*, *vt* to betroth. — *n* faith pledged; contract of marriage. — *adj* **affi'anced** betrothed, engaged to be married. [O.Fr. *afiance*.]

affidavit *af-i-dā'vit*, *n* a written declaration on oath. [L.L. *affīdāvit*, 3rd pers. sing. perf. of *affīdāre*, to pledge one's faith.]

affiliate *ə-fil'i-āt*, *vt* to adopt or attach as a member or branch; to impute paternity of; to assign the origin of. — *vi* to become closely connected, to associate; to fraternise. — *n* (*ə-fil'i-ət*) an affiliated person, an associate; a branch, unit or subsidiary of an organisation. — *n* **affilia'tion**. — *adj* **affil'iable**. [L. *affīliātus*, adopted — *ad*, to, *fīlius*, a son.]

affine *a-fīn'* or *a'*, *n* a relation, esp. by marriage. — *adj* **affined'** related; bound by some tie. [O.Fr. *affin* — L. *affīnis*, neighbouring — *ad*, to, at, *fīnis*, a boundary.]

affinity *ə-fin'i-ti*, *n* relationship by marriage; relation of sponsor and godchild; natural or fundamental relationship, esp. common origin; attraction, esp. chemical attraction; a spiritual attraction between two persons; a person whose attraction for another is supposed to be of this kind. — *adj* **affin'itive**. — **affinity card** a credit card linked to a particular charity, to which the issuing bank pays a fee on issue and subsequent donations according to the credit level. [Ety. as for **affine**.]

affirm *ə-fûrm'*, *vt* to assert confidently or positively; to ratify (a judgment); to confirm or stand by (one's own statement); to declare one's commitment to; to state in the affirmative (*logic*); to declare formally, without an oath (*law*). — *vi* to make an affirmation. — *adj* **affirm'able**. — *n* **affirm'ance** affirmation; assertion; confirmation. — *adj* and *n* **affirm'ant**. — *n* **affirmation** (*af-ər-mā'shən* or *-ûr-*) assertion; that which is affirmed; a positive judgment or proposition; a solemn declaration in lieu of an oath. — *adj* **affirm'ative** affirming or asserting; positive, not negative; (of an answer, etc.) agreeing, saying 'yes'; dogmatic. — *n* the affirmative mode; an affirmative word, proposition or utterance. — *adv* **affirm'atively**. — *adj* **affirm'atory**. — *n* **affirm'er**. — *adv* **affirm'ingly**. — **affirmative action** (chiefly *US*) positive steps taken to ensure that minority groups and women are not discriminated against, esp. as regards employment. [O.Fr. *afermer* — L. *affirmāre* — *ad*, to, *firmus*, firm.]

affix *ə-fiks'*, *vt* to fix to something; to subjoin; to attach; to append; to add (to something). — *n* (*af'iks*) an addition to a root, stem or word, whether *prefix*, *suffix* or *infix*, to produce a derivative or an inflected form; any appendage or addition. [L. *affīgere*, *-fīxum* — *ad*, to, *figĕre*, to fix.]

afflict *ə-flikt'*, *vt* to distress grievously; to harass; to vex. — *adj* **afflict'ed** harassed by disease of body or mind (with *with*); suffering. — *n* and *adj* **afflict'ing** distressing. — *n* **afflic'tion** state or cause of grievous distress. — *adj* **afflict'ive** causing distress. [L. *afflīgĕre*, *-flīctum*, to overthrow, cast down — *ad*, to, *flīgĕre*, to dash to the ground.]

affluent *af'lōō-ənt*, *adj* inflowing; abounding; wealthy. — *n* an inflowing stream. — *n* **aff'luence** inflow; abundance; wealth. — *adv* **aff'luently**. — *n* **aff'luentness**. — **affluent society** a society in which the ordinary person can afford many things once regarded as luxuries. [L. *affluĕre* — *ad*, to, *fluĕre*, *fluxum*, to flow.]

afforce *ə-förs'*, (*law*) *vt* to strengthen (e.g. a jury by addition of skilled persons). — *n* **afforce'ment**. [O.Fr. *aforcer* — L.L. *exfortiāre* — L. *ex*, out, *fortis*, strong.]

afford *ə-förd'*, *vt* to yield, give, provide; to bear the expense, or disadvantage, of (having the necessary money or other resources or security of position). — *adj* **afford'able**. [M.E. *aforthen* — O.E. *geforthian*, to further or cause to come forth.]

affray *ə-frā'*, *n* a disturbance, breach of the peace; a brawl, fight or fray. [O.Fr. *afrayer* — L.L. *exfridāre*, to break the king's peace — L. *ex*, out of, O.H.G. *fridu*, peace.]

affricate *af'ri-kət* or *-kāt*, (*phon*) *n* a consonant sound beginning as a plosive and passing into the corresponding fricative. — *adj* **affric'ative**. — *adj* **aff'ricāted**. — *n* **affricā'tion**. [L. *affricāre*, *-ātum*, to rub against — *ad*, to, *fricāre*, to rub.]

affright *ə-frīt*, *vt* to frighten. [O.E. *āfyrhtan* — *ā-* (intensive) and *fyrhtan*, to frighten.]

affront *ə-frunt'*, *vt* to meet face to face; to face; to confront; to insult to one's face. — *n* a contemptuous treatment; an open insult; indignity. — *adj* **affront'ed** insulted or offended, esp. in public. — *n* and *adj* **affront'ing**. — *adv* **affront'ingly**. — *adj* **affront'ive**. [O.Fr. *afronter*, to slap on the forehead — L.L. *affrontāre* — L. *ad*, to, *frōns*, *frontis*, forehead.]

AFG *abbrev* for Afghanistan (I.V.R.).

Afghan *af'gan*, *n* a native or citizen, or the language, of Afghanistan (also **Afghan'i**); (without *cap*) a heavy knitted or crocheted woollen blanket or shawl. — **Afghan hound** an ancient breed of hunting and sheep dog of Afghanistan and northern India, kept as a pet in the West.

aficionado *a-fish-yo-nä'dō*, *n* an amateur; an ardent follower, fan: — *pl* **aficiona'dos**. [Sp.]

afield *ə-fēld'*, *adv* to, in, or on the field; to or at a distance. [**a-**[1] and **field**.]

afire *ə-fīr'*, *adj* and *adv* on fire; in a state of inflammation. [**a-**[1] and **fire**.]

aflame *ə-flām'*, *adj* and *adv* in a flaming or glowing state. [**a-**[1] and **flame**.]

aflatoxin *af-lə-toks'in*, *n* a (possibly carcinogenic) toxin produced in foodstuffs by species of the mould Aspergillus. [*A*spergillus *fla*vus and **toxin** — L. *aspergĕre*, to sprinkle, *flavus*, yellow.]

AFL-CIO *abbrev* for American Federation of Labor and Congress of Industrial Organisations.

afloat *ə-flōt'*, *adv* and *adj* in a floating state; at sea; unfixed; in circulation. [**a-**[1] and **float**.]

AFM *abbrev* for: Air Force Medal; audio frequency modulation.

afoot *ə-fŏŏt'*, *adv* and *adj* on foot; astir; actively in being. [**a-**[1] and **foot**.]

afore *ə-för'*, *combining form* denoting before. — *adv* **afore'hand** beforehand; before the regular time for accomplishment; in advance. — *adj* **afore'mentioned** previously mentioned, aforesaid. — *adj* **afore'said** said or named before. — *adj* **afore'-thought** thought of or meditated before; premeditated. — *n* premeditation. [O.E. *onforan* — *on*, *foran*; see **before**.]

a fortiori *ā för-ti-ör'ī* or *ä för-ti-ör'ē*, (L.) with stronger reason.

Afr. *abbrev* for Africa; African.

afraid *ə-frād'*, *adj* struck with fear, fearful (with *of*); timid; reluctantly inclined to think (that); regretfully admitting. [Past p. of **affray**.]

afreet. See **afrit**.

afresh *ə-fresh'*, *adv* anew. [Pfx. *a-*, of, and **fresh**.]

African *af'rik-ən*, *adj* of Africa. — *n* a native of Africa; a Negro or other person of black race, esp. one whose people live now, or lived recently, in Africa. — *n* **Africanisā'tion** or **-z-**. — *vt* **Af'ricanise** or **-ize** to make African; to exclude people of other races from, replacing them with Africans. — Also *vi.* — *n* **Af'ricanism** an African characteristic. — *n* **Af'ricanist** someone who is learned in matters relating to Africa. — **African violet** a plant from tropical Africa (*Saintpaulia ionantha*), commonly with violet-coloured flowers but not related to the violet. [L. *Africānus*.]

Afrikaans *af-ri-käns'*, *n* one of two official languages of South Africa (it developed from 17th-cent. Dutch). — *n* **Afrikan'er** a person born in South Africa of white parents (esp. of Dutch descent). — Also *adj.* — *n* **Afrikan'erdom** the nationalistic feeling or the political ascendancy, of the Afrikaners in South Africa. [Ety. as for **African**.]

afrit or **afreet** *ä-frēt'* or *af'rēt*, *n* an evil demon in Arabian mythology. [Ar. *'ifrīt*, a demon.]

Afro *af'rō*, (*colloq*; sometimes without *cap*) *adj* a shortening for African; (of a hairstyle) characterised by thick, bushy curls standing out from the head, as worn by some Blacks (also *n*). — **Afro-** *combining form* African (and). — *adj* **Afro-Amer'ican** to do with or relating to American(s) of African descent. — Also *n.* — *adj* **Afro-Asian** (*-āzh'yən*) of or consisting of, Africans and Asians; of Asian origin but African citizenship; of mixed Asian and African blood; (of language) belonging to a group spoken in southwest Asia and north Africa. — *adj* **Afro-Caribbē'an** of or relating to (the culture, music, dance, etc. of) people of African descent in or from the Caribbean area. — *n* **Afro-jazz'** jazz showing evidence of influence of African music. — *n* **Afro-rock'** rock music showing evidence of influence of African music.

aft *äft*, *adj* or *adv* behind; near or towards the stern of a vessel or aircraft. [O.E. *æftan*.]

after *äf'tər*, *prep* and *adv* behind in place; later in time than; following in search of; in imitation of; in proportion to, or in agreement with; concerning; subsequent to, or subsequently, afterwards; in the manner of, or in imitation of; according to; in honour of; with the name, or a name derived from the name, of. — *adj* behind in place; later in time; more towards the stern (in this sense as if the *compar* of **aft**). — *conj* later than the time when. — *npl* **af'ters** (*colloq*) the dessert or other course following a main course. — *adv* **af'terward** (chiefly *US*) or **af'terwards** at a later time; subsequently. — **af'terbirth** the placenta and membranes expelled from the uterus after a birth; a posthumous birth; **af'terburner** the device used in afterburning; **af'terburning** reheat, the use of a device to inject fuel into the hot exhaust gases of a turbojet in order to obtain increased thrust; **af'tercare** care subsequent to a period of treatment, corrective training, etc. — Also *adj.* — **af'ter-crop** a second crop from the same land in the same year; **after-dinn'er** the time following dinner. — *adj* belonging to that time, esp. before leaving the table. — **af'ter-effect** an effect that comes after an interval; **af'tergame** a second game played in the hope of reversing the issue of the first; means employed after the first turn of affairs; **af'terglow** a glow remaining after a light source has faded, esp. that in the sky after sunset; **af'tergrowth** a later growth; an aftermath; **af'ter-image** an image that persists for a time after one looks at an object; **af'ter=life** a future life; later life; a life after death; **af'termath** later consequences (of a particular incident or occurrence), esp. if bad; a second mowing of grass in the same season. — *adj* **af'ter-mentioned** mentioned subsequently. — **afternoon'** the time between noon and evening. — Also *adj* **af'ternoon**. — *adj* **af'tersales** after a sale has been completed, usually with reference to servicing the goods, installation etc. — **af'tershave** a lotion for men, for use after shaving; **af'tershock** one of several minor shocks following the main shock of an earthquake; **af'tertaste** a taste that remains or comes after eating or drinking. — *adj* **af'ter-tax** (of profit) remaining after (esp. income) tax has been paid. — **af'ter-thought** a thought or thing thought of after the occasion; a later thought or reflection or modification. — **after a fashion** see under **fashion**; **after all** when everything is taken into account; in spite of everything. [O.E. *æfter*, in origin a comparative from *af* (*æf*), off.]

aftermost *äf'tər-mōst* or *-məst*, or **aftmost** *äft'*, *adj* (*superl* of **aft**) nearest the stern; hindmost. [O.E. *æftemest*, a double superlative.]

afterward, afterwards. See under **after**.

AG *abbrev* for: Adjutant-General; *Aktiengesellschaft* (Ger.), joint stock company; (or **A-G**) Attorney-General.

Ag (*chem*) *symbol* for silver. [L. *argentum*.]

aga or **agha** *ä'gə* or *ä-gä'*, *n* a Turkish commander or chief officer. — **Aga Khan** (*kän*) the head of the Ismaili Muslims. [Turk. *aga*, *aghā*.]

Agadah. See **Haggadah**.

again *ə-gen'* or *ə-gān'*, *adv* once more; in return; in response or consequence; back; further; on the other hand; to the same amount in addition. — **again and again** repeatedly. [O.E. *ongēan*, *ongegn*.]

against *ə-genst'* or *ə-gānst'*, *prep* opposite to; in opposition or resistance to; in protection from; in or into contact or collision with or pressure upon; in anticipation of; in contrast or comparison with; in exchange for; instead of. [**again**, with genitive ending *-es*, and *-t* as in **whilst, betwixt, amongst**.]

agamic *a-gam'ik*, or **agamous** *ag'ə-məs*, *adj* asexual; parthenogenetic. — *n* **agamogenesis** (*-jen'*) reproduction without sex, as in lower animals and in plants. [Gr. *a-* (privative) and *gamos*, marriage.]

agapanthus *a-gə-pan'thəs*, *n* any of several plants of a genus of lily native to South Africa, with clusters of blue flowers. [Gr. *agapē*, love, *anthos*, flower.]

agape[1] *ag'ə-pē*, *n* selfless Christian brotherly love; the love of God for man; a feast in token and celebration of these loves: — *pl* **ag'apae** (*-pē*). [Gr. *agapē*, love.]

agape[2] *ə-gāp'*, *adj* or *adv* with gaping mouth. [**a-**[1] and **gape**.]

agar *āgär* or **agar-a'gar** *n* a jelly prepared from seaweeds of various kinds used in bacteria-culture, medicine, glue-making, silk-dressing, and cooking; any of the seaweeds concerned. [Malay.]

agaric *ag'ər-ik* or *əg-ar'ik*, *n* a fungus, properly one of the mushroom family, but loosely applied. — *adj* **agar'ic**. [Gr. *agarikon*.]

agate *ag'it* or *-āt*, *n* a banded variegated chalcedony; a marble used in games, made of this material or of variegated glass. [Fr., — Gr. *achātēs*, said to be so called because first found near the river *Achates* in Sicily.]

agave *a-gā'vē*, *n* any plant of an aloe-like American genus of amaryllids. — Also called *American aloe* and *maguey*. [L. *Agāvē*, Gr. *Agauē*, daughter of Cadmus, fem. of *agauos*, illustrious.]

age *āj*, *n* duration of life; the time during which a person or thing has lived or existed; the time of life reached; mature years; legal maturity; the time of being old; equivalence in development to the average of an actual age; a period of time, esp. any great division of world, human, or individual history; (esp. in *pl*) a long time, however short (*colloq*). — *vi* to grow old; to develop the characteristics of old age. — *vt* to make to seem old or to be like the old; to mature: — *pr p* **aging** or **ageing** (*āj'ing*); *pa t* and *pa p* **aged** (*ājd*). — *adj* **aged** (*āj'id*) advanced in age, old; (*ājd*) of the age of. — *npl* (*āj'id*; usu. with *the*) old people. — *n* **agedness** (*āj'id-nis*). — *n* **age'ing** or **ag'ing** the process of growing old or developing qualities of the old; maturing; change in properties that occurs in certain metals at atmospheric temperature after heat treatment or cold working. — *n* **age'ism** discrimination on grounds of age. — *n* and *adj* **age'ist**. — *adj* **age'less** never growing old, perpetually young; timeless. — **age'-bracket** the people between particular ages, taken as a group; **age group** a group of people of a similar age. — **be** or **act your age!** don't be childish; **be ages with** (*Scot*) to be the same age as; **of age** old enough to be deemed legally mature (with respect to voting, crime, contracts, marriage, etc.); **over age** too old; **under age** too young; not yet of age. [O.Fr. *aäge* (Fr. *âge*) — L. *aetās*.]

agency. See under **agent**.

agenda *ə-* or *a-jen'də*, *npl* (often treated as *nsing*) (a list of) things to be done; a programme of business for discussion at a meeting. [L. neuter pl. of *agendus*, to be done, gerundive of *agĕre*, to do.]

agent *ā'jənt*, *n* a person or thing that acts or exerts power; any natural force acting on matter; a person authorised or delegated to transact business for another; a sales representative for a business; a secret agent, spy. — *adj* acting; of an agent. — *n* **agency** (*ā'jən-si*) the operation or action of an agent; instrumentality, operation; the office or business of an agent; such a business putting employers and those requiring employment in contact with each other (e.g. a recruitment agency or nursing agency). — *adj* **agen'tial** (*-shəl*) pertaining to an agent or agency. [L. *agēns*, *-entis*, pres. p. of *agĕre*, to do.]

agent provocateur *a-zhā prō-vo-ka-tœr*, *n* (Fr.) a person employed to lead others, by pretending sympathy with them, into committing unlawful acts.

agglomerate *ə-glom'ər-āt*, *vt* to make into a ball; to collect into a mass. — *vi* to grow into a mass. — *adj* (*-rət* or *-rāt*) agglomerated; clustered; gathered in a head (*bot*). — *n* (*-rət* or *-rāt*) a volcanic rock consisting of irregular fragments. — *adj* **agglom'erated**. — *n* **agglomerā'tion**. — *adj* **agglom'erative**. [L. *agglomerāre*, *-ātum* — *ad*, to, *glomus*, *glomeris*, a ball.]

agglutinate *ə-gloo͞t'in-āt*, *vt* to glue together; to cause to cohere or clump. — *vi* to cohere as if glued; to clump. — *adj* (*-nət* or *-nāt*) agglutinated. — *adj* **agglut'inable**. — *adj* **agglut'inant**. — *n* an agglutinating agent. — *n* **agglutinā'tion** the act of agglutinating; an agglutinated mass; the clumping of bacteria, blood corpuscles, protozoa, etc. (*biol*); a type of word-formation process in which words are inflected by the addition of one or more meaningful elements (each expressing a single element of meaning) to a stem (*linguis*). — *adj* **agglut'inative** tending, or having power, to agglutinate. — **agglutinating** or **agglutinative languages** languages in which words are inflected by agglutination. [L. *agglūtināre* — *ad*, to, *glūten*, *-inis*, glue.]

aggrandise or **-ize** *ə-gran'dīz*, *vt* to make greater, or make to seem greater. — *n* **aggrandisement** or **-z-** (*ə-gran'diz-mənt*). [Fr. *agrandir* — L. *ad*, to, *grandis*, large.]

aggravate *ag'rə-vāt*, *vt* to make more grievous or worse; to irritate, annoy (*colloq*). — *adj* **agg'ravated** (*law*) of an offence, made more serious (e.g. by violence). — *adj* **agg'ravating**. — *adv* **agg'ravatingly**. — *n* **aggravā'tion**. [L. *aggravāre*, *-ātus* — *ad*, to, *gravis*, heavy.]

aggregate *ag'ri-gāt*, *vt* to collect into a mass or whole, assemble; to add as a member to a society; to amount to (*colloq*). — *vi* to accumulate. — *adj* (*-gət* or *-gāt*) formed of parts that combine to make a whole; formed into a single mass or cluster (*bot*). — *n* (*-gət* or *-gāt*) an assemblage; a mass; a total; any material mixed with cement to form concrete; a collection of elements having a common property that identifies the collection (*math*). — *adv* **agg'regately**. — *n* **aggregā'tion**. — *adj* **agg'regātive**. [L. *aggregāre*, *-ātum*, to bring together, as a flock — *ad*, to, *grex*, *gregis*, a flock.]

aggress *ə-gres'*, *vi* to make a first attack; to begin a quarrel. — *n* **aggression** (*-gresh'ən*) a first act of hostility or injury; the use of armed force by a state against the sovereignty, territorial integrity or political independence of another state; self-assertiveness, either as a good characteristic or as a sign of emotional instability. — *adj* **aggress'ive** making the first attack, or prone to do so; discourteously hostile or self-assertive; offensive as opposed to defensive; showing energy and initiative. — *adv* **aggress'ively**. — *n* **aggress'iveness**. — *n* **aggress'or** the person who or force which attacks first. [L. *aggredī*, *-gressus* — *ad*, to, *gradī*, to step.]

aggrieve *ə-grēv'*, *vt* to pain or injure; to distress. — *adj* **aggrieved'** injured, distressed; having a grievance. [O.Fr. *agrever*, lit. to press heavily upon — L. *ad*, to, *gravis*, heavy.]

aggro *ag'rō*, (*slang*) *n* short form of **aggravation**, and also associated with **aggression**, meaning aggressive behaviour or troublemaking, esp. between gangs, racial groups, etc.

agha. See **aga**.

aghast *ə-gäst'*, *adj* stupefied with horror. [Now obsolete *agast* — O.E. *gǣstan*, to terrify.]

agile *aj'īl* or in U.S. *aj'əl*, *adj* nimble, active; quick-moving and supple. — *adv* **ag'ilely**. — *n* **agility** (*ə-jil'i-ti*) nimbleness; swiftness and suppleness. [Fr., — L. *agilis* — *agĕre*, to do or act.]

agio *aj'i-ō* or *aj'ō*, *n* the amount of deviation from the fixed par of exchange between the currencies of two countries; the sum payable for the convenience of exchanging one kind of money for another, e.g. silver for gold, paper for metal; the difference in exchange between worn or debased coinage and coinage of full value; agiotage: — *pl* **ag'ios**. — *n* **agiotage** (*aj'ə-tij*) speculative manoeuvres in stocks and shares; stock-jobbing; money-changing; agio. [It. *agio*, convenience.]

agitate *aj'i-tāt*, *vt* to disturb, perturb; to excite; to discuss, or keep up the discussion of; to stir violently; to keep moving. — *vi* to stir up public feeling. — *adj* **ag'itāted**. — *adv* **ag'itātedly**. — *n* **agitā'tion**. — *adj* **ag'itātive**. — *n* **ag'itātor** a person who excites or keeps up a social or political agitation; an apparatus for stirring. [L. *agitāre* — *agĕre*, to put in motion.]

agitato *äj-it-ä'tō*, (*mus*) *adj* agitated; restless and wild. — Also *adv*. [It.]

agitprop *aj'it-prop*, *n* (often with *cap*) pro-communist agitation and propaganda. — Also *adj*. [Russ. *Agitpropbyuro*, office of *agitatsiya*, agitation, and *propaganda*.]

aglet *ag'lit* or **aiglet** *āg'lit*, *n* the metal tag on the end of a lace or string; an ornamental tag or other metal appendage; an aiguillette. [**aiguillette**.]

aglitter *ə-glit'ər*, *adj* and *adv* in a glitter, sparkling. [**a-**[1] and **glitter**.]

aglow *ə-glō'*, *adj* and *adv* glowing. [**a-**[1] and **glow**.]

AGM or **agm** *abbrev* for annual general meeting.

agma *ag'mə*, *n* (the phonetic symbol ŋ for) a velar nasal consonant, as the *ng* in *thing* or the *n* in *think*. [Gr., fragment, nasalised g.]

agnail. See **hangnail**.

agnate *ag'nāt*, *adj* related on the father's side or through a male ancestor; related generally. — *n* a person related in this way. — *adj* **agnatic** (*-nat'*) or **agnat'ical**. — *adv* **agnat'ically**. — *n* **agnā'tion**. [L. *agnātus* — *ad*, to, *(g)nāscī*, to be born. See **cognate**.]

agnostic *ag-* or *əg-nos'tik*, *n* a person who believes that we know nothing of things beyond material phenomena — that a Creator, creative cause, and unseen world are unknown or unknowable things. — Also *adj*. — *n* **agnos'ticism**. [Coined by T.H. Huxley in 1869 from Gr. *agnostos*, unknown, unknowable.]

Agnus Dei *ag'nəs* or *än'yo͞os dā'ē*, *n* a part of the Roman Catholic mass beginning with these words; music for it; a figure of a lamb emblematic of Christ, bearing the banner of the cross. [L., lamb of God.]

ago *ə-gō'*, *adv* gone; past; since. [O.E. *āgān*, past p. of *āgān*, to pass away.]

agog *ə-gog'*, *adj* and *adv* in excited eagerness. [Perh. O.Fr. *en gogues*, frolicsome.]

agonic *ə-gon'ik*, *adj* making no angle. — **agonic line** the line of no magnetic variation, along which the magnetic needle points directly north and south (*geol*). [Gr. *agōnos* — **a-**[2] and *gōniā*, angle.]

agony *ag'ə-ni*, *n* extreme suffering; a violent mental struggle, anguish; the death struggle. — *vi* **ag'onise** or **-ize** to struggle, contend; to suffer agony; to worry intensely (*colloq*). — *vt* to subject to agony. — *adj* **ag'onised** or **-z-** suffering or expressing anguish. — *adv* **ag'onisedly** or **-z-** (*-īz-id-li*). — *adj* **ag'onising** or **-z-** causing agony; intensely painful. — *adv* **ag'onisingly** or **-z-**. — **agony aunt** a person, usu. a woman, who gives advice in an agony column, or on radio or T.V.; **agony column** the part of a newspaper or magazine in which readers submit, and receive advice about, personal problems; the part of a newspaper containing special advertisements, as for missing friends and the like; **agony uncle**. [Gr. *agōniā*, contest, agony.]

agora[1] *ag'ə-rə*, *n* an assembly, place of assembly, market-place in ancient Greece. — *n* **agoraphō'bia** morbid fear of (crossing) open places. — *adj* and *n* **agoraphō'bic**. [Gr. *agorā*, assembly, market-place, *phobos*, fear.]

agora[2] *ag-ə-rä'*, *n* a monetary unit of Israel, worth 1/100 of an Israeli shekel: — *pl* **agorot** (*-rot'*). [Heb. *agōrāh* — *āgōr*, to collect.]

agouti or **agouty** *ə-go͞o'tē*, *n* a small South American rodent related to the guinea-pig. [Fr., — Sp. *aguti* — Guaraní *acuti*.]

AGR *abbrev* for advanced gas-cooled reactor (see **advance**).

agr. or **agric.** *abbrev* for agriculture.

agraffe *ə-graf'*, *n* a hooked clasp used by stonemasons to hold blocks together. [Fr. *agrafe* — *à*, to, *grappe* — O.H.G. *krapfo*, hook.]

agranulocytosis *a-gran-ū-lō-sī-tō'sis* or **agranulosis** *a-gran-ū-lō'sis*, *n* a blood disorder in which there is a marked decrease in granulocytes, with lesions of the mucous membrane and skin. [**a-**[2], **granulocyte**, and **-osis**.]

agraphia *a-graf'i-ə*, *n* loss of power to write, from brain disease or injury. — *adj* **agraph'ic**. [**a-**[2] and Gr. *graphein*, to write.]

agrarian *əg-rā'ri-ən*, *adj* relating to land, or its management or distribution. — *n* **agrā'rianism** equitable division of lands; a political movement in favour of change in conditions of property in land. [L. *agrārius* — *ager*, a field.]

agree *ə-grē'*, *vi* to concur (with *with* and *in*, *on* or *about*); to accede or assent (to); to be consistent (with); to suit, do well or be compatible (with); to harmonise; to take the same gender, number, case, or person (with *with*; *gram*). — *vt* to arrange with consent of all; to concede (that); to decide jointly (to do, that); to consent (to do): — *pr p* **agree'ing**; *pa t* and *pa p* **agreed'**. — *n* **agreeabil'ity**. — *adj* **agree'able** pleasant, affable; willing, consenting (*colloq*); in harmony; suitable. — *adv* in accordance. — *n* **agree'ableness**. — *adv* **agree'ably**. — *n* **agree'ment** a compact, contract, treaty; concord, harmony; conformity. [O.Fr. *agréer*, to accept kindly — L. *ad*, to, and *grātus*, pleasing.]

agrément *a-grā-mã*, (Fr.) *n* the approval by a state of a diplomatic representative sent to it. — *npl* **agréments** (*-mã*) amenities; courtesies, charms, blandishments; embellishments, such as grace notes and trills (*mus*).

agri- *ag-ri-* or **agro-** *ag-rō-*, *combining form* pertaining to fields, land use, or agriculture. — *n* **ag'ribusiness** or **ag'robusiness** all the operations of supplying the market with farm produce taken together, including growing, provision of farm machinery, distribution, etc. — *n* **agrobiol'ogy** the study of plant nutrition and soil yields. — *adj* **agrobiolog'ical**. — *n* **agrobiol'ogist**. — *n* **agrochem'ical** a chemical intended for agricultural use. — Also *adj*. — *n* **agrofor'estry** any system of land use which integrates the cultivation of trees and shrubs and the raising of agricultural crops and/or animals on the same land. — *n* **agroind'ustry** the area of production that serves the needs of both agriculture and industry.

agriculture *ag'ri-kul-chər*, *n* the art or practice of cultivating the land. — *adj* **agricult'ural**. — *n* **agricult'uralist** or **agricult'urist** a person skilled in agriculture; a farmer. [L. *ager*, (Gr. *agros*) field, *cultūra*, cultivation.]

agrimony *ag'ri-mən-i*, *n* a perennial herb of a genus (*Agrimonia*) of the rose family, with small yellow flowers and bitter taste and a rootstock which provides a yellow dye; extended to other plants, esp. **hemp'-agrimony** (*Eupatorium cannabinum*), a composite. [L. *agrimōnia* (a blunder or misreading) — Gr. *argemōnē*, long prickly-headed poppy.]

agro-, **agrobiology**, etc. See under **agri-**.

agronomy *ag-ron'ə-mi*, *n* rural economy. — *adj* **agronom'ic**. — *nsing* **agronom'ics** the science dealing with the management and productivity of land. — *n* **agron'omist**. [Fr. *agronomie*.]

agrostology *ag-ros-tol'ə-ji*, *n* the study of grasses. — *adj* **agrostological** (*-tə-loj'i-kl*). — *n* **agrostol'ogist**. [Gr. *agrōstis*, dog's-tooth grass.]

aground *ə-grownd'*, *adv* in or to a stranded condition; on the ground. [**a-**[1] and **ground**.]

ague *ā'gū*, *n* a fever with hot and cold fits; malaria; a shivering fit. — *adj* **agued** (*ā'gūd*) struck with ague. — *adj* **ā'gūish**. — *adv* **ā'gūishly**. [O.Fr. (*fièvre*) *ague* — L. (*febris*) *acūta*, sharp (fever).]

AH *abbrev* (in dates) for *anno Hegirae* (L.), in the year of Hegira (i.e. from the flight of Mohammed in A.D. 622, 13 Sept.).

ah *ä*, *interj* expressing surprise, joy, pity, complaint, objection, etc.

aha *ə-hä'*, *interj* expressing exultation, pleasure, surprise or contempt. [**ah** and **ha**.]

ahead *ə-hed'*, *adv* further on; in advance; forward; headlong. [**a-**[1] and **head**.]

ahem *ə-həm'*, *ə-hem'* or *ə-hm'*, *interj* used to draw attention to oneself, or to express a reservation, as though clearing the throat.

ahimsa *ə-him'sə*, *n* the duty of sparing animal life; non-violence. [Sans. *ahiṁsā*.]

ahistorical *ā-his-tor'i-kəl, adj* not historical; taking no account of, or not related to, history. [**a-**[2] and **historical**.]

-aholic or **-oholic** *-ə-hol'ik*, (*facetious*) *sfx* having an addiction to (something) as in *workaholic, clothesoholic*. — **-ahol'ism** or **-ohol'ism** (*-izm*) used as noun suffix. [By analogy, from alc*oholic*, alc*oholism*.]

ahoy *ə-hoi'*, (*naut*) *interj* used to hail another vessel, etc. [**ah** and **hoy**[2].]

AI *abbrev* for: artificial insemination; artificial intelligence.

ai[1] *ä'ē*, *n* the three-toed sloth. [Tupí *ai*, representing the animal's cry.]

ai[2]. See **ayu**.

AID *abbrev* for: Agency for International Development (*US*); artificial insemination by donor (now known as **DI**).

aid *ād*, *vt* to help. — *n* help; assistance, as in defending an action; that which helps; an auxiliary; a helper; an apparatus, etc., that gives help, e.g. *hearing-aid, navigational aid*; money, etc., donated to relieve poor or disaster-stricken countries. — *adj* **aid'ed**. — *n* **aid'er**. — *adj* **aid'ful**. — *n* **aid'ing**. — *adj* **aid'less**. — **aid and abet** (*law*) to assist and encourage, esp. in committing a crime; **in aid of** (*colloq*) intended to achieve; in support of. [O.Fr. *aider* — L. *adjūtāre*.]

aide *ād*, *n* a confidential assistant to a person of senior rank e.g. an ambassador or president; an aide-de-camp. — **aide-de-camp** (*ed-* or *ād-də-kã'*) an officer who attends a general, governor, etc. and acts as a personal assistant: — *pl* **aides-de-camp** (*ed-* or *ād-*). [Fr., assistant, assistant on the field.]

aide-mémoire *ed-mā-mwär*, (Fr.) *n* an aid to the memory, a reminder; a memorandum-book; a written summary of a diplomatic document.

AIDS *ādz*, *n* a condition brought about by a virus which causes the body's immune system to become deficient, leaving the sufferer very vulnerable to infection. — **AIDS-related complex** a viral condition marked esp. by fever and swollen lymph-nodes, that may develop into AIDS. [Acronym for *a*cquired *i*mmune *d*eficiency *s*yndrome.]

aiglet. See **aglet**.

aigrette *ā'gret* or *ā-gret'*, *n* an egret plume; any ornamental feather plume; a spray of jewels. [Fr., egret.]

aiguille *ā-gwēl'*, *n* a sharp, needle-like peak of rock; a slender boring-tool. — *n* **aiguillette'** a tagged point of braid hanging from the shoulder in some uniforms. [Fr., a needle — L. *acūla*, dimin. of *acus*, a needle.]

AIH *abbrev* for artificial insemination by husband.

aikido *ī-kē'dō*, *n* a Japanese combative sport using locks and pressure against joints. [Jap., — *ai*, to harmonise, *ki*, breath, spirit, *dō*, way, doctrine.]

ail *āl*, *vt* (*impers*) to trouble, afflict, be the matter with; to have the matter with one. — *vi* to be sickly or indisposed. — *adj* **ail'ing** unwell; in poor health. — *n* **ail'ment** indisposition; disease, esp. if not very serious. [O.E. *eglan*, to trouble.]

aileron *āl'* or *el'ə-rɔ̃* or *-ron*, *n* a flap on an aeroplane wingtip for lateral balancing. [Fr. dimin. of *aile* — L. *āla*, a wing.]

ailuro- *ī-lo͞or'ə-* or **ailur-** *ī-lo͞or'-*, *combining form* denoting cat. — *n* **ailur'ophile** (*-fīl*) a cat lover or fancier. — *n* **ailurophilia** (*-fil'i-ə*). — *adj* **ailurophil'ic**. — *n* **ailur'ophobe** (*-fōb*) a cat hater; a person with an abnormal fear of cats. — *n* **ailurophō'bia**. — *adj* **ailuropho'bic**. [Gr. *ailouros*, cat.]

aim *ām*, *vt* to point, level or direct, with (or as if with) a view to hitting an object; to purpose or try (to do). — *vi* (with *at*) to direct a course; to level a weapon; to direct a blow or missile; to direct a remark with personal or special application; to direct one's intention and endeavours with a view to attaining. — *n* an act or manner of aiming; an object or purpose aimed at; design, intention. — *adj* **aim'less**. — *adv* **aim'lessly**. — *n* **aim'lessness**. — **aim off** (*rifle shooting*) to aim slightly off the target to allow for wind or other factor; **take aim** to aim deliberately.

ain't *ānt*, (*colloq*) contracted form of *are not*, used also for *am* or *is not*; also for *have not*.

aioli or **aïoli** *ī-ō'lē*, *n* a garlic-flavoured mayonnaise. [Prov. *ai*, garlic, *oli*, oil — L. *allium*, garlic and *oleum*, oil.]

air *ār*, *n* the gaseous mixture (chiefly nitrogen and oxygen) of which the earth's atmosphere is composed; the medium through which sound waves travel (*radio*); the medium in which aircraft operate; a light breeze; the aura or atmosphere surrounding or created by anything; bearing, outward appearance, manner, look; an assumed or affected manner; (in *pl*) an affectation of superiority; exposure, publicity; a melody or tune; the chief, usually upper, part or tune (*mus*). — *adj* of or pertaining to the air; affecting or regulating (the) air; by means of (the) air; operated by air; of aircraft; carried out, or conveyed, by aircraft. — *vt* to expose to the air; to ventilate; to warm and dry; to give an airing to, to voice; to make public knowledge, to spread. — *vi* to take an airing; to become aired; to be broadcast (*TV* and *radio*). — *n* **air'er** a person who airs; a frame on which clothes are dried. — *adv* **air'ily** in an airy manner; jauntily. — *n* **air'iness**. — *n* **air'ing** exposure to air or heat, to general notice or open debate; a short excursion in the open air. — *adj* **air'less** without air; without free communication with the outer air; stuffy. — *adv* **air'ward** or **air'wards** up into the air. — *adj* **air'y** consisting of or relating to air; having sufficient (fresh) air; like air; unsubstantial; sprightly, jaunty. — **air'-ambulance** an aircraft used to take patients from remote places to hospital; **air'-arm** the branch of the fighting services that uses aircraft; **air bag** a safety device in a motor car, etc. consisting of a bag that inflates to protect the occupants in a collision; an air-filled bag for another purpose, e.g. raising sunken craft; **air base** a base of operations for aircraft; **air'-bed** an inflated mattress; **air'-bladder** a sac containing gas; a fish's swim bladder, serving to regulate buoyancy, etc. — *adj* **air'borne** carried by air; borne up in the air. — **air'-brake** a brake worked by compressed air; a means of reducing the speed of an aircraft; **air'-brush** a device for spraying paint, etc., powered by compressed air, or for touching up or toning down a photograph. — *adj* **air'-brushed**. — **air'-bubble** a bubble of air; **air'burst** the explosion of a bomb, etc. in the air. — *adj* designed to explode in the air. — **Air'bus®** (also without *cap*) a very large passenger jet aircraft used for short flights; **air-chief-mar'shal** an air force officer ranking with an admiral or general; **air-comm'odore** an air force officer ranking with a commodore or brigadier; **air-compress'or** (*eng*) a machine which draws in air at atmospheric pressure, compresses it, and delivers it at higher pressure. — *vt* **air-condi'tion** to equip, e.g. a building, with devices for air-conditioning. — *adj* **air-condi'tioned**. — **air-condi'tioning** (devices for) the bringing of air to the desired state of purity, temperature and humidity; **air-corr'idor** in an area where flying is restricted, a narrow strip along which flying is allowed; **air'-cover** protection given by fighter aircraft to other forces during a military operation; the protecting aircraft; **aircraft** *nsing* (also *pl*) any structure or machine for travelling in the air; **air'craft-carrier** a vessel from which aircraft can take off and on which they may alight; **air'-craftman** or **air'craftsman** an air force member of lowest rank; **aircraftwoman** or **aircraftswoman** lowest rank in the W.R.A.F.; **air'-crew** the crew of an aircraft; **air'-cushion** a cushion that can be inflated; a protective barrier, e.g. between a hovercraft and land or water, formed by down-driven air; **air dam** on a motor vehicle, a front spoiler; **air'=**

drop (*mil*) a landing of men or supplies by parachute; **air'field** an open expanse where aircraft may land and take off; **air'foil** (*NAm*) an aerofoil; **air force** a force organised for warfare in the air; **air'frame** the body of an aircraft as opposed to its engines; **air freight** transport of freight by air; the cost of this. — Also *vt*. — **air frost** (*meteorol*) a screen temperature of below 0°C; **air'-gun** a gun that discharges missiles by means of compressed air; **air'head** (*slang*) an idiot, featherbrain; **air'hole** a hole for the passage of air; a hole in ice where animals come up to breathe; an air-pocket; **air'-hostess** a female member of an aircraft crew, responsible for attending to the comfort of the passengers; **air'-lane** a route normally taken by aircraft because of steady winds; **air letter** a letter sent by airmail; **air lieutenant** a rank in the Zimbabwean Air Force equivalent to a flying officer in the Royal Air Force; **air'lift** a transport operation carried out by air, esp. in an emergency. — Also *vt*. — **air'line** a route or system of traffic by aircraft; a company operating such a system. — Also *adj*. — **air'liner** a large passenger aircraft; an aircraft operating in an airline; **air loadmaster** one of a team of usu. three men in charge of winching operations on a helicopter; **air'lock** a bubble in a pipe obstructing flow of liquid; a small chamber in which pressure of air can be raised or lowered, through which communication is made between a caisson where the air is compressed and the outer air (*civ eng*); **air'mail** mail conveyed by air. — *vt* to send by airmail. — Also *adj*. — **air'man** a person who flies; an aircraft pilot, technician or navigator, *specif* in the RAF someone below officer rank: — *fem* **air'woman; air'manship** the art of handling aircraft; **air-mar'shal** an air force officer ranked with a vice-admiral or a lieutenant-general; **air'-mechanic** a person who tends and repairs aircraft; **air'-passage** the passage by which air enters and leaves the lungs; **air-pir'acy** the hijacking of an aircraft; **air'plane** (chiefly *NAm*) an aeroplane; **air play** the broadcasting of a song, singer, record, etc. over the radio; **air'-pocket** a region of rarefied or down-flowing air, in which aircraft drop; **air'port** an aerodrome usu. with a custom-house, used as a station for transport of passengers and cargo; **air'-power** military power in terms of aircraft; **air'-pump** an instrument for pumping air out or in; **air'-raid** an attack on a place by aircraft; **air rifle** a rifle that discharges missiles by means of compressed air; **air'-sac** an outgrowth of the lung in birds, helping respiration or lightening the body; **Air Scout** a member of a branch of the Scouts with special interest in air activities; **air'screw** the propeller of an aircraft; **air'ship** a mechanically driven dirigible aircraft, lighter than air; **air shot** in golf or cricket, a stroke that fails to connect with the ball; **air'-sickness** nausea affecting travellers by air. — *adj* **air'sick.** — *adj* and *n* **air'side** (of, in or relating to) that part of an airport having direct access to the apron, and off-limits to non-travelling public and unauthorised personnel, the area usu. controlled by an airport authority (**go** or **pass airside** to enter this restricted area). — **air'space** the part of the atmosphere above a particular territory, state, etc.; the space used, or required by, an aircraft in manoeuvring; **air'stream** a flow of air; **air'-strike** an attack with aircraft; **air'strip** a temporary or emergency landing-place for aircraft; a runway; **air terminal** a terminus to or from which passengers are conveyed from or to an airport; the terminal building(s) of an airport. — *adj* **air'tight** impermeable to air; impenetrable (*fig*). — **air'time** the amount of broadcasting time on radio or television allotted to a particular topic, type of material, commercial advertisement, etc.; the time at which the broadcasting of a programme, etc. is due to begin; **air-vice-mar'shal** an air force officer ranking with a rear-admiral or major-general; **air'wave** a channel for broadcasting; **air'way** a passage for air; a radio channel; an organised route for air travel; **air'-worthiness.** — *adj* **air'worthy** in fit condition for safe flying. — *adj* **airy-fair'y** fanciful, flimsy, insubstantial. — **air-sea rescue** combined use of aircraft and high-speed launches in sea rescue; **air-traffic control** the system of regional centres and airport units which instruct aircraft exactly on what route to follow, height to fly, etc.; **give oneself airs** to put on a superior manner; **in the air** prevalent in a vague or indefinite form; **off the air** not broadcasting, or being broadcast, for a period of time; **on the air** in the act of broadcasting; broadcast by radio; **up in the air** undecided; excited or angry. [O.Fr. (and Fr.) *air* — L. *āēr* — Gr. *āēr*.]

Airedale *ār'dāl* or **Airedale terrier** *ter'i-ər*, *n* a large terrier of a breed orig. from *Airedale* in Yorkshire.

aisle *īl*, *n* a side division of the nave or other part of a church or similar building, generally separated off by pillars; a passage between rows of seats e.g. in an aircraft or a theatre, cinema, etc. — *adj* **aisled** (*īld*) having aisles. [O.Fr. *ele* — L. *āla*, a wing; confused with **isle** and **alley**.]

aitch *āch*, *n* the eighth letter of the alphabet (H, h). — **drop one's aitches** to fail to pronounce initial aitches on words, formerly considered a sign of lack of education. [O.Fr. *ache*.]

aitchbone *āch'bōn*, *n* (in cattle) the bone of the rump; the cut of beef over it. [An *aitchbone* is for *a nachebone* — O.Fr. *nache*, buttock and **bone**.]

ajar *ə-jär'*, *adv* and *adj* partly open. [O.E. *on*, on, *cerr*, a turn.]

AK *abbrev* for: Alaska (U.S. state); Knight of (the Order of) Australia.

aka or **AKA** *abbrev* for also known as.

akene *a-kēn'*, *n*. Same as **achene**.

akimbo *ə-kim'bō*, *adj* and *adv* with hand on hip and elbow out. [M.E. *in kenebow*, poss. in a keen (sharp) bow or bend.]

akin *ə-kin'*, *adj* related by blood; of a similar nature. [**a-**[1] and **kin**.]

akinesia *ā-kin-ē'zi-ə* or *-ē'shə*, or **akinesis** *ā-kin-ē'sis*, (*pathol*) *n* the lack, loss or impairment of the power of voluntary movement. [Gr. *akinesia*, lack of motion — **a-**[2] and *kinein*, to move.]

AL *abbrev* for: Alabama (U.S. state); Albania (I.V.R.).

Al (*chem*) *symbol* for aluminium.

Ala. *abbrev* for Alabama (U.S. state).

à la *a la*, *prep* in the manner of, e.g. *à la James Joyce*; in cooking, prepared with or in the manner of (a person or place), e.g. *à la Dubarry*, with cauliflower, *à la Florentine*, with spinach, etc. [Fr. — contraction of *à la mode de*.]

ala *ā'lə*, *n* a winglike structure, as e.g. a membranous outgrowth on a fruit or a leafy expansion running down the stem from a leaf (*bot*); any flat winglike process, esp. of bone (*zool*): — *pl* **alae** (*ā'lē*). — *adj* **ā'lar** or **ā'lary** pertaining to a wing. — *adj* **ā'late** or **ā'lated** winged, having an ala. [L. *āla*, wing.]

alabaster *al'ə-bäs-tər* or *al-ə-bäs'tər*, *n* a soft semi-transparent massive gypsum, widely used for ornamental purposes. — *adj* of or like alabaster. — *adj* **alabas'trine.** [Gr. *alabastros*, said to be from *Alabastron*, a town in Egypt.]

à la carte *a la kärt* or *ä lä kärt*, with each dish charged individually at the price shown on the menu; with the freedom to pick and choose (*fig*). [Fr., according to the bill of fare.]

alacrity *ə-lak'ri-ti*, *n* briskness; cheerful readiness; promptness. [L. *alacritās*, *-ātis* — *alacer*, *alacris*, brisk.]

Aladdin's cave *ə-lad'inz kāv*, *n* a place full of wonderful treasures (*fig*). — **Aladdin's lamp** a charmed object able to grant all one's wishes. [Aladdin, a character in *Arabian Nights*.]

alae See **ala.**

à la maître d'hôtel *a la metr' dō-tel,* in cooking, served plain with a parsley garnish. [Fr., in the style of a house-steward or hotel-keeper.]

à la mode *a la mod* or *mōd,* fashionable; of beef, larded and stewed with vegetables (*cookery*); of desserts, served with ice-cream (*US*). [Fr. *à la mode,* according to the fashion.]

à la poupée *a la pōō-pā,* (Fr.) of the printing of an engraving or etching, with inks of different colours being spread on the plate with paper or cloth pads (*poupées*) before the impression is taken.

alar, alary. See **ala.**

alarm *ə-lärm',* *n* a fear-stricken state; apprehension of danger; a warning of danger; a mechanical device for arousing, warning or giving notice; the noise made by such a device; orig., a call to arms. — *vt* to startle, agitate; to strike with fear. — *adj* **alarmed'.** — *adv* **alarm'edly.** — *adj* **alarm'ing.** — *adv* **alarm'ingly.** — *n* **alarm'ism.** — *n* **alarm'ist** a scaremonger, or someone who is easily alarmed. — Also *adj.* — **alarm'-bell; alarm'-clock** a clock that can be set to ring an alarm at a chosen time; **alarm'-radio** a clock radio. — **sound the alarm** to give the signal to prepare for an emergency. [O.Fr. (and Fr.) *alarme* — It. *all'arme,* to (the) arms.]

Alas. *abbrev* for Alaska (U.S. state).

alas *ə-läs',* *interj* (now somewhat *archaic* or *mock-heroic*) expressing grief or misfortune. [O.Fr. *ha las, a las* (mod. Fr. *hélas*); *ha,* ah, *las,* wretched, weary — L. *lassus,* wearied.]

alate. See **ala.**

alb *alb, n* a long white sleeved vestment worn esp. by R.C. clergy. [O.E. *albe* — L.L. *alba* — L. *albus,* white.]

albacore *al'bə-kör, n* a large tuna with long pectoral fins. [Port. *albacor* — Ar. *al,* the, *bukr,* young camel.]

Albanian *al-bā'ni-ən, adj* of or pertaining to the S.E. European Republic of *Albania.* — *n* a native or citizen of Albania; the language of the Albanians.

albatross *al'bə-tros, n* a large, long-winged sea-bird with remarkable powers of flight; a hole in three below par (*golf*); used symbolically to mean an oppressive and inescapable fact, influence, etc. (from the dead bird hung round the neck of the sailor in Coleridge's *Ancient Mariner*). [Perh. influenced by L. *albus,* white.]

albedo *al-bē'dō, n* a measure of the reflecting power of an object (e.g. a planet), expressed as the proportion of incident light it reflects: — *pl* **albe'dos.** [L. *albēdō,* whiteness — *albus,* white.]

albeit *öl-bē'it, conj* even if, although. [**all be it.**]

albescent *al-bes'ənt, adj* becoming white; whitish. — *n* **albesc'ence.** [L. *albēscēns, -entis,* pres. p. of *albēscere,* to grow white.]

albino *al-bē'nō* or in U.S. *al-bī'nō, n* a person or other animal with abnormally white skin and hair and pink irises; a plant lacking in pigment: — *pl* **albi'nos.** — *n* **al'binism** (*-bin-*) or **albinoism** (*-bē'*). — *adj* **albinotic** (*al-bin-ot'ik*). [Port., white Negro or albino — L. *albus,* white.]

albugo *al-bū'gō, n* leucoma: — *pl* **albū'gos.** — *adj* **albugineous** (*-jin'i-əs*) like the white of an egg or of the eye. [L. *albūgō, -inis,* whiteness.]

album *al'bəm, n* a blank book for the insertion of photographs, autographs, scraps, postage-stamps, etc.; a printed book of selections, esp. of music; a book-like container for gramophone records; a long-playing gramophone record: — *pl* **al'bums.** — **al'bum-leaf** a short musical composition. [L. neut. of *albus,* white.]

albumen *al'bū-mən* or *al-bū'mən, n* the white of an egg; the nutritive material surrounding the yolk in the eggs of higher animals, a mixture of proteins (*zool*); any tissue within the seed-coat other than the embryo itself — endosperm and perisperm, serving as a store of food for the young plant (*bot*). — *vt* **albū'menise,** **albū'minise** or **-ize** (*phot*) to cover or impregnate with albumen or an albuminous solution. — *n* **al'būmin** (or *al-bū'min*) a protein of various kinds soluble in pure water, the solution coagulable by heat. — *adj* **albū'minous** like or containing albumen or albumin. — *n* **albūminūr'ia** presence of albumin in the urine. [L. *albūmen, -inis* — *albus,* white.]

albumin, albuminise, etc. See **albumen.**

alburnum *al-bûrn'əm, n* sapwood, the soft wood between inner bark and heartwood. — *adj* **alburn'ous.** [L. *albus,* white.]

alchemy *al'kə-mi, n* the infant stage of chemistry, aimed chiefly towards transmuting other metals into gold, and discovering the elixir of life; a transmuting potency (*fig*). — *adj* **alchemic** (*-kem'ik*) or **alchem'ical.** — *n* **al'chemist.** [Ar. *al-kīmīā* — *al,* the, and *kīmīā* — late Gr. *chēmeiā, chȳmeiā,* the art of transmutation.]

alcheringa *al-chə-ring'gə* or **alchera** *al'chə-rə, n* dreamtime. [Aboriginal.]

alcohol *al'kə-hol, n* a liquid generated by the fermentation of sugar or other saccharine matter and forming the intoxicating element of fermented liquors; a general term for a class of hydrocarbon compounds analogous to common (or ethyl) alcohol, in which a hydroxyl group is substituted for an atom of hydrogen. — *adj* **alcohol'ic** of, like, containing, or due to alcohol. — *n* a person addicted to excessive drinking of alcohol. — *n* **alcholīsā'tion** or **-z-.** — *vt* **al'coholīse** or **-ize** to convert into or saturate with alcohol. — *n* **al'coholism** the condition suffered by an alcoholic; alcoholic poisoning. — *n* **alcoholom'eter** an instrument for measuring the proportion of alcohol in solutions. — *n* **alcoholom'etry.** [Ar. *al-koh'l* — *al,* the, *koh'l,* antimony powder used in the East to stain the eyelids.]

alcove *al'kōv, n* a recess in a room, e.g. for a bed, seating, shelving; any recess, e.g. a covered outdoor shelter in a wall. [Sp. *alcoba,* a place in a room railed off to hold a bed — Ar. *al,* the, *qobbah,* a vault.]

Ald. *abbrev* for Alderman.

aldehyde *al'di-hīd, n* a volatile fluid with a suffocating smell, obtained by the oxidation of alcohol; a compound differing from an alcohol in having two atoms fewer of hydrogen. [Contr. for *alcohol dēhydrogenātum,* alcohol deprived of hydrogen.]

al dente *al den'tā,* (*cookery*) *adj* of pasta, firm to the teeth. [It., to the tooth.]

alder *öl'dər, n* any tree of the genus **Alnus,** related to the birches, usually growing in moist ground; extended to various other trees or shrubs. — *adj* **al'dern** made of alder. [O.E. *alor.*]

alderman *öl'dər-mən, n* in English boroughs, a civic dignitary next in rank to the mayor, elected by fellow councillors (chiefly *hist*); a superior member of an English county council (chiefly *hist*); a member of the governing body of a borough or of its upper house, elected by popular vote (*NAm*): — *pl* **al'dermen.** — *adj* **aldermanic** (*-man'ik*). — *adj* **al'dermanlike** or **al'dermanly** pompous and portly. — *n* **al'dermanry.** — *n* **al'dermanship.** [O.E. *aldorman* (West Saxon *ealdorman*) a nobleman of highest rank, governor or high official — *ald* (*eald*) old, and noun-forming suffix *-or.*]

Alderney *öl'dər-ni, n* a small dairy cow, formerly of a breed kept in *Alderney,* now loosely including Jersey and Guernsey. — Also *adj.*

aldose *al'dōs,* (*chem*) *n* any of a class of monosaccharide sugars which contain an aldehyde group. [*ald*ehyde.]

aldrin *al'drin, n* a chlorinated hydrocarbon, used as a contact insecticide. [From K. *Alder,* German chemist (1902–58).]

ale *āl, n* an alcoholic beverage made from an infusion of malt by fermentation; the name applied to beers made by a brewing process in which yeast ferments on the top of the liquid. — **ale'-house** (*colloq*) a house in which ale is sold, a pub; **ale'wife** a fish related to the herring, common off the North East of America: — *pl* **ale'wives**. [O.E. (Anglian) *alu*.]

aleatory *ā'li-ə-tər-i*, *adj* depending on contingencies; used of the element of chance in poetic composition, etc.; aleatoric (*mus*). — *n* aleatoric music. — *adj* **aleatoric** (*ā-li-ə-tör'ik*) in which chance influences the choice of notes (*mus*); aleatory. [L. *āleātōrius* — *āleātor*, a dicer — *ālea*, a die.]

Alec, alec, Aleck. See under **smart**.

alee *ə-lē'*, (*naut*) *adv* on or toward the lee side. [O.N. *ā*, on, *hlē*, lee.]

Alemannic *al-ə-man'ik*, *n* the High German dialect of Switzerland, Alsace, etc. [L. *Alemanni*, an ancient people of South West Germany.]

alert *ə-lûrt'*, *adj* watchful, wide awake; brisk, sharp, lively. — *n* a danger warning; the time for which it lasts; a condition of readiness or expectancy. — *vt* to make alert. — *adv* **alert'ly**. — *n* **alert'ness**. — **on the alert** on the watch; wakefully attentive. [Fr. *alerte* — It. *all'erta*, on the watch.]

alexanders *al-ig-zän'dərz*, *n* an umbelliferous plant (genus *Smyrnium*), the stems formerly eaten as celery is now. [O.E. *alexandre*.]

Alexandrian *al-ig-zän'dri-ən*, *adj* relating to *Alexandria* in Egypt, its school of philosophy, its poetry, or the general character of its culture and taste, erudite and critical rather than original in inspiration — sometimes with a suggestion of decadence; relating to *Alexander* the Great or any other of the same name. — Also *n*. — *n* and *adj* **Alexan'drīne** Alexandrian. — *n* **alexan'drīne** a verse of six iambs (in English), or in French of 12 and 13 syllables in alternate couplets. — Also *adj*.

alexandrite *al-ek-zan'drīt*, *n* a dark green mineral, a kind of chrysoberyl. [Discovered on the day of majority of the Cesarevich later *Alexander* II.]

alexia *a-lek'si-ə*, *n* loss of power to read; word-blindness. — *adj* **alex'ic**. [N.L. — **a-**[2] and Gr. *legein*, to speak, confused with L. *legĕre*, to read.]

alexin *a-lek'sin*, *n* a body present in the blood serum, which uniting with an antiserum gives protection against disease. [Gr. *alexein*, to ward off.]

ALF *abbrev* for Animal Liberation Front, an organisation dedicated to freeing animals from cruel or exploitative captivity.

Alf *alf*, *n* a classic example of a narrow-minded, ignorant and male-chauvinist man. — Also *adj*.

alfalfa *al-fal'fə*, *n* a variety of, or (esp. *US*) another name for the fodder plant, lucerne. [Sp. *alfalfa* — Ar. *alfaćfaćah*.]

alfresco *al-fresk'ō*, *adv* and *adj* in the fresh or cool air; on fresh or moist plaster (*painting*). [It.; see **fresco, fresh**.]

alg. *abbrev* for algebra or algebraic.

alga *al'gə*, *n* a seaweed; any member of the Algae: — *pl* **algae** (*al'jē* or *-gē*). — *npl* **Algae** (*bot*) the seaweeds and allied forms. — *adj* **al'gal** (*-gəl*). — *n* **al'gicide** (*-ji-sīd*) a substance used to destroy algae. — *n* **al'gin** (*-jin*) sodium alginate, a gummy nitrogenous organic compound obtained from seaweeds. — *n* **al'ginate** a salt of alginic acid. — *adj* **algin'ic** (as **alginic acid**, an acid obtained from certain seaweeds, used in plastics, medicine, as a food-thickening agent, etc.). — *adj* **al'goid** (*-goid*) of the nature of or resembling an alga. — *adj* **algolog'ical**. — *n* **algol'ogist**. — *n* **algol'ogy** the study of algae. [L. *alga*, seaweed.]

algebra *al'ji-brə*, *n* a method of calculating by symbols — by means of letters employed to represent quantities, and signs to represent their relations, thus forming a kind of generalised arithmetic; in modern mathematics, any of a number of systems using symbols and involving reasoning about relationships and operations. — *adj* **algebraic** (*-brā'ik*) or **algebrā'ical**. — *adv* **algebrā'ically**. — *n* **algebrā'ist** a person skilled in algebra. [It. and Sp., — Ar. *al-jebr*, resetting (of anything broken), hence combination.]

Algerian *al-jē'ri-ən*, *adj* of Algeria or Algiers. — *n* a native of Algeria.

algesia *al-jē'zi-ə* or *-si-*, *n* sensitivity to pain. — *n* **algē'sis** the sensation of pain. [N.L. — Gr. *algēsis* — *algein*, to suffer.]

-algia *al'ji-ə*, *combining form* denoting pain (in a particular part or because of a particular thing). [Gr. *algos*, pain.]

algicide. See **alga**.

algid *al'jid*, *adj* cold, chill — esp. applied to a cold fit in disease. — *n* **algid'ity**. [L. *algidus*, cold.]

alginate, algology, etc. See **alga**.

ALGOL or **Algol** *al'gol*, *n* a type of high-level computer programming language. [*Algo*rithmic *l*anguage.]

Algonkian *al-gong'ki-ən* or **Algonquian** also *-kwi-*, *n* a family of North American Indian languages, including Natick, Shawnee, Ojibwa, Cheyenne, etc., spoken over a wide area; a member of a tribe speaking one of these languages. — Also *adj*. [Am. Eng. — **Algonquin**.]

Algonquin *al-gong'kwin* or **Algonkin** *-kin*, *n* a leading group of North American Indian tribes in the valley of the Ottawa and around the northern tributaries of the St Lawrence; a member of this group; their language. — Also *adj*. [Micmac Indian *algoo-making*, at the place of spearing fish.]

algorism *al'gə-rizm*, *n* the Arabic system of numeration; arithmetic; an algorithm. [L.L. *algorismus* — Ar. *al-Khwārazmi*, the native of Khwārazm (Khiva), i.e. the 9th-cent. mathematician Abu Ja'far Mohammed ben Musa.]

algorithm *al'gə-ridhm*, *n* a rule for solving a mathematical problem in a finite number of steps; a set of prescribed computational procedures for solving a problem or achieving a result (*comput*); a step-by-step method for solving a problem. — *adj* **algorith'mic**. — **algorithmic language** see **ALGOL**. [**algorism**.]

alias *ā'li-əs*, *adv* otherwise. — *n* an assumed name: — *pl* **a'liases**. [L. *aliās*, at another time, otherwise — *alius*, other.]

alibi *al'i-bī*, *n* the plea in a criminal charge of having been elsewhere at the relevant time; the fact of being elsewhere; an excuse for failure (*colloq*). [L. *alibī*, elsewhere, orig. locative — *alius*, other.]

Alice *al'is*, *n* the main character in the children's fantasies *Alice's Adventures in Wonderland* (1865) and *Through the Looking-glass* (1872) by Lewis Carroll. — **Alice band** a wide hair-band of coloured ribbon or other material. — *adj* **Al'ice-in-Wonderland** as if happening in a dream or fantasy; unreal.

alicyclic *al-i-sīk'lik*, *adj* having properties of aliphatic organic compounds but containing a ring of carbon atoms instead of an open chain. [**aliphatic** and **cyclic**.]

alidad *al'i-dad* or *al-i-dad'*, also **alidade** *-dād*, (*surveying*) *n* a revolving index for reading the graduations of an astrolabe, quadrant or similar instrument, or for taking the direction of objects. [Ar. *al 'idādah*, the revolving radius — *'adid*, humerus.]

alien *ā'li-ən* or *ā'lyən*, *adj* belonging to something else; foreign, from elsewhere; extraneous; repugnant or offensive; inconsistent (with *to*); incompatible or irreconcilable. — *n* a foreigner or outsider; a resident neither native-born nor naturalised; an extra-terrestrial; a plant introduced by man but maintaining itself. — *n* **alienabil'ity**. — *adj* **a'lienable** (*law*) capable of being transferred to another. — *vt* **a'lienate** to transfer; (*law*) to estrange, to distance by taking away friendship or contact. — *n* **alienā'tion** estrangement; mental or emotional detachment; the state of not being involved. — *n* **a'lienātor**. — *n* **alienee'** (*law*) a person to whom property is transferred. — *n* **a'lienor** (*law*) a person who transfers property. [L. *aliēnus* — *alius*, other.]

aliform *ā'li-förm* or *al'i-förm*, *adj* wing-shaped. [L. *āla*, wing, *forma*, shape.]

alight[1] *ə-līt'*, *vi* to dismount or descend; to perch or settle; to land, come to rest; to come by chance (upon something): — *pa t* and *pa p* **alight'ed** or **alit'**. [O.E. *ālīhtan*. See **light**[3].]

alight[2] *ə-līt*, *adj* on fire; lit up. [**a-**[1] and **light**[1].]

align *ə-līn'*, *vt* to arrange in line; to make (e.g. a view or policy) fit or tally (with *with*). — *vi* to agree or fall into line; to be arranged on or in a line. — *n* **align'ment** setting in a line or lines; a row arranged in this way; taking of side, or a side taken, politically, etc. — **alignment chart** a nomogram, esp. one comprising three scales in which a line joining values on two determines a value on the third. [Fr. *aligner* — L. *ad*, to, *līneāre*, to line.]

alike *ə-līk'*, *adj* the same in appearance or character. — *adv* equally. [O.E. *gelīc*, combined with O.N. *ālīkr*, O.E. *onlīc*; see **like**[1].]

aliment *al'i-mənt*, *n* nourishment; food; provision for maintenance, alimony (*Scot*). — *vt* to support, sustain (*Scot*); to provide aliment for. — *adj* **alimental** (*-ment'l*) supplying food. — *adj* **aliment'ary** pertaining to aliment; nutritive. — *n* **alimentā'tion**. — *adj* **aliment'ative**. — **alimentary canal** the internal passage from the mouth to the anus. [L. *alimentum* — *alĕre*, to nourish.]

alimony *al'i-mən-i*, *n* an allowance for support made by one spouse to the other pending or after their divorce or legal separation. [L. *alimōnia* — *alĕre*, to nourish.]

aline *ə-līn'*, (*NAm*) *vt* and *vi* to align. — *n* **aline'ment**.

A-line *ā'līn*, *adj* (of clothing) narrow at the top and widening evenly to a full hem-line. [**A** and **line**[2].]

aliphatic *al-i-fat'ik*, (*chem*) *adj* fatty; belonging to the open-chain class of organic compounds, or methane derivatives (opp. to *aromatic*). [Gr. *aleiphar*, *aleiphatos*, oil.]

aliquant *al'i-kwənt*, (*math*) *adj* such as will not divide a number without a remainder, thus 5 is an aliquant part of 12. [L. *aliquantum*, somewhat.]

aliquot *al'i-kwot*, (*math*) *adj* such as will divide a number without a remainder. [L. *aliquot*, some, several.]

alit. See **alight**[1].

aliunde *ā-li-un'de*, (*law*) *adv* from another source. — Also *adj*. [L., from elsewhere.]

alive *ə-līv'*, *adj* living; vigorous; existing; lively, animated; (of a wire, etc.) live; sensitive, cognisant (with *to*). — **alive and kicking** strong and active; full of vigour; **alive with** swarming with. [O.E. *on līfe*, in life.]

alkali *al'kə-lī*, (*chem*) *n* a substance which, dissolved in water, forms a solution containing hydroxyl ions and with a pH of more than 7: — *pl* **al'kalies** or **al'kalis**. — *adj* of, pertaining to, containing or forming an alkali. — *n* **alkalesc'ence**. — *n* **alkalesc'ency**. — *adj* **alkalesc'ent** tending to become alkaline; slightly alkaline. — *adj* **al'kaline** (*-līn* or *-lin*) having the properties of an alkali; containing much alkali. — *n* **alkalinity** (*-lin'*) the quality of being alkaline; the extent to which a substance is alkaline. — *vt* **al'kalinize** or **al'kanize** to make alkaline. — *n* **al'kaloid** any of various nitrogenous organic bases found in plants, having specific physiological action. — *adj* pertaining to or resembling alkali. — **alkali metals** the univalent metals of the first group of the periodic system, lithium, sodium, potassium, rubidium, caesium, francium, forming strong basic hydroxides; **alkaline earth** an oxide of any of the alkaline earth metals; an alkaline earth metal; **alkaline earth metals** the bivalent metals of the second group of the periodic system, calcium, strontium, barium, and sometimes magnesium and radium. [Ar. *alqalīy*, the calcined ashes.]

alkane *al'kān*, *n* the general name for a hydrocarbon of the methane series, of general formula C_nH_{2n+2}. [*alk*yd and meth*ane*.]

alkanet *al'kə-net*, *n* a Mediterranean plant (genus *Alkanna*) of the borage family; a red dye obtained from its root; extended to various related plants (*Anchusa*, etc.). [Sp. *alcaneta* (dimin.) — Ar. *al-hennā*, the henna.]

alkene *al'kēn*, (*chem*) *n* the general name for an unsaturated hydrocarbon of the ethylene series, of general formula C_nH_{2n}. [*alk*yl and eth*ene*.]

alkie or **alky** *al'ki*, (*colloq*) *n* an alcoholic.

alkyd *al'kid*, *n* any of a group of synthetic resins used in paints and protective coatings and in adhesives. — Also **alkyd resin** (*rez'in*). [*alky*l and aci*d*.]

alkyl *al'kil*, (*chem*) *n* the general name for a monovalent hydrocarbon radical. [Ger. *Alk*ohol, alcohol and **-yl**.]

alkyne *al'kīn*, (*chem*) *n* the general name for a hydrocarbon of the acetylene series, of general formula C_nH_{2n-2}. [*alk*yd and eth*yne*.]

all *öl*, *adj* comprising every individual one (e.g. *all men*); comprising the whole extent, etc., of (e.g. *all winter*); any whatever; (preceding 'the') as many as there are, or as much as there is (e.g. *all the men, all the cheese*); also used following *pl pers pronoun*, or sometimes *npl* (e.g. *we all laughed, the guests all came*); the greatest possible (e.g. *with all haste, in all sincerity*); every. — *n* the whole; everybody; everything; one's whole possessions or utmost efforts. — *adv* wholly; entirely; quite, completely; without limit, infinitely; on all sides; on each side, apiece. — *combining form* infinite, infinitely; universal; completely, wholly; by all; having all for object. — *n* **all'ness** the condition of being all. — Possible compounds are without limit and only a selection can be given. — *adj* **all'-American** representative of the whole of America, esp. in some admirable quality; typically American (in behaviour, appearance, etc.); consisting entirely of U.S. or American members. — **All Blacks** the New Zealand international rugby team; **all-clear'** a signal that the reason for sheltering, or (*fig*) for inactivity, is past. — *adj* **all'-day** lasting all day. — *adj* **all-elec'tric** using only electricity for heating and lighting. — **All-Hall'ows** All Saints' Day, 1 November; **all'heal** the great valerian or other plant thought to have healing properties. — *adj* **all-import'ant** essential; crucial. — *adj* **all-in'** including everything; (of wrestling) with no restrictions on holds, freestyle. — *adj* **all'night** lasting or open, etc. all night. — *adj* **all'-or-nothing** that must be gained, accepted, etc. completely or not at all. — *adj* **all'-out** using maximum effort; of a strike, with everyone participating. — *adj* **all'-over** over the entire surface, body, etc. — *adj* **all-play-all'** (of a competition) in which every competitor plays against every other in turn. — *adj* **all-pow'erful** supremely powerful; omnipotent. — *adj* **all-pur'pose** that can be used for any purpose, in any circumstances, etc. — *adj* **all-risks'** (of insurance) covering all risks except a number specifically excluded (as e.g. war risks, damage due to depreciation, etc.). — *adj* **all'-round** including or applying to all; adequate, complete or competent on all sides. — **all-round'er** a person who shows ability in many sports or many aspects of a particular sport, esp. cricket; a person who shows an ability in or who has an involvement in many kinds of work, etc. (also *adj*); **all-round'ness**. — *adj* **all'-star** having a cast or team all of whom are stars. — *adj* **all'-time** of all time to date. — *n* and *adj* **all'-up** (of loaded aircraft, etc.) total (weight). — **after all** when everything has been considered; in spite of all that, nevertheless; **all along** everywhere along; all the time; **all at once** suddenly; **all but** everything short of, almost; **All Fools' Day** April Fools' Day, 1 April; **all for** (*colloq*) strongly in favour of; **all found** (usu. of a price) all in, with everything included; **All Hallows' Day** All Saints' Day; **all in** exhausted; everything included; **all in all** all things considered, all or everything together; that which someone is wholly wrapped up in; **all of** (*colloq*) as long or as far, etc. as; the whole distance, time, etc. of; **all out** at full power or speed; **all over** everywhere; over the whole of; covered with (*colloq*); thoroughly, entirely; very characteristically; **all over the place** all awry, or in a disorganised muddle; **all over with** finished, done with, completely at an end with; **all right** a colloq. phrase expressing agreement or approval; **All Saints' Day** 1 November, a Christian festival in honour of the saints collectively; **All Souls' Day** 2 November, a R.C. day of prayer for souls in Purgatory; **all systems go** everything (is) in working order, starting up, etc. (also *fig*); **all that** (usu. after a negative or a question) so, that, as... as all that; **all the best** a phrase used to wish someone good luck, etc.; **all there** (*colloq*) completely sane; alert; **all the same** see under **same**; **all-time high** or **low** a high or low level never before reached; **all-time record** a record exceeding all others in all times; **all told** including every person, thing, etc.; taking everything into account; **all up with** at an end with; beyond any hope for; **and all that** and all the rest of it, *et cetera*; **as all that** to that extent; **at all** in the least degree; in any way; in any circumstances; used also merely to give emphasis; **be all over someone** to be excessively, and sometimes irritatingly, friendly and attentive to someone one is with; **once and for all** once and once only, finally; **when all is said and done** after all; all things considered. [O.E. (Anglian) *all*.]

alla breve *al'ə* or *äl'lä brā'vā*, (*mus*) taking the minim as the main unit, not the crotchet, e.g. two beats to the bar instead of four. [It., according to the breve (there being orig. a breve to the bar).]

Allah *al'ä*, (*Islam*) *n* the name of God. [Ar. *allāh* — *alilāh*, the God.]

allantois *a-lan'tō-is*, *n* a membranous sac-like appendage with respiratory, nutritive or excretory functions in the embryos of mammals, birds, and reptiles. — *adj* **allanto'ic**. — *adj* **allan'toid** (*-toid*). — *n* the allantois. [Irregularly formed from Gr. *allās*, *-āntos*, a sausage, *eidos*, form.]

allay *ə-lā'*, *vt* to put down, quell; to calm, alleviate, abate; to reduce; to alloy, temper. — *vi* to abate. — *n* **allay'er**. — *n* **allay'ing**. [O.E. *ālecgan*.]

allege *ə-lej'*, *vt* to assert with a view to subsequent proof, hence without proof; to bring forward in argument or plea; to cite or quote in discussion. — *n* **allegation** (*al-i-gā'shən*) the act of alleging; that which is alleged; an unproved or unaccepted assertion. — *adj* **alleged** (*ə-lejd'*). — *adv* **allegedly** (*-lej'əd-li*). — *n* **alleg'er**. [O.Fr. *esligier*, to clear at law — L. *ex*, from, *lītigāre*, to sue.]

allegiance *ə-lē'jəns*, *n* the relation or obligation of subject to sovereign or state; loyalty (to a person or cause). [L. *ad*, to, and **liege**.]

allegory *al'i-gər-i*, *n* a narrative, picture, etc. intended to be understood symbolically. — *adj* **allegoric** (*-gor'ik*) or **allegor'ical**. — *adv* **allegor'ically**. — *vt* **all'egorise** or **-ize** to put in the form of an allegory; to treat as allegory. — *vi* to use allegory. — *n* **allegorīsā'tion** or **-z-**. — *n* **all'egoriser** or **-z-**. — *n* **all'egorist**. [Gr. *allēgoriā* — *allos*, other, *agoreuein*, to speak.]

allegro *a-lā'grō*, (*mus*) *adv* and *adj* with brisk movement; lively and rather fast. — *n* an allegro piece or movement: — *pl* **alle'gros**. — *adv* and *adj* **allegret'to** somewhat brisk (less so than allegro). — Also *n* (*pl* **allegret'tos**). [It., — L. *alacer*, brisk.]

allele *al-ēl'*, *n* shortened form of **allelomorph** (*al-ēl'ō-mörf*) any one of the two or more possible forms of a gene; a gene considered as the means of transmission of an allele. — *adj* **allelomor'phic**. — *n* **allelomor'phism**. [Gr. *allēlōn*, of one another, *morphē*, form.]

alleluia or **alleluiah** *al-i-lōō'yä*. Same as **hallelujah**.

allemande *al'i-mand*, *al'mand* or *al-mād*, (*mus*) *n* a smooth-running movement of moderate tempo, in common time, coming after the prelude in a classical suite; a German dance in 2–4 time; a movement affecting change of order in a dance. [Fr. *allemande* (*fem.*), Ger.]

allergy *al'ər-ji*, *n* an altered or acquired state of sensitivity; an abnormal reaction of the body to substances normally harmless; hypersensitivity to certain antigens etc.; (*colloq*) dislike, repugnance. — *n* **all'ergen** any substance that induces an allergic reaction. — *adj* **allergen'ic** causing an allergic reaction. — *adj* **allergic** (*ə-lûr'jik*) (of the body) reacting in an abnormally sensitive manner; suffering from an allergy (to). — *n* an allergic person. [Ger. *Allergie* — Gr. *allos*, other, *ergon*, work.]

alleviate *ə-lēv'i-āt*, *vt* to make light; to mitigate. — *n* **allēviā'tion**. — *n* **allēv'iātor**. — *adj* **allēv'iative**. — *adj* **allēviā'tory**. [L.L. *alleviāre*, *-ātum* — L. *ad*, to, *levis*, light.]

alley *al'i*, *n* a narrow lane; a back lane; a long narrow enclosure, or rink, for bowls or skittles; a walk in a garden or shrubbery: — *pl* **all'eys**. — **all'eyway** a narrow passage or alley. [O.Fr. *alee* (Fr. *allée*), a passage, from *aller*, to go.]

allheal. See **all**.

alliaceous *al-i-ā'shəs*, *adj* garlic-like. [L. *allium*, garlic.]

alliance. See **ally**.

alligator *al'i-gā-tər*, *n* a reptile of a mainly American family related to the crocodile but with a shorter, broader snout and other characteristics. — **alligator pear** the avocado pear. [Sp. *el*, the, *lagarto*, lizard.]

alliteration *ə-* or *a-lit-ər-ā'shən*, *n* the recurrence of the same initial sound (not necessarily letter) in words in close succession, as 'the low last edge of the long lone land' (Swinburne). — *vi* **allit'erate** to begin with the same sound; to constitute alliteration; to practise alliteration. — *adj* **allit'erative**. [L. *ad*, to, *lītera*, *littera*, a letter.]

allium *al'i-əm*, *n* a plant of the genus **Allium** to which onions, leeks, garlic, etc. belong. [L., garlic.]

allo- *a-lō-* or *a-lə-*, *combining form* denoting: other; one of a group constituting a structural unit; different; from outside. [Gr. *allos*, other.]

allocarpy *al'ō-kär-pi*, (*bot*) *n* fruiting after cross-fertilisation. [**allo-** and Gr. *karpos*, fruit.]

allocate *al'ō-kāt* or *al'ə-kāt*, *vt* to apportion or assign; to locate. — *adj* **all'ocable** or **allocāt'able**. — *n* **allocā'tion** the act of allocating; a share allocated; apportionment, allotment; an allowance made upon an account. [L. *allocāre* — *ad*, to, *locāre*, *-ātum*, to place.]

allochthonous *al-ok'thə-nəs*, (*science*) *adj* having moved or been moved from another environment, away from its native location. [**allo-** and Gr. *chthon*, ground.]

allocution *al-ō-kū'shən*, *n* an exhortation; a formal address. [L. *allocūtiō*, *-ōnis* — *ad*, to, and *loquī*, *locūtus*, to speak.]

allogamy *al-og'ə-mi*, (*bot*) *n* cross-fertilisation. — *adj* **allog'amous**. [**allo-** and Gr. *gamos*, marriage.]

allometry *al-om'ə-tri*, *n* (the study of) the growth of a part of the body relative to that of other parts or of the whole body, in one organism or comparatively in a number of different organisms. — *adj* **allomet'ric**. [**allo-** and Gr. *metron*, measure.]

allomorph *al'ō-mörf*, (*linguis*) *n* one of two or more forms of the same morpheme. [**allo-** and Gr. *morphē*, form.]

allonym *al'ō-nim*, *n* another person's name adopted as a pseudonym by a writer. — *adj* **allon'ymous**. [Fr. — Gr. *allos*, other, *onyma* = *onoma*, name.]

allopathy *al-op'ə-thi*, *n* orthodox medical practice, treatment of diseases by drugs, etc., whose effect on the body is the opposite of that of the disease, as distinct from *homoeopathy*. — *n* **all'ōpath**. — *adj* **allopathic** (*al-ō-path'ik*). — *n* **allop'athist**. [Ger. *Allopathie*, coined by Hahnemann (1755–1843) — Gr. *allos*, other, *pathos*, suffering.]

allophone *al'ō-fōn*, (*linguis*) *n* one of two or more forms of the same phoneme. — *adj* **allophonic** (*-fon'ik*). [**allo-** and Gr. *phōnē*, sound.]

allopurinol *al-ō-pūr'in-ol*, *n* a drug used in the treatment of gout, reducing the formation of uric acid. [**allo-**, **purin** and *-ol* — L. *oleum*, oil.]

allosaur *al'ō-sör*, *n* a large, lizard-hipped, carnivorous dinosaur of the genus *Allosaurus*. [**allo-** and Gr. *sauros*, lizard.]

allosteric *al-ō-ster'ik* or *-stēr'ik*, (*biol*) *adj* (of an enzyme the activity of which may be) influenced by a combination with another substance; pertaining to the inhibition or stimulation of activity caused by such a combination. — *n* **allos'tery**. [**allo-** and **steric**.]

allot *ə-lot'*, *vt* to distribute in portions; to parcel out; to assign; to divide as by lot: — *pr p* **allott'ing**; *pa t* and *pa p* **allott'ed**. — *n* **allot'ment** the act of allotting; a part or share allotted; a piece of ground let out for spare-time cultivation under a public scheme. — *n* **allottee'** a person to whom something is allotted. [O.Fr. *aloter* — *à*, to, and the root of **lot**.]

allotropy *al-ot'rə-pi*, *n* the property (esp. in chemical elements, as carbon) of existing in more than one form. — *n* **allotrope** (*al'ə-trōp*) an allotropic form. — *adj* **allotrop'ic**. — *n* **allot'ropism**. — *adj* **allot'ropous** having nectar accessible to all kinds of insects (*bot*); (of insects) short-tongued, as those that visit allotropous flowers. [**allo-** and Gr. *tropos*, turn, habit.]

allow *ə-low'*, *vt* to permit; to assign, grant or give, esp. periodically; to concede, acknowledge; to assume as an element in calculation or as something to be taken into account; to admit or agree as due. — *vi* to permit; to make allowance for. — *n* **allowabil'ity**. — *adj* **allow'able**. — *n* **allow'ableness**. — *adv* **allow'ably**. — *n* **allow'ance** that which is allowed; a limited portion or amount allowed, allotted or granted; a ration or stint; money allowed to meet expenses or in consideration of special conditions; a sum periodically granted; a taking into account in calculation or excuse, as in *make allowances for*. — *vt* to put upon an allowance; to supply in limited quantities. — *adj* **allowed'** permitted; licensed; acknowledged. [O.Fr. *alouer*, to praise, bestow.]

alloy *al'oi* or *ə-loi'*, *n* a mixture of metals; extended to a mixture of metal with non-metal; the baser ingredient in such a mixture (esp. in gold or silver); anything added in a mixture that impairs or debases the main ingredient. — *vt* to mix (metal); to mix with a less valuable metal; to impair or debase by being present; to temper or qualify. — *vi* to become alloyed. [Fr. *aloi* (n.), *aloyer* (vb.) — L. *alligāre* — *ad*, to, *ligāre*, to bind.]

allspice *äl'spīs*, *n* pimento or Jamaica pepper, supposed to combine the flavours of cinnamon, nutmeg and cloves (see also **calycanthus**).

allude *ə-lo͞od'* or *-lūd'*, *vi* (with *to*) to convey an indirect reference in passing; to refer without explicit mention, or with suggestion of further associations; to refer. — *n* **allu'sion** (*-zhən*) indirect reference. — *adj* **allu'sive** (*-siv*) alluding; hinting; referring indirectly. — *adv* **allu'sively**. — *n* **allu'siveness**. [L. *allūdĕre* — *ad*, at, *lūdĕre*, *lūsum*, to play.]

allure *ə-lūr'* or *-lo͞or'*, *vt* to entice, seduce or attract. — *n* **allure'** or **allure'ment**. — *n* **allur'er**. — *adj* **allur'ing**. — *adv* **allur'ingly**. [O.Fr. *alurer* — *à*, to, *lurer*, to lure.]

allusion, etc. See **allude**.

alluvia, alluvial. See **alluvium**.

alluvion *ə-lo͞o'vi-ən* or *-lū'*, *n* land gradually gained from a river or the sea by the washing up of sand and earth; the formation of such land. [L. *alluviō*, *-ōnis*; see **alluvium**.]

alluvium *ə-lo͞o'vi-əm* or *-lū'*, *n* matter transported in suspension and deposited by rivers or floods: — *pl* **allu'via**. — *adj* **allu'vial**. [L. neut. of *alluvius*, washed up — *ad*, to, *luĕre*, to wash.]

ally *ə-lī'*, *vt* to join in relation of marriage, friendship, treaty, co-operation or assimilation: — *pr p* **ally'ing**; *pa t* and *pa p* **allied'**. — *n* **a'lly** a member of or party to an alliance; a state or sovereign joined in league for co-operation in a common purpose; a person who co-operates or helps, a supporter; anything near to another in classification or nature: — *pl* **a'llies**. — *n* **allī'ance** the state of being allied; union, or combination by marriage, treaty, etc.; a group of allies; a subclass or group of families (*bot*). — *adj* **a'llied** (or *-līd'*). [O.Fr. *alier* — L. *alligāre*.]

allyl *al'il*, (*chem*) *n* an organic radical (C_3H_5) whose sulphide is found in oil of garlic. [L. *allium*, garlic, and Gr. *hȳlē*, matter.]

almacantar *al-mə-kan'tər* or **almucantar** *al-mū-kan'tər*, (*astron*) *n* a circle of altitude, parallel to the horizon; an instrument for determining a star's passage across an almacantar. [Ar. *almuqantarāt*, the sundials — *al*, the, *qantarah*, bridge.]

alma mater *al'mə mā'tər* or *al'ma mä'ter*, (L.) *n* a term applied by former students to their university, school or college. [L., bountiful mother.]

almanac *öl'mə-nak*, *n* a register of the days, weeks and months of the year, with astronomical events, anniversaries, etc. published annually; an annual publication containing a variety of factual information. [App. from an Ar. word *al-manākh*.]

almandine *al'man-dīn* or *-dēn*, *n* precious (red iron-alumina) garnet. [L.L. *alabandīna* — *Alabanda*, a town in Caria, where it was found.]

almighty *öl-mīt'i*, *adj* omnipotent; irresistible; invincible; mighty. — Also *adv*. — **the Almighty** God. [O.E. *ælmihtig*.]

almond *ä'mənd*, *n* the fruit, and esp. the kernel, of a tree related to the peach, with a dry husk instead of flesh; anything of the shape of an almond (an ellipse pointed at one end). — *adj* made of or flavoured with almond. [O.Fr. *almande* — L. *amygdala* — Gr. *amygdalē*.]

almoner *ä'mən-ər* or *al'mən-ər*, *n* a distributor or giver of alms (*archaic*); a medical social worker attached to a hospital (no longer official title). [O.Fr. *aumoner*, *aumonier* — L.L. *eleēmosynārius* (adj.); see **alms**.]

almost *öl'mōst* or *-məst*, *adv* very nearly. [**all** and **most** (in sense of nearly).]

alms *ämz*, *nsing* and *pl* relief given out of pity to the poor. — **alms'-house** a house endowed for the support and lodging of the poor. [O.E. *ælmysse*, through L.L. from Gr. *eleēmosynē* — *eleos*, compassion.]

almucantar. See **almacantar**.

Alnus. See **alder**.

aloe *al'ō*, *n* any member of a mainly South African genus **Aloe** (*al'ō-ē*), mostly of trees and shrubs, of the lily family, extended to the so-called *American aloe* (see **agave**); (usu. in *pl* form but treated as *sing*) a bitter purgative drug, condensed from the juice of leaves of various species of Aloe. — **aloe vera** (*ver'ə* or *vē'rə*) (also with *caps*) a variety of aloe plant or esp. the juice of its leaves (thought to have healing and other qualities) used in cosmetics, etc. [Directly and through O.E. *aluwan*, *alewan* (pl.) — L. *aloē*.]

aloft *ə-loft'*, *adv* on high; overhead; above; on the top; high up. [O.N. *ā lopti*, in the sky — *ā*, on, in, to, *lopt* (see **loft**).]

alogia *ə-lōj'ē-ə*, *n* inability to speak, due to brain lesion. [**a-**[1] and Gr. *logos*, speech.]

alogical *a-loj'i-kl* or *ā-*, *adj* outside the domain of logic. [**a-**[1] and **logical**.]

aloha *ä-lō'ə* or *-lō'hä*, *interj* greetings; farewell. [Hawaiian, love, kindness.]

alone *ə-lōn'*, *adj* single; solitary; unaccompanied; by oneself; unique. — *adv* singly. — *n* **alone'ness.** — **go it alone** (*colloq*) to act on one's own, without help. [**all** and **one.**]

along *ə-long'*, *adv* by or through the length; lengthwise; at full length; throughout; onward; together, in company or conjunction. — *prep* lengthwise by, through, or over; by the side of. — *prep* and *adv* **along'side** beside; side by side (with); close to the side (of). [O.E. *andlang* — pfx. *and-*, against, and *lang*, long.]

aloof *ə-lo͞of'*, *adv* with avoidance or detachment; with reserve suggesting consciousness of superiority; apart; some way off (from); without participation. — *adj* distant, withdrawn. — *adv* **aloof'ly.** — *n* **aloof'ness.** [**a-**[1] and **loof** — **luff**, windward.]

alopecia *al-ō-pē'si-ə* or *-shə*, *n* baldness, hair loss. [Gr. *alōpekiā*, fox-mange, a bald spot, *alōpēx*, fox.]

aloud *ə-lowd'*, *adv* audibly; loudly. [**a-**[1] and **loud.**]

ALP *abbrev* for Australian Labor Party.

alp *alp* or *älp*, *n* a high mountain; a mountain pasture; (in *pl* with *cap*) the mountain ranges of Switzerland and neighbouring countries. — *adj* **Alp'ine** or **alp'ine** (*-īn*) of the Alps or other mountains; growing on mountain tops. — *n* an alpine plant. — *n* **alp'inism** (*-in-*) the art or practice of mountain-climbing. — *n* **alp'inist.** [L. *Alpēs*, the Alps.]

alpaca *al-pak'ə*, *n* a domesticated animal related to the llama; cloth made of its long silky wool. [Sp., prob. from Quechua.]

alpha *al'fə*, *n* the first letter of the Greek alphabet (Α, α); the first or brightest star of a constellation; the beginning; in classification, the first or one of the first grade. — *adj* short for **alphabetical** (*colloq* or *comput*); in chemical classification, designating one of two or several isomeric forms of a compound. — **al'pha-blocker** a drug used to cause blood-vessels to dilate, esp. in muscle; **alpha particle** (*phys*) a helium nucleus given off by radioactive substances; **alpha ray** (*phys*) a stream of alpha particles; **alpha rhythm** or **wave** one of the principal slow waves recorded on electroencephalogram indicating normal relaxed brain activity. — **alpha and omega** beginning and end. [Gr. *alpha* — Heb. *āleph*.]

alphabet *al'fə-bet*, *n* a system of letters, esp. arranged in conventional set order; first elements, basics. — *adj* **alphabet'ic** or **alphabet'ical** relating to or in the order of an alphabet. — *adv* **alphabet'ically.** — *vt* **al'phabetise** or **-ize** to arrange alphabetically. — **alphabet soup** a confusing or off-putting series or mass of strings of letters, esp. the abbreviations of names of official bodies (*fig*, after a type of soup with letter-shaped noodles in it). [Gr. *alphabētos* — *alpha*, *bēta*, the first two Greek letters.]

alphanumeric *al-fə-nū-mer'ik* or **alphanumer'ical** *-əl*, *adj* consisting of, or (of a machine) using, both letters and numbers. — *adv* **alphanūmer'ically.** — Also **alphamer'ic** or **alphamer'ical.** [**alpha** and **numeric.**]

alphasort *al'fə-sört*, *vt* to sort into alphabetical order. [**alpha** and **sort.**]

alpine, etc. See **alp.**

already *öl-red'i*, *adv* previously, or by the time in question. [**all** and **ready.**]

alright *öl-rīt'*. An alternative, less acceptable, spelling of **all right.**

Alsatian *al-sā'shən*, *n* a German sheep-dog of wolflike breed, often used by police and security officers because of its strength and fierceness (also called **German shepherd, German shepherd dog** or **German Police dog**); a native of Alsace (a district in N.E. France). [L. *Alsatia*, Alsace.]

alsike *al'sik*, *n* a white or pink-flowered clover. [From *Alsike*, near Uppsala, a habitat.]

also *öl'sō*, *adv* likewise; further. — **al'so-ran** a horse that *also ran* in a race but did not get a 'place'; a person of a similar degree of importance. [O.E. *all swā*, all so.]

alstroemeria *al-strə-mē'ri-ə*, *n* a plant of the South American genus *Alstroemeria* of the amaryllis family with inverted leaves. [C. *Alströmer*, 18th-cent. Swedish botanist.]

alt *alt*, (*mus*) *n* a high tone, in voice or instrument. — **in alt** in the octave above the treble stave beginning with G. [L. *altus*, high.]

Altaic *al-tā'ik*, *n* a family of languages, forming one branch of Ural-Altaic, and consisting of Turkic, Mongolic and Tungusic. — Also *adj.*

altar *ölt'ər*, *n* a block or table for making sacrifices on; a table used for mass or the eucharist; the communion table; a scene of worship or marriage ceremony (*fig*); a ledge on a dry-dock wall. — **alt'ar-cloth** the covering of the altar; **alt'arpiece** a work of art placed above and behind an altar; **alt'ar-rails** in a church or chapel, rails separating the presbytery from the rest of the chancel; **alt'ar-stone** a stone serving as an altar; a consecrated slab forming, or inserted in, the top of an altar. — **high altar** the principal altar; **lead to the altar** to marry (a woman). [L. *altāre* — *altus*, high.]

alter *öl'tər*, *vt* to make different; to modify. — *vi* to become different. — *n* **alterabil'ity.** — *adj* **al'terable.** — *n* **alterā'tion.** — *adj* **al'terātive** able to cause change. — *n* a medicine or treatment that changes bodily functions. — *adj* **al'tered** (of a rock) changed in mineral composition by natural forces. [L. *alter*, one of two, the other of two.]

altercate *öl'tər-kāt*, *vi* to dispute heatedly, argue. — *n* **altercā'tion.** — *adj* **al'tercātive.** [L. *altercārī*, *-ātus* — *alter*, other.]

alter ego *al'tər eg'ō* or *ē'gō*, *n* one's second self (see **second**); a trusted, intimate friend: — *pl* **alter egos.** [L., lit. other I.]

alternate *öl'tər-nāt*, also *al'-*, *vt* to cause to follow by turns or one after the other (properly of two things). — *vi* to follow or interchange (with each other; properly of two things); to happen by turns, change by turns. — *n* a deputy, substitute; an alternative. — *adj* **alternate** (*öl-tûr'nət*; in U.S. *öl'-*) arranged or coming one after the other by turns; every other or second; sometimes used with the sense 'alternative'; (of leaves) placed singly with change of side at each node; (of angles) placed one after the other on either side of a line (*geom*). — *n* **alter'nance** (or **al'ternance**) alternation, interchange or variation; training by alternate periods of theoretical and practical work. — *adj* **alter'nant** (or **al'ternant**) alternating. — *n* a spelling or sound variant that does not affect meaning (allomorph or allophone); a type of determinant (*math*). — *adj* **al'ternating.** — *n* **alternā'tion** the act of alternating; alternate succession; interchange; reading or singing antiphonally. — *n* **al'ternātor** a generator of alternating current. — **alternate energy** see **renewable energy**; **alternating current** an electric current that periodically reverses its direction. [L. *alternāre*, *-ātum* — *alter*, one or other of two.]

alternative *öl-tûr'nə-tiv*, *n* either of a pair, or any of a set, of possibilities, esp. of choice; a choice between them; one of them, esp. other than the one in question. — *adj* possible as an alternative; considered by some as preferable to the existing state or form of something, as being less conventional or less materialistic, and more in harmony with nature, as *alternative society*, *alternative technology*, *alternative energy*, *alternative medicine*, etc. — *adv* **alter'natively** with an alternative; by way of alternative. — **Alternative Service Book** a modernised version of the liturgy of the Church of England, used as an alternative to the Book of Common Prayer. [**alternate.**]

althaea or (esp. in U.S.) **althea** *al-thē'ə, n* a plant of the marshmallow and hollyhock genus **Althaea** (or **Althea**) which is sometimes extended to the hibiscus genus and applied (without *cap*) esp. to the rose of Sharon. [Gr. *althaiā*, marshmallow.]

althorn *alt'hörn, n* a tenor saxhorn. [**alt**.]

although *öl-dhō', conj* though (esp., but not necessarily, in stating matter of fact). [**all** and **though**.]

altimeter *al-tim'i-tər, al'ti-mē-tər* or *öl', n* an instrument for measuring height, by means of differences in atmospheric pressure or (*radio altimeter*) by means of the time taken for a radio wave from an aircraft to be reflected back. [L. *altus*, high, and **meter**[1].]

altissimo *al-tis'(s)i-mō, (mus) adj* very high. — **in altissimo** in second octave above treble stave beginning with G. [It., superl. of *alto*, high.]

altitude *al'ti-tūd, n* height, esp. above sea-level; angle of elevation (of a star, etc.) above the horizon; length of the perpendicular from apex to base of a triangle; a high point or position. — *adj* **altitūd'inal** pertaining to altitude; found at high level. — **altitude sickness** same as **mountain sickness**. [L. *altitūdō, -inis*, — *altus*, high.]

alto *al'tō, (mus) n* a high falsetto male voice; countertenor; contralto, the lowest female voice; the part sung by a countertenor or contralto; an instrument of corresponding compass; the possessor of a countertenor or contralto voice: — *pl* **al'tos**. — Also *adj*. [It., — L. *altus*, high.]

altocumulus *al-tō-kū'mū-ləs, n* cumulus cloud forming at 2400–6000 m. (8000–20 000ft): — *pl* **altocu'muli** (*-lī*). [N.L. — L. *altus* high, and **cumulus**.]

altogether *öl-tŏŏ-gedh'ər* or *-tə-gedh'ər, adv* wholly; completely; without exception; in total; all things considered. — **the altogether** (*colloq*) the nude. [**all** and **together**.]

alto-rilievo *äl-tō-rēl-yä'vō, n* high relief; figures projected by at least half their thickness from the background on which they are sculptured. — Partly anglicised as **alto-relievo** (*al-tō-ri-lē'vō*). [It. See **relief**.]

altostratus *al-tō-strā'təs* or *-strä'təs, n* cloud forming a continuous layer at 2400–6000 m. (8000–20 000ft): — *pl* **altostra'ti** (*-tī*). [N.L. — L. *altus* high, and **stratus** under **stratum**.]

altrices *al-trī'sēz, npl* birds whose young are hatched very immature and have to be fed in the nest by the parents. — *adj* **altricial** (*-trish'l*). [L. *altrīcēs* (pl. of *altrix*), feeders, nurses.]

altruism *al'trŏŏ-izm, n* the principle of living and acting for the interest of others. — *n* **al'truist**. — *adj* **altruist'ic**. — *adv* **altruist'ically**. [Fr. *altruisme*, formed by Comte from It. *altrui*, someone else.]

ALU (*comput*) *abbrev* for arithmetic and logic unit.

alula *al'ū-lə, n* in birds, the bastard-wing. [L. dimin. of *āla*, wing.]

alum *al'əm, n* double sulphate of aluminium and potassium, with 24 molecules of water, crystallising in transparent octahedra; any like compound of a trivalent metal (esp. aluminium) and a univalent metal or radical. [L. *alūmen, -inis*.]

aluminium *al-ū-min'i-əm* or in N.Am. **aluminum** *ə-lŏŏ'mi-nəm, n* an element (symbol **Al**; atomic no. 13), a light silvery malleable and ductile metal. — *n* **alumina** (*ə-lū'mi-nə* or *ə-lŏŏ'mi-nə*) oxide of aluminium. — *vt* **alu'minise** or **-ize** to treat (a metal) so as to form an aluminium alloy on its surface; to coat (e.g. glass) with aluminium. [**alum**.]

aluminous *ə-lū'min-əs* or *ə-lŏŏ'min-əs, adj* of the nature of, or containing, alum or alumina. [**alum**.]

alumnus *al-um'nəs, n* a former pupil or student: — *pl* **alum'nī**: — *fem* **alum'na** (*pl* **alum'nae** *-nē*). [L., foster-son, pupil — *alĕre*, to nourish.]

alveolus *al-vē'ə-ləs, al'vi-* or *al-vi-ō'ləs, n* a pit, small depression or dilatation; a tooth socket; one of the clustered cells at the termination of a bronchiole in the lungs: — *pl* **alveoli**. — *adj* **alve'olar** (or *-ōl'*, or *al'*) of an alveolus; produced with the tongue against the roots of the upper teeth (*phon*); pitted. — *adj* **alvē'olate** (or *al'vi-*) pitted; honeycombed; inserted in an alveolus. — *n* **al'veole** an alveolus. — *n* **alveolitis** (*al-vi-ə-lī'tis*) inflammation of the alveoli in the lungs. — **alveolar arch** the part of the jaw in which the teeth are inserted. [L. *alveolus*, dimin. of *alveus*, a hollow.]

always *öl'wāz, adv* every time; ever; continually; in any case. [**all** and **way**[2].]

alyssum *al'is-əm* or *ə-lis', n* a plant of the *Alyssum* genus of low-growing cruciferous plants with white, yellow or mauve flowers; a mass of such plants. — **sweet alyssum** a white scented perennial of a related genus. [Gr. *alysson*, a plant reputed to cure madness — **a-**[2] and Gr. *lyssa*, madness.]

Alzheimer's disease *alts'hī-mərz diz-ēz', n* an illness affecting the brain and causing dementia in the middle-aged or elderly. [Named after Alois *Alzheimer* (1864–1915), German neurologist.]

AM *abbrev* for: amplitude modulation; Associate Member; Member of (the Order of) Australia.

Am. *abbrev* for: Amateur; America; American.

Am (*chem*) *symbol* for americium.

am *am* or *əm*, used as *1st pers sing* of the verb *to be*. [O.E. *am, eam*.]

a.m. or **am** *abbrev* for *ante meridiem* (L.), before noon (in the morning).

AMA *abbrev* for: American Medical Association; Association of Metropolitan Authorities; Australian Medical Association.

amadavat. See **avadavat**.

amadou *am'ə-dŏŏ, n* tinder made from fungi (genus *Polyporus*) growing on trees, used also as a styptic. [Fr.]

amalgam *ə-mal'gəm, n* a mixture of mercury with other metal; any soft mixture; a mixture or blend. [L.L. *amalgama*, perh. — Gr. *malagma*, an emollient.]

amalgamate *ə-mal'gəm-āt, vt* to mix with mercury; to merge. — *vi* to unite in an amalgam; to come together as one; to blend. — *n* **amalgamā'tion** a blending or merging; a union of diverse elements. — *adj* **amal'gamātive**. [**amalgam**.]

amanita *am-ən-ī'tə, n* a mushroom of the *Amanita* genus, including the fly agaric (q.v.) and other poisonous kinds. [Gr. *amānītai* (pl.), a kind of fungus.]

amanuensis *ə-man-ū-en'sis, n* a literary assistant, esp. one who writes to dictation or copies from manuscript: — *pl* **amanuen'sēs**. [L. *āmanuēnsis* — *ā*, from, *manus*, hand.]

amarant *am'ər-ant* or **amaranth** *am'ər-anth, n* a fabled never-fading flower, emblem of immortality; any species of **Amarant'us** or **Amaran'thus** the love-lies-bleeding genus, with richly-coloured long-lasting spikes. — *n* **am'aranth** a highly-nutritious S. American cereal (also **grain amaranth**); a type of dye used for colouring foodstuffs. [Gr. *amarantos* — *a-* (*see* **a-**[2]) and *marainein*, to wither; the *th* forms from confusion with *anthos*, flower.]

amaryllis *am-ə-ril'is, n* any plant of the bulbous S. Afr. genus *Amaryllis*, esp. the belladonna lily. [*Amaryllis*, a girl's name, in the Gr. and L. poets, and others.]

amass *ə-mas', vt* and *vi* to gather in great quantity; to accumulate. [Fr. *amasser* — L. *ad*, to, and *massa*, a mass.]

amateur *am'ə-tər, -tūr* or *-tûr', n* a person who practises something for the love of it, not as a profession; a person who takes part in sport for pleasure (opp. to *professional*); a dilettante; someone whose understanding of, or ability in, a particular art, etc. is superficial or inexpert. — Also *adj*. — *adj* **amateur'ish** imperfect and defective in execution; performed without professional skill. — *adv*

amateur'ishly. — *n* **amateur'ishness** or **am'ateurism**. [Fr., — L. *amātor*, *-ōris*, a lover.]

amatol *am'ə-tol*, *n* a high explosive composed of *am*monium nitrate and trinitro*tol*uene.

amatory *am'ə-tər-i*, *adj* relating to or causing love; amorous. — *adj* **amato'rial** (*-tö'*). — *adv* **amato'rially**. [L. *amātōrius*.]

amaurosis *am-ö-rō'sis*, *n* blindness caused by disease of the optic nerves. — *adj* **amaurotic** (*-rot'ik*). [Gr. *amaurōsis* — *amauros*, dark.]

amaze *ə-māz'*, *vt* to overwhelm with astonishment or wonder. — *adv* **amaz'edly**. — *n* **amaz'ement** astonishment mingled with wonder. — *adj* **amaz'ing**. — *adv* **amaz'ingly** (often hyperbolically). [O.E. *āmasian* (found in the past p. *āmasod*).]

Amazon *am'ə-zon* or *-zən*, *n* in Greek story, one of a nation of women warriors, located near the Black Sea; one of a legendary race of female warriors of S. America; (the following usu. without *cap*) a female soldier; a strong, vigorous or aggressive woman. — Also *adj*. — **am'azon-ant** a European and American ant which enslaves the young of other species. [Gr. *Amāzōn*, *-onos*, in folk-etymology referred to *a-*, without, *māzos*, breast, with the explanation that Amazons cut off the right breast lest it should get in the way of the bowstring.]

Amazonian *am-ə-zō'ni-ən*, of or relating to the River Amazon in S. America; (also without *cap*) of, relating to or resembling an Amazon. [**Amazon**.]

ambassador *am-bas'ə-dər*, *fem* **ambassadress** *-drəs*, *n* a diplomat of the highest rank, sent by one sovereign or State to another as a permanent representative; a messenger or agent. — *adj* **ambassadorial** (*-dö'ri-əl*). — *n* **ambass'adorship**. — **ambass'ador-at-large** an ambassador not accredited to any particular foreign government; **ambassador extraordinary** an ambassador sent on a special occasion, as distinguished from the resident ambassador. [Fr. *ambassadeur* — L. *ambactus*, a slave or servant.]

amber *am'bər*, *n* a yellowish fossil resin; the orange traffic-light, which acts as a cautionary signal between red (stop) and green (go). — *adj* made of amber; amber-hued — clear brownish yellow. — *adj* **am'berous** or **am'bery**. — *n* **am'broid** or **am'beroid** pressed amber, a synthetic amber formed by heating and compressing pieces of natural amber too small to be of value in themselves, sometimes along with other resins. — **am'berjack** a large Atlantic game-fish having golden markings when young. [Fr. *ambre* — Ar. *'anbar*, ambergris.]

ambergris *am'bər-grēs*, *n* an ash-grey strongly-scented substance originating in the intestines of the spermaceti whale and used in the manufacture of perfumes. [Fr. *ambre gris*, grey amber.]

ambi- *am-bi-*, *pfx* round, both, on both sides. [L., — *ambo*, both.]

ambiance. See **ambient**.

ambidextrous *am-bi-deks'trəs*, *adj* able to use both hands equally well; on both sides; double-dealing. — *n* **ambidexterity** (*-ter'i-ti*) or **ambidex'trousness**. — *adv* **ambidex'trously**. [**ambi-**, and L. *dexter*, right.]

ambient *am'bi-ənt*, *adj* going round; (of e.g. air temperature) surrounding; enveloping. — *n* that which encompasses; the air or sky. — *n* **ambience** (*am'bi-əns*) or **ambiance** (*ā-bē-ās*) environment; surrounding influence; atmosphere; the use or disposition of accessories in art. [L. *ambiēns*, *-entis*, pres. p. of *ambīre* — pfx. *ambi-*, about, *īre*, to go.]

ambiguous *am-big'ū-əs*, *adj* doubtful; undetermined; of intermediate or doubtful nature; indistinct; wavering; having more than one possible meaning; equivocal. — *n* **ambigū'ity** doubtful or double meaning; an equivocal expression. — *adv* **ambig'uously**. — *n* **ambig'uousness**. [L. *ambiguus* — *ambigĕre*, to go about, waver — pfx. *ambi-*, both ways, *agĕre*, to drive.]

ambilateral *am-bi-lat'ə-rəl*, *adj* relating to or involving both sides. [**ambi-** and L. *latus*, *lateris*, side.]

ambisexual *am-bi-seks'ū-əl*, *adj* (esp. of sexual characteristics, e.g. pubic hair) common to both sexes. [**ambi-** and **sexual**.]

Ambisonics® *am-bi-son'iks*, *nsing* (also without *cap*) a system of high-fidelity sound reproduction using multiple channels which electronically reproduces ambient sound as perceived by the human ear. [**ambi-** and **sonics**.]

ambit *am'bit*, *n* circuit; scope; compass; precincts; confines. [L. *ambitus*, a going round — pfx. *ambi-*, round, *itus*, going.]

ambition *am-bish'ən*, *n* aspiration after success or advancement; the object of aspiration. — *adj* **ambi'tionless**. — *adj* **ambitious** (*am-bish'əs*) full of ambition; strongly desirous (of, to do); aspiring; indicating ambition; pretentious. — *adv* **ambi'tiously**. — *n* **ambi'tiousness**. [L. *ambitiō*, *-ōnis*, canvassing — pfx. *ambi*, about, and *īre*, *itum*, to go.]

ambivalence *am-biv'ə-ləns* or **ambivalency** *-i*, *n* coexistence in one person of opposing emotional attitudes towards the same object. — *adj* **ambiv'alent**. [**ambi-**, and L. *valēns*, *-entis*, pres. p. of *valēre*, to be strong.]

amble *am'bl*, *vi* to move, as a horse, by lifting together both legs on one side alternately with those on the other side; to move at an easy pace; to go like an ambling horse; to ride an ambling animal. — *n* an ambling pace. — *n* **am'bler**. — *n* and *adj* **am'bling**. [Fr. *ambler* — L. *ambulāre*, to walk about.]

amblyopia *am-bli-ō'pi-ə*, *n* impaired sight without any apparent damage to the eye. [Gr. *amblyōpiā* — *amblys*, dull, *ops*, eye.]

Amblystoma *am-blis'to-mə*, *n* a genus of tailed amphibians in the gill-less or salamandroid suborder, called axolotl in the larval stage. [Gr. *amblys*, blunt, *stoma*, mouth.]

amboceptor *am'bə-sep-tər*, *n* (*biochem*) in immunisation, an antibody acting as a double receptor, linking both with the antigen and with the complement. [L. *amber* both, and **receptor**.]

ambroid. See **amber**.

ambrosia *am-brō'z(h)i-ə* or *-z(h)ə*, *n* the food (later, the drink) of the Greek gods, which conferred everlasting youth and beauty; the anointing oil of the gods; any fragrant or delicious food or beverage; something sweet and pleasing; bee-bread. — *adj* **ambrō'sial** fragrant; delicious; immortal; heavenly. — *adv* **ambrō'sially**. — *adj* **ambrō'sian**. [Gr. *ambrosiā* — *ambrotos*, immortal — **a-**[2], and *brotos*, for *mbrotos*, mortal.]

ambry *am'bri* or **aumbry** *öm'bri*, *n* a recess for church vessels. [O.Fr. *almerie* — L. *armārium*, a chest, safe — *arma*, arms, tools.]

ambulance *am'bū-ləns*, *n* a vehicle or (**air ambulance**) helicopter, etc., for conveying sick or injured. — *adj* **am'bulant** walking; able to walk; moving from place to place; allowing or calling for walking. — *n* a walking patient. — *adj* **am'bulatory** (*-ə-tər-i*) of or for walking; moving from place to place, not stationary; subject to change (*legal*). — **am'bulance-chaser** a lawyer on the look-out for accidents in order to instigate actions for damages (*US*); **am'bulanceman** or **am'bulancewoman** a male or female member of the crew of an ambulance. [L. *ambulāre*, *-ātum*, to walk about.]

ambuscade *am-bəs-kād'*, *n* an ambush. — *vt* and *vi* to ambush. [Fr. *embuscade* or Sp. *emboscada*; see **ambush**.]

ambush *am'bo͝osh*, *n* a lying in wait to attack by surprise; a place of lying in wait; a person or troop lying in wait. — *vt* and *vi* to attack from ambush. — **ambush bug** (*US*) any of several insects of the *Phymatidae* that prey on other insects from a place of concealment, e.g. within a flower. [O.Fr. *embusche* — *embuscher* — L.L. *imboscāre* — *im*, in, *boscus* (unattested), bush.]

am-dram *am-dram'*, (*colloq*) *n* (usu. *sing*) amateur dramatics. — Also *adj*.

ameba, amebic, etc. U.S. spelling of **amoeba, amoebic,** etc.

ameer. See **amir.**

ameliorate *ə-mē'lyə-rāt*, *vt* and *vi* to improve. — *n* **amēliorā'tion.** — *adj* **amē'liorātive.** [Fr. *améliorer* — L. *ad*, to, *melior*, better.]

amen *ä-men'* or *ā-men'*, *interj* so let it be (said esp. at the end of a prayer). [Heb. *āmēn*, true, truly, retained in Gr. and English translations.]

amenable *ə-mēn'ə-bl* or (esp. in U.S.) *ə-men'ə-bl*, *adj* ready to be led or won over; liable or subject. — *n* **amenabil'ity** or **amen'ableness.** — *adv* **amen'ably.** [Fr. *amener*, to lead — *à* — L. *ad*, to, *mener*, to lead — L.L. *mināre*, to lead, to drive (as cattle).]

amend *ə-mend'*, *vt* to free from fault or error; to correct; to improve; to alter in detail, with a view to improvement, as a bill before parliament; to rectify; to cure; to mend. — *vi* to grow or become better; to reform; to recover. — *adj* **amend'able.** — *adj* **amend'atory** corrective. — *n* **amend'er.** — *n* **amend'ment** correction; improvement; an alteration or addition to a document, agreement, etc.; an alteration proposed on a bill under consideration; a counter-proposal or counter-motion put before a meeting. — **make amends** to supply a loss; to compensate (for). [Fr. *amender* — L. *ēmendāre* — *ē*, out of, and *mendum*, a fault.]

amenity *ə-mē'ni-ti* or *ə-men'i-ti*, *n* pleasantness, as in situation, climate, manners, disposition; a pleasing feature, object, characteristic; a facility (usu. *pl*); civility. — **amenity bed** a hospital bed, the occupant of which pays for amenities such as privacy while still receiving free medical treatment. [L. *amoenus*, pleasant.]

amenorrhoea or in U.S. **amenorrhea** *a-* or *ā-men-ō-rē'ə*, *n* failure or absence of menstruation. [**a-**[2] and Gr. *mēn*, month, *rhoiā*, a flowing.]

ament *ā'mənt* or *ə-ment'*, *n* a person who fails to develop mentally; a sufferer from amentia. — *n* **amentia** (*a-men'shi-ə* or *ā-men'shi-ə*) mental deficiency. [L. *āmēns*, *-entis* — *ā*, from, *mēns*, *mentis*, mind.]

amentum *a-men'təm*, *n* a catkin: — *pl* **amen'ta.** — Also **a'ment.** [L., thong.]

Amer. *abbrev* for: America; American.

Amerasian *am-ər-ā'shən*, *n* a person fathered by an American serviceman in Vietnam or Korea, or, more generally, anyone of mixed American and Asian parentage. — Also *adj*. [*American* and **Asian.**]

American *ə-mer'i-kən*, *adj* pertaining to America, esp. to the United States. — *n* a native or citizen of America; the English language as spoken in America. — *vt* **Amer'icanise** or **-ize** to make American. — *n* **Amer'icanism** a custom, characteristic, word, phrase, or idiom characteristic of Americans; condition of being an American citizen; (advocacy of) American policies, political attitudes, etc.; devotion to American institutions. — **American aloe** agave; **American eagle** the bald eagle; **American Express® card** a type of credit card issued by a commercial company; **American football** an American game of football, somewhat resembling British rugby football, played with an elliptical ball between teams of eleven players (unlimited substitution being allowed), scoring being by points won for touch-downs and goals; **American Indian** a member of the native race of America; **American pit bull terrier** an American breed of pit bull terrier (q.v. at **pit**[1]); **American plan** (in a hotel, etc.) the system of including meals in the charge for a room (see also **European plan**); **American tiger** a jaguar; **American tournament** see **round robin** under **round**. [From *America*, perh. so called from Richard *Ameryk*, Sheriff of Bristol, who financed John Cabot's voyage; also said to be from Amerigo (L. *Americus*) Vespucci.]

americium *am-ər-ish'i-əm*, *n* a radioactive metallic element (atomic no. 95; symbol **Am**), obtained artificially in *America*.

Amerind *am'ər-ind* or **Amerindian** *am-ər-ind'i-ən*, *n* and *adj* American Indian.

amethyst *am'ə-thist*, *n* a bluish violet quartz used as a gemstone; its colour. — *adj* of, or coloured like, amethyst. [Gr. *amethystos* (lit. not drunken, the stone being supposed to prevent drunkenness) — *a-* (privative) and *methyein*, to be drunken.]

Amex *a'meks*, *abbrev* for: American Express®; American Stock Exchange.

Amharic *am-har'ik*, *n* a Semitic language, the official language of Ethiopia. — Also *adj*. [*Amhara* district of Ethiopia.]

amiable *ām'i-ə-bl*, *adj* of sweet and friendly disposition; lovable. — *n* **āmiabil'ity** or **ām'iableness.** — *adv* **ām'iably.** [O.Fr. *amiable*, friendly — L. *amīcābilis* — *amīcus*, friend; confused in meaning with O.Fr. *amable*, lovable.]

amianthus *am-i-anth'əs* or more correctly **amiantus** *-ant'əs*, *n* the finest fibrous asbestos, which can be made into cloth unaffected by fire. [Gr. *amiantos* (*lithos*), undefiled (stone) — *a-* (privative) and *miainein*, to soil.]

amicable *am'ik-ə-bl*, *adj* in friendly spirit. — *n* **amicabil'ity** or **am'icableness.** — *adv* **am'icably.** [L. *amīcābilis* — *amīcus*, a friend — *amāre*, to love.]

amice[1] *am'is*, *n* a strip of fine linen, worn formerly on the head, now on the shoulders, by a priest at mass. [O.Fr. *amit* — L. *amictus*, cloak — *amb-*, about, and *jacĕre*, to throw.]

amice[2] *am'is* or **almuce** *al-mūs'*, *n* a furred hood or hooded cape with long ends hanging down in front, worn by certain religious orders. [O.Fr. *aumuce.*]

amicus curiae *a-mī'kus kū'ri-ē* or *a-mē'ko͝os ko͞o'ri-ī*, (L.) *n* a person or group not directly involved in a case who may be represented by request or permission of the court; counsel representing such: — *pl* **amī'cī** (or *-mē'kē*). [L., lit. friend of the court.]

amid *ə-mid'*, *prep* in the midst of; among. — *adv* **amid'ships** in, near or towards the middle of a ship lengthwise. [O.E. *on middan* (dat. of adj.), in middle.]

amide *am'īd*, *n* a derivative of ammonia in which an acid radical takes the place of one or more of the three hydrogen atoms. — *n* **amido-group** (*ə-mē'dō-*) the group NH_2 in such combination. [From **ammonia.**]

amidst *ə-midst'* *prep* amid. [**amid**; the *s* is a later adverbial genitive ending, the *t* as in **amongst, betwixt,** etc.]

Amidol® *am'i-dol*, *n* a colourless chemical $(C_6H_3(NH_2)_2(OH).2HCl)$ used as a photographic developer.

amine *am'īn* or *-ēn*, *n* a derivative of ammonia (NH_3) in which one or more hydrocarbon radicals take the place of one or more of the three hydrogen atoms. — **amino-ac'id** (*a-mē-nō-*) a fatty acid in which the amino-group takes the place of a hydrogen atom of the hydrocarbon radical; **amino-group'** the group NH_2 in such combination. [From **ammonia.**]

aminobutene *a-mē-nō-bū'tēn*, *n* a pain-relieving drug, less addiction-forming than morphine. [**amine** and *butene* (an alkene hydrocarbon).]

amir or **ameer** *a-mēr'* or *ə-mēr'*, *n* the title borne by certain Muslim princes. [Ar. *amīr*; see **admiral, emir.**]

Amish *ä'mish* or *am'ish*, *adj* of or belonging to a strict U.S. Mennonite sect. — Also *npl*. [Ger. *amisch*, after 17th-cent. Swiss bishop, J. *Amman* or *Amen.*]

amiss *ə-mis'*, *adv* astray; wrongly; improperly; faultily. — **come amiss** to be unwelcome or untoward;

take amiss to take offence at (strictly, by misinterpretation). [**a-**[1] and **miss**[1].]

amitosis *am-i-tō'sis*, (*biol*) *n* cell-division without mitosis. — *adj* **amitotic** (*-tot'ik*). — *adv* **amitot'ically.** [**a-**[2] and Gr. *mitos*, thread.]

amitryptyline *am-i-trip'tə-lēn*, *n* an antidepressant drug, also used to treat enuresis. [From *am*ino, *trypt*amine (a hallucinogenic substance), meth*yl*, with ending *-ine*.]

amity *am'i-ti*, *n* friendship; goodwill; friendly relations. [Fr. *amitié* — L. *amicus*, a friend.]

ammeter *am'i-tər*, *n* an instrument for measuring electric current usu. in amperes. [From **ampere**, and Gr. *metron*, measure.]

ammo *am'ō*, *n* a familiar contraction of **ammunition**.

ammonia *amō'ni-ə* or *ə-mō'ni-ə*, *n* a pungent compound of nitrogen and hydrogen (NH_3) first obtained in gaseous form from *sal ammoniac*; its solution in water, strictly ammonium hydroxide (*liquid ammonia*). — *adj* **ammō'niac** or **ammonī'acal** of ammonia. — *adj* **ammō'niated** combined or impregnated with ammonia. [N.L. derived from sal *ammoniac* — L. *sal* salt and *ammoniacus* of Ammon; see **ammonite**.]

ammonite *am'ən-īt*, *n* a fossil cephalopod of many kinds, with coiled chambered shell resembling a ram's horn. — *n* **amm'onoid** a member of the order *Ammonoidea*, to which the ammonites and related cephalopods belong. [Gr. *Ammōn*, *-ōnos*, the ram-headed god of ancient Egypt.]

ammonium *a-mō'ni-əm* or *ə-mō'ni-əm*, *n* a univalent radical, NH_4, resembling the alkali metals in chemical behaviour. [Ety. as for **ammonia**.]

ammunition *am-ū-nish'ən*, *n* things used for charging firearms — missiles or propellants (*colloq* **am'mo**); orig. military stores generally; explosive military devices; anything that can be used in fighting (*lit* and *fig*). — *vt* to supply with ammunition. [Obs. Fr. *amunition*, app. from *l'amunition* for *la munition*; see **munition**.]

amnesia *am-nē'zhyə*, *n* the loss of memory. — *n* **amne'siac** a person who suffers from amnesia. — Also *adj*. — *adj* and *n* **amne'sic**. [Gr. *amnēsiā*.]

amnesty *am'nəs-ti*, *n* a general pardon; a period during which offenders may admit to certain crimes or infringements without penalty. — *vt* to give amnesty to. [Gr. *amnēstiā*, forgetfulness.]

amnion *am'ni-ən*, *n* the innermost membrane enveloping the embryo of reptiles, birds and mammals: — *pl* **am'nia**. — *combining form* **amnio-** amnion; amniotic. — *n* **amniocentesis** (*am-ni-ō-sin-tē'sis*) the insertion of a hollow needle into the uterus of a pregnant woman to withdraw a sample of the amniotic fluid to test for foetal abnormalities, etc. — *adj* **amniot'ic**. — *n* **amniot'omy** surgical rupture of the amnion during, or in order to induce, labour. — **amniotic fluid** the fluid within the amnion in which the embryo is suspended. [Gr.]

amoeba or in U.S. **ameba** *ə-mē'bə*, *n* a protozoon of ever-changing shape: — *pl* **amoe'bae** (*-bē* or *-bī*) or **amoe'bas**. — *n* **amoebī'asis** infection (esp. of the colon) by amoebae. — *adj* **amoe'bic**. — *adj* **amoe'biform**. — *adj* **amoe'boid**. [Gr. *amoibē*, change.]

amok *ə-mok'* or **amuck** *ə-muk'*, *adj* and *adv* in a frenzy, esp. in phrase **run amok**, to rush about wildly, attacking anyone in one's path (also *fig*). [Malay *amoq*, frenzied.]

among *ə-mung'* or **amongst** *ə-mungst'*, *prep* of the number of; amid. [O.E. *on-gemang*, lit. in mixture, crowd — *gemengan*, to mingle: for *-st* see **against**.]

amontillado *ä-mon-til-yä'dō* *n* a light medium-dry sherry orig. from *Montilla*: — *pl* **amontilla'dos**. [Sp.]

amoral *ā-mor'əl*, also *a-mor'əl*, *adj* non-moral, outside the domain of morality. — *n* **amor'alism** refusal to recognise the validity of any system of morality. — *n* **amor'alist**. [**a-**[2] and **moral**.]

amorance *am'ər-əns*, *n* (*psychol*) the state of being in love; romantic love. — *adj* **am'orant**. [L. *amor*, love.]

amorist *am'ər-ist*, *n* a lover; a ladies' man; a person who writes of love; a seeker of sexual adventures or experiences. — *n* **am'orism**. [L. *amor*, love.]

amoroso *am-or-ō'sō*, (*mus*) *adj* tender; (of sherry) sweet, full-bodied. — Also *adv*. — Also *n*. — *n* a lover; a ladies' man: — *pl* **amoro'sos**: — *fem* **amoro'sa**. [It.]

amorous *am'ər-əs*, *adj* inclined to love, esp. sexual love; in love; fond; relating to love. — *adv* **am'orously**. — *n* **am'orousness**. [O.Fr. *amorous* (Fr. *amoureux*) — L.L. *amōrōsus* — *amor*, love.]

amorphous *ə-mör'fəs*, *adj* without definite shape or structure; shapeless; without crystalline structure. — *n* **amor'phism**. [Gr. *amorphos*, shapeless — *a-* (privative) and *morphē*, form.]

amortise or **-ize** *ə-mör'tīz* or *-tiz*, *vt* to pay off (a debt) esp. through a sinking-fund. — *n* **amortisā'tion** or **-z-**. [L.L. *a(d)mortizāre* — Fr. *à*, to, *mort*, death.]

amount *ə-mownt'*, *vi* to come in total; to come in meaning or substance (with *to*). — *n* the whole sum; principal and interest together; quantity; value, import, equivalence. [O.Fr. *amonter*, to ascend — L. *ad*, to, *mōns*, *montis* a mountain.]

amour *ə-mōōr'*, *n* a love affair (now usu. discreditable); a loved one. [Fr., — L. *amor*, *amōris*, love.]

amour-propre *a-mōōr-propr'*, (Fr.) *n* self-esteem, sometimes in exaggerated form, shown in readiness to take offence at slights.

amp *amp*, *n* short for **ampere**.

ampelopsis *am-pi-lop'sis*, *n* a plant of the genus of climbing shrubs *Ampelopsis*: — *pl* **ampelop'ses** (*-sēz*). [Gr. *ampelos*, vine, *opsis*, appearance.]

ampere *am'per* or *-pēr'*, (*electr*) *n* the SI and MKSA unit of current, defined as that which, flowing in two parallel conductors, each infinitely thin and long, one metre apart in a vacuum, will produce a force between the conductors of 2×10^{-7} newtons per metre length (**international ampere** a unit formerly defined by means of the rate of deposition of silver from a solution of silver nitrate and slightly less than the practical unit in use; now the same as the unit just defined). — *n* **am'perage** current in amperes. [From A. M. *Ampère* (1775–1836), French physicist.]

ampersand *am'pərs-and*, *n* the character (&; originally ligatured *E* and *T*, for L. *et*) representing *and*. [*and per se*, *and* — that is, &, by itself, means 'and'.]

Ampex® *am'peks*, *n* a system of magnetic recording of television signals. — *vt* to record by Ampex.

amphetamine *am-fet'ə-mēn*, *n* a synthetic, potentially habit-forming drug used to stimulate the central nervous system or as a decongestant. [*a*lpha *m*ethyl *phene*t*hyl* + *amine*.]

amphi- *am-fi-*, *pfx* indicating both, on both sides (or ends) or around. [Gr.]

amphibian *am-fi'bi-ən*, *adj* amphibious; of the **Amphibia**, a class of cold-blooded vertebrates typically gill-breathing in the larval state and lung-breathing or skin-breathing as adults — frogs, toads, newts, salamanders, caecilians. — *n* a member of the Amphibia; an aeroplane designed to alight on land or water; a vehicle for use on land or water. [N.L. — Gr; see **amphibious**.]

amphibious *am-fib'i-əs*, *adj* living, or adapted to life, or use, on land and in or on water; (of military operations) in which troops are conveyed across the sea or other water in landing barges, assault-craft, etc., and land on enemy-held territory; of double, doubtful, or ambiguous nature. [Gr. *amphibios* — *amphi*, on both sides, *bios*, life.]

amphibole *am'fi-bōl*, *n* any mineral of a group of dark-coloured, rock-forming silicates, including hornblende. — *n* **amphib'olite** a rock composed essentially of amphibole. [Gr. *amphibolos*, ambiguous, on account of the resemblance between hornblende and tourmaline.]

amphibology *am-fi-bol'ə-ji*, *n* a phrase or sentence ambiguous not in its individual words but in its construction; the use of such ambiguities. — *adj* **amphibol'ic** or **amphibological** (*-bə-loj'i-kl*). — *adj* **amphib'olous** (*-ə-ləs*). [Gr. *amphibolos* — *amphi*, on both sides, *ballein*, to throw.]

amphimixis *am-fi-mik'sis*, *n* fusion of gametes; sexual reproduction; combination of characters from both parents. — *adj* **amphimic'tic**. [Gr. *amphi*, on both sides, *mīxis*, intercourse, mixing.]

amphipod *am'fi-pod*, *n* one of the **Amphip'oda**, an order of small sessile-eyed crustaceans with swimming feet and jumping feet — sand-hoppers, etc. — *adj* **amphip'odous**. [**amphi-**, and Gr. *pous*, *podos*, a foot.]

amphitheatre *am'fi-thē-ə-tər*, *n* a building with rows of seats one above another, around an open space; a similar configuration of hill slopes; one of the galleries in a theatre. — *adj* **amphithe'atral** or **amphitheatrical** (*-at'ri-kl*). — *adv* **amphitheat'rically**. [Gr. *amphitheātron* — *amphi*, on both sides, *theātron*, theatre.]

ampholyte *am'fō-līt*, *n* an *ampho*teric electro*lyte*.

amphora *am'fə-rə*, *n* a two-handled jar used by the Greeks and Romans for holding liquids: — *pl* **am'phorae** (*-rē* or *-rī*). [L. *amphora* — Gr. *amphoreus*, *amphiphoreus* — *amphi*, on both sides, and *phoreus*, a bearer.]

amphoteric *am-fō-ter'ik*, *adj* of both kinds; acting both ways, e.g. as acid and base, electropositive and electronegative. [Gr. *amphoteros*, both.]

ample *am'pl*, *adj* spacious; wide; large enough; abundant; liberal; copious; full or somewhat bulky in form. — *n* **am'pleness**. — *adv* **am'ply** (*-pli*). [Fr. — L. *amplus*, *amplificāre*, *amplitūdō*.]

amplexus *am-plek'səs*, *n* the clasping of the female of certain amphibians by the male, as part of the mating process; the period of this. [L., encircling, embrace.]

amplify *am'pli-fī*, *vt* to make more copious in expression; to add to; to increase loudness of (sound), strength of (current), etc.: — *pr p* **am'plifying**; *pa p* and *pa t* **am'plified**. — *n* **amplificā'tion** enlargement. — *n* **am'plifier** a person who amplifies; a lens that enlarges the field of vision; a device for giving greater loudness. [Ety. as for **ample**.]

amplitude *am'pli-tūd*, *n* largeness; abundance; width; range; extent of vibratory movement (from extreme to extreme, or from mean to extreme); the angular distance from the east point of the horizon at which a heavenly body rises, or from the west point at which it sets. — **amplitude modulation** (*telecomm*) modulation in radio transmission by varying the amplitude of the carrier wave — cf. *frequency modulation*. [Ety. as for **ample**.]

amplosome *am'plə-sōm*, *n* the short or stocky type of human figure. [L. *amplus*, large, Gr. *sōma*, body.]

ampoule or in U.S. **ampule** *am'pōōl* (also *-pōōl*), *n* a small sealed glass etc. container for a hypodermic dose, etc. [Fr.; see **ampulla**.]

ampulla *am-pōōl'ə*, *n* a small two-handled ancient Roman flask; a vessel for holy oil, as at coronations; cruet for the wine and water used at the altar; any small membranous vesicle (*biol*); the dilated end of a semicircular canal in the ear: — *pl* **ampull'ae** (*-ē*). — See also **ampoule**. [L. irreg. dimin. of *amphora*, a flagon.]

amputate *am'pūt-āt*, *vt* to cut off, as a limb. — *n* **amputā'tion**. — *n* **am'putātor**. — *n* **amputee'**. [L. *amputāre*, *-ātum* — *amb-*, around, and *putāre*, *-ātum*, to lop.]

amrit *am'rət*, *n* a sacred sweetened water used in the Sikh baptismal ceremony; the ceremony itself. [Punjabi, — Sans. *amṛta*, immortal.]

amt. *abbrev* for amount.

amtrack *am'trak*, *n* an amphibious tracked military motor landing-vehicle. [**am** for *am*phibious, and **track**.]

Amtrak *am'trak*, *n* a U.S. corporation (the National Railroad Passenger Corporation) managing passenger rail-travel between major U.S. cities. [*Am*erican *Tra*vel and Trac*k*.]

amu *abbrev* for atomic mass unit.

amuck. See **amok**.

amulet *am'ū-let* or *am'ū-lit*, *n* a charm carried about the person. — *adj* **amulet'ic**. [L. *amulētum*.]

amuse *ə-mūz'*, *vt* to occupy pleasantly; to entertain or divert; to excite mirth in. — *adj* **amus'able**. — *adj* **amused'**. — *adv* **amus'edly**. — *n* **amuse'ment** distraction of attention; a pleasant feeling of the ludicrous; that which amuses; a mechanical or other device for amusement at a fairground, amusement arcade, etc.; recreation; pastime. — *n* **amus'er**. — *adj* **amus'ing** mildly funny; diverting; entertaining. — *adv* **amus'ingly**. — **amusement arcade** a public hall, etc. with gambling machines, video games, etc.; **amusement park** a public park with fairground rides, sideshows, etc. [Fr. *amuser* — *à*, to, *muser*, to stare.]

amyl *am'il*, *n* an alcohol radical, C_5H_{11}. — *n* **am'ylase** (*-ās*) any of the enzymes that play a part in hydrolysis of starch and similar substances. — **amyl nitrate** a liquid added to diesel fuel to improve its ignition quality, also inhaled to heighten sexual pleasure; **amyl nitrite** a fruity-smelling, amber-coloured liquid, inhaled medicinally as a vasodilator. [From the first syllable of Gr. *amylon*, starch, fine meal, and *hȳlē*, matter, from having been first obtained from fusel-oil made from starch.]

amylum *am'il-əm*, (*chem*) *n* starch. — *adj* **amylā'ceous**. — *adj* **am'yloid**. — *n* in any of several pathological conditions, an intercellular deposit of starch-like material in the tissues. — *adj* **amyloid'al**. — *n* **amyloidō'sis** the condition of the body in which amyloid is deposited in the tissues. — *n* **amylop'sin** an enzyme in pancreatic juice that converts starch into sugar. [Gr. *amylon*, the finest flour, starch; lit. unmilled — *a-* (privative) and *mylē*, a mill.]

amyotrophy *a-mi-ot'rə-fi*, *n* atrophy of the muscles. — *adj* **amyotroph'ic**. [Gr. *a-*, not, *mys*, muscle, *trophē*, nourishment.]

Amytal® *am'i-təl*, *n* a white crystalline powder used as a sedative. — Also without *cap*.

an *an* or *ən*, *adj* one; the indefinite article, used before a vowel sound, and by some (now rarely) before an unstressed syllable beginning with a sounded *h*. [O.E. *ān*; see **one**.]

an-. See **a-**[2].

-ana *-ä'nə* or *-ā'nə*, also **-iana** *-i-ä'nə* or *-ā'nə*, *sfx* denoting things belonging to, or typical of, such as sayings, anecdotes, small objects, etc., e.g. Victori*ana* (generally used in reference to the time of Queen Victoria rather than to Victoria herself). [L. neut. pl. ending of adjectives in *-anus*.]

anabaptist *an-ə-bap'tist*, *n* a name given by opponents to a person who holds that baptism should be of adults only and therefore that those baptised in infancy must be baptised again; (with *cap*) someone of a Protestant sect of German origin (1521) rejecting infant baptism and seeking establishment of a Christian communism. [Gr. *ana-*, again, and *baptizein*, to dip.]

anabas *an'a-bas*, *n* a fish of the *Anabas* genus to which belongs the climbing perch, an East Indian fish that often leaves the water. [Gr. *anabās*, aorist p. of *anabainein*, to climb.]

anabiosis *an-ə-bī-ō'sis*, *n* returning to life after apparent death; the ability to do this; a state of suspended animation. — *adj* **anabiot'ic**. [Gr. *anabiōsis* — *ana*, up, back, *bios*, life.]

anableps *an'ə-bleps*, *n* a fish of the *Anableps* genus of bony fishes with open air-bladders, and projecting eyes divided in two for vision in air and water. [Gr. *ana*, up, *blepein*, to look.]

anabolism *an-ab'əl-izm*, *n* chemical building up of complex substances in living matter (opp. to *katabolism*). — *adj* **anabolic** (*an-ə-bol'ik*). — **anabolic steroids** steroids used to increase the build-up of body tissue, esp. muscle, illegally used by some athletes. [Gr. *anabolē*, a heaping up — *ana*, up, *bolē*, a throw.]

anachronism *ə-nak'rə-nizm*, *n* an error assigning a thing to an earlier or (less strictly) to a later age than it belongs to; anything out of keeping with chronology. — *adj* **anachron'ic**. — *adj* **anachronist'ic**. — *adj* **anach'ronous**. — *adv* **anachron'ically**. — *adv* **anachronist'ically**. — *adv* **anach'ronously**. [Gr. *ana-*, backwards, *chronos*, time.]

anacoluthia *an-ə-ko-lōō'thi-ə* or *-lū'thi-ə*, *n* an error in syntax when the latter part of a sentence does not grammatically fit the earlier. — *n* **anacolu'thon** an instance of anacoluthia; anacoluthia: — *pl* **anacolu'tha**. [Gr. *anakolouthiā*, *anakolouthon* — *an-* (privative) and *akolouthos*, following.]

anaconda *an-ə-kon'də*, *n* a gigantic South American water-boa. [Perh. from a Sinhalese name for another snake in Sri Lanka.]

anacoustic zone *an-ə-kōōst'ik zōn*, *n* a zone of absolute silence in space. [**an-** and **acoustic**.]

anacrusis *an-ə-krōō'sis*, (*prosody*) *n* one or more short syllables introductory to the normal rhythm of a line: — *pl* **anacru'ses** (*-sēz*). — *adj* **anacrustic** (*-krus'tik*). [Gr. *anakrousis*, a pushing back, striking up a tune — *ana*, up, back, *krouein*, to strike.]

anadromous *an-ad'rə-məs*, *adj* (of fishes) ascending rivers periodically for spawning (opp. to *catadromous*). [Gr. *anadromos*, running up — *ana*, up, *dromos*, a run.]

anaemia or in U.S. **anemia** *an-ēm'i-ə*, *n* lack of red blood corpuscles or of haemoglobin — a condition marked by paleness and weakness. — *adj* **anaem'ic** suffering from anaemia; sickly, spiritless, washed-out, lacking in body (*fig*). — **pernicious anaemia** a severe form of anaemia characterised by abnormalities in the red blood corpuscles, etc. [Gr. *anaimiā* — *an-* (privative) and *haima*, blood.]

anaerobe *an'ār-ōb*, *n* an organism that lives in absence of free oxygen. — *adj* **anaerobic** (*-ob'ik* or *-ōb'ik*) or **anaerobiotic** (*-ō-bī-ot'ik*) living in the absence of free oxygen; of a process, etc., requiring the absence, or not requiring the presence, of free oxygen; effected by anaerobes, as a biochemical change; involving the activity of anaerobes. — *adv* **anaerob'ically** or **anaerobiot'ically**. — *n* **anaerobio'sis** life in the absence of oxygen. [Gr. *an-* (privative) and, *āēr*, air, *bios*, life.]

anaesthesia (or in U.S. **anesthesia**, etc.) *an-əs-thē'zi-ə*, also **anaesthe'sis** *-sis*, *n* loss of feeling; insensibility, general or local. — *adj* **anaesthetic** (*-thet'ik*) producing or connected with insensibility. — *n* an anaesthetic agent. — *adv* **anaesthet'ically**. — *nsing* **anaesthet'ics** the science of anaesthesia. — *n* **anaesthetīsā'tion** or **-z-**. — *vt* **anaes'thetise** or **-ize**. — *n* **anaesthetist** (*-ēs'thə-tist*) a person who administers anaesthetics. — **general anaesthetic** one which produces insensibility in the whole body, usually causing unconsciousness; **local anaesthetic** one producing insensibility in only the relevant part of the body. [Gr. *anaisthēsiā*, insensibility, *anaisthētos*, insensible.]

anagen *an'ə-jen*, *n* the growing phase of a hair follicle. — *adj* **anagen'ic**. [N.L. — Gr. *ana* up, and *genesis*.]

anaglyph *an'ə-glif*, *n* an ornament in low relief; a picture composed of two prints, in complementary colours, seen stereoscopically through spectacles of these colours. — *adj* **anaglyph'ic**. — *n* **anaglypta** (*a-na-glip'tə*) a type of plain white wallpaper that has a heavily embossed pattern. — Also *adj*. — *adj* **anaglyp'tic**. [Gr. *anaglyphos*, *anaglyptos*, in low relief — *ana*, up, back, *glyphein*, to engrave, carve.]

anagoge *an-ə-gō'ji* or **an'agogy** *n* mystical interpretation. — *adj* **anagogic** (*-goj'ik*) pertaining to mystical interpretation; of the strivings in the unconscious towards morally high ideals. — *adj* **anagog'ical**. — *adv* **anagog'ically**. [Gr. *anagōgē*, leading up, elevation — *ana*, up, *agein*, to lead.]

anagram *an'ə-gram*, *n* word or phrase formed by the letters of another in a different order. — *adj* **anagrammat'ic** or **anagrammat'ical**. — *adv* **anagrammat'ically**. [Gr. *ana-*, back, *gramma*, letter.]

anal, anally. See **anus**.

anal. *abbrev* for: analogy; analysis.

analeptic *an-ə-lep'tik*, *adj* restoring vigour; restoring to consciousness, esp. after anaesthesia. — *n* a restorative medicine. [Gr. *analēptikos*, restorative — *ana*, up, and the root *lab* of *lambanein*, to take.]

analgesia *an-al-jē'zi-ə*, *n* insensibility to pain. — *n* **analgesic** (*-jē'sik*) an anodyne. — *adj* producing analgesia. [Gr. *analgēsiā* — *an-* (privative) and *algeein*, to feel pain.]

analogue or in U.S. **analog** *an'ə-log*, *n* that which is analogous to something else, e.g. protein substances prepared to resemble meat; that which has a similar function (distinguished from a *homologue*) (*biol*); a variable physical quantity which is similar to some other variable in that variations in the former are in the same proportional relationship as variations in the latter, often being used to record or represent such changes (also *adj*); a watch with the traditional face and hands (also *adj*; opp. to *digital*). — *adj* **analog'ical**. — *adv* **analog'ically**. — **analogue computer** a type of computer in which varying electrical currents or voltages, etc., are used to represent proportionally other quantities (e.g. forces, speeds) in working out problems about these qualities; **analogue transmission** (*telecomm*) the transmission of signals and messages by means of radio waves, without first converting them to a computerised form as in *digital transmission*. [Gr. *analogon* — *analogos*, proportionate.]

analogy *an-al'ə-ji*, *n* an agreement or correspondence in certain respects between things otherwise different; a resemblance of relations; parallelism; relation in general; a likeness; proportion, or the equality of ratios (*math*); agreement in function, as distinguished from *homology* or agreement in origin (*biol*); a resemblance by virtue of which a word may be altered on the model of another class of words, as *strove*, *striven*, remodelled upon *drove*, *driven*, etc. (*philol*). — *adj* **anal'ogous** (*-gəs*) having analogy; having some correspondence or resemblance; similar in certain circumstances or relations (with *to*); positively electrified by heating. — *adv* **anal'ogously**. — *n* **anal'ogousness**. [Gr. *analogiā* — *ana*, according to, and *logos*, ratio.]

analysand. See **analysis**.

analyse or **analyze** *an'ə-līz*, *vt* to resolve or separate a thing into its elements or component parts; to ascertain those parts; to trace a thing or things to the source or cause; to discover the general principles underlying individual phenomena by doing this; to resolve a sentence into its syntactic elements (*gram*): — spellings with **-z-** in following words are chiefly U.S. — *adj* **analysable** or **-z-** (*an-ə-līz'ə-bl*). — *n* **an'alyser** or **-z-** a person who analyses; a device that analyses. [Gr. *analȳein*, to unloose, *ana*, up, *lȳein*, to loose.]

analysis *ən-al'is-is*, *n* the action or process of analysing; a table or statement of the results of analysing; use of algebraical methods; psychoanalysis: — *pl* **anal'yses** (*-sēz*). — Opp. to *synthesis*. — *n* **analysand** (*ən-al'i-zand*) a person undergoing psychoanalysis. — *n* **an'alyst** (*-list*) a person skilled in or practising analysis, esp. chemical or economic; a psychoanalyst; analytical chemistry. — **in the last analysis** when all inessentials are excluded from the problem, or the situation. [Gr. *analўsis* — *analўein*; see **analyse**.]

analytic *an-ə-lit'ik*, *adj* pertaining to, performing, or inclined to analysis; resolving into first principles. — *n* (often *pl* in form) analytical logic; analytical geometry. — *adj* **analyt'ical**. — *adv* **analyt'ically**. — **analytical chemistry** (*loosely* **analysis**) chemistry concerned with determination of the constituents of chemical compounds, or mixtures of compounds; **analytical geometry** co-ordinate geometry; **analytical languages** those that use separate words instead of inflexions; **analytical logic** logic which is concerned with analysis. [**analyse**.]

anamnesis *an-am-nēs'is*, *n* the recalling to memory of things past; a patient's account of his or her medical history: — *pl* **anamnē'ses** (*-sēz*). — *adj* **anamnes'tic**. [Gr. *anamnēsis* — *ana*, up, back, *mimnēskein*, to remind, recall to memory.]

anandrous *an-an'drəs*, (*bot*) *adj* without stamens. [Gr. *anandros*, lacking men — *an-* (privative) and *anēr*, *andros*, a man.]

ananthous *an-an'thəs*, (*bot*) *adj* without flowers. [Gr. *ananthēs* — *an-* (privative) and *anthos*, a flower.]

anapaest or **anapest** *an'ə-pēst*, (*prosody*) *n* a foot of two short (or unstressed) syllables followed by a long (or stressed) syllable — a dactyl reversed. — *adj* **anapaes'tic** or **anapaes'tical**. [Gr. *anapaistos*, struck back — *ana*, back, *paiein*, to strike.]

anaphora *ən-af'ə-rə*, *n* the rhetorical device of beginning successive sentences, lines, etc., with the same word or phrase; the use of a word (such as *it*, *do*) to avoid repetition of a preceding word or group of words; the offering of the Eucharistic elements. — *adj* **anaphoric** (*an-ə-for'ik*) or **anaphor'ical** (*-əl*) referring to a preceding word or group of words. — *adv* **anaphor'ically**. [Gr. *anaphorā*, a carrying back, reference — *ana*, back, *pherein*, to bear.]

anaphrodisiac *an-af-rō-diz'i-ak*, *adj* tending to diminish sexual desire. — *n* an anaphrodisiac agent. [Gr. *an-* (privative) and *aphrodīsiakos*, sexual.]

anaphylaxis *an-ə-fil-aks'is*, *n* an increased susceptibility to injected foreign material, protein or non-protein, brought about by a previous introduction of it. — Also **anaphylax'y**. — *adj* **anaphylac'tic** or **anaphylac'toid** having a resemblance to anaphylaxis. [Gr. *ana*, back, *phylaxis*, protection.]

anaplasty *an'ə-pläs-ti*, *n* the repairing of superficial lesions by the use of adjacent healthy tissue, as by transplanting a portion of skin. — *adj* **anaplas'tic**. [Gr. *ana*, again, *plassein*, to form.]

anaptyxis *an-əp-tik'sis*, (*phon*) *n* the development of a vowel between consonants. — *adj* **anaptyc'tic**. [Gr. *anaptyxis*, gape — *ana*, back, *ptyssein*, to fold.]

anarchy *an'ər-ki*, *n* complete absence of law or government; a harmonious condition of society in which government is abolished as unnecessary; utter lawlessness; chaos; complete disorder. — *adj* **anarch'ic** or **anarch'ical**. — *adv* **anarch'ically**. — *vt* **anarchise** or **-ize** (*an'ər-kīz*) to make anarchic. — *n* **an'archism** the teaching of the anarchists. — *n* **an'archist** a person whose ideal of society is one without government of any kind; someone who seeks to bring about such a condition by terrorism. — Also *adj*. — *adj* **anarchist'ic**. — *n* **anarcho-syn'dicalism** syndicalism (q.v.). — *n* and *adj* **anarcho-syn'dicalist**. [Gr. *anarchiā*, leaderlessness, lawlessness — *an-* (privative) and *archē*, government.]

anastigmat *an-as'tig-mat* or *an-ə-stig'mat*, *n* an anastigmatic lens. — *adj* **anastigmat'ic** (*an-ə-*) free from astigmatism. — *n* **anastig'matism**. [**an-** and **astigmatic**.]

anastomosis *an-as-tə-mō'sis*, *n* communication by cross-connections to form a network: — *pl* **anastomō'ses** (*-sēz*). — *vi* **anas'tomose** to intercommunicate in such a way. — *adj* **anastomot'ic**. [Gr. *anastomōsis*, outlet — *ana*, back, *stoma*, mouth.]

anastrophe *a-* or *ə-nas'trə-fi*, (*rhet*) *n* inversion. [Gr. *anastrophē* — *ana*, back, and *strephein*, to turn.]

anat. *abbrev* for anatomy.

anathema *a-nath'i-mə* or *ə-nath'i-mə*, *n* a solemn ecclesiastical curse or denunciation involving excommunication; a curse or execration; a person or thing cursed ecclesiastically or generally; an object of abhorrence: — *pl* **anath'emas**. — *adj* **anathematical** (*-mat'i-kl*). — *n* **anathematisation** or **-z-** (*-mə-tī-zā'shən*). — *vt* and *vi* **anath'ematise** or **-ize**. [Gr. *anathĕma*, a thing dedicated or accursed, for *anathēma*, a votive offering.]

Anatolian *an-ə-tōl'i-ən*, *adj* of *Anatolia*, now the major part of Turkey; of or denoting any or all of an extinct family of languages belonging to, or closely related to, the Indo-European family. — *n* a native or inhabitant of Anatolia; the Anatolian family of languages.

anatomy *ə-nat'ə-mi*, *n* the art of dissecting any organised body; the science of the physical structure of an animal or plant learned by dissection; physical frame or structure; the human body (*colloq*); dissection; analysis (*fig*). — *adj* **anatomic** (*an-ə-tom'ik*) or **anatom'ical**. — *adv* **anatom'ically**. — *vt* **anat'omise** or **-ize** to dissect; to lay open minutely (*fig*). — *n* **anat'omist** a person skilled in anatomy. [Gr. *anatomē*, dissection — *ana*, up, *tomē*, a cutting.]

anatto. See **annatto**.

anbury *an'bər-i*, *n* a soft bloody wart on horses, etc. (also **angleberry** *ang'gl-bər-i*); a disease in turnips, cabbages, etc., due to a slime-fungus. [Perh. for *angberry* — O.E. *ange*, narrow, painful, and **berry**.]

ANC *abbrev* for African National Congress.

ancestor *an'sis-tər*, *n* someone from whom a person is descended; a forefather; a plant or animal from which another type has evolved; a person or thing regarded as the forerunner of another: — *fem* **an'cestress**. — *adj* **ancestral** (*an-ses'trəl*) of or relating to ancestors; inherited or derived from ancestors. — *n* **an'cestry** a line of ancestors; lineage. — **an'cestor-worship**. [O.Fr. *ancestre* — L. *antecēssor* — *ante*, before, *cēdĕre*, *cēssum*, to go.]

anchor *ang'kər*, *n* an implement for mooring a ship to the bottom, or for holding a balloon to the ground, or the like; anything that gives stability or security (*fig*); often short for anchor-man. — *vt* to fix by an anchor; to fasten. — *vi* to cast anchor; to stop or rest. — *n* **anch'orage** the act of anchoring; a place of or for anchoring; rest or support to the mind (*fig*); duty imposed for anchoring. — *adj* **anch'orless**. — **Anchor Boys** the most junior section of the Boys' Brigade; **anchor escapement** or **recoil escapement** a clock escapement in which the pallets push the escape-wheel slightly backwards at the end of each swing, causing a recoil of the pendulum; **anchor leg** the last stage of a relay-race; **anch'or-man** the man at the back of a team in a tug-of-war; the man who runs the last stage of a relay-race; a person on whom the success of an activity depends, esp., on television, the person responsible for smooth running of a dialogue or discussion between or among others; **anchor plate** a heavy, usu. steel, plate set into the ground or foundations to which bracing for a structure is fixed; **anch'or-stock** the cross-bar of an anchor, which causes one or other of the flukes to turn to the bottom. — **at anchor** anchored; **cast anchor** to let down the anchor; **weigh anchor** to take up the anchor. [O.E. *ancor* — L. *ancŏra*.]

anchorite *ang'kə-rīt*, *n* a man or woman who has withdrawn from the world, esp. for religious reasons; a recluse. — *n* **anch'orage** a recluse's cell. — *n* **anch'oress** or **anc'ress** a female anchorite. [Gr. *anachōrētēs* — *ana*, apart, *chōreein*, to withdraw.]

anchorage. See **anchor** and **anchorite.**

anchovy *an'chə-vi* or *-chō-*, also *an-chō'vi*, *n* a small edible Mediterranean fish of the herring family, often used for making sauce, paste, etc. — *n* **anchoveta** (*-vet'ə*; *Sp Am*) a small Pacific anchovy, used for bait. — **an'chovy-pear** the fruit of a W. Indian tree, often pickled. [Sp. and Port. *anchova*.]

anchylose, etc. See **ankylose,** etc.

ancient *ān'shənt*, *adj* very old; of former times; of long standing; belonging or relating to times long past, esp. before the downfall of the Western Roman Empire (A.D. 476). — *n* an aged man; an elder or senior; someone who lived in ancient times — usu. in *pl* and applied esp. to the Greeks and Romans. — *adv* **an'ciently.** — **ancient history** (*colloq, fig*) information, news or gossip which, contrary to the expectations of the teller, one is already well aware of; something no longer of importance; **ancient monument** an old and historic building etc. scheduled for preservation, esp. under government control. [Fr. *ancien* — L.L. *antiānus*, former, old — L. *ante*, before.]

ancillary *an-sil'ər-i* or *an'sil-ər-i*, *adj* auxiliary; supplementary; subsidiary; subordinate; (of computer equipment) additional in any way, not necessarily connected to the central processing unit. — Also *n*. [L. *ancilla*, a maid-servant.]

ancipitous *an-sip'i-təs* or **ancip'ital,** (*bot*) *adj* two-edged and flattened. [L. *anceps*, *-cipitis*, two-edged, double — *ambi-*, on both sides, *caput*, *capitis*, head.]

ancress. See **anchorite.**

AND *and*, (*comput*) *n* a logic circuit that has two or more inputs and one output, the output signal being 1 if all its inputs are 1, and 0 if any of its inputs is 0. [**and**[1].]

AND *abbrev* for Andorra (I.V.R.).

and[1] *and*, *ənd*, *ən* or *n*, *conj* indicating addition; also; also of another kind; used to introduce a consequence or aim; used to introduce a question expressive of surprise, realisation, wonder, incredulity, etc.; used to join identical words to indicate repetition, progression or continuity. — **and all** not without; **and how** (*colloq*) I should think so indeed; **and then some** (*colloq*) and even more. [O.E. *and*, *ond*; cf. Ger. *und*, and L. *ante*, before, Gr. *anti*, against.]

and[2] *and*, *n* the sign ampersand; a use of the word 'and'; something added.

Andalusian *an-də-lōō'syən*, *-shyən*, *-zyən* or *-zhyən*, *n* a native of *Andalusia* (Sp. *Andalucía*), in Spain. — Also *adj*.

andante *an-dan'tā*, (*mus*) *adv* and *adj* moving with moderately slow, even expression. — *n* a movement or piece composed in andante time. — *adj*, *adv* and *n* **andantino** (*mus*; *an-dan-tē'nō*) (a movement, etc.) somewhat slower than andante; now more usu. intended for somewhat quicker: — *pl* **andanti'nos.** [It., pres. p. of *andare*, to go.]

Andean *an-dē'ən* or **Andine** *an'dīn*, *adj* of, or like, the *Andes* Mountains.

andiron *and'ī-ərn*, *n* an iron bar to support the end of a log in a fire; a fire-dog. [O.Fr. *andier*; early confused with **iron.**]

Andrew *an'drōō*, *n* one of the twelve Apostles, patron saint of Scotland. — **St Andrew's cross** a saltire, or cross of equal shafts crossed diagonally; the saltire of Scotland, white on a blue ground.

andro- *an-drō-* or *an-dro'-*, sometimes **andr-,** *combining form* denoting: man; male. — *adj* **androcentric** (*an-drō-sent'rik*) male-centred, centring on the man. — *adj* **androdioecious** (*-dī-ē'shəs*) having hermaphrodite and male flowers on separate plants (see **dioecious**). — *n* **androecium** (*an-drē'shi-əm* or *-si-əm*) stamens collectively (Gr. *oikion*, house). — *n* **androgen** (*an'drō-jən*) any one of the male sex hormones; a synthetic compound with similar effect. — *adj* **androgen'ic** of or relating to an androgen. — *n* and *adj* **an'drogyne** (*-jīn*) hermaphrodite (Gr. *gynē*, woman). — *adj* **androgynous** (*an-droj'i-nəs* or *-drog'*) having the characteristics of both male and female in one individual; having both male and female flowers (*bot*). — *n* **androg'yny** hermaphroditism. — *n* **an'droid** a robot in human form. — *n* **androl'ogy** the branch of medicine which deals with the functions and diseases peculiar to men. — *adj* **andromonoecious** (*an-drō-mon-ē'shəs*) having hermaphrodite and male flowers on the same plant (see **monoecious**). — *n* **androsterone** (*ən-dros'tə-rōn* or *an-dro-stē'rōn*; from *ster*ol) a male sex-hormone, found in the testes and in urine. [Gr. *anēr*, *andros*, man, male.]

Andromeda *an-drom'i-də*, *n* a genus of shrubs of the heath family; (without *cap*) a plant of this genus; a northern constellation lying between Cassiopeia and Pegasus. — *n* **andromedotoxin** (*an-drom'i-dō-tok-sin*) a vegetable drug obtained from Andromeda, used in relief of high blood pressure. [*Andromeda*, in Greek myth, a maiden delivered by Perseus from a sea-monster.]

anecdote *an'ik-dōt*, *n* a short narrative of an incident of private life; such narratives. — *n* **an'ecdōtage** anecdotes collectively.. — *adj* **anecdōt'al.** — *n* **anecdōt'alist** or **an'ecdōtist** a person who relates anecdotes. — *adv* **anecdot'ally.** [Gr. *an-* (privative) and *ekdotos*, published.]

anemia *ə-nē'myə*, (*US*) *n* anaemia. — *adj* **ane'mic.**

anemo- *ə-nem-ō-* or *an-i-mo'-*, *combining form* denoting wind. — *n* **anemogram** (*ə-nem'o-gram*) an anemographic record. — *n* **anem'ograph** (*-gräf*) an instrument for measuring and recording the pressure and velocity of the wind. — *adj* **anemographic** (*-graf'ik*). — *n* **anemology** (*ani-mol'ə-ji*) the science of the winds. — *n* **anemometer** (*-mom'i-tər*) a wind-gauge. — *adj* **anemometric** (*-mō-met'rik*). — *n* **anemom'etry.** — *n* **anemophō'bia** fear of wind or draughts. [Gr. *anemos*, wind.]

anemone *ə-nem'ə-ni*, *n* windflower; any member of the genus *Anemone* of the crowfoot family; a sea-anemone. [Gr. *anemōnē*.]

anencephaly *an-ən-sef'ə-li* or *-kef'ə-li*, *n* congenital absence of all or part of the brain. — Also **anencephalia** (*-āl'yə*). — *adj* **anencephal'ic.** [**an-**; and see **encephalon.**]

aneroid *an'ə-roid*, *adj* dispensing with the use of liquid. — *n* an aneroid barometer. [Fr. *anéroïde* — Gr. *a-* (privative) and *nēros*, wet, *eidos*, form.]

anesthesia *an-əs-thē'zyə*, (*US*) *n* anaesthesia. — *adj* and *n* **anesthet'ic.** — *vt* **anes'thetize.** — *n* **anes'thetist.**

anestrus *an-ēs'trəs* or **anestrum** *an-ēs'trəm*, (*US*) *n* anoestrus. — *adj* **anes'trous.**

aneurin *an'ū-rin* or *ə-nū'rin*, *n* vitamin B_1, deficiency of which affects the nervous system. — Also called **thiamine.** [**a-**[2] and Gr. *neuron*, nerve.]

aneurysm or **aneurism** *an'ūr-izm*, *n* dilatation of an artery (*pathol*); any abnormal enlargement. — *adj* **aneurys'mal** or **aneuris'mal.** [Gr. *aneurysma* — *ana*, up, *eurys*, wide.]

anew *ə-nū'* or in U.S. *-nōō'*, *adv* afresh; again. [**of** and **new.**]

angary *ang'gər-i*, (*law*) *n* a belligerent's right to seize and use neutral or other property (subject to compensation). [Gr. *angareiā*, forced service — *angaros*, a courier.]

angel *ān'jl*, *n* a divine messenger; a ministering attendant or guardian spirit; a person possessing the qualities attributed to these — gentleness, purity, etc.; a radar echo of unknown origin; a financial backer or adviser (*colloq*). — *adj* **angelic** (*an-jel'ik*) or **angel'ical.** — *adv* **angel'ically.** — **an'gel-cake** or **an'gel-food** a cake made of flour, sugar and white of egg; **angel dust** (*colloq*) the drug phencyclidine, a hallucinogen; **an'gel-fish** a tropical American river-fish of the family *Cichlidae*, with a much compressed, almost circular body but crescent-shaped owing to the long fin filaments, the whole banded with changing black vertical stripes; applied also to several other fishes; **angels-on-horse'back** oysters and bacon on toast. [Gr. *angelos*, a messenger.]

Angeleno *an-jel-ē'nō, n* a native or citizen of Los Angeles: — *pl* **Angele'nos.**

angelica *an-jel'i-kə, n* (with *cap*) a genus of umbelliferous plants with large leaves and double-winged fruit, once regarded as a defence against poison and pestilence; a garden plant by some included in the genus as *A. archangelica*, by others called *Archangelica officinalis*; its candied leaf-stalks and midribs used as decoration for cakes, etc. [Med. L. *herba angelica* angelic herb.]

angelus *an'ji-ləs*, (*Christian relig*) *n* a short devotional exercise in honour of the Incarnation, repeated three times daily; the bell rung in Roman Catholic countries at morning, noon and sunset to invite the faithful to recite the angelus. [From the introductory words, '*Angelus* domini nuntiavit Mariae'.]

anger *ang'gər, n* hot displeasure, often involving a desire for retaliation; wrath. — *vt* to make angry; to irritate. [O.N. *angr*.]

Angevin *an'ji-vin, adj* of *Anjou*, in France; relating to the Plantagenet house that reigned in England from 1154 to 1485, descended from Geoffrey V, Count of Anjou. — *n* a native of Anjou; a member of the house of Anjou.

angina *an-jī'nə, n* short for angina pectoris; any inflammatory affection of the throat, such as quinsy, croup, etc. — *adj* **anginal** (*an-jī'nl*). — **angina pectoris** a disease of the heart marked by paroxysms of intense pain, radiating from the breastbone mainly towards the left shoulder and arm. [L. *angīna*; see **anguish**.]

angio- *an-ji-ō-, combining form* referring to the blood vessels. — *n* **angiogen'esis** the development of blood vessels and heart tissue in the embryo. — *n* **angiogram** *an'ji-ō-gram*, a photograph made by angiography. — *n* **angiog'raphy** the art or process of making X-ray photographs of blood-vessels by injecting the vessels with a substance opaque to the rays. — *n* **angioma** (*an-ji-ō'mə*) a benign tumour composed of blood or lymph vessels: — *pl* **angiō'mas** or **angiō'mata.** — *n* **angioplas'ty** surgery of the blood vessels. [Gr. *angeion*, a case, vessel.]

angiosperm *an'ji-ō-spûrm, n* a plant of the **Angiosperm'ae,** one of the main divisions of flowering plants, in which the seeds are in a closed ovary, not naked as in gymnosperms. — *adj* **angiosperm'al** or **angiosperm'ous**. [Gr. *angeion*, case, *sperma*, seed.]

Angle *ang'gl, n* a member or descendant of the German tribe (O.E. *Engle*) from Schleswig that settled in Northumbria, Mercia and East Anglia. — *adj* **Ang'lian** of the Angles. — *n* an Angle; the English dialect of the Angles. [L. *Anglus*.]

angle[1] *ang'gl, n* a corner; the distance or change in direction between two lines or surfaces diverging from the same point, measured in degrees (°), radians, right angles or (of angular velocity) revolutions; the inclination of two straight lines, or of two curves measured by that of their tangents, or of two planes measured by that of perpendiculars to their intersection (*geom*); the spread of a cone, a number of meeting planes or the like, measured by the area on the surface of a sphere subtending it at the centre (*geom*); an outlying corner or nook; a point of view; a frame (*snooker*, etc.); an angle shot (*squash*). — *vt* to put in a corner; to put in the jaws of a billiard pocket; to move, drive, direct, turn, adjust or present at an angle; to present (news, etc.) in such a way as to serve a particular end. — *vi* to proceed at an angle or by an angular course. — *adj* **ang'led** having angles; biased. — *adv* **ang'lewise.** — **ang'ledozer** a bulldozer whose blade may be angled or tilted to the left or right; **angle iron** an L-shaped piece of iron or steel used in structural work; **angle shot** a shot taken with a camera tilted above or below the horizontal (*cinematography*); a shot which hits first the side wall, then the front wall, without touching the floor (*squash*). [Fr., — L. *angulus*.]

angle[2] *ang'gl, vi* to fish with rod and line (for); to try to gain by some artifice (with *for*). — *vt* to angle for. — *n* **ang'ler** a person who fishes with rod and line, esp. for sport; the devil-fish or *fishing-frog*, a wide-mouthed voracious fish that attracts its prey by waving filaments attached to its head; extended to related kinds, some of them remarkable for the dwarf males parasitic on the female. — *n* **ang'ling.** [O.E. *angul*, hook.]

angleberry. See **anbury.**

Anglican *ang'gli-kən, adj* of or characteristic of the Church of England and churches in communion with it; English (esp. *US*). — Also *n*. — *n* **Ang'licanism** the principles of the Church of England; attachment to English institutions, esp. the English Church. [Med. L. *Anglicanus* — L. *Anglus*, Angle.]

anglicise or **-ize** *ang'li-sīz*, to make English. — *vi* to assume or conform to English ways. — *n* **anglicisa'tion** or **-z-**. — *n* **ang'licism** (*-sizm*) an English idiom or peculiarity. — *n* **ang'licist** or **ang'list** a person who has a scholarly knowledge of the English language, literature and culture. [Ety. as for **Anglican**.]

Anglo *ang'glō, adj* of British extraction; (esp. *US*) Anglo-American. — Also *n*: — *pl* **Ang'los.**

Anglo- *ang-glō-, combining form* English; British; esp. conjointly English or British and something else. — *n* **Anglo-Cath'olic** a person who regards himself or herself as a Catholic of Anglican pattern; a High-Churchman. — Also *adj*. — *n* **Anglo-Cathol'icism**. — *adj* **Anglocen'tric** taking English or British affairs, institutions, culture, etc. as a norm, focus, etc. in one's outlook or behaviour. — *n* **Anglo-I'rish** the English language as spoken in Ireland; Irish people of English descent; people of mixed English and Irish descent. — *adj* of England or Britain and Ireland; of the Anglo-Irish people or speech. — (All the following also with *cap*) *n* **ang'lophile** (*-fīl*) a friend and admirer of England and things English (Gr. *philos*, friend). — Also *adj*. — *n* **anglophil'ia**. — *adj* **anglophil'ic**. — *n* **ang'lophobe** a person who fears or dislikes England and things English (Gr. *phobos*, fear). — Also *adj*. — *n* **anglophō'bia**. — *adj* **anglophō'biac** or **anglophobic** (*-fōb'* or *-fob'*). — *adj* **Ang'lophone** (sometimes without *cap*) of a state, person, etc., speaking or using English (esp. as opp. to French) in everyday affairs. — *n* an English-speaking (esp. as opp. to French-speaking) person, esp. in a state, etc. where English is not the only language spoken. — *adj* **Anglophon'ic** (sometimes without *cap*). — *n* **Anglo-Sax'on** Old English, the English language before 1100 or 1150 A.D.; plain English, often implying forthright use of English words that are usually taboo in ordinary conversation (*colloq*); one of the Germanic settlers in England and Scotland, including Angles, Saxons and Jutes, or of their descendants; a Saxon of England, distinguished from the Old Saxons of the Continent; a white native speaker of English. — Also *adj*. [L. *Anglus*.]

Angora *ang-gö'rə, adj* (sometimes without *cap*) of an Angora breed or yarn, etc. — *n* (in all meanings sometimes without *cap*) an Anatolian goat; its long silky wool (the true mohair); cloth made from it; a silky-haired rabbit; an Angora cat; yarn or material partly or wholly of Angora rabbit hair. — **Angora cat** a silky-haired kind of cat similar to the Persian and possibly no longer existing as a pure breed, the term now being treated by some as an obsolete term for Persian cat. [Angora, former name of Ankara, now the capital city of Turkey.]

Angostura *ang-gos-tū'rə, n* a town (now Ciudad Bolivar) on the narrows (Sp. *angostura*) of the Orinoco in Venezuela. — **Angostura bitters**® a brand of aromatic bitters first made in Angostura sometimes used as a flavouring in alcoholic drinks.

angry *ang'gri, adj* excited with anger; inflamed; of threatening aspect. — *adv* **ang'rily**. — *n* **ang'riness**. — **angry young man** a young man loud in disgust at what his elders have made of society (popularised by *Look Back in Anger*, play, 1956, by John Osborne, one of a group of writers of the period to whom the term was applied). [**anger**.]

Angst or **angst** *angst, n* anxiety, esp. a general feeling of anxiety produced by awareness of the uncertainties and paradoxes inherent in the state of being human. — *adj* **Angst'-** or **angst'-ridden**. [Ger. *Angst*, Dan. *angst*, fear, anxiety.]

Ångström or **angstrom** *ang'* or *ong'strəm, n* a unit (10^{-10} metres) used in expressing wavelengths of light, ultraviolet rays, X-rays, molecular and atomic distances. — Formerly, but not now usu., **Ångström** (or **angstrom**) **unit**. [Anders J. *Ångström* (1814–74), Swedish physicist.]

anguish *ang'gwish, n* excessive pain of body or mind; agony. — *vt* to afflict with anguish. — *vi* to suffer anguish. — *adj* **ang'uished**. [O.Fr. *angoisse*, choking — L. *angustia*, tightness, narrowness.]

angular *ang'gū-lər, adj* having an angle or corner; measured by an angle; stiff in manner, the opposite of easy or graceful (*fig*); bony and lean in figure. — *n* **angūlarity** (*-lar'i-ti*). — **angular velocity** the rate at which an object rotates round a fixed point or axis, measured as the rate of change in the angle turned through by the line between the object and the point or axis. [L. *angularis* — *angulus*, **angle**[2].]

anharmonic *an-här-mon'ik, adj* not harmonic. [**an-**; Gr. *harmonikos*, harmonic.]

anhedonia *an-hi-dō'ni-ə, (psychol) n* the inability to feel pleasure; the loss of interest in formerly pleasurable pursuits. [**an-**; Gr. *hēdonē*, pleasure.]

anhedral *an-hē'drəl, adj* crystalline in internal structure but not in outward form; having a downward (negative) dihedral angle (*aeronautics*).

anhelation *an-hi-lā'shən, n* shortness of breath. [L. *anhēlātiō, -ōnis* — *anhēlāre*, to gasp.]

anhydride *an-hī'drīd, n* a compound representing in its composition an acid *minus* water. — *n* **anhy'drite** a mineral, anhydrous calcium sulphate. — *adj* **anhy'drous** free from water. [**an-**; Gr. *hydōr*, water.]

aniconic *an-ī-kon'ik, adj* symbolising without aiming at resemblance; pertaining to aniconism. — *n* **ani'conism** (*-kən-izm*) worship or veneration of an object that represents a god without being an image of him. — *n* **ani'conist**. [**an-**; Gr. *eikōn*, image.]

anil *an'il, n* indigo, the plant or dye. [Port. — Ar. *an-nil*, the indigo plant — Sans. *nīlī*, indigo.]

aniline *an'il-ēn, -in* or *-īn, n* a product of coal tar extensively used in dyeing and other industrial arts, first obtained from *anil*. — Also *adj* (as in *aniline dye*).

animadvert *an-im-ad-vûrt', vi* to take cognisance (*law*; usu. with *on* or *upon*); to take note; to comment critically (on); to express censure. — *n* **animadver'sion**. — *n* **animadvert'er**. [L. *animus*, the mind, *ad*, to, and *vertĕre*, to turn.]

animal *an'i-məl, n* an organism having life, sensation, and voluntary motion — typically distinguished from a plant, which has life, but apparently not sensation or voluntary motion; often, a lower animal — one below man; a mammal; a brutish or sensual man; loosely or colloquially, a person, thing, organisation, etc. — *adj* of, of the nature of, derived from, or belonging to an animal or animals; brutal, sensual. — *adj* **animal'ic** of or pertaining to animals. — *n* **an'imalism** exercise or enjoyment of animal life, as distinct from intellectual; the state of being actuated by mere animal appetites; brutishness, sensuality; the theory that man is a mere animal being. — *n* **an'imalist** a person who practises or believes in animalism. — *n* **animality** (*-al'i-ti*) animal nature or life; status of an animal or of a lower animal. — *adv* **an'imally** physically. — **animal liberationist** a member or supporter of any body dedicated to ending the exploitation of animals by human beings; **animal magnetism** see under **magnet**; **animal righter** a person who believes in (and fights for) **animal rights**, the rights of animals to exist without being exploited by humans; **animal spirits** nervous force; exuberance of health and life; cheerful buoyancy of temper; **an'imal-worship**; **an'imal-worshipper**. — **there is** (or **there ain't**) **no such animal** (*colloq*) there is no such person, creature or thing. [L. *animal* — *anima*, air, breath, life, soul.]

animalcule *an-im-al'kūl, n* a microscopic animal: — *pl* **animal'cūles** or **animal'cūla**. — *adj* **animal'cūlar**. [L. *animalculum*, dimin. of *animal*.]

animate *an'im-āt, vt* to give life to; to enliven; to put spirit into; to actuate; to record still drawings etc. on film or video tape in such a way that the images appear to move. — *adj* (*-mit*) living; having animal life. — *adj* **an'imated** lively; full of spirit; endowed with life; moving as if alive. — *adv* **an'imatedly**. — *adj* **an'imating**. — *adv* **an'imatingly**. — *n* **animā'tion** the act or process of animating; the state of being alive; liveliness; vigour. — *n* **an'imatism** primitive attribution of life to natural phenomena and natural objects, but not, as in *animism*, belief that spirits reside in them. — *n* **an'imātor** a person who enlivens or animates something; an artist who makes drawings for animated cartoons. — *adj* **animatron'ic** of or like something animated by animatronics. — *nsing* **animatron'ics** the art of animating a lifelike figure of a person, animal, etc. by electronic means. — **animated cartoon** a film, video tape etc. produced from drawings, each successive drawing showing a very slight change of position so that a series of them gives the effect of a definite movement. [L. *animāre, -ātum* — *anima*, air, breath, life.]

animism *an'im-izm, n* the attribution of a soul to natural objects and phenomena. — *n* **an'imist**. — *adj* **animis'tic**. [L. *anima*, the soul.]

animosity *an-im-os'i-ti, n* strong dislike; enmity. [L. *animōsitās*, fullness of spirit.]

animus *an'im-əs, n* intention; actuating spirit; hostility; in Jungian psychology, the male component of the female personality. [L. *animus*, spirit, soul.]

anion *an'ī-ən, n* an ion that seeks the anode; an electronegative ion. — *adj* **anion'ic**. [Gr. *ana*, up, *iōn*, going, pres. p. neut. of *ienai*, to go.]

anise *an'is, n* a plant (*Pimpinella*) whose aromatic seeds, of a flavour similar to liquorice, are used in making cordials, etc. — *n* **an'iseed** the seed of anise; anisette. — *n* **anisette** (*an-i-zet'*) a cordial or liqueur prepared from anise seed. [Gr. *anīson*, anise.]

aniso- *an-ī-sō-* or *an-ī-so'-, combining form* denoting unequal. — *adj* **anisotrop'ic** not isotropic, showing differences of property or of effect in different directions. — *n* **anisot'ropy**. [Gr. *anisos*, unequal — *an-*, not, *isos*, equal.]

ankh *angk, n* a T-shaped cross with a loop above the horizontal bar — the symbol of life. [Egyp., life.]

ankle *angk'l, n* the joint connecting the foot and leg. — *adj* **ank'led** having ankles. — *n* **ank'let** (*-lit*) an ornamental or supporting ring or chain for the ankle. — **ank'le-biter** (*Austr slang*) a child; **ank'le-boot** a boot reaching above the ankle; **ank'le-chain** a chain worn as decoration round the ankle; **ankle sock** a sock reaching to and covering the ankle; **ankle strap** (a shoe with) a strap which fastens round the ankle. [O.E. *anclēow*.]

Ankole *ang-kō'lē, n* a breed of large cattle with long horns. — Also *adj*. [*Ankole*, plateau region in Uganda.]

ankylosaur *ang'kə-lə-sör*, *n* any of the **Ankylosauria** (*-sör'i-ə*), a suborder of bird-hipped plant-eating dinosaurs of the Cretaceous period, with short legs and flattened heavily-armoured bodies, including **Ankylosaur'us** which gave its name to the suborder. [N.L. — Gr. *ankylos*, crooked, *sauros*, lizard.]

ankylosis or **anchylosis** *ang-ki-lō'sis*, *n* the fusion of bones or skeletal parts; the fixation of a joint by fibrous bands or union of bones. — *vt* and *vi* **ank'ylose** or **anch'ylose** (of a joint or bones) to stiffen or fuse. — *adj* **ank'ylosed** or **anch'ylosed.** — **ankylosing spondylitis** rheumatoid arthritis of the spine. [Gr. *ankylōsis*, stiffening of a joint — *ankyloein*, to crook.]

ankylostomiasis or **anchylostomiasis** *ang-ki-lō-sto-mī'ə-sis*, *n* hook-worm disease or miner's anaemia, caused by a parasitic round-worm or threadworm. [Gr. *ankylos*, crooked, *stoma*, mouth.]

anlage *än'lä-gə*, (*biol*) *n* the primordium, the source or first discernible rudiment of an organ. [Ger.]

anme *abbrev* for *anonyme* (Fr.), limited liability.

annal *an'əl*, *n* a year's entry in a chronicle; (in *pl*) records of events listed under the years in which they happened; historical records generally; yearbooks. — *vt* **ann'alise** or **-ize** to record. — *n* **ann'alist** a writer of annals. — *adj* **annalist'ic.** [L. *annālis*, yearly — *annus*, a year.]

annates *an'āts*, (*RC*) *npl* the first-fruits, or one year's income of a benefice, paid to the Pope. [L.L. *annāta* — L. *annus*, a year.]

annatto or **anatto** *a-* or *ə-nat'ō*, *n* a bright orange colouring matter obtained from the fruit pulp of a tropical American tree, *Bixa orellana*: — *pl* **annatt'os** or **anatt'os.**

anneal *ə-nēl'*, *vt* to heat and cool gradually (glass, metals), esp. in order to temper or toughen; to strengthen. — Also *vi*. — *n* **anneal'er.** — *n* **anneal'ing.** [Pfx. *an-*, on, and O.E. *ǣlan*, to burn.]

annectent *ə-nek'tənt*, (*biol*) *adj* connecting, linking, having characteristics that are intermediate between those of two other species, genera, etc. [L. *annectĕre* — *ad*, to, *nectĕre*, to tie.]

annelid *an'ə-lid*, *n* a member of the **Annelida** (*ə-nel'i-də*) a class comprising the red-blooded worms, having a long body composed of numerous rings. [L. *annellus*, *ānellus*, dimin. of *ānulus*, a ring.]

annex *ə-neks'*, *vt* to add to the end; to join or attach; to take permanent possession of; to purloin, appropriate (*colloq*); to affix; to append. — *n* (*an'eks*) something added; a supplementary building — sometimes (as Fr.) **annexe** (*a-neks'* or *an'eks*). — *n* **annexā'tion** (*an-*). [L. *annectĕre*, *annexum* — *ad*, to, *nectĕre*, to tie.]

annihilate *ə-nī'(h)il-āt*, *vt* to reduce to nothing; to put out of existence; to crush or wither by look or word (*fig*); to defeat completely (*colloq* and *fig*); to cause to annihilate (*phys*). — *vi* to undergo annihilation (*phys*). — *n* **annīhilā'tion** reduction to nothing; the process by which a particle and its corresponding antiparticle, e.g. an electron and a positron, combine and are spontaneously transformed into radiation (**annihilation radiation**) (*phys*). — *adj* **annī'hilātive.** — *n* **annī'hilātor.** [L. *annihilāre*, *-ātum* — *ad*, to, *nihil*, nothing.]

anniversary *an-i-vûrs'ə-ri*, *adj* returning, happening or commemorated about the same date every year; relating to annual recurrence or celebration. — *n* the day of the year on which an event happened or is celebrated as having happened in a previous year; the celebration proper to recurrence, esp. a mass or religious service. [L. *anniversārius* — *annus*, a year, and *vertĕre*, *versum*, to turn.]

anno Domini *an'ō dom'in-ī* or *-in-ē*, (L.) in the year of our Lord. — *n* advancing old age (*colloq*).

annotate *an'ō-tāt*, *vt* to make notes upon. — *vi* to append notes. — *n* **annōtā'tion** the making of notes; a note of explanation; comment. — *n* **ann'ōtātor.** [L. *annotāre* — *ad*, to, *notāre*, *-ātum*, to mark.]

announce *ə-nowns'*, *vt* to declare; to give public notice of; to make known. — *n* **announce'ment.** — *n* **announc'er** a person who announces; a person who reads the news and announces other items in the programme (*TV* and *radio*). [O.Fr. *anoncer* — L. *annuntiāre* — *ad*, to, *nuntiāre*, to report.]

annoy *ə-noi'*, *vt* and *vi* to trouble; to vex; to tease; to harm, esp. in military sense. — *n* **annoy'ance** that which annoys; the act of annoying; the state of being annoyed. — *adj* **annoyed'** (with *at* or *with*). — *n* **annoy'er.** — *adj* **annoy'ing.** — *adv* **annoy'ingly.** [O.Fr. *anoier* (noun *anoi*, mod. *ennui*) — L.L. *inodiāre*.]

annual *an'ū-əl*, *adj* yearly; coming every year; lasting or living for a year; requiring to be renewed every year; performed in a year; being, or calculated as, the total for one year. — *n* a plant that lives for one year only; a publication appearing yearly, esp. an illustrated gift-book; a yearbook. — *vt* **ann'ualise** or **-ize** to convert to, or calculate on, a yearly rate, amount, etc. — *adv* **ann'ually.** [L.L. *annuālis* — L. *annus*, a year.]

annuity *ə-nū'i-ti*, *n* a payment (generally of uniform amount) falling due in each year during a given term, such as a period of years or the life of an individual, the capital sum not being returnable. — *n* **annū'itant** a person who receives an annuity. [Fr. *annuité* — L.L. *annuitās*, *-ātis* — L. *annus*, year.]

annul *ə-nul'*, *vt* to make null; to reduce to nothing; to abolish: — *pr p* **annull'ing**; *pa t* and *pa p* **annulled'.** — *n* **annul'ment.** [Fr. *annuler* — L.L. *annūllāre* — L. *ad*, to, *nūllus*, none.]

annular *an'ū-lər*, *adj* ring-shaped; cutting in a ring; ring-bearing. — *n* the ring-finger. — *n* **annūlarity** (*-lar'i-ti*). — *adj* **ann'ūlate** or **ann'ulated** ringed. — *n* **ann'ūlet** a little ring; a small flat fillet encircling a column, etc. (*archit*). [L. *annulāris*, for *ānulāris* — *ānulus*, a ring — dimin. of *ānus*, a rounding or ring.]

annunciate *ə-nun'si-āt* or *ə-nun'shi-āt*, *vt* to proclaim. — *n* **annunciā'tion** (*-si-*) proclamation; esp. (with *cap*) that of the angel to the Virgin Mary, or its anniversary, 25 March (**Annunciā'tion-day** Lady-day). — *adj* **annun'ciative.** — *n* **annun'ciātor** a device giving audible or visual information, e.g. indicating where a bell or telephone is being rung. [L. *annuntiāre*, *-ātum* — *ad*, to, *nuntiāre* — *nuntius*, a messenger; *c* from mediaeval spelling of Latin; cf. **announce.**]

Anobium *a-nō'bi-əm*, *n* a genus of small beetles of the family **Anobiidae** (*a-nō-bī'i-dē*), a number of species of which bore in dry wood. [N.L. — Gr. *ano*, upwards, *bios*, life.]

anode *an'ōd*, *n* the electrode by which an electric current enters an electrolyte or gas (opp. to *cathode*); in high vacuum, the electrode to which electrons flow. — *vt* **an'odise** or **-z-** to give a protective or decorative coat to (a metal) by using it as an anode in electrolysis. — *adj* **anōd'al.** — *adj* **anodic** (*an-od'ik*) of an anode; upwards on the genetic spiral (*bot*). [Gr. *anodos*, way up — *ana*, up, *hodos*, way.]

anodyne *an'ō-dīn*, *n* a medicine that allays pain; something that relieves mental distress; something that prevents, soothes, or avoids argument, criticism, or controversy. — *adj* allaying pain or mental distress; preventing, soothing, or avoiding argument, criticism, or controversy; harmless, innocent. [Gr. *anōdўnos* — *an-*, without, *ŏdўnē*, pain.]

anoestrus or in U.S. **anestrus** *an-ēs'trəs*, *n* a (sometimes prolonged) period of sexual inactivity between periods of oestrus. — *adj* **anoes'trous.** [**an-** and **oestrus.**]

anoint *ə-noint'*, *vt* to smear with ointment or oil; to consecrate with oil. — *n* **anoint'ment.** [Fr. *enoint*, past p. of *enoindre* — L. *inungĕre*, *inunctum* — *in*, on, *ung(u)ĕre*, to smear.]

anomaly *ə-nom'ə-li, n* irregularity; deviation from rule; the angle measured at the sun between a planet in any point of its orbit and the last perihelion, the point in its orbit when it is nearest to the sun (*astron*). — *adj* **anomalis'tic** or **anomalis'tical** anomalous; departing from established rules; irregular. — *adv* **anomalis'tically.** — *adj* **anom'alous** irregular; deviating from rule; (of vision) relatively insensitive to one or more colours. — **anomalistic year** see under **year**. [Gr. *anōmalos* — *an-* (privative) and *homalos*, even — *homos*, same.]

anomie or **anomy** *an'ə-mē, n* in society or in an individual, a condition of hopelessness caused by or characterised by breakdown of rules of conduct and loss of belief and sense of purpose. — *adj* **anomic** (*ə-nom'ik*). [Fr., — Gr. *anomia*, or *-iē*, lawlessness — *an-*, without, *nomos*, law.]

anon *ə-non'*, (now only *literary*) *adv* immediately; soon; at another time; coming (in reply to a call). [O.E. *on*, in, *ān*, one.]

anon. *abbrev* for anonymous.

anonymous *ə-non'i-məs, adj* lacking a name; without name of author, real or feigned; lacking distinctive features or individuality. — *n* **anonym** (*an'*) a person whose name is not given; a pseudonym. — *vt* **anon'ymise** or **-ize** to remove the name(s) and any other identifying feature(s) from; to make anonymous. — *n* **anonym'ity.** — *adv* **anon'ymously.** [Gr. *anōnymos* — *an-*, without, and *onyma* = *onoma*, name.]

Anopheles *an-of'əl-ēz, n* a genus of germ-carrying mosquitoes; (without *cap*) a mosquito of this genus. — *adj* **anoph'eline** relating to Anopheles. — *n* a mosquito of this genus. [Gr. *anōphelēs*, hurtful — *an-*, without, *ophelos*, help.]

Anoplura *an-o-plōō'rə, npl* an order or suborder of insects, the bugs. [Gr. *anoplos*, unarmed, *ourā*, tail.]

anorak *an'ə-rak, n* a usu. hooded waterproof outer jacket. [Greenland Eskimo word for a fur coat.]

anorexia *an-or-ek'si-ə, n* lack of appetite: anorexia nervosa. — *adj* **anorec'tic** causing a lack of appetite; relating to, or suffering from, anorexia (nervosa). — *n* an anorectic substance. — Also *n* and *adj* **anoret'ic.** — *adj* **anorex'ic** relating to, or suffering from, anorexia (nervosa); relating to anorexics. — *n* a person suffering from anorexia (nervosa). — **anorexia nervosa** (*nûr-vō'sə* or *nûr-vō'zə*; *psychol* or *med*) a condition characterised by loss of appetite and aversion to food due to emotional disturbance, leading to marked emaciation, etc. and death. [Gr. *an-*, without, not, *orexis*, longing — *oregein*, to reach out.]

anosmia *an-oz'mi-ə, n* the loss of sense of smell. [Gr. *an-*, without, not, *osmē*, smell, *-ia*.]

another *ə-nudh'ər, adj* and *pron* a different or distinct (thing or person); one more; a second; one more of the same kind; any other. — **one another** a compound reciprocal pronoun usu. regarded as interchangeable with 'each other', but by some restricted to cases where more than two individuals are involved; **one with another** taken all together, taken on an average. [Orig. **an other**.]

anoxia *an-ok'si-ə, n* deficient supply of oxygen to the tissues. — *adj* **anox'ic.** [**an-**, *oxygen* and *-ia*.]

ANS *abbrev* for autonomic nervous system.

ans. *abbrev* for answer.

ansate *an'sāt* or **ansated** *an'sāt-id, adj* having a handle. [L. *ansātus* — *ansa*, handle.]

Anschluss *an'shlŏŏs*, (Ger.) *n* union, esp. the political union of Germany and Austria in 1938.

anserine *an'sər-īn, adj* of the goose or the goose family; stupid. [L. *anserīnus* — *anser*, goose.]

answer *än'sər, n* that which is said, written, or done in meeting a charge, combating an argument, objection, or attack; that which is called for by a question or questioning state of mind; the solution of a problem; an acknowledgment; a return in kind; anything given, sent or said in return; an immediate result or outcome in definite relation to the act it follows; a repetition or echo of a sound; restatement of a theme by another voice or instrument (*mus*). — *vt* to speak, write, or act in answer to or against; to say or write as an answer; to give, send, afford, or be an answer to; to behave in due accordance with; to be in proportion to or in balance with; to give a conclusive or satisfactory answer to; to serve the purpose of; to fulfil; to recompense satisfactorily; to be punished for. — *vi* to give an answer; to behave in answer; to be responsible; to suffer the consequences; to be in conformity; to serve the purpose; to succeed; to react. — *adj* **an'swerable** able to be answered; accountable; suitable; equivalent; in due proportion. — *n* **answerabil'ity.** — *adv* **an'swerably.** — *n* **an'swerer.** — **answerphone** (*än'sə-fōn*) or **answering machine** a device that automatically answers incoming telephone calls, plays a pre-recorded message to the callers and records their messages on audio tape; **answering service** a commercial service which answers telephone calls, takes messages, etc. for its clients when they are not available. — **answer back** (*colloq*) to answer someone who expects silent submission; to answer pertly; **answer to** or **to the name of** to show sign of accepting as one's name; to have as one's name (*colloq*). [O.E. *andswaru* (noun), *andswarian* (verb) — *and-*, against, *swerian*, to swear.]

ant *ant, n* a small hymenopterous insect (having four transparent wings), of proverbial industry; loosely, a termite. — *n* **ant'ing** the introduction by birds of live ants or other stimulants into their plumage, possibly as a pleasurable means of cleaning it and their skin. — **ant'bear** the great ant-eater, found in swampy regions in S. America; the aardvark of S. Africa; **ant'-eater** any one of a S. American family of edentates (mammals having no front teeth or no teeth at all), feeding chiefly on ants; a pangolin; an aardvark; an echidna. — *npl* **ant'-eggs** or **ants''-eggs** pupae of ants. — **ant'-hill** a hillock raised as a nest by ants or by termites; anything like an ant-hill in terms of crowdedness, bustle, etc. (*fig*); **ant'-lion** a neuropterous insect (having four net-veined wings) whose larva traps ants in a funnel-shaped sand-hole. — **have ants in one's pants** (*colloq*) to be restless, impatient, needlessly hurrying. [O.E. *ǣmete*.]

antacid *ant-as'id, adj* counteracting acidity of the stomach. — *n* a medicine that counteracts acidity. [**anti-** and **acid**.]

antagonist *an-tag'ə-nist, n* someone who contends or struggles with another; an opponent; a muscle that opposes the action of another; in an organism, something that has an opposite effect. — Also *adj*. — *n* **antagonīsā'tion** or **-z-.** — *vt* **antag'onise** or **-ize** to counteract the action of; to arouse opposition in. — *n* **antag'onism** opposition; hostility; production of opposing effects, e.g. in a living body; interference with the growth of another organism, as by using up the food supply or producing an antibiotic substance. — *adj* **antagonist'ic.** — *adv* **antagonis'tically.** [Gr. *antagōnistēs* — *anti*, against, *agōn*, contest.]

Antarctic *ant-ärk'tik, adj* opposite the Arctic; of, near or relating to the south pole. — *n* the south polar regions. — **Antarctic Circle** the parallel of latitude 66°32′S, bounding the region of the earth surrounding the south terrestrial pole. [Gr. *antarktikos* — *anti*, opposite, and *arktikos*; see **Arctic.**]

ante *an'ti, n* a fixed stake put down by a poker player, usu. before the deal; advance payment. — *vt* to stake; to pay. — **up** (or **raise**) **the ante** (*colloq* and *fig*) to increase the costs or risks involved in, or the demands requiring to be met before, some action. [L., before.]

ante- *an'ti-, pfx* before. [L. *ante*, old form *anti*; conn. with Gr. **anti-**.]

antecedent *an-ti-sē'dənt, adj* going before in time; prior. — *n* that which precedes in time; an ancestor;

the noun or its equivalent to which a relative pronoun refers (*gram*); the conditional part of a hypothetical proposition (*logic*); the numerator term of a ratio (*math*); (in *pl*) previous principles, conduct, history, etc. — *n* **antecē'dence.** — *adv* **antecē'dently.** [L. *antecēdēns, -entis* — *ante*, before, *cēdĕre*, to go.]

antechamber *an'ti-chām-bər*, *n* a chamber or room leading to a more important apartment. [Fr. *antichambre* — L. *ante*, before, and *camera*, a vault.]

antechoir *an'ti-kwīr*, *n* the space in front of the choir in a church. [L. *ante*, before, and **choir.**]

antedate *an'ti-dāt*, *n* a date assigned which is earlier than the actual date. — *vt* to date before the true time; to assign to an earlier date; to bring about at an earlier date; to be of previous date to; to accelerate; to anticipate. [L. *ante*, before, and **date**[1].]

antediluvian *an-ti-di-lo͞o'vi-ən* or *-di-lū'vi-ən*, *adj* existing or happening before Noah's Flood; resembling the state of things before the Flood; very old-fashioned, primitive. — *n* someone who lived before the Flood; a person who lives to be very old. — *adj* **antedilu'vial.** — *adv* **antedilu'vially.** [L. *ante*, before, *dīlūvium*, flood.]

antefix *an'ti-fiks*, *n* (usu. in *pl*) an ornament concealing the ends of roofing tiles: — *pl* **an'tefixes** or **antefix'a** (L.). — *adj* **antefix'al.** [L. *ante*, before, in front, and *figĕre, fixum*, to fix.]

antelope *an'ti-lōp*, *n* any one of a group of hollow-horned cud-chewing animals closely related to goats. [O.Fr. *antelop* — Med. L. *antalopus* — Late Gr. *antholops*.]

ante meridiem *an'ti mer-id'i-em*, (L.) before noon.

antenatal *an-ti-nā'tl*, *adj* before birth. — **antenatal clinic** a clinic for the purpose of treating and giving advice to pregnant women. [L. *ante*, before, *nātālis*, natal, *nātus*, born.]

antenna *an-ten'ə*, *n* a feeler or horn in insects, crustaceans, and myriapods; (in wireless communication) a structure for sending out or receiving electric waves; an aerial: — *pl* **antenn'ae** (*-ē*) or **antenn'as** (*radio*). [L. *antemna, antenna*, yard (of a mast).]

antependium *an-ti-pend'i-əm*, *n* a hanging for the front of an altar. [L. *ante*, before, and *pendēre*, to hang.]

ante-post *an'ti-pōst*, *adj* (of betting) ending before the runners come under starter's orders. [L. *ante*, before, and **post**[1].]

anterior *an-tē'ri-ər*, *adj* before, in time or place; in front; towards the bract or away from the axis (*bot*). — *n* **anteriority** (*-or'i-ti*). — *adv* **antē'riorly.** [L. *antĕrior* (compar.) — *ante*, before.]

anteroom *an'ti-ro͞om*, *n* a room leading into another larger room; a waiting-room; an officers' mess sitting-room. [L. *ante*, before, and **room.**]

anteversion *an-ti-vûr'shən*, (*med*) *n* the tipping forward of a bodily organ. — *vt* **antevert'.** [L. *ante*, before, and *vertĕre, versum*, to turn.]

anthelion *an-thē'li-ən*, *n* a luminous coloured ring seen on a cloud or fog-bank opposite the sun: — *pl* **anthe'lia.** [Gr. *ant(h)ēlios, -on*, — *anti*, opposite, *hēlios*, the sun.]

anthelminthic *an-thel-min'thik*, or **anthelmintic** *an-thel-min'tik*, *adj* destroying or expelling worms. — *n* a drug used for that purpose. [Gr. *anti*, against, and *helmins, helminthos*, a worm.]

anthem *an'thəm*, *n* a composition for a church choir, commonly with solo passages, usually set to a passage from the Bible; any song of praise or gladness; loosely applied to an officially recognised national hymn or song (as *national anthem*). [O.E. *antefn* — Gr. *antiphōna* (pl.) sounding in answer. See **antiphon.**]

anther *an'thər*, (*bot*) *n* that part of a stamen that contains the pollen. — *n* **antherid'ium** the gametangium in which male gametes are produced: — *pl* **antherid'ia.** [Gr. *anthēra*, a medicine made from flowers, esp. their inner parts — *anthos*, flower.]

antho- *an-tho-* or *an-thə-*, *combining form* denoting flower. — *n* **anthocarp** (*an'thō-kärp*; Gr. *karpos*, fruit) a fruit resulting from many flowers, e.g. the pineapple (*bot*); a fruit of which the perianth or the torus forms part (*bot*). — *adj* (*bot*) **anthocarp'ous.** — *adj* **anthophilous** (*an-thof'i-ləs*) loving, frequenting, or feeding on flowers. — *n* **an'thophore** (*-thō-fōr*; *bot*) an elongation of the receptacle between calyx and corolla. — *npl* **Anthozō'a** (Gr. *zōia*; *zool*) animals; the *Actinozoa*, a class of coelenterates including sea-anemones, corals, etc. [Gr. *anthos*, flower.]

anthology *an-thol'ə-ji*, *n* a choice collection of writings, songs or paintings etc. — *vt* and *vi* **anthol'ogise** or **-ize.** — *n* **anthol'ogist.** [Gr. — orig. a collection of Gr. epigrams — Gr., a flower gathering.]

Anthony *an'tən-i*, *n* a 4th-century saint. — **St Anthony's cross** a cross in the form of a T, a tau-cross; **St Anthony's fire** (*popularly*) an inflammatory disease, erysipelas; **St Anthony's nut** earth-nut or pignut.

anthophilous, etc. See **antho-.**

anthracene *an'thrə-sēn*, *n* a product of coal-tar distillation ($C_{14}H_{10}$), a source of dyestuffs. [Ety. as for **anthrax**, with sfx. *-ene*.]

anthracite *an'thrə-sīt*, *n* hard lustrous coal that burns nearly without a flame or smoke, consisting almost entirely of carbon. — *adj* **anthracitic** (*an-thrə-sit'ik*) of or of the nature of anthracite. [Gr. *anthrakitēs*, a kind of coal; cf. **anthrax.**]

anthracosis *an-thrə-kō'sis*, *n* a diseased state of the lung due to breathing coal-dust. [**anthrax** and **-osis.**]

anthrax *an'thraks*, *n* a deadly disease due to a bacillus, most common in sheep and cattle but communicable to human beings; a sore caused by the disease; a carbuncle, a malignant boil. — *adj* **anthracic** (*an-thras'ik*). — *adj* **anthracoid** (*an'thrə-koid*) like anthrax. [Gr. *anthrax, -akos* charcoal, coal, carbuncle (stone or boil).]

anthrop- *an-throp-* or **anthropo-** *an-thro-pō-*, *combining form* denoting man or human. — *adj* **anthropic** (*an-throp'ik*) or **anthrop'ical** human. — *adj* **anthropocentric** (*an-thrō-pō-sent'rik*; Gr. *kentron*, centre) centring the universe in human beings. — *adj* **an'thropoid** like a human being; applied esp. to the highest apes — gorilla, chimpanzee, orang-utan, gibbon, but also to the higher Primates generally — human beings, apes, monkeys, but not lemurs. — *n* an anthropoid ape. — *adj* **anthropoid'al.** — *adj* **anthropological** (*an-thrō-po-loj'i-kl*). — *adv* **anthrōpolog'ically.** — *n* **anthropol'ogist.** — *n* **anthropol'ogy** the scientific study of human beings and their way of life. — *adj* **anthropomet'ric.** — *n* **anthropometry** (*an-thro-pom'i-tri*) measurement of the human body. — *n* **anthropomorph'ism** conception or representation of a god as having the form, personality, or attributes of a human being; ascription of human characteristics to what is not human, esp. an animal. — *adj* **anthropomorph'ous** formed like or resembling a human being. — *n* **anthropophagy** (*an-thrə-pof'ə-ji*) cannibalism. — *n* **anthropophō'bia** a morbid fear of people. — *n* **anthropos'ophist.** — *adj* **anthroposoph'ical.** — *n* **anthropos'ophy** (Gr. *sophiā*, wisdom) the knowledge of the nature of human beings; human wisdom; esp. the spiritualistic doctrine of Rudolf Steiner (1861–1925). [Gr. *anthrōpos*, man (in general sense).]

anthurium *an-thū'ri-əm*, *n* a member of the *Anthurium* genus of tropical American plants with showy leaves and flowers. [Gr. *anthos*, flower, *oura*, tail.]

anti *an'ti* or in U.S. also *an'tī*, *prep* opposed to, against. — *n* and *adj* (a person who is) opposed to anything. [Gr. *anti*, against, instead of, etc.]

anti- *an'ti-* or in U.S. also *an'tī-*, *pfx* denoting: (1) acting against, counteracting, resisting, resistant to; (2) opposed to; (3) opposite or reverse. [Gr. *anti*, against.]

Words with the prefix **anti-** are listed in the following text or in the separate panel.

anti-aircraft *an-ti-ār'kräft*, *adj* intended for use against hostile aircraft. [**anti-** (1).]
antiballistic *an-ti-bə-lis'tik*, *adj* (of a missile, etc.) designed to destroy a ballistic missile. [**anti-** (1).]
antibiosis *an-ti-bī-ō'sis*, *n* antagonistic relation between associated organisms; inhibition of growth by a substance produced by another organism. [**anti-** (1) and Gr. *biosis*, way of life.]
antibiotic *an-ti-bī-ot'ik*, *adj* inimical to life; inhibiting the growth of another organism, used esp. of a substance produced by micro-organisms or synthetically which, in dilute solution, has the capacity to inhibit the growth of, or to destroy, micro-organisms causing infectious diseases; of, or relating to antibiosis. — *n* an antibiotic substance. [**anti-** (1) and Gr. *biosis*, way of life; adj. *biōtikos* — *bios*, life.]
antibody *an'ti-bod-i*, *n* a defensive substance produced in an organism in response to the action of a foreign body such as the toxin of a parasite. [**anti-** (1).]
antic *ant'ik*, *n* (usu. in *pl*) a fantastic action or trick; a caper. — *vi* to cut capers. [It. *antico*, ancient — L. *antīquus*; orig. used of the fantastic decorations found in the remains of ancient Rome. See also **antique**.]
anticathode *an-ti-kath'ōd*, *n* the target of an X-ray tube, on which the cathode rays are focused and from which X-rays are emitted. [**anti-** (3).]
anticatholic *an-ti-kath'ə-lik*, *adj* opposed to the Catholic or the Roman Catholic Church, to Catholics, or to what is catholic. [**anti-** (2).]
anti-chip *an-ti-chip'*, *adj* (of paint etc.) resistant to chipping. [**anti-** (1).]
Antichrist *an'ti-krīst*, *n* an opponent of Christ; the great opposer of Christ and Christianity expected by the early Church; applied by some (e.g. Protestant extremists) to the Pope. — *adj* **antichristian** (*an-ti-kris'chən*) relating to Antichrist; opposed to Christianity. [Gr. *Antichristos* — *anti-*, against, *Christos*, Christ.]
anticipate *an-tis'ip-āt*, *vt* to forestall (a person or thing); to use, spend or deal with in advance or before the due time; to realise beforehand; to foresee or count upon as certain; to expect; to precede; to advance to an earlier time, bring on sooner. — *vi* to be before the normal time; to do anything before the appropriate time. — *adj* **antic'ipant** anticipating, anticipative. — Also *n*. — *n* **anticipā'tion** act of anticipating; assignment to too early a time; introduction of a tone or tones of a chord before the whole chord (*mus*); intuition; foretaste; previous notion; presentiment; prejudice; imagining beforehand; expectation. — *adj* **anti'cipātive**. — *adv* **anti'cipātively** or **anti'cipatorily**. — *n* **antic'ipātor**. — *adj* **anti'cipatory**. [L. *anticipāre*, *-ātum* — *ante*, before, *capĕre*, to take.]
anticlerical *an-ti-kler'i-kl*, *adj* opposed to the clergy or their power. — *n* a member of an anticlerical party. — *n* **anticler'icalism**. [**anti-** (2).]
anticlimax *an-ti-klī'maks*, *n* the opposite of climax; a disappointment; a ludicrous drop in impressiveness after a progressive rise. — *adj* **anticlīmac'tic**. — *adv* **anticlīmac'tically**. [**anti-** (3).]
anticline *an'ti-klīn*, *n* (*geol*) an arch-like fold dipping outwards from the fold-axis. — *adj* **anticlīn'al** sloping in opposite directions; perpendicular to the surface near the growing-point (*bot*). — *n* an anticline. [**anti-** (1) and Gr. *klinein*, to lean.]
anticlockwise *an-ti-klok'wīz*, *adv* in the opposite direction to that of the hands of a clock. [**anti-** (3).]
anticoagulant *an-ti-kō-ag'ū-lənt*, *n* a drug that hinders clotting of blood. — Also *adj*. [**anti-** (1).]
anticonvulsant *an-ti-kən-vul'sənt*, *n* a drug used to control convulsions e.g. in treating epilepsy. — Also *adj*. [**anti-** (1).]
anticyclone *an-ti-sī'klōn*, *n* a rotatory outflow of air from an area of high pressure. — *adj* **anticyclonic** (*-klon'ik*). [**anti-** (3).]
antidepressant *an-ti-di-pres'ənt*, *n* a drug used to counteract depression. — Also *adj*. [**anti-** (1).]
antidesiccant *an-ti-des'i-kənt*, *n* a chemical which prevents or inhibits the drying-out of a plant, etc. [**anti-** (1).]
anti-devolutionist *an-ti-dē-* or *an-ti-de-vəl-ōō'shən-ist* or *-ū'shən-ist*, *n* a person who is opposed to devolution. [**anti-** (2).]
antidote *an'ti-dōt*, *n* something which counteracts poison; anything that prevents an evil (with *against*, *for*, or *to*; *fig*). — *adj* **antido'tal**. [Gr. *antidotos* — *didonai*, to give.]
anti-establishment *an-ti-es-tab'lish-mənt*, *adj* opposed to the opinions and values of the establishment in society. — *n* the people who are opposed to such opinions, etc. [**anti-** (1).]
anti-fade *an-ti-fād'*, *adj* resistant to fading. [**anti-** (1).]
anti-feedant *an-ti-fēd'ənt*, *n* any of a number of substances present in some species of plants which make the plants resistant to insect pests. [**anti-** (1).]
anti-flash *an-ti-flash'*, *adj* protecting against the flash of explosions, etc. [**anti-** (1).]
antifreeze *an'ti-frēz*, *n* a substance, e.g. ethylene glycol, with low freezing point put into water to lower its freezing point, esp. used in the radiator of an internal-combustion engine to prevent freezing up. [**anti-** (1).]
antigen *an'ti-jen*, *n* any substance that stimulates the production of an antibody. — *adj* **antigen'ic**. — *adv* **antigen'ically**. [**anti-** (1) and Gr. *gennaein*, to engender.]
anti-hero *an'ti-hē-rō*, *n* a principal character who lacks noble qualities and whose experiences are without tragic dignity: — *fem* **anti-heroine** (*-her'ō-in*). — *adj* **anti-heroic** (*-hi-rō'ik*). [**anti-** (3).]
antihistamine *an-ti-his'tə-mēn*, *n* any of a group of drugs that prevents the action of histamines in allergic conditions. [**anti-** (1).]
antihypertensive *an-ti-hī-pər-ten'siv*, *adj* (of a drug or other measure) used to lower the blood pressure. — *n* an antihypertensive drug. [**anti-** (1).]

Some words with **anti-** prefix; see **anti-** entry for numbered senses

antibil'ious *adj* (1).
antifric'tion *adj* (1).
anti-inflamm'atory *adj* (1).
antimalā'rial *adj* (1).
antimicrō'bial *adj* (1).
antimonarch'ical *adj* (2).
antimon'archist *n* (2).
anti-na'tional *adj* (2).
anti-roll' *adj* (1).
antiship' *adj* (1).
antisub'marine *adj* (1).
antivī'ral *adj* (1).

antiknock *an-ti-nok'*, *n* a substance that prevents knock or detonation in internal-combustion engines. [**anti-** (1).]
anti-lock *an-ti-lok'*, *adj* (of a braking system) designed to prevent the wheels of a vehicle locking when the brakes are applied. [**anti-** (1).]
antilogarithm *an-ti-log'ə-ridhm* or *-rithm*, *n* a number of which a particular number is the logarithm (*abbrev* **an'tilog**). [**anti-** (3).]
antilogy *an-til'ə-ji*, *n* a contradiction. — *adj* **antilogous** (*an-til'ə-gəs*) of the contrary kind; negatively electrified by heating. [Gr. *antilogiā*, contradiction.]
antilymphocyte serum *an-ti-lim'fə-sīt sē'rəm*, *n* serum used to prevent defensive action of lymphocytes, e.g. in cases where they would reject an organ transplanted into the body. [**anti-** (1).]
antimacassar *an-ti-mə-kas'ər*, *n* a covering for chair-backs, etc., to protect them from being soiled (orig. by hair oil), or for ornament. [**anti-** (1) and *macassar* an oil once used for the hair.]
anti-marketeer *an-ti-mär-ki-tēr'*, *n* a British person who opposed Britain's entry into or opposes British membership of the European Common Market. [**anti-** (2).]
antimatter *an-ti-mat'ər*, *n* extraterrestrial matter (not as yet discovered) that would consist of particles similar to those of terrestrial matter but of opposite electrical charge or, in the case of the neutron, reversed magnetic polarity. [**anti-** (3).]
antimony *an'ti-mən-i*, *n* a brittle, bluish-white element (atomic no. 51; symbol **Sb**, for stibium) of metallic appearance. — *adj* **antimonial** (*an-ti-mō'ni-əl*) of, relating to, or containing, antimony. — *n* a drug containing antimony. — *adj* **antimonic** (*an-ti-mon'ik*) containing pentavalent antimony. — *adj* **antimō'nious** containing trivalent antimony. [L.L. *antimōnium*, prob. from some Arabic word.]
antinephritic *an-ti-ne-frit'ik*, *adj* acting against diseases of the kidney. [**anti-** (1).]
antineutrino *an-ti-nū-trē'nō*, *n* the antiparticle of the neutrino. — *n* **antineutron** (*an-ti-nū'tron*) an uncharged particle that combines with the neutron with mutual annihilation and emission of energy. [**anti-** (3).]
anting. See **ant**.
antinode *an'ti-nōd*, (*phys*) *n* a point of maximum disturbance midway between nodes. — *adj* **antinōd'al.** [**anti-** (3).]
antinomian *an-ti-nō'mi-ən*, *n* a person who denies the obligatoriness of moral law; a person who believes that Christians are emancipated by the gospel from the obligation to keep the moral law, faith alone being necessary. — Also *adj*. — *n* **antino'mianism**. — *adj* **antinomic** (*an-ti-nō'mik*) or **antino'mical** of, relating to, of the nature of, or involving, antinomy. — *n* **antinomy** (*an-tin'ə-mi*) a contradiction in a law; a conflict of authority; conclusions discrepant though apparently logical. [**anti-** (1) and Gr. *nomos*, law.]
anti-novel *an'ti-nov-l*, *n* a type of novel of the mid-twentieth century which largely discards plot and character and concerns itself with tiny inner dramas on the border of consciousness. [**anti-** (3).]
antioxidant *an-ti-ok'si-dənt*, *n* a substance that prevents or inhibits oxidation. [**anti-** (1).]
antipapal *an-ti-pā'pəl*, *adj* opposed to the pope or the papal system. — See also **antipope**. [**anti-** (2).]
antiparticle *an'ti-pär-ti-kl*, *n* the 'pair' of an elementary particle, particle and antiparticle being mutually destructive. [**anti-** (3).]
antipasto *an-ti-päs'tō*, (It.) *n* an hors d'œuvre, an appetiser.
antipathy *an-tip'əth-i*, *n* opposition in feeling; aversion; repugnance; incompatibility; mutual opposition; an object of antipathy. — *adj* **antipathet'ic** or **antipathet'ical.** — *adv* **antipathet'ically.** — *adj* **antipathic** (*an-ti-path'ik*) belonging to antipathy; opposite; contrary. — *n* **antip'athist**. [**anti-** (1) and Gr. *pathos*, feeling.]
anti-personnel *an-ti-pûr-sən-el'*, *adj* intended to destroy military personnel and other persons but not necessarily equipment etc. [**anti-** (1).]
antiperspirant *an-ti-pûr'spi-rənt*, *n* a substance that helps to stop perspiration when applied to the skin. — Also *adj*. [**anti-** (1).]
antiphiloprogenitive *an-ti-fil-ō-prō-jen'i-tiv*, *adj* intended to prevent the production of offspring. [**anti-** (1).]
antiphlogistic *an-ti-flə-jist'ik*, *adj* acting against heat, or inflammation. — *n* a medicine to allay inflammation. [**anti-** (1).]
antiphon *an'ti-fon*, *n* alternate chanting or singing; a species of church music sung by two parties each responding to the other — also **antiphony** (*an-tif'ən-i*). — *adj* **antiph'onal**. — *n* a book of antiphons or of anthems. — Also **antiph'onary** and **antiph'oner**. — *adv* **antiph'onally.** — *adj* **antiphonic** (*an-ti-fon'ik*) or **antiphon'ical** mutually responsive. — *adv* **antiphon'ically.** [Gr. *anti*, in return, and *phōnē*, voice: a doublet of **anthem.**]
antiphrasis *an-tif'rə-sis*, (*rhet*) *n* the use of words in a sense opposite to the literal one. — *adj* **antiphrastic** (*an-ti-fras'tik*) or **antiphras'tical** involving antiphrasis; ironical. [Gr., — *anti*, against, *phrasis*, speech.]
antipodes *an-tip'ə-dēz*, *npl* (also *sing*) (sometimes with *cap*) Australia and New Zealand, as being so related to Great Britain or Europe; a point or place diametrically opposite to another on the surface of the earth or of any globular body or sphere; a pair of points or places so related to each other; those who live on the other side of the globe, or on opposite sides, standing feet to feet; the exact opposite of a person or a thing. — *adj* **antip'odal,** esp. of the Antipodes. — *adj* **antipodē'an**. [Gr. *antipŏdēs*, pl. of *antipous*, with feet opposite — *pous*, *podos*, a foot.]
antipole *an'ti-pōl*, *n* the opposite pole; direct opposite. [**anti-** (3).]
antipope *an'ti-pōp*, *n* a pontiff set up in opposition to one asserted to be canonically chosen, such as those who resided at Avignon in the 13th and 14th centuries. — See also **antipapal**. [**anti-** (3).]
antiproton *an-ti-prō'ton*, *n* a particle comparable to the proton but negatively charged. [**anti-** (3).]
antipruritic *an-ti-proo-rit'ik*, *n* a substance that reduces itchiness. — Also *adj*. [**anti-** (1).]
antipsychotic *an-ti-sī-kot'ik*, *adj* (of a drug) alleviating psychosis. — *n* an antipsychotic drug. [**anti-** (1).]
antipyretic *an-ti-pī-ret'ik*, *adj* counteracting fever. — *n* an antipyretic agent. [Gr. *anti-*, against, *pyretos*, fever — *pyr*, fire.]
antiq. *abbrev* for: antiquarian; antiques; antiquities.
antiquark *an'ti-kwärk*, *n* the antiparticle (not as yet discovered) corresponding to the quark. [**anti-** (3).]
antiquary *an'ti-kwər-i*, *n* a person who studies, collects, or deals in relics of the past, but not usually very ancient things — curiosities rather than objects of serious archaeological interest. — *adj* **antiquarian** (*an-ti-kwā'ri-ən*) connected with the study of antiquities. — *n* an antiquary. — *n* **antiquā'rianism.** [L. *antīquārius* — *antīquus*, old.]
antique *an-tēk'*, *adj* ancient; of a good old age; old-fashioned; savouring of bygone times; after the manner of the ancients. — *n* anything very old; an old relic; a piece of old furniture or other object sought by collectors. — *vt* to alter the appearance of (wood, leather, etc.) so that it seems very old. — *vt* **antiquate** (*an'ti-kwāt*) to make antique, old, or obsolete; to put out of use. — *adj* **an'tiquated.** — *n* **antique'ness.** — *n* **antiquitarian** (*an-tik-wi-tā'ri-ən*) a person attached to old ways or beliefs. — *n* **antiq'uity** ancient times, esp. the times of the ancient Greeks and Romans; great age; ancient style; the people of

old time; a relic of the past. [L. *antīquus*, old, ancient — *ante*, before; infl. by Fr. *antique*.]

anti-racism *an-ti-rās'izm*, *n* opposition to prejudice and persecution on grounds of race, and support for policies that promote equality among and tolerance between groups of different racial origins. — *adj* and *n* **anti-ra'cist**. [**anti-** (2).]

antirrhinum *an-ti-rī'nəm*, *n* a plant of the snapdragon genus *Antirrhinum*. [Latinised from Gr. *antirrīnon*, snapdragon — *anti*, like, mimicking, *rhīs*, *rhīnos*, nose.]

antiscorbutic *an-ti-skör-būt'ik*, *adj* acting against scurvy. — *n* a remedy for or something that prevents scurvy developing. [**anti-** (1).]

anti-Semite *an-ti-sem'īt* or *-sēm'īt*, *n* a hater of Semites, esp. Jews, or of their influence. — *adj* **anti-Semitic** (*an-ti-sim-it'ik*). — *n* **anti-Semitism** (*an-ti-sem'it-izm* or *an-ti-sēm'it-izm*). [**anti-** (2).]

antisepsis *an-ti-sep'sis*, *n* destruction, or inhibition of growth, of bacteria. — *adj* **antisep'tic**. — *n* an antiseptic agent. — *n* **antisep'ticism** antiseptic treatment. — *adv* **antisep'tically**. — *vt* **antisepticise** or **-ize** (*an-ti-sep'ti-sīz*). [Gr. *anti-*, against, *sēpsis*, putrefaction.]

antiserum *an'ti-sēr-əm*, *n* a serum which contains antibodies: — *pl* **antiser'ums** or **antiser'a**. [*anti*body and **serum**.]

antisocial *an-ti-sō'shl*, *adj* opposed to the good of society, or the principles of society; disinclined to mix in society; without social instincts. — *adv* **antiso'cially**. — *n* **antiso'cialism**. — *n* **antiso'cialist** an opponent of socialism. — *n* **antisociality** (*an-ti-so-shi-al'i-ti*) unsociableness; opposition to the principles of society. [**anti-** (2).]

antispasmodic *an-ti-spaz-mod'ik*, *adj* preventing or alleviating spasms or convulsions. — *n* a remedy for spasms. [**anti-** (1).]

antistatic *an-ti-stat'ik*, *adj* having the property of counteracting static electricity. — Also *n*. [**anti-** (1).]

antistrophe *an-tis'trə-fi* or *-trō-fi*, *n*. See **strophe**.

antisyzygy *an-ti-si'zi-ji*, *n* union of opposites. [Gr. *antisyzygīā* — *anti-*, against, opposite, *syzygīā*, union, coupling.]

antithesis *an-tith'i-sis*, *n* a figure in which thoughts or words are balanced in contrast; a thesis or proposition opposing another; opposition; the direct opposite: — *pl* **antith'eses** (*-sēz*). — *adj* **antithet'ic** or **antithet'ical**. — *adv* **antithet'ically**. [Gr. *antithesis* — *thesis*, placing.]

antitoxin *an-ti-tok'sin*, *n* a substance that neutralises toxin formed in the body. — *adj* **antitox'ic**. [**anti-** (1).]

antitrade *an'ti-trād*, *n* a wind that blows in the opposite direction to the trade wind — that is, in the northern hemisphere from south-west, and in the southern hemisphere from north-west. [**anti-** (3).]

antitrust *an-ti-trust'*, *adj* (mainly *US*) of legislation, etc., directed against the adverse effects of monopolies on commerce. [**anti-** (1).]

antitussive *an-ti-tus'iv*, *adj* tending to alleviate or suppress coughing. — *n* an antitussive agent. [**anti-** (1) and L. *tussis*, a cough.]

antitype *an'ti-tīp*, *n* that which corresponds to the type; that which is prefigured by the type. — *adj* **antityp'al** or **antitypic** (*an-ti-tip'ik*) or **antityp'ical**. [**anti-** (3).]

antivenin *an-ti-ven'in* or **antivenene** *an-ti-ven-ēn'*, *n* an antitoxin counteracting esp. snake venom. [**anti-** (1).]

antivivisection *an-ti-viv-i-sek'shən*, *n* opposition to vivisection. — *n* **antivivisec'tionism**. — *n* **antivivisec'tionist**. [**anti-** (2).]

antler *ant'lər*, *n* a bony outgrowth from the frontal bone of a deer, normally one of a pair. — *adj* **ant'lered**. — **ant'ler-moth** a moth, with antler-like markings on the wings, its larvae very destructive to pastures. [O.Fr. *antoillier*.]

antonomasia *ant-on-o-mā'zi-ə*, *n* use of an epithet, or the name of an office or attributive, for a person's proper name, e.g. his lordship for an earl; and conversely, e.g. a Napoleon for a great conqueror. [Gr. *antonomasiā* — *onomazein*, to name, *onoma*, a name.]

antonym *ant'ə-nim*, *n* a word opposite in meaning to another. [Gr. *onyma* = *onoma*, a name.]

antrorse *an-trörs'*, (*biol*) *adj* turned up or forward. [From *anterus*, hypothetical positive of L. *anterior*, front, and L. *versus*, turned.]

ANU *abbrev* for Australian National University.

anuria *an-ū'ri-ə*, *n* failure in secretion of urine. [Gr. *an-* (privative), *ouron*, urine.]

anus *ā'nəs*, *n* the opening of the alimentary canal through which undigested residues are voided from the body. — *adj* **ā'nal**. — *adv* **ā'nally**. [L. *ānus*, *-ī*, a ring.]

anvil *an'vil*, *n* an iron block on which smiths hammer metal into shape; the incus of the ear, a bone in the middle ear shaped like an anvil. — **anvil secateurs** secateurs with two straight blades, the cutting blade closing against a blunt flat blade. [O.E. *anfilte*, *onfilti*.]

anxious *ang(k)'shəs*, *adj* uneasy with fear and desire regarding something doubtful; solicitous; eager (for something or to do something). — *n* **anxiety** (*ang(g)-zī'i-ti*) state of being anxious; a state of chronic apprehension as a symptom of mental disorder. — *adj* **anxiolytic** (*angk-si-ō-lit'ik*) of a drug, reducing anxiety and tension. — Also *n*. — *adv* **an'xiously**. — *n* **an'xiousness**. [L. *anxius* — *angĕre*, to press tightly. See **anger, anguish**.]

any *en'i*, *adj* and *pron* one (unspecified); some; whichever, no matter which. — *adv* at all, to an appreciable extent. — *n* and *pron* **an'ybody** any single person; a person of any account. — *adv* **an'yhow** in any way whatever; in any case, at least; indifferently, carelessly. — *n* and *pron* **an'yone** (or **any one**) anybody at all; anybody whatever. — *adv* **an'yroad** (*colloq*) anyway. — *n* and *pron* **an'ything** a thing (unspecified), as opposed to nothing. — *adv* to any extent. — *adv* **an'ytime** at any time. — *adv* **an'yway** in any manner; anyhow; in any case. — *adv* **an'ywhere** in or to any place. — *adv* **an'ywise** in any manner; to any degree. — **any amount** a lot (*colloq*); **any day** in any circumstances; **any more** any longer; **any old** any, with connotations of indifference, lack of thought, etc.; **any old how** without any special care; **any old thing** anything at all; **at any rate** whatever may happen; at all events; **like anything** very much; with great vigour. [O.E. *ǣnig* — *ān*, one.]

ANZAAS *an'zəs* or *an'zas*, *abbrev* for Australian and New Zealand Association for the Advancement of Science.

Anzac *an'zak*, *n* any Australian or New Zealand soldier. — Also *adj*. — **Anzac Day** 25 April, a public holiday in Australia and New Zealand in memory of the Anzac landing in Gallipoli (1915). [Orig. a member of the *A*ustralian and *N*ew *Z*ealand *A*rmy *C*orps during World War I.]

Anzus *an'zəs*, *abbrev* for (the alliance between) Australia, New Zealand and the United States.

AO *abbrev* for: Army Order; Officer of (the Order of) Australia.

AOB or **aob** *abbrev* for any other business.

AOC *abbrev* for Air Officer Commanding; (of wine) appellation d'origine contrôlée.

AOCB *abbrev* for any other competent business.

AONB *abbrev* for Area of Outstanding Natural Beauty (protected area).

aor. *abbrev* for aorist.

aorist *ā'ər-ist*, (*gram*) *n* a tense, esp. in Greek, expressing simple past time, with no implications of continuance, repetition, or the like. — *adj* **aorist'ic.** [Gr. *aoristos*, indefinite — *a-*, not, and *horistos*, limited.]

aorta *ā-ör'tə*, *n* the main artery that carries oxygenated blood from the heart. — *adj* **aor'tal** or **aor'tic.** — *n* **aortī'tis** inflammation of the aorta. [Gr. *aortē* — *aeirein*, to raise up.]

aoudad *ä'ōō-dad*, *n* a North African wild sheep. [Native name in French spelling.]

AP *abbrev* for Associated Press.

apace *ə-pās'*, *adv* at a quick pace; swiftly. [**a-**[1] and **pace**[1].]

Apache *ə-pa'chi*, *n* a Red Indian of a group of tribes in Arizona, New Mexico, etc. [Perh. Zuñi *āpachu*, enemy.]

apagoge *ap-ə-gō'jē*, *n* reduction to absurdity, indirect proof by showing the falsehood of the opposite. — *adj* **apagogic** (*ap-ə-go'jik*) or **apago'gical.** — *adv* **apago'gically.** [Gr. *apagōgē*, leading away, *apagein*, to lead off.]

apart *ə-pärt'*, *adv* separately; aside; asunder, parted; separate; out of consideration. — *n* **apart'ness.** — **set apart** to separate; to devote; **take apart** (*slang*) to reprimand severely; **tell apart** to distinguish, see the difference between. [Fr. *à part* — L. *ad partem*, to the side.]

apartheid *a-pärt'hāt* or *a-pär'tīd*, *n* segregation and separate development (of races); (also *fig*, of e.g. segregation of the sexes). [Afrik.]

apartment *ə-pärt'mənt*, *n* a single room in a house, a public room or bedroom; a flat, a set of rooms usu. on one floor of a building (usu. used as a dwelling; mainly *NAm*). — *adj* **apartmental** (*ə-pärt-ment'əl*). [Fr. *appartement*, a suite of rooms forming a complete dwelling — L. *ad*, to, and *partīre*, *partīrī*, to divide.]

apatetic *ap-ə-tet'ik*, *adj* of an animal's coloration or marking which closely resembles that of another species or of its surroundings. [Gr. *apatētikos*, deceitful.]

apathy *ap'əth-i*, *n* lack of feeling, passion, or interest; indifference. — *adj* **apathet'ic** or **apathet'ical.** — *adv* **apathet'ically.** [Gr. *apatheia* — *a-*, without, *pathos*, feeling.]

Apatosaurus *ə-pat-ə-sör'əs*, *n* the scientific name for Brontosaurus. [Gr. *apatē*, deceit, *sauros*, lizard.]

ape *āp*, *n* a monkey; a large monkey without a tail or with a very short one; a mimic; an imitator. — *vt* to mimic; to imitate. — *n* **ape'dom.** — *n* **ape'hood.** — *n* **ap'ery** conduct of one who apes; any ape-like action; a colony of apes. — *adj* **ap'ish** like an ape; imitative; foppish. — **ape'man** any of several extinct primates thought to have been intermediate in development between man and the higher apes. — **go ape** (*US slang*) to go crazy (with *over* or *for*). [O.E. *apa*.]

apepsy *a-pep'si* or **apepsia** *a-pep'si-ə*, *n* weakness of digestion. [Gr. *apepsiā*, indigestion; *a-*, without, not, *peptein*, to digest.]

aperçu *a-per-sü*, *n* a summary exposition; a brief outline; a glimpse; an immediate intuitive insight. [Fr. *aperçu*, survey, sketch — lit. (past p. of *apercevoir*) perceived.]

aperient *ə-pē'ri-ənt*, *n* and *adj* laxative. — *adj* **aperitive** (*ə-per'i-tiv*) laxative. — *n* same as **apéritif**; an aperitive medicine. [L. *aperīre*, *apertum*, to open.]

aperiodic *ā-pē-ri-od'ik*, *adj* not periodic; coming to rest without oscillation. — *n* **aperiodicity** (*ā-pē-ri-ə-dis'i-ti*). [**a-**[2] and **periodic.**]

apéritif or **aperitif** *ə-per-i-tēf'* or *ə-per'i-tēf*, *n* a drink taken as an appetiser. [Fr., — L.L. *aperitīvus* — *aperīre*, to open.]

aperture *ap'ər-chər*, *n* an opening; a hole; the diameter of the opening through which light passes in an optical instrument. [L. *apertura* — *aperīre*, to open.]

apery. See **ape.**

apetalous *ə-pet'əl-əs*, *adj* (*bot*) without petals. — *n* **apet'aly.** [**a-**[2] and Gr. *petalon*, a leaf.]

APEX *ā'peks*, *abbrev* for: advance purchase excursion (a reduced airline fare); Association of Professional, Executive, Clerical and Computer Staff.

apex *ā'peks*, *n* summit, tip, or point; a vertex (*geom*); the culminating point, climax of anything: — *pl* **ā'pexes** or **apices** (*āp'i-sēz* or *ap'i-sēz*). [L. *ăpex*, *ăpĭcis*, a tip.]

apfelstrudel *ap-fəl-shtrōō'dəl* or *ap-fəl-strōō'dəl*, *n* a sweet pastry containing apples, spices, etc. [Ger.]

aphaeresis or **apheresis** *a-fē'ri-sis*, (*gram*) *n* the taking away of a sound or syllable at the beginning of a word. [Gr. *aphairesis*, a taking away, *apo*, away, and *haireein*, to take.]

aphagia *ə-fā'j(i)-ə*, *n* inability to swallow; (of imago of certain insects) inability to feed. [Gr. *a-* (privative) and *phagia* — *phagein*, to eat.]

aphasia *a-fā'zhi-ə* or *a-fā'zi-ə*, *n* inability to express thought in words, or inability to understand the spoken or written words of others, because of some brain disorder. — *n* and *adj* **aphā'siac.** — *adj* **aphasic** (*a-fā'zik*). [Gr. *a-* (privative) and *phasis*, speech — *phanai*, to speak.]

aphelion *a-fē'li-ən*, *n* a planet's furthest point in its orbit from the sun: — *pl* **aphē'lia.** — *adj* **aphē'lian** or **aphē'lic.** [Gr. *apo*, from, *hēlios*, sun.]

apheliotropic *a-fē-li-ə-trop'ik*, *adj* turning away from the sun. — *n* **apheliot'ropism.** [Gr. *apo*, from, *hēlios*, sun, and *tropikos*, pertaining to turning.]

apheresis. See **aphaeresis.**

aphesis *af'i-sis*, *n* the gradual and unintentional loss of an unaccented vowel at the beginning of a word, as in *squire* from *esquire* — a special form of aphaeresis. — *adj* **aphetic** (*ə-fet'ik*). — *vt* **aph'etise** or **-ize.** [Gr. *aphesis*, letting go — *apo*, from, *hienai*, to send.]

aphis *āf'is* or **aphid** *āf'id*, *n* a small insect that sucks plant juices e.g. a greenfly: — *pl* **aph'ides** (*āf'i-dēz*) or **aph'ids.** — *adj* **aphid'ical.** — *n* **aphicide** (*af'i-sīd*) or **aphidicide** (*af-id'i-sīd*) an aphis killer.

aphonia *a-fō'ni-ə* or **aphony** *af'ə-ni*, *n* loss of voice from hysteria, disease of larynx or vocal cords, etc. — *adj* **aphonic** (*ə-fon'ik*) or **aphonous** (*af'ə-nəs*) voiceless. [Gr. *a-* (privative) and *phōnē*, voice.]

aphorism *af'ər-izm*, *n* a concise statement of a principle in any science; a brief, pithy saying; an adage. — *vi* **aph'orise** or **-ize.** — *n* **aph'oriser** or **-z-.** — *n* **aph'orist.** — *adj* **aphoris'tic.** — *adv* **aphoris'tically.** [Gr. *aphorizein*, to define — *apo*, from, *horos*, a limit.]

aphotic *a-fō'tik*, *adj* lightless. [Gr. *a-* (privative) and *phōs*, *phōtos*, light.]

aphrodisiac *af-rə-diz'i-ak*, *adj* exciting sexually. — *n* something that arouses sexual desire, e.g. a food or a drug. — *n* **aphrodis'ia** sexual desire, esp. violent. — *adj* **Aphrodis'ian** belonging to Aphrodite. [Gr. *aphrodīsiakos* — *Aphrodītē*, the goddess of love.]

aphtha *af'thə*, *n* the disease thrush; a small whitish ulcer on the surface of a mucous membrane: — *pl* **aphthae** (*af'thē*). — *adj* **aph'thous.** [Gr. *aphtha*, mostly in pl. *aphthai*.]

aphyllous *a-fil'əs*, (*bot*) *adj* without leaves. — *n* **aphyll'y.** [Gr. *a-* (privative) and *phyllon*, a leaf.]

apian *ā'pi-ən*, *adj* relating to bees. — *adj* **apiarian** (*ā-pi-ā'ri-ən*) relating to beehives or beekeeping. — *n* **ā'piarist** a beekeeper. — *n* **a'piary** (*ā'pi-ər-i*) a place where bees are kept. — *n* **ā'piculture** beekeeping. — *n* **āpicul'turist.** [L. *ăpis*, a bee, *ăpiārium*, a bee-house.]

apical *ap'ik-l* or *āp'ik-l*, *adj* of or at the apex; denoting a sound articulated with the tip of the tongue (*phon*). — *adv* **ap'ically.** — *npl* **ap'ices** see **apex.** [See **apex.**]

apiculture. See **apian.**

apiece *ə-pēs'*, *adv* for each piece, thing, or person; to each individually. [**a-**[1] and **piece.**]

apish. See **ape**.

aplacental *a-plə-sen'tl*, *adj* without placenta. [**a-**[2] and **placental**.]

aplasia *a-plā'zhi-ə* or *a-plā'zi-ə*, *n* imperfect development or absence of an organ or part. — *adj* **aplastic** (*a-plas'tik*). — **aplastic anaemia** a form of anaemia caused by malfunctioning of the bone marrow. [**a-**[2] and N.L. *-plasia* — Gr. *plasis*, moulding.]

aplenty *ə-plen'ti*, *adv* in plenty. [**a-**[1] and **plenty**.]

aplomb *ə-plom'*, *n* self-possession, coolness. [Fr. *aplomb*, composure; balance, perpendicular.]

apnoea or **apnea** *ap-nē'ə*, *n* a cessation of breathing. [Gr. *apnoia* — *a-* (privative) and *pno(i)ē*, breath.]

apo. *abbrev* for apogee.

Apoc. *abbrev* for: Apocalypse; Apocrypha; Apocryphal.

Apocalypse *a-pok'əl-ips*, *n* the last book of the New Testament, otherwise the Revelation of St John; (without *cap*) any book purporting to reveal the future or last things; a revelation or disclosure. — *adj* **apocalypt'ic** pertaining to the Apocalypse; prophetic of disaster or of the end of the world. — *adj* **apocalypt'ical**. — *adv* **apocalypt'ically**. [Gr. *apokalypsis*, an uncovering — *apo*, from, *kalyptein*, to cover.]

apocarpous *ap-ō-kär'pəs*, (*bot*) *adj* having the carpels separate. [Gr. *apo*, from, *karpos*, fruit.]

apochromatic *ap-ə-krō-mat'ik*, *adj* relatively free from chromatic and spherical aberration. — *n* **apochro'mat** an apochromatic lens or instrument. — *n* **apochro'matism**. [Gr. *apo*, from, *chrōma*, *-atos*, colour.]

apocope *ə-pok'ə-pē*, *n* the cutting off of the last sound or syllable of a word. — *vt* **apoc'opate**. — *n* **apocopā'tion**. [Gr. *apokopē* — *apo*, off, *koptein*, to cut.]

apocrine *ap'ə-krīn*, (*biol*) *adj* (of a gland) whose product is formed by the breakdown of part of its active cells. [Gr. *apo*, off, *krīnein*, to separate.]

apocrypha *ə-pok'rif-ə*, *npl* hidden or secret things; applied specially to certain books or parts of books included in the Septuagint and Vulgate translations of the Old Testament but not accepted as canonical by Jews or Protestants, and to later books (the Apocrypha of the New Testament) never accepted as canonical or authoritative by any considerable part of the Christian Church: — *nsing* **apoc'ryphon**. — *adj* **apoc'ryphal** of the Apocrypha; of doubtful authority; spurious; fabulous. [Gr., things hidden — *apo*, from, *kryptein*, to hide.]

apodictic *ap-ə-dik'tik* or **apodeictic** *ap-ə-dīk'tik*, *adj* necessarily true; demonstrative without demonstration; beyond contradiction. — *adj* **apodic'tical** or **apodeic'tical**. — *adv* **apodic'tically** or **apodeic'tically**. [Gr. *apodeiktikos* — *apodeiknynai* (*apo* and *deiknynai*), to demonstrate.]

apodosis *ə-pod'ə-sis*, (*gram*) *n* the consequent clause in a conditional sentence (opp. to *protasis*). [Gr. *apodosis* — *apo*, back, *didonai*, to give.]

apogaeic. See **apogee**.

apogamy *ə-pog'ə-mi*, (*bot*) *n* omission of the sexual process in the life-history — the sporophyte developing either from an unfertilised egg-cell or some other cell. — *adj* **apog'amous**. — *adv* **apog'amously**. [Gr. *apo*, from, *gamos*, marriage.]

apogee *ap'ō-jē*, *n* a heavenly body's point of greatest distance from the earth; culmination (*fig*; opp. to *perigee*.) — *adj* **apogaeic** (*ap-ə-jē'ik*). — *adj* **apogē'al**. — *adj* **apogē'an**. [Gr. *apogaion* — *apo*, from, *gaia*, or *gē*, the earth.]

apolitical *ā-pəl-it'ik-əl*, *adj* indifferent to political affairs; uninvolved in politics. — *adv* **apolit'ically**. — *n* **apolitical'ity**. — *n* **apolit'icism**. [**a-**[2] and **political**.]

Apollo *ə-pol'ō*, *n* the Greek sun-god, patron of poetry and music, medicine, archery, etc.; (sometimes without *cap*) an extremely handsome young man: — *pl* **Apoll'os**. [Gr. *Apollōn*, *-ōnos*, L. *Apollō*, *-inis*.]

apologetic *ə-pol-ə-jet'ik*, *adj* regretfully acknowledging fault. — *n* a defence, vindication. — *adj* **apologet'ical**. — *adv* **apologet'ically**. — *nsing* **apologet'ics** the defensive argument or method, esp. the defence of Christianity. — *n* **apologia** (*ap-ə-lō'ji-ə*) a written defence or vindication. — *vi* **apologise** or **-ize** (*ə-pol'ə-jīz*) to put forward a defence; (now usu.) to express regret for a fault. — *n* **apologist** (*ə-pol'ə-jist*) a defender by argument. — *n* **apology** (*ə-pol'ə-ji*) a defence, justification, apologia; an explanation with expression of regret; a regretful acknowledgment of a fault; a poor specimen hardly worthy of its name. [Gr. *apologia*, defence, *apologos*, a tale — *apo*, off, *logos*, speaking.]

aponeurosis *ap-ō-nū-rō'sis*, *n* a flat thin tendon. — *adj* **aponeurotic** (*ap-ō-nū-rot'ik*). [Gr. *aponeurōsis* — *apo*, off, *neuron*, tendon.]

apophatic *a-pə-fat'ik*, (*theol*) *adj* (of a description of God) using negatives, i.e., saying what God is not.

apophlegmatic *ap-ə-fleg-mat'ik*, (*med*) *adj* promoting the discharge of mucus. — *n* an apophlegmatic agent. [Gr. *apophlegmatikos* — *apo*, off; see **phlegm**.]

apophthegm or **apothegm** *ap'ə-them*, *n* a pithy saying, more short, pointed, and practical than the aphorism need be. — *adj* **apophthegmatic** or **apothegmatic** (*ap-ə-theg-mat'ik*), **apophthegmat'ical** or **apothegmat'ical**. — *adv* **apophthegmat'ically** or **apothegmat'ically**. [Gr. *apophthegma* — *apo*, forth, *phthengesthai*, to utter.]

apophyge *a-pof'i-jē*, *n* the curve where a column merges in its base or capital. [Gr. *apophygē*, escape.]

apophysis *a-pof'i-sis* or *a-pof'i-zis*, *n* an outgrowth or protuberance, esp. on a bone, on the end of a pine-cone scale or on a moss stalk below the capsule (*biol*); a branch from a mass of igneous rock (*geol*): — *pl* **apoph'yses** (*a-pof'i-sēz*). [Gr., offshoot — *apo*, off, *phyein*, to grow.]

apoplexy *ap'ə-pleks-i*, *n* sudden loss of sensation and motion, generally the result of haemorrhage or thrombosis in the brain. — *adj* **apoplec'tic** of apoplexy; infuriated (*colloq*). — *adj* **apoplec'tical**. [Gr. *apoplēxiā* — *apo-* (expressing completeness) and *plēssein*, to strike.]

aport *ə-pört'*, (*naut*) *adv* on or towards the port side. [**a-**[1] and **port**[3].]

aposematic *ap-ə-sē-mat'ik*, *adj* (of animal coloration) warning. [Gr. *apo*, away from, *sēma*, *sēmatos*, sign.]

apospory *ə-pos'pə-ri*, (*bot*) *n* omission of spore-formation in the life-history — the gametophyte developing vegetatively from the sporophyte. — *adj* **apos'porous**. [Gr. *apo*, away from, and **spore**.]

apostasy *ə-post'ə-si*, *n* abandonment of one's religion, principles, or party; a revolt from ecclesiastical obedience, from a religious profession, or from holy orders; defection. — *n* **apost'ate** (*ə-post'āt* or *ə-post'it*) a person who has apostatised; a renegade. — Also *adj*. — *adj* **apostatic** (*ap-ō-stat'ik*) or **apostat'ical**. — *vi* **apostatise** or **-ize** (*ə-pos'tə-tīz*). [Gr. *apostasiā*, a standing away — *apo*, from, *stasis*, a standing.]

a posteriori *ā pos-tē-ri-ō'rī* or *ä pos-ter-i-ō'rē*, *adj* applied to reasoning from experience, from effect to cause; inductive; empirical; gained from experience; — opp. to *a priori*. — Also *adv*. [L. *ā*, from, *posteriōrī*, abl. of *posterior*, coming after.]

apostle *ə-pos'l*, *n* someone sent to preach the gospel; esp. one of Christ's twelve chosen followers; someone who first introduces Christianity in a country; a principal champion or supporter of a new system, or of a cause; the highest in the fourfold ministry of the Catholic Apostolic Church; one of the twelve officials forming a presiding high council in the Mormon Church. — *n* **apos'tleship**. — *n* **apost'o-**

late (*ə-post'ə-lāt*) the office of an apostle. — *adj* **apostolic** (*ap-əs-tol'ik*) or **apostol'ical**. — *adv* **apostol'ically**. — *n* **apostolicism** (*ap-əs-tol'i-sizm*). — *n* **apostolicity** (*ə-post-ə-lis'i-ti*) the quality of being apostolic. — **Apostles' Creed** the oldest form of Christian creed that exists, early ascribed to the apostles; **apostle spoons** silver spoons with handles ending in figures of the apostles, once a common baptismal present; **apostolical succession** the derivation of holy orders by unbroken chain of transmission from the apostles through bishops — the theory of the Catholic Church; the assumed succession of a ministry so ordained to apostolic powers and privileges; **apostolic see** the see of Rome, the diocese of the Pope; **apostolic vicar** the cardinal representing the Pope in extraordinary missions. [Gr. *apostolos*, someone sent away, *apo*, away, *stellein*, to send.]

apostrophe[1] *ə-pos'trə-fi*, *n* (in *rhet*) a sudden turning away from the ordinary course of a speech to address some person or object present or absent. — *adj* **apostrophic** (*ap-ə-strof'ik*). — *vt* **apos'trophise** or **-ize** to address by apostrophe. [Gr. *apo*, from, *strophē*, a turning.]

apostrophe[2] *ə-pos'trə-fi*, *n* a mark (') showing (among other uses) the omission of a letter or letters in a word; a sign of the possessive case in modern Eng. [Gr. *apostrophos*, turning away, elision; confused with **apostrophe**[1].]

apothecary *ə-poth'i-kər-i*, *n* a legal description for licentiates of the Society of Apothecaries, licensed to dispense prescribed drugs; orig. a druggist or pharmacist. — **apothecaries' measure** liquid units of capacity (fluid ounce, etc.) used by pharmacists before 1969; **apothecaries' weight** a pre-1969 system based on the troy ounce. [L.L. *apothēcarius* — Gr. *apothēkē*, a storehouse — *apo*, away, and *tithenai*, to place.]

apothegm, etc. See **apophthegm**.

apothem *ap'ə-them*, *n* the perpendicular from the centre to any of the sides of a regular polygon. [Gr. *apo*, away from, *thema*, that which is placed.]

apotheosis *ə-poth-i-ō'sis*, *n* a deification; glorification: — *pl* **apotheoses** (*ə-poth-i-ō'sēz*). — *vt* **apoth'eosise** or **-ize**. [Gr. *apotheōsis* — *apo-* (expressing completion) and *theos*, a god.]

app. *abbrev* for: apparent; apparently; appendix; apprentice.

appal *ə-pöl'*, *vt* to horrify, dismay: — *pr p* **appall'ing**; *pa t* and *pa p* **appalled'**. — *adj* **appall'ing**. — *adv* **appall'ingly**. [Perh. from O.Fr. *apalir*, *apallir*, to wax pale, make pale. See **pall**[2] and **pale**[2].]

Appaloosa *a-pə-lōō'sə*, *n* a North American breed of horse, usu. white or grey with dark spots. [Prob. the *Palouse* Indians.]

appanage or **apanage** *ap'ən-ij*, *n* a provision for maintenance, esp. of a king's younger child; dependent territory; a perquisite; an adjunct or attribute. [Fr. *apanage* — L. *ad*, and *panis*, bread.]

apparat *ä'pə-rät*, *n* the political machine of the Communist party. — *n* **apparatchik** (*ä-pə-räch'ik*) a member of the Soviet bureaucracy or Communist party machine elsewhere; a Communist agent; a party official in any political party: — *pl* **apparat'chiki**. [Russ., apparatus.]

apparatus *ap-ə-rā'təs* or *ap-ə-ra'təs*, *n* things prepared or provided, material; set of instruments, tools, natural organs, etc.; a machine or piece of equipment with a particular purpose; materials (such as various readings) for the critical study of a document (**apparatus criticus** *ap-ə-rā'təs krit'i-kəs* or *ap-a-rä'tŏŏs krit'i-kŏŏs*): — *pl* **appara'tuses** or **appara'tus** (L. *appārātūs*). [L. *appārātus*, *-ūs* — *ad*, to, *pārāre*, *-ātum*, to prepare.]

apparel *ə-par'əl*, *vt* to dress, clothe; to adorn: — *pr p* **appar'elling**; *pa t* and *pa p* **appar'elled**. — *n* attire, dress. — *n* **appar'elment**. [O.Fr. *apareiller* — L. *ad*, to, *pār*, equal.]

apparent *ə-par'ənt*, or *ə-pār'ənt*, *adj* that may be seen; obvious; conspicuous; seeming; obtained by observation without correction, distinguished from *true* or from *mean*. — *n* **appar'ency** apparentness; position of being heir-apparent. — *adv* **appar'ently**. — *n* **appar'entness**. — **apparent (solar) time** true time, as shown e.g. on a sundial, as opposed to mean (solar) time. [L. *appārens*, *-entis*, pres. p. of *appārēre*; see **appear**.]

apparition *ap-ə-rish'ən*, *n* an appearing; an appearance; reappearance e.g. of a heavenly body after occultation; that which appears; a phantom; a ghost. — *adj* **appari'tional**. [**appear**.]

apparitor *ə-par'i-tər*, *n* an officer in attendance on an ecclesiastical court; a university beadle. [L. *appāritor*. See **appear**.]

appeal *ə-pēl'*, *vi* to call upon, have recourse to (with *to*); to refer (to a witness or superior authority); to make supplication or earnest request (to a person for a thing); to ask for (aid, charity etc.) by making a demand on people's feelings; to resort for verification or proof (to some principle or person); to attract one's interest or enjoyment; to demand another judgment by a higher court; to remove to another court; to ask for the umpire's decision esp. as to whether a player is out (*cricket*). — *vt* to remove to a higher court (*archaic* except in U.S.). — *n* recourse; an act of appealing; a supplication; removal of a cause to a higher tribunal; an evocation of sympathetic feeling, interest or enjoyment. — *adj* **appeal'able** (of a decision) that can be appealed against or referred to a superior tribunal. — *adj* **appeal'ing** making an appeal; imploring; calling forth sympathy; attractive. — *adv* **appeal'ingly**. — *n* **appeal'ingness**. — **Court of Appeal** a section of the English High Court of Justice; **Court of Criminal Appeal** an English Court created in 1907 for appeal in criminal cases. [O.Fr. *apeler* — L. *appellāre*, *-ātum*, to address, call by name; also to appeal to, impeach.]

appear *ə-pēr'*, *vi* to become visible; to present oneself formally before an authority or tribunal, hence to act as the representative or counsel for another; to come into view, to come before the public; to perform (on stage or on film etc.); to be published; to be manifest; to seem. — *n* **appear'ance** the act of appearing, e.g. in court to prosecute or answer a charge; the publication of a book; the effect of appearing conspicuously, show, parade; the condition of that which appears, form, aspect; outward look or show; a natural phenomenon; an apparition. — *n* **appear'er**. — **keep up appearances** to keep up an outward show, often with intent to conceal absence of the inward reality; **put in an appearance** to appear in person, *often* only briefly; **to all appearance(s)** so far as appears to any one. [O.Fr. *apareir* — L. *appārēre* — *ad*, to, *pārēre*, *pāritum*, to come forth.]

appease *ə-pēz'*, *vt* to pacify; to propitiate by concessions; to satisfy; to quiet; to allay. — *adj* **appeas'able**. — *n* **appease'ment**. — *adv* **appeas'ingly**. [O.Fr. *apeser*, to bring peace — L. *ad*, to, *pāx*, *pācis*, peace.]

appellant *ə-pel'ənt*, *n* a person who appeals; a person who impeaches. — *adj* **appell'ate** relating to appeals. — *n* **appellation** (*ap-ə-lā'shən*) that by which anything is called; name, esp. one attached to a particular person. — *adj* **appellā'tional**. — *n* **appellative** (*ə-pel'ə-tiv*) a common as distinguished from a proper name; a designation. — *adj* common (as distinguished from proper); of or pertaining to the giving of names. — *adv* **appell'atively**. [L. *appellāre*, *-ātum*, to call.]

appellation contrôlée *a-pel-a-syõ kõ-trō-lā* or **appellation d'origine contrôlée** (*dor-ē-zhēn*), (Fr.)

in the labelling of French wines, a guarantee that the wine conforms to certain specified conditions of origin, strength, etc. — Also *abbrev* **AOC.**

append *ə-pend'*, *vt* to hang on (to something); to add. — *n* **append'age** something appended; esp. one of the paired jointed structures of arthropods — antennae, jaws or legs. — *adj* **append'ant** attached, annexed, consequent. — *n* an adjunct, quality. [L. *ad*, to, *pendĕre*, to hang.]

appendicectomy *ə-pen-di-sek'tə-mi* or (esp. in U.S.) **appendectomy** *a-pen-dek'tə-mi*, *n* surgical removal of the vermiform appendix. [Ety. as for **append** with Gr. *ektomē*, cutting out.]

appendicitis *ə-pen-di-sī'tis*, *n* inflammation of the vermiform appendix.

appendicular. See **appendix.**

appendix *ə-pen'diks*, *n* something appended or added; a supplement; an addition to a book or document, containing explanatory matter that is not essential to its completeness; a prolongation or projection; the vermiform appendix (*anat*): — *pl* **append'ixes** or **appendices** (*ə-pen'di-sēz* or *ə-pen'di-siz*). — *adj* **appendicular** (*a-pen-dik'ū-lər*) of the nature of or belonging to an appendix. — **appendix vermiformis** or **vermiform appendix** a small blind tube leading off the caecum, part of the large intestine (*anat* and *zool*). [Ety. as for **append.**]

apperception *ap-ər-sep'shən*, *n* the mind's perception of itself as a conscious agent; an act of voluntary consciousness, accompanied with self-consciousness; the assimilation of a new sense-experience to a mass already in the mind. — *adj* **appercep'tive.** — *adj* **appercipient** (*ap-ər-sip'i-ənt*). — *vt* **apperceive** (*ap-ər-sēv'*). [L. *ad*, to, and **perception** and **perceive.**]

appertain *ap-ər-tān'*, *vi* to belong, as a possession, a right, or attribute. — *adj* **appertain'ing** proper, appropriate (with *to*). — *adj* **apper'tinent** appertaining. [O.Fr. *apartenir*, *apertenir* — L. *ad*, to, *pertinēre*, to belong.]

appetent *ap'i-tənt*, *adj* eagerly desirous; craving; longing. — *n* **app'etence** or **app'etency.** [L. *appetēns*, *-entis*, pres. p. of *appetĕre* — *ad*, to, *petĕre*, to seek.]

appetite *ap'i-tīt*, *n* physical craving, accompanied with uneasy sensation (e.g. hunger, thirst or sexual desire); natural desire; inclination; desire for food; hunger (with *for*). — *n* **app'etiser** or **-z-** something, esp. food or drink, to whet the appetite. — *adj* **app'etising** or **-z-.** — *adv* **app'etisingly** or **-z-.** [O.F. *apetit* — L. *appetitus* — *appetĕre*; see **appetent.**]

applaud *ə-plöd'*, *vt* to express approval of by clapping the hands or otherwise; to extol; to commend. — *vi* to clap the hands or otherwise express approval. — *n* **applaud'er.** — *adj* **applaud'ing.** — *adv* **applaud'ingly.** — *n* **applause** (*ə-plöz'*) clapping of hands or other sign of approval; general approbation; loud praise; acclamation. [L. *applaudĕre*, *-plausum* — *ad*, to, *plaudĕre*, to clap.]

apple *ap'l*, *n* the fruit of the apple-tree; extended to other fruits (as pineapple, custard-apple) or even galls (oak-apple); the fruit of the forbidden tree in the Garden of Eden (*Bible*). — **app'le-blossom; app'le-cart; app'le-jack** (*US*) apple brandy, distilled from fermented apple juice; **apple-pie'** a pie made with apples; **apple-tart'** a tart made with apples; **app'le-tree** a tree (*Pyrus malus*) of the rose family, closely related to the pear-tree. — **apple of the eye** the pupil of the eye; something especially dear; **apple-pie bed** a bed prepared as a practical joke, e.g. with sheets doubled up, so as to be impossible or painful to get into; **apple-pie order** perfect order; **apples and pears** (*rhyming slang*; often shortened to **apples**) stairs; **the Big Apple** see **big; upset the apple-cart** to throw plans into confusion. [O.E. *æppel.*]

Appleton layer *ap'əl-tən lā'ər*, *n* an ionised region in the atmosphere, about 150 miles up, that acts as a reflector of radio waves. [From the physicist Sir Edward *Appleton.*]

applicable . . . to **. . . applied.** See **apply.**

appliqué *a-plē'kā*, *n* work applied to, or laid on, another material, either of metalwork or of lace or the like. — Also *adj.* [Past p. of Fr. *appliquer*, to apply.]

apply *ə-plī'*, *vt* to lay or put in contact; to administer; to bring to bear; to put to use; to show the reference or relevance of; to assign; to wield or ply; to direct; to devote (to a pursuit); to lay on as appliqué; to cover with appliqué. — *vi* to suit or agree; to have recourse; to offer oneself as a candidate; to make or lodge a request; to be relevant; to hold good; to give close attention: — *pr p* **apply'ing;** *pa t* and *pa p* **applied'.** — *adj* **applī'able** applicable. — *n* **applī'ance** application; apparatus. — *n* **applicability** (*ap-li-kə-bil'i-ti*). — *adj* **applicable** (*ap'lik-ə-bl* or *ə-plik'ə-bl* in *adj* and *adv*) that may be applied; suitable. — *adv* **app'licably.** — *n* **app'licant** a person who applies; a petitioner; a candidate for a post. — *adj* **app'licate** put to practical use, applied. — *n* **applicā'tion** the act of applying, administering, or using; a thing applied; a formal request for a post, etc.; an appeal or petition; diligence; close thought or attention; employment, use of anything in special regard to something else; a particular type of problem or process (*comput*); a bringing to bear; the lesson or moral of a fable; employment of a word with assignment of meaning; a kind of needlework, appliqué. — *adj* **app'licātive** put into actual use in regard to anything; practical. — *n* **app'licator** a device or tool for applying something. — *adj* **applicatory** (*ap'li-kə-tə-ri*) having the property of applying. — *adj* **applied** (*ə-plīd'*) placed with a flat surface against or close to something; turned to use. — **application(s) package** (or **program**) (*comput*) a package or program designed to cope with a particular job, such as payroll-processing, vehicle-scheduling, warehouse control, etc.; **applied arts** see **useful** under **use**[2]; **applied mathematics** mathematics applied to observed facts of nature, or to practical life; **applied science** science put to use for a purpose, generally utilitarian, other than its own end (opposed to *pure*). [O.Fr. *aplier*, and its source, L. *applicāre*, *-ātum* — *ad*, to, *plicāre*, to fold.]

appoggiatura *äp-pod-jä-tōō'rä*, (*mus*) *n* a leaning note — a grace-note written in smaller size taking its time at the expense of the following note; a similar note with a stroke through the tail, played very quickly. [It. — *appoggiare*, to lean upon.]

appoint *ə-point'*, *vt* to fix; to settle; to assign, grant; to fix the time of; to engage to meet; to name to an office; to ordain; to prescribe; to destine, devote. — *adj* **appoint'ed** fixed; furnished; equipped. — *n* **appointee'** a person appointed to a job, position or office. — *adj* **appoint'ive** (*US*) filled by appointment. — *n* **appoint'ment** engagement, esp. for a meeting, consultation, etc.; direction; nomination; an office to which one is or may be nominated; (now usu. in *pl*) equipment, article of equipment. [O.Fr. *apointer* — *à point*, to (the) point.]

apportion *ə-pōr'shən*, *vt* to portion out; to divide in just shares; to adjust in due proportion. — *n* **appor'tionment.** [L. *ad*, to, and **portion.**]

appose *ə-pōz'*, *vt* to apply, e.g. a seal to a document; to place side by side. [Fr. *apposer* — L. *ad*, to, *pausāre*, to cease, rest; confused and blended in meaning with words from *pōnĕre*, *pŏsitum*, to put.]

apposite *ap'ə-zit*, *adj* apt; to the purpose. — *adv* **app'ositely.** — *n* **app'ositeness.** — *n* **apposition** (*ap-ə-zish'ən*) application; juxtaposition; the position of a word parallel to another in syntactic relation (*gram*); growth by deposition on the surface (*bot*). — *adj* **apposi'tional.** — *adj* **appositive**

(*ə-poz'i-tiv*) placed in apposition. [L. *appŏsitus*, past p. of *appōnĕre*, to put to — *ad*, to, *pōnĕre*, to put.]

appraise *ə-prāz'*, *vt* to set a price on; to value with a view to sale or (in U.S.) payment of customs duty; to estimate the worth of. — *adj* **apprais'able**. — *n* **apprais'al** appraisement. — *n* **appraise'ment** a valuation; estimation of quality. — *n* **apprais'er** a person who values property; a person who estimates quality. — *adj* **apprais'ive**. — *adv* **apprais'ively**. [Later form of **apprise**[2].]

appreciate *ə-prē'shi-āt*, *vt* to estimate justly; to be fully sensible of all the good qualities in; to estimate highly; to perceive; to raise in value, to advance the quotation or price of, as opp. to *depreciate*. — *vi* to rise in value. — *adj* **apprē'ciable** capable of being estimated; perceptible. — *adv* **apprē'ciably**. — *n* **apprēciā'tion** the act of setting a value, esp. on a work of literature or art; just — and also favourable — estimation; a sympathetic critical essay; increase in value. — *adj* **apprē'ciative** characterised by or implying appreciation. — *adv* **apprē'ciatively**. — *n* **apprē'ciātor** a person who appreciates, or estimates justly. — *adj* **apprē'ciatory** (*ə-prē'shyə-tər-i*). [L.L. *appretiāre*, *-ātum* — *ad*, to, and *pretium*, price.]

apprehend *ap-ri-hend'*, *vt* to lay hold of; to arrest; to be conscious of by the senses; to lay hold of by the intellect; to catch the meaning of; to understand; to recognise; to consider; to look forward to, esp. with fear. — *n* **apprehensibil'ity**. — *adj* **apprehens'ible**. — *n* **apprehen'sion** act of apprehending or seizing; arrest; conscious perception; conception; ability to understand; fear. — *adj* **apprehens'ive** pertaining to the laying hold of sensuous and mental impressions; intelligent, clever; having an apprehension or notion; fearful; anticipative of something adverse. — *adv* **apprehens'ively**. — *n* **apprehens'iveness**. [L. *appraehendĕre* — *ad*, to, *praehendĕre*, *-hēnsum*, to lay hold of.]

apprentice *ə-prent'is*, *n* someone bound by formal agreement to a skilled person to learn a craft; a mere novice. — Also *adj*. — *vt* to bind as an apprentice. — *n* **apprent'icement**. — *n* **apprent'iceship** the state of an apprentice; a time of training for a trade, or for any activity. — **serve an apprenticeship** to undergo the training of an apprentice. [O.Fr. *aprentis* — *aprendre*, to learn — L. *appraehendĕre*; see **apprehend**.]

apprise[1] *ə-prīz'*, *vt* to give notice to; to inform. [Fr. *apprendre*, past p. *appris*; see **apprehend**.]

apprise[2] or **apprize** *ə-prīz'*, *vt* to value, appreciate. [O.Fr. *appriser*, *aprisier* — *à*, to, and *prisier*, to price, prize. See **appraise**.]

appro. See under **approbation** and **approve**.

approach *ə-prōch'*, *vt* to bring near; to come near to in any sense; to come into personal relations or seek communication with; to resemble. — *vi* to come near. — *n* a drawing near; play on drawing near the putting-green (also **approach'-stroke** or **approach'-shot**, etc.; *golf*); an avenue or means of access; approximation; attitude towards, way of dealing with; (usu. *pl*) advances towards personal relations. — *n* **approachabil'ity**. — *adj* **approach'able**. [O.Fr. *aprochier*, L.L. *adpropiāre* — L. *ad*, to, *prope*, near.]

approbation *ap-rə-bā'shən*, *n* a formal sanction; approval. — **on approbation** (or *colloq* **on appro** *ap'rō*) on approval. [L. *approbāre*, *-ātum*; see **approve**.]

appropriate *ə-prō'pri-āt*, *vt* to make to be the private property of anyone; to take to oneself as one's own; to filch; to set apart for a purpose, assign; to suit (with *to*). — *adj* (*-pri-ət*) set apart for a purpose; peculiar (with *to*); suitable (with *to* or *for*). — *adv* **apprō'priately**. — *n* **apprō'priateness**. — *n* **apprōpriā'tion**. — *adj* **apprō'priative**. — *n* **apprō'priativeness**. — *n* **apprō'priātor**. — **appropriate technology** (the development, adaptation or upgrading of) local or locally appropriate industries (e.g. spinning, weaving, pottery, etc. in developing countries) as an alternative to expensive and inappropriate imported technologies. [L. *appropriāre*, *-ātum* — *ad*, to, *proprius*, one's own; see **proper**.]

approve *ə-prōōv'*, *vt* to confirm; to sanction or ratify; to think well of, to be pleased with; to commend. — *vi* to judge favourably, to be pleased (with *of*). — *adj* **approv'able** deserving approval. — *n* **approv'al** approbation. — *adv* **approv'ingly**. — **approved school** (between 1933 (Scotland 1937) and 1969) a state boarding school for young people who had broken the law or who were pronounced to be in need of care and protection. — **on approval** (or *colloq* **on appro** *ap'rō*) subject to approval; without obligation to buy. [O.Fr. *aprover* — L. *approbāre* — *ad*, to, and *probāre*, to test or try.]

approx. *abbrev* for: approximate; approximately.

approximate *ə-proks'im-ət*, *adj* close together; nearest or next; approaching correctness. — *vt* (*ə-proks'im-āt*) to bring near; to come or be near to. — *vi* to come near (to), approach. — *adj* **approx'imal** close together; next to. — *adv* **approx'imately**. — *n* **approximā'tion** an approach; an imprecise account, calculation, etc.; a result in mathematics not rigorously exact, but so near the truth as to be sufficient for a given purpose. — *adj* **approx'imative** (*-i-mā-tiv* or *-i-mə-tiv*) approaching closely. — **very approximate** very nearly exact; but by some used to mean very rough. [L. *approximāre*, *-ātum* — *ad*, to, *proximus*, nearest.]

appurtenance *ə-pûr'tən-əns*, *n* something that appertains; an appendage or accessory; a right belonging to a property (*law*). — *adj* and *n* **appur'tenant**. [A.Fr. *apurtenance* — O.Fr. *apertenance* — *apertenir*. See **appertain**.]

APR *abbrev* for annual percentage rate.

Apr. *abbrev* for April.

apraxia *a-praks'i-ə*, *n* an inability, not due to paralysis, to perform voluntary purposeful movements of parts of the body, caused by brain lesion. [Gr., inaction.]

après-ski or **apres-ski** *a-pre-skē* or *-prā-*, *n* (the evening period of, or clothes, etc. suitable for) social activity after skiing. — Also *adj*. [Fr.]

apricot *ā'pri-kot* or *-kət*, also *a'pri-*, *n* a fruit of the plum genus, roundish, orange-coloured, with a downy skin and a rich aromatic flavour; its colour; the tree that bears it. [Formerly *apricock* — Port. *albricoque* — Ar. *al-birqūq*.]

April *ā'pril* or *-prəl*, *n* the fourth month of the year. — **April fool** a person who is hoaxed, deceived, or made a fool of on April 1; a hoax or trick played on that day. — **April Fools' Day** 1 April, the day on which tricks are traditionally played and fools made. [L. *Aprīlis*.]

a priori *ā prī-ö'rī* (L. *ä prē-ör'ē*) the term applied to reasoning from what is prior, logically or chronologically, e.g. reasoning from cause to effect; from a general principle to its consequences, or even from observed fact to another fact or principle not observed. — *n* **apriō'rism**. — *n* **apriority** (*-or'i-ti*). [L. *ā*, from, *priōrī* (abl.), preceding.]

apron *ā'prən*, *n* a piece of cloth, leather etc. worn in front, esp. to protect clothes from dirt or damage; anything resembling an apron in shape or use; a stage or part of stage in front of the proscenium arch, projecting to greater or less extent into the auditorium (also **a'pron-stage**); a rim, border, etc.; ground surface at entrance to a hangar, lock, airport terminal, etc.; an extent of e.g. gravel, sand, spread outward from a source (*geol*). [M.E. *napron* — O.Fr. *naperon* — *nappe*, cloth, table-cloth (*an apron* from *a napron*; cf. **adder**[1]).]

apropos *a-prō-pō'* or *-prə-*, *adv* to the purpose; appropriately; in reference to (with *of*); by the way, incidentally. — *adj* to the purpose. [Fr. *à propos*. See etys. for **propose** and **purpose**.]

apse *aps*, *n* a semicircular or polygonal recess, esp. at the east end of a church choir. — *adj* **ap'sidal** of an apse or apsis. — *n* **aps'is** (*astron*) in an orbit, the point of greatest or least distance from the central body (also called **apse**): — *pl* **apsides** (*ap'si-dēz* or *əp-sī'dēz*). [L. *apsis*, *-īdis* — Gr. *hapsis* (*apsis*), *-īdos*, a felly, wheel, arch, loop.]

apso. See **lhasa apso**.

APT *abbrev* for advanced passenger train.

apt *apt*, *adj* fitting; fit, suitable; apposite, appropriate; tending (to); liable, ready or prone; likely (to); ready or quick to learn. — *n* **ap'titude** natural ability, readiness to learn (with *for*); tendency (with *to*); fitness. — *adv* **apt'ly**. — *n* **apt'ness**. [L. *aptus*, fit, suitable.]

apt *abbrev* for apartment.

apterous *ap'tər-əs*, *adj* wingless. [Gr. *a*-, without, *pteron*, feather, wing.]

apteryx *ap'tər-iks*, *n* a member of a flightless genus (*Apteryx*) of birds, the kiwis: — *pl* **ap'teryxes**. — *adj* **apterygial** (*-tər-ij'i-əl*) lacking paired fins or other limbs. [Gr. *a*-, without, *pteryx*, *-ygos*, wing.]

aptitude, aptly, aptness. See **apt**.

AQ *abbrev* for achievement quotient.

aq. *abbrev* for: *aqua* (L.), water, solution, liquid (*chem* and *pharm*); aqueous.

aqua- *ak-wə-*, *ak-wa-* or **aqui-** *ak-wi-*, *combining form* denoting water. [L. *aqua*, water.]

aquaculture *ak'wə-kul-chər* or **aquiculture** *ak'wi-*, *nsing* or *npl* the practice of using the sea, lakes, rivers, etc. for fish-farming, shellfish cultivation, the growing of plants, etc. [**aqua-** and **culture**.]

aqualung *ak'wə-lung*, *n* a lightweight, self-contained diving apparatus with compressed-air supply carried on the back. [**aqua-** and **lung**.]

aquamarine *ak-wə-mə-rēn'*, *n* a transparent pale green beryl, a gemstone; its colour. — *adj* bluish-green. [L. *aqua marīna*, sea water — *mare*, the sea.]

aquaplane *ak'wə-plān*, *n* a board on which a person stands and is towed behind a motorboat. — *vi* to ride on an aquaplane; (of a car, etc.) to travel or skid on a film of water which has built up between the tyres and the road surface. — *n* **a'quaplaner**. — *n* **a'quaplaning**. [**aqua-**.]

aquarelle *ak-wə-rel'*, *n* (a) painting in transparent watercolours. — *n* **aquarell'ist**. [Fr., — It. *acquerella*, *acquarella*.]

aquarium *ə-kwā'ri-əm*, *n* a tank or (a building containing) a series of tanks for keeping aquatic animals or plants: — *pl* **aquā'riums** or **aquā'ria**. — *adj* **aquā'rian**. — *n* a person who keeps an aquarium (*US* **aquā'rist**).

Aquarius *ə-kwā'ri-əs*, *n* the Water-bearer, a sign of the zodiac, and a constellation once coincident with it; a person born between 20 Jan. and 19 Feb., under the sign of Aquarius. [L. *aquārius*, *-a*, *-um*, adj. — *aqua*, water.]

aquatic *ə-kwat'ik* or *-kwot'*, *adj* living, growing, practising sports, taking place, in or on water. — *n* an aquatic plant, animal, or sportsperson. — *nsing* or *npl* **aquat'ics** water sports. [L. *aquāticus* — *aqua*, water.]

aquatint *ak'wə-tint*, *n* a method of etching on copper with resin and nitric acid. — *vt* and *vi* to engrave in aquatint. [It. *acqua tinta*, dyed water.]

aquavit *äk'wə-vēt* or *ak'*, *n* a Scandinavian spirit made from potatoes or grain, flavoured with caraway seeds. [Dan., Sw., Norw. *akvavit* — Med. L. *aqua vītae*, water of life, alcohol.]

aqueduct *ak'wi-dukt*, *n* an artificial channel or pipe for conveying water, most commonly understood to mean a bridge across a valley; a bridge carrying a canal; a small passage in an animal body (*zool*). [L. *aqua*, water, *dūcĕre*, *ductum*, to lead.]

aqueous *ā'kwi-əs*, *adj* of water; watery; deposited by water. [L. *aqua*, water.]

aqui-. See **aqua-**.

aquifer *ak'wi-fər*, (*geol*) *n* any formation containing water sufficient to supply wells, etc. [N.L. — L. *aqua*, water, *ferre*, to carry.]

Aquila *ak'wi-lə*, *n* the golden eagle genus. — *adj* **aq'uiline** (*-līn*) of the eagle; hooked like an eagle's beak. [L. *aquila*, eagle.]

aquiver *ə-kwiv'ər*, *adv* or predicative *adj* in a quivering state. [**a-**[1] and **quiver**[1].]

AR *abbrev* for: airman recruit (*US*); annual return (*finance*); Arkansas (U.S. state); army regulation; autonomous region (or republic).

Ar. *abbrev* for: Arab; Arabian; Arabic.

Ar (*chem*) *symbol* for argon.

Arab *ar'əb*, *n* one of the Semitic people inhabiting Arabia and neighbouring countries; a horse of a native Arabian breed popular for its grace and speed; a neglected or homeless boy or girl (usu. **street** or **city Arab**). — *adj* Arabian. — *adj* **Arabian** (*ə-rā'bi-ən* or *-byən*) of or belonging to Arabia or the Arabs. — *n* a native of Arabia. — *adj* **Arabic** (*ar'əb-ik*) relating to Arabia, or to its language. — *n* the language or script of the Arabs; see also **gum**. — *n* **Ar'abist** someone learned in, or studying, Arabic culture, history, language, etc. — **Arabian camel** a one-humped camel; **Arabian Gulf** an arm of the Arabian Sea founded by Iran, Iraq, Kuwait, Saudi Arabia, Qatar and the United Arab Emirates; (*loosely*) this entire region, including the above-named countries; **Arabian** or **Arabic numerals** the numerals in ordinary use in arithmetic, brought from India to Europe by the Arabs. [L. *Arabs*, *Arabis* — Gr. *Araps*, *Arabos*.]

Arab. *abbrev* for: Arabian; Arabic.

arabesque *ar-ə-besk'*, *n* a short musical composition with decorative qualities; a posture in ballet dancing in which one leg is stretched out backwards parallel with the ground and the body is bent forward from the hips; a fantastic painted or sculptured ornament consisting of foliage and other forms curiously intertwined. [Fr., — It. *arabesco*, in the Arabian style.]

arabica *ə-rab'i-kə*, *n* coffee produced from the shrub *Coffea arabica*, grown esp. in Brazil and other S. American countries.

arable *ar'ə-bl*, *adj* (of land) fit for ploughing and crop production. [L. *arābilis* — *arāre*, to plough.]

araceous. See **Arum**.

Arachnida *a-rak'ni-də*, *npl* the class of arthropods which includes spiders, scorpions, mites, etc. — *n* **arach'nid** any member of the class. — *n* and *adj* **arach'nidan**. — *adj* **arach'noid** like a cobweb. — *n* the arachnoid membrane. — *adj* **arachnoi'dal**. — *adj* **arachnolog'ical**. — *n* **arachnol'ogist** a person who studies the Arachnida. — *n* **arachnol'ogy**. — *n* **arachnophō'bia** fear of spiders. — *n* **arach'nophobe**. — **arachnoid membrane** one of the three coverings of the brain and spinal cord. [Gr. *arachnē*, spider.]

aralia *ə-rā'li-ə*, *n* a plant of the *Aralia* genus of the ivy family much grown as decorative plants. — *adj* **araliā'ceous**.

Aramaic *ar-ə-mā'ik*, *n* any of a group of Semitic languages (including that spoken by Christ) once used in *Aramaea* (roughly, modern Syria) in commerce and government. — Also *adj*. [Gr. *Aramaios*.]

arame *ə-rä'mi*, *n* a type of edible seaweed, looking like black bootlaces. [Jap.]

aramid fibre *ar'ə-mid fī'bər*, *n* an exceptionally strong lightweight synthetic fibre much used in composite materials. [*ar*omatic poly*amid*e **fibre**.]

Aran *a'rən*, *adj* (of knitwear) made in a style or with a pattern that originated in the *Aran* Islands, off the west coast of Ireland.

arapaima *ar-ə-pī'mə, n* a gigantic S. American river-fish, sometimes reaching *c* 200 kg (4 cwt.). [Tupí origin.]

araucaria *a-rö-kā'ri-ə, n* a tree of the monkey-puzzle genus *Araucaria*, of coniferous trees of S. America and Australasia. [*Arauco*, in S. Chile.]

arb *ärb*, (*colloq*; *stock exchange*) *n* short for arbitrageur.

arbiter *är'bi-tər, n* a judge; an umpire, or a person chosen by parties to decide between them. — Also *fem* **ar'bitress.** — *adj* **ar'bitrable.** — *n* **ar'bitrage** (*-trij*) arbitration; traffic in bills of exchange or stocks designed to profit by different prices in different markets, or from price changes due to mergers, takeovers, etc. (also *vi*). — *n* **arbitrageur** (*-tra-zhœr'*) a person who carries out arbitrage (*colloq* short form **arb**). — *n* **arbit'rament** the decision of an arbiter; power of decision. — *vi* and *vt* **ar'bitrate** to decide or determine; to refer to arbitration; to judge as arbiter. — *n* **arbitrā'tion** the decision of an arbiter; *specif* in industrial relations, the submission by disputing parties of their case to an arbiter for an independent decision. — *n* **ar'bitrātor** an arbiter. — **Arbitration Court** (*Austr* and *NZ*) a tribunal for the settlement of industrial disputes. [L.]

arbitrary *är'bi-trər-i, adj* arising from accident rather than from rule; capricious; not bound by rules; despotic, absolute. — *adv* **ar'bitrarily.** — *n* **ar'bitrariness.** [L. *arbitrārius* — *arbiter.*]

arbitrate, arbitration, etc. See **arbiter.**

arbor[1] *är'bər, n* a shaft, beam, spindle or axis in a mechanical device. [L. *arbor*, tree.]

arbor[2]. See **arbour.**

arboreal *är-bö'ri-əl, adj* of, or of the nature of, trees; tree-dwelling. — *adj* **arbo'reous** of or belonging to trees; treelike; in the form of a tree; wooded. — *n* **arboresc'ence** a treelike growth; a treelike crystalline formation. — *adj* **arboresc'ent** growing, formed or branched like a tree. [L. *arbor*, tree.]

arboretum *är-bor-ē'to͝om, n* a botanic garden of trees: — *pl* **arborē'ta.** [N.L. — L. *arbor*, tree.]

arboriculture *är'bər-i-kul-chər, n* the culture of trees, esp. for ornamental and scientific purposes. — *adj* **arboricul'tural.** — *n* **arboricul'turist.**

arborist *är'bər-ist, n* a person who studies trees. [L. *arbor*, tree.]

arbour or in U.S. **arbor** *är'bər, n* a retreat or bower of trees or climbing plants; a pergola (esp. *US*). [A.Fr. *herber* — L. *herbārium* — *herba*, grass, herb; meaning changed through confusion with L. *arbor*, tree.]

ARC *abbrev* for AIDS-related complex.

arc *ärk, n* a part of the circumference of a circle or other curve; a luminous discharge of electricity across a gap between two conductors or terminals. — *adj* (*math*) denoting an inverse hyperbolic or trigonometrical function (as in **arc sine** (or **arcsin'**), **arc cosine** (or **arccos'**), **arc tangent** (or **arctan'**)). — *vi* to form an arc: — *pr p* **arc'ing** or **arck'ing**; *pa t* and *pa p* **arced'** or **arcked'.** — *n* **arc'ing** or **arck'ing.** — **arc'second** (*astron*) a unit of angle measurement, $\frac{1}{3600}$ of a degree; **arcwelding** see **weld[2].** [L. *arcus*, a bow.]

arcade *är-kād', n* a row of arches, open or closed, on columns or pilasters; a walk with an arch over it; a covered passageway lined with shops. — *adj* **arcād'ed.** — *n* **arcād'ing.** [Fr., — L.L. *arcāta*, arched.]

Arcadian *är-kād'i-ən, adj* pastoral; simple, innocent. — *n* **Arcād'ianism.** [Of *Arcadia* in ancient Greece and the simple rural pursuits of its people.]

arcane *är-kān', adj* secret; mysterious. — *adv* **arcane'ly.** — *n* **arcane'ness.** [L. *arcānus*, secret — *arca*, a chest.]

arccos *abbrev* for arc cosine (see under **arc**).

arch[1] *ärch, n* a structure of wedge-shaped stones or other pieces supporting each other by mutual pressure and able to sustain an overlying weight; anything of a similar form; an archway; the bony structure of the foot between the heel and the toes, normally having an upward curve. — *vt* to cover or provide with an arch. — *vt* and *vi* to bend in the form of an arch. — *adj* **arched** having the form of an arch; covered with an arch. — **arch'way** an arched or vaulted passage. — **dropped** or **fallen arch** a flattened foot arch. [O.Fr. *arche* — L. *arcus*, bow.]

arch[2] *ärch, adj* waggish, mischievous; roguish; cunning, shrewd. — *adv* **arch'ly.** — *n* **arch'ness.** [**arch-**, in words such as *arch*-fiend, etc.]

arch. *abbrev* for: archaic, archaism; archipelago; architect, architectural, architecture.

arch- *ärch-* (or *ärk-* in direct borrowings from Greek), *pfx* first or chief; often used to give emphasis in an odious sense. — *n* **arch'-enemy** a chief enemy; Satan. — *n* **arch-fiend'** Satan; an utterly evil creature or spirit. — *n* **arch-vill'ain** someone supremely villainous. [O.E. *arce-*, *ærce-*, through L. from Gr. *archi-* — *archos*, chief.]

archae-, arche- *är-ki-*, or **archaeo-, archeo-** *är-ki-ō-* or *-o-*, *combining form* denoting: ancient, primitive; pertaining to archaeology. [Gr. *archaios*, ancient — *archē*, beginning.]

Archaean *är-kē'ən*, (*geol*) *adj* and *n* (of or relating to) the oldest geological period, early Pre-Cambrian. [Gr. *archaios*, ancient — *archē*, beginning.]

archaeol. *abbrev* for archaeology.

archaeology, also (esp. *NAm*) **archeology** *är-ki-ol'ə-ji, n* the study of human antiquities, usu. as discovered by excavation. — *adj* **archaeolog'ical** (also **archeol-**) — *adv* **archaeolog'ically** (also **archeol-**). — *n* **archaeol'ogist** (also **archeol'ogist**). [L.L. — Gr. *ar haiologia*, the study of antiquity.]

archaeometry *är-ki-om'ə-tri, n* the use of scientific methods in archaeology. — *adj* **archaeomet'ric.** — *n* **archaeom'etrist.** [**archaeo-** and *-metry* — Gr. *metron*, a measure.]

archaeopteryx *är-ki-op'tə-riks, n* a Jurassic fossil bird of the **Archaeopteryx** genus, with a long bony tail. [Gr. *archaios*, ancient, *pteryx*, wing.]

archaic *är-kā'ik, adj* not absolutely obsolete but no longer in general use; old-fashioned, savouring of the past. — *adv* **archā'ically.** — *n* **ar'chāism** an archaic word or phrase. — *n* **ar'chāist.** — *adj* **archāist'ic** affectedly or imitatively archaic. [Gr. *archaikos* — *archaios*, ancient.]

archangel *ärk'ān-jl* or *ärk-ān'jəl, n* an angel of the highest order. — *adj* **archangelic** (*-an-jel'ik*). [Gr. *archangelos* — *archos*, chief, *angelos*, messenger.]

archbishop *ärch-bish'əp, n* a metropolitan bishop who superintends the bishops in his province, and also exercises episcopal authority in his own diocese. — *n* **archbish'opric** the office or jurisdiction of, or area governed by, an archbishop. [O.E. *ærcebiscop*; see **arch-** and **bishop.**]

archdeacon *ärch-dē'kən, n* the ecclesiastical dignitary having the chief supervision of a diocese or part of it, next under the bishop. — *n* **archdeac'onry** the office, jurisdiction or residence of an archdeacon. [O.E. *ærcedīacon*; see **arch-** and **deacon.**]

archdiocese *ärch-dī'ə-sis* or *-sēs, n* an archbishop's diocese.

archduke *ärch'dūk* or *ärch-dūk'*, (*hist*) *n* the title of certain early reigning dukes of importance, and of princes of the imperial house of Austria: — *fem* **archduchess** (*ärch-duch'is*) a princess of the imperial house of Austria; a wife or widow of an archduke. — *adj* **archdū'cal.** — *n* **archduch'y** or **archduke'dom.** [**arch-** and **duke.**]

archegonium *ärk-i-gō'ni-əm*, (*bot*) *n* the flask-shaped female reproductive organ of mosses and ferns, and (in a reduced form) of flowering plants: — *pl* **archego'nia.** [Gr. *archegonos*, founder of a race.]

archeology, etc. See **archaeology.**

archer *ärch'ər*, *n* a person who shoots with a bow and arrows; (with *cap*; with *the*) the constellation and sign of the zodiac Sagittarius. — Also *fem* **arch'eress**. — *n* **arch'ery** the art or sport of shooting with the bow; a company of archers. — **arch'er-fish** a fish that catches insects by shooting water at them from its mouth. [O.Fr. *archier* — L. *arcārius* — *arcus*, a bow.]

archetype *ärk'i-tīp*, *n* the original pattern or model, prototype. — *adj* **archetȳp'al** or **archetyp'ical**. [Gr. *archetypon*, — *arche-* and *typos*, a model.]

archidiaconal *är-ki-dī-ak'ə-nəl*, *adj* of an archdeacon. [Gr. *archidiākonos*; see **deacon**.]

archiepiscopal *är-ki-i-pis'kə-pəl*, *adj* of an archbishop. — *n* **archiepis'copacy** or **archiepis'copate** the dignity or province of an archbishop. [Gr. *archiepiskopos*, archbishop.]

archil *är'chil* or *är'kil*, *n* a red or violet dye made from various lichens; a lichen that yields it, esp. a species of Roccella. — Also **or'chil**. [O.Fr. *orchel*, *orseil* (Fr. *orseille*).]

Archimedean *ärk-i-mē-dē'ən* or *-mē'di-ən*, *adj* pertaining to *Archimedes*, a celebrated Greek mathematician of Syracuse (*c* 287–212 B.C.). — **Archimedean screw** a machine for raising water, etc., in its simplest form a tube bent spirally turning on its axis; **principle of Archimedes** that a body weighed when immersed wholly or partly in a fluid shows a loss of weight equal to the weight of fluid it displaces.

archipelago *ärk-i-pel'ə-gō*, *n* a sea abounding in islands such as the Aegean, and hence a group of islands: — *pl* **archipel'agoes** or **archipel'agos**. — *adj* **archipelagic** (*-pi-laj'ik*). [*Archipelago*, the Aegean Sea — It. *arcipelago* — Gr. *archi-*, chief, *pelagos*, sea.]

archit. *abbrev* for architect, architectural or architecture.

architect *ärk'i-tekt*, *n* a designer of buildings; a designer of ships (*naval archit*); a maker or a contriver. — *vt* to plan or design as an architect. — *adj* **architecton'ic** pertaining to architecture; constructive; controlling or directing; pertaining to the arrangement of knowledge. — *npl* **architecton'ics** the science of architecture; the systematic arrangement of knowledge. — *adj* **architec'tural** (*-chər-əl*). — *adv* **architec'turally**. — *n* **arch'itecture** one of the fine arts, the art of designing buildings; style of building; structures or buildings collectively; the art or science of building; the overall design of the software and esp. the hardware of a computer; organisation, framework, structure. [Gr. *architektōn*, master-builder — *archi-*, chief, *tektōn*, a builder.]

architrave *ärk'i-trāv*, (*archit*) *n* the lowest division of the entablature resting immediately on the abacus of the column; the collective name for the various parts, jambs, lintels, etc., that surround a door or window; the moulding round an arch. — *adj* **arch'itraved**. [It. — Gr. *archi-*, chief, and L. *trabs*, *trabis*, a beam.]

archive *ärk'īv*, *n* (usu. in *pl*) a repository of public records or of records and monuments generally; public records; (rare in *sing*) a historic document; files of data stored on tape or disk (*comput*). — *vi* and *vt* to keep archives or store in archives. — *adj* **archīv'al** (or *ärk'i-vəl*). — *n* **archivist** (*ärk'i-vist*) a keeper of archives or records. [Fr., — L.L. *archī(v)um* — Gr. *archeion*, magisterial residence — *archē*, government.]

archivolt *är'ki-vōlt*, (*archit*) *n* the under-curve of an arch, intrados; the moulding on it. [It. *archivolto* — *arco*, an arch, *volta*, vault.]

ARCIC *abbrev* for Anglican-Roman Catholic International Commission.

arco saltando *är'kō säl-tän'dō*, (*mus*) with rebounding bow. — *n* a quick staccato. — **arco** or **coll'arco** (*mus*) with the bow (a direction marking the end of a pizzicato passage). [It.]

arcsin *abbrev* for arc sine (see under **arc**).

arctan *abbrev* for arc tangent (see under **arc**).

Arctic *ärk'tik*, *n* (usu. with *the*) the area lying north of the Arctic Circle or north of the timber line. — *adj* **arc'tic** (also with *cap*) relating to the Arctic or to the north; extremely cold. — **Arctic Circle** the parallel of latitude 66°32′N, bounding the region of the earth around the north pole. [Orig. relating to the Great Bear (the northern constellation) — Gr. *arktos*, a bear.]

arctoid *ärk'toid*, *adj* bear-like. [Gr. *arktos*, a bear.]

arctophile *ärk'tə-fīl*, *n* a lover or collector of teddy-bears. [Gr. *arktos*, bear, and **-phile**.]

ARD (*med*) *abbrev* for acute respiratory disease (of any type).

Ardas *ur-das'*, *n* in the Sikh religion, a short direct prayer to God (similar in status to the Lord's Prayer in Christianity). [Punjabi, supplication.]

ardent *ärd'ənt*, *adj* burning, fiery; zealous, burning with emotion. — *n* **ard'ency**. — *adv* **ard'ently**. — *n* **ard'our** warmth of passion or feeling; eagerness, enthusiasm. — **ardent spirits** distilled alcoholic liquors. [L. *ardēns*, *-entis*, pres. p. of *ardēre*, to burn.]

arduous *ärd'ū-əs*, *adj* laborious; difficult to accomplish; steep, difficult to climb. — *adv* **ard'uously**. — *n* **ard'uousness**. [L. *arduus*, steep, high.]

are[1] *är*, *n* the unit of the metric land measure, 100 sq. metres. [Fr., — L. *ārea*, a site, space, court.]

are[2] *är*, used as plural of the present indicative of the verb *to be*. [Old Northumbrian *aron*.]

area *ā'ri-ə*, *n* a space or piece of ground; a portion of surface; a region (*lit* and *fig*); part of a building, city, etc. designated a special purpose or character; a sunken space alongside the basement of a building (in U.S. **a'reaway**); the measure of a regional or surface extent. — *adj* **ā'real**. — **area code** (*US*) a three-digit number used before the local telephone number when dialling long-distance telephone calls. [L. *ārea*, an open empty place, etc.]

areca *ar'i-kə* or *ə-rē'kə*, *n* a tree belonging to the betel-nut genus of palms (*Areca*). [Port., — Malayalam *adekka*.]

areg. See **erg**[2].

arena *ə-rē'nə*, *n* an area enclosed by seating, in which public sporting contests or entertainments take place; orig. part of the ancient amphitheatre strewed with sand for combats; any sphere of action (*fig*). — **arena stage** a stage which can have audience all round it (see **theatre-in-the-round** under **theatre**). [L. *arēna*, sand.]

arenaceous *ar-i-nā'shəs*, *adj* sandy; composed of sand or quartz grains (*geol*); with shells composed of agglutinated sand-grains (*zool*); sand-growing (*bot*). [L. *arēna*, sand.]

aren't *ärnt*. Contraction of **are not** or (*colloq*; as interrogative) **am not**.

areola *a-rē'ō-lə*, *n* a small space marked off by lines, or a slightly sunken spot (*biol*); an interstice in a tissue (*physiol*); any circular spot such as that around the nipple (*physiol*); the part of the iris of the eye bordering on the pupil (*physiol*): — *pl* **arē'olae** (*-lē*). — *adj* **arē'olar**. — *adj* **arē'olate** or **arē'olated** divided into small areas. — *n* **arēolā'tion**. — *n* **areole** (*ar'i-ōl*) an areola; a spiny or hairy spot on a cactus. [L. *āreola*, dimin. of *ārea*.]

arête *a-ret'*, *n* a sharp ridge; esp. in French Switzerland, a rocky edge on a mountain. [Fr., — L. *arista*, an ear of corn, fish-bone, spine.]

argali *är'gə-li*, *n* the great wild sheep of Asia. [Mongol.]

argentiferous *är-jən-tif'ə-rəs*, (*mineralogy*) *adj* containing silver. [L. *argentum*, silver, *ferre*, to bear.]

Argentine *är'jən-tīn*, *adj* of or belonging to Argentina, a republic in S. America, or to its people. — *n* a native or citizen of Argentina.

argentine *är'jən-tīn, adj* of or like silver. — *n* white metal coated with silver; a small smelt with silvery sides. [L. *argentum*, silver.]

argie-bargie. See under **argue.**

argil *är'jil, n* potter's clay; pure clay or alumina. — *adj* **argillā'ceous** clayey. — *n* **ar'gillite** a hardened clay rock. [L. *argilla* — Gr. *argillos*, white clay — *argēs*, white.]

arginine *ar'ji-nīn, n* one of the essential amino-acids.

argol *är'gol, n* a hard, generally reddish, crust formed on the sides of wine-vessels, from which cream of tartar and tartaric acid are obtainable. [Prob. conn. with Gr. *argos*, white.]

argon *är'gon, n* a colourless, odourless inert gas (atomic no. 18; symbol **Ar**). [Gr. *ārgon*, inactive — *a-* (privative) and *ergon*, work.]

argot *är'gō, n* slang, orig. that of thieves and vagabonds; cant. [Fr.]

argue *är'gū, vt* to discuss with reasoning; to persuade or bring by reasoning (into or out of course of action); to seek to show by reasoning; to give reason to believe; to prove or indicate. — *vi* to contend with reasoning; to contradict, dispute; to offer reasons. — *adj* **ar'gūable.** — *adv* **ar'gūably.** — *n* **ar'gūer.** — *n* **ar'gūment** a reason or series of reasons offered or possible as proof or inducement (with *for* or *against*); exchange of such reasons; debate; matter of debate or contention; a summary of subject-matter; a quantity upon which another depends, or under which it is to be sought in a table (*math*); the angle between a vector and its axis of reference (*math*); proof, evidence. — *n* **argūmentā'tion** reasoning; a sequence or exchange of arguments. — *adj* **argūment'ative** controversial; fond of or prone to arguing. — *adv* **argūment'atively.** — *n* **argūment'ativeness.** — *vi* **argy-bar'gy** or **argie-bar'gie** to argue tediously or vexatiously. — *n* argumentative wrangling. [Fr. *arguer* — L. *argūtāre* — *argūere*, to show, accuse; *argūmentum*, proof, accusation, summary of contents.]

argus *är'gəs, n* an East Indian pheasant of the genus *Argusianus* with a long colourful tail with eye-spots; a butterfly with many eye-spots on the wings (as some *Lycaenidae* and *Satyridae*). — **argus tortoise beetle** a black-spotted, reddish, tortoise-shaped beetle that feeds on plants of the convolvulus family. [*Argus* (of Gr. mythology) who had a hundred eyes.]

argy-bargy. See under **argue.**

aria *ä'ri-ə, (mus) n* an air or melody, esp. an accompanied vocal solo in a cantata, oratorio or opera; a regular strain of melody followed by another in contrast and complement, and then repeated *da capo*. [It., from root of **air.**]

arid *ar'id, adj* dry; parched; barren; (of a region or climate) having so little rainfall as to support only desert or semi-desert vegetation; meagre, lifeless. — *n* **arid'ity** or **ar'idness.** — *adv* **ar'idly.** [L. *aridus.*]

ariel *ā'ri-əl, n* a kind of gazelle. [Ar. *aryil.*]

Aries *ā'ri-ēz, n* the Ram, a constellation giving its name to a sign of the zodiac; a person born between 22 March and 20 April, under the sign of Aries. [L. *ariēs, -etis*, ram.]

arietta *ar-i-et'ə, (mus) n* a little aria or air. [It., dimin. of *aria.*]

aright *ə-rīt', adv* in a right way; rightly. [**a-**[1] and **right.**]

aril *är'il, (bot) n* a covering or appendage of some seeds, an outgrowth of the funicle; sometimes, a caruncle (*false aril*). — *adj* **ar'illary, ar'illate** or **ar'illated.** [L.L. *arillus*, raisin.]

arioso *a-ri-ō'sō, adj* and *adv* in the melodious manner of an aria, or between aria and recitative. — Also *n*: — *pl* **ario'sos** or **ario'si** (*-sē*). [It. *aria.*]

aris *ar'is, (Cockney slang) n* arse. [Short for 'Aristotle', rhyming slang for 'bottle', which is in turn short for 'bottle and glass', rhyming slang for 'arse'.]

arise *ə-rīz', vi* to rise up; to originate (with *from, out of*); to come into being, view, or activity: — *pa t* **arose** (*ə-rōz'*); *pa p* **arisen** (*ə-riz'n*).

arista *ə-ris'tə, (biol) n* a bristly process from the glume of certain grasses, an awn; a bristle-like appendage on some insects' antennae. — *adj* **aris'tate** (or *ar'is-tāt*) awned. [L. *arista*, an awn.]

aristo *a'ris-tō* or *ə-ris'tō, (colloq) n* short for aristocrat.

aristocracy *ar-is-tok'rə-si, n* government by, or political power of, a privileged order; a state governed in this way; a nobility or privileged class; a class of people holding privileged status in any field. — *n* **aristocrat** (*ar'is-tə-krat* or *ə-ris'tə-krat*) a member of the or an aristocracy; a person who has the characteristics of or attributed to an aristocracy, esp. a grand or a haughty person; one of the, or the, best of its kind. — *adj* **aristocrat'ic** belonging to aristocracy; having the character that belongs to, or is thought to befit, aristocracy. — *adv* **aristocrat'ically.** — *n* **aristocratism** (*-tok'rə-tizm*) the spirit of, or belief in, aristocracy. [Gr. *aristokratiā* — *aristos*, best, *kratos*, power.]

Arita *a-rē'tə, n* a Japanese porcelain manufactured from the early 17th cent. at *Arita* near Nagasaki.

arith. *abbrev* for arithmetic or arithmetical.

arithmetic *ə-rith'mə-tik, n* the science of numbers; the art of calculating in figures. — *adj* **arithmetic** (*ar-ith-met'ik*) or **arithmet'ical.** — *adv* **arithmet'ically.** — *n* **arithmetician** (*-mə-tish'n* or *ar'ith-mə-*). — **arithmetic and logic unit** (*comput*) the part of a central processing unit that carries out arithmetic and logical operations required by an input command; **arithmetic progression** a series increasing or diminishing by a common difference, as 7, 10, 13, 16, 19, 22; or 12, $10\frac{1}{2}$, 9, $7\frac{1}{2}$, 6; **arithmetic mean** see **mean**[2]. [Gr. *arithmētikē*, of numbers — *arithmos*, number.]

arithmo- *ar-ith-mō-, combining form* denoting number or numbers. [Gr. *arithmos*, number.]

Ariz. *abbrev* for Arizona (U.S. state).

ark *ärk, n* in Jewish history, the wooden coffer in which the Tables of the Law were kept; a large floating vessel, as Noah's in the biblical Flood (Genesis vi–viii); a toy representing Noah's ark with animals inside it. — **out of the Ark** (*colloq*) utterly old-fashioned, antediluvian. [O.E. *arc* — L. *arca*, a chest.]

arkose *är-kōs', n* a sandstone rich in feldspar grains, formed from granite, etc. [Fr.]

arm[1] *ärm, n* the human forelimb from shoulder to hand; an upper limb in other bipedal mammals; a similar member in other animals, e.g. a tentacle; a narrow projecting part; an inlet; a branch; a rail or support for the arm as on a chair; (in clothing) a sleeve. — *adj* **armed** (usu. in composition) having an arm or arms, as in *one-armed*. — *n* **arm'ful.** — *adj* **arm'less.** — *n* **arm'let** a little arm; a ring or band round the arm. — **arm'band** a band of cloth worn round the sleeve; **arm'chair** a chair with arms. — *adj* **arm'chair** amateur; stay-at-home; conducted from (the comfort or security of) home. — *n* and *adj* **arm'-chancing** see **chance one's arm** under **chance.** — **arm'hole** the hole in a garment through which the arm is put. — *adv* **arm-in-arm'** with arms interlinked. — **arm'lock** (in *wrestling*, etc.; also *fig*) a hold by the arms (also *vt*); **arm'pit** the hollow under the shoulder. — **at arm's length** at a distance (*lit* and *fig*), not showing friendliness or familiarity but careful detachment; (of negotiations, etc.) in which each party preserves its independent ability to bargain (*adj* **arms'-length,** e.g. in shareholding, having broad and ultimate control, without involvement in policy decisions, etc.); **in arms** carried or young enough to be carried as a child; **right arm** the main support or assistant; **the long arm of the law** the far-reaching power and influence of the law — esp. the police force; **within arm's reach** able to be reached easily, i.e. from where one is sitting; **with open arms** with a hearty welcome. [O.E. *arm*.]

arm[2] *ärm*, *n* a weapon; a branch of the fighting forces; (in *pl*) weapons of offence and defence; (in *pl*) hostilities; (in *pl*) fighting, soldiering; (in *pl*) heraldic insignia, coats-of-arms. — *vt* to provide with weapons, means of protection, armature, or (*fig*) equipment; to make (a bomb, etc.) ready to explode; to strengthen with a metal plate or otherwise (as of a vehicle). — *vi* to take up arms. — *adj* **armed** provided with arms or a means of defence; (of an animal, etc.) having a protective armour. — **arms race** competition among nations in building up armaments. — **bear arms** to serve as a soldier; (also **give arms**) to show armorial bearings (*heraldry*); **in arms** armed; quartered (*heraldry*); **lay down one's arms** to surrender or submit; **take up arms** to resort to fighting; **under arms** armed; **up in arms** protesting hotly; ready and keen to resist. [Fr. *armes*, from L. *arma* (pl.).]

armada *är-mä'də* (sometimes *är-mā'də*), *n* a fleet of armed ships, esp. that sent by Philip II of Spain against England in 1588. [Sp., fem. past p. of *armar* — L. *armāre*, to arm.]

armadillo *ärm-ə-dil'ō*, *n* an American edentate mammal whose body is covered with bands of bony plates: — *pl* **armadill'os**. [Sp., dimin. of *armado*, armed.]

Armageddon *är-mə-ged'n*, *n* the great symbolical battlefield of the Apocalypse, scene of the final struggle between the powers of good and evil (*Bible*); a great, or esp. the ultimate, war or battle of nations. [*Harmagedōn* or *Armageddōn* given as Heb. name in Revelations xvi. 16.]

Armagnac *är-mä-nyak*, *n* a dry brandy distilled in S.W. France. [Name of district.]

Armalite® *ar'mə-līt*, *n* a low-calibre, high-velocity assault rifle with an automatic and semi-automatic facility.

armament *är'mə-mənt*, *n* a force equipped for war; total means of making war; munitions, esp. for warships; defensive equipment. [L. *armāmenta*, tackle, equipment.]

armature *är'mə-chər*, *n* armour; any defensive apparatus; a wooden or wire support around which a sculpture, model, etc., is constructed; a piece of iron set across the poles of a magnet; a moving part in a magnetic circuit to indicate the presence of electric current; a rotor, the metal part (wound with current-carrying wire) that in a generator turns to produce a current, and in a motor provides the current that produces torque. [L. *armātūra*, armour.]

Armenian *är-mē'nyən*, *adj* belonging to *Armenia*, in Western Asia, or its people or language, or their branch of the Christian Church. — *n* a native of Armenia; one of the Armenian people; the language of the Armenians.

armiger *är'mi-jər*, (*heraldry*) *n* a person entitled to a coat-of-arms; an esquire. — *adj* **armi'geral** or **armi'gerous**. [L., an armour-bearer — *arma*, arms, *gerĕre*, to bear.]

armilla *är-mil'ə*, *n* a frill on a mushroom stalk (*bot*); a bracelet (*archaeol*). — *adj* **armill'ary** (or *är'mil-ər-i*). — **armillary sphere** (*astron*) a skeleton sphere made up of hoops to show the motions of the heavenly bodies. [L. *armilla*, an armlet.]

armistice *är'mi-stis*, *n* a suspension of hostilities; a truce. — **Armistice Day** 11 November 1918, the day fighting ended in World War I, kept since as an anniversary, from 1946 as Remembrance Sunday (q.v. under **remember**). [Fr., — L.L. *armistitium* — L. *arma*, arms, *sistĕre*, to stop.]

armlet. See under **arm[1]**.

armorial *är-mör'i-əl*, *adj* of heraldic arms. — *n* a book of coats-of-arms. — *n* **ar'morist** a person skilled in heraldry. — *n* **ar'mory** heraldry; see also **armour**. — **armorial bearings** the design in a coat-of-arms.

armour or in U.S. **armor** *är'mər*, *n* defensive dress, esp. of metal, chain-mail, etc.; protective covering; armoured vehicles; heraldic insignia. — *n* **ar'mory** (*US*) armoury; drill hall and headquarters of an army unit; an arsenal. — *adj* **ar'moured** protected by armour. — *n* **ar'mourer** a maker, repairer or custodian of arms and armour. — *adj* **ar'mourless.** — *n* **ar'moury** a collection of arms and armour; a place where arms are kept; armour collectively. — *adj* **ar'mour-clad** clad in armour. — *n* an armoured ship. — **armoured-car', -crui'ser, -train'**, etc.; **ar'mour-plate** a defensive plate for a ship, tank, etc. — *adj* **armour-plat'ed.** [O.Fr. *armure* — L. *armātūra* — *arma*, arms.]

army *ärm'i*, *n* a large body of people armed for war and under military command; a body of people banded together in a special cause, sometimes, as the 'Salvation Army', in imitation of military methods; a great number, a host (used esp. of insects). — **army ant** any of several kinds of stinging ants which move about in vast numbers; **army corps** (*kör*) a miniature army comprising all arms of the service; **army list** a list of all commissioned officers; **army worm** the larva of a small fly (*Sciara*) that collects in vast armies; the larva of any of several (esp. N. Am. and E. Afr.) types of moth that can move in multitudes from field to field destroying crops. [Fr. *armée*, past p. fem. of *armer* — L. *armāre*, *-ātum* to arm.]

arna *är'nä*, *n* the Indian water-buffalo, *Bubalus bubalis*. [Hindi.]

arnica *är'ni-kə*, *n* a tincture of the flowers of a composite plant (*Arnica montana*) applied to sprains and bruises (but not to open wounds).

aroid. See **Arum.**

aroma *ə-rō'mə*, *n* a spicy fragrance; flavour or peculiar charm (*fig*). — *n* **aromather'apy** a method of treating bodily ailments using essential plant oils. — *n* **aromather'apist.** — *adj* **aromatic** (*ar-ō-mat'ik*) fragrant; spicy; belonging to the closed-chain class of organic compounds, or benzene derivatives (opp. to *aliphatic*; *chem*). — Also *n*. [L., from Gr. *arōma*, *-atos*, spice.]

arose. See **arise.**

around *ə-rownd'*, *prep* on all sides of; round or round about; somewhere near; in existence or circulation (*colloq*). — *adv* on every side; in a circle; round about, on the move. — **get around to** (*colloq*) to reach the point of (doing something); **have been around** (*colloq*) to be experienced, or sophisticated. [**a-[1]** and **round.**]

arouse *ə-rowz'*, *vt* and *vi* to rouse; to stimulate. — *n* **arous'al.** — *n* **arous'er.** [Pfx. *a-* (intensive) and **rouse.**]

ARP *abbrev* for air raid precautions.

arpeggio *är-ped'jō* or *-jyō*, (*mus*) *n* a chord of which the notes are performed, not simultaneously, but in rapid (normally upward) succession; the notes of a chord played or sung, esp. as an exercise, in rapid ascending or descending progression, according to a set pattern: — *pl* **arpegg'ios.** — *vt* **arpegg'iate** (*-ji-āt*) to perform or write in arpeggios. — *n* **arpeggiā'tion.** [It. *arpeggiare*, to play the harp — *arpa*, harp.]

arquebus *är'kwi-bus* or **harquebus** *här'*, *n* an old-fashioned handgun. — *n* **arquebusier** (*-bus-ēr'*) a soldier armed with an arquebus. [Fr. *arquebuse* — Du. *haakbus* — *haak*, hook, *bus*, box, barrel of a gun.]

arr. *abbrev* for: arranged (by); arrival, arrived, arrives, arriving, etc.

arraign *ə-rān'*, *vt* to call to account; to put upon trial; to accuse publicly. — *n* **arraign'er.** — *n* **arraign'ment.** [O.Fr. *aresnier* — L.L. *arratiōnāre* — L. *ad*, to, *ratiō*, *-ōnis*, reason.]

arrange *ə-rānj'*, *vt* to set in a rank or row; to put in order; to settle or work out; to adapt for other instruments or voices (*mus*). — *vi* to come to an agreement (with *to*); to make plans (with *to* or *for*). —

n **arrange'ment.** — *n* **arrang'er.** [O.Fr. *arangier* — *à* (L. *ad*, to), and *rangier, rengier*; see **range.**]

arrant *ar'ənt, adj* downright, unmitigated, out-and-out; notorious; rascally. — *adv* **arr'antly.** [A variant of **errant.**]

arras *ar'əs, n* a hanging screen of tapestry for a wall. [After type orig. made at *Arras* in France.]

array *ə-rā', n* an imposing, purposeful, or significant arrangement; an arrangement of terms in rows and columns, (esp. if square) a matrix (*math*); dress or equipage (usu. *archaic*). — *vt* to put in order, arrange; to empanel (jurors) (*law*); to dress, adorn or equip. — *n* **array'ment.** [A.Fr. *arai*, O.Fr. *arei*, array, equipage.]

arrears *ə-rērz', npl* (occasionally *sing*) that which remains unpaid or undone; total unpaid debt; the condition of being in arrears. — **in arrears** behindhand, esp. in the payment of rent, etc. [O.Fr. *arere, ariere* (Fr. *arrière*) — L. *ad*, to, *retrō*, back, behind.]

arrest *ə-rest', vt* to apprehend by legal authority; to seize by warrant, take into custody; to catch, fix (e.g. the attention); to bring to a standstill, check. — *n* seizure by warrant; stoppage, failure (as e.g. of a mechanism or an organ); the act of arresting. — *adj* **arrest'able** (of an offence) such that the offender may be arrested without warrant; liable to arrest. — *n* **arrestee'** a person prevented by arrestment from making payment or delivery to another until the arrester's claim upon that other is secured or satisfied. — *n* **arrest'er** a person who, or a thing which, arrests; a person who makes an arrestment (also **arrest'or**). — *adj* **arrest'ive** tending to arrest. — *n* **arrest'ment** a checking, stopping; detention of a person arrested till liberated on bail, or by security (*law*); a process which prohibits a debtor from handing over to his or her creditor money or property until a debt due by that creditor to a third party (the arrester) is paid or secured (*Scots law*). — **arrester gear** shock-absorbing transverse cables on an aircraft-carrier's deck for the arrester hook of an alighting aircraft to catch on; **arrester hook** a hook put out from an aircraft alighting on an aircraft-carrier, to catch on the arrester gear. — **arrest of judgment** a delay between conviction and sentence because of possible error; **cardiac arrest** a heart attack or heart failure; **under arrest** having been apprehended by legal authority, held in custody. [O.Fr. *arester* — L. *ad*, to, *restāre*, to stand still.]

arrhythmic *ā-rith'mik* or *-ridh'mik, adj* having an irregular or interrupted rhythm. — *n* **arrhyth'mia** (*med*) irregularity of the heart-beat. [**a-**[2] and **rhythmic.**]

arris *ar'is*, (*building*, etc.) *n* a sharp edge on stone, metal, etc. at the meeting of two surfaces. — **arris gutter** a V-shaped gutter, usu. of wood; **arris rail** a wooden, etc. rail of triangular section; **arris tile** an angular roof-tile for use where hips or ridges intersect. [See **arête.**]

arrive *ə-rīv', vi* to reach any place; to attain to any object (with *at*); to achieve success or recognition. — *n* **arriv'al** the act of arriving; a person who or thing that arrives. [O.Fr. *ariver* — L.L. *adrīpāre* — L. *ad*, to, *rīpa*, shore.]

arrivederci *är-ē-vəd-er'chē*, (It.) *interj* goodbye until we meet again.

arriviste *a'rē-vēst, n* a person 'on the make'; a parvenu, upstart; a self-seeker. — *n* **a'rrivisme.** [Fr.]

arrogance *ar'ə-gəns, n* undue assumption of importance; conceit, self-importance. — *adj* **arr'ogant** overbearing; conceited, self-important. — *adv* **arr'ogantly.** — *vt* **arrogate** (*ar'ə-gāt*) to claim as one's own, esp. proudly or unduly; to ascribe, attribute or assign (to another). — *n* **arrogā'tion** an act of arrogating; undue assumption. [L. *arrogāre* — *ad*, to, *rogāre, -ātum*, to ask or claim.]

arrondissement *ä-rɔ̃-dēs'mã, n* in France a subdivision of a department or a municipal subdivision of some large cities, esp. Paris. [Fr., — *arrondir*, to make round.]

arrow *ar'ō, n* a straight, pointed missile, made to be shot from a bow or blowpipe; any arrow-shaped mark or object; (in *pl*) darts (*colloq*). — *vt* to indicate, show the position of, by use of an arrow. — *adj* **arr'owy** of or like arrows. — **arr'ow-head** the head or pointed part of an arrow; **arr'owroot** a West Indian plant, *Maranta arundinacea* or a nutritious starch from its rhizome; extended to other plants and their starch; **arr'ow-shot** the range of an arrow; **arr'owwood** a species of *viburnum*, or other shrubs or trees formerly used by American Indians to make arrows. [O.E. *arwe.*]

arroyo *ə-roi'ō*, (*US*) *n* a rocky ravine; dry watercourse: — *pl* **arroy'os.** [Sp.]

arse *ärs* or in U.S. **ass** *as*, (*vulg*) *n* the buttocks; impudence, cheek (*Austr*). — *n* **arse'hole** or in U.S. **ass'hole** the anus (*vulg*); a worthless, contemptible, etc. person (*vulg slang*). — **arse licker** or **arse'-licker** (*vulg slang*) an extremely obsequious person; **arse'-licking.** — **arse around** or **about** (*vulg slang*) to mess around, do nothing in particular. [O.E. *ærs.*]

arsenal *ärs'i-nl* or *ärs'nl, n* a magazine or factory for naval and military weapons and ammunition; a storehouse (*fig*). [It. *arzenale, arsenale* — Ar. *dār aççināʻah*, workshop.]

arsenic *ärs'ə-nik* or *ärs'nik, n* the chemical element (symbol **As**; atomic no. 33); a poison, the trioxide of the element (As_2O_3; **white arsenic**). — *n* **ar'senate** or **arseniate** (*-sē'ni-āt*) a salt of arsenic acid. — *adj* **arsenic** (*är-sen'ik*), **arsen'ical** or **arsē'nious** composed of or containing arsenic. — *n* **ar'senide** a compound of arsenic with a metal. — *n* **ar'senite** a salt of arsenious acid. — *n* **arsine** (*är'sēn, -sin* or *-sīn*) the poisonous gas, hydride of arsenic (AsH_3); a compound in which one or more hydrogen atoms of AsH_3 are replaced by an alkyl radical, etc. [Gr. *arsenikon*, yellow orpiment.]

arson *är'sn, n* the crime of feloniously setting fire to houses, haystacks, or similar property. — *n* **ar'sonist.** [O.Fr. — L. *arsiō, -ōnis* — *ardēre, arsum*, to burn.]

art[1] *ärt, n* practical skill, or its application, guided by principles; application of skill to production of beauty (esp. visible beauty) and works of creative imagination, as in *the fine arts*; drawing and painting, and often sculpture; a branch of learning, esp. one of the *liberal* arts, as in *faculty of arts, master of arts*; skill or knowledge in a particular department; a skilled profession or trade, craft, or branch of activity; human skill and agency (opp. to *nature*); magic or occult knowledge or influence; a method or knack of doing a thing; cunning, artifice, craftiness. — *adj* of, for, or concerned with, painting, sculpture, etc. (as in *art gallery, art historian*); intended to be decorative or artistic; produced with studied artistry, not arising spontaneously by chance. — *adj* **art'ful** cunning, clever; skilful, masterly. — *adv* **art'fully.** — *n* **art'fulness.** — *n* **art'iness.** — *adj* **art'less** simple; guileless, unaffected. — *adv* **art'lessly.** — *n* **art'lessness.** — *adj* **art'y** (*colloq*), or less commonly **art'sy**, artistic, or aspiring to be. — **art deco** (*dek'ō*) the style of decorative art characteristic of the 1920s and 1930s, developing the curvilinearity of art nouveau into more streamlined geometrical forms; **art form** an accepted medium of artistic expression; a set form or arrangement in poetry or music; **art nouveau** (*är noo-vō'*) a decorative form of art (*c* 1890–1910) in which curvilinear forms are important and fundamentally unrelated images are often combined in a single design; **art paper** a type of paper for illustrations, coated with a composition containing china clay; **arts student** a student in the faculty of arts; **art student** a student of painting, sculpture, etc.; **art union** (*Austr* and *NZ*) a lottery; **art'work** the illustrations and other decorative material in a publication. — *adj* **arty-craft'y** to do with, or esp. involved in, arts and crafts; self-consciously artistic. — *adj* **arty-fart'y** (*derog colloq*) arty or artistically highbrow. — **fine art** general term for aesthetic works of art; the fine arts (see below); an operation or practice requiring special craftsmanship (*colloq*); **get something down to a fine art** to become very skilled at something through practice; **soft art** (and **soft sculpture**) works of art (and sculpture) constructed from textiles or other soft materials; **the fine arts** painting, poetry, music, etc. [L. *ars*, *artis*.]

art[2] *ärt*, (*archaic*, *liturgical*, *formal* or *poetic*) used as 2nd pers. sing. pres. indic. of the verb *to be*. [O.E.]

art. *abbrev* for: article; artificial; (also **arty**) artillery.

artefact or **artifact** *är'ti-fakt*, (esp. *archaeol*) *n* a thing made by human workmanship. — *adj* **artefac'tual**. [L. *arte*, by art (abl. of *ars*), *factum*, made.]

artery *är'tər-i*, *n* a tube or vessel that conveys blood from the heart; any main channel of communication or movement. — *adj* **arterial** (-*tē'ri-əl*). — *n* **artērialisā'tion** or **-z-**. — *vt* **artēr'ialise** or **-ize** to make arterial. — *n* **artēriosclerō'sis** (*med*) hardening of the arteries. — *adj* **artēriosclerotic** (-*ot'ik*). — **arterial road** a main traffic road from which lesser routes branch. [L. *artēria* — Gr. *artēriā*, windpipe, artery.]

artesian *är-tē'zyən*, *-zhən* or *-zhyən*, *adj* of a type of well in which water rises in a borehole by hydrostatic pressure from a basin whose outcrop is at a higher level. [*Artesian*, of Artois in N. France (such wells being in early use there).]

artful. See **art**[1].

arthralgia *är-thral'ji-ə* or *-jə*, (*pathol*) *n* pain in a joint. — *adj* **arthral'gic**. — *n* **arthritis** (*är-thrī'tis*) inflammation of a joint. — *adj* **arthritic** (-*thrit'ik*) of or near a joint; of or of the nature of arthritis. — *n* a person suffering from arthritis. [Gr. *arthron*, a joint, *algos*, pain.]

arthrodesis *är-thrō-dē'sis*, (*med*) *n* the immobilising of a joint in the body by the surgical fusion of the bones. [Gr. *arthron*, joint, *desis*, binding together.]

arthropathy *är-throp'ə-thi*, (*med*) *n* disease of the joints. [Gr. *arthron*, joint, *patheia*, suffering.]

arthroplasty *är'thrō-plas-ti*, (*med*) *n* surgical repair of a joint; replacement of a joint by an artificial joint. [Gr. *arthron*, joint, *plastos*, moulded.]

arthropod *är'thrō-pod*, *n* any member of the **Arthropoda** (*är-throp'od-ə*), a major division of the animal kingdom, with segmented bodies and jointed appendages — crustacea, arachnids, millipedes, centipedes, insects, etc. — *adj* **arthrop'odal**. [Gr. *arthron*, joint, *pous*, *podos*, a foot.]

arthroscopy *är-thros'ko-pi*, (*med*) *n* examination of a joint with an endoscope. [Gr. *arthron*, joint, *skopeein*, to look.]

Arthurian *är-thū'ri-ən*, *adj* relating to King *Arthur*, a ruler of the Britons, whose court is the centre of many legends, but who himself perhaps existed; pertaining to the legends.

artic *är-tik'* or *är'tik*, (*colloq*) *n* short for articulated lorry.

artichoke *är'ti-chōk*, *n* a thistlelike perennial plant with large scaly heads and edible receptacles. — **Jerusalem artichoke** a totally different plant, a species of sunflower with edible tubers like potatoes, Jerusalem being a corruption of It. *girasole* sunflower. [North It. *articiocco* — Old Sp. *alcarchofa*.]

article *är'ti-kl*, *n* a separate element, member or part of anything; a particular object or commodity; an item; a single clause or term; a distinct point in an agreement, or (in *pl*) an agreement viewed as a set of these (as in *articles of apprenticeship*, etc.); a literary composition in a newspaper, periodical, encyclopaedia, etc., dealing with a subject distinctly and independently; the adjective *the* (*definite article*), *a* or *an* (*indefinite article*) or the equivalent in another language (*gram*). — *vt* to bind by articles of apprenticeship. — *adj* **ar'ticled** bound as apprentice. — *adj* **artic'ūlable**. — *adj* **artic'ūlar** belonging to the joints; at or near a joint. — *adj* **artic'ūlate** jointed; composed of distinct parts; composed of recognisably distinct sounds, as human speech; clear, lucid; able to express one's thoughts with ease. — *vt* to attach by a joint; to connect by joints; to form into distinct sounds, syllables, or words. — *vi* to form a joint or correlation (with); to speak distinctly. — *adj* **artic'ūlated**. — *adv* **artic'ūlately**. — *n* **artic'ūlateness**. — *n* **articūlā'tion** jointing; distinctness, or distinct expression in speech; a joint; a segment. — *n* **artic'ūlātor**. — *adj* **artic'ūlatory**. — **articulated lorry** a lorry made easier to manoeuvre by having its (sometimes detachable) front section flexibly attached to the rear section so that it can move at an angle to it. — **articles of faith** the binding statement of points of belief of a Church, etc.; **articles of war** the code of regulations for the government and discipline of armed services. [L. *articulus*, a little joint, *articulāre*, *-ātum*, to provide with joints, to utter distinctly — *artus*, joint.]

artifact. See **artefact**.

artifice *är'ti-fis*, *n* contrivance or trickery; an ingenious expedient; skill. — *n* **artif'icer** a mechanic (esp. *mil*, *navy*); a person who creates skilfully; a craftsman; a contriver. — *adj* **artificial** (*är-ti-fish'l* or *är'ti-fish-l*) synthetic (opp. to *natural*); fictitious, factitious, feigned, made in imitation (opp. to *real*); contrived (opp. to *spontaneous*); made by man; affected in manners. — *n* **artificiality** (-*fish-i-al'i-ti*). — *adv* **artific'ially**. — *n* **artific'ialness**. — **artificial insemination** the injection of semen into the uterus otherwise than by sexual union; **artificial intelligence** the use of computers in such a way that they perform functions normally associated with human intelligence, such as learning, adapting, self-correction and decision-taking; **artificial kidney** a kidney machine; **artificial language** an invented language functioning not as the native speech of its users, but as a computer language or means of international communication; **artificial respiration** stimulation of respiration manually or mechanically by forcing air in and out of the lungs. [L. *artificium* — *artifex*, *-ficis*, an artificer — *ars*, *artis*, and *facĕre*, to make.]

artillery *är-til'ər-i*, *n* offensive weapons of war, now esp. the heavier kinds, e.g. cannon; a branch of the military service using such weapons; the science of handling guns. — *n* **artill'erist** a person skilled in artillery; a gunner. — **artill'ery-man** a soldier of the artillery. [O.Fr. *artillerie* — *artiller*, to arm.]

artiness. See **art**[1].

artiodactyl *är-ti-ō-dak'til*, *adj* even-toed. — *n* a member of the **Artiodac'tyla** or even-toed ungulate mammals, in which the third and fourth digit form a symmetrical pair and the hind-foot bears an even number of digits (cf. **perissodactyl**.) [Gr. *artios*, even in number, *daktylos*, finger or toe.]

artisan *ärt-i-zan'* or *ärt'i-zan*, *n* a handicraftsman or mechanic, a skilled workman. — *adj* **artis'anal** (or *ärt'*). [Fr. — It. *artigiano*, ult. from L. *artitus*, skilled.]

artist *ärt'ist*, *n* a person who practises or is skilled in an art, now esp. a fine art; a person who has the qualities of imagination and taste required in art; a painter or draughtsman; a performer, esp. in music; a person good at, or given to, a particular activity, such as *booze artist* (esp. *Austr* and *US slang*). — *adj* **artist'ic** or **artist'ical**. — *adv* **artist'ically**. — *n* **art'istry** artistic pursuits; artistic workmanship, quality or ability. — **artistic temperament** the emotional and capricious temperament ascribed to artists. [Fr. *artiste* — L. *ars*, *artis*, art.]

artiste *är-tēst'*, *n* a public performer, entertainer; someone adept in a manual art. [Fr.]

artless, artsy, arty, arty-farty. See under **art**[1].

arugula *ə-ro͞o'gə-lə*, *n* rocket, a Mediterranean herb used in salads. [It. dialect, ult. from L. *eruca*, a colewort.]

Arum *ā'rəm*, *n* a flower of the cuckoo-pint or wake-robin genus; (without *cap*) any of several related plants. — *adj* **araceous** (*a-rā'shəs*) or **aroid** (*ā'roid*). — **arum lily** *Zantedeschia aethiopica*, having a yellow spadix enclosed in a large white bract. [L. *arum* — Gr. *aron*.]

arundinaceous *ə-run-di-nā'shəs*, *adj* of or like a reed. [L. *arundināceus* — *arundō*, *-inis*, a reed.]

Aryan *ā'ri-ən*, *adj* Indo-Germanic, Indo-European; now generally of the Indian, or Indian and Iranian, branch of the Indo-European languages; speaking one of these languages; in Nazi politics, Caucasian, esp. of northern European type and esp. as opp. to Jewish. — *n* the parent Indo-European language; a speaker of an Aryan language. — *vt* **Ar'yanise** or **-ize.** [Sans. *ārya*, noble.]

aryl *ar'il*, (*chem*) *n* any aromatic univalent hydrocarbon radical. [**aromatic** and Gr. *hȳlē*, matter.]

arytaenoid or **arytenoid** *ar-i-tē'noid*, *adj* pitcher-shaped. — *n* a cartilage or a muscle of the larynx. [Gr. *arytainoeidēs* — *arytaina*, a cup, *eidos*, form.]

AS *abbrev* for: Advanced Supplementary (examination); Anglo-Saxon; antisubmarine; Assistant Secretary.

As (*chem*) *symbol* for arsenic.

as[1] *az* or *əz*, *adv* in whatever degree, proportion or manner; to whatever extent; in that degree; to that extent; so far; however; specifically. — *conj* or almost *prep* for instance; in the manner, character, part or aspect of; in so far as; whereas. — *conj* because, since; while, when; as if. — *pron* who, which, that (after *such*, *so*, *same*, or where a statement is treated as antecedent). — **as from** or **as of** from (a specified time); **as if** or **as though** as it would be if; **as it were** so to speak; in some sort; **as many as** all who; **as much** the same; just that; **as now** or **as then** just as at this, or that, time; **as was** formerly; in a former state; **as well** also; in addition; equally well, suitably, happily, etc.; **as yet** up to this moment; until now; **as you were** a military order to return to the former position; **so as to** with the purpose or consequence specified. [O.E. *all-swā* (*eall-swā*), all so, wholly so.]

as[2] *as*, (*Roman antiq*) *n* a Roman unit of weight, a pound of 12 ounces; a copper coin, orig. a pound in weight, ult. half an ounce: — *pl* **ass'es**. [L. *ās*, *assis*, a unit.]

ASA *abbrev* for: Advertising Standards Authority; Amateur Swimming Association; American Standards Association, used e.g. (*phot*) to label film speeds.

asana *ä'sə-nə*, *n* any of the positions taught in yoga. [Sans. *āsana*.]

ASAP or **asap** *abbrev* for as soon as possible.

asbestos *az-bes'tos*, *n* a fine fibrous form of certain minerals, capable of being woven into incombustible cloth; (commercially) *chrysotile*, a fibrous serpentine. — *adj* **asbes'tic** or **asbes'tine** of or like asbestos. — *n* **asbestō'sis** a lung disease caused by inhaling asbestos dust. [Gr., (lit.) unquenchable — *a-*, not, *sbestos*, extinguished.]

ascarid *as'kə-rid*, *n* any nematode worm of the parasitic genus **As'caris** that infests the small intestines. [Gr. *askaris*, pl. *askarides*.]

ascend *ə-send'* or *a-send'*, *vi* to go up, mount, rise. — *vt* to go up, mount, climb; to trace back in time or ancestry. — *n* **ascend'ancy** or **ascend'ency** dominating influence. — *n* **ascend'ant** or less commonly **ascend'ent** (*astrol*) the part of the ecliptic just risen or about to rise at any instant (a planet in this was supposed to influence a person born at the time); (from the phrase **in the ascendant**) a position of pre-eminence; a person who rises or mounts; a rise, up-slope. — *adj* rising; just risen above the horizon; predominant. — *n* **ascend'er** a person who or thing which ascends; (the upper part of) a letter such as b, d, h, k (*printing*, etc.). — *adj* **ascend'ible** (also **ascend'able**) scalable. — *adj* **ascend'ing** rising; curving up from a prostrate to an erect position (*bot*). — *n* **ascension** (*-sen'shən*) ascent; an ascent to heaven, esp. Christ's. — *n* **ascent'** a going up; advancement; a going back in time or ancestry; a way up; an up-slope. — **Ascen'sion-day** or **Ascension Day** (*Christian relig*) Holy Thursday, ten days before Whitsunday, commemorating Christ's Ascension. — **ascend the throne** to become king or queen. [L. *ascendĕre*, *ascēnsum* — *ad*, to, *scandĕre*, to climb.]

ascertain *as-ər-tān'*, *vt* to find out for certain; to verify, prove. — *adj* **ascertain'able.** — *n* **ascertain'ment.** [O.Fr. *acertener* — *à*, to, *certain*, certain.]

ascetic *a-* or *ə-set'ik*, *n* a person who rigidly avoids ordinary bodily gratifications for conscience's sake; a person who aims to compass holiness through mortification of the flesh; a strict hermit; a person who lives a life of austerity. — *adj* **ascet'ic** or **ascet'ical** rigorous in mortifying the flesh; of asceticism; recluse. — *adv* **ascet'ically.** — *n* **ascet'icism** (*-sizm*). [Gr. *askētikos* — *askētēs*, one who is in training — *askeein*, to work, exercise, train.]

asci. See **ascus**.

ascidium *a-sid'i-əm*, *n* a pitcher-shaped leaf or part of a leaf: — *pl* **ascid'ia.** — *n* **ascid'ian** a sea-squirt, shaped like a double-mouthed flask. [Gr. *askidion*, dimin. of *askos*, a leather bag, wine-skin.]

ASCII *as'ki*, (*comput*) *abbrev* for American Standard Code for Information Interchange, a binary code used by VDUs, printers, etc. to represent characters.

ascites *a-sī'tēz*, (*pathol*) *n* dropsy of the abdomen. — *adj* **ascit'ic** (*-sit'ik*) or **ascit'ical.** [Gr. *askītēs* — *askos*, belly.]

ascomycete, ascospore. See under **ascus**.

ascorbic *ə-skör'bik*, *adj* antiscorbutic — only in **ascorbic acid** vitamin C. [**a-**[2] and **scorbutic.**]

ascot *as'kot*, *n* a type of necktie with broad ends that are tied to lie one across the other. [The race-course at *Ascot*, England, well-known for the fashionable dress of spectators.]

ascribe *ə-* or *a-skrīb'*, *vt* to attribute, impute or assign. — *adj* **ascrīb'able.** — *n* **ascription** (*-skrip'shən*) act, expression or formula of ascribing or imputing, e.g. that ascribing glory to God at the end of a Christian sermon. [L. *ascrībĕre* — *ad*, to, *scrībĕre*, *scrīptum*, to write.]

ascus *as'kəs*, (*bot*) *n* an enlarged cell, commonly elongated, in which usually eight spores are formed: — *pl* **asci** (*as'ī*). — *n* **as'comycete** (*as'kō-mī-sēt*) any one of the **Ascomycetes** (*-sē'tēz*), one of the main divisions of the fungi, characterised by formation of asci. — *n* **as'cospore** a spore formed in an ascus. [Gr. *askos*, bag.]

Asdic *az'dik*, *n* an apparatus for detecting and locating a submarine or other underwater object by means of ultrasonic waves echoed back from the submarine, etc. [*A*llied (or *A*nti-) *S*ubmarine *D*etection *I*nvestigation *C*ommittee.]

ASE *abbrev* for Association for Science Education.

ASEAN or **Asean** *a'si-ən*, *abbrev* for Association of South East Asian Nations.

aseismic *a-*, *ā-* or *ə-sīz'mik*, *adj* free from earthquakes. [**a-**[2] and **seismic.**]

asepalous *a-*, *ā-* or *ə-sep'ə-ləs*, *adj* without sepals. [**a-**[2] and **sepal.**]

aseptic *ā-sep'tik*, also *a-* or *ə-sep'tik*, *adj* not liable to, or preventing, decay or putrefaction; involving or accompanied by measures to exclude micro-organisms. — *n* an aseptic substance. — *n* **asep'ti-**

cism (*-sizm*) aseptic treatment. — *n* **asep'sis** freedom from sepsis or blood-poisoning; the process of rendering, or condition of being, aseptic; exclusion of micro-organisms: — *pl* **asep'ses** (*-sēz*). — *vt* **asep'ticise** or **-ize** (*-ti-sīz*) to make aseptic; to treat with aseptics. [Gr. *asēptos* — *a-*, not, *sēpein*, to cause to decay.]

asexual *ā-seks'ū-əl*, also *a-* or *ə-seks'ū-əl*, *adj* without sex; not involving sexual activity. — *n* **asexūality** (*-al'i-ti*). — *adv* **asex'ūally**. [**a-**[2] and **sexual**.]

ASH *abbrev* for Action on Smoking and Health.

ash[1] *ash*, *n* a well-known timber tree of the olive family; its wood which is white, tough, and hard. — *adj* **ash'en**. [O.E. *æsc*.]

ash[2] *ash*, *n* (often in *pl*) the dust or remains of anything burnt; (also **volcanic ash** or **ashes**) volcanic dust, or a rock composed of it; (in *pl*) the remains of a human body when burnt. — *adj* **ash'en** of the colour of ash; (of the face) very pale. — *adj* **ash'y**. — **ash'bin, -bucket** or **-can** a receptacle for ashes and other household refuse. — *adj* **ash-blond'** (of hair) of a pale, silvery blond colour; having hair of this colour: — *fem* (also *n*) **ash-blonde'**. — **ash'-pan** a tray fitted underneath the grate of a fireplace to receive the ashes; **ash'-tray** a small tray or saucer for tobacco ash and cigarette ends; **Ash Wednesday** (*Christian relig*) the first day of Lent, named from the ancient custom of sprinkling ashes on the head to show penance and mourning. — **the Ashes** (*cricket*) the test-match series between England and Australia, or the trophy the teams vie to 'bring back' or retain respectively (following a mock 'In Memoriam' notice for English cricket in the *Sporting Times* after the Australian victory in 1882. [O.E. *asce*.]

ashamed *ə-shāmd'*, *adj* affected with shame (with *of* an action or person; with *for*, meaning on behalf of, a person; also with *that*). — *adv* **ashamed'ly** (or *ə-shām'id-li*). — *n* **ashamed'ness** (or *ə-shām'id-nis*). — *adj* **asham'ing**. [Pfx. *a-*, (intensive) and O.E. *sc(e)amian*, to shame.]

ashen, etc. See **ash**[1,2].

ashet *ash'it*, (now chiefly *Scot*) *n* a large meat-plate or serving-dish. [Fr. *assiette*.]

ashlar or **ashler** *ash'lər*, *n* a squared stone used in building or facing a wall; masonry of such stones. — Also *adj*. — *vt* to face with ashlar. [O.Fr. *aiseler* — L. *axillāris* — *axilla*, dimin. of *axis*, axle, plank.]

ashore *ə-shōr'*, *adv* on, or on to, the shore or land (from the sea). [**a-**[1] and **shore**[1].]

ashram *äsh'rəm*, *n* usu. in India, a hermitage, or a place of retreat for a religious group. [Sans. *āśrama*.]

Asian *ā'shən*, *ā'shi-ən*, *ā'shyən*, also *-zh-* or **Asiatic** *-i-at'ik*, *adj* belonging to *Asia* (esp. Asia Minor). — *n* a native of Asia or person of Asian descent. — *adj* **Asianic** (*-an'ik*) Asian, esp. of a group of non-Indo-European languages of Asia and Europe.

aside *ə-sīd'*, *adv* on or to one side; privately; apart. — *n* words spoken in an undertone, so as not to be heard by some person present; words spoken by an actor which the other persons on the stage are supposed not to hear; an indirect effort of any kind. — **aside from** apart from; **set aside** to quash (a judgment); to put to one side (*lit* or *fig*). [**a-**[1] and **side**.]

asinine *as'in-īn*, *adj* of or like an ass; idiotic. — *n* **asininity** (*-in'i-ti*). [L. *asinīnus* — *asinus*, ass.]

ASIO *āz'* or *az'i-ō*, *abbrev* for Australian Security Intelligence Organisation.

ask *äsk*, *vt* to beg, request; to make a request of; to inquire; to inquire of; to invite; to seek. — *vi* to make a request (for); to inquire (*after* a person, etc.; *about* a matter, etc.). — *n* **ask'er**. — **asking price** a price set by the seller of an article before bargaining has begun. — **ask for it** (*colloq*) to behave in a way likely to bring trouble on oneself; **I ask you!** would you believe it, don't you agree — usu. expressing criticism; **if you ask me** in my opinion. [O.E. *ascian*, *acsian*.]

askance *ə-skans'*, *adv* sideways; awry; obliquely. — **look askance at** to look at with disdain, disapproval, envy, or (now usu.) suspicion.

asker. See **ask**.

askew *ə-skū'*, *adv* or *adj* at or to an oblique angle; awry. [App. **a-**[1] and **skew**[1].]

ASL *abbrev* for American Sign Language, the N. Am. system of hand and arm movements used by the deaf to replace spoken words.

aslant *ə-slänt'*, *adv* or *adj* on the slant, slantwise. — *prep* slantwise across, athwart (*Scot*). [**a-**[1] and **slant**.]

asleep *ə-slēp'*, *adv* or *adj* in or to a sleeping state; dead (*euph*); (of limbs) numbed, sometimes with tingling or prickly feeling. [**a-**[1] and **sleep**.]

ASLEF *az'lef*, *abbrev* for Associated Society of Locomotive Engineers and Firemen.

ASM *abbrev* for air-to-surface missile.

-asm. See **-ism**.

asocial *a-* or *ā-sō'shl*, *adj* not social; antisocial. [**a-**[2] and **social**.]

asp *asp* or *äsp*, *n* a venomous snake of various kinds including *Vipera aspis* of Southern Europe, Cleopatra's asp (prob. the horned viper), the biblical asp (prob. the Egyptian juggler's snake, *Naja haje*), and the cobra. [L., — Gr. *aspis*.]

asparagus *əs-par'ə-gəs*, *n* any plant of the genus *Asparagus* (having leaves reduced to scales) some cultivated as ornamental plants, and one species for its young shoots eaten as a delicacy. [L., — Gr. *asparagos*.]

aspartame *əs-pär'tām*, *n* an artificial sweetener, 200 times sweeter than sucrose.

aspect *as'pekt*, *n* a view, standpoint; direction of facing; appearance presented; way of viewing; surface facing a particular direction, face, side, elevation; the situation of one planet with respect to another, as seen from the earth (*astron*); in some languages, a verbal form expressing simple action, repetition, beginning, duration, etc. (*gram*); attitude (*aeronautics*). — *adj* **aspec'tual** (*gram* and *astron*) of or relating to aspect. [L. *aspectus*.]

aspen *asp'ən* or *äsp'ən*, also *-in*, *n* the trembling poplar. [O.E. *æspe*.]

asperges *ə-spûr'jez* or *-jēz*, (*RC*) *n* a short service introductory to the mass in which holy water is sprinkled. — *n* **aspergill** (*as'pər-jil*) a holy water sprinkler. — Also **aspergillum** (*-jil'əm*): — *pl* **aspergill'a** or **aspergill'ums**. [L. *aspergere*, to scatter or sprinkle upon.]

aspergillosis *as-pər-jil-ō'sis*, *n* a disease, fatal to birds and also occurring in domestic animals and man, caused by any of various moulds, esp. species of **Aspergillus**, a genus of minute moulds occurring on decaying substances. [Aspergillus (— L. *aspergĕre*, to scatter or sprinkle upon) and **-osis**.]

asperity *as-per'i-ti*, *n* roughness; harshness; acrimony, bitterness. [L. *asper*.]

asperse *as-pûrs'*, *vt* to slander or accuse falsely. — *n* **asper'sion** calumny; slander. — *adj* **asper'sive**. [L. *aspergĕre*, *aspersum* — *ad*, to, *spargĕre*, to sprinkle.]

asphalt *as'falt*, *n* a black or dark-brown, hard, bituminous substance, occurring naturally and as a residue in petroleum distillation, etc.; a mixture of this with rock chips or other material, used for paving, roofing, etc. — *vt* to lay, cover or impregnate with asphalt. — *n* **as'phalter** a person who lays asphalt. — *adj* **asphalt'ic**. [Gr. *asphaltos*, from an Eastern word.]

aspheric *ə-* or *ā-sfer'ik*, *adj* not spherical; (of a surface) not forming part of a sphere. [**a-**[2] and **spheric**.]

asphodel *as'fə-del* or *-fo-del*, *n* a plant of the lily family; various other plants, esp. bog-asphodel. [Gr. *asphodelos*; cf. **daffodil**.]

asphyxia *as-fik'si-ə*, (*med*) *n* stoppage or suspension of the vital functions owing to any cause interfering with respiration and preventing oxygen from reaching the body tissue. — *n* and *adj* **asphyx'iant** (a chemical substance) producing asphyxia. — *vt* **asphyx'iate** to produce asphyxia in. — *adj* **asphyx'iāted**. — *n* **asphyxiā'tion**. — *n* **asphyx'iātor**. [Gr. *asphyxiā* — *a-*, without, *sphyxis*, pulse.]

aspic *as'pik*, *n* a clear savoury meat- or fish-jelly used as a glaze or to mould fish, game, hard-boiled eggs, etc. [Perh. from *aspic*, asp, because it is 'cold as an aspic' (Fr. proverb).]

aspidistra *as-pid-ist'rə*, *n* a plant of the *Aspidistra* genus of plants of the asparagus group of Liliaceae — often grown indoors, having long, tough, evergreen leaves. [Perh. Gr. *aspis*, a shield.]

aspire *əs-* or *as-pīr'*, *vi* (with *to*, *after*, or an infinitive) to desire eagerly; to aim at, or strive for, high things; to tower up. — *n* **aspīr'ant** (or *as'pir-ənt*) a person who aspires (with *after* or *for*); a candidate. — *vt* **aspirate** (*as'pir-āt*) to pronounce with a full breathing, i.e. the sound of *h*, as in *house* (*phon*); to follow (a stop) by an audible breath (*phon*); to replace (a consonant) by another sound, normally a fricative, when there is a combination with the sound *h* or the letter *h* (*gram*, *phon*, etc.); to draw (gas, fluid, etc.) out of a cavity by suction; to inhale (*med*). — Also *vi*. — *n* (*as'pir-it* or *-ət*) the sound represented by the letter *h*; a consonant sound, a stop followed by an audible breath; a mark of aspiration, the rough breathing (ʻ) in Greek; a letter representing an aspirate sound. — Also *adj*. — *n* **aspirā'tion** eager desire; (usu. in *pl*) lofty hopes or aims; pronunciation of a sound with a full breathing; an aspirated sound; drawing a gas, liquid or solid, in, out, or through. — *adj* **aspirā'tional** relating to the aspirations or aims of a person or of people. — *n* **as'pirātor** an apparatus for drawing air or other gases through bottles or other vessels; an instrument for removing fluids or solids from cavities of the body (*med*). — *adj* **aspiratory** (*as-pīr'ə-tə-ri* or *as'pir-ə-tə-ri*) relating to breathing. — *adj* **aspīr'ing** desiring, aiming at, etc. — *adv* **aspīr'ingly**. — *n* **aspīr'ingness**. [L. *aspīrāre*, *-ātum* — *ad*, to, *spīrāre*, to breathe.]

aspirin *as'pər-in* or *as'prin*, *n* a drug (acetyl-salicylic acid) used for relieving rheumatic pains, neuralgia, etc.

Ass. or **Assoc.** *abbrev* for Association.

ass[1] *as* or *äs*, *n* a small, usu. grey, long-eared animal of the horse genus; a dull, stupid fellow (*colloq*). [O.E. *assa* — L. *asinus*.]

ass[2]. See **arse**.

assagai. See **assegai**.

assai *äs-sä'ē* or *as'ī*, (*mus*) *adv* very. [It., — L. *ad*, to, *satis*, enough.]

assail *ə-sāl'*, *vt* to attack. — *adj* **assail'able**. — *n* **assail'ant** a person who attacks. — *n* **assail'er**. — *n* **assail'ment**. [O.Fr. *asaillir* — L. *assilīre* — *ad*, upon, *salīre*, to leap.]

assassin *ə-* or *a-sas'in*, *n* a person who, usu. for a reward, or for political reasons, kills by surprise or secretly. — *vt* **assass'inate** to murder by surprise or secret assault; to murder (esp. a prominent person) violently, often publicly; to destroy by treacherous means, as a reputation (*fig*). — *n* **assassinā'tion**. — *n* **assass'inātor**. [In 11–13 cent. Persia and Syria, a member of the military and religious order (notorious for secret murders) supporting the Old Man of the Mountain — Ar. *hashshāshīn*, hashish-eaters.]

assault *ə-sölt'*, *n* a sudden attack; a storming, as of a town; in English law, an unlawful attempt to apply force to the person of another — when force is actually applied the act amounts to *battery*; an attack of any sort by arguments, appeals, etc. — *vt* to make an assault or attack upon. — *adj* used in attack; preparing, or prepared, for attack. — *n* **assault'er**. — **assault course** a course laid out with obstacles that must be negotiated, used for training soldiers, etc. [O.Fr. *asaut* — L. *ad*, upon, *saltus*, a leap, *salīre*, to leap. See **assail**.]

assay *a-* or *ə-sā'*, *vt* to put to the proof, make trial of; to test; to determine the proportion of a metal, or other component, in; to give as result. — *vi* to adventure, make an attempt; to practise assaying (of ores, etc.). — *n* (sometimes *as'ā*) a test or trial; a determination of proportion of metal; a specimen used for the purpose; experiment; experience. — *adj* **assay'able**. — *n* **assay'er** a person who assays metals. — *n* **assay'ing**. [O.Fr. *assayer*, noun *assai*; see **essay**.]

assegai or **assagai** *as'ə-gī*, *n* a slender spear of hard wood tipped with iron, some for hurling, some for thrusting with — used in S. Africa. — *vt* to kill or wound with an assegai. [Through Fr. or Port. from Ar. *azzaghāyah* — *az* = *al*, the, *zaghāyah*, a Berber word.]

assemble *ə-sem'bl*, *vt* to call or bring together; to collect; to put together the parts of. — *vi* to meet together. — *n* **assem'blage** a collection of persons or things; the whole collection of remains found on an archaeological site; all the flora and fauna of one type in an ecosystem (*biol*); (also *a-sä-bläzh*) (putting together) a sculptural or other work of art consisting in whole or in part of selected objects, usu. objects made for another purpose. — *n* **assem'bler** someone who or that which assembles; a program that converts a program in assembly language into one in machine-code (*comput*). — *n* **assem'bly** the act of assembling; the putting together of parts; a company assembled; a formal ball or meeting for dancing and social intercourse; a meeting for religious worship or the like; a deliberative or legislative body, esp. in some legislatures a lower house. — **assembly hall** a hall, e.g in a school, in which assemblies are held; **assembly language** a program language more like a natural language than is machine-code (*comput*); **assembly line** a serial arrangement of workers and apparatus for passing on work from stage to stage in assembling a product; **assem'blyman** or **assem'blywoman** a member of an assembly or lower house; **assembly room** a public ballroom or room for entertainments. — **General Assembly** in Scotland, Ireland and the United States, the highest court of the Presbyterian Church; in England and Wales, the highest court of the United Reformed Church; **Legislative Assembly** or **House of Assembly** the lower or only house of some legislatures. [Fr. *assembler* — L.L. *assimulāre*, to bring together — *ad*, to, *similis*, like. See **assimilate**.]

assemblé *ä-sä-blā*, *n* a ballet dancer's leap with extended leg followed by crossing of legs. [Fr. *assembler*, to bring together.]

assembly. See **assemble**.

assent *a-* or *ə-sent'*, *vi* to express agreement or acquiescence (with *to*). — *n* an agreeing or acquiescence; compliance. — *n* **assent'er**. — *adj* **assentient** (*ə-sen'shənt*) or **assent'ive**. — *adv* **assent'ingly**. — *n* **assent'iveness**. — *n* **assent'or** a person who subscribes a candidate's nomination paper in addition to proposer and seconder. — **royal assent** the sovereign's formal acquiescence in a measure which has passed the Houses of Parliament. [L. *assentārī*, to flatter, frequentative of *assentīrī*, to assent, agree.]

assert *ə-sûrt'*, *vt* to declare positively, affirm; to insist; to vindicate or defend by arguments or measures (now used only with cause as object, or reflexively). — *adj* **assert'able**. — *n* **assert'er** or **assert'or** a champion, defender; a person who makes a positive statement. — *n* **asser'tion** (*-shən*). — *adj* **assert'ive** asserting or confirming confidently; positive; dogmatic. — *adv* **assert'ively**. — *n* **assert'iveness**. — **assert oneself** to defend one's rights or opinions, sometimes with unnecessary zeal; to thrust oneself forward. [L. *asserĕre*, *assertum*, to lay hands on, claim — *ad*, to, *serĕre*, to join.]

assess *ə-ses'*, *vt* to fix the amount of, as a tax; to tax or fine; to fix the value or profits of, for taxation (with *at*); to estimate or judge. — *adj* **assess'able.** — *n* **assess'ment** act of assessing; a valuation for the purpose of taxation; a tax. — *n* **assess'or** a person who assesses; a legal adviser who sits beside a magistrate; a person who assesses taxes, or value of property, income, etc., for taxation; a person appointed as an associate in office with another. — *adj* **assessorial** (*as-es-ör'i-əl*). — *n* **assess'orship.** — **assessment centre** a place where young offenders are detained so that their individual needs can be assessed and recommendations formulated about their future. [L. *assidēre*, *assessum*, to sit by, esp. of judges in a court, from *ad*, to, at, *sedēre*, to sit.]

asset *as'et*, *n* an item of property; something advantageous or well worth having. — **ass'et-stripping** (now usu. *derog*) the practice of acquiring control of a company and selling off its assets; **ass'et-stripper.** [Formed as false sing. of **assets.**]

assets *as'ets*, *npl* the property of a deceased or insolvent person, considered as chargeable for all debts, etc.; the entire property of all sorts belonging to a merchant or to a trading association. [From the A.Fr. law phrase *aver assetz*, to have enough, O.Fr. *asez*, enough.]

asseverate *ə-* or *a-sev'ər-āt*, *vt* to declare solemnly. — *n* **asseverā'tion.** [L. *assevērāre*, *-ātum* — *ad*, to, *sevērus*, serious; see **severe.**]

asshole. See **arse.**

assiduity *as-id-ū'i-ti*, *n* persistent application or diligence; (in *pl*) constant attentions. — *adj* **assiduous** (*ə-sid'ū-əs*) constant or unwearied in application. — *adv* **assid'ūously** unremittingly. — *n* **assid'ūousness.** [L. *assiduus* — *ad*, to, at, *sedēre*, to sit.]

assign *ə-sīn'*, *vt* to allot, share out; to designate, appoint; to put forward, adduce; to make over, transfer; to ascribe, refer; to specify; to fix, determine. — *n* (*law*) a person to whom any property or right is made over. — *adj* **assign'able.** — *n* **assignation** (*as-ig-nā'shən*) an appointment to meet, used e.g. of secret meetings between lovers and mostly in a bad sense; the making over of any right to another (*Scots law*). — *n* **assignee** (*as-īn-ē'*) a person to whom any right or property is assigned; a trustee of a sequestrated estate. — *n* **assignment** (*-sīn'mənt*) act of assigning; anything assigned; the writing by which a transfer is made (*law*); a task allotted. — *n* **assignor** (*as-i-nör'*; *law*) a person who makes over. [Fr. *assigner* — L. *assignāre*, to mark out — *ad*, to, *signum*, a mark or sign.]

assimilate *ə-sim'il-āt*, *vt* to make similar or like (with *to* or *with*); to take fully into the mind, experience effects of (e.g. knowledge); to receive and accept fully within a group, absorb; to convert into a like substance, as food in the body; to modify (a speech sound), making it more like a neighbouring sound in a word or sentence. — *vi* to be incorporated or absorbed (into); to become like (with *to*). — *adj* **assim'ilable.** — *n* **assimilā'tion.** — *n* **assimilā'tionist** a person who advocates a policy of assimilation, esp. of racial groups (also *adj*). — *adj* **assim'ilātive** having the power or tendency to assimilate. [L. *assimilāre*, *-ātum* — *ad*, to, *similis*, like.]

assist *ə-sist'*, *vt* to help (*with* work, etc., or *in* a matter, etc.). — *vi* to help (with *with* or *in*). — *n* **assis'tance** help; relief. — *n* **assis'tant** a person who assists; a helper. — *adj* helping. — *n* **assis'tantship.** — *adj* **assis'ted** for which help (e.g. financial aid, additional power) is supplied. [Fr. *assister* — L. *assistĕre*, to stand by — *ad*, to, *sistĕre*, to set, take one's stand.]

assize *ə-sīz'*, *n* a legislative sitting (*hist*); (in *pl*) periodical sittings of judges on circuit in England and Wales, with a jury (until 1972 when crown courts replaced them). [O.Fr. *assise*, assembly of judges, set rate — *asseoir* — L. *assidēre* — *ad*, to, *sedēre*, to sit.]

Assoc. See **Ass.**

associate *ə-sō'shi-āt* or *-si-āt*, *vt* to join, connect or link; to connect in one's mind; to make a colleague or partner. — *vi* to consort, keep company (with *with*); to combine or unite. — *adj* (*-ət* or *-āt*) associated; connected; confederate; joined as colleague or junior colleague. — *n* (*-ət* or *-āt*) a person joined or connected with another; a colleague, companion, friend, partner or ally; a person admitted to a society without full membership. — *n* **associabil'ity.** — *adj* **asso'ciable** (*-shi-ə-bl* or *-shə-bl*). — *n* **assō'ciateship.** — *n* **associā'tion** (*-si-* or *-shi-ā'shən*) an act of associating; union or combination; a society of persons joined to promote some object or cause; a set of species of plants or animals characteristic of a certain habitat (*biol*); loose aggregation of molecules (*chem*); (also **association football**; *colloq* **soccer**) the game as formulated by the Football Association (formed 1863), with eleven players a side (as opp. to *Rugby* football); connection of thoughts or of feelings; (usu. in *pl*) thought, feeling or memory, more or less permanently connected with e.g. a place, an occurrence, something said; a relationship between the EEC and certain other countries, e.g. in Africa and the Caribbean, being more than just a trade agreement but with the associated members not enjoying membership of the EEC. — *n* **associa'tionism** (*psychol*) the theory which considers association of ideas to be the basis of all mental activity. — *adj* **assō'ciātive** tending to association. — *n* **associativity** (*-ə-tiv'i-ti*). — **associate professor** in U.S., Australia and New Zealand, a university or college teacher immediately below professor in rank. — **association of ideas** mental linkage that facilitates recollection — by similarity, contiguity, repetition. [L. *associāre*, *-ātum* — *ad*, to, *socius*, a companion.]

assonance *as'ən-əns*, *n* a correspondence in sound; vowel-rhyme, coincidence of vowels without regard to consonants, as in *mate* and *shape*, *feel* and *need*; extended to correspondence of consonants with different vowels; resemblance, correspondence. — *adj* **ass'onant.** — **assonantal** (*-ant'əl*). — *vi* **ass'onate** to correspond in vowel sound; to practise assonance. [L. *assonāre*, *-ātum* — *ad*, to, *sonāre*, to sound.]

assort *ə-sört'*, *vt* to distribute in classes, classify; to class, rank. — *vi* to match, or be in a class with (with *with*). — *adj* **assort'ative** (*-ə-tiv*). — *adj* **assort'ed** classified, arranged in sorts; made up of various sorts. — *n* **assort'er.** — *n* **assort'ment** an act of assorting; a quantity or number of things assorted; a variety. [Fr. *assortir* — L. *ad*, to, *sors*, *sortis*, a lot.]

ASSR *abbrev* for Autonomous Soviet Socialist Republic (an administrative division within the Soviet Union).

Asst or **asst** *abbrev* for Assistant or assistant.

assuage *ə-swāj'*, *vt* to soften, mitigate or allay. — *n* **assuage'ment.** — *n* and *adj* **assuag'ing.** — *adj* **assuā'sive** (*-siv*) soothing; mitigating. [O.Fr. *assouager* — L. *ad*, to, *suāvis*, mild.]

assume *ə-sūm'* or *-sōōm'*, *vt* to adopt, take in; to take for granted; to take up, take upon oneself; to claim or pretend to possess. — *vi* to make undue claims; to be arrogant. — *adj* **assum'able.** — *adv* **assum'ably.** — *adj* **assumed'** taken as the basis of argument; appropriated, usurped; pretended. — *adv* **assum'edly.** — *adj* **assum'ing** haughty; arrogant. — *n* assumption; arrogance; presumption. — *conj* (often with *that*) if it can be taken for granted that. — *adv* **assum'ingly.** — *n* **assumption** (*-sum'shən* or *-sump'shən*) an act of assuming; taking for granted; supposition; that which is taken for granted or supposed; arrogance; taking upon oneself; a taking up bodily into heaven, esp. (with *cap*) of the Virgin Mary (*Christian relig*). — Also *adj*. — *adj* **assump'tive** of the nature of an assumption; gratuitously assumed; apt, or too apt, to assume. [L. *assūmĕre, assūmptum* — *ad*, to, *sūmĕre*, to take.]

assure *ə-shōōr'*, *vt* to make sure or secure; to give confidence; to tell positively; to insure. — *adj* **assur'able.** — *n* **assur'ance** confidence; feeling of certainty; self-confidence; composure; audacity; positive declaration; insurance, now esp. life-insurance (i.e. against certainties rather than risks); security; the securing of a title to property; a promise; a surety or warrant. — *adj* **assured'** certain; confident; beyond doubt; secured; pledged; insured; self-confident; brazen, barefaced. — *n* a person whose life or property is insured; the beneficiary of an insurance policy. — *adv* **assur'edly** certainly, in truth, undoubtedly (also *interj*). — *n* **assur'edness.** — *n* **assur'er** a person who gives assurance; an insurer or underwriter; a person who insures his or her life. [O.Fr. *aseürer* (Fr. *assurer*) — L.L. *adsēcūrāre* — *ad*, to, *sēcūrus*, safe; see **sure.**]

assurgent *ə-sûr'jənt*, *adj* rising, ascending; rising in a curve to an erect position (*bot*). — *n* **assur'gency** the tendency to rise. [L. *ad*, to, *surgĕre*, to rise.]

Assyrian *a-* or *ə-sir'i-ən*, *adj* of Assyria. — *n* an inhabitant or native of Assyria; the Semitic language of ancient Assyria; a modern form of an Aramaic dialect still spoken, Syriac. — *n* **Assyriol'ogist.** — *n* **Assyriol'ogy** the science of Assyrian antiquities. [Gr. *Assyrios* — *Assyriā*.]

AST *abbrev* for Atlantic Standard Time, one of the standard time zones in N. Am., and the time in it.

astatic *a-stat'ik*, *adj* having no tendency to stand in a fixed position; without polarity, as a pair of magnetic needles set in opposite directions (*phys*). — *n* **astatine** (*as'tə-tēn*) a radioactive chemical element (atomic no. 85; symbol **At**) of the halogen series. [Gr. *astatos*, unstable.]

aster *as'tər*, *n* a starlike figure, as in mitotic cell-division (*biol*); (with *cap*) a genus of Compositae, a family of flowers with showy radiated heads, white to lilac-blue or purple, flowering in late summer and autumn, hence often called Michaelmas daisies; a plant of this genus or a related form; extended to the related **China aster** (*Callistephus hortensis*) brought from China to France by a missionary in the 18th century. [Gr. *astēr*, a star.]

asterisk *as'tə-risk*, *n* a star-shaped mark (*) used as a reference to a note, as a mark of omission, as a mark of a word or root inferred to have existed but not recorded, and for other purposes. — *vt* to mark with an asterisk. — *adj* **as'terisked.** [L.L. *asteriscus*, a small star — Gr. *asteriskos*, dimin. of *astēr*, a star.]

asterism *as'tə-rizm*, *n* a group of stars; three asterisks placed to direct attention to a passage; in some minerals the property of showing by reflected or transmitted light a star-shaped luminous figure. [Gr. *asterismos*, a constellation.]

asteroid *as'tə-roid*, *n* a minor planet. — *adj* resembling a star, starfish, or aster. — *adj* **asteroid'al.** [Gr. *asteroeidēs*, starlike.]

astern *ə-stûrn'*, (*naut* and *aeronautics*) *adv* in or towards the stern; behind. [**a-**[1] and **stern**[2].]

asthenia *as-thē'ni-ə* or *-thi-nī'ə*, *n* debility. — *adj* **asthenic** (*-then'ik*) of or relating to asthenia; lacking strength; of a slender type, narrow-chested, with slight muscular development (*anthrop*); belonging to a type thought prone to schizophrenia, having a small, light trunk and disproportionately long limbs (*psychol*). — *n* a person of asthenic type. [Gr. *astheneia* — *a-*, without, *sthenos*, strength.]

asthma *as'mə*, also *asth'*, *ast'* and in U.S. usu. *az'mə*, *n* a chronic disorder of the organs of respiration, characterised by difficulty of breathing, wheezing, and a tightness in the chest. — *adj* **asthmatic** (*-mat'ik*). — *adv* **asthmat'ically.** [Gr. *asthma, -atos* — *aazein*, to breathe with open mouth.]

astigmatism *ə-stig'mə-tizm*, *n* a defect in an eye, lens or mirror, by which rays from one point are not focused at one point. — *adj* **astigmatic** (*a-stig-mat'ik*). — *adv* **astigmat'ically.** [Gr. *a-*, without, not, *stigma, -atos*, a point.]

astilbe *as-til'bi*, *n* a plant of the *Astilbe* genus of perennial plants of the family *Saxifragaceae*, with clusters of red or white flowers. [Gr. *a-*, without, not, *stilbos*, glittering.]

astir *ə-stûr'*, *adv* on the move; out of bed, up and about; excited, roused; in motion. [**a-**[1] and **stir**[1].]

astonish *əs-ton'ish*, *vt* to amaze, stun; to impress with sudden surprise or wonder. — *adj* **aston'ished** amazed, stunned. — *adj* **aston'ishing** very wonderful, amazing. — *adv* **aston'ishingly.** — *n* **aston'ishment** amazement; wonder; a cause for astonishment. [Ult. from L. *ex*, out, *tonāre*, to thunder.]

astound *əs-townd'*, *vt* to amaze, to strike dumb with astonishment. — *adj* **astound'ed** stunned; dazed; amazed. — *n* **astound'ing.** — *adv* **astound'ingly.** [From the past p. of old verb *astone*, to astonish.]

astr. or **astron.** *abbrev* for astronomical or astronomy.

astraddle *ə-strad'l*, *adv* with legs wide apart. [**a-**[1] and **straddle.**]

astragal *as'trə-gəl*, *n* a small semicircular moulding round a column or elsewhere (*archit*); one of the bars that hold the panes of a window (*archit*; *Scot*). [Gr. *astragalos*, a vertebra, ankle-bone, moulding.]

astrakhan *as-trə-kan'*, *n* lambskin with a curled wool from the Middle East; a rough fabric made in imitation of it. — *adj* made of astrakhan; (of a lamb) of the type suitable for astrakhan production. [*Astrakhan*, a city in the U.S.S.R. on the Caspian Sea.]

astral *as'trəl*, *adj* belonging to the stars; starry; star-shaped. — **astral body** an astral counterpart of the physical body; a ghost or wraith. [L. *astrālis* — *astrum*, a star.]

astray *ə-strā'*, *adv* out of the right way, off course; away from correct behaviour, wrong; lost, out of correct place. [**a-**[1] and **stray.**]

astride *ə-strīd'*, *adv* in a striding position; with a leg on each side. — *prep* astride of; on either side of. [**a-**[1] and **stride.**]

astringent *ə-strin'jənt*, *adj* contracting, drawing together, styptic; having power to constrict or contract organic tissues; (of e.g. manner) sharp, austere, severe. — *n* an astringent agent, e.g. a cosmetic preparation to tone the skin. — *adv* **astrin'gently.** [L. *astringĕre, astrictum* — *ad*, to, *stringĕre*, to draw tight.]

astro- *as-trō-* or *as-tro'-*, *combining form* denoting: star; astrology. — *n* **as'trodome** a small transparent observation dome on the top of the fuselage of an aeroplane; a sports centre covered by a huge translucent plastic dome, orig. one at Houston, Texas. — *n* **astrometereol'ogy** the study of the influence, or supposed influence, of the stars, planets, etc. on climate and weather. — *n* **astronaviga'tion** the navigation of aircraft, spacecraft or sailing craft by means of observation of the stars. — *adj* **astrophys'ical.** — *n* **astrophys'icist.** — *nsing* **astrophys'ics** the science of the chemical and physical condition of the stars and of interstellar matter. [Gr. *astron*, star.]

astrol. *abbrev* for astrological or astrology.

astrology *as-trol'ə-ji*, *n* the study of the supposed influence of the movements and positions of the stars and planets on human and terrestrial affairs. — *adj* **astrolog'ical.** — *adv* **astrolog'ically.** [L. *astrologia*, (early) astronomy — Gr. *astron*, *logos*, discourse.]

astrometeorology, astronavigation, astrophysics. See under **astro-**.

astrometry *as-trom'ə-tri, n* the precise measurement of position in astronomy. [**astro-** and **-metry**.]

astronaut *as'trə-nöt, n* a person trained to engage in space travel. — *nsing* **astronaut'ics** the science of space travel. [**astro-** and *-naut* (— L. *nautes*, a sailor).]

astronomy *as-tron'ə-mi, n* the study of the celestial bodies and the heavens in all scientific aspects. — *n* **astron'omer** a scientist in the field of astronomy. — *adj* **astronom'ic** or **astronom'ical** relating to astronomy; prodigiously great, like the distance of the stars. — **astronomical unit** the earth's mean distance from the sun (*c* 92.9 million miles) used as a measure of distance within the solar system; **astronomical year** see under **year**. [L. *astronomia* — Gr. *astron*, star, *nomos*, law.]

Astroturf® *as'trō-tûrf, n* an artificial surface for sports pitches, etc., having a woven, grasslike pile on a rubber base (used esp. for American or Association football). — Also *adj*.

astute *as-* or *əs-tūt'* or in U.S. *əs-tōōt', adj* shrewd; perceptive, sagacious; wily. — *adv* **astute'ly**. — *n* **astute'ness**. [L. *astūtus* — *astus*, craft.]

asunder *ə-sun'dər, adv* apart; into parts; separately. [**a-**[1] and **sunder**.]

ASW *abbrev* for antisubmarine warfare.

asylum *ə-sī'ləm, n* a place of refuge for debtors and for those accused of crime; an institution for the care or relief of the unfortunate such as the blind or (*old-fashioned*) mentally ill; (any place of) refuge or protection: — *pl* **asy'lums**. — **political asylum** protection given to a person by one country from arrest in another; refuge provided by a country to a person leaving their own without the permission of its government. [L. *asȳlum* — Gr. *asȳlon* (neut.) inviolate — *a-*, without, *sȳlon*, *sȳlē*, right of seizure.]

asymmetry *ā-* or *a-sim'ə-tri, n* lack of symmetry, irregularity of form. — *adj* **asymmetric** (*-et'rik*) or **asymmet'rical**. — *adv* **asymmet'rically**. [Gr. *asymmetriā* — *a-*, without, *symmetriā*, symmetry.]

asymptote *a'sim-tōt*, (*math*) *n* a line, or sometimes a curve, that continually approaches a curve but never meets it. — *adj* **asymptotic** (*-tot'ik*) or **asymptot'ical**. — *adv* **asymptot'ically**. [Gr. *asymptōtos* — *a-*, not, *syn*, together, *ptōtos*, apt to fall.]

asynchronism *ā-* or *a-sing'krə-nizm, n* lack of synchronism or correspondence in time. — Also **asyn'chrony**. — *adj* **asyn'chronous**. [Gr. *a-*, not, *syn*, together, *chronos*, time.]

asyndeton *a-sin'də-ton*, (*gram, rhet*) *n* a sentence or construction in which the conjunctions are omitted. — *adj* **asyndet'ic**. [Gr. *asyndeton* — *a-*, not, *syndetos*, bound together.]

asynergy *a-* or *ā-sin'ûr-ji*, (*med*) *n* lack of coordination in action, as of muscles. [Gr. *a-*, not, *syn*, together, *ergon*, work.]

asystole *ā-* or *a-sis'to-lē*, (*med*) *n* inability of the heart to empty itself by contracting. — Also **asys'tolism**. [Gr. *a-*, without, *systolē*, contraction.]

AT *abbrev* for: administrative trainee; alternative technology; appropriate technology.

At (*chem*) *symbol* for astatine.

at *at* or *ət, prep* denoting (precise) position in space or time, or some similar relation, such as amount, response, occupation, aim, activity. — **at it** occupied in a particular way, doing a particular thing; up to some criminal activity (*colloq*); having sexual intercourse (*colloq*); **at that** see **that**; **get someone at it** to make someone excited, worked up or agitated; **where it's at** see **where**. [O.E. *æt*.]

ATA *abbrev* for: Air Transport Association (*US*); Air Transport Auxiliary.

atabrin or **atebrin** *at'ə-brin, n* mepacrine.

atactic. See **ataxia**.

ataman *at'a-man, n* a Cossack headman or general — a hetman: — *pl* **at'amans**. [Russ., — Ger. *Haupt*, head, *Mann*, man.]

ataraxia *at-ə-rak'si-ə* or **ataraxy** *at'ə-rak-si*, (*med*) *n* a state of calmness, tranquillity. — *adj* and *n* **atarac'tic** or **atarax'ic** tranquillising (drug). [Gr. *ataraxiā* — *a-*, not, *tarassein*, to disturb.]

atavism *at'əv-izm, n* appearance of ancestral, but not parental, characteristics; reversion to an ancestral, or to a primitive, type. — *adj* **atavist'ic**. [L. *atavus*, a great-great-great-grandfather, an ancestor — *avus*, a grandfather.]

ataxia *a-tak'si-ə* or **ataxy** *a-tak'si* or *at'aks-i, n* inability to co-ordinate voluntary movements (*med*; see **locomotor ataxy** under **locomotor**); lack of order. — *adj* **atact'ic** or **atax'ic**. [Gr. *ataxiā*, disorder.]

ATC *abbrev* for: air-traffic control; Air Training Corps; automatic train control.

ate *et* or *āt, pa t* of **eat**.

atebrin. See **atabrin**.

atelectasis *a-tel-ek'tə-sis*, (*med*) *n* incomplete inflation of a lung at birth; the collapse of a lung in an adult. — *adj* **atelectatic** (*-tat'ik*). [Gr. *atelēs*, incomplete, *ektasis*, stretching out.]

atelier *at'əl-yā, n* a workshop, esp. an artist's studio. [Fr.]

a tempo *ä tem'pō*, (*mus*) in time, i.e. revert to the previous or original tempo. [It.]

atheism *ā'thi-izm, n* disbelief in the existence of a god. — *n* **a'theist**. — *adj* **atheist'ic** or **atheist'ical**. — *adv* **atheist'ically**. [Gr. *atheos* — *a-*, without, *theos*, god.]

athematic *ath-i-mat'ik, adj* without a thematic vowel (*gram, linguis*); not using themes as a basis (*mus*). — *adv* **athemat'ically**. [**a-**[2] and **thematic**.]

Athene *a-thē'nē* or **Athena** *-nə, n* the Greek goddess of wisdom, the protecting goddess of Athens. — *n* **Athenaeum** (*ath-ə-nē'əm*) a temple of Athene; an ancient institution of learning, or literary university; a name sometimes taken by a literary institution, library, etc. — *adj* **Athenian** (*a-thē'ni-ən*) of Athens. — *n* a native or citizen of Athens or Attica.

athermancy *ath-ûr'mən-si*, (*phys*) *n* impermeability to radiant heat. — *adj* **ather'manous**. [**a-**[2] and Gr. *thermainein*, to heat.]

atheroma *ath-ər-ō'mə*, (*med*) *n* a cyst with porridge-like contents; a thickening of the inner coat of arteries. — *adj* **atherōm'atous**. — *n* **atherosclerō'sis** arteriosclerosis, or a form or stage of it. — *n* and *adj* **atherosclerotic** (*-ot'ik*). [Gr. *athērōma* — *athērē* or *athărē*, porridge.]

athetosis *ath-ə-tō'sis*, (*med*) *n* involuntary movement of fingers and toes due to a lesion of the brain. — *adj* **ath'etoid**. — *n* a spastic who has involuntary movements. [N.L. — Gr. *athetos*, without position, set aside, *athetēsis*, rejection.]

athlete *ath'lēt, n* a person who takes part in physical exercise, esp. contests of strength, speed, endurance or agility; a person who is active and vigorous. — *adj* **athletic** (*-let'ik*) relating to athletics; strong, vigorous; of a long-limbed, large-chested, muscular type of body (*anthrop*). — *adv* **athlet'ically**. — *n* **athlet'icism** (*-i-sizm*) practice of, training in, or devotion to, athletics. — *npl* or *nsing* **athlet'ics** athletic sports. — *nsing* the practice of athletic sports. — **athlete's foot** a contagious disease of the foot, caused by a fungus; **sexual athlete** see under **sex**. [Gr. *athlētēs* — *athlos*, contest.]

at-home. See under **home**.

-athon *-ə-thon* or **-thon**, *combining form* used to denote something long in terms of time and endurance, usu. a prolonged fund-raising event, e.g. *telethon, talkathon*. [After mar*athon*.]

athwart *ə-thwört', adv* sideways; transversely; awry; wrongly; perplexingly. — *prep* across. [**a-**[1] and **thwart**.]

atingle *ə-ting'gl, adj* and *adv* in a tingle, tingling. [a-[1] and **tingle**.]

Atlantean, Atlantes. See **Atlas**.

Atlantic *at-* or *ət-lan'tik, n* the Atlantic Ocean, extending from the Arctic to the Antarctic separating the continents of Europe and Africa from North and South America. — *adj* of, bordering on, relating to, the Atlantic Ocean. [Gr. *Atlas, Atlantos*, Atlas.]

Atlas *at'ləs, n* the Titan who bore the heavens on his shoulders (*Gr mythol*); the African mountain range into which, in Greek mythology, Atlas was transformed: — *pl* **Atlantes** (*at-lan'tēz*) a figure of a man serving as a column in a building. — *adj* **Atlantē'an** of Atlas; gigantic.

atlas *at'ləs, n* a book of maps, plates or the like; the vertebra supporting the skull (*anat*): — *pl* **at'lases**. [**Atlas**, whose figure used to appear on title-pages of atlases.]

ATM *abbrev* for automated (or automatic) teller machine.

atman *ät'mən*, (*Hinduism*) *n* the divine within the self. [Sans. *ātman*, self, soul.]

atmolysis *at-mol'i-sis*, (*chem* and *phys*) *n* a method of separating mixed gases by their different rates of passage through a porous septum. — *vt* **at'molyse** or **at'molyze** (*-līz*). [Gr. *atmos*, vapour, *lysis*, loosing.]

atmosphere *at'məs-fēr, n* the gaseous envelope that surrounds the earth or any of the celestial bodies; any gaseous medium; a unit of atmospheric pressure equal to the pressure exerted by a column of mercury 760 millimetres in height at 0°C, practically the same as standard atmosphere (see **standard**); a feeling of space and distance in a picture; any surrounding influence or pervading feeling (*fig*). — *adj* **atmospheric** (*-fer'ik*) or **atmospher'ical** of or depending on the atmosphere; having a perceptible atmosphere (e.g. of a place, music, etc.). — *adv* **atmospher'ically**. — *npl* **atmospher'ics** noises interfering with radio reception, due to electric disturbances in the ether. [Gr. *atmos*, vapour, *sphairă*, a sphere.]

atoll *at'ol* or *ə-tol', n* a coral island consisting of a circular belt of coral enclosing a central lagoon. [Name in Maldive Islands.]

atom *at'əm, n* the smallest particle in an element that can take part in a chemical reaction, consisting of a nucleus and one or more orbiting electrons; anything very small. — *adj* **atomic** (*ə-tom'ik*) pertaining to atoms; obtained by means of atomic fission, as **atomic energy** or **power**; driven by atomic power; heated by atomic power. — *adj* **atom'ical**. — *n* **atomicity** (*at-əm-is'i-ti*) the state or fact of being composed of atoms; the number of atoms in a molecule; valency. — *n* **atomisā'tion** or **-z-**. — *vt* **at'omise** or **-ize** to reduce to atoms; to reduce (a liquid or solid) to a fine spray or minute particles; to destroy by bombing. — *n* **at'omīser** or **-z-** an instrument for discharging liquids in a fine spray. — **atom** (or **atomic**) **bomb** a bomb in which the nuclei of uranium or plutonium atoms bombarded by neutrons split with explosive transformation of part of their mass into energy; **atomic energy** nuclear energy; **atomic mass unit** 1/12 of the mass of an atom of carbon-12; **atomic number** the number of units of charge of positive electricity on the nucleus of an atom of an element; **atomic pile** a device for the controlled release of nuclear energy, e.g. a lattice of small rods of natural uranium embedded in a mass of pure graphite which serves to slow down neutrons; **atomic theory** the hypothesis that all atoms of the same element are alike and that a compound is formed by union of atoms of different elements in some simple ratio; **atomic warfare** warfare using atomic bombs; **atomic weight** relative atomic mass (q.v.); **a'tom-smasher** (*colloq*) an apparatus for breaking up the atom, an accelerator. [Gr. *atomos* — *a-* (privative) and *tomos*, verbal adj. of *temnein*, to cut.]

atonal, etc. See **atony**.

atone *ə-tōn', vi* to make amends or reparation (with *for*); to make up for deficiencies. — *n* **atone'ment** the act of atoning; expiation; reparations; the reconciliation of God and man by means of the incarnation and death of Christ (*Christian theol*). — *n* **aton'er**. [**at one**.]

atony *at'ən-i, n* lack of muscle tone; debility; lack of stress or accent (*prosody*). — *adj* **atonal** (*ā-tō'nl* or *a-*; *mus*) not referred to any scale or tonic. — *n* **atonality** (*at-ə-nal'i-ti*). — *n* **atō'nalism**. — *adj* **atonic** (*a-ton'ik*) without tone; unaccented (*prosody*); debilitated. — *n* **atonic'ity** (*-is'*) debility, weakness. [Gr. *atoniā* — *a-* (privative) and *tonos*, tone, strength.]

atop *ə-top', adv* on or at the top. — *prep* on top of. [**a-**[1] and **top**[1].]

ATP *abbrev* for Automatic Train Protection.

Atracurium *a-trə-kū'ri-əm, n* a muscle-relaxing drug used in surgery.

atrium *ā'* or *ä'tri-əm, n* the entrance hall or chief apartment of an ancient Roman house; a central courtyard; a cavity or entrance (*zool*); either of the two upper cavities of the heart into which blood passes from the veins: — *pl* **a'tria**. — *adj* **a'trial**. [L. *ātrium*.]

atrocious *ə-trō'shəs, adj* extremely cruel or wicked; heinous; very grievous; execrable. — *adv* **atrō'ciously**. — *n* **atrō'ciousness**. — *n* **atrocity** (*ə-tros'i-ti*) atrociousness; an atrocious act. [L. *ātrōx*, *ătrōx*, *-ōcis*, cruel.]

atrophy *at'rəf-i, n* wasting away; degeneration; diminution of size and functional activity by disuse; emaciation. — *vt* and *vi* to (cause to) suffer atrophy; to waste away. — *adj* **at'rophied**. [Gr. *a-* (privative) and *trophē*, nourishment.]

atropin *at'ro-pin* or **atropine** (also *-pīn*), *n* a poisonous alkaloid found in deadly nightshade, used in medicine. [N.L. *Atropa belladonna*, — Gr. *Atropos* the Fate that cut the thread of life; see **belladonna**.]

Att. *abbrev* for Attorney.

attach *ə-tach', vt* to bind or fasten; to connect, associate; to join in action, function or affection; to seize (property) or to arrest (a person) (*law*). — *vi* to adhere, to be fastened; to be attributable (to). — *adj* **attach'able**. — *adj* **attached'**. — *n* **attach'ment** act or means of fastening; a bond of fidelity or affection; seizure of goods or person by legal process; a piece, etc. that is to be attached. [O.Fr. *atachier*, from *a* (— L. *ad*), and perh. the root of **tack**[1].]

attaché *ə-tash'ā, n* a junior member of an ambassador's staff; an attaché-case. — **atta'ché-case** a small rigid rectangular leather receptacle for documents, etc. [Fr., attached.]

attack *ə-tak', vt* to act against with violence; to assault; to criticise severely; to begin (a task or activity) vigorously; to begin to affect or act destructively upon. — *vi* to take the initiative in attempting to score (*sport*). — *vt* and *vi* (*mus*) to begin (a phrase or piece). — *n* an assault or onset; the offensive part in any contest; the beginning of active operations on anything; severe criticism or calumny; sudden onset or episode of illness; a performer's approach to a piece, dance, etc. or mode of beginning with respect to crispness, verve, and precision (*mus, ballet*, etc.); used collectively to designate the players in a team who are in attacking positions. — *adj* **attack'able**. — *n* **attack'er**. [Fr. *attaquer*.]

attain *ə-tān', vt* to reach or gain by effort; to accomplish. — *vi* to come or arrive. — *adj* **attain'able**. — *n* **attainabil'ity** or **attain'ableness**. — *n* **attain'ment** act of attaining; the thing attained; acquisition; (in *pl*) acquirements in learning. [O.Fr. *ataindre* — L. *attingĕre* — *ad*, to, *tangĕre*, to touch.]

attainder *ə-tān'dər*, *n* act of attainting; loss of civil rights through conviction for high treason (*law*); a stain, disgrace. [O.Fr. *ataindre* — see **attain**.]

attaint *ə-tānt'*, *vt* to convict; to deprive of rights by conviction for treason (*law*); to accuse; to disgrace, stain. [O.Fr. *ataint* — *attaindre*; see **attain**.]

attar *at'ər*, *n* a very fragrant essential oil made in Bulgaria and elsewhere, chiefly from the damask rose. [Pers. *atar*.]

attempt *ə-temt'*, *vt* to try, endeavour (to do, or with *n* of action). — *vi* to make an attempt or trial. — *n* an endeavour; a personal assault; any act that can fairly be described as one of a series which, if uninterrupted and successful, would constitute a crime (*law*). — *n* **attemptabil'ity**. — *adj* **attempt'able**. [O.Fr. *atempter* — L. *attentāre* — *ad*, *temptāre*, *tentāre*, to try — *tendĕre*, to stretch.]

attend *ə-tend'*, *vt* to wait on; to be present at; to go regularly to (a school, etc.). — *vi* to listen (to); to apply oneself, direct one's mind and efforts (with *to*). — *n* **attend'ance** the act of attending; presence; gathering of persons attending. — *adj* **attend'ant** giving attendance; accompanying. — *n* a person who attends or accompanies; a servant. — *n* **attendee'** used in the sense of 'attender' of a person attending a conference, attendance centre, etc. — *n* **attend'er**. — **attendance allowance** a grant paid to a person who needs the constant attendance of a nurse; **attendance centre** a centre where a young offender may be required to attend regularly, instead of serving a prison sentence. [L. *attendere*.]

attention *ə-ten'shən*, *n* an act of attending; steady application of the mind; heed; civility, courtesy; (in *pl*) courtship; the position of standing rigidly erect with hands by the sides and heels together (*mil*). — *interj* a cautionary word calling for someone's attention; an order to come to attention (*mil*). — *adj* **atten'tional** (*psychol*, etc.) relating to attention or concentration. — **attention span** the length of time for which a person can concentrate. — **draw (someone's) attention to** to direct (someone's) notice towards. [L. *attentiō*, *-ōnis*.]

attentive *ə-ten'tiv*, *adj* full of attention; courteous, mindful. — *adv* **attent'ively**. — *n* **attent'iveness**. [Ety. as for **attention**.]

attenuate *ə-ten'ū-āt*, *vt* to make thin or lean; to break down into finer parts; to reduce in density; to reduce in strength or value. — *vi* to become thin or fine; to grow less. — *n* **atten'uant** anything that attenuates. — Also *adj*. — *adj* **atten'uate** or **atten'uated** thin; thinned; dilute, rarefied; tapering. — *n* **attenuā'tion** process of making slender; reduction of intensity, density, force, or (of bacteria) virulence; in homoeopathy, the reduction of the active principles of medicines to minute doses; reduction in magnitude, amplitude, or intensity, arising from absorption or scattering (*nuc*, *telecom*). — *n* **atten'uator**. [L. *attenuāre*, *-ātum* — *ad*, to, *tenuis*, thin.]

attest *ə-test'*, *vt* to testify or bear witness to; to affirm by signature or oath; to give proof of, to manifest. — *vt* and *vi* to enrol for military service. — *vi* to bear witness (to). — *adj* **attest'able**. — *n* **attestation** (*at-es-tā'shən*) an act of attesting; administration of an oath. — *adj* **attest'ative**. — *adj* **attest'ed** certified free from the tubercle bacillus. — *n* **attest'er** or **attest'or**. [L. *attestārī* — *ad*, to, *testis*, a witness.]

Att.-Gen. *abbrev* for Attorney-General.

Attic *at'ik*, *adj* of Attica or Athens; chaste, refined, classical, in taste, language, etc., like the Athenians. — **Attic salt** refined, dry wit. [Gr. *Attikos* — *Attikē*, Attica.]

attic *at'ik*, (*archit*) *n* a low storey or structure above the cornice of the main part of an elevation; a room in the roof of a house. [The structure was supposed to be in the Athenian manner; see **Attic**.]

attire *ə-tīr'*, *vt* to dress, array or adorn. — *n* dress; any kind of covering. [O.Fr. *atirer*, put in order — *à tire*, in a row — *à* (L. *ad*), to, *tire*, *tiere*, order, dress; see **tier**.]

attitude *at'i-tūd*, *n* posture or position; a posture or position expressing some thought or feeling; a habitual mode of thought or feeling; a studied or affected posture; a position on one leg with the other leg extended behind (*ballet*); of an aircraft, the angles made by its axes with the relative airflow or with the horizontal; the tilt of a vehicle measured in relation to the surface of the earth as horizontal plane (*space flight*). — *adj* **attitud'inal**. — *vi* **attitud'inise** or **-ize** to assume affected attitudes. — *n* **attitud'iniser** or **-z-**. — *n* **attitud'inising** or **-z-**. — **strike an attitude** to assume a position or figure indicative of a feeling or emotion not really felt. [Fr. *attitude* or It. *attitudine* — L. *aptitūdō*, *-inis* — *aptus*, fit.]

atto- *at-ō-*, *pfx* one million million millionth, 10^{-18}. [Dan., Norw. *atten*, eighteen.]

attorney *ə-tûr'ni*, *n* a person legally authorised to act for another; a person legally qualified to manage cases in a court of law; a solicitor: — *pl* **attor'neys**. — *n* **Attorney-Gen'eral** the chief law-officer for England, the Republic of Ireland, a dominion, colony, etc.; in the United States, the head of the Department of Justice; also the legal adviser of a State governor. — **attorney at law** or **public attorney** a professional and duly qualified legal agent; **attorney in fact** or **private attorney** one duly appointed by power of attorney to act for another in matters of contract, money payments, and the like; **letter, warrant** or **power of attorney** a formal instrument by which one person authorises another to perform certain acts for him them. [O.Fr. *atorné*, past p. of *atorner*, — L.L. *attornāre*, to assign; see **turn**.]

attract *ə-trakt'*, *vt* to cause to approach otherwise than by material bonds; to draw (a crowd, attention, financial investment, etc.); to allure; to entice; to be liable to (tax) (*legal*, etc.). — *adj* **attract'able**. — *n* **attract'ant** something that attracts, esp. that effects communication in insects and animals. — *adv* **attract'ingly**. — *n* **attrac'tion** act of attracting; an attracting force; that which attracts. — *adj* **attract'ive** having the power of attracting; alluring. — *adv* **attract'ively**. — *n* **attract'iveness**. — *n* **attract'or**. — **Great Attractor** a powerful gravitational force of uncertain origin pulling certain galaxies, including our own, towards its source. [L. *attrahĕre*, *attractum* — *ad*, to, *trahĕre*, to draw.]

attrib. *abbrev* for: attributive; attributively.

attribute *ə-trib'ūt*, *vt* to ascribe, assign, or consider as belonging. — *n* (*at'rib-ūt*) that which is attributed; that which is inherent in, or inseparable from, anything; a quality or property; a virtue; a conventional symbol. — *adj* **attrib'utable**. — *n* **attribution** (*at-ri-bū'shən*) act of attributing; that which is attributed. — *adj* **attrib'utive** expressing an attribute; (of an adjective) placed immediately before or immediately after the noun it qualifies (*gram*). — *n* a word added to another to denote an attribute (*gram*). — *adv* **attrib'utively**. [L. *attribuĕre*, *-tribūtum* — *ad*, to, *tribuĕre*, to give.]

attrite *ə-trīt'*, *adj* worn by rubbing or friction; repentant through fear of punishment, not yet from the love of God (*theol*). [L. *attrītus* — *atterĕre* — *ad*, to, *terĕre*, *trītum*, to rub.]

attrition *ə-tri'shən*, *n* rubbing together; wearing down; imperfect sorrow for sin, arising from fear of punishment rather than love of God (*theol*); the wearing down of an adversary, resistance, resources, etc. (*fig*). — *adj* **attri'tional**. [**attrite**.]

attune *ə-tūn'* or in U.S. *-tōōn'*, *vt* to put in tune; to make tuneful (one's voice, song, etc.); to make to harmonise or accord; to accustom or acclimatise. — *n* **attune'ment**. [L. *ad*, to, and **tune**.]

Atty *abbrev* for Attorney.
At. wt. *abbrev* for atomic weight.
atypical *a-* or *ā-tip'i-kl, adj* not typical. [**a-**[2] and **typical**.]
AU *abbrev* for Ångström unit; astronomical unit.
Au (*chem*) *symbol* for gold.
auberge *ō-berzh', n* an inn. — *n* **aubergiste** (*ō-ber-zhēst'*) an innkeeper. [Fr., of Gmc. origin; see **harbour**.]
aubergine *ō'ber-jēn* or *-zhēn, n* the fruit of the egg-plant, the brinjal; its purple colour. — *adj* of this colour. [Fr. dimin. of *auberge*, a kind of peach — Sp. *alberchigo* — Ar. *al*, the, Sp. *pérsigo* — L. *persicum*, a peach.]
aubrieta *ö-brē'tə* or **aubrietia** *ö-brē'shyə, n* a plant of the purple-flowered Mediterranean genus (*Aubrieta*) of trailing cruciferous plants. [After Claude *Aubriet* (*c* 1665–1742), naturalist-painter.]
auburn *ö'bûrn, adj* reddish brown; orig. light yellow. [L.L. *alburnus*, whitish — L. *albus*, white.]
au courant *ō ko͞o-rã*, (Fr.) *adj* well up in the facts or situation.
auction *ök'shən, n* a public sale at which goods are sold to the highest bidder; auction bridge. — *vt* to sell by auction. — *adj* **auc'tionary.** — *n* **auctioneer'** a person who sells or is licensed to sell by auction. — **auction bridge** a form of bridge in which players bid to choose trumps. — **Dutch auction** a kind of auction at which the salesman starts at a high price, and comes down until someone bids; any of several other unconventional or informal types of auction. [L. *auctiō, -ōnis*, an increasing — *augēre, auctum*, to increase.]
audacious *ö-dā'shəs, adj* daring; bold; impudent. — *adv* **audā'ciously.** — *n* **audā'ciousness** or **audacity** (*ö-das'i-ti*). [Fr. *audacieux* — L. *audāx* — *audēre*, to dare.]
audible *öd'i-bl, adj* able to be heard. — *n* **audibil'ity** or **aud'ibleness.** — *adv* **aud'ibly.** [L. *audīre*, to hear.]
audience *öd'ī-əns, n* a ceremonial interview; an assembly of hearers or spectators; the listeners to a radio programme, viewers of a television programme, or even readers of a book, magazine, author, etc. [L. *audientia*, — *audīre*, to hear.]
audile *ö'dil* or *-dīl, adj* pertaining to hearing. — *n* a person inclined to think in terms of sound. [Ety. as for **audible**.]
audio *öd'i-ō, n* reproduction of recorded or broadcast sounds (also *adj*); short for **audiotypist** or **audiotyping**: — *pl* **aud'ios.** [Ety. as for **audible**.]
audio- *ö-di-ō-, combining form* pertaining to sound, esp. broadcast sound; pertaining to, using, or involving, audio-frequencies. — *n* **aud'io-engineer** a person concerned with the transmission and reception of broadcast sound. — *n* **audio-fre'quency** a frequency of oscillation which, when the oscillatory power is converted into a sound pressure, is perceptible by the ear. — *n* **aud'iogram** a tracing produced by an audiograph. — *n* **aud'iograph** a machine used to test a patient's hearing by transmitting sound waves directly to the inner ear. — *n* **audiol'ogist.** — *n* **audiol'ogy** the science of hearing esp. with reference to the diagnosis and treatment of hearing defects. — *n* **audiom'eter** an instrument for measuring differences in hearing; one for measuring intensities of sounds which, for specified frequencies, are perceivable by the ear. — *n* **aud'iotyping.** — *n* **aud'iotypist** a typist able to type directly from material reproduced by a dictating machine. — *adj* **audiovis'ual** concerned simultaneously with seeing and hearing. — **audiovisual aids** material such as pictures, closed-circuit TV, teaching machines, etc. used in the classroom. [Ety. as for **audible**.]
audit *öd'it, n* an examination of accounts by an authorised person or persons; a statement of account; a check or examination; an evaluation of a specified quantity or quality, as in *energy audit*, *efficiency audit*. — *vt* to examine and verify by reference to vouchers, etc. — *n* **aud'itor** a hearer; a person who audits accounts: — *fem* **aud'itress.** [L. *audītus*, hearing.]
audition *öd-ish'ən, n* a trial performance by an applicant for an acting, etc., position (also *vt* and *vi* with *for*); the sense, or an act, of hearing; mode of hearing. — *adj* **aud'itive** or **aud'itory** of, or related to, hearing. [Ety. as for **audit**.]
auditorium *ö-dit-ör'i-əm, n* in a theatre, or the like, the space allotted to the audience; the reception-room of a monastery: — *pl* **auditor'iums** or **auditor'ia.** [L. *audītōrius*, concerning a hearing.]
AUEW *abbrev* for Amalgamated Union of Engineering Workers. — **AUEW-TASS** (*-tas*) *abbrev* for Amalgamated Union of Engineering Workers Technical, Administrative and Supervisory Section.
au fait *ō fe*, (Fr.) well-acquainted with a matter; well-informed, expert (with *with*).
Aufl. *abbrev* for *Auflage* (Ger.), edition.
au fromage *ō fro-mäzh*, (Fr.) with cheese.
Aug. *abbrev* for August.
aug. *abbrev* for augmentative.
auger *ö'gər, n* a carpenter's tool for boring; an instrument for boring holes in the ground. — **au'ger-bit** an auger that fits into a carpenter's brace. [From *nauger* (*an auger* for *a nauger*) — O.E. *nafugār* — *nafu*, a nave of a wheel, *gār*, a piercer.]
aught *öt, n* ought; anything. [O.E. *ā-wiht* contr. to *āht* (whence **ought**), and shortened to *aht* (whence **aught**); *ā-wiht* is from *ā, ō*, ever, and *wiht*, creature, whit, wight.]
augm. *abbrev* for augmentative.
augment *ög-ment', vt* to increase; to make larger. — *vi* to grow larger. — *adj* **augment'able.** — *adj* **augment'ative** having the quality or power of augmenting; (of an affix or derivative) increasing the force of the original word (*gram*; also *n*). — *n* **augmentā'tion** increase; addition; the repetition of a melody in notes of greater length than the original (*mus*). — *adj* **augment'ed.** — *n* **augment'er** or **augment'or** a nerve that increases the rate of activity of an organ. — **augmented interval** (*mus*) one increased by a semitone. [L. *augēre*, increase.]
Augmentin® *ög-men'tin, n* a drug administered along with an antibiotic that prevents the antibiotic from being metabolised, and thus ensures its potency.
au gratin *ō gra-tẽ*, (Fr.) cooked covered with bread-crumbs or grated cheese, or with both.
augur *ö'gər, n* among the ancient Romans, a person who sought knowledge of secret or future things by observing the flight and the cries of birds; a diviner; a soothsayer. — *vt* to predict from signs. — *adj* **au'gural** (*ög'ū-rəl* or *-yər-əl*). — *n* **au'gurship.** — *n* **au'gūry** the art or practice of auguring; an omen. — **augur well (or ill) for** to be an encouraging (or discouraging) sign with respect to. [L.; prob. from *avis*, bird.]
August *ö'gəst, n* the eighth month of the year. [After the Roman emperor *Augustus*.]
august *ö-gust', adj* venerable; imposing; sublime; majestic. — *adv* **august'ly.** — *n* **august'ness.** [L. *augustus* — *augēre*, to increase, honour.]
Augustan *ö-gust'ən, adj* pertaining to the Emperor *Augustus*, or to the time in which he reigned (31 B.C.–A.D. 14) — the most brilliant age in Roman literature; hence pertaining to any similar age, as the reign of Anne in English, and that of Louis XIV in French, literature; classic; refined.
Augustine *ö'gəst-in, ö-gust'in* or **Augustinian** *-tin'i-ən, n* a person of any order of monks or nuns whose rule is based on the writings of St. Augustine; someone who holds the opinions of St Augustine, esp. on predestination and irresistible grace (*theol*). — *adj* **Augustin'ian** of or relating to St. Augustine. — *n* **Augustin'ianism.** — **Augustinian (or Austin) friars** or **hermits** the fourth order of mendicant

friars, wearing a black habit, but not to be confused with the Black Friars or Dominicans.

Aujeszky's disease *ow-yes'kis di-zēz'*, *n* a disease of pigs, with symptoms similar to those of rabies. [*Aujeszky*, a Hungarian scientist (d. 1933), who identified it.]

auk *ök*, *n* a short-winged, heavy-bodied bird of the family *Alcidae*. — *n* **auk'let** one of the smaller birds of the family. — **great auk** large, flightless auk, extinct *c* 1844; **little auk** an auk (*Plautus alle*) of the North Atlantic and Arctic Oceans. [O.N. *ālka*.]

au lait *ō lā*, (Fr.) with milk.

auld *öld*, (*Scot*) *adj* old. — **auld lang syne** lit. old long since, long ago. [O.E. *ald*.]

aumbry. See **ambry**.

au mieux *ō myø*, (Fr.) on the best of terms.

au naturel *ō na-tü-rel*, (Fr.) in the natural state; cooked plainly.

aunt *änt*, *n* a father's or mother's sister, or an uncle's wife or a great-aunt (used with *cap* as a title either before a woman's first name or independently); a woman to whom one can turn for advice, sympathy, practical help, etc. (*fig*); (usu. in dimin., with *cap*) a title sometimes used by children for female friends of their parents; (in dimin., with *cap*) a facetious name for the British Broadcasting Corporation or (*Austr*) the Australian Broadcasting Corporation. — *dimin* **aunt'ie** or **aunt'y**. — *adj* **aunt'ly**. — **Aunt Sally** a pastime in which sticks or balls are thrown at a dummy; a target for abuse (*fig*). [O.Fr. *ante* — L. *amita*, a father's sister.]

au pair *ō per*, (Fr.) orig. by mutual service without payment; used of an arrangement whereby girls perform light domestic duties in exchange for board and lodging and pocket-money. — *n* an au pair girl.

aura *ö'rə*, *n* a subtle emanation, esp. that essence which is claimed to emanate from all living things and to provide an atmosphere for occult phenomena; an air or distinctive character (*fig*); the peculiar sensations that precede an attack of epilepsy, hysteria, and certain other ailments (*pathol*): — *pl* **aurae** (*ö'rē*) or **au'ras**. — *adj* **au'ral**. [L. *aura*, a breeze.]

aural *ö'rəl*, *adj* pertaining to the ear. — *adv* **au'rally**. [L. *auris*, ear.]

aureate *ö'ri-ət*, *adj* gilded; golden; floridly rhetorical. [L. *aurum*, gold.]

aureola *ö'rē'ə-lə* or **aureole** *ö'ri-ōl*, *n* a crown, or an increment to the ordinary blessedness of heaven, gained by virgins, martyrs, and doctors (*theol*); the gold or coloured disc or ring round the head or whole body in a picture, symbolising glory; a glorifying halo (*fig*); a halo or corona around the sun or moon, or the clear space within it (*meteorol*); any halo-like appearance. [L. *aureola corona*, golden crown.]

Aureomycin® *ö-ri-ō-mī'sin*, *n* tradename for *chlortetracycline*, an antibiotic used against typhus and other diseases, obtained from Strepto*myces aureo*-faciens.

au revoir *ō rə-vwär*, (Fr.) goodbye until we meet again.

auric *ö'rik*, *adj* pertaining to gold; containing trivalent gold (*chem*). [L. *aurum*, gold.]

auricle *ör'i-kl*, *n* the external ear; an earlike appendage to an atrium in the heart, or the atrium itself; an earlike lobe of a leaf, etc. — *adj* **aur'icled** having appendages like ears. — *adj* **auric'ūlar** pertaining to the ear; known by hearing, or by report; told privately. — *adv* **auric'ūlarly**. — *adj* **auric'ūlate** (*-lət*) or **auric'ūlated** (*-lāt-id*) ear-shaped. — **auricular confession** confession to a priest. [L. *auricula*, dimin. of *auris*, the ear.]

auriferous *ör-if'ər-əs*, *adj* bearing or yielding gold. [L. *aurifer* — *aurum*, gold, *ferre*, to bear; *facĕre*, to make.]

auriscope *ö'ris-kōp*, *n* an instrument for examining the ear. [L. *auris*, ear, and **-scope**.]

aurist *ö'rist*, *n* a specialist in diseases of the ear. [L. *auris*, ear.]

aurochs *ör'* or *owr'oks*, *n* the extinct urus or wild ox; (erroneously) the European bison. [O.H.G. *ûr-ohso* — *ûr* (adopted into L. as *ūrus*, into Gr. as *ouros*), and *ohso*, ox.]

Aurora *ö-rö'rə*, *n* the dawn; the goddess of dawn; (without *cap*) a luminous atmospheric phenomenon of electrical character seen in and towards the Polar regions, with a tremulous motion, and streamers of light: — *pl* **auro'ras** or **auro'rae**. — *adj* **auro'ral**. — **aurora borealis** (*bö-ri-ā'lis* or *-ä'lis*) or **aurora septentrionalis** (*sep-ten-tri-on-ā'lis*) the northern aurora or northern lights; **aurora australis** (*ös-trā'lis*) the southern lights, a similar phenomenon in the southern hemisphere. [L. *Aurōra*.]

aurous *ö'rəs*, *adj* containing univalent gold. [L. *aurum*, gold.]

AUS *abbrev* for Australia, including Papua New Guinea (I.V.R.).

auscultation *ös-kəl-tā'shən*, *n* listening to internal bodily sounds as an aid to diagnosis, usu. with a stethoscope. — *vt* and *vi* **aus'cultate** to examine by auscultation. — *n* **aus'cultātor** a person who practises auscultation; an instrument for the purpose. — *adj* **auscultatory** (*-kul'tə-tə-ri*). [L. *auscultāre*, to listen.]

Auslese *ows'lā-zə*, (Ger.) *n* choice, selection; wine made from selected bunches of grapes.

auspice *ös'pis*, *n* an omen, esp. a good one; augury; (in *pl*) patronage. — *vt* **auspicate** (*ös'pi-kāt*) to foreshow; to initiate or inaugurate with hopes of good luck. — *adj* **auspicious** (*-pish'əs*) having good auspices or omens of success; favourable; fortunate; propitious. — *adv* **auspi'ciously**. — *n* **auspi'ciousness**. [Fr., — L. *auspicium* — *auspex*, *auspicis*, a bird-seer, from *avis*, bird, and *specĕre*, to look, to observe; see **augur**.]

Aussie *oz'i* or *os'i*, (*slang*) *n* and *adj* Australian.

Aussiedler *ows'sēd-lər*, (Ger.) *n* an immigrant. [Lit. out-settler.]

austere *ös-tēr'*, *adj* harsh; severe; stern; grave; severe in self-discipline; severely simple, without luxury. — *adv* **austere'ly**. — *n* **austere'ness**. — *n* **austerity** (*os-ter'it-i*) quality of being austere; severity of manners or life; harshness; asceticism; severe simplicity of style, dress or habits. — *adj* evincing or adopted in austerity. [L. *austērus* — Gr. *austēros* — *auein*, to dry.]

Austin. See **Augustine**.

Austr. *abbrev* for: Australia; Australian.

austral *ös'trəl*, *adj* (also with *cap*) southern. — *n* a unit of currency in Argentina. [L. *austrālis* — *Auster*, the south wind.]

Australasian *os-* or *ös-trə-lā'zhən*, *adj* pertaining to Australasia, or the lands that lie south-east of Asia. — *n* a native or inhabitant of one of these. [**Austral** and **Asian**.]

Australian *ös-trā'li-ən*, *adj* of, or pertaining to, Australia. — *n* a person native to or resident in Australia. — *n* **Austrā'lianism** an Australian idiom; feeling for Australia. — **Australia Day** (a public holiday celebrating) the anniversary of the founding of the colony of New South Wales on 26 January 1788; **Australian rules** or **Australian rules football** an Australian version of football played by eighteen a side with an oval ball (familiarly called **rules**). [L. *austrālis*, southern — *Auster*, south wind.]

Australopithecus *os-trəl-ō-pith'ə-kəs* or *-pi-thē'kəs*, *n* a genus of extinct primates, represented by skulls, etc., found in southern Africa. — *adj* and *n* **australopithecine** (*-pith'ə-sīn*). — **Australopithecus robustus** a proto-human species which lived between two and three million years ago. [**Austral**, and Gr. *pithēkos*, ape.]

Austrian *ös'tri-ən*, *adj* of or pertaining to *Austria*. — *n* native or citizen of Austria.

AUT *abbrev* for Association of University Teachers.

aut-. See **auto-**.

autacoid *ö'tə-koid, n* an internal secretion that excites or inhibits action in various tissues; a hormone or chalone. [Gr. *autos*, self, *akos*, drug.]

autarchy *öt'är-ki, n* absolute power; despotism. — *adj* **autar'chic** or **autar'chical**. — *n* **aut'archist**. [Gr. *autos*, self, *archein*, to rule.]

autarky *öt'är-ki, n* self-sufficiency. — *adj* **autar'kic** or **autar'kical**. — *n* **aut'arkist**. [Gr. *autarkeiā* — *autos*, self, *arkeein*, to suffice.]

authentic *ö-then'tik, adj* genuine; authoritative; true, entitled to acceptance, of established credibility; (of writing) trustworthy, as setting forth real facts; in existentialism, used to describe the way of living of someone who takes full cognisance of the meaninglessness of the world yet deliberately follows a consistent course of action. — *adv* **authen'tically**. — *vt* **authen'ticate** to make authentic; to prove genuine; to give legal validity to; to certify the authorship of. — *n* **authenticā'tion**. — *n* **authen'ticātor**. — *n* **authenticity** (*ö-thən-tis'i-ti*) the quality of being authentic; the state of being true or in accordance with fact; genuineness. — **authentic cadence** (*mus*) a perfect cadence. [Gr. *authentikos*, warranted — *autos*, self.]

author *öth'ər, n* a person who brings anything into being; a beginner of any action or state of things; the original writer of a book, article, etc. — *fem* **auth'oress**. — *vt* to write or originate. — *adj* **authorial** (*-thö'*). — *adj* **auth'orish**. — *n* **auth'orship**. [Through Fr. from L. *auctor* — *augēre*, *auctum*, to increase, produce.]

authorise or **-ize** *öth'ər-īz, vt* to give authority to; to sanction; to justify; to establish by authority. — *adj* **authorīs'able** or **-z-**. — *n* **authorisā'tion** or **-z-**. — **Authorised Version** the English translation of the Bible completed in 1611. [O.Fr. *autoriser*.]

authority *ö-thor'it-i, n* legal power or right; power derived from office, character or prestige; weight of testimony; permission; a person or body holding power; an expert; a passage or book referred to in witness of a statement; the original bestower of a name (*biol*). — *adj* **authoritā'rian** setting authority above liberty. — Also *n*. — *n* **authoritā'rianism**. — *adj* **authoritative** (*ö-thor'it-āt-iv* or *ö-thor'it-ət-iv*) having the sanction or weight of authority; dictatorial. — *adv* **author'itatively**. — *n* **author'itativeness**. [L. *auctōritas, -ātis* — *auctor*.]

autism *öt'izm, n* absorption in imaginative activity directed by the thinker's wishes, with loss of contact with reality; an abnormality of childhood development affecting language and social communication. — *adj* **autis'tic**. — *adv* **autis'tically**. [Gr. *autos*, self.]

auto *ö'tō, n* (chiefly *US*) short for **automobile**: — *pl* **au'tos**.

auto- *ö-tō-* or **aut-** *öt-, combining form* denoting: (1) self; (2) same; (3) self-caused; (4) automobile; (5) automatic. [Gr. *autos*, self.]

autoantibody *ö-tō-an'ti-bod-i*, (*med*) *n* an antibody produced in reaction to an antigenic constituent of the body's own tissues. [**auto-** (1).]

Autobahn or **autobahn** *ow'tō-bän* also *ö'tə-*, (Ger.) *n* a motorway.

autobiography *ö-tō-bi-og'rə-fi, n* a person's life written by him- or herself. — *n* **autobiog'rapher**. — *adj* **autobiographic** (*-ō-graf'ik*) or **autobiograph'ical** (*-l*). — *adv* **autobiograph'ically**. [Gr. *autos*, self, *bios*, life, *graphein*, to write.]

autobus *ö'tō-bus, n* a motor-bus. [**auto-** (4) and **bus**.]

autocar *ö'tō-kär, n* a motor car. [**auto-** (4) and **car**.]

autocephalous *ö-tō-sef'ə-ləs, adj* having its own governing body; independent. — *n* **autoceph'aly** the condition of being autocephalous. [Gr. *autos*, self, *kephalē*, head.]

autochanger *ö'tō-chān-jər* or **au'tochange** *n* (a record-player having) a device by means of which records are dropped from a stack one at a time on to the turntable. [**auto-** (5).]

autochthon *ö-tok'thon, n* one of the earliest inhabitants of a country; an aboriginal: — *pl* **autoch'thons** or **autoch'thonēs**. — *adj* **autoch'thonous** (of flora or fauna) indigenous; formed in the region where found (*geol*); found in the place of origin. — *n* **autoch'thonism** or **autoch'thony**. [Gr. *autochthōn*, sprung from the soil — *autos*, self, *chthōn*, *chthonos*, soil.]

autoclave *ö'tō-klāv, n* a strong, sealed vessel for carrying out chemical reactions under pressure and at high temperatures, or one in which super-heated steam under pressure is used for sterilising or cooking. [Fr., self-fastening apparatus — Gr. *autos*, self, perh. L. *clāvis*, key or *clāvus*, nail.]

autocrat *ö'tō-krat, n* a ruler with absolute power; a dictatorial person. — *n* **autocracy** (*-tok'rə-si*) an absolute government by one person; despotism. — *adj* **autocrat'ic**. — *adv* **autocrat'ically**. [Gr. *autokratēs* — *autos*, self, *kratos*, power.]

autocross *ö'tō-kros, n* a motor race round a grass field. [**auto-** (4).]

autocue *ö'tō-kū, n* a device showing a television speaker the text of what he or she has arranged to say. [**auto-** (5).]

auto-da-fé *ö-tō-da-fā', n* the public declaration of the judgment passed on heretics in Spain and Portugal by the Inquisition; the infliction of the punishment that immediately followed, esp. the public burning of the victims: — *pl* **autos-da-fé**. [Port. *auto da fé* (Sp. *auto de fe*); *auto* — L. *actum*, act; *da*, of the — L. *de*, of; and *fé* — L. *fidēs*, faith.]

autodestruct *ö-tō-di-strukt', adj* (of a craft, missile, etc.) capable of destroying itself; pertaining to the function of self-destruction. — *vi* to destroy itself. [**auto-** (1).]

autodidact *ö'-tō-dī'dakt, n* a self-taught person. — *adj* **autodidact'ic**. — *n* **autodidact'icism**. [Gr. *autodidaktos* — *autos*, self, *didaktos*, taught.]

autoerotic *ö-tō-ə-rot'ik, adj* relating to sexual excitement or gratification gained from one's own body, with or without external stimulation. — *n* **autoerot'icism** or **autoer'otism**. [**auto-** (1) and Gr. *erōtikos*, amorous — *erōtaein*, to love.]

autoexposure *ö-tō-eks-pō'zhər, n* a system for automatically adjusting the aperture and/or shutter speed of a camera according to the lighting conditions. [**auto-** (5).]

autofocus *ö'tō-fō-kəs, n* a device which automatically focuses a camera lens on the subject being photographed. — Also *adj*. [**auto-** (5).]

autogamy *ö-tog'ə-mi, n* self-fertilisation. — *adj* **autog'amous** or **autogamic** (*ö-tō-gam'ik*). [Gr. *autogamos*, breeding alone — *autos*, self, *gamos*, marriage.]

autogenesis *ö-to-jen'is-is, n* the production of life from inanimate matter; spontaneous generation. — *adj* **autogen'ic** pertaining to autogenesis; self-generated. — *nsing* **autogen'ics** (also **autogenic training**) a system of relaxation teaching voluntary control of bodily tension, etc. — *n* **auto'geny** autogenesis. [Gr. *autogenēs* — *genos*, offspring.]

autogenous *ö-toj'ə-nəs, adj* self-generated; independent; (of a graft, vaccine, etc.) produced from tissue, bacteria, etc. from the patient's own body; (of a joint) made without flux, etc., by melting edges together (*metalwork*). [Ety. as for **autogenesis**.]

autogiro or **autogyro** *ö-tō-jī'rō, n* an aircraft whose chief support in flight is derived from the reaction of the air upon freely-revolving horizontal rotors: — *pl* **autogi'ros** or **autogy'ros**. [Orig. trademark; invented by Juan de la Cierva; Sp., — Gr. *autos*, self, *gyros*, circle.]

autograft *ö'tō-gräft*, *n* a graft from one part to another of the same body. — Also *vt*. [**auto-** (2) and **graft**[1].]

autograph *ö'tō-gräf*, *n* one's own handwriting; a signature; an original manuscript. — *vt* to write with one's hand; to write one's signature in or on, to sign. — *adj* of painting, sculpture, etc., done personally by the artist, not by a pupil or follower. — *adj* **autographic** (*-graf'*). — *adv* **autograph'ically**. — *n* **autography** (*ö-tog'rə-fi*) the act of writing with one's own hand; reproduction of the outline of a writing or drawing by facsimile. — **autograph album** or **book** one in which to collect signatures, etc. [Gr. *autographos*, written with one's own hand — *autos*, self, *graphein*, to write.]

autoguide *ö'tō-gīd*, *adj* and *n* (of) a system whereby information on traffic conditions is collected by roadside sensors and relayed to drivers via receivers in their vehicles. [**auto-** (4) or (5).]

autogyro. See **autogiro**.

autoharp *ö'tō-härp*, *n* a kind of zither, with button-controlled dampers, which produces chords. [**auto-** (5).]

auto-immunisation or **-z-** *ö-tō-im-ū-nī-zā'shən*, *n* production by a living body of antibodies which attack constituents of its own tissues, perh. the cause of certain serious diseases (**auto-immune diseases**). — *n* **auto-immun'ity**. [**auto-** (1).]

auto-intoxication *ö-tō-in-toks-i-kā'shən*, *n* poisoning by substances produced within the body. — *n* and *adj* **auto-intox'icant**. [**auto-** (1).]

autologous *ö-tol'ə-gəs*, *adj* making use of blood or tissue obtained from (and stored for re-use in the treatment of) the same patient, prior to or during an operation or transfusion; derived from the same individual. [**auto-** and *-logous* (on the model of *homologous*).]

autolysis *ö-tol'is-is*, *n* the breaking down of tissue by the organism's own enzymes. — *vt* and *vi* **aut'olyse** or **-lyze** (*-līz*) to (cause to) undergo autolysis. — *adj* **autolyt'ic**. — **autolysed yeast powder** a flavour-enhancer derived from yeast. [Gr. *autos*, self, *lysis*, loosening.]

automat *ö'to-mat*, (*NAm*) *n* a cafeteria in which hot or cold food and drink is obtained from slot machines; a slot machine of this kind. [Ety. as for **automation**.]

automate *ö'tō-māt*, *vt* to apply automation to. [Back-formation from **automation**.]

automatic *ö-tə-mat'ik*, *adj* working by itself without direct and continuing human operation; (of a firearm) reloading itself from an internal magazine, or able to continue firing as long as there is pressure on the trigger; of (the gears of) a motor vehicle, operated by automatic transmission; (of a telephone system) worked by automatic switches; (of behaviour, reactions, etc.) done, etc., without thinking, mechanical; occurring as a matter of course. — *n* an automatic firearm, machine, etc.; the position of the switches, etc. on a machine, etc., that allows it to operate automatically. — *adv* **automat'ically**. — *n* **automaticity** (*-tis'i-ti*). — **automatic defibrillator** a small battery-powered device implanted in the body which senses and corrects abnormal heart rhythms; **automatic drive** automatic transmission; **automatic pilot** (also **au'topilot**) a device which can be set to steer an aircraft or ship on a chosen course; used (*fig*) of an automatism that takes over one's actions or behaviour in fatigue, abstraction, etc.; **automatic teller** see **automatic teller machine**; **automatic transmission** in a motor vehicle, power transmission by fluid drive, allowing gears to change automatically; **automatic writing** writing performed without the volition of the writer. — **automatic** (or **automated**) **teller machine** (also with *caps*; abbrev. **ATM**) an electronic panel set into the exterior wall of a bank, etc. which, on the insertion of one's cash card and the keying of one's personal identification number, dispenses cash or information about one's bank or building society account; **Automatic Train Protection** (abbrev. **ATP**) a system which automatically stops or slows down a train in response to a signal or speed restriction; **Automatic Vehicle Identification** (abbrev. **AVI**) a system for toll roads which recognises electronically-tagged vehicles and automatically charges the owner's account. [Gr. *automatos*, self-moving — *autos*, self.]

automation *ö-to-mā'shən*, *n* a high degree of mechanisation in manufacture, the handling of material between processes being automatic and the whole being automatically controlled. [Ety. as for **automatic**.]

automatism *ö-tom'ə-tizm*, *n* automatic or involuntary action; power of self-moving; power of initiating vital processes from within the cell, organ or organism, independent of any direct or immediate external stimulus; the self-acting power of the muscular and nervous systems, by which movement is effected without intelligent determination; action without conscious volition; suspension of control by the conscious mind, so that ideas may be released from the unconscious — a technique of surrealism (*art*). — *n* **autom'atist** a person who acts automatically. [Ety. as for **automatic**.]

automaton *ö-tom'ə-tən*, *n* a self-moving machine, or one that moves by concealed machinery; a living being regarded as without consciousness; a person who acts by routine, without intelligence: — *pl* **autom'atons** or **autom'ata**. [Ety. as for **automatic**.]

automobile *ö'tō-mō-bēl*, *n* a motor car. — *npl* **automobil'ia** collector's items of motoring interest. [Gr. *autos*, self; L. *mōbilis*, mobile.]

automotive *ö-tō-mō'tiv*, *adj* self-propelling; pertaining to automobiles; pertaining to the motor car trade. [Gr. *autos*, self, L.L. *motivus*, causing to move.]

autonomy *ö-ton'əm-i*, *n* the power or right of self-government, esp. partial self-government; (in the philosophy of Kant) the doctrine that the human will carries its guiding principle within itself. — *adj* **autonomic** (*ö-tō-nom'ik*) self-governing; pertaining to the autonomic nervous system; spontaneous (*bot*, *zool*). — *nsing* **autonom'ics** the study of self-regulating systems for process control. — *n* **auton'omist**. — *adj* **auton'omous** (of a country, etc.) wholly or partially self-governing; independent; (of the will) guided by its own principles (*philos*); autonomic (*bot*, *zool*). — **autonomic nervous system** system of nerve fibres, innervating muscles, glands, etc., whose actions are automatic. [Gr. *autonomos* — *nomos*, law.]

autopilot. See **automatic pilot** under **automatic**.

autopista *ow'tō-pēs-ta*, (Sp.) *n* a motorway.

autoplasty *ö'tō-plas-ti*, *n* grafting of healthy tissue from another part of the same body. — *adj* **autoplas'tic**. [Gr. *autos*, self, *plastos*, formed.]

autopsy *ö'top-si* or *ö-top'si*, *n* a post-mortem examination. — Also *vt*. — *adj* **autopt'ic** or **autopt'ical**. — *adv* **autopt'ically**. [Gr. *autos*, self, *opsis*, sight.]

autoradiograph *ö-tō-rā'di-ō-gräf*, *n* in tracer work, the record of a treated specimen on a photographic plate caused by radiations from the radio-isotope used. — *adj* **autoradiograph'ic**. — *n* **autoradiography** (*-og'rəf-i*) the production of autoradiographs. [**auto-** (1).]

auto-reverse *ö-tō-ri-vûrs'*, *n* and *adj* (a facility provided in a cassette player for) reversing the tape direction so as to play the following side on completion of the first, without turning the tape over manually. [**auto-** (5) and (1).]

autorickshaw *ö-tō-rik'shö*, *n* a light, three-wheeled vehicle powered by a motorcycle engine, used in India, etc. [**auto-** (4).]

autoroute *ō-tō-rōōt*, (Fr.) *n* a motorway.

autosome *ö'tō-sōm*, *n* a chromosome other than a sex-chromosome. — *adj* **autosom'al**. [Gr. *autos*, self, *sōma*, body.]

autostrada *ow'tō-strä-da*, (It.) *n* a motorway.

auto-suggestion *ö-tō-sə-jes'chən*, (*psychol*) *n* a mental process similar to suggestion, but originating in a belief in the subject's own mind. [**auto-** (3).]

autoteller *ö'tō-tel-ər*, *n* an automatic telling machine. [**auto-** (5).]

autotimer *ö'tō-tīm-ər*, *n* a device on a cooker, etc. that can be adjusted in advance to turn the apparatus on or off at a desired time. [**auto-** (5).]

autotomy *ö-tot'ə-mi*, (*zool*) *n* reflex separation of part of the body. [Gr. *autos*, self, *tomē*, cut.]

autotoxin *ö-tō-tok'sin*, *n* a poisonous substance formed within the organism against which it acts. [Gr. *autos*, self, and **toxin**.]

autotrophic *ö-tō-trof'ik*, (*biol*) *adj* capable of building up food materials from inorganic matter. — *n* **au'totroph** an autotrophic organism. [Gr. *autos*, self, *trophē*, food.]

autotype *ö'tō-tīp*, *n* a true impress or copy of the original; a process of printing from a photographic negative in a permanent pigment. — *vt* to reproduce by such a process. — *n* **autotypog'raphy** a process by which drawings made on gelatine are transferred to a plate from which impressions may be taken. [**auto-** (2).]

autrefois acquit *ōt-rə-fwä a-kē* or **autrefois convict** *kō-vē*, (*law*) *n* a defence plea, arguing that a defendant cannot be charged a second time with an offence of which he or she has been acquitted, or an offence of which he or she has been found guilty. [Fr.]

autumn *ö'təm*, *n* the third season of the year, when fruits are gathered in, generally (in the northern hemisphere) from August or September to October or November; astronomically, from the autumnal equinox to the winter solstice; a period of harvest or of maturity. — *adj* **autum'nal** (*ö-tum'nəl*) pertaining to autumn; blooming in autumn; beyond the prime; withering or withered. — *adv* **autum'nally**. — *adj* **au'tumny** (*-tə-mi*; *colloq*) autumn-like. — **autumn crocus** a species of *Colchicum*, meadow-saffron. [L. *autumnus*.]

auxesis *ök-sē'sis*, *n* increase in size; growth resulting from an increase in cell size. — *adj* **auxet'ic**. — *n* something that promotes auxesis. [Gr. *auxēsis*, increase.]

auxiliary *ög-zil'yər-i*, *adj* helping; subsidiary; peripheral (*comput*). — *n* a helper; a subordinate or assistant person or thing; an auxiliary verb (*gram*); (esp. in *pl*) a soldier serving with another nation; a naval vessel not used for combat. — **auxiliary verb** (*gram*) a verb that helps to form the mood, tense or voice of another verb. [L. *auxiliāris* — *auxilium*, help — *augēre*, to increase.]

auxin *öks'in*, *n* any of a number of growth-promoting substances present in minute quantities in plants. [Gr. *auxein*, to increase.]

AV *abbrev* for audio-visual; (or **A.V.**) Authorised Version.

Av. *abbrev* for Avenue (in street names).

av. See **ave**.

avadavat *av-ə-də-vat'* or **amadavat** *am-*, *n* an Indian songbird related to the weaver birds. [From *Ahmadabad*, whence they were sent to Europe as cagebirds.]

avail *ə-väl'*, *vt* to be of value or service to; to benefit (used reflexively with *of* in the sense of make use, take advantage). — *vi* to be of use; to answer the purpose. — *n* effectual advantage (esp. in phrases such as *of*, *to no avail*, *of any avail*). [L. *ad*, to, *valēre*, to be worth, to be strong.]

available *ə-väl'ə-bl*, *adj* at one's disposal; accessible; within reach; obtainable; to be had or drawn upon; valid (*law*). — *n* **availabil'ity** or **avail'ableness**. — *adv* **avail'ably**. [**avail** and **-able**.]

avalanche *av'ə-länsh* or *-länch*, *n* a hurtling mass of snow, with ice and rock, descending a mountainside; a snow-slip, as from a roof; an overwhelming influx; a shower of particles resulting from the collision of a high-energy particle with matter (*nuc*). — *vt* and *vi* to carry or come down as or like an avalanche. [Fr. dialect, *avaler*, to descend — *à* (L. *ad*), to, *val* (L. *vallis*), valley.]

avant-garde *av-ã-gärd'*, *n* those who create or support the newest ideas and techniques in an art, etc. — Also *adj*. — *n* **avant-gard'ism** avant-garde theory or practice, or support of these. — *n* **avant-gard'ist** a member of the avant-garde. [Fr. *avant-garde*, vanguard.]

avarice *av'ər-is*, *n* eager desire for wealth; covetousness. — *adj* **avaricious** (*-ish'əs*). — *adv* **avari'ciously**. — *n* **avari'ciousness**. [Fr., — L. *avāritia* — *avārus*, greedy — *avēre*, to pant after.]

avast *ə-väst'*, (*naut*) *interj* hold fast! stop! [Prob. Du. *houd vast*, hold fast.]

avatar *a-və-tär'*, *n* the descent of a Hindu deity in a visible form; incarnation; supreme glorification of any principle (*fig*). [Sans. *ava*, away, down, and root *tar-*, to pass over.]

avdp. or **avoir.** *abbrev* for avoirdupois.

ave *ā'vē*, *ä'vi* or *ä'vā*, (*RC liturgical* or *formal*) *interj* be well and happy; hail. — *n* an address or prayer to the Virgin Mary, in full, **ave Maria** (*ä'vā mə-rē'ə*) or **ave Mary**, the Hail Mary, or angelic salutation (Luke i. 28). [Imper. of L. *avēre*, to be well.]

ave. or **av.** *av*, *abbrev* for: avenue; average.

avenge *ə-venj'* or *-venzh'*, *vt* to take vengeance on someone on account of. — *adj* **aveng'ing**. — *n* **aveng'er**. [O.Fr. *avengier* — L. *ad*, to, *vindicāre*, to claim. See **vengeance**.]

avens *av'ənz*, *n* any plant of the rosaceous genus *Geum* (**water avens** *Geum rivale*; **wood avens** herb-bennet); also the related sub-alpine **mountain avens** (*Dryas octopetala*). [O.Fr. *avence*.]

aventurine *a-ven'chə-rin*, *n* a brown, spangled kind of Venetian glass; a kind of quartz enclosing spangles of mica or haematite (also called **gold'stone**). [It. *avventura*, chance — because of the accidental discovery of the glass.]

avenue *av'ən-ū* or in U.S. *-ōō*, *n* the principal approach to a country-house, usually bordered by trees; a double row of trees, with or without a road; a wide and handsome street, with or without trees; any passage or entrance into a place; means of access or attainment (*fig*). [Fr., — L. *ad*, to, *venīre*, to come.]

aver *ə-vûr'*, *vt* to declare to be true; to affirm or declare positively; to prove or justify (*law*): — *pr p* **averr'ing**; *pa p* **averred'**. — *n* **aver'ment** positive assertion; a formal offer to prove a plea (*law*); the proof offered (*law*). [Fr. *avérer* — L. *ad*, *vērus*, true.]

average *av'ər-ij*, *n* arithmetical mean value of any quantities; estimation of such a mean; (*loosely*) ordinary or prevailing value, common run; expense or loss by damage of ship or cargo; equitable distribution of expense or loss. — *adj* mean; prevailing, ordinary. — *vt* to obtain the average of; to amount to on an average; to do on an average. — *vt* and *vi* to even out to an average. — **average adjuster** an assessor employed by an insurance company in marine claims. — **law of averages** (*popularly*) a proposition stating that the mean of a situation is maintained by the averaging of its extremes. [Cf. Fr. *avarie*, It. *avaria*, duty on goods.]

averse *ə-vûrs'*, *adj* disinclined (with *to*; but some prefer *from*); reluctant; turned away from the main axis (*bot*). — *adv* **averse'ly**. — *n* **averse'ness** or **aver'-**

sion dislike; hatred; the object of dislike. — *adj* **aver'sive** showing aversion; with purpose, or result, of averting. — **aversion therapy** treatment of a person suffering from a compulsive form of behaviour by associating his or her thoughts about it with something unpleasant such as the administration of an electric shock. [L. *āvertěre*, *āversus* — *ab*, from, *vertěre*, to turn.]

avert *ə-vûrt'*, *vt* to turn aside; to prevent; to ward off. — *adj* **avert'ed.** — *adj* **avert'ible** capable of being averted. [Ety. as for **averse.**]

Avertin® *ə-vûr'tin*, *n* tradename of the anaesthetic *tribromoethanol*.

Aves *ā'vēz*, (L.) *ä'vās* or *-wās*, *npl* birds as a class of vertebrates. [L. *avis*, bird.]

Avesta *ə-ves'tä*, *n* the Zoroastrian holy Scriptures. — *adj* **Aves'tan** or **Aves'tic** of the Avesta or its East Iranian language. — *n* the language of the Avesta, also called Zend. [Pehlevi *Avîstâk*, lore.]

avgas *av'gas*, (*US*) *n* any kind of *av*iation *gas*oline.

avgolemono *av-gə-le'mə-nō*, (Gr.) *n* soup made from chicken stock, lemon juice and egg yolks.

AVI *abbrev* for Automatic Vehicle Identification.

avian *ā'vi-ən*, *adj* of or pertaining to birds. [L. *avis*, bird.]

aviary *ā'vi-ə-ri*, *n* a large cage or the like for keeping birds. — *n* **a'viarist** a person who keeps an aviary. [L. *aviārium* — *avis*, bird.]

aviate *ā'vi-āt*, *vi* to fly mechanically, navigate the air, a back-formation from **aviation.** — *n* **āviā'tion** the art or practice of mechanical flight. — *n* **ā'viātor** an airman or airwoman in the general sense. — *n* **aviatrix** (*ā-vi-ā'triks*) a female pilot. [Ety. as for **Aves.**]

aviculture *ā'vi-kul-chər*, *n* bird-rearing; bird-fancying. — *n* **avicul'turist.** [L. *avis*, bird, *cultūra*, — *colěre*, to cultivate.]

avid *av'id*, *adj* greedy; eagerly desirous. — *n* **avid'ity.** — *adv* **av'idly.** [L. *avidus.*]

avidin *a'vi-din*, *n* a protein found in egg-white which combines with biotin and prevents its absorption. [From *avid* and biot*in*.]

avifauna *ā'vi-fö-nə*, *n* the bird-life of a region. [N.L. — L. *avis*, bird, and **fauna.**]

avionics *ā-vi-on'iks*, *nsing* the science concerned with the development and use of electronic and electrical devices for aircraft. — *adj* **avio'nic.** [*avi*ation electr*onics*.]

avitaminosis *ā-vit-ə-min-ōs'is*, *n* lack of vitamins or a condition due to this. [**a-²**, **vitamin,** and **-osis.**]

AVM *abbrev* for: Air Vice-Marshal; automatic vending machine.

avocado *a-və-kä'dō*, *n* a tropical tree of the laurel family; (also **avocado pear** (*pār*)) its pear-shaped fruit; (also **alligator pear**); the colour of the skin of the fruit, blackish-green; the colour of the flesh of the fruit, yellowish-green: — *pl* **avoca'dos.** — Also *adj.* [Sp. *aguacate* — Aztec *ahuacatl.*]

avocation *av-ə-kā'shən*, *n* properly, a diversion or distraction from one's regular employment; improperly used for **vocation,** business which calls for one's time and attention. [L. *āvocātiō*, *-ōnis*, a calling away — *ab*, from, *vocāre*, to call.]

avocet *av'ə-set*, *n* a black and white wading bird (genus *Recurvirostra*) with a long, slender, upturned bill. [Fr. *avocette*, It. *avosetta.*]

Avogadro's constant or **number** *a-və-gä'drōz konst'ənt* or *num'bər*, *n* the number of specified elementary units (e.g. molecules) in a mole of any substance. — **Avogadro's law, rule** or **hypothesis** the law that at equal temperature and pressure equal volumes of gases contain the same number of molecules. [A. *Avogadro* (1776–1856), Italian physicist.]

avoid *ə-void'*, *vt* to evade; to shun. — *adj* **avoid'able.** — *n* **avoid'ance.** [A.Fr. *avoider*, O.Fr. *esvuidier* — L. *ex*, out, and root of **void.**]

avoirdupois *av-ər-də-poiz'*, *av'* or *av-wär-dū-pwä'*, *n* (*abbrev* **avdp.** or **avoir.**) a system of weights in which the lb. equals 16 oz.; (esp. *facetiously*) weight; heaviness or stoutness. — *adj* of the system of weights. [O.Fr. *aveir de pes*, to have weight — L. *habēre*, to have, *dē*, from, *pēnsum*, that which is weighed.]

avoision *ə-voi'zhən*, *n* a portmanteau-word coined by the Institution of Economic Affairs in 1979 to represent a compromise, and blurring of the moral distinction between, tax *avoi*dance (legal) and tax eva*sion* (illegal).

avow *ə-vow'*, *vt* to declare; to acknowledge; to maintain. — *adj* **avow'able.** — *n* **avow'ableness.** — *n* **avow'al** a positive declaration; an acknowledgment; a frank confession. — *adj* **avowed'.** — *adv* **avow'edly.** — *n* **avow'er.** [O.Fr. *avouer*, orig. to swear fealty to — L. *ad*, to, and L.L. *vōtāre* — L. *vōtum*, a vow: with sense affected by L. *advocāre*. See **vow.**]

avulsion *ə-vul'shən*, *n* forcible separation; tearing away; sudden removal of land by change of a river's course, whereby it remains the property of the orig. owner (opp. to **alluvion**). [L. *āvellěre*, *āvulsum*, to pluck or tear away.]

avuncular *ə-vung'kū-lər*, *adj* of or suitable to an uncle; benign, kindly. [L. *avunculus*, an uncle.]

AWACS *ā'waks*, *abbrev* for airborne warning and control system.

await *ə-wāt'*, *vt* to wait or look for; to be in store for; to attend. [O.N.Fr. *awaitier* — *à*, tō; see **wait.**]

awake *ə-wāk'*, *vt* to rouse from sleep; to rouse from inaction. — *vi* to cease sleeping; to rouse oneself from sleep or indifference: — *pa t* **awoke'** or **awaked'**; *pa p* **awōk'en, awoke'** or **awaked'.** — *adj* not asleep; vigilant; aware, cognisant (with *to*). — *vt* **awak'en** to awake; to rouse into interest or attention; to call to a sense of sin (*theol*). — *vi* to awake; to spring into being. — *adj* **awak'ening** becoming awake; rousing; revivifying, reanimating. — *n* a becoming awake, aware or active; a throwing off of indifference or ignorance; a rousing. — *n* and *adj* **awak'ing.** — **be awake to** to be fully aware of. [O.E. *āwæcnan* (past tense *āwōc*, past p. *āwacen*), confused with *āwacian* (past tense *āwacode*). See **wake¹** and **watch.**]

award *ə-wörd'*, *vt* to give officially as a payment or prize; to determine such payment, etc.; to grant. — *n* judgment; final decision, esp. of arbitrators; that which is awarded; a prize. [O.Fr. *ewarder*, *eswarder* — L. *ex*, in sense of thoroughly, and the root of **ward** and **guard.**]

aware *ə-wār'*, *adj* wary; informed; conscious (with *of*). — *n* **aware'ness** state of being aware; consciousness, esp. a dim form. [O.E. *gewær* — *wær*, cautious.]

awash *ə-wosh'*, *adv* on a level with the surface of the water; afloat at the mercy of the waves. — *adj* having the surface covered with water; full of (with *with*). [**a-¹** and **wash.**]

away *ə-wā'*, *adv* onward; continuously; without hesitation, stop, or delay; forthwith; out of the place in question; not at home; on the opponents' ground (*sport*; also *adj*); at or to a distance; off; in or into an averted direction; out of existence, life, or consciousness; with effect of removal or elimination; far; with omission of verb = go or (with *with*) take away (usu. *imper*). — *n* in football pools, a match won by a team playing on the opponents' ground. — *interj* go away!; get out! — **away from it all** in or into a place which is remote from the bustle of life; **do away with** to abolish; **explain away** to explain so as to make the thing explained seem not to exist; **fall away** to dwindle; to waste away; to lose enthusiasm and leave gradually; to slope down; **fire away** to go on, proceed now without further delay; **make away with** to destroy; to murder; to steal. [O.E. *aweg*, *onweg* — *on*, on, *weg*, way.]

AWE *abbrev* for Atomic Weapons Establishment.

awe *ö*, *n* reverential wonder or fear; dread. — *vt* to strike with or influence by reverence or fear. — *adj* **awed** (*öd*) awe-stricken. — *adj* **awe'some** awed; awe-inspiring; dreadful; amazing, great, impressive (*slang*). — *adv* **awe'somely**. — *n* **awe'someness**. —**awe'-inspiring**; **awe'-stricken** or **awe'-struck** struck with awe. [O.N. *agi*.]

aweather *ə-wedh'ər*, (*naut*) *adv* towards the weather or windward side (opp. to *alee*). [**a-**[1].]

aweigh *ə-wā'*, (*naut*) *adv* in the process of being weighed, as an anchor just raised from the bottom. [**a-**[1] and **weigh**[1].]

awful *ö'fəl*, *adj* very bad; unpleasant; inspiring awe. — *adv* very (*colloq*, esp. *Scot*). — *adv* **aw'fully** badly; reprehensibly; very, extremely. [**awe**.]

awhile *ə-(h)wīl'*, *adv* for some time; for a short time. [O.E. *āne hwīle*, a while (dative).]

awkward *ök'wərd*, *adj* clumsy; ungraceful; embarrassed; difficult to deal with; embarrassing. — *adj* **awk'wardish**. — *adv* **awk'wardly**. — *n* **awk'wardness** clumsiness; embarrassing or inharmonious quality or condition. [Prob. O.N. *afug*, turned the wrong way, and sfx. *-ward*.]

awl *öl*, *n* a pointed instrument for boring small holes. [O.E. *æl*.]

awn *ön*, *n* the beard of barley, or similar bristly growth. — *adj* **awned**. [O.N. *ögn* or a lost O.E. cognate.]

awning *ön'ing*, *n* a covering, usu. canvas, to shelter from the sun or weather. — *vt* **awn** to shelter with an awning.

awoke *ə-wōk'*, *pa t* of **awake**.

AWOL *ā'wol*, *abbrev* for absent, or absence, without official leave.

AWRE *abbrev* for Atomic Weapons Research Establishment.

awry *ə-rī'*, *adj* twisted to one side; distorted, crooked; wrong; perverse. — *adv* askew; unevenly; perversely; erroneously. — **look awry** to look askance at anything. [**a-**[1] and **wry**.]

AWU *ā'wōō*, *abbrev* for atomic weight unit.

axe or in U.S. **ax** *aks*, *n* a tool for hewing or chopping, with edge and handle in the same plane; a stone-dressing hammer; ruthless cutting down of expenditure (*fig*): — *pl* **ax'es**. — *vt* to hew or strike with an axe; to dismiss as superfluous; to cut down, reduce (*fig*); to dispense with (*fig*). — **axe'-breaker** (*Austr*) any of several kinds of hard-wooded tree. — **axe to grind** a private purpose to serve. [O.E. *æx*.]

axel *aks'l*, (*figure skating*) *n* a jump from one skate to the other, incorporating one and a half (or **double axel**) two and a half turns in the air. [*Axel* Paulsen (1855–1938), a Norw. skater.]

axerophthol *aks-ər-of'thol*, *n* vitamin A. [**a-**[2] and **xerophthalmia**.]

axes. See under **axe, axis**.

axial, axile. See under **axis**.

axilla *ak-sil'ə*, *n* the armpit (*anat*); axil (*bot*): — *pl* **axillae** (*-ē*). — *n* **ax'il** the angle between leaf and stem. — *adj* **ax'illar** or **ax'illary**. [L. *āxilla*, the armpit.]

axiology *aks-i-ol'ə-ji*, *n* the science of the ultimate nature, reality, and significance of values. — *adj* **axiological** (*-ə-loj'i-kl*). — *n* **axiologist** (*-ol'ə-jist*). [Gr. *axios*, worthy, *logos*, discourse.]

axiom *aks'i-əm*, *n* a self-evident truth; a universally received principle; an assumption made for the purpose of argument. — *adj* **axiomat'ic** or **axiomat'ical**. — *adv* **axiomat'ically**. — *nsing* **axiomat'ics** the study of axioms and axiom systems. [Gr. *axiōma*, *-atos* — *axioein*, to think worth, to take for granted — *axios*, worthy.]

axis *ak'sis*, *n* a line about which a body rotates, or about which a figure is conceived to revolve; a straight line about which the parts of a figure, body or system are symmetrically or systematically arranged; a fixed line adopted for reference in co-ordinate geometry, curve-plotting, crystallography, etc.; the second vertebra of the neck (*zool*); the main stem or root, or a branch in relation to its own branches and appendages (*bot*); an alliance of powers, as if forming together an axis of rotation — esp. of Germany and Italy (1936): — *pl* **axes** (*ak'sēz*). — *adj* **ax'ial** relating to, or of the nature of, an axis. — *adv* **ax'ially**. — *adj* **ax'ile** (*ak'sīl*) coinciding with an axis. — **axis of incidence** the line passing through the point of incidence of a ray perpendicularly to the refracting surface; **axis of refraction** the continuation of the same line through the refracting medium; **axis of the equator** the polar diameter of the earth which is also the axis of rotation. [L. *axis*.]

axle *aks'l*, *n* the rod in the hub of a wheel on which the wheel turns; a pivot or support of any kind. — **ax'le-box** the box in which the axle end turns. [More prob. O.N. *öxull* than a dimin. from O.E. *eax*.]

Axminster *aks'min-stər*, *n* a variety of cut-pile carpet, the tufts of pile each being inserted separately into the backing during its weaving. — Also *adj*. [*Axminster* in Devon, where it originated.]

axolotl *aks'ə-lot-l*, *n* the larval form of Amblystoma, commonly retaining its larval character throughout life, though capable of breeding. [Aztec.]

axon *ak'son*, *n* an extension of a nerve cell or neuron which in most cases transmits impulses away from the cell. [N.L. — Gr. *axōn*, axis.]

ay. See **aye**.

ayatollah *a-yə-tol'ə* or *-tō'lə*, *n* (sometimes with *cap*) a Muslim religious leader of the Shiah sect; an ideological leader or policy-maker. [Ar. *ayatollah*, sign of God — *āya*, sign, *ollāh*, God.]

aye or **ay** *ī*, *adv* yea; yes; indeed. — *n* a vote in the affirmative; a person who votes affirmatively. — *interj* **aye aye** expressing affirmation or agreement (*naut*). — **the ayes have it** (in Parliament) affirmative votes are in the majority. [Prob. dialect *aye*, ever, or **yea**.]

Aylesbury *ālz'bər-i*, *n* a breed of ducks much valued as food. — Also *adj*. [*Aylesbury*, a market town in Buckinghamshire.]

Ayrshire *ār'shər*, *n* a breed of reddish-brown and white dairy cattle. — Also *adj*. [*Ayrshire*, a former Scottish county, where they originated.]

ayu *ä'ū* or *ī'ōō*, also **ai** *ī*, *n* a small edible Japanese fish (*Plecoglossus altevis*). — Also called **sweet'fish**. [Jap.]

Ayurveda *ä-yŏŏr-vā'də*, *n* the body of classical Indian medical teaching. — *adj* **ayurve'dic**. [Sanskrit, knowledge of long life.]

AZ *abbrev* for Arizona (U.S. state).

az-. See **azo-**.

azalea *a-zā'li-ə*, *n* a plant of the *Azalea* genus closely related to, or subgenus of, *Rhododendron*, shrubby plants, with five stamens and annual leaves. [Gr. *azaleos*, dry; reason for name uncertain.]

azan *ä-zän'*, *n* the Muslim call to public prayer made five times a day by a muezzin. [Ar. *'adhan*, invitation.]

Azania *a-zā'ni-ə* or *-zä'ni-ə*, *n* a name given by some black activists to South Africa. — *adj* **Aza'nian**.

Azapo *a-za'pō*, *abbrev* for Azanian People's Organisation.

azathioprine *az-ə-thī'ə-prēn*, *n* a synthetic drug used in transplant surgery to suppress the body's immune system. [**azo-**, **thio-** and **purin**.]

azeotrope *ə-zē'ə-trōp*, *n* any liquid mixture which distils over without decomposition in a certain ratio, the boiling-point of the mixture differing from that of any constituent. — *adj* **azeotrop'ic** (*-trop'*). [Gr. *a-* (privative), *zeein*, to boil, and *tropos*, a turn.]

Azerbaijani *a-zər-bī-jä'ni* or *-zhä'ni*, *n* a native or inhabitant of the Soviet Socialist Republic of Azerbaijan; the Turkic language of Azerbaijan; a speaker of Azerbaijani in the neighbouring state of Iran. — Also *n*.

azide *a'* or *ā'zīd*, *n* a salt or an ester derived from hydrazoic acid. [**az-** and *-ide*.]

azimuth *az'im-əth*, *n* the arc of the horizon between the meridian of a place and a vertical circle passing through any celestial body. — *adj* **az'imuthal** (or *-mūdh'* or *-mūth'*) pertaining to the azimuth. [Ar. *as-sumūt*, *as* = *al*, the, *sumūt*, pl. of *samt*, direction. See **zenith**.]

azine *ā'zēn* or *-zin*, *n* any six-membered organic compound containing one or more nitrogen atoms. [**azo-**.]

azo- or **az-** *ā-z(o)-* or *az-(o)-*, *combining form* denoting nitrogen. — *n* **azo-ben'zene** a yellow or orange crystalline substance used in dyeing. — *n* **azo-com'pound** a compound in which two nitrogen atoms are each attached to (usu.) a carbon atom. — *n* **az'o-dye** a dye containing an azo-compound. [*azote*, an old name for nitrogen.]

azoic *a-zō'ik*, *adj* without life; before the existence of animal life; containing no organic traces (*geol*). [Gr. *a-* without, *zōē*, life.]

azolla *a-zol'ə*, *n* a fern of the *Azolla* genus of tiny water ferns. [N.L., app. formed from Gr. *azein*, to dry, *ollynai*, to destroy.]

azonal *ā-* or *a-zōn'əl*, *adj* not arranged in zones or regions. — *adj* **azonic** (*a-zon'ik*) not limited to a zone, not local. [Gr. *a-*, without, *zōnē*, a belt.]

AZT *abbrev* for azidothymidine, a drug used in the treatment of AIDS.

Aztec *az'tek*, *n* one of a people dominant in Mexico before the Spanish conquest; the language of this people, Nahuatl. — Also *adj*.

azure *azh'ər*, *ā'zhər* or *ā'zhūr*, *adj* of a faint blue; sky-coloured; blue (*heraldry*). — *n* a delicate blue colour; the sky. [O.Fr. *azur* — L.L. *azura* — Ar. (*al*) *lazward*, Pers. *lājward*, lapis lazuli, blue colour.]

azygous *az'i-gəs*, *adj* not yoked or joined with another; unpaired (*anat*). — *n* **azygy** (*az'i-ji*). [Gr. *azygos* — *a-*, without, *zygon*, a yoke.]

azymous *az'i-məs*, *adj* unfermented; unleavened. — *n* **az'yme** (*-īm* or *-im*) unleavened bread used in the Eucharist. [Gr. *azȳmos* — *a-*, without, *zȳmē*, leaven.]

B

B or **b** *bē*, *n* the second letter in the modern English alphabet; the seventh note of the scale of C major (*mus*); the subsidiary series of paper sizes, ranging from B0 (1000 × 1414 mm.) to B10 (31 × 44 mm.); something of a second class or order (such as a road of secondary importance), or a class arbitrarily designated B; one of the four types of blood in the ABO blood group system; a designation indicating lesser importance, secondary billing, etc. (such as the **B'-side** of a record, or a **B'-movie**).

B or **B.** *abbrev* for: Bachelor; Baron; bass (*mus*); Belgium (I.V.R.); bishop (*chess*); Britain; British.

B *symbol* for baryon number (*phys*); black (on lead pencils to indicate softness); boron (*chem*).

B *symbol* for magnetic flux density.

B- (*aeronautics*) *pfx* used to designate a bomber plane.

b or **b.** *abbrev* for: barrel(s); billion; book; born; bowled (*cricket*).

b *abbrev* for breadth.

BA *abbrev* for: Bachelor of Arts; Booksellers' Association (of Great Britain and Ireland); British Academy, a body promoting literary and social studies; British Airways.

Ba (*chem*) *symbol* for barium.

BAA *abbrev* for British Airports Authority.

baa *bä*, *n* the cry of a sheep. — *vi* to bleat. — *n* **baa'ing.** [Imit.]

BAAS *abbrev* for British Association for the Advancement of Science.

baas *bäs*, (*SAfr*) *n* master, overseer, sir (esp. as used by a black South African addressing a white). — *n* **baas'skap** the condition in which one section of the population is treated as a master race; the theory used to justify this. [Afrik. — Du.]

baba *bä'bä*, *n* a small cake, leavened with yeast, with or without fruit, soaked in a rum syrup. — Also **rum baba** or **baba au rhum** (*ō rom*). [Fr. — Pol. *baba*, 'old woman'.]

babaco *bə-bak'ō*, *n* a subtropical five-sided fruit related to papaya, orig. from Ecuador.

babacoote *bab'ə-ko͞ot*, *n* a large lemur, the indri or a closely related species. [Malagasy *babakoto*.]

Babbitt metal or **Babbitt's metal** *bab'it* or *bab'itz met'l*, *n* a soft anti-friction alloy (tin, with copper antimony, and usu. lead). [Isaac *Babbitt* (1799–1862), the Massachusetts inventor.]

babble *bab'l*, *vi* to speak like a baby; to make a continuous murmuring sound like a brook, etc.; to talk incessantly; to tell secrets. — *vt* to say in a confused, uncontrolled or unthinking way; to divulge by foolish talk. — *n* idle senseless talk; confused murmuring, as of a stream. — *n* **babb'ler.** — *n* and *adj* **babb'ling.** — *adj* **babb'ly.** [Prob. imit.]

babe *bāb*, *n* a form of **baby**.

Babel *bā'bl*, *n* (also without *cap*) a confused sound of voices; (also without *cap*) a scene of confusion; a foolishly conceived lofty structure. — *n* **Bā'beldom.** — *n* **Bā'belism.** — *adj* **Bā'belish** or **Bab'elesque.** [Heb. *Bābel*, prob. Assyr. *bāb-ili*, gate of God.]

babiche *ba-bēsh'*, *n* thongs or laces made of rawhide. [Fr.-Can., from Algonquian.]

babiroussa, babirussa or **babirusa** *bä-bi-ro͞o'sə*, *n* a wild hog found esp. in Sulawesi, Indonesia, with great upturned tusks in the male. [Malay *bābi*, hog, *rūsa*, deer.]

baboo. See **babu**.

baboon *bə-bo͞on'*, *n* a large monkey, with a long face, doglike tusks, and a tail; a clumsy, brutish person. — *adj* **baboon'ish.** [M.E. *babewyn*, grotesque figure, baboon — O.Fr. *babuin*.]

babouche, babuche or **baboosh** *bə-bo͞osh'*, *n* an Oriental heelless slipper. [Fr., — Ar. *bābūsh* — Pers. *pā*, foot, *pūsh*, covering.]

babu or **baboo** *bä'bo͞o*, *n* a title for Hindus in some parts of India corresponding to Mr; an Indian clerk, etc. educated to some extent in English (esp. *hist*). — Also *adj*. [Hind. *bābū*.]

babuche. See **babouche.**

babushka *bə-bo͞osh'kə*, *n* a triangular headscarf tied under the chin; a grandmother, granny. [Russ. *bábushka*, grandmother, dimin. of *baba*, old woman.]

baby *bā'bi*, *n* an infant, young child; an unborn child; a young animal; a babyish person; something small of its kind; a girl, girlfriend (*colloq*); an inexperienced person; one's pet project, machine, etc.; one's own responsibility. — *vt* to treat as a baby. — Also *adj*. — *n* **ba'byhood.** — *adj* **ba'byish.** — **ba'by-batterer** a person who indulges in **ba'by-battering** in instances of the **battered baby syndrome** (q.v. under **batter**[1]); **baby boom** (*colloq*) (a period of) increase in the birth-rate; **baby boomer** a person born during a baby boom, esp. that which followed World War II; **ba'by-bouncer** or **-jumper** a harness or seat suspended from springs, elastic straps, etc. in which a young baby can amuse itself; **Baby Buggy®** a light, collapsible pushchair for a baby or toddler; **baby face** a young-looking face, esp. one plump and smooth like a baby's; someone with such a face; **baby grand** a small grand piano, about 2 metres in length; **Ba'bygro®** an all-in-one stretch-fabric suit for a baby: — *pl* **Ba'bygros; ba'by-minder** a person who takes in infants to look after for pay. — *vi* (and esp. in U.S. *vt*) **ba'by-sit** to act as baby-sitter (to). — **ba'by-sitter** a person who looks after a baby or child to relieve the usual attendant; **ba'by-sitting; ba'by-snatcher** a person who steals a baby, e.g. from its pram; **ba'by-snatching; ba'by-talk** the speech of babies learning to talk, or an adult's imitation of it; **ba'by-walker** a wheeled frame with a canvas, etc. seat for supporting a baby learning to walk. — **be left holding the baby** to be left in the lurch with an irksome responsibility; **throw out the baby with the bathwater** to get rid of the essential along with the superfluous. [Prob. imit.]

Babylon *bab'i-lon*, *n* a place of sorrowful exile; a place, etc. of luxury and decadence, used (*derog*) formerly by Protestants in reference to the Roman Catholic Church, more recently by Rastafarians of western culture. — *adj* **Babylō'nian** of Babylon; huge, gigantic.

BAC *abbrev* for British Aircraft Corporation.

baccalaureate *bak-ə-lö'ri-āt*, *n* the university degree of bachelor or a diploma of lesser status awarded by a college, etc. — *adj* **baccalau'rean.** [L.L. *baccalaureus*, altered from *baccalārius*. See **bachelor.**]

baccarat or **baccara** *bak'ə-rä*, *n* a French card game played by betters and a banker.

Bacchus *bak'əs, n* the Greek and Roman god of wine. — *n* **bacchanal** (*bak'ə-nəl*) a worshipper, priest or priestess, of Bacchus; a drunken reveller; a dance, song, or revel in honour of Bacchus. — *adj* relating to drinking or drunken revels. — *npl* **bacchanā'lia** or **bacch'anals** feasts in honour of Bacchus; drunken revels. — *n* **bacchanalian** (*-nā'li-ən*) a drunken reveller. — *adj* bacchanal. — *n* **bacchanā'lianism.** — *n* and *adj* **bacchant** (*bak'ant*) a priest or votary of Bacchus; a reveller; a drunkard. — *n* **bacchante** (*bə-kant'*, *bak'ant* or *ba-kant'i*) a priestess of Bacchus; a female bacchanal. — *adj* **Bacch'ian** or **Bacchic** (*bak'ik*) relating to Bacchus; jovial; drunken. [L. *Bacchus*, Gr. *Bakchos*.]

baccy *bak'i* or **bacco** *bak'o*, colloq. short forms of **tobacco.**

Bach. or **bach.** *abbrev* for Bachelor or bachelor.

bachelor *bach'əl-ər, n* an unmarried man; a person who has taken his or her first degree at a university; a young unmated bull-seal or other male animal. — *n* **bach** or **batch** (*Austr* and *NZ colloq*) a bachelor. — *vi* to live as a bachelor; to do for oneself. — Also *vt* with *it*. — *n* **bach'elordom** or **bach'elorhood.** — *n* **bach'elorship** the degree of bachelor. — **bachelor flat** or (*slang*) **pad** a flat or other residence for an unmarried person; **bach'elor-girl** a young unmarried woman who supports herself; **bachelor's-butt'ons** a double-flowered yellow or white buttercup; also applied to other plants. — **Bachelor of Arts** (*abbrev* **BA**) or **Bachelor of Science** (*abbrev* **BSc**) a university or college degree conferred upon a student who has successfully completed an undergraduate course in the arts/humanities or the sciences/social sciences respectively; a man or woman who has received such a degree. [O.Fr. *bacheler* — L.L. *baccalārius*.]

bacillus *bə-sil'əs, n* (with *cap*) a genus of rod-shaped bacteria; a member of the genus; (*loosely*) any rod-shaped bacterium; (*popularly*) any disease-causing bacterium: — *pl* **bacill'ī.** — *adj* **bacill'ar** or **bacill'ary** (also *bas'il-ər-i*) of the shape or nature of a bacillus, rodlike. — *n* **bacill'icide** a substance which destroys bacilli. — *adj* **bacill'iform.** [L.L. *bacillus*, dimin. of *baculus*, a rod.]

back *bak, n* the rear part of the body in man (*specif* between the neck and the buttocks), and the upper part in four-legged animals; the rear part, or the side remote from that presented or habitually seen; the underside of a leaf or of a violin; part of the upper surface of the tongue opposite the soft palate; the convex side of a book, opposite to the opening of the leaves; the thick edge of a knife, etc.; the upright hind part of a chair, bench, etc.; something added to the rear or far side; one of the players behind the forwards — *full back* (who guards the goal), *half back* and *three-quarter back* (*football, etc.*). — *adj* rearward, situated at or towards the back of; remote; reversed; made by raising the back of the tongue (*phon*); belonging to the past. — *adv* to or towards the back; to or towards the place from which one came; to a former state or condition; behind; behind in time; in return; again; ago. — *vt* to help or support; to support (a horse, an opinion, etc.) by placing a wager or bet on; to countersign or endorse; to provide a back or a backing for; to lie at the back of; to form the back of; to cause to move backward or in the opposite direction. — *vi* to move or go back or backwards; (of the wind) to change counter-clockwise. — *adj* **backed** having a back. — *n* **back'er.** — *n* **back'ing** support at the back; support for an enterprise; musical accompaniment, esp. of a popular song; a body of helpers; anything used to form a back or line the back; the action of putting or going back; a counter-clockwise change of wind. — *adj* and *adv* **backward** (*bak'wərd*) towards the back; on the back; towards the past; from a better to a worse state; in a direction opposite to the normal. — *adj* keeping back; shy, bashful; unwilling; retarded, slow in development; dull or stupid (*colloq*). — *n* **backwardā'tion** percentage paid by a seller of stock for keeping back its delivery till the following account. — *adv* **back'wardly.** — *n* **back'wardness.** — *adv* **back'wards** backward. — **back'ache** pain in the back. — *adj* **back'-bench** of or sitting on the **back benches**, the seats in parliament occupied by members who do not hold office. — *vt* **back'bite** to speak ill of or unkindly of (someone) in their absence (also *vi*). — **back'biter; back'biting.** — Also *adj*. — **back'blocks** (*Austr* and *NZ*) remote, sparsely populated country; the back part of a livestock station, far from water; **back'-board** a board fastened across the back to straighten the body; a piece of rigid material to which the basket is attached, marked to contrast with the surface behind it (*basketball*); **back'bone** the spinal column; a main support or axis; mainstay; firmness of character. — *adj* **back'boned.** — *adj* **back'boneless.** — **back'-breaker** a very heavy job. — *adj* **back'breaking.** — **back burner** the rear burner on a stove, used esp. for keeping a pot simmering that needs no immediate attention; (*fig*; orig. *US*) low-priority or pending status (**keep, place** or **put on the back burner** to set aside, postpone work on, or keep in reserve for later consideration or action). — *vi* and *vt* **back-cal'culate** to make a calculation as to an earlier condition, situation, etc. (esp. as to the level of a person's intoxication) based on data recorded at a later time. — **back'-calculation; back'chat** answering back; repartee. — Also *vi*. — **back'-cloth** or **back'drop** the painted cloth or curtain at the back of the stage; the background to any situation, activity, etc. — *vi* and *vt* **back'-comb** to give (the hair) a puffed-out appearance by combing the underlying hairs towards the roots and smoothing the outer hairs over them. — **back'-country** remote, thinly-populated districts. — Also *adj*. — **back'-court** (*lawn tennis*) that part of the court lying behind the service-line. — Also *adj*. — **back'-crawl** a swimming stroke similar to the crawl, performed on the back. — *vt* **back-date'** to put an earlier date on; to count as valid retrospectively from a certain date. — **back door** a door in the back part of a building. — *adj* **back'-door** unworthily secret; clandestine. — **backdown** see **back down** below; **back'-draught** a backward current; **backdrop** see **back-cloth; back-end'** the rear end; **back'fill** the material used in backfilling. — *vt* and *vi* to refill (e.g. foundations or an excavation) with earth or other material. — **back'fire** ignition of gas in an internal-combustion engine's cylinder at the wrong time. — *vi* (*bak-fīr'*) to have a backfire; to go wrong (*colloq*). — **back foot** (*cricket*) the batsman's foot furthest from the bowler (**off the back foot** (of a stroke) played with the weight on the back foot, defensive in stance; also *adj* **back'-foot**). — **back'-formātion** the making of a word from one that is taken to be a derivative; **back garden** or **back green** a garden or green, at the back of a house; **back'ground** the space behind the principal figures of a picture; that against which anything is, or ought to be, seen (*fig*); upbringing and previous history; environment; a place of obscurity, the shadows (*fig*). — *adj* in the background (*lit* or *fig*). — **background radiation** low-level radiation from substances present in the environment; **back'hand** the part of the court to the left of a right-handed player, or the right of a left-handed player (*tennis*); a stroke made with the hand turned backwards; handwriting with the letters sloping backwards. — Also *adj*. — *adj* **back'-handed** backhand; (of a compliment, etc.) indirect, dubious, sarcastic, insincere. — **back-hand'er** a blow with the back of the hand; a bribe (*colloq*); **back'land** a piece of land at the back of an established property, *specif* when viewed or used as an area for building development;

back'lash reaction or consequence, esp. if violent; the jarring or recoiling motion of ill-fitting machinery; **back'list** books previously published which a publisher keeps in print, as opposed to newly published books; **back'-load** a load taken on by a lorry for a return journey. — *vi* to obtain a back-load. — **back'-loading; back'log** a reserve or accumulation of business, stock, work, etc., that will keep one going for some time (*colloq*); **back'-number** a copy or issue of a newspaper or magazine of a previous date; a person or thing out of date or past the useful stage (*fig*); **back'pack** a pack carried on the back, a rucksack. — *vi* to carry a pack on the back esp. as a hiker. — **back'packer; back'packing; back'pay** pay that is overdue. — *vi* **back-ped'al** to press the pedals back, as in slowing a fixed-wheel bicycle; to hold back; to reverse one's course of action. — **back-ped'alling.** — *adj* **back'room** (of persons) doing important work behind the scenes, esp. in secret (*colloq*). — *vi* **back'scratch.** — **back'scratcher** a clawed instrument for scratching the back; someone who practises backscratching; **back'scratching** doing favours in return for favours, for the advantage of both parties; servile flattery; **back'-shift** a group of workers whose time of working overlaps or comes between the day-shift and the night-shift; the time when this group is on duty; **back'side** the back or hinder side or part of anything; the rear part of an animal; the buttocks (*colloq*); **back'-slang** slang in which every word is pronounced as if spelt backwards. — *adj* **back'=slapping** vigorously, demonstratively cheery. — *n* such an approach, manner or behaviour towards associates. — *vi* **back'slide** to slide or fall back in faith or morals, or work etc. — **back'slider; back'sliding.** — *vi* **back'space** (or *-spās'*) to move the carriage of a typewriter one or more spaces back by means of a particular key. — *n* the key used for backspacing (also **back'spacer** or **backspace key**); the act of backspacing. — **back'spin** a rotary movement against the direction of travel of a ball (in golf, billiards, etc.) imparted to reduce its momentum on impact. — *adj* and *adv* **backstage'** (*lit* and *fig*) behind the scenes, unobserved by the public. — **back'stairs** servants' or private stairs of a house. — *adj* secret or underhand. — **back'stays** ropes or stays extending from the topmast-heads to the sides of a ship, and slanting a little backward; any stay or support at the back; **back'stitch** a method of sewing in which, for every new stitch, the needle enters behind, and comes out in front of, the end of the previous one; **back'stop** a screen, wall, etc. acting as a barrier in various sports or games, e.g. shooting, baseball, etc.; (the position of) a player, e.g. in baseball who stops the ball; something providing additional support, protection, etc.; **back street** a street away from the main road in a town or city, esp. as part of a poorer, less fashionable area; **back'-stroke** back-crawl; a swimming-stroke with circular movements of the arms and legs, performed on the back; **back'swing** (*sport*) (in a swing of a club, racket, etc.) the first stage, in which it is swung back and away from the ball. — *vi* **back'track** to go back on one's course. — **back'tracking; back-up** support; a copy taken of data being worked on, stored on another disk against the possibility of damage to or loss of the working disk (*comput*); **back'wash** a receding wave; a backward current; a reaction, repercussion or aftermath; **back'water** a pool or belt of water connected with a river but not in the line of its present course or current; a place unaffected by the movements of the day (*fig*); a backward current of water; swell of the sea caused by a passing ship; **back'woods** the forest beyond the cleared country; **backwoods'man; backyard'** a yard behind a house. — *adj* (of a person) operating a small business from domestic premises, as *backyard mechanic*, or practising unofficially or illegally. — **back down** to abandon one's opinion or position (*n* **back'down**); **back of** (*US*) behind; **back out** to move out backwards; to evade an obligation or undertaking; **back-seat driver** someone free of responsibility but full of advice; a person controlling from a position from which he or she ought not to control; **back=street abortion** an abortion performed by an unqualified person operating illicitly; **back-to=back'** with backs facing each other; (of houses) built thus (also *n*); following in close sequence (*colloq*); **back to front** the wrong way round, with the back where the front should be; reversed, in mirror image; in the wrong order, with matters that should be deferred being discussed or dealt with first; completely, thoroughly; **back up** to give support to; **bend, fall** or **lean over backwards** (*colloq*) to go even to the point of personal discomfort or inconvenience so as to be accommodating or to please; **break the back of** to overburden; to accomplish the hardest part of; **get off someone's back** to stop pestering or bothering someone; **know (something) backwards** to have a thorough knowledge of (something); **on the back of** close behind; **put one's back into** to put great effort into; **set** or **put one's** (or **someone's**) **back up** to show resentment or arouse resentment; **take a back seat** to withdraw into obscurity or subordination; **talk through the back of one's neck** see **neck.** [O.E. *bæc.*]

backgammon *bak-gam'ən* or *bak'gam-ən*, *n* a game for two players, using a board with dice and fifteen men or pieces each. — *vt* to defeat at backgammon. [**back,** because the pieces are sometimes taken up and obliged to go *back*, i.e. re-enter at the table, and M.E. *gamen*, play.]

backsheesh, backshish. See **baksheesh.**

backward, backwards, etc. See **back.**

baclava. See **baklava.**

bacon *bā'kn*, *n* pig's flesh (now the back and sides) salted or pickled and dried, used as a foodstuff. — *n* **ba'coner** a pig suitable for bacon production. — **bring home the bacon** (*colloq*) to achieve an object, successfully accomplish a task; to provide material support; **save (some)one's bacon** (to enable someone) to come off unscathed from a difficult situation. [O.Fr. *bacon.*]

Baconian *bā-kō'ni-ən*, *adj* pertaining to Francis *Bacon* (1561–1626) or his philosophy, or to Roger *Bacon* (d. *c* 1292) or his teaching, or to the theory that Francis Bacon wrote Shakespeare's plays. — Also *n.*

bacteria *bak-tē'ri-ə*, *npl* a class of microscopic unicellular or threadlike plants, agents in putrefaction, nitrogen fixation, etc., and the cause of many diseases: — *nsing* **bactē'rium** any member of the class, esp. a rod-shaped one. — *n* **bacteraemia** or in U.S. **bacteremia** (*-ē'mi-ə*) the presence of bacteria in the blood. — *adj* **bactē'rial.** — *adj* **bactēricī'dal.** — *n* **bactē'ricide** a substance that destroys bacteria. — *adj* **bactēriolog'ical.** — *n* **bactēriol'ogist.** — *n* **bactēriol'ogy** the scientific study of bacteria. — *n* **bactēriolȳ'sin** (or *-ol'i-sin*) an antibody that destroys bacteria. — *n* **bactēriol'ysis** destruction of bacteria by an antibody (Gr. *lysis*, dissolution). — *adj* **bactēriolyt'ic.** — *n* **bacteriophage** (*bak-tē'ri-ō-fāj* or *-fäzh*) any of a large number of virus-like agents, present in the atmosphere, soil, water, living things, etc., whose function is to destroy bacteria. — *n* **bactērios'tasis** inhibition of the growth of bacteria. — *n* **bactē'riostat** an agent that inhibits their growth. — *adj* **bactēriostat'ic.** [Gr. *baktērion*, dimin. of *baktron*, a stick.]

Bactrian camel *bak'tri-ən kam'əl*, *n* a two-humped camel native to central Asia. [Of *Bactria*, now nearly corresponding to Balkh, a district of N. Afghanistan.]

baculovirus *bak'ū-lō-vī-rəs*, *n* a type of virus only found to attack insects. [L. *baculus*, a rod, and **virus**.]

bad *bad*, *adj* (*compar* **worse**, *superl* **worst**) ill or evil; wicked; hurtful; incorrect, faulty; poor, unskilful; worthless; unfavourable; painful; unwell; spurious; severe; having serious effects; good, attractive (*slang*, orig. *US*). — *n* something evil, wicked, hurtful, etc. — *n* **badd'ie** or **badd'y** (*colloq*) a criminal person or villain, esp. as portrayed in films, television or radio shows. — *adj* **badd'ish** somewhat bad. — *adv* **bad'ly** in a faulty or unskilful way; unfavourably; severely; to a marked extent; very much. — *n* **bad'ness.** — **bad blood** angry or hostile feeling; **bad debt** a debt that cannot be recovered; **bad lands** the barren waste region in South Dakota; (usu. **bad'lands**) any similar region; **bad language** swearing. — *adj* **bad'ly-off** poorly provided for, esp. in terms of money. — *vt* **bad'mouth** (*colloq*) to criticise, malign. — **bad news** any unwelcome, upsetting or irritating event, or a report of such; someone or something troublesome, irritating, etc. (*slang*). — *adj* **bad-tem'pered.** — **bad trip** (*colloq*) an episode of terrifying hallucinations and physical discomfort resulting from taking a drug, esp. LSD. — **go bad** to decay; **go to the bad** to go to moral ruin; **in someone's bad books** unpopular with someone; **to the bad** in a bad condition; in deficit.

bade *bad* or (*poetic*) *bād*, *pa t* of **bid** (both verbs).

badge *baj*, *n* a mark or emblem showing rank, membership of a society, etc.; any distinguishing mark or symbol. [M.E. *bage*.]

badger *baj'ər*, *n* a burrowing, nocturnal, hibernating animal of the otter and weasel family; extending to other animals — hyrax, wombat, ratel; a paint-brush (or other brush) made of badger's hair. — *vt* to pester or worry. — **badg'er-baiting** or **-drawing** the sport of setting dogs to draw out a badger from a barrel or artificial earth, etc. [Prob. from **badge** and the noun-forming sfx. *-ard*, in reference to the white mark like a badge on its forehead.]

badinage *bad'in-äzh*, *n* light playful talk; banter. [Fr. *badinage* — *badin*, playful or bantering.]

badminton *bad'min-tən*, *n* a game played with shuttlecocks on a court with a high net, with the object of making the shuttlecock strike the ground in the opponent's court; a cooling summer drink of claret, sugar and soda-water. [*Badminton* in Gloucester.]

BAe. *abbrev* for British Aerospace.

Baedeker *bā'di-kər*, *n* any of the series of travellers' guidebooks published by Karl *Baedeker* (1801–59) or his successors; any similar guidebook.

BAF *abbrev* for British Athletics Federation.

baff *baf*, (*golf*) *vt* to strike the ground with the sole of the club in playing, and so to send the ball up in the air. — *n* **baffy** (*baf'i*) a club like a brassy, but with a somewhat shorter shaft and a more sloping face.

baffle *baf'l*, *vt* to frustrate, confound, bewilder, or impede perplexingly; to regulate or divert (liquid, gas, sound waves, etc.). — *n* a plate or similar device for regulating or diverting the flow of liquid, gas, sound waves, etc. (also **baff'le-board, baff'le-plate** or **baff'ler**). — *n* **baff'lement.** — *n* **baff'ler.** — *adj* **baff'ling.** — *adv* **baff'lingly.** — **baff'legab** (*slang*) the professional verbal diarrhoea of many politicians and salespeople, characterised by prolix abstract circumlocution and/or a profusion of abstruse technical terminology, used as a means of persuasion, pacification or obfuscation. [Perh. Scot.; but cf. Fr. *bafouer*, or earlier *beffler*, from O.Fr. *befe*, mockery.]

BAFTA *baf'ta*, *abbrev* for British Academy of Film and Television Arts.

bag *bag*, *n* a sack, pouch, receptacle for carrying or containing; a bagful; measure of (a specified) quantity for produce; a game-bag, hence the quantity of fish or game secured, however great; an udder, or other natural pouch; an unattractive, slovenly or immoral woman (*slang*); a person's line or vocation (*slang*); (in *pl*) loose, wide-legged trousers (*colloq*); a quantity of drugs, esp. heroin in a paper or other container (*drug-taking slang*). — *vi* to bulge, swell out; to sag. — *vt* to put into a bag (esp. of game); hence to kill (game); to seize, secure or steal; to denigrate (*Austr*): — *pr p* **bagg'ing**; *pa p* **bagged.** — *n* **bag'ful**: — *pl* **bag'fuls.** — *adj* **bagged** (*bagd*) in a bag; bulged slackly. — *adv* **bagg'ily.** — *adj* **bagg'y** loose like a bag; bulged. — **bag lady** a homeless female derelict who carries her possessions, accumulated scavengings, etc. around with her in a shopping bag (or usu. several); **bag'man** a man who carries a bag; a man who collects or distributes money on behalf of another by dishonest means or for a dishonest purpose (*US*); a swagman (*Austr*); **bag'-net** a bag-shaped net for catching fish; **bag'-wash** (a laundry that offers) a laundry service by which rough unfinished washing is done. — **bag and baggage** completely, as in *to clear out bag and baggage*; **bag of bones** an emaciated living being; **bag of tricks** the whole outfit; **bags** or **bags I** (*slang*) I lay claim to; **bags of** (*slang*) plenty of; **in the bag** secured or as good as secured; **let the cat out of the bag** to disclose a secret. [M.E. *bagge*, perh. Scand.]

bagatelle *bag-ə-tel'*, *n* a trifle, trinket; a piece of music in a light style; a game played on a board with balls, usu. nine, and a cue or spring, the object being to put the balls into numbered holes or sections. [Fr., — It. *bagatella*, a conjuror's trick, a trifle.]

bagel *bā'gəl*, *n* a hard leavened roll in the shape of a doughnut. [Yiddish *beygel* — Ger. *Beugel*.]

baggage *bag'ij*, *n* traveller's luggage; the tents, provisions, etc. of an army; a worthless woman (*colloq*). — **bagg'age-car** (*US*) a railway luggage-van; **baggage reclaim** the process whereby (esp. long-distance) travellers collect their baggage on arrival at their destination; the area in an airport terminal, etc. where travellers collect their baggage after arrival; **bagg'age-train** a train of baggage-animals, wagons, etc. [O.Fr. *bagage* — *baguer*, to bind up.]

bagpipes *bag'pīps*, *npl* (also *nsing* **bag'pipe**) a wind-instrument consisting of a *bag* fitted with *pipes*. — *n* **bag'piper.** — *n* **bag'piping.**

BAgr. or **BAgric.** *abbrev* for Bachelor of Agriculture.

baguette *bag-et'*, *n* a long narrow French loaf of white bread with a thick crust; a precious stone cut in the shape of a long rectangle; a small moulding like an astragal (*archit*). [Fr., rod, dimin. — L. *baculum*.]

bah *bä*, *interj* expressing disgust or contempt. [Fr.]

Bahai or **Baha'i** *bə-* or *bä-hä'ē*, *n* an adherent of a religion (orig. Persian) following the teaching of *Baha*-Ullah, who claimed to be the bringer of a new revelation from God; the religion itself. — Also *adj.* — *n* **Baha'ism.** — *n* **Baha'ist** or **Baha'ite.**

Bahasa Indonesia *bə-hä'sə in-də-nē'zi-ə*, *-zhi-ə* or *-zhyə*, *n* the Indonesian language. — **Bahasa Malaysia** Malay. [Malay, Indonesian *bahasa*, language.]

baht *bät*, *n* the monetary unit of Thailand (100 *satang*). [Thai *bāt*.]

BAI *abbrev* for *Baccalaureus in Arte Ingeniaria* (L.), Bachelor of Engineering.

baignoire *ben-wär*, *n* a theatre box on a level with the stalls. [Fr., bath.]

bail[1] *bāl*, *n* the (usu. monetary) security given to procure the release of an accused person to assure his or her subsequent appearance in court; release from custody on the strength of such security; a person who gives or becomes such security. — *vt* to set someone free by giving security for them; to release on the security of another; to deliver (goods) in trust upon a contract. — *adj* **bail'able.** — *n* **bailee'** a person to whom goods are bailed. — *n* **bail'er** a variant spelling of **bailor** (*US*). — *n* **bail'ment** a delivery of goods in trust; the action of bailing a prisoner. — *n* **bail'or** a person who bails goods to a bailee. — **bail'bond** a bond given by a prisoner and his or her surety upon being bailed. — **bail out** (*colloq*) to stand bail for (a prisoner); to assist out of (financial) difficulties (*n* **bail'-out**); **forfeit** or (*colloq*) **jump bail** to fail to reappear in court at the designated time after being released on bail; **stand, go** or **give bail** to provide the bail for a prisoner. [O.Fr. *bail*, custody, handing over, *baillier*, to control, guard, hand over.]

bail[2] or **bayle** *bāl*, *n* a barrier; a pole separating horses in an open stable. — *vt* **bail** to confine. [O.Fr. *baile*, perh. from *baillier*, to enclose; or L. *baculum*, a stick.]

bail[3] *bāl*, *n* one of the crosspieces on the top of the wicket in cricket. [Prob. conn. with **bail**[2].]

bail[4] *bāl*, *n* on a typewriter, teleprinter, etc., a hinged bar that holds the paper against the platen. [Prob. conn. with **bail**[2].]

bail[5] (also **bale**) *bāl*, *n* a bucket or other vessel for ladling out water from a boat. — *vt* to clear of water with a bail or bails; to ladle (often with *out*). — *n* **bail'er**. — **bale** or **bail out** to escape from an aeroplane by parachute; to escape from a potentially difficult situation. [Fr. *baille*, bucket.]

bail[6] *bāl*, *n* a hooplike handle, as of a kettle, etc. [Prob. O.N. *beygla*, hoop.]

bailey *bāl'i*, *n* the outer wall of a feudal castle; hence the outer court, or any court within the walls. [Fr. *baille*, palisade, enclosure.]

Bailey bridge *bā'li brij*, *n* a prefabricated bridge constructed speedily for emergency use. [Designed during World War II by Sir Donald *Bailey*.]

bailie *bāl'i*, *n* in Scotland, the title of a magistrate who presides in borough court — elected by the town council from among the councillors (now mainly *hist*). — *n* **bail'ieship**. — Also **baill'ie** and **baill'ieship**. [O.Fr. *bailli*, *baillif*; see **bailiff**.]

bailiff *bāl'if*, *n* an agent or land-steward; a sheriff's officer; the first civil officer in Jersey and Guernsey; formerly any king's officer, e.g. sheriff, mayor, etc., and surviving in certain cases as a formal title. — *n* **bail'iwick** (*law*) the jurisdiction of a bailiff; jurisdiction in general. [O.Fr. *baillif*. See **bail**[1].]

baillie. See **bailie**.

Baily's beads *bā'liz bēdz*, (*astron*) *npl* bright spots, visible during the last seconds before a total eclipse of the sun. [Detected in 1836 by the astronomer F. *Baily*.]

bain-marie *ban-ma-rē'* or *bɛ̃-ma-rē*, *n* a vessel of hot or boiling water into which another vessel is placed to cook slowly or keep hot (*cookery*); a water-bath (*chem*). [Fr., bath of Mary — L. *balneum Mariae*.]

Bairam *bī'räm* or *bī-räm'*, *n* the name of two Muslim festivals — the *Lesser Bairam* lasting three days, after the feast of Ramadan, and the *Greater*, seventy days later, lasting four days. [Pers.]

bairn *bārn*, (*Scot* and *Northern Eng*) *n* a child. [O.E. *bearn* — *beran*, to bear.]

bait *bāt*, *n* food put on a hook to allure fish or make them bite; any allurement or temptation; a rage (*slang*). — *vt* to set with food as a lure; to tempt; to set dogs on (a bear, bull, etc.); to persecute, harass; to exasperate (esp. with malice), tease. — *n* **bait'er**. — *n* **bait'ing**. [M.E. *beyten* — O.N. *beita*, to cause to bite — *bita*, to bite.]

baize *bāz*, *n* a coarse woollen cloth with a long nap, used mainly for coverings, linings, etc.; a table cover of such cloth, esp. the covering of card- and snooker tables, etc. — *vt* to cover or line with baize. [Fr. *baies*, pl. (fem.) of *bai* — L. *badius*, bay-coloured.]

Bajan *bājən*, (*colloq*) *adj* Barbadian. [Corrupted short form.]

bajra *bäj'rə* or *-rä*, also **bajri** or **bajree** *bäj'rē*, *n* a kind of Indian millet. [Hind.]

bake *bāk*, *vt* to dry, harden or cook by the heat of the sun or fire; to make or cook in an oven. — *vi* to become firm through heat; to be very hot (*colloq*); to work as a baker: — *pr p* **bāk'ing**. — *n* **bāk'er**. — *n* **bāk'ery** a bakehouse; a baker's shop. — *n* **bāk'ing** the process by which bread (or cake, etc.) is baked; the quantity baked at one time. — **baked Alaska** a pudding consisting of ice-cream, and usu. cake, covered with meringue baked rapidly; **baked beans** beans boiled and baked, now generally used of a variety tinned in tomato sauce; **bake'house** a house or place used for baking in; **bake'ware** heat-resistant dishes suitable for use in baking; **bak'ing-powder** a mixture (e.g. tartaric acid and sodium bicarbonate) giving off carbon dioxide, used as a raising agent in baking; **bak'ing-soda** sodium bicarbonate. [O.E. *bacan*.]

Bakelite® *bā'kəl-īt*, *n* a synthetic resin with high chemical and electrical resistance, made by condensation of cresol or phenol with formaldehyde. [From its inventor, L. H. *Baekeland* (1863–1944).]

Baker day *bā'kər dāy*, (*colloq*) *n* a periodic in-service training day for teachers, on which students do not attend school. [Kenneth *Baker*, Secretary of State for Education, 1986–89.]

Bakewell pudding *bāk'wel pŏŏd'ing* or **tart** (*tärt*), *n* a pastry base spread with jam and a filling made of eggs, sugar, butter and ground almonds. [*Bakewell* in Derbyshire.]

baklava or **baclava** *bak'lə-və*, *n* a Turkish dessert made of layers of flaky pastry, honey, nuts, etc. [Turk.]

baksheesh, bakhshish, backsheesh or **backshish** *bak'* or *buk'shēsh*, *n* a gift of money in India, Turkey, etc., a gratuity or tip. [Pers. *bakhshīsh*.]

bal. (*bookkeeping*) *abbrev* for balance.

Balaclava cap *bal-ə-klä'və kap* or **helmet** (*hel'mit*), *n* a warm knitted hat covering the head and neck, with an opening for the face. [*Balaklava* in Crimea.]

balalaika *ba-lə-lī'kə*, *n* a Russian musical instrument, like a guitar, with a triangular body and usu. three strings. [Russ.]

balance *bal'əns*, *n* equilibrium; what is needed to produce equilibrium, a counterpoise; harmony among the parts of anything; equality or just proportion of weight or power; the sum required to make the two sides of an account equal, hence the surplus, or the sum due on the account; the remainder; the act of weighing two things; an instrument for weighing, usu. formed of two dishes or scales hanging from a beam supported in the middle; a contrivance that regulates the speed of a clock or watch. — *vt* to set or keep in equilibrium; to counterpoise; to compare; to settle, as an account; to weigh in a balance; to examine and test so as to make the debtor or creditor sides of an account agree (*bookkeeping*). — *vi* to have equal weight or power, etc.; to be or come to be in equilibrium; to hesitate or fluctuate. — *adj* **bal'anced** poised so as to preserve equilibrium; well-arranged, stable; well-adjusted, composed. — *n* **bal'ancer**. — **bal'ance-sheet** a summary and balance of accounts; **bal'ance-wheel** a wheel in a watch or chronometer which regulates the beat or rate. — **balance of mind** sanity; **balance of payments** the difference over a stated period between a nation's total receipts (in all forms) from foreign countries and its total payments to foreign countries; **balance of power** a state of equilibrium of forces in which no nation or group of nations has the resources to go to war with another or others with likelihood of success; **balance of trade** the difference in value between a country's imports and exports; **in the balance** unsettled; undecided; **off balance** unstable, esp. mentally or emotionally; in a state of unreadiness to respond to an attack, challenge, etc.; **on balance** having taken everything into consideration. [Fr., — L. *bilanx*, having two scales — *bis*, double, *lanx*, *lancis*, a dish or scale.]

balancé *bal-ã-sã*, (Fr.) *n* in ballet, a rocking step taking the weight from one foot to the other.

balata *bal'ə-tə*, *n* the gum of the bully-tree of South America, used as a substitute for rubber and gutta-percha. [Prob. Tupí.]

balboa *bäl-bō'ə*, *n* the monetary unit of Panama (100 centésimos). [Vasco Nuñez de *Balboa*, *c* 1475–1517.]

balcony *bal'kə-ni*, *n* a stage or platform projecting from the wall of a building, supported by pillars or consoles, and surrounded with a balustrade or railing; in theatres, usu. the gallery immediately above the dress circle (in *US* the dress circle itself). — *adj* **bal'conied**. [It. *balcone* — *balco*, of Gmc. origin.]

bald *böld*, *adj* without hair, feathers, etc., on the head (or on other parts of the body); bare, unadorned; lacking in literary grace or charm, blunt; undisguised, plain. — *adj* **bald'ing** going bald. — *adj* **bald'ish** somewhat bald. — *adv* **bald'ly** plainly, without tact or euphemism. — *n* **bald'ness**. — **bald'-eagle** the American white-headed eagle, used as the national emblem. — *adj* **bald'-faced** having white on the face (e.g. of a horse). — *adj* **bald'-headed**. — *adv* (*slang*) without restraint; out and out. — **bald as a coot** see **coot**. [Perh. **balled**, rounded.]

baldachin or **baldaquin** *böl'də-kin*, *n* a canopy over a throne, pulpit, altar, etc.; in R.C. processions, a canopy carried over the priest who carries the host. [It. *baldacchino*, Fr. *baldaquin*, a canopy, — It. *Baldacco*, Baghdad, from where the silk brocade of which they were made came.]

balderdash *böl'dər-dash*, *n* idle senseless talk; anything jumbled together without judgment.

baldric or **baldrick** *böld'rik*, *n* a warrior's belt or shoulder sash, for supporting a sword or bugle, etc. [Cf. M.H.G. *balderich*, girdle.]

bale[1] *bāl*, *n* a bundle (e.g. of straw, cotton), or package of goods. — *vt* to make into bales. — *n* **bal'er**. [M.E. *bale*.]

bale[2]. See **bail**[5].

balection. See **bolection**.

baleen *bə-* or *ba-lēn'*, *n* horny plates growing from the palate of certain whales, the whalebone used commercially. — Also *adj*. [O.Fr. *baleine* — L. *balaena*, whale.]

baleful *bāl'fəl*, *adj* lugubrious, sorrowful; malignant, hurtful; of evil influence. — *adv* **bale'fully**. — *n* **bale'fulness**. [O.E. *bealu*.]

balk or **baulk** *bölk*, *vi* to pull up, or stop short at a difficulty; to jib; to refuse a jump, etc.; to refrain, desist. — *vt* to shirk, avoid; to decline; to ignore, pass over; to put a stumbling-block in the way of; to thwart, frustrate, foil. — *n* a check, frustration; a disappointment; failure to take a jump or the like; part of a billiard table marked off by the balkline; a forbidden action of the pitcher in baseball; a squared timber; a tie-beam of a house, stretching from wall to wall, esp. when laid so as to form a loft (the **balks**); an unploughed ridge. — *n* **balk'er**. — *n* **balk'iness**. — *n* and *adj* **balk'ing**. — *adv* **balk'ingly**. — *adj* **balk'y** apt to balk; perverse, refractory. — **balk'line** a line drawn across a billiard table; a boundary line for the preliminary run in a jumping competition etc. [O.E. *balca*, ridge.]

Balkanise or **-ize** (also without *cap*) *böl'kən-īz*, *vt* to reduce to the condition of the *Balkan* peninsula which was divided in the late 19th and early 20th centuries into a number of mutually hostile territories. — *n* **Balkanisātion**, **balkanisātion** (or *-z-*).

ball[1] *böl*, *n* anything spherical or nearly so; a rounded or matted mass; any rounded protuberant part of the body, e.g. the ball of the foot; a round or oval object used in sports (of varying size, shape and composition according to the sport); a throw or delivery of the ball at cricket, etc.; a game played with a ball, esp. (*US*) baseball or football; (in *pl*) testicles (*vulg*); (in *pl*) nonsense (also *interj*; *vulg*); (in *pl*) guts, courage (*slang*, esp. *US*). — *vt* to form into a ball. — *vi* to gather into a ball. — *adj* **balled** formed into a ball. — *n* **ball'ing**. — *adj* **ball-and-claw'** see **claw-and-ball** under **claw**. — **ball'-barrow** a wheelbarrow with a ball-shaped wheel; **ball-bear'ing** a device for lessening friction by making a revolving part turn on loose steel balls; one of the balls so used; **ball'-boy** or **ball'-girl** (*tennis*) a boy or girl who collects balls that are out of play, supplies balls to the server, etc.; **ball'-breaker** or (*US*) **ball'-buster** (*vulg slang*) a person, or a task, job, etc. that is excessively demanding; a woman who is ruthless, demanding or demoralising in her treatment of men. — *n* and *adj* **ball'-breaking** or **-busting**. — **ball'cock** the stopcock of a cistern turned by a floating ball that rises and falls with the water; **ball'game** any game played with a ball, esp. (*US*) baseball or football; a situation, as in *a new ball-game* (*colloq*); **ball lightning** a slowly-moving luminous ball occasionally seen during a thunderstorm; **ball park** (*US*) a baseball field; a sphere of activity (*colloq*). — *adj* (*US*) **ball'park** approximate (esp. in the phrase *ballpark figures*). — **ball'-player** (*US*) a baseball-player; **ball'point** or **ballpoint pen** a fountain-pen having a tiny ball rotating against an inking cartridge as its writing tip. — **ballsed-up**, **balls-up** see **balls up** below. — **ball and socket** (*med* and *eng* etc.) a joint formed of a ball partly enclosed in a cup-shaped cavity, allowing rotation on various axes; **ball of fire** a lively, dynamic person; **balls up** (*vulg*) to make a muddle or mess of; to throw into confusion (*n* **balls'-up**; *adj* **ballsed'-up**); **keep the ball rolling** to keep things going; **make a balls** or **balls-up of** (*vulg*) to do badly, make a thorough mess of; **no ball** (*cricket* etc.) a delivery of the ball adjudged contrary to rule; **on the ball** properly in touch with the situation; on the alert; **play ball** see **play**; **set**, **start** or **get the ball rolling** to make the first move; to start things going; **the ball at one's feet** success in one's grasp; an opportunity ready to be taken; **the ball's in your court** the responsibility for the next move is yours. [M.E. *bal* — O.N. *böllr*.]

ball[2] *böl*, *n* an assembly for dancing. — **ball'-dress**; **ball'room**. — Also *adj*. — **have a ball** to enjoy oneself very much (*colloq*). [O.Fr. *bal* — *baller*, to dance — L.L. *ballāre*.]

ballad *bal'əd*, *n* a slow, sentimental song; a simple narrative poem in short stanzas (usu. of four lines, of eight and six syllables alternately); a popular song, often scurrilous, referring to contemporary persons or events (now chiefly *hist*; orig. a song accompanying a dance). [O.Fr. *ballade* — L.L. *ballāre*, to dance.]

ballade *ba-läd'*, *n* a poem of one or more triplets of stanzas, each of seven, eight, or ten lines, including refrain, followed by an envoy, the whole on three (or four) rhymes; sometimes (*loosely*) any poem in stanzas of equal length; an ill-defined form of instrumental music, often in six-eight or six-four time. [An earlier spelling of **ballad**, with old pronunciation restored.]

ballast *bal'əst*, *n* heavy material used to weigh down and steady a ship or balloon; broken stone or other material used as the bed of a road or railway; that which makes anything steady. — *vt* to load with ballast; to make or keep steady. [Prob. Old Sw. *barlast* — *bar*, bare, *last*, load.]

ballerina *bal-ə-rē'nə*, *n* a female ballet-dancer: — *pl* **balleri'ne** (*-nā*) or **balleri'nas**. [It.]

ballet *bal'ā*, *n* a theatrical performance of dancing with set steps and pantomimic action; (a suite of) music for it; a troupe giving such performances; the art or activity of dancing in this way. — *adj* **balletic** (*bal-et'ik*) of the art of ballet. — *adv* **ballet'ically**. — **ball'et-dancer**; **ball'et-dancing**; **ball'et-master**

or **ball'et-mistress** a man or woman who directs or teaches ballet. [Fr.; — dimin. of *bal*, a dance.]

ballistic *bə-lis'tik*, *adj* projectile; relating to projectiles. — *nsing* **ballis'tics** the science of projectiles. — **ballistic missile** a guided missile that ends in a ballistic descent, the guidance being only for part of its course. [L. *ballista*, a military engine in the form of a crossbow for heavy missiles, — Gr. *ballein*, to throw.]

ballocks. See **bollocks.**

balloon *bə-lo͞on'*, *n* an apparatus for travel (or for carrying weather-recording instruments, etc.) in the air, supported by buoyancy rather than mechanically-driven, consisting of a large bag that is filled with gas, and a cabin or basket beneath; a toy consisting of an inflatable, usu. coloured rubber bag; anything inflated, empty (*fig*); an ornamental ball on a pillar, etc. (*archit*); a balloon-shaped drawing enclosing words spoken in a strip cartoon. — *adj* of or like a balloon. — *vi* to ascend or travel in, or as if in, a balloon; to puff out like a balloon; (of an aeroplane) to rise up in the air (as a result of landing on a firm surface, or increased airspeed, etc.). — *vt* to inflate; to send high in the air. — *n* **balloon'ing.** — *n* **balloon'ist.** — **when the balloon goes up** when the trouble starts. [It. *ballone*, augmentative of *balla*, ball.]

ballot *bal'ət*, *n* a little ball, ticket or paper used in voting; a secret vote or method of voting by putting a ball or ticket or paper into an urn or box; in U.S. extended to open voting. — *vi* to vote by ballot; to draw lots: — *pr p* **ball'oting**; *pa t* and *pa p* **ball'oted.** — **ball'ot-box** a box for putting ballots into; **ball'ot-paper** a paper on which a ballot vote is recorded; **ball'ot-rigging** dishonest manipulation of a ballot. [It. *ballotta*, dimin. of *balla*, ball.]

ballpeen (or **ballpein) hammer** *böl'pēn ham'ər*, *n* a hammer with a rounded peen (q.v.), used esp. for beating metal.

ballsy *böl'zi*, (*slang*, esp. *US*) *adj* gutsy, tough and courageous. [**balls** (slang).]

bally *bal'i*, (*slang*) *adj* a euphemism for **bloody**, but almost meaningless.

ballyhoo *bal-i-ho͞o'*, (*slang*) *n* noisy propaganda; fuss, commotion. — *vt* to create loud publicity, make a ballyhoo, about: — *pr p* **ballyhoo'ing**; *pa t* and *pa p* **ballyhooed'**.

balm *bäm*, *n* an aromatic substance; a fragrant and healing ointment; aromatic fragrance; anything that heals or soothes pain; a tree yielding balm; a plant, with an aroma similar to that of lemon, or one of various other garden herbs. — *adj* **balm'ily.** — *n* **balm'iness.** — *adj* **balm'y** fragrant; mild and soothing; bearing balm. [O.Fr. *basme* — L. *balsamum*. See **balsam.**]

balmoral *bal-mor'əl*, *n* a flat Scottish bonnet; a kind of boot lacing in front. [*Balmoral*, royal residence in Aberdeenshire.]

baloney or **boloney** *ba-* or *bə-lō'ni*, (*slang*) *n* deceptive talk; nonsense. [Thought to be from *Bologna* (*sausage*).]

balsa *böl'sə* or *bäl'sə*, *n* corkwood, a tropical American tree (*Ochroma lagopus*) of the silk-cotton family, with very light wood; a raft or float. [Sp., raft.]

balsam *böl'səm*, *n* a plant of the genus *Impatiens*; a liquid resin or resinous oily substance, esp. balm of Gilead; any healing agent (*fig*). — *adj* **balsamic** (*-sam'ik*). — *adj* **balsamif'erous** producing balsam. — *adj* **bal'samy** fragrant. — **balsam fir** an American fir (*Abies balsamea*); **balsam of Peru** and **balsam of Tolu** see **Peru** and **Tolu**; **Canada balsam** a turpentine from the balsam fir. [L. *balsamum* — Gr. *balsamon*.]

Balt *bölt*, *n* the Baltic provinces or states; a native or inhabitant of these regions; a speaker of a Baltic language. — *adj* **Balt'ic** of the sea separating Scandinavia from Germany and Russia; of the western division of the Baltoslavs. — *n* the Baltic languages. — *n* **Balt'oslav.** — *adj* **Balt'oslav, Balt'oslavic** or **Balt'oslavonic** of a family of Indo-European languages including the Slavonic languages with Lettish, Lithuanian, and (extinct) Old Prussian. [From the *Baltic Sea* — L. *Baltia*, Scandinavia.]

balthazar or **balthasar** *bal'thə-zär*, *n* a very large wine-bottle, in capacity usu. taken to equal 16 ordinary bottles (12·80 litres or 2·75 gallons). [Coined in reference to Daniel v. 1.]

Baltimore *böl'tim-ör*, *n* a common orange and black N. American bird, called also *Baltimore oriole*, *firebird*, etc. [From Lord *Baltimore*, whose livery was orange and black.]

baluster *bal'əs-tər*, *n* a small pillar supporting a stair rail or a parapet coping, often circular in section and curvaceous in outline. — *adj* (of a vessel, its stem or handle) like a baluster in shape. — *adj* **bal'ustered.** — *n* **bal'ustrade** a row of balusters joined by a rail or coping. [Fr. *balustre* — L.L. *balaustium* — Gr. *balaustion*, pomegranate flower; from its shape.]

bambino *bam-bē'nō*, *n* a child: — *pl* **bambi'nos** or **bambi'ni** (*-nē*). [It.]

bamboo *bam-bo͞o'*, *n* a gigantic tropical and subtropical grass with hollow-jointed woody stem; the stem, used esp. for making furniture. [Perh. Malay *bambu*.]

bamboozle *bam-bo͞o'zl*, *vt* to deceive; to confound or mystify. — *n* **bamboo'zlement.**

bampot *bam'pot*, (*Scot*) *n* an idiot, fool.

ban[1] *ban*, *n* sentence of banishment; a prohibition; a denunciation; a curse; a vague condemnation. — *vt* to forbid or prohibit; to anathematise. [O.E. *gebann*, proclamation, *bannan*, to summon: cf. **banns.**]

ban[2] *ban*, *n* a Romanian coin making up one hundredth part of a leu: — *pl* **bani** (*ban'ē*). [Rum.]

banal *bə-näl'*, *bā'nəl* or *bə-nal'* *adj* commonplace, trivial, flat. — *n* **banal'ity** cliché, triteness, triviality. — *adv* **banal'ly.** [Fr.]

banana *bə-* or *ba-nä'nə*, *n* a treelike herbaceous plant or its nutritious yellow fruit which grows in hanging bunches. — **bana'na-bender** (*Austr colloq*) a Queenslander; **banana republic** (*derog*) any of the small republics in the tropics depending on exports of fruit and on foreign investment; hence any small country dependent on foreign capital; **banana skin** (*fig*) something which causes a slip-up or a downfall; **banana split** a dish composed of a banana halved lengthways, ice-cream, and other ingredients. — **be** or **go bananas** (*slang*) to be or go crazy; **top banana** the star entertainer in a line-up (esp. of comedians); the most important person in a group, organisation, etc. (*colloq*). [Sp. or Port., from the native name in Guinea.]

Banbury cake *ban'bər-i kāk*, *n* a kind of mince-pie made in *Banbury*, Oxfordshire.

band[1] *band*, *n* that by which loose things are held together; a tie or connecting piece; (in *pl*) shackles, bonds, fetters. — **band'-stone** a stone set transversely in a wall to bind the structure. [M.E. *band*, *bond* — O.N. *band*.]

band[2] *band*, *n* a flat strip (of cloth, rubber, metal, etc.) to bind round or reinforce etc. anything; a stripe crossing a surface distinguished by its colour or appearance; a flat strip between mouldings, or dividing a wall surface; a belt for driving machinery; (in *pl*) the pair of linen strips hanging down in front from the collar, worn by some Protestant clergymen and by barristers and advocates; a group or range of frequencies or wavelengths between two specified limits (*radio*, *electronics*); in sound reproduction, a separately recorded section of a record or tape; a group of close-set lines esp. in a molecular spectrum (*phys*); a particular range, between an upper and lower limit, of e.g. intelligence, wealth, etc. — *n*

band'age a strip of cloth for winding round an injured part of the body; an adhesive plaster for protecting a wound or cut. — *vt* to bind with a bandage. — *adj* **band'ed** fastened as with a band; striped with bands; formed into bands. — *n* **band'-ing** the division of children in the final year of primary school into three groups according to ability, in order to obtain an even spread in the mixed-ability classes usual in comprehensive schools. — **band'-box** (or *ban'boks*) a light kind of box for holding caps, millinery, etc. — *adj* (esp. *US*) very neat and tidy, spruce; delicate. — **band'brake** or **band'-clutch** a brake or clutch in the form of a flexible band that can be tightened about a wheel or drum; **band'-saw** an endless saw, a toothed steel belt; **band'-wheel** a wheel on which a strap or band runs; **band'width** the width of a band or range of radio frequencies. [M.E. *bande* — O.Fr. *bande*.]

band[3] *band, n* a number of persons bound together for any common purpose; a body of musicians, esp. performers on wind and percussion instruments. — *vt* to bind together. — *vi* to associate, assemble, confederate. — **band'master** the conductor of a band; **bands'man** a member of a band of musicians; **band'stand** a structure for accommodating a band of musicians; **band'wagon** the car that carries the band in a circus procession; a fashionable movement, a trend enjoying current success. — **Band of Hope** an association pledged to lifelong abstinence from alcoholic drinks; **jump** or **leap on the band-wagon** to join in any popular and currently successful movement in the hope of gaining advantage from it. [Fr. *bande*, of Gmc. origin.]

bandage. See under **band**[2].

Band-aid® *band'ād, n* a type of sticking-plaster for covering minor wounds. — *adj* (usu. without *cap*; of policies, etc.) makeshift, temporary.

bandana or **bandanna** *ban-dan'ə, n* a silk or cotton coloured handkerchief, with spots or diamond prints, orig. from India. [Hind. *bā̃dhnū*, a mode of dyeing.]

B and B or **B & B** *abbrev* for bed and breakfast (see under **bed**).

bandeau *ban'dō* or *ban-dō', n* a band to bind the hair, worn around the head: — *pl* **bandeaux** (*ban'dōz* or *-dōz'*). [Fr.]

banderilla *ban-* or *bän-dä-rēl'yä, n* a dart with a streamer, stuck by bullfighters in the bull's neck. — *n* **banderillero** (*ban-* or *bän-dä-rēl-yä'rō*) a bullfighter who uses banderillas: — *pl* **banderille'ros**.

banderol or **banderole** *ban'də-rōl, n* a small banner or streamer; a flat band with an inscription (*archit*). [Fr.]

bandicoot *ban'di-kōōt, n* the largest species of rat, found in India and Sri Lanka; a member of the genus *Perameles* of small marsupials. [Telugu *pandikokku*, pig-rat.]

bandit *ban'dit, n* an outlaw; a brigand; (*airmen's slang*) an enemy plane: — *pl* **ban'dits** or **banditti** (*ban-dit'ē*). — *n* **ban'ditry**. — **one-armed bandit** a fruit-machine, so called from the similarity to an arm of the lever pulled to operate it, and the heavy odds against the user. [It. *bandito*.]

bandog *ban'dog, n* an aggressive dog kept chained or tied up; a cross between an American pit bull terrier and a mastiff, rottweiler or Rhodesian ridgeback, bred for exceptional ferocity. [M.E. *band-dogge*; **band**[1] and **dog**.]

bandoleer or **bandolier** *ban-dō-lēr', n* a shoulder belt, esp. for carrying ammunition. — *adj* **bandoleered'** or **bandoliered'** wearing a bandoleer. [O.Fr. *bandouillere* — It. *bandoliera* — *banda*, a band.]

bandwagon. See **band**[3].

bandy[1] *ban'di, vt* to beat to and fro; to toss from one to another (esp. words *with* anyone); to pass a story, or information, etc. from mouth to mouth (with *about*); to give and take (blows or reproaches): — *pr p* **ban'dying**; *pa t* and *pa p* **ban'died**. — *n* **ban'dying**.

bandy[2] *ban'di, adj* bent wide apart at the knee; having bandy or crooked legs. — *adj* **ban'dy-legged**. [Poss. **bandy**[1].]

bane *bān, n* a source or cause of evil, misery, etc.; poison; destruction or death. — *adj* **bane'ful** destructive; pernicious; poisonous. — *adv* **bane'-fully**. [O.E. *bana*, a murderer; O.N. *bani*, death.]

bang[1] *bang, n* a heavy blow; a sudden loud noise; an explosion; a thrill, burst of activity, sudden success (*fig*); an act of sexual intercourse (*slang*); an injection of a drug (*slang*). — *vt* to beat; to strike violently; to slam (e.g. a door); to have sexual intercourse with (*slang*); to inject a drug (*slang*). — *vi* to make a loud noise; to slam. — *adv* with a bang; abruptly; absolutely (as in *bang up-to-date*). — *adj* complete, total (used for emphasis, as in *the whole bang lot*). — *n* **bang'er** something that bangs; an explosive firework; a decrepit old car (*colloq*); a sausage (*slang*). — **bang goes** (*colloq*) that's the end of; **bang off** (*colloq*) immediately; **bang on** (*colloq*) right on the mark; to speak at length, esp. assertively and repetitiously; **bang to rights** orig., caught red-handed (*criminals' slang*); certainly, absolutely, no doubt (*colloq*); **bang up** (*slang*) to imprison, *specif* to shut up in a cell; **Big Bang** see under **big**; **go with a bang** to go well, be a success. [O.N. *banga*, to hammer.]

bang[2] *bang, n* hair cut square across the brow (often in *pl*). — *vt* to cut square across. — *adj* **banged** wearing the hair in such a way. — **bang'-tail** a tail with the end tuft squared; an animal whose tail hair is banged. [An Americanism, poss. from the phrase *bang off*.]

bang[3]. Same as **bhang**.

bangle *bang'gl, n* a circlar bracelet worn on the arm or leg. — *adj* **ban'gled** wearing bangles. [Hind. *bàngrī*, *bànglī*.]

bania *ban'yə*, **banian** or **banyan** *ban'yən* or *-yan, n* an Indian fig-tree with vast rooting branches; a loose jacket, gown, or undergarment worn in India. [Port. *banian*, perh. through Ar. *banyān*, from Hind. *baniyā*.]

banish *ban'ish, vt* to condemn to exile; to drive away; to expel. — *n* **ban'ishment** exile. [Fr. *bannir*, *baniss-* — L.L. *bannīre*, to proclaim.]

banister *ban'is-tər, n* a stair-rail with its supports (often in *pl*). [**baluster**.]

banjax *ban-jaks'* or *ban'jaks*, (*slang*) *vt* to ruin, destroy. [Anglo-Irish; poss. combination of **bang**[1] and **smash**.]

banjo *ban'jō* or *ban-jō', n* a musical instrument played with the fingers or with a plectrum — having a long neck, a circular body of stretched parchment like a drum, and usu. five strings of catgut and wire; applied to various tools or devices shaped like a banjo: — *pl* **ban'jos** or **ban'joes**. — *n* **ban'joist** (*-ist*). [Negro pronunciation of *bandore*, an Elizabethan stringed instrument.]

bank[1] *bangk, n* a mound or ridge; an upward slope; the edge of a river, lake, etc.; the raised border of a road, railway cutting, etc.; the coal-face in a mine; a shoal or shallow, raised area of seabed; a mass of cloud or mist; the tilt of an aeroplane. — *vt* to enclose with a bank; to deposit or pile up; to cover (a fire) so as to lessen the rate of combustion. — *vt* and *vi* (of aircraft) to tilt in turning. [M.E. *banke*, prob. Scand.]

bank[2] *bangk, n* a tier or rank, e.g. of oars, keys on a typewriter, etc.; a range of apparatus or equipment; a working table in various crafts. [O.Fr. *banc*.]

bank[3] *bangk, n* an institution for the keeping, lending etc., of money; a moneybox for savings; a stock of money, fund, or capital; in games of hazard, the money that the proprietor or other, who plays against all, has before them; a pool to draw cards from; any store of material or information; any supply, reserve or pool (of workers, resources etc.). — *vt* to deposit in a bank. — *vi* to have a bank account; to count, rely (on) (*colloq*). — *adj* **bank'able.** — *n* **bank'er** a person who keeps a bank; a person employed in banking business; a certainty, something that can be banked on or betted on. — Also *adj*. — *n* **bank'ing** the business of the banker. — *adj* pertaining to a bank. — **bank'-bill** a bill drawn by one bank upon another; **bank'-book** a book in which record is kept of money deposited in or withdrawn from a bank; **banker's card** a card issued by a bank guaranteeing the honouring of any cheque up to a specified value; **banker's order** a standing order (q.v.); **bank-hol'iday** a day on which banks are legally closed — in England observed as a general holiday; **bank'-note** a note issued by a bank, which passes as money, being payable to the bearer on demand; **bank'roll** money resources. — **break the bank** in gambling, to win from the management the sum fixed as the limit it is willing to lose on any one day; **clearing bank** a bank which is a member of the London Clearing-house; **joint-stock bank** one whose capital is subscribed by a large number of shareholders; **merchant bank** one whose functions include financing transit of goods and providing financial and commercial advice. [Fr. *banque* — It. *banca*.]

banket *bang-ket'*, (*SAfr*; *geol*) *n* a gold-bearing pebbly conglomerate. [Du. *banketje*, almond rock.]

bankrupt *bangk'rupt*, *n* a person who fails in business; an insolvent person. — *adj* insolvent; destitute (with *of*). — *vt* to make bankrupt; to have (a person) declared bankrupt; to ruin or impoverish (*fig*). — *n* **bank'ruptcy** (*bangk'rupt-si*). [Fr. *banque-route*, It. *banca rotta* — *banca*, bank, and *rotto*, *-a* — L. *ruptus*, broken.]

banner *ban'ər*, *n* strictly, a square flag bearing a coat of arms; a military standard; a flag bearing some device, often carried on two poles, or hanging from a cross-piece, used in processions, etc. — *adj* **bann'ered** furnished with banners. — **banner headline** a large-type headline running right across a newspaper page. [O.Fr. *banere* — L.L. *bandum*, *bannum*.]

bannock *ban'ək*, (chiefly *Scot*) *n* a flat (orig. home-made) cake of oatmeal, barley, or pease-meal, usu. baked on a griddle. [O.E. *bannuc*.]

banns *banz*, *npl* a proclamation of intended marriage. — **forbid the banns** to make formal objection to a projected marriage. [**ban**[1].]

banquet *bangk'wit*, *n* a feast. — *vt* to give a feast to. — *vi* to feast: — *pr p* **banq'ueting**; *pa t* and *pa p* **banq'ueted.** — *n* **banq'ueter.** — *n* **banqueteer'.** — *n* **banq'ueting.** — **banq'ueting-hall; banq'ueting-house.** [Fr., — *banc*, bench.]

banquette *bang-ket'*, *n* a raised way inside a parapet (*archit*); a built-in wall-sofa used instead of individual seats, e.g. in a restaurant. [Fr.; It. *banchetta*, dimin. of *banca*, seat.]

banshee *ban'shē*, (orig. *Ir folklore*) *n* a female spirit who wails and shrieks before a death in the family to which she is attached. [Ir. *bean sidhe*, Old Ir. *ben síde*, woman of the fairies.]

bantam *ban'təm*, *n* a small variety of the common domestic fowl; a small man, esp. a soldier. — *adj* of bantam breed; little and combative. — **ban'tamweight** a weight category applied variously in boxing and wrestling; a sportsman of the specified weight for the category (e.g. in professional boxing above flyweight, **jun'ior-bantamweight** (maximum 52 kg./115 lb.), **ban'tamweight** (maximum 54 kg./118 lb.) and **su'per-bantamweight** (maximum 55 kg./122 lb.)) [Prob. *Bantam* in Java.]

banter *ban'tər*, *vt* to joke at; to mock in fun. — *n* humorous ridicule; joking. — *n* **ban'terer.** — *n* and *adj* **ban'tering.** — *adv* **ban'teringly.**

Bantu *ban'tōō*, *n* a name given to a large group of African languages and the peoples speaking them in South and Central Africa; official name for African peoples of South Africa. — Also *adj*. — *n* **Ban'tustan** the coined name for a semi-independent region, or homeland, of South Africa populated and administered by Bantus; a region of similar status elsewhere.

banyan. See **bania.**

banzai *bän'zä-ē*, *interj* a Japanese battle-cry and salute to the emperor; a Japanese exclamation of joy uttered on happy occasions. [Jap. *banzai*, 10 000 years, forever.]

baobab *bā'ō-bab*, *n* a gigantic tropical Western African tree. [Prob. Afr.]

BAOR *abbrev* for British Army of the Rhine.

Bap. or **Bapt.** *abbrev* for Baptist.

bap *bap*, (*Scot* and *Northern Eng*) *n* a large, flat and elliptical breakfast roll.

bap. or **bapt.** *abbrev* for baptised.

baptise or **baptize** *bapt-īz'*, *vt* to administer baptism to; to christen, give a name to; to name at launching and break a bottle of wine on the bow of. — *n* **baptism** (*bap'tizm*) immersion in or sprinkling with water as a religious ceremony; an experience regarded as initiating someone into a society, group, etc. — *adj* **baptis'mal.** — *adv* **baptis'mally.** — *n* **bapt'ist** a person who baptises; (with *cap*) a member of a Christian sect which approves only of baptising by immersion, and that only of persons who profess their faith in Christ. — *n* **bap'tistery** or **bap'tistry** a place for administration of baptism, whether a separate building or part of a church. — **baptism of fire** any trying ordeal, such as a first experience of being under fire (*fig*); **clinical baptism** baptism administered to the sick; **conditional** (or **hypothetical**) **baptism** baptism administered conditionally when it is doubtful whether the person was previously baptised validly or at all; **private baptism** baptism elsewhere than in church. [Gr. *baptizein* — *baptein*, to dip.]

bapu *bä'pōō*, *n* spiritual father. [Hindi.]

Bar. *abbrev* for Barrister.

bar[1] *bär*, *n* a rod, strip or oblong block of any solid substance; a strong rod or long piece used as a lever, door fastening, barrier, part of a gate or grate, etc.; a crossbar; a bolt; a barrier; an obstruction or impediment; that which completely puts an end to an action or claim; in salary statements, a level beyond which one cannot rise unless certain conditions, concerning e.g. the amount of advanced work one does, are met; a bank or shoal as at the mouth of a river or harbour; a counter across which liquor or food is served; (one room in) a public-house; a rail or similar structure marking off a space, as in a house of parliament, or that at which prisoners are arraigned in court; (usu. with *cap*) barristers or advocates collectively; a ballet-dancer's exercise rail (usu. **barre**); an addition to a medal, a strip of metal below the clasp; a ridge; a stripe, esp. transverse; a horizontal band across a shield (*heraldry*); a vertical line across the staff marking off a measure (see also **double-bar**; *mus*); the measure itself (*mus*); a counter at which one particular article of food, clothing, etc., is sold, or one particular service is given. — *vt* to fasten, secure, shut (out or in), furnish or mark with a bar or bars; to hinder; to obstruct; to exclude the possibility or validity of; to preclude; to divide into bars: — *pr p* **barr'ing**; *pa t* and *pa p* **barred.** — *prep* except, but for. — *n* **barr'ing.** — *prep* except for; leaving out of consideration. — **bar'-bell** a bar weighted at the ends for gymnastic exercises; **bar'-chart** or **bar'-graph** a graph showing comparative quantities by means of oblong sections produced to the appropriate length; **bar code** an arrangement, readable by computer, of thick and thin parallel lines, e.g. printed on, and giving coded details of, goods in a supermarket, etc. — *adj* **bar'-coded.** — **bar'keeper** keeper of a refreshment bar or toll-bar; **bar lunch** a light meal or snack available in a bar; **bar'-magnet** a permanent magnet in the form of a straight bar; **bar'maid, bar'man** or **bar'person** a woman, man or person who serves at a bar in a public-house etc.; **bar'-room** a room in which there is a bar, a taproom; **bar'-tender** a barman or barmaid. — **at the bar** in court; in practice as a barrister or advocate; **bar none** (*colloq*) with no exceptions; **behind bars** in prison; **called to the bar** admitted as barrister or advocate in the U.K.; **called within the bar** made Queen's (or King's) counsel in the U.K. [O.Fr. *barre* — L.L. *barra*.]

bar² *bär*, (*meteorol*) *n* a unit used in expressing atmospheric pressure (millibar equals a thousand dynes per square centimetre): — *pl* **bar**. [Gr. *baros*, weight.]

bar. *abbrev* for baritone.

barathea *bar-ə-thē'ə*, *n* a soft woollen fabric of worsted, or of worsted and silk, etc.

BARB or **Barb** *bärb*, *abbrev* for Broadcasters' Audience Research Board.

barb¹ *bärb*, *n* the beardlike jag near the point of an arrow, fish-hook, etc.; one of the threadlike structures forming a feather's web; a sting (*fig*); a wounding or wittily-pointed remark; a woven linen covering for the throat and breast (and sometimes the lower part of the face) worn by women in the Middle Ages, still part of the habit of certain orders of nuns. — *vt* to arm with barbs. — *adj* **barb'ate** bearing a hairy tuft. — *adj* **barb'ated** barbed; bearded. — *n* **barb'el** a freshwater fish of the carp family with beardlike appendages at its mouth; such an appendage. — *n* **barb'et** a tropical bird with bristly beak; a kind of poodle. — *n* **barbicel** (*bär'bi-sel*) a tiny hook on the barbule of a feather. — *n* **barb'ule** a small barb; a fish's barbel; a hairlike structure on the barb of a feather. [L. *barba*, a beard.]

barb² *bärb*, *n* a horse of a racing breed related to the Arab; a dark-coloured fancy pigeon. [From *Barbary*, where the breeds originated.]

Barbadian *bär-bā'di-ən*, *adj* of the West Indian island of *Barbados*. — Also *n*.

barbarous *bär'bər-əs*, *adj* falling short of the standard of correctness, classical purity, and good taste; unscholarly; corrupt or ungrammatical or unidiomatic; uncultured; uncivilised; brutal; harsh. — *n* **barbār'ian** someone without taste or refinement; a somewhat uncivilised man; a cruel man. — Also *adj*. — *adj* **barbaric** (*bär-bar'ik*) uncivilised; characteristic of barbarians; rude; tastelessly ornate and ostentatious; wild and harsh. — *n* **barbarisation** or **-z-** (*bär-bər-ī-zā'shən*). — *vt* **bar'barise** or **-ize** to make barbarous; to corrupt (e.g. a language). — *n* **bar'barism** savagery, brutal or uncivilised behaviour; rudeness of manners; a form of speech offensive to scholarly taste. — *n* **barbarity** (*bär-bar'i-ti*) savageness; cruelty. — *adv* **bar'barously**. — *n* **bar'barousness**. [Gr. *barbaros*, foreign, lit. stammering, from the unfamiliar sound of foreign tongues.]

Barbary *bär'bər-i*, *n* the country of the *Berbers*, in North Africa. — **Barbary ape** a type of macaque, the only European monkey; **Barbary sheep** a North African wild sheep.

barbecue *bär'bi-kū*, *vt* to grill over an open fire, usu. of charcoal, often adding a highly seasoned sauce to the food. — *n* a framework for barbecuing food over an open fire; a portable grill for cooking thus; food cooked in this way; a party, esp. held out of doors, where food is so cooked. [Sp. *barbacoa* — Haitian *barbacòa*, a framework of sticks set upon posts.]

barbel. See **barb¹**.

barber *bär'bər*, *n* a person who shaves beards, cuts and styles men's hair, etc. — *vt* to shave or cut the hair of. — **bar'ber-shop** or **bar'bershop** a type of music originating in the U.S., played, or esp. sung, in close harmony, usu. in quartets. — Also *adj*. — **barber's pole** the barber's sign, a pole striped spirally, generally red and white. [O.Fr. *barbour* — L. *barba*, a beard.]

barberry *bär'bər-i*, *n* a thorny shrub (*Berberis*) of various species, most with yellow flowers and red berries, common in ornamental hedges. [L.L. *berberis*.]

barbet. See **barb¹**.

barbican *bär'bi-kən*, *n* a projecting watchtower over the gate of a castle or fortified town; esp. the outwork intended to defend the drawbridge. [O.Fr. *barbacane*.]

barbicel. See **barb¹**.

barbie *bär'bi*, *n* (*Austr*; *colloq*) a barbecue.

barbituric *bärb-it-ū'rik*, (*chem*) *adj* applied to an acid which is the source of barbiturates. — *n* **barb'itone** or **barb'ital** a derivative of barbituric acid used as a sedative and hypnotic. — *n* **barbit'urate** a salt or ester of barbituric acid used as a sedative or hypnotic drug. [From the lichen Usnea *barbata* and *uric* acid.]

Barbour® *bär'bər* or **Bar'bour® jacket** (*jak'ət*) (also **Bar'bour® coat** (*kōt*)), *n* a strong waterproof jacket (or coat) esp. made of waxed cotton.

barbs *barbz*, (*slang*) *npl* short for **barbiturates**.

barbule. See **barb¹**.

barcarole or **barcarolle** *bär'kə-rōl* or *bär-kə-rol'*, *n* a gondolier's song; a musical composition of a similar character. [It. *barcarola*, a boat-song — *barca*, a boat.]

BArch. *abbrev* for Bachelor of Architecture.

bard¹ *bärd*, *n* a Celtic poet and singer; a poet (*literary*); a poet whose work has won a competition at the Eisteddfod. — *adj* **bard'ic**. [Gael. and Ir. *bard*.]

bard² *bärd*, *n* piece of bacon or pork fat used to cover meat or game during cooking to prevent drying-out. — *vt* to cover a piece of meat or game with bards. [Fr. *barde* — Sp. *albarda*, pack-saddle.]

bare *bār*, *adj* naked; open to view; uncovered, bareheaded; unsheathed; unarmed; threadbare, worn; unprovided or scantily provided; poor; scanty; mere; unadorned; empty. — *vt* to strip or uncover. — *adv* **bare'ly** nakedly; plainly; explicitly; openly; hardly, scarcely; just and no more; not quite. — *n* **bare'ness**. — *adj* **bār'ish** somewhat bare. — *adj* and *adv* **bare'back** without saddle. — *adj* **bare'backed** with bare back; unsaddled. — *adj* **bare'boat** in shipping, used of a charter or hire in which the chartering company is totally responsible for manning, supplies, maintenance and insurance. — *adj* **bare'faced** impudent, shameless; beardless; with the face uncovered. — *adv* **barefacedly** (*bār-fāst'li* or *bār-fās'id-li*). — **bare'facedness**. — *adj* and *adv* **bare'foot** or **barefoot'ed** having the feet bare. — *adj* and *adv* **barehead'ed**. — *adj* and *adv* **bare-knuck'le** without gloves on; fiercely aggressive. — *adj* and *adv* **bare'legged**. — **barefoot doctor** orig. in China, an agricultural worker trained in the basic principles of health, hygiene and first-aid. [O.E. *bær*.]

barege or **barège** *bä-rezh'*, *n* a light, mixed dress-fabric. [*Barèges* in Hautes-Pyrénées.]

barf *bärf*, (*slang*) *vi* to vomit. [Orig. U.S.]

bargain *bär'gən*, *n* a contract or agreement; a favourable transaction; an advantageous purchase. — *vi* to make a contract or agreement; to haggle; to count (*on*), or make allowance (*for* a possibility). — *vt* to lose by bad bargaining (with *away*). — *n* **bar'gainer**. — **bar'gain-basement** or **-counter** places in a shop where bargains are promised; **bar'gain-hunter** a person who goes shopping to find bargains. — **into the bargain** as well, in addition; **make the best of a bad bargain** to do one's best in an adverse situation; **strike a bargain** to come to terms. [O.Fr. *bargaine*.]

barge *bärj, n* a flat-bottomed freight boat, used on rivers and canals; a lighter; a large pleasure or state boat. — *vi* to move clumsily; to bump (*into*); to push one's way rudely. — *n* **barg'ee** a bargeman. — **barge'man** manager of a barge; **barge'master** proprietor of a barge; **barge'pole** a pole for propelling a barge. — **barge in** to intrude; to interfere; **not touch with a bargepole** to refuse to have anything to do with. [O.Fr. *barge* — L.L. *barga*.]

barge-board *bärj'bōrd, n* a board along the edge of a gable. — *npl* **barge'-stones** those making up the sloping edge of a gable. [Perh. L.L. *bargus*, a gallows.]

baric. See **barium.**

barite. See under **baryta.**

baritone *bar'i-tōn, n* a deep-toned male voice between bass and tenor; a singer with such a voice; a baritone saxophone. — *adj* of the pitch and compass of a baritone. [Gr. *barytonos*, deep sounding.]

barium *bā'ri-əm, n* a metallic element (atomic no. 56; symbol **Ba**) present in baryta. — *adj* **bā'ric.** — **barium meal** a mixture of barium sulphate administered to render the alimentary canal opaque to X-rays. [See **baryta.**]

bark[1] *bärk, n* the abrupt cry of a dog, wolf, etc.; report of a gun. — *vi* to utter a bark; to advertise wares noisily. — *vt* to utter abruptly and peremptorily; to make by barking. — *n* **bark'er** a dog; a barking dog; a tout advertising wares, a show, etc. in a loud voice to attract custom. — **bark up the wrong tree** to follow a false scent; **chief barker** the title of the president of the Variety Club of Great Britain; **his bark is worse than his bite** his speech may be bad-tempered or fierce, but his actual deeds are not so bad. [O.E. *beorcan*.]

bark[2] or **barque** *bärk, n* a ship of small size, square-sterned, without head-rails; technically, a three-masted vessel whose mizzen-mast is fore-and-aft-rigged (instead of being square-rigged like the fore and main masts); any boat or sailing ship (*poetic*). [Fr. *barque* — L.L. *barca*.]

bark[3] *bärk, n* the rind or covering of the trunk and branches of a tree; that used in tanning or dyeing; that used in medicine (cinchona); an outer covering or skin. — *vt* to strip or peel bark or skin from; to encrust. — *vi* to form a bark. — *adj* **bark'less.** — *adj* **bark'y.** — **bark'-beetle** any beetle of the family *Scolytidae*, tunnellers in and under bark. — *adj* **bark'-bound** compressed by failure to shed the bark. [O.N. *börkr*.]

barley *bär'li, n* a hardy grass (*Hordeum vulgare* and other species); its grain used for food, and for making malt liquors and spirits. — **bar'leycorn** the grain from which malt is made; a single grain of barley; **barley sugar** sugar candied by melting and cooling (formerly by boiling with a decoction of barley); **barley water** a liquid produced by boiling down pearl barley in water, usu. sweetened and flavoured as a cold drink. — **pearl barley** the grain stripped of husk and pellicle, and completely rounded by grinding; **pot barley** the grain deprived by milling of its outer husk, used in making broth, etc. [O.E. *bærlic*, of barley.]

barm *bärm, n* froth of fermenting liquor; yeast. — *adj* **barm'y** frothy; fermenting; mentally unsound (*slang*); also **balmy** (*bä'mi*). — *n* **barm'iness.** — *adj* **barm'y-brained.** [O.E. *beorma*.]

bar mitzvah, bar mizvah or **bar mitsvah** *bär mits'və, n* (sometimes with *caps*; also hyphenated or as one word) in the Jewish religion, a boy attaining the age (usu. 13 years) of religious responsibility; the festivities held in recognition of this event. [Heb., son of the law.]

barn *bärn, n* a building in which grain, hay, etc., are stored. — *vt* to store in a barn. — **barn dance** a social gathering at which square-dances and other traditional country-dances are danced; **barn'-door** the door of a barn; (*humorously*) any broad target; **barn owl** a species of owl, generally buff-coloured above and white below; **barn'-stormer** a strolling player (as type of ranting actor); a peripatetic public speaker. — *vi* **barn'storm** to tour usu. country areas giving theatrical performances; to travel about speaking at meetings, usu. for election purposes. — Also *vt*. — *n* **barn'yard.** — Also *adj* as in **barnyard fowl.** [O.E. *bere-ern*, contr. *bern*, from *bere*, barley, *ern*, a house.]

barnacle[1] *bär'nə-kl, n* a crustacean that adheres to rocks and ship bottoms etc.; a companion not easily shaken off; a barnacle-goose. — **bar'nacle-goose** a wild black and white goose of N. Europe once believed to develop from the **goose'-barnacle,** a barnacle that attaches itself, esp. to floating wood, by a thick stalk. [O.Fr. *bernaque* — L.L. *bernaca*.]

barnacle[2] *bär'nə-kl, n* an instrument put on a restless horse's nose to keep him quiet. [O.Fr. *bernac*.]

barney *bär'ni*, (*colloq*) *n* a rough noisy quarrel.

barogram *bar'ō-gram, n* a tracing produced by a barograph. [Gr. *baros*, weight, and **-gram.**]

barograph *bar'ō-gräf, n* a recording barometer. [Gr. *baros*, weight, and **-graph.**]

barometer *bə-rom'i-tər, n* an instrument for measuring atmospheric pressure; a weather glass; an indicator of change (e.g. in public opinion; *fig*). — Also *adj*. — *adj* **barometric** (*bar-ō-met'rik*) or **barome'trical** (*-kl*). — *adv* **baromet'rically.** — *n* **barometry** (*ba-rom'ət-ri*). [Gr. *baros*, weight, *metron*, measure.]

baron *bar'ən, n* a title of rank, the lowest in the British peerage; a foreign noble of similar grade; the head of any organisation or institution who is regarded as wielding despotic power (e.g. a *press baron*); formerly a peer or great lord of the realm generally. — *n* **bar'onage** the whole body of barons; a list or book of barons. — *n* **bar'oness** a baron's wife, or a lady holding a baronial title in her own right. — *adj* **baronial** (*bə-rō'ni-əl*) pertaining to a baron or barony; applied to a turreted style of architecture favoured by the Scottish land-holding class. — *n* **bar'ony** the territory of a baron; in Ireland, a division of a county; in Scotland, a large freehold estate, or manor, even though not carrying with it a baron's title and rank; the rank of baron. [O.Fr. *barun, -on* — L.L. *barō, -ōnis*, man.]

baronet *bar'ən-et, n* the lowest British hereditary title, ranking below a baron. — *n* **bar'onetage** the whole body of baronets; a list or book of baronets. — *n* **bar'onetcy** the rank or title of baronet. — *adj* **baronet'ical.** [Dimin. of **baron.**]

barony. See under **baron.**

baroque *bə-rok'* or *bə-rōk', n* a bold, vigorous, exuberant style in architecture, decoration, and art generally, that arose with the Counter-Reformation and prevailed in Louis XIV's time, degenerating into ornamental extravagance; a comparable style in music, or literature. — *adj* in baroque style; whimsical; flamboyant; sometimes rococo. [Fr. *baroque*, from Port. and Sp.; of architecture, from It.]

baroscope *bar'ō-skōp, n* an instrument for indicating changes in the density of the air. [Gr. *baros*, weight, *skopeein*, to look at.]

barostat *bar'ō-stat, n* an automatic device for regulating pressure, e.g. in an aircraft. [Gr. *baros*, weight, and **-stat.**]

barouche *ba-rōōsh'* or *bə-rōōsh', n* a double-seated four-wheeled horse-drawn carriage with a collapsible top. [Ger. *Barutsche* — It. *baroccio* — L. *bis*, twice, *rota*, a wheel.]

barque. See **bark**[2].

barrack[1] *bar'ək, n* a building for soldiers, esp. in garrison (generally in *pl*); a huge plain, often bleak, building, esp. for housing many people. — *vt* and *vi* to lodge in barracks. — *adj* **barr'ack-room** (of humour, etc.) somewhat coarse. — **barrack-room lawyer** an argumentative soldier given to disputing military procedure; hence any insistent but unqualified giver of advice. [Fr. *baraque* — It. *baracca*, or Sp. *barraca*, tent.]

barrack[2] *bar'ək*, *vt* and *vi* to make a hostile demonstration (against), esp. by cheering ironically, at a cricket-match, etc. — *vi* (with *for*; *Austr* and *NZ*) to support, shout encouragement to. — *n* **barr'acker**. — *n* and *adj* **barr'acking**. [Perh. two separate words — Aboriginal Austr. *borak*, for the first sense and poss. Northern Ir. dialect *barrack*, meaning 'to brag', for the second sense.]

barracouta *bar-ə-ko͞o'tə*, *n* an edible fish from the southern hemisphere; (also **barracoo'ta** or **barracuda** *bar-ə-ko͞o'də*) a voracious West Indian fish similar to the grey mullets. [Sp. *baracuta*.]

barrage *bar'äzh*, *n* an artificial bar across a river; the forming of such a bar: a barrier formed by continuous shower of projectiles along a fixed or a moving line (curtain-fire), or by captive balloons, or mines, or otherwise; a heavy or continuous fire (as of questions, criticisms, etc.); a heat or round to select contestants, or decide a dead-heat (*sport*). — **barr'age-balloon**. [Fr. *barrage* — *barre*, bar.]

barramundi *bar-ə-mun'di*, *n* an Australian river-fish, valued as a food; any of several other Australian river-fish, and the Australian lung-fish. [Aboriginal.]

barre *bär*, *n* a horizontal rail fixed to the wall at waist-level, which ballet-dancers use to balance themselves while exercising (sometimes **bar**). [Fr.]

barrel *bar'əl*, *n* a wooden vessel made of curved staves bound with hoops; its contents or its capacity; a revolving drum; a cylinder; a tube e.g. of a gun; a button on a braided coat; the trunk of a horse, etc. — *vt* to put in barrels. — *n* **barr'elage**. — *n* **barr'elful** (*pl* **barr'elfuls**) as much as a barrel will hold. — *adj* **barr'elled** having a barrel or barrels; put in barrels. — *adj* **barrel-chest'ed** having a large, rounded, projecting ribcage. — **barr'el-house** a cheap saloon; **barr'el-organ** a mechanical instrument for playing tunes by means of a revolving drum set with pins turned by a handle; **barrel roll** (*aerobatics*) a complete revolution on the longitudinal axis; **barrel vault** a vault with a simple hemicylindrical roof (*adj* **barrel-vault'ed**). — **have someone over a barrel** to be in a position to get whatever one wants from someone. [Fr. *baril*.]

barren *bar'ən*, *adj* incapable of bearing offspring; not producing fruit, seed, crops, vegetation, etc.; infertile; unproductive; arid; jejune. — *n* (in *pl* with *cap*) in North America, plateaux with small trees but no timber. — *n* **barr'enness**. [O.Fr. *barain*, *brahain*, *brehaing*.]

barricade *bar'ik-ād*, *n* a temporary fortification raised to block a street; a barrier. — *vt* to block; to close or enclose with a barricade. [Fr. *barricade* or Sp. *barricada*.]

barrier *bar'i-ər*, *n* a defensive stockade or palisade; a fence or other structure to bar passage or prevent access; a separating or restraining obstacle. — *vt* to shut by means of a barrier. — **barrier cream** an ointment for the skin used to prevent dirt from entering the pores and as a protection against oils and solvents; **barrier reef** a coral-reef fringing a coast with a navigable channel inside. [O.Fr. *barriere* — L.L. *barrāria* — *barra*.]

barrio *bar'i-ō*, *n* esp. in U.S., a Spanish-speaking, usu. poor, community or district: — *pl* **barr'ios**. [Sp., district, quarter.]

barrister *bar'is-tər*, *n* a lawyer who is qualified to plead at the bar in a law-court (in Scotland called *advocate*). — *adj* **barristerial** (*bar-is-tē'ri-əl*). — *n* **barr'istership**. [From L.L. *barra*, bar (i.e. orig. of the Inns of Court).]

barrow[1] *bar'ō*, *n* a small usu. hand-propelled cart used to convey a load. — **barr'ow-boy** a street-trader with wares displayed on a barrow; **barr'ow-tram** the shaft of a barrow. [O.E. *bearwe* — *beran*, to bear.]

barrow[2] *bar'ō*, *n* a hill or hillock (*obs* except in place names); an ancient earth-built grave-mound, tumulus. [O.E. *beorg*.]

Bart *abbrev* for Baronet.

barter *bär'tər*, *vt* to give in exchange (with *for* or *away*). — *vi* to trade by exchange of commodities. — *n* trade by direct exchange of goods. — *n* **bar'terer**. [Prob. O.Fr. *barat*.]

Bartholin's glands *bär'tə-linz glandz*, (*physiol*) *npl* a pair of mucus-secreting glands in the vagina. [Discovered by Caspar *Bartholin* (1655–1738), a Danish anatomist.]

bartisan or **bartizan** *bär'ti-zan* or *bär-ti-zan'*, *n* a parapet or battlement; a projecting gallery on a wall-face; (*erron*) a corbelled corner turret. — *adj* **bar'tisaned** (or *bar-ti-zand'*). [App. first used by Scott, who found a reading *bertisene*, for *bratticing*; see **brattice**.]

Bart's *bärts*, *abbrev* for St Bartholomew's Hospital, London.

barycentric *bar-i-sen'trik*, *adj* pertaining to the centre of gravity. [Gr. *barys*, heavy, *kentron*, centre.]

barye *bär'ē*. Same as **microbar**.

baryon *bar'i-on*, *n* any one of the heavier class of subatomic particles, which includes protons and neutrons (opp. to *lepton*). [Gr. *barys*, heavy.]

barysphere *bar'is-fēr*, *n* the heavy core of the earth within the lithosphere. [Gr. *barys*, heavy, *sphairă*, sphere.]

baryta *bə-rī'tə*, *n* barium monoxide. — *n* **bary'tes** (*bə-rī'tēz*) heavy spar, barium sulphate (also **barite** *bā'rīt*); (*loosely*) baryta. — *adj* **barytic** (*ba-rit'ik*) of or containing baryta or barium. — **baryta paper** paper coated on one side with an emulsion of barium sulphate and gelatine. [Gr. *barys*, heavy.]

BAS *abbrev* for: Bachelor of Agricultural Science; British Antarctic Survey.

basal. See under **base**[1].

basalt *bas'ölt*, *n* a dark-coloured igneous rock; a type of pottery similar in appearance to the rock. — *adj* **basalt'ic**. [L. *basaltēs* — Gr. *basanītēs* (*lithos*), touchstone.]

bascule *bas'kūl*, *n* an apparatus of which one end rises as the other sinks. — **bascule bridge** a bridge that rises when a counterpoise sinks in a pit. [Fr. *bascule*, see-saw.]

base[1] *bās*, *n* that on which a thing rests; foot, bottom; foundation, support; the part, e.g. of an organ of a plant or animal, nearest the place of attachment; the foot of a pillar (*archit*); the lower part of a shield (*heraldry*); a number on which a system of numeration or of logarithms is founded; the chief ingredient; an ingredient of a mixture that plays a subsidiary but important part, such as giving bulk; in dyeing, a mordant; a starting-point; a standard against which comparisons can be made; a base-line; a fixed station in games such as baseball; a place from which operations are conducted or on which they depend; home or headquarters; a substance that reacts with an acid to form a salt, or dissolves in water forming hydroxyl ions (*chem*); that element in words to which suffixes and prefixes are added. — *vt* to found or place on a base: — *pr p* **bās'ing**; *pa p* **based** (*bāst*). — *adj* **bās'al** pertaining to or situated at the base; at the lowest level; (*loosely*) fundamental. — *adj* **base'less** without a base or foundation. — *n* **base'lessness**. — *n* **base'ment** an underlying support; the lowest storey of a building beneath the principal one, esp. one below ground level. — *adj* **basilar** (*bas'il-ar*) basal. — **basal anaesthesia** anaesthesia acting as a basis for further and deeper anaesthesia; **basal metabolism** the level of metabolism occurring in an individual in a resting state; **base'ball** a team game, played nine-a-side with bat and ball, the players on the batting side making a circuit of four bases on the field; a ball for the game; **base'baller; base'-line** an accurately measured line used as a base for triangulation; a line at the end of the court (*lawn tennis*); a line joining bases (*baseball*); **base'plate** the foundation plate of a piece of heavy machinery; **base rate** the rate, determined by a bank, on which it bases its lending rates of interest; **Basic English** a reduced English vocabulary of 850 words for teaching foreigners or for use as an auxiliary language; (without *cap*) English using few and simple words. — **base out** see **bottom out; get to** (or **make**) **first base** (*US colloq*) to complete the first stage in a process; **off base** (*US colloq*) wrong, mistaken. [Fr. *base* — L. *basis* — Gr. *basis* — root of *bainein*, to go.]

base² *bās*, *adj* low in place, value, estimation, or principle; mean; vile; worthless; debased; servile as opposed to *free* (*law*); humble. — *adv* **base'ly.** — *n* **base'ness.** — *adj* **base'-born** low-born; illegitimate. — **base coin** spurious coin; **base metal** any metal other than the precious metals; a metal that alters on exposure to air (opp. to *noble metal*). — *adj* **base'-minded** of a low mind or spirit; mean. [Fr. *bas* — L.L. *bassus*, thick, squat.]

baseball, basement. See under **base¹**.

basenji *bə-sen'jē*, *n* a smallish, erect-eared, curly-tailed African hunting dog that rarely barks. [Bantu, *pl.* of *mosenji, musengi*, native.]

BASF *abbrev* for *Badische Anilin und Soda-Fabrik* (a German chemical company).

bash *bash*, *vt* to beat, batter; to smash; to attack harshly or maliciously, physically or verbally. — *n* a heavy blow; mark of a blow; a party (*colloq*). — *n* **bash'er** a person who, or thing that, bashes (sometimes used as *sfx*). — *n* **bash'ing** (often used as *sfx*, as in *queer-bashing, union-bashing*) the activity of making harsh or malicious physical or verbal attacks on individuals or (members of) groups one dislikes. — **have a bash** (*colloq*) to have a try; to make an attempt (at). [Prob. Scand.]

bashful *bash'fōōl*, *adj* easily confused; modest; shy, lacking confidence. — *adv* **bash'fully.** — *n* **bash'fulness.** — *adj* **bash'less** unashamed. [See **abash.**]

basho *bash'ō*, *n* in sumo wrestling, a tournament: — *pl* **bash'o.** [Jap.]

Basic or **BASIC** *bā'sik*, *n* a computer language using a combination of simple English and algebra. [*B*eginners' *A*ll-purpose *S*ymbolic *I*nstruction *C*ode.]

basic *bā'sik*, *adj* belonging to or of the nature of a base; fundamental; simple, plain, without extras; containing excess of a base; poor in silica (opp. to *acid*; *geol*). — *n* (in *pl*) fundamental principles. — *adv* **ba'sically** with reference to what is basic; fundamentally, essentially. — *n* **basicity** (*bās-is'it-i*). — **basic process** a steel-making process with a furnace lined with material rich in metallic oxides; **basic slag** a by-product of the basic process rich in lime, used as manure. [**base¹**].

basidium *bas-id'i-əm*, *n* a fungal fructification from which spores (usually four) are loosed: — *pl* **basid'ia.** — *adj* **basid'ial.** — *npl* **Basidiomycetes** (*ba-sid-i-ō-mī-sē'tēz*) one of the main groups of fungi, characterised by the possession of basidia, including the familiar toadstools as well as rusts and smuts. [Gr. *basis*, basis, and dimin. ending, *-idion*.]

basil *baz'il*, *n* an aromatic labiate plant (*Ocimum*), used for seasoning food; extended to calamint and other labiates. [O.Fr. *basile* — L. *basilisca*, representing Gr. *basilikon*, lit. royal, perh. with reference to *basiliskos*, cobra, as a reputed cure for snakebite.]

basilar. See **base¹**.

basilica *bə-sil'i-kə*, *n* a large oblong hall, with double colonnades and commonly a semicircular apse, used for judicial and commercial purposes; a magnificent church formed out of such a hall, or built after its plan; a Roman Catholic church with honorific privileges; orig. a royal palace. — *adj* **basil'ical** royal. — *adj* **basil'ican** of a basilica. [Gr. *basilikos, -ē, -on*, royal — *basileus*, king.]

basin *bā'sn*, *n* wide open vessel or dish; a sink, washbasin; a basinful; any hollow place containing water, such as a dock; the area drained by a river and its tributaries. — *n* **ba'sinful** as much as will fill a basin: — *pl* **ba'sinfuls.** — **have a basinful** (*colloq*) to have an excess of. [O.Fr. *bacin* — L.L. *bachinus*.]

basis *bās'is*, *n* the foundation, or that on which a thing rests; the groundwork or first principle; the fundamental ingredient: — *pl* **bases** (*bās'ēz*). [See **base¹**.]

bask *bäsk*, *vi* to lie in the warmth or sunshine (often *fig*). — **basking shark** a large but harmless shark that shows its great dorsal fin as it basks. [O.N. *bathask*, to bathe.]

basket *bäs'kit*, *n* a receptacle of plaited or interwoven twigs, rushes, canes or other flexible materials; a basketful; a net used as goal at basketball; a goal scored in basketball; a collection of similar or related ideas or things; a bastard (*euph*). — *n* **bas'ketful** as much as fills a basket: — *pl* **bas'ketfuls.** — *n* **bas'ketry** basketwork. — **bas'ketball** a team game in which goals are scored by throwing a ball into a raised horizontal net; the ball used in the game; **bas'ket-chair** a wicker chair; **bas'ket-maker; bas'ket-making; bas'ket-stitch** (*knitting*) groups of plain and purl stitches alternating vertically and horizontally, resembling basketwork in effect; **bas'ketweave** a form of weaving using two or more strands in the warp and weft; **bas'ketwork** articles made of interlaced twigs, canes, etc.; the art of making these. — **basket of currencies** (*econ*) a name for the special monetary unit composed of various European currencies in fixed proportions, used as a standard against which to assess the value of any particular currency, or as a currency in its own right.

basmati rice *bas-mat'i rīs*, *n* a long grain, naturally perfumed rice.

Basque *bäsk*, *n* a member of a people inhabiting the western Pyrenees, in Spain and France; their language; (without *cap*) a short-skirted jacket, or a continuation of a bodice a little below the waist; a close-fitting (under-)bodice. — *adj* **Basque** of the Basques or their language or country. [Fr.]

bas-relief *bas-ri-lēf'* or *ba'ri-lēf*, or (It.) **basso-rilievo** *bäs-sō-rēl-yā'vō*, (*popularly*) **-relievo** *bas-ō-ri-lē'vō*, *n* sculpture in which the figures do not stand far out from the ground on which they are formed. [Fr. and It. See **base²** and **relief.**]

bass¹ *bās*, *n* the low part in music; a bass singer — often in Italian form **basso** (*bäs'sō*): — *pl* **bas'sos** or **bassi** (*bā'si*); a bass instrument, esp. (*colloq*) a double-bass; low frequency sound as output from an amplifier, etc. — *adj* (of a musical instrument or voice) low in pitch and compass. — *n* **bass'ist** a person who plays a double-bass or a bass guitar. — *adj* **bass'y** somewhat bass; predominantly bass. — **bass'-bar** a strip of wood on the belly of a violin, etc., under the bass foot of the bridge, to distribute the vibrations; **bass clef** (*mus*) the F clef, in which the note F below middle C is written on the fourth line of the stave; **bass drum** the large drum of an orchestra or band; **bass fiddle** (*colloq*) a double-bass; **bass guitar** an electric guitar similar in sound and range to the double-bass. [See **base²**.]

bass² or **basse** *bas*, *n* a European sea-fish of the sea-perch family; extended to other sea and freshwater fishes. [O.E. *bærs*.]

basset *bas'it*, *n* a low-set, smooth-coated hound with long ears (also **bass'et-hound** or **basset hound**); an outcrop (*geol*). — **basset horn** (It. *corno di bassetto*) the richest and softest of all wind instruments, similar to a clarinet in tone and fingering, but with a twice-bent wooden tube. — *n* **bass'et=hornist.** [Fr., — *bas*, low.]

bassinet *bas'i-net*, *n* a kind of basket with a hood used as a cradle; a similarly shaped pram; a bed in hospital, with necessary equipment, for care of a baby. [Fr. dimin. of *bassin*, a basin.]

basso. See **bass**[1].

bassoon *bə-sōōn'*, *n* a woodwind instrument, its compass from B flat below the bass stave to C or F in the treble. — *n* **bassoon'ist.** [It. *bassone*, augm. of *basso*, low.]

basso profundo *bä-sō prō-fŏŏn'dō*, (It.) *n* a deep bass voice or singer.

basso-rilievo. See **bas-relief.**

bast *bast*, *n* phloem, the conductive material in a plant; inner bark, esp. of lime; fibre; matting. [O.E. *bæst.*]

bastard[1] *bas'tərd* or *bäs'tərd*, *n* a child born of parents not married to each other; a recalcitrant person or thing, an unpleasant person, an unfortunate person, or almost meaninglessly, a chap (*vulg*). — *adj* born to parents not married to each other; not genuine; resembling, but not identical with, the species bearing the name; of abnormal shape or size; false. — *n* **bastardisā'tion** or **-z-.** — *vt* **bas'tardise** or **-ize** to reduce to a lower state or condition. — *n* **bast'ard-ism** bastardy. — *adj* **bas'tardly.** — *n* **bas'tardy** the state of being a bastard. — **bas'tard-wing** three, four, or five feathers on the first digit (corresponding to the thumb) of a bird's wing. [O.F. *bastard* (Fr. *bâtard*), child of the pack-saddle (O.Fr. *bast*).]

bastard[2] *bas'tərd*, (*SAfr*) *n* a person of mixed white and coloured parentage, whether legitimately born or not. [Du. *bastaard*, bastard.]

baste[1] *bāst*, *vi* to beat with a stick. — *n* **bāst'ing.** [Prob. conn. with O.N. *beysta*, Dan. *böste*, to beat.]

baste[2] *bāst*, *vt* to drop fat or butter over, as in roasting.

baste[3] *bāst*, *vt* to tack in sewing. [O.Fr. *bastir* — O.H.G. *bestan*, to sew.]

Bastille *bas-tēl'*, *n* an old fortress and state prison in Paris, demolished in the Revolution (July 1789). [Fr. a tower, — O.Fr., *bastir* (Fr. *bâtir*), to build.]

bastinado *bast-in-ād'ō*, *vt* to beat with a baton or stick, esp. on the soles of the feet (an Eastern punishment): — *pr p* **bastinād'oing** or **bastinād'ing**; *pa p* **bastinād'oed** or **bastinād'ed.** — *n* **bastinade'.** — *n* **bastinād'o**: — *pl* **bastinād'oes.** [Sp. *bastonada*, Fr. *bastonnade* — *baston*, *baton*; cf. **baton, batten**[2].]

bastion *bast'yən*, *n* a kind of tower at the angle of a fortification; a defence (*fig*). — *adj* **bast'ioned.** [Fr., — It. *bastione* — *bastire*, to build.]

Basuto *ba-sōō'tō*, *n* the Bantu people of Lesotho (formerly Basutoland); one of these people (*pl* **Basu'tos**); their language (also **Sotho**).

BASW *abbrev* for British Association of Social Workers.

BAT *abbrev* for British-American Tobacco Company.

bat[1] *bat*, *n* a flattish club for striking the ball in cricket; a club for baseball; in tennis, etc., a racket (*colloq*); something shaped like a bat e.g. the signalling devices used by a batman to guide aircraft; a batsman or batswoman; a blow. — *vt* and *vi* to hit with a bat (in cricket, etc.); to hit as if with a bat: — *pr p* **batt'ing**; *pa t* and *pa p* **batt'ed.** — *n* **batt'er.** — *n* **batt'ing** the management of a bat in playing games; cotton fibre prepared in sheets, for quilts, etc. — **bat'man** a man on an aerodrome or aircraft carrier who assists planes to taxi to position using a pair of lightweight bats; (see also separate entry); **bats'man,** *fem* **bats'woman** the person who wields the bat at cricket, etc.; **bats'manship.** — **off one's own bat** by one's own efforts; on one's own initiative. [Perh. from O.E. *bat* (a doubtful form), prob. Celt. *bat*, staff.]

bat[2] *bat*, *n* a flying mammal with wings attached mainly to its arms and hands, but extending along its sides to the hind-feet and tail, usu. nocturnal. — *adj* **bats** (*colloq*) crazy. — *adj* **batt'y** batlike; bat-infested; crazy (*colloq*). — **batwing sleeve** a sleeve that is very wide at the armhole and tight at the wrist. — **have** (or **be**) **bats in the belfry** (*colloq*) to be crazy or slightly mad; **like a bat out of hell** (*colloq*) very quickly. [M.E. *bakke*, app. from Scand.]

bat[3] *bat*, *vt* to flutter, esp. an eyelid. — **not bat an eye** or **eyelid** to show no surprise or emotion.

bat. or **batt.** *abbrev* for: battalion; battery.

batata *bə-tä'tə*, *n* the sweet-potato. [Sp. from Haitian.]

batch *bach*, *n* the quantity of bread baked, or of anything made or got ready, at one time; a set; a group of similar objects or people. — *vt* to collect into, or treat in, batches. — *adj* **batch'ing.** — **batch processing** (*comput*) a method of processing data in which similar items of data are collected together for processing at one time. [From the root of **bake.**]

bate[1] *bāt*, *vt* and *vi* to abate; to lessen, diminish; to blunt. — **with bated breath** (holding one's breath) in fear or suspense. [Aphetic form of **abate.**]

bate[2]. Same as **bait**, a rage (*slang*).

bateau *bä-tō'*, *n* a light river-boat, esp. on Canadian rivers: — *pl* **bateaux** (*ba-tōz'*). [Fr.]

bateleur *bat'lər*, *n* a short-tailed African eagle. [Fr., mountebank, app. from its characteristic movements.]

BATF *abbrev* for Bureau of Alcohol, Tobacco and Firearms (U.S.).

Bath *bäth*, *n* a famous city in Somerset, with Roman *baths*. — *n* **Bath bun** a rich sweet bun; **Bath chair** (also without *cap*) a large wheeled chair for invalids; **Bath Oliver** a plain biscuit invented by Dr W. Oliver of Bath.

bath *bäth*, *n* water for immersing the body; an act of bathing; a receptacle or a house for bathing; (in *pl*) a building containing baths for the use of the public, and a swimming pool; a place for undergoing medical treatment by means of bathing; the act of exposing the body to vapour, mud, sunlight, etc.; a liquid or other material (as sand), or a receptacle, in which anything is immersed for heating, washing, or steeping (*chem*): — *pl* **baths** (*bädhz*, also *bäths*). — *vt* to give a bath to; to wash (oneself) in a bath. — *vi* to take a bath. — **bath'cube** bath-salts in the form of a solid cube; **bath'house** or **bath'-house; bath'robe** a towelling loose-fitting garment worn esp. before and after bathing or swimming; dressing-gown (*US*); **bath'room** a room containing a bath, and usu. a washbasin and lavatory; esp. in N. Am., a lavatory; **bath'-salts** a usu. sweet-smelling substance used in baths to soften and perfume the water; **bath'tub.** — **Order of the Bath** an English order of knighthood, so named from the bath before installation. [O.E. *bæth*; Ger. *Bad.*]

bathe *bādh*, *vt* to wash as in a bath; to wash or moisten, with any liquid; to moisten, suffuse, encompass. — *vi* to take a dip or swim; to bask. — *n* the act of bathing; a swim or dip. — *n* **bāth'er** someone who bathes; (in *pl*; *Austr* and *NZ*) a swimming costume. — **bāth'ing-box** or **-hut** a small structure for bathers to undress and dress in; **bāth'ing-costume, -dress** or **-suit** a swimming costume. [O.E. *bathian.*]

bathetic. See **bathos.**

bath mitzvah, bath mizvah or **bath mitsvah** *bäth mits'və*, (sometimes with *caps*; also hyphenated or as one word) esp. in the U.S., a girl of the Jewish religion attaining the age (usu. 12 to 13 years) of religious responsibility; the festivities held in recognition of this event. [Heb., daughter of the law.]

batholite *bath'ō-līt*, *n* a mass of igneous rock that has risen from a great depth. — *adj* **batholithic** (*bath-ō-lith'ik*) or **batholitic** (*bath-ō-lit'ik*). [Gr. *bathos*, depth, *lithos*, a stone.]

bathometer *bath-om'it-ər*, *n* a bathymeter. [Gr. *bathos*, depth, *metron*, measure.]

bathos *bā' thos, n* a ludicrous descent from the elevated to the ordinary in writing or speech. — *adj* **bathetic** (*bə-thet' ik*). [Gr. *bathos*, depth.]

bathy- *bath-i-, combining form* denoting deep. — *adj* **bathyal** (*bath' i-əl*) of ocean depths of between 200 and 2000 metres. — *n* **bathymeter** (*bath-im' ət-ər*; Gr. *metron*, measure) a sounding instrument. — *adj* **bathymet'ric** or **bathymet'rical**. — *n* **bathym'etry** the science of sounding seas and lakes. — *n* **bath'ysphere** (Gr. *sphaira*, sphere) a submersible observation chamber (**bath'yscaph, -scaphe**, or **-scape** are later types). [Gr. *bathys*, deep.]

batik *bat' ik, n* an orig. Indonesian method of producing designs on cloth by covering with wax, for each successive dipping, those parts that are to be protected from the dye; fabric patterned by this method. [Malay.]

batiste *ba-tēst', n* a fine fabric of linen, cotton or wool. [Fr., cambric — *Baptiste*, the original maker; or from its use in wiping the heads of children after baptism.]

batman *bat' mən, n* an officer's attendant. — See also under **bat**[1]. [Fr. *bât*, pack-saddle.]

baton *bat' ən* or *bat' n, n* a staff of office, e.g. that of a marshal; a policeman's truncheon; a short stick passed on from one runner to the next in a relay-race; a light wand used by the conductor of an orchestra; a knobbed staff carried, tossed and twirled by a drum major, etc., at the head of a marching band, etc.; a baton round. — **baton charge** a swift forward movement of police against a hostile crowd with truncheons drawn for use. — *vt* **bat'on-charge**. — **baton gun** a gun which fires **baton rounds**, plastic bullets, used in riot-control. — **under the baton of** (of choirs and orchestras) conducted by. [Fr. *bâton*.]

batsman, batswoman. See **bat**[1].

batt. See **bat**. (abbrev).

battalion *bə-tal' yən, n* a body of soldiers consisting of several companies; a body of men drawn up in battle array. [Fr. *batallion* — It. *battaglione*; see **battle**.]

batten[1] *bat' n, vi* to thrive at the expense of (with *on*); to grow fat; to feed abundantly (on; *lit* and *fig*). [O.N. *batna*, to grow better.]

batten[2] *bat' n, n* a piece of sawn timber used for flooring, support of laths, etc.; a strip of wood fastened across parallel boards, or used to fasten down hatches aboard ship, etc.; a row of electric lamps or a strip of wood carrying them. — *vt* to fasten or furnish with battens. — *n* **batt'ening** battens forming a structure. — **batten down the hatches** to prepare for a crisis (*fig*); orig. to secure the hatches on a ship against bad weather. [**baton**.]

Battenberg *bat' ən-bûrg* or **Battenburg cake** (*kāk*), *n* a kind of cake usu. made in pink and yellow squares and covered with marzipan. [Perh. from *Battenberg*, a village in W. Germany.]

batter[1] *bat' ər, vt* to beat with successive blows; to wear with beating or by use; to attack with artillery. — *n* ingredients (usu. flour and eggs) beaten along with some liquid (e.g. milk) into a paste (*cookery*); paste for sticking. — *adj* **batt'ered** suffering frequent violent assaults (in particular **battered baby** (or **child**) a baby (or child) suffering such attacks at the hands of its parents, or **battered wife** a woman who suffers such attacks by her spouse); covered or treated with batter. — **batt'ering-ram** a large beam used for battering down walls. — **battered baby** (or **child**) **syndrome** a collection of symptoms found in a baby or young child, caused by violence on the part of the parent or other adult suffering from social and psychological disturbance. [O.Fr. *batre* — L.L. *battěre* (L. *ba(t)tuěre*), to beat.]

batter[2] *bat' ər*, (*building*) *n* slope (e.g. of the face of a structure) upwards and backwards. — *vi* to slope in this way.

batter[3]. See **bat**[1].

battery *bat' ər-i, n* the act of battering; a number of cannon with their equipment; the place on which cannon are mounted; a unit of artillery or its personnel; a combination of Leyden jars, lenses, or other apparatus; a series of two or more electric cells arranged to produce, or store, electricity; a single voltaic or solar cell; an attack against a person, beating, wounding, or threatening by touching clothes or body (*law*); an arrangement of tiers of cages in which hens are kept; an arrangement of similarly restrictive compartments for rearing pigs or cattle intensively; an apparatus for preparing or serving meals. — **battery of tests** (*psychol*) a set of tests covering various factors relevant to some end purpose, e.g. job selection.

batting. See **bat**[1].

battle *bat' l, n* a contest between opposing armies; a fight or encounter. — *vi* to fight; to struggle; to contend (with *against* or *with*). — *vt* to contest. — *n* **batt'ler**. — **batt'le-axe** a kind of axe once used in battle; a formidable woman (*colloq*); **battle-axe block** (or **section**) (*Austr* and *NZ*) a plot of land without a street frontage, with access to and from the street via a drive or lane; **batt'le-cruiser** a large cruiser with battleship qualities; **batt'le-cry** a war-cry, slogan; **batt'ledress** a simplified military uniform, close-fitting at the waist, allowing freedom of movement; **battle fatigue** (*psychol*) psychological disorder caused by stress of combat; **batt'lefield** or **batt'leground** the place on which a battle is or was fought; **battle royal** a general mêlée. — *adj* **batt'le-scarred** scarred in battle. — **batt'leship** a warship of the first class. — **do battle** (often *fig*) to fight; **half the battle** anything that brings one well on the way to success; **join battle** to engage in fighting. [Fr. *bataille* — L. *battuālia*, fighting.]

battledore *bat' l-dör, n* a light bat for striking a ball or shuttlecock. [Perh. Sp. *batidor*, a beater, a washing beetle.]

battlement *bat' l-mənt, n* a wall or parapet with embrasures for shooting through. [O.Fr. *batailler*, movable defences.]

battology *bat-ol' ə-ji, n* futile repetition in speech or writing. — *adj* **battolog'ical**. [Gr. *battologiā*, stuttering.]

batty, batwing sleeve. See **bat**[2].

bauble *bö' bl, n* a trifling piece of finery; a jester's sceptre. [O.Fr. *babel, baubel*, toy, trinket.]

baud *böd', n* a unit of signalling speed (*teleg*); speed at which computers pass information (e.g. by telephone line) to other computers etc. (*comput*).

baudekin *böd' i-kin*. Same as **baldachin**.

baudric or **baudrick** *böd' rik*. Same as **baldric**.

bauera *bow' ə-rə, n* a plant of the *Bauera* genus of evergreen shrubs with pink flowers found in Australia. [F. and F.A. *Bauer*, 19th-cent. Austrian botanical painters.]

Bauhaus *bow' hows, n* a German school of art and architecture (1919–33) having as its aim the integration of art and technology in design. [Lit. building-house.]

bauhinia *bō-hin' i-ə, n* a plant of the *Bauhinia* genus of tropical trees. [J. and G. *Bauhin*, 17th-cent. Swiss botanists.]

baulk. See **balk**.

bauxite *bök' sīt* or *bök'-zīt, n* a clay compound containing aluminium. — *adj* **bauxitic** (*bök-sit' ik*). [From Les *Baux*, near Arles, and *-ite*.]

bawble. Same as **bauble**.

bawd *böd, n* a woman who keeps a brothel. — *adv* **bawd'ily**. — *n* **bawd'iness**. — *n* **bawd'ry** procuring; unchastity; lewd talk. — *adj* **bawd'y** lewd. — *n* lewd talk. — **bawd'y-house** a brothel. [Prob. M.E. *bawdstrot*, pander — O.Fr. *baldestrot*, prob. — *bald*, bold, gay, and the root of **strut**.]

bawl *böl, vt* and *vi* to shout or cry out very loudly. — *n* a loud cry or shout. — *n* **bawl'er**. — *n* **bawl'ing**. — **bawl out** (*colloq*) to reprimand bullyingly.

[Perh. L.L. *baulāre*, to bark, but cf. Icel. *baula*, to low like a cow — O.N. *baula*, a cow.]

bay[1] *bā, adj* reddish brown inclining to chestnut (of horses, usu. with a black mane and tail). — *n* a bay horse. [Fr. *bai* — L. *badius*, chestnut-coloured.]

bay[2] *bā, n* an inlet of the sea with a wider opening than a gulf; an inward bend of the shore; a similar recess in a land form, e.g. in a mountain range. — **bay salt** coarse-grained salt, orig. from sea-water. — **the Bay State** Massachusetts. [Fr. *baie* — L.L. *baia*, a harbour.]

bay[3] *bā, n* the space between two columns, timbers, walls, etc.; any recess or stall; a space for a vehicle to park; a space where vehicles can be loaded and unloaded (also **loading bay**); a passing-place in a military trench; a side-line in a railway station (also **bay'-line**); a compartment (e.g. bomb bay) or section of an aircraft. — **bay window** any window forming a recess. — *adj* **bay-win'dowed**. [O.Fr. *baee* — *baer*, to gape, be open; prob. conn. with **bay**[2].]

bay[4] *bā, n* the laurel tree; extended to other trees and shrubs, species of *Magnolia*, *Myrica*, etc.; (in *pl*) an honorary garland or crown of victory, originally of laurel; literary renown. — **bay'berry** the berry of the bay tree, or of candle-berry; a tree (*Pimenta acris*) related to allspice; **bay leaf** the dried leaf of the laurel tree used as a flavouring agent in cooking; **bay rum** an aromatic liquid prepared from the leaves of *Pimenta acris* used medicinally and cosmetically; this liquid mixed with certain other substances. [O.Fr. *baie*, a berry — L. *bāca*.]

bay[5] *bā, n* barking, baying (esp. of a dog in pursuit); the combined cry of hounds in conflict with a hunted animal; the last stand of a hunted animal when it faces the hounds at close quarters. — *vi* to bark (esp. of large dogs). — *vt* to bark at; to utter by baying; to bring to bay. — **bay at the moon** to make a futile gesture; **keep at bay** to prevent from coming closer; **stand** (or **be**) **at bay** to face the dogs at close quarters; to face one's pursuers. [Partly O.Fr. *abai*, barking, *bayer*, to bark, partly O.Fr. *bay*, open-mouthed suspense — L.L. *badāre*, to open the mouth.]

bayadère *bä-yä-der', n* a Hindu dancing-girl; a horizontally-striped woven fabric. [Fr., — Port. *bailadeira*.]

bayle. See **bail**[2].

bayonet *bā'ə-nit, n* a stabbing instrument of steel fixed to the muzzle of a firearm; (also **bayonet fitting**) a type of fitting for a light bulb, camera lens, etc., in which prongs on its side fit into slots to hold it in place. — *vt* to stab with a bayonet; to force at the point of the bayonet. — **bayonet joint** or **socket**, etc. one with, or for, a bayonet fitting. [Fr. *baïonnette*, perh. from *Bayonne*, in France; or from O.Fr. *bayon*, arrow.]

bayou *bī'ōō, (US) n* the marshy offshoot of a lake or river. [Perh. Fr. *boyau*, gut, or Choctaw *bāyuk*, little river.]

bazaar or **bazar** *bə-zär', n* an Eastern marketplace or exchange; a fair in imitation of an Eastern bazaar, often selling goods in aid of charity; sometimes, a big shop. [Pers. *bāzār*, a market.]

bazooka *bə-zōō'kə, n* an anti-tank gun for rocket-driven projectiles; a rocket launcher situated on the wing of an aeroplane. [Invented name.]

bazouki. See **bouzouki**.

BB *abbrev* for Boys' Brigade. — *symbol* for very black (on lead pencils).

bb *abbrev* for books.

BBB *symbol* for blacker than a BB pencil (on a pencil).

BBBC *abbrev* for British Boxing Board of Control.

BBC *abbrev* for British Broadcasting Corporation.

BBFC *abbrev* for British Board of Film Censors.

BC *abbrev* for: Battery Commander; (or **B.C.**) before Christ (used in dating to indicate the number of years before the year once thought to be that of Christ's birth); Board of Control; British Columbia (Canadian province).

BCC *abbrev* for British Council of Churches.

B-cell *bē'-sel, (immun) n* a type of lymphocyte that matures in the bone marrow, and produces antibodies. [*b*one marrow and **cell**.]

BCG or **bcg** *abbrev* for bacillus of Calmette and Guérin, a strain of the tubercle bacillus, used for inoculation.

BCh. *abbrev* for *Baccalaureus Chirurgiae* (L.), Bachelor of Surgery.

BCL *abbrev* for Bachelor of Civil Law.

BCom. or **BComm.** *abbrev* for Bachelor of Commerce.

BCS *abbrev for* British Computer Society.

BD *abbrev* for: Bachelor of Divinity; bank draft; bills discounted.

bd *abbrev* for: board; bond; bound.

BDA *abbrev* for British Dental Association.

Bde *abbrev* for Brigade.

BDH *abbrev* for British Drug Houses.

BDI *abbrev* for *Bundesverband des Deutschen Industrie* (Ger.), Federation of German Industry.

BDS *abbrev* for: Bachelor of Dental Surgery; Barbados (I.V.R.).

bds *abbrev* for boards.

BE *abbrev* for: Bachelor of Engineering; Board of Education.

Be *(chem) symbol* for beryllium.

be *bē, vi infin* to live; to exist; to have the state or quality mentioned: — *pr p* **bē'ing**; *pa p* **been** (*bēn* or *bin*); *pr subj* **be**; for *pr t* see **am, art**[2]**, is, are**; for *pa t* see **was, were.** — **be-all and end-all** the supreme aim or issue. [O.E. *bēon*.]

b e *abbrev* for bill of exchange.

be- *bi-, pfx* used: (1) to form words with the sense of around, on all sides, in all directions, thoroughly; (2) to form verbs from adjectives and nouns; (3) formerly, to make intransitive verbs transitive, as in *bespeak*. [O.E. *bi-*, weak form of *bī*.]

BEAB *abbrev* for British Electrical Approvals Board.

beach *bēch, n* the shore of a sea or of a lake, esp. when sandy or pebbly. — *vt* to drive or haul up on a beach. — *adj* **beached** having a beach; driven on a beach. — *adj* **beach'y** pebbly. — **beach'-ball** a large usu. inflatable, colourful ball for playing games on a beach; **beach'comber** (*-kōm-ər*) a long rolling wave; a loafer about the wharfs in Pacific seaports: a settler on a Pacific island who maintains himself by pearl-fishery, or by gathering jetsam, etc. on beaches; **beach'combing; beach'head** an area held on an enemy's shore for the purpose of landing; **beach'master** an officer in charge of disembarking troops; **beach'-rescue** a person employed to save beach bathers in difficulties. [Orig. a dialect word for shingle.]

beacon *bē'kən, n* a fire on high ground lit as a signal, e.g. to warn of danger; a hill on which it could be lighted; an erection with or without a light marking a rock or shoal in navigable waters; a light to guide airmen; a sign marking a street crossing — e.g. a **Belisha** (*bə-lē'shə* or *bə-lish'ə*) **beacon** named after the Minister of Transport 1934; a wireless transmitter in which the radiation is concentrated in one or more narrow beams, so as to act as a guide to shipping or aircraft; anything that warns of danger. — *vt* to act as a beacon to; to light up; to mark by beacons. [O.E. *bēacn*, a beacon, a sign.]

bead *bēd, n* a little ball strung with others in a rosary, for counting prayers; a similar ball or the like pierced for stringing to form a necklace, etc.; a beadlike drop; the front-sight of a gun; a narrow moulding orig. of semi-circular section, sometimes broken into beadlike parts, now in various shapes, used esp. for covering small gaps; the flange of a tyre. — *vt* to furnish with beads or beading. — *vi* to form a bead or beads. — *adj* **bead'ed** having beads or a bead; in beadlike form. — *n* **bead'ing** bead (moulding); work in beads. — *adj* **bead'y** beadlike, small and bright (as eyes); covered with beads or bubbles. — **draw a bead on** (*US*) to take aim at. [O.E. *gebed*, prayer; see **bid**[2].]

beadle *bēd'l*, *n* a mace-bearer; a petty officer of a church, college, etc.; a parish officer with the power of punishing petty offenders; in Scotland, the church-officer attending on the minister. [O.E. *bydel* — *bēodan*, to proclaim, to bid; affected by O.Fr. form *bedel*.]

beady. See **bead**.

beagle *bē'gl*, *n* a small hound; a spy; a bailiff; a small kind of shark. — *vi* to hunt with beagles. — *n* **bea'gler**. — *n* **bea'gling**.

beak *bēk*, *n* a bird's bill; a hard or sharp snout; a nose (*jocularly*); a pointed process or projection; a magistrate, schoolmaster, or schoolmistress (*slang*). — *adj* **beaked** (*bēkt*). — *adj* **beak'y**. — [O.Fr. *bec* — L. *beccus* (recorded by Suetonius), a cock's bill.]

beaker *bēk'ər*, *n* a large drinking-bowl or cup, or its contents; a deep glass or other vessel used by chemists, generally with a lip for pouring; a usu. plastic tumbler; one of a set of similar cylindrical-shaped objects, a child's toy. [O.N. *bikarr*.]

beam *bēm*, *n* a large and straight piece of timber or iron forming one of the main structural members of a building, etc.; any of the transverse pieces of framing extending across a ship's hull; the greatest width of a ship or boat; breadth; the part of a balance from which the scales hang; the stem, or main part of a deerhorn, an anchor or a plough; a cylinder of wood in a loom; a shaft or ray of light or other radiations; a gleam; a raised horizontal bar on which gymnasts perform balancing exercises (*gymnastics*). — *vt* to send forth; to place on a beam; to transmit or direct, e.g. by beam system. — *vi* to shine; to smile radiantly. — *n* **beam'er**. — *adv* **beam'ily** radiantly. — *n* **beam'iness** radiance; breadth. — *n* and *adj* **beam'ing**. — *adv* **beam'ingly**. — *adj* **beam'ish** radiant. — *adj* **beam'less** without beams; emitting no rays. — *adj* **beam'y** shining; radiant. — **beam'-ends** the ends of the transverse beams of a ship; **beam'-engine** a steam-engine with a beam connecting the piston-rod and the crank of the wheel-shaft. — **off (or on) the beam** off (or on) the course shown by a radio beam; off (or on) the right track (*fig*); **on her beam-ends** (of a ship) so much inclined to one side that the beams become nearly vertical; **on one's beam-ends** in acute distress, destitute; **on the port (or starboard) beam** applied to any distant point out at sea, at right angles to the keel, and on the left (or right) side. [O.E. *bēam*, tree, stock of a tree, ray of light.]

BEAMA *abbrev* for British Electrical and Allied Manufacturers' Association.

bean *bēn*, *n* the name of several kinds of leguminous plants and their seeds, esp. the common, or broad bean and the French kidney, or haricot bean; applied also to the seeds of other plants, from their beanlike form, such as coffee; a coin (*colloq*); the head (*colloq*). — *vt* (*colloq*) to hit on the head. — *n* **bean'ery** (*US slang*) a cheap restaurant. — *n* **bean'o** (*colloq*) a beanfeast, a disturbance, a jollification: — *pl* **bean'os**. — **bean'-bag** a small cloth bag containing dried beans or the like, used in games; a large cushion filled e.g. with chips or balls of plastic foam, used as seating (also **beanbag chair**); **bean'feast** an annual dinner given by employers to their workers at which beans used to be prominent; a jollification; **bean'pole** a supporting pole up which a bean plant climbs; a tall, very thin person (*colloq*); **bean sprout** the young shoot of the mung bean or certain other beans, used as a vegetable esp. in Chinese cookery; **bean'stalk** the stem of a bean plant. — **full of beans** in high spirits; **know how many beans make five** (*colloq*) to be fully alert, know what's what; **old bean** see under **old**. [O.E. *bēan*, Ger. *Bohne*.]

bear[1] *bār*, *vt* to carry; to have; to convey; to remove from the board in the final stage of the game (*backgammon*); to sustain or support; to thrust or drive; to endure; to purport; to afford; to behave or conduct (oneself); to bring forth, give birth to (*pa p* **born** (*börn*) in passive uses). — *vi* to suffer; to be patient; to have reference (with *on* or *upon*); to press (with *on* or *upon*); to lie in, or take, a direction; to be capable of sustaining weight; to be productive: — *pr p* **bear'ing**; *pa t* **bore**; *pa p* **borne** (*börn*). — *adj* **bear'able**. — *n* **bear'ableness**. — *adv* **bear'ably**. — *n* **bear'er** someone who or that which bears; the actual holder of a cheque or the like; a person who helps to carry a body to the grave; a carrier or messenger; formerly in India a personal, household or hotel servant. — *n* **bear'ing** demeanour; direction; a supporting surface; relation; that which is borne upon an escutcheon; the part of a machine that bears friction, esp. part of a shaft or axle and its support (sometimes in *pl*; see **ball-bearing**). — Also *adj*. — **bearer bond** or **bearer share, security**, etc. a bond, etc. the title to which is held by the person in possession of it; **bearing rein** a fixed rein between the bit and the saddle, by which a horse's head is held up and its neck made to arch. — **bear away** to sail away; to carry away; **bear down** to overthrow; to press downwards; (with *upon* or *towards*) to sail with the wind (towards); (with *upon*) to approach (someone or something) rapidly and purposefully; **bear hard (or heavily) upon** (*lit* and *fig*) to press heavily on; to oppress, afflict; **bear in mind** to remember (that); to think of, take into consideration; **bear in upon** (usu. in *passive*) to impress upon, or to make realise, esp. by degrees; **bear out** to corroborate; **bear up** to keep up one's spirits; **bear with** to make allowance for; **bring to bear** to bring into operation (with *against* or *upon*); **find** (or **lose**) **one's bearings** to ascertain (or to become uncertain of) one's position or orientation. [O.E. *beran*.]

bear[2] *bār*, *n* a heavy carnivorous animal with long shaggy hair and hooked claws; any rude, rough or ill-bred fellow; a person who sells stocks for delivery at a future date, anticipating a fall in price (*stock exchange*; opp. to *bull*); the name of two constellations, the Great and Little Bear (Ursa major and minor). — *vi* to speculate for a fall. — *adj* **bear'ish** like a bear in manners; inclining towards, or anticipating a fall in prices (*stock exchange*). — *adv* **bear'ishly**. — *n* **bear'ishness**. — **bear garden** a turbulent gathering; formerly an enclosure for **bear'-baiting**, the former sport of setting dogs to worry a bear; **bear'skin** the skin of a bear; a shaggy woollen cloth for overcoats; the high fur cap worn by the Guards in England. [O.E. *bera*.]

beard *bērd*, *n* the hair that grows on the chin and adjacent parts of a grown man's face; the tuft on the lower jaw of a goat, seal, etc.; a fish's barbel; an awn or threadlike spike as on the ears of barley (*bot*); a tuft of hairs; a barb of a hook, an arrow, etc.; the gills of an oyster, etc. — *vt* to oppose to the face. — *adj* **beard'ed**. — *adj* **beard'less**. [O.E. *beard*.]

béarnaise *bā-ar-nez* or **béarnaise sauce** (*sös*), *n* (also with *cap*) a sauce made from egg yolks, butter, shallots, tarragon, chervil and wine vinegar. [Fr. *béarnaise* (fem. of *béarnais*) of Béarn, region of south-western France.]

beast *bēst*, *n* an irrational animal, as opposed to man; a four-footed animal; a brutal person; anything beastly (*colloq*). — *n* **beast'ie** (orig. *Scot*) a dimin. form of **beast**, the four-footed animal; an insect, spider, etc. (*colloq*). — *n* **beast'liness**. — *adj* **beast'like** (also *adv*). — *adj* **beast'ly** like a beast in actions or behaviour; bestial; foul; sensual; vile, disagreeable (*colloq*). — *adv* brutishly; abominably, frightfully (*colloq*). [O.Fr. *beste* — *L. bestia*.]

beastings. Same as **beestings.**

beat *bēt*, *vt* to strike repeatedly; to batter; to whip up or switch; to flap; to strike (bushes, undergrowth etc.) in order to rouse game; to thrash; to defeat, to frustrate; to be too difficult for; to outdo, excel; to spread flat and thin by beating with a tool (as gold); to mark (time) with a baton, etc. — *vi* to give strokes repeatedly; to pulsate; to impinge; to mark time in music; to sail as close as possible to directly into the wind: — *pr p* **beat'ing**; *pa t* **beat**; *pa p* **beat'en** or now rarely **beat**. — *n* a recurrent stroke, its sound, or its moment; accent; pulsation, esp. that heard when two notes nearly in tune are sounded together; a round or course, such as a policeman's; an area of land or stretch of riverbank on which sportsmen hunt or fish; a place of resort. — *adj* weary; fatigued; relating to beatniks (*colloq*). — *adj* **beat'able.** — *adj* — **beat'en** made smooth or hard by beating or treading; trite; worn by use; exhausted (*Austr* and *NZ*; *colloq*). — *n* **beat'er** a person or thing which beats or strikes; a person who rouses or beats up game; a crushing or mixing instrument. — *n* **beat'-ing.** — *n* **beatnik** (*bēt'nik*) a young person whose behaviour, dress etc., are unconventional. — **beat music** popular music with a very pronounced rhythm. — *adj* **beat'-up** dilapidated through excessive use. — **beat a retreat** to retreat, orig. to beat the drum as a signal for retreat (**beat the retreat** to perform the military ceremony (**beating the retreat**) consisting of marching and military music usu. performed at dusk (orig. marking the recall of troops to their quarters)); **beat down** of a buyer, to try to reduce (the price of goods), to persuade (the seller) to settle for less; **beat it** (*slang*) to make off hastily or furtively; (as *imper*) go away!; **beat off** to drive back; **beat one's brains** to puzzle one's brains about something; **beat one's breast** (*fig*) to show extravagant signs of grief; **beat out** to flatten or reduce in thickness by beating; **beat someone to it** to manage to do something before someone else can; **beat the bounds** to trace out boundaries in a perambulation, certain objects in the line of journey being formally struck; **beat the clock** to do or finish something within the time allowed; **beat up** to pound or whip into froth, paste, a mixture, etc.; to put up as by beating the bushes; to subject to a violent and brutal attack (*colloq*; also in U.S. **beat up on**); to disturb; to arouse; to go about in quest of anything; to make way against wind or tide; **take a beating** to suffer physical or verbal chastisement; **take some** (or **a lot of**) **beating** (*colloq*) to be of very high quality, i.e. to be difficult to excel. [O.E. *bēatan*, past t. *bēot*.]

beatify *bi-at'i-fī*, *vt* to make blessed or happy; to declare to be in the enjoyment of eternal happiness in heaven. — *adj* **beatific** (*bē-ə-tif'ik*) or **beatif'ical** making supremely happy. — *adv* **beatif'ically.** — *n* **beatificā'tion** the act of beatifying; a declaration by the Pope that a person is blessed in heaven, authorising a certain definite form of public reverence payable to him — the first step to canonisation (*RC*). [L. *beātus*, blessed, *facĕre*, to make.]

beatitude *bi-at'i-tūd*, *n* happiness of the highest kind; a title given to patriarchs in the Orthodox Churches; (in *pl*) sayings of Christ in Matthew v, declaring certain classes of person to be blessed (*Christian relig*). [L. *beātitūdō* — *beātus*, blessed.]

beatnik. See under **beat.**

beau[1] *bō*, *n* a man attentive to dress or fashion; a dandy; a lover: — *pl* **beaux** (*bōz*). [Fr. *beau*, *bel* — L. *bellus*, fine, gay.]

beau[2] *bō*, (Fr.) *adj* beautiful, handsome, fine. — **beau geste** (*zhest*) gracious gesture; **beau monde** (*mɔ̃d*) the gay or fashionable world.

Beaufort *bō'fərt*, *adj* devised by Sir Francis *Beaufort* (1774–1857), Irish-born British admiral and hydrographer. — **Beaufort scale** a scale of wind velocity, with 0 for calm, 12 for hurricane.

beauty *bū'ti*, *n* the quality that gives pleasure to the sight, or aesthetic pleasure generally; a particular grace or excellence; a beautiful person, esp. a woman; also applied collectively; a very fine specimen of its kind. — *n* **beaut** (*slang*) someone or something exceptionally beautiful or remarkable. — *adj* and *interj* (esp. *Austr*) excellent, fine. — *adj* **beauteous** (*bū'ti-əs*) a poetic word for beautiful. — *adv* **beau'teously.** — *n* **beau'teousness.** — *n* **beautician** (*bū-tish'ən*) a person engaged in women's hairdressing, facial make-up, manicuring, etc. — *n* **beautificā'tion.** — *n* **beau'tifier** a person who or something which beautifies or makes beautiful. — *adj* **beau'tiful** fair; with qualities that give delight to the senses, esp. the eye and ear, or which awaken admiration in the mind. — *adv* **beau'tifully.** — *vt* **beau'tify** to make beautiful; to grace; to adorn. — **beauty contest** a competition held for the selection of a beauty queen; **beauty parlour** an establishment for the hairdressing, manicuring, face-massaging, etc., of women; **beauty queen** a girl who is voted the most attractive or best-proportioned in a competition; **beauty sleep** the sleep before midnight, considered the most refreshing; **beauty spot** a patch placed on the face to heighten beauty; a birthmark resembling such a patch; a foil to set off something else; a scene of outstanding beauty. [O.Fr. *biaute* (Fr. *beauté*) — L.L. *bellitās*, *-ātis* — L. *bellus*.]

beaux arts *bō-zär*, (Fr.) *npl* fine arts.

beaver *bēv'ər*, *n* an amphibious rodent (*Castor*); its valuable fur; a hat of beaver fur or a substitute material; a glove of beaver fur; a heavy woollen cloth; a boy belonging to the most junior branch of the scout movement (also **Beaver Scout**). — **beaver away** (*colloq*) to work very hard (at). [O.E. *befer*, *beofor*.]

bebop *bē'bop*, *n* a variety of jazz music (from about 1940) which added new harmonies, melodic patterns, and rhythms to accepted jazz characteristics. — Also **bop.** — Also *vi*. [Imit. of two quavers in the rhythm.]

becalm *bi-käm'*, *vt* to make calm, still or quiet. — *adj* **becalmed'** motionless from lack of wind. [**be-** (1).]

became *bi-kām'*, *pa t* of **become.**

because *bi-koz'* or *bi-köz'*, *adv* and *conj* for the reason that; on account (of). [**by** and **cause.**]

béchamel *bā'shə-mel*, **béchamel sauce** (*sös*) or **bechamel** *besh'ə-mel*, *n* a white sauce flavoured with onion and herbs and sometimes enriched with cream. [Fr.; from name of steward of Louis XIV.]

bêche-de-mer *besh'də-mer*, *n* the trepang or sea slug, much esteemed in China as a food delicacy. [Fr., — Port. *bicho do mar*, 'sea-worm', the sea slug.]

Becher's Brook *bē'cherz brŏŏk*, *n* a notoriously difficult jump in the English Grand National steeplechase; a particularly difficult or critical obstacle, problem or possible stumbling-block.

beck[1] *bek*, *n* a brook. [O.N. *bekkr*.]

beck[2] *bek*, *n* a sign with the finger or head. — **at someone's beck and call** always ready to obey or wait upon someone. [A contr. of **beckon.**]

becket *bek'it*, (*naut*) *n* a loop of rope having a knot at one end and an eye at the other; a large hook, or a wooden bracket used to keep loose tackle or spars in a convenient place. [Perh. Du. *bogt*, *bocht*, a bend of rope.]

beckon *bek'n*, *vt* and *vi* to nod or (now usu.) make a summoning sign (to). [O.E. *bīecnan* — *bēacn*, a sign.]

become *bi-kum'*, *vi* to come to be; to be the fate (followed by *of*). — *vt* to suit or befit; to grace; to adorn fittingly; to look well in: — *pa t* **became'**; *pa p* **become'.** — *adj* **becom'ing.** — *adv* **becom'ingly.** — *n* **becom'ingness.** [O.E. *becuman*; see **come.**]

becquerel *bek'ə-rel* or *bek-ə-rel'*, *n* the derived SI unit of radioactivity, symbol **Bq**, equal to one disintegration per second. [A.H. *Becquerel* (1852–1908), Fr. physicist.]

BEd. *abbrev* for Bachelor of Education.

bed *bed*, *n* a couch or place to sleep on; a mattress; a bedstead; a garden plot; a layer of oysters, etc.; a place in which anything rests; conjugal union, sexual relationship, the marriage-bed, matrimonial rights and duties; the channel of a river; sea or lake bottom; a layer or stratum. — *vt* to put to bed; to provide, or make, a bed for; to have sexual intercourse with; to plant in a bed; to lay in layers or on a surface; to embed. — *vi* to go to bed: — *pr p* **bedd'ing**; *pa p* **bedd'ed.** — *adj* **bedd'able** sexually attractive. — *n* **bedd'er** a plant suitable for a flower bed. — *n* **bedd'ing** mattress, bedclothes, etc.; litter for cattle; stratification (*geol*). — **bed'bug** the common bug; **bed'chamber** a bedroom; **bed'clothes** sheets, blankets, etc., for a bed; **bed'cover** an upper covering for a bed; **bedd'y-bye** or **-byes** bed, as a place to sleep (used in speaking to children or *facetiously*); **bed'fellow** a sharer of a bed; a colleague; something or someone that associates with another; **bed'-jacket** a light jacket worn when sitting up in bed; **bed'-linen** sheets and pillow-cases; **bed'pan** a utensil into which a person confined to bed can urinate and defecate; a warming-pan; **bed'-plate** (*mech*) the metal base to which the frame of a machine, engine, etc. is attached; **bed'-post** a corner support of a bedstead. — *adj* **bed'ridden** confined to bed by age or sickness; worn out. — **bed'rock** the solid rock underneath superficial formations; fundamental principles (*fig*); the lowest state. — *adj* bottom, lowest; basic, fundamental. — **bed'-roll** a sleeping-bag or bedclothes rolled up so as to be easily carried by a camper, etc.; **bed'room** a room with a bed; a sleeping apartment; room in bed, sleeping space. — *adj* (esp. of a comedy or farce) involving or hinting at sexual activity between people in a bedroom, in night-clothes, etc. — **bed'-sheet** a cotton, nylon, etc. sheet for a bed; **bed'side** position by a bed. — Also *adj*. — **bedside book** one esp. suitable for reading in bed; **bedside manner** that assumed by a doctor at a sickbed; **bed-sitt'ing-room** a combined bedroom and sitting-room, e.g. in lodgings (shortened to **bed'-sit** or **bed'-sitter**); **bed'socks** warm socks for wearing in bed; **bed'sore** an ulcer arising from long confinement to bed, esp. over the bony prominences; **bed'spread** a coverlet put over a bed by day; **bed'stead** a frame for supporting a bed; **bed'straw** any plant of the genus *Galium* (once used as straw for mattresses); **bed'-table** a table for use by a person in bed; **bed'time** the time for going to bed. — *adj* to do with, or suitable for, bedtime. — **bed'-wetting** the accidental passing of urine in bed. — **bed and board** food and lodging; full connubial relations; **bed and breakfast** (at a hotel, etc.) overnight accommodation with breakfast (*adj* **bed-and-break'fast** (*stock exchange*) in which shares are sold one day and rebought the next to establish a gain or a loss for tax purposes); **bed down** to (cause to) settle down, esp. in a makeshift bed, for sleep; **bed of roses** any easy or comfortable place; **bed out** to plant out in a flower-bed, etc.; **get out of bed on the wrong side** to start the day in a bad mood; **go** or **put to bed** (of newspapers, magazines, etc.) to go to or send to press; **lie in the bed one has made** to have to accept the consequences of one's own actions; **make a bed** to put a bed in order; **take to one's bed** to go to bed because of illness, grief, age, etc. [O.E. *bed(d)*.]

bedazzle *bi-daz'l*, *vt* to dazzle or overpower by any strong light: — *pa p* **bedazz'led**, stupefied, besotted. — *n* **bedazz'lement.** [**be-** (1).]

beddable. See **bed.**

bedeck *bi-dek'*, *vt* to deck or ornament. [**be-** (1).]

bedeguar *bed'i-gär*, *n* a soft spongy gall found on the branches of sweet-brier and other roses, also called the sweet-brier sponge. [Fr. *bédeguar* — Pers. and Ar. *bādā-war*, lit. wind-brought.]

bedel or **bedell.** Old spellings of **beadle**, still used at Oxford and Cambridge.

bedevil *bi-dev'l*, *vt* to throw into confusion; to play the devil with; to torment; to treat with devilish malignity; to possess as a devil: — *pr p* **bedev'illing**; *pa t* and *pa p* **bedev'illed.** — *n* **bedev'ilment.** [**be-** (2).]

bedew *bi-dū'*, *vt* to moisten gently, as with dew. [**be-** (2).]

bedlam *bed'ləm*, *n* a place of uproar, a madhouse; pandemonium. — *adj* fit for a madhouse. [From the priory St Mary of *Bethlehem*, in London, afterwards a madhouse (Bethlehem Royal Hospital).]

Bedlington *bed'ling-tən* or **Bedlington terrier** (*ter'i-ər*), *n* a long-bodied lightly-built terrier, fastest of its kind. [*Bedlington*, near Morpeth, where it was first bred.]

Bedouin or **Beduin** *bed'o͞o-in* or *bed'win*, *n* (also without *cap*) a tent-dwelling nomad Arab: — *pl* **Bed'ouin** or **Bedouins.** — Also *adj*. — *n* and *adj* **Bedu** (*bed'o͞o*) (a) Bedouin. [Fr. *bédouin* — Ar. *badāwin*, dwellers in the desert.]

bedraggle *bi-drag'l*, *vt* to soil by dragging in the wet or dirt. — *adj* **bedragg'led.** [**be-** (1).]

Beds. *abbrev* for Bedfordshire.

Bedu, Beduin. See **Bedouin.**

bee *bē*, *n* a four-winged insect that makes honey; a gathering of persons to unite their labour for the benefit of one individual or family, or for some joint amusement, exercise or competition (as *quilting-bee*, *husking-bee* or *spelling-bee*; a busy person; (usu. in *pl*) a lump of a type of yeast. — **bee balm** a species of *Monarda*, a plant of the mint family; **bee'-bread** the pollen collected by bees as food for their young; **bee'-eater** any bird of a brightly-plumaged family allied to the kingfishers; **bee'-flower** a flower pollinated by bees; **bee'-glue** propolis, resin-like material gathered by bees from trees; **bee'hive** a case or box in which bees are kept (*adj* dome-shaped, like an old-fashioned beehive, as **beehive hairstyle, beehive tomb**); **bee'keeper; bee'keeping; bee'-kite** the honey-buzzard; **bee'line** see **make a beeline for** below; **bee'-moth** a moth whose larvae are very destructive to young bees; **bee'-orchis** an orchid whose flower resembles a bee; **bees'wax** the wax secreted by bees and used by them in constructing their cells, greatly valued as an ingredient in polish for wood. — *vt* to polish with beeswax. — **bees'wing** a filmy crust of tartar formed in port and some other wines after long keeping. — **a bee in one's bonnet** a whimsical or crazy fancy on some point; an obsession; **make a beeline for** to take the most direct way towards (like the honey-laden bee's way home); **the bee's knees** (*colloq*) someone or something, particularly good, admirable, etc. [O.E. *bēo*.]

Beeb *bēb*, *n* colloq. for **BBC** — British Broadcasting Corporation.

beech *bēch*, *n* a common forest tree of the genus *Fagus* with smooth grey bark; extended to the related genus *Nothofagus* and to many trees not related; the wood of such a tree. — **beech'-fern** a fern of the polypody family; **beech'-marten** the stone-marten; **beech'-mast** the mast or nuts of the beech-tree, which yield a valuable oil, **beech'-oil; beech'-wood** a wood of beech-trees; beech timber. [O.E. *boece*, *bēce*.]

beef *bēf*, *n* the flesh of domestic cattle as food; extended to that of some other animals, such as the horse; muscle; vigorous muscular force; a complaint; an argument or quarrel. — *adj* of beef. — *vi* to grumble. — *adj* **beef'y** like beef; fleshy, muscular; stolid. — **beef'burger** a round flat cake of finely chopped meat, usu. fried or grilled; **beef'cake** (a picture of a) muscle-man; brawn as distinct from brain; **beef cattle** cattle reared mainly for their meat, as opposed to *dairy cattle* reared mainly for milk production; **beef'eater** the ox-bird or ox-pecker; a consumer of beef; a yeoman of the guard; a warder of the Tower of London; **beef olive** a thin slice of beef rolled round a savoury stuffing and usu. stewed; **beef'steak** a thick slice of beef for broiling or frying; **beef-tea'** stimulating rather than nutritious food for invalids; juice of beef strained off, after simmering in water; **beef tomato** a particularly large variety of tomato. — **beef up** (*colloq*) to add strength to, to reinforce. [O.Fr. *boef* (Fr. *bœuf*) — L. *bōs*, *bovis*.]

been *bēn* or *bin*, *pa p* of **be**.

beep *bēp*, *n* the sound made by the horn of a car, etc., or an electronic device. — *vi* and *vt* to (cause to) make such a sound. — *n* **beep'er**. [Imit.]

beer *bēr*, *n* an alcoholic beverage made by fermentation, in which the yeast settles to the bottom (cf. **ale**), from malted barley flavoured with hops; the generic name of malt liquor, including ale and porter; a glassful, etc., of this to drink. — *adj* **beer'y** of, or affected by, beer. — *n* **beer'iness**. — **beer'-barrel**; **beer'-bottle**; **beer'-engine** or **beer'-pump** a machine for drawing beer up from the casks to the bar; **beer'-garden** a garden with tables where beer and other refreshments may be purchased; **beer'hall** (*SAfr*) a large public drinking place for non-whites; **beer'-mat** a small, usu. cardboard table-mat for a beer-glass, etc.; **beer'-money** money given in lieu of beer and spirits; a gratuity; **beer'-parlor** or **-parlour** (*Can*) a public room in a hotel, etc., where beer is served; **beer'-up** (*Austr slang*) a drinking-bout. — **beer and skittles** idle enjoyment; **bitter beer** pale ale, a highly hopped beer made from the very finest selected malt and hops (**mild** or **sweet** ale being of greater gravity or strength, and comparatively lightly hopped); **dry beer** see under **dry**; **small beer** orig. weak beer; something trifling or unimportant, esp. when compared with something else. [O.E. *bēor*.]

beestings *bēst'ingz*, *n* the first milk drawn from a cow after calving. [O.E. *bȳsting*, *bēost*.]

beet *bēt*, *n* a plant with a succulent root, used as food and as a source of sugar. — **beet'root** the root of the beet plant; **beet sugar**. [O.E. *bēte* — L. *bēta*.]

beetle[1] *bē'tl*, *n* any insect of the Coleoptera, an order in which the forewings are reduced to hard and horny covers for the hindwings; a game in which a drawing of a beetle is made up gradually from its component parts, body, head, etc., according to the throw of dice, the object being to produce a completed drawing; (esp. with *cap*) a particular variety of small Volkswagen car with rounded roof and bonnet, resembling a beetle (*colloq*). — *vi* to jut, to overhang; to scurry (*colloq*). — *adj* **beet'ling** jutting; prominent; overhanging. — *adj* **beet'le-browed** with overhanging or prominent brows. — **beetle brows**; **beet'le-crusher** (*slang*) a big heavy foot or boot; a policeman; an infantryman; **beetle drive** a progressive game of beetle. — **beetle off** to scurry away like a beetle (*colloq*); **black beetle** the cockroach (properly not a beetle). [M.E. *bityl* — O.E. *bitula*, *bitela* — *bītan*, to bite.]

beetle[2] *bē'tl*, *n* a heavy wooden mallet used for driving in wedges, crushing or beating down paving-stones, or the like; a wooden pestle-shaped utensil for mashing potatoes, beating linen, clothes, etc. [O.E. *bīetl* — *bēatan*, to beat.]

beetroot. See **beet**.

beeves *bēvz*, *npl* cattle, oxen. [See **beef**.]

BEF *abbrev* for British Expeditionary Force.

bef. *abbrev* for before.

befall *bi-fōl'*, *vt* (or *vi* with *dative*) to fall or happen to; to occur to. — *vi* to happen or come to pass; to fall in one's way: — *pr p* **befall'ing**; *pa t* **befell'**; *pa p* **befall'en**. [O.E. *bef(e)allan*; see **fall**[1].]

befinned *bi-find'*, *adj* having fins. [**be-** (2)].

befit *bi-fit'*, *vt* to be fitting, or suitable to or for. — *vi* to be correct or fitting: — *pr p* **befitt'ing**; *pa p* **befitt'ed**. — *adj* **befitt'ing**. — *adv* **befitt'ingly**. [**be-** (1).]

before *bi-fōr*, *prep* in front of; ahead of; in the presence or sight of; under the consideration or cognisance of; previous to; previous to the expiration of; in preference to; superior to. — *adv* in front; sooner; earlier; in the past; formerly. — *conj* previous to the time when. — *adv* **before'hand** before a particular time; in advance or anticipation; by way of preparation; in advance of one's needs. — *adj* **before-men'tioned**. — **before Christ** see abbrev. **BC**; **before the wind** in the direction in which the wind is blowing, and hence helped along by it. [O.E. *beforan*. See **fore**.]

befoul *bi-fowl'*, *vt* to make foul; to soil or make dirty. [**be-** (2).]

befriend *bi-frend'*, *vt* to commence a friendship with; to act as a friend to. — *n* **befriend'er**. [**be-** (2).]

befuddle *bi-fud'l*, *vt* to reduce to a confused condition (esp. through drink). [**be-** (1).]

beg[1]. Same as **bey**.

beg[2] *beg*, *vi* to ask for alms or charity, esp. habitually; to sit up on the hindquarters, as a dog does for a reward. — *vt* to ask for earnestly; to beseech; to pray: — *pr p* **begg'ing**; *pa t* and *pa p* **begged** (*begd*). — *n* **beggar** (*beg'ər*) a person who begs; a person who lives by begging; (hyperbolically) one who is in need, esp. of money; an impoverished person; often used playfully and even affectionately. — *vt* to reduce to beggary; to exhaust or impoverish; to go beyond the resources of, as of description or imagination (*fig*). — *n* **begg'arliness**. — *adj* **begg'arly**. — *n* **begg'ary** extreme poverty. — *n* and *adj* **begg'ing**. — *adv* **begg'ingly**. — **begg'ar-man**; **beggar-my-neigh'bour** a game that continues till one player has gained all the others' cards; profit-making at the expense of others (also *adj*); **begg'ing-bowl** a bowl carried by beggars, esp. certain orders of monks, in which to receive food, money, etc.; **begg'ing-letter** a letter soliciting charity, esp. money. — **beg the question** to avoid giving an answer, esp. by means of assuming that a premise as yet unproved is true; **go begging** or **a-begging** to lack a purchaser, occupant, etc.

began *bi-gan'*, *pa t* of **begin**.

beget *bi-get'*, *vt* to produce or cause; to produce offspring (of humans, and commonly of the father); to produce as an effect, to cause: — *pr p* **begett'ing**; *pa t* **begot'** (or *archaic*, esp. *Bible* **begat'**); *pa p* **begott'en** or **begot'**. — *n* **begett'er**. [O.E. *begitan*, to acquire; see **get**.]

beggar. See **beg**[2].

begin *bi-gin'*, *vi* to come into being; to originate; to perform the first act; to open or commence; to have an opening or commencement. — *vt* to perform the first act of; to start: — *pr p* **beginn'ing**; *pa t* **began'** (now rarely **begun'**); *pa p* **begun**. — *n* **beginn'er** a person who begins; a person who is in the early stages of learning to do anything. — *n* **beginn'ing** origin; a start; a commencement of action; an opening or first part; a rudiment. — **to begin with** firstly; at first. [O.E. *beginnan*, from **be-** (3) and *ginnan*, to begin.]

beglamour *bi-glam'ər*, *vt* to invest with glamour; to bedazzle, infatuate or impress with glamour. [**be-** (2).]

begone *bi-gon'*, *interj* be gone; be off; get away.

begonia *bi-gō'ni-ə*, *n* a plant of the *Begonia* genus of tropical, esp. American, pink-flowered plants cultivated in greenhouses. [Named from Michel *Bégon* (1638–1710), patron of botany.]

begorra or **begorrah** *bi-gor'ə*, *interj* (esp. *facetious*) an Anglo-Irish modification of **by God**.

begot *bi-got'*, **begotten** *bi-got'n*. See **beget**.

begrime *bi-grīm'*, *vt* to soil with grime. [**be-** (2).]

begrudge *bi-gruj'*, *vt* to grudge or envy; to envy someone's possession of. [**be-** (1).]

beguile *bi-gīl'*, *vt* to charm; to cheat or deceive; to spend (time) pleasantly; to trick into some course of action. — *n* **beguile'ment**. — *n* **beguil'er**. — *adv* **beguil'ingly**. [**be-** (1) and obs. transitive verb *guile*.]

beguine *bə-gēn'*, *n* a dance of French West Indian origin or its music, in bolero rhythm. [Fr.]

begum *bā'gəm* or *bē'gəm*, *n* a Muslim princess or lady of rank; a deferential title given to any Muslim lady. [Urdu *begam*; cf. **beg**[1], **bey**.]

begun *bi-gun'*, *pa p* (sometimes *pa t*) of **begin**.

behalf *bi-häf'*, *n* sake, account; part. — **on** (in U.S. **in**) **behalf of**, or **on** (in U.S. **in**) **someone's behalf** speaking, acting, etc. for (usu. someone else). [M.E. *behalve* — O.E. *be healfe*, by the side.]

behatted *bi-hat'id*, *adj* wearing a hat. [**be-** (2).]

behave *bi-hāv'*, *vt* to conduct (oneself) well; to conduct or manage (commonly with *oneself*) in a given manner. — *vi* to conduct oneself (towards); to conduct oneself well; to act in a particular manner; to function: — *pa t* and *pa p* **behaved'**. — *n* **behaviour** or in N.Am. **behavior** (*bi-hāv'yər*) conduct; manners or deportment, esp. good manners; manner of action; response to stimulus (*physiol*). — *adj* **behāv'ioural** or in N.Am. **behāv'ioral** of or relating to behaviour. — *adv* **behāv'iourally** or in N.Am. **behāv'iorally**. — *n* **behāv'iourism** or in N.Am. **behāv'iorism** a psychological method which uses the objective observation of conduct in other beings under certain stimuli as the basis for all its theories and conclusions. — *n* **behāv'iourist** or in N.Am. **behāv'iorist** an adherent of behaviourism. — **behavioural enrichment** the creation of a mentally stimulating environment for a captive animal, e.g. in a zoo, with provision of objects for the animal to investigate and play with; **behavioural science** a science which studies the behaviour of human beings or other organisms (e.g. psychology, sociology); **behaviour therapy** a means of treating a neurotic symptom (e.g. a phobia) by training the patient in new behaviour and gradually conditioning him or her to react normally. — **on** (or **upon**) **one's best behaviour** consciously trying to be as well-behaved as possible. [**be-** (1) and **have**.]

behead *bi-hed'*, *vt* to cut off the head of. — *n* **behead'ing**. [**be-** (1), meaning off or away.]

beheld *bi-held'*, *pa t* and *pa p* of **behold**.

behest *bi-hest'*, *n* command; request. [O.E. *behǣs*, a promise.]

behind *bi-hīnd'*, *prep* at the back of (in position, or supporting); in the place or state left by; at the far side of; after (in time, rank, order); inferior to, or less far advanced than. — *adv* at the back, in the rear; backward, less advanced; past; in arrears. — *n* the rump, the buttocks (*euph*). — *adj* and *adv* **behind'-hand** tardy; in arrears. — **behind someone's back** without someone knowing (when they might feel entitled to know); **come from behind** to progress from the rear of a field of contestants into a winning position; **put something behind one** to resign something (usu. unpleasant) to the past and consider it finished. [O.E. *behindan*.]

behold *bi-hōld'*, *vt* (*literary* or *Bible*) to look at; to view or see. — *vi* (*literary* or *Bible*) to look: — *pa t* and *pa p* **beheld'**. — *imper* or *interj* see; lo; observe. — *adj* **behold'en** bound in gratitude (to); under an obligation (to). — *n* **behold'er**. [O.E. *behaldan*, to hold, observe.]

behove *bi-hōv'* or (esp. *US*) **behoove** *-hōōv'*, *vt* and *vi* to be fit, right, or necessary — now only used impersonally with *it*. [O.E. *behōfian*, to be fit, to stand in need of.]

beige *bāzh*, *adj* greyish buff with a slight hint of pink. — *n* a woollen fabric of undyed wool. [Fr.]

beigel *bā'gəl*, *n* an alternative spelling of **bagel**.

beignet *ben'yā*, *n* a fritter; a deep-fried ball of choux pastry. [Fr.]

being *bē'ing*, *n* existence; substance; essence; any person or thing existing. — *adj* existing or present. — *adj* **bē'ingless**. — **the Supreme Being** God. [Verbal noun and pres. p. of **be**.]

bejabers *bi-jā'bərz*, *interj* (esp. *facetious*) an Anglo-Irish modification of **by Jesus**.

bejewel *bi-jōō'əl*, *vt* to adorn with jewels. — *adj* **bejew'elled**. [**be-** (2).]

bel *bel*, *n* a measure for comparing noises, electric currents, etc., the number of bels being the logarithm to the base 10 of the ratio of the intensity of one compared to the other. [From Graham *Bell* (1847–1922), telephone inventor.]

belabour *bi-lā'bər*, *vt* to beat soundly; to assail verbally. [**be-** (1).]

Bel & Dr. (*Bible*) *abbrev* for (the Apocryphal Book of) Bel and the Dragon.

belated *bi-lāt'id*, *adj* coming or happening too late; out of date. — *n* **belāt'edness**. [**be-** (2).]

belay *bi-lā'*, *vt* to make fast; to secure by a turn (of a rope) about a cleat, belaying pin, point of rock, etc.; to beset; to besiege: — *pa t* and *pa p* **belayed'**. — *interj* enough; stop. — *n* a turn of a rope in belaying; a cleat or point etc. about which a belay is made. — **belaying pin** a pin for belaying ropes about. [O.E. *belecgan*.]

bel canto *bel kan'tō*, (It.) *adv* a manner of operatic singing that emphasises beauty of tone.

belch *belch*, *vt* and *vi* to void (wind) from the stomach through the mouth; to eject violently; to pour forth, as the smoke from a volcano, chimney, etc. — *n* an act of belching. [O.E. *bealcian*; Du. *balken*.]

beleaguer *bi-lēg'ər*, *vt* to lay siege to; to pester. — *n* **beleag'uerment**. [Du. *belegeren*, to besiege — *be-*, *leger*, camp.]

belemnite *bel'əm-nīt*, *n* a fossil pointed like a dart, being the internal shell of a cephalopod mollusc. [Gr. *belemnitēs* — *belemnon*, a dart.]

bel esprit *be-les-prē*, (Fr.) *n* a wit or genius: — *pl* **beaux esprits** (*bō-zes-prē*).

belfry *bel'fri*, *n* the part of a steeple or tower in which bells are hung; a bell-tower, sometimes standing apart from other buildings; a movable wooden tower, used in the Middle Ages in attacking a fortification. — *adj* **bel'fried** having a belfry. [Orig. and properly a watchtower, from O.Fr. *berfroi* — M.H.G. *berchfrit* — *bergan*, to protect, *frid*, *frit*, a tower.]

Belg. *abbrev* for: Belgian; Belgium.

Belgian *bel'jən*, *adj* of *Belgium*, a country of Europe. — *n* a native or citizen of Belgium. — *adj* **Bel'gic** of the *Belgae*, a tribe who in ancient times possessed Belgium, or of Belgium. — **Belgian hare** a hare-like breed of domestic rabbit. [L. *Belga*, *Belgicus*.]

belie *bi-lī'*, *vt* to show the untruth of; to present falsely, misrepresent or falsify; to fail to fulfil or justify: — *pr p* **bely'ing**; *pa t* and *pa p* **belied'**. — *n* **belī'er**. [**be-** (3).]

believe *bi-lēv'*, *vt* to regard as true; to accept as true what is said by (someone); to think (followed by a noun clause). — *vi* to be firmly convinced; to have (esp. religious) faith (with *in* or *on*). — *n* **belief'** conviction of the truth of anything; faith; the opinion or doctrine believed. — *adj* **belief'less**. — *adj* **believ'able**. — *n* **believ'er** a person who believes; a person who is an adherent of Christianity, Islam, or any other religion. — *adj* **believ'ing** trustful; having belief. — *adv* **believ'ingly**. — **be unable** (or **hardly able**) **to believe one's eyes** or **ears** to receive with incredulity what one has just seen or heard; **I believe so** I think so; **make believe** see under **make**; **to the best of my belief** as far as I know. [M.E. *bileven* — *bi-*, *be*, *leven*.]

Belisha beacon. See **beacon**.

belittle *bi-lit'l*, *vt* to make small; to cause (a person, their opinions, etc.) to appear small, to disparage. — *n* **belitt'lement**. — *adj* **belitt'ling**. [**be-** (2).]

bell *bel*, *n* an instrument for giving a ringing sound, typically a hollow vessel of metal with flared mouth struck by a tongue or clapper, but taking many other forms; a flower corolla shaped like an ordinary bell; anything bell-shaped; the sound of a bell; a signal or intimation by bell; a stroke or double stroke of a bell to indicate the number of half-hours of a four-hour watch that have elapsed — 'two bells', 'three bells', etc., meaning that two, three, etc. half-hours have passed (*naut*). — *vt* to provide with a bell, esp. in **bell the cat** (q.v. below). — *vt* and *vi* to (cause to) flare out in the shape of a bell. — *adj* **belled** shaped like a bell. — **bell'-bird** any of various birds with bell-like notes. — *adj* **bell'-bottomed** (of trousers) widening greatly towards the ankle. — **bell'-boy** (chiefly *US*) a bellhop; **bell'-buoy** a buoy carrying a bell, rung by the movement of waves; **bell end** a rounded end, esp. to the back of a tent; **bell'-flower** a campanula; **bell'-founder** a person who casts bells in a foundry; **bell'-foundry; bell'-glass** a bell-shaped glass for sheltering flowers, etc.; **bell'-heather** a variety of erica with bell-shaped flowers; **bell'hop** a hotel porter or page; **bell'-housing** a tapered outer casing of part of a vehicle's transmission; **bell'-jar** a bell-shaped glass cover, placed over apparatus in laboratories to confine gases, etc.; **bell'-metal** the metal of which bells are made — an alloy of copper and tin; **bell'-pull** a cord or handle used in ringing a bell; **bell'-push** a button used in ringing an electric or spring bell; **bell'-ringer** a person who rings a bell on stated occasions; a performer on church bells or musical hand-bells; **bell'-ringing; bell'-rope**. — *adj* **bell'-shaped**. — **bell'-tent** a bell-shaped tent; **bell'-tower** a tower built to contain one or more bells, a campanile; **bell'-turret** a turret containing a chamber for a bell, usually crowned with a spire; **bell'-wether** the leading sheep of a flock, on whose neck a bell is hung; a ringleader (*fig*); a setter of a standard, pattern or trend, a leader (*econ* etc.). — **bell, book, and candle** a phrase popularly used in reference to the articles employed in a form of excommunication; **bells and whistles** (*slang*) additional, largely decorative rather than functional, features; **bells of Ireland** an annual plant that has white flowers with green bell-shaped calyces, sometimes preserved for use in dried-flower arrangements; **bell the cat** to undertake the leading part in any hazardous enterprise, from the ancient fable of the mice who proposed to hang a warning bell round the cat's neck; **clear as a bell** (of a sound) distinct and pure in tone; **give someone a bell** (*slang*) to telephone someone; **sound as a bell** in perfect condition, health, etc. [O.E. *belle*.]

belladonna *bel-ə-don'ə*, *n* the deadly nightshade, all parts of which are narcotic and poisonous from the presence of atropine; the drug prepared from it. — **belladonna lily** a pink-flowered South African amaryllis. [It. *bella donna*, fair lady; one cosmetic property of belladonna is to enlarge the pupil of the eye.]

bellarmine *bel'är-mēn*, (*antiq*) *n* a large jug with a big belly, decorated with a bearded face, said to represent Cardinal *Bellarmine* (1542–1621), made in mockery by Dutch Protestants.

belle[1] *bel*, *n* a handsome woman; the chief beauty of a place or occasion. [Fr. *belle* (*fem*) — L. *bellus*, *-a*, *-um*.]

belle[2] *bel*, (Fr.) *adj fem* of **beau**. — **belle amie** (*be-la-mē*) a female friend or mistress; **belle laide** (*bel led*) a woman considered pretty or charming because of her ugliness. — Also *adj*. — **la belle époque** (*la-bel-ā-pok*; also with *caps*) 'the fine period', the time of security and gracious living for the well-to-do, ended by World War I.

belles-lettres *bel-let'r'*, *npl* polite or elegant literature, including poetry, fiction, criticism, aesthetics, etc. — *n* **bellet'rist** or **bellett'rist**. [Fr., lit. fine letters.]

bellicose *bel'ik-ōs*, *adj* contentious, warlike. — *adv* **bell'icosely**. — *n* **bellicosity** (*-kos'i-ti*). [L. *bellicōsus*.]

bellied. See **belly**.

belligerent *bil-ij'ər-ənt*, *adj* aggressive; waging war; recognised legally as waging war. — *n* a country, person, etc. waging war; one recognised as doing so. — *n* **bellig'erence**. — *n* **bellig'erency**. — *adv* **bellig'erently**. [L. *belligerāre*, to wage war — *bellum*, war, *gerĕre*, to wage.]

bellow *bel'ō*, *vi* to roar like a bull; to make any violent outcry. — *vt* to roar out. — *n* the roar of a bull; any deep, loud sound or cry. — *n* **bell'ower**. [M.E. *belwen*; O.E. *bylgian*, to roar.]

bellows *bel'ōz*, *npl* or *nsing* an instrument for producing a current of air to encourage a fire, or sound an organ, accordion, etc. (also **pair of bellows**); a telescopic sleeve connected between a camera body and lens, used when focusing on small, close objects. — *adj* in the form of a bellows, allowing for expansion, as in the tongue of a boot, etc. — **bellows to mend** (esp. in sporting parlance) shortness of breath, e.g. in a horse. [Ety. as for **belly**.]

belly *bel'i*, *n* the part of the body between the breast and the thighs, containing the bowels; the stomach, as the receptacle of food; the bowels proper; the womb or uterus; the deep interior of anything; the bulging part of anything, as of a bottle, or any concave or hollow surface, as of a sail; the front or under surface of e.g. an animal, as opp. to the *back*; in a violin or a leaf, the upper surface; a sound-board (*mus*). — *adj* ventral, abdominal. — *vi* to swell or bulge (often with *out*): — *pa t* and *pa p* **bellied** (*bel'id*). — *adj* **bell'ied** bulging; puffed out. — *combining form* **-bellied** with a particular kind of belly (as in *pot-bellied*). — *n* **bell'yful** a sufficiency; more than enough. — *n* and *adj* **bell'ying**. — **bell'y-ache** a pain in the belly; a persistent complaint or whine (*slang*). — *vi* (*slang*) to complain whiningly. — **bell'y-band** a saddle-girth: a band fastened to the shafts of a vehicle, and passing under the belly of the horse drawing it; **bell'y-button** (*colloq*) the navel; **bell'y-dance** a sensuous Eastern dance, performed by a woman, with very pronounced movement of the abdomen and hips; **bell'y-dancer; bell'y-flop** an inexpert dive in which one lands face down, flat on the water; a belly-landing. — Also *vi*. — **bell'y-landing** (of an aircraft) a landing without using the landing-wheels; **bell'y-laugh** a deep, unrestrained laugh. — **belly up to** (*US slang*) to go directly or purposefully towards; **go belly up** (*slang*; esp. *US*) to die (as a dead fish, floating belly upwards); of a business, etc., to fail. [M.E. *bali*, *bely* — O.E. *bælig*, *belig*, *bælg*, *belg*, bag.]

belong *bi-long'*, *vi* to pertain (to); to be the property (of; with *to*); to be a part or appendage (of), or in any way connected (with) (with *with* or *to*); to have a proper place (in); to be entirely suitable; to be a native or inhabitant, or member (of). — *n* **belong'er** (*sociol*) a person of conservative, middle-class values and lifestyle, conforming to social norms. — *npl* **belong'ings** possessions; personal effects. [M.E. *bi-*, *be-longen*, intensive of *longen*. See **long**.]

Belorussian or **Byelorussian** *byel-ə-rush'ən*, *adj* White Russian, of a region to the west of Moscow; of its language or people. — Also *n*. [Russ. *Belorossiya* — *beliy*, white.]

beloved *bi-luv'id*, also *bi-luvd'*, *adj* much loved, very dear (often compounded with *well-*, *best-*, etc.). — *n* (*bi-luv'id*) a person who is much loved. [Obs. *belove*, to love — **be-** (1).]

below *bi-lō'*, *prep* beneath in place, rank or quality; underneath; not worthy of. — *adv* in a lower place; downstairs; on earth as regarded from heaven, or in hell as regarded from earth (*fig*). — adj and *adv* **below-stairs'** downstairs; in or belonging to the servants' quarters. — *adj* **below-the-line'** of or pertaining to that part of the government's spending and revenue not allowed for in its original estimates; of or pertaining to business spending or income which, because of its unusual nature, is listed separately from the normal financial details on a company's accounts. [M.E. *bilooghe* — *bi*, by, *looghe*, low.]

bel paese *bel pä-ä'zē*, *n* a mild Italian cheese. [Formerly a trademark.]

belshazzar. See **balthazar**.

belt *belt*, *n* a girdle, zone or band (*geog*); a band of leather or other material worn around the waist; a band of flexible material used to transmit motion in machinery; a broad stripe of anything, different in colour or material from what surrounds it; something which confines or restrains; a band worn around the waist awarded in recognition of a specific (grade of) achievement in some sports, etc. (see **black, Lonsdale**); a sharp blow, impact or shock (*colloq*). — *vt* to award a belt, or to invest formally with one, as in conferring knighthood; to encircle with a belt; to thrash with a belt; to hit hard (*colloq*). — *vi* (*slang*) to go very quickly. — *adj* **belt'ed** wearing, marked with, or having a belt. — *n* **belt'er** something outstanding, or strikingly good or bad (*colloq*); a song for belting out (*colloq*). — *n* **belt'ing** belts collectively; material for making belts; a beating. — *adj* **belt-and-bra'ces** giving double security or double the chances of success. — *n* **belt'way** (*US*) a ring-road. — **belt out** (*colloq*) to sing, play or send out vigorously or with great enthusiasm; **belt up** (*slang*) to be quiet; **hit**, etc., **below the belt** to hit, etc., an opponent's body lower than the waist (forbidden in some sports); hence to deliver a mean blow, attack unfairly (*fig*); **tighten one's belt** to reduce one's demands or expenditure, to economise (*n* **belt'-tightening**); **under one's belt** (*fig*) firmly and irrevocably secured or in one's possession. [O.E. *belt* — L. *balteus*.]

Beltane *bel'tān*, *n* an ancient Celtic festival, held at the beginning of May; the first day of May (Old Style) — one of the four old quarter-days of Scotland. — Also *adj*. [Gael. *bealltainn, beilteine*.]

beluga *bi-lōō'gə*, *n* the white whale, one of the dolphin family, found in Arctic seas; the great Russian sturgeon, a source of caviar. [Russ. *beliy*, white.]

belvedere *bel'vi-dēr* or *-dēr'*, *n* a pavilion or raised turret or lantern on the top of a house, built to provide a view, or to admit the breeze; a summer-house on high ground. [It. *belvedere* — *bel*, beautiful, *vedere*, to see.]

belying. See **belie**.

BEM *abbrev* for British Empire Medal.

bemoan *bi-mōn'*, *vt* to lament, bewail (the loss of). — *vi* to grieve. — *n* **bemoan'er**. — *n* **bemoan'ing**. [**be-** (1).]

bemuse *bi-mūz'*, *vt* to put into confusion; to puzzle. — *adj* **bemused'**. [**be-** (1).]

ben[1] *ben*, *n* a mountain peak. [Gael. *beinn*.]

ben[2] *ben*, (*Scot*) *prep* and *adv* in or toward the inner or better room or rooms (of). — *n* the inner or better room or rooms of a house (as opp. to the *but* or kitchen through which formerly one had to pass first). — **a but and ben** a two-roomed house. [M.E. *binne* — O.E. *binnan*, within.]

bench *bench* or *bensh*, *n* a long (usu. wooden) seat with or without a back; a work-table or working-place; a judge's seat; the body or assembly of judges; a tribunal; (esp. in football) a seat for officials and non-players at a match; a level ledge in the slope of masonry or earthwork; a terrace (*geol*); (in a greenhouse or conservatory) a raised bed or a platform with sides for holding potted plants; a platform on which dogs are shown. — *vt* to place on or furnish with benches; to take (a player) out of a game; to put plants on greenhouse benches; to show (dogs). — *combining form* used to denote the particular area in Parliament where MPs sit, and their respective prominence (as in *front bench, back bench*). — *n* **bench'er** a senior member of an inn of court. — *n* **bench'ership**. — **bench fees** laboratory fees paid by scientific, medical and technical students; **bench'mark** a surveyor's mark cut on a rock, etc. indicating a point of reference in levelling; anything taken or used as a point of reference or comparison, a standard, criterion, etc. — Also *adj*. — **bench-warr'ant** one issued by a judge rather than a justice or magistrate. — **raise to the bench** to make a judge or bishop. [O.E. *benc*.]

bend *bend*, *vt* to force into (or out of) a curved or angled form; to curve; to bow, turn (the body) downwards; to subject (to one's will, etc.); to dispose or incline to a point of view; to aim or direct (one's attention, etc.); to fasten (*naut*). — *vi* to curve; to stoop; to bow (down) the body; to give way, yield or show flexibility; to turn in a given direction; to incline to a point of view: — *pa t* and *pa p* **bent**; also **bend'ed**. — *n* a knot by which one rope or string is tied to another, or to itself after passing through a ring, etc.; a parallel band crossing a shield from top to bottom (a **bend-sin'ister**, a mark of illegitimacy, runs from top right to bottom left) (*heraldry*); an act of bending; state of being bent; a bent thing; a place of bending, as in a road, arm, etc.; a bow or stoop. — *adj* **bend'ed** (only in **on bended knee**). — *n* **bend'er** a person or machine that bends; a (drunken) spree (*slang*); a temporary shelter consisting of a shell of woven branches covered with tarpaulins or plastic sheeting (*colloq*). — *n* and *adj* **bend'ing**. — *adv* **bend'wise** (*heraldry*) diagonally. — *adj* **bend'y** divided into bends (*heraldry*); full of, characterised by, curves or bends (*colloq*); flexible (*colloq*). — *n* and *adj* **bent** see **bent**[1]. — **bent'wood** wood artificially curved for chair-making, etc. — Also *adj*. — **bend over backwards** see **back**; **round the bend** (*colloq*) crazy, mad; **the bends** decompression sickness, also known as *caisson disease*. [O.E. *bendan*, to constrain, bind, fetter, string (as a bow), *bend*, bond, fetter.]

beneath *bi-nēth'*, *adv* and *prep* below; in a lower position so as to be under, or nearly so, or to be covered (by); inside, behind, at the back (of). — *prep* in a manner or of a type unworthy of, unbecoming to. [O.E. *beneothan*.]

Benedict. See **eggs Benedict** at **egg**[1].

Benedictine *ben-i-dik'tin* or *-tīn*, *adj* pertaining to St *Benedict* (480–543), or his monastic rule. — *n* a monk or nun of the order founded by him at Monte Cassino; (*-tēn*) a cordial or liqueur resembling Chartreuse, distilled at Fécamp in Normandy, formerly by Benedictine monks.

benediction *ben-ə-dik'shən*, *n* any blessing; a solemn invocation of the divine blessing on men or things; a blessing pronounced at the end of a religious service; a brief and popular service in the Roman Catholic Church; grace before or after a meal; blessedness. — *adj* **benedic'tional**. — *adj* **benedict'ive**. — *adj* **benedict'ory**. — *n* **Benedict'us** the canticle, a non-metrical hymn, used in the Roman and Anglican services. [L. *benedīcĕre, -dictum* — *bene*, well, *dicĕre*, to say, speak.]

Benedictus. See **benediction**.

benefaction *ben-i-fak'shən*, *n* the act of doing good; a good deed done or benefit conferred; a grant or endowment. — *n* **ben'efactor** (or *-fak'*) a person who confers a benefit; a person who aids financially e.g. an institution, a patron: — *fem* **ben'efactress** (or *-fak'trəs*). — *adj* **benefac'tory**. [L. *benefactiō, -ōnis.*]

benefice *ben'i-fis, n* a church living, an area from which an income is obtained, esp. in return for the spiritual care of its inhabitants. — *adj* **ben'eficed** possessing a benefice. — *n* **beneficence** (*bi-nef'i-səns*) active goodness; kindness; charity; a charitable gift. — *adj* **benef'icent**. — *adv* **benef'icently**. — *adj* **beneficial** (*ben-i-fish'l*) useful; advantageous; enjoying the use of and profits from property (*law*). — *adv* **benefic'ially**. — *n* **benefic'iary** a holder of a benefice; a person who receives a gift or advantage; a person who enjoys, or has the prospect of enjoying, any interest or estate held in trust by others. [L. *beneficus*, kindly, beneficent, *beneficium*, a service, benefit — *bene*, well, *facĕre*, to do.]

benefit *ben'i-fit, n* any advantage, natural or other; a performance, match, etc., whose proceeds go to one of the company, a player, or some other particular person or cause (also *adj*); a right in the form of money or services enjoyed under social security or insurance schemes; a kindness; a favour. — *vt* to do good to; to be to the advantage of. — *vi* to obtain advantage or good (with *from* or *by*): — *pr p* **ben'efiting**; *pa t* and *pa p* **ben'efited**. — **benefit of the doubt** presumption of innocence when culpability is uncertain; **benefit society** a friendly society. [M.E. *benfet* — A.Fr. *benfet* — L. *benefactum.*]

Benelux *ben'ə-luks, n* a name for (the economic union between) *Be*lgium, the *Ne*therlands and *Lux*embourg.

Benesh *ben'esh, n* a system of notation for detailing movements in dancing, introduced in 1955 by Joan and Rudolf *Benesh*.

benevolence *bi-nev'ə-ləns, n* disposition to do good; generosity; an act of kindness; a kind of forced loan or contribution, levied by kings without legal authority (*Eng hist*). — *adj* **benev'olent** charitable, generous, kindly, well disposed. — *adv* **benev'olently**. [O.Fr. *benivolence* and L. *benevolentia.*]

BEng. *abbrev* for Bachelor of Engineering.

Bengal *ben-göl'* or *beng-göl'*, *n* a striped cotton woven in the *Bengal* region, or an imitation of it. — *adj* from Bengal — modern Bangladesh, and West Bengal (Indian state); made of Bengal. — *n* and *adj* **Bengalese** (*ben-gə-lēz'* or *beng-*) a person from Bengal: — *pl* **Bengalese'**. — *adj* **Bengali** (*ben-gö'li* or *beng-*) of or belonging to Bengal. — *n* a person from Bengal; the language of Bengal, the official language of Bangladesh.

benighted *bi-nī'tid, adj* lost in intellectual or moral darkness; ignorant. [**be-** (2) and **night**.]

benign *bi-nīn', adj* favourable, esp. in astrology (as opp. to *malign*); kindly and gracious; of a mild type (as opp. to *malignant*; *med*); (of climate) salubrious, mild or warm. — *n* **benignancy** (*bi-nig'nən-si*). — *adj* **benig'nant** kind and gracious; benign. — *adv* **benig'nantly**. — *n* **benig'nity**. — *adv* **benign'ly** (*-nīn'*). [O.Fr. *benigne* — L. *benīgnus.*]

benison *ben'i-zən* or *-sən, n* a benediction, blessing, esp. of God. [O.Fr. *beneiçun* — L. *benedictiō, -ōnis.*]

Benjamin *ben'jə-min, n* a youngest son; a favourite child. [As in Genesis xlii.]

benjamin *ben'jə-min, n* gum benzoin. — Also **gum benjamin**. — **ben'jamin-tree** a variety of tree found in Java and Sumatra; the American spice-bush. [**benzoin**.]

bennet *ben'it*. See **herb bennet** at **herb**.

benny[1] *ben'i*, (*slang*) *n* an overcoat.

benny[2] *ben'i*, (*slang*) *n* an amphetamine tablet. [Abbrev. of **Benzedrine**.]

bent[1] *bent, pa t* and *pa p* of **bend**. — *adj* curved; having a bend; intent, determined (*on* or *upon* doing something); morally crooked, or criminal (*colloq*); homosexual, or otherwise sexually deviant (*derog slang*); stolen (*slang*). — *n* tendency, trend, inclination; leaning or bias, natural inclination of the mind; the extent to which a bow may be bent; capacity of endurance. [**bend**.]

bent[2] *bent, n* any stiff or wiry grass; the old dried stalks of grasses; a genus of grasses, slender and delicate in appearance, some useful as pasture-grasses and for hay. — Also **bent'-grass**. [O.E. *beonet.*]

Benthamism *ben'thəm-izm, n* the social and political teaching of Jeremy *Bentham* (1748–1832), whose leading principle is summed up in the phrase, 'the greatest happiness of the greatest number'. — *n* **Ben'thamite**.

benthos *ben'thos, n* the flora and fauna of the sea-bottom, or of lakes. — *adj* **ben'thic**. — **benthopelagic** (*-thō-pi-laj'ik*) (of marine or lake fauna) living just above the bottom. — *n* **ben'thoscope** a submersible sphere from which to study deep-sea life. [Gr. *benthos*, depth.]

bentonite *ben'tən-īt, n* a valuable clay, consisting mainly of montmorillonite, widely used in industry as a bond, filler, etc., and also as a clarifying agent in wine-making. [Fort *Benton*, Montana, where it was found.]

ben trovato *ben trō-vä'tō*, (It.) *adj* aptly invented.

ben venuto *ben ven-ōō't'ō*, (It.) *adj* welcome.

bentwood. See **bend**[1].

benumb *bi-num', vt* to make insensible or powerless; to stupefy (now chiefly of *cold*); to deaden the feelings of or in; to paralyse generally. — *adj* **benumbed'**. — *n* **benumbed'ness**. — *n* **benumb'ment**. [**be-** (2).]

Benzedrine® *ben'zi-drēn, n* a tradename for amphetamine.

benzene *ben'zēn, n* the simplest of the aromatic series of hydrocarbons, its molecule consisting of a ring or closed chain of six carbon atoms each with a hydrogen atom attached — formerly called benzine, benzol, names now used differently (see below). — *n* **ben'zal** or **benzyl'idine** a radical whose oxide is **benzal'dehyde** or oil of bitter almonds. — *n* **benzine** (*ben'zēn*) a mixture of hydrocarbons obtained by destructive distillation of petroleum, used as a solvent, motor fuel, etc.; improperly, benzene. — *n* **benzocaine** (*ben-zō-kā'in* or *ben'zō-kān*) a drug used as a local anaesthetic and in the treatment of gastritis (**benzine** and **cocaine**). — *n* **benzodiazepine** (*ben-zō-dī-az'ə-pēn, -pin* or *-pīn*) one of a group of tranquillising and soporific drugs. — *n* **ben'zol** or **ben'zole** crude benzene, used as a motor-spirit; improperly, benzene. — *n* **ben'zoline** benzine; impure benzene. — *n* **benzpyrene** (*benz-pī'rēn*) a cancer-inducing hydrocarbon found in coal-tar and present in small quantities in smoke, including tobacco smoke (**benzene** and **pyrene**). — *n* **benzylidine** see **benzal** above. — **benzene hexachloride** (known as **BHC**) a very toxic variety of insecticide. [From **benzoin**.]

benzoin *ben'zō-in* or *-zoin, n* gum benjamin, the aromatic and resinous juice of a tree of Java and Sumatra, used in perfumery, in pastilles, for incense and friar's balsam. — *adj* **benzo'ic**. — **benzoic acid** an acid found in benzoin and other gums. [In the 16th cent., *benjoin.*]

bequeath *bi-kwēdh', vt* to leave by will to another person (strictly, of personal property); to give to posterity, to leave behind; to commit or entrust to anyone. — *adj* **bequeath'able**. — *n* **bequeath'al**. — *n* **bequeath'ment**. [O.E. *becwethan* — pfx. *bi-, be-*, and *cwethan*, to say.]

bequest *bi-kwest', n* act of bequeathing; that which is bequeathed, a legacy. [M.E. *biqueste* — O.E. pfx. *bi-, be-*, and *cwethan*, to say.]

berate *bi-rāt', vt* to scold or chide severely. [**be-** (1).]

Berber *bûr'bər, n* a member of one of the Muslim peoples of North Africa; the language of the Berbers. — Also *adj*. [Ar. *barbar.*]

berberis *bûr'bər-is, n* any shrub of the barberry genus (*Berberis*). [Latinised from Ar.; see **barberry.**]

berceuse *ber-sœz', n* a cradle song; a musical composition in similar rhythm. [Fr.]

bereave *bi-rēv', vt* to widow, orphan, or deprive by death of some dear relative or friend; to deprive or rob of something valued generally: — *pa t* and *pa p* **bereaved'** (usu. by death), **bereft'** (usu. in general sense). — *adj* **bereaved'**. — *n* **bereave'ment** loss by death of a relative or friend. [O.E. *berēafian*, to plunder.]

beret *ber'i, n* a flat, round, woollen cap worn by Basques and others. [Fr. *béret.*]

berg[1] *bûrg* or *berhh, n* a hill or mountain. — **bergfall** (*bûrg'föl* or *berk'fäl*) fall of mountain-rock (Ger., mountain fall); **bergschrund** (*berk'shrŏŏnt*) a crevasse formed where a glacier or snowfield moves away from a mountain wall (Ger., mountain cleft); **berg wind** in S. Africa, a hot, dry wind blowing from the mountains towards the coastal regions. [Ger. *Berg*, Du. *berg*, hill.]

berg[2] *bûrg, n* short for **iceberg**.

bergamot[1] *bûr'gə-mot, n* a kind of citron or orange, whose aromatic rind yields oil of bergamot, used in perfumery; the essence so extracted; a mint of similar smell.

bergamot[2] *bûr'gə-mot, n* a fine pear. [Fr., — It., — Turk. *begarmudi*, prince of pears.]

bergère *ber-zher', adj* denoting a type of easy chair or sofa with cane back and arms. [Fr., shepherdess.]

beribboned *bi-rib'ənd, participial adj* decorated with ribbons. [**be-** (2).]

beriberi *ber'i-ber-i, n* an Eastern disease caused by lack of vitamin B_1. [Sinh. *beri*, weakness.]

berk or **burk** *bûrk*, (*slang*) *n* a fool. [Short for Cockney rhyming slang *Berkeley Hunt*, for *cunt*.]

Berkeleian *bärk-lē'ən, bärk'li-ən* or in U.S. *bûrk'-, adj* pertaining to Bishop *Berkeley* (1685–1753), who maintained that the world we see depends for its existence on being perceived. — *n* a follower of Berkeley. — *n* **Berkelei'anism** (or *bärk'*).

berkelium *bər-kē'li-əm, n* an element (atomic no. 97; symbol **Bk**), prepared in a cyclotron at *Berkeley*, California.

Berks. *bärks, abbrev* for Berkshire.

berley or **burley** *bûr'li*, (*Austr*) *n* bait, groundbait; leg-pulling, humbug (*colloq*).

berlin *bûr'lin, bər-lēn'* or *-lin', n* an old four-wheeled covered carriage, with a seat at the rear covered with a hood (also **ber'line**); a closed motor car with the driver's seat partitioned off. [From the city of *Berlin*.]

berm *bûrm, n* a narrow ledge or path beside a road, etc.; the area of level ground between the raised mound of a barrow or other earthwork and the ditch surrounding it (*archaeol*). [Fr. *berme.*]

Bermudan *bər-mū'dən* or **Bermudian** *-di-ən, adj* and *n* (a native or inhabitant) of Bermuda. — **Bermuda grass** (*bər-mū'də*) a type of grass native to Southern Europe, now growing widely in warm countries, with wiry roots, used in lawns and for binding sand dunes; **Bermuda rig** a sailing rig in which there is a large fore-and-aft sail fixed directly to a tall mainmast. — *adj* **Bermuda rigged**. — **Bermuda shorts** shorts, for men or women, reaching almost to the knee. — Also **Bermu'das**. — **Bermuda Triangle** the area between Florida, the Bahamas, and Cuba where ships and aeroplanes are alleged to mysteriously disappear.

berry *ber'i, n* any small succulent fruit; a simple fruit with the seed-enclosing wall succulent throughout (thus excluding strawberry, raspberry and blackberry, which are not) (*bot*); a coffee-bean; a cereal grain; a lobster's or crayfish's egg. — *vi* to gather berries. — *adj* **berr'ied** having berries. — *n* **berr'ying**. [O.E. *berie.*]

berserk *ber-sûrk'* or *-zûrk'* or **berserk'er** *-ər, n* a Norse warrior who was filled with a frenzied and irresistible fury at the sight of the field of battle. — *adj* **berserk'** violently frenzied or angry (usu. with *go*). — *adv* **berserk'ly**. [O.N. *berserkr.*]

berth *bûrth, n* a place allotted to a ship at anchor or at a wharf; a room or sleeping-place in a ship, railway sleeping-carriage, etc.; any allotted or assigned place; a situation or place of employment, usu. a comfortable one. — *vt* and *vi* to moor (a ship). — *vt* to provide with a berth for sleeping or working. — *n* **berth'age** accommodation, or dues paid, for mooring or anchoring. — **give a wide berth to** to keep well away from generally.

beryl *ber'il, n* a precious stone occurring in hexagonal crystals, of which emerald and aquamarine are varieties, a silicate of beryllium and aluminium, green, colourless, yellow or blue, once thought to have magical properties. — *adj* pale greenish. — *n* **beryll'ia** the oxide of **beryll'ium**, a metallic element (atomic no. 4; symbol **Be**), used as a moderator for slowing down neutrons in nuclear reactors, and industrially to harden alloys, etc. — *n* **berylliō'sis** a disease caused by exposure to the fumes or dust from beryllium salts, in which tissue is formed esp. in the lungs. [O.Fr. *beryl* — L. *bēryllus* — Gr. *bēryllos.*]

beseech *bi-sēch, vt* to entreat, to implore; to ask or pray earnestly to (God, etc.): — *pa t* and *pa p* **besought** (*bi-söt'*) or **beseeched'**. — *n* **beseech'er**. — *n* and *adj* **beseech'ing**. — *adv* **beseech'ingly**. [**be-** (1), and M.E. *sechen*; see **seek.**]

beset *bi-set', vt* to surround with hostile intentions, to attack or lay siege to; to assail mentally, perplex, endanger, with problems, temptations, obstacles, etc.; to occupy so as to allow no-one to go out or in: — *pr p* **besett'ing**; *pa t* and *pa p* **beset'**. — *n* **besett'er**. — *adj* **besett'ing**. [O.E. *besettan* — *settan*, to set.]

beside *bi-sīd', prep* by the side of, next to, near; outside of; as distinct from, compared with. — *adv* nearby; besides; to the side. — *adv* **besides'** in addition; moreover. — *prep* over and above; as well as. — **beside oneself** having lost self-control, irrational (with anger, worry, etc.); **beside the mark, point** or **question** irrelevant (and therefore inconsequential). [O.E. *besīdan*, by the side (dat.).]

besiege *bi-sēj', vt* to attack violently with the intent of capturing; to attack with armed forces; to throng round in large numbers; to pester (*colloq*). — *n* **besieg'er**. — *n* and *adj* **besieg'ing**. [**be-** (1).]

B. ès L. (*Fr.*) *abbrev* for *Bachelier ès Lettres*, Bachelor of Letters.

besmear *bi-smēr', vt* to smear or daub (with); to besmirch. [**be-** (1).]

besmirch *bi-smûrch', vt* to soil, as with smoke or dirt; to sully (a reputation, etc.). [**be-** (1).]

besom *bē'zəm, n* a bunch of twigs for sweeping; a broom made of these; any cleansing or purifying agent (*fig*). [O.E. *besema.*]

besotted *bi-sot'id, adj* infatuated (with). — *adv* **besott'edly**. — *n* **besott'edness**. [**be-** (2).]

besought *bi-söt', pa t* and *pa p* of **beseech**.

bespangle *bi-spang'gl, vt* to adorn with spangles, or with anything sparkling or shining. [**be-** (1).]

bespatter *bi-spat'ər, vt* to spatter or sprinkle with dirt or anything wet; to defame (*fig*). — *adj* **bespatt'ered**. [**be-** (1).]

bespeak *bi-spēk', vt* to stake a claim to beforehand; to order or apply for; to request; to betoken (a quality): — *pa t* **bespoke'** (or *archaic* **bespake'**); *pa p* **bespōk'en**, also **bespoke'** (see also **bespoke**, below). [**be-** (3).]

bespeckle *bi-spek'l, vt* to mark with speckles or spots. — *adj* **bespeck'led**. [**be-** (1).]

bespectacled *bi-spek'tə-kəld, adj* wearing, or as if wearing, spectacles. [**be-** (2).]

bespoke *bi-spōk'*, *adj* (esp. of clothes) specially tailored or designed to the client's measurements, requirements, etc.; (of a tailor, etc.) making clothes to order. [Past p. of **bespeak.**]

besprinkle *bi-spring'kl*, *vt* to sprinkle over. [**be-** (1).]

B. ès S. (Fr.) *abbrev* for *Bachelier ès Sciences*, Bachelor of Sciences.

Bessarabian *bes-ə-rā'bi-ən*, *adj* of *Bessarabia*, a region of the S.W. U.S.S.R. — *n* a native or citizen of Bessarabia; a type of carpet from this region.

Bessemer *bes'əm-ər*, *adj* pertaining to the steel-making process invented by Sir Henry *Bessemer* (1813–98). — **Bessemer converter** a type of furnace used in the Bessemer process; **Bessemer process** a process for making steel from molten pig-iron.

best *best*, *adj* (*superl* of **good**) good in the greatest degree; first; highest; most excellent in any way. — *n* one's utmost endeavour, the limit of one's ability; the highest perfection; the most advantageous or excellent share, part, success, or lot (as the *best of the bargain, the best of three* — tosses, games, etc.); (one's) smartest clothing, etc. — *adv* (*superl* of **well**) to the highest degree of quality, excellence, etc.; better than anyone else. — *vt* (*colloq*) to win against, to outdo or outwit. — **best-before date** the date (stamped, etc. on a package esp. with the wording 'best before (e.g.) 15 August') up to which a manufacturer can guarantee the good quality of a consumer (usu. food) product; **best boy** (*NAm*) the chief assistant to the head lighting electrician on a film or television production crew; **best boy** or **girl** (*colloq*) a favourite friend of the opposite sex; **best buy** (a) most highly recommended purchase from those available; **best end** a cut of lamb, etc. from the part of the neck nearest the ribs; **best man** the groom's (male) attendant and ring-keeper at a wedding; **best part** larger part; **bestsell'er** a book that has sold many copies, overall or in a given season; the writer of such a book. — **(all) for the best** likely to have the best ultimate outcome; **all the best** see under **all**; **at best** assuming the most favourable conditions; **for the best** done with the best of intentions; **have the best of it** to finish ahead in a contest; **I had best** or **I were best** I should (be well advised to); **make the best of** to obtain the best results from (a poor, unpromising, etc. situation); **put one's best foot forward** see under **foot**; **six of the best** see under **six**; **with the best of them** as successfully or well as anyone. [O.E. *betst*, *betest*; see **better.**]

bestial *best'i-əl*, *adj* like an animal; rude, unrefined; sexually depraved. — *vt* **best'ialise** or **-ize** to make bestial. — *n* **best'ialism** lack of the human capacity for reasoning. — *n* **bestiality** (*-al'i-ti*) behavioural likeness to animals; disgusting vice, esp. copulation between an animal and a person. [L. *bestiālis* — *bestia*, beast.]

bestiary *best'i-ər-i*, *n* a book of a type popular in the Middle Ages, describing animals, both real and fabled, allegorised for moral teaching purposes. [L.L. *bestiārium*, a menagerie — *bestia*, a beast.]

bestir *bi-stûr'*, *vt* to cause to begin lively action; to arouse into activity. [**be-** (1).]

bestow *bi-stō'*, *vt* to give or confer (a reward, distinction, etc.); to endow with (a particular quality). — *n* **bestow'al.** — *n* **bestow'er.** [**be-** (1).]

bestraddle *bi-strad'l*, *vt* to bestride. [**be-** (3).]

bestrew *bi-stroo'*, *vt* to cover loosely (with something strewn or scattered over): — *pa p* **bestrewed'** or **bestrewn'** (*with*). [**be-** (1).]

bestride *bi-strīd'*, *vt* to stand or sit across in an imposing manner; to defend or protect, from the sense of standing over a fallen person to defend them; to stride over: — *pa t* **bestrode'**; *pa p* **bestridd'en.** — *adj* **bestrīd'able.** [**be-** (3).]

besuited *bi-soo'tid*, *adj* wearing a suit. [**be-** (2).]

bet *bet*, *n* a prediction of the result of anything yet to be decided, often gambled on with money or other stakes; the stakes to be lost or won on the result of a doubtful outcome. — *vt* and *vi* to lay or stake (money, etc.), as a bet: — *pr p* **bett'ing**; *pa t* and *pa p* **bet** or **bett'ed.** — *n* **bett'er** a person who bets — also **bett'or.** — *n* **bett'ing.** — **a better bet** a more hopeful proposition or possibility; **an even bet** an equal chance; **you bet** (*slang*) certainly.

bet. *abbrev* for between.

beta *bē'tə*, *n* the second letter (Β, β) of the Greek alphabet; in classification, the second or one of the second grade, the grade below alpha; (in a constellation) a star second in brightness (with *cap*). — *adj* (in chemical classification) designating one of two or more isomeric forms of a compound. — *n* **be'tatron** (Gr. *-tron*, agent sfx.) a type of particle accelerator, for accelerating electrons — used in medicine and industry. — **be'ta-blocker** a drug that reduces heart-rate and interferes with the action of stress hormones such as adrenaline, used to treat e.g. high blood-pressure and angina; **beta-carotene** (*-kar'ə-tēn*) a nutrient found in yellow and orange fruits and vegetables; **Beta fibre** a high-fibre product of sugar-beet used as a dietary supplement to aid the absorption of cholesterol; **beta rays** streams of **beta particles**, electrons, given off by radium and other radioactive substances; **beta-thalassemia** (*-thal-ə-sē'mi-ə*) a genetic disorder of the haemoglobin. [Gr. *bēta*; see **B.**]

betaine *bē'tə-in* or *-ēn*, *n* a crystalline, sweet-tasting alkaloid occurring in sugar-beet and other plants, also found in animals. [L. *bēta*, beet, and *-ine.*]

betake *bi-tāk'*, (*literary*) *vt* to take (oneself) to, to go (with *self*): — *pa t* **betook'**; *pa p* **betāk'en.** [**be-** (1).]

bête *bet*, (Fr.) *n* a brute, a stupid person. — *n* **bêtise** (*bet-ēz*) stupidity; a blunder, a stupid action. — **bête noire** (*nwär*; *lit*, black beast) a person or thing that one especially dislikes, fears, is bad at, etc.

betel *bē'tl*, *n* the leaf of the **be'tel-pepper**, a climbing plant, which is chewed in the East along with betel-nuts and lime. — **be'tel-nut** the seed from the orange-coloured fruits of the betel-pepper. [Through Port. from Malayalam *vettila.*]

Beth Din *bāt dēn* or *beth din*, *n* a Jewish court, in London presided over by the Chief Rabbi. [Heb. *bēth*, house, *dīn*, judgment.]

bethink *bi-thingk'*, (*literary*) *vt* to think about or call to mind; to recollect (generally followed by a reflexive pronoun and *of*). — *vi* to consider: — *pa t* and *pa p* **bethought** (*bi-thöt'*). [O.E. *bithencan.*]

betide. See **woe betide you**, etc. at **woe.**

betimes *bi-tīmz'*, (*literary*) *adv* in good time, early; speedily, soon. [**be-** (1) and **time.**]

bêtise. See **bête.**

betoken *bi-tō'kən*, *vt* to show by a sign; to be an omen of; to mean, to symbolise. [**be-** (1).]

béton *bā'tɔ̃*, *n* lime concrete; concrete. [Fr.]

betony *bet'ən-i*, *n* a common red- or purple-flowered plant growing in woods, of great repute in ancient and mediaeval medicine; extended to various plants. [Fr. *bétoine* — L. *betonica, vettonica.*]

betook *bi-took'*, *pa t* of **betake.**

betray *bi-trā'*, *vt* to give knowledge of treacherously (to an enemy); to disclose in breach of trust; to deceive (someone innocent and trustful), to seduce; to show signs of. — *n* **betray'al** (an) act of betraying. — *n* **betray'er** a traitor; the seducer of an innocent girl. [**be-** (1) and O.Fr. *trair* (Fr. *trahir*) — L. *tradĕre*, to deliver up.]

betroth *bi-trōdh'* or *-trōth'*, *vt* to contract, or promise, to marry. — *n* **betroth'al** an engagement to marry; a ceremonious declaration of such an engagement. — *n* and *adj* **betrothed'** (a person) promised in marriage. [**be-** (2), and **troth** or **truth.**]

better *bet'ər, adj* (*compar* of **good**) good in a greater degree; preferable; improved; more suitable; larger; kinder; stronger in health; completely recovered from illness, etc. — *adv* (*compar* of **well**) well in a greater degree; more fully, completely, expertly, etc.; over or more. — *n* a person superior in quality or rank (esp. in *pl*). — *vt* to make better; to surpass, to do better than. — *adj* **bett'ered.** — *n* **bett'ering** amelioration, improvement. — **bett'erment** improvement, esp. in standard of life, status, or value of property. — *n* **bett'erness.** — **bett'er-ball** a form of stroke-play golf in which all players play a drive but thereafter each pair plays only one ball alternately, a four-ball; **better half** a jocular or patronising term for a wife. — **be better than one's word** to do more than one had promised; **be the better for** to be improved as a result of; **better off** in superior circumstances; more fortunate; richer; **for better (or) for worse** whatever the result may be; **get the better of** to gain the advantage over, overcome; **had better** see under **have**; **have seen** or **known better days** to be worse off or in worse condition now than formerly; **the better part of** more than half of, the majority of; **think better of** to revise one's decision about, esp. to decide against; to have a higher opinion of. [O.E. *bet* (adv.), *betera* (adj.) better.]

between *bi-twēn', prep* in, to, through or across the space that separates; intermediate to; involving; indicating a choice of alternatives; by combined action or influence of; from one to another of; in joint possession of (generally, two). — *adv* in or to an intermediate place; at spacial or temporal intervals. — *n* **between'ness** state of being between. — **between'-decks** the space between any two decks of a ship (also *adv*). — *adv* **between'time, between'times** or **between'whiles** at intervals. — **between ourselves** or **between you and me** (*slang* **and the cat** or **doorpost** or **bedpost**, etc.) or **between us two** in confidence; **between the devil and the deep blue sea** in a desperate dilemma or position; **go'-between** see **go**[1]. [O.E. *betwēonum*, and *betwēon* — *be*, by, and *twēgen*, *twā*, twain, two.]

betwixt *bi-twikst', prep* and *adv* between. — **betwixt and between** in a middling, undecided position. [O.E. *betweox* — *twā*, two, and the sfx. *-ix*, -ish, with added *-t*, as in *against* and *amidst*.]

beurre *bœr*, (Fr.) *n* butter. — **beurre manié** (*ma-nyā*) a butter and flour mixture for thickening sauces; **beurre noir** (*nwär*) butter heated until it browns.

beurré *bœ-rā, n* a soft pear of various kinds. [Fr., buttery.]

BeV *abbrev* for billion electron-volts, where billion = one thousand million.

bevatron *bev'ə-tron, n* a type of proton accelerator (see **accelerator** under **accelerate**). [From **BeV** and Gr. agent sfx. *-tron*.]

bevel *bev'l, n* a slant or inclination of a surface; an instrument opening like a pair of compasses, and adjustable for measuring angles. — *adj* having the form of a bevel; slanting. — *vt* to form so as to have a bevel or slant: — *pr p* **bev'elling**; *pa t* and *pa p* **bev'elled.** — *adj* **bev'elled** cut to an oblique angle, sloped off. — *n* **bev'eller.** — *n* **bev'elling.** — **bev'el-gear** or **bev'el-wheels** (*mech*) wheels working on each other in different planes, the cogs of the wheels being bevelled or at oblique angles to the shafts. [From the older form of Fr. *beveau*, bevel (instrument).]

beverage *bev'ər-ij, n* any liquid for drinking, esp. tea, coffee, hot milk, etc. — *adj* **bevv'ied** (*slang*) drunk. — *n* **bevv'y** or **bev'y** (*slang*) (an) alcoholic drink; a drinking session. — **beverage room** (*Can*) a beer parlour. [O.Fr. *bevrage*, *beivre* — L. *bibĕre*, to drink.]

bevy *bev'i, n* a company or flock (of larks, quails, swans, roes, or ladies).

bewail *bi-wāl', vt* to lament; to mourn loudly over (esp. the dead). — *vi* to emit lamenting sounds. — *n* and *adj* **bewail'ing.** [**be-** (1).]

beware *bi-wār', vi* (usu. with *of*, or with *that* or *lest*) to be on one's guard, to be careful. — *vt* to be on one's guard against. [**be** and *ware*, an archaic word meaning cautious.]

bewhiskered *bi-wis'kərd* or *-hwis'kərd, adj* having whiskers on the face. [**be-** (2).]

Bewick's swan *bū'iks swon, n* a small white swan native to N. Asia and N.E. Europe, that winters occasionally in W. Europe. [T. *Bewick* (d. 1828), Eng. wood-engraver, illustrator of *History of British Birds*.]

bewig *bi-wig', vt* to cover with or dress in a wig. — *adj* **bewigged'.** [**be-** (2).]

bewilder *bi-wil'dər, vt* to perplex, confuse. — *adj* **bewil'dered** confused. — *adj* **bewil'dering.** — *adv* **bewil'deringly.** — *n* **bewil'derment.** [**be-** (1) and obs. Eng. *wildern* — O.E. *wilddēoren*, wilderness — *wild*, wild, *dēor*, beast.]

bewitch *bi-wich', vt* to affect by witchcraft (mostly malignantly); to fascinate or charm. — *adj* **bewitch'ing** charming by witchcraft; enchanting (*loosely*). — *adv* **bewitch'ingly.** — *n* **bewitch'ment.** [**be-** (1).]

bey *bā, n* a Turkish governor. [Turk.]

beyond *bi-yond', prep* on the farther side of; farther on in comparison with; out of reach of; above, superior to, better than; apart from, in addition to. — *adv* farther away; into the hereafter. — *n* (with *the*) the unknown; the hereafter. — **beyond measure** too great to be measured; **beyond one** more than one is able to do; outside one's comprehension; **go beyond** to surpass, go further than; **the back of beyond** a place of extreme remoteness. [O.E. *begeondan* — *be-*, and *geond*, across, beyond; see **yon**.]

bezel *bez'l, n* the part of the setting of a precious stone which encloses it; an oblique side or face of a cut gem; the grooved rim in which a watch-glass is set, etc.; a sloped cutting edge (of e.g. a chisel). [From an O.Fr. word represented by mod. Fr. *biseau*.]

bezique *bi-zēk', n* a card game for two, three, or four people, played with two packs, from which all cards below the seven have been removed; the winning combination at this game of the knave of diamonds and queen of spades. [Fr. *bésigue*.]

bf *abbrev* for: brought forward (as in accounts, etc.); bloody fool (*vulg*).

BFPO *abbrev* for British Forces Post Office (abroad).

BG *abbrev* for Bulgaria (I.V.R.).

BH *abbrev* for British Honduras (I.V.R.).

bhajan *buj'ən, n* a Hindu religious song. [Sans.]

bhajee or **bhagee** *bä'jē, n* (in Indian cookery) an appetiser consisting of vegetables cooked in batter.

bhakti *buk'ti, n* (in Hinduism) devotion to a god, as a path to salvation; a form of yoga. [Sans., portion.]

bhang *bang, n* a narcotic and intoxicant, leaves and shoots of hemp. [Hind. *bhā̃g*.]

bharal *bur'əl, n* the blue sheep of the Himalaya. — Also **burrhel** or **burhel.** [Hind.]

BHC *abbrev* for **benzine hexachloride.**

bhindi *bin'di, n* the okra, frequently used in Indian cookery. [Hindi.]

bhp *abbrev* for brake horse-power.

BHS *abbrev* for British Home Stores (a department store).

Bi (*chem*) *symbol* for bismuth.

bi *bī*, (*colloq*) *adj* short for **bisexual.**

bi-, *bī-* or sometimes **bin-** *bin-* before a vowel, *pfx* denoting two, twice, double. [L. *bis*, twice, *bīnī*, two by two, for *duis*, *duīnī*.]

biannual *bī-an'ū-əl, adj* happening, etc. twice a year, half-yearly; happening, etc. every two years, two-yearly. — *adv* **biann'ually.** [L. *bi-*, twice, *annus*, year.]

bias *bī'əs, n* a one-sided inclination of the mind; a prejudice; any special influence that sways one's thinking; an unevenness or imbalance, esp. in distribution or sampling of statistics; a bulge or greater weight on one side of a bowl (in the game of bowling), making it turn to one side; a slanting line or cut across the grain of a material; the voltage applied to certain electronic components to cause them to function in a given direction only. — *adj* cut slantwise. — *adv* slantwise. — *vt* to prejudice or influence, esp. unfairly; to affect so as to cause movement etc. in one direction rather than another; to cut on the slant: — *pr p* **bī'asing** (also **bī'assing**); *pa t* and *pa p* **bī'ased** (also **bī'assed**). — *n* **bī'asing.** — **bias binding** (a long narrow folded piece of) material cut slantwise and used for finishing hems, seams etc., in sewing. [Fr. *biais*, slant.]

biathlon *bī-ath'lon, n* an international competition consisting of both cross-country skiing and shooting. — *n* **biath'lete.** [L. *bi-*, twice, Gr. *athlon*, a contest.]

biaxial *bī-aks'i-əl, adj* having two (optic, etc.) axes. — Also **biax'al.** [**bi-** and **axial.**]

Bib. *abbrev* for Bible.

bib *bib, n* a cloth or plastic napkin put under a child's chin; (of an apron, overalls, etc.) the front part above the waist; a vest bearing their number worn by competition athletes, etc.; a fish of the cod and haddock genus with a large chin barbel. — *n* **bibb'er** a tippler, drinker; chiefly used as a combining form, as (*Bible*) *wine-bibber*. — *n* **bib'ful** see **spill a bibful** below. — **best bib and tucker** (*colloq*) best clothes; **spill a bibful** (*slang*) to give away a secret, make an embarrassing revelation.

bibelot *bēb'lō, n* a knick-knack. [Fr.]

bibl. *abbrev* for: biblical; bibliographical; bibliography.

Bible *bī'bl, n* (also **bible**) (the book containing) the Scriptures of the Old and New Testaments; (also **bible**) a comprehensive book regarded as the ultimate authority on its subject. — *adj* **biblical** (*bib'li-kəl*) of, like or relating to the Bible. — *adv* **bib'lically.** — *n* **bib'licism** (*-sizm*) biblical doctrine, learning or literature; literal interpretation and acceptance of the Bible. — *n* **bib'licist** or **bib'list** a person skilled in biblical learning; a person who interprets and accepts the Bible literally. — **Bible belt** those areas of the Southern U.S.A. of predominantly fundamentalist and puritanical Christian religious dogma; **Bible paper** very thin strong paper for printing; **Bi'ble-thumper** a vigorous, aggressive or dogmatic Christian preacher; **Bi'ble-pounding** or **Bi'ble-thumping.** [Fr., — L.L. *biblia*, fem. sing., earlier neut. pl., from Gr. *biblia*, books, esp. the canonical books.]

bibli- *bib-li-, combining form* denoting book or books. — *n* **bibliographer** (*-og'rə-fər*) the compiler of a bibliography. — *adj* **bibliographic** (*-ə-graf'ik*) or **bibliograph'ical** (*-əl*). — *n* **bibliog'raphy** study, description or knowledge of books, in regard to their outward form, authors, subjects, editions, and history; a list of books on a particular subject or by a single author; a list of the works referred to in the process of writing a book, article etc. — *n* **bib'liophil** (*-fil*) or **bib'liophile** (*-fīl*; Gr. *philos*, friend) a lover or collector of books. — Also *adj*. — *n* **biblioph'ilism.** — *n* **biblioph'ily.** — *n* **bibliophō'bia** hatred of books. [Gr. *biblion*, book; cf. **Bible.**]

biblio. or **bibliog.** *abbrev* for bibliography.

bibulous *bib'ū-ləs, adj* addicted to strong drink. — *adv* **bib'ulously.** — *n* **bib'ulousness.** [L. *bibulus* — *bibĕre*, to drink.]

bicameral *bī-kam'ər-əl, adj* (of a legislative body) having two chambers. — *n* **bicam'eralism.** — *n* **bicam'eralist** an advocate of the bicameral parliamentary system. [L. *bi*, twice, *camera*, chamber.]

bicarbonate *bī-kär'bən-āt, n* an acid salt of carbonic acid; sodium bicarbonate, used in baking-powder or as an antacid digestive remedy (*colloq* short form **bi'carb**). [**bi-** and **carbonate.**]

BICC *abbrev* for British Insulated Callender's Cables.

bicentenary *bī-sen-tēn'ər-i*, or *-ten'* or (esp. *NAm*) **bicentennial** *bī-sen-ten'i-əl, adj* happening every two hundred years; pertaining to a two-hundredth anniversary. — *n* a two-hundredth anniversary. [L. *bi-*, twice, *centum*, a hundred, *annus*, a year.]

biceps *bī'seps, n* a large muscle at the front of the upper arm or a similar one on the back of the thigh. — *adj* **bicipital** (*-sip'*) of or relating to the biceps; two-headed. [L. *biceps*, two-headed — *bis*, twice, and *caput*, head.]

bichord *bī'körd, adj* (of a musical instrument) having paired strings in unison for each note. [**bi-** and **chord**[2].]

bicker *bik'ər, vi* to argue in a petty way. — *n* a fight, a quarrel.

biconcave *bī-kon'kāv, adj* concave on both sides. [**bi-** and **concave.**]

biconvex *bī-kon'veks, adj* convex on both sides. [**bi-** and **convex.**]

bicultural *bī-kul'chə-rəl, adj* of, having, containing or consisting of two distinct cultures. — *n* **bicul'turalism.** [**bi-** and **cultural.**]

bicuspid *bī-kus'pid, adj* having two cusps. — *n* a tooth located between the molars and the canine teeth, a premolar. — *adj* **bicusp'idate.** [**bi-** and **cuspid.**]

bicycle *bī'si-kl, n* a vehicle with two wheels, one directly in front of the other, driven by pedals or (**mo'tor-bicycle**) a motor. — *vi* to ride a bicycle. — *n* **bī'cyclist.** — **bicycle chain** the chain transmitting motion from the pedals to the wheels of a bicycle; **bicycle clip** a metal clip for holding a cyclist's trousers closely to his or her leg to avoid fouling the wheels, etc.; **bicycle polo** see under **polo**[1]; **bicycle pump** a hand pump for inflating bicycle tyres. [L. *bi-*, twice, Gr. *kyklos*, a circle, wheel.]

bid[1] *bid, vt* to offer, esp. to offer to pay at an auction; to propose winning (a given number of tricks in certain card games). — *vi* to make an offer or proposal: — *pr p* **bidd'ing**; *pa t* **bade** (*bad*; also *bād*) or **bid**; *pa p* **bidd'en** or **bid.** — *n* an offer of a price; a risky attempt or proposal; a call (at cards). — *adj* **bidd'able** easily persuaded or controlled, docile. — *n* **bidd'er.** — *n* **bidd'ing** command or request. — **bid fair** to seem likely; **bid in** (of an owner or his or her agent) in an auction, to overbid the highest offer; **bid up** to raise the market price of (something) artificially, by means of specious bids, etc. [O.E. *bēodan.*]

bid[2] *bid, vt* to invite; to command; to greet with, say as a greeting. — Tenses are as in the preceding verb, with which it has been confused. — *n* **bidd'ing** a prayer requesting something, e.g. blessing. [O.E. *biddan.*]

biddy *bid'i, n* an old woman (*slang* and *derog*).

bide *bīd, vi* (*Scot* or *archaic*) to wait; to dwell; to remain. — *vt* to await (*obs* except in **bide one's time,** to await a favourable moment): — *pa t* **bīd'ed** or **bode**; *pa p* **bīd'ed.** [O.E. *bīdan*; but sometimes for **abide.**]

bidet *bē'dā, n* a basin on a low pedestal, for washing the genital and anal areas, etc. [Fr., pony.]

bi-directional *bī-dī-rek'shə-nəl, adj* operating in two directions; printing the lines of a text alternately left to right and right to left (*comput*, etc.).

bidon *bē'dɔ̃, n* a vessel for holding liquids, such as a wooden cup, water-bottle, tin-can or oil-drum. — *n* **bidonville** (*bē'don-vēl* or *bē-dɔ̃-*) in a French-speaking country, a shanty town with dwellings made from oil-drums. [Fr.]

bien *byɛ̃*, (Fr.) *adv* well. — **bien-aimé** (*byɛ̃-ne-mā*) well-beloved; **bien élevé** (*-nā-ləv-ā*) well brought up, well-mannered; **bien-être** (*-netr*) a sense of well-being; **bien pensant** (*pā-sā*) right-thinking; orthodox; **bienséance** (*-sā-ãs*) propriety; (in *pl*) the proprieties.

biennial *bī-en'i-əl* or *-en'yəl*, *adj* lasting two years; happening or appearing once every two years. — *n* a plant that flowers and fruits only in its second year, then dies. — *adv* **bienn'ially**. [L. *biennium*, two years — *bi-*, twice, *annus*, a year.]

bier *bēr*, *n* a carriage or frame of wood for bearing a dead person to the grave. [O.E. *bǣr*.]

bierkeller *bēr'kel-ər*, *n* a German or German-style bar, selling beer. [Ger., beer cellar.]

bifacial *bī-fā'shl*, *adj* having two faces; having two dissimilar sides. [**bi-** and **facial**.]

biff *bif*, (*colloq*) *n* a blow. — *vt* to strike hard.

bifid *bif'id* or *bī'fid*, *adj* divided into two parts by a deep split. [L. *bifidus* — *bi-*, twice, *findĕre*, to cleave or split.]

bifocal *bī-fō'kəl*, *adj* composed of parts of different focal lengths. — *npl* **bifō'cals** spectacles with bifocal lenses, for both long- and short-sightedness. [**bi-** and **focal**.]

bifoliate *bī-fō'li-āt*, *adj* having two leaves or leaflets. — *adj* **bifō'liolate** having two leaflets. [L. *bi-*, twice, *folium*, leaf.]

bifurcate *bī'fər-kāt* or *-fûr'*, *adj* having two prongs or branches. — *vi* (*bī'fər-kāt*) to divide into two branches. — *n* **bifurcā'tion**. — *adj* **bī'furcated**. [L. *bifurcus* — *bi-*, *bis*, twice, *furca*, a fork.]

big *big*, *adj* (*compar* **bigg'er**; *superl* **bigg'est**) large or great; grown-up; older (as in *big sister*, *big brother*); magnanimous (usu. *facetious*); loud; very or most important, as the *Big Three*, *Big Four*, etc., (leaders, countries, organisations, etc.); pregnant (esp. *Bible*). — *adv* (*colloq*) boastfully or ambitiously, as in *talk big*; greatly or impressively. — *adj* **bigg'ish**. — *n* **bigg'y** or **bigg'ie** (*colloq*) a large or important person or thing. — *n* **big'ness**. — **Big Bang** or **big bang** the explosion of a small dense mass which some scientists believe to have been the origin of the universe; the changes in the system and rules of the British Stock Exchange instituted on 27 October 1986, in effect deregulating many of its practices and abolishing the distinction between jobbers and brokers. — *adj* **big-bell'ied** having a big belly; pregnant (with). — **Big Brother** a dictator, as in George Orwell's *Nineteen Eighty-four* (1949); a powerful leader or organisation, perceived as ubiquitous and sinister; **big bucks** or **big money** (*slang*) large amounts of money; **big business** large business enterprises and organisations, esp. collectively; **Big C** (*colloq*) cancer; **big Daddy** or **big White Chief** (*colloq*; both also **Big**) a paternalistic or domineering head of an organisation, etc.; **big deal** (*colloq*) used as a scornful response to an offer, boast, etc.; **big dipper** a roller-coaster at a fair (orig. *US*); (with *caps*) the constellation Great Bear (esp. *NAm*); **big end** in an internal-combustion engine, the larger end of the connecting-rod; **big fish** a powerful person, esp. one in a criminal organisation thought worthy of capture; **big'foot** in the U.S. and Canada, a hairy primate reputed to inhabit wilderness areas, and said to be between 6 and 15 feet tall; **big guns** (*colloq*) the important, powerful persons in an organisation, etc.; **big'-head** (*colloq*) a conceited person. — *adj* **big-head'ed**. — **big'horn** the Rocky Mountain goat or sheep; **big money** see **big bucks** above; **big'mouth** (*slang*) a talkative and often boastful person. — *adj* **big'-mouthed**. — **big name** (*colloq*) a celebrity; **big noise** (*colloq*) an important person. — *vt* **big'-note** (*Austr colloq*) to boast about oneself, try to make oneself seem important; **big shot** see **bigwig** below; **big stick** (*colloq*) a display of force, as threat or means of persuasion. — *adj* **big-tick'et** (*US colloq*) expensive. — **big'-time** (*colloq*) the top level in any pursuit, esp. show-business; — *adj* at the top level; important. — **big toe** see **toe**; **big top** a large circular tent used for circus performances; **big wheel** a Ferris wheel; **Big White Chief** see **big Daddy** above; **big'wig** or **big shot** (*colloq*) a powerful person, a person of some importance. — **go over big (with)** (*colloq*) to impress greatly; **in a big way** vigorously, enthusiastically; **too big for one's boots** conceited, self-important. [M.E. *big*,— Du. *bigge*.]

bigamy *big'ə-mi*, *n* the custom, crime, or fact of having two legal wives or husbands at once. — *n* **big'amist** a person who has committed bigamy. — *adj* **big'amous**. — *adv* **big'amously**. [L. *bi-*, twice, Gr. *gamos*, marriage.]

bight *bīt*, *n* a wide bay; a bend or coil (in a rope, etc.) [O.E. *byht*.]

bigot *big'ət*, *n* a person blindly and obstinately devoted to a particular set of ideas, creed or political party, and dismissive towards others. — *adj* **big'oted** having the qualities of a bigot. — *n* **big'otry** blind or excessive zeal, esp. in religious, political or racial matters. [O.Fr.]

bijection *bī-jek'shən*, (*math*) *n* a mapping function that is both an injection and a surjection. [**bi-**, and *-jection* from L. *jacere*, to throw.]

bijou *bē'zhoo͞*, *n* a trinket; a jewel: — *pl* **bijoux** (*bē'zhoo͞z*). — *adj* small and elegant. — *n* **bijouterie** (*bē-zhoo͞t'ər-ē*) jewellery, esp. trinkets. [Fr.]

bike *bīk*, *n* and *vi* colloq. for **bicycle** or **motorbike**. — *n* **bī'ker**. — *n* **bī'kie** (*Austr* and *NZ colloq*) a member of a gang of motorcycle riders. — *n* **bī'king**. — **bike'way** (*NAm*) a lane, road, etc. exclusively for pedal bicycles. — **on your bike** (*slang*) a contemptuous expression of dismissal.

bikini *bi-kē'ni*, *n* a brief swimming-costume, in two separate parts. [From *Bikini*, an atoll of the Marshall Islands, scene of atom-bomb experiments; the bikini's effects on men were reputed to be similar.]

bilabial *bī-lā'bi-əl*, *adj* two-lipped; (of a sound) produced by contact or approximation of the two lips, e.g. b or w (*phon*). — *n* a bilabial consonant. — *adj* **bīlā'biate** (*bot*) two-lipped, like some corollas. [L. *bi-*, twice, *labium*, a lip.]

bilateral *bī-lat'ər-əl*, *adj* having or involving two sides; affecting two parties or participants mutually. — *n* **bilat'eralism** two-sidedness; equality in value of trade between two countries. — *adv* **bilat'erally**. [L. *bi-*, twice, *latus*, *-eris*, side.]

bilberry *bil'bər-i*, *n* a whortleberry shrub; its dark-blue berry. [Cf. Dan. *böllebær*.]

bile *bīl*, *n* a thick bitter fluid secreted by the liver; irritability, ill temper. — *adj* **biliary** (*bil'yər-i*) of the bile, the bile ducts or the gall-bladder. — *adj* **bilious** (*bil'yəs*) pertaining to or affected by bile; irritable, bad-tempered; (of colours) very unpleasant, sickly. — *adv* **bil'iously**. — *n* **bil'iousness**. — **bile'-ducts** the ducts that convey the bile to the small intestine. [Fr., — L. *bīlis*.]

bilge *bilj*, *n* the bulging part of a cask; the broadest part of a ship's bottom; filth, dirty water etc. such as collects there; rubbish, drivel (*slang*). — *vi* (of a ship) to spring a leak in the bilge. — *adj* **bilg'y** having the appearance and disagreeable smell of bilge-water. — **bilge'-keel** a ridge along the bilge of a ship to prevent or reduce rolling; **bilge'-pump**; **bilge'-water**.

Bilharzia *bil-här'zi-ə* or *-tsi-ə*, *n* a genus of parasitic worms with adhesive suckers, infesting human and other blood, with two larval stages, first in water-snails and then in man. — *n* **bilhar'zia**, **bilharzī'asis** or **bilharziō'sis** a disease (also known as schistosomiasis) caused by these worms, common in tropical countries, esp. Egypt and other parts of Africa. [From Theodor *Bilharz* (1825–62), an expert in parasitic worms.]

biliary. See **bile**.

bilingual *bī-ling'gwəl*, *adj* expressed in two languages; speaking two languages, esp. as mother tongues or with similar fluency. — *n* **bīling'ualism**. — *n*

bīling'uist. — *adv* **biling'ually**. [L. *bilinguis* — *bi*-, twice, *lingua*, tongue.]

bilious. See **bile**.

bilk *bilk*, *vt* to elude; to cheat; to avoid paying (someone) what is due. — *n* **bilk'er**. [At first a term in cribbage.]

bill[1] *bil*, *n* a concave battle-axe with a long wooden handle; a kind of hatchet with a long blade and wooden handle in the same line with it, often with a hooked point, used in pruning. — **bill'hook** a bill or hatchet with a curved point. [O.E. *bil*.]

bill[2] *bil*, *n* the beak of a bird, or anything similar in shape or function; a sharp promontory; the point of an anchor fluke (*naut*). — *vi* to touch bills, as doves do; hence, to caress or talk fondly. — *combining form* **-billed** having a bill of the stated type. — *n* and *adj* **bill'ing**. — **bill'board** (*naut*) a board used to protect a ship's planking from damage by the bills when the anchor is weighed. [O.E. *bile*.]

bill[3] *bil*, *n* a written account of money owed; a draft of a proposed law; a written agreement to pay a sum of money at a fixed date; a bank-note (*NAm*); a poster advertising an event, product, etc.; (often as a *combining form*, as in *playbill*, *handbill*) a slip of paper serving as an advertisement; a list of performers, etc. in order of importance; a programme of entertainment. — *vt* to send an invoice to; to announce or advertise. — *adj* **billed** (*bild*) named in a list or advertisement. — *n* **bill'ing** the making out or sending of bills or invoices; the (total amount of) money received from customers or clients; precedence of naming in an announcement or poster, as *top billing*, *second billing*, etc. — **bill'board** a board on which large advertising posters are stuck; **bill'-fold** (*NAm*) a soft case or wallet for paper money; **bill'poster** or **bill'sticker** a person who sticks up bills or posters. — **bill of costs** an account of a solicitor's charges and outgoings in the conduct of the client's business; **bill of exchange** a document employed by the parties to a business transaction whereby payment is made through a mutually convenient third party, thereby avoiding the cost and complications of foreign exchange; **bill of fare** a list of dishes or articles of food, a menu; **bill of health** an official certificate of the state of health on board a ship before sailing; **bill of indictment** a statement of a charge made against a person; **bill of lading** a paper signed by the master of a ship, by which he makes himself responsible for the safe delivery of the goods specified therein; a certificate stating that specified goods are aboard a vessel; **bill of rights** see under **right**; **bill of sale** in English law, a formal deed assigning personal property; **clean bill of health** a certificate stating that there is no illness on board a ship; a statement that a person is healthy; a statement that an organisation, etc. is in good condition (*fig*); **double** (or **triple**) **bill** a programme of entertainment consisting of two (or three) main items, esp. films; **fill the bill** see under **fill**; **top the bill** to head the list of performers, to be the star attraction. [L.L. *billa* — L. *bulla*, a knob, a seal, hence a document bearing a seal, etc.; cf. **bull**[2].]

billabong *bil'ə-bong*, (*Austr*) *n* a cut-off loop of a river, replenished only by floods; an offshoot from a river (strictly one that does not rejoin it). [Aboriginal *billa*, river, *bung*, dead.]

billboard. See **bill**[2, 3].

billet[1] *bil'it*, *n* a note or letter assigning quarters to soldiers or others; the quarters requisitioned; an allocated sleeping- or resting-place; a job or occupation. — *vt* to quarter or accommodate, e.g. soldiers: — *pr p* **bill'eting**; *pa t* and *pa p* **bill'eted**. [O.Fr. *billette*, dimin. of *bille*; see **bill**[3].]

billet[2] *bil'it*, *n* a small log of wood; a bar of metal; an ornament in Norman architecture in the form of short cylinders with spaces between. [Fr. *billette* — *bille*, the young trunk of a tree.]

billet-doux *bil-i-dōō'* or *bē-yā-dōō'*, *n* a love-letter: — *pl* **billets-doux'** (same pronunciation as the singular form). [Fr. *billet*, letter, *doux*, sweet.]

billiards *bil'yərdz*, *nsing* any of various games played with a cue and balls on a rectangular table, the table in the most common version having pockets at the sides and corners, into which the balls can be struck. — **bill'iard-ball**; **bill'iard-cue**; **bill'iard-table**. [Fr. *billard* — *bille*, a stick, hence a cue.]

billion *bil'yən*, *n* in Britain, France (since 1948), etc., a million millions (unit and twelve ciphers); in N.Am., often now in Britain, one thousand millions (unit and nine ciphers). — *n* **billionaire'**. — *adj* and *n* **bill'ionth**. [**bi**- and **million**.]

billow *bil'ō*, *n* a great wave; a wave, the sea (*poetic*). — *vi* to roll or swell in great waves or clouds; to bulge (out), as a sail in the wind. — *adj* **bill'owed**. — *adj* **bill'owing**. — *adj* **bill'owy**.

billy *bil'i*, *n* a cylindrical container for boiling water, cooking, etc. (*Austr* and *NZ*; also **bill'y-can**); a truncheon (*NAm*): — *pl* **bill'ies**.

billycock *bil'i-kok*, *n* a hard felt hat.

billy-goat *bil'i-gōt*, *n* a he-goat.

billy-o or **billy-oh** *bil'i-ō*, in phrase **like billy-o(h)**, vigorously, rapidly, fiercely.

bilobar *bī-lō'bər*, **bilobate** *bī-lō'bāt* or **bilobed** *bī'lōbd*, *adj* having two lobes. — *adj* **bilobular** (*bī-lob'ū-lər*) having two lobules. [L. *bi*-, twice, and **lobe** or **lobule**.]

biltong *bil'tong*, (*SAfr*) *n* sun-dried lean meat. [Du. *bil*, buttock, *tong*, tongue.]

BIM *abbrev* for British Institute of Management.

bimbashi *bim-bä'shē*, *n* a military officer (in Turkey or Egypt). [Turk. *bin*, thousand, *baš*, head.]

bimbo *bim'bō*, (*slang*) *n* a person, usu. a woman, esp. one who is young and highly physically attractive but dim, naïve or superficial: — *pl* **bim'bos**. [It., child.]

bimetallic *bī-mi-tal'ik*, *adj* composed of, or using, two metals; (of a monetary system) in which gold and silver are on precisely the same footing as regards mintage and legal tender. — *n* **bimetallism** (*bī-met'əl-izm*) such a system. — *n* and *adj* **bimet'allist**. — **bimetallic strip** a strip, formed by bonding two metals one of which expands more than the other, which bends with change of temperature, used in thermostatic switches, etc.

bimonthly *bī-munth'li*, *adj* or *adv* (happening, etc.) once every two months; (happening, etc.) twice a month. [L. **bi**- and **month**.]

bin *bin*, *n* a receptacle for rubbish; a receptacle for storing e.g. corn; a stand or case with compartments in which to store bottled wine in a wine-cellar; the wine contained in it; (short for **loony bin**) a lunatic asylum (*slang*); gaol (*slang*); a pocket (*slang*). — *vt* to put (e.g. bottled wine) into a bin: — *pr p* **binn'ing**; *pa t* and *pa p* **binned**. — **bin'-liner** a usu. plastic bag for lining a rubbish bin or dustbin. [O.E. *binn*, a manger.]

bin-. See **bi-**.

binary *bī'nər-i*, *adj* composed of two; twofold. — *n* a binary system or star. — **binary fission** (*biol*) division of an organism or cell into two parts; **binary operation** in mathematics, combining two elements from a collection of elements in such a way as to give another element from the same collection (e.g. addition or multiplication in the ordinary number system); **binary scale** the scale of mathematical notation whose base is 2 (instead of 10); **binary system** a system using the binary scale of mathematical notation; a system in which numbers are expressed by using two digits only, viz. 1 and 0; two stars revolving about their mutual centre of gravity (also **binary star**); **binary weapon, munition**, etc. a bomb or shell loaded with two separate canisters of non-toxic chemicals, the chemicals combining at the time of firing to produce a lethal gas. [L. *bīnārius* — *bīnī*, two by two, *bis*, twice.]

binaural *bīn-ö'rəl, adj* having, employing or relating to two ears; (of reproduction of sound) using two sound channels. — *adv* **binaur'ally**. [L. *bīnī*, two by two, *auris*, ear.]

bind *bīnd, vt* to tie or fasten together; to pass or put something round; to restrain; to fix; to sew a border on; to tie up or bandage; to fasten together the sections of and put a cover on (a book); to impose an obligation on; to oblige by oath or promise; to contract as an apprentice; to hold or cement firmly; to cause (dry ingredients) to cohere by adding a small amount of liquid (*cookery*); to constipate. — *vi* to become bound: — *pa t* and *pa p* **bound** (*bownd*). — *n* in music, the mark for indicating that a note is to be held, not repeated (of the same form as the slur or legato mark); a difficult or annoying situation, a bore (*slang*). — *n* **bind'er** a person who binds (books, sheaves, etc.); anything that binds, such as a rope, a bandage, a cementing agent, a tie-beam, a header in masonry, or a case or file for binding loose papers in; an attachment to a reaping-machine for tying the bundles of grain cut and thrown off; a reaping-machine provided with one. — *n* **bind'ery** a book-binder's place of work. — *adj* **bind'ing** restraining; obligatory. — *n* the act of someone who binds; anything that binds; the covering of a book. — **bind'weed** any of various weeds which trail along the ground and twine themselves about other plants, trees, etc. (esp. one of the genus *Convolvulus*). — **be bound up in** to be wholly devoted to or occupied with; **bind over** to subject to legal constraint (esp. not to disturb the peace); **I'll be bound** I'll bet, I'm certain. — See also **bound**[1] and **bounden**. [O.E. *bindan*.]

binge *binj* or *binzh*, (*colloq*) *n* a bout of overindulgence, esp. in eating or drinking. — *vi* to overindulge in this way. — *n* **bin'ger**.

bingo *bing'gō, n* a game in which numbers are called at random which may then be covered on players' cards, prizes being won by the first to cover all or certain of the numbers displayed on a card (cf. **housey-housey** under **house**, **lotto** under **lottery**, **tombola**). — *interj* the exclamation made by the first player to finish in this game; an exclamation expressing a sudden discovery, unexpectedness, etc. — **bingo hall**.

binnacle *bin'ə-kl*, (*naut*) *n* the casing in which a ship's compass is kept. [Formerly *bittacle* — Port. *bitācola* — L. *habitāculum*, a dwelling-place — *habitāre*, to dwell.]

binocular *bī-* or *bi-nok'ū-lər, adj* with two eyes; suitable for use with two eyes; stereoscopic. — *n* a binocular telescope (usu. (*a pair of*) *binoculars*). [L. *bīnī*, two by two, *oculus*, an eye.]

binomial *bī-nōm'i-əl, adj* (*alg*) consisting of two terms, as $a+b$. — *n* a binomial expression. [L. *bi-*, twice, *nōmen*, a name, a term.]

bint *bint*, (*derog slang*) *n* a girl or woman (with various shades of meaning). [Ar., daughter.]

bio- *bī-ō-, combining form* signifying: life; living organisms; living tissue — as in e.g. the following. — *n* **bioassay** (*bī-ō-ə-sā'* or *-as'ā*) the assessment of the strength and effect of a drug or other substance by testing it on a living organism and comparing the results with the known results of another drug, etc. — *nsing* **bio-astronaut'ics** the science dealing with the effects of travel in space on living organisms. — *n* **bioavailabil'ity** the extent to which a drug, etc., after administration (e.g. by mouth), is available to the tissue it is intended to act on. — *adj* **bioavail'-able**. — *n* **biocat'alyst** a substance, e.g. an enzyme, that produces or speeds up a biochemical reaction. — *adj* and *n* **biochem'ical**. — *n* **biochem'ist**. — *n* **biochem'istry** the chemistry of living things, physiological chemistry. — *n* **bioclimatol'ogy** an older name for **biometeorology**. — *adj* **biodegrād'able** (of substances) able to be broken down by bacteria. — *n* **biodegradā'tion** (also **biodeteriorā'tion**). — *adj* **biodestruct'ible** biodegradable. — *adj* **biodynam'ic** dealing with the activities of living organisms; (of a system of land cultivation) fertilising with organic materials only. — *nsing* **biodynam'ics**. — *n* **bioecol'ogy** the branch of ecology dealing with the interrelationship of plant and animal life. — *nsing* **bioenerget'ics** the biology of energy relationships in living organisms or energy changes produced by them; see also **Reichian therapy**. — *n* **bio-engineer'ing** see **biological engineering** under **biology**. — *nsing* **bioeth'ics** the study of the ethical problems produced by medical and scientific research, etc. — *n* **biofeed'back** the clinical control of body functions in response to monitoring by electronic instruments such as an electrocardiograph. — *n* **bi'ogas** domestic or commercial gas obtained by treating naturally-occurring materials. — *n* **biogen'esis** the derivation of living things from living things only; biogeny. — *adj* **biogenet'ic** or **biogen'ic** relating to biogeny, or to biogenesis. — *adj* **biogenous** (*-oj'ə-nəs*) parasitic. — *n* **biog'eny** the course of organic evolution or development of the individual or the race. — *n* **bioluminesc'ence** the emission of light by living organisms. — *n* **bi'omass** the quantity or weight of living material (animals, plants, etc.) in a unit of area; living material as a source of energy. — *n* **biomatē'rial** suitable material from which to produce artificial body parts that are to be in direct contact with living tissue. — *nsing* **biomechan'ics** the mechanics of movements in living creatures. — *adj* **biomed'ical** of or pertaining to both biology and medicine; applied to the study of the effects of stress, esp. space travel, on living organisms. — *n* **biomed'icine**. — *adj* **biometeorolog'ical**. — *n* **biometeorol'ogy** the effect of weather and climate on plants, animals and man. — *adj* **biomet'ric**. — *n* **biometrician** (*-trish'ən*). — *n* **biom'etry** the statistical or quantitative study of biology (also *nsing* **biomet'rics**). — *adj* **bionom'ic**. — *nsing* **bionom'ics** (Gr. *nomos*, law) the study of the relations between the organism and its environment; ecology. — *adj* **biopsycholog'ical**. — *n* **biopsychol'ogy** the branch of psychology, or of biology, which deals with the interaction of mind and body, and the effects of this interaction. — *npl* **bi'orhythms** physiological, emotional and intellectual rhythms or cycles, supposed to cause variations in mood or performance. — *n* **bi'oscope** a cinematographic apparatus or theatre or (*SAfr*) a cinema. — *n* **bi'osphere** the part of the earth and its atmosphere in which living things are found. — *n* **biosyn'thesis** the production of chemical substances by a living organism. — *adj* **biosynthet'ic**. — *n* **biō'ta** the flora and fauna of a region. — *adj* **biotechnolog'ical**. — *n* **biotechnol'ogist**. — *n* **biotechnol'ogy** the utilisation of living organisms (e.g. bacteria) in industry, etc., e.g. in the creation of energy, destruction of waste, and the manufacture of various products; ergonomics (*NAm*). — *n* **bi'otype** within a species, a distinct subgroup. [Gr. *bios*, life.]

bio *bī'ō, n* short for **biography**: — *pl* **bi'os**.

biography *bī-og'rə-fi, n* a written account or history of the life of an individual; the art of writing such accounts. — *n* **biographee'** the subject of a biography. — *n* **biog'rapher** a person who writes biography. — *adj* **biographic** (*bī-ō-graf'ik*) or **biograph'ical** (*-kəl*). — *adv* **biograph'ically**. [**bio-** and Gr. *graphein*, to write.]

biol. *abbrev* for biology.

biology *bī-ol'ə-ji, n* the science of living things; the life sciences collectively, including botany, anatomy and physiology, zoology, etc. — *adj* **biological** (*bī-ō-loj'i-kəl*) of or pertaining to biology; physiological; effected by living organisms or by enzymes. — *adv* **biolog'ically**. — *n* **biol'ogist**. — **biological clock** an in-built mechanism which regulates the physiological rhythms and cycles of living organisms; **biological control** a method of reducing the numbers of a pest (plant, animal or parasite) by introducing or encouraging one of its enemies; **biological engineering** the provision of (electrical, electronic, etc.) aids for bodily functions, e.g. hearing aids, artificial limbs and joints, etc. (also **bioengineering**); the manipulation of living cells so as to promote their growth in a desired way; **biological warfare** methods of warfare involving the use of disease bacteria. [**bio-** and **-logy**.]

bionic *bī-on'ik*, *adj* relating to or using bionics; superhuman (*colloq*). — *nsing* **bion'ics** the study of methods of working of living creatures and the application of the principles observed to the design of computers and other machines; (*loosely*) the replacement of parts of the body by electronic and/or mechanical devices, such as powered limbs, heart valves, etc.

biont *bī'ont*, *n* a living organism. — *adj* **bion'tic**. [Gr. *bios*, life, *ōn* (stem *ont-*) from *einai*, to be.]

-biont *-bī-ont*, *combining form* signifying an organism belonging to a particular habitat or environment. — *adj combining form* **-bion'tic.** [Ety. as for **biont**.]

biopic *bī'ō-pik*, *n* a film, usu. an uncritically admiring one, telling the life-story of a celebrity. [*Bio*graphical *pic*ture.]

biopsy *bī'op-si*, *n* the surgical removal of tissue or fluid from a living body for diagnostic examination; such examination.

-biosis *-bi-ō'sis*, *combining form* denoting a specific way of living. — *adj combining form* **-biotic** (*-bī-ot'ik*). [Gr. *biōsis*, way of life; adj. *biōtikos*.]

biotic *bī-ot'ik*, *adj* pertaining to life. — *adv* **biot'ically**. [Gr. *biōtikos*.]

biotin *bī'ō-tin*, *n* one of the members of the vitamin B complex (also known as vitamin H). [Gr. *biotos*, means of living.]

bipartisan *bī-pärt-i-zan'*, *adj* pertaining to, supported by, or consisting of members of, two parties. [**bi-** and **partisan**.]

bipartite *bī-pärt'īt*, *adj* divided into two parts; (of e.g. a document) having two corresponding parts; (of e.g. an agreement) affecting two parties. — *n* **bipartition** (*-tish'ən*) division into two parts. [L. *bi-*, *bis*, twice, *partītus*, divided — *partīre*, *-īrī*, to divide.]

biped *bī'ped*, *n* an animal with two feet. — *adj* **bi'ped** or **bipedal** (*bī-ped'əl* or *-pē'dəl*) having two feet; using two feet for walking. — *n* **biped'alism**. [L. *bipēs*, *-pedis* — *bi-*, twice, *pēs*, *pedis*, foot.]

biphenyl *bī-fē'nīl*, *n* and *adj*. Same as **diphenyl**.

bipinnate *bī-pin'āt*, (*bot*) *adj* pinnate with each pinna itself pinnate. [**bi-** and **pinnate**.]

biplane *bī'plān*, *n* an aeroplane or glider with two sets of wings, one above the other. [**bi-** and **plane**[2].]

BIPM *abbrev* for *Bureau International des Poids et Mesures* (Fr.), International Bureau of Weights and Measures.

bipolar *bī-pō'lər*, *adj* having two poles or extremities (*lit* and *fig*). — *n* **bipolar'ity**. [**bi-** and **polar**.]

birch *bûrch*, *n* a hardy forest-tree (*Betula*), with smooth white bark and very durable wood; a rod for punishment, consisting of a birch twig or twigs. — *vt* to flog. — *adj* **birch** or **birch'en** made of birch. — **birch fly** see **blackfly**; **birch rod** a birch for punishment. [O.E. *berc*, *bierce*.]

bird *bûrd*, *n* a warm-blooded, egg-laying, feathered vertebrate of the class *Aves*, having forelimbs modified into wings; a general name for a feathered animal (orig. applied to the young); a person (*slang*); a prison sentence (*slang*; from **bird-lime**, rhyming slang for 'time'); a girl, esp. one's girlfriend (*slang*). — *vi* to shoot at, seek to catch or snare birds. — *n* **bird'er** (*colloq*) a bird-watcher. — *n* **bird'ie** (*dimin*) a little bird; the achievement of a hole in golf in one stroke less than par. — *n* **bird'ing** hunting or snaring birds; bird-watching. — **bird'bath** a basin set up for birds to bathe in. — *adj* **bird'-brained** (*colloq*) flighty, silly. — **bird'cage** a cage of wire or wicker for holding birds; **bird'call** an instrument for imitating birds' notes; **bird'-cherry** a small wild cherry tree; its astringent fruit; **bird'-dog** a dog trained to find or retrieve birds for hunters; **bird'-fancier** a person who breeds cage-birds, or keeps them for sale. — *adj* **bird'-hipped** (of dinosaurs) having a pelvis slightly similar to a bird's, the pubis extending backwards to lie parallel with the upper pelvis, ornithischian. — **bird impact** bird strike; **bird'-lime** a sticky substance for catching birds; see also **bird** *n*, above; **bird'man** an ornithologist or a person otherwise concerned with birds; **bird'-nesting** see **bird's-nesting** below; **bird'seed** seed (hemp, etc.) for cage-birds; a thing trifling in amount, chicken feed (*slang*); **bird's'-eye** a kind of primrose, of speedwell, or of tobacco. — *adj* such as might be seen by a flying bird; having markings like birds' eyes. — **bird'shot** pellets suitable for shooting birds; **bird's'-nest** the nest in which a bird lays and hatches her eggs; a name given to several plants from their appearance, esp. *Monotropa* and *Neottia* (bird's-nest orchid); **bird's'-nesting** or **bird'-nesting** seeking and robbing birds' nests; **bird'-spider** any of various large spiders preying on small birds, found in tropical America; **bird strike** collision of a bird or birds with an aircraft resulting in aircraft damage; **bird'-table** a table, inaccessible to cats, for wild birds to feed on; **bird'watcher; bird'-watching** observation of birds in their natural habitat; **bird'-wing** or **birdwing butterfly** any of various very large brightly coloured butterflies of south-east Asia. — **a bird in the hand is worth two in the bush** a certainty is not to be thrown away for a poor chance of something better; **a little bird told me** I heard from a source I will not reveal; **bird of paradise** see under **paradise; bird-of-paradise flower** any of various plants of the genus *Strelitzia*, found in S. America and southern Africa, with flowers resembling bird's heads; **bird's-eye view** a general view from above; a general view of a subject; **birds of a feather** see under **feather; do bird** (*slang*; see **bird** *n*, above) to serve a prison sentence; **(strictly) for the birds** (*slang*) not to be taken seriously, of little value; **get the bird** (i.e. the goose) in stage slang, to be hissed; hence, to be dismissed. [O.E. *brid*, the young of a bird, a bird.]

birefringent *bī-rə-frin'jənt*, (*mineralogy*) *adj* doubly refracting, as Iceland spar is. — *n* **birefrin'gence**. [**bi-**, and *refringent*, an old word meaning refracting.]

biretta *bir-et'ə*, *n* a square cap worn by clergy — by priests, black; bishops, purple; cardinals, red. [It. *berretta* — L.L. *birretum*, cap.]

biriyani or **biryani** *bir-yä'ni* or *bi-ri-yä'ni*, *n* a spicy rice dish. [From Urdu.]

Biro® *bī'rō*, *n* a kind of ballpoint pen: — *pl* **Bi'ros**. [L. *Biró*, Hungarian inventor.]

birth *bûrth*, *n* the process of being born; the act of bearing young; coming into the world; dignity of family; origin. — **birth certificate** an official document giving the date and place of one's birth and the names of one's parents; **birth control** the control of reproduction by contraceptives; **birth'-mark** a mark, e.g. a pigmented area or spot, on one's body at birth; **birth pill** a contraceptive pill; **birth'place** the place of one's birth; **birth control** the control of reproduction by contraceptives; **birth'-rate** the proportion of live births to population; **birth'right** the right or privilege to which one is entitled by birth; native rights; **birth sign** the sign of the zodiac under which one was born; **birth'-stone** a gemstone associated with one's birth sign. [Prob. O.N. *byrthr*.]

birthday *bûrth'dā*, *n* the day on which one is born; its anniversary. — *adj* relating to the day or anniversary of one's birth. — **birth'day-book** a book in which to record the birthdays of one's friends and relatives; **birthday honours** titles, etc. conferred on the sovereign's official birthday; **birth'day-suit** complete nakedness. — **official birthday** a day on which a sovereign or ruler's birthday is officially celebrated. [**birth** and **day**.]

biryani. See **biriyani.**

BIS *abbrev* for Bank for International Settlements.

bis *bis, adv* twice; a direction indicating that a part is to be repeated (*mus*). [L.]

biscacha. Same as **viscacha.**

biscuit *bis'kit, n* a small, thin, crisp cake made of unleavened dough; an unsweetened scone eaten with meat or gravy (*US*); pottery that has been fired but not yet glazed; a square mattress (*mil*). — *adj* pale brown in colour. — *adj* **bis'cuity** like a biscuit in flavour or texture. — **take the biscuit** to surpass everything else (*ironic*). [O.Fr. *bescoit* (mod. *biscuit*) — L. *bis*, twice, *coquĕre, coctum*, to cook or bake.]

bise *bēz, n* a cold north or north-east wind prevalent at certain seasons in and near Switzerland. [Fr.]

bisect *bī-sekt', vt* and *vi* to divide into two (usu. equal) parts. — *n* **bisec'tion.** — *n* **bisec'tor** a line that divides an angle, etc., into two equal parts. [L. *bi-*, twice, *secāre, sectum*, to cut.]

bisexual *bī-seks'ū-əl, adj* hermaphrodite; attracted sexually to both sexes. [L. **bi-** and **sexual.**]

bish *bish*, (*colloq*) *n* a blunder, mistake.

bishop *bish'əp, n* in the Roman Catholic and Orthodox churches and in the Anglican Communion, a senior clergyman consecrated for the spiritual direction of a diocese, usu. under an archbishop; in the early Christian, and certain modern Protestant, churches, a spiritual overseer of a local church or group of churches; a chessman whose move is in a diagonal line; a hot drink of mulled red wine flavoured with bitter oranges; any of several kinds of colourful African weaver bird (also **bish'op-bird**). — *n* **bish'opric** the office and jurisdiction of a bishop; a diocese. — **bishop's cap** a genus (*Mitella*) of the saxifrage family, with one-sided inflorescences. — **bishop sleeve** a full sleeve drawn in tightly at the wrist. [O.E. *biscop* — L. *episcopus* — Gr. *episkopos*, overseer.]

bisk. See **bisque**[1].

bismuth *bis'* or *biz'məth, n* a brittle reddish-white element (atomic no. 83; symbol **Bi**). [Ger. *Bismuth, Wissmuth* (now *Wismut*).]

bison *bī'sn* or *bī'zn, n* a large wild ox with shaggy hair and a fatty hump — the European bison, almost extinct in the wild, and the American, commonly called buffalo in America. [From L. *bisōn, -ontis*, prob. of Gmc. origin.]

Bispa *bis'pə, abbrev* for British Independent Steel Producers' Association.

bisque[1] or **bisk** *bisk, n* a rich shellfish soup, made with wine and cream. [Fr.]

bisque[2] *bisk, n* a kind of unglazed white porcelain; pottery that has undergone the first firing before being glazed. [See **biscuit.**]

bisque[3] *bisk, n* a term in tennis, golf, etc., for the handicap whereby a player allows a weaker opponent (at the latter's choice of time) to score a point in a set, deduct a stroke at a hole, take an extra turn in croquet, etc. [Fr.]

bistable *bī'stā-bl, adj* (of a valve or transistor circuit) having two stable states. [**bi-**.]

bister. See **bistre.**

bistort *bis'tört, n* a plant of the dock family with twisted rootstock. — Also called **snakeweed.** [L. *bistorta* — *bis*, twice, *tortus, -a, -um*, twisted.]

bistoury *bis'tər-i, n* a narrow surgical knife for making incisions. [Fr. *bistouri.*]

bistre or **bister** *bis'tər, n* a pigment of a warm brown colour made from the soot of wood, esp. beechwood. — *adj* **bis'tred.** [Fr. *bistre.*]

bistro *bē'strō, n* a small bar or restaurant: — *pl* **bis'tros.** [Fr. slang.]

bisulphate *bī-sul'fāt, n* an acid sulphate. — *n* **bīsul'phide** a disulphide.

bit[1] *bit, n* a bite, a morsel; a small piece; $12\frac{1}{2}$ cents (*US*; used only in **two, four** or **six bits**); the smallest degree; a brief space of time; a small tool for boring (see **brace**); the boring-piece of a drilling-machine; the part of the bridle that the horse holds in its mouth; the part of a key that engages the lever of the lock. — *vt* to put the bit in the mouth of; to curb or restrain: — *pr p* **bitt'ing;** *pa p* **bitt'ed.** — *adj* **bit'sy** (*colloq*) prettily small. — *adj* **bitt'y** scrappy, disjointed, made up of odds and ends; not forming an artistic whole. — **bit'-part** a small part in acting; **bit player** an actor who plays bit-parts. — **a bit** or **a bit of** somewhat, rather, as in *a bit of a fool, a bit stupid*; **a bit of all right** (*slang*) a person or thing highly approved of; **a bit off** (*colloq*) in bad taste; **a bit on the side** (*slang*) (one's partner in) extramarital sexual relations; **bit by bit** piecemeal; gradually; **bits and bobs** or **bits and pieces** odds and ends; **do one's bit** to do one's due share; **take** or **get the bit in** (or **between) one's teeth** to throw off control; to take up or have a tenacious or keen interest (in) or occupation (with something). [From **bite.**]

bit[2] *bit*, the smallest unit of information in computers and communications theory. [Contracted *b*inary dig*it*.]

bitch *bich, n* the female of the dog, wolf, and fox; a woman, very rarely a man (*abusively*); a malicious or arrogant woman; an act of grumbling (*slang*). — *vi* (*slang*) to complain, talk bitchily. — *vt* (*slang*) to mess up, spoil (often *bitch up*). — *n* **bitch'ily.** — *n* **bitch'iness.** — *adj* **bitch'y.** [O.E. *bicce.*]

bite *bīt, vt* and *vi* to seize or tear with the teeth; to puncture with the mouth-parts, as an insect does; to cut or penetrate; to eat into chemically; to take effect; to grip; to deceive, to take in (now only in passive); to accept something offered as bait (also *fig*): — *pa t* **bit;** *pa p* **bit** or **bitt'en.** — *n* a grasp by the teeth; the manner in which the teeth come together; a puncture by an insect; the wound or sore caused by this; a nibble at the bait; something bitten off; a mouthful; biting quality; grip; pungency; incisiveness; corroding action. — *n* **bīt'er** a person who bites; an animal with a habit of biting; a fish apt to take the bait. — *n* **bit'ing.** — *adj* which bites; sharp, cold; sarcastic. — **bite in** (*etching*) to eat out the lines of with acid; **bite off more than one can chew** to overestimate one's capacities; to undertake something one cannot achieve; **bite someone's head off** to speak to someone unnecessarily angrily; **bite the bullet** to submit bravely to something unpleasant; to face up to an unpalatable fact or situation; **bite the dust** to fall, to die; **put the bite on** to extort money from; **what's biting you?** what is the matter with you? [O.E. *bītan.*]

bitonal *bī-tōn'əl, adj* using two musical keys simultaneously. — *n* **bitonal'ity.** [**bi-**.]

bitter *bit'ər, adj* having a taste like that of quinine or hops; sharp; painful; acrimonious; broodingly resentful. — *n* any substance having a bitter taste, esp. a type of ale. — *adj* **bitt'erish.** — *adv* **bitt'erly.** — *n* **bitt'erness.** — *npl* **bitt'ers** a liquid prepared from bitter herbs or roots, and used to aid digestion or stimulate appetite, or to flavour drinks. — **bitter-app'le** a type of cucumber, the colocynth; **bitter lemon** a lemon-flavoured soft drink; **bitter orange** the Seville orange, bitter when ripe, used for making marmalade, etc.; **bitt'ersweet** the woody nightshade, whose stems when chewed taste first bitter, then sweet; a mixture of sweet and bitter (also *fig*; also *adj*); **bitter vetch** see **vetch.** — **a bitter pill to swallow** something which is difficult or unpleasant to accept, such as an unwelcome fact. [O.E. *biter* — *bītan*, to bite.]

bittern *bit'ərn, n* a marsh bird of the heron family. [M.E. *bittour, botor* — O.Fr. *butor*.]

bitty. See **bit**[1].

bitumen *bit'ū-mən* or *bi-tū'mən, n* the name applied to various inflammable mineral substances, such as naphtha, petroleum, asphalt; one of these, a tarry substance used to surface roads and roofs. — *vt* **bitū'minate** to mix with or make into bitumen (also **bitū'minise** or **-ize**). — *n* **bituminisā'tion** or **-z-**. — *adj* **bitū'minous** impregnated with bitumen. — **bituminous coal** coal that flames in burning, from richness in volatile hydrocarbons. [L. *bitūmen, -inis*.]

bivalent *bī-vā'lənt* or *biv'ə-lənt, adj* having a valency of two (*chem*); pertaining to one of a pair of homologous chromosomes (also *n*). — *n* **bivā'lence** or **bivā'lency**. [L. *bi-*, twice, and **-valent**.]

bivalve *bī'valv, n* an animal having a shell in two valves or parts, like the oyster; a seed vessel of a similar kind. — *adj* having two valves. [L. *bi-*, twice, *valva*, a folding-door.]

bivouac *biv'ōō-ak, vi* to pass the night in the open air or in a makeshift camp; to make such a camp: — *pr p* **biv'ouacking**; *pa p* **biv'ouacked**. — *n* a makeshift camp or camping-place; the making of or staying in this. — Also (*slang*) *n* and *v* **bivv'y**. [Fr., — Ger. *Beiwacht*, additional watch.]

bi-weekly *bī-wēk'li, adj* occurring or appearing once every two weeks, or twice a week. — Also *adv*. — *n* a periodical issued twice a week, or once every two weeks.

bi-yearly *bī-yēr'li, adj* and *adv* (happening, issued, etc.) twice a year, or every two years.

biz *biz*. Slang for **business**.

bizarre *bi-zär', adj* odd; fantastic. [Fr., — Sp. *bizarro*, gallant, brave.]

bizcacha. See **viscacha**.

Bk (*chem*) *symbol* for berkelium.

bk *abbrev* for: bank; book.

bkg *abbrev* for banking.

bkpg *abbrev* for bookkeeping.

bks *abbrev* for: barracks; books.

BL *abbrev* for: Bachelor of Law; Bachelor of Letters; British Legion; British Leyland; British Library.

bl *abbrev* for: bale; barrel; bill of lading.

blab *blab, vi* to talk idly; to tell tales. — *vt* to let out (a secret): — *pr p* **blabb'ing**; *pa p* **blabbed**. — *n* **blabb'er** or **blabber'mouth** a person who blabs, esp. one who reveals secrets. — *n* and *adj* **blabb'ing**. [M.E. *blabbe*.]

black *blak, adj* of the darkest colour; reflecting no light; used as a classification of pencil-leads to indicate softness in quality and darkness in use; obscure; dismal; sullen; horrible; foul, dirty; malignant; unlucky; dark-haired; wearing dark armour or clothes; (of coffee or tea) without milk or cream; illicit; (of income) not reported in tax returns; unofficial; under trade-union ban; (the following senses often with *cap*) dark-skinned, of African, West Indian or Australian Aboriginal descent; of African, Asian or mixed descent (esp. *SAfr*); (of an area or state) inhabited or controlled by Black people; of, belonging to, or relating to, Black people. — *n* black colour or absence of colour; a dark-skinned person, esp. of African, West Indian or Australian Aboriginal descent; a black pigment; a smut; smut fungus; black clothes. — *vt* to make black; to soil or stain; to put under trade-union ban. — *vt* **black'en** to make black; to defame. — *vi* to become black. — *n* **black'ing** a substance used for blacking leather, etc. — *adj* **black'ish**. — *n* **black'ness**. — *adj* **black-and-blue'** livid in colour because of bruising. — *adj* **black-and-white'** partly black, partly white; drawing or drawn in black on a white ground; not in colour (*cinematography, phot, TV*); consisting of extremes, not admitting any middle ground. — **black art** magic. — *vt* **black'ball** to vote against by putting a black ball into a ballot-box; to ostracise; to vote against, veto. — **black-bee'tle** a cockroach; **black belt** a belt showing the highest grade of proficiency in some martial arts; a person who has attained this grade; **black'berry** the fruit of the bramble. — *vi* to gather blackberries. — **black'bird** a species of thrush, the male of which is black; a grackle or other bird of the *Icteridae* (*US*); **black'board** a board painted black, for writing on; **black body** a body that absorbs all incident radiation, reflecting none; **black book** a book recording the names of persons deserving punishment (see also **in someone's black books** below); **black bottom** an American dance of late 1920s; **black box** a type of seismograph for registering underground explosions; a unit of electronic equipment in package form which records all the flight details in an aircraft; a device or unit, esp. electronic, whose internal workings need not be understood by the user (*comput*, etc.); **black bread** dark, coarse rye-bread. — *adj* **black'-browed** sullen. — **black'buck** an Indian antelope, the male of which is dark-coloured; **black'cap** a warbler, the male of which has a black crown; **black'cock** see **black grouse**; **black comedy** a play in which, under fantasy and grotesque humour, the hopeless world of reality is clearly seen; a comedy about dreadful events; **Black Country** the industrial Midland counties of England; **blackcurr'ant** the small black berry of a garden shrub of the gooseberry genus; **black death** (also with *caps*) a deadly epidemic of bubonic plague that swept over Asia and Europe, reaching England in 1348; **black diamond** same as **carbonado**; (in *pl*) coal; **black economy** economic activity involving payment in kind or cash not declared for tax purposes; **black eye** an eye of which the iris is dark; a discoloration around the eye due to a blow or fall; **black-eye(d) bean** or **pea** a leguminous plant (*Vigna sinensis*) indigenous to Asia but cultivated elsewhere and used like French beans; a similar plant (*Vigna catjang*); **black-eyed Susan** a N. Am. composite plant of the *Rudbeckia* genus, with dark centres and yellow or orange rays; a tropical African climbing plant (*Thunburgia alata*) that has yellow flowers with purple centres; **black'fellow** an Australian Aboriginal; **black'fly** a thrips or aphid; any of several black- or grey-bodied insects of the *Simuliidae*, hump-backed blood-suckers (also known as **birch fly** and **buffalo gnat**); **Black'foot** a member of a tribe of Algonquin American Indians: — *pl* **Blackfoot** or **-feet**. — Also *adj*. — **Black Friar** (also without *caps*) a Dominican, from his black mantle (over a white woollen habit); **black Friday** Good Friday; an unlucky Friday; **black gram** see **urd**; **black grouse** a large northern European grouse, the male of which (**blackcock**) is black with a lyre-shaped tail (the female is called a **greyhen**); **black gold** (*colloq*) oil; **blackguard** (*blag'ärd*) a contemptible scoundrel; **black'head** an accumulation of sebum in a pore or hair follicle; an infectious disease of turkeys, pheasants and other fowl. — *adj* **black-heart'ed** having an evil disposition. — **black hole** a field of such strong gravitational pull that matter and energy cannot escape from it, presumed to exist where a massive star has collapsed (*astron*); **black ice** a thin layer of transparent ice on a road; **black'jack** vingt-et-un, or a game like it; a combination of an ace and a face-card in the game of blackjack; **black knight** a company making an unwelcome bid to take over another; **black'lead** a black mineral (plumbago, not lead) used in making pencils, etc.; **black'leg** a worker continuing to work during a strike or one taking a striker's place. — *vi* to work as a blackleg. — **black letter** the Old English (also called Gothic) type (𝔅𝔩𝔞𝔠𝔨-𝔩𝔢𝔱𝔱𝔢𝔯); **black light** invisible infrared or ultraviolet light; **black'list** a list of defaulters or persons against whom a warning is necessary, or who are liable to loss of employment or lack of full recognition because of their (usu. political) views. — *vt* **black'list** to put on a blacklist. — **black lung** a lung disease of miners, pneumoconiosis; **black magic** see under **magic**; **black Maria** (*mə-rī'ə*) a prison van; **black mark** something known or noted to one's discredit; **black market** surreptitious trade in rationed goods; buying and selling that is against the law or official regulations (e.g. illegal traffic in drugs); **black-marketeer'**; **black mass** a travesty of the mass, practised in devil-worship; **Black Monk** (also without *caps*) a Benedictine; **black nationalism** a movement aimed at increasing Black self-determination and reducing White influence in all areas with a Black population; **black nationalist; black'out** total extinction or concealment of lights; a failure or cut in electrical power; sudden loss of consciousness, or failure of the mind to work; a complete stoppage or suppression (of news, communications, etc.); a stoppage in the transmission of television programmes; **black paper** an unofficial document similar in form to a government white paper, criticising official policy; **black powder** gunpowder; **Black Power** (also without *caps*) a militant movement to increase the influence of Black people, esp. in predominantly white countries; **black-pudd'ing** a blood-pudding (q.v.); **Black Rod** the usher of the chapter of the Garter and of the House of Lords; **black sheep** a disreputable member of a family or group; **Black'shirt** a member of a Fascist organisation, esp. in the Nazi SS and in Italy during World War II; **black'smith** a smith who works in iron; **black spot** the name given to disease of various plants, e.g. roses; a small area which has bad conditions or a bad record; **Black Stone** a piece of black basalt sacred to Muslims, believed to have been given to Abraham by the angel Gabriel; **black stump** (*Austr* and *NZ*) a mythical distance-marker (esp. in **beyond the black stump** in the far outback); **black swan** a swan with black plumage and red beak, native to Australia; **black'thorn** a dark-coloured thorn bush bearing sloes; **black tie** a man's black bow tie worn with a dinner-jacket. — *adj* (of an occasion) formal, at which a dinner-jacket should be worn. — **black velvet** champagne and stout; **black widow** a very venomous American and Far Eastern spider, the female with a black body and the habit of eating her mate. — **black in the face** purple through strangulation, passion, or effort; **black out** to obliterate with black; to extinguish or cover all lights; suddenly to lose consciousness; to suppress (news or radio communication); **in black and white** in writing or in print; in art, etc., in no colours but black and white; **in someone's black books** having incurred someone's displeasure; in trouble or disgrace (in a certain person's eyes); **in the black** solvent, out of debt; making a profit. [O.E. *blæc*, black.]

blackmail *blak'māl*, *n* hush-money extorted under threat of exposure, often baseless; such extortion. — *vt* to extort money from (a person); to force by threats (into doing something). — *n* **black'mailer**. — **blackmail selling** the practice of refusing to further the sale of property unless the purchaser fulfils certain conditions, such as arranging the mortgage with a given company. [**black**, and *mail*, an obsolete term for a payment of money.]

bladder *blad'ər*, *n* a thin distended or distensible bag; any such bag in the animal body, esp. the receptacle for urine. — *adj* **bladd'ered**. — *adj* **bladd'ery**. — **bladd'er-worm** the asexual state of a tapeworm or cestode; **bladd'erwrack** a common brown seaweed with bladders. [O.E. *blǣdre* — *blāwan*, to blow.]

blade *blād*, *n* the flat or expanded part of a leaf or petal, esp. a leaf of grass or corn; the cutting part of a knife, sword, etc.; the flat part of an implement, not necessarily having a cutting edge; the flat part of an oar; the paddle-like part of a propeller; the free outer part of the tongue. — *adj* **blad'ed**. — **blade'-bone** the flat bone at the back of the shoulder, the scapula. [O.E. *blæd*.]

blag *blag*, (*slang*) *vt* and *vi* to rob; to scrounge, wheedle. — *n* a theft, robbery.

blah *blä*, (*slang*) *n* bunkum; pretentious nonsense. — Also **blah-blah'**. — *vi* to talk stupidly or insipidly. — *adj* **blah** (*slang*) dull or insipid. [Poss. imit.]

blain *blān*, *n* a boil or blister. [O.E. *blegen*.]

BLAISE *blāz*, *abbrev* for British Library Automated Information Service.

blame *blām*, *vt* to find fault with; to censure; to impute fault to; to accuse of causing. — *n* imputation of a fault; culpability; responsibility for what is amiss. — *adj* **blā'mable** or **blame'able.** — *n* **blā'mableness** or **blame'ableness**. — *adv* **blā'mably** or **blame'ably**. — *adj* **blamed** (*US slang*) damned, confounded (also *adv*). — *adj* **blame'ful** deserving blame. — *adv* **blame'fully**. — *n* **blame'fulness**. — *adj* **blame'less** without blame; guiltless; innocent. — *adv* **blame'lessly**. — *n* **blame'worthiness**. — *adj* **blame'worthy** deserving blame; culpable. — **be to blame** to be the cause (of something bad). [Fr. *blâmer*, O.Fr. *blasmer* — Gr. *blasphēmeein*, to speak ill.]

blanch *blänch*, *vt* to whiten; to immerse (fruit, vegetables, etc.) briefly in boiling water (*cookery*). — *vi* to grow white. [Fr. *blanchir* — *blanc*, white.]

blancmange *blə-mäzh'* or *-mönzh'*, *n* a flavoured milk dessert thickened with cornflour or gelatine and set in a mould. [Fr. *blancmanger* — *blanc*, white, *manger*, food.]

blanco *blangk'ō*, (*mil*) *n* an opaque white, khaki, etc. substance for treating uniform belts, etc. — *vt* to treat with blanco. [*Blanco*, a trademark — Fr. *blanc*, white.]

bland *bland*, *adj* smooth; mild; without distinctive characteristics; not irritating or stimulating; polite, suave; ironical. — *adv* **bland'ly**. — *n* **bland'ness**. [L. *blandus*.]

blandish *bland'ish*, *vt* to flatter and coax, to cajole. — *n* **bland'ishment**. [Fr. *blandir*, *blandissant* — L. *blandīrī*.]

blank *blangk*, *adj* without writing or marks, as white paper is; empty; featureless; expressionless; nonplussed; sheer; (of verse) unrhymed. — *n* a paper without writing; a lottery-ticket that brings no prize; an empty space, a void or vacancy; a lapse of memory or concentration; the white mark in the centre of a target (*archery*); a form of document having blank spaces to be filled up (*archaic* except in *US*); a roughly shaped piece to be fashioned into a manufactured article; a dash in place of an omitted word; a blank cartridge. — *vt* to make blank; (esp. with *off*) to seal (an opening) with a plug, etc.; to prevent (one's opponent in a game) from making any score (*NAm*). — *vt* and *vi* to produce blanks during a manufacturing process. — *n* **blank'ing**. — *adv* **blank'ly**. — *n* **blank'ness**. — **blank cartridge** one without a bullet; **blank cheque** a signed cheque in which the sum is not filled in; complete freedom to act as one thinks best (*fig*); **blank verse** unrhymed verse esp. of five feet. — **draw a blank** (*colloq*) to get no result, to fail. [Fr. *blanc*.]

blanket *blangk'it*, *n* a covering, generally woollen, for a bed, etc.; a covering generally; fertile material put round a nuclear reactor core to breed new fuel; a rubber or plastic sheet used in offset printing to transfer the image from the plate to the paper; coverage; something that conceals or obscures. — *vt* to cover, obstruct, or extinguish with, or as with, a blanket. — *adj* applying generally or covering all cases. — *n* **blank'eting** cloth for blankets. — **blanket bath** the washing of a sick person in bed; **blanket spray** a spray of pesticide, etc. covering everything in a given area; **blanket stitch** a stitch used esp. for the edge of a blanket; **blank'etweed** a rapidly-spreading green filamentous alga that forms in ponds. — **on the wrong side of the blanket** illegitimately; **wet blanket** a damper of spirits; a killjoy. [O.Fr. *blankete*, dimin. of *blanc*, white.]

blanquette *blä-ket*, (Fr.) *n* a ragout of e.g. chicken or veal made with a white sauce.

blare *blär*, *vi* to sound loudly, usu. harshly, as for example a trumpet does. — *n* a loud, harsh noise. [M.E. *blaren*.]

blarney *blär'ni*, *n* flattery or cajoling talk. — *vt* to cajole. [*Blarney* Castle, near Cork, where a stone difficult to reach is said to confer the gift of persuasive talk on those who kiss it.]

blasé *blä'zā*, *adj* indifferent to pleasure, etc. because of familiarity; surfeited with enjoyments. [Fr. past p. of *blaser*, to cloy.]

blaspheme *blas-fēm'*, *vt* to speak impiously of or contemptuously of God or sacred things. — *vi* to speak profanely or impiously; to curse and swear. — *n* **blasphem'er**. — *adj* **blasphemous** (*blas'fi-məs*). — *adv* **blas'phemously**. — *n* **blas'phemy** impious or profane speaking or behaviour. — **blasphemous libel** (*law*) blasphemy against the Christian faith. [Gr. *blasphēmiā*; see ety. for **blame**.]

blast *bläst*, *n* a blowing or gust of wind; a forcible stream of air; a sound of a wind instrument, car horn, etc.; an explosion or detonation; a shock-wave of air caused by this; any scorching, withering or pernicious influence; a blight. — *vi* to emit blasts, blow; to use explosives; to curse. — *vt* to blow up; to destroy or damage with an explosive; to blow into; to strike with a blast; to blight, wither, scorch; to curse. — *adj* **blast'ed**. — *n* **blast'er**. — *n* and *adj* **blast'ing**. — **blast'-furnace** a smelting furnace into which hot air is blown; **blast'-furnaceman**; **blast'-off** the (moment of) launching of a rocket-propelled missile or space capsule (*vt* and *vi* **blast off**). — **in** or **at full blast** in a state of maximum activity. [O.E. *blǣst*.]

-blast *-blast*, *combining form* denoting: developing; budding; immature. [Gr. *blastos*, bud.]

blasto- *blas-tō-*, *combining form* denoting a sprout, bud, germ. — *n* **blas'tocyst** the blastula in mammals. — *n* **blas'tocoel** or **blas'tocoele** (*-sēl*) the cavity inside a blastula. — *n* **blas'tomere** (Gr. *meros*, part) a cell formed in an early stage of the cleavage of a fertilised ovum. — *n* **blas'tosphere** (Gr. *sphaira*, sphere) a blastula. [Ety. as for **-blast**.]

blastula *blas'tū-lə*, *n* a hollow sphere of cells, one cell thick, formed in the cleavage of a fertilised ovum. — *adj* **blast'ūlar**. — *n* **blastulā'tion**. [Ety. as for **-blast**.]

blatant *blā'tənt*, *adj* clamorous; obtrusive; unashamedly obvious; flagrant. — *adv* **blat'antly**. [Prob. a coinage of Spenser.]

blather. See **blether**.

blaze[1] *blāz*, *n* a burst of light or of flame; a fire; an area of brilliant light or colour; a bursting out or active display. — *vi* to burn with a strong flame; to throw out a brilliant light; to be furious (*colloq*). — *npl* **blaz'es** the fires of hell, in imprecations like **to blazes**; also **like blazes** with fury. — **blaze away** to fire a rapid and repeated stream of bullets; to work very hard (*colloq*); **blaze up** to burst into flames; to become furious (*colloq*). [O.E. *blæse*, torch.]

blaze[2] *blāz*, *n* a white mark on an animal's face; a mark on a tree made by chipping the bark or otherwise. — *vt* to mark (a tree or a track) with a blaze. — **blaze the trail** (*lit* and *fig*) to show the way as a pioneer. [Perh. Du. *bles* or O.N. *blesi*; or **blaze**[1].]

blaze[3] *blāz*, *vt* to proclaim, to spread (news). [Connected with O.N. *blāsa*, to blow; confused with **blazon**.]

blazer *blā'zər*, *n* a light jacket, often in the colours or with the badge of a club, school, etc. [**blaze**[1].]

blazon *blā'zn* or (in *heraldry*) *blaz'n*, *vt* to make public; to display ostentatiously; to depict or to explain in heraldic terms (*heraldry*). — *n* a coat-of-arms, heraldic bearings (also *fig*); the science or rules of coats-of-arms. — *n* **blaz'oner**. — *n* **blaz'onry** the art of drawing or of deciphering coats-of-arms; heraldry. [Fr. *blason*, a shield, confused with **blaze**[3].]

bldg *abbrev* for building.

bleach *blēch*, *vt* to make pale or white; to whiten (e.g. textile fabrics); to clean or disinfect with bleach. — *vi* to grow white. — *n* the process or act of bleaching; a bleaching agent. — *n* and *adj* **bleach'ing**. — **bleaching powder** a compound of calcium, chlorine and oxygen ($CaOCl_2$). [O.E. *blǣcan*.]

bleak[1] *blēk*, *adj* dull and cheerless; desolate; cold, unsheltered. — *adv* **bleak'ly**. — *n* **bleak'ness**. [Apparently O.N. *bleikr*, answering to O.E. *blǣc*, *blāc*, pale, shining, black; cf. **bleach**.]

bleak[2] *blēk*, *n* a small silvery river-fish whose scales yield a pigment used in making artificial pearls. [O.N. *bleikja*, or a lost equivalent O.E. word.]

blear *blēr*, *vt* to dim; to blur; to dim the sight of; to hoodwink. — *adj* **bleared**. — *n* **blear'iness**. — *adj* **blear'y** (of the eyes) blurred, dim, watery; dull with sleep, drowsy. — *adj* **blear'y-eyed**. [Cf. Ger. *Blerr*, soreness of the eyes.]

bleat *blēt*, *vi* to cry like a sheep; to complain, grumble; to talk nonsense. — *n* a sheep's cry or similar quavering sound; a complaint, grumble. — *n* **bleat'er** (*colloq*) a complainer. — *n* and *adj* **bleat'ing**. [O.E. *blǣtan*; imit.]

bleb *bleb*, *n* a transparent blister of the cuticle; a bubble, as in water. [Prob. imit.]

bled *bled*, *pa t* and *pa p* of **bleed**.

bleed *blēd*, *vi* to lose blood or sap; to ooze or drop like blood; (of paint or dye) to run; (of printed matter) to overrun the edge of the page; to have money, etc., extorted from one; to feel great pity (*fig*). — *vt* to draw blood from, esp. surgically; to draw sap from; to print, or to trim the printed sheet, so that the text, etc. runs off the page; to extort or extract from; to draw off (liquid or gas) from a closed system or holder: — *pa t* and *pa p* **bled**. — *n* **bleed'er** a person who bleeds; a haemophiliac (*colloq*); a (nasty) person (*slang*). — *n* **bleed'ing** a discharge of blood or sap; the act or process of drawing off blood; diffusion or running of colouring matter. — *adj* emitting blood, sap or other liquid; bloody (*colloq*); full of compassion. — **bleeding heart** a name given to various plants of the genera *Dicentra*, *Colocasia*, etc.; a contemptuous name for a do-gooder; **bleed nipple** or **valve** a valve to enable liquid or gas to be drawn from a closed system or tank. — **bleed like a pig** or **stuck pig** to bleed copiously. [O.E. *blēdan*. See **blood**.]

bleep *blēp*, *vi* to give out a high sound or radio signal. — *vt* to contact (a person) by activating his or her bleeper. — *n* a high-pitched sound or signal; a bleeper. — *n* **bleep'er** a detecting device that bleeps on receiving a certain radio or other signal; such a device, carried by e.g. a doctor, by which he or she can be contacted. [Imit.]

blemish *blem'ish*, *n* (*lit* and *fig*) a stain or defect. — *vt* to mark with any deformity; to tarnish; to spoil. [O.Fr. *blesmir*, *blemir*, to stain.]

blench *blench*, *vi* to shrink or start back; to flinch. [O.E. *blencan*.]

blend *blend*, *vt* to mix together, esp. intimately or harmoniously. — *vi* to be mingled; to harmonise; to shade off. — *n* a mixture; a portmanteau word. — *n* **blend'er**. — *n* **blend'ing**. [M.E. *blenden*.]

blende *blend*, *n* a mineral, zinc sulphide. [Ger. *Blende* — *blenden*, to deceive, from its resemblance to galena.]

blenny *blen'i*, *n* a member of the genus *Blennius* of fish, usually slimy. [Gr. *blennos*, mucus.]

blepharism *blef'ər-izm*, *n* spasm of the eyelid. — *n* **blepharī'tis** inflammation of the eyelid. — *n*

blepharoplas'ty plastic surgery of the eyelids. — *n* **blepharospa'sm** blepharism. [Gr. *blepharon*, eyelid.]

blesbok *bles'bok*, *n* a South African antelope with a blaze on its forehead. [Du. *bles*, blaze, *bok*, goat.]

bless *bles*, *vt* to consecrate; to make the sign of the cross over (*Christian relig*); to extol as holy, to pronounce holy or happy; to invoke divine favour upon; to wish happiness to; to make joyous, happy or prosperous; to glorify; to approve officially: — *pa p* **blessed** (*blest*) or **blest**. — *adj* **bless'ed** or **blest** happy; prosperous; in heaven; beatified; (*euph*) accursed, confounded. — *adv* **bless'edly**. — *n* **bless'edness**. — *n* **bless'ing** a wish or prayer for happiness or success; any means or cause of happiness; a gift from God; a form of invoking the favour of God at a meal; official approval. — **blessed sacrament** (*Christian relig*) the consecrated Host. — **be blessed with** to have the good fortune to possess; **a blessing in disguise** something proving unexpectedly advantageous. [O.E. *blēdsian*, *blētsian*, *bletsian*, to bless, prob. from *blōd*, blood.]

blest *blest*, *pa p* of **bless**. — Also *adj*.

blether (*Scot*) *bledh'ər* or **blather** (*US* and *dialect*) *bladh'ər*, *vi* to talk garrulous nonsense; to chat, gossip. — *n* a person who blethers; (often in *pl*) garrulous nonsense; a chat. — *n* and *adj* **bleth'ering**. [M.E. *blather* — O.N. *blathra*, to talk foolishly, *blathr*, nonsense.]

blew *blo͞o*, *pa t* of **blow**[2].

blewits *blū'its*, *n* a kind of edible mushroom of the *Tricholoma* family, lilac-coloured when young. [Perh. from **blue**.]

blight *blīt*, *n* a disease in plants which shrivels or withers them; a cause of blight; anything that injures, destroys, depresses or frustrates; a blighted state, decay, setback. — *vt* to affect with blight; to shrivel; to frustrate. — *adj* **blight'ed** affected with blight; spoiled, ruined; (of a, usu. urban, area) becoming a slum. — *n* **blight'er** a cause of blighting; a term of (usu. playful) abuse, scamp, beggar, wretch (*slang*). — *n* and *adj* **blight'ing**. — **planning blight** a fall in value, and consequent neglect, of property in an area, caused by uncertainty about its planned future.

blimey *blī'mi*, *interj* expressing surprise or annoyance (*slang*). — Also **cor blimey** or **gorbli'mey**. [Corruption of (*God*) *blind me*.]

blimp *blimp*, *n* a small type of airship-like, heavier-than-air, craft for scouting, advertising, etc.; an incurably conservative stout elderly military officer, as Colonel *Blimp* of the cartoonist David Low (1891–1963), or any other person of similar views; soundproof housing for a sound-film camera. — *adj* **blimp'ish** like Colonel Blimp.

blind *blīnd*, *adj* without sight; dark; obscure; invisible; concealed; not directed, or affording no possibility of direction, by sight or by foresight; without previous knowledge; ignorant or undiscerning; unobserving; voluntarily overlooking; without an opening; (in flying) using instruments only, without seeing one's course or receiving radio directions; (of plants) failing to produce expected growth or flowers. — *n* something intended to blind one to the facts; a window-screen; an awning; a stake put up without seeing one's cards (*poker*). — *vt* to make blind; to darken, obscure, or deceive; to dazzle; to make matt. — *vi* to curse, swear (*slang*). — *adj* **blind'ed** deprived of sight; without intellectual discernment. — *n* **blind'er** a person who or something which blinds; a spectacular sporting performance (*colloq*); a drinking spree (*colloq*). — *n* and *adj* **blind'ing**. — *adv* **blind'ly**. — *n* **blind'ness**. — **blind-all'ey** a cul-de-sac; a situation, job, etc. which does not offer any prospect of improvement or advancement (also *adj*); **blind'-coal** anthracite (as burning without flame); coal partly carbonised by an igneous intrusion; **blind date** an appointment with someone one has not seen or met before; the partner (to be) met in this way. — *adj* **blind-drunk'** so drunk as to be like a blind man. — *adj* **blind'fold** having the eyes bandaged so as not to be able to see. — Also *adv*. — *vt* to cover the eyes of. — *n* a piece of fabric, a handkerchief, etc. used for covering up the eyes. — **blind'-gut** the caecum; **blindman's-buff'** a game in which a blindfold player tries to catch the others; **blind'-side** the side on which a person is blind to danger; weak point; (usu. **blind side**) the part of the field between the scrum, etc. and the touch-line nearer it (*rugby*); **blind spot** the spot on the retina where the optic nerve joins and where there are no visual cells; a region of understanding in which one's intuition and judgment always fail; **blind'worm** a slow-worm. — **bake blind** to bake a pastry case without a filling; **not a blind bit of** (*colloq*) not any; **the blind leading the blind** the ignorant trying to instruct the ignorant. [O.E. *blind*.]

blini *blē'ni* or *blin'i*, *n* a small buckwheat pancake, as eaten esp. with caviar and sour cream: — *pl* **bli'ni** or **bli'nis**. [Russ.; see **blintz**.]

blink *blingk*, *vi* to close both eyes momentarily; to wink; to see obscurely; to look with the eyes half-closed; to shine unsteadily. — *n* a glimpse, glance, or wink; a gleam, esp. momentary. — *n* **blink'er** a leather flap to prevent a horse from seeing sideways or backwards. — *vt* to obscure or limit the vision of (*lit* and *fig*). — *adj* or *intensive adv* **blink'ing** (*slang*) used to add force or emphasis, prob. as a substitute for *bloody*. — **on the blink** (of an electrical or electronic device) (going) out of order. [Cf. **blench**.]

blintz *blints*, *n* a thin filled pancake. [Yiddish *blintse* — Russ. *blin*, pancake (pl. *blini*).]

blip *blip*, *n* a sharp tap or blow; the image of an object on a radar screen, usu. a bright spot or sudden sharp peak on a line; an unforeseen phenomenon claimed or expected to be temporary (chiefly *econ*); the small, high sound made by a radar instrument. — *vi* to produce a blip. — *vt* to tap or hit sharply.

bliss *blis*, *n* the highest happiness; the special happiness of heaven. — *adj* **bliss'ful**. — *adv* **bliss'fully**. — *n* **bliss'fulness**. [O.E. *blīths* — *blīthe*, blithe.]

blister *blis'tər*, *n* a thin bubble or bladder on the skin, often containing watery matter; a similar spot elsewhere (e.g. on a leaf, metal or paint). — *vt* to raise a blister or blisters on; to burn with scathing words (*fig*). — *vi* to develop blisters. — *adj* **blis'tery**. — *adj* **blis'tering** (of criticism) virulent, cruel (*fig*); painfully intense or strenuous; (of the weather) very hot; (of an action, pace, etc.) hard, fast. — **blister card** or **pack** a bubble pack; **blister copper** copper at an intermediate stage of production, about 98% pure. [M.E.; most prob. O.Fr. *blestre*, conn. with O.N. *blāstr*, *blāsa*, to blow.]

blithe *blīdh*, *adj* cheerful; merry; joyfully heedless. — *adv* **blithe'ly**. — *n* **blithe'ness**. [O.E. *blīthe*, joyful. See **bliss**.]

blith'ering *blidh'ər-ing*, (*slang*) *adj* used as an expression of contempt. [Form of **blethering**.]

BLit. or **BLitt.** *bē-lit'*, *abbrev* for *Baccalaureus Lit(t)erarum* (L.), Bachelor of Letters or Bachelor of Literature.

blitz *blits*, *n* an attack or bombing from the air (also **blitzkrieg** *blits'krēg*); any sudden, overwhelming attack (also **blitzkrieg**); an intensive campaign (*colloq*); a burst of intense activity, in order to achieve something (*colloq*). — *vt* to attack or damage (as if) by an air-raid; to deal with or complete by a burst of intense activity (*fig*). [Ger. *Blitzkrieg*, lightning war, the German method in 1939 — *Blitz*, lightning, *Krieg*, war.]

blizzard *bliz'ərd*, *n* a blinding storm of wind and snow.

BLLD *abbrev* for British Library Lending Division.

bloat *blōt*, *vt* to swell or puff out. — *vi* to swell or dilate; to grow turgid. — *n* a disease of ruminants in which the abdomen is distended (also **bloat'ing**). — *adj* **bloat'ed** swollen (often as a result of gluttony); swollen with riches (*fig*).

bloater *blōt'ər*, *n* a herring partially dried in smoke, esp. at Yarmouth.

blob *blob*, *n* a drop or globule; anything soft and round; a round spot; zero. [Imit.]

bloc *blok*, *n* a combination of parties, nations, or other units to achieve a common purpose. [Fr.]

block *blok*, *n* a mass of wood or stone, etc., usu. flat-sided; a piece of wood or other material used as a support, or as a mould, or for printing from, or as a toy; (in *pl*) starting blocks; a pulley with its framework or the framework alone; a compact mass, group or set; a group of buildings bounded by intersecting streets; an obstruction; the head (esp. in phrase *knock someone's block off*); an impassive person; a psychological barrier preventing intellectual development, progress, etc.; an instance of, or a cause of, blockage or blocking; a bloc; (also **licence block**) a section of sea within which a company is licensed to explore for and extract oil or gas; a cylinder block; a chopping-block; a pad of writing or drawing paper. — *adj* in a block or lump; comprising a number grouped and dealt with together. — *vt* to enclose or shut up; to restrict; to obstruct; to make inactive; to shape as on a block, or to sketch out roughly (often with *in* or *out*); to stop (a ball) with one's bat resting upright on the ground (*cricket*); to print (usu. a fabric) from a block. — *n* **blockade'** cutting a place off by surrounding it with troops or by ships; obstruction. — *vt* to block up by troops or ships. — *n* **block'age** an act or instance of obstructing, or the state of being obstructed. — *adj* **blocked**. — *n* **block'er** (*med*) a substance, used as a drug, that prevents the production, or the operation, of some other substance in the body. — *n* **block'ing** interruption of a train of thought, esp. by unpleasant thoughts rising in the mind. — **block'board** board made up of plywood veneer enclosing thin strips of wood; **block'buster** a bomb or explosive charge able to destroy a number of buildings simultaneously; a forceful or powerful thing or person; an expensively produced and commercially successful film, etc. — *n* and *adj* **block'busting**. — **block capital** a capital letter written in imitation of type; **block grant** a fixed general grant made by the central government to a local authority for all its services; **block'head** a stupid person; **block'house** a small temporary fort; a house constructed of squared logs; a shelter of reinforced concrete, etc. used as an observation post and control centre for rocket launches, etc.; **block letter** a block capital; block type; **block release** release from employment for a period in order to complete a course of study; **block vote** a vote by a delegate at a conference, counted as the number of people he or she represents; **block'-work** hollow blocks of precast concrete used for building. — **do one's block** (*Austr* and *NZ colloq*) to be very angry; **on the block** up for auction. [Fr. *bloc*, probably Gmc.]

bloke *blōk*, *n* a man (*slang*); the commander (*naut*).

blond (usu. in *fem* **blonde**) *blond*, *n* a person of fair complexion and light-coloured hair (opp. to *brunette*). — *adj* (of hair) between pale gold and light chestnut in colour; having fair hair and usu. a fair complexion. [Fr.]

blood *blud*, *n* the oxygenating fluid (red in the higher animals) circulating in the body; descent, good birth; relationship, kindred; the blood-royal (as in *princes of the blood*); temperament; bloodshed or murder; the supposed seat of passion — hence temper, anger (as in *his blood is up*), etc. — *vt* to bleed; to smear with blood; to initiate into blood sports or to war (also *fig*). — *adj* **blood'ed** having blood; of pure blood, pedigreed; initiated. — *adj* **blood'less** without blood; dead; anaemic; without bloodshed. — *n* **blood'lessness**. — **blood agar** agar-agar for growing bacteria, to which blood has been added before the jelly set. — *adj* **blood-and-thund'er** sensational, melodramatic. — **blood bank** a supply of blood plasma, or the place where it is kept; **blood'-bath** a massacre (also *fig*); **blood'-brother** a brother by blood; a man who has entered a close and binding friendship with another, among some peoples involving ceremonies involving the mixing of blood; **blood count** the number of red or white corpuscles in the blood. — *adj* **blood'curdling** exciting horror with a physical feeling as if the blood had curdled. — **blood donor** a person who gives blood for use in transfusion; **blood doping** or **packing** the practice of temporarily increasing the oxygen-carrying capacity of an athlete's blood by re-injecting red blood cells previously drawn off; **blood group** any of various types of blood identified and defined by their antigenic structures, esp. one of the four types of human blood (designated O, A, B, AB); **blood'heat** the temperature of human blood (37°C, about 98°F); **blood'-horse** a horse of the purest and most highly prized blood, origin, or stock; a thoroughbred; **blood'hound** a large hound, noted for its powers of following a scent; a detective (*fig*); **blood'letting** bleeding by opening a vein; bloodshed; **blood'-line** (of animals, etc.) all the individuals in a family line over a number of generations, esp. as considered with regard to some characteristic or other; **blood'lust** desire for bloodshed; **blood'-money** money earned by laying or supporting a capital charge against anyone, esp. if the charge is false or made by an accomplice; money paid to a hired assassin; money paid or accepted for doing something shameful; compensation formerly paid to the next of kin of a victim who has been killed; **blood oath** (*Austr*) an interjection expressing surprise or anger; **blood orange** a variety of orange with red or red-streaked pulp; **blood packing** see **blood doping**; **blood'-plate** a platelet; **blood'-poisoning** a name popularly, but loosely, used of pyaemia and septicaemia; **blood pressure** the pressure of the blood on the walls of the blood-vessels, varying with age and physical condition; **blood'-pudding** a pudding made with blood and other materials; **blood'-relation** one related by common ancestry; **blood-roy'al** royal descent; **blood'shed** the shedding of blood; slaughter. — *adj* **blood'shot** (of the eye) red or inflamed with blood. — **blood sports** those involving the killing of animals — fox-hunting and the like. — *adj* **blood'stained** stained with blood; guilty of murder. — **blood'stock** pedigree horses collectively; **blood'stone** a green chalcedony with bloodlike spots of red jasper; haematite; **blood'stream** the blood flowing through the body; something playing a similarly vital part (*fig*); **blood'-sucker** an animal that sucks blood, esp. a leech; an extortioner; a person who sponges on another; **blood test** an examination of a small specimen of blood; **blood'thirstiness** eager desire to shed blood. — *adj* **blood'thirsty**. — **blood transfusion** the taking of blood from the veins of one person and subsequent injection of it into those of another; **blood type** blood group; **blood'-typing** the classification of blood according to blood groups, or the identification of the blood group to which a sample of blood belongs; **blood'-vessel** a vein or artery. — **after** or **out for (someone's) blood** having murderous intentions (towards someone) (*lit* and *fig*); **first blood** the first drawing of blood in a fight (also *fig*); **fresh** or **new blood** new members in any association of people, to add vitality and new ideas; **in hot** or **cold blood** under or free from excitement or sudden passion; **in one's blood** in one's character, inborn; **make someone's blood boil** to arouse someone's fury. [O.E. *blōd*.]

bloody *blud'i, adj* of the nature of blood; stained with blood; murderous, cruel. — *adj* or *adv* employed as an intensifier, sometimes expressing anger but often almost meaningless. — *vt* to make bloody: — *pr p* **blood'ying**; *pa t* and *pa p* **blood'ied**. — *adv* **blood'ily**. — *n* **blood'iness**. — **bloody Mary** a cocktail consisting of vodka, tomato juice and seasoning. — *adj* **bloody-mind'ed** liking bloodshed, cruel; in a mood of, or inclined to show, aggressive obstinacy. — **bloody-mind'edness**.

bloom[1] *blōōm, n* a blossom or flower (also collectively); the state of being in flower; the prime or highest perfection of anything; the first freshness of beauty of anything; rosy colour; the glow on the cheek; a powdery, waxy, or cloudy surface or appearance; a sudden rapid multiplication of plankton, algae, etc.; an efflorescence. — *vi* to bear flowers; to come into flower; to be in a state of beauty or vigour; to flourish. — *vt* to give a bloom to. — *adj* **bloom'ing** flowering; flourishing; fresh and youthful; bright; euphemistically for bloody (*slang*). [O.N. *blōm.*]

bloom[2] *blōōm, n* a mass or bar of iron or steel in an intermediate stage of manufacture. [O.E. *blōma.*]

bloomer *blōōm'ər, n* an absurd and embarrassing blunder (*slang*); a longish crusty loaf of white bread with rounded ends and a number of slashes across the top. [**bloom[1]**.]

bloomers *blōōm'ərz, npl* a loose undergarment similar to knickers, having legs gathered above the knee; women's loose baggy trousers, short and gathered below the knee or long and gathered at the ankle. [Amelia *Bloomer* (1818–94), American social reformer, who advocated a costume for women which had a short full skirt and bloomers (trousers).]

bloop *blōōp, n* a howling sound on a soundtrack or made by a radio. — *vi* to make such a sound. — *n* **bloo'per** a radio that makes such a sound; a stupid mistake (*slang*). [Imit.]

blossom *blos'əm, n* a flower or bloom, esp. one that precedes edible fruit (also *collectively*); the state of being in flower (*lit* and *fig*). — *vi* (often with *out*) to put forth blossoms or flowers; to flourish and prosper. — *n* **bloss'oming**. — *adj* **bloss'omy** covered with flowers, flowery. [O.E. *blōstm, blōstma.*]

blot[1] *blot, n* a spot, as of a drop of ink; a stain in reputation; a blemish. — *vt* to obliterate, destroy (with *out*); to spot or smudge; to disgrace; to blemish; to dry with blotting-paper: — *pr p* **blott'ing**; *pa t* and *pa p* **blott'ed**. — *n* **blott'er** a person who blots; a sheet, pad, or book of blotting-paper. — *n* **blott'y** blotted; smudged. — **blott'ing-paper** absorbent paper, used for absorbing ink. — **blot one's copybook** to blemish one's record, esp. by an indiscretion or error.

blot[2] *blot, n* a piece liable to be taken at backgammon; exposure of a piece; a weak place in anything. [Cf. Dan. *blot*, Du. *bloot*, naked, exposed.]

blotch *bloch, n* an irregular discoloration; any plant disease characterised by blotching. — *vt* to mark or cover with blotches. — *adj* **blotched**. — *n* **blotch'iness**. — *n* and *adj* **blotch'ing**. — *adj* **blotch'y**. [Prob. formed on **blot[1]**.]

blotto *blot'ō, (slang) adj* helplessly drunk. [**blot[1]**.]

blouse *blowz, n* a woman's usu. loose-fitting garment for the upper part of the body; a short, loose jacket gathered into a waistband, part of a soldier's or airman's battledress; a loose belted outer garment worn by (esp. French) workmen. — *vt* to arrange in loose folds. [Fr.]

blouson *blōō'zon, n* a loose outer garment fastened at the waist by a belt, drawstring, etc. [Fr.]

blow[1] *blō, n* a stroke or knock; a sudden misfortune or calamity. — *adj* **blow-by-blow'** (of a story or description) very detailed. — **at a blow** by a single action, suddenly; **come to blows** (of people quarrelling) to start fighting. [Found from the 15th century; perh. from **blow[2]** or conn. with Ger. *bläuen*, to beat.]

blow[2] *blō, vi* to produce a current of air; (of air or wind) to move (often *impers*); to breathe hard; to spout, as whales do; to boast; (of insects) to deposit eggs; to blow up (also *vt*); (of an electric fuse) to melt (also *vt*). — *vt* to force air on to or into; to shape (glass, etc.) by blowing air into it; to drive by a current of air; to sound, as a wind-instrument; to destroy or force by explosive; to fan or kindle; (of insects) to deposit eggs on; to squander (*slang*); to fail to succeed with or in when one has the chance (*slang*; usu. with *it*): — *pa t* **blew** (*blōō*); *pa p* **blown** (*blōn*), in imprecations **blowed** (*blōd*). — *n* a blast; an insect egg; cannabis (*Br slang*); cocaine (*Am slang*). — *n* **blow'er** a person who blows; a machine for producing a blast of air; a speaking-tube, telephone, or similar means of sending messages (*colloq*); a communication system (*colloq*). — *n* **blow'ie** (*Austr* and *NZ colloq*) a blowfly. — *adj* **blown** out of breath, tired; swollen; stale, worthless. — *adj* **blow'y** windy; gusty. — **blow'down** an accident in a nuclear reactor. — *vt* **blow'-dry** to arrange (hair) by simultaneously brushing and drying it with a hand-held hair-drier. — Also *n*. — **blow'fly** a flesh-fly (*Sarcophaga*); a bluebottle (*Calliphora*); **blow'hard** a boastful person. — Also *adj*. — **blow'hole** a whale's nostril; a hole in ice to which seals, etc., come to breathe; a vent for escape of gas, etc.; a natural vent from the roof of a cave up to the ground surface, through which air and water are forced by rising tides; **blow'job** (*slang*) fellatio; **blow'lamp** a portable lamp producing a jet of very hot flame; **blow'-moulding** a process used in fabricating plastic objects, the molten thermoplastic being blown against the sides of the mould; **blow'-out** a feast (*slang*); a tyre burst (*colloq*); a violent escape of oil and gas from an oil-well; **blow-out preventer** a valve in the wellhead of an oil-well to prevent blow-outs; **blow'pipe** a pipe through which air is blown on a flame, to increase its heat; a long straight tube from which an arrow, pellet, etc., is blown by the breath; a glass-blower's tube; **blow'-torch** a blowlamp; **blow'-up** an explosion; an enlargement of (part of) a photograph, illustration, etc. — **blow away** (*slang*) to kill, murder; **blow hot and cold** to be favourable and unfavourable by turns, to be irresolute; **blow in** to turn up casually; **blow off** to allow (steam, etc.) to escape; (of steam, etc.) to escape forcibly; **blow one's** or **someone's mind** (*slang*) to go, or cause to go, into a state of ecstasy under the influence of a drug or of an exhilarating experience; **blow one's stack** or **top** (*colloq*) to explode in anger; **blow out** to extinguish by blowing; to force outwards by an explosion; (of a tyre) to burst (*colloq*); (of an oil-well) to emit an uncontrolled jet of oil and gas; **blow over** to pass away, as a storm, a danger or a scandal; **blow someone's cover** (*slang*) to reveal someone's identity; **blow the whistle on** (*slang*) to inform on (a person); **blow up** to destroy by explosion; to explode; to finish in disaster; to inflate; to scold; to lose one's temper; to enlarge (e.g. an illustration). [O.E. *blāwan.*]

blowzy or **blowsy** *blow'zi, adj* fat and ruddy, or flushed with exercise; dishevelled; coarse, rowdy. [Cant or dialect *blowze*, a beggar's woman.]

BLRD *abbrev* for British Library Reference Division.

blub *blub, (colloq) vi* to weep, sob: — *pr p* **blubb'ing**; *pa t* and *pa p* **blubbed**. [Short for **blubber**.]

blubber *blub'ər, n* the fat of whales and other sea animals; excessive fat; a bout of weeping. — *vi* to weep effusively. [M.E. *blober, bluber*; prob. imit.]

bludge *bluj* (*slang*; esp. *Austr* and *NZ*) *vi* and *vt* to scrounge. — *vi* to loaf about; to evade work or other responsibility. — *n* **bludg'er**.

bludgeon *bluj'n*, *n* a short stick with a heavy striking end. — *vt* to beat with a bludgeon; to assail heavily; to coerce (*colloq*).

blue[1] *bloo͞*, *adj* of the colour of the unclouded sky; livid; greyish; dismal; depressed; learned, pedantic (as in *blue-stocking*); indecent or obscene; dressed in blue; symbolised by blue; politically conservative or right-wing. — *n* the colour of blue things; a blue object; the sky; the sea; a blue pigment; (also **wash'ing-blue**) a blue powder or liquid (indigo, Prussian blue, etc.) used in laundries; a present or past representative of Oxford or Harrow (dark blue), or Cambridge or Eton (light blue), in sports; a similar representative of any university; the badge awarded to him or her, or the honour of wearing it; a butterfly of the family *Lycaenidae*; (in *pl*) depression; (in *pl* usu. construed as *sing*) a slow, sad song orig. an American Negro folksong, characteristically with three four-bar lines and blue notes, or any similar composition (sometimes neither slow nor sad). — *vt* to make blue; to treat with blue. — *vi* to turn blue. — *n* **blue'ness.** — *adj* **blues'y.** — *adj* **blu'ish.** — **blue baby** a baby with congenital cyanosis; **Blue'beard** a villainous character in European folklore, who murdered his wives in succession; (also without *cap*) any similar wife-murderer; **blue'bell** (*bloo͞'bel*) in S. England the wild hyacinth; in Scotland and N. England the harebell; **blue'berry** the fruit of *Vaccinium vacillans* and other American species; **blue'-bird** a small American bird related to the warblers; **blue blood** aristocratic blood (Sp. *sangre azul*); **blue book** a report or other paper printed by parliament (from its blue paper wrapper); **blue'bottle** the blue cornflower; a large fly (*Calliphora*) with metallic blue abdomen, a blowfly; a policeman (*slang*); the Portuguese man-of-war (*Austr* and *NZ*); **blue-breast** see **bluethroat; blue'-cheese** cheese with veins of bluish mould; **blue'-chip** a term applied to the most reliable industrial shares, or to anything of high value or prestige. — *adj* **blue-coll'ar** relating to manual work or workers. — **blue duck** a species of duck found in the mountains of New Zealand; **Blue Ensign** a blue flag with the Union Jack in one corner, flown by the Naval Reserve and certain yachts and merchant vessels; **blue film** or **movie** a pornographic film; **blue flag** one awarded to beaches meeting European Community standards of cleanness; **blue fox** an arctic fox; its fur; **blue funk** (*slang*) great terror; **blue'grass** a slightly glaucous permanent grass of Europe and North America, esp. Kentucky; a simple style of country music, originating in Kentucky and popular in the southern U.S.; **blue ground** a greyish-blue decomposed agglomerate in which diamonds are found; **blue gum** any of several species of Eucalyptus, esp. *E. globulus*; **blue hare** the mountain hare; **blue'jacket** a seaman in the navy; **blue jay** an American jay (*Cyanocitta cristata*); **blue john** ornamental fluorspar; **blue moon** a very long but quite indeterminate time — from the rare occurrence of the moon appearing to be blue because of dust particles in the atmosphere; **blue mould** a fungus that turns bread, cheese, etc., blue; **blue movie** see **blue film; blue murder** (*colloq*) extreme activity or commotion; **blue note** a flattened note, usu. third or seventh, characteristic of the blues; **blue pencil** a pencil of the colour traditionally used for correcting, emending, etc. — *vt* **blue-pen'cil** to correct, edit, or censor (as if) with a blue pencil. — **Blue Peter** a blue flag with a white rectangle hoisted when a ship is about to sail; a call for trumps in whist; **blue pointer** a large voracious shark found off the coast of Australia, the mako shark; **blue'print** a photographic print, white upon blue, on paper sensitised with ferric salts, produced from a photographic negative or a drawing on transparent paper; a detailed plan of work to be done, or a guide or model provided by agreed principles or rules or by conclusions from earlier experiment. — Also *vt.* — **blue ribbon** or **riband** the ribbon of the Order of the Garter; any very high distinction or prize; **blue sheep** the bharal. — *adj* **blue sky** or **skies** (of research, etc.) having no immediate practical application; (of stocks, securities) financially unsound or fraudulent. — **blue'-stocking** a learned woman, esp. one inclining to pedantry; **blue'throat** or **blue'breast** a songbird of Europe and Asia, the male of which has a blue throat; **blue tit** a small bird with blue wings and tail and a blue-topped head; **blue'-tongue** (*Austr*) a rouse-about; a lizard of the genus *Tiliqua*; **blue water** open sea; **blue whale** a migratory rorqual of the southern hemisphere, the biggest living animal. — **blue-eyed boy** a favourite who can do no wrong; **blue-sky laws** (*US*) laws to prevent fraud in the sale of stocks (against capitalising of blue skies stocks); **full blues** full formal naval uniform (*Navy slang*); **out of the blue** from the cloudless sky; entirely unexpectedly; **shout, scream** or **cry blue murder** to shout loudly in pain, alarm or rage; **the Blues** the Royal Horse Guards; **true blue** a person unswervingly faithful, esp. to a political party of blue persuasion (*adj* **true'-blue**). [M.E. *blew* — O.Fr. *bleu*, of Gmc. origin.]

blue[2] *bloo͞*, *vt* to squander. [Prob. for **blow.**]

bluff[1] *bluf*, *adj* steep or upright in front; rough and hearty in a good-natured way; outspoken; (of the shape of a body) such that, when it moves through air or other fluid, it leaves behind it a large disorderly wake and experiences a large drag (opp. of *streamlined*). — *n* a high steep bank. — *adv* **bluff'ly.** — *n* **bluff'ness.** [Perh. Du. *blaf* (obs.), broad, flat; or M.L.G. *blaff*, even, smooth.]

bluff[2] *bluf*, *vt* or *vi* to deceive or seek to deceive by concealment of weakness or show of self-confidence or threats (orig. in poker to conceal poor cards). — *n* a bluffing act or behaviour. — *n* **bluff'er.** — **call someone's bluff** to expose or challenge someone's bluff. [Perh. Du. *bluffen*, to brag, boast.]

blunder *blun'dər*, *vi* to make a gross mistake; to flounder about. — *vt* to utter thoughtlessly; to mismanage, bungle; to achieve, put or make by blundering. — *n* a gross mistake. — *n* **blun'derer.** — *adj* **blun'dering.** — *adv* **blun'deringly.** [M.E. *blondren*; prob. conn. with **blend.**]

blunderbuss *blun'dər-bus*, (*hist*) *n* a short handgun with a wide bore. [Du. *donderbus* — *donder*, thunder, *bus*, a box, gun-barrel, gun.]

blunge *blunj*, (*pottery*) *vt* to mix (clay or the like) with water. — *n* **blung'er.** [From *bl*end and pl*unge*.]

blunt *blunt*, *adj* having a dull edge or point; rough; outspoken; dull. — *vt* and *vi* to make or become dull. — *adj* **blunt'ish.** — *adv* **blunt'ly.** — *n* **blunt'ness.**

blur *blûr*, *n* an ill-defined spot or smear; a confused impression. — *vt* to blot; to make indistinct in outline. — *vi* to make blurs: — *pr p* **blurr'ing;** *pa t* and *pa p* **blurred.** [Perh. a variety of **blear.**]

blurb *blûrb*, *n* a publisher's commendatory description of a book, commonly printed on the jacket; any brief commendatory advertisement. — *vt* (*US colloq*) to praise, describe, state, etc. in a blurb. [Attributed to Gelett Burgess, American author.]

blurt *blûrt*, *vt* to utter suddenly or unadvisedly (with *out*). — *n* and *adj* **blurt'ing.** [Prob. imit.]

blush *blush*, *n* a red glow on the skin caused by shame, modesty, etc.; any reddish colour or suffusion. — *adj* pinkish. — *vi* to show shame or confusion by growing red; to grow red. — *n* **blush'er** a person who blushes; a cosmetic, usu. pinkish, applied to the cheeks to add colour to them. — *n* and *adj* **blush'ing.** — *adv* **blush'ingly.** [Cf. O.E. *blyscan*, to shine.]

bluster *blus'tər*, *vi* to blow boisterously; to storm, rage; to bully or swagger. — *vt* to utter loudly or boastfully; to bully by a show of temper. — *n* a blast or roaring of e.g. the wind; bullying or boasting language; a storm of anger. — *n* **blust'erer.** — *n* and *adj* **blus'tering.** — *adv* **blus'teringly.** — *adj* **blus'terous** noisy; boastful. — *adj* **blus'tery** stormy. [Cf. E. Frisian *blüstern*, to bluster.]

blutwurst *bloōt'voōrst*, *n* blood-pudding. [Ger.]

Blvd *abbrev* for Boulevard.

BM *abbrev* for: Bachelor of Medicine; British Museum.

BMA *abbrev* for: British Medical Association; British Midland Airways.

BMATT (sometimes *bē'mat*) *abbrev* for British Military Advisory and Training Team.

BMEWS (sometimes *bē'mūz*) *abbrev* for ballistic missile early warning system.

BMJ *abbrev* for British Medical Journal.

BML *abbrev* for British Museum Library.

BMus. *abbrev* for Bachelor of Music.

BMW *abbrev* for *Bayerische Motoren Werke* (Ger.), Bavarian motor works.

BMX *bē'em-eks*, *n* cycle racing on a rough artificial track; a BMX bike. — **BMX bike** a small bicycle designed for BMX racing, also used for stunt-riding. [Abbrev. for *bicycle motocross*.]

Bn *abbrev* for Baron.

bn *abbrev* for: battalion; billion.

BNB *abbrev* for British National Bibliography.

BNEC *abbrev* for British National Export Council.

BNFL *abbrev* for British Nuclear Fuels Limited.

BNOC (sometimes *bē'nok*) *abbrev* for British National Oil Corporation.

b.o. *abbrev* for: body odour (also **B.O.**); branch office; buyer's option.

bo[1] (*pl* **bos**), **boh** *bō* or **boo** *boō*, *interj* an exclamation used in fun, to startle someone. — **not be able to say boo to a goose** to be inarticulate from extreme meekness.

bo[2]. See **bo tree.**

boa *bō'ə*, *n* (with *cap*) a genus, mainly South American, of large snakes that kill their prey by pressure; popularly any large constricting snake; a long, serpentlike coil of fur, feathers, or the like worn round the neck by ladies. — **boa constrictor** properly the name of one species; popularly any boa, python or similar snake. [L. *bŏa*, a kind of snake.]

boar *bör*, *n* the male pig. — **wild boar** a wild pig of Europe and Asia, having prominent tusks. [O.E. *bār*.]

board *börd*, *n* a broad and thin strip of timber; a table; provision of meals (with or without lodging); a council-table; a council or authorised body; a slab, etc. prepared for playing a game (such as a chess-board) or other special purpose (such as a notice-board, blackboard, surfboard); (in *pl*) the stage; a sheet of stiff or laminated paper; a flat sheet of composite material, such as *chipboard*, *plasterboard*, etc.; a rectangular piece forming the side of a book-binding. — *vt* to cover with boards; to supply with food (and bed) at fixed terms; to enter (a ship, train, bus, etc.). — *vi* to receive food (and lodging). — *n* **board'er** a person who receives board; a person who boards a ship. — *n* **board'ing** the act of covering with boards; a structure or collection of boards; the act of boarding a ship. — **boarding card** see **boarding pass**; **board'-game** a game (e.g. chess, snakes-and-ladders) which is played with pieces, counters, etc. on a specially designed board; **board'ing-house** a house where boarders are kept; **boarding pass** or **card** a card allowing one to board an aircraft, ship, etc.; **board'ing-school** a school in which board and lodging are provided for pupils; **board'room** a room for meetings of a board of directors; **board'sailor**; **board'sailing** sail-boarding; **board'walk** a footpath made of boards. — **above board** openly; **go by the board** to go over the side of a ship; to be discarded or ignored; to meet disaster; **on board** aboard; **sweep the board** to take all the cards; to win everything; **take on board** to receive, accept (new notions, additional responsibilities, etc.). [O.E. *bord*, board, the side of a ship.]

boart. See **bort.**

boast *bōst*, *vi* to talk conceitedly; to brag (with *of*). — *vt* to brag of; to speak proudly or confidently of, esp. justifiably; to possess with pride. — *n* an expression of pride; a brag; the cause of boasting. — *n* **boast'er.** — *adj* **boast'ful** given to bragging. — *adv* **boast'fully.** — *n* **boast'fulness.** — *n* **boast'ing.** [M.E. *bōst*.]

boat *bōt*, *n* a small rowing, sailing or motor vessel; a ship; a boat-shaped utensil (as *sauce-boat*). — *vi* to sail about in a boat. — *vt* to put or convey in a boat; (with *it*) to go in a boat. — *n* **boat'er** a person who boats; a straw hat. — *n* **boat'ing.** — **boat'-builder** a person or firm that constructs boats; **boat'-deck** a ship's top deck, on which the small boats are carried; **boat'-hook** a hook fixed to a pole used for pulling or pushing off a boat; **boat'house** a house or shed for a boat; **boat'-load**; **boat'man** a man who has charge of a boat; a rower; **boat neck** a high slit-shaped neckline extending on to the shoulders. — *adj* **boat'-necked.** — **boat people** refugees, esp. from Vietnam, who set off in boats to find a country that will admit them; **boat'race** a race in rowing-boats; **boat'-train** a train run in connection with a ship. — **in the same boat** (of people) in the same unfavourable circumstances; **push the boat out** (*colloq*) to entertain, celebrate, etc., lavishly; **take to the boats** to escape in lifeboats from a sinking ship (also *fig*). [O.E. *bāt*.]

boatswain (often **bosun, bo'sun, bo's'n** or **bos'n**) *bō'sn*, *n* the foreman of a crew (warrant-officer in the navy) who looks after a ship's boats, rigging, flags, etc. — **boatswain's call, pipe** or **whistle** see under **whistle**; **boatswain's chair** a wooden seat slung from ropes, for a person working on a ship's side, rigging, etc.; **boatswain's mate** a boatswain's assistant. [**boat** and **swain.**]

bob[1] *bob*, *vi* to move quickly up and down; to curtsey; to ride a bobsled. — *vt* to move in a short jerking manner; to execute with a bob; to cut (hair) square across; to dock, to bobtail: — *pr p* **bobb'ing**; *pa t* and *pa p* **bobbed.** — *n* a short jerking motion; a curtsey; anything that moves with a bob or swing; the weight of a pendulum, plumb-line, or anything similar; a knot of hair; bobbed or docked hair; any small roundish body; a short line at or near the end of the stanza; a bobsled; a term (also **plain bob**) used in bell-ringing for a method of change-ringing. — **bob'cat** a kind of lynx; **bob'sled** or **-sleigh** a short sledge; a racing sledge for two or more people, with a continuous seat, steering mechanism, and brakes; **bob'tail** a short or cut tail; an animal with a bobbed tail (also *adj*); a word applied in contempt to the rabble, as in *rag-tag and bobtail*. — Also *vt*. — *adj* **bob'tailed** with tail cut short. — **bob up** to appear suddenly. [Poss. Gael. *baban*, *babag*.]

bob[2] *bob*, (*slang*) *n* a shilling or 5 pence: — *pl* **bob.**

bobbin *bob'in*, *n* a reel or spool for winding yarn, wire, etc. — **bobb'in-lace** lace made on a pillow with bobbins; **bobb'in-net** or **bobb'inet** a fine machine-made netted lace. [Fr. *bobine*.]

bobble *bob'əl*, *n* a bobbing motion; the movement of disturbed water; a woolly ball for trimming clothes, etc. — *vt* and *vi* to bob rapidly or continuously; (orig. *US*) to fumble or bungle. — **bobb'le-hat** a usu. knitted tapering hat with a bobble at the top. [**bob**[1].]

bobby *bob'i*, (*slang*) *n* a policeman. [Familiar form of *Robert*, from Sir Robert Peel, Home Secretary at the passing of the Metropolitan Police Act, 1828.]

bobby calf *bob'i käf*, *n* a calf slaughtered before it has been weaned.

bobby-dazzler *bob'i-daz-lər*, (*colloq*) *n* anything overwhelmingly excellent, striking or showy, esp. a woman; a young girl who sets out to make an impression.

bobby-pin *bob'i-pin*, *n* a hairgrip.

bobbysock *bob'i-sok*, (*colloq*) *n* an ankle sock, esp. as worn by teenage girls.

bobcat. See **bob**[1].

bobolink *bob'ō-lingk*, *n* a N. Am. songbird. [At first *Bob Lincoln*, from its note.]

bobsled, bobsleigh. See **bob**[1].

bobstays *bob'stāz*, (*naut*) *npl* ropes or stays used to hold the bowsprit down to the stem or cut-water, and counteract the strain of the foremast stays.

bobtail. See **bob**[1].

bob-white *bob-wīt'* or *-hwīt*, *n* an American quail. [Imit.]

boche or **bosche** *bosh*, (*derog*) *n* World War I slang (orig. French) for a German, esp. a German soldier. — Also with *cap*.

bock *bok*, (Fr., from Ger.) *n* a strong German beer — from *Einbocker bier*, *Eimbockbier* — beer from Einbeck (Eimbeck); now often a glass or mug of beer (holding quarter of a litre).

BOD *abbrev* for biochemical oxygen demand.

bod *bod*, (orig. *services slang*) *n* a person. [Contraction of **body**.]

bode[1] *bōd*, *vt* to portend; to be a prediction of; to foretell; to have a presentiment of. — *vi* to be an omen (good or bad). [O.E. *bodian*, to announce — (*ge*)*bod*, a message.]

bode[2] *bōd*. See **bide**.

bodega *bo-dē'gə*, or Sp. *bō-dā'ga*, *n* a wine-shop; a warehouse for storing and maturing wine. [Sp. — L. — Gr. *apothēkē*, a storehouse.]

bodgie *boj'i*, (*Austr* and *NZ*) *n* a young Australian male of the 1950s, similar in dress and behaviour to the British Teddy boy; something that is a fake, useless, or fraudulent (also *adj*). [Perhaps from dialect *bodge*, to work or do something carelessly or clumsily.]

Bodhisattva *bō-di-sat'wə* or *-və*, or *bo-*, (*Buddhism*) *n* a person who postpones entry into nirvana in order to help others; a future Buddha. [Sans. — *bodhi*, enlightenment, *sattva*, existence.]

bodhi tree. See **bo tree**.

bodhrán *bow-rän'* or *bō'rən*, *n* a shallow one-sided drum, common in Irish and Scottish folk music. [Irish Gaelic.]

bodice *bod'is*, *n* a woman's outer garment covering the waist and bust; the close-fitting waist or body of a woman's gown; a stiffened inner garment (*archaic*). — **bod'ice-ripper** a romantic (historical) novel involving violence. [Orig. pl. of **body**.]

bodkin *bod'kin*, *n* a large blunt needle; a small dagger; a small instrument for pricking holes, for fastening up hair, for correcting type, etc. [Poss. connected with Welsh *bidog*, dagger.]

body *bod'i*, *n* the whole frame of a human or a lower animal; the main part of an animal, as distinguished from the limbs; the main part of anything; the part of a vehicle which carries the load or passengers; a corpse; matter, as opposed to spirit; substance or substantial quality; fullness, as of flavour in a wine; solidity; opacity of a paint or pigment; a mass; a person (*colloq*); a number of persons united by something they have in common: — *pl* **bod'ies**. — *vt* (usu. with *forth*) to give form to; to embody: — *pr p* **bod'ying**; *pa t* and *pa p* **bod'ied**. — *adj* **bod'ily** of the body, esp. as opposed to the mind. — *adv* in the flesh; as a whole. — **bodily function** any of the processes or activities performed by or connected with the body, such as breathing, hearing, and digesting; **bod'y-bag** a bag made of heavy material in which a dead body (esp. that of a war casualty or accident victim) is transported; **body blow** in boxing, a blow to the body; a serious setback; **bod'y-builder** a person who by an exercise and dietary regime builds up the size and strength of the muscles; an apparatus for exercising muscles; a nutritious food; a person who makes vehicle bodies. — *n* and *adj* **bod'y-building**. — **bod'y-cavity** the cavity in which the viscera of the higher animals lie, the coelom; **bod'y-check** (*sport*) a deliberate obstruction of an opposing player's movements, permitted in e.g. lacrosse and ice-hockey, not in soccer (also *vt*); **bod'y-checking; body clock** the biological clock; **bod'yguard** a guard consisting of one person or several people, to accompany and give physical protection to someone; **body language** communication of information by means of conscious or unconscious gestures, attitudes, facial expressions, etc.; **bod'yline** body-line bowling (see below); **body packer** (*slang*) someone who smuggles drugs by swallowing them or otherwise hiding them in their body; **body politic** the collective body of the people in its political capacity; **bod'ypopping** a form of dancing with robotlike movements; **bod'yshell** bodywork; **body shop** a vehicle body repair or construction shop; **bod'y-snatcher** a person who secretly disinters dead bodies for dissection; **body stocking** a one-piece, skin-tight undergarment for women; **bod'ysuit** a close-fitting one-piece garment for women; **bod'y-warmer** a padded sleeveless jacket; **bod'ywork** the metal outer frame of a motor vehicle. — **body and soul** one's entire self; **body-line bowling** in cricket, fast bowling delivered at the batsman's body (also **bod'yline**); **in a body** (acting) all together. [O.E. *bodig*.]

Boer *bōōr*, (chiefly *hist*) *n* a S. African of Dutch descent, orig. one engaged in farming. — Also *adj*. [Du.; see **boor**.]

boff *bof*, (*slang*; esp. *US*) *n* a punch; a hearty laugh; an entertainment. — *vi* and *vt* to hit, esp. with the fist. — *vi* to copulate. [Perh. imit.]

boffin *bof'in*, (orig. *services slang*) *n* a research scientist, esp. one employed by armed forces or government.

Bofors gun *bō'förz* or *-förs gun*, a single- or double-barrelled, quick-firing anti-aircraft gun. [From *Bofors*, Sweden, where orig. made.]

bog *bog*, *n* spongy, usu. peaty, ground; a marsh; a lavatory (*slang*). — *n* **bogg'iness**. — *adj* **bogg'y**. — **bog'-asphodel** a yellow-flowered bog-plant; **bog'-bean** buckbean, a marsh plant; **bog-iron** see **bog-ore; bog'land; bog'-moss** sphagnum; **bog'-myrtle** sweet-gale, a bog plant; **bog'oak** trunks of oak embedded in bogs and preserved from decay; **bog'-ore** or **bog'-iron** an iron ore found in boggy land; **bog'-spavin** distension of the capsule of the hock-joint of the horse; **bog'trotter** (*slang*, often *derog*) an Irishman. — **bog down** to encumber with an overwhelming amount of work, a difficult task, etc. [Ir. and Gael. *bogach*; *bog*, soft.]

bogey[1] *bō'gi*, (*golf*) *n* the score, for a given hole or for the whole course, of an imaginary good player, Colonel *Bogey*, fixed as a standard — now usu. a score of one stroke above the par for any hole. [Perh. **bogy**.]

bogey[2]. See **bogie, bogy**.

boggle *bog'l*, *vi* to start, draw back with fright; to hesitate or evade; (of one's mind, esp. in *the mind boggles*) to be unable to imagine or grasp something, to be astounded by something (*colloq*). — *n* **bogg'ler**. [**bogle**.]

bogie or **bogey** *bō'gi*, *n* a low heavy truck, a trolley; a railway coach; a pivoted undercarriage, as in a locomotive engine.

bogle *bō'gl*, *n* a spectre or goblin; a scarecrow (also **tatt'ie-bogle**); a bugbear, or source of terror. [Scot.; possibly connected with **bug**[1].]

bogong *bō'gong*, *n* a noctuid moth eaten by Australian Aborigines. — Also **bugong** (*bōō'*). [Aboriginal.]

bogus *bō'gəs*, *adj* counterfeit, spurious. [An American cant word.]

bogy or **bogey** *bō'gi*, *n* a goblin; a bugbear or special object of dread; the devil; a policeman (*slang*): — *pl*

bō'gies or **bō'geys**. — *n* **bō'gyism** or **bō'geyism**. — **bo'gy-man** or **bo'gey-man** the Devil or other frightening being with whom to threaten children. [Perhaps a form of **bogle**.]

boh. See **bo**[1].

bohea *bō-hē'*, *n* black tea; the lowest quality of black tea. [From the *Wu-i* hills in China.]

Bohemian *bō-hē'mi-ən*, *n* a native or inhabitant of Bohemia, formerly a kingdom, now part of Czechoslovakia; a gypsy; (also without *cap*) an artist or writer, or indeed anyone, who sets social conventions aside. — Also *adj*. — *n* **Bohē'mianism** (also without *cap*). [Fr. *bohémien*, a gypsy, from the belief that these wanderers came from *Bohemia*.]

boil[1] *boil*, *vi* to pass rapidly from liquid into vapour with violent evolution of bubbles; to bubble up as if from the action of heat; to be heated in boiling liquid; to be hot; to be excited or angry. — *vt* to heat to a boiling state; to cook, dress, clean or otherwise treat by boiling. — *n* the act or condition of boiling. — *n* **boil'er** a person who boils; that in which anything is boiled ; a vessel in which steam is generated; a vessel in which water is heated for circulation; a (usu. old) fowl, best cooked by boiling. — *n* **boil'ing**. — *adj* at boiling-point; very hot; bubbling; extremely angry. — **boil'ing-point** the temperature at which a liquid, esp. water, boils; the point of emotion, esp. anger, where control is lost; **boiled sweet** a sweet of boiled sugar, flavouring, and often colouring; **boil'er-maker**; **boiler suit** a workman's overall garment. — **boil down** to reduce in bulk by boiling; to extract the substance of; **boil down to** (*fig*) to mean, to signify when reduced to essentials; **boil over** to bubble over the sides of the containing vessel; to break out into unrestrained indignation; **come to the boil** to reach boiling-point; to reach a critical state; **on the boil** boiling; active. [O.Fr. *boillir* — L. *bullīre* — *bulla*, a bubble.]

boil[2] *boil*, *n* an inflamed swelling. [O.E. *bȳl*.]

boisterous *bois'tər-əs*, *adj* noisy and exuberant; wild; turbulent; stormy. — *adv* **bois'terously**. — *n* **bois'terousness**. [M.E. *boistous*.]

boko *bō'kō*, (*slang*) *n* the nose: — *pl* **bō'kos**.

bolas *bō'läs*, *n* (properly *pl*) a South American missile, consisting of two or more balls or stones strung together, swung round the head and hurled so as to entangle an animal. — **bolas spider** a spider that catches its prey with a sticky drop on the end of a line thrown like a bolas. [Sp., balls.]

bold *bōld*, *adj* daring; forward or impudent; presumptuous; executed vigorously; striking, noticeable, well marked. — *adv* **bold'ly**. — *n* **bold'ness**. — *adj* **bold'-faced** impudent; (of type) having a heavy face. — **be so bold as to** to venture, take the liberty; **bold as brass** utterly unabashed, cheeky. [O.E. *bald*.]

bole[1] *bōl*, *n* the trunk of a tree. [O.N. *bolr*.]

bole[2] *bōl*, *n* a friable earthy clay, usually red. [Gr. *bolos*, a clod.]

bolection or **balection** *bō-* or *bə-lek'shən*, *n* a moulding around a panel, projecting beyond the surface of the framing.

bolero *bə-lā'rō*, *n* a Spanish national dance; a tune to which it may be danced; (usu. *bol'ə-rō*) a jacketlike bodice, coming barely to the waist: — *pl* **boleros**. [Sp.]

bolide *bō'līd*, *n* a large meteor, esp. one that bursts; a fireball. [Fr., — L. *bolis*, *-idis* — Gr. *bolīs*, missile.]

bolivar *bol-ē'vär*, *n* the standard monetary unit of Venezuela (100 *céntimos*). [From Simón *Bolívar* (1783–1830).]

boliviano *bol-ē-vi-ä'nō*, *n* a Bolivian dollar (100 centavos): — *pl* **bolivia'nos**.

boll *bōl*, *n* a swelling; a knob; a round capsule, as in cotton, flax, poppy, etc. — *vi* to swell, to form bolls. — *adj* **bolled** (*bōld*) swollen, podded. — **boll'-weevil** a weevil whose larvae infest cotton-bolls; **boll'-worm** a moth caterpillar that destroys cotton-bolls, etc. [A form of **bowl**[2] — O.E. *bolla*.]

bollard *bol'ərd*, *n* a short post on a wharf or ship, etc., round which ropes are secured; one of a line of short posts preventing the passage of motor vehicles. [Prob. **bole**[1].]

bolletrie *bol'ə-trē*. Same as **bully-tree**.

bollock *bol'ək*, (*slang*) *vt* to reprimand severely. — *n* **boll'ocking**. [Connection with **bollocks** uncertain.]

bollocks *bol'əks* or **ballocks** *bol'*, also *bal'*, *npl* (now generally considered *vulg*) testicles. — *nsing* (*slang*) nonsense; a muddle, mess. — *vt* to make a botch of. [O.E. *beallucas*, testicles.]

bolo *bō'lō*, (esp. *US*) *n* in boxing, a long sweeping uppercut: — *pl* **bo'los**. — Also **bolo punch**.

Bologna *bol-ōn'yä*, *adj* of the town of *Bologna* in Italy. — *adj* and *n* **Bologn'ese** (or *-ēz'*). — **Bologna sausage**. — **spaghetti (alla) bolognese** see **spaghetti**. [L. *Bonōnia*.]

bolometer *bō-lom'i-tər*, *n* an instrument for measuring radiant energy. — *adj* **bolomet'ric**. — *n* **bolom'etry**. [Gr. *bolē*, stroke, ray, *metron*, a measure.]

boloney. See **baloney**.

Bolshevik or **bolshevik** *bol'shə-vik*, *n* a member of the Russian Majority (or Extreme) Socialist party (*hist*); a violent revolutionary Marxist communist; an anarchist, agitator, troublemaker (used loosely as a term of disapproval). — Also *adj*. — *n* and *adj* colloq. contraction **bol'shie** or **bol'shy**. — *n* **bol'shevism**. — *n* **bol'shevist**. — Also *adj*. [Russ. — *bolshe*, greater, *-vik*, agent suffix.]

bolster *bōl'stər*, *n* a long, sometimes cylindrical, pillow or cushion; a pad; anything similar in form or use, esp. any piece of mechanism acting as a support against pressure; a form of cold chisel. — *vt* (also with *up*) to support; to hold up. — *adj* **bol'stered** supported; swelled out. — *n* and *adj* **bol'stering**. [O.E. *bolster*.]

bolt[1] *bōlt*, *n* a bar or rod that slides into a hole or socket to fasten a door, etc.; a heavy screw or pin with a head; a thunderbolt; a roll of a definite measure (of cloth, etc.); an arrow, esp. for a crossbow. — *vt* to fasten with a bolt; to swallow hastily; to cause to rush out, run away, take flight; to connect or join (*fig*). — *vi* to spring, dart; to run away, escape; (of a horse) to run out of control; (of a plant) to flower and go to seed. — *n* **bolt'er**. — **bolt'hole** a hole into which a bolt slides; a secret passage or way of escape; a refuge from danger; a secluded, private place. — *adj* **bolt'-on** additional, supplementary. — **bolt'-rope** a rope sewed all round the edge of a sail to prevent it from tearing. — **bolt from the blue** an unexpected event; **bolt upright** upright, and straight as an arrow; **have shot one's bolt** to be unable to do more than one has done. [O.E. *bolt*.]

bolt[2]. See **boult**.

Boltzmann constant *bōlts'mən kon'stənt*, (*phys*) *n* the ratio of the gas constant to Avogadro's constant. [Ludwig *Boltzmann* (1844–1906), Austrian physicist.]

bolus *bō'ləs*, *n* a rounded mass; a large pill. [L. *bōlus* — Gr. *bōlos*, a lump.]

bomb *bom*, *n* a hollow case containing explosive, incendiary, smoke-producing, poisonous, or other offensive material; a piece of programming, inserted into software, that can be activated to sabotage the system (*comput*); (also **volcanic bomb**) a rounded mass of lava thrown out by a volcano; an old worn-out car (*Austr* and *NZ colloq*). — *vi* to throw, discharge, or drop bombs; (sometimes with *out*) to be a flop, fail (*slang*). — *vt* to attack, injure, or destroy with bombs. — *n* **bomber** (*bom'ər*) a person who bombs or plants bombs; a bombing aeroplane. — Also *adj*. — **bomb'-disposal** the act of removing and detonating unexploded bombs; **bomber jacket**

a short jacket with zipped front and elasticated waist. — *adj* **bomb'-proof** proof or secure against the force of bombs. — **bomb'shell** a bomb; (now only *fig*) a sudden and surprising piece of news; **bomb'-site** an area which has been laid waste by air-raid(s). — **go like a bomb** to go very well or very quickly; **make a bomb** (*colloq*) to make or earn a great deal of money. [Fr. *bombe*, prob. — L. *bombus* — Gr. *bombos*, humming sound.]

bombard *bom-bärd'*, *vt* to attack with artillery; to batter or pelt; to subject to a succession of blows or impingements; to assail, e.g. with questions (*fig*); to subject, e.g. an atom, to a stream of particles at high speed (*phys*). — *n* **bombardier** (*bom-* or *bum-bər-dēr'*) the lowest non-commissioned officer in the British artillery. — *n* **bombardment** (*bom-bärd'mənt*). — **bombardier beetle** a beetle that explosively discharges an acrid volatile fluid. [O.Fr. *bombard*, an old cannon for firing stones or shot; see also ety. for **bomb**.]

bombasine or **bombazine** *bom'bə-zēn* or *-zēn'*, *n* twilled or corded fabric of silk or cotton and worsted. [Fr. *bombasin*.]

bombast *bom'bast*, *n* bumptiously pompous language. — *adj* **bombas'tic** pompous; inflated. — *adv* **bombas'tically**. [L.L. *bombax*, cotton — Gr. *bombȳx*, silk.]

Bombay duck *bom'bā duk*, *n* a fish, the bummalo.

bombe *bom* or *bɔ̃b*, *n* a dessert, usually ice-cream frozen in a round or melon-shaped mould. [Fr.]

bombé *bom'bā* or *bɔ̃-bā*, *adj* (of furniture) having a rounded, convex front. [Fr., bulging, convex.]

bomber. See **bomb**.

bombilate *bom'bil-āt* or **bombinate** *bom'bin-āt*, *vi* to hum, buzz, drone, boom. — *n* **bombilā'tion** or **bombinā'tion**. [L. *bombilāre*, *bombināre*.]

bombo *bom'bō*, (*Austr colloq*) *n* cheap wine, plonk.

bon *bɔ̃*, (Fr.) *adj* good. — **bon appetit** (*bo-na-pə-tē*) good appetite, said politely to those who are (about to start) eating; **bon goût** (*gōō*) good taste; **bonjour** (*-zhōōr*) good day; good morning; **bon mot** (*pl* **bons mots**) (*mō*) a witty saying; **bonsoir** (*-swär*) good evening; **bon ton** (*tɔ̃*) the height of fashion; **bon vivant** (*vē-vɑ̃*) a jovial companion; a person who lives well, esp. one who enjoys fine food; **bon viveur** (*vē-vœr*; not used in Fr.) a bon vivant, esp. a man-about-town; **bon voyage** (*vwä-yäzh*) may you have a good journey.

bona fide *bō'nə fīd*, *fī'də* or *-di*, also *bo'nä fi'dā*, *adj* genuine. — **bona fides** (*fī'dēz* or *fid'ās*) good faith; genuineness; evidence or proof of genuineness. [L.]

bonanza *bon-an'zə*, *n* a rich mine or vein of gold (*NAm*); a large amount of gold; any source of wealth or stroke of luck. [Sp., good weather (at sea).]

bonbon *bon'bon* or *bɔ̃-bɔ̃*, *n* a confection, a sweet. — *n* **bonbonnière** (*bɔ̃-bon-yer'*) a fancy box or dish for holding sweets. [Fr., reduplication of *bon*, good.]

bonce *bons*, *n* a large marble; the head (*slang*).

bond[1] *bond*, *n* something that binds; a link, connection, union or (*chem*) attraction; a written obligation to pay a sum or to perform a contract; a debenture, a security issued by the government or a company when borrowing money; a mortgage (*Scots law*); any constraining or cementing force or material; in building, the overlapping connection of one stone or brick with another; (in *pl*) imprisonment, captivity; the condition of goods retained in a warehouse, called a **bonded warehouse** or **store**, until duties are paid. — *vt* to connect, secure, or bind with a bond; to put in a condition of bond; to cause to adhere (to). — *vi* to form an emotional bond. — *adj* **bond'ed** secured by bond. — *n* **bond'er** a bondstone or header. — *n* **bond'ing** an act of bonding; the forming of the attachment between a mother and her newborn child (*psychol*). — **bond'-holder** a person who holds bonds of a private person or public company; **bond paper** a superior kind of paper; **bonds'man** (*law*) a surety; **bond'stone** a stone that reaches a considerable distance into or entirely through a wall, binding it together. [A variant of **band** — O.E. *bindan*, to bind.]

bond[2] *bond*, *adj* in a state of servitude. — *n* **bond'age** captivity; slavery; a sexual practice in which the partners derive additional pleasure through, or by applying, physical restraint or binding. — *adj* (of usu. black leather clothes or accessories) aggressive-looking, with chains, metal studs, buckles, etc. — **bond'maid**, **bond'-woman** or **bonds'woman** a female slave; **bond'man** or **bonds'man** a male slave; **bond'manship**; **bond'servant** a slave; **bond'-service** the condition of a bondservant; slavery; **bond'-slave** a slave. [O.E. *bonda*, a husbandman, a householder.]

bondsman. See **bond**[1, 2].

bone *bōn*, *n* a hard substance forming the skeleton of the higher animals; a separate piece of the skeleton; a piece of whalebone; (in *pl*) the skeleton or anything resembling it in any way; (in *pl*) mortal remains. — *vt* to take the bones out of, e.g. meat. — *adj* **boned** having bones; having the bones removed. — *adj* **bone'less** lacking bones; spineless (*fig*). — *n* **bō'niness**. — *n* **bō'ner** (*slang*) a howler, a blunder. — *adj* **bō'ny** full of, consisting of, or like bones; thin. — **bone'-ash** or **bone'-earth** the remains of bones burned in an open furnace; **bone china** china in the making of which calcium phosphate, as in bone-ash, is used; **bone'-dust** ground or pulverised bones, used in agriculture; **bone'head** a blockhead; **bone'-lace** lace woven with bobbins, once often made of bones; **bone'-meal** ground bones used as fertiliser and as animal feed; **bone'-oil** a liquid got in dry distillation of bones; **bone'setter** a person who treats broken or dislocated bones, esp. when not surgically qualified; **bone'shaker** a colloq. name for earlier forms of bicycle; any uncertainly reliable, crazy vehicle; **bone-spav'in** a bony excrescence or hard swelling on the inside of the hock of a horse; **bone-tur'quoise** blue fossil bone or tooth used as turquoise; **bony fishes** the Teleostei, an order of fishes including most of the living forms. — **bare bones** the essentials (of a subject); **bone dry** as dry as a bone; **bone idle** utterly idle; **bone of contention** something that causes strife; **bone to pick** a difference to be cleared up (with somebody); **bone up on** (*slang*) to study or collect information about (a subject); **close to (or near) the bone** offensively pointed; on the verge of indecent; **feel in one's bones** to know instinctively, without proof; **make no bones of** or **about** to have no scruples about; to make no fuss or difficulty about; **near the bone** see **close to the bone** above; **(never) make old bones** (not) to live to old age; **to the bone** to the inmost part; to the minimum; **work one's fingers to the bone** to work until one is exhausted. [O.E. *bān*.]

bonfire *bon'fīr*, *n* a large fire in the open air on occasions of public celebration, or for burning garden refuse, etc. — originally a fire in which bones were burnt. — **Bonfire night** November 5, Guy Fawkes night (see **guy**[2]). [**bone** and **fire**.]

bong *bong*, *n* a deep hollow or ringing sound. — *vi* to make such a sound. — Also *vt*. [Imit.]

bongo *bong'gō* or **bongo drum** (*drum*), *n* small Cuban drum played with the fingers — generally used in pairs: — *pl* **bon'gos** or **bongo drums**. [Am. Sp. *bongó*.]

bonhomie or **bonhommie** *bon'o-mē*, *n* easy good nature. — *adj* **bon'homous**. [Fr.]

bonism *bon'izm*, *n* the doctrine that the world is good, but could be perfected. — *n* **bon'ist**. [L. *bonus*, good.]

bonito *bo-nē'tō*, *n* any of several large fish of the mackerel family: — *pl* **boni'tos**. [Sp.]

bonk *bongk*, *n* a blow or thump, or its sound; an act of sexual intercourse (*vulg*). — *vt* to hit or thump; to have sexual intercourse with (*vulg*). [Imit.]

bonkers *bong'kərz*, (*slang*) *adj* crazy; slightly drunk.

bonne *bon*, *fem* of **bon** (Fr.) *adj* good. — *n* a French maid or nursemaid. — **bonne chance** (*shãs*) good luck; **bonne compagnie** (*kɔ̃-pa-nyē*) good society; **bonne foi** (*fwa*) good faith; **bonne grace** (*gräs*) good grace, gracefulness; **bonne mine** (*mēn*) good appearance, pleasant looks.

bonnet *bon'it*, *n* a woman's head-covering, tied on by ribbons, etc.; a soft cap; an additional part laced to the foot of jibs, or other fore-and-aft sails, to gather more wind (*naut*); a wire cowl over a chimney-top; the cover of a motor car engine, or of various parts of machinery, etc.; the second stomach of a ruminant. — *vt* to put a bonnet on. — *adj* **bonn'eted**. — **bonn'et-monkey** an Indian macaque (from the appearance of the head); **bonnet-rouge** (Fr.; *bon-ā-rōōzh*) the red cap of liberty of the French Revolution, in the form of a Phrygian cap. [O.Fr., — L.L. *bonnetum*, orig. the name of a material.]

bonny or **bonnie** *bon'i*, *adj* comely, pretty; plump; healthy-looking. — *n* a sweetheart. — Also *adv*. — *adv* **bonn'ily**. — *n* **bonn'iness**.

bonsai *bon'sī* or *bōn'sī*, *n* a dwarf tree growing in a pot, produced by special methods of cultivation (*pl* **bon'sai**); the art of growing such trees. [Jap. *bon*, tray, bowl, *sai*, cultivation.]

bonspiel *bon'spēl*, *n* a curling match. [From Du. *spel*, play.]

bontebok *bon'tə-bok*, *n* a South African antelope. [Du. *bont*, particoloured, *bok*, goat.]

bonus *bō'nəs*, *n* something good or desirable gained or given with something else; a premium beyond the usual interest for a loan; an extra dividend to shareholders; a policy-holder's share of profits; an extra payment to a workforce or staff. — **bonus issue** an issue of additional shares to a company's shareholders, representing a capitalisation of reserves. [L. *bonus*, good.]

bonze *bonz*, *n* a Buddhist priest. [Jap. *bonzô* or *bonzi*, a priest.]

bonzer *bon'zər*, (*Austr colloq*) *adj* very good.

boo[1] or **booh** *bōō*, *n* and *interj* a sound expressing disapprobation or contempt. — *vt* and *vi* to show disapproval (of) by making such a sound. — **boo-hoo** (*-hōō'*) the sound of noisy weeping. — *vi* to weep noisily.

boo[2]. See **bo**[1].

boob[1] *bōōb*, (*colloq*) *vt* to bungle. — *vi* to blunder. — *n* a blunder (also **booboo** *bōō'bōō*). — **boob'-tube** (*slang*) a television set. [**booby**.]

boob[2] *bōōb*, (*slang*) *n* a female breast (usu. in *pl*). — **boob'-tube** (*slang*) a woman's clinging garment covering the torso from waist to armpit.

booboo. See **boob**[1].

booby *bōō'bi*, *n* a stupid person; a type of gannet. — **boo'by-prize** a prize for the least successful in a competition, etc.; **boo'by-trap** a harmless-looking object which on being touched sets off an explosion; a form of practical joke, e.g. when something is made to fall upon someone entering a door. — *vt* to set up a booby-trap in or on. [Perh. Sp. *bobo*, a dolt.]

boodle *bōōd'l*, *n* counterfeit money; money obtained by political or official corruption; spoil; a crowd, pack. [Perh. Du. *boedel*, property.]

boogie-woogie *bōōg-i-wōōg'i*, *n* a jazz rhythm in which the piano has a constantly repeated figure in the bass. — *n* **boog'ie** boogie-woogie; dancing to pop music. — *vi* to dance to pop music: — *pr p* **boog'ieing**; *pa t* and *pa p* **boog'ied**. [From U.S. slang *boogie*, a Negro performer, and *woogie*, invented to rhyme.]

booh. See **boo**[1].

book *bŏŏk*, *n* sheets of paper, etc., bound or otherwise fastened together, either printed, written on, or blank; a large-scale literary composition; a division of a volume or composition; (with **the**) the Bible; a record of bets made with different people; any source of instruction (*fig*); a libretto; a script; (in *pl*) formal accounts of transactions. — *vt* to write or enter in a book; to engage or reserve in advance; (of the police) to take the name of, for an alleged offence; to arrest; (of a referee) to enter a player's name in a notebook for an offence (*football*). — *vi* to make a reservation in advance. — *adj* **book'able**. — *n* **book'ie** (*colloq*) a bookmaker. — *n* **book'ing** a reservation of e.g. a room in a hotel, a theatre seat, a seat on a plane, train, etc. — *adj* **book'ish** relating to books; fond of books, studious; acquainted only with, and experienced only through, books. — *n* **book'ishness**. — *n* **book'let** a small book. — **book'binder** a person who binds books; **book'binding**; **book'case** a piece of furniture with shelves for books; **book club** a society that buys, circulates on loan, or prints books for its members. — *adj* **booked-out'** or **booked-up'** full up; unable to accept further reservations, bookings or appointments. — **book'-end** a prop for the end of a row of books; **book'ing-clerk** a person who sells tickets; **book'ing-hall**; **book'ing-office** an office where reservations are made or tickets sold; **book'keeper**; **book'keeping** the keeping of accounts in a regular and systematic manner; **book'-learning** learning got from books, as opposed to practical knowledge; **book'maker** a person who accepts bets at race-courses, etc. and pays out the winnings; **book'mark** or **book'marker** a strip of leather, etc., or other object, for marking a particular opening in, or one's current place in, a book; **book'plate** a decorative label usually pasted inside the cover of a book, bearing the owner's name or other distinguishing information; **book'-post** an arrangement in the Post Office for the transmission of books; **book price** or **value** the officially-recorded value, not necessarily the market value, of a commodity; **book'rest** a support for a book, a bookstand; **book'seller** a person who sells books; **book'selling**; **book'shelf** a shelf for books; **book'-shop** a shop where books are sold; **book'stall** a stall or stand where books are sold; **book'stand** a bookstall; a stand or support for holding up a book in reading; **book'store** (*US*) a bookshop; **book'-token** a voucher to be exchanged for books of a stated price, given as a gift; **book value** see **book price**; **book'work** study from books, theoretical as opposed to practical work; work on account books, etc.; **book'worm** a grub that eats holes in books; a person who is devoted to reading. — **be on the books** to have one's name in an official list as a member, a customer, etc.; **book in** to reserve a place or room (at); to register at a hotel; **book of words** (*colloq*) directions for use; **book through** to book as a whole a journey to be made in parts; **bring to book** to bring to account; **closed book** a subject completely unknown or uncomprehended; **get one's books** to be dismissed; **in someone's good (**or **bad) books** favourably (or unfavourably) regarded by someone; **read like a book** to understand thoroughly (usu. a person's character or motives); **suit one's book** to be agreeable to or favourable to one; **take a leaf out of someone's book** to profit by someone's example; **throw the book at** (*colloq*) to administer a lengthy and detailed reproof to. [O.E. *bōc*, book.]

Boolean algebra *bōō'lē-ən al'ji-brə*, *n* an algebra closely related to logic in which the symbols used do not represent arithmetical quantities. [Named after George *Boole* (1815–64).]

boom[1] *bōōm*, *n* an inflatable barrier used to contain oil from spillages, etc.; a pole by which a sail is stretched; a chain or bar stretched across a harbour; a barrier of floating logs; a long beam. [Du. *boom*, beam, tree.]

boom[2] *bōōm*, *vt* to make a hollow sound or roar. — *n* a hollow roar. — **boom'-box** (*slang*) a powerful portable radio and cassette recorder with built-in speakers, a ghetto-blaster. [From a L.G. root; like **bomb**, of imit. origin.]

boom[3] *bōōm*, *vi* to become suddenly prosperous; to increase sharply in value. — *n* a sudden increase of activity in business, etc.; a sudden rise in price or value. — *n* and *adj* **boom'ing**. — **boom town** one which has expanded rapidly and prospered because of e.g. the arrival of a valuable new industry. [Prob. from **boom**[2].]

boomerang *bōōm'ə-rang*, *n* a curved missile used by the natives of Australia, sometimes so balanced that it returns towards the thrower; an act that recoils upon the agent (*fig*). — *vi* to recoil in such a way (*fig*). [Aboriginal.]

boon[1] *bōōn*, *n* a gift, favour. [O.N. *bōn*, prayer.]

boon[2] *bōōn*, *adj* jovial, convivial, or kind (as a *boon companion*). [Fr. *bon* — L. *bonus*, good.]

boondocks *bōōn'doks*, (*US colloq*) *npl* wild or remote country; a dull provincial place. — Also **boo'nies**. [Tagálog *bundok*, mountain.]

boong *bōōng*, (*offensive*) *n* an Aborigine; a New Guinea native. [Aborigine word.]

boonies *bōō'niz*. See **boondocks**.

boor *bōōr*, *n* a coarse person; a Dutch colonist in South Africa (*hist*). — *adj* **boor'ish** awkward or rude. — *adv* **boor'ishly**. — *n* **boor'ishness**. [Du. *boer*; perh. partly O.E. *būr*, *gebūr*, farmer.]

boost *bōōst*, *vt* to push up; to raise, e.g. morale or price; to advertise or promote; to supplement or increase supply, strength etc.; to push (a spacecraft) into orbit by means of a booster. — Also *n*. — *n* **boost'er** a person or thing which boosts; a keen supporter (*US*); an auxiliary motor in a rocket; any device to increase the effect of another mechanism; an additional dose of a vaccine to increase or renew the effect of the original dose.

boot[1] *bōōt*, *n* a covering for the foot and lower part of the leg, made of leather, rubber, etc.; a compartment in a motor car for luggage, etc.; an instrument of torture for the leg. — *vt* to put boots on; to kick; to turn out, dismiss (with *out*; *colloq*); to start up (a computer) (often with *up*); to load the initial programs on (a computer) (often with *up*). — *adj* **boot'ed** having boots on, equipped for riding. — *n* **bootee** (*bōō'tē* or *-tē'*) a short boot; an infant's knitted boot. — *n* **boots** a hotel servant who cleans boots, runs messages, etc. — **boot'black** a person whose job is to clean and polish shoes; **boot boy** same as **bovver boy**. — *adj* **boot'-faced** with an unsmiling, expressionless face. — **boot'lace** a lace for fastening boots; **bootlace tie** a very thin stringlike necktie; **boot'leg** the leg of a high boot. — *vt* to smuggle (alcoholic drink); to make, or deal in (illicit goods, e.g. alcoholic drink, records). — Also *vi*. — *adj* made or sold illicitly. — **boot'legger; boot'legging; boot'licker** a toady (*US* **boot'lick;** also *vt*); **boot'licking; boot'maker; boot'making; boot sale** same as **car boot sale; boot'strap** (*comput*) the piece of software that boots or boots up; **boot virus** (*comput*) a computer virus in the sector of a floppy disc used in booting up. — **bet one's boots** to be quite certain; **boot and saddle** the signal for mounting; **boots and all** (*Austr* and *NZ*) without reservation; **die in one's boots** to die a sudden death, not in bed; **get the boot** (*slang*) to be dismissed; **have one's heart in one's boots** to have lost courage; **lick someone's boots** to try to ingratiate oneself with someone by obsequious behaviour; **pull oneself up by one's bootstraps** to get on by one's own efforts; **put the boot in** or **put in the boot** (*slang*) to resort to physical or verbal bullying; to attack unfairly; **the boot is on the other foot** or **leg** responsibility (now) lies the other way. [O.Fr. *bote* — L.L. *botta*, *bota*.]

boot[2] *bōōt*, *vt* to profit or give advantage to. — *adj* **boot'less** without profit; useless. — *adv* **boot'lessly**. — *n* **boot'lessness**. — **to boot** in addition. [O.E. *bōt*, compensation, amends.]

booth *bōōdh* or *bōōth*, *n* a hut or small shop of simple construction; a covered stall at a fair or market; a partly-enclosed compartment, as one in which to vote, telephone, or eat in a restaurant. [O.N. *būth*, or a cognate word.]

booty *bōōt'i*, *n* spoil taken in war or by force. [O.N. *bȳti*, share — *bȳta*, to divide.]

booze *bōōz*, (*colloq*) *vi* to drink deeply or excessively. — *n* intoxicating liquor; a drinking bout. — *adj* **boozed**. — *n* **booz'er** a person who boozes; a public house (*slang*). — *adv* **booz'ily**. — *adj* **booz'ing** drinking; for drinking. — *adj* **booz'y** or **booz'ey** inclined to booze; drunken. — **booze'-up** a drinking bout (*slang*).

bop[1] *bop*, *n* short for **bebop**, of which it was a development in the 1950s. — *vi* (*colloq*) to dance to pop music. — *n* **bopp'er**.

bop[2] *bop*, (*slang*) *n* a blow. — *vt* to strike. [Imit.]

bor. *abbrev* for borough.

bora *bö'rə*, *n* a strong north-east wind in the upper Adriatic. [Venetian variant of It. *borea* — L. *boreas*.]

boracic. See **borax**.

borage *bur'ij* or *bor'ij*, *n* a blue-flowered, bristly, aromatic herb. [L.L. *borrāgō*.]

borane. See **boron**.

borax *bö'raks*, *n* a mineral found on alkaline lake shores. — *adj* **bo'ric** or **boracic** (*bo-ras'ik*) of or relating to borax or boron. — *n* **bo'rate** a salt of boric acid. — **boric, boracic** or **orthoborac'ic acid** an acid (H_3BO_3) obtained by dissolving borax, and also found native in mineral springs in Italy. [Fr. and L.L. *borax* — Ar. *būraq*.]

borazon. See **boron**.

borborygmus *bör-bə-rig'məs*, *n* the sound of flatulence in the intestines. — *adj* **borboryg'mic**. [Gr. *borborygmos*.]

Bordeaux *bör-dō'*, *n* claret, wine of *Bordeaux* region, S.W. France. — **Bordeaux mixture** a mixture of lime and copper sulphate, used to kill fungus and insect parasites on plants.

bordello *bör-del'ō*, *n* a house for prostitution: — *pl* **bordell'os**. [It.; O.Fr. *bordel*, a cabin — L.L. *borda*.]

border *börd'ər*, *n* the edge or margin of anything; the boundary of a country, etc., esp. (*cap* — also in *pl*, with **the**) that between England and Scotland; a flower-bed in a garden; a piece of ornamental edging or trimming. — *adj* of or on the border. — *vi* to come near or to be adjacent (with *on*, *upon*, *with*). — *vt* to furnish with a border; to bound. — *adj* **bord'ered**. — *n* **bord'erer** a person who dwells or was born on the border of a country. — **Border collie** a breed of medium-sized, usu. black and white, collie dog; **bord'erland** a border region. — *adj* belonging to the undefined margin between two things. — *adj* **bord'erline** marginal, doubtfully or just coming within the definition of a quality, condition, etc. — Also *n*. — **Border Leicester** a sheep of a breed developed by cross-breeding Leicesters and Cheviots; **Border terrier** a small rough-haired terrier, originally from the Borders. [O.Fr. *bordure*; from root of **board**.]

bordure *bör'dūr* or *-jōōr*, (*heraldry*) *n* a border surrounding a shield. [Ety. as for **border**.]

bore[1] *bör*, *vt* to pierce so as to form a hole; to weary or annoy with tediousness. — *vi* to form a hole or borehole by drilling or piercing. — *n* a hole made by boring; the size of the cavity of a tube; in Australia, an artesian well; a person, thing, or activity that wearies; something that causes annoyance, a nuisance (*colloq*). — *n* **bore'dom** tedium. — *n* **bor'er**. — *adj* **bor'ing**. — *n* the act of making a hole in anything; a hole made by boring; (in *pl*) the chips produced by boring. — **bore'hole** a bore in the earth's crust for investigation or for water, oil, etc. [O.E. *borian*.]

bore[2] *bör*, *pa t* of **bear**[1].

bore[3] *bör*, *n* a tidal flood that rushes with great violence up the estuaries of certain rivers, an eagre. [O.N. *bāra*, a wave or swell.]

Boreas *bor'* or *bör'i-as*, *n* the North Wind. — *adj* **bō'real** of the North Wind or the North; (with *cap*) of the northern and mountainous parts of the Northern hemisphere; (with *cap*) of a post-glacial period when the climate of Europe and North America resembled that of the present Boreal region. [L., Gr. *Bŏrĕas*.]

borecole *bör'kōl*, *n* kale. [Du. *boerenkool*, lit. peasant's cabbage.]

boric. Same as **boracic** — see **borax**.

boride. See **boron**.

born *börn*. See **bear**[1]. — **born again** having received new spiritual life (*adj* **born'-again**); **born fool, born mimic** etc., someone whose folly, mimic ability, etc., is innate; **born to be** destined to be; **in (all) one's born days** in one's whole lifetime; **not born yesterday** not young in experience, not a fool.

borne *börn*, *pa p* of **bear**, to carry.

borné *bor'nā*, *adj* limited, narrow-minded. [Fr. past p. of *borner*, to limit.]

Bornholm disease *börn'hōm diz-ēz'*, *n* a rare infectious disease caused by a virus, named from the Baltic island *Bornholm*, where it was first described.

boron *bö'ron*, *n* a non-metallic element (atomic no. 5; symbol **B**), present in borax and boric acid. — *n* **borane** (*bör'ān*) any boron hydride, efficient as high-energy fuel. — *n* **borazon** (*bör'a-zon*) a man-made substance, a compound of boron and nitrogen, hard as diamond. — *n* **boride** (*bör'īd*) any of a class of substances made by combining boron chemically with a metal. — *n* **borosil'icate** a salt of boric and silicic acids, used in making heat- and chemical-resistant glass. [**borax**.]

borough *bur'ə*, *n* a town with a corporation and special privileges granted by royal charter; a town that sends representatives to parliament; one of the local government divisions of London or New York. — **borough court** formerly, an inferior court dealing with minor offences, etc., presided over by local magistrates; **close** or **pocket borough** a borough whose representation was in the nomination of some person — common before 1832; **county borough** a borough (by Acts of 1888, 1926, 1958, respectively above 50 000, 75 000, 100 000, inhabitants) with some of the characters of a county — abolished 1974; **rotten borough** one which still returned members to parliament although the constituency had disappeared — all abolished in 1832. — The Scottish terms are grouped under **burgh**. [O.E. *burg*, *burh*, a city.]

borrow *bor'ō*, *vt* and *vi* to obtain on loan or trust; to adopt from a foreign source; to derive from another (with *from* or *of*). — *vi* (*golf*) to allow for slope or wind, esp. by putting the ball uphill of the hole. — *n* (*golf*) a slope on a green. — *adj* **borr'owed** taken on loan; counterfeit; assumed. — *n* **borr'ower**. — *n* and *adj* **borr'owing**. — **borrowed time** an unexpected extension of life, or of the time allowed for some activity; **borrow hole** or **pit** (*civ eng*) a pit formed by the excavation of material to be used elsewhere for embanking, etc. [O.E. *borgian* — *borg*, *borh*, a pledge, security.]

borsch *börsh* or **borscht** *börsht*, *n* a Russian soup with beetroot, etc. — Also **bortsch** (*börch*), etc. [Russ. *borshch*.]

borstal or **borstall** *bör'stəl*, *n* formerly, an establishment for the detention of young adult delinquents, now replaced by a range of more or less similar detention systems. [From the first reformatory of the kind, at *Borstal*, a suburb of Rochester, Kent.]

bort or **boart** *bört*, *n* diamond fragments or dust; a coarse diamond or crystalline form of carbon, used industrially for cutting or as an abrasive. [Fr.]

bortsch or **bortscht.** See **borsch**.

borzoi *bör'zoi*, *n* a dog like a huge greyhound, but with a long, soft coat. [Russ. *borzii*, swift.]

bosbok or **boschbok; boschveld.** See under **bush**[1].

bosche. See **boche**.

Bose-Einstein statistics. See **boson**.

bosh *bosh*, *n* nonsense; foolish talk. — Also *interj*. [Turk. *bosh*, worthless.]

bosk *bosk*, (*literary*) *n* a thicket. — *adj* **bosk'y** woody or bushy; shady. [**bush**[1].]

bo's'n or **bos'n.** See **boatswain**.

bosom *bo͝oz'əm*, *n* the breast of a human being; the part of the dress that covers it; (sometimes in *pl*) a woman's breasts; the imagined seat of the passions and feelings, the heart; any close or secret receptacle or location. — *adj* (*attributively*) confidential, intimate. — *adj* **bos'omed**. — *adj* **bos'omy** (of a woman) having large breasts. [O.E. *bōsm*.]

boson *bō'son*, *n* any of a class of subatomic particles whose behaviour is governed by **Bose-Einstein statistics**, according to which, under certain conditions, particles of the same kind will accumulate in each low-energy quantum mechanical state. [S.N. *Bose* (1894–1974), Indian physicist.]

boss[1] *bos*, *n* a knob or stud; a thickened part of a shaft, for strengthening or to allow attachment of other parts (*mech*); a wheel or propeller hub; a raised ornament in wood or leatherwork or (*archit*) at the intersection of ribs in a vault. — *vt* to ornament with bosses. — *adj* **bossed** embossed. — *adj* **boss'y**. [O.Fr. *boce* (Fr. *bosse*).]

boss[2] *bos*, (*colloq*) *n* a chief or leader; a master, manager or foreman; the person who pulls the wires in political intrigues. — *adj* chief; excellent. — *vt* to manage or control; to domineer over (usu. with *about* or *around*). — *adv* **boss'ily**. — *n* **boss'iness**. — *adj* **boss'y**. — *nsing* **boss'yboots** (*colloq*) a person who enjoys telling others what to do. [New York Dutch *baas*, master.]

boss[3] *bos*: **boss'-eyed** with one good eye; squint-eyed; out of true.

bossa nova *bos'ə nō'və*, *n* a style of dancing originating in Brazil, or the music for it. [Port. *bossa*, trend, tendency, *nova*, new.]

Boston terrier *bos'tən ter'i-ər*, *n* a breed of dog arising from a cross between a bulldog and a bull-terrier. [From *Boston*, U.S.A.]

bosun or **bo'sun.** See **boatswain**.

bot[1] or **bott** *bot*, *n* the maggot of a botfly, parasitic in the intestines of the horse and other animals; (in *pl*) the diseased condition caused by this. — **bot'fly** a name for various flies that lay their eggs on horses, etc.

bot[2] *bot*, (*Austr colloq*) *n* a cadger. — *vi* and *vt* to cadge. — **on the bot** cadging. [**bot**[1].]

bot. *abbrev* for: botanical, botany; bottle.

botany *bot'ən-i*, *n* the science of plants; the plants of an area; fine wool, orig. from Botany Bay, Australia (sometimes with *cap*; also *adj*). — *adj* **botan'ic** or **botan'ical**. — *n* **botan'ical** a drug made from vegetable matter. — *adv* **botan'ically**. — *n* **bot'anist** a person skilled in botany. [Gr. *botanē*, grass, fodder.]

BOTB *abbrev* for British Overseas Trade Board.

botch *boch*, *n* a clumsy patch; badly finished work. — *vt* to patch or mend clumsily; to put together unsuitably or unskilfully; to bungle (often with *up*). — *vi* to bungle. — *n* **botch'er** a bungler. — *n* **botch'ery**. — *n* and *adj* **botch'ing**. — *adj* **botch'y** marked with or full of botches.

botfly. See **bot**[1].

both *bōth*, *adj* and *pronoun* the two; the one and the other. — *adv* or *conj* as well (sometimes of more than two). [O.N. *bāthar*.]

bother *bodh'ər*, *vt* to perplex or tease; to worry or concern; to fluster; to pester. — *vi* to stir oneself; to worry or be concerned (about). — *n* petty trouble, difficulty or perplexity. — *interj* expressing irritation. — *n* **botherā'tion** (*colloq*). — *adj* **both'ersome**. — **I** or **they** etc. **cannot be bothered** I or they etc. consider it too much trouble (to do something); I or they etc. find (someone or something) annoying (with *with*). [Perh. Anglo-Irish for **pother**, or from Ir. *bodhair*, to annoy or deafen.]

bothy or **bothie** *both'i*, *n* a humble cottage or hut; a one-roomed hut or temporary dwelling; in Scotland, a barely furnished dwelling for farm-servants. — **both'yman**. [Cf. **booth**.]

botoné or **bottony** *bot'ən-i*, (*heraldry*) *adj* having buds or knobs at the extremity, applied to a cross with each arm terminated in three buds, like a trefoil. [O.Fr.]

bo tree *bō trē* or **bodhi tree** (*bō'di*), *n* in India and Sri Lanka the pipal, holy tree of the Buddhists, under which Buddha found enlightenment, planted near every temple. [Sinhalese *bo*, from Pali *bodhi*, perfect knowledge.]

bott. See **bot**[1].

botte *bot*, (Fr.) *n* a pass or thrust in fencing.

bottega *bot-tā'gä*, (It.) *n* the studio of an artist and the artist's assistants or apprentices.

bottle *bot'l*, *n* a narrow-necked hollow vessel for holding liquids, esp. of glass or plastic; the contents of such a vessel; liquor or drinking; a glass or plastic container with a teat for feeding milk to a baby; courage, firmness of resolve (*slang*). — *vt* to enclose in bottles; to preserve in bottles or jars; to block the entrance of (*fig*); to enclose, block or store up (*fig*). — *adj* **bott'led** enclosed or preserved in bottles or jars; shaped or protuberant like a bottle; kept in restraint; drunk (*slang*). — *n* **bott'leful** as much as fills a bottle: — *pl* **bott'lefuls**. — *n* **bott'ler** a person or machine that bottles. — **bottle bank** a purpose-built skip in which empty glass bottles, jars, etc. may be deposited for collection for recycling; **bott'le-blond** or *fem* **bott'le-blonde** someone whose blond(e) hair-colouring came out of a bottle (i.e. is artificial, not natural); **bott'le-brush** a brush for cleaning bottles, with bristles standing out from a central axis; a name given to various plants of a similar appearance. — *vt* **bott'le-feed** to feed milk to from a bottle rather than the breast. — **bott'le-gas** or **bottled gas** liquefied butane or propane gas in containers for use in lighting, cooking, heating, etc. — *adj* and *n* **bott'le-green** dark green. — **bott'leneck** a narrow place in a road where traffic is apt to be congested (often *fig*); **bott'lenose** a bottle-nosed toothed whale (*Hyperoodon*) or dolphin (*Tursiops*). — *adj* **bott'le-nosed** with a nose or snout shaped like a bottle. — **bott'le-o** or **-oh** (*Austr*) a dealer in used bottles (from his cry); **bott'le-opener** a device for opening bottles; **bott'le-party** a more or less improvised drinking party where each person brings a bottle. — **bottle off** to draw from the cask and put into bottles; **bottle out** (*slang*) to lose one's nerve and withdraw (from e.g. a contest); **bottle up** to enclose as in a bottle; to hold back. [O.Fr. *bouteille*, dimin. of *botte*, a vessel for liquids — L.L. *butis*, a vessel.]

bottom *bot'əm*, *n* the lowest part or surface of anything; that on which anything rests or is founded; the part of the body one sits on; the bed of the sea, a river, etc.; the seat of a chair; the less dignified or important end; the foot of a page, hill, etc.; the lower part of a ship; fundamental character or ingredient; staying power. — *adj* lowest. — *vt* to ground or base (esp. with *on* or *upon*). — *vi* to find bottom; to found, rest. — *adj* **bott'omed**. — *adj* **bott'omless**. — *adj* **bott'ommost** (*-mōst* or *-məst*) nearest the bottom. — *n* **bott'omry** (*law*) the practice of obtaining a loan (to finance a sea voyage) using the ship as security. — **bottom drawer** the drawer or any supposed place in which a young woman keeps articles for use after her marriage; **bott'om-fish** a fish that feeds on the bed of the sea, a lake, etc. (also *collectively*); **bottom line** the final line of a financial statement, showing net profit or loss; the essential factor in a situation; **at bottom** fundamentally; **at the bottom of** the real origin or cause of; **bet one's bottom dollar** to bet all one has; **bottom out** (*US* **base out**) of prices, etc., to reach and settle at the lowest level, esp. just before a rise; **from the bottom of one's heart** with heartfelt sincerity; **get to the bottom of** to investigate exhaustively; **the bottom has fallen out of the market** there has been a sudden reduction in the market demand (for something); **touch** or **hit bottom** to reach the lowest point. [O.E. *botm*.]

botty *bot'i*, *n* a child's or slang word for (a person's) **bottom**.

botulism *bot'ū-lizm*, *n* severe or often fatal poisoning by tinned or other food carrying a **botulinum toxin**, a powerful bacterial poison produced by the *Bacillus botulinus* (or *Clostridium botulinum*) organism. [L. *botulus*, sausage, from the shape of the bacteria.]

bouclé *bōō'klā*, *n* a yarn having the threads looped to give a bulky effect; a fabric made of such a yarn. — Also *adj*. [Fr., curled, looped.]

boudoir *bōōd'wär*, *n* a lady's private room. [Fr., — *bouder*, to pout, to be sulky.]

bouffant *bōō-fã*, *adj* (of a hairstyle or the style of an article of clothing) puffed out, full, bulging. [Fr.]

bougainvillaea or **bougainvillea** *bōōg-ən-vil'i-ə* or *-vil-ē'ə*, *n* any member of a tropical American genus of plants (*Bougainvillaea* or *Bougainvillea*), frequently trained over trellises, with triplets of flowers almost concealed by rosy or purple bracts. [From the first French circumnavigator of the globe, Louis Antoine de *Bougainville* (1729–1811).]

bough *bow*, *n* a branch of a tree. [O.E. *bōg*, *bōh*, an arm, the shoulder.]

bought. See **buy**.

bougie *bōō'zhē*, (*med*) *n* an instrument (orig. of waxed linen) for distending contracted mucous canals, or for calibration, applying medication, etc. [Fr., a wax candle — *Bougie* in Algeria.]

bouillabaisse *bōō-yä-bes'*, *n* a Provençal thick, spiced soup made of fish and vegetables. [Fr.]

bouillon *bōō'yɔ̃*, *n* a strong broth. [Fr.; see **boil**[1].]

Boul. *abbrev* for Boulevard.

boulder *bōld'ər*, *n* a large stone rounded by the action of water; a mass of rock transported by natural agencies from its native bed (*geol*). — *adj* containing boulders. — **bould'er-clay** a stiff stony mass of finely ground rock, usu. containing boulders and pebbles, formed as a ground moraine under land-ice.

boule. See **buhl**.

boules *bōōl*, *npl* a French form of bowls, pétanque. [Fr.]

boulevard *bōōl'vär* or *bōōl'ə-vär*, also *-värd*, *n* a broad road, walk, or promenade bordered with trees; a broad main road. [Fr. (orig. applied to a road formed on the demolished fortification of a town) — Ger. *Bollwerk*; see **bulwark**.]

boulle. See **buhl**.

boult or **bolt** *bōlt*, *vt* to sift through coarse cloth; to examine by sifting. — *n* **boult'er** or **bolt'er** a sieve; a machine for separating bran from flour. [O.Fr. *bulter*.]

bounce *bowns*, *vi* to jump or spring suddenly; to spring up or back like a ball; to burst (into or out of a room, etc.); to come back to one, as a cheque that cannot be cashed. — *vt* to cause to rebound; to turn out, eject, dismiss; to hustle, force. — *n* a leap or spring; springiness; resilience, vitality. — *n* **bounc'er** someone who, or that which, bounces; a ball bowled so as to bounce and rise sharply off the ground (*cricket*); a person employed to eject undesirable people from a club, dance-hall, etc., or to prevent them from entering. — *adv* **boun'cily**. — *n* **boun'ciness**. — *adj* **bounc'ing** large and heavy; energetic; hearty. — *adj* **bounc'y** prone to bouncing or full of bounce; lively, cocky; vigorous, resilient. — **bounce back** to recover quickly and easily. [Du. *bonzen*, to strike, from *bons*, a blow.]

bound[1] *bownd*, *pa t* and *pa p* of **bind**. — *combining form* restricted to, or by, e.g. *housebound*, *stormbound*. — **bound to** obliged to (a person, etc.); certain to (do something) (perh. partly from **bound**[4]).

bound[2] *bownd*, *n* a limit; (in *pl*) the limit of that which is reasonable or permitted; (in *pl*) a borderland, land generally within certain understood limits, the district. — *vt* to set bounds to; to limit, restrain or surround. — *adj* **bound'ed** restricted, cramped; surrounded. — *adj* **bound'less** having no limit; vast. — *n* **bound'lessness**. — **out of bounds** not to be visited, entered, etc.; in such a prohibited place. [O.Fr. *bonne* — L.L. *bodina*.]

bound[3] *bownd*, *vi* to spring or leap. — *n* a spring or leap. — *n* **bound'er** a person who bounds; a person whose moral conduct is objectionable. — *adj* **bound'ing**. — **by leaps and bounds** by startlingly rapid stages. [Fr. *bondir*, to spring, in O.Fr. to resound — L. *bombitāre*.]

bound[4] *bownd*, *adj* ready to start (for); on the way to (with *for*, or following an *adv*, e.g. *homeward bound*; also as *combining form* e.g. in *southbound*). — See also **bound**[1]. [O.N. *būinn*, past p. of *būa*, to prepare.]

boundary *bownd'ər-i* or *bownd'ri*, *n* a limit; a border; termination, final limit; a hit to the limit of the ground (*cricket*); a score for such a hit (four or six runs). [**bound**[2].]

bounden *bownd'n*, *adj* obligatory. [Archaic past p. of **bind**.]

bounty *bown'ti*, *n* generosity in bestowing gifts; the gift bestowed; money offered as an inducement to enter the army, or as a premium. — *adj* **boun'teous** or **boun'tiful** generous in giving. — *adv* **boun'teously** or **boun'tifully**. — *n* **boun'teousness** or **boun'tifulness**. — **bounty hunter** a person who hunts down wanted criminals, or anything for which a reward has been offered. — **Lady Bountiful** the charitable great lady of a district. [O.Fr. *bontet* (*bonté*), goodness — L. *bonitās*, *-ātis* — *bonus*, good.]

bouquet *bōō'kā* or *bōō-kā'*, *n* a bunch of flowers; the perfume given off by wine; a compliment, praise. — **bouquet garni** (*bŏŏk'ā gär-nē'*) a bunch or sachet of herbs used as flavouring, removed before the dish is served (Fr., garnished bouquet). [Fr. *bouquet*, dimin. of *bois*, a wood.]

Bourbon *bûr'bən*, *n* (also without *cap*) maize whisky (orig. made in *Bourbon* County, Kentucky). — **Bourbon biscuit** two chocolate-flavoured pieces of biscuit with chocolate cream between. [From the *Bourbon* royal line of France and Spain.]

bourdon *bōōr'dən*, *n* a drone bass of a bagpipe; a bass stop in an organ or harmonium. [See **burden**[2].]

bourgeois *bōōrzh'wä*, *n* a member of the middle class; a merchant or shopkeeper; a person with capitalist, materialistic or conventional values. — *adj* middle-class; conventional; humdrum; conservative; materialistic. — *n* **bourgeoisie** (*bōōr'zhwä-zē* or *-zē'*) the middle class of citizens, esp. seen as capitalistic, materialistic, etc. [Fr. *bourgeois*, a citizen.]

bourguignon *bōōr-gē-nyɔ̃*, (*cookery*) *adj* (of meat dishes) stewed with onion, mushrooms and Burgundy wine. [Fr., Burgundian.]

bourkha. Same as **burk(h)a**.

bourree *bōōr'ā* or *bōōr-ā'*, *n* a brisk dance in duple time, originating in Auvergne or in the Basque provinces; a musical composition in the same rhythm. [Fr.]

bourse *bōōrs*, *n* an exchange where merchants meet for business; a stock exchange, esp. (with *cap*) that in Paris. [Fr.]

bout *bowt*, *n* a turn or round; a spell or stint; in boxing or wrestling, a contest; a fit or attack (of an illness). [*bought*, a bend, twist.]

boutique *bōō-tēk'*, *n* a small shop, or a department in a shop, selling fashionable clothes, etc.; a small specialist business or agency operating within a larger business sphere, esp. advertising, accountancy or investment services; about 1960, used esp. for a small, expensive, exclusive dress shop for women. — *adj* small, specialist, exclusive. [Fr.]

bouzouki *bōō-zōō'ki*, *n* a plucked metal-stringed instrument, used esp. in Greece. — Also **bazou'ki** (*bə-*). [Mod. Gr.]

bovine *bō'vīn*, *adj* of or pertaining to cattle; stupid, dull. — **bovine somatotrophin** a hormone drug that increases milk production in cattle; **bovine spongiform encephalopathy** an infectious degenerative brain disease of cattle, orig. caused by cattle feed processed from scrapie-infected sheep remains. [L. *bōs*, *bovis*, an ox or cow.]

Bovril® *bov'ril*, *n* a concentrated beef extract used to make drinks, to flavour meat dishes, etc. [L. *bōs*, *bovis*, ox, cow.]

bovver boy *bov'ər boi*, *n* a member of a gang of hooligans in the habit of engaging in street fights using heavy, hobnailed boots (**bovver boots**) to kick their opponents; a troublemaker, esp. one who uses rough methods. [Prob. Cockney pronunciation of **bother**.]

bow[1] *bow*, *vi* to bend; to bend the neck or body in greeting, acknowledging a compliment, etc.; to submit (to). — *vt* to bend or incline downwards; to crush down; to express by a bow. — *n* a bending of the neck or body as a formal or respectful greeting, or to acknowledge applause, etc. — *adj* **bowed** (*bowd*) bent forward, esp. in the back. — **bow out** to withdraw or retire from a place, situation, etc.; **take a bow** to acknowledge applause or recognition. [O.E. *būgan*, to bend.]

bow[2] *bō*, *n* a piece of flexible wood or other material for shooting arrows, bent by means of a string stretched between its ends; anything of a bent or curved shape, such as the rainbow; a rod strung with horsehair, by which the strings of a violin, etc., are played; a knot with one or two loops; a looped knot of ribbons; a bow tie; a single movement (up or down) or stroke of the bow in playing an instrument. — *vi* to handle the bow in playing. — *vt* to play with a bow; to mark (for stringed instruments) which notes should be played downbow and which upbow. — *npl* **bow'-compasses** a small pair of compasses, often with a bow-shaped spring instead of a hinge. — *adj* **bow'-fronted** having a convex front. — **bow'head** the right whale, of the Arctic, with a large head and arched jaw; **bow'-leg** a bandy leg like a bow. — *adj* **bow'-legged** (*-legd* or *-leg-id*). — **bow'man** an archer; **bow'-saw** a saw with a narrow blade stretched like a bowstring in a strong bow-shaped frame (also **log'-saw**); a saw with a narrow blade stretched in an H-shaped frame and held taut by tightening a cord at the opposite end of the frame; **bow'shot** the distance to which an arrow can be shot from a bow; **bow'string** the string by which a bow is drawn; a horizontal tie on a bridge or girder. — *adj* of, for or having a bowstring. — **bow tie** a necktie tied in a looped knot, often for formal wear; **bow-win'dow** a window projecting in a curve. [O.E. *boga*.]

bow[3] *bow*, *n* the forepart of a ship — often used in *pl*, the ship being considered to have starboard and port bows, meeting at the stem. — *n* **bow'er** or **bow'er-anchor** an anchor at the bow or forepart of a ship. — **bow'-oar** the oar nearest the bow; **bow'-wave** the wave created by the bow of a moving ship; a shock wave (*fig*). — **on the bow** within 45° of the point right ahead. [From a L.G., Du. or Scand. word for shoulder; see **bough.**]

bowdlerise or **-ize** *bowd'lər-īz, vt* to expurgate a book or writing, by removing whatever might be considered indelicate, esp. to do so unnecessarily. — *n* **bowdlerisā'tion** or **-z-**. — *n* **bowd'leriser** or **-z-**. — *n* **bowd'lerism.** [From Dr T. *Bowdler* (1754–1825), who published an expurgated Shakespeare in ten volumes in 1818.]

bowel *bow'əl, n* an interior part of the body; (in *pl*) the entrails, intestines; (in *pl*) the innermost, interior part of anything. [O.Fr. *boel* — L. *botellus*, a sausage, an intestine.]

bower[1] *bow'ər, n* a shady enclosure or recess in a garden, an arbour. — **bow'er-bird** an Australian bird that makes a bower adorned with colourful feathers, shells, etc. [O.E. *būr*, a chamber.]

bower[2] or **bower-anchor**. See **bow**[3].

bowie knife *bō'i* (in U.S. *bōō'i*) *nīf, n* a strong, one-edged dagger-knife with a blade about twelve inches long. [From Colonel *Bowie*, died 1836, who popularised it, and perhaps invented it.]

bowl[1] *bōl, n* a heavy wooden ball with a bias (q.v.); (in *pl*) a game played by rolling such balls on a green towards a jack; (in *pl*) sometimes the game of skittles (ninepins) or American bowls (tenpins). — *vi* to play at bowls; to roll or trundle (esp. with *on* or *along*); to travel swiftly and smoothly in a wheeled vehicle (usu. with *along*); to pitch the ball to the batsman at the wicket (*cricket*); to be bowler. — *vt* to roll or trundle; to deliver by bowling (*cricket*); to put out by hitting the wicket with a bowled ball (also with *out*; *fig* to overcome). — *n* **bowl'er** a person who plays at bowls or bowls in cricket. — *n* **bowl'ing.** — **bowl'ing-alley** a long narrow covered place for ninepin- or tenpin-bowling; **bowl'ing-green** a smooth grassy plot for bowls. — **bowl over** to knock down; to overwhelm, thoroughly impress or delight. [Fr. *boule* — L. *bulla*.]

bowl[2] *bōl, n* a vessel, characteristically of approximately hemispherical shape, for domestic use; a round drinking-cup, more wide than deep; the round hollow part of anything; a large bowl-shaped structure, stadium, etc. [O.E. *bolla*.]

bowler[1] *bō'lər* or **bowler hat** (*hat*), *n* a stiff felt hat with a roundish brim. [Said to be name of a hatter who made it in 1850.]

bowler[2]. See **bowl**[1].

bowline *bō'lin,* (*naut*) *n* a rope from the weather side of the square sails to the port or starboard bow, to keep the sail close to the wind; (also **bowline knot**) a simple knot making a loop at the end of a rope which will not slip. [M.L.G. *bōlīne*, M.Du. *boechlijne*.]

bowser *bow'zər, n* a light tanker used for refuelling aircraft on an airfield (also with *cap*); a petrol pump (*Austr* and *NZ*). [Orig. tradename.]

bowsprit *bō'sprit,* (*naut*) *n* a strong spar projecting over the bows of a ship. [M.L.G. *bōgsprēt*, M.Du. *boechspriet*.]

bowwow *bow'wow, n* a dog (*childish* or *facetious*); (*bow-wow'*) a dog's bark. [Imit.]

box[1] *boks, n* an evergreen shrub or small tree with hard smooth yellowish wood, often used to border garden-walks and flower-beds (also **box'-tree** or **box'-wood**); its wood (also **box'wood**); extended to various other plants, esp. the Eucalyptus. [O.E. *box* — L. *buxus* — Gr. *pyxos*, the box-tree.]

box[2] *boks, n* a case or receptacle for holding anything, usu. four-sided; a compartment; a ruled-off space; an old square pew or similar enclosure, e.g. a *sentry-box, signal-box, witness-box*, etc.; in a theatre, a small enclosure with several seats; a small house or lodge, as a *shooting-box*, etc.; the driver's seat on a carriage; a light, padded shield covering the genitals (*cricket*); a pitcher's standing-place (*baseball*); part of a page enclosed within lines, etc.; the contents of a box; a present usu. of (Christmas) money to tradesmen; a fund; a stock or package of unit trusts (*finance*). — *vt* to put into or provide with boxes; to enclose, confine (often with *in* or *up*). — *n* **box'ful** as much as a box will hold: — *pl* **box'fuls.** — *n* **box'iness.** — *adj* **box'y.** — **box-cam'era** a simple box-shaped camera; **box'car** (*US*) a box-wagon; **box'-girder** a hollow, square or rectangular, girder; **Boxing Day** the day after Christmas, when boxes or presents were traditionally given to employees, etc.; the first weekday after Christmas, observed as a public holiday; **box junction** an area at a crossroads or other road-junction, marked with yellow criss-crossed lines, into which a vehicle may not move unless its exit is clear; **box'-kite** a kite composed of open-ended boxes; **box number** a number to which replies to advertisements may be sent; **box'-office** in a theatre, etc., the office at which seats may be booked; receipts from a play, etc.; ability to draw an audience; attraction as judged by the box-office. — Also *adj.* — **box'-pleat** a type of double pleat formed by folding the cloth into two pleats facing opposite directions; **box'room** a room (esp. a small room) in which boxes, etc., are stored; **box'-seat** a driver's seat on a coach; a seat in a box in a theatre, etc.; a commanding or favourable position (*Austr colloq*); **box van** a motor van with a box-shaped goods compartment; **box'-wagon** a closed railway wagon. — **the box** (*colloq*) television; **the whole box and dice** (*Austr* and *NZ*) the whole lot. [O.E. *box* — L. *buxem*, accus. of *buxis* — Gr. *pyxis*, a box.]

box[3] *boks, n* a blow on the head or ear with the hand. — *vt* to strike with the hand or fist. — *vi* to fight with the fists. — *n* **box'er** a person who boxes or is skilled in boxing; a medium-sized, smooth-haired dog of a breed, with bulldog blood, developed in Germany; (*hist*; with *cap*) a member of a Chinese society hostile to foreigners. — *n* **box'ing.** — **boxer shorts** loose shorts as worn by boxers; loose-fitting underpants for men, with an elasticated waistband and front opening; **box'ing-glove** a padded glove worn in boxing. — **box clever** to act in a clever or cunning way. [Possibly connected with Gr. *pyx*, with the fist.]

boy *boi, n* a male child; a lad; a son; a young man generally; in some countries, a native or coloured servant or labourer (as a form of address *offensive* in S. Africa); (in *pl*) a group of men with whom a man is friendly or familiar (*colloq*); a man with a particular function, skill, etc., as in *backroom boy*. — *interj* same as **oh boy.** — *n* **boy'hood.** — *adj* **boy'ish.** — *adv* **boy'ishly.** — *n* **boy'ishness.** — **boy'friend** a girl's favourite boy for the time being; a male lover in a romantic or sexual relationship; **Boys' Brigade** an organisation of boys for the promotion of habits of obedience, reverence, discipline and self-respect; **Boy Scout** see **Scout.** — **boys in blue** (*facetious*) the police; **boys will be boys** one must expect and put up with foolish or childish behaviour; **oh boy** an expression of pleasure, enthusiasm, etc. [M.E. *boi*.]

boyar *bo-yär'* or *boi'är, n* a member of the old Russian aristocracy next in rank to the ruling princes, before the reforms of Peter the Great. [Russ. *boyarin*.]

boycott *boi'kot, vt* to refuse to take part in, deal with, handle by way of trade, etc.; to shut out from all social and commercial intercourse. — *n* an act of boycotting. — *n* **boy'cotter.** [From Captain *Boycott* of County Mayo, who was so treated by his neighbours in Dec. 1880.]

Boyle's law. See under **law.**

boyo *boi'ō,* (*slang*; orig. *Ir* and *Welsh*) *n* a boy, young man. [**boy.**]

bozo *bō'zō,* (*US slang*) *n* a man, fellow, now esp. a rather dim-witted one. [Prob. Sp. dialect *boso* — Sp. *vosotros*, you (pl.).]

BP *abbrev* for: bills payable (also **B/P**); blood pressure; British Petroleum; British Pharmacopoeia.
Bp *abbrev* for Bishop.
bp *abbrev* for: (also **b/p**) bills payable; birthplace; bishop; boiling point.
BPC *abbrev* for British Pharmaceutical Codex.
BPharm. *abbrev* for Bachelor of Pharmacy.
BPhil. *abbrev* for *Baccalaureus Philosophiae* (L.), Bachelor of Philosophy.
bpi (*comput*) *abbrev* for bits per inch.
b. pl. *abbrev* for birthplace.
bps (*comput*) *abbrev* for bits per second.
Bq *symbol* for becquerel.
BR *abbrev* for: (also **B/R**) bills receivable; Brazil (I.V.R.); British Rail.
Br. *abbrev* for: Britain; British; Brother.
Br (*chem*) *symbol* for bromine.
br. *abbrev* for: branch; bridge; brother; brown.
br *abbrev* for: bank rate; bedroom; (also **b/r**) bills receivable.
bra *brä*, *n* short for **brassière**. — *adj* **bra'less** not wearing a brassière.
braaivleis *brī'flās*, (*SAfr*) *n* a barbecue party. [Afrik. *braai*, to grill, *vleis*, meat.]
brace *brās*, *n* anything that draws together and holds tightly; an instrument of wood or iron used by carpenters and metal-workers for turning boring tools; a mark ({ or }) connecting words, lines, staves of music, indicating that they are taken together, and also used as a bracket in algebra; a pair or couple (esp. of game shot); (in *pl*) a combination of straps for supporting the trousers; (often in *pl*) an appliance made of wire fitted over the teeth to straighten them. — *vt* to tighten or strengthen, to give firmness to; to tone up. — *n* **brāc'er**. — *adj* **brāc'ing** giving strength or tone. — **brace-and-bit'** a brace with the drilling bit in place. [O.Fr. *brace* (Fr. *bras*), the arm, power — L. *brāchium*, *bracchium*, Gr. *brachīōn*.]
bracelet *brās'lit*, *n* an ornament for the wrist; a handcuff (*colloq*). [Fr. dimin., — L. *brāchiāle* — *brāchium*; see ety. for **brace**.]
brachial *brāk'* or *brak'i-əl*, *adj* of the arm. — *n* **brachiā'tion** the use of arms as a supplementary means of locomotion. [L. *brāchium*; see ety. for **brace**.]
brachiopod *brak'i-ō-pod*, *n* a member of a class **Brachiopoda** (*-op'o-də*) of shelled animals related to worms, having usually two long armlike processes serving to waft food particles to the mouth. [Gr. *brachīōn*, an arm, *pous*, *podos*, a foot.]
Brachiosaurus *brak-i-ō-sö'rəs*, *n* a genus of huge lizard-hipped plant-eating dinosaurs, unusual in that their front legs were longer than their back legs; (without *cap*) a member of the genus. [Gr. *brachīōn*, an arm, *sauros*, a lizard.]
brachy- *brak-i-*, *combining form* signifying short. [Gr. *brachys*, short.]
bracken *brak'ən*, *n* the commonest British fern, abundant on hillsides, etc.
bracket *brak'it*, *n* a projecting support; a small shelf fastened to a wall; one of the marks used to enclose words or mathematical symbols, etc. (*printing*); a bracketed group; a group or category defined and demarcated by certain limiting parameters, as in *income bracket*. — *vi* to support by brackets; to enclose by brackets; to group, e.g. in an honour list, implying equality. — **bracket clock** a rectangular clock with an internal pendulum, designed to stand on a table or wall-bracket; **brack'et-creep** an inflationary phenomenon whereby a salary rise makes a taxpayer less well off by pushing him or her into a higher tax bracket. [Fr. *braguette* — Sp. *bragueta* — L. *brāca*, sing. of *brācae*, breeches.]
brackish *brak'ish*, *adj* saltish, rather salt. — *n* **brack'ishness**. [Du. *brak*, brackish.]
bract *brakt*, *n* a leaf (often modified) that bears a flower in its axil. — *adj* **bract'eal**. — *n* **bract'eate** (*archaeol*) a thin-beaten plate of gold or silver. — *adj* of metal beaten thin; having bracts. — *adj* **bract'eolate** having bracteoles. — *n* **bract'eole** a small leaf on the axis of a flower. — *adj* **bract'less**. [L. *bractea*, a thin plate of metal, gold-leaf.]
brad *brad*, *n* a small tapering nail with a side projection instead of a head. — **brad'awl** a small boring tool. [O.N. *broddr*, spike.]
brady- *brad-i-*, *combining form* signifying slow. — *n* **bradycard'ia** (Gr. *kardiā*, heart) slowness of heartbeat. [Gr. *bradys*, slow.]
brae *brā*, (*Scot*) *n* the slope bounding a riverside plain; a hill-slope. [O.N. *brā*, eyelid; cf. **brow**.]
brag *brag*, *vi* and *vt* to boast or bluster: — *pr p* **bragg'ing**; *pa t* and *pa p* **bragged**. — *n* a boast or boasting; something one boasts of or is proud of; a card game like poker. — *adv* **bragg'ingly**.
braggadocio *brag-ə-dō'shi-ō* or *-chiō*, *n* a braggart or boaster (also with *cap*); empty boasting: — *pl* **braggado'cios**. [From *Braggadochio* in Spenser's *Faerie Queene*.]
braggart *brag'ərt*, *adj* boastful. — *n* a vain boaster. — *adj* **bragg'artly**. [Fr. *bragard*, vain, bragging.]
Brahma[1] *brä'mə*, *n* a large, orig. Chinese breed of fowl, modified in Europe and America, having feathered legs. — Also *adj*. [*Brahmaputra*, whence it is said to have been brought.]
Brahma[2] *brä'mə*, *n* the first god of the Hindu triad, the creator of the Universe. — *n* **Brah'man** (*-mən*) or **Brah'min** one of the highest or priestly caste among the Hindus; (**Brahmin**; *derog*, esp. *US*) a highly cultured person. — *adj* **Brahmanic** (*-man'ik*), **Brahman'ical**, **Brahmin'ic**, **Brahmin'ical** or **Brah'minee**. — *n* **Brah'manism** or **Brah'minism** one of the religions of India, worship of Brahma. — **brahmin** (*US* **Brahman**) **bull** or **cow** the zebu, or zebu cross.
Brahms and Liszt *brämz and list*, (*rhyming slang*) *adj* pissed, drunk.
braid *brād*, *vt* to plait, intertwine; to thread, wind about or through; to trim, bind or outline with braid. — *n* a plait, especially of hair; a fabric woven in a narrow band; an interweaving, plaiting. — *adj* **braid'ed**. — *n* **braid'ing** plaiting; manufacture of braid; work in braid; braids collectively. [O.E. *bregdan*, to move quickly, flash, change colour, plait, weave.]
brail *brāl*, *n* one of the ropes used to truss up a sail (*naut*). — *vt* to haul in (e.g. a sail) by pulling upon the brails. [O.Fr. *brail* — L. *brācāle*, a waist-belt — *brācae*, breeches.]
Braille *brāl*, *n* a kind of raised type for the blind, having arbitrary signs consisting of varying combinations of six points on the following basic arrangement (⠿). — Also *adj*. — *n* **braill'er** a machine for writing in Braille. — *n* **Braill'ist** a person who can transcribe Braille. [From Louis *Braille* (1809–52), the inventor.]
brain *brān*, *n* (sometimes in *pl*) in vertebrates, that part of the central nervous system that is contained within the skull; in invertebrates, the nervous ganglia near the head end of the body; the seat of the intellect and of sensation; the intellect; (in *pl*) intelligence, common sense; a person of exceptional intelligence (*colloq*); (in *pl*) person(s) who plan and control an enterprise. — *vt* to dash out the brains of; to hit hard over the head (*colloq*). — *adj* **brained** having brains (esp. in *combining form* **-brained**). — *adj* **brain'less** without brains or understanding; silly. — *adj* **brain'y** (*colloq*) well endowed with brains; intellectual. — *n* **brain'iness**. — **brain'case** the cranium; **brain'child** an original thought or work: — *pl* **brain'children**; **brain damage** a general term covering all injury or disease of the brain, temporary or permanent. — *adj* **brain'-dead**. — **brain death** the cessation of function of the brain, thought by some doctors to be the true indication of death,

rather than the cessation of the heartbeat (also called **cerebral death**); **brain drain** the continuing loss of citizens of high intelligence and creativity through emigration; **brain fever** encephalitis, inflammation of the brain; **brain'pan** braincase; **brain stem** the stemlike part of the brain connecting the spinal cord with the cerebral hemispheres, and controlling certain major functions, e.g. the operation of the heart and lungs and the ability to be conscious; **brain'-storm** a sudden disturbance of the mind; a sudden inspiration; **brain'storming** (orig. *US*) the practice of thrashing out a problem, developing a strategy, etc. by intensive group discussion in which ideas are put forward in an extempore manner; **brains trust** a committee of experts; a number of reputedly well-informed persons chosen to answer questions of general interest in public and without preparation; **brain'-teaser** a difficult puzzle or problem; **brain'-washing** the subjection of a person to systematic indoctrination or mental pressure to make them change their views, confess to a crime, etc. — *vt* **brain'wash.** — **brain'-wave** an electrical impulse produced by the brain; a sudden bright idea; an access of cleverness. — **on the brain** as an obsession; **pick someone's brains** see under **pick.** [O.E. *brægen*.]

braise *brāz*, *vt* to stew in a closed vessel. [Fr. *braiser*.]

brake[1] *brāk*, *n* a thicket.

brake[2] *brāk*, *n* a device for applying resistance to the motion of a body either to slow it down (e.g. a vehicle brake) or to absorb and measure the power developed by an engine, etc.; any means of stopping or slowing down (*fig*); an instrument for breaking flax or hemp; a harrow; a kind of vehicle (see **break**[2]). — *vt* to slow down or stop with, or as if with, a brake. — *vi* to apply or operate a brake, esp. on a vehicle; to be slowed down or stopped by a brake. — *adj* **brake'less.** — **brake'-block** a block pressed against a wheel as brake; **brake horsepower** the effective or useful power of a motor, measured by brake applied to the driving shaft; **brake'-shoe** the rubbing part of a brake; **brakes'man** (in U.S. **brake'man**) the man whose business it is to manage the brake of a railway train; **brake'-van** the carriage in which the brake is worked; **brake'-wheel** the wheel to which a brake is applied. [From the root of **break.**]

bramble *bram'bl*, *n* the blackberry bush, a wild prickly shrub of the raspberry genus; any of various rough prickly shrubs; a blackberry (*Scot*). — *n* **bram'bling** a bird closely related to the chaffinch. — *adj* **bram'bly.** — **bram'ble-bush** a blackberry bush or thicket. [O.E. *brēmel*.]

bran *bran*, *n* the refuse of grain; the inner husks of corn sifted from the flour; the coarser part of anything. — *adj* **brann'y.** — **bran'-mash; bran'-tub** a tub of bran from which Christmas presents, etc., are drawn. [O.Fr. *bran*.]

branch *bränch* or *bränsh*, *n* a shoot or armlike limb of a tree; anything like a limb of a tree; any offshoot from a main trunk, such as a minor road, railway line, etc. (also *adj*); a subdivision, a section or department of a subject; any subordinate division of a business, subsidiary shop, office, etc. (also *adj*). — *vt* to divide into branches. — *vi* to spread out as a branch (with *out*, *off*, *from*), or in branches. — *adj* **branched.** — *n* and *adj* **branch'ing.** — *adj* **branch'less.** — *adj* **branch'y.** — **branch'-line** a subsidiary railway line. [Fr. *branche* — L.L. *branca*, an animal's paw.]

branchia *brangk'i-ə*, *n* a gill: — *pl* **branch'iae** (*-ē*). — *adj* **branch'ial.** — *adj* **branch'iate** having branchiae. [L. *branchia* — Gr. *branchion* (pl. *-a*).]

brand *brand*, *n* a piece of wood burning or partly burned; an instrument for branding; a mark burned into anything with a hot iron; a trademark; a particular class of goods (as if distinguished by a trademark); a general name for the fungoid diseases or blights of grain crops (*bunt*, *mildew*, *rust*, and *smut*). — *vt* to burn or mark with a hot iron, or otherwise. — *adj* **brand'ed.** — *n* **brand'ling** a type of worm, reddish with lighter bands, used e.g. as bait for fishing. — **brand'-image** the impression that the public has of a product or (*fig*) person; **brand'ing-iron; brand'-iron** a gridiron; an iron to brand with; a trivet or tripod to set a pot or kettle on; **brand'-name** a tradename identifying a particular manufacturer's products. — *adj* **brand'-new** completely new. [O.E. *brand*, *brond*, O.N. *brandr*, from root of **burn**[2].]

brandade *brã-däd*, *n* a Provençal dish made of salt fish cooked with olive oil, garlic and cream. [Fr.]

brandish *brand'ish*, *vt* to wave or flourish (e.g. a weapon). — *n* a waving or flourish. [Fr. *brandir*, *brandiss-* from root of **brand.**]

brandling. See **brand.**

brandy *brand'i*, *n* an alcoholic liquor distilled from wine; a glass of this. — *adj* **bran'died** heartened or strengthened with brandy. — **brandy butter** butter with brandy and sugar beaten in; **bran'dy-glass** a short-stemmed drinking-glass with a globular bowl; **brand'y-snap** a thin crisp biscuit flavoured with ginger and orig. brandy. [Formerly *brand-wine* — Du. *brandewijn* — *branden*, to burn, to distil, *wijn*, wine.]

brant-goose. See **brent-goose.**

brash[1] *brash*, *n* angular fragments of rock, which occasionally form the basement bed of alluvial deposits; clippings of hedges or trees. — *adj* **brash'y.** [Prob. Fr. *brèche*.]

brash[2] *brash*, *n* an eructation or belching of acid water from the stomach — water brash. [Prob. onomatopoeic.]

brash[3] *brash*, *adj* reckless, impetuous (*US*); forward, bumptious; bold; (of wood) brittle (*US*).

brasier. Same as **brazier.**

brass *bräs*, *n* an alloy of copper and zinc; effrontery (*slang*); money (*slang*); an article or fixture of brass; a monumental plate of brass, commonly with an effigy; (*collectively*) the brass wind-instruments or their players in an orchestra or band. — *adj* made of brass. — *adv* **brass'ily.** — *n* **brass'iness.** — *n* **brass'y** (a stroke with) a brass-soled wooden golf club (also **brass'ie;** also *adj*). — *adj* like brass; brazen-faced. — **brass band** a band of players of (mainly) brass wind instruments; a small military band. — *adj* **brass'-faced** (*colloq*) impudent, shameless. — **brass farthing** a whit; **brass'-founder** a person who casts objects in brass; **brass hat** (*mil slang*) a staff officer (with gold braid on his hat); **brass neck** (*colloq*) effrontery; **brass plate** a name plate on a professional person's office door, usu. made of brass; a symbol of membership of the professional class; **brass'-rubbing** the process of copying the design on a brass plate, etc., on to paper by laying the paper over the brass and rubbing it with coloured wax, chalk, etc.; the copy so obtained; **brass tacks** details of practical business. — **brass (someone) off** (*slang*) to make (someone) annoyed or fed up; **brassed off; top brass** those in authority at the top (also **the brass**). [O.E. *bræs*.]

brassard *bras'ärd* or **brassart** *bras'ərt*, *n* a piece of armour for the arm (*hist*); an armband or armlet; a symbolic band for the arm. [Fr. — *bras*, arm.]

brasserie *bras'ə-rē*, *n* a bar serving food; a simple restaurant. [Fr., brewery.]

brassica *bras'i-kə*, *n* a plant of the turnip and cabbage genus (*Brassica*) of Cruciferae. [L., cabbage.]

brassière or **brassiere** *bras'-*, *braz'i-er*, or in U.S. sometimes *brə-zēr'*, *n* a woman's undergarment to support or cover the breasts. [Fr.]

brat *brat*, *n* a contemptuous name for a child; an annoying child. — *adj* **bratt'y.** — **brat pack** (*colloq*; esp. *derog*) a group of successful and popular young (usu. teenage male) stars working in a creative field, esp. cinema, with a rowdy, high-spirited image; **brat**

packer a member of the brat pack. [O.E. *bratt*, prob. Old Ir. *brat*, plaid, Gael. *brat*, apron.]

brattice *brat'is*, *n* a wooden partition or lining; a partition to control ventilation in a mine; a covered gallery on a castle wall, commanding the wall-face below; in mediaeval siege operations, a fixed tower of wood. [O.Fr. *breteshe* — L.L. *bretachia*.]

bratwurst *brat'vŏŏrst*, *n* a type of German sausage. [Ger.]

bravado *brav-ä'dō*, *n* a display of bravery; a boastful threat: — *pl* **brava'dos** or **brava'does.** [Sp. *bravada*.]

brave *brāv*, *adj* daring, courageous; noble; making a fine appearance; excellent. — *vt* to meet boldly; to defy; to face (out). — *n* a brave soldier, esp. a North American Indian warrior. — *adv* **brave'ly.** — *n* **brav'ery** courage; heroism. — **brave new world** a desirable or perfect future society (from Shakespeare's *Tempest* V, i, 183), usu. used sardonically, *specif* by Aldous Huxley as the title of his novel (1932) portraying a society where scientific, etc., progress has produced a repressive, totalitarian régime rather than a utopia. [Fr. *brave*; It. and Sp. *bravo*.]

bravo *brä'vō*, *interj* well done, excellent: — *pl* **bra'vos** or **bra'voes.** [Sp. and It.]

bravura *brä-vōō'rə*, *n* spirit and dash in execution (*mus*); a florid air with difficult and rapid passages (*mus*); a brilliant or daring display. — Also *adj*. [It.]

braw *brö*, (*Northern*) *adj* fine, splendid; dressed finely. [Scots form of **brave.**]

brawl[1] *bröl*, *n* an unruly, rowdy punch-up. — *vi* to fight rowdily; to make a disturbance. — *n* **brawl'er.** — *n* and *adj* **brawl'ing.** [M.E. *bralle*.]

brawn *brön*, *n* muscle, esp. of the arm or calf of the leg; thick flesh; muscular strength; a preparation of meat made from pig's head and ox-feet, cut up, boiled and pickled. — *n* **brawn'iness.** — *adj* **brawn'y** fleshy; muscular; strong. [O.Fr. *braon*, flesh (for roasting).]

bray[1] *brā*, *vt* to break, pound, or grind small, as in a mortar. — *n* **bray'er** an instrument for grinding or spreading ink in printing. [O.Fr. *breier* (Fr. *broyer*).]

bray[2] *brā*, *n* the cry of the ass; any harsh grating sound. — *vi* to cry like an ass; to give out harsh sounds. [O.Fr. *brai*, *brait*; *braire* — L.L. *bragīre*.]

Braz. *abbrev* for: Brazil; Brazilian.

braze[1] *brāz*, *vt* to cover with, or make like, brass. — *adj* **brā'zen** of or belonging to brass; impudent. — *vt* to face (out) impudently. — *adv* **brā'zenly.** — *n* **brā'zenness** or **brā'zenry** effrontery. — *n* **brazier** (*brāz'yər*, *brāzh'ər* or *brāzh'yər*) a worker in brass. — *adj* **bra'zen-faced** shameless; impudent. [**brass.**]

braze[2] *brāz*, *vt* to join with hard solder. — *n* **brazier** (*brāz'yər*, *brāzh'yər* or *brāzh'ər*) a vessel or tray for hot coals. [O.Fr. *braser*, to burn; perh. influenced by **brass.**]

brazier. See **braze**[1, 2].

brazil *brə-zil'* or **brazil-wood** *-wŏŏd*, *n* the hard reddish wood of the East Indian sappan tree or other species of *Caesalpinia*, used in dyeing; also that of *Guaiacum*. — *n* **Brazil'ian** a native or citizen of Brazil, in South America. — *adj* from or of Brazil. — *n* **braz'ilin** a dyestuff obtained from brazil-wood. — **Brazil nut** the white, oily, edible, hard-shelled seed of a large Brazilian tree. [O.Fr. *bresil* — L.L. *brasilium*, a red dye-wood brought from the East. When a similar wood was discovered in South America the country became known as *terra de brasil*, land of red dye-wood.]

BRCS *abbrev* for the British Red Cross Society (see **The Red Cross** under **red**).

BRE *abbrev* for: Bachelor of Religious Education (chiefly *US*); Building Research Establishment.

breach *brēch*, *n* a break; an opening, or discontinuity; a breaking of a law, contract, covenant, promise, etc.; a quarrel; a broken condition or part of anything; a gap made in a fortification. — *vt* to make a breach or opening in. — **breach of promise** often used simply for breach of promise of marriage; **breach of the peace** a violation of the public peace by riot, etc. [O.E. *bryce*, *brice*, related to **break**[1].]

bread *bred*, *n* a food made of a baked paste of flour or meal, usu. with yeast or other raising agent; food; livelihood; money (*slang*). — *vt* to cover (a cutlet, etc.) with breadcrumbs before cooking. — *adj* **bread'ed.** — **bread-and-butt'er** bread sliced and buttered; livelihood. — *adj* connected with making a living or with the consumption of bread-and-butter; materialistic, practical; ordinary, routine; descriptive of a letter of thanks for hospitality. — **bread'-basket** a basket for holding bread; the stomach (*slang*; also *fig*); **bread'board** a board on which bread is cut; a board on which temporary or experimental electronic circuits may be laid out; **bread'crumb** (usu. in *pl*) bread crumbled down e.g. as a dressing (when commercially produced usu. coloured orange) for fish, etc. — *vt* to cover with breadcrumbs. — **bread'fruit** the fruit of a tree of the South Sea Islands, which when roasted forms a good substitute for bread; **bread'head** (*slang*) a drug dealer who is not an addict; someone motivated by money alone; **bread knife** a large serrated knife for cutting bread; **bread sauce** a thick milk-based sauce made with bread(crumbs); **bread'-stick** a long, thin stick of bread dough baked until crisp; **bread'-winner** the person who earns a living for a family. — **bread buttered on both sides** very fortunate circumstances; **know which side one's bread is buttered on** to know how to act for one's best interests; **on the breadline** at subsistence level, with just enough to make ends meet (from **breadline,** a queue of poor or down-and-out people waiting for free food, esp. from government sources); **take the bread out of someone's mouth** to deprive someone of the means of living. [O.E. *brēad*.]

breadth *bredth*, *n* extent from side to side; width; liberality of mind. — *adv* **breadth'ways** or **breadth'wise** in terms of breadth; broadside on. [O.E. *brǣdu*.]

break[1] *brāk*, *vt* to divide, part, or sever, wholly or partially; to rupture; to shatter; to destroy the continuity or integrity of; to interrupt (a fall, journey, etc.); to bruise or penetrate the surface of; to crush; to break a bone in, or separate the bones of; to subject, overcome or wear out; to tame or habituate to obedience (also with *in*); to cure (of a habit); to violate (e.g. a law, promise, bounds, or prison); to set aside (e.g. a will); to impart (esp. with delicacy); to make bankrupt; to degrade or cashier; to improve on (a particular time, number of strokes, etc., for a course or distance); to unfurl. — *vi* to separate; to come apart, or go to pieces, esp. suddenly; to give way; to start away; to burst forth (usu. with *out*); to force a passage (with *out* or *through*); to pass suddenly into a condition or action (e.g. into laughter, revolt, sweat, spots); to open or come into view (e.g. day, hope, a scene); (of news) suddenly to become generally known; (of the voice) to crack; to collapse; (of a wave) to burst into foam; to sever a connection; to fall out (with a friend); to change direction (e.g. a cricket-ball on pitching); to break the balls (*billiards*, etc.; see below); (of the weather) to change suddenly, esp. after a settled period; (of cloud, etc.) to disperse: — *pa t* **broke**; *pa p* **brō'ken,** or less usu. **broke.** — *n* an act of breaking; the state of being broken; an opening; a pause, interval, or interruption; a consecutive series of successful strokes (*billiards*, *croquet*); the number of points so scored at billiards; a continuous run of anything; the deviation of a ball on striking the pitch (*cricket*); an instance of breaking service (*tennis*); a chance (as in *an even break*, a fair or equal chance); a good chance. — *adj* **break'able.** — Also *n* (in *pl*) items that can be (easily) broken. — *n* **break'ableness.** — *n* **break'-age** the act of breaking or its consequences; a broken place. — *n* **break'er** a person or machine that breaks; a wave broken on rocks or shore; someone who broadcasts on Citizens' Band radio (*slang*). — *n* and *adj* **break'ing.** — **break'away** revolt, defection; withdrawal, secession; a stampede or stampeding animal (*Austr*). — *adj* having seceded, defected, etc. — **break'dance** or **break'dancing** a form of dance to rock or disco music using some routines drawn from gymnastics; **break'down** a stoppage through accident; collapse; disintegration; an analysis. — *adj* assisting after a breakdown, etc. — *n* and *adj* **break'-even** see **break even** below. — **break'-in** an illegal (and sometimes violent) entering of a building; **break'ing-point** the point at which a person, relationship, situation, etc. breaks down under stress. — *adj* **break'neck** headlong; very fast, usu. dangerously so. — **break-out** see **break out** below; **break point** a point giving one the opportunity to break service (*tennis*); (also **break'-point**) a point at which a computer program will stop running to allow checking, etc.; **break'through** a forcible passage through a barrier; the solving of a problem, esp. scientific, after much effort, opening the way to further developments; any comparable success; **break'time** (at school, etc.) recess, break between work periods; **break'-up** dissolution; **break'water** a barrier against the force of waves. — **break a record** see under **record; break a strike** see **strike-breaker** under **strike; break away** to go away or escape abruptly; to sever connection forcibly or abruptly; **break camp** to dismantle and pack one's tents, etc.; **break cover** (of e.g. a fox) to burst forth from concealment; **break down** to demolish; to crush; to collapse; to fail completely; to analyse; **break even** to avoid making a loss but fail to make a profit (*n* and *adj* **break'-even**); **break forth** to burst out, issue; **break ground** see under **ground**[2]; **break in** to make (shoes, etc.) less stiff by use (see also **break** *vt* above); **break in, in on** or **into** to enter violently; to interpose abruptly; **breaking and entering** house-breaking, illegal entry into property; **break off** to detach by breaking; to put an abrupt end to; to stop abruptly; **break out** to appear suddenly; to escape (*n* **break'-out**); to suddenly become active; to become covered with (a rash, etc.; with *in*); **break service** or **break someone's serve** to win a game in which one's opponent is serving (*tennis*, etc.); **break someone's heart** to crush someone emotionally, esp. by failing them in love; **break the balls** (or simply **break**) to open the game by striking the red ball or giving a miss, or to continue the game this way when a similar position occurs (*billiards*); to open the game by striking one of the red balls (*snooker*); **break the ice** (*fig*) to get through first difficulties, esp. restraint on first meeting; **break through** to force a passage through (a barrier); **break up** to break open; to break in pieces; to go to pieces; to put an end to; to disperse; to dig or plough up; to decay in health or faculties; **break wind** to let out flatulence from the bowels; **break with** to cease relations with, esp. to quarrel with; to stop adhering to (tradition, a habit). [O.E. *brecan*.]

break[2] or **brake** *brāk*, *n* a long wagonette; a carriage frame all wheels and no body, used in breaking in horses; an estate car. [**break,** *vt*.]

breakfast *brek'fəst*, *n* the first meal of the day. — Also *adj*. — *vi* to take breakfast. [Orig. a break or breaking of a fast.]

bream *brēm*, *n* a freshwater fish of the carp family, with high-arched back; extended to other fishes. [O.Fr. *bresme* (Fr. *brême*) — O.H.G. *brahsema*.]

breast *brest*, *n* the forepart of the human body between the neck and the belly; one of the two mammary glands in women (or rudimentary in men), forming soft protuberances on the chest; the corresponding part of any animal; the part of a jacket, etc. which covers the breast: a swelling slope. — *vt* to set the breast against; to oppose manfully; to mount. — *adj* (usu. as *combining form*) **breast'ed** having (a certain type of) breast(s). — **breast'bone** the sternum, the bone running down the middle of the breast, to which the first seven ribs are attached; **breast cancer** a malignant tumour of the breast. — *vt* **breast'-feed** to give milk to from the breasts rather than from a bottle. — **breast'-feeding.** — *adv* **breast-high'** high as the breast. — **breast'plate** a plate or piece of armour for the breast; **breast'stroke** a swimming-stroke performed breast-down, with circling movements of the arms and legs; **breastsummer** or **bressummer** (*bres'ə-mər*) a summer or beam supporting the whole, or a great part, of the front of a building in the manner of a lintel; **breast'work** a hastily constructed earthwork. — **double-** and **single-breasted** see under **double** and **single; make a clean breast of** to make a full confession of. [O.E. *brēost*.]

breath *breth*, *n* the air drawn into and then expelled from the lungs; power of breathing; life; a single act of breathing; breathing without vibrating the vocal cords (*phon*); the time occupied by a single act of breathing; a very slight breeze. — *vt* **breath'alyze** (*breth'ə-līz*) (in U.K. usu. **breath'alyse**) to test with a breathalyser. — *n* **breath'alyzer** (in U.K. usu. **breath'alyser**) a device which indicates the amount of alcohol in a person's breath, by means of a plastic bag containing alcohol-sensitive crystals which change colour when a certain concentration of alcohol vapour is blown through them. — *adj* **breath'less** out of breath; with the breath held or taken away, from excitement, interest, etc.; breezeless. — *adv* **breath'lessly.** — *n* **breath'lessness.** — *adj* **breath'y** (of a speaking voice) accompanied by much unvocalised breath; (of a singer or instrument-player) without proper breath control, causing impure sound. — *adv* **breath'ily.** — *n* **breath'iness.** — *adj* **breath'taking** astounding. — **breath'-test** a test carried out on a person's breath, by breathalyser or other device, to determine how much alcohol that person has consumed. — **below** or **under one's breath** in a low voice; **catch one's breath** to rest until one is no longer out of breath; to stop breathing for an instant; **out of breath** having difficulty in breathing; panting from exertion, etc.; **waste one's breath** to talk to no avail, profitlessly; **take someone's breath away** to leave someone breathless through astonishment, delight, etc; **with bated breath** scarcely breathing or with breath restrained out of suspense, fear or reverence. [O.E. *brǣth*.]

breathe *brēdh*, *vi* to draw in or expel breath or air to or from the lungs or other respiratory organs; to respire; to take breath, to rest or pause; to live, continue to draw breath. — *vt* to draw into or expel from the lungs; to infuse; to give out as breath; to utter softly, whisper. — *adj* **breathable** (*brēdh'ə-bl*). — *n* **breath'er** someone who breathes or lives; a spell of exercise; a rest to recover breath. — *n* **breath'ing** the act of breathing; respite; one or other of two signs used in Greek to signify presence ('rough breathing') or absence ('smooth breathing') of the aspirate. — **breath'ing-space** time to breathe or rest; a brief respite. — **breathe again** to be relieved after an anxious moment or time; **breathe down someone's neck** to keep too insistently close to someone, esp. when supervising them; **breathe freely** to be at ease; **breathe one's last** to die. [From **breath.**]

breccia *brech'yə*, (*geol*) *n* a rock composed of angular fragments. — *adj* **brecciated** (*brech'i-ā-tid*) reduced to or composed of breccia. [It.]

bred *bred*, *pa t* and *pa p* of **breed.**

breech *brēch*, *n* (almost always in *pl*, **breeches** *brich'iz*; in *NAm*, etc. also **britches**) a garment worn by men on the lower parts of the body — strictly, as distinguished from trousers, coming to just below the knee, but often used generally for trousers; the lower or back part of anything, esp. of a gun (*pl* in these senses pronounced *brēch'iz*). — *n* **breeching** (*brich'-ing*) a part of a horse's harness attached to the saddle, coming round the breech and hooked to the shafts; a strong rope attached to the breech of a gun to secure it to a ship's side. — **breech birth** or **delivery** one in which the buttocks come first; **breech'es-buoy** a life-saving apparatus enclosing the person like a pair of breeches; **breech'-loader** a firearm loaded by introducing the charge at the breech instead of the muzzle. — *adj* **breech'-loading**. [O.E. *brēc*, *pl.* of *brōc*.]

breed *brēd*, *vt* to generate or bring forth; to cause or promote the generation of, or the production of breeds of; to train or bring up; to cause or occasion. — *vi* to produce offspring; to be produced or brought forth, to originate: — *pa t* and *pa p* **bred**. — *n* that which is bred, progeny or offspring; a strain, variety or race; a kind, type. — *n* **breed'er**. — *n* **breed'ing** the act of producing; upbringing; manners. — Also *adj*. — **breeder reactor** a nuclear reactor capable of creating more fissile material than it consumes in maintaining the chain reaction; **breed'ing-ground** a place where animals, etc. go to breed; an attitude, environment, etc. which fosters or creates (esp. something considered undesirable) (*fig*). [O.E. *brēdan*, to cherish, keep warm.]

breeks *brēks*, *npl* Scots form of **breeches**, trousers.

breeze[1] *brēz*, *n* a light wind; something delightfully easy (*slang*). — *vi* to blow as or like a breeze; to go briskly and cheerily (*slang*); to do, achieve, etc. something with ease (with *through*). — *adj* **breeze'-less**. — *adv* **breez'ily**. — *n* **breez'iness**. — *adj* **breez'y** fanned with or subject to breezes; bright, lively, exhilarating. — **breeze up sale** (*horse-racing*) a horse sale at which prospective purchasers can watch (usu. young, untried) horses go through their paces over a short distance. [Old Sp. *briz*, north-east wind.]

breeze[2] *brēz*, *n* furnace refuse used in making **breeze brick, breeze blocks** and **breeze concrete** for building. [Perh. O.Fr. *brese*.]

bregma *breg'mə*, *n* the part of the skull where the frontal and the two parietal bones join — sometimes divided into the right and left bregmata: — *pl* **breg'mata**. [Gr.]

bremsstrahlung *bremz'shträ-lo͝ong*, (*phys*) *n* electromagnetic radiation produced when an electron collides with, or is deflected by, a positively charged nucleus. [Ger. *bremsen*, to brake, *Strahlung*, radiation.]

Bren *bren* or **Bren gun** (*gun*) *n* (also without *cap*) a light machine-gun. [First manufactured in *Br*no, in Czechoslovakia, and then in *En*field, in England.]

brent-goose *brent'go͞os* or **brant-goose** *brant'*, *n* a small wild goose, with black head, neck, long wing feathers and tail, the belly white, the rest slaty-grey, often confused with the barnacle goose. — Also **brent barnacle**. [Prob. *branded*, brindled.]

bressummer. See **breastsummer**.

Bret. *abbrev* for Breton.

brethren *bredh'rən*. See under **brother**.

Breton *bret'ən*, *n* a native of Brittany (*Bretagne*), France; the Celtic tongue of Brittany; (also without *cap*; also **Breton hat**) a hat with a rounded crown and turned-up brim. — *adj* of Brittany.

breve *brēv*, *n* the mark of a short vowel (as in *ĕ*), opp. to *macron*; an obsolescent note, |𝅜|, twice as long as the longest now used (the **semibreve**), but half (or in 'perfect' time one-third) as long as the obsolete long (*mus*). [L. *brevis*, short.]

brevet *brev'it*, *n* a military commission entitling an officer to take rank (temporarily) above that for which he or she receives pay. — *vt* to confer such rank on: — *pr p* **brev'eting**; *pa t* and *pa p* **brev'eted** (those who pronounce it *bri-vet'* write **brevett'ing** and **brevett'ed**). [Fr., — L. *brevis*, short.]

breviary *brēv'i-ər-i*, *n* a book containing the daily service of the R.C. Church. [L. *brĕviārium* — *brevis*, short.]

brevity *brev'it-i*, *n* shortness; conciseness. — **brevity code** a code in which a single symbol is substituted for a group of words. [Poss. A.Fr. *brevete*, shortness, influenced by L. *brevitās*, *brevitātis*, — L. *brevis*, short.]

brew *bro͞o*, *vt* to prepare by infusion, boiling and fermentation, as beer from malt and other materials, or by infusion, mixing, or boiling, without fermentation, as for tea or punch; to contrive or plot. — *vi* to perform the operation of brewing ale or beer, etc.; to be gathering or forming. — *n* a brewing; a brewage; a variety of making of a brewed beverage; a concoction, mixture. — *n* **brew'age** something brewed; mixed liquor. — *n* **brew'er** a person who brews. — *n* **brew'ery** a place used for brewing. — *n* **brew'ing** the act of making liquor from malt; the quantity brewed at once. — **brew'pub** a combined pub and small-scale brewery, serving its own real ale; **brewer's droop** (*colloq*) in a man, inability to get an erection when drunk; **brewers'** (or **brewer's**) **yeast** a yeast used in brewing (esp. *Saccharomyces cerevisiae*) also used medically as a source of the vitamin B complex vitamins. [O.E. *brēowan*.]

Brezhnev Doctrine *brezh'nev dok'trin*, *n* the Soviet doctrine which arose during the leadership of Leonid *Brezhnev* (d.1982), that the Soviet Union has the right to intervene in the internal affairs of another communist country to counter a perceived threat to socialism.

briar. See **brier**[1,2].

Briard *brē-är'* or *brē-ärd'*, *n* a large, heavy, hairy dog of a French breed. [*Brie*, district in N.E. France.]

bribe *brīb*, *n* something offered to someone to influence their judgment unduly or to persuade them to behave in a certain way. — *vt* to influence by offering a bribe; to gain over, win over, by bribery. — *vi* to practise bribery. — *n* **brīb'er**. — *n* **brīb'ery** the act of giving or taking bribes. [O.Fr. *bribe*, a lump of bread.]

bric-à-brac or **bricabrac** *brik'ə-brak*, *n* old curiosities, knick-knacks, or other treasured odds and ends. [Fr.]

brick *brik*, *n* baked clay; a shaped block of baked clay, generally rectangular; a brick-shaped block of other material, often compressed; a child's building block of wood, etc.; a good, kind person (*colloq*). — *adj* made of brick or bricks. — *vt* (with *in*, *up*, etc.) to fill with brick or bricks; to cover with brick or bricks or something that has the appearance of brick or bricks; to wall in with brick or bricks. — *n* (*colloq*) **brick'ie** a bricklayer. — *n* **brick'ing** brickwork; imitation brickwork. — *adj* **brick'y**. — **brick'bat** a piece of brick, esp. if used as a missile; a critical remark (*fig*); **brick'-kiln** a kiln in which bricks are made; **brick'-layer** in the building trade, a person who lays and builds with bricks; **brick'laying; brick'maker; brick'making**. — *adj* **brick-red'** of the colour of an ordinary red brick. — **brick'work** work constructed in brick; bricklaying; **brick'works** a factory producing bricks. — **a brick short of a load** (*colloq*) not quite sane; **drop a brick** to say or do something horrifyingly tactless or indiscreet; **like a ton of bricks** heavily and promptly; **like banging** or **knocking one's head against a brick wall** said of a laborious but unrewarding attempt, e.g. to persuade, inform, etc.; **make bricks without straw** to try to do a piece of work without the materials necessary for it; to make something that will not last. [Fr. *brique*, from the root of **break**.]

bridal *brīd'əl*, *adj* belonging to or relating to a bride or a wedding; nuptial. [O.E. *brȳdealo*, lit. bride-ale; see **bride** and **ale** (feast).]

bride *brīd*, *n* a woman about to be married or newly married. — **bride'groom** a man about to be married or newly married; **brides'maid** a girl or young unmarried woman who attends the bride at a wedding; **bride'wealth** or **bride'-price** in tribal societies, etc., a price paid (usu. in kind) to a bride's family by the bridegroom. [O.E. *brȳd*.]

bridge[1] *brij*, *n* a structure spanning a river, road, etc. giving communication across it by foot, road, rail, etc.; the narrow raised platform from which the captain of a ship gives directions; a thin upright piece of wood supporting the strings in a violin or similar instrument; the bony upper part of the nose; a support for a billiard cue; a bridge-like structure by which false teeth are borne by natural teeth or roots; in the theatre, a platform that rises above the stage; anything that connects across a gap; a type of electrical circuit for measuring resistance, etc. — *vt* to be or to build a bridge over; to connect the extremities of (a gap) (*fig*); to make an electrical connection between. — *n* **bridg'ing** the process of making, or the construction forming, a bridge; a brace or braces fixed between joists to strengthen them; provision of credit necessary for a business transaction. — Also *adj*. — **bridge'-builder** a person who builds bridges; a person who tries to reconcile hostile parties, etc., esp. in diplomacy; **bridge'-building; bridge'head** a fortification covering the end of a bridge nearest to the enemy's position; any advanced position seized in enemy territory; **bridging loan** a short-term loan, usu. for a fairly large sum and at a relatively high rate of interest, providing bridging for a business transaction, esp. house purchase. — **cross a bridge when one comes to it** not to bother about a future problem until it affects one. [O.E. *bryg*.]

bridge[2] *brij*, *n* any of various card games, for two pairs of players, developed from whist — see **auction bridge** and **contract bridge**; orig. a variety (**bridge whist**) in which the dealer or dealer's partner chose the trump suit, or no-trumps, and the dealer played his or her partner's hand as a dummy. [Earlier known as *bridge whist*, *biritch*.]

bridie *brī'di*, (*Scot*) *n* a meat turnover.

bridle *brī'dl*, *n* an apparatus put on a horse's head by which to control it; any curb or restraint; a movement expressing resentment, scorn or vanity — a throwing back of the head with a forward tilt, like a horse pulled up by the bridle. — *vt* to put a bridle on; to manage by a bridle; to check or restrain. — *vi* to make the movement described (usu. with *at* the thing taken amiss). — *adj* **brī'dled**. — **bri'dle-path** or **-road** a path or way for those riding or leading horses on. [O.E. *brīdel*.]

Brie *brē*, *n* a white, soft cheese made in *Brie*, N.E. France.

brief *brēf*, *n* a summary of a client's case for the instruction of counsel (*law*); a writ; a short statement of any kind; instructions; a lawyer, esp. a barrister (*slang*); (in *pl*) close-fitting legless underpants. — *adj* short; concise; insubstantial, barely adequate. — *vt* to issue instructions to. — *n* **brief'ing** the action, or an instance, of making or giving a brief; instructions. — *adj* **brief'less**. — *adv* **brief'ly**. — *n* **brief'ness**. — **brief'-case** a small case for carrying briefs, or for other papers, etc. — **hold a brief** (*law*) to be retained as counsel; to assume the attitude of advocate rather than judge; **hold no brief for** not to support or advocate; **in brief** in few words; **papal brief** a papal document issued without some of the solemnities proper to a papal bull. [Fr. *bref* — L. *brevis*, short.]

brier[1] or **briar** *brīr* or *brī'ər*, *n* a prickly shrub; a wild rose bush. — **sweet brier** eglantine, a wild rose with scented leaves. [O.E. (Anglian) *brēr* (W. Saxon *brǣr*).]

brier[2] or **briar** *brī'ər*, *n* the white heath, a southern European shrub; a tobacco-pipe made out of its woody root. [Fr. *bruyère*, heath.]

Brig. *abbrev* for Brigadier.

brig *brig*, *n* a two-masted, square-rigged vessel; a place of detention on board ship (*US navy*); a prison (*US slang*). [Shortened from **brigantine**.]

brigade *brig-ād'*, *n* a body of troops consisting of a group of regiments, battalions, or batteries commanded by a general officer; a band of people more or less organised. — *n* **brigadier** (*brig-ə-dēr'*) (in the British army and Royal Marines) a general officer between colonel and major-general in rank, having command of a brigade; a brigadier general (*US colloq*). — **brigadier general** (*US army*) an officer ranking above colonel and below major general. [Fr. *brigade* — It. *brigata* — L.L. *briga*, strife.]

brigand *brig'ənd*, *n* a bandit or freebooter. — *n* **brig'andage** or **brig'andry**. [Fr., — It. *brigante* — L.L. *briga*, strife.]

brigantine *brig'ən-tēn*, *n* a two-masted vessel, with the main mast of a schooner and the foremast of a brig. [Fr. *brigantin* — It. *brigantino*, pirate ship.]

Brig. Gen. *abbrev* for Brigadier General.

bright *brīt*, *adj* shining; full of light; vivid; clear; cheerful; vivacious; clever; illustrious. — *adv* brightly. — *vt* and *vi* **bright'en** to make or grow bright or brighter; to clear up; to cheer up. — *adv* **bright'ly**. — *n* **bright'ness**. — **bright and early** very early; in good time; **the bright lights** the places of entertainment in a city centre. [O.E. *byrht*, *beorht*.]

brill[1] *bril*, *n* a fish related to the turbot, spotted with white.

brill[2] *bril*, (*colloq*) *adj* short for **brilliant**, excellent.

brilliant *bril'yənt*, *adj* sparkling, glittering; splendid; superlatively bright, having a dazzling hard lustre; of outstanding or conspicuous ability or intelligence; performing or performed in a showy manner or with great display of technical skill; very good, excellent (*colloq*); brilliant-cut. — *n* a brilliant-cut diamond or other gem. — *vt* and *vi* to cut and polish the smaller triangular facets on a diamond. — *n* **brill'iance** or **brill'iancy**. — *adv* **brill'iantly**. — *n* **brill'iantness**. — *adj* **brill'iant-cut** (of gems) cut in a many-faceted form resembling two truncated cones base to base. [Fr. *brillant*, pres. p. of *briller*, to shine.]

brilliantine *bril'yən-tēn*, *n* perfumed hair oil for making the hair glossy. [Fr. *brillant*, shining.]

brim *brim*, *n* the upper edge of a vessel or of a similarly-shaped cavity; the rim of a hat. — *vi* to be or become full to the brim: — *pr p* **brimm'ing**; *pa t* and *pa p* **brimmed**. — *adj* **brim-full'** full to the brim; brimming with tears. — *adj* **brim'less**. — *adj* **brimmed** brim-full; having a brim. — *adv* and *adj* **brimm'ing**. [M.E. *brymme*.]

brimstone *brim'stən*, *n* sulphur. — **brimstone butterfly** a common yellow butterfly of the cabbage white genus. [Lit. burning stone; from O.E. *brȳne*, a burning — *byrnan*, to burn, and **stone**.]

brinded *brin'did*, **brindled** *brin'dld* or **brindle** *brin'dl*, *adj* marked with spots or streaks. — *n* **brin'dle** the state of being brindled. [See **brand**.]

brine *brīn*, *n* very salt water. — *adj* **brīn'ish** like brine; somewhat salt. — *adj* **brīn'y** pertaining to brine or to the sea; salt. — **brine'-pan** or **-pit** a pan or pit in which brine is evaporated to obtain salt; a salt spring. — **the briny** (*colloq*) the sea. [O.E. *brȳne*, a burning.]

bring *bring*, *vt* to fetch; to cause to come; to persuade or force (oneself); to bring forward, cite or institute (e.g. an argument, charge, action): — *pa t* and *pa p* **brought** (*bröt*). — *n* **bring'er**. — *n* **bring'ing**. — **bring about** to bring to pass or effect; to turn round; **bring down** to overthrow; to lower; to humble; to shoot; **bring the house down** to provoke or receive a general, enthusiastic burst of applause; **bring forth** to give birth to or produce; **bring forward** to advance; in bookkeeping (used in *pa p* **brought forward**), to transfer (a partial sum) to the head of the next column; **bring home** to prove; to impress; **bring in** to introduce; to pronounce (a verdict); **bring off** to bring away (e.g. by a boat from a ship); to rescue; to achieve or succeed; **bring on** to induce; to cause to advance; to advance the growth of (plants); **bring oneself to** to persuade or steel oneself to (do something unpleasant); **bring out** to make clear or prominent; to put e.g. a book, a play, a singer before the public; **bring round** to restore from illness or unconsciousness; to win over; **bring to** to restore to consciousness; to bring to a standstill (*naut*); **bring up** to rear or educate; to introduce to notice; to make prominent; to vomit; **bring up the rear** to come last. [O.E. *bringan*, to carry, bring.]

brinjal *brin'jäl* or *-jöl*, *n* in India, the egg-plant, or its fruit. [Sans. *vātiṅgaṇa*, through Pers., Ar. and Port.]

brink *bringk*, *n* the edge or border of a steep place or of a river (often *fig*). — **brink'manship** or **brinks'-manship** the action or art of going to the very edge of, but not into, war or other disaster in pursuit of a policy. — **on the brink of** (*fig*) on the point of, very near. [Prob. Dan. *brink*, declivity.]

brio *brē'ō*, *n* liveliness, vivacity, spirit. [It.]

brioche *brē-osh'*, *n* a type of light, soft loaf or roll rich with butter and eggs. [Fr.]

briquette or **briquet** *bri-ket'*, *n* a brick-shaped block made of coal-dust, for use as fuel; a small brick-shaped slab. [Fr. *briquette*, dimin. of *brique*, **brick**.]

brisé *brē-zā*, (*ballet*) *n* a movement in which the dancer jumps off one foot, strikes the feet or legs together and lands on two feet. — **brisé volé** (*vol-ā*, Fr. past p. of *voler*, to fly) a brisé performed with each leg alternately, completed by landing on one foot: — *pl* **brisés volés** (*brē-zā volā* or *volāz*). [Fr., of *briser*, to break.]

brisk *brisk*, *adj* full of life and spirit; promptly active; sharp, abrupt. — *adv* **brisk'ly.** — *n* **brisk'ness.** [First found in Shakespeare's time; poss. Welsh *brysg*, brisk of foot; perh. Fr. *brusque*.]

brisket *bris'kit*, *n* the breast of an animal, esp. the part next to the ribs; meat from this part of an animal. [Perh. conn. with Fr. *brechet*, *brichet*.]

brisling *bris'ling*, *n* a Norwegian sprat. [Norw., sprat.]

bristle *bris'l*, *n* a short stiff hair. — *vi* to stand erect (like bristles); to be full or thickly packed (with *with*; *fig*); to have or set bristles erect; to show rage or resistance (*fig*). — *vt* to cover (as with bristles); to make bristly; to make (e.g. bristles) erect: — *pr p* **brist'ling**; *pa t* and *pa p* **brist'led.** — *adj* **brist'led** having or fitted with bristles. — *n* **brist'liness.** — *adj* **brist'ly.** [Conn. with O.E. *byrst*.]

Bristol *bris'tl*, *n* a city in the county of Avon. — *npl* **bris'tols** breasts (see **titty**[1]; *Cockney rhyming slang* from *Bristol city*). — **Bristol fashion** in good order.

Brit *brit*, *n* (*colloq* shortening of **British**) a British person.

Brit. *abbrev* for: Britain; Britannia; British; Briton.

Britannia *bri-tan'yə* or *-i-ə*, *n* a seated female figure with a trident and helmet, representing Britain or the British Commonwealth. — **Britannia metal** an alloy, mainly tin with copper, antimony, lead or zinc or a mixture of these, similar to pewter. [L. *Britannia*, *Brittan(n)ia*, Great Britain or the British Islands.]

Britannic *brit-an'ik*, *adj* pertaining to Britannia or Britain (*archaic*, but surviving officially in *Britannic majesty*).

britches. See **breech.**

British *brit'ish*, *adj* pertaining to Britain, to its former or present inhabitants or citizens, or to its empire or commonwealth of nations. — *n* the British people; the language of the ancient Britons. — *n* **Brit'ishism** or **Brit'icism** (*-sizm*) an expression characteristic of the English spoken in Britain. — **Brit'isher** (orig. *US*) a native or citizen of Britain. — *n* **Brit'ishness.** — **British disease** extreme militancy in industrial relations, esp. excessive use of strikes; **British plate** a kind of German silver; **British Summer Time** the time adopted in Britain during the summer, one hour ahead of Greenwich Mean Time (to give extra daylight in the evenings); **British thermal unit** the amount of heat required to raise the temperature of 1 lb of water by 1° F, equivalent to 1055.06 joules. [O.E. *Brettisc* — *Bret*, a Briton, Welshman.]

Briton *brit'ən*, *n* a native or citizen of Great Britain or of any of the associated states; one of the Brythonic inhabitants of Britain before the coming of the English, or one of their present representatives the Welsh. [L. *Brittō*, *-ŏnis*, or *-ōnis*; see **Brython.**]

brittle *brit'l*, *adj* apt to break; easily broken; frail; sharp, edgy. — *n* a type of hard toffee made with caramelised sugar and nuts. — *n* **britt'leness.** — **brittle bones** an inherited disease characterised by abnormal fragility of the bones; **britt'le-star** a member of a class of echinoderms like starfish with long snaky sharply differentiated arms. [O.E. *brēotan*, to break.]

BRN *abbrev* for Bahrain (I.V.R.).

Bro. *abbrev* for Brother.

broach *brōch*, *vt* to pierce (e.g. a cask), to tap; to open up or begin; to start to speak about. — *vi* and *vt* to (cause a sailing-ship to) veer dangerously when running downwind, so as to lie beam on to the waves (also *n*). — *n* a tapering, pointed instrument, used chiefly for boring or rounding holes; a spit; (also **broach'-spire**) a church spire without parapets, consisting of a tall octagonal and a low square pyramid interpenetrating each other; a visible corner of the square pyramid in such a spire. — *n* **broach'er.** [Fr. *broche*, a spit or pointed rod.]

broad *bröd*, *adj* wide; large, spacious, free or open; widely diffused; covering a wide range, spectrum, etc.; giving prominence to main elements, or harmony of the whole, without insisting on detail; liberal-minded; slow and full-toned; strongly marked in pronunciation or dialect; coarse, indelicate; (of money) denoting the less liquid categories (e.g. M2, M3, see under **M**), such as that in an account, etc., realisable only with several months' notice. — *n* the broad part; (in East Anglia) a lake-like expansion of a river; a woman or, sometimes, a prostitute (*NAm slang*). — Also *adv*. — *vt* and *vi* **broad'en** to make or grow broad or broader. — *adv* **broad'ly.** — *n* **broad'ness.** — **broad-arr'ow** a mark (↑) used on government property, or generally. — *adj* **broad'-based** including a wide range of opinions, subjects, political groups, etc. — **broad bean** a plant, *Vicia faba*, of the pea family, or one of its large flat edible seeds which grow in pods. — *adj* **broad'brush** rough; not worked out in detail (*colloq*). — *adj* **broad'cast** scattered or sown over the general surface; dispersed widely; communicated generally, by word of mouth, pamphlets, radio, TV, or any other means; by means of broadcast. — *adv* in all directions. — *n* something sown by broadcasting; general dissemination; the sending out of material by radio or TV for reception by the public. — *vt* and *vi* to scatter, send out or disseminate freely by any means, esp. by radio or TV transmission: — *pa t* and *pa p* **broad'cast.** — *n* **broad'caster.** — *n* **broad'-casting.** — **Broad Church** a party within the Church of England favouring a broad and liberal interpretation of dogmatic definitions and creed subscription; (esp. without *cap*) a political or other group, party, etc. that is similarly liberal-minded or all-inclusive. — *adj* **broad'-church.** — **broad'-cloth** a fine, fulled woollen or worsted cloth; **broad daylight** clear, open daylight. — *adj* **broad'-gauge** see under **gauge.** — *adj* **broad'-leaf** or **-leaved** having broad leaves, not needles. — *adj* **broad'loom** (of carpet) woven on a wide loom. — *adj* **broad=**

mind'ed liberal; tolerant. — **Broad Scots** older or dialect forms of the Scottish tongue, a development of Old English; **broad'sheet** a sheet of paper printed usu. on one side only; a newspaper of large format, measuring approx. 40 × 60 cm. (about 16 × 24 inches); **broad'side** all the guns on one side of a ship of war; their simultaneous discharge; a critical attack (*fig*); **broad'sword** a cutting sword with a broad blade. — *adv* **broad'ways** or **-wise**. — **as broad as it is long** six of one and half a dozen of the other. [O.E. *brād*.]

brocade *brōk-ād'* or *brok'ād*, *n* a heavy silk fabric with a raised (or apparently raised) design on it. — *adj* **brocād'ed** woven or worked in the manner of brocade; dressed in brocade. [It. *broccato*, Fr. *brocart*, from It. *broccare*, Fr. *brocher*, to prick, stitch.]

broccoli *brok'ə-li*, *n* a hardy variety of cauliflower; (also **sprouting broccoli**) a variety of this with purple or green floret buds, and their stalks, eaten as a vegetable. [It.; pl. of *broccolo*, a sprout, dimin. of *brocco*, a skewer, a shoot.]

broch *brohh*, *n* a dry-built circular tower of the late Iron Age with galleries in the thickness of the wall, common in the north of Scotland, very rare in the south. [Scots — O.N. *borg*.]

brochure *brō'shoōr* or *brō-shoōr'*, also *bro'*, *n* a pamphlet, information or publicity booklet. [Fr., — *brocher*, to stitch — *broche*, a needle.]

brock *brok*, *n* a badger. [O.E. *brocc* — Celt. (as Gael. *broc*).]

Brocken spectre *brok'ən spek'tər*, the shadow of an observer, enlarged and often surrounded by coloured lights, thrown onto a bank of cloud — a phenomenon sometimes encountered on mountain-tops. [*Brocken*, a peak in the Harz mountains, E. Germany.]

brocket *brok'it*, *n* a stag in its second year, with its first, dagger-shaped, horns; a small S. American deer with short unbranched horns. [Fr. *brocard* — *broque*, a spike.]

broderie anglaise *brod-rē ā-glez* or *brō'də-ri ā'glāz*, *n* open-work embroidery. [Fr., English embroidery.]

Broederbond (*SAfr*) *broō'-* or *broŏ'dər-bont*, *n* an organisation of Nationalist Afrikaners, highly secret until recent years, with membership in key public and professional positions, etc. [Afrik. — Du. *broeder*, brother, *bond*, band, fellowship.]

brogue[1] *brōg*, *n* a stout shoe. [Ir. *brōg*, dimin. *brògan* and Gael. *bròg*, a shoe.]

brogue[2] *brōg*, *n* a dialectal accent, esp. Irish. [Perh. **brogue**[1], but Ir. *barróg*, hold, grip, speech impediment, is also suggested.]

broil[1] *broil*, *n* a noisy quarrel; a confused disturbance. [Fr. *brouiller*, to trouble.]

broil[2] *broil*, *vt* to cook over hot coals; to grill. — *vi* to be extremely hot, or (*NAm*) enraged. — *n* **broil'er** a very hot day; a quickly-reared young chicken sold ready for broiling (also *adj*). [O.Fr. *bruillir* or *bruller*, to burn.]

brokage. See **broker**.

broke *brōk*, *pa t* of **break**. — *adj* bankrupt, without money; hard up (*colloq*). — **go for broke** to make an all-out bid or supreme effort, or to gamble everything (in order to gain something).

broken *brō'kən*, *pa p* of **break**. — *adj* interrupted; incomplete, fragmentary; infringed, violated; humbled or crushed; dispersed, routed; (of a horse) trained to saddle or bridle; with surface interrupted; variegated; arpeggiated (*mus*); bankrupt; (of a language) spoken badly or haltingly, as by a learner. — *adv* **brō'kenly**. — *n* **brō'kenness**. — *adj* **bro'ken-down** disintegrated; decayed; ruined in character or strength. — *adj* **broken-heart'ed** crushed emotionally; greatly depressed or hurt, esp. by disappointmemt in love. — **broken home** the home of children whose parents are divorced or have separated; **broken man** a man whose life is completely shattered. — *adj* **broken-wind'ed** (of e.g. a horse) having short breath or disordered respiration.

broker *brōk'ər*, *n* a person employed to buy and sell for others; a secondhand dealer; a go-between, negotiator or intermediary; a stockbroker. — *vi* **broke** or (*US*) **brok'er** to bargain, negotiate. — *n* **brōk'erage** or **brōk'age** the business of a broker; commission for transacting business for others; a broker's office. — *n* **brōk'ing**. — **brō'ker-dealer** (*stock exchange*) since 27 Oct. 1986, a firm or person officially combining the jobs of stockbroker and stockjobber. [M.E. *brocour* — A.Fr. *brocour*. The original meaning seems to be tapster; cf. **broach**.]

brolly *brol'i*, (*colloq*) *n* an umbrella. [A clipped form.]

brome-grass *brōm'gräs*, *n* a grass (*Bromus*) strongly resembling oats. [Gr. *bromos*, a kind of oats.]

bromelain *brom'ə-lān* or **brom'elin** *-lin*, *n* an enzyme, obtained from the juice of the pineapple plant, that breaks down proteins, used medically and in skin care products, etc. [L. *bromēlia*, pineapple.]

bromine *brō'mēn*, *-min* or *-mīn*, *n* a non-metallic chemical element (atomic no. 35; symbol **Br**), a red liquid giving off an irritating, poisonous brown vapour. — *n* **brō'mate** a salt of bromic acid, $HBrO_3$. — *adj* **brō'mic**. — *n* **brō'mide** a salt of hydrobromic acid, HBr; a dull platitudinous person (from the use of bromides as sedatives); a platitude; a type of monochrome photographic print, loosely applied to other types. — *adj* **brōmid'ic** conventionally commonplace. — **bromide paper** a paper with a sensitive surface containing silver bromide, used in printing from a negative (*photog*). [Gr. *bromos*, stink.]

bronchi, bronchia, etc. See **bronchus**.

broncho. See **bronco**.

broncho- *brong-kō-*, *combining form* relating to the bronchi. — *n* **bron'cho-constrictor** or **bron'cho-dilator** any drug that causes the bronchi to narrow or expand. — *n* **bronch'oscope** an instrument which, when passed down into the bronchi, allows their examination, the removal of foreign bodies, etc. — *adj* **bronchoscop'ic** or **bronchoscop'ical**. — *adv* **bronchoscop'ically**. — *n* **bronchos'copy**.

bronchus *brongk'əs*, *n* either of the main forks of the windpipe (*anat*): — *pl* **bronch'i** (*-ī*). — *npl* **bronch'ia** the small branches of the bronchi. — *adj* **bronch'ial** pertaining to the bronchi, or the bronchia. — *n* **bronch'iole** (*-ōl*) any of the minute branches of the bronchi. — *adj* **bronchitic** (*-it'ik*) pertaining to or suffering from bronchitis. — *n* a person suffering from bronchitis. — *n* **bronchitis** (*-ī'tis*) inflammation of the lining of the bronchial tubes. [Gr. *bronchos*, windpipe; *bronchia*, bronchia.]

bronco or **broncho** *brong'kō*, (*US*) *n* a half-tamed horse: — *pl* **bron'cos** or **bron'chos**. [Sp. *bronco*, rough, sturdy.]

Brontosaurus *bron-tə-sör'əs*, *n* a popular (and former) name for Apatosaurus, a genus of lizard-hipped, quadripedal, herbivorous dinosaurs, found as fossils in Wyoming and Colorado; (without *cap*) a member of this genus (also **bront'osaur**). [Gr. *brontē*, thunder, *sauros*, lizard.]

Bronx cheer *brongks chēr*, (*US*) *n* a vulgar sound of disapproval, a raspberry. [From the *Bronx* borough of New York City.]

bronze *bronz*, *n* an alloy of copper and tin; now also applied to a copper alloy without tin; anything cast in bronze; the colour of bronze; a bronze medal. — *adj* made of bronze; coloured like bronze. — *vt* and *vi* to make or become bronze-like. — *adj* **bronzed** coated with bronze; bronze-coloured, sunburned. — *n* **bronz'er**. — *n* **bronz'ing**. — *adj* **bronz'y**. — **Bronze Age** a prehistoric condition or stage of culture (coming between the Stone Age and the Iron

Age) marked by the use of bronze as the material for tools and weapons; **bronze medal** in athletics competitions, etc., the medal awarded as third prize. [Fr., — It. *bronzo, bronzino*.]

brooch *brōch*, *n* an ornamental clasp with a joined pin fitting into a hook. [Fr. *broche*, a spit; see **broach**.]

brood *bro͞od*, *n* something bred; offspring, children or family; the number hatched, produced or cherished at once; the condition of breeding or brooding. — *adj* for breeding (as in *brood mare*, etc.). — *vt* to sit on or cover in order to breed or hatch; to hatch; to cover, e.g. with wings; to meditate moodily on. — *vi* to sit as a hen on eggs; to hang envelopingly (over); to think anxiously for some time; to meditate silently (with *on*, *over*). — *n* **brood'er**. — *n* **brood'iness**. — *adv* **brood'ingly**. — *adj* **brood'y** inclined to sit or incubate; apt to brood or to breed; feeling keen or inclined to have a baby. [O.E. *brōd*; cf. **breed**.]

brook[1] *bro͝ok*, *n* a small stream. [O.E. *brōc*.]

brook[2] *bro͝ok*, *vt* to bear or endure. [Earlier sense, to enjoy — O.E. *brūcan*, to use, enjoy.]

brooklime *bro͝ok'līm*, *n* a speedwell plant that grows in brooks and ditches. [**brook**[1] and O.E. *hleomoc*, brooklime.]

broom *bro͞om*, *n* a yellow-flowering papilionaceous shrub, *Cytisus scoparius*, or a related kind; a brush made of its twigs or of anything similar; a long-handled domestic sweeping brush. — *vt* to sweep with a broom. — **broom'ball** a team game played on ice using broom-shaped sticks and a plastic ball; **broom'stick** the handle of a broom. — **new brooms sweep clean** people newly appointed to a position work very conscientiously, or try to sweep away abuses, old attitudes, old methods, etc. [O.E. *brōm*.]

Bros. (sometimes *bros*), *abbrev* for Brothers.

brose *brōz*, *n* a food made by pouring boiling water or milk on oatmeal or peasemeal, seasoned with salt and butter. — **Atholl brose** a mixture of whisky and honey and sometimes oatmeal. [Scot.]

broth *broth*, *n* water in which vegetables and meat, etc. have been boiled, used as soup or (in *med science* often with other substances added) as a medium for culture of bacteria. [O.E. *broth* — *brēowan*, to brew.]

brothel *broth'l*, *n* a house or establishment where prostitution is practised. — **brothel creeper** (*colloq*) a man's soft shoe with thick crêpe sole. [M.E. *brothel*, worthless person — O.E. *brothen*, ruined; influenced in meaning by *bordel* (archaic), a house of prostitution.]

brother *brudh'ər*, *n* a male in relation to another person of either sex born of the same parents or (*half-brother*) parent; anyone closely united with or resembling another who is associated in common interests, occupation, etc.; a fellow-member of a religious order, a guild, etc.; a fellow-creature; a fellow-citizen; someone of the same religion as another; a kinsman (*Bible*): — *pl* **broth'ers** or **breth'ren**, the latter esp. used in the sense of fellow-members and in the names of certain bodies. — *adj* associated in any relation (also as a *combining form*, as in **brother-man'**). — *n* **broth'erhood** the state of being a brother; an association of men for any purpose. — *n* **broth'erliness**. — *adj* **broth'erly** like a brother; kind or affectionate. — **broth'er-in-law** the brother of a husband or wife; a sister's husband; a husband's or wife's sister's husband: — *pl* **broth'ers-in-law**. [O.E. *brōthor*, pl. *brēther*.]

brought *bröt*, *pa t* and *pa p* of **bring**.

brouhaha *bro͞o-hä'hä* or *bro͞o'hä-hä*, *n* fuss, excitement, clamour, or an instance of this. [Fr.; perh. from Heb.]

brow *brow*, *n* the eyebrow; the ridge over the eyes; the forehead; the edge of a hill; a pit-head; aspect, appearance (*fig*). — *vt* **brow'beat** to bear down (on) with stern looks or speech; to bully. [O.E. *brū*.]

brown *brown*, *adj* of a dark, woody, or dusky colour, tending towards red or yellow; dark-complexioned; tanned or sunburnt. — *n* a dark-reddish earthy or woody colour. — *vt* to give a brown colour to; to roast until brown. — *vi* to become brown. — *n* **brown'ie** a drudging domestic goblin (*folklore*); (with *cap*; in full **Brownie Guide**) a member of the junior section of the Girl Guides, having (until 1990) a brown uniform; (a square piece of) a kind of rich, chewy chocolate cake containing nuts (*US*); a kind of currant bread (*Austr* and *NZ*). — *n* **brown'ing** the process of making or becoming brown; a preparation for this purpose. — *adj* **brown'ish**. — *n* **brown'ness**. — *adj* **brown'y** of a brownish colour. — **brown algae** or **seaweeds** one of the main divisions of the algae. — *vt* and *vi* **brown-bag'** (*US*) to bring (one's lunch, or alcohol) in a brown paper bag or something similar. — **brown bear** the common bear of Europe and Asia; **brown bread** any dark-coloured bread, esp. that made of unbolted flour, e.g. wholemeal. — *adj* (*rhyming slang*) dead. — **brown coal** lignite; **brown dwarf** see under **dwarf**; **brown fat** heat-producing fat cells of a brownish colour, found in various parts of the body, e.g. between the shoulder-blades, thought to be activated by overeating and thus to have a bearing on weight-gain; **brown'field (site)** (a site) previously developed to some extent (as opp. to **greenfield**); **brown goods** a term covering types of electrical equipment orig. wooden-cased, such as audio and TV (as opp. to traditionally white kitchen appliances such as refrigerators and washing-machines); **brownie point** (sometimes *ironic*) a commendation for doing well; **brown'out** (esp. *US*) reduction in electrical power, etc., a partial blackout; **brown owl** the tawny owl; (with *caps*; correctly **Brownie Guider**) a woman who has charge of a group of Brownies; **brown paper** coarse and strong paper used chiefly for wrapping; **brown rice** rice hulled but not polished; **Brown'shirt** a member of Hitler's organisation of storm-troopers; a Nazi; **brown stout** a kind of dark ale; **brown study** reverie; absent-mindedness; **brown sugar** unrefined or partially refined sugar; **brown trout** a kind of trout common in Europe, dark-coloured on the back and lighter underneath. — **browned off** (*slang*) fed up; bored; dejected. [O.E. *brūn*.]

Brownian *brown'i-ən*, (*phys*) *adj* pertaining to Robert *Brown* (1773–1858), who drew attention to **Brownian movement** or **motion**, an agitation of particles in a colloid solution caused by impact of molecules in the surrounding medium.

browse *browz*, *vi* to feed on rough shoots of plants; to read in a casual or haphazard way. — *vt* to browse on. — *n* a browsing. — *n* **brows'er**. — *n* **brows'ing**. [O.Fr. *brouster* (Fr. *brouter*) — *broust*, a sprout.]

BRS *abbrev* for British Road Services.

BRU *abbrev* for Brunei (I.V.R.).

brucellosis *bro͞o-səl-ō'sis*, *n* a disease of animals, also called **contagious abortion** (q.v. at **abortion**), communicable to man as undulant fever. [Sir David *Bruce*, bacteriologist, and *-ella*, *-osis*.]

bruchid *bro͞o'kid*, *n* and *adj* (a beetle) of the family **Bruch'idae** whose larvae live on peas, beans, etc. [Gr. *brouchos*, locust.]

brucine *bro͞os'ēn*, *n* an alkaloid, less physiologically active than strychnine.

bruhaha. A spelling of **brouhaha**.

bruise *bro͞oz*, *vt* to crush by beating or pounding without breaking the surface; to pound; to mark and discolour part of the surface of e.g. the skin of a person, fruit, etc.; to hurt by unkind words. — *vi* to be injured physically or in feelings. — *n* an injury with discoloration of the human skin made by anything blunt and heavy; a similar injury to fruit or plants. — *n* **bruis'er** a person who or thing that bruises; a prize-fighter, or a big, strong, aggressive person generally (*colloq*). — *n* and *adj* **bruis'ing**. [O.E. *brȳsan*, to crush, combined with O.Fr. *brisier*, *bruiser*, *bruser*, to break.]

bruit *brōōt*, *n* something reported widely; a murmur heard in auscultation (*med*). — *vt* to spread about, report or rumour; to make famous. [Fr. *bruit*.]

brûlé *brü-lā*, (*cookery*) *adj* with a coating of caramelised sugar. [Fr., burnt.]

Brum *brum*, (*colloq*) *n* Birmingham. — *n* **Brumm'ie** a person from Birmingham.

brumby *brum'bi*, (*Austr*) *n* a wild horse.

brume *brōōm*, *n* fog. [L. *brūma*, winter.]

brunch *brunch* or *brunsh*, *n* a compromise between *br*eakfast and l*unch*. [Portmanteau word.]

brunette *brōōn-et'*, *n* a woman or girl with brown or dark hair. — *adj* (of hair-colouring) brown. [Fr. dimin. of *brun*, brown.]

brunt *brunt*, *n* the force of a blow; the chief stress or crisis of anything; the shock of an onset or contest.

brush *brush*, *n* an instrument set with bristles or similar for grooming, cleansing or for applying friction or a coating of some material; a tuft; a bushy tail; a bundle of wires, strips, or the like, making electrical contact between surfaces in relative motion; an application of a brush; a grazing contact; a skirmish; lopped or broken twigs; an assemblage of shrubs and small trees; an area covered with thickets. — *vt* to pass a brush over, groom or sweep with a brush; to touch or rub as if with a brush; to remove by a sweeping motion (with *off* or *away*). — *vi* to use a brush; to pass with light contact. — *adj* **brushed** smoothed, rubbed, straightened, etc. with a brush; (of cloth) with the surface roughened or raised. — *n* **brush'er**. — *n* **brush'ing**. — *adj* **brush'y** like a brush; covered with brush. — **brush'-fire** a fire of dry bushes, etc., which usually spreads quickly and dangerously; **brush'-off** (*colloq*) a curt or discourteous dismissal or act of ignoring; a rebuff; **brush-up** see **brush up** below; **brush'wood** loppings and broken branches; underwood or stunted wood; **brush'work** work done with a brush; a painter's manner of using a brush. — **brush aside** or **off** to ignore or dismiss; **brush up** to freshen one's appearance; to clean and tidy; to renew one's knowledge of (a subject; sometimes with *on*) (*n* **brush'-up**). [O.Fr. *brosse*, brushwood.]

brusque *brōōsk* or *brusk*, *adj* blunt and abrupt in manner. — *adv* **brusque'ly**. — *n* **brusque'ness**. — *n* **brusquerie** (*brōōs'kə-rē*). [Fr.]

Brussels *brus'əlz*, *n* the capital city of Belgium. — **Brussels lace** a fine lace with sprigs applied on a net ground; **Brussels sprout** a variety of the common cabbage with sprouts like miniature cabbages.

brut *brōōt*, (Fr.) *adj* (of wines) raw, unsweetened.

brute *brōōt*, *adj* belonging to the lower animals; irrational; rude; crude. — *n* one of the lower animals, esp. the larger mammals; a brutal person; a large articulated goods trolley used on railway stations; a very large high-intensity spotlight. — *adj* **brut'al** like a brute; unfeeling; inhuman; stupidly cruel or sensual. — *n* **brutalisā'tion** or **-z-**. — *vt* **brut'alise** or **-ize** to make like a brute, to degrade; to treat with brutality. — *n* **brut'alism** deliberate crudeness of style in art, architecture, literature, etc. — *n* and *adj* **brut'alist**. — *n* **brutal'ity**. — *adv* **brut'ally**. — *n* **brute'ness** a brutelike state; brutality. — *adj* **brut'ish** brutal. — *adv* **brut'ishly**. — *n* **brut'ishness**. — **brute fact** a fact alone, presented without explanation; **brute force** sheer physical strength. [Fr. *brut*, rough, crude — L. *brūtus*, dull, irrational.]

bruxism *bruks'izm*, *n* habitual grinding of the teeth. [Gr. *brychein*, to gnash.]

bry- *brī-* or **bryo-** *brī-ō-*, *combining form* denoting moss. [Gr. *bryon*, a moss, liverwort.]

bryology *brī-ol'ə-ji*, *n* the study of mosses. — *adj* **bryological** (*-ə-loj'i-kl*). — *n* **bryol'ogist**. [Gr. *bryon*, moss, liverwort, *logos*, discourse.]

bryony *brī'ə-ni*, *n* a wild climbing plant (also called **white bryony**) of the gourd family, common in English hedgerows. — **black bryony** a climbing plant of the yam family, similar to bryony in habit and disposition. [L. *bryōnia* — Late Gr. *bryōniā*.]

bryophyte *brī'ō-fīt*, *n* a member of one of the main groups of the vegetable kingdom, mosses and liverworts. [Gr. *bryon*, a moss, a liverwort, *phyton*, plant.]

Brython *brith'on*, *n* a Celt of the group to which Welsh, Cornish and Bretons belong. — *adj* **Brython'ic**. [Welsh *Brython*, Briton — introduced in philological use by Sir John Rhys (1840–1915).]

BS *abbrev* for: Bachelor of Science (*US*); Bachelor of Surgery; British Standard(s); Building Society; bullshit (*US slang*).

bs *abbrev* for: balance sheet; bill of sale; bullshit (*US slang*).

BSB *abbrev* for British Satellite Broadcasting, a company formerly licensed to broadcast programmes by satellite.

BSC *abbrev* for: British Steel Corporation; Broadcasting Standards Council.

BSc. *abbrev* for Bachelor of Science.

BSE *abbrev* for bovine spongiform encephalopathy.

BSI *abbrev* for British Standards Institution, an organisation which lays down minimum standards of quality and issues standard specifications for a wide range of manufactured goods.

BSL *abbrev* for British Sign Language.

BSM *abbrev* for British School of Motoring.

BST *abbrev* for: bovine somatotrophin; British Summer Time.

BT *abbrev* for British Telecom.

Bt *abbrev* for Baronet.

BTA *abbrev* for British Tourist Authority.

BTCV *abbrev* for British Trust for Conservation Volunteers.

BTEC *abbrev* for Business and Technician Education Council.

BTU *abbrev* for: Board of Trade unit (1kWh); British thermal unit (also **Btu** or **btu**).

bu. *abbrev* for bushel(s).

bub *bub* or **bubby** *bub'i*, (*US*) *n* boy (in addressing). [Cf. Ger. *Bube*, boy.]

buba *bōō'bə*, (*med*) *n* another name for **yaws**.

bubble *bub'l*, *n* a globule of liquid or solidified liquid blown out with gas; anything empty and insubstantial; an unsound or fraudulent scheme; a bubbling noise. — *adj* insubstantial; deceptive; fleeting, transient; like a bubble in shape and lightness. — *vi* to rise in bubbles; to give off bubbles; to make sounds as of rising and bursting bubbles; (with *with*) to show (great joy, rage, etc.). — *adj* **bubb'ly**. — *n* (*colloq*) champagne. — **bubble-and-squeak'** left-over potato, meat and cabbage, etc. fried together; **bubble bath** a cosmetic preparation that makes foam in bath-water; **bubb'le-car** a midget motor car resembling a bubble in its rounded line and windowed top; **bubb'le-chamber** (*phys*) a device for showing the path of a charged particle by the string of bubbles left in its track — a variant of the cloud-chamber; **bubb'le-gum** a kind of chewing-gum that can be blown into large bubbles. — *adj* **bubb'le-headed** frivolous, flighty. — **bubble memory** (*comput*) a memory composed of minute moving pockets of magnetism that represent, by their presence or absence in relation to fixed points, bits (q.v.) of digital information; **bubble pack** a type of packaging in which goods are enclosed in a transparent bubble of plastic, etc. backed by card. — **bubble over** to show uncontrolled anger, mirth, etc.; **bubble under** to hover just below a significant point or division, as on a scale. [Cf. Sw. *bubbla*, Du. *bobbel*.]

bubo *bū'bō*, (*med*) *n* an inflammatory swelling of the lymph nodes, esp. in the groin or armpit: — *pl* **bū'boes**. — *adj* **bubonic** (*-bon'ik*) relating to or characterised by buboes. — *n* **bubonocele** (*bū-*

bon'ō-sēl; Gr. *kēlē*, tumour) a hernia in the groin, with related swelling. — **bubonic plague** a form of plague characterised by buboes. [L. *būbō* — Gr. *boubōn*, the groin, a bubo.]

buccal *buk'əl*, *adj* of, towards or pertaining to the cheek; pertaining to the mouth, oral. [L. *bucca*, cheek.]

buccaneer or **buccanier** *buk-ən-ēr'*, *n* one of the piratical adventurers in the West Indies during the 17th century, who plundered chiefly Spanish ships. — *vi* to act as a buccaneer. — *n* and *adj* **buccaneer'ing**. — *adj* **buccaneer'ish**. [Fr. *boucanier* — *boucan*, a Carib wooden gridiron (used by French settlers in the West Indies).]

buck[1] *buk*, *n* the body of a cart. — **buck'board** a board or rail projecting over cart-wheels; a plank on four wheels, with a light seat to hold two persons (*US*); **buck'cart** a buckboard; a cart with boards projecting over the wheels. [O.E. *būc*, body.]

buck[2] *buk*, *n* the male of the deer, goat, hare and rabbit (cf. *doe*); a male fallow deer; a lively young man; an act of bucking; a dollar (*US, Can, Austr, NZ; slang*); a counter or marker (*cards*). — *vi* (of a horse or mule) to attempt to throw (from its back) by rapid jumps into the air, coming down with the back arched, head down, and forelegs stiff. — *vt* to throw by bucking; to resist; to cheer, invigorate, tone up (*slang*; usu. with *up*). — *n* **buck'er** an animal that bucks. — **buck'-eye** the American horse-chestnut; a native of the state of Ohio (*US*). — *adj* (*US*) flashy, showy; corny. — **buck'horn** or **buck's'-horn** the material of a buck's horn as used for handles, etc.; **buck-passing** see **pass the buck** below; **buck'saw** a large saw consisting of a blade set in an H-shaped frame tightened by a cord, used with a saw-buck; **buck'-shot** a large kind of shot, used in shooting deer; **buck'skin** a soft leather made of deerskin or sheepskin; a strong twilled woollen cloth, cropped of nap; (in *pl*) breeches or a suit of buckskin. — *adj* made of or like the skin of a buck. — **buck'thorn** a genus (*Rhamnus*) of shrubs whose berry supplies the sap-green used by painters; **buck'tooth** a projecting tooth. — **bucks (or bucks') party** (*Austr colloq*) a stag party; **buck up** (*slang*) to rouse oneself; to cheer up; to improve; to stimulate; **make a fast buck** (*colloq*) to earn some money quickly or easily but not necessarily honestly; **pass the buck** (*slang*) to shift the responsibility to someone else (from the practice of passing the marker to the next dealer in some forms of poker) (*n* **buck'-passing**); **the buck stops here** the final responsibility rests here. [O.E. *buc*, *bucca*.]

buckaroo or **buckeroo** *buk'ə-rōō* or *-rōō'*, (*US*) *n* a cowboy. [Sp. *vaquero*.]

buckbean *buk'bēn*, *n* a marsh plant (*Menyanthes trifoliata*) of the gentian family. — Also called **bog'bean**. [Flem. *bocks boonen*, goat's beans.]

bucket *buk'it*, *n* a waste-paper bin (*colloq*); a bucketful; (a glass of) alcoholic drink (*Scot colloq*); a vessel for drawing or holding water, etc.; one of the compartments on the circumference of a water-wheel; one of the scoops of a dredging-machine. — *vt* to lift or carry in a bucket. — *vt* and *vi* to drive or ride very hard or bumpily. — *vi* (of rain) to pour heavily (*colloq*). — *n* **buck'etful** as much as a bucket will hold: — *pl* **buck'etfuls**. — *n* **buck'eting**. — **bucket seat** a round-backed, often forward-tipping, seat for one in a motor car, aeroplane, etc.; **bucket shop** (*colloq*) the office of an outside broker — a mere agent for bets on the rise or fall of prices of stock, etc.; any agency operating along similar lines, e.g. one dealing in unsold airline tickets; **buck'et-wheel** a contrivance for raising water by means of buckets attached to the circumference of a wheel. — **kick the bucket** (*slang*) to die (perh. from dialect *bucket*, a beam from which slaughtered animals are hung). [Prob. connected with O.E. *būc*, a pitcher, or O.Fr. *buket*, a pail.]

buckle *buk'l*, *n* a (usu. metal or plastic) fastening for a strap or band, consisting of a rim and a tongue; a crisped, curled or warped condition. — *vt* and *vi* to connect or fasten with a buckle; to bend or warp. — *n* **buck'ler** a small shield used in parrying. — **buckle down** or **buckle to** to apply oneself zealously (to); **buckle under** to give in or collapse, under strain. [Fr. *boucle*, the boss of a shield, a ring — L.L. *buccula*, dimin. of *bucca*, a cheek.]

Buckley's *buk'liz* or **Buckley's chance** (*chäns*), (*Austr colloq*) *n* no chance at all.

bucko *buk'ō*, *n* a swaggerer, a domineering bully (orig. *naut slang*); a young lad, chap (chiefly *Ir*): — *pl* **buck'oes**. [**buck**[2].]

buckram *buk'rəm*, *n* a coarse open-woven fabric of jute, cotton or linen made very stiff with size. — *adj* made of buckram. [O.Fr. *boquerant*.]

Bucks. *abbrev* for Buckinghamshire.

bucksaw. See **buck**[2].

Buck's fizz or **buck's fizz** *buks fiz*, *n* champagne (or sparkling white wine) and orange juice. [*Buck's* Club (in London) and **fizz**.]

buckshee *buk-shē'*, *adj* free, gratuitous; spare, extra. [**baksheesh**.]

buckshot ... to ... **bucktooth**. See **buck**[2].

buckwheat *buk'wēt* or *-hwēt*, *n* a cereal used in Europe for feeding horses, cattle and poultry, in America made into cakes for the breakfast table. [Prob. Du. *boekweit*, or Ger. *Buchweizen*, beech-wheat, from the shape of the seeds.]

bucolic *bū-kol'ik* or **bucol'ical** *-əl*, *adj* pertaining to the tending of cattle; pastoral; rustic, countrified. — *n* **bucol'ic** a pastoral poem or poet; a rustic. [L. *būcolicus* — Gr. *boukolikos* — *boukolos*, a herdsman.]

bud[1] *bud*, *n* a rudimentary shoot of a plant; a protuberance that develops asexually into a new individual (*biol*); the first visible rudiment of a limb, horn, etc.; something undeveloped or immature; a young person (as a term of endearment). — *vt* to put forth as buds; to graft by inserting a bud under the bark of another tree. — *vi* to put forth buds; to come as a bud; to be in or issue from the bud: — *pr p* **budd'ing**; *pa t* and *pa p* **budd'ed**. — *n* **budd'ing**. — *adj* in bud; beginning to develop or show talent in a particular way (as *a budding poet*). — **in bud** putting forth buds; **nip in the bud** to destroy or put a stop to (something) at its very beginning. [M.E. *budde*.]

bud[2]. See **buddy**.

Buddha *bōōd'ə*, *n* a title applied to Sakyamuni or Gautama, the founder of a religion of spiritual purity; a general name for any one of a series of teachers of whom he is one. — *n* **Budd'hism** the religion founded by the Buddha. — *n* **Budd'hist** a believer in Buddhism. — *adj* **Budd'hist** or **Buddhist'ic**. [Sans. *buddha*, wise, from *bodhati*, he understands.]

buddleia *bud'li-ə*, *n* a plant of the *Buddleia* genus of shrubs and trees with showy clusters of purple or orange flowers. [Named in honour of Adam *Buddle* (d. 1715), botanist.]

buddy *bud'i*, *n* brother (*US*); a pal, one's most constant companion; someone who volunteers to help and care for a person suffering from AIDS. — Also (esp. as *US* form of address) **bud**. [Prob. from same root as *butty*, a comrade.]

budge *buj*, *vi* and *vt* to move or stir. — *n* **budg'er**. [Fr. *bouger* — L. *bullīre*, to bubble.]

budgerigar *buj'ər-i-gär* or *-gär'*, *n* a cage and aviary bird, an Australian parrakeet. — *familiarly* **budgie** (*buj'i*). [Aboriginal.]

budget *buj'it*, *n* (often with *cap*) a financial statement and programme put before parliament by the Chancellor of the Exchequer; a plan of domestic expenditure or the like. — *adj* cheap, economical, inexpensive. — *vi* to prepare a budget. — *vt* to provide for in a budget: — *pr p* **budg'eting**; *pa t* and *pa p* **budg'eted**. — *adj* **bud'getary**. — **budget account** a special bank account, into which money is paid regularly by the bank from a customer's main account and from which payment of previously agreed recurring expenses, e.g. fuel bills, T.V. licence, is made; an account with a shop, into which the customer makes regular payments to cover purchases at the shop. — **budget for** to allow for, when planning one's expenditure. [Fr. *bougette*, dimin. of *bouge*, a pouch — L. *bulga*.]

budgie. See **budgerigar**.

budo *bōō'dō*, *n* the system or philosophy of the martial art. [Jap., the way of the warrior.]

buff *buf*, *n* white leather from which the grain surface has been removed, used for army accoutrements; orig. buffalo hide; a military coat; the colour of buff, a light yellow; the bare skin; a buff-stick or buff-wheel; (in *pl*) certain regiments in the British army, from their former buff-coloured facings; an enthusiast, fan (*colloq*). — Also *adj*. — *vt* to polish with a buff. — *n* **buff'er** a person who buffs or polishes. — **buff'-leather**; **buff'-stick** or **buff'-wheel** a stick or wheel covered with buff-leather or the like, and charged with an abrasive for polishing. — **in the buff** naked. [Fr. *buffle*, a buffalo.]

buffalo *buf'ə-lō*, *n* a name for certain large animals of the cattle family; the American bison (*US*); a bison: — *pl* **buff'aloes**. — **buffalo gnat** see **blackfly**. [It. *buffalo*, through L. from Gr. *boubalos*.]

buffer *buf'ər*, *n* a mechanical apparatus for deadening the force of a concussion, as in railway carriages; a ship's fender; something or someone that acts as a protection against impact, shock or damage; a fellow, esp. a dull or ineffectual fellow (as in *old buffer*); a substance or mixture which opposes change of hydrogen-ion concentration in a solution (*chem*); a temporary store into which data can go while awaiting transfer e.g. from computer to printer, acting as an adjusting mechanism between processes of different speeds (*comput*). — *vt* to treat with a buffer. — *vi* to use, or be used as, a buffer. — *adj* **buff'ered**. — **buffer state** or **zone** a neutral country or zone lying between two others whose relations are or may become strained; **buffer stock** stock held in reserve to minimise the effect of price fluctuations or unreliable deliveries. [O.Fr. *buffe*, a blow.]

buffet[1] *buf'it*, *n* a blow with the fist; a slap; a stroke, esp. heavy and repeated, as of the wind, fortune, etc. — *vt* to strike with the hand or fist; to knock or push about roughly, to batter; to struggle against, beat back. — *vi* to deal heavy blows. — *n* **buff'eting** a striking with the hand, boxing; contention; repeated blows; irregular oscillation of any part of an aircraft, caused and maintained by an eddying wake from some other part. [O.Fr. *buffet* — *buffe*, a blow, esp. on the cheek.]

buffet[2] *bōōf'ā*, *n* a refreshment counter or bar; a meal set out on a table, etc., from which the diners serve themselves; (*buf'it*) a sideboard. — Also *adj*. — **buffet car** (*bōōf'ā kär*) a railway coach with light meal or snack service. [Fr. *buffet*.]

buffoon *buf-ōōn'*, *n* a person who sets out to amuse others by jests, grimaces, etc.; a fool. — *n* **buffoon'ery**. [Fr. *bouffon* — It. *buffone*; *buffare*, to jest.]

bug[1] *bug*, *n* a name applied loosely to certain insects, and specifically to one that infests houses and beds; any insect or small animal (*US*); a disease-germ; a viral disease (*colloq*); a craze, obsession; an enthusiast; a snag, a defect, a fault (*colloq*); a hidden microphone; a light vehicle stripped of everything inessential; a lunar excursion module (see **module**). — *vt* to plant a concealed listening device in; to annoy, irritate (*slang*). — *adj* **bugged**. — *n* and *adj* **bugg'ing**. [Perh. O.E. *budda*, beetle.]

bug[2] *bug*, (*US*) *vi* to start or bulge: — *pr p* **bugg'ing**; *pa t* and *pa p* **bugged**. — *adj* **bug'-eyed** with eyes protruding in astonishment, etc.

bug[3] *bug*, (*US*) *vi* to leave. — **bug out** to desert, esp. in panic. [Perh. from **bugger (off)**.]

bugbear *bug'bār*, *n* an object of terror, dislike, or annoyance. [M.E. *bugge*, prob. Welsh *bwg*, a hobgoblin.]

bugger *bug'ər*, *n* someone guilty of bestiality and unnatural, i.e. anal, sexual intercourse; a term of abuse for a man or child, often quite colourless or even kindly (*vulg colloq*); a rogue, scamp — applied inoffensively to child or animal (*US*); a difficult or unpleasant task, etc. (*vulg colloq*). — *vt* to have unnatural sexual, i.e. anal, intercourse with; (the following all *vulg colloq*) to exhaust; to frustrate, ruin the plans of; to spoil, prevent success in (also with *up*). — *vi* (with *off*; *vulg colloq*) to go away quickly. — *interj* (*vulg colloq*) used to express annoyance. — *n* **bugg'ery** (*law*) bestiality, unnatural sexual, esp. anal, intercourse. — **bugger about** (*vulg colloq*) to potter about, do nothing useful; **bugger all** (*vulg colloq*) none, nothing. [Fr. *bougre* — L. *Bulgarus*, Bulgarian.]

buggy *bug'i*, *n* a light carriage or gig of several kinds — in North America, a one-horse, four-wheeled vehicle with one seat, — in England, two-wheeled, — in India, hooded; a child's push-chair; a light, very basic vehicle.

bugle *bū'gl*, *n* (also **bū'gle-horn**) a horn used as a drinking vessel or hunting-horn: a treble instrument with or without keys, usu. made of copper, like the trumpet, but having the bell less expanded and the tube shorter and more conical, used more for signalling than music. — *vi* to sound a bugle. — *n* **bū'gler** a person who plays the bugle. — *n* **bū'glet** a small bugle. — **bū'gle-band**; **bū'gle-call**. [O.Fr. *bugle* — L. *būculus*, dimin. of *bōs*, an ox.]

bugloss *bū'glos*, *n* a name for several plants of the borage family. [Fr. *buglosse* — L. *būglōssa* — Gr. *bouglōssos* — *bous*, ox, *glōssa*, tongue.]

bugong. See **bogong**.

buhl *bōōl*, *n* a complicated form of inlay, gold, silver, or brass and pewter, ivory and mother-of-pearl in tortoiseshell, etc., forming panels for furniture decoration; furniture decorated in this way. — Also **boulle** or **boule**. [From Charles André *Boulle* (1642–1732), a cabinetmaker in the service of Louis XIV.]

build *bild*, *vt* to erect (e.g. a house, bridge, etc.); to construct (e.g. a railway, etc.); to establish (*fig*); to base (e.g. hopes) (on); to form (combinations) (*cards*). — *vi* to depend (with *on* or *upon*): — *pa t* and *pa p* **built**. — *n* form; make. — *n* **build'er** a person who builds, or controls the work of building. — *n* **build'ing** the art or process of erecting houses, etc.; a substantial structure for giving shelter, e.g. a house, office-block; used as a collective noun for a gathering of rooks. — *adj* **built** formed or shaped. — **builders' merchant** a trader who supplies building materials; **build'ing-block** a hollow or solid block made of concrete or other material, larger than a brick; **building society** a society that advances money to its members as mortgages for homes, and provides interest-bearing accounts for savers; **build'-up** a building up, increasing, strengthening; the amount of this; a working up of favourable publicity; preliminaries leading up to a climax in a story, speech, etc. — *adj* **built'-in** formed as part of a main structure, esp. if recessed; present as part of one's genetic inheritance; inherent; included (as part of a deal, etc.); very firmly fixed. — *adj* **built'-up** (of an area) covered with buildings. — **build in** to enclose or fix by building; **build up** to close up (e.g. a door) by building work; to cover with buildings; to create, or be created, or to increase, gradually (e.g. a concentration of troops, a reputation, voltage, tension); to put together from parts already made; to edify spiritually. [O.E. *gebyld*, past p. of an assumed *byldan*, to build — *bold*, a dwelling.]

bulb *bulb*, *n* a subterranean bud with swollen leaf-bases in which reserve materials are stored; a protuberance or swelling; part of the brain called the medulla oblongata (*med*); a dilatation or expansion of a glass tube; the glass of an electric light. — *vi* to form bulbs; to bulge out or swell. — *adj* **bulb'ar.** — *adj* **bulbed.** — *adj* **bulbif'erous** (of a plant) producing bulbs. — *adj* **bulb'ous** bulging; swollen. [L. *bulbus* — Gr. *bolbos*, an onion.]

bulbul *bo͝ol'bo͝ol*, *n* any bird of the family *Pycnonotidae* of Africa and Asia; in Persian poetry, the nightingale; a sweet singer. [Ar.]

Bulg. *abbrev* for Bulgaria or Bulgarian.

Bulgarian *bul-gā'ri-ən*, *adj* of *Bulgaria* or its language. — *n* a native or citizen of Bulgaria; the Slavonic language of Bulgaria.

bulge *bulj*, *n* a protuberance, swelling; a temporary increase. — *vi* and *vt* to swell out. — *adj* **bul'ging** swelling out; overfull. — *adj* **bul'gy.** [O.Fr. *boulge*, prob. L. *bulga*, a leather knapsack: a Gallic word; cf. **bilge.**]

bulgur or **bulghur** *bo͝ol'* or *bul'gər*, *n* a form of cooked, broken wheat. — Also **bulg(h)ur wheat.** [Turk.]

bulimia *bū-lim'i-ə*, (*med*) *n* abnormal hunger or appetite (also *fig*); bulimia nervosa. — *adj* and *n* **bulim'ic.** — **bulimia nervosa** (*nər-vō'sə* or *-zə*) a pathological condition, an eating disorder in which binge eating is followed by depression and guilt, self-induced vomiting and purging, etc. [Gr. *boulīmiā* — *bous*, ox, *līmos*, hunger.]

bulk *bulk*, *n* a cargo; the belly, trunk, or body; a hull or hold; volume or size; great size; the greater part; any huge body or structure; mass. — *vi* to be in bulk; to fill out (with *out* or *up*); to be of weight or importance. — *vt* to put or hold in bulk; (often with *out* but also with *up*) to cause to swell, make greater in size. — *adv* **bulk'ily.** — *n* **bulk'iness.** — *adj* **bulk'y** having bulk; filling much space; unwieldy. — **bulk buying** large-scale purchase of a commodity, esp. on preferential terms and by a single buyer on behalf of a body of consumers; guaranteed purchase by one country of all or most of another's output of a commodity; **bulk carrier** a vessel carrying cargo, such as grain, that is not in the form of separate packages. — **bulk large** to be prominent or intrusive; **load in bulk** to put cargo in loose; **sell in bulk** to sell cargo as it is in the hold; to sell in large quantities. [Prob. (hypothetical) O.N. *bulki*, heap or cargo, confused with O.E. *buc*, belly.]

bulkhead *bulk'hed*, *n* any of the partitions separating one part of the interior of a ship, aircraft, etc. from another; a protecting barrier or structure.

bull[1] *bo͝ol*, *n* a male whale, walrus, elephant, moose, etc.; an uncastrated male of the cattle family; (with *cap*) Taurus (*astron*); a person who seeks to raise the price of stocks, and speculates on a rise (opp. to *bear*); a bull's-eye, (a shot that hits) the centre of a target; nonsense (*slang*); spit and polish (*mil slang*). — *adj* male; massive; favourable to the bulls, rising (*stock exchange*). — *vt* to try to raise the price of; to polish (*mil slang*). — *vi* to brag (*slang*); to talk rubbish (*slang*). — *adj* **bull'ish** like a bull; obstinate; inclining towards rising prices (*stock exchange*); optimistic, upbeat (*colloq*). — *adv* **bull'ishly.** — *n* **bull'ishness.** — *n* **bull'ock** an ox or castrated bull. — **bull ant** short for **bulldog ant; bull'bar** (*Austr*) a strong metal bar or frame on the front of a vehicle to protect it from damage if struck by an animal; **bull'-calf** a male calf; a stupid fellow, a lout; **bull'dog** a breed of dogs of great courage, formerly used for baiting bulls; a person of obstinate courage. — *vt* to attack like a bulldog; to wrestle with and throw (a steer, etc.) (*US*). — **bulldog ant** a black or red Australian ant with a vicious sting; **bulldog clip** a clip with a spring, used for holding papers, etc. together or to a board; **bull'dust** euph. for **bullshit** (*Austr* and *NZ*); fine dust, as on outback roads (*Austr*); **bull'fight** a popular spectacle in Spain, Portugal, Southern France, and Latin America, in which a bull is goaded to fury by mounted men armed with lances, and killed by a specially skilful swordsman; **bull'fighter; bull'fighting; bull'finch** a plump red-breasted finch; (perh. for *bull-fence*) a kind of high, thick hedge hard to jump; **bull'frog** a large frog; **bull'head** the miller's thumb, a small river fish with a large, flat head; extended to various similar fishes. — *adj* **bull'-headed** impetuous and obstinate. — **bull'-horn** a loudhailer; **bull'-mastiff** a cross between the bulldog and the mastiff, the mastiff strain predominating. — *adj* **bull'-necked** thick-necked. — *adj* **bull'-nosed** with a blunt nose, like a bull's. — **bull'-pen** a pen for a bull; a similar enclosure for prisoners (*US*); a part of the ground where pitchers warm up (*baseball*); **bull point** (*colloq*) a key point, a salient point; **bull'-ring** the enclosure for bull-fighting or bull-baiting; a ring for a bull's nose; **bull'-roarer** an oblong slip of wood, whirled at the end of a string to give a loud whirring noise; **bull session** (esp. *US*) an informal discussion esp. between men; **bull's'-eye** the central boss formed in making a sheet of spun glass; a thick lens, or round piece of glass, as in a lantern; a round opening or window; the centre of a target; a shot that hits it; a big round hard peppermint sweet; **bull'shit** (*vulg slang*) nonsense; deceptive humbug. — *vi* and *vt* to talk nonsense (to), often with the intention of deceiving. — **bull'shitter; bull's wool** (*Austr colloq*) any fibrous bark; euph. for **bullshit; bull=terr'ier** a breed of dog with a smooth, short-haired coat, orig. a cross between bulldog and terrier; **bull'whip** or **bull'whack** a heavy short-handled whip. — **a bull in a china shop** a person who lacks the delicacy that the situation calls for; **bull into** to plunge hastily into; **take the bull by the horns** to grapple boldly with a danger or difficulty. [M.E. *bole*, prob. O.N. *bole, boli.*]

bull[2] *bo͝ol*, *n* an edict of the pope with his seal affixed. [L. *bulla*, a knob, a leaden seal.]

bulla *bo͝ol'ə*, *n* a seal attached to a document. — *adj* **bull'ate** blistered or puckered; bubble-like; knobbed; inflated. [L. *bulla.*]

bullace *bo͝ol'is*, *n* a shrub closely allied to the sloe. [Cf. O.Fr. *beloce.*]

bullate. See **bulla.**

bulldoze *bo͝ol'dōz*, *vt* to intimidate; to bully; to level and clear by bulldozer; to demolish as if by bulldozer; to force or push through against opposition (*fig*). — *n* **bull'dozer** a person who bulldozes; a powerful, heavy tractor with a vertical blade at the front used for levelling and clearing land.

bullet *bo͝ol'it*, *n* a projectile, now esp. a round or conical one fired from any kind of small-arm; a plumb or sinker in fishing. — **bull'et-head** a round head; an obstinate fellow (*US*). — *adj* **bull'et=headed.** — *adj* **bull'et-proof** proof against bullets. [Fr. *boulette*, dimin. of *boule*, a ball — L. *bulla.*]

bulletin *bo͝ol'i-tin*, *n* an official report of public news, or of a patient's progress; a periodical publication of a society, etc. — **bulletin board** a noticeboard, esp. (*comput*) an electronic one containing messages, advertisements, and interchange of information. [Fr., — It. *bullettino.*]

bullet-tree or **bulletrie.** Same as **bully-tree.**

bullion *bo͝ol'yən*, *n* gold or silver in the mass and uncoined; occasionally, precious metal, coined and uncoined. [Perh. conn. with L.L. *bulliō, -ōnis*, a boiling.]

bullock. See **bull**[1].

bully[1] *bo͝ol'i*, *n* a cruel tormentor of the weak. — *adj* excellent. — *vt* to oppress cruelly; to threaten in a noisy way: — *pr p* **bull'ying**; *pa t* and *pa p* **bull'ied**. — *interj* good. — **bull'y-boy** a ruffian hired to beat or intimidate someone. — **bully for you** (or **him**, etc.; often *ironic*) good for you (or him, etc.). [Perh. Du. *boel*, a lover.]

bully[2] *bŏŏl'i* or **bully-beef** *bŏŏl'i-bēf*, *n* canned or pickled beef. [Prob. Fr. *bouilli*, boiled beef, influenced by **bull**[1].]

bully-off *bŏŏl'i-of*, *n* and *v* the old term for **pass-back** in hockey.

bullyrag *bŏŏl'i-rag*, *vt* to assail with abusive language or horseplay; to badger.

bully-tree *bŏŏl'i-trē*, *n* a name for several West Indian trees of the *Sapota* genus yielding good timber, edible fruits, and balata. — Also **bull'et-tree**, **bull'etrie** and **boll'etrie**. [Perh. from **bullace**; perh. from **balata**.]

bulrush *bŏŏl'rush*, *n* a name given to two distinct tall marsh or water plants — the reedmace or cat's-tail, and clubrush, a plant of the sedge family. [Perh. **bole**[1] or **bull**[1] in sense of massive or coarse, and **rush**[2].]

bulwark *bŏŏl'wərk*, *n* a fortification or rampart; a breakwater or sea-wall; the side of a ship projecting above the deck; any means of defence or security. — *vt* to defend; to fortify. [Cf. Ger. *Bollwerk*.]

bum[1] *bum*, *n* the buttocks (*colloq*); the anus (*vulg*). — *vt* (*vulg*) to have anal intercourse with. — **bum bag** a small bag on a belt, as orig. used by skiers, etc.; **bum'freezer** (*slang*) an Eton jacket; a waist-length jacket; **bum'sucker** (*vulg*) a toady; **bum'sucking**. [Cf. **bump** in sense of swelling.]

bum[2] *bum*, *vi* to hum or make a murmuring sound, like a bee: — *pr p* **bumm'ing**; *pa t* and *pa p* **bummed**. — *n* a humming sound. — *n* **bumm'er** a person or thing that bums. [Imit.]

bum[3] *bum*, (*NAm slang*) *n* a (drunken) spree; a dissolute fellow; a sponger. — *adj* worthless; despicable; dud; wrong, false. — *vi* to loaf; to sponge; to live dissolutely. — *vt* to cadge: — *pr p* **bumm'ing**; *pa t* or *pa p* **bummed**. — *n* **bumm'er** a dissolute fellow; a loafer; a sponger; a dismal failure (*colloq*); something worthless (*colloq*); a disappointment (*colloq*); a bad trip (q.v.) on drugs (*colloq*); a nasty experience (*colloq*). — **bum steer** (*slang*) something misleading, false or worthless, a dud. — **give someone the bum's rush** (*slang*) to eject someone by force; to dismiss someone summarily, esp. from one's employment.

bumbershoot *bum'bər-shŏŏt*, (*US facetious*) *n* an umbrella. [Alteration of *umbre*lla, with para*chute*.]

bumble *bum'bl*, *vi* to bungle; to utter indistinctly; to bustle about blunderingly. — *n* confusion; indistinct utterance; a bungler; an idler. — **bum'ble-bee** a large wild loud-humming bee, a humble-bee. [Frequentative of **bum**[2].]

bumf or **bumph** *bumf*, (*colloq*) *n* papers, official papers, documents (*disparagingly*); lavatory paper. [Short for *bum-fodder*, **bum**[1] and **fodder**.]

bummalo or **bumalo** *bum'ə-lō*, *n* the Bombay duck, a small Indian fish related to the salmon, dried and eaten as a relish: — *pl* **bumm'alo** or **bum'alo**. [Marathi *bombīl*.]

bummer. See **bum**[2, 3].

bump *bump*, *vi* to make a heavy or loud noise; to knock dully; to jolt; to move joltingly; (of a cricket-ball) to bound high on striking the pitch. — *vt* to strike with a dull sound; to strike against; to dislodge, knock, shove; in boat-racing, to overtake and impinge upon — the bumper consequently taking the place of the bumped in rank; to turn away (a passenger who holds a valid reservation for a seat on a particular flight) because the airline has allowed too many seats to have been booked. — *n* a dull heavy blow; a thump; (in *pl*) a series of thumps against the ground administered esp. to a child celebrating his or her birthday, by others holding him or her by the arms and legs; a high rebound of a cricket-ball; a jolt; a lump or swelling; a protuberance on the head confidently associated by phrenologists with qualities or propensities of mind; hence (*colloq*) faculty. — *n* **bump'er** any thing or person that bumps; a bar on a motor car to lessen the shock of collision; a railway buffer (*US*); a pad fitted round the inside of a cot to stop a baby bumping herself or himself; a bumping race; a cup or glass filled to the brim for drinking a toast; anything large or generous in measure; a crowded house at a theatre or concert. — *adj* full to overflowing; unusually large or plentiful. — *vi* to drink bumpers. — *n* **bump'iness**. — *adj* **bump'y**. — **bumping race** a boat-race in which the boats seek to bump, not to pass. — **bump into** to happen to meet (someone); **bump off** (*slang*) to kill, murder; **bump start** to start a car by pushing it and engaging the gears while it is moving (*n* **bump'-start**); **bump up** (*colloq*) to raise (prices); to increase the size of; **with a bump** with an unpleasant suddenness. [Imit.]

bumph. See **bumf**.

bumpkin *bump'kin*, *n* an awkward, clumsy rustic; a clown. — *adj* **bump'kinish**. [Prob. Du. *boomken*, a log.]

bumptious *bump'shəs*, *adj* offensively self-important. — *adv* **bump'tiously**. — *n* **bump'tiousness**. [Prob. formed from **bump**.]

bun *bun*, *n* a kind of sweet cake; hair formed into a rounded mass. — **bun'-fight** (*colloq*) a tea-party; a noisy occasion or assembly. [Perh. from O.Fr. *bugne*, a swelling.]

BUNAC *bū'nak*, *abbrev* for British Universities North America Club.

bunch *bunch* or *bunsh*, *n* a number of things aggregated or fastened together; a cluster; a handful of e.g. flowers; something in the form of a tuft or knot. — *vi* to swell out in a bunch; to cluster, form a tight group. — *vt* to make a bunch of; to concentrate. — *adj* **bunched** humped, protuberant; lumpy. — *n* **bunch'iness**. — *n* **bunch'ing** the act of drawing together into a bunch; too close grouping together of cars on a motorway, etc. (esp. after a long gap), of ships arriving in port, etc. — *adj* **bunch'y** growing in bunches or like a bunch; bulging. — **bunch of fives** see under **five**.

bunco. See **bunko**.

buncombe. See **bunkum**.

bundle *bun'dl*, *n* a number of things loosely bound together; a bunch; a loose parcel, esp. one contained in a cloth; a strand of conducting vessels, fibres, etc. (*biol*); a definite measure or quantity, as two reams of paper, twenty hanks of linen yarn, etc. — *vt* to make into bundles; to put hastily or unceremoniously; to hustle. — *vi* to go hurriedly or in confusion (with *away*, *off*, *out*). — **bundle of fun** an exuberant and entertaining person (often *ironic* of one who is not); **go a bundle on** (*slang*) to like or be enthusiastic about. [Conn. with **bind** and **bond**[1].]

bundu *bŏŏn'dŏŏ*, (*SAfr*) *n* a remote uncultivated region. [Bantu.]

Bundy® *bun'di*, (*Austr*) *n* a time-clock in a factory, etc.

bung[1] *bung*, *n* the stopper of the hole in a barrel; a large cork. — *vt* to stop up or enclose with a bung (also *fig*). — **bung'hole** a hole for a bung; **bung'-vent** a small hole in a bung to let gases escape, etc.

bung[2] *bung*, (*slang*) *vt* to throw or shove carelessly and hurriedly.

bung[3] *bung*, (*Austr colloq*) *adj* dead; bust; ruined. — **go bung** to die; to fail, go bust; to go phut. [Aboriginal.]

bungalow *bung'gə-lō*, *n* a lightly-built house, properly with a veranda and one storey; (*loosely*) a one-storey house. [Hindi *baṅglā*, (house) in the style of Bengal, house.]

bungee jumping *bun'ji jump'ing*, *n* the sport of jumping from a height with strong rubber ropes or cables attached to the ankles to ensure that the jumper bounces up before reaching the ground or other surface.

bungle *bung'gl, n* anything clumsily done; a gross mismanagement. — *vi* to act in a clumsy manner. — *vt* to make or mend clumsily; to mismanage grossly; to make a failure of because of a lack of skill. — *n* **bung'ler**. — *adj* **bung'ling** clumsy, awkward; unskilfully or badly done. — Also *n*. — *adv* **bung'lingly**. [Prob. onomatopoeic.]

bunion *bun'yən, n* a lump or inflamed swelling on the first joint of the big toe. [Poss. It. *bugnone*, a botch.]

bunk[1] *bungk, n* a box or recess in a ship's cabin, a sleeping-berth anywhere; one of a pair of narrow beds one above the other (also **bunk bed**). — *vi* to occupy a bunk. — *n* **bunk'er** a compartment for fuel on a ship; the fuel-oil carried by a ship for its own use; a sand-pit or sandy gap in turf, esp. as a hazard in a golf course. — *vt* to fuel; to play into a bunker. — *vi* to fuel. — *adj* **bunk'ered** in a bunker; in difficulties. — **bunk'house** a building containing sleeping accommodation for labourers on a ranch, etc. [Cf. O.N. *bunki*, Scand. *bunke*, heap.]

bunk[2] *bungk*, (*slang*) *n* fleeing, running away (esp. in the phrase **to do a bunk**). — *vi* to flee; (with *off*) to do a bunk, to play truant.

bunk[3]. See **bunkum**.

bunker[1] *bung'kər, n* an underground bombproof shelter. [Ger.]

bunker[2]. See **bunk**[1].

bunko or **bunco** *bung'kō*, (*US*) *n* a form of confidence-trick by which a simple person is swindled or taken somewhere and robbed: — *pl* **bun'kos** or **bun'cos**. — *vt* to rob or swindle in such a way.

bunkum or (esp. *US*) **buncombe** *bung'kəm*, also **bunk** *bungk, n* bombastic speech-making intended for the newspapers rather than to persuade the audience; humbug; claptrap. [From *Buncombe*, a county in North Carolina, whose congressman is said to have gone on talking in Congress, explaining apologetically that he was 'only talking for Buncombe'.]

bunny *bun'i, n* a pet name for a rabbit. — **bunn'y-girl** (sometimes with *caps*) a night-club hostess provocatively dressed in a brief, close-fitting costume with a white fluffy tail, and wearing rabbitlike ears; **bunn'y-hug** a 20th-century American dance.

Bunsen burner *bun'sən* or *bŏŏn'sən bûrn'ər, n* a gas-burner in which a plentiful supply of air is caused to mingle with the gas before ignition, so that a smokeless flame of low luminosity but great heating power is the result. [From the inventor R. W. *Bunsen* (1811–99), a German chemist.]

bunt[1] *bunt, n* a disease of wheat; the fungus (*Tilletia*) that causes it. — *adj* **bunt'ed**. — *adj* **bunt'y**.

bunt[2] *bunt, n* the bagging part of a fishing-net, a sail, etc. — *vi* (of a sail, etc.) to belly. — **bunt'line** a rope passing from the foot-rope of a square sail to prevent bellying in furling.

bunt[3] *bunt, vi* to push with the horns, butt; to spring, rear; to block a ball with the bat (*baseball*; also *vt* and *n*). — *n* a push. — *n* **bunt'ing** pushing.

bunting[1] *bunt'ing, n* a thin worsted material for ships' colours; flags, cloth decorations.

bunting[2] *bunt'ing, n* any of a family of small finchlike birds.

bunting[3]. See **bunt**[3].

buntline. See **bunt**[2].

buoy *boi* (also in U.S. often *bōō'ē*, and in derivatives below *bōō'y-*), *n* a floating secured mark, serving (by its shape, colour, light, sound, etc.) as a guide or as a warning. — *vt* to furnish or mark with buoys or marks; to keep afloat, bear up, or sustain (usu. with *up*); to raise, lift (usu. with *up*). — *vi* to rise. — *n* **buoy'age** a series of buoys or floating beacons to mark the course for ships; the provision, or system, of buoys. — *n* **buoy'ancy** capacity for floating lightly on water or in the air; loss of weight owing to immersion in a fluid; lightness of spirit, cheerfulness (*fig*). — *adj* **buoy'ant** tending to float or to buoy up; light, cheerful, and elastic; (of share prices, sales, profits, etc.) tending to rise; (of a firm) with rising profits, etc. — *n* **buoy'antness**. [Du. *boei*, buoy, fetter, through Romance forms from L. L. *boia*, a collar of leather.]

BUPA *bōō'pə* or *bū'-*, *abbrev* for British United Provident Association.

BUR *abbrev* for Burma, now called Myanmar (I.V.R.).

bur. See **burr**[1,2].

Burberry *bûr'bər-i, n* a kind of waterproof cloth; a raincoat made of this cloth. [From *Burberrys*, trademark of Burberrys Ltd., the manufacturers.]

burble *bûrb'l, n* a murmur. — *vt* and *vi* to murmur; to gurgle; to talk excitedly and rather incoherently (*colloq*). — *n* **burb'ling**. [Prob. onomatopoeic.]

burbot *bûr'bət, n* a freshwater fish, like the ling, with a longish barbel on its lower jaw. [Fr. *bourbotte*, *barbotte* — L.L. *borba*, mud, or L. *barba*, a beard.]

burden[1] *bûr'dən, n* a load; weight; cargo; a ship's carrying capacity (still often **burthen** (*bûr'dhən*)); that which is grievous, oppressive, or difficult to bear; an obligation; any restriction, limitation, or encumbrance affecting a person or property (*Scots law*); (in *pl*) a boat's floorboards. — *vt* to load; to oppress; to encumber. — *adj* **bur'denous** or **bur'densome** heavy; oppressive. — **burden of proof** the obligation to prove one's contention. [O.E. *byrthen* — *beran*, to bear.]

burden[2] *bûr'dən, n* bourdon or bass; part of a song repeated at the end of every stanza, a refrain; the leading idea of anything. [Fr. *bourdon*, a humming tone in music — L.L. *burdō*, a drone bee; confused with **burden**[1].]

burdock. See **burr**[1].

bureau *bū'rō* or *bū-rō'*, *n* a writing-table combined with chest of drawers; a chest of drawers (*US*); a room or office where such a table is used; a department or office for the transacting of business, such as collecting and supplying information; a government department: — *pl* **bureaux** or **bureaus** (*-ōz*). [Fr. *bureau* — O.Fr. *burel*, russet cloth — L. *burrus*, red.]

bureaucracy *bū-rok'rə-si, n* a system of government by officials, responsible only to their departmental chiefs; any system of administration in which matters are hindered by excessive adherence to minor rules and procedures. — *n* **bur'eaucrat** a government official; someone who practises or favours bureaucracy. — *adj* **bureaucrat'ic**. — *adv* **bureaucrat'ically**. — *n* **bureaucratisā'tion** or **-z-**. — *vt* **bureauc'ratise** or **-ize** to form into a bureaucracy; to make bureaucratic. [**bureau**, and Gr. *kratos*, power.]

bureau de change *bü-rō də shãzh*, (Fr.) *n* an office where currency can be exchanged.

burette *bū-ret'*, *n* a graduated glass tube with a tap, for measuring liquids run off; a cruet for religious ceremonies. [Fr.]

burgee *bûr'jē, n* a swallow-tailed flag or pennant.

burgeon *bûr'jən, vi* to put forth sprouts or buds; to grow. [Fr. *bourgeon*, a bud, shoot.]

burger *bûr'gər*, (*colloq*) *n* short for **hamburger**, **cheeseburger**, etc. — **-burger** used as a combining form as in *beefburger* or *cheeseburger*, to denote (a bread roll containing) a fried or grilled cake of meat, etc., made of, or accompanied by, the particular food mentioned.

burgess *bûr'jis, n* a freeman or citizen of a borough. [O.Fr. *burgeis*.]

burgh *bûr'ə*, a spelling of **borough**, used for Scottish burghs, otherwise archaic. — *adj* **burghal** (*bûrg'l*). — *n* **burgher** (*bûrg'ər*) a freeman or citizen of a borough (or burgh); a townsman. — **parliamentary burgh** one whose boundaries, as first fixed in 1832 for parliamentary representation, were adopted later for municipal purposes; a burgh which by itself or in combination elects a member of parliament; often applied to one that has ceased to do so; **royal burgh** a corporate body deriving its existence, constitution, and rights from a royal charter, actual or presumed to have existed. [See **borough.**]

burglar *bûrg'lər, n* a person who enters a building as a trespasser (before 1969, by night) to commit a felony, e.g. to steal. — *vt* **burg'larise** or **-ize** (*US colloq*). — *n* **burg'lary.** — *vi* **burgle** (*bûr'gl*; a back-formation from **burglar**) to commit burglary. — *vt* to enter as a burglar. — **aggravated burglary** burglary involving the use of weapons or explosives.

burgomaster *bûr'gō-mäs-tər, n* the chief magistrate of an Austrian, Dutch, Flemish or German town. [Du. *burgemeester*; Ger. *Bürgermeister*, lit. borough-master.]

burgoo *bûr-go͞o'* or *bûr'go͞o, n* a sailor's dish of boiled oatmeal with salt, butter and sugar; a stew or thick soup for American picnics.

burgundy *bûr'gən-di, n* a French wine (generally red), made in *Burgundy*; a similar wine made elsewhere. — **Burgundy mixture** a fungicide composed of copper sulphate, sodium carbonate, and water.

burhel. Same as **bharal.**

burial *ber'i-əl, n* the act of burying. — **bur'ial-ground** a ground set apart for burials; **bur'ial-place** a burial-ground; the place where anyone is buried. [O.E. *byrgels*, a tomb; see **bury.**]

burin *bū'rin, n* a kind of chisel of tempered steel, used in copper engraving; the distinctive style of an engraver; a palaeolithic flint tool. — *n* **bur'inist** an engraver. [Fr.; from the root of **bore**[1].]

burk. See **berk.**

burka or **burkha** *bo͝or'kə, n* a loose garment, with veiled eyeholes, covering the whole body. [Urdu *burqa'* — Ar.]

burl[1] *bûrl, n* a small knot in thread; a knot in wood. [O.Fr. *bourle*, tuft of wool.]

burl[2] *bûrl*, (*Austr* and *NZ colloq*) *n* an attempt, shot. [Prob. Scot. *birl*, *burl*, a twist, turn.]

burlap *bûr'lap, n* a coarse canvas of jute or hemp for wrappings, or a lighter material, e.g. of flax, for wall-coverings, etc. — sometimes in *pl*.

burlesque *bûr-lesk', n* ludicrous imitation; a piece of literature, of acting, or other performance that mocks its original by grotesque exaggeration or by combining the dignified with the low or the familiar; an entertainment combining often coarse jokes, striptease, songs, and dancing (*US*); a playful or jocular composition (*mus*). — *adj* of the nature of burlesque; practising burlesque. — *vt* to mock by burlesque; to make a burlesque of. [It. *burlesco*; prob. from L.L. *burra*, a flock of wool, a trifle.]

burley. See **berley.**

burly *bûr'li, adj* big and sturdy. — *n* **bur'liness.** [M.E. *borlich*.]

Burman *bûr'mən, adj* relating to *Burma* (since 1989, the Republic of Myanmar). — *n* a person belonging to the majority ethnic group of Myanmar. — *adj* **Burmese** (*bûr'mēz* or *-mēz'*) Burman. — *n* the official language of Myanmar; (until 1989) a native or citizen of Burma.

burn[1] *bûrn*, (now chiefly *Scot*) *n* a small stream or brook. [O.E. *burna*, brook, spring; cf. Du. *born*, Ger. *Born*.]

burn[2] *bûrn, vt* to consume or injure by fire or great heat; to produce an effect of heat on (as to bake pottery, calcine lime, scorch food, wither grass); to oxidise; to use (up), e.g. uranium, in a nuclear reactor (usu. with *up*); to corrode; to make by fire or analogous means. — *vi* to be burnt; to be on fire; to give out heat or light; to glow; to feel excess of heat; to be inflamed with passion: — *pa t* and *pa p* **burnt** or **burned.** — *n* a hurt or mark due to burning; the firing of a rocket engine in order to produce thrust; a very fast ride, etc. on a motorcycle, in a speed-boat, etc.; pain felt in a muscle, experienced during demanding exercise. — *n* **burn'er** a person who, or thing that, burns; a fixture or part of a lamp, gas-jet or gas cooker from which a flame comes. — *n* **burn'ing** the act of consuming by fire; conflagration; inflammation; a quantity burned at one time; controlled expenditure of rocket propellant for course adjustment purposes. — *adj* very hot; scorching; ardent; excessive. — Also *adv.* — **burn'ing-glass** a convex lens concentrating the sun's rays at its focus; **burn'ing-mirror** a concave mirror for producing heat by concentrating the sun's rays; **burning question** or **issue** one keenly discussed; **burn-out** see **burn out** below; **burnt almonds** almonds in burnt sugar; **burnt cork** charred cork used for blacking the face. — Also (with *hyphen*) *vt.* — **burnt cream** crème brûlée; **burnt-off'ering** something offered and burned on an altar as a sacrifice; **burnt sienna** see under **sienna; burn'-up** the using up of fuel in a nuclear reactor. — **burn a hole in one's pocket** said of money when one is eager to spend it; **burn down** to burn to the ground; **burned out** ineffective, exhausted; **burned up** (*US slang*) angry; **burn in** to fix and make durable by intense heat; to imprint indelibly; **burn one's boats** to cut oneself off from all chance of retreat; to stake everything on success; **burn one's fingers** or **get one's fingers burnt** to suffer as a result of interfering, embarking in speculations, etc.; **burn out** to destroy or drive out by burning; to burn till the fire dies down from lack of fuel; to (cause to) become ineffective through overwork, exhaustion, etc. (*n* **burn'-out**); **burn the candle at both ends** see under **candle; burn the midnight oil** to study late into the night; **burn up** to consume completely by fire; to be burned completely; to increase in activity of burning; to make short or easy work of; to become or make angry (*US slang*); **(money) to burn** (money) in great abundance. [O.E. the transitive weak verb *bærnan*, *bærnde*, *bærned*, has been confused with the intransitive strong verb *beornan*, *byrnan*, *barn*, *bornen*; cf. Ger. *brennen*, to burn.]

burnet *bûr'nit, n* the name of two closely related rosaceous plants, the *great burnet*, a meadow plant, and *common* or *salad burnet* found on the Chalk and sometimes used in salad, etc., both with close aggregates of brownish-purple flowers; the burnet moth. — **burnet moth** a moth of the *Zygaenidae*, esp. of the genus *Arthrocera*, with red-spotted or red-streaked forewings. [O.Fr. *burnete*, *brunette*; see **brunette.**]

burnish *bûrn'ish, vt* to polish; to make bright by rubbing. — *n* polish; lustre. — *n* **burn'isher.** — *n* **burn'ishing.** — *n* **burn'ishment.** [Fr. *brunir*, *bruniss-*, to burnish — *brun*, brown.]

burnous *bûr-no͞os'* or **burnouse** *-no͞oz', n* a mantle with a hood much worn by the Arabs. [Fr., — Ar. *burnus*.]

burnt *bûrnt, pa t* and *pa p* of **burn**[2]. — Also *adj.*

buroo *bə-ro͞o'* or **broo** *bro͞o*, (*Scot* and *Ir*) *n* the office at which people receive unemployment benefit; unemployment benefit. — **on the buroo** or **broo** unemployed and receiving unemployment benefit. [**bureau.**]

burp *bûrp, vi* to belch (*colloq*). — Also *n.* — *vt* to rub or pat a baby's back after it has been fed, in order to cause it to belch. [Imit.]

burr[1] or **bur** *bûr, n* the prickly seed-case or head of certain plants, which sticks to clothes or animals; any impediment or inconvenient adherent; any lump, ridge, etc., more or less sharp, an excrescence on a tree, or markings representing it in wood; a knot in thread; a knob at the base of a deer's horn; the rough edge to a line made by an engraving tool, which, when the plate is inked, gives a further quality to the line; waste raw silk; the sweetbread or pancreas; the name for various tools and appliances, such as the triangular chisel for clearing the corners of mortises, etc.; the blank driven out of a piece of sheet-metal by a punch; a partly vitrified brick. — *adj* **burr'y.** — **bur'dock** a composite plant with hooked involucral bracts and docklike leaves; any species of *Xanthium*. — **burr in the throat** something seeming to stick in the throat, producing a choking sensation. [Cognate with Dan. *borre*, a bur.]

burr[2] or **bur** *bûr*, *n* the rough sound of *r* pronounced in the throat, as by many Northumberland people. — *vi* to whisper hoarsely, to murmur. [Usually associated with **burr**[1] but perh. imit.]

burra sahib *bur'ə sä'ib*, *n* in India, a title of respect for the head of a family, a superior officer, etc. [Hind. *bara*, great, and **sahib**.]

burro *bōōr'ō*, *n* a donkey: — *pl* **burr'os.** [Sp.]

burrow *bur'ō*, *n* a hole in the ground dug esp. by certain animals for shelter or defence; a passage, hole, or gallery dug or eaten through wood, stone, etc.; a refuge. — *vi* to make holes underground as rabbits do; to work one's way through earth, etc.; to dwell in a concealed place. — *vt* to make a burrow in; to make by burrowing. [Prob. a variant of **borough** — O.E. *beorgan*, to protect.]

bursa *bûr'sə*, *n* a pouch or sac, esp. one containing viscid lubricating fluid at points of friction (*zool*): — *pl* **bur'sae** (*-sē*). — *adj* **bur'sal** relating to a bursa; fiscal. — *n* **bur'sar** a treasurer; in Scotland, a student or pupil maintained at a university or school by funds derived from endowment. — *adj* **bursarial** (*-sā'ri-əl*). — *n* **bur'sarship** the office of a bursar. — *n* **bur'sary** the treasury of a college or monastery; in Scotland, a scholarship. — *n* **bursī'tis** inflammation of a bursa. [L.L. *bursa*, a purse — Gr. *byrsa*, skin or leather.]

burst *bûrst*, *vt* to break into pieces; to break open or cause to give way suddenly or by violence; to make by bursting; to tear apart the perforated sheets of continuous stationery. — *vi* to fly open or in pieces, esp. owing to a force from within; to give way suddenly; to break forth or away; to force a way; to break suddenly into being, or into some condition, activity, or expression of feeling: — *pa t* and *pa p* **burst.** — *n* an act, occasion, or result of bursting; a sudden outbreak; a hard gallop; a spurt; a drunken bout; a measure of the strength of an envelope. — *n* **burst'er** a person or thing that bursts; *specif* a machine which bursts continuous stationery. — **burst binding** an unsewn book binding in which the gathered sections are perforated at the fold and glue is made to penetrate through the perforations; **burst'-up** a complete break; disruption; commotion; collapse; failure. [O.E. *berstan*; see also **bust**[2].]

burthen. See **burden**[1].

Burton *bûr'tn*, *n* a drink (of beer). — **gone for a Burton** (*airmen's slang*) drowned, dead; absent; missing; no longer in existence. [A town in Staffordshire famous for its beer.]

bury *ber'i*, *vt* to hide in the ground; to cover; to consign (a dead body) to the grave, the sea, etc.; to hide or blot out of remembrance: — *pr p* **bur'ying**; *pa t* and *pa p* **bur'ied.** — **bur'ying-beetle** a beetle of the genus *Necrophorus* that buries small animals as food for its larvae; **bur'ying-ground** a plot of ground set apart for burying the dead; a graveyard; **bur'ying-place.** — **bury the hatchet** to renounce enmity. [O.E. *byrgan*, to bury.]

bus *bus*, *n* an omnibus; a car, aeroplane, etc. (*slang*); a number of conductors forming a circuit or route along which data or power may be transmitted (also **highway** or **trunk**; *comput*): — *pl* **bus'es** or (less commonly) **buss'es.** — *vt* to transport by bus. — *vi* to go by bus; (in a restaurant, etc.) to clear dirty dishes from tables, replenish supplies of needed items, and otherwise assist the waiting staff. — *n* **bus'ing** or (less commonly) **buss'ing** the transporting by bus of people from one district to another, esp. children to school, to achieve a more even racial, etc. balance. — **bus'-conductor**; **bus'-driver**; **bus'-fare**; **bus'man** the driver or conductor of a bus; **bus'-stop** a stopping-place for a bus, for passengers to board it or alight; the post or sign usu. marking such a place. — **busman's holiday** a holiday spent in activities similar to one's work; **miss the bus** (*fig*) to lose an opportunity. [Short for **omnibus.**]

bus. *abbrev* for business.

busby *buz'bi*, *n* a fur hat with a bag hanging on its right side, worn esp. by hussars. [Prob. Hung.]

bush[1] *bŏŏsh*, *n* a woody plant between a tree and an undershrub in size; a shrub thick with branches; anything of bushy tuftlike shape; forest; wild uncultivated country (even though treeless); such country covered with bushes; the wild. — *adj* **bushed** (*slang*) bewildered; tired. — *n* **bush'iness.** — *adj* **bush'y** full of or like bushes; thick and spreading. — *n* (*Austr* and *NZ colloq*) someone who lives in the country as distinct from the town. — **bush'-baby** a small S. African lemur; **bush'buck** a small S. African antelope, or any other of the same genus (*Tragelaphus*). — Also (Du.) **boschbok** (*bos'bok*), (Afrik.) **bosbok** (*bos'bok*); **bush'-cat** the serval; **bush'fire** (esp. *Austr* and *NZ*) a fire in forest or scrub; **bush'-fly** a small black Australian fly (*Musca vetustissima* or other species), swarms of which are a great nuisance to people and animals in the bush; **bush'-fruit** a fruit growing on a bush, such as gooseberry or raspberry; **bush'-lawyer** a prickly trailing plant (*Rubus cissoides*); someone who feigns a knowledge of law (*Austr*); **bush'man** a settler, or traveller, in uncleared land; a woodsman; (with *cap*) one of a now almost extinct nomadic, short-statured, yellowish-brown, aboriginal race of huntsmen in S. Africa. — Also *adj.* — **bush'master** a venomous S. American snake (*Lachesis muta*); **bush pilot** an airline pilot operating over uninhabited country; **bush'ranger** a lawless person, often an escaped criminal, who takes to the bush and lives by robbery (*Austr*); **bush shirt** or **bush jacket** a cotton, etc., garment with four patch pockets and a belt; **bush sickness** a disease of cattle, sheep and goats, caused by a mineral deficiency in pastures (*Austr* and *NZ*); **bush telegraph** (*facetious*) the rapid transmission of news among primitive communities by drum-beating, etc.; gossip, rumour; **bush'veld** or **boschveld** (*bos'*) veld made up largely of woodland. — *vi* **bush'walk** to walk or hike through the bush as a leisure activity (*Austr*). — Also *n.* — **bush'walker**; **bush'walking.** — *vi* **bush'whack** to range through the bush; to fight in guerrilla warfare; to travel through woods, esp. by clearing a way to do so. — *vt* to ambush. — **bush'whacker** a guerrilla fighter; a sniper; **bush'whacking.** — **beat about the bush** to go round about a subject, to avoid coming to the point; **go bush** (*Austr*) to go off into the bush; to leave town or one's usual haunts; to abandon civilised life. [M.E. *busk*, *busch* — O.N. *buskr*. Some uses are from the corresponding Du. *bosch*.]

bush[2] *bŏŏsh*, *n* the metal box or lining of any cylinder in which an axle works. — *vt* to furnish with a bush. — **bush'-metal** hard brass, gunmetal, a composition of copper and tin, used for journals, bearings, etc. [Du. *bus* — L. *buxus*, box-tree.]

bushel *bŏŏsh'əl*, *n* a dry measure of 8 gallons, no longer official, for grain, fruit, etc.; a container for this quantity. — **hide one's light under a bushel** to keep quiet about or conceal one's talents or abilities. [O.Fr. *boissiel* — root of **box**[2].]

bushido *bōō'shi-dō*, *n* a Japanese code of chivalry. [Jap. *bushi*, warrior, *dō*, doctrine.]

business *biz'nis*, *n* employment; a trade, profession, or occupation; a task or errand incumbent or undertaken; a matter requiring attention; dealings, commercial activity; a commercial or industrial concern; one's concerns or affairs; a matter or affair; action as distinguished from dialogue (*theat*); a thing, used quite indefinitely (*colloq*); (*biz'i-nis*, also written **busyness**) the state of being busy. — Also *adj* (*biz'nis*). — *adj* **bus'iness-like** methodical, systematic, practical. — **business card** a card carried by business people, with their name and designation, and the name, address, telephone number and description, etc. of their firm; **business end** (*colloq*) the end or part of something that actually functions or does the work (as *business end of a fork*); **bus'inessman**, *fem* **bus'inesswoman** someone engaged in commercial transactions. — **like nobody's business** (*colloq*) keenly, energetically; **make it one's business** to undertake to accomplish something or see it done; **mean business** to be in earnest; **mind one's own business** to confine oneself to one's own affairs; **send someone about their business** to dismiss someone unceremoniously; **the business** (*slang*) exactly what is required, the right person, etc. for the job. [**busy**.]

busk *busk*, *vi* to play as a wandering musician or actor. — *n* **busk'er** a wandering musician or actor. — *n* **busk'ing**. [Prob. Sp. *buscar*, to seek.]

bust[1] *bust*, *n* a sculpture representing the head and breast of a person; the upper front part of the human body, esp. a woman's. — *adj* **bust'ed** breasted; adorned with busts. — *adj* **bust'y** (*colloq*; of a woman) having a large bust. [Fr. *buste*; It. and Sp. *busto*.]

bust[2] *bust*, (*colloq*) *vt* and *vi* to break, shatter; to make or become bankrupt. — *vt* to arrest: — *pa t* and *pa p* **bust'ed** or **bust**. — *n* a drinking bout; a police raid (*slang*). — *adj* ruined, penniless. — *n* **bust'er** (*colloq*) something large; a frolic; a roisterer; a horse-breaker; a form of address to a man or boy; a strong south wind (*Austr*); someone or something that destroys or shatters, esp. as *combining form* as in *blockbuster*. — *n* esp. as *combining form* **bust'ing**. — **busted flush** see under **flush**[4]; **bust'-up** a quarrel or disruption; a disturbance or brawl. — **go bust** to become bankrupt. [Orig. a colloq. form of **burst**.]

bustard *bust'ərd*, *n* any bird of the genus *Otis*, usually ranked with cranes. [Fr. *bistard* — L. *avis tarda*, slow bird (a misnomer).]

bustier *bü-styā*, (Fr.) *n* a strapless long-line brassière or tight-fitting bodice.

bustle[1] *bus'l*, *vi* to busy oneself noisily or fussily; to be full of or busy with (with *with*). — *n* hurried activity; stir; tumult. — *n* **bust'ler**. [M.E. *bustelen*.]

bustle[2] *bus'l*, *n* a frame or pad for causing a skirt to hang back from the hips; a car boot (*colloq*).

busy *biz'i*, *adj* fully employed; active; diligent; meddling; fussily active; (of a telephone line) engaged; (of a picture or design) unrestful because having too much detail. — *n* (*slang*) a detective. — *vt* to make busy; to occupy: — *pr p* **bus'ying**; *pa t* and *pa p* **bus'ied**. — *adv* **bus'ily**. — *n* **bus'yness** the state of being busy (see **business**). — **bus'ybody** a person who meddles in others' affairs; **busy Lizzie** a popular fast-growing pot-plant of the *Impatiens* genus, usu. with pink or white flowers. [O.E. *bysig*.]

but[1] *but*, *prep* except. — *conj* on the other hand; in contrast; nevertheless; unless, if not; otherwise than (that); introducing emphasis, as in *nobody, but nobody, must go*; except that (merging in *prep*); that not (developing into a negative *relative pron*). — *adv* only. — *n* an objection; an outer room (*Scot*). — Also *adj*. — **anything but** certainly not; **but and ben** see **ben**[2]; **but for** or **but that** were it not for, or that. [O.E. *be-ūtan*, *būtan*, without — *be*, by, and *ūtan*, out — near, and yet outside.]

butadiene *bū-tə-dī'ēn*, *n* (L. *dis*, twice) a hydrocarbon, C_4H_6, used in making synthetic rubber. — *n* **bu'tane** a hydrocarbon of the methane series, C_4H_{10}, widely used as a fuel (see **bottle-gas**). [**butyl**.]

Butazolidin® *bū-ta-zol'i-din*, *n* phenylbutazone (q.v.). — sometimes shortened to **bute** (*būt*; *slang*; also with *cap*).

butch *bōōch*, *n* an aggressively tough man (*slang*); the 'male' partner in a homosexual or lesbian relationship (*slang*). — *adj* tough; aggressively masculine. [Am. boy's nickname.]

butcher *bōōch'ər*, *n* a person whose business is to slaughter animals for food, or who deals in their flesh; a person who delights in bloody deeds. — *vt* to slaughter and prepare (animals) for sale as food; to put to a bloody death, to kill cruelly; to spoil, as a bad actor does or the like (*fig*). — *n* **butch'ering**. — *n* **butch'er's** (orig. **butcher's hook**; *Cockney rhyming slang*) a look. — *n* **butch'ery** great or cruel slaughter; a slaughterhouse. — **butch'er-bird** a shrike; a bird of the genus *Cracticus* (*Austr*). [O.Fr. *bochier*, *bouchier*, one who kills he-goats — *boc*, a he-goat; **buck**[2].]

bute or **Bute**. See **Butazolidin**.

butler *but'lər*, *n* a servant in charge of liquors, plate, etc.; an officer in a royal household. — *vi* to act as butler. — Also **butt'le** (back-formation). — *n* **but'lery** the butler's pantry. [Norm. Fr. *butuiller* — L.L. *buticulārius*. See **bottle**.]

butment. Same as **abutment**.

butt[1] *but*, *vt* to strike with the head, as a goat, etc. does. — *vi* to strike with the head (also with *at* or *against*); to go or drive head first. — *n* a push or blow with the head. — *n* **butt'er** an animal that butts. — **butt in** to interfere, thrust oneself into a conversation, etc. [O.Fr. *boter*, to push, strike.]

butt[2] *but*, *n* a large cask; a wine butt = *c* 573 litres (126 gallons), a beer and sherry butt = *c* 491 litres (108 gallons). [Cf. Fr. *botte*, Sp. *bota*, L.L. *butta*.]

butt[3] *but*, *n* a mark or mound for archery practice; a mound behind targets; someone who is made an object of ridicule; a hiding-place for grouse-shooters. [Fr. *but*, goal.]

butt[4] *but*, *n* the thick and heavy end; the stump; a tree-trunk; the part of a hide from or towards the rear of an animal; thick leather; the fag-end of a cigar or cigarette; the buttocks (*US colloq*); the wooden, etc. handle or steadying shoulder-part of a pistol or rifle; a remnant; the square end of a plank meeting another. — *vi* to abut; to meet end to end. — **butted** or **butt joint** a joint formed between the squared ends of the two jointing pieces, which come together but do not overlap; **butt'-end**; **butt welding** welding the seam formed by joining two butt-ends. [Poss. conn. with **butt**[3] and **abut**.]

butter[1] *but'ər*, *n* an oily substance obtained from cream by churning; extended to various substances resembling or containing it; flattery. — *vt* to spread over with butter, mortar or other soft substance; to flatter (usu. with *up*). — *adj* **butt'ery** like butter; smeared with butter or the like. — **butt'er-bean** an American bean akin to the French bean; **butt'er-cloth** or **-mus'lin** a loose-woven cloth suitable for wrapping butter; **butt'ercup** a crowfoot (*Ranunculus*), esp. of one of those species that have golden-yellow cup-shaped flowers; **butt'er-dish** or **-plate** a dish or plate for holding butter at table; **butt'er-fat** the fat contained in butter, chiefly glycerides of palmitic and oleic acids. — *adj* **butt'er-fingered** prone to let things slip. — **butt'er-fingers** (*nsing*) someone who lets a ball, etc., they ought to catch, slip through their fingers; **butt'erfly** a general name for any of the daylight Lepidoptera, roughly distinguished from moths by their clubbed antennae; a frivolous, flighty person (*fig*); butterfly stroke: — *pl* **butt'erflies**. — *adj* light, flighty, like a butterfly. — **butt'erfly-screw** or **butt'erfly-nut** a screw or nut, turned by winged finger-grips; **butterfly stroke** a swimming-stroke performed lying on one's front, the arms working simultaneously with an overarm action; **butterfly valve** a disc-shaped valve in a carburettor, etc.; a valve consisting of two hinged plates; **butt'er-knife** a blunt knife for taking butter from a butter dish; **butt'ermilk** the milk that remains after the butter has been separated from the cream by churning; **butter-muslin** see **butter-cloth** above; **butt'ernut** the oily nut of the North American white walnut; the tree itself; its light-coloured close-grained wood; an edible nut of the souari (*Caryocar*) tree of Guiana (also called **soua'ri-nut**); **butter oil** a dairy product consisting almost entirely of milk fat; **butt'er-pat** a pat of butter; a wooden instrument for working butter into shape; **butt'erscotch** a kind of toffee containing much butter. — **butterflies in the stomach** nervous tremors in the stomach; **butter up** to flatter. [O.E. *butere*; Ger. *Butter*; both from L. *būtȳrum* — Gr. *boutȳron*.]

butter². See **butt¹**.

buttery¹ *but'ər-i*, *n* a storeroom, often in a college, for provisions, esp. liquors. — **butt'ery-bar** the ledge for holding tankards in the buttery; **butt'ery-hatch** a half-door over which provisions are handed from the buttery. [Fr. *bouteillerie*, lit. a place for bottles; see also **butler** and **bottle.**]

buttery². See **butter¹**.

buttle. See **butler**.

buttock *but'ək*, *n* either side of the rump or protuberant part at the back of the body above the legs; a cut of meat from the buttock, e.g. silverside; a throw by use of the buttock (*wrestling*). — *vt* to throw in this way. [Dimin. of **butt⁴**.]

button *but'n*, *n* a knob or disc, used as a fastening, ornament, or badge; a knob, e.g. that at the end of a foil, that for winding a watch, that to which a violin tailpiece is looped; a bud; the head of an unexpanded mushroom (also **button mushroom**); a pimple; the knob of an electric bell, etc.; anything of small value. — *adj* like a button, used e.g. of small varieties of vegetables, blooms, etc. of a compact, globular shape. — *vt* to fasten by means of buttons; to close up tightly. — *vi* to be capable of being fastened with buttons. — *nsing* **butt'ons** a page in a hotel, etc. — *adj* **butt'ony** decorated with buttons; like a button or buttons. — *adj* **butt'oned-up** (*slang*) uncommunicative. — **button cell** or **button cell battery** a small, flat, circular battery, used to power a watch, etc.; **butt'onhole** the slit through which a button is passed; a flower or flowers for wearing in the buttonhole of a lapel. — *vt* to make buttonholes in; to sew with a stitch suitable for the protection of edges (*buttonhole-stitch*); to detain in talk. — **butt'on-hook** a hook for pulling buttons through buttonholes in boots, gloves, etc.; **button mushroom** see **button** above. — **buttoned up** (*slang*) successfully fixed up; safe in hand; ready for action; see also **buttoned-up** above. [Fr. *bouton*, any small projection, from *bouter*, to push.]

buttress *but'rəs*, *n* a projecting support built on to the outside of a wall; any support or prop. — *vt* to prop or support, with, or as if with, a buttress. [App. O.Fr. *bouterez* — *bouter*, to push, bear against.]

butty *but'i*, (*Northern*) *n* a sandwich, snack.

butyl alcohol *bū'til al'kə-hol*, *n* any of four isomeric alcohols of formula $C_4H_9{\cdot}OH$, used as solvents, etc. [**butyric**.]

butyric *bū-tir'ik*, *adj* pertaining to or derived from butter. — *n* **bū'tyrate** a salt of **butyric acid**, a volatile fatty acid, one isomer of which gives rancid butter its smell. [See **butter¹**.]

buxom *buks'əm*, *adj* (of a woman) plump and comely. — *n* **bux'omness**. [M.E. *buhsum*, pliable, obedient — O.E. *būgan*, to bow, yield, and sfx. *-sum*, (see **-some¹**).]

buy *bī*, *vt* to purchase for money; to bribe; to obtain in exchange for something; to accept, believe (*slang*): — *pr p* **buy'ing**; *pa t* and *pa p* **bought** (*böt*). — *n* something purchased. — *adj* and *n* **buy'able**. — *n* **buy'er** a person who buys; a person employed to buy goods (e.g. for a store or company). — **buyers' (**or **buyer's) market** one in which buyers control the price, because supply exceeds demand. — **a good buy** (*colloq*) a wise purchase; a bargain; **buy in** to collect a stock of by buying; to buy back for the owner at an auction (*n* **buy'-in**); **buy into** to pay for a share or interest in; **buy off** to buy exemption or release for; to get rid of by paying; **buy out** to dispossess or take over possession from by payment (*n* **buy'-out**); to buy off; **buy over** to win over by payment; to bribe; **buy up** to purchase the whole stock of; **have bought it** (*slang*) to have been killed; **I'll buy that** I'll accept that explanation though it seems surprising. [O.E. *bycgan*, *bohte*, *boht*; Goth. *bugjan*.]

buzz *buz*, *vi* to make a noise like that of insects' wings; to murmur; to move quickly (*slang*). — *vt* to utter with a buzzing sound; to make a telephone call to (*colloq*); to whisper or spread secretly; to transmit by Morse over a telephone wire by means of a key; to throw (*slang*); to fly very low over or very close to; to interfere with in flight by flying very near to (*aeronautics*). — *n* the noise of bees and flies; a humming sound; a voiced hiss; a whispered report; a telephone call (*colloq*); a pleasant feeling, stimulation (*colloq*); enthusiasm (*colloq*); a craze, fad (*colloq*). — *n* **buzz'er** a person who buzzes; an apparatus that makes a buzzing sound. — *n* and *adj* **buzz'ing**. — *adv* **buzz'ingly**. — *adj* **buzz'y**. — **buzz bomb** a flying bomb; **buzz'-saw** (*US*) a circular saw; **buzz word** (*colloq*) a well-established term in the jargon of a particular subject, science, etc., its use conveying the impression of specialised knowledge and of being very up-to-date. — **buzz off** (*slang*) to go away. [From the sound.]

buzzard *buz'ərd*, *n* a large bird of prey of the genus *Buteo*; extended to some others, such as the *honey-buzzard* and *turkey-buzzard*. [Fr. *busard*.]

BV *abbrev* for: *Beata Virgo* (L.), Blessed Virgin; *Bene vale* (L.), farewell; *Besloten Vennootschap* (Du.), limited company.

BVM *abbrev* for Blessed Virgin Mary.

BVM & S *abbrev* for Bachelor of Veterinary Medicine and Surgery.

bwana *bwä'nä*, *n* master; sir. [Swahili.]

BWB *abbrev* for British Waterways Board.

BWR *abbrev* for boiling-water reactor.

BWV *abbrev* for *Bach Werke Verzeichnis* (Ger.), catalogue of Bach's works.

by¹ *bī*, *prep* at the side of; near to; along a route passing through, via; past; (in oaths) in the presence of, or with the witness of; through (denoting the agent, cause, means, etc.); to the extent of; in quantity measurable in terms of; in accordance with; in respect of; (of time) not after; during (day, night, etc.); multiplied into, or combined with another dimension of; in succession to; (of horses, etc.) sired by. — *adv* near; aside; away; past; in reserve. — *n* and *adj* see **bye¹**. — **by'-blow** a side blow or side-stroke; **by'-election** a parliamentary election for a seat during the sitting of parliament; **by'-end** a subsidiary aim; **by'-form** a subsidiary form; a form varying from the usual one; **by'-going** the action of passing by (esp. in **in the by-going,** in passing). — *adj* **by'gone** (*-gon*). — *npl* **by'gones** past happenings or grievances; ornaments, household articles, etc., of former times which are not fine enough, or not old enough, to be valued as antiques (also in *sing*). — **by'-lane** a side lane or passage out of the common road; **bylaw** and **bye-law** see separate entry; **by'line** a line at the head of a newspaper or magazine article telling by whom it is written; **by'-name** or **by'name** a nickname; another name by which a person is known; **by'pass** a road, route or passage for carrying traffic, fluids, electricity, etc., round an obstruction, congested place, etc. **(cardio-**

pulmonary bypass a method whereby (in cardiac surgery) circulation and oxygenation of blood is maintained artificially, bypassing the heart and lungs). — *vt* to supply with a bypass; to direct (e.g. fluid) along a bypass; to go round and beyond by a bypass; to ignore, leave out (*fig*); to evade. — **by'= passage** a side passage; **by'path** a secluded or indirect path; **by'-play** action subordinate to and apart from the main action of a play; **by'-plot** a subsidiary plot; **by'-product** a product formed in the process of making something else; **by'road** a minor or side road; **by'stander** someone who stands by or near one; a looker-on; **by'-street** an obscure street; **by'way** a private, secluded or obscure way; **by'word** a common saying, proverb; an object of scorn; a person noted for a specified characteristic. — **by and by** at some future time; before long, presently; in the course of time; **by and large** whether close-hauled or before the wind (*naut*); speaking generally; on the whole; **by oneself** alone; **by the by** (or **bye**) or **by the way** in passing, incidentally; **let bygones be bygones** let past quarrels be ignored. — See also **bye**[1]. [O.E. *bī*, *bi*, *big*; Ger. *bei*, L. *ambi-*.]

by[2]. See **bye**[1].

bye[1] or **by** *bī*, *n* anything of minor importance, a side issue, a thing not directly aimed at; the state of a player who has not drawn an opponent, and passes without contest to the next round (*games*); (in golf) the holes remaining after the match is decided, played as a subsidiary game; a run made from a ball bowled but not struck or touched by the batsman (*cricket*). — *adj* subsidiary; part; indirect. — See also **by**[1]. [See **by**[1].]

bye[2] *bī* or **bye-bye** *bī'bī* or *bə-bī'*, colloq. forms of **goodbye**.

bye-law. See **bylaw**.

Byelorussian. See **Belorussian**.

by-going, bygones, by-lane. See **by**[1].

bylaw or **bye-law** *bī'lö*, *n* the law of a local authority or private corporation; a supplementary law or an inferred regulation. [O.N. *bȳjar-lög*; from O.N. *būa*, to dwell.]

byline, by(-)name. See **by**[1].

BYO *abbrev* for bring your own, esp. bring your own alcohol.

BYOB *abbrev* for bring your own bottle, beer or (*colloq*) booze.

bypass ... to ... **by-product**. See **by**[1].

byre *bīr*, (mainly *Scot*) *n* a cowhouse. [O.E. *bȳre*.]

byroad. See **by**[1].

Byronic *bī-ron'ik*, *adj* possessing the characteristics of Lord *Byron* (1788–1824), or of his poetry, overstrained in sentiment or passion, cynical and libertine.

byssus *bis'əs*, *n* a fine yellowish flax; linen made from it (the 'fine linen' of the Bible); the bundle of filaments by which some shellfish attach themselves. [L., — Gr. *byssos*, a fine flaxen substance.]

bystander, bystreet. See **by**[1].

byte *bīt*, (*comput*) *n* a set of usu. eight binary digits (bits) considered as a unit. [Poss. from *b*inar*y* digi*t* *e*ight, or from **bit**[2] and **bite**.]

byway, byword. See **by**[1].

Byzantine *biz-an'tīn*, *bīz-an'tīn* or *-tin*, or *biz'ən-*, *adj* relating to *Byzantium* (Constantinople, now Istanbul); rigidly hierarchic; intricate, tortuous. — *n* an inhabitant of Byzantium. — *n* **Byzan'tinist** a person who studies, or is an expert on, Byzantine history, affairs, etc. — **Byzantine Church** the Eastern or Greek Orthodox Church; **Byzantine Empire** the Eastern or Greek Empire from A.D. 395 to 1453. [Gr. *Bȳzantion*.]

C

C or **c** *sē*, *n* the third letter in the modern English alphabet, in origin a rounded form of the Greek *gamma*; one of the notes of the musical scale, the sound on which the system is founded — the keynote of the natural scale, C major, having neither flats nor sharps.

C or **C.** *abbrev* for: clubs (*cards*); Conservative; Cuba (I.V.R.).

C *symbol* for: carbon (*chem*); century (preceding numeral, e.g. C20, twentieth century); common time, four crotchets in a bar (*mus*); coulomb; (Roman numeral) 100.

C symbol for electrical capacitance.

°C *symbol* for: degree(s) Celsius; degree(s) centigrade.

c or **c.** *abbrev* for: *caput* (L.), chapter; carat; caught; cent(s); centi-; centime(s); *circa* (L.), about; cold.

¢ *symbol* for cent(s).

© *symbol* for copyright.

CA *abbrev* for: California (U.S. state); Central America; Chartered Accountant (Scotland and Canada); chief accountant; Consumers' Association; County Alderman.

Ca (*chem*) *symbol* for calcium.

ca *abbrev* for: cases; *circa* (L.), about.

CAA *abbrev* for Civil Aviation Authority.

CAB *abbrev* for: Citizens' Advice Bureau; Civil Aeronautics Board (U.S.).

cab *kab*, *n* a taxicab; the driver's shelter on a lorry, etc.; a public carriage, orig. horse-drawn, now usu. motor-driven. — *n* **cabb'y** or **cabb'ie** a familiar dimin. of **cab'man**, a man who drives a horse cab, or of **cab'-driver** a taxi-driver. — **cab'-rank** or **cab'-stand** a place where cabs stand for hire. [**cabriolet**.]

cabal *kə-bal'*, *n* a small party united for some secret design; the plot itself. — *vi* to form a party for a secret purpose; to intrigue: — *pr p* **caball'ing**; *pa t* and *pa p* **caballed'**. — *n* **caball'er**. [Fr. *cabale*; from Heb. *qabbālāh*; see **cabbala**.]

cabala, etc. See **cabbala**.

caballero *kab-al-yār'ō*, *n* a Spanish gentleman: — *pl* **caballer'os**. [Sp., — L. *caballārius*, horseman — *caballus*, horse.]

cabana *kə-ban'ə* or *-ban'yə*, (esp. *US*) *n* a small tentlike cabin on the beach or by a swimming-pool; a cabin or chalet. [Sp. *cabaña*.]

cabaret *kab'ə-rā*, *n* a restaurant, etc. where entertainment is provided; the kind of entertainment given there, e.g. a song-and-dance or comedy routine. [Fr., tavern; prob. for *cabaneret* — *cabane*, a hut.]

cabbage *kab'ij*, *n* a vegetable (*Brassica oleracea*) of the Cruciferae genus; the edible terminal bud of various palms; a dull, inactive person; a brain-damaged or mentally subnormal person (*colloq*). — *adj* **cabb'agy**. — **cabb'age-butterfly** or **cabbage-white'** a large white butterfly (*Pieris*) whose larvae feed on the leaves of cabbage and similar plants; **cabb'age-fly** a fly whose maggots damage cabbage roots; **cabb'age-lettuce** a lettuce with a cabbage-like head; **cabb'age-moth** a moth whose larva feeds on cabbage; **cabb'age-palm** or **cabb'age-tree** *Oreodoxa oleracea* or other palm with an edible cabbage; **cabb'age-rose** a rose that has a bunchy cabbage-like flower; **cabb'age-tree** the cabbage-palm of coastal areas of Eastern Australia; a New Zealand tree with bushy heads of grass-shaped leaves; any cabbage-palm; **cabb'age-worm** the larva of the cabbage-butterfly or of the cabbage-moth. [Fr. *caboche*, head — L. *caput*.]

cabbala or **cabala** *kab'ə-lə* or *kə-bä'lə*, *n* a secret traditional lore of Jewish rabbis, who read hidden meanings into the Bible. — *n* **cabb'alism** the science of the cabbala. — *n* **cabb'alist** an expert or specialist in the cabbala. — *adj* **cabbalist'ic** or **cabbalist'ical** relating to the cabbala; having a hidden meaning. — Also **cab'alism**, **cab'alist**, etc. [Heb. *qabbālāh*, tradition, *qibbēl*, to receive.]

cabbie, cabby. See **cab**.

cabin *kab'in*, *n* a hut or cottage; (in a ship) a small room used for living accommodation or an office; (on a small boat) a shelter for the crew and passengers; (in an airliner) the section of the aircraft for carrying passengers and luggage. — *vt* to shut up in a cabin or in a cramped space. — **cab'in-boy** a boy who serves the officers or cabin passengers of a ship; **cabin class** the class between tourist and first class; **cabin crew** the members of an aircraft crew who look after the passengers; **cabin cruiser** a power-driven boat with full provision for living on board; **cabin passenger** a passenger having cabin accommodation. [Fr. *cabane* — L.L. *capanna*.]

cabinet *kab'i-nət* or *kab'nət*, *n* a case for storing or displaying articles of value; a cupboard or drawer for storage; a small room, closet or private apartment; (usu. with *cap*) a select inner group of the ministers who govern a country. — **cab'inetmaker** a maker of cabinets and other fine furniture; **cab'inetmaking** the occupation or art of the cabinetmaker; **cabinet minister** a member of a cabinet; **cab'inet-pudding** a cakelike pudding; **cab'inet-wood**. [Dimin. of **cabin**.]

cable *kā'bl*, *n* a strong rope or chain for hauling or tying anything, esp. a ship's anchor; a cable-length; electrical wiring for a building, an electrical appliance, etc.; a cablegram; cable television. — Also *adj*. — *vt* and *vi* to provide with a cable; to tie up; to telegraph or send by cable; to provide with cable television. — *n* **cā'bling** a bead or moulding like a thick rope. — **cā'ble-car** a car suspended from a moving cable, used as a method of transport up mountains, across valleys, etc.; a car on a cable-railway; **cā'blegram** a telegram sent by cable; **cā'ble-length** or **cā'ble's-length** a tenth of a nautical mile, approx. 183 m. (200 yards) or 100 fathoms (in U.S. approx. 219 m. (720 ft.) or 120 fathoms); **cā'ble-moulding** a bead or moulding carved in imitation of a thick rope; **cā'ble-stitch** a series of stitches producing a pattern suggestive of cables; **cable television** the transmission of television programmes by cable to individual subscribers; **cāble-tram'way** or **-rail'way** one along which cars or carriages are drawn by an endless cable; **cā'blevision** cable television; **cā'bleway** a structure for transport of material in cars suspended from a cable. [Fr., — L.L. *caplum*, a halter — L. *capĕre*, to hold.]

cabochon *ka-bō-shɔ̃*, *n* a precious stone polished but uncut, or cut **en** (*ã*) **cabochon**, i.e. rounded on top and flat on the back, without facets. — Also *adj*. [Fr., *caboche* — L. *caput*, head.]

caboodle *kə-bōō'dl*, (*slang*) *n* a crowd or collection.

caboose *kə-bōōs'*, *n* a ship's kitchen; a car, usu. at the rear of a train for the train crew or workmen (*US*); someone bringing up the rear (*US*); a hut. [Du. *kombuis*.]

cabotage *kab'o-tij*, *n* right of control over air traffic within its territory, exercised by a particular country; coastal trading. [Fr.]

cabriole *kab'ri-ōl*, *n* a capriole. — *adj* (of furniture legs) curved, often like an animal's paw. — *n* **cabriolet** (*-lā'*) a light carriage with two wheels; a motor car with folding top; a small armchair of curved design (18th-century). [Fr., — L. *capra*, a goat.]

cacao *kə-kä'ō* or *kə-kā'ō*, *n* a tropical American tree (*Theobroma cacao*) or its seeds from which cocoa and chocolate are made. [Mex. *cacauatl*, cacao tree.]

cachalot *kash'ə-lot* or *-lō*, *n* the sperm-whale. [Fr.]

cache *kash*, *n* a hiding-place for treasure, provisions, ammunition, etc.; a collection of stores hidden away. — *vt* to hide. [Fr. *cacher*, to hide.]

cachet *kash'ā*, *n* an official seal; any distinctive stamp (*fig*), esp. something showing or conferring prestige; a capsule enclosing a medicine. [Fr.]

cachexy *ka-kek'si* or **cachexia** *-si-ə*, *n* a bad state of body or mind. — *adj* **cachec'tic** or **cachec'tical**. [L., — Gr. *kachexiā* — *kakos*, bad, *hexis*, condition.]

cachinnate *kak'in-āt*, *vi* to laugh loudly. — *n* **cachinnā'tion**. — *adj* **cachinn'atory** (or *kak'*). [L. *cachinnāre*, to laugh loudly.]

cacholot. Same as **cachalot**.

cachou *ka-shōō'*, *n* a pill or lozenge made of extract of liquorice, cashew-nut, or similar, used by some smokers in the hope of sweetening the breath. [Fr.]

cachucha *kə-chōō'chə*, *n* a lively Spanish dance in 3–4 time, like the bolero. [Sp.]

cacique *ka-sēk'*, *n* a West Indian chief; in Spain or Latin America, a political boss. — *n* **caciqu'ism** government by a cacique. [Haitian.]

cack-handed *kak-hand'id*, (*slang*) *adj* left-handed; clumsy. — *n* **cack-hand'edness**. [Dialect *cack*, excrement, — L. *cacāre*, to defecate.]

cackle *kak'l*, *n* the sound made by a hen or goose; talk or laughter of similar sound or value. — *vi* to make such a sound. — Also *vt*. — *n* **cack'ler**. — **cut the cackle** (*slang*) to stop the useless talk. [M.E. *cakelen*.]

caco- *kak-ō-*, *combining form* denoting bad. [Gr. *kakos*, bad.]

cacodyl *kak'ō-dil*, *n* a colourless stinking liquid, composed of arsenic, carbon and hydrogen. — *adj* **cacodyl'ic**. [Gr. *kakōdēs*, stinking, *hȳlē*, matter.]

cacoepy *kak-ō'ə-pi*, *n* bad or wrong pronunciation. [Gr. *kakos*, bad, *epos*, word.]

cacoethes *kak-ō-ē'thēz*, *n* a bad habit, itch or yen. [Gr. *kakoēthēs*, *-ēs*, ill-disposed — *kakos*, bad, *ēthos*, habit.]

cacography *kak-og'rə-fi*, *n* bad handwriting or spelling. — *n* **cacog'rapher**. — *adj* **cacographic** (*-ō-graf'ik*) or **cacograph'ical**. [Gr. *kakos*, bad, *graphē*, writing.]

cacology *ka-kol'ə-ji*, *n* faulty vocabulary or pronunciation. [Gr. *kakos*, bad, *logos*, speech.]

cacomistle *ka'kə-mis-əl* or **cacomixl** *ka'kə-miks-əl*, *n* a small carnivore found in south-west U.S. and Mexico. [Mex. Sp., — Nahuatl *tlaco*, half, *miztli*, cougar.]

cacophony *ka-kof'ə-ni*, *n* a disagreeable sound; discord of sounds. — *adj* **cacoph'onous**, **cacophonic** (*-ō-fon'ik*), **cacophon'ical** or **cacophonious** (*-fō'ni-əs*) harsh-sounding. [Gr. *kakos*, bad, *phōnē*, sound.]

cactus *kak'tus* or *-təs*, *n* a name given to any plant of the American family **Cactā'ceae** whose stems store water and do the work of leaves, which are generally reduced to spines; (also **cactus dahlia**) a type of double-flowered dahlia: — *pl* **cac'tī** or **cac'tuses**. — *adj* **cactā'ceous**. — *adj* **cac'tiform**. [L., — Gr. *kaktos*, a prickly plant found in Sicily.]

cacuminal *ka-kū'mi-nəl*, (*phon*) *adj* produced by turning the tip of the tongue up and back, retroflex. — *n* a cacuminal sound. [L. *cacūmen*, *-inis*, top, point, tip.]

CAD (often *kad*) *abbrev* for: compact audio disc; computer-aided design.

cad *kad*, (*old-fashioned* or *facetious*) *n* a man who lacks the instincts of a gentleman, a scoundrel. — *adj* **cadd'ish**. — *n* **cadd'ishness**. [Short for **cadet**.]

cadastral *ka-das'trəl*, *adj* pertaining to a **cadastre** (*ka-das'tər*) or public register of the lands of a country for fiscal purposes; applied also to a survey on a large scale. [Fr., — L.L. *capitastrum*, register for a poll tax — L. *caput*, the head.]

cadaver *kə-dav'ər* or *-dā'vər*, *n* a corpse. — *adj* **cadav'eric**. — *adj* **cadav'erous** corpselike; sickly-looking; gaunt. — *n* **cadav'erousness**. [L. *cadāver*, a dead body — *cadĕre*, to fall (dead).]

caddice. See **caddis**.

caddie or **caddy** *kad'i*, *n* a person who attends a golfer at play, carrying the clubs. — *vi* to act as caddie; to carry clubs. — **caddie (or caddy) car** a device for taking a bag of golf clubs round the course — also **caddie (or caddy) cart**. [**cadet**.]

caddis or **caddice** *kad'is*, *n* the larva of the **cadd'is-fly** which lives in water in a **cadd'is-case**, a silken sheath covered with fragments of wood, stone, etc. — Also **cadd'is-worm**.

caddy[1] *kad'i*, *n* a small box for holding tea; any storage container (*US*). [Malay *kati*, the weight of a small packet of tea.]

caddy[2]. See **caddie**.

cade *kād*, *n* a lamb or colt brought up by hand, a pet lamb. — Also *adj*.

cadence *kā'dəns*, *n* the fall of the voice; rise and fall of sound, modulation; rhythm; a succession of chords closing a musical period. — *adj* **cā'denced** rhythmical. — *n* **cā'dency** rhythm; the relative status of younger sons (*heraldry*). — *adj* **cadential** (*kə-den'shəl*). [Fr. — L. *cadĕre*, to fall.]

cadenza *kä-dent'sa* or *kə-den'zə*, (*mus*) *n* an outstanding virtuoso passage or flourish given by a solo voice or instrument towards the end of a movement. — *adj* **cadential** (*kə-den'shəl*). [It. *cadenza* — L. *cadĕre*, to fall.]

cadet *kə-* or *ka-det'*, *n* a person undergoing training for one of the armed forces; in New Zealand, a newcomer gaining experience in farming; a trainee (*US*). — *n* **cadet'ship**. — **cadet corps** an organised body undergoing military training. [Historically, a younger son or brother, generally sent away for military training — Fr. *cadet*.]

cadge *kaj*, *vt* and *vi* to sponge (money, etc.); to beg or go about begging. — *n* **cadg'er**. [Prob. connected with **catch**.]

cadi *kä'di* or *kā'di*, *n* a magistrate in Muslim countries. [Ar. *qādī*, a judge.]

Cadmean victory *kad-mē'ən vik'tər-i*, *n* one very costly to both sides. [From *Cadmus*, in Greek mythology, who sowed a dragon's teeth from which sprang soldiers who fought each other until only five were left.]

cadmium *kad'mi-əm*, *n* an element (atomic no. 48; symbol **Cd**), a white metal, occurring in zinc ores, used in magnets, metal-plating and as a control in nuclear reactors. — **cadmium yellow** cadmium sulphide used as a pigment. [Gr. *kadmiā*, *kadmeiā* (*gē*), Cadmean (earth), calamine.]

cadre *kad'r*, *käd'ri*, *kad'ər* or *käd'ər*, *n* a framework, esp. the permanent skeleton of a military unit; any nucleus of key people; (prob. from Fr. through Russ.) a cell of trained Communist leaders; a member of such a cell. [Fr.]

caduceus *ka-dū'si-us*, (*mythol*) *n* the rod of Hermes, messenger of the gods, — a wand surmounted with two wings and entwined by two serpents: — *pl* **cadū'ceī**. — *adj* **cadū'cean**. [L. *cādūceus*, related to Gr. *kērȳkeion*, a herald's wand — *kēryx*, *-ykos*, a herald.]
caducous *ka-dū'kəs*, (*bot*) *adj* (of e.g. leaves or flowers) falling early. [L. *cadūcus* — *cadĕre*, to fall.]
CAE *abbrev* for: College of Advanced Education (*Austr*); computer-aided engineering.
Caecilia *sē-sil'i-ə*, *n* a genus of legless burrowing Amphibia with hidden eyes. — *adj* **caecil'ian**. — *n* any member of the class to which Caecilia belongs. [L. *caecus*, blind.]
caecum or in U.S. **cecum** *sē'kəm*, (*anat*) *n* a blind sac; a sac or bag having only one opening, connected with the intestine of an animal: — *pl* **cae'ca** or in U.S. **cec'a**. — *adj* **cae'cal** or in U.S. **cec'al**. [L., neut. of *caecus*, blind.]
Caenozoic *sē-nō-zō'ik*. Same as **Cainozoic**.
caerulean. See **cerulean**.
Caesar *sē'zər*, *n* an absolute monarch, an autocrat, from the Roman dictator Gaius Julius *Caesar* (100–44 B.C.); (also without *cap*) a Caesarean operation, delivery or birth (*colloq*). — *adj* **Caesarean** or **Caesarian** (*-ā'ri-ən*) relating to Julius Caesar; relating to (a birth carried out by) Caesarean section. — *n* an adherent of Caesar, an imperialist. — *n* **Cae'sarism**. — *n* **Cae'sarist**. — *n* **Cae'sarship**. — **Caesarean section** or **operation** delivery of a child by cutting through the walls of the abdomen (perh. from *caedĕre*, to cut — connected with the tradition that the first bearer of the cognomen *Caesar* was delivered this way).
caesium or in U.S. **cesium** *sēz'i-əm*, *n* an element (atomic no. 55; symbol **Cs**), a silver-white, soft alkaline metal; used in the form of compounds or alloys in photoelectric cells, etc. [L. *caesius*, bluish grey.]
caesura or **cesura** *si-zū'rə*, (*prosody*) *n* division of a foot between two words; a pause in a line of verse (generally near the middle): — *pl* **caesu'ras** or **caesu'rae**. — *adj* **caesū'ral**. [L. *caesūra* — *caedĕre*, *caesum*, to cut off.]
café or **cafe** *kaf'ā* or *ka'fi*, *n* a coffee-house or small modest restaurant. — **café au lait** (*ō le*) coffee made with hot milk; coffee with milk added; **café noir** (*nwär*) black coffee (i.e. without milk); **café society** fashionable society. [Fr. *café*, coffee(-house).]
cafeteria *ka-fi-tē'ri-ə*, *n* a restaurant with a counter for self-service. [Cuban Sp., a tent in which coffee is sold.]
cafetière *kaf-tyār'*, *n* a coffee percolator or similar coffee-maker e.g. a jug with a filter plunger. [Fr.]
caff *kaf*, (*slang*) *n* a café or cafeteria.
caffeine *kaf'ēn* or *kaf-ē'in*, *n* an alkaloid present in coffee and tea, a weak stimulant to the nervous system. — *adj* **caff'einated** containing caffeine. — *n* **caff'einism** or **caffeism** (*kaf'ē-izm*) an unhealthy condition caused by excessive caffeine. [Fr. *caféine*; see **coffee**.]
CAFOD *kaf'od*, *abbrev* for Catholic Fund for Overseas Development.
caftan *kaf'tən* or *kaf-tan'*, *n* a long-sleeved Persian or Turkish garment, reaching to the ankles and often tied with a sash; a similar long, loose garment with wide sleeves. [Turk. *qaftān*.]
cage *kāj*, *n* a box or compartment wholly or partly of open-work for confining captive animals; a frame with a platform or platforms used in hoisting in a vertical shaft; a wire guard; any structure resembling a bird's cage. — *vt* to imprison in a cage: — *pr p* **cag'ing**; *pa t* and *pa p* **caged**. — *adj* **caged** confined. — *n* **cage'ling** a bird that is or has been kept in a cage. — **cage'bird** a bird of a kind habitually kept in a cage; **cage'work** open-work like the bars of a cage. — **cage in** to imprison (usu. *fig*). — **rattle someone's** (or **the**) **cage** (*colloq*) to stir (someone) up, provoke (someone's) anger or irritation. [Fr., — L. *cavea*, a hollow place.]
cagey or **cagy** *kāj'i*, (*colloq*) *adj* not frank, secretive; artfully shy, wary, chary. — *adv* **cag'ily**. — *n* **cag'iness** or **cag'eyness**.
cagoule or **kagoule** *kə-gōōl'*, *n* a lightweight, weatherproof anorak, often knee-length. [Fr. *cagoule*, a monk's hood.]
cagy. See **cagey**.
cahoots *kə-hōōts'*, *npl* esp. in the phrase **in cahoots** (*colloq*), in collusion (with).
CAI *abbrev* for computer-aided (or -assisted) instruction.
caiman. Same as **cayman**.
Cain *kān*, *n* in the Bible, Adam's son, murderer of Abel (Gen. iv.), hence allusively a murderer. — **raise Cain** to make a determined or angry fuss.
Cainozoic *kī-nō-zō'ik*, (*geol*) *adj* and *n* Tertiary. [Gr. *kainos*, new, *zōē*, life.]
caique or **caïque** *kä-ēk'*, *n* a light skiff as used on the Bosporus. [Fr., — Turk. *kaik*, a boat.]
cairn *kārn*, *n* a heap of stones, esp. one raised over a grave, or as a landmark on a mountain-top or path; a small variety of Scottish terrier (also **cairn terrier**). — *adj* **cairned** marked with cairns. — *n* **cairngorm'** or **cairngorm'-stone** brown or yellow quartz found among the Cairngorm Mountains in Scotland. [Gael. *càrn*.]
caisson *kā'sən* or *kə-sōōn'*, *n* a tumbril or ammunition wagon; a strong case for keeping out the water while the foundations of a bridge are being built; an apparatus for lifting a vessel out of the water for repairs or inspection; the pontoon or floating gate used to close a dry dock. — **caisson disease** see **decompression sickness** under **decompress**. [Fr., from *caisse*, a case or chest. (See **case**[1].)]
cajole *kə-jōl'*, *vt* to coax (into); to cheat by flattery (into or out of). — *n* **cajole'ment** coaxing in order to delude; wheedling; flattery. — *n* **cajol'er**. — *n* **cajol'ery**. [Fr. *cajoler*, to chatter.]
Cajun *kā'jən*, *n* a descendant of the French-speaking Acadians deported to Louisiana in 1755; the language of the Cajuns. — *adj* of or pertaining to Cajun or the Cajuns; belonging to or characteristic of Cajun traditions (esp. in reference to their lively syncopated music or spicy cookery). [Corruption of **Acadian**.]
cake *kāk*, *n* a breadlike composition enriched with additions such as sugar, spices, currants, peel, etc.; a separately made mass of such composition; a piece of dough that is baked; a small loaf of fine bread; any flattened mass baked, such as *oatcake*, or formed by pressure or drying, as of soap, clay, snow, blood; cattle cake. — *vt* and *vi* to form into a cake or hard mass. — *n* and *adj* **cāk'ing**. — *adj* **cāk'y** or **cāk'ey**. — **cake hole** (*slang*) mouth; **cake'walk** a dance developed from the prancing movement once performed by American Negroes in competition for a cake; something accomplished with supreme ease. — **a piece of cake** (*colloq*) something very simple to do; **cakes and ale** vaguely, all the good things of life; **go** or **sell like hot cakes** see under **hot**; **have one's cake and eat it** or **eat one's cake and have it** to have the advantage of both alternatives; **take the cake** (*slang*) to carry off the honours, be the ultimate (*ironically*) e.g. in idiocy, or intolerable behaviour; to top it all. [O.N. *kaka*.]
CAL (often *kal*) *abbrev* for computer-aided (or -assisted) learning.
Cal. *abbrev* for (great or large) calorie.
cal. *abbrev* for: calendar; calibre; (small or gram-) calorie.
calabash *kal'ə-bash*, *n* a gourd, or its shell used as a vessel, tobacco-pipe, etc.; the fruit of the calabash tree or its shell similarly used. — **calabash tree** a tropical American tree (*Crescentia cujete*) with large

melonlike fruit. [Fr. *calebasse* — Sp. *calabaza* — Pers. *kharbuz*, melon.]

calaboose *kal'ə-bōōs* or *-bōōs'*, (*US slang*) *n* a prison. [Sp. *calabozo*.]

calabrese *kal-ə-brā'zā*, *n* a kind of green sprouting broccoli. [It., Calabrian.]

calamander *kal-ə-man'dər*, *n* a hard and valuable cabinet-wood of the ebony genus, brownish with black stripes, brought from India and Sri Lanka. [Prob. Sinh.]

calamari *kä-lä-mär'i* or *kal-ə-mär'i*, *n* in Italian cookery, squid. [It., pl. of *calamaro*, squid; see ety. for **calamary**.]

calamary *kal'ə-mər-i*, *n* any of various species of squid. [L. *calamārius* — *calamus* — Gr. *kalamos*, pen, from the shape of their internal shell.]

calamine *kal'ə-mīn* or *-min*, *n* a mineral, zinc carbonate. — **calamine lotion, ointment** or **powder** a soothing lotion, ointment or powder for the skin, containing zinc carbonate or oxide. [Fr. — L.L. *calamīna*, prob. — L. *cadmia*; see **cadmium**.]

calamint *kal'ə-mint*, *n* a plant of an aromatic genus allied to mint and thyme. [Fr. — Gr. *kalaminthē*.]

calamity *kə-lam'i-ti*, *n* a great misfortune; affliction. — *adj* **calam'itous** disastrous, tragic, dreadful. — *adv* **calam'itously**. — *n* **calam'itousness**. [Fr. *calamité* — L. *calamitās*, *-ātis*.]

calamus *kal'ə-məs*, *n* a member of a genus of palms whose stems make canes or rattans; a quill (*zool*); the reed pen used by the ancients in writing: — *pl* **cal'amī**. [L. — Gr. *kalamos*, reed, cane, pen.]

calando *kä-län'dō*, (*mus*) *adj* and *adv* gradually slower and weaker. [It., falling off.]

calandria *kal-an'dri-ə*, *n* a sealed vessel used in the core of certain types of nuclear reactor.

calash *kə-lash'*, *n* a light low-wheeled carriage with a folding top; a large hood with hoops fashionable for ladies in the 18th cent. [Fr. *calèche*; of Slav. origin.]

calc-. See **calci-**.

calcaneum *kal-kā'ni-əm* or **calcaneus** *-kā'ni-əs*, (*anat*) *n* the heel-bone. — *adj* **calca'neal** or **calca'nean**. [L. *calcāneum*, the heel — *calx*, the heel.]

calcar *kal'kär*, *n* a spurlike projection, esp. from the base of a petal (*bot*); a bird's spur (*zool*). — *adj* **cal'carate** bearing one or more spurs. — *adj* **calcar'iform** spur-shaped. — *adj* **cal'carine** spurlike. [L., a spur — *calx*, the heel.]

calcareous *kal-kā'ri-əs*, *adj* chalky; limy. — **calcareous tufa** see **tufa**. [L. *calcārius*, from *calx*, lime.]

calceiform *kal-sē'i-förm* or **calceolate** *kal'sē-ə-lāt*, (*bot*) *adj* slipper-shaped. [L.L. *calceus*, a shoe — *calx*, the heel.]

calceolaria *kal-si-ō-lā'ri-ə*, *n* any plant of the South American genus *Calceolaria*, largely cultivated for the beauty of the slipperlike flowers. slipperwort. [L. *calceolus*, dimin. of *calceus*, a shoe.]

calces. See **calx**.

calci- *kal-si-* or **calc-** *kals-*, *combining form* denoting calcium or limestone. — See **calcium**.

calciferol, etc. See **calcium**.

calcify *kal'si-fī*, *vt* and *vi* to make or become limy, by secretion, deposition or substitution. — *adj* **calcif'ic** calcifying or calcified. — *n* **calcificā'tion** the process of calcifying, a changing into lime. [**calcium**.]

calcine *kal'sīn*, *kal-sīn'* or *kal'sin*, *vt* to reduce to a calx by the action of heat; to subject to prolonged heating, esp. so as to oxidise, or so as to drive off water and carbon dioxide. — *adj* **cal'cinable**. — *n* **calcinā'tion**. [Med. L. *calcināre* — L. *calx*, *calcis*, lime.]

calcite *kal'sīt* or **calcspar** *kalk'spär*, *n* a mineral, calcium carbonate crystallised in the hexagonal system, the main constituent of limestone and many marbles, etc.

calcitonin *kal-si-tō'nin*, *n* a hormone which regulates the amount of calcium in the blood and so inhibits loss of this element from bones. [*calc*ium and *tone*, plus suffix *-in*.]

calcium *kal'si-əm*, *n* a metallic element (atomic no. 20; symbol **Ca**) present in lime, chalk, gypsum, etc. — *adj* **cal'cic** containing calcium. — *adj* **cal'cicole** or **calcic'olous** growing on limestone or limy soils. — *n* **calcif'erol** vitamin D_2. — *adj* **calcif'erous** containing lime. — *adj* **cal'cifuge** (*-fūj*) or **calcif'ugous** (*-ū-gəs*) avoiding limestone. — *adj* **calcigerous** (*-sij'ə-rəs*) containing lime. — **calc-sin'ter** see **tufa**. [L. *calx*, *calcis*, lime, limestone.]

calculate *kal'kū-lāt*, *vt* to count or reckon; to think out, esp. mathematically. — *vi* to make a calculation; to estimate. — *adj* **cal'culable**. — *adv* **cal'culably**. — *adj* **cal'culāted** thought out; reckoned; computed; fitted, likely, of such a nature as probably (to). — *adj* **cal'culāting** that calculates; deliberately selfish and scheming; shrewd, circumspect. — *n* **calculā'tion** the art or process of calculating; an estimate; a forecast, projection. — *adj* **calculā'tional** or **cal'culātive** relating to calculation. — *n* **cal'culātor** a person who or thing that calculates; an electronic device that performs arithmetical calculations; a book, table, etc. for obtaining arithmetical results. — **calculated risk** a possibility of failure, the degree of which has been estimated and taken into account before a venture is undertaken; **calculating machine**. [L. *calculāre*, *-ātum*, to reckon using little stones — *calculus*, dimin. of *calx*, a stone.]

calculus *kal'kū-ləs*, *n* a system of computation used in the higher branches of mathematics (*pl* **cal'culuses**); a stonelike concretion which forms in certain parts of the body (*pl* **cal'culī**). — *adj* **cal'cular** pertaining to the mathematical calculus. — *adj* **cal'culary, cal'culose** or **cal'culous** pertaining to or affected with stone or with gravel. — **differential calculus** a method of treating the values of ratios of differentials or the increments of quantities continually varying; **integral calculus** the summation of an infinite series of differentials; **predicate calculus** a notation system by means of which the logical structure of simple propositions may be represented; **propositional calculus** a notation system in which symbols representing propositions and logical constants are used to indicate the logical relations between propositions. [L.; see ety. at **calculate**.]

caldera *käl-dā'rə*, (*geol*) *n* a volcanic crater of great size. [Sp., cauldron.]

caldron. See **cauldron**.

Caledonian *kal-i-dō'ni-ən*, *adj* pertaining to ancient *Caledonia*, to the Highlands of Scotland, Scotland generally, or (*geol*) to a mountain-forming movement well developed in Scotland. — *n* a Scot. [L. *Călēdŏnia*.]

calefaction *kal-i-fak'shən*, *n* the act of heating; the state of being heated. — *adj* **calefacient** (*-fā'shənt*) warming. — *n* a medicinal preparation that warms the area it is applied to. — *adj* **calefac'tory** warming. [L. *calefacĕre* — *calēre*, to grow hot, *facĕre*, *factum*, to make.]

calendar *kal'ən-dər*, *n* the way in which the natural divisions of time are arranged with respect to each other for the purposes of civil life; an almanac or table of months, days and seasons, or of special facts, etc.; a list of events, appointments, etc. — *vt* to place in a calendar or list; to analyse and index. — *adj* as found on a calendar. — *n* **cal'endarer**. — *n* **calendarisa'tion** or **-z-**. — *vt* **cal'endarise** or **-ize** in accounting, to divide (something, e.g. a budget) into equal units of time within a year (usu. months). — *n* **cal'endarist**. — *adj* **calen'dric** or **calen'drical** of, pertaining to, or like a calendar in some way or another. — **perpetual calendar** see under **perpetual**. [*L. calendārium*, an account-book, *kalendae*, calends.]

calender *kal'ən-dər, n* a machine with bowls or rollers for finishing the surface of cloth, paper, etc., by combined moisture, heat and pressure; a person who calenders (properly a calendrer). — *vt* to dress in a calender. — *n* **cal'endering.** — *n* **cal'endrer.** — *n* **cal'endry** a place where calendering is done. [Fr. *calandre* — L. *cylindrus* — Gr. *kylindros*, roller.]

calendric, calendrical. See **calendar.**

calends *kal'əndz, npl* among the ancient Romans, the first day of each month. [L. *kalendae* — *calāre*, Gr. *kaleein*, to call (because the beginning of the month was proclaimed).]

calendula *ka-len'dū-lə, n* any plant of the genus *Calendula*, the marigold genus. [L. *kalendae*, calends (but the connection is not obvious).]

calenture *kal'ən-chər, n* a tropical fever or delirium caused by heat; heatstroke. [Fr. — Sp. *calentura* — L. *calēns, -entis* — *calēre*, to be hot.]

calf[1] *käf, n* the young of the cow, elephant, whale, and certain other mammals; calfskin leather; an iceberg in relation to its parent glacier: — *pl* **calves** (*kävz*) or (of calfskin) **calfs.** — *vt* and *vi* **calve** (*käv*) to bring forth a calf; to detach (an iceberg). — *adj* **calf'-bound** bound in calfskin. — **calf'-love** a boy's or girl's amorous attachment; **calf's'-foot** or **calves''-foot** the foot of the calf, used in making a jelly; **calf'skin** the skin of the calf, making a good leather for bookbinding and shoes. — **half'-calf** a bookbinding in which the back and corners are in calfskin; **in** or **with calf** (of cows) pregnant; **smooth calf** a binding in plain or undecorated calf leather. [O.E. (Anglian) *cælf*.]

calf[2] *käf, n* the thick fleshy part at the back of the leg below the knee: — *pl* **calves** (*kävz.*) [O.N. *kālfi*.]

calibre or **caliber** *kal'i-bər, n* the diameter of the bore of a gun or tube; character, capacity (*fig*). — *vt* **cal'ibrāte** to determine the calibre of, or the true values answering to the graduations of; to mark calibrations on. — *n* **calibrā'tion** the act of calibrating; one of a series of marks indicating values. — *n* **cal'ibrātor.** — *adj* **cal'ibred** or **cal'ibered.** [Fr. *calibre*, the bore of a gun.]

caliche *kä-lē'chā, n* sodium nitrate, calcium carbonate, and other minerals occurring as concretions in the soil of arid regions. [Sp.]

calico *kal'i-kō, n* a cotton cloth first brought from *Calicut* in India; plain white unprinted cotton cloth, bleached or unbleached; coarse printed cotton cloth: — *pl* **cal'icos** or **cal'icoes.** — *adj* made of calico; with bright or spotted design, as associated with calico.

Calif. *abbrev* for California (U.S. state).

calif. See **caliph.**

californium *kal-i-för'ni-əm, n* a made-made element (atomic no. 98; symbol **Cf**). [First produced at the University of *California*.]

calipash *kal'i-pash, n* the part of a turtle close to the upper shell, a dull greenish fatty gelatinous substance. — *n* **cal'ipee** the light-yellowish portion of flesh from the turtle's belly. [Prob. from W.Indian words.]

caliper *kal'i-pər, n* (in a braking assembly) the part that presses (the brake pads) against the disc or wheel. [Conn. with **callipers.**]

calipers. See **callipers.**

caliph *kal'if* or *kā'lif, n* a successor of Mohammed; the spiritual leader of Islam. — Also **calif, kalif** or **khalif.** — *adj* **cal'iphal.** — *n* **cal'iphate** the office, rank, government or empire of a caliph. [Fr. *calife* — Ar. *khalīfah*, a successor.]

calisthenics. See **callisthenics.**

calk[1]. See **caulk.**

calk[2] *kök, n* a pointed piece on a horseshoe to prevent slipping. — *vt* to provide with a calk. [O.E. *calc*, shoe — L. *calx*, a heel.]

calk[3] or **calque** *kök* or *kalk, vt* to copy by rubbing the back with colouring matter and then tracing with a blunt point. — *n* (usu. **calque**; *kalk*) a loan-translation (q.v.). [L. *calcāre*, to tread — *calx*, the heel.]

call *köl, vi* to cry aloud (often with *out*); to make a short visit (with *on, for* or *at*); to make a telephone call; to demand a show of hands after repeated raising of stakes (*poker*). — *vt* and *vi* (*cards*) to declare (trump suit, etc.). — *vt* to name; to summon; to rouse; to designate or reckon; to select for a special office, e.g. to the bar; to telephone; to read out the names in (a roll); to demand the repayment of (a debt, loan, redeemable bonds, etc.); to apply (an offensive name) to (*colloq*); to make a call (*sport*); to broadcast a commentary on (a race, etc.) (*Austr* and *NZ*). — *n* a summons or invitation (to the witness-box, the telephone, to the stage or rehearsal, etc.); a sense of vocation; a demand; a short visit; a signal by trumpet, bell, etc.; a telephone connection or conversation, or a request for one; occasion, cause (*colloq*); a declaration or undertaking, or the right to make it in turn (*cards*); a decision on the status of a shot, articulated by an umpire or (esp. in *tennis*) a line judge (*sport*); a cry, esp. of a bird; an invitation to the pastorate of a congregation; an option of buying within a certain time certain securities or commodities at a stipulated price (*stock exchange*; also called **call option**); the money paid to secure such an option; one instalment of the payment for newly issued securities. — *n* **call'er.** — *n* **call'ing** vocation. — **call'-bird** a bird trained to lure others into snares by its call; **call'-box** a public telephone box; **call'-boy** a boy who calls the actors when they are required on stage; **call'-girl** a prostitute on call by telephone; **calling card** a visiting card; **call money** (*finance*) money called in for repayment; **call option** see **call** above; **call'-out** see **call out** below; **call sign** or **signal** (*communications*) a combination of letters and numbers, identifying a particular ship, aircraft, transmitter, etc.; **call'-up** an act of calling up, esp. conscription into the armed forces. — **call attention to** to point out; **call back** to recall; to visit again; to telephone again; **call by** (*colloq*) to visit in passing; **call for** to come for and take away with one; to ask loudly for; to demand; to require (*adj* **called'-for** required, necessary; **not called for** uncalled-for); **call forth** to evoke; **call in** to bring in from public use (old currency notes, etc.); to demand repayment of (a debt, etc.); to call to one's help (e.g. a doctor, the police); to withdraw from circulation; to withdraw (e.g. an application); **call in (or into) question** to challenge, throw doubt on; **call off** to summon away; to withdraw or back out; to cancel or abandon; **call of nature** (*euph*) the need to urinate, etc.; **call on** or **upon** to invoke, appeal to; to make a short visit to; **call out** to summon to service, bring into operation; to instruct (members of a trade union) to come out on strike; to request or arrange a visit (e.g. of a repairman, service engineer; *n* and *adj* **call'-out**); **call over** to read aloud (a list); **call the shots** (orig. *US*) or **call the tune** to say what is to happen, to order, or be in command; **call to mind** to recollect, or cause to recollect; **call to order** to call upon (participants) to observe the rules of debate; (of a chairman) to announce that a formal meeting is starting; **call up** to summon, to a tribunal, to service, to memory, etc.; **on call** ready to a answer a summons; **pay a call** (*colloq euph*) to go to the lavatory, respond to a call of nature; **within call** within calling distance. [O.E. *ceallian* and O.N. *kalla*].

calla *kal'ə, n* a marsh plant of the arum family; (also **calla lily**) the arum lily.

callanetics *kal-ə-net'iks, nsing* a system of physical exercise designed to tone the muscles. [From U.S. *Callan* Pinckney, who developed the system in the 1970s; sfx. *-etics* as in ath*letics*.]

caller *käl'ər* or *köl'ər*, (*Scot*) *adj* fresh; cool. [Prob. the same as **calver**.]

calligram or **calligramme** *kal'igram*, *n* a design using the letters of a word. [*calli*graphy and *-gram*.]

calligraphy *kə-lig'rə-fi*, *n* fine penmanship; a characteristic style of writing. — *n* **callig'rapher**. — *adj* **calligraphic** (*kal-i-graf'ik*) or **calligraph'ical**. — *n* **callig'raphist**. [Gr. *kallos*, beauty, *graphein*, to write.]

Calliope *kə-lī'ə-pi* or *kal-ī'o-pē*, (*Gr mythol*) *n* the Muse of epic poetry; (without *cap*) a set of steam-whistles played by a keyboard (*US*). [Gr. *Kalliŏpē*.]

callipers or (esp. in U.S.) **calipers** *kal'i-pərz*, *npl* compasses with legs suitable for measuring the inside or outside diameter of bodies. — *adj* **call'iper**. — *vt* to measure with callipers. — **calliper** or **calliper splint** a splint fitted to the leg, so that the patient may walk without any pressure on the foot. — See also **caliper**. [**calibre**.]

callisthenics or (esp. in U.S.) **calisthenics** *kal-is-then'iks*, *npl* exercises for cultivating gracefulness and strength. — *adj* **callisthen'ic** or **calisthen'ic**. [Gr. *kallos*, beauty, *sthenos*, strength.]

callous *kal'əs*, *adj* hardened; unfeeling, cruel. — *n* **callos'ity** thickening of the skin; callousness. — *adv* **call'ously**. — *n* **call'ousness** lack of feeling, brutality. [L. *callōsus* — *callus*, hard skin.]

callow *kal'ō*, *adj* unfledged, unbearded; inexperienced. [O.E. *calu*.]

callus *kal'əs*, *n* a thickening of the skin; new material by which fractured bones are consolidated (*pathol*); soft tissue that forms over a cut surface (*bot*). [L.]

calm *käm*, *adj* still or quiet; (of a person or an action) serene, tranquil, assured; cool, impudent (*colloq*). — *n* absence of wind (also in *pl*); repose; serenity of feelings or actions. — *vt* and *vi* (also **calm down**) to make or become calm; to quiet. — *vt* to becalm. — *n* and *adj* (*med*) **calmative** (*kal'* or *kä'*). — *adj* **calmed** (*kämd*). — *adv* **calm'ly**. — *n* **calm'ness**. [Fr. *calme* (It. *calma*), from L.L. *cauma* — Gr. *kauma*, noonday heat.]

calomel *kal'ō-mel*, *n* mercurous chloride, used in medicine as a purgative. [Fr., apparently from Gr. *kalos*, beautiful, *melās*, black.]

calorie *kal'ər-i*, *n* the amount of heat needed to raise a gram of water 1° centigrade in temperature (*small* or *gram-calorie*); (sometimes with *cap*) the amount of heat needed to raise a kilogram of water 1° centigrade in temperature (*great*, *large*, *kilogram-calorie* or *kilocalorie*; = 1000 small calories) (used in expressing the heat- or energy-producing value of foods). — *adj* **calorif'ic** causing heat; heating. — *n* **calorificā'tion**. — *n* **calorim'eter** an instrument for measuring heat (not temperature) or thermal constants. — *n* **calorim'etry**. — **calor gas**® (sometimes with *caps*) a type of gas for cooking, heating, etc. usually sold in large metal containers for use where there is no permanent supply of gas; **calorific value** (of a food or fuel) the number of heat units got by complete combustion of unit mass. [L. *calor*, heat.]

calotype *kal'ō-tīp*, *n* an early kind of photography. — *n* **cal'otȳpist**. [Gr. *kalos*, beautiful, *typos*, an image.]

calque. See **calk**[3].

caltha *kal'thə*, *n* a plant of the *Caltha* genus of flowers to which the marsh marigold belongs. [L.]

caltrop *kal'* or *köl'trop*, *n* an old military weapon, an iron ball with four spikes so arranged that when it is on the ground one spike always stands upright, used to obstruct the enemy; a name for several plants with fruits so shaped, e.g. (esp. in *pl*) water chestnut. [O.E. *coltetræppe*, *calcatrippe* — L. *calx*, heel, and the root of **trap**.]

calumet *kal'ū-met*, *n* the peace-pipe of the N. American Indians, a tobacco-pipe smoked in token of peace. [Norman Fr. *calumet*, shepherd's pipe — L. *calamus*, reed.]

calumny *kal'əm-ni*, *n* false accusation; slander. — *vt* **calumniate** (*kə-lum'ni-āt*) to accuse falsely; to slander. — *vi* to spread evil reports. — *n* **calumniā'tion**. — *n* **calum'niātor**. — *adj* **calum'niātory** or **calum'nious** of the nature of calumny; slanderous. — *adv* **calum'niously**. [L. *calumnia*, prob. conn. with *calvī*, to deceive.]

Calvados *kal'və-dos* or *-dos' n* a brandy made from cider or apple-pulp, esp. in the Calvados department of Normandy.

Calvary *kal'və-ri*, *n* the name of the place where Jesus was crucified; a representation of Christ's crucifixion, or a series of scenes connected with it (*Christian relig*). — **Calvary cross** (*heraldry*) a Latin cross on three steps. [L. *calvāria*, skull.]

calve. See **calf**[1].

calver *kal'vər*, *vt* to prepare (salmon or other fish) when alive or freshly caught. — *adj* **cal'vered**. [Cf. **caller**.]

calves. See **calf**[1, 2].

Calvinism *kal'vin-izm*, *n* the doctrines of the great Genevan religious reformer, John *Calvin* (1509–1564), esp. on particular election, predestination, the incapacity for true faith and repentance of the natural man, efficacious grace, and final perseverance (continuance of the saints in a state of grace until the final state of glory). — *n* **Cal'vinist**. — *adj* **Calvinist'ic** or **Calvinist'ical**.

calvities *kal-vish'i-ēz*, (*med*) *n* baldness. [L. *calvitiēs* — *calvus*, bald.]

calx *kalks*, *n* the substance of a metal or mineral that remains after strong heating: — *pl* **calxes** (*kalk'siz*) or **calces** (*kal'sēz*). [L. *calx*, *calcis*, lime.]

calycanthus *kal-i-kan'thəs*, *n* a shrub of the small N. American genus, *Calycanthus*, including *Carolina allspice* or *strawberry shrub*. [N.L.]

calyciform ... to ... **calycoideous**. See **calyx**.

calypso *ka-lip'sō*, *n* a W. Indian folk-song, usually dealing with current events, usually made up as the singer goes along: — *pl* **calyp'sos**. — *n* **calypso'-nian** a writer or singer of calypsos. [Poss. from 17th–18th cent. W. African *kaiso*, ceremonial song.]

calyx *kā'liks* or *kal'iks*, *n* the outer covering of a flower, its separate leaves termed sepals (*bot*); applied to various cuplike structures, such as the cup of a coral (*biol*; by confusion with *calix*, a cup or chalice): — *pl* **ca'lyces** (*-sēz*) or **ca'lyxes**. — *adj* **calyciform** (*kal-is'i-förm*) having the form of a calyx. — *adj* **calyc'inal** or **calycine** (*kal'i-sīn*) pertaining to a calyx. — *adj* **cal'ycoid** or **calycoi'deous** like a calyx. [Gr. *kalyx*, a covering — *kalyptein*, to cover.]

calzone *kal-tsō'ne*, *n* a large pasty-shaped pastry roll filled with cheese, tomato, etc., like a closed pizza: — *pl* **calzo'ni** or **calzo'nes**. [It.]

CAM (often *kam*) *abbrev* for computer-aided manufacturing or manufacture.

cam *kam*, (*mech*) *n* an eccentric projection on a revolving shaft, shaped so as to give some desired linear motion to another part. — **cam'shaft** or **cam'-wheel** a shaft or wheel bearing a cam or cams. [Du. *kam*, cam, comb.]

camaraderie *kam-ə-räd'ə-rē*, *n* good fellowship; the intimacy of comradeship. [Fr.]

camarilla *kam-ə-ril'ə*, *n* a body of secret intriguers; a small room. [Sp. dimin. of *cámara*, a chamber.]

camaron *kam-ar-ōn'* or *kam'ə-ron*, *n* a kind of freshwater crustacean resembling a crayfish. [Sp. *camarón*, a shrimp — L. *cam(m)arus*, a sea-crab.]

camber *kam'bər*, *n* a slight convexity on an upper surface (as on a road, a beam, the deck of a ship, etc.). — *vt* and *vi* to arch slightly. [Fr. *cambre* — L. *camerāre*, to vault.]

Camberwell beauty *kam'bər-wel bū'ti*, *n* a large and beautiful butterfly, first recorded in England in 1748 at *Camberwell*.

cambist *kam'bist*, *n* a person skilled in the science of financial exchange. — *n* **cam'bism** or **cam'bistry**. [It. *cambista* — L. *cambīre*, to exchange.]

cambium *kam'bi-əm*, (*bot*) *n* a layer or cylinder of meristem by whose differentiation into xylem and phloem new wood and bast are formed. — *adj* **cam'bial**. — *adj* **cam'biform**. [L.L. — L. *cambīre*, to change.]

Cambodian *kam-bō'di-ən*, *adj* of or pertaining to *Cambodia* (officially called *Kampuchea* from 1975 to 1979), a country of S.E. Asia. — *n* a native of Cambodia; its language.

Cambrian *kam'bri-ən*, *adj* pertaining to *Cambria* or Wales; Welsh; the geological system (well represented in Wales) next above the Archaean. — *n* an inhabitant of Cambria, or Wales; the Cambrian system. [Latinised from Welsh *Cymry*, Welshmen, *Cymru*, Wales.]

cambric *kam'brik*, *n* a fine white linen, orig. manufactured at *Kamerijk* (Cambrai) in French Flanders; a cotton imitation.

Cambs. *abbrev* for Cambridgeshire.

camcorder *kam'kör-dər*, *n* a video *cam*era and sound *recorder* combined in one unit.

came *kām*, *pa t* of **come**.

camel *kam'əl*, *n* an animal of Asia and Africa with one or two humps on its back, used as a beast of burden and for riding; a watertight structure for raising a vessel in shallow water; a humped type of aeroplane; a light yellowish-brown colour. — *adj* of the colour camel. — *n* **cameleer'** a person who drives or rides a camel. — *n* **cam'elid** an animal of the **Camel'idae**, the camel family of artiodactyls. — Also *adj*. — *adj* **cam'elish** like a camel, obstinate. — *n* **cam'eloid** of the camel family. — Also *n*. — *adj* **cam'el-backed** hump-backed. — **cam'el-corps** troops mounted on camels; **camel hair** or **camel's hair** the hair of the camel; the hair of the squirrel's tail used for paint-brushes; **camel spin** (*skating*) a type of spin in which one leg is extended horizontally behind the skater. [L. *camēlus* — Gr. *kamēlos* — Phoenician or Heb. *gāmāl*.]

camellia *ka-mēl'yə* or *-mel'yə*, *n* any shrub of the *Camellia* genus of evergreen shrubs closely related to tea, native to eastern Asia, grown for the singular beauty of their flowers. [Named from *Camellus*, a Jesuit, who collected plants in the Philippine Islands.]

camelopard *kam-el'ō-pärd* or *kam'əl-ō-pärd*, *n* the giraffe. [L. *camēlopardus* — Gr. *kamēlos*, the camel, *pardălis*, the panther.]

Camembert *kam'əm-ber* (Fr. *kam-ã-ber*), *n* a soft rich cheese made near *Camembert*, in Normandy.

cameo *kam'i-ō*, *n* a gem with a figure (usu. head or bust in profile) carved in relief, esp. one in which a differently coloured lower layer serves as ground; a short literary piece; a small rôle in a play or film: — *pl* **cam'eos**. — *adj* miniature, small and perfect of its kind. — **cam'eo-part** or **-rôle**; **cameo ware** pottery with relief figures against a different colour. [It. *cammeo* — L.L. *cammaeus*.]

camera *kam'ər-ə*, *n* the photographer's apparatus, for recording an outside image on a light-sensitive plate or film; the apparatus that receives the image of the scene and converts it into electrical impulses for transmission (*TV*); a judge's private chamber: — *pl* **cam'eras**. — *adj* **cam'eral**. — *adj* **cam'erāted** chambered; vaulted. — *n* **camerā'tion**. — **cam'eraman** a photographer, esp. for the press, television or cinema; **camera obscura** (*ob-skūr'ə*; L., dark chamber) a dark chamber in which an image of outside objects is projected on a screen. — *adj* **cam'era-ready** (*printing*) (of copy, artwork, etc.) ready to be photographed for plate-making. — *adj* **cam'era-shy** (*colloq*) not liking to be photographed. — **cam'erawork**. — **in camera** in a (judge's private) room; in secret; **on camera** in front of a camera, being filmed. [Orig. a vaulted room, — L. *camera*, Gr. *kamarā*, vault.]

camerlengo *kam-ər-leng'gō* or **camerlingo** *-ling'gō*, *n* a papal treasurer: — *pl* **camerleng'os** or **camerling'os**. [It.]

cami- *kam'i-*, *combining form* short for **camisole**. — *npl* **cam'iknickers** combined camisole and knickers. — *n* **cam'i-top**.

camion *kam'i-ən*, *n* a heavy lorry or wagon. [Fr.]

camisole *kam'i-sōl*, *n* a loose undergarment, a bodice usu. with thin shoulder straps rather than sleeves; a sleeved jacket, a woman's loose negligée or jacket. [Sp. and Prov. *camisa*, shirt — L. *camisia*.]

camlet *kam'lit*, *n* a cloth perhaps originally of camel's hair, but now chiefly of wool and goat's hair. [Fr. — L.L. *camelotum* — L. *camēlus*.]

camomile or **chamomile** *kam'ō-mīl*, *n* a name for several plants related to chrysanthemum, or their dried flowers, used medicinally for the stomach, as a tonic, etc. — **camomile (or chamomile) tea** medicinal tea made with dried camomile flowers. [Fr. *camomille* — L. *chamomilla* — Gr. *chamaimēlon*, lit. earth-apple, from the apple-like smell of its blossoms.]

camouflage *kam'ōō-fläzh* or *kam'ə-fläzh*, *n* any device or means (esp. visual) for disguising, or for deceiving an adversary; the use of such a device or means. — *vt* and *vi* to deceive, counterfeit, disguise. — **camouflage suit** one made of material designed to camouflage the soldier in the field. [Fr. *camouflet*, a whiff of smoke intentionally blown in the face, an affront.]

camp[1] *kamp*, *n* a place on which a tent or tents or the like are pitched; a collection of temporary dwellings, or their inhabitants collectively; temporary quarters of an army, tribe, travellers, holidaymakers, or others; an old fortified site; a permanent military station; a party or side. — *vi* to encamp, or pitch tents; to lodge in a camp (often with *out*, i.e. in the open). — *n* **camp'er** a person who camps; a motor vehicle purpose-built, or which can be converted, for use as temporary living accommodation. — **camp-bed'**, **-chair'**, **-stool'**, etc. a portable folding bed, etc.; **camp'-fire** the fire of an encampment; a reunion, lodge, or section, of certain organisations; **camp-foll'ower** a non-combatant who follows in the train of an army, as servant, etc.; a person associated with a (political, etc.) group without actually being a member; **camp'ground** (*US*) or **camp'site** a ground suitable, or specially laid out, for camping. — **camp on** (*telecomm*) to put (a telephone call) through to an engaged extension, to be connected automatically when the extension is free; **camp out** to live temporarily in a tent or in the open air; to stay temporarily in improvised accommodation. [L. *campus*, a plain.]

camp[2] *kamp*, *adj* theatrical, affected, exaggerated; effeminately homosexual; characteristic of homosexuals. — *n* absurd extravagance in manner, deliberate (**high camp**) or without full awareness of the effect. — Also *vi*. — *adj* **camp'y**. — **camp up** to make exaggerated, etc.; **camp it up** to show camp qualities ostentatiously.

campaign *kam-pān'*, *n* the time during which an army keeps the field; the operations of that time; an organised series of operations in the advocacy of some cause or object. — *vi* to serve in or conduct a campaign. — *n* **campaign'er**. [Fr. *campagne* — L. *campania* — *campus*, a field.]

campaniform *kam-pan'i-förm*, (*biol*) *adj* bell-shaped, dome-shaped. [L.L. *campana*, a bell and **-form**.]

campanile *kam-pan-ē'lā*, *n* a bell-tower, esp. a tall one detached from the church. [It., from *campana*, a bell.]

campanology *kam-pən-ol'ə-ji*, *n* the subject or science of bells or bell-ringing. — *adj* **campano-**

log'ical. — *n* **campanol'ogist.** [L.L. *campana*, a bell, and **-ology**.]

campanula *kam-pan'ū-lə*, *n* a plant of the *Campanula* genus (giving its name to a family **Campanulā'ceae** commonly known as bell-flowers or bells, the best-known being the harebell or Scottish bluebell. — *adj* **campanūlā'ceous.** [N.L. — L.L. *campana*, a bell.]

campanulate *kam-pan'ū-lāt*, *adj* bell-shaped. [L.L. *campana*, a bell.]

camphor *kam'fər*, *n* a solid essential oil, derived from the camphor laurel (a species of cinnamon tree) of Taiwan, etc., or synthetically manufactured, having a peculiar aromatic taste and smell; any similar compound. — *adj* **camphorā'ceous** like camphor. — *vt* **cam'phorate** to impregnate with camphor. — *adj* **camphoric** (*-for'ik*) pertaining to camphor. [Fr. *camphre* — L.L. *camphora* — Ar. *kāfūr*.]

campion *kam'pi-ən*, *n* any plant of the genera *Lychnis* (or *Melandryum*) and *Silene*.

campus *kam'pəs*, *n* college grounds (and buildings), or a college, or a self-contained division of a university; a university; the academic world. [L., field.]

campylobacter *kam'pil-ō-bak-tər*, *n* a bacterium that is a common cause of food poisoning in humans, and also of abortion in cattle and sheep. — *n* **campylobactēriō'sis** infection with campylobacter. [Gr. *kampylos*, bent, *bacterion*, a litte rod (from its shape).]

CAMRA *kam'rə*, *abbrev* for Campaign for Real Ale.

cam-wood *kam'-wŏŏd*, *n* the wood of a West African tree, at first white, turning red on exposure to air, used as a red dye. [Perh. from African name *kambi*.]

Can. *abbrev* for: Canada; Canadian.

can[1] *kan*, *vt* (*obs* in *infinitive* except in Scots) to be able; to have sufficient power; to have skill in: — *3rd person* **can**; *pa t* **could**. [O.E. *cunnan*, to know (how to do a thing), to be able; pres. indic. *can*. See **con**[2], **ken, know**; also **cannot, can't, couthy.**]

can[2] *kan*, *n* a tin, vessel of tin-plate in which meat, fruit, etc., are sealed up; a vessel for holding or carrying liquids, generally of tinned iron, with a handle over the top; a container for various things, such as ashes or rubbish (*US*), or film in quantity; a jacket in which a fuel rod is sealed in an atomic reactor; (with *the*) jail (*slang*); a lavatory (*slang*); (in *pl*) headphones (*slang*). — *vt* to put into tins to preserve; to store in containers; to stop, put an end to (*US colloq*): — *pr p* **cann'ing**; *pa p* and *pa t* **canned**. — *adj* **canned** packed in tins; (of music) recorded for reproduction; drunk (*slang*). — *n* **can'ful** as much as a can will hold: — *pl* **can'fuls.** — *n* **cann'er.** — *n* **cann'ery** a place where provisions are tinned. — **can bank** the equivalent of a bottle bank (q.v.) for cans; **can'-opener** a tin-opener. — **can of worms** an unpredictable and potentially difficult situation or problem; **carry the can** (*slang*) to take the blame. [O.E. *canne*.]

Canadian *kə-nā'di-ən*, *adj* pertaining to *Canada*. — *n* a native or citizen of Canada. — **Canada Day** a Canadian public holiday, the anniversary of the union of the provinces, 1 July 1867 (formerly called **Dominion Day**); **Canada goose** a common wild goose (*Branta canadensis*) of N. America.

canaille *kan-äy'*, *kan-ī'* or *kən-āl'*, *n* the mob, the vulgar rabble. [Fr., — L. *canis*, a dog.]

canakin. See **cannikin**.

canal *kə-nal'*, *n* an artificial watercourse, esp. for navigation; a duct that conveys fluids (*biol*); a groove. — *adj* **canalicular** (*kan-ə-lik'ū-lər*) like or pertaining to a canaliculus. — *adj* **canalic'ulate** or **canalic'ulated** channelled, grooved. — *n* **canalic'ulus** (*anat*) a small furrow or channel: — *pl* **canalic'ulī**. — *n* **canalisation** or **-z-** (*kan-əl-ī-zā'shən*) the construction of canals; formation of an artificial channel; conversion into a canal; direction into a fixed channel (*lit* and *fig*). — *vt* **can'alise** or **-ize** to make a canal through; to convert into a canal; to direct into a fixed channel (*lit* and *fig*). — **canal'-boat** a boat for canal traffic; **canal'-rays** (*phys*) positive rays, a stream of positively electrified particles through a perforation in the cathode of a vacuum-tube. [L. *canālis*, a water pipe.]

canapé *ka'nə-pi* or *ka-na-pā*, *n* a small biscuit or piece of pastry or bread, etc., with a savoury filling or spread, usu. served with drinks. [Fr., a (covered) sofa, a canapé.]

canard *ka-när'* or *ka-närd'*, *n* a false rumour; a second wing fitted near the nose of an aircraft, esp. one smaller than the main wing and acting as the horizontal stabiliser; an aircraft with such a wing. — *adj* denoting such a wing, aircraft configuration, etc. [Fr., lit. duck.]

canary *kə-nā'ri*, *n* a songbird (finch) found in the Canary Islands, bright yellow in domestic breeds; a light sweet wine from the *Canary* Islands. — *adj* canary-coloured, bright yellow. — **canā'ry-grass** a grass whose seed **(canā'ry-seed)** is used to feed canaries.

canasta *kə-nas'tə*, *n* a card game of the rummy type, originating in S. America. [Sp., basket.]

canaster *kə-nas'tər*, *n* a roughly-broken kind of tobacco (so called from the rush basket in which it was originally brought from Spanish America). [Sp. *canastro* — Gr. *kanastron*.]

cancan *kan'kan*, *n* a stage dance of French origin, orig. considered very improper because of the high-kicking. [Fr. *cancan*, chatter, scandal, the cancan.]

cancel *kan'sl*, *vt* to annul or suppress; to abolish or wipe out; to counterbalance or compensate for; to cross out; (often with *out*) to remove as balancing each other, e.g. like quantities from opposite sides of an equation. — *vi* (with *out*) to neutralise each other: — *pr p* **can'celling**; *pa t* and *pa p* **can'celled.** — *n* the suppression of a printed leaf or sheet; the part so cancelled, or (usually) the new one substituted. — *adj* **can'cellate** or **cancellat'ed** marked with a lattice-like pattern, reticulated; spongy (*anat*). — *n* **cancellā'tion** cancelling; crosswise marking. [L. *cancellāre*, to cross out.]

cancellarial *kan-səl-ār'i-əl* or **cancellarian** *-ār'i-ən*, *adj* relating to a chancellor. — *n* **cancellā'riate** chancellorship. [L. *cancellārius*; see **chancellor.**]

Cancer *kan'sər*, *n* the genus to which the edible crab belongs; a constellation (the Crab) between Gemini and Leo, and a sign of the zodiac (once coincident with it); a person born between 23 June and 23 July, under the sign of Cancer; (without *cap* in the following senses) loosely any malignant new growth or tumour; properly a carcinoma or disorderly growth of cells which invade adjacent tissue and may spread to other parts of the body; the condition caused by this; any corroding evil (*fig*). — *vi* **can'cerate** to become cancerous. — *n* **cancerā'tion.** — *adj* **can'cerous** of, like or affected with cancer. — *n* **cancerphobia** or **cancerophobia** (*-fō'bi-ə*) excessive fear of contracting, or that one may have, cancer. — *adj* **cancriform** (*kang'kri-förm*) crab-shaped; like cancer. — *n* **cancroid** (*kang'kroid*) crablike; cancerlike. — Also *n*. — See also **tropic**. [L., crab.]

CAND *abbrev* for Campaign Against Nuclear Dumping.

candela *kan-del'ə* or *-dē'lə*, *n* a unit of luminous intensity. [**candle.**]

candelabrum *kan-di-la'brəm* or *-lä'brəm*, *n* a branched and ornamented candlestick or lampstand: — *pl* **candela'bra** (also used as a false *sing* with *pl* **candela'bras**). — **candelabrum tree** any of several African trees with branches arranged like a candelabrum. [L. *candēlābrum* — *candēla*, candle.]

candescent *kan-des'ənt*, *adj* glowing; white-hot. — *n* **candesc'ence**. [L. *candēscere* — *candēre*, to glow.]

C and G *abbrev* for City and Guilds (of London Institute).

candid *kan'did, adj* frank, ingenuous; unposed, unrehearsed, informal; fair, impartial. — *adv* **can'didly.** — *n* **can'didness.** [L. *candidus*, white.]

candidate *kan'di-dāt, n* a person who seeks or is nominated for any office or honour, so called because, at Rome, the applicant used to dress in white; a person or thing apparently suitable for a particular end; an examinee. — *n* **can'didature, can'didateship** or **can'didacy** (*-də-si*). [L. *candidātus* — *candidus*, white.]

candied. See **candy.**

candle *kan'dl, n* a cylinder of wax, tallow, or the like surrounding a wick, burned to give light; something resembling this in appearance or function; a candela. — *vt* to test (e.g. an egg) by holding it up before a candle or other light. — **can'dle-berry** wax myrtle or bayberry of the spurge family, or its fruit; **can'dle-dipping** the method of making candles by dipping instead of moulding; **can'dle-end** the end-piece of a burnt-out candle; **can'dle-holder** a candlestick or candelabrum; **can'dle-light** the light of a candle; illumination by candles; **can'dle-power** the illuminating power of a source of light; **can'dlestick** a portable stand for a candle; **can'dlewick** the wick of a candle; a cotton tufted material used for bedspreads, etc.; **can'dle-wood** the wood of various West Indian and Mexican resinous trees. — **burn the candle at both ends** to exhaust oneself by attempting to do too much, usu. by going to bed late and getting up early for work; **do a candle** (of a parachute) to fail to inflate; **not fit to hold a candle to** not to be compared with; **the game is not worth the candle** the thing is not worth the labour or expense of it. [O.E. *candel* — L. *candēla*, from *candēre*, to glow.]

Candlemas *kan'dl-məs, (Christian relig) n* the church festival of the purification of the Virgin Mary, on 2 February, when candles are blessed. [**candle** and **mass**[2].]

candour or in U.S. **candor** *kan'dər, n* sincerity; frankness. [Fr. *candeur* — L. *candor*, whiteness, from *candēre*, to shine.]

C and W *abbrev* for country and western (music).

candy *kan'di, n* a sweet of sugar boiled and crystallised (also **sugar-can'dy**) any form of confectionery (*US*). — *vt* to preserve or coat with sugar; (of sugar or the like) to crystallise; to encrust. — *vi* to crystallise; to become encrusted. — *adj* **can'died** encrusted with candy or sugar; sugared, flattering (*fig*). — **candy floss** a fluffy ball of spun, coloured and flavoured sugar sold on the end of a stick; something insubstantial or ephemeral. — Also *adj.* — **candy stripe** a textile fabric pattern, consisting of narrow coloured stripes on a white background. [Fr. *candi*, from Ar. *qandah*, candy.]

candytuft *kan'di-tuft, n* a cruciferous plant with flowers in tufts, the outer petals larger than the inner. [*Candia* (Crete), where the species originated, and **tuft.**]

cane *kān, n* the stem of one of the small palms (e.g. calamus or rattan) or the larger grasses (e.g. bamboo or sugar-cane), or raspberry or the like; wicker, rattan, etc. used to weave baskets or light furniture; a slender stick used as a support for plants, etc.; a slender rod for beating; a walking-stick. — *vt* to beat with a cane; to make or weave (e.g. chairs) with canes. — *n* **can'ing** a thrashing with a cane; a severe beating or defeat (*colloq*). — *adj* **can'y** like, made of, or abounding in cane. — *adj* **cane'-bottomed** having a seat of interwoven cane strips. — **cane'-brake** a thicket of canes; **cane'-chair** a chair made of rattan; **cane'fruit** fruit borne on canes, such as raspberries and blackberries; **cane'-mill** a mill for crushing sugar-cane; **cane'-sugar** sucrose, esp. that obtained from the sugar-cane; **cane'-toad** (*Austr*) the large toad (*Bufo marinus*) introduced to, and now abundant in, Queensland; **cane'-work** strips of cane woven to form chair-backs, baskets, etc.; the craft of weaving cane. [Fr. *canne* — L. *canna* — Gr. *kannē*, a reed.]

canellini. See **cannellini.**

cangle *kang'l, (Scot) n* noise, disturbance. — *vi* to argue, wrangle. [Cf. Norw. *kjangle*, to quarrel.]

canine *kan'īn* or *kān'īn, adj* like or pertaining to the dog or related species. — *n* any animal of the dog tribe; a canine tooth. — *n* **caninity** (*kə-* or *kā-nin'i-ti*). — *n* **Ca'nis** the dog genus, typical of the family **Can'idae.** — **canine appetite** a huge appetite; **canine tooth** a sharp-pointed tooth between the incisors and the premolars. [L. *canīnus* — *canis*, a dog.]

canister *kan'is-tər, n* a box or case, usu. of metal, for holding tea, shot, etc. [L. *canistrum*, a wicker-basket; Gr. *kanastron* — *kannē*, a reed.]

canities *ka-nish'i-ēz, n* whiteness of the hair. [L.]

canker *kang'kər, n* an ulcer; ulceration; a fungus disease in trees; inflammation in horses' feet; irritation and ulceration in dogs' and cats' ears; an abscess or ulcer in birds; anything that corrupts, consumes, irritates or decays; a canker-worm. — *vt* to eat into, corrupt or destroy; to infect or pollute; to make sour and ill-conditioned. — *vi* to grow corrupt; to decay. — *adj* **cank'ered** malignant, soured, crabbed. — *adv* **cank'eredly.** — *n* **cank'eredness.** — *adj* **cank'erous** corroding like a canker. — *adj* **cank'ery** affected with canker. — **cank'er-worm** a larva that cankers or eats into plants. [L. *cancer*, a crab, gangrene.]

canna, cannae. See **cannot.**

cannabis *kan'ə-bis, n* (with *cap*) the hemp genus; a plant of this genus, esp. common hemp or Indian hemp; a mood-altering drug obtained from these. — *adj* **cann'abic.** — *n* **cann'abin** a resin obtained from the dried leaves and flowers of the cannabis plant, containing the active principle of the drug. — *n* **cann'abinoid** any one of a number of substances found in cannabin, having narcotic or mood-altering properties. — **cannabis resin** cannabin. [Gr. *kannabis*].

cannel *kan'l, n* a bituminous coal that burns with a bright flame, used for making oils and gas. — Also **cann'el-coal.** [Prob. form of **candle.**]

cannellini or **canellini** *kan-ə-lē'nē, n* a kind of white kidney bean used in French and Italian cooking. — Also **cannellini bean.**

cannelloni *kan-ə-lō'nē, n* hollow tubes of pasta, served stuffed with cheese, meat, etc. [It.]

cannelure *kan'i-lūr, n* a groove or a fluting; a groove round the cylindrical part of a bullet. [Fr.]

cannibal *kan'i-bl, n* any eater of the flesh of its own species. — *adj* relating to or practising cannibalism. — *vt* **cann'ibalise** or **-ize** to repair (a vehicle, aircraft, etc.) with parts taken from other vehicles, etc.; to take (parts), or take parts from (aircraft), for such repairs. — *n* **cannibalisa'tion** or **-z-.** — *n* **cann'ibalism** the practice of eating one's own kind. — *adj* **cannibalist'ic.** [Sp. *Caníbal*, *Caríbal*, Carib.]

cannon *kan'ən, n* a great gun usu. mounted on wheels (*hist*; *pl* **cann'ons** or **cann'on**); a rapid-firing, large-calibre gun fitted to an aeroplane, ship or helicopter gunship (*pl* **cann'ons** or **cann'on**); a cannon bone; a stroke in which the cue-ball hits both the red and the opponent's ball (*billiards*). — *vi* to cannonade; to make a cannon (*billiards*); to strike on the rebound; to collide. — *vt* to collide with. — *n* **cannonade'** an attack with heavy artillery. — *vt* to attack or batter with heavy artillery. — **cann'onball** a ball to be shot from a cannon (*hist*); something resembling this in appearance, weight or force. — *vi* to move rapidly with great force. — **cannon bone** the bone below the knee or hock in hoofed mammals; **cann'on-fodder** men regarded merely as material to be expended in war; **cann'on-shot** a cannonball; the distance to which a cannon will propel a ball. [Fr. *canon* — L. *canna*, a reed.]

cannot *kan'ət, vb* can not (contracted to **can't** *känt*, *Scots* **canna** *kan'ä* or *kan'ə*, **cannae** *kan'ä*). [**can**[1] and **not**.]

cannula *kan'ū-lə*, (*med*) *n* a surgical tube, or the breathing-tube inserted in the windpipe after tracheotomy: — *pl* **cann'ulae** (*-ū-lē*) or **cann'ulas**. — *adj* **cann'ular**. — *adj* **cann'ulate**. [Dimin. of L. *canna*, a reed.]

canny *kan'i, adj* knowing; skilful; shrewd; sparing in money matters; good, nice (*Scot* and *Northern*); well, fortunate (*Scot*); sly or pawky. — Also *adv*. — *adv* **cann'ily**. — *n* **cann'iness**. [App. conn. with **can**[1].]

canoe *kə-nōō', n* a narrow, flat-bottomed boat propelled by paddling (orig. made of a hollowed tree-trunk). — *vi* to paddle a canoe. — *n* **canoe'ing**. — *n* **canoe'ist**. [Sp. *canoa* — Haitian *canoa*.]

canon[1] *kan'ən, n* a law or rule, esp. in ecclesiastical matters; a general rule or principle; standard or criterion; the books of the Bible accepted as the standard or rule of faith by the Jewish or Christian faiths; works forming any similar standard; the recognised genuine works of any author; a type of musical composition constructed according to a rule, one part following another in imitation; a list of saints canonised. — *adj* **canonic** (*kə-non'ik*) or **canon'ical** of the nature of, according to, or included in a canon; regular; ecclesiastical. — *adv* **canon'ically**. — *npl* **canon'icals** the official dress of the clergy, regulated by the church canons. — *n* **canonicity** (*kan-ən-is'i-ti*) the state of belonging to the canon. — *n* **canonisā'tion** or **-z-**. — *vt* **can'onise** or **-ize** to enrol in the canon or list of saints. — *n* **can'onist** a person learned in canon law. — *adj* **canonist'ic**. — **canonical hours** set hours for prayer; **canon law** a digest of the formal decrees of councils, and of patriarchal decisions as to doctrine and discipline. [Gr. *kanōn*, a straight rod — *kannē*, a reed.]

canon[2] *kan'ən, n* a member of a body of clergymen serving a cathedral or other church and living under a rule; a clerical dignitary belonging especially to a cathedral, enjoying special emoluments, and obliged to reside there part of the year. — *n* **can'oness** a member of a community of women living under a rule; a woman holding a prebend or canonry, often living in the secular world. — *n* **can'onry** the benefice of a canon. — **canon regular** a member of either of two orders of clergy intermediate between monks and secular clergy. [O.E. *canonic* — L. *canonicus* — *canōn*; see **canon**[1].]

canoodle *kə-nōōd'l*, (*slang*) *vi* to embrace amorously.

canopy *kan'ə-pi, n* a covering hung over a throne or bed; a ceremonial covering held over the head; any overhanging covering, such as the sky; the topmost layer of branches in a forest; a rooflike projection over a tomb, stall, etc.; the transparent cover over the cockpit of an aircraft; the overhead fabric part of a parachute. — *vt* to cover with a canopy: — *pr p* **can'opying**; *pa t* and *pa p* **can'opied**. [Gr. *kōnōpion*, a couch with a mosquito curtain — *kōnōps*, a mosquito.]

Cant. *abbrev* for: Canterbury; Canticles.

cant[1] *kant, vi* to use the language of thieves, etc.; to talk in an affectedly solemn or hypocritical way. — *n* a hypocritical or affected or perfunctory style of speech or thought; the language peculiar to a sect; odd or peculiar talk of any kind; slang; affected use of religious phrases or sentiments. — Also *adj*. — *n* **cant'er**. — *adj* **cant'ing** whining, pretending to piety. [L. *cantāre*, frequentative of *canĕre*, to sing.]

cant[2] *kant, n* an inclination from the level; a toss or jerk which tilts anything; a sloping or tilted position or face. — *vt* and *vi* to turn on the edge or corner; to tilt or toss suddenly; to tilt, slope. — *adj* **cant'ed** tilted, sloping. — *n* **cant'ing**. — **cant'-board** a sloping board; **cant'dog** or **cant'-hook** a metal hook on a long handle, for rolling logs; **cant'-rail** a timber supporting the roof of a railway carriage. [Prob. conn. with Du. *kant*; Ger. *Kante*, corner.]

can't. See **cannot**.

Cantab. *kan'tab, abbrev* for *Cantabrigiensis* (L.), of Cambridge.

cantabile *kan-tä'bē-lā*, (*mus*) *adj* easy and flowing. — Also *n*. [It., suitable for singing.]

Cantal *kan'tal* or *kä'tal, n* a hard, full-fat French cheese made from cow's milk, from the *Cantal* department of the Auvergne.

cantaloupe or **cantaloup** *kan'tə-lōōp, n* a small, ribbed musk melon; in U.S. extended to other varieties. [Fr., — It. *Cantalupo*, near Rome, where it was first grown in Europe.]

cantankerous *kən-tang'kər-əs, adj* irascible; contrary, stubborn. — *adv* **cantan'kerously**. — *n* **cantan'kerousness**. [M.E. *contek*, strife.]

cantata *kan-tä'tə, n* a choral work, a short oratorio or opera intended for concert performance only. [It., — L. *cantāre*, frequentative of *canĕre*, to sing.]

cantate *kan-tä'tā* or *kan-tā'tē, n* the 98th Psalm, from its opening words in Latin, 'Cantate Domino'.

canteen *kan-tēn', n* a flask for carrying liquids, used by soldiers, etc.; a set of cooking utensils for soldiers, campers, etc.; a box containing a set of knives, forks and spoons; a set of cutlery; a refreshment-house or small shop for soldiers; a restaurant attached to a factory, office, etc. — **wet (or dry) canteen** one in which alcoholic drinks are (or are not) sold. [Fr. *cantine* — It. *cantina*, a cellar.]

canter *kan'tər, n* an easy gallop. — *vi* to move at an easy gallop. — *vt* to make (a horse, etc.) canter. [Orig. *Canterbury-gallop*, from the easy pace at which the pilgrims rode to Canterbury.]

canterbury *kan'tər-bər-i, n* a stand with divisions in it for holding books, music, etc.: — *pl* **can'terburys** or **can'terburies**. — **Canterbury bells** or **bell** a flower (*Campanula medium*) with large blue, white or pink bells.

cantharides *kan-thar'i-dēz, npl* a blistering agent and stimulant made from the dried bodies of the Spanish fly, formerly also used as an aphrodisiac. — Also **Spanish fly**. — *adj* **canthar'idal, cantharid'ian** or **canthar'idine** the active principle of cantharides. [Gr. *kantharidĕs*, pl. of *kantharis*, an insect used for blistering.]

canthus *kan'thəs, n* the angle at the junction of the eyelids: — *pl* **can'thī**. [Gr. *kanthos*.]

canticle *kan'ti-kl, n* a song; a non-metrical hymn, esp. one used in church service as the *Benedicite*; a short canto; (in *pl*; usu. with *cap*) the Song of Solomon. [L. *canticum*, dimin. *canticulum*.]

cantilena *kan-ti-lē'nə, n* a ballad or light song; a vocal or instrumental melody; a singing exercise. [L. *cantilēna*.]

cantilever *kan'ti-lēv-ər* or *-lēv'ər, n* a support fixed at one end and free at the other. — *adj* **can'tilevered**. — **cantilever bridge** one composed of arms projecting from the piers and connected together in the middle of the span. [Perh. **cant**, angle, and **lever**.]

cantillate *kan'ti-lāt, vt* and *vi* to chant, intone. — *n* **cantillā'tion**. — *adj* **can'tillatory**.

cantina *kan-tē'nə, n* a bar, saloon; a wine-shop. [Sp. and It.]

cantle *kan'tl, n* a corner, edge or slice of anything; the raised hind part of a saddle. [**cant**[2], edge.]

canto *kan'tō, n* a division of a long poem; the part that carries the melody (*mus*): — *pl* **can'tos**. [It., — L. *cantus* — *canĕre*, to sing.]

canton *kan'tən* or *kan-ton', n* a division of territory, constituting in Switzerland a separately governed region, in France a subdivision of an arrondissement. — *vt* to divide into cantons; (*mil* pronunciation *kən-tōōn'*) to allot quarters to: — *pr p* **can'toning**;

pa t and *pa p* **can'toned**. — *adj* **can'tonal** pertaining to or divided into cantons. — *vt* **can'tonise** or **-ize** to divide (a town etc.) into separate areas according to the religions, ethnic origins, etc. of the inhabitants. — *n* **cantonisa'tion** or **-z-**. — *n* **canton'ment** (*mil* pronunciation *kən-tōōn'mənt*) the temporary quarters of troops taking part in manoeuvres or active operations. [O.Fr. *canton*; It. *cantone*, corner, district — *canto*, a corner: cf. **cant**^{2}.]

Cantonese *kan-ton-ēz'*, *adj* belonging to or typical of *Canton*, a city in S. China; esp. of a style of cooking originating there. — *n* a native of Canton; the dialect of Chinese spoken in Southern China and Hong Kong: — *pl* **Cantonese'**.

cantor *kan'tör*, *n* the leader of the singing in a church, a precentor; in a synagogue, the person who chants the liturgy and leads the congregation in prayer. [L., singer, *canĕre*, to sing.]

cantrip *kan'trip*, (*Scot*) *n* a freak or wilful piece of trickery; a witch's spell.

Cantuar. *kan'tū-är*, *abbrev* for: *Cantuaria* (L.), Canterbury; *Cantuariensis* (L.), of Canterbury.

Canuck *kə-nuk'*, (*Can colloq*; often *derog*) *n* a French-Canadian.

canvas *kan'vəs*, *n* a coarse cloth made of cotton, hemp or other material, used for sails, tents, etc., and for painting on; the sails of a ship; a piece of stretched canvas, painted or to be painted; the covered front or back of a racing-boat (whence **a canvas-length, win by a canvas**) (*rowing*); open-weave material on which embroidery or tapestry is worked. — *vt* to cover with canvas. — **can'vas-stretcher** a wooden frame on which canvas is stretched for oil-painting; **can'vas-work** embroidery on canvas, or on cloth over which canvas has been laid to guide the stitches. — **under canvas** having the sails unfurled, under sail; living in a tent. [O.Fr. *canevas* — L. *cannabis* — Gr. *kannabis*, hemp.]

canvass *kan'vəs*, *vt* to examine; to discuss; to solicit votes, orders, contributions, etc., from. — *vi* to solicit votes, etc. (with *for*); to go from person to person seeking information. — *n* close examination; a seeking or solicitation of votes, information, etc. — *n* **can'vasser**. [**canvas**.]

cany. See **cane**.

canyon *kan'yən*, *n* a deep gorge or ravine. [Sp. *cañón*, a hollow, from root of **cannon**.]

canzone *kant-sō'nā* or **canzona** *kan-zō'nə*, *n* a song or air resembling a madrigal but less strict: — *pl* **canzo'ni** (*-nē*) or **canzo'nas**. — *n* (*dimin*) **canzonet** (*kan-zō-net'*) or **canzonetta** (*kan-tsō-net'ə*): — *pl* **canzonet'te** (*-tā*). [It., a song, L. *cantiō*, *-ōnis* — *canĕre*, to sing.]

caoutchouc *kow'chŏŏk*, *n* india-rubber, gum elastic; the latex of rubber trees. [Fr., — Carib *cahuchu*.]

CAP (sometimes *kap*) *abbrev* for Common Agricultural Policy.

cap *kap*, *n* a flat brimless hat, usu. with a peak; an official or symbolic headdress or one appropriated to a special class or use, academic, athletic, etc.; membership of a team symbolised by a cap; an artificial covering for a tooth, replacing the natural enamel; a caplike covering of any kind; a percussion cap (q.v.) for a toy gun; the top of a toadstool; the uppermost or terminal part of anything; (also **Dutch cap**) a contraceptive diaphragm. — *vt* to cover the end or top of; to touch with a cap in conferring a degree; to admit to membership of a team; to outdo or surpass by following with a better; to set a limit to (esp. local authority budgets). — *vt* and *vi* to salute by raising the cap: — *pr p* **capp'ing**; *pa p* and *pa t* **capped** (*kapt*). — *n* **capp'er**. — *n* **capp'ing** the action of the verb *cap*; a covering; a graduation ceremony. — **cap pistol** a toy gun using a percussion cap; **cap rock** a stratum of (usu. impervious) rock overlying oil- or gas-bearing strata; **cap sleeve** a short sleeve, just covering the shoulder; **cap'stone** a coping stone; the horizontal stone of a dolmen (*archaeol*); a flat stone acting as a cap e.g. to a shaft. — **cap and bells** the marks of a professional jester; **cap and collar mortgage** one having a minimum (*collar*) and maximum (*cap*) rate of interest; **cap in hand** submissively; supplicatingly; **cap of liberty** the conical cap given to a Roman slave on enfranchisement, and for this reason popular during the French revolution, now the symbol of republicanism; **cap verses** to quote verses in turn, according to rule; **set one's cap at** (of a woman) to set oneself to captivate (a man); **the cap fits** the allusion is felt to apply; **throw up one's cap** to make this gesture (*lit* or *fig*) in token of immoderate joy; **to cap it all** as a (usu. unpleasant) climax. [O.E. *cæppe* — L.L. *cappa*, a cape or cope.]

cap. (sometimes *kap*) *abbrev* for: capital; *capiat* (L.), let him (or her) take.

capable *kā'pə-bl*, *adj* having practical ability; able (often with *of*); qualified. — *n* **capabil'ity** the quality or state of being capable; (usu. in *pl*) a feature capable of being used or developed; ability for the action indicated, because provision and preparation have been made; manufacturing facilities, such as factories or plant. — *n* **cā'pableness**. — **capable of** able, good, well-made, etc., enough to, or bad, foolish, etc., enough to (followed by a verbal noun or other action noun); susceptible of. [Fr., — L.L. *capābilis* — L. *capĕre*, to hold, take.]

capacious *kə-pā'shəs*, *adj* including much; roomy; wide; extensive. — *adv* **capā'ciously**. — *n* **capā'ciousness**. [L. *capāx*, see **capacity**.]

capacitance *kə-pas'i-təns*, *n* the property that allows a system to store an electric charge; the value of this expressed in farads (q.v.). — *n* **capac'itor** an electrical device having large capacitance, usu. consisting of conductors separated by an insulator. [**capacity**.]

capacity *kə-pas'i-ti*, *n* power of holding, containing, absorbing or grasping; room; volume; ability; power of mind; the character in which one does something; legal competence; maximum possible output or performance; capacitance; possession of industrial plant, technology, etc., with resulting ability to produce goods. — *adj* attaining the full capacity. — *vt* **capac'itate** to make capable; to qualify. — *n* **capacitā'tion**. — **capacity for heat** power of absorbing heat; **legal capacity** the power to alter one's rights or duties by the exercise of free will, or responsibility for one's acts; **to capacity** to the utmost capacity, the fullest extent possible. [Fr. *capacité* — L. *capāx*, *-ācis*, able to receive — *capĕre*, to hold.]

caparison *kə-par'i-sən*, *n* a rich cloth laid over a war-horse; dress and ornaments generally. — *vt* to cover (e.g. a horse) with a cloth; to dress very richly. — *adj* **capar'isoned**. [Fr. *caparaçon* — L.L. *cappa*.]

cape^1 *kāp*, *n* a covering for the shoulders attached to a coat or cloak; a sleeveless cloak. — *n* **cape'let** a small cape. [O.Fr. *cape* — L.L. *cappa*.]

cape^2 *kāp*, *n* a head or point of land jutting into the sea or a lake. — **Cape Coloured** (*SAfr*) a person of mixed race, mainly in the W. Cape area; **Cape doctor** a south-east wind in the Cape; **Cape Dutch** a former name for Afrikaans (q.v.); **Cape gooseberry** a S. American plant of the potato and nightshade genus with bladdery calyx; its edible fruit; **Cape hyacinth** see **hyacinth**; **Cape Sparrow** see **mossie**^{2}. — **the Cape** Cape of Good Hope; Cape Province, Capetown, and Cape Peninsula. [Fr. *cap* — L. *caput*, the head.]

capelet. See **cape**^{1}.

capelin *kap'ə-lin* or **caplin** *kap'lin*, *n* a small fish of the smelt family, abundant off Newfoundland, much used as bait. [Fr. *capelan*.]

caper^1 *kā'pər*, *n* a thorny S. European shrub with edible flower-buds — also **cap'er-bush**; the flower-bud, pickled. — **cā'per-sauce** a sauce for boiled mutton, etc., made with capers. [L. *capparis* — Gr. *kapparis*.]

caper[2] *kā'pər*, *vi* to leap or skip like a goat; to dance playfully; to frolic. — *n* a leap; a gambol; an escapade; any activity or pursuit (*colloq*); an illegal or questionable act (*slang*). — *n* **cā'perer.** — **cut a caper** or **capers** to gambol. [L. *caper* (masc.), *capra* (fem.), a goat.]

caper[3]. See **capercailzie.**

capercailzie or **capercaillie** *cap-ər-kā'lzi*, *-lyi* or *-li*, *n* a large European grouse, the male of which has dark plumage and a fan-shaped tail. — Also **cap'er.** [Gael. *capull coille*, horse of the wood.]

capillaceous *kap-il-ā'shəs*, *adj* hairlike; having numerous fine filaments. [Ety. as for **capillary.**]

capillary *kə-pil'ə-ri*, sometimes *kap'*, *adj* having to do with hair; hairlike; of very small bore; relating to capillary attraction. — *n* a fine-bored tube; a minute vessel such as those that connect arteries with veins. — *n* **capillarity** (*-lar'i-ti*) capillary quality; capillary attraction. — **capillary attraction** the force that causes liquids to rise in capillary tubes and wicks, to spread through blotting-paper, etc.; **capillary matting** highly absorbent matting made of fine filaments, used in capillary watering; **capillary watering** a system of plant watering using capillary attraction of water through a wick, sand, etc. [L. *capillus*, hair.]

capita. See **caput, per capita.**

capital[1] *kap'it-l*, *adj* principal; excellent; relating to capital; involving the death penalty; placed at the head; (of a letter) of the form and size which begins a sentence or name. — *n* the chief or most important thing; the chief town or seat of government; a capital letter; the property, equipment and/or money used for carrying on a business. — *interj* excellent. — *n* **capitalīsā'tion** or **-z-.** — *vt* **cap'italise** or **-ize** to provide with capital; to convert into capital or money; to turn to account; to print or write with capital letters or an initial capital letter. — *vi* to turn to one's advantage (with *on*). — *n* **cap'italism** the condition of possessing capital; the economic system which generates and gives power to capitalists. — *n* **cap'italist** a person who derives income and power from capital. — *adj* relating to capitalism. — *adj* **capitalist'ic.** — *adv* **cap'itally** chiefly; principally; excellently (*colloq*); by capital punishment. — **capital assets** fixed capital (see below); **capital expenditure** spending on capital assets; expenditure from which benefits may be expected in the long term; **capital gains** profits from the sale of bonds or other assets; **capital goods** goods to be used in production, not for consumption. — *adj* **capital-intens'ive** requiring a comparatively large amount of capital relative to the amount of labour involved. — **capitalisation issue** an issue of shares given free by a company to its shareholders (in proportion to the size of their holdings) in order to capitalise reserves, a bonus issue; **capital murder** a murder punished by the death penalty; **capital punishment** the death penalty; **capital sum** a lump sum payable on an insurance policy; **capital territory** the part of a country in which the capital city is situated. — **capital transfer tax** a tax payable on gifts of money or property over a certain value, made either during the lifetime of the giver or after his or her death; **circulating** or **floating capital** that which constantly changes hands, such as wages paid to workmen, raw material used; **fixed capital** buildings, machines, tools, etc.; **make capital out of** to turn to advantage; **working capital** capital needed to carry on a business; assets after debts have been paid. [O.Fr. *capitel* — L. *capitālis* — *caput*, the head.]

capital[2] *kap'it-l*, *n* the head or top part of a column, etc. [L. *capitellum*, dimin. of *caput*, head.]

capitalism, etc. See **capital**[1].

capitation *kap-i-tā'shən*, *n* a poll tax; the levying of this. — **capitation allowance** or **grant** an allowance or grant of so much a head; **capitation fee** a payment made to a general practitioner for each patient on his or her list. [L. *capitātus*, headed, *capitātiō*, *-ōnis*, poll tax — *caput*, head.]

Capitol *kap'it-ol* or *-əl*, *n* the temple of Jupiter at Rome, built on the *Capitoline* hill; the house where Congress or a state legislature meets (*US*). — *adj* **capitō'lian** or **capit'oline.** [L. *Capitōlium* — *caput*, the head.]

capitular[1] *kə-pit'ūl-ər*, *n* a statute passed in a chapter or ecclesiastical court; a member of a chapter. — *adj* relating or belonging to a chapter in a cathedral. — *adv* **capit'ularly.** — *n* **capit'ulary** a collection of ordinances. [See ety. for **chapter.**]

capitular[2]. See **capitulum.**

capitulate[1] *kə-pit'ūl-āt*, *vi* to yield or surrender, esp. on certain conditions. — *n* **capit'ulant** a person who capitulates. — *n* **capitulā'tion.** — *adj* **capit'ulatory.** [L.L. *capitulātus*, past p. of *capitulāre*, to arrange under heads — *capitulum*, a chapter.]

capitulate[2]. See **capitulum.**

capitulum *kə-pit'ū-ləm*, (*bot*) *n* a close head of sessile flowers: — *pl* **capit'ula.** — *adj* **capit'ular** or **capit'ulate.** [L., dimin. of *caput*, head.]

caplet *kap'lət*, *n* a solid medicinal tablet with a hard coating (of a soluble material as used to make capsules), usu. made in elongated oval shape to ease swallowing. [*cap*sule and tab*let*.]

caplin. See **capelin.**

capo *cap'ō* (*pl* **cap'os**), in full **capotasto** *kapō-tas'tō* (*pl* **capotas'tos**), *n* a movable bridge secured over the fingerboard and strings of a lute or guitar, to alter the pitch of all the strings together. [It. *capo tasto*, head stop.]

capon *kā'pn*, *n* a castrated cock fattened for eating. — *vt* **cā'ponise** or **-ize.** [O.E. *capun*.]

capot *kə-pot'*, *n* the winning of all the tricks at the game of piquet, and scoring forty. — *vt* to score capot against. [Fr.]

capotasto. See **capo.**

capote *kə-pōt'*, *n* a long kind of cloak or mantle. [Fr. dimin. of *cape*, a cloak; see **cape**[1].]

cappuccino *ka-pōō-chē'nō*, *n* coffee with a little milk; white coffee, esp. from a machine, topped with froth: — *pl* **cappuccin'os.** [It., Capuchin.]

capriccio *kä-prē'chō* or *kə-prē'chi-ō*, (*mus*) *n* a kind of free composition, not keeping to the rules for any particular form: — *pl* **capri'ccios** or **capricci** (*-prē'chē*). — *adv* **capriccioso** (*-ō'sō*) in a free style. [It., perh. from L. *caper*; see **caper**[2].]

caprice *kə-prēs'*, *n* a change of humour or opinion without reason; a whim; changeableness; a capriccio (*mus*). — *adj* **capricious** (*kə-prish'əs*) full of caprice; changeable. — *adv* **capri'ciously.** — *n* **capri'ciousness.** [Fr., perh. from L. *caper*; see **caper**[2].]

Capricorn *kap'ri-körn*, *n* a constellation and a sign of the zodiac represented as a horned goat or monster; a person born between 23 December and 19 January, under the sign of Capricorn. — See also **tropic.** [L. *capricornus* — *caper*, a goat, *cornū*, a horn.]

caprine *kap'rīn*, *adj* goatlike. [L. *caprīnus* — *caper*, a goat.]

capriole *kap'ri-ōl*, *n* a caper; a leap without advancing (*dressage*). — *vi* to leap, caper. [O.Fr. *capriole* — It. *capriola* — L.; see **cabriole, caper**[2].]

caps. *kaps*, *abbrev* for capitals (in printing or writing).

capsicum *kap'si-kəm*, *n* (with *cap*) a tropical shrubby genus of the potato family, yielding a fleshy, many-seeded fruit; the fruit of one species, eaten as a vegetable (also called *green*, *red* or *sweet pepper*); the dried seeds of other species, yielding paprika and cayenne pepper. [Perh. L. *capsa*, a case.]

capsid[1] *kap'sid*, *n* the outer protein shell of some viruses. [L. *capsa*, case.]

capsid[2] *kap'sid* or **capsid bug** (*bug*), *n* any of several small active plant pests. [Gr. *kapsis*, gulping — *kaptein*, to gulp down.]

capsize *kap-sīz'*, *vt* to overturn (esp. a boat). — *vi* to be overturned. — *n* an overturning. — *adj* **capsiz'able**.

capstan *kap'stən*, *n* an upright machine turned by bars or otherwise so as to wind a cable around it; the revolving shaft which controls the spin of a tape in a tape-recorder, etc.; (also **capstan lathe**) a lathe with a revolving turret holding several tools which can be used in succession. — **capstan table** a round-topped, often revolving table. [Fr. *cabestan*, *capestan*, through L.L. forms from L. *capĕre*, to take, hold.]

capsule *kap'sūl*, *n* a dry seedcase which splits to release seeds (*bot*); a fibrous or membranous covering (*zool*); a gelatine case for holding a dose of medicine; a metallic or other container; a self-contained spacecraft or a part of one; a similar craft used on or under water. — *adj* **cap'sular** in the form of, or resembling, a capsule; brief, condensed. — *adj* **cap'sulate** contained in or made into a capsule. — *vt* **cap'sulise** or **-ize** to condense. [Fr., — L. *capsula*, dimin. of *capsa*, a case — *capĕre*, to hold.]

Capt. *abbrev* for Captain.

captain *kap'tin*, *n* a head or chief officer; the commander of a ship; the commander of a company of troops; in the navy, an officer of the rank below commodore and above commander; in the army (in U.S. also the Air Force) an officer of the rank below major and above lieutenant; the senior pilot of a civil aircraft; the leader of a team or club; the head boy of a school. — *vt* to lead or act as captain. — *n* **cap'taincy** the rank or commission of a captain; the period of office of a captain; the leadership or rule of a captain. — *n* **cap'tainship**. — **captain-gen'eral** the commander of an army; **captain's chair** a wooden armchair with back and arms in one semicircular piece supported on vertical spindles. — **captain of industry** a great industrial employer. [O.Fr. *capitaine* — L.L. *capitāneus*, chief — L. *caput*, head.]

caption *kap'shən*, *n* a heading, legend or accompanying wording of an article, chapter, illustration or cinematograph picture, etc. — *vt* to give a caption (heading, etc.) to. [L. *captiō*, *-ōnis* — *capĕre*, to take.]

captious *cap'shəs*, *adj* ready to catch at faults or take offence; peevish. — *adv* **cap'tiously**. — *n* **cap'tiousness**. [L. *captiōsus* — *captiō*; see **caption**.]

captive *kap'tiv*, *n* a prisoner; a person or animal kept in confinement. — *adj* confined; kept in bondage; (of an animal) living its whole life in a zoo or other controlled habitat; restrained by a line (as a balloon); charmed or subdued by anything (*fig*); pertaining to captivity; that cannot refuse what is offered (as a *captive audience*, *market*, etc.). — *vt* **cap'tivate** to charm; to engage the affections of. — *adj* **cap'tivating**. — *n* **captiv'ity**. — **captive bolt** or **captive bolt pistol** a gunlike device which fires a rod, used in slaughtering animals; **captive time** time during which a person is not working but must be available at the place of work. [L. *captīvus* — *capĕre*, *captum*, to take.]

capture *kap'chər*, *n* the act of taking; the thing taken; an arrest. — *vt* to take as a prize; to take by force; to succeed in representing (something intangible or elusive) in a fixed or permanent form; (of an atomic or nuclear system) to acquire an additional particle (*phys*). — *n* **cap'tor** or **cap'turer**. [L. *captūra* — *capĕre*, *captum*, to take.]

Capuchin *kap'ū-chin* or *kap-ōō-shēn'*, *n* a friar of a strict Franciscan order; (without *cap*) a cloak like a Capuchin's; (without *cap*) a capuchin monkey. — **capuchin monkey** a S. American monkey with hair like a cowl. [Fr. *capuche*, cowl — L.L. *cappa*.]

caput *kap'ut* or *-ət*, *n* a head; a knob, esp. a bony protuberance: — *pl* **cap'ita**. [L.]

capybara *kap-i-bä'rə*, *n* the largest living rodent, a native of South America, resembling a large guinea pig. [Port. from Tupí.]

Car. *abbrev* for *Carolus* (L.), Charles.

car *kär*, *n* a self-propelled wheeled vehicle designed to carry passengers (also **motor car**); a wheeled vehicle of a specified type (as *jaunting car*, *tramcar*, etc.); a railway carriage, esp. of a specified type (as *dining-car*, *sleeping-car*, etc.); any railway carriage, wagon or truck (*US*); the part of a balloon, cable-car or airship that carries passengers and load; a chariot or cart (*poetic*). — **car'-coat** a short coat designed for wearing in a car; **car ferry** a ferry boat designed so that cars can be driven on and off; **car'load** as much as a car will carry; **car'park** an open space or a building for parking cars; **car'phone** a portable telephone for use in a car; **car pool** an arrangement by which several car owners take turns in giving lifts to each other; **car'port** a covered parking space, esp. a space under a roof projecting from a building. — *adj* **car'-sick** affected with nausea by the movement of a car. — **car-sickness**; **car'-wash** a place specially equipped for the automatic washing of cars. — **car boot sale** a sale at which goods are sold direct from the boots of the owners' cars. [O.Fr. *carre* — L.L. *carra*, a Celt. word, seen in Ir. *carr*.]

carabineer, carabinier. See **carbine**.

carabiniere *kä-rä-bē-nyā'rā*, (It.) *n* a policeman armed with a rifle: — *pl* **carabinie'ri** (*-rē*).

caracal *kar'ə-kal*, *n* the desert lynx of N. Africa and S. Asia. [Fr.]

caracol or **caracole** *kar'ə-kōl*, (*dressage*) *n* a half-turn or wheel. — *vi* to turn half-round. [Fr. *caracole* — It. *caracollo* — Sp. *caracol*, a spiral snail shell.]

caracul. See **karakul**.

carafe *kə-raf'*, *n* a water-bottle or wine-flask for the table; the amount contained in a carafe. [Fr., prob. from. Ar. *gharafa*, to draw water.]

carambole *ka'rəm-bōl*. See **carom**.

caramel *kar'ə-mel*, *n* a dark-brown substance produced from sugar by loss of water on heating, used in colouring and flavouring food and drink; a chewy sweet made with sugar, butter, etc. — *adj* made of or containing caramel; of the colour of caramel. — *n* **caramelisā'tion** or **-z-**. — *vt* and *vi* **car'amelise** or **-ize**. [Fr., — Sp. *caramelo*.]

carapace *kar'ə-pās*, *n* the shell of the crab, tortoise, etc.; official dress or reserved manner used as a protection against outside influences. — *adj* **carapā'cial** (*-shl*). [Fr., — Sp. *carapacho*.]

carat *kar'ət*, *n* a unit of weight (metric carat = 200 milligrams) used for gems; (also **karat**) a unit used in expressing fineness of gold, 24-carat gold being pure gold. [Fr., — Ar. *qīrāt*, perh. from Gr. *keration*, a carob-seed used as a weight.]

caravan *kar'ə-van* or *-van'*, *n* a company travelling together for security, esp. in crossing the desert; a company of people; a covered van; a house on wheels. — *vi* to travel in a caravan: — *pr p* **car'avanning**; *pa p* and *pa t* **car'avanned**. — *n* **caravaneer'** the leader of a caravan. — *n* **caravanette'** a motorised mobile home. — *n* **car'avanner** a caravaneer; a person who stays in a caravan, esp. for holidays. — *n* **caravanserai** (*-van'sə-rī*) a kind of unfurnished inn or extensive enclosed court where caravans stop. — **caravan site** or **park** an open space laid out for caravans. [Pers. *kārwān*, caravan; *kārwānsarāī* (*sarāī*, inn).]

caravel *kar'ə-vel*, *n* a light Mediterranean sailing-ship. [Fr. *caravelle*.]

caraway *kar'ə-wā*, *n* an umbelliferous plant with aromatic fruits (**caraway seeds**) used as a tonic and condiment. [Prob. Sp. *alcaravea* (*carvi*), Ar. *karwiyā* — Gr. *karon*.]

carb *kärb*, (*colloq*) *n* short for **carburettor**.

carbide *kär'bīd*, *n* a compound of carbon with another element, esp. calcium carbide. [**carbon**.]

carbine *kär'bīn*, *n* a short light rifle. — *n* **carbineer'**, **carabineer'**, **carbinier'** or **carabinier'** a soldier armed with a carbine. [Fr. *carabine*.]

carbohydrate *kär-bō-hī'drāt*, *n* a compound of carbon, hydrogen and oxygen, the last two being in the same proportion as in water; extended to similar compounds, the sugars and starches which form the main source of energy in food. [See **carbon** and **hydrate**.]

carbolic *kär-bol'ik*, *n* (in full **carbolic acid**) phenol. [L. *carbō*, coal, *oleum*, oil.]

carbon *kär'bən*, *n* a non-metallic element (atomic no. 6; symbol **C**), widely diffused, occurring uncombined as diamond and graphite; a piece of carbon (esp. an electrode or a lamp-filament), or of carbon paper; a carbon copy; a carbonado diamond. — Also *adj*. — *adj* **carbonā'ceous** coaly; containing much carbon; like carbon. — *n* **car'bonate** a salt of carbonic acid, H_2CO_3. — *vt* to combine or impregnate with carbon dioxide; to carbonise. — *n* **carbonā'tion**. — *adj* **carbonic** (*-bon'ik*) pertaining to carbon. — *n* **carbonisā'tion** or **-z-**. — *vt* **car'bonise** or **-ize** to reduce to carbon; to char or coke; to cover with carbon. — *vi* to become carbonised. — **carbon arc** an arc between two carbon electrodes, used for high-intensity lighting; **carbon black** a form of finely divided carbon produced by partial combustion of hydrocarbons; **carbon copy** a duplicate of writing or typed matter made by interleaving **carbon paper**, a paper coated with a pigment made of carbon or other material; any exact duplicate; **carbon dating** estimating the date of death of organic material from the amount of carbon-14 still present in it; **carbon dioxide** an oxide of carbon (CO_2), a colourless, odourless, incombustible gas, present in the atmosphere, which in solution in water forms **carbonic acid** (H_2CO_3), a weak acid; **carbon fibres** very fine filaments of carbon used in bundles, bound together by resin, to form strong, lightweight materials; **car'bon-14** a radioactive isotope of carbon used e.g. as a tracer element in biological studies or in dating archaeological material; **carbon monoxide** (CO) a colourless, odourless, very poisonous gas which burns with a blue flame to form carbon dioxide; **carbon steel** steel containing carbon, with different properties according to the quantity of carbon used; **carbon tetrachloride** (CCl_4) a solvent, etc.; **car'bon-12** an isotope of carbon with a mass of 12, used as a standard in determining relative atomic and molecular weight. — **carbon dioxide snow** dry ice (see **ice**). [Fr. *carbone* — L. *carbō*, *-ōnis*, coal, charcoal.]

carbonado *kär-bən-ā'dō*, *n* a variety of crystalline carbon, black, opaque, harder than diamond, used in drilling, etc. — Also called **black diamond, carbon**. [Port., carbonated.]

carboniferous *kär-bən-if'ər-əs*, *adj* producing carbon or coal; (with *cap*; *geol*) belonging to the **Carboniferous System**, one of the main divisions of the Palaeozoic rocks, following the Devonian and preceding the Permian. [**carbon**.]

carbonyl *kär'bə-nil*, (*chem*) *n* the radical CO. — *vt* **carbonylate** (*kär-bon'i-lāt*) to introduce the carbonyl group into. — *n* **carbonylā'tion**. [**carbon**, and Gr. *hyle*, matter.]

Carborundum® *kär-bər-un'dum*, *n* a silicon carbide, used as a substitute for corundum in grinding, etc. [**carbon** and **corundum**; a trademark in some countries.]

carboxyl *kär-boks'il*, *n* the radical COOH. — *adj* **carboxylic** (*-bok-sil'ik*). [**carbon**, **oxygen**, Gr. *hȳlē*, matter.]

carboy *kär'boi*, *n* a large glass or plastic bottle, with basketwork or other casing, for dangerous chemicals. [Pers. *qarābah*.]

carbuncle *kär'bung-kl*, *n* a mythical self-luminous gem; a fiery-red precious stone; a pimple, esp. on the face or neck; a local inflammation of the skin and subcutaneous tissues, caused by bacterial infection. — *adj* **car'buncled** set with the gem carbuncle; afflicted with carbuncles. — *adj* **carbun'cular** belonging to or like a carbuncle; red; inflamed. [L. *carbunculus*, dimin. of *carbō*, a coal.]

carburet *kär'bū-ret* or *-ret'*, **car'burate** *-āt* or **car'burise** or **-ize** *vt* to combine with carbon; to charge with carbon compounds. — *n* **carburā'tion** or **carburetion** (*-rā'shən* or *-resh'ən*) or **carburīsā'tion** or **-z-**. — *adj* **car'buretted** (or *-ret'id*). — *n* **car'burettor, car'buretter**, or in U.S. **car'buretor** or **car'bureter** (also *-ret'ər*) an apparatus for charging a gas with carbon compounds, esp. part of an internal-combustion petrol engine in which air is mixed with volatile fuel in the desired proportion. [Fr. *carbure* — L. *carbō*, coal.]

carcajou *kär'kə-jōō*, *n* the wolverine. [Canadian Fr., prob. from an Indian name.]

carcase or **carcass** *kär'kəs*, *n* a dead body of an animal, esp. one to be used as meat; (*disrespectfully*) a live human body; the framework of anything; a ruin. — **carcase (or carcass) meat** raw meat as prepared for the butcher's shop, not tinned. [O.Fr. *carquois* (Fr. *carcasse*), a skeleton.]

carcinogen, carcinogenic. See **carcinoma**.

carcinoma *kär-si-nō'mə*, *n* a cancer: — *pl* **carcinō'mata** or **carcinō'mas**. — *adj* **carcinō'matous**. — *n* **carcin'ogen** (*-jen*) a substance that encourages the growth of cancer. — *n* **carcinogen'esis**. — *adj* **carcinogen'ic**. — *n* **carcinogenic'ity**. — *n* **carcinō'sis** or **carcinōmatō'sis** spread of cancer in the body. [Gr. *karkinōma* — *karkinos*, crab.]

CARD (sometimes *kärd*) *abbrev* for Campaign Against Racial Discrimination.

Card. *abbrev* for Cardinal.

card[1] *kärd*, *n* a small piece of cardboard or stiff paper; one with figures for playing a game; one with a greeting, invitation, message, etc.; a small piece of cardboard or plastic carrying information, in print or on a magnetic strip; the programme of races at a race-meeting; a comical or eccentric person; (in *pl*) a game played with cards. — *vt* to return on a scoring-card (*golf*); to enter in a card index. — *adj* **card'-carrying** openly expressing membership of or support for a party or group. — **card catalogue** a card index; **card column** (*comput*) one of the eighty vertical columns of a punched card; **card file** a card index; **card'-game** a game played with playing-cards; **card'-holder** a person who has a membership card; **card index** one with entries on separate cards. — *vt* **card-in'dex**. — **card mechanic** see under **mechanic**; **card'punch** (*comput*) a machine which perforates cards to record data; **card reader** (*comput*) a device which reads the data on a punched card and converts it to a form suitable for storage or processing; **card'-sharp** or **-sharper** a person who cheats at cards; **card'-table** a table for playing cards on; **card'-vote** a voting system that gives each delegate's vote a value in proportion to the number he or she represents. — **a card up one's sleeve** an advantageous factor or argument kept in reserve; **cards on the table** one's resources and moves freely laid open; **get one's cards** to be dismissed; **house of cards** an erection of playing-cards in storeys; any flimsy or precarious structure, scheme, etc.; **on the cards** not improbable; **play one's cards well (or badly)** to make (or not to make) the best of one's chances; **show one's cards** to expose one's secrets or designs; **the cards are stacked against (someone or something)** the circumstances, facts, are ranged against (a person, an argument, etc.); **throw**

up (or **in**) **the cards** to give in; to confess defeat. [Fr. *carte* — L. *c(h)arta* — Gr. *chartēs*, paper.]

card[2] *kärd*, *n* an instrument for combing wool or flax. — *vt* to comb (wool, etc.). — *n* **card'er**. [Fr. *carde* — L. *carduus*, a thistle.]

cardamom or **cardamum** *kär'də-məm*, *n* the capsules of several tropical plants of the ginger family, which form an aromatic spice. — Also **card'amon**. [L. *cardamōmum* — Gr. *kardamōmon*.]

cardan joint *kär'dan joint*, *n* a type of universal joint invented by Geronimo *Cardano* (1501–76), Italian mathematician.]

cardboard *kärd'börd*, *n* a thin, stiff, finely-finished pasteboard; a rougher, thicker material made from paper pulp and used to make cartons or boxes. — *adj* made of cardboard; flimsy, insubstantial; stiff. — *adj* **card'boardy**. — **cardboard city** an area in which homeless people gather, using cardboard boxes, etc. for shelter. [**card**[1] and **board**.]

cardi or **cardy** *kär'di*, (*colloq*) *n* a cardigan.

cardiac *kär'di-ak*, *adj* belonging to the heart or to the upper end of the stomach. — *n* a person with cardiac disease. — *adj* **cardiacal** (*-dī'ə-kl*) cardiac. — **cardiac arrest** stopping of the heartbeat; **cardiac failure** heart-failure; **cardiac massage** manual stimulation of the heart, directly or by pressure on the chest wall, to restart circulation. [L. *cardiacus* — Gr. *kardiakos* — *kardiā*, heart.]

cardialgia or **cardialgy**. See under **cardio-**.

cardigan *kär'di-gən*, *n* a knitted woollen jacket, named after Lord *Cardigan* (1797–1868). — *adj* **car'diganed** wearing a cardigan.

cardinal *kär'di-nl*, *adj* of fundamental importance; of a deep scarlet colour, like a cardinal's cassock or hat. — *n* one of the princes of the church constituting the sacred college at Rome, to whom pertains the right of electing a new pope. — *n* **car'dinalate** or **car'dinalship** the office or dignity of cardinal. — *n* (*math*) **cardinal'ity** the property of having a cardinal number; the cardinal number associated with a given set. — *adv* **car'dinally** fundamentally. — **car'dinal-bishop, car'dinal-priest** and **car'dinal-deacon** the three orders of cardinal in the sacred college; **cardinal numbers** numbers expressing how many (1, 2, 3, distinguished from *ordinals*); **cardinal points** north, south, east and west; **cardinal virtues** justice, prudence, temperance and fortitude. [L. *cardinālis* — *cardō*, *cardinis*, a hinge.]

cardio- *kär-di-ō-*, or before a vowel **cardi-** *combining form* denoting heart. — *n* **cardialgia** (*-di-al'ji-ə*) or **car'dialgy** heartburn. — *n* **car'diogram** a tracing obtained from a cardiograph. — *n* **car'diograph** an instrument for recording movements of the heart. — *n* **cardiog'rapher** a person who uses a cardiograph. — *n* **cardiog'raphy**. — *n* **cardiol'ogist**. — *n* **cardiology** (*-ol'ə-ji*) the science that deals with the structure, function, and diseases of the heart. — *adj* **cardiopul'monary** pertaining to the heart and lungs. — *adj* **cardiorespir'atory** relating to the action of the heart and lungs. — *adj* **cardiothoracic** (*-thö-ra'sik*) relating to the heart and chest. — *adj* **cardiovascular** (*-vas'kū-*) pertaining to or involving the heart and blood-vessels. — *n* **cardī'tis** inflammation of the heart. [Gr. *kardiā*, heart.]

cardoon *kär-dōōn'*, *n* a Mediterranean plant closely related to the true artichoke, its leafstalks and ribs eaten like celery. [Obs. Fr. *cardon* — L. *carduus*, a thistle.]

Cards. *abbrev* for Cardiganshire, a former county (now part of Dyfed).

cardy. See **cardi**.

CARE *kār*, *abbrev* for Cooperative for American Relief Everywhere.

care *kār*, *n* affliction; anxiety; heedfulness; heed; charge, oversight; medical or social welfare services; an object of anxiety or watchfulness. — *vi* to be anxious; to be inclined; to be concerned; to mind; to have a liking or fondness; to provide for, look after, watch over (with *for*). — *adj* **care'ful** full of care; heedful; painstaking, thorough. — *adv* **care'fully**. — *n* **care'fulness**. — *adj* **care'less** without care; heedless, unconcerned. — *adv* **care'lessly**. — *n* **care'lessness**. — *n* **car'er** a person who cares; a person who takes responsibility for another, dependent, person. — *adj* **car'ing** compassionate; concerned professionally with social, medical, etc. welfare (as in the *caring professions*, i.e. social workers, nurses, etc.). — **care assistant** a person employed to look after children or old or disabled people in a home, hospital, etc. — *adj* **care'free** free from anxiety. — **care label** a label on a garment, giving washing, etc., instructions; **care order** a court order placing a child in care. — *vt* and *vi* **care'take** to act as caretaker (for a property, etc.). — **care'taker** a person put in charge of anything, esp. a building. — *adj* exercising temporary supervision or control, as in *caretaker government*. — **care'worker** a person employed to help look after dependent people in their own homes. — *adj* **care'worn** worn or vexed with care. — **care of** to be delivered to the custody of, or at the address of; **for all I** (or **you**, etc.) **care** it is a matter of indifference to me, you, etc.; **have a care** to take care; **I**, etc., **couldn't care less** I, etc., do not care in the least; **in care** (of a child) in the guardianship of a local authority or other official organisation; (of an elderly person) in an old people's home or geriatric ward; **in care of** (*US*) care of (see above); **take care** to be careful or cautious; **take care of** to look after with care; to make the necessary arrangements regarding (*colloq*). [O.E. *caru*.]

careen *kə-rēn'*, *vt* to turn over on the side, esp. for repairing or cleaning. — *vi* to heel over; to rush along (*erron*; for *career*). — *n* a heeling position. — *n* **careen'age** a place where ships are careened; the cost of careening. [L. *carīna*, keel.]

career *kə-rēr'*, *n* a rush; progress through life; one's profession or occupation; progress or advancement in this. — *adj* having a career; dedicated to a career. — *vi* to rush wildly; to move or run rapidly. — *n* **career'ism**. — *n* **career'ist** a person intent on his or her own advancement. — Also *adj*. — **career break** a period away from one's career for study, childcare, etc.; **career diplomat** one who has risen through the profession, rather than a political appointee; **careers master** or **mistress** a schoolteacher who advises pupils on their choice of career; **career woman** a woman who attaches great importance to her job, to promotion, etc. [Fr. *carrière*, a racecourse — L.L. *carrāria*, carriage-road — *carrus*, wagon.]

caress *kə-res'*, *vt* to touch affectionately; to fondle. — *n* a gentle or affectionate touch. — *n* and *adj* **caress'ing**. — *adv* **caress'ingly**. [Fr. *caresser* — It. *carezza*, an endearment — L. *cārus*, dear.]

caret *kar'ət*, *n* (in proofreading, etc.) a mark, ʎ to show where to insert something omitted. [L., 'there is lacking'.]

cargo *kär'gō*, *n* the goods carried by a ship or aeroplane; any load to be carried: — *pl* **car'goes**. — *vt* to load, weigh down (with *with*). — **cargo cult** a type of religion in certain South Pacific islands based on the belief that ancestors or spirits will return in ships or aircraft bringing products of modern civilisation and thus make the islanders rich and independent; **cargo cultist**. [Sp., — root of **car**.]

cariacou *kar'i-ə-kōō* or **carjacou** *kär'jə-kōō*, *n* any deer of the American genus or subgenus *Cariacus*, including the Virginian deer. [Tupí, *cariacu*.]

Carib *kar'ib*, *n* a member of a race inhabiting parts of Central America and northern South America; their language. — Also *adj*.

Caribb. *abbrev* for Caribbean.

Caribbean *kar-i-bē'ən* or in U.S. *kər-ib'i-ən*, *adj* of or pertaining to the Caribs or their language; of or pertaining to the West Indies or their inhabitants or culture. — Also *n.*

caribou *kar'i-bōō, n* the American reindeer. [Can. Fr.]

caricature *kar'i-kə-tūr* or *-chōōr, n* a likeness of anything so exaggerated or distorted as to appear ridiculous. — *vt* to turn into ridicule by distorting a likeness; to burlesque. — *adj* **caricatūr'al**. — *n* **caricatūr'ist**. [It. *caricatura* — *caricare*, to load, from the root of **car**.]

CARICOM *kar'i-kom, abbrev* for *Cari*bbean *Com*munity.

caries *kā'ri-ēz, n* decay, esp. of teeth. [L. *cariēs*.]

CARIFTA *kar-if'tə, abbrev* for *Cari*bbean *F*ree *T*rade *A*rea.

carillon *kə-ril'yən* or *kar'il-yən, n* a set of bells for playing tunes; a mechanism for playing them; a melody played on them; an instrument or organ-stop imitating a peal of bells. — *vi* to play a carillon. — *n* **carill'onneur** (also *-nûr'*) or **carill'onist** (also *kar'*). [Fr., — L.L. *quadriliō, -ōnis*, a quaternary, as formerly rung on four bells.]

carina *kə-rī'nə, (biol) n* a keel or keel-like ridge. — *adj* **carinate** (*kar'i-nāt*) keeled. [L. *carīna*, a keel.]

carioca *kar-ē-ō'kə, n* a Brazilian dance or its tune, a maxixe or variety of it; (with *cap*) a native of Rio de Janeiro. — Also *adj.* [Port.]

cariole or **carriole** *kar'i-ōl, n* a small open carriage; a light cart. [Fr. *carriole* — root of **car**.]

carjacou. See **cariacou**.

carline *kär'lin, n* any plant of a genus (*Carlina*: **Carline thistle**) closely related to the true thistles. [From *Carolus* or *Karl*, Charlemagne.]

Carlovingian. See **Carolingian**.

Carmelite *kär'mi-līt, n* a White Friar, or friar of the mendicant order of Our Lady of Mount *Carmel*, in Palestine (now Israel), founded there *c*1156; a member of a contemplative order of nuns, founded in 1452. — Also *adj.*

carminative *kär'min-ə-tiv* or *kär-min'ə-tiv, adj* expelling flatulence. — *n* a medicine with that effect. [L. *cārmināre*, to card, comb out — *cārmen*, a card for wool.]

carmine *kär'mīn* or *kär'min, n* the red colouring matter of the cochineal insect; its colour. — *adj* of that colour. [Fr. *carmin* — same root as **crimson**.]

carnage *kär'nij, n* extensive or indiscriminate killing of people. [Fr., — It. *carnaggio*, carnage — L. *carō, carnis*, flesh.]

carnahuba. See **carnauba**.

carnal *kär'nl, adj* fleshly; sensual; unspiritual; bodily; sexual. — *vt* **car'nalise** or **-ize** to sensualise. — *n* **car'nalism**. — *n* **car'nalist** a sensualist. — *n* **carnality** (*-nal'i-ti*). — *adv* **car'nally**. — **carnal knowledge** (*law*) sexual intercourse. [L. *carō, carnis*, flesh.]

carnation *kär-nā'shən, n* a colour ranging from light pink to deep crimson; a double-flowering variety of the clove-pink. — *adj* of the colour carnation. [L. *carnātiō, -ōnis*, fleshiness.]

carnauba or **carnahuba** *kär-nä-ōō'bə* or *-now'bə, n* a Brazilian palm; its yellowish wax. [Braz.]

carneous *kär'ni-əs* or **carnose** *kär'nōs, adj* fleshy; of or like flesh. — *n* **carnos'ity** a fleshy excrescence growing in and obstructing any part of the body. [Ety. as for **carnal**.]

carnet *kär'nā, n* a customs or other permit; a book of tickets, vouchers, or the like. [Fr.]

carnival *kär'ni-vl, n* a festive occasion, often with a procession, sideshows, etc.; riotous feasting, merriment or amusement; a feast observed by Roman Catholics just before the fast of Lent; a fairlike entertainment. [It. *carnevale*, apparently from L. *carnem levāre*, to put away flesh.]

Carnivora *kär-niv'ə-rə, npl* an order of flesh-eating mammals. — *n* **car'nivore** (*-vōr*) a carnivorous animal. — *adj* **carniv'orous** flesh-eating. — *adv* **carniv'orously**. — *n* **carniv'orousness**. [L. *carō, carnis*, flesh, *vorāre*, to devour.]

carnose, carnosity. See **carneous**.

carob *kar'ob* or *-əb, n* a Mediterranean tree; its edible fruit; a substitute for chocolate prepared from the fruit. [Fr. *carobe* — Ar. *kharrūbah*.]

carol *kar'əl, n* a song of joy or praise; a Christmas song or hymn. — *vi* to dance or sing a carol; to sing or warble. — *vt* to praise or celebrate in song: — *pr p* **car'olling**; *pa p* and *pa t* **car'olled**. — *n* **car'oller**. [O.Fr. *carole*.]

Carolean. See **Caroline**.

Caroline *kar'ō-līn, adj* belonging to the time of Charles I or II (also **Carolean** *-lē'ən*); belonging to the time of any other Charles or of Charlemagne. — **Caroline minuscule** see **Carolingian**. [L. *Carolus*, Charles.]

Carolingian *kar-ə-lin'ji-ən* or **Carlovingian** *kär-lō-vin'ji-ən, adj* relating to a dynasty of Frankish kings, so called from *Karl* (L. *Carolus*) the Great or Charlemagne (742–814). — **Carolingian** (or **Caroline**) **minuscule** a script developed in France at the time of Charlemagne.

carom *kar'əm, n* and *vi* a shortened form of **carambole** (*kar'əm-bōl*), the same as **cannon** in billiards.

carotene *kar'ō-tēn* or **carotin** *kar'ō-tin, n* any of a number of reddish-yellow pigments widely distributed in plants, precursors of vitamin A. — *n* **carotenoid** or **carotinoid** (*kar-ot'in-oid*) any of a group of pigments similar to carotenes, some of which are precursors of vitamin A. [L. *carōta*, carrot, and sfx. *-ene*.]

carotid *kə-rot'id, adj* relating to the two great arteries of the neck. [Gr. *karōtidĕs* (pl.) — *karos*, sleep, the ancients supposing that deep sleep was caused by compression of them.]

carouse *kə-rowz', n* a drinking-bout; a noisy revel. — *vi* to hold a drinking-bout; to drink freely and noisily. — *n* **carous'al** a carouse; a feast. — *n* **carous'er**. — *adv* **carous'ingly**. [Ger. *gar aus*, quite out, i.e. empty the glass.]

carousel or in U.S. **carrousel** *kar-ə-sel', n* a merry-go-round (*US*); a rotating magazine, e.g. for slides in a projector; a rotating conveyor, e.g. for luggage. [Fr. *carrousel*.]

carp[1] *kärp, vi* to find fault (with *at*); to nag about trivialities. — *n* **carp'er**. — *n* and *adj* **carp'ing** cavilling; fault-finding. — *adv* **carp'ingly**. [Most prob. Scand., O.N. *karpa*, to boast, modified in meaning through likeness to L. *carpĕre*, to pluck, deride.]

carp[2] *kärp, n* an edible freshwater fish. [O.Fr. *carpe* — L.L. *carpa*.]

carpal. See **carpus**.

carpel *kär'pl, n* a modified leaf forming the whole or part of the female parts of a flower. — *adj* **car'pellary**. [Gr. *karpos*, fruit.]

carpenter *kär'pint-ər, n* a worker in timber as used in building houses, etc. — *vi* to do the work of a carpenter. — *vt* to make by carpentry. — *n* **car'pentry** the trade or work of a carpenter. — **car'penter-bee** or **-ant** a bee or ant that excavates its nest in wood. [O.Fr. *carpentier*, from the root of **car**.]

carpet *kär'pit, n* the woven, felted or tufted covering of floors, stairs, etc.; a smooth, or thin, surface or covering; a prison sentence of three months (*slang*). — *vt* to cover with or as if with a carpet; to have up for reprimand: — *pr p* **car'peting**; *pa p* and *pa t* **car'peted** — *n* **car'peting** the material of which carpets are made; carpet, or carpets. — **car'pet-bag** a bag used when travelling, made of carpeting; **car'petbagger** a person who comes to a place for political or other ends, having no previous connection with it; **carpet beetle** any of several beetles or their larvae which are harmful to carpets and fabrics; **car'pet-bombing** systematic bombing of a whole area; **carpet shark** a shark with a spotted back like a patterned carpet; **car'pet-slipper** a slipper whose upper was orig. made of carpeting; **car'pet-snake** a variegated python of Australia; **car'pet-sweeper** an apparatus with a revolving brush and a dustpan, for sweeping carpets; **carpet tile** one of a number of squares of carpeting which are laid together in such a way as to form an area of carpet. — **carpet-bag steak** a beefsteak stuffed with oysters; **on the carpet** under discussion; up before someone in authority for reprimand; at or near ground level (*airmen's slang*); **sweep under the carpet** to hide from someone's notice, put out of one's mind (unpleasant problems or facts). [O.Fr. *carpite* — L.L. *carpeta*, *-pita*, coarse fabric made from rags pulled to pieces — L. *carpĕre*, to pluck.]

carpus *kär'pəs*, *n* the wrist, or corresponding part of the forelimb. — *adj* **car'pal** pertaining to the carpus. — *n* a bone of the carpus. — **carpal tunnel syndrome** numbness and pain in the fingers caused by compression of the nerve as it passes through the carpal tunnel (between the bones of the wrist and the tendons). [Latinised from Gr. *karpos*, wrist.]

carrageen or **carragheen** *kar-ə-gēn'*, *n* a purplish-red North Atlantic seaweed used for making soup and a kind of blancmange, and as an emulsifying and gelling agent — also called *Irish moss*. — *n* **carragee'nan** or **carraghee'nin** a colloid prepared from red algae, used in food processing, pharmaceuticals, etc. [Prob. Ir. *carraigín*, little rock.]

carrel or **carrell** *kar'əl*, *n* a desk or alcove in a library for private study. [See **carol**.]

carriage *kar'ij*, *n* the act or cost of carrying; a four-wheeled horse-drawn vehicle for passengers; a railway passenger-coach; a wheeled support of a gun; the structures on which an aeroplane lands; a carrying part of a machine; bearing, deportment. — **carriage clock** a small portable clock, usu. with a case with a handle on top; **carr'iage-drive** a road for carriages through parks, etc.; **carriage driving** the competitive sport of driving a carriage and horse(s). — *adv* **carriage-free'** without charge for transport. — *adv* **carriage-for'ward** without prepayment of carriage. — **carriage horse** a horse that draws a carriage. — *adv* **carriage-paid'** with prepayment of carriage. — **carriage trade** trade from the wealthy; **carr'iageway** a road, or part of a road, used by vehicles. [See ety. for **carry**.]

carrick bend *kar'ik bend*, (*naut*) *n* a knot for joining two ropes.

carrier. See **carry**.

carriole. See **cariole**.

carrion *kar'i-ən*, *n* the dead and putrid body or flesh of any animal; anything vile. — *adj* relating to, or feeding on, putrid flesh. — **carrion beetle** a beetle of the family *Silphidae*, which feeds on carrion; **carr'ion-crow** the common crow. [Fr. *charogne* — L.L. *carōnia* — L. *carō*, *carnis*, flesh.]

carrot *kar'ət*, *n* a plant having a tapering root of a reddish or yellowish colour; the root itself, which is edible and sweet; an incentive, enticement. — *adj* **carr'oty** carrot-coloured (esp. of hair). — **carrot and stick** incentive and punishment, as alternative methods of persuasion. [Fr. *carotte* — L. *carōta*.]

carrousel. See **carousel**.

carry *kar'i*, *vt* to convey; to bear; to lead or transport; to take by force; to effect; to gain; to behave or conduct oneself; (of money) to be sufficient for; to pass, by a majority; to add to another column (*arith*); (of a newspaper) to publish (e.g. an item of news), or to publish as a regular feature; to do the work of, cover up the deficiencies of (another); to keep (merchandise, etc.) in stock; to maintain; to be sufficient to maintain; to be pregnant with. — *vi* (of a voice, a gun, etc.) to reach, indicating its range; to be pregnant: — *pr p* **carr'ying**; *pa p* and *pa t* **carr'ied**. — *n* the distance a golf ball goes when struck till it touches the ground; range; an act of carrying; the portage of a boat; land across which a boat has to be carried between one navigable stream or stretch and another. — *n* **carr'ier** a person who or an organisation that carries, esp. for hire; anything that carries; an instrument for carrying; a passenger aircraft; a basket, framework, or the like, for carrying luggage, as on a bicycle; a person who or animal that transmits disease (without suffering from it) by harbouring germs, or a virus, etc.; a vehicle for communicating a signal in cases where the medium cannot convey the actual signal (as speech, etc., in radio transmission); non-active material mixed with, and chemically identical to, a radioactive compound (*nuc*); a carrier-pigeon; a carrier bag; an aircraft carrier. — **carrier bag** a strong paper or plastic bag for carrying shopping, etc.; **carr'ier-pigeon** a pigeon with homing instincts, used for carrying messages; **carrier rocket** a rocket used to carry, e.g. a satellite into orbit; **carr'ycot** a small portable cot for a baby. — **carry all before one** to bear down all obstacles; **carry away** to carry off; to deprive of self-control by exciting the feelings; to transport; **carry back** to set (a loss) against the previous year's profit, in order to lessen the total tax liability (*n* **carr'y-back**); **carry forward** to transfer written or printed matter to the next page, or figures to the next column; **carry off** to cause the death of; to kidnap, abduct; to gain, or to win, as a prize; to cause to pass muster; **carry on** to manage; to continue; to proceed; to complain or behave unrestrainedly (*n* **carr'y-on** or **carry'ing-on**); to flirt (*with*); **carry out** to accomplish; **carry over** to bring into the other (political, etc.) party; to take (e.g. an account) to a new page; to postpone to next occasion; to postpone payment of (an account) to the next accounting period; **carry the can** to accept responsibility for a misdemeanour; **carry the day** to be successful; to win the day; **carry through** to support through difficulties; to accomplish; **carry weight** to possess authority; to have force. [O.Fr. *carier* — L.L. *carricāre*, to cart — L. *carrus*, a car.]

cart *kärt*, *n* a horse-drawn vehicle used for farm purposes, or for conveying heavy loads; a light two-wheeled horse-drawn vehicle with springs; any similar vehicle drawn by some other animal, or by hand. — *vt* to convey in a cart; to carry, esp. with difficulty (often with *around*). — *n* **cart'age** the act or cost of carting. — **cart'-horse** a (usu. heavy) draught-horse; **cart'load** as much as a cart can carry; **cart'road, cart'-track** or **cart'way** a road or way by which carts may pass; **cart'wheel** the wheel of a cart; a sideways somersault with arms and legs extended. — *vi* to make a sideways somersault. — **cart'wright** a carpenter who makes carts. — **cart off** (*colloq*) to remove; **in the cart** in an awkward predicament; in trouble; **put the cart before the horse** to reverse the natural or sensible order of things.

carte. See under **quart**[2].

carte-blanche *kärt-blăsh*, *n* freedom of action. [Fr., lit. blank paper.]

cartel *kär-təl'*, *n* a political alliance or bloc; a combination of firms formed to control a market. — *n* **cartelisā'tion** or **-z-**. — *vt* and *vi* **car'telise** or **-ize**. [Fr., — L. *c(h)arta*; see **card**[1].]

Cartesian *kär-tē'zi-ən* or *-zhyən*, *adj* relating to the French philosopher René *Descartes* (1596–1650), or his philosophy, or mathematical methods. — *n* a follower of Descartes. — *n* **Cartēs'ianism**. — **Cartesian co-ordinates** co-ordinates of a point which have reference to two fixed lines that cross each other in a plane, or to three meeting surfaces; **Cartesian devil, diver** or **bottle-imp** a scientific toy named after Descartes, a glass container with a floating figure that sinks when the top of the container is pressed.

Carthusian *kär-thū'zi-ən* or *-thōō'zi-ən*, *n* a monk or (since 1229) a nun of an order founded by St Bruno in 1086, noted for its strictness; a scholar of the Charterhouse School. — *adj* of or pertaining to the order or the school. [L. *Cartusiānus*, Chatrousse, near which their first monastery was founded.]

cartilage *kär'ti-lij*, *n* gristle, a firm pearly white substance, often (*temporary cartilage*) converted later into bone. — *adj* **cartilaginous** (*-laj'*). [Fr., — L. *cartilāgō, -inis*.]

cartogram *kär'tə-gram*, *n* a map presenting statistical information in diagrammatic form. [**carto-(graphy)** and **-gram**.]

cartography *kär-tog'rə-fi*, *n* map-making. — *n* **cartog'rapher**. — *adj* **cartographic** (*-tō-graf'ik*) or **cartograph'ical**. — *n* **cartol'ogy** the science of maps and charts. — *adj* **cartolog'ical**. [L. *c(h)arta* — Gr. *chartēs*, a sheet of paper, and Gr. *graphein*, to write.]

cartomancy *kär'tō-mən-si*, *n* divination by playing-cards. [L.L. *carta*, a card, Gr. *manteiā*, divination.]

carton *kär'tən*, *n* a small container made of cardboard, waxed paper, plastic, etc. [Fr.; see **cartoon**.]

cartoon *kär-tōōn'*, *n* a preparatory drawing; any large sketch or design on paper; a comic or satirical drawing; a strip cartoon; a cinematograph film made by photographing a succession of drawings. — *vt* to caricature by a cartoon. — *n* **cartoon'ist**. [Fr. *carton* or It. *cartone*, L. *charta*; see **card**[1].]

cartouche *kär-tōōsh'*, *n* a scroll-like ornament with rolled ends (*archit*); in hieroglyphics, an ancient Egyptian oval figure enclosing royal or divine names. — Also **cartouch'**. [Fr., — It. *cartoccio* — L. *c(h)arta* — Gr. *chartēs*, paper.]

cartridge *kär'trij*, *n* a case containing the charge for a gun (**blank cartridge** with powder only; **ball cartridge** with a bullet as well); a small container holding e.g. film for a camera, ink for a pen; a type of cassette of magnetic tape. — **car'tridge-belt** a belt having pockets for individual cartridges or clips of cartridges for a gun; **car'tridge-pāper** a light-coloured, strong paper for drawing or printing on. [Ety. as for **cartouche**.]

caruncle *ka-* or *kə-rung'kl*, *n* a small fleshy growth, e.g. a cockscomb. — *adj* **carun** or **carun'culous**. [Fr. — L. *caruncula*.]

carve *kärv*, *vt* to cut (wood, ivory, etc.) into forms, patterns, etc.; to make or shape by cutting; to cut up (meat) into slices or pieces. — *vi* to exercise the art or perform the act of carving. — *adj* **carv'en** (*literary*) carved. — *n* **carv'er**. — *n* **carv'ery** a type of buffet-service restaurant where the main course meat is carved from the joint on request. — *n* **carv'ing** the act or art of sculpture, esp. in wood or ivory; a carved form, shape or figure; the act or art of cutting up meat at table. — **carv'ing-knife** a large knife for carving meat. — **carve out** to hew out; to gain by one's exertions (*fig*); **carve up** (*slang*) to divide, esp. illegal profits; to injure a person, esp. by slashing with a razor (*n* **carve'-up**). [O.E. *ceorfan*, to cut.]

caryatid *kar-i-at'id*, *n* a female figure used instead of a column to support a ceiling or entablature: — *pl* **caryat'ids** or **caryat'ides** (*-i-dēz*). — *adj* **caryat'ic**. — *adj* **caryat'idal**. — *adj* **caryatidē'an**. — *adj* **caryatid'ic**. [Gr. *Karyātis*, a priestess of Artemis at *Karyai* (*Caryae*), pl. *Karyātidĕs*.]

Casanova *kas-ə-nō'və*, *n* a man conspicuous for his amorous adventures and success with women, as was Giovanni Jacopo *Casanova* de Seingalt (1725–98).

casbah. Same as **kasbah**.

cascade *kas-kād'*, *n* a waterfall; a trimming of lace or other material falling in loose waves like a waterfall; apparatus connected in series, each piece operating the next one in turn or acting on the output of the preceding one. — *vi* to fall in cascades; to form or cause a cascade. [Fr., — It. *cascata* — L. *cadĕre*, to fall.]

cascara *kas-kä'rə*, *n* a Californian buckthorn (*bot*); the bark of the cascara, used as a tonic and laxative. [Sp. *cáscara*, bark.]

CASE *kās*, *abbrev* for: computer-aided (or computer-assisted) software engineering; Confederation for the Advancement of State Education.

case[1] *kās*, *n* a covering, box, or sheath containing something; the contents of such a box, etc., as in *a case of wine*; the boards and back of a hardback book. — In combination denoting a box or other container, as in *suitcase*, *bookcase*, etc. — *vt* to enclose in a case. — *n* **cās'ing** the act of putting on a case; an outside covering of any kind, as of boards, plaster, etc.; a suitcase or briefcase, or other container or covering; a strong rigid pipe or tube lining a well, shaft, etc. — *adj* **case'-bound** (of a book) with a hard cover. — *vt* **case'-harden** to harden on the surface (*metall*); to make callous or insensitive, through previous experiences (*fig*). — **case'-hardening**; **case'maker** a person who makes covers for books; **case'-worm** caddis-worm; **lower-case** see under **low**[2]; **upper-case** see under **up**. [O.N.Fr. *casse* (mod. Fr. *châsse* and *caisse*) — L. *capsa* — *capĕre*, to take.]

case[2] *kās*, *n* that which happens, an event or occurrence; state or condition; subject of question, investigation or inquiry; (an instance of) a person or animal having a disease; (records relating to) a person under medical treatment or being dealt with by a social worker, etc.; an odd or humorous character (*slang*); a legal statement of facts, either in total or as presented by the defence or the prosecution; a lawsuit; a plausible contention, something to be said for a position or action, a point; (any of the specific types of) grammatical relation of a noun, pronoun, or (in some languages) adjective to other words in the sentence, and/or its variation in form to express that relation. — *vt* (*slang*) to reconnoitre or examine, usu. with a view to burglary. — **case'book** a book recording medical, legal, etc. cases which are valuable as examples for reference; **case history** a record of ancestry, environment, personal history, previous illness etc., for use in diagnosis and treatment, or for some other purpose; **case'-law** law as decided in previous cases; **case'load** the number of cases a doctor, social worker, etc. has to deal with at a particular time; **case'-study** a study based on the analysis of one or more cases or case histories; (the gathering and organising of information for) a case history; **case'-work** the study of individuals or families, their environment and history, often together with supervision and guidance; **case'-worker**. — **case in point** an example of what is under discussion; **in any case** anyway, however; whatever happens; **in case** in order to be safe, make sure, etc.; in the event that; lest; **make out one's case** to give reasons for one's statements or position; **the case** the fact, the reality. [O.Fr. *cas* — L. *cāsus* — *cadĕre*, to fall.]

casein *kā'sēn* or *kā'si-in*, *n* a protein obtained from milk, forming the basis of cheese.

casemate *kās'māt*, *n* any bombproof vaulted chamber, e.g. in a ship. — *adj* **case'mated**. [Fr.]

casement *kās'mənt*, *n* the case or frame of a window; a window that opens on vertical hinges (also **casement window**). — *adj* **case'mented** having casements.

cash *kash*, *n* coins or paper money, available or ready money. — *adj* using cash; paid by cash. — *vt* to turn into or exchange for money. — *n* **cashier** (*-ēr'*) a person who has charge of the receiving and paying of money. — *adj* **cash'less** operated, paid for, conducted, performed, etc. using credit cards or computer transfers, without the use of cash. — **cash'account** an account to which nothing is carried but cash; **cash'-book** a book in which account is kept of the receipts and expenditure of money; **cash'-box**;

cash card a card, issued by a bank or building society, that allows the holder to use a cash dispenser; **cash crop** a crop intended for sale, not for consumption by the producer; **cash desk** a table, etc., with a till where money is taken for goods purchased; **cash dispenser** a machine which dispenses money on the insertion of a special plastic card; **cash flow** the movement of money in and out of a business; **cash limit** a limit set on the total amount of money a company, institution, etc., may spend; **cash machine** a cash dispenser; **cash point** the place in a shop, supermarket, etc. where money is taken for goods purchased; a cash dispenser; **cash-reg'ister** a till that automatically and visibly records the net amount of money put in. — **cash and carry** sale for cash, with delivery performed by the buyer; a usu. large shop which trades in this way, often at wholesale prices; **cash down** with payment at the time of purchase; **cash in** to exchange for money; **cash in on** to take advantage of (an opportunity or situation); **cash in one's (checks** or**) chips** to exchange counters for money on leaving a gaming table; to die (*slang*); **cash up** to count the money taken in a shop, etc., usu. at the end of each day. [O.Fr. *casse*, a box.]

cashew *kə-shōō'* or *kash'ōō*, *n* a spreading tropical American tree with kidney-shaped nuts **(cash'ew= nuts)** whose kernels are used as food. [Tupí *caju*.]

cashier[1] *kash-ēr'*, *vt* to dismiss from a post, esp. in the forces, in disgrace. — *n* **cashier'ing** or **cashier'-ment** dismissal. [Du. *casseren*, to cashier — L. *cassus*, void, empty.]

cashier[2]. See **cash**.

cashmere *kash'mēr*, *n* (a fabric made from) fine soft *Kashmir* goats' hair; any similar product. — Also *adj*.

casino *kə-sē'nō*, *n* an establishment for gambling, mainly in the forms of roulette and card and dice games; a card-game in which players match cards in hand with others on the table (also **cassi'no**): — *pl* **casi'nos**. [It.]

cask *käsk*, *n* a round hollow container for liquor, made of wooden staves bound with hoops; the quantity contained in such a vessel. — *vt* to put in a cask. [Sp. *casco*, skull, helmet, cask.]

casket *käsk'it*, *n* a small case for holding jewels, etc.; a coffin (esp. *NAm*).

casque *käsk*, *n* a helmet; a helmet-like horny protuberance, as on the beak of some birds. [Ety. as for **cask**.]

Cassandra *kəs-an'drə*, (*Gr mythol*) *n* a daughter of Priam, king of Troy, loved by Apollo, who gave her the gift of prophecy, but not of being believed, hence anyone who expresses gloomy views of the future and is not listened to.

cassata *ka-sä'tə*, *n* an (orig. Italian) ice-cream containing nuts and candied fruit. [It.]

cassava *kə-sä'və*, *n* a plant of tropical America, whose roots yield a nourishing starch. — Also **manioc**, **yucca** or **tapioca**. [From a Taino (language of extinct W.Indian tribe) name.]

casserole *kas'ə-rōl*, *n* a stew-pan; a covered pot in which food is both cooked and served; a dish of food which has been cooked in this way. — *vt* to cook in a casserole. [Fr.]

cassette *kas-et'*, *n* a light-tight container for X-ray film, or one for photographic film for loading into a camera, etc.; a plastic case containing a reel of magnetic recording tape. — **cassette recorder** or **cassette player** a machine which records on to or plays magnetic tape cassettes; **cassette single** or **cassing'le** a magnetic tape cassette containing only two tracks, as on a single record. [Fr., dimin. of *casse*, case.]

cassis *ka-sēs'*, *n* a syrupy blackcurrant drink or flavouring. [Fr.]

cassiterite *ka-sit'ə-rīt*, *n* a brown mineral, a dioxide of tin. [Gr. *kassiteros*, tin.]

cassock *kas'ək*, *n* a long robe or outer coat worn by clergy and choristers; a shorter garment worn by Scottish ministers. — *adj* **cass'ocked**. [Fr. *casaque* — It. *casacca*.]

cassoulet *ka-sōō-lā*, (Fr.) *n* a stew consisting of beans and various kinds of meat.

cassowary *kas'ə-wər-i*, *n* any member of a genus of flightless birds, found esp. in New Guinea, closely related to the emu. [Malay *kasuārī* or *kasavārī*.]

cast *käst*, *vt* to throw or fling; to throw (a fishing-line) into the water; to throw off, shed, drop; to throw down, project (a shadow); to voice (doubts, etc.); to reckon, calculate, add up; to mould or shape (metal, etc., or artifacts from it); to appoint (an actor *for* a part or *as* a character); to assign the parts in (a play, etc.). — *vi* to throw a fishing-line into the water: — *pa t* and *pa p* **cast**. — *n* the act of casting; a throw of anything, as a fishing-line; the thing thrown, esp. in angling; the distance thrown; a squint, as of the eye; matter ejected by a bird, earthworm, etc.; a throw or turn of fortune, a chance; a mould; a rigid casing for holding a broken limb while the bone sets; form, manner, stamp or quality (esp. of a person); the company of actors playing rôles in a given play, etc.; an overall shade or tinge of colour. — *adj* moulded; rejected, cast off. — *n* **cast'ing** the act of casting or moulding; something which is cast or moulded; a mould. — **cast'away** a person shipwrecked in a desolate place. — *adj* worthless, rejected. — **casting couch** (*facetious*) a couch on which actresses are said to be seduced with the promise of a part in a film, play, etc.; **casting director** a person responsible for casting actors for all the parts in a film, TV production, play etc.; **cast'ing-vote** a chairman's deciding vote in case of deadlock; **cast-i'ron** an iron-carbon alloy distinguished from steel by its containing substantial amounts of cementite or graphite, meaning it is unsuitable for working and must be cast. — *adj* hard, rigid; unarguable, incontestable. — *adj* **cast'-off** rejected, laid aside, given away, no longer wanted, etc. — *n* anything, esp. clothing, given or thrown away, no longer wanted, etc.; the act or result of casting off manuscript or typewritten copy. — **cast-steel'** steel that has been cast, not shaped by mechanical working. — **cast about** to look about, to search (for), literally or in one's mind; **cast a horoscope** or **nativity** to make an astrological calculation of someone's future; **cast an eye** or **a glance** to look briefly and informally; **cast a spell (upon)** to speak or put under an enchantment; **cast a vote** to record or make a vote; **cast back** to direct one's thoughts towards the past; **cast down** to deject or depress mentally; **cast loose** to set loose or adrift; **cast off** to reject; to release (a boat) from moorings; (in knitting, etc.) to eliminate stitches; to estimate the amount of printed matter that manuscript or typewritten copy will make when typeset; **cast on** (in knitting, etc.) to make stitches; **cast up** to mention as a reproach; to turn up or arrive by chance. [O.N. *kasta*, to throw.]

castanets *kas-tə-nets'*, *npl* (a pair of) hollow shell-shaped pieces of ivory or hard wood, struck by the finger to produce a clicking sound — an accompaniment to Spanish dances and guitars. [Sp. *castañeta* — L. *castanea*, a chestnut.]

caste *käst*, *n* a social class in India; an exclusive social class. — *adj* **caste'less** having no caste. — **caste'=mark** a mark indicating a person's caste, worn on the forehead (also *fig*). — **lose caste** to descend in social rank. [Port. *casta*, breed, race — L. *castus*, pure, unmixed.]

castellan and **castellated**. See **castle**.

caster. See **castor**.

castigate *kas'tig-āt*, *vt* to punish or scold; to criticise severely. — *n* **castigā'tion**. — *n* **cas'tigātor**. — *adj* **cas'tigatory** (*-ə-tər-i*). [L. *castīgāre*, *-ātum*.]

Castilian *kas-til'yən, adj* of, or typical of, Castile. — *n* a person born or living in Castile; the language of Castile, standard Spanish. [Sp. *Castellano*.]

castle *käs'l, n* a fortified house or fortress; the residence of a prince or nobleman, or a large country mansion generally; a rook in chess. — *vi* (*chess*) to move the king two squares (on the first rank) towards either castle and place the castle on the square the king has passed over. — *n* **castellan** (*kas'təl-an*) the governor or keeper of a castle. — *adj* **castellated** (*kas'tel-āt-id*) having turrets and battlements like a castle. — *adj* **cas'tled** provided with castles. — **castle-guard'** the guard for the defence of a castle. — **castles in the air** or **in Spain** imaginary or unrealistic hopes or plans. [O.E. *castel* — L. *castellum*, dimin. of *castrum*, a fortified place.]

castor or **caster** *käst'ər, n* a small solid swivelling wheel attached to furniture for mobility; a container with a perforated top for sprinkling sugar, etc. — **castor (**or **caster) sugar** white granulated sugar finely crushed. [Ety. as for **cast**.]

castor-oil *käs-tər-oil', n* a medicinal and lubricating oil obtained from the seeds of a tropical African plant, the **castor-oil plant**.

castrate *kas-trāt', vt* to remove the testicles from; to render powerless, lacking in impact, etc. — *adj* **castrat'ed** gelded; rendered ineffective, expurgated. — *n* **castrā'tion**. — *n* **castrato** (*kas-trä'tō*; from It.) a male singer castrated in boyhood so as to preserve a soprano or alto voice: — *pl* **castra'ti** (*-tē*). [L. *castrāre, -ātum*.]

casual *kazh'ū-əl* or *kaz'ū-əl, adj* accidental; unforeseen; occasional; off-hand; (of sexual relations) lacking in depth of feeling of commitment; negligent, careless; unceremonious, relaxed, free and easy; (of a worker) employed only according to demand, without permanent employment. — *n* an occasional employee. — *vt* **cas'ualise** or **-ize** to turn (regular workers) into casual workers. — *n* **casualīsa'tion** or **-z-**. — *adv* **cas'ually**. — *n* **cas'ualness**. — *npl* **cas'uals** slip-on flat-heeled shoes; loose-fitting, comfortable and informal clothing. — **casual clothes** informal clothing; **casual labour** seasonal workers without permanent employment; **casual labourer**. [L. *cāsuālis* — *cāsus*; see **case²**.]

casualty *kazh'ū-əl-ti* or *kaz'ū-əl-ti, n* a person injured or killed; an accident; the casualty department of a hospital; a person lost to one side in a conflict, by wounds, death, desertion, etc. (*mil*); a thing damaged or destroyed. — **casualty department** or **ward** a hospital department or ward, where accident and emergency patients are (first) treated. [Ety. as for **casual**.]

casuist *kaz'ū-ist, n* a person who studies and resolves cases involving moral conscience; often, a person who argues plausibly but falsely in such cases. — *adj* **casūist'ic** or **casūist'ical**. — *adv* **casūist'ically**. — *n* **cas'ūistry** the science of resolving cases concerned with moral conscience; plausible but flawed reasoning. [Fr. *casuiste* — L. *cāsus*; see **case²**.]

casus belli *kä'zo͞os be'lē* or *kā'səs be'lī*, (L.) *n* something which causes, involves or justifies war.

CAT *kat, abbrev* for: College of Advanced Technology; computer-aided (or computer-assisted) testing; computerised axial tomography.

cat¹ *kat, n* a carnivore of the genus *Felis*, esp. the small domesticated kind or any of the smaller wild species; a spiteful woman (*derog*); short for **cat-o'-nine'-tails**, a whip with nine knotted tails or lashes, once used in the army and navy; a man, chap (*slang*); short for **caterpillar** (tractor). — *vt* to lash with a cat-o'-nine-tails. — *n* **cat'hood** the state of being a cat or having the nature of a cat. — *n* **cat'kin** a spike or tuft of closely-gathered small flowers, as in the willow, hazel, etc. — *adj* **cat'like** like a cat; noiseless, stealthy. — *n* **catt'ery** a place where cats are bred, or cared for in their owners' absence. — *adj* **catt'ish** or **catt'y** like a cat; spiteful. — *adv* **catt'ishly** or **catt'ily**. — *n* **catt'ishness** or **catt'iness**. — **cat'amount** any of various large wild cats, esp. applied to the puma and lynx; **catamoun'tain** as the catamount, but esp. applied to the leopard and panther. — *adj* **cat-and-dog'** constantly quarrelling. — *adj* **cat-and-mouse'** used of harassing or toying with an opponent, victim, etc. before finally killing, defeating or otherwise disposing of them; also of waiting and watching for the right moment to attack and dispose of one's opponent. — **cat'-burglar** a burglar who employs stealth and agility for his or her purposes; **cat'call** a shrill whistle or cry expressing disapproval or dissatisfaction, esp. at an artiste's performance. — *vi* to make a catcall. — *vt* to direct catcalls at. — **cat'fish** a type of fish with catlike whiskers near its mouth; **cat'-flap** a small door set into a larger door to allow a cat entry and exit; **cat'gut** a kind of cord made from the intestines of sheep and other animals and used for violin strings, some surgical ligatures, etc.; **cat'house** a brothel (*slang*); **cat litter** a granular absorbent material used to line a tray on which a cat may urinate and defecate; **cat'mint** or **cat'nip** a mint-like plant attractive to cats; **cat'nap** a brief sleep, esp. without lying down; **cat's-cra'dle** a pastime in which a string looped about the fingers and passed from player to player is altered from one symmetrical pattern to another; **cat's-eye'®** a small reflector set into a road surface; a name for various minerals giving the appearance of a cat's eye when polished; **cat's'-paw** a light breeze (*naut*); a person who is used by another; **cat's'-tail** a catkin; a bulrush; **cat'suit** a type of close-fitting one-piece trouser suit for women; **cat'walk** a narrow footway, as on a bridge, above the stage in a theatre, or for the models at a fashion show. — **Cheshire cat** (*chesh'ər kat*) a cat famous for grinning, like the one in Lewis Carroll's *Alice's Adventures in Wonderland*; **enough to make a cat laugh** enough to make even the least likely person inclined to laugh; **like a cat on hot bricks** or **on a hot tin roof** (*colloq*) uneasy, restive; very nervous; **like something the cat brought** or **dragged in** bedraggled, slovenly in dress, scruffy, etc.; **no room to swing a cat** without even a minimum of space, very cramped; **not have a cat in hell's chance** (*slang*) to have no chance at all; **play cat-and-mouse with** to deal with in a cat-and-mouse way; **put the cat among the pigeons** to stir up a great deal of trouble; **rain cats and dogs** (*colloq*) to pour down heavily; **see which way the cat jumps** to watch how things are going to turn out before committing oneself; **the big cats** lions, tigers, leopards, etc.; **the cat's pyjamas** or **whiskers** (*slang*) the very thing that is wanted, the ideal thing; anything very good. [O.E. *cat*.]

cat² *kat, n* short for **catamaran** and **catalytic converter**.

cat. *abbrev* for: catalogue; catechism.

catachresis *kat-ə-krē'sis*, (*rhet*) *n* misapplication of a word. — *adj* **catachrestic** (*-kres'tik*) or **catachres'tical** (*-əl*). — *adv* **catachres'tically**. [Gr. *katachrēsis*, misuse.]

cataclasm *kat'ə-klazm, n* a disruption, a breaking down. — *adj* **cataclas'mic**. [Gr. *kataklasma* — *kata*, down, *klaein*, to break.]

cataclysm *kat'ə-klizm, n* a flood of water or other major disaster; a great revolution or change, esp. in the life of an entire people. — *adj* **cataclys'mic**. — *adv* **cataclys'mically**. [Gr. *kataklysmos* — *kata*, downward, *klyzein*, to wash.]

catacomb *kat'ə-kōm* or *-ko͞om, n* an underground excavation used as a burial-place, esp. near Rome, where many of the early Christian victims of persecution were buried; any place built with crypt-like recesses. [It. *catacomba* — L.L. *Catacumbas*.]

catadioptric *kat-ə-dī-op'trik*, *adj* employing both reflection and refraction, as the construction of some long-focal-length photographic lenses. [**catoptric** and **dioptric**.]

catadromous *kət-ad'rəm-əs*, *adj* (of fishes) descending periodically for spawning to the lower parts of a river or to the sea (opp. to *anadromous*). [Gr. *kata*, down, *dromos*, a run.]

catafalque *kat'ə-falk*, *n* a temporary tomb-like structure used in funeral ceremonies or processions. [Fr., — It. *catafalco*.]

Catalan *kat'ə-lan*, *adj* of or belonging to *Catalonia*; of or concerning Catalan. — *n* a person born or living in Catalonia; the language spoken in Catalonia.

catalectic *kat-ə-lek'tik*, (*prosody*) *adj* lacking one syllable in the last foot. — *n* **catalex'is.** [Gr. *katalēktikos*, incomplete — *katalēgein*, to stop.]

catalepsy *kat'ə-lep-si*, *n* a state where one is more or less completely incapacitated, with severe bodily rigidity; cataplexy in animals. — *adj* and *n* **catalep'tic.** — *adv* **catalep'tically.** [Gr. *katalēpsis*, seizure, catalepsy — *kata*, down, *lēpsis*, taking, seizure.]

catalexis. See **catalectic.**

catalo. Same as **cattalo.**

catalogue *kat'ə-log* (or in N.Am. often **cat'alog**), *n* a systematic list of names, books, pictures, etc. — *vt* to put into a catalogue; to make a catalogue of. — *n* **cat'aloguer** (or in N.Am. often **cat'aloger**). — *vt* **cat'aloguise** or **-ize** (or in N.Am. often **cat'alogize**). [Gr. *katalogos*, from *kata*, in order, *legein*, to reckon.]

catalysis *kə-tal'i-sis*, *n* the chemical influence of a substance which is not itself permanently changed. — *vt* **cat'alyse** or **-yze** (*-līz*) to subject to catalysis; to act as a catalyst with respect to. — *n* **cat'alyser** or **-z-** a catalysing agent; a catalytic converter. — *n* **cat'alyst** (*-list*) a catalysing agent; a catalytic converter; a person who causes or promotes change by their presence in a situation or their input to it (*fig*). — *adj* **catalytic** (*-lit'ik*) or **catalyt'ical.** — *adv* **catalyt'ically.** — **catalytic converter** a device fitted to the exhaust of a motor vehicle to remove certain impurities from the exhaust gases. [Gr. *katalysis* — *kata*, down, *lyein*, to loosen.]

catamaran *kat'ə-mə-ran* or *kat-ə-mə-ran'*, *n* a boat, esp. a sailing boat, with two hulls; a raft of logs lashed together. [Tamil *kaṭṭu-maram*, tied wood.]

catamite *kat'ə-mīt*, *n* a boy kept for homosexual purposes. [L. *catamītus*.]

catamount, catamountain. See under **cat**[1].

cataplasm *kat'ə-plazm*, *n* a plaster or poultice. [Gr. *kataplasma*.]

cataplexy *kat'ə-plek-si*, *n* a condition of immobility induced by extreme emotion, e.g. shock (*med*); a physical state resembling death, adopted by some animals to discourage predators. — *adj* **cataplec'tic.** [Gr. *kataplēxis*, amazement — *kata*, down, *plēssein*, to strike.]

catapult *kat'ə-pult*, *n* (in ancient history) a war machine for throwing boulders, etc.; a small forked stick having an elastic string fixed to the two forks, used for firing small stones; any similar device, as for launching aeroplanes from an aircraft-carrier. — *vt* and *vi* to shoot out from, or as if from, a catapult. — **catapult fruit** one that shoots out its seeds. [L. *catapulta* — Gr. *katapeltēs*.]

cataract *kat'ə-rakt*, *n* a waterfall; an opaque condition of the lens of the eye, painless and unaccompanied by inflammation; the area rendered opaque, which is surgically removable. [L. *cataracta* — Gr. *kataraktēs*, portcullis, waterfall.]

catarrh *kat-är'*, *n* a discharge of fluid owing to inflammation of a mucous membrane, esp. of the nose, often chronic. — *adj* **catarrh'al** or **catarrh'ous.** [L. *catarrhus* — Gr. *katarrhous* — *kata*, down, *rheein*, to flow.]

catastrophe *kət-as'trə-fi*, *n* a sudden disaster; a sudden and violent upheaval in some part of the surface of the earth (*geol*); an unfortunate conclusion, outcome, etc.; a final event; the climax of the action of the plot in a play or novel. — — *adj* **catastrophic** (*kat-ə-strof'ik*). — *adv* **catastroph'ically.** — *n* **catas'trophism** the old theory of geological change by vast, unconnected catastrophes and new creations. — *n* **catas'trophist.** [Gr. *kata*, down, *strophē*, a turning.]

catatonia *kat-ə-tō'ni-ə*, *n* a type of schizophrenia characterised by periodic states of rigidity or immobility. — *adj* and *n* **catatonic** (*-ton'ik*). [Gr. *kata*, down, *tonos*, stretching, straining.]

catawba *kə-tö'bə*, *n* an American variety of grape; a wine made from it. [*Catawba* River in Carolina.]

catcall. See under **cat**[1].

catch *kach*, *vt* to take hold of (esp. a thing in motion); to gather (the ball) after the batsman has hit it and before it touches the ground (*cricket*); to dismiss (a batsman) thus; to hear (*colloq*); to understand; to seize, having chased (a person, etc.); to trap or ensnare when hunting, fishing, etc.; to entangle or fasten on(to); to come upon, to happen to see; to meet (*colloq*); to be in time for; to take as a means of transport; to strike, hit; to get (a disease, etc.) by infection or contagion; to succeed in reproducing (someone's qualities or likeness, etc.) by painting, photography or imitation. — *vi* to become entangled or fastened; (of a fire, or of anything to be burned) to catch light: — *pa t* and *pa p* **caught** (*köt*). — *n* seizure; an act of catching, esp. the ball at cricket, etc.; a clasp, or anything that fastens or holds; that which is caught; a person who is considered worth catching as a marriage partner; a sudden advantage taken; a concealed difficulty or disadvantage; in someone's voice, an indistinctness caused by strong emotion; a children's game in which a ball, etc. is thrown and caught in turn; a round for three or more voices, often deriving comic effect by the interweaving of the words. — *adj* **catch'able** capable of being caught. — *n* **catch'er.** — *adj* **catch'ing** infectious (*med* or *fig*); captivating, attractive. — *n* **catch'ment** the water collected from a river etc. catchment area; the pupils collected from a school catchment area. — *adj* **catch'y** attractive; readily taking hold in the mind, as a tune, etc. may be. — *adj* **catch'-all** covering or dealing with a number of instances, eventualities or problems, esp. ones not covered or dealt with specifically by other provisions. — *n* a clause, statement etc. of this type; **catch-as-catch-can'** a style of wrestling in which any hold is allowed. — Also *adj* and *adv*. — **catch'-basin** or **catch'-pit** a trap for dirt in a drain; **catch'-crop** a secondary crop grown before, after, or at the same time as, and on the same piece of ground as, a main crop; **catch'-drain** a drain on a hillside to catch the surface water; **catch fencing** protective safety fencing surrounding a motor race-track; **catch'fly** a name for a species of campion and several of bladder-campion with sticky stems for catching insects; **catchment area** the area from which a river or reservoir is fed (also **catchment basin**); the area from which the pupils for a school are drawn, or the locality served by another public facility, e.g. a hospital; **catch'penny** a worthless thing made only for profit. — Also *adj.* — **catch'-phrase** a phrase that becomes popular and is much repeated; a slogan; **catch points** railway points which can derail a train to prevent it accidentally running onto a main line. — *adj* **Catch 22** (title of novel by J. Heller, 1961) denoting an absurd situation in which one can never win, being constantly balked by a clause, rule, etc. which itself can change to block any change in one's course of action — or being faced with a choice of courses of action, both or all of which would have undesirable consequences. — *n* such a situation; **catch'word** the word at the head of the page in a dictionary or encyclopaedia; (in typed correspondence, etc.) the first word of a page given at the bottom of the preceding page; any word or phrase taken up and repeated esp. as the watchword or slogan of a political party; an actor's cue. — **catch at** to make a hasty attempt to catch; **catch cold (at)** to suffer a financial or other misfortune (as a result of making an unwise investment); **catch fire** or **light** to become ignited; to become inspired by passion or enthusiasm; **catch hold of** to seize; **catch it** (*colloq*) to get a scolding or the like; **catch me** or **him**, etc., an emphatic colloquial phrase implying that there is not the remotest possibility of my or his (etc.) doing the thing mentioned; **catch on** to comprehend; to become fashionable, catch the popular imagination; **catch one's breath** see under **breath**; **catch one's death** see under **death**; **catch someone's drift** to follow what someone is talking about; **catch out** to detect in error or deceit; **catch sight of** to get a glimpse of; **catch up** to draw level (with) and sometimes overtake; **catch up** or **away** to snatch or seize hastily. [From O.Fr. *cachier* — L.L. *captiāre* from *captāre*, intensive of *capĕre*, to take; see **chase**[1].]

catchup or **catsup**. See **ketchup**.

cat-cracker *kat'krak-ər*, *n* (in full, **catalytic cracker**) an industrial plant in which the chemical breaking down of petroleum is speeded up by the use of a catalyst. — *n* **cat'-cracking**.

catechise or **-ize** *kat'i-kīz*, *vt* to instruct by question and answer, esp. in the Christian faith; to examine systematically by questioning. — *adj* **catechetic** (*-ket'ik*) or **catechet'ical** relating to catechism or oral instruction in the first principles, esp. of Christianity. — *adv* **catechet'ically**. — *n* **cat'e-chiser** or **-z-**. — *n* **cat'echīsing** or **-z-**. — *n* **cat'echism** any comprehensive system of teaching drawn up in form of question and answer; a set of questions; a thorough examination by questions. — *n* **cat'echist** a person who catechises; a teacher of catechumens; an indigenous teacher in a mission church. — *adj* **catechis'tic, catechis'tical** or **catechis'mal** pertaining to a catechist or catechism. [L. *catēchismus*, formed from Gr. *katēchizein*, *katēcheein*, to din into the ears — *kata*, back, *echē*, a sound.]

catechu *kat'i-choo* or *-shoo*, *n* a dark extract from certain Indian plants (acacia, betel-nut, etc.) which are rich in tannin. — *n* **catecholamine** (*-kō'lə-mēn* or *-chō'*) any of several compounds (e.g. adrenaline and noradrenaline) that mimic the action of the nerves supplying the involuntary muscles, and that are derivatives of catechu. [Cf. Malay *cachu*.]

catechumen *kat-i-kū'mən*, *n* a person who is being taught the rudiments of Christianity. — *adj* **cat-echūmen'ical**. — *adv* **catechūmen'ically**. — *n* **catechū'menism** or **catechū'menship**. [Gr. *katēchoumenos*, being taught, pres. p. pass. of *kat-ēcheein*, to teach; cf. **catechise**.]

category *kat'i-gər-i*, *n* a class or order of things, people, etc. possessing similar characteristics; (in *pl*) the highest classes under which objects of philosophy can be systematically arranged, understood as an attempt at a comprehensive classification of all that exists (*philos*). — *adj* **categorial** (*ka-tə-gör'i-əl*) of or pertaining to a category. — *adv* **categor'ially**. — *adj* **categorical** or **categoric** (*-gor'*) positive; absolute; without exception. — *adv* **categor'ically** absolutely; without qualification; particularly definitely. — *n* **categor'icalness** the quality of being absolute and unqualified. — *vt* **cat'egorise** or **-ize** to place in a particular category or list; to class. — *n* **cat'-egorist**. — **categorical imperative** in the ethics of Kant, the absolute unconditional command of the moral law obliging people to act responsibly. — **category-A** and **category-B prisoner** a prisoner of a certain degree of dangerousness and for whom a certain degree of security is required, A being the most dangerous category. [Gr. *katēgoriā*, assertion, predication, accusation.]

catena *kə-tē'nə*, *n* a chain or connected series: — *pl* **cate'nae** (*-nē*) or *cate'nas*. — *adj* **catenarian** (*kat-i-nā'ri-ən*) of, or of the nature of, a chain or a catenary. — *n* **catē'nary** (or *kat'*) the curve formed by a flexible cord hanging freely between two points of support; the arrangement of pylons and cables through which electricity is supplied on some electrified railway lines. — *adj* relating to, or like, a chain. — *vt* **catenate** (*kat'i-nāt*) to connect as in or by a chain. — *adj* linked as in a chain. — *n* **catenā'tion**. [L. *catēna*, chain.]

cater *kā'tər*, *vi* to provide food, entertainment, etc. (for); to provide the requirements of (a person, occasion, etc.; with *to* or *for*). — *vt* (*NAm*) to provide food, entertainments, etc. for (an occasion). — *n* **cā'terer**. — *n* **cā'teress**. — *n* **cā'tering**. [Ult. from L. *captāre*, to seize.]

cater-cornered *kat'ər-kör-nərd*, (*NAm*) *adj* diagonal; diagonally opposite (from). — *adv* diagonally. [Dialect — Fr. *quatre*, four, and **cornered**.]

caterpillar *kat'ər-pil-ər*, *n* a butterfly or moth grub; extended to other insect larvae; (from **Caterpillar**®) a tractor or other (esp. earth-moving) vehicle running on endless articulated tracks consisting of flat metal plates. [See **cat**[1] and **pile**[1].]

caterwaul *kat'ər-wöl*, *n* the shriek or cry emitted by a domestic cat when on heat. — *vi* to make such a noise; to make any discordant sound similar to this; to quarrel like cats. — *n* **cat'erwauling**. [Ety. as for **cat**[1], and **waul**.]

catfish and **catgut**, etc. See under **cat**[1].

Cath. *abbrev* for Catholic.

cath. *abbrev* for cathedral.

cathartic *kath-ärt'ik* or **cathartical** *-ärt'ik-əl*, *adj* cleansing, purifying; having the power of cleansing the bowels (*med*); purgative; causing emotional or psychological catharsis. — *n* **cathart'ic** a purgative medicine. — *vt* **cath'arise** or **-ize** to render absolutely clean. — *n* **cathar'sis** purification; evacuation of the bowels (*med*); purification of the emotions, as by the drama according to Aristotle; the purging of the effects of pent-up emotion and repressed thoughts, by bringing them to the surface of consciousness (*psychol*): — *pl* **cathar'ses** (*-sēz*). [Gr. *kathartikos*, fit for cleansing, *katharos*, clean.]

cathectic. See **cathexis**.

cathedral *kə-thē'drəl*, *n* the principal church of a diocese, containing the bishop's throne. — *adj* belonging to a seat of authority or a cathedral; having a cathedral. — *n* **cathedra** (*-thē'drə* or *-thed'rə*) a bishop's throne. — See also **ex cathedra**. [L. *cathēdra*, *cathĕdra* — Gr. *kathĕdrā*, a seat.]

Catherine-wheel *kath'ə-rin-hwēl*, also *kath'rin* and *wēl*, *n* a rotating firework; a rose-window (*archit*). [From St *Catherine* of Alexandria (4th cent.), who miraculously escaped torture on a wheel.]

catheter *kath'i-tər*, *n* a tube for admitting or removing gases or liquids through channels of the body, esp. for removing urine from the bladder. — *n* **catheter-isā'tion** or **-z-** insertion of a catheter. — *n* **cath'eterism** use of the catheter. — *n* **cathet-om'eter** an instrument for measuring small differences in the level of liquids in tubes. [Gr. *kathetos*, perpendicular, *kathetēr*, a catheter.]

cathexis *kə-thek'sis*, (*psychol*) *n* a charge of mental energy attached to any particular idea or object: — *pl* **cathex'es** (*-sēz*). — *adj* **cathec'tic**. [Gr. *kathexis*, holding.]

cathode *kath'ōd*, *n* the electrode of an electrolytic cell at which positively charged ions are discharged into the exterior electric circuit; the positive terminal or electrode of a dry battery; in valves and tubes, the source of electrons. — See **anode**. — *adj* **cath'odal**.

— *adj* **cathod'ic.** — *n* **cathod'ograph** a photograph by X-rays. — *n* **cathodog'rapher.** — *n* **cathodog'raphy.** — **cathode-ray oscilloscope** a machine on which can be displayed the repeated and transient waveforms of current or voltage, radio waveforms, etc.; **cathode rays** streams of negatively charged particles (electrons) proceeding from the cathode of a vacuum tube; **cathode-ray tube** a device in which a narrow beam of electrons, which can be deflected by magnetic and/or electrostatic fields, acts on a fluorescent screen or photographic surface — used in television sets, etc. [Gr. *kathodos*, a going down — *kata*, down, *hodos*, a way.]

catholic *kath'ə-lik, adj* (with *cap*) belonging to the Christian Church before the great schism between East and West, or to any church claiming to be historically related to it, esp. after the schism the Western church, after the Reformation the Church of Rome (Roman Catholic); (with *cap*) relating to the Roman Catholics; liberal (opp. of exclusive); general, embracing the whole body of Christians; universal. — *n* (with *cap*) an adherent of the R.C. Church. — *vt* and *vi* **cathol'icise** or **-ize** (also with *cap*) to make or become Catholic. — *n* **catholicisa'tion** or **-z-** (also with *cap*). — *n* **Cathol'icism** the beliefs, dogma of the R.C. Church. — *n* **catholicity** (*-is'i-ti*) universality; liberality or breadth of view(s). — *n* **cathol'icon** (*-kon*) a universal remedy, a panacea. — **Catholic emancipation** the relief of the Roman Catholics, granted in 1829, from certain penal regulations and restrictions. [Gr. *katholikos*, universal — *kata*, throughout, *holos*, the whole.]

cation *kat'ī-ən, (phys) n* an ion that travels towards the cathode; a positively-charged ion. [Gr. *kata*, down, *iōn*, neut. — pres. p. of *ienai*, to go.]

catkin, catmint, catnip, etc. See under **cat**[1].

catoptric *kat-op'trik, adj* relating to reflection. — *nsing* **catop'trics** the part of optics which is concerned with reflected light. [Gr. *katoptron*, a mirror.]

CAT scanner *kat skan'ər, n* short for **computerised axial tomography scanner** (qq.v. under **compute**).

catsup. See **ketchup.**

cattalo *kat'ə-lō, n* a cross between the bison ('buffalo') and the domestic cow: — *pl* **catt'alos** or **catt'aloes.** [From *catt*le and buff*alo*.]

cattle *kat'l, npl* beasts of pasture, esp. cows, bulls, and oxen. — **cattle cake** a concentrated, processed food for cattle, in the form of blocks or cakes; **cattle grid** (or in U.S. **cattle guard**) a frame of spaced bars covering a trench or depression in a road where it passes through a fence, crossable by motor vehicles or pedestrians but not by hoofed animals; **catt'le-lifter** a stealer of cattle; **catt'le-lifting; catt'leman** a person who tends cattle, or who rears them on a ranch; **cattle prod** a rod or goad, usu. electrified, for driving cattle, etc.; **cattle show** an exhibition of cattle or other domestic animals in competition for prizes. [O.Fr. *catel, chatel* — L.L. *captāle*, L. *capitāle* — *caput*, the head.]

Caucasian *kö-kā'zhi-ən* or *-zi-ən, n* a person belonging to that one of the main racial divisions of mankind which is native to Europe, North Africa and western and central Asia; a member of the white race; a white person; a native of the *Caucasus* or the country around it. — *adj* of or pertaining to a Caucasian or Caucasians in any of the above senses; pertaining to the Caucasus or the country around it; of or pertaining to the languages spoken in the Caucasus which do not belong to the Indo-European, Semitic, or Ural-Altaic groups (*linguis*).

caucus *kö'kəs, n* any small group which acts as (semi-)autonomous body within a larger group or organisation, esp. (*derog*) one which is excessively influential. — *vi* to hold a caucus.

caudal *kö'dl, (zool) adj* pertaining to the tail. — *adj* **cau'dad** towards the tail. — *adj* **cau'dāte** or **cau'dated** tailed. [L. *cauda*, tail.]

caudex *kö'deks, (bot) n* the stem of a tree, esp. of a palm or tree-fern: — *pl* **caud'ices** (*-i-sēz*) or **caud'exes.** [L.]

caudillo *kow-dēl'yō, n* in Spanish-speaking countries, a leader; a head of state: — *pl* **caudil'los.** [Sp.]

caught *köt, pa t* and *pa p* of **catch.**

caul *köl, n* the membrane sometimes covering the head of infants at birth; a net or covering for the head. [O.Fr. *cale*, a little cap.]

cauldron or **caldron** *köl'drən, n* a very large pot for boiling or heating liquids. [O.Fr. *caudron* — L. *caldārium* — *calidus*, hot — *calēre*, to be hot.]

cauliflower *ko'li-flowr, n* a variety of cabbage with an edible white flower-head. — **cauliflower ear** an ear permanently swollen and misshapen by injury, esp. from repeated blows. [L. *caulis*, cabbage; and **flower.**]

caulk or **calk** *kök, vt* to render (planks, etc. of a boat) watertight by pressing suitable material into the seams. — *n* **caulk'er.** — *n* **caulk'ing.** — **caulk'ing-iron** an instrument like a chisel used for pressing tarred rope (oakum) into the seams of ships. [O.Fr. *cauquer*, to press — L. *calcāre*, to tread — *calx*, heel.]

cause *köz, n* that which produces an effect; that by or through which anything happens; a motive; an ideal or heartfelt belief in the name of which people band together to do something; sake, advantage; a legal action between contending parties. — *vt* to produce; to bring about the existence of; to bring about the occurrence of. — *conj* (*dialect* or *colloq*) because (usu. **'cause**). — *adj* **caus'al** being the cause, that causes; relating to a cause or causes. — *n* **causal'ity** the relationship between cause and effect; the mechanics of the cause of something. — *adv* **caus'ally.** — *n* **causā'tion** the act of causing; the bringing about of an effect; causality. — *adj* **caus'ative** causal; of the nature of, or expressing causation. — *n* a form of verb expressing or implying causation. — *adv* **caus'atively.** — *adj* **cause'less** without cause; without just or reasonable cause. — *adv* **cause'lessly.** — *n* **cause'lessness.** — *n* **caus'er.** — **first cause** the original cause or creator of all, God; **have** or **show cause** to have or give reasons for a certain course of action; **make common cause** (often with *with*) to unite for a common purpose; **natural causes** causes (of death) such as old age or disease, as opp. to violence or accident; **secondary causes** causes derived from a primary or first cause. [Fr. — L. *causa*.]

cause célèbre *kōz sā-lebr', (Fr.) n* a very notable or famous trial; a notorious controversy or highly controversial person.

causerie *kōz'ər-ē, n* a talk or gossip; a paragraph of chat about literature or art. [Fr.]

causeway *köz'wā, n* a raised road or path through a marsh or across water; a pathway paved with stone. — *adj* **cause'wayed.** [M.E. *causee* — O.Fr. *caucie* — L.L. *via calciāta*, a trodden way.]

caustic *kös'tik, adj* burning; corroding; of e.g. remarks, bitter, severe, cutting (*fig*); pertaining to, or of the shape of, a caustic (*math* or *phys*). — *n* a substance that has a corroding or disintegrating action on the skin and flesh; an envelope of light rays proceeding from a fixed point and reflected or refracted by a curve (*math*); a caustic curve or caustic surface (*phys*). — *adv* **caus'tically.** — *n* **causticity** (*-tis'i-ti*) or **caus'ticness** quality of being caustic. — **caustic ammonia** ammonia as a gas, or in solution; **caustic curve** a curve in the shape of a caustic, the form of a plane section through a caustic surface (*phys*); **caustic lime** quicklime, lime containing no water; **caustic potash** potassium hydroxide; **caustic soda** sodium hydroxide, used in making soap; **caustic surface** a caustic-shaped surface, the envelope of rays of light reflected or refracted by a curved surface (*phys*). [L. *causticus* — Gr. *kaustikos* — *kaiein*, to burn.]

cauterise or **-ize** *kö'tər-īz*, *vt* to burn with a caustic substance, a hot metal implement, etc., esp. so as to destroy infected tissue in a wound; to sear (*fig*). — *n* **cau'ter** or **cau'tery** burning or destroying with caustics, a hot iron, etc.; a burning iron, caustic, etc. for burning or destroying tissue. — *n* **cau'terant** a cauterising substance. — *n* **cauterīsā'tion** or **-z-**. — *adj* **cau'terīsing** or **-z-**. — *n* **cau'terism**. [Fr. *cautériser* — L.L. *cautērizāre* — Gr. *kautēr*, a hot iron — *kaiein*, to burn.]

caution *kö'shən*, *n* heedfulness, carefulness; a warning; a warning that what a person says may be used as evidence (*law*); an amusing or astonishing person or thing (*colloq*). — *vt* to warn to take care; to give (someone) a caution (*law*). — *adj* **cau'tionary** containing a caution or cautions. — *n* **cau'tioner**. — *adj* **cautious** (*kö'shəs*) possessing or using caution; watchful, heedful; prudent. — *adv* **cau'tiously**. — *n* **cau'tiousness**. — **caution money** money paid in advance as security for good behaviour. [Fr. — L. *cautiō*, *-ōnis* — *cavēre*, to beware.]

cavalcade *kav-əl-kād'* or *kav'əl-kād*, *n* a procession of people on horseback or in vehicles; a parade. — *vi* to proceed in a cavalcade. [Fr., through It. and L.L. — L. *caballus*, a horse.]

cavalier *kav-əl-ēr'*, *n* a knight; (with *cap*) a Royalist (supporter of the King) in the English Civil War; a gallant or gentleman accompanying a lady. — *adj* haughty, supercilious, devil-may-care, incautious; like a cavalier. — *adv* **cavalier'ly** off-hand, haughtily, with supercilious disregard or curtness. — *adj* cavalier. [Fr. — It. *cavallo*; see **cavalcade**.]

cavalry *kav'əl-ri*, *n* (a troop of) mounted soldiers. — *n* **cav'alryman**. — **cavalry twill** see **twill**. [Fr. *cavallerie* — It. *cavalleria* — L. *caballārius*, horseman — *caballus*, horse.]

cavatina *kav-ə-tē'nə*, *n* a simple melody with no second part or da capo; (*loosely*) a short operatic air, of a smooth and melodious character. [It.]

cave[1] *kāv*, *n* a hollow in a rock; a small faction of seceders from a political party (from the Cave of Adullam; *Bible*: 1 Samuel xxii, 1–2). — *vt* to hollow out. — *vi* to inhabit a cave (usu. temporarily). — *n* **ca'ver** a person who explores caves. — *n* **ca'ving** cave-exploration. — **cave'-bear** a Pleistocene bear of which fossils have been found in caves; **cave'-dweller** a person who lives in a cave, esp. one of the Stone Age people of prehistoric times; **cave'man** a cave-dweller; a modern male with primitive and chauvinist ways (*colloq*). — **cave in** to slip, to subside, to collapse inwards (*n* **cave'-in**); to yield to outside pressure, to give way, collapse (*fig*). [Fr., — L. *cavus*, hollow.]

cave[2] *kāv'i*, (*schoolboy slang*) *interj* beware. — **keep cave** to keep watch. [L. *căvē*, imper. sing., *căvĕat*, 3rd sing. pres. subjunctive of *căvēre*, to take care.]

caveat *kav'i-at* or *kāv'i-at*, *n* a precondition (*law*); a warning. — **caveat actor** (*ak'tör*) let the doer beware; **caveat emptor** (*emp'tör*) it is the buyer's responsibility. [L.]

cavendish *kav'ən-dish*, *n* tobacco moistened and pressed into rectangular cakes.

cavern *kav'ərn*, *n* a deep hollow place in rocks, a large cave. — *vt* to put in a cavern; to hollow out. — *adj* **cav'erned** full of caverns. — *adj* **cav'ernous** like a cavern in size, huge; hollow; full of caverns. — *adv* **cav'ernously**. [L. *caverna* — *cavus*, hollow.]

caviare or **caviar** *kav'i-är* or *kav-i-är'*, *n* salted roe of the sturgeon fish; something whose flavour is too fine for the common taste (*fig*).

cavil *kav'il*, *vi* to make petty, trifling objections (with *at* or *about*): — *pr p* **cav'illing**; *pa t* and *pa p* **cav'illed**. — *n* a frivolous, petty objection. — *n* and *adj* **cav'illing**. — *n* **cav'iller**. [O.Fr. *caviller* — L. *cavillārī*, to practise jesting.]

cavity *kav'it-i*, *n* a hollow space; a decayed hollow in a tooth. — *vi* **cav'itate** to form hollows. — *n* **cavitā'tion** the formation of cavities in a structure, or of gas bubbles in a liquid, or of a vacuum, or of a partial vacuum as between a body moving in a fluid and the fluid; a cavity. — *adj* **cav'itied**. — **cavity wall** a wall consisting of two layers with a space between. [L. *cavitās* — *cavus*, hollow.]

cavort *kə-vört'*, *vi* to frolic, bound about joyfully. [Explained as a corruption of **curvet**.]

cavy *kāv'i*, *n* a member of the guinea pig genus of rodents. [*Cabiai*, native name in French Guiana.]

caw *kö*, *vi* to cry as a crow. — *n* the cry of a crow. — *n* **caw'ing**. [From the sound.]

cay *kā*, *n* a low islet, the same as **key**[2]. [Sp. *cayo*.]

cayenne *kā-en'*, *n* a very strong, pungent red pepper **(cayenne pepper)** made from several species of chilli. — *adj* **cayenned'** seasoned with cayenne.

cayman *kā'mən*, *n* any of several Central and South American animals related to crocodiles and alligators: — *pl* **cay'mans**. — Also **cai'man**. [Sp. *caimán*.]

cayuse *kī-ūs'*, (*NAm*) *n* an Indian pony used by cowboys. [Am. Ind.]

CB *abbrev* for: Citizens' Band (radio); Companion of the (Order of the) Bath; confined (or confinement) to barracks.

Cb (*chem*) *symbol* for columbium (now niobium).

CBC *abbrev* for Canadian Broadcasting Corporation.

CBE *abbrev* for Commander of the (Order of the) British Empire.

CBer *sē-bē'ər*, *n* short for Citizens' Band radio user.

CBI *abbrev* for Confederation of British Industry.

CBS *abbrev* for Columbia Broadcasting System.

CBSO *abbrev* for City of Birmingham Symphony Orchestra.

CC *abbrev* for: Cape Coloured (see **cape**[2]); closed circuit (transmission); County Council; Cricket Club.

cc *abbrev* for: *capita* (L.), chapters; cubic centimetre(s).

CCCP. See **USSR**.

CCD *abbrev* for charge coupled device.

CCF *abbrev* for Combined Cadet Force.

CD *abbrev* for: Civil Defence; compact disc; contagious disease or diseases; *Corps Diplomatique* (Fr.), Diplomatic Corps.

Cd *abbrev* for coefficient of drag.

Cd (*chem*) *symbol* for cadmium.

cd *abbrev* for candela.

CDN *abbrev* for Canada (I.V.R.).

Cdr *abbrev* for Commander.

CD-ROM *sē-dē-rom'*, *abbrev* for compact disc read-only memory.

CDSO *abbrev* for Companion of the Distinguished Service Order.

CDT *abbrev* for craft, design, technology.

CDV *abbrev* for Civil Defence Volunteers.

CE *abbrev* for: chemical engineer; chief engineer; Church of England; civil engineer; Common Entrance; Common Era; *Communauté européene* (Fr.), the mark required as the manufacturer's declaration of conformity with EC toy safety regulations on all toys since Jan.1990; Council of Europe.

Ce (*chem*) *symbol* for cerium.

cease *sēs*, *vt* and *vi* to stop; to end. — *n* end; cessation. — *adj* **cease'less** without ceasing; continuous. — *adv* **cease'lessly**. — *n* **ceas'ing**. — **cease'-fire** an order to cease firing; an agreed end to active hostilities. [Fr. *cesser* — L. *cēssāre*, to give over — *cēdĕre*, to yield.]

cebadilla. See **sabadilla**.

ceca, cecal, cecum. See **caecum**.

cedar *sē'dər*, *n* a large evergreen coniferous tree remarkable for the durability and fragrance of its wood; applied also to many more or less similar trees; the wood of these trees, cedarwood. — *adj* made of cedar. — *adj* **cē'dared** covered with cedars. — **ce'darwood** (also *adj*). [L. *cedrus* — Gr. *kedros*.]

cede *sēd*, *vt* to yield or give up to another person, country etc. — *vi* to give way, yield. [L. *cēdĕre*, *cēssum*, to yield, to give up.]

cedilla *se-dil'ə*, *n* a mark (orig. a subscript Z) placed under the letter c (thus ç), formerly used in Spanish to indicate that the letter had the sound of (Spanish) *z* where that of *k* would be expected, still used esp. in French and Portuguese to indicate an *s*-sound as before *a*, *o*, *u*, and in other languages used under various letters to denote other sounds, e.g. Turkish s (*sh*) and c (*ch*). [Sp., dimin. from *zēta*, the Greek name of *z*; see **z**.]

CEDO *abbrev* for Centre for Education Development Overseas.

cee *sē*, *n* the third letter of the alphabet (C, c); anything shaped like it. — **cee'-spring** or **c'-spring** a spring in the shape of a C to support the frame of a carriage.

Ceefax® *sē'faks*, *n* the teletext service of the British Broadcasting Corporation. [**see** and **facts**.]

CEGB *abbrev* for Central Electricity Generating Board (privatised in January 1990 and split into four new companies: *PowerGen*, *Nuclear Electric*, *National Grid* and *National Power*).

CEI *abbrev* for Council of Engineering Institutions.

ceilidh *kā'li*, *n* in Scotland and Ireland, an informal evening of song, story and dancing. [Gael., a visit.]

ceiling *sē'ling*, *n* the inner roof of a room; the highest altitude at which an aircraft can fly; the height above the ground of the base of the cloud-layer; an upper limit. — *adj* **ceil'inged** having a ceiling. — *n* **ceilom'eter** an instrument for measuring the cloud ceiling.

cel *n*. See **cell**.

cel. *abbrev* for celebrated.

celandine *sel'ən-dīn*, *n* either of two plants (**greater celandine** and **lesser celandine**) supposed to flower when the swallows came, and to perish when they went. [O.Fr. *celidoine* — Gr. *chelīdonion* — *chelīdōn*, a swallow.]

celebrate *sel'i-brāt*, *vt* to mark by solemn ceremonies, as a festival or an event; to perform with proper rites and ceremonies, as a mass, a marriage, or other pleasant occasion; to publish the praises of; to make famous. — *vi* to do something enjoyable because of a feeling of pleasure at some event, achievement, etc. — *n* **cel'ebrant** a person who celebrates; the principal person officiating at a rite or ceremony. — *adj* **cel'ebrated** distinguished; famous. — *n* **celebrā'tion**. — *n* **cel'ebrātor**. — *adj* **cel'ebratory**. — *n* **celebrity** (*si-leb'ri-ti*) fame; notoriety; a person of distinction or fame (*slang abbrev* **celeb'**). [L. *celebrāre*, *-ātum* — *celeber*, frequented.]

celerity *si-ler'i-ti*, *n* quickness, rapidity of motion or thought. [Fr. *célérité* — L. *celeritās* — *celer*, quick.]

celery *sel'ər-i*, *n* a plant with a flat-topped flower-head whose blanched leafstalks are eaten cooked or uncooked. — *n* **celeriac** (*si-ler'i-ak*) a variety of celery with a root like a turnip. [Fr. *céleri* — Gr. *selīnon*, parsley.]

celesta *si-les'tə* or **celeste** *si-lest'*, *n* a keyboard instrument in which the hammers strike steel plates over wooden resonators. [Fr. *céleste*, heavenly.]

celestial *si-lest'yəl*, *adj* heavenly; living in heaven; in the visible sky, the heavens. — *n* an inhabitant of heaven. — *adv* **celest'ially**. [Through Fr. from L. *caelestis* — *caelum*, heaven.]

celiac. See **coeliac**.

celibacy *sel'i-bəs-i*, *n* the unmarried state, esp. as adhered to because of a vow; abstention from sexual intercourse. — *adj* **cel'ibate** (*-bit*) living as a single person; abstaining from sexual intercourse. — *n* a person who is unmarried, or bound by a vow not to marry. [L. *caelebs*, single.]

cell *sel*, *n* a mass of living matter, the smallest unit capable of independent existence, walled or unwalled, by itself or associated with others; a small room in a prison, monastery, etc.; a vessel with electrodes and an electrolyte, for generating an electric current by chemical action, esp. a dry battery; a unit group, esp. of espionage personnel, terrorists, political activists, etc.; a small monastery or nunnery dependent on another; one compartment of a comb in a hive; a hermit's one-roomed dwelling; a small cavity (*biol*); (a radio transmitter serving) one of the geographical areas into which Britain is divided for the coverage of cellular radio (q.v.); a celluloid (also **cel**); the unit of storage in computing. — *n* **cell'a** the inner chamber of an ancient temple: — *pl* **cell'ae** (*-ē*). — *adj* **celled** having cells, cellular. — *adj* **cellif'erous** having or producing cells. — *adj* **cell'ūlar** consisting of, characterised by, or containing cells or compartments; relating to or involving cells in the body; porous; having an open texture. — *n* **cell'ule** a little cell. — *adj* **cellū-lif'erous** having or producing little cells. — *n* **cell'ūlite** deposits of fat, not responsive to dieting or exercise, which give the skin a dimpled, pitted appearance. — *n* **cellūlī'tis** spreading infection of sub-surface tissue with pus-forming bacteria. — *n* **cell'ūloid** a type of plastic which is elastic, very strong, and usu. transparent or translucent; a sheet of this material; one of the drawings which make up a film cartoon, usu. composed on a sheet of celluloid. — *n* **cell'ūlose** a carbohydrate forming the chief component of cell-walls in plants and in wood. — *adj* **cellūlōs'ic** containing, or derived from cellulose. — *n* a compound or substance containing cellulose. — **cell'-division** (*biol*) the process in which cells each split into two new cells, so increasing in number during growth or reproduction; **cell'phone** or **cellular phone** a pocket telephone for use in a cellular radio system; **cellular (**or **cell-mediated) immunity** an acquired immunity in which white corpuscles from the lymph glands play a major part; **cellular radio** a system of radio communication based on a network of roughly hexagonal geographical cells each served by a transmitter, the receiving equipment automatically tuning in to each in turn as it moves across the cells' borders. [O.Fr. *celle* — L. *cella*, conn. with *celāre*, to cover.]

cella. See **cell**.

cellar *sel'ər*, *n* any underground room or vault; a room for storing wine, beer, coal, etc., usu. below ground level; a stock of wine. — *vt* to store in a cellar. — *n* **cell'arage** (a quantity of) cellar space; a charge for storing in cellars. — *n* **cell'arer** or **cell'arist** a person who is in charge of a cellar; an officer in a monastery who looks after the provisions. — *n* **cell'aret** a case, cupboard or drawer for holding bottles of wine, etc. — **cell'ar-book** a record of wines kept in a cellar; **cell'ar-flap** a plate covering an entrance to a cellar; **cell'arman** a person responsible for a cellar. [O.Fr. *celier* — L. *cellārium* — *cella*.]

cello *chel'ō*, *n* a shortened form of **violoncello** (sometimes written **'cello**): — *pl* **cell'os**. — *n* **cell'ist** or **'cell'ist** for **violoncellist**.

cellophane® *sel'ō-fān*, *n* a tough, transparent, paper-like wrapping material made from viscose. [*cell*ulose and Gr. *phainein*, to show.]

cellphone, cellular, cellulite, celluloid, cellulose. See under **cell**.

celom. See **coelom**.

Celsius *sel'si-əs*, *adj* pertaining to the centigrade scale used in the thermometer constructed by Anders *Celsius* (1701–44) in which the freezing-point of water is 0° and the boiling-point is 100° (to convert degrees Celsius to Fahrenheit multiply by $\frac{9}{5}$ and add 32).

Celt *kelt* or *selt*, *n* a Gaul (*hist*); extended to include members of other Celtic-speaking or recently Celtic-speaking peoples. — Also **Kelt**. — *adj* **Celt'ic** or

Kelt'ic pertaining to the Celts; of a branch of the Indo-European family of languages including Breton, Welsh, Cornish, Irish, Gaelic, Manx. — *n* **Celt'icism** or **Kelt'icism** a Celtic idiom or custom. — *n* **Celtomā'nia** or **Keltomā'nia.** — **Celtic cross** a Latin cross, as used conventionally for Christian memorials etc., with a broad circle around the point of intersection of the crossbar and the upright; **Celtic Sea** the area of sea to the south of Ireland and west of Cornwall. [L. *Celtae*; Gr. *Keltoi* or *Keltai*.]

Celt. *abbrev* for Celtic.

cembalo *chem'bə-lō*, *n* a musical instrument with strings struck by hammers, a dulcimer; a harpsichord or pianoforte: — *pl* **cem'balos.** — *n* **cem'balist.** [It.; see **cymbal.**]

cement *si-ment'*, *n* anything that makes two substances or objects stick together; mortar; glue; material used for dental fixings; a bond or union; the bony substance forming the outer layer of the root of a tooth, cementum. — *vt* to unite with cement; to join firmly. — *n* **cementation** (*sē-mən-tā'shən*) the act of cementing; the process of impregnating the surface of one substance with another by surrounding it with powder and heating, as in steel-making. — *n* **cemen'tum** the boney outer covering of the root of a tooth. — *adj* **cemen'tatory** or **cementi'tious** having the quality of cementing or uniting firmly. [O.Fr. *ciment* — L. *caementum*, chip of stone used to fill up in building a wall, *caedimentum* — *caedĕre*, to cut.]

cemetery *sem'i-tri*, *n* a burial-ground for the dead. [L.L. *coemētērium* — Gr. *koimētērion*, sleeping-place.]

cen. *abbrev* for: central; century.

CEng. *sē-eng'*, *abbrev* for Chartered Engineer.

cenobite. See **coenobite.**

cenotaph *sen'ə-täf*, *n* an empty tomb; a monument in honour of one or more people buried elsewhere. [Gr. *kenotaphion* — *kenos*, empty, *taphos*, a tomb.]

cenote *si-nō'ti*, *n* a deep, natural hole in the ground with a pool at the bottom of it, esp. in the Yucatan peninsula, often used by the Mayas as a place of sacrifice. [Sp. — Maya *conot*, *tyonot*.]

Cenozoic *sē-nō-zō'ik*. Same as **Cainozoic.**

cense *sens*, *vt* to burn incense in front of. [Ety. as for **incense**[2].]

censer *sens'ər*, *n* a ceremonial container in which incense is burned. [O.Fr. *censier*, *encensier* (mod. *encensoir*) — *incendĕre*, *incēnsum*, to burn.]

censor *sen'sər*, *n* a magistrate who kept account of the property of Roman citizens, imposed taxes, and watched over their morals (*hist*); an official with similar functions elsewhere; an official who examines books, papers, telegrams, letters, films, etc., with powers to delete material, or to forbid publication, delivery, or showing; an unconscious inhibitive mechanism in the mind, that prevents what is painful to the conscious from emerging from the subconscious (*psychol*). — *vt* to subject to censorship or to censorial examination or condemnation. — *adj* **censorial** (*-ö'ri-əl*) pertaining to a censor, or to the correction of public morals. — *adj* **censo'rian** censorial. — *adj* **censo'rious** expressing censure; fault-finding. — *adv* **censo'riously.** — *n* **censo'riousness.** — *n* **cen'sorship** the work of a censor, censoring; the office of censor; the time during which a censor holds office. [L. *cēnsor*, *-ōris*.]

censure *sen'shər*, *n* an opinion or judgment (formerly general, now unfavourable only); blame. — *vt* to form or give an unfavourable opinion or judgment of; to blame. — *adj* **cen'surable** deserving censure; blamable. — *n* **cen'surableness.** — *adv* **cen'surably.** [L. *cēnsūra* — *cēnsēre*, to estimate.]

census *sen'səs*, *n* an official enumeration of inhabitants with statistics relating to them. — *vt* to carry out a census of. [L. *cēnsus*, *-ūs*, a register.]

cent *sent*, *n* a hundredth part, esp. of a dollar; a coin of that value. — *n* **cent'al** a weight of 100 lb. — **per cent** by the hundred, per hundred. [L. *centum*, a hundred.]

cent. *abbrev* for: central; *centum* (L.), a hundred; century.

centaur *sen'tör*, *n* a mythical being, half man, half horse. — *adj* **centau'rian.** [Gr. *kentauros*.]

centavo *sen-tä'vō*, *n* a Spanish American coin and monetary unit: — *pl* **centa'vos.** [Sp.]

centenary *sen-tēn'ər-i* (also *-ten'* or *sen'*), *n* a hundred; a century or hundred years; a hundredth anniversary. — *adj* pertaining to a hundred or to a centennial. — *n* **centenā'rian** a person who is a hundred years old or more. [L. *centēnārius* — *centēnī*, a hundred each — *centum*.]

centennial *sen-ten'i-əl*, *adj* happening once in every hundred years; lasting a hundred years. — *n* (*NAm*) a hundredth anniversary, a centenary. [L. *centum*, a hundred, *annus*, a year.]

center. The U.S. spelling of **centre.**

centering. See **centring.**

centesimal *sen-tes'i-məl*, *adj* hundredth; having divisions of a hundredth, as e.g. a centigrade thermometer. — *adv* **centes'imally.** [L. *centēsimus* — *centum*.]

centi- *sen-ti-*, *combining form* signifying 1/100 of the unit named. [L. *centum*, a hundred.]

centigrade *sen'ti-grād*, *adj* having a hundred degrees, as e.g. the **Celsius** scale. [L. *centum*, a hundred, *gradus*, a step, a degree.]

centigram or **centigramme** *sen'ti-gram*, *n* the hundredth part of a gram(me). [Fr., — L. *centum*, a hundred, and **gram(me)**.]

centilitre or in U.S. **centiliter** *sen'ti-lē-tər*, *n* the hundredth part of a litre, 10 cubic centimetres. [Fr., — L. *centum*, a hundred, and **litre.**]

centime *sā'tēm* or *sā-tēm'*, *n* a coin and monetary unit (of France etc.), 1/100 of a franc. [Fr., — L. *centesimum*, a hundredth.]

centimetre or in U.S. **centimeter** *sen'ti-mē-tər*, *n* a linear measure, the hundredth part of a metre. — **centimetre-gram-second** (*abbrev* **CGS** or **cgs**) **system** a system of scientific measurement with the centimetre, etc. as units of length, mass, time. [Fr., — L. *centum*, a hundred, and **metre**[2].]

centipede *sen'ti-pēd*, *n* any carnivorous flattened animal with many joints, most of which bear one pair of legs. [L. *centum*, a hundred, *pēs*, *pedis*, a foot.]

centner *sent'nər*, *n* a unit of weight equivalent to 50 kg. or 100 lb. [Ger., — L. *centēnārius*.]

cento *sen'tō*, *n* a poem or other writing manufactured by putting together verses or passages written by one author, or several authors: — *pl* usu. **cen'tos.** — *n* **cen'toist** or **cen'tonist.** [L. *centō*, *-ōnis*, Gr. *kentrōn*, patchwork.]

central, etc. See **centre.**

centre or in U.S. **center** *sen'tər*, *n* the middle point of anything, esp. a circle or sphere; the middle area of anything; a fixed point of reference; the point toward which all things move or are drawn; a nucleus or focal point; a place, institution, etc. devoted to a specified activity; a player in a central position (*Rugby football*, etc.); in soccer etc., a centre-forward; (in U.S. **center**) the player in the centre of the offensive line, who starts the play by passing the ball through his legs to a backfield player; a political party, or its members, having moderate opinions; a rod with a conical tip for supporting a workpiece in a lathe or other machine tool (*mach*). — *vt* to place on or collect to a centre. — *vi* to be placed in the middle; to have a centre; to lie or move in relation to a centre (often with *on*, or *upon*, *round* or *around*): — *pr p* **cen'tring** or in U.S **cen'tering**; *pa t* and *pa p* **cen'tred** or in U.S. **cen'tered.** — *adj* pertaining to the political centre. — *adj* **cen'tral** belonging to, in, or near, the centre; principal, dominant, most important, essential. — *n* **centralisā'tion** or **-z-**

cen'tralism. — *n* **cen'tralism** the tendency or policy of administering by the sovereign or central government matters which would be otherwise under local management. — *n* **cen'tralist** (also *adj*). — *vt* and *vi* **cen'tralise** or **-ize** to draw to or concentrate at a centre. — *n* **centrality** (*-tral'i-ti*) central position; dominance, quality of being essential, principal. — *adv* **cen'trally.** — *n* **cen'treing** see separate article **centring.** — *adj* **cen'tric** relating to, placed in, or containing the centre. — *combining form* **-cen'tric** having a specific type of centre. — *adj* **cen'trical.** — *adv* **cen'trically.** — *n* **cen'tricalness.** — *n* **centricity** (*-tris'i-ti*). — *n* **cen'tring** see separate article. — *n* **cen'trism** the practice of sticking to the middle ground in politics; the holding of moderate, non-extreme political opinions. — *adj* and *n* **cen'trist.** — **central forces** forces causing an acceleration towards or from a fixed point, the **centre of force**; **central heating** a system of heating a house or building by water, steam or warm air conducted throughout the building from one point; **central locking** in a motor vehicle, the automatic locking of all the doors as the driver's door is locked; **cen'tre-bit** a joiner's tool, turning on a centre, for boring circular holes; **cen'treboard** a movable plate, fitted to drop below the keel of a racing yacht; **cen'trefold** a set of photographs or an illustration printed across a centre spread; the (usu. female) subject of such a centre spread in glamour or pornographic magazines; **centre-for'ward** in association football and hockey, the central player among the forwards; **centre-half'** the central player among the half-backs; **cen'trepiece** something placed at the centre as a focal point, esp. an ornament for the middle of a table, ceiling, etc.; a central character or feature in a story, film, etc.: **centre spread** the two facing centre pages of a newspaper, magazine, etc.; an article or set of photographs printed on these. — **central nervous system** (*zool*) the main centres of the nervous system with their associated nerve cords; **central processor** or **central processing unit** the part of a computer which performs the logical and arithmetical operations on the data and which controls other units of the computer system; **central to** essential, most important for the understanding or working of; **centre of attraction** the point to which bodies tend by the force of gravity or the like; **centre of excellence** a focal point, esp. a university (or one of its departments) for work at the highest level (in a particular subject); **centre of force** see **central forces** above; **centre of gravity** the point at which the weight of a body acts; **centre stage** in or to the centre of a theatre stage; at or to the focal point (of e.g. political attention; *fig*). [Fr., — L. *centrum* — Gr. *kentron*, a sharp point.]

centri- *sen-tri-* or **centro-** *sen-tro-*, *combining form* denoting centre.

centric, etc. See **centre**.

centrifugal *sen-trif'ū-gəl*, *sen'* or *-fū'*, *adj* tending away from a centre; using, or produced by centrifugal force. — *vt* **centrif'ugalise** or **-ize** (also *sen'* or *-fū'*) to subject to centrifugal force. — *adv* **centrifugally.** — *n* **cen'trifuge** (*-fūj*) a machine which, by rapid rotation, separates substances of different densities — used in industry, biochemistry, etc. — *vt* to subject to such rotation. — *n* **centrifugation** (*-fū-gā'shən*) or **centrifugence** (*-trif'ū-jəns*, *sen'* or *-fū'*) centrifugal tendency or force. — **centrifugal force** the resistance of a revolving body, by virtue of its inertia, to an acceleration towards the centre, equal and opposite to centripetal force; **centrifugal machine** a centrifuge. [Gr. *kentron* and L. *centrum* (from Gr.) a sharp point, and L. *fugere*, to flee.]

centring or in U.S. **centering** *sen'tring*, (*archit*) *n* the framework upon which an arch or vault of stone, brick, or iron is supported during its construction. — Also **cen'treing.**

centripetal *sen-trip'i-tel* or *sen-tri-pē'tel*, *adj* tending towards a centre. — **centripetal force** a force acting on a revolving body, causing it to tend inward towards a centre, equal and opposite to centrifugal force. [Gr. *kentron* and L. *centrum* (from Gr.), a sharp point, and L. *petere*, to seek.]

centrum *sen'trəm*, *n* the main part of a vertebra.

centuple *sen'tū-pl*, *adj* hundredfold. — *vt* to multiply or increase a hundred times. — *n* **centuplicā'tion.** — *adj* **centū'plicate.** — *n* one of a hundred similar things or copies. — *vt* to centuple. [L. *centuplus* and *centuplex* — *centum*, *plicāre*, to fold.]

century *sen'tū-ri*, *n* a set or series of a hundred, as of Roman soldiers, runs at cricket, or consecutive years (esp. reckoned from the conventionally accepted date of Christ's birth). — *n* **centū'rion** in the Roman army, the commander of a century; a person who has scored or achieved a hundred in any way. [L. *centuria*, a century — *centum*, a hundred.]

CEO *abbrev* for Chief Executive Officer.

cep *sep*, *n* a type of edible mushroom. [Fr. *cèpe*, — L. *cippus*, a stake.]

cephal- *sef-əl-*, *si-fal-*, *kef-al-* or *ki-fal-*, *combining form* signifying head. — *adj* **ceph'alad** (*zool*) towards the head. — *adj* **ceph'alate** having a head. — *adj* **cephal'ic** of, or belonging to, the head; for curing pains in the head. — *n* a remedy for head-pains. — **-cephal'ic** and **-ceph'alous** adjective combining forms. — *adj* **ceph'alous** having a head. — *n* **cephalag'ra** gout in the head. — *n* **cephalal'gia** (*med*) headache. — *adj* **cephalal'gic.** — *n* **cephalī'tis** inflammation of the brain. — *n* **ceph'alopod** (*-pod*) a member of the **Cephalopoda** (*-op'od-ə*), the highest class of molluscs, usu. large animals, exclusively living in the sea, with the foot modified into arms surrounding the mouth, e.g. cuttlefish, etc. — *n* **cephalospō'rin** any of a group of widely effective antibiotics derived from certain types of fungi. *n* **cephalothro'ax** (in some crustaceans) part of the body formed by the fusion of the head and thorax. — **cephalic index** the ratio of the breadth to the length of the skull expressed as a percentage; **cephalic presentation** the usual position of a child in the womb just before birth, head downwards. [Gr. *kephalē*, head.]

ceramic *si-ram'ik*, *adj* pertaining to a ceramic or to ceramics; made of a ceramic. — *n* any product that is first shaped and then hardened by means of heat, or the material from which it is formed (esp. potter's clay, but also many modern materials of quite different composition). — *nsing* **ceram'ics** the potter's art; the science of ceramic materials. — *n* **ceram'ist** or **ceram'icist** a person who makes a scientific study of clays and other ceramic materials, or who puts them to practical use. — *n* **cer'met** a combination of *cer*amic particles and a *met*al matrix; a type of electronic resistor made of such material. [Gr. *keramos*, potter's earth.]

cerate and **cerated**. See **cere**.

ceratitis. Same as **keratitis** (see under **keratin**).

ceratoid *ser'ə-toid*, (*anat*) *adj* horny. [Gr. *keratoeidēs* — *keras*, horn, *eidos*, form.]

Ceratopsian *ser-ə-top'si-ən*, *n* a member of a large group of dinosaurs of the late Cretaceous period, being four-footed, herbivorous, horned and beaked. — Also *adj*. [Gr. *keras*, horn, *ops*, face.]

cercus *sûr'kəs*, (*anat*) *n* a tail-like appendage. — *adj* **cer'cal** pertaining to a tail. [Gr. *kerkos*, tail.]

cere *sēr*, *vt* to cover with wax. — *n* the bare waxlike patch at the base of the upper part of a bird's beak. — *adj* **cērā'ceous** waxy. — *n* **cēr'ate** a paste or stiff ointment containing wax (*med*). — *adj* **cēr'ated** (of a bird) having a cere. — *adj* **cēr'eous** waxy. — **cere'-cloth** or **cerement** (*sēr'mənt*) a cloth dipped in melted wax to wrap a dead body in. [L. *cēra*, wax.]

cereal *sē'ri-əl*, *adj* (of crops etc.) relating to edible grain. — *n* a grain used as food, such as wheat, barley, etc.; a food prepared from such grain, esp. any of various breakfast foods. [L. *Cĕrēs*, *-eris*, Roman goddess of tillage and corn.]

cerebellum *ser-i-bel'əm*, *n* the lower back part of the brain, whose function is to co-ordinate voluntary movements and maintain balance: — *pl* **cerebell'a** or **cerebell'ums**. — *adj* **cerebell'ar**, **cerebell'ic** or **cerebell'ous**. [L., little brain, dimin. of *cerebrum*.]

cerebrum *ser'i-brəm* (in U.S. also *si-rē'brəm*), *n* the front and larger part of the brain. — *adj* **cer'ebral** (in *U.S.* also *sə-rē'brəl*) pertaining to the brain or the cerebrum; intellectual, as opposed to practical. — *vi* **cer'ebrate** to display brain action. — *n* **cerebrā'tion** action of the brain, esp. unconscious. — *adj* **cer'ebric** (or *sər-eb'rik*) cerebral. — *adj* **cereb'riform** brain-shaped. — *n* **cerebrī'tis** inflammation of the cerebrum. — *adj* **cerebrōspīn'al** relating to the brain and spinal cord together. — *adj* **cerebrōvas'cūlar** relating to the cerebrum and its blood-vessels. — **cerebral death** see **brain death** under **brain**; **cerebral haemorrhage** haemorrhage of the blood-vessels in the brain; **cerebral hemispheres** the two large divisions of the cerebrum; **cerebral palsy** a form of congenital paralysis marked by lack of muscular co-ordination, etc.; **cerebrospinal fever** meningitis; **cerebrovascular accident** a paralysing stroke. [L. *cerebrum*, the brain.]

cerement and **cereous**. See **cere**.

ceremony *ser'i-mə-ni*, *n* a rite, a formal act, custom etc.; such rites, acts, etc., regarded collectively; pomp, formality, etc. — *adj* **ceremonial** (*-mō'ni-əl*) relating to ceremony or a ceremony. — *n* pomp; ceremonies collectively. — *n* **ceremō'nialism** adherence to outward formality and custom. — *adv* **ceremō'nially**. — *adj* **ceremō'nious** full of ceremony; particular in observing formalities; precise. — *adv* **ceremō'niously**. — *n* **ceremō'niousness**. — **master of ceremonies** a person who directs the form and order of the ceremonies to be observed on some public occasion; a compère; **stand on ceremony** to be particular about observing formalities; **without ceremony** informally; without formalities. [L. *caerimōnia*, sanctity.]

cerge *sûrj*, *n* a large wax candle burned before an altar. [O.Fr., — L. *cēreus* — *cēra*, wax.]

cerise *sər-ēs'* or *-ēz'*, *n* and *adj* light and clear red. [Fr., cherry.]

cerium *sē'ri-əm*, *n* a metallic element (atomic no. 58; symbol **Ce**). [Named from the planet *Ceres* discovered about the same time.]

cermet. See under **ceramic**.

CERN *sûrn*, *abbrev* for *Conseil Européen pour la Recherche Nucléaire* (Fr.), European Organisation for Nuclear Research.

cerograph *sē'rō-gräf*, *n* a writing on wax; printing by means of engraving on a plate spread with wax. — *adj* **cērographic** (*-graf'ik*) or **cērograph'ical**. — *n* **cērographist** (*-rog'rə-fist*). — *n* **cērog'raphy**. [Gr. *kēros*, wax, *graphein*, to write.]

ceroplastic *sē-rō-plas'tik*, *adj* pertaining to wax modelling. — *nsing* **ceroplas'tics** the art of wax modelling. [Gr. *kēros*, wax, *plastikos*, plastic — *plassein*, to mould.]

cert *sûrt*, *n*. See **certain**.

cert. or **certif.** *abbrev* for: certificate; certificated; certify.

certain *sûr'tn*, *adj* sure; not to be doubted; resolved, fixed, decided, determined; inevitable; some (indeterminate number or quantity of). — *adv* **cer'tainly** without doubt, undoubtedly; in a resolved, fixed, etc. manner. — *interj* yes, of course. — *n* **cer'tainty** (*slang* **cert**, sometimes in the phrase **dead cert**). — *n* **cer'titude** (a) certainty. — **for certain** certainly; **in a certain condition** (*euph*) pregnant. [O.Fr., — L. *certus* — *cernĕre*, to decide.]

certif. See **cert.** (*abbrev*).

certificate *sər-tif'i-kət* or *-kāt*, *n* a written declaration, official or formal, of some fact; a printed statement of qualification(s) or recognised professional status. — *vt* to award a certificate to. — *adj* **cer'tifiable** (*-fī-ə-bl*) capable of being certified (esp. as insane). — *adv* **cer'tifīably**. — *adj* **certif'icated** (of e.g. a teacher) holding a certificate of training and fitness. — *n* **certificā'tion**. — *adj* **certif'icātory**. — *n* **cer'tifīer**. — *vt* **cer'tify** to declare certain; to guarantee; to inform reliably; to declare in writing; to declare (someone) insane: — *pr p* **cer'tifying**; *pa p* **cer'tified**. [Fr. *certificat* — L. *certificāre*, *certus*, certain, *facĕre*, to make.]

certiorari *sûr-shi-ō-rā'rī*, *n* a writ by which cases are removed from inferior courts into the High Court of Justice. [L.L. *certiōrārī*, to be informed of — *certior*, compar. of *certus*, certain.]

certitude. See **certain**.

cerulean or **caerulean** *si-rōō'li-ən*, *adj* sky-blue; dark-blue; sea-green. [L. *caerŭleus*, dark blue or green.]

cerumen *si-rōō'men*, *n* ear wax. — *adj* **ceru'minous**. [L. *cēra*, wax.]

ceruse *sē'rōōs* or *si-rōōs'*, *n* white lead. — *n* **cē'rusite** or **cē'russite** naturally-occurring lead carbonate. [Fr., — L. *cērussa*, conn. with *cēra*, wax.]

cervelat *sûr'və-lä*, *n* a kind of smoked sausage, made of pork. [Fr. — It. *cervellata*.]

cervine *sûr'vīn*, *adj* relating to deer; like deer; fawn-coloured. [L. *cervīnus* — *cervus*, a stag.]

cervix *sûr'viks*, *n* the neck of an organ, esp. the uterus. — *adj* **cervical** (*sûr'vi-kl* or *sər-vī'kl*). — **cervical smear** the collection of a sample of cells from the neck of the womb and the examination of these cells under a microscope, as a test for early cancer. [L. *cervīx*, *cervīcis*, neck.]

Cesarean. Esp. U.S. spelling of **Caesarean**.

cesarevitch or **cesarewitch**, and **cesarevna**. See under **tsar**.

cesium. See **caesium**.

cessation *ses-ā'shən*, *n* a ceasing or stopping; a rest; a pause. [L. *cessātiō*, *-ōnis*. See **cease**.]

cesser *ses'ər*, (*law*) *n* the cessation of a term or liability when an obligation is fulfilled. [Fr. *cesser*, to cease.]

cession *sesh'ən*, *n* a yielding up, ceding. — *n* **cess'ionary** a person to whom an assignment of (e.g. property) has been legally made. [L. *cēssiō*, *-ōnis*; see **cede**.]

cesspit *ses'pit* or **cesspool** *-pōōl*, *n* a pit or pool for collecting sewage or filthy water.

c'est-à-dire *set-a-dēr'* or *sāt-*, (Fr.) that is to say.

c'est la vie *se* (or *sā*) *la vē*, (Fr.) that's life.

cestode *ses'tōd*, *n* a tapeworm or bladder-worm. — *n* **ces'toid** a cestode. — Also *adj*. — *n* and *adj* **cestoid'ean**. [Gr. *kestos*, a girdle, a strap, *eidos*, form.]

cesura. See **caesura**.

Cetacea *si-tā'shi-ə* or *-shyə*, *npl* an order of mammals living in water and having fishlike form, including the toothed whales (sperm whales, bottle-noses, dolphins, etc.) and the baleen whales (right whale, hump-backs, rorquals). — *n* and *adj* **cetā'cean**. — *adj* **cetā'ceous**. — *n* **cete** (*sēt*) a whale or sea-monster. — *n* **cetol'ogy** the study of whales. [Gr. *kētos*, a sea-monster.]

cetane *sē'tān*, *n* a paraffin hydrocarbon found in petroleum. — **cetane number** a measure of the ignition quality of diesel engine fuel. [sperma*ceti* and chem. sfx. *-ane*.]

cete[1] *sēt*, *n* a collective noun for a company of badgers.

cete[2]. See under **Cetacea**.

ceteris paribus *set'ər-is par'i-bus* or *kā'tə-rēs pa'ri-bŏŏs*, (L.) other things being equal.

cetology. See under **Cetacea**.

cet. par. *abbrev* for ceteris paribus.

cetyl alcohol *sē'til* (or in U.S. *sē'təl*) *al'kə-hol*, *n* a waxy crystalline solid used in detergents and pharmaceuticals. [So called because compounds of it occur in spermaceti; Gr. *kētos*, a sea-monster, *hȳlē*, *matter*.]

cevadilla. See **sabadilla.**

Cf (*chem*) *symbol* for californium.

cf. *abbrev* for *confer* (L.), compare.

CFA *abbrev* for *Communauté financière africaine*, as in **CFA franc** (*abbrev* **CFAFr**), standard monetary unit in various African countries (former French overseas territories).

CFC *abbrev* for chlorofluorocarbon.

cfi or **cf and i** *abbrev* for cost, freight, (and) insurance.

CFP *abbrev* for *Comptoirs français du Pacifique*, as in **CFP franc** (*abbrev* **CFPFr**), standard monetary unit in French Polynesia, New Caledonia (French Pacific overseas territories).

cg *abbrev* for centigram(s) or centigramme(s).

c.g. *abbrev* for centre of gravity.

CGI or **CGLI** *abbrev* for City and Guilds (of London) Institute.

CGPM *abbrev* for *Conférence Générale des Poids et Mesures* (Fr.), General Conference of Weights and Measures.

CGS *abbrev* for: centimetre-gramme-second (also **cgs**); Chief of the General Staff.

CGT *abbrev* for Capital Gains Tax.

CH *abbrev* for: Companion of Honour; *Confederatio Helvetica* (L.), Switzerland (also I.V.R.).

Ch. *abbrev* for: Champion; Chaplain; Chapter; Chief; China; Chinese; Chronicles (*Bible*); Church.

ch *abbrev* for central heating.

ch. *abbrev* for: chain (linear measure); chapter; child; children.

cha *chä*, (*colloq*) *n* tea; rolled tea. [Chin. *ch'a*.]

Chablis *shab'lē*, *n* a very dry white Burgundy wine made at *Chablis*, department of Yonne, in France.

chabouk *chä'bŏŏk*, *n* a horse-whip. [Pers. *chābuk*.]

cha-cha *chä'-chä* or **cha-cha-cha** *chä'-chä-chä*, *n* an orig. W. Indian dance, a later form of the mambo.

chaconne *sha-kon'* or *shə-kon'*, *n* an old dance, with slow movements; music for this dance, a series of variations on a ground bass, in triple time. [Fr., — Sp. *chacona* — Basque *chucun*, pretty.]

chacun à son goût *sha-kœ̃n a sɔ̃ gōō*, (Fr.) each person to his own taste. — Also **à chacun son goût**.

chadar, chaddar, chador, chuddah or **chuddar** *chud'ə* or *-ər*, *n* the large veil worn by Muslim and Hindu women, covering head and body; a cloth spread over a Muslim tomb. [Pers. *chaddar*, Hindi *caddar*, a square cloth.]

chaeta *kē'tə*, *n* a hard bristle on the body of the earthworm and other invertebrates: — *pl* **chaetae** (*kē'tē*) — *n* **chaetopod** (*kē'tō-pod*) a worm (as the earthworm) of the class **Chaetop'oda**, that crawls with the help of bristles. [Gr. *chaitē*, hair, spine.]

chafe *chāf*, *vt* to heat, fret, irritate or wear by rubbing; to cause to fret or rage. — *vi* to heat, irritate, etc. by rubbing; to fret or rage (with *against* or *at*). — *n* an irritation caused by rubbing. [Fr. *chauffer* — L. *calefacĕre* — *calēre*, to be hot, *facĕre*, to make.]

chafer *chāf'ər*, *n* any of several kinds of beetle, e.g. the cockchafer. [O.E. *cefer*.]

chaff *chäf* or *chaf*, *n* husks of corn which has been threshed or winnowed; cut hay and straw; strips of metallic foil, bits of wire, etc. fired into or dropped through the air to deflect radar signals and so interfere with detection; rubbish, or worthless matter; light banter, badinage. — *vt* to banter with. — *n* and *adj* **chaff'ing.** — *adv* **chaff'ingly.** [O.E. *ceaf*.]

chaffinch *chaf'inch* or *-insh*, *n* a little songbird of the finch family, the male having a pinkish body and grey head. [Said to delight in *chaff*; and see **finch**.]

chagrin *shag'rin* or *shə-grin'*, *n* vexation; annoyance; embarrassment. — *vt* to vex, annoy or embarrass. — *adj* **chagrined'**. [Fr. *chagrin*, shagreen, rough skin, ill-humour.]

chain *chān*, *n* a series of links or rings passing through one another; a linked series, e.g. of house-buyers; a mountain range; a string of islands; something that binds; a connected course or train (of events); a linear measure of 100 links, or 66 feet; a series (of shops, hotels, restaurants, etc.) under the same management; a number of atoms linked in succession (*chem*); (in *pl*) fetters, bonds, confinement or restriction generally; (in *pl*) circular apparatus consisting of metal links fitted to the wheels of a car in icy conditions to prevent skidding. — *vt* to fasten (also **chain up** or **down**); to fetter; to restrain; to measure, with chain or tape (*surveying*). — *adj* **chained** bound or fastened, with or as with a chain; fitted with a chain. — *adj* **chain'less** without chains; unfettered, unrestricted. — *n* **chain'let** a small chain. — **chain'brake** a cut-off device on a chainsaw, activated automatically if the chainsaw kicks back; **chain'-breaker** a method or device for avoiding or resolving the problems created by a chain of house-buyers and -sellers each awaiting action on the part of others earlier or later in the sequence; **chain'-bridge** a suspension bridge; **chain'-drive** transmission of power by chain-gear. — *adj* **chain'-driven.** — **chain'-gang** a gang of convicts wearing leg-irons, often chained together; **chain'-gear** or **-gearing** gears consisting of an endless chain and (generally) sprocket-wheels; **chain-let'ter** a letter soliciting (among other things) the sending by the recipient of similar letters to other people; **chain-light'ning** forked or zigzag lightning; **chain-mail'** armour of connected links, much used in Europe in the 12th and 13th centuries; **chain'-pier** a pier supported by chains like a chain-bridge; **chain reaction** a process in which each reaction is in turn the stimulus of a further similar reaction; **chain'saw** a power saw with teeth linked in an endless chain. — *vt* and *vi* **chain-smoke'** to smoke (cigarettes, etc.) non-stop, lighting each from its predecessor. — **chain'-smoker; chain'stitch** a knitting or sewing stitch resembling the links of a chain; **chain'-store** one of a series of shops, esp. department stores, under the same management; **chain'wheel** a toothed wheel, as on a bicycle, which meshes with a chain to transmit motion. [O.Fr. *chaeine* — L. *catēna*.]

chair *chār*, *n* a movable seat for one person, with a back to it; the seat or position of a person in authority, as a judge, a bishop, or the person presiding over any meeting; a chairman; a professorship; the instrument or the punishment of death by electrocution (with *the*). — *vt* to conduct (a meeting) as chairman, etc.; to carry publicly in triumph; to place in a seat of authority. — **chair'-bed** a chair capable of being turned into a bed. — *adj* **chair'borne** (*colloq*) working at a desk. — *adj* **chair'bound** unable to walk; confined to a wheelchair. — **chair'lift** a set of seats suspended from cables used to take skiers uphill; **chair'man** a person (male or female) who takes the chair, or presides, at an assembly or meeting (also **chair'person**; *fem* **chair'woman**); **chair'manship.** [Fr. *chaire* — L. — Gr. *kathedrā*.]

chaise *shāz*, *n* a light open carriage for one or more persons; a chaise-longue. — **chaise-longue'** (*lɔ̃g'*) a couch with a back at one end only and a short armrest. [Fr., a form of *chaire*; see **chair**.]

chakra *chak'ra*, *n* amongst the Sikhs, a disc-shaped knife used as a missile; a discus representing the sun, as in portrayals of Hindu gods; in yoga, a centre of spiritual power in the body. [Sans. *cakra*, wheel.]

chalaza *ka-lā'zə*, (*bot*) *n* in a bird's egg, the string that holds the yolk-sac in position; the base of the ovule. [Gr. *chalaza*, hail, lump.]

chalcedony *kal-sed'ə-ni* or *kal'*, *n* a beautiful mineral composed of silica, usually banded, translucent, of waxy lustre, generally white or bluish-white, consisting of crystalline fibres. — *adj* **chalcedonic** (*-si-don'ik*). [Gr. *chalkēdōn*.]

chalcography *kal-kog'rə-fi*, *n* the art of engraving on copper or brass. — *n* **chalcog'rapher** or **chalcog'raphist**. [Gr. *chalkos*, copper, *graphein*, to write.]

chalcopyrite *kal-kō-pī'rīt*, *n* copper-pyrites, a yellow double sulphide of copper and iron. [Gr. *chalkos*, copper, and **pyrite**.]

chalet *shal'ā*, *n* a summer hut used by Swiss herdsmen in the Alps; a wooden villa; a small house, usu. of wood, built for use by holidaymakers, etc. [Fr.]

chalice *chal'is*, *n* a cup or bowl; a communion-cup. [O.Fr. *chalice* — L. *calix*, *calicis*.]

chalk *chök*, *n* white soft rock, composed of calcium carbonate; a substitute for this used for writing, etc.; a piece of this. — *vt* to write, rub, mark, or manure, with chalk. — *n* **chalk'iness**. — *adj* **chalk'y**. — **chalk'board** (esp. *NAm*) a blackboard; **chalk'face** (*colloq*, usu. **at the chalkface**) the classroom, as the centre of the teacher's activities; **chalk'pit** a pit in which chalk is dug; **chalk'stone** a stone or piece of chalk; (in *pl*) the white concretions formed round the joints in chronic gout. — **as like (or as different) as chalk and cheese** completely unalike; **by a long chalk** by a considerable distance or degree; **chalk and talk** the formal, traditional teaching method of writing on the blackboard and expounding; **chalk out** to trace out, as with chalk, to plan; **chalk up** to make a special (esp. mental) note of; to record (a score, etc.); to charge or ascribe (to e.g. a person); **not know chalk from cheese** to be unable to tell apart things which are completely different; **the Chalk** (*geol*) the uppermost part of the Cretaceous system in England. [O.E. *cealc* — L. *calx*, limestone.]

challah *hä'lə*, *n* a variety of Jewish bread, usu. plaited. [Heb. *hallāh*.]

challenge *chal'inj*, *vt* to call on (someone) to settle a matter by fighting or by any kind of contest; to put under stress, examination or test; to accuse; to object to; to administer a challenge to (*med*). — *n* a summons to a contest of any kind, but esp. a duel; a calling into question of anyone or anything; an objection to a juror; the demand for identification and authority made by a sentry; an accusation; a difficulty which stimulates interest or effort; a task, undertaking, etc. to test one's powers and capabilities to the full; the administration to an immunised subject of a substance which could cause an allergic reaction or infection, in order to test the effectiveness of the immunisation (*med*). — *adj* **chall'engeable** that may be challenged. — *adj* **chall'enged** (esp. *NAm*) handicapped, impaired, as in *physically challenged*. — *n* **chall'enger**. — *adj* **chall'enging**. — *adv* **chall'engingly**. [O.Fr. *chalenge*, a dispute, claim — L. *calumnia*, a false accusation — *calvī* or *calvĕre*, to deceive.]

chalone *kāl'* or *kal'ōn*, *n* an internal secretion which inhibits action when a hormone excites it. — *adj* **chalon'ic**. [Gr. *chalaein*, to relax.]

chalumeau *shal-ū-mō'* or *shal-ü-mō'*, *n* an early reed instrument that developed into the clarinet; the lowest register of the clarinet: — *pl* **chalumeaux** (*-mōz'*). [Fr., — O.Fr. *chalemel* — L.L. *calamellus*, dimin. of *calamus*, a pipe, a reed.]

Chalybean *kal-ib-ē'ən* or *ka-lib'i-ən*, (*metall*) *adj* well tempered. — *adj* **chalyb'eate** containing iron. — *n* a water or other liquid containing iron. [Gr. *chalyps*, *chalybos*, steel, or *Chalyps*, one of the *Chalybĕs*, a nation famous for steel.]

chamaeleon. See **chameleon**.

Chamb. *abbrev* for Chamberlain.

chamber *chām'bər*, *n* a room; the place where an assembly meets; a house of a legislature, e.g. the French Chamber of Deputies; an assembly or body of people met for some purpose, as a chamber of commerce; a compartment; a cavity; the back end of the bore of a gun, where a bullet or cartridge is placed prior to firing; (in *pl*) a suite of rooms in a building occupied separately, esp. by lawyers; (in *pl*) a judge's room for hearing cases not taken into court; a chamberpot. — *vt* to put in a chamber; to confine. — *adj* **cham'bered** confined; having rooms or space separated by a succession of walls; (of a shell) having partitions. — **chamber concert** a concert of chamber music; **cham'bermaid** a female servant who looks after bedrooms in hotels, etc.; **chamber music** music, performed by a small group such as a quartet, suitable for a room rather than a theatre or a large hall; **cham'berpot** a vessel for urine etc., used in the bedroom. — **chamber of commerce** (sometimes with *caps*) a group of businessmen working together to promote local trade. [Fr. *chambre* — L. *camera* — Gr. *kamarā*, a vault, a room.]

chamberlain *chām'bər-lin*, *n* an officer appointed by a monarch, nobleman, or corporation, to perform domestic and ceremonial duties or to act as factor or steward. — *n* **cham'berlainship**. — **Lord Chamberlain** an officer of high standing in the royal household. [O.Fr. *chambrelenc*.]

chambray *shöm'brā*, *n* a fine cotton or linen fabric, with interwoven white and coloured threads. [Orig. U.S.; related to **cambric**.]

chambré *shã-brā*, (*Fr.*) *adj* (of wine) at room temperature.

chameleon or **chamaeleon** *kə-mēl'yən*, *n* a small lizard famous for changing its colour; an inconstant, changeable or readily adaptable person (*fig*). — Also *adj*. — *adj* **chameleonic** (*-i-on'ik*). — *adj* **chamel'eon-like**. [L. *chamaeleōn* — Gr. *chamaileōn* — *chamai*, on the ground (i.e. dwarf) and *leōn*, a lion.]

chamfer *cham'fər*, *n* a bevel or slope made by paring off the edge of anything orig. right-angled; a groove, channel or furrow. — *vt* to cut or grind off bevel-wise, as a corner; to channel or make furrows on; to flute, as a column. — *adj* **cham'fered**. [Fr. *chanfrein* — L. *cantum frangĕre*, to break the edge or side.]

chamois *sham'wä*, *n* a goatlike antelope inhabiting high mountains in southern and central Europe: — *pl* **chamois** (*sham'wä*); (*sham'i*) a soft kind of leather orig. made from its skin (see also **shammy**). [Fr.]

chamomile. See **camomile**.

champ[1] *champ*, *vi* to make a snapping noise with the jaws while chewing. — *vt* to bite or chew; to munch; to crush; to mash. — *n* the act of champing; (esp. in Northern Ireland) a dish made of potatoes, leeks and spring onions. — **champ at the bit** to show signs of impatience while waiting for something (*fig*). [Poss. onomatopoeic; conn. with **jam**[2].]

champ[2] *champ*, (*slang*) *n* short form of **champion**.

champagne *sham-pān'*, *n* a white sparkling wine, strictly from *Champagne* in France; the amber-like colour of white champagne; (*loosely*) a wine similar to that from Champagne.

champers *sham'pərz*, (*colloq*) *n* champagne.

champerty *cham'pər-ti*, (*law*) *n* an illegal bargain whereby the one party is to assist the other in a suit, and is to share in the proceeds. [Norm. Fr. — L. *campī pars*, part of the field.]

champignon *sham'pin-yɔ̃*, *n* a mushroom or other edible fungus, esp. the fairy-ring champignon.

champion *cham'pi-ən*, *n* someone who defends a cause; a successful combatant; a person who fights in single combat, sometimes for another (*hist* or *archaic*); (in sports) a competitor who has excelled all others; a hero. — *adj* acting or ranking as champion, first; excellent (*colloq*). — *vt* to defend; to support. — *n* **cham'pioness**. — *n* **cham'pionship** a contest held to decide who is the champion; the position of honour gained by being champion; the act of championing. [Fr., — L.L. *campiō*, *-ōnis* — L. *campus*, a plain, a place for games.]

champlevé *shã-lə-vā*, *n* enamel work done with vitreous powders in channels cut in a metal base. — Also *adj*. [Fr.]

Chanc. *abbrev* for: Chancellor; Chancery.
chance *chäns, n* that which happens or results fortuitously, or without assignable cause; fortune; an unexpected event; risk; opportunity; possibility of something happening; (sometimes in *pl*) probability. — *vt* to risk. — *vi* to happen; (with *up* or *on*) to happen to find or meet. — *adj* happening by chance. — *adj* **chance'ful**. — *adj* **chance'less**. — *n* **chanc'er** (*colloq*) a person prepared to take risks for self-advancement. — *adj* **chanc'y** risky, uncertain. — **an eye to the main chance** awareness of the opportunity for self-enrichment; **by chance** accidentally; **chance one's arm** to take a chance, often recklessly (*adj* **arm'-chancing**); **chance upon** to find by chance; **chance would be a fine thing** (*colloq*) some hope!; **even chance** equal probability for or against; **no chance** or **not a chance** that is not going to happen; **stand a good chance** to have a reasonable expectation; **take one's chance** to accept what happens; to risk an undertaking. [O.Fr. *cheance* — L.L. *cadentia* — L. *cadĕre*, to fall.]
chancel *chän'sl, n* the eastern part of a church, orig. separated from the nave by a screen of latticework. [O.Fr., — L. *cancellī*, lattices.]
chancellor *chän'səl-ər, n* a chief minister; the president, or a judge, of a court of chancery or other court; the titular head of a university. — *n* **chan'cellorship**. — *n* **chan'cellery** or **chan'cellory** the position, department, etc. of a chancellor. — **Chancellor of the Exchequer** the chief minister of finance in the British government; **Lord Chancellor** or **Lord High Chancellor** the Speaker of the House of Lords, presiding judge of the Chancery Division, keeper of the Great Seal. [Fr. *chancelier* — L.L. *cancellārius*, orig. an officer that had charge of records, and stood near the *cancelli* (L.), cross-bars surrounding the judgment seat.]
chance-medley *chäns-med'li, n* unintentional homicide in which the killer is not entirely without blame; action with an element of chance. [O.Fr. *chance medlée*, mingled chance.]
Chancery *chän'sər-i, n* a division of the High Court of Justice; a court of record generally; the office of a chancellor; (without *cap*) the offices of an embassy or legation. — **in chancery** (of an estate, etc.) in litigation; in an awkward predicament (*slang*). [Fr. *chancellerie*.]
chancre *shang'kər*, (*med*) *n* the hard swelling that constitutes the primary lesion in syphilis. — *n* **chanc'roid** a non-syphilitic ulceration of the genital organs due to venereally contracted infection. — *adj* **chanc'roid**. — *adj* **chanc'rous**. [Fr.; a form of **canker**.]
chancy. See **chance**.
chandelier *shan-di-lēr', n* a lighting fixture, suspended from the ceiling and often branched, holding a number of light bulbs. [Fr., — L.L. *candēlārius*, a candle-maker, *candēlāria*, a candlestick — L. *candēla*, a candle.]
chandler *chand'lər, n* a maker of candles; a dealer in candles, oil, soap, etc.; a dealer generally (as in *corn-chandler, ship-chandler*). — *n* **chand'lering**. — *n* **chand'lery** goods sold by a chandler. [Ety. as for **chandelier**.]
change *chānj, vt* to alter or make different; to put or give for another; to cause to move from one state to another; to exchange. — *vi* to undergo change; to change one's clothes or vehicle. — *n* the act of changing; alteration or variation of any kind; a shift; variety; money given for money of a different kind, or in adjustment of a payment; (*collectively*) coins of low value; satisfaction (*colloq*). — *n* **changeabil'ity** or **change'ableness** fickleness; the power of being changed. — *adj* **change'able** subject or prone to change; fickle; inconstant; admitting possibility of change. — *adv* **change'ably**. — *adj* **change'ful** full of change; changeable. — *adv* **change'fully**. — *n* **change'fulness**. — *adj* **change'less** without change; constant. — *n* **change'ling** a surreptitious substitute; a child substituted for another, esp. one supposed to be left by the fairies. — *n* **chāng'er**. — **change'-over** transition to a new system or condition; **change-ringing** see **ring the changes** below. — **change colour** to blush or turn pale; **change down** (*autos*) to change to a lower gear; **change of heart** a change of attitude, viewpoint, or opinion, often resulting in the reversal of a decision; **change of life** the menopause; **change one's mind** to form a different opinion; **change one's tune** to change one's attitude or opinions; to change one's manner of speaking; **change up** (*autos*) to change to a higher gear; **ring the changes** to go through all the possible permutations in ringing a peal of bells (*n* **change'-ringing**); to do, use, etc. a limited number of things repeatedly in varying ways, order, etc.; **small change** (*collectively*) coins of low value; a petty thing. [Fr. *changer* — L. *cambīre*, to barter.]
channel *chan'l, n* the bed of a stream of water; a strait or narrow sea; a navigable passage; a passage for conveying a liquid; a groove or furrow; a gutter; means of passing or conveying; (in *pl*) means of communication; a one-way path for a signal; a path for information in a computer; a narrow range of frequencies, part of a frequency band, for the transmission of radio and television signals without interference from other channels. — *vt* to make a channel; to furrow; to convey (through); to direct (into a particular course; *lit* and *fig*): — *pr p* **chann'elling**; *pa t* and *pa p* **chann'elled**. — *adj* **chann'elled**. — **channel seam** a seam on clothing outlined by stitching running along both sides; **channel seaming**. — **the Channel** the English Channel. [O.Fr. *chanel, canel* — L. *canālis*, a canal.]
chanoyu *chä'no-ū, n* a Japanese tea ceremony. [Jap., hot water for tea.]
chanson *shā'sõ, n* a song. — **chanson de geste** (*də zhest*) an old French epic poem. [Fr.]
chant *chänt, vt* to recite in a singing manner; to intone; to sing; to celebrate in song. — *n* song; melody; a kind of church music, in which prose is sung. — *n* **chant'er** or **chant'or** a singer; a precentor; (in a bagpipe) the pipe with fingerholes, on which the melody is played. — *n* **chant'ress**. — *n* **chant'ry** an endowment, or chapel, for the chanting of masses. — *n* **chanty** see **shanty²**. [Fr. *chanter* — L. *cantāre* — *canĕre*, to sing.]
chanterelle *chan-tər-el', n* a yellowish edible fungus. [Fr., dimin. from Gr. *kantharos*, cup.]
chanteuse *shan'tōōs* or *-tōōz*, also *shā-tøz, n* a female nightclub singer. [Fr.]
chantey. See **shanty²**.
chanticleer *chant'i-klēr* or *chant-i-klēr', n* a cock. [From the name of the cock in the old fable of *Reynard the Fox* — O.Fr. *chanter*, to sing, *cler*, clear.]
chantie. Same as **shanty²**.
Chantilly *shan-ti'li* or *shā-tē-yē, n* a delicately patterned silk or linen lace. — Also **Chantilly lace** (*lās*). — *adj* (of cream) sweetened and whipped, and usu. flavoured with vanilla; prepared or served with such cream. [*Chantilly*, France, where the lace was first made.]
chantor, chantress, chantry. See **chant**.
chanty¹. See **shanty²**.
chanty² *chan'ti*, (*Scot slang*) *n* a chamberpot.
Chanukah, Chanukkah. See **Hanukkah**.
chaos *kā'os, n* the shape of matter before it was reduced to order; disorder; shapeless mass. — *adj* **chaot'ic** confused. — *adv* **chaot'ically**. — **chaos theory** the theory that the universe is not ordered according to the accepted laws of physics. [Gr.]
Chap. *abbrev* for: Chaplain; Chapter.
chap¹ *chap, vi* to crack. — *vt* to cause to crack or divide. — *n* a crack; a crack or split in the skin, caused by exposure to cold. — *adj* **chap'less**. — *adj* **chapped**

cracked, of a heavy soil in dry weather, or of the skin in cold weather. [M.E. *chappen*.]

chap[2] *chap, n* a fellow (*colloq*): — *fem* (*facetious*) **chap'ess** or **chapp'ess**. — *n* **chapp'ie** a familiar dimin. of **chap**. — *n* **chap'man** an itinerant dealer; a pedlar. [O.E. *cēap*, trade, *cēapman*, trader.]

chap[3] *chap, n* a chop or jaw; a cheek. — *adj* **chap'fallen** same as **chopfallen**. [Cf. **chop**[3].]

chaparajos *shap-ə-rā'ōs*, or *chä-pä-rä'hhos*, also **chaparejos** *-rā'* or *-rē'*, *npl* cowboy's leather riding leggings (short form **chaps**). [Mex. Sp.]

chaparral *shap-ə-ral'* or *chäp-ä-räl'*, *n* dense tangled brushwood. — **chaparral cock** a type of cuckoo of the Californian and Mexican chaparral that runs along the ground. [Sp., — *chaparro*, evergreen oak, one of its constituents.]

chapati or **chapatti** *chəp-ät'i, n* a thin flat loaf of unleavened bread. [Hind.]

chapel *chap'l, n* a place of Christian worship subordinate to a regular church, or attached to a house or institution; a cell of a church containing its own altar; a place of worship of Nonconformists in England, Roman Catholics or Episcopalians in Scotland, etc.; a chapel service; a printing office, or an association or trade union of workmen relating to it. — *adj* Nonconformist. — *n* **chap'elry** the jurisdiction of a chapel. — **chap'el-master** a director of music; **chapel royal** the oratory of a royal palace. — **chapel of ease** a chapel for worshippers at some distance from the parish church; **father** or **mother of the chapel** the president of a printing office or chairman or chairwoman of a printers' association or trade union branch. [O.Fr. *capele* — L.L. *cappella*, dimin. of *cappa*, a cloak or cope; orig. from the cloak of St Martin.]

chaperon or **chaperone** *shap'ə-rōn, n* a kind of hood or cap; (esp. formerly) an older woman who accompanies, and usu. supervises, a younger one on social occasions, etc. — *vt* to attend in such a capacity. — *n* **chap'eronage**. [Fr., a large hood — *chape*, a hooded cloak — L.L. *cappa*; see **cape**[1].]

chapess. See **chap**[2].

chaplain *chap'lin, n* a clergyman attached to an institution, establishment, organisation, or family. — *n* **chap'laincy**. — *n* **chap'lainry**. — *n* **chap'lainship**. [O.Fr. *chapelain* — L.L. *cappellānus* — *cappella*; see **chapel**.]

chaplet *chap'lit, n* a garland or wreath for the head; a circlet of gold, etc.; a string of beads used in counting prayers, one-third of a rosary in length; anything in a string; a metal support of a cylindrical pipe. — *adj* **chap'leted**. [O.Fr. *chapelet* — *chape*, a headdress.]

chapman, chappess, chappie. See **chap**[2].

Chaps *chaps, abbrev* for Clearing house automated payment system.

chaps. See **chaparajos**.

chapter *chap'tər, n* a main division of a book, or of anything; a subject or category generally; a series or sequence (of events); a division of the Acts of Parliament of a session; an assembly of the canons of a cathedral or collegiate church, or the members of a religious or military order (from the custom of reading a chapter of the rule or of the Bible); its members collectively; an organised branch of a society or fraternity. — *vt* to put into chapters. — **chap'ter-house** a building used for meetings of a cathedral, church, etc. chapter. — **chapter and verse** the exact reference to the passage of the authority of one's statements. [O.Fr. *chapitre* — L. *capitulum*, dimin. of *caput*, the head.]

char[1] or **charr** *chär, n* a small fish (*Salvelinus*) of the salmon family, found in mountain lakes and rivers. [Prob. Celt.; cf. Gael. *ceara*, red, blood-coloured.]

char[2] *chär, vt* to reduce to carbon. — *vt* and *vi* to scorch: — *pr p* **charr'ing**; *pa t* and *pa p* **charred**. — *n* a substance, e.g. charcoal, resulting from charring.

char[3] *chär, n* an occasional piece of work, an odd job; a charwoman. — *vi* to do odd jobs of work; to do house-cleaning: — *pr p* **charr'ing**; *pa t* and *pa p* **charred**. — **char'woman** or **char'lady** a woman hired to do rough cleaning. [O.E. *cerran*, *cierran*, to turn.]

char[4] *chär*, (*slang*) *n* tea. [Cockney spelling of **cha**.]

charabanc *shar'ə-bang* or *-bã*, *n* formerly, a long open vehicle with rows of seats set across its width; more recently, (now used rarely, esp. *facetiously*) a tourist coach. [Fr. *char à bancs*, carriage with benches.]

character *kar'ək-tər, n* a letter, sign, figure, stamp, or distinctive mark; a mark of any kind, a symbol in writing, etc.; one of a set of symbols, e.g. letters of the alphabet, numbers, punctuation marks, that can be arranged in groups to represent data for processing (*comput*); any essential or distinguishing feature; a quality; nature; the aggregate of distinctive qualities which constitutes personal or national individuality; esp. moral qualities; the reputation of possessing these; a person noted for eccentricity or well-marked personality; a personality as created in a play or novel or appearing in history; a person (*slang*). — *n* **characterīsā'tion** or **-z-**. — *vt* **char'acterise** or **-ize** to describe by distinctive qualities; to be a distinguishing mark or quality of. — *n* **characteris'tic** that which marks or constitutes the character; the integral part of a logarithm. — *adj* **characteris'tic** or **characteris'tical**. — *adv* **characteris'tically**. — *adj* **char'acterless** without character or distinctive qualities. — **character actor** an actor who plays character parts; **character assassination** the destruction of a person's reputation by slander, rumour, etc.; **characteristic radiation** the wavelength of radiation that characterises a particular substance; **character part** a stage or film rôle portraying an unusual or eccentric personality type; **character sketch** a short description of the main traits in a person's character. — **in character** in harmony with the part assumed, appropriate; in keeping with the person's usual conduct or attitudes; dressed for the part; **out of character** not in character. [Fr. *caractère* — Gr. *charaktēr*, from *charassein*, to cut, engrave.]

charade *shə-räd'* or in U.S. usu. *-rād'*, *n* an acted riddle in which the syllables and the whole are uttered or represented in successive scenes; a piece of ridiculous pretence. [Fr., perh. — Prov. *charrada*, chatter, or Sp. *charrada*, clownishness.]

charcoal *chär'kōl, n* charred wood, or coal made by charring wood; a carbon-containing material produced by the partial combustion, with air excluded, of wood or other substances; a stick of this material for drawing. — *n* and *adj* (also **charcoal grey**) (of) a dark grey colour. [**char**[2] and **coal**.]

chard *chärd, n* the edible leafstalk of cardoon, artichoke, or a variety (*Swiss chard*) of white beet. [L. *carduus*, thistle.]

chardonnay *shär-do-nā', n* a type of grape used in making dry white wine; the wine itself. [Fr.]

charge *chärj, vt* to load, to put something into, to fill; to load heavily, burden; to fill completely; to cause to accumulate electricity; to give a task to, to order, command; to accuse; to place a bearing upon (with *with*; *heraldry*); to exact or demand from, to ask as the price; to set down as a liability against; to attack at a rush; to put forward an accusation (that). — *vi* to make an attack. — *n* that which is loaded or laid on; cost or price; the load of powder, fuel, etc., for a gun, furnace, etc.; an attack or onset; care, custody; the object of care; an accumulation of electricity; a command; an accusation (*law*); a device borne on a shield (*heraldry*); (in *pl*) expenses. — *adj* **charge'able** liable to be charged; open to accusation; blamable. — *n* **charge'ableness**. — *adv* **charge'ably**. — *adj* **charge'less**. — *n* **char'ger** a flat dish capable of holding a large joint, a platter; a war-horse. — **charge account** an account in which goods obtained are entered to be paid for later. — *vt* **charge'-cap.** — **charge'-capping** the setting by central government of an upper limit on the community charge that can be levied by a local authority; **charge'card** a card issued by an organisation, e.g. a chain-store, that allows its holder to buy goods on credit; **charge'-hand** or **charge'-man** the leader of a group of workmen; **charge'-nurse** a nurse in charge of a ward; **charge'-sheet** a police list of accused and the charges against them. — **bring a charge** to accuse (with *against*; *law*); **charge down** (in Rugby football) to run towards (a kicked ball) and block it; **give in charge** to hand over to the police; **in charge** in control or authority, responsible (often with *of*); **take charge of** to assume the care of. [Fr. *charger* — L.L. *carricāre*, to load — L. *carrus*, a wagon; see **car, cargo.**]

chargé-d'affaires *shär-zhā-dä-fer'*, *n* a diplomatic agent of lesser rank: — *pl* **chargés-d'affaires'** (*shär-zhā-*). [Fr.]

charily, chariness. See **chary.**

chariot *char'i-ət*, *n* a car used in ancient warfare or racing; a ceremonial carriage. — *n* **charioteer'** someone who drives a chariot. [Fr., dimin. of *char*, a car.]

Charis *kar'is*, *n* any one of the three **Char'ites** (*-tēz*), the Graces, Greek goddesses of whatever imparts graciousness to life, — *Euphrosyne*, *Aglaia* and *Thalia*.

charisma *kə-riz'mə* or **charism** *kar'izm*, *n* a spiritual power given by God; personal quality or gift that enables an individual to impress and influence many of his or her fellows. — *adj* **charismat'ic** of, pertaining to, or having a charisma or charism. — **charismatic movement** a non-denominational religious movement based on a belief in the divinely-inspired gifts of speaking in tongues, healing, prophecy, etc. [Gr. *charis*, *-itos*, grace.]

charity *char'i-ti*, *n* the disposition to think favourably of others, and do them good; almsgiving; a usu. non-profit-making foundation, institution, or cause, devoted to caring for those in need of help, etc.; universal love (*NT*). — *adj* **char'itable** of or relating to, showing, inspired by charity; (of an institution, etc.) having the status of, being in the nature of, a charity. — *n* **char'itableness.** — *adv* **char'itably.** [Fr. *charité* — L. *cāritās*, *-ātis* — *cārus*, dear.]

charivari *shär-i-vär'i*, *n* a cacophonous mock serenade, orig. to newly-weds, using pans, lids etc; a cacophony. [Fr., — L.L. *caribaria*, a headache.]

charlatan *shär'lə-tən*, *n* someone who pretends to have, esp. medical, knowledge; a quack. — *adj* **charlatanic** (*-tan'ik*) or **charlatan'ical.** — *n* **char'latanism.** — *n* **char'latanry.** [Fr., — It. *ciarlatano* — *ciarlare*, to chatter.]

Charley or **Charlie** (also without *cap*) *chär'li*, *n* an inefficient, ineffectual person, a fool (often in the phrase *a proper Charlie*). [From the name *Charles*.]

charlotte *shär'lət*, *n* a kind of deep tart containing cooked apple or other fruit. — **charlotte russe** (*rüs*) a custard or cream enclosed in a kind of sponge-cake. [From the name.]

charm *chärm*, *n* a spell; something thought to possess occult power, as an amulet, a metrical form of words, etc.; a trinket; power of fascination; attractiveness; (in *pl*) personal attractions; that which can please irresistibly; in particle physics, (the quantum number used to account for) the unusual properties and behaviour of certain elementary particles. — *vt* to influence by a charm; to subdue by secret influence; to enchant; to delight; to allure. — *adj* **charmed** bewitched; delighted; protected as by a special charm; (in particle physics) having charm. — *n* **charm'er.** — *adj* **charm'ful** abounding in charms. — *adj* **charm'ing** highly pleasing; delightful; fascinating. — *adv* **charm'ingly.** — *adj* **charm'less.** — *adv* **charm'lessly.** — **charm offensive** a method of trying to get what one wants by overwhelming with reasonableness, attractive offers, etc. [Fr. *charme* — L. *carmen*, a song.]

Charollais or **Charolais** *shar'ō-lā*, *n* a breed of cattle and, more recently, of sheep named after an old district of France (Charolais) of which Charolles is the capital.

Charon *kā'rən*, (*Gr mythol*) *n* the ferryman who rowed the shades of the dead across the river Styx.

charoset or **charoseth.** See **haroset** or **haroseth.**

charr. See **char**[1].

chart *chärt*, *n* a marine map, showing part of a sea or other water, with the islands, coasts, soundings, currents, etc.; an outline map, curve, or a tabular statement giving information of any kind; (usu. in *pl*) the lists of the ten, twenty, etc. most popular records, i.e. those which have sold the most copies, each week. — *vt* to map. — *n* **chart'ist** a person who makes and/or studies charts of past performances, esp. of stocks and shares, with a view to forecasting future trends. — *n* **chart'ism** (see also **Chartism**, separate entry). — *adj* **chart'less.** — *adj* **chart'-busting** (*slang*; esp. of records) very successful. — **chart'-buster; chart'house** or **chart'-room** the room in a ship where charts are kept. [O.Fr. *charte* — Gr. *chartēs*, a sheet of paper.]

charter *chärt'ər*, *n* any formal writing in evidence of a grant, contract, or other transactions, conferring or confirming titles, rights, or privileges, etc.; the formal deed by which a sovereign guarantees the rights and privileges of his or her subjects; a document creating a borough or other corporation; a patent; a grant. — *vt* to establish by charter; to let or hire, as a ship, on contract. — *adj* hired (as in *charter plane*); made in a hired aeroplane (as in *charter flight*). — *adj* **chart'ered** granted or protected by a charter; privileged; licensed; hired by contract. — *n* **chart'erer.** — **chartered accountant, engineer** or **surveyor**, etc. a person qualified under the regulations of the relevant institute or professional body which has a royal charter. [O.Fr. *chartre* — Gr. *chartēs*, a sheet of paper.]

Charterhouse *chärt'ər-hows*, *n* a Carthusian monastery; the famous hospital and school instituted in London in 1611, on the site of a Carthusian monastery. [See **Carthusian.**]

Chartism *chärt'izm*, *n* a movement in Great Britain for the extension of political power to the working-classes. — *n* **Chart'ist.** — Also *adj*. [See **charter.**]

chartist, chartism. See **chart.**

Chartreuse *shär-trœz'*, *n* a Carthusian monastery, esp. the original one, La Grande Chartreuse near Grenoble in France; (sometimes without *cap*) a famous liqueur, usu. green, sometimes yellow, long manufactured there by the monks from aromatic herbs and brandy. [See **Carthusian.**]

chary *chā'ri*, *adj* cautious; wary (of doing, saying, giving, etc.). — *adv* **chār'ily.** — *n* **chār'iness.** [O.E. *cearig* — *cearu*, care.]

Charybdis *kə-rib'dis*, *n* (in the *Odyssey*) a dangerous monster that dwelt under a rock, later a whirlpool on the Sicilian side of the Straits of Messina — with **Scylla** providing the proverbial alternatives of evil or disaster. — See **Scylla.**

chase[1] *chās*, *vt* to pursue; to hunt; to seek; to drive away; to put to flight; to follow with a chaser or chasse. — *vi* (*colloq*) to hurry (about, around or after). — *n* pursuit; a hunting; (with *the*) the sport of hunting. — *n* **chas'er** a pursuer; a hunter; a horse for steeplechasing; a drink of a different kind taken after another, contrasting or complementary, sort (*colloq*). — **chase rainbows** to pursue an impossible aim; **give chase** to set off in pursuit; **wild-goose chase** any foolish or profitless pursuit of the unattainable. [O.Fr. *chacier*, *chasser* — L. *capěre*, to take.]

chase[2] *chās, vt* to enchase, to decorate by engraving. — *n* **chās'er**. — *n* **chās'ing** the art of engraving on the outside of raised metalwork; the art of cutting the threads of screws. [Short for **enchase**.]

Chasid, Chasidic, etc. See **Hasid**.

chasm *kaz'əm, n* a yawning or gaping hollow; a gap or opening. — *adj* **chas'med**. — *adj* **chasmic** (*kaz'-mik*). — *adj* **chas'my**. [Gr. *chasma*, from *chainein*, to gape.]

chasse *shas, n* a dram or liqueur taken after coffee. — Also **chasse-café'**. [Fr. *chasser*, to chase.]

chassé *shas'ā, n* a gliding step in dancing. — *vi* to make such a step. [Fr.]

chasseur *shas-œr', n* a hunter or huntsman; one of a select body of French light infantry or cavalry; a liveried attendant. — *adj* (*cookery*) of or cooked in a sauce containing mushrooms, shallots, white wine, etc. [Fr., — *chasser*, to hunt; see **chase**[1].]

Chassid, Chassidic, etc. See **Hasid**.

chassis *shas'ē* or *shas'i, n* the structural framework of a motor car to which the working parts and body may be attached; an aeroplane's landing-carriage: — *pl* **chassis** (*shas'ēz* or *-iz*). [Fr. *chassis*, frame.]

chaste *chāst, adj* sexually virtuous; modest; refined and pure in taste and style. — *adv* **chaste'ly**. — *vt* **chasten** (*chās'n*) to free from faults by punishing; to punish; to purify or refine; to restrain or moderate. — *adj* **chās'tened** purified; modest; tempered. — *n* **chās'tener**. — *n* **chaste'ness**. — *n* **chās'tenment**. — *vt* **chastise** (*chas-tīz'*) to inflict punishment upon for the purpose of correction; to reduce to order or to obedience. — *adj* **chastīs'able**. — *n* **chastisement** (*chas'tiz-mənt*). — *n* **chastity** (*chas'ti-ti*) sexual purity; virginity. — **chastity belt** a device said to have been worn e.g. by wives of absent crusaders, to prevent their having sexual intercourse; a device made in modern times according to its supposed design. — Also *fig*. [O.Fr. *chaste* — L. *castus*, pure.]

chasuble *chaz'ū-bl* or *chas', n* a sleeveless vestment worn by the priest while celebrating mass. [Fr. — L.L. *casubula* — L. *casula*, dimin. of L. *casa*, a hut.]

chat[1] *chat, vi* to talk easily or familiarly. — *vt* (often with *up*) to talk to informally and often flirtatiously in order to gain something: — *pr p* **chatt'ing**; *pa t* and *pa p* **chatt'ed**. — *n* familiar, easy talk. — *n* **chatt'iness**. — *adj* **chatt'y** fond of chatting; informal, relating to chat. — **chat'line** a telephone service enabling callers to participate in general conversation with other callers; **chat'-show** (*colloq*) a radio or television programme in which invited personalities talk informally with their host (also **talk'-show**). [From **chatter**.]

chat[2] *chat, n* a genus of small birds in the thrush family, including the stonechat. [From the sound of their voice.]

château *shat'ō, n* a castle; a great country-seat, esp. in France; a vineyard estate around a castle, house, etc., esp. in Bordeaux: — *pl* **chât'eaux** (*-tōz*). — *n* **châtelain** (*shat'ə-lẽ*) a castellan. — *n* **chât'elaine** (*shat'ə-len*) a female keeper or mistress of a castle or a large household; an ornamental bunch of short chains bearing keys, scissors, etc., attached to the waist-belt. — *adj* **château bottled** (of wine) bottled on the estate in which it has been produced. [Fr. (O.Fr. *chastel*) — L. *castellum*, dimin. of *castrum*, a fort.]

chattel *chat'l, n* any kind of property which is not freehold. — **goods and chattels** all personal movable possessions. [O.Fr. *chatel* — L.L. *captāle* — L. *capitāle*, etc., property, goods.]

chatter *chat'ər, vi* to talk idly or rapidly; (of birds) to utter a succession of rapid short notes; of the teeth when one shivers, to make a clicking sound. — *n* a noise like that made by a magpie, or by teeth striking together; idle talk. — *n* **chatt'erer**. — *n* **chatt'ering**. — **chatt'erbox** someone who talks or chatters incessantly. [From the sound.]

chatty. See **chat**[1].

chauffeur *shō'fər* or *-fœr', n* a person employed to drive a motor car: — *fem* **chauffeuse** (*-fœz*). — *vi* and *vt* to drive, act as a chauffeur (for). [Fr., stoker.]

chauvinism *shō'vin-izm, n* an absurdly extravagant pride in one's country, with a corresponding contempt for foreign nations; extravagant attachment to any group, place, cause, etc. — *n* **chau'vinist**. — *adj* **chau'vinist**. — *adj* **chauvinist'ic**. — **male chauvinist (pig)** see **male**. [From Nicolas *Chauvin*, an ardent veteran of Napoleon's.]

ChB *abbrev* for *Chirurgiae Baccalaureus* (L.), Bachelor of Surgery.

CHD *abbrev* for coronary heart disease.

cheap *chēp, adj* low in price or cost; charging low prices; of a low price in relation to the value; easily obtained; of little value; paltry; inferior; vulgar. — Also *adv*. — *vt* **cheap'en** to make cheap, to lower the price of; to lower the reputation of; to beat down the price of. — *n* **cheap'y** or **cheap'ie** (*colloq*) something which is low in price or cost. — Also *adj*. — *adv* **cheap'ly**. — *n* **cheap'ness**. — *adj* **cheap'o** (*colloq*; usu. *derog*) cheap, esp. with connotations of inferiority or tawdriness. — **cheap labour** labour paid at a poor rate; **cheap'skate** (*slang*) a miserly person. — **cheap and nasty** offensively inferior and of low value; **dirt cheap** ridiculously cheap; **on the cheap** cheap or cheaply. [O.E. *cēap*, price, a bargain, *ceapian*; O.N. *kaupa*, Ger. *kaufen*, to buy.]

cheat *chēt, n* someone who cheats; a fraud; a deception; a card-game in which deception is allowed. — *vt* to deceive, defraud or impose upon. — *vi* to be deceitful. — *n* **cheat'er**. — *n* **cheating**. [**escheat**.]

check *chek, vt* to bring to a stop; to restrain or hinder; to rebuke; to verify, often by comparison; to tick (*US*); to deposit or receive in exchange for a check; to mark with a pattern of crossing lines; to place in check (*chess*). — *vi* to come to a stop; to make investigations. — *n* anything that checks; a sudden stop, repulse or rebuff; restraint; control; a mark put against items in a list; an order for money (usually written **cheque** except in U.S.); a means of verification or testing; a restaurant bill; a counter used in games at cards (hence *pass in one's checks* = to die); a pattern of cross lines forming small squares, as in a chessboard; any fabric woven with such a pattern; a position in which a player is forced either to move or to guard his king (*chess*). — *adj* divided into small squares by crossing lines. — *n* **check'er** someone who hinders, rebukes or scrutinises; (in *pl*; *US*) the game of draughts. — **check book** (*US*) a cheque book; **check digit** (*comput*) a digit carried in computer processes to discover errors, check accuracy, etc.; **checked square** a square in a crossword that belongs to the solution of two clues; **check'erboard** a checked board on which checkers or draughts is played; **check'list** a list for verification purposes; a comprehensive list; an inventory; **check'mate** (O.Fr. *eschec mat* — Ar. *shāh māt(a)*, the king is dead); a check given to the adversary's king when in a position in which it can neither be protected nor moved out of check, so that the game is finished (*chess*); defeat. — *vt* to put in checkmate (*chess*); to defeat. — **check'out** the cash desk where goods bought in a supermarket, etc. are paid for; the act of checking out (see below); **check'point** a place where an official check of documents, etc. is made; **check'-rein** a strap hindering a horse from lowering its head; **check'-up** a medical examination, esp. one of a series of regular examinations; a testing scrutiny; **check'-weigher** or **check'-weighman** a person who on the part of the men checks the weight of coal sent up to the pit-mouth. — **check in** and **check out** to record one's arrival and departure from work; to perform the necessary business at a hotel office, airport, etc., on arriving, and leaving (*n* **check'-in**

and **check'-out**); **check off** to mark off on a list as having arrived, been completed, etc.; to deduct (trade union dues) from a worker's pay before he or she receives it (*US*; *n* **check'-off**); **check out** (*colloq*) to test, examine, investigate (*n* **check'-out**); see also at **check in**; **check up** to investigate; to examine and test (often with *on*). — **hold** (or **keep**) **in check** to restrain, keep back. [O.Fr. *eschec*, *eschac*, through Ar. from Pers. *shāh*.]

checker. See **check**; also **cheque**.

Cheddar *ched'ər*, *n* a kind of cheese first made at *Cheddar* in Somerset.

cheek *chēk*, *n* the side of the face below the eye, the fleshy wall of the mouth; effrontery, impudence (*colloq*); a side-post of a door, window, etc.; a buttock (*colloq*). — *vt* (*colloq*) to address insolently. — *adv* **cheek'ily**. — *adj* **cheek'y** (*colloq*) rude; saucy. — **cheek'bone** the bone above the cheek; **cheek'-pouch** an expansion of the cheek, forming a bag, as in monkeys, etc. — **cheek by jowl** side by side; **turn the other cheek** see under **turn**. [O.E. *cēce*, *cēace*, cheek, jaw.]

cheep *chēp*, *vi* to chirp, as a young bird. — *n* a sound of cheeping. [Imit.]

cheer *chēr*, *n* disposition, frame of mind (with *good*, etc.); joy; a shout of approval or welcome. — *vt* to comfort; to encourage; to applaud. — *vi* to shout encouragement or applause. — *n* **cheer'er**. — *adj* **cheer'ful** in, of, resulting in, or accompanied by good spirits. — *adv* **cheer'fully**. — *n* **cheer'fulness**. — *adv* **cheer'ily**. — *n* **cheer'iness**. — *interj* **cheerio'** or **cheer'o** a bright informal goodbye: — *pl* **cheerios'** or **cheer'os**. — *adj* **cheer'less** without comfort, gloomy. — *n* **cheer'lessness**. — *interj* **cheers!** (*colloq*) good health! (used when drinking a toast); thank you!; cheerio, goodbye! — *adj* **cheer'y** cheerful; promoting or resulting in cheerfulness. — **cheer'leader** (esp. *US*) a person who directs organised cheering, as at team games. — **cheer up** (*colloq*) to make or become more cheerful. [O.Fr. *chiere*, face — L.L. *cara*, the face.]

cheerio. See under **cheer**.

cheese[1] *chēz*, *n* a kind of food, made from the curd of milk, separated from the whey, of a soft, creamy consistency or pressed into a solid or semi-solid mass; a solid mass of such food; a flavoured kind of food, with the consistency of soft cheese; the flattened cheese-shaped disc used in skittles. — *n* **chees'iness**. — *adj* **chees'y** having the nature, often the smell, of cheese; (of a grin) wide (*colloq*); artificial, insincere (*colloq*). — **cheese'board** a flat board, etc. on which cheese is served; a collection of cheeses served on such a board; **cheese'burger** a hamburger cooked with cheese on top of it; **cheese'-cake** a kind of cake having a base of pastry or biscuit crumbs, with a filling of cream cheese, sugar, eggs, flavouring, etc.; female shapely charms, esp. when photographically displayed in magazines, etc. (*slang*); **cheese'cloth** a loose-woven cloth suitable for pressing cheeses; a stronger type of loosely-woven cotton cloth used for making shirts, etc.; **cheese'-paring** parsimony, miserliness. — *adj* mean and parsimonious. — **cheese'-press** a machine in which curds for cheese are pressed; **cheese straw** a long thin biscuit flavoured with cheese; **cheese'wire** a thin wire used for cutting cheese. — **green cheese** cheese not yet dried; **hard cheese** (*slang*) hard luck. [O.E. *cēse*, *cȳse*, curdled milk — L. *cāseus*.]

cheese[2] *chēz*, *n* anything of excellent quality. — **big cheese** (*slang*) a person of importance. [Prob. Pers. and Hindi *chīz*, thing.]

cheese[3] *chēz*, (*slang*) *vt* in the phrases **cheese it** to stop, run off; **cheesed off** (also **cheesed**) fed up.

cheetah *chē'tə*, *n* an animal like the leopard, found in Africa and S.W. Asia, used in hunting. [Hindi *cītā* — Sans. *citraka*, *citrakāya*, having a speckled body.]

chef *shef*, *n* a usu. male cook, esp. a head-cook (in full **chef de cuisine** (*də kwē-zēn*) the head of a kitchen). — **chef d'œuvre** (*shā dœvr'*) a masterpiece: — *pl* **chefs d'œuvre** (*shā-*). [Fr. head, chief; see **chief**.]

cheiro- *kī'rō-* or *kī-ro'-*, also **chiro-** *combining form* signifying hand. — *n* **cheirog'nomy** or **chirog'nomy** palmistry. — *n* **cheirog'raphy** or **chirog'raphy** handwriting, penmanship. — *n* **chei'rōmancy** or **chi'rōmancy** (*-man-si*) fortune-telling by the hand. — *n* **cheirop'teran** or **chirop'teran** a member of the **Cheirop'tera** (or **Chirop'tera**) the order of bats. [Gr. *cheir*, hand.]

Chekhovian *che-kō'vi-ən*, *adj* pertaining to the Russian writer Anton *Chekhov* (1860–1904), or to (the style of) his stories and plays.

chela[1] *kē'lə*, *n* (*zool*) the prehensile claw of an arthropod: — *pl* **chē'lae** (*-ē*). — *adj* **chē'late**. — *n* (*chem*) a co-ordination compound (e.g. haemoglobin) in which a central metallic ion is attached to an organic molecule at two or more positions. — *vi* to form a chelate. — *n* **chēlā'tion**. — *n* **chēlā'tor**. — *adj* **chēlif'erous** (*zool*) having a chela or chelae. — **chelation therapy** the treatment of heavy metal (e.g. lead) poisoning or certain other diseases by substances (**chelating agents**) which combine chemically with the toxic substances and render them harmless. [Latinised from Gr. *chēlē*.]

chela[2] *chā'lə*, *n* a novice in Buddhism; a disciple of a religious teacher or leader. — *n* **che'laship**. [Hindi *celā*, servant, disciple.]

chelicera *kē-lis'ə-rə*, *n* a biting appendage in arachnids: — *pl* **chēlic'erae** (*-rē*). [Gr. *chēlē*, a crab's claw, *keras*, horn.]

cheliferous. See **chela**[1].

cheloid. See **keloid**.

Chelonia *ki-lō'ni-ə*, *n* an order of reptiles with horny shell and horny beak, tortoises and turtles. — *adj* and *n* **chelō'nian**. [Gr. *chelōnē*, a tortoise.]

Chelsea *chel'sē*, *n* a district of London. — **Chelsea bun** a rolled bun filled with currants and raisins; **Chelsea pensioner** an elderly, often disabled, ex-soldier, connected with the Chelsea Royal Hospital.

chem. *abbrev* for: chemical; chemistry.

chemin de fer *shə-mɛ̃ də fer*, *n* a variety of the card game baccarat. [Fr. railway.]

chemise *shə-mēz'*, *n* a woman's shirtlike undergarment; a straight dress, a smock. [Fr. *chemise* — L.L. *camisia*, a nightgown, surplice.]

chemistry *kem'is-tri*, *n* the science of the properties of substances elementary and compound, and the laws of their combination and action one upon another. — *adj* **chemiat'ric** relating to medicine or physicians. — *adj* **chem'ical** relating to chemistry; versed in or studying chemistry. — *n* a substance obtained by chemical means or used in chemical operations. — *adv* **chem'ically**. — *n* **chemiluminesc'ence** luminescence arising from chemical processes, e.g. that of the glow-worm. — *n* **chem'ism** chemical action. — *n* **chem'ist** a person skilled in chemistry; a manufacturer of or dealer in chemicals and drugs; a pharmacist. — (The following words in **chemo-** usu. *kē-*, esp. in U.S.) **chemōpsychī'atry** treatment of mental illness by drugs; **chemōrecep'tor** a sensory nerve-ending, receiving a chemical stimulus; **chemōsyn'thesis** (*bot*) the formation of organic material by some bacteria by means of energy derived from chemical changes; **chemōtherapeu'tics** (*nsing*) or more commonly **chemōther'apy** treatment of infectious diseases or cancer by means of chemical compounds. — **chemical closet** or **toilet** a kind of toilet containing deodorising and liquefying chemicals, used when running water is not available; **chemical dependency** addiction to alcohol and/or drugs; **chemical engineering** design, construction, and operation of chemical plant and works, esp. in industrial chemistry; **chemical warfare** warfare involving the use of irritating or asphyxiating gases, oil flames, etc. [See **alchemy**.]

chenille *shə-nēl'*, *n* a thick, velvety cord of silk or wool resembling a woolly caterpillar; a velvet-like material used for table-covers, etc. [Fr. *chenille*, caterpillar — L. *canicula*, a hairy little dog, *canis*, a dog.]

cheong-sam *chong'-sam*, *n* a tight-fitting high-necked dress with slits at the sides. [Chin. (Cantonese), long dress.]

cheque or in U.S. **check** *chek*, *n* a money order on a bank. — **cheque book** a book of cheque forms; **cheque card** a card issued by a bank to a client, undertaking payment of cheques up to a certain limit. — **blank cheque** a cheque signed by the drawer without having the amount indicated; concession of power without limit (*fig*); **cheque book diplomacy** negotiations where financial considerations are the most important element; **cheque book journalism** news, articles, etc., based on information bought, usu. at a high price; **crossed cheque** an ordinary cheque with two transverse lines drawn across it, which have the effect of making it payable only through a bank account. [See **check**.]

chequer *chek'ər*, *n* alternation of colours as on a chessboard (see also **checker**). — *vt* to mark in squares of different colours; to variegate; to interrupt. — *adj* **cheq'uered** or **check'ered** variegated, like a chessboard; varying in character; eventful, with alternations of good and bad fortune. — *adv* **cheq'uerwise**. — **chequered flag** the black and white flag shown to the winner and subsequent finishers in a motor race; **cheq'uer-work** any pattern having alternating squares of different colours. [See **check**.]

cherish *cher'ish*, *vt* to protect and treat with affection; to nurture, nurse; to entertain in the mind. — *n* **cher'ishment**. [Fr. *chérir*, *chérissant* — *cher*, dear — L. *cārus*.]

chernozem *chûr'nō-zem*, *n* a very fertile soil of sub-humid steppe, consisting of a dark topsoil over a lighter calcareous layer. [Russ., black earth.]

Cherokee *cher'ə-kē*, *n* (a member of) a tribe of Iroquoian Indians; the language of the Cherokee.

cheroot *shə-rōōt'*, *n* a cigar not pointed at either end. [Fr. *cheroute*, Tamil *shuruttu*, a roll.]

cherry *cher'i*, *n* a small stone-fruit; the tree that bears it; extended to many fruits resembling it in some way; the new ball (*cricket slang*); the hymen or virginity (*slang*). — *adj* like a cherry in colour, usually bright red; ruddy. — **cherry brandy** a liqueur made by steeping Morello cherries in brandy; **cherr'y-laurel** a species of cherry with evergreen laurel-like leaves; **cherr'y-picker** a crane-like device consisting of a platform at the end of a long arm with an elbow-like joint in it, the platform being raised as the arm is raised; **cherry-pie'** a pie made of cherries; the common heliotrope; **cherr'y-plum** a plum of flavour approaching a cherry; **cherr'y-stone** the hard endocarp of the cherry, the stone; **cherry tomato** a more or less cherry-sized red tomato. — **have (**or **take) two bites (**or **a second bite) at the cherry** (*colloq*) to have (or take) a second chance or opportunity. [O.E. *ciris* — L. *cerasus* — Gr. *kerasos*, a cherry-tree.]

chert *chûrt*, (*geol*) *n* a compact flinty chalcedony.

cherub *cher'əb*, *n* a winged creature with human face, represented as associated with Jehovah; a celestial spirit; a chubby-faced person, esp. a child: — *pl* **cher'ubs** or **cherubim** (*cher'ə-bim* or *-ū-bim*) or **cher'ubims**. — *adj* **cherubic** (*-ōō'bik*), **cheru'bical** or **cherubim'ic** angelic. — *adv* **cheru'bically**. [Heb. *k'rub*, pl. *k'rubim*.]

chervil *chûr'vil*, *n* a plant (*Anthriscus cerefolium*) cultivated as an aromatic pot-herb; also other species of *Anthriscus* (*common*, *wild* and *rough chervil*); extended to sweet cicely (*sweet chervil*). [O.E. *cerfille* — L. *caerefolium* — Gr. *chairephyllon*.]

chess *ches*, *n* a game of skill for two, played with figures or men of different kinds which are moved on a chequered board. — **chess'board** the board on which chess is played; a chequered design; **chess'man**. [O.Fr. *eschès* — Pers. *shāh*, a king.]

chessel *ches'l*, *n* a cheese mould. [**cheese**[1].]

chest *chest*, *n* a large strong box; the part of the body between the neck and the abdomen, the thorax; a treasury; a chestful. — *adj* **chest'ed** having a chest; placed in a chest. — *n* **chest'ful**. — *adj* **chest'y** of the quality of the chest-voice; suggestive of disease of the chest (*colloq*); self-important (*slang*). — **chest freezer** a long, low freezer which opens at the top; **chest'-note** in singing or speaking, a deep note; **chest'-protector** a covering to keep the chest warm; **chest'-register**, **chest'-tone** or **chest'-voice** the lowest register of the voice. — **chest of drawers** a piece of furniture made up of a case in which drawers slide; **off one's chest** (*colloq*) off one's mind; admitted, stated, declared openly. [O.E. *cyst* — L. *cista* — Gr. *kistē*.]

chesterfield *chest'ər-fēld*, *n* a long overcoat; a heavily padded sofa. [Lord *Chesterfield*.]

chestnut *ches'nut*, *n* a tree of genus *Castanea*, esp. the *Spanish* or *Sweet Chestnut*; its edible nut, encased (three together) in a prickly husk; its hard timber; the **horse-chestnut** (*Aesculus hippocastanum*), its fruit or nut; a chestnut horse; a stale joke or cliché (*slang*). — *adj* of chestnut colour, reddish-brown. [O.Fr. *chastaigne* — L. *castanea* — perh. from *Castana*, in Thessaly.]

chevalet *shə-va'lā* or *she'*, (*mus*) *n* the bridge of a stringed instrument. [Fr. dimin. of *cheval*, a horse.]

cheval-glass *shə-val'-gläs*, *n* a large glass or mirror supported on a frame and able to swivel in it. [Fr. *cheval*, horse, stand.]

chevalier *shev-ə-lēr'*, *n* a cavalier; a knight; a gallant. [Fr., — L.L. *caballārius* — L. *caballus*, a horse.]

cheven *chev'ən*, *n* the chub. [Fr. *chevin*, *chevanne*.]

Cheviot *chē'vi-ət* or *chev'i-ət*, *n* a hardy breed of short-woolled sheep reared on the *Cheviot* Hills; a cloth made from their wool.

chevron *shev'rən*, *n* a rafter; the representation of two rafters of a house meeting at the top (*heraldry*); a V-shaped band on the sleeve, a mark of non-commissioned rank or (in army and R.A.F., inverted) of long service and good conduct. — *adj* **chev'roned**. — **chevron board** a road sign consisting of a line of horizontal V-shapes, used to indicate a sharp change in direction. [Fr. *chevron*, rafter — L. *capreolus*, dimin. of *caper*, a goat.]

chevrotain *shev'rō-tān* or *-tən*, *n* a mouse deer, any member of an Asian tropical family of small deerlike animals. [Fr., dimin. of *chèvre* — L. *capra*, she-goat.]

chevy. See **chivvy**.

chew *chōō*, *vt* to bruise and grind with the teeth; to masticate; to meditate, reflect (*fig*). — *n* the action of chewing; a quid of tobacco. — *adj* **chew'y** soft, able to be chewed, like toffee. — **chew'ing-gum** a preparation made from chicle gum, produced by the sapodilla plum tree, sweetened and flavoured. — **chew out** (*colloq*) to tell off, reprimand; **chew the cud** (of cows, etc.) to masticate a second time food that has already been swallowed and passed into the first stomach; to ruminate in thought (*fig*; also **chew over**); **chew the rag** or **the fat** (*slang*) to keep on arguing the point. [O.E. *cēowan*; cf. **jaw**.]

Cheyenne *shī-an'* or *-en'*, *n* (a member of) a tribe of N. American Indians now living in Montana and Oklahoma; the Algonkian language of the tribe. [Can. Fr. — Siouan (Dakota) *Shahiyena*, people who speak unintelligibly.]

chez *shā*, *prep* at the home or establishment of. [Fr.]

chi *kī* or *hhē*, *n* the twenty-second letter (Χ, χ) of the Greek alphabet, representing an aspirated *k* sound. [Gr. *chei*, *chī*.]

chiack or **chyack** *chī'ak*, (*Austr colloq*) *vt* to tease, deride, jeer at. — Also *n*. — *n* **chī'acking.** [Brit. obs. slang, to greet, salute.]

Chianti *kē-an'ti* or *-än'ti*, It. *kyän'tē*, *n* a red (or white) wine of Tuscany. [*Chianti* Mountains.]

chiaroscuro *kyär-ō-sko͞o'rō*, *n* management of light and shade in a picture; a monochrome painting; the effect of light and shade (also *fig*): — *pl* **chiaroscu'ros.**

chiasm *kī'azm* or **chiasma** *kī-az'mə*, (*anat*) *n* a decussation or intersection, esp. that of the optic nerves. — *n* **chīas'mus** (*rhet*) contrast by parallelism in reverse order, as *Do not live to eat, but eat to live*. — *adj* **chīas'tic.** [Gr. *chiasma*, a cross-shaped mark, *chiastos*, laid crosswise, like the Greek letter X (*chi, chei*).]

chic *shēk*, *n* style, elegance; artistic skill. — *adj* having chic; smart and fashionable. — *adv* **chic'ly.** [Fr.]

chicane *shi-kān'*, *n* a trick or artifice; a series of sharp bends on a motor-racing track. — *n* **chicā'nery** trickery or artifice, esp. in legal proceedings; quibbling. — *n* **chicā'ning** quibbling. [Fr. *chicane*, sharp practice at law.]

chicano *chi-kä'nō* or *shi-*, *n* (*US*, sometimes considered *derog*; also with *cap*) an American of Mexican descent: — *pl* **chica'nos.** — Also *adj*. [Sp. *mejicano*, Mexican.]

chichi or **chi-chi** *shē'shē* or *chē'chē*, *adj* stylish, chic, self-consciously fashionable; fussy, precious, affected. — *n* something that is, or quality of being, chichi. [Fr.]

chick *chik*, *n* the young of birds, esp. of the hen; a child, as a term of endearment; a girl or young woman (*slang*). — *n* **chick'en** the young of birds, esp. of the domestic fowl; the domestic fowl; the flesh of a fowl (not always young); a prairie chicken; a youthful person, esp. a girl; a faint-hearted person (*colloq*); a type of sometimes competitive game in which one dares to perform some physically dangerous activity (*colloq*). — *adj* (*colloq*) cowardly, frightened. — *vi* (*colloq*) to show fear. — *n* **chick'ling** a little chicken. — **chick'en-feed** poultry food; small change (*colloq*); something of little value (*colloq*). — *adj* **chicken-heart'ed** or **-liv'ered** timid, cowardly. — **chick'en-pox** a contagious febrile disease, chiefly of children, rather like a mild form of smallpox; **chick'en-run** an enclosure for hens; **chick'en-wire** wire-netting; **chick'-pea** see **chickling**[1]; **chick'weed** one of the commonest of weeds, much relished by fowls and cagebirds. — **chicken-and-egg situation** one in which it is impossible to tell which is the cause and which the effect; **chicken out** (*colloq*; often with *of*) to desert or quit through cowardice; **the chickens have come home to roost** see under **roost**[1]. [O.E. *cicen*; cf. Du. *kieken*, Ger. *Küken*.]

chickadee *chik-ə-dē'*, *n* an American titmouse. [From its note.]

chickling[1] *chik'ling*, *n* a species of pea (also **chickling vetch**). — **chick'-pea** gram, a plant of the pea family; its edible seed. [Fr. *chiche* — L. *cicer*, chick-pea.]

chickling[2]. See under **chick.**

chicle *chik'l* or *chik'li*, *n* the gum of the sapodilla tree, chewing-gum. [Sp., — Mex.]

chicly. See **chic.**

chicory *chik'ə-ri*, *n* a blue-flowered composite; its carrot-like root (ground to mix with coffee). [Fr. *chicorée* — L. *cichorēum* — Gr. *kichorion*.]

chide *chīd*, *vt* to scold, rebuke, reprove by words: — *pr p* **chīd'ing**; *pa t* **chid** or sometimes **chīd'ed**; *pa p* **chid** or **chidd'en**, sometimes **chīd'ed.** — *n* **chīd'ing** scolding. [O.E. *cīdan*.]

chief *chēf*, *adj* head; principal, highest, first; outstanding, important (with *compar* **chief'er**, *superl* **chief'est**). — *adv* chiefly. — *n* a head or principal person; a leader; the principal part or top of anything; the greater part; generally one-third of the area of the shield (*heraldry*). — *n* **chief'dom** or **chief'ship** state of being chief; sovereignty. — *n* **chief'ess** a female chief. — *adj* **chief'less.** — *n* **chief'ling.** — *adv* **chief'ly** in the first place; principally; for the most part. — *n* **chief'tain**, *fem* **chief'tainess**, the head of a clan; a leader or commander. — *n* **chief'taincy** or **chief'tainry.** — *n* **chief'tainship.** — **Chief Constable** (in Britain) an officer commanding the police force in an administrative area. — **-in-chief** *combining form* denoting at the head, as in *commander-in-chief*. — **chief of staff** (*mil*) a senior staff officer; (with *cap*) the senior officer of each of the armed forces; **in chief** borne in the upper part of the shield (*heraldry*); of a tenure, held directly from the sovereign; most importantly. [Fr. *chef* — L. *caput*, the head.]

chiffchaff *chif'chaf*, *n* a small warbler. [Imit.]

chiffon *shif'on* or *shē'fɔ̃*, *n* (in *pl*) trimmings, or other adornments; a thin fine clothing fabric of silk, nylon, etc. — *n* **chiffonier** (*shif-ən-ēr'*) an ornamental cabinet. [Fr., rag, adornment — *chiffe*, rag.]

chigger. See **chigoe.**

chignon *shē'nyɔ̃*, *n* a fold or roll of hair worn on the back of the head and neck. [Fr.]

chigoe *chig'ō* or **chigger** *chig'ər*, *n* a tropical American, African and Indian flea which buries itself, esp. beneath the toenails; the larva of a harvest-mite (*Trombicula*) of America, Europe, and Asia, that burrows in the skin. — Also called **jigg'er.** [W. Ind. name.]

chihuahua *chi-wä'wä*, *n* a very small dog (1 kg. (2 lb.) or so) with big eyes and pointed ears. [*Chihuahua* in Mexico.]

chilblain *chil'blān*, *n* a painful red swelling, esp. on hands and feet in cold weather. [**chill** and **blain.**]

child *chīld*, *n* a very young person (up to the age of sixteen for the purpose of some acts of parliament, under fourteen in criminal law); a son or daughter; one standing in a relationship of adoption or origin (to a person, place, etc.); disciple; (in *pl*) offspring; (in *pl*) descendants; (in *pl*) inhabitants: — *pl* **children** (*chil'drən*). — *n* **child'hood** the state of being a child; the time of being a child. — *adj* **child'ish** of or like a child; silly; trifling. — *adv* **child'ishly.** — *n* **child'ishness** what is natural to a child; puerility. — *adj* **child'less.** — *adj* **child'like.** — **child abuse** physical or mental cruelty to or neglect of a child by a parent or guardian; **child'bearing** the act of bringing forth children. — *adj* **child'-bearing.** — **child benefit** an allowance granted by the government to parents for children; **child'birth** the giving birth to a child; **child'care; child endowment** (*Austr*) family allowance from a government source; **child'minder** a person, usu. untrained but often listed on an official register, who looks after children. — *adj* **child'-proof** or **child-resis'tant** not able to be damaged, opened, worked, etc., by a child. — **child's play** something very easy to do; **child'-study** the psychology and physiology of children; **child welfare** health and wellbeing of young children as an object of systematic social work. — **second childhood** the childishness of old age; **with child** (*archaic* or *literary*) pregnant. [O.E. *cild*, pl. *cild*, later, *cildru*, *-ra*.]

Childermas *chil'dər-məs*, *n* Innocents' Day, a festival (28 Dec.) to commemorate the slaying of the children by Herod. [O.E. *cildra*, genitive pl. of *cild*, child and *mæsse*, mass.]

Chile *chil'i*, *adj* of Chile. — *n* and *adj* **Chil'ean.** — **Chile** (or **Chilean**) **pine** the monkey-puzzle; **Chile saltpetre** sodium nitrate.

chili or **chile** *chil'i*. Variant forms of **chilli.**

chiliad *kil'i-ad*, *n* the number 1000; 1000 of anything (e.g. years). [Gr. *chīlias*, *-ados* — *chīlioi*, 1000.]

chill *chil*, *n* coldness; a cold that causes shivering; anything that damps or disheartens. — *adj* shivering with cold; slightly cold; opposite of *cordial*. — *vi* to grow cold. — *vt* to make chill or cold; to preserve by cold. — *adj* **chilled** made cold; preserved by cold. — *n* **chill'er**. — *adv* **chill'ily**. — *n* **chill'iness**. — *n* and *adj* **chill'ing**. — *n* **chill'ness**. — *adj* **chill'y** cold; chilling; sensitive to cold. — **chill factor** the degree by which weather conditions, e.g. wind (as in **wind-chill factor**), increase the effect of low temperatures. — **take the chill off** to warm slightly. [O.E. *cele*, *ciele*, cold; see **cold**, **cool**.]

chilli *chil'i*, *n* the pod of the capsicum, extremely pungent and stimulant, used in sauces, pickles, etc., and dried and ground to form cayenne pepper; chilli con carne (*colloq*): — *pl* **chill'is** or **chill'ies**. — Also **chili** or **chile**. — **chilli con carne** (*kon kär'nā*) a dish of minced meat, beans and chillis, originating in Mexico. [Nahuatl.]

chimb. See **chime**[2].

chime[1] *chīm*, *n* a set of bells tuned in a scale; (often in *pl*) the ringing of such bells in succession; a definite sequence of bell-like notes sounded as by a clock; the harmonious sound of bells or other musical instruments; agreement of sound or of relation; harmony; rhyme; jingle. — *vi* to sound a chime or in chime; to accord or agree; to jingle. — *vt* to strike, or cause to sound in chime; to indicate by chiming. — **chime in** to join in, in agreement. [M.E. *chimbe*, prob. O.Fr. *cymbale* — L. *cymbalum*, a cymbal.]

chime[2] or **chimb** *chīm*, *n* the rim formed by the ends of the staves of a cask. [Cognate with Ger. *Kimme*, edge.]

chimer *chim'ər* or **chimere** *chi-mēr'*, *n* a long sleeveless tabard; the upper robe worn by a bishop. [O.Fr. *chamarre*.]

chimera or **chimaera** *kī-* or *ki-mē'rə*, *n* (often with *cap*) a fabulous, fire-spouting monster, with a lion's head, a serpent's tail, and a goat's body; any idle or wild fancy; a picture of an animal having its parts made up of various animals; an organism made up of two genetically distinct tissues. — *n* **chimaer'id** a fish of the genus *Chimaera* or related genera of the family **Chimaer'idae** (*-i-dē*). — *adj* **chimeric** (*-mer'ik*) or **chimer'ical** of the nature of a chimera; wild; fanciful; pertaining to an organism made up of genetically distinct tissues. — *adv* **chimer'ically**. [L., — Gr. *chimaira*, a she-goat.]

chimney *chim'ni*, *n* a passage for the escape of fumes, smoke, or heated air from a fireplace or furnace; a glass tube surrounding a lamp flame; a volcanic vent; a cleft in a rock-face just large enough for a mountaineer to enter and climb. — **chim'ney-breast** the part of a wall that projects into a room and contains the fireplace and chimney; **chim'ney-corner** or **chim'ney-nook** in old chimneys, the space between the fire and the side-wall of the fireplace; the fireside, commonly spoken of as the place for the aged and infirm; **chim'ney-piece** a shelf over the fireplace; **chim'ney-pot** a cylindrical pipe at the top of a chimney; **chim'ney-stack** a group of chimneys carried up together; a chimney-stalk; **chim'ney-stalk** a very tall chimney; **chim'ney-sweep** a person who sweeps or cleans chimneys; **chim'ney-top** the top of a chimney. [Fr. *cheminée* — L. *camīnus*, a furnace.]

chimpanzee *chim-pən-zē'*, *n* one of the African anthropoid apes: — often shortened to **chimp**. [W. Afr.]

Chin. *abbrev* for: China; Chinese.

chin *chin*, *n* the jutting part of the face below the mouth. — *adj* **chin'less** having a receding chin; upper-class and not very clever, esp. in *chinless wonder* (*facetious*). — **chin'strap** the strap on a helmet, etc. that goes under the chin. — *n* and *vi* **chin'wag** (*slang*) talk. — **keep one's chin up** to keep cheerful in a difficult situation (usu. reduced to **chin up!** in exhortation); **take it on the chin** to be courageous in misfortune. [O.E. *cin*; Gr. *genys* (jaw).]

china *chī'nə*, *n* articles of porcelain brought from China in 16th cent.; Chinese porcelain or, esp., Western imitation or version of it; mate (*Cockney rhyming slang* from *china plate*). — *adj* made of china; (with *cap*) of, from, etc., China. — *n* **Chinese** (*chī-nēz'*) a native or citizen of China (*pl* **Chīnese'**); the language of China. — *adj* (in names of commodities, sometimes without *cap*) of, concerning or relating, etc. to China, its language or its people. — **china clay** fine white clay used in making porcelain, etc.; **China goose** the Chinese goose; **Chi'naman** a Chinese (*derog*); **China tea** a kind of tea grown in China and smoke-cured; **Chi'natown** a Chinese quarter in a town; **Chinese block** see **Chinese temple block**; **Chinese boxes** a set of boxes nesting one inside another, so that when one opens one box, one finds yet another to open inside it; **Chinese cabbage** either of two kinds of plant, *Brassica chinensis* or *Brassica pekinensis*, with edible leaves; **Chinese checkers** a board game similar to draughts; **Chinese goose** the largest living goose (*Anser*, or *Cygnopsis*, *cygnoides*), domesticated in East Asia; **Chinese gooseberry** a subtropical vine with edible fruit that is commonly called **kiwi fruit**; **Chinese lantern** a paper lantern; **Chinese leaves** Chinese cabbage; **Chinese puzzle** a very difficult puzzle or problem; **Chinese wall** or **walls** the strict demarcation barriers which must exist between e.g. the corporate finance and investment advisory departments of a bank, etc. in order to ensure that privileged information available to one department is not available to the other and so prevent conflicts of interest from arising. — **Chinese temple block** or **Chinese block** a percussion instrument consisting of a hollow wooden block that is struck with a hammer. [Prob. from the *Ch'in* dynasty, third cent. B.C.]

Chinagraph® *chī'nə-gräf*, *n* a kind of pencil that writes on glass, porcelain, etc. [**china** and **-graph**.]

chinch *chinch*, *n* the bed-bug in America. [Sp. *chinche* — L. *cimex*.]

chincherinchee *ching-kə-rin-chē'* or **chinkerinchee** *chin-kə-rin'chē*, *n* a white-flowered S.African plant of the star-of-Bethlehem genus. — Also (*colloq*) **chinks**. [Said to be imit. of the flower-stalks rubbing together in the wind.]

chinchilla *chin-chil'ə*, *n* a small rodent of South America valued for its soft grey fur; the fur itself; (with *cap*) a breed of rabbits, or of cats, with soft grey fur. [Sp.]

chin-chin *chin-chin'*, (*colloq*) *interj* hello; good-bye; good health! (as a toast). [Anglo-Chin. — Chin. *ts'ing ts'ing*.]

chindit *chin'dit*, *n* a member of General Wingate's commando force in Burma during World War II. [Burmese *chinthey*, a griffin, the force's badge.]

chine[1] *chīn*, *n* a piece of the backbone and adjoining parts (esp. of a pig) for cooking; a ridge crest. — *vt* to break the back of. [O.Fr. *eschine*, prob. from O.H.G. *scina*, pin, thorn.]

chine[2] *chīn*, *n* a ravine. [O.E. *cinu*, a cleft.]

chiné *shē-nā'*, *adj* mottled, with the pattern printed on the warp. [Fr., dyed in a (supposedly) Chinese way.]

Chinese. See under **china**.

Chink *chingk*, **Chinkie** or **Chinky** *chingk'i*, (*colloq* and *offensive*) *n* and *adj* Chinese. — *n* **chink'ie** or **chink'y** (*colloq*) a meal of Chinese food. [**China**.]

chink[1] *chingk*, *n* a cleft, a narrow opening. — *vi* to crack. — *vt* to fill up cracks. — *adj* **chink'y** full of chinks. — **chink in someone's armour** a significant weakness. [App. formed upon M.E. *chine*, a crack — O.E. *cinu*, a cleft.]

chink[2] *chingk*, *n* the clink, as of coins; money (*slang*). — *vi* to emit a sharp sound. — *vt* to clink together. [Imit.]

chinkerinchee, chinks. See **chincherinchee.**

chino *chē'nō*, (orig. *US*) *n* strong khaki-like twilled cotton; (in *pl*) trousers made of it: — *pl* **chi'nos.** [Am., — Sp.]

chinoiserie *shē-nwä-zə-rē* or *-zrē*, (Fr.) *n* Chinese objects, decoration, behaviour, etc.

Chinook *chin-ōōk'*, *n* a warm dry wind blowing down the eastern side of the Rocky Mountains, making winter grazing possible; also a warm moist wind from the Pacific.

chintz *chints*, *n* a cotton printed generally in several colours on a white or light ground. — *adj* **chintz'y** covered with, or like, chintz; cheap, gaudy. [Orig. pl. — Hindi *chīt*, spotted cotton cloth.]

chip *chip*, *vt* to strike with small sharp cutting blows; to strike small pieces off the surface of (also with *at*); to remove by chipping (often with *away* or *off*); to slice or pare; to cut as with an adze; to chaff, tease (*colloq*). — *vi* to become chipped; to play a chip-shot: — *pr p* **chipp'ing;** *pa t* and *pa p* **chipped.** — *n* an act of chipping; a piece chipped off, esp. a flattish fragment; a small fragment of stone (also **chipp'ing**); a surface flaw; a thin slice of fruit, etc.; a potato-chip; a potato-crisp (*NAm*); a thin strip of wood, used for making boxes, baskets, etc.; a chip-basket; a small, flat piece of wood, plastic, etc. used to represent money in certain games; a minute piece of silicon or other semiconducting material on which one or more microcircuits can be formed (also **microchip** or **silicon chip**); a hit or kick which sends a ball high into the air over a short distance (*sport*). — *n* **chipp'ing** see **chip** above. — *adj* **chipp'y** abounding in chips; dry as a chip; touchy, quarrelsome, aggressive (*Can colloq*); having a chip on one's shoulder (see below; *colloq*). — *n* (a meal from) a chip-shop (*colloq*; also **chipp'ie**). — *n* **chips** (*slang*) a carpenter (also **chipp'y**); money. — *npl* fried potato-chips (*colloq*). — **chip'-basket** a fruit basket of interwoven chips; a metal basket in which potato-chips are placed for frying; **chip'board** reconstructed wood made by consolidation of chips from woodland trimmings, workshop waste, etc., with added resin; **chip'-shop** a restaurant selling take-away meals of fish and chips, etc.; **chip'-shot** (*golf*) a short lofted approach. — **chip in** to enter the game by putting chips on the table; to interpose; to pay part of the cost of something (*colloq*); **chip off the old block** someone with the characteristics of their father; **chip on one's shoulder** a defiant manner, as if daring anyone to knock it off; readiness to take offence; bitterness, grievance; **have had one's chips** to have died; to have had one's chance; to have been beaten; **when the chips are down** at a critical moment when it is too late to alter the situation. [M.E. *chippen*; M.L.G., M.Du. *kippen*, to hatch by chipping shell.]

chipmunk *chip'mungk*, *n* a North American squirrel. [From Am.Ind. name.]

chipolata *chip-ə-lä'tə*, *n* a small, slim sausage. [Fr., — It. *cipolla*, onion.]

Chippendale *chip'ən-dāl*, *adj* applied to a style of furniture, after the name of a well-known cabinet-maker of the 18th cent.; also applied to a style of book-plates.

chipper *chip'ər*, *adj* briskly cheerful; well, fit. [Perh. Northern dialect *kipper*, lively.]

chirality *kī-ral'i-ti*, *n* the property of a chemical of existing in left-handed and right-handed structural forms; the handedness of such a chemical. — *adj* **chī'ral.** [Gr. *cheir*, hand.]

chiro-. See **cheiro-.**

Chiron *kī'rən*, *n* name given to a body thought to be a minor planet with an orbit between Saturn and Uranus, but now reckoned to be a very large comet. [Gr., name of mythological teacher.]

chiropodist *ki-rop'ə-dist*, *n* a person who treats minor ailments of the feet, e.g. corns, verrucas. — *adj* **chiropō'dial.** — *n* **chirop'ody.** [App. Gr. *cheir*, hand, and *pous*, *podos*, foot; but *cheiropodēs* means having chapped feet.]

chiropractic *kī-rə-prak'tik*, *n* a method of healing concerned with disorders of the locomotor system, which relies upon the removal of nerve interference by manual adjustment of the spinal column, etc.; a chiropractor. — *n* **chīroprac'tor** a person who practises chiropractic. [Gr. *cheir*, hand, *prāktikos*, concerned with action — *prattein*, to do.]

chirp *chûrp*, *n* the sharp thin sound of certain birds and insects. — *vi* to make such a sound; to talk in a cheerful and lively strain. — *vt* to urge by chirping. — *n* **chirp'er.** — *adv* **chirp'ily.** — *n* **chirp'iness.** — *adj* **chirp'ing.** — *adj* **chirp'y** lively; merry. [Imit.]

chirr *chûr*, *vi* to chirp like a cricket or grasshopper. [Imit.]

chirrup *chir'əp*, *vi* to chirp; to make a sound with the mouth to urge on a horse; to cheer up. — *adj* **chirr'upy** cheerful. [Lengthened form of **chirp**, associated with **cheer up.**]

chisel *chiz'l*, *n* a tool with the end bevelled to a cutting edge, in literature esp. the tool of the sculptor. — *vt* to cut, carve, etc. with a chisel; to cheat (*slang*): — *pr p* **chis'elling;** *pa t* and *pa p* **chis'elled.** — *adj* **chis'elled** cut with a chisel; having sharp outlines, as cut by a chisel (*fig*). — *n* **chis'elling.** [O.Fr. *cisel* — L. *caedĕre*, to cut.]

chit[1] *chit*, *n* a short informal letter, a note; a bill which one signs and pays at a later date; a receipt; an order or pass; testimonial. — Also **chitt'y.** [Hindi *citthī*.]

chit[2] *chit*, *n* a child; a girl (*slightingly*). — *adj* **chitt'y.** — *adj* **chitt'y-faced.** [*kit*, contr. of **kitten.**]

chitchat *chit'chat*, *n* chatting or idle talk; prattle; gossip. — *vi* to chat, gossip. [A reduplication of **chat**[1].]

chitin *kī'tin*, *n* the substance which forms most of the hard parts of arthropods. — *adj* **chī'tinous.** [Fr. *chitine* — Gr. *chĭtōn*, a tunic.]

chiton *kī'ton*, *n* the tunic worn by ancient Greeks; (with *cap*) a genus of marine molluscs with shell of movable plates. [Gr. *chitōn*, a tunic.]

chitterling *chit'ər-ling*, *n* (also in *pl*) the smaller intestines of a pig or other edible animal.

chiv *chiv* or **shiv** *shiv*, (*slang*) *n* and *vt* knife. [From older *chive*, knife (*thieves' slang*) or perh. Romany *chiv*, blade.]

chivalry *shiv'əl-ri*, *n* the usages and qualifications of chevaliers or knights; bravery and courtesy; the system of knighthood in feudal times and its social code; a body of knights; noblemen, knights collectively. — *adj* **chivalric** (*-al'rik*) or **chiv'alrous** pertaining to chivalry; bold; gallant. — *adv* **chiv'alrously.** — *n* **chiv'alrousness.** [Fr. *chevalerie* — *cheval* — L.L. *caballus*, a horse.]

chive *chīv*, *n* a herb like the leek and onion, with tufts of leaves (used in cooking) and clustered bulbs. [Fr. *cive* — L. *cēpa*, an onion.]

chivvy, chivy *chiv'i* or **chevy** *chev'i*, *vt* to harass, pester; to urge on. [Perh. from the Border ballad of battle, *Chevy Chase.*]

chlamys *klam'is*, *n* (in ancient Greece) a short cloak for men; a purple cope: — *pl* **chlam'ydes** (*-i-dēz*). — *adj* **chlam'ydate** (*zool*) having a mantle. — *adj* **chlamyd'eous** (*bot*) having a perianth. — *n* **chlamydia** (*klə-mid'i-ə*) any micro-organism of the genus *Chlamydia* resembling viruses and bacteria, which cause disease in man and birds; a sexually transmitted disease caused by *Chlamydia trachomatis.* — *n* **Chlamydō'mōnas** a genus of freshwater algae. — *n* **chlam'ydospore** a thick-walled spore. — *adj* **chlamyd'ial.** [Gr. *chlamys*, pl. *chlamydĕs*.]

chloasma *klō-az'mə*, *n* a skin disease marked by yellowish-brown patches. [Gr. *chloasma*, greenness, yellowness — *chloē*, verdure.]

chloracne *klör-ak'ni, n* a type of disfiguring skin disease resembling acne in appearance, caused by contact with chlorinated hydrocarbons.

chlorine *klö'rēn, -rin* or *-rīn, n* a yellowish-green gas (symbol **Cl**; atomic no. 17) with a peculiar and suffocating odour, used in bleaching, disinfecting, and poison gas warfare. — *n* **chlor'al** (or *-al'*) a limpid, colourless, oily liquid ($CCl_3{\cdot}CHO$), of penetrating odour, formed when anhydrous alcohol is acted on by dry chlorine gas; (*loosely*) *chloral hydrate*, a white crystalline substance used as a hypnotic. — *n* **chlo'ralism** the habit, or the morbid effects, of using chloral hydrate. — *n* **chloram'bucil** (*-bū-sil*) an oral drug used to treat some cancers, e.g. leukaemia. — *n* **chlo'rate** a salt of chloric acid. — *adj* **chlo'ric** or **chlo'rous** of or from chlorine. — *n* **chlo'rīde** a compound of chlorine with another element or radical; bleaching powder (*chloride of lime*), not a true chloride. — *vt* **chlo'ridise** or **-ize** to convert into a chloride; to cover with chloride of silver (*phot*). — *vt* **chlor'inate** to treat with chlorine (as in sterilisation of water or extraction of gold from ore). — *n* **chlorinā'tion.** — *vt* **chlo'rinise** or **-ize** to chlorinate. — *n* **chlo'rite** a salt of chlorous acid (*chem*); a general name for a group of minerals, hydrated silicates of magnesia, iron and alumina. — *adj* **chlorit'ic** pertaining to, of the nature of, or containing, the mineral chlorite. — *n* **chlorofluorocar'bon** (usu. in *pl*) one of certain gases which can be used e.g. as propellants for aerosols, as cooling agents, and in the manufacture of polystyrene foam, but they cause irreparable damage to the ozone layer around the earth. — *n* **chloroform** (*klor'ə-förm*) a limpid, mobile, colourless, volatile liquid ($CHCl_3$) with a characteristic odour and a strong sweetish taste, used to induce unconsciousness. — *vt* to administer chloroform to. — *n* **chlor'oformer** or **chloroform'ist.** — *n* **Chloromy'cetin**® (or *-mī-sēt'in*) a drug used against typhoid, cerebrospinal meningitis, etc. — *n* **chlorophyll** or **chlorophyl** (*klor'ə-fil*) the ordinary green colouring matter of vegetation. — *n* **chlo'roplast** a chlorophyll-bearing plastid. — *n* **chloroprene** a colourless fluid derived from acetylene and hydrochloric acid. — *n* **chlorō'sis** properly *green sickness*, a form of anaemia affecting young women; blanching of the green parts of a plant, esp. for want of iron (*bot*). — *adj* **chlorot'ic** pertaining to or affected by chlorosis. — *n* **chlorprō'mazine** a tranquillising drug. — **chloric acid** ($HClO_3$), a monobasic acid, a vigorous oxidising agent. [Gr. *chlōros*, pale green.]

ChM *abbrev* for *Chirurgiae Magister* (L.) Master of Surgery.

CHO *abbrev* for Confederation of Healing Organisations.

choc *chok*, (*colloq*) *n* and *adj* a short form of **chocolate.** — **choc'-ice** or **choc'-bar** an ice-cream with a chocolate covering.

chocaholic or **chocoholic** *chok-ə-hol'ik, n* a person who is addicted to chocolate. [*choc*olate, and **-aholic** or **-oholic.**]

chock *chok, vt* to fasten as with a block or wedge. — *n* a wedge to prevent movement; a log. — *adj* **chock-a-block'** or **chock-full'** quite full. — *adj* **chock'-tight** very tight. [See **choke.**]

chocoholic. See **chocaholic.**

chocolate *chok'ə-lit* or *chok'lət, n* a paste made of the ground seeds of *Theobroma cacao* (cocoa), with sugar and flour or similar material; a sweet made of, or covered with, the paste; a beverage made by dissolving the paste, or a powder prepared from it, in hot water or milk. — *adj* chocolate-coloured, dark reddish-brown; made of or flavoured with chocolate. — *adj* **choc'olaty** or **choc'olatey.** — *adj* **choc'olate-box** pretty-pretty or over-sentimental, esp. of a painting. [Sp. *chocolate*; from Nahuatl, *chocólatl*, a mixture containing chocolate.]

Choctaw *chok'tö, n* an American Indian of a tribe formerly chiefly in Mississippi; the tribe, or its language; (sometimes without *cap*) a skating movement, forward on the edge of one foot, then backward on the opposite edge of the other. [Choctaw *Chahta.*]

choice *chois, n* the act or power of choosing; the thing chosen; an alternative; a preference; the preferable or best part; variety from which to choose. — *adj* worthy of being chosen; select; appropriate. — *adv* **choice'ly** with discrimination or care. — *n* **choice'ness** particular value; excellence; nicety. — **by, for** or **from choice** by preference; **Hobson's choice** the choice of a thing offered or nothing (from *Hobson*, a Cambridge horse keeper, who lent out the horse nearest the stable door, or none at all); **make choice of** to select; **take one's choice** to take what one wishes. [Fr. *choix* — *choisir*; cf. **choose.**]

choir *kwīr, n* a chorus or band of singers, esp. those belonging to a church; the part of a church appropriated to the singers; a group of instruments of the same class playing together. — **choir'boy, choir'-girl** or **choir'man** a boy, girl or man who sings in a choir; **choir'master** the director of a choir; **choir school** a school usu. maintained by a cathedral to educate boys who also sing in the choir; **choir'-screen** a screen of latticework, separating the choir from the nave. — *npl* **choir'-stalls** fixed seats in the choir of a church, generally of carved wood. [Fr. *chœur* — L. *chorus* — Gr. *choros*; see **chorus.**]

choke *chōk, vt* to stop or interfere with the breathing of (whether by compression, blocking, fumes, emotion, or otherwise); to injure or suppress by obstruction, overshadowing, or deprivation of air, etc.; to constrict; to block; to clog; to obstruct. — *vi* to be choked; to die (*slang*); to lose one's nerve when facing an important challenge. — *n* a complete or partial stoppage of breath; the sound of choking; a constriction; a device to prevent the passage of too much petrol, oil, gas, electric current, etc. — *adj* **choked** (*colloq*) angry; upset. — *n* **chōk'er** that which or someone who chokes; a large neck-cloth; a very high collar; a close-fitting necklace or jewelled collar. — *n* **chokey** see separate entry **choky.** — *adj* **chōk'y** tending to, or inclined to, choke. — **choke'-damp** carbon dioxide or other suffocating gas in mines; **chok'ing-coil** a coil of thick wire, used to limit the supply of electric light. — **choke back** or **down** to repress as if by a choking action; **choke off** to get rid of; to deter by force, to discourage; **choke up** to fill completely; to block up.

choky or **chokey** *chō'ki, n* a prison; a toll-station. [Hindi *caukī.*]

cholangiography *kol-an-ji-og'rə-fi, n* the examination by X-ray of the gall bladder and bile-ducts. [Gr. *cholē*, bile, *angeion*, case, vessel.]

cholecyst *kō'li-sist, n* the gall bladder. — *n* **cholecystec'tomy** excision of the gall bladder. — *n* **cholecystī'tis** inflammation of the gall bladder. — *n* **cholecystos'tomy** or **cholecystot'omy** surgical opening of the gall bladder. [Gr. *cholē*, bile, *kystis*, a bladder.]

choler *kol'ər, n* the bile; anger, irascibility. — *adj* **chol'eric** full of choler; passionate. — *adv* **chol'erically** (also *-er'ik-əl-i*). [Gr. *cholerā* — *cholē*, bile, partly through Fr.]

cholera *kol'ər-ə, n* a highly infectious and deadly disease characterised by bilious vomiting and purging. — *adj* **choleraic** (*kol-ər-ā'ik*). [Gr. *cholerā* — *cholē*, bile.]

choleric. See **choler.**

cholesterol *ko-les'tər-ol, n* an alcohol ($C_{27}H_{45}OH$), occurring abundantly in gallstones, nerves, bloodstream, etc., a white crystalline solid, thought to be a cause of arteriosclerosis. — *adj* **cholester'ic.** [Gr. *cholē*, bile, *stereos*, solid.]

choli *chō'lē*, *n* a short, short-sleeved blouse often worn under a sari. [Hindi *colī*.]

cholic *kol'ik* or *kōl'ik*, *adj* pertaining to bile, as **cholic acid** ($C_{24}H_{40}O_5$) got from bile. — *n* **chol'ine** (*kō'lin* or *-lēn'*) an alcohol ($C_5H_{15}NO_2$) found in bile, used in the synthesis of lecithin, etc., and in preventing accumulation of fat in the liver. [Gr. *cholē*, bile.]

chomp *chomp*, (*colloq*) *vt* and *vi* to munch with noisy enjoyment. — *n* the act or sound of munching thus. [Variant of **champ**[1].]

chondrus *kon'drəs*, *n* a cartilage; a chondrule: — *pl* **chon'drī**. — *adj* **chon'dral**. — *n* **chondre** (*kon'dər*) a chondrule. — *n* **chondrificā'tion** formation of chondrin or development of or change into cartilage. — *vt* and *vi* **chon'drify** to change into cartilage. — *n* **chon'drin** a firm elastic, translucent, bluish-white gelatinous substance, the ground-substance of cartilage. — *n* **chon'drite** a meteorite containing chondrules. — *adj* **chondrit'ic**. — *adj* **chon'droid** like cartilage. — *n* **chon'drule** a rounded granule found in meteorites and in deep-sea deposits. [Gr. *chondros*, a grain, grit, cartilage.]

choo-choo *choo'choo*, *n* a child's word for a railway train. [Imit.]

chook *chook*, (*colloq*, esp. *Austr*) *n* a hen, chicken. [Imit.]

choose *chooz*, *vt* to take or pick out in preference to another thing; to select; to will or determine; to think fit. — *vi* to make a choice (between, from, etc.): — *pa t* **chose** (*chōz*); *pa p* **chos'en**. — *n* **choos'er**. — *adj* **choos'ey** or **choos'y** (*colloq*) difficult to please, fastidious. — **not much to choose between** each about equally good or bad; **pick and choose** to select with care or at leisure; **the chosen people** the Israelites (1 Chronicles xvi. 13). [O.E. *cēosan*, Du. *kiesen*.]

chop[1] *chop*, *vt* to cut with a sudden blow (away, down, off, etc.); to cut into small pieces; to reduce greatly or abolish (*colloq*). — *vi* to hack; to crack or fissure; to take a direction (running into **chop**[2]): — *pr p* **chopp'ing**; *pa t* and *pa p* **chopped**. — *n* an act of chopping; chopped food; a piece cut off; a slice of mutton or pork, containing a rib; a crack; a sharp downward blow; (with *the*) dismissal (*colloq*). — *n* **chopp'er** someone who or that which chops; a cleaver; a helicopter (*slang*); (in *pl*) teeth (*slang*). — *n* and *adj* **chopp'ing**. — *adj* **chopp'y** full of chops or cracks; (of the sea, etc.) running in irregular waves. — **chop'-house** a house where mutton-chops and beefsteaks are served; an eating-house; **chopp'ing-block** or **chopp'ing-board** one on which material to be chopped is placed; **chopp'ing-knife** a knife for chopping up food. — **chop at** to aim a blow at; **chop in** to break in, interrupt; **chop up** to cut into small pieces; **for the chop** (*slang*) about to be dismissed; **get the chop** (*slang*) to be dismissed from one's job, etc.; to be killed. [A form of **chap**[1].]

chop[2] *chop*, *vt* and *vi* to change direction (running into **chop**[1]): — *pr p* **chopp'ing**; *pa t* and *pa p* **chopped**. — *n* an exchange; a change. — **chop-log'ic** chopping of logic; someone who chops logic. — **chop and change** to change about; **chop logic** to argue contentiously; **chops and changes** vicissitudes. [Connection with **chop**[1] and with **chap**[2] is not clear.]

chop[3] *chop*, *n* the chap or jaw. — *adj* **chop'fallen** lit. having the chop or lower jaw fallen down; cast-down, dejected. — **lick one's chops** (*colloq*) to await eagerly or greedily. [See **chap**[3].]

chop[4] *chop*, *n* in China and India, a seal; a brand; a sealed document. — **first chop** best quality; **no chop** no good. [Hindi *chāp*, seal, impression.]

chop-chop *chop-chop'*, *adv* promptly. [Pidgin Eng.]

chopstick *chop'stik*, *n* (usu. in *pl*) either of two small sticks used, esp. by the Chinese, instead of a fork. [**chop-chop**, and **stick**[2].]

chop-suey *chop-soo'i*, *n* a miscellaneous Chinese-style dish, fried in sesame-oil. [Chin., mixed bits.]

choral, chorale. See **chorus**.

chord[1] *körd*, (*mus*) *n* the simultaneous union of sounds of a different pitch. — *adj* **chord'al**. [From **accord**.]

chord[2] *körd*, *n* a string of a musical instrument (*poetic*); a sensitive area of the emotions (*fig*); a straight line joining any two points on a curve (*geom*); a cord (see **spinal, vocal**); the straight line joining the leading and the trailing edges of an aerofoil section (*aeronautics*). — *adj* **chord'al**. — *npl* **Chordāt'a** the highest phylum or division of the animal kingdom, including the vertebrates — animals possessing a notochord. — *n* **chor'date** a member of the Chordata. — Also *adj*. — *n* **chordophone** (*kör'dō-fōn*; *mus*) a stringed instrument. — *adj* **chordophonic** (*-fon'ik*). — *n* **chordotomy** see **cord**. — **strike a chord** to prompt a feeling of recognition, familiarity, etc. [Gr. *chordē*, a string, intestine.]

chore *chör*, *n* a household task; an unenjoyable task. [Form (orig. U.S.) of **char**[3].]

chorea *ko-rē'ə*, *n* St Vitus's dance, a nervous disease, causing irregular involuntary movements of the limbs or face. [L., — Gr. *choreiā*, a dance.]

choreography, choreographer, etc. See under **chorus**.

choria. See **chorion**.

choriamb *kor'i-amb*, *n* (in verse) a foot of four syllables, the first and last long, the others short. — *adj* and *n* **choriam'bic**. [Gr. *choriambos* — *choreios*, a trochee, *iambos*, iambus.]

choric. See under **chorus**.

chorion *kö'ri-on*, *n* the outer foetal envelope: — *pl* **cho'ria**. — *adj* **cho'rioid**. — *adj* **cho'roid**. [Gr. *chorion*.]

chorist, etc. See under **chorus**.

chorizo *cho-rē'zō*, *n* a dry, highly-seasoned sausage, made from pork. [Sp.]

chorography *kö-rog'rə-fi*, *n* geography; topography. — *adj* **chorographic** (*-ro-graf'ik*) or **chorograph'ical**. — *adj* **chorolog'ical**. — *n* **chorol'ogist**. — *n* **chorol'ogy** the science of geographical distribution. [Gr. *chōrā*, region, country.]

choroid. See **chorion**.

chortle *chört'l*, *vi* to chuckle; to utter a low, deep laugh. — Also *n*. [Coined by Lewis Carroll in 1872.]

chorus *kö'rəs*, *n* a band of singers and dancers; in Greek plays, a number of persons, or a person, who between the episodes danced, and chanted comment and counsel; a company of singers; a composition which is sung by a chorus; the combination of voices in one simultaneous utterance; a refrain, in which the company may join. — *vt* to sing or say together: — *pr p* **cho'rusing**; *pa t* and *pa p* **cho'rused**. — *adj* **chor'al** pertaining to a chorus or a choir. — *n* (*ko-räl'*; often altered to **chorale'**) a simple harmonised composition with slow rhythm; a psalm or hymn tune. — *adv* **chor'ally** in the manner of a chorus; suitable for a choir. — *adj* **choric** (*kor'ik* or *kö'rik*). — *n* **chorist** (*kor'ist* or *kö'rist*) or **chor'ister** a member of a choir. — *vt* **chor'eograph** to compose or arrange (a dance, dances, etc.). — *vi* to practise choreography. — *n* **chor'eograph** or **choreographer** (*kor-i-og'rə-fər*). — *adj* **choreographic** (*-graf'ik*). — *n* **choreog'raphy** or **choreg'raphy** the art, or the notation, of dancing, esp. ballet-dancing; the art of arranging or composing dances, esp. ballets; the arrangement of a ballet. — *n* **choreol'ogist**. — *n* **choreol'ogy** the study of ballets and their history. — **chor'us-girl** a woman employed to sing or dance in a chorus on the stage; **chorus master** the director of a choir. [L., — Gr. *choros*, dance; see also **choir**.]

chose, chosen. See **choose**.

chou *shōō*, *n* a soft rosette; a cream bun; dear, pet: — *pl* **choux** (*shōō*). — **choux pastry** very light, rich pastry. [Fr.]
chough *chuf*, *n* the red-legged crow, or any bird of the genus *Fregilus* or *Pyrrhocorax*. [Perh. from its cry.]
choux. See **chou**.
chow *chow*, *n* food; a Chinese mixed condiment; a mixed fruit preserve; a dog of a Chinese breed. — *adj* mixed, miscellaneous. [Pidgin Eng., food.]
chowder *chow'dər*, *n* a stew or thick soup made of fish with vegetables; a similar soup made with other main ingredients. [Fr. *chaudière*, a pot.]
chow-mein *chow-mēn'* or *-mān'*, *n* fried noodles; a Chinese-style dish of seasoned shredded meat and vegetables, served with fried noodles. [Chin., fried noodles.]
CHP *abbrev* for combined heat and power.
Chr. *abbrev* for: Christ; Christian.
chrematist *krē'mə-tist*, *n* a political economist. — *adj* **chrematis'tic** pertaining to finance, money-making, or political economy. — *nsing* **chrematis'tics** the science of wealth. [Gr. *chrēmatistēs*, a money-getter.]
chrism *krizm*, *n* consecrated or holy oil; unction; a chrisom. — *adj* **chris'mal** pertaining to chrism. — *n* a case for containing chrism; a veil used in christening. — *n* **chris'om** or **christ'om** a white cloth or robe (also **chris'om-cloth**) put on a child newly anointed with chrism after its baptism. [O.Fr. *chresme* (Fr. *chrême*) — Gr. *chrīsma* — *chrīein*, to anoint.]
Christ *krīst*, *n* the Anointed, a name given to Jesus; a Messiah. — *vt* **christen** (*kris'n*) to baptise in the name of Christ; to give a name to; to use for the first time (*colloq*). — *n* **Christendom** (*kris'n-dəm*) that part of the world in which Christianity is the received religion; the whole body of Christians. — *n* **christening** (*kris'ning*) the ceremony of baptism. — *n* **Christian** (*kris'chən*) a believer in the religion based on the teachings of Christ or one so classified; a follower of Christ; a person whose behaviour is considered becoming to a follower of Christ; often a vague term of approbation, a decent, respectable person. — *adj* relating to Christ or his religion; in the spirit of Christ. — *n* **christianīsā'tion** or **-z-**. — *vt* **christ'ianise** or **-ize** to make Christian; to convert to Christianity. — *n* **christ'ianiser** or **-z-**. — *n* **Christ'ianism**. — *n* **Christianity** (*kris-ti-an'i-ti*) the religion of Christ; the spirit of this religion. — *adj* **Christ'ianlike**. — *adj* **Christ'ianly**. — Also adv. — *n* **Christ'ianness**. — *adj* **Chrīst'like**. — *n* **Chrīst'-liness**. — *adj* **Chrīst'ly** like Christ. — **Christian era** the era counted from the date formerly assigned to the birth of Christ; **Christian name** the name given at christening; the personal name as distinguished from the surname; **Christian Science** a religion which includes spiritual or divine healing, founded in 1866 by Mrs Eddy; **Christian Scientist**. [O.E. *Crīst* — Gr. *Chrīstos* — *chrīein*, to anoint.]
Christadelphian *kris-tə-del'fi-ən*, *n* a member of a small religious body believing in conditional immortality. [Gr. *Chrīstos*, Christ, *adelphos*, brother.]
Christiania *kris-ti-än'i-ə*, also **Chris'tie** or **Chris'ty** (also without *caps*) *n* a turn with skis parallel executed when descending at speed. [Former name of Oslo.]
Christmas *kris'məs*, *n* an annual festival, orig. a mass, in memory of the birth of Christ, held on 25 December (**Christmas Day**); the season at which it occurs. — Also *adj*. — *adj* **Christ'massy** or **Christ'masy**. — **Christmas box** a box containing Christmas presents; a Christmas gift, often of money, to tradesmen, etc.; **Christmas cake** a rich fruit-cake, usu. iced, made for Christmas; **Christmas card** a card sent to one's friends at Christmas; **Christmas daisy** the aster; **Christmas Eve** 24 December; **Christmas pudding** a rich, spicy fruit-pudding, eaten at Christmas; **Christ'mas-tide** or **Christ'mas-time** the season of Christmas; **Christmas tree** a tree, usu. fir, set up in a room or a public place, and loaded with Christmas gifts and/or decorations. [**Christ** and **mass**[2].]
Christology *kris-tol'ə-ji*, *n* that branch of theology which is concerned with the nature and person of Christ. — *adj* **Christological** (*-to-loj'i-kl*). — *n* **Christol'ogist**. [Gr. *Chrīstos*, *logos*, discourse.]
christom *kriz'əm*. See **chrisom** under **chrism**.
Christy. See **Christiania**.
chroma *krō'mə*, *n* quality of colour; a hue. — *n* **chrō'mate** a salt of chromic acid. — *adj* **chrōmat'ic** pertaining to, or consisting of, colours; coloured; relating to notes in a melodic progression, which are raised or lowered by accidentals, without changing the key of the passage, and also to chords in which such notes occur (*mus*). — *adv* **chrōmat'ically**. — *n* **chrōmaticity** (*-tis'*) the colour quality of light depending on hue and saturation. — *nsing* **chrō-mat'ics** the science of colours. — *n* **chrō'matin** a readily stained substance in the nucleus of a cell. — *adj* **chrōmatograph'ic**. — *n* **chrōmatog'raphy** methods of separating substances in a mixture which depend on selective adsorption, partition between non-mixing solvents, etc., using a **chrōmat'ograph**, and which present the substances as a **chrōmat'o-gram**, such as a series of visible bands in a vertical tube. — *n* **chrome** chromium or a chromium compound. — Also *adj*. — *vt* in dyeing, to treat with a chromium solution; to plate with chromium. — *adj* **chrō'mite** a mineral, a double oxide of chromium and iron. — *n* **chrō'mium** a metallic element (atomic no. 24; symbol **Cr**) remarkable for the beautiful colour of its compounds. — *n* **chrō'mōsome** a rod-like portion of the chromatin of a cell nucleus, performing an important part in mitotic cell-division, and in the transmission of hereditary characters. — *adj* **chrōmosō'mal**. — *n* **chrōmakey** (*TV*) a special effect in which a coloured background can be removed from a picture and a different background substituted. — **chromatic aberration** blurring of an optical image, with colouring of the edges, caused by light of different wavelengths being focused at different distances; **chromatic scale** (*mus*) a scale proceeding by semitones; **chrome-plat'ing** electroplating with chromium; **chrome-steel'** an alloy steel containing chromium; **chrome-yell'ow** a pigment of lead chromate; **chromic acid** an acid of chromium (H_2CrO_4), of an orange-red colour, much used in dyeing and bleaching; **chromosome number** the number of chromosomes in a cell nucleus, constant for any given species. [Gr. *chrōma*, *-atos*, colour.]
Chron. (*Bible*) *abbrev* for (the Books of) Chronicles.
chron. *abbrev* for: chronicle; chronological; chronology.
chron- *kron'*, *krən-* or **chrono-** *-o-*, *-ə-* or *kron-o'*, *combining form* denoting time. — *adj* **chron'ic** lasting a long time; (of a disease) deep seated or long continued (as opp. to *acute*); deplorable (*slang*). — *n* a chronic invalid. — *adj* **chron'ical** chronic. — *adv* **chron'ically**. — *n* **chronic'ity**. — *n* **chron'ograph** an instrument for taking exact measurements of time, or for recording graphically the moment or duration of an event. — *n* **chronog'rapher** a chronicler. — *n* **chronog'raphy** chronology. — *n* **chronol'oger**. — *adj* **chronolog'ic** or **chrono-log'ical**. — *adv* **chronolog'ically**. — *n* **chron-ol'ogist**. — *n* **chronol'ogy** the science of computing time; a scheme of time; order of time. — *n* **chron-om'eter** an instrument for accurate measurement of time. — *adj* **chronomet'ric** or **chronomet'rical**. — *n* **chronom'etry** the art of measuring time by means of instruments; measurement of time. — *n* **chrō'non** (*phys*) a unit of time — that required for a photon to travel the diameter of an electron, 10^{-24} seconds. — *n* **chron'oscope** an instrument used for

measuring extremely short intervals of time, esp. in determining the velocity of projectiles. — **chronological age** age in years, etc. (opp. e.g. to *mental age*). [Gr. *chronos*, time.]

chronicle *kron'i-kl*, *n* a bare record of events in order of time; a history; a story, account; (in *pl*, with *cap*) the name of two of the Old Testament books. — *vt* to record as a chronicle. — *n* **chron'icler** a writer of a chronicle. — **chronicle play** a drama which follows closely historical events and characters. [A.Fr. *cronicle* — L. — Gr. *khronika*, annals.]

chrys- *kris-* or **chryso-** *kris-ō-* or *-ə-*, *combining form* denoting gold. — *n* **chrys'alid** or **chrys'alis** orig. a golden-coloured butterfly pupa; a pupa generally; a pupa case: — *pl* **chrysalides** (*kris-al'i-dēz*), **chrys'-alises** or **chrys'alids.** — *n* **chrysan'themum** (*kris-* or *kriz-*) a plant of the *Chrysanthemum* genus of composite plants to which belong the corn marigold and ox-eye daisy; any of several cultivated plants of the genus, with colourful double flower-heads (often shortened to **chrysanth'**). — *adj* **chryselephant'-ine** made of gold and ivory. — *n* **chrysober'yl** a mineral, beryllium aluminate, of various shades of greenish-yellow or gold colour. — *n* **chrys'olite** olivine, esp. yellow or green precious olivine. — *n* **chrys'oprase** (*-prāz*) a green chalcedony. [Gr. *chrȳsos*, gold.]

chthonian *thō'ni-ən* or **chthonic** *thon'ik*, *adj* pertaining to the underworld and the deities inhabiting it; ghostly. [Gr. *chthōn*, *chthŏnos*, the ground.]

chub *chub*, *n* a small fat river-fish of the carp family. — *adj* **chubbed** or **chubb'y** short and thick, plump. — *n* **chubb'iness.**

chuck[1] *chuk*, *n* the call of a hen, a clucking noise; a chicken (dimin. **chuck'ie**); a word of endearment. — *vi* to call (as a hen does). [A variant of **cluck.**]

chuck[2] *chuk*, *n* a gentle blow under the chin; a toss or throw, hence dismissal (*colloq*). — *vt* to tap under the chin; to toss; to pitch; to abandon or dismiss. — **chucker-out'** (*colloq*) a person who expels undesirable people. — **chuck it** (*colloq*; sometimes with *in*) to stop, give over; **chuck out** (*colloq*) to expel (a person); to throw away, get rid of; **chuck up** (*colloq*) to give up; to give in; to vomit. [Fr. *choquer*, to jolt.]

chuck[3] *chuk*, *n* a lump or chunk; an instrument for holding an object so that it can be rotated, as on a lathe; food (*slang*); a cut of beef, the neck and shoulder blade.

chuckle[1] *chuk'l*, *n* a quiet laugh. — *vi* to laugh in a quiet, suppressed manner, in derision or enjoyment. — *n* **chuck'ling.** [Cf. **chuck[1]**.]

chuckle[2] *chuk'l*, *adj* clumsy. — **chuck'le-head** a loutish fellow. — *adj* **chuck'le-headed** stupid; awkward, clumsy. [Prob. **chock,** a log.]

chuddah, chuddar. Variants of **chadar.**

chuff *chuf* or **chuff-chuff** *chuf'chuf*, *vi* to make a series of puffing sounds, as a steam locomotive does; to move while making such sounds. [Imit.]

chuffed *chuft*, (*colloq*) *adj* very pleased. [Dialect *chuff*, chubby.]

chug *chug*, *n* a rapid explosive noise, as of an internal-combustion engine. — *adj* **chugg'ing.** — *vi* **chug** to make a chugging noise; (of a vehicle) to move while making such a noise. [Imit.]

chukker or **chukka** *chuk'ər* or *-ə*, *n* a period of play in polo. [Hindi *cakkar*, a round.]

chum *chum*, *n* a friend or associate. — *vi* to be or become a chum. — *vt* to be or become a chum to; to accompany. — *adj* **chumm'y** sociable. — **chum up with** to become intimate with. [Perh. a mutilation of *chamber-fellow*.]

chump *chump*, *n* an end lump of wood, mutton, etc.; a thick lump; a blockhead; the head. — **off one's chump** out of one's mind. [Perh. related to **chunk.**]

chunder *chun'dər*, (*Austr slang*) *vi* to vomit. — Also *n*.

chunk *chungk*, *n* a thick piece of anything, such as wood, bread, etc. — *adj* **chunk'y** in chunks; short and broad; (of sweaters, etc.) thick and heavy. [Perh. related to **chuck[3]**.]

Chunnel *chun'l*, (*colloq*) *n* (also without *cap*) the tunnel underneath the English Channel, connecting England and France. [*Ch*annel t*unnel*.]

chunter *chun'tər*, (*colloq*) *vi* (often with *on*) to mutter; to grumble; to chatter unceasingly. [Imit.]

chupati, chupatti. Same as **chapati, chapatti.**

church *chûrch*, *n* a building set apart for public worship, esp. that of a parish, and esp. that of an established or once established form of religion; a church service; the whole body of Christians; the clergy; any particular sect or denomination of Christians; any body professing a common creed. — *adj* of the church; ecclesiastical; belonging to the established church (*colloq*). — *vt* to perform a service in church with (e.g. a woman after childbirth). — *adj* **church'less.** — *adj* **church'ly** concerned with the church; ecclesiastical. — *adv* **church'ward** or **church'wards.** — *adj* **church'y** obtrusively devoted to the church; savouring of church. — **Church Army** an organisation of the Church of England, resembling the Salvation Army; **church'goer** a person on the way to, or who habitually goes to, church; **church'going** the act or habit of going to church; **church'man** a clergyman or ecclesiastic; a member or upholder of the established church; **church-off'icer** a church attendant; **church-parade'** a uniformed parade of a military or other body for the purpose of churchgoing; **church-ser'vice** a religious service in a church; the form followed; a book containing it; **church'-warden** an officer who represents the interests of a parish or church; **church'woman** a female member or upholder of a church, esp. the Anglican Church; **church'yard** a burial-ground round a church. [O.E. *cirice*, *circe* — Gr. *kȳriakon*, belonging to the Lord — *kȳrios*, lord.]

Churchillian *chûr-chil'i-ən*, *adj* of, in the manner of, or resembling Sir Winston *Churchill* (1874–1965), British prime minister.

churinga *cho͞o-ring'gə*, *n* a sacred amulet. [Austr. Aboriginal.]

churl *chûrl*, *n* an ill-bred, surly fellow. — *adj* **churl'ish** rude; surly; ungracious. — *adv* **churl'ishly.** — *n* **churl'ishness.** [O.E. *ceorl*, a countryman.]

churn *chûrn*, *n* an apparatus used for the production of butter from cream or from whole milk; a large milk-can suggestive of an upright churn. — *vt* to agitate so as to obtain butter; to stir or agitate violently (often with *up*); to turn over persistently (ideas in the mind); to engage in excessive and unnecessary buying and selling of (shares, etc.) or cancelling and purchasing of (insurance policies, etc.). — *vi* to perform the act of churning; to move restlessly and with violence. — *n* **churn'ing** the act of making butter; the quantity of butter made at once. — **churn'-milk** buttermilk. — **churn out** to produce continuously with effort. [O.E. *cyrin*.]

churr *chûr*, *n* a low sound made by certain birds and insects. — *vi* to make this sound. [Prob. imit.]

chute[1] or **shoot** *sho͞ot*, *n* a waterfall, rapid; a passage or sloping trough for sending down goods, water, logs, rubbish, etc.; a slide in a park, etc. [Fr. *chute*, fall, combined with **shoot.**]

chute[2] *sho͞ot*, (*colloq*) *n* short for **parachute.** — *n* **chut'ist** a parachutist.

chutney *chut'ni*, *n* a condiment (orig. East Indian), of mangoes, chillies, etc.; an imitation made with home-grown materials, such as apples. [Hindi *catnī*.]

chutzpah *hho͝ot'spə*, *n* effrontery, nerve. [Yiddish.]

chyack. See **chiack.**

chyle *kīl*, (*med*, *zool*) *n* a white fluid, mainly lymph mixed with fats derived from food in the body. [Gr. *chȳlos*, juice — *cheein*, to pour.]

chyme *kīm*, *n* the pulp to which food is reduced in the stomach. — *n* **chymificā'tion** the act of being formed into chyme. — *vt* **chym'ify** to form into chyme. — *adj* **chym'ous.** [Gr. *chȳmos*, chyme, juice — *cheein*, to pour.]

CI *abbrev* for: Channel Islands; Côte d'Ivoire, Ivory Coast (I.V.R.).

Ci *symbol* for curie.

CIA *abbrev* for Central Intelligence Agency (U.S.).

Cia *abbrev* for *Compagnia* (It.), Company.

ciao *chow, interj* an informal greeting used on meeting or parting: — *pl* **ciaos.** [It.]

CIB *abbrev* for Chartered Institute of Bankers.

ciborium *si-bö'ri-əm, n* a vessel closely resembling a chalice in which the host is deposited; a canopy supported on four pillars over the high altar: — *pl* **cibo'ria.** [L., a drinking-cup.]

cicada *si-kä'də* or *-kā'də* or **cicala** *-kä'lə, n* an insect remarkable for its loud chirping sound. [L. *cicāda*; It. *cicala*.]

cicatrice *sik'ə-tris, n* a scar over a healed wound; a scar in the bark of a tree; the mark left where a leaf, etc., has been attached: — *pl* **cicatrī'cēs.** — Also **cicatrix** (*sik-ā'triks* or *sik'ə-triks*): — *pl* **cic'a-trixes.** — *n* **cicatrīsā'tion** or **-z-** the process of healing over. — *vt* **cic'atrīse** or **-ize** to help the formation of a cicatrix on; to scar. — *vi* to heal. [L. *cicātrīx, -īcis*, a scar.]

cicely *sis'ə-li, n* a name for several plants related to chervil, esp. *Myrrhis odorata* (sweet cicely). [L. and Gr. *seseli*.]

cichlid *sik'lid, n* any fish of the family *Cich'lidae*, to which the angel-fish of the Amazon belongs. — *adj* **cich'loid.** [Gr. *kichlē*, a kind of wrasse.]

CID *abbrev* for: Council of Industrial Design; Criminal Investigation Department.

-cide *-sīd, combining form* denoting: (1) killing, murder; (2) killer, murderer. — **-cī'dal** adjective combining form. [L. *caedere*, to kill.]

cider or **cyder** *sī'dər, n* an alcoholic drink made from apples. — *adj* **cī'dery.** — **ci'der-and** a mixture of cider and spirits; **ci'der-cup** a drink of sweetened cider, with other ingredients; **ci'der-press** an apparatus for pressing the juice from apples. [Fr. *cidre* — L. *sīcera* — Gr. *sikera*, strong drink — Heb. *shēkār*.]

ci-devant *sē-də-vã*, (Fr.) *adj* and *adv* before this, former, formerly.

CIE *abbrev* for: Companion of the (Order of the) Indian Empire; *Córas Iompair Éireann* (Ir.), Transport Organisation of Ireland.

Cie *abbrev* for *Compagnie* (Fr.), Company.

cif *abbrev* for cost, insurance, freight.

cigar *si-gär', n* a roll of tobacco-leaves with a pointed end for smoking. — *n* **cigarette** (*sig-ə-ret'*) finely-cut tobacco rolled in thin paper (*colloq* shortened forms **cig, cigg'ie** and **cigg'y**). — *n* **cigarillo** (*sig-ə-ril'ō*) a small cigar: — *pl* **cigarill'os.** — **cigarette'-card** a picture card formerly given away with a packet of cigarettes; **cigarette'-end** or **-butt** the unsmoked remnant of a cigarette; **cigarette'-holder** (or **cigar'-holder**) a mouthpiece for a cigarette (or cigar); **cigarette'-lighter** a mechanical contrivance for lighting cigarettes; **cigarette'-paper** paper for making cigarettes. — *adj* **cigar'-shaped** cylindrical with tapered ends. [Sp. *cigarro*.]

CII *abbrev* for Chartered Insurance Institute.

cilium *sil'i-əm, n* a hairlike lash on a cell; a flagellum (*biol*): — *pl* **cil'ia.** — *adj* **cil'iary.** — *adj* **cil'iate** or **cil'iated** bearing a cilium or cilia; fringed with hairs. [L. *cilium*, eyelash.]

cill *sil*, (*building*) *n* an old variant of **sill**, now usual in the trade.

CIM *abbrev* for: Commission on Industry and Manpower; computer-integrated manufacture.

C-in-C *abbrev* for Commander-in-chief.

cinch *sinch, n* a saddle-girth (*US*); a secure hold (*colloq*); a certainty (*colloq*); something easy (*colloq*). — *vi* to tighten the cinch. — *vt* to bind firmly, esp. with a belt around the waist; to make sure of (*colloq*); to pull (clothing) in tightly at the waist. [Sp. *cincha* — L. *cingula*.]

cinchona *sing-kō'nə, n* any tree of the *Cinchona* genus yielding the bark from which quinine and related by-products are obtained — also called *Peruvian bark*; the dried bark of these trees. — *adj* **cinchonaceous** (*-kən-ā'shəs*) or **cinchonic** (*-kon'ik*). — *n* **cinch'onine** an alkaloid obtained from cinchona bark. [Said to be so named from the Countess of *Chinchón*, who was cured of a fever by it in 1638.]

cincture *singk'chər, n* a girdle or belt; a moulding round a column. — *vt* to gird, encompass. — *adj* **cinc'tured** having a cincture. [L. *cinctūra* — *cingĕre, cinctum*, to gird.]

cinder *sin'dər, n* the refuse of burned coals; an ember; anything charred by fire; a fragment of lava. — *vi* and *vt* to turn to cinder(s). — *n* **Cinderell'a** a scullery-maid; the despised and neglected one of a set. — Also *adj*. — *adj* **cin'dery.** — **cin'der-cone** a hill of loose volcanic materials; **cin'der-path** (or **-track**) a path (or racing-track) laid with cinders. [O.E. *sinder*, slag.]

cine- or **ciné-** *sin-i-, combining form* denoting cinema or cinematograph. — *n* **cin'e-camera** or **cin'é-camera** a camera for taking moving photographs. — *n* **cin'e-film** film suitable for use in a cine-camera. — *n* **cin'eplex** a multiple-cinema complex. — *n* **cin'e-projector** (or **cin'é-**). — *n* **Cinerama**® (*-ə-rä'mə*) a method of film projection on a wide curved screen to give a three-dimensional effect — the picture is photographed with three **cineram'ic** cameras. — *n* **ciné vérité** cinéma vérité.

cinéaste, cineaste or **cineast** *sin'ē-ast, n* a person who takes an artistic interest in, or who makes, motion pictures. [Fr.]

cinema *sin'ə-mə* or *-mä, n* a building in which motion pictures are shown; (with *the*) motion pictures collectively, or as an art; material or method judged by its suitability for the cinema. — *adj* **cinemat'ic** pertaining to, suitable for, or savouring of, the cinema. — **cin'ema-goer** a person who goes (regularly) to the cinema; **cin'ema-organ** an organ with showier effects than a church organ; **Cin'ema-Scope**® name of one of the methods of film projection on a wide curved screen to give a three-dimensional effect — the picture is photographed with a special type of lens; **cinéma vérité** realism in films sought by photographing scenes of real life. [**cinematograph**.]

cinematograph *sin-ə-mat'ə-gräf, n* apparatus for projecting a series of instantaneous photographs so as to give a moving representation of a scene, with or without reproduction of sound; an exhibition of such photographs. — *n* **cinematog'rapher.** — *adj* **cinematograph'ic** or **cinematograph'ical.** — *n* **cinematog'raphist.** — *n* **cinematog'raphy** the art of making motion pictures. [Fr. *cinématographe* — Gr. *kīnēma, -atos*, motion, *graphein*, to write, represent.]

cine-projector, cineplex, Cinerama®. See **cine-**.

cineraria[1] *sin-ə-rā'ri-ə, n* a brightly-flowered variety of plants, with ashy down on the leaves. [L. *cinerārius*, ashy — *cinis, cineris*, ash.]

cineraria[2]. See **cinerarium** under **cinerary.**

cinerary *sin'ə-rə-ri, adj* pertaining to ashes; for containing ashes of the dead. — *n* **cinerā'rium** a place for depositing the ashes of the dead: — *pl* **cinerā'ria.** — *n* **cinerā'tion.** — *n* **cinerā'tor.** — *n* **cinē'rea** grey nerve matter. — *adj* **cinē'real** ashy; cinerary. — *adj* **cinē'reous** ashy-grey; ashy. — *adj* **cineri'tious** ashy-grey; pertaining to grey nerve matter. [L. *cinereus*, ashy — *cinis, cineris*, ash.]

cinnabar *sin'ə-bär, n* a mineral, sulphide of mercury, called vermilion when used as a pigment. — *adj* vermilion-coloured. — *adj* **cinnabaric** (*-bär'ik*). — *adj* **cinn'abarine** (*-bə-rēn*). [Gr. *kinnabari*, from Pers.]

cinnamon *sin'ə-mən, n* the spicy bark of a lauraceous tree of Sri Lanka; the tree; a light yellowish brown. — Also *adj*. [Gr. *kinnamōmon*, later *kinnamon* — Heb. *qinnāmōn*.]

cinque *singk, n* the number five as on dice. — **cinque'foil** a flower with five petals (*heraldry*); a similar figure formed by cusps in a circular window or the head of a pointed arch (*archit*); species of the genus *Potentilla* (*bot*); the five-bladed clover (*bot*). — **Cinque Ports** the five ancient ports on the south of England lying opposite to France — Sandwich, Dover, Hythe, Romney, and Hastings (later associated with Winchelsea, Rye, and a number of subordinate ports). [Fr.]

cinquecento *ching'kwe-chen-tō, n* the 16th century — the art and architecture of the Renaissance period. — Also *adj*. [It., five hundred, *mil*, one thousand, being understood.]

CIO. See **AFL-CIO**.

CIOB *abbrev* for Chartered Institute of Building.

CIPA *abbrev* for Chartered Institute of Patent Agents.

CIPFA *abbrev* for Chartered Institute of Public Finance and Accountancy.

cipher (or sometimes **cypher**) *sī'fər, n* a secret code; an interweaving of the initials of a name; any person or thing of little value, a nonentity; any of the Arabic numerals; formerly, the character 0 (*arith*). — *vt* to write in cipher; to calculate. — *n* **cī'phering**. — **cī'pher-key** a key to a cipher or piece of secret writing. [O.Fr. *cyfre*, Fr. *chiffre* — Ar. *cifr*, zero, empty.]

CIPM *abbrev* for *Comité International des Poids et Mesures* (Fr.), International Committee of Weights and Measures.

cipollino *chē-pol-lē'nō, n* a marble with green bands: — *pl* **cipolli'nos**. [It. *cipolla*, an onion.]

CIR *abbrev* for Commission on Industrial Relations.

cir. or **circ.** *abbrev* for *circa*, *circiter* or *circum* (L.), about.

circa *sûr'kə, prep* and *adv* about, around. [L.]

circadian *sûr-kā'di-ən, adj* esp. in *circadian rhythm*, pertaining to any biological cycle (e.g. of varying intensity of metabolic or physiological process, or of some feature of behaviour) which is repeated, usu. approx. every 24 hours. [From L. *circa*, about, *di(em)*, day, and sfx. *-an*.]

circinate *sûr'sin-āt, adj* ring-shaped; rolled inwards (*bot*). [L. *circināre*, *-ātum*, make round.]

circiter *sûr'si-tər, prep* (with dates) about, around. [L.]

circle *sûr'kl, n* a plane figure bounded by one line every point of which is equally distant from a fixed point called the centre; the circumference of the figure so defined; a circular object; a ring; a planet's orbit; a parallel of latitude; a series ending where it began; a group of things in a circle; a company surrounding or associating with the principal person; those of a certain class or group. — *vt* to move round; to encompass; to draw a circle around. — *vi* (often with *round* or *around*) to move in a circle; to stand in a circle. — *adj* **cir'cled** circular; encircled. — *n* **cir'cler**. — *n* **cir'clet** a little circle; a little circular band or hoop, esp. a metal headband. — *n* and *adj* **cir'cling** moving in a circle. — **come full circle** to return to the beginning; to regain or turn out to be in a former state; **go round in circles** to get no results in spite of effort; not to get anywhere; **great** (or **small) circle** a circle that is the intersection of a sphere by a plane passing through (or not passing through) the centre of the sphere; **reasoning in a circle** assuming what is to be proved as the basis of the argument; **run round in circles** to act in too frenzied a way to achieve anything useful. [O.E. *circul* — L. *circulus*, dimin. of *circus*.]

circs *sûrks*, (*slang*) *npl* a shortened form of **circumstances**.

circuit *sûr'kit, n* a journey round; a way round; perimeter; a roundabout way; an area enclosed; the path, complete or partial, of an electric current; a round made in the exercise of a calling, esp. by judges; the judges making the round; a district in which such a round is made, as by Methodist preachers, commercial travellers; a group of theatres, cinemas, etc., under common control, through which an entertainment circulates; the venues visited in turn and regularly by sports competitors, performers, etc.; a motor-racing track. — *vt* to go round. — *adj* **circuitous** (*-kū'i-təs*) roundabout. — *adv* **circū'itously**. — *n* **circū'itousness**. — *n* **circuitry** (*sûr'kit-ri*) the detailed plan of a circuit, as in radio or television, or its components. — *n* **circū'ity** motion in a circle; an indirect course. — **circuit board** a printed circuit board (see under **print**); **cir'cuit-breaker** a switch or other device for interrupting an electric circuit; **circuit judge** a judge in a county or crown court; **circuit training** a form of athletic training consisting of repeated series of exercises. [Fr., — L. *circuitus* — *circuīre* — *circum*, round, *īre*, to go.]

circular *sûr'kū-lər, adj* of or pertaining to a circle; in the form of a circle; round; ending in itself; recurring in a cycle; addressed to a circle of persons. — *n* an intimation sent to a number of persons. — *vt* **cir'cularise** or **-ize** to make circular; to send circulars to. — *n* **circularity** (*-lar'i-ti*). — *adv* **cir'cularly**. — **circular file** (*comput*) one in which each item has a pointer to the next, the last leading back to the first; **circular letter** a letter of which copies are sent to several persons; **circular saw** a power-driven saw in the shape of a flat disc with a serrated edge. [L. *circulāris*.]

circulate *sûr'kū-lāt, vt* to make to go round as in a circle; to spread. — *vi* to move round; to be spread about; to repeat in definite order (of decimals). — *adj* **cir'culable** capable of being circulated. — *n* and *adj* **cir'culating**. — *n* **circulā'tion** the act of moving in a circle or in a closed path (as the blood); spreading or moving about; dissemination; the sale of a periodical; the money in use at any time in a country. — *adj* **cir'culātive** or **cir'culatory** circulating. — *n* **cir'culātor**. — **circulating library** one from which books are circulated among subscribers; **circulatory system** the system of blood and lymph vessels, including the heart. — **in** (or **out of) circulation** in (or out of) general use, activity, etc. [L. *circulāre*, *-ātum*.]

circum- *sûr'kəm-*, *sər-kum'-* or *sûr-kəm-*, *combining form* denoting around. [L. *circum*.]

circumambient *sûr-kəm-am'bi-ənt, adj* going round about, encompassing. — *n* **circumam'bience**. — *n* **circumam'biency**. [L. *ambīre*, to go round.]

circumambulate *sûr-kəm-am'bū-lāt, vi* to walk round about. — *n* **circumambulā'tion**. [L. *circum*, around, *ambulāre*, *-ātum*, to walk.]

circumcentre *sûr'kem-sen-tər, n* the centre of the circumscribed circle or sphere. [**circum-**.]

circumcise *sûr'kəm-sīz, vt* to cut or cut off all or part of the foreskin (of a male) or all or part of the clitoris (of a female), often as a religious rite; to purify (*fig*). — *n* **cir'cumciser**. — *n* **circumcision** (*-sizh'n*) the act of circumcising; the state of being circumcised. [L. *circumcīdĕre*, *-cīsum* — *caedĕre*, to cut.]

circumference *ser-kum'fər-əns, n* the boundary-line, esp. of a circle; compass; distance round. — *adj* **circumferential** (*-en'shl*). — *n* **circum'ferentor** (*-en-tər*) an instrument for measuring horizontal angles, consisting of a graduated circle, sights, and a magnetic needle; a graduated wheel for measuring the circumference of wheels. [L. *circum*, around, *ferre*, to carry.]

circumflect *sûr-kəm-flekt', vt* to bend round; to mark with a circumflex. — *n* **cir'cumflex** an accent (ˆ) originally denoting a rising and falling of the voice on a vowel or syllable. — Also *adj*. — *n* **circumflexion**

(*-flek'shən*) a bending round. [L. *circum*, around, *flectĕre*, *flexum*, to bend.]

circumfluence *sər-kum'flōō-əns*, *n* a flowing round; the engulfing of food by surrounding it (as by protozoa, etc.). [L. *circum*, around, *fluĕre*, to flow.]

circumfuse *sûr-kəm-fūz'*, *vt* to pour around. — *participial adj* **circumfused'**. — *adj* **circumfus'ile** molten. — *n* **circumfusion** (*-fū'zhən*). [L. *circum*, around, *fundĕre*, *fūsum*, to pour.]

circumlittoral *sûr-kəm-lit'ə-rəl*, *adj* adjacent to the shoreline. [L. *circum*, around, *littus*, for *lītus*, *-oris*, shore.]

circumlocution *sûr-kəm-lō-kū'shən*, *n* expressing an idea in more words than are necessary; an instance of this; evasive talk. — *vi* **circumlocūte'** to use circumlocution. — *n* **circumlocū'tionist** a person who does this. — *adj* **circumlocutory** (*-lok'ū-tər-i*). [L. *circum*, around, *loquī*, *locūtus*, to speak.]

circumlunar *sûr-kəm-lōō'nər* or *-lū'*, *adj* situated or moving round the moon. [L. *circum*, around, *lūna*, the moon.]

circumnavigate *sûr-kəm-nav'i-gāt*, *vt* to sail or fly right round. — *adj* **circumnav'igable**. — *n* **circumnavigā'tion**. — *n* **circumnav'igātor**. [**circum-**.]

circumpose *sûr-kəm-pōz'*, *vt* to place round. — *n* **circumposi'tion** the act of placing round. [L. *circumpōnĕre*, by analogy with *impose*, etc.]

circumscribe *sûr-kəm-skrīb'*, *vt* to draw a line round; to describe a curve or figure touching externally; to enclose within certain limits, to curtail, abridge. — *adj* **circumscrīb'able**. — *n* **circumscrīb'er**. — *n* **circumscription** (*-skrip'shən*) limitation; the line that limits; the act of circumscribing; an inscription running round; a defined district. — *adj* **circumscrip'tive** marking the external form or outline. [L. *circum*, around, *scrībĕre*, *scrīptum*, to write.]

circumsolar *sûr-kəm-sō'lər*, *adj* situated or moving round the sun. [L. *circum*, around, *sōl*, the sun.]

circumspect *sûr'kəm-spekt*, *adj* looking round on all sides watchfully; cautious; prudent. — *n* **circumspec'tion** watchfulness; caution; examining. — *adj* **circumspec'tive** looking around; wary. — *adv* **cir'cumspectly**. — *n* **cir'cumspectness**. [L. *circum*, around, *specĕre*, *spicĕre*, *spectum*, to look.]

circumstance *sûr'kəm-stəns*, *n* the logical surroundings of an action; an attendant fact; an accident or event; ceremony; detail; (in *pl*) the state of one's affairs. — *vt* to place in particular circumstances. — *adj* **circumstantial** (*-stan'shl*) consisting of details; minute. — *n* **circumstantiality** (*-stan-shi-al'i-ti*) the quality of being circumstantial; minuteness in details; a detail. — *adv* **circumstan'tially**. — *npl* **circumstan'tials** incidentals; details. — *vt* **circumstan'tiate** to prove by circumstances; to describe exactly. — **circumstantial evidence** evidence which is not positive nor direct, but which is gathered inferentially from the circumstances in the case; **in good** (or **bad**) **circumstances** prosperous (or unprosperous); **in** or **under no circumstances** never; **in** or **under the circumstances** conditions being what they are. [L. *circum*, around, *stāns*, *stantis*, standing — *stāre*, to stand.]

circumterrestrial *sûr-kəm-ti-res'tri-əl*, *adj* situated or moving round the earth. [L. *circum*, around, *terrestris*, — *terra*, the earth.]

circumvent *sûr-kəm-vent'*, *vt* to go round; to encompass; to surround so as to intercept or capture; to get round, or to outwit. — *n* **circumven'tion**. — *adj* **circumvent'ive** deceiving by artifices. [L. *circum*, around, *venīre*, *ventum*, to come.]

circumvolve *sûr-kəm-volv'*, *vt* to roll round. — *vi* to revolve. — *n* **circumvolution** (*-lōō'* or *-lū'*) a turning or rolling round; anything winding or sinuous. [L. *circum*, around, *volvĕre*, *volūtum*, to roll.]

circus *sûr'kəs*, *n* orig. a circular building for the exhibition of games; a place, building, or tent for the exhibition of feats of horsemanship and other performances; a show of this kind or the company of performers (also *fig*); a group of houses arranged in the form of a circle; an open place at a street junction; a natural amphitheatre; a group of people who travel around putting on a display (such as a *flying circus*), often in the form of a competition (such as a *tennis circus*); a noisy entertainment or scene. — *adj* **cir'cussy** or **cir'cusy**. [L. *circus* — Gr. *kirkos*.]

ciré *sē'rā*, *n* (a fabric with) a highly glazed finish. [Fr. past p. of *cirer*, to wax.]

cire perdue *sēr per-dü*, (Fr.) *n* lit. 'lost wax', a method of casting in metal, the mould being formed round a wax model which is then melted away.

cirl *sûrl* or **cirl bunting** (*bun'ting*), *n* a species of bunting. [It. *cirlo*.]

cirque *sûrk*, (*geog*) *n* a deep round hollow, a natural amphitheatre, formed by glaciation. [Fr. — L. *circus* — Gr. *kirkos*.]

cirrate, cirriform, etc. See **cirrus**.

cirrhosis *si-rō'sis*, *n* a wasting of the proper tissue of the liver, accompanied by abnormal growth of connective tissue. — *adj* **cirrhot'ic**. [Gr. *kirrhos*, tawny — from the colour of the liver so diseased.]

cirripede *sir'i-pēd* or **cirriped** *sir'i-ped*, *n* one of the **Cirripē'dia**, a subclass of marine Crustacea which includes the barnacles. [L. *cirrus*, a curl, *pēs*, *pedis*, foot.]

cirrus *sir'əs*, *n* the highest form of clouds, consisting of curling fibres; a tendril (*bot*); any curled filament (*zool*): — *pl* **cirr'ī**. — *adj* **cirr'ate** or **cirr'iform** like a cirrus. — *adj* **cirr'igrade** moving by cirri. — *adj* **cirr'ose** with tendrils. — *adj* **cirr'ous** having a cirrus. — **cirro-cū'mulus** a cloud of small white flakes or ripples (also called *mackerel sky*); **cirro-stratus** (*strä'tōōs*) a high thin sheet of haze-like cloud. [L., a curl, tuft.]

CIS *abbrev* for Chartered Institute of Secretaries.

Cisalpine *sis-alp'in* or *-īn*, *adj* on this (i.e. the Roman) side of the Alps. — *adj* **Cisatlan'tic**. — *adj* **cislu'nar** on this side of the moon, i.e. between the moon and the earth. — *adj* **cispon'tine** on this side of the bridges, in London, north of the Thames. [L. *cis*, on this side.]

ciselure *sēz'lōōr*, *n* the art or operation of chasing (metal); the chasing upon a piece of metalwork. — *n* **cis'eleur** (*-lər*) a chaser. [Fr.]

cislunar, cispontine. See under **Cisalpine**.

cissy *sis'i*, (*slang*) *n* an effeminate person. — Also *adj*. [Partly from the name *Cecily*, partly from **sister**; cf. **sis**.]

cist *sist*, *n* a tomb consisting of a stone chest covered with stone slabs. — *adj* **cist'ed** containing cists. — *adj* **cist'ic** like a cist. [See ety. for **chest**.]

Cistercian *sis-tûr'shən*, *n* a member of the order of monks established in 1098 in the forest of Cîteaux (*Cistercium*), in France — an offshoot of the Benedictines. — Also *adj*.

cistern *sis'tərn*, *n* an artificial reservoir or tank for holding water or other liquid; a natural reservoir. [L. *cisterna* — *cista*, a chest.]

cistic. See **cist**.

cistus *sis'təs*, *n* any plant of the rock-rose genus (*Cistus*) of shrubby plants: — *pl* **cis'tuses**. [Gr. *kistos*, rock-rose.]

CIT *abbrev* for Chartered Institute of Transport.

cit. *abbrev* for: citation; citizen.

citadel *sit'ə-dəl*, *n* a fortress in or near a city. [It. *cittadella*, dimin. of *città*, a city; see **city**.]

cite *sīt*, *vt* to call or summon; to summon to appear in court; to quote; to name; to adduce as proof. — *adj* **cīt'able**. — *n* **cīt'al** summons to appear. — *n* **citā'tion** (*sīt-* or *sit-*) an official summons to appear; a document containing the summons; the act of quoting; the passage or name quoted; mention in dispatches; official recognition of achievement. — *adj* **cit'atory** having to do with citation; addicted to citation. — *n* **cīt'er.** [L. *citāre, -ātum*, to call, intensive of *ciēre, cīre*, to make to go.]

CITES *abbrev* for Convention on International Trade in Endangered Species (of Wild Fauna and Flora).

cithara *sith'ə-rə, n* an ancient Greek musical instrument differing from the lyre in its flat shallow sound-chest. — *n* **cith'arist** a player on it. — *adj* **citharist'ic.** — *n* **cith'er, cith'ern** or **citt'ern** an early modern metal-stringed musical instrument, played with a plectrum; the Tirolese zither. [L., — Gr. *kitharā*; cf. **guitar, zither.**]

citify. See **city.**

citizen *sit'i-zən* or *-zn, n* an inhabitant of a city; a member of a state; a townsman; a freeman: —*fem* **cit'izeness.** — *vt* **cit'izenise** or **-ize** to make a citizen of. — *n* **cit'izenry** the general body of citizens. — *n* **cit'izenship** the state of being or of having rights and duties of a citizen; conduct in relation to these duties. —**citizen's arrest** an arrest, legally allowable, made by a member of the public; **Citizens' Band** (orig. *US*) a band of radio frequencies on which the public are permitted to broadcast personal messages, etc.; **Citizens' Band radio** (also **CB radio**). [M.E. *citesein* — O.Fr. *citeain*; see **city.**]

citron *sit'rən, n* the fruit of the citron tree, resembling a lemon; the tree that bears it, considered to be the parent of the lemon and lime-fruit. — *n* **cit'range** (*-rənj*) a hybrid between citron and orange. — *n* **cit'rate** a salt of citric acid. — *adj* **cit'ric** derived from the citron (**citric acid** the acid to which lemon and lime juice owe their sourness, $C_6H_8O_7$). — *n* **cit'rin** the water-soluble vitamin P, found in citrus fruits, etc. — *adj* **cit'rous.** — *n* **cit'rus** a citron tree; (with *cap*) a genus of the *Rutaceae* family including the citron, lemon, orange, etc. — **citron tree; citrus fruits** citrons, lemons, limes, oranges, grapefruit. [L. *citrus*, from which comes also Gr. *kitron*, a citron.]

cittern. Same as **cither.** [See under **cithara.**]

city *sit'i, n* a large town; an incorporated town that has or had a cathedral; in various countries a municipality of higher rank, variously defined; the business centre or original area of a large town; (often with *cap*) the centre of British financial affairs, most banks, etc., being in the City of London. — *n* **citificā'tion.** — *vt* **cit'ify** to give the characteristics or attitudes of the city, or city culture, to (a person, etc.). — **city desk** the desk or (*fig*) the department or field of work of a city editor; **city editor** the financial editor of a newspaper; **city farm** a farm established within an urban area in order to let city children learn about agriculture; **city fathers** the magistrates; the town or city council; **city hall** a town hall; **cit'yscape** a view or picture of a city (following *landscape*); **city-slick'er** a city-dweller perceived as over-sophisticated and untrustworthy; **city state** a sovereign state consisting of a city with a small surrounding territory. — **city of God, heavenly city,** etc., the ideal of the Church of Christ in glory; **city technology college** a secondary school set up in an inner-city district, funded by central government and (local) industry, specialising in teaching scientific and technological subjects; **Eternal City** Rome; **Holy City** Jerusalem. [Fr. *cité*, a city — L. *civitās, -ātis*, the state — *cīvis*, a citizen.]

civ. *abbrev* for: civil; civilian.

civet *siv'it, n* a perfume obtained from the **civet** or **civet cat,** a small catlike carnivore of Africa, India, etc. [Fr. *civette* — Ar. *zabād.*]

civic *siv'ik, adj* pertaining to a city or citizen. — *adv* **civ'ically.** — *nsing* **civ'ics** the science of citizenship. — **civic centre** a place in which the chief public buildings of a town are grouped. [L. *cīvicus* — *cīvis*, citizen.]

civil *siv'il, adj* pertaining to the community; polite (in any degree short of discourtesy); pertaining to ordinary life, not military; pertaining to the individual citizen; relating to private relations amongst citizens, and such suits as arise out of these, as opposed to *criminal* (*law*). — *n* **civil'ian** a person engaged in civil as distinguished from military and naval pursuits. — Also *adj.* — *vt* **civil'ianise** or **-ize** to convert from military to civilian use; to replace military personnel in (a factory, etc.) by civilians. — *adv* **civ'illy.** — **civil aviation** non-military flying, esp. commercial airlines and their operation; **civil defence** a civilian service for the wartime protection of the civilian population against the effects of enemy attack by air, etc.; **civil disobedience** refusal to obey laws and regulations, pay taxes, etc., used as non-violent means of forcing concessions from government; **civil engineer** a person who plans and builds railways, docks, etc.; **civil engineering; civil law** (as opp. to *criminal law*) the law laid down by a state regarding the rights of the inhabitants, esp. that founded on Roman law; **civil liberty** (often in *pl*) personal freedom of thought, word, action, etc.; **civil list** the expenses of the sovereign's household (**civil list pensions** those granted by royal favour); **civil marriage** one performed by a civil magistrate, not by a clergyman; **civil rights** (often with *caps*) the rights of a citizen to personal freedom, i.e. political, racial, legal, social, etc. — Also *adj.* — **civil servant** a person who works in the **civil service,** the paid service of the state (other than military, naval, legislative and judicial); **civil war** a war between citizens of the same state. [L. *cīvīlis* — *cīvis*, citizen.]

civilise or **-ize** *siv'il-īz, vt* to reclaim from barbarism; to instruct in arts and refinements. — *adj* **civilīs'able** or **-z-**. — *n* **civilīsā'tion** or **-z-** the state of being civilised; culture; cultural condition or complex. — *adj* **civ'ilised** or **-z-** (having) advanced beyond the primitive savage state; refined in interests and tastes; sophisticated, self-controlled and well-spoken. — *n* **civ'ilīser** or **-z-**. [See **civil.**]

civility *si-vil'i-ti, n* politeness; polite attentions. [**civil.**]

civvy *siv'i,* (*slang*) *n* and *adj* civilian; (in *pl* **civv'ies**) civilian clothes. — **civvy street** (*colloq*) civilian life after the Services.

CJD *abbrev* for Creutzfeldt-Jakob disease.

Cl (*chem*) *symbol* for chlorine.

clack *klak, vi* to make a noise as of a hard, flat thing flapping; to chatter. — *n* a noise of this kind; an instrument making it; the sound of chattering voices; the tongue (*colloq*). — *n* **clack'er.** [Prob. imit.]

clad *klad, pa t* and *pa p* of **clothe.** — *adj* clothed, or covered. — *vt* to cover one material with another, e.g. one metal with another (as in a nuclear reactor), or brick or stonework with a different material (in building). — *n* **cladd'er.** — *n* **cladd'ing.**

clade *klād,* (*biol*) *n* a group of organisms that have evolved from a common ancestor. — *n* **clād'ism** adherence to cladistic theories. — *n* **clād'ist.** — *adj* **cladistic** (*klə-dis'tik*). — *nsing* **cladist'ics** a taxonomic theory which classifies organisms according to the shared characteristics which distinguish a group from other groups. [Gr. *klados*, branch.]

cladode *klad'ōd,* (*bot*) *n* a branch with the appearance and functions of a leaf. [Gr. *klados*, a shoot.]

claim *klām, vt* to demand as a right; to maintain or assert; to call for. — *vi* to make a claim (*on* one's insurance policy, etc.). — *n* a demand for something supposed due; a right or ground for demanding; the thing claimed, esp. a piece of land appropriated by a miner or other; a call, shout. — *adj* **claim'able.** — *n* **claim'ant** or **claim'er** a person who makes a claim. — **claim'-jumper** a person who takes possession of another's mining claim; **claims assessor** an assessor employed by an insurance company, usu. in motor accident claims. — **lay claim to** to assert a right to. [O.Fr. *claimer* — L. *clāmāre*, to call out.]

clairaudience *klār-öd'i-əns*, *n* the alleged power of hearing things not present to the senses. — *n* and *adj* **clairaud'ient.** [Fr. *clair* — L. *clārus*, clear, and **audience.**]

clairvoyance *klār-voi'əns*, *n* the alleged power of seeing things not present to the senses. — Also **clairvoy'ancy.** — *n* and *adj* **clairvoy'ant.** [Fr. *clair* — L. *clārus*, clear, and Fr. *voir* — L. *vidēre*, to see.]

clam^{1} *klam*, *n* a gripping instrument. [O.E. *clam*, fetter.]

clam^{2} *klam*, *n* an edible shellfish of various kinds; a scallop or scallop-shell; a very reticent person (*colloq*). — *vi* to gather clams: — *pr p* **clamm'ing;** *pa t* and *pa p* **clammed.** — **clam'bake** a baking of clams on hot stones, with potatoes, etc., popular at picnic parties in U.S.; such a party; any informal party; **clam-chow'der** chowder made with clams; **clam'-shell.** — **clam up** (*colloq*) to become silent. [**clam**^{1}.]

clamant *klam'ənt* or *klām'ənt*, *adj* calling aloud or earnestly. — *n* **clam'ancy** urgency. — *adv* **clam'antly.** [L. *clāmāre*, to cry out.]

clamber *klam'bər*, *vi* and *vt* to climb with difficulty, grasping with hands and feet (often with *up* or *over*). — *n* the act of clambering. [From the root of **climb.**]

clammed, clamming. See **clam**^{2}.

clammy *klam'i*, *adj* sticky; moist and adhesive. — *adv* **clamm'ily.** — *n* **clamm'iness.** [Dialect *clam*, dampness — O.E. *clæman*, to anoint.]

clamour or in U.S. **clamor** *klam'ər*, *n* loud continuous outcry; uproar; any loud noise; persistent expression of dissatisfaction. — *vi* to cry aloud in demand (often with *for*); to make a loud continuous outcry. — *adj* **clam'orous** noisy, boisterous. — *adv* **clam'orously.** — *n* **clam'orousness.** — *n* **clam'ourer.** [L. *clāmor*, *-ōris.*]

clamp^{1} *klamp*, *n* a piece of timber, iron, etc., used to fasten things together or to strengthen any framework; any instrument for holding; a wheel clamp. — *vt* to bind with a clamp; to grasp or press firmly; to put (on) authoritatively, impose; to fit a wheel clamp to (a car). — **clamp down on** to suppress, or suppress the activities of, firmly (*n* **clamp'down**). [From a root seen in O.E. *clam*, fetter.]

clamp^{2} *klamp*, *n* a heavy tread. — *vi* to tread heavily. [Prob. from the sound.]

clan *klan*, *n* a tribe or collection of families subject to a single chieftain, commonly bearing the same surname, and supposed to have a common ancestor; a clique, sect; a collective name for a number of persons or things. — *adj* **clann'ish** closely united and keeping aloof from others, like the members of a clan. — *adv* **clann'ishly.** — *n* **clann'ishness.** — *n* **clan'ship** association of families under a chieftain; feeling of loyalty to a clan. — **clans'man** or **clans'woman** a male or female member of a clan. [Gael. *clann*, offspring, tribe — L. *planta*, a shoot.]

clandestine *klan-des'tin*, *adj* concealed or hidden; private; sly. — *adv* **clandes'tinely.** — *n* **clandes'tineness** or **clandestin'ity.** [L. *clandestīnus* — *clam*, secretly.]

clang *klang*, *vi* to produce a loud deep ringing sound. — *vt* to cause to clang. — *n* a ringing sound, like that made by striking large pieces of metal. — *n* **clang'er** a singularly ill-timed remark or comment; a stupid mistake. — *n* and *adj* **clang'ing.** — *adj* **clangorous** (*klang'gər-əs*). — *adv* **clang'orously.** — *n* **clang'our** or in U.S. **clang'or** a clang; a loud ringing noise. — *vi* to make a clangour. — **drop a clanger** (*colloq*) to say something tactless; to make a stupid blunder. [L. *clangĕre*, to sound; *clangor*, noise of birds or wind instruments.]

clank *klangk*, *n* a metallic sound, less prolonged than a clang, such as is made by chains hitting together. — *vi* or *vt* to make or cause to make a clank. — *n* **clank'ing.** [Prob. formed under the influence of **clink**^{1} and **clang.**]

clap^{1} *klap*, *n* the noise made by two things striking together suddenly, esp. the hands; a slap; a pat (*Scot*); a sudden blow or stroke (*lit* and *fig*); a burst of sound, esp. thunder. — *vt* to strike together so as to make a noise; to applaud with the hands; to bang; to pat (*Scot*); to fasten or close promptly; to put suddenly, throw (e.g. into prison). — *vi* to strike the hands together; to stike or slam with a noise; to applaud: — *pr p* **clapp'ing;** *pa t* and *pa p* **clapped.** — *n* **clapp'er** a person who claps; a thing that claps, such as the tongue of a bell; an instrument for making a striking noise, such as a rattle; the tongue (*slang*). — *vi* to make a noise like a clapper. — *vt* to ring by pulling on a clapper. — *n* and *adj* **clapp'ering.** — *n* **clapp'ing** applause; the noise of striking. — **clap'board** (*US*) a thin board used in covering wooden houses; **clapom'eter** (*colloq*) a device for measuring audience reaction in quiz shows, etc. — *adj* **clapped-out'** (*colloq*) tired, exhausted; finished, of no more use. — **clapp'erboard** (or **-boards**) a hinged board (or set of hinged boards) clapped together in front of the camera before and after shooting a piece of film, so as to help synchronise sound and vision; **clap'trap** flashy but insincere or empty words; nonsense; **claptrapp'ery.** — **clap eyes on** to catch sight of; **clap hold of** to seize roughly; **like the clappers** (*colloq*) at top speed. [O.N. *klappa*, to pat.]

clap^{2} *klap*, (*slang*) *n* gonorrhoea. — *vt* to infect with gonorrhoea. [Cf. Du. *klapoor.*]

claque *klak*, *n* an institution for securing the success of a performance, by prearranged applause; a body of hired applauders. — *n* **claqueur** (*kla-kûr'*) a member of a claque. [Fr., — *claquer*, to clap.]

claret *klar'ət*, *n* originally applied to wines of a light-red colour, but now used in Britain for the dark-red wines of Bordeaux; a dark red colour (also *adj*). — **clar'et-cup** a drink made up of iced claret, brandy, sugar, etc.; **clar'et-jug** a fancy jug for holding claret. [Fr. *clairet* — *clair* — L. *clārus*, clear.]

clarify *klar'i-fī*, *vt* to make clear, easily understood; to make clear or pure, esp. butter, etc. — *vi* to become clear: — *pr p* **clar'ifying;** *pa t* and *pa p* **clar'ified.** — *n* **clarificā'tion.** — *n* **clar'ifīer.** [L. *clārus*, clear, *facĕre*, to make.]

clarinet *klar-in-et'* or *klar'i-net*, *n* a wind instrument, usually of wood, in which the sound is produced by a single thin reed, the range of pitch being approximately that of the violin. — *n* **clarinett'ist.** — **bass clarinet** one pitched an octave lower than the ordinary clarinet. [Fr., — L. *clārus*, clear.]

clarino *kla-rē'nō*, *n* the highest register of the trumpet in baroque music; an organ stop imitating this; a trumpet, a clarion: — *pl* **clari'ni** or **clarin'os.** — *adj* relating to the trumpet's highest register.

clarion *klar'i-ən*, *n* a kind of trumpet whose note is clear and shrill; the sound of a trumpet, or a sound resembling that of a trumpet. — **clarion call** (*fig*) a stirring summons (to duty, etc.). [Fr. *clairon* — *clair* — L. *clārus*, clear.]

clarity *klar'i-ti*, *n* clearness. [M.E. *clarte* — L. *clāritās.*]

clary *klā'ri*, *n* a plant of the sage genus with pale-blue flowers and large coloured bracts; extended to others of the genus. [L.L. *sclarea.*]

clash *klash*, *n* a loud noise, such as is caused by the striking together of sheets of metal; noisy opposition or contradiction; an outbreak of fighting. — *vi* to dash noisily together; to meet in opposition; to disagree; (of events) to coincide disturbingly; (of colours) to jar visually when placed together. — *vt* to strike noisily against. — *n* **clash'ing.** [Imit.]

clasp *kläsp*, *n* a fastening; a bar on the ribbon of a medal; an embrace; a grasp. — *vt* to fasten with a clasp; to enclose and hold in the hand or arms; to embrace. — *n* **clas'per** that which clasps; the tendril of a plant; a clasping organ (*zool*). — *n* **clasp'ing**. — **clasp'-knife** a knife whose blade folds into the handle. [M.E. *clapse*.]

class *kläs*, *n* a rank or order of persons or things; high rank or social standing; the system or situation in any community in which there is division of people into different social ranks; a number of students or scholars who are taught together, or are in the same year of their course; a group of students graduating together (in a certain year, e.g. *class of* 1989) (*US*); a scientific division or arrangement in biological classification; a grade (of merit in examination, accommodation in a ship or railway train, etc.); style, quality (*colloq*). — *vt* to form into a class or classes; to arrange methodically. — *vi* to take rank. — *adj* (*slang*) of high class. — *adj* **class'able** or **class'ible** capable of being classed. — *adj* **classed**. — *n* **class'iness** (*colloq*) the quality of being classy. — *n* **class'ism** prejudice or discrimination on grounds of social class. — *adj* **class'ist** motivated or influenced by classism. — *adj* **class'less** having no class distinctions; not belonging to any social class; not confined to any particular category. — *adj* **class'y** (*colloq*) of or characteristic of high or upper class. — **class'-book** a book used in class teaching. — *adj* **class'-conscious** clearly or acutely conscious of membership of a social class. — **class-con'scious-ness; class-distinc'tion; class'-fellow** or **class'mate** a student in the same class at school or college; **class'room** a room in which a class is held; **class'-war** hostility or hostilities between different social ranks or classes, esp. between the working class and the combined middle and upper classes. — **in a class of** (or **on**) **its own** so good as to be without an equal. [L. *classis*, a division of the Roman people.]

class. *abbrev* for: classical; classification.

classic *klas'ik n* any great writer, composer or work; something of established excellence; something quintessentially typical or definitive; any of five flat races (e.g. the Derby) for three-year-olds, or other established sporting event; something delightful, such as a good story (*colloq*); (in *pl*) Greek and Latin studies. — *adj* **class'ic** or **class'ical** (usu. **classic**) of the highest class or rank, esp. in literature or art; (**classical**) of orchestral and chamber music, etc., as opposed to jazz, folk music, etc.; (usu. **classical**) used of the best Greek and Roman writers; (usu. **classical**) pertaining to Greek and Latin studies; (usu. **classical**; i.e. opposed to *romantic*) in style like the authors of Greece and Rome or the old masters in music; chaste, refined, restrained, in keeping with classical art; (usu. **classic**) having literary or historical associations; traditionally accepted, long or well established; (usu. **classic**) excellent, definitive (*slang*); (usu. **classic**) of clothes, made in simple tailored style that does not soon go out of fashion. — *n* **classical'ity**. — *adv* **class'ically**. — *n* **class'ical-ness**. — *vt* **class'icise** or **-ize** to make classic or classical. — *vi* to imitate a classical style in literature, music, etc. — *n* **class'icism** (*-sizm*) a classical idiom; (in literature, music, etc.) a principle, character, or tendency such as is seen in Greek classical literature, marked by beauty of form, good taste, restraint, and clarity (opposed to *romanticism*). — *n* **class'icist** a person educated in the classics, or devoted to their being used in education; a person who is for classicism rather than romanticism. — **classic car** a motor car of classic design, esp. one manufactured between 1925 and 1942; **classic races** the five chief annual horse-races — the Two Thousand Guineas, One Thousand Guineas, Derby, Oaks, and St Leger. [**class**.]

classify *klas'i-fī*, *vt* to arrange in classes; to make secret for security reasons: — *pr p* **class'ifying**; *pa p* **class'ified**. — *adj* **class'ifīable** (or *-fī'ə-bl*). — *adj* **classif'ic** denoting classes. — *n* **classificā'tion** the act or a system of arranging in classes. — *adj* **classificā'tory**. — *adj* **class'ified** arranged in classes; (of a road) in a class entitled to receive a government grant; (of information) secret. — *n* **class'ifier**. — **classified advertisements** advertisements in a newspaper or periodical grouped according to the goods or services offered. [L. *classis*, a class, division, *facĕre*, to make.]

clastic *klas'tik*, (*geol*) *adj* (of sedimentary rock) composed of fragments of older rock, fragmental. [Gr. *klastos* — *klaein*, to break.]

clathrate *klath'rit* or *-rāt*, *adj* lattice-shaped (*biol*); (of a molecular compound) having one component enclosed in the cavities of the crystals of another component (*chem*). [L. *clāthrāre*, to provide with a lattice.]

clatter *klat'ər*, *n* a repeated rattling noise; a repetition of abrupt, sharp sounds. — *vi* to make rattling sounds. — *vt* to cause to rattle. — *n* **clatt'erer**. — *adv* **clatt'eringly**. [O.E. *clatrung*, clattering (verbal noun).]

claudication *klö-di-kā'shən*, (*med*) *n* a limp, limping. [L. *claudicātio*, *-ōnis* — *claudus*, lame.]

clause *klöz*, *n* a group of words that contains a subject and its finite verb (*gram*); an article or part of a contract, will, act of parliament, etc. — *adj* **claus'al**. — *adj* **claus'ūlar** pertaining to, or consisting of, a clause or clauses. — **dependent clause** a clause which cannot stand in isolation as a sentence in itself (opp. to *independent clause*). [Fr. *clause* — L. *claudere*, to shut.]

claustral *klös'trəl*. Same as **cloistral**.

claustrophobia *klos-* or *klös-trə-fō'bi-ə*, *n* a pathological dread of confined spaces. — *n* **claus'tro-phobe** a sufferer from claustrophobia. — *adj* **claustrophōb'ic**. [L. *claustrum*, an enclosed space, and **phobia**.]

claustrum *klös'trəm*, (*anat*) *n* a thin layer of grey matter in the brain hemispheres: — *pl* **claus'tra**. [L. *claustrum*, an enclosed place.]

clausular. See **clause**.

clavate *klā'vāt*, *klav'āt* or **clavated** *-id*, *adj* (*biol*) club-shaped. [L. *clāva*, a club.]

clave[1] *klāv*, *pa t* of **cleave**[2].

clave[2] *klä'vā*, *n* one of a pair of small wooden cylinders held in the hands and struck together to mark S. American dance rhythm. [Sp., key to code, etc., clef — L. *clāvis*, key.]

clavichord *klav'i-körd*, *n* an old keyboard stringed instrument in which the tangent striking the string to produce the sound also determines the vibrating length. [L. *clāvis*, a key, *chorda*, a string.]

clavicle *klav'i-kl* or **clavicula** *klav-ik'ū-lə*, *n* the collar-bone. — *adj* **clavic'ūlar**. [Fr. *clavicule* — L. *clāvicula*, dimin. of *clāvis*, a key.]

clavier *klä-vēr'*, *n* a stringed keyboard instrument, esp. the clavichord or the pianoforte; the keyboard of a musical instrument. [Fr. (or Ger. *Klavier*, — Fr.), — L. *clāvis*, a key.]

claw *klö*, *n* the hooked nail of a bird, mammal or reptile, or the creature's foot with a number of such nails; the leg of a crab, insect, etc., or its pointed end or pincer; anything shaped or used like a claw. — *vt* to scratch, tear, scrape, seize (with or as if with claws). — *adj* **clawed** having claws. — *adj* **claw'less**. — *adj* **claw-and-ball'** (of furniture) having feet carved to represent an animal's claw holding a ball (also **ball-and-claw'**). — **claw'back** an arrangement by which financial benefit is partially recouped in extra taxation; a similar arrangement extended to other situations; **claw'-hammer** a hammer with one part of the head divided into two claws, for drawing nails. — **claw back** to recoup money by means of taxation, etc. [O.E. *clawu*.]

clay *klā*, *n* earth in very fine particles, tenacious and impervious (*agri*); a tenacious ductile earthy material, hydrated aluminium silicates more or less impure (*chem* and *min*); earth in general; the human body. — *adj* **clay'ey** made of clay; covered with clay; like clay. — *adj* **clay'ish** of the nature of clay. — **clay'-court** a type of hard-surfaced tennis court; **clay'pan** (*Austr*) a shallow depression in clay soil, holding water after rain; **clay pigeon** a disc thrown from a trap and shot at as a substitute for a pigeon; **clay'-pipe** a tobacco-pipe of baked clay; **clay'-pit** a pit from which clay is dug. — **feet of clay** (*fig*) faults and weaknesses of character not at first suspected. [O.E. *clæg*.]

claymore *klā'mōr*, *n* a large sword formerly used by the Scottish Highlanders. [Gael. *claidheamhmór* — Gael. and Ir. *claidheamh*, sword, *mór*, great.]

clean *klēn*, *adj* free from dirt, stain, or anything that contaminates; pure, fresh; guiltless; honest, uncorrupted; neat in execution, unerring; having nothing of an incriminating nature on one's person (*slang*); (of a driving licence) without any endorsements for motoring offences; (of e.g. an athlete) clear of drugs when tested; complete; free of radioactive fallout; of a design that causes little turbulent wake (*aerodynamics*). — *adv* quite, entirely; smoothly; without mishap. — *vt* to make clean, or free from dirt, corruption, contamination, etc. — *n* an act of cleaning; a lift of the weight to the shoulders, where it is held with arms bent (*weight-lifting*). — *n* **clean'er**. — *n* and *adj* **clean'ing** (the act of) making clean. — *n* **cleanliness** (*klen'li-nəs*) habitual cleanness or purity. — *adj* **cleanly** (*klen'li*) clean in habits and person; pure; neat. — *adv* (*klēn'li*) in a clean manner. — *n* **cleanness** (*klēn'nəs*). — *adj* **clean-cut'** neat, well-shaped; with a neat, respectable appearance. — **clean hands** freedom from guilt or corruption; **cleaning lady** or **woman** a woman employed to clean a house, premises, etc. — *adj* **clean-limb'ed** with shapely limbs; trim. — *adj* **clean-liv'ing** morally upright; respectable. — **clean room** a sterile, dust-free environment created to minimise risk of contamination for delicate scientific procedures, manufacturing, etc. — *adj* **clean-shav'en** with all facial hair shaved off. — **clean'skin** (*Austr*) an unbranded animal (also **clear'skin**); a person with a clean police record (*colloq*); **clean'-up** an act of thorough cleaning; the stamping out of an evil (see also **clean up** below). — **a clean sheet** or **slate** a fresh start; **a clean sweep** a complete change; the winning or gaining of all the prizes, votes, etc. (usu. with *of*); **clean as a whistle** very clean or cleanly; completely emptied; **clean bowled** (*cricket*) bowled out by a ball which hits the stumps without hitting the bat; **clean out** to clean the inside of; to take away all someone's money from (someone) (*colloq*); **clean up** to make clean; to free from vice, corruption, etc.; to make (large profits) (*n* and *adj* **clean'-up**); **come clean** (*slang*) to confess or to divulge everything; **make a clean break** to sever a relationship, etc. completely; **show a clean pair of heels** or **take to one's heels** to run away; **take (someone) to the cleaners** (*slang*) to take all, or a great deal of, a person's money, etc.; to beat or criticise (someone) severely. [O.E. *clæne*.]

cleanse *klenz*, *vt* to make clean or pure. — *adj* **cleans'able**. — *n* **cleans'er** a person who, or that which, cleanses; cleansing-cream, lotion or the like. — *n* **cleans'ing**. — **cleans'ing-cream** a type of cream used to remove make-up from the face; **cleansing department** the section of local administration that deals with the collecting and disposing of refuse and the cleaning of streets. [O.E. *clænsian*.]

clear *klēr*, *adj* pure, bright, undimmed, unclouded, undulled; free from obstruction, difficulty, complication, contents, blame or accusation; disengaged; plain, obvious; distinct; without blemish, defect, drawback or diminution; lucid; transparent; not coded; not blocked. — *adv* in a clear manner; plainly; wholly; quite; out of the way (of). — *vt* to make clear; to empty; to free from obscurity, obstruction or guilt; to free, acquit or vindicate; to leap, or pass by or over; to make as profit; to settle, as a bill; to decode; to unscramble; to declare free from security, etc., restrictions; to pass (a cheque, etc.) through a clearing bank; to pass through (customs, etc.). — *vi* to become clear; to grow free, bright or transparent. — *n* **clear'age** a piece of land cleared. — *n* **clear'ance** the act of clearing; general removal or emptying; eviction from lands; removal of hindrances; intervening space; play between parts, as of a machine; a declaration of freedom from restrictions. — *n* **clear'er** someone or something that clears; a clearing bank. — *n* **clear'ing** the act of making clear; a tract of land cleared of wood, etc., for cultivation; the method by which bankers change cheques and drafts, and arrange the differences. — *adv* **clear'ly** in a clear manner; distinctly; obviously. — *n* **clear'ness**. — **clearance sale** a sale of goods at reduced prices in order to make room for new stock. — *adj* **clear-cut'** sharp in outline; free from obscurity. — *adj* **clear-eyed'** clear-sighted, discerning. — **clear felling** the wholesale felling of all the trees in a particular area. — *adj* **clear-head'ed** having a clear understanding. — **clearing bank** a bank that is a member of the London Bankers' Clearing House, through which it makes credit and cheque transfers to and from other banks; **clearing house** an office where financial clearing business is done; a central source or pool of information, etc. — *adj* **clear-sight'ed** having clearness of sight; discerning. — **clear-sight'edness**; **clear'story** see **clerestory**; **clear'way** a stretch of road on which motorists are not allowed to stop. — **clear off** to get rid of, dispose of; to go away, esp. in order to avoid something (*colloq*); **clear one's throat** to give a slight cough; **clear out** to get rid of; to empty; to empty out, sort through, tidy up (e.g. a room or cupboard), throwing away unwanted material (*n* **clear'-out**); (of a ship) to clear and leave port; to take oneself off; **clear the air** to simplify the situation and relieve tension; **clear the decks** (*fig*) to clear away everything surplus, so as to prepare for action; **clear the way** to make the way open; **clear up** to make or to become clear; to explain (a mystery, misunderstanding, etc.); **in the clear** free of suspicion; out of a difficulty; solvent. [Fr. *clair* — L. *clārus*, clear.]

clearcole *klēr'kōl*, *n* a priming coat consisting of size or glue with whiting. [Fr. *claire colle*, clear glue.]

cleat *klēt*, *n* a wedge; a piece of wood, etc., nailed across anything to keep it in its place or give it an additional strength; a piece attached to parts of a ship for fastening ropes. — *vt* to strengthen with a cleat; to fasten to or by a cleat. [From a supposed O.E. *clēat*.]

cleavage *klē'vij*, *n* a split; the hollow between a woman's breasts, esp. as shown by a low-cut dress; a tendency to split, esp. (in rocks and minerals) in certain directions; mitotic cell-division (*biol*). [**cleave**[1].]

cleave[1] *klēv*, *vt* to divide, to split; to separate with violence; to go or cut through. — *vi* to split apart; to crack: — *pr p* **cleav'ing**; *pa t* **clōve** or **cleft**; *pa p* **clōv'en** or **cleft**. — *adj* **cleav'able**. — *n* **cleav'ableness**. — *n* **cleav'er** a person who or that which cleaves; a butcher's chopper. — *adj* **cleav'ing** splitting. — *n* a cleft. — **in a cleft stick** (*fig*) in a difficult situation; in a dilemma. [O.E. *clēofan*.]

cleave[2] *klēv*, *vi* to stick or adhere; to unite: — *pa t* **cleaved** or (*archaic*) **clāve**; *pa p* **cleaved**. — *n* **cleav'ers** or **clivers** (*kliv'ərz*) goose-grass which cleaves to fur or clothes by its hooks. — *n* and *adj* **cleav'ing**. [O.E. *clifian*.]

clef *klef*, (*mus*) *n* a character placed on the stave by which the absolute pitch of the notes is fixed. [Fr. *clef*, key — L. *clāvis*.]

cleft[1] *kleft, pa t* and *pa p* of **cleave**[1].

cleft[2] *kleft, n* an opening made by cleaving or splitting; a crack, fissure or chink. — *adj* split, divided. [Cf. Ger. *Kluft*, Dan. *klyft*, a hole.]

cleg *kleg, n* a gadfly, horse-fly. [O.N. *kleggi*.]

cleistogamy or **clistogamy** *klīs-tog'ə-mi, (bot) n* production of small flowers, often simplified and inconspicuous, which do not open, and in which self-pollination occurs. — *adj* **cleistogamic** *(-tə-gam'ik)* or **cleistog'amous**. [Gr. *kleistos*, closed, *gamos*, marriage.]

clematis *klem'ə-tis* or *klə-mā'tis, n* any of several temperate climbing plants of the buttercup family, of the genus *Clematis*, including traveller's-joy. [L., — Gr. *klēmatis*, a plant, prob. periwinkle — *klēma*, a twig.]

clement *klem'ənt, adj* mild; gentle; kind; merciful. — *n* **clem'ency** the quality of being clement; mildness; readiness to forgive. — *adv* **clem'ently**. [Fr., — L. *clēmēns, -entis*.]

clementine *klem'ən-tēn* or *-tīn, n* a type of orange either a variety of tangerine or perh. a hybrid of orange and tangerine.

clench *klench* or *klensh, vt* to close tightly; to grasp; to clinch. [Same as **clinch**.]

clepsydra *klep'si-drə, n* an instrument for measuring time by the trickling of water, a water-clock. [L., — Gr. *klepsydrā* — *kleptein*, to steal, *hydōr*, water.]

clerestory or (esp. in U.S.) **clearstory** *clēr'stö-ri, (archit) n* an upper storey or part with its own row of windows — esp. the storey above the triforium in a church. [**clear** (prob. in sense of lighted) and **storey**.]

clergy *klûr'ji, n* the ministers of the Christian or other religion collectively. — **cler'gyman** one of the clergy, a regularly ordained minister; **cler'gy-woman** a woman who is a minister of religion. [Fr. *clergé* — L. *clēricus* — Gr. *klērikos* — *klēros*, a lot, a heritage, then the clergy.]

cleric *kler'ik, n* a clergyman. — *adj* **cler'ical** belonging to the clergy; of, done by or relating to a clerk, office worker, or to general office work. — *n* **cler'icalism** undue influence of the clergy; sacerdotalism. — *n* **cler'icalist**. — *npl* **cler'icals** clerical garb. — **clerical collar** the white collar worn by many Christian clergymen, fastening behind the neck. [L.L. *clericūs*, a priest, clerk.]

clerihew *kler'i-hū, n* a jingle that humorously sums up the life and character of some notable person in two short couplets. [Started by E. *Clerihew* (Bentley) in his *Biography for Beginners* (1905).]

clerisy *kler'i-si, n* scholars, educated people as a class. [Ger. *Klerisei* — Med. L. *clēricia*.]

clerk *klärk* (or in U.S. *klûrk*), *n* a person employed to deal with correspondence, accounts, records, etc. in an office; a record- or account-keeper, esp. for a law court or legislative body; a shop assistant (*US*); a hotel receptionist (*US*); a lay minister (*C of E*). — *vi* to act as clerk. — *adj* **clerk'ish** like a clerk. — *adj* **clerk'ly** scholarly. — *adv* in a scholarly manner. — *n* **clerk'ship**. — **clerk of the course** (in horse- or motor-racing) an official in charge of administration; **clerk of works** or **clerk of the works** a person who superintends the erection and maintenance of a building, etc. [O.E. *clerc*, a priest — L.L. *clēricus*; see ety. for **clergy**.]

clever *klev'ər, adj* dexterous, deft; able; bright, intelligent; ingenious; skilful. — *n* **clev'erness**. — *adj* **clev'erish** somewhat clever. — *adv* **clev'erly**. — *adj* **clever-clev'er** flaunting a superficial knowledgeableness; too clever. — **clever dick** (*slang*) a person who thinks him- or herself clever. [Orig. dialect; poss. conn. with M.E. *clivers*, claws.]

clevis *klev'is, n* a U-shaped piece of metal through which tackle may pass, fixed at the end of a beam.

clew or **clue** *klōō, n* a thread that guides through a labyrinth; the corner of a sail *naut*. — *vt* to coil up into a clew or ball; to tie up to the yards (usu. with *up*; *naut*); to fix up (*fig*). — *npl* **clew'-lines** (*naut*) ropes on the smaller square sails by which they are clewed up for furling. [O.E. *cliwen*.]

clianthus *kli-an'thəs, n* any of several plants of the Australian genus *Clianthus*, shrubs or vines with hanging red flowers. [L., — G. *kleos*, glory, *anthos*, flower.]

cliché *klē'shā, n* a stereotyped phrase, or literary tag; something hackneyed as idea, plot, situation; an electrotype or stereotype plate (*printing*). — *adj* **cli'ché-ridden, cli'ché'd** or **cli'chéed** filled with clichés. [Fr.]

click *klik, n* a short, sharp ticking sound; anything that makes such a sound (such as a latch for a gate); a clucking sound characteristic of certain South African native languages. — *vi* to make a light, sharp sound; to fit into place opportunely or successfully, esp. to succeed in coming into relations of sociability with a person of the other sex (*slang*). — *n* **click'er**. — **click beetle** any of various beetles (*Elateridae*), which can flip over with a clicking sound if on their back; **click'-clack** a persistent clicking noise; **clickety-click'** or **-clack'** a continuous, usu. regular, clicking sound. [Dimin. of **clack**.]

client *klī'ənt, n* a person who employs a lawyer or other professional adviser; a customer; a vassal, dependant, etc. — *n* **clī'entage** the whole number of one's clients; the client's relation to the patron. — *adj* **clīental** *(-ent'l)*. — *n* **clientèle** *(klē-ā-tel')* or **clientele** *(klī'ən-tel)* a following; all the clients of a lawyer, shopkeeper, etc. — *n* **clī'entship**. — **client state** a state which depends on another for protection, economic aid, etc. [L. *cliēns, -entis*, a dependant upon a *patrōnus* (protector).]

cliff *klif, n* the steep side of a mountain; a high steep rock. — *adj* **cliffed'** or **cliff'y** having cliffs; craggy. — **cliff-face'** the sheer or steep front of a cliff; **cliff'hanger** a tense, exciting adventure or contest; an ending line of an episode of a serial, etc. that leaves one in suspense; a serial, film, etc. that keeps one in suspense. — *vi* **cliff'hang**. — *n* and *adj* **cliff'-hanging**. [O.E. *clif*; Du. *clif*; O.N. *klif*.]

climacteric *klī-mak'tər-ik* or *klī-mak-ter'ik, n* a critical period in human life, in which some great bodily change takes place, esp. the menopause or the equivalent in men; a critical time. — *adj* pertaining to such a period; critical. — *adj* **climacter'ical**. [Gr. *klīmaktēr* — *klīmax*, a ladder.]

climactic, climactical. See **climax**.

climate *klī'mit* or *-māt, n* the condition of a country or place with regard to temperature, moisture, etc. (also *fig*); the character of something (*fig*). — *adj* **clī'matal**. — *adj* **clīmatic** *(-mat'ik)* or **climat'ical**. — *vt* **clī'matise** or **-ize** see **acclimatise**. — *adj* **clīmatograph'ical**. — *n* **clīmatog'raphy** a description of climates. — *adj* **clīmatolog'ical**. — *n* **clīmatol'ogist**. — *n* **clīmatol'ogy** the science of climates, or an investigation of the causes on which the climate of a place depends. — **climate of opinion** the critical atmosphere or complex of opinions prevalent at a particular time or in a particular place. [Fr. *climat* — L. *clima* — Gr. *klima, -atos*, slope.]

climax *klī'maks, n* (of a story, play, piece of music, etc.) the most interesting and important or exciting part; a culmination; sexual orgasm; the arranging of discourse in order of increasing strength (*rhet*); (*loosely*) the last term of the rhetorical arrangement; the relatively stable culmination of a series of plant and animal communities developing in an area (also **climax community**). — *vi* to ascend in a climax; to culminate (in). — *adj* **climact'ic** or **climact'ical** pertaining to a climax. — *adv* **climact'ically**. [Gr. *klīmax, -akos*, a ladder — *klīnein*, to slope.]

climb *klīm, vi* or *vt* to ascend or mount by clutching with the hands and feet; to ascend with difficulty; to mount; (of plants) to ascend by means of tendrils or otherwise; extended to similar downward movement: — *pa t* and *pa p* **climbed**. — *n* an act of climbing; an ascent. — *adj* **climb'able**. — *n* **climb'er**. — *n* and *adj* **climb'ing**. — *n* **climb'-down** see **climb down** below. — **climb'ing-frame** a wooden or metal structure on or through which children can climb; **climbing iron** a metal frame with a horizontal spike, worn strapped to the feet as an aid in climbing trees, telegraph poles, etc. — **climb down** to abandon a firmly stated opinion or resolve, or an excessive or overweening demand, position or attitude. [O.E. *climban*.]

clime *klīm*, (chiefly *poetic*) *n* a country, region, tract. [**climate**.]

clinch *klinch* or *klinsh*, *vt* to settle or confirm (*fig*); to drive home (an argument; *fig*); to fasten or rivet a nail by bending and beating down the point. — *vi* to grapple. — *n* an act of clinching; an embrace (*colloq*); the fastening of a nail by beating it back. — *n* **clinch'er** someone who or something that clinches; a decisive argument. — *adj* **clinch'er-built** same as **clinker-built** (see **clink**[3]). [Same as **clench**.]

cline *klīn*, (*biol*) *n* a gradation of differences of form, etc., seen e.g. within one species over a specified area of the world. [See **clino-**.]

cling *kling*, *vi* to stick close by adhesive surface or by clasp; to adhere in interest or affection; to hold to an opinion: — *pa t* and *pa p* **clung**. — *n* adherence. — *adj* **cling** or **cling'stone** (of peaches, etc.) having the pulp adhering firmly to the stone. — *n* **cling'er**. — *n* **cling'iness**. — *adj* **cling'y** tending to cling; sticky. — **cling'film** a type of transparent plastic film used to wrap food, seal food containers, etc. — *adj* **cling'stone** see **cling** (*adj*) above. [O.E. *clingan*.]

clinic *klin'ik*, *n* a private hospital or nursing-home; an institution, or a department of one, or a group of doctors, for treating patients or for diagnosis or giving advice; any group meeting for instruction, often remedial, in a particular field; the instruction of medicine or surgery at the bedside of hospital patients; a session of such instruction. — Also *adj*. — *adj* **clin'ical** hospital-like; concerned with, based on, observation; strictly objective; analytical; plain, functional in appearance. — *adv* **clin'ically**. — *n* **clinician** (*-ish'ən*) a doctor, etc. who works directly with patients; a doctor, etc. who runs, or works in, a clinic. — **clinical death** a state of the body in which the brain has entirely ceased to function, though artificial means can be used to maintain the action of the heart, lungs, etc.; **clinical medicine** or **surgery** medicine or surgery as taught by clinics; **clinical lecture** one given to students at the bedside of the sick; **clinical thermometer** one for taking the temperature of patients. [Gr. *klīnikos* — *klīnē*, a bed.]

clink[1] *klingk*, *n* a ringing sound made by striking metal, glass, etc. — *vt* to cause to make a short, soft ringing sound. — *vi* to make a short, soft ringing sound; to go with a clink. — **clink'stone** phonolite (from its metallic clink when struck). [A form of **click** and **clank**.]

clink[2] *klingk*, (*slang*) *n* prison. [App. orig. *Clink* prison in Southwark.]

clink[3] *klingk*, *vt* to clinch; to rivet. — *adj* (*slang*) **clink'ing**. [Northern form of **clinch**.]

clinker[1] *kling'kər*, *n* the incombustible residue of fused ash raked out of furnaces; furnace slag; the cindery crust of some lava flows; a hard brick (also **klink'er**). [Du. *klinker* (the brick); **clink**[1].]

clinker[2] *kling'kər*, *n* a nail used as a protective stud in footwear. — *adj* **clink'er-built** made of planks which overlap those below and are fastened with clinched nails. [**clink**[3].]

clinker[3] *kling'kər*, (*slang*) *n* someone or something that is popular, well liked, or exceedingly good. [**clink**[1].]

clino- *klī-nō-*, *combining form* signifying oblique, reclining. — *n* **clinometer** (*klīn-* or *klin-om'i-tər*) any of various instruments for measuring slope, elevation or inclination. — *adj* **clinomet'ric**. — *n* **clinom'etry**. [Gr. *klīnein*, to lean — *klīnē*, a bed.]

Clio *klī'ō*, (*Gr mythol*) *n* the Muse of history. [Gr. *Kleiō*, proclaimer.]

cliometrics *klī-ō-met'riks*, *nsing* the application of statistical analysis of data in economic history. [**Clio** and econo*metrics*.]

clip[1] *klip*, *vt* to cut with shears; to cut off; to trim or cut off the hair, twigs, ends, edges, etc. of; to cut out (a magazine article, etc.); to excerpt a section from (a film, etc.); to reduce or curtail; to shorten (a sound); to abbreviate (a word) esp. in speech, as 'sec' for 'second'; to punch a piece from (a ticket, etc.); to cheat, overcharge (*colloq*); to hit sharply. — *vi* to go at a good speed: — *pr p* **clipp'ing**; *pa p* **clipped**. — *n* an act of clipping; the thing removed by clipping; yield of wool; a sharp, stinging blow; a piece taken from a film for separate showing. — *adj* **clipped**. — *n* **clipp'er** a person who clips; a clipping instrument; a swift mover, *specif* a fast sailing-vessel. — *n* **clipp'ing** the act of clipping, esp. the edges of coins; a small piece clipped off, a shred or paring; a newspaper cutting. — *adj* fast-going. — **clip'-joint** a place of entertainment, e.g. a night-club, where customers are overcharged or cheated. — **clip the wings** to cut the feathers of a bird's wings to prevent it from flying; to restrain ambition (*fig*); to deprive of the means of rising. [Prob. from O.N. *klippa*, to cut.]

clip[2] *klip*, *vt* to encircle, hold firmly, or embrace. — *n* a device for gripping, clasping, fastening or holding things together; a container for ammunition which is clipped on to a rifle, etc. — **clip'board** a firm board to which papers can be clipped in order to take notes easily. — *adj* **clip'-on** fastening on to something by means of a clip. [O.E. *clyppan*, to embrace.]

clip-clop. See **clop**.

clique *klēk*, *n* an exclusive group of people; a faction; a coterie — used generally in a bad sense. — *adj* **cliqu'ey**, **cliq'uy** or **cliqu'ish** relating to a clique; exclusive. — *n* **cliqu'iness** or **cliqu'ishness**. — *n* **cliqu'ism** the tendency to form cliques. [Fr.; prob. conn. with **click**.]

clistogamy. See **cleistogamy**.

clitic *klit'ik*, (*linguis*) *adj* (of a word, e.g. French 'me', 'te', 'le') not capable of being stressed, usually pronounced as though part of the preceding or following word. — Also *n*. [Back-formation from **proclitic**, **enclitic**.]

clitoris *kli'* or *klī'tə-ris*, *n* a small elongated erectile organ at the front of the vulva in females, the counterpart, in miniature, of the male penis. — *adj* **clit'oral**. — *n* **clitoridec'tomy** surgical removal of part or all of the clitoris, female circumcision. [Gr. *kleitoris*.]

CLit. *abbrev* for Companion of Literature (awarded by the Royal Society of Literature, London).

clivers. See **cleavers**.

Clo. *abbrev* for Close (in street names).

cloaca *klō-ā'kə*, *n* a sewer; a cavity in birds and reptiles, in which the intestinal and urinary ducts terminate: — *pl* **cloacae** (*klō-ā'sē*). — *adj* **clōā'cal**. [L. *cloāca* — *cluēre*, to purge.]

cloak *klōk*, *n* a loose outer garment; a covering; that which conceals; a disguise, pretext. — *vt* to clothe with a cloak; to cover; to conceal (usu. with *with* or *in*). — *adj* **cloak-and-dagg'er** concerned with plot and intrigue esp. espionage. — **cloak'room** a room for keeping coats and hats; a lavatory. [O.Fr. *cloke*, *cloque* — L.L. *cloca*, a bell, a horseman's bell-shaped cape.]

clobber[1] *klob'ər*, (*slang*) *n* clothing, gear.

clobber[2] *klob'ər*, (*slang*) *vt* to hit very hard; to attack, cause to suffer (*fig*); to defeat overwhelmingly.

cloche *klosh, n* a bell-shaped glass cover under which plants are forced; a lady's close-fitting hat. [Fr. — L.L. *cloca, clocca*, a bell.]

clock[1] *klok, n* a machine for measuring time, strictly one with a bell; a speedometer (*colloq*). — *vt* to time by a clock or stop-watch; to achieve (a certain officially attested time for a race); to hit (*slang*); to observe, notice (*slang*); to turn back the mileometer of (a car) so that it registers a lower figure than the actual mileage (*n* **clock'ing** this (illegal) practice). — *vi* to register a time by a recording clock. — *adv* **clock'wise** in the direction in which the hands of a clock move. — **clock card** a card on which the hours worked by an employee are recorded by a time-clock; **clock'maker; clock'-radio** an electronic apparatus combining the functions of alarm-clock and radio, esp. for bedside use — also **alarm'-radio; clock tower** a usu. square tower having a clock at the top with a face on each exterior wall; **clock'work** the works or machinery of a clock; steady, regular machinery like that of a clock. — *adj* automatic. — **against the clock** making an effort to overcome shortage of time or achieve the shortest time; **beat the clock** to finish a job, etc., before the time limit runs out; **clock in, out, on** or **off** to register time of coming or going, in, out, on or off; **clock up** (*colloq*) to reach (a certain speed, score, etc.); **like clockwork** as smoothly as if driven by clockwork (*fig*); **o'clock** (for earlier **of the clock**) as reckoned or shown by the clock; in a direction corresponding to that shown by the hour-hand of a horizontal clock; **put back the clock** or **put the clock back** to return to an earlier time and its conditions; **put the clock** (or **clocks) back** or **forward** to alter the clocks to allow for the change from or to summer time; **round the clock** for the whole of the twenty-four hours; **watch the clock** to wait eagerly for one's work-time to finish, i.e. to skimp one's work, or do no more than is necessary (*n* **clock'-watcher;** *n* **clock'-watching**). [M.E. *clokke*, prob. through O.Fr. from L.L. *cloca, clocca*, a bell.]

clock[2] *klok, n* an ornament on the side of a stocking. — *adj* **clocked** ornamented with such clocks.

clod *klod, n* a thick round mass or lump, that sticks together, esp. of earth or turf; a concreted mass; a stupid person. — *adj* **clodd'ish.** — *n* **clodd'ishness.** — *adj* **clodd'y** earthy. — **clod'hopper** a dolt; a heavy, clumsy shoe (*slang*). — *adj* **clod'hopping** boorish. [A later form of **clot.**]

clog *klog, n* a wooden shoe; a shoe with a wooden sole; a heavy block of wood fastened to a person or animal to restrict movement; an obstruction. — *vt* to choke up with an accumulation (often with *up*); to obstruct, impede; to fasten a clog to. — *adj* **clogged** choked up, blocked; encumbered. — *n* **clogg'er** a person who makes clogs. — *n* **clogg'iness.** — *adj* **clogg'y** lumpy, sticky. — **clog'dance** a dance performed with clogs, the clatter keeping time to the music. — **pop one's clogs** (*slang*) to die. [M.E. a block of wood.]

cloisonné *klwäz-on-ā, kloi-zon'ā* or *-ā', adj* decorated in enamel, in compartments formed by small fillets of metal. — *n* work of this kind. [Fr. — *cloison*, a partition.]

cloister *klois'tər, n* a covered arcade forming part of a monastic or collegiate establishment; a place of religious retirement, a monastery or nunnery; an enclosed place; monastic life. — *vt* to confine in a cloister; to confine within walls. — *adj* **clois'tered** dwelling in or enclosed by cloisters; sheltered from reality and the full experience of life. — *adj* **clois'tral** pertaining or confined to a cloister; secluded. [O.Fr. *cloistre* (O.E. *clauster*) — L. *claustrum* — *claudĕre, clausum*, to shut.]

clomp *klomp, n* and *vi* same as **clump.**

clone *klōn*, (*biol*) *n* the whole stock of individuals derived asexually from one sexually produced; any of such individuals; a person or thing closely similar to another, a copy or replica (*colloq*). — *vt* to reproduce as a clone; to produce a clone or clones of. — *adj* **clō'nal.** [Gr. *klōn*, shoot.]

clonic. See **clonus.**

clonk *klongk, n* the sound of something heavy falling on to a surface. — *vi* to make or go with such a sound. — *vt* to hit. [Imit.]

clonus *klō'nəs, n* a spasm of alternate contractions and relaxations of the muscles. — *adj* **clonic** (*klon'ik*). [Latinised from Gr. *klŏnos*, tumult.]

clop *klop, n* the sound of a horse's hoof-tread. — *adv* with a clop. — *vi* to make or go with such a sound. — Also **clip-clop'** and **clop-clop'.** [Imit.]

cloqué *klo-kā', n* an embossed fabric. — Also *adj.* [Fr.]

close[1] *klōs, adj* shut up; with no opening; confined, unventilated; stifling; narrow; stingy; near, in time or place (often with *to* or *by*); intimate; compact; crowded; hidden; reserved; private; secret; thorough, in detail. — *adv* in a close manner; tightly; nearly; densely; secretly. — *n* an enclosed place; a narrow passage off a street, esp. leading to a tenement stairway or courtyard; a small, quiet, esp. dead-end road; the precinct of a cathedral. — *adv* **close'ly.** — *n* **close'ness.** — *adj* **close-band'ed** closely united. — **close call** a narrow escape; **close company** a firm controlled by five, or fewer, people; **close corporation** a corporation which fills up its own vacancies, without outside interference; **close encounter** a direct personal confrontation with an extraterrestrial being (also *fig*). — *adj* **close-fist'ed** or **close-hand'ed** penurious, covetous. — *adj* **close'-fitting** (of clothes) designed to fit tightly. — *adj* **close'-grained** with the particles, fibres, etc., close together, compact. — **close harmony** (*mus*) harmony in which the notes of chords lie close together. — *adj* **close'-knit** (of communities, etc.) closely connected, bound together. — *adj* **close-lipped'** or **-mouthed'** reticent, saying little. — **close season** or **time** a time of the year when it is illegal to kill certain game or fish — the breeding season; a prohibited or inactive period in any sport; **close shave** or **close thing** a close call; **close'-up** a photograph or film taken near at hand and thus detailed and big in scale; a close scrutiny. — **close on** almost, nearly; **close to the chest** without revealing one's intentions. [Fr. *clos*, shut — L. *claudĕre, clausum*, to close, shut up.]

close[2] *klōz, vt* to complete, conclude; to end, terminate; to block, make impassable or impenetrable; to forbid access to; to place (a door, etc.) so as to cover an opening, to shut; to put an end to discussion of; to cease operating or trading; to make close, draw or bring together, narrow; to unite; (of ships) to come or pass near to. — *vi* to come to an end; to cease operating or trading; to come together; to unite; to narrow; to agree (with). — *n* the manner or time of closing; a stop; a cadence; the end. — *adj* **closed** shut; blocked; not open to traffic; with permanent sides and top; having a lid, cover, etc.; exclusive, having few contacts outside itself (e.g. *a closed community*); not open to all, restricted; continuous and finishing where it began. — *n* **clos'er.** — *n* **clos'ing** ending; enclosing; coming together, agreement. — *n* **clos'ure** the act of closing; something that closes or fastens; the end. — **closed book** (*fig*) a mystery; something about which one knows nothing. — *adj* **closed chain** (*chem*) having a molecule in which the atoms are linked ringwise, like a chain with the ends united. — **closed circuit** (*television*) a system in which the showing is for restricted not general viewing; **closed shop** an establishment in which only members of a trade union, or of a particular trade union, will be employed; the principle or policy implied in such a regulation; **closed syllable** one ending in a consonant; **closing price** the value of shares on the stock-market when business stops for the day; **clos'ing-time** the time at which business stops, esp. in public houses. — **behind (or with) closed doors** in private, the public being excluded, as in court cases, etc. (*adj* **closed-door'**); **close a bargain** to make an agreement; **close down** to come to a standstill or stoppage of work; to give up business (*n* **close'-down**); **close in upon** to surround and draw near to; **close on** to catch up with; **close one's eyes to** to ignore purposely; **close ranks** (of soldiers drawn up in line) to stand closer together in order to present a more solid front to the enemy; to unite, make a show of solidarity in the face of a common danger; **close with** to accede to; to grapple with; **with closed doors** see **behind closed doors** above. [Fr. *clore, clos* — L. *claudĕre, clausum.*]

closet *kloz'it, n* a recess or cupboard off a room; a small private room; a privy; a horizontal band one-half the width of a bar (*heraldry*). — *adj* secret, private. — *vt* to shut up in, as if in, or take into a closet; to conceal: — *pr p* **clos'eting**; *pa t* and *pa p* **clos'eted.** — **closet queen** (*slang*) a homosexual who does not openly admit his homosexuality; **closet-strat'egist** a mere theorist in strategy. — **come out of the closet** to admit openly of a practice, tendency, habit, etc. previously kept a close secret (esp. homosexuality). [O.Fr. *closet*, dimin. of *clos*, an enclosure; see **close**[1].]

clostridium *klost-rid'i-əm, n* any of several species of ovoid or spindle-shaped bacteria including those causing botulism and tetanus. [N.L., — Gr. *klostēr*, a spindle, and dimin. sfx. *-idium.*]

closure. See **close**[2].

clot *klot, n* a mass of soft or solidified fluid matter, such as blood; a fool. — *vt* and *vi* to form into clots: — *pr p* **clott'ing**; *pa t* and *pa p* **clott'ed.** — *vt* **clott'er** to coagulate. — *n* **clott'iness.** — *n* **clott'ing** coagulation. — *adj* **clott'y.** — **clotted cream** a famous Devonshire delicacy, thick cream made from scalded milk. [O.E. *clott*, a clod of earth.]

cloth *kloth, n* woven material from which garments or coverings are made; a piece of this material, for a particular use, e.g. floorcloth, tablecloth; (with *the*) the clerical profession, the clergy; sails: — *pl* **cloths** (*kloths*). — **cloth cap** a flat cap. — *adj* **cloth'-eared** (*slang*) deaf, usu. because inattentive. — **cloth of gold** cloth with threads of gold and silk or wool. [O.E. *clāth*, cloth.]

clothe *klōdh, vt* to cover with a garment; to provide with clothes; to invest, equip (*fig*); to cover: — *pr p* **clothing** (*klōdh'ing*): — *pa t* and *pa p* **clothed** (*klōdhd*) or **clad**. — *npl* **clothes** (*klōdhz*; *colloq klōz*) garments or articles of dress; bedclothes. — *n* **clothier** (*klō'dhi-ər*) a person who makes or sells cloth or clothes. — *n* **clo'thing** clothes, garments; covering. — **clothes'-brush** a brush for clothes. — *adj* **clothes'-conscious** concerned about one's clothes and appearance. — **clothes'-horse** a frame for hanging laundry on to air or to dry; **clothes'-line** a rope or wire, etc. for hanging washing on to dry; **clothes'-moth** any of various moths whose larvae feed on wool or fur; **clothes'-peg** or **clothes'-pin** a wooden or plastic clip to hold washing on a clothes-line; **clothes'-pole** a pole from which clothes-lines are hung; **clothes'-press** a cupboard, often with drawers, for storing clothes; an apparatus for pressing clothes; **clothes'-prop** a pole with a notched end for raising or supporting a clothes-line; **clothes'-sense** dress-sense. [O.E. *clāthian* — *clāth*, cloth.]

cloture *klō'chər* or (Fr.) *klō-tür, n* closure; the limitation of a debate in a legislative assembly, usu. by calling for an immediate vote (*US*). — Also *vt.* [Fr. *clôture.*]

cloud *klowd, n* a mass of fog, consisting of minute particles of water, often in a frozen state, floating in the atmosphere; anything unsubstantial (*fig*); a great number of anything; anything that obscures as a cloud does; a dark or dull spot; a great volume of dust or smoke; anything gloomy, overhanging or ominous. — *vt* to overspread with clouds; to darken; to defame; to stain with dark spots or streaks; to dull. — *vi* to become clouded or darkened. — *adj* **cloud'ed** hidden by clouds; darkened, indistinct, dull (*fig*); variegated with spots. — *adv* **cloud'ily.** — *n* **cloud'iness.** — *n* **cloud'ing** a cloudy appearance. — *adj* growing dim. — *adj* **cloud'less** unclouded, clear. — *adv* **cloud'lessly.** — *adj* **cloud'y** darkened with, or consisting of, clouds; obscure; gloomy; stained with dark spots. — **cloud base** the under-surface of a cloud or clouds; the height of this above sea-level; **cloud'berry** a low plant related to the bramble, with an orange-red berry; **cloud'burst** a sudden downpour of rain over a small area; **cloud-cuck'oo-land** an imaginary situation or land esp. as the product of impractical or wishful thinking; **cloud ceiling** the height of the cloud base above the ground; **cloud'-chamber** an apparatus in which the path of charged particles is made visible by means of water-drops condensed on gas ions; **cloud'-seeding** the induction of rainfall by scattering particles, e.g. dry ice, silver iodide, on clouds from aircraft. — **on cloud nine** (*colloq*) intensely happy; **under a cloud** in trouble, disgrace, or disfavour; **with one's head in the clouds** in a dreamy impractical way or state. [O.E. *clūd*, a hill, then a cloud.]

clout *klowt, n* influence, power (*colloq*); a blow or cuff; a piece of cloth; a garment. — *vt* to hit with great force; to cuff; to mend with a patch. [O.E. *clūt.*]

clove[1] *klōv, pa t* of **cleave**[1]. — **clove'-hitch** a kind of hitch knot, used to connect ropes of different thicknesses, or a rope to an object.

clove[2] *klōv, n* a division of a bulb (e.g. of garlic). [O.E. *clufu*; cf. **cleave**[1].]

clove[3] *klōv, n* the flower-bud of the **clove'-tree** dried as a spice, and yielding an essential oil, **oil of cloves**, used in medicine; (in *pl*) a cordial obtained from it. — **clove-gill'yflower** or **clove'-pink** a variety of pink (flower), smelling of cloves. [Fr. *clou*, nail, from its shape — L. *clāvus*, a nail.]

cloven *klōv'n, adj* split; divided. — *adj* **cloven-foot'ed** or **-hoofed'** having the hoof divided, as the ox or sheep. — **the cloven hoof** applied to any indication of devilish agency or temptation, from the early representation of the devil with cloven hoofs. [Past p. of **cleave**[1].]

clover *klō'vər, n* any of a genus (*Trifolium*) of papilionaceous plants, with heads of small flowers and trifoliate leaves, affording rich pasturage. — *adj* **clov'ered** covered with clover. — *adj* **clov'ery** abounding in clover. — **clov'er-grass** clover; **clov'erleaf** a traffic arrangement in which one road passes over the top of another and the roads connecting the two are in the pattern of a four-leafed clover; any interlinked arrangement of this shape. — Also *adj.* — **live in clover** to live luxuriously or in abundance. [O.E. *clāfre* (usu. *clǣfre*).]

clown *klown, n* a comic entertainer, esp. in the circus, with colourful clothes and make-up; a person who behaves in a comical way; a stupid person (*colloq*); a rude, clumsy or boorish person. — *vi* to play the clown. — *n* **clown'ery** a clown's performance. — *n* **clown'ing.** — *adj* **clown'ish** of or like a clown. — *adv* **clown'ishly.** — *n* **clown'ishness.** [Perh. — L. Ger., cf. Fris. *klönne, klünne.*]

cloy *kloi, vt* to satiate to the point of disgust. — *vi* to become distasteful from excess; to cause distaste, esp. by being too sweet or rich. — *adj* **cloyed.** — *adj* **cloy'ing.** [Aphetised from *accloy* — O.Fr. *encloyer* — L.L. *inclāvāre*, to drive in a nail.]

cloze *klōz*, (*educ*) *adj* denoting a type of exercise in which the reader is required to supply words that have been deleted from a text, as a test of comprehension in reading. [Formed from **closure**.]

CLP *abbrev* for Constituency Labour Party.

CLR *abbrev* for computer language recorder.

CLT *abbrev* for computer language translator.

club *klub*, *n* a heavy tapering stick, knobby or thick at one end, used to strike with; a cudgel; a bat used in certain games; an instrument for playing golf, with a wooden, iron, or aluminium head, or a wooden head with brass sole; a playing card with black trefoil pips; a combination; a clique, set; an association of persons for social, political, athletic, or other ends; an association of persons who possess premises or facilities which all members may use; a clubhouse, or the premises occupied by a club; a nightclub. — *vt* to beat with a club; to use a heavy object as a club. — *vi* (esp. with *together*) to join together for some common end; to combine together; to share in a common expense. — *adj* **clubb'able** or **club'able** sociable. — *adj* **clubbed** enlarged at the end like a club. — *n* **clubb'ing** beating; combination; a thickening, as of finger-ends; the frequenting of nightclubs. — *adj* **clu'bby** characteristic of a club; sociable; exclusive, cliquey. — **club'-face** the face of a golf club; **club-foot'** a deformed foot. — *adj* **club-foot'ed**. — **club'-head** the head of a golf club; **club'house** a building for the accommodation of a club; **club'land** the area around St James's in London, where many of the old-established clubs are; an area or region containing a large number of nightclubs or working-men's clubs; **club'-line** (*printing*) a short line at the end of a paragraph; **club'man** a man who carries a club; a member of a club; a frequenter of clubs, man-about-town; **club'-room** the room in which a club meets; **club'root** a fungal disease which attacks the roots of plants of the Cruciferae; **club'rush** any sedge of the genus *Scirpus*; **club sandwich** a sandwich of three slices of bread or toast containing two fillings; **club soda** soda water; **club'woman**. — **in the club** or **in the pudding club** (*slang*) pregnant; **join the club** (*colloq*) we are all in the same position; me too. [O.N. and Sw. *klubba*; same root as **clump**.]

cluck *kluk*, *n* the call of a hen to her chickens; any similar sound. — *vi* to make such a sound. — *adj* **cluck'y** (*Austr slang*) obsessed with babies, broody. [Imit.]

clue[1] *kloo͞*, *n* anything that points to the solution of a mystery. — *adj* **clue'less** without a trace; ignorant; stupid. — *adj* **clued-up'** (*colloq*) (well-)informed. — **clue in** (*colloq*) to inform; **not have a clue** to have no information; to have no idea, no notion at all. [See **clew**.]

clue[2]. See **clew**.

clump *klump*, *n* a shapeless mass of anything; a cluster; a clot; a thick additional sole; a heavy tread; a blow. — *vi* to walk heavily; to clot; to cluster. — *vt* to put in a clump; to beat. — *n* **clump'iness**. — *adj* **clump'ing** (*colloq*) clumsy. — *adj* **clump'y** having many clumps; heavy. [Prob. Scand.]

clumsy *klum'zi*, *adj* badly made; unwieldy; awkward; ungainly. — *adv* **clum'sily**. — *n* **clum'siness**. [M.E. *clumsen*, to be stiff or numb.]

clung *klung*, *pa t* and *pa p* of **cling**.

clunk *klungk*, *n* a metallic noise; a thump. — *vi* to fall with this sound. [Imit.]

cluster *klus'tər*, *n* a number of things of the same kind growing or joined together; a bunch; a mass; a crowd; a statistically significant number of people within a sample having given characteristics. — *vi* to grow in or gather into clusters. — *vt* to collect into clusters; to cover with clusters. — *adj* **clus'tered** grouped. — *adj* **clus'tering**. — *adj* **clus'tery**. — **clus'ter-bean** a legume grown for forage; **clus'ter-bomb** a bomb that opens on impact to throw out a number of small bombs; **cluster graft** an organ transplant in which the patient receives more than one organ; **cluster marketing** advertising, etc. aimed at people with specific characteristics; **cluster physics** the physics of very small numbers of atoms; **clust'er-pine** the pinaster, a pine with clustered cones. [O.E. *clyster*.]

clutch[1] *kluch*, *vt* to close the hand upon; to hold firmly; to seize or grasp. — *vi* to make a snatching movement (with *at*). — *n* a grasping hand (often in *pl*); a device by which two shafts or rotating members may be connected or disconnected either while at rest or in relative motion; the pedal in a motor vehicle which controls this device; grasp; a snatching movement; (in *pl*) power, control. — **clutch bag** a kind of handbag without strap or handle, carried in the hand or under the arm. [O.E. *clyccan*, to clench.]

clutch[2] *kluch*, *n* a brood of chickens; a sitting of eggs; (*loosely*) a number, group. — *vt* to hatch.

clutter *klut'ər*, *n* a clotted or confused mass; a disorderly accumulation; confusion; irregular interference on a radar screen from echoes, rain, buildings, etc. — *vi* to crowd together. — *vt* to litter, clog with superfluous objects, material, etc. (often with *up*). [From **clot**; influenced by **cluster** and **clatter**.]

Clydesdale *klīdz'dāl*, *adj* (of a breed of cart-horses) originating in *Clydesdale*, the area of Scotland through which the Clyde flows. — *n* a Clydesdale horse. — *adj* **Clyde'side** relating to *Clydeside*, the area along the Clyde estuary; or to shipbuilding, formerly its main industry. — *n* **Clyde'sider** an inhabitant of Clydeside.

clypeus *klip'i-əs*, *n* the shield-like part of an insect's head. — *adj* **clyp'eal** of the clypeus. — *adj* **clyp'eate** or **clyp'ēiform** buckler-shaped. [L. *clipeus* (*clypeus*), a round shield.]

CM *abbrev* for: *Chirurgiae Magister* (L.), Master of Surgery; Corresponding Member.

Cm (*chem*) *symbol* for curium.

cm. *abbrev* for: *carat metrique* (Fr.), metric carat; *causa mortis* (L.), by reason of death; centimetre(s).

CMEA *abbrev* for Council for Mutual Economic Assistance.

CMG *abbrev* for Companion of (the Order of) St. Michael and St. George.

CMHR *abbrev* for combustion modified highly resilient.

CMI *abbrev* for computer-managed instruction.

CML *abbrev* for computer-managed learning.

CMS *abbrev* for Church Missionary Society.

CMV *abbrev* for cytomegalovirus.

CNAA *abbrev* for Council for National Academic Awards.

CNAG *abbrev* for Comunn na Gàidhlig, the national agency concerned with the development of Gaelic.

CND *abbrev* for Campaign for Nuclear Disarmament.

CNN *abbrev* for Cable News Network (U.S.).

CNR *abbrev* for Canadian National Railway.

CNRS *abbrev* for *Centre National de la Recherche Scientifique* (Fr.), National Centre for Scientific Research.

CNS *abbrev* for central nervous system.

CO *abbrev* for: Colombia (I.V.R.); Colorado (U.S. state); combined operations; Commanding Officer; Commonwealth Office; conscientious objector; Crown Office.

Co. *abbrev* for: Company; County.

Co (*chem*) *symbol* for cobalt.

c/o *abbrev* for care of.

co-. See **com-**.

coacervate *kō-as'ər-vāt* or *-ûr'vāt*, *vt* to heap; to cause to mass together. — *n* (also **coacervā'tion**) a reversible aggregation of particles into liquid droplets before flocculation. [L. *coacervāre*, *-ātum* — *acervus*, heap.]

coach *kōch*, *n* a large, closed, four-wheeled carriage, esp. one for state occasions or one plying for conveyance of passengers; a railway carriage; a bus for tourists and sightseers; a private tutor; a professional trainer in athletics, football, etc. — *vt* to tutor, instruct, prepare for an examination, sporting event, etc. — *vi* to go by coach; to act as tutor or instructor. — *n* **coach'ing** travelling by coach; tutoring; instruction. — **coach'builder** a person who builds the bodies of cars, lorries, railway carriages, etc.; **coach'-building**. — *adj* **coach'-built** (of prams) of solid construction and upholstered. — **coach'-horse** a horse used for drawing a coach; **coach'-house** a building to keep a coach in; **coach'-line** an ornamental line along the body of a motor vehicle, building, etc.; **coach'load** the number of people a coach can carry; **coach'man** the driver of a coach; a servant employed to drive a carriage; **coach party** a group of people travelling by coach; **coach tour** a holiday or outing on which people travel from place to place by coach; **coach'-work** the fine work of a motor car body. [Fr. *coche* — Hung. *kocsi*, from *Kocs*, in Hungary.]

coaction *kō-ak'shən*, *n* joint action; mutual relations. — *adj* **cōac'tive** acting together. — *n* **cōactiv'ity**. [**co-** and **action**.]

coad. *abbrev* for coadjutor.

coadjutant *kō-aj'ə-tənt*, *adj* mutually helping. — *n* a person who helps another. — *n* **coadj'utor** a helper, assistant, esp. of a bishop; an associate: — *fem* **coadj'utress** or **coadj'utrix**. — *n* **coadj'utorship**. [L. *adjūtor*, a helper — *ad*, to, *juvāre*, to help.]

co-agent *kō-ā'jənt*, *n* a joint agent. — *n* **co-ā'gency**.

coagulate *kō-ag'ū-lāt*, *vt* to make to curdle, clot or set by a chemical reaction. — *vi* to curdle, clot or set irreversibly. — *n* **cōagūlabil'ity**. — *adj* **cōag'ūlable**. — *n* **cōag'ūlant** a substance that causes coagulation. — *n* **cōagūlā'tion**. — *adj* **cōag'ūlātive**. — *n* **cōag'ulator**. — *adj* **cōag'ūlatory**. — *n* **cōag'ūlum** what is coagulated. [L. *coāgulāre*, *-ātum* — *agĕre*, to drive.]

coal *kōl*, *n* a firm, brittle, generally black combustible carbonaceous rock derived from vegetable matter; a piece of this rock; a piece of charcoal, esp. glowing; a cinder; an ember. — *vi* to take in coal. — *vt* to supply with coal. — *n* **coal'er** a ship or train carrying or transporting coal. — *adj* **coal'y** of or like coal; covered with coal. — **coal'-bed** a stratum of coal. — *adj* **coal'-black** black as coal, very black. — **coal'-bunker** a box, recess or compartment for holding coal; **coal'-cellar** a cellar or similar place for storing coal; **coal'-cutter** a machine for undercutting a coal-bed; **coal'-dust** coal in fine powder; **coal'-face** the exposed surface of coal in a mine; **coal'-field** a district containing coal strata. — *adj* **coal'-fired** burning or fuelled by coal. — **coal'fish** coley; **coal'-gas** the mixture of gases produced by the distillation of coal, used for lighting and heating; **coal'-hole** a small coal-cellar; a hole in the pavement for filling a coal-cellar; **coal'man** a man who sells or carries coal; **Coal Measures** (*geol*) the uppermost division of the Carboniferous; **coal'-merchant** a dealer in coal; **coal'mine** a mine from which coal is dug; **coal'miner**; **coal'-scuttle** a fireside container for coal; **coal'-tar** a thick, black, opaque liquid formed when coal is distilled; **coal'-tit** (also **cole'-**) a small species of tit with a dark back and black head. — **carry coals to Newcastle** to take a thing where it is already most abundant; **haul** or **call over the coals** to reprimand; **heap coals of fire on someone's head** to excite someone's remorse and repentance by returning good for evil (from the Bible: Romans xii. 20). [O.E. *col*.]

coalesce *kō-ə-les'*, *vi* to grow together or unite into one body. — *n* **coalesc'ence**. — *adj* **coalesc'ent**. [L. *coalēscĕre* — *alēscĕre*, to grow up.]

coalition *kō-ə-lish'ən*, *n* combination or alliance short of union, esp. of states or political parties. — *adj* **cōali'tional**. — *n* **cōali'tioner** or **cōali'tionist**. — *n* **cōali'tionism**. — **coalition government** government by a coalition of parties. [L. *coalitiō*, ety. as for **coalesce**.]

coaming *kōm'ing*, (*naut*) *n* (usu. in *pl*) raised work around the edges of the hatches of a ship to keep water out.

Coanda effect *kō-an'də i-fekt'*, *n* the tendency of liquid, when it encounters a curved surface, to run along it. [Henri Marie *Coanda*, 1885–1972, French engineer.]

coapt *kō-apt'*, *vt* to adjust. — *n* **coaptā'tion**. [L. *coaptāre* — *aptāre*, to fit.]

coarse *kōrs*, *adj* common, base, inferior; rough; rude; uncivil; harsh; gross; large in grain, fibre or mesh, etc.; without refinement. — *adv* **coarse'ly**. — *vt* and *vi* **coars'en** to make or become coarse. — *n* **coarse'ness**. — *adj* **coars'ish** somewhat coarse. — **coarse fish** freshwater fish other than those of the salmon family, but including the grayling, which, though of a salmon family, is classed as a coarse fish, because of its time of spawning (opp. to *game fish*); **coarse fishing**. — *adj* **coarse'-grained** large in grain; coarse in nature (*fig*); gross. [From phrase 'in course', hence *ordinary*.]

coast *kōst*, *n* the border of land next to the sea; the seashore; an act or spell of coasting. — *vi* to sail along or near a coast; to travel downhill on a sledge, on a cycle without pedalling or in a motor car out of gear; to glide; to succeed or proceed without effort. — *vt* to sail by or near to. — *adj* **coast'al**. — *n* **coast'er** a vessel engaged in coasting; a container or mat for a decanter or glasses on a table. — *adj* **coast'ing** keeping near the coast; trading between ports in the same country. — *n* the act of sailing, or of trading, along the coast; sliding downhill. — *adv* **coast'ward** or **coast'wards** toward the coast. — *adv* **coast'-wise** along the coast. — *adj* carried on along the coast. — **coast'guard** an organisation which keeps watch along the coast for prevention of smuggling, for life-saving, defence, etc.; a member of this; **coast'line** the line or boundary of a coast; shoreline. — *adj* **coast-to-coast'** covering the whole country, nationwide. — **the coast is clear** there is no obstacle or danger in the way. [O.Fr. *coste* (Fr. *côte*) — L. *costa*, rib, side.]

coat *kōt*, *n* an outer garment with sleeves; an overcoat; the hair or wool of an animal; any covering; a membrane or layer, as of paint, etc. — *vt* to clothe; to cover with a coat or layer. — *n* **coat'ee** a short close-fitting coat, esp. for a baby. — *n* **coat'er** a worker, machine, etc., that applies a layer or covering. — *n* **coat'ing** a covering, layer; cloth for coats. — **coat'-hanger** a curved piece of wood, etc., with a hook, by which clothes may be hung and kept in shape; **coat'rack** or **coat'stand** a rack or stand with pegs for hanging coats on; **coat tails** the long back-pieces of a tail-coat. — **coat of arms** the family insignia embroidered on the outer garment worn over the hauberk, or coat of mail; the heraldic bearings of a person, family, or organisation; **coat of mail** a piece of armour for the upper part of the body, made of metal scales or rings linked one with another; **turn one's coat** to change one's principles, or to turn from one party to another. [O.Fr. *cote* (Fr. *cotte*) — L.L. *cottus*, *cotta*, a tunic.]

coati *kō-ä'tē*, *-ti* or *kə-wä'tē*, *n* an American carnivorous mammal related to the raccoons. — Also **coati-mun'di** or **-mon'di**. [Tupí.]

co-author *kō-ö'thər*, *n* a joint author.

coax[1] *kōks*, *vt* to persuade by fondling or flattery; to humour or soothe; to manipulate patiently. — *n* **coax'er**. — *adv* **coax'ingly**. [Obs. *cokes*, a simpleton.]

coax[2] or **co-ax** *kō'aks*, *n* short for coaxial cable.

coaxial *kō-ak'si-əl*, *adj* having the same axis. — *adv* **coax'ially**. — **coaxial cable** a cable consisting of one or more **coaxial pairs**, each a central conductor within an outer tubular conductor.

cob[1] *kob, n* a short-legged strong horse; a male swan (also **cob'-swan**); a lump; a rounded object; a cobloaf; a corncob; a cobnut. — **cob'loaf** a rounded, round-headed or misshapen loaf; **cob'nut** a large hazelnut. [Perh. conn. with **cop**[1].]

cob[2] *kob, n* a kind of composition of clay and straw for building. — **cob'-wall; cob cottage**.

cobalt *kō'bölt, n* a metallic element (atomic no. 27; symbol **Co**), having similarities to nickel; a blue pigment prepared from it — also **cōbalt-blue'**. — *adj* of this deep-blue colour. — **cobalt-60** a radioactive isotope of cobalt used in the gamma-ray treatment of cancer. — *adj* **cobalt'ic**. — *adj* **cobaltif'erous**. — *n* **cō'baltite** a mineral containing cobalt, arsenic and sulphur (also **cobalt glance**). — **cobalt bomb** a suggested bomb consisting of a hydrogen bomb encased in cobalt — made more dangerous than ever by the cobalt-60 dust released. [Ger. *Kobalt*, from *Kobold*, a demon, a nickname given by the German miners.]

cobber *kob'ər*, (*Austr colloq*) *n* mate, chum, buddy.

cobble[1] *kob'l* or **cobblestone** *kob'l-stōn, n* a rounded stone, esp. formerly used in paving. — *vt* to pave with cobblestones.

cobble[2] *kob'l, vt* to mend shoes; to patch up, assemble, put together, or mend coarsely (often with *together* or *up*). — *n* **cobb'ler** a person who cobbles or mends shoes; an iced drink made up of wine or spirits, sugar, lemon, etc.; a (usu. fruit) pie with a thick pastry crust; (in *pl*; *slang*) nonsense. — *n* **cobb'lery**. — *n* **cobb'ling**.

co-belligerent *kō-bi-lij'ə-rənt, adj* co-operating in warfare. — Also *n*.

Cobol *kō'bōl* or *-bol, n* a computer programming language, for commercial use, which uses English words. [*Co*mmon *b*usiness *o*riented *l*anguage.]

cobra *kō'brə* or *kob'rə, n* a poisonous snake, found in India and Africa, which dilates its neck so as to resemble a hood. — *adj* **cob'ric**. — *adj* **cob'riform** like or akin to the cobra. [Port., snake.]

cobweb *kob'web, n* a spider's web or net; any snare or device intended to entrap; anything flimsy or easily broken; anything that obscures. — *adj* **cob'webby**.

coca *kō'kə, n* a Peruvian shrub whose leaves contain cocaine. [Sp. — Quechua *coca*.]

Coca-Cola® *kō-kə-kō'lə, n* a carbonated soft drink first made in the U.S. (often shortened to **Coke**). — **coca-colonisā'tion** (*facetious*) the invasion of other parts of the world by American culture.

cocaine *ko-kān', n* an alkaloid obtained from coca-leaves or produced synthetically; an addictive narcotic used medicinally as a local anaesthetic. — *n* **cocain'ism** a morbid condition induced by addiction to cocaine. — *n* **cocain'ist**. [**coca**.]

coccid, etc. See under **coccus**.

coccus *kok'əs, n* a one-seeded portion of a dry fruit that breaks up (*bot*); a spherical bacterium; (with *cap*) a genus of hemipterous insects of a family **Coccidae** (*kok'si-dē*): — *pl* **cocci** (*kok'sī*). — *adj* **coccal** (*kok'əl*). — *n* **coccid** (*kok'sid*) any of the Coccidae. — Also *adj*. — *n* **coccidioidomycosis** (*-i-oi-dō-mī-kō'sis*) infection resulting from the inhalation of the spores of the fungus *Coccidioides immitis*, occurring either as an influenza-like respiratory illness, or as a severe, progressive disease affecting the skin, viscera, nervous system and lungs. — *n* **coccidium** (*kok-sid'i-əm*) a protozoan parasite of the order **Coccid'ia**: — *pl* **coccid'ia**. — *n* **coccidiosis** (*kok-sid-i-ō-sis*) a contagious infection of birds and animals by coccidia. — *n* **coccid'iostat** any of various drugs used to prevent the development of coccidium-caused diseases, often added to feed-stuffs or drinking-water. [L., — Gr. *kokkos*, a berry.]

coccyx *kok'siks* (*anat*) *n* the terminal triangular bone of the vertebral column: — *pl* **coccyges** (*kok-sī'jēz*). — *adj* **coccygeal** (*kok-sij'i-əl*) or **coccyg'ian**. [Gr. *kokkyx, -ȳgos*, cuckoo, coccyx (as resembling its bill).]

cochineal *koch'i-nēl* or *-nēl', n* a scarlet dyestuff consisting of the dried bodies of a Coccus insect gathered from a cactus in Mexico, the West Indies, etc.; the insect itself. [Sp. *cochinilla*, dimin. of L. *coccinus*, scarlet — *coccum*, a berry.]

cochlea *kok'li-ə, n* anything spiral-shaped, esp. a snail-shell; the spiral cavity of the ear (*anat*). — *adj* **coch'lear** (*-li-ər*) pertaining to the cochlea of the ear. — *adj* **coch'leāte** or **coch'leated** twisted spirally. [L. *coc(h)lea*, a shell, screw — Gr. *kochlias*, a snail.]

cock[1] *kok, n* a male bird, esp. of the domestic fowl (often in composition, as in **cock'bird, cock-rob'in, cock-sparr'ow**); a male crab, lobster or salmon; a weathercock; (sometimes as *old cock*) a familiar form of address to a man (*slang*); anything set erect; a tap; part of the lock of a gun, held back by a spring, which, when released by the trigger, produces the discharge; a penis (*vulg*); nonsense (*colloq*). — *vt* to set erect or upright (often with *up*); to set up the brim of; to draw back, as the cock of a gun; to turn up or to one side; to tilt up knowingly, inquiringly or scornfully. — *vi* to strut; to swagger. — *adj* **cocked** set erect; turned up or to one side; (of a gun) with the cock drawn back, ready to fire. — *n* **cock'erel** a young cock. — *adv* **cock'ily**. — *n* **cock'iness**. — *adj* **cock'y** self-important, bumptious; pert. — **cock-a-doodle-doo'** the crow of a cock. — *vt* to crow. — *adj* **cock-a-hoop'** in exultant spirits. — *adj* **cock'-and-bull** (of a story) fabricated and incredible. — **cock'-crow** early morning, when cocks crow; **cocked hat** an old-fashioned three-cornered hat; **cock'eye** a squinting eye. — *adj* **cock'eyed** having a cockeye; off the straight, awry (*colloq*); tipsy (*colloq*). — **cock'fight** a fight or contest between game-cocks; a fight; **cockhorse'** a child's imaginary or toy horse; **cock'pit** a pit or enclosed space where game-cocks fought; a frequent battleground; a sheltered depression in the deck of a yacht or small ship, from which it is steered; (in aircraft) a compartment in the fuselage for the pilot; the driver's seat in a racing car; **cock-sparr'ow** a male sparrow; a small, lively person; **cock'spur** a spur on the leg of a game-cock; a type of catch used on casement windows; **cockspur grass** an invasive grass of warmer, orig. only tropical, climates. — *adj* **cock'sure** quite sure, self-confident, esp. offensively. — **cock'-up** (*colloq*) a muddle, mess, confusion. — **cock of the walk** a person who is, or thinks himself, the most important in a group; **go off at half cock** (*colloq*) to begin too soon, when not properly prepared; **knock into a cocked hat** to give a profound beating; **live like fighting cocks** to have every luxury. [O.E. *coc*.]

cock[2] *kok, n* a small pile of hay, dung, etc. — *adj* **cocked** heaped up in cocks. [Cf. O.N. *kökkr*, a lump.]

cockade *kok-ād', n* a rosette worn on the hat as a badge. [Fr. *cocarde* — *coq*, cock.]

cockatoo *kok-ə-tōō', n* any of a number of large crested parrots of the Australian region. — *n* **cockatiel** or **cockateel** (*-tēl'*) a small crested parrot of Australia. [Malay *kakatua*.]

cockatrice *kok'ə-trīs* or *-tris, n* a fabulous monster like a serpent; a cock-like monster with a dragon's tail (*heraldry*). [O.Fr. *cocatris*.]

cockboat *kok'bōt, n* a ship's small boat; a small frail boat.

cockchafer *kok'chāf-ər, n* a large greyish-brown beetle, destructive to vegetation. [**cock**[1] and **chafer**.]

cocker *kok'ər* or **cocker spaniel** (*span'yəl*), *n* a small breed of spaniel with long silky ears, as used when shooting woodcock.

cockerel, cockeye, cockeyed, cockhorse. See **cock**[1].

cockle[1] *kok'l, n* a cornfield weed, esp. now the *corn-cockle*, a tall pink-flowered variety similar to campion.. [O.E. *coccel*.]

cockle[2] *kok'l, n* a large bivalve mollusc with thick, ribbed, heart-shaped, equal-valved shell; its shell; a bivalve shell generally. — *adj* **cock'led** shelled like a cockle. — **cock'leshell** the shell of a cockle; a frail boat. — **cockles of one's heart** one's inmost heart. [Fr. *coquille* — Gr. *konchylion* — *konchē*, a cockle.]

cockney *kok'ni, n* (often with *cap*) a person born in London, strictly, within hearing of Bow Bells; London dialect, esp. of the East End. — *adj* (often with *cap*) characteristic of a Cockney. — *n* **cock'neydom** the domain of Cockneys. — *n* **cock'neyism** a Cockney idiom or characteristic. [M.E. *coken-ey*, cock's egg, hence, an oddity; or perh. with Fr. *coquin*, a rogue — L. *coquus*, a cook.]

cockroach *kok'rōch, n* an orthopterous insect, the so-called black beetle. [Sp. *cucaracha*, woodlouse, cockroach.]

cocktail *kok'tāl, n* a mixed drink containing spirits and other liquors; an appetiser consisting of e.g. seafood with a sauce; a mixture of substances generally. — *adj* (of food items) suitable to be served with cocktails. — **cocktail bar** or **lounge** a bar or room in a hotel or restaurant where cocktails and other spirits are served; **cocktail dress** one for semi-formal wear; **cocktail shaker** or **mixer** a container for mixing cocktails; **cocktail stick** a small wooden or plastic stick for a cherry, olive, small sausage, etc., when eaten with drinks. — **fruit cocktail** a salad of finely-diced fruit. [**cock**[1] and **tail**[1].]

cocky. See **cock**[1].

coco *kō'kō, n* a tropical seaside palm-tree with curving stem (also **co'co palm, co'conut-palm** and **co'co-tree**), producing the coconut: — *pl* **cō'cos**. — **co'conut** a large edible nut, yielding **coconut-butt'er** or **coconut-oil'**, and **coconut-milk'**; **co'conut ice** a kind of sweet made of coconut and sugar; **co'conut-matting** matting made from the husk of the coconut; **co'conut-shy** a fairground throwing game with coconuts as targets or as prizes. [Port. and Sp. *coco*, a bugbear; applied to the nut from the three marks at the end of it, which form a grotesque face.]

cocoa *kō'kō, n* the seed of the cacao or chocolate tree; a powder made from the seeds; a drink made from the powder. — **co'coa-beans** the seeds, esp. when dried and fermented; **co'coa-butter** or **co'coa-fat** a fat obtained from the seeds (different from *coconut*-butter). [**cacao**.]

COCOM or **Cocom** *kō'kom, abbrev* for Coordinating Committee for Multilateral Export Controls.

cocoon *ko-kōōn', n* the silken sheath spun by many insect larvae in passing into the pupa stage and by spiders for their eggs; the capsule in which earthworms and leeches lay their eggs; a preservative covering for military and other equipment; a cosy, secure place or situation. — *vt* to wrap or preserve carefully as in a cocoon. — *n* **cocoon'ery** a place for keeping silkworms when feeding and spinning cocoons. [Fr. *cocon*, from *coque*, a shell — L. *concha*, a shell.]

cocotte *ko-kot', n* a small fireproof dish, usu. for an individual portion.

cod[1] *kod* or **codfish** *kod'fish, n* a food-fish (*Gadus morrhua*) of northern seas; any fish of the genus *Gadus* or the family *Gadidae*. — *n* **cod'ling** a small cod. — **cod'-fisher; cod'-fishery; cod'-fishing**. — **cod-liver oil** a medicinal oil extracted from the fresh liver of the common cod or related fish.

cod[2] *kod*, (*slang*) *n* a jest; a hoax. — *adj* mock; done, intended, etc. as a joke or take-off. — *vt* to hoax; to poke fun at: — *pr p* **codd'ing**; *pa t* and *pa p* **codd'ed**.

Cod. *abbrev* for Codex.

c.o.d. *abbrev* for cash (or collect) on delivery.

coda *kō'də, n* a passage forming the completion of a piece, rounding it off to a satisfactory conclusion (*mus*); any similar passage or piece in a story, dance sequence, etc. [It., — L. *cauda*, a tail.]

coddle *kod'l, vt* to pamper, mollycoddle; to cook (esp. eggs) lightly.

code *kōd, n* a collection or digest of laws; a system of rules and regulations (*specif* regarding education); established principles or standards (of art, moral conduct, etc.); a system of signals; a system of words, letters, or symbols which represent sentences or other words, to ensure economy or secrecy in transmission; a set of rules and characters for converting one form of data to another (*comput*); the characters of the resulting representation of data (*comput*); the pattern of holes in a punched card or paper tape which represents a character or instructions. — *vt* to codify; to express in code. — *n* **codificā'tion** (*kod-* or *kōd-*). — *n* **codifīer** (*kōd'* or *kod'*) or **cōd'ist** a person who codifies. — *vt* **codify** (*kōd'* or *kod'*) to put into the form of a code; to systematise: — *pr p* **cod'ifying**; *pa t* and *pa p* **cod'ified**. — *n* and *adj* **cod'ing**. — **code'-book** a book containing the words, symbols, etc., of a code or codes; **code'-breaker** a person who tries to interpret secret codes; **code'-breaking; code'-name** or **-number** a name or number used for convenience, economy, secrecy, etc. — *adj* **code'-named**. — **code of conduct** or **practice** an established method or set of rules for dealing with, behaving in, etc., a particular situation. [Fr. *code*; see **codex**.]

codeine *kō'dēn, n* an alkaloid, obtained from opium, used as an analgesic and sedative. [Gr. *kōdeia*, poppy-head.]

co-dependant or (esp. in U.S.) **co-dependent** *kō-di-pend'ənt*, (*psychol*) *n* a person who seeks to fulfil his or her own emotional needs by caring for a dependant. — *n* **co-depend'ency**. — *adj* **co-depend'ent**.

codex *kō'deks, n* a manuscript volume: — *pl* **codices** (*kōd'i-sēz*). — *n* **cōdicol'ogy** the study of manuscript volumes. — *adj* **cōdicolog'ical**. [L. *cōdex* or *caudex, -icis*, trunk of a tree, set of tablets, a book.]

codger *koj'ər, n* a man, a chap, esp. if old or strange. [Prob. a variant of **cadger**.]

codicil *kod'i-sil, n* a supplement to a will. — *adj* **codicill'ary**. [L. *cōdicillus*, dimin. of *cōdex*.]

codicology. See **codex**.

codification, etc. See **code**.

codling[1] *kod'ling* or **codlin** *kod'lin, n* an elongated apple.

codling[2]. See **cod**[1].

codon *kō'don*, (*biol*) *n* a triplet of bases in the messenger-RNA molecule, which determines a particular amino-acid in protein synthesis. [**code**, *-on*.]

codpiece *kod'pēs, n* a pouch once worn by men in the front of tight hose or breeches. [O.E. *codd*, a small bag, and **piece**.]

co-driver *kō'-drī-vər, n* one of two alternating drivers, esp. in a race or rally.

codswallop or **cod's-wallop** *kodz'wol-əp*, (*colloq*) *n* nonsense, rubbish.

coeducation *kō-ed-ū-kā'shən, n* education of the sexes together. — *n* **co'ed** a girl or woman educated at a coeducational institution (usu. *US*); a coeducational school. — *adj* **co'ed** or **coeducā'tional**.

coefficient *kō-if-ish'ənt, n* that which acts together with another thing; a numerical or literal expression for a factor of a quantity in an algebraic term (*math*); a numerical constant used as a multiplier to a variable quantity, in calculating the magnitude of a physical property (*phys*).

coelacanth *sē'lə-kanth, n* any of a group of fishes of very great antiquity. [From Gr. *koilos*, hollow, *akantha*, spine.]

Coelenterata *sə-len-tər-ā'tə* or *sē-*, *npl* a phylum of many-celled animals, radially symmetrical, with a single body-cavity, the enteron. — *adj* and *n* **coelen'terate**. [Gr. *koilos*, hollow, *enteron*, intestine.]

coeliac or (esp. in U.S.) **celiac** *sē'li-ak*, *adj* relating to the abdomen; pertaining to coeliacs, coeliac disease, etc. — *n* a person suffering from coeliac disease. — **coeliac disease** a disease of the intestines in which a sensitivity to gluten prevents the proper absorption of nutrients. [Gr. *koiliakos* — *koiliā*, the belly.]

coelom or (esp. in U.S.) **celom** *sē'lōm* or *-lom*, *n* the body-cavity, or space between the intestines and the body-wall in animals above the Coelenterates. — *npl* **Coelō'mata** animals possessing a coelom. — *adj* **coe'lomate** having a coelom. — *n* a coelomate animal. — *adj* **coelomat'ic** or **coelom'ic**. [Gr. *koilōma, -atos*, a cavity.]

coelurosaur *sēl'ū-rə-sör*, *n* a bipedal carnivorous dinosaur of the Triassic and Cretaceous periods, thought to be the ancestor of archaeopteryx.

coenobite or **cenobite** *sēn'o-bīt*, *n* a monk who lives in a community. — *adj* **coenobitic** (*-bit'ik*) or **coenobit'ical** (*-əl*). — *n* **coen'obitism**. — *n* **coen-ō'bium** a religious community; a colony of unicellular organisms (*biol*): — *pl* **coenō'bia**. [Gr. *koinōbion* — *koinos*, common, *bios*, life.]

coequal *kō-ē'kwəl*, *adj* equal with another of the same rank or dignity. — *n* a person or thing of the same rank. — *n* **cōequality** (*-i-kwol'*). — *adv* **coē'qually**.

coerce *kō-ûrs'*, *vt* to restrain by force; to compel. — *adj* **cōer'cible**. — *adv* **cōer'cibly**. — *n* **cōer'cion** restraint; government by force. — *n* **cōer'cionist**. — *adj* **cōer'cive** having power to coerce; compelling; tending to or intended to coerce. — *adv* **cōer'cively**. — *n* **cōer'civeness**. — *n* **coerciv'ity** the coercive force needed to demagnetise a material that is fully magnetised. — **coercive force** the reverse magnetising force required to bring the magnetisation of a ferromagnetic material to zero. [L. *coercēre* — *arcēre*, to shut in.]

coetaneous *kō-i-tā'ni-əs*, *adj* of the same age; contemporary. [L. *aetās, aetātis*, age.]

coeval *kō-ē'vəl*, *adj* of the same age. — *n* a person or thing of the same age; a contemporary. [L. *coaevus* — *aevum*, age.]

co-exist *kō-igz-ist'* or *-egz-ist'*, *vi* to exist at the same time or together. — *n* **co-exist'ence**. — *adj* **co-exist'ent**. — **peaceful co-existence** a living side by side in mutual toleration.

co-extend *kō-iks-tend'* or *-eks-*, *vi* to extend equally. — *n* **co-exten'sion**. — *adj* **co-exten'sive**.

C of A *abbrev* for Certificate of Airworthiness.

C of E *abbrev* for: Church of England; Council of Europe.

coffee *kof'i*, *n* a powder made by roasting and grinding the seeds of a tree (*Coffea arabica, robusta*, etc.) of the madder family; a drink made from the powder. — **coffee bar** or **shop** a small restaurant where coffee, tea, cakes, etc. are served; **coff'ee-bean** the seed of the coffee-tree; **coffee break** a break for coffee during the working day; **coff'ee-cup** a (usu. small) cup for coffee; **coffee essence** concentrated liquid coffee extract; **coffee grounds** the sediment left after coffee has been infused; **coff'ee-house** a house where coffee and other refreshments are sold; **coff'ee-housing** gossiping while a covert is drawn (*hunting*); talking during a game, esp. in order to distract or mislead players (*cards*); **coff'ee-maker**; **coff'ee-mill** a machine for grinding coffee-beans; **coffee morning** a morning social gathering, often in aid of charity, at which coffee is drunk; **coff'ee-pot** a pot in which coffee is prepared and served; **coffee service** or **set** a set of utensils for serving and drinking coffee; **coff'ee-table** a small low table; **coff'ee-tree**; **coff'ee-whitener** whitener (q.v.) for coffee. — **coffee-table book** a large, expensive, illustrated book of the kind one would set out on a coffee-table for visitors to admire; **white** or **black coffee** coffee with or without milk respectively. [Turk. *kahveh* — Ar. *qahwah*, orig. meaning wine.]

coffer *kof'ər*, *n* a chest for holding money or treasure; a deep panel in a ceiling. — *vt* to hoard up. — *adj* **coff'ered**. — **coff'er-dam** a watertight structure allowing underwater foundations to be built dry. [O.Fr. *cofre*, a chest — L. *cophinus*, a basket — Gr. *kophinos*, a basket.]

coffin *kof'in*, *n* a box for a dead body. — *vt* to place in a coffin. — **coff'in-bone** a bone enclosed in a horse's hoof. — **drive a nail in one's coffin** to do something tending to hasten death or ruin. [O.Fr. *cofin* — L. *cophinus* — Gr. *kophinos*, a basket.]

C of I *abbrev* for Church of Ireland.

C of S *abbrev* for: Chief of Staff; Church of Scotland.

cog *kog*, *n* a projection on a toothed wheel; a cog-wheel; an unimportant person in a large organisation (*fig*). — **cog'-wheel** a toothed wheel. [M.E. *cogge*.]

cog. *abbrev* for cognate.

COGB *abbrev* for Certified Official Government Business.

COGENE *kō'jēn*, *abbrev* for Committee on Genetic Experimentation (of the International Council of Scientific Unions).

cogener *kō'ji-nər*, *n* a variant of **congener**.

cogent *kō'jənt*, *adj* powerful; convincing. — *n* **cō'gence** or **cō'gency** convincing power. — *adv* **cō'gently**. [L. *cōgēns, -entis*, pres. p. of *cōgĕre* — *coagĕre*, to drive.]

cogitate *koj'i-tāt*, *vi* to turn a thing over in one's mind; to meditate; to ponder. — *adj* **cog'itable**. — *n* **cogitā'tion** deep thought; meditation. — *adj* **cog'itātive** having the power of thinking; given to cogitating. [L. *cōgitāre, -ātum*, to think deeply — *co-*, *agitāre*, to put in motion.]

Cognac *kon'yak*, *n* a French brandy made near *Cognac*, in Charente.

cognate *kog'nāt*, *adj* of the same family, kind or nature; derived from the same ancestor, root or other original; related or allied. — *n* someone related by blood, a kinsman. — *n* **cog'nateness** or **cognā'tion**. — **cognatic succession** the succession to the throne of the eldest child, irrespective of sex. [L. *cognātus* — *co-*, *(g)nāscī*, to be born.]

cognition *kog-nish'ən*, *n* a knowledge; apprehension; knowing, in the widest sense, including sensation, perception, etc. (*psychol*). — *adj* **cognisable** or **-z-** (*kog'niz-ə-bl*; also *kon'iz-*) that may be known or understood; that may be judicially investigated. — *adv* **cog'nisably** or **-z-**. — *n* **cog'nisance** or **-z-** (or *kon'iz-*) knowledge or notice, judicial or private; observation; jurisdiction; that by which one is known, a badge. — *adj* **cog'nisant** or **-z-** (or *kon'iz-*) having cognisance or knowledge of. — *vt* **cognise'** or **-ize'** to become conscious of. — *adj* **cognit'ional**. — *adj* **cog'nitive** capable of, or pertaining to, cognition. — *adv* **cog'nitively**. — *n* **cognitiv'ity**. — **take cognisance of** to recognise, take into consideration. [L. *cognitiō, -ōnis* — *cognōscĕre*, *cognitum* — *co-*, *(g)nōscĕre*, to know.]

cognomen *kog-nō'mən*, *n* a surname; a nickname; a name; the last of the three names of a Roman, indicating the house or family to which he belonged. [L. *cognōmen, -inis* — *co-*, *(g)nōmen*, a name.]

cognoscente *ko-nyō-shent'ā*, *n* someone professing a critical knowledge of works of art, music, literature, etc.; a connoisseur: — *pl* **cognoscent'i** (*-ē*). [It. (mod. *conoscente*) — L. *cognōscĕre*, to know.]

cognovit *kog-nō'vit*, (*law*) *n* an acknowledgment by a defendant that the plaintiff's cause is just. [L. *cognōvit actiōnem*, (he) has confessed the action.]

cohabit *kō-hab'it*, *vi* to live together esp. as husband and wife, or as if husband and wife. — *n* **cohab'itant** someone dwelling with others. — *n* **cohabitā'tion**

living together; government by a head of state and a ruling party of opposing views. — *n* **cohabitee'** or **cohab'itor** (*colloq* short form **co'hab**). [L. *co-habitāre* — *co-*, *habitāre*, to dwell.]

co-heir *kō-ār'*, *n* a joint heir: — *fem* **co-heir'ess**. — *n* **coheritor** (*kō-her'it-ər*) a co-heir.

cohere *kō-hēr'*, *vi* to stick together; to be consistent. — *vt* to fit together in a consistent, orderly whole. — *n* **cohēr'ence** or **cohēr'ency** a tendency to cohere; a sticking together; consistency. — *adj* **cohēr'ent** sticking together; connected; consistent in thought or speech; (of a system of units) such that one unit multiplied or divided by another gives a third unit in the system exactly; (of beam of radiation) showing definite, not random, relationships between points in a cross-section. — *adv* **cohēr'ently**. — *n* **cohēr'er** an apparatus for detection of electric waves by reduced resistance of imperfect contact, as if by cohesion. — *n* **cohesibil'ity** (*-hēz-*). — *adj* **co-hēsible** (*-hēz'*) capable of cohesion. — *n* **cohē'sion** (*-zhən*) the act of sticking together; a form of attraction by which particles of bodies stick together; concrescence of similar parts (*bot*); logical connection. — *adj* **cohē'sive** (*-siv* or *-ziv*) having the power of cohering; tending to unite into a mass. — *adv* **cohe'sively**. — *n* **cohe'siveness**. [L. *cohaerēre*, *-haesum* — *co-*, *haerēre*, stick.]

coheritor. See **co-heir**.

coho or **cohoe** *kō'hō*, *n* a Pacific salmon: — *pl* **co'hos** or **co'hoes**.

cohog. Same as **quahog**.

cohort *kō'hört*, *n* a tenth part of a Roman legion; any band of warriors; a group of individuals; (*popularly*) a companion or follower. [L. *cohors*, *-tis*, an enclosed place, a multitude enclosed, a company of soldiers.]

COHSE *kō'zi*, *abbrev* for Confederation of Health Service Employees.

COI *abbrev* for Central Office of Information.

coif *koif*, *n* a covering for the head, esp. worn by women. — *vt* to provide with a coif; to dress (the hair). — *n* **coiffeur** (*kwä-fœr'*) a hairdresser: — *fem* **coiffeuse** (*-œz'*). — *n* **coiffure** (*kwä-für'*) a style of hairdressing. — Also *vt*. [Fr. *coiffe* — L.L. *cofia*, a cap.]

coil *koil*, *vt* to wind in rings; to enclose in twists. — *vi* to wind. — *n* a coiled object; one of the rings into which anything is coiled; a wire wound spirally to conduct electricity; a contraceptive device consisting of a metal or plastic coil fitted in the uterus. [O.Fr. *coillir* (Fr. *cueillir*) — L. *colligĕre* — *col-*, together, *legĕre*, to gather.]

coin *koin*, *n* a piece of metal legally stamped and current as money; money. — *vt* to convert into money; to stamp; to invent, fabricate, esp. a new word. — *n* **coin'age** the act of coining money; the currency; the pieces of metal coined; the invention, or fabrication, of something new, esp. a word or phrase; what is invented. — *n* **coin'er** a person who coins money; a maker of counterfeit coins; an inventor. — *n* **coin'ing** minting; invention. — **coin'-box** a telephone which one operates by putting coins in a slot. — *adj* **coin-op'erated**, **coin'-op** or **coin-in-the-slot'** (of a machine) operated by inserting a coin in a slot. — **coin a phrase** to use a new phrase or expression (usu. *ironic*, i.e. to repeat a cliché); **coin money** to make money rapidly; **pay someone in his (**or **her) own coin** to give tit for tat; to give as good as one got. [Fr. *coin*, a wedge (see **quoin**), also the die to stamp money — L. *cuneus*, a wedge.]

coincide *kō-in-sīd'*, *vi* to occupy the same place or time; to agree; to correspond; to be identical. — *n* **coincidence** (*kō-in'si-dəns*) fact, event, or condition of coinciding; the occurrence of events simultaneously or consecutively in a striking manner but without any causal connection between them. — *n* **coin'cidency**. — *adj* **coin'cident**. — *adj* **coincid-ental** (*-dent'l*). — *adv* **coincident'ally**. — *adv* **coin'cidently**. [L. *co-*, *incidĕre* — *in*, in, *cadĕre*, to fall.]

co-insurance *kō'in-shōō'rəns*, *n* insurance jointly with another, esp. when the insurer bears part of the risk.

coir *koir*, *n* the strong fibre of coconut husk. [From Tamil or Malayalam.]

coition *kō-ish'ən* or **coitus** *kō'it-əs*, *n* sexual intercourse. — *adj* **cō'ital**. — **coitus interruptus** (*in-tə-rup'təs*) coitus intentionally interrupted by withdrawal before semen is ejaculated; **coitus reservatus** (*rez-ûr-vä'təs*) coitus in which ejaculation is avoided. [L. *coitiō*, *-ōnis* — *co-*, together, *īre*, *ĭtum*, to go.]

coke[1] *kōk*, *n* a form of fuel obtained by the heating of coal in confined space whereby its more volatile constituents are driven off; the residue when any substance (e.g. petrol) is carbonised. — *vt* and *vi* to make into, or become, coke. — *adj* **cō'ky** like coke. — **coking coal** bituminous coal good for coking.

coke[2] *kōk*, *n* cocaine (*slang*); (®; with *cap*) Coca-Cola.

COL *abbrev* for computer-oriented language.

Col. *abbrev* for: Colonel; Colorado (U.S. state); (the Letter to the) Colossians (*Bible*).

col *kol*, *n* a depression or pass in a mountain-range (*geog*); a region between two anticyclones giving a similar figure when represented in contour (*meteorol*). [Fr., — L. *collum*, a neck.]

col. *abbrev* for column.

col-. See **com-**.

cola or **kola** *kō'lə*, *n* (with *cap*) a genus of W. African trees producing nuts used in drugs and for flavouring soft drinks; a soft drink so flavoured. [Afr. name.]

colander *kul'ən-dər*, *n* a perforated vessel used as a strainer in cookery. [L. *cōlāre*, to strain.]

colatitude *kō-lat'i-tūd*, *n* the complement of the latitude. [**co(mplement)** and **latitude**.]

colchicum *kol'ki-kəm*, *n* a plant of the *Colchicum* genus of the family *Liliaceae* including meadow saffron; its corm and seeds, used for gout and rheumatism and yielding colchicine: — *pl* **col'chica** or **col'chicums**. — *n* **col'chicine** (*-chi-* or *-ki-sēn*) an alkaloid used to produce polyploidy, etc. [L., — Gr. *kolchikon*, meadow saffron.]

cold *kōld*, *adj* giving or feeling a sensation that is felt to be the opposite of hot; chilly; low in temperature; without passion or zeal; spiritless; unfriendly; indifferent; reserved; (of colours) suggesting cold rather than heat, as blue or grey; without application of heat; used of operations formerly requiring heat, e.g. **cold-cast'ing**, **-forg'ing**, **-mould'ing** and **-weld'ing**; (in marketing, politics, etc.) involving contacting people thought to be potential customers or supporters, without the contact having been prearranged or primed, and with no knowledge of the people's likely reactions or opinions, as in **cold calling** or **cold canvassing**. — *n* a relative absence of heat; the feeling or sensation caused by the absence of heat; coldness; a spell of cold weather; a catarrhal inflammation of the mucous membrane of the respiratory organs, caused by a virus, usu. accompanied by hoarseness and coughing; catarrh; chillness. — *adj* **cold'ish**. — *adv* **cold'ly**. — *n* **cold'ness**. — *n* and *adj* **cold'blood** (of) a horse belonging to the heavy draught breeds (cf. *warmblood*). — *adj* **cold-blood'ed** having body-temperature depending upon environment, as fishes; without feeling; (of persons or actions) hard-hearted. — *adv* **cold-blood'edly**. — *n* **cold-blood'edness**. — **cold cathode** (*electr*) an electrode from which electron emission results from high-potential gradient at the surface at normal temperatures; **cold'-chisel** a strong and finely-tempered chisel for cutting cold metal; **cold'-cream** a creamy ointment used to remove make-up or as a cooling dressing for the skin;

cold cuts slices of cold cooked meat; **cold feet** loss of nerve; cooling off of courage or ardour; **cold fish** a person with no emotion; **cold'-frame** or **cold'-house** a plant frame, greenhouse, without artificial heat; **cold front** the surface of an advancing mass of cold air where it meets a retreating mass of warmer air; **cold fusion** nuclear fusion without prior heating, i.e. effected at normal room temperature. — *adj* **cold-heart'ed** lacking feeling; indifferent. — *adv* **cold-heart'edly**. — *n* **cold-heart'edness**. — *vt* **cold-should'er** to give the cold shoulder to (see below). — **cold snap** a sudden spell of cold weather; **cold sore** a blister or group of blisters on or near the mouth, caused by a viral infection (*herpes simplex*); **cold steel** cutting or stabbing weapons, as opp. to bullets; **cold storage** storage and preservation of goods in refrigerating chambers; abeyance (*fig*); **cold turkey** sudden withdrawal of narcotics (also *fig*); **cold water** water at its natural temperature in ordinary conditions. — *vt* **cold'-work** to shape (metals) at or near atmospheric temperature by rolling, pressing, etc. — **catch cold** to contract a cold; to make an unexpected loss; **cold as charity** a proverbial phrase expressing ironically great coldness or indifference; **come in from the cold** to gain acceptance or recognition after a period of isolation or neglect; **give** or **show the cold shoulder** to show studied indifference; to rebuff; **in a cold sweat** (as if) sweating with fear; **in cold blood** with deliberate intent, not under the influence of passion; **leave one cold** to fail to impress; **leave out in the cold** to neglect, ignore; **pour** or **throw cold water on** to discourage. [O.E. *cald*.]

cole *kōl*, *n* a general name for all sorts of cabbage. — **cole'-seed** the seed of rape; rape; **cole'slaw** cabbage salad; **cole'-wort** cabbage, esp. varieties with no heart. [O.E. *cawel*; from L. *cōlis*, *caulis*, a stem, esp. of cabbage.]

Coleoptera *kol-i-op'tər-ə*, *npl* an order of insects having the forewings hard or horny, serving as wing-cases for the functional wings — the beetles. — *adj* **coleop'teral** or **coleop'terous**. — *n* **coleop'terist** a person who studies beetles. [Gr. *koleos*, a sheath, *pteron*, a wing.]

coleoptile *kol-i-op'tīl*, (*bot*) *n* a protective sheath around the first leaves of cereals. [Gr. *koleos*, a sheath, *ptilon*, a feather.]

coleslaw. See **cole**.

cole-tit. See under **coal**.

coleus *kō'li-əs*, *n* a plant of the *Coleus* genus with variegated coloured leaves often used for indoor decoration. [Gr. *koleos*, a sheath.]

coley *kō'li*, *n* an edible fish of the cod family.

colic *ko'lik*, *n* severe spasmodic pain and flatulent distension of the abdomen, without diarrhoea. — *adj* **col'icky** like, suffering from or causing colic. [**colon**[2].]

coliform *kō'li-förm*, *adj* like a sieve. [L. *cōlāre*, to strain.]

coliseum. See **colosseum** under **colossus**.

colitis. See **colon**[2].

coll. *abbrev* for: colleague; collector; college; colloquial.

collaborate *kəl-ab'ər-āt*, *vi* to work in association (sometimes invidiously, with an enemy). — *n* **collaborā'tion**. — *adj* **collab'orative**. — *n* **collab'orātor**. — *n* **collaborā'tionist** (in invidious sense). [L. *collabōrāre*, *-ātum* — *labōrāre*, to work.]

collage *kol-äzh'*, *n* a picture made from scraps of paper and other odds and ends pasted up; any work put together from assembled fragments. — *n* **collag'ist**. [Fr., pasting.]

collagen *kol'ə-jen*, *n* a protein in fibrous connective tissue, readily turned into gelatine. — *adj* **collag'enous**. [Gr. *kolla*, glue, and *gen-*, the root of *gignesthai*, to become.]

collapse *kəl-aps'*, *n* a falling away or breaking down; any sudden or complete breakdown or prostration. — *vi* to cave in; to close or fold up; to break down; to go to ruin; to lose heart. — *n* **collapsibil'ity** or **collaps'ability**. — *adj* **collaps'ible** or **collaps'able** (of furniture) capable of being folded or dismantled. [L. *collāpsus* — *col-*, together, *lābī*, *lāpsus*, to slide or fall.]

collar *kol'ər*, *n* something worn round the neck by a person, horse, dog, etc.; the neck or (sometimes detachable) neckband of a garment; the part of an animal's skin or coat, or a bird's feathers, round the neck; a marking around an animal or bird's neck; a surrounding band; the junction of root and stem in a plant; a piece of meat rolled up and tied; a joint of bacon from the neck. — *vt* to seize by the collar; to put a collar on; to seize or arrest (*slang*). — *n* **collarette'** a small collar for a garment. — **coll'ar-beam** a horizontal piece of timber connecting or bracing two opposite rafters, to prevent sagging; **coll'ar-bone** the clavicle, a bone connecting the shoulder blade and breastbone; **collared dove** a dove of Europe and Asia, having a black stripe around the back of the neck; **coll'ar-stud** a stud for fastening a shirt collar. — **have one's collar felt** to be arrested (*slang*). [O.Fr. *colier* — L. *collāre* — *collum*, the neck.]

collard *kol'ərd*, *n* cole-wort. [**cole-wort**.]

collat. *abbrev* for: collateral; collaterally.

collate *kol-āt'*, *vt* to bring together for comparison; to examine and compare, e.g. books, and esp. old manuscripts; to place sheets of a book or document in order for binding or stapling; to examine with respect to completeness and sequence of sheets, etc; to merge two or more files, sets of records, etc. — *adj* **collā'table**. — *n* **collā'tion** the act of collating; a light repast between meals. — *n* **collā'tor** a person who collates or compares; a machine which merges sets of punched cards or separates cards from a set; a machine which puts copied or printed sheets into sequential sets. [L. *collātum*, used as supine of *conferre* — pfx. *col-* and *lātum* (*ferre*, to bring).]

collateral *kol-at'ər-l*, *adj* side by side; running parallel or together; corresponding; descended from the same ancestor, through a different line. — *n* a collateral relation; a contemporary; a rival; collateral security. — *adv* **collat'erally**. — **collateral security** an additional and separate security for repayment of money borrowed. [L. *col-*, *latus*, *lateris*, a side.]

colleague *kol'ēg*, *n* a person associated with another in some employment. — *n* **coll'eagueship**. [Fr. *collègue* — L. *collēga* — *col-*, *legēre*, to choose.]

collect *kəl-* or *kol-ekt'*, *vt* to assemble or bring together; to put (one's thoughts) in order; to receive payment of; to call for and remove. — *vi* to come together; to accumulate. — *n* **collect** (*kol'ekt*) a short prayer. — *adj* and *adv* (*-ekt'*; *US*) (of a telephone call, telegram, etc.) paid for by the recipient. — *adj* **collect'able** or **collect'ible** of interest to a collector. — *n* one of a set of toys or ornaments each purchasable separately but priced and marketed in such a way as to encourage the purchase of all or much of the range. — *adj* **collect'ed** gathered together; (of a poet's or other writer's works) assembled in one volume, one set of volumes, etc.; composed, cool. — *adv* **collect'edly**. — *n* **collect'edness** self-possession; coolness. — *n* and *adj* **collect'ing**. — *n* **collec'tion** the act of collecting; the gathering of contributions, esp. of money; the money collected; an accumulation; an assemblage; a book of selections; a regular removal of rubbish for disposal, letters for posting, etc.; composure. — *adj* **collect'ive** considered as forming one mass or sum; congregated; common; expressing a number or multitude (*gram*). — *n* a gathering, assemblage; a unit of organisation in a collectivist system; (*loosely*) a group of people who run a business, etc., for their mutual benefit, often with no specifically designated jobs. — *adv* **collect'ively**. — *vt* **collect'ivise** or **-ize** to give a collectivist organisation to. — *n* **collect'ivism** the economic theory that industry should be carried on with a collective capital — a form of socialism; a system embodying this. — *n* and *adj* **collect'ivist**. — *n* **collectiv'ity**. — *n* **collect'or** that which, or someone who, collects; a person who seeks to acquire and set together examples or specimens. — **collect'ing-box** a field-naturalist's box for specimens; a box for receiving money contributions; **collective bargaining** negotiation on conditions of service between an organised body of workers on one side and an employer or association of employers on the other; **collective farm** a state-controlled farm consisting of a number of small-holdings operated on a co-operative basis; **collective noun** a singular noun referring to a group of people or things; **collective responsibility** the convention that all decisions of a cabinet, etc. are presented and treated as being unanimous; **collective unconscious** (*psychol*) the part of the unconscious mind that originates in ancestral experience; **collector's item** or **piece** an object beautiful, valuable, interesting, etc. enough to be included in a collection. — **collect on delivery** cash on delivery (*US*). [L. *colligĕre, collēctum — legĕre*, to gather.]

colleen *kol'ēn* or *kol-ēn'*, *n* a girl. [Irish *cailín*.]

college *kol'ij*, *n* an organised body of persons with a specific function, often having exclusive privileges; a body or society that is a member of a university or is co-extensive with a university; an institution for higher, professional or vocational education; a literary, political or religious institution; the premises housing a college. — *n* **coll'eger** a member of a college; one of the foundationers at Eton College. — *adj* **collegial** (*kə-lē'ji-əl*) pertaining to a college or university, or to a collegium. — *n* **collegial'ity** sharing by bishops in papal decision-making. — *adj* **collē'giate** pertaining to or resembling a college; containing a college, e.g. a town; instituted like a college; corporate. — **college pudding** a kind of steamed dried fruit pudding; **collegiate (**or **collegial) church** a church having a college or chapter, consisting of a dean or provost and canons, attached to it; in Scotland, a church occupied by two or more pastors of equal rank (also **collegiate charge**). — **college of cardinals** the whole body of cardinals, electors of the pope; **college of education** a college for training teachers. [Fr. *collège* — L. *collēgium*, from *col-*, and *legĕre*, to gather.]

collegium *ko-lēj'i-əm*, *n* college of cardinals; an administrative board: — *pl* **colle'gia** or **colle'giums**. [L. *collēgium*; see **college**.]

collenchyma *kol-eng'ki-mə*, (*bot*) *n* the strengthening tissue of thick-cornered cells. [Gr. *kolla*, glue, *en*, in, *chyma*, that which is poured.]

Colles' fracture *kol'is frak'chər*, *n* a fracture of the radius near the wrist, with backward displacement of the hand. [Abraham *Colles*, 1773–1843, Irish surgeon.]

collet *kol'it*, *n* a ring or collar; the collar of a plant; the part of a piece of jewellery which contains the stone. [Fr., — L. *collum*.]

collide *kə-līd'*, *vi* to dash together; to clash. — *vt* to cause to collide. — *n* **collī'der**. — *n* **collision** (*-lizh'n*) the state of being struck together; a violent impact, a crash; conflict; opposition; clashing. — **collision course** a course which, if persisted in, will result in a collision (*lit* and *fig*); **elastic collision** a collision in which both kinetic energy and momentum are conserved (*phys*); a collision in which the bombarding particle does not excite or break up the struck nucleus, and is simply scattered (**elastic scattering**) (*nuc*); **inelastic collision** a collision in which momentum, but not kinetic energy, is conserved (*phy*); a collision in which there is a change in the total energies of the particles involved, the resultant scattering being termed **inelastic scattering** (*nuc*). [L. *collīdĕre, collīsum — col-, laedĕre*, to strike.]

collie or **colly** *kol'i*, *n* a long-haired, intelligent breed of sheepdog, originating in Scotland.

collier *kol'yər*, *n* a coalminer; a ship that carries coal; a sailor in such a ship. — *n* **coll'iery** a coalmine. [**coal**.]

colligate *kol'i-gāt*, *vt* to bind together. — *n* **colligā'tion** conjunction; bringing together under a general principle or conception. [L. *colligāre, -ātum — col-, ligāre*, to bind.]

collimate *kol'i-māt*, *vt* to make parallel; to adjust accurately parts of (an optical instrument, as a surveying telescope). — *n* **collimā'tion**. — *n* **coll'imātor** a device for obtaining a beam of parallel rays of light or a beam of particles moving in parallel paths; a subsidiary telescope for collimating other instruments. [*collīmāre*, a wrong reading for L. *collīneāre*, to bring into line with — *col-*, together, *līnea*, a line.]

collinear *ko-lin'i-ər*, *adj* in the same straight line.

Collins *kol'ins*, *n* a cocktail made with a spirit, lemon or lime juice, sugar and soda water (also without *cap* e.g. **vodka collins, whiskey collins**). — **John Collins** or **Tom Collins** this made with gin.

collision. See **collide**.

collocate *kol'ō-kāt*, *vt* to place together; to set; to arrange. — *n* **collocā'tion**. [L. *collocāre, -ātum*, — *col-, locāre*, to place.]

collocutor, collocutory. See **colloquy**.

collodion *kol-ō'di-ən*, *n* a gluey solution of nitrated cotton (or cellulose nitrates) in alcohol and ether, used in surgery and photography. [Gr. *kollōdēs — kolla*, glue, *eidos*, form, appearance.]

collogue *kə-lōg'*, *vi* to converse confidentially. [Prob. from L. *colloquī*, to speak together.]

colloid *kol'oid*, *n* a substance in a state in which, though apparently dissolved, it cannot pass through a membrane; a substance that readily assumes this state; a colloidal system. — *adj* **colloid'al**. — **colloidal system** a dispersed substance plus the material in which it is dispersed. [Gr. *kolla*, glue, *eidos*, form.]

colloq. *abbrev* for: colloquial; colloquially.

colloquy *kol'ə-kwi*, *n* a speaking together; mutual discourse; conversation. — *n* **collocutor** (*kol-ok'ū-tər*). — *adj* **colloc'ūtory**. — *adj* **colloquial** (*kə-lō'kwi-əl*) pertaining to or used in common conversation. — *n* **collō'quialism** a form of expression used in familiar talk. — *adv* **collō'quially**. — *n* **collō'quium** a conference; a meeting for discussion; a seminar: — *pl* **collō'quia** or **collo'quiums**. [L. *colloquium — col-, loquī*, to speak.]

collotype *kol'ō-tīp*, *n* a printing process using a hardened gelatine plate, used in book illustration; a print produced by this process. [Gr. *kolla*, glue, and **type**.]

collude *kol-ūd'* or *-ōōd'*, *vi* to conspire, esp. in a fraud. — *n* **collud'er**. — *n* **collu'sion** the act of colluding; a secret agreement to deceive; conspiracy. — *adj* **collu'sive** pertaining to a collusion; conspiratorial. — *adv* **collu'sively**. [L. *collūdĕre, collūsum*, from *col-*, and *lūdĕre*, to play.]

colly. See **collie**.

collywobbles *kol'i-wob-lz*, (*facetious*) *n* abdominal pain or disorder; nervous stomach, or a state of apprehensiveness generally. [Prob. **colic** and **wobble**.]

coloboma *kol-o-bō'mə*, *n* a fissure in the eyeball or in one of its parts. [N.L. — Gr. *kolobōma*, a mutilation — *kolobos*, maimed.]

Colobus *kol'ō-bəs*, *n* an African genus of monkeys, almost thumbless; (without *cap*) any of several monkeys of the genus: — *pl* **col'obi** (*-bī* or *-bē*) or

col'obuses. — *adj* **col'obid.** [Gr. *kolobos*, maimed.]

colocynth *kol'o-sinth*, *n* a kind of bitter gourd; a cathartic drug obtained from it. [Gr. *kolokynthis*.]

colon[1] *kō'lən*, *n* the punctuation mark (:), used to indicate a distinct clause of a sentence, to introduce a list, spoken or reported words, etc., or, in figures, to indicate ratio. [Gr. *kōlon*, a limb, member.]

colon[2] *kō'lən*, *n* the large intestine from the caecum to the rectum. — *n* **colitis** (*ko-lī'tis*) inflammation of the colon. — *adj* **colon'ic.** — *adj* **colorec'tal** pertaining to the colon and rectum. — *n* **colos'tomy** (*kə-*) the making of an artificial anus by surgical means. [Gr. *kŏlon*, the large intestine.]

colonel *kûr'nəl*, *n* a senior army officer, usu. a staff officer; (*loosely*) a form of address to a lieutenant-colonel. — *n* **col'onelcy** (*-si*) the office or rank of colonel. — *n* **col'onelship** colonelcy; the quality of being a colonel. — **colonel-in-chief'** an honorary colonel, in Britain generally a member of the Royal Family. [Older Fr. and Sp. *coronel* — It. *colonello*, the leader of a *colonna*, or column — L. *columna*.]

colonial, etc. See **colony.**

colonic. See **colon[2].**

colonnade *kol-ən-ād'*, *n* a range of columns placed at regular intervals; a similar row, as of trees. — *adj* **colonnād'ed.** [Fr., — L. *columna*.]

colony *kol'ən-i*, *n* a name vaguely applied to a state's dependencies overseas or abroad (distinguished from a *dominion*); a body of persons settled in a foreign country, or forming a separate ethnic, cultural or occupational group; the settlement so formed; the place they inhabit; a number of organisms, esp. of one kind, living together as a community (*biol*); a group or company of Beaver Scouts. — *adj* **colonial** (*kə-lō'ni-əl*) pertaining to, of the nature of, or dating from the time when a territory was, a colony. — *n* an inhabitant, citizen, or member of a colony, a colonist. — *n* **colō'nialism** a trait of colonial life or speech; the colonial system (see below); policy of obtaining, or maintaining hold over, colonies, esp. with the purpose of exploiting them. — *adj* and *n* **colōn'ialist.** — *adv* **colōn'ially.** — *n* **colonīsā'tion** or **-z-** the act or practice of colonising; state of being colonised. — *vt* **col'onise** or **-ize** to plant or establish a colony in; to form into a colony; (of plants, animals, etc.) to spread into a new habitat. — *vi* to settle. — *n* **col'onist** an inhabitant of a colony; a voter set up for election purposes; a weed of cultivated ground (*bot*). — **colonial animals** organisms consisting of numerous individuals in bodily union; **colonial system** the theory that the settlements abroad should be treated as proprietary domains exploited for the benefit of the mother country. [L. *colōnia* — *colōnus*, a husbandman — *colĕre*, to till.]

colophon *kol'ə-fon* or *-fən*, *n* an inscription at the end of a book, often naming the author and printer, with place and date of execution, etc.; a publisher's imprint or device, with name, date, etc. [L. *colophōn* — Gr. *kolophōn*, summit, finishing touch.]

colophony *kol-of'ə-ni* or *kol'*, *n* rosin. [Gr. *kolophōniā* from *Kolophōn*, Colophon, in Asia Minor.]

color. U.S. spelling of **colour.**

Colorado beetle *kol-ər-ä'dō bē'tl*, *n* an American beetle, yellow with black stripes, a potato pest. [*Colorado*, the U.S. state.]

coloration. See under **colour.**

coloratura *kol-or-ət-ōō'rə*, (*mus*) *n* florid vocal passages. — *adj* florid. — **coloratura soprano** a high and flexible soprano voice, capable of singing coloratura passages; a singer with such a voice. [It., colouring.]

colorectal. See under **colon[2].**

colorific, etc. See under **colour.**

Coloss. (*Bible*) *abbrev* for (the Letter to the) Colossians.

colossal *kə-los'əl*, *n* like a colossus; gigantic.

colossus *kəl-os'əs*, *n* a person or organisation of gigantic power and influence (*fig*); orig. a gigantic statue, esp. that of Apollo at (but not astride of) the entrance of the harbour of Rhodes: — *pl* **coloss'i** (*-ī*) or **coloss'uses.** — *n* **colossē'um** or **colisē'um** a large stadium or place of entertainment (after Vespasian's amphitheatre at Rome, which was the largest in the world). [L., — Gr. *kolossos*.]

colostomy. See **colon[2].**

colostrum *ko-los'trəm*, *n* a mammal's first milk after giving birth. [L.]

colour, also (esp. in U.S.) **color** *kul'ər*, *n* a sensation of light induced in the eye by electromagnetic waves of a certain frequency — the colour being determined by the frequency; a property whereby bodies have different appearances to the eye through surface reflection or absorption of rays; hue, one of the constituents into which white light can be decomposed; appearance of blood in the face; race or race-mixture other than Caucasian; appearance; plausibility; reason, pretext; tint; shade; paint; vividness; timbre (*mus*); variety; (in *sing* or *pl*) a flag, ensign, or standard; (in *pl*) a symbol of membership of a party, club, college, team, etc.; in particle physics, any of six varieties of a particular characteristic of quarks and antiquarks, used to define possible combinations of these particles in baryons and mesons. — *vt* to put colour on; to stain; to paint; to set in a favourable light; to exaggerate; to disguise; to misrepresent. — *vi* to take on colour; to blush. — *n* **col'orant** or **col'ourant** a substance used for colouring. — *n* **colorā'tion** or **colourā'tion** colouring; mode of colouring; disposition of colours. — *adj* **colorif'ic** (*kol-* or *kul-*) producing colours. — *n* **colorim'eter** (*kol-* or *kul-*) an instrument for comparison of colours. — *n* **colorim'etry.** — *adj* **col'oured** having colour; (of the complexion) other than white; (*loosely*; often *derog*) belonging to a dark-skinned race; (usu. with *cap*) in South Africa, of mixed racial descent — partly Caucasian, partly of darker race; (also with *cap*) in South Africa, of one of the official racial groups, neither white nor African; not of Caucasian race. — *n* (usu. with *cap*) in South Africa, a person of mixed racial descent speaking either English or Afrikaans as the mother tongue; (also with *cap*) in South Africa, a member of one of the official racial groups, one who is neither white nor African; (in *pl*) coloured items for washing, as opposed to whites. — *n* **col'ourer.** — *adj* **col'ourful** full of colour; vivid. — *n* **col'ouring** any substance used to give colour; the actual colours of anything, and their arrangement; manner of applying colours; appearance, esp. a person's hair and skin colour; tone. — *n* **colourisa'tion** or **-z-.** — *vt* **col'ourise** or **-ize** to add colour to a film made in black-and-white. — *n* **col'ourist** a person who colours or paints; someone who excels in colouring. — *adj* **col'ourless** without colour; transparent; pale; neutral; lacking distinctive character. — *adj* **col'oury** having much colour. — **colour bar** social discrimination between whites and other races. — *adj* **col'our-blind** unable to distinguish some colours from others, or to see them at all. — **colour blindness; colour code** a system of identification, e.g. of electrical wires, by different colours. — *vt* **col'our-code** to mark with different colours for identification. — **coloured pencil** one containing a coloured lead as distinct from graphite or blacklead. — *adj* **col'ourfast** (of material, etc.) with colours that will not run when washed. — **colour film** a film for making colour photographs; **colour scheme** general conception of combination of colours in a design; **col'our-sergeant** the sergeant who guards the colours of a regiment; **colour supplement** or **magazine** an illustrated magazine printed in colour and published as a usu. weekly part of a newspaper. — Also **colour-sup, -supp** or **-mag** (*colloq*). — *adj* of a style often pictured in such a magazine, i.e. expensive and rather exclusive. — *n* **col'our-way** a combination of colours. — **colour in** to fill in an area on a piece of paper, etc. with colour; **false colours** a false pretence; **give colour** to give plausibility; **high colour** ruddiness of complexion; **in one's true colours** as one really is; **lose colour** to lose one's good looks; to become pale; to appear less probable (*fig*); **nail one's colours to the mast** to commit oneself to some party or plan of action; **off colour** faded; indisposed; past one's best; slightly indecent; **see the colour of a person's money** to be sure that a person has money to pay for an article about to be bought. [O.Fr. *color* — L. *color*, *-ōris*.]

colposcope *kol'pō-skōp*, *n* an instrument for examining the neck of the uterus, esp. for early signs of cancer. — *adj* **colposcop'ical**. — *adv* **colposcop'ically**. — *n* **colpos'copy** an examination using a colposcope. [Gr. *kolpos*, the womb, *skopein*, to see.]

Colt *kōlt*, *n* a pistol invented by Samuel *Colt* (1814–62).

colt *kōlt*, *n* a young horse; an awkward, somewhat clumsy person; an inexperienced youth; esp. in sports and games, a young, inexperienced player. — *adj* **colt'ish** like a colt; frisky. — **colts'foot** a plant with clusters of small flowers, shaggy stalk and large soft leaves. [O.E. *colt*.]

colter. See **coulter**.

columbine *kol'əm-bīn*, *adj* of or like a dove; dove-coloured. — *n* any plant of the buttercup genus, with coloured sepals and spur-shaped petals, giving the appearance of a bunch of pigeons. — *n* **columbā'rium** a dovecot; a niche for a sepulchral urn: — *pl* **columbar'ia**. — *n* **col'umbary** a dovecot. [L. *columba*, a dove.]

column *kol'əm*, *n* an upright cylinder, used as support or adornment; any upright body or mass like a column; a body of troops forming a long, narrow procession; a vertical row of figures, etc.; a vertical section of a page or of a table of information; a particular section in a newspaper, often habitually written by the same person; a bundle of nerve-fibres; the central part of an orchid. — *adj* **columnal** (*kə-lum'nl*) or **colum'nar** pertaining to columns; like a column; formed or arranged in columns. — *n* **columnist** (*kol'əm-nist* or *-ist*) a person who writes a regular column in a newspaper etc. — **column inch** a measure used in newspapers, etc., being an area one column wide by one inch deep. [L. *columna*, rel. to *celsus*, high; Gr. *kolōnē*, a hill.]

Com. *abbrev* for: Commander; Commissioner; Committee; Commodore; Commonwealth; Communist.

com. *abbrev* for: comedy; commerce; committee; common; commune.

com- *kom-*, **con-** *kon-* or **co-** *ko-* or *kō-*, also, by assimilation, **col-** *kol-* or **cor-** *kor-*, *pfx* denoting: together, with; similar; used as intensive, as in *consolidate*, *constant*. [L. *com*, old form of *cum*, with.]

coma[1] *kō'mə*, *n* a deeply unconscious state following medical trauma; stupor. — *adj* **com'atose** affected with coma; extremely drowsy (*facetious*). [Gr. *kōma*, *-atos*.]

coma[2] *kō'mə*, *n* a tuft (*bot*); the head of a tree; the cloudlike envelope of the head of a comet (*astron*); (the manifestation of) a defect in an optical system (e.g. in a telescope) in which the image of a point appears as a blurred pear-shaped patch (*optics*): — *pl* **com'ae** (*-ē*). — *adj* **cō'mal**, **cō'mate**, **cō'mose** or **cō'mous**. [Gr. *kŏmē*, hair of head.]

comatose. See **coma**[1].

comb[1] *kōm*, *n* a toothed implement or part of a machine, for separating, arranging and cleaning hair, wool, flax, etc.; anything of similar form; the fleshy crest on the head of some birds; the top or crest of a wave, of a roof, or of a hill, etc.; a regular structure made by bees for storing honey, honeycomb. — *vt* to separate, arrange or clean by means of a comb or as if with a comb; to search thoroughly. — *vi* to break with white foam, as the top of a wave. — *adj* **combed**. — *n* **comb'er** someone who or that which combs wool, etc.; a long foaming wave. — *npl* **comb'ings** hairs or wool fibres combed off. — *adj* **comb'less**. — **comb out** to arrange (hair) by combing after rollers, etc. have been removed; to remove (tangles, etc.) from hair by combing; to search thoroughly for and remove. [O.E. *camb*.]

comb[2] or **combe**. See **coomb**.

combat *kom'bat*, *vi* to contend or struggle. — *vt* to fight against, to oppose; to contest; to debate: — *pr p* **com'bating**; *pa t* and *pa p* **com'bated**. — *n* a struggle; a fight; fighting, military action. — *adj* **com'batable**. — *adj* **com'batant** disposed to combat; taking part or liable to take part in military action. — *n* a person who takes part in (a) combat. — *adj* **com'bative** inclined to quarrel, aggressive. — *n* **com'bativeness**. — **combat fatigue** same as **battle fatigue**; **combat jacket** a jacket (in the style of those) worn by soldiers when fighting, usu. khaki with camouflage markings. [Fr. *combattre*, to fight — L. pfx. *com-*, mutual, and *bātuĕre*, to strike.]

comber. See under **comb**[1].

combine *kəm-bīn'*, *vt* to join together; to unite chemically (with) to form a new compound. — *vi* to come into close union (with); to co-operate; to unite and form a new compound (*chem*). — *n* (*kom'bīn*) a syndicate, a trust, an association of trading companies; a combine harvester. — *n* **combinabil'ity**. — *adj* **combinate** (*kom'bin-āt*) combined. — *n* **combinā'tion** the act of combining; union, joining of individual things; chemical union, forming a new compound; a motorcycle with sidecar (also **motorcycle combination**); a group of persons united for a purpose; in mathematics, a possible set of a given number of things selected from a given number; the series of letters or numbers that must be dialled to open a combination lock. — *npl* **combinā'tions** (*colloq* shortened form **coms** or **combs** (*komz*)) a warm undergarment covering the whole body, with long sleeves and legs. — *adj* **com'binātive**. — *adj* **combinato'rial** concerned with arrangements (*math*). — *adj* **combin'atory**. — *adj* **combīned**. — *adj* **combīn'ing**. — *n* **combo** (*kom'bō*) a small jazz or dance band; any combination (*colloq*): — *pl* **com'bos**. — **combination lock** a lock used on safes, suitcases, etc., with numbered dials which must be turned in a special order a certain number of times, or to a certain number, to open it; **combination oven** an oven which functions as both a microwave and as a conventional oven; **combine harvester** a combined harvesting and threshing machine. [L. *combīnāre*, to join — *com-*, *bīnī*, two and two.]

combs *komz*. Short for **combinations**.

combust *kəm-bust'*, *vt* to burn up. — *n* **combustibil'ity**. — *adj* **combust'ible** liable to catch fire and burn; excitable. — *n* something that will catch fire and burn. — *n* **combust'ibleness** quality of being combustible. — *n* **combust'ion** (*-yən*) burning; the action of fire on combustible substances; oxidation or similar process with production of heat. — **spontaneous combustion** burning caused by heat generated in the substance or body itself. [L. *combūrĕre*, *combūstum*, to consume — *com-* (intensive) and *ūrĕre*, to burn.]

Comdr *abbrev* for Commander.

Comdt *abbrev* for Commandant.

come *kum*, *vi* to move toward the place that is the point of view of the speaker or writer (the opposite of *go*); to draw near; to arrive at a certain state or condition; to issue, to happen, to turn out; to become; to amount (to); to reach; to begin to be in some condition; to achieve a sexual orgasm, to ejaculate (*slang*); to be had, got, gained; (only *3rd pers sing*; esp. in *subjunctive*) when (a certain time) comes (as in

Come five o'clock, I shall be exhausted). — *vt* (*colloq*) to act the part of, assume the behaviour of, as in *Don't come the innocent with me*; (with *it*) to try to impress, assert one's authority over, etc.: — *pr p* **com'ing**; *pa t* **came** (*kām*); *pa p* **come**. — *interj* (or *imper*) expressive of encouragement, protest or reproof (often in phrases **come come** or **come now**). — *n* **com'er** a person who comes; a person who shows promise (*colloq*). — *n* **com'ing** arrival or approach; (esp. with *cap*) the Advent, or the hoped-for return (also **Second Coming**) of Christ. — *interj* or *pr p* used as a promise of arrival. — *adj* future; of future importance. — *adj* **come-at'-able** (*colloq*) accessible. — **come'-back** a return, esp. to a former activity or good, popular, successful, etc., state; a revival; a retort, rejoinder; cause or ability to complain; recrimination; **come'down** a descent; a disappointment or deflation; a degradation; **come-hith'er** an invitation to approach; allure. — *adj* of a look, manner, etc., inviting (esp. sexually). — **come'-on** (*colloq*) encouragement, esp. sexual; persuasion; **comeupp'ance** (*colloq*) deserved rebuke or punishment. — **all comers** anyone that arrives, volunteers, etc.; **as it comes** however it is made, in any way whatsoever; **come about** to happen; to turn to face the opposite way (*naut*); **come again?** (*colloq*) what did you say?; pardon?; **come and go** to fluctuate; to have freedom of movement and action; **come at** to reach; to attack; to approach; **come away** to become detached; **come back** to return to popularity, office, etc.; to retort; **come by** to come near; to pass by; to obtain; **come down** to descend; to be reduced; to lose esp. financial status; to emerge from the state induced by a hallucinogenic or addictive drug; **come down on** or **upon** to be severe with; **come down with** to become ill with (a disease); **come for** to arrive in order to collect; to attack; **come forward** to identify oneself (e.g. to the police); **come home** to return to one's house; to touch one's interest or feelings closely, to affect (with *to*); **come in** to enter; to reply to a radio signal or call; **come in for** to receive as, or as if as, one's share; to receive incidentally; **come into** to inherit; **come of** to be a descendant of; to be the consequence of, arise from; **come of age** to reach full legal age; **come off** to become detached; to obtain a specified type of result (with *best*, *worst*, etc.); to prove successful; **come off it!** (*colloq*) don't be ridiculous!; **come on** to advance; to thrive, succeed; to proceed; to begin; often in *imper* as a challenge or invitation to attack; **come on stream** (of oil wells) to start regular pumping (also *fig*, esp. of computers); **come on strong** (*colloq*) to speak or act forcefully or aggressively; **come out** to emerge; to result (well, etc.); to be published; to become known or evident; to enter society; to declare openly one's homosexuality (*slang*); to stop work, strike; to declare oneself (against or in favour of); **come out with** to utter; **come over** to befall; to come into the mind of; to experience a certain feeling (as in *to come over faint*; *colloq*); **come round** to come by a circuitous path; to happen in due course; to veer; to become favourable (in opinion, etc.); to recover consciousness after a faint, etc.; **come short of** to fail to attain; **come to** to amount to, to total; to recover consciousness; **come to grief** to meet with disaster; **come to oneself** to return to one's normal state of mind; **come to pass** (esp. *Bible*) to happen; **come true** to be fulfilled, to happen; **come under** to be included under; **come undone** or **unfastened**, etc. to become detached, loose, etc.; **come up** to be raised in discussion, etc.; **come up against** to encounter (an obstacle, difficulty); **come upon** to meet; to find; **come up with** to suggest; to overtake; **have it coming** (*colloq*) to have no chance of avoiding, or to get, one's just deserts; **how come?** how does it happen that?; **to come** future. [O.E. *cuman*.]

Comecon *kom'i-kon*, *n* a Communist organisation, the *Co*uncil for *M*utual *Econ*omic Aid, or Assistance.

comedo *kom'i-dō*, *n* a blackhead, a black-tipped, white mass often found in blocked skin pores: — *pl* **com'edos**. — *adj* **comedogen'ic** causing blackheads. [L. *comedō*, *-ōnis*, glutton — *comedĕre*, to eat up, from its wormlike appearance.]

comedy *kom'i-di*, *n* a dramatic production having a pleasant or humorous character; works of this type, collectively; a story with a happy ending; an incident of a comic or humorous nature. — *n* **comedian** (*kə-mē'di-ən*) a person who acts in or writes comedies; an entertainer who tells jokes, etc.: — *fem* **comedienne** (*kə-mē-di-en'*; orig. French, and still sometimes spelt **comédienne**). — *adj* **comē'dic** (or *-med'*) of or pertaining to comedy. — *n* **comedy of manners** (a) satirical comedy dealing with the manners or fashions of a social class. [Fr. *comédie* — L. *cōmoedia* — Gr. *kōmōidiā*.]

comely *kum'li*, *adj* pleasing; graceful; handsome or pretty. — *adv* in a pleasing or graceful manner. — *n* **come'liness**. [Conn. with O.E. *cȳmlic* — *cȳme*, suitable, *lic*, like.]

comestible *kom-est'ibl*, *adj* eatable. — *n* (usu. in *pl*) food. [Fr., — L. *comedĕre*, to eat up.]

comet *kom'it*, *n* a heavenly body with a very eccentric orbit, having a definite nucleus, a cloudlike light surrounding the nucleus, and commonly a luminous tail turned away from the sun. [Gr. *komētēs*, long-haired — *komē*, hair.]

comfit *kum'fit*, *n* a sweetmeat; a sugar-coated seed or almond. [Fr. *confit*; see ety. for **confection**.]

comfort *kum'fərt*, *vt* to relieve from pain or distress; to soothe, cheer, console. — *n* relief; encouragement; ease, a degree of luxury; freedom from annoyance; whatever gives ease, consolation, enjoyment, etc.; a subject of satisfaction. — *adj* **com'fortable** imparting or enjoying comfort; easy (*fig*); having enough money to live well. — *adv* **com'fortably**. — *n* **com'forter** a person who gives comfort; a long narrow woollen scarf; a dummy teat; a bed quilt (*US*). — *adj* **com'fortless**. — *n* **com'fortlessness**. — *adj* **com'fy** (*colloq*) comfortable. — **cold comfort** little, if any, comfort. [O.Fr. *conforter* — L. *con-* (intensive) and *fortis*, strong.]

comfrey *kum'fri*, *n* a rough plant related to borage, formerly used in healing. [O.Fr. *confirie*.]

comic *kom'ik*, *adj* relating to comedy; raising mirth or laughter; droll. — *n* the quality or element that arouses mirth or laughter; an actor of humorous parts; a humorous entertainer on stage, in clubs, on TV, etc.; an amusing person (*colloq*); a paper or magazine, esp. for children, with illustrated stories, strip cartoons, etc. (orig. comic, later also serious, even horrific; also **comic book**). — *adj* **com'ical** funny, amusing. — *n* **comical'ity** or **com'icalness**. — *adv* **com'ically**. — **comic strip** a cartoon made up of a series of drawings, a strip cartoon. [Ety. as for **comedy**.]

comice *kom'is*, *n* a variety of pear (also **comice pear**).

COMINT *kom'int*, *abbrev* for *Com*munications *In*telligence, that branch of military intelligence concerned with monitoring and intercepting communications transmitted by the enemy. — Cf. **ELINT**.

comity *kom'i-ti*, *n* courteousness; civility. — **comity of nations** (L. *comitas gentium*) the international courtesy by which effect is given (within limits) to the laws of one state within the territory of another state. [L. *cōmitās*, *-ātis* — *cōmis*, courteous.]

comm. *abbrev* for: commander; commentary; communication.

comma *kom'ə*, *n* a phrase (*rhet*); in punctuation, the sign (,) that marks the smallest division of a sentence; the smallest or slightest interval, break or discontinuity. — **comma bacillus** the micro-organism that causes cholera. — **inverted commas** a set of double or single superscript commas used to introduce and close a quotation, the introductory one(s) being inverted (". ." or '. .'). [L., — Gr. *komma*, a section of a sentence, from *koptein*, to cut off.]

command *kəm-änd'*, *vt* to order; to exercise supreme (esp. military) authority over; to demand; to have within sight, range, influence, or control. — *vi* to have chief authority; to govern. — *n* an order; authority, power; control; the thing or people under one's authority; a military division under separate control; ability or understanding; a signal or message activating a mechanism or setting in motion a sequence of operations by instruments, esp. computers; a command paper. — *n* **commandant** (*kom-ən-dant'* or *kom'*) an officer who has the command of a place or of a body of troops. — *n* **commandant'ship**. — *vt* **commandeer'** to seize for military use; to take over for one's own use, without asking. — *n* **command'er** a person who commands; an officer in the navy next in rank under a captain; a high-ranking police officer in charge of a district; a member of a higher class in an order of knighthood. — *n* **command'ership**. — *adj* **command'ing** dominating, impressive, authoritative; strategic. — *adv* **command'ingly**. — *n* **command'ment** a command; one of the Biblical rules by which Christians believe life should be lived. — *n* **command'o** a unit of a special service brigade, esp. the Royal Marines, equivalent to a battalion (*mil*); a soldier serving in such a unit: — *pl* **command'os**. — **command economy** an economy in which there is no private sector, and all production decisions are taken by the state; **commander-in-chief'** the officer in supreme command of an army, or of the entire forces of a state; **command module** the part of a spacecraft from which operations are directed; **command paper** a government document, orig. presented to parliament by command of the monarch; **command performance** a performance before royalty; **command post** a military unit's (temporary) headquarters. — **at one's command** available for use; **ten commandments** the ten commands given by God to Moses on Mount Sinai, as described in the Old Testament book of Exodus. [Fr. *commander* — L.L. *commandāre* (L. *commendāre*) — L *mandāre*, to entrust.]

commedia dell'arte *ko-mā'dē-a de-lär'te*, *n* Italian Renaissance comedy, with stock characters.

comme il faut *kom ēl fō*, (Fr.) as it should be; correct; approved by the fashionable world; genteel.

commemorate *kəm-em'ə-rāt*, *vt* to signify remembrance of by a solemn or public act; to celebrate; to preserve the memory of. — *adj* **commem'orable**. — *n* **commemorā'tion** preserving the memory of some person or thing, esp. by a solemn ceremony. — *adj* **commem'orative** or **commem'oratory** tending or serving to commemorate. — *n* **commem'orātor**. [L. *commemorāre*, *-ātum*, to remember — *com-* (intensive) and *memor*, mindful.]

commence *kəm-ens'*, *vi* and *vt* to begin; to originate. — *n* **commence'ment** the beginning. [O.Fr. *com(m)encier* — L. *com-* (intensive) and *initiāre*, to begin.]

commend *kəm-end'*, *vt* to commit as a charge or responsibility; to recommend as worthy; to praise. — *adj* **commend'able** praiseworthy. — *n* **commend'ableness**. — *adv* **commend'ably**. — *n* **commendation** (*kom-ən-dā'shən*) the act of commending; praise; a public award for praiseworthy action. — *adj* **commend'atory** commending; containing praise or commendation. [L. *commendāre* — *com-* (intensive) and *mandāre*, to trust.]

commensal *kə-men'səl*, *adj* eating at the same table; living together for mutual benefit (*biol*). — *n* a person whom one eats with, esp. in the forces; an organism living in partnership (not parasitism) with another. — *n* **commen'salism** or **commensal'ity**. — *adv* **commen'sally**. [L. *com-*, together, *mēnsa*, a table.]

commensurable *kəm-en'shə-rə-bl* or *-sū-*, (*math*) *adj* having a common measure; capable of being measured exactly by the same unit; in due proportion. — *n* **commensurabil'ity** or **commen'surableness**. — *adv* **commen'surably**. — *adj* **commen'surate** equal in measure or extent; in due proportion (with *with*). — *adv* **commen'surately**. — *n* **commen'surateness**. — *n* **commensurā'tion**. [L. *com-*, *mēnsūra*, a measure — *mētīrī*, *mēnsus*, to measure.]

comment *kom'ənt* or *-ent*, *n* a note conveying illustration or explanation; a remark, observation or criticism. — *vi* to make critical or explanatory notes (on); to make remarks, observations, etc. — *vt* to say in comment. — *n* **comm'entary** a comment; a remark; a series or book of comments or critical notes; a continuous description of a sport, event, etc., broadcast on television or radio (also **running commentary**). — *vi* **comm'entate** to give a running commentary. — *n* **comm'entātor** a person who comments; the writer of a critical commentary; a broadcaster of a running commentary. — *n* **comm'enter** or **comm'entor**. — **no comment** (*colloq*) I have nothing to say (usu. to a newspaper or television reporter). [L. *commentārī*, to devise, contrive — *com-* and *mēns*, *mentis*, the mind.]

commerce *kom'ûrs*, *n* interchange of merchandise on a large scale between nations or individuals; trade or traffic. — *adj* **commer'cial** (*-shl*) pertaining to commerce; having profit as the main aim; commercially viable. — *n* a commercially-sponsored advertisement on radio or TV; a commercial vehicle. — *n* **commercialese'** business jargon. — *vt* **commer'cialise** or **-ize** to make profit the main aim of; to turn (something) into a source of profit (often *derog*). — *n* **commer'cialism** commercial attitudes and aims; an expression characteristic of commercial language. — *n* **commer'cialist**. — *n* **commerciality** (*-shi-al'i-ti*). — *adv* **commer'cially**. — **commercial traveller** a travelling sales representative of a business concern; **commercial vehicle** generally, a goods-carrying vehicle; by some, understood to include passenger-carrying vehicles such as buses. [Fr., — L. *commercium* — *com-*, mutual, *merx*, *mercis*, merchandise.]

commie *kom'i*, (*colloq derog*) *n* and *adj* short form of **communist**.

comminate *kom'in-āt*, *vt* to threaten. — *n* **comminā'tion** (an instance of) threatening, denunciation; a recital of God's threats against sinners. — *adj* **comm'inative** or **comm'inatory** threatening punishment. [L. *comminārī*, *-ātum* — *com-*, (intensive) and *minārī*, to threaten.]

commingle *kəm-ing'gl*, *vt* and *vi* to mingle or mix together. — *adj* **comming'led**.

comminute *kom'in-ūt*, *vt* to reduce to minute particles; to pulverise. — *n* **comminū'tion**. [L. *comminuěre*, *-ūtum*, to break into pieces.]

commis *ko'mi*, *n* an agent, deputy; an apprentice waiter, steward or chef. [Fr.]

commiserate *kəm-iz'ər-āt*, *vi* to feel or express compassion for; to express sympathy (with). — *n* **commiserā'tion** pity, sympathy. [L. *com-*, with, *miserāri*, to deplore — *miser*, wretched.]

commissar *kom-i-sär'* or *kom'*, *n* a commissary (officer); (also **People's Commissar**) formerly, in the Soviet Union, a head of a government department (since 1946 called **minister**); (also **political commissar**) in the Soviet Union, a Communist Party official responsible for political education, encouragement of party loyalty, etc., esp. in military units. — *n* **commissā'riat** the department charged with the furnishing of provisions, e.g. for an army; the office of a commissary or of a commissar; a body of commissars. — *n* **commissar'ship**. [L.L. *commissārius* — *committěre, commissum*.]

commissary *kom'is-ər-i, n* a store supplying equipment and provisions to the military (*US*); (the supply of) provisions (*US*); a restaurant or canteen, esp. in a film studio (orig. *US*); an officer who furnishes provisions, etc. to an army; an officer representing a bishop; a deputy. — *adj* **commissā'rial** pertaining to a commissary. [Ety. as for **commissar**.]

commission *kəm-ish'ən, n* the act of committing; the state of being commissioned or committed; that which is committed; a document, etc., conferring authority, or the authority itself, esp. that of a military, naval or air officer, or a justice of the peace; a percentage paid to an agent; a body of people appointed to perform certain duties; an order for a piece of work, esp. a work of art. — *vt* to give a commission to or for; to empower; to appoint; to put into service. — *vi* to be put into service. — *n* **commissionaire** (*-ār'*) a uniformed doorkeeper or messenger. — *adj* **commiss'ioned**. — *n* **commiss'ioner**. — *n* **commiss'ionership**. — **commissioned officer** one appointed by commission. — **High Commission** an embassy representing one country of the British Commonwealth in another such country; **High Commissioner** the chief representative in a High Commission; **in** (or **out of**) **commission** (of warships, etc.) prepared (or unprepared) for service; in (or not in) usable or working condition. [Ety. as for **commit**.]

Commissr *abbrev* for Commissioner.

commissure *kom'is-ūr, n* a joint; a joining surface; a bundle of nerve-fibres connecting two nerve-centres. — *adj* **commiss'ūral** (or *-sū'*). [L. *commissūra*, a joining.]

commit *kə-mit', vt* to give in charge or trust; to consign, send; to become guilty of, perpetrate; to involve (esp. oneself); to pledge, promise: — *pr p* **committ'ing**; *pa t* and *pa p* **committ'ed**. — *n* **commit'ment** the act of committing; an order for sending to prison; imprisonment; an obligation (to be) undertaken; declared attachment to a doctrine or cause. — *n* **committ'al** commitment; imprisonment; (the ceremony of) the placing of a coffin in a grave, crematorium furnace or the sea; a pledge, actual or implied. — *adj* **committ'ed** having entered into a commitment; (of literature) written from, or (of an author) writing from, a fixed standpoint or with a fixed purpose, religious, political, or other. — *n* **committ'ee** a group selected from a more numerous body (or the whole body) by which some special business is conducted; (*kom-i-tē'*) a person to whom something is committed; a person charged with the care of a lunatic or imbecile (*law*). — *n* **committ'eeship**. — **commit oneself** to make a definite decision or judgment (on); to make a definite agreement; **commit to memory** to learn by heart, memorise. [L. *committěre* — *com-*, with, *mittěre*, to send.]

commix *kə-miks', vt* and *vi* to mix together. — *n* **commix'ture** the act of mixing together; the state of being mixed; the compound formed by mixing.

commn *abbrev* for commission.

commode *kə-mōd', n* a small sideboard; an ornamental chest of drawers; a chair containing a chamberpot. [Ety. as for **commodious**.]

commodious *kə-mō'di-əs, adj* roomy, spacious; comfortable. — *adv* **commo'diously**. — *n* **commo'diousness**. [L. *commodus* — *com-*, together, *modus*, measure.]

commodity *kə-mod'i-ti, n* an article of trade; (in *pl*) goods, produce. [O.Fr. *commodité* — L. (see **commodious**).]

commodore *kom'ə-dör, n* an officer of a rank between an admiral and a captain; the senior captain in a fleet of merchant ships; the president of a yacht-club; a commodore's ship.

common *kom'ən, adj* belonging equally to more than one; mutual; public; general; usual; frequent; ordinary; easily got or obtained; of little value; vulgar; of low degree. — *n* a tract of open land, used by all the inhabitants of a town, parish, etc.; a right to take something from the land of another person (*law*). — *adj* **comm'onable** held in common, mutually. — *n* **comm'onage** the right of pasturing on a common with others; the right of using anything in common; a common. — *n* **commonal'ity** frequency, widespreadness. — *n* **comm'onalty** the general body of the people; the common people. — *n* **comm'oner** a person who is not a noble. — *n* **comm'oning** the conversion of land to common. — *adv* **comm'only** in a common manner; meanly, vulgarly; ordinarily; usually, frequently, often; generally. — *n* **comm'onness**. — *npl* **comm'ons** the common people; (with *cap*) their representatives — i.e. the lower House of Parliament or **House of Commons**; common land, kept for the mutual benefit of ordinary people; food in general, rations. — **Common Era** same as **Christian era**; **common gender** the gender of a noun or pronoun having one form for both male and female, such as L. *bōs*, bull or cow, Eng. *student*; **common ground** a subject of mutual interest, agreement, etc.; **comm'onhold** a freehold held in common by a number of owners, who have joint responsibility for managing the property (e.g. a block of flats); **common-law marriage** in England, any of various informal types of marriage ceremony given legal recognition till 1753, some of which if performed abroad, are still legally valid; loosely, the bond between a man and woman living together as husband and wife but not legally married; **common market** an association of countries as a single economic unit with internal free trade and common external tariffs; (with *caps*) see **European Economic Community**; **common noun** a name that can be applied to all the members of a class (opp. to *proper* noun). — *adj* **common-or-gar'den** ordinary. — **comm'onplace** a platitude, pointless remark. — *adj* frequent, common, usual; lacking distinction; hackneyed, overused. — **commonplace book** a note or memorandum book; **common room** (in schools, colleges, etc.) a room to which the students or teachers have common access; **common school** (*US*) a public elementary school; **common sense** average understanding; good sense or practical wisdom. — *adj* **commonsense'** or **commonsens'ical**. — **common stair** an interior stair giving access to several independent flats or dwellings; **common time** (*mus*) four beats or two beats to the bar rhythm. — **common of pasture** (*law*) the ancient right to graze animals on common land; **in common** together (with); shared or possessed equally; **make common cause with** to cast in one's lot with; to adopt the same interests and aims as; **short commons** (*colloq*) meagre rations; **the common good** the interest of the community at large; **the common people** the people in general. [Fr. *commun* — L. *commūnis*.]

commonweal *kom'ən-wēl, n* the common good, welfare of the community. — *n* **comm'onwealth** (*-welth*) the public or whole body of the people; a group of states united by a strong but elastic link, as *the British Commonwealth*; a form of government in which the power rests with the people; a state or dominion. — **Commonwealth Day** the second Monday in March, kept as a day of celebration in the British Commonwealth. [See **wealth**.]

commotion *kə-mō'shən, n* a violent motion or moving; excited or tumultuous action, physical or mental; agitation; tumult, noise, disturbance. [L. *com-* (intensive) and *movēre, mōtum*, to move.]

Communautaire *ko-mo͞o-no-tār'*, (Fr.) *adj* of, in or pertaining to a spirit or attitude in keeping with the principles and aims of the European Community. — Also **Commu'nitaire**.

commune[1] *kom'ūn*, *n* in France, etc., a small territorial division; in some communist countries, an agricultural community; a group of people living together as a group, sharing all possessions, income, etc., mutually. — *adj* **communal** (*kom'ū-nl* or *kə-mū'*) pertaining to a commune or a community; owned in common, shared equally. — *n* **commūnalīsā'tion** or **-z-**. — *vt* **commū'nalise** or **-ize** (or *kom'*) to make communal. — *n* **commū'nalism**. — *n* **commū'nalist**. — *adv* **comm'ūnally** (or *kə-mū'*). [Fr. *commune*.]

commune[2] *kə-mūn'* or *kom'ūn*, *vi* to converse or talk together; to have intercourse, esp. spiritual, e.g. with nature; to receive Holy Communion. — *n* and *adj* **commūn'ing**. [O.Fr. *communer*, to share.]

communicate *kə-mū'ni-kāt*, *vt* to impart, inform, tell; to reveal, demonstrate; to bestow. — *vi* to succeed in conveying one's meaning to others; to have something in common (with another person); to have communication, correspondence, verbal or written contact (with *with*); to have a means of communication; to partake of Holy Communion. — *adj* **commū'nicable** that may be communicated (esp. of a disease). — *adv* **commū'nicably**. — *n* **commū'nicant** a person who partakes of Holy Communion. — *n* **commūnicā'tion** (an act of) communicating; that which is communicated; (a piece of) correspondence; a means of communicating, a connecting passage or channel; (in *pl*) means of giving and receiving information, as the press, cinema, radio and television; a means of transporting, esp. troops and supplies. — *adj* **commū'nicātive** inclined to communicate or give information. — *adv* **commū'nicātively**. — *n* **commū'nicātor**. — *adj* **commū'nicātory** imparting knowledge. — **communique** or **communiqué** (*kom-ū'ni-kā*) an official announcement, esp. from a long distance. — **communicating door** a door which gives access from one room, etc. to another; **communication cord** a cord in the wall or ceiling of a railway train which can be pulled in an emergency to stop the train; **communications satellite** an artificial satellite in orbit around the earth, used to relay radio, television and telephone signals; **communication (or communications) theory** the theory of the transmitting of information, esp. to, from or between machines. [L. *commūnicāre*, *-ātum* — *commūnis*, common.]

communion *kəm-ūn'yən*, *n* the act of communing; spiritual intercourse or contact; fellowship; union of a number of people in a religious service; the body of people uniting in such a service; (**Holy Communion**) the sacrament commemorating the Last Supper (*Christian relig*). — **commun'ion-cloth, -cup** and **-table** those used at a service of Holy Communion. [L. *commūniō*, *-ōnis*, from *commūnis*, common.]

communique or **communiqué**. See under **communicate**.

communism *kom'ūn-izm*, *n* a theory according to which society should be classless, private property should be abolished, and land, factories, etc. collectively owned and controlled; a system of government adhering to these principles; (often with *cap*) Marxian socialism as understood in Russia. — *n* **comm'ūnist** a believer in communism. — *adj* of, or pertaining to, communism; believing in or favouring communism. — *adj* **commūnist'ic** believing in or favouring communism; of or favouring communal living and ownership.

community *kəm-ūn'i-ti*, *n* a body of people in the same locality; the public in general; people having common rights, etc.; a body of people leading a common life, or under socialistic or similar organisation; a monastic body; a common possession or enjoyment; agreement. — *adj* of, for, or by a local community. — *n* **communitā'rian** a member of a community; an advocate of living in communities. — **community care** care of the elderly, sick, terminally ill, etc. in their own homes rather than in hospital or old people's homes; **community centre** a place where members of a community may meet for social and other activities; **community charge** a tax which replaced the former rating system, levied to pay for local government services and facilities, poll tax; **community property** property owned equally by each partner in a marriage; **community service** unpaid work for the community, often done by minor criminals as an alternative to imprisonment under a **community-service order**; **community work** a form of social work based on the needs of local people and communities; **community worker**. [O.Fr. *communité* — L. *commūnitās*, *-ātis* — *commūnis*, common.]

commute *kə-mūt'*, *vt* to exchange; to exchange (esp. the death sentence) for a punishment less severe; to pay off (e.g. a debt being paid by instalments) early by a single payment, by a simpler or more convenient method, etc.; to change (electric current) from alternating to direct or vice versa. — *vi* to travel regularly, esp. daily to work, between suburban home and town office. — *n* **commūtabil'ity**. — *adj* **commūt'able** that may be commuted or exchanged. — *vt* **commūtate** (*kom'*; *electr*) to commute. — *n* **commūtā'tion** the act of commuting (a sentence, payment or current); change or exchange of one thing for another. — *adj* **commū'tative** (or *kom'ū-tā-tiv*) relating to exchange; interchangeable; such that $x^*y = y^*x$ — where * denotes a binary operation (*math*). — *adv* **commūtatively**. — *n* **comm'ūtātor** an apparatus for reversing electric currents. — *n* **commūt'er** a person who travels daily between home and work. — **commuter belt** an area surrounding a large city or town, from which people commute to work. [L. *commūtāre* — *com-*, with, *mūtāre*, to change.]

comose and **comous**. See **coma**[2].

comp *komp*, *n* short form of **compositor**.

comp. *abbrev* for: (or **compar.**) comparative; compare; compound; compounded.

compact[1] *kəm-pakt'*, *adj* closely placed or fitted together; tightly grouped, not spread out; (of a person) smallish; firm; close; brief; (of a car) medium-sized and economical (*NAm*). — *n* **compact** (*kom'*) a small case containing face-powder for carrying in the handbag (also **powder compact**); a compact car (*NAm*). — *vt* (*-pakt'*) to press closely together; to consolidate. — *adj* **compact'ed**. — *adv* **compact'edly**. — *n* **compact'edness**. — *adv* **compact'ly**. — *n* **compac'tion** the act of compacting, or state of being compacted; sediments compacted by pressure from above (*geol*); an area formed by dumping rock waste, etc., pressing it together by means of heavy machines, and causing or allowing grass to grow over the whole. — *n* **compact'ness**. — *n* **compact'or** a machine which crushes solid waste into the ground. — **compact disc** a small audio disc from which digitally-recorded sound can be read by laser, a laser disc. [L. *compāctus*, past p. of *compingĕre* — *com-*, *pangĕre*, to fix.]

compact[2] *kom'pakt*, *n* a mutual bargain or agreement; a league, treaty, or union. — *adj* (*kom-pakt'*) united (e.g. in a league). [L. *compactum* — *com-pacīscī*, from *com-*, with, *pacīscī*, to bargain.]

compander *kom-pan'dər*, (*electronics*, *telecomm*) *n* a device for compressing the volume range of the transmitted signal and re-expanding it at the receiver, to increase the signal/noise ratio. — *adj* **compan'ded**. — *n* **compan'ding**. [*com*pressor and ex*pander*.]

companion[1] *kəm-pan'yən*, *n* a person who keeps company or frequently associates with another, voluntarily or as a profession; a member of an order of knighthood, esp. in a lower grade; one of a pair or set of things; an often pocket-sized book on a particular subject. — *adj* of the nature of a companion; accompanying. — *adj* **compan'ionable** suitable to be a companion; agreeable. — *adv* **compan'ionably.** — *adj* **compan'ioned** having a companion. — *n* **compan'ionhood.** — *adj* **compan'ionless.** — *n* **compan'ionship** the state of being a companion; company, fellowship; a body of companions. [Fr. *compagnon*, from L.L. *compānium*, a mess — L. *com-*, with, and *pānis*, bread.]

companion² *kəm-pan'yən*, (*naut*) *n* the skylight or window-frame through which light passes to a lower deck or cabin. — **compan'ion-hatch** the covering of an opening in a deck; **compan'ionway** a staircase from the deck to a cabin. [Du. *kompanje*, quarterdeck.]

company *kum'pə-ni*, *n* a person or people with whom one associates; any assembly of people, or of animals and birds; a group of people associated for trade, etc.; a society; a subdivision of a regiment; the crew of a ship; a group of actors working together; a collective noun for a flock of widgeon; fellowship; social intercourse. — *adj* (*attrib*) belonging to, relating to, or associated with, a commercial company. — **bad company** unsuitable, esp. criminal, companions or associates. — **be good** (or **bad**) **company** to have (or lack) companionable qualities; **in company** in the presence of people outside one's immediate family or intimate acquaintance; **keep company** to associate (with *with*); **know a man by his company** to determine a man's character by the quality of his friends; **part company** to separate, go different ways (*lit* or *fig*). [Fr. *compagnie*; same root as **companion¹**.]

compar. *abbrev* for: comparative; comparison.

compare *kəm-pār'*, *vt* to put (as if) side by side so as to ascertain how far things agree or disagree (often with *with*); to liken or represent as similar (with *to*); to give the degrees of comparison of (*gram*). — *vi* to make comparison; to relate (well, badly, etc.) in comparison. — *n* **comparabil'ity.** — *adj* **comparable** (*kom'pər-ə-bl*). — *n* **com'parableness.** — *adv* **com'parably.** — *adj* **comparative** (*kəm-par'ə-tiv*) pertaining to or making comparison; estimated by comparing with something else; relative, not positive or absolute; (of adjectives and adverbs) expressing more, greater degree (*gram*; also *n*). — *adv* **compar'atively.** — *n* **compar'ator** any device for comparing accurately, so as e.g. to detect deviations from a standard or to confirm identity. — *n* **comparison** (*-par'i-sən*) the act of comparing; the capacity of being compared; a comparative estimate; a simile or figure of speech by which two things are compared; the inflection of an adjective or adverb to express different relative degrees of its quality (*gram*). — **comparability study** a comparison of wages, conditions, etc. in different jobs, or the same job in different areas, usu. in order to determine future levels of wages; **comparison microscope** a microscope in which there are two objective lenses, so that images from each can be examined side by side. — **beyond compare** without any rival or equal; **compare notes** to share or exchange one's ideas (with someone else). [L. *comparāre*, to match, from *com-*, *parāre*, to make or esteem equal — *par*, equal.]

compartment *kəm-pärt'mənt*, *n* a partitioned-off or marked-off division of an enclosed space or area; a closed-off division of a railway carriage; a division of anything. — *n* **compartmentalisā'tion** or **-z-**. — *vt* **compartment'alise** or **-ize** to divide into categories or into units, esp. units with little intercommunication. — *adv* **compartment'ally.** [Fr. *compartiment* — L. *com-* (intensive) and *partīrī*, to divide — *pars*, *partis*, a part.]

compass *kum'pəs*, *n* an instrument consisting of a magnetised needle, used to find directions; (in *pl*) a pair of jointed legs, for describing circles, etc. (also **pair of compasses**); a circuit or circle; limit; range of pitch of a voice or instrument; circumference; girth. — *vt* to pass or go round; to surround or enclose; to grasp, comprehend; to bring about, accomplish, achieve, or obtain. — *adj* **com'passable** capable of being compassed. — **com'pass-card** the circular dial of a compass; **compass rose** the circular design showing the principal directions on a map or chart; **com'pass-saw** one for cutting in curves; **compass-win'dow** a semicircular bay window. [Fr. *compas*, a circle.]

compassion *kəm-pash'ən*, *n* fellow-feeling, or sorrow for the sufferings of another; pity. — *adj* **compass'ionable** pitiable. — *adj* **compass'ionate** inclined to pity or mercy; merciful. — *adv* **compass'ionately.** — **compassionate leave** or **discharge**, etc., leave, discharge, etc. in exceptional circumstances for personal reasons; **compassion fatigue** progressive disinclination to show charity or compassion, usu. due to the sheer volume of deserving cases. [Fr., — L.L. *compassiō*, *-ōnis* — *com-*, with, *patī*, *passus*, to suffer.]

compatible *kəm-pat'i-bl*, *adj* consistent (with), congruous; capable of co-existence; admissible in combination; able to be transplanted into another's body without rejection (*med* and *biol*); able to form grafts, or capable of self-fertilisation (*bot*); (of drugs) able to be used simultaneously without undesirable side-effects or interaction (*chem*). — *n* something (esp. a computer) which is compatible with others. — *n* **compatibil'ity** or **compat'ibleness.** — *adv* **compat'ibly.** [Fr., — L. *com-*, with, *patī*, to suffer.]

compatriot *kəm-pāt'ri-ət* or *-pat'*, *n* a fellow-countryman. — Also *adj*. — *adj* **compatriotic** (*-ot'ik*). [Fr. *compatriote* — L. *compatriōta*.]

compeer *kom'pēr* or *kəm-pēr'*, *n* a person who is the equal of another; a companion. [L. *compār* — *com-* (intensive) and *pār*, equal.]

compel *kəm-pel'*, *vt* to drive or urge on forcibly (to); to oblige; to force: — *pr p* **compell'ing**; *pa t* and *pa p* **compelled'**. — *adj* **compell'able.** — *adj* **compell'ing** forcing attention, fascinating. [L. *com-* (intensive) and *pellĕre*, *pulsum*, to drive.]

compendium *kəm-pen'di-əm*, *n* a shortening or abridgment; an abstract or collection of extracts; a collection of board-games in one box: — *pl* **compen'diums** or **compen'dia.** — *adj* **compen'dious** concise but comprehensive. — *adv* **compen'diously.** — *n* **compen'diousness.** [L. *compendium*, what is weighed together, or saved — *com-*, together, *pendĕre*, to weigh.]

compensate *kom'pən-sāt*, *vt* to make (esp. financial) amends to, or to recompense; to counterbalance. — *vi* to make amends (for). — *n* **compensā'tion** the act of compensating; amends, esp. financial, for loss, injury, etc.; the neutralisation of opposing forces (*phys*); the process of compensating for sense of failure or inadequacy by concentrating on achievement or superiority, real or imagined, in some other sphere; the defence mechanism involved in this (*psychol*). — *adj* **compensā'tional, com'pensātive** (or *kəm-pen'sə-tiv*) or **compen'satory** (also *-sā'*) giving compensation. — *n* **com'pensātor.** [L. *com-* (intensive) and *pēnsāre*, frequentative of *pendĕre*, to weigh.]

compère *kɔ̃-per* or *kom'per*, *n* a person who introduces and interlinks items of an entertainment. — *vt* to act as compère to. [Fr., godfather.]

compete *kəm-pēt'*, *vi* to seek or strive for something in rivalry with others; to contend for a prize. — *n* **competition** (*kom-pi-tish'ən*) the act of competing; rivalry in striving for the same goal; a match or trial of ability; those things or people with which or whom others are competing. — *adj* **competitive** (*kəm-pet'i-tiv*) pertaining to or characterised by competition; (of e.g. price) such as to give a chance of successful result in conditions of rivalry, reasonably cheap. — *n* **compet'itiveness.** — *n* **compet'itor** a person who competes; a rival or opponent. — **in competition** competing (with). [L. *competĕre*, to strive together — *com-*, *petĕre*, to seek, strive after.]

competent *kom'pi-tənt*, *adj* suitable; legally qualified; sufficiently good; efficient. — *n* **com'petence** or **com'petency** suitability, fitness; efficiency; capacity, ability; legal power or capacity. — *adv* **com'petently**. [L. *competĕre*, to come together, be convenient — *com-*, *petĕre*, to seek.]

compile *kəm-pīl'*, *vt* to write or compose by collecting the materials from other books; to draw up or collect; (in *golf*, etc.) to put together (a score of). — *n* **compilā'tion** (*-pil-* or *-pīl-*) the act of compiling; the thing compiled, esp. a collection of audio recordings. — *n* **com'pilātor** a person who compiles. — *adj* **compī'latory**. — *n* **compile'ment** a compilation. — *n* **compīl'er** a person who compiles; a complex program which translates instructions in a program-language into machine code (*comput*) (cf. **interpreter**). [Fr. *compiler*.]

complacent *kəm-plā'sənt*, *adj* showing satisfaction, esp. when self-satisfied, usu. with insufficient regard to problems, dangers, etc. — *n* **complā'cence** or **complā'cency** (self-)satisfaction. — *adv* **complā'cently**. [L. *complacēre* — *com-* (intensive) and *placēre*, to please.]

complain *kəm-plān'*, *vi* to express grief, pain, unfavourable opinion (at, about); to express a sense of injury; to make a mournful sound; to indicate that one has an illness (with *of*). — *vt* to utter as a complaint. — *n* **complain'ant** a person who complains; a person who raises a suit, a plaintiff (*law*). — *n* **complain'er** a complainant. — *n* and *adj* **complain'ing**. — *adv* **complain'ingly**. — *n* **complaint'** an instance, or the act, of complaining; an expression of grief and dissatisfaction; finding fault; the thing complained about; a grievance; a disease or illness, an ailment. [Fr. *complaindre* — L.L. *complangĕre* — L. *com-* (intensive) and *plangĕre*, to bewail.]

complaisant *kəm-plā'zənt*, *adj* wishing to please; obliging. — *n* **complais'ance** desire to please, esp. in excess; an obliging manner or attitude. — *adv* **complais'antly**. [Fr., *complaire* — L. *complacēre*.]

complement *kom'pli-mənt*, *n* that which completes or fills up; that amount by which an angle or arc falls short of a right angle or quadrant; that which is added to certain verbs to make a complete predicate; either of any pair of colours which together give white; full number or quantity; all members of a set not included in a given subset (*math*); a series of proteins in blood serum that combine with antibodies to destroy antigens (*immun*). — *vt* **complement** (*-ment'* or *kom'pli-mənt*) to be the complement of. — *adj* **complement'al** completing. — *adv* **complement'arily**. — *n* **complementar'ity** a concept which accepts the existence of superficially inconsistent views of an object or phenomenon (*phys*). — *adj* **complement'ary** completing; together making up a whole, a right angle, ten, an octave, or white; (of medical treatment, therapies, etc.) not mainstream, alternative. [L. *complēmentum* — *com-* (intensive) and *plēre*, to fill.]

complete *kəm-plēt'*, *adj* free from deficiency, not lacking any part; perfect; finished; entire, whole; fully equipped; consummate, fully skilled. — *vt* to finish; to make perfect or entire. — *vi* to finish. — *adj* **complēt'able**. — *adj* **complēt'ed**. — *adv* **complete'ly**. — *n* **complete'ness**. — *n* **complē'tion**. [L. *complēre*, *-ētum*, to fill up — *com-* (intensive) and *plēre*, to fill.]

complex *kom'pleks*, *adj* composed of more than one, or of many parts; not simple or straightforward; intricate; difficult. — *n* a complex whole; a group of (repressed and forgotten) ideas or impressions to which are ascribed abnormal mental conditions and abnormal bodily conditions due to mental causes (*psychol*); loosely applied to the mental condition itself; a complex chemical substance; a collection of interrelated buildings, units, etc., forming a whole, such as a *sports complex*. — *vt* to complicate; to combine into a complex. — *n* **complex'edness**, **com'plexness** or **complex'ity** the state of being complex; complication. — *vt* and *vi* **complex'ify** to make or become complex or complicated. — *n* **complexificā'tion**. — **complex number** the sum of a real and an imaginary number; **complex sentence** one consisting of a principal clause and one or more subordinate clauses. [L. *complex* — *com-*, together, and root of *plicāre*, to fold.]

complexion *kəm-plek'shən*, *n* colour or look of the skin, esp. of the face; general appearance, temperament, or texture; general character or nature (*fig*). — *adj* **complex'ioned** having a certain complexion. — *adj* **complex'ionless** colourless; pale. [Fr., — L. *complexiō*, *-ōnis*, a combination, physical structure of body — *com-*, and *plectĕre*, to plait.]

compliance *kəm-plī'əns*, *n* yielding; agreement, complaisance; assent; submission; under the deregulated stock-market, self-policing by securities firms to ensure that the rules to prevent information passing between departments with potentially conflicting interests are being obeyed. — *adj* **complī'ant** yielding; flexible, submissive; civil. — *adv* **complī'antly**. [See **comply**.]

complicate *kom'pli-kāt*, *vt* to make complex; to entangle. — *adj* (*bot*) folded together. — *adj* **com'plicated** intricate, complex; difficult, confused. — *n* **complicā'tion** an intricate blending or entanglement; a complexity; (usu. in *pl*) further disease or illness starting during treatment of or recovery from an existing medical condition; something which causes or adds to difficulty or confusion. — **complicated fracture** a fracture where there is some other injury (e.g. a dislocation). [L. *com-*, together, *plicāre*, *-ātum*, to fold.]

complicity *kəm-plis'i-ti*, *n* the state or condition of being an accomplice.

complier. See **comply**.

compliment *kom'pli-mənt*, *n* an expression of admiration or praise; (usu. in *pl*) an expression of formal respect or civility. — *vt* (*-ment'* or *kom'pli-mənt*) to pay a compliment to; to express respect for; to praise; to flatter; to congratulate. — *adj* **compliment'ary** conveying, or expressing, civility or praise; using compliments; given free. — *n* **com'plimenter**. — **compliments of the season** greetings appropriate to special times, such as Christmas, etc.; **left-handed compliment** a remark intended to seem a compliment, but in reality the reverse; **pay** or **present one's compliments** to give one's respects or greeting. [Fr. *compliment* — L. *complīmentum*.]

complin or **compline** *kom'plin*, *n* in the Christian liturgy, the seventh and last service of the day, at 9 p.m., completing the set hours for prayer. [O.Fr. *complie* — L. *complēta* (*hōra*).]

comply *kəm-plī'*, *vi* to yield to the wishes of another; to agree or consent to (with *with*). — *n* **complī'er**. — *adj* **comply'ing** compliant, yielding, flexible. [It. *complire*, to fulfil, to suit, to offer courtesies — L. *complēre*, to fulfil.]

compo *kom'pō*, *n* a mortar of cement; a mixture of whiting, resin, and glue for ornamenting walls: — *pl* **com'pos**. — **compo rations** (*mil*) rations for use in the field when no fresh food is available.

component *kəm-pō'nənt*, *adj* making up; forming one of the elements or parts. — *n* one of the parts or elements of which anything is made up, or into which it may be broken down. — *adj* **componential** (*-nen'shəl*). [L. *compōnĕre*.]

comport *kəm-pört'*, *vi* to agree, suit (with *with*). — *vt* (*reflexive*) to bear; to behave. — *n* **comport'ment** behaviour. [L. *comportāre* — *com-*, with, *portāre*, to carry.]

compose *kəm-pōz'*, *vt* to form by putting together or being together; to put in order or at rest; to settle or soothe; to design artistically; to set up for printing; to create (esp. in music and literature). — *vi* to write (esp.) music; to set type. — *adj* **composed'** settled; quiet; calm. — *adv* **compōs'edly.** — *n* **compōs'edness.** — *n* **compōs'er** a writer or author, esp. of music. — *n* **composure** (*kəm-pōzh'yər* or *-pōzh'ər*) calmness. [Fr. *composer* — L. *com-*, with, *pausāre*, to cease, rest; confused and blended in meaning with words from *pōnĕre*, *positum*, to place.]

composite *kom'pə-zit* or (*formerly* and *NAm*) *-poz'*, *adj* made up of distinct parts or elements; belonging to the **Compositae** (*kəm-poz'i-tē*), a large family related to the campanulas but having small flowers crowded together in heads on a common axis surrounded by bracts so as to resemble single flowers; (of a proposal, etc.) combining points from several sources. — *n* a composite thing; something made up of distinct parts or diverse elements; a composite portrait (esp. *NAm*); a plant of the Compositae. — *vt* (*-zīt*) to pool and combine (proposals from various sources, e.g. local branches of a political party) so as to produce a satisfactory list for discussion at a higher, esp. national, level. — *n* **com'positeness.** — *n* **composi'tion** the act or art of composing; the nature or proportion of the ingredients (of anything); a thing composed; a work of art, esp. in music; an exercise in writing prose or verse; arrangement of parts; combination; an artificial mixture, esp. one used as a substitute; mental or moral make-up. — *adj* **composi'tional.** — *adj* **compositive** (*-poz'*). — *n* **compos'itor** a person who sets up type for printing. — *adj* **compos'itous** (*bot*) composite. — **composite portrait** a blend of several portraits; a photograph printed from several negatives representing different persons or the same person at different times. [L. *compositus*, *compostus* — *com-*, together, *pōnĕre*, to place.]

compos mentis *kom'pos men'tis*, (L.) of sound mind, sane.

compost *kom'post*, *n* mixture; manure consisting of a mixture of decomposed organic substances. — *vt* to treat with compost; to convert into compost. — *n* **com'poster** an apparatus for converting garden waste into compost. — **com'post-heap** a pile of plant refuse, soil, and often chemical fertiliser, which decomposes to form compost. [Ety. as for **composite.**]

composure. See **compose.**

compot or **compote** *kom'pot* or *kom'pōt*, *n* fruit preserved in syrup; stewed fruit. [Fr. *compote.*]

compound¹ *kəm-pownd'*, *vt* to make up; to combine (*chem*); to settle or adjust by agreement; to agree for a consideration not to prosecute (a felony); to intensify, make worse or greater. — *vi* to agree, or come to terms. — *adj* (*kom'*) mixed or composed of a number of parts; so united that the whole has properties of its own which are not necessarily those of its constituents (*chem*); not simple, dealing with numbers of various denominations of quantity, etc., or with processes more complex than the simple process (*arith*). — *n* a mass made up of a number of parts; a word made up of two or more words; a compound substance (*chem*). — *n* **compound'er.** — **compound eye** in insects, etc., an eye made up of many separate units; **compound interest** interest added to the principal at the end of each period (usu. a year) to form a new principal for the next period, thus giving further interest on the interest to date; **compound sentence** (*gram*) one containing more than one principal clause; **compound time** (*mus*) time in which each bar is made up of two or more simple measures. [O.Fr. *compundre* from L. *compōnĕre* — *com-*, together, *pōnĕre*, to place.]

compound² *kom'pownd*, *n* an enclosure round a house or factory (esp. in India), or for housing labourers (S. Africa), prisoners, or detainees. [Malay *kampong*, *kampung*, enclosure.]

comprehend *kom-pri-hend'*, *vt* to grasp with the mind, to understand; to comprise or include. — *n* **comprehensibil'ity** or **comprehen'sibleness.** — *adj* **comprehen'sible** capable of being understood. — *adv* **comprehen'sibly.** — *n* **comprehen'sion** understanding; power of the mind to understand. — *adj* **comprehen'sive** having the quality or power of comprehending or containing much; including everything, complete. — *n* a comprehensive school. — *adv* **comprehen'sively.** — *n* **comprehen'siveness.** — *n* **comprehensivīsā'tion** or **-z-** the act or process of converting schools to comprehensives. — *vt* **comprehen'sivise** or **-ize.** — **comprehensive school** a secondary school, serving a particular area, that provides education for pupils of all ability levels. [L. *comprehendĕre*, *-hēnsum* — *com-*, *prehendĕre*, to seize.]

compress *kəm-pres'*, *vt* to press together; to force into a narrower space; to condense or concentrate. — *n* (*kom'*; *med*) a pad used to apply pressure to any part of the body; a folded cloth applied to the skin. — *adj* **compressed'** pressed together; compacted; laterally flattened or narrowed (*biol*). — *n* **compressibil'ity.** — *adj* **compress'ible** that may be compressed. — *n* **compress'ibleness.** — *n* **compression** (*kəm-presh'ən*) the act of compressing; the state of being compressed or condensed; flattening; deformation by pressure; the stroke that compresses the gases in an internal-combustion engine. — *adj* **compress'ional.** — *adj* **compress'ive** tending to compress. — *n* **compress'or.** — *n* **compressure** (*-presh'ər*). — **compressed air** air at more than atmospheric pressure; **compression-ignition engine** an internal-combustion engine in which ignition of the liquid fuel injected into the cylinder is performed by the heat of compression of the air charge. [L. *compressāre* — *com-*, together, *pressāre*, to press.]

comprise *kəm-prīz'*, *vt* to contain, include; to consist of (often, incorrectly, with *of*). — *adj* **comprīs'able.** — *n* **comprīs'al** the act, condition, or fact of comprising. [Fr. *compris*, past p. of *comprendre* — L. *comprehendĕre.*]

compromise *kom'prə-mīz*, *n* a settlement of differences by concession on each side; anything of intermediate or mixed kind, neither one absolute nor another. — *vt* to settle by concession on each side; to involve or bring into question; to expose to risk of injury, suspicion, censure or scandal. — *vi* to make a compromise. [Fr. *compromis* — L. *comprōmittĕre*, *-missum* — *com-*, together, *prōmittĕre*, to promise.]

Compsognathus *komp-sog'nə-thəs*, *n* one of the smallest known dinosaurs, lizard-hipped, walking on two feet, and carnivorous. [Gr. *kompsos*, elegant, *gnathos*, jaw.]

comptroller. See under **control.**

compulsion *kəm-pul'shən*, the act of compelling; force; a strong irrational impulse. — *adj* **compul'sive** having the power to compel; pertaining to compulsion; (of a person) driven by, (of an action) caused by, a specific, constant and irresistible impulse; (*loosely*) irresistible, fascinating. — *adv* **compul'sively.** — *adv* **compul'sorily.** — *adj* **compul'sory** obligatory; compelling. — *n* an exercise comprising specified compulsory figures, movements, or dances, e.g. in ice-skating. — **compulsory purchase** enforced purchase by a public authority of property needed for public purposes. [L. *compulsāre*, frequentative of *compellere*; see **compel.**]

compunction *kəm-pungk'shən*, *n* remorse tinged with pity, regret. — *adj* **compunc'tious.** [O.Fr., —

L. *compunctiō, -ōnis* — *com-* (intensive) and *pungěre, punctum*, to prick.]

compute *kəm-pūt'*, *vt* to calculate, esp. with a computer; to estimate. — *adj* **comput'able** calculable. — *n* **comput'er** a calculator; a machine or apparatus, mechanical, electric or electronic, for carrying out (esp. complex) calculations, dealing with numerical data or with stored items of other information; also used for controlling manufacturing processes, or co-ordinating parts of a large organisation. — *n* **computā'tion** the act of computing; (a) calculation; an estimate. — *adj* **computā'tional** involving calculation. — *n* **computerese'** (*facetious*) computer language; the jargon used by people who deal with computers. — *vt* **comput'erise** or **-ize** to bring computer(s) into use to control (a process, operation, or system of operations formerly done by manual or mechanical means); to process (data) by computer. — *n* **computerisā'tion** or **-z-**. — **computerised axial tomography scanner** a machine which produces X-ray pictures of sections of the body with the assistance of a computer (shortened to **CAT scanner**); **computer crime** or **fraud** crime such as embezzlement, committed through the manipulation of company finances, etc., by computer; **computer game** a game on cassette for playing on a home computer, the player attempting to manipulate moving images on the screen by operating certain keys or a joystick; **computer graphics** diagrammatic or pictorial matter produced by computer, on a screen or in printed form; **computer language** a system of alphabetical or numerical signs used for feeding information into a computer; **computer literacy**. — *adj* **computer-lit'erate** competent, or fully versed, in the use of computers. — **computer science** the sciences connected with computers, e.g. computer design, programming, data processing, etc.; **computer scientist**; **computer typesetting** the use of computers to process keyed material, outputting justified, hyphenated, etc. lines, the output being either a new tape to be used on a typesetting or filmsetting machine or, in many systems, the final product on paper or film; **computer virus** see under **virus**. [L. *computāre* — *com-* (intensive) and *putāre*, to reckon.]

comrade *kom'rid* or *kum'rid*, *n* a close companion; an intimate associate or friend; a fellow-soldier; in some socialist and communist circles used as a term of address, or prefixed to a name; a communist (*derog slang*). — *adj* and *adv* **com'radely**. — *n* **com'radeship**. [Sp. *camarada*, a roomful, a room-mate — L. *camera*, a room.]

coms *komz*, *npl* short for **combinations**.

COMSAT or **comsat** *kom'sat*, *abbrev* for *com*munications *sat*ellite.

Con. *abbrev* for Consul.

con[1] *kon*, *adv* and *n* a contraction of L. *contrā*, against, as in **pro and con**, for and against.

con[2] *kon*, *vt* to study carefully, scan, pore over; to commit to memory: — *pr p* **conn'ing**; *pa t* and *pa p* **conned**. — *n* **conn'er**. — *n* **conn'ing**. [Another form of **can**[1], O.E. *cunnan*, to know.]

con[3] or **conn** *kon*, (*naut*) *vt* to direct the steering of. — Also *vi*. — *n* **conn'er**. — *n* **conn'ing**. — **conn'ing-tower** the wheel-house of a submarine or warship. [Older forms *cond, condue*, etc. — Fr. *conduire* — L. *condūcěre*.]

con[4] *kon*, (*slang*) *adj* short for **confidence**, as in **con game** or **con trick**, a swindle, **con man** or **woman** a swindler, esp. one with a persuasive way of talking. — *vt* **con** to swindle; to trick; to persuade by dishonest means. — *n* a trick, swindle.

con[5] *kon*, (*slang*) *n* a prisoner. [Abbrev. of **convict**.]

con. *abbrev* for: conclusion; *contra* (L.), against; conversation.

con-. See **com-**.

con amore *kon am-ö're*, (It.) with love; very earnestly.

con brio *kon brē'ō*, (It.; esp. *mus*) with spirit.

conc. *abbrev* for: concentrated; concentration.

concatenate *kən-kat'ə-nāt*, *vt* to chain or link together; to connect in a series. — *n* **concatenā'tion** a series of links united; a series of things depending on or resulting from each other. [L. *con-*, *catēna*, a chain.]

concave *kon'kāv* or *kon-kāv'*, *adj* curved inwards (opp. to *convex*). — *vt* and *vi* to make or become hollow. — *adv* **con'cavely** (or *-kāv'*). — *n* **concavity** (*kən-kav'i-ti*) the quality of being concave; a hollow. — *adj* **concāvō-con'cave** or **doub'le-concave** concave on both sides. — *adj* **concāvō-con'vex** concave on one side, and convex on the other. [L. *concavus*, from *con-* (intensive) and *cavus*, hollow.]

conceal *kən-sēl'*, *vt* to hide completely or carefully; to keep secret; to disguise; to keep from telling. — *n* **conceal'er**. — *n* **conceal'ment**. [O.Fr. *conceler* — L. *concēlāre*, from *con-* (intensive) and *cēlāre*, to hide.]

concede *kən-sēd'*, *vt* to yield or give up; to admit, allow (that). — *vi* to make a concession; to admit defeat. — *n* **conced'er**. [L. *concēděre, -cēssum* — *con-*, wholly, *cēděre*, to yield.]

conceit *kən-sēt'*, *n* overbearing self-esteem, vanity; a witty thought, esp. far-fetched, affected or (over-)ingenious. — *adj* **conceit'ed** egotistical, vain. — *adv* **conceit'edly**. — *n* **conceit'edness**. [From **conceive** on the analogy of **deceive, deceit**.]

conceive *kən-sēv'*, *vt* to receive into or form in the womb; to form in the mind; to imagine or think. — *vi* to become pregnant; to think. — *n* **conceivabil'ity** or **conceiv'ableness**. — *adj* **conceiv'able**. — *adv* **conceiv'ably**. [O.Fr. *concever* — L. *concipěre, conceptum*, from *con-*, together, *capěre*, to take.]

concentrate *kon'sən-trāt*, *vt* to bring towards, or collect at, a common centre; to focus; to direct (attention, etc.) exclusively upon the matter in hand; to condense, to increase the quantity of in a unit of space. — *vi* to move towards a common centre; to direct one's thoughts or efforts towards one goal. — *n* a product of concentration; something in concentrated form. — *adj* **con'centrate** concentrated. — *n* **concentrā'tion** the act of concentrating; the condensing of anything; the number of molecules or ions to a unit of volume; the keeping of the mind fixed on something. — **concentration camp** a prison camp for people (esp. civilians) obnoxious to the authorities. [A lengthened form of **concentre**.]

concentre *kən-sent'ər*, *vi* to tend to or meet in a common centre; to be concentric. — *vt* to bring or direct to a common centre or point. — *adj* **concen'tric** or **concen'trical** having a common centre. — *adv* **concen'trically**. — *n* **concentricity** (*kon-sən-tris'i-ti*). [Fr. *concentrer* — L. *con-*, *centrum* — Gr. *kentron*, point.]

concept *kon'sept*, *n* a thing thought of, a general notion; an idea, invention. — *n* **concep'tion** the act of conceiving; the fertilisation of an ovum; the formation, or power of forming in the mind, of a concept, plan, thought, etc.; a concept; (often in negative expressions) a notion, thought, idea. — *adj* **concep'tual** pertaining to conception or concepts. — *n* **conceptualisā'tion** or **-z-**. — *vt* **concep'tualise** or **-ize** to form a concept, idea, notion or mental picture of. — *vi* to form concepts; to think abstractly. — *n* **concep'tualism** the doctrine in philosophy that universals exist only in the mind. — *n* **concep'tualist**. — *adj* **conceptualis'tic**. — *n* **concep'tus** (*-təs*) the foetus and surrounding tissue forming in the uterus immediately on fertilisation: — *pl* **concep'tuses**. — **concept car** a prototype car produced by a manufacturer to illustrate a general idea or genre of vehicle. [L. *concipĕre, -ceptum*, to conceive.]

concern *kən-sûrn'*, *vt* to relate or belong to; to have to do with, deal with, have as subject matter; to affect or interest; to involve by interest, occupation or duty; to trouble, make anxious; to bother (oneself) with. — *n* that which relates or belongs to one; affair; business; interest; regard; anxiety; a business establishment; in Quaker terminology, a spiritual directive to act in a given matter. — *adj* **concerned'** involved; taking an active interest in current social, etc., problems; troubled, anxious. — *adv* **concern'edly**. — *n* **concern'edness**. — *prep* **concern'ing** regarding; about. — **as concerns** with regard to. [L. *concernĕre*, to distinguish, (later) to have respect to.]

concert *kon'sərt*, *n* union or agreement in any undertaking; harmony, esp. musical; a musical performance. — *vt* (*kən-sûrt'*) to construct or devise together. — *adj* **concerted** (*-sûrt'*) mutually planned or orchestrated; arranged in parts (*mus*). — *n* **concerto** (*kon-chûr'tō*) a composition for solo instrument(s) and orchestra in sonata form: — *pl* **concer'tos**. — **con'cert-goer** a habitual attender of concerts; **concert-grand'** a grand piano suitable for concerts; **con'cert-hall**; **con'cert-master** the leader of an orchestra; **concert party** a small group of performers, entertainers, etc., often at a private function; a group of people working together to buy shares which are later to be used as if they are a single holding. — **in concert** working or conspiring together; performing at a concert venue. [It. *concertare*, to sing in concert.]

concertina *kon-sər-tē'nə*, *n* a musical instrument consisting of a pair of bellows, usually hexagonal, the sounds produced (when the bellows are squeezed and buttons pressed) by free vibrating reeds of metal, as in the accordion; anything of similar folded-up shape. — *vi* and *vt* to collapse or fold up like a concertina: — *pr p* **concerti'naing**; *pa p* and *pa t* **concerti'naed**. [Ety. as for **concert**, plus dimin. affix.]

concession *kən-sesh'ən*, *n* the act of conceding; the thing conceded; a grant; the right, granted under government licence, to drill for oil or gas in a particular area; (the right to conduct) a branch of one business within a branch or on the premises of a larger one; a reduced-price ticket (for the elderly, schoolchildren, the unwaged, etc. — *n* **concessionaire'** a person who has obtained a business concession. — *adj* **concess'ionary**. — *adj* **concess'ive** implying concession. [Ety. as for **concede**.]

conch *kongk* or *konch*, *n* the name for various marine molluscs, and their shells; such a shell used as a trumpet; a concha; a shell-like device for kneading and mixing chocolate during manufacture: — *pl* **conchs** (*kongks*) or **conches** (*kon'chiz*). — *n* **concha** (*kong'kə*) the semi-dome of an apse (*archit*); the outer ear, or its cavity: — *pl* **conchae** (*kong'kē* or *-chē*). — *adj* **conch'ate** or **conch'iform** shaped like a shell, esp. one valve of a bivalve shell. — *adj* **concholog'ical**. — *n* **conchol'ogist**. — *n* **conchol'ogy** the study of molluscs and their shells. [L. *concha* — Gr. *konchē*, a cockle or mussel.]

conchiglie *kon-kē'lē-e*, *npl* shell-shaped pasta. [It.]

conchy or **conchie** *kon'shi*, (*derog slang*) *n* a *conscientious* objector; an over-conscientious person (*Austr*).

concierge *kɔ̃-si-erzh'*, *n* a warden; a janitor; a porter (male or female). [Fr.]

conciliate *kən-sil'i-āt*, *vt* to gain, or win over; to reconcile, bring together (esp. opposing sides in an industrial dispute). — *vi* to make friends, having been hostile. — *n* **concilia'tion** the act or process of conciliating. — *adj* **concil'iative** (or *-ā-tiv*). — *n* **concil'iātor**. — *adj* **concil'iatory**. [L. *conciliāre, -ātum* — *concilium*, council.]

concise *kən-sīs'*, *adj* cut short; brief but pertinent. — *adv* **concise'ly**. — *n* **concise'ness** or **concision** (*-sizh'ən*) the quality of being concise; terseness. [L. *concīsus*, past p. of *concīdĕre* — *con* (intensive) and *caedĕre*, to cut.]

conclave *kon'klāv*, *n* the room in which cardinals meet to elect a pope; the body of cardinals; any close or secret assembly. [L. *conclāve* — *con-*, with, *clāvis*, a key.]

conclude *kən-klōōd'*, *vt* to close; to end; to decide (that); to settle or arrange finally; to infer. — *vi* to end; to form a final judgment. — *adj* **conclud'ed** finished; settled. — *adj* **conclud'ing** final, closing. — *n* **conclu'sion** (*-zhən*) the act of concluding; the end, close, or last part; inference, resultant assumption; judgment. — *adj* **conclusive** (*-klōō'siv*) or **conclu'sory** final; convincing. — *adv* **conclus'ively**. — *n* **conclus'iveness**. — **in conclusion** finally. [L. *conclūdĕre, conclūsum* — *con-* (intensive) and *claudĕre*, to shut.]

concoct *kən-kokt'*, *vt* to fabricate; to plan, devise; to prepare or mature. — *n* **concoct'er** or **concoct'or**. — *n* **concoc'tion** the action of concocting; something fabricated or made up from separate parts, e.g. a story, a lie, a food dish or drink; preparation of a medical prescription, etc. [L. *concoquĕre, concoctum* — *con-*, together, *coquĕre*, to cook, to boil.]

concomitant *kən-kom'i-tənt*, *adj* occurring along with, because of, or in proportion to (something else). — *n* someone who or something that necessarily accompanies. — *adv* **concom'itantly**. [L. *con-* (intensive) and *comitāns, -antis*, pres. p. of *comitārī*, to accompany.]

concord *kon'körd* or *kong'-*, *n* the state of being of the same opinion or feeling; harmony; agreement; a combination of sounds satisfying to the ear (opp. to *discord*). — *vi* **concord'** (*kən-*) to agree; to harmonise. — *n* **concord'ance** agreement; an index of the words or passages of a book or author. — *adj* **concord'ant** harmonious, united. — *adv* **concord'antly**. — *n* **concord'at** a pact or agreement, esp. between the pope and a secular government. [Fr. *concorde* — L. *concordia* — *concors*, of the same heart, from *con-* and *cor, cordis*, the heart.]

concourse *kon'körs* or *kong'*, *n* a large hall; an open space, esp. in a railway station, airport, etc., for transit, meeting, etc.; an assembly of people for some event. [Fr. *concours* — L. *concursus* — *con-*, *currĕre*, to run.]

concrescence *kən-kres'əns*, (*med*) *n* a coalescence or growing together. — *adj* **concresc'ent**. [L. *concrēscentia* — *con-*, *crēscĕre*, to grow.]

concrete *kon'krēt*, *adj* formed into one mass; real, actual, specific, not abstract, able to be experienced; made of concrete. — *n* a mixture of sand, gravel, etc., and cement, used in building; a solid mass formed by parts growing or sticking together. — *vt* (*-krēt'*) to form into a solid mass; (*kon'*) to cover or fix with concrete. — *vi* (*-krēt'*) to harden. — *adv* **con'crētely**. — *n* **con'crēteness** (or *-krēt'*). — *n* **concretion** (*-krē'shən*) a concreted mass; a nodule or lump formed within a rock by materials rearranging themselves about a centre (*geol*); a solid mass formed within an animal or plant body (*med*). — *adj* **concrē'tionary**. — *n* **concretisā'tion** or **-z-**. — *vt* **con'cretise** or **-ize** to render concrete or actual, to realise, bring about. — *n* **con'cretism** regarding, representing, abstract things as concrete. — *n* and *adj* **con'cretist**. — **concrete jungle** (*facetious*) an area of bleakly ugly (esp. high-rise) buildings; **con'crete-mixer** a machine with a large revolving drum for mixing concrete; **concrete music** same as **musique concrète**; **concrete poetry** an art form which seeks to introduce a new element into poetry by means of visual effects such as special arrangements of the letters of the poem on the printed page. [L. *concrētus* — *con-*, together, *crēscĕre*, *crētum*, to grow.]

concubine *kong'kū-bīn*, (esp. *Bible*) *n* a woman who cohabits with a man without being married. — *n* **concubinage** (*kon-kū'bin-ij*) the state of living together as man and wife without being married. — *adj* **concū'binary**. [Fr., — L. *concubīna* — *con-*, together, *cubāre*, to lie down.]

concupiscence *kən-kū'pis-əns*, *n* a violent desire, sexual appetite, lust. — *adj* **concū'piscent**. [L. *concupīscentia* — *concupīscĕre* — *con-* (intensive) and *cupĕre*, to desire.]

concur *kən-kûr'*, *vi* to agree; to assent; to coincide; to meet in one point; to run together: — *pr p* **concurr'ing**; *pa p* and *pa t* **concurred'**. — *n* **concurrence** (*-kur'*) agreement; assent; the meeting of lines in one point; coincidence. — *adj* **concurr'ent** running, coming, acting, or existing together or simultaneously; coinciding; accompanying; meeting in the same point. — *adv* **concurr'ently**. — *adj* **concurr'ing** agreeing. [L. *concurrĕre* — *con-*, *currĕre*, to run.]

concuss *kən-kus'*, *vt* to affect with concussion; to disturb; to shake. — *n* **concussion** (*-kush'*) a violent blow, esp. on the head; the resulting injury to the brain, causing temporary or partial loss of consciousness; a violent shock caused by the sudden contact of two bodies. [L. *concussus*, past p. of *concutĕre* — *con-*, together, *quatĕre*, to shake.]

condemn *kən-dem'*, *vt* to pronounce guilty; to judge unfavourably or blame; to sentence (to imprisonment or death); to give up (to some fate); to pronounce (esp. a building or machine) unfit for use. — *n* **condemnation** (*kon-dəm-nā'shən*) the state of being condemned; (something said or written in) the act of condemning. — *adj* **condem'natory** expressing or implying condemnation. — *adj* **condemned'** pronounced to be wrong, guilty, or worthless; belonging or relating to one who is sentenced to punishment by death (e.g. *condemned cell*); declared dangerous or unfit. [L. *condemnāre*, from *con-* (intensive) and *damnāre*, to hurt.]

condense *kən-dens'*, *vt* to reduce to a smaller extent or volume; to render more dense, intense, or concentrated; to subject to condensation (*chem*). — *vi* to become condensed. — *n* **condens'āte** a product of condensation. — *n* **condensā'tion** (*kon-*) the act of condensing; water which, having vaporised, returns to its liquid state, e.g. on a cold window; the union of two or more molecules of the same or different compounds with the elimination of water, alcohol, or other simple substances (*chem*); loosely applied to almost any reaction in which a product of higher molecular weight than the original substance is obtained. — *n* **condens'er** an apparatus for reducing vapours to a liquid form; a mirror or lens for focusing light; a capacitor. — **condensation trail** see **contrail**; **condensed milk** milk reduced and thickened by evaporation, and sugared. [L. *condēnsāre* — *con-* (intensive) and *dēnsus*, dense.]

condescend *kon-di-send'*, *vi* to act graciously to inferiors; to deign (to do something) (*facetious*); to stoop to what is unworthy of one. — *adj* **condescend'ing** gracious to inferiors; offensively patronising. — *adv* **condescend'ingly**. — *n* **condescen'sion**. [L. *con-* (intensive) and *dēscendĕre*, to descend — *dē*, down from, *scandĕre*, to climb.]

condign *kən-dīn'*, *adj* (usu. of punishment) well deserved. [L. *condīgnus* — *con-* (intensive) and *dīgnus*, worthy.]

condiment *kon'di-mənt*, *n* a seasoning, esp. salt or pepper. [L. *condīmentum* — *condīre*, to preserve, to pickle.]

condition *kən-dish'ən*, *n* the state in which things exist, e.g., the *human condition*; a particular quality of existence, good, bad, etc.; a prerequisite, prior requirement; a term of a contract; (in *pl*) circumstances; that which must be true for a further statement to be true (*logic*); a clause in a will, etc, which requires something to happen before the will is enacted (*law*). — *vt* to restrict, limit; to put into the required state; to prepare, train (a person or animal) for a certain activity or for certain conditions of living; to secure by training (a certain behavioural response to a stimulus which would not normally cause it) (*psychol*). — *adj* **condi'tional** depending on conditions; expressing a condition or conditions. — *n* **conditional'ity**. — *adv* **condi'tionally**. — *adj* **condi'tioned** having a certain condition, state, or quality; caused by psychological conditioning. — *n* **condi'tioner** a person, substance, or apparatus that brings something (esp. hair) into a good or required condition. — *n* **condi'tioning**. — **conditioned reflex** or **response** a reflex response to a stimulus which depends upon the former experience of the individual (*psychol*); **in** or **out of condition** in good or bad condition; physically fit or unfit. [L. *condiciō* (wrongly *conditiō*), *-ōnis*, an agreement — *condīcĕre*, — *con-*, together, *dīcĕre*, to say.]

condo *kon'dō*, (*NAm*) *n* short for **condominium**.

condole *kən-dōl'*, *vi* to grieve (with another person); to express sympathy in sorrow. — *adj* **condol'atory** expressing condolence. — *n* **condol'ence** (usu. in *pl*) an expression of sympathy with another's sorrow. [L. *con-*, with, *dolēre*, to grieve.]

condom *kon'dom* or *-dəm*, *n* a contraceptive rubber sheath for the penis.

condominium *kon-də-min'i-əm*, *n* joint sovereignty; a country whose government is controlled by two or more other countries; a block of apartments in which each apartment is separately owned (*NAm*); such an apartment (*NAm*). [L. *con-*, together, *dominium*, lordship.]

condone *kən-dōn'*, *vt* to forgive; to pass over without blame, overlook intentionally, excuse. — *adj* **condon'able**. — *n* **condonā'tion** (*kon-*). [L. *con-* (intensive) and *dōnāre*, to give.]

condor *kon'dör* or *-dər*, *n* a large South American vulture. [Sp. *cóndor* — Quechua *cuntur*.]

conduce *kən-dūs'*, *vi* to help to bring about, contribute (towards a result). — *adj* **conduc'ive** leading or tending; favourable to or helping towards something. — **conducive to** helping towards or encouraging. [L. *con-*, together, *dūcĕre*, to lead.]

conduct *kən-dukt'*, *vt* to lead or guide; to convey (water, blood, sap, etc.); to direct; to manage (one's life, business affairs, etc.); to behave (esp. oneself); to carry, transmit, allow to pass (*electr*; also *vi*); to beat time for and co-ordinate (an orchestra, piece of music, etc.; also *vi*). — *n* (*kon'dukt*) the act or method of leading or managing; behaviour; guidance; management. — *n* **conduct'ance** a conductor's power of conducting electricity, the reciprocal of the resistance. — *n* **conductibil'ity**. — *adj* **conduct'ible** capable of conducting (heat, etc.); capable of being conducted or transmitted. — *n* **conduc'tion** the act or property of conducting or transmitting; transmission (of e.g. heat) by a conductor. — *adj* **conduct'ive** having the quality or power of conducting or transmitting. — *n* **conductiv'ity** the power of transmitting heat, electricity, etc.; the power of a specific substance to conduct electricity. — *n* **conduct'or** a person or thing that conducts; a leader; a manager; a director of an orchestra or choir; a person sometimes in charge of taking fares on a bus, etc. but not driving it (*fem* **conduc'tress**); a railway guard (*NAm*); anything which has the property of transmitting electricity, heat, etc. — *n* **conduct'orship** the office of conductor. — **safe-con'duct** see under **safe**. [L. *conductus* — *condūcĕre*.]

conduit *kon'dit*, also *kon'dū-it* or *-dwit*, *n* a channel or pipe conveying water or other fluid, or covering electric wires, etc.; a means of transmission or communication (*fig*). [Fr. *conduit* — L. *conductus* — *condūcĕre*, to lead.]

condyle *kon'dil* or *-dīl*, *n* a protuberance at the end of a bone for articulation with another bone. — *adj* **con'dylar** or **con'dyloid**. [Gr. *kondylos*, knuckle.]

cone *kōn*, *n* a solid figure with a point and a base in the shape of a circle or ellipse (*geom*); a volcanic hill; the typical flower (or fruit) of certain trees, e.g. the pine, fir, etc., woody and more or less conical; an ice-cream cornet, often including the ice-cream; one of a series of plastic bollards shaped like geometrical cones, placed round obstacles, etc. in the road in order to divert traffic. — *vt* to shape like a geometrical cone. — *vi* to bear cones. — *adj* **conic** (*kon'ik*) or **con'ical** having the form of, or pertaining to, a cone. — *n* a conic section. — *adv* **con'ically**. — *nsing* **con'ics** the geometry of the cone and its sections. — *adj* **cō'niform** in the form of a cone. — **conic section** a figure made by the intersection of a cone by a plane. — **cone off** to close off (e.g. one carriageway of a motorway) with plastic cones. [Gr. *kōnos*.]

coney. See **cony**.

confabulate *kən-fab'ū-lāt*, *vi* to chat (*colloq* **confab'** (*kon-*)); to imagine experiences to compensate for loss of memory (*psychiatry*). — *adj* **confab'ūlar**. — *adj* **confab'ūlatory**. — *n* **confabūlā'tion** a chat (*colloq* **con'fab**); the act or process of confabulating (*psychiatry*). — *n* **confab'ūlātor**. [L. *cōnfābulārī* — *con-*, *fābulārī*, to talk.]

confection *kən-fek'shən*, *n* composition, compounding, mixing; a sweetmeat; a light, frothy entertainment (*fig*). — *n* **confec'tionary** a place where confectionery is made or kept. — *adj* pertaining to or of the nature of confectionery. — *n* **confec'tioner** a person who makes or sells confectionery, sweet cakes or sweetmeats; a sweet-shop. — *n* **confec'tionery** confectioners' work or art; sweetmeats in general. [L. *cōnficĕre*, *cōnfectum*, to make up together — *con-*, *facĕre*, to make.]

confederate *kən-fed'ər-ət*, *adj* leagued together; allied (esp., with *cap*, the seceding American states of the Civil War). — *n* a person united in a league; (with *cap*) a supporter of the seceding states in the U.S. Civil War; an ally; an accomplice. — *vi* and *vt* (*-āt*) to league together or join in a league. — *n* **confed'eracy** a league or alliance; people or states united by a league; a conspiracy. — *n* **confederā'tion** a league; an alliance, esp. of princes, states, etc.; an association of more or less autonomous states united permanently by a treaty. [L. *cōnfoederāre*, *-ātum* — *con-* and *foedus*, *foedĕris*, a league.]

confer *kən-fûr'*, *vt* to give or bestow (esp. a privilege or honour); to compare (*obs*) — in use as abbrev. **cf**. — *vi* to talk or consult together: — *pr p* **conferr'ing**; *pa t* and *pa p* **conferred'**. — *n* **conferee'** a person with whom one confers; a person on whom something is bestowed; a person taking part in a conference. — *n* **conference** (*kon'*) the act of conferring; an appointed meeting or series of meetings for instruction or discussion. — *n* **confer'ment** bestowal; a thing bestowed. — **in conference** attending a meeting; engaged, busy. [L. *cōnferre* — *con-*, together, *ferre*, to bring.]

conférence *kō-fā-rās*, (Fr.) *n* a lecture. — *n* **conférencier** (*-rā-syā*) a lecturer.

confess *kən-fes'*, *vt* to acknowledge fully (esp. something wrong); to own up to or admit; to make known, as sins to a priest; to hear a confession from, as a priest. — *vi* to make confession (esp. to a priest). — *n* **confession** (*kən-fesh'ən*) acknowledgment, admission of a crime or fault; the thing confessed; a statement of religious belief; acknowledgment of sin to a priest. — *n* **confess'ional** the seat or enclosed recess where a priest hears confessions; the institution of confession. — *adj* pertaining to confession. — *n* **confess'or** a priest who hears confessions and grants absolution; a person who makes a statement, esp. a declaration of religious faith: — *fem* **confess'oress**. — *n* **confess'orship**. — *adj* **confessed** admitted; avowed, declared; evident. — *adv* **confess'edly**. — **confess to** to admit, acknowledge. [Fr. *confesser* — L. *cōnfitērī*, *cōnfessus* — *con-* (signifying completeness) and *fatērī*, to confess.]

confetti *kən-fet'i*, *npl* small pieces of coloured paper flung at brides and bridegrooms. [It.]

confide *kən-fīd'*, *vi* to trust wholly or have faith (with *in*); to impart secrets to someone as confidences (with *in*). — *vt* to tell with reliance upon secrecy. — *n* **confidant** (*kon-fi-dant'*) a person confided in or entrusted with secrets, esp. in love affairs; a close friend: — *fem* **confidante'**. — *n* **confidence** (*kon'fi-dəns*) firm trust or belief; faith; trust in secrecy; self-assurance, self-belief; assuredness, esp. in the outcome of something; admission to knowledge of secrets or private affairs; a confidential communication. — *adj* **con'fident** trusting firmly; having full belief; (esp. self-)assured, bold. — *adj* **confidential** (*-den'shl*) given in confidence; admitted to a person's confidence; private. — *n* **confidential'ity**. — *adv* **confiden'tially**. — *adv* **con'fidently**. — *n* **confīd'er**. — *adj* **confīd'ing** trustful. — *adv* **confīd'ingly**. — **confidence trick** a swindler's trick, whereby a person is induced to hand over money to the swindler for something they will never receive. — **in confidence** secretly, as a secret; **in one's confidence** trusted by the person in question with confidential matters. [L. *cōnfīdĕre* — *con-* (signifying completeness) and *fīdĕre*, to trust.]

configuration *kən-fig-ū-rā'shən*, *n* external figure, shape or arrangement; outline; relative position or aspect, esp. of planets; spatial arrangement of atoms in a molecule (*chem*); Gestalt, the organised whole (*psychol*). — *adj* **configurā'tional**. — *vt* **config'urate** or **config'ure** to shape, arrange. [L. *cōnfigūrāre*, to form.]

confine *kon'fīn*, *n* a border, boundary, or limit (generally in *pl*).— *vt* **confine'** to limit, enclose, bound; to imprison. — *adj* **confin'able**. — *adj* **confined'** limited; imprisoned; narrow, small. — *n* **confine'ment** the state of being shut up; restraint; imprisonment. — *adj* **confin'ing** bordering; limiting. — **be confined** to be limited; to be imprisoned; to be restrained to bed or indoors in childbirth. [L. *cōnfīnis*, bordering — *con-*, together, *fīnis*, the end.]

confirm *kən-fûrm'*, *vt* to strengthen; to fix or establish; to ratify; to verify, give proof of the truth or justification of; to put through a ceremony to admit to full religious communion. — *adj* **confirm'able**. — *n* **con'firmand** a candidate for religious confirmation. — *n* **confirmā'tion** a making firm or sure; convincing proof; the rite by which persons are admitted to full communion in many churches. — *adj* **confirm'ative** tending to confirm. — *adj* **confirm'atory** giving additional strength to; confirming. — *adj* **confirmed'** settled; inveterate, habitual, addicted. — *n* **confirm'er**. — *n* **confirm'ing**. [O.Fr. *confermer* — L. *cōnfirmāre* — *con-* (intensive) and *firmāre* — *firmus*, firm.]

confiscate *kon'fis-kāt*, *vt* to appropriate to or seize for the state, as a penalty; to take possession of by authority. — *adj* forfeited. — *adj* **con'fiscable** (or *-fis'*). — *adj* **confiscatory** (*kon'fis-kā-tər-i* or *kən-fis'kə-tər-i*) of the nature of confiscation. — *n* **confiscā'tion** the act of confiscating. — *n* **con'fiscātor** a person who confiscates. [L. *cōnfiscāre*, *-ātum* — *con-*, together, *fiscus*, a basket, purse, treasury.]

conflagrate *kon'flə-grāt*, *vt* and *vi* to burn up. — *n* **conflagrā'tion** a great burning or fire; a war or other major disturbance (*fig*). [L. *cōnflagrāre* — *con-* (intensive) and *flagrāre*, to burn.]

conflate *kən-flāt'*, *vt* to fuse; to combine (e.g. two different readings of a text) into one, often by means of parentheses. — *n* **conflā'tion.** [L. *cōnflāre*, *-ātum*, to blow together.]

conflict *kon'flikt*, *n* unfortunate coincidence or opposition; violent collision; (a) struggle, contest, war, etc. — *vi* (*kən-flikt'*) to fight; to contend; to be in opposition; to clash, be unfortunately simultaneous. — *adj* **conflict'ing** clashing, competing; contradictory. — **in conflict** incompatible, or irreconcilable (with). [L. *cōnflīgĕre*, *-flīctum* — *con-*, together, *flīgĕre*, to strike.]

confluence *kon'flōō-əns*, *n* a flowing together; a meeting-place, esp. of rivers; the act of meeting together. — *adj* **con'fluent** flowing together; running into one; uniting. — *n* a stream uniting and flowing with another. — *adv* **con'fluently.** [L. *cōnfluĕre* — *con-*, together, *fluĕre*, *fluxum*, to flow.]

conform *kən-förm'*, *vt* to make like or of the same form or type; to adapt. — *vi* to be or become of the same form or type (often with *to*); to comply (with *to*); to obey (with *with*). — *adj* **conform'able** corresponding in form or type; compliant, agreeable; (of rock layers etc.) as originally laid down (*geol*). — *adv* **conform'ably.** — *n* **conformā'tion** particular form, shape, or structure; adaptation. — *n* **conform'er** or **conform'ist** a person who complies with social, etc., norms. — *n* **conform'ity** similarity to the norm; compliance; consistency with a standard. — **in conformity with** in accordance with. [L. *cōnfōrmāre* — *con-*, *fōrmāre* — *fōrma*, form.]

confound *kən-fownd'*, *vt* to overthrow, defeat; to confuse, fail to distinguish between; to throw into disorder; to perplex; to astonish; used in the imperative as a mild curse. — *adj* **confound'ed** confused; astonished; damned, blasted (a term of disapproval; *colloq*). [O.Fr. *confondre* — L. *cōnfundĕre*, *-fūsum* — *con-*, together, *fundĕre*, to pour.]

confraternity *kon-frə-tûr'ni-ti*, *n* a brotherhood, esp. a religious or charitable one; a clan; brotherly friendship. [L. *con-*, together, *frāter*, brother.]

confrère *kɔ̃-frer*, *n* a colleague; a fellow-member or associate. — *n* **confrérie** (*kɔ̃-frā-rē*) a brotherhood. [Fr., — L. *con-*, together, *frāter*, brother.]

confront *kən-frunt'*, *vt* to come or be face to face with; to face in opposition; to bring face to face; to compare. — *n* **confrontā'tion** (*kon-*) the bringing of people face to face; continued hostile attitude, with hostile acts but without declaration of war. — *adj* **confrontā'tional** involving, causing, etc. confrontation. — *n* **confrontā'tionism** the favouring of confrontation as a political means. [Fr. *confronter* — L. *con-*, together, *frōns*, *frontis*, forehead.]

confuse *kən-fūz'*, *vt* to perplex; to throw into disorder; to fail to distinguish; to pour or mix together so that things cannot be distinguished. — *adj* **confu'sable** or **confu'sible** liable to be confused. — Also *n*. — *adj* **confused'** perplexed; disordered. — *adv* **confu'sedly** in a confused manner; disorderly. — *n* **confū'sion** (*-zhən*) the state of being confused; disorder; perplexity; turmoil. [**confound.**]

confute *kən-fūt'*, *vt* to prove to be false; to refute. — *adj* **confūt'able.** — *n* **confūtā'tion** (*kon-*). [L. *cōnfūtāre*.]

Cong. *abbrev* for: Congregation; Congregational; Congress.

conga *kong'gə*, *n* a Cuban dance, usu. performed by several people moving in single file; music for it. — Also *vi*. — **conga drum** a narrow bass drum beaten with the hands. [Am. Sp., of the Congo.]

congé *kɔ̃-zhā* or **congee** *kon'ji*, *n* permission to depart; a dismissal. [Fr. *congé*.]

congeal *kən-jēl'*, *vi* to pass from fluid to solid, e.g. by cooling; to coagulate; to stiffen (also *fig*). — *vt* to freeze; to change from fluid to solid by cold; to solidify, e.g. by cooling. — *adj* **congeal'able.** — *n* **congeal'ment** the act or process of congealing. — *n* **congelation** (*kon-ji-lā'shən*) the act or process of congealing; anything congealed. [L. *congelāre* — *con-* (intensive) and *gelū*, frost.]

congee. See **congé**.

congener *kon'ji-nər*, *n* something of the same kind or nature, esp. a plant or animal of the same genus; a secondary product in an alcoholic drink that helps to determine its flavour, colour and power to intoxicate. — *adj* **congeneric** (*-ner'ik*) or **congener'ical** (*-əl*) of the same genus, origin, or nature; of the congeners of an alcoholic beverage. [L. *con-*, with, *genus*, *generis*, kind.]

congenial *kən-jē'ni-əl*, *adj* pleasant, friendly or agreeable; of the same spirit or tastes; kindred, sympathetic; to one's taste; suitable. — *n* **congēniality** (*-al'i-ti*). — *adv* **congē'nially.** [L. *con*, with, *geniālis*, see **genial**[1].]

congenital *kən-jen'i-təl*, *adj* (of diseases or deformities) dating from birth, but not hereditary; complete or absolute, as if from birth (esp. in the phrase *congenital idiot*). — *adv* **congen'itally.** [L. *congenitus*, — *con-*, together, *gignĕre*, *genitum*, to beget.]

conger *kong'gər*, *n* a large sea-fish of the eel family. — Also **conger-eel'**. [L., — Gr. *gongros*.]

congeries *kon-jer'i-ēz* or *-jēr'*, *n* a collection, mass or heap: — *pl* **conger'ies.** [L. *congeriēs* — *con-*, together, *gerĕre*, *gestum*, to bring.]

congest *kən-jest'*, *vt* to bring together, or heap up; to accumulate; to cause congestion in. — *vi* to become overcrowded. — *adj* **congest'ed** overcrowded; packed closely together; clogged. — *adj* **congest'ible.** — *n* **congestion** (*-jes'chən*) an overcrowded condition; an accumulation of blood in any part of the body; fullness. — *adj* **congest'ive** indicating congestion or tending to become congested. [L. *congerĕre*, *congestum* — *con-*, together, *gĕrere*, *gestum*, to bring.]

conglomerate *kən-glom'ər-it*, *adj* gathered into a mass; bunched; composed of pebbles cemented together (*geol*). — *vt* and *vi* (*-āt*) to gather into a ball. — *n* (*-it*) a conglomerate rock (*geol*); a miscellaneous mass or collection; an industrial group made up of companies which often have diverse and unrelated interests. — *n* **conglomerā'tion** the state of being conglomerated; a collection or jumble of things. [L. *conglomerāre*, *-ātum* — *con-*, together, *glomus*, *glomeris*, a ball of thread.]

congrats *kən-grats'*, (*colloq*) *interj* short for congratulations.

congratulate *kən-grat'ū-lāt*, *vt* to express pleasure in sympathy with; to felicitate; to consider clever (esp. *reflexive*). — *n* **congratūlā'tion.** — *adj* **congrat'ūlative** or **congrat'ūlatory** (or *-lā*) expressing congratulation. — *n* **congrat'ūlator.** [L. *congrātulārī*, *-ātus* — *con-* (intensive) and *grātulārī* — *grātus*, pleasing.]

congregate *kong'grə-gāt*, *vi* to flock together. — *vt* to gather together; to assemble. — *adj* **con'gregated** assembled. — *n* **con'gregant** a member of a (esp. Jewish) congregation. — *n* **congrega'tion** a body of people actually or habitually attending a particular church; an assemblage of people or things; the act of congregating; a board charged with some department of administration in the Roman Catholic Church; a name given to certain religious orders without solemn vows; an academic assembly. — *adj* **congregā'tional** pertaining to a congregation; (with *cap*) pertaining to the Independent Church. — *n* **Congregā'tionalism** a form of church government in which each congregation is independent in the management of its own affairs — also called *Independency*. — *n* **Congregā'tionalist.** — **Congregation for the Doctrine of the Faith** see **Inquisition.** [L. *congregāre*, *-ātum* — *con-*, together, *grex*, *gregis*, a flock.]

congress *kong'gres*, *n* an assembly of delegates, ambassadors, etc.; (with *cap*) the federal legislature of the United States; the act of meeting together;

intercourse. — *vi* to meet in congress. — *adj* **congressional** (*-gresh'*). — *n* **Con'gressman**, *fem* **Con'gresswoman**, a member of Congress, esp. of the House of Representatives. [L. *con-*, together, *gradi, gressus*, to step, to go.]

congruence *kong'groo-əns, n* suitability or appropriateness; agreement; the quality of being congruent (*geom*). — *adj* **con'gruent** suitable; agreeing or corresponding; congruous; identical in shape (*geom*). — *n* **congru'ity** agreement between things; consistency; suitability. — *adj* **con'gruous** suitable or appropriate; consistent. — *adv* **con'gruously**. — *n* **con'gruousness**. [L. *congruĕre*, to run together.]

conia. See **coniine**.

conic, conical. See **cone**.

conidium *kon-id'i-əm*, (*bot*) *n* an asexual spore not produced in a sporangium: — *pl* **conid'ia**. — *adj* **conid'ial**. [Gr. *konis*, dust.]

conifer *kon'i-fər* or *kōn'*, *n* any tree of the group *Coniferae*, including yews, pines, firs, etc., which typically bear cones. — *adj* **conif'erous** cone-bearing; of the conifer family. [L. *cōnus*, a cone, *ferre*, to bear.]

coniform. See **cone**.

coniine *kō'ni-ēn, n* a highly poisonous liquid alkaloid found in hemlock (*Conium*). — Also **cō'nia** or **cō'nine**. [Gr. *kōneion*, hemlock.]

conj. *abbrev* for: conjunction; conjunctive.

conjecture *kən-jek'chər, n* an opinion without proof; an opinion formed on slight or defective evidence or none at all; a guess. — *vi* to guess. — *vt* to make conjectures regarding; to conclude by conjecture. — *adj* **conject'urable**. — *adj* **conject'ural** involving conjecture; given to conjecture. — *adv* **conject'urally**. [L. *conjicĕre, conjectum*, to throw together — *con-, jacĕre*, to throw.]

conjoin *kən-join'*, *vt* to join together; to combine. — *vi* to unite. — *adj* **conjoined'** united; in conjunction. — *adj* **conjoint'** joined together; united. — *adv* **conjoint'ly**. [Fr. *conjoindre* — L. *con-, jungĕre, junctum*, to join.]

conjugal *kon'joo-gəl, adj* pertaining to marriage. — *n* **conjugality** (*-gal'i-ti*). — *adv* **con'jugally**. — **conjugal rights** the right of sexual relations with a spouse. [L. *conjugālis* — *conjux*, a husband or wife — *con-*, together, *jugum*, a yoke.]

conjugate *kon'joo-gāt, vt* to give the various inflections or parts of (a verb) (*gram*); to unite (*biochem*). — *vi* to undergo inflection (*gram*); to unite (*biochem*). — *adj* (*-gət* or *-gāt*) joined, connected or coupled; occurring in pairs (*bot*); reciprocally related (*math*); having the same root, cognate (*gram*). — *n* (*-gət*) a word with the same root as another word; anything joined or connected with, or related to, something else. — *n* **con'jugant** (*biol*) one of a pair of cells or organisms undergoing conjugation. — *adj* **con'jugated** conjugate; (of atoms, groups, bonds, or the compounds in which they occur) showing a special type of mutual influence, esp. characterised by an arrangement of alternate single and double bonds between carbon atoms. — *adj* **conjugā'tional** or **con'jugative**. — *n* and *adj* **con'jugating**. — *n* **conjugā'tion** the set of all the inflectional forms of a verb (*gram*); inflection in verbs (*gram*); the act of joining; union. — **conjugated protein** a biochemical compound in which a protein is combined with a non-protein. [L. *conjugāre, -ātum* — *con-*, together, *jugāre* — *jugum*, a yoke.]

conjunct *kən-junkt'* or *kon'junkt, adj* conjoined; joint. — *n* **conjunc'tion** connection, union; combination; simultaneous occurrence in space or time; a word that connects sentences, clauses, and words (*gram*); one of the aspects of the planets, when two bodies have the same celestial longitude or the same right ascension (formerly when they were in the same sign) (*astrol*). — *adj* **conjunc'tional**. — *adv* **conjunc'tionally**. — *n* **conjunctiva** (*kon-jungkt-ī'və*) the mucous membrane on the front of the eye and the inner eyelid. — *adj* **conjunctī'val** of the conjunctiva. — *adj* **conjunc'tive** closely united; serving to join; connective (*anat*); being a conjunction, or related to (the use of) conjunctions (*gram*). — *adv* **conjunc'tively**. — *n* **conjunc'tiveness**. — *n* **conjunctivitis** (*-iv-ī'tis*; *med*) inflammation of the conjunctiva. — *adv* **conjunct'ly** conjointly; in union. — *n* **conjunc'ture** a combination of circumstances, esp. one leading to a crisis. [L. *conjunctiō, -ōnis* — *conjungĕre*; see **conjoin**.]

conjure *kun'jər, vi* to practise magic tricks, esp. for public entertainment. — *vt* (usu. *kən-jŏŏr'*) to implore earnestly; (*kun'jər*) to compel (a spirit) by incantations; to call before the imagination (often with *up*); to render, effect, cause to be or become, by magic (often with *out, away*, etc.). — *n* **conjurā'tion** a magic trick; the performing of magic tricks; a solemn appeal or entreaty. — *n* **conjurer** or **conjuror** (*kun'* or *kon'*) a person who performs magic tricks. — *n* **con'juring** the performing of magic tricks. — **to conjure with** regarded as influential, powerful or important (esp. in the phrase *a name to conjure with*). [Fr. *conjurer* — L. *conjūrāre*, to swear together — *con-, jūrāre*, to swear.]

conk[1] *kongk, n* (*slang*) the nose. — *n* **conk'er** a strung snail-shell or usu. horse chestnut used in the game of **conkers**, in which each seeks to break their opponent's by hitting it with their own; a horse chestnut. [**conch**.]

conk[2] *kongk*, (*slang*) *vi* to get out of order, fail or break down (esp. with *out*); to fall asleep or collapse from exhaustion (with *out*).

conk[3] *kongk*, (*slang*) *n* the head; a blow on the head. — *vt* to strike (a person) on the head.

Conn. *abbrev* for Connecticut (U.S. state).

conn *vt* and *vi*. See **con**[3].

conn. *abbrev* for: connected; connection.

connate *kon'āt, adj* inborn; innate; allied; congenital (*med*); united in growth (*biol*). — *n* **connā'tion** (*biol*) union, esp. of similar parts or organs. [L. *con-, nāscī, nātus*, to be born.]

connatural *kon-ach'ər-əl, adj* of the same or similar nature; congenital (*med*). [Ety. as for **connate**.]

connect *kən-ekt'*, *vt* to tie or fasten together; to establish a relation between; to associate. — *vi* to be or become joined; to be significant or meaningful (*colloq*); to hit (a target) with a blow, a kick, etc. (*colloq*); to have or develop an understanding or rapport (*NAm*); to find a source of illicit drugs (*slang*). — *adj* **connect'able** or **connect'ible**. — *adj* **connect'ed** joined; linked; coherent; related. — *adv* **connect'edly**. — *n* **connect'er** or **connect'or**. — *n* **connection** or **connexion** (*-ek'shən*) the act of connecting; that which connects; context; relation; coherence; the opportunity to change trains, buses, etc.; a relative, esp. a distant one, or one by marriage; (in *pl*) a friend or relative in a position of power or influence; a supplier of narcotic drugs (*slang*). — *adj* **connect'ive** binding together (*anat*). — *adv* **connect'ively**. — *n* **connectiv'ity**. — **connecting rod** a rod attached to two parts of a machine to allow motion in one part to cause motion in the other part, esp. such a rod connecting a piston to a crankshaft; **connective tissue** any of several kinds of animal tissue — e.g. bone, cartilage, ligaments. — *adj* **well-connect'ed** related to people of a social position considered important. — **in connection with** concerning. [L. *con-* and *nectĕre, nexum*, to tie.]

connexion. See **connect**.

conning-tower. See **con**[3].

conniption *kən-ip'shən*, (*NAm slang*) *n* a fit of rage or hysteria (also **conniption fit**). [Poss. Ger. *knipsen*, to snap, click.]

connive *kən-īv'*, *vi* to plot or conspire (often with *with*); to agree to take no notice of a crime, a wrongdoing, etc. (often with *at*); to have a private understanding (often with *with*). — *n* **conniv'ance.** — *n* **conniv'er.** [L. *connīvēre, cōnīvēre*, to wink.]

connoisseur *kon-əs-ûr'* or *kon'*, *n* a person with well-informed knowledge and appreciation, esp. of fine food and wine or in the arts. [Fr. *connoître* (*connaître*) — L. *cognōscĕre*, to know.]

connote *kon-ōt'*, *vt* to signify secondarily; to imply as inherent attribute(s); to include as a condition. — *vt* **connotate** (*kon'ō-tāt*) to connote. — *n* **connotā'tion** an association or implication additional to the idea, object, etc. denoted. — *adj* **conn'otātive** (also *-nō'tə-tiv*) or **connō'tive.** [L. *con-*, with, *notāre*, to mark.]

connubial *kən-ū'bi-əl*, *adj* pertaining to marriage. — *n* **connubiality** (*-al'i-ti*). — *adv* **connū'bially.** [L. *con-*, with, *nūbĕre*, to marry.]

conoid. See **cone.**

conquer *kong'kər*, *vt* to overcome or vanquish (also *fig*); to gain control of by force or with an effort (also *fig*). — *vi* to be the victor. — *adj* **con'querable.** — *n* **con'querableness.** — *adj* **con'quering.** — *n* **con'queror** a person who conquers; a victor. — *n* **conquest** (*kong'kwest*) the act of conquering; that which is conquered or acquired by physical or moral force; the act of gaining the affections of another; the person whose affections have been gained. [O.Fr. *conquerre* — L. *conquīrĕre, conquaerĕre* — *con-* (intensive) and *quaerĕre*, to seek.]

conquistador *kong-kēs-ta-dör'* or *-kwis'*, *n* a conqueror, applied to the conquerors of Mexico and Peru: — *pl* **conquis'tadors** or **conquistadores** (*-dör'es*). [Sp., — L. *conquīrĕre*.]

con-rod *kon'rod*, *n* short for **connecting-rod.**

cons. *abbrev* for: consecrated; consigned; consignment; consolidated; consonant; constable; constitution, constitutional; construction; consulting.

consanguine *kon-sang'gwin*, *adj* related by blood; of the same family or descent — also **consanguin'eous.** — *n* **consanguin'ity** relationship by blood; a close relationship or connection. [L. *cōnsanguineus* — *con-*, with, *sanguis* or *sanguīs*, blood.]

conscience *kon'shəns*, *n* moral sense; scrupulousness, conscientiousness. — *adj* **con'scienceless.** — *adj* **con'scient** aware; conscious. — *adj* **conscientious** (*-shi-en'shəs*) regulated by a regard to conscience; scrupulous; tending to take great care, show diligence, etc. — *adv* **conscien'tiously.** — *n* **conscien'tiousness.** — **conscience clause** a clause in a law, contract, etc. which allows people with moral objections not to obey, be bound, etc.; **conscience money** money given to relieve the conscience as compensation for a wrongdoing; **conscientious objector** a person who objects on grounds of conscience, esp. to military service. — **freedom of conscience** the right to hold religious or other beliefs without persecution; **good (or bad) conscience** an approving (or reproving) conscience; **in all conscience** certainly; by all that is right and fair (*colloq*); **on one's conscience** causing feelings of guilt; **prisoner of conscience** a person imprisoned on account of their political beliefs. [Fr., — L. *cōnscientia*, knowledge — *cōnscīre*, to know well, in one's own mind.]

conscious *kon'shəs*, *adj* having the feeling or knowledge of something; aware; having consciousness. — *n* the conscious mind. — In combination **-conscious** being very aware of and concerned about, e.g. *clothes-conscious, cost-conscious.* — *adv* **con'sciously.** — *n* **con'sciousness** the waking state of the mind; the knowledge which the mind has of anything; awareness; thought. — **con'sciousness-raising** development of (esp. public) awareness of social and political issues. — Also *adj.* [L. *cōnscius* — *cōnscīre*, to know; see **conscience.**]

conscribe *kən-skrīb'*, *vt* to enlist by conscription. — *adj* **conscript** (*kon'skript*) enrolled, registered, esp. compulsorily. — *n* someone enrolled compulsorily, esp. in the armed forces. — *vt* (*kən-skript'*) to enlist compulsorily. — *n* **conscrip'tion** compulsory enrolment for service; the obtaining of recruits by compulsion. [L. *cōnscrībĕre*, to enrol.]

consecrate *kon'si-krāt*, *vt* to render holy or venerable; to set apart for a holy use; to devote (time, energy, etc.). — *adj* consecrated; sanctified; devoted. — *n* **consecrā'tion** the act of rendering holy. — *adj* **con'secrātive.** — *n* **con'secrātor.** — *adj* **consecratory** (*-krā'tər-i*). [L. *cōnsecrāre, -ātum*, to make wholly sacred.]

consecutive *kən-sek'ū-tiv*, *adj* following in regular order or one after another; expressing consequence (*gram*). — *n* **consecution** (*kon-si-kū'shən*) a train of consequences or deductions; a series of things that follow one another. — *adv* **consec'utively.** — *n* **consec'utiveness.** [L. *cōnsequī* — *con-* (intensive) and *sequī*, to follow.]

consensus *kən-sen'səs*, *n* agreement of various parts; agreement in opinion; unanimity; (*loosely*) trend of opinion. — *adj* **consen'sual** existing by or based only on consent (*legal*); (of a part of the body) reacting to stimulation of another part (*med*). — *adv* **consen'sually.** — **consensual contract** a contract requiring merely the consent of the parties. [L. *cōnsēnsus* — *cōnsentīre*; see **consent.**]

consent *kən-sent'*, *vi* to agree; to give permission; to be of the same mind; to comply. — *vt* to agree. — *n* agreement; permission. — *n* **consentience** (*kən-sen'shəns*) agreement. — *adj* **consen'tient** agreeing. — **consenting adult** a person over the age of 21, legally able to enter into a homosexual relationship (also *fig*). — **age of consent** the age at which a person is legally competent to give consent to certain acts, esp. sexual intercourse; **with one consent** unanimously. [L. *cōnsentīre* — *con-*, *sentīre*, to feel, to think.]

consequence *kon'si-kwəns*, *n* that which follows or comes after as a result or inference; effect; importance; social standing; the relation of an effect to its cause (*logic*); (in *pl*) a game describing the meeting of a man and a woman and its consequences, each player writing a part of the story, not knowing what the others have written. — *adj* **con'sequent** following, esp. as a natural effect or deduction. — *n* that which follows; the natural effect of a cause. — *adj* **consequential** (*-kwen'shl*) following as a result, esp. an indirect result; significant, important; self-important. — *n* **consequen'tialism** (*ethics*) the principle stating that the morality of an action is judged according to how good or bad its consequences are. — *adv* **consequen'tially.** — *adv* **con'sequently.** — **in consequence (of)** as a result (of); **of no consequence** trivial, unimportant; **take the consequences** to accept the (often unpleasant) results of one's actions. [Fr., — L. *cōnsequī* — *con-* (intensive) and *sequī*, to follow.]

conservative *kən-sûr'və-tiv*, *adj* tending to support the preservation of established views, customs, institutions, etc.; opposed to change; traditional; moderate; cautious; (with *cap*) belonging or pertaining to the Conservative Party. — Also *n.* — *n* **conser'vatism** opposition to innovation; (with *cap*) the policies and principles of the Conservative Party. — *adv* **conser'vatively** traditionally; in a traditional way; moderately or cautiously. — *n* **conser'vativeness** conventionality; moderation. — **Conservative Party** in the U.K., Canada and Australia, the political party advocating support for established customs and institutions, opposing socialism, and usu. favouring free enterprise. [Ety. as for **conserve.**]

conserve *kən-sûrv'*, *vt* to keep in a safe, whole or undamaged state; to retain; to preserve. — *n* (also *kon'*) something preserved, e.g. fruits in sugar. — *adj* **conser'vable.** — *n* **conser'vancy** in the U.K., a court or board having authority to preserve the fisheries, etc., of a river; the act of preserving; esp. official care of a river, forest, etc. — *adj* **conser'vant**. — *n* **conservā'tion** (*kon-*) the act of conserving (esp. old buildings, flora and fauna, the environment). — *adj* **conservā'tional**. — *n* **conservā'tionist** a person who is actively interested in conservation, esp. of the environment or natural resources. — *n* **conservatoire** (*kɔ̃-ser-va-twär* or *kən-sûr'və-twär*) or **conservatō'rium** a school of music. — *n* **con'servātor** (or *kən-sûr'və-tər*) a person who preserves from injury or violation; a guardian or custodian. — *n* **conser'vatory** a storehouse; a greenhouse or place in which exotic plants are kept; a school of music. — *n* **conser'ver**. — **conservation area** an area designated as being of special architectural or historic interest, and therefore protected from any alterations which would destroy its character. — **conservation of mass and energy** the principle that the sum of the total amount of mass and energy in a given isolated system is constant. [L. *cōnservāre* — *con-*, *servāre*, to keep.]

consider *kən-sid'ər*, *vt* to look at attentively or carefully; to think or deliberate on; to take into account; to attend to; to regard as; to think, hold the opinion (that). — *vi* to think seriously or carefully; to deliberate. — *adj* **consid'erable** more than a little; of some importance; worthy of being considered. — *n* **consid'erableness**. — *adv* **consid'erably**. — *n* and *adj* **consid'erate** (*-it*) thoughtful for the feelings and interests of others. — *adv* **consid'erately**. — *n* **consid'erateness** thoughtfulness for others. — *n* **considerā'tion** careful thought; something considered; motive or reason; considerateness; importance; recompense, payment. — *adj* **consid'ered** carefully thought out, deliberate. — *prep* **consid'ering** in view of. — *conj* seeing that. — *adv* everything considered. — **in consideration of** because of; as payment for; **take into consideration** to allow for; **under consideration** being considered or dealt with. [L. *cōnsīderāre*.]

consign *kən-sīn'*, *vt* to entrust; to commit; to transmit; to transfer; to devote. — *adj* **consign'able**. — *adj* **consigned'** given in trust. — *n* **consignee** (*kon-sīn-ē'*) a person to whom anything is consigned or entrusted. — *n* **consign'er** or **consign'or**. — *n* **consign'ment** a thing consigned; a set of things consigned together; the act of consigning. [L. *cōnsignāre*, to attest.]

consist *kən-sist'*, *vi* to be composed (of); to exist (in); to lie (in); to be compatible. — *n* **consist'ence** substance. — *n* **consist'ency** degree of density or thickness; agreement with something previously stated or shown. — *adj* **consist'ent** free from contradiction; fixed or steady; not fluid; agreeing together, compatible; true to principles. — *adv* **consist'ently**. — *adj* **consistō'rial** or **consistō'rian**. — *n* **con'sistory** (or *-sist'*) a spiritual or ecclesiastical court. [L. *cōnsistere* — *con-*, together, *sistere*, to set, stand.]

console[1] *kən-sōl'*, *vt* to give solace or comfort to; to cheer in distress. — *adj* **consōl'able**. — *n* **consolā'tion** solace; alleviation of misery; a comforting circumstance. — *adj* **consolatory** (*kən-sol'ə-tər-i* or *-sōl'*) comforting. — *n* **console'ment**. — *n* **consol'er**. — **consolā'tion-match, -prize, -race**, etc., a match, prize, race, etc., for the otherwise unsuccessful. [L. *cōnsōlārī* — *con-* (intensive) and *sōlārī*, to comfort.]

console[2] *kon'sōl*, *n* the key-desk of an organ; a panel or cabinet with dials, switches, etc., control unit of an electrical, electronic, or mechanical system. [Fr.]

consolidate *kən-sol'i-dāt*, *vt* to make solid; to form into a compact mass; to unite into one; to merge; to rearrange and strengthen (*mil*). — *vi* to grow solid or firm; to unite. — *adj* **consol'idated**. — *n* **consolidā'tion**. — *adj* **consol'idative**. — *n* **consol'idator**. [L. *cōnsolidāre*, *-ātum* — *con-* (intensive) and *solidus*, solid.]

consols *kon'solz*, *npl* government securities without a maturity date. [Abbrev. of *Consolidated Annuities*.]

consommé *kɔ̃-som-ā* or *kən-som'ā*, *n* a clear soup made from meat by slow boiling. [Fr.]

consonant *kon'sən-ənt*, *n* any speech sound other than a vowel; a letter of the alphabet representing such a sound. — *adj* consistent (with); suitable; harmonious. — *n* **con'sonance** a state of agreement; agreement or unison of sounds. — *n* **con'sonancy** harmony. — *adj* **consonantal** (*-ant'*). — *adv* **con'sonantly**. [L. *cōnsonāre*, to harmonise — *con-*, *sonāre*, to sound.]

consort *kon'sört* or *-sərt*, *n* a partner; a companion; a wife or husband, esp. of a reigning monarch; an accompanying ship. — *vi* **consort'** to associate or keep company (with); to agree. — *adj* **consort'ed** associated. — *n* **consort'er**. — *n* **consortium** (*kon-sör'ti-əm*, *-shəm* or *-shi-əm*) a combination of several banks, business concerns, or other bodies; association; fellowship: — *pl* **consor'tia** or (esp. *NAm*) **consor'tiums**. — **in consort** in company; in harmony. [L. *cōnsors*, *-sortis* — *con-*, *sors*, a lot.]

conspectus *kən-spek'təs*, *n* a comprehensive view or survey; a synopsis. [L. *cōnspectus* — *cōnspicĕre*, to look at.]

conspicuous *kən-spik'ū-əs*, *adj* catching the eye; noticeable; prominent or attracting attention. — *n* **conspic'uousness**. — *adv* **conspic'uously**. — **conspicuous consumption** extravagant, ostentatious spending on luxury goods in order to impress other people. [L. *cōnspicuus* — *cōnspicĕre* — *con-* (intensive) and *specĕre*, to look.]

conspire *kən-spīr'*, *vi* to plot or scheme together; to act together to one end. — *n* **conspiracy** (*-spir'ə-si*) the act of conspiring; a banding together for a purpose, often secret, usu. unlawful; a plot; joint action, concurrence. — *n* **conspir'ator** a person who conspires. — *adj* **conspiratō'rial**. — *adv* **conspirato'rially**. — **conspiracy of silence** an agreement not to talk about a particular matter. [L. *cōnspīrāre* — *con-*, together, *spīrāre*, to breathe.]

constable *kun'stə-bl* or *kon'*, *n* a policeman or policewoman of the lowest rank; the warden of a castle. — *n* **constabulary** (*kən-stab'ū-lər-i*) an organised body of constables; a police force. — *adj* of or pertaining to constables. — **special constable** a person sworn in by law officers to preserve the peace, or to execute warrants on special occasions. [O.Fr. *conestable* — L. *comes stabulī*, count or companion of the stable.]

constant *kon'stənt*, *adj* fixed; unchangeable; firm; continual; faithful. — *n* (*math*) a fixed quantity. — *n* **con'stancy** fixedness; unchangeableness; faithfulness. — *adv* **con'stantly**. [L. *cōnstāns*, *-stantis*, from *cōnstāre*, to stand firm — *con-* (intensive) and *stāre*, to stand.]

constatation *kon-stə-tā'shən*, *n* a statement, assertion; ascertaining, verification. [Fr. *constater*.]

constellate *kon'stəl-āt* or *kən-stel'āt*, *vt* to cluster; to compel or affect by stellar influence. — *vi* to cluster together. — *n* **constellā'tion** a group of stars; any group of people, ideas, factors in a situation, etc.; in astrology, a particular disposition of the planets, supposed to influence the course of human life or character. — *adj* **constell'atory**. [L. *con-*, with, *stellāre* — *stella*, a star.]

consternate *kon'stər-nāt*, *vt* to fill with dismay or confusion. — *n* **consternā'tion** dismay or amazement, often causing confusion or lack of understanding. [L. *cōnsternāre*, *-ātum* — *con-*, wholly, *sternĕre*, to strew.]

constipate *kon'stip-āt*, *vt* to cause an irregular and insufficient action of the bowels of; to deprive of vigour (*fig*). — *adj* **con'stipated**. — *n* **constipā'tion**. [L. *cōnstīpāre*, *-ātum*, to press together.]

constitute *kon'stit-ūt, vt* to form or make up; to establish; to set up; to appoint. — *n* **constituency** (*kən-stit'ū-ən-si*) the whole body of voters, or a district or population, represented by a member of parliament, etc.; a set of people supporting, patronising, or forming a power-base for, a business organisation, pressure group, etc. — *adj* **constit'uent** constituting or forming; essential; component; electing; constitution-making. — *n* an essential part; one of those who elect a representative, esp. in a parliament; an inhabitant of the constituency of a member of parliament, etc. — *n* **constitū'tion** (*kon-*) a system of laws and customs established by the sovereign power of a state for its own guidance; an established form of government; the act of constituting; the natural condition of body or mind; disposition; molecular structure, taking into account not only the kinds and numbers of atoms but the way in which they are linked (*chem*). — *adj* **constitū'tional** conforming to the constitution or frame of government; existing subject to fixed laws; inherent in the natural make-up or structure of a person or thing. — *n* a walk for the benefit of one's health. — *vt* **constitū'tionalise** or **-ize** to make constitutional. — *n* **constitū'tionalism** adherence to the principles of the constitution. — *n* **constitū'tionalist** or **constitu'tionist** a person who favours a constitution or the constitution. — *n* **constitutional'ity**. — *adv* **constitū'tionally**. — *adj* **con'stitutive** that constitutes or establishes; having power to constitute; essential; component. [L. *con-* (intensive) and *statuĕre*, to make to stand, to place.]

constrain *kən-strān', vt* to force, compel; to confine; to restrict by a condition. — *adj* **constrain'able**. — *adj* **constrained'** forced, compelled; lacking ease and spontaneity of manner. — *adv* **constrain'edly**. — *n* **constraint** compulsion; confinement; a restricting condition. [O.Fr. *constraindre*.]

constrict *kən-strikt', vt* to press together; to contract; to cramp; to limit. — *adj* **constrict'ed**. — *n* **constric'tion** a pressing together; contraction; tightness; something constricted. — *adj* **constrict'ive**. — *n* **constrict'or** something which constricts or draws together; a muscle that compresses an organ or structure; a snake that crushes its prey in its folds. [L. *cōnstringĕre*.]

construct *kən-strukt', vt* to build up; to make; to put together the parts of; to compose; to compile; to put in grammatical relation. — *adj* constructed. — *n* (*kon'strukt*) a thing constructed, esp. in the mind; an image or object of thought constructed from a number of sense-impressions or images (*psychol*). — *adj* **construct'able** or **construct'ible**. — *n* **construct'er** or **construct'or**. — *n* **construc'tion** the act of constructing; anything constructed; a building; the syntactic relations of words in a sentence (*gram*); a word or group of words (*gram*); interpretation; meaning. — *adj* **construc'tional**. — *adj* **construct'ive** capable of, tending towards, or concerned in, constructing; representing positive advice (opp. of *destructive*). — *adv* **construct'ively**. — *n* **construct'iveness**. — *n* **construct'ivism** or **construc'tionism** a non-representational style of art using man-made industrial materials and processes such as twisting and welding. [L. *cōnstruĕre*, to build.]

construe *kən-stroo'* or *kon'stroo, vt* to interpret; to infer; to construct grammatically; to analyse the grammatical structure of. — *vi* to be capable of grammatical analysis. [L. *cōnstruĕre, constructum*, to pile together.]

consubstantial *kon-sub-stan'shl, adj* of the same substance, nature, or essence, esp. (*Christian theol*) of the Trinity. — *vt* and *vi* **consubstan'tiate** (*-shi-āt*) to unite in one common substance or nature, esp. (*Christian theol*) bread and wine and the body of Christ. — *n* **consubstantiā'tion** the doctrine of the actual, substantial presence of the body and blood of Christ co-existing in and with the bread and wine used at the Lord's Supper (cf. **transubstantiation**). — *n* **consubstantiā'tionist**. [L. *con-*, with, and **substantial**.]

consuetude *kon'swi-tūd, n* custom; familiarity. — *adj* **consuetū'dinary** customary. [L. *cōnsuētūdō, -inis*, custom.]

consul *kon'səl, n* an agent for a foreign government appointed to attend to the interests of its citizens and its commerce; one of the two chief magistrates in the Roman republic. — *adj* **con'sular** (*-sū-lər*) pertaining to a consul. — *n* **con'sulate** (*-sūl-* or *-səl-*) the office, residence or jurisdiction of a consul or consuls. — *n* **con'sulship** the office, or term of office, of a consul. [L. *cōnsul*.]

consult *kən-sult', vt* to ask advice of; to look up for information or advice; to consider (wishes, feelings, etc.). — *vi* to consider jointly (with *with*). — *n* **consult'ancy** an agency which provides professional advice; the post of consultant. — *n* **consultant** (*kən-sult'ənt*) a person who gives professional advice or takes part in consultation; the most senior grade of doctor in a given speciality in a hospital; a person who seeks advice or information. — Also *adj*. — *n* **consultā'tion** (*kon-səl-* or *-sul-*) deliberation, or a meeting for deliberation, esp. of physicians or lawyers. — *adj* **consult'ative** or **consult'ive** of or pertaining to consultation, esp. of bodies without vote on the decision. — *n* **consult'atory** or **consult'ory** of the nature of consultation. — *n* **consultee'** the person consulted. — *n* **consult'er**. — *adj* **consult'ing** (of a physician, lawyer, etc.) competent to give professional advice to others in the same field. — *n* **consult'or**. — **consult'ing-room** the room in which a doctor sees a patient. [L. *cōnsultāre*, intensive of *cōnsulĕre*, to consult.]

consume *kən-sūm'* or *-soom', vt* to use up; to devour; to waste or spend; to destroy by wasting, fire, evaporation, etc.; to exhaust. — *vi* to waste away. — *adj* **consum'able**. — *n* (usu. in *pl*) something that can be consumed. — *n* **consum'er** a person who consumes; a person who uses an article produced (opp. of *producer*). — *n* **consum'erism** (the promotion of) the protection of the interests of buyers of goods and services against defective or dangerous goods, etc.; the theory that a steady growth in the consumption of goods is necessary for a sound economy. — *n* **consum'erist**. — *adj* **consum'ing** wasting or destroying; engrossing. — **consumer durables** consumer goods for domestic use and designed to last a fairly long time; **consumer research** the study of the needs and preferences of consumers. [L. *cōnsūmĕre, -sūmptum*, to destroy — *con-* (signifying completeness) and *sūmĕre*, to take.]

consummate *kon'sum-āt, -səm-* or *-sū-, vt* to raise to the highest point; to perfect or finish; to make (marriage) legally complete by sexual intercourse. — *adj* (*kən-sum'āt* or *-it*, or *kon'sū-*) complete, supreme or perfect of its kind; skilled or competent. — *adv* **consumm'ately** perfectly; with accomplishment. — *n* **consummā'tion** the act of completing; perfection; the subsequent intercourse which makes a marriage legally valid. [L. *cōnsummāre, -ātum*, to perfect.]

consumption *kən-sump'shən* or *kən-sum'shən*, the act or process of consuming or using up; the quantity consumed; wasting of the body; an earlier name for pulmonary tuberculosis. — *adj* **consump'tive** wasting away; pertaining or inclined to the disease consumption. — *n* a person affected by consumption. — *adv* **consump'tively**. — *n* **consump'tiveness** or **consumptiv'ity** (*kon-*). [**consume**.]

cont. or **contd** *abbrev* for continued.

contact *kon'takt*, *n* touch; meeting; association; means or occasion of communication; a person one can call upon for assistance, information, introductions, etc., in a business or other organisation; a person who has been exposed to contagion; meeting in a point without intersection (*math*); close approximation allowing passage of electric current or communication of disease; a place or part where electric current may be allowed to pass. — *adj* involving contact; caused or made active by contact. — *vt* and *vi* (also *kon-takt'*) to bring or to come into contact; to get in touch with, or establish a connection with. — *adj* **contact'able** able to be contacted. — **contact lens** a lens, usu. of plastic material, worn in contact with the eyeball, instead of spectacles; **contact man** (*colloq*) an intermediary in transactions, esp. shady ones. [L. *contingĕre*, *contactum*, to touch — *con-*, wholly, *tangĕre*, to touch.]

contagion *kən-tā'jən*, *n* transmission of a disease by direct contact with an infected person or object; a disease or poison transmitted in this way; the means of transmission; the transmission of an emotional state, e.g. excitement; a harmful influence. — *adj* **contā'gious** communicable by contact; carrying disease or other contagion; spreading easily (*fig*; *colloq*). — *adv* **contā'giously**. — *n* **contā'giousness**. [L. *contāgiō*, *-ōnis* — *con-*, *tangĕre*, to touch.]

contain *kən-tān'*, *vt* to have within, enclose; to comprise, include; to restrain; to keep fixed; to hold back; to keep in check. — *adj* **contain'able**. — *n* **contain'er** something which contains goods, etc. for storage; a large boxlike receptacle of standard shape and size in which goods are enclosed for transport on a lorry, train or ship. — *n* **containerisā'tion** or **-z-**. — *vt* **contain'erise** or **-ize** to put (freight) into standard sealed containers; to use such containers for (e.g. a transport operation). — *n* **contain'ment** the act of containing; the act or policy of preventing the spread beyond certain limits of a power or influence regarded as hostile, by means other than war; the successful result of this. — **container ship** a ship designed for the most efficient stowing and transport of such containers; **container terminal** a port, railway station, etc., or part of one, set aside and equipped for handling containers. [O.Fr. (Fr.) *contenir* — L. *continēre* — *con-*, *tenēre*, to hold.]

contaminate *kən-tam'i-nāt*, *vt* to pollute, esp. by radioactivity; to infect; to defile by touching or mixing with; to corrupt. — *adj* **contam'inable**. — *n* **contam'inant**. — *n* **contaminā'tion**. [L. *contāmināre*, *-ātum* — *contāmen*, pollution.]

contango *kən-tang'gō*, (*stock exchange*) *n* a percentage paid by the buyer to the seller of stock for keeping back its delivery to the next settling-day: — *pl* **contang'os**. [Arbitrarily from **continue**.]

contemn *kən-tem'*, *vt* to despise. — *adj* **contem'nible**. [L. *contemnĕre*, *-temptum*, to value little.]

contemplate *kon'tem-plāt*, *vt* to consider or look at attentively; to meditate on or study; to intend. — *vi* to think seriously; to meditate (on, upon). — *n* **contemplā'tion** attentive viewing or consideration; matter for thought; purpose; meditation; a meditative condition of mind. — *adj* **con'templātive** (or *kən-tem'plə-*) given to contemplation. — *n* a person leading a life of religious contemplation. — *adv* **con'templatively** (or *-tem'*). — *n* **con'templativeness** (or *-tem'*). — *n* **con'templātor**. — **contemplative life** (*theol* and *philos*) life devoted to meditation (opp. to *active life*). — **in contemplation of** in the expectation of; bearing in mind as a possibility. [L. *contemplārī*, *-ātus*, — *con-* (intensive) and *templum*, temple.]

contemporaneous *kən-tem-pə-rā'ni-əs*, *adj* living, happening or being at the same time. — *n* **contemporaneity** (*-ə-nē'i-ti*) or **contemporā'neousness**. — *adv* **contemporā'neously**. — *n* **contem'porariness**. — *adj* **contem'porary** belonging to the same time (with); of the same age; (*loosely*) present-day, esp. up-to-date, fashionable, etc. — *n* a person who lives at the same time as another. — *vt* **contem'porise** or **-ize** to make contemporary in mind. [L. *con-*, *tempus*, *-oris*, time.]

contempt *kən-tempt'*, *n* scorn (with *for*); disgrace; disregard of the rule of law, or authority, as in *contempt of court*, *contempt of Parliament*. — *n* **contemptibil'ity** or **contempt'ibleness**. — *adj* **contempt'ible** despicable. — *adv* **contempt'ibly**. — *adj* **contempt'ūous** haughty or scornful. — *adv* **contempt'ūously**. — *n* **contempt'uousness**. [**contemn**.]

contend *kən-tend'*, *vi* to strive; to struggle in emulation or in opposition; to dispute or debate (with *against*, *for*, *with* or *about*). — *vt* to maintain in dispute (that). — *n* **contend'er**. — *adj* **contend'ing**. — *n* **conten'tion** debate; strife; a point argued. — *adj* **conten'tious** in, or relating to, dispute; controversial; quarrelsome; given to dispute. — *adv* **conten'tiously**. — *n* **conten'tiousness**. [L. *contendĕre*, *-tentum* — *con-* (intensive) and *tendĕre*, to stretch.]

content[1] *kon'tent*, *n* that which is contained; the substance; (in *pl*) the things contained; (in *pl*) a list of chapters, etc., in a book; capacity. — **content word** a word which has a meaning independent of its context (opp. to *function word*). [**contain**.]

content[2] *kən-tent'*, *adj* satisfied; quietly happy. — *n* peace of mind; satisfaction. — *vt* to make content. — *adj* **content'ed** content. — *adv* **content'edly**. — *n* **content'ment**. [Fr., — L. *contentus*, contained, hence, satisfied — *con-*, *tenēre*, to hold.]

conterminous *kən-tûr'min-əs*, *adj* adjacent, meeting along a common boundary; meeting end to end. [L. *conterminus*, neighbouring — *con-*, *terminus*, a boundary.]

contest *kən-test'*, *vt* to call in question or make the subject of dispute; to strive to gain. — *vi* to contend. — *n* (*kon'*) a struggle for victory; a competition; strife; a debate, dispute, argument. — *adj* **contest'able**. — *n* **contest'ant** a person who takes part in a contest. — *n* **contestā'tion**. — *adj* **contest'ed**. — *n* **contest'er**. — *adj* **contest'ing**. [Fr. *contester* — L. *contestārī*, to call to witness.]

context *kon'tekst*, *n* the parts of a piece of writing or speech which precede and follow a particular word or passage and may fix, or help to fix, its true meaning; associated surroundings, setting. — *adj* **context'ūal**. — *n* **contextūalisā'tion** or **-z-**. — *vt* **context'ūalise** or **-ize** to place in context. — *adv* **context'ūally**. — *n* **context'ure** structure; fabric. [L. *contextus*, *contexĕre* — *con-*, *texĕre*, *textum*, to weave.]

contiguous *kən-tig'ū-əs*, *adj* touching, adjoining; near; next (to) in space or time. — *n* **contigū'ity** or **contig'uousness**. — *adv* **contig'uously**. [L. *contiguus* — *contingĕre*, to touch on all sides — *con-*, wholly, *tangĕre*, to touch.]

continent *kon'ti-nənt*, *n* a vast landmass not broken up by seas; one of the great divisions of the land surface of the globe; the mainland portion of one of these; (usu. with *cap*) the mainland of Europe, as distinct from Britain. — *adj* able to control the movements of one's bladder and bowels; restraining within due bounds, or absolutely abstaining from, the indulgence of pleasure (esp. sexual); temperate; virtuous. — *n* **con'tinence** or **con'tinency** ability to control one's bladder and bowels; self-restraint or (esp. sexual) abstinence; chastity. — *adj* **continen'tal** (*-ent'l*) of, characteristic of, or of the nature of, a continent or the mainland of Europe as distinct from Britain. — *n* a native or inhabitant of a continent, esp. the mainland of Europe. — *adv* **con'tinently**. — **continental breakfast** a light breakfast of rolls and coffee; **continental divide** a range of mountains forming the watershed of a continent; **continental drift** (*geol*) the hypothetical slow drifting apart of land masses, as e.g. in A. L. Wegener's theory of the formation of world continents from one original landmass; **continental quilt** a duvet; **continental shelf** a gently sloping zone, under relatively shallow seas, offshore from a continent or island. [L. *continēns, -entis* — *continēre*, to contain.]

contingent *kən-tin'jənt, adj* dependent on something else; liable but not certain to happen; accidental. — *n* an event liable but not certain to occur; a share, quota or group, esp. of soldiers. — *n* **contin'gency** a possible future event; a chance happening or concurrence of events; something dependent on such (also *adj*); chance; uncertainty. — *adv* **contin'gently**. — **contingency plans** plans or arrangements made in case a particular situation should arise. [L. *contingēns, -entis* — *con-*, mutually, *tangĕre*, to touch.]

continue *kən-tin'ū, vt* to draw out or prolong; to extend; to maintain; to go on with; to resume; to adjourn (*legal*); to be a prolongation of. — *vi* to remain in the same place or state; to last or endure. — *adj* **contin'uable**. — *adj* **contin'ual** without interruption; unceasing; persistent. — *adv* **contin'ually**. — *n* **contin'uance** duration; uninterrupted succession; stay; adjournment (*legal*). — n **contin'uant** (*phon*) a consonant sound which is produced on an uninterrupted flow of breath. — Also *adj*. — *n* **continuā'tion** going on; persistence; constant succession; extension; resumption; a further instalment. — *adj* **contin'ued** uninterrupted; unceasing; extended; resumed; in instalments. — *n* **continū'ity** the state of being continuous or consistent; uninterrupted connection; a complete scenario of a cinema film; the ordering or arrangement of film or television shots and scenes, or of parts of a radio broadcast, in a correct or consistent way. — *n* **continuo** (*kon-tin'ū-ō*) a bass part as written for a keyboard instrument, with or without an accompaniment; the instruments playing this part: — *pl* **contin'uos**. — *adj* **contin'uous** joined together in space or time without interruption. — *adv* **contin'uously**. — *n* **contin'uousness**. — *n* **contin'ūum** that which is continuous; that which must be regarded as continuous and the same and which can be described only relatively: — *pl* **contin'ua**. — **continuing education** part-time courses of study for adult students; **continuity girl** or **man** a person employed on the set of a cinema film to ensure continuity, esp. in matters of costume, make-up, props, etc., between different shots; **continuous assessment** the assessment of the progress of a pupil or student by intermittent checks, e.g. class tests, essays, etc., throughout the year; **continuous creation** the notion of creation as going on always, not as a single act at one particular time; **continuous stationery** (*comput*) stationery consisting of a long sheet of paper with regular perforations, usu. folded fan-wise and fed through a printer. [L. *continuāre* — *continuus*, joined, connected, from *continēre*, to hold together.]

contort *kən-tört', vt* to twist or turn violently. — *adj* **contort'ed** twisted. — *n* **contor'tion** a violent twisting; deformation. — *adj* **contor'tional**. — *n* **contor'tionism**. — *n* **contor'tionist** a gymnast who practises contorted postures; a person who twists words and phrases. — *adj* **contort'ive**. [L. *con-* (intensive) and *torquēre, tortum*, to twist.]

contour *kon'tōōr, n* outline, shape or surface; general character or aspect; a contour line. — *vt* to mark with contour lines; to follow the contour lines of. — *adj* **con'toured** (of chairs, etc.) shaped to fit the lines of the human body. — **contour cultivation, farming** and **ploughing** the ploughing (and planting) of sloping land along the contour lines to counter erosion; **contour line** a line on a map, etc. linking points on the ground which are all at the same height above sea-level. [Fr. *contour*.]

contr. *abbrev* for: contracted; contraction.

contra *kon'tra* or *-trə, adv* and *prep* against. — *n* an argument against; the other side.

contra- *kon-tra-* or *-trə, pfx* denoting: against; contrary. [L. *contrā*.]

contraband *kon'trə-band, adj* forbidden by law to be imported or exported; prohibited. — *n* illegal trade; smuggled or prohibited goods. [Sp. *contrabanda* — It. *contrabbando* — L. *contrā*, L.L. *bandum*, ban.]

contrabass *kon-trə-bās, n* the double-bass. [It. *contra(b)basso* — pfx. *contra-* indicating an octave lower, and *basso*, bass.]

contrabassoon *kon-trə-bas-ōōn', n* a metal or wooden instrument, like a bassoon but sounding an octave lower. [*contra-* (see **contrabass** above), and **bassoon**.]

contraception *kon-trə-sep'shən, n* prevention of conception by artificial or natural means. — *n* **contracep'tive** a drug, device or other means of contraception. — Also *adj*. [L. *contrā*, against, and **(con)ception**.]

contract *kən-trakt', vt* to draw together; to lessen; to shorten; to effect by agreement; to come into, become the subject of; to incur; to catch (a disease); to bargain for; to betroth. — *vi* to shrink; to become less; to become shorter; to make a contract (with *with* or *for*). — *n* (*kon'trakt*) an agreement on fixed terms; a bond; a betrothal; a written statement representing an agreement; an undertaking; in criminal circles, an undertaking to kill a particular person, esp. for an agreed sum of money (*slang*). — *n* **contractabil'ity**. — *adj* **contract'able** (*kən-*) able to be contracted, esp. of a disease or habit. — *n* **contract'ed** drawn together; shortened; narrow; engaged to be married. — *adv* **contract'edly**. — *n* **contract'edness**. — *n* **contractibil'ity**. — *adj* **contract'ible** capable of being contracted or shortened. — *adj* **contract'ile** tending or having the power to contract or draw in. — *n* **contractil'ity** (*kon-*). — *n* **contrac'tion** (*kən-*) the act of contracting; a word shortened in speech or spelling; a symbol for shortening; a tightening of the muscles or muscle fibres. — *adj* **contrac'tional** or **contrac'tionary** having the effect of contracting. — *adj* **contract'ive** tending to contract. — *n* **contract'or** a person who, or a company which, engages to carry out work or furnish supplies at a stated rate; one of the parties to a bargain or agreement. — *adj* **contract'ūal**. — **contract bridge** a development of auction bridge, in which tricks beyond the number bid for count only like honours. — **contract in** to agree to participate on certain conditions; **contract out** to decide not to participate in a pension scheme, etc.; to withdraw from an obligation, agreement, etc.; to arrange that certain conditions shall not apply; to offer (work previously carried out by in-house staff, in a school, hospital, etc.) to private contractors. [L. *contractus* — *con-*, together, *trahĕre, tractum*, to draw.]

contradict *kon-trə-dikt', vt* to deny what is affirmed by; to assert the contrary of; to deny; to be contrary to in character. — *adj* **contradict'able**. — *n* **contradic'tion** the act of contradicting; a statement asserting the contrary; denial; inconsistency. — *adj* **contradict'ive** contradicting or tending to contradict. — *adv* **contradict'ively**. — *n* **contradict'or**. — *adv* **contradict'orily**. — *n* **contradict'oriness**. — *adj* **contradict'ory** affirming the contrary; inconsistent. — *n* (*logic*) either of two propositions such that both cannot be true, or both cannot be false. — **contradiction in terms** a group of words containing a contradiction. [L. *contrādīcĕre, -dictum* — *contrā-*, against, *dīcere*, to say.]

contradistinguish *kon-trə-dis-ting'gwish, vt* to distinguish by contrasting different qualities or conditions. — *n* **contradistinc'tion.** [L. *contrā*, against, and **distinguish.**]

contraflow *kon'trə-flō*, *n* a system of traffic regulation on motorways, when one carriageway is closed and the other is arranged for two-way traffic. [L. *contrā*, against, and **flow.**]

contrail *kon'trāl*, *n* a trail of condensed vapours left by a high-flying aircraft. — Also **vapour trail.** [**con-(densation)** and **trail.**]

contraindicate *kon-trə-in'di-kāt*, (*med*) *vt* to point to (a particular treatment or procedure) as unsuitable. — *n* **contrain'dicant.** — *n* **contraindicā'tion.** — *adj* **contraindic'ative.** [L. *contrā*, against, and **indicate.**]

contralto *kən-tral'tō* or *-träl'tō*, *n* the lowest musical voice in women; a singer with such a voice; a part for such a voice: — *pl* **contral'ti** (*-tē*) or **contral'tos.** — Also *adj*. [It., *contra-*, and **alto.**]

contraption *kən-trap'shən*, *n* a contrivance. [Perh. *contrivance adaption.*]

contrapuntal, contrapuntist. See **counterpoint.**

contrary *kon'trə-ri*, *adj* opposite; contradictory; (usu. *kən-trā'ri*) perverse. — *n* an extreme opposite; a proposition related to another in such a way that both cannot be true though both may be false (*logic*). — *n* **contrariety** (*-rī'i-ti*) (an) opposition; (an) inconsistency. — *adv* **contrarily** (*kon'* or *-trā'*). — *n* **contrariness** (*kon'* or *-trā'*). — *adv* **con'trariwise** (or *-trā'* or *-tra'*) in the contrary way; on the other side; on the other hand. — **on the contrary** quite the opposite, not at all; **to the contrary** to the opposite effect. [L. *contrārius* — *contrā*, against.]

contrast *kən-träst'*, *vi* to stand in opposition. — *vt* to set in opposition to, in order to show difference. — *n* (*kon'träst*) opposition or unlikeness in things compared; a contrasting person or thing; the (degree of) difference in tone between the light and dark parts of a photograph or a television picture. — *adj* **contrast'ive.** — *adj* **con'trasty** (*phot*; of prints or negatives) showing a high degree of contrast. — **contrast medium** a suitable substance used in diagnostic radiology in order to give contrast. [Fr. *contraster* — L. *contrā*, opposite to, *stāre*, to stand.]

contrasuggestible *kon-trə-suj-est'i-bl*, (*psychol*) *adj* responding to suggestion by believing or doing the opposite. [L. *contrā*, against, and **suggestible.**]

contrate *kon'trāt*, *adj* (of wheels, esp. in watchmaking) having cogs parallel to the axis. [L. *contrā*, opposite.]

contravene *kon-trə-vēn'*, *vt* to infringe; to oppose. — *n* **contraven'tion.** [L. *contrā*, against, *venīre*, *ventum*, to come.]

contretemps *kɔ̃-tr'-tã*, *n* something happening inopportunely or at the wrong time; anything embarrassing; a hitch. [Fr. *contre*, against, *temps*, time.]

contribute *kən-trib'ūt* or *kon'*, *vt* to give along with others; to give for a common purpose; to add towards a common result, to a fund, etc.; to write and send for publication with others. — *vi* to give or bear a part; to be a contributor. — *adj* **contrib'utable** payable; subject to contribution. — *n* **contribū'tion** (*kon-*) the act of contributing; something contributed; a levy or charge imposed on a number of people; anything given for a common purpose or done towards a common end; a written composition supplied to a periodical, etc. — *adj* **contrib'utive** giving a share; helping. — *n* **contrib'utor.** — *adj* **contrib'utory** giving or given to a common purpose or fund; having partial responsibility; (of a pension scheme) to which the employee makes a contribution as well as the employer. — **contributory negligence** failure to take adequate precautions against an accident, etc., resulting in partial legal responsibility for injury, damage, etc. [L. *con-*, *tribĕre*, *-ūtum*, to give.]

contrite *kən-trīt'* or *kon'trīt*, *adj* with the spirit broken by a sense of sin; wholly penitent; (of an action) showing a sense of guilt or sin. — *adv* **contritely.** — *n* **contriteness.** — *n* **contrition** (*kon-trish'ən*) remorse; deep sorrow for past sin and resolve to avoid future sin (*Christian relig*). [L. *contrītus* — *conterĕre* — *con-*, wholly, *terĕre*, to bruise.]

contrive *kən-trīv'*, *vt* to plan; to invent; to bring about or effect; to manage or arrange; to plot. — *adj* **contriv'able.** — *n* **contriv'ance** an invention; the act of contriving; a deceitful plan. — *adj* **contrived'** laboured; artificially intricate. [O.Fr. *controver* — *con-* (intensive) and *trover*, to find.]

control *kən-trōl'*, *n* restraint; authority; command; regulation; a check; a means of operating, regulating, directing or testing; a station for doing so; a scientific experiment performed without variables to provide a standard of comparison for other experiments (also **control experiment**); a subject or group of subjects (**control group**) providing such a standard of comparison; a disembodied spirit or other agency supposed to direct a spiritualistic medium. — *adj* pertaining to control. — *vt* to check; to restrain; to govern; to command or operate: — *pr p* **contrōll'ing**; *pa t* and *pa p* **contrōlled'**. — *n* **contrōllabil'ity.** — *adj* **controll'able.** — *n* **controll'er** an official authorised to control some activity or department; an apparatus for regulating; a person who supervises financial affairs or examines financial accounts (also **comptroll'er**). — *n* **controll'ership.** — **control character** (*comput*) one which, in a suitable context, produces a particular effect, e.g. start, delete, etc.; **controlling interest** a number of shares sufficient to ensure control over the running of a company; **control panel** or **board** a panel or board containing dials, switches and gauges for operating and monitoring electrical or other apparatus; **control register** (*comput*) one which stores the instructions controlling the operation of a computer for one cycle; **control room** a room in which control instruments are placed, e.g. in a broadcasting station; **control tower** a building at an airport, aerodrome, etc. from which take-off and landing instructions are given; **control unit** (*comput*) the part of a computer which interprets instructions and controls the execution of a program. [Fr. *contrôle*, from *contre-rôle*, a duplicate register — L. *contrā*, against, *rotulus*, a roll.]

controvert *kon'trə-vûrt*, *vt* to oppose; to argue against; to dispute. — *adj* **controver'sial** (*-shəl*) relating to controversy; arousing controversy. — *n* **controver'sialist** a person given to controversy. — *adv* **controver'sially.** — *n* **con'troversy** (also *kən-trov'*) contention; dispute; a war of opinions, in books, pamphlets, etc.; a debate. — *adj* **controvert'ible.** — *adv* **controvert'ibly.** [L. *contrā*, against, *vertĕre*, to turn.]

contumacious *kon-tū-mā'shəs*, *adj* opposing lawful authority with contempt; obstinate; stubborn. — *adv* **contumā'ciously.** — *n* **contumā'ciousness.** — *n* **con'tumacy** (*-məs-i*) obstinate disobedience or resistance; refusal to comply with the orders of a court of law. [L. *contumāx*, *-ācis*, insolent.]

contumely *kon'tūm-li* or *-i-li*, *n* scornful insolence; a scornful insult. — *adj* **contumē'lious.** [L. *contumēlia.*]

contuse *kən-tūz'*, *vt* to bruise (the body). — *n* **contusion** (*-tū'zhən*) a bruise; the act of bruising; the state of being bruised. — *adj* **contū'sive** tending to bruise. [L. *contundĕre*, *contūsum* — *con-* (intensive) and *tundĕre*, to bruise.]

conundrum *kən-un'drəm*, *n* a riddle, esp. one whose answer is a play on words; any puzzling question.

conurbation *kon-ûr-bā'shən*, *n* a dense cluster of neighbouring towns considered as a single unit in some respects, e.g. industrial, economic, administrative. [L. *con-*, together, *urbs*, city.]

conv. *abbrev* for conventional.

convalesce *kən-vəl-es'*, *vi* to regain health, esp. by resting. — *n* **convalesc'ence** gradual recovery of health and strength; the period during which this takes place. — *adj* **convalesc'ent** gradually recovering health; promoting or encouraging convalescence. — Also *n*. [L. *con-* (intensive) and *valēscēre* — *valēre*, to be strong.]

convection *kən-vek'shən*, *n* a transmission, esp. that of heat or electricity through liquids or gases by means of currents; vertical movement, esp. upwards, of air or atmospheric conditions (*meteorol*). — *adj* **convec'tional.** — *adj* **convec'tive.** — *n* **convec'tor** a device for heating by convection. [L. *convectiō*, *-ōnis*, bringing together — *con-*, *vehěre*, to carry.]

convene *kən-vēn'*, *vi* to come together; to assemble. — *vt* to call together; to summon before a court, etc. — *adj* **convēn'able.** — *n* **convēn'er** or **convēn'or** a person who convenes a meeting; a person who chairs a committee. [Fr. *convenir* — L. *convenīre* — *con-*, together, *venīre*, to come.]

convenient *kən-vēn'yənt*, *adj* suitable; handy; commodious. — *n* **convēn'ience** suitability; an advantage; any means or device for promoting (esp. domestic) ease or comfort; a lavatory or water-closet, esp. (**public convenience**) a building containing several for use by the public. — *adv* **convēn'iently.** — **convenience food** food (partly) prepared before sale so as to be ready, or almost ready, for the table; **convenience store** (*NAm*) a small grocery shop, often part of a chain, that stays open after normal shopping hours. — **at one's (earliest) convenience** (on the first occasion or at the earliest time) when it is suitable or opportune. [L. *convenīre*.]

convent *kon'vənt*, *n* a closed community of people, usu. women, devoted to a religious life; the house in which they live, a monastery or (now usu.) nunnery. — *adj* **convent'ual** belonging to a convent. — *n* a monk or nun. [Through Fr. from L. *convenīre*, *conventum*, to come together.]

conventicle *kən-vent'i-kl*, *n* a secret, illegal or forbidden religious meeting; the building where such a meeting takes place. [L. *conventiculum*, a secret meeting of monks.]

convention *kən-ven'shən*, *n* an assembly, esp. of representatives or delegates for some common object; fashion; established usage; a meeting of political party delegates for nominating a candidate (*US*); any temporary treaty; an agreement; the act of convening; in card games, a mode of play in accordance with a recognised code of signals. — *adj* **conven'tional** customary; growing out of tacit agreement or custom; bound or influenced by convention; formed or adopted by convention; (of weapons, warfare and energy sources) not nuclear. — *vt* **conven'tionalise** or **-ize** to make conventional. — *n* **conven'tionalism** adherence to, or advocacy of, that which is established; something conventional. — *n* **conven'tionalist.** — *n* **conventional'ity** the state of being conventional; something which is established by use or custom. — *adv* **conven'tionally.** — *n* **conventioneer'** (*NAm*) a person attending a convention. [**convene.**]

converge *kən-vûrj'*, *vi* to tend towards or meet in one point, value, quality, etc.; (of animals) to undergo convergence. — *n* **conver'gence** the act or point of converging (also **conver'gency**); the property of having a limit, for infinite series, sequences, products, etc. (*math*); the independent development, in animals not related evolutionarily, of similar physical features or characteristics. — *adj* **conver'gent** meeting or tending to meet in a point; coming nearer together (also *fig*). [L. *con-*, *vergěre*, to bend, to incline.]

converse *kən-vûrs'*, *vi* to talk (with, about); to commune spiritually (with). — *adj* **convers'ant** (also *kon'*) acquainted by study; familiar. — *n* **conversā'tion** talk; an instance of communication by talking. — *adj* **conversā'tional.** — *n* **conversā'tionalist** or **conversā'tionist** a person who enjoys or excels in conversation. — **conversation piece** an object that arouses comment by its novelty; a painting of a number of people in their usual environment, engaged in their usual pastimes, etc. [Fr. *converser* — L. *conversārī*, to turn about, go about — *con-* (intensive) and *versāre*, to keep turning.]

convert *kən-vûrt'*, *vt* to change or turn from one thing, condition, opinion, party or religion to another; to cause to acquire faith in a particular religion; to change into the converse; to alter into something else; to exchange for an equivalent. — *vi* to undergo conversion; to be convertible (from one form into another); to switch (religious or political) allegiance. — *n* (*kon'vûrt*) a person who is converted, esp. to a particular religious faith. — *adj* **con'verse** (or *-vûrs'*) reversed in order or relation. — *n* (only *kon'*) that which is the opposite of another; a proposition in which the subject and predicate have changed places (*logic*); a proposition in which that which is given and that which is to be proved in another proposition are interchanged (*math*). — *adv* **converse'ly.** — *n* **conver'sion** a change from one condition, use, opinion, party, religion or spiritual state to another; something, esp. a building, adapted for a different purpose. — *n* **convert'er.** — *n* **convertibil'ity.** — *adj* **convert'ible** that may be converted; (of currency) that may be freely converted into other currencies, or into gold (or dollars) at a fixed price. — *n* anything convertible; a car with a folding top. — *adv* **convert'ibly.** [L. *convertěre*, *conversum* — *con-*, *vertěre*, to turn.]

convex *kon'veks* or *kon-veks'*, *adj* rising into a round form on the outside (opp. of *concave*). — *n* a convex figure, surface, body or part. — *n* **convex'ity** roundness of form on the outside; a convex part or figure. — *n* **con'vexness** (or *-veks'*). — *adv* **con'vexly** (or *-veks'*). — *adj* **convexo-con'cave** (or *-kāv'*) convex on one side, and concave on the other. — *adj* **convexo-con'vex** (or *-veks'*) convex on both sides. [L. *convexus*, vaulted.]

convey *kən-vā'*, *vt* to carry; to transmit; to impart; to steal; to communicate (ideas, etc.); to make over in law. — *adj* **convey'able.** — *n* **convey'ance** the act or means of conveying; a vehicle of any kind; the act of transferring property (*legal*). — *n* **convey'ancer** a person who prepares deeds for the transference of property. — *n* **convey'ancing.** — *n* **convey'or** or **convey'er** a person or thing that conveys in any sense; a mechanism for continuous transport of materials, packages, goods in process of manufacture, etc. (also **convey'or-belt**). [O.Fr. *conveier* — L. *con-*, *via*, a way.]

convict *kən-vikt'*, *vt* to prove guilty; to pronounce guilty. — *n* (*kon'*) a person convicted or found guilty of crime; a person who has been condemned to penal servitude. — *n* **convic'tion** the state of being convinced; strong belief; the act of convincing; the act or an instance of proving guilty. — **carry conviction** to be convincing. [Ety. as for **convince.**]

convince *kən-vins'*, *vt* to influence the mind of by evidence; to satisfy as to truth or error. — *adj* **convinc'ible.** — *adj* **convinc'ing** producing conviction; certain, positive, beyond doubt; (of a victory, etc.) by a large or significant margin. — *adv* **convinc'ingly.** [L. *convincěre*, *con-* (signifying completeness) and *vincěre*, *victum*, to conquer.]

convivial *kən-viv'i-əl*, *adj* social; jovial; feasting or drinking in company; relating to a feast. — *n* **conviv'ialist.** — *n* **convivial'ity.** — *adv* **con-**

viv'ially. [L. *convīvium*, a living together, a feast — *con-*, together, *vīvěre*, to live.]

convoke *kən-vōk'*, *vt* to call together; to assemble (also **convocate** *kon'vō-kāt*). — *n* **convocā'tion** a large (esp. formal) assembly, e.g. of members of a university court; the act of convoking; a synod of clergy of either the provinces of Canterbury or York (*C of E*). — *adj* **convocā'tional.** [L. *convocāre* — *con-*, together, *vocāre*, *-ātum*, to call.]

convolve *kən-volv'*, *vt* to roll together, or one part on another. — *adj* **convolute** (*kon'və-lo͞ot* or *-lūt*) rolled together, or one part on another (also **con'voluted**); coiled laterally (*bot*); (of a shell) having the inner whorls concealed or overlapped by the outer (*zool*). — *adj* **con'voluted** (of argument, style of speech or writing) intricate, difficult to understand; unclear; convolute, rolled together. — *n* **convolution** (*-lo͞o'* or *-lū'*) a twist or coil; a fold or sinuosity, esp. of the brain surface. [L. *con-*, together, *volvěre*, *-ūtum*, to roll.]

convolvulus *kən-vol'vū-ləs*, *n* any of a large number of twining or trailing plants of the genus *Convolvulus*, including bindweed. [L. *convolvěre*; see ety. for **convolve.**]

convoy *kon'voi*, *vt* to accompany (vehicles, esp. ships) for protection; to escort. — *n* the act of convoying; a ship or ships of war guarding a fleet of merchant-vessels; the ships protected in this way; an escort; any group of vehicles, esp. lorries, travelling together; a supply of stores, etc., under escort. [Fr. *convoyer*; see **convey.**]

convulse *kən-vuls'*, *vt* to agitate violently; to affect by spasms (also *fig*). — *n* **convul'sion** any violent involuntary contraction of the muscles of the body; any violent disturbance; (in *pl*) fits of uncontrollable laughter (*colloq*). — *adj* **convuls'ive.** — *adv* **convuls'ively.** — *n* **convuls'iveness.** [L. *con-* (intensive) and *vellěre*, *vulsum*, to pluck, to pull.]

cony or **coney** *kō'ni*, *n* a rabbit; rabbit-skin. [Prob. through O.Fr. *conil*, from L. *cunīculus*, a rabbit.]

coo[1] *ko͞o*, *vi* to make a sound like a dove; (of lovers) to speak fondly. — *vt* to murmur softly or ingratiatingly. — *n* the sound made by doves. — *n* and *adj* **coo'ing.** — *adv* **coo'ingly.** [Imit.]

coo[2] *ko͞o*, (*slang*) *interj* expressive of surprise.

cooee or **cooey** *ko͞o'ē*, *n* a call to attract attention. — *vi* to utter the call. — *interj* attracting attention. — **within cooee** (*Austr* and *NZ colloq*) nearby. [Aboriginal.]

cook *ko͝ok*, *vt* to prepare as food by heat; to subject to great heat; to manipulate for any purpose, or falsify (accounts, etc.). — *vi* to practise cookery; to undergo cooking. — *n* a person who undertakes or is skilled in cooking. — *adj* **cook'able.** — *n* **cook'er** a stove, special vessel, or other apparatus for cooking; a variety (e.g. of apple) suitable for cooking. — *n* **cook'ery** the art or practice of cooking food. — *adj* **cook-chill'** (of foods and meals) cooked then packaged and stored in a refrigerated state, requiring re-heating before serving. — *n* the process of preparing food in this way. — **cook'ery-book** a book of recipes for cooking dishes; **cook'house** a building or room for cooking in, esp. in a camp or on a ship; **cook'ing-apple**, etc., an apple, etc., esp. suitable for cooking; **cook'ing-range** a stove adapted for cooking several things at once; **cook'ware** pans, dishes, etc., used for cooking. — **cook someone's goose** (*colloq*) to spoil someone's plans; **cook the books** (*colloq*) to falsify accounts, etc.; **cook up** (*colloq*) to concoct (a story, an excuse, etc.); **what's cooking?** (*slang*) what is happening?; what is being planned? [O.E. *cōc*, a cook — L. *coquus.*]

cookie *ko͝ok'i*, *n* a small sweet biscuit or cake; a bun (*Scot*); a person (esp. in the phrase *a smart cookie*) (*NAm*). — **that's how** (or **that's the way**) **the cookie crumbles** that's what the situation is; that's the way things usually happen. [Du. *koekje*, a cake.]

Cook's tour *ko͝oks to͞or*, (*colloq*) *n* a rapid but extensive tour; a wide-ranging superficial inspection. [Thomas *Cook* (1808–92), English travel agent.]

cool *ko͞ol*, *adj* slightly cold; free from excitement; calm; not zealous, ardent or cordial; indifferent; impudent; unemotional and relaxed; (of jazz music) restrained, economical and relaxed; (of amounts, esp. of money) exact; not less than; excellent (*colloq*, esp. *NAm*). — *vt* to make cool; to allay or moderate, as heat, excitement, passion, etc. — *vi* (often with *down*) to grow cool. — *n* that which is cool; coolness; calmness and self-possession. — *n* **cool'ant** a cooling agent, esp. a liquid. — *n* **cool'er** anything that cools; a vessel in which something is cooled; jail (*slang*). — *adj* **cool'ish.** — *adv* **cool'ly** in a cool manner; with composure; indifferently; impudently. — *n* **cool'ness.** — **cool box** or **bag** an insulated box or bag used to keep food, etc., cool. — *adj* **cool-head'ed** not easily excited; capable of acting with composure. — **cool'ing-tower** a large structure in which water heated industrially is cooled for re-use. — **cool it** (*slang*) to calm down, act in a relaxed fashion; **cool off** to become less angry and more amenable to reason (*n* and *adj* **cool'ing-off'**); to grow less passionate (*n* and *adj* **cool'ing-off**); **cool one's heels** to be kept waiting; **keep one's cool** (*colloq*) to remain calm, keep one's head; **lose one's cool** to become flustered. [O.E. *cōl.*]

coolabah or **coolibah** *ko͞ol'ə-bä*, *n* any of several species of Australian eucalyptus tree. [Aboriginal.]

coolamon *ko͞o'lə-mon*, (*Austr*) *n* a wooden or bark vessel used by Australian Aborigines to hold liquids, etc. [Aboriginal.]

coolie or **cooly** *ko͞ol'i*, *n* a hired native labourer in India and China (*offensive*); in South Africa, an Indian (*offensive*). [Prob. *Kolī*, a tribe of W. India; or Tamil, *kūli*, hire.]

coolly, etc. See **cool.**

coomb, coombe, comb or **combe** *ko͞om*, *n* a short deep valley; a hollow in a hillside. [O.E. *cumb*, a hollow.]

coon *ko͞on*, *n* the raccoon (*colloq*); a Negro (*offensive slang*). [U.S.; for **raccoon.**]

coop *ko͞op*, *n* a wicker basket; a box or cage for poultry or small animals; a confined, narrow place, esp. a prison cell. — *vt* (often with *up*) to confine in a coop or elsewhere.

co-op *kō-op'* or *kō'op*, (*colloq*) *n* short for **co-operative society** or **co-operative store.**

cooper *ko͞op'ər*, *n* a person who makes barrels, casks, etc. — *vt* to repair or make (barrels, etc.). — *n* **coop'erage** the work or workshop of a cooper; the sum paid for a cooper's work. [L.G., — L.L. *cūpārius* — *cūpa*, cask.]

co-operate (also **coop-** in all words) *kō-op'ər-āt*, *vi* to work together. — *n* **co-operā'tion** joint operation; assistance; willingness to help; combination in co-operative societies. — *adj* **co-op'erative** (also *n*). — *adj* **co-op'erant.** — *n* **co-op'erātor.** — **co-operative society** a commercial enterprise from which the profits are passed on to workers and customers; **co-operative store** the shop of a co-operative society. [**co-** and **operate.**]

co-opt *kō-opt'*, *vt* to elect into any body by the votes of its members. — *n* **co-optā'tion** or **co-op'tion.** — *adj* **co-op'tative** or **co-op'tive.** [L. *cooptāre*, *-ātum* — *co-*, together, *optāre*, to choose.]

co-ordinate (also **coor-** in all words) *kō-ör'di-nāt*, *vt* to place or classify in the same order or rank; to adjust the relations or movements of; to combine or integrate harmoniously; to harmonise; to match. — *n* an element of the same order as another; each of a system of two or more magnitudes used to define the position of a point, line, or surface by reference to a fixed system of lines, points, etc.; (in *pl*) outer garments in harmonising colour, material and pattern (cf. *separates*). — *adj* of the same order or rank;

pertaining to or involving co-ordination or co-ordinates. — *adv* **co-or'dinately**. — *n* **co-or'dinateness** the quality of being matched or harmonised. — *n* **co-ordinā'tion** ordered action together; balanced or skilful movement. — *adj* **co-or'dinative**. — *n* **co-or'dinator**.

coot *kōōt*, *n* a short-tailed waterfowl, with a characteristic white spot on the forehead (and so called *bald*, as in the phrase *bald as a coot*); a foolish person (*colloq*). [M.E. *cote*.]

cop[1] *kop*, *n* a conical ball of thread on a spindle; a top or head of anything. — *adj* **copped** rising to a cop or head. [O.E. *cop*, summit.]

cop[2] *kop*, (*slang*) *vt* to capture; to catch; to acquire or get. — *n* a policeman; a capture. — *n* **copp'er** (*slang*) a policeman. — **cop'-shop** (*slang*) police station. — **cop out** (*slang*) not to take responsibility for, to refuse to participate in (*n* **cop'-out**); **not much cop** (*slang*) of little worth, not very good. [Perh. Fr. *caper*, to seize — L. *capĕre*, *captum*, to take.]

copaiba *kō-pī'bä* or **copaiva** *kōpī'vä*, *n* a transparent aromatic resin obtained from S. American trees of the genus *Copaifera*, much used in medicine and perfumery, etc. [Sp. and Port. from Tupí.]

copal *kō'pəl*, *n* a hard resin obtained from many tropical trees and used to make varnishes and lacquers. [Sp., — Nahuatl *copalli*, resin.]

copartner *kō-pärt'nər*, *n* a joint partner. — *n* **co-part'nership**.

cope[1] *kōp*, *n* a semicircular, sleeveless hooded cloak worn over the alb or surplice in some Christian ceremonies; anything cloak-like. — *vt* to cover as with a cope. — *n* **cop'ing** the covering course of masonry of a wall. — **cope'-stone** or **cop'ing-stone** a stone that copes or tops a wall. [M.E. *cape*.]

cope[2] *kōp*, *vi* (esp. with *with*) to contend; to deal (with) successfully. [Fr. *couper* — L. *colaphus*, a blow with the fist.]

cope[3] *kōp*, *vt* to cut (a piece of moulding) so that it fits over another piece. — **cop'ing-saw** a narrow saw blade held under tension in a wide, U-shaped metal frame, used for cutting curves. [Fr. *couper*, to cut.]

copeck. See **kopeck**.

copepod *kō'pi-pod*, *n* a member of the **Copep'oda**, a class of Crustacea, minute animals with oarlike swimming feet. [Gr. *kōpē*, handle, oar, *pous*, *podos*, foot.]

Copernican *ko-pûr'ni-kən*, *adj* relating to *Copernicus*, the famous Polish astronomer (1473–1543), or to his system, which stated that the earth and other planets revolve around the sun.

copier. See **copy**.

coping. See **cope**[1].

co-pilot or **copilot** *kō'pī-lət*, *n* a second pilot in an aircraft.

copious *kō'pi-əs*, *adj* plentiful; overflowing; abounding. — *adv* **cō'piously**. — *n* **cō'piousness**. [L. *cōpiōsus* — *cōpia*, plenty — *co-* (intensive) and *ops*, *opis*, wealth.]

copita *ko-pēt'ə*, *n* a tulip-shaped sherry glass. [Sp.]

copolymer *kō-pol'i-mər*, *n* a substance polymerised along with another, the result being a chemical compound, not a mixture. — *vt* **copol'ymerise** or **-ize**. — *n* **copolymerisā'tion** or **-z-**.

copper[1] *kop'ər*, *n* a reddish moderately hard metallic element (atomic no. 29; symbol **Cu**, for L. *cuprum*), perh. the first metal used by man; a coin, made orig. of copper; a copper vessel; a boiler (orig. of copper) for laundry, etc.; any of several kinds of copper-coloured butterfly. — *adj* made of copper; copper-coloured. — *vt* to cover with copper. — *n* **copp'ering** the act of sheathing with copper; a covering of copper. — *adj* **copp'erish**. — *adj* **copp'ery**. — **copper beech** a variety of the common beech with purplish, copper-coloured leaves. — *vt* **copp'er-bottom** to cover the bottom of with copper. — *adj* **copp'er-bottomed** having the bottom covered with copper; sound, reliable, esp. financially. — **copp'erhead** a venomous snake of the eastern U.S. similar to the rattlesnake; a similar Australian snake; **copp'erplate** a plate of polished copper on which something has been engraved; an impression taken from the plate; faultless handwriting; **copper pyrītēs** a yellow double sulphide of copper and iron; **copp'ersmith** a smith who works in copper; **copp'er-work** work in copper; (also *nsing* **copp'er-works**) a place where copper is wrought or manufactured. [O.E. *copor* — L.L. *cuper* — L. *cuprum*, a form of *cyprium* (*aes*), Cyprian (brass), because found in *Cyprus*.]

copper[2]. See **cop**[2].

copperas *kop'ər-əs*, *n* ferrous sulphate. [Fr. *couperose*, perh. — L. *cuprī rosa*, rose of copper, or *aqua cuprōsa*, copper water.]

coppice *kop'is* or **copse** *kops*, *n* a wood of small growth for periodical cutting; a wood of sprouts from cut stumps. — *vt* to make into a coppice. — *n* **copp'icing**. — *adj* **cop'sy**. — **copse'wood**. [O.Fr. *copeiz*, wood, newly cut — L.L. *colpare*, to cut.]

copra *kop'rə*, *n* the dried kernel of the coconut, yielding coconut oil. [Port., from Malayalam.]

copro- *kop-ro-*, *combining form* denoting: dung; obscenity. — *n* **coprol'ogy** the obscene in literature and art. — *adj* **coproph'agous** (*-gəs*) (of certain beetles) feeding on dung. — *n* **coproph'agy** (*-ji*). — *n* **coprophil'ia** morbid pleasure in dung or filth. — *adj* **coproph'ilous** delighting in dung or filth; growing on or in dung. [Gr. *kopros*, dung.]

copse, copsewood and **copsy**. See **coppice**.

Copt *kopt*, *n* a Christian descendant of the ancient Egyptians. — *adj* **Copt'ic**. — *n* the language of the Copts. [Gr. *Aigyptios*, Egyptian.]

copter *kop'tər*, (*colloq*) *n* short for helicopter.

copula *kop'ū-lə*, *n* that which joins together; the word joining the subject and predicate (*logic* or *linguis*). — *adj* **cop'ular**. — *vi* **cop'ulāte** to have sexual intercourse (with). — *vt* to unite. — *n* **copulā'tion**. — *adj* **cop'ulatory**. [L. *cōpula* — *co-*, *apĕre*, to join.]

copy *kop'i*, *n* an imitation; a transcript; a reproduction; that which is imitated or reproduced; a single specimen of a book, magazine, newspaper, etc.; matter (e.g. a newspaper article) for printing; something newsworthy. — *vt* to write, paint, etc. in the manner of; to imitate closely; to transcribe; to reproduce or duplicate. — *vi* to make a copy of another's work and pass it off as one's own: — *pr p* **cop'ying**; *pa t* and *pa p* **cop'ied**. — *n* **cop'ier**. — *n* **cop'yist** a person whose job is to copy documents. — **cop'ybook** a writing or drawing book of models printed for imitation; a collection of copies of documents. — *adj* conventional or commonplace; (of an example, operation, etc.) perfect, or carried out flawlessly. — **cop'y-cat** (*colloq*) a term applied in resentful derision to an imitator. — *adj* imitated; done in imitation. — **cop'yholder** an assistant who reads copy to a proofreader; **cop'yright** the sole right to reproduce a literary, dramatic, musical or artistic work. — *adj* protected by copyright. — *vt* to secure the copyright of. — *adj* **cop'yrightable**. — **cop'y-taster** a person who selects items for publication or broadcast from the range of material submitted by reporters, etc.; **cop'y-typing**; **cop'y-typist** a typist who copies written, printed, etc. matter, not working from shorthand or recorded sound; **cop'ywriter** a writer of copy (esp. advertisements) for the press. [Fr. *copie*, from L. *cōpia*, plenty; in L.L. a transcript.]

coq au vin *kok-ō-vɛ̃*, (Fr.) *n* a dish of chicken cooked in red wine, with herbs, garlic, etc. [Fr., cock in wine.]

coquet or **coquette** *ko-* or *kō-ket'*, *vi* to flirt; to dally: — *pr p* **coquett'ing**; *pa p* and *pa t* **coquett'ed**. — *n* **cō'quetry** (*-kit-ri*) the act of coquetting; the attempt to attract admiration, without serious affection; deceit in love; any artful prettiness. — *n* **coquette'** a woman who flirts. — Also *adj*. — *adj* **coquett'ish** practising coquetry; typical of a coquette. — *adv* **coquett'ishly**. — *n* **coquett'ishness**. [Fr. *coqueter* — *coquet*, dimin. of *coq*, a cock.]

coquille *ko-kē'*, *n* (often in *pl*) a scallop; a dish or pastry case in the shape of a scallop or shell. [Fr., — L. *conchȳlium*, — Gr. *konchylion*, a cockle or mussel.]

Cor. *abbrev* for: (the Letters to the) Corinthians (*Bible*); Coroner.

cor *kör*, (*colloq*) *interj* an expression of surprise. — **cor blimey** a form of **gorblimey**. [Vulg. form of God.]

cor-. See **com-**.

coracle *kor'ə-kl*, *n* a small oval rowing-boat made by stretching hides over a wickerwork frame, used in Wales and Ireland. [Conn. with Welsh *corwg*, anything round.]

coral *kor'əl*, *n* a rocklike substance of various colours deposited on the bottom of the sea, formed from the skeletons, mostly calcareous, of some invertebrates of the classes *Anthozoa* and *Hydrozoa*; the invertebrates themselves; (in *pl*) a necklace of coral; a deep orange-pink colour. — *adj* made of coral, esp. red coral; like coral in colour; of a deep orange-pink. — *adj* **corallā'ceous** like, or having the qualities of, coral. — *adj* **corallif'erous** containing coral. — *adj* **coralliform** (*-al'*) having the form of coral. — *adj* **corallig'enous** producing coral. — *adj* **cor'alline** of, like, or containing coral. — *n* **cor'allite** the skeleton of a simple coral or of one polyp; a fossil coral. — *adj* **cor'alloid** in the form of coral; resembling coral. — **cor'al-fish** any of several kinds of tropical, spiny-finned fish which inhabit coral reefs; **coral-is'land** or **coral-reef'** a small island or reef formed by the growth and deposit of coral; **coral-rock'** limestone composed of coral. [L. *corallum* — Gr. *korallion*.]

cor anglais *kör ā'glā*, *n* an oboe set a fifth lower than the ordinary oboe. [Fr., English horn.]

corbel *kör'bəl*, (*archit*) *n* a projection from the face of a wall, supporting a weight. — *adj* **cor'belled** or in U.S. **cor'beled**. — *n* **cor'belling** or in U.S. **cor'beling**. — **corbel-ta'ble** a row of corbels and the parapet or cornice they support. — **corbel out** or **off** to (cause to) project on corbels. [O.Fr. *corbel* — L.L. *corvellus*, dimin. of *corvus*, a raven.]

corbicula *kör-bik'ū-lə*, *n* the pollen basket of bees, consisting of the dilated posterior tibia with its fringe of long hairs: — *pl* **corbic'ulae** (*-lē*). — *adj* **corbic'ulate**. [L. dimin. of *corbis*, a basket.]

corbie *kör'bi*, (*Scot*) *n* a raven; a crow. — **cor'bie-steps** the small stonework steps on the slopes of a gable, crow-steps. [O.Fr. *corbin* — L. *corvus*, a raven.]

cord *körd*, *n* a small rope or thick string; a part of the body resembling a cord (as spinal cord, umbilical cord); a measure of cut wood (128 cubic feet), orig. determined by the use of a cord or string; a raised rib on cloth; ribbed cloth, esp. corduroy (also *adj*); (in *pl*) corduroy trousers; a flex for an electrical apparatus. — *vt* to bind with a cord. — *n* **cord'age** a quantity of cords or ropes, as the rigging of a ship, etc. — *adj* **cord'ed** fastened with cords; ribbed; (of wood) piled in cords. — *n* **cord'ing** the act of binding; cordage. — *n* **cord'ite** a cord-like smokeless explosive. — *adj* **cord'less** (of an electrical device) operating without a flex; battery-powered. — *n* **cordot'omy** cutting in certain parts of the spinal cord to relieve great pain (also **chordot'omy**). [Fr. *corde* — L. *chorda*; see **chord**[2].]

cordate *kör'dāt*, *adj* heart-shaped; having the base indented next to the petiole (*bot*). — *adj* **cord'iform** heart-shaped. [L. *cor*, *cordis*, the heart.]

cordial *kör'di-əl*, *adj* friendly; hearty; sincere; affectionate; reviving the heart or spirits. — *n* a soft drink with a fruit base, usu. diluted before being drunk; a medicine or drink for refreshing the spirits; anything which revives or comforts the heart. — *n* **cordiality** (*-al'i-ti*) or **cor'dialness**. — *adv* **cor'dially**. [Fr., — L. *cor*, *cordis*, the heart.]

cordiform. See **cordate**.

cordillera *kör-dil-yā'rə*, *n* a chain of mountains, esp. the chain including the Andes and the Rocky Mountains. [Sp., — Old Sp. *cordilla* — L. *chorda*, cord.]

cordite. See under **cord**.

cordon *kör'dən*, *n* a cord or ribbon bestowed as a badge of honour; a line of police, soldiers, etc., or a system of road-blocks, encircling an area so as to prevent or control passage into or out of it; a row of stones along the line of a rampart (*fort*); a single-stemmed fruit-tree. — *vt* (often with *off*) to close (off) an area with a cordon of men, ring of barriers, etc. [Fr.]

cordon bleu *kor-dɔ̃ blø*, (Fr.) *n* blue ribbon; a cook of the highest excellence. — *adj* (of a cook or cookery) of a very high standard.

cordon sanitaire *kor-dɔ̃ sa-nē-ter*, (Fr.) *n* a line of sentries posted to restrict passage into and out of an area and so keep contagious disease within that area; neutral states keeping hostile states apart; a barrier (*lit* or *fig*) isolating a state, etc.

cordotomy. See under **cord**.

cordovan *kör'də-vən*, *n* goatskin leather, orig. from *Cordoba* in Spain.

corduroy *kör'də-roi* or *-roi'*, *n* a ribbed cotton fabric made after the fashion of velvet; (in *pl*) corduroy trousers. — *adj* made of corduroy. [Perh. Fr. *corde du roi*, king's cord or perh. **cord** and obs. *duroy*, a coarse woollen fabric.]

CORE *kör*, *abbrev* for Congress of Racial Equality (U.S.)

core *kör*, *n* in an apple, pear, etc. the central casing containing the seeds; the innermost or most essential part of something (also *adj*); the central part of the earth (*geol*); a cylindrical sample of rock, soil, etc. extracted by a drill; the lump of stone or flint remaining after flakes have been struck off it (*archaeol*); the part of a nuclear reactor containing the fissile material (*phys*); (also **magnetic core**) a small ferromagnetic ring which, charged or uncharged by electric current, can thus assume two states corresponding to the binary digits 0 and 1 (*comput*); a computer memory. — *vt* to take out the core of (an apple, etc.). — *adj* **cored** having the core removed; cast by means of a core; having a core. — *n* **cor'er** a device for removing the core of an apple, etc. — **core times** see **flexitime** under **flex**.

co-relation, co-relative. Same as **correlation** and **correlative**.

coreligionist *kō-rə-lij'ən-ist*, *n* a follower of the same religion as another.

coreopsis *kor-i-op'sis*, *n* a plant of the *Coreopsis* genus of annual or perennial composite plants mostly native to America, some species of which are cultivated for their showy flowers. [Gr. *koris*, a bug, *opsis*, appearance, from the shape of the seed.]

co-respondent *kō-rə-spond'ənt*, (*legal*) *n* a man or woman charged with adultery, and proceeded against along with the wife or husband who is the *respondent*.

corf *körf*, *n* a coalminer's basket, now usu. a trolley or wagon; a cage for fish or lobsters: — *pl* **corves** (*körvz*). [Du., — L. *corbis*, basket.]

Corfiot or **Corfiote** *kör'fi-ət*, *n* a native or citizen of Corfu. — Also *adj*.

CORGI *körgi*, *abbrev* for Confederation for the Registration of Gas Installers.

corgi *kör'gi*, *n* a Welsh breed of dog, with a foxlike head and short legs. [Welsh *corr*, dwarf, *ci*, dog.]

coriaceous. See **corium**.

coriander *kor-i-an'dər*, *n* a European umbelliferous plant whose leaves and seeds are used as a flavouring in food. [Fr. *coriandre* — L. *coriandrum* — Gr. *koriannon*.]

Corinthian *kor-inth'i-ən*, *adj* of *Corinth* in Greece; of an ornate style of Greek architecture, with acanthus capitals. — *n* a native or inhabitant of Corinth.

Coriolis effect *kor-i-ō'lis i-fekt'*, (*phys*) *n* the deflection (to the right in the Northern hemisphere, left in the Southern) and acceleration of bodies, etc. moving relative to the earth's surface, caused by the earth's rotation. [First studied by G.B. *Coriolis* (1792–1843).]

corium *kō'ri-əm*, *n* (*anat*) the inner skin, under the epidermis. — *adj* **coriā'ceous** leathery. [L. *corium* — Gr. *chorion*, skin, leather.]

cork *körk*, *n* the outer bark of the cork-tree, an oak found in S. Europe, N. Africa, etc.; a stopper made of cork; a tissue of close-fitting, thick-walled cells, almost airtight and watertight, forming bark or covering the surfaces of wounds (*bot*); a piece of cork; a fisherman's float made of cork. — *adj* made of cork. — *vt* to stop with a cork; to bottle up or repress (with *up*). — *n* **cork'age** a charge made in a restaurant, etc. for serving wine not bought on the premises. — *adj* **corked** (of wine) tainted as if by the cork, generally in fact by a fungus which develops on the cork. — *n* **cork'er** a person or thing that is an excellent example (of something) (*slang*); a person or device that inserts corks. — *n* **cork'iness**. — *adj* **cork'ing** (*slang*) surpassing; excellent. — *adj* **cork'y** of or resembling cork; (of wine) corked (*NAm*). — **cork'-oak** a S. European species of oak; **cork'-screw** a screw for drawing corks from bottles. — *adj* like a corkscrew in shape. — *vi* to move in a spiral manner; **cork'-tree** the cork-oak; **cork'wood** very light wood; applied to many trees with light wood, e.g. balsa. [Perh. from Sp. *alcorque*, cork slipper, which may be from L. *quercus*, oak.]

corm *körm*, *n* a bulb-like plant of which the crocus is an example. [Gr. *kormos*, the lopped trunk of a tree.]

cormorant *kör'mə-rənt*, *n* a member of a genus of shiny black web-footed sea-birds of great voracity. [Fr. *cormoran*, from L. *corvus marīnus*, sea crow.]

Corn. *abbrev* for: Cornish; Cornwall.

corn[1] *körn*, *n* collectively seeds of cereal plants, or the plants themselves — esp. (in England) wheat, (in Scotland and Ireland) oats and (in N. America) maize; a grain or hard particle; a kernel or small hard seed; something old-fashioned or hackneyed. — *adj* of, for, pertaining to, made from, growing among or feeding on, corn; granular. — *vt* to preserve with salt or brine. — *adj* **corned** salted (e.g. **corned beef** — also **corn'-beef**). — *adj* **corn'y** (*colloq*) of, like or abounding in corn; old-fashioned; uninteresting from frequent use; dull; over-sentimental. — **corn'-borer** a European moth whose larvae have become a maize pest in America; **corn'brash** (*geol*) a clayey limestone whose presence in soil affords good growth for cereal crops; **corn bread** or **cake** (*US*) bread or cake made of maize meal; **corn bunting** a common brown bunting (*Emberiza calandra*) of Europe and Asia; **corn'-chandler** a retailer of grain; **corn'-chandlery**; **corn circle** see **crop circle**; **corn cob** the woody core of a maize ear; **corn'crake** a small wading bird with characteristic cry, inhabiting cornfields; **corn dolly** a decorative figure made of plaited straw; **corn exchange** a building where trade in corn is (or was) carried on. — *adj* **corn'-fed** fed on corn; well fed. — **corn'-flag** a gladiolus; **corn'flakes** toasted flakes of maize, eaten esp. as a breakfast cereal; **corn'flour** finely ground maize, rice, or other grain, used esp. for thickening sauces; **corn'flower** a beautiful blue-flowered cornfield weed of the Compositae family; **corn law** a law regulating trade in grain, esp. (in *pl* with *cap*) laws that restricted importation to Britain by a duty, repealed in 1846; **corn pone** (*US*) maize-bread, often baked or fried; a maize loaf; **corn rent** rent paid in corn, not money; **corn'row** a hairstyle, esp. Afro-Caribbean, in which the hair is arranged in tightly braided flat rows; **corn shuck** (*NAm*) the leaves enclosing a maize ear; **corn'-shucking** the removal of corn shucks; a group of people gathered together for this purpose; **corn'starch** (*NAm*) cornflour; **corn'-thrips** a minute insect that sucks the sap of grain; **corn'-weevil** a small weevil, destructive in granaries; **corn whisky** an American whisky made from maize. — **corn cob pipe** a tobacco-pipe with the bowl made of a maize cob. — **corn on the cob** a cob of maize with grains still attached, boiled whole and eaten as a vegetable. [O.E. *corn*.]

corn[2] *körn*, *n* a small hard growth chiefly on the toe or foot, resulting from an increase of thickness of cuticle, caused by pressure or friction. — *adj* **cor'neous** horny. — *adj* **cornic'ulate** horned; horn-shaped. — *adj* **corn'y** of or pertaining to horns or corns; having corns; horny. — **corn plaster** a remedial plaster for corns. — **tread on someone's corns** to hurt someone's feelings. [L. *cornū*, a horn.]

cornea *kör'ni-ə*, *n* the transparent horny membrane that forms the front covering of the eye. — *adj* **cor'neal**. — **corneal lens** a contact lens covering the transparent part of the eye only. [L. *cornea* (*tēla*), horny (tissue).]

cornel *kör'nəl*, *n* any tree of the genus *Cornus*, particularly the cornelian-cherry or cornelian-tree, a small tree (*Cornus mas*) of middle and southern Europe. [L.L. *cornolium* — L. *cornus*, cornel.]

cornelian *kör-nē'li-ən* or **carnelian** *kär-nē'li-ən-* *n* a fine kind of quartz, generally translucent red. [Fr. *cornaline* — L. *cornū*, a horn, or *cornum*, cornelian-cherry.]

corneous. See **corn**[2].

corner *kör'nər*, *n* the point where two lines or several planes meet; an angular projection or recess; a secret or confined place; an awkward or embarrassing position; a difficulty; a free shot, taken from the corner of the field, given to the opposite side when a player in football or hockey plays the ball over their own goal-line; an operation by which the whole of a stock or commodity is bought up so that the buyers may resell at their own price. — *vt* to supply with corners; to put in a corner; to put in a fix or difficulty; to form a corner against; to get control of (a market for a particular commodity) by forming a corner. — *vi* to turn a corner. — *adj* **corn'ered**. — *adv* **corn'erwise** with the corner in front; diagonally. — **corn'erstone** a stone that unites the two walls of a building at a corner; the principal stone, esp. the corner of the foundation of a building; something of prime importance. — **fight** or **stand one's (own) corner** to defend strongly or maintain one's (own) position, stand, argument, etc.; **(just) round the corner** close at hand; soon to be attained, reached, etc.; **turn the corner** to go round the corner; to get past a difficulty or danger; to begin to pick up; **within the four corners of** contained in. [O.Fr. *corniere* — L. *cornū*, horn.]

cornet *kör'nit*, *n* a treble brass valve instrument, more tapering than the trumpet; a cornet-player; any funnel-shaped object, e.g. a piece of gold for assaying, an ice-cream-filled wafer cone, or a cream-filled pastry. — *n* **cor'netist** or **cornett'ist** a cornet-player. — *n* **cornettino** (*-tē'nō*) an instrument of the cornet family with a compass a fourth above that of a cornet (also **small cornet**). — *n* **corne'tto** or **corn'ett** a woodwind instrument with a mouthpiece like a trumpet's. [Fr. *cornet*, dimin. of *corne* — L. *cornū*, horn.]

cornice *kör'nis*, *n* a projecting moulding along the top of a building, window, etc.; a plaster moulding round a ceiling; a moulded ridge for supporting picture-hooks; the uppermost member of the entablature, surmounting the frieze (*classical archit*). — *vt* to furnish with a cornice. — *adj* **cor'niced**. [Fr., — It., poss. — Gr. *korōnis*, a curved line, cf. L. *corōna*.]

corniche *kor-nēsh'*, *n* a coast road built along a cliff-face. [Fr.]

corniculate. See under **corn**[2].

Cornish *kör'nish*, *adj* pertaining to Cornwall. — *n* the Celtic language of Cornwall, dead since the late 18th cent. — **Cornish pasty** a pasty (**pasty**[2]) with meat and vegetables.

cornucopia *kör-nū-kō'pi-ə*, *n* the horn of plenty — according to one fable, the horn of the goat that suckled Jupiter, placed among the stars as an emblem of plenty (*Gr mythol*); an ornamental vase in the shape of a horn; an abundant source of supply. — *adj* **cornucō'pian**. [L. *cornū cōpiae* — *cornū*, horn, *cōpia*, plenty.]

corny. See **corn**[1,2].

corolla *kor-ol'ə* or *-ōl'ə*, (*bot*) *n* the inner circle or whorl of the floral envelopes. — *adj* **corollā'ceous**. [L. *corolla*, dimin. of *corōna*, a crown.]

corollary *kər-ol'ə-ri* or in U.S. *kor'ə-lā-ri*, *n* an easy inference; a natural consequence or result. [L. *corollārium*, a garland, money for a garland, a tip — *corolla*.]

corona *ko-rō'nə* or *kə-*, *n* the large, flat, projecting member of a cornice crowning the entablature (*archit*); the trumpet of a daffodil, etc.; a coloured ring round the sun or moon, distinguished from the halo by having a red outer part; a round pendent chandelier: — *pl* **corō'nas** or **corō'nae** (*-ē*). — *n* **cor'onal** (*-ə-nl*) a circlet for the head; a small crown or garland. — *adj* **corō'nal** pertaining to a crown, a corona, or to the top of the head; like a crown. — *adj* **cor'onary** (*-ən-ə-ri*) coronal; surrounding a part (**coronary arteries** those that supply the muscle of the heart-wall with blood; so **coronary circulation**). — *n* a coronary thrombosis. — *adj* **cor'onāte** or **cor'onated** applied to shells with a row of projections round the apex. — *n* **coronā'tion** the ceremony of crowning a monarch. — **coronary thrombosis** stoppage of a branch of a coronary artery by a clot of blood. [L. *corōna*, a crown.]

coroner *kor'ə-nər*, *n* an officer whose chief duty is to enquire into the causes of accidental or suspicious deaths. [O.Fr. *corouner* — L. *corōna*, crown.]

coronet *kor'ə-nit*, *n* a small crown worn by the nobility; an ornamental headdress; the lowest part of a horse's pastern, just above the coffin bone. — *adj* **cor'oneted**. [O.Fr. *coronete*, dimin. of *corone*, crown — L. *corōna*.]

corozo *kor-ō'sō*, *n* a South American short-stemmed palm whose seed (**corozo nut**) gives vegetable ivory: — *pl* **corō'zos**. [Sp. from an Ind. language.]

Corp. *abbrev* for: Corporal; Corporation.

corpora. See **corpus**.

corporal[1] *kör'pə-rəl*, *n* a non-commissioned officer ranking next below a sergeant. — *n* **cor'poralship**. [Fr. *caporal* — It. *caporale* — *capo*, the head — L. *caput*, the head.]

corporal[2] *kör'pə-rəl* or *-prəl*, *adj* belonging or relating to the body; having a body; material, not spiritual. — *n* in Catholic and episcopal churches, the cloth on which the bread and wine of the Eucharist are laid out and with which the remains are covered. — *n* **corporality** (*-al'i-ti*). — *adv* **cor'porally**. — **corporal punishment** punishment inflicted on the body, e.g. flogging or hanging. [L. *corpus*, *corporis*, the body.]

corporate *kör'pə-rət*, *adj* legally united into a body so as to act as an individual; belonging or pertaining to a corporation; united. — *n* a company, as opposed to a private individual (*finance*). — *adv* **cor'porately**. — *n* **cor'porateness**. — *n* **corpora'tion** a body or society authorised by law to act as one individual unit; a town council; a company (*NAm*); a belly, esp. a pot-belly (*colloq*). — *n* **cor'poratism** (the policy of) control of a country's economy through the combined power of large businesses, etc. — *n* and *adj* **cor'poratist**. — **corporate hospitality** the entertaining by business companies of potential clients, esp. by wining and dining them at prestigious sporting events; **corporation aggregate** a corporation consisting of several people; **corporation sole** a corporation consisting of one person and his or her successors; **corporation tax** a tax levied on the income of companies. [L. *corpus*, *corporis*, the body.]

corporeal *kor-pō'ri-əl*, *adj* having a body or substance; material; not spiritual. — *n* **corpo'realism** materialism. — *n* **corpo'realist**. — *n* **corporeality** (*-al'i-ti*). — *adj* **corpo'really**. [L. *corpus*, the body.]

corps *kör*, *n* a division of an army forming a tactical unit; a branch or department of an army; a set of people working more or less together: — *pl* **corps** (*körz*). [Fr., — L. *corpus*, body.]

corps de ballet *kor də ba-le*, (Fr.) *n* the company of ballet dancers at a theatre. — **corps d'élite** (*kor dā-lēt*) (Fr.) a small number of people picked out as being the best in any group. — **corps diplomatique** (*dē-plō-ma-tēk*) (Fr.) the diplomatic corps.

corpse *körps*, *n* a dead human body. — *vi* (*theat slang*) (of an actor on stage) to begin to laugh, or to forget one's lines, etc. — *vt* (*theat slang*) to cause (an actor) to corpse. [L. *corpus*, the body.]

corpus *kör'pəs*, *n* a body of literature, law, etc.; any special structure in the body; the main part of anything: — *pl* **cor'pora** (*-pə-rə*). — *n* **cor'pūlence** or **cor'pūlency** fleshiness of body; excessive fatness. — *adj* **cor'pūlent**. — *adv* **cor'pūlently**. — *n* **cor'puscle** (*-pus-l*; sometimes *-pus'l*) a cell or other minute body suspended in fluid, esp. a red or white cell in the blood; a minute particle (also **corpus'cule**). — *adj* **corpus'cular**. — **corpus callosum** (*kə-los'əm*; L. *callosus*, callous, hard-skinned) in humans and higher mammals, a connecting column of nerve fibre between the two cerebral hemispheres: — *pl* **corpora callosa**; **corpus cavernosum** (*ka-vər-nō'səm*; L. *cavernosus*, cavernous, hollow) a section of erectile tissue in the penis or clitoris: — *pl* **corpora cavernosa**; **Corpus Christi** (*kris'tē*) the Christian festival in honour of the Eucharist, held on the Thursday after the festival of the Trinity; **corpus delicti** (*di-lik'tī*; *law*) the essential facts of the crime charged, e.g. in a murder trial, that somebody is actually dead and has been murdered; **corpus luteum** (*lōō'ti-əm*) a mass of yellow tissue that develops in a Graafian follicle after the discharge of an ovum, secreting progesterone: — *pl* **corpora lutea**; **corpus vile** (*vī'lē*) a person or thing considered so expendable as to be a fit object for experimentation, regardless of the consequences: — *pl* **corpora vilia** (*vil'i-ə*). [L. *corpus*, the body.]

corr. *abbrev* for: correspond; corrupted; corruption.

corrade *ko-* or *kə-rād'*, (*geol*) *vt* to wear away through the action of loose solid material, e.g. pebbles in a stream or wind-borne sand. — *n* **corrasion** (*-rā'zhən*). [L. *corrādĕre*, to scrape together — *con-*, together, *rādĕre*, *rāsum*, to scratch.]

corral *kə-ral'* or *ko-*, *n* a pen for cattle; an enclosure to drive hunted animals into; a defensive ring of wagons. — *vt* to pen; to form into a corral: — *pr p* **corrall'ing**; *pa t* and *pa p* **corralled'**. [Sp.]

correct *kə-rekt'*, *vt* to make right or supposedly right; to remove or mark faults or supposed faults from or in; to do this and evaluate; to set (a person) right; to punish; to counterbalance; to bring into a normal state. — *adj* right; according to standard; free from faults. — *adj* **correct'able** or **correct'ible**. — *adv* **correct'ly**. — *n* **correc'tion** emendation or would-be emendation; amendment; punishment; quantity to be added to bring to a standard or balance an error; a period of reversal or counteraction during a strong market trend (*US finance*). — *adj* **correc'tional**. — *n* **correct'itude** correctness of conduct or behaviour. — *adj* **correct'ive** of the nature of or by way of correction; tending to correct; correcting. — *n* that which corrects. — *n* **correct'ness**. — *n* **correct'or** a person who, or that which, corrects; a director or governor; a proofreader. — *adj* **cor-rect'ory** corrective. [L. *corrigĕre, corrēctum* — *cor-* (intensive) and *regĕre*, to rule.]

correlate *kor'i-lāt, vi* to be related to one another. — *vt* to bring into relation with each other; to establish relation or correspondence between. — *n* either of two things so related that one implies the other or is complementary to it. — *adj* **correlā'table**. — *n* **correlā'tion** the state or act of correlating; mutual relation, esp. of phenomena regularly occurring together; interdependence, or the degree of it. — *adj* **correlative** (*-el'ə-tiv*). — *n* a person or thing correspondingly related to another person or thing. — *adv* **correl'atively**. — *n* **correl'ativeness** or **correlativ'ity**. [L. *cor-*, with, and **relate**.]

corres. *abbrev* for corresponding.

correspond *kor-i-spond', vi* to answer, suit, agree (with *to* or *with*); to communicate, esp. by letter. — *n* **correspond'ence** or **correspond'ency** relation of agreement, part to part, or one to one; communication by letter; a body of letters; suitability; harmony. — *adj* **correspond'ent** answering; agreeing; suitable. — *n* a person with whom communication is kept up by letters; a person who contributes letters, or is employed to send special reports (e.g. *foreign correspondent, war correspondent*) to a periodical. — *adv* **correspond'ently**. — *adj* **cor-respond'ing** similar, comparable, matching; suiting; carrying on correspondence by letters; correspondent; answering. — *adv* **correspond'ingly**. — *adj* **correspon'sive** corresponding; answering. — **correspondence course** or **school**, etc., one conducted by postal correspondence. [L. *cor-*, with, *respondēre*, to respond.]

corrida *kō-rē'dhä*, (Sp.) *n* a bullfight. — Also **corrida de toros** (*dā tō'rōs*).

corridor *kor'i-dör, n* a passageway or gallery communicating with separate rooms or dwellings in a building or compartments in a railway train; a strip of territory or airspace by which a country, etc. has access to a particular place, e.g. a port, or providing access through another's land for a particular purpose. — **corridors of power** (*fig*) the higher reaches of government administration. [Fr., — It. *corridore* — It. *correre*, to run — L. *currĕre*.]

corrie *kor'i, n* a semicircular mountain recess or cirque. [Gael. *coire*, a cauldron.]

corrigendum *kor-i-jen'dəm, n* something which requires correction: — *pl* **corrigen'da**, used esp. for corrections to be made in a book. [L., gerundive of *corrigĕre*, to correct.]

corrigent *kor'i-jənt, adj* corrective. — *n* something with corrective properties or function, esp. a drug to counteract or reduce undesirable effects of others in a formula. — *adj* **corr'igible** that may be corrected; open to correction. — *n* **corrigibil'ity**. [L. *cor-rigĕre*; see **correct**.]

corroborate *kər-ob'ə-rāt, vt* to confirm; to make more certain. — *adj* **corrob'orable**. — *adj* **cor-rob'orative** tending to confirm. — *n* that which corroborates. — *n* **corroborā'tion** confirmation. — *n* **corrob'orātor**. — *adj* **corrob'oratory** corroborative. [L. *cor-* (intensive) and *rōborāre, -ātum*, to make strong; see **robust**.]

corroboree *kə-rob'ə-rē, n* a ceremonial dance of Australian Aborigines; a song for such a dance; a festive gathering. — *vi* to hold a corroboree. [Aboriginal.]

corrode *kər-ōd', vt* to eat away by degrees, esp. chemically; to rust. — *vi* to be eaten away. — *adj* **corrōd'ent** having the power of corroding. — *n* something which corrodes. — *n* **corrōsibil'ity**. — *adj* **corrōs'ible** (also **corrōd'ible**). — *n* **corrosion** (*-rō'zhən*) the act or process of eating or wasting away. — *adj* **corrōs'ive** having the quality of eating away. — *n* that which has the power of corroding. — *adv* **corrōs'ively**. — *n* **corrōs'iveness**. [L. *cor-* (intensive) and *rōdĕre, rōsum*, to gnaw.]

corrugate *kor'ə-* or *kor'oo-gāt, vt* to wrinkle or draw into folds. — *n* **corrugā'tion** the act of wrinkling or state of being wrinkled; a wrinkle. — **corrugated iron** sheet iron bent by ridged rollers into a wavy form for strength; **corrugated paper** a wrinkled paper used as wrapping material. [L. *cor-* (intensive) and *rūgāre, -ātum*, to wrinkle — *rūga*, a wrinkle.]

corrupt *kər-upt', vt* to taint, destroy the purity of; to pervert; to debase; to spoil; to bribe. — *vi* to rot, go bad; to lose purity, spoil. — *adj* defiled; depraved; dishonest, venal; of the nature of, or involving, bribery; bribed; not genuine or pure; rotten, putrid; debased or made very faulty in transcription; (of a computer program or data in store) containing errors arising e.g. from a fault in the hardware or software. — *n* **corrupt'er**. — *n* **corruptibil'ity**. — *adj* **corrupt'ible** liable to be corrupted. — *n* **cor-rupt'ibleness**. — *adv* **corrupt'ibly**. — *n* **corrup'-tion** the quality of being corrupt; a corrupt action; bribery; dishonesty; rottenness; impurity. — *n* **corrup'tionist** a person who defends or who practises corruption. — *adj* **corrupt'ive**. — *adv* **corrupt'ly**. — *n* **corrupt'ness**. [L. *cor-* (intensive) and *rumpĕre, ruptum*, to break.]

corsage *kör-säzh', n* the bodice of a woman's dress; a small bouquet to be worn there. [O.Fr., — *cors* — L. *corpus*, the body.]

corsair *kör'sār, n* a privateer (esp. of Barbary); a pirate. [Fr. *corsaire* — L. *cursus*, a running — *currĕre*, to run.]

corselet. See **corslet**.

corset *kör'sit, n* a close-fitting stiff inner bodice; stays; a stiff belt coming down over the hips; the controls imposed by the Bank of England to restrict banks' capacity to lend money (*colloq*). — *vt* to supply with a corset: — *pr p* **cor'seting**; *pa t* and *pa p* **cor'seted**. — *n* **corsetier** (*kor-sə-tyā*, also *-tēr'*), *fem* **cor-setière** (*kor-sə-tyer*, also *-tēr'*) a maker or seller of corsets. — *n* **cor'setry** corsets; the making or selling of corsets. [Dimin. of O.Fr. *cors* — L. *corpus*, the body.]

corslet or **corselet** *körs'lit, n* a cuirass, a protective body-covering of leather, or steel, etc.; a modified corset, or combined belt and brassière. — *adj* **cors'leted**. [Fr. *corselet*, dimin. of O.Fr. *cors* — L. *corpus*, the body.]

cortège *kör-tezh', n* a train of attendants; a procession, such as a funeral procession. [Fr., — It. *corte*, court.]

cortex *kör'teks, n* the bark or skin of a plant between the epidermis and the vascular bundles (*bot*); the outer layer of an organ, esp. of the brain (*zool*): — *pl* **cortices** (*kör'ti-sēz*) or sometimes **cor'texes**. — *adj* **cor'tical** pertaining to the cortex; external. — *adj* **cor'ticāte** or **cor'ticāted** furnished with bark. — *n* **corticoster'oid** or **cor'ticoid** any of the steroids, e.g. cortisone, extracted from the adrenal cortex. [L. *cortex, cortĭcis*, bark.]

cortisone *kör'ti-zōn* or *-sōn, n* 'compound E', a steroid isolated from the adrenal cortex, or prepared from ox bile, etc., an anti-inflammatory agent.

corundum *kə-run'dəm, n* a mineral consisting of alumina, second in hardness only to the diamond — varieties include sapphire, ruby and emery. [Tamil *kurundam*.]

coruscate *kor'əs-kāt, vi* to sparkle; to throw off flashes of light. — *adj* **coruscant** (*-rus'*) flashing. — *adj* **cor'uscating** (esp. *fig*, of wit). — *n* **coru-scā'tion** a glittering; sudden flash of light. [L. *coruscāre,-ātum*, to vibrate, glitter.]

corvée *kör-vā', (hist) n* the obligation to perform gratuitous labour (such as the maintenance of roads) for the sovereign or feudal lord. [Fr.,— L. *corrogāre* — *cor-*, together, *rogāre*, to ask.]

corves. See **corf.**

corvette *kör-vet'*, *n* an escort ship specially designed for protecting convoys against submarine attack; formerly a flush-decked vessel, with one tier of guns. [Fr., — Sp. *corbeta* — L. *corbīta*, a slow-sailing ship.]

Corvus *kör'vəs*, *n* the crow genus, typical of the family **Cor'vidae** and subfamily **Corvī'nae**. — *n* **cor'vid** (*zool*) a member of the Corvidae. — *adj* **cor'vine** (*-vīn*). [L. *corvus*, a raven.]

corybant *kor'ə-bant*, *n* a priest of the goddess Cybele, whose rites were accompanied with noisy music and wild dances (*Gr mythol*); a reveller. — *adj* **cory-ban'tic** wildly excited. — *n* **cor'ybantism.** [Gr. *korybās, korybantos.*]

corymb *kor'imb*, (*bot*) *n* a flattish-topped raceme. — *adj* **cor'ymbose** (or *kor-imb'ōz*). [L. *corymbus* — Gr. *korymbos*, a cluster.]

coryza *ko-rī'zə*, *n* a cold in the head; nasal catarrh. [L., — Gr. *koryza.*]

CoS *abbrev* for Chief of Staff.

cos[1] *kos*, *n* a crisp, long-leaved lettuce. — Also **cos lettuce.** [Introduced from the Aegean island of Cos (Gr. *Kōs*).]

cos[2] *kos* or *kōz*, *n* short for **cosine.**

'cos *koz* or *kəz*, (*colloq*) *adv* and *conj* because.

Cosa Nostra *kō'zə nos'trə*, *n* the Mafia organisation, esp. in U.S. [It., 'our thing'.]

cosecant *kō-sek'ənt* or *kō-sēk'ənt*, *n* one of the six trigonometrical functions of an angle, the reciprocal of the sine — identical with the secant of the complementary angle (short form **cosec** *kō'sek*).

cosech *kōs-ek'*, *n* short for *h*yperbolic *cosec*ant.

coseismal *kō-sīz'məl* or **coseismic** *kō-sīz'mik*, *adj* experiencing an earthquake shock simultaneously. [L. *co-*, together, Gr. *seismos*, earthquake.]

cosh[1] *kosh*, (*slang*) *n* a bludgeon, truncheon, lead-pipe, piece of flexible tubing filled with metal or the like, used as a weapon. — Also *vt*. [Prob. Romany, from *koshter*, a stick.]

cosh[2] *kosh* or *kos-āch'*, *n* short for *h*yperbolic *cos*ine.

COSHH *abbrev* for Control of Substances Hazardous to Health.

co-signatory *kō-sig'nə-tə-ri*, *adj* uniting with others in signing. — *n* someone who does so.

cosine *kō'sīn*, *n* one of the six trigonometrical functions of an angle, the ratio of the base to the hypotenuse — identical with the sine of the complementary angle (short form **cos** *kos* or *kōz*).

COSLA *koz'lə*, *abbrev* for Convention of Scottish Local Authorities.

cosmetic *koz-met'ik*, *adj* purporting to improve beauty, esp. that of the complexion; correcting defects of the face, etc., or making good particular deficiencies (e.g. *cosmetic surgery*); involving or producing an apparent or superficial concession, improvement, etc. without any real substance to it. — *n* (usu. in *pl*) a preparation for the improvement of beauty, etc. — *n* **cosmē'sis** cosmetic surgery or treatment. — *adj* **cosmet'ical.** — *adv* **cosmet'ic-ally.** — *n* **cosmeti'cian** a person who produces, sells, or is skilled in the use of, cosmetics (sometimes *fig*). — *vt* **cosmet'icise** or **-ize** to give cosmetic treatment to. — *n* **cosmet'icism.** — *n* **cos-metol'ogy** the art or profession of applying cosmetics or hairdressing, or of carrying out plastic surgery. [Gr. *kosmētikos* — *kosmeein*, to adorn — *kosmos*, order.]

cosmos[1] *koz'mos*, *n* any plant of the American genus of composites (*Cosmos*) related to the dahlia. [Gr. *kosmos*, ornament.]

cosmos[2] *koz'mos*, *n* the world or universe as an orderly or systematic whole (opp. to chaos); a complex but orderly system. — *adj* **cos'mic** relating to the cosmos; universal. — Also **cos'mical.** — *adv* **cos'mically.** — **cosmical constant** same as **cosmological constant; cosmic rays** highly penetrating rays from interstellar space, consisting of protons, electrons, positrons, etc. [Gr. *kosmos*, order, world, universe.]

cosmogony *koz-mog'ə-ni*, *n* a theory or myth of the origin of the universe, esp. of the stars, nebulae, etc. — *adj* **cosmogon'ic** or **cosmogon'ical.** — *n* **cosmog'onist** a person who speculates on the origin of the universe. [Gr. *kosmogonia* — *kosmos*, order, the universe and root of *gignesthai* to be born.]

cosmography *koz-mog'rə-fi*, *n* the science of the constitution of the universe; a description of the world or universe. — *n* **cosmog'rapher.** — *adj* **cosmograph'ic** or **cosmograph'ical.** [Gr. *kosmographia* — *kosmos*, order, the universe, *graphein*, to write.]

cosmology *koz-mol'əji*, *n* the science of the universe as a whole; a treatise on the structure and parts of the system of creation. — *adj* **cosmolog'ical.** — *n* **cosmol'ogist.** — **cosmological constant** a constant introduced by Einstein into his General Relativity equations to produce a solution in which the universe would be static — abandoned by him when the universe was later shown to be expanding, but still retained in various theoretical cosmological models with a value close to or equal to zero; **cosmological principle** according to the cosmology of general relativity, the principle that, at a given time, the universe would look the same to observers in other nebulae as it looks to us. [Gr. *kosmos*, order, the universe, *logos*, discourse.]

cosmonaut *koz'mə-nöt*, *n* an astronaut, *specif* a Soviet astronaut. [Russ. *kosmonaut*, — Gr. *kosmos*, the universe, *nautes*, a sailor.]

cosmopolitan *koz-mə-pol'i-tən*, *n* a citizen of the world; someone free from local or national prejudices. — *adj* belonging to, representative of, etc., all parts of the world; unprejudiced. — *n* **cosmo-pol'itanism.** — *n* and *adj* **cosmop'olite** (a) cosmopolitan. [Gr. *kosmopolītēs* — *kosmos*, the world, *polītēs*, a citizen, *polis*, a city.]

cosponsor *kō'spon-sər*, *vt* to sponsor jointly. — Also *n*.

Cossack *kos'ak*, *n* one of a people in south-eastern Russia, formerly serving as cavalry. — **Cossack hat** a brimless hat of fur or similar material. [Turk. *quzzāq*, freebooter.]

cosset *kos'it*, *vt* to fondle; to pamper: — *pr p* **coss'eting;** *pa t* and *pa p* **coss'eted.** — *n* a hand-reared lamb or other pet. [Perh. O.E. *cot-sǣta*, *cot-setla*, cot-dweller.]

cost *kost*, *vt* or *vi* to be obtainable at a price of; to involve an expenditure of; to require to be outlaid, suffered or lost: — *pa t* and *pa p* **cost.** — *vt* to estimate the cost of production of: — *pa t* and *pa p* **cos'ted.** — *n* what is or would have to be outlaid, suffered or lost to obtain anything; (in *pl*) the expenses of a lawsuit. — *n* **cost'liness.** — *adj* **cost'ly** high-priced; valuable. — **cost'-accountant** a person who analyses and classifies elements of cost, as material, labour, etc., or who devises systems of doing this; **cost'-accounting** (*vt* **cost'-account**). — *adj* **cost-effec'tive** giving adequate return for outlay. — **cost-effec'tiveness** or **cost efficiency.** — *adj* **cost'-free** free of charge. — Also *adv*. — **cost plus** a work contract where payment is based on the actual production cost plus an agreed percentage of that cost as profit. — *adj* **cost-plus'.** — **cost price** the price the merchant pays for goods bought; **cost push** (*econ*) inflation due to rising production costs. — **at all costs** no matter what the cost or consequences may be; **cost-benefit analysis (or assessment)** the comparison of the cost of a particular course of action with the benefits (to be) derived from it; **cost of living** the total cost of goods ordinarily required in order to live up to one's usual standard; **cost of living index** an official figure showing the cost of living at a certain date compared with that at another date taken as a standard; **prime cost** the price of production, without regard to profit or overhead expenses. [O.Fr. *couster* (Fr. *coûter*) — L. *cōnstāre*, to stand at.]

costa *kos'tə, n* a rib-like structure, vein, ridge: — *pl* **cos'tae** (*-ē*). — *adj* **cos'tal** of or near the ribs, the costa, or the side of the body. — *adj* **cos'tāte** or **cos'tated** having or resembling ribs. [L. *costa*, a rib.]

co-star *kō'stär, n* a cinema, TV etc. star appearing with other stars. — *vi* to appear with other stars: — *pr p* **co'-starring**; *pa t* and *pa p* **co'-starred**.

costard *kos'tərd, n* a large kind of apple. [Perh. L. *costa*, a rib.]

costate, costated. See **costa**.

costermonger *kos'tər-mung-gər* or **coster** *kos'tər, n* a seller of fruit and other wares from a barrow. [Orig. *costardmonger* — **costard** and **monger**.]

costive *kos'tiv, adj* constipated. — *adv* **cos'tively**. — *n* **cos'tiveness**. [Fr. *constipé*; see **constipate**.]

costmary *kost'mār-i, n* a composite plant of southern Europe, grown in gardens for its fragrant leaves. [L. *costum* — Gr. *kostos*, costus, and *Maria*, the Virgin Mary.]

costume *kos'tūm, n* a manner of dressing; dress, garb; a woman's outer dress as a unit; fancy dress; (a piece of) clothing for a particular purpose, as in *swimming-costume*. — *vt* (*kos-tūm'* or in U.S. *-tōōm'*) to dress. — *adj* **costumed'**. — *n* **costum'er** or **costum'ier** a person who makes or deals in costumes. — **costume drama, piece** or **play** one in which the actors wear the costumes of an earlier era; **costume jewellery** jewellery made of paste rather than real gemstones, worn for adornment only. [Fr., — It. *costume* — L. *cōnsuētūdō, -inis*, custom.]

Costus *kos'təs, n* a genus of plants of the ginger family; (without *cap*) an aromatic root wrongly assigned to it. [Latinised from Gr. *kostos*.]

cosy *kō'zi, adj* snug; comfortable. — *n* a covering used for a teapot, to keep the tea warm (also **tea'-cosy**); a similar covering for a boiled egg. — *adv* **cō'sily**. — *n* **cō'siness**. — **cosy along** (*colloq*) to reassure, often with falsehoods; **cosy up** (*colloq*, esp. *US*; with *to* or *with*) to try to gain someone's favour or friendship.

cot[1] *kot*, (*poetic*) *n* a small dwelling, a cottage. [O.E. *cot*.]

cot[2] *kot, n* a small bed, esp. one with high sides for a young child; a swinging bed of canvas (for officers, the sick, etc.) (*naut*); a hospital bed. — **cot death** the sudden, unexplained death in sleep of an apparently healthy baby. — Also called **sudden infant death syndrome**. [Anglo-Ind., — Hindi *khāṭ*.]

cot[3] *kot, n* short for cotangent.

cot[4]. See **cote**.

cotangent *kō-tan'jənt, n* one of the six trigonometrical functions of an angle, the reciprocal of the tangent — identical with the tangent of the complementary angle.

cote *kōt* or **cot** *kot, n* a place, shelter, for animals (as in *dovecote* or *dovecot*, *sheepcote*). [O.E. *cote*; cf. **cot**[1].]

coterie *kō'tə-ri, n* a social, literary or other exclusive circle. [Fr.; orig. a number of peasants holding land jointly from a lord — L.L. *cota*, a cot.]

coth *koth, n* short for *h*yperbolic *cot*angent.

co-tidal *kō-tīd'l, adj* having high tide at the same time.

cotillion *ko-til'yən* or **cotillon** *ko-tē'yɔ̃, n* a sort of lively dance with varied steps; a formal (esp. a coming-out) ball (*US*). [Fr., petticoat — *cotte*, a coat.]

Cotinga *kō-ting'gə, n* a tropical American genus of bright plumaged passerine birds; (without *cap*) any bird of its family, **Cotingidae** (*-tin'ji-dē*). [Of Tupí origin.]

cotoneaster *ko-tō-ni-as'tər, n* a plant of the *Cotoneaster* genus of shrubs or small trees related to hawthorn. [L. *cotōnea*, quince.]

cotta *kot'ə, n* a short surplice. [L.L.]

cottage *kot'ij, n* a small dwelling-house; a country residence; a public lavatory used by homosexuals for soliciting (*slang*). — *n* **cott'ager** a person who lives in a cottage, esp. a rural labourer. — *adj* **cott'agey**. — *n* **cott'aging** (of male homosexuals) soliciting in public lavatories. — **cottage cheese** soft white loose cheese made from skim-milk curds; **cottage hospital** a small, rural hospital without resident doctors; **cottage industry** one in which the work is done wholly or largely by people in their own homes; **cottage loaf** a loaf consisting of a smaller lump on the top of a bigger one; **cottage piano** a small upright piano; **cottage pie** shepherd's pie. [L.L. *cottagium* — O.E. *cot*; see **cot**[1].]

cotter *kot'ər, n* a pin or wedge for fastening and tightening. — *n* **cott'er-pin** a pin for keeping a cotter in place.

cotton *kot'n, n* a soft substance like fine wool, the long hairs covering the seeds of the cotton-plant; the plant itself, individually or collectively; yarn or cloth made of cotton. — *adj* made of cotton. — *adj* **cott'ony**. — **cotton belt** (sometimes with *caps*) the region in the south-eastern United States in which much cotton is produced; **cott'on-boll** the pod of the cotton-plant; **cotton cake** cakes or pellets of compressed cotton-seed, used as an animal feed; **cotton candy** (*US*) candy floss; **cott'on-gin** a machine for separating the seeds from the fibre of cotton; **cott'on-mill** a factory where cotton is spun or woven. — *adj* **cott'on-picking** (*US slang*; sometimes *facetious*) used as a relatively mild pejorative. — **cott'on-plant** one of various species of *Gossypium*, yielding cotton; **cott'on-press** a press for compressing cotton into bales; **cott'on-seed** the seed of the cotton-plant, yielding a valuable oil; **cott'ontail** any of several species of rabbits of the genus *Sylvilagus*, the ordinary U.S. rabbit; **cott'on-wood** any one of several American species of poplar; **cotton-wool'** loose cotton pressed in a sheet as an absorbent or protective agent, for stuffing, etc.; a protected, cushioned or cosseted state (*fig*); padding, waffle; cotton in its raw or woolly state. — **cotton on to** (*slang*) to understand, get the hang of. [Fr. *coton* — Ar. *qutun*.]

cotyledon *kot-i-lē'dən, n* a seed-leaf (*bot*); (with *cap*) a genus of S. African plants; a plant of this genus. — *adj* **cotylē'donary** like a seed-leaf. — *adj* **cotylē'donous** pertaining to or having cotyledons. [Gr. *kotylēdōn* — *kotylē*, a cup.]

coucal *kōō'käl, n* any member of a genus (*Centropus*) of common bush-birds in Africa, India and Australia, the lark-heeled cuckoos. [Imit.]

couch[1] *kowch, vt* to lay down; to cause to lie down; to arrange in language, to express; to depress or remove (a cataract in the eye); to level. — *vi* to lie down for the purpose of sleep, concealment, etc. — *n* a kind of sofa with half back and one raised end; any sofa; any place for rest or sleep; a bed, esp. for daytime use, e.g. one on which a doctor's or psychiatrist's patient lies for examination. — *adj* **couch'ant** lying down with head up (*heraldry*). — *n* **couch'ing** embroidery in which the surface is covered with threads and these are secured by stitches forming a pattern. — **couch potato** (*slang*, orig. *US*) a person whose leisure time is spent sitting shiftlessly in front of the television or video. [Fr. *coucher*, to lay down — L. *collocāre*, to place.]

couch[2] *kowch, kōōch* or **couch grass** (*gräs*), *n* a grass related to wheat, a troublesome weed owing to its creeping rootstocks. [A variant of **quitch**.]

couchette *kōō-shet', n* a sleeping-berth on a continental train or a cross-channel boat, convertible from and into ordinary seating. [Fr.]

coudé *koo-dā'*, (*astron*) *adj* (of a reflecting telescope) in which one or more plane mirrors reflect the light down the polar axis. [Fr., bent like an elbow.]

cougar *koo'gär* or *-gər*, *n* a puma. [Fr. *couguar* — Port. *cucuarana*, adapted from a Tupí-Guaraní name.]

cough *kof*, *vi* to expel air with a sudden opening of the glottis and a characteristic harsh sound. — *vt* to expel by coughing. — *n* the act or the sound of coughing; an ailment of which coughing is a symptom. — *n* **cough'er**. — *n* **cough'ing**. — **cough'-drop** or **cough'-lozenge** a medicated lozenge to relieve a cough; **cough'-mixture** a liquid medicine to relieve a cough. — **cough up** (*slang*) to pay out, hand over, under compulsion. [M.E. *coughen*.]

could *kood*, *pa t* of **can**[1]. — **could be** (*colloq*) perhaps, maybe. [M.E. *coude, couth* — O.E. *cūthe* for *cunthe*, was able; *l* is inserted from the influence of *would* and *should*.]

coulée *koo-lā'*, *n* a lava-flow; a ravine (*NAm*). [Fr. *couler*, to flow.]

coulis *koo-lē*, (Fr.) *n* a thin purée of fish, fowl or vegetables.

coulisse *koo-lēs'*, *n* a piece of grooved wood, as the slides in which the side-scenes of a theatre run — hence (in *pl*) the wings. [Fr. *couler*, to glide, to flow — L. *cōlāre*, to strain.]

couloir *kool-wär'*, *n* a gully. [Fr., passage.]

coulomb *koo-lom'*, *n* the MKSA and SI unit of electric charge (static or as a current), supplied by one ampere flowing for one second. — *n* **coulom'eter** a voltameter. — *adj* **coulomet'ric**. [From the Fr. physicist, C. A. de *Coulomb* (1736–1806).]

coulter or (esp. in U.S.) **colter** *kōl'tər*, *n* the iron cutter in front of a ploughshare. [O.E. *culter* — L. *culter*, knife.]

coumarin or **cumarin** *koo'mə-rin*, *n* a crystalline compound ($C_9H_6O_2$) obtained from tonkabeans, woodruff, etc. used for scenting tobacco, flavouring, etc. — *adj* **coumaric** (*-mar'ik*). [Tupí *cumarú*, tonkabean.]

council *kown'sl* or *-sil*, *n* an assembly called together for deliberation, advice, administration or legislation; the people making up such an assembly; the body directing the affairs of a town, county, parish, etc.; an assembly of ecclesiastics met to regulate doctrine or discipline; a governing body in a university; a committee that arranges the business of a society. — Also *adj*. — *n* **coun'cillor** or in U.S. **coun'cilor** a member of a council. — **coun'cil-chamber** the room where a council is held; **council estate** an area set apart for council-houses; **coun'cil-house** a house in which a council meets; a house erected by a municipal council; **council tax** a tax based on and banded according to property value, with discount for people living alone, proposed to replace poll tax. — **Council of Ministers** in the EEC, the decision-making body comprising ministers of the member countries; **council of war** a conference of officers called to consult with the commander (also *fig*); **in council** in the council-chamber; in consultation; **legislative council** a council to assist a governor, with power to make laws. [Fr. *concile* — L. *concilium*.]

counsel *kown'sl*, *n* advice; consultation; deliberation; a person who gives counsel, a barrister or advocate. — *vt* to advise; to warn: — *pr p* **coun'selling**; *pa t* and *pa p* **coun'selled**. — *adj* **couns'ellable**. — *n* **coun'selling** (a service consisting of) helping people to adjust to or deal with personal problems, etc. by enabling them to discover for themselves the solution to the problems while receiving sympathetic attention from a counsellor; (sometimes) the giving of advice on miscellaneous problems. — Also *adj*. — *n* **coun'sellor** or in U.S. **coun'selor** a person who counsels; a person involved in counselling; a barrister. — *n* **coun'sellorship** or in U.S. **coun'selorship**. — **counsel of perfection** an impractical ideal; **keep counsel** to keep a secret; **Queen's Counsel** (abbrev. **QC**) or **King's Counsel** (abbrev. **KC**) a barrister or advocate appointed by letters-patent — the office is honorary, but gives the right of precedence in all the courts. [Fr. *conseil* — L. *consilium*, advice — *consulĕre*, to consult.]

count[1] *kownt*, *n* on the Continent, a noble equal in rank to an earl. — *n* **count'ess** a lady of the same rank as a count or earl; the wife of a count or earl. — *n* **count'ship**. [O.Fr. *conte* — L. *comes, comitis*, a companion — *con-*, with, *īre*, to go.]

count[2] *kownt*, *vt* to number, sum up; to name the numerals up to; to take into account, reckon as significant or to be recognised; to reckon, esteem, consider. — *vi* to number; to be numbered; to be of account; to be recognised in reckoning; to have a certain value; to reckon; to name the numerals in order. — *n* the act of numbering; reckoning; the number counted; the counting of the seconds (by a referee) in which a fallen man may get up and resume fighting (also **count'-out**; *boxing*); esteem, consideration, account; a particular charge in an indictment (*law*). — *adj* (of a noun) which is able to form a plural. — *adj* **count'able** capable of being counted; to be counted; accountable; (of a noun) count. — *adj* **count'ed** accounted, reckoned. — *n* **count'er** a person who or that which counts; that which indicates a number; a disc or similar, used in reckoning or (in *games*) as a substitute for a coin or a marker of one's position on a board; a table or raised surface over which goods are laid, money counted, food is served, etc. — *adj* **count'less** that cannot be counted; innumerable. — **count'-down** a descending count or counted check to a moment of happening regarded as zero, as in the firing of a rocket; **count'ing-frame** a frame having moveable beads, used for elementary counting, etc., an abacus. — *adj* **count'line** (of a confectionery bar) made as an individual line (e.g. a filled or chocolate-covered combination bar), as distinct from moulded chocolate. — **count-out** see **count** above; **count out** (of a meeting, esp. of the House of Commons) to bring to an end by pointing out that a quorum is not present; (in children's games) to eliminate players by counting while repeating a rhyme; to judge (a boxer) defeated by counting the maximum allowable seconds in which to resume. — **keep count** to keep an accurate numerical record (of); **lose count** to fail to keep count (of); **out for the count** (*fig*) unconscious, or completely exhausted; **over the counter** (*adj* **over-the-count'er**) (of goods, esp. drugs) legally sold direct to the customer; involving trading in shares not on the official Stock Exchange list; **under the counter** hidden from customers' sight (*adj* **under-the-count'er** reserved for the favoured customer; sold, or procured, illegally or secretly). [O.Fr. *cunter* (Fr. *compter*) — L. *computāre*.]

countenance *kown'tən-əns*, *n* the face; the expression of the face; favour, approbation; acquiescence, sanction. — *vt* to favour, approve or sanction. [O.Fr. *contenance* — L. *continentia*, restraint, demeanour — *continēre*, to contain.]

counter[1] *kown'tər*, *adv* the opposite way; in opposition. — *adj* contrary; opposing; opposite. — *n* that which is counter or opposite; the part of a ship's stern from the lower moulding to the waterline (*naut*). — *vt* to contradict; to meet or answer by a stroke or move; to strike while receiving or parrying a blow (*boxing*). — **run counter to** to move in the opposite direction to; to act or happen in a way contrary to (instructions, expectations, etc.). [Partly aphetic for **encounter**, partly directly from A.Fr. *countre*, O.Fr. (Fr.) *contre* — L. *contrā*, against.]

counter[2]. See **count**[2].

counter- *kown-tər-*, *combining form* signifying against. — *n* **coun'ter-attack** an attack in reply to an attack. — Also *vt* and *vi*. — *n* **coun'ter-attraction** attraction in an opposite direction; a rival show. — *vt* **counterbal'ance** to balance by weight on the opposite side; to act against with equal weight, power or influence. — *n* **coun'terbalance** an equal weight, power or agency working in opposition. — *n* **coun'ter-bid** a bid made in opposition to another bid. — *n* **coun'ter-bidder**. — *n* **coun'terblast** a defiant pronouncement or denunciation. — *n* **coun'terblow** a return blow. — *n* **coun'terbluff** actions or words intended as a bluff, made in opposition to someone else's bluff. — *n* **coun'ter-bore** a straight-sided widening of the end of a bored hole; a drill for making this. — *vt* to form a counter-bore in. — *vt* **coun'tercharge** a charge brought forward in opposition to another charge. — Also *vi*. — *vt* **countercheck'** to check by opposing, separate or additional means. — *n* **coun'tercheck** a check in opposition or addition to another. — *n* **coun'ter-claim** (esp. *law*) a claim brought forward as a partial or complete set-off against another claim. — *adv* **coun'ter-clockwise** in a direction contrary to that of the hands of a clock. — *n* **coun'ter-culture** a way of life deliberately different from that which is normal or expected. — *n* **counter-esp'ionage** espionage directed against the enemy's spy system or action taken to counter it in one's own country. — *n* **coun'ter-force** an opposing force. — *n* **counter-insur'gency** action taken against insurgents. — Also *adj*. — *n* **counter-intell'igence** activities (e.g. censorship, camouflage, use of codes, etc.) aimed at preventing an enemy from obtaining information, or the organisation that carries these out. — *n* **counter-irr'itant** an irritant used to relieve another irritation. — *vi* **coun'termarch** to march back or in a direction contrary to a former one. — *n* a marching back or in a direction different from a former one. — *n* **coun'termeasure** an action intended to counteract the effect of another action or happening. — *n* **coun'ter-move** or **-movement** a contrary move or movement. — *n* **coun'ter-offensive** counter-attack; an attack by the defenders. — *vt* **coun'ter-plot** to plot against in order to frustrate another plot. — *n* a plot or stratagem opposed to another plot. — *adj* **counter-produc'tive** acting against productivity, efficiency or usefulness. — *n* **coun'ter-proposal** one which proposes an alternative to a proposal already made. — *n* **Counter-Reforma'tion** (*hist*) a reform movement within the Roman Catholic Church, following and counteracting the Reformation. — *n* **counter-revolu'tion** a subsequent revolution counteracting the effect of a previous. — *n* and *adj* **counter-revolu'tionary** (a person) opposing a particular revolution or opposed to revolutions. — *n* **coun'terscarp** (*fort*) the side of the ditch nearest to the besiegers and opposite to the scarp. — *n* **coun'tershaft** an intermediate shaft driven by the main shaft. — *vt* **countersign'** to sign on the opposite side of a writing; to sign in addition to the signature of a superior, to attest the authenticity of a writing. — *n* (*kownt'ər-sīn*) a military private sign or word, which must be given in order to pass a sentry. — *n* **counter-sig'nature** a name countersigned to a writing. — *vt* **coun'tersink** to bevel the edge of (a hole), as for the head of a screw-nail; to set the head or top of on a level with, or below, the surface of the surrounding material. — *n* **coun'ter-tenor** the highest alto male voice (so called because a contrast to tenor). — *n* **coun'ter-weight** weight in an opposite scale; a counterbalancing influence or force. [A.Fr. *countre*, O.Fr. *contre* — L. *contrā*, against.]

counteract *kown-tər-akt'*, *vt* to act counter or in opposition to; to neutralise. — *n* **counterac'tion**. — *adj* **counterac'tive**. [**counter-** and **act**.]

counterfeit *kown'tər-fit* or *-fēt*, *vt* to imitate; to copy without authority; to forge. — *n* something false or copied, or that pretends to be true and original. — *adj* pretended; made in imitation; forged; false. — *n* **coun'terfeiter**. — *adv* **coun'terfeitly**. [O.Fr. *contrefet*, from *contrefaire*, to imitate — L. *contrā*, against, *facĕre*, to do.]

countermand *kown-tər-mänd'*, *vt* to give a command in opposition to one already given; to revoke. — *n* (*kownt'*) a revocation to a former order. — *adj* **countermand'able**. [O.Fr. *contremander* — L. *contrā*, against, *mandāre*, to order.]

counterpane *kown'tər-pān*, *n* a coverlet for a bed. [O.Fr. *contrepoint* — *coultepointe* — L. *culcita puncta*, a stitched pillow; see **quilt**.]

counterpart *kown'tər-pärt*, *n* the part that answers to, fits into or completes another part, having the qualities which the other lacks; a duplicate, close or exact copy. [**counter-**.]

counterpoint *kown'tər-point*, *n* the art of combining melodies (*mus*); a melody added to another (*mus*); an opposite point. — *vt* to write in counterpoint; to set in contrast for effect. — *adj* **contrapunt'al**. — *n* **contrapunt'ist** a composer skilled in counterpoint. [Fr. *contrepoint* and It. *contrappunto* — L. *contrā*, against, *punctum*, a point, from the pricks, points or notes placed against those of the melody; in some senses **counter-** and **point**.]

counterpoise *kown'tər-poiz*, *vt* to poise or weigh against or on the opposite side; to act in opposition to with equal effect. — *n* an equally heavy weight in the other scale. [**counter-**.]

countervail *kown-tər-vāl'*, *vt* to act against with equal effect; to be of equal value to; to compensate. [O.Fr. *contrevaloir* — *contre* (— L. *contra*, against), *valoir*, to be of avail (— L. *valere*, to be strong).]

country *kun'tri*, *n* a region; a state; a nation; rural districts as distinct from town; the land of one's birth or citizenship; country music. — *adj* belonging to the country; rural; rustic. — *adj* **coun'trified** or **coun'tryfied** like or suitable for the country in style; like a person from the country in style or manner. — **country-and-west'ern** a popularised form of music deriving from the rural folk-music of the United States. — Also *adj*. — **country club** a club in the country which has facilities for sport, leisure and social activities; **country cousin** a relative from the country, unaccustomed to town sights or manners; **country-dance'** a dance as practised by country people; a type of dance either for an indefinite number of couples in a circle or two lines, or for groups of fixed numbers of couples in two lines, having a precise and sometimes complex pattern of movements; **country-dan'cing**; **coun'try-folk** fellow-countrymen; rural people; **country gentleman** a landed proprietor who resides on his estate in the country; **country-house'** or **-seat'** a large house, or property, in the country; **coun'tryman** a man who lives in the country; a man belonging to the same country, fellow-countryman; **country music** the folk-music of the rural areas of the United States; country-and-western music; both of these taken together; **coun'tryside** a district or part of the country; rural districts in general; **country town** a small town in a rural district. — *adj* **countrywide'** all over the country. — **coun'trywoman** a woman who lives in the country; a woman of the same country. — **go to the country** (*politics*) to appeal to the community by calling a general election. [O.Fr. *contrée* — L.L. *contrāta*, *contrāda*, an extension of L. *contrā*, over against.]

county *kown'ti*, *n* a portion of a country separated for administrative, parliamentary or other purposes, a shire. — *adj* of a, or the, county; of county family. — **county council** a council for managing the public affairs of a county; **county councillor**; **county court** the highest court of law within a county; **county cricket** cricket played in matches between clubs representing counties; **county family** a family of nobility or gentry (**coun'ty-people**) with estates and a seat in the county; **county hall** the administrative centre of a county; **county town** the town in which the public business of the county is transacted. [**count[1]**.]

coup *kōō*, *n* a blow, stroke; a clever and successful stroke in a board or card game; a masterstroke, clever and successful stratagem (*fig*); a coup d'état. — **coup de foudre** (*də fōō-dr'*) a sudden and astonishing happening; love at first sight; **coup de grâce** (*də gräs*) a finishing blow to put out of pain; a finishing stroke generally; **coup de main** (*də mẽ*) a sudden overpowering attack; **coup d'état** (*dā-tä*) a violent or subversive stroke of state policy; **coup de théâtre** (*də tā-ätr'*) a sudden and sensational turn of events, e.g. in a play; **coup d'oeil** (*dœy*) a general view at a glance. [Fr., — L.L. *colpus* — L. *colaphus* — Gr. *kolaphos*, a blow.]

coupe[1] *kōōp*, (Fr.) *n* a dessert, usu. made with ice-cream and often fruit, served in a glass bowl; a glass container for serving such a dessert, usu. with a shallow bowl and a short stem.

coupe[2] *kōōp*, (*US*) *n* a coupé (motor car).

coupé *kōō-pā'*, *n* a four-wheeled carriage seated for two inside, with a separate seat for the driver; a two-door motor car with a roof sloping towards the back. [Fr., past p. of *couper*, to cut.]

couple *kup'l*, *n* two of a kind joined together, or connected; two, a pair; two people considered as partners, esp. a man and a woman; that which joins two things together, a link. — *vt* to join together. — *vi* to pair sexually. — *n* **coup'ledom**. — *n* **coup'ler** someone who or that which couples or unites; an organ mechanism by which stops of one manual can be played from another or from the pedals. — *n* **coup'let** a pair, couple; a twin; two successive lines that rhyme with each other (*poetry*). — *n* **coup'ling** that which connects; an appliance for transmitting motion in machinery, or for connecting vehicles as in a railway train. — **a couple of** (*loosely*) two or three; a few. [O.Fr. *cople* — L. *cōpula*.]

coupon *kōō'pon* or *-pən*, *n* a billet, check, or other slip of paper cut off from its counterpart; a separate ticket or part of a ticket; a voucher certifying that payments will be made, services performed, goods sold, etc.; a piece cut from an advertisement entitling one to some privilege; a printed betting form on which to enter forecasts of sports results. [Fr. *couper*, to cut off.]

courage *kur'ij*, *n* the quality that enables people to meet danger without giving way to fear; bravery; spirit. — *interj* take courage. — *adj* **courageous** (*kə-rā'jəs*) full of courage; brave. — *adv* **courā'geously**. — *n* **courā'geousness**. — **Dutch courage** artificial courage induced by drinking; **pluck up courage** or **take one's courage in both hands** to nerve oneself; to gather boldness; **the courage of one's convictions** courage to act up to, or consistently with, one's opinions. [O.Fr. *corage* (Fr. *courage*), from L. *cor*, the heart.]

courant *kōō-rant'*, *adj* (*heraldry*) in a running attitude. — *n* **courante** or **courant** (*kōō-ränt'*) an old dance with a kind of gliding step; music for it. [Fr., pres. p. of *courir*, to run; see **current**.]

courgette *kōōr-zhet'*, *n* a small marrow. [Fr. *courge*, gourd.]

courier *kōō'ri-ər*, *n* a messenger, esp. one employed to deliver special or urgent messages or items; a state or diplomatic messenger; an official guide and organiser who travels with tourists; a title of certain newspapers. [Fr., lit. a runner — L. *currĕre*, to run.]

course *kōrs*, *n* the path in which anything moves; the ground over which a race is run, golf is played, etc.; a channel for water; the direction pursued; regular progress from point to point; a habitual method of procedure; a prescribed series, sequence, process or treatment, as of lectures, training, pills, etc.; each of the successive divisions of a meal — soup, fish, etc.; a range of bricks or stones on the same level in building. — *vt* to run, chase or hunt after; to use in coursing. — *vi* to run; to move with speed, as in a race or hunt. — *n* **cours'er** a swift horse; a person who courses or hunts; a swift running bird. — *n* **cours'ing** hunting esp. of hares with greyhounds, by sight rather than by scent. — **course'work** work that goes to make up an educational course. — **in due course** eventually; at a suitable later time; **in the course of** during; in the process of; undergoing (something); **in the course of time** eventually; with the passing of time; **of course** by natural consequence; indisputably; it must be remembered (often used to introduce a comment on a preceding statement); **run (or take) its** or **their course** to proceed or develop freely and naturally, usu. to a point of completion or cessation; **the course of nature** or **the normal**, etc. **course of events** the usual way in which things happen or proceed. [Fr. *cours* — L. *cursus*, from *currĕre, cursum*, to run.]

court *kōrt*, *n* an enclosed space, such as one surrounded by houses; a piece of ground or floor on which certain games are played; a division marked off by lines on such a place; the palace of a sovereign; the body of persons who form the sovereign's suite or council; an assembly of courtiers; a hall of justice (*law*); the judges and officials who preside there; any body of persons assembled to decide causes; a sitting of such a body. — *vt* to pay attentions to; to woo; to solicit; to seek. — *n* **court'ier** someone who frequents courts or palaces; a person who courts or flatters. — *n* **court'ing** wooing. — *n* **court'liness**. — *adj* **court'ly** having manners like those of, or befitting, a court; politely stately; fair and flattering. — *n* **court'ship** the act or process of wooing a woman in order to persuade her to become one's wife; the period of time over which this is carried out; courtly behaviour. — **court'-day** a day on which a judicial court sits; **court'-house** a building where the law-courts are held; **courtly love** a conception and tradition of love, originating in late mediaeval European literature, in which the knight sublimates his love for his lady in submission, service and devotion; **court-mar'tial** a court held by officers of the army, navy or air force for the trial of offences against service law: — *pl* **courts-mar'tial** or (*colloq*) **court-mar'tials**. — *vt* to try before a court-martial: — *pr p* **court-mar'tialling**; *pa t* and *pa p* **court-mar'tialled**. — **court order** a direction or command of a justiciary court; **court'-roll** the record of a court of justice; **court'room** a room in a court-house in which lawsuits and criminal cases are heard; **court shoe** a ladies' dress shoe without straps or laces; **court tennis** the game of tennis, distinguished from lawn tennis (also **real** or **royal tennis**); **court'yard** a court or enclosed ground attached to a house. — **go to court** to institute legal proceedings against someone; **hold court** to preside over admiring followers, etc.; **laugh someone out of court** see under **laugh**; **out of court** without a trial in a law-court; without claim to be considered. [O.Fr. *cort* (Fr. *cour*) — L.L. *cortis*, a courtyard — L. *cors, cohors,-tis*, an enclosure.]

court bouillon *kōōr bōō-yɔ̃'*, *n* a seasoned stock made with water, vegetables and wine or vinegar, in which fish is boiled. [Fr. *court*, short — L. *curtus*, and **bouillon**.]

Courtelle® *kōōr-tel'*, *n* a synthetic acrylic wool-like fibre.

courteous *kûrt'yəs*, *adj* polite, considerate or respectful in manner and action; obliging. — *adv* **court'eously**. — *n* **court'eousness**. — *n* **courtesy** (*kûrt'ə-si*) courteous behaviour; an act of civility or respect. — **courtesy title** a title really invalid, but allowed by the usage of society — as for children of peers. [O.Fr. *corteis, cortois*; see **court**.]

courtesan or **courtezan** *kûrt'i-zan, kört'* or *-zan', n* a mistress or prostitute, esp. to a man of status or wealth. [Fr. *courtisane* — It. *cortigiana*, orig. a woman of the court.]

couscous or **kouskous** *ko͞os'ko͞os, n* granulated wheat flour; a N. African dish of steamed couscous with meat, vegetables, etc. [Fr., — Ar. *kuskus* — *kaskasa*, to pound.]

cousin *kuz'n, n* the son or daughter of an uncle or aunt; formerly a kinsman generally; a person belonging to a group related by common ancestry, etc.; something kindred or related to another. — *n* **cous'inhood** or **cous'inship**. — *adj* **cous'inly**. — *n* **cous'inry** cousins collectively. — **cousin-ger'man** a first cousin; **first cousin** the child of one's aunt or uncle, a full cousin; **first cousin once removed** the son or daughter of a cousin-german — sometimes loosely called *second cousin*; **second cousin** the child of one's parent's first cousin; (*loosely*) a first cousin once removed. [Fr., — L. *consōbrīnus* — *con-* (signifying connection) and *sobrīnus*, applied to the children of sisters, from the root of *soror*, a sister.]

couthie or **couthy** *ko͞oth'i, adj* friendly, kindly; comfortable; snug. [Prob. O.E. *cūth*, known.]

couture *ko͞o-tür', n* dressmaking or dress designing. — *n* **couturier** (*ko͞o-tür'yā*), *fem* **couturière** (*-yer'*) a dressmaker or dress designer. [Fr.]

couvade *ko͞o-väd', n* a custom among certain peoples in many parts of the world for the father to take to his bed at the birth of a child, and submit to certain restrictions of food, etc. [Fr. *couver*, to hatch.]

covalency *kō-vā'lən-si, n* the union of two atoms by the sharing of a pair of electrons, one from each atom — cf. **electrovalency**. — *adj* **covā'lent**. [L. *co-*, together, and **valency**.]

cove[1] *kōv, n* a small inlet of the sea; a bay; a cavern or rocky recess; the moulding covering the junction of wall and ceiling (also **cō'ving**.). [O.E. *cofa*, a room.]

cove[2] *kōv*, (*Austr colloq; old Br slang*) *n* a fellow, a customer.

coven *kuv'in* or *-ən, n* a gathering of witches; a gang of thirteen witches. [See **covin**.]

covenant *kuv'ə-nənt, n* a mutual agreement; the writing containing the agreement; an engagement entered into between God and a person or a people — a dispensation, testament. — *vi* to enter into an agreement. — *vt* to agree to; to stipulate. — *adj* **cov'enanted** agreed to by covenant; bound by covenant; holding a position under a covenant or contract. — *n* **covenantee'** the person to whom a covenant is made. — *n* **cov'enanter** (usu. in Scotland *kuv-ə-nant'ər*) a person who signed or adhered to the *Scottish National Covenant* of 1638 (the *Solemn League and Covenant* of 1643 was in effect an international treaty between Scotland and England for securing civil and religious liberty). — *n* **cov'enantor** that party to a covenant who subjects him- or herself to the penalty of its breach. — **covenant of grace** or **redemption** (*Christian theol*) that by which life is freely offered to sinners on condition of faith in Christ. [O.Fr., — L. *con-*, together, *venīre*, to come.]

Coventry *kov'* or *kuv'ənt-ri, n* a city in the West Midlands of England. — **send to Coventry** to ostracise, esp. to refuse to talk to.

cover *kuv'ər, vt* to put or spread something on, over or about; to come or be on, over or about; to hide; to clothe; to protect; to screen; to suffice for; to provide for or against; to comprise; to traverse; to take as field of operations; to play a higher card upon; to put down a stake of equal value in betting; to copulate with (esp. of a stallion); to command with a weapon; (of a journalist) to report on (a news story). — *n* something which covers or is intended to cover; a bedcover; a lid; the binding of a book; an envelope, esp. one with a stamp and postmark, as *first-day cover*; undergrowth, thicket, concealing game, etc.; a pretext or disguise; an apparently genuine identity, job, etc. used as a front, esp. by spies; the protection provided by an insurance policy; the funds available to cover liabilities; a confederate; a table setting for a person (thus *cover charge*); a cover version; a cover point. — *adj* intended to conceal the true nature or identity of a person, organisation, etc. — Also used in composition. — *n* **cov'erage** the area or (*fig*) amount covered or included; the group or section of the community reached by an advertising medium; the (extent of) reporting of a topic, event, etc. on television, in the press, etc.; insurance cover. — *adj* **cov'ered**. — *n* **cov'ering**. — **cov'erall** a boiler suit (*US*; often in *pl*); a one-piece garment for babies, covering arms, legs and body. — *adj* covering or including everything. — **cover charge** a charge per person made by a restaurant, in addition to charge for food; **cover crop** a subsidiary crop grown partly to protect the soil; **cover drive** (*cricket*) a drive past cover point; **cover girl** a girl pictured on a magazine cover; **covering letter** a letter to explain documents enclosed with it; **cover note** (*insurance*) a note certifying that the holder has a current insurance policy or has insurance coverage while his or her policy is being prepared; **cover point** in cricket, etc., (the position of) the player who supports (and stands to the right of) point; in lacrosse, (the position of) one of the defending players; **cov'erslip** a loose cover for a duvet; **cover version** a recording of a song, etc. which has previously been recorded by someone else. — **cover for** to act in the place of (someone who is absent, etc.); **cover up** to cover completely; to conceal, withhold information (*colloq*; *n* **cov'er-up**). [Fr. *couvrir* (It. *coprire*) — L. *cooperīre* — *co-* and *operīre*, to cover.]

coverlet *kuv'ər-lit, n* a bedcover. [Fr. *couvrir*, to cover, *lit* (L. *lectum*), a bed.]

covert *kuv'* or *kōv'ərt, adj* concealed; secret. — *n* a feather covering the quill-bases of wings and tail of a bird; (usu. pronounced *kuv'ər*) a cover for game. — *adv* **cov'ertly** in a secret, stealthy or concealed manner. — *n* **cov'erture** covering, shelter; disguise. [M.E., covered, — O.Fr. past p. of *covrir*, to cover.]

covet *kuv'it, vt* to desire or wish for eagerly; to wish for (something belonging to another): — *pr p* **cov'eting**; *pa t* and *pa p* **cov'eted**. — *adj* **cov'etable**. — *adj* **cov'eted**. — *adv* **cov'etingly**. — *adj* **cov'etous** inordinately desirous; avaricious. — *adv* **cov'etously**. — *n* **cov'etousness**. [O.Fr. *coveit(i)er* (Fr. *convoiter*) — L. *cupiditās, -ātis* — *cupěre*, to desire.]

covey *kuv'i, n* a brood or hatch of partridges; a small flock of game birds; a party or set of people. [O.Fr. *covée* — L. *cubāre*, to lie down.]

covin *kōv'in* or *kuv'in, n* a conspiracy; a coven. [O.Fr. covin — L.L. *convenium* — *con-*, together, *venīre*, to come.]

coving. See **cove**[1].

cow[1] *kow*, the female of the bovine animals; the female of certain other animals, such as the elk, elephant, whale, etc.; an ugly, ungainly, slovenly, or objectionable woman (*vulg*). — **cow'bell** a bell for a cow's neck; **cow'berry** the red whortleberry; **cow'bird** or **cow blackbird** an American bird that accompanies cattle, and drops its eggs into other birds' nests; **cow'boy** a man who has the charge of cattle on a ranch (*US*); any rather rough male character in stories, etc. of the old American West, such as a gunfighter or a man involved in fighting Indians; a rodeo performer (*US*); a young inexperienced lorry-driver, or anyone who drives an unsafe or overloaded lorry (*slang*); an often inadequately qualified person providing inferior services (*colloq derog*). — Also *adj*. — **cowboy boots** high-heeled, pointed boots, usu. with ornamental stitching etc. worn by, or reminiscent of styles worn by, cowboys and ranchers; **cow'-calf** a female calf; **cow'catcher** (*US*) an apparatus on the front of a railway engine to throw off obstacles; **cow-cher'vil, -pars'ley** or **-weed** wild chervil; **cow'-dung; cow'girl** a young woman who dresses like and does the work of a cowboy; **cow'grass** perennial red clover; **cow'hand** a cowboy (*US*); **cow'herd** a person who herds cows; **cow'hide** the hide of a cow, esp. that made into leather; **cow'house** a building in which cows are kept, a byre; **cow'lick** a tuft of turned-up hair on the forehead (also **cow's lick**); **cow'man** a man who tends cows; a man who owns a cattle ranch (*US*); **cow-parsley** see **cow-chervil**; **cow-pars'nip** an umbelliferous plant, hogweed used as fodder; **cow'-pat** a flat roundish lump of cow-dung; **cow'poke** (*US colloq*) a cowboy; **cow'pox** a disease that appears in pimples on the teats of the cow, its vaccine used to immunise against smallpox; **cow'puncher** (*US colloq*) a cowboy; **cow'shed** a cowhouse; **cow's lick** see **cowlick**; **cow-weed** see **cow-chervil**. — **till the cows come home** for an unforeseeably long time. [O.E. *cū*.]

cow[2] *kow*, *vt* to subdue the spirit of; to keep under. — *adj* **cowed** abjectly depressed or intimidated. [Perh. from O.N. *kūga*; Dan. *kue*, to subdue.]

cowage. See **cowhage**.

coward *kow'ərd*, *n* a reprehensibly faint-hearted person; a person who lacks courage; someone who brutally takes advantage of the weak or attacks the undefended. — *n* **cow'ardice** (*-is*) lack of courage; timidity; brutal conduct towards the weak or undefended. — *n* **cow'ardliness**. — *adj* **cow'ardly** having the character of a coward; characteristic of, or to be expected of, a coward. [O.Fr. *couard* — L. *cauda*, a tail.]

cower *kow'ər*, *vi* to crouch or cringe in fear. — **cower away** to shrink back in fear. [Cf. O.N. *kūra*, Dan. *kure*, to lie quiet.]

cowhage, cowage *kow'ij* or **cowitch** *kow'ich*, *n* a tropical leguminous climbing plant; the stinging hairs on its pod, used medicinally as a vermifuge; its pods. [Hindi *kavāc*.]

cowl *kowl*, *n* a large, loose hood esp. of the kind worn by a monk; a monk's hooded habit; a cover, usu. revolving, fitted over a chimney to improve ventilation; the part of a motor vehicle to which the windscreen and instrument panel are fixed; a cowling. — *adj* **cowled** wearing a cowl. — *n* **cowl'ing** the metal casing round an aeroplane engine. — *adj* **cowl'-necked** (of a dress, sweater, etc.) having a collar which lies in loose folds round the neck and shoulders as a monk's cowl does. [O.E. *cugele*.]

co-worker *kō-wûr'kər*, *n* an associate; someone who works with one on a project, etc. [**co-**.]

cowrie or **cowry** *kow'ri*, *n* a mollusc of a large genus (*Cypraea*) of gasteropods; the shell of the mollusc, in certain primitive societies used as money or invested with magic qualities. [Hindi *kaurī*.]

cowslip *kow'slip*, *n* a species of primrose, with fragrant yellow flowers arranged in umbels. [O.E. *cūslyppe* — *cū*, cow-dung.]

cox *koks*, *n* a shortened form of **coxswain**. — *vt* and *vi* to act as coxswain in a boat. — *adj* **coxed** having a cox. — *adj* **cox'less**.

coxa *koks'ə*, *n* the hip (*anat*); the segment of an arthropod's leg closest to its body (*zool*): — *pl* **cox'ae** (*-ē*). — *adj* **cox'al**. — *n* **coxal'gia** (*-ji-ə*) pain in the hip. [L.]

coxcomb *koks'kōm*, *n* a foolishly vain or conceited man; a strip of red cloth notched like a cock's comb, which professional fools used to wear. — *n* **cox'combry** the behaviour of a coxcomb. [**cock's comb**.]

coxiness. See **cock**[1].

coxswain *kok'sn* or *kok'swān*, *n* the helmsman of a lifeboat; (usu. **cox**) the steersman of a racing eight or four (*rowing*); a petty officer in charge of a boat and crew. [Obs. *cock*, a boat (cf. **cockboat**) and **swain**.]

Coy. (*mil*) *abbrev* for Company.

coy *koi*, *adj* bashful; affectedly shy. — *adv* **coy'ly**. — *n* **coy'ness**. [Fr. *coi* — L. *quiētus*, quiet.]

coyote *koi'ōt*, *koi-ōt'(i)*, *kī-ōt'i* or *kī'ōt*, *n* a prairie-wolf, a small wolf of N. America: — *pl* **coyo'tes** or **coyo'te**. [Mex. *coyotl*.]

coypu *koi'pōō*, *-pōō'* or *-pū*, *n* a large South American aquatic rodent yielding nutria fur. [Native name.]

cozen *kuz'n*, (*old*) *vt* to cheat. — *n* **coz'enage** deceit. — *n* **coz'ener**. [Perh. Fr. *cousiner*, to claim kindred; see **cousin**.]

cp *abbrev* for candle-power (q.v.).

cp. *abbrev* for compare.

CPAC *abbrev* for Consumer Protection Advisory Committee.

CPAG *abbrev* for Child Poverty Action Group.

Cpd *abbrev* for compound.

CPG *abbrev* for Coronary Prevention Group.

CPGB *abbrev* for Communist Party of Great Britain.

CPI *abbrev* for consumer price index, a method of demonstrating the inflation rate.

Cpl *abbrev* for Corporal.

CPO *abbrev* for: Chief Petty Officer; Crime Prevention Officer.

cpp *abbrev* for current purchasing power.

CPR *abbrev* for Canadian Pacific Railway.

CPRE *abbrev* for Campaign for the Protection of Rural England.

CPRS *abbrev* for Central Policy Review Staff, a former body (1971–83) reviewing and reporting on British Government strategy, also known as the **Government Think-Tank**.

CPS *abbrev* for Crown Prosecution Service.

cps (*phys*) *abbrev* for cycles per second.

CPSA *abbrev* for Civil and Public Services Association.

CPU (*comput*) *abbrev* for central processing unit.

CQ (*radio*) *symbol* transmitted by an amateur operator to establish communication with any other amateur operator.

Cr *abbrev* for Councillor.

Cr (*chem*) *symbol* for chromium.

cr. *abbrev* for: credit; creditor; crown.

crab[1] *krab*, *n* any of the marine decapod crustaceans, having a wide, flat carapace in which the abdomen is folded under the cephalothorax; its flesh as a food; (with *cap*) the sign of the zodiac and constellation Cancer; a portable winch; a crab-louse. — *vi* to fish for crabs. — *adj* **crabb'y** crablike. — *adj* **crab'like**. — *adv* and *adj* **crab'wise** with sideways motion like a crab's. — **crab'-louse** a crab-shaped louse infesting the hair of the pubis, etc.; **Crab Nebula** the expanding cloud of gas in the constellation of Taurus, being the remains of a supernova observed in 1054 A.D.; **crab'-yaws** yaws tumours on the soles and palms. — **catch a crab** (*rowing*) to sink the oar too deeply, or not deeply enough, in the water and fall backwards in consequence. [O.E. *crabba*.]

crab[2] *krab*, *n* a wild bitter apple; a sour-tempered person. — **crab'-apple; crab'stick** a walking-stick or cudgel made of crab-apple wood; **crab'-tree**.

crabbed *krab'id*, *adj* ill-natured, perverse or irascible; (of handwriting) cramped or difficult to decipher. — *adv* **crabb'edly**. — *n* **crabb'edness**. — *adj* **crabb'y** bad-tempered, ill-natured. — *adv* **crabb'ily**. — *n* **crabb'iness**. [**crab**[1] intermixed in meaning with **crab**[2].]

crack *krak*, *vt* and *vi* to (cause e.g. a whip to) make a sharp sudden sound; to split; to break partially or suddenly; to fracture, the parts remaining in contact; to (cause to) give way under strain, torture, etc.; (of petroleum, etc.) to break into simpler molecules. — *vt* to break open (a safe, etc.); to solve the mystery of (a code, etc.); to utter in jest; to hit with a resounding noise. — *vi* (of the voice) to change tone or register suddenly. — *n* a sudden sharp splitting sound; a partial fracture; a flaw; a sharp, resounding blow; an expert; a quip or gibe; a try (*slang*); a highly addictive form of cocaine mixed with other substances (usu. baking powder) and sold and used in small pelletlike pieces. — *adj* (*colloq*) excellent; expert. — *adj* **cracked** split; damaged; crazy (*informal*). — *n* **crack'er** a person or thing that cracks; a thin crisp biscuit; a colourful tubular package that comes apart with a bang, when the ends are pulled, to reveal a small gift, motto, etc.; a small, noisy firework; the apparatus used in cracking petroleum; something exceptionally good or fine of its type (*colloq*). — *adj* **crack'ers** (*colloq*) crazy; unbalanced. — *adj* **crack'ing** (*colloq*) (of speed, etc.) very fast; very good. — **cracked wheat** wheat coarsely ground, boiled and then dried for use as a cereal food, bulgur; **crack'erjack** a person or thing of highest excellence. — Also *adj.* — *adj* **crack'jaw** hard to pronounce. — **crack'pot** a crazy person. — Also *adj.* — **at the crack of dawn** at daybreak; very early in the morning; **crack a bottle, can,** etc. to open or drink a bottle, can, etc.; **crack a joke** to utter a joke with some effect; **crack down on** to take firm action against (*n* **crack'down**); **crack the whip** to assert authority suddenly or forcibly; **crack up** (*colloq*) to praise; to fail suddenly or to go to pieces; to distress considerably; **fair crack of the whip** a fair opportunity; **get cracking** to get moving quickly. [O.E. *cracian*, to crack.]

crackle *krak'l*, *vi* to make a slight but sustained cracking noise as a wood fire does; to rustle loudly. — *n* a slight cracking or loud rustling; a kind of porcelain, purposely cracked in the kiln as a form of decoration. — *n* **crack'ling** the rind of roast pork. — *adj* **crack'ly** producing a cracking or rustling noise; brittle, crisp. [Frequentative of **crack**.]

cracknel *krak'nəl*, *n* a light, brittle biscuit; (in *pl*) crisply fried pieces of fat pork (*NAm*). [M.E. *krakenelle*, perh. O.Fr. *craquelin*.]

-cracy *-krə-si*, *sfx* used to indicate rule, government (by a particular group, etc.) as in *democracy*, *mobocracy*. — *sfx* **-crat** (*-krat*) person supporting, or partaking in, government (by a particular group, etc.). — *adj sfx* **-cratic** or **-cratical**. [Gr. *-kratia*, from *kratos*, power.]

cradle *krā'dl*, *n* a small bed for a baby, usu. on rockers or suspended; (with *the*) infancy (*fig*); the place of origin or nurture of a particular thing or person; a stand, rest or holder for supporting something; a suspended platform or trolley which can be raised and lowered and from which work can be carried out on the side of a ship, building, etc.; a framework, esp. one for keeping bedclothes from pressing on a patient, or one under a ship for launching; a rocking box for gold-washing; a wooden pronged attachment for a scythe, for combining the operations of gathering and cutting. — *adj* having been so since infancy, as in *a cradle Catholic*. — *vt* to lay or rock in a cradle; to hold and rock lovingly; to wash (soil containing gold) in a rocking box; to nurture. — *vt* and *vi* in the game of lacrosse, to keep (the ball) in the net of one's stick while running, by means of a rocking action. — *n* **crā'dling** (*archit*) a wooden or iron framework within a ceiling. — **cra'dle-snatcher** a person who marries someone much younger; **cra'dlesong** a lullaby. — **from the cradle to the grave** throughout one's life. [O.E. *cradol*.]

craft *kräft*, *n* cunning; dexterity; art; creative artistic activity involving construction, carving, weaving, sewing, etc. as opposed to drawing (also **craft'work**); a skilled trade; the members of a trade, as a body; an occupation; a ship of any kind (orig. small), an air vehicle or a space vehicle: — *pl* **craft**. — *vt* to make or construct, esp. with careful skill. — *adv* **craft'ily**. — *n* **craft'iness**. — *adj* **craf'ty** cunning; wily. — **craft shop** a shop in which materials and tools for creative activities such as embroidery, basketry, model-making, etc. are sold; **crafts'man** a person engaged in a craft; **crafts'manship**; **crafts'person** (*pl* **crafts'people**); **crafts'woman**; **craft'work** see **craft** above. [O.E. *cræft*.]

crag *krag*, *n* a rough steep rock or point, a cliff. — *adj* **cragg'ed** craggy. — *n* **cragg'edness** or **cragg'iness**. — *adj* **cragg'y** full of crags or broken rocks; rough; rugged. — *n* **crag-and-tail'** (*geol*) a hill-form with steep declivity at one end and a gentle slope at the other. — **crags'man** a skilled or experienced rock-climber. [App. conn. with Gael. *creag*, *carraig*.]

crake *krāk*, (*dialect*) *n* a crow, raven; a corncrake. [Cf. **corncrake, croak**.]

cram *kram*, *vt* to press closely together; to stuff; to fill to superfluity; to overfeed; to teach or learn, hastily for a certain occasion (e.g. an examination or lawsuit). — *vi* to eat greedily; to prepare for an examination, etc. by hasty and intensive learning: — *pr p* **cramm'ing**; *pa t* and *pa p* **crammed**. — *n* a crush. — *adj* **cramm'able**. — *adj* **crammed**. — *n* **cramm'er** a person or machine that crams poultry; someone who, or an establishment that, crams pupils or a subject. — *adj* **cram'-full**. [O.E. *crammian*.]

crambo *kram'bō*, *n* a game in which one person gives a word to which another finds a rhyme. [Prob. from L. *crambē repetīta*, cabbage served up again.]

cramp[1] *kramp*, *n* an involuntary and painful contraction of a voluntary muscle or group of muscles; (in *pl*) acute abdominal pain; restraint. — *vt* to affect with spasms; to confine; to hamper. — *adj* **cramped** (of handwriting) small and closely written; compressed; restricted, without enough room, confined. — *adj* **cramp'ing** restricting, confining. — **bather's cramp** paralysis attacking a bather; **writer's cramp** a disorder affecting writers, the muscles refusing to obey when an attempt to write is made. — **cramp someone's style** to restrict someone's movements or actions. [O.Fr. *crampe*.]

cramp[2] *n* a cramp-iron; a contrivance with a movable part that can be screwed tight to press things together, a clamp. — *vt* to fasten with a cramp-iron. — **cramp'-iron** a piece of metal bent at both ends for binding things together. [M.Du. *krampe*, a hook.]

crampon *kram'pon*, *n* a grappling-iron; a spiked contrivance attached to boots for climbing rock-faces or telegraph poles, or for walking on ice. [**cramp**[2].]

cran *kran*, *n* a measure of capacity for herrings just landed in port — $37\frac{1}{2}$ gallons. [Prob. Gael. *crann*, a measure.]

cranberry *kran'bər-i*, *n* the red acid berry of a small evergreen shrub growing in peaty bogs and marshy grounds, or the larger berry of an American species, both made into jellies, sauces, etc.; the shrub itself.

crane *krān*, *n* any bird of the *Gruidae*, large wading birds with long legs, neck, and bill; a machine for raising heavy weights, usu. having a rotating boom from the end of which the lifting gear is hung; a travelling platform for a film camera. — *vt* to raise with a crane; to stretch one's neck as a crane does. — *vi* to stretch out the neck. — **crane'-fly** a fly with very long legs, the daddy-long-legs; **cranes'bill** or **crane's'-bill** any wild species of the Geranium genus, from the beaked fruit. [O.E. *cran*.]

cranium *krā'ni-əm*, *n* the skull; the bones enclosing the brain: — *pl* **crā'niums** or **crā'nia**. — *adj* **crā'nial**. — *n* **crāniol'ogist**. — *n* **crāniol'ogy** the study of skulls; phrenology. — *n* **crāniom'eter** an instrument for measuring the skull. — *n* **crāniom'etry**. — *n* **crāniot'omy** the act of crushing the skull of the dead foetus in obstructed deliveries (*obstetrics*); incision of the skull esp. for the purpose of neurosurgery. — **cranial index** the breadth of a skull as a percentage of the length. [L.L. *crānium* — Gr. *krānion*, the skull.]

crank[1] *krangk, n* an arm on a shaft for communicating motion to or from the shaft (*mach*); a handle on this principle for starting a motor (also **crank'handle** or **start'ing-handle**); a person of eccentric or faddy habits and tastes (*derog*); an irascible person (*NAm*). — *vi* to turn a crank (often with *up*). — *vt* to turn (a shaft) using a crank; to start (a motor) with a crank. — *adv* **crank'ily**. — *n* **crank'iness**. — *adj* **crank'y** eccentric, faddy or full of whims (*derog*); crabbed, ill-tempered (*NAm*); shaky, unsteady. — **crank'case** a boxlike casing for the crankshaft and connecting-rods of some types of reciprocating-engine; **crank'-shaft** the main shaft of an engine or other machine, which carries a crank or cranks for the attachment of connecting rods. [O.E. *cranc*.]

crank[2] *krangk*, (*drug-taking slang*) *n* any amphetamine drug. — **crank up** to inject narcotics. [From motoring image.]

crannog *kran'og*, (*archaeol*) *n* a Celtic lake-dwelling, typically a tiny island artificially enlarged and fortified. [Ir., — O.Ir. *crann*, tree.]

cranny *kran'i, n* a fissure; a chink; a secret place. — *adj* **crann'ied** having crannies or fissures. [Fr. *cran*, a notch.]

crap[1] *krap, n* excrement (*vulg*); rubbish (*slang*); nonsense (*slang*). — *vi* to defecate (*vulg*). — *adj* **crapp'y**. [M.E. *crappe*, chaff — M.Du. *krappe*, prob. from *krappen*, to tear off.]

crap[2]. See **craps**.

crape *krāp, n* a thin silk fabric, tightly twisted in manufacture so as to have a finely wrinkled appearance, dyed black, for use as mourning; a band of this for putting round a mourner's hat or arm. — *adj* made of crape. [O.Fr. *crespe* — L. *crispus*, crisp.]

craps *kraps, nsing* a gambling game in which a player rolls two dice (also **crap**). — *n* **crap** a losing throw in craps. — **crap out** to make a losing throw in craps (*US*); to fail (*US*); **shoot craps** to play craps.

crapulence *krap'ū-ləns, n* sickness caused by excessive drinking; intemperance. — *adj* **crap'ulent**. — *adj* **crap'ulous**. [L. *crāpula*, intoxication.]

craquelure *krak'ə-lūr* or *-lōōr, n* the fine cracking that occurs in the varnish or pigment of old paintings; this effect or pattern. [Fr.]

crases. See **crasis**.

crash[1] *krash, n* a noise as of things breaking or being crushed by falling; the shock of two bodies meeting; a collision between vehicles, etc.; the failure of a commercial undertaking; economic collapse; a fall or rush to destruction; the complete breakdown of a computer system or program; the disagreeable after-effects of a high (*drug-taking slang*). — *adj* involving suddenness, speed or short-term intensive effort. — *vt* and *vi* to dash, or fall, to pieces with a loud noise; to move with a harsh noise; to collide or cause to collide with another vehicle, etc.; to fall or cause (an aircraft) to fall violently to earth or into the sea, usu. with extensive damage; to gatecrash (*colloq*); to have or cause (a computer system or program) to have a complete breakdown. — *vi* to come to grief, fail disastrously; to suffer the unpleasant after-effects of a high (*drug-taking slang*). — *adj* **crash'ing** (*colloq*) extreme, overwhelming, esp. in *a crashing bore*. — **crash barrier** a protective barrier usu. of steel placed e.g. along the edge of a road or the central reservation of a motorway; **crash course** a short but intensive programme of instruction; **crash'-helmet** a padded safety headdress for motorcyclists, racing motorists, etc. — *vi* and *vt* **crash-land'** in an emergency, to land (an aircraft) abruptly, with resultant damage. — **crash-land'ing; crash'-mat** a thick mattress used by athletes and gymnasts to absorb the impact of landing after a jump, etc.; **crash'-matting; crash'pad** a place providing temporary sleeping accommodation (*slang*). — *adj* **crash'-proof** designed to withstand a crash. — **crash out** (*slang*) to fall asleep; to become unconscious. [Imit.]

crash[2] *krash, n* a coarse strong linen. [Perh. from Russ. *krashenina*, coloured linen.]

crasis *krā'sis, n* the mingling or contraction of two vowels into one long vowel, or into a diphthong (*gram*): — *pl* **crā'sēs** (*-sēz*). [Gr. *krāsis*, mixture.]

crass *kras, adj* grossly stupid, tactless or insensitive. — *adv* **crass'ly**. — *n* **crass'ness**. [L. *crassus*.]

-crat, -cratic, -cratical. See **-cracy**.

crate *krāt, n* a strong metal, plastic, wooden or wickerwork case with partitions, for carrying breakable or perishable goods; a decrepit aeroplane or car (*colloq*). — *vt* to pack in a crate. [L. *crātis*, a wickerwork hurdle.]

crater *krāt'ər, n* the bowl-like mouth of a volcano; a hole in the ground where a meteorite has fallen, or a shell, mine or bomb exploded; a circular rimmed depression in the surface of the moon; a large, two-handled bowl for mixing wine in (*archaeol*). [L., — Gr. *krātēr*, a mixing bowl.]

cravat *krə-vat', n* a formal neckerchief worn esp. by men as an alternative to a tie. [Fr. *cravate* — introduced in 1636 from the *Cravates* or Croatians.]

crave *krāv, vt* to beg earnestly; to require; to long for. — *vi* to long (with *for* or *after*). — *n* **crav'ing** a longing. [O.E. *crafian*, to crave.]

craven *krā'vən, n* a coward; a spiritless fellow. — *adj* cowardly; spiritless. — *adv* **crav'enly**. — *n* **crav'enness**. [M.E. *cravant*, perh. — L. *crepare*, crack.]

craw *krö, n* the crop, throat, or first stomach of fowls; the crop of insects; the stomach of animals generally. [M.E. *crawe*.]

crawfish. See **crayfish**.

crawl *kröl, vi* to move slowly with the body on or close to the ground; to move on hands and knees; to creep; to move slowly or stealthily; to behave abjectly or obsequiously; to be covered with crawling things (with *with*); to swim using the crawl stroke. — *n* the act of crawling; a slow pace; an alternate overhand swimming stroke. — *n* **crawl'er** someone who or that which crawls; an abject or obsequious person; a sluggish person; a creeping thing. — *n* **crawl'ing**. — *adj* creeping; lousy, verminous. — *adj* **craw'ly** (*colloq*) with, or like the feeling of, something crawling over one; creepy. — **crawler lane** on an uphill stretch of motorway, an extra lane for the use of slow-moving vehicles. [M.E., perh. — O.N. *krafla*, creep.]

crayfish *krā'fish* or **crawfish** *krö'fish, n* a large freshwater crustacean. [M.E. *crevice* — O.Fr. *crevice* — O.H.G. *krebiz*, a crab.]

crayon *krā'ən, n* a pencil made of chalk, wax or pipe-clay, variously coloured, used for drawing; a drawing done with crayons. — *vt* and *vi* to draw with a crayon. [Fr. *crayon* — *craie*, chalk.]

craze *krāz, vt* or *vi* to develop or cause (pottery or metal) to develop a series of fine cracks. — *n* a fashion or fad. — *adj* **crazed** deranged, demented; covered with fine cracks. — *adv* **crāz'ily**. — *n* **crāz'iness**. — *adj* **crāz'y** demented, deranged; ridiculous, stupid; exuberantly wild in behaviour (*colloq*); extravagantly enthusiastic or passionate (with *about*; *colloq*); composed of flat, irregular pieces. — **crazy golf** a form of putting in which balls have to be hit past, through or over obstacles such as humps, tunnels, bends, etc. to reach the hole; **crazy paving** paving composed of irregularly shaped slabs of stone or concrete, used for ornamental effect on terraces, garden paths, etc.; **crazy quilt** a patchwork quilt made up haphazardly of irregular pieces of material sewn together. [M.E., break, — O.N.]

creak *krēk, vi* to make a sharp grating or squeaking sound, as of an unoiled hinge, or sagging floorboard. — *n* a grating noise. — *adv* **creak'ily**. — *adj* **creak'y**. [From the sound.]

cream *krēm*, *n* the oily substance that rises to the surface of milk, yielding butter when churned; the colour of this substance, yellowish-white; the best part of anything; the pick of a group of things or people; a food largely made of cream, or like cream in consistency or appearance, as in *ice-cream*; a cream-like substance, e.g. *face-cream* or *hand cream*, for skin. — *vt* to take off the cream from (milk), to skim; to select (the best) from a group, etc. (with *off*); to beat to the consistency of cream (e.g. a mixture of sugar and butter in cake-making); to treat with cream. — *vi* to form cream; to gather like cream. — *adj* of the colour of cream, yellowish-white; prepared with cream; (of sherry) sweet. — *n* **cream'er** a device for separating cream from milk; a small jug for cream (esp. *NAm*); a substitute for milk, in powder form, for use in coffee, etc. — *n* **cream'ery** an establishment where butter and cheese are made from milk; a shop selling milk, butter, etc. — *n* **cream'iness.** — *adj* **cream'y** full of cream, or like cream in appearance, consistency, etc. — **cream'-bun** or **-cake** a kind of bun or cake, filled with cream or an imitation of it; **cream-cheese'** soft white cheese, made with cream. — *adj* **cream'-coloured.** — **cream cracker** a crisp, unsweetened type of biscuit; **cream jug** a small jug for serving cream or milk. — *adj* **cream'-laid** (of laid paper) cream or white in colour. — **cream puff** a confection of puff pastry filled with cream; **cream soda** (esp. *US*) a vanilla-flavoured fizzy drink. — *adj* **cream'-wove** (of wove paper) cream or white in colour. — **cream of chicken, mushroom,** etc. **soup** chicken, mushroom, etc. soup made with milk or cream; **cream of tartar** a white crystalline compound, potassium hydrogen tartrate. [O.Fr. *cresme*, *creme* — L.L. *cramum*, of Celt. origin, infl. by ecclesiastical *chrisma*, unction.]

crease *krēs*, *n* a mark made by folding, pressing or crumpling; such a mark pressed centrally and longitudinally into a trouser-leg; a wrinkle or line on the face; any of the three lines that regulate the positions of batsman or bowler at the wicket (*cricket*). — *vt* to make a crease or creases in; to graze with a bullet. — *vi* to become creased. — *vt* and *vi* (*colloq*) to double up with laughter (often with *up*). — *n* **creas'er.** — *adj* **creas'y** full of creases; liable to crease. — *adj* **crease-resist'ant** or **-resist'ing** (of a fabric) not becoming creased in normal wear.

create *krē-āt'*, *vt* and *vi* to bring into being or form out of nothing; to bring into being by force of imagination; to make, produce or form; to design. — *vt* to invest with a new form, office or character; to institute; to be the first actor to play (a certain role). — *vi* (*slang*) to make a fuss. — *n* **creation** (*krē-ā'shən*) the act of creating; (with *cap* and **the**) God's act of creating the universe (*Christian relig*); that which is created; the world, the universe; a specially designed, or particularly striking, garment. — *n* **creā'tionism** the theory that everything that exists had its origin in special acts of creation by God (opp. to *evolutionism*). — *n* **creā'tionist.** — *adj* **creā'tive** having power to create; creating; showing or relating to imagination or originality; (esp. of accounting or accountancy) characterised by an imaginative re-interpretation or dubious manipulation of established rules of procedure, for personal benefit or for ease of operation (*euph*). — *adv* **creā'tively.** — *n* **creā'tiveness.** — *n* **creativity** (*krē-ə-tiv'*) state or quality of being creative; ability to create. — *n* **creā'tor** someone who creates; a maker; (with *cap* and **the**) the Supreme being, God. — *n* **creā'torship.** — *adj* **creatural** (*krē'chər-əl*) or **crea'turely** pertaining to a creature or thing created. — *n* **creature** (*krē'chər*) an animate being, esp. an animal; a human being, in this sense often used in contempt or compassion; something created, whether animate or inanimate; a person completely under one's control, a dependant, instrument, or puppet. — **creative accountancy** or **accounting** see **creative** above; **creature comforts** material comforts such as food, drink, a place to sleep, etc.; [L. *creāre*, *-ātum*, to create, *creātūra*, a thing created.]

creatine *krē'ə-tin* or *-tēn*, *n* a constant and characteristic constituent of the striped, i.e. voluntary muscle of vertebrates ($C_4H_9N_3O_2$). [Gr. *kreas*, *kreatos*, flesh.]

creative, creator, creature. See under **create.**

crèche *kresh*, *n* a public nursery for children; a model representing the scene of Christ's nativity. [Fr. *crèche*, manger.]

-cred *-kred*, (*slang*) *combining form* denoting one's *cred*ibility or ability to inspire confidence on the basis of one's record, as in *street-cred*, one's reputation among the urban population.

credal. See **creed.**

credence *krē'dəns*, *n* belief; trust; the small table beside the altar on which the bread and wine are placed before being consecrated (also **credence shelf, credence table** and **credenza** (*krə-den'zə*)). — *n* **creden'tial.** — *npl* **credentials** (*kri-den'shlz*) evidence of competence, taken as one's entitlement to authority, etc.; letters of introduction, certificates, etc. entitling one to trust. [L.L. *crēdentia*, trust — L. *crēdĕre*, to believe.]

credenza. See **credence.**

credible *kred'ibl*, *adj* capable of being believed; seemingly worthy of belief or of confidence; reliable. — *n* **credibil'ity** the quality of deserving belief; the amount of confidence placed in one on the basis of one's record. — *n* **cred'ibleness.** — *adv* **cred'ibly.** — **credibility gap** the discrepancy between what is claimed or stated and what is, or seems likely to be, the case. [L. *crēdībilis*, believable, — *crēdĕre*, to believe.]

credit *kred'it*, *n* belief; esteem, reputation or honour; distinction; good character; acknowledgment or recognition of something contributed or achieved; sale on trust; time allowed for payment; a balance in a person's favour in an account; an entry in an account making acknowledgment of a payment; the side of an account on which such entries are made; a sum placed at a person's disposal in a bank up to which he or she may draw; certified completion of a course of study counting towards a final pass; (in *pl*) credit titles; (in *pl*) a list of acknowledgments in a book, etc. — *vt* to believe; to trust; to enter on the credit side of an account; to ascribe to (with *to* or *with*); to mention in the credit titles. — *adj* **cred'itable** trustworthy; bringing credit or honour; praiseworthy. — *n* **cred'itableness.** — *adv* **cred'itably.** — *n* **cred'itor** a person to whom a debt is due. — **credit card** a card obtainable from a credit card company which, in places where the card is recognised, enables the holder to have purchases, services, etc. debited to an account kept by the company; a similar card issued by other organisations, or by certain banks, some for use only with a cheque book; **credit rating** (an assessment of) the level of a person's or business's creditworthiness; **credit scoring** the calculation of a person's credit rating by adding up points awarded according to the person's age, marital status, occupation, address, etc.; **credit titles** (or, more frequently, **cred'its**) acknowledgments of the work of participators shown at the beginning or end of a cinema film, television programme, etc.; **credit union** a non-profit-making co-operative savings association which makes loans to its members at low interest; **cred'itworthiness** entitlement to credit as judged from earning capacity, promptness in debt-paying, etc. — *adj* **cred'itworthy.** — **be a credit to someone,** etc. to be proof of time, trouble, etc. well-invested in one by someone, etc.; **give credit for** to acknowledge as having (a quality, etc.). [O.Fr. *crédit* — L. *crēditum*, loan, — *crēdĕre*, to believe.]

credo *krē'dō*, *n* a belief or set of beliefs; (with *cap*) the Apostles' Creed or Nicene Creed or a musical setting of either: — *pl* **crē'dōs**. [L., I believe.]

credulity *kri-dū'li-ti*, *n* disposition to believe without sufficient evidence; credulousness. — *adj* **credulous** (*kred'ū-ləs*) apt to believe without sufficient evidence; unsuspecting. — *adv* **cred'ūlously**. — *n* **cred'ūlousness**. [L. *crēdŭlus*, over-trustful, — *crēdĕre*, to believe.]

creed *krēd*, *n* a summary of articles of religious belief; any system of belief or set of principles. — *adj* **creed'al** or **cred'al**. — **the Creed** the Apostles' Creed or the Nicene Creed. [O.E. *crēda* — L. *crēdō*, I believe.]

creek *krēk*, *n* a small inlet or bay, or the tidal estuary of a river; a small river or brook (*NAm* and *Austr*). — **up the creek** (*slang*) in dire difficulties. [Prob. Scand., O.N. *kriki*, a nook.]

creel *krēl*, *n* a basket, esp. a fish basket.

creep *krēp*, *vi* to move with the belly on or near the ground; to move or advance slowly or stealthily; to slip or encroach very gradually; to develop insidiously; to grow along the ground or on supports, as a vine does; to fawn or cringe; (of the flesh) to have a shrinking sensation, as a concomitant of horror, etc.; to undergo creep (*metall*): — *pa t* and *pa p* **crept**. — *n* the act of creeping; a slow slipping or yielding to stress; crystallisation or rise of a precipitate on the side of a vessel above the surface of a liquid; gradual alteration of shape under stress (*metall*); a narrow passage; a cringing, unassertive or otherwise unpleasant person (*slang*). — *n* **creep'er** something or someone that creeps; a creeping plant; a small bird that runs up trees, a tree-creeper (*NAm*); an implement for dragging deep water; a crêpe-soled, or other soft-soled, shoe (*colloq*); a wheeled board on which one may lie and move about while working under a vehicle e.g. as a mechanic; a ball bowled so as to stay low (*cricket*). — *adj* **creep'ing**. — *adv* **creep'ingly**. — *adj* **creep'y** mysterious, rather eerie or chilling. — *n* **creepy-crawl'y** a crawling insect (also *adj*). — **creeping Jesus** (*slang*) a cringingly sanctimonious person. — **the creeps** a feeling of horror or revulsion. [O.E. *crēopan*.]

cremate *kri-māt'*, *vt* to burn (a dead body). — *n* **cremā'tion**. — *n* **cremāt'or** a person who undertakes cremations; a furnace for cremation; an incinerator. — *n* **crematō'rium** a place for cremating dead bodies. — *adj* **crem'atory** (*-ə-tər-i*). — *n* a crematorium. [L. *cremāre*, *-ātum*, to burn.]

creme *krēm*, *n* a form of **cream**, used *specif* for skin creams, frequently used in proprietary names.

crème or **crême** *krem*, (Fr.) *n* cream — applied to various creamy substances. — **crème caramel** (*kar-a-mel*) an egg custard baked in a dish lined with caramel; **crème de menthe** (*də māt*) a peppermint-flavoured liqueur.

crème de la crème *krem də la krem*, (Fr.) *n* cream of the cream, the very best.

crenate *krēn'āt* or **crenated** *kren-āt'id*, (*bot*) *adj* (of e.g. a leaf) having rounded teeth between sharp notches. — *n* **crēnā'tion**. — *n* **crenature** (*krē'* or *kren'*). [From an inferred L. *crēna*, a notch.]

crenellate *kren'i-lāt*, (*archit*) *vt* to furnish with battlements. — *adj* **cren'ellated**. — *n* **crenellā'tion**. [Fr. *créneler*, from an inferred L. *crēna*, a notch.]

creole *krē'ōl* or *krē-ōl'*, *n* (usu. with *cap*) strictly applied in the former Spanish, French, and Portuguese colonies of America, Africa and the East Indies to natives of pure European blood (as opp. to immigrants born in Europe or to coloured natives); (usu. with *cap*) a native, but not aboriginal or indigenous; (*loosely*; usu with *cap*) a native of mixed blood; (usu. with *cap*) applied to the native French or Spanish stock in Louisiana (*US*); (usu. with *cap*) a colonial patois (French, Spanish, etc.) (also **creolised** or **creolized language**) a language formerly a pidgin which has developed and become the accepted language of a region. — *adj* (sometimes with *cap*) pertaining to a Creole or creole. — *n* **crēōlisā'tion** or **-z-** the development of a pidgin into a creole. [Fr. *créole* — Sp. *criollo*, dimin. of *criado*, nursling.]

creosote *krē'ə-sōt*, *n* an oily liquid obtained by distillation of wood-tar used as an antiseptic; a somewhat similar liquid obtained from coal-tar, used to preserve wood (**creosote oil** or **coal-tar creosote**). — *vt* to treat with creosote. [Gr. *kreas*, flesh, *sōtēr*, saviour — *sōzein*, to save.]

crêpe or **crepe** *krāp*, *n* any of several finely wrinkled fabrics similar to **crape** (q.v.); rubber rolled in thin crinkly sheets (**crêpe rubber**); (usu. **crêpe**) a thin pancake. — *n* **cre'piness**. — *adj* **cre'py** or **cre'pey** (of the skin) wrinkled. — **crêpe-de-chine** (*də shēn*; also **crepe-**) a crape-like fabric, orig. of silk; **crêpe paper** thin crinkled paper. — *adj* **crêpe'-soled** soled with crêpe rubber. — **crêpe suzette** (*sü-zet*) a thin pancake in a hot orange- or lemon-flavoured sauce, usu. flambéed: — *pl* **crêpes suzettes** (*krāp sü-zet*). [See **crape**.]

crepitate *krep'i-tāt*, *vi* to crackle, snap; to rattle; (of beetles) to discharge an offensive fluid. — *adj* **crep'itant** crackling. — *n* **crepitā'tion** the act of crepitating; crackling; a crackling sound detected in the lungs in certain diseases, e.g. pneumonia. [L. *crepitāre*, frequentative of *crepāre*, to crack, rattle.]

crepitus *krep'i-təs*, (*med*) *n* the grating detectable in an arthritic joint when moved, or that produced by a fractured bone at the point of fracture, if disturbed. [L., a creaking or rattling.]

crept *krept*, *pa t* and *pa p* of **creep**.

crepuscular *kri-pus'kū-lər*, *adj* of or relating to twilight; dim, dark; (of certain animals) active, or appearing, at twilight. [L. *crepusculum*, twilight.]

Cres. *abbrev* for Crescent.

cresc. (*mus*) *abbrev* for crescendo.

crescendo *kresh-en'dō*, (*mus*) *adj* and *adv* gradually increasing in loudness. — *n* increase of loudness; a passage of increasing loudness; a high point, a climax: — *pl* **crescen'dos**. [It., increasing.]

crescent *kres'ənt*, *n* (more usu. **the crescent moon**) the waxing moon; a figure like the moon in its first or last quarter; the Turkish (orig. Byzantine) standard or emblem; the Turkish power; the Muslim faith; a curved street or terrace; a crescent-shaped roll, a croissant. [L. *crēscēns*, *-entis*, pres. p. of *crescĕre*, to grow.]

cresol *krēs'ol*, *n* a compound present in coal-tar and creosote used as an antiseptic. [From *creos*ote and alcoh*ol*.]

cress *kres*, *n* a name for many pungent-leaved cruciferous plants of various genera, used as a garnish, or in salads. [O.E. *cresse*, *cerse*.]

cresset *kres'it*, (*hist*) *n* an iron basket in which oil or pitch could be burnt for lighting purposes, usu. placed on top of a pole; a torch generally. [O.Fr. *cresset*, *crasset* — Old Du. *kruysel*, a hanging lamp.]

crest *krest*, *n* the comb or tuft on the head of a cock or other bird; a long narrow ridge forming the summit of anything, as a roof-ridge or the top of a hill or wave; a ridge along the surface of a bone (*anat*); a plume of feathers or other ornament on the top of a helmet; an accessory figure orig. surmounting the helmet in a coat of arms, also used separately as a device on personal effects (*heraldry*). — *vi* to culminate, reach a high point. — *vt* to surmount (a hill or wave). — *adj* **crest'ed** having a crest; having an elevated appendage like a crest (*bot*). — *adj* **crest'-fallen** dejected or cast-down. — **on (or riding) the crest of a wave** enjoying a run of success. [O.Fr. *creste* — L. *crista*.]

cretaceous *kri-tā'shəs, adj* composed of or like chalk; (with *cap*) belonging to the uppermost system of the Secondary or Mesozoic rocks. [L. *crētāceus* — *crēta*, chalk.]

cretin *kret'in, n* a child suffering from a congenital deficiency of thyroid hormone, which, if untreated, can lead to mental deficiency and incomplete physical development; a person having these conditions as a result of such a deficiency; an idiot (*colloq*). — *n* **cret'inism**. — *adj* **cret'inous**. [Fr. *crétin* — L. *christiānus*, human creature.]

cretonne *kret-on'* or *kret'on, n* a strong printed cotton fabric used for curtains or for covering furniture. [Fr., prob. from *Creton* in Normandy.]

Creutzfeldt-Jakob disease *kroits'felt yak'ōb di-zēz', n* a rare progressive neurological disease characterised by dementia, wasting of muscle tissue and spasticity, affecting esp. the elderly. [H.G. *Creutzfeldt* and A.M. *Jakob*, 20th-cent. neurologists.]

crevasse *kri-vas', n* a crack or split in a glacier; a fissure in a river embankment (*US*). — *vt* to make a fissure in (a dyke, etc.) (*US*). [O.Fr. *crevace* — L. *crepāre*, to creak, break.]

crevice *krev'is, n* a narrow crack or split, esp. in a rock. [See **crevasse**.]

crew[1] *kroo, n* a set, gang; a ship's company; the oarsmen and steersman manning a racing boat; a group or team of people with individual duties, in charge of a bus, train or aeroplane. — *vi* to act as a crew member on a ship, etc. (esp. with *for*). — **crew cut** an extremely short, upstanding style of haircut; **crew neck** a round, close-fitting style of neck on a jersey (*adj* **crew'-necked**). [O.Fr. *creue*, increase — *croistre*, to grow.]

crew[2] *kroo, pa t* of **crow**.

crewel *kroo'əl*, a fine worsted yarn used for embroidery and tapestry. — **crew'elwork**. [M.E.]

crib *krib, n* a child's bed usu. with slatted sides, a cot (esp. *US*); a manger or fodder-receptacle; a representation, esp. a model of the scene around the manger that served as a bed for the newborn Christ; a stall for oxen; a rudimentary dwelling; a country cottage (*NZ*); a timber framework for a dam, a pier foundation; a mine-shaft lining, etc.; a container for grain; an act of stealing, or something stolen, from another's work, a plagiarism; a key, or baldly literal translation, used as an aid by students, etc.; the discarded cards at cribbage, used by the dealer in scoring. — *vt* to put in a crib; to steal (another's work), to plagiarise: — *pr p* **crib'bing**; *pa t* and *pa p* **cribbed**. — **crib'-biting** (in horses) a harmful habit of seizing the edge of the manger in the teeth and swallowing air. [O.E. *cribb*, manger.]

cribbage *krib'ij, n* a card game in which each player discards a certain number of cards for the *crib*, and scores by holding certain combinations and by bringing the sum of the values of cards played to certain numbers. — **cribb'age-board** a scoring-board for cribbage, with holes for pegs. [*crib*, discarded cards; see **crib**.]

crick *krik, n* a spasm or cramp of the muscles, esp. of the neck. — *vt* to produce a crick in. [Prob. imit.]

cricket[1] *krik'it, n* a jumping insect, related to the grasshopper and locust, the male of which makes a chirping sound by rubbing its forewings together. [O.Fr. *criquet*.]

cricket[2] *krik'it, n* an outdoor game played with bats, a ball, and wickets, between two sides of eleven each. — *vi* to play at cricket. — *n* **crick'eter**. — *n* and *adj* **crick'eting**. — **not cricket** (*colloq*) not fair play. [Fr. *criquet*, goalpost.]

cricoid *krī'koid*, (*anat*) *adj* ring-shaped. — *n* a cartilage of the larynx. [Gr. *krikoeides* — *krikos*, a ring, *eidos*, form.]

cri de cœur *krē də kœr*, (Fr.) *n* a cry from the heart — heartfelt, passionate entreaty, complaint or reproach.

cried, crier, cries. See **cry**.

crikey *krī'ki*, (*slang*) *interj* a mild oath or expression of surprise. [Euph. for *Christ*.]

crim. con. (*law*) *abbrev* for criminal conversation (q.v. under **crime**).

crime *krīm, n* a violation of law, esp. if serious; an act punishable by law; such acts collectively or in the abstract; an act gravely wrong morally; sin; something deplorable (*colloq*). — *adj* **criminal** (*krim'*) relating to crime; guilty of crime; violating the law. — *n* a person who is guilty of crime. — *n* **criminal'ity** the condition of being a criminal; guiltiness. — *adv* **crim'inally**. — *n* **criminol'ogist**. — *n* **criminol'ogy** the science dealing with crime and criminals. — **crime sheet** (*mil*) a record of offences; **crime wave** a sharp rise in the level of criminal activity; **criminal conversation** (often **crim. con.**) adultery; **criminal court**; **criminal law** that part of the law dealing with offences, offenders and punishment; **criminal lawyer**. [Fr., — L. *crīmen, -inis*.]

crime passionel *krēm pa-syo-nel*, (Fr.) *n* a crime due to (sexual) passion.

criminal, etc., **criminologist**, etc. See under **crime**.

crimp *krimp, vt* to press into folds or ridges; to put tight waves or curls into (the hair) with curling tongs; to bend into shape; to thwart or hinder (*US*). — *n* a curl or wave; a bend or crease. — *n* **crimp'er** a person or device that crimps or corrugates; a hairdresser (*slang*). — *adj* **crimp'y** frizzy. [O.E. *gecrympan*, to curl.]

Crimplene® *krim'plēn, n* (a crease-resistant, synthetic fabric made from) a thick polyester yarn.

crimson *krim'zn, n* a deep red colour, tinged with blue; red in general. — *adj* deep red. — *vt* to dye crimson. — *vi* to become crimson; to blush. [M.E. *crimosin* — O.Fr. *cramoisin*; from Ar.]

cringe *krinj, vi* to stoop in servility; to cower in fear; to behave timidly and obsequiously; to fawn or flatter with mean servility; (*loosely*) to wince or flinch. — *n* a servile obeisance. — *n* **crin'ger**. — *n* and *adj* **crin'ging**. — *adv* **crin'gingly** in an obsequious manner. [Rel. to O.E. *crincan, cringan*, to shrink.]

cringle *kring'gl, n* a small piece of rope worked into the bolt-rope of a sail, and containing a metal ring or thimble. [L.G. *Kringel*, little ring.]

crinkle *kringk'l, vt* to twist, wrinkle, crimp. — *vi* to wrinkle up, curl. — *n* a wrinkle; (also **crink'ly**) paper money, money in general (*slang*). — *adj* **crink'ly** wrinkly. [Rel. to O.E. *crincan*; see **cringe**.]

crinoid *krī'noid* or *krin'oid, n* the feather-star or sea-lily, an echinoderm with cap-shaped body and branching arms. [Gr. *krĭnoeides*, like a lily.]

crinoline *krin'ə-lin* or *-lēn, n* orig. a stiff fabric of horsehair and flax used to distend women's skirts; a hooped petticoat or skirt made to project all round by means of steel wire. — *adj* **crin'olined**. [Fr., *crin* — L. *crinis*, hair, and *lin* — L. *linum*, flax.]

crinum *krī'nəm, n* any of various plants of the Amaryllis family, characterised by luxuriant clusters of lily-like flowers. [Gr. *krĭnon*, a lily.]

cripes *krīps*, (*slang*) *interj* expression of surprise or worry. [Euph. for *Christ*.]

cripple *krip'l, n* a lame person; a person damaged, disabled or deficient in some way, as an *emotional cripple*; a bracket attached to a ladder on the ridge of a roof to support scaffold boards. — *vt* to make lame or disable; to impair, undermine or curtail with disastrous effect. — *adj* **cripp'led**. [O.E. *crypel*; conn. with **creep**.]

crise *krēz*, (Fr.) *n* a peak of emotional distress, an emotional crisis: — *pl* **crises** (*krēz*). — **crise de nerfs** (*də ner*) an attack of nerves, hysterics.

crisis *krī'sis, n* a crucial or decisive moment; a turning-point, e.g. in a disease; a time of difficulty or distress;

an emergency: — *pl* **crises** (*krī'sēz*). [Gr. *krisis*, a decision, judgment.]

crisp *krisp*, *adj* curling closely; so dry as to break or crumble easily, brittle; (of pastry) short; (of weather) fresh and bracing; firm, the opposite of limp or flabby; (of wording) neat, terse, well-turned; (of manner) firm, decisive, authoritarian. — *vt* and *vi* to make or become crisp. — *n* (usu. in *pl*) a thin slice of potato fried till crisp, a potato-crisp; a piece of food fried or roasted to crispness. — *adj* **crisp'āte** (*bot* and *zool*) having a wavy edge. — *n* **crisp'er** a compartment of a refigerator in which to keep lettuce, etc. fresh. — *adv* **crisp'ly**. — *n* **crisp'ness**. — *adj* **crisp'y**. — **crisp'bread** a brittle, unsweetened type of biscuit of rye or wheat. [O.E., — L. *crispus*.]

criss-cross *kris'-kros*, *n* a network of crossing lines. — *adj* consisting of a network of crossed lines. — *adv* crosswise. — *vt* and *vi* to cross repeatedly. [From *christ-cross*, a Latin cross used to introduce the alphabet in old learning books.]

crista *kris'tə*, *n* a crest; a ridge or fold (*biol*): — *pl* **cris'tae** (-*ē*). — *adj* **crist'ate** crested. [L.]

cristobalite *kris-tō'bə-līt*, *n* one of the principal forms of silica, produced from quartz at high temperatures, occurring in volcanic rocks, slags, etc. [Cerro San *Cristóbal* in Mexico, where it was discovered.]

crit *krit*, (*colloq*) *n* short for **criticism**.

criterion *krī-tē'ri-ən*, *n* a means or standard of judging; a test; a rule, standard, or canon: — *pl* **critē'ria**. — **crite'rion referencing** the practice of judging examinees individually according to their acquisition of skills, without reference to achievements by their peers. [Gr. *kritērion* — *kritēs*, a judge.]

critic *krit'ik*, *n* someone who assesses the quality of something, a judge; a professional reviewer of literature, art, drama or music; a person skilled in textual studies, and the ascertainment of the original words where readings differ; a fault-finder. — *adj* **crit'ical** at or relating to a turning-point, transition or crisis; decisive, crucial; (*loosely*) seriously ill; relating to criticism; rigorously discriminating; captious. — *n* **critical'ity**. — *adv* **crit'ically**. — *n* **crit'icalness**. — *n* **crit'icaster** a petty critic. — *adj* **criticisable** or **-z-** (-*sī'zə-bl*). — *vt* **crit'icise** or **-ize** to analyse and pass judgment on; to find fault with, to censure. — *n* **crit'icism** the art of judging, esp. in literature or the fine arts; a critical judgment or observation. — **critical mass** (*nuc*) the minimum amount of fissile material needed to sustain a chain reaction; **critical temperature** that temperature above which a gas cannot be liquefied by pressure alone. — **critical path analysis** the working out with the aid of a computer of the sequence of operations that must be followed in order to complete a complex piece of work in the minimum time. [Gr. *kritikos* — *krīnein*, to judge.]

critique *kri-tēk'*, *n* a critical analysis or commentary, a review; the art of criticism. — *vt* to discuss or analyse critically. [Fr., — Gr. *kritikē* (*technē*), the art of criticism.]

critter or **crittur** *krit'ər*, (*dialect* and *colloq*; now esp. *US*) *n* creature; animal.

croak *krōk*, *vi* (of a frog or raven) to utter a low hoarse sound; to speak similarly hoarsely; to grumble or talk dismally; to die (*slang*). — *vt* to utter (words) hoarsely; to kill (*slang*). — *n* the sound, or a sound similar to that, of a frog or raven. — *n* **croak'er** an animal or bird that croaks; a grumbler; a tropical sea-fish that emits croaking noises. — *adv* **croak'ily**. — *n* **croak'ing**. — *adj* **croak'y**. [Imit.]

Croat *krō'at*, *n* a native or inhabitant of Croatia in Yugoslavia; the language of Croatia. — Also *adj*. — *adj* **Croatian** (-*ā'shən*) belonging to Croatia or its people. — *n* a Croat; the Croat language. [Serbo-Croatian *Hrvat*.]

croc *krok*, (*colloq*) *n* short for **crocodile**.

crochet *krō'shā*, *n* decorative work consisting of intertwined loops, executed in wool or thread with a small hook. — *vi* and *vt* to work in crochet: — *pr p* **crocheting** (*krō'shā-ing*); *pa t* and *pa p* **crocheted** (*krō'shād*). — *n* **cro'cheting**. [Fr. *crochet* — *croche*, *croc*, a hook.]

crocidolite *krō-sid'ə-līt*, *n* a fibrous mineral consisting mainly of silicate of iron and sodium, called *blue asbestos*. [From Gr. *krokis*, *-idos*, nap of cloth, *lithos*, stone.]

crock[1] *krok*, *n* a pot or jar; a potsherd. — *n* **crock'ery** earthenware; all types of domestic pottery. [O.E. *croc*; perh. of Celt. origin.]

crock[2] *krok*, (*colloq*) *n* a broken down or decrepit person or thing. [Cf. Norw. and Sw. *krake*, a poor beast.]

crockery. See **crock**[1].

crocket *krok'it*, (*archit*) *n* an ornament on the sloping sides of a pediment, pinnacle, etc., usu. like curled leaves or flowers. [See **croquet**.]

crocodile *krok'ə-dīl*, *n* a large, long-tailed tropical reptile with powerful tapering jaws and a thick skin covered with bony plates; leather from crocodile skin; a double file of school pupils taking a walk. — **crocodile clip** a clip for making electrical connections, with serrated jaws that interlock; **crocodile tears** hypocritical grief — from the old story that crocodiles (which have large lachrymal glands) shed tears over the hard necessity of killing animals for food. [L. *crocodīlus* — Gr. *krokodeilos*, a lizard.]

crocus *krō'kəs*, *n* a bulbous iridaceous plant with brilliant yellow, purple, or white flowers: — *pl* **cro'cuses**. [L. *crocus* — Gr. *krokos*, saffron.]

Croesus *krē'səs*, *n* a very rich man. [*Croesus*, king of Lydia, of fabulous wealth.]

croft *kroft*, *n* in Scotland, a small piece of arable land esp. adjoining a dwelling; a small farm. — *n* **croft'er** someone who runs or farms a croft. — *n* **croft'ing**. [O.E.]

Crohn's disease *krōnz diz-ēz'*, *n* a chronic inflammatory disease esp. affecting the distal portion of the small bowel, causing scarring and thickening of the bowel wall. [B. *Crohn* (born 1884), U.S. physician.]

croissant *krwä'sã*, *n* a crescent-shaped breadroll made with a large quantity of butter and having a flaky consistency. [Fr.]

croix de guerre *krwä də ger*, (Fr.) *n* a military decoration for heroism in action.

Cro-Magnon *krō-mag'nən* or *krō-man'yɔ̃*, *adj* pertaining to an early type of Homo sapiens, long-skulled but short-faced, of late Palaeolithic times. [From *Cro-Magnon*, in Dordogne, where the first skulls of this race were found.]

cromlech *krom'lehh* or *-lek*, *n* a stone circle; formerly applied to a dolmen. [Welsh *cromlech* — *crom*, curved, circular, *llech*, a stone.]

Cromwellian *krom-wel'i-ən*, *adj* of or relating to Oliver *Cromwell*, Puritan and Lord Protector of the Commonwealth (1653–58). — *n* a supporter of Cromwell.

crone *krōn*, *n* an old woman (*derog*). [Perh. O.Fr. *carogne*, carrion, hag, directly or through Du.]

cronk *krongk*, (*Austr colloq*) *adj* ill; of poor quality; fraudulent. [From **crank**[1].]

crony *krō'ni*, *n* an intimate companion. — *n* **crō'nyism** (*US colloq*) the practice of appointing friends to well-paid posts regardless of their fitness for the posts. [Said to be orig. university slang — Gr. *chronios*, long-continued, perennial.]

crook *kro͝ok*, *n* a bend, or something bent; a staff bent at the end, as a shepherd's or bishop's; a professional swindler or thief; a curved tube used to lower the pitch of a wind instrument; a curved tube carrying the mouthpiece of a bassoon. — *adj* (*Austr* and *NZ colloq*) ill; inferior; nasty, unpleasant. — *vt* and *vi* to bend or form into a hook. — *adj* **crook'ed** bent;

containing an angle or series of angles; twisted, contorted; not straight, tipped at an angle; dishonest or illegal (*colloq*); (often *kro͞okt*) angry with (with *on*) (*Austr* and *NZ*). — *adv* **crook'edly**. — *n* **crook'edness**. — **go crook** (*Austr colloq*) to lose one's temper; **go crook on** or **at** (*Austr* and *NZ colloq*) to upbraid, rebuke. [Prob. O.N. *krōkr*, hook.]

croon *kro͞on*, *vi* to sing or hum in an undertone. — *vt* and *vi* to sing softly in a sentimentally contemplative manner. — Also *n*. — *n* **croon'er**. — *n* **croon'ing**. [Cf. Du. *kreunen*, to groan.]

crop *krop*, *n* a hunting whip with loop instead of lash; an act or mode of cutting; style of cutting or wearing short hair; the total quantity produced, cut, or harvested; the total growth or produce; a cultivated plant, collectively; a number, quantity (of products, ideas, etc.) produced or appearing at a time, a supply; a season's yield; the craw, a dilatation of a bird's oesophagus; a similar structure in another animal; an outcrop. — *vt* to cut off the top, ends, margins, or loose parts of; to cut short; to mow, reap, or gather; to bite off in eating; to raise crops on; to cut the hair of. — *vi* to yield a crop; to come to the surface (with *up* or *out*); hence, to come (up) casually, as in conversation: — *pr p* **cropp'ing**; *pa t* and *pa p* **cropped**. — *n* **cropp'er** someone who or that which crops; a plant that yields a crop; a person who raises a crop for a share of it; a fall (*colloq*); a failure (*colloq*). — *n* **cropp'ing** the act of cutting off; the raising of crops. — **crop circle** a swirled and flattened circle in a field of arable crop, formed in a spiral pattern and thought to be a natural phenomenon caused by particular meteorological conditions on an undulating landscape (also called **corn circle**); **crop'dusting** the spraying of crops with fungicides or insecticides from the air; **crop'duster** a person who or aeroplane that does this. — *adj* **crop'-eared** having ears cropped, or hair cropped to show the ears. — **crop'land** land used for growing crops; **crop'-marks** (*archaeol*) variations in the depth or colour of a crop growing in a field, which, viewed from the air, can show the presence of a structure beneath the soil. — **come a cropper** (*colloq*) to have a fall. [O.E. *crop*, the top shoot of a plant, the crop of a bird.]

croquet *krō'kā*, *n* a game in which wooden balls are driven by means of long-handled mallets, through a series of hoops. — *vt* to drive away by striking another ball in contact. [N.Fr. *croquet*, a dialect form of *crochet*, dimin. of *croc*, *croche*, a crook.]

croquette *krō-ket'*, *n* a ball or round cake, usu. of minced and seasoned meat, fish or potato, coated in breadcrumbs and fried. [Fr., — *croquer*, to crunch.]

crosier or **crozier** *krō'zhyər* or *-zyər*, *n* the pastoral staff or crook of a bishop or abbot; (*erroneously*) an archbishop's cross. — *adj* **cro'siered**. [M.E. *crose* or *croce* — L.L. *crocia*, a crook.]

cross *kros*, *n* a gibbet on which the Romans exposed criminals, typically consisting of two pieces of timber, one placed tranversely to the other; (with *cap*) the particular one on which Christ suffered; (with *cap*) the symbol of the Christian religion, or of the crusades; a representation of Christ's cross; any object, figure, or mark formed by two parts or lines transverse to each other, with or without elaboration; such a mark used instead of a signature by an illiterate person; such a mark used to symbolise a kiss in a letter; a monument not always in the form of a cross, where proclamations are made, etc.; a place in a town or village where such a monument stands or stood; a cross-shaped pendant or medal; a crossing or crossway; anything that crosses or thwarts; adversity or affliction in general, or a burden or cause of suffering, as in *bear one's cross*; mixing of breeds; a hybrid; something intermediate in character between two other things; a transverse pass, esp. towards the opposing team's goal (*football*, etc.). — *adj* lying across or crosswise; transverse; oblique; adverse; interchanged; peevish; angry, displeased (with); hybrid; balancing, neutralising. — *adv* and *prep* across. — *vt* to mark with a cross; to make the sign of the cross over; to set something, or draw a line, across; to place crosswise; to cancel by drawing cross lines; to pass from one side to the other of; to pass transversely, esp. in the direction of the opposing team's goal (*football*, etc.); to extend across; to interbreed; to draw two lines across (a cheque), thereby restricting it to payment through a bank; to obstruct; to thwart; to annoy; to bestride. — *vi* to lie or pass across; to meet and pass; to interbreed. — *adj* **crossed**. — *n* **cross'ing** the act of making the sign of the cross; the act of going across; a place where a roadway, etc., may be crossed; intersection; act of thwarting; cross-breeding. — *adv* **cross'ly**. — *n* **cross'ness**. — *adv* **cross'wise** across. — **cross'bar** a transverse bar; a kind of lever. — *adj* **cross'-barred**. — **cross'beam** a large beam stretching across a building and serving to hold its sides together; **cross'bench** a bench laid crosswise; a bench in Parliament on which independent members in Parliament sometimes sit. — *adj* independent; impartial. — **cross'bencher**; **cross'bill** a finch of the genus *Loxia* with mandibles crossing near the points; **cross'bones** a figure of two thigh-bones laid across each other — forming with the skull a conventional emblem of death or piracy; **cross'bow** a weapon for shooting bolts, formed of a bow placed crosswise on a stock; **cross'bower** or **cross'bowman**. — *adj* **cross'bred**. — **cross'breed** a breed produced by crossing; the offspring of a cross; **cross'breeding**; **cross-butt'ock** a particular throw over the hip in wrestling. — *vt* **cross'-check** to test the accuracy of e.g. a statement by consulting various sources of information. — Also *vi* and *n*. — **cross'-claim** a claim made by the defendant against the plaintiff. — *adj* and *adv* **cross-coun'try** through fields, woods, over hills, etc., rather than by road, esp. (of running, skiing, etc.) over a long distance. — *adj* **cross-cul'tural** pertaining to the differences between cultures; bridging the gap between cultures. — **cross'-current** (in the air, sea, or a river) a current flowing across the main current; **cross'cut** a crosswise cutting; a short way across from one point to another. — *vt* (*-kut'*) to cut across. — **crosscut saw** a large saw worked by two men, one at each end, for cutting beams crosswise; **cross'cutting** (*cinema* and *TV*) cutting and fitting together film sequences so that in the finished picture the action moves from one scene to another and back again, thus increasing dramatic tension; **cross'-dāting** (*archaeol*) dating one site, level, etc., by comparison with others; **cross'-dressing** transvestism; wearing unisex clothes; **crossed line** a telephone line connected in error to a different line or circuit; **cross-examinā'tion**. — *vt* **cross-exam'ine** to question minutely, or with a view to checking evidence already given; to subject to examination by the other side. — **cross'-eye**. — *adj* **cross'-eyed** squinting. — *vt* **cross'-fade** (*TV* and *radio*) to cause (a sound source or picture) to fade away while gradually introducing another (also *vi*). — **cross'-fertilisātion** the fecundation of a plant by pollen from another; fruitful interaction of ideas from e.g. different cultures. — *adj* **cross'field** (*football*; of a pass, etc.) usu. long and transverse in direction. — **cross'fire** (*mil*) the crossing of lines of fire from two or more points (also *fig*). — *adj* **cross'-grained** having the grain or fibres crossed or intertwined; perverse; contrary; intractable. — *adv* across the grain; perversely. — **cross'-hatching** (in drawing, etc.) shading by intersecting sets of parallel lines; **cross-infec'tion** infection of an already ill or injured person with germs unrelated to his or her own complaint, liable to occur e.g. in hospitals where a variety of diseases are being treated; infection from one species to another. — *vt* **cross-infect'**. — **cross'-kick** a crossfield kick; **cross-lat'eral** a person affected with cross-laterality. — Also *adj*. — **cross-lateral'ity** a mixture of physical one-sidedness, as the combination of a dominant left eye with a dominant right hand. — *adj* **cross'-leaved** having leaves in four rows, set crosswise. — *adj* **cross'-legged** having the legs crossed. — Also *adv*. — *adj* **cross'-magnetic** diamagnetic. — *vt* **cross'-match** to test (blood samples from a donor and a recipient) for compatibility. — **cross'over** a road passing over the top of another; a place or point at which a crossing or transfer is made. — *adj* **cross'-party** covering or drawn from all political parties. — **cross'patch** an ill-natured person; **cross'piece** a piece of material of any kind crossing another; **cross-ply tyre** tyre in which the plies of fabric in the carcass are wrapped so as to cross each other diagonally; **cross'-pollination** transfer of pollen from one flower to the stigma of another; **cross-pur'pose** a contrary purpose; (in *pl*) a game in which answers to questions are transferred to other questions; (in *pl*) confusion in conversation or action by misunderstanding. — *vt* **cross-ques'tion** to cross-examine. — **cross-ref'erence** a reference in a book to another title or passage. — *vi* and *vt* **cross-refer'**. — **cross'-rib** an arch supporting a vault; **cross'road** a road crossing the principal road, a bypath; a road joining main roads; (often in *pl*) a place where roads cross; (in *pl*) a stage at which an important decision has to be made. — *adj* **cross'roads**. — **cross-ruff'** (*cards*) alternate ruffing by partners, each leading a suit that the other lacks; **cross'-section** a transverse section; a comprehensive representation. — *vt* to make a cross-section of. — *adj* **cross-sec'tional**. — **cross'-staff** a surveying instrument consisting of a staff surmounted with a frame carrying two pairs of sights at right angles; **cross'-stitch** a stitch in the form of a cross; needlework of such stitches; **cross'-talk** interference of one telephone conversation with another; backchat; repartee; **cross'way** a way that crosses another or links others; **cross'wind** a wind blowing across the path of, e.g. an aeroplane; **cross'word** or **crossword puzzle** a type of puzzle invented in America in 1913, in which a square with blank spaces is to be filled with letters which, read across or down, will give words corresponding to clues given. — **cross one's fingers** or **keep one's fingers crossed** to place one finger across another in the hope of ensuring good luck; **cross one's heart (and hope to die)** to emphasise that one is being truthful by making the sign of a cross over one's heart; **cross someone's lips** to be uttered by someone; **cross someone's mind** to flash across someone's mind; **cross someone's palm** to put a coin in someone's hand; **cross someone's path** to come in someone's way; to thwart someone; **cross swords** to enter into a dispute (with); **on the cross** diagonally. [O.E. *cros* — O.N. *kross* — L. *crux*, *crucis*.]

crosse *kros*, *n* the stick with which the game of lacrosse is played, having at its top end a network of leather thongs enclosed in a triangular frame. [Fr.]

crotch *kroch*, *n* a fork, as of a tree; the bifurcation of the human body; the corresponding area in e.g. a pair of trousers; the human genital area. — *adj* **crotched**.

crotchet *kroch'it*, *n* a note in music, equal to half a minim, ♩; a crooked or perverse fancy; a whim, or conceit. — *adj* **crotch'eted** or **crotch'ety** having crotchets or peculiarities; short-tempered. [Fr. *crochet*, dimin. of *croche*, a hook; see **crochet**.]

croton *krō'tən*, *n* any plant of the *Croton* genus of tropical plants of the spurge family. — **croton oil** a powerful purgative obtained from the seeds of *Croton tiglium*. [Gr. *krŏtōn*, a sheep-tick, which the seed resembles.]

crouch *krowch*, *vi* to squat or lie close to the ground; to bend low with legs doubled; to cringe; to fawn. — *vt* to bend. — *n* act or position of crouching. [Possibly connected with **crook**.]

croup¹ *kro͞op*, *n* inflammation of the larynx and trachea in children, associated with difficulty in breathing and a peculiar ringing cough; a burr. — *vi* to croak or speak hoarsely. — *n* **croup'iness**. — *adj* **croup'ous**. — *adj* **croup'y**. [From the sound made.]

croup² or **croupe** *kro͞op*, *n* the rump of a horse; the place behind the saddle. [Fr. *croupe*, a protuberance.]

croupier *kro͞o'pi-ər* or *-pi-ā*, *n* a person who officiates at a gaming-table, collecting the stakes and paying the winners. [Fr., one who rides on the croup.]

croupous, croupy. See **croup¹**.

croûte *kro͞ot*, *n* a thick slice of fried bread for serving entrées. — *n* **croû'ton** (*-tɔ̃* or *-ton*) a small cube of fried bread. — **en croûte** (*cookery*) wrapped in pastry and baked. [Fr. *croûte*, crust.]

crow *krō*, *n* any of several large black birds of the genus *Corvus*, esp. *C. corone* (the so-called *carrion crow*); extended to other birds of this genus, esp. the rook; the defiant or triumphant cry of a cock; a child's inarticulate cry of joy. — *vi* to croak; to utter a crow; to boast, swagger, triumph (often with *over*): — *pa t* **crew** (*kro͞o*) or **crowed**. — **crow'-bar** a large iron bar usu. bent at the end, to be used as a lever; **crow'foot** a buttercup, sometimes extended to other plants (*pl* in this sense **crow'foots**); crow's-foot; **crow's'-foot** one of the wrinkles produced by age, spreading out from the corners of the eyes; **crow's'-nest** (*naut*) an elevated shelter for a man on the lookout. — *npl* **crow'-steps** step-like stonework on a gable. — **as the crow flies** in a straight line; **stone the crows** (*slang*) an expression of amazement, horror, etc. [O.E. *crāwe*, a crow, *crāwan*, to crow.]

crowd *krowd*, *n* a number of persons or things closely pressed together, without order; the rabble; multitude; a social set. — *vt* to gather into a lump or crowd; to fill by pressing or driving together; to compress; to thrust, put pressure on. — *vi* to press on; to press together in numbers; to swarm. — *adj* **crowd'ed**. — **crowd'-puller** a person, event, etc., attracting a large audience. [O.E. *crūdan*, to press.]

crown *krown*, *n* a circular head ornament, esp. as a mark of honour; the diadem or state-cap of royalty; kingship; the sovereign; governing power in a monarchy; honour; the top of anything, e.g. a head, hat, tree, arch; the visible part of a tooth; a substitute for this, made of gold or synthetic material, etc., fitted over a broken or bad tooth; (in gem-cutting) the upper of the two conical surfaces of a brilliant; the junction of root and stem of a plant; a short rootstock; a clasping metal cap for a bottle; chief ornament; completion or consummation; a coin orig. stamped with a crown, esp. a 5 shilling piece; used to translate various coin names, such as krone. — *vt* to cover or invest with a crown; to cap; to invest with royal dignity; (in draughts) to convert into a king or crowned man by the placing of another draught on the top on reaching the crown-head; to adorn; to dignify; to complete happily; to hit on the head (*slang*). — *adj* **crowned**. — *n* **crown'ing**. — *adj* **crown'less**. — **crown agent** a solicitor in Scotland who prepares criminal prosecutions; (with *caps*) one of a British body of business agents operating internationally, appointed by the Ministry for Overseas Development; **crown'-cap** a lined metal cap for a bottle; **crown colony** colony administered directly by the home government; **crown courts** the system of courts in England and Wales that administer criminal jurisdiction; **crown Derby** a late 18th-century porcelain made at Derby, marked with a crown; **crowned head** a monarch;

crown'-glass alkali-lime glass; window-glass formed in circular plates or discs; **crown'-green** a bowling-green with the centre higher than the edges; **crown'-head** (in draughts) the back row of squares, where a man is crowned; **crown-jew'el** a jewel pertaining to the crown or sovereign; **crown'-land** land belonging to the crown or sovereign; **Crown Office** the administrative office of the Queen's Bench Division of the High Court; the office in which the great seal is affixed; **crown-of-thorns starfish** or **Crown of Thorns** a starfish that eats living coral; **crown prince** the heir apparent to the crown; **crown princess** the female heir to a throne; the wife of a crown prince; **crown roast** roast ribs of lamb or pork arranged in a circle like a crown; **crown'-wheel** a wheel with teeth set at right angles to its plane; **crown witness** a witness for the crown in a criminal prosecution instituted by it. [O.Fr. *corone* — L. *corōna*; cf. Gr. *korōnos*, curved.]

crozier. See **crosier**.

CRT *abbrev* for cathode ray tube.

cru *krü*, (Fr.) *n* a vineyard or group of vineyards.

cruces. See **crux**.

crucial *kro͞o'shəl*, *adj* testing or decisive; essential, very important; very good (*slang*); crosslike; of the nature of a crux. [**crux**.]

crucian or **crusian** *kro͞o'shən*, *n* the German carp, without barbels. [L.G. *karusse* (Ger. *Karausche*) — L. *coracīnus* — Gr. *korakīnos*, a black perch-like fish — *korax*, raven.]

cruciate *kro͞o'shi-āt*, *adj* cross-shaped; crossing. [L. *crux*, *crucis*, a cross.]

crucible *kro͞o'si-bl*, *n* an earthen pot for melting ores, metals, etc. [L.L. *crucibulum*.]

crucifer *kro͞o'si-fər*, *n* a cross-bearer in a procession; a member of the Cruciferae. — *npl* **Crucif'erae** (*bot*) a family of dicotyledons, with cross-shaped flowers, including cabbage, turnip, cress, wallflower. — *adj* **crucif'erous** bearing or marked with a cross; with four petals placed crosswise; of the Cruciferae. [L. *crux*, *crucis*, a cross, *ferre*, to bear.]

cruciform *kro͞o'si-förm*, *adj* cross-shaped. [L. *crux*, *crucis*, a cross, *fōrma*, shape.]

crucify *kro͞o'si-fī*, *vt* to expose or put to death on a cross; to fasten to a wheel or the like, as a military field punishment; to subdue completely; to mortify; to torment; to treat harshly or cruelly; to hold up to scorn or ridicule: — *pr p* **cru'cifying**; *pa t* and *pa p* **cru'cified**. — *n* **cru'cifier** someone who crucifies. — *n* **cru'cifix** a figure or picture of Christ fixed to the cross. — *n* **crucifixion** (*-fik'shən*). [O.Fr. *crucifier* — L. *crucifīgĕre*, *crucifīxum* — *crux*, cross, *fīgĕre*, to fix.]

crud *krud* or *kro͝od*, (*slang*) *n* dirt, filth, esp. if sticky; radioactive waste; a contemptible person. — *adj* **crudd'y** dirty; contemptible. [**curd**.]

crude *kro͞od*, *adj* raw, unprepared: not reduced to order or form; unfinished; undigested; immature; unrefined; coarse, vulgar, rude; inartistic. — *n* crude oil. — *adv* **crude'ly**. — *n* **crude'ness**. — *n* **crud'ity** rawness; unripeness; that which is crude. — **crude oil** petroleum in its unrefined state. [L. *crūdus*, raw.]

crudités *krü-dē-tā*, (Fr.) *npl* raw fruit and vegetables served as an hors d'œuvre.

cruel *kro͞o'əl*, *adj* disposed to inflict pain, or pleased at suffering; devoid of pity, merciless, savage; severe. — *adv* **cru'elly**. — *n* **cru'elty**. — *adj* **cruel-heart'ed** delighting in cruelty. [Fr. *cruel* — L. *crūdēlis*.]

cruet *kro͞o'it*, *n* a small jar or bottle for sauces and condiments for the table; a vessel for wine, oil, or water for religious ceremonies. [A.Fr., dimin. of O.Fr. *cruye*, jar, from root of **crock**[1].]

cruise *kro͞oz*, *vi* to sail to and fro; (of a vehicle, aircraft, etc.) to progress smoothly at a speed economical in fuel, etc.; to wander about seeking something (with *about*, etc.; *colloq*); to go round public places looking for a sexual partner (*slang*). — *n* a sailing to and fro; a wandering voyage in search of an enemy or for the protection of vessels or for pleasure or health; a land journey of similar character. — *n* **cruis'er** someone who or that which cruises; a speedy warship, specially for cruising; a privateer; a cruising yacht; a cruiser-weight boxer. — **cruise missile** a subsonic guided missile using the air for support; **cruis'er-weight** a boxer between middle and heavy, a light-heavyweight (see **heavyweight**); **cruise'way** a canal for exclusively recreational use. [Du. *kruisen*, to cross.]

crumb *krum*, *n* a small bit or morsel of bread; a small particle of anything; the soft part of bread; a worthless person (*slang*). — *vt* to break into crumbs; to put crumbs in or on; to remove crumbs from. — *vi* to crumble. — *adj* **crumb'y** in crumbs; soft. — *adj* **crum'my** crumby; not good, worthless, inferior, unpleasant, out of sorts, etc. (*colloq*). [O.E. *cruma*.]

crumble *krum'bl*, *vt* to break into crumbs. — *vi* to fall into small pieces; to decay. — *n* a crumb; that which crumbles easily; a sweet dish consisting of a layer of stewed fruit covered with a crumbled mixture of flour, butter and sugar. — *npl* **crum'blies** (*slang*) very old people. — *adj* **crum'bly**. [Orig. dimin. of **crumb**.]

crumbs *krumz*, (orig. *schoolchildren's slang*) *interj* expressing surprise, dismay, etc. [Euph. for *Christ*.]

crumhorn. See **krummhorn**.

crummy. See **crumb**.

crump *krump*, (*mil slang*) *n* (the sound of) an exploding bomb, etc. — *vi* to make such a sound. [Imit.]

crumpet *krum'pət*, *n* a soft, unsweetened griddle cake; the head (*slang*); a girl (*slang*); women, female company (*slang*). [O.E. *crump* — *crumb*, crooked.]

crumple *krump'l*, *vt* to crush into irregular wrinkles; to wrinkle; to cause to collapse. — *vi* to wrinkle; to collapse. — *adj* **crump'led**. — *n* **crump'ling**. — **crumple zones** the front and rear portions of a motor car designed to crumple and absorb the impact in a collision while the passenger area remains intact. [O.E. *crump*, crooked.]

crunch *krunch*, *vt* to crush with harsh noise, with the teeth, under foot, etc.; to chew anything hard, and make such a noise. — *vi* to make such a noise; to chew with, or as with, such a noise. — *n* the act or sound of crunching; (with *the*) the real testing or critical moment, trial of strength, time or cause of difficulty, etc. (*colloq*); a crisis, emergency (*colloq*). — *n* **crunch'iness**. — *adj* **crunch'y**. — **number cruncher** and **number crunching** see under **number**.

crupper *krup'ər*, *n* a strap of leather fastened to the saddle and passing under the horse's tail to keep the saddle in its place; the hind part of a horse. [O.Fr. *cropiere* — *crope*, the croup.]

crusade *kro͞o-sād'*, *n* any one of many mediaeval military expeditions under the banner of the cross to recover the Holy Land from the Muslims; any daring or romantic undertaking; concerted action to further a cause. — *vi* to go on a crusade. — *n* **crusād'er** someone engaged in a crusade. [Fr. *croisade* — Prov. *crozada* — *croz* — L. *crux*, a cross.]

cruse *kro͞oz*, also *kro͞os*, *n* an earthen pot; a small cup or bottle. [Cf. O.N. *krūs*; Ger. *Krause*.]

crush *krush*, *vt* to break or bruise; to squeeze together; to beat down or overwhelm; to subdue; to ruin. — *vi* to become broken or crumpled under pressure. — *n* a violent squeezing; a close crowd of persons or things; a drink made from fruit juice; a narrowing passage for cattle; an infatuation (with *on*), or its object (*slang*). — *adj* **crush'able**. — *adj* **crushed**. — *n* **crush'er**. — *adj* **crush'ing**. — *adv* **crush'ingly**. — **crush bar** a bar in a theatre for selling drinks in the intervals of a play, etc.; **crush'-barrier** a barrier erected to restrain a crowd. [O.Fr. *croissir*.]

crusian. See **crucian**.

crust *krust*, *n* the hard rind or outside coating of anything; the outer part of bread; a dried-up scrap of bread; a livelihood (*slang*); the covering of a pie, etc.; the solid exterior of the earth; the dry scaly covering on a skin lesion; a layer of sediment on the side of the bottle in some wines and ports. — *vt* to cover with a crust or hard case. — *vi* to gather into a hard crust. — *adj* **crust'al** pertaining to a crust, esp. the earth's. — *adj* **crust'ate** or **crustāt'ed** covered with a crust. — *n* **crustā'tion** an adherent crust. — *adv* **crust'ily.** — *n* **crust'iness.** — *adj* **crust'less.** — *adj* **crust'y** of the nature of or having a crust, as port or other wine; having a hard or harsh exterior; hard; snappy; surly. [L. *crusta*, rind.]

Crustacea *krus-tā'shə* or *-shi-ə*, *npl* a large class of arthropod animals with hard shells, almost all aquatic — crabs, lobsters, shrimps, sand-hoppers, woodlice, water-fleas, barnacles, etc. — *adj* and *n* **crustā'cean.** — *adj* **crustā'ceous** crusty. [L. *crusta*, shell.]

crutch *kruch*, *n* a staff with a cross-piece at the head to place under the arm of a lame person; any support of like form; a bifurcation, crotch; a small figure inserted to show the number to be carried (*arith*). — *vt* to support; to prop; to clip wool from the hindquarters of (a sheep) (*Austr*). — *vi* to go on crutches. [O.E. *crycc*.]

crux *kruks*, *n* something that occasions difficulty or perplexity (*fig*); that on which a decision turns; the essential point, as of a problem: — *pl* **crux'es** or **cruces** (*kroo'sēz*). [L. *crux, crucis*, a cross.]

cruzado *kroo-zä'dō*, *n* the monetary unit of Brazil (100 centavos): — *pl* **cruza'dos.**

cry *krī*, *vi* to utter a shrill loud sound, esp. one of pain or grief; to weep; to bawl. — *vt* to utter loudly; to exclaim; to proclaim or make public; to offer for sale by crying out: — *3rd pers sing* **cries**; *pr p* **cry'ing**; *pa t* and *pa p* **cried** (*krīd*). — *n* any loud sound, esp. of grief or pain; a call or shout; a fit of weeping; a particular sound uttered by an animal; prayer; clamour; a watchword, battle-cry or slogan; a street call of wares for sale or services offered: — *pl* **cries.** — *n* **crī'er** someone who cries, esp. an official maker of proclamations. — *n* **cry'ing** the act of calling loudly; weeping. — *adj* calling loudly; claiming notice and usu. redress, as in *a crying shame*. — **cry'-baby** someone who cries childishly. — **a far cry** a great distance; **cry for the moon** to beg, or sigh, for something unattainable; **crying in the wilderness** voicing opinions or making suggestions that are not (likely to be) heeded; **cry off** to withdraw from an agreement; **cry one's eyes (**or **heart) out** to weep copiously or bitterly; **cry out** to give a shout or shriek, e.g. of alarm, pain, etc.; **cry out for** to be in urgent or obvious need of; **cry out to be (done, used,** etc.) to be someone or something that very much ought to be (done, used, etc.); **cry over spilt milk** to waste time in bemoaning what is irreparable; **cry stinking fish** to decry one's own goods; **cry up** to praise; **for crying out loud** (*slang*) an expression of frustration, impatience, etc.; **great cry and little wool** much ado about nothing; **in full cry** in full pursuit; **within cry of** within hearing distance. [Fr. *crier* — L. *quirītāre*, to scream.]

cryo- *krī-ō-* or *krī-o'-*, *combining form* denoting frost or ice. — *n* **cryobiol'ogy** the biology of organisms below their normal temperature. — *adj* **cryobiolog'ical.** — *n* **cryobiol'ogist.** — *n* **cry'ogen** (*-jen*) a substance used for obtaining low temperatures, a freezing mixture. — *adj* **cryogen'ic** pertaining to the science of cryogenics, or to work done, apparatus used, or substances kept, at low temperatures. — *nsing* **cryogen'ics** the branch of physics concerned with phenomena at very low temperatures. — *n* **cryogeny** (*-oj'ə-ni*) refrigeration; cryogenics. — *n* **cry'olite** an ice-stone or Greenland spar, sodium aluminium fluoride, earliest source of aluminium. — *n* **cryom'eter** a thermometer for low temperatures. — *adj* **cryomet'ric.** — *adj* **cryon'ic.** — *nsing* **cryon'ics** the practice of preserving human corpses by freezing them, with the idea that advances in science may enable them to be revived at some future time. — *adj* **cryophil'ic** (*biol*) able to thrive at low temperatures. — *n* **cry'ostat** apparatus for achieving or demonstrating cooling by evaporation; any apparatus for maintaining a low temperature. — *n* **cryosur'gery** surgery using instruments at very low temperatures. — *n* **cryother'apy** medical treatment using extreme cold. — **cryonic suspension** cryonics. [Gr. *kryos*, frost.]

crypt *kript*, *n* an underground chapel or cell. — *adj* **cryp'tal** pertaining to, or of the nature of, a crypt. [L. *crypta* — Gr. *kryptē* — *kryptein*, to hide.]

crypt- *kript-* or **crypto-** *-ō-* or *-o-*, *combining form* denoting hidden. — *n* **cryptanal'ysis** the art of deciphering codes, etc. — *n* **cryptan'alyst.** — *n* **crypto-Chris'tian.** — *n* **crypto-comm'unist.** — *adj* **cryptocryst'alline** with crystalline structure visible only under the microscope. — *n* **cryp'togam** any member of the class of flowerless plants. — *adj* **cryptogā'mian.** — *adj* **cryptogamic** (*-gam'ik*). — *adj* **cryptog'amous.** — *n* **cryptog'amist.** — *n* **cryptog'amy.** — *adj* **cryptogen'ic** (of diseases) of unknown origin. — *n* **cryp'togram** or **cryp'tograph** anything written in cipher. — *n* **cryptog'rapher** or **cryptog'raphist.** — *adj* **cryptograph'ic.** — *n* **cryptog'raphy.** — *adj* **cryptolog'ical.** — *n* **cryptol'ogist.** — *n* **cryptol'ogy** secret language; the scientific study of codes. — *n* **cryp'tonym** a secret name. — *adj* **crypton'ymous.** [Gr. *kryptos*, hidden.]

cryptic *krip'tik*, *adj* hidden; secret; unseen; mysteriously obscure. — *adv* **cryp'tically.** [L.L. *crypticus* — Gr. *kryptikos*, *kryptos* hidden.]

cryptosporidium *krip-tō-spō-rid'i-əm*, *n* a micro-organism of the genus *Cryptosporidium*, a cause of gastrointestinal disorders in humans and animals: — *pl* **cryptosporid'ia.** — *n* **cryptosporidiō'sis** a disease caused by infection by cryptosporidia. [**crypto-** and *sporidium*, a type of spore.]

crystal *kris'tl*, *n* rock-crystal, a clear quartz, like ice; a body, generally solid, whose atoms are arranged in a definite pattern, outwardly expressed by geometrical form with plane faces; a crystalline element, of piezoelectric or semiconductor material, functioning as e.g. a transducer, oscillator, etc. in an electronic device; a globe of rock-crystal or the like in which one may see visions (also **crystal ball**); anything bright and clear; a superior glass of various kinds; cut glass. — *adj* composed of or like crystal. — *adj* **crys'talline** (*-īn* or *-in*) like crystal or a crystal; composed of crystal, crystals, or parts of crystals; having the structure of a crystal. — *n* a crystalline substance. — *n* **crystallin'ity.** — *adj* **crystallī'sable** or **-z-.** — *n* **crystallīsā'tion** or **-z-.** — *vt* and *vi* **crys'tallise** or **-ize** to form into crystals; to make or become definite or concrete; (esp. of fruit) to coat with sugar crystals. — *n* **crys'tallite** a small, imperfectly formed or incipient crystal; a minute body in glassy igneous rocks. — *n* **crystallog'rapher.** — *adj* **crystallograph'ic.** — *n* **crystallog'raphy** the science of the structure, forms and properties of crystals. — *n* **crys'talloid** a substance in a state in which it dissolves to form a true solution which will pass through a membrane; a minute crystalline particle of protein (*bot*). — *adj* like a crystal; of the nature of a crystalloid. — *adj* **crys'tal-clear** very or completely clear. — **crys'tal-gazer; crys'tal-gazing** gazing in a crystal or the like to obtain visual images, whether in divination or to objectify hidden contents of the mind; **crystalline lens** the transparent refractive body of the eye; **crystal set** a simple radio receiver using only a crystal detector; **crystal violet** an antiseptic dye. [O.Fr. *cristal* — L. *crystallum* — Gr. *krystallos*, ice — *kryos*, frost.]

CS *abbrev* for: Chemical Society; Christian Science; Civil Service; Clerk to the Signet; Court of Session; Czechoslovakia (I.V.R.). — See also **CS gas**.

Cs (*chem*) *symbol* for caesium.

c/s *abbrev* for cycles per second (hertz).

CSA *abbrev* for Confederate States of America.

CSCE *abbrev* for Conference on Security and Co-operation in Europe.

CSE *abbrev* for Certificate of Secondary Education.

CSEU *abbrev* for Confederation of Shipbuilding and Engineering Unions.

CS gas *sē'es gas*, *n* an irritant gas that affects vision and respiration, synthesised in 1928 by Corson and Stoughton and used in riot control.

CSIRO *abbrev* for Commonwealth Scientific and Industrial Research Organisation.

CSM *abbrev* for Committee on Safety of Medicines.

CSO *abbrev* for community-service order.

CSP *abbrev* for: Chartered Society of Physiotherapists; Council for Scientific Policy.

c-spring. See **cee-spring**.

CST (*NAm*) *abbrev* for Central Standard Time.

CSU *abbrev* for Civil Service Union.

CSV *abbrev* for community service volunteer.

CSYS *abbrev* for Certificate of Sixth Year Studies.

CT *abbrev* for: Connecticut (U.S. state); same as **CAT** (see under **compute**).

Ct *abbrev* for Court (in addresses, etc.).

ct *abbrev* for: carat; cent; court.

CTC *abbrev* for: city technical college; city technology college; Cyclists' Touring Club.

CTCC *abbrev* for Central Transport Consultative Committee.

ctene *tēn*, *n* a comblike swimming organ in the Ctenophora. — *adj* **cteniform** (*tēn'* or *ten'*) or **cten'oid** comb-shaped. — *npl* **Ctenoph'ora** a class of Coelenterates — beautifully delicate, free-swimming marine organisms, moving by means of meridionally placed comblike plates. — *n* and *adj* **ctenoph'oran**. — *n* **cten'ophore** any member of the Ctenophora. [Gr. *kteis*, *ktenos*, comb.]

CTOL *abbrev* for conventional take-off and landing.

CTT *abbrev* for capital transfer tax.

Cu (*chem*) *symbol* for *cuprum* (L.), copper.

cu. or **cub.** *abbrev* for cubic.

cub[1] *kub*, *n* the young of certain animals such as foxes, etc.; a young boy or girl (playful or contemptuous, esp. of the ill-conditioned, unmannerly, raw or conceited); (in full **Cub Scout**) a member of the junior section of the Scout Association; a beginner, novice, apprentice. — *vt* and *vi* to bring forth (cubs): — *pr p* **cubb'ing**; *pa t* and *pa p* **cubbed**.

cub[2] *kub*, *n* a cattle-pen; a chest. — *n* **cubb'y** or **cubb'y-hole** a snug enclosed place. [Prob. from L.G.]

Cuban *kū'bən*, *adj* pertaining to *Cuba* or its people. — *n* a native of Cuba. — **Cuban heel** (on footwear) a medium high heel without curves.

cubby-hole. See **cub**[2].

cube *kūb*, *n* a solid body having six equal square faces, a solid square; the third power of a quantity (*math*). — *vt* to raise to the third power (*math*); to cut into cubes; to calculate the amount or contents of in cubic units. — *adj* **cū'bic** or **cū'bical** pertaining to a cube; solid; (**cubic**) of or involving the third power or degree (*math*). — *adv* **cū'bically**. — *n* **cū'bicalness**. — *adj* **cū'biform**. — *n* **cū'bism** a modern movement in painting, which seeks to represent several aspects of an object seen from different standpoints arbitrarily grouped in one composition, making use of cubes and other solid geometrical figures. — *n* and *adj* **cū'bist**. — *n* **cū'boid** a rectangular parallelepiped esp. one whose faces are not all equal. — *adj* **cū'boid** or **cū'boidal** resembling a cube in shape. — **cube root** (*math*) the quantity of which the given quantity is the cube. [Fr., — L. *cubus* — Gr. *kybos*, a die.]

cubeb *kū'beb*, *n* the dried berry of *Piper cubeba*, a Sumatran climbing pepper shrub — used as a drug. [Fr. *cubèbe* — Ar. *kabābah*.]

cubic. See **cube**.

cubicle *kū'bi-kl*, *n* a bedroom; part of a dormitory or other large room which is partitioned off; a cell; a small compartment used for dressing and undressing as at a clinic, swimming pool, etc. [L. *cubiculum* — *cubāre*, to lie down.]

cubic zirconia. See under **zircon**.

cubism, etc. See **cube**.

cubit *kū'bit*, *n* an old measure, the length of the arm from the elbow to the tip of the middle finger. [L. *cubitum*, the elbow.]

cuboid, etc. See **cube**.

cuckold *kuk'əld*, *n* a man whose wife has proved unfaithful. — *vt* to make cuckold. — *n* **cuck'oldom** or **cuck'oldry** the state of a cuckold; the act of making a cuckold. [O.Fr. *cucuault* — *cucu*, cuckoo.]

cuckoo *kŏŏ'kŏŏ*, *n* a bird (*Cuculus canorus*) that cries *cuckoo*, noted for depositing its eggs in the nests of other birds; any bird of this or related genera; a silly person. — *adj* (*colloq*) silly. — **cuck'oo-clock** a clock in which the hours are told by a cuckoo-call; **cuck'oo-flower** a species of the *Cardamine* genus — lady's-smock; ragged Robin; **cuck'oo-pint** (*-pint* or *-pīnt*) the wake-robin, *Arum maculatum*; **cuck'oo-spit** or **-spittle** a froth secreted by frog-hoppers on plants, surrounding the larvae and pupae. [Imit.]

cucullate *kū'kul-āt* or *-kul'* or **cucullated** *-id*, *adj* hooded; shaped like a hood. [L. *cucullatus* — *cucullus*, a hood.]

cucumber *kū'kum-bər* or *-kəm-*, *n* a creeping plant with bristly lobed leaves and tendrils; its long cylindrical fruit, used as a salad and pickle. — **cool as a cucumber** calm, imperturbable. [L. *cucumis*, *-eris*.]

cucurbit *kū-kûr'bit*, *n* a chemical vessel used in distillation (orig. shaped like a gourd); a cucurbitaceous plant. — *adj* **cucur'bital** or **cucurbitā'ceous** pertaining to the **Cucurbitā'ceae** a family of sympetalous dicotyledons, including gourd, melon, etc.; gourd-like. [L. *cucurbita*, a gourd.]

cud *kud*, *n* food brought back from the first stomach of a ruminating animal to be chewed again. — **cud'-weed** a woolly composite plant of the genus *Gnaphalium*, or a related plant. — **chew the cud** (*colloq*) to meditate, to reflect. [O.E. *cwidu*.]

cuddie. See **cuddy**[2].

cuddle *kud'l*, *vt* to hug; to embrace; to fondle. — *vi* to lie close and snug together. — *n* a close embrace. — *adj* **cudd'lesome** or **cudd'ly** pleasant to cuddle, being e.g. attractively plump, soft, etc.; suggestive of, conducive to, cuddling.

cuddy[1] *kud'i*, *n* a small cabin or cookroom, in the forepart of a boat or lighter; in large vessels, the officers' cabin under the poop-deck.

cuddy[2] or **cuddie** *kud'i*, (*Scot* and *dialect*) *n* a donkey; a horse; a stupid person. [Perh. *Cuthbert*.]

cudgel *kuj'l*, *n* a heavy staff; a club. — *vt* to beat with a cudgel: — *pr p* **cudg'elling**; *pa t* and *pa p* **cudg'elled**. — *n* **cudg'eller**. — *n* **cudg'elling**. [O.E. *cycgel*.]

cue[1] *kū*, *n* the last words of an actor's speech serving as a hint to the next speaker; any hint. — *vt* to give a cue to; to insert (e.g. a film sequence, sound effect, etc.) into a script: — *pr p* **cue'ing** or **cū'ing**; *pa t* and *pa p* **cued**. — **cue someone in** (orig. *US slang*) to inform (someone); **on cue** just at the right moment. [According to some from Fr. *queue*, tail (see next word); in 17th cent. written Q, and derived from L. *quando*, when, i.e. when the actor was to begin.]

cue[2] *kū*, *n* a twist of hair at the back of the head; a rod used in playing billiards, etc. — *vt* to form a cue in (hair); to hit (a ball) with a cue (also *vi*): — *pr p* **cue'ing** or **cū'ing**; *pa t* and *pa p* **cued.** — *n* **cue'ist** a billiard-player. — **cue'-ball** the ball struck by the cue. [Fr. *queue* — L. *cauda*, a tail.]

cuesta *kwes'tə*, *n* a hill ridge having a steep scarp on one side and a gradual slope on the other, caused by denudation of gently dipping hard rock strata. [Sp.]

cuff[1] *kuf*, *n* a light blow with the open hand. — *vt* to strike with the open hand; to beat.

cuff[2] *kuf*, *n* the end of the sleeve near the wrist; a covering for the wrist; a handcuff; a turned-up fold at the bottom of a trouser leg (*NAm* and *Austr*). — **cuff'-link** either of a pair of usu. decorative fasteners, orig. consisting of two buttons linked together, now usu. one button-like object attached to a pivoting bar, used for fastening a shirt cuff. — **off the cuff** unofficially and offhand; improvised; **on the cuff** (*US*) on tick; on the house. [Prob. cognate with **coif.**]

cui bono? *kī* or *kwē bō'nō* or *koo'ē bo'nō*, (L.) for whose benefit is it?; who is the gainer?

cuirass *kwi-ras'*, *n* a defensive breastplate and back-plate fastened together; a breastplate alone. — *vt* to furnish with a cuirass. — *n* **cuirassier** (-*ēr'*) a horse-soldier wearing a cuirass. [Fr. *cuirasse* — *cuir*, leather — L. *corium*, skin, leather.]

cuish. See **cuisse.**

cuisine *kwē-zēn'*, *n* cookery; a kitchen or cooking department. — *n* **cuisin'ier** (-*yā*) a cook. — **cuisine minceur** (*mɜ̃-sœr*; Fr., slenderness) a style of cooking characterised by imaginative use of light, simple ingredients. [Fr., — L. *coquīna* — *coquĕre*, to cook.]

cuisse *kwis* or **cuish** *kwish*, *n* thigh armour. [Fr. *cuisse* — L. *coxa*, hip.]

cul-de-sac *kool'də-sak* or *kul'*, *n* a street, etc. closed at one end; a blind-alley. [Fr. *cul*, bottom — L. *cūlus*; Fr. *de*, of, *sac*, sack.]

Culex *kū'leks*, *n* the typical genus of **Culic'idae** or gnats; (without *cap*) an insect of this genus: — *pl* **culices** (*kū'li-sēz*). — *adj* **culiciform** (-*lis'*). — *n* **cu'licine.** — *n* **cu'licid.** [L. *culex*, -*icis*.]

culinary *ku'lin-ər-i*, *adj* pertaining to the kitchen or to cookery; used in the kitchen. [L. *culīnārius* — *culīna*, a kitchen.]

cull *kul*, *vt* to select; to pick out and destroy, as inferior or superfluous members of a group, e.g. of seals, deer. — *n* an act of culling; an unsuitable animal eliminated from a flock or herd. — *n* **cull'er.** — *n* **cull'ing.** [Fr. *cueillir*, to gather — L. *colligĕre*, to gather together.]

cullet *kul'it*, *n* waste glass, melted up again with new material. [Fr. *collet* — L. *collum*, neck.]

cullis *kul'is*, *n* a roof gutter or groove. [Fr. *coulisse.*]

culm[1] *kulm*, *n* a grass or sedge stem. — *vi* to form a culm. — *adj* **culmif'erous** having a culm. [L. *culmus*, a stalk.]

culm[2] *kulm*, *n* coal-dust; anthracite dust. — *adj* **culmif'erous** producing culm.

culmen *kul'men*, *n* the top ridge of a bird's bill. [L., a summit.]

culmiferous. See **culm**[1,2].

culminate *kul'min-āt*, *vi* to reach the highest point (with *in*); to be on, or come to, the meridian, and thus the highest (or lowest) point of altitude (*astron*). — *vt* to bring to the highest point. — *adj* **cul'minant** at its highest point. — *n* **culminā'tion** the act of culminating; the top; the highest point; transit of a body across the meridian (*astron*). [L.L. *culmināre*, -*ātum* — *culmen*, or *columen*, -*inis*, a summit.]

culottes *kū-lot'* or *koo-*, *npl* a divided skirt. [Fr. *culotte*, breeches.]

culpable *kul'pə-bl*, *adj* faulty; criminal. — *n* **culpabil'ity** or **cul'pableness** liability to blame. — *adv* **cul'pably.** — *adj* **cul'patory** expressive of blame. [L. *culpa*, a fault.]

culprit *kul'prit*, *n* a person at fault; a criminal. [From the fusion in legal phraseology of *cul.* (*culpable*, *culpābilis*), and *prit*, *prist*, ready.]

cult *kult*, *n* a system of religious belief; a sect; an unorthodox or false religion; a great, often excessive, admiration for a person or idea; the person or idea giving rise to such admiration; (with *of*) a fad. — *adj* applied to objects associated with pagan worship; pertaining to, or giving rise to, a cult, extremely fashionable. — *adj* **cult'ic** or **cult'ish** pertaining to, characteristic of a cult. — *n* **cult'ism** adherence to a cult. — *n* **cult'ist.** [L. *cultus* — *colĕre*, to worship.]

cultigen *kul'ti-jen*, *n* a cultivated type of plant of uncertain origin.

cultivate *kul'ti-vāt*, *vt* to fill or produce by tillage; to prepare for crops; to devote attention to; to civilise or refine. — *adj* **cul'tivable** or **cultivāt'able.** — *n* **cultivar** (*kul'ti-vär*) a plant variety produced from a naturally occurring species, that has been developed and maintained by cultivation (*culti*vated *var*iety). — *n* **cultivā'tion** the art or practice of cultivating; civilisation; refinement. — *n* **cul'tivātor** a person who cultivates; an agricultural implement — a grubber. [L.L. *cultivāre*, -*ātum* — L. *colĕre*, to till, to worship.]

culture *kul'chər*, *n* cultivation; the state of being cultivated; refinement; the result of cultivation; a type of civilisation; the attitudes and values which inform a society; a crop of experimentally-grown bacteria or the like. — *vt* to cultivate; to improve. — *adj* **cul'turable.** — *n* **cul'tural.** — *adv* **cul'turally.** — *adj* **cul'tured** cultivated; well educated; refined. — *adj* **cul'tureless.** — *n* **cul'turist** a devotee of culture; a person who grows cultures in a laboratory. — **cultural anthropology** social anthropology; **cultural** or **culture shock** disorientation caused by an abrupt change from one environment, culture, ideology, etc., to another; **cultured pearl** a pearl grown round a small foreign body deliberately introduced into an oyster's shell; **culture medium** a nutritive substance on which cultures can be grown; **culture vulture** a derogatory term for one who has an extravagant interest in the arts. [L. *cultūra* — *colĕre.*]

culvert *kul'vərt*, *n* an arched channel for carrying water beneath a road, railway, etc. [Perh. from Fr. *couler*, to flow.]

cum *kum*, *prep* combined with; with the addition of (as *cum-dividend*, of shares, including the right to the next dividend); used as a combining form to indicate dual function, nature, etc., as in *kitchen-cum-dining-room*. [L.]

cumarin. See **coumarin.**

cumbersome *kum'bər-səm*, *adj* unwieldy, awkward, unmanageable. — *n* **cum'brance** encumbrance, hindrance, burden. — *adj* **cum'brous** hindering; obstructing; unwieldy. [App. O.Fr. *combrer*, to hinder — L.L. *cumbrus*, a heap — L. *cumulus*, a heap.]

cumec *kū'mek*, (*eng*) *n* short for *cu*bic *me*tre per se*c*ond, a unit for measuring volumetric rate of flow.

cumin or **cummin** *kum'in* or *kū'min*, *n* an umbelliferous plant of the Mediterranean region, with seeds like caraway, used for flavouring and valuable as carminatives. [O.E. *cymen* — L. *cumīnum* — Gr. *kymīnon.*]

cummerbund *kum'ər-bund*, *n* a waist-belt, a sash. [Pers. *kamarband*, a loin-band.]

cummin. See **cumin.**

cumquat *kum'kwot*, *n.* Same as **kumquat.**

cumulate *kūm'ū-lāt*, *vt* and *vi* to heap together; to accumulate. — *adj* **cum'ulate** or **cum'ulated** heaped up. — *n* **cumulā'tion** accumulation. — *adj* **cum'ulative** increasing by successive additions. — *adv* **cum'ulatively.** — **cumulative vote** a system by which a voter may distribute a number of votes at will among the candidates, giving more than one to a candidate if he or she chooses. [L. *cumulāre*, *-ātum* — *cumulus*, a heap.]

cumulus *kū'mū-ləs*, *n* a heap; a kind of cloud consisting of rounded heaps with a darker horizontal base: — *pl* **cū'mulī**. — *adj* **cū'muliform**. — *adj* **cū'mulose**. — **cūmulo-cirr'us** a delicate cirrus-like cumulus; **cūmulo-nim'bus** a cumulus discharging showers. [L. *cumulus*, a heap.]

cuneal *kū'ni-əl* or **cuneate** *kū'ni-āt*, *adj* wedge-shaped. — *adj* **cuneat'ic** cuneiform. — *adj* **cunei-form** (*kū-nē'i-förm*, *kūn'i-i-förm* or *kū'ni-förm*) wedge-shaped — specially applied to the old Hittite, Babylonian, Assyrian and Persian writing, of which the characters were impressed by the wedge-shaped facets of a stylus. — *n* cuneiform writing. [L. *cuneus*, a wedge.]

cunjevoi *kun'ji-voi*, (*Austr*) *n* a sea squirt; a large-leaved araceous plant. [Aboriginal.]

cunnilingus *kun-i-ling'gəs*, *n* oral stimulation of the female genitalia. [L. *cunnus*, vulva, *lingĕre*, to lick.]

cunning *kun'ing*, *adj* knowing; skilful; artful; crafty. — *n* knowledge; skill; faculty of using stratagem to accomplish a purpose; craftiness; artifice. — *adv* **cunn'ingly**. — *n* **cunn'ingness** the quality of being cunning; artfulness, slyness. [O.E. *cunnan*, to know.]

cunt *kunt*, (*vulg*) *n* the female genitalia; a woman regarded as a sexual object; an unpleasant, contemptible person. [M.E. *cunte*.]

CUP *abbrev* for Cambridge University Press.

cup *kup*, *n* a drinking-vessel, usu. roughly hemispherical; a hollow; a cup-shaped structure (*biol*); either of the two cup-shaped supports for the breasts in a brassière; a cupful; a dry or liquid measure used in cooking; half a pint (*US*); the liquid contained in a cup; a mixed beverage made with wine (as *claret-cup*); an ornamental vessel offered as a prize; a competition with such a vessel as a prize; the hole, or its metal lining, on the green (*golf*); the chalice, or the consecrated wine, at the Eucharist. — *vt* to form into a cup; to lodge in or as if in a cup. — *vi* to become cup-shaped: — *pr p* **cupp'ing**; *pa t* and *pa p* **cupped**. — *n* **cup'ful** as much as fills a cup: — *pl* **cup'fuls**. — *n* **cup'pa** (*colloq*) a cup of tea. — **cup'-and-ball** a ball and socket joint; the game of catching a tethered ball in a cup on the end of a stick; **cup'-cake** a small round cake baked in a foil or paper case; **cup'-mark** a cup-shaped hollow made by prehistoric man on rocks, standing-stones, etc.; **cup'-tie** (*sport*) one of a series of games to determine the winners of a cup. — **there's many a slip 'twixt cup and lip** failure is possible at the last moment. [O.E. *cuppe* — L. *cūpa*, *cuppa*, a tub.]

cupboard *kub'ərd*, *n* an item of furniture, or a recess fitted with a door, used for storage. — *vt* to store. — **cup'board-love** hypocritical show of affection for material gain.

cupel *kū'pəl*, *n* a small vessel used by goldsmiths in assaying precious metals. — *vt* to assay in a cupel: — *pr p* **cū'pelling**; *pa t* and *pa p* **cū'pelled**. — *n* **cūpellā'tion** recovery of precious metal in assaying. [L. *cūpella*, dimin. of *cūpa*; see **cup**.]

Cupid *kū'pid*, *n* the Roman love-god, identified with Greek Eros; (without *cap*) a winged figure of a young boy representing the love-god (*art*, etc.). — *adj* **cūpid'inous** full of desire, esp. amorous. — *n* **cūpid'ity** covetousness. [L. *Cūpīdo*, *-inis* — *cupĕre*, to desire.]

cupola *kū'pə-lə*, *n* a spherical vault, or concave ceiling, on the top of a building; the internal part of a dome; a lantern on the top of a dome; an armoured dome or turret to protect a gun; a furnace used in iron-foundries. — *vt* to furnish with a cupola. — *adj* **cū'pola'd** or **cū'polaed**. — *adj* **cū'polar**. — *adj* **cū'polated**. [It., — L. *cūpula*, dimin. of *cūpa*, a cask.]

cuppa. See **cup**.

cupreous *kū'pri-əs*, *adj* of, containing, or like copper. — *adj* **cū'pric** of or containing bivalent copper. — *adj* **cūprif'erous** yielding copper. — *adj* **cū'prous** of or containing univalent copper. — *n* **cū'pro-nickel** an alloy of copper and nickel. [L. *cupreus* — *cuprum*; see **copper**[1].]

cupule *kū'pūl*, *n* a small cup in a liverwort containing gemmae (*bot*); a cup-shaped envelope on the fruit of some trees, e.g. oak, beech, chestnut. — *adj* **cū'pūlar** or **cū'pūlate** cup-like; pertaining to a cupule. — *adj* **cūpūlif'erous** bearing cupules. [L. *cūpula*, dimin. of *cūpa*, tub.]

cur *kûr*, *n* a worthless dog, of low breed; a contemptible scoundrel. — *adj* **curr'ish**. — *adv* **curr'ishly**. — *n* **curr'ishness**. [M.E. *curre*.]

cur. or **curt.** *abbrev* for current (this month).

curaçao or **curaçoa** *kōō-rä-sä'ō*, *kū'rə-sō* or *kū-ra-sō'*, *n* a liqueur flavoured with bitter orange peel. [*Curaçao*, island in W. Indies, where first made.]

curacy. See **curate**[1].

curare or **curari** *kū-* or *kōō-rä'ri*, *n* a paralysing poison extracted from wourali root, etc., by S. American Indians for arrows — now a source of valuable drugs. — *n* **cura'rine** a highly poisonous alkaloid derivative, used, e.g. in surgery, as a muscle relaxant. — *vt* **cu'rarise** or **-ize**. [Port. from Carib *kurari*.]

curassow *kū'rə-sō* or *kū-räs'ō*, *n* a large turkey-like S. American bird. [From the island of *Cura cao*.]

curate[1] *kūr'it*, *n* a clergyman in the Church of England, assisting a rector or vicar. — *n* **cur'acy** (*-ə-si*) or **cur'ateship** the office, employment, or benefice of a curate. — **curate's egg** anything of which only parts are excellent. [L.L. *cūrātus*, L. *cūra*, care.]

curate[2] *kūr-āt'*, *vt* to act as curator for (e.g. an exhibition or museum). [Back-formation from **curator**.]

curative. See **cure**.

curator *kūr-ā'tər* (in Scots law *kūr'ə-tər*), *n* a person who has the charge of anything; a superintendent, esp. of a museum: — *fem* **curā'trix**. — *adj* **curatorial** (*-ə-tö'ri-əl*). — *n* **curā'torship**. [L. *cūrātor*.]

curatory. See **cure**.

curb *kûrb*, *n* a chain or strap attached to the bit for restraining a horse; another spelling for **kerb** (chiefly *US*); a check or restraint. — *vt* to furnish with or guide by a curb; to restrain or check. [Fr. *courbe* — L. *curvus*, bent.]

curcuma *kûr-kū'mə*, *n* any plant of the *Curcuma* genus of the ginger family yielding turmeric. — *n* **cur'cumine** the colouring matter of turmeric. [Ar. *kurkum*, saffron.]

curd *kûrd*, *n* milk thickened or coagulated by acid; the cheese part of milk, as distinguished from the whey; any substance of similar consistency; the flowering head of cauliflower, broccoli, etc. — *vt* and *vi* to curdle. — *n* **curd'iness**. — *vt* and *vi* **curd'le** to turn into curd; to coagulate; to thicken. — *adj* **curd'y**. — **curd cheese** a mild white cheese made from skimmed milk curds. [Prob. Celt.]

cure *kūr*, *n* that which heals; a remedy, or course of remedial treatment; a means of improving a situation; a course or method of preserving or arresting decomposition; the total quantity cured; treatment by which a product is finished or made ready for use; care of the sick; an act of healing. — *vt* to heal or make better; to preserve as by drying, salting, etc.; to finish by means of chemical change, or to use heat or chemicals in the last stage of preparing (a thermosetting plastic). — *vi* to undergo a process or course of curing. — *adj* **cūr'able**. — *n* **cūr'ableness**. — *n* **cūrabil'ity**. — *adj* **cūr'ative** or **cūr'atory** tending to cure. — *adj* **cūre'less**. — *n* **cūr'er**. — **cūre'-all** a panacea. [O.Fr. *cure* — L. *cūra*, care.]

curé *kū'rā*, *n* a parish priest in France. [Fr.; see **curate**[1].]

curettage *kū-ret'ij*, *n* scraping of a body cavity by means of a surgeon's instrument known as a **curette'**. — *vt* **curette'** to scrape with a curette. — *n* **curette'ment** curettage. [Fr. *curer*, to clean, clear.]

curfew *kûr'fū*, *n* a regulation obliging persons to be indoors within certain hours; the ringing of a bell at a certain hour as a traditional custom, or the bell itself; the time of curfew; in feudal times, the ringing of a bell as a signal to put out all fires and lights. — **cur'few-bell**. [O.Fr. *covrefeu*; *couvrir*, to cover, *feu*, fire.]

curia *kū'ri-ə*, *n* the court of the papal see. [L. *cūria*, one of the divisions of a Roman tribe, a senate, a court.]

curie *kū-rē'* or *kū'rē*, *n* a unit of radioactivity, defined as 3.7×10^{10} disintegrations per second (becquerels), or the quantity of a radioactive substance which undergoes this number of disintegrations; orig., the quantity of radon in radioactive equilibrium with a gram of radium. — *n* **curium** (*kū'*) a chemical element (atomic no. 96; symbol **Cm**). [After Marie and Pierre *Curie*, discoverers of radium.]

curio *kū'ri-ō*, *n* any article of bric-à-brac, or anything considered rare and curious: — *pl* **cū'rios**. [For **curiosity**.]

curious *kū'ri-əs*, *adj* anxious to learn; inquisitive; singular; rare; odd. — *n* **curiosity** (*-os'i-ti*) state or quality of being curious; inquisitiveness; that which is curious; anything rare or unusual. — *adv* **cū'riously**. — *n* **cū'riousness**. [Fr. *curieux* — L. *cūriōsus*.]

curium. See **curie**.

curl *kûrl*, *vt* to twist into ringlets; to coil; to cause to move in a curve. — *vi* to shrink into ringlets; to move in curves; to writhe; to eddy; to play at the game of curling. — *n* a ringlet of hair, or what is like it; a wave, bending, or twist; a plant disease in which leaves curl; a curled condition. — *adj* **curled**. — *n* **curl'er** someone who, or that which, curls; a player at the game of curling. — *n* **curl'iness**. — *n* **curl'ing** a game common in Scotland, consisting in sliding heavy smooth stones along a sheet of ice. — *adj* **curl'y**. — **curl'ing-īrons** or **curl'ing-tongs** an instrument used for curling the hair; **curl'ing-pond** a pond on which curling is played; **curl'ing-stone** a heavy stone with a handle, used in playing curling; **curl'-paper** a paper twisted into the hair to give it curl; **curl'y-greens** kale. — *adj* **curl'y-headed**. — **curl up** (*colloq*) to be embarrassed; **out of curl** lacking energy, limp. [M.E. *crull*.]

curlew *kûr'lōō* or *-lū*, *n* a moorland bird of the woodcock family with long curved bill and long legs, and plaintive whistling cry. [O.Fr. *corlieu*; prob. from its cry.]

curlicue *kûr'lə-kū*, *n* a fancy twist or curl. [**curly** and **cue**[1].]

curmudgeon *kər-muj'ən*, *n* an avaricious, ill-natured, churlish fellow; a miser. — *adj* and *adv* **curmud'geonly**.

curmurring *kər-mûr'ing*, *n* a rumbling sound, esp. that made in the bowels by flatulence. [Imit.]

currach or **curragh** *kur'ə* or *kur'əhh*, *n* a long-shaped boat of similar construction to a coracle. [Ir. *curach*.]

currajong. See **kurrajong**.

currant *kur'ənt*, *n* a small black raisin or dried seedless grape (imported from eastern Mediterranean countries); extended to several species of the genus *Ribes* (*black*, *red*, *white*, *flowering currant*), and to various other plants, and their fruits. — *adj* **curr'anty**. — **curr'ant-bread** a sweetened bread with some (grape) currants in it; **curr'ant-bun** or **-loaf** a dark spiced cake full of currants; **curr'ant-cake** a cake with currants in it; **curr'ant-jelly** a jelly made from red or black currants; **curr'ant-wine**. [*Corinth*.]

currawong *kur'ə-wong*, *n* any of several Australian birds of the genus *Strepera*, with a distinctive, resounding call. [Aboriginal.]

current *kur'ənt*, *adj* belonging to the period of time now passing, up-to-date; present; generally or widely received; passing from person to person. — *n* a running or flowing; a stream; a portion of water or air moving in a certain direction; a flow of electricity; course. — *n* **curr'ency** circulation; that which circulates, esp. the money of a country; general estimation; up-to-dateness. — *adv* **curr'ently**. — *n* **curr'entness**. — **current account** a bank account on which one is usu. not paid interest and from which money may be withdrawn by cheque, etc.; **pass current** to be received as genuine. [L. *currēns*, *-entis* — pres. p. of *currĕre*, to run.]

curricle *kur'i-kl*, *n* a two-wheeled open chaise, drawn by two horses abreast. [L. *curriculum*, course, race, racing chariot — *currĕre*, to run.]

curriculum *kə-rik'ū-ləm*, *n* a course, esp. the course of study at a university, etc.: — *pl* **curric'ula** or **curric'ulums**. — *adj* **curric'ular** of or relating to a curriculum or to courses of study. — **curriculum vitae** (*kə-rik'ūl-əm vī'tē*, *kōōr-ik'ŏŏ-lŏŏm vē'tī* or *wē'tī*) (a biographical sketch of) the course of someone's life esp. details of education and achievements. [Ety. as for **curricle**.]

curried, **currier**. See **curry**[2].

currish, **currishly**, etc. See **cur**.

curry[1] *kur'i*, *n* a meat or other dish prepared with turmeric and mixed spices. — *vt* to make a curry of. — **curr'y-powder** ground spices and turmeric. [Tamil *kari*, sauce.]

curry[2] *kur'i*, *vt* to dress (leather); to rub down and dress (a horse); to beat; to scratch: — *pr p* **curr'ying**; *pa t* and *pa p* **curr'ied**. — *n* **curr'ier** a person who curries or dresses tanned leather. — *n* **curr'ying**. — **curr'y-comb** an iron instrument or comb used for currying or cleaning horses. — **curry favour** to seek to ingratiate onself. [O.Fr. *correier*, *conrei*, outfit, from L. *con-*, with, and the root seen in **array**.]

curse *kûrs*, *vt* to invoke or wish evil upon; to blaspheme; to afflict with; to damn; to excommunicate. — *vi* to utter abuse; to swear. — *n* an invocation or wishing of evil or harm; evil invoked on another person; the excommunication sentence; an imprecation; any great evil; (with *the*) menstrual period (*colloq*). — *adj* **curs'ed** under a curse; hateful. — *adv* **curs'edly**. — *n* **curs'edness**. — *n* **curs'er**. — *n* **curs'ing**. [O.E. *cursian* — *curs*, a curse.]

cursive *kûr'siv*, *adj* (of handwriting) written with a running hand; flowing; (of a typeface) designed to imitate handwriting. — *adv* **cur'sively**. [L.L. *cursīvus* — L. *currĕre*, to run.]

cursor *kûr'sər*, *n* a sliding part of a measuring instrument; one of several (usu. flashing) devices appearing on a VDU screen used to indicate position, e.g. of the next input character. — *adj* **curso'rial** adapted for running. — *adv* **cur'sorily** (*-sər-*). — *n* **cur'soriness**. — *adj* **cur'sory** running quickly over; hasty; superficial. [L. *cursor*, pl. *cursōrēs*, a runner.]

curt *kûrt*, *adj* short; concise; discourteously brief or summary. — *adv* **curt'ly**. — *n* **curt'ness**. [L. *curtus*, shortened.]

curtail *kər-tāl'*, *vt* to cut short; to cut off a part of; to abridge. — *n* **curtail'ment**. [Old spelling *curtal*, O.Fr. *courtault* — L. *curtus*, shortened.]

curtain *kûr'tən*, *n* hanging drapery at a window, around a bed, etc.; the part of a rampart between two bastions (*fort*); a screen of cloth or metal concealing the stage, or restricting the spread of fire (*theat*); the fall of the curtain, close of a scene or act (*theat*); a protective barrier in general. — *vt* to enclose or furnish with curtains; (with *off*) to separate with, or as if with, a curtain. — **curtain call** a summons from the audience to appear at the end of a scene;

cur'tain-raiser a short play preceding the main performance; an event which precedes and foreshadows a more important event; **curtain speech** a speech made in front of a theatre curtain; **curtain wall** a wall that is not load-bearing, e.g. does not support a roof. — **be curtains (for)** (*colloq*) to be the end or death (of); **behind the curtain** away from public view; **draw the curtain** to draw it aside, so as to show what is behind, or to draw it in front of anything so as to hide it. [O.Fr. *cortine* — L.L. *cortīna*.]

curtsy or **curtsey** *kûrt'si*, *n* a formal indication of respect (by women) made by bending the knees. — *vi* to make or 'drop' a curtsy. [**courtesy**.]

curvaceous, curvate, etc. See **curve**.

curve *kûrv*, *n* anything bent; a line that is not straight; a line (including a straight line) answering to an equation; a graph; the curved line on a graph representing the rise and fall of measurable data, e.g. birth-rate; a curved surace; (in *pl*) the rounded contours of a woman's body (*colloq*). — *vt* to bend; to form into a curve. — *vi* to bend; to move in a curve. — *adj* **curvaceous** or **curvacious** (*kûr-vā'shəs*; *colloq*) (of a woman) having shapely curves. — *adj* **cur'vāte** or **curvat'ed** curved or bent in a regular form. — *n* **curvā'tion**. — *adj* **cur'vative** (*-və-tiv*). — *n* **cur'vature** (*-və-chər*) a curving or bending; the continual bending, or the amount of bending, from a straight line; the reciprocal of the radius at any point. — *adj* **curved**. — *adj* **curvicau'date** having a crooked tail. — *adj* **curvicos'tate** having curved ribs. — *adj* **curvifō'liate** having curved leaves. — *adj* **cur'viform**. — *adj* **curvilin'eal** or **curvilin'ear** bounded by curved lines. — *n* **curvilinear'ity**. — *adj* **cur'ving**. — *adj* **curv'y**. [L. *curvus*, crooked.]

curvet *kûr'vet* or *kər-vet'*, *n* a light leap of a horse in which the forelegs are raised together, next the hindlegs with a spring before the forelegs touch the ground. — *vi* (*kər-vet'* or *kûr'vet*) to leap in curvets; to frisk: — *pr p* **curvett'ing** or **cur'veting**; *pa t* and *pa p* **curvett'ed** or **cur'veted**. [It. *corvetta*, dimin. of *corvo* — L. *curvus*.]

curvicaudate, curvilineal, etc. See **curve**.

cusec *kū'sek*, (*eng*) *n* short for *cu*bic feet per *sec*ond, a unit for measuring volumetric rate of flow.

cush. See **cushion**.

cushat *kush'ət*, (*Scot*) *n* the ringdove or wood-pigeon. [O.E. *cūscute*, perh. from its note, and *scēotan*, to shoot.]

cushion *ko͝osh'ən*, *n* a case filled with some soft, elastic material, e.g. feathers or foam rubber, for resting on; a pillow; a pad; the elastic lining of the inner side of a billiard-table (*colloq* **cush**); a body of steam remaining in the cylinder of a steam-engine, acting as a buffer to the piston; anything that serves to a deaden a blow. — *vt* to seat on, or provide with, a cushion; to serve as a cushion for or against; to suppress (complaints) by ignoring. — *adj* **cush'ioned** furnished with a cushion, padded; having cushion-tyres. — *adj* **cush'iony** like a cushion, soft. — **cush'ion-tyre** or **-tire** a cycle tyre of rubber tubing, with rubber stuffing. [O.Fr. *coissin* — L. *coxīnum*, *coxa*, hip, or perh. L. *culcita*, mattress, cushion.]

Cushite or **Kushite** *ko͝osh'īt*, *n* a group of languages of eastern Africa; (a member of) a race speaking any of these languages. — *adj* of or relating to the languages or the race. — Also **Cushitic** or **Kushitic** (*-it'*). [*Cush*, an ancient kingdom in the Nile valley, and **-ite**.]

cushy *ko͝osh'i*, (*slang*) *adj* easy and comfortable. [Perh. Hind. *khush*, pleasant, *khushī*, happiness.]

cusp *kusp*, *n* a point; the point or horn of the moon, etc.; a toothlike meeting of two branches of a curve, with sudden change of direction; a toothlike ornament common in Gothic tracery (*archit*); a prominence on a tooth; a division between signs of the zodiac (*astrol*). — *adj* **cus'pate**. — *adj* **cusped**. — *adj* **cus'pid**. — *adj* **cus'pidal**. — *adj* **cus'pidate** or **cus'pidated** (*biol*) having a rigid point. [L. *cuspis*, *-idis*, a point.]

cuspidor or **cuspidore** *kus'pi-dör*, (*US*) *n* a spittoon. [Port., — L. *conspuĕre*, to spit upon.]

cuss *kus*, (*slang*) *n* a curse; a fellow. — *vt* and *vi* to curse. — *adj* **cuss'ed** cursed; obstinate. — *n* **cuss'edness** contrariness. — **cuss'-word**. [**curse**; prob. sometimes associated with **customer**.]

custard *kus'tərd*, *n* a baked mixture of milk, eggs, etc., sweetened or seasoned (now usu. **egg custard**); a cooked mixture of similar composition, thickened with cornflour. — **cus'tard-apple** the fruit of a W. Indian tree with eatable pulp, like a custard; **custard-pie comedy** slapstick, esp. of early U.S. films in which comedians threw custard pies at each other; **custard powder** a flavoured preparation containing cornflour, sugar, etc. for using with milk to make custard; **custard tart** a tart containing custard. [Earlier *custade*, a corruption of *crustade*, a pie with a crust; see **crust**.]

custody *kus'tə-di*, *n* a watching or guarding; care; security; imprisonment. — *adj* **custō'dial**. — *n* **custō'dian** a person who has care, esp. of some public building. — *n* **custō'dianship**. [L. *custōdia*, guard, *custōs*, *-ōdis*, a keeper.]

custom *kus'təm*, *n* what one is accustomed to doing; usage; frequent repetition of the same act; regular trade or business; any of the distinctive practices and conventions of a people or locality; a tax on goods; (in *pl*) duties on imports and exports; (in *pl*) the collecting authorities. — *adj* (esp. *US*) made to order. — *adv* **cus'tomarily**. — *n* **cus'tomariness**. — *adj* **cus'tomary** according to use and wont; usual; holding or held by custom. — *n* **cus'tomer** a person who usually frequents a certain place of business; a buyer; a person (*slang*). — *vt* **cus'tomise** or **-ize** to make in such a way as to suit specified individual requirements. — *adj* **cus'tomised** or **-z-**. — *adj* **cus'tom-built** or **cus'tom-made** built (as e.g. a motor car) or made to a customer's order. — **cus'tom-house** the place, esp. at a port, where customs or duties on exports and imports are collected. — **customs union** a group of states having free trade between themselves, and a common tariff policy toward non-member states. [O.Fr. *custume*, *costume* — L. *cōnsuētūdō*, *-inis* — *cōnsuēscĕre*, to accustom.]

cut *kut*, *vt* to penetrate with a sharp edge, make an incision in; to cleave or pass through; to divide; to carve, hew, make or fashion by cutting; to sever; to reap; to excise; to intersect; to divide (a pack of cards) by lifting the upper portion at random; to expose (a card or suit) in this way; (in tennis, golf, etc.) to strike obliquely, imparting spin to; to reduce, lessen or abridge; to wound, hurt, or affect deeply; to shorten; to pass intentionally without greeting; to renounce, give up; to stay away from; to make (a sound recording, e.g. a disc); to grow (teeth) through the gums. — *vi* to make an incision; to intersect; to strike obliquely; to be cut; to dash, go quickly; to run away, to be off (*slang*); (in film-making) to cease photographing; (of a film) to change rapidly to another scene: — *pr p* **cutt'ing**; *pa t* and *pa p* **cut**. — *n* a cleaving or dividing; an excavation for a road, railway, etc.; a cross passage; a stroke or blow; (in various games) a particular stroke, generally implying obliquity and spin; (in cricket) a stroke to the off side with horizontal bat; a reduction or diminution; an act of unkindness; the result of fashioning by cutting, carving, etc. (e.g. clothes, hair, gemstones); the act, or outcome, of cutting a pack of cards; an incision or wound; an excision; a piece cut off; total quantity cut; a varying unit of length for cloth and yarn; an engraved block or the picture from it; manner of cutting, or fashion; a rake-off or share (*slang*); in films, the action of cutting or its result. — *adj* (*slang*) (of a drug) adulterated or diluted. — *n* **cutt'er** a person or thing that cuts; a tailor who measures and cuts out the cloth; a small vessel with one mast, a mainsail, a forestay-sail, and a jib set to bowsprit-end; a powerful motor-launch which may be armed; a medium-sized pig carcase, from which joints and fillets are taken. — *n* **cutt'ing** a dividing or lopping off; an incision; a piece cut from a newspaper; a piece of a plant cut off for propagation; an open excavation for road, railway, etc.; editing of film or recording. — *adj* (of a remark, etc.) intended to be cruel or hurtful; (of wind) penetrating. — **cut'away** a coat with the skirt cut away in a curve in front; a model or picture showing the interior workings of something, with the overlying parts removed; (in films or television) a shot of action that is related to, or happening simultaneously to, the central events. — *adj* having parts cut away. — **cut'back** a going back in a plot to earlier happenings; a reduction or decrease, esp. in expenditure, workforce, production, etc.; **cut flowers** flowers cut from their plants for display in vases, etc.; **cut glass** flint glass shaped by cutting or grinding; **cut'-in** the act of cutting in; **cut'-off** that which cuts off or shortens; the point at which something ceases to operate or apply (also *adj*); **cut'-out** the act of cutting out; something which has been cut out; a safety device, e.g. for breaking an electric circuit. — *adj* **cut'-over** (*US*) (of land) having had its timber removed. — *adj* **cut'-price** at a reduced rate. — **cut'-throat** an assassin; a ruffian; an open razor. — *adj* murderous; ruinous. — **cutting edge** a part or area (of an organisation, branch of study, etc.) that breaks new ground, effects change and development, etc.; **cut'-water** the forepart of a ship's prow. — **a cut above** something distinctly better; **cut a dash** to have a striking appearance; **cut and cover** a method of forming a tunnel by making an open cutting, arching it over, and covering in; **cut and dry** or **cut and dried** ready made, fixed beforehand; **cut and run** to be off quickly; **cut and thrust** (in fencing) the use of the edges and the point of the weapon; swift, shrewd, and cleverly-calculated action or reaction, argument, etc. (*adj* **cut-and-thrust'**); **cut back** to prune close to the stem; to revert to a previous scene; to reduce; **cut both ways** (of a decision, action, situation, etc.) to have or result in both advantages and disadvantages; **cut corners** to turn corners by the quickest way, not keeping close to the edge of the road; to do something (e.g. a piece of work) with the minimum of effort and expenditure and therefore often imperfectly; **cut dead** to refuse to recognise; **cut down** to bring down by cutting; to reduce, curtail; **cut down to size** to cause (a person) to feel less important or to be less conceited; **cut in** to interpose; to deprive someone of a dancing partner; to intercept on the telephone; to take one's place in a line of traffic in front of an overtaken vehicle, etc.; to come into a game by cutting a card; to give a share; **cut it fine** to take risks by calculating too narrowly; **cut it out** (*colloq*) to make an end of it, leave off; **cut loose** to break free from constraints; **cut off** to sever; to isolate; to put an end to prematurely; to intercept; to stop; (of an electrical device) to stop working, usu. automatically, esp. as a safety measure; to disinherit; **cut off with a shilling** to bequeath only a shilling; to disinherit; **cut one's coat according to one's cloth** to adapt oneself to circumstances; **cut one's losses** to have done with an unprofitable matter; **cut one's teeth (on)** (*colloq*) to gain experience (by means of); to practise (on); **cut out** to shape; to debar; to supplant; to pass out of a game on cutting a card; to pass out of a line of traffic in order to overtake; (of an engine) suddenly to stop functioning; **cut out for** naturally fitted for; **cut short** to abridge; to make short by cutting; to silence by interruption; **cut teeth** to have teeth grow through the gums, as an infant; **cut up** to cut into pieces; to criticise severely; to turn out (well or ill) when divided into parts; (in *passive*) to be deeply distressed; **cut up rough** to take something amiss, become difficult or angry.

cutaneous *kū-tā'ni-əs, adj* of or pertaining to the skin. [N.L. *cutāneus* — L. *cutis*, skin.]

cute *kūt, adj* daintily or quaintly pleasing. — *adv* **cute'ly**. — *adj* **cute'sy** (esp. *US*) sentimentally or affectedly cute, twee. — *n* **cū'tie** or **cū'tey** a smart girl; something cute. — **cū'tie-pie** (*slang*) someone cute or sweet, a poppet. [Aphetic form of **acute**.]

cuticle *kū'ti-kl, n* the outermost or thin skin; the dead skin at the edge of finger- and toenails; the waxy or corky layer on the epidermis in plants (*bot*); the protective outer covering of many invertebrates, e.g. insects (*zool*). — *adj* **cūtic'ular**. [L. *cutīcula*, dimin. of *cutis*, skin.]

cutis *kū'tis*, (*anat* and *zool*) *n* the true skin, as distinguished from the cuticle. [L., skin.]

cutlass *kut'ləs, n* a short, broad sword, with one cutting edge, once used in the navy. [Fr. *coutelas*, augmentative from L. *cultellus*, dimin. of *culter*, a ploughshare, a knife.]

cutler *kut'lər, n* a person who makes or sells knives. — *n* **cut'lery** implements for eating food; edged or cutting instruments in general; the business of a cutler. [Fr. *coutelier* — L. *culter*, knife.]

cutlet *kut'lit, n* rib and the meat belonging to it or similar piece of mutton, veal, etc.; other food made up in the shape of a cutlet. [Fr. *côtelette*, dimin. of *côte*, from L. *costa*, a rib.]

cuttle *kut'l, n* a cephalopod mollusc remarkable for its power of ejecting a black, inky liquid (also **cutt'lefish**); extended to other cephalopods. — **cutt'le-bone** or **cuttlefish bone** the internal shell of the cuttlefish, used for making tooth-powder, for polishing metals, etc. [O.E. *cudele*.]

cuvée *kü-vā* or *ko͞o-vā', n* a vat of blended wine of uniform quality. [Fr.]

CV *abbrev* for: *chevaux* (Fr.), as in **2CV** *deux chevaux*, two horsepower (car); Cross of Valour (*Austr* and *Can*).

cv *abbrev* for: (or **CV**) curriculum vitae; *cursus vitae* (L.), course, progress of life.

cva *abbrev* for cerebrovascular accident.

CVO *abbrev* for Commander of the (Royal) Victorian Order.

cwm *ko͞om, n* the Welsh name for a valley or glen; a cirque (*geol*). [Welsh, cf. **coomb**, and Fr. *combe*.]

CWO or **cwo** *abbrev* for cash with order.

CWS *abbrev* for Co-operative Wholesale Society.

cwt *abbrev* for hundredweight(s). [*c* for L. *centum*, a hundred, and *wt* for *weight*.]

CY *abbrev* for Cyprus (I.V.R.).

cyan *sī'an, n* a greenish blue; printers' blue ink. — *adj* of a greenish blue colour. — **cyan-** or **cyano-** (*sī-ən-ə-* or *-ō-*) *combining form* denoting blue or dark blue; relating to, or indicating, cyanide or cyanogen. — *n* **cyan'amide** the amide of cyanogen, a white crystalline substance ($NCNH_2$); loosely applied to **calcium cyanamide** (NCNCa), a fertiliser. — *n* **cyanate** (*sī'ən-āt*) a salt of cyanic acid. — *adj* **cyan'ic** of or belonging to cyanogen. — *n* **cy'anide** a direct compound of cyanogen with a metal. — *vt* to treat with a cyanide. — *n* **cy'aniding** extraction of gold or silver from ore by means of potassium cyanide. — *n* **cy'anin** a plant pigment, blue in the cornflower, but red in the rose because of its reaction with acids. — *n* **cy'anine** any of a group of dyes used as sensitisers in photography. — *vt* **cy'anise** or **-ize** to turn into cyanide. — *n* **cy'anite** same as **kyanite**. — *n* **cyanoac'rylate** any of several strong, fast-setting adhesives derived from acrylic acid. — *n* **cyanocobal'amin** (*cobalt* and *vitamin*) vitamin B_{12}, which has a large and complicated molecule, in one form including a cyanide group, in all forms including a cobalt atom. — *n* **cyan'ogen** (*-jen*) a compound of carbon and nitrogen (CN)$_2$ forming a colourless, poisonous gas with an almond-like odour, an essential ingredient of Prussian blue. — *adj* **cy'anosed** (*colloq*). — *n* **cyanō'sis** abnormal blueness of the skin. — *adj* **cyanot'ic.** — *n* **cyan'otype** blueprint. — **cyanic acid** an acid composed of cyanogen, oxgen and hydrogen (HCNO). [Gr. *kyanos*, blue.]

cybernetics *sī-bər-net'iks, nsing* the comparative study of automatic communication and control in functions of living bodies and in mechanical electronic systems (such as in computers). — *adj* **cybernet'ic.** — *n* **cybernet'icist** (*-sist*). [Gr. *kybernētēs*, a steersman.]

cycad *sī'kad, n* one of an order of gymnospermous plants superficially resembling ferns and palms. — *adj* **cycadā'ceous.** [Formed from supposed Gr. *kykas*, a misreading of *koīkas*, accus. pl. of *koīx*, doum-palm.]

cycl-. See **cyclo-.**

cyclamate *sik'la-māt* or *sīk'*, *n* any of a number of very sweet substances derived from petrochemicals, formerly used as sweetening agents in food, soft drinks, etc.

cyclamen *sik'lə-mən, n* a plant of the S. European *Cyclamen* genus, related to the Primulas, with nodding flowers and bent-back petals. [Gr. *kyklamīnos*.]

cycle *sī'kl, n* a period of time in which events happen in a certain order, and which constantly repeats itself; a recurring series of changes; an imaginary circle or orbit in the heavens; a series of poems, romances, etc., centring in a figure or event; a group of songs with related subjects; a bicycle or tricycle; complete series of changes in a periodically varying quantity, e.g. an alternating current, during one period; sequence of computer operations which continues until a criterion for stoppage is reached, or the time of this. — *vt* to cause to pass through a cycle of operations or events; to transport or accompany on a cycle. — *vi* to move in cycles; to ride on a cycle. — *adj* **cy'clic** or **cy'clical** pertaining to or containing a cycle; recurring in cycles; arranged in a ring or rings. — *n* **cyclical'ity.** — *adv* **cy'clically.** — *n* **cy'clicism.** — *n* **cyclic'ity.** — *n* **cy'cling.** — *n* **cy'clist** a person who rides on a cycle. — *n* **cy'cloid** a figure like a circle; a curve traced by a point on the circumference of a circle which rolls along a straight line. — *adj* nearly circular; cyclothymic; characterised by swings of mood (*psychol*). — *adj* **cycloid'al.** — *n* **cyclō'sis** circulation: — *pl* **cyclō'ses** (*-sēz*). — **cy'cleway** a track or path, often running alongside a road, constructed and reserved for cyclists; **cyclic compound** a closed-chain or ring compound in which the ring consists of carbon atoms only (*carbocyclic compound*) or of carbon atoms linked with one or more other atoms (*heterocyclic compound*). — **cycle per second** see **hertz.** [Gr. *kyklos*, circle.]

cyclo *sī'klō*, (*colloq*) *n* a trishaw: — *pl* **cy'clos.** [**cycle.**]

cyclo- *sīk-lō-* or **cycl-** *sīkl-*, *combining form* denoting: cycle; ring; circle; cyclic compound. — **cy'clo-cross** a pedal-bicycle race over rough country in the course of which bicycles have to be carried over natural obstacles. [Gr. *kyklos*, circle.]

cycloid. See under **cycle.**

cyclone *sī'klōn, n* a system of winds blowing spirally inwards towards a centre of low barometric pressure; (*loosely*) a wind-storm; a separating apparatus, a kind of centrifuge. — *adj* **cyclon'ic.** [Gr. *kyklōn*, contr. pres. p. of *kykloein*, to whirl round.]

cyclonite *sī'klə-nīt, n.* See **RDX.**

cyclopaedia or **cyclopedia** *sī-klō-pē'di-ə, n* a shortened form of **encyclopaedia.** — *adj* **cyclopae'dic** or **cyclope'dic.**

cyclopropane *sī-klō-prō'pān, n* a cyclic hydrocarbon C_3H_6, a general anaesthetic. [**cyclo-** and **propane.**]

Cyclops *sī'klops, n* one of a fabled race of giants who lived chiefly in Sicily, with one eye in the middle of the forehead (*pl* **Cy'clops, Cyclō'pes** or **Cy'clopses**); (without *cap*) a one-eyed monster (*pl* **cyclō'pes**). [Gr. *kyklōps*, pl. *kyklōpes* — *kyklos*, a circle, *ōps*, an eye.]

cyclorama *sī-klō-rä'mə, n* a circular panorama; a curved background in stage and cinematograph sets, used to give impression of sky distance, and for lighting effects. — *adj* **cycloram'ic.** [**cyclo-** and Gr. *horāma*, view.]

cyclosis. See under **cycle.**

cyclospermous *sī-klō-spûr'məs*, (*bot*) *adj* with embryo bent round the endosperm. [**cyclo-** and Gr. *sperma*, seed.]

Cyclostomata *sī-klō-stō'mə-tə, npl* a class of animals with fixed open mouth, including the lampreys. — *n* **cy'clostome** a member of the class. — *adj* **cyclostomous** (*-klos'to-məs*). [**cyclo-** and Gr. *stŏma*, mouth.]

cyclostyle *sī'klō-stīl, n* an apparatus for multiplying copies of a writing by use of a pen with a small puncturing wheel. — Also *vt.* [**cyclo-.**]

cyclothymia *sī-klō-thī'mi-ə, n* a temperament inclined to alternation of high and low spirits. — *n* **cy'clothyme** a person with such a temperament. — *adj* **cyclothy'mic.** [**cyclo-** and Gr. *thymos*, spirit.]

cyclotron *sī'klō-tron, n* a type of particle accelerator (see **accelerator** under **accelerate**) for accelerating the heavier atomic particles (such as protons), used in the treatment of cancer. [**cyclo-** and **-tron** (3).]

cyder. Same as **cider.**

cyesis *sī-ē'sis, n* pregnancy: — *pl* **cyē'ses** (*-sēz*). [Gk. *kyēsis*.]

cygnet *sig'nit, n* a young swan. [Dimin. from L. *cygnus*, ult. — Gr. *kyknos*, a swan.]

cylinder *sil'in-dər, n* a solid figure of uniform cross-section generated by a straight line remaining parallel to a fixed axis and moving round a closed curve — ordinarily in a circle perpendicular to the axis (giving a *right circular cylinder*); a roller-shaped object; a cylindrical part, solid or hollow, such as a rotating part of a printing press, or the tubular chamber in which a piston works (*mech*). — *adj* **cylin'dric** or **cylin'drical.** — *adv* **cylin'drically.** — *n* **cylindricity** (*-dris'i-ti*). — *adj* **cylin'driform.** — *n* **cylin'drite** a mineral of cylindrical habit, compound of tin, lead, antimony and sulphur. — *n* **cyl'indroid** a body like a cylinder. — Also *adj.* — **cyl'inder-block** a casing in which the cylinders of an internal-combustion engine are contained; **cyl'inder-head** the closed end of the cylinder of an internal-combustion engine; **cylinder lock** a type of lock comprising a movable cylinder which can be rotated inside a fixed cylinder only when the correct key is inserted. — **firing** (or **working,** etc.) **on all cylinders** working at full strength or perfectly; in good condition. [Gr. *kylindros*, roller, *kylindein*, to roll.]

Cym. *abbrev* for Cymric.

cymbal *sim'bəl, n* a hollow brass plate-like musical instrument, beaten with a stick, etc. or against another of a pair. — *n* **cym'balist** a cymbal-player. — *n* **cym'balo** the dulcimer: — *pl* **cym'baloes** or **cym'balos.** — *adj* **cym'biform** boat-shaped. [L. *cymbalum* — Gr. *kymbalon* — *kymbē*, the hollow of a vessel.]

cyme *sīm*, (*bot*) *n* a young shoot; any sympodial inflorescence, the main shoot ending in a flower, the subsequent flowers growing on successive lateral branches. — *adj* **cym'oid.** — *adj* **cym'ose.** — *adj* **cym'ous.** [L. *cȳma*, *cīma* — Gr. *kȳma*, a sprout.]

Cymric *kim'rik* or *kum'*, *adj* Welsh. — *n* **Cym'ry** the Welsh. [Welsh *Cymru*, Wales.]

cynic *sin'ik* or **cynical** *sin'ik-əl, adj* disinclined to recognise or believe in goodness or selflessness; lit., doglike, snarling, surly. — *n* **Cyn'ic** one of a sect of philosophers founded by Antisthenes of Athens (born *c* 444 B.C.), characterised by an ostentatious contempt for riches, arts, science, and amusements — so called from their morose manners; (without *cap*) a morose or snarling man; (without *cap*) someone who takes a pessimistic view of human motives and actions. — *n* **cyn'icism** (*-i-sizm*) contempt for and suspicion of human nature; heartlessness, misanthropy; a cynical remark. — *adv* **cyn'ically.** — *n* **cyn'icalness.** [Gr. *kynikos*, doglike — *kyōn, kynos*, dog, or perh. from *Kynosarges*, the gymnasium where Antisthenes taught.]

cynosure *sin'* or *sīn'ō-shōōr, n* the dog's tail, or Lesser Bear (*Ursa Minor*), the constellation containing the North Star; the North Star itself; hence anything that strongly attracts attention or admiration. [Gr. *kyōn, kynos*, a dog, *ourā*, a tail.]

cypher. See **cipher.**

cypress *sī'prəs* or *-pris, n* a coniferous tree (*Cupressus*), whose branches used to be carried at funerals; hence a symbol of death; extended to various other trees, esp. in America to the swamp-growing deciduous conifer. [O.Fr. *ciprès* (Fr. *cyprès*) — L. *cupressus* — Gr. *kyparissos*.]

Cyprian *sip'ri-ən, adj* of the island of Cyprus; a Cypriot. — *n* **Cyp'riot** or **Cyp'riote** a native of Cyprus.

Cyprinus *si-prī'nəs, n* the carp genus of fishes, giving name to the family **Cyprinidae** (*si-prin'i-dē*). — *adj* **cyprine** (*sip'rīn*). — *n* **Cyprin'odont** (Gr. *odous, odontous*, tooth) any of several esp. marine types of soft-finned tropical or subtropical fishes related to the carp, but with toothed jaws, including guppies and sword-tails. — Also *adj.* — *adj* **cyp'rinoid** (*-rin-oid*) resembling the carp. [L. — Gr. *kyprīnos*, a kind of carp.]

Cypriot or **Cypriote**. See **Cyprian**.

cypripedium *sip-ri-pē'di-əm, n* a plant of the *Cypripedium* genus of orchids, lady's slipper: — *pl* **cypripē'dia.** [Gr. *Kypris*, Aphrodite, *podion*, a little foot, modified by L. *pēs*, foot.]

Cyrillic *sir-il'ik, adj* pertaining to the alphabet attributed to St Cyril (9th cent.), distinguished from the other Slavonic alphabet, the Glagolitic.

cyst *sist, n* a bladder or baglike structure, whether normal or containing morbid matter (*anat* or *pathol*); a membrane enclosing an organism in a resting stage (*biol*). — *adj* **cyst'ic** or **cyst'iform.** — *n* **cystī'tis** inflammation of the bladder. — *n* **cys'tocele** hernia of the bladder. — *n* **cyst'oscope** an instrument for examining the inside of the bladder; — *n* **cysto'scopy.** — *n* **cystot'omy** the operation of cutting into the bladder. — **cystic fibrosis** (*fī-brō'sis*) a hereditary disease, appearing in infancy or childhood, characterised by too great production of mucus and of fibrous tissue, and the presence of cysts, conditions which interfere with digestion, breathing, etc. [L.L. *cystis* — Gr. *kystis*, a bladder.]

cystine *sis'tēn* or *-tin, n* an amino-acid, $C_6H_12O_4N_2S_2$, found in most proteins, esp. keratin. — *n* **cysteine** (*sis'tē-ēn* or *-in*) an amino-acid, $C_3H_7O_2NS$. [**cyst.**]

cyto- *sī-tō-, combining form* denoting cell. — *n* **cyt'ochrome** any of a group of substances in living cells, of great importance in cell oxidation. — *n* **cyt'ode** a protoplasm body without nucleus. — *n* **cytodiagnos'is** medical diagnosis following the close examination of the cells of the body tissues or fluids, e.g. the smear test for cervical cancer. — *n* **cytodifferentiā'tion** the process of specialisation, in cell development. — *n* **cytogen'esis** cell formation. — *adj* **cytogenet'ic.** — *adv* **cytogenet'ically.** — *n* **cytogenet'icist.** — *nsing* **cytogenet'ics** genetics in relation to cytology. — *adj* **cyt'oid** cell-like. — *n* **cytokīn'in** any of numerous substances which regulate plant growth by inducing cell division. — *adj* **cytolog'ical.** — *n* **cytol'ogist.** — *n* **cytol'ogy** that part of biology that deals with cells. — *n* **cytol'ysis** (Gr. *lysis*, loosening) dissolution of cells. — *n* **cytomegalovī'rus** any of a group of viruses containing DNA, the cause of various diseases in humans including one characterised by cell enlargement in the brain, liver, lungs, etc. of newborn babies. — *n* **cytom'eter** any of various devices for counting cells. — *adj* **cytomet'ric.** — *n* **cytom'etry.** — *n* **cyt'oplasm** the protoplasm of a cell apart from that of the nucleus. — *n* **cytoskel'eton** the internal fibrous structure within cytoplasm, determining the shape of a cell, and influencing its movement. — *adj* **cytoskel'etal.** — *adj* **cytotox'ic.** — *n* **cytotoxic'ity.** — *n* **cytotox'in** a substance poisonous to cells. [Gr. *kȳtos*, vessel, hollow.]

czar, czardom, czarevich, czarevna, czarina, etc. See **tsar,** etc.

Czech *chek, n* a member of a westerly branch of the Slavs, the Bohemians, and sometimes also the Moravians; a Czechoslovak; the language of the Czechs, Bohemian, closely allied to Polish. — Also *adj.* — *n* **Czechoslō'vak** a native or citizen of *Czechoslovakia*; a member of the Slavic people including the Czechs and the Slovaks. — Also *adj.* — *adj* **Czechoslovak'ian.** [Polish.]

D

D or **d** *dē, n* the fourth letter in the modern English alphabet; the second note in the natural scale (*mus*); anything shaped like the letter; the semicircular marking on a billiards table. — **D-day** (*dē'dā*) the opening day (6 June 1944) of the Allied invasion of Europe in World War II; any critical day of action; **D'-mark** Deutsche mark (see **mark**[2]); **D'-notice** a notice officially sent to newspapers, etc., asking them not to publish certain information; **D'-ring** a metal ring or clip in the shape of a capital D, used in various kinds of harness or as trimming on garments.

D or **D.** *abbrev* for: *Deutschland*, Federal Republic of Germany (I.V.R.); diamonds (*cards*); dinar. — **3-D** *abbrev* for three-dimensional (see **dimension**).

D *symbol* for: deuterium (*chem*); (Roman numeral) 500.

d or **d.** *abbrev* for: day; dead; deci-; degree; *dele* (L.), delete; *denarius* or *denarii* (L.), a penny or pence (before 1971); deserted; died; duke.

'd *d*, a shortened form of **had** or **would**.

DA *abbrev* for: dinar; Diploma in Anaesthetics; Diploma of Art; District Attorney (*US*); duck's arse (hairstyle).

da *abbrev* for deca-.

dab[1] *dab, vt* to strike gently with something soft or moist; to smear: — *pr p* **dabb'ing**; *pa t* and *pa p* **dabbed**. — *n* a gentle blow; a small lump of anything soft or moist; (usu. in *pl*) a fingerprint (*slang*); a species of flatfish. — *n* **dabb'ity** (*Scot*) a cheap pottery figure sold at fairgrounds, etc. — **dab'chick** the little grebe. [Cf. early Mod. Du. *dabben*, to pinch.]

dab[2] *dab, n* an expert person. — Also *adj*. — **a dab hand at** an expert at.

dabble *dab'l, vt* to shake about in liquid; to spatter with moisture. — *vi* to play in liquid with hands or feet; to do anything in a trifling or small way. — *n* the act of dabbling. — *n* **dabb'ler**. — *n* and *adj* **dabb'ling**. — *adv* **dabb'lingly**. [Frequentative of **dab**[1].]

dabchick. See **dab**[1].

da capo *dä kä'pō, (mus)* an indication in music that the performer must return to the beginning of the piece and conclude at the double bar marked *Fine* (abbrev. **DC**). [It., from the head or beginning.]

dace *dās, n* a small river fish of the carp family and chub genus. [M.E. *darce* — O.Fr. *dars* — L.L. *dardus*, a dart.]

dacha *dä'chə, n* a country house or cottage in Russia. [Russ., orig. gift (esp. from a ruler).]

dachshund *daks'ho͝ond, n* a dog of German origin, with long body and very short legs. [Ger. *Dachs*, badger, *Hund*, dog.]

dacoit *da-koit', n* one of a gang of robbers in India and Burma (now Myanmar). — *n* **dacoit'y** robbery by gang-robbers, brigandage. [Hind. *dākait, dakait*, a robber.]

Dacron® *dak'ron* or *dāk'ron, n* U.S. name for **Terylene®**.

dactyl *dak'til, (prosody) n* a foot of three syllables, one long followed by two short like the joints of a finger. — *adj* **dactyl'ic**. — *adv* **dactyl'ically**. [Gr. *daktylos*, a finger.]

dad *dad, n*. See **daddy**.

Dada *dä'dä* or **Dadaism** *dä'dä-izm, n* a short-lived (from 1916 to *c* 1920) movement in art and literature which sought to abandon all form and throw off all tradition. — *n* **Da'daist**. — *adj* **Dadais'tic**. [Fr., *dada*, hobby-horse, a name said to have been arbitrarily chosen by the German writer Hugo Ball.]

daddy *dad'i, n* father (*childish* or *colloq*; often as a form of address); the oldest or most important person or thing (*slang*). — Also **dad**. — **daddy-long'-legs** the crane-fly.

dado *dā'dō, n* the cubic block forming the body of a pedestal (*classical archit*); a skirting of wood along the lower part of the walls of a room, often merely represented by wallpaper, painting, etc.: — *pl* **dā'dos** or **dā'does**. — *vt* to provide with a dado. [It.]

daedal or **dedal** *dē'dəl, adj* formed with art; displaying artistic or inventive skill; intricate, varied. — *adj* **Daedalian** (*dē-dā'li-ən*) of, pertaining to, or resembling the work of *Daedalus*, mythical designer of the Cretan labyrinth (*Gr mythol*); (without *cap*) daedal.

daemon *dē'mən* or **daimon** *dī'mōn, n* a spirit holding a middle place between gods and men, a good genius. — *adj* **daemonic** or **daimonic** (*-mon'ik*) supernatural; inspired. [Gr. *daimōn, -onos*, a spirit, a genius; see **demon**.]

daffodil *daf'ə-dil, n* a yellow-flowered narcissus; often (*colloq*) **daff** or **daff'y**. — *adj* pale yellow. [M.E. *affodille* — O.Fr. *asphodile* — Gr. *asphodelos*, asphodel; the *d* is unexplained.]

daffy[1] *daf'i, (colloq) adj* daft, crazy.

daffy[2]. See **daffodil**.

daft *däft, (colloq) adj* silly; weak-minded; insane; unreasonably merry; very fond (of) or enthusiastic (about) (*colloq*). — *adv* **daft'ly**. — *n* **daft'ness**. [O.E. *gedæfte*, mild, meek. See **deft**.]

dag[1] *dag, n* a dirt-clotted tuft of wool on a sheep (also **dag'lock**); a scruffy, untidy, slovenly person (*Austr colloq*); a person, esp. an adolescent, who is, or feels, socially awkward or graceless (*Austr colloq*). — *vt* to cut off a sheep's dags. — *adj* **dagg'y** (*Austr* and *NZ colloq*) scruffy, dishevelled.

dag[2] *dag, (Austr colloq) n* a person who is rather eccentric or comically entertaining (see also **dag**[1]). [Br. dialect *dag*, a dare.]

dagga *dag'ə* or *duhh'ə, n* Indian hemp (called true dagga); an African labiate plant (*Leonotis leonurus*) or other species (Cape or red dagga) smoked as a narcotic, called the love-drug. [Hottentot *dachab*.]

dagger *dag'ər, n* a knife or short sword for stabbing at close quarters; an obelus, a mark of reference † (*printing*). — **dagg'erboard** (*naut*) a light, narrow, completely removable centreboard. — **at daggers drawn** in a state of hostility; **double dagger** a (third-level) reference mark, used esp. to refer to a footnote, ‡, diesis (*printing*); **look daggers** to look in a hostile manner. [M.E.; cf. Fr. *dague*.]

daglock. See **dag**[1].

dago *dā'gō, (offensive) n* a person of Spanish, Portuguese or Italian origin: — *pl* **dā'goes**. [Prob. Sp. *Diego*.]

daguerreotype *də-ger'ō-tīp, n* a method of photography by mercury vapour development of silver iodide exposed on a copper plate; a photograph taken by this method. — *vt* to photograph by that process. [Fr., from Louis *Daguerre* (1789–1851).]

dagwood. Same as **dogwood** (see under **dog**).

dahl. See **dal**.

dahlia *dāl'yə* or in U.S. *däl'yə*, *n* any plant of a Mexican genus (*Dahlia*) of perennial garden composites with large brightly-coloured flowers and tuberous roots. [From Anders *Dahl*, an 18th-cent. Swedish botanist.]

daikon *dī'kon*, *n* a long white Japanese root vegetable of the radish family, similar to a mooli. [Jap.]

Dáil *doil* or **Dáil Eireann** (*ār'ən*), *n* the lower house of the legislature of the Republic of Ireland. [Ir., 'assembly (of Ireland)'.]

daily *dā'li*, *adj* and *adv* every day. — *n* a daily paper; a non-resident servant; (in *pl*) film rushes (*US*). — **daily bread** one's living, livelihood; **daily double** (in horse racing) a single bet on the winners of two races on the same day; **daily dozen** (*colloq*) physical exercises done regularly, usu. every morning. [**day**.]

daimon. See **daemon**.

dainty *dān'ti*, *adj* pleasant to the palate; delicate; tasteful; genteel; fastidious. — *n* that which is dainty, a delicacy, esp. a small cake. — *adv* **dain'tily**. — *n* **dain'tiness**. [M.E. *deintee*, anything worthy or costly — O.Fr. *daintié*, worthiness — L. *dignus*, worthy.]

daiquiri *dī'kə-ri* or **daquiri** *dak'ə-ri*, *n* a cocktail containing rum and lime-juice. [Cuban place name.]

dairy *dā'ri*, *n* a place where milk is kept, and butter and cheese made; a shop where milk and other dairy produce is sold; a company which processes or supplies milk or milk products. — *n* **dai'rying**. — **dairy cattle** cattle reared mainly for the production of milk, as distinct from *beef cattle*, reared primarily for their meat products; **dai'ry-farm**; **dai'rymaid**; **dai'ryman**; **dairy products** milk and its derivatives, butter, cheese, etc. [M.E. *deye* — O.E. *dǣge*, a dairymaid.]

dais *dās* or *dā'is*, *n* a raised floor at the upper end of a hall where the high table, throne, etc. stands; a platform for the use of speakers, etc. [O.Fr. *deis* — L.L. *discus*, a table — L. — Gr. *diskos*, a disc.]

daisy *dā'zi*, *n* a composite wild or garden plant with a yellow disc and white rays; extended to other plants, as the *Michaelmas daisy*, *ox-eye daisy*, etc.; a general term of admiration, often ironical. — **dai'sy-chain** a string of daisies each threaded through the stem of the next; **dai'sy-cutter** a horse that does not lift its feet high; a cricket-ball skimmed along the ground; **dai'sy-wheel** a horizontal, wheel-shaped device with printing characters at the end of the spokes. — **fresh as a daisy** bright and vigorous, with strength and spirits unimpaired; **pushing up the daisies** (*slang*) dead (and buried). [O.E. *dæges ēage*, day's eye.]

Dakin's solution *dā'kinz səl-* or *sol-ōō'shən*, also *-ū'shən*, *n* a dilute solution of sodium hypochlorite and boric acid used as an antiseptic. [From Henry *Dakin*, British chemist (1880–1952).]

dal, dahl or **dhal** *däl*, *n* any of various dried split pulses; a purée of pulse. [Hind. *dal*, to split.]

Dalai Lama *dä'lī läm'ə*, *n* the head of the Tibetan Buddhist hierarchy. [Mongolian *dalai*, ocean, Tibetan *lama*, high priest.]

dale *dāl*, *n* the low ground between hills; the valley through which a river flows. — **dales'man** *specif* a man of the dales of Yorkshire. [O.E. *dæl*, reinforced by O.N. *dalr*.]

Dalek *dä'lek*, *n* a mobile mechanical creature with a harsh, staccato voice. [From a children's television series.]

dali *dä'li*, *n* a tropical American tree related to nutmeg, yielding staves etc., and wax seeds. [Native name.]

dally *dal'i*, *vi* to lose time by idleness or trifling; to play (with); to exchange caresses: — *pr p* **dall'ying**; *pa t* and *pa p* **dall'ied**. — *n* **dall'iance** dallying, toying or trifling; mutual exchange of embraces; delay. — *n* **dall'ier** a trifler. [O.Fr. *dalier*, to chat.]

Dalmatian *dal-mā'shən*, *adj* belonging to *Dalmatia* (now a part of Yugoslavia). — *n* a native or inhabitant of Dalmatia; a breed of large, short-haired dog, white with dark spots (also *adj*).

dalmatic *dal-mat'ik*, *n* a loose-fitting, wide-sleeved ecclesiastical vestment, worn specially by deacons in the R.C. Church, also sometimes by bishops. [L.L. *dalmatica*, a robe worn by persons of rank.]

dal segno *däl sān'yō*, an indication in music that the performer must return to the sign :𝄋: (abbrev. **DS**). [It. *dal segno*, from the sign.]

dalton *döl'tən*, *n* another name for **atomic mass unit** (q.v. under **atom**). — *n* **Dal'tonism** (also without *cap*) colour-blindness; inability to distinguish red from green. [From the chemist and physicist John *Dalton* (1766–1844), who described his own case of colour-blindness.]

Daltonism[1] *döl'tən-izm*, *n* a school method (the Dalton plan) by which each pupil pursues separately a course suited to them, in monthly instalments. [First tried in 1920 at *Dalton*, Massachusetts.]

Daltonism[2]. See **dalton**.

dam[1] *dam*, *n* an embankment to restrain water; the water so confined; a restraint (*fig*). — *vt* to keep back by a bank: — *pr p* **damm'ing**; *pa t* and *pa p* **dammed**. [Gmc.]

dam[2] *dam*, *n* a mother, usu. of cattle, horses, etc. [A form of **dame**.]

dam[3] *dam*, a *colloq* form of **damn** or **damned**. — *adj* **dam'fool** stupid, ridiculous. — *interj* **damm'it** damn it. — **near as dammit** see under **near**.

damage *dam'ij*, *n* hurt, injury, loss; the value of what is lost; cost (*colloq*); (in *pl*) the financial reparation due for loss or injury sustained by one person through the fault or negligence of another. — *vt* to harm. — *vi* to be harmed. — *adj* **dam'ageable**. — *n* **damageabil'ity**. — *adv* **dam'agingly**. [O.Fr. (Fr. *dommage*) — L. *damnum*, loss.]

damascene *dam'ə-sēn* or *dam-ə-sēn'*, *n* a Damascus or damascened sword; inlay of metal (esp. gold) or other materials on steel, etc.; the structure or surface appearance of Damascus steel. — *vt* to decorate (esp. steel) by inlaying or encrusting; to ornament with the watered or wavy appearance of Damascus steel, or in imitation of it. — **Damascus blade** a sword made from Damascus steel; **Damascus steel** a hard steel, repeatedly folded and hammered, giving a wavy surface pattern. [From *Damascus*, famous for its steel and (see **damask**) silk work.]

damask *dam'əsk*, *n* material, originally of silk, now usually of linen, with a woven pattern; Damascus steel or its surface appearance; the red colour of the damask rose. — *vt* to figure (cloth); to damascene. — *adj* of the colour of a damask rose. — **damask plum** the damson; **damask rose** a fragrant pink or red variety of rose; **dam'ask-steel** Damascus steel. [From *Damascus* (see **damascene**).]

dame *dām*, *n* the mistress of a house, a matron (now usu. jocular or patronising); a woman (*slang*); the comic vulgar old woman of the pantomime, usu. played by a male actor; a noble lady; (the title of) a lady of the same rank as a knight; a title given to members of certain orders of nuns, esp. Benedictine. [Fr. *dame* — L. *domina*, a lady.]

damfool. See **dam**[3].

dammar or **dammer** *dam'ər*, *n* a copal used for making varnish, obtained from various conifers. [Malay *damar*.]

dammit. See **dam**[3].

damn *dam*, *vt* to censure; to sentence to eternal punishment; to doom; to curse or swear at. — *n* an interjection expressing annoyance, disgust or impatience (*colloq*); something of little value (*colloq*); a curse. — *adj* **damnable** (*dam'nə-bl*) deserving or tending to damnation; hateful; pernicious. — *n*

damnabil'ity or **dam'nableness**. — *adv* **dam'nably**. — *n* **damnation** (*-nā'shən*) condemnation; the punishment of the impenitent in the future state (*theol*); eternal punishment. — *adj* **dam'natory** (*-nə-tər-i*) consigning to damnation. — *adj* **damned** (*damd*; *poetic dam'nid*) sentenced to everlasting punishment (**the damned** *damd*, those so sentenced); hateful; used to express surprise (as in *I'll be damned!*). — *adv* very, exceedingly. — *n* **damnification** (*dam-ni-fi-kā'shən*) infliction of injury or loss. — *vt* **dam'nify** to cause loss to. — *adj* **damning** (*dam'ing* or *-ning*) exposing to condemnation. — **damn all** (*colloq*) nothing at all; **damn with faint praise** to condemn in effect by expressing too cool approval; **do one's damnedest** (*damd'əst*; *colloq*) to do one's very best. [Fr. *damner* — L. *damnāre*, to condemn — *damnum*, loss.]

damp *damp*, *n* vapour, mist; moist air; (in mines, etc.) any gas other than air; a gloom; discouragement. — *vt* to wet slightly; to discourage; to check; to make dull; to slow down the rate of burning (of a fire) (often with *down*). — *adj* moist. — *vt* and *vi* **damp'en** to make or become damp or moist; to stifle (*fig*). — *n* **damp'er** someone who or something that damps; a depressive influence; a door or shutter for shutting off or regulating a draught; a device for diminishing the amplitude of vibrations or cycles; a mute (*mus*); (in a piano, harpsichord, etc.) the pad which silences a note after it has been played; a kind of unleavened bread (orig. *Austr*); a cake of this. — *n* **damp'ing** reduction in vibration through dissipation of energy (*phys*); diminution in sharpness of resonance through the introduction of resistance (*electronics*). — *adj* **damp'ish**. — *n* **damp'ishness**. — *adv* **damp'ly**. — *n* **damp'ness**. — **damp'-course** a layer of moisture-proof material in a masonry wall. — *adj* **damp'-proof** impervious to moisture. — **damp-proof course** a damp course; **damp squib** something that fails to go off with the expected bang (*lit* and *fig*). [M.E. *dampen*.]

damsel *dam'zəl*, *n* (*archaic* or *poetic*) a young girl or unmarried woman. — **dam'selfish** a small brightly-coloured tropical fish of the family *Pomacentridae*; **dam'selfly** an insect of the order *Odonata*, resembling the dragonfly. [O.Fr. *dameisele* — L.L. *domicella*, dimin. of L. *domina*, lady.]

damson *dam'zən*, *n* a rather small, oval, dark-purple plum. — **damson cheese** a thick damson jam. [Shortened from *Damascene* — *Damascus*.]

Dan. *abbrev* for: (the Book of) Daniel (*Bible*); Danish.

dan[1] *dan*, *n* in Japanese combative sports, a level of proficiency (usu. 1st rising to 10th); a person who has gained such a level. [Jap.]

dan[2] *dan*, *n* a small sea marker-buoy. — Also **dan buoy**.

dance *däns*, *vi* to move rhythmically, esp. to music; to spring. — *vt* to cause to dance or jump; to perform, execute, esp. a dance. — *n* a sequence of steps or rhythmic movements, usu. to music; the tune to which dancing is performed; the musical form of a dance-tune; a meeting for dancing; a series of dance-like movements performed by birds, etc., e.g. as a mating display. — *adj* **dance'able**. — *n* **danc'er**. — *n* **danc'ing**. — **dance'-band**; **dance'-hall** a public hall for dancing; **dance'-music**; **dance'-tune**; **danc'ing-girl** a woman who entertains, in a club, etc. by dancing. — **dance attendance** to wait assiduously (on); **dance of death** a series of allegorical paintings symbolising the universal power of death, represented as a skeleton; **dance to someone's tune** to conform to someone's wishes; **lead someone a (merry) dance** to keep someone involved unnecessarily in a series of perplexities and vexations. [O.Fr. *danser*, from Gmc.]

D and C *abbrev* for dilatation and curettage (an operation which cleans out a body cavity, esp. the womb).

dandelion *dan'di-lī-ən*, *n* a common yellow-flowered composite with jagged-toothed leaves. [Fr. *dent de lion*, lion-tooth.]

dander *dan'dər*, *n* anger; passion. — **get someone's** (or **one's**) **dander up** or **raise someone's** (or **one's**) **dander** to make or become angry.

Dandie Dinmont *dan'di din'mənt*, *n* a short-legged rough-coated terrier of Scottish Border breed. [From *Dandie Dinmont* in Scott's *Guy Mannering*.]

dandify, etc. See **dandy**.

dandle *dan'dl*, *vt* to fondle (a baby), toss (it) in the arms or dance (it) lightly on the knee. — *n* **dand'ler**.

dandruff *dand'ruf* or *-rəf*, *n* a scaly scurf on the skin under the hair.

dandy *dan'di*, *n* a man who pays great attention to his dress; a dandy-roll. — *adj* (*colloq*) smart, fine — a word of general commendation. — *vt* **dan'dify** to dress up. — *adv* **dan'dily**. — *adj* **dan'dyish**. — *n* **dan'dyism**. — **dan'dy-brush** a stiff-bristled brush for grooming a horse; **dan'dy-roll** a wire-gauze cylinder that impresses the ribs and watermark on paper.

Dane *dān*, *n* a native or citizen of Denmark; a Scandinavian invader of Britain in the 9th–10th cent.; a Great Dane. — *adj* **Danish** (*dān'ish*) belonging to Denmark. — *n* the language of the Danes; a Danish pastry. — **Danish blue** a blue-veined, strongly-flavoured cheese; **Danish pastry** a flaky confection of sweetened dough, containing jam or other fillings and often iced. [Dan. *Daner* (pl.).]

danegeld *dān'geld* or **danegelt** *dān'gelt*, *n* a tax imposed in England in the 10th cent., to buy off the Danes or to defend the country against them (*hist*); payment or concessions made to avoid trouble. [O.E. *Dene*, Danes, *geld*, payment.]

Danelaw or **Danelagh** *dān'lö*, (*hist*) *n* that part of England, N.E. of Watling Street, occupied (9th–11th cent.) by the Danes; (without *cap*) the Danish law which prevailed there. [O.E. *Dena lagu*, Danes' law.]

danger *dān'jər*, *n* peril, hazard or risk; insecurity. — *adj* **dan'gerous** full of danger; unsafe; insecure. — *adv* **dan'gerously**. — *n* **dan'gerousness**. — **danger money** extra money paid for doing a more than usually perilous job; **dangerous drugs** certain specific drugs, including morphine, cocaine, heroin, etc., to the dispensing of which stringent regulations apply. — **in danger of** liable to; on the point of; **on the danger list** (in a hospital, etc.) categorised as being dangerously ill (also *fig*). [O.Fr. *dangier*, absolute power, hence power to hurt, — L.L. *dominium*, feudal authority.]

dangle *dang'gl*, *vi* to hang loosely or with a swinging motion. — *vt* to cause to dangle; to show as an enticement. — *n* **dang'ler**. — *n* and *adj* **dang'ling**. [Cf. Dan. *dangle* — O.N. *dingla*.]

Danish. See **Dane**.

dank *dangk*, *adj* unpleasantly moist, wet. — *adj* **dank'ish**. — *n* **dank'ness**.

danse macabre *dãs ma-käbr'*, (Fr.) *n* dance of death (q.v.).

danseur *dã-sœr*, *n* a male ballet dancer. — *n* **danseuse** (*dã-sœz*) a female dancer; a female ballet dancer. [Fr.]

Dantean *dan'ti-ən* or **Dantesque** *dan-tesk'*, *adj* like (the work of) the Italian poet *Dante* Alighieri (1265–1321); sublime; austere.

dap *dap*, *vi* to bounce; to dip gently into water; to fish with a fly bounced gently on the surface.

daphne *daf'ni*, *n* any plant of the *Daphne* genus of shrubs, including spurge-laurel. [Gr. *daphnē*, sweet bay.]

Daphnia *daf'ni-ə*, *n* a genus of water flea. — *n* **daph'nid** (*-nid*) any member of the genus. [Gr. *Daphne*.]

dapper *dap'ər*, *adj* little and active; neat; spruce. — *n* **dapp'erness**. [Du. *dapper*, brave.]

dapple *dap'l, adj* marked with spots or splotches; mottled. — *vt* to variegate with splotches of colour or shade. — *adj* **dapp'led.** — *adj* and *n* **dapple-grey'** (an animal, esp. a horse) of a pale grey colour with darker spots.

daquiri. See **daiquiri.**

Darby and Joan *där'bi ənd jōn,* a devoted elderly married couple. — **Darby and Joan Club** a social club for elderly people. [Poss. from characters in an 18th-cent. song.]

dare *dār, vi* and *vt* to be bold enough (to); to venture: — *3rd pers sing* **dares,** or before infinitive often **dare;** *pa t* and *pa p* **dared;** *pa t* (*rarely*) **durst,** esp. in subjunctive mood. — *vt* to challenge; to defy; to face: — *3rd pers sing* **dares;** *pa t* and *pa p* **dared.** — *n* an act of daring or a challenge to perform it. — *adj* **dar'ing** bold; courageous; fearless. — *n* boldness. — *adv* **dar'ingly.** — **dare'-devil** a rash, venturesome person. — *adj* unreasonably rash and reckless. — **dare'-devilry.** — **I dare say** or **I daresay** I suppose. [O.E. *durran.*]

dariole *da'rē-ōl* or *dar'yōl, n* a shell of pastry, etc., or small round mould; a dish comprising such a shell and its filling; one prepared in such a mould. [Fr.]

dark *därk, adj* without light; black, or somewhat blackish; (of hair and skin colouring) not of a fair or light hue; gloomy; (of a theatre) closed; secret; sinister. — *n* absence of light; nightfall; a state of ignorance. — *vt* **dark'en** to make dark or darker; to render ignorant; to sully. — *vi* to grow dark or darker. — *n* **dar'kie** see **darky.** — *adj* **dark'ish.** — *adv* **dark'ly.** — *n* **dark'ness.** — *n* **dark'y** or **dark'ie** (*offensive*) a black or coloured person. — **Dark Ages** the period of European history from the 5th to the 9th or 12th (or 15th) century, once considered a time of intellectual darkness; **Dark Continent** Africa; **darkfield microscope** an ultramicroscope (q.v.); **dark horse** (in racing) a horse whose capabilities are not known; a person whose abilities or motives are not known; a candidate not brought forward till the last moment (esp. *US*); **dark-lant'ern** a lantern whose light can be covered; **dark meat** the darker meat from the legs, etc. of poultry (cf. *white meat*); **dark'room** a room for developing and printing photographs free from such light as would affect photographic plates; **dark star** a star that emits no visible light, and can be detected only by its radio waves, gravitational effect, etc. — **darken someone's door** (often with *negative*, often implying unwelcomeness) to appear as a visitor; **in the dark** ignorant, unaware; **keep it dark** to conceal it; **prince of darkness** Satan. [O.E. *deorc.*]

darling *där'ling, n* a dearly-loved person (often as a form of address); a favourite. — *adj* beloved; sweet, delightful (*colloq*). [O.E. *dēorling*; see **dear.**]

darn[1] *därn, vt* to mend by interwoven stitches. — *n* a darned place. — *n* **darn'er** a person who darns; a darning-needle. — *n* **darn'ing.** — **darning egg** or **mushroom** a smooth, carved object, usu. wooden, to support material being darned; **darn'ing-needle.**

darn[2] *därn* and **darned** *därnd,* minced forms of **damn** and **damned.**

darnel *där'nəl, n* a species of rye-grass; perh. the tares of the Bible. [Poss. connected with O.Fr. *darne*, stupid, from its supposed narcotic properties.]

darshan *där'shən,* (*Hinduism*) *n* a blessing conferred by seeing or touching a great or holy person. [Hindi.]

dart *därt, n* a pointed weapon or toy for throwing with the hand; anything that pierces; a tapering fold sewn on the reverse of material in order to shape it; (in *pl*) a game in which darts are thrown at a board; a sudden forward movement; (in some snails) a calcareous needle supposed to be used as a sexual stimulus. — *vt* to hurl suddenly; to send or shoot out. — *vi* to move, start or shoot out rapidly. — *n* **dart'er** a person or thing which darts; a freshwater diving bird related to the cormorants; an archer-fish; applied also to various small American fishes of the perch family. — *adj* **dart'ing.** — *adv* **dart'ingly.** — **dart'-board** the target used in the game of darts. [O.Fr. *dart*; cf. O.E. *daroth.*]

Darwinism *där'win-izm, n* the theory of the origin of species propounded by Charles *Darwin* (1809–82). — *adj* and *n* **Darwin'ian** or **Dar'winist.**

dash *dash, vt* to throw, thrust or drive violently; to break by throwing together; to bespatter; to frustrate; to confound; to modify by diluting or mixing. — *vi* to rush; to smash against. — *n* a violent striking; a rush; a violent onset; a blow; a splash; a splash of colour; a stroke of the pen or similar mark; a mark (—) at a break in a sentence or elsewhere; a euphemism for damn (sometimes represented by this sign); a staccato mark; an acute accent used in algebra and in lettering or diagrams as a discriminating mark; a long element in the Morse code; verve; ostentation; a small quantity of added ingredient; a dashboard in a motor vehicle. — *n* **dash'er.** — *adj* **dash'ing** spirited; showy; stylish. — *adv* **dash'ingly.** — **dash'board** a board in front of the driver of a horse-drawn vehicle to keep off splashes of mud; the instrument panel of a motor vehicle or small aircraft; **dash'-pot** a device for damping vibration by a piston moving in a cylinder containing liquid. — **dash off** to throw off or produce hastily; to leave abruptly; **dash out** to knock out by striking against something. [M.E. *daschen, dassen*, to rush, or strike with violence.]

dasheen *da-shēn', n* the taro plant. [Poss. Fr. *de Chine*, of China.]

dashiki or **dasheki** *da-shē'ki, n* a type of loose shirt worn in Africa, and also in the U.S. [W. African.]

dassie *das'i,* (*SAfr*) *n* the hyrax. [Du. *dasje*, dimin. of *das*, badger.]

das'tardly *das'tərd-li, adj* despicable; cowardly. — *n* **das'tardliness.** [Prob. connected with **dazed.**]

dasyphyllous *das-i-fil'əs,* (*bot*) *adj* having crowded, thick or woolly leaves. [Gr. *dasys*, bushy, *phyllon*, leaf.]

dasyure *das'i-ūr, n* any marsupial of the flesh-eating genus **Dasyu'rus** (called native cat) or the family **Dasyu'ridae** (Tasmanian devil, Tasmanian wolf, etc.). [Gr. *dasys*, shaggy, *ourā*, tail.]

DAT, Dat, dat *dat.* See **digital audio tape** under **digit.**

dat. *abbrev* for dative.

data *dā'tə* (or in U.S. and technical Eng. *dä'tə*), *npl* (commonly treated as *nsing*) facts given, from which others may be inferred: — *sing* **da'tum** (q.v.). — *n* **datamā'tion** shortened term for automatic data processing. — **da'tabank** or **da'tabase** a body of information stored in a computer, and from which particular pieces of information can be retrieved when required; **da'tabus** or **data highway** (*comput*) a path for transferring data; **data communications** the sending of computer encoded data by means of telecommunications; **data processing** see under **process.** — **direct data capture** or **data capture** the putting of information into a form that can be fed directly into a computer. [L. *dăta*, things given.]

datacomms *dā* or *dä'tə-komz, n* short for *data communications.*

Datapost® *dā* or *dä'tə-pōst, n* an express service for parcels and packages provided by the Royal Mail.

date[1] *dāt, n* a statement of time, or time and place, of writing, sending, or executing (as on a letter, book, document, etc.); a particular day of the month; the time of an event; an appointment or engagement (*colloq*); the person dated (in the last sense of the *vt*). — *vt* to affix a date to; to ascertain the date of; to suggest the date of; to make an appointment with (*colloq*); to go out with (a member of the opposite sex), esp. regularly (*colloq*). — *vi* to have begun (at a specified time); to be typical of a particular time; to become old-fashioned. — *adj* **dāt'able** or **dāt'e-able**. — *adj* **dat'ed** old-fashioned, out of date. — *adj* **date'less**. — *n* **dāt'er**. — *n* and *adj* **dāt'ing**. — **date'-coding** marking in code on the container a date after which food should not be used; **date line** short for International Date Line; **date'-line** a line giving the date and location (as on a newspaper); **date'-stamp** a device for stamping the date on documents, etc.; the impression made by this. — **out of date** see under **out**; **to date** until now; **up to date** aware of and following modern trends, having the latest knowledge and information, etc.; adapted or corrected to the present time; modern. [O.Fr. *date* — L. *dătum*, given.]

date[2] *dāt*, *n* the fruit of the date-palm. — **date'-palm** a palm (tree) of N. Africa and S.W. Asia. [Fr. *datte* — Gr. *daktylos*, a finger, a date.]

DATEC *dā'tek*, *abbrev* for data and telecommunications.

Datel® *dā'tel*, *n* a facility provided by British Telecom for the transfer of data between computers. [*da*ta and *tel*ex.]

Datin. See **Datuk**.

dative *dāt'iv*, (*gram*) *adj* expressing an indirect object. — *n* the dative case; a word in the dative. — *adj* **dātī'val**. [L. *dātīvus* — *dăre*, to give.]

Datuk *da-to͝ok'*, *n* a member of a senior chivalric order in Malaysia: — *fem* **Datin** (*da-tēn'*). [Malay *datu*, chief.]

datum *dā'təm*, *sing* of **data** (q.v.). — **dā'tum-line**, **-level** or **-plane** the horizontal base-line from which heights and depths are measured; **datum point** a reference point against which measurements and comparisons can be made. [L. *dătum*, given — *dăre*, to give.]

datura *də-tū'rə*, *n* any plant of the thorn-apple genus (*Datura*) of the potato family, with strongly narcotic properties; the poison derived from these plants. [Hind. *dhatūrā*.]

dau. *abbrev* for daughter.

daub *dōb*, *vt* to smear; to paint crudely. — *n* a crude painting. — *n* **daub'er**. — *n* **daub'ing**. — *adj* **daub'y** sticky. [O.Fr. *dauber*, to plaster — L. *dealbāre*, to whitewash.]

daube *dōb*, (Fr.) *n* a meat stew.

daughter *dö'tər*, *n* a female in relation to her parent; a female descendant; a woman (generally). — *adj* proceeding or formed, as from a parent; (of a cell) formed by division (*biol*). — *n* **daugh'terliness**. — *adj* **daugh'terly**. — **daughter board** (*comput*) a printed circuit board, or anything similar, which plugs into a motherboard; **daugh'ter-in-law** a son's wife: — *pl* **daugh'ters-in-law**. [O.E. *dohtor*.]

daunt *dönt*, *vt* to frighten; to discourage; to subdue. — *n* **daunt'er**. — *adj* **daunt'less** not to be daunted, resolute, bold. — *adv* **daunt'lessly**. — *n* **daunt'lessness**. [O.Fr. *danter* — L. *domitāre*.]

dauphin *dö'fin*, (*hist*) *n* the eldest son of the king of France (1349–1830). — *n* **dauphine** (*dö-fēn'*) or **dau'phiness** his wife. [O.Fr. *daulphin* — *Delphinus*, family name of the lords of the Viennois.]

davenport *dav'n-pört*, *n* a small ornamental writing-desk; a large sofa. [Prob. from the maker.]

davidia *da-vid'i-ə*, *n* a shrub or small tree (*Davidia involucrata*), native to China, with heart-shaped leaves and conspicuous white bracts.

Davis apparatus *dā'vis ap-ər-ā'təs*, *n* a device making possible escape from a crippled submarine, invented by Sir Robert *Davis* (1890–1965).

davit *dav'it* or *dā'vit*, *n* one of a pair of erections for hoisting and lowering, e.g. on a ship, for lowering a boat. [App. from the name *David*.]

Davy *dā'vi* or **Davy-lamp** *-lamp*, *n* the safety-lamp used in coalmines, invented by Sir Humphry *Davy* (1778–1829).

Davy Jones *dā'vi jōnz*, *n* a sailor's familiar name for the (malignant) spirit of the sea, the devil. — **Davy Jones's locker** the sea, as the grave of men drowned at sea.

daw *dö*, *n* a bird of the crow family, esp. a jackdaw. [M.E. *dawe*.]

dawdle *dö'dl*, *vi* to waste time by trifling; to act or move slowly. — *n* **daw'dler**. — *adv* **daw'dlingly**.

dawn *dön*, *vi* to become day; to begin to grow light; to begin to appear. — *n* **dawn** or **dawn'ing** daybreak; beginning. — **dawn chorus** the singing of birds at dawn; **dawn raid** a stock market operation in which a large proportion of a company's shares are suddenly bought at a price much higher than their prevailing market rate. — **dawn on** to begin to become evident to or be understood by. [Appears first as **dawning**, prob. from O.N.; cf. Sw. and Dan. *dagning*.]

day *dā*, *n* the time of light, from sunrise to sunset, morning till night; twenty-four hours, from midnight to midnight; the time the earth takes to make a revolution on its axis; the hours devoted to work (*working-day*); a day set apart for a purpose, as for receiving visitors; lifetime; time of existence, vogue or influence; daylight. — **day'-bed** a kind of couch or sofa; a hospital bed for a day-patient; **day'-boat** a small pleasure-boat with no sleeping accommodation; **day'-book** a book for entering the transactions of each day; **day'-boy** or **-girl** see **day scholar** below; **day'break** dawn; **day care** daytime supervision and help given by trained nursing and other staff to a group of pre-school children, or elderly or handicapped people; **day centre** or **day care centre** a centre which provides social amenities and/or supervision for elderly or handicapped people, vagrants, alcoholics, petty offenders, etc.; **day'dream** a pleasant fantasy or reverie. — Also *vi*. — **day'dreamer**; **day'-lābour** labour paid by the day; **day'-lābourer**; **day'light** the light of day; a clear space; **daylight-sav'ing** increasing the amount of daylight available for work or play by advancing the clock, usu. by one hour (**Daylight Saving Time** the time adopted for daylight-saving purposes); **day'-lily** a liliaceous plant whose blossoms last only for a day. — *adj* **day'long** during the whole day. — **day'-nursery** a place where young children are cared for while their parents work. — *adj* **day'-old** one day old. — **day'-patient** a hospital patient who attends for treatment (e.g. minor surgery) and goes home the same day; **day-release'** a system by which workers are freed from employment during the day so as to attend an educational course. — Also *adj*. — **day-return'** a usu. reduced rail or bus fare for a journey to a place and back on the same day; a ticket for this type of journey; **day room** a room used as a communal living-room in a school hospital, hostel, etc.; **day'-sailor** a day-boat powered by sail; **day'-scholar** a pupil who attends a boarding-school during school hours, but lives at home (also **day'-boy** or **day'-girl**); **day'-school** a school held during the day, as opposed both to a night-school and to a boarding-school; **day'-shift** a group of workers that takes its turn during the day; the daytime period of work; **day'star** the morning star; the sun; **day'time** the time of daylight; day (as opp. to evening and night). — Also *adj*. — *adj* **day-to-day'** daily, routine. — **day trip** a trip made to somewhere and back within one day; **day'-tripper**. — **at the end of the day** (*fig*) when all is said and done; **call it a day** to announce a decision to leave off; **day about** on alternate days; **day by day** daily; **day in, day out** for an indefinite succession of days; **day of action** a day designated by an organisation for industrial action, demonstrations, etc. in support of a cause; **day off** a day's holiday; **day out** a day spent away from home for pleasure; **days of grace** days allowed for payment of bills, etc., beyond the day named; **from day to day** concerned only with the present; **have had its** (or **one's**) **day** to have become worn out or useless; **in this day and age** at the present time; **knock** or **beat the (living) daylights out of** (*colloq*) to beat severely; **make someone's day** to make the day (pleasurably) memorable for someone; **one day** or **one of these (fine) days** at some indefinite time in the future; **scare the (living) daylights out of** (*colloq*) to terrify; **see daylight** to arrive at some comprehension, illumination, prospect of a solution; **that will be the day** (*colloq*) that is very unlikely; **the day** the time spoken of or expected; **the other day** not long ago; **the time of day** the hour of the clock; a greeting; **win the day** to gain the victory. [O.E. *dæg*.]

Dayak. See **Dyak.**

dayglo *dā'glō*, *adj* of a luminously brilliant green, yellow, pink or orange. [*Day-glo®*, a brand of paint.]

daze *dāz*, *vt* to stun, to stupefy. — *n* a state of bewilderment. — *adj* **dazed** (*dāzd*). — *n* **da'zer.** — *adv* **dazedly** (*dāz'id-li*). — **in a daze** stunned. [O.N. *dasa-sk* (refl.), to be breathless.]

dazzle *daz'l*, *vt* to daze or overpower with strong light; to stun by brilliancy, beauty or cleverness. — *vi* to be dazzled. — *n* the act of dazzling; that which dazzles. — *n* **dazz'ler.** — *n* and *adj* **dazz'ling.** — *adv* **dazz'lingly.** [Frequentative of **daze.**]

dB *abbrev* for decibel.

dBA *symbol* for acoustic decibel.

DBE *abbrev* for Dame (Commander of the Order) of the British Empire.

dbl. *abbrev* for double.

DBS *abbrev* for: direct broadcast (or broadcasting) by satellite; direct broadcast (or broadcasting) satellite.

DC *abbrev* for: *da capo* (*mus*); District Commissioner; District of Columbia (U.S.); Doctor of Chiropractic.

DCC *abbrev* for digital compact cassette (q.v. under **digit**).

DCh. *abbrev* for *Doctor Chirurgiae* (L.), Doctor of Surgery.

DCL *abbrev* for Doctor of Civil Law.

DCM *abbrev* for Distinguished Conduct Medal.

DCMG *abbrev* for Dame Commander of (the Order of) St. Michael and St. George.

DCVO *abbrev* for Dame Commander of the (Royal) Victorian Order.

DD *abbrev* for: direct debit (or **dd, d/d**); *Divinitatis Doctor* (L.), Doctor of Divinity; *dono dedit* (L.), gave as a gift (or **dd**).

D/D or **dd** *abbrev* for: days after date; day's date.

dd, d/d. See **DD, D/D.**

DDR *abbrev* for (until Oct. 1990) *Deutsche Demokratische Republik* (Ger.), German Democratic Republic (East Germany; also I.V.R.).

DDS *abbrev* for: digital data storage; Doctor of Dental Surgery.

DDT *abbrev* for dichlorodiphenyltrichloroethane, an insecticide.

DE *abbrev* for: Delaware (U.S. state); Department of Employment.

de- *dē-* or *di-*, *pfx* (1) meaning down from, away; (2) indicating a reversal of process, or deprivation; (3) used intensively. [L., or Fr. — L.]

DEA *abbrev* for Drug Enforcement Administration (U.S.).

deacon *dē'kən*, *n* (in Episcopal churches) a member of the order of clergy under priests; (in some Presbyterian churches) an officer, man or woman, as distinct from the elders, who attends to the secular affairs of the church; (in Congregational and some other churches) an officer who advises the pastor, distributes the bread and wine at communion, and dispenses charity. — *n* **dea'coness** a female servant of the Christian society in the time of the apostles; one of an order of women in some Protestant churches whose duties are pastoral, educational, social and evangelical. — See also **diaconate.** [L. *diāconus* — Gr. *diākonos*, servant.]

deactivate *dē-ak'tiv-āt*, *vt* to diminish or stop the activity of. — *n* **deactiva'tion.** [**de-** (2).]

dead *ded*, *adj* no longer alive; inanimate; (of a ball) at rest, out of play; (of a golf ball) within a certain putt, or into the hole; out of use; obsolete; inactive; cold and cheerless; dull; numb; insensitive; unproductive; as good as dead; inelastic; without vegetation; utter, complete, absolute (*slang*); unerring. — *adv* in a dead manner; absolutely; utterly; directly; exactly (*colloq*). — *n* the time of greatest stillness, e.g. *the dead of night*. — *vt* **dead'en** to make dead; to deprive partly of vigour, sensibility or sensation; to blunt; to lessen; to make soundproof. — *n* **dead'ener.** — *n* and *adj* **dead'ening.** — *n* **dead'liness.** — *adj* **dead'ly** causing death; fatal; implacable; very great (*colloq*). — *adv* in a manner resembling death; extremely (*colloq*). — *n* **dead'ness.** — *adj* **dead-and-alive'** dull, inactive. — **dead'-beat** (*colloq*) a down-and-out (see also **dead beat** below). — **dead'-bolt** or **-lock** one moved by turning the key or knob without intervention of a spring; **dead centre** in a reciprocating engine or pump, either of the positions at the top and bottom of a piston stroke, at which the crank and connecting-rod are in line and there is no actual turning effect (usu. **top** or **bottom dead centre**); a non-rotating centre in the tailstock of a lathe; **dead duck** (*colloq*) a plan, idea, person, etc., that has no chance of success or survival; **dead-end'** a pipe, passage, etc., closed at one end; a blind-alley (*lit* and *fig*). — *adj* leading nowhere (*lit* and *fig*). — **dead'-eye** (*naut*) a round, flattish wooden block with a rope or iron band passing around it, and pierced with three holes for a lanyard; **dead'-fall** a trap with a weight that falls when its support is removed; **dead'-head** a person who enjoys privileges without paying, e.g. in a theatre, etc.; an ineffective, unproductive person. — *vt* to remove the withered heads of flowers, in order to encourage further growth. — **dead-heat'** a race in which two or more competitors are equal; the result of this, a tie. — Also *vi*. — **dead language** one no longer spoken; **dead-lett'er** a letter undelivered and unclaimed at the post-office; a law or ordinance made but not enforced; **dead-letter box** or **drop** a place where secret messages, etc. may be left for later collection; **dead'-lights** storm-shutters for a cabin window; **dead'line** the closing date, last possible time; **dead'lock** the case when matters have become so complicated that all is at a complete standstill; see also **dead-bolt.** — *vi* and *vt* to reach or bring to a standstill because of difficulties, etc. — **dead loss** a complete loss; a useless ally or endeavour (*fig*); **deadly nightshade** belladonna; **deadly sin** a mortal sin (see under **seven**); **dead'-march** a piece of solemn music played at funeral processions, esp. of soldiers. — *npl* **dead'-men** (*colloq*) empty bottles after a party or drinking-bout. — **dead'-nettle** a labiate plant superficially like a nettle but stingless. — *adj* **dead'pan** expressionless; emotionless; dead serious or mock serious. — **dead point** another (e.g. *eng*) name for **dead centre; dead-reck'oning** an estimation of a ship's place simply by the logbook; **dead ringer** (*slang*) a person who (or a thing which) looks exactly like someone (or something) else; **dead-set'** a complete standstill, as of a gundog pointing at game. — *adj* absolutely determined. — **dead spit** the exact image; **dead-weight'** unrelieved weight; a heavy and oppressive burden; the difference in a ship's displacement loaded and light; **dead wood** useless material or personnel. — **dead as a dodo, a doornail, a herring** or **mutton** absolutely dead; **dead beat** (*colloq*) quite overcome, exhausted; **dead drunk** completely drunk; **dead man's handle** a device, e.g. on an electric train, which allows current to pass only so long as there is pressure on it; **dead man's pedal** a foot-operated safety device on the same principle, used esp. on diesel trains; **dead set** see under **set; dead against** or **dead set against** utterly opposed to; **dead to the world** very soundly asleep; unconscious; **leave for dead** to abandon, presuming dead; to surpass spectacularly (*colloq*); **over my dead body** when I am beyond caring, and not until then; **the dead** those who are dead. [O.E. *dēad*; from root of **die.**]

deaf *def, adj* with no, or with impaired, hearing; not willing to hear or take notice. — *vt* **deaf'en** to make deaf; to stun (with noise). — *adj* **deaf'ening** making deaf (with noise); very loud. — *adv* **deaf'ly.** — *n* **deaf'ness.** — **deaf'-aid** a hearing-aid; **deaf-mute'** a person who is both deaf and dumb (considered *offensive* by some deaf people). — **deaf alphabet** a system of representing the letters of the alphabet by signs made with the hands (also **deaf-and-dumb alphabet,** a name now deprecated); **deaf language** sign language used by the deaf (also **deaf-and-dumb language,** a name now deprecated). — **turn a deaf ear** to pretend not to have heard; to ignore. [O.E. *dēaf*.]

deal[1] *dēl, n* a portion, an indefinite quantity; the act of distributing cards; a business transaction (esp. a favourable one); treatment. — *vt* to divide, to distribute; to deliver. — *vi* to transact business (in); to act; to distribute cards: — *pa t* and *pa p* **dealt** (*delt*). — *n* **deal'er** a person who deals (cards) or whose turn it is to deal, or who has dealt the hand in play; a trader. — *n* **deal'ership** the state of being a dealer; dealers as a group. — *n* **deal'ing** (often in *pl*) manner of acting towards others; business transactions. — **deal with** to have to do with; to take action in regard to. [O.E. *dǣlan* — *dǣl*, a part.]

deal[2] *dēl, n* a fir or pine board of a standard size; soft wood. — *adj* made of deal. [M.L.G. *dele*.]

de-alcoholise or **-ize** *dē-al'kə-hə-līz, vt* to reduce the amount of alcohol in wine, beer, etc.

dealt. See **deal**[1].

dean[1] or **dene** *dēn, n* a small valley. [O.E. *denu*, a valley; cf. **den.**]

dean[2] *dēn, n* a dignitary in cathedral and collegiate churches who presides over the canons; a rural dean; the chief cardinal-bishop of the College of Cardinals; the president of a faculty in a college or of the *Faculty of Advocates*; a resident fellow of a college who has administrative and disciplinary functions; the senior member of a corps or body. — *n* **dean'ery** the office of a dean; a group of parishes presided over by a dean; a dean's house. — **rural dean** a clergyman who, under the bishop, has the special care and inspection of the clergy in certain parishes. [O.Fr. *deien* — L.L. *decānus* or Gr. *dekānos*, a chief of ten.]

dear *dēr, adj* high in price; costly; characterised by high prices; highly valued; beloved; a conventional form of address used in letter-writing. — *n* a person who is dear or beloved; an affectionate form of address. — Also **dear'ie** or **dear'y.** — *adv* at a high price. — *adv* **dear'ly** affectionately; earnestly; at great cost. — *n* **dear'ness.** — **dear me, dearie** (or **deary) me** an expression of dismay, etc.; **dear knows** an expression of ignorance; **oh dear** an expression of surprise, sorrow, pity or dismay. [O.E. *dēore, dȳre*.]

dearth *dûrth, n* scarcity; want; famine; barrenness. [**dear.**]

death *deth, n* the state of being dead; extinction or cessation of life; manner of dying; mortality; a cause of death; the end or destruction of something; a thing considered as fearsome or painful, etc. as death; spiritual lifelessness. — *adj* **death'less** never dying; everlasting. — *n* **death'lessness.** — *adj* **death'like.** — *n* **death'liness.** — *adj* **death'ly** deadly; deathlike. — **death'-adder** a poisonous Australian snake; **death'-agony** the struggle often preceding death; **death'-bed** the bed on which one dies; **death'-blow** a blow that causes death; **death'-cap** or **-cup** a very poisonous toadstool often mistaken for an edible mushroom; **death'-cell** a prison cell for condemned prisoners awaiting execution; **death certificate** a legal certificate on which a doctor states the fact and usu. cause of a person's death. — *adj* **death'-dealing.** — **death duty** (often in *pl*) duty paid on inheritance of property (now replaced by **inheritance tax** (q.v.)); **death'-knell** the ringing of a bell to announce a death; something that announces the end of one's hopes, ambitions, etc. (*fig*); **death'-mask** a plaster cast taken from the face after death; **death penalty** the legal taking of a person's life as punishment for crime; **death'-rate** the proportion of deaths to the population; **death'-rattle** a rattling in the throat that sometimes precedes death; **death row** (*US*) the part of a prison containing death-cells; **death's'-head** the skull of a human skeleton, or a figure of it; **death's-head moth** a hawk-moth with pale markings on the back of the thorax somewhat like a skull; **death squad** an unofficial terrorist group who murder those whose views or activities they disapprove of, often operating with the tacit or covert support of the government of the country; **death star** a small thin star-shaped metal plate with sharpened points, used as a missile; **death'-throe** the dying agony; **death'trap** an unsafe structure or place that exposes one to great danger of death; **death'-warrant** an order from the authorities for the execution of a criminal; **death'-watch** a vigil, watch kept beside a dying person; **deathwatch beetle** a beetle found in buildings which makes a ticking noise; **death wish** (*psychol*) a wish, conscious or unconscious, for death for oneself or another. — **at death's door** very near to death; **catch one's death (of cold)** (*colloq*) to catch a very bad cold; **death on** fatal to; fond of; good at; **do (or put) to death** to kill; to cause to be killed; **in at the death** having caught up on a hunted animal before the dogs have killed it; present at the finish, crux, climax, etc. of anything (*fig*); **jaws of death** the point of death; **like death warmed up** or **over** (*colloq*) very unwell; **like grim death** tenaciously; **sign one's own death-warrant** to do something that makes one's downfall inevitable; **to death** until dead; to a state of exhaustion; **to the death** to the very end. [O.E. *dēath*.]

deb *deb*. Colloq. form of **débutante.**

debacle or **débâcle** *di-bak'l* or *dā-bäk'l', n* a complete break-up or collapse; a breaking-up of ice on a river; a sudden flood of water leaving its path strewed with debris (*geol*); a stampede. [Fr. *débâcle*; *dé-, des-, bâcler*, to bar.]

debag *di-bag', (colloq) vt* to remove the trousers of, as a prank or punishment. — *n* **debagg'ing.** [**de-** (2).]

debar *di-bär', vt* to exclude; to hinder: — *pr p* **debarr'ing;** *pa t* and *pa p* **debarred'.** — *n* **debar'ment.** [**de-** (3).]

debark *di-bärk', vt* or *vi* to disembark. — *n* **dēbarka'tion** or **dēbarcā'tion.** [Fr. *débarquer* — *des-*, away, *barque*, a ship.]

debase *di-bās', vt* to lower; to make mean or of less value; to adulterate. — *adj* **debased'** degraded. — *n* **debās'edness.** — *n* **debase'ment** degradation. — *n* **debās'er.** — *adj* **debās'ing.** — *adv* **debās'ingly.** [**de-** (1).]

debate *di-bāt', n* argument; a formal discussion, esp. in parliament or some other forum. — *vt* to argue about. — *vi* to deliberate; to consider; to join in debate. — *adj* **debāt'able** or **debate'able** liable to be disputed; open to argument; contentious. — *n* **debāt'er.** [O.Fr. *debatre* — L. *dē, batuĕre* to beat.]

debauch *di-böch', vt* to corrupt with lewdness; to seduce; to vitiate. — *vi* to overindulge. — *n* a fit or period of intemperance or lewdness. — *adj* **debauched'** corrupt; profligate. — *adv* **debauch'edly.** — *n* **debauch'edness.** — *n* **debauchee** (*di-böch-ē'* or *-bösh-ē'*) a person indulging in debauchery. — *n* **debauch'er.** — *n* **debauch'ery** excessive intemperance; habitual lewdness. — *n* **debauch'ment.** [O.Fr. *desbaucher*, to corrupt — *des-*, *baucher*, to hew.]

debenture *di-ben'chər*, *n* a written acknowledgment of a debt; a security issued by a company for money borrowed on the company's property, having a fixed rate of interest and usually fixed redemption rates; a certificate entitling an exporter of imported goods to a repayment of the duty paid on their importation. — *adj* **debent'ured** (of goods) entitled to a debenture. [L. *dēbentur*, there are due — the first word of the receipt.]

debilitate *di-bil'i-tāt*, *vt* to make weak; to impair the strength of. — *n* **debilitā'tion.** — *adj* **debil'itating.** — *adj* **debil'itative.** — *n* **debil'ity** weakness and languor. [L. *dēbilitāre*, *-ātum* — *dēbilis*, weak.]

debit *deb'it*, *n* a debt or something due; an entry on the debtor side of an account, recording a sum owing (*bookkeeping*). — *vt* to charge with a debt; to enter on the debtor side of an account. — **debit card** a card used by a purchaser by means of which money is directly transferred from his or her account to the retailers. [L. *dēbitum*, what is due, — *dēbēre*, to owe.]

de-blur *dē-blûr'*, *vt* to make (blurred photographs) sharp, esp. with the aid of computers: — *pr p* **de-blurr'ing;** *pa t* and *pa p* **de-blurred'.** [**de-** (2).]

debonair *deb-ə-nār'*, *adj* of good appearance and manners; elegant; courteous. — *adv* **debonair'ly.** — *n* **debonair'ness.** [Fr. *de*, of, *bon*, good, and the old word *aire* (masc.), manner, origin.]

debouch *di-bowch'* or *di-bōōsh'*, *vi* to issue or emerge, to march or flow out from a narrow pass or confined place. — *n* **debouch'ment** an act or place of debouching. [Fr. *déboucher* — *de*, from, *bouche*, mouth.]

débridement *dā-brēd'mənt* or *di-*, (*med*) *n* the removal of foreign matter or dead or infected tissue from a wound. — *vt* **débride'** to clean or treat (a wound) by débridement; to remove (dead tissue, etc.) by débridement. [Fr., lit. unbridling.]

debrief *dē-brēf'*, *vt* to gather information from a soldier, astronaut, etc., on return from a mission. — *n* **debrief'ing.** [**de-** (2).]

debris or **débris** *deb'rē*, *dəb-rē'* or *dāb'rē*, *n* wreckage; ruins; rubbish; a mass of rocky fragments. [Fr., from *briser*, related to **bruise.**]

debt *det*, *n* what one owes to another; what one becomes liable to do or suffer; a state of obligation or indebtedness; a duty; a sin (*Bible*). — *n* **debt'or** a person who or country, body, etc. that owes a debt. — **debt bondage** a system (often amounting to virtual slavery) whereby a person is obliged to work for a money-lender in an attempt to pay off debt. — **bad debt** a debt of which there is no prospect of payment; **debt of honour** a debt not recognised by law, but considered morally binding — esp. a gambling or betting debt; **floating debt** miscellaneous public debt, like exchequer and treasury bills; **in someone's debt** under an obligation (not necessarily pecuniary) to someone; **national debt** see under **nation.** [O.Fr. *dette* — L. *dēbitum*, *dēbēre*, to owe.]

debug *dē-bug'*, *vt* to remove concealed listening devices from; to find faults or errors in and remove them from (esp. a machine or computer program); to remove insects from (*colloq*). [**de-** (2).]

debunk *dē-bungk'*, *vt* (*slang*) to clear of bunk or humbug; to remove the whitewash from (a reputation); to show up (e.g. a theory) as false. [**de-** (2).]

debus *dē-bus'*, *vt* and *vi* to unload from or get out of a bus or other vehicle: — *pr p* **debuss'ing;** *pa t* and *pa p* **debussed'.** [**de-** (1).]

début *dā-bü'*, *n* a beginning or first attempt; a first appearance before the public, or in society. — *vi* to start, make a first appearance. — *n* **dé'butante** (*-tãt* or *deb'ū-tənt*) a young woman making her first appearance in society (shortened colloquially to **deb**); a female performer making her first appearance. — *adj* **debb'y** (*colloq*) of or like a deb or debs. [Fr. *début*, a first stroke — *de*, from, *but*, aim, mark.]

Dec. *abbrev* for December.

dec. *abbrev* for deceased.

deca- *dek-ə-*, *pfx* signifying ten. [Gr. *deka.*]

decade *dek'ād* or *dek-ād'*, *n* a series of ten years; any group or series of ten. — *adj* **dec'adal.** [Gr. *dekas*, *-ados* — *deka*, ten.]

decadence *dek'ə-dəns* or **decadency** *dek'ə-dən-si*, *n* a decline from a superior state, standard or time; a state of decay. — *adj* **dec'adent** decaying, declining; lacking in moral, physical or artistic vigour. — *n* a degenerate person. — *adv* **dec'adently.** [Fr. *décadence* — L.L. *dēcadentia* — L. *dē*, down, *cadĕre*, to fall.]

decaffeinate *dē-kaf'i-nāt*, *vt* to extract most or all of the caffeine from (coffee, tea or cola). — *n* **decaff** (*dē'kaf* or *di-kaf'*; *colloq*) decaffeinated coffee. [**de-** (2).]

decagon *dek'ə-gon*, *n* a plane figure of ten angles and sides. — *adj* **decagonal** (*-ag'ən-əl*). [Gr. *deka*, *gōniā*, an angle.]

decagramme or **decagram** *dek'ə-gram*, *n* [Fr. *décagramme* — Gr. *deka*, ten, and **gramme** (see **gram**[2]).]

decahedron *dek-ə-hē'drən*, *n* a solid figure having ten faces. — *adj* **decahē'dral.** [Gr. *deka*, ten, *hedrā*, a seat.]

decal *dē'kal* or *dek'al*, *n* a transfer (picture or design). [From Fr. *décalquer*, to trace, copy.]

decalcify *dē-kal'si-fī*, *vt* to deprive of lime. — *n* **decalcificā'tion.** [**de-** (2).]

decalitre *dek'ə-lēt-ər*, *n* ten litres, 2·20 imperial gallons, 2·64 U.S. gallons. [Fr. *décalitre* — Gr. *deka*, ten, *lītrā*, a pound.]

decalogue *dek'ə-log*, *n* the ten commandments (see under **command**). [Gr. *deka*, ten, *logos*, a discourse.]

decametre *dek'ə-mēt-ər*, *n* ten metres. [Fr. *décamètre* — Gr. *deka*, ten, *metron*, a measure.]

decamp *di-kamp'*, *vi* to make off, esp. secretly; to break camp. — *n* **decamp'ment.** [Fr. *décamper.*]

decanal *dek-ān'əl*, *adj* pertaining to a dean or deanery. [L.L. *decānus*, *-i.*]

decant *di-kant'*, *vt* to pour off, leaving sediment; to pour from one vessel into another; to move (people) to another area, etc. — *n* **decant'er** an ornamental stoppered bottle for holding decanted liquor. [Fr. *décanter* — L. *dē*, from *canthus*, beak of a vessel.]

decapitate *di-kap'i-tāt*, *vt* to behead. — *n* **decapitā'tion.** [L.L. *dēcapitāre* — L. *dē*, from, *caput*, the head.]

Decapoda *di-kap'ə-də*, *npl* an order of higher crustaceans with ten feet (including pincers) — crabs, lobsters, shrimps, prawns, etc.; an order of cephalopods with ten arms. — *n* **dec'apod** a member of either of these orders. — Also *adj.* — *adj* **decap'odal, decap'odan** or **decap'odous.** [Gr. *deka*, ten, *pous*, *podos*, a foot.]

decarbonise or **-ize** *dē-kär'bən-īz*, *vt* to remove carbon or carbon dioxide from (also **decar'būrise** or **-ize; decar'bonate**). — *n* **decarbonā'tion.** — *n* **decarbonīsā'tion** or **-z-.** — *n* **decarburīsā'tion** or **-z-.** [**de-** (2).]

decasyllable *dek-ə-sil'ə-bl*, *n* a line of verse, or a word, of ten syllables. — *adj* **decasyllabic** (*-ab'ik*). [Gr. *deka*, ten, *syllabē*, a syllable; see **syllable.**]

decathlon *dek-ath'lon, n* a two-day contest of ten events at the modern Olympic Games. — *n* **decath'-lete.** [Gr. *deka,* ten, *athlon,* a contest.]

decay *di-kā', vi* to fall away from a state of health or excellence; to waste away; to rot. — *vt* to cause to waste away; to impair. — *n* a falling into a worse or less perfect state; a wearing away; rotting; bad or rotten matter (e.g. in a tooth); disintegration of a radioactive substance. — *adj* **decayed'** rotten; reduced in circumstances, impoverished. [O.Fr. *decair* — L. *dē,* from, *cadĕre* to fall.]

decease *di-sēs', n* death. — *vi* to die. — *adj* **de-ceased'** dead; lately dead. — *n* (*sing* or *pl*) the dead person (or persons) in question. [O.Fr. *deces* — L. *dēcessus,* departure, death.]

decedent *di-sē'dənt,* (*US law*) *n* a deceased person. [L. *dēcēdēns, -entis,* pres. p. of *dēcēdĕre,* to depart.]

deceit *di-sēt', n* the act of deceiving; anything intended to mislead another; fraud; falseness. — *adj* **de-ceit'ful** full of deceit; disposed or tending to deceive; insincere. — *adj* **deceit'fully.** — *n* **deceit'fulness.** [O.Fr. *deceite* — L. *dēcipĕre, dēceptum,* to deceive.]

deceive *di-sēv', vt* to mislead or cause to err; to cheat. — *n* **deceiv'er.** [Fr. *décevoir* — L. *dēcipĕre, dēceptum,* to deceive.]

decelerate *dē-sel'ər-āt, vt* and *vi* to slow down. — *n* **decelerā'tion.** — *n* **decel'erator.** — *n* **decelero-m'eter** an instrument for measuring deceleration. [L. *dē,* down, *celer,* swift.]

December *di-sem'bər, n* the twelfth month of the year. [L. *December* — *decem,* ten (because formerly the tenth month).]

decemvir *di-sem'vər, n* a member of a body of ten men; esp. of those who drew up the Laws of the Twelve Tables at Rome (451–450 B.C.): — *pl* **decem'virs** or **decem'viri** (L. *dek'em-wi-rē* or *-vi-rī*). — *adj* **decem'viral.** — *n* **decem'virate** a body of ten men in office; the term of office of decemvirs. [L. *decem,* ten, *vir,* a man.]

decency. See **decent.**

decennary *di-sen'ər-i* or **decennium** *di-sen'i-əm, n* a period of ten years. — *adj* **decenn'ial** consisting of, or happening every, ten years. [L. *decem,* ten, *annus,* a year.]

decent *dē'sənt, adj* becoming; seemly; proper; modest; moderate; fairly good; passable; showing tolerant or kindly moderation; nice, pleasant. — *n* **dē'cency** comformity to accepted moral and ethical standards; fairness; considerateness; (in *pl*) the conventions of respectable behaviour. — *adv* **dē'-cently.** [L. *decēns, -entis,* pres. p. of *decēre,* to be becoming.]

decentralise or **-ize** *dē-sen'trəl-īz, vt* to withdraw from the centre; to transform by transferring functions from a central government, organisation or head to local centres. — *n* **decentralisā'tion** or **-z-.** [**de-** (2).]

deception *di-sep'shən, n* an act of deceiving; the state of being deceived; a means of deceiving or misleading; a trick; an illusion. — *adj* **decep'tive** tending to deceive; misleading. — *adv* **decep'tively.** — *n* **decep'tiveness.** — **deceptive cadence** (*mus*) same as **interrupted cadence.** [O.Fr. — L.L. *dēceptiō, -ōnis* — *dēcipĕre,* to deceive.]

deci- *des -i-, pfx* signifying one-tenth. [L. *decimus,* tenth.]

decibel *des'i-bel, n* the tenth part of a bel — a unit more commonly used than **bel** (q.v.). [L. *deci-,* and **bel.**]

decide *di-sīd', vt* to determine; to end; to settle; to resolve. — *vi* to make up one's mind. — *adj* **decid'able** capable of being decided. — *adj* **de-cid'ed** determined; clear, unmistakable; resolute. — *adv* **decid'edly.** — *n* **decid'er** someone who, or that which, decides; an action, etc. that proves decisive, such as the winning goal in a match (*colloq*). [O.Fr. *decider* — L. *dēcīdĕre* — *dē,* away, *caedĕre,* to cut.]

deciduous *di-sid'ū-əs, adj* liable to be shed at a certain period; shedding all the leaves together (opp. to *evergreen*; *bot*); shedding wings (as some insects). — *n* **decid'uousness.** [L. *dēciduus* — *dēcĭdĕre* — *dē,* from, *cadĕre,* to fall.]

decilitre *des'i-lē-tər, n* a tenth part of a litre.

decillion *di-sil'yən, n* a million raised to the tenth power; in American notation, a thousand raised to the eleventh power. — *adj* and *n* **decill'ionth.** [L. *decem,* ten, and **million.**]

decimal *des'i-məl, adj* numbered or proceeding by tens. — *n* a decimal fraction. — *n* **decimalisā'tion** or **-z-.** — *vt* **dec'imalise** or **-ize** to convert to a decimal system, esp. the metric system. — *adv* **dec'imally.** — **decimal currency** one in which the basic unit is divided into ten (or a multiple of ten) parts; **decimal fraction** a fraction expressed by continuing ordinary decimal notation into negative powers of ten, a point being placed after the unit figure; **decimal notation** a system of writing numbers based on ten and powers of ten, our ordinary system; **decimal places** the number of figures written after the point **(decimal point)** which separates the unit and the decimal fraction; **decimal system** a system in which each unit is ten times the next below it, esp. the metric system of weights and measures. [L. *decima* (*pars*), a tenth (part).]

decimate *des'i-māt, vt* to take or destroy the tenth part of; (*loosely*) to reduce very heavily. — *n* **decimā'tion.** — *n* **dec'imātor.** [L. *decimāre, -ātum* — *decimus,* tenth — *decem,* ten.]

decimetre *des'i-mē-tər, n* a tenth of a metre.

decipher *di-sī'fər, vt* to read or transliterate or interpret from secret, unknown or difficult writing; to make out. — *n* **decīpherabil'ity.** — *adj* **decī'pherable.** — *n* **decī'pherer.** — *n* **decī'pher-ment.** [**de-** (2).]

decision *di-sizh'ən, n* the act or product of deciding; settlement; judgment; the quality of being decided in character. — *adj* **decisive** (*-sīs'iv*) having the power of deciding; showing decision; final; positive. — *adv* **decī'sively.** — *n* **decī'siveness.** — **decision table** (*logic* and *comput*) a table comprising four sections showing a number of conditions and actions to be taken if these are or are not met, indicating the action to be taken under any condition or set of conditions. [See **decide.**]

deck *dek, vt* to clothe; to adorn; to provide with a deck. — *n* a horizontal platform extending from one side of a vessel to the other, thereby joining the sides together, and forming both a floor and a covering (*naut*); a floor, platform or tier, as in a bus, bridge, etc.; the ground (*slang*); a pile of things laid flat; a pack of cards; the part of a pack used in a particular game, or the undealt part; the turntable of a record-player; that part of a tape-recorder or computer in which the magnetic tapes are placed, and the mechanism for running them; a set of punched cards. — *adj* **decked** (*dekt*) adorned, decorated. — *n* **deck'er** the person or thing that decks; a vessel, vehicle or other structure that has a deck or decks (used only as a combining form, as in *three-decker*). — *n* **deck'ing** adornment; a platform. — **deck'-chair** a chair, usually folding and made of canvas, such as passengers sit or lie on deck in; **deck'-hand** a person employed on deck; an ordinary sailor; **deck'house** a house, room or box on deck; **deck'-passage** a passage securing only the right of being on deck, without cabin accommodation; **deck'-passenger; deck'-quoits** quoits as played on a ship's deck, with rope rings; **deck'-tennis** lawn tennis modified for playing on board ship. — **clear the decks** to tidy up, remove encumbrances, esp. in preparation for action (orig. naval action, now often *fig*); **deck out** to adorn, decorate; **hit the deck** (*slang*) to lie, fall, or be pushed down quickly.

[Verbal meanings — Du. *dekken*, to cover; noun meanings — M.Du. *dec*, roof, covering.]

deckle *dek'l*, *n* (in paper-making) a contrivance for fixing the width of sheet; a deckle-edge. — *adj* **deckled** (*dek'ld*) deckle-edged. — **deck'le-edge** the raw or ragged edge of handmade paper or an imitation of it. [Ger. *Deckel*, lid.]

decko. See **dekko.**

declaim *di-klām'*, *vi* to make a set or rhetorical speech; to harangue; to recite. — *vt* to utter, repeat or recite declamatorily. — *n* **declaim'ant.** — *n* **declaim'er.** — *n* and *adj* **declaim'ing.** — *n* **declamation** (*dek-lə-mā'shən*) the act of declaiming; a set speech in public; display in speaking. — *adv* **declamatorily** (*di-klam'ə-tə-ri-li*). — *adj* **declam'atory** of the nature of declamation; appealing to the passions; noisy and rhetorical. [L. *dēclāmāre* — *de-* (intensive) and *clāmāre*, to cry out.]

declare *di-klār'*, *vt* to make known; to announce; to assert; to make a full statement of (e.g. goods at customs); to expose and claim a score for (*bezique*, etc.); to announce one's choice of trump-suit or no trump (*bridge*). — *vi* to make a statement; to announce one's decision or sympathies; to show cards in order to score; to end an innings voluntarily before ten wickets have fallen (*cricket*). — *adj* **declār'able** capable of being declared, exhibited or proved. — *n* **declār'ant** a person who makes a declaration. — *n* **declaration** (*dek-lə-rā'shən*) the act of declaring; that which is declared; a written affirmation; a formal announcement (e.g. of war); in common law, the pleading in which the plaintiff in an action at law sets forth his or her case against the defendant. — *adj* **declarative** (*di-klar'ə-tiv*) or **declar'atory** making a statement or declaration. — *adv* **declar'atively** or **declar'atorily.** — *adj* **declāred'** avowed, stated. — *adv* **declā'redly** avowedly. — *n* **declār'er.** [L. *dēclārāre* (partly through Fr. *déclarer*).]

declass *dē-kläs'*, *vt* to remove or degrade from one's class. — *adj* **déclassé**, *fem* **déclassée** (*dā-klä-sā*; Fr.) having lost caste or social standing. [Fr. *déclasser*.]

declassify *dē-klas'i-fī*, *vt* to take off the security list; to remove from a classification. [**de-** (2).]

declension *di-klen'shən*, *n* a system of cases and case-endings (*gram*); a class of words similarly declined; a statement in order of the cases of a word; a falling off; decay; descent. — *adj* **declen'sional.** [See **decline.**]

decline *di-klīn'*, *vi* to bend or turn away; to deviate; to refuse; to bend or slope down; to fail or decay, e.g. in health or fortune; to draw to an end. — *vt* to bend down; to turn away from; to refuse; to give the various cases of (*gram*). — *n* a falling off; deviation; decay; a period of gradual deterioration; a downslope. — *adj* **declīn'able** having inflection for case. — *n* **declinā'tion** (*-klin-*) the act of declining (*US*); a sloping or bending downwards; deviation; the angular distance of a heavenly body from the celestial equator (*astron*). — *n* **declinom'eter** an instrument for measuring declination in various senses, esp. the **declination of the compass** or **magnetic declination** (i.e. the deviation of the magnetic needle from the true north), or the declination or dip of a compass needle (see **dip of the needle**). — **on the decline** in the process of becoming less, deteriorating. [L. *dēclīnāre* (partly through Fr. *décliner*).]

declivity *di-kliv'i-ti*, *n* a place that slopes downward (opp. of *acclivity*); inclination downwards. — *adj* **decliv'itous.** [L. *dēclīvitās, -ātis* — *dē*, downward, *clīvus*, sloping.]

declutch *dē-kluch'*, *vi* to release the clutch (of a motor vehicle). [**de-** (2).]

Deco or **deco** *dek'ō*, *adj* pertaining to art deco (q.v.).

decoct *di-kokt'*, *vt* to extract the substance of by boiling. — *n* **decoc'tion** an extract of anything obtained by boiling. [L. *dēcoquĕre*, *dēcoctum* — *dē*, down, *coquĕre*, to cook.]

decode *dē-kōd'*, *vt* to translate from a code. — *vt* and *vi* (*linguis*) to convert from sound or writing to meaning, or from a foreign language to one's own language. — *n* **decō'der.** [**de-** (2).]

decoke *dē-kōk'*, (*colloq*) *vt* to decarbonise (an internal-combustion engine). [**de-** (2).]

decollate *dē-kol'āt*, *vt* to separate continuous stationery into separate sheets or forms. [L. *dēcollāre*, to behead — *dē*, from, *collum*, the neck.]

décolleté *dā-kol'tā*, *adj* wearing a low-cut dress; (of clothes) low-cut. — *n* **décolletage** (*dā-kol-täzh'*) a low-cut neckline; a dress with this; the exposure of the neck and shoulders in such a dress. [Fr., past p. of *décolleter*, to bare the neck and shoulders — *collet*, collar.]

decolonise or **-ize** *dē-kol'ə-nīz*, *vt* to release from being a colony, grant independence to. — *n* **decolonisā'tion** or **-z-**. [**de-** (2).]

decolour or **decolor** *dē-kul'ər*, *vt* to deprive of colour — also **decol'ourise, decol'orise** or **-ize.** [L. *dēcolōrāre* — *dē*, from, *color*, colour.]

decommission *dē-kəm-ish'ən*, *vt* to take out of commission or operation, e.g. a warship or atomic reactor. — *n* **decommiss'ioner.** — *n* **decommis-s'ioning.** [**de-** (2).]

decompose *dē-kom-pōz'*, *vt* to separate the component parts of; to resolve into elements. — *vi* to decay, rot. — *n* **decompōsabil'ity.** — *adj* **decompōs'able.** — *n* **decompōs'er.** [Fr. *décomposer* — pfx. *dé-* (L. *dis-*, apart), *composer*; see ety. for **compose.**]

decomposition *di-kom-pə-zish'ən*, *n* the act or state of decomposing; decay. [Fr. pfx. *dé-* (L. *dis-*), apart, and **composition.**]

decompress *dē-kəm-pres'*, *vt* to release from pressure. — *n* **decompression** (*-presh'ən*) the act or process of releasing from pressure; the gradual reduction of pressure on persons (such as divers, construction workers, etc.) on returning to normal atmospheric conditions; any operation to relieve excessive pressure (*surg*). — *adj* **decompress'ive.** — *n* **decompress'or.** — **decompression chamber** a chamber in which pressure can be reduced gradually to atmospheric pressure, or in which a person can be subjected gradually to decreased atmospheric pressure; **decompression sickness** bends, a painful, and sometimes fatal, disorder affecting divers, etc. who are too suddenly subjected to decreased air pressure, caused by the formation of nitrogen bubbles in the body as nitrogen comes rapidly out of solution from the blood and other body fluids. [**de-** (2).]

decongest *dē-kən-jest'*, *vt* to relieve or end the congestion of. — *n* **deconges'tant** (*med*) an agent that relieves congestion. — *n* **decongest'ion** (*-yən*). — *adj* **deconges'tive.** [**de-** (2).]

deconsecrate *dē-kon'si-krāt*, *vt* to deprive of the character given by consecration; to secularise. — *n* **deconsecrā'tion.** [**de-** (2).]

deconstruction *dē-kən-struk'shən*, *n* a method of critical analysis applied esp. to literary texts, which, questioning the ability of language to represent reality adequately, asserts that no text can have a fixed and stable meaning and that readers must eradicate all philosophical or other assumptions when approaching a text. — *vt* **deconstruct'.** — *n* and *adj* **deconstruc'tionist.** [**de-** (2).]

decontaminate *dē-kən-tam'in-āt*, *vt* to free from contamination. — *n* **decontam'inant.** — *n* **decontaminā'tion.** — *adj* **decontam'inative.** — *n* **decontam'inātor.** [**de-** (2).]

decontrol *dē-kən-trōl'*, *vt* to remove (esp. official) control from. — *n* removal of control. [**de-** (2).]

décor *dā'kör*, *n* scenery and stage embellishments; ornament; the general decorative effect (colour scheme, furnishings, etc.) of a room. [Fr., decoration.]

decorate *dek'ə-rāt*, *vt* to ornament, to beautify; to paint, put wallpaper on (a house, etc.); to honour with a badge or medal. — *adj* **dec'orated**. — *n* **decorā'tion** ornament; the applied paint and wallpaper in e.g. a house; the badge of an order; a medal; (in *pl*) flags, bunting, paper chains, etc., put out or hung at a time of celebration. — *adj* **dec'orative** (*-rə-tiv*) ornamental. — *adv* **dec'oratively**. — *n* **dec'orativeness**. — *n* **dec'orātor** a person who decorates, esp. houses. — **Decorated style** (*archit*) a style of Gothic architecture, elaborate and richly decorated, which prevailed till near the end of the 14th century. [L. *decorāre*, *-ātum* — *decēre*, to be becoming.]

decorous *de'kə-rəs*, *adj* suitable; proper; decent. — *adv* **dec'orously**. — *n* **dec'orousness**. — *n* **decō'rum** propriety of conduct; decency. [L. *decōrus*, becoming.]

decoupage or **découpage** *dā-ko͞o-päzh'*, *n* the craft (originating in the 18th century) of applying decorative paper cut-outs to e.g. wood surfaces; a picture produced in this way. [Fr. *découper*, to cut out.]

decouple *dē-kup'l*, *vt* to reduce or prevent unwanted coupling within (a circuit or circuits) (*electr*); to separate from, end the connection with. — *n* **decoup'ling**. [**de-** (2).]

decoy *di-koi'*, *vt* to lure into a trap. — *n* (*dē'koi*) anything intended to lure into a snare (*lit* and *fig*); an apparatus of hoops and network for trapping wild ducks; a person, etc. employed to allure others into a snare. [Perh. Du. *de*, the, *kooi*, a cage.]

decrease *di-krēs'*, *vi* to become less. — *vt* to make less. — *n* (*dē'krēs*) a growing less; loss. — *adv* **decreas'ingly**. [O.Fr. *decrois*, a decrease — L. *dēcrēscĕre* — *dē*, from, *crēscĕre*, to grow.]

decree *di-krē'*, *n* an order by someone in authority; an edict or law; a judicial decision; a predetermined purpose (*theol*). — *vt* to decide or determine by sentence in law; to appoint. — *vi* to make a decree: — *pr p* **decree'ing**; *pa t* and *pa p* **decreed'**. — **decree absolute** a final decree; in a divorce, that which makes the partners free to marry again; **decree nisi** (*-nīsī*; L. *nisi*, unless) a provisional decree which will be made absolute in due time unless cause is shown to the contrary (granted esp. in divorce cases). [O.Fr. *decret* and L. *dēcrētālis* — L. *dēcrētum* — *dēcernĕre*, to decide.]

decrement *dek'ri-mənt*, *n* the act or state of decreasing; the quantity lost by decrease; the decrease in value of a variable (*math*); the ratio of each amplitude to the previous one in an oscillator (*phys*). — *vt* to decrease the value of by a given amount. [L. *dēcrēmentum*.]

decrepit *di-krep'it*, *adj* worn out by the infirmities of old age; in the last stage of decay. — *n* **decrep'itness** or **decrep'itude** the state of being decrepit or worn out with age. [L. *dēcrepitus*, noiseless, very old.]

decrepitate *di-krep'i-tāt*, (*phys*) *vi* to crackle (like salts when heated). — *vt* to roast so as to cause a continual crackling, to calcine. — *n* **decrepitā'tion**. [L. *dē-* (intensive) and *crĕpitāre*, to rattle.]

decrescendo *dē-krə-shen'dō*, (*mus*; It.) *n*, *adj* and *adv* (a) becoming quieter, diminuendo: — *pl* **decrescend'os**. [It., pres. p. of *decrescere*, to decrease.]

decretal *di-krē'təl*, *n* a decree, esp. a papal edict; (in *pl*; often with *cap*) the second part of the canon law, the decrees of various popes concerning points of ecclesiastical law. — *adj* pertaining to a decree or decretal. [L. *dēcretālis*; see ety. for **decree**.]

decriminalise or **-ize** *dē-krim'in-əl-īz*, *vt* to make (a practice, etc.) no longer a criminal offence. — *n* **decriminalisā'tion** or **-z-**. [**de-** (2).]

decry *di-krī'*, *vt* to condemn; to criticise as worthless: — *pr p* **decry'ing**; *pa t* and *pa p* **decried'**. — *n* **decrī'al**. — *n* **decrī'er**. [Fr. *dé-*, *des-* (L. *dis-*), and *crier*, to cry.]

decrypt *dē-kript'*, *vt* to decode. — *n* **decryp'tion**. [**de-** (2) and **crypt-**.]

dectet *dek-tet'*, *n* a group of ten (musicians, lines of verse, etc.); a composition for ten musicians. [L. *decem*, ten, and **quartet**, **quintet**, etc.]

decumbent *di-kum'bənt*, *adj* lying down; lying flat but having a rising tip (*bot*). — *n* **decum'bence** or **decum'bency**. [L. *dē*, down, *-cumbĕre* (in compounds only), to lie.]

decuple *dek'ū-pl*, *adj* tenfold. — *n* a number repeated ten times. — *vt* to make tenfold, multiply by ten. [Fr. *décuple* — L. *decuplus*.]

decurve *dē-kûrv'*, (*biol* and *bot*) *vi* to curve downwards. — *n* **decurvā'tion**. — *adj* **decurved'**. [**de-** (1).]

decussate *di-kus'āt*, *vt* to divide in the form of an X. — *vi* to cross in such a form; to intersect. — *adj* **decuss'ate** or **decuss'ated** crossed; arranged in pairs which cross each other, like some leaves. — *adv* **decuss'ately**. — *n* **decussā'tion** (*dek-*). [L. *decussis*, a coin of ten *asses* (*decem asses*) marked with X, ten.]

DEd. *dē-ed'*, *abbrev* for Doctor of Education.

dedal. See **daedal**.

dedans *də-dã*, *n* an open gallery at the end of the service side of a court in real tennis; spectators (collectively) at a tennis match. [Fr.]

dedicate *ded'i-kāt*, *vt* to set apart and devote to some (esp. sacred) purpose; to devote wholly or chiefly; to inscribe or give orally in tribute (to anyone); to inaugurate or open (*US*). — *adj* devoted. — *adj* **ded'icated** consecrated, religiously devoted; giving one's whole interest and work to a particular cause or belief; single-minded, determined; manufactured or set aside for a specific purpose, as a *dedicated calculator*, or made to work in conjunction with another specific piece of equipment, as a *dedicated flash-gun*. — *n* **dedicatee** (*ded-i-kə-tē'*) a person to whom a thing is dedicated. — *n* **dedicā'tion** the act of dedicating; the state of being dedicated; an address or tribute to a patron, mentor, etc., prefixed to a book. — *adj* **dedicā'tional**, **ded'icatory** (*-kə-* or *-kā-*) or **ded'icative**. — *n* **ded'icātor**. — **Feast of Dedication** another name for **Hanukkah**. [L. *dēdicāre*, *-ātum* — *dē*, down, *dicāre*, to declare.]

dedifferentiation *dē-dif-ər-en-shi-ā'shən*, (*biol* and *med*) *n* a change by which specialised or heterogeneous tissue reverts to a generalised or homogeneous form. [**de-** (2).]

dedramatise or **-ize** *dē-drä'mə-tīz*, *vt* to play down or deny the importance of, lessen or minimise the tension or friction caused by. [**de-** (2).]

deduce *di-dūs'*, *vt* to work out logically (that); to infer from what precedes or from premises, clues, remarks, etc. — *n* **deduce'ment**. — *adj* **dedūc'ible** that may be deduced or inferred. — *n* **dedūcibil'ity** or **dedūc'ibleness**. — *vt* **deduct** (*-dukt'*) to take away, subtract. — *n* **deductibil'ity**. — *adj* **deduct'ible**. — *n* **deduc'tion** the act of deducing; the thing deduced; the inference of a particular truth from a general truth previously known, as distinguished from *induction*, leading from particular truths to a general truth; the act of deducting; the thing or amount deducted. — *adj* **deduct'ive** (of thought or reasoning) concerned with deduction from premises or accepted principles. — *adv* **deduct'ively**. [L. *dēdūcĕre*, *dēductum* — *dē*, from, *dūcĕre*, to lead.]

dee *dē*, *n* the fourth letter of the alphabet (D or d); anything shaped like it. — *n* (*euph*) a substitute for **damn**.

deed *dēd*, *n* something done, an act; an exploit, esp. heroic; a legal transaction, esp. involving the transfer of property; the documentary evidence of it, signed, sealed and delivered. — *vt* to transfer (property). — **deed poll** a deed executed by one party, esp. one by which a person changes his or her name. — **in deed** in reality. [O.E. *dǣd* — *dōn*, to do.]

dee-jay or **deejay** *dē'jā* or *dē-jā'*, (*colloq*) *n* a phonetic representation of the initials **DJ**, abbrev. of **disc-jockey**. — *vi* to act as a dee-jay.

deem *dēm*, *vt* or *vi* to judge; to think; to believe. — *n* **deem'ster** a judge — now only in the Isle of Man. — *n* **dempster** (*dem'stər*) formerly in Scotland, an officer who repeated the sentence after the judge. [O.E. *dēman*, to form a judgment — *dōm*, judgment.]

de-emphasise or **-ize** *dē-em'fə-sīz*, *vt* to take the emphasis away from, treat or consider as of little or less importance. [**de-** (2).]

deep *dēp*, *adj* extending or placed far down or far from the outside; great in extent from top to bottom; penetrating a (relatively) long way; greatly recessed; very distant; greatly involved; engrossed (in); difficult to understand; very secret; wise and perceptive; cunning; profound; intense; heartfelt; sunk low; low in pitch; in the outfield, (relatively) not close to the wickets (*cricket*). — *adv* in a deep manner; at or to a great depth or distance from the top of something; far (in time); intensely, profoundly. — *n* that which is deep; the sea (*poetic*); a deep place. — *vt* **deep'en** to make deeper in any sense; to increase. — *vi* to become deeper. — *adv* **deep'ly**. — *n* **deep'ness**. — See also **depth**. — *adj* **deep'-dyed** thoroughgoing, extreme (in a bad sense). — *adj* **deep-felt'**. — **deep-freeze'** storage of foodstuffs, or other perishable substances, at very low temperature; the appliance in which the material is stored. — Also *vt*. — *vt* **deep-fry'** to fry food completely submerged in fat or oil. — **deep kiss** a French kiss, a kiss using the tongue; **deep kissing**. — *adj* **deep'-laid** secretly plotted or devised. — **deep litter** a method of keeping hens in a henhouse with a deep layer of peat material on the floor. — *adj* **deep-root'ed** (*lit* and *fig*). — *adj* (*attrib*) **deep'-sea** pertaining to the deeper parts of the sea. — *adj* **deep-seat'ed** not superficial, ingrained. — *adj* **deep'-set** (esp. of eyes) set deeply (into the face). — **Deep South** a region of the U.S., roughly Georgia, Alabama, Mississippi and Louisiana; **deep space** the area of space beyond the moon's orbit; **deep structure** (*linguis*) the underlying grammatical concepts and relationships of words in a sentence from which its *surface structure* (q.v.) derives; **deep therapy** the treatment of disease by deep X-rays or gamma rays; **deep throat** (*colloq*) a highly confidential informant. — *adj* **deep-toned'** having a deep tone or timbre. — **go in, dive in** or **be thrown in at the deep end** to plunge, or be plunged, straight into an activity, job, etc., with little or no experience or preparation; **go off the deep end** (*colloq*) to express strong feelings without restraint; to lose one's temper completely; **in deep water** in difficulties; **two deep, three deep,** etc., in two, three, etc., layers or rows. [O.E. *dēop*.]

deer *dēr*, *n* any of the family of even-toed hoofed animals characterised by the possession of antlers by the males at least — including stag, reindeer, etc.: — *pl* **deer**. — **deer'-fence** a very high fence that deer cannot jump over; **deer'-forest** a wild tract of wooded land reserved for deer; **deer'horn** or **deer'-horn** a deer's antler or its material; **deer'-hound** a large rough-coated greyhound; **deer'-lick** a spot of salt ground to which deer come to lick the earth; **deer'-park**; **deer'skin** skin of the deer, or the leather made from it; **deer'stalker** a person who stalks deer; a sportsman's helmet-shaped cap; **deer'stalking**. [O.E. *dēor*.]

def. *abbrev* for: defendant; definition.

deface *di-fās'*, *vt* to destroy or mar the face or external appearance of, to disfigure. — *n* **deface'ment**. — *n* **defā'cer**. — *adv* **defā'cingly**. [O.Fr. *desfacer* — L. *dis-*, away, *faciēs*, face.]

de facto *dā* or *dē fak'tō*, (L.) actual, if not rightful or legally recognised (e.g. *the de facto ruler*); in fact, actually. — *n* (*Austr*) a de facto husband or wife.

defalcate *dē'fal-kāt*, *vi* to embezzle money held on trust. — *n* **defalcā'tion**. — *n* **de'falcator**. [L. *dē*, from, *falcāre*, to cut — *falx*, *falcis*, a sickle.]

defame *di-fām'*, *vt* to take away or destroy the good fame or reputation of; to say malicious things about. — *n* **defamation** (*def-ə-mā'shən*) the act of defaming; slander or libel. — *adv* **defamatorily** (*di-fam'ə-tər-i-li*). — *adj* **defam'atory**. [O.Fr. *diffamer* — L. *diffāmāre* — *dis-*, away, *fāma*, report.]

defat *dē-fat'*, *vt* to remove fat or fats from: — *pr p* **defatt'ing**; *pa t* and *pa p* **defatt'ed**. [**de-** (2).]

default *di-fölt'*, *n* neglect to do what duty or law requires; failure to fulfil a financial obligation. — *vi* to fail through neglect of duty; to fail to appear in court when called upon; to fail to fulfil a financial obligation (with *on* or *in*). — *n* **default'er** a person who defaults, esp. financially; a military offender. — **by default** because of failure to do something; **in default of** in the absence of; for lack of; **judgment by default** judgment given against a person because he or she fails to plead or make an appearance in court. [O.Fr. *defaute* (noun) and *default* (3rd pers. sing. of *defaillir*) — L. pfx. *dē-* and *fallĕre*; see **fault**.]

defeasance *di-fēz'əns*, (*law*) *n* a rendering null or void. — *adj* **defeas'ible** that may be annulled. — *n* **defeasibil'ity** or **defeas'ibleness**. [O.Fr. *defesance* — *desfaire*; see **defeat**.]

defeat *di-fēt'*, *vt* to win a victory over; to get the better of; to frustrate, prevent; to ruin. — *n* overthrow, as of an army in battle; loss of a game, race, etc.; a frustration of plans; ruin. — *n* **defeat'ism** readiness, inclination to accept defeat. — *n* **defeat'ist**. — Also *adj*. [O.Fr. *defait* — *desfaire*, to undo — L. *dis-* (negative) and *facĕre*, to do.]

defecate *def'i-kāt*, *vt* to clear of dregs or impurities. — *vi* to emit excrement. — *n* **defecā'tion**. — *n* **def'ecātor**. [L. *dēfaecāre*, *-ātum*, to cleanse — *dē*, from, *faex*, *faecis*, dregs.]

defect *dē'fekt* or *di-fekt'*, *n* a deficiency; a lack; an imperfection; a blemish; a fault. — *vi* (*di-fekt'*) to desert one's country or a cause, transferring one's allegiance (to another). — *n* **defec'tion** (an act of) desertion; a failure to carry out a duty; (an act of) revolt. — *adj* **defect'ive** having defects; lacking in some necessary quality; imperfect; faulty; insufficient; incomplete in inflexions or forms (*gram*). — *n* a person who is subnormal in physical or mental powers. — *adv* **defect'ively**. — *n* **defect'iveness**. — *n* **defect'or** a person who deserts or betrays their country, etc. [L. *dēficĕre*, *dēfectum*, to fail — *dē*, down, *facĕre*, to do.]

defence or in U.S. **defense** *di-fens'*, *n* (an act of) defending; capability or means of resisting an attack; protection; a protective piece of armour; vindication, justification (for an action, etc.); a defendant's plea or argument (*law*); the defending party in legal proceedings; the members of a (football, hockey, etc.) team who are in defending positions, e.g. halves, backs, goalkeeper. — *adj* **defence'less** or in U.S. **defense'less**. — *adv* **defence'lessly** or in U.S. **defense'lessly**. — *n* **defence'lessness** or in U.S. **defense'lessness**. — *vt* **defend** (*di-fend'*) to keep off anything hurtful from; to guard or protect; to maintain against attack; to act as lawyer for (a defending party). — *vi* to have, and act on, the responsibility for preventing scoring (*sport*). — *adj* **defend'able**. — *n* **defend'ant** a person accused or sued (*law*). — *n* **defend'er** a person who defends; a player who defends the goal, etc.; the holder of a championship, etc., who seeks to maintain his or her title; a person sued or accused (*Scots law*). — *n* **defensibil'ity**. — *adj* **defens'ible** capable of being defended. — *adv* **defens'ibly**. — *adj* **defens'ive** defending; cautious, attempting to justify one's actions; in a state or posture of defence. — *adv* **defens'ively**. — **defence'man** or in U.S. **defense'man** in ice-hockey and lacrosse, a player (other than the goalkeeper) who defends the goal; **defence mechanism** an unconscious mental process by which an individual excludes ideas or experiences painful to them (*psychiatry*); a response by the body in reaction to harmful organisms (*med*). — **defender of the faith** a title borne by the sovereigns of England since Henry VIII, on whom it was conferred in 1521 for his book against Luther; **stand** or **be on the defensive** to be in the position of defending oneself, not attacking. [L. *dēfenděre*, *dēfēnsum*, to ward off.]

defenestration *dē-fen-is-trā'shən*, *n* (an act of) flinging someone out of a window. [L. *dē*, from, *fenestra*, window.]

defense. See **defence**.

defer[1] *di-fûr'*, *vt* to delay to another time: — *pr p* **deferr'ing**; *pa t* and *pa p* **deferred'**. — *n* **defer'ment**. — *adj* **deferr'able** or **defer'able**. — *n* **deferr'al**. — *n* **deferr'er**. — **deferred payment** payment by instalments; **deferred sentence** a legal sentence which is delayed until such time as the criminal's conduct can be examined; **deferred shares** shares not entitling the holder to a full share of profits. [L. *differre* — *dis-*, asunder, *ferre*, to bear, carry.]

defer[2] *di-fûr'*, *vi* to yield (to the wishes or opinions of another person, or to authority): — *pr p* **deferr'ing**; *pa t* and *pa p* **deferred'**. — *n* **deference** (*def'ər-əns*) a deferring or yielding; respectful compliance or acknowledgment; submission. — *adj* **deferential** (*-en'shl*) showing deference. — *adv* **deferen'tially**. [L. *dēferre* — *dē*, down, *ferre*, to bear.]

defiance *di-fī'əns*, *n* the act of defying; a challenge to combat; aggressiveness; brave or bold contempt of opposition. — *adj* **defī'ant** full of defiance, insolently bold. — *adv* **defī'antly**. [**defy**.]

defibrillator *dē-fib'ri-lā-tər* or *-fīb'*, (*med*) *n* a machine which applies an electric current to the chest or heart to stop irregular contractions, or fibrillation, of the heart. [**de-** (2).]

deficient *di-fish'ənt*, *adj* lacking (in); less than complete; defective. — *n* **defic'iency** defect; shortage; the amount which is lacking for completeness. — *adv* **defic'iently**. — **deficiency disease** a disease due to lack of necessary substances (esp. vitamins) in the diet, such as rickets, scurvy, beriberi, pellagra. [L. *dēficěre*.]

deficit *def'i-sit* or *-fis'*, *n* shortfall esp. of revenue, as compared with expenditure; the amount of a shortfall. [Fr. *déficit* — L. *dēficit* (3rd pers. sing. pres. indic. of *dēficěre*, to lack.]

defied, defier, etc. See **defy**.

defilade. See **defile**[1].

defile[1] *di-fīl'*, *vi* to march in single file. — *n* (*dē'fīl* or *di-fīl'*) a long narrow pass, in which troops can march only in single file; a gorge. — *vt* **defilade** (*def-i-lād'*) to plan a fortification so as to protect it or those in it from raking crossfire. — Also *n*. [Fr. *défiler* — L. *dis-*, *fīlum*, a thread.]

defile[2] *di-fīl'*, *vt* to befoul; to pollute or corrupt; to violate. — *n* **defile'ment** (an act of) defiling; foulness. — *n* **defīl'er**. [L. *dē*, and O.E. *fȳlan* — *fūl*, foul; confused with O.Fr. *defouler*, to trample, violate.]

define *di-fīn'*, *vt* to fix (the bounds or limits of); to determine with precision; to describe accurately; to fix or describe the meaning of. — *n* **definabil'ity**. — *adj* **defīn'able**. — *adv* **defīn'ably**. — *n* **defin'er**. — *adj* **definite** (*def'i-nit*) defined; having distinct limits; fixed; certain, sure; exact; clear; referring to a particular person or thing (*gram*; see also **article**). — *adv* **def'initely** in a definite manner; yes indeed, certainly (*colloq*). — *n* **def'initeness**. — *n* **defini'tion** a description of a thing according to its properties; an explanation of the exact meaning (of a word, term or phrase); sharpness of outline, visual clarity. — *adj* **defini'tional**. — *adj* **definitive** (*di-fin'i-tiv*) defining or limiting; positive; final; most authoritative, expert or complete. — *n* (*gram*) an adjective used to limit the extent of meaning of a noun, e.g. *this*, *that*. — *adv* **defin'itively**. — *n* **defin'itiveness**. [L. *dēfīnīre*, *-ītum*, to set bounds to — *dē*, *fīnis*, a limit.]

deflagrate *def'lə-grāt*, *vi* and *vt* to burn suddenly, generally with flame and crackling noise. — *adj* **deflagrable** (*dē-flag'*) which deflagrates; deflagrating readily. — *n* **deflagrā'tion**. [L. *dēflagrāre* — *dē*, down, *flagrāre*, to burn.]

deflate *dē-flāt'*, *vt* and *vi* to collapse or cause to collapse due to emptying of gas; (of one's hopes, ego, etc.) to reduce in extent due to disappointment, criticism, etc.; (of an economy) to cause deflation in or to suffer from deflation. — *n* **deflā'ter** or **deflā'tor**. — *n* **deflā'tion** the act or process of deflating; the state of being deflated; a financial condition in which there is a decrease in the amount of money available relative to its buying power (opp. to *inflation*; *econ*); removal of loose soil material by the wind. — *adj* **deflā'tionary**. — *n* **deflā'tionist** someone who favours deflation of currency. — Also *adj*. [L. *dē*, from, *flāre*, to blow.]

deflect *di-flekt'*, *vi* and *vt* to turn aside; to swerve or deviate from a correct line or proper course. — *n* **deflec'tion** (an act of) bending or turning away; deviation. — *adj* **deflec'tive** causing deflection. — *n* **deflec'tor** a device for deflecting a flame, electric arc, etc. [L. *dē*, from, down, *flectěre*, *flexum*, to bend, turn.]

deflower *di-flowr'*, *vt* to strip of flowers; to deprive of grace and beauty, or of virginity; to rape (*euph*). — *n* **deflower'er**. [O.Fr. *desflorer* — L. *dē*, from, *flōs*, *flōris*, a flower.]

defoliate *di-fō'li-āt*, *vt* to strip of leaves. — *n* **defō'liant** a chemical preparation used to remove leaves. — *n* **defō'liātor**. [L.L. *dēfoliāre*, *-ātum* — *dē*, off, *folium*, a leaf.]

deforest *dē-for'ist*, *vt* to strip of forests. — *n* **deforestā'tion**. [**de-** (2).]

deform *di-förm'*, *vt* to alter or injure the form of; to disfigure; to change the shape of without breaking into pieces. — *vi* to become altered in shape without breaking into pieces. — *n* **deformabil'ity**. — *adj* **deform'able**. — *n* **dēforma'tion**. — *adj* **deformed'** misshapen, disfigured, etc. — *adv* **deform'edly**. — *n* **deformed'ness**. — *n* **deform'er**. — *n* **deform'ity** the state of being deformed; lack of proper shape; ugliness, disfigurement; anything that destroys beauty; an ugly feature or characteristic. [L. *dēfōrmis*, ugly — *dē*, from, *fōrma*, beauty.]

defraud *di-fröd'*, *vt* to deprive by fraud (of); to cheat or deceive. — *n* **defraud'er**. [L. *dēfraudāre* — *dē*, from, *fraus*, *fraudis*, fraud.]

defray *di-frā'*, *vt* to pay, provide the means to pay: — *pr p* **defray'ing**; *pa t* and *pa p* **defrayed'**. — *adj* **defray'able**. — *n* **defray'al** or **defray'ment**. — *n* **defray'er**. [O.Fr. *desfrayer* — *des-* (L. *dis-*), *frais*, expenses.]

defreeze *dē-frēz'*, *vt* to thaw out, defrost (esp. frozen foods). [**de-** (2).]

defrock *dē-frok'*, *vt* to depose from priesthood; to remove from a comparable position in some other sphere. [**de-** (2) and (*vt*) *frock* to invest with priestly office.]

defrost *dē-frost'*, *vt* to remove frost or ice from; to thaw out. — Also *vi*. — *n* **defrost'er** a device for defrosting esp. a windscreen. [**de-** (2).]

deft *deft*, *adj* handy, clever, dexterous, esp. in movement. — *adv* **deft'ly**. — *n* **deft'ness**. [O.E. *gedæfte*, meek — *dæftan*, *gedæftan*, to prepare, make fit.]

defunct *di-fungkt'*, *adj* having finished the course of life, dead; finished, no longer working or in use. [L. *dēfungī*, *dēfunctus*, to finish.]

defuse *dē-fūz'*, *vt* to remove the fuse of (a bomb, etc.), so making it harmless. — Also *fig*.

defy *di-fī'*, *vt* to challenge; to brave, dare; to flout, or to resist (e.g. authority, convention, an order, a person): — *pr p* **defy'ing**; *pa t* and *pa p* **defied'**; *3rd pers sing present indicative* **defies'**. — *n* **defī'er**. [O.Fr. *defier* — L.L. *diffīdāre*, to renounce faith or allegiance.]

deg. *abbrev* for degree or degrees.

dégagé *dā-ga-zhā*, (Fr.) *adj* unembarrassed, unconstrained, easy; uninvolved. [Past p. of Fr. *dégager*, to disentangle.]

degas *dē-gas'*, *vt* to remove gas from; to eject or emit in the form of a gas. [**de-** (2).]

degauss *dē-gows'*, *vt* to protect against magnetic mines by equipment for neutralising a ship's magnetic field; to remove the magnetic field from (esp. a television tube). [**de-** (2).]

degenerate *di-jen'ər-it*, *adj* having neglected the high qualities of mankind, become base, immoral, etc. — *n* a person who is degenerate. — *vi* (*-āt*) to decline from a more moral, desirable, etc. state; to grow worse in quality or standard. — *n* **degen'eracy** the act or process of becoming degenerate; the state of being degenerate. — *adv* **degen'erately**. — *n* **degen'erateness**. — *n* **degenerā'tion** the act or process of degenerating. — *adj* **degen'erative** tending or causing to degenerate. [L. *dēgenerāre,-ātum*, to depart from its kind — *dē*, from, down, *genus*, *genĕris*, kind.]

degrade *di-grād'*, *vt* to lower in grade or rank; to deprive of office or dignity; to lower in character, value or position, or in complexity; to wear down, erode (*geol*); to decompose (*chem*). — *vi* to decompose (*chem*). — *adj* **degrād'able** able to decompose chemically or biologically. — *n* **degradation** (*deg-rə-dā'shən*) becoming degraded; disgrace; a lowering in dignity; degeneration; wearing down, erosion; decomposition (*chem*). — *adj* **degrād'ed** reduced in rank; base, degenerate, declined in quality or standard; low. — *adj* **degrād'ing** morally debasing; disgraceful. [O.Fr. *degrader* — L. *dē*, down, *gradus*, a step. See **grade**.]

degrease *dē-grēs'*, *vt* to strip or cleanse of grease. — *n* **degreas'ant** a substance which removes grease. [**de-** (2).]

degree *di-grē'*, *n* a gradation on a scale, or that which it measures; a unit of temperature; the 360th part of a revolution or circle; one of a series of advances or steps; relative position; rank; extent, amount; a mark of distinction conferred by universities and some colleges, either earned by examination or research or granted as a mark of honour; 60 geographical miles; nearness (of relationship); comparative amount (of criminality, severity, etc.); one of the three stages (*positive*, *comparative* and *superlative*) in the comparison of an adjective or adverb; the highest sum of exponents in any term (*alg*); the number of points in which a curve may be met by a straight line. — **by degrees** by small amounts, gradually; **degree of freedom** (*phys*) any one of the independent variables defining the state of a system (e.g. temperature, pressure, concentration); a capability of variation (a system having two variables one of which is dependent on the other has one *degree of freedom*); **first, second** and **third degree burn** (*med*) the three categories of seriousness of a burn, third degree being most serious; **first, second** and **third degree murder** (*NAm*) the three categories of criminality of (and therefore severity of punishment for) a murder, first degree being most serious; **forbidden degrees** the degrees of blood relationship between which marriage is not allowed; **third degree** a method of extracting a confession by bullying or torture; any ruthless interrogation; **to a degree** to a certain extent; to a great extent, to extremes. [Fr. *degré* — L. *dē*, down, *gradus*, a step.]

dehisce *di-his'*, *vi* to gape, burst open (*bot*, etc.). — *n* **dehisc'ence**. — *adj* **dehisc'ent**. [L. *dĕhīscēns*, pres. p. of *dĕhīscĕre* — *dē* (intensive) and *hīscĕre*, inceptive of *hiāre*, to gape.]

dehorn *dē-hörn'*, *vt* to remove the horns from; to prune (a tree). — *n* **dehorn'er**. [**de-** (2).]

dehumanise or **-ize** *dē-hū'mən-īz*, *vt* to deprive of specifically human qualities, render inhuman. [L. *dē*, from, down, and **humanise**.]

dehydrate *dē-hī'drāt* or *dē'*, *vt* to remove water from chemically; to remove moisture from, to dry; to deprive of strength, interest, etc. (*fig*). — *vi* to lose water. — *n* **dēhydrā'tion** loss or withdrawal of moisture; excessive loss of water from the tissues of the body (*med*); the removal of water from oil or gas. — *n* **dēhy'drātor** or **dēhy'drater** (or *dē'*). [L. *dē*, from, Gr. *hydōr*, water.]

dehypnotise or **-ize** *dē-hip'nə-tīz*, *vt* to bring out of a hypnotic trance. — *n* **dehypnotisā'tion** or **-z-**. [**de-** (2).]

de-ice *dē-īs'*, *vt* to dislodge ice from (aircraft surfaces, windscreens, etc.), or to treat them so as to prevent its formation. — *n* **dē-īc'er** any means of doing this, whether a fluid, a paste, or a mechanical or pneumatic device. [**de-** (2).]

deictic. See **deixis**.

deify *dē'i-fī* or *dā'i-fī*, *vt* to exalt to the rank of a god; to worship as a deity; to make godlike: — *pr p* **dē'ifying**; *pa t* and *pa p* **de'ified**. — *adj* **deif'ic** or **deif'ical** making, or treating as if, godlike or divine. — *n* **deificā'tion**. — *n* **de'ifīer**. [Fr. *déifier* — L. *deificāre* — *deus*, a god, *facĕre*, to make.]

deign *dān*, *vi* to condescend, stoop (to doing something). [Fr. *daigner* — L. *dīgnārī*, to think worthy — *dīgnus*, worthy.]

dei gratia *dā'ē grä'ti-a* or *dē'ī grā'shi-ə*, (L.) by the grace of God.

deindustrialise or **-ize** *dē-in-dus'tri-əl-īz*, *vt* to disperse or reduce the industrial organisation and potential of a nation, area, etc. — *n* **deindustrialisā'tion** or **-z-**. [**de-** (2).]

deist *dē'ist* or *dā'ist*, *n* a person who believes in the existence of God, but not in a divinely revealed religion. — *n* **de'ism**. — *adj* **deist'ic** or **deist'ical**. [L. *deus*, a god.]

deity *dē'i-ti* or *dā'i-ti*, *n* godhood; divinity; a god or goddess; (with *cap* and **the**) the Supreme Being, God. [Fr. *déité* — L.L. *deitās* — L. *deus*, god.]

deixis *dīk'sis*, (*gram*) *n* the use of words relating to the time and place of utterance, e.g. personal pronouns and demonstrative adverbs, adjectives and pronouns. — *adj* **deictic** (*dīk'tik*) designating words relating to the time and place of utterance (also *n*); proving directly (*logic*). — *adv* **deic'tically**. [Gr. *deiknynai*, to show.]

déjà vu *dā-zhä vü*, *n* an illusion of having experienced before something that is really being experienced for the first time, a form of the memory disorder paramnesia (*psychiatry*); in any of the arts, unoriginal material, old stuff. [Fr., already seen.]

deject *di-jekt'*, *vt* to depress the spirits of. — *adj* **deject'ed**. — *adv* **deject'edly**. — *n* **deject'edness** or **dejec'tion**. [L. *dējicĕre*, *-jectum* — *dē*, down, *jacĕre*, to cast.]

de jure *dā jōō'rā*, (L.) by right; rightful.

dekalogy *di-kal'ə-ji*, *n* a group of ten novels. [Gr. *deka*, ten, *logos*, discourse, by analogy with **trilogy**.]

dekko or **decko** *dek'ō*, (*slang*) *n* a look: — *pl* **dekk'os** or **deck'os**. — *vi* to look. — **have** or **take a dekko** to have a (quick) look. [Hind. *dekho*, imperative of *dekhnā*, to see.]

Del. *abbrev* for Delaware (U.S. state).

del. *abbrev* for: delegate; *delineavit* (L.), (he or she) drew it.

delaminate *dē-lam'i-nāt*, *vi* to split into single layers. — *n* **deliminā'tion**. [L. *dēlamināre* — *dē*, *lāmina*, a layer.]

delay *di-lā'*, *vt* to put off to another time; to defer; to hinder or retard (e.g. an engine's timing). — *vi* to pause or linger: — *pr p* **delay'ing**; *pa t* and *pa p* **delayed'**. — *n* a putting off or deferring; the (amount of) time during which something is put off; a pause; a hindrance; a device by which the operation of a mechanism can be timed to take place after an interval. — *n* **delay'er**. — **delayed action** the operation of a switch, detonation of explosives, etc. some time after the mechanism has been set; **delayed drop** (*aeronautics*) a parachute descent in which the parachutist deliberately delays pulling the rip-cord. [O.Fr. *delaier*.]

dele *dē'li*, *imper vt* delete, a direction in proofreading to remove a letter or word, indicated by *δ* or other sign. [L. *dēlē*, imperative of *dēlēre*, to delete.]

delectable *di-lekt'ə-bl*, *adj* delightful; very pleasing. — *n* **delect'ableness** or **delectabil'ity**. — *adv* **delect'ably**. — *n* **delectā'tion** (*dē-*) delight, enjoyment. [Fr., — L. *dēlectābilis* — *dēlectāre*, to delight.]

delegate *del'i-gāt*, *vt* to send as a representative; to entrust or commit (to a subordinate). — *n* (*-gət*) a person who is delegated; a deputy or representative; a person elected to Congress to represent a territory (e.g. Guam or American Samoa), as distinguished from the representatives of the States (*US*). — *adj* delegated, deputed. — *adj* **del'egable**. — *n* **del'egacy** the act or system of delegating; a delegate's appointment or authority; a body of delegates. — *n* **delegā'tion** delegating; a deputation, a body of delegates. [L. *dē*, away, *lēgāre*, *-ātum*, to send as ambassador.]

delete *di-lēt'*, *vt* to erase; to destroy. — *n* **delē'tion**. [L. *dēlēre*, *dēlētum*, to blot out.]

deleterious *del-i-tē'ri-əs*, *adj* harmful or destructive. — *adv* **deletē'riously**. — *n* **deletē'riousness**. [Gr. *dēlētērios*, hurtful.]

delf or **delph** *delf*, also **delft** *delft*, *n* (in full **Delft'-ware**) a kind of earthenware originally made at *Delft*, Holland.

deli. Short for **delicatessen**.

deliberate *di-lib'ər-āt*, *vt* to consider, think about carefully. — *vi* to consider the reasons for and against anything; to reflect, think; to debate. — *adj* (*-it*) well considered, not impulsive; intentional; (of movement) slow and careful; slow in determining. — *adv* **delib'erately** in a deliberate manner. — *n* **delib'erateness**. — *n* **deliberā'tion** the act of deliberating; mature reflection; calmness, coolness. — *adj* **delib'erative** proceeding or acting by deliberation. — *adv* **delib'eratively**. — *n* **delib'erativeness**. — *n* **delib'erātor**. [L. *dēlīberāre*, *-ātum* — *dē-* (intensive) and *lībrāre*, to weigh.]

delicate *del'i-kit*, *adj* gently pleasing to the senses, esp. the taste; not strong; dainty; discriminating or perceptive; of a fine, slight texture or construction; tender; not robust, esp. in health; (of a colour) pale; requiring careful handling (*lit* and *fig*); refined in manners; gentle, polite. — *n* **del'icacy** (*-kə-si*) the state or quality of being delicate; refinement; tenderness, weakness (esp. of health); anything delicate or dainty, esp. to eat; a special culinary luxury. — *adv* **del'icately**. — *n* **del'icateness**. [L. *dēlicātus*.]

delicatessen *del-i-kə-tes'n*, *npl* or *nsing* prepared foods, esp. cooked meats, pâtés, and unusual or foreign foods; (as *nsing*; *colloq* short form **del'i**) a shop selling these. [Ger. pl. of Fr. *délicatesse*, delicacy.]

delicious *di-lish'əs*, *adj* pleasing to the senses, esp. taste; giving exquisite pleasure. — *adv* **deli'ciously**. — *n* **deli'ciousness**. [L. *dēliciōsus* — *dēliciae* or *dēlicium*, delight.]

delight *di-līt'*, *vt* to please greatly. — *vi* to have or take great pleasure (with *in*); to please greatly. — *n* a great degree of pleasure; extreme satisfaction; that which gives great pleasure. — *adj* **delight'ed** greatly pleased. — *adv* **delight'edly**. — *n* **delight'edness**. — *adj* **delight'ful** causing, or full of, delight. — *adv* **delight'fully**. — *n* **delight'fulness**. [O.Fr. *deliter* — L. *dēlectāre*.]

Delilah *di-lī'lə*, *n* the Philistine woman who tricked Samson (*Bible*); a courtesan; a temptress.

delimit *di-lim'it* or **delimitate** *di-lim'i-tāt*, *vt* to determine or mark the limit or limits of. — *n* **delimitā'tion**. — *adj* **delim'itative**. [L. *dēlīmitāre* — *dē* (intensive) and *līmitāre*; see **limit**.]

delineate *di-lin'i-āt*, *vt* to mark out with, or as if with, lines; to represent by a sketch or picture; to draw; to describe. — *adj* **delin'eable**. — *n* **delineā'tion** the act of delineating; a sketch, representation or description. — *adj* **delin'eative**. — *n* **delin'eātor**. [L. *dēlīneāre*, *-ātum* — *dē*, down, *līnea*, a line.]

delineavit *di-lin-i-ā'vit* or *-ä'wit*, (L.) (he or she) drew (this), sometimes added to the signature of the artist or draughtsman on a drawing.

delinquent *di-ling'kwənt*, *adj* failing in duty; of or concerning a bad debt or debtor. — *n* a person who fails in his or her duty, esp. to pay a debt; an offender, esp. a young criminal; a person lacking in moral and social sense. — *n* **delin'quency** failure in or omission of duty, esp. financial; a fault; crime, the state of being delinquent. — *adv* **delin'quently**. [L. *dēlinquēns*, *-entis*, pres. p. of *dēlinquĕre* — *dē-* (intensive) and *linquĕre*, *lictum*, to leave.]

deliquesce *del-i-kwes'*, *vi* to melt and become liquid by absorbing moisture, as certain salts, etc. — *n* **deliquesc'ence**. — *adj* **deliquesc'ent**. [L. *dēliquēscĕre* — *dē-* (intensive) and *liquēscĕre*, to become fluid.]

delirious *di-lir'i-əs*, *adj* wandering in the mind, esp. through fever or other illness; tremendously pleased, happy or excited. — *adv* **delir'iously**. — *n* **delir'iousness**. — *n* **delir'ium** the state of being delirious, esp. through fever; wild excitement, happiness or wild enthusiasm. — **delirium tremens** (*trē'menz* or *tre'*; *colloq abbrev* **DT's**) a delirious disorder of the brain produced by over-absorption of alcohol, often marked by convulsive or trembling symptoms and hallucination. [L. *dēlīrus*, crazy — *dēlīrāre*, lit. to turn aside — *dē*, from, *līra*, a furrow; *tremēns*, the pres. p. of *tremĕre*, to tremble.]

deliver *di-liv'ər*, *vt* to liberate or set free (from restraint or danger); to rescue (from evil or fear); to give up, output, discharge; to hand over, distribute or convey to the addressee; to communicate, to pronounce (a speech, message, etc.); to unleash, throw out (a blow, a ball, etc.); to assist (a mother) at the birth (of). — *adj* **deliv'erable**. — *n* **deliv'erance** liberation; release; the utterance of a judgment or authoritative opinion. — *n* **deliv'erer**. — *n* **deliv'ery** the act of delivering; the act or manner of speaking in public, of discharging a shot, of throwing a cricket ball, etc.; a distribution; the route, or a round, of distribution; (the manner of) an act of giving birth. — **deliver the goods** (*slang*) to carry out what is required or promised. [Fr. *délivrer* — L. *dē*, from, *līberāre*, to set free.]

dell *del*, *n* a deep hollow or small valley, usually covered with trees. [O.E.]

delouse *dē-lows'*, *vt* to free from lice. [**de-** (2).]

delph. See **delf**.

Delphic *del'fik*, *adj* relating to *Delphi*, a town of ancient Greece, or to its famous oracle; (also without *cap*) like an oracle, esp. if ambiguous or difficult to interpret. — Also **Del'phian**. — *adv* **del'phically**. [Gr. *Delphikos*.]

delphinium *del-fin'i-əm*, *n* any plant of the *Delphinium* genus of flowers, including the larkspurs: — *pl* **delphin'iums** or **delphin'ia**. [Latinised from Gr.

delphīnion, larkspur, dimin. of *delphīs*, dolphin (from the appearance of the flowers).]

delt. Short for **deltoid muscle**.

delta *del'tə*, *n* the fourth letter (Δ δ) of the Greek alphabet, equivalent to *d*; an alluvial area at the mouth of a stream or river, Δ-shaped in the case of the Nile, where the flow splits into several channels; in classification, the fourth or one of the fourth grade, the grade below gamma. — *adj* **deltā'ic** pertaining to a delta. — *adj* **del'toid** of the form of the Greek Δ; triangular. — *n* a deltoid muscle. — *adj* and *n* **del'ta-wing** (a jet aeroplane) with triangular wings. — **deltoid muscle** the large triangular muscle of the shoulder. [Gr., — Heb. *daleth*, a tent-door.]

deltiology *del-ti-ol'ə-ji*, *n* the study and collection of picture postcards. — *n* **deltiol'ogist**. [Gr. *deltion*, small writing-tablet.]

delude *di-lōōd'*, *vt* to deceive, or cause to accept what is false as true. — *adj* **delud'able**. — *adj* **delud'ed**. — *n* **delud'er**. [L. *dēlūdĕre*, to play false.]

deluge *del'ūj*, *n* a great flow of water; a flood, esp. the original biblical flood of Noah; an overwhelming flow or quantity (*fig*). — *vt* to inundate; to overwhelm with or as if with water. [Fr. *déluge* — L. *dīluvium* — *dīluĕre* — *dis-*, away, *luĕre*, to wash.]

delusion *di-lōō'zhən*, *n* the act of deluding; the state of being deluded; a hallucination; a false belief (esp. *psychiatry*). — *adj* **delu'sional** pertaining to or afflicted with delusions. — *adj* **delu'sive** (*-siv*) or **delu'sory** apt, or tending, to delude; deceptive. — *adv* **delu'sively**. — *n* **delu'siveness**. [**delude**.]

de luxe *də lüks'*, *di lōōks'* or *luks'*, *adj* sumptuous, luxurious; having refinements or superior qualities. [Fr., of luxury.]

delve *delv*, *vi* to dig, esp. with the hands; to research deeply (with *into*). — *n* **delv'er**. [O.E. *delfan*, to dig.]

demagnetise or **-ize** *dē-mag'nit-īz*, *vt* to deprive of magnetic properties. — *n* **demagnetīsā'tion** or **-z-**. — *n* **demag'netiser** or **-z-**. [**de-** (2).]

demagogue *dem'ə-gog*, *n* a leader of the people; a popular orator who appeals to the baser emotions of his or her audience. — *adj* **demagogic** or **demagogical** (*-gog'* or *-goj'*). — *n* **demagogism** or **demagoguism** (*dem'ə-gog-ism*). — *n* **dem'agoguery** (*-gog-*) or **dem'agogy** (*-goj-i*). [Gr. *dēmagōgos* — *dēmos*, people, *agōgos*, leading.]

demand *di-mänd'*, *vt* to claim; to ask for peremptorily or authoritatively; to require, insist upon. — *n* asking for what is due; peremptory asking for something, insistence upon something; a claim; desire shown by consumers; the amount of any article, commodity, etc. that consumers will buy. — *adj* **demand'able**. — *n* **demand'ant** someone who demands; a plaintiff (*law*). — *n* **demand'er**. — *adj* **demand'ing** requiring much attention, effort, etc. — **in (great) demand** much sought after, desired; **on demand** whenever required. [Fr. *demander* — L. *dē-* (intensive) and *mandāre*, to put into one's charge.]

demanning *dē-man'ing*, *n* the deliberate reduction of the number of employees in a particular industry, etc. — *vt* **deman'**: — *pr p* **demann'ing**; *pa t* and *pa p* **demanned'**. [**de-** (2).]

demarcation *dē-märk-ā'shən*, *n* the act of marking off or setting boundaries; separation; a fixed limit; in trade unionism, the strict separation of the area of work of one craft or trade from that of another. — Also **demarkā'tion**. — *vt* **dē'marcate** to mark off or limit; to separate. — **demarcation dispute** a disagreement between trade unions in a particular factory or industry about which union's members are responsible for performing a particular task. [Sp. *demarcación* — *de*, from, *marcar*, to mark.]

démarche *dā-märsh*, (Fr.) *n* a step or measure (esp. diplomatic).

dematerialise or **-ize** *dē-mə-tē'ri-əl-īz*, *vt* and *vi* to become or cause to become invisible, to vanish, cease to exist. — *n* **dematerialisā'tion** or **-z-**. [**de-** (2).]

deme *dēm*, (*biol*) *n* a group of plants or animals that are closely related and live in a single distinct locality. [Gr. *dēmos*, people.]

demean[1] *di-mēn'*, *vt* to bear, behave, conduct (*reflexive*). — *n* **demeanour** or in U.S. **demean'or** (*di-mēn'ər*) behaviour; manner towards another person. [O.Fr. *demener* — *de-* (intensive) and *mener*, to lead.]

demean[2] *di-mēn'*, *vt* to lower in status, reputation, or (often *reflexive*) dignity.

demented *di-ment'id*, *adj* out of one's mind; insane; crazy (*colloq*); suffering from dementia. — *adv* **dement'edly**. — *n* **dement'edness**. — *n* **dementia** (*di-men'shi-ə*; *psychol*) any form of insanity characterised by the failure or loss of mental powers; the organic deterioration of intelligence, memory and orientation, often with advancing age. — **dementia praecox** or **precox** (*prē'koks*) schizophrenia. [L. *dēmēns*, *dēmentis*, out of one's mind — *dē*, from, *mēns*, the mind.]

demerara *dem-ə-rā'rə* or *-rä'rə*, *n* a type of brown sugar with large crystals; a type of rum. [*Demerara* in Guyana.]

demerge *dē-mûrj'*, *vi* (of companies, etc.) to undergo a reversal of a merger, to become separate again. — *n* **demer'ger**. [**de-** (2).]

demerit *dē-* or *di-mer'it*, *n* a fault or defect (esp. in a person); a mark given for a fault or offence, esp. in schools or the army, etc. (*NAm*). [L. *dēmerērī*, *dēmeritum*, to deserve fully, later understood as to deserve ill.]

demersal *di-mûrs'əl*, *adj* living underwater; found on or near the bottom. [L. *dē*, down, *mergĕre*, *mersum*, to plunge.]

demesne *di-mēn'* or *-mān'*, *n* a manor-house with lands adjacent to it not let out to tenants; any estate of land. [Form of **domain**.]

demi- *dem-i-*, *combining form* denoting half or half-sized. — *n* **dem'igod** a person whose nature is partly divine, esp. a hero fabled to be, or idolised as, the offspring of a god and a mortal: — *fem* **dem'igoddess**. — *n* **demi-monde** (*dem'i-mond*) a class of women in an unrespectable social position, the kept mistresses of society men; the shady section of a profession or group. — *n* **demi-mondaine** (*-ān'*) a woman member of the demi-monde. — Also *adj*. — *n* **demi-pension** (*də-mē-pā-syɔ̃*; Fr. *pension*, boarding-house) the provision of bed, breakfast and one other meal, in hotels, etc., half board. — *n* **demi-semiquaver** (*dem-i-sem'i-kwā-vər*; *mus*) a note equal in time to half of a semiquaver. [Fr. *demi* — L. *dīmidium* — *di-*, apart, *medius*, the middle.]

demijohn *dem'i-jon*, *n* a glass bottle with a wide body and narrow neck often with handles, used esp. for holding wine. [Fr. *dame-jeanne*, Dame Jane.]

demilitarise or **-ize** *dē-mil'i-tər-īz*, *vt* to release from military control, remove forces from. — *n* **demilitarīsā'tion** or **-z-**. [**de-** (2).]

demineralise or **-ize** *dē-min'ə-rə-līz*, *vt* to remove salts from (water or the body). — *n* **demineralisā'tion** or **-z-**. [**de-** (2).]

demise *di-mīz'*, *n* death, esp. of a sovereign or a distinguished person (*euph*); a transferring by lease; a transfer of the crown or of an estate to a successor. — *vt* to give to a successor; to bequeath by will; to transfer by lease. — *adj* **demī'sable**. [O.Fr. *demise*, past p. of *desmettre*, to lay down — L. *dis-*, aside, *mittĕre*, *missum*, to send.]

demist *dē-mist'*, *vt* to clear (e.g. a car windscreen) of condensation. — Also *vi*. — *n* **demist'er** a mechanical device which does this, usu. by blowing hot air. [**de-** (2).]

demitasse *dem'i-tas*, *n* (the quantity contained by) a small cup of, or for, (esp. black) coffee. [Fr., half-cup.]

demo *dem'ō*, (*colloq*) *n* short for **demonstration**, esp. in the sense of a public expression of feeling: — *pl* **dem'os.**

demobilise or **-ize** *di-mōb'il-īz*, *vt* to take out of action; to disband; to discharge from the army (*colloq*). — *n* **demobilisā'tion** or **-z-**. — *n* and *vt* **demob'** (*pr p* **demobb'ing**; *pa t* and *pa p* **demobbed'**) colloq. shortening of **demobilisation** and **demobilise.** — Also *adj.* [**de-** (2).]

democracy *di-mok'rə-si*, *n* a form of government in which the supreme power is vested in the people collectively, and is administered by them or by officers appointed by them; the common people; a state of society characterised by recognition of equality of rights and privileges for all people; political, social or legal equality. — *n* **democrat** (*dem'ə-krat*) a person who adheres to or promotes democracy as a principle; (sometimes with *cap*) a member of the Democratic party in the United States, the party generally inclining to look to marginally left of centre; a member of any British, Irish, German, etc. political party with *Democratic* in its title (*colloq*). — *adj* **democrat'ic** or **democrat'ical** relating to democracy; insisting on, advocating or upholding equal rights and privileges for all. — *adv* **democrat'ically.** — *vt* **democratise** or **-ize** (*di-mok'*) to make democratic. — *n* **democratīsā'tion** or **-z-**. [Fr. *démocratie* — Gr. *dēmokratiā* — *dēmos*, the people, *kratos*, strength.]

démodé *dā-mo-dā*, (Fr.) *adj* out of fashion.

demoded *dē-mōd'id*, *adj* (*disparagingly*) no longer in fashion. [**de-** (2).]

demodulate *dē-mod'ū-lāt*, (*radio*) *vt* to perform demodulation on (a wave). — *n* **demodulā'tion** the inverse of modulation, a process by which an output wave is obtained that has the characteristics of the original modulating wave. — *n* **demod'ulator.** [**de-** (2).]

demography *di-mog'rə-fi*, *n* the study of population. — *n* **demog'rapher.** — *adj* **demographic** (*dem-ə-graf'ik*). [Gr. *dēmos*, the people, *graphein*, to write.]

demoiselle *dəm-wä-zel'*, *n* a young lady (*archaic* or *facetious*); a graceful variety of crane (*ornithol*); a dragonfly; a fish related to the wrasses. [Fr.; see **damsel.**]

demolish *di-mol'ish*, *vt* to ruin, lay waste; to destroy, put an end to, cause to collapse. — *n* **demoli'tion** (*dem-ə-*) the act of pulling down; ruin. — *n* **demoli'tionist.** [Fr. *démolir* — L. *dēmōlīri*, to throw down.]

demon *dē'mən*, *n* an evil spirit, a devil; sometimes like **daemon,** a friendly spirit or good genius; a person of great energy, enthusiasm or skill (*fem* **dē'moness**). — Also *adj.* — *adj* **demoniac** (*di-mōn'i-ak*). — *n* a person possessed by a demon or evil spirit. — *adj* **demoniacal** (*dē-mə-nī'ə-kl*) pertaining to or like demons or evil spirits; influenced by demons. — *adv* **demonī'acally.** — *adj* **demonic** (*di-mon'ik*) demoniac. — *n* **dē'monism** a belief in, or worship of, demons. — *n* **dē'monist.** — *n* **dēmonol'ater** (*-ol'ə-tər*). — *n* **dēmonol'atry** the worship of demons. — *adj* **dēmonolog'ic** or **demonolog'ical.** — *n* **dēmonol'ogist.** — *n* **dēmonol'ogy** an account of, or the study of, demons and their ways. [L. *daemōn* — Gr. *daimōn*, a spirit, genius; in N.T. and Late Greek, a devil; see **daemon.**]

demonetise or **-ize** *dē-mon'i-tīz* or *-mun'*, *vt* to remove from currency as money. — *n* **demonetīsā'tion** or **-z-**. [**de-** (2).]

demonstr. *abbrev* for demonstrative (also **demon.** or **demons.**).

demonstrate *dem'ən-strāt*, *vt* to make apparent; to give proof of; to prove with certainty; to teach, expound, explain or exhibit by practical means. — *vi* to act as a demonstrator. — *adj* **demon'strable** (or *dem'ən-*). — *n* **demon'strableness** or **demonstrabil'ity.** — *adv* **dem'onstrably** (or *di-mon'*). — *n* **demonstrā'tion** a pointing out, indication; proof beyond doubt; expression (of the feelings) by outward signs; a public expression of feelings (esp. of protest), as by a mass-meeting, a procession, etc.; a movement to exhibit military intention, or to deceive an enemy; a practical lesson, explanation or exhibition. — Also *adj.* — *adj* **demon'strative** pointing out, indicating (as a *demonstrative adjective*); making evident; proving with certainty; of the nature of proof; given to showing one's feelings openly. — *adv* **demon'stratively.** — *n* **demon'strativeness.** — *n* **dem'onstrātor** a person who proves beyond doubt; a teacher or assistant who helps students with practical work; a person who travels about exhibiting the uses and merits of a product; a person who takes part in a public protest demonstration; a vehicle or other product or piece of merchandise used for demonstration to customers. [L. *dēmōnstrāre*, *-ātum* — *dē-* (intensive) and *mōnstrāre*, to show.]

demoralise or **-ize** *dē-mor'əl-īz*, *vt* to lower the morale of, to deprive of spirit and confidence; to corrupt morally. — *n* **demoralīsā'tion** or **-z-**. [**de-** (2).]

demote *di-mōt'*, *vt* to reduce in rank. — *n* **demō'tion.** [On the analogy of **promote; de-** (2).]

demotic *di-mot'ik*, *adj* pertaining to the people; popular; pertaining to a simplified kind of writing different from the hieratic, or priestly, kind and from hieroglyphics (*Egyp antiq*). — *n* **demot'icist** or **demot'ist** a student of demotic script. [Gr. *dēmos*, people.]

demotivate *dē-mōt'i-vāt*, *vt* to cause a loss of motivation (in or for someone, etc.). [**de-** (2).]

demount *dē-mownt'*, *vt* to take down from a support, place of display, etc.; to take (e.g. a building) to pieces in such a way that it can be reassembled. — *adj* **demount'able.** [**de-** (2) and **mount,** to set in position.]

dempster. See under **deem.**

demulcent *di-mul'sənt*, *adj* soothing. — *n* a medicine that soothes irritation. [L. *dēmulcēns*, *-entis* — *dē*, down, *mulcēre*, to stroke, to soothe.]

demur *di-mûr'*, *vi* to object; to hesitate from uncertainty or before difficulty: — *pr p* **demurr'ing;** *pa t* and *pa p* **demurred'.** — *n* **demurr'al** hesitation or refusal. — *adj* **demurr'able.** — *n* **demurr'age** undue delay or detention of a vessel, railway wagon, etc.; compensation for such detention. — *n* **demurr'er** a person who demurs; an objection (*law*); a plea in law that, even if the opponent's facts are as he or she says, they still do not support his or her case (*law*). [Fr. *demeurer* — L. *dēmorārī*, to loiter, linger.]

demure *di-mūr'*, *adj* sober, staid (in dress or manners); modest, chaste; affectedly modest. — *adv* **demure'ly.** — *n* **demure'ness.** [O.Fr. *meur* (Fr. *mûr*) — L. *matūrus*, ripe.]

demy *dem'i* or *di-mī'*, *n* before metrication, a size of printing and writing paper approximating to *A2* 420 × 594 mm. [Fr. *demi* — L. *dīmidium*, half.]

demyelinate *dē-mī'ə-lin-āt*, (*med*) *vt* to destroy the myelin of (nerve fibres). — *n* **demyelinā'tion.** [**de-** (2).]

demystify *dē-mis'ti-fī*, *vt* to make no longer mysterious or obscure. — *n* **demystificā'tion.** [**de-** (2).]

demythologise or **-ize** *dē-mith-ol'ə-jīz*, *vt* to remove mythology from (esp. the Bible) in order to arrive at the basic meaning. [**de-** (2).]

den *den*, *n* the hollow lair of a wild beast; a pit, cave; a haunt of vice or misery; a private domestic room or office for work or pleasure (*colloq*). — **den mother** (*US*) an adult female leader of a Cub Scout group; any adult female protective figure in general. [O.E. *denn*, a cave, lair.]

denarius *di-nā'ri-əs*, *n* the chief ancient Roman silver coin, divided into ten *asses*: — *pl* **dena'rii** (*-ri-ī*).

[L. *dēnārius* — *dēnī*, ten by ten.]

denary *dēn'ər-i, adj* containing or having as a basis the number ten. [Ety. as for **denarius**.]

denationalise or **-ize** *dē-nash'ən-əl-īz, vt* to return from state to private ownership; to deprive of national rights or character. — *n* **denationalisā'tion** or **-z-**. [**de-** (2).]

denaturalise or **-ize** *dē-nach'ər-əl-īz, vt* to make unnatural; to deprive of naturalisation as a citizen. — *n* **dēnaturalīsā'tion** or **-z-**. [**de-** (2).]

denature *dē-nā'chər*, also **denaturise** or **-ize** *dē-nā'chər-īz, vt* to change the nature or properties of (e.g. a protein by heat or other treatment); to render (alcohol, etc.) unfit for human consumption; to add (non-radioactive material) to radioactive material, in order to prevent its being used in an atomic bomb (*nuc*). — *n* **denā'turant** a substance used to denature another. [**de-** (2).]

denazify *dē-nät'si-fī, vt* to free from Nazi influence and ideology. — *n* **denazificā'tion**. [**de-** (2).]

dendrite *den'drīt, n* a branching projection of a nerve-cell; a treelike crystalline mass or crystal. — *adj* **dendrit'ic**. — *adj* **dendrochronolog'ical**. — *n* **dendrochronol'ogist**. — *n* **dendrochronology** (*den-drō-kron-ol'ə-ji*) the fixing of dates in the past by comparative study of the annual growth rings in ancient trees. — *n* **dendroclimatol'ogy** the study of growth rings in trees as evidence of climatic change. — *adj* **den'droid** or **dendroid'al** treelike, having branches. — *n* **dendrol'atry** the worship of trees. — *adj* **dendrolog'ical**. — *n* **dendrol'ogist**. — *n* **dendrol'ogy** a treatise on trees; (the science or study of) the natural history of trees. [Gr. *dendron*, tree.]

dene[1] or **dean** *dēn, n* a small valley. [See **dean**[1].]

dene[2] *dēn, n* a sandy tract of land, a dune.

denegation *den-i-gā'shən, n* a denial. [L. *dēnegāre, -ātum*, to deny.]

DEng. *dē-eng', abbrev* for Doctor of Engineering.

dengue *deng'gi, n* an acute tropical epidemic fever, seldom fatal. [Apparently Swahili, *dinga*.]

deniable, denial, denier, etc. See **deny**.

denier *den'i-ər, n* a unit of silk, rayon, and nylon yarn weight. [Fr. — L. *dēnārius*.]

denigrate *den'i-grāt, vt* to blacken (esp. a reputation). — *n* **denigrā'tion**. — *n* **den'igrātor**. [L. *dē-* (intensive) and *nigrāre*, to blacken — *niger*, black.]

denim *den'im, n* coloured twilled cotton fabric for jeans, overalls, etc.; (in *pl*) a garment (esp. a pair of jeans) made of denim. [Fr. *de*, of, and *Nîmes*, town in S. France.]

denitrate *dē-nī'trāt, vt* to free from nitric acid or other nitrogen compounds. — *n* **denītrā'tion** or **denītrificā'tion** removal of nitrogen or its compounds. — *n* **denī'trificātor**. — *vt* **denī'trify**. [**de-** (2).]

denizen *den'i-zn, n* an inhabitant (human or animal); a person admitted to the rights of a citizen (of a given place); a wild plant, probably foreign, that keeps its footing when it has been introduced; a naturalised foreign word or expression. [O.Fr. *deinzein* — *deinz, dens* (Fr. *dans*), within.]

denominate *di-nom'in-āt, vt* to give a name to, to call. — *n* **denominā'tion** the act of naming; a name or title; a class or group, esp. of units in weights, money, etc.; (of coins, etc.) an allotted value; a collection (of individual plants, etc.) called by the same name; a religious sect. — *adj* **denominā'tional**. — *adv* **denominā'tionally**. — *adj* **denom'inative** giving or having a title. — *adv* **denom'inatively**. — *n* **denom'inātor** the lower number in a vulgar fraction, which names the parts into which the whole number is divided (*arith*). — **common denominator** a number that is a multiple of each of the denominators of a set of fractions; something that makes comparison, communication, agreement, etc., between things or people possible. [L. *dē-* (intensive) and *nōmināre*, to name — *nōmen*, name.]

denote *di-nōt', vt* to note or mark off (a limit, border, etc.); to indicate by a sign; to signify or mean. — *n* **dēnotā'tion**. — *adj* **denō'tative**. — *adv* **denō'tatively**. [Fr. *dénoter* — L. *dēnotāre, -ātum* — *dē* (intensive) and *notāre*, to mark.]

dénouement *dā-nōō'mā, n* the unravelling of a plot or story; the issue, event or outcome (of a sequence of events). [Fr., — L. *dis-*, *nodāre*, to tie.]

denounce *di-nowns', vt* to inform against or accuse publicly; to condemn (esp. an argument or theory); to notify formally termination of (treaties, etc.). — *n* **denounce'ment** denunciation. — *n* **denounc'er**. [Fr. *dénoncer* — L. *dēnuntiāre*.]

de novo *dē nō'vō* or *dā nō'wō*, (L.) anew, again from the beginning.

dense *dens, adj* thick, closely-spaced, compact; extremely stupid (*colloq*). — *adv* **dense'ly**. — *n* **dense'ness**. — *n* **densim'eter** an instrument for measuring the relative density or the closeness of grain of a substance. — *adj* **densimet'ric**. — *n* **densim'etry**. — *n* **densitom'eter** an instrument for measuring the optical transmission or reflecting properties of a material, or the strength of colour of a photographic image. — *adj* **densitomet'ric**. — *n* **densitom'etry**. — *n* **dens'ity** the quality or degree of being thick, closely-spaced or compact; the proportion of a mass to its bulk or volume; the quantity of matter per unit of bulk. [L. *dēnsus*, thick, dense.]

dent *dent, n* a hollow in a surface, caused by a blow. — *vt* to make such a hollow in; to do injury to (someone's pride, etc.). [Variant of **dint**.]

dent. *abbrev* for: dental; dentist; dentistry.

dental *dent'əl, adj* pertaining to or concerned with the teeth or dentistry; produced by the aid of the teeth. — *n* (*phon*) a sound pronounced by applying the tongue to the teeth or (*loosely*) the gums. — *adj* **dent'ate** or **dent'ated** toothed; notched; having a tooth-shaped pattern. — *n* **dent'icle** a small toothlike structure; a dentil. — *adj* **dentic'ulāte** or **dentic'ulated** notched; having dentils. — *n* **denticulā'tion**. — *adj* **dent'iform** having the shape of a tooth or of teeth. — *n* **dent'ifrice** (*-fris*; L. *fricāre*, to rub) a substance used in rubbing or cleaning the teeth — toothpaste or tooth-powder. — *n* **dent'il** a denticle; one of a series of square blocks or projections forming decoration on a cornice. — *adj* **dentilin'gual** (L. *lingua*, tongue; of a sound; *phon*) formed between the teeth and the tongue, as *th* in *thin* and *this*. — *n* a consonant sound so formed. — *n* **dent'ine** (*-ēn*) or **dent'in** the substance of which teeth are mainly composed. — *n* **dent'ist** a person qualified to treat diseases and malformations of, and injuries to, teeth. — *n* **dent'istry** the art or work of a dentist. — *n* **denti'tion** the cutting or growing of teeth; the shape, number, and typical arrangement of the teeth in a given species. — *n* **dent'ure** a set of (esp. artificial) teeth. — **dental floss** see **floss**. [L.L. *dentālis* — *dēns, dentis*, a tooth; dimin. *denticulus*.]

denuclearise or **-ize** *dē-nū'klēr-īz, vt* to remove nuclear weapons from (a country, state, etc.). — *n* **denuclearīsā'tion** or **-z-**. [**de-** (2).]

denude *di-nūd', vt* to make nude or naked; to strip (esp. an area of land). — *n* **denudation** (*den-ū-dā'shən* or *dē-nū-*) a making nude or bare; the wearing away of rocks whereby the underlying rocks are laid bare (*geol*). [L. *dēnūdāre* — *dē-* (intensive) and *nūdāre, -ātum*, to make naked.]

denunciate *di-nun'si-āt* or *-shi-āt, vt* to denounce. — *n* **denunciā'tion** any formal declaration; the act of denouncing. — *n* **denun'ciātor**. — *adj* **denun'ciatory** containing, or of the nature of, a denunciation. [L. *dēnunciāre* or *dēnuntiāre*; see **denounce**.]

Denver boot *den'vər bōōt*, (*slang*) *n* a wheel-clamp. [From *Denver*, U.S., its original place of use.]

deny *di-nī', vt* to declare not to be true; to disown, reject (e.g. a relative, former ally, etc.); to refuse (esp. a request); to refuse to admit; to refuse a visitor (access to): — *pr p* **deny'ing**; *pa t* and *pa p* **denied'**. — *n* **denīabil'ity**. — *adj* **denī'able**. — *adv* **denī'ably**. — *n* **denī'al** the act of denying; (a statement of) refusal; rejection. — *n* **denī'er**. — **deny oneself** to refuse to allow oneself pleasure (in). [Fr. *dénier* — L. *dēnegāre* — *dē-* (intensive) and *negāre*, to say no.]

Deo *dā'ō* or *dē'ō*, (L.) to, for, or with God. — **Deo gratias** (*grä'ti-äs* or *-shi-äs*) thanks to God; **Deo volente** (*vo-len'tā* or *wo-*) God willing.

deoch-an-doruis *dohh-ən-do'ris*, *n* a stirrup cup, a parting drink. [Gael. *deoch*, drink, *an*, the, *doruis*, genitive of *dorus*, door.]

deodar *dē'ō-där*, *n* a cedar tree of the Himalayas, much praised by Indian poets; its hard, sweet-smelling wood. [Sans. *deva-dāru*, divine tree.]

deodorise or **-ize** *dē-ō'dər-īz*, *vt* to take the (usu. unpleasant) odour or smell from; to make inoffensive by euphemism, evasion, etc. (fig). — *n* **deō'dorant**, also **deō'doriser** or **-z-** a substance that destroys or conceals unpleasant smells; by extension, a container for this. — *n* **deō-dorīsā'tion** or **-z-**. [**de-** (2).]

deontology *dē-on-tol'ə-ji*, *n* the study of duty, ethics. — Also *nsing* **deon'tics**. — *adj* **deon'tic**. — *adj* **deontological** (*-tə-loj'*). — *n* **deontol'ogist**. [Gr. *deon*, *-ontos*, neuter pres. p. of *deein*, to be necessary, to behave, *logos*, discourse.]

deoxidate *dē-oks'i-dāt*, *vt* to remove oxygen from, or reduce (*chem*). — Also **deox'idise** or **-ize**. — *n* **deoxidā'tion**, also **deoxidīsā'tion** or **-z-**. — *n* **deox'idīser** or **-z-** a substance that deoxidises. — *vt* **deoxygenate** (*dē-oks'ij-ən-āt*) to remove oxygen from. — Also **deox'ygenise** or **-ize**. — *pfx* **deoxy-** or **desoxy-** containing less oxygen. — **deoxyribonucleic acid** (*dē-oks-i-rī-bō-nū-klē'ik*) an acid present in the chromosomes of all plant and animal cells, the means of passing on hereditary characteristics. [**de-** (2).]

Dep. or **dep.** *abbrev* for: department; deputy.

dep. *abbrev* for: depart or departs; departure; deposed.

depart *di-pärt'*, *vi* to go away; to quit or leave; to die (*euph*). — *n* **depart'er**. — *n* **depart'ure** the act of departing; a going away from a place; deviation (from a normal course of action, etc.); the distance in nautical miles travelled by a ship due east or west; a death (*euph*). — **a new departure** a change of purpose, method or activity, a new course of procedure; **the departed** (*euph*) a person (or people) who has (or have) died. [Fr. *départir* — L. *dis-*, apart, *partīre* (*partīrī*), to part, to divide.]

department *di-pärt'mənt*, *n* a special or allotted function, sphere of activity, duty or expertise; a section of an administration, of a university, office or other organisation; a section of a large shop or store, selling a particular type of goods; a division of a country, esp. a département of France. — *adj* **departmental** (*dē-pärt-ment'l*). — *vt* **department'alise** or **-ize** to form into separate departments; to deal with (a large amount of work, etc.) by allotting a specific share to different departments. — *n* **departmentalisā'tion** or **-z-**. — *n* **department'alism** too strict division of work among departments with little intercommunication. — *adv* **department'ally**. — **department store** a large shop selling a great variety of goods in different departments. [Fr. *département* — *départir*; see **depart**.]

département *dā-pär-tə-mâ*, *n* any of the regional government divisions into which France is split. [Fr.]

depend *di-pend'*, *vi* to be sustained by or connected with anything; to rely (on). — *adj* **depend'able** that may be depended on; reliable. — *adv* **depend'ably**. — *n* **depend'ant** a person who depends on another for (esp. financial) support or otherwise. — *n* **depend'ence** the state of being dependent; reliance, trust. — *n* **depend'ency** a foreign territory dependent on a country, a kind of subordinate colony without self-government. — *adj* **depend'ent** depending, relying, contingent, relative. — **depending on** or **dependent on** according as. [Fr. *dépendre* — L. *dēpendēre* — *dē*, from, *pendēre*, to hang.]

depersonalise or **-ize** *dē-pûr'sən-əl-īz*, *vt* to take away the characteristics or personality of; to make impersonal, dehumanise. — *n* **dēpersonalisā'tion** or **-z-**. [**de-** (2).]

depict *di-pikt'*, *vt* to paint or draw; to make a likeness of; to describe (esp. minutely). — *n* **depict'er** or **depict'or**. — *n* **depic'tion**. — *adj* **depict'ive**. [L. *dēpingĕre*, *dēpictum* — *dē-* (intensive) and *pingĕre*, to paint.]

depilate *dep'i-lāt*, *vt* to remove the hair from. — *n* **depilā'tion** the removal or loss of hair. — *n* **dep'ilātor**. — *n* **depilatory** (*di-pil'ə-tər-i*) an application (e.g. a cream) for removing superfluous hairs. — *adj* possessing this ability. [L. *dēpilāre*, *-ātum* — *dē*, out, *pilus*, hair.]

deplane *dē-plān'*, (*US*) *vi* to disembark from an aeroplane. [**de-** (2) and **plane²**.]

deplete *di-plēt'*, *vt* to empty, reduce, exhaust, use up. — *n* **deplē'tion**. [L. *dēplēre*, *dēplētum*, to empty — *dē-* (negative) and *plēre*, to fill.]

deplore *di-plör'*, *vt* to express strong disapproval or disgust at; to feel or express deep grief for. — *adj* **deplor'able** lamentable, causing great regret; hopelessly bad. — *n* **deplor'ableness** or **deplorabil'ity**. — *adv* **deplor'ably**. [L. *dēplōrāre* — *dē-* (intensive) and *plōrāre*, to weep.]

deploy *di-ploi'*, *vt* to open out or extend; to spread out and place strategically (forces). — *vi* (of e.g. a body of troops) to take up strategic positions. — *n* **deploy'ment**. [Fr. *déployer* — L. *dis-*, apart, *plicāre*, to fold.]

deplume *dē-plōōm'*, *vt* to strip of plumes or feathers. [**de-** (2).]

depolarise or **-ize** *dē-pō'lər-īz*, (*phys*) *vt* to deprive of polarity. — *n* **depolarīsā'tion** or **-z-**. [**de-** (2).]

depoliticise or **-ize** *dē-po-lit'i-sīz*, *vt* to remove the political nature or awareness from. [**de-** (2).]

depolymerise or **-ize** *dē-pol'i-mər-īz*, *vt* to break a large molecule into simpler ones that have the same basic formula. — *vi* to decompose in this way. — *n* **depolymerisā'tion** or **-z-**. [**de-** (2).]

deponent *di-pō'nənt adj* (*gram*) (of a verb) having a passive form but active meaning. — *n* a deponent verb; a person who makes a deposition, esp. under oath, or whose written testimony is used as evidence in a court of justice. [L. pres. p. *dēpōnēns*, *-entis* — *dē*, down, *pōnĕre*, to place, lay.]

depopulate *dē-pop'ū-lāt*, *vt* to rid of people, remove the population from. — *vi* to become devoid of people. — *n* **depopulā'tion**. [L. *dēpopulārī*, *-ātus*, to swarm over a country, said of hostile people (L. *populus*) — hence to ravage, later understood as to deprive of people.]

deport¹ *di-pört'*, *vt* to expel (e.g. as an undesirable alien or foreigner). — *n* **deportā'tion** (*dē-*). — *n* **deportee'** (*dē-*). [Fr. *déporter* — L. *dēportāre* — *dē-*, away, *portāre*, *-ātum*, to carry.]

deport² *di-pört'*, *vt* (*reflexive*) to behave. — *n* **deport'ment** behaviour; physical bearing, stance, gait; manners. [O.Fr. *deporter* — L. *dē-* (intensive) and *portāre*, to carry.]

depose *di-pōz'*, *vt* to remove from a high office or post. — *vi* to give testimony. — *adj* **depōs'able**. — *n* **depōs'er**. [Fr. *déposer* — L. *dē*, from, *pausāre*, to pause, (later) to place.]

deposit *di-poz'it*, *vt* to put or set down; to place; to lay; to entrust (esp. money); to lodge as a pledge, give (esp. money) as security; to lay down as a coating, bed, vein, etc. (*geol*). — *n* that which is deposited or put down; a sum of money paid to secure an article, service, etc., the remainder of the cost being paid later; an accumulation by sedimentation, precipitation, or other natural means (*geol*); something entrusted to another's care, esp. money put in a bank; the state of being deposited. — *n* **depos'itary** a person with whom anything is left for safe keeping; a guardian — also **depos'itory**. — *n* **depos'itor**. — *n* **depos'itory** a place where anything is deposited for safe keeping — also **depos'itary**. — **deposit account** a bank account in which money is placed to gain interest, and for which cheques are not used. [L. *dēpŏsitum*, placed.]

deposition *dē-pə-zish'ən*, *n* the act of deposing; declaration, written sworn testimony to be used as a substitute for the production of the witness in open court; the act or process of depositing. — *adj* **deposi'tional**. [**deposit**; blended with root of **depose**.]

depot *dep'ō*, *n* a storehouse; a military post where stores are kept and recruits trained; the headquarters of a regiment; a place where buses or tram-cars are kept; a bus or train station (*NAm*). [Fr. *dépôt* — L. *dēpōnĕre*, to put down.]

deprave *di-prāv'*, *vt* to make morally bad or worse; to corrupt. — *adj* **deprāved'** corrupt. — *n* **depravity** (*di-prav'i-ti*) a corrupt state of moral character; extreme wickedness; the hereditary tendency of man to sin (*theol*). [L. *dēprāvāre* — *dē-* (intensive) and *prāvus*, bad.]

deprecate *dep'ri-kāt*, *vt* to disparage, belittle; to argue or protest against; to express disapproval of. — *adj* **dep'recating** expressing disparagement, contempt, disapproval. — *n* **deprecā'tion**. — *adj* **dep'recātive** or **dep'recātory**. — *n* **dep'recātor**. — *adv* **dep'recātorily**. [L. *dēprecārī*, *-ātus* — *dē*, away, *precārī*, to pray.]

depreciate *di-prē'shi-āt*, *vt* to lower the worth of; to undervalue, be contemptuous of the value of. — *vi* to fall in value. — *adv* **deprē'ciātingly**. — *n* **depreciātion** (*-si-ā'shən* or *-shi-*) falling in value; disparagement, ridicule. — *adj* **deprē'ciative** or **deprē'ciatory** tending to depreciate or lower. — *n* **deprē'ciātor**. [L. *dēpretiāre*, *-ātum* — *dē*, down, *pretium*, price.]

depredation *dep-ri-dā'shən*, *n* the act of plundering; the state of being ravaged; (usu. in *pl*) hardship, damage. — *n* **dep'redātor**. [L. *dēpraedārī*, *-ātus* — *dē-* (intensive) and *praedārī* — *praeda*, plunder.]

depress *di-pres'*, *vt* to press down; to lower; to cause to sink; to deject or cast a gloom over. — *n* **depress'ant** anything which lowers activity or spirits; a sedative. — Also *adj*. — *adj* **depressed'** pressed down; lowered; flattened or slightly hollowed; dejected; (of a market, trade, etc.) reduced, not flourishing. — *adj* **depress'ing** tending to depress, esp. in spirits. — *n* **depression** (*di-presh'ən*) a sinking; a lowering; a region of low barometric pressure; a hollow; dejection; a condition of reduced trade activity and prosperity. — *adj* **depress'ive** tending to depress; (of a person) suffering from periods of depression. — *n* a person suffering from periods of depression. — *n* **depress'or** something which lowers activity; a muscle that draws down; a surgical instrument for pressing down. — **depressed area** a region suffering from reduced trade, and often consequently one of specially heavy unemployment, poor housing, etc. [L. *dēprimĕre*, *-pressum* — *dē*, down, *premĕre*, to press.]

depressurise or **-ize** *dē-presh'ər-īz*, *vt* to reduce the air pressure in (e.g. an aircraft cabin), esp. suddenly. — *n* **depressurisā'tion** or **-z-**. [**de-** (2).]

deprive *di-prīv'*, *vt* to take possession away from; to keep from enjoyment (of). — *n* **deprivā'tion** (*dep-ri-*) the act of depriving; the state of being deprived; a loss. — *adj* **deprived'** having had something taken away (with *of*); suffering from hardship, esp. the lack of good educational, social, medical, etc. facilities. [L.L. *dēprīvāre*, to degrade — L. *dē*, from, *prīvāre*, to deprive.]

Dept. or **dept.** *abbrev* for: department; deputy.

depth *depth*, *n* deepness; the measure of deepness down or inwards; a deep place; intensity (of e.g. feeling); the innermost or intensest part, as in *depth of winter*; difficulty of understanding, obscurity; extent of wisdom and penetration of mental powers. — **depth'-bomb** or **depth'-charge** a powerful bomb that explodes under water (dropped over or near submarines); **depth psychology** the psychology of the unconscious mind; **depth psychologist**. — **in depth** extensive(ly) and thorough(ly) (*adj* **in-depth'** see **in**); (of defence) consisting of several successive lines; **out of one's depth** in water where one cannot touch the bottom with one's head above the surface; in a situation, etc., beyond one's understanding; **the depths** the lowest pitch of humiliation and misery.

depute *di-pūt'*, *vt* to appoint or send as a substitute or agent; to send with a special commission; to give (one's authority) to someone else. — In combination (*dep'ūt*) in Scotland, appointed deputy (as in *sheriff-depute*). — *n* **deputation** (*dep-ū-tā'shən*) the act of deputing; the person or persons deputed or appointed to transact business on another's behalf; a representative body of people sent to state a case in a dispute. — *vt* **dep'ūtise** or **-ize** to appoint as deputy. — *vi* to act as deputy. — *n* **dep'ūty** a person deputed or appointed to act for another; a delegate or representative, or substitute; a legislator, member of a chamber of deputies; a person who attends to safety arrangements in a coalmine. [L. *dēputāre*, to prune, (later) to select.]

der. *abbrev* for: derivation; derivative; derived.

deracinate *dē-ras'i-nāt*, *vt* to root up. — *n* **deracinā'tion**. [Fr. *déraciner* — L. *dē*, from, L.L. *rādicīna*, dimin. of L. *rādix*, a root.]

derail *di-rāl'*, (*lit* and *fig*) *vt* to cause to leave the rails. — *vi* to go off the rails. — *n* **derail'ment**. [**de-** (2).]

dérailleur *dā-ra-yœr* or **dérailleur gear** (*gēr*), *n* a variable bicycle-gear depending on a mechanism by means of which the chain can be transferred from one sprocket wheel to another of different size. [Fr. *dérailler*, to derail.]

derange *di-rānj'*, *vt* to put out of place or order; to put into disarray, confusion; to make insane. — *adj* **deranged'** disordered, disarrayed; insane. — *n* **derange'ment** disorder, disarray; insanity. [Fr. *déranger* — *dé-* (L. *dis-*), apart, *ranger*, to rank.]

derate *dē-rāt'*, *vt* to relieve (wholly or partially) from paying local rates; to reduce the maximum capacity ratings of electrical equipment to allow for deterioration, etc. — *n* **derat'ing**. [**de-** (2).]

deration *dē-ra'shən*, *vt* to free from rationing. [**de-** (2).]

Derby *där'bi*, *n* a horse-race held annually on Epsom Downs (instituted by Earl of *Derby*, 1780); (often without *cap*) any race attracting much interest, or a keen sporting contest, esp. one between neighbouring teams; (*dûr'bi*; *US*; often without *cap*) a bowler hat.

derecognise or **-ize** *dē-rek'əg-nīz*, *vt* to withdraw recognition from (esp. a trade union). — *n* **derecogni'tion**. [**de-** (2).]

deregister *dē-rej'is-tər*, *vt* to remove from a register. — *n* **deregistrā'tion**. [**de-** (2).]

deregulate *dē-reg'ū-lāt*, *vt* to free from regulations or controls. — *n* **deregulā'tion**. [**de-** (2).]

derelict *der'i-likt*, *adj* forsaken; abandoned, falling in ruins. — *n* anything (esp. a ship) forsaken or abandoned; a person abandoned by society, a down-and-out. — *n* **derelic'tion** the act of forsaking (esp. duty), unfaithfulness or remissness; the state of being abandoned; land regained from under water by a change of waterline. [L. *dērelinquĕre*, *-lictum* — *dē* (intensive), *re-*, behind, *linquĕre*, to leave.]

derequisition *dē-rek-wi-zi'shən, vt* to return (something that has been used for a military purpose) to civilian use. [**de-** (2).]

derestrict *dē-ri-strikt', vt* to free from restriction (esp. a road from a speed limit). — *n* **derestric'tion**. [**de-** (2).]

deride *di-rīd', vt* to laugh at; to mock. — *n* **derid'er**. — *adj* **derisible** (*-riz'*). — *n* **derision** (*di-rizh'ən*) the act of deriding; mockery. — *adj* **derisive** (*di-rīs'iv*) mocking. — *adv* **derī's'ively**. — *n* **derī's'iveness**. — *adj* **derī's'ory** mocking; ridiculous, insulting. [L. *dērīdēre, -rīsum* — *dē* (intensive) and *rīdēre*, to laugh.]

de rigueur *də rē-gœr*, (Fr.) absolutely essential, required by strict etiquette, or by fashion, etc.

derision, derisive, etc. See under **deride**.

deriv. *abbrev* for: derivation; derivative; derived.

derive *di-rīv', vt* to proceed, draw, take, obtain or receive (from a source or origin); to infer; to trace to or from an origin. — *vi* to descend, issue, originate. — *adj* **derīv'able**. — *n* **derivā'tion** the act of deriving; the tracing of a word to its root; source, origin; that which is derived; descent or evolution; a sequence of statements showing how a certain result must follow from other statements already accepted, as in a mathematical formula, logical progression, etc. — *adj* **derivā'tional**. — *adj* **derivative** (*di-riv'ə-tiv*) derived or taken from something else; (sometimes *derog*) unoriginal, based on something already in existence. — *n* that which is derived; a word formed from another word, esp. by prefixation or suffixation; a differential coefficient (*math*); (in *pl*) futures and options (*stock exchange*). — *adv* **deriv'atively**. [Fr. *dériver* — L. *dērīvāre* — *dē*, down, from, *rīvus*, a river.]

derm *dûrm, n* the true skin, below the outer layer — also **der'ma** or **der'mis**. — *n* **dermabrā'sion** a cosmetic operation in which the facial skin is scrubbed, peeled away and allowed to heal. — *adj* **der'mal** or **der'mic** pertaining to the skin; consisting of skin. — *n* **dermatī'tis** inflammation of the skin. — *n* **dermatograph'ia** a type of nettle-rash in which the physical allergy causes stroking or scratching, etc. to raise a red weal on the skin. — *adj* **dermatograph'ic**. — *adj* **dermatolog'ical**. — *n* **dermatol'ogist**. — *n* **dermatol'ogy** the branch of science that concerns itself with the skin. — *n* **derm'atome** a surgical instrument for cutting layers of skin, esp. for grafting; the part of an embryonic somite, or skin segment, that produces the dermis; the area of skin supplied with nerves from a single spinal root. — *n* **dermatomyosī'tis** a disease characterised by inflammation of the skin and muscles, and wasting of the muscles. — *adj* **dermatoplas'tic**. — *n* **dermatoplas'ty** a plastic operation on the skin, esp. grafting. — *n* **dermatō'sis** any skin disease: — *pl* **dermatō'ses** (*-sēz*). — *n* **der'moid** a cyst of congenital origin, containing such structures as hair, skin and teeth, occurring usu. in the ovary. [Gr. *derma, -atos*, the skin.]

derogate *der'ō-gāt, vi* and *vt* to lessen by taking away; to detract. — *n* **derogā'tion** a taking from; detraction. — *adj* **derog'ative**. — *adv* **derog'atively**. — *adv* **derogatorily** (*di-rog'ə-tər-i-li*). — *n* **derog'atoriness**. — *adj* **derog'atory** detracting; injurious, insulting, adversely critical. [L. *dērogāre,-ātum*, to repeal part of a law — *dē*, down, from, *rogāre*, to propose a law.]

derrick *der'ik, n* a mechanism for hoisting materials, by a boom hung from a central post; a framework or tower over a borehole or the like. [From *Derrick*, a 17th-century hangman.]

derrière *der-i-er'*, (Fr.) *n* the behind, buttocks.

derring-do *der-ing-doo'*, (*false archaic*) *n* daring action(s). — [Spenser mistook Lydgate's *dorryng do*, i.e. daring (to) do (misprinted *derrynge do*) for a noun.]

derringer *der'in-jər, n* a short American pistol. [Inventor's name.]

derris *der'is, n* any plant of a tropical genus (*Derris*) of plants related to peas and beans, whose roots yield an insecticide powder. [Gr. *derris*, a leather coat.]

derry *der'i*, (*slang*, esp. *Austr*) *n* a feeling of dislike or resentment, esp. in the phrase **have a derry on (someone)**.

derv *dûrv, n* diesel engine fuel oil. [From *d*iesel *e*ngined *r*oad *v*ehicle.]

dervish *dûr'vish, n* (sometimes with *cap*) a member of one of numerous Muslim fraternities, professing poverty and leading an austere life. [Turkish *dervīsh* — Pers. *darvish*, a dervish — lit., a poor man.]

DES *abbrev* for Department of Education and Science.

desalinate *dē-sal'in-āt, vt* to remove salt from (esp. sea water). — Also **desal'inise** or **-ize**. — *n* **desalinā'tion**. — *n* **desal'inātor**. — *n* **desalinisā'tion** or **-z-**. [**de-** (2).]

descale *dē-skāl', vt* to remove scales from (esp. fish); to scrape away an encrustation from. [**de-** (2).]

descant *des'kant, n* an accompaniment above and harmonising with the main melody (*mus*). — *adj* (of a musical instrument) having a higher register and pitch than most others of the same family. — *vi* **descant'** to sing a descant. [O.N.Fr. *descant* — L. *dis-*, apart, *cantus*, a song.]

descend *di-send', vi* to climb down; to move from a higher to a lower place or condition; to move from general to particular topics, details, etc.; to make an invasion (often with *on* or *upon*); to be derived (from); (of the testes) to move from the abdominal cavity into the scrotum at maturity. — *vt* to move down upon, to traverse downwards. — *n* **descend'ant** a person who descends, i.e. offspring from an ancestor. — *adj* **descend'ed** derived by ancestry or other relationship. — *adj* **descend'ent** going down; proceeding from an ancestor. — *n* **descend'er** the part of a letter such as *j* or *p* that comes below the line on which *x* sits (*printing*). — *adj* **descend'ible** (also **descend'able**) that may descend or be descended; capable of transmission by inheritance, heritable. — *n* **descent'** an act of descending; transmission by succession, inheritance; motion or progress downward; slope; a raid or invasion; derivation from an ancestor; a generation, a degree in genealogy; descendants collectively. [Fr. *descendre* — L. *dēscendĕre* — *dē*, down, *scandĕre*, to climb.]

deschool *dē-skool', vt* and *vi* to free children from the restrictions of traditional classroom learning and a set curriculum, and educate them in a less formal way, esp. at home. — *n* **deschool'er**. — *n* **deschool'ing**. [**de-** (2).]

descramble *dē-skram'bəl, vt* to unscramble, decipher. [**de-** (2).]

describe *di-skrīb', vt* to trace out or delineate; to give an account of, recount the physical appearance or details of. — *adj* **descrīb'able**. — *n* **describ'er**. — *n* **description** (*di-skrip'shən*) the act of describing; an account of anything in words; sort, class or kind (*loosely*). — *adj* **descrip'tive** containing description. — *adv* **descrip'tively**. — *n* **descrip'tiveness**. — *n* **descrip'tivism** the use of, or belief in, descriptive linguistics (see below); a theory of ethics by which only empirical statements are acceptable. — **descrip'tor** (*comput*) a symbol or form of words that identifies a particular subject in a storage system, or gives information on how particular material is stored; a key word or a heading. — **descriptive geometry** the study of three-dimensional figures when projected onto a two-dimensional surface; **descriptive linguistics** the study of the description of a language structure as it occurred individually at a particular time, i.e. with no reference to its history, any other language, etc. [L. *dēscrībĕre* — *dē*, down, *scrībĕre, scrīptum*, to write.]

descry *di-skrī'*, *vt* to discover by looking; to espy: — *pr p* **descry'ing**; *pa t* and *pa p* **descried'**. [App. two words: O.Fr. *descrire* for *descrivre* — L. *dēscrīběre* (see **describe**), and O.Fr. *descrier*, *decryer*, to proclaim, announce.]

desecrate *des'i-krāt*, *vt* to make no longer consecrated; to profane, damage (something sacred). — *n* **des'ecrater** or **des'ecrator**. — *n* **desecrā'tion** the act of desecrating; profanation, damage (of anything sacred). [Coined on the analogy of **consecrate** — L. *dē*, from.]

desegregate *dē-seg'ri-gāt*, *vt* to abolish racial segregation in. — *n* **desegregā'tion**. — *n* and *adj* **desegregā'tionist**. [**de-** (2).]

deselect *dē-si-lekt'*, *vt* (of a political party at constituency or ward level) not to select (the candidate who is already an M.P., or councillor) as candidate for re-election; (of a selection panel or other body) not to reselect (e.g. an athlete) for a place on a team, to represent a country, county or the like. — *n* **deselec'tion**. [**de-** (2).]

desensitise or **-ize** *dē-sen'sit-īz*, *vt* and *vi* to make or become less sensitive. — *n* **desensitīsā'tion** or **-z-**. — *n* **desen'sitiser** or **-z-**. [**de-** (2).]

desert[1] *di-zûrt'*, *n* anything which is deserved; a reward; merit. [O.Fr., past p. of *deservir*; see **deserve**.]

desert[2] *di-zûrt'*, *vt* to leave; to forsake. — *vi* to run away; to leave a service, e.g. the army, without permission. — *n* **desert'er** someone who deserts or quits a service without permission. — *n* **deser'tion** an act of deserting; the state of being deserted; wilful abandonment of a legal or moral obligation. [L. *dēserěre*, *dēsertum* — *dē-* (negative) and *serěre*, to bind.]

desert[3] *dez'ərt*, *adj* uninhabited; uncultivated. — *n* a desolate or barren tract, usu. with little or no water; a waste; a place of solitude. — *n* **desertificā'tion**, **desertīsā'tion** or **-z-** the deterioration or reversion of land to desert conditions, owing to overgrazing, erosion, etc. — **desert boots** laced suede ankle-boots with rubber soles; **desert pea** (usu. **Sturt's desert pea**) an Australian pea with a predominantly scarlet flower; **desert rat** (from the divisional sign, a jerboa) a soldier of the British 7th Armoured Division who served in N. Africa in 1941–42. [O.Fr. *desert* — L. *dēsertum* — *dēserěre*, to desert, unbind.]

deserve *di-zûrv'*, *vt* to be entitled to by merit; to warrant, be worthy of. — *vi* to be worthy of reward. — *adj* **deserved'**. — *adv* **deserv'edly**. — *n* **deserv'edness**. — *n* **deserv'er**. — *adj* **deserv'ing** worthy. — *adv* **deserv'ingly** according to what is deserved; justly. [O.Fr. *deservir* — L. *dēservīre* — *dē* (intensive) and *servīre*, to serve.]

desex *dē-seks'*, *vt* to deprive of sexual character or quality. [**de-** (2).]

déshabillé. Same as **dishabille**.

desiccate *des'i-kāt*, *vt* to dry; to preserve by drying. — *vi* to grow dry. — *adj* **des'iccant** or **desiccative** (*di-sik'ə-tiv*) drying; having the power of drying. — *n* a drying agent. — *n* **desiccā'tion** the act or process of drying up; the state of being dried up. — *n* **des'iccātor** an apparatus for drying. [L. *dēsiccāre*, *-ātum*, to dry up.]

desideratum *di-sid-ər-ä'təm* or *-zid-*, *n* something desired or much wanted: — *pl* **desidera'ta**. [L. *dēsīderāre*, *-ātum*, to long for.]

design *di-zīn'*, *vt* to draw; to plan and execute artistically; to form a plan of; to contrive, invent; to set apart or intend. — *n* a drawing or sketch; a plan in outline; a plan or scheme formed in the mind; a plot; intention. — *adj* **design'able**. — *adv* **design'edly** by design; intentionally. — *n* **design'er** a person who provides designs or patterns; a draughtsman; a person who designs sets for plays, operas, films, etc. — *adj* of or pertaining to a designer; designed by (and bearing the name of) a known fashion designer; designed or created to follow the fashionable trend or image (*loosely*; slightly *derog*); custom-made, for a particular, specific purpose. — *adj* **design'ing** artful; scheming. — *n* the art of making designs or patterns. — *adv* **design'ingly**. — **design engineer** a designer in engineering. — **by design** intentionally. [Fr. *désigner* — L. *dēsignāre*, *-ātum* — *dē-*, off, *signum*, a mark.]

designate *dez'ig-nāt*, *vt* to mark out so as to make known; to show, indicate; to be a name or label for; to appoint or nominate. — *adj* nominated to but not yet in possession of an office (used after the noun, as in *chairman designate*). — *n* **designā'tion** a showing or pointing out; a name, a title; a mode of address descriptive of occupation, standing, etc.; nomination to office. — *n* **des'ignātor**. [Ety. as for **design**.]

desire *di-zīr'*, *vt* to long for; to wish for. — *n* an earnest longing or wish; a prayer or request; the object desired; lust. — *adj* **desīr'able** worthy of desire or approval; pleasing, agreeable. — *n* a desirable person or thing. — *n* **desīrabil'ity** or **desīr'ableness**. — *adv* **desīr'ably**. — *adj* **desīr'ous** (usu. with *of*) full of desire, wanting; eager. [Fr. *désirer* — L. *dēsīderāre*.]

desist *di-zist'*, *vi* to stop (doing something). [L. *dēsistěre* — *dē-*, away from, *sistěre*, to cause to stand.]

desk *desk*, *n* a sloping or flat table for writing or reading, often fitted with drawers, etc.; a counter in a public place for information, registration, etc.; a department of a newspaper office, e.g. *the news desk*; a music-stand; a pulpit or lectern. — *adj* **desk'-bound** confined to a desk, i.e. doing paperwork and administration rather than active or practical work. — *adj* **desk'top** (of a computer, etc.) designed for use on a desk. — *n* such a computer; **desk'-work** work done at a desk, e.g. by a clerk or author. — **desktop publishing** (a system for) the production on a desktop computer of all the pre-press stages of publication, i.e. typesetting, design, layout, illustration, etc. [M.E. *deske* — L. *discus* — Gr. *diskos*.]

deskill *dē-skil'*, *vt* to remove the element of human skill from (a job, process, operation, etc.) through automation, computerisation, etc. [**de-** (2).]

désœuvré *dāz-œv-rā*, (Fr.) *adj* unoccupied; at a loose end.

desolate *des'ə-lāt*, *vt* to make lonely or forlorn; to make extremely sad; to deprive of inhabitants; to lay waste. — *adj* (*-lit*) comfortless, dreary, forlorn; extremely sad; lonely; totally lacking in inhabitants; laid waste. — *adv* **des'olately**. — *n* **des'olateness**. — *n* **des'olāter** or **des'olātor**. — *n* **desolā'tion**. [L. *dēsōlāre*, *-ātum* — *dē-* (intensive) and *sōlāre*, to make alone.]

desorption *dē-sörp'shən*, *n* release from an adsorbed state. — *vt* **desorb'**. [**de-** (2).]

despair *di-spār'*, *vi* to be without hope (of). — *n* hopelessness; anything which causes despair. — *adj* **despair'ing** apt to despair; full of despair. — *adv* **despair'ingly**. [O.Fr. *desperer* — L. *dē-* (negative) and *spērāre*, to hope.]

despatch. See **dispatch**.

desperado *des-pər-ä'dō*, *n* a desperate person, reckless of danger; a wild ruffian: — *pl* **despera'dos** or **despera'does**. [Old Sp. — L. *dēspērātus*.]

desperate *des'pər-it*, *adj* in a state of despair; hopeless; despairingly reckless; extremely bad; extremely anxious or eager (for, to do, etc.) (*colloq*). — *adv* **des'perately**. — *n* **des'perateness**. — *n* **desperā'tion** a state of despair; despairing; disregard of danger, recklessness. [**despair**.]

despicable *dis-pik'ə-bl* or *des'pik-*, *adj* deserving to be despised; contemptible. — *n* **despicabil'ity** or **despic'ableness** (or *des'pik-*). — *adv* **despic'ably** (or *des'*). [**despise**.]

despise *di-spīz'*, *vt* to look down on with contempt, hate. — *n* **despīs'er**. [O.Fr. *despire* (*despis-*) — L. *dēspicěre* — *dē*, down, *specěre*, to look.]

despite *di-spīt'*, *prep* in spite of; notwithstanding. [O.Fr. *despit* (mod. *dépit*) — L. *dēspectus* — *dēspicĕre*; see **despise**.]

despoil *di-spoil'*, *vt* to plunder completely; to strip; to rob. — *n* **despoil'er**. — *n* **despoil'ment**. [O.Fr. *despoiller* (mod. *dépouiller*; see next word).]

despoliation *di-spōl-i-ā'shən*, *n* despoiling. [L. *dēspoliāre* — *dē-* (intensive) and *spolium*, spoil.]

despondency *di-spond'ən-si*, *n* lack of hope, dejection. — *adj* **despond'ent**. — *adv* **despond'ently**. [L. *dēspondēre*, to resign — *dē*, away, *spondēre*, to promise.]

despot *des'pot*, *n* a person invested with absolute power; a tyrant. — *adj* **despotic** (*dis-pot'ik*) or **despot'ical** pertaining to or like a despot; having absolute power; tyrannical. — *adv* **despot'ically**. — *n* **des'potism** absolute power; a state governed by a despot. [O.Fr. *despot* — Gr. *despotēs*, a master.]

dessert *diz-ûrt'*, *n* a final course of a meal, pudding or other sweet item; fruit, sweetmeats, etc. served at the end of a meal. — **dessert'spoon** a spoon used for eating desserts, smaller than a tablespoon and larger than a teaspoon; **dessert'spoonful**: — *pl* **dessert'spoonfuls**. [O.Fr. *dessert* — *desservir*, to clear the table.]

destabilise or **-ize** *dē-stā'bil-īz*, *vt* to make unstable or less stable (*lit* and *fig*). — *n* **destā'biliser** or **-z-**. [**de-** (2).]

de-Stalinise or **-ize** *dē-stä'li-nīz*, *vt* to remove the influence of Joseph *Stalin* (from Russian politics, etc.). — *n* **de-Stalinīsā'tion** or **-z-**.

destine *des'tin*, *vt* (often by fate) to ordain or appoint to a certain use or state; to intend. — *n* **destinā'tion** the purpose or end to which anything is destined or appointed; the place to which one is going. — *n* **des'tiny** the purpose or end to which any person or thing is appointed; unavoidable fate. [Fr. *destiner* — L. *dē-* (intensive) and root of *stāre*, to stand.]

destitute *des'ti-tūt*, *adj* in utter poverty; entirely lacking in (with *of*). — *n* **destitu'tion** the state of being destitute; poverty. [L. *dēstituĕre*, *-ūtum* — *dē-*, away, *statuĕre*, to place.]

destroy *di-stroi'*, *vt* to pull down; to defeat or kill; to ruin; to put an end to: — *pr p* **destroy'ing**; *pa t* and *pa p* **destroyed'**. — *adj* **destroy'able**. — *n* **destroy'er** a person or thing that destroys; a small, fast-moving warship. [O.Fr. *destruire* (Fr. *détruire*) — L. *dē-*, down, *struĕre*, to build.]

destruction *di-struk'shən*, *n* the act or process of destroying; overthrow; physical or moral ruin; death; a cause of destruction. — *vt* **destruct'** to destroy a rocket or missile in flight. — Also *vi*. — *adj* **destruc'tible** capable of being or liable to be destroyed. — *n* **destructibil'ity**. — *adj* **destruc'tive** causing or concerned with destruction; (of e.g. criticism) unhelpfully negative (opp. of *constructive*). — *adv* **destruc'tively**. — *n* **destruc'tiveness**. — *n* **destruc'tor** (*di-*) a furnace for burning up refuse. — **destructive distillation** the decomposition of solid substances by heating, and the subsequent collection of the volatile substances produced. [L. *dēstruĕre*, *-structum*; see **destroy**.]

desuetude *di-sū'i-tūd* or *des'wi-tūd*, *n* disuse; discontinuance. [L. *dēsuētūdō* — *dē* (negative) and *suēscĕre*, to become used.]

desultory *des'əl-tər-i* or *-tri*, *adj* jumping from one thing to another; without rational or logical connection; rambling. — *adv* **des'ultorily**. — *n* **des'ultoriness**. [L. *dēsultōrius* — *dēsultor*, a vaulter, — *dē*, from, *salīre*, to jump.]

detach *di-tach'*, *vt* to unfasten; to take away or separate; to withdraw; to send off on special service (*mil*). — *vi* to separate. — *adj* **detach'able**. — *adj* **detached'** unconnected; separate; impartial; aloof; free from care, passion, ambition, and worldly bonds. — *adv* **detach'edly**. — *n* **detach'ment** the state of being detached; the act of detaching; that which is detached, e.g. a unit of troops from the main body. [Fr. *détacher* — O.Fr. pfx. *des-* (L. *dis-*), apart, and root of **attach**.]

detail *di-tāl'* or *dē'tāl*, *vt* to relate minutely; to enumerate; to set apart for a particular service. — *vi* to give details about anything. — *n* (*dē'tāl* or (esp. *NAm*) *di-tāl'*) a small or unimportant part; an item; too much attention to relatively unimportant particulars; (chiefly *mil*) a small body set apart for special duty. — *adj* **detailed** giving full particulars; exhaustive. — **go into detail** to study, discuss, etc., a matter deeply, considering the particulars; **in detail** point by point. [Fr. *détailler* — *de-* (intensive) and *tailler*, to cut.]

detain *di-tān'*, *vt* to hold back; to delay; to stop; to keep; to keep in custody. — *adj* **detain'able**. — *n* **detainee'** a person kept in custody. — *n* **detain'er** the holding of what belongs to another (*law*); a warrant to a sheriff to keep in custody a person already in confinement. — *n* **detain'ment** detention. [O.Fr. *detenir* — L. *dētinēre*.]

detect *di-tekt'*, *vt* to discover; to discern; to find out (esp. something elusive or secret). — *adj* **detect'able** or **detect'ible**. — *n* **detec'tion** the discovery of something hidden or not easily observed; the state of being found out. — *adj* **detect'ive** employed in or concerned with detection. — *n* a policeman, usually not in uniform, or other person (*private detective*) who investigates cases of crime or watches the behaviour of suspected persons. — *n* **detec'tor** an apparatus for detecting something, e.g. smoke, tampering with a lock, pressure of electric currents, electric waves, etc. — **detective story** one in which clues to the detection of a criminal are set forth and unravelled. [L. *dētegĕre*, *-tēctum* — *dē-* (negative) and *tegĕre*, to cover.]

detention *di-ten'shən*, *n* the act of detaining; the state of being detained; confinement, or restriction of liberty, esp. of an offender. — **detention centre** a place of confinement for young offenders. [L. *dētinēre*, *dētentum* — *dē*, from, *tenēre*, to hold.]

détente *dā-tāt*, (Fr.) *n* relaxation of strained relations (esp. between countries).

deter *di-tûr'*, *vt* to frighten from; to hinder or prevent: — *pr p* **deterr'ing**; *pa t* and *pa p* **deterred'**. — *n* **deter'ment**. — *n* **deterrence** (*di-ter'əns*). — *adj* **deterrent** (*di-ter'ənt*) serving to deter. — *n* anything that deters; (*specif*) a nuclear weapon. [L. *dēterrēre* — *dē*, from, *terrēre*, to frighten.]

deterge *di-tûrj'*, *vt* to cleanse (e.g. a wound). — *n* **deterg'ent** that which cleanses; a cleansing agent, esp. (commonly) a soapless cleanser. — *adj* (also **deters'ive**) cleansing; purging. [L. *dētergēre*, *dētersum* — *dē*, off, *tergēre*, to wipe.]

deteriorate *di-tē'ri-ə-rāt*, *vt* to make worse. — *vi* to grow worse. — *n* **detēriorā'tion** the act of making worse; the process of growing worse. [L. *dēteriōrāre*, *-ātum* — *dēterior*, worse.]

determine *dē-tûr'min*, *vt* to limit; to fix or settle; to define; to decide; to resolve; to cause to resolve; to put an end to (*law*). — *vi* to come to a decision; to come to an end (*law*). — *adj* **deter'minable**. — *n* **deter'minacy** (*-ə-si*). — *adj* **deter'minant** serving to determine. — *n* that which serves to determine; the sum of all the products got by taking one from each row and column of a square block of quantities, each product being reckoned positive or negative according as an even or an odd number of transpositions reduces it to the order of the rows (or of the columns) — used for the solution of equations and other purposes (*math*). — *adj* **deter'mināte** determined or limited; fixed; decisive; (of a plant) having the main stem and branches ending in flowers. — *adv* **deter'minately**. — *n* **determinā'tion** the act of determining; the condition of being determined; that which is determined or resolved on; end (*law*); direction to a certain end; resolution; fixedness of purpose; decision of character. — *adj* **deter'minātive** that determines, limits or defines. — *adj* **deter'mined** ascertained; fixed; firm in purpose; resolute. — *adv* **deter'minedly.** — *n* **deter'miner** someone who, or that which, determines; a limiting adjective or modifying word such as *each*, *my*, etc. (gram). — *n* **deter'minism** the doctrine that all things, including the will, are determined by causes — the converse of free-will. — *n* **deter'minist.** [L. *dētermināre*, *-ātum* — *dē* (intensive) and *terminus*, a boundary.]

deterrent. See **deter.**

detest *di-test'*, *vt* to hate intensely. — *adj* **detest'able** extremely hateful; abominable. — *n* **detestabil'ity** or **detest'ableness.** — *adv* **detest'ably.** — *n* **detestā'tion.** [Fr., — L. *dētestāri* — *dē* (intensive) and *testāri*, to execrate.]

dethrone *di-thrōn'*, *vt* to remove from a throne. — *n* **dethrone'ment.** — *n* **dethron'er.** — *n* **dethron'ing.** [**de-** (2).]

detonate *det'ə-nāt*, *vt* and *vi* to explode or cause to explode rapidly and loudly. — *n* **detonā'tion** an explosion with report; in an internal-combustion engine, premature combustion of part of the mixture, causing knocking or pinking. — *n* **det'onātor** a substance that detonates; a substance or contrivance whose explosion initiates that of another explosive. [L. *dētonāre*, *-ātum* — *dē*, down, *tonāre*, to thunder.]

detour *dē'tŏŏr*, *n* a deviation; a circuitous way. — Also *vt* and *vi.* [Fr. *dé-* (L. *dis-*) apart, *tour*, turning.]

detoxicate *dē-toks'i-kāt* or **detoxify** *-toks'i-fī*, *vt* to rid of poison or its effects. — *n* **detox'icant** a substance that detoxicates. — Also *adj.* — *n* **detoxicā'tion** or **detoxificā'tion.** — **detoxification centre** a centre for the cure of alcoholism. [**de-** (2).]

detract *di-trakt' vt* to distract. — *vi* to take away (with *from*); to reduce in degree; to diminish. — *n* **detract'or.** — *n* **detrac'tion** depreciation; slander. — *adj* **detract'ive** tending to detract; derogatory. — *adv* **detract'ively.** [L. *dētrahĕre* — *dē*, from, *trahĕre*, *tractum*, to draw.]

detrain *dē-trān'*, *vt* to set down out of a railway train. — *vi* to alight from a train. — *n* **detrain'ment.** [**de-** (2).]

detribalise or **-ize** *dē-trī'bə-līz*, *vt* to cause to lose tribal characteristics, customs, etc., usu. in favour of an urban way of life. — *n* **detribalīsā'tion** or **-z-.** [**de-** (2).]

detriment *det'ri-mənt*, *n* diminution; damage; loss; a thing that causes diminution, damage or loss. — *adj* **detrimental** (*-ment'l*). — *adv* **detriment'ally.** [L. *dētrīmentum* — *dē*, off, *terĕre*, *trītum*, to rub.]

detritus *di-trī'təs*, *n* a mass of substance gradually worn off solid bodies; an aggregate of loosened fragments, esp. of rock; accumulated debris. — *adj* **detrī'tal.** — *n* **detrition** (*di-trish'ən*) wearing away. [L. *dētrītus*, worn — *dē*, off, *terĕre*, *trītum*, to rub.]

de trop *də trō*, (Fr.) superfluous; in the way.

detumescence *dē-tū-mes'əns*, *n* diminution of swelling (opp. to *intumescence*). [**de-** (2).]

deuce[1] *dūs* or in NAm *dōōs*, *n* a card or die with two spots; a situation ('forty all') in which one side must gain two successive points to win the game, or ('five all', 'games all') two successive games to win the set (*lawn tennis*); a throw of two at dice. [F. *deux*, two — L. *duōs*, accus. of *duo*, two.]

deuce[2] *dūs*, *n* in exclamatory phrases, the devil. — *adj* **deuced** (*dū'sid* or *dūst*) (as an intensifier) damned, absolute, etc. — *adv* confoundedly; extremely. — Also **deuc'edly.** [Prob. from the **deuce**[1], the lowest throw at dice.]

deus *dē'əs* or *dā'ōōs*, (*L.*) *n* god: — *pl* **di** (*dī* or *dē*). — **deus ex machina** (usu. *eks mak'in-a*, sometimes *mə-shē'nə*) a god brought on the stage by a mechanical device; a contrived and inartistic solution of a difficulty in a plot.

Deut. (*Bible*) *abbrev* for (the Book of) Deuteronomy.

deuter- *dū-tər-* or **deutero-** *dū-tər-ō-*, *combining form* denoting second or secondary. — *vt* **deu'terate** to add deuterium to, or to replace hydrogen by deuterium in (molecules). — *n* **deuterā'tion.** — *n* **deu'teride** a hydrogen compound containing another element. — *n* **deuterium** (*-tē'ri-əm*) heavy hydrogen, an isotope of hydrogen of double mass. — *n* **deu'teron** the nucleus of heavy hydrogen, of mass 2, carrying unit positive charge. — *n* **Deuteronomy** (*-on'ə-mi*) the fifth book of the Pentateuch. — **deuterium oxide** heavy water.

Deutschmark *doich'märk* or **Deutsche Mark** *doich'ə märk*, *n* the standard monetary unit (100 pfennig) of Germany (and of West Germany prior to unification). [Ger.]

deutzia *dūt'si-ə* or *doit'si-ə*, *n* any of the plants of the genus *Deutzia*, with panicles of white flowers, introduced from China and Japan. [After Jan *Deutz*, 18th-cent. Dutch naturalist.]

devalue *dē-val'ū*, *vt* to reduce the value of. — Also *vi* (esp. of currency). — *vt* **deval'uate.** — *n* **devaluā'tion.** [**de-** (2).]

devanagari *dā-və-nä'gə-ri*, *n* the script in which Sanskrit and Hindi are usually written and printed. — Also with *cap.* [Sans. *devanāgari*, town script of the gods; see **nagari.**]

devastate *dev'əs-tāt*, *vt* to lay waste; to plunder; to shock or greatly disappoint (*colloq*). — *adj* **dev'astating** ravaging; overpoweringly effective (*colloq*). — *adv* **dev'astatingly.** — *n* **devastā'tion** the act of devastating; the state of being devastated; havoc. — *n* **dev'astātor.** [L. *dēvastāre*, *-ātum* — *dē-* (intensive) and *vastāre*, to lay waste.]

develop *di-vel'əp*, *vt* to bring out what is latent or potential in; to bring to a more advanced or more highly organised state; to work out the potentialities of; to elaborate; to cause to grow or advance; to evolve; to contract (a disease); to make more available; to exploit the natural resources of (a region); to build on or prepare (land) for building on; to bring into a position useful in attack (*chess*); to express in expanded form (*math*); to unroll into a plane surface (*geom*); to render visible the image on a negative by the use of chemicals (*phot*). — *vi* to open out; to evolve; to advance through successive stages to a higher, more complex, or more fully grown state: — *pr p* **devel'oping**; *pa t* and *pa p* **devel'oped.** — *adj* **devel'opable.** — *adj* **devel'oped.** — *n* **devel'oper** a person who develops, esp. property; a reagent for developing photographs. — *n* **develop'ment** the act or process of developing; the state of being developed; a gradual unfolding or growth; evolution; the expression of a function in the form of a series (*math*); elaboration of a theme, or that part of a movement in which this occurs (*mus*); new situations that emerge. — *adj* **development'al.** — *adv* **development'ally.** — **development area** a region of heavy unemployment where new industry is given official encouragement. [Fr. *développer*, opp. to *envelopper*, of obscure origin.]

Devi *dā'vē*, *n* in India, used as a title for a married woman (following her name). [Sans., goddess.]

deviate *dē'vi-āt*, *vi* to turn aside from a certain course; to diverge, differ, from a standard, mean value, etc. — *n* (*dē'vi-ət*; *psychol*) a person who deviates much from the norm, esp. sexually; a deviant. — *n* **dē'viance** or **dē'viancy.** — *n* **dē'viant** someone who deviates from the norm, esp. sexually. — Also *adj.* — *n* **dēviā'tion.** — *n* **dē'viātor.** — *adj* **dēviā'tory.** — **deviation of the compass** departure of the mariner's compass from the magnetic meridian, owing to the ship's magnetism or other local causes; **standard deviation** the square root of the variance of a number of observations (*math*). [L. *dēviāre*, *-ātum* — *dē*, from, *via*, a way.]

device *di-vīs'*, *n* that which is devised or designed; contrivance; a plan or scheme; an emblem; a motto. — **leave someone to their own devices** to leave someone alone, not distracting or interfering with them. [O.Fr. *devise*; see **devise**.]

devil *dev'l* or *-il*, *n* an evil spirit; (with *cap*) the supreme spirit of evil; a wicked person; a reckless, lively person; (usu. pitying) a fellow; an animal, thing, problem, etc. difficult to deal with; a person who excels or exceeds in anything; a printer's devil; a drudge (esp. *legal* or *literary*); a dust-storm; fighting spirit; a machine of various kinds, esp. for tearing; used as a mild oath. — *vt* to season highly and broil. — *vi* to perform another person's drudgery; to do very menial work: — *pr p* **dev'illing** or in N.Am. **dev'iling**; *pa t* and *pa p* **dev'illed** or in N.Am. **dev'iled.** — *adj* **dev'ilish** fiendish, malignant; very bad. — *adv* (*colloq*) very, exceedingly. — *adv* **dev'ilishly.** — *n* **dev'ilment** frolicsome mischief. — *n* **dev'ilry.** — **dev'il-fish** the giant ray of the United States; the octopus. — *adj* **dev'il-may-care** reckless, audacious. — **devil's advocate** a person who states the case against a proposal, course of action, etc., usu. for the sake of argument; advocatus diaboli, the Promoter of the Faith, an advocate at the papal court whose duty it is to propose objections against a canonisation (*RC*); **dev'il's-bit** a species of scabious with a rootstock as if bitten off; **devil's books** playing cards; **devil's coach-horse** a large dark-coloured beetle; **devil's darning-needle** a dragonfly or damselfly (*colloq*); **devil's food cake** (chiefly *US*) a kind of chocolate cake; **devils-on-horse'back** prunes wrapped in bacon, grilled, and served on toast; **devil's picture-books** (also in *sing*) same as **devil's books; devil's tattoo** see **tattoo**[1]. — **between the devil and the deep blue sea** faced with alternatives which are equally undesirable; **devil a bit, a one, a thing,** etc., not at all, not one, etc.; **devil take the hindmost** every man for himself; **go to the devil** to become ruined; (*interj*) go away!; **play the devil** to make havoc (with); **printer's devil** the youngest apprentice in a printing-office; a printer's errand-boy; **raise hell** or **raise the devil** see under **raise; talk of the devil** here comes the person we were talking of; **the devil and all** much ado; turmoil; **the devil to pay** serious trouble (as a consequence of an action, etc.). [O.E. *dēofol, dēoful* — L. *diabolus* — Gr. *diabolos*, from *diaballein* to throw across, to slander.]

devious *dē'vi-əs*, *adj* deceitful; tortuous of mind; winding; roundabout; out of the way; remote; erring. — *adv* **dē'viously.** — *n* **dē'viousness.** [L. *dēvius*; see **deviate.**]

devise *di-vīz'*, *vt* to contrive; to scheme; to compose; to bequeath (*law*). — *vi* to consider; to scheme. — *n* the act of bequeathing; a will; property bequeathed by will. — *adj* **devīs'able.** — *n* **devīs'al.** — *n* **devisee** (*dev-ī-zē'*) a person to whom property is bequeathed. — *n* **devīs'er.** — *n* **devīs'or** someone who bequeaths property by will. [O.Fr. *deviser, devise* — L.L. *dīvīsa*, a division of goods, a mark, a device.]

devitalise or **-ize** *dē-vī'tə-līz*, *vt* to deprive of vitality or life-giving qualities. — *n* **devitalīsā'tion** or **-z-.** [**de-** (2).]

devoid *di-void'*, *adj* (with *of*) destitute, free; empty. [O.Fr. *desvoidier* — L. *dis-*, away, *viduāre*, to deprive.]

devoir *dev'wär*, *n* (esp. in *pl*) a courtesy; an act of civility. [Fr., — L. *dēbēre*, to owe.]

devolution *dēv-ə-lōō'shən, dev-* or *-lū'*, *n* a passing from one person to another; a handing over of powers; a modified home rule, the delegation of certain powers to regional governments by a central government. — *adj* **devolu'tionary.** — *n* **devolu'tionist.** [**devolve.**]

devolve *di-volv'*, *vt* to pass on; to hand down; to deliver over, esp. powers to regional governments by a central government. — *vi* to roll down; to fall or pass over in succession (with *on*). — *n* **devolve'ment.** [L. *dēvolvĕre, -volūtum* — *dē*, down, *volvĕre*, to roll.]

Devonian *di-vō'ni-ən*, *adj* belonging to *Devonshire*; belonging to a period between the Silurian and the Carboniferous (*geol*). — *n* a native of Devonshire; the Devonian rock system. — **Devon minnow** an angler's lure that imitates a swimming minnow; **Devonshire cream** clotted cream.

dévot *dā-vō*, *fem* **dévote** *dā-vot*, (Fr.) *n* a devotee.

devote *di-vōt'*, *vt* to set apart or dedicate; to give up wholly (to). — *adj* **devōt'ed** given up (to); strongly attached (to); zealous. — *adv* **devōt'edly.** — *n* **devōt'edness.** — *n* **devotee** (*dev-ə-tē'* or *dev'*) someone wholly or superstitiously devoted, esp. to religion; a votary; someone strongly and consistently interested in something (with *of*). — *n* **devō'tion** the act of devoting; the state of being devoted; consecration; giving up of the mind to the worship of God; piety; prayer; strong affection or attachment; ardour; faithful service; (in *pl*) prayers. — *adj* **devō'tional.** — *n* **devōtional'ity** or **devō'tionalness.** — *adv* **devō'tionally.** [L. *dēvovēre, dēvōtum* — *dē*, away, *vovēre*, to vow.]

devour *di-vowr'*, *vt* to swallow greedily; to eat up; to consume or waste with violence or wantonness; to take in eagerly by the senses or mind. — *n* **devour'er.** — *adj* **devour'ing.** — *adv* **devour'ingly.** — *n* **devour'ment.** [O.Fr. *devorer* — L. *dēvorāre* — *dē* (intensive) and *vorāre*, to swallow.]

devout *di-vowt'*, *adj* given up to religious thoughts and exercises; pious; solemn; earnest. — *adv* **devout'ly.** — *n* **devout'ness.** [O.Fr. *devot* — L. *dēvōtus*; see **devote.**]

dew *dū*, *n* moisture deposited from the air on cooling, esp. at night, in minute specks upon the surface of objects; a similar deposit or exudation of other kinds; early freshness. — *vt* to moisten (as) with dew (*poetic*). — *adv* **dew'ily.** — *n* **dew'iness.** — *adj* **dew'y.** — **dew'berry** a kind of bramble or blackberry having a bluish, dew-like bloom on the fruit; **dew'claw** a rudimentary inner toe, esp. on a dog's leg; **dew'drop; dew'fall** the deposition, or time of deposition, of dew; **dew'point** the temperature at which a given sample of moist air becomes saturated and forms dew; **dew'-pond** a hollow supplied with water by mist. — *adj* **dew'y-eyed** fresh, innocent and trusting (often *ironic*). [O.E. *dēaw*; cf. O.N. *dögg*, Ger. *Tau* dew.]

dewan or **diwan** *dē-wän'*, *n* in India, a financial minister; a state prime minister. [Pers. *dīwān*; see **divan.**]

Dewar flask *dū'ər fläsk*, *n* (sometimes without *cap*; also **dew'ar**) a type of vacuum flask. [From Sir James *Dewar* (1842–1923), its inventor.]

dewater *dē-wö'tər*, *vt* to drain or pump water from (e.g. coal). [**de-** (2).]

Dewey decimal system or **classification** *dū'i des'i-məl sis'tim* or *klas'i-fi-kā'shən*, *n* a system of library classification, based on the division of books into numbered classes, with further subdivision shown by numbers following a decimal point. — Also **decimal classification.** [Invented by Melvil *Dewey* (1851–1931), U.S. librarian.]

dewlap *dū'lap*, *n* the pendulous skin under the throat of oxen, dogs, etc.; the fleshy wattle of the turkey. [Prob. **dew** and O.E. *læppa*, a loose hanging piece.]

Dexedrine® *dek'sə-drēn*, *n* dextroamphetamine.

dexter *deks'tər*, (*heraldry*) *adj* on the right-hand side; of that side of the shield on the right-hand side of the bearer, the spectator's left. [L., right.]

dexterity *deks-ter'i-ti*, *n* skill of manipulation, or skill generally; adroitness. — *adj* **dex'terous** or **dex'trous** adroit; skilful. — *adv* **dex'terously** or

dex'trously. — *n* **dex'terousness** or **dex'trousness.**

dextral *deks'trəl, adj* right; turning to the right; of the right-hand side of the body; lying right-side-up. — *n* **dextral'ity.** — *adv* **dex'trally.** [L. *dexter*, right.]

dextran *deks'trən, n* a carbohydrate formed in sugar solutions, a substitute for blood plasma in transfusion. [**dextro-**.]

dextrin or **dextrine** *deks'trin, n* a gummy mixture obtained from starch by heating or otherwise, used as a thickener in foods and in adhesives.

dextro- *deks-trō-, combining form* denoting to or towards the right. — *n* **dextroamphet'amine** or **dexamphet'amine** the dextrorotatory isomer of amphetamine, used as a stimulant. — *n* **dextrocar'dia** (Gr. *kardiā*, a heart) a condition in which the heart lies in the right side of the chest, not the left. — *n* **dextrophos'phate** an anticoagulant and cholesterol-lowering drug whose usefulness in AIDS research is currently being tested. — *n* **dextrorōtā'tion.** — *adj* **dextrorō'tatory** rotating to the right (clockwise). [L. *dexter*; Gr. *dexious*, Sans. *dakṣina*, on the right, on the south.]

dextrorse *deks-trörs'* or *deks'*, (*biol*) *adj* rising spirally and turning to the left, i.e. crossing an outside observer's field of view from left to right upwards (like a screw-nail). [L. *dextrōrsus*, towards the right — *dexter*, *vertĕre*, to turn.]

dextrose *deks'trōz* or *-ōs, n* glucose.

DF *abbrev* for Defender of the Faith.

DFC *abbrev* for Distinguished Flying Cross.

DFM *abbrev* for Distinguished Flying Medal.

DG *abbrev* for: *Dei gratia* (L.), by the grace of God; Director-General.

dg *abbrev* for decigram(s).

DGFT *abbrev* for Director General of Fair Trading.

dhal. See **dal.**

dharma *där'mə* or *dûr', n* virtue or righteousness arising from observance of social and moral law (*Hinduism*); truth as laid down in the Buddhist scriptures; the law. [Sans.]

dhobi *dō'bi, n* an Indian washerman. — **dhobi itch** a tropical allergic dermatitis. [Hindi *dhobī*.]

dhoti *dō'ti* or **dhooti** *dōō'ti, n* the Hindu loincloth; a cotton fabric used for this. [Hindi *dhotī*.]

dhow *dow, n* an Arab lateen-sailed vessel of the Indian Ocean.

DHSS *abbrev* for (until 1989) Department of Health and Social Security (now **DSS** — Department of Social Services).

dhurra. See **durra.**

DI *abbrev* for donor insemination (q.v. under **donation**).]

di- *dī-, pfx* denoting two, twice or double. — See also **dis-**. [Gr. *dis*, twice.]

dia. *abbrev* for diameter.

dia- *dī-a-* or *-ə-, pfx* denoting: through; across; during; composed of. [Gr.]

diabetes *dī-ə-bē'tēz, n* any of several diseases marked by an excessive discharge of urine, notably **diabetes insip'idus** a disease caused by a disorder of the pituitary gland leading to malfunction of the kidney, and **diabetes mellī'tus** (L., honied) caused by insulin deficiency or, rarely, an excess of insulin, with excess of sugar in the blood and urine. — *adj* **diabetic** (*-bet'ik*) relating to, or suffering from, diabetes; for the use of diabetics. — *n* a person suffering from diabetes. — *n* **diabetol'ogist** a doctor specialising in the study and treatment of diabetes and the care of diabetics. [Gr. *diabētēs*, a siphon, *dia*, through, *bainein*, to go.]

diable *dē-äbl'* or *dē-abl', n* an unglazed earthenware casserole with a handle and a wide base tapering up to a narrow neck. [Fr.]

diablerie *dē-äb'lə-rē, n* magic; the black art; sorcery; mischief. [Fr. *diable*; see **devil.**]

diabolic *dī-ə-bol'ik, adj* of the devil; satanic; like a devil; extremely cruel. — *adj* **diabol'ical** (*colloq*) very shocking, annoying or difficult; outrageous; (as an intensifier) complete or absolute. — *adv* **diabol'ically.** [Gr. *diabolikos* — *diabolos*; see **devil.**]

diabolo *di-a'bol-ō, n* a game in which a two-headed top is spun, tossed, and caught on a string attached to two sticks, held one in each hand. [Gr. *diaballō*, I throw over, toss.]

diachronic *dī-ə-kron'ik, adj* of the study of a subject (esp. a language) through its historical development (opp. of *synchronic*). — *adv* **diachron'ically.** — *n* **diachronism** (*dī-ak'*). — *adj* **diachronist'ic** or **diach'ronous.** [**dia-** and Gr. *chronos*, time.]

diacid *dī-as'id, adj* having two replaceable hydrogen atoms; capable of replacing two hydrogen atoms of an acid. [**di-** and **acid.**]

diaconate *dī-ak'ə-nāt, n* the office or period of service of a deacon. — *adj* **dīac'onal** pertaining to a deacon. [**deacon.**]

diacritic *dī-ə-krit'ik* or **diacrit'ical** *-əl, adj* distinguishing — used of marks (e.g. accents, cedillas, etc.) attached to letters to indicate modified sound, value, etc. — *n* **diacrit'ic** such a mark. [Gr. *diakritikos* — *dia*, between, *kritikos*, see **critic.**]

diadem *dī'ə-dem, n* a crown or jewelled headband; regal power; a crowning glory. [O.Fr. *diademe* — Gr. — *dia*, round, *deein*, to bind.]

diaeresis or **dieresis** *dī-er'i-sis* or *-ēr', n* a mark (¨) placed over a vowel-letter, esp. the second of two adjacent ones to show that it is to be pronounced separately, as in *naïf*; a pause or break where the end of the word coincides with the end of a foot (*prosody*): — *pl* **diaer'eses** or **dier'eses** (*-ēz*). [Gr. *diairesis*, separation.]

diagnosis *dī-əg-nō'sis, n* the identification of a disease by means of its symptoms; a formal determining description, esp. of a plant: — *pl* **diagnō'ses** (*-ēz*). — *n* **diagnosabil'ity.** — *adj* **dī'agnosable** (or *-nō'*). — *vt* **dī'agnose** (or *-nōz'*, or (esp. in U.S.) *-nōs* or *-nōs'*) to ascertain from symptoms, as of a disease. — *adj* **diagnos'tic** of, or useful in, diagnosis; distinguishing; differentiating. — *n* that by which anything is known; a symptom. — *nsing* **diagnos'tics** diagnosis as a branch of medicine. — *n* **diagnosti'cian** (*-nos-tish'ən*) a person skilled in diagnosis. [Gr., *dia*, between, *gnōsis*, knowing.]

diagonal *dī-ag'ə-nəl, adj* through the corners, or joining two vertices that are not adjacent, of a polygon; (of a plane) passing through two edges, not adjacent, of a polyhedron; slantwise. — *n* a straight line or plane drawn in this way. — *adv* **diag'onally.** [L. *diagōnālis*, from Gr. *dia*, through, *gōniā*, a corner.]

diagram *dī'ə-gram, n* a figure or plan intended to explain rather than represent actual appearance; an outline figure or scheme; a curve symbolising a set of facts; a record traced by an automatic indicator. — *adj* **diagrammatic** (*-grə-mat'ik*). — *adv* **diagrammat'ically.** [Gr. *diagramma* — *dia*, round, *graphein*, to write.]

dial *dī'əl, n* a graduated plate on which a movable index shows the value of some quantity measured, or can be set to make an adjustment (as in getting a telephone connection, tuning a radio); the face of a watch or clock; an instrument for showing the time of day by the sun's shadow (as in *sundial*); the numbered plate on a telephone, and the movable disc fitted on top; a face (*slang*). — *vt* to measure or indicate or get into communication with by dial. — *vi* to use a telephone dial: — *pr p* **di'alling;** *pa t* and *pa p* **di'alled.** — *n* **di'aller.** — *n* **di'alling** the art of constructing sundials; the science which explains the measuring of time by the sundial; surveying by dial. — **dialling code** a group of numbers dialled to obtain the desired exchange in an automatic dialling system; **dialling tone** or in U.S. **dial tone** the continuous sound heard on picking up a telephone receiver which indicates that one may begin dialling. [L.L. *diālis*, daily — L. *diēs*, a day.]

dial. *abbrev* for dialect.

dialect *dī'ə-lekt*, *n* a variety or form of a language peculiar to a district or social class, esp. (but not necessarily) one which is not a literary or standard form; a peculiar manner of speaking; any of two or more variant forms of a particular computer language. — *adj* **dialect'al.** — *adv* **dialect'ally.** — *n* **dialectol'ogist.** — *n* **dialectol'ogy.** [Through Fr. and L. from Gr. *dialektos*, speech, manner of speech, peculiarity of speech — *dia*, between, *legein*, to speak.]

dialectic *dī-ə-lek'tik* or **dialectical** *-lek'tik-əl*, *adj* pertaining to discourse or to dialectics. — *n* **dialec'tic** (also **dialec'tics**, *nsing*) a debate which seeks to resolve the conflict between two opposing theories, rather than disprove any one of them; the art of discussing, esp. that branch of logic which teaches the rules and modes of reasoning. — *adv* **dialec'tically.** — *n* **dialecti'cian** a person skilled in dialectics; a logician. [Gr. *dialektikos*.]

dialogue or in U.S. (sometimes) **dialog** *dī'ə-log*, *n* conversation between two or more people, esp. of a formal or imaginary nature; the lines spoken by characters in plays, films, novels, etc.; an exchange of views in the hope of ultimately reaching agreement. — *vi* (esp. *NAm*) to take part in a dialogue (often with *with*). — *adj* **dialog'ic** (*-loj'*). — *n* **dial'ogist** a writer or speaker of dialogues. — *adj* **dialogist'ic** or **dialogist'ical.** [Fr., — L. *dialogus* — Gr. *dialogos*, a conversation.]

dialysis *dī-al'i-sis*, *n* the separation of substances by diffusion through a membranous septum or partition (*chem*); removal of impurities from the blood by a kidney machine (q.v.) (*med*): — *pl* **dial'yses** (*-sēz*). — *adj* **dialysable** or **-z-** (*dī-ə-līz'ə-bl*). — *vt* **dialyse** or in U.S. **-yze** (*dī'ə-līz*) to separate by dialysis. — *vi* to use a kidney machine. — *n* **di'alȳser** or **-z-**. — *adj* **dialytic** (*-lit'ik*). [Gr. *dialysis* — *dia*, apart, *lyein*, to loose.]

diam. *abbrev* for diameter.

diamagnetic *dī-ə-mag-net'ik*, *adj* applied to any substance of which a rod suspended between the poles of a magnet arranges itself across the lines of force. — *n* **diamag'net** a diamagnetic substance. — *adv* **diamagnet'ically.** — *n* **diamag'netism.** [**dia-** and **magnetic.**]

diamanté *dē-a-mā-tā* or *dī-ə-man'ti*, *adj* decorated with glittering particles. — *n* a fabric decorated in this way. — *adj* **diamantine** (*dī-ə-man'tīn*) of, or resembling, diamonds. [Fr., *diamant*, diamond.]

diameter *dī-am'i-tər*, *n* a straight line passing through the centre of a circle or other figure, terminated at both ends by the circumference; the measure through or across. — *adj* **diam'ētral** or **diametric** (*di-ə-met'rik*) in the direction of a diameter; pertaining to the diameter; as of opposite ends of a diameter (as in *diametrical opposition*). — *adv* **diam'etrally.** — *adv* **diamet'rically.** [Through Fr. and L. from Gr. *diametros* — *dia*, through, across, *metron*, a measure.]

diamond *dī'ə-mənd*, *n* a highly prized gemstone, and the hardest of all minerals, consisting of carbon crystallised in the cubic system; a rhombus; a card of a suit distinguished by pips of this shape; a baseball field, or the part between bases. — *adj* resembling, made of, or marked with diamonds; lozenge-shaped, rhombic. — *adj* **dī'amonded.** — **di'amond-back** a N. American terrapin with diamond-shaped markings on its shell; a N. American rattlesnake with diamond-shaped markings; **diamond bird** any of several small insectivorous Australian songbirds; **diamond dove** a small Australian dove with white markings on the wings, often kept in cage or aviary; **diamond jubilee** a sixtieth anniversary (of marriage, **diamond-wedd'ing**); **diamond snake** a carpet snake with diamond-shaped markings. — **rough diamond** an uncut diamond; a person of great worth, but of rough appearance and unpolished manners. [M.E. *diamaunt* — O.Fr. *diamant* — L.L. *diamas, -antis* — Gr. *adamas, -antos*; see **adamant.**]

diandrous *dī-an'drəs*, *adj* (of a flower or flowering plant) having two stamens. [Gr. *dis*, twice, *anēr, andros*, a man, male.]

dianthus *dī-an'thəs*, *n* any plant of the genus (*Dianthus*) of herbaceous flowers to which carnations and pinks belong. [Poss. Gr. *Dios anthos*, Zeus's flower; or *dianthēs*, flowering in succession.]

diapason *dī-ə-pā'zən* or *-sən*, *n* the whole range or compass of tones; a standard of pitch; a full volume of various sounds in concord; a foundation-stop of an organ (*open* or *stopped diapason*) extending through its whole compass. [Gr. *dia pasōn chordōn symphōniā*, concord through all the notes.]

diapause *dī'ə-pöz*, *n* in insects and the embryos of some animals, a period of suspended animation and growth. [Gr. *diapausis*, pause.]

diaper *dī'ə-pər*, *n* (esp. in U.S.) a baby's nappy; linen or cotton cloth with a square or diamond pattern, used chiefly for table linen and towels; the pattern itself. [O.Fr. *diaspre, diapre* — Gr. *dia*, through, *aspros*, white.]

diaphanous *dī-af'ə-nəs*, *adj* transparent; translucent; light and delicate. — *adv* **dīaph'anously.** — *n* **dīaph'anousness.** [Gr. *diaphanēs* — *dia*, through, *phainein*, to show, shine.]

diaphoresis *dī-ə-for-ē'sis*, (*med*) *n* sweat, esp. artificially induced. — *adj* **diaphoretic** (*-et'ik*) promoting sweating. — *n* a diaphoretic substance. [Gr. *diaphorēsis*, sweating.]

diaphragm *dī'ə-fram* or *-frəm*, *n* a thin partition or dividing membrane esp. the muscular structure separating the chest from the abdomen; a metal plate with a central hole, for cutting off side-rays in optical instruments; a strengthening or stiffening plate (*eng*); (in a telephone) a thin vibrating disc that converts electrical signals into sound waves and vice versa; a contraceptive device consisting of a thin rubber or plastic cap placed over the mouth of the cervix. — *adj* **diaphragmat'ic** (*-frag-*). [Gr. *diaphragma*, partition, midriff.]

diapositive *dī-ə-poz'i-tiv*, *n* a transparent photographic positive; a slide. [**dia-** and **positive.**]

diarchy *dī'är-ki*, *n* a form of government in which two people, states or bodies are jointly vested with supreme power. — *adj* **diarch'al** or **diarch'ic.** [Gr. *di-*, twice, *archein*, to rule.]

diarrhoea or in U.S. **diarrhea** *dī-ə-rē'ə*, *n* a persistent purging or looseness of the bowels; an excessive flow of anything (*fig*). — *adj* **diarrhoe'al** or **diarrhoe'ic**, or in U.S. **diarrhē'al** or **diarrhē'ic.** [Gr. *diarroia* — *dia*, through, *rhoiā*, a flow.]

diary *dī'ə-ri*, *n* a book for making daily records, noting engagements, etc.; a daily record. — *vt* **diarise** or **-ize** (*dī'ə-riz*) to enter in a diary. — *vi* to keep a diary. [L. *diārium* — *diēs*, day.]

diascope *dī'ə-skōp*, *n* an optical projector used for showing transparencies on a screen; a slide projector. [**dia-** and Gr. *skopeein*, to view.]

diaspora *dī-as'por-ə*, *n* (with *cap*) dispersion, used collectively for the dispersed Jews after the Babylonian captivity, and also in the apostolic age for the Jews living outside of Palestine, now, for Jews outside Israel; a similar dispersion or migration of other peoples or communities. — Also *adj*. [Gr. *diasporā* — *dia*, through, *speirein*, to scatter.]

diastase *dī'ə-stās*, (*biol*) *n* an enzyme that converts starch into sugar, produced in germinating seeds and in pancreatic juice. — *adj* **diastā'sic** or **diastatic** (*-stat'ik*). [Gr. *diastasis*, division.]

diaster *dī-as'tər*, (*biol*) *n* in cell-division, a stage in which the daughter chromosomes are situated in two groups near the poles of the spindle, ready to form the daughter nuclei. [Gr. *di-*, twice, *astēr*, a star.]

diastole *dī-as'tə-lē*, (*physiol*) *n* dilatation of the heart, auricles and arteries (opp. to *systole*, or contraction). — *adj* **diastolic** (*dī-ə-stol'ik*). [Gr. *diastolē* — *dia*, apart, *stellein*, to place.]

diatessaron *dī-ə-tes'ə-ron* or *-rən*, *n* an arrangement of the four Gospels as a single narrative. [Gr. *dia tessarōn*, through, or composed of, four.]

diathermic *dī-ə-thûr'mik*, *adj* permeable by, or able to conduct, radiant heat. — Also **diather'mal, diather'manous** and **diather'mous**. — *n* **diather'macy, diather'mancy** or **diathermanē'ity** permeability by or conductibility of radiant heat. — *n* **di'athermy** heating of internal parts of the body by electric currents. [Gr. *dia*, through, *thermē*, heat.]

diathesis *dī-ath'i-sis*, *n* a particular condition or habit of body, esp. one predisposing to certain diseases. — *adj* **diathetic** (*dī-ə-thet'ik*). [Gr. *diathesis* — *dia*, apart, *tithenai*, to place.]

diatom *dī'ə-təm*, *n* one of a class of microscopic unicellular algae with flinty shells in two halves, fitting like box and lid. — *adj* **diatomā'ceous**. — *n* **dī'atomist** a person who studies diatoms. — *n* **diatomite** (*dī-at'əm-īt*) diatomaceous earth, a powdery siliceous deposit. [Gr. *diatomos*, cut through.]

diatomic *dī-ə-tom'ik*, *adj* consisting of two atoms; having two replaceable atoms or groups; bivalent. [**di-** and **atom**.]

diatonic *dī-ə-ton'ik*, *adj* proceeding by the tones and intervals of the natural scale in Western music. — *adv* **diaton'ically**. [Gr. *diatonikos* — *dia*, through, *tonos*, tone.]

diatribe *dī'ə-trīb*, *n* an abusive or bitter harangue. [Gr. *diatribē*, a discourse, pastime.]

diazepam *dī-ā'zə-pam*, *n* a drug used as a tranquilliser and muscle relaxant.

diazo *dī-az'ō*, *adj* (of compounds) containing two nitrogen atoms and a hydrocarbon radical; (of a photocopying process) using a diazo compound decomposed by exposure to light (also **dye'line**). — *n* a copy made by the diazo method: — *pl* **diaz'os** or **diaz'oes**. [**di-** and **azo-**.]

dib[1] *dib*, *vi* to dip; to fish by letting the bait bob up and down on the surface of the water: — *pr p* **dibb'ing**; *pa t* and *pa p* **dibbed**. [Prob. a form of **dab**[1].]

dib[2] *dib*, *n* one of the small bones of a sheep's leg; (in *pl*) a children's game, played by throwing up such small bones or stones (**dib'-stones**) from the palm and catching them on the back of the hand — also *jacks* or in Scots *chuckie-stanes* or *chucks*; (in *pl*) money (*slang*).

dibasic *dī-bā'sik*, *adj* capable of reacting with two equivalents of an acid; (of acids) having two replaceable hydrogen atoms. [**di-** and **basic**.]

dibble *dib'l* or **dibber** *dib'ər*, *n* a pointed tool used for making holes for seeds or plants. — *vt* **dibb'le** to plant with a dibble. — *vi* to make holes; to dip the bait lightly in and out of the water (*angling*). — *n* **dibb'ler** someone who or that which dibbles; a dibber; a small carnivorous Australian marsupial with a long snout and a short hairy tail. [Prob. connected with **dab**[1].]

dice[1], **dicey** and **dicing**. See **die**[2].

dice[2] *dīs*, (*Austr colloq*) *vt* to reject.

dicephalous *dī-sef'ə-ləs*, *adj* two-headed. [Gr. *dikephalos* — *di-*, double, *kephalē*, a head.]

dichloralphenazone *dī-klör-əl-phen'ə-zōn*, *n* a drug used as a hypnotic and sedative. [**di-**, *chloral* hydrate, and *phenazone*, an antipyretic drug.]

dichlorodiphenyltrichloroethane *dī-klö-rō-dī-phe-nil-trī-klö-rō-ēth'ān*, *n* known as **DDT**, a white powder orig. used to kill lice and thus prevent the spread of typhus; effective also against other insects, but having long-term disadvantages.

dichotomy *dīk-ot'ə-mi*, *n* a division into two strongly contrasted groups or classes; repeated branching (*bot*). — *vt* and *vi* **dichot'omise** or **-ize**. — *n* **dichot'omist**. — *adj* **dichot'omous** or **dichot'omic**. — *adv* **dichot'omously**. [Gr. *dichotomiā* — *dicha*, in two, *tomē*, a cut.]

dichroism *dī'krō-izm*, *n* the property of showing different colours exhibited by doubly refracting crystals when viewed in different directions by transmitted light. — *adj* **dichrō'ic** or **dichrōit'ic**. [Gr. *dichroos*, two-coloured — *di-*, twice, *chroā*, colour.]

dichromate *dī-krō'māt*, *n* a salt of **dichromic acid** containing two chromium atoms. — Also **bīchrō'mate**. [**di-** and **chromate**.]

dichromatic *dī-krō-mat'ik*, *adj* having two colours; able to see two colours and two only, as in red-green colour-blind persons who see only blue and yellow. — *n* a person who has dichromatic vision. — *n* **dichrō'matism**. — *adj* **dichrō'mic** dichroic; dichromatic. [Gr. *di-*, twice, *chrōma*, *-atos*, colour.]

dichromic. See **dichromate, dichromatic**.

dick *dik*, (*slang*) *n* a detective; a penis (*vulg*). — **dick'head** (*vulg*) an idiot; a fool; someone despised. — **clever Dick** a know-all. [*Dick*, for Richard.]

dickens *dik'ənz*, *n* the deuce, the devil, as in *what the dickens, play the dickens*. [App. *Dickon*, Richard, as a substitute for **devil**.]

Dickensian *dik-en'zi-ən*, *adj* pertaining to Charles *Dickens* (1812–70), the novelist; pertaining to those conditions, esp. squalid social or working conditions, described in his novels.

dicker *dik'ər*, *n* haggling or bargaining; petty trade by barter, etc. — *vi* to haggle; to hesitate or dither.

dickey, dicky or **dickie** *dik'i*, *n* a false shirt front; the driver's seat in a carriage; a seat at the back of a carriage; a folding seat at the back of a motor car. [Perh. from dialect *dick*, a leather apron; perh. Du. *dek*, a cover.]

dicky[1] *dik'i*, (*colloq*) *adj* shaky; not in good condition. [Poss. from *Tom and Dick*, Cockney rhyming slang for *sick*.]

dicky[2]. See **dickey**.

dicky-bird *dik'i-bûrd*, *n* a small bird (*childish*); a word (*rhyming slang*). [*Dick*, for Richard.]

diclinous *dī'kli-nəs* or *-klī'*, (*bot*) *adj* having the stamens and pistils in separate flowers, whether on the same or on different plants. — *n* **dī'clinism**. [Gr. *di-*, twice, double, *klīnē*, a bed.]

dicotyledon *dī-kot-i-lē'dən*, (*bot*) *n* (often shortened to **dī'cot**) a plant having embryos with two seed-leaves or cotyledons. — *adj* **dicotylē'donous**. [Gr. *di-*, twice, and **cotyledon**.]

dicrotic *dī-krot'ik*, *adj* (of the pulse) having two beats to one beat of the heart. — Also **dī'crotous**. — *n* **dī'crotism**. [Gr. *di-*, twice, double, *krotos*, beat.]

dict. *abbrev* for: dictation; dictator; dictionary.

dicta. See **dictum**.

Dictaphone® *dik'tə-fōn*, *n* a recording apparatus for dictating letters, etc. [L. *dictāre*, to dictate, Gr. *phōnē*, sound.]

dictate *dik-tāt'*, *vt* to say or read for another to write; to lay down with authority; to command. — *vi* to give orders; to behave dictatorially. — *n* (*dik'tāt*) an order, rule or direction. — *n* **dictā'tion** the act, art, or practice of dictating; speaking or reading of words for a pupil, secretary, etc., to write; the words dictated; overbearing command. — *n* **dictā'tor** a person invested with absolute authority, orig. an extraordinary Roman magistrate; someone who or that which dictates. — *adj* **dictatorial** (*dik-tə-tö'ri-əl*) like a dictator; absolute; overbearing. — *adv* **dictatō'rially**. — *n* **dictā'torship**. — *adj* **dic'tatory**. [L. *dictāre*, *-ātum*, frequentative of *dīcĕre*, to say.]

diction *dik'shən*, *n* enunciation; manner of speaking or expressing; choice of words. [L. *dictio*, *-ōnis* — *dicĕre*, *dictum*, to say.]

dictionary *dik'shən-ə-ri, n* a book containing the words of a language alphabetically arranged, with their meanings, etymology, etc.; a lexicon; a work containing information on any area of knowledge, alphabetically arranged. [L.L. *dictiōnārium.*]

Dictograph® *dik'tō-graf, n* an instrument for transmitting speech from room to room, with or without the speaker's knowledge, usu. by means of a small concealed microphone. [L. *dictum*, thing said, Gr. *graphein*, to write.]

dictum *dik'təm, n* a popular maxim; an authoritative saying: — *pl* **dic'ta.** [L.]

did *did, pa t* of **do**[1].

didactic *dī-* or *di-dak'tik, adj* intended to teach; instructive (sometimes pedantically or dictatorially so); preceptive. — *adv* **didac'tically.** — *n* **didac'ticism** (*-sizm*). — *nsing* **didac'tics** the art or science of teaching. [Gr. *didaktikos* — *didaskein*, to teach.]

diddle *did'l, vt* to cajole, swindle; to waste time, to dawdle (*NAm*). — *n* **didd'ler.**

diddy *did'i,* (*colloq*) *adj* small; tiny.

didgeridoo *dij-ər-i-dōō', n* an Australian Aboriginal musical instrument, consisting of a very long tube producing a low-pitched resonant sound. [Aboriginal word.]

didicoy, diddicoy or **didicoi** *did'i-koi, n* an itinerant tinker or scrap dealer, not a true gypsy. [Romany.]

dido *dī'dō,* (*US colloq*) *n* an antic or caper; a frivolous or mischievous act: — *pl* **dī'does** or **dī'dos.**

didymium *di-* or *dī-dim'i-əm, n* a supposed element discovered in 1841, later resolved into neodymium and praseodymium. [Gr. *didymos*, twin, from its constant association with *lanthanum.*]

didymous *did'i-məs,* (*biol*) *adj* twin; twinned; growing in pairs; composed of two parts slightly connected. [Gr. *didymos*, twin.]

die[1] *dī, vi* (or *vt* with object *death*) to lose life; to perish; to wither; (of an engine) to stop working; esp. **be dying** hyperbolically, to languish, suffer long or be very eager (for), or to be overcome by the effects (of): — *pr p* **dy'ing**; *pa t* and *pa p* **died** *dīd.* — *adj* **die'away** languishing. — **die'-hard** an irreconcilable conservative; a resolute, obstinate or dauntless person. — Also *adj.* — **die away** to disappear by degrees; to become gradually inaudible; **die back** (*bot*) to die by degrees from the tip backwards (*n* **die'back**); **die down** to subside; to die above ground, leaving only roots or rootstocks; **die game** to keep up one's spirit to the last; **die hard** to struggle hard against death, to be long in dying; to be difficult to suppress, eradicate or persuade (*n* and *adj* **die'hard**); **die off** to die quickly or in large numbers; **die out** to become extinct, to disappear; **die the death** (*theat slang*) to arouse no response from one's audience; **never say die** never give up. — See also **dying.** [Prob. from a lost O.E. (Anglian) *dēgan.*]

die[2] *dī, n* (also **dice** *dīs*) a small cube with faces numbered or otherwise distinguished, thrown in games of chance, etc.; (also **dice**) a small cubical piece; (also **dice**) hazard; a stamp for impressing coin, etc.; applied to various tools for shaping things by stamping or cutting: — *pl* (in games of chance, cookery, etc.) **dice**; (in stamping and shaping) **dies** (*dīz*). — *vi* **dice** to play with dice; to take great risks. — *vt* to cut into dice; to chequer: — *pr p* **dīc'ing**; *pa t* and *pa p* **diced.** — *adj* **diced** cut into dice. — *adj* **dīc'ey** (*colloq*) risky; tricky; uncertain in result. — *vt* **die'-cast** to shape (metal or plastic) by casting in a metal mould. — **die'-casting**; **die'-sinker**; **die'sinking** the engraving of dies for embossing, etc. — **dice with death** to take great risks; **no dice** no answer, or a negative answer; no success; **straight as a die** (i.e. a gaming die; *fig*) completely honest; **the die is cast** an irrevocable step has been taken; there is no turning back now. [O.Fr. *de*, pl. *dez*, from L.L. *dadus* = L. *datus*, given or cast.]

dieldrin *dēl'drin, n* a crystalline organochlorine compound used as a contact insecticide. [O. *Diels* (1876–1954), Ger. chemist, and **aldrin.**]

dielectric *dī-i-lek'trik, adj* non-conducting; transmitting electric effects without conducting. — *n* a substance, solid, liquid or gas capable of supporting an electric stress, and hence an insulator. — **dielectric heating** the heating of a non-conducting substance as a result of loss of power in dielectric. [Gr. *dia*, through, and **electric.**]

diene *dī'ēn, n* an organic compound containing two double bonds between carbon atoms. [**di-**, and *-ene* as in **alkene, benzene,** etc.]

dieresis. Same as **diaeresis.**

dies *dī'ēz* or *dē'ās,* (*L.*) *n* day: — *pl* **dies.** — **dies irae** (*īr'ē* or *ēr'ī*) the day of wrath; the day of judgment (from a Latin hymn); the hymn itself, used in the Mass for the dead; **dies non** (*non* or *nōn*) a day on which judges do not sit, or one on which normal business is not transacted.

diesel *dēz'l, n* diesel oil; a locomotive, train, etc., driven by a diesel engine; a diesel engine. — **diesel engine** a compression-ignition engine in which the oil fuel is introduced into the heated compressed-air charge as a jet of liquid under high pressure; **diesel oil** heavy fuel oil used in diesel engines. [Rudolph *Diesel* (1858–1913), German engineer.]

diesis *dī'i-sis, n* the difference between a major and a minor semitone (*mus*); the double-dagger (‡) (*printing*): — *pl* **dī'eses** (*-sēz*). [Gr. *diesis*, a quarter-tone.]

diet[1] *dī'ət, n* a planned or prescribed selection of food, esp. one designed for weight-loss or the control of some disorder; the food habitually consumed by a person or animal. — *vt* to prescribe a diet for or put on a diet. — *vi* to take food according to rule, esp. in order to lose weight. — *adj* **dī'etary** pertaining to a diet or the rules of a diet. — *n* a course of diet; an allowance of food, esp. in large institutions. — *n* **dī'eter.** — *adj* **dīetet'ic** or **dīetet'ical** pertaining to diet. — *adv* **dīetet'ically.** — *nsing* **dīetet'ics** the study of, or rules for regulating, diet. — *n* **dīetitian** or **dīetician** (*-ish'ən*) an authority on diet. — **dietary fibre** fibrous substances in fruits, vegetables and cereals which keep bowel movements regular and are thus thought to help prevent certain diseases — also called **roughage**; **diet sheet** a list of permitted foods for a person on a diet. [Fr. *diète* — L.L. *diaeta* — Gr. *diaita*, mode of living, diet.]

diet[2] *dī'ət, n* a national, federal, or provincial assembly, council, or parliament; the proceedings under a criminal libel (*Scots law*). [O.Fr. *diete* — L.L. *diēta* — Gr. *diaita*; or from L. *diēs*, a (set) day.]

diethyl *dī-eth'il, adj* having two ethyl groups. [**di-.**]

diff. *abbrev* for: difference; different.

differ *dif'ər, vi* to be unlike, distinct or various (used by itself, or followed by *from*); to disagree (with *with*, sometimes *from*). — *n* **diff'erence** dissimilarity; the quality distinguishing one thing from another; a contention or quarrel; the excess of one quantity or number over another; differentia; a distinguishing mark; a modification to distinguish the arms of a branch from those of the main line (*heraldry*). — *adj* **diff'erent** distinct; separate; unlike; not the same (with *from*, also *to*); out of the ordinary (*colloq*); novel. — *n* **differentia** (*-en'shi-ə*; L.) in logic, that property which distinguishes a species from others: — *pl* **differen'tiae** (*-shi-ē*). — *adj* **differen'tial** (*-shəl*) constituting or pertaining to a difference or differentia; discriminating; pertaining to infinitesimal differences (*math*). — *n* an infinitesimal difference; a differential gear; a price or wage difference. — *adv* **differen'tially.** — *vt* **differentiate** (*-en'shi-āt*) to make different, cause to develop difference(s); to classify as different; to constitute a difference between; to obtain the differential coefficient of (*math*). — *vi* to become different by specialisation; to distinguish (*from* or *between*). — *n*

differentiā'tion the act of distinguishing; description of a thing by giving its differentia; a change by which what was generalised or homogeneous became specialised or heterogeneous; the act or process of differentiating, or determining the ratio of the rates of change of two quantities, one of which is a function of the other (*math*). — *n* **differen'tiātor.** — *adv* **diff'erently.** — **differential calculus** see **calculus; differential coefficient** the ratio of the rate of change of a function to that of its independent variable; **differential equation** one involving total or partial differential coefficients; **differential gear** a gear enabling one driving wheel of a motor vehicle to move faster than another, e.g. when cornering; **differential motion** a mechanical movement in which the velocity of a driven part is equal to the difference of the velocities of two parts connected to it; **differential pricing** pricing that differs according to method of payment (as e.g. discount for cash or extra charge for credit transactions), legal in U.K. from March 1991. — **agree to differ** to agree to accept amicably a difference of opinion without further argument; **difference of opinion** a matter about which two or more people or groups disagree; **with a difference** with something special; in a special way. [L. *differe* — *dif-* (for *dis-*), apart, *ferre*, to bear.]

difficult *dif'i-kəlt*, *adj* not easy; hard to do; requiring labour and pains; hard to please; not easily persuaded; unmanageable; hard to resolve or extricate oneself from; potentially embarrassing. — *adv* **diff'icultly** (mainly *chem*). — *n* **diff'iculty** the quality or fact of being difficult; a difficult situation; laboriousness; an obstacle; an objection; that which cannot be easily understood or believed; embarrassment of affairs; a quarrel. — **make difficulties** to be hard to please; to make objections. [L. *difficilis* — *dis-* (negative) and *facilis*, easy.]

diffident *dif'i-dənt*, *adj* lacking in self-confidence; overly shy or modest. — *n* **diff'idence.** — *adv* **diff'idently.** [L. *diffīdĕre*, to distrust.]

diffract *di-frakt'*, *vt* to break up; to subject to diffraction. — *n* **diffrac'tion** the spreading of light or other rays passing through a narrow opening or by the edge of an opaque body or reflected by a grating, etc., with interference phenomena, coloured and other. — *adj* **diffrac'tive.** — *n* **diffractom'eter** an instrument used in the examination of the crystal structure of matter by means of diffraction of X-rays, or of the atomic structure of matter by means of diffraction of electrons or neutrons. [L. *diffringĕre*, *diffrāctum* — *dis-*, asunder, *frangĕre*, to break.]

diffuse[1] *di-fūz'*, *vt* to send out in all directions; to scatter; to circulate; to publish. — *vi* to spread. — *n* **diffūs'er.** — *n* **diffūsibil'ity.** — *adj* **diffūs'ible.** — *n* **diffū'sion** a spreading or scattering abroad; extension; distribution; mixture through each other of gases or liquids in contact; spread of cultural elements from one region or community to another (*anthrop*). — *adj* **diffū'sive** (*-siv*). — *adv* **diffū'sively.** — *n* **diffū'siveness** or **diffūsiv'ity.** — **diffused lighting** lighting that, being evenly distributed, produces no glare. [L. *diffundĕre*, *diffūsum* — *dif-* (*dis-*), asunder, *fundĕre*, to pour out.]

diffuse[2] *di-fūs'*, *adj* diffused; widely spread; wordy; not concise. — *adv* **diffuse'ly.** — *n* **diffuse'ness.** [Root as above.]

dig *dig*, *vt* to excavate; to turn up with a spade or otherwise; to get or put by digging; to poke or thrust; to understand or approve (*old slang*). — *vi* to use a spade; to seek (for) by digging (*lit* and *fig*); to burrow; to mine; to lodge (*colloq*); to study hard (*NAm colloq*): — *pr p* **digg'ing**; *pa t* and *pa p* **dug.** — *n* an act or course of digging; an archaeological excavating expedition; an excavation made by archaeologists; a poke; a taunt. — *adj* **digg'able.** — *n* **digg'er** a person or animal that digs; a miner, esp. a goldminer; an Australian or New Zealand soldier; an Australian colloq. form of address; a machine for digging. — *npl* **digg'ings** places where mining is carried on, esp. for gold; digs. — *npl* **digs** (*colloq*) accommodation; lodgings. — **digg'er-wasp** a burrowing wasp of various kinds; **digging stick** a primitive tool, a pointed stick, sometimes weighted, for digging the ground. — **dig a pit for** (*fig*) to set a trap for; **dig in** to cover over by digging; to work hard; to begin eating (*colloq*); **dig oneself in** to entrench oneself; to establish oneself in a position; **dig one's heels in** to refuse to be moved or persuaded; **dig out** to unearth (*lit* and *fig*); **dig up** to remove from the ground by digging; to excavate; to obtain by seeking (*colloq*). [Prob. O.Fr. *diguer*, to dig; of Gmc. origin.]

digamma *dī-gam'ə*, *n* vau, the obsolete sixth letter (Ϝ, Ͷ, ϝ) of the Greek alphabet with the sound of the English *w*. [Gr. *di-*, twice, and *gamma*, from its form like one capital *Γ* over another.]

digastric *dī-gas'trik*, *adj* fleshy at each end, as one of the muscles of the lower jaw is. [Gr. *di-*, double, *gastēr*, the belly.]

digest[1] *di-jest'* or *dī-*, *vt* to dissolve in the stomach; to think over, to take in gradually, the meaning and implications of; to prepare or classify in the mind; to soften by heat and moisture (*chem*); to distribute and arrange. — *vi* to be dissolved in the stomach; to be softened by heat and moisture. — *n* **digest'er** a vessel in which strong extracts are made from animal and vegetable substances. — *n* **digestibil'ity.** — *adj* **digest'ible.** — *n* **digestion** (*di-jest'yən*) the dissolving of the food in the stomach; mental assimilation; exposing to slow heat, etc. (*chem*); orderly arrangement. — *adj* **digest'ive** pertaining to digestion; promoting digestion. — *n* something which promotes digestion; (also **digestive biscuit**) a round, semi-sweet biscuit, the basic ingredient of which is meal. — *adv* **digest'ively.** — **digestive tract** the alimentary canal. [L. *dīgerĕre*, *dīgestum*, to dissolve.]

digest[2] *dī'jest*, *n* a body of laws collected and arranged; a synopsis; an abstract; a periodical abstract of news or current literature. [L. *dīgesta*, neut. pl. of *dīgestus*, past p. of *dīgerĕre*, to carry apart, to arrange.]

digit *dij'it*, *n* a figure, esp. one used in arithmetic to represent a number; a finger or toe; a finger's breadth as a unit of measurement (1.9 cm. or 3/4 in.). — *adj* **dig'ital** showing numerical information by a set of digits to be read off, instead of by a pointer on a dial, etc.; (of electronic circuits) responding to and producing signals which at any given time are at any one of a number of possible discrete levels, generally either one of two levels; of continuous data (e.g. sound signals), separated into discrete units to facilitate transmission, processing, etc., or of the transmission, etc. of sound, etc. in this form; pertaining to the fingers, or to arithmetical digits. — *n* **digitalin** (*dij-i-tā'lin* or *dij'it-ə-lin*) a glucoside or mixture of glucosides obtained from digitalis leaves, used as a heart-stimulant. — *n* **Digitā'lis** the foxglove genus; (without *cap*) dried foxglove leaves used as a drug. — *adj* **dig'itate** or **dig'itated** (of leaves) consisting of several fingerlike sections. — *adv* **dig'itately.** — *n* **digitā'tion** fingerlike arrangement; a fingerlike division. — *adj* **digit'iform** formed like fingers. — *adj* **dig'itigrade** walking on the toes. — *n* an animal that walks on its toes. — *n* **digitīsā'tion** or **-z-.** — *vt* **dig'itise** or **-ize** to put (data) into digital form, e.g. for use in a digital computer. — *n* **dig'itiser** or **-z-.** — **digital audio tape** (abbrev. **DAT, Dat** or **dat**) a magnetic audio tape on which sound has been recorded digitally; this form of recorded sound, affording greater clarity and compactness, and less distortion than conventional recording; **digital clock** or **watch** a clock or watch without a conventional face, on which the time is indicated directly by numbers; **digital compact cassette** (abbrev. **DCC**) a digital audio tape, in standard cassette format, that is played via a fixed-head tape recorder; this form of recorded sound; **digital compact disc** compact disc (q.v.); **digital computer** an electronic calculating machine using arithmetical digits, generally binary or decimal notation; **digital recording** a digital means of storing and transmitting information electronically (e.g. in sound recording as on compact disc, digital audio tape, digital compact cassette); **digitising board, pad, table** or **tablet** a device consisting of a flat surface on which diagrams may be drawn with a special stylus, the co-ordinates of the position of the stylus at any given point on the diagram being digitised for storage, etc. [L. *digitus*, finger, toe.]

diglot *dī'glot, adj* bilingual. — *n* a bilingual person or book. [Gr. *diglōttos* — *di-*, double, *glōtta*, tongue.]

dignify *dig'ni-fī, vt* to invest with honour; to exalt; to lend an air of dignity to: — *pr p* **dig'nifying**; *pa t* and *pa p* **dig'nified.** — *adj* **dig'nified** marked or consistent with dignity; exalted; noble. [L.L. *dīgnificāre* — *dīgnus*, worthy, *facĕre*, to make.]

dignity *dig'ni-ti, n* the state of being dignified; elevation of mind or character; grandeur of bearing or appearance; elevation in rank, place, etc.; degree of excellence; preferment; high office. — *n* **dig'nitary** someone in a high position or rank, esp. in government or the church. — **beneath one's dignity** degrading, at least in one's own estimation; **stand on one's dignity** to assume a manner that asserts a claim to be treated with respect. [Fr. *dignité* — L. *dīgnitās, -ātis* — *dīgnus*, worthy.]

digraph *dī'gräf, n* two letters expressing a single sound, as *ph* in *digraph.* [Gr. *di-*, twice, *graphē*, a mark, a character — *graphein*, to write.]

digress *dī-gres', vi* to depart from the main subject; to introduce irrelevant matter. — *n* **digression** (*-gresh'ən*) a departure from the main point; a part of a discourse not about the main subject. — *adj* **digress'ional** or **digress'ive.** — *adv* **digress'ively.** [L. *dīgredī, digressus* — *dī-* (*dis-*), aside, *gradī*, to step.]

dihedral *dī-hē'drəl, adj* bounded by two planes, or two plane faces. — *n* a dihedral angle. — *n* **dihē'dron** the limiting case of a double pyramid when the vertices coincide. — **dihedral angle** the angle made by the wing of an aeroplane with the horizontal axis. [Gr. *di-*, twice, *hedrā*, a seat.]

dihydric *dī-hī'drik, adj* having two hydroxyl groups. [**di-**.]

dik-dik *dik'dik, n* a name for several very small E. African antelopes, of the genus *Madoqua.* [Said to be a name in Ethiopia.]

dike[1] or **dyke** *dīk, n* a trench, or the earth dug out and thrown up; a ditch; a mound of earth raised to prevent flooding; a wall (*Scot*); an igneous mass injected into a fissure in rocks, sometimes weathered out into wall-like forms (*geol*); a lavatory (*Austr* and *NZ slang*). — *vt* to provide with a dike. — *vi* to make a dike. — *n* **dīk'er.** [O.E. *dīc.*]

dike[2] or **dyke** *dīk*, (*slang*) *n* a lesbian. — *adj* **dīk'ey** or **dyk'ey.**

diktat *dik-tät'* or *-tat', n* a harsh settlement forced on the defeated or powerless; an order or statement allowing no opposition. [Ger., something dictated.]

dilapidate *di-lap'i-dāt, vt* to pull down stone by stone; to cause to go to ruin. — *adj* **dilap'idated** in a state of disrepair or ruin. — *n* **dilapidā'tion** the state of ruin; (in *pl*) damage done to a building during tenancy (*law*); (in *pl*) money paid at the end of an incumbency by the incumbent for putting the parsonage, etc., in good repair (*eccles*). — *n* **dilap'idātor.** [L. *dīlapidāre* — *dī-*, asunder, *lapis, lapidis*, a stone.]

dilate *dī-lāt'* or *di-lāt', vt* to spread out in all directions; to expand; to enlarge. — *vi* to widen; to expand; to speak at length. — *n* **dilātabil'ity.** — *adj* **dilāt'able.** — *n* **dilatation** (*-lə-tā'shən*) or **dilā'tion** expansion; a transformation which produces a figure similar to, but not congruent with, the original (*math*). — *n* **dil'atātor** an instrument or a muscle that expands. — *adj* **dilāt'ed** expanded and flattened. — *n* **dilāt'or** a dilatator; someone who dilates (also **dilāt'er**). — *adj* **dilāt'ive.** [L. *dīlātus* — *dī-* (*dis-*), apart, *lātus*, wide.]

dilatory *dil'ə-tə-ri, adj* slow; given to procrastination; tending to delay. — *adv* **dil'atorily.** — *n* **dil'atoriness.** [L. *dīlātōrius.* See **dilate.**]

dildo or **dildoe** *dil'dō, n* an object serving as an erect penis substitute: — *pl* **dil'dos** or **dil'does.**

dilemma *di-* or *dī-lem'ə, n* a position where each of two alternative courses (or of all the feasible courses) is eminently undesirable; (*loosely*) a predicament; a problem; a form of argument in which the maintainer of a certain proposition is committed to accept one of two propositions each of which contradicts his original contention (the argument was called a 'horned syllogism', hence the **horns of a dilemma** (*logic*). — *adj* **dilemmat'ic.** — **on the horns of a dilemma** in a dilemma (see comments above). [L., — Gr. *dilēmma* — *di-*, twice, double, *lēmma*, an assumption — *lambanein*, to take.]

dilettante *dil-et-an'ti, n* a person who loves the fine arts but in a superficial way and without serious purpose; a dabbler in art, science or literature: — *pl* **dilettan'ti** (*-tē*). — Also *adj.* — *adj* **dilettan'tish.** — *n* **dilettan'tism** or **dilettan'teism.** [It., pres. p. of *dilettare* — L. *dēlectāre*, to delight.]

diligent *dil'i-jənt, adj* steady and earnest in application; industrious. — *n* **dil'igence** steady application; industry; a French or continental stagecoach (also pronounced *dē-lē-zhās*; *hist*). — *adv* **dil'igently.** [Fr., — *dīligēns, -entis*, pres. p. of L. *dīligĕre*, to choose.]

dill[1] *dil, n* an umbelliferous Eurasian herb, the fruits or 'seeds' of which are used in condiments and as a carminative. — **dill pickle** pickled cucumber flavoured with dill; **dill'-water** a medicinal drink prepared from the seeds. [O.E. *dile.*]

dill[2] *dil*, (*Austr colloq*) *n* a fool. [Prob. **dilly**[2].]

dilly[1] *dil'i*, (*colloq*) *n* an excellent or very pleasing person or thing. — Also *adj.* [Perh. contr. of **delightful.**]

dilly[2] *dil'i*, (*Austr colloq*) *adj* foolish, silly. [Prob. **daft** and **silly.**]

dilly-dally *dil-i-dal'i*, (*colloq*) *vi* to loiter or trifle. [Reduplication of **dally**; cf. **shilly-shally.**]

dilute *di-lūt', vt* to diminish the concentration of, by mixing, esp. with water; to make thinner or more liquid; to make less strong, powerful or forceful; (of labour) to increase the proportion of unskilled to skilled in. — *vi* to become mixed. — *adj* diminished in concentration by mixing. — *adj* **diluent** (*dil'ū-ənt*) diluting. — *n* that which dilutes. — *adj* **dilut'able.** — *n* a drink such as a fruit squash which is diluted before being drunk. — *n* **dilut'ee** an unskilled worker introduced into a skilled occupation. — *n* **dilute'ness.** — *n* **dilut'er** or **dilut'or.** — *n* **dilu'tion.** [L. *dīluĕre, dīlūtum* — *dī-*, away, *luĕre*, to wash.]

diluvium *dil-ū'vi-əm* or *dil-ōō', n* an inundation or flood; a loose glacial deposit of sand, gravel, etc. — *adj* **dilu'vial** or **dilu'vian** pertaining to a flood, esp. Noah's; caused by a deluge. — *n* **dilu'vialist** someone who explains geological phenomena by the biblical flood. — *n* **dilu'vialism.** [L. *dīluvium*, a deluge — *dīluĕre*, to wash away.]

dim *dim, adj* not bright or distinct; obscure; not seeing clearly; mentally dull, stupid (*colloq*). — *vt* to make dark; to obscure. — *vi* to become dim: — *pr p* **dimm'ing**; *pa t* and *pa p* **dimmed.** — *adv* **dim'ly.** — *n* **dimm'er** a device for regulating the supply of light. — *adj* **dimm'ish** somewhat dim. — *n* **dim'ness.** —

dim'wit (*colloq*) a stupid person. — **a dim view** (*colloq*) an unfavourable view; **dim out** to reduce the lighting (of) gradually (*n* **dim'-out**). [O.E. *dimm*.]

dime *dīm*, *n* the tenth part of an American and Canadian dollar, 10 cents; a coin of this value; a small sum of money. — **dime novel** a cheap novel, usu. sensational; **dime store** (*US*) a shop selling cheap goods — orig. costing not more than a dime. — cheap, commonplace. [Fr., orig. *disme*, from L. *decima* (*pars*) a tenth (part).]

dimension *dī-* or *di-men'shən*, *n* measure in length, breadth or thickness (the three dimensions of space); scope, extent (also *fig*); size; the sum of the indices in a term (*alg*); a factor or aspect. — *vt* to give the dimensions of; to make to specified dimensions. — *adj* **dimen'sional** concerning dimension. — *In combination* denoting of so many dimensions, as in *three-dimensional*. — *adj* **dimen'sionless.** — **dimension work** masonry in stones of specified size. — **fourth dimension** an additional dimension attributed to space; (in relativity theory, etc.) time; **new dimension** a fresh aspect; **third dimension** depth, thickness; a rounding out, completeness, given by added detail, etc. (*fig*). [Fr., — L. *dīmēnsiō*, *-ōnis* — *dīmētīrī*, *dīmēnsus* — *dī* (*dis-*), apart, *mētīrī*, to measure.]

dimer *dī'mər*, *n* a compound whose molecule has twice as many atoms as another compound of the same empirical formula (the *monomer*). — *adj* **dīmeric** (*-mer'ik*). — *n* **dīmerisā'tion** or **-z-**. — *vt* **dī'merise** or **-ize.** [**di-** and mono*mer*.]

dimerous *dim'ə-rəs*, *adj* consisting of two parts; with two members in each whorl (*bot*); having two-jointed tarsi (*entom*). — *adj* **dimeric** (*dī-mer'ik*) bilaterally symmetrical; dimerous. — *n* **dimerism** (*dim'ər-izm*). [Gr. *di-*, double, twice, *meros*, a part.]

dimeter *dim'i-tər*, (*prosody*) *adj* containing two measures. — *n* a verse of two measures. [L., — Gr. *dimetros* — *di-*, twice, *metron*, a measure.]

dimidiate *di-mid'i-ət*, *adj* divided into halves. — *n* **dimidiā'tion.** [L. *dīmidiāre*, *-ātum*, to halve — *dīmidius*.]

dimin. *abbrev* for diminutive.

diminish *di-min'ish*, *vt* to make less; to take a part from; to degrade or belittle. — *vi* to grow or appear less; to subside. — *adj* **dimin'ishable.** — *adj* **dimin'ished** made smaller; lessened; humbled; of a semitone less than perfect or minor (*mus*). — *n* and *adj* **dimin'ishing.** — *adv* **dimin'ishingly.** — *n* **dimin'ishment.** — **diminished responsibility** limitation in law of criminal responsibility on the grounds of mental weakness or abnormality, not merely of actual insanity. — **law of diminishing returns** the fact that there is a point beyond which any additional amount of work, expenditure, taxation, etc. results in progressively smaller output, profits, yields, etc. [Coined from archaic *minish*, to lessen, in imitation of L. *dīminuĕre*, to break in pieces — *minuĕre*, to make less.]

diminuendo *di-min-ū-en'dō*, (*mus*) *adj* and *adv* letting the sound die away. — Also *n*: — *pl* **diminuen'does** or **diminuen'dos.** [It., — L. *dēminuendus*, gerundive of *dēminuĕre*, to lessen (see **diminish**).]

diminution *dim-in-ū'shən*, *n* a lessening; decrease. — *adj* **dimin'utive** of a diminished size; very small; contracted. — *n* a word formed from another to express a little one of the kind (*gram*); one of the smaller ordinaries, of the same shape as one of the larger ones (*heraldry*). — *adv* **dimin'utively.** — *n* **dimin'utiveness.** [**diminish**.]

dimissory *dim'is-ə-ri* or *di-mis'ə-ri*, *adj* sending away or giving leave to depart. [L. *dīmissōrius* — *dīmittĕre*, *dīmissum* — *dis-*, apart, *mittĕre*, to send.]

dimity *dim'i-ti*, *n* a stout white cotton, striped or figured in the loom by weaving with two threads. [Gr. *dimitos* — *di-*, twice, *mitos*, a thread.]

dimmer, dimming, etc. See **dim**.

dimorphism *dī-mör'fizm*, *n* the occurrence of two forms in the same species (*biol*); the property of crystallising in two forms (*chem*). — *adj* **dimor'phic** or **dimor'phous.** [Gr. *di-*, twice, *morphē*, form.]

dimple *dim'pl*, *n* a small hollow, esp. on a person's cheeks or chin. — *vi* to form dimples. — *adj* **dim'pled.** — *adj* **dim'ply.** [App. cognate with Ger. *Tümpel*, pool.]

dim sum *dim sum*, *n* a selection of Chinese foods, often eaten as an appetiser, usu. including steamed dumplings with various fillings. [Chin.]

DIN *din*, *n* a unit of measurement of the speed of photographic film; a standard system of plugs and sockets used to connect domestic audio and video equipment. [Abbrev. Ger. *D*eutsch *I*ndustrie *N*orm, German Industry Standard.]

din *din*, *n* a loud continued jarring noise. — *vt* to assail (the ears) with noise: — *pr p* **dinn'ing**; *pa t* and *pa p* **dinned.** — **din into** (*colloq*) to instil knowledge into (a person) by forceful repetition. [O.E. *dynn*, *dyne*.]

dinar *dē-när'*, *n* the monetary unit of Yugoslavia, and of Algeria, Tunisia, Iraq and other Arab countries; an ancient Arab gold coin of 65 grains' weight. [L. *dēnārius*.]

dine *dīn*, *vi* to take dinner; to feast (on). — *vt* to provide with a dinner. — *n* **din'er** a person who dines; a dining-car on a train; a small, inexpensive restaurant (esp. *US*). — *n* **dinette'** an alcove or other part of a room or kitchen set apart for meals. — **din'er-out** a person who is often invited to dinner parties; **din'ing-car** a railway carriage in which meals are served; **din'ing-hall; din'ing-room; din'ing-table.** — **dine off** or **on** to have as one's dinner; **dine out** to dine somewhere other than at home, usu. in a restaurant; **dine out on** to be invited to dinner, or (*loosely*) to enjoy social success, on the strength of one's possession of e.g. interesting information. [O.Fr. *disner*, prob. — L. *dis-*, expressing undoing, *jējūnus*, fasting.]

DIng. *abbrev* for *Doctor Ingeniariae* (L.), Doctor of Engineering.

ding *ding*, *vi* to ring; to sound; to keep sounding. — *vt* to reiterate to a wearisome degree. — *n* **ding'-dong** the sound of bells ringing; monotony; sameness; an argument or fight. — *adj* and *adv* like a bell ringing; keenly contested. — *vt* and *vi* to ring; to nag. [Imit.]

Ding an sich *ding an zihh*, (Ger.; *philos*) *n* the thing-in-itself, the noumenon.

dingbat *ding'bat*, (*US slang*) *n* something whose name one has forgotten, or does not want to use; a foolish or eccentric person; a tramp; money. — *adj* **ding'-bats** (*Austr* and *NZ colloq*) daft, crazy. — **the dingbats** (*Austr* and *NZ colloq*) delirium tremens. [Perh. **ding** and **bat**[1].]

dinge. See **dingy**.

dinges *ding'əs*, (*SAfr colloq*) *n* an indefinite name for any person or thing whose name one cannot or will not remember. [Du., — Afrik. *ding*, thing.]

dinghy *ding'gi*, *n* a small open boat, propelled by oars, sails or an outboard motor; any collapsible rubber boat, esp. one kept for use in emergencies. [Hind. *dingī*, a small boat.]

dingle *ding'gl*, *n* a wooded hollow; a dell.

dingo *ding'gō*, *n* the wild dog of Australia; a cheat or coward (*Austr slang*): — *pl* **ding'oes.** [Name in obs. Aboriginal dialect.]

dingy *din'ji*, *adj* dim or dark; shabby and dirty-looking; dull; soiled. — *n* **dinge** dinginess. — *vt* to make dingy. — *n* **din'giness.**

dinkum *ding'kəm*, (*Austr* and *NZ colloq*) *adj* real, genuine; square, honest. — Also *adv*. — Emphatically **fair dinkum**. — Also **dink'y-di** or **-die**. [Eng. dialect *dinkum*, a fair share of work.]

dinky[1] *ding'ki*, (*colloq*) *adj* neat; dainty; trivial, insignificant (*US*). [Scot. *dink*, neat.]

dinky[2] *ding'ki*, (*colloq*) *n* double- (or *d*ual-)*i*ncome *n*o *k*ids — acronym applied to a member of a young, childless (usu. married) couple both earning a good salary, who thus enjoy an affluent lifestyle: — *pl* **dink'ies.** — Also *adj.*

dinner *din'ər*, *n* the chief meal of the day, at midday or (usu.) in the evening; a formal meal or public banquet, often in celebration of a person or event. — *vi* to dine. — **dinn'er-dance** a dance following a formal dinner; **dinn'er-hour; dinn'er-jacket** a man's tailless dress-jacket, usu. black; **dinner lady** a woman who cooks and/or serves meals in a school canteen; **dinner party** a party at which dinner is served; **dinn'er-service** or **-set** a complete set of plates and dishes for several people at dinner; **dinn'er-wagon** a sideboard in two tiers, for holding dishes, etc.; orig. a shelved trolley for a dining-room. [**dine.**]

dinosaur *dī'nə-sör*, *n* any extinct (Mesozoic) reptile of the order **Dinosaur'ia** in length from two to eighty feet; a chance survivor of a type characteristic of a bygone era (*fig*). — *adj* (*fig*) **dinosaur'ic.** [Gr. *deinos*, terrible, *sauros*, lizard.]

dinothere *dī'nə-thēr*, *n* any extinct elephantine mammal of the genus *Deinotherium*, with downward-curving tusks. [Gr. *deinos*, terrible, *thērion*, wild beast.]

dint *dint*, *n* the mark of a blow (often **dent**); force (as in *by dint of*). — *vt* to make a dint in. [O.E. *dynt*, a blow.]

diocese *dī'ə-sis* or *-sēs*, *n* the circuit or extent of a bishop's jurisdiction. — *adj* **diocesan** (*dī-os'i-sn* or *-zn*) pertaining to a diocese. — *n* a bishop in relation to his diocese; one of the clergy in the diocese. [Through Fr. and L. from Gr. *dioikēsis* — *dioikeein*, to keep house.]

diode *dī'ōd*, (*electronics*) *n* the simplest electron tube with heated cathode and anode; a two-electrode semiconductor device evolved from primitive crystal rectifiers. [Gr. *di-*, twice, *hodos*, way.]

dioecious *dī-ē'shəs*, (*biol*) *adj* having the sexes in separate individuals or creatures; not hermaphrodite; having male and female flowers on different plants. — *n* **dioe'cism** (*-sizm*). [Gr. *di-*, twice, *oikos*, a house.]

Dionysia *dī-ə-niz'i-ə* or *-nis'*, *npl* dramatic and orgiastic festivals in honour of *Dionȳsos* (Bacchus), Greek god of wine. — *adj* **Dionys'iac** or **Dionys'ian.**

Diophantine *dī-ə-fan'tīn*, *adj* pertaining to the Alexandrian mathematician *Diophantos* (*c* A.D. 275). — **Diophantine equations** (*math*) indeterminate equations for which integral or rational solutions are required.

dioptric *dī-op'trik* or **dioptrical** *di-op'trik-əl*, *adj* pertaining to dioptrics or a dioptre. — *n* **diop'tre** or (esp. in U.S.) **diop'ter** a unit of measurement of the power of a lens, the reciprocal of the focal distances in metres, negative for a divergent lens. — *nsing* **diop'trics** the part of optics that deals with refraction. [Gr. *dioptrā*, a levelling instrument, *diop-tron*, a spyglass.]

diorama *dī-ə-rä'mə*, *n* an exhibition of translucent pictures seen through an opening with lighting effects; a miniature three-dimensional scene with figures; a display of e.g. a stuffed animal in a naturalistic setting, in a museum, etc.; a miniature film or television set. — *adj* **dioram'ic.** [Gr. *dia*, through, *horāma*, a sight.]

diorite *dī'ə-rīt*, *n* a crystalline granular igneous rock composed of plagioclase and hornblende. — *adj* **diorit'ic.** [Gr. *diorizein*, to distinguish — *dia*, through, *horos*, a boundary.]

dioxide *dī-ok'sīd*, *n* an oxide with two atoms of oxygen in the molecule. [**di-** and **oxide.**]

dioxin *dī-ok'sin*, *n* an extremely toxic poison found in weedkillers and bleaching agents, known to cause cancer, skin, liver and kidney disease, and birth defects.

Dip. *abbrev* for Diploma, as e.g. **Dip. Ed.**, Diploma in Education, **Dip. Tech.**, Diploma in Technology, **Dip. SW**, Diploma in Social Work.

dip *dip*, *vt* to immerse for a time; to lower; to lower and raise again (as a flag); to cause (headlights) to shine below the eye-level of oncoming motorists; to baptise by immersion; to lift by dipping (usu. with *up*); to dye or clean by dipping; to involve in money difficulties (*colloq*); to mortage; to pawn. — *vi* to plunge and emerge; to sink; to reach down into something; to enter slightly; to look cursorily; to incline downwards; to dip snuff (see below): — *pr p* **dipp'ing**; *pa t* and *pa p* **dipped.** — *n* the act of dipping; a hollow; a sag; that which is taken by dipping; an inclination downwards; a sloping; (of the headlights of a car, etc.) the state of being dipped; the angle a stratum of rock makes with a horizontal plane (*geol*); the angle between the horizontal and the earth's magnetic field; magnetic dip; a short swim; a liquid in which anything is dipped (such as sheep, garments, etc.); a creamy mixture into which bread, biscuits, etc., are dipped; a candle made by dipping a wick in tallow; a pickpocket (*slang*). — *n* **dipp'er** someone who, or that which, dips; a ladle; a bucket or scoop of a dredge or excavator; a contrivance for directing motor car headlights upwards or downwards (also **dip'-switch**); a dipping bird esp. the water ouzel; a nickname for a Baptist. — *n* **dipp'ing** the action of the verb; snuff-dipping. — **dip'-circle** or **dipp'ing-needle** an instrument for determining magnetic dip; **dip'-net** a long-handled net for dipping up fish; **dip'stick** a rod for measuring depth of liquid in a sump, etc.; a stupid or foolish person (*colloq*); **dip'-switch** see **dipper** above. — **dip in** to take a share; **dip into** to take or use (e.g. money from a fund); to read cursorily in; **dip of the horizon** the angle of the visible horizon below the level of the eye; **dip of the needle** the angle a balanced magnetic needle makes with the horizontal plane; **dip snuff** orig., in the southern U.S., to rub the gums and teeth with a wet stick dipped in snuff; to suck a pinch or small bag of snuff held between one's cheek and gum (*ns* **snuff'-dipper; snuff'-dipping**). [O.E. *dyppan*, causal of *dȳpan*, to plunge in.]

dipeptide *dī-pep'tīd*, (*chem*) *n* a peptide formed by the combination of two amino-acids. [**di-** and **peptide** (see **pepsin**).]

diphenyl *dī-fē'nil*, *n* a hydrocarbon, $C_{12}H_{10}$, consisting of two phenyl groups, used as a fungicide, in dye manufacture, etc. (also **bīphē'nyl**). — *adj* having two phenyl groups, esp. replacing hydrogen. [**di-** and **phenyl.**]

diphtheria *dif-thē'ri-ə* or *dip-*, *n* an infectious throat disease in which the air-passages become covered with a leathery membrane. — *adj* **diphtheric** (*-ther'ik*) or **diphtheritic** (*-thər-it'ik*). — *adj* **diph'-theroid.** [Fr. *diphthérie*, *diphthérite* (now *diphtérie*) — Gr. *diphtherā*, leather.]

diphthong *dif'thong* or *dip-*, *n* two vowel-sounds pronounced as one syllable (as in *out*); (*loosely*) a digraph; the ligature *æ* or *œ*. — *adj* **diphthongal** (*-thong'gəl*). — *adv* **diphthong'ally.** — *vt* **diph'-thongise** or **-ize** (*-gīz*). [Gr. *diphthongos* — *di-* twice, *phthongos*, sound, vowel.]

dipl- *dip-l-* or **diplo-** *dip-lō-*, *combining form* signifying double. — *n* **diplococcus** (*dip-lə-kok'əs*) (*bacteriol*) a coccus which divides by fission, the two resulting individuals remaining paired. — *n* **Diplod'ocus** (Gr. *dokos*, beam, bar, from its appearance) a gigantic, quadrupedal, herbivorous dinosaur of the sauropod group, remains of which have been found in the Jurassic rocks of the Rocky Mountains. — *adj* **dip'loid** (Gr. *eidos*, form; *biol*) having the full or unreduced number of chromosomes characteristic of the species, as in body cells (opp. to *haploid*). — *n* **diploid'y.** [Gr. *diploos*, double.]

Diplock court *dip'lok kört, n* in Northern Ireland, a court of law which sits without a jury.

diploma *di-plō'mə, n* a document conferring some honour or privilege, as a university degree, etc. — *vt* to furnish with a diploma. — *n* **diplomate** (*dip'lə-māt*) someone who holds a diploma. [L., - Gr. *diplōma*, a letter folded double — *diploos*, double.]

diplomacy *di-plō'mə-si, n* the art of negotiation, esp. in relations between states; tact in management of people concerned in any affair. — *n* **diplomat** (*dip'lə-mat*) a person employed or skilled in diplomacy. — *nsing* **diplomat'ics** the science of deciphering ancient writings, as charters, etc.; palaeography. — *adj* **diplomat'ic** pertaining to diplomacy; tactful and skilful in negotiating or dealing with people. — *adv* **diplomat'ically.** — *vi* **diplo'matise** or **-ize** to practise diplomacy. — *n* **diplo'matist** a diplomat. — *n* **diplomatol'ogy** the study or science of diplomatics, charters, decrees, etc. — **diplomatic bag** a bag used for sending documents, etc., to and from embassies, free of customs control; the contents of such a bag; **diplomatic corps** the whole body of foreign diplomats resident in any capital; **diplomatic immunity** immunity from local laws and taxation enjoyed by diplomats abroad; **diplomatic relations** formal relations between states marked by the presence of diplomats in each other's country. [Fr. *diplomatie* (pronounced *-sie*) — *diplomate*, *diplomatique*, ult. from L. (see **diploma**).]

Dipodidae *dī-pod'i-dē, npl* the jerboa family of rodents. [Gr. *dipous*, two-footed — *di-*, twice, *pous*, *podos*, a foot.]

dipody *dip'ə-di, (prosody) n* a double foot. [Gr. *di-*, double, *pous*, *podos*, foot.]

dipolar *dī-pō'lər, adj* having two poles. — *n* **di'pole** two equal and opposite electric charges, or magnetic poles of opposite sign, set a small distance apart; a body or system containing either of these; a type of radio or television aerial. [**di-** and **polar.**]

dippy *dip'i, (colloq) adj* crazy; insane.

dipsomania *dip-sō-mā'ni-ə, n* an intermittent pathological craving for alcoholic stimulants. — *n* **dipsomā'niac** someone who suffers from dipsomania (*colloq* **dip'sō**: — *pl* **dip'sōs**). [Gr. *dipsa*, thirst, *maniā*, madness.]

Diptera *dip'tər-ə, n* the genus of two-winged insects or flies; (without *cap*) any insect of the genus. — *adj* **dip'teral** two-winged; with a double colonnade (*archit*). — *n* **dip'teran** a dipterous insect. — *n* **dip'terist** a student of flies. — *adj* **dip'terous** with two wings or winglike expansions. [Gr. *dipteros*, two-winged, *di-*, twice, *pteron*, a wing.]

diptych *dip'tik, n* a double-folding wooden writing-tablet; a pair of pictures, esp. with a religious theme, painted on hinged wooden panels. [Gr. *diptychos* — *di-*, *ptychē*, a tablet, a fold.]

Dir. *abbrev* for Director.

dire *dīr, adj* dreadful; calamitous in a high degree; urgent; portentous. — *adj* (*poetic*) **dire'ful.** — *adv* **dire'fully.** — *n* **dire'fulness.** [L. *dīrus.*]

direct *dī'rekt* or *di-rekt', adj* straight; straightforward; by the shortest way; forward, not backward or oblique; immediate; without intervening agency or interposed stages; in the line of descent; outspoken; sincere; unambiguous; unsophisticated in manner; (of a dye) fixing itself without a mordant. — *n* (*mus*) an indication of the first note or chord of the next page or line. — *adv* straight; by the shortest way; without deviation, intervening agency or interposed stages. — *vt* to keep or lay straight; to point or aim; to point out the proper course to; to guide; to order; to address, mark with the name and residence of a person; to plan and superintend (the production of a film or play). — *vi* to act as director of a film, stage-play, etc. — *n* **direc'tion** aim at a certain point; the line or course in which anything moves or on which any point lies; guidance; command; the body of persons who guide or manage a matter; the work of the director of a film, stage-play, etc. — *adj* **direc'tional** relating to direction in space. — *adj* **direc'tionless** not moving, looking, etc. in any particular direction; aimless. — *adj* **direct'ive** having the power or a tendency to direct. — *n* a general instruction. — *n* **directiv'ity** the property of being directional. — *adv* **direct'ly** in a direct manner; without intermediary; immediately (in time and otherwise). — *conj* (often with *that*; *colloq*) as soon as. — *n* **direct'ness.** — *n* **direct'or** a person who directs; a person who directs the shooting of a cinema film; a manager or governor; a member of a board conducting the affairs of a company; a counsellor; part of a machine or instrument which guides the motion. — *n* **direct'orate** a body of directors; the office of director. — *adj* **directorial** *-tö'*). — *adj* **direct'ory** containing directions; guiding. — *n* a body of directions; a guide; a book with the names and residences of the inhabitants of a place; (with *cap*) the *Directoire*, or French Republican government of 1795–99. — *n* **direc'torship.** — *n* **direct'rix** a line serving to describe a conic section, which is the locus of a point whose distances from focus and directrix have a constant ratio (*geom*): — *pl* **directrices** (*-trī'sēz*). — **direct access** same as **random access**; (see under **random**); **direct action** coercive methods of attaining industrial or political ends as opp. to pacific, parliamentary, or political action; **direct current** an electric current flowing in one direction only; **direct debit** an arrangement by which a creditor can claim payment direct from the payer's bank account; **direct drilling** the ploughing and sowing of a field in one operation; **directional aerial** one that can receive or transmit radio waves in one direction only; **direc'tion-finder** a radio receiver that determines the direction of arrival of incoming waves, used esp. in navigation; **direc'tion-indicator** an aerial navigation device in which needles of actual and desired course overlap when the aircraft is on its true course; **direct labour** labour employed directly, not through a contractor; **direct method** a method of teaching a foreign language through speaking it, without translation, and without formal instruction in grammar; **direct object** a word or group of words denoting that upon which the action of a transitive verb is directed; **direct'or-general** a chief administrator of a usu. non-commercial organisation; **director's chair** a light folding chair with a seat and back of canvas or similar material and arm-rests; **direct speech** speech reported as spoken, in the very words of the speaker (L. *ōrātiō rēcta*); **direct tax** one levied directly on individuals or organizations, rather than on goods or services. — **directed-energy weapon** a weapon whose destructive force consists of beams of light, electromagnetic pulses, subatomic particles, or the like; **direct-grant school** until 1979, a fee-paying school which received a state grant on condition that it took a specified number of non-fee-paying pupils. [L. *dīrigĕre*, *dīrēctum* — *dī-*, apart, *regĕre*, to rule.]

Directoire *dē-rek-twär, (hist) n* the French Directorate of 1795–99. — *adj* after the fashion in dress or furniture then prevailing; (of knickers) knee-length, with elastic at the waist and knee. [Fr.; see **direct.**]

directrix. See under **direct.**

dirge *dûrj, n* a funeral song or hymn; a slow and mournful piece of music. [Contr. from *dīrige* (imper. of L. *dīrigĕre*, to direct), the first word of an antiphon sung in the office for the dead.]

dirham *dûr-ham', də-ram'* or *dē'ram, n* the monetary unit of Morocco (100 centimes); a coin equal to this in value; a coin used in several N. African and Middle Eastern countries, with varying value. [Ar., Pers., and Turk. forms of the Greek *drachmē*, a drachma or dram.]

dirigible *dir'i-ji-bl* or *-rij'*, *adj* that can be directed. — *n* a navigable balloon or airship. — *adj* **dir'igent** directing. [**direct.**]

dirigisme *dē-rēzh-ēzm'*, *n* control by the State in economic and social spheres. — *adj* **dirigiste** (*-ēst'*). [Fr., — It. *dirigismo*.]

diriment *dir'i-mənt*, (*law*) *adj* nullifying. [L. *dirimĕre*.]

dirk *dûrk*, *n* a Highland dagger; a sidearm worn by midshipmen and naval cadets (*hist*). [Orig. Scots, in form *durk*.]

dirndl *dûrn'dl*, *n* an Alpine peasant woman's dress with close-fitting bodice and full skirt; an imitation of this, esp. a full skirt with a tight, often elasticated waistband. [Ger. dialect, dimin. of *dirne*, girl.]

dirt *dûrt*, *n* any filthy substance, such as dung, mud, etc.; foreign matter adhering to anything; loose earth; a mixture of earth, gravel and cinders, used as a surface for race-tracks, etc.; rubbish; obscenity; a worthless or despised person or thing; spiteful gossip. — *adv* **dirt'ily.** — *n* **dirt'iness.** — *adj* **dirt'y** marked with dirt; soiled; foul, filthy; of a colour, not bright or clear; stormy; obscene; unclean in thought or conversation; despicable; showing anger or reproof; mean; sordid; dishonest, treacherous. — *vt* to soil with dirt; to sully: — *pr p* **dirt'ying**; *pa t* and *pa p* **dirt'ied.** — *adj* **dirt-cheap'** very cheap. — **dirt farmer** (*US*) someone who farms his or her own land, esp. without hired help; **dirt'-road** a soft road, unpaved and unmacadamised; **dirt'-track** a rough unsurfaced track; a motorcycle racing-track, with earthy or cinder surface; **dirty bomb** one that produces a large amount of radioactive contamination; **dirty dog** (*slang*) a dishonest or contemptible person; **dirty linen** (*colloq*) personal problems or grievances (esp. in the phrase *wash one's dirty linen in public*); **dirty look** (*colloq*) a look of anger, disapproval or reproof; **dirty money** money earned by base means; in dock labour, extra pay for unloading offensive cargo; extra pay for any unpleasant, dirty, etc. task; **dirty trick** a dishonest or despicable act; a political intrigue (esp. in the phrase *dirty-tricks campaign* or *operation*); **dirty word** an obscene word; a word for something (such as a feeling, principle, or belief) that is regarded with disfavour at the present time; **dirty work** work that dirties the hands or clothes; dishonourable practices, esp. undertaken on behalf on another; foul play; **dirty old man** (*colloq*) a man whose sexual aspirations and actions are considered appropriate only to a younger man. — **do the dirty on** to play a low trick on, cheat; **eat dirt** to acquiesce submissively in a humiliation; **throw dirt** to besmirch a reputation. [M.E. *drit*, prob. O.N. *drit*, excrement.]

dis- *dis-* or **di-** *di-*, *pfx* (1) meaning in two, asunder, apart; (2) meaning 'not' or a reversal; (3) indicating a removal or deprivation; (4) used intensively. [L. *dis-*, *dī-*.]

disa *dī'sə* or *dī'zə*, *n* a plant of a genus (*Disa*) of African orchids with dark green leaves; an orchid of certain other genera.

disable *dis-ā'bl*, *vt* to cripple or incapacitate; to deprive of power; to weaken; to disqualify legally. — *adj* **disā'bled** physically handicapped; designed or intended for people with physical handicaps. — *n* **disā'blement.** — *n* **disabil'ity** a handicap, esp. physical; lack of legal power or qualification; a disqualification. — [**dis-** (2).]

disabuse *dis-ə-būz'*, *vt* to undeceive or set right. [**dis-** (2).]

disaccord *dis-ə-körd'*, *vi* to be at discord; not to agree. — Also *n*. [**dis-** (2).]

disadvantage *dis-əd-vänt'ij*, *n* an unfavourable circumstance or condition; loss; damage. — *adj* **disadvan'taged** deprived of the resources and privileges, usu. social, enjoyed by the majority of people; in unfavourable conditions relative to other (specified) people. — *adj* **disadvantageous** (*dis-ad-vənt-ā'jəs*) involving or bringing disadvantage; unfavourable. — *adv* **disadvantā'geously.** — *n* **disadvantā'geousness.** [**dis-** (2).]

disaffect *dis-ə-fekt'*, *vt* to take away the affection of; to make discontented or unfriendly: — *pa p* and *adj* **disaffect'ed** ill-disposed or alienated; tending to break away. — *adv* **disaffect'edly.** — *n* **disaffect'edness.** — *n* **disaffec'tion** the state of being disaffected; lack of affection or friendliness; alienation; ill-will; political discontent or disloyalty. [**dis-** (3).]

disaffiliate *dis-ə-fil'i-āt*, *vt* and *vi* to end an affiliation (to); to separate oneself (from). — *n* **disaffiliā'tion.** [**dis-** (2).]

disaffirm *dis-ə-fûrm'*, *vt* to contradict; to repudiate or reverse (*law*). — *n* **disaffirmā'tion** (*dis-a-*). [**dis-** (2).]

disafforest *dis-ə-for'ist*, *vt* to bring out of the operation of forest laws; to take away the legal status of a forest from; to clear of forest, disforest. — *n* **disafforestā'tion** or **disaffor'estment.** [L. *dis-*, reversal, and L.L. *afforestāre*, to make into a forest.]

disaggregate *dis-ag'ri-gāt*, *vt* to separate (something) into its component parts. — *n* **disaggregā'tion.** [**dis-** (1).]

disagree *dis-ə-grē'*, *vi* to differ or be at variance; to dissent; to quarrel; to be opposed; to prove unsuitable or a source of annoyance, as of food disagreeing with the stomach. — *adj* **disagree'able** not amicable; unpleasant; offensive. — *n* **disagree'ableness** or **disagreeabil'ity.** — *adv* **disagree'ably.** — *n* **disagree'ment** absence of agreement; difference; unsuitableness; dispute. [**dis-** (2).]

disallow *dis-ə-low'*, *vt* not to allow; to refuse to sanction; to deny the authority, validity, or truth of; to reject, to forbid. — *adj* **disallow'able.** — *n* **disallow'ance.** [**dis-** (2).]

disambiguate *dis-am-big'ū-āt*, *vt* to take away the ambiguity from; to make unambiguous. — *n* **disambigua'tion.** [**dis-** (3).]

disamenity *dis-ə-mē'ni-ti* or *-men'-*, *n* a disadvantage or drawback (e.g. of a property or district). [**dis-** (3).]

disanalogy *dis-an-a'lə-ji*, *n* a non-correspondence; an aspect or feature in which something is not analogous to something else. — *adj* **disanal'ogous** (*-gəs*). [**dis-** (2).]

disappear *dis-ə-pēr'*, *vi* to vanish from sight; to become lost; to cease to exist, be felt, etc. — *n* **disappear'ance.** [**dis-** (3).]

disappoint *dis-ə-point'*, *vt* to frustrate the hopes or expectations of; to prevent the fulfilment of. — *vi* to cause disappointment. — *adj* **disappoint'ed** saddened by the frustration of hopes, etc.; balked. — *adj* **disappoint'ing** causing disappointment. — *n* **disappoint'ment** the defeat of one's hopes or expectations; frustration; the vexation accompanying failure. [O.Fr. *desapointer*, *des-* (L. *dis-*), away, *apointer*, to appoint.]

disapprobation *dis-ap-rō-bā'shən*, *n* disapproval. — *adj* **disapp'robātive** or **disapp'robātory.** [**dis-** (2).]

disapprove *dis-ə-prōōv'*, *vt* and *vi* to give or have an unfavourable opinion (of); to reject. — *n* **disapprov'al.** — *adv* **disapprov'ingly.** [**dis-** (2).]

disarm *dis-ärm'*, *vt* to deprive of arms; to render defenceless; to deprive of the power to hurt; to conciliate or placate (*fig*); to deprive of suspicion or hostility; to reduce to a peace footing. — *vi* to disband troops, reduce national armaments, etc. — *n* **disarm'ament** the reduction of national armaments; the act of disarming or the state of being disarmed. — *n* **disarm'er** someone who or that which disarms; a person in favour of reducing national armaments. — *adj* **disarm'ing** charming; tending to placate. [**dis-** (3).]

disarrange *dis-ə-rānj'*, *vt* to undo the arrangement of; to put into disorder. — *n* **disarrange'ment.** [**dis-** (2).]

disarray *dis-ə-rā'*, *vt* to break the array of; to throw into disorder. — *n* lack of array or order; untidiness. [**dis-** (2), (3).]

disarticulate *dis-är-tik'ūl-āt*, *vt* to separate the joints of. — *vi* to separate at a joint. — *n* **disarticulā'tion.** [**dis-** (1).]

disassemble *dis-ə-sem'bl*, *vt* to take (a machine, etc.) apart. — *n* **disassem'bly.** [**dis-** (1).]

disassociate *dis-ə-sō'shi-āt*, *vt* (with *from*) to disconnect; to dissociate. — *n* **disassociā'tion.** [**dis-** (2).]

disaster *diz-äs'tər*, *n* a great and sudden misfortune; an adverse or unfortunate event; a calamity. — *adj* **disas'trous** calamitous, ruinous; gloomy, foreboding disaster. — *adv* **disas'trously.** — **disaster area** an area in which there has been a disaster (e.g. flood, explosion), requiring special official aid; (*loosely*) any place where a misfortune has happened; anything which is untidy, ugly, disadvantageous, etc. (*colloq*); **disaster movie** a film which has as its main theme or focus of action a disaster or catastrophe. [O.Fr. *desastre* — L. *dis-*, with evil sense, *astrum*, star.]

disattribution *dis-at-ri-bū'shən*, *n* the act of adjudging a work of art, etc. to be no longer the product of a particular artist, etc.; an instance of this. [**dis-** (2).]

disattune *dis-ə-tūn'*, *vt* to put out of harmony. [**dis-** (2).]

disavow *dis-ə-vow'*, *vt* to disclaim knowledge of, or connection with; to disown; to deny. — *n* **disavow'al.** [O.Fr. *desavouer*, *des-*, away, *avouer*, to avow.]

disband *dis-band'*, *vt* to disperse, break up (a group, unit, etc.). — *vi* to break up. — *n* **disband'ment.** [O.Fr. *desbander*, to unbind, *des-* (signifying reversal) and *bander*, to tie.]

disbar *dis-bär'*, (*law*) *vt* to expel from the Bar. — *n* **disbar'ment.** [**dis-** (3).]

disbelieve *dis-bə-lēv'*, *vt* to believe to be false; to refuse to believe. — *vi* to have no faith (*in*). — *n* **disbelief'.** — *n* **disbeliev'er.** [**dis-** (2).]

disbench *dis-bench'* or *-bensh'*, (*law*) *vt* to deprive of the status of a member of a governing body in the Inns of Court. [**dis-** (3).]

disbenefit *dis-ben'i-fit*, *n* a drawback, disadvantage, loss, inconvenience, etc.; absence or loss of a benefit. [**dis-** (2), (3).]

disbud *dis-bud'*, *vt* to remove buds from. [**dis-** (3).]

disburden *dis-bûr'dn*, *vt* to rid of a burden; to free; to unload or discharge. [**dis-** (3).]

disburse *dis-bûrs'*, *vt* to pay out. — *n* **disburse'ment** a paying out; that which is paid. [O.Fr. *desbourser*, *des-* (L. *dis-*), apart, *bourse*, a purse.]

disc *disk*, *n* any flat thin circular body or structure; a circular figure, as that presented by the sun, moon and planets; the enlarged torus of a flower; a layer of fibrocartilage between vertebrae, the slipping of which (*slipped disc*) causes pressure on spinal nerves and hence pain; a gramophone record; (usu. as **disk**) a magnetic disc or a disc file (see entry at **disk**). — *adj* **disc'oid** or **discoid'al.** — *n* **discog'raphy** collection, description, etc., of gramophone records; the history or description of musical recording; a list of recordings by one composer or performer. — *n* **discog'rapher.** — *n* **disc'ophile** (*-ō-fīl*) someone who makes a study of and collects gramophone records. — **disc brake** one in which the friction is obtained by pads hydraulically forced against a disc on the wheel; **disc harrow** or **plough** a harrow or plough in which the soil is cut by inclined discs; **disc'-jockey** a person who introduces and plays records (esp. of popular music) on a radio or television programme, etc.; **disc parking** a system according to which the motorist is responsible for affixing to their car special disc(s) showing their time of arrival and the time when permitted parking ends; **disc player** a machine for playing videodiscs; a wheel on a motor vehicle, etc. in which the hub and rim are connected by solid metal, rather than by spokes. [Gr. *diskos*.]

discalced *dis-kalst'*, *adj* without shoes, bare-footed, or wearing only sandals, as a branch of the Carmelite order of friars and nuns noted for their austerity. — *n* and *adj* **discal'ceate.** [L. *discalceātus* — *dis-* (negative) and *calceus*, a shoe.]

discapacitate *dis-kə-pas'i-tāt*, *vt* to incapacitate. [**dis-** (2).]

discard *dis-kärd'*, *vt* and *vi* to reject; to get rid of as unwanted; (of cards) to throw away as not needed or not allowed by the game; in whist, etc., to throw down a (useless) card of another suit when one cannot follow suit and cannot or will not trump. — *n* (also *dis'*) the act of discarding; the card or cards thrown out of the hand; abandonment; a cast-off, anything discarded. [**dis-** (3).]

discarnate *dis-kär'nit* or *-nāt*, *adj* disembodied; separated from its or the body. [**dis-** (1), and L. *carō*, *carnis*, flesh.]

discern *di-sûrn'* or *-zûrn'*, *vt* to make out; to distinguish by the eye or understanding. — *n* **discern'er.** — *adj* **discern'ible.** — *adv* **discern'ibly.** — *adj* **discern'ing** discriminating; showing acute judgment. — *n* **discern'ment** the power or faculty of discriminating; judgment; acuteness. [L. *discernĕre* — *dis-*, thoroughly, *cernĕre*, to sift, perceive.]

discharge *dis-chärj'*, *vt* to free from or relieve of a charge of any kind (burden, explosive, electricity, liability, accusation, etc.); to set free; to acquit; to dismiss from employment; to fire (as a gun); to pour out; to emit or let out; to perform (as a task or duty); to pay; to distribute (as weight). — *vi* to unload; to become released from a charged state; to allow escape of contents; to flow away or out. — *n* (usu. *dis'chärj*) the act of discharging; release from a charge of any kind; unloading; liberation; acquittal; dismissal; outflow; rate of flow; emission; payment; performance; that which is discharged. — *n* **discharg'er** someone who discharges; an apparatus for discharging, esp. electricity; an apparatus for firing an explosive. — **discharge'-tube** a tube in which an electric discharge takes place in a vacuum or in a gas at low pressure. [O.Fr. *descharger* — *des-*, apart, *charger*; see **charge.**]

dischuffed *dis-chuft'*, (*colloq*) *adj* displeased; disappointed. [**dis-** (2).]

disciple *dis-ī'pl*, *n* a person who follows or believes in the doctrine of another; a person who professes to receive instruction from another; a follower, esp. one of the twelve apostles of Christ. — *n* **discī'pleship.** [Fr., — L. *discipulus*, from *discĕre*, to learn.]

discipline *dis'i-plin*, *n* training designed to engender self-control and an ordered way of life; the state of self-control achieved by such training; a branch of learning or field of study; a branch of sport; subjection to control; punishment. — *vt* to subject to discipline; to train; to educate; to bring under control; to chastise. — *adj* **disc'iplinable.** — *adj* **disc'iplinal** (or *-plī'*). — *n* **disciplinā'rian** a person who enforces strict discipline. — *adj* disciplinary; advocating or practising strict discipline. — *adj* **disc'iplinary** pertaining to or of the nature of discipline. — *n* **disc'ipliner.** [Ety. as for **disciple.**]

disclaim *dis-klām'*, *vt* to renounce all claim to; to refuse to acknowledge or be responsible for; to repudiate; to reject. — *vi* to make a disclaimer. — *n* **disclaim'er** a denial, disavowal or renunciation. [O.Fr. *disclaimer* — L. *dis-*, apart, *clāmāre*, to cry out.]

disclose *dis-klōz'*, *vt* to lay open; to bring to light; to reveal. — *n* **disclō'sure** (*-zhər*) the act of disclosing; that which is disclosed or revealed. — **disclosing**

tablet a tablet which, when chewed, reveals by means of a coloured dye areas of plaque to be removed from the teeth. [O.Fr. *desclos* — L. *dis-*, apart, *claudĕre*, *clausum*, to shut.]

disco *dis'kō*, *n* short for **discothèque**: — *pl* **dis'cos**. — *adj* suitable, or specially produced, for discothèques, as in *disco dancing*, *disco dress*, *disco music*. — *vi* (*colloq*) to go to a disco; to dance to disco music: — *pr p* **disc'oing**; *pa t* and *pa p* **disc'oed**. — *n* **dis'coer** a person who frequents discos.

discographer, discography, discoid, discoidal, etc. See under **disc**.

discolour or in U.S. **discolor** *dis-kul'ər*, *vt* to change or spoil the natural colour of; to mark with other colours, to stain; to dirty or disfigure. — *vi* to become discoloured. — *n* **discolorā'tion** or **discolourā'tion**. — *adj* **discol'oured** or in U.S. **discol'ored**. [O.Fr. *descolorer* — L. *dis-*, apart, *colōrāre* — *color*, colour.]

discombobulate *dis-kəm-bob'ū-lāt*, (*NAm slang*) *vt* to disconcert or upset.

discomfit *dis-kum'fit*, *vt* to disconcert or to balk: — *pr p* **discom'fiting**; *pa t* and *pa p* **discom'fited**. — *n* **discom'fiture**. [O.Fr. *desconfit* — L. *dis-* (negative), *conficĕre*, to prepare.]

discomfort *dis-kum'fərt*, *n* lack of comfort; uneasiness; slight pain. — *vt* to deprive of comfort; to make uneasy. [O.Fr. *desconforter* — *des-* (privative) and *conforter*, to comfort; see **comfort**.]

discommode *dis-kə-mōd'*, *vt* to inconvenience. — *adj* **discommō'dious**. — *adv* **discommō'diously**. [**dis-** (2), obs. verb *commode*, to suit.]

discompose *dis-kəm-pōz'*, *vt* to deprive of composure; to disturb or agitate; to disarrange or disorder. — *n* **discompō'sure** (*-zhər* or *-zhyər*). [**dis-** (2).]

disconcert *dis-kən-sûrt'*, *vt* to throw into confusion; to disturb; to frustrate; to put out of countenance, embarrass. — *n* **disconcer'tion** confusion. — *n* **disconcert'ment**. [Obs. Fr. *disconcerter* — *des-*, apart, *concerter*, to concert.]

disconformable *dis-kən-förm'ə-bl*, *adj* not similar or consistent; of strata, with their original relative positions disturbed; not conformable. — *n* **disconform'ity** lack of conformity. [**dis-** (2).]

disconnect *dis-kən-ekt'*, *vt* and *vi* to break the connection, esp. electrical (between). — *adj* **disconnect'ed** separated; loosely united, as of a discourse. — *adv* **disconnect'edly**. — *n* **disconnec'tion** or **disconnex'ion**. [**dis-** (1).]

disconsolate *dis-kon'sə-lit*, *adj* beyond consolation or comfort; very sad or disappointed. — *adv* **discon'solately**. — *n* **discon'solateness**. [L. *dis-* (negative) and *consōlārī*, *consōlātus*, to console.]

discontent *dis-kən-tent'*, *n* lack of contentment; dissatisfaction. — *vt* to deprive of contentment; to stir up to ill-will. — *adj* **discontent'ed** dissatisfied. — *adv* **discontent'edly**. — *n* **discontent'edness**. — *n* **discontent'ment**. [**dis-** (2), (3).]

discontiguous *dis-kon-tig'ū-əs*, *adj* not contiguous, not in contact. — *n* **discontigū'ity**. [**dis-** (2).]

discontinue *dis-kən-tin'ū*, *vt* to cease to continue; to put an end to; to stop. — *vi* to cease. — *n* **discontin'uance** or **discontinuā'tion** a breaking off or ceasing. — *n* **discontinu'ity** (*-kon-*). — *adj* **discontin'uous** not continuous; broken off; separated; interrupted by intervening spaces. — *adv* **discontin'uously**. [O.Fr. *discontinuer* — L. *dis-*, reversal, *continuāre*, to continue.]

discophile. See under **disc**.

discord *dis'körd*, *n* disagreement, strife (opp. of *concord*); difference or contrariety of qualities; a combination of inharmonious sounds; uproarious noise. — *vi* **discord'** to disagree. — *n* **discord'ance** or **discord'ancy**. — *adj* **discord'ant** without concord or agreement; inconsistent; contradictory; harsh; jarring. — *adv* **discord'antly**. [O.Fr. *descord* — L. *discordia* — *dis-*, apart, *cor*, *cordis*, the heart.]

discotheque or **discothèque** *dis'kə-tek*, *n* a club or party where music for dancing is provided by records; the equipment and records used to provide such music (*colloq* **dis'co**, q.v.) [Fr., a record-library — Gr. *diskos*, disc, *thēkē*, case, library.]

discount *dis'kownt*, *n* a deduction made for prompt payment of an account, or according to some other negotiated agreement; the rate or percentage of the deduction granted; the amount by which the price of a share or stock unit is below the par value. — *vt* **discount'** to disregard, or reject as unimportant; to reduce the effect of (e.g. an extravagant statement, a fabulous story or an event foreseen); to sell at a reduced price; to pay (rarely to receive) beforehand the present worth of (a bill of exchange). — *vi* to practise discounting. — *adj* **discount'able**. — *n* **discount'er**. — **discount house** a company trading in bills of exchange, etc.; **discount rate** the rate at which a discount is granted; the rate at which banks can borrow funds using bills as security; bank rate (*NAm*); **discount store** a shop where goods are sold at less than the usual retail price. — **at a discount** at a reduced price; not sought after; depreciated in value; (of shares) below par. [O.Fr. *descompter*, *des-*, away, *compter*, to count.]

discountenance *dis-kown'tən-əns*, *vt* to refuse support to; to discourage; to show disapproval of; to abash. — *n* cold treatment; disapprobation. [O.Fr. *descontenancer* — *des-*, reversal, *contenance*, countenance.]

discourage *dis-kur'ij*, *vt* to take away the courage of; to dishearten; to oppose by showing disfavour. — *n* **discour'agement** act of discouraging; that which discourages; dejection. — *n* and *adj* **discour'aging** disheartening, depressing. — *adv* **discour'agingly**. [O.Fr. *descourager*. See **courage**.]

discourse *dis-kōrs'* or *dis'kōrs*, *n* speech or language generally; conversation; a treatise; a speech; a sermon. — *vi* to talk or converse; to reason; to treat formally (with *on*). — *adj* **discours'al**. [Fr. *discours* — L. *discursus* — *dis-*, away, *currĕre*, to run.]

discourteous *dis-kûrt'yəs*, *adj* lacking in courtesy; uncivil. — *adv* **discourt'eously**. — *n* **discourt'eousness**. — *n* **discourt'esy** discourteousness; a discourteous remark or act. [**dis-** (2).]

discover *dis-kuv'ər*, *vt* to find or find out, esp. for the first time; to make known; to reveal. — *adj* **discov'erable**. — *n* **discov'erer** a person who makes a discovery, esp. of something never before known. — *n* **discov'ery** the act of finding out; the thing discovered; gaining knowledge of the unknown; exploration or reconnaissance (as in **voyage of discovery**). — **discovery well** an exploratory oil well which proves to yield a commercially viable amount of oil. [O.Fr. *descouvrir*, *des-* (L. *dis-*), away, *couvrir*, to cover; see **cover**.]

discredit *dis-kred'it*, *n* ill-repute; disgrace; a person or thing bringing these. — *vt* to disgrace; to deprive of credibility; to refuse to believe in. — *adj* **discred'itable** bringing discredit; disgraceful. — *adv* **discred'itably**. [**dis-** (2), (3).]

discreet *dis-krēt'*, *adj* careful in one's actions and choice of words, esp. able to keep secrets; tactful; prudent; modest; unpretentious. — *adv* **discreet'ly**. — *n* **discreet'ness**. [O.Fr. *discret* — L. *discrētus* — *discernĕre*, to separate, to perceive.]

discrepancy *dis-krep'ən-si*, *n* disagreement, variance of facts or sentiments. — *adj* **discrep'ant** contrary, disagreeing. [L. *discrepāns*, *-antis*, different to sound.]

discrete *dis-krēt'*, *adj* separate; discontinuous; consisting of distinct parts; referring to distinct objects. — *adv* **discrete'ly**. [L. *discrētus*; cf. **discreet**.]

discretion *dis-kresh'ən*, *n* quality of being discreet; prudence; liberty to act at pleasure. — *adj* **dis-**

cre'tional or **discre'tionary** left to discretion; unrestricted. — *adv* **discre'tionally** or **discre'tionarily**. — **age** or **years of discretion** the age at which one's judgment becomes mature; **at discretion** according to one's own judgment; **be at someone's discretion** to be under someone's power or control. [O.Fr. *discrecion* — L. *discrētiō, -ōnis*.]

discriminate *dis-krim'i-nāt*, *vt* to note the difference of or between; to distinguish. — *vi* to make or note differences or distinctions; to distinguish (with *between*); (with *in favour of* or *against*) to treat differently, esp. because of one's feelings or prejudices about a person's sex, race, religion, etc. — *n* (*-nət*) a special function of the roots of an equation, expressible in terms of the coefficients — zero value of the function showing that at least two of the roots are equal. — *adj* **discrim'ināting** noting distinctions; gifted with judgment and penetration. — *adv* **discrim'inātingly**. — *n* **discriminā'tion** the act or process of discriminating; judgment; good taste; the selection of a signal having a particular characteristic (frequency, amplitude, etc.) by the elimination of all the other input signals (*telecomm*). — *adj* **discrim'inative** discriminatory. — *n* **discrim'inātor** a person who, or thing which, discriminates; a device which affects the routing and/or determines the fee units for a call originating at a satellite exchange (*telecomm*). — *adj* **discrim'inatory** biased, unfair, revealing prejudice; making fine distinctions. — **positive discrimination** discrimination in favour of those who were formerly discriminated against, esp. in the provision of social and educational facilities and employment opportunities. [L. *discrīmināre, -ātum* — *discrīmen*, that which separates.]

discursive *dis-kûr'siv*, *adj* (of writing or speaking style) proceeding from one subject to another with no formal plan, given to digression, roving, desultory; intellectual, rational, rather than intuitive (*philos*). — *adv* **discur'sively**. — *n* **discur'siveness**. [Med. L. *discursīvus* — L. *discursus*, conversation.]

discus *dis'kəs*, *n* a heavy wooden disc, thickening towards the centre, thrown for distance in athletic contests, orig. in ancient Greece. [L., — Gr. *diskos*.]

discuss *dis-kus'*, *vt* to examine in detail, in speech or writing; to talk or argue about in conversation, to debate. — *adj* **discuss'able** or **discuss'ible**. — *n* **discussion** (*dis-kush'ən*) debate, argument or conversation; a detailed treatment in speech or writing. [L. *discutĕre, discussum*, to break up.]

disdain *dis-dān'*, *vt* to think unworthy; to scorn. — *n* a feeling of contempt, generally tinged with superiority; haughtiness. — *adj* **disdain'ful**. — *adv* **disdain'fully**. — *n* **disdain'fulness**. [O.Fr. *desdaigner*. with *des-* (L. *dis-*) for L. *dē* in L. *dēdīgnārī* — *dīgnus*, worthy.]

disease *diz-ēz'*, *n* an unhealthy state of body or mind; a disorder, illness or ailment with distinctive symptoms, caused e.g. by infection; unhealthiness, or a specific ailment, in plants; a social evil (*fig*). — *adj* **diseased'** affected with disease. — *n* **diseas'edness**. [O.Fr. *desaise* — *des-*, not, *aise*, ease.]

diseconomy *dis-ə-kon'ə-mi*, *n* (an instance of) something which is economically wasteful or unprofitable. [**dis-** (2).]

disembark *dis-im-bärk'*, *vt* to set ashore; to take out of a ship. — *vi* to leave a ship; to land. — *n* **disembarkā'tion**. [O.Fr. *desembarquer* — *des-* (L. *dis-*), *embarquer*.]

disembarrass *dis-im-bar'əs*, *vt* to free from an embarrassment, burden or complication (with *of*). — *n* **disembarr'assment**. [**dis-** (2).]

disembody *dis-im-bod'i*, *vt* to remove or free (a spirit) from the body. — *adj* **disembod'ied**. — *n* **disembod'iment**. [**dis-** (3).]

disembogue *dis-im-bōg'*, *vt* (usu. *reflexive*) and *vi* (of a river, etc.) to discharge at the mouth (with *into*). — *n* **disembogue'ment**. [Sp. *desembocar* — L. *dis-*, not, *in*, into, *bucca*, mouth.]

disembowel *dis-im-bow'əl*, *vt* to take out the bowels of; to tear out the inside of. — *n* **disembow'elment**. [**dis-** (3).]

disenchant *dis-in-chänt'*, *vt* to free from enchantment, to disillusion. — *n* **disenchant'ment**. [**dis-** (2).]

disencumber *dis-in-kum'bər*, *vt* to free from an encumbrance; to disburden. — *n* **disencum'brance**. [**dis-** (2).]

disendow *dis-in-dow'*, *vt* to take away the endowments of (esp. of an established church). — *adj* **disendowed'**. — *n* **disendow'ment**. [**dis-** (3).]

disenfranchise *dis-in-fran'chīz* or *-shīz*, *vt* to disfranchise; to deprive of suffrage. — *n* **disenfran'chisement** (*-chiz-* or *-shis-*). [**dis-** (2).]

disengage *dis-in-gāj'*, *vt* to free from being engaged; to separate; to set free; to release. — *vi* to come loose. — *adj* **disengaged'** at leisure, without engagement. — *n* **disengage'ment**. [O.Fr. *desengager* — *des-* (L. *dis-*, negative), *engager*, to engage.]

disentail *dis-in-tāl'*, *vt* to break the entail of (an estate); to divest. — *n* the act of disentailing. [**dis-** (2).]

disentangle *dis-in-tang'gl*, *vt* to free from entanglement or disorder; to unravel; to disengage or set free. — *n* **disentang'lement**. [**dis-** (2).]

disentomb *dis-in-tōōm'*, *vt* to take out from a tomb. [**dis-** (2).]

disequilibrium *dis-ek-wi-lib'ri-əm*, *n* lack of balance, esp. in economic affairs: — *pl* **disequilib'ria**. [**dis-** (2).]

disestablish *dis-is-tab'lish*, *vt* to undo the establishment of; to deprive (a church) of established status. — *n* **disestab'lishment**. [**dis-** (2).]

disesteem *dis-is-tēm'*, *n* lack of esteem; disregard. — *vt* to disapprove of; to dislike. [**dis-** (2).]

diseur *dē-zør*, *fem* **diseuse** *dē-zøz*, (Fr.) *n* a reciter or entertainer.

disfavour or in U.S. **disfavor** *dis-fā'vər*, *n* the state of being out of favour or disapproved of; hostility, disapproval or dislike; a disobliging act. — *vt* to be hostile to, to disapprove or oppose. [**dis-** (2).]

disfigure *dis-fig'ər*, *vt* to spoil the appearance of, to blemish or mar; to deface; to deform or distort. — *n* **disfig'urement**. [O.Fr. *desfigurer* — L. *dis-*, not, *figūrāre*, to figure.]

disforest *dis-for'ist*, *vt* to strip of trees, to deforest; to disafforest (*law*). [**dis-** (2).]

disfranchise *dis-fran'chīz* or *-shīz*, *vt* to deprive of a franchise, or of rights and privileges, esp. that of voting for a member of parliament. — *n* **disfran'chisement**. [**dis-** (2).]

disgorge *dis-görj'*, *vt* to eject from the throat; to vomit; to discharge in great volume or with violence; to give up, esp. reluctantly. — *n* **disgorge'ment**. [O.Fr. *desgorger*, *des*, away, *gorge*, throat.]

disgrace *dis-grās'*, *n* the state of being out of favour; a cause of shame, something or someone shameful; disrepute or dishonour. — *vt* to put out of favour; to bring disgrace or shame upon. — *adj* **disgrace'ful** bringing disgrace; causing shame; dishonourable. — *adv* **disgrace'fully**. — *n* **disgrace'fulness**. — *n* **disgra'cer**. — **in disgrace** out of favour; shamed. [Fr. *disgrâce* — L. *dis-*, not, *grātia*, favour, grace.]

disgruntle *dis-grun'tl*, (*colloq*) *vt* to disappoint or displease. — *adj* **disgrun'tled** out of humour, discontented, sulky. — *n* **disgrun'tlement**. [**dis-** (4), and dialectal *gruntle*, to complain.]

disguise *dis-gīz'*, *vt* to change the appearance or character of; to conceal the identity of, e.g. by dress intended to deceive, or by a counterfeit manner and appearance; to mask or hide (facts or feelings); to misrepresent. — *n* dress intended to disguise the wearer; a false appearance; a misleading representation. — *adj* **disguis'able**. — *adj* **disguised'**. — *n*

disguis'er. [O.Fr. *desguisier* — *des-* (L. *dis-*, not), *guise*, manner; see **guise**.]

disgust *dis-gust'*, *n* loathing or extreme disapproval, distaste or annoyance; (*formerly*) distaste, disfavour, displeasure. — *vt* to cause disgust in. — *adj* **disgust'ed**. — *adv* **disgust'edly**. — *n* **disgust'edness**. — *adj* **disgust'ing**. — *adv* **disgust'ingly**. — *n* **disgust'ingness**. — **in disgust** with or because of a feeling of disgust. [O.Fr. *desgouster* — *des-* (L. *dis-*, not) and *gouster* — L. *gustāre*, to taste.]

dish *dish*, *n* a flat or shallow vessel for holding or serving food; a dishful; the food in a dish; food prepared in a particular way for the table; a hollow, a concavity; (also **dish aerial**) a microwave aerial in the form of a parabolic reflector, used for radar or radio telescopes and for satellite broadcast reception; a good-looking person, esp. of the opposite sex (*colloq*). — *vt* to put in a dish, for serving at table; to make concave; to outwit, circumvent (*colloq*); to ruin (*colloq*). — *adj* **dished** having a concavity; (of a pair of wheels on a car, etc.) sloping in towards each other at the top; completely frustrated (*colloq*). — *n* **dish'ful**. — *adj* **dish'y** (*colloq*) good-looking, attractive. — **dish aerial** see **dish** above; **dish'-cloth** a cloth for washing, drying or wiping dishes; **dish'-cover** a cover for a dish to keep its contents hot; **dish'-rag** a dish-cloth; **dish'-towel** a cloth for drying dishes, a tea-towel (esp. *US* and *Can*); **dish'-washer** a machine which washes dishes, cutlery, etc.; a person employed to wash dishes; **dish'-water** water in which dishes have been washed; a liquid deficient in strength or cleanliness. — **dish out** to serve out; to share (food) among several people; to give, give out (*colloq*; usu. *disparagingly*, esp. with *it*, of rough treatment, punishment, etc.); **dish up** to serve up, esp. *fig* of old materials presented anew. [O.E. *disc*, a plate, a dish, a table — L. *discus* — Gr. *diskos*.]

dishabille *dis-ə-bēl'*, *n* careless attention to one's dress, appearance, etc.; a state of undress. — Also **déshabillé** (*dā-zä-bē-yā*). [Fr. *déshabillé*, past p. of *déshabiller*, to undress — *des-* (L. *dis-*), apart, *habiller*, to dress.]

disharmony *dis-här'mə-ni*, *n* lack of harmony; discord; disagreement, dissent; incongruity. — *adj* **disharmonious** (*-mō'*). — *adv* **disharmō'niously**. [**dis-** (2).]

dishearten *dis-härt'n*, *vt* to deprive of courage, or spirits; to discourage or demoralise; to depress. — *adj* **disheart'ened**. — *adj* **disheart'ening**. — *adv* **disheart'eningly**. [**dis-** (2).]

dishevel *di-shev'l*, *vt* to ruffle (hair) or disarrange (clothing): — *pr p* **dishev'elling**; *pa t* and *pa p* **dishev'elled**. — *adj* **dishev'elled** (of a person) untidy or bedraggled in appearance; (of hair) hanging loose, or merely untidy. — *n* **dishev'elment**. [O.Fr. *discheveler* — L. *dis-*, in different directions, *capillus*, the hair.]

dishonest *dis-on'ist*, *adj* not honest; lacking integrity; disposed to cheat; insincere. — *adv* **dishon'estly**. — *n* **dishon'esty**. [O.Fr. *deshoneste*.]

dishonour or in U.S. **dishonor** *dis-on'ər*, *n* lack of respect or honour; disgrace or shame; something that brings discredit; an affront. — *vt* to deprive of honour; to disgrace; to cause shame to; to seduce; to degrade; to refuse the payment of (a cheque). — *adj* **dishon'ourable** or in U.S. **dishon'orable** not in accordance with a sense of honour; disgraceful. — *n* **dishon'ourableness** or in U.S. **dishon'orableness**. — *adv* **dishon'ourably** or in U.S. **dishon'orably**. — *n* **dishon'ourer** or in U.S. **dishon'orer**. — **dishonorable discharge** dismissal from the U.S. armed forces for serious misconduct such as theft or desertion. — **dishonorably discharged**. [O.Fr. *deshonneur*.]

dishorn *dis-hörn'*, *vt* to deprive of horns. [**dis-** (3).]

dishy. See **dish**.

disillusion *dis-i-lōō'zhən* or *-lū'*, *vt* to destroy the illusions of, to disenchant; to disabuse. — *n* disillusionment. — *adj* **disillu'sioned** disenchanted, disabused of an illusion; often, bereft of comfortable beliefs whether they were false or true. — *n* **disillu'sionment**. [**dis-** (3).]

disincentive *dis-in-sen'tiv*, *n* a discouragement to effort; a deterrent. — Also *adj*. [**dis-** (2).]

disinclination *dis-in-kli-nā'shən*, *n* lack of inclination; unwillingness. — *vt* **disincline** (*-klīn'*) to render unwilling, reluctant or averse. — *adj* **disinclined'** not inclined; averse. [**dis-** (2).]

disincorporate *dis-in-kör'pə-rāt*, *vt* to deprive of corporate rights. — *n* **disincorporā'tion**. [**dis-** (2).]

disinfect *dis-in-fekt'*, *vt* to rid of disease-causing bacteria, etc. by cleaning, esp. with a chemical. — *n* **disinfect'ant** a chemical, etc. that destroys bacteria. — Also *adj*. — *n* **disinfec'tion**. — *n* **disinfect'or**. [**dis-** (2).]

disinfest *dis-in-fest'*, *vt* to rid (a place, animal, etc.) of vermin. — *n* **disinfestā'tion**. [**dis-** (2).]

disinflation *dis'in-flā-shən*, (*econ*) *n* return to the normal condition after inflation; deflation which reduces or stops inflation. — *adj* **disinflā'tionary**. [**dis-** (2).]

disinformation *dis-in-fər-mā'shən*, *n* deliberate leakage of misleading information. [**dis-** (2).]

disingenuous *dis-in-jen'ū-əs*, *adj* not ingenuous; not frank or open; crafty, devious. — *adv* **disingen'uously**. — *n* **disingen'uousness**. [**dis-** (2).]

disinherit *dis-in-her'it*, *vt* to cut off from hereditary rights; to deprive of an inheritance. — *n* **disinher'itance**. [**dis-** (3).]

disintegrate *dis-in'ti-grāt*, *vt* and *vi* to separate into parts; to break up; to crumble. — *n* **disintegrā'tion** the act or state of disintegrating; a process in which a nucleus ejects one or more particles, esp. in spontaneous radioactive decay (*nuc*). — *n* **disin'tegrātor** a machine for crushing or pulverising. [**dis-** (1).]

disinter *dis-in-tûr'*, *vt* to remove from a grave or from the earth; to dig up or bring to light; to bring out of obscurity: — *pr p* **disinterr'ing**; *pa t* and *pa p* **disinterred'**. — *n* **disinter'ment**. [**dis-** (2).]

disinterest *dis-in'tər-ist*, *n* impartiality, freedom from prejudice; lack of interest, unconcern. — *vt* to free from interest. — *adj* **disin'terested** not influenced by private feelings or considerations; not deriving personal advantage; impartial; unselfish, generous; (revived from obsolescence) uninterested. — *adv* **disin'terestedly**. — *n* **disin'terestedness**. [**dis-** (2).]

disinvest *dis-in-vest'*, *vi* and *vt* to remove investment (from; with *in*). — *n* **disinvest'ment**. [**dis-** (2).]

disjoin *dis-join'*, *vt* and *vi* to separate, disconnect. [O.Fr. *desjoindre* — L. *disjungĕre* — *dis-*, apart, *jungĕre*, to join.]

disjoint *disjoint'*, *vt* and *vi* to disconnect or come apart at the joints; to dislocate or disunite. — *adj* **disjoint'ed** (of discourse, a narrative, etc.) incoherent; lacking connection or continuity; separated at the joints. — *adv* **disjoint'edly**. — *n* **disjoint'edness**. [O.Fr. *desjoinct* — *desjoindre*, to disjoin.]

disjunct *dis-jungkt'*, also *dis'jungkt*, *adj* disjoined. — *n* (*logic*) one of the propositions in a disjunction; a disjunctive proposition. — *n* **disjunc'tion** the act of disjoining; disunion; separation; a compound statement comprising propositions connected by an element denoting 'or' (*logic*). — *adj* **disjunct'ive** disjoining; tending to separate; (of conjunctions) indicating an alternative or opposition (*gram*); relating to, containing, forming, or being part of, a disjunction (*logic*). — *n* a disjunctive word or element. — *adv* **disjunct'ively**. — *n* **disjunct'ure** disjunction. [O.Fr. *desjoinct* — *desjoindre*, to disjoin.]

disk *disk*, *n* a disc (esp. *US*); a magnetic disc (*comput*). — *n* **diskette'** (*comput*) a small floppy magnetic disk. — **disk capacity** (*comput*) the amount of storage space on a disk; **disk drive** a computer peripheral with a head that records data on, and retrieves data from, disks; **disk file** or **store** (*comput*) a random access device consisting of disks coated with magnetisable material, on which data is stored in tracks. — **disk operating system** (abbrev. **DOS**) software that manages the storage and retrieval of information on disk on personal computers.

dislike *dis-līk'*, *vt* to have an aversion to, to find unpleasant or disagreeable; to disapprove of. — *n* aversion; disapproval; distaste. — *adj* **dislike'able** or **dislī'kable**. [**dis-** (2) and **like²**.]

dislocate *dis'lō-kāt*, *vt* to displace (a bone) from its joint, to put out of joint; to disrupt, disorganise or disturb. — *adv* **dis'locatedly**. — *n* **dislocā'tion** a dislocated joint; displacement; disorganisation; derangement (of traffic, plans, etc.); a fault (*geol*). [L.L. *dislocāre*, *-ātum* — L. *dis-*, apart, *locāre*, to place.]

dislodge *dis-loj'*, *vt* to prise, knock or force out of position; to drive from a place of hiding or of defence. — *n* **dislodge'ment** or **dislodg'ment**. [O.Fr. *desloger* — *des-*, apart, *loger*, to lodge.]

disloyal *dis-loi'əl*, *adj* not loyal; unfaithful. — *adv* **disloy'ally**. — *n* **disloy'alty**. [O.Fr. *desloyal* — L. *dis-*, not, *lēgālis*, legal.]

dismal *diz'məl*, *adj* gloomy; dreary; sorrowful; lugubrious; depressing. — *adv* **dis'mally**. — *n* **dis'malness**. — **dismal Jimmy** an uncompromising pessimist. [O.Fr. *dismal* — L. *diēs malī*, evil, unlucky days.]

dismantle *dis-man'tl*, *vt* to pull down, take to bits; to demolish; to undo the structure of (an organisation, etc.), in consequence of a decision to terminate it; to raze the fortifications of; to strip of furniture, fittings or equipment. — *n* **disman'tlement**. — *n* **disman'tler**. [O.Fr. *desmanteller* — *des-*, away, *mantel*, a mantle.]

dismast *dis-mäst'*, *vt* to topple the mast or masts of (a sailing ship). [**dis-** (3).]

dismay *dis-* or *diz-mā'*, *vt* to appal or alarm; to discourage. — *n* alarm or consternation. — *adj* **dismay'ing**. [App. through O.Fr. — L. *dis-*, not, and O.H.G. *magan*, to have might or power.]

dismember *dis-mem'bər*, *vt* to cut up or tear (a body) limb from limb; to tear to pieces; to divide up, break up. — *n* **dismem'berment**. [O.Fr. *desmembrer*.]

dismiss *dis-mis'*, *vt* to send away or allow to go; to discharge from employment, to sack; to discard, dispose of (a suggestion, topic, etc.); to reject, to put out of court (a case or claim) (*law*); to put out (a batsman or a team) for a stated number of runs (*cricket*). — *vi* (*imper*) as a military command, to fall out. — *n* **dismiss'al**. — *adj* **dismiss'ible**. — *adj* **dismiss'ive**. [**dis-** (3) and L. *mittěre*, *missum*, to send; L. *dimissus*.]

dismount *dis-mownt'*, *vi* to get down from a horse, bicycle, etc. — *vt* to remove from a stand, framework, setting, etc. [O.Fr. *desmonter*.]

Disneyesque *diz-ni-esk'*, *adj* in the style of the characters, etc. appearing in the cartoon films of Walt *Disney* (1901–66), American cartoonist and film producer; fantastical, whimsical, unreal. — *vt* **Dis'neyfy** to present or process the history of, or facts concerning (a site, etc.) by means of video films or other visual aids, esp. simplistically for the convenience of the tourist, instead of encouraging exposure to the actual environment: — *pr p* **Dis'neyfying**; *pa t* and *pa p* **Dis'neyfied**. — *n* **Disneyficā'tion**.

disobedient *dis-ō-bēd'yənt*, *adj* neglecting or refusing to obey. — *n* **disobed'ience**. — *adv* **disobed'iently**. [**dis-** (2).]

disobey *dis-ə-bā'*, *vt* and *vi* to neglect or refuse to obey. [O.Fr. *desobeir* — *des-*, not, *obeir*, to obey.]

disoblige *dis-ə-blīj'*, *vt* to refuse or fail to oblige; to disregard the wishes of; to offend or injure thereby; to inconvenience (*colloq*). — *adj* **disoblīg'ing** not obliging; not careful to attend to the wishes of others; unaccommodating; unkind. — *adv* **disoblīg'ingly**. — *n* **disoblīg'ingness**. [**dis-** (2).]

disorder *dis-ör'dər*, *n* lack of order; a state of confusion; disturbance among the public, crowd violence, rioting, etc.; a malfunctioning of the body, an ailment or illness. — *vt* to disarrange, reduce to confusion; to disturb the balance of (the mind, etc.); to disturb the health of, produce disease in. — *adj* **disor'dered** confused, deranged. — *n* **disor'derliness**. — *adj* **disor'derly** untidy, in a state of confusion; irregular; lawless, unruly; causing a disturbance of the peace (*law*). — **disorderly conduct** (*law*) any of several minor infringements of the law likely to cause a breach of the peace; **disorderly house** a brothel or gambling establishment, in either of which disorderly behaviour might be expected. [O.Fr. *desordre* — *des-*, not, *ordre*, order.]

disorganise or **-ize** *dis-ör'gən-īz*, *vt* to disarrange or disrupt; to disturb the system or structure of. — *adj* **disor'ganised** or **-z-** disordered; unsystematic, muddled. — *n* **disorganisā'tion** or **-z-**. [**dis-** (2).]

disorient *dis-ö'ri-ənt*, *vt* to confuse as to direction, cause (someone) to lose his or her bearings. — Also **diso'rientate**. — *n* **disorientā'tion**. [**dis-** (2).]

disown *dis-ōn'*, *vt* to refuse to own or acknowledge as belonging to oneself; to deny any connection with; to repudiate. — *n* **disown'er**. — *n* **disown'ment**. [**dis-** (2).]

disparage *dis-par'ij*, *vt* to talk slightingly of, to belittle. — *n* **dispar'agement**. — *n* **dispar'ager**. — *adv* **dispar'agingly**. [O.Fr. *desparager* — *des-* (negative) and *parage*, equality, rank.]

disparate *dis'pər-it* or *-āt*, *adj* essentially unalike, and therefore incapable of being compared. — *n* (in *pl*) things too unalike to be compared. — *adv* **dis'parately**. — *n* **dis'parateness**. [L. *disparātus* — *dis-*, not, *parāre*, to make ready; infl. by *dispar*, unequal.]

disparity *dis-par'i-ti*, *n* inequality; unlikeness so great as to render comparison difficult and union unsuitable. [L. *dispar*, unequal — *dis-*, not, *par*, equal.]

dispassionate *dis-pash'ə-nət*, *adj* calm, cool, unemotional; not affected by personal feelings, unprejudiced, fair, impartial. — *adv* **dispass'ionately**. [**dis-** (2).]

dispatch or **despatch** *dis-pach'*, *vt* to send off (mail, a person to do a task, etc.); to kill or put to death; to dispose of; to perform or deal with speedily. — *n* the sending away of mail, a messenger, etc.; dismissal; rapid performance of a task, etc.; haste, promptitude; death, e.g. by execution or murder; that which is dispatched, as a message, esp. telegraphic; (in *pl*) state papers or other official papers (diplomatic, military, etc.). — *n* **dispatch'er**. — **dispatch'-box** or **-case** a box or case for holding dispatches or valuable papers; **dispatch'-rider** a carrier of dispatches, on horseback or motorcycle. — **mentioned in dispatches** as a distinction, commended in official military dispatches for bravery, etc. [It. *dispacciare* or Sp. *despachar* — L. *dis-*, apart, and root of *pangěre*, *pactum*, to fasten.]

dispel *dis-pel'*, *vt* to drive away and scatter; to cause to disappear: — *pr p* **dispell'ing**; *pa t* and *pa p* **dispelled'**. [L. *dispellěre* — *dis-*, away, *pellěre*, to drive.]

dispensable, dispensary and **dispensation**. See **dispense**.

dispense *dis-pens'*, *vt* to deal out or distribute; to administer (justice, etc.); to make up (medicine) for distributing or administering. — *adj* **dispen'sable** able to be dispensed with, expendable, inessential;

able to be dispensed. — *n* **dispensabil'ity**. — *n* **dispen'sableness**. — *n* **dispen'sary** a place where medicines, etc. are dispensed and medical care given, e.g. in a hospital or school; a charitable organisation for dispensing medicine and medical advice. — *n* **dispensā'tion** the act of dispensing or dealing out; administration (of justice, etc.); licence or permission to neglect a rule, esp. of church law in the Roman Catholic Church; the regulation or ordering of events by God, Providence or nature; a divinely-ordained religious system specific to a community or period. — *adj* **dispen'satory** granting dispensation. — *n* a directory listing the composition, application and uses of medical drugs. — *n* **dispens'er** a person who dispenses, esp. a pharmacist who dispenses medicines; a container or machine that gives out a commodity in prearranged quantities. — **dispense with** to disregard, forgo or waive; to do without. [Fr. *dispenser* — L. *dis-*, not, pēnsāre, to weigh.]

disperse *dis-pûrs'*, *vt* to scatter in all directions; to spread; to diffuse; to drive asunder; to cause to vanish, to dissipate; to suspend (particles) in a medium so as to form a colloid (*phys*). — *vi* to separate; to spread abroad; to vanish. — *n* **disper'sal** dispersion; distribution; the spread of a species to new areas. — *n* **disper'sant** a substance that effects dispersion. — *adv* **dispers'edly**. — *n* **dispers'edness**. — *n* **dispers'er**. — *n* **dispersion** (*dis-pûr'shən*) a scattering, or state or process of being scattered; the removal of inflammation (*med*); the spreading out of rays owing to different refrangibility (*phys*); the range of deviation of values of a variable from the average (*statistics*); the state of a finely divided colloid; a substance in that state; the diaspora. — *adj* **disper'sive** tending or serving to disperse. [L. *dīspergĕre*, *dīspersum* — *dī-*, asunder, apart, *spargĕre*, to scatter.]

dispirit *dis-pir'it*, *vt* to dishearten; to discourage. — *adj* **dispir'ited** dejected, discouraged. — *adv* **dispir'itedly**. — *n* **dispir'itedness**. — *adj* **dispir'iting** disheartening. — *adv* **dispir'itingly**. [**dis-** (2).]

displace *dis-plās'*, *vt* to put out of place; to disarrange; to remove from an office or post; to supplant, replace or supersede. — *adj* **displace'able**. — *n* **displace'ment** a putting or being out of place; a supplanting or superseding; the difference between the position of a body at a given time and that occupied at first; the quantity of water displaced by a ship afloat or an immersed body; the disguising of emotional feelings by unconscious transference from one object to another (*psychol*). — **displaced person** a person forced from his or her country by war, revolution, persecution or oppression, a refugee or stateless person. [O.Fr. *desplacer* — *des-* (negative) and *place*, place.]

display *dis-plā'*, *vt* to unfold or spread out; to exhibit; to set out ostentatiously; to present (advertising copy, etc.) in an eye-catching way (*printing*). — *n* a displaying or unfolding; an exhibition or demonstration; presentation of advertising copy, etc. so as to attract attention, through appropriate deployment of typefaces, use of space, etc. (*printing*); ostentatious show; an animal's or bird's behaviour when courting, threatening intruders, etc., in which the crest is raised, feathers spread, etc.; the 'picture' on a cathode-ray tube screen making the information visible (*electronics*). — *adj* **displayed'**. — *n* **display'er**. [O.Fr. *despleier* — *des-* (negative) and *plier*, *ploier* — L. *plicāre*, to fold.]

displease *dis-plēz'*, *vt* to offend; to annoy, irritate; to be disagreeable to. — *vi* to raise aversion. — *adj* **displeased'** vexed, annoyed. — *adj* **displeas'ing** disagreeable; giving offence. — *adv* **displeas'ingly**. — *n* **displeas'ingness**. — *n* **displeasure** (*dis-plezh'ər*) the condition of feeling displeased; anger, annoyance; a cause of irritation. [O.Fr. *desplaisir* — *des-* (negative) and *plaisir*, to please.]

disport *dis-pört'*, (*literary*) *vt* (usu. *reflexive*) to divert or amuse (oneself). — *vi* to play about, frolic or gambol. [O.Fr. (*se*) *desporter*, to carry (oneself) away from one's work, to amuse (oneself) — L. *dis-*, away, *portāre*, to carry.]

dispose *dis-pōz'*, *vt* to arrange or settle; to distribute, place in order, or arrange in position; to incline (with *to* or *towards*). — *vi* to ordain what is to be. — See also **dispose of** below. — *n* **disposabil'ity**. — *adj* **dispō'sable** able to be disposed of; intended to be thrown away or destroyed after use; (of assets, etc.) available for one's use. — *n* a product intended for disposal after use. — *n* **dispō'sal** the act of disposing of or dealing with something; arrangement, disposition, deployment; the act or process of getting rid of something; the act of bestowing, transferring or assigning property, etc. — *adj* **disposed'** inclined; liable, having a tendency (with *to*); (used after *well*, *ill*, *kindly*, etc.) having friendly, unfriendly, etc. feelings (with *to* or *towards*). — *n* **dispō'ser**. — **disposable income** one's net income after tax has been paid, available for spending, saving, investing, etc. — **at one's disposal** at one's service, available for one's use; under one's management or control, to deploy as one wishes; **dispose of** to deal with, esp. finally and decisively; to sell, transfer, part with or give away; to get rid of or throw away; to prove (an adversary, argument or claim) wrong; to consume (food, etc.), esp. in haste; to kill. [Fr. *disposer* — *dis-*, apart, *poser*, to place — L. *pausāre*, to pause, (later) to place.]

disposition *dis-pə-zish'ən*, *n* an arrangement, deployment or distribution; a natural tendency or inclination; temperament, personality; the act of, or a scheme for, dealing with affairs, etc., bestowing or assigning property, etc. [Fr., — L., from *dis-*, apart, *pōnĕre*, *positum*, to place.]

dispossess *dis-pə-zes'*, *vt* to deprive of property, land, etc. — *adj* **dispossessed'** deprived of possessions, property, etc.; deprived of one's home, country or rights. — *n* **dispossession** (*dis-pə-zesh'ən*). — *n* **dispossess'or**. [**dis-** (2).]

dispraise *dis-prāz'*, *n* the expression of an unfavourable opinion; blame, reproach. — *vt* to blame or censure. [O.Fr. *despreisier* — *des-* (negative) and *preisier*, to praise.]

disproof *dis-prōōf'*, *n* the disproving of something; evidence or argumentation that disproves something, refutation. [**dis-** (2).]

disproportion *dis-prə-pör'shən*, *n* lack of appropriate proportion; lack of balance, symmetry or equality. — *adj* **dispropor'tional**. — *adv* **dispropor'tionally**. — *adj* **dispropor'tionate** out of proportion; not of the appropriate size or amount (usu. too large or too much) in relation to something. — *adv* **dispropor'tionately**. — *n* **dispropor'tionateness**. [**dis-** (2).]

disprove *dis-prōōv'*, *vt* to prove to be false or wrong: — *pa p* **disproved'** or **disproven** (*-prō'vən* or *-prōō'vən*). — *adj* **dispro'vable**. — *n* **dispro'val**. [O.Fr. *desprover*; see **prove**.]

dispute *dis-pūt'*, *vt* to argue about; to contend for, fight or quarrel over; to call in question or oppose by argument. — *vi* to argue or debate (with *about* or *over*). — *n* an argument; a debate; a quarrel. — *adj* **dis'putable** (also *-pū'tə-bl*) that may be called in question; of doubtful certainty. — *n* **disputabil'ity** or **dis'putableness**. — *adv* **dis'putably**. — *n* **dis'putant** a contestant in a debate, or party in an argument. — *adj* engaged in debate or argument. — *n* **dispu'ter**. — *n* **disputā'tion**. — *adj* **disputā'tious** or **dispu'tative** inclined to dispute, cavil or controvert. — *adv* **disputā'tiously** or **disput'atively**. — n **disputā'tiousness** or **dispu'tativeness**. — **beyond, past** or **without dis-**

pute indubitably, certainly; **in dispute** being debated or contested. [O.Fr. *desputer* — L. *disputāre* — *dis-*, apart, *putāre*, to think.]

disqualify *dis-kwol'i-fī, vt* to render or declare unsuitable, unfit or unable to do a particular thing; to debar: — *pr p* **disqual'ifying**; *pa p* and *pa t* **disqual'ified**. — *adj* **disqualifī'able**. — *n* **disqualificā'tion** the act of disqualifying or state of being disqualified; anything that disqualifies or incapacitates. [**dis-** (3).]

disquiet *dis-kwī'ət, n* uneasiness, restlessness; anxiety. — *vt* to make uneasy or anxious; to disturb or upset. - *adj* **disquī'eting**. — *adv* **disquī'etingly**. — *n* **disquī'etude** a feeling of anxiety or unease. [**dis-** (2).]

disquisition *dis-kwi-zish'ən, n* a carefully or minutely argued examination of a topic; an essay. — *adj* **disquisi'tional** or **disquisi'tionary** pertaining to or of the nature of a disquisition. [L. *disquīsītiō, -ōnis* — *dis-* (intensive) and *quaerěre*, to seek.]

disrate *dis-rāt'*, (*naut*) *vt* to reduce (e.g. a petty officer) to a lower rating or rank. [**dis-** (3).]

disregard *dis-ri-gärd', vt* to pay no attention to; to ignore; to dismiss as unworthy of attention. — *n* lack of attention; neglect; lack of respect. — *adj* **disregard'ful**. — *adv* **disregard'fully**. [**dis-** (2).]

disrelish *dis-rel'ish, vt* not to relish; to dislike. — *n* distaste, dislike or disgust. [**dis-** (2).]

disremember *dis-ri-mem'bər*, (*dialect* or *US colloq*) *vt* to fail to remember or recall, to forget. [**dis-** (2).]

disrepair *dis-ri-pār', n* a worn-out or dilapidated condition; an unsatisfactory working condition; the state of needing to be repaired. [**dis-** (2).]

disrepute *dis-ri-pūt', n* bad repute; discredit. — *adj* **disrep'utable** unreliable or untrustworthy; disgraceful; not respectable; shabby, dingy, not presentable. — *n* **disrep'utableness**. — *adv* **disrep'utably**. [**dis-** (2).]

disrespect *dis-ri-spekt', n* lack of respect; discourtesy; incivility. — *adj* **disrespect'ful** showing disrespect; irreverent; uncivil. — *adv* **disrespect'fully**. — *n* **disrespect'fulness**. [**dis-** (2).]

disrobe *dis-rōb'*, (esp. *literary*) *vt* and *vi* to take robes off; to undress. — *vt* to remove the covering or concealment from; to divest of authority. [**dis-** (2), (3).]

disrupt *dis-rupt', vt* and *vi* to interrupt (growth, progress, etc.); to upset or throw into disorder or confusion; to split or burst. — *n* **disrupt'er** or **disrupt'or**. — *n* **disrup'tion** interruption, disturbance or upheaval; a breach, division or split; (with *cap*) in Scottish ecclesiastical history, the separation of the Free Church from the Established Church for the sake of spiritual independence (1843). — *adj* **disrup'tive** having an upsetting or unsettling effect; obstreperous, unruly. — *adv* **disrupt'ively**. [L. *disruptus, dīruptus* — *dīrumpěre* — *dis-*, apart, *rumpěre*, to break.]

diss[1] *dis, n* an Algerian reedy grass used for cordage, etc. [Ar. *dīs*.]

diss[2] *dis*, (*rapper slang*) *vt* to reject or dismiss with contempt. [App. abbrev. of **disrespect**.]

dissatisfy *dis-sat'is-fī, vt* to fail to satisfy; to disappoint; to make discontented; to displease. — *n* **dissatisfac'tion**. — *adj* **dissat'isfied** discontented; not pleased. [**dis-** (2).]

dissect *di-sekt', vt* to cut into small pieces; to cut (a dead animal or plant) into parts for the purpose of minute examination; to analyse or criticise minutely. — *adj* **dissect'ed** deeply cut into narrow segments (*bot*); cut up by valleys (*geol*). — *adj* **dissect'ible**. — *n* **dissec'tion** the act or the art of cutting in pieces a plant or animal in order to ascertain the structure of its parts. — *n* **dissect'or**. — **dissecting microscope** a form of microscope that allows dissection of the object under examination; **dissecting room** or **table** a room in which, or table on which, anatomical dissection is practised. [L. *dissecāre, dissectum* — *dis-*, apart, *secāre*, to cut.]

disseise or **disseize** *dis-sēz'*, (*law*) *vt* to dispossess, esp. wrongfully. — *n* **disseis'in** or **disseiz'in** wrongful dispossession. [**dis-** (3).]

disselboom *dis'əl-bōōm*, (*SAfr*) *n* the single shaft of an ox-wagon or other cart or wagon. [Du. *dissel*, shaft, *boom*, beam.]

dissemble *di-sem'bl, vt* to disguise or mask (one's true feelings or character). — *vi* to pretend; to assume a false appearance; to play the hypocrite; to dissimulate. — *n* **dissem'blance**. — *n* **dissem'bler**. [L. *dissimulāre* — *dissimilis*, unlike — *dis-*, not, *similis*, like.]

disseminate *di-sem'i-nāt, vt* to sow or scatter abroad; to propagate; to diffuse. — *adj* scattered. — *n* **disseminā'tion**. — *n* **dissem'inātor**. — **disseminated sclerosis** an older name for **multiple sclerosis**. [L. *dissēminare, -ātum* — *dis-*, apart, *sēminare*, to sow.]

dissent *di-sent', vi* not to assent; to disagree, to differ (with *from*); to break away from an established church and adopt new religious beliefs or practices. — *n* the act of dissenting; difference of opinion; a protest by a minority; a differing or separation from an established church. — *n* **dissen'sion** disagreement; discord; strife. — *n* **dissent'er** someone who disagrees; (with *cap*) someone, esp. a Protestant, who refuses to conform to the established church, a nonconformist. — *adj* **dissen'tient** (*-shənt*) declaring dissent; disagreeing. — *n* a person who disagrees; a person who declares his or her dissent. — *adj* **dissent'ing**. — *adv* **dissent'ingly**. [L. *dissentīre, dissēnsum* — *dis-*, apart, *sentīre*, to think.]

dissepiment *di-sep'i-mənt*, (*bot* and *zool*) *n* a septum, a partition. — *adj* **dissepimental** (*-ment'l*). [L. *dissaepīmentum*, a partition.]

dissertation *dis-ər-tā'shən, n* a formal discourse; a treatise. — *adj* **dissertā'tional**. [L. *dissertāre*, intensive of *disserěre*, to discuss.]

disservice *dis-sûr'vis, n* injury, sometimes done in an attempt to help; mischief; a bad turn. [O.Fr. *desservir* — L. *dis-*, not, *servīre*, to serve.]

dissever *di-sev'ər, vt* and *vi* to sever; to part in two; to separate. — *n* **dissev'erance, disseverā'tion** or **dissev'erment**. — *adj* **dissev'ered**. [O.Fr. *dessevrer* — L. *dis-*, apart, *sēparāre*, to separate.]

dissident *dis'i-dənt, adj* dissenting. — *n* a dissenter, esp. one who disagrees with the aims and procedures of the government. — *n* **diss'idence** disagreement. [L. *dissidēns, -entis*, pres. p. of *dissidēre* — *dis-*, apart, *sedēre*, to sit.]

dissimilar *di-sim'il-ər, adj* not similar; unalike, different. — *n* **dissimilarity** (*-ar'*). — *adv* **dissim'ilarly**. [**dis-** (2).]

dissimilate *di-sim'i-lāt, vi* and *vt* (esp. of sounds, *philol*) to become or make dissimilar. — *n* **dissimilā'tion** the process of becoming or rendering dissimilar; katabolism. [**dis-** (2).]

dissimilitude *dis-i-mil'i-tūd, n* the quality of being unalike, dissimilarity. [**dis-** (2).]

dissimulate *di-sim'ū-lāt, vt* to conceal or disguise (one's real feelings, etc.), to dissemble. — *vi* to practise dissimulation, play the hypocrite. — *n* **dissimulā'tion**. — *n* **dissim'ulātor**. [L. *dissimulāre, -ātum*, to dissimulate — *dis-*, not, *similis*, like.]

dissipate *dis'i-pāt, vt* to scatter or disperse; to squander; to waste; to dispel. — *vi* to separate or disperse, and disappear; to waste away. — *adj* **diss'ipated** dissolute, intemperate, indulging unrestrainedly in frivolous pleasure. — *adv* **diss'ipatedly**. — *n* **dissipā'tion** intemperate, extravagant or dissolute living; the process of dissipating or being dissipated; the wasteful spending of something. — *adj* **diss'ipātive** tending to dissipate or disperse. [L. *dissipāre*, *-ātum* — *dis-*, apart, *supāre*, to throw.]

dissociate *di-sō'shi-āt* or *-si-āt*, *vt* to separate; to treat or regard as separate and distinct; (*reflexive*) to distance (oneself), declare (oneself) to be unconnected with something (with *from*). — *vi* and *vt* to undergo or subject to dissociation. — *n* **dissociā'tion** (*-sō-shi-* or *-sō-si-*) the act of dissociating or process or state of being dissociated; separation into simpler constituents, esp. a reversible separation caused by heat, or separation into ions (*chem*); the splitting off from consciousness of certain ideas and their accompanying emotions, leading to fragmentation of the personality into independent identities, as in cases of split or multiple personality (*psychol*). — *adj* **dissō'ciative**. [L. *dissociāre*, *-ātum* — *dis-*, apart, *sociāre*, to associate.]

dissoluble *dis-ol'ū-bl*, *adj* capable of being dissolved, soluble. — *n* **dissolūbil'ity**. [L. *dissolūbilis* — *dissolvěre*, to dissolve.]

dissolute *dis'ə-lōōt* or *-lūt*, *adj* loose, esp. in morals, debauched, intemperate, licentious. — *n* a dissolute person. — *adv* **diss'olutely**. — *n* **diss'oluteness**. [L. *dissolūtus*, lax — *dissolvěre*, to loosen.]

dissolution *dis-ə-lōō'shən* or *-lū'shən*, *n* break-up, disintegration into parts; decay and death; the annulment or ending of a partnership or relationship; the dispersal of an assembly, as of Parliament before an election. [L. *dissolūtiō*, *-ōnis*, a breaking-up — *dissolvěre*.]

dissolve *di-zolv'*, *vt* and *vi* to (cause to) go into solution; to (cause to) become liquid, to melt; to separate or break up, and disperse; to terminate or dismiss (an assembly, such as Parliament) or be terminated or dismissed. — *vt* to annul or terminate (e.g. a partnership or marriage). — *vi* to collapse or subside emotionally, e.g. into tears; to fade away; to fade out one scene gradually while replacing it with another (also *n*; *cinema* and *TV*). — *n* **dissolvabil'ity**. — *adj* **dissol'vable**. — *n* **dissol'vent** a less common word for solvent. — *adj* having power to dissolve or disperse. [L. *dissolvěre* — *dis-*, apart, *solvěre*, *-ūtum*, to loose.]

dissonant *dis'ə-nənt*, *adj* (of sounds, esp. musical) discordant, inharmonious; jarring, clashing, incompatible, conflicting, contradictory or incongruous. — *n* **diss'onance** or **diss'onancy** (a chord or interval containing) a combination of sounds that calls for resolution (*mus*); discordancy, disharmony; incongruity, incompatibility, disagreement. — *adv* **diss'onantly**. [L. *dissonāns*, *-antis* — *dis-*, apart, *sonāre*, to sound.]

dissuade *di-swād'*, *vt* to deter, esp. through advice or argument, to persuade not to do something (with *from*). — *n* **dissuā'der**. — *n* **dissuā'sion** (*-zhən*). — *adj* **dissuā'sive** (*-siv*) tending to dissuade. — *adv* **dissuā'sively**. [L. *dissuādēre* — *dis-*, apart, *suādēre*, *suāsum*, to advise.]

dissyllable. A variant of **disyllable**.

dissymmetry *dis-sim'i-tri*, *n* lack of symmetry; the symmetry of an object and its mirror-image, or of the right and left hands, etc., enantiomorphy. — *adj* **dissymmetric** or **dissymetrical** (*-et'*). — *adv* **dissymmet'rically**. [**dis-** (2).]

distaff *dis'täf*, *n* the stick that holds the bunch of flax, tow or wool in spinning; women's work (*literary*). — **distaff side** the female part, line, side, or branch of a family or descent, the male equivalent being the *spear-side*. [O.E. *distæf*, from the root found in L.G. *diesse*, the bunch of flax on the staff; and *stæf*, staff.]

distal *dis'təl*, *adj* farthest from the point of attachment (opp. to *proximal*; *anat* and *zool*); farthest from the centre (opp. to *mesial*; *dentistry*). — *adv* **dis'tally**. [Formed from **distance** on the analogy of *central*.]

Distalgesic® *dis-tal-jē'zik*, *n* a pain-killing drug in tablet form, containing paracetamol. [*Dis*tillers' Co. Ltd and an*algesic*.]

distance *dis'təns*, *n* the gap or interval between two points in space or time; the extent of such a gap or interval; remoteness or separation in space or time; a remote place or time; the remotest part of one's field of vision, or the equivalent part in a picture; progress, headway; aloofness of manner; the scheduled duration of a boxing match, etc.; in horse-racing, a point 240 yards back from the winning post (*Br*), or a final stretch of the course (*US*), which a horse, in heat-races, must reach by the time the winner has covered the whole course, in order to run in the final heat. — *adj* (*athletics*) (of races) over a long distance. — *vt* to place at a distance; to hold (oneself) aloof (with *from*); to leave at a distance behind. — **distance education** or **teaching** the provision of educational courses, e.g. by television or correspondence course, for students unable to attend in person the educational institution concerned; **distance learning** the following of such educational courses; **middle distance** the part of a scene between the foreground and the furthest part. — **go the distance** to complete what one has started (*colloq*); to endure to the end of a (boxing, etc.) bout; **keep someone at a distance** to treat someone with aloofness; **keep one's distance** to abstain from familiarity, to keep aloof. [L. *dīstantia*, distance — *dīstans*, as **distant**.]

distant *dis'tənt*, *adj* at a certain distance; at a great distance; remote, in time, place, resemblance or connection; indistinct; reserved or aloof in manner. — *adv* **dis'tantly**. — *n* **dis'tantness**. [Fr., — L. *dīstāns*, *-antis* — *dī-*, apart, *stāns*, *stantis*, pres. p. of *stāre*, to stand.]

distaste *dis-tāst'*, *n* disrelish, repugnance or dislike (with *for*). — *adj* **distaste'ful** unpleasant, unpalatable or disagreeable. — *n* **distaste'fulness**. [**dis-** (2).]

distemper[1] *dis-temp'ər*, *n* a mode of painting in size, water glass, or other watery medium giving body to the pigment; paint of this kind for indoor walls, stage, scenery, etc. — *vt* to paint in distemper. [L. *dis-* (reversal) and *temperāre*, to regulate, mix in proportion.]

distemper[2] *dis-temp'ər*, *n* any of several infectious diseases affecting animals, esp. a viral illness (**canine distemper**) of dogs, foxes, ferrets and mink. [Archaically, a bodily or mental ailment, — O.Fr. *destemprer*, to derange — L. *dis-*, apart, *temperāre*, to regulate.]

distend *dis-tend'*, *vt* and *vi* to swell up, expand, inflate, (as though) as a result of increasing internal pressure. — *n* **distensibil'ity**. — *adj* **disten'sible**. — *n* **disten'sion**. [L. *distenděre* — *dis-*, apart, *tenděre*, *tēnsum* or *tentum*, to stretch.]

distich *dis'tik*, (*prosody*) *n* two lines of verse forming a unit complete in sense, a couplet. — *adj* **dis'tichous** (*bot*) arranged in, or having, two opposite vertical rows. [Gr. *distichos* — *di-*, twice, *stichos*, a line.]

distil or in U.S. **distill** *dis-til'*, *vi* to fall in drops; to flow gently; to evaporate and condense again; to use a still. — *vt* to let fall or cause to fall in drops; to convert from liquid into vapour by heat, and then to condense again; to extract as an essence or concentrate by evaporation and condensation; to accumulate or amass little by little in pure form (*fig*); to reduce to essentials by sorting and sifting (*fig*): — *pr p* **distill'ing**; *pa t* and *pa p* **distilled'**. — *adj* **distill'able**. — *n* **dis'tilland** that which is to be, or is being, distilled. — *n* **dis'tillāte** the product of distillation. — *n* **distillā'tion** the process of distilling. — *adj* **distill'atory** of or for distilling. — *n* **distill'er**. — *n* **distill'ery** a place where distilling, esp. of alcoholic spirits, is carried on. — **destructive distillation** the collection of volatile matters released when a substance is destroyed by heat in a close vessel (as coal is in making gas); **fractional distillation** the separation by distilling of liquids having different boiling-points, the heat being gradually increased and the collecting vessel changed; **vacuum distillation** distillation under reduced pressure (effecting a lowering of the boiling-point). [O.Fr. *distiller* — L. *dēstillāre*, *-ātum* — *dē*, down, *stillāre*, to drop — *stilla*, a drop.]

distinct *dis-tingkt'*, *adj* separate; different; well-defined; clear; definite, unmistakable. — *adv* **distinct'ly** clearly; definitely, unmistakably. — *n* **distinct'ness**. [L. *dīstinctus*, separate.]

distinction *dis-tingk'shən*, *n* separation or division; discrimination; a distinguishing mark or character; difference; a mark or honorific recognition of excellence; an honour; discriminating favour; noticeable eminence; outstanding merit; impressive and meritorious individuality. [L. *dīstinctio*, *-ōnis*, separation, distinction.]

distinctive *dis-tingk'tiv*, *adj* marking out as different, distinguishing; characteristic, readily recognisable, serving to identify. — *n* a distinctive feature. — *adv* **distinct'ively**. — *n* **distinct'iveness**. [*dīstinct-*, stem of past p. of L. *dīstinguĕre*, and sfx. *-ive*.]

distingué *dē-stē̃-gā*, (Fr.) *adj* distinguished; striking: — *fem* **distinguée**.

distinguish *dis-ting'gwish*, *vt* to mark off, set apart, differentiate (often with *from*); to recognise by characteristic qualities; to make out, identify; to separate by a mark of honour; to make eminent or known; to conduct (oneself) noticeably well. — *vi* to make or show distinctions or differences, to recognise a difference (often with *between*). — *adj* **disting'uishable**. — *adv* **disting'uishably**. — *adj* **disting'uished** illustrious, eminent; dignified in appearance or manner; remarkable (with *for*). — *adj* **disting'uishing** peculiar, serving to identify. [L. *dīstinguĕre*, *dīstinctum* — *dī-*, apart, *stinguĕre*, orig. to prick.]

distort *dis-tört'*, *vt* to twist or pull awry, spoil the natural shape of, deform; to misrepresent (statements, facts, etc.); to pervert, warp; to alter or make indistinct (a signal or sound) in transmission or reproduction (*radio* and *telecomm*). — *adj* **distort'ed**. — *n* **distortion** (*-tör'shən*) the process of distorting or being distorted; deformation; misrepresentation; change of waveform in course of transmission resulting in loss of clarity (*radio* and *telecomm*); warping, perversion. [L. *dis-*, apart, *torquēre*, *tortum*, to twist.]

distract *dis-trakt'*, *vt* to draw the attention of (someone) away from something, divert someone('s attention) in another or several other directions; to confuse; to harass; to render crazy, madden; to divert, amuse, entertain. — *adj* **distract'ed** confused, bewildered; harassed; crazy, mad, maddened. — *adv* **distract'edly**. — *n* **distract'edness**. — *n* **distractibil'ity**. — *adj* **distract'ible**. — *adj* **distract'ing**. — *adv* **distract'ingly**. — *n* **distrac'tion** the state of being distracted; perplexity; agitation; madness; that which distracts; a diversion, amusement; recreation, relaxation. [L. *distrahĕre*, *-tractum* — *dis-*, apart, *trahĕre*, to draw.]

distrain *dis-trān'*, (*law*) *vt* to seize (esp. goods for debt, esp. for non-payment of rent or rates). — *vi* to seize the goods of a debtor. — *adj* **distrain'able**. — *n* **distrainee'** a person whose property has been distrained. — *n* **distrain'er** or **distrain'or**. — *n* **distrain'ment**. — *n* **distraint'** seizure of goods. [O.Fr. *destraindre* — L. *dī-*, apart, *stringĕre*, to draw tight.]

distrait *dēs-tre*, (Fr.) *adj* absent-minded.

distraught *dis-tröt'*, *adj* distracted; frantic, e.g. with grief or worry. [Modified form of **distract**, in its earlier sense 'distracted'.]

distress *dis-tres'*, *n* extreme pain or suffering, esp. mental or emotional; that which causes suffering; calamity, misfortune; acute poverty; exhaustion; peril; difficulty; act of distraining goods (*law*). — *vt* to afflict with (esp. mental or emotional) pain or suffering; to harass; to grieve; to reduce financially, impoverish; to impart an antique appearance to (furniture), age artificially, by knocking, scraping, etc.; to distrain (*law*). — *adj* **distressed'** suffering mentally or physically; impoverished; (of furniture) deliberately battered so as to appear antique. — *n* **distress'er**. — *adj* **distress'ful**. — *adv* **distress'fully**. — *n* **distress'fulness**. — *adj* **distress'ing**. — *adv* **distress'ingly**. — **distressed area** a depressed area, affected by severe unemployment; **distress signal** a radio signal or flare put out by a ship in distress. — **in distress** (of a ship or aircraft) in danger, needing help. [O.Fr. *destresse* — L. *dīstringĕre*.]

distribute *dis-trib'ūt* or *dis'*, *vt* to divide amongst several; to deal out or allot; to classify; to disperse about a space; to spread out; to separate (type) and put back in compartments (*printing*); to use (a term) with full extension, including every individual to which it is applicable (*logic*). — *adj* **distrib'utable**. — *adj* **distrib'utary**. — *n* an off-flow from a river that does not return to it (e.g. in a delta). — *n* **distributee'** (*US law*) a person who shares in the estate of a deceased person. — *n* **distributer** see **distributor**. — *n* **distribu'tion** the act or process of distributing; dispersal; division; range; allotment; classification; the application of a general term to all the objects denoted by it (*logic*); the manner in which the products of industry are shared among the people (*econ*); the range of values of a variable presented in terms of frequency (*statistics*). — *adj* **distribu'tional**. — *adj* **distrib'utive** that distributes, separates or divides; giving to each his own; referring individually to all members of a group, as the words *each*, *every*, *either*, *neither* (*gram*); (of a general term) applying to all objects denoted by it (*logic*). — *n* a distributive word such as *each* or *every* (*gram*). — *adv* **distrib'utively**. — *n* **distrib'utiveness**. — *n* **distrib'utor** or **distrib'uter** someone who, or that which, distributes; an agent, or middleman, between manufacturer and retailer; a device in a petrol engine whereby high tension current is transmitted in correct sequence to the sparking plugs. — **distributed processing** (*comput*) the distribution of processing power away from the centre to other terminals. [L. *distribuĕre* — *dis-*, apart, *tribuĕre*, *tribūtum*, to allot.]

district *dis'trikt*, *n* a portion of territory defined for political, judicial, educational, or other purposes (such as a registration district, a militia district, the District of Columbia); generally, an area, locality or region; in local government, an administrative subdivision of a Scottish region or of an English or Welsh county; a constituency (*US*). — *vt* to divide into districts. — **district attorney** (*US*) a public prosecutor for a district; **district council** in British local government, the council elected to govern a district; **district court** (*US*) the federal court for a district; **district heating** the distribution of heat from a central source to buildings in the surrounding area; **district nurse** a nurse appointed to attend patients in their own homes. [Fr., — L.L. *dīstrictus*, jurisdiction — *dīstringĕre*, to stretch out.]

distrust *dis-trust'*, *n* lack of trust; lack of faith or confidence; doubt. — *vt* to have no trust in; to disbelieve; to doubt. — *n* **distrust'er**. — *adj* **distrust'ful** full of distrust; apt to distrust; suspicious. — *adv* **distrust'fully**. — *n* **distrust'fulness**. [**dis-** (2), (3).]

disturb *dis-tûrb'*, *vt* to interrupt; to inconvenience; to throw into confusion; to agitate, upset. — *n* **disturb'ance** interruption; a commotion or fracas; derangement; agitation; interference, molestation (*law*). — *adj* **disturbed'** worried; confused, esp. emotionally, maladjusted. — *n* **disturb'er**. — *adj*

disturb'ing. [O.Fr. *destourber* — L. *dis-*, apart, *turbāre*, to agitate.]

disulfiram *dī-sul-fē'rəm*, *n* a drug used to treat chronic alcoholism, acting by inducing nausea, etc., if alcohol is taken.

disulphide *dī-sul'fīd*, *n* a sulphide containing two atoms of sulphur to the molecule. [**di-**.]

disunion *dis-ūn'yən*, *n* lack of union, dissension, disagreement; separation, estrangement. — *vt* **disunite'** to separate from union, detach, divide; to estrange, drive apart. — *vi* to part, separate. — *n* **disu'nity** lack of unity, dissension. [**dis-** (2), (1).]

disuse *dis-ūs'* or *dis'ūs*, *n* the state of being no longer used, observed or practised; neglect, desuetude. — *adj* **disused** (*dis-ūzd'*) no longer used; no longer observed or practised. [**dis-** (2), (3).]

disyllable or **dissyllable** *dī-sil'ə-bl*, *n* a word of two syllables. — *adj* **disyllabic** (*-lab'ik*). [Gr. *di-*, twice, *syllabē*, a syllable.]

ditch *dich*, *n* a trench dug in the ground for drainage, or irrigation, or to serve to mark a boundary; any long narrow depression carrying water; the border of a bowling-green. — *vi* to make, repair or clean a ditch or ditches; (of an aircraft or pilot) to come down in the sea (*colloq*). — *vt* to dig a ditch in or around; to drain by ditches; to drive (a vehicle) into a ditch or crash deliberately; to abandon, or get rid of (*slang*); to escape from or leave (a person) in the lurch (*slang*); to bring (an aircraft) down in the sea (*colloq*). — *n* **ditch'er** a man or machine that makes, cleans or repairs ditches. — **ditch'-water** stagnant foul water such as is found in ditches, proverbially dull. [O.E. *dīc*, whence also **dike**[1].]

dither *didh'ər*, *vi* to waver, vacillate. — *n* a state of irresolution. — *n* **dith'erer**. — *adj* **dith'ery**. — **all of a dither** nervous, agitated. [Prob. imit.]

dithyramb *dith'i-ram* or *-ramb*, *n* in ancient Greece, a wild, impassioned choral hymn sung in honour of Bacchus; a poem or piece of writing in wildly rapturous or bombastic vein. — *adj* **dithyram'bic** of or like a dithyramb; rapturous; wild and boisterous. — *adv* **dithyram'bically**. [Gr. *dīthyrambos*.]

ditsy or **ditzy** *dit'si*, (*US colloq*) *adj* amiably eccentric, scatterbrained; precious, affected.

dittany *dit'ə-ni*, *n* an aromatic plant of the genus *Dictamnus*, native to Crete, formerly held to have medicinal value. [O.Fr. *dictame* — Gr. *diktamnos*; prob. from Mt. *Diktē* in Crete.]

ditto *dit'ō*, (in writing abbreviated to **do.** or replaced by ditto marks (q.v. below)) *n* that which has been said; the same thing: — *pl* **ditt'os**. — *adv* as before, or aforesaid; in the same manner, likewise; (as assenting rejoinder) same here. — *vt* to duplicate, echo: — *pr p* **ditt'oing**; *pa t* and *pa p* **ditt'oed**. — **ditto marks** a sign " written immediately below a word, etc., to show that it is to be understood as repeated. [It. *ditto* — L. *dictum*, said, past p. of *dīcĕre*, to say.]

dittography *di-tog'rə-fi*, *n* unintentional repetition of letters or words by a scribe or printer in copying a manuscript. [Gr. *dittos*, double, *graphein*, to write.]

ditty *dit'i*, *n* a simple song or poem. [O.Fr. *ditie* — L. *dictāre*, to dictate.]

ditty-bag *dit'i-bag* or **ditty-box** *-boks*, *n* a sailor's bag for personal belongings.

ditzy. See **ditsy**.

diuretic *dī-ū-ret'ik*, *adj* increasing the flow of urine. — *n* a medicine that increases the flow of urine. — *n* **diurē'sis** increased, or excessive, excretion of urine. [Gr. *diourētikos* — *dia*, through, *ouron*, urine.]

diurnal *dī-ûr'nəl*, *adj* daily; relating to or performed in or lasting a day; belonging to the daytime; (of animals) active during the day; (of flowers) open during the day. — *adv* **diur'nally**. [L. *diurnālis* — *diēs*, a day; cf. **journal**[1].]

Div. *abbrev* for Division.

div *div*, *n* short for **dividend**.

div. *abbrev* for: divide; division; divine; divorce or divorced.

diva *dē'vä*, *n* a great female singer, esp. an operatic prima donna. [It., — L. *dīva*, goddess.]

divalent *dī-vā'lənt*, *adj* having a valency of two, i.e. capable of uniting with two atoms of hydrogen or their equivalent. — *n* **divā'lency**. [Gr. *di-*, twice, L. *valēre*, to be worth.]

divan *di-van'*, *n* a couch without back or sides; a bed of similar design (also **divan'-bed**); in some Muslim countries, a council chamber, court of justice, or council of state. [Ar. and Pers. *dīwān*, a long seat.]

divaricate *dī-var'i-kāt*, (*biol*) *vi* to part into two branches, to fork; to diverge. — *adj* widely divergent, spreading apart. — *n* **divaricā'tion**. [L. *dīvaricāre*, *-ātum* — *dis-*, apart, *varicāre*, to spread the legs — *varus*, bent apart.]

dive *dīv*, *vi* to plunge headfirst into, or down through water or down through the air; (of a submarine) to submerge; (of an aircraft) to descend steeply, nose-first; to go headlong into a recess, etc., or suddenly investigate the interior of a container, etc. (with *into*); to involve oneself whole-heartedly (with *into*). — *vt* to plunge, dip: — *pa t* **dived** or in U.S. **dove** (*dōv*). — *n* a plunge; a swoop; a headlong descent; a refuge; a resort, e.g. a bar, generally disreputable (*slang*); a faked knockout (*boxing*). — *n* **div'er** a person who dives or can dive; a person who dives for pearls; a person who works from a diving-bell or in a diving-suit beneath water; any member of a genus (*Gavia*) of ducklike diving birds; (*loosely*; esp. *formerly*) any of various diving birds, such as the auk, grebe, penguin, etc. — *n* and *adj* **di'ving**. — *vt* and *vi* **dive'-bomb** to attack with, or as if with, a dive-bomber; to discharge bombs while diving. — **dive'-bomber** an aeroplane that discharges a bomb while in a steep dive; **dive'-bombing**; **di'ving-bell** a hollow vessel or chamber, orig. bell-shaped, open at the bottom and supplied with air by a tube from above, in which one may descend into and work under water; **di'ving-board** a board for diving from; **di'ving-suit** a watertight costume for a diver, with a detachable helmet and air supply. [O.E. *dȳfan*, *dūfan* — O.N. *dȳfa*.]

diverge *di-* or *dī-vûrj'*, *vi* to tend from a common point in different directions; to vary from the standard; to deviate, differ; (of a mathematical series) to increase indefinitely. — *vt* to deflect, cause to diverge. — *n* **diverg'ence** or **diverg'ency** the act, or amount, of diverging; the condition of being divergent; the flow of air away from a particular region, usu. associated with fine weather (*meteorol*); the property of an infinite series, of having no limit, etc. (*math*); the turning outward of the eyes in focusing on a distant object (*physiol*); initiation of a chain reaction in which more neutrons are released than are absorbed and lost (*nuc*). — *adj* **diverg'ent** diverging; (of thought or thinking) following unconventional routes, so as to produce a variety of solutions in problem-solving (*psychol*). — *adv* **diverg'ently**. — *adj* **diverg'ing**. [L. *dī-*, apart, *vergĕre*, to incline.]

divers *dī'vərz*, (*archaic* or *literary*) *adj* sundry; several; more than one. [L. *dīversus*, turned different ways, contrary, different.]

diverse *dī'vərs* or *dī-vûrs'*, *adj* various, assorted; multiform; different, distinct. — *adv* **di'versely** or **diverse'ly**. — *adj* **diversifī'able**. — *n* **diversificā'tion**. — *adj* **diver'sified**. — *vt* **divers'ify** to give variety to, vary, variegate or modify; to make (investments) in securities of different types so as to lessen risk of loss; to engage in production of a variety of (manufactures, crops). — Also *vi*: — *pr p* **diver'sifying**; *pa t* and *pa p* **diver'sified**. — *n* **diver'sion** act of diverting or turning aside; something which diverts; amusement, recreation; something done to turn the attention of an opponent; an official detour to avoid (part of) a road which is temporarily closed. — *adj* **diver'sionary** of the nature of a diversion, designed to distract the attention of an opponent. — *n* **diver'sity** state of being diverse; variety; difference, dissimilarity. [L. *dīversus*, different, various.]

divert *dī-* or *di-vûrt'*, *vt* to turn aside; to change the direction of; to distract from business or study; to amuse. — *adj* **divert'ible.** — *n* **divertibil'ity.** — *adj* **divert'ing** tending to divert; amusing, entertaining. — *adv* **divert'ingly.** [Fr., — L. *dīvertĕre* — *dī-*, aside, *vertĕre*, to turn.]

diverticulum *dī-vər-tik'ū-ləm*, (*anat*) *n* a sac or pouch formed e.g. by herniation in the wall of a tubular organ esp. the intestines: — *pl* **dīvertic'ula.** — *adj* **dīvertic'ular.** — *n* **dīverticulī'tis** inflammation of one or more diverticula. — *n* **dīverticulō'sis** the presence of several diverticula in the intestines. [L. *dīverticulum*, a byway, retreat.]

divertimento *di-vûr-ti-men'tō*, (*mus*) *n* an entertaining piece of music, esp. a suite for orchestra or chamber ensemble: — *pl* **divertimen'ti** (*-tē*). [It.]

divertissement *dē-ver-tēs'mã*, (Fr.) *n* a short entertainment, e.g. a ballet interlude, between the acts of a play, or between plays; generally, a diversion or entertainment.

Dives *dī'vēz*, *n* the rich man at whose gate Lazarus lay (*Bible*: Luke xvi. 19); a rich person. [L. *dīves*, rich (man), understood as a proper name.]

divest *dī-vest'*, *vt* to remove clothes from, strip (with *of*); to strip or deprive (with *of*); to disencumber or free (oneself) (with *of*). — *n* **divest'iture, dives'ture** or **divest'ment.** [O.Fr. *desvestir*, from L. *dēvestīre* — *dē*, away from, *vestīre*, to clothe.]

divi. See **divvy.**

divide *di-vīd'*, *vt* to split up, or mark off, into parts; to separate, part; to distinguish, set apart; to classify; to share, distribute, allot or deal out; to ascertain how many times a quantity is contained in (*math*); to be a boundary or a subject of difference between; to keep apart; to set at variance, cause disagreement between; to sever; to cause to vote for and against a motion. — *vi* to separate; to fall apart; to branch; to vote for and against a motion; to be capable of division; to be contained a specified number of times in another number (with *into*). — *n* an area of high land between two river systems, a watershed (esp. *NAm*); something that divides or separates, a gap or split. — *n* **divī'der** someone who or that which divides; a screen or partition (also **room'-divider**); (in *pl*) a kind of compasses for measuring. — **divided highway** (*US*) a dual carriageway; **divided skirt** wide-legged knee-length trousers for women, having the appearance of a skirt, culottes. [L. *dīvidĕre*, *dīvīsum* — *dis-*, apart, root *vid*, to separate.]

dividend *div'i-dend*, *n* a number that is to be divided by another; the share of a sum divided that falls to each individual, by way of interest or otherwise; the sum payable to creditors of an insolvent estate (*law*). — **dividend stripping** a method of evading tax on dividends by a contrived arrangement between a company liable to tax and another in a position to claim repayment of tax; **div'idend-warrant** a certificate entitling to payment of dividend. — **declare a dividend** to announce the sum per cent a trading concern is prepared to pay its shareholders. [L. *dīvidendum*, to be divided, *dīvidĕre*.]

dividivi *div'i-div-i*, *n* the curved pods of a small tropical American tree (*Caesalpinia coriaria*) used for tanning and dyeing; the tree itself. [Carib name.]

divine *di-vīn'*, *adj* belonging to or proceeding from a god; holy; transcendently good, beautiful or accomplished; wonderful, splendid (*colloq*). — *n* a theologian. — *vt* to foresee or foretell as if divinely inspired; to guess; to prognosticate; to search for (underground water, etc.), esp. with a divining-rod. — *vi* to profess or practise divination; to have forebodings. — *n* **divinā'tion** the art or practice of divining; seeking to know the future or unknown things, by supernatural means; instinctive prevision; prediction; conjecture. — *n* **divī'ner** a person who divines or professes divination; a conjecturer. — *adj* **divi'natory** relating to divination, conjectural. — *adv* **divīne'ly.** — *n* **divīne'ness.** — **divine right** the concept that monarchs rule by the authority of God rather than by consent of the people; any authority supposed to be unquestionable; **divī'ning-rod** a rod, usually of hazel, used by those professing to discover water or metals underground. [O.Fr. *devin*, soothsayer, and L. *dīvīnus* — *dīvus*, a god.]

diving. See **dive.**

divinity *di-vin'i-ti*, *n* godhead; the nature or essence of a god; a celestial being; a god; the science of divine things; theology. [O.Fr. *devinite* — L. *dīvīnitās,-tātis*; see **divine.**]

divisible *di-viz'i-bl*, *adj* capable of being divided or separated; capable of being divided without remainder (*math*). — *n* **divisibil'ity** or **divis'ibleness.** — *adv* **divis'ibly.** [L. *dīvīsībĭlis* — *dīvīdĕre*, to divide.]

division *di-vizh'ən*, *n* act of dividing; state of being divided; that which divides; a partition; a barrier; a portion or section; one of a set of graded classes or groups; one of the parts of a territorial, business, etc., unit, divided for administrative, etc., purposes; an army unit (usually half an army corps) containing almost all branches of the service; separation; the taking of a vote; difference in opinion, etc.; disunion; the process of finding how many times one quantity is contained in another (*math*); a taxonomic grouping, the equivalent of a phylum (*bot*). — *adj* **divisional** (*-vizh'*) relating to or marking a division or separation (also **divis'ionary**); relating or belonging to a part of a larger unit. — **division lobby** see under **lobby.** [L. *dīvīsiō, -ōnis* — *dīvīdĕre*, to divide.]

divisive *di-vī'ziv*, *adj* tending to divide or separate; tending to create dissension. — *adv* **divī'sively.** — *n* **divī'siveness.** [L.L. *dīvīsīvus* — *dīvīdĕre*, to divide.]

divisor *di-vī'zər*, (*math*) *n* the number that divides the dividend; a number that divides another without remainder, a factor. [L. *dīvīsor* — *dīvīdĕre*, to divide.]

divorce *di-vörs'*, *n* the legal dissolution of a marriage or the decree that dissolves it; complete separation or severance (*fig*). — *vt* to dissolve the marriage of; to obtain a divorce from; to separate, sever. — *vi* to separate by divorce. — *adj* **divorce'able.** — *n* **divorcee'** a divorced person. — Also **divorcé** *masc* and **divorcée** *fem* (*di-vör'sā*; Fr.). [Fr., — L. *dīvortium* — *dīvortĕre* or *divertere*, (of a woman) to leave one's husband.]

divot *div'ət*, *n* a thin sod, cut for roofing, etc. (*Scot*); a small piece of turf gouged out by a golfer's club-head, or by a horse's hoof.

divulge *dī-vulj'* or *di-*, *vt* to reveal, disclose, make public. — *n* **dīvulgā'tion, divul'gence** or **divulge'ment.** [L. *dīvulgāre* — *dī-*, abroad, *vulgāre*, to publish — *vulgus*, the common people.]

divvy or **divi** *div'i*, (*slang*) *n* a dividend; a share. — **divvy up** to divide (spoils, etc.); to go shares: — *pr p* **divv'ying**; *pa t* and *pa p* **divv'ied.** [Abbrev. of **divide, dividend.**]

Diwali *di-wä'lē*, *n* the Hindu or Sikh festival of lamps held in October or November. [Hindi *divālī*.]

diwan. See **dewan.**

dixie or **dixy** *diks'i*, *n* a military cooking-pail or camp-kettle. [Perh. Hindi *degcī* — Pers. *degcha*, dimin. of *dīg*, large metallic cooking utensil.]

Dixieland *dik'si-land*, *n* an early style of jazz in New Orleans, played by small combinations of instruments. [*Dixie*, name given to southern states of U.S.]

DIY *abbrev* for do-it-yourself (q.v. under **do**[1]).

dizygotic *dī-zī-got'ik*, (*biol*) *adj* developed from two zygotes or fertilized eggs. — **dizygotic twins**

fraternal twins, i.e. ones which have developed from two zygotes. [Gr. *di-*, twice, and **zygote**.]

dizzy *diz'i*, *adj* giddy; confused, bewildered; (of a height) so elevated as to cause giddiness in anyone looking down (often *fig*); generally, giddy-making, confusing, bewildering; silly (*colloq*). — *vt* to make dizzy; to confuse: — *pr p* **dizz'ying**; *pa t* and *pa p* **dizz'ied**. — *adv* **dizz'ily**. — *n* **dizz'iness**. — *adj* **dizz'ying** making one dizzy. — *adv* **dizz'yingly**. [O.E. *dysig*, foolish.]

DJ *dē-jā'*, *n* a dee-jay, disc-jockey; a dinner-jacket (*colloq*).

djellaba or **djellabah** *jə-lä'bə* or *jel'ə-bə*, *n* a cloak with a hood and wide sleeves. — Also **jella'ba** or **jell'abah**. [Ar. *jallabah, jallāb*.]

djinn, djinni. See **jinn**.

DK *abbrev* for Denmark (I.V.R.).

dl *abbrev* for decilitre(s).

DLit. or **DLitt**. *abbrev* for *Doctor litterarum* or *litteraturae* (L.), Doctor of Letters or of Literature.

DM *abbrev* for Deutschmark or Deutsche Mark.

DMus. *abbrev* for Doctor of Music.

DMZ *abbrev* for demilitarised zone.

DNA *abbrev* for deoxyribonucleic acid (q.v.). — **DNA profiling** genetic fingerprinting (see under **genetic**).

DNB *abbrev* for Dictionary of National Biography (a reference work containing the biographies of famous British people).

do[1] *dōō* or *də*, *vt* to put in some condition; to render; to confer; to bestow; to perform; to accomplish; to finish; to exhaust; to work at; to perform work upon; to beat up, thrash (*slang*); to prepare, set in order; to cook; to cheat, or overreach (*slang*); to raid, rob (*slang*); to treat; to make the round of, see the sights of (*colloq*); to spend in prison. — *vi* to act, be active; to behave; to fare; to thrive; to suffice; to be just good enough; to serve (with *for*); to arrange, devise or effect in respect of something or someone (with *with* or *about*): — *3rd pers sing* **does** (*duz*); *pa t* **did**; *pr p* **do'ing**; *pa p* **done** (*dun*). — *Do* serves as a substitute for a verb that has just been used. It is used as an auxiliary verb (where there is no other auxiliary), with an infinitive in negative, interrogative, emphatic, and rhetorically inverted sentences, etc., but these uses are limited with the verbs *have* and *do*. — *n* a feast, celebration; a swindle, hoax (*slang*): — *pl* **do's** or **dos**. — *adj* **do'able** able to be done. — *n* **do'er** a person who does, or habitually does, anything; a busy, active or energetic person; a person who prefers taking action, or practical steps, to contemplation and discussion; a healthy farm animal (*NZ*); a horse in respect of its appetite, as in *a good doer* (*horse-racing*). — *adj* **do'ing** active (as in *up and doing*). — *n* (*colloq*) a scolding; thrashing; severe treatment; the agency or handiwork of someone seen as instrumental in something; (in *pl*) activities, behaviour; (in *pl*) fancy dishes or adjuncts; (in *pl*) what's-its-name (*slang*). — **done** *pa p* of **do**. — *adj* utterly exhausted; finished, completed; cooked to a degree suitable for eating; (of behaviour, etc.) socially acceptable. — *interj* (used in clinching a bargain, etc.) agreed. — **do'-gooder** a slighting name for someone who tries to benefit others by social reforms, etc., implying that his or her efforts are unwelcome, self-righteous or ineffectual; **do-good'ery** (*derog*); **do-good'ism** (*derog*). — *adj* **do-it-yourself'** designed to be built, constructed, etc. by an amateur rather than by someone specially trained. — Also *n*. — **do-it-yourself'er**; **do'-nothing** a lazy or idle person; **do-noth'ingism**; **do-noth'ingness**. — **all done** completely finished, used up; **be** or **have done with** to finish with, end contact or dealings with; **do away with** to abolish, destroy; **do by** to act towards; **do down** to cheat, get the better of (*colloq*); **do for** to suit; to provide for; to ruin; to kill (*colloq*); to do domestic work for (*colloq*); **do in** to exhaust; to ruin, to murder; **do or die** to make a final desperate attempt to do or achieve something, no matter what the cost or consequences (*adj* **do-or-die'**); **do out** (*colloq*) to clean thoroughly (a room, etc.); **do out of** to deprive of by cheating; **do over** to cover over, as with paint; to beat up (*slang*); to re-do, repeat (*US*); **do's and don'ts** advice or rules for action, esp. in particular circumstances; **do something, etc. for** to improve, enhance; **do to death** to murder; to repeat too often; **do up** to fasten up; to put up, make tidy, arrange, tie up; to redecorate; to apply cosmetics to; to dress, array (oneself) becomingly; to fatigue utterly; **do well** to prosper; to be wise, sensible (to take a particular step); **do without** not to be dependent on, to dispense with; **have done** to desist; to stop it; to have no more dealings; **have to do with** to have any sort of connection with; **have you done?** (*colloq*) are you finished?; **how do you do?** a conventional phrase used on greeting; **I, etc. can't be doing with** I, etc. can't abide, have no patience with; **make do (with)** see under **make**; **nothing doing** no; **that's done it** it is completed; (*interj* indicating dismay) it is spoilt, ruined; **what are you, etc. doing with (something)?** why have you, etc. got (something)? [O.E. *dōn, dyde, gedōn*.]

do[2]. See **doh**.

do *abbrev* for ditto.

DOA *abbrev* for dead on arrival (esp. at hospital).

doat. See **dote**.

dob *dob* (*Austr colloq*) *vt* (usu. with *in*) to inform on or betray. [Br. dialect *dob*, to put down.]

d.o.b *abbrev* for date of birth.

dobbin *dob'in*, *n* a workhorse. [An altered dimin. of *Robert*.]

Doberman (or Dobermann) pinscher *dōb'ər-mən pin'shər*, *n* a breed of terrier — large, smooth-coated, with long forelegs. [*Dobermann*, the first breeder, and Ger. *Pinscher*, terrier.]

Dobro® *dō'brō*, *n* an acoustic steel guitar with metallic resonator, of a type usu. laid flat on the knee to play, particularly associated with country music and producing a wavering sound.

Dobson unit *dob'sən ū'nit*, *n* a unit of measurement of the ozone layer, expressed in terms of its hypothetical thickness at sea-level pressure, 100 Dobson units representing a thickness of one millimetre.

DOC *abbrev* for District Officer Commanding.

doc *dok*, *n* a familiar contraction of **doctor**.

docent *dō-sent'* or *dō'sent*, *n* a teacher or lecturer at a college or university. [Ger. *Dozent*, university teacher.]

DOCG *abbrev* for *Denominazione di Origine Controllata Garantita* (It.), a designation of wines, guaranteeing quality, strength, etc.

dochmius *dok'mi-əs*, (*prosody*) *n* a foot of five syllables, typically with first and fourth short, the rest long. — *adj* **doch'miac**. [L. — Gr. *dochmios*.]

docile *dō'sīl* or in U.S. *dos'l*, *adj* obedient, compliant, submissive; easy to teach or train, willing to learn. — *n* **docil'ity** (*-sil'*). [Fr., — L. *docilis* — *docēre*, to teach.]

dock[1] *dok*, *n* a weed with large leaves and a long root. [O.E. *docce*.]

dock[2] *dok*, *vt* to cut short, to curtail; to cut off the whole or part of (an animal's tail); to cut the tail off (an animal); to reduce (someone's pay), or deduct (a certain amount) from it. — *n* the solid part of a tail, or the part left after docking. [M.E. *dok*, prob. — O.N. *dokkr*, stumpy tail.]

dock[3] *dok*, *n* (often used in *pl*) an artificial basin for the reception of vessels and cargo; the waterway between two wharves or two piers; a wharf or pier; in a railway station, the place of arrival and departure of a train. — *vt* to place in a dock; to bring into dock; to equip with docks; to join (spacecraft) together in space. — *vi* to enter a dock; to join together in space.

— *n* **dock'age** accommodation in docks for ships; dock-dues. — *n* **dock'er** a dockside labourer whose job is to load and unload ships. — *n* **dock'ing.** — **dock'-dues** payments for use of a dock; **dock'land** a district round about docks; **dock'-master** the person superintending a dock; **dock'side** the area alongside a dock; **dock'yard** a naval establishment with docks, building-slips, stores, etc. — **dry dock** a dock from which the water can be pumped, in order to effect repairs to the underside of a ship (*vt* **dry'-dock** to put in dry dock); **in the dock** (*facetious*; of a vehicle) undergoing repairs and so unavailable for use. [M.Du. *docke.*]

dock⁴ *dok, n* the enclosure for the accused in a court of law. — **in the dock** on trial in a court of law; under attack, facing criticism (with *for*). [Flem. *dok*, cage, hatch, sty.]

docket *dok'it, n* a bill or ticket affixed to anything indicating its contents, a label; a list or register of cases in court, or of legal judgments, or (*US*) business to be transacted; a custom-house certificate of payment; a summary of the contents of a document, etc. — *vt* to fix a label to; to enter in a book; to mark the contents of papers on the back; to summarise the contents of (a document, etc.): — *pr p* **dock'eting;** *pa t* and *pa p* **dock'eted.** [Perh. a dimin. of **dock²**, to curtail.]

Doc Martens® *dok mär'tənz, npl* a make of lace-up, esp. black leather, boots with light thick resilient soles.

doctor *dok'tər, n* a licensed medical practitioner; a person holding a doctorate, the most senior academic degree in any subject; a dentist or veterinary surgeon (*NAm*); one of a small number of especially revered early ecclesiastical writers (also **Doctor of the Church**); a mender or repairer of something; a ship's cook; a name for various contrivances for removing defects in manufacture; an angler's fly. — *vt* to treat, as a doctor does; to patch up, repair; to sophisticate, tamper with, falsify; to spay, castrate (*colloq*). — *vi* to practise medicine. — *adj* **doc'toral** relating to the academic degree of doctor. — *n* **doc'torate** the academic degree of doctor. — *adj* **doc'torly** appropriate to a doctor, showing a doctor's skill or concern. — **doc'tor-fish** a sea-surgeon; **Doctors' Commons** before the establishment of the Divorce Court and Probate Court in 1857, the college of the doctors of civil law in London, incorporated by royal charter in 1768. — **go for the doctor** (*Austr colloq*) to make an all-out effort, give one's all; **what the doctor ordered** (*colloq*) the very thing that's needed. [L., a teacher — *docēre*, to teach.]

doctrinaire *dok-tri-nār', adj* preoccupied with theory, inclined to carry principles to logical but unworkable extremes; impractical; dogmatic. [Fr., — L.L. *doctrīnārius.*]

doctrine *dok'trin, n* a body of religious, political, etc. teaching; a guiding principle, belief or precept. — *adj* **doctrī'nal.** — *adv* **doctrī'nally.** [L. *doctrīna* — *docēre*, to teach.]

docudrama *dok'ū-drä-mə, n* a play or film reproducing real events and characters. [*documentary drama.*]

document *dok'ū-mənt, n* a paper esp. of an official character, affording information, proof or evidence of anything. — *vt* to support or prove by documents or evidence; to furnish (a ship) with documents. — *n* **document'alist** a specialist in documentation; a collector and classifier of documents. — *adv* **document'arily.** — *n* **documentarisā'tion** or **-z-**. — *vt* and *vi* **document'arise** or **-ize** to present in, or make documentaries. — *n* **documen'tarist** a person who makes documentaries. — *adj* **document'ary** relating to, or found in, documents; (of TV programmes, etc.) aiming at presenting reality. — *n* a film, radio or TV programme about real people or events, without fictional colouring or professional actors. — *n* **documentā'tion** preparation, setting forth, or use of documentary evidence and authorities; documents or other material provided in support, amplification or authentication. — **document reader** (*comput*) a form of optical character-reader which converts the characters into code and feeds them automatically into the computer. [Fr., — L. *documentum* — *docēre*, to teach.]

dodder¹ *dod'ər, n* a leafless, twining, pale parasitic plant of or related to the convolvulus family. [M.E. *doder.*]

dodder² *dod'ər, vi* to shake, totter, or progress unsteadily, as a result of age. — *n* **dodd'erer** (*derog*) a feeble, senile person. — *adj* **dodd'ering** (*derog*) decrepit in body and feeble in mind, senile. — *adj* **dodd'ery** unsteady with age.

doddle *dod'l*, (*colloq*) *n* something very easily accomplished. [Poss. — *doddle*, toddle or dawdle.]

dodeca- *dō-dek-ə-*, *combining form* denoting twelve. — *n* **dodec'agon** (Gr. *gōniā*, an angle) a plane figure with twelve angles and sides. — *n* **dodecahedron** (*-hē'dron*; Gr. *hedrā*, a seat) a solid figure, having twelve faces. — *adj* **dodecahē'dral.** — *adj* **dodecaphon'ic** (*mus*; Gr. *phōnē*, voice) twelve-tone. — *adj* **dodecasyllab'ic.** — *n* **dodecasyll'able** (*prosody*) a line of twelve syllables. [Gr. *dōdeka*, twelve.]

dodge *doj, vt* to evade (a blow, etc.) by a sudden shift of place or position; to evade by astuteness or deceit. — *vi* to move out of the way of a blow, etc.; in change-ringing, to make two bells change order in the sequence (*bell-ringing*). — *n* an evasion; a trick, ruse, stratagem; an instance of dodging (*bell-ringing*). — *n* **dodg'er** a shirker; a clever trickster; a screen on a ship's bridge for shelter in rough weather; food, esp. bread (*dialect* and *Austr colloq*); an advertising leaflet (*US*). — *adj* **dodg'y** (*colloq*) difficult to do or carry out; risky; uncertain, unstable, unreliable. — **dodge the column** (*slang*) to evade one's duties.

Dodgems® *doj'əmz, n* (also without *cap*) a fairground amusement in which drivers of small electric cars within an enclosure try to bump others without being bumped.

dodo *dō'dō, n* a clumsy flightless bird, about the size of a turkey (native to Mauritius) which became extinct about the end of the 17th century; an old-fashioned or stupid person (*colloq*): — *pl* **do'does** or **do'dos.** [Port. *doudo*, silly.]

DOE *abbrev* for Department of the Environment.

doe *dō, n* the female of the smaller deer such as the fallow deer or roe-deer; extended to the female of the antelope, kangaroo, rabbit, hare, and some other animals. — *adj* **doe'-eyed** having large, dark eyes like those of a deer. — **doe'-skin** the skin of a female fallow deer; a smooth, close-woven, woollen cloth. [O.E. *dā*; Dan. *daa*, deer.]

doek *dŏŏk*, (*SAfr*) *n* a square cloth for tying round the head, worn by African women. [Afrik., cloth.]

doer, does, etc. See **do¹**.

doff *dof, vt* to take off, remove (a piece of one's clothing); to lift (one's hat) in greeting someone. [**do¹** and **off.**]

dog *dog, n* an animal of the genus *Canis*, which includes the wolf and fox; the domestic species, diversified into a large number of breeds; a male of this and of other species; a mean scoundrel; generally a fellow; either of the two constellations, the Greater and the Lesser Dog; an andiron; a hook for holding logs; a gripping appliance of various kinds; a cock, as of a gun; (in *pl*) greyhound races (*colloq*); a boring or unattractive woman (*US slang*). — *adj* (and in combination) of dogs; male (opp. to *bitch*); spurious, base, inferior, as in *dog Latin*. — *adv* (esp. in combination) utterly. — *vt* to follow as a dog; to track and watch constantly; to worry, plague, infest: — *pr p* **dogg'ing;** *pa t* and *pa p* **dogged.** — *adj* **dogg'ed** stubbornly persevering or determined; pertinacious. — *adv* **dogg'edly.** — *n* **dogg'edness.**

— *n* **dogg'iness**. — *adj* **dogg'ish** like a dog; characteristic of dogs; churlish. — *adv* **dogg'ishly**. — *n* **dogg'ishness**. — *adj* **dogg'y** fond of dogs; of, for, or characteristic of a dog or dogs. — *n* (also **dogg'ie**) dimin. of **dog**. — **dog'berry** the fruit of the dogwood; **dog'-biscuit** a hard kind of biscuit for dogs; **dog'cart** a two-wheeled horse-vehicle with seats back to back, orig. used to carry sporting dogs; **dog'-collar** a collar for a dog; a clerical collar fastened behind; **dog'days** the period when the Dogstar rises and sets with the sun (generally reckoned as 3 July to 11 August). — *adj* **dog'-eared** of pages of a book, turned down like the ears of a dog; shabby, scruffy. — **dog-eat-dog'** ruthless pursuit of one's own interests. — Also *adj*. — **dog'-end** (*slang*) a cigarette-end; **dog'-fancier** a breeder or seller of dogs; **dog'fight** a fight between dogs; any confused fight; a fight between fighter aircraft, esp. at close quarters; **dog'fish** a small shark of various kinds; **dog'gy-bag** a bag used by diners to carry home leftover food from a restaurant (for their pets); **dog'gy-paddle** or **dog'-paddle** a simple swimming stroke with alternate arm movements, similar to the swimming action of a dog; **dog'-handler** a policeman, etc., in charge of a specially trained dog; **dog'-house** (esp. *US*) a kennel; a place of disgrace (*fig*); **dog-Latin** spurious or sham Latin; **dog'-leg** a sharp bend, like that in a dog's hind leg; something so bent, e.g. (*golf*) a hole with a bent fairway. — *adj* (also **dog'legged**) bent like a dog's hind leg. — **dog'-rose** a species of wild rose; **dog's age** (*colloq*) a long time; **dog's'-body** (orig. *naut slang*) junior naval (or other) officer; (usu. **dogs'body**) someone who does menial, monotonous work for others; **dog's breakfast** or **dinner** anything very untidy; **dog'-sled** one pulled by a team of dogs; **dog's life** a wretched, miserable life; **dog's'-meat** scraps and refuse sold as food for dogs; **dog's'-nose** gin and beer, or a similar mixture; **dog's'-tail-grass** a common British pasture grass; **Dog'star** Sirius, in the constellation of the Greater Dog, the brightest star in the heavens, from which are named the dogdays; **dog's'-tongue** hound's-tongue, a plant of the borage family; **dog's'-tooth** a broken-check pattern used extensively in the weaving of tweeds; **dog tag** a metal identity disc for a dog or (*colloq*) a soldier. — *adj* **dog'-tired** or **dog'-weary** completely worn out. — **dog'tooth** a moulding in later Norman architecture, consisting of a series of ornamental square pyramids; **dog'-violet** a scentless wild violet; **dog'-watch** (*naut*) on board ship, a watch 4–6 p.m. or 6–8 p.m., of two hours only, instead of four; **dog'wood** the wild cornel, a small tree with white flowers and purple berries, the shoots and leaves turning red in autumn. — **dog in the manger** a person who will not let others enjoy what he or she has no personal use for; **dogs of war** (*fig*) troops, aggressors, mercenaries, warlike people; **go to the dogs** to be ruined; **hot dog** a roll containing a hot sausage; **like a dog's dinner** (*slang*) very smart, dressed up flamboyantly; **put on the dog** (*NAm*) to put on airs, behave showily. [Late O.E. *docga*.]

doge *dōj* or *dō'jā*, *n* the chief magistrate in republican Venice and Genoa. [L. *dux*, a leader.]

dogger[1] *dog'ər*, *n* a two-masted Dutch fishing-vessel. [Du.]

dogger[2] *dog'ər*, (*geol*) *n* a concretion, esp. of ironstone; a sandy ironstone or ferruginous sandstone; (with *cap*) part of the Middle Jurassic.

doggerel *dog'ər-əl*, *n* irregular measures in burlesque poetry; trivial poetry of poor quality. — *adj* irregular in rhythm; of poor quality. — Also **dogg'rel**.

doggo *dog'ō*, (*colloq*) *adv* hidden. [Poss. from **dog**.]

doggone *dog-gon'*, (*US*) *interj* expressing vexation (*adj* and *adv* **doggone'** or **doggoned'**), from **dog on (it)**, God damn (it).

dogie or **dogy** *dō'gi*, (*US*) *n* a motherless calf.

dogma *dog'mə*, *n* a settled opinion; a principle or doctrine; a doctrine laid down with authority. — *adj* **dogmat'ic** or **dogmat'ical** pertaining to a dogma; asserting something as if it were a dogma; asserting positively; overbearing. — *adv* **dogmat'ically**. — *nsing* **dogmat'ics** (*theol*) the statement of Christian doctrines, systematic theology. — *vi* **dog'matise** or **-ize** (*-mə-tīz*) to state one's opinion dogmatically or arrogantly. — *n* **dog'matiser** or **-z-**. — *n* **dog'matism** dogmatic or positive assertion of opinion. — *n* **dog'matist** a person who makes positive assertions. — *n* **dogmatol'ogy** the science of dogma. [Gr. *dogma*, *-atos*, an opinion — *dokeein*, to think, seem.]

doh or **do** *dō*, (*mus*) *n* in sol-fa notation, a syllable representing the first note of the scale: — *pl* **dohs**, **dos** or **do's**. [Perh. L. *Dominus*, Lord, *do* having replaced the syllable *ut* used by the It. originator.]

dohyo *dō'yō*, *n* in sumo wrestling, the ring or marked area in which the wrestlers compete. [Jap.]

DoI *abbrev* for Department of Industry.

doily *doi'li*, *n* a small lace or lacy paper, etc. ornamented napkin, often laid on or under dishes. — Also **doy'ley** or **doyly**. [From *Doily* or *Doyley*, a famous haberdasher.]

dojo *dō'jō*, *n* a place where judo, karate, etc. are taught or practised: — *pl* **do'jos**. [Jap.]

dol. *abbrev* for: dolce (*mus*); dollar.

Dolby® *dol'bi*, *n* an electronic device which reduces the amount of extraneous noise on recorded or broadcast sound. [R. *Dolby* (born 1933), its inventor.]

dolce *dol'chā*, *adj* and *adv* sweet or sweetly (esp. of music). — *n* a soft-toned organ-stop. — **dolce far niente** (*fär nē-en'tā*; It. sweet doing nothing) pleasant idleness; **dolce vita** (*vē'ta*) a life of wealth, pleasure and self-indulgence. [It., — L. *dulcis*.]

doldrums *dol'drəmz*, *npl* those parts of the ocean near the equator where calms and light but unpredictable winds prevail; a state of inactivity or stagnation; low spirits. [Prob. conn. with obs. *dold*, stupid, or *dol*, dull.]

dole[1] *dōl*, *n* a share; something given in charity; state pay to unemployed (*colloq*). — *vt* (usu. with *out*) to deal out in small portions. — **on the dole** (*colloq*) living on unemployment or other benefit. [O.E. *dāl*; cf. **deal**[1].]

dole[2] *dōl*, *n* pain; grief; great sadness, depression (*archaic* and *poetic*). — *adj* **dole'ful** full of grief; melancholy, depressed. — *adv* **dole'fully**. — *n* **dole'fulness**. [O.Fr. *doel* (Fr. *deuil*), grief — L. *dolēre*, to feel pain.]

dolerite *dol'ər-īt*, (*geol*) *n* a basic igneous rock like basalt in composition but coarser grained. — *adj* **doleritic** (*-it'ik*). [Fr. *dolérite* — Gr. *doleros*, deceptive.]

dolicho- *dol-i-kō-*, *combining form* denoting long. — *adj* **dolichocephalic** (*-sif-al'ik*; Gr. *kephalē*, the head) long-headed — having a breadth of skull (from side to side) less than 75 (or 78) per cent of the length (front to back) — opp. to *brachycephalic*. — Also **dolichoceph'alous**. — *n* **dolichoceph'aly** or **dolichoceph'alism**. [Gr. *dolichos*, long.]

doll[1] *dol*, *n* a puppet; a toy in the form of a baby or other human being; an overdressed and rather silly woman; a young woman. — *vi* and *vt* to dress in a showy way (often with *up*). — *adj* **doll'ish**. — *n* **doll'ishness**. — *n* **doll'y** (dimin. of **doll**) an attractive young girl (also **dolly girl** or **doll'ybird**); a slow, easy catch (*cricket*) or shot. — Also *adj*. — **doll's'-house** (*US* **doll'-house**); **doll'y-mixture** a mixture of small brightly-coloured sweets; one of these sweets. [From *Dolly*, familiar dimin. of *Dorothy*.]

doll[2] *dol*, (*horse-racing*) *n* a hurdle used as a barrier on a race-course to exclude certain areas from use by riders. — **doll off** or **doll out** to mark off by means of dolls.

dollar *dol'ər, n* a silver coin (= 100 cents) of U.S., Canada, Australia, New Zealand, Mexico, Hong Kong, etc. — **dollar area** those countries as a whole whose currencies are linked to the U.S. dollar; **dollar diplomacy** diplomacy dictated by financial interests; diplomacy that uses financial power to increase political power; **dollar gap** the excess of imports from a country with dollar currency over exports to it, necessitating settlement by dollar exchange or in gold. [Ger. *T(h)aler*, short for *Joachimsthaler* because first coined at the silver-mines in Joachimsthal (Joachim's dale) in Bohemia.]

dollop *dol'əp, n* a lump.

dolly[1]. See **doll**[1].

dolly[2] *dol'i, n* an implement used to wash ore (*mining*); a tool for holding the head of a rivet; a trolley, truck or platform on wheels or rollers; a wooden stick or shaft, used to stir clothes in a wash-tub (*old*). — *vt* to use a dolly on; to wheel or roll with a dolly. — **dolly camera** a camera moving on a dolly; **dolly shot** a shot taken with a dolly camera; **dolly switch** a switch, for an electric light, etc., consisting of a pivotal lever pushed up and down vertically; **doll'y-tub** a tub for washing clothes or ores with a dolly. [Ety. as for **doll**[1].]

Dolly Varden *dol'i vär'dən, n* a large hat, one side bent downwards, abundantly trimmed with flowers; a large American fish of the char genus. [Named from a character in Dickens's *Barnaby Rudge*.]

dolma *dol'mə, n* a vine or cabbage leaf with a savoury stuffing: — *pl* **dol'mas** or **dolmades** (Gr., *-mä'des*). [Turk.]

dolman sleeve *dol'mən slēv, n* a kind of sleeve which tapers from a very wide armhole to a tight wrist. [Turk. *dōlāmān*, a Turkish robe with slight sleeves.]

dolmen *dol'mən, n* a stone table; a prehistoric structure, possibly a tomb, of erect unhewn stones, supporting a flattish stone. [Fr. *dolmen*, perh. — Breton *dol*, *taol*, table, *men*, stone.]

dolomite *dol'ə-mīt, n* a mineral, double carbonate of calcium and magnesium; a rock composed of that mineral, magnesian limestone. — *adj* **dolomitic** (*-mit'ik*). [After the Fr. geologist D. Guy de *Dolomieu* (1750–1801).]

dolour or in U.S. **dolor** *dol'ər*, also *dōl'ər*, (*poetic*) *n* pain, grief or anguish. — *adv* **dolorō'sō** (It.; *mus*) sorrowfully. — *adj* **dol'orous** full of pain or grief; doleful. — *adv* **dol'orously**. — *n* **dol'orousness**. [O.Fr., — L. *dolēre*, to grieve.]

dolphin *dol'fin, n* any of a group of animals of the whale kind, about 2.5–3 m. (8–10 ft.) long, with a beak-like snout; sometimes used loosely in the U.S. to include the porpoise; fish about 1.5 m. (5 ft.) in length noted for the brilliancy of its colours when dying (also **dol'phin-fish**); a buoy or pile for mooring; a structure of piles used to protect a harbour entrance, etc. — *n* **dolphinarium** (*-ā'ri-əm*) an aquarium for dolphins: — *pl* **dolphinā'riums** or **dolphinā'ria** (*-ə*). [O.Fr. *daulphin* — L. *delphinus* — Gr. *delphīs*, *-phīnos*.]

dolt *dōlt, n* a dull or stupid person. — *adj* **dolt'ish** dull, stupid. — *adv* **dolt'ishly**. — *n* **dolt'ishness**. [For **dulled** or blunted.]

DOM *abbrev* for: *Deo optimo maximo* (L.), to God, best and greatest; *Dominus omnium magister* (L.), God the master of all; Dominican Republic (I.V.R.); dirty old man.

Dom *dom, n* the Portuguese form of *Don*; also a title given to certain Catholic dignitaries and members of some monastic orders, esp. the Benedictine. [L. *dominus*, lord.]

Dom. *abbrev* for: Dominical; Dominican; Dominion; *Dominus* (L.), Lord.

dom. *abbrev* for domestic.

-dom *-dom* or *-dəm, sfx* forming nouns, denoting: dominion, power, state or condition; a group of people (with a specified characteristic, e.g. *officialdom*). [O.E. *dōm*, judgment; Ger. *-tum*.]

domain *dō-mān', n* an estate or territory that is owned or governed by a person, a family or a ruler; ownership; the scope or range of any subject or sphere of knowledge; a public park or recreation area (*Austr* and *NZ*); an aggregate to which a variable belongs (*math*). — *adj* **domain'al** or **domā'nial**. [Fr. *domaine* — L. *dominicum* — *dominus*, a master.]

dome *dōm, n* a structure, usually hemispherical, over a large building; a large cupola; a head (*colloq*); anything with a hemispherical shape. — *vt* to cover with a dome; to make into the shape of a dome. — *vi* to become dome-shaped. [L. *domus*, a house.]

Domesday-book or **Doomsday-book** *do͞omz'dā-bo͝ok, n* a book compiled around 1086 by order of William the Conqueror, containing a survey of all the lands in England, their value, owners, etc. — so called from its authority in judgment (O.E. *dōm*) on the matters contained in it.

domestic *dō-* or *də-mes'tik, adj* belonging or relating to home or family; enjoying or accustomed to being at home; private; tame; not foreign. — *n* a servant in the house. — *adj* **domes'ticable** capable of being domesticated. — *adv* **domes'tically**. — *vt* **domes'ticate** to make domestic or familiar; to tame. — *adj* **domes'ticated** adapted to or content with home life and activities; tamed. — *n* **domesticā'tion**. — *n* **domes'ticātor**. — *n* **domesticity** (*dō-* or *do-mis-tis'i-ti*) domestic or domesticated state; home life. — **domestic architecture** the architecture of mansions, dwelling-houses, cottages, etc.; **domestic economy** the principles of running a household efficiently; **domestic science** the household skills of cooking, sewing, etc. [L. *domesticus* — *domus*, a house.]

domicile *dom'i-sīl* or *-sil* or **domicil** *dom'i-sil, n* a dwelling-place; one's legally recognised place of residence. — *vt* **dom'icile** (*-sīl*) to establish in a fixed residence. — *adj* **dom'iciled**. — *adj* **domiciliary** (*-sil'*) of or relating to domicile; dealing with or available to people in their own homes. — **domiciliary visit** an authorised visit to a private house for the purpose of searching it; a visit made by a doctor, etc. to a patient's or client's home. [Fr., — L. *domicilium* — *domus*, a house.]

dominant *dom'in-ənt, adj* prevailing; predominant; having a commanding position; of an ancestral character, appearing in the first generation of cross-bred offspring to the exclusion of the alternative character in the other parent, which may yet be transmitted to later generations (*genetics*). — *n* the fifth above the tonic (*mus*); a dominant gene or the character determined by it; one of the prevailing species in a plant community. — *n* **dom'inance** or **dom'inancy** ascendancy; the state of being dominant. — *adv* **dom'inantly**. [L. *dominans*, *-antis*, pres. p. of *dominārī*, to be master.]

dominate *dom'in-āt, vt* to have command or influence over, to govern; to prevail over; to tower over; to command a view of; to be predominant or very noticeable in; to project one's personality, influence, etc. strongly over. — Also *vi*. — *n* **dominā'tion** government; absolute authority; tyranny. — *n* **dom'inātor**. [L. *dominārī*, *-ātus*, to be master — *dominus*, master.]

domineer *dom-in-ēr', vi* (often with *over*) to rule imperiously; to command arrogantly; to be overbearing. — *adj* **domineer'ing** overbearing, authoritarian. [Prob. from O.Fr. *dominer* — L. *dominārī*.]

dominical *do-min'i-kl, adj* (*Christian relig*) belonging to the Lord (as the Lord's Prayer or the Lord's Day). — **dominical letter** one of the first seven letters of the alphabet, used in calendars to mark the Sundays throughout the year. [L.L. *dominicālis* — *dominus*, lord, master.]

Dominican *do-min'i-kən, adj* belonging to St *Dominic* or to the Dominicans. — *n* a friar or monk of the order of St Dominic, founded in 1215, preaching friars or *Black Friars*, from their black mantle.

dominie *dom'i-ni, n* a schoolmaster, a tutor (esp. *Scot*). [L. *domine*, voc. of *dominus*, master.]

dominion *də-min'yən, n* sovereignty; rule, power or authority; a domain or territory with one ruler, owner or government; a completely self-governing colony, not subordinate to but freely associated with the mother country; control. [L.L. *dominiō, -ōnis* — *dominus*, master.]

domino *dom'i-nō, n* one of the usu. twenty-eight oblong pieces with which the game of **dom'inoes** (*-nōz*) is played, divided into two compartments, each of which is a blank or marked with from one to six spots; a long cloak of black silk with a hood, used at masked balls, or its wearer; a mask: — *pl* **dom'inoes** or **dom'inos**. — **domino theory** the theory that one event sets off a series of similar events, thus exhibiting the **domino effect**, from the fall of one domino standing on end causing the whole row to fall in turn. [App. Sp. *dominó, dómino*, in some way conn. with L. *dominus*, master.]

don[1] *don, n* (with *cap*) a Spanish title, corresponding to English Sir, Mr (*fem* **Doña** (*dōn'ya*), Italian form **Don'na**); a Spanish nobleman, a Spaniard; a fellow of a college or university; any member of the teaching staff of a college or university; an expert (*Austr* and *NZ*). — *adj* **donn'ish** pertaining to or acting like a college don. — **Don Juan** (*hwän* or *jōō'ən*) a legendary Spanish licentious nobleman; an attractive libertine and profligate. [Sp., — L. *dominus*.]

don[2] *don, vt* to do or put on: — *pr p* **donn'ing**; *pa t* and *pa p* **donned**. [**do**[1] and **on**.]

donation *dō-nā'shən, n* an act of giving; that which is given, a gift of money or goods. — *vt* **dōnate'** to give as a gift; to contribute, esp. to charity. — *n* **dō'native** (or *don'*) a gift; a gratuity; a benefice presented by the founder or patron without reference to the bishop. — *adj* vested or vesting by donation. — *n* **dōnā'tor** someone who makes a gift, a donor. — *n* **dōnee'** the person to whom a gift is made. — *n* **dō'ning** (*colloq*) the act of donating (as blood). — *n* **dō'nor** a giver; a benefactor; a person who (or animal which) provides blood or semen, or tissue or organs for use in transplant surgery. — **donor card** a card carried by a person specifying parts of the body that may be used in transplant surgery in the event of the carrier's death; **donor insemination** artificial insemination using semen from a donor. [Fr. — L. *dōnāre, -ātum* — *dōnum*, a gift.]

donder *don'ə*, (*SAfr slang*) *vt* to beat up, thrash. — *n* a scoundrel, rogue. [Afrik., to thrash — Du. *donderen*, to swear, bully.]

done. See **do**[1].

donee. See under **donation**.

doner kebab. See under **kebab**.

dong[1] *dong, n* a deep ringing sound, as that of a large bell. — Also *vi.* [Imit.]

dong[2] *dong*, (*vulg*; *orig* and *chiefly US*) *n* the penis.

donga *dong'gə*, (orig. *SAfr*) *n* a gully made by soil erosion. [Zulu, bank, side of a gully.]

dongle *dong'gl, n* a device plugged into a computer which prevents the use of software on a different machine.

doning. See under **donation**.

donjon *dun'jən, n* a strong central tower in ancient castles, to which the garrison retreated when hard pressed. [A doublet of **dungeon**.]

donkey *dong'ki, n* an ass; a stupid person; a person used by drug dealers to carry drugs being smuggled through customs (*slang*): — *pl* **don'keys**. — **don'key-engine** a small auxiliary engine; **donkey jacket** a strong jacket, with shoulders of leather or (usu.) a substitute, and patch pockets; **donkey vote** (*Austr*) in a preferential system of voting, a vote accepting the order of candidates on the ballot paper; such votes collectively; **don'key-work** drudgery. — **argue** or **talk the hindlegs off a donkey** to argue or talk persistently and therefore usu. persuasively; **donkey's years** a long time (a pun on *ears*). [Perh. from *Duncan*.]

Donna. See under **don**[1].

Donnybrook or **donnybrook** *don'i-brŏŏk, n* a rowdy brawl or assembly. [From the fair at *Donnybrook*, Dublin.]

donor. See under **donation**.

don't *dōnt*, for **do not**. — *n* something that must not be done. — **don't-know'** (the answer given by) a person whose mind is not made up with regard to some, esp. political, issue.

donut. Same as **doughnut**.

doodah *dōō'dä* or (esp. in U.S.) **doodad** *dōō'dad, n* a small ornament or trinket; a gadget. — **all of a doodah** very agitated. [From **do**[1].]

doodle *dōōd'l, vi* to scrawl or scribble meaninglessly. — *n* something doodled. — *n* **dood'ler**.

doodlebug *dōōd'l-bug, n* the larva of an ant-lion or other insect (used in divination in America; *US*); any instrument, scientific or unscientific, used by prospectors to indicate the presence of minerals; a flying bomb (*war slang*).

doolally *dōō-lal'i*, (*slang*) *adj* mentally unbalanced; crazy. [Deolali, a town near Bombay.]

doom *dōōm, n* destiny, fate; ruin; catastrophe; death; final judgment. — *vt* to pronounce judgment on; to condemn to destiny or catastrophe. — **doom'-merchant** (*colloq*) a pessimist; someone who continually expects and forecasts disaster; **dooms'day** the day of doom, the last judgment; a day of reckoning; **doom'watch** pessimism about the contemporary situation and about the future, esp. of the environment; observation of the environment to prevent its destruction by pollution, over-population, etc.; a generally pessimistic view of the future. — Also *adj* and *vi.* — **doom'watcher; doom'-watching**. — **Doomsday-book** see **Domesday-book**. — **crack of doom** the last trump; **till doomsday** forever. [O.E. *dōm*, judgment.]

doona *dōō'nə*, (*Austr*) *n* a continental quilt. [Orig. a trademark.]

door *dör, n* the usual entrance into a house, room or passage; a frame for closing up the entrance; a means of approach or access. — **door'bell; door'keeper; door'knob; door'knock** (*Austr*) a fundraising appeal in which agents go from door to door soliciting donations. — Also *adj* and *vi.* — **door'knocker** a knocker on a door; a person who doorknocks (*Austr*); **door'-man** a porter, doorkeeper (also **doors'man**); **door'mat** a mat for wiping shoes on at a door; an uncomplaining person whom others treat inconsiderately (*colloq*); **door'nail** a stud for a door; **door'post** the jamb or side-piece of a door; **door'-step** a step at a door; a thick slice of bread (*colloq*). — *vt* to go from door to door round (an area), e.g. canvassing in an election; esp. of journalists, to pester someone, by waiting on their doorstep: — *pr p* **door'stepping**; *pa t* and *pa p* **door'stepped**. — **door'stepper; door'stepping; door'stop** a wedge to prevent a door swinging shut; a knob fixed to floor or wall to prevent a door opening too far. — *adj* **door'-to-door'** calling at each house in an area in order to sell, canvass, etc. (also *adv*). — **door'way** an opening where there is or might be a door. — **close (**or **open) the door to** to make impossible (or possible); **doorstep selling** going from house to house to (try to) sell goods or services; **lay at someone's door** to blame someone (for); **next door (to)** in the next house; near or bordering upon; **on one's doorstep** close to one's house, etc.; **out-of-doors** see under **out**; **show someone the door** to turn someone out of the house. [O.E. *duru* (fem.) and *dor* (neut.).]

dopa *dō'pə, n* a naturally-occurring amino-acid, a form of which, L-dopa is used in the treatment of Parkinson's disease. [From *di*oxy*p*henyl*a*lanine, a former name for the compound.]

dope *dōp, n* a thick liquid, semi-liquid, or pasty material; lubricating grease; aeroplane varnish; a substance added to improve the efficiency or modify the properties of anything; opium; a drug, esp. one administered to an athlete, a racehorse or taken by an addict; drug-taking; confidential or fraudulent information in advance (*colloq*); information in general (*colloq*); anything supplied to dull, blind, or blunt the conscience, feeling, or insight; a fool (*colloq*). — *vt* to give or apply dope to; to drug; to add impurities to (a semiconductor) to modify or improve its properties (*electronics*). — *vi* to take dope. — *n* **dōp'ant** (*electronics*) a substance used in doping. — *adj* **dope'y** or **dōp'y** stupefied; stupid. — *n* **dōp'ing** (*electronics*) the addition of known impurities to a semiconductor, to achieve the desired properties in diodes and transistors. — **dope'-fiend** a drug addict. [Du. *doop*, a dipping, sauce; *doopen*, to dip.]

doppelgänger *dop'l-geng-ər, n* an apparition, a ghostly double of a human person. [Ger., lit. double-goer.]

dopplerite *dop'lər-īt, n* a black elastic substance (calcium salts of humus acids) found in peat beds. — **Doppler effect** or **shift** an observed change of wavelength when a source of vibrations is moving towards or from the observer, used in e.g. **Doppler radar** to determine velocities of observed objects. [From Christian *Doppler* (1803–53), an Austrian physicist.]

dorado *də-rä'dō, n* the coryphene, a large edible marine fish, so called from its iridescent gold/blue colour when dying: — *pl* **dora'dos.** [Sp. from *dorar*, to gild — L. *deaurāre, -ātum*.]

Dorian mode *dō'ri-ən mōd, n* a mode of ancient Greek music, traditionally of a stirring, solemn, simple and martial quality; an authentic mode of old church music, extending from d to d with d as its final. [L. *Dōrius* — Gr. *Dōrios* — *Dōris*, an area of Ancient Greece.]

Doric *dor'ik, adj* denoting one of the Greek orders of architecture, distinguished by its simplicity and massive strength. — *n* an Ancient Greek dialect; any dialect imagined to resemble it, esp. Scottish. [L. *Dōricus* — Gr. *Dōrikos* — *Dōris*, an area of Ancient Greece.]

dork *dörk*, (*US slang*) *n* an idiot, an object of contempt. — *adj* **dork'y.** [Orig. a penis.]

dorm *dörm*, (*colloq*) *n* short for **dormitory.**

dormant *dör'mənt, adj* sleeping; hibernating; (of seeds, etc.) alive but not active or growing; (of volcanoes) inactive but not extinct; torpid, lethargic; resting; not used, in abeyance (as a title). — *n* **dor'mancy.** [O.Fr. *dormant*, pres. p. of *dormir* — L. *dormīre*, to sleep.]

dormer *dör'mər, n* a dormer window. — **dormer window** a small window with a gable, projecting from a sloping roof (orig. a dormitory window). [O.Fr. *dormeor* — L. *dormīre*, to sleep.]

dormie. See **dormy.**

dormitory *dör'mi-tər-i, n* a large room with many beds, whether in separate cubicles or not; a college hostel (*US*); a small town or a suburb (also **dormitory town** or **suburb**), the majority of whose residents work elsewhere. [L. *dormītōrium* — *dormīre*, to sleep.]

Dormobile® *dör'mə-bēl, n* a type of van equipped for living and sleeping in.

dormouse *dör'mows, n* any member of a family of rodents, in form and habit resembling a small squirrel: — *pl* **dor'mice.** [Perh. conn. with L. *dōrmīre*, to sleep (from their hibernation), and prob. **mouse.**]

dormy or **dormie** *dör'mi*, (*golf*) *adj* as many holes up or ahead as there are yet to play. [Perh. conn. with L. *dormīre*, to sleep; the player who is *dormy* cannot lose even by going to sleep.]

dorp *dörp, n* a Dutch or S. African village or small town; a town considered as provincial and backward (*colloq*; *derog*). [Du., Afrik.; O.E. *thorp*.]

dorsal *dör'sl, adj* relating or belonging to the back. — *n* a dorsal fin; a dorsal vertebra. — *adv* **dor'sally.** — *n* **dorsiflex'ion** a bending backwards; a bending of the back, a bow. — *adj* **dor'sigrade** walking on the back of the toes. [L. *dorsum*, the back.]

dory[1] *dö'ri, n* a golden-yellow fish of the mackerel family, officially called sea-wolf. — Also called **John Dory.** [Fr. *dorée*, from *dorer*, to gild.]

dory[2] *dö'ri*, (esp. *US*) *n* a small boat, with flat bottom, sharp bow and stern, especially suited for surf-riding.

DOS *dos*, (*comput*) *abbrev* for disc operating system.

dos-à-dos *dō-za-dō', n* a seat on which people sit back to back; (*dō-sē-dō'*) a square-dance figure in which dancers pass each other back to back: —*pl* **dos-à-dos.** — Also **dosi-do'**: — *pl* **dosi-dos'.** [Fr.]

dose *dōs, n* the quantity of medicine, electric current, X-rays, etc., administered at one time; a portion, esp. a measured portion, of something given or added; anything disagreeable or medicinal to be taken; a bout, esp. of an illness or something unpleasant. — *vt* to give doses to. — *n* **dōs'age** the practice, act or method of dosing; the regulation of dose; the proper size of dose. — *n* **dōsim'eter** an instrument for measuring radiation. — *n* **dōsim'etry.** — **dose equivalent** a quantity of absorbed radiation dosage, measured in sieverts or (esp. formerly) in rems, being the value of the absorbed dose (q.v. below) adjusted to take account of the different effects different types of radiation have on the human body, etc. — **absorbed dose** the amount of radiation absorbed by a body, etc., measured in grays or (esp. formerly) rads. [Fr., — Gr. *dŏsis*, a giving — *didonai*, to give.]

dosh *dosh*, (*slang*) *n* money.

dosi-do. See **dos-à-dos.**

doss *dos*, (*slang*) *n* a sleep; a bed, sleeping-place. — *vi* to sleep; to go to bed. — *n* **doss'er** someone who lodges in a doss-house, or wherever possible. — **doss'-house** a very cheap lodging-house. — **doss down** to go to bed in a doss-house, or in a makeshift bed elsewhere. [Perh. from *doss*, a dialectal Eng. name for a hassock.]

dossier *do'si-ā, do-syā'* or *dos'i-ər*, (*legal*) *n* a bundle of documents relating to a person or case; a brief. [Fr., — *dos* — L. *dorsum*, back.]

dot[1] *dot, n* a very small spot; a symbol representing the short element in Morse and other codes. — *vt* to mark with a dot or dots; to scatter with objects; to hit (*slang*); to place, stand, etc. at irregular spaced intervals: — *pr p* **dott'ing**; *pa t* and *pa p* **dott'ed.** — *n* **dott'iness.** — *adj* **dott'y** crazed (*colloq*). — **dotted line** a line composed of dots or dashes that (on printed forms, etc.) one is instructed to sign on, tear along, etc.; **dotted note** or **rest** (*mus*) one whose length is increased by one half by a dot placed after it; **dotted rhythm** one characterised by dotted notes; **dot matrix** (*comput*) a method of printing using a rectangular matrix consisting of lines of pins, a selection of which is used to make each letter shape. — **dot and carry** (*arith*) to set down the units and carry over the tens to the next column; **dot one's i's and cross one's t's** to pay great attention to detail; **on the dot (of)** exactly (at) (a given time); **the year dot** (*colloq*) the very beginning of time. [O.E. *dott*, head of a boil.]

dot[2] *dot, n* a woman's dowry. — *adj* **dō'tal.** [Fr., — L. *dōs, dōtis*.]

dote or **doat** *dōt, vi* to show excessive love (with *upon* or *on*); to be weakly affectionate. — *n* **dōt'age** the childishness of old age. — *n* **dōt'ard** a person showing the weakness of old age. [Cf. Old Du. *doten*, to be silly.]

dotterel *dot'ər-əl*, *n* a kind of plover, named from its apparent stupidity in allowing itself to be approached and caught; a stupid fellow. [Ety. as for **dote**, with sfx. *-rel*.]

douane *dōō-än'* or *dwän*, *n* a custom-house. — *n* **douanier** (*dwä-nyā'*) a custom-house officer. [Fr., — Ar. *dīwān*.]

Douay Bible *dōō'ā bī'bl*, *n* an English Roman Catholic translation of the Bible done at *Douai*, France in 1609–10.

double *dub'l*, *adj* twice as much; of about twice the weight, size or quality; twofold; two of a sort together; in pairs; paired; for two people; folded once; sounding an octave lower. — *adv* to twice the extent; twice over; two together. — *vt* to multiply by two; to make twofold; to make twice as much or as many; to be the double of; in acting, to play by doubling; to be a substitute for or counterpart of; to raise the scores at stake in (a hand at bridge); to sound in another octave; to line (*heraldry*); to fold; to clench. — *vi* to increase to twice the quantity; to turn sharply back on one's course; to act as substitute; in acting, to play two different parts in the same piece; in bridge, to make a double (bid). — *n* a quantity twice as much; a score of twice the amount shown, as in the outer ring of a dartboard; a combination of two things of the same kind (as a binary star); (in *pl*) a game with two players on each side (*tennis*, etc.); two faults in succession (*tennis*); a bid which, if successful, increases one's score for the hand and, if unsuccessful, increases one's penalty (*bridge*); a win, or a defeat, in two events on the same programme; a combined bet on two races, stake and winnings from the first being bet on the second; a duplicate; an actor's substitute; a quick pace (short for **double-quick**); an exact counterpart. — *n* **doub'leness** the state of being double; duplicity. — *n* **doub'leton** (the possession of) two cards of a suit in a hand. — *adv* **doub'ly**. — **double act** (*theat*) a variety act for two people; the two entertainers; **double-a'gent** an agent secretly acting simultaneously for two opposing powers; **double axel** (*skating*) an axel incorporating two and a half turns. — *adj* **double-banked'** having two men at each oar, or having two tiers of oars one above the other, as in ancient galleys. — *adj* **double-barr'elled** having two barrels; (of a surname) hyphened; (of a compliment) ambiguous. — **double-bass'** the largest and lowest-pitched instrument of the violin family, playing an octave below the cello; **double bed** a bed wide enough for two people; **double bill** see under **bill**[3]; **double bind** (*psychiatry*) a situation in which conflicting cues are given so that any choice of behaviour will be considered wrong. — *adj* **double-blind'** denoting a comparative experiment, trial, etc. in which the identities of the control group are known neither to the subjects nor to the experimenters; **double bond** (*chem*) a covalent bond involving the sharing of two pairs of electrons; **double-bott'om** or **double-bottom lorry** an articulated lorry pulling a trailer. — *adj* **double-breast'ed** (of a coat) having two fronts, one to be folded over the other. — *vt* and *vi* **double-check'** to check a second time. — Also *n*. — **double chin** a chin with a fold of flesh; **double concerto** a concerto for two solo instruments; **double cream** a cream with a higher fat content than single cream; **doub'le-cross** a betrayal or deceiving of someone for whom one was supposed to be betraying or deceiving someone else. — *vt* to betray by double-cross. — **double-cross'er**; **double-dagg'er** a diesis (‡); **double-deal'er** a deceitful person; **double-deal'ing** duplicity; **double-deck'er** a ship having two decks; a bus, tram-car, etc., in two storeys or tiers; a sandwich having three pieces of bread and two layers of filling; a novel, film, etc., in two separate parts. — *vi* **double-declutch'** (*autos*) to change into a different gear by first changing to neutral, increasing the engine speed, then engaging the chosen gear, disengaging the clutch at both stages. — **double-decomposi'tion** a chemical action in which two compounds exchange some of their constituents. — *adj* **double-dens'ity** (*comput*) of a disc which can record double the normal number of bytes. — **double door** or **doors** a door consisting of two parts hung on opposite posts; **double-dotted note** or **rest** (*mus*) one whose length is increased by three-quarters by two dots placed after it; **double-dotted rhythm** one characterised by double-dotted notes; **double-Dutch'** incomprehensible talk. — *adj* **doub'le-dyed** twice-dyed; deeply imbued. — **doub'le-eagle** a heraldic representation of an eagle with two heads, as in the old arms of Russia and Austria. — *adj* **double-edged'** having two edges; cutting or working both ways. — **double-en'try** (*bookkeeping*) a method by which two entries are made of each transaction; **double exposure** (*phot*) accidental or deliberate superimposition of one image on another; **double fault** (*tennis*, etc.) two faults served in succession, causing the loss of a point. — *vi* **double-fault'**. — **double feature** a cinema programme involving two full-length films. — *adj* **double-fig'ure**. — **double figures** a score, total, etc. of any number equal to or greater than 10 but less than 100; **double first** a university degree with first-class honours in two different subjects; a person who has such a degree. — *adj* **double-front'ed** (of a house) having main-room windows on both sides of the front door. — **double-glaz'ing** a double layer of glass in a window with an air-space between the layers to act as insulation. — *adj* **double-glazed'**. — **double Gloucester** (*glos'tər*) a Gloucestershire cheese of extra richness; **double-head'er** a coin with a head on each side (*colloq*); two games played on the same day (*sport*; *NAm*); **double helix** the DNA molecule, two spirals coiled round an axis; **double jeopardy** second trial for the same offence. — *adj* **double-joint'ed** having loose joints admitting some degree of movement backward. — *adj* **double-locked'** locked with two locks or bolts; locked by two turns of the key. — *adj* **double-mean'ing** ambiguous. — Also *n*. — **double negative** a construction consisting of two negatives, esp. when only one is logically required. — *vt* and *vi* **double-park'** to park (a car, etc.) alongside vehicles already parked at the kerb. — **double pneumonia** pneumonia of both lungs. — *adj* and *adv* **double-quick'** at a pace approaching a run; very fast. — **doub'le-speak** double-talk; **double standard** a principle, etc. applied in such a way as to allow different standards of behaviour to different people, groups, etc.; (in *pl*) the practice of advocating (for others) certain moral, etc. standards not followed by oneself; bimetallism; **double star** (*astron*) a binary star; two unrelated stars appearing close together when seen through a telescope; **double-stopp'ing** (*mus*) see **stopping** under **stop**; **double-take'** a reaction, usu. delayed, caused by surprise or admiration; **doub'le-talk** talk that sounds relevant but means nothing; ambiguous, deceptive talk; **doub'lethink** the faculty of simultaneously harbouring two conflicting beliefs — coined by George Orwell in his book *Nineteen Eighty-Four* (1949); **double time** payment to a worker at twice the usual rate; a time twice as fast as the previous time (*mus*); a fast marching pace (*US*). — *adj* **double-tongued'** deceitful. — **double vision** seeing two images of the same object, because of lack of co-ordination between the two eyes; **double-u** (*dub'l-ū*) the twenty-third letter of the alphabet (W, w); **double wedding** one involving two couples; **double zero option** see **zero-zero option**. — **at the double** very quickly;

double back to go back in the direction one has just come, usu. not by the same path; **double or quits** in gambling, the alternative, left to chance, of doubling or cancelling payment (*adj* **double-or-quits'**); **double up** to fold double; to bend over (as with laughter); to share with another. [O.Fr. *doble* — L. *duplus*, double.]

double entendre *dōōbl' ā-tā'dr'*, *n* (the use of) a word or phrase with two meanings, one usu. more or less indecent. [Fr. of 17th cent., superseded now by (*mot*) *à double entente*.]

doublet *dub'lit*, *n* a close-fitting garment for the upper part of the body — with *hose*, the typical masculine dress in the 14th–17th centuries; a thing that is repeated or duplicated; one of a pair, esp. one of two words orig. the same but varying in spelling and meaning, e.g. *balm*, *balsam*. [O.Fr., dimin. of *double*.]

doubletree *dub'l-trē*, *n* the horizontal bar on a vehicle to which the whippletree (with harnessed animals) is attached.

doubloon *dub-lōōn'*, *n* an obsolete Spanish gold coin. [Sp. *doblón*, — *doble*, double.]

doubt *dowt*, *vi* to be undecided in opinion. — *vt* to be uncertain about; to question; to incline to believe only with uncertainty or fear; to distrust; to suspect (*archaic*; also *reflexive*). — *n* uncertainty of opinion; a suspicion; a thing doubtful or questioned. — *adj* **doubt'able.** — *n* **doubt'er.** — *adj* **doubt'ful** feeling doubt; subject to doubt; not clear; insecure; not confident; not likely or not certain to participate, co-operate, etc. — *n* a doubtful person or thing. — *adv* **doubt'fully.** — *n* **doubt'fulness.** — *n* and *adj* **doubt'ing.** — *adv* **doubt'ingly.** — *adj* **doubt'less** without doubt; certainly; no doubt (often only allowing for the possibility). — *adv* **doubt'lessly.** — **doubting Thomas** a doubter or sceptic; someone who needs proof before believing something (from the doubting of *Thomas*, in the Bible: John, xx. 25). — **beyond doubt** or **beyond a shadow of a doubt** certain or certainly; **in doubt** not certain, undecided; **no doubt** surely. [O.Fr. *douter* — L. *dubitāre*.]

douceur *dōō-sûr'*, *n* a conciliatory present, bribe or tip. [Fr. *doux*, *douce*, mild — L. *dulcis*, sweet.]

douche *dōōsh*, *n* a jet of water directed upon or into the body from a pipe, etc.; an apparatus for producing such a jet. — *vt* and *vi* to use a douche (on). [Fr., — It. *doccia*, a water pipe.]

dough *dō*, *n* a mass of flour or meal moistened and kneaded, but not baked; money (*slang*). — *n* **dough'iness.** — *adj* **dough'y** like dough; soft; (of complexion) pallid, pasty. — **dough'-boy** or **dough'-ball** a boiled flour dumpling; **dough'nut** sweetened dough fried in fat; an accelerating tube in the form of a toroid (*nuc*); a toroidal assembly of enriched fissile material for increasing locally the neutron intensity in a reactor (*nuc*). — *vi* to practise doughnutting. — **dough'nutting** the surrounding of a speaker in parliament by other members to give an impression to television viewers esp. of a packed house. [O.E. *dāh*, dough.]

doughty *dow'ti*, *adj* able, strong; brave. — *adv* **dough'tily.** — *n* **dough'tiness.** [O.E. *dyhtig*, valiant.]

Douglas fir *dug'ləs fûr*, *n* a tall western American coniferous timber tree. [David *Douglas* (1798–1834), who introduced it to Britain.]

doum-palm *dowm'* or *dōōm'-päm*, *n* an African palm with a branched stem and a fruit tasting of gingerbread. [Ar. *daum*, *dūm*.]

dour *dōōr*, *adj* obstinate; sullen; grim. — *n* **dour'ness.** [App. L. *dūrus*, hard.]

doura. See **durra.**

douroucouli *dōō-rōō-kōō'lē*, *n* a nocturnal monkey, any monkey of the S. American genus *Nyctipithecus*. [S. Am. name.]

douse[1] or **dowse** *dows*, *vt* to plunge into water. — *vi* to fall suddenly into water.

douse[2] or **dowse** *dows*, *vt* to put out, extinguish (as a light). — *n* **dous'er** a shutter for cutting off light in a cinema projector. [Perh. conn. with **dout.**]

dout *dowt*, *vt* to put out, extinguish. — *n* see **dowt.** — *n* **dout'er.** [**do**[1] and **out.**]

dove *duv*, *n* a pigeon, (often combined, as in *ring-dove*, *turtledove*) used esp. of the smaller species; an old term of endearment; an emblem of innocence, gentleness, also of the Holy Spirit (*Bible*: Matthew iii. 16); in politics, industrial relations, etc., a person who seeks peace and conciliation rather than confrontation or war (opp. to *hawk*). — **dove'-colour** a greyish, bluish, pinkish colour; **dove'cot** or **dove'-cote** a small building or structure in which pigeons breed; a pigeon-house; **dove'tail** a tenon shaped like a dove's spread tail, for fastening boards; a joint of alternate tenons and mortises of that shape. — *vt* and *vi* to fit by or as if by one or more dovetails. — **dove'tailing.** [O.E. *dūfe*, in *dūfe-doppa*, a diving bird.]

dovekie *duv'ki*, *n* the little auk or rotch; the black guillemot. [Dimin. of **dove.**]

dowager *dow'ə-jər*, *n* a widow with a jointure or dower; a title given to a widow to distinguish her from the wife of her husband's heir (also *adj*); an elderly usu. wealthy woman of imposing appearance. [O.Fr. *douagere* — L. *dōtāre*, to endow.]

dowdy *dowd'i*, *adj* (esp. of a woman) wearing dull-looking, clumsy, ill-shaped clothes. — *adv* **dowd'ily.** — *n* **dowd'iness.**

dowel *dow'əl*, *n* a pin for fastening things together by fitting into a hole in each. — *vt* to fasten by means of dowels. — *n* **dow'elling** long, thin, usu. wooden rod of circular section. [Prob. rel. to Ger. *Döbel*, *Dübel*, a plug.]

dower *dow'ər*, *n* a jointure; a dowry; an endowment. — *vt* to give a dowry to; to endow. — **dow'er-house** the house set apart for the widow, usu. on her late husband's estate. [O.Fr. *douaire* — L. *dōtāre*, to endow.]

Dow-Jones average or **index** *dow-jōnz' av'ər-ij* or *in'deks*, *n* an indicator of the relative prices of stocks and shares on the New York stock exchange. [Charles H. *Dow* (1851–1902) and Edward D. *Jones* (1856–1920), American economists.]

down[1] *down*, *n* soft feathers; a soft covering of fluffy hair. — *n* **Down'ie**® a duvet. — *n* **down'iness.** — *adj* **down'y** covered with or made of down; like down. [O.N. *dūnn*.]

down[2] *down*, *n* a treeless upland; (in *pl*) an undulating upland tract of pasture-land, esp. in S.E. England (**the Downs**); the roadstead off E. Kent. [O.E. *dūn*, a hill — Celt. *dun*.]

down[3] *down*, *adv* to a lower position, level or state; away from a centre (capital city, university, etc.); southward; in a low or lowered position or state; below; on or to the ground; downstairs; under the surface; from earlier to later times; from greater to less; to a standstill, exhaustion, or conclusion; to a final state of subjection, silence, etc.; at a disadvantage; ill; behindhand; in writing or record, in black and white; on the spot, immediately in cash; against or hostile to (with *on* or *upon*); broken, not operational (*comput*). — *adj* directed towards or having a lower position or level; depressed; broken, not operational (*comput*). — *prep* in a descent along, through or by; to or in a lower position on or in; along in the direction of the current of a river; along. — *n* a descent; a low place; a time of comparative bad luck; an act of throwing or putting down; a feeling of dislike; one of four consecutive periods of play, during which a team must score or advance the ball 9 m. (10 yd.) in order to retain possession (*Am football*). — *vt* to knock, throw, shoot or put down; to overthrow; to depress. — *interj* ordering (esp. a dog) to go or stay down; (with *with*) expressing a wish for the downfall of someone or something. — *n* **down'er** (*slang*) a depressant drug; any depressing experience, etc. — *adv* **down'ward** (*-wərd*) or **down'wards** (*-wərdz*) from higher to lower; from source to outlet; from more ancient to modern; in the lower part. — *adj* **down'ward**. — *adv* **down'wardly**. — *adj* **down-and-out'** at the end of one's resources (*n* **down'-and-out**). — *adj* **down-at-heel'** generally shabby. — **down'beat** a downward movement of a conductor's baton; an accented beat. — *adj* (*colloq*) relaxed, unworried; depressed; pessimistic. — **down'bow** (*mus*) a movement of the bow over the strings beginning at the nut end. — *adj* **down'cast** dejected. — **down'-draught** a current of air downwards; **down'fall** failure, humiliation, ruin; a heavy fall of rain; **down'force** aerodynamically-caused downward force in a car, etc. which e.g. improves its roadholding; **down'grade** a downward slope or course. — *adj* and *adv* downhill. — *vt* **downgrade'** to reduce in status, etc.; to belittle, underrate. — *adj* **downheart'ed** dejected. — *adj* **down'hill** descending, sloping. — *adv* **downhill'**. — *adj* **down'-home** (*US colloq*) characteristic of the southern U.S. states; characteristic of the country or country-dwellers; homemade; friendly. — **down'-line** the line of a railway leading from the capital, or other important centre, to the provinces. — *vt* **download'** (*comput*) to transfer (data or programs) from one computer to another. — *adj* **down-mar'ket** of (buying, selling or using) commodities relatively low in price, quality or prestige. — Also *adv*. — *adv* and *adj* **down'most** superlative of *down*. — **down payment** a deposit on an article, service, etc.; **down'pipe** a drainpipe which takes rainwater from the gutter of a roof; **down'pour** a heavy fall of rain, etc. — *adv* **down'right** in plain terms; utterly. — *adj* plain-spoken; brusque; utter, out-and-out (as in *downright madness*); thorough. — **down'rush** a rushing down (as of gas, hot air, etc.); **down'side** the adverse or disadvantageous aspect of a situation (also *adj*). — *vt* **down'size** to reduce in size (esp. a workforce by redundancy); to design or make a smaller model of (a car etc.). — *adv* **downstage'** towards the footlights (also *adj*). — *adv* **downstairs'** in or towards a lower storey; in the servants' quarters. — *n* a lower storey, usu. the ground floor. — *adj* **down'stair** or **down'stairs**. — *adv* **downstream'** with the current. — *adj* **down'stream** further down the stream; going with the current. — **down'swing** a downward trend in volume of trade, etc.; the part of the swing where the club is moving down towards the ball (*golf*). — *adj* **down-to-earth'** sensible; practical; realistic. — *adj* and *adv* **down'-town** in or towards the lower part or (esp. *US*) the business and shopping centre of the town. — *n* this part of a town. — **down'-train** a railway train which leaves from the chief terminus; **down'trend** a downward trend. — *adj* **down'trodden** trampled on; tyrannised over. — **down'turn** a downward trend, decline. — *adj* and *adv* **down'wind** in the direction in which the wind is blowing; in or to a position (relative to someone or something) in this direction (often with *of*). — **down in the mouth** in low spirits; **down on one's luck** in unfortunate circumstances; **down tools** to stop work, strike; **down under** in or to Australia and New Zealand; **go down** (often with *with*) to be received (well or badly) (by); (often with *with*) to be acceptable (to); (with *with*) to contract (illness); **go downhill** to deteriorate (in health, prosperity, morality); **up and down** alternately well and ill; to and fro. [M.E. *a-down, adun* — O.E. *of dūne*, from the hill.]

Downie®. See under **down**[1].

Downing Street *down'ing strēt*, (*colloq*) *n* the British Government. [*Downing Street* in London, containing the official residences of the British Prime Minister and the Chancellor of the Exchequer.]

Down's syndrome *downz sin'drōm*, *n* a congenital disease caused by chromosomal abnormality, in which there is mental deficiency and a broadening and flattening of the features. — Formerly known as **Mongolism**. [John L. H. *Down*, (1828–96), English physician.]

dowry *dow'ri*, *n* the property which a woman brings to her husband at marriage; a natural endowment. [See **dower**.]

dowse[1] *dows*, *vt* and *vi*. See **douse**[1,2].

dowse[2] *dowz*, *vi* to look for water with a divining-rod. — *n* **dows'er** a person who divines water.

dowt or **dout** *dowt*, (*Scot*) *n* a cigarette-end. [From **dout**.]

doxology *doks-ol'ə-ji*, (*Christian relig*) *n* a hymn or liturgical formula ascribing glory to God. [Gr. *doxa*, opinion, reputation, glory, *logos*, discourse.]

doxy *dok'si*, *n* a woman of loose character.

doyen *doi'ən* or *dwä-yã fem* **doyenne** *doi-en'* or *dwä-yen*, *n* a senior member (of an academy, diplomatic corps, class, profession, etc.). [Fr. — L. *decānus*.]

doyley. See **doily**.

doz. (sometimes *duz*) *abbrev* for dozen.

doze *dōz*, *vi* to sleep lightly, or to be half-asleep; to be in a dull or stupefied state. — *n* a short light sleep. — *n* **dō'zer**. — *n* **dō'ziness**. — *adj* **dō'zy** drowsy; not alert, stupid (*colloq*).

dozen *duz'n*, *n* a set of twelve; also used, esp. in *pl*, for a less exact number: — *pl* **doz'en** when preceded by a numeral, otherwise **doz'ens**. — *adj* and *n* **doz'enth**. — **baker's, devil's** or **long dozen** thirteen; **daily dozen** see under **daily**; **half-a-doz'en** six; approximately six; **round dozen** a full dozen. [O.Fr. *dozeine* — L. *duodecim*.]

dozer. Colloq. for **bulldozer** (see **bulldoze**).

DP *abbrev* for: data processing; displaced person.

DPA *abbrev* for: Data Protection Authority; Discharged Prisoners' Aid.

DPH *abbrev* for Diploma in Public Health.

DPh. or **DPhil.** *abbrev* for Doctor of Philosophy.

dpi (*comput*) *abbrev* for dots per inch.

DPP *abbrev* for Director of Public Prosecutions.

dpt *abbrev* for department.

DR *abbrev* for dry riser.

Dr *abbrev* for: debtor; Doctor; Driver; Drummer.

Dr. *abbrev* for: drachma; Drive (in street names).

dr. *abbrev* for: dram; drawer.

drab[1] *drab*, *n* a low, sluttish woman; a whore.

drab[2] *drab*, *adj* dull and monotonous. — *n* a grey or dull-brown colour; cloth of this colour. — *adv* **drab'ly**. — *n* **drab'ness**. [Perh. Fr. *drap*, cloth — L.L. *drappus*.]

drachm *dram*, *n* a drachma; a dram.

drachma *drak'mə*, *n* in ancient Greece, a weight, and a silver coin of different values; the standard unit of modern Greek currency (100 *leptae*). [Gr. *drachmē* — *drassesthai*, to grasp with the hand.]

Draconian *drə-* or *drā-kō'ni-ən*, **Draconic** (*-kon'ik*), also **dracōn'ian** or **dracon'ic** *adj* extremely severe, as were the laws of *Draco*, an Athenian magistrate in 621 B.C.

draff *dräf*, *n* dregs; the refuse of malt after brewing.

draft *dräft*, *n* anything drawn; a plan; a preliminary sketch; the selecting of a smaller body (of people, animals, things) from a larger; the body so selected (esp. *mil*); conscription (*US*); an order for the payment of money; (occasional and *US*) a draught (in various senses). — *vt* to draw an outline of; to draw up in preliminary form; to draw off, detach. — *n* **draft'er** or **draught'er** someone who drafts; a draught-horse. — **draft'-dodger** (*US colloq*) someone who avoids conscription; **draft'-horse, draft'-ox, drafts, drafts'man, drafts'manship** see under **draught**. [**draught**.]

drag *drag, vt* to draw by force; to draw slowly; to pull roughly and violently; to explore with a dragnet or hook; to apply a drag to. — *vi* to hang so as to trail on the ground; to move slowly and heavily; to lag; to give the feeling of being unduly slow or tedious: — *pr p* **dragg'ing**; *pa t* and *pa p* **dragged**. — *n* anything dragged; an act of dragging; a dragging effect; the component of the aerodynamic force on a body travelling through a fluid (esp. a vehicle travelling through air) that lies along the longitudinal axis; a net or hook for dragging along to catch things under water; a heavy harrow; a brake, esp. an iron shoe that drags on the ground; any obstacle to progress; a tedious, dreary occupation or experience (*slang*); a trail of scent left by an animal, or a trail of broken undergrowth caused by an animal dragging off its prey; an artificial scent dragged on the ground for foxhounds to follow; a short 'draw' on a cigarette (*slang*); (the wearing of) transvestite clothing, now usu. women's dress worn by a man (*slang*; also *adj*). — *n* **drag'ster** a car for drag-racing. — **drag'net** a net to be dragged along the bottom of water or the ground; a systematic police search for a wanted person; **drag'-parachute** a small parachute attached to the rear of an aircraft, which opens on landing to assist deceleration; **drag'-queen** a homosexual who likes wearing women's clothes; **drag race** a motor car or motorcycle contest in acceleration, with standing start and over a quarter-mile course. — **drag by** to pass slowly; **drag on** to continue slowly and tediously; **drag one's feet** or **heels** to hang back deliberately in doing something; **drag out** to prolong unnecessarily or tediously. [Northern — O.E. *dragan* or O.N. *draga*.]

dragée *drä'zhā, n* a sweet enclosing a nut or fruit; a medicated sweet; a chocolate drop; a small silvered ball for decorating a cake. [Fr.]

draggle *drag'l, vt* or *vi* to make or become wet and dirty, as if by dragging along the ground; to trail. [Frequentative of **drag**.]

dragoman *drag'ō-mən, n* an interpreter or guide in Eastern countries: — *pl* **drag'ōmans**. [Fr., from Ar. *tarjumān* — *tarjama*, to interpret.]

dragon *drag'ən, n* a fabulous winged scaly-armoured fire-breathing monster, often a guardian of treasure, ravaging a country when its hoard is rifled; a fierce, intimidating or watchful person; a paper kite; applied to various plants. — *n* **drag'onet** a fish. — **drag'onfly** a long-bodied often brilliantly-coloured insect that lives on prey; **drag'on's-blood** a red resinous exudation from the dragon-tree and many other trees, used for colouring varnishes, etc.; **drag'on-tree** a large tree growing in the Canary Islands, having a thick trunk and producing dragon's-blood. — **chase the dragon** (*slang*) to smoke heroin by heating it and inhaling the fumes. [Fr., — L. *dracō, -ōnis* — Gr. *drakōn, -ontos*.]

dragonnade *drag-ən-ād', n* the persecution of French Protestants under Louis XIV by means of dragoons; any persecution by military means (usu. in *pl*). [Fr., from *dragon*, dragoon.]

dragoon *drə-gōōn', n* a heavy cavalryman (as opp. to hussars and lancers), a term surviving in the names of certain regiments. — *vt* to compel by military bullying; to compel by force. [Fr. *dragon*, dragon, dragoon.]

drain *drān, vt* to draw off by degrees; to filter; to draw off water, sewage or other liquid from; to instal a drain or drainage in; to make dry; to drink dry; to exhaust. — *vi* to flow off gradually; to lose liquid, esp. gradually; to discharge. — *n* a watercourse; a channel allowing liquid to drain; a ditch or sewer; expenditure that exhausts or diminishes. — *n* **drain'age** act, process, method or means of draining; means of discharging water; the system of drains in a town. — *n* **drain'er** a device on which articles are placed to drain. — **drain'age-basin** the area of land that drains into one river; **drain'ing-board** a sloping surface beside a sink, where dishes, etc. are placed to drain when washed; **drain'pipe** a pipe to carry away waste water or rainwater; (in *pl*; *colloq*) very narrow trousers. — **down the drain** (*slang*) gone, lost; wasted. [O.E. *drēahnian*.]

drake *drāk, n* the male of the duck.

Dralon® *drā'lon, n* a type of acrylic fibre.

dram *dram, n* a contraction of **drachm**; $\frac{1}{16}$th of an ounce avoirdupois; formerly (still *US*) apothecaries' measure of $\frac{1}{8}$th of an ounce; a small drink of alcohol, esp. whisky; a tipple. [Through Fr. and L., from Gr. *drachmē*; see **drachma**.]

drama *drä'mə, n* a composition showing life and action intended for representation by actors; the total range of dramatic literature; theatrical entertainment; a dramatic situation, or series of exciting, tense, tragic, etc. events. — *adj* **dramat'ic** (*drə-mat'ik*) belonging to or of drama; appropriate to or in the form of drama; with the force and vividness of a drama; impressive or important because of speed, size, suddenness, etc. — *adv* **dramat'ically**. — *n* (usu. *sing*) **dramat'ics** the acting, production, study of plays; a show of excessive, exaggerated emotion (*colloq*). — *n* **dramatīsā'tion** or **-z-** the act of dramatising; the dramatised version of a novel or story. — *vt* **dram'atise** or **-ize** to compose in, or turn into, the form of a drama or play; to exaggerate the importance of or emotional nature of. — *n* **dram'atist** a writer of plays. — **drama documentary** see **faction**[2]; **dramatic irony** a situation, etc. in a play, the irony of which is clear to the audience but not to the characters; **dramatis persōnae** (*-ē* or *-ī*) the characters of a drama or play. [L., — Gr. *drama, drāmatos* — *drāein*, to do.]

Dramamine® *dram'ə-mēn, n* a drug used esp. to treat travel sickness.

dramaturgy *dram'ə-tûr-ji, n* the principles of dramatic composition; theatrical art. — *n* **dram'aturge** or **dram'aturgist** a playwright. — *adj* **dramatur'gic** or **dramatur'gical**. [See ety. for **drama**, and Gr. *ergon*, a work.]

Drambuie® *dram-bōō'i* or *-bū'i, n* a Scotch whisky liqueur. [**dram**, and Gael. *buidhe*, yellow, golden, or agreeable, pleasant.]

drank *drangk, pa t* of **drink**.

drape *drāp, vt* to cover as with cloth; to hang cloth in folds about; to put (oneself) in a casual and graceful pose. — *n* a hanging or curtain (*US* and *theat*). — *n* **drāp'er** a dealer in cloth, textiles and clothing. — *n* **drāp'ery** cloth, textiles, etc.; hangings; the business of a draper; the representation of clothes and hanging folds of cloth (*art*): — *pl* **drāp'eries**. [O.Fr. *draper*, to weave, drape.]

drastic *dras'tik, adj* forcible, powerful in action; violent; unsparing; great and quick or sudden; dramatic; bad, unpleasant; extreme. — *adv* **dras'tically**. [Gr. *drastikos* — *drāein*, to act, to do.]

drat *drat, interj* used to express vexation. — *adj* **dratt'ed**. [From **God rot**.]

draught *dräft, n* a current of air; the act of drawing or pulling; the thing or quantity drawn; the act of drinking; the quantity drunk in one breath; a dose of liquor or medicine; a chosen detachment of men (usu. **draft**); the depth to which a ship sinks in the water; a thick disc used in the game of draughts (also **draughts'man**); (in *pl*) a game played by two persons moving draughtsmen alternately on a chequered board; the outline of a picture, or a preliminary sketch or plan (usu. **draft**). — *adj* on draught. — *vt* to sketch out or make a preliminary plan of or attempt at (also **draft**); occasionally for **draft** in sense of draw off, set apart from a larger body. — *n* **draught'iness**. — *adj* **draught'y** full of draughts or currents of air. — **draught'-animal, draught'-horse, draught'-ox**, etc., one used for drawing heavy loads; **draught-bar** see **drawbar**;

draught'board a chessboard used for playing draughts. — *adj* **draught'-proof** sealed, filled, etc. to prevent draughts. — Also *vt.* — **draught'proofing; draughts'man** a piece used in playing draughts; someone skilled or employed in drawing; someone who draughts or draws up documents (in this sense usu. **draftsman**); **draughts'manship.** — **feel the draught** (*fig*) to be unpleasantly aware of being short of money; **on draught** (of liquor) sold from the cask. [O.E. *draht* — *dragan*, to draw; see **drag, draw.**]

Dravidian *drə-vid'i-ən, adj* belonging to a dark, long-headed, wavy-haired race of Southern India; belonging to a group of languages in Southern India, including Tamil, Malayalam, Kannada, Telugu, etc. — Also *n.* [Sans. *Drāvida*, an ancient province of Southern India.]

draw *drö, vt* to pull or drag along; to bring forcibly towards or after one; to pull into position; to pull back; to take at random from a number; to entice, attract; to encourage to talk freely (usu. **draw out**); to inhale; to take out; to unsheathe; to cause to flow out; to extract by pulling; to eviscerate; to deduce; to lengthen; to receive or take from a source or store; to demand by a draft; to get by lot; to trace; to construct in linear form; to make a picture of by drawing lines; to describe; to put into shape; to write out (as a cheque); to require as depth of water for floating; to finish without winning or losing; to glance (*cricket*); to hit (the ball) too much to the left (if right-handed) or to the right (if left-handed) (*golf*); to deliver (a bowl) so that it moves in a curve to the point aimed for (*bowls*); to deliver gently (*curling*); to force one's opponents to play (all their cards of a suit, esp. trumps) by continually leading cards of that suit (*bridge*, etc.); to hit (the cue ball) so that it recoils after striking another ball (*billiards*, etc.). — *vi* to pull; to practise drawing; to move; to make one's way, go; (of a flue, etc.) to have a good current of air; to draw a card, a sword, lots; to infuse; to end a game without winning or losing; to move in a curve to the point aimed for (*bowls*): — *pa t* **drew** (*droo*); *pa p* **drawn.** — *n* the act of drawing; assignment by lot of prizes, opponents in a game, etc.; anything drawn; a drawn or undecided game; an attraction. — *adj* **draw'able.** — *n* **drawee'** the person on whom a bill of exchange is drawn. — *n* **draw'er** a person or thing that draws; (*drör*) a thing drawn out, as the sliding box in a **chest of drawers**; (in *pl*) a close undergarment for the lower part of the body and the legs. — *n* **draw'ing** the art of representing objects or forms by lines drawn, shading, etc.; a picture in lines; the act of assigning by lot; the act of pulling, etc. — *adj* **drawn** pulled together; neither won nor lost; strained, tense; unsheathed; eviscerated. — **draw'-back** a disadvantage; a receiving back some part of the duty on goods on their exportation; **draw'bar** a sliding bar; a bar used in coupling railway vehicles; **drawbar outfit** a lorry, whether or not articulated, with a trailer; **draw'bridge** a bridge that can be drawn up or let down as required; **draw'-down** a reduction, diminution; **draw hoe** a hoe designed for pulling soil towards one, having a flat blade at about right angles to the handle; **draw'ing-board** a slab on which paper can be pinned for drawing on; the planning stage of a project, etc. (*fig*); **draw'ing-master; draw'ing-pin** a short broad-headed pin; **draw'ing-room** see separate article; **drawn'-thread work** or **drawn work** ornamental work done by pulling out some of the threads of a fabric; **draw'-sheet** a hospital sheet that can be drawn out from under a patient; **draw'-string** a string, cord, etc., in a casing in, or threaded through, material, by which the material may be drawn or gathered up. — *adj* having or closed by such a string. — **at daggers drawn** openly hostile; **draw a blank** to get no result; lit., to get a lottery ticket that wins no prize; **draw back** to recoil; to withdraw; **draw, hang, and quarter** see under **hang; draw in** to reduce, contract; to become shorter; **draw near** to approach; **draw off** to cause to flow from a barrel, etc.; to withdraw; **draw on** to approach; to pull on; **draw on** or **upon** to make a draught upon; to make a demand upon (e.g. patience, resources); to draw one's weapon against; **draw out** to lengthen; to entice into talk and self-expression; (of an army, etc.) to leave the place; **draw rein** to slacken speed, to stop; **draw stumps** to end play in cricket by removing the wickets; **draw the line** to fix a limit; to find finally and positively unacceptable; **draw the teeth of** to make harmless; **draw up** to form in regular order; to compose, put into shape; to stop; **out of the top drawer** of top grade, esp. socially. [O.E. *dragan*; cf. **drag.**]

drawing-room *drö'ing-room, n* a living room or sitting-room. — *adj* suitable for the drawing-room. [Orig. *withdrawing-room* (to which the company withdrew after dinner).]

drawl *dröl, vi* to speak in a slow lengthened tone. — *vt* to say in a slow and sleepy manner. — *n* a slow, lengthened utterance. — *n* **drawl'er.** [Conn. with **draw.**]

drawn *drön, pa p* of **draw.** — Also *adj.*

dray[1] *drā, n* a low strong cart for heavy goods; a timber sledge. — **dray'-horse; dray'man.** [Cf. O.E. *dræge*, dragnet — *dragan*, to draw; see **drag, draw.**]

dray[2]. Same as **drey.**

dread *dred, n* great fear; awe; an object of fear or awe. — *adj* dreaded; inspiring great fear or awe. — *vt* to fear greatly; to reverence. — *adj* **dread'ed** (now usu. *facetiously*; with **the**) fearsome, terrifying. — *adj* **dread'ful** producing great fear or awe; terrible; very bad, unpleasant (*colloq*). — *adv* **dread'fully** in a dreadful way; very (much) (*colloq*). — *n* **dread'fulness.** — **dread'locks** the long-plaited hairstyle adopted by Rastafarians; **dread'nought** a thick cloth, or a garment made of it; a powerful type of battleship or battle-cruiser (dating from 1905–6). — **penny dreadful** a cheap sensational serial, book, etc. [M.E. *dreden* — O.E. *ondrǣdan*, to fear.]

dream *drēm, n* a train of thoughts and images experienced during sleep, a vision; something only imaginary; a distant hope or ideal, prob. unattainable. — *vi* to experience dreams during sleep; to think idly (with *of*); to think (of) as possible, contemplate as imaginably possible. — *vt* to see or imagine in, or as in, a dream: — *pa t* and *pa p* **dreamed** or **dreamt** (*dremt*). — *n* **dream'er.** — *adv* **dream'ily.** — *n* **dream'iness.** — *adj* **dream'less.** — *adv* **dream'lessly.** — *n* **dream'lessness.** — *adj* **dream'y** full of dreams; given to dreaming; appropriate to dreams; dreamlike; lovely (*colloq*). — **dream'boat** (*slang*) someone wonderful and desirable — usu. of the opposite sex; **dream'-land** the land of dreams, reverie, or imagination; **dream ticket** (orig. *US*; esp. a pair of candidates considered) the ideal or optimum electoral ticket; **dream'time** in the mythology of Australian Aboriginals, the time when the earth and patterns of life on earth took shape; **dream'-world** a world of illusions. — **dream up** to plan in the mind, often unrealistically; **go like a dream** to work, progress, etc. ideally well. [M.E. *dream, drēm.*]

dreary *drēr'i, adj* gloomy; cheerless. — *adj* **drear** dreary. — *n* **drear'iness.** — *adv* **drear'ily.** [O.E. *drēorig*, mournful, bloody — *drēor*, gore.]

dreck *drek*, (*slang*) *n* rubbish, trash. — *adj* **dreck'y.** [Yiddish *drek*, Ger. *Dreck*, dirt, filth, dung.]

dredge[1] *drej, n* a bag-net for dragging along the bottom of the sea to collect oysters, biological specimens, mud, etc.; a machine for deepening a harbour, canal, river, etc., for excavating under water or on land, or for raising alluvial deposits and washing them for minerals. — *vt* and *vi* to gather, explore or deepen with a dredge. — *n* **dredg'er** a boat, ship or raft equipped for dredging; a machine for dredging; someone who dredges. [Conn. with **drag, draw.**]

dredge[2] *drej, vt* to sprinkle. — *n* **dredg'er** a container with perforated lid for dredging. [O.Fr. *dragie*, sugar-plum — Gr. *tragēmata*, dessert.]

dregs *dregz, npl* impurities in liquor that fall to the bottom, the grounds; dross; the most worthless part of anything. — *n* **dregg'iness.** — *adj* **dregg'y** containing dregs; muddy; foul. [O.N. *dregg*.]

drek. Same as **dreck**.

drench *drench* or *drensh, vt* to soak; to wet thoroughly; to force a drench upon (an animal). — *n* a dose of liquid medicine forced down the throat (of an animal). [O.E. *drencan*, to cause to drink.]

Dresden china, porcelain or **ware** *drez'dən chī'nə, pōrs'lin* or *wār, n* fine decorated china made in Saxony (Royal Saxon porcelain factory established at Meissen, 1710).

dress *dres, vt* to clothe; to apply suitable materials to; to finish or trim; to add seasoning to (food); to set in order, prepare, arrange; to treat, tend; to draw (fowl); to manure; to adorn; to tie (a fly) (*angling*). — *vi* to put on clothes; to put on finer, more elaborate, or more formal clothes; to come into line: — *pa t* and *pa p* **dressed.** — *n* the covering or decoration of the body; a woman's one-piece skirted garment; style of clothing; ceremonial or formal clothing. — *adj* pertaining to (formal) evening dress. — *n* **dress'er** someone who dresses; a medical student who dresses wounds; a person who assists an actor to dress (*theat*); a tool or machine for dressing; a sideboard, esp. with a high back and shelves; a chest of drawers or dressing-table (*US*). — *n* **dress'ing** material used to cover a wound; the action of someone who dresses; sauce or (*US*) stuffing used in preparing a dish for the table, etc.; manure or the like, applied to land; a substance used to give stiffness and gloss to cloth. — *adj* **dress'y** showy; indicating care in dressing. — **dress'-circle** the first gallery of a theatre; **dress'-coat** a fine black coat with narrow or cutaway skirts, worn in full dress; **dress'ing-case** a case for toiletry items; **dress'ing-down** a severe scolding; a thrashing; **dress'ing-gown** a loose garment worn before or whilst dressing, etc.; **dress'ing-room; dress'ing-station** a place where wounded are collected and tended by members of a field-ambulance; **dress'ing-table; dress'-length** enough (material) to make a dress; **dress'maker** a person who makes clothes; a person who makes clothes for women and children as a living (*vi* **dress'make** colloq. back-formation); **dress'-making; dress'-rehearsal** a full rehearsal in costume with everything as for the performance. — Also *fig.* — **dress sense** sense of style in dress, knowledge of what suits one; **dress'-shield** a piece of material that protects the armpit of a dress against sweat; **dress'-shirt, dress'-suit** and **dress'-tie** those for formal evening dress; **dress uniform** a formal, ceremonial uniform. — **dress down** to reprimand severely; to thrash; to dress deliberately informally; **dress up** to dress for a part; to masquerade; to treat so as to make appear better, more interesting, etc., than it really is; to dress elaborately; **evening dress** or **full dress** the costume prescribed by fashion for evening receptions, dinners, balls, etc.; **get dressed** to put one's clothes on. [O.Fr. *dresser*, to prepare — an inferred L.L. *dīrectiāre*, to straighten; see **direct.**]

dressage *dres'äzh, n* training of a horse in deportment and response to controls; this equestrian discipline practised in competition; the manoeuvres practised. [Fr.]

drew *drōō, pa t* of **draw.**

drey or **dray** *drā, n* a squirrel's nest.

drib *drib, n* a drop; a trickle; a small quantity. — Also **dribb'let** or **drib'let.** — **dribs and drabs** small quantities at a time. [Rel. to **drip.**]

dribble *drib'l, vi* to fall in small drops; to trickle; to slaver, like an infant or an idiot. — *vt* to let fall in drops; to give out in small portions. — *vt* and *vi* to move the ball forward little by little, tricking opponents (*football, hockey*, etc.). — Also *n.* — *n* **dribb'ler.** — *adj* **dribb'ly.** [Frequentative of **drib.**]

dried, drier, dries, driest. See **dry.**

drift *drift, n* a heap of matter (e.g. snow) driven together; floating materials driven by water; a streaming movement; the direction in which a thing is driven; the meaning or implication of words used; a slow current caused by the wind; passive travel with the current, wind, etc.; abandonment to external influences; a group of animals driven or herded; loose superficial deposits, esp. glacial or fluvio-glacial (*geol*); a horizontal or oblique excavation or passage (*mining*, etc.). — *vt* to carry by drift; to cause or allow to drift; to pierce or tunnel. — *vi* to be floated along; to be driven into heaps; to leave things to circumstance; to wander around, or live, without any definite aim. — *n* **drift'age.** — *n* **drift'er** someone who, or that which, drifts; an aimless, shiftless person; a fishing-boat that uses a drift-net. — **drift'-ice** floating masses of ice drifting before the wind; **drift'-net** a net which is allowed to drift with the tide; **drift'wood** wood drifted by water. [M.E.; O.N. *drift*, snowdrift; root as **drive.**]

drill[1] *dril, vt* to bore, pierce; to make with a drill; to exercise (soldiers, pupils, etc.) by repeated practice; to pierce with a bullet or bullets (*slang*); to sow in rows. — *n* a tool for boring holes in stone, metal, teeth, or other hard substances; a large boring instrument used in mining, etc.; training exercise, or a session of it; correct procedure or routine (*colloq*); a ridge with seed or growing plants on it (turnips, potatoes, etc.); the plants in such a row; the machine for sowing the seed; a type of shellfish which bores into the shells of oysters. — *n* **drill'er.** — **drill bit** a removeable cutting and boring head in a drill; **drilling platform** a floating or fixed offshore structure supporting a drilling rig; **drilling rig** or **drill rig** the complete apparatus and structure required for drilling an oil rig; **drill'-sergeant** a sergeant who drills soldiers; **drill'ship** a free-floating ship-shaped drilling platform. [Prob. borrowed from Du. *drillen*, to bore.]

drill[2] *dril, n* a W. African baboon, smaller than the mandrill. [Perh. a W. Afr. word.]

drill[3] *dril, n* a stout twilled linen or cotton cloth. [Ger. *Drillich*, ticking.]

drily. See under **dry.**

drink *dringk, vt* to swallow (a liquid) as from a glass, bowl, etc.; to absorb, soak up; to take in through the senses. — *vi* to swallow (a liquid); to drink alcohol; to drink alcohol to excess: — *pr p* **drink'ing;** *pa t* **drank;** *pa p* **drunk.** — *n* an act of drinking; a quantity drunk; something to be drunk; a beverage; intoxicating liquor, alcohol. — *adj* **drink'able.** — *n* **drink'ableness.** — *n* **drink'er** a person who drinks; a tippler. — *n* **drink'ing.** — *adj* fit to drink; for drinking. — *adj* **drink-drive'** pertaining to drink-driving. — *vi* to drive under the influence of alcohol. — **drink-dri'ver** someone who drives a vehicle after having drunk more than the legally permitted amount of alcohol. — *n* and *adj* **drink-dri'ving.** — **drink'ing-fountain; drinking-up time** in a public house, the few minutes allowed after official closing time for customers to finish their last drinks before leaving. — **drink in** to absorb (rain, etc.), as dry land does; to take in eagerly (something seen, said, etc.); **drink (someone, the others,** etc.,) **under the table** to continue drinking and remain (comparatively) sober after (someone, the others, etc.) have completely collapsed; **drink to** or **drink (to) the health of** to drink wine, etc., with good wishes for the health, prosperity, etc. of; **drink up** to empty by drinking; to finish drinking; **strong drink** alcoholic liquor; **the drink** (*slang*) the sea; a bribe. — See also **drunk**. [O.E. *drincan*; Ger. *trinken*.]

drip *drip*, *vi* to fall in drops; to let fall drops. — *vt* to let fall in drops: — *pr p* **dripp'ing**; *pa t* and *pa p* **dripped**. — *n* a falling in drops; that which falls in drops; a projecting edge on a roof, sill, etc.; a device for passing a fluid slowly and continuously, esp. into a vein of the body (also **drip'-feed**); the material so passed; a weak, pathetic person (*colloq*); drivel, esp. sentimental (*slang*). — *n* **dripp'ing** that which falls in drops, esp. fat from meat in roasting. — *adj* **drip-dry'** (of a material or garment) which, when allowed to dry by dripping, requires no, or little, ironing. — Also *vi* and *vt*. — **drip'-feed** a drip (see above). — *vt* to treat (a patient, etc.) with a drip. — **drip'stone** a projecting moulding over doorways, etc., serving to throw off the rain. [O.E. *dryppan* — *drēopan*.]

drisheen *dri-shēn'*, *n* a type of Irish sausage made with sheep's blood. [Ir. *drisìn*.]

drive *drīv*, *vt* to control or guide the movements or operations of; to convey or carry in a vehicle; to urge or force in or through; to push; to provide motive power to; to compel; to send away with force, e.g. a ball, esp. (*golf*) to play from the tee or with a driver, (*cricket*) to hit strongly down the pitch, and (*tennis*) to return forcibly underarm; to urge or hurry along; to chase; to excavate (e.g. a tunnel). — *vi* to control an engine, vehicle, draught-animal, etc.; to press forward with violence; to be forced or driven along; to go in a motor vehicle or carriage; to aim or tend towards a point (with *at*); to strike with a sword, the fist, etc. (with *at*): — *pr p* **drīv'ing**; *pa t* **drōve**, *pa p* **driv'en**. — *n* an excursion in a vehicle; a road for driving on, esp. the approach to a house within its own grounds; a driving stroke (*sport*); impulsive force; power of getting things done; the chasing of game towards the shooters; pushing sales by reducing prices; an organised campaign to attain any end; a meeting in order to play certain games, e.g. whist; apparatus for driving. — *n* **drivabil'ity** or **driveabil'ity**. — *adj* **driv'able** or **drive'able**. — *n* **driv'er** a person who or thing which drives, in all senses; a club used in golf to propel the ball from the tee. — *adj* **driv'erless**. — **drive'-in** a refreshment stop, store, cinema, etc., where patrons are catered for while still remaining in their motor cars. — Also *adj*. — **driving licence** an official licence to drive a motor vehicle; **driv'ing-mirror** a small mirror in which a driver can see what is behind his or her vehicle; **driving seat** the seat in a vehicle in which the driver sits; a position of control; **driving test** a test of ability to drive safely, esp. an official and obligatory test; **driv'ing-wheel** a main wheel that communicates motion to other wheels; one of the main wheels in a locomotive. — **drive a coach and horses through** (*colloq*) to demolish (an argument, etc.) by demonstrating the obvious faults in it; to brush aside, ignore completely; **drive home** to force (e.g. a nail) completely in; to make completely understood or accepted. [O.E. *drīfan*, to drive.]

drivel *driv'l*, *vi* to dribble, slaver like an infant; to speak like an idiot: — *pr p* **driv'elling**; *pa t* and *pa p* **driv'elled**. — *n* slaver; nonsense. — *n* **driv'eller**. [M.E. *drevelen*, *dravelen*; O.E. *dreflian*.]

driven. See **drive**.

drizzle *driz'l*, *vi* to rain in fine drops. — *vt* to shed in fine drops; to cover in fine drops or in mist. — *n* a small, light rain. — *adj* **drizz'ly**. [Frequentative of M.E. *dresen* — O.E. *drēosan*, to fall.]

drogue *drōg*, *n* a conical canvas sleeve open at both ends, used as one form of sea-anchor, or to check the way of an aircraft, etc.; (or **drogue parachute**) a parachute used to reduce speed of a falling object; a funnel device on the end of the hose of a tanker aircraft; a wind-sock; an air target of similar shape. — **drogue bomb** an improvised terrorist bomb, made with a grenade or plastic explosive, using a plastic bag or similar as a drogue to stabilise it when thrown.

droit *drwä* (before a vowel *drwät*; Eng. *droit*), *n* right, legal claim. [Fr.]

droll *drōl*, *adj* odd; amusing; laughable. — *n* **droll'ery** drollness; a jest. — *n* **droll'ness**. — *adv* **drolly** (*drōl'li*). [Fr. *drôle*, prob. from Du. *drollig*, odd — *trold*, a hobgoblin.]

dromedary *drom'* or *drum'i-dər-i*, *n* a one-humped Arabian camel. [L.L. *dromedārius* — Gr. *dromas*, *dromados*, running.]

drone *drōn*, *n* the male of the honey-bee; a lazy person, living off the labour of others; a deep humming sound; a bass-pipe of a bagpipe; a monotonous speaker or speech; an aircraft piloted by remote control. — *vi* to emit a monotonous humming sound; (with *on*) to talk at length in a monotonous or expressionless way. — *vt* to say in such a tone. — **drone'-pipe** a pipe producing a droning sound. [O.E. *drān*, bee.]

drongo *drong'gō*, *n* any member of a family of glossy-black fork-tailed insect-catching birds of the Old World tropics; a nitwit, a no-hoper (*Austr slang*): — *pl* **drong'oes** or **drong'os**. [From Malagasy.]

droog *dro͞og*, *n* a gang-member, *specif* a violent hooligan of the type portrayed by Anthony Burgess in his novel *A Clockwork Orange* (1962). — *adj* **droog'ish** (of dress, behaviour, etc.) reminiscent of a droog. [Coined by Burgess after Russ. *drug*, a friend.]

drool *dro͞ol*, *vi* to slaver; to drivel; to show effusive or lascivious pleasure (with *over*). — *n* drivel. [**drivel**.]

droop *dro͞op*, *vi* to hang down; to grow weak or faint; to decline. — *vt* to let hang down. — *n* a drooping position. — *adv* **droop'ily**. — *n* **droop'iness**. — *adj* **droop'y**. [O.N. *drūpa*, to droop.]

drop *drop*, *n* a small rounded blob of liquid that hangs or falls at one time; a very small quantity of liquid; anything hanging like a drop; a small, round sweet; a curtain dropped between acts (also **drop'-curtain**); (in *pl*) a medicine taken in drops; a fall; a vertical descent or difference of level; a landing by parachute; an instance of dropping anything. — **drop-** used (in combination) of something that drops or is used in or for dropping. — *vi* to fall or let fall in drops; to fall suddenly, steeply or sheer; to sink; to lapse; to diminish; to subside into a condition, come gradually to be. — *vt* to let fall; to let go, relinquish, abandon, part with; to let fall in drops; to spot, bespatter, sprinkle; to cause to fall; to omit; to lower; (of an animal) to give birth to; to say casually; to write and send (a note) in an offhand manner; to hole, etc. (a ball); to score (a goal) with a drop-kick; to set down from a vehicle or ship; to cease to associate with; to lose (a sum of money, a game as part of a contest); to take one more (shot, stroke) than par (*golf*); to bring down by a shot: — *pr p* **dropp'ing**; *pa t* and *pa p* **dropped**. — *n* **drop'let** a little drop. — *n* **dropp'er** a person who or thing which drops; a tube or contrivance for making liquid come out in drops. — *n* **dropp'ing** something which is dropped; (usu. in *pl*) dung, excrement. — **drop'-forging** the process of shaping metal parts by forging between two dies, one fixed to the hammer and the other to the anvil of a steam or mechanical hammer (*n* and *vt* **drop'-forge**); **drop'-goal** (*Rugby football*) a goal secured by a drop-kick; **drop'-hammer** or **drop'-press** a swaging, stamping, or forging machine; **drop'-kick** a kick made when the ball rebounds from the ground after dropping from the hand (*Rugby football*; also *vt*). — *adj* **drop'-leaf** (of a desk or table) with a hinged leaf (or leaves) which can be raised or dropped to horizontal position, but lies vertical when not in use. — **drop'-out** a drop-kick taken following the defender's touchdown (*Rugby football*); a person who has withdrawn from an academic course or from conventional society; a patch which fails to record data on a magnetic tape (*comput*); **drop'-scene** a drop-curtain; **drop'-scone** a scone made like a pancake; **drop'-shot** (*tennis*, etc.) a ball made to drop close to the net; **drop tank** (*aeronautics*) a tank, esp. for fuel, that can be dropped during flight; **drop'-wort** a species of spiraea with beadlike root tubercles. — **a drop in the ocean** an infinitesimally small quantity; **at the drop of a hat** immediately; on the smallest provocation; **drop a brick** see under **brick**; **drop away** or **off** to depart, disappear; **drop in** to come, fall, set, etc. in, or arrive, casually, unintentionally, or one by one (*n* and *adj* **drop'-in**); **drop off** to fall asleep; to become less, to diminish; **drop out** to disappear from one's place; to make a drop-kick (*Rugby football*); to withdraw, esp. from an academic course or from conventional life in society; **let drop** to disclose inadvertently, or seemingly so. [O.E. *dropa*, a drop, *dropian*, *droppian*, to drop.]

dropsy *drop'si*, *n* an abnormal accumulation of watery fluid in any part of the body. — *adj* **drop'sical.** [Aphetic for *hydropsy* — Gr. *hydōr*, water.]

Drosophila *dros-of'i-lə*, *n* a genus of small yellow flies — fruit-flies — which breed in fermenting fruit juices and are used in genetic experiments; (without *cap*) any fly of the genus. [Gr. *drosos*, dew, moisture, *phileein*, to love.]

dross *dros*, *n* the scum of melting metals; waste matter, refuse; small or waste coal. — *n* **dross'iness.** — *adj* **dross'y.** [O.E. *drōs*.]

drought *drowt*, *n* dryness; shortage of rain or of water; thirst. — *adj* **drought'y.** [O.E. *drūgath*, dryness — *drūgian*, to dry.]

drove *drōv*, *pa t* of **drive.** — *n* a number of cattle, or other animals, driven or herded together; a crowd, or horde, moving together. — *n* **drov'er** someone whose occupation is to drive cattle. — *n* **drov'ing** the occupation of a drover; the action of herding cattle, etc. [O.E. *drāf*, *drīfan*, to drive.]

drown *drown*, *vi* to die of suffocation in liquid. — *vt* to kill by suffocation in liquid; to submerge; to flood; to extinguish; to make indistinguishable or imperceptible. — **drown someone out** (*colloq*) to make someone inaudible by making a louder noise. [M.E. *drounen*.]

drowse *drowz*, *vi* to doze, sleep lightly. — *vt* to make heavy with sleep, cause to doze; to pass in a half-sleeping state. — *n* a half-sleeping state. — *adv* **drows'ily.** — *n* **drows'iness.** — *adj* **drows'y** sleepy; heavy; dull; inducing sleep. [App. O.E. *drūsian*, to be sluggish.]

drub *drub*, *vt* to beat or thrash: — *pr p* **drubb'ing**; *pa t* and *pa p* **drubbed.** — *n* **drubb'ing** a cudgelling; (in games) a thorough defeat. [Perh. Ar. *daraba*, to beat, bastinado — *darb*, a beating.]

drudge *druj*, *n* a person who does heavy monotonous work; a menial servant. — *vi* to do dull, laborious or lowly work. — *n* **drudg'ery** the work of a drudge; uninteresting toil; hard or humble labour. [Perh. from root of O.E. *drēogan*, to perform, undergo.]

drug *drug*, *n* any substance used in the composition of medicine, to cure or prevent a disease; a narcotic substance, esp. an addictive one; a poisonous or stupefying substance; something one is intoxicated by or craves for (*fig*). — *vt* to mix or season with drugs; to administer a drug to; to poison or stupefy with drugs. — *vi* to administer drugs or medicines; to take drugs, esp. narcotics, habitually: — *pr p* **drugg'ing**; *pa t* and *pa p* **drugged.** — *n* **drugg'ie** (*colloq*) a drug addict. — *n* **drugg'ist** a person who deals in drugs; a pharmacist (*US*). — **drug'-addict** a habitual taker of (non-medicinal) drugs; **drug'-pusher** a pusher, someone who peddles narcotics illegally; **drug'-runner** someone who smuggles drugs; **drug'-running**; **drug'-store** (esp. *US*) a chemist's shop (usu. selling a variety of goods, including refreshments). [O.Fr. *drogue*.]

drugget *drug'it*, *n* a woven and felted coarse woollen fabric, as used as protective covering for a floor or carpet. [O.Fr. *droguet*.]

druid *drōō'id*, *n* (also with *cap*) a priest among the ancient Celts of Britain, Gaul and Germany; an Eisteddfod official. — *adj* **druid'ic** or **druid'ical.** — *n* **dru'idism** the doctrines which the druids taught; the ceremonies they practised. [L. pl. *druidae*, from a Celt. stem *druid-*.]

drum[1] *drum*, *n* a percussion instrument, a skin stretched on a frame; anything shaped like a drum; the tympanum of the ear; the upright part of a cupola (*archit*); a cylinder, esp. a revolving cylinder; a magnetic drum (*comput*; see under **magnet**); a cylindrical barrel; a house (*slang*). — *vi* to beat a drum; to beat rhythmically. — *vt* to expel to the sound of a drum or drums (with *out*; esp. *mil*; also *fig*); to summon, call together (with *up*); to impress or stress by repetition: — *pr p* **drumm'ing**; *pa t* and *pa p* **drummed.** — *n* **drumm'er** a person who drums; a commercial traveller (esp. *US*); a swagman (*Austr*). — **drum'beat**; **drum brake** a type of brake in which two shoes grip the inside of the brake drum; **drum'head** the head or skin of a drum; the top part of a capstan; (also **drumhead cabbage**) a type of flat-headed cabbage. — *adj* (*mil*) improvised in the field (as of a court-martial). — **drum-ma'jor** the marching leader of a military band; **drum majorette** a girl who heads a marching band, usu. twirling a baton, in a parade, etc.; a majorette; **drum'stick** the stick with which a drum is beaten; the tibia of a dressed fowl. — **beat** or **bang the drum** to indulge in publicity. [From a Gmc. root found in Du. *trom*, Ger. *Trommel*, a drum; prob. imit.]

drum[2] *drum*, *n* in Scotland and Ireland, a ridge, drumlin. — *n* **drum'lin** (*geol*) a usu. oval ridge formed under the ice-sheet of the Glacial Period. [Ir. and Gael. *druim*, back.]

drunk *drungk*, *pa p* of **drink.** — *adj* intoxicated (also *fig*). — *n* a drunk person. — *n* **drunk'ard** a person who frequently drinks to excess; a habitual drinker. — *adj* **drunk'en** given to excessive drinking; resulting from intoxication; drunk. — *adv* **drunk'enly.** — *n* **drunk'enness.**

drupe *drōōp*, *n* any fleshy fruit with a stone. — *adj* **drupā'ceous.** — *n* **drup'el** or **drupe'let** a little drupe, forming part of a fruit, as in the raspberry. [L. *drūpa* — Gr. *dryppā*, an olive.]

Druse, Druze or **Druz** *drōōz*, *n* (one of) a people inhabiting chiefly a mountainous district in the south of Syria, whose religion contains elements found in the Koran, the Bible, Gnosticism, etc. — Also *adj*. [Perh. from *Darazi*, an early exponent of the religion.]

druse *drōōz*, *n* a rock cavity lined with crystals, a geode. [Ger. *Druse* — Czechoslovakian *druza*, a piece of crystallised ore.]

dry *drī*, *adj* (*compar* **drī'er**, *superl* **drī'est**) without water or liquid, contained or adhering; free from or deficient in moisture, sap or rain; thirsty; out of water; failing to yield water, or milk, or other liquid; (of a fruit) not fleshy; not green; (of e.g. toast) unbuttered; (of wines etc.) free from sweetness and fruity flavour; (of beer) brewed by a method that removes the bitter taste, aftertaste and smell of traditional beer; legally forbidding the liquor trade (*colloq*); frigid, precise, formal; (of humour) quiet, restrained, uttered in a matter-of-fact way, as if not intended to be humorous; (of manner) distantly unsympathetic; (of a cough) not producing catarrh; (of natural gas) containing only small amounts of liquid constituent. — *vt* to free from or empty of water or moisture (often with *off*). — *vi* to become dry (often with *off*); to evaporate entirely: — *pr p*

dry'ing; *pa t* and *pa p* **dried**; *3rd pers sing pr t* **dries**. — *n* a person who favours strict adherence to hardline right-wing Conservative policies (*Br politics*). — *n* **drī'er** or **dry'er** someone who, or that which, dries; a machine for extracting moisture from cloth, grain, etc.; a drying agent for oils, paint, etc. — *adv* **drī'ly** or **dry'ly**. — *adj* **dry'ish**. — *n* **dry'ness**. — **dry battery** (*electr*) a battery composed of dry-cells; **dry'-cell** an electric cell in which the electrolyte is not a liquid but a paste. — *vt* **dry'-clean** to clean (clothes, etc.) using e.g. a petroleum-based solvent rather than water. — *vt* **dry'-cure** to cure by drying. — *vt* **dry'-dock** see **dry dock** at **dock**[3]. — *adj* **dry'-eyed** tearless. — *adj* **dry'-fly** (of fishing) without sinking the fly in the water. — *npl* **dry'-goods** drapery, etc. distinguished from groceries, hardware, etc. — **dry hole** a well which does not yield commercially viable quantities of oil or gas; an unsuccessful project (*fig*); **dry ice** and **dry-iced** see **ice**; **drying-up cloth** a cloth or towel for drying dishes, a dish-towel; **dry land** land as opposed to sea; **dry measure** a system of measure by bulk, used for grain, etc.; **dry'mouth** xerostomia; **dry'-plate** a sensitised photographic plate, with which a picture may be made without the preliminary use of a bath; **dry point** a sharp needle by which fine lines are drawn in copperplate engraving; a plate or impression produced with it; **dry riser** a vertical pipe with an outside access through which water can be pumped from the street to the individual floors of a building in the event of a fire; **dry rot** a decay of timber caused by fungi which reduce it ultimately to a dry brittle mass; **dry run** a practice exercise (*mil*); a rehearsal. — *adj* and *adv* **dry'-shod** without wetting the shoes or feet. — **dry ski** an adaptation of a ski with which one can practise skiing on a dry surface; **dry skiing**. — *adj* **dry'-stone** built of stone without mortar. — **dry suit** a close-fitting air- and watertight synthetic suit for wearing in esp. cold water, that retains warmth by a layer of air, and allows clothing to be worn under it; **dry-wall'er** a person who builds walls without mortar. — **cut and dry** or **dried** see under **cut**; **dry out** (*colloq*) to take or give a course of treatment to cure oneself or another person of alcoholism; **dry up** to dry thoroughly or completely; to cease to produce liquid (water, milk, etc.); to forget one's lines or part (as an actor, etc.; *colloq*); to stop talking (*slang*); **high and dry** see under **high**; **the dry** (sometimes with *cap*; *Austr colloq*) the dry season in central and northern Australia. [O.E. *drȳge*.]

dryad *drī'ad* or *-əd*, (*Gr mythol*) *n* a wood nymph. [Gr. *drўas*, *-ados*, — *drȳs*, oak tree.]

DS *abbrev* for: dal segno (*mus*); disseminated sclerosis; Doctor of Surgery.

DSC *abbrev* for Distinguished Service Cross.

DSc *abbrev* for *Doctor Scientiae* (L.), Doctor of Science.

DSM *abbrev* for Distinguished Service Medal.

DSO *abbrev* for (Companion of the) Distinguished Service Order.

dsp *abbrev* for *decessit sine prole* (L.), died without issue.

DSS *abbrev* for Department of Social Security.

DST *abbrev* for Daylight Saving Time.

DT *abbrev* for data transmission.

DTh. or **DTheol.** *abbrev* for *Doctor Theologiae* (L.), Doctor of Theology.

DTI *abbrev* for Department of Trade and Industry.

DTP *abbrev* for desktop publishing.

DT's or **dt's** (*colloq*) *abbrev* for delirium tremens.

Du. *abbrev* for Dutch.

dual *dū'əl*, *adj* twofold; consisting of two; expressing or representing two things (*gram*). — *n* a grammatical form indicating duality; a word in the dual number. — *vt* to make (a road) into dual carriageway. — *n* **dū'alism** (*philos*) the view which seeks to explain the world by the assumption of two radically independent and absolute elements — e.g. (1) the doctrine of the entire separation of spirit and matter, thus being opposed both to *idealism* and to *materialism*, (2) the doctrine of two distinct principles of good and evil, or of two divine beings of these characters. — *adj* **dūalis'tic**. — *adv* **dūalis'tically**. — *n* **duality** (*dū-al'i-ti*) doubleness; state of being double. — *adv* **dū'ally**. — **dual carriageway** a road consisting of two separated parts, each for use of traffic in one direction only; **dual control** joint control or jurisdiction. — *adj* **dual-control'** able to be operated by either or both of two persons. — **dual personality** a condition in which the same individual shows at different times two very different characters. — *adj* **dual-pur'pose** serving or intended to serve two purposes. [L. *duālis* — *duo*, two.]

dub[1] *dub*, *vt* to confer knighthood upon (from the ceremony of striking the shoulders with the flat of a sword); to confer any name or dignity upon; to rub a softening and waterproof mixture into (leather); to dress (a fly) for fishing: — *pr p* **dubb'ing**; *pa p* **dubbed**. — *n* **dubb'ing** or **dubb'in** a preparation of grease for softening leather. [O.E. *dubbian*, to dub a knight.]

dub[2] *dub*, *vt* to give (a film) a new soundtrack, e.g. one in a different language; to add sound effects or music; to transfer (recorded music, etc.) to a new disc or tape; to combine so as to make one record (music, etc., from more than one source, e.g. a live performance and a recording). — **dub poet**; **dub poetry** a style of poetry, of W. Indian origin, performed spontaneously in reggae rhythm to dubbed or recorded music. [Abbrev. of **double**.]

dubbin, dubbing. See **dub**[1].

dubious *dū'bi-əs*, *adj* doubtful, causing or having doubt; uncertain; of uncertain result or outcome; arousing suspicion or disapproval. — *n* **dūbiety** (*-bī'i-ti*) doubt. — *adv* **dū'biously**. — *n* **dū'biousness**. [L. *dubius*.]

ducal *dū'kəl*, *adj* pertaining to a duke. — *adv* **dū'cally**. [Fr., — L.L. *ducālis* — L. *dux*, leader.]

ducat *duk'ət*, *n* a gold or silver coin of varying values, formerly much used on the Continent. [O.Fr., — It. *ducato* — L.L. *ducātus*, a duchy.]

duce *dōō'chā*, *n* the title assumed by the Italian dictator Mussolini. [It., leader — L. *dux*.]

Duchenne muscular dystrophy *dü-shen' mus'kū-lər dis'trə-fi*, *n* (short form **Duchenne**) an esp. common and severe form of muscular dystrophy, which strikes children under 10 years old. [Guillaume *Duchenne*, French physician 1806–75.]

duchess *duch'əs* or *-es*, *n* the wife or widow of a duke; a woman of the same rank as a duke in own right. [O.Fr. *duchesse*.]

duchesse *duch'es* or *dü-shes'*, *n* a table-cover or centrepiece. — **duchesse lace** Flemish pillow lace with designs in cord outline; **duchesse potatoes** piped shapes of mashed potato, butter, milk and egg-yolk baked until light brown. [Fr., duchess.]

duchy *duch'i*, *n* the territory of a duke, a dukedom. [O.Fr. *duché* — L.L. *ducātus*.]

duck[1] *duk*, *n* a kind of coarse cotton, linen, etc. cloth used for small sails, sacking, etc. [Du. *doek*, linen cloth.]

duck[2] *duk*, *vt* to dip for a moment in water; to avoid (*colloq*). — *vi* to dip or dive; to lower the head suddenly; to cringe, yield. — *n* a quick plunge, dip; a quick lowering of the head or body. — *n* **duck'er**. — *n* **duck'ing**. — **duck'ing-stool** (*hist*) a stool or chair in which offenders were tied and ducked in the water. — **duck out of** to shirk, avoid (responsibilities, etc.). [M.E. *douken* from an assumed O.E. *dūcan*, to duck, dive.]

duck[3] *duk*, *n* any bird of the family *Anatidae*, characterised by short webbed feet, a small hind-toe not reaching the ground, netted scales in front of the lower leg, and a long bill; the female duck as distinguished from the male *drake*; in cricket (orig. *duck's egg* for zero (O) on a scoring-sheet), no runs; a darling, sweetheart (used loosely as a term of address; *colloq*); an oscillating shape used in wave-power technology. — *n* **duck'ling** young duck. — *n* **ducks** or **duck'y** (*colloq*) a term of endearment. — *adj* **duck'y.** — **duck'bill** a platypus. — *adj* **duck'-billed.** — **duck'-board** a board with slats nailed across it, used for walking in excavations, etc., on swampy ground, or as steps in repair work on roofs. — *adj* **duck'-footed.** — **duck'-hawk** moor-buzzard or marsh-harrier; (*US*) peregrine falcon; **duck'-pond; duck's arse** (or, in U.S., **ass**) a hairstyle in which the hair is swept back to a point on the neck resembling a duck's tail. — *vi* **duck'shove** (*Austr* and *NZ colloq*) to jump a queue; to cheat; to steal; to avoid responsibilities. — **duck'shover** (*Austr* and *NZ colloq*); **duck soup** (*US slang*) something very easy, a cinch; **duck'weed** any plant of a family of monocotyledons most of which consist of a small flat green floating plate. — **Bombay duck** a small Indian fish, the bummalo, dried and eaten as a relish; **break one's duck** (*cricket*) to make one's first run; **lame duck** an inefficient or helpless person or organisation; anything disabled; a defaulter; **make** or **play ducks and drakes** to make flat stones skip on the surface of water; to squander, waste (with *of* or *with*); **sitting duck** an easy target, helpless victim; **wild duck** the mallard, esp. the hen-bird. [O.E. *dūce* , a duck.]

duck[4] *duk*, *n* a kind of amphibious military transport vehicle or landing craft. [From manufacturers' code initials, DUKW.]

duct *dukt*, *n* a tube conveying fluids in animal bodies or plants; a pipe for an electric cable; a hole, pipe or channel for carrying a fluid; an air-passage. — *vt* to carry along, or as if along, a duct. — *adj* **duct'less.** — **ductless glands** masses of glandular tissue that lack ducts and discharge their products directly into the blood. [L. *ductus* — *dūcĕre*, to lead.]

ductile *duk'tīl* or *-til*, *adj* yielding; capable of being drawn out into threads; easily led. — *n* **ductility** (*-til'i-ti*) capacity of being drawn out without breaking. [Fr., — L. *ductilis* — *dūcere*, to lead.]

dud *dud*, (*colloq*) *n* any useless or ineffective person or thing; a bomb or projectile that fails to go off; a counterfeit; a failure. — Also *adj.*

dude *dūd* or *do͞od*, (orig. *US slang*) *n* a fellow; a man from the city, holidaying out West; a man much concerned with dressing smartly. — *adj* **du'dish.** — *n* **du'dism.** — **dude ranch** a ranch run as a holiday resort or for training in ranching; **dude up** to dress up flashily.

dudgeon *duj'ən*, *n* offended indignation, as in the phrase *in high dudgeon.*

due *dū*, *adj* owed; that ought to be paid or done to another; proper; appointed, under engagement (to be ready, arrive, etc.) — *adv* exactly, directly. — *n* something which is owed; what one has a right to or has earned; fee, toll, charge or tribute; (in *pl*) subscription to a club or society. — **due date** the date on which a bill of exchange, etc. must be paid. — **due to** caused by; owing to, because of (a use still deprecated by some, but now almost standard); (of horses) pregnant by; **give someone his (**or **her) due** to be fair to someone; **give the devil his due** to acknowledge some commendable quality, etc., in someone otherwise disapproved of; **in due course** in the ordinary way when the time comes. [O.Fr. *deü*, past p. of *devoir* to owe.]

duel *dū'əl*, *n* a prearranged fight between two people, under fixed conditions and generally on an affair of honour; single combat to decide a quarrel; any fight or struggle between two parties. — *vi* to fight in a duel: — *pr p* **dū'elling;** *pa t* and *pa p* **dū'elled.** — *n* **dū'eller.** — *n* **dū'elling.** — *n* **dū'ellist.** [It. *duello* — L. *duellum.*]

duenna *dū-en'ə*, *n* a lady who acts the part of governess or chaperons a younger. [Sp. *dueña* — L. *domina*, fem. of *dominus*, lord.]

duet *dū-et'*, *n* a composition in music for two performers; the performance or performers of such; any action involving two parties. — *vi* to perform a duet: — *pr p* **duett'ing;** *pa t* and *pa p* **duett'ed.** — *n* **duett'ist.** [It. *duetto*, dimin. of *duo* — *due*, two — L. *duo.*]

duff[1] *duf*, *n* a stiff flour pudding boiled in a bag. [A form of **dough.**]

duff[2] *duf*, *vt* to make to look new; to alter brands on (stolen cattle); to steal cattle. — *n* (*slang*) **duff'ing, duffing-up'** or **duffing-o'ver.** — **duff up** or **over** (*slang*) to beat up. [Perh. a back-formation from **duffer.**]

duff[3] *duf*, *vt* to misplay by hitting the ground behind the ball (*golf*); to bungle. [Back-formation from **duffer.**]

duff[4] *duf*, (*colloq*) *adj* no good; broken, not working. [Prob. **duff**[3].]

duffel or **duffle** *duf'l*, *n* a thick, coarse woollen cloth, with a thick nap. — **duffel (**or **duffle) bag** a canvas bag, cylindrical in shape, orig. used for a sailor's kit; **duffel (**or **duffle) coat** a jacket or coat, usu. hooded, made of duffel. [Du., from *Duffel*, a town near Antwerp.]

duffer *duf'ər*, *n* an unskilful or worthless person; someone who fakes up sham articles or duffs cattle.

duffle. See **duffel.**

dug[1] *dug*, *n* a nipple or udder of a cow or similar. [Cf. Sw. *dægga*, Dan. *dægge*, to suckle.]

dug[2] *dug*, *pa t* and *pa p* of **dig.** — **dug'out** a boat made by hollowing out the trunk of a tree; a rough dwelling or shelter dug out of a slope or bank or in a trench; a (usu. sunken) shelter or covered bench area beside a sports pitch in which players, etc. wait when not in the game.

dugong *do͞o'gong*, *n* a herbivorous marine mammal, up to 3 m. long, with flipperlike forelimbs. [Malayan *dūyong.*]

duiker or **duyker** *dī'kər*, also *dā'kər*, *n* a small S. African antelope; (as *dī'kər*) a cormorant (*SAfr*). [Du., diver (from plunging into the bush, or into the sea).]

duke *dūk*, *n* a sovereign prince of a small state; a nobleman of the highest order; (*do͞ok*; *slang*) the fist. — *n* **duke'dom.** [O.Fr. *duc* — L. *dux, ducis*, a leader — *dūcĕre*, to lead.]

DUKW. See **duck**[4].

dulcet *duls'it*, *adj* sweet; melodious, harmonious. — *n* **Dul'citone**® a keyboard instrument in which graduated tuning-forks are struck by hammers. [L. *dulcis*, sweet.]

dulcimer *dul'si-mər*, *n* a musical instrument like a flat box, with sounding-board and wires stretched across bridges. [Sp. *dulcemele* — L. *dulce melos*, a sweet song.]

dulia *dū-* or *do͞o-lī'ə*, (*RC*) *n* the inferior veneration accorded to saints and angels (as opp. to **hyperdulia,** accorded to the Virgin Mary, and **latria,** accorded to God alone). [Gr. *douleiā*, servitude.]

dull *dul*, *adj* slow to learn or to understand; lacking sharpness in hearing (or another sense); insensible; without life or spirit; uninteresting; slow-moving; lacking brightness or clearness; cloudy; muffled; blunt. — *vt* to make dull. — *vi* to become dull. — *n* **dull'ard** a dull and stupid person. — *adj* **dull'ish.** — *n* **dull'ness** or **dul'ness.** — *adv* **dully** (*dul'li*). [Rel. to O.E. *dol*, foolish, and *dwellan*, to err.]

dulse *duls*, *n* an edible red seaweed, esp. *Rhodymenia palmata.* [Gael. *duileasg.*]

duly *dū'li*, *adv* properly; fitly; at the proper time. [**due.**]

duma *dōō'mə*, *n* an elected council, esp. (*hist*) the Russian parliament of 1906–17. — *n* **dum'aist** a duma member. [Russ. *duma*, of Gmc. origin.]

dumb *dum*, *adj* without the power of speech; silent; soundless; stupid (orig. *US* after Ger. or Du.). — *adv* **dumb'ly**. — *n* **dumb'ness**. — **dumb'bell** a double-headed weight swung in the hands to develop the muscles; someone stupid (*US*); **dumb blonde** (in films, etc.) a blonde-haired beauty of limited intelligence; **dumb'-cluck** a fool. — *vt* **dumbfound'** or **dumfound'** to strike dumb; to astonish. — **dumb'-piano** a soundless keyboard for piano practice; **dumb'-show** gesture without words; pantomime. — *adj* **dumb'struck** silent with astonishment. — **dumb terminal** (*comput*) an input or output terminal which has no independent processing capability; **dumb'-waiter** a movable platform used for conveying food, dishes, etc., at meals; a stand with revolving top for holding dessert, etc.; a small lift for food and dishes. — **strike dumb** to silence with astonishment. [O.E. *dumb*; Ger. *dumm*, stupid, Du. *dom*.]

dumbo *dum'bō*, (*colloq*) *n* a dimwit. [**dumb**.]

dumdum *dum'dum*, *n* a soft-nosed expanding bullet, first made at *Dum Dum* near Calcutta.

dummy *dum'i*, *n* a sham or counterfeit article taking the place of a real one; a block, lay-figure or mannequin; a dumb person; an unprinted model of a book; a rubber teat for an infant; an exposed hand of cards; the imaginary player of such a game or hand; a feint of passing or playing the ball (*Rugby football*, etc.). — *vt* and *vi* to sell the dummy (to; see below). — *adj* silent; sham, feigned. — **dummy run** an experimental run; a try-out or testing. — **sell the dummy** (*Rugby football*, etc.) to deceive an opponent by a feint of passing or playing the ball (also *fig*). [**dumb**.]

dump *dump*, *vt* to set down heavily or with a thump; to unload; to tip (esp. rubbish); to get rid of; to transfer data held in computer memory to a printer or disk (*comput*); to land and sell at prices below cost of production in the exporting country — or (according to some) in the importing country (*econ*). — *n* a place for the discharge of loads, or for rubbish; a deposit or store (*mil*); a dirty, dilapidated place; a printout or other copy of data held in computer memory. — *n* **dump'er** someone who, or that which dumps; a dumper truck; (in surfing) a wave that crashes suddenly downwards with great force, causing surfers to fall. — **dump'bin** in a shop, a display stand or a container for e.g. bargain items; **dump (**or **dumper) truck** a lorry which can be emptied by raising the front of the carrier to allow the contents to slide out the back. — **dump on** (*US slang*) to do down, belittle; to take advantage of. [Cf. Dan. *dumpe*, Norw. *dumpa*, to fall abruptly.]

dumpling *dump'ling*, *n* a kind of thick pudding or mass of paste; a dumpling-shaped person or animal; a silly person.

dumps *dumps*, *npl* low spirits. — **down in the dumps** (*colloq*) depressed. [Prob. rel. to O.Du. *domp*, mist; or Ger. *dumpf*, gloomy.]

dumpy *dump'i*, *adj* short and thick. — *n* a dumpy person or animal. — *n* **dump'iness**. [18th-cent.; perh. from **dumpling**.]

dun[1] *dun*, *adj* greyish brown; mouse-coloured; dingy; dusky. — *n* a dun colour; a horse of dun colour. — **dun'-bird** the pochard, esp. the female; **dun'-diver** the goosander, esp. the female or young male. [O.E. *dun*.]

dun[2] *dun*, *vt* to importune for payment; to plague, pester, harass: — *pr p* **dunn'ing**; *pa t* and *pa p* **dunned**. — *n* someone who duns; a demand for payment. [Perh. rel. to **din**.]

dun[3] *dun*, *n* a hill; a fortified mound. [Celt.; in many place names.]

dunce *duns*, *n* a slow learner; a stupid person. — **dunce's cap** a tall conical hat, once worn at school to indicate stupidity. [*Dunses*, schoolmen who opposed classical studies on the revival of learning (named after *Duns* Scotus (d. 1308), their leader.]

dunderhead *dun'dər-hed*, *n* a stupid person. — *adj* **dun'derheaded**. — *n* **dun'derheadedness**.

Dundonian *dun-dō'ni-ən*, *n* and *adj* (a person) belonging to, coming from or born in Dundee, Scotland.

dune *dūn*, *n* a low hill of sand, esp. on the seashore. — **dune'-buggy** (orig. *US*) a usu. small car with large tyres, used for driving on beaches. [Fr., — O.Du. *duna*; cf. **down**[2].]

dung *dung*, *n* excrement; manure. — *vt* to manure with dung. — *vi* to void excrement. — **dung'-beetle** a scarabaeid beetle generally; **dung'-fly** any of a number of small two-winged flies that breed on dung or decaying vegetable matter; **dung'-fork** a fork used for moving stable manure; **dung'-heap** or **dung'-hill** a heap of dung; any squalid situation or place. [O.E.]

dungaree *dung-gə-rē'* or *dung'gə-rē*, *n* a coarse Indian calico; (in *pl*) work overalls made of it, esp. loose trousers with a bib front and shoulder straps; (in *pl*) a similar garment for casual wear. [Hindi *dūgrī*.]

dungeon *dun'jən*, *n* a close, dark prison; a cell under ground; orig. the principal tower of a castle. [O.Fr. *donjon* — L.L. *domniō*, *-ōnis*.]

dunk *dungk*, *vt* and *vi* to dip cake, etc., that one is eating in one's coffee or other beverage. — *n* **dunk'er**. [Ger. *tunken*, to dip.]

dunlin *dun'lin*, *n* the red-backed sandpiper. [Dimin. of **dun**[1].]

dunnage *dun'ij*, *n* loose wood laid in the bottom of a ship's hold to keep the cargo out of the bilge-water, or wedged between parts of the cargo to keep them steady.

dunnart *dun'ärt*, *n* a marsupial mouse of Australia and Papua New Guinea (genus *Sminthopsis*). [Aboriginal.]

dunnite *dun'īt*, *n* a kind of explosive based on ammonium picrate. [From its inventor, the U.S. army officer, Col. B. W. *Dunn* (1860–1936).]

dunno *də-nō'*. Colloq. contraction of **(I) don't know**.

dunnock *dun'ək*, *n* the hedge-sparrow. [Dimin. of **dun**[1].]

dunny *dun'i*, (*colloq* or *dialect*) *n* a lavatory (*Austr* and *NZ*); an outside lavatory (*Scot*).

duo *dōō'ō* or *dū'ō*, *n* a duet; two persons, etc., associated in some way (e.g. a pair of musicians or variety artists): — *pl* **dū'os**. [It., — L. *duo*, two.]

duodecennial *dū-ō-di-sen'yəl*, *adj* occurring every twelve years. [L. *duodecim*, twelve, *annus*, year.]

duodecimal *dū-ō-des'i-ml*, *adj* computed by twelves; twelfth. — Also *n*. — **duodecimal system** a number system whose base is twelve. [L. *duodecim*, twelve — *duo*, two, *decem*, ten.]

duodecimo *dū-ō-des'i-mō*, *adj* formed of sheets folded so as to make twelve leaves. — *n* a book of such sheets — usu. written 12mo. [L. *in duodecimō*, in twelfth.]

duodenum *dū-ō-dē'nəm*, *n* the first portion of the small intestine (so called because about twelve fingers'-breadth in length): — *pl* **duodē'na**. — *adj* **duodē'nal**. — *n* **duodēnec'tomy** excision of the duodenum. — *n* **duodēnī'tis** inflammation of the duodenum. [Formed from L. *duodēnī*, twelve each.]

duologue *dū'ō-log*, *n* a dialogue between two actors. [L. *duo* (or Gr. *dyo*), two, Gr. *logos*, discourse.]

duomo *dwō'mō*, (It.) *n* a cathedral: — *pl* **duō'mos** or **duō'mi** (*-ē*).

duopoly *dū-op'ə-li*, *n* a situation in which two companies, etc., monopolise trading in a commodity. [L. *duo* (or Gr. *dyo*), two, and mono*poly*.]

duotone *dū'ō-tōn*, *n* and *adj* (a drawing, print, etc.) done in two tones or colours. [L. *duo*, two, and **tone**.]

DUP *abbrev* for Democratic Unionist Party (the Protestant nationalist party of Northern Ireland).

dup. *abbrev* for duplicate.

dupe *dūp*, *n* a person who is cheated. — *vt* to deceive; to trick. — *n* **dūpabil'ity**. — *adj* **dū'pable**. — *n* **dū'per**. — *n* **dū'pery** the art of deceiving others. [Fr.]

dupion *dū'pi-ən* or *-on*, *n* a double cocoon, made by two silkworms spinning together; a kind of coarse silk made from these cocoons. [Fr. *doupion*, from It. *doppione*, double.]

duple *dū'pl*, *adj* double, twofold; having two beats in the bar (*mus*). [L. *duplus*, double.]

duplex *dū'pleks*, *adj* twofold, double; having some part doubled; allowing communication, transmission, in both directions simultaneously (*comput* and *teleg*). — *n* a duplex apartment or house. — *n* **du'plexer** (*telecomm* and *radar*) a system allowing the use of the same aerial for transmission and reception. — **duplex apartment** a flat on two floors; **duplex house** (*US*) a house, divided either horizontally or vertically, providing accommodation for two families. [L. *duplex*, *-icis*.]

duplicate *dū'pli-kit*, *adj* double; twofold; like, equivalent or alternative. — *n* another (esp. subsidiary or spare) thing of the same kind; a copy or transcript; the condition of being in two copies. — *vt* (*dū'pli-kāt*) to double; to copy; to repeat. — *n* **dūplicā'tion**. — *adj* **dū'plicative**. — *n* **dū'plicātor** a copying machine. — **in duplicate** in two copies, or original accompanied by a copy. [L. *duplicāre*, *-ātum* — *duo*, two, *plicāre*, to fold.]

duplicity *dū-plis'i-ti*, *n* doubleness, esp. in conduct or intention; insincerity; double-dealing. — *adj* **duplic'itous**. [L. *duplex*, *-icis*, double.]

dura *dū'rə*, *n* short for **dura mater**.

durable *dūr'ə-bl*, *adj* able to last or endure; hardy; permanent. — *n* something that will endure, esp. (in *pl*) goods that do not need replacing frequently. — *n* **durabil'ity** or **dur'ableness**. — *adv* **dur'ably**. — *n* **durā'tion** continuance in time; time indefinitely; power of continuance; length of time. — *adj* **durā'tional**. — **for the duration** (*colloq*) as long as the war (or the situation under discussion) continues. [L. *dūrāre*, to harden, endure, last.]

Duralumin® *dūr-al'ū-min*, *n* a strong, light, aluminium alloy containing copper. [L. *dūrus*, hard, and *aluminium*.]

dura mater *dū'rə mā'tər* or L. *do͞o'ra mä'ter*, (*anat*) *n* the exterior membrane of the brain and spinal column. [L. *dūra māter*, hard mother, a translation of the Ar. name.]

duramen *dū-rā'mən*, (*bot*) *n* heartwood. [L. *dūrāmen*, hardness — *dūrus*, hard.]

duration, etc. See under **durable**.

durbar *dûr'bär*, *n* a reception or levee; an Indian court (*hist*). [Pers. *darbār*, a prince's court, lit. a door of admittance.]

duress *dūr-es'* or *dūr'es*, *n* coercion illegally exercised; compulsion, pressure; constraint, force; imprisonment. [O.Fr. *duresse* — L. *dūritia* — *dūrus*, hard.]

durian *do͞o'ri-ən* or *dū'*, *n* a tall Indian and Malayan fruit-tree with leaves like a cherry's; its large fruit, with hard rind and foul-smelling but pleasant-tasting pulp. [Malay *dūrī*, thorn.]

during *dū'ring*, *prep* throughout the time of; in the course of. [Orig. pres. p. of obs. *dure*, to last.]

durmast *dûr'mäst*, *n* a European oak bearing sessile acorns, noted for its tough wood. [Perh. a blunder for *dun mast*.]

durra, doura or **dhurra** *do͞o'rə*, *n* Indian millet, a grass related to sugar-cane, much cultivated for grain in Asia and Africa, or other species of the genus. [Ar. *dhurah*.]

durst *dûrst*, see **dare**. [O.E. *dorste*, past tense of *durran*, to dare.]

durum *dū'rəm* or **durum wheat** (*hwēt* or *wēt*), *n* a kind of spring wheat, grown esp. in Russia, N. Africa and N. America, whose flour is used in making spaghetti, etc. [L. *trīticum dūrum*, hard wheat.]

dusk *dusk*, *n* twilight; partial darkness; darkness of colour. — *adj* darkish; of a dark colour. — *vt* and *vi* to make or become dusky. — *adv* **dusk'ily**. — *n* **dusk'iness**. — *adj* **dusk'y** partially dark or obscure; dark-coloured; gloomy. [O.E. *dox*, dark.]

dust *dust*, *n* fine particles of solid matter, esp. earth, powdery matter or dirt; a cloud of this; the earth; the grave; a debased or shabby condition; a disturbance, a brawl (*colloq*). — *vt* to free from dust (also *vi*); to sprinkle. — *n* **dust'er** a cloth or brush for removing dust; a sprinkler; a dustcoat. — *adv* **dust'ily**. — *n* **dust'iness**. — *adj* **dust'less**. — *adj* **dust'y** covered or sprinkled with dust; like dust; contemptible, bad (as in the phrases *not so dusty* and *a dusty answer*; *slang*). — **dust'-bath** the action of birds in rubbing dust into their feathers, prob. to get rid of parasites; **dust'bin** a receptacle for household rubbish; a repository for anything unwanted, unimportant, etc. (*fig*); **dust'-bowl** a drought area subject to dust-storms; **dust'cart** a vehicle for taking away household rubbish; **dust'coat** an overall; a light overcoat; **dust cover** the jacket of a book; a dustsheet; **dusting powder** fine powder, esp. talcum powder; **dust jacket** dust cover; **dust'man** a man employed to remove household rubbish; **dust'pan** a pan or shovel for removing dust, etc. swept from the floor. — *adj* **dust'proof** impervious or inaccessible to dust. — **dust'sheet** a cloth for protecting furniture from dust; **dust'-storm** a small storm in which a whirling column of dust or sand travels across a dry country; **dust'-up** (*colloq*) a quarrel, a brawl; **dusty answer** an unsatisfying, unfruitful or sordid response (*fig*). — **bite the dust** see under **bite**; **throw dust in someone's eyes** (*fig*) to deceive someone. [O.E. *dūst*.]

Dutch *duch*, *adj* pertaining to the Netherlands, its people, or language. — *n* the language of the Netherlands; (in *pl*) the people of the Netherlands. — **Dutch'man** a native or citizen of the Netherlands: — *pl* **Dutch'men**; *fem* **Dutch'woman**: — *pl* **Dutch'women**. — **Dutch auction** see under **auction**; **Dutch barn** a storage barn consisting of a roof on a steel framework; **Dutch cap** see **cap**; **Dutch courage** see under **courage**; **Dutch doll** a wooden doll with jointed legs; **Dutch hoe** a hoe with blade attached as in a spade; **Dutch oven** a heavy, covered cooking-pot used by burying in coals; a heavy stewpot or casserole; **Dutch treat** an occasion (e.g. a meal or an entertainment) when each person pays for himself or herself; **Dutch uncle** someone who criticises or reprimands one unsparingly. — **double Dutch** any unknown or unintelligible language; **Dutch elm disease** a fungal, usu. fatal, disease of elm trees, spread by bark beetles, causing a gradual withering; **go Dutch** (*colloq*) to pay each for himself or herself; **I'm a Dutchman** an expression used ironically to show disbelief and rejection of an earlier statement. [Ger. *deutsch*, (lit.) belonging to the people — O.H.G. *diutisc*.]

dutch *duch*, (*Cockney slang*) *n* a wife. [Prob. **duchess**.]

duty *dū'ti*, *n* that which is due; what one is bound by any (esp. moral) obligation to do; one's proper business; service, attendance; supervision of pupils out of school hours; performance of function or service; the work done by a machine under given conditions, or for a specified amount of energy supplied; respect, deference; tax on goods, etc. — *adj* **dū'teous** devoted to duty; obedient. — *adv* **dū'teously**. — *n* **dū'teousness**. — *adj* **dū'tiable** subject to custom duty. — *adj* **dū'tied** subjected to duties and customs. — *adj* **dū'tiful** attentive to duty; respectful; expressive of a sense of duty. — *adv* **dū'tifully**. — *n* **dū'tifulness**. — *adj* **duty-bound'**

obliged by one's feeling of duty; honour-bound. — *adj* **duty-free'** free from tax or duty. — *n* (*colloq*) a shop, usu. at an airport or on board a ship, where duty-free articles are on sale; an article on sale at such a shop; **duty officer** the officer on duty at any particular time. — *adj* **duty-paid'** on which duty has been paid. — **do duty for** to serve as, to act as substitute for; **on duty** performing one's duties, or liable to be called upon to do so, during a specified period of time (opp. to **off duty**). [A. Fr. *dueté* — O.Fr. *deü*, due.]

duumvir *dōō-, dū-um'vir* or *-vər*, *n* one of two associated in the same post: — *pl* **duum'virs** or **duum'viri** (*-ī*; L. *dōō-ōōm-wir'ē*). — *adj* **duum'viral.** — *n* **duum'virate** an association of two men in one post; a government by duumvirs. [L. *duumvirī*, for *duovirī* — *duo*, two, *vir*, a man.]

duvet *dōō'vā* (Fr. *dü-vā*), *n* a quilt stuffed with eiderdown, swan's-down or man-made fibres, used on a bed in place of blankets, etc. [Fr.]

duvetyn, duvetyne or **duvetine** *dū'və-tēn* or *duv'tin*, *n* a soft fabric with a nap, made of cotton, wool, silk or rayon, and often used for women's clothes. [Fr. *duvetine* — *duvet*, down.]

dux *duks*, (esp. *Scot*) *n* the top academic prize-winner in a school or class. [L., a leader.]

duyker. See **duiker.**

DV *abbrev* for *Deo volente* (L.), God willing.

Dv. *abbrev* for Drive (in street names).

DVLA *abbrev* for Driver and Vehicle Licensing Agency (*formerly* Centre).

dwarf *dwörf*, *n* an abnormally small person, esp. (in general but non-technical usage) a person with abnormally short limbs but normal body and head; an animal or plant much below the ordinary height; anything very small of its kind; a small manlike being, esp. a metal-worker (*folklore*); a small star of high density and low luminosity (**white, red, brown dwarf,** etc. according to colour): — *pl* **dwarfs** or (*rare*) **dwarves.** — *adj* dwarfed; very small. — *vt* to hinder from growing; to make to appear small. — *vi* to become dwarfed. — *adj* **dwarfed.** — *adj* **dwarf'ish** like a dwarf; very small. — *adv* **dwarf'ishly.** — *n* **dwarf'ishness.** — *n* **dwarf'ism** condition of being a dwarf. [O.E. *dweorg.*]

dwell *dwel*, *vi* to abide or reside (*formal* or *archaic*); to remain; to rest attention (on): — *pr p* **dwell'ing;** *pa t* and *pa p* **dwelt** or **dwelled.** — *n* a pause, hesitation in the working of a machine (*eng*); a part of a cam shaped so as to allow a pause in operation at the point of maximum lift (*eng*). — *n* **dwell'er.** — *n* **dwell'ing** (*formal* or *archaic*) the place where one dwells; a house; habitation. — **dwell'ing-house** a house used as a dwelling, in distinction from a place of business or other building; **dwell'ing-place.** [O.E. *dwellan*, to go astray, delay, tarry.]

dwile *dwīl*, *n* a floorcloth or mop. [Cf. Du. *dweil*, a mop.]

dwindle *dwind'l*, *vi* to grow less; to waste away; to grow feeble; to become degenerate. [O.E. *dwīnan*, to fade.]

DY *abbrev* for Benin (*formerly* Dahomey) (I.V.R.).

Dy (*chem*) *symbol* for dysprosium.

dyad *dī'ad*, *n* a pair of units treated as one; a bivalent atom, radical or element (*chem*). — *adj* **dyad'ic.** [Gr. *dyas, -ados* — *dyo*, two.]

Dyak or **Dayak** *dī'ak*, *n* a member of any of the indigenous, generally non-Muslim tribes of the interior of Borneo; their languages and dialects. [Malay *dayak*, up-country.]

dybbuk *dib'ək*, (*Jewish folklore*) *n* an evil spirit, or the soul of a dead person, that enters the body of a living person and controls his or her actions. [Heb. *dibbūq.*]

dye *dī*, *vt* to stain; to give a new colour to: — *pr p* **dye'ing;** *pa t* and *pa p* **dyed.** — *n* stain; a colouring liquid; colour produced by dyeing. — *adj* **dy'able** or **dye'able.** — *adj* **dyed.** — *n* **dye'ing.** — *n* **dy'er** a person whose trade is to dye cloth, etc. — **dyeline** (*dī'līn*) see **diazo; dye'stuff** a substance used in dyeing; **dye'wood** any wood from which material is obtained for dyeing; **dye'-work** or **-works** an establishment for dyeing. — **dye in the wool** to dye (the wool) before spinning, to give a more permanent result; **dyed-in-the-wool** (*fig*) (too) fixed in one's opinions or attitudes. [O.E. *dēagian*, to dye, from *dēag, dēah*, colour.]

dying *dī'ing*, *pr p* of **die**[1]. — *adj* occurring immediately before death, e.g. *dying words*; pertaining to death; declining; last, final.

dyke, dykey. See **dike**[1,2].

dyn. *abbrev* for: dynamo; dynamometer; dyne.

dynamic *dīn-am'ik* or *din-*, *adj* relating to force; relating to dynamics; relating to the effects of forces in nature; relating to activity or things in movement; relating to dynamism; causal; forceful, very energetic. — *n* a moving force; any driving force instrumental in growth or change (esp. social). — *adj* **dynam'ical.** — *adv* **dynam'ically.** — *n* **dynam'icist** a person who studies dynamics. — *nsing* **dynam'ics** the science of matter and motion, mechanics, sometimes restricted to kinetics; (often as *npl*) (signs indicating) varying levels of loudness (*mus*). — *vt* **dyn'amise** or **-ize** to make dynamic. — *n* **dyn'amism** dynamic quality; a theory which explains the phenomena of the universe by some immanent energy; operation of force; quality of restless energy. — *n* **dyn'amist.** — *adj* **dynamis'tic.** [Gr. *dy̆namikos* — *dy̆namis*, power.]

dynamite *dīn'ə-mīt*, *n* explosive consisting of absorbent matter, such as porous silica, saturated with nitroglycerine; something highly dangerous to deal with; someone or something excellent or thrilling (*slang*). — *vt* to blow up with dynamite (also *fig*). — *n* **dyn'amiter.** [Gr. *dynamis*, power.]

dynamo *dīn'ə-mō*, *n* contraction for **dynamo-electric machine,** a machine for generating electric currents by means of the relative movement of conductors and magnets: — *pl* **dyn'amos.** — *adj* **dynamoelec'tric** or **dynamoelec'trical.** — *n* **dynamom'eter** an instrument for measuring force, or (brake horse-)power. — *adj* **dynamomet'ric** or **dynamomet'rical.** — *n* **dynamom'etry.** — *n* **dyn'amotor** an electrical machine with two armature windings, one acting as a motor and the other as a generator, and a single magnetic field, for converting direct current into alternating current. — *n* **dyn'atron** (*electronics*) a four-electrode thermionic valve used to generate continuous oscillation. [Gr. *dy̆namis*, power.]

dynast *din'ast* or *-əst*, also (*US*) *dīn'*, *n* a ruler. — *adj* **dynas'tic** or **dynas'tical** relating to a dynasty. — *adv* **dynast'ically.** — *n* **dyn'asty** (*-əs-ti*) a succession of kings of the same family, or of members of any powerful family or connected group. [Fr. *dynastie*, or L.L. *dynastīa* — Gr. *dy̆nasteia*, power, dominion — *dy̆nasthai*, to be able.]

dyne *dīn*, *n* the force which (in the centimetre-gram-second system), acting on a mass of one gramme, produces an acceleration of one centimetre per second per second, equal to 10^{-5} of a newton. [Gr. *dy̆namis*, force.]

dys- *dis-*, *pfx* signifying ill, bad or abnormal. [Gr.]

dysarthria *dis-är'thri-ə*, (*med*) *n* impaired ability to articulate speech resulting from damage to the central or peripheral nervous system. [**dys-**, and Gr. *arthron*, a joint.]

dysentery *dis'ən-tər-i* or *-tri*, (*med*) *n* a term formerly applied to any condition in which inflammation of the colon was associated with the frequent passage of bloody stools; now confined to *amoebic dysentery* and to *bacillary dysentery*. — *adj* **dysenteric** (*-ter'ik*). [Gr. *dysenterīa* — *dys-*, amiss, *enteron*, intestine.]

dysfunction *dis-fungk'shən* or *-fung'shən*, *n* impairment or abnormality of the functioning of an organ. — *adj* **dysfunc'tional**. [**dys-** and **function**.]

dysgenic *dis-jen'ik*, (*zool*) *adj* unfavourable to racial improvement. [**dys-** and the root of Gr. *gennaein*, to beget.]

dysgraphia *dis-graf'i-ə*, *n* inability to write, due to brain damage or other cause. — *adj* **dysgraph'ic**. [**dys-** and Gr. *graphein*, to write.]

dyskinesia *dis-kin-ē'zi-ə*, *n* lack of control over bodily movements; impaired performance of voluntary movements. [**dys-** and Gr. *kīnēsis*, movement.]

dyslexia *dis-leks'i-ə*, *n* word-blindness, great difficulty in learning to read or spell, unrelated to intellectual competence and of unknown cause. — *adj* and *n* **dyslec'tic** or **dyslex'ic**. [**dys-** and Gr. *lexis*, word.]

dyslogistic *dis-lə-jis'tik*, *adj* disapproving, reproachful, abusive. — *adv* **dyslogis'tically**. [**dys-** and Gr. *logos*, discourse.]

dysmenorrhoea or (esp. in U.S.) **dysmenorrhea** *dis-men-ō-rē'ə*, *n* difficult or painful menstruation. — *adj* **dysmenorrhoe'al** or **dysmenorrhe'al**, **dysmenorrhoe'ic** or **dysmenorrhe'ic**. [**dys-** and Gr. *mēn*, month, *rhoiā*, flow.]

dysmorphophobia *dis-mör-fō-fō'bi-ə*, *n* abnormal fear of any personal physical deformity. [**dys-**, **morpho-** and **phobia**.]

dyspareunia *dis-pä-rōō'ni-ə*, *n* painful or difficult coitus. [**dys-** and Gr. *para*, beside, *eunē*, a bed.]

dyspepsia *dis-pep'si-ə*, *n* indigestion. — *n* **dyspep'tic** a person suffering from dyspepsia. — *adj* suffering from, pertaining to, or arising from, indigestion; bad-tempered. — *adv* **dyspep'tically**. [Gr. *dyspepsiā* — *dys-*, ill, *pepsis*, digestion.]

dysphagia *dis-fā'ji-ə*, *n* difficulty in swallowing. — *adj* **dysphagic** (*-faj'ik*). [**dys-** and Gr. *phagein* (aorist), to eat.]

dysphasia *dis-fāz'i-ə* or *-fā'zhə*, *n* difficulty in expressing or understanding thought in spoken or written words, caused by brain damage. [**dys-** and Gr. *phasis*, speech.]

dysphemism *dis'fə-mizm*, *n* the replacing of a mild or inoffensive word or phrase by an offensive one; the offensive word or phrase substituted. — *adj* **dysphemis'tic**. [**dys-** and **(eu)phemism**.]

dysphoria *dis-fö'ri-ə*, *n* uneasiness; absence of feeling of wellbeing. — *adj* **dysphor'ic**. [Gr. *dysphŏriā*, affliction, pain — *dys-*, ill, and the root of *pherein*, to bear.]

dysplasia *dis-plā'zi-ə*, *n* abnormal development or growth of a cell, tissue, organ, etc. — *adj* **dysplas'tic**. [**dys-** and Gr. *plāsis*, moulding.]

dyspnoea or (esp. in U.S.) **dyspnea** *disp-nē'ə*, *n* difficult or laboured breathing. — *adj* **dyspnoe'al** or **dyspne'al**, **dyspnoe'ic** or **dyspne'ic**. [Gr. *dyspnoia* — *dys-*, ill, *pnoē*, breathing.]

dyspraxia *dis-prak'si-ə*, *n* an impaired ability to perform deliberate actions. [**dys-** and Gr. *prāxis*, doing.]

dysprosium *dis-prōz'i-əm*, *n* a metallic element of the rare earths (atomic no. 66; symbol **Dy**). [Gr. *dysprositos*, difficult to reach — *dys-*, ill, difficult, *pros*, to, *ienai*, to go.]

dysrhythmia *dis-ridh'mi-ə*, *n* abnormal or defective rhythm. [**dys-** and Gr. *rhythmos*, rhythm.]

dysthymia *dis-thī'mi-ə*, *n* abnormal anxiety and despondency. — *n* **dysthȳ'miac** a sufferer from dysthymia. — *adj* **dysthȳ'mic**. [**dys-** and Gr. *thymiā*, despair.]

dystocia *dis-tō'shi-ə*, *n* abnormal or difficult labour or childbirth. [**dys-** and Gr. *tokos*, birth.]

dystonia *dis-tō'ni-ə*, (*med*) *n* a disorder of muscle tone, causing muscle spasm. — *adj* **dystonic** (*-ton'ik*). [**dys-** and Gr. *tonos*, tension.]

dystrophy *dis'trə-fi*, (*biol*) *n* impaired or imperfect nutrition; any of several disorders in which there is wasting of muscle tissue, etc. — *adj* **dystrophic** (*-tro'fik*). — *n* **dys'trophin** a protein essential to normal muscle function, found to be lacking in muscular dystrophy sufferers. — **muscular dystrophy** see under **muscle**. [**dys-** and Gr. *trophē*, nourishment.]

dysuria *dis-ū'ri-ə*, (*med*) *n* a difficulty or pain in passing urine. — *adj* **dysū'ric**. [Gr. *dysouriā* — *dys-*, bad, *ouron*, urine.]

DZ *abbrev* for Algeria (I.V.R.; from the Arabic name *al-Djazā'ir*).

dz. *abbrev* for dozen.

dzho, dzo. See **zho**.

E

E or **e** *ē*, *n* the fifth letter in the modern English alphabet; in music, the third note or sound of the natural diatonic scale, the major third above the tonic C.

E or **E.** *abbrev* for: East; electromotive force (*phys*); energy (*phys*); English; European (as in *E number*); exa- (SI prefix; see Appendix); Spain (i.e. *España*; I.V.R.). — **E'-boat** (*e*nemy *boat* or Ger. *Eilboot* — *Eile*, speed) a fast German motor torpedo-boat; **E. coli** see **Escherichia coli; E'-fit**® a form of identikit, the image being composed on screen and adjustable by fine degrees; **e'-mail** or **E'-mail** electronic mail (q.v.); **E-layer** or **E-region** see **Kennelly-Heaviside layer; E number** an identification code required by EEC law for food additives such as colourings and preservatives, consisting of the letter E followed by a number.

E *symbol* for (mediaeval Roman numeral) 250.

each *ēch*, *adj* and *pron* every one separately considered. — **each other** one another, by some restricted in application to two; **each way** (in betting) for a win and for a place. [O.E. *ǣlc* — *ā*, ever, *gelīc*, alike.]

eager *ē'gər*, *adj* excited by desire; keen (to do something); keen to obtain (with *for*). — *adv* **ea'gerly.** — *n* **ea'gerness.** — **eager beaver** an enthusiast; a zealous person; a person too eager for work. [O.Fr. *aigre* — L. *ācer*, *ācris*, sharp.]

eagle *ē'gl*, *n* a name given to many large birds of prey; a military standard carrying the figure of an eagle; a U.S. gold coin bearing an eagle on its reverse, formerly one worth 10 dollars, now one available in denominations of 5, 10, 25 and 50 dollars; a hole at golf played in two strokes less than par. — *n* **ea'glet** a young or small eagle. — *adj* **ea'gle-eyed** or **ea'gle-sighted** sharp-eyed; discerning. — **ea'gle-owl** any of a number of large horned owls of the genus *Bubo*. [O.Fr. *aigle* — L. *aquila*.]

eagre *ā'gər* or *ē'gər*, *n* a bore or sudden rise of the tide in a river.

EAK *abbrev* for Kenya (i.e. East Africa Kenya; I.V.R.).

ear[1] *ēr*, *n* the organ of hearing, or just the external part of this; the sense or power of hearing; the faculty of distinguishing sounds, esp. of a different pitch; attention; anything projecting or shaped like an ear. — *adj* **eared.** — *n* **ear'ful** (*colloq*) a rough scolding, a reprimand; as much talk or gossip as one's ears can stand. — *n* **ear'ing** (*naut*) one of a number of small ropes to fasten the upper corner of a sail to the yard. — *adj* **ear'less.** — **ear'ache** pain in the ear; **ear'drops** medicinal drops for the ear; pendant earrings; **ear'drum** the tympanic membrane, a thin partition between the outer ear and the organs of the middle ear, which vibrates as sound waves strike it; the cavity of the middle ear, the tympanum; **ear'flap** one of two coverings for the ears, attached to a cap, to protect them from cold or injury; **ear'-hole** the aperture of the ear; **ear'lobe** the soft lower part of the ear; **ear'mark** an owner's mark on an animal's ear; a distinctive mark. — *vt* to put an earmark on; to set aside, or intend, for a particular purpose. — **ear'muffs** a pair of ear coverings, worn for warmth, joined by a band across the head; **ear'phone** a headphone; **ear'piece** the part of a telephone, etc. to which one puts one's ear. — *adj* **ear'-piercing** shrill, deafening. — *n* the piercing of the lobe of the ear for the purpose of inserting earrings. — **ear'plug** a plug of soft material inserted into the outer ear to exclude unwanted sound, water, etc.; **earring** (*ēr'ing*) a piece of jewellery hung from, or fixed on or in, the earlobe; **ear'shot** the distance at which a sound can be heard. — *adj* **ear'-splitting** ear-piercing, deafening. — **ear'-trumpet** a trumpet-shaped tube held to the ear to assist hearing; **ear'wax** a waxy substance secreted by the glands of the ear. — **about one's ears** said of something falling about one (as a house), or assailing one all around (also *fig*); **a thick ear** (*colloq*) a blow on the ear, by way of chastisement; **a word in someone's ear** a private word with someone; **be all ears** to be listening eagerly; **fall on deaf ears** (of a remark, request, etc.) to be ignored; **give ear** to attend (with *to*); **go in (at) one ear and out (at) the other** to make no permanent impression; **have** or **keep one's ear to the ground** to keep oneself well informed about what is going on around one; **have someone's ear** to be sure of someone's favourable attention; **lend an ear** to listen (with *to*); **make a pig's ear of** see under **pig**; **make someone's ears burn** to discuss someone in his or her absence; **out on one's ear** (*colloq*) turned out, dismissed; **pin back one's ears** to listen attentively; **play by ear** to play on a musical instrument without the help of written music; **set by the ears** to set at variance, cause dissension between; **turn a deaf ear** to refuse to listen (with *to*); **up to one's ears in** or **over head and ears in** deeply involved in; **walls have ears** someone may be listening; **wet behind the ears** (*colloq*) naive, immature. [O.E. *ēare*.]

ear[2] *ēr*, *n* a spike, e.g. of corn. — *vi* to put forth ears. — *adj* **eared** (of corn) having ears. [O.E. *ēar*.]

earcon *ēr'kon*, (*comput*) *n* an audio signal given by a computer, e.g. indicating what task it is performing, as distinct from an *icon*, or visual signal. [Artificial coinage, from *ear* and *icon*.]

earl *ûrl*, *n* a British nobleman ranking between a marquess and a viscount: — *fem* **count'ess.** — *n* **earl'dom** the land or status of an earl. — **Earl Marshal** an English officer of state, president of the College of Heralds. [O.E. *eorl*, a warrior, hero.]

early *ûr'li*, (*compar* **ear'lier**, *superl* **ear'liest**) *adv* near the beginning (of a time, period, or series); soon; in good time; beforehand; before the appointed time. — *adj* belonging to or happening in the first part of time, period, series or sequence; belonging to or happening in the first stages of development; beforehand; ready, advanced, or on the spot in good time; happening in the remote past or near future; (of temperatures, figures, etc.) low. — *n* **ear'liness.** — **early bird** the proverbial catcher of the (early) worm; an early riser; **early closing** observance of a weekly half-holiday by the shopkeepers of a town; **Early English** the form of Gothic architecture in which the pointed arch was first employed in Britain. — **earlier on** previously; **early and late** at all times; **early on** before much time has elapsed; **early warning system** a system of advance warning or notice, esp. of nuclear attack; **it's early days** (*colloq*) it's too soon to know, have a result, etc.; **keep early hours** to rise and go to bed early. [O.E. *ǣrlīce* (adv.) — *ǣr*, before.]

earn *ûrn*, *vt* to gain by labour; to acquire; to deserve. — *n* **earn'er** a person who earns; something that brings a good income or profit (*slang*). — *npl* **earn'ings** money, etc. that has been earned; the profits from a venture; income from investments. — **earn out** to make enough money from sales to recover costs or make a profit. [O.E. *earnian*, to earn.]

earnest[1] *ûr'nist*, *adj* sincere in intention; serious, esp. over-serious, in disposition; determined, whole-hearted; impassioned, fervent. — *n* used in the expression **in earnest** (see below). — *adv* **ear'nestly**. — *n* **ear'nestness**. — **in all earnestness** most sincerely; urgently; **in earnest** serious, not joking; in a determined or unequivocal way; in reality. [O.E. *eornost*, seriousness.]

earnest[2] *ûr'nist*, *n* payment given in token of a bargain made; a pledge; first-fruits. [M.E. *ernes* — O.F. *erres*, pledges — Gr. *arrabon*, pledge — Heb. *'ērābōn*.]

earth *ûrth*, *n* the third planet in order from the sun (often with *cap*); the matter on the surface of the globe; soil, a mixture of disintegrated rock and organic material in which plants are rooted; dry land, as opposed to sea; the world; the inhabitants of the world; dirt; a burrow, esp. of a fox; an electrical connection with the earth; an old name for certain oxides of metals (see **rare earth**). — *vt* to connect to earth electrically; to heap earth round, or partially cover (a plant) with earth (with *up*). — *adj* **earth'en** made of earth or clay. — *n* **earth'iness**. — *n* **earth'liness**. — *n* **earth'ling** (*literary*, esp. *science fiction*; often with *cap*) a person who lives on or comes from the planet earth. — *adj* **earth'ly** belonging to the earth; vile; worldly; (with neg., interrog., etc.) conceivably possible, as in *no earthly use*, *what earthly reason*, etc. — *n* (*colloq*; with neg.) chance (for *earthly chance*). — *adj* **earth'ward** moving towards earth, earth-directed. — *adv* (also **earth'wards**) towards earth. — *adj* **earth'y** consisting of, relating to, or resembling earth; coarse, gross, crude or unrefined. — *adj* **earth'born** born from or on the earth. — *adj* **earth'bound** restricted or confined to the earth (*lit* and *fig*); heading towards earth. — **earth'-closet** a closet in which earth is used to deodorise faecal matter; **earth'enware** coarse pottery; **earth'-house** an underground stone-lined gallery associated with the Iron Age, which may have functioned as a storehouse or possibly dwelling, a souterrain; **earth-light** see **earth-shine**; **earth'man** or **earth'woman** esp. in science fiction, a man or woman who lives on the planet earth; **earth mother** the earth personified as a goddess; a woman, typically plump and fertile, who seems to symbolise motherhood. — *adj* **earth'=motherly**. — **earth'-movement** elevation, subsidence, or folding of the earth's crust; **earth'mover** a bulldozer or other piece of mobile equipment designed to shift large quantities of soil, etc. — *adj* **earth'moving**. — **earth'nut** the edible root tuber of *Conopodium flexuosum*, a woodland umbelliferous plant; the peanut; **earth'quake** a succession of vibrations that shake the earth's surface, caused by the shifting of tectonic plates or by volcanic activity; a disruptive event, an upheaval (*fig*); **earth science** any of the sciences dealing with the earth, e.g. geography, geology. — *adj* **earth'shaking** or **earth'shattering** of great importance or consequence. — **earth'-shine** or **earth'-light** the faint light visible on the part of the moon not illuminated by the sun; **earth'-tremor** a slight earthquake; **earthwoman** see **earthman**; **earth'work** a fortification built of earth; an embankment; work of excavation and embanking; **earth'worm** the common worm. — **cost the earth** (*colloq*) to be very expensive; **down** or **back to earth** back to reality (*adj* **down-to-earth** see under **down**[3]); **go to earth** to seek a hole or hiding-place (also *fig*); **on earth** used for emphasis in phrases such as *how on earth*, *why on earth*, etc.; absolutely, without exception, as in *best on earth*; **run to earth** to search out, find; **the Earthshaker** (*mythol*) Poseidon, the Greek god responsible for causing earthquakes. [O.E. *eorthe*.]

earwig *ēr'wig*, *n* a long-bodied insect with an abdomen terminating in pincers, once supposed to creep into the ear. — *vt* to try to influence (someone) through confidential communications and insinuations. [O.E. *ēarwicga* — *ēare*, ear, *wicga*, insect, beetle.]

ease *ēz*, *n* freedom from difficulty; naturalness; unconstrained manner; freedom from pain or disturbance; rest from work, relaxation; quiet, peace. — *vt* to free from pain, trouble or anxiety; to make comfortable, relax; to relieve; to calm; to move gently; to manoeuvre little by little; to loosen, relax. — *vi* to become less acute or severe (often with *off* or *up*); to move very gradually; to be in increasing demand (*econ*). — *adj* **ease'ful** giving ease, relaxing; quiet, restful. — *n* **ease'ment** (*law*) the right to use something (esp. land) not one's own or to prevent its owner from making an inconvenient use of it. — *adv* **eas'ily**. — *n* **eas'iness**. — *adj* **eas'y** not difficult; convenient; at ease; free from pain; tranquil; unconstrained, natural; giving ease; yielding; (of financial circumstances) not straitened, comfortable; not tight; not strict; in plentiful supply; (of a market) not showing unusually great activity. — Also *adv* (esp. *colloq*). — *interj* a command to lower, to go gently, to stop rowing, etc. — *adj* **easy-care'** (esp. of materials) easy to look after, clean, etc. — **eas'y-chair** an armchair for resting comfortably in. — *adj* **easy-go'ing** unhurried, leisurely; placid, relaxed, tolerant. — **easy listening** a category of modern popular music comprising pleasant but undemanding songs and tunes. — Also *adj*. — **easy meat, game** or **mark** a person or thing that is easy to beat, fool, persuade, hit, destroy, etc.; **easy money** money made without much exertion or difficulty; **easy street** (*colloq*) a situation of comfort or affluence; **easy terms** hire-purchase. — **an easy touch** see under **touch**; **at ease** free from anxiety; in a comfortably relaxed frame of mind or physical attitude; (of soldiers) standing with feet apart, not at attention; **be easy** (*colloq*) to be quite willing to fall in with one arrangement or another; **chapel of ease** see under **chapel**; **easy does it!** take your time, do it slowly, carefully; **easy on the eye** (*colloq*) good to look at; **go easy on** to be lenient with; to use sparingly; **ill at ease** anxious; embarrassed, uneasy; uncomfortable; **stand at ease** (a command to soldiers, etc.) to stop standing at attention, stand with feet apart; **stand easy** (a command to soldiers, etc.) to adopt an even more relaxed position than 'at ease'; **take it easy** to avoid exertion; to be in no hurry; **take one's ease** to make oneself comfortable, relax. [O.Fr. *aise*, ult. — L. *adjacēns*, neighbouring.]

easel *ēz'l*, *n* a usu. three-legged collapsible frame for supporting a blackboard or a picture during painting. [Du. *ezel*, or Ger. *Esel*, a donkey.]

easily, easiness. See **ease**.

east *ēst*, *n* that part of the heavens where the sun rises at the equinox; one of the four cardinal points of the compass; the east part of a region. — *adj* and *adv* toward the rising of the sun; (blowing) from the east. — *adj* **east'bound**. — *adj* **east'erly** situated in the east; coming from the east; looking toward the east. — *adv* on the east; toward the east. — *n* an east wind. — *adj* **east'ern** toward the east; connected with, or belonging to, the east; dwelling in the east. — *n* **east'erner** a native or inhabitant of the east. — *adj* **east'ernmost** situated furthest east. — *adv* **east'ward** or **east'wards** toward the east. — *adj* **east'ward**. — *adj* **east'bound** bound for the east;

travelling east. — *adj* **east-by-north'** (or **-south'**) $11\frac{1}{4}$ degrees north (or south) from due east; **East End** the eastern part of London or some other town, often an area inhabited by people of the poorer classes; **East-end'er; Eastern Church** or **Eastern Orthodox Church** the churches which follow the ancient rite of the East and accept the first seven councils, rejecting papal supremacy — also **Orthodox Church, Greek Church, Greek Orthodox Church, Orthodox Eastern Church; East Indian, East Indies** see under **Indian; east-north-(**or **south)-east'** $22\frac{1}{2}$ degrees north (or south) from east. — **the East** the countries between the Balkans and China (see also **Near East, Middle East, Far East**); in mid-to-late 20th-century politics, the countries, chiefly of the eastern hemisphere, under communist rule. [O.E. *ēast*.]

Easter *ēst'ər*, *n* a Christian festival commemorating the resurrection of Christ, held on the Sunday after the first full moon following the spring equinox, 21 March. — **Easter Day** the day of this festival (also **Easter Sunday**); **Easter egg** a painted, decorated, stained or artificial (esp. made of chocolate) egg, given as a present at Easter; **East'ertide** the days around Easter; the fifty days from Easter to Whitsuntide (*eccles*). [O.E. *ēastre*; perh. from *Eostre* (*Eastre*), a goddess whose festival was held at the spring equinox.]

EAT *abbrev* for Tanzania (i.e. East Africa Tanzania; I.V.R.).

easy. See **ease**.

eat *ēt*, *vt* to take into the body by the mouth as food; to bite, chew and swallow; to include or tolerate in one's diet; to consume (often with *up*); to corrode, destroy (often with *away*); to upset, irritate, worry (*colloq*). — *vi* to take food; to take a meal, e.g. at a stated time; to make inroads, make a hole, gnaw (with *into* or *through*): — *pr p* **eat'ing**; *pa t* **ate** (*et* or *āt*); *pa p* **eaten** (*ē'tən*). — *n* (in *pl*; *colloq*) food. — *adj* **eat'able**. — *n* anything used as food (chiefly in *pl*). — *n* **eat'er** a person, animal or thing that eats; a variety (e.g. of apple) suitable for eating uncooked. — *n* **eat'ery** (*slang*) a restaurant. — **eat'ing-apple**, etc., one suitable for eating uncooked; **eat'ing-house** a restaurant. — **eat away** to destroy gradually; to gnaw (sometimes with *at*); **eat humble-pie** see **humbles**; **eat into** to consume, make inroads into; **eat one's hat** an undertaking promised on conditions one thinks very improbable; **eat one's heart out** to pine away, brooding over misfortune; **eat one's words** to take back what one has said; **eat out** to have a meal away from home, usu. in a restaurant; **eat up** to devour entirely; to consume, absorb; (esp. in *passive*) to obsess, preoccupy wholly. [O.E. *etan*.]

EAU *abbrev* for Uganda (i.e. East Africa Uganda; I.V.R.).

eau *ō*, *n* the French word for water, used in English in various combinations. — **eau de Cologne** a perfume, first made at Cologne in 1709; **eau de Javelle** see **Javel water; eau de Nil** (*də nēl*; water of the Nile) a pale-green colour, Nile green; **eau de vie** (*də vē*; water of life) brandy.

eaves *ēvz*, *npl* the projecting edge of the roof. — *vi* **eaves'drop** to listen surreptitiously to others' conversation. — Also *vt*: — *pr p* **eaves'dropping**; *pa t* and *pa p* **eaves'dropped**. — **eaves'dropper; eaves'dropping**. [O.E. *efes*, the clipped edge of thatch.]

EAZ *abbrev* for Tanzania (i.e. East Africa Zanzibar; I.V.R.).

EB *abbrev* for epidermolysis bullosa (q.v. under **epidermis**); Epstein-Barr (virus).

ebb *eb*, *n* the going back of the tide. — *vi* to flow back; to sink; to decline. — **ebb'tide** the ebbing tide. — **at a low ebb** (*fig*) in a low or weak state. [O.E. *ebba*.]

ebony *eb'ən-i*, *n* a kind of wood almost as heavy and hard as stone, usually black, that takes a high polish; a tree yielding it; a black person (*US old derog*), now black people in general, their concerns and sensibilities. — *adj* made of ebony; black as ebony. — *vt* and *vi* **eb'onise** or **-ize** to make or become like ebony. — *n* **eb'onite** black vulcanised rubber, vulcanite. [L. *(h)ebenus* — Gr. *ebenos*.]

EBU *abbrev* for European Broadcasting Union.

ebullient *i-bul'yənt*, *adj* enthusiastic, exuberant; boiling. — *n* **ebull'ience** or **ebull'iency**. — *adv* **ebull'iently**. — *n* **ebullition** (*eb-ə-lish'ən*) the act of boiling; an outbreak. [L. *ēbulliēns*, *-entis* — *ēbullīre* — *ē*, out, *bullīre*, to boil.]

eburnean *eb-ûr'ni-ən*, *adj* of or like ivory. [L. *eburneus* — *ebur*, ivory.]

EC *abbrev* for: East Caribbean; East Central; Ecuador (I.V.R.); European Community.

ecad *ek'ad*, (*bot*) *n* an organism that has adapted to its environment. [Gr. *oikos*, home, and *-ad*, towards.]

écarté[1] *ā-kär'tā*, *n* a game in which cards may be exchanged for others. [Fr., discarded — *é-* (L. *ēx*, out of, from), *carte*, a card.]

écarté[2] *ā-kär'tā*, (*ballet*) *n* a position in which the arm and leg are extended to the side. [Fr., spread, separated.]

eccentric *ek-sen'trik*, *adj* (of behaviour, etc.) odd or unconventional; unusual, departing from the norm; not positioned centrally; with the axis to one side, not at the centre; (of superimposed circles) not concentric, not having the same centre. — *n* an eccentric person; a contrivance for taking an alternating rectilinear motion from a revolving shaft (*mech*). — *adv* **eccen'trically**. — *n* **eccentricity** (*-sən-tris'*) peculiarity of conduct; oddness, unusualness; the condition of being eccentric; in a conic section, the constant ratio of the distance of a point on the curve from the focus to its distance from the directrix (*geom*). [Gr. *ek*, out of, *kentron*, centre.]

Eccl. or **Eccles.** (*Bible*) *abbrev* for (the Book of) Ecclesiastes.

Eccles cake *ek'lz kāk*, *n* a round cake of sweet pastry containing dried fruit. [*Eccles* in Lancashire.]

ecclesia *i-klē'zi-ə*, *n* a popular assembly, esp. of Athens, where the people exercised full sovereignty; applied to the ancient Jewish congregation, and to the early Christian Church. [Gr. *ekklēsia* — *ek*, out, *kalein*, to call.]

ecclesiastic *i-klē-zi-as'tik*, *n* someone consecrated to the church, a priest or clergyman. — *adj* relating to the church or to the clergy (also **ecclesias'tical**). — *adv* **ecclesias'tically**. [Gr. *ekklēsiastikos*, relating to the ecclesia.]

ecclesiology *i-klē-zi-ol'ə-ji*, *n* the science of church forms and traditions and of church architecture and decoration. — *adj* **ecclesiolog'ical**. — *n* **ecclesiol'ogist**. — **ecclesiastical year** see **year**. [Gr. *ekklēsia*, congregation or church, *logos*, discourse.]

Ecclus. (*Bible*) *abbrev* for (the Apocryphal Book of) Ecclesiasticus.

eccrine *ek'rīn*, *adj* (of a gland, esp. the sweat glands) secreting externally. — *n* **eccrinology** (*ek-ri-nol'ə-ji*) the branch of physiology that relates to the secretions. [Gr. *ek*, out of, *krīnein*, to separate, secrete.]

ecdysis *ek'di-sis*, (*zool*) *n* the act of casting off an outer skin or shell by an insect. [Gr. *ekdysis* — *ek*, out of, *dyein*, to put on.]

ECG *abbrev* for electrocardiogram or electrocardiograph.

échappé *ā-sha-pā*, (Fr.; *ballet*) *n* a double leap from two feet, starting in fifth position, landing in second or fourth, and finishing in fifth.

echelon *esh'ə-lon*, *n* a stepped or staggered arrangement of troops, ships, planes, etc.; a particular level in the hierarchy of an organisation. [Fr. *échelon* — *échelle*, ladder, stair.]

echeveria *ech-ə-vē'ri-ə, n* a succulent plant of a genus (*Echeveria*) of the *Crassulaceae* family. [*Echeveri*, 19th-cent. Mexican botanical artist.]

echidna *i-kid'nə, n* an Australian toothless, spiny, egg-laying, burrowing monotreme animal. [Gr. *echidna*, viper.]

echinoderm *i-kī'nə-dûrm, n* any one of a phylum of radially symmetrical marine animals, having the body-wall strengthened by calcareous plates, and moving usually by tube-feet — starfishes, sea-urchins, brittle-stars, sea cucumbers, and crinoids. — *adj* **echinoder'mal** or **echinoder'matous**. [Gr. *echīnos*, hedgehog, sea-urchin, *derma*, skin.]

echinus *e-kī'nəs, n* a sea-urchin. — *adj* **echī'noid** like a sea-urchin. — *n* a sea-urchin. [Gr. *echīnos*, a hedgehog, sea-urchin.]

echo *ek'ō, n* the sending back or reflection of sound or other waves; the repetition of sound by reflection; a reflected sound; (in *pl*) reverberations, repercussions; a repetition; an imitation; an imitator; something that reminds one of something else; a memory evoked; the signal emitted by an object being scanned by radar; the visual signal from such an object, appearing on screen; conventional play to indicate what cards one holds (*cards*): — *pl* **ech'oes**. — *vi* to reflect sound; to be sounded back; to resound; to play a card as echo. — *vt* to send back (sound or other waves); to send back the sound of; to repeat; to imitate: — *pr p* **ech'ōing**; *pa t* and *pa p* **ech'oed**. — *n* **ech'ōer**. — *adj* **echō'ic** of the nature of an echo; onomatopoeic (*philol*). — *n* **echolalia** (*ek-ō-lā'li-ə*; Gr. *laliā*, talk) senseless or compulsive repetition of words heard (*psychiatry*). — **echo chamber** a room in which sound can be echoed, for recording or radio effects, or when measuring acoustics; **echo location** determining (as a bat does) the position of objects by means of supersonic vibrations echoed from them; **ech'o-sounding** a method of measuring depth of water, locating shoals of fish, etc., by noting the time for return of an echo from the bottom, or bottom and shoal, etc. [L., — Gr. *ēchō*, a sound.]

echo virus *ek'ō vī'rəs, n* any of a group of viruses which can cause respiratory and intestinal diseases and meningitis. [*e*nteric *c*ytopathogenic *h*uman *o*rphan virus.]

éclair *ā-klār'* or *i-klār', n* a cake, long in shape but short in duration, with cream filling and usu. chocolate icing. [Fr. *éclair*, lightning.]

eclampsia *i-klamp'si-ə*, (*med*) *n* acute toxaemia occurring in late pregnancy, associated with high blood pressure, oedema and convulsive fits. — *adj* **eclamp'tic**. [Gr. *eklampsis* — *eklampein*, to flash forth violently (as a fever) — *ek*, out of, *lampein*, to shine.]

éclat *ā-klä', n* striking effect; showy splendour; distinction, celebrity; applause. [Fr. *éclat*, from O.Fr. *esclater*, to break, to shine.]

eclectic *ek-lek'tik, adj* selecting or borrowing from a variety of styles, systems, theories, etc.; characterised by such selection or borrowing; choosing the best out of everything; broad, the opposite of exclusive. — *n* a person who adopts eclectic methods, e.g. in philosophy. — *adv* **eclec'tically**. — *n* **eclec'ticism** (*-sizm*). [Gr. *eklektikos* — *ek*, from, *legein*, to choose.]

eclipse *i-klips', n* the total or partial obscuring of the light of a heavenly body, either when another passes directly in front of it (a *solar eclipse* occurring when the moon passes between the sun and the earth) or when it passes into the shadow of another (a *lunar eclipse* occurring when the earth passes between the sun and the moon); a throwing into the shade; darkness. — *vt* to hide wholly or in part; to darken; to throw into the shade, to cut out or surpass. — *n* **eclip'tic** the great circle in which the plane containing the centres of the earth and sun cuts the celestial sphere; the apparent path of the sun's annual motion among the fixed stars. — *adj* pertaining to an eclipse or the ecliptic. [O.Fr. — Gr. *ekleipsis*, failure — *ek*, out of, *leipein*, to leave.]

eclogue *ek'log, n* a pastoral poem often in the form of a dialogue. [L. *ecloga* — Gr. *eklogē*, a selection.]

eclosion *i-klō'zhən, n* the emergence, esp. of an insect from its pupal case or a larva from its egg. — *vi* **eclose'**. [Fr. *éclosion* — L., *ex-*, *claudĕre*, to shut.]

eco- *ēk-ō-* or *ek-ə-*, *combining form* signifying ecology or ecological (as in *eco-catastrophe*, *eco-politics*).

ecocide *ē'kō-sīd, n* the destruction of the aspects of the environment which enable it to support life. [**eco-**.]

eco-freak *ē'kō-frēk, n* a person concerned with the state of, and the protection of, the environment, an environmentalist. [**eco-**.]

eco-friendly *ē-kō-frend'li, adj* ecologically acceptable, in harmony with, or not threatening to, the environment. [**eco-**.]

eco-label *e'kō-lā-bl, n* a label used by manufacturers of products claiming to be environmentally acceptable, specifying to the consumer the exact nature of their ecological soundness. — *n* **e'co-labelling**. [**eco-**.]

ecology *ē-kol'ə-ji* or *ek-ol'*, also *ik-*, *n* (the scientific study of) the relationships that plants, animals and human beings have to their environment and to each other. — *adj* **ecological** (*e-* or *ē-kə-loj'i-kəl*). — *adv* **ecolog'ically**. — *n* **ecol'ogist**. [Gr. *oikos*, house, *logos*, discourse.]

econometrics *i-kon-ə-met'riks, nsing* statistical analysis of economic data and their interrelations. — *adj* **economet'ric** or **economet'rical**. — *n* **econo-met'rist** or **econometri'cian**. [*econo*my and Gr. *metron*, measure.]

economy *ē-*, *i-* or *e-kon'ə-mi, n* the administration of the material resources of an individual, community or country; the state of these resources; a frugal and judicious expenditure of money; the efficient use of something, e.g. speech, effort, etc.; an organised system; the regular way of operating, of e.g. nature. — *adj* pertaining to a cheaper class of air or sea travel; (of packets of goods, etc.) of a larger size, so costing less than several small sizes (of packets, etc.). — *adj* **economic** (*ē-kə-nom'ik* or *ek-ə-*) relating or having reference to economy or to economics; relating to industry or business; operated at, or capable of yielding, a profit; economical. — *adj* **econom'ical** thrifty; frugal; careful; economic. — *adv* **econom'ically**. — *nsing* or *npl* **econom'ics** (see also **home economics** under **home**); pecuniary position and management; financial or economic aspects. — *nsing* political economy. — *n* **econo-misā'tion** or **-z-** the act of economising. — *vi* **econ'omise** or **-ize** to manage with economy; to spend money carefully; to save (often with *on*). — *n* **econ'omīser** or **-z-**. — *n* **econ'omist** an expert on or student of political economy. [L. *oeconomia* — Gr. *oikonomiā* — *oikos*, a house, *nomos*, a law.]

ecosphere *ē'kō-sfēr, n* the parts of the universe, or esp. the earth, in which life is possible. [**eco-**.]

écossaise *ā-ko-sez', n* orig. a dance or dance-tune of Scottish origin in 3-4 or 2-4 time; later a lively country-dance or its music in 2-4 time. [Fr., fem. of *écossais*, Scottish.]

ecosystem *ē'kō-sis-təm, n* a unit consisting of a community of organisms and their environment. [**eco-**.]

ecotoxic *ē-kō-tok'sik, adj* poisonous to plants or animals, deleterious to the environment. — *n* **eco-toxicol'ogist**. — *n* **ecotoxicol'ogy** the study of the destructive effect of waste materials, etc. on the environment. [**eco-**.]

ecru *e-*, *ā-kroo'* or *-krü', n* unbleached linen; its colour. — *adj* of the colour of unbleached linen, greyish yellow. [Fr. *écru* — L. *ex-* (intensive) and *crūdus*, raw.]

ECSC *abbrev* for European Coal and Steel Community.

ecstasy *ek'stə-si*, *n* a state of exalted pleasure or happiness, rapture; an access of any strong emotion, e.g. rage; (often with *cap*) a drug taken for its stimulant and hallucinogenic properties, *methylenedioxymethamphetamine* (*slang*); a trance-like state of temporary mental alienation and altered or diminished consciousness. — *adj* **ecstat'ic** causing ecstasy; amounting to ecstasy; rapturous. — *n* a person given to bouts of ecstasy; a user of the drug ecstasy. — *adv* **ecstat'ically**. [Gr. *ekstasis* — *ek*, from, and root of *histanai*, to make to stand.]

ECT *abbrev* for electroconvulsive therapy.

ecto- *ek-tō-* or *-tə-*, *combining form* signifying outside, often opp. to **endo-**, **ento-**. — See also **exo-**. [Gr. *ektos*, outside.]

ectoblast *ek'tə-bläst*, *n* the epiblast of an embryo. — *adj* **ectoblas'tic**. [**ecto-** and Gr. *blastos*, shoot, bud.]

ectoderm *ek'tə-dûrm*, *n* the external germinal layer of epiblast of the embryo, or any part of the mature animal derived from it (also **ex'oderm**). — *adj* **ectoderm'al** or **ectoderm'ic**. [**ecto-** and Gr. *derma*, skin.]

ectoenzyme *ek'tō-en-zīm*, *n* an exoenzyme. [**ecto-**.]

ectomorph *ek'tə-mörf*, *n* a person of thin, light body build. — *adj* **ectomorph'ic**. — *n* **ec'tomorphy**. [*ecto*derm (an ectomorph having a prevalence of structures formed from this) and Gr. *morphē*, shape.]

ectopic *ek-top'ik*, (*pathol*) *adj* in an abnormal position. — **ectopic pregnancy** the development of a foetus outside the uterus, esp. in a Fallopian tube. [Gr. *ek*, from, *topos*, place.]

ectoplasm *ek'tə-plazm*, *n* the outer layer of cytoplasm of a cell (*biol*); matter said by spiritualists to emanate from the body of a medium during a trance. — *adj* **ectoplas'mic**. [**ecto-** and Gr. *plasma*, something moulded.]

ECU, Ecu or **ecu** *ā'kū* or *ek'ū*, *n* short for **European currency unit**, a unit of currency whose rate is based on a range of European currencies within the EMS — used e.g. as a reserve currency and seen as the notional single European currency. — **hard ECU, Ecu** or **ecu** an ECU existing as a true international currency managed by the EMF, based on the narrow band of the ERM and not devaluing against any other European currency. [Acronym.]

ecumenic *ek-* or *ē-kū-men'ik*, or **ecumenical** *-men'ik-əl*, *adj* general, universal, belonging to the entire Christian Church; of or relating to the ecumenical movement. — *adv* **ecumen'ically**. — *n* **ecumen'icalism** or **ecumen'icism** (*-i-sizm*) or **ecumen'ism** (or *i-kū'mə-nizm*) the doctrines and practice of the Christian ecumenical movement. — *nsing* **ecumen'ics** the study of ecumenical awareness and the ecumenical movement in the Christian church. — **ecumenical movement** a movement within the Christian church towards unity on all fundamental issues of belief, worship, etc. [L. *oecumenicus* — Gr. *oikoumenikos* — *oikoumenē* (*gē*), inhabited (world).]

ECUSA or **Ecusa** *i-kōō'sə*, *abbrev* for Episcopal Church of the United States of America.

eczema *ek'si-mə*, *n* a skin disease characterised by redness, severe itching and the formation of tiny vesicles that ooze and crust. — *adj* **eczematous** (*-sem'ə-təs* or *-zem'*). [Gr. *ekzeein* — *ek*, out of, *zeein*, to boil.]

Ed. *abbrev* for Editor.

ed. *abbrev* for: edited; edition.

edacious *i-*, *ē-* or *e-dā'shəs*, (*literary* or *facetious*) *adj* given to eating; gluttonous. — *adv* **edā'ciously**. — *n* **edā'ciousness** or **edacity** (*i-das'i-ti*). [L. *edāx*, *edācis* — *edĕre*, to eat.]

Edam *ē'dam*, *n* a type of mild Dutch cheese, shaped into globes with a red outer skin. [After *Edam* near Amsterdam.]

edaphic *i-daf'ik*, (*bot* or *ecol*) *adj* relating to the soil. — *n* **edaphology** (*ed-ə-fol'ə-ji*). [Gr. *edaphos*, ground.]

eddy *ed'i*, *n* a current running back, contrary to the main stream, thus causing a circular motion or small whirlpool; a similarly whirling motion of smoke, mist or wind. — *vi* to move round and round: — *pr p* **edd'ying**; *pa t* and *pa p* **edd'ied**. — **eddy current** an electric current caused by varying electromotive forces which are due to varying magnetic fields, giving rise to heating in motors, transformers, etc. — Also called **Foucault current** (*fōō-kō'*).

edelweiss *ā'dəl-vīs*, *n* a small Alpine plant of the same family as the daisy and dandelion, the flowers of which have a collar of white woolly leaves. [Ger. *edel*, noble, *weiss*, white.]

edema, edematose, edematous. See **oedema**.

Eden *ē'dən*, *n* the garden in which Adam and Eve lived before the Fall (*Bible*); a paradise. — *adj* **Edenic** (*-den'*). [Heb. *ēden*, delight, pleasure.]

edentate *ē-den'tāt*, *adj* without teeth; without front teeth. — *n* a member of the **Edentā'ta**, an order of mammals of Central and S. America having no front teeth or no teeth at all — sloths, ant-eaters, armadillos. [L. *ēdentātus*, toothless — *ē*, out of, *dēns*, *dentis*, a tooth.]

edge *ej*, *n* the border of anything; a rim; the brink; the intersection of the faces of a solid figure; a ridge or crest; the cutting edge of an instrument; keenness; incisiveness, trenchancy; sharpness of mind or appetite. — *vt* to put an edge or border on or round; to border, form or be a border for; to trim the edge of; to move or push little by little, esp. edgeways or sideways; to strike with the edge of the bat (*cricket*). — *vi* to move sideways; to move gradually. — (In combination) **-edged** having an edge or edges of the stated kind or number, as in *sharp-edged*, *two-edged*. — *n* **edg'er** a garden tool for trimming the edge of a lawn; someone or something that edges. — *adv* **edge'ways** or **edge'wise** sideways; with edge foremost or uppermost; in the direction of the edge. — *n* **edg'iness** the state of being on edge. — *n* **edg'ing** a border, esp. decorative, round something, e.g. a garment; (a strip of) material, e.g. lace, for using as an edge-trimming. — *adj* **edg'y** irritable, on edge. — **edge (or edged) tool** a tool with a sharp edge. — **edge out** to remove or get rid of gradually; to defeat by a small margin; **get a word in edgeways** to get a word in with difficulty; **have the edge on** or **over** to have the advantage over; **on edge** in an irritable or jumpy state; nervous or tense with anticipation; **set someone's teeth on edge** to set up a disagreeable sensation in the teeth and mouth, as sour fruit does; to cause to wince, irritate acutely. [O.E. *ecg*.]

edible *ed'i-bl*, *adj* able or fit to be eaten. — *n* something for food. — *n* **edibil'ity** or **ed'ibleness**. [L. *edibilis* — *edĕre*, to eat.]

edict *ē'dikt*, *n* something proclaimed by authority; an order issued by a king or lawgiver. — *adj* **edict'al**. — *adv* **edict'ally**. [L. *ēdictum* — *ē*, out of, *dīcĕre*, *dictum*, to say.]

edifice *ed'i-fis*, *n* a large building or house. [Fr. *édifice* — L. *aedificium* — *aedificāre*, to build — *aedēs*, a temple, house, *facĕre*, to make.]

edify *ed'i-fī*, *vt* to strengthen spiritually; to improve the mind of: — *pr p* **ed'ifying**; *pa t* and *pa p* **ed'ified**. — *n* **edificā'tion** instruction; progress in knowledge or in goodness. — *n* **ed'ifier**. — *adj* **ed'ifying** instructive; improving. — *adv* **ed'ifyingly**. [L. *aedificāre*, to build — *aedēs*, a temple, house, *facĕre*, to make.]

edit *ed'it*, *vt* to prepare (a writer's work or works) for publication; to correct and improve (a piece of text, etc.) ready for publication; to reword; to censor or bowdlerise; to be the editor of (a newspaper or periodical); to compile (a work of reference); to prepare for broadcasting; to make up the final version of a motion picture by selection, rearrangement, etc., of material photographed previously. — *n* **edi'tion** one of the different forms in which a book is published; the form given to a text by its editor; the number of copies of a book printed at a time, or at different times without alteration; a number of identical articles (e.g. copies of a work of art) issued at one time; reproduction. — *n* **ed'itor** a person who edits books, etc.; someone who is in charge of a newspaper, periodical, etc., or a section of it. — *adj* **editō r'ial** of or belonging to an editor. — *n* an article in a newspaper written by an editor or leader writer. — *vi* **editor'ialise** or **-ize** to introduce personal opinions or bias into reporting; to expound one's views in an editorial or in the style of one. — *n* **editorialisā'tion** or **-z-**. — *adv* **editor'ially**. — *n* **ed'itorship**. — **edit out** to remove (a piece of film, tape, text, etc.) during editing. [L. *ēdĕre, ēdĭtum* — *ē*, from, *dăre*, to give.]

educate *ed'ū-kāt*, *vt* to bring up and instruct; to teach; to train. — *adj* **ed'ucable**. — *n* **educabil'ity** or **educātabil'ity**. — *adj* **ed'ucated** having had a (good) education; cultivated, knowledgeable, refined in judgment or taste; (of a guess) authoritative, backed by experience, to be accorded credence. — *n* **educā'tion** bringing up or training, of e.g. a child; instruction, teaching; strengthening of the powers of body or mind; culture. — *adj* **educā'tional**. — *adv* **educā'tionally**. — *n* **educā'tionalist** or **educa'tionist** a person skilled in methods of educating or teaching; a person who promotes education. — *adj* **ed'ucātive** of or relating to education; tending to teach. — *n* **ed'ucātor**. — *adj* **educatory** (*ed'* or *-kā'tə-ri*). [L. *ēducāre, -ātum*, to rear — *ēdūcĕre* — *ē*, from, *dūcĕre*, to lead.]

educe *i-dūs'*, *vt* to draw out, extract or elicit; to develop; to infer. — *n* **educe'ment**. — *adj* **educ'ible**. — *n* **eduction** (*i-duk'shən*). [L. *ēdūcĕre, ēductum* — *ē*, from, *dūcĕre*, to lead.]

edulcorate *i-dul'kə-rāt*, *vt* to free from soluble particles by washing. — *adj* **edul'corant**. — *n* **edulcorā'tion**. — *adj* **edul'corātive**. — *n* **edul'corātor**. [L. *ē-* (intensive) and *dulcōrāre*, to sweeten.]

Edwardian *ed-wörd'i-ən*, *adj* belonging to or characteristic of the reign of (any) King *Edward*, esp. Edward VII; (of a motor car) built in the period 1905 to 1918, coming between veteran and vintage cars. — Also *n*.

-ee *-ē*, *sfx* signifying: the person affected by some action, e.g. *evacuee*, *interviewee*; a person in a particular situation, e.g. *absentee*; a person performing some action, e.g. *attendee*, *standee* (esp. *US*). [Fr. past p. sfx. *-é* or *-ée* — L. *-ātus*, *-āta*.]

EEC *abbrev* for European Economic Community.

EEF *abbrev* for Engineering Employers' Federation.

EEG *abbrev* for electroencephalogram or electroencephalograph.

eek *ēk*, *interj* of fright, used conventionally in children's comics, etc. [Representative of a shriek or squeal.]

eel *ēl*, *n* any fish of the *Anguillidae*, *Muraenidae*, or other family of *Apodes*, fishes with long smooth cylindrical or ribbon-shaped bodies, scaleless or nearly so, without pelvic fins; extended to various other fishes of similar form, such as the **sand eel** (or launce) and **electric eel**; a devious, evasive person, a slippery character. — *adj* **eel'y**. — **eel'grass** or **eel'wrack** grasswrack (*Zostera*), a grasslike flowering plant of the pondweed family, growing in seawater; **eel'pout** (*-powt*) the burbot, a freshwater edible fish; the blenny, a small fish with a slimy tapering body; **eel'worm** a nematode worm. [O.E. *ǣl*.]

e'en *ēn*. A poetic contraction of **even**[1,2].

EEO *abbrev* for Energy Efficiency Office.

EEPROM (*comput*) *abbrev* for electronically erasable progammable read-only memory.

e'er *ār*. A poetic contraction of **ever**.

eerie *ē'ri*, *adj* unnatural, mysterious, weird or chilling. — *adv* **ee'rily**. — *n* **ee'riness**. [Scot. — O.E. *ærg* (*earg*), timid.]

EETPU *abbrev* for Electrical, Electronic, Telecommunication and Plumbing Union.

eff *ef*, *euphemism* for **fuck**, esp. in *adj* **eff'ing** and *vi* **eff off**. — **eff'ing and blinding** swearing.

efface *i-* or *e-fās'*, *vt* to obliterate, wear away; to rub out, erase; to keep (oneself) out of view, make (oneself) inconspicuous. — *adj* **efface'able**. — *n* **efface'ment**. [Fr. *effacer* — L. *ex*, out, *faciēs*, face.]

effect *i-fekt'*, *n* the result of an action; the impression produced; purport; reality; (in *pl*) goods, property; (in *pl*) sound, and also lighting, devices contributing to the illusion of the place and circumstance in which the action is carried on (*theatre*, *cinema*, etc.). — *vt* to produce; to accomplish, bring about. — *n* **effec'ter**. — *adj* **effec'tible**. — *adj* **effec'tive** having power to effect; causing something; successful in producing a result or effect; powerful; serviceable; actual; in force. — *n* and *adj* (a soldier, or a body of soldiers) ready for service. — *adv* **effec'tively**. — *n* **effec'tiveness**. — *n* and *adj* **effec'tor** (*biol*) (an organ or substance) that effects a response to stimulus. — *adj* **effec'tual** successful in producing the desired effect. — *n* **effectual'ity** or **effec'tualness**. — *adv* **effec'tually**. — *vt* **effec'tuate** to accomplish. — *n* **effectuā'tion**. — **for effect** so as to make a telling impression; **give effect to** to carry out, perform; **come**, etc. or **put**, etc. **into effect** to become or make operative; **in effect** in truth, really; substantially; in operation, operative; **take effect** to begin to operate; to come into force; **to that effect** with the previously indicated purport. [O.Fr., — L. *effectus* — *ex*, out, *facĕre*, to make.]

effeminate *i-fem'in-ət*, *adj* womanish or unmanly. — *n* **effem'inacy** (*-ə-si*) or **effem'inateness**. — *adv* **effem'inately**. [L. *effēminātus* — *effēmināre*, to make womanish.]

effendi *e-fen'di*, *n* in Turkey, a former title for civil officials, now used orally with the force of *Mr*; generally, in the Eastern Mediterranean, a title of respect for educated or high-ranking people. [Turk.; from Gr. *authentēs*, an absolute master.]

efferent *ef'ə-rənt*, *adj* conveying outward or away, as in (*zool*) **efferent nerve**, a nerve carrying impulses away from the central nervous system. — *n* **eff'erence**. [L. *ē*, from, *ferēns*, *-entis*, pres. p. of *ferre*, to carry.]

effervesce *ef-ər-ves'*, *vi* (of a liquid) to give off gas bubbles, esp. with a faint hissing noise, to fizz; to froth up; to behave or talk vivaciously. — *n* **effervesc'ence**. — *adj* **effervesc'ent** bubbling or fizzing from the escape of gas; lively, vivacious, exuberant. [L. *effervēscĕre* — *ex* (intensive) and *fervēre*, to boil.]

effete *e-fēt'*, *adj* exhausted, enfeebled, debilitated; degenerate, decadent. — *adv* **effete'ly**. — *n* **effete'ness**. [L. *effētus*, weakened by having brought forth young — *ex*, out, *fētus*, the bringing forth of young.]

efficacious *ef-i-kā'shəs*, *adj* able to produce the result intended or desired. — *adv* **efficā'ciously**. — *n* **efficā'ciousness**, **efficacity** (*-kas'i-ti*) or **eff'icacy** (*-kə-si*) the power of producing an effect; effectiveness. [L. *efficāx*, *-ācis* — *efficĕre*, to accomplish.]

efficient *i-fish'ənt*, *adj* capable, competent, proficient, working with speed and economy; effective. — (In combination) **-effi'cient** economical in the use or consumption of a particular resource, as in *energy-*

efficient. — *n* **effi'ciency** the quality of being efficient; the ratio of a machine's output of energy to input. — *adv* **effi'ciently**. [Fr., — L. *efficiēns*, *-entis*, pres. p. of *efficěre*, to accomplish.]

effigy *ef'i-ji*, *n* a likeness or figure of a person; the head or impression on a coin. — **burn** or **hang in effigy** to burn or hang a figure of a person (to express disapproval). [L. *effigiēs* — *effingěre* — *ex* (intensive) and *fingěre*, to form.]

effing. See **eff**.

effleurage *ef-lə-räzh'*, *n* a stroking movement in massage. [Fr., glancing, grazing.]

effloresce *ef-lo-res'*, *vi* to blossom forth; to become covered with a powdery crust (*chem*); to form a powdery crust. — *n* **effloresc'ence** production of flowers; the time of flowering; a rash or eruption on the skin; a powdery surface crust; the formation of such a crust. — *adj* **effloresc'ent**. [L. *efflōrēscěre* — *ex*, out, *flōrēscěre*, to blossom.]

effluent *ef'lōō-ənt*, *adj* flowing out. — *n* liquid industrial waste; outflow from sewage during purification; a stream that flows out of another stream or lake. — *n* **eff'luence**. [L. *effluēns*, *-entis*, pres. p. of *effluěre* — *ex*, out, *fluěre*, to flow.]

effluvium *e-flōō'vi-əm*, *n* disagreeable vapours rising from decaying matter; an unpleasant exhalation generally: — *pl* **efflu'via**. — *adj* **efflu'vial**. [L.L., — L. *effluěre* (see **effluent**).]

efflux *ef'luks*, *n* the act of flowing out; that which flows out. — Also **effluxion** (*e-fluk'shən*). [L. *effluěre* — *ex*, out, *fluěre*, *fluxum*, to flow.]

effort *ef'ərt*, *n* exertion of body or mind; an attempt; a struggle; a piece of work produced by way of attempt; anything done, produced or accomplished. — *adj* **eff'ortful**. — *adj* **eff'ortless** appearing easy, showing no sign of effort. [Fr., — L. *ex*, out, *fortis*, strong.]

effrontery *i-frunt'ər-i*, *n* shameless impudence or audacity. [Fr. *effronterie* — L. *ex*, out, without, *frōns*, *frontis*, forehead.]

effulgent *i-ful'jənt*, *adj* giving off a brilliant light, shining, radiant. — *n* **efful'gence**. — *adv* **efful'gently**. [L. *effulgēre* — *ex*, out, *fulgēre*, to shine.]

effuse *i-fūz'*, *vt* to pour forth; to spread out. — *adj* (*i-fūs'*) loosely spreading (*bot*); (of shells) with the lips separated by a groove. [L. *effūsus*, past p. of *effunděre*, to pour out, shed.]

effusion *i-fū'zhən*, *n* an unrestrained outpouring of words, esp. expressing warmth or enthusiasm; a literary, esp. poetic, outpouring (often *derog*); the act of pouring, or process of being poured, out; something poured over or shed. [L. *effūsio*, *-ōnis*, an outpouring — *effunděre*, to pour out.]

effusive *i-fū'ziv*, *adj* expressing feelings, esp. of warmth and enthusiasm, in a copious, gushing manner (*rather derog*); poured out at the surface in a state of fusion, volcanic (*geol*). — *adv* **effus'ively**. — *n* **effus'iveness**. [L. *effūsus* — *effunděre*, to pour out, and sfx. *-ive*.]

EFL *abbrev* for English as a Foreign Language.

EFTA *abbrev* for European Free Trade Association, a body committed to free trade between its member countries (currently Austria, Finland, Iceland, Norway, Sweden, Switzerland) and to the creation of a single European market.

EFTPOS or **Eftpos** *eft'pos*, *abbrev* for electronic funds transfer at point of sale.

EFTS *abbrev* for electronic funds transfer system.

e.g. or **eg** *abbrev* for *exempli gratia* (L.), for example.

egalitarian *i-gal-i-tā'ri-ən*, *n* and *adj* (a person) believing in, and upholding, the principle of equality among people. — *n* **egalitā'rianism**. [Fr. *égalitaire* — *égal*, equal — L. *aequalis*, equal.]

egg[1] *eg*, *n* an oval body laid by the female of birds, reptiles, fish, insects and certain other animals, from which the young is hatched, esp. that laid by a hen, used as food; an ovum or female gamete (also **egg'-cell**); a zygote, the fertilised ovum, or the organism growing within it. — *n* **egg'er** or **egg'ar** a large brown moth whose cocoons are egg-shaped. — *adj* **egg'y** savouring of, or covered with, eggs. — **egg-and-anch'or**, **egg-and-dart'** and **egg-and-tongue'** ornaments, esp. found in cornice mouldings, in the form of eggs alternating with anchors, darts or tongues; **egg-and-spoon race** a race in which each competitor carries an egg in a spoon; **egg'-beater** an egg-whisk; a helicopter (esp. *NAm colloq*); **egg'-box** a protective partitioned container for holding (esp. six) eggs; **egg'-cosy** a cover for keeping a boiled egg hot; **egg'cup** a cup-shaped holder for holding a boiled egg at table; **egg custard** see **custard**; **egg'-flip** a drink made of ale, wine, spirits or milk, with eggs, sugar, spice, etc.; **egg'-head** (*colloq*) an intellectual; **egg'nog** a drink of eggs and hot beer, spirits, etc.; **egg'-plant** the aubergine or brinjal, an East Indian annual plant with edible egg-shaped fruit; **egg'-plum** a yellowish egg-shaped plum; **egg'shell** the hard calcareous covering of a bird's egg; a very thin kind of porcelain. — *adj* thin and delicate; (of paint, etc.) having only a slight gloss. — **egg'-slice** a utensil for lifting fried eggs out of a pan; **egg'-spoon** a small spoon used for eating boiled eggs out of the shell; **egg'-timer** a small sand-glass for timing the boiling of eggs; **egg'-tooth** a hard point on the beak by which an unhatched bird or reptile breaks the eggshell; **egg'wash** a thin mixture of egg and milk (or water) used as a glaze for pastry; **egg'-whisk** an instrument for beating raw eggs. — **a bad egg** (*colloq*) a worthless person; **eggs Benedict** (*ben'i-dikt*) a slice of ham and a poached egg placed on a slice of toast and covered with hollandaise sauce; **good egg!** (*colloq*) an exclamation of approval; **have** or **put all one's eggs into one basket** to risk all on one enterprise; **have, get,** or **be left with, egg on one's face** (*slang*) to be left looking foolish; **teach one's grandmother to suck eggs** to presume to teach someone older and wiser than oneself; to teach someone something that he or she knows already. [O.N. *egg*.]

egg[2] *eg*, *vt* (with *on*) to incite, urge on. [O.N. *eggja* — *egg*, an edge.]

eggar, egger, eggy. See **egg**[1].

eglantine *eg'lən-tīn* or *-tin*, *n* a fragrant species of wild rose, the sweet-brier. [Fr., — O.Fr. *aiglent*, as if from a L. *aculentus*, prickly.]

ego *eg'ō* or *ē'gō*, *n* the 'I' or self — that which is conscious and thinks; an image of oneself; egotism. — *adj* **egocen'tric** self-centred; regarding or regarded from the point of view of the ego. — *n* **egocentri'city**. — *n* **eg'ōism** the doctrine that we have proof of nothing but our own existence (*philos*); the theory of self-interest as the principle of morality (*ethics*); over-concern for one's own wellbeing, selfishness; preoccupation with oneself, self-centredness, egotism. — *n* **eg'ōist**. — *adj* **egōis'tic** or **egois'tical**. — *adv* **egōis'tically**. — *n* **egomā'nia** morbid egotism. — *n* **egomā'niac**. — *adj* **egomanī'acal** (*-mən-*). — *n* **eg'otism** a frequent use of the pronoun I; thinking or speaking too much of oneself; self-exaltation. — *n* **eg'otist**. — *adj* **egotis'tic** or **egotis'tical**. — *adv* **egotis'tically**. — **ego ideal** (*psychol*) one's personal standards, ideals, ambitions, etc. acquired as one recognises parental and other social standards; one's idealised picture of oneself; **e'go-trip** (*slang*) an action or experience that inflates one's good opinion of oneself; **e'go-tripper**. — **massage someone's ego** (*facetious*) to flatter someone, rub someone up the right way. [L. *ego*, *egō*, and Gr. *egō*, I.]

egregious *i-grē'jəs*, *adj* outrageous; notorious. — *adv* **egrē'giously**. — *n* **egrē'giousness**. [L. *ēgregius*, chosen out of the flock — *ē*, out of, *grex*, *gregis*, a flock.]

egress *ē'gres*, *n* the act of going out; departure; the way out; the power or right to depart. — *n* **egression** (*i-gresh'ən*) the act of going out; departure. [L. *ēgredī*, *ēgressus* — *ē*, out of, *gradī*, to go.]

egret *ē'grit*, *n* a white heron of any of several species. [Variant of **aigrette**.]

Egyptian *ē-jip'shən*, *adj* belonging to Egypt, a country of N.E. Africa. — *n* a native or citizen of Egypt. — *adj* **Egyptolog'ical**. — *n* **Egyptol'ogist**. — *n* **Egyptol'ogy** the science of Egyptian antiquities.

eh *ā*, *interj* expressing inquiry, failure to hear, or slight surprise.

EHO *abbrev* for environmental health officer.

EIA *abbrev* for environmental impact assessment.

Eid al-Adha, Eid al-Fitr. See **Id-al-Adha, Id-al-Fitr.**

eider *ī'dər*, *n* a northern sea-duck, sought after for its fine down (also **ei'der-duck**). — **ei'derdown** the soft down of the eider, used for stuffing quilts; a quilt. [Prob. through Sw. from O.N. *æthar*, genitive of *æthr*, an eider.]

eidetic *ī-det'ik*, (*psychol*) *adj* (of a mental image) extraordinarily clear and vivid, as though actually visible; (of a person, or memory) reproducing, or able to reproduce, a vividly clear visual image of what has been previously seen. — *n* a person with this ability. — *adv* **eidet'ically**. [Gr. *eidētikos*, belonging to an image — *eidos*, form.]

eigen- *ī-gən-*, *combining form* signifying proper, own. — *n* **ei'gen-frequency** one of the frequencies with which a particular system may vibrate. — *n* **ei'gentone** a tone characteristic of a particular vibrating system. — *n* **ei'genvalue** any of the possible values for a parameter of an equation for which the solutions will be compatible with the boundary conditions. [Ger. *eigen*, own.]

eight *āt*, *n* the cardinal number one above seven; a symbol (8, viii, etc.) representing that number; a set of eight things or persons (syllables, leaves, oarsmen, etc.); an eight-oar boat; a card with eight pips; a shoe or other article of a size denoted by 8; the eighth hour after midday or midnight. — *adj* of the number eight; eight years old. — *adj* **eighth** (*ātth*) last of eight; next after the seventh; equal to one of eight equal parts. — *n* an eighth part; a person or thing in eighth position; an octave (*mus*). — *adv* **eighthly** (*ātth'li*). — *n* **eight'some** a group or set of eight; a Scottish reel for eight dancers (also **eightsome reel**). — *adj* **eight'fold** amounting to eight times as much; divided into eight parts. — *adv* by eight times as much. — **figure of eight** a figure shaped like an 8, e.g. made on the ice in skating, etc.; **one over the eight** (*colloq*) one alcoholic drink too many; **piece of eight** an old Spanish coin worth eight reals; **the eights** annual boatraces between the various Oxford colleges. [O.E. *æhta*.]

eighteen *ā-tēn'* or *ā'tēn*, *n* eight and ten; **(18)** a certificate designating a film suitable only for persons of eighteen and over. — Also *adj*. — *adj* **eigh'teenth** (or *-tēnth'*) last of eighteen; next after the seventeenth; equal to one of eighteen equal parts. — *n* an eighteenth part; a person or thing in eighteenth position. — *adv* **eighteenth'ly**. [O.E. (Mercian) *æhtatēne*.]

eightfold, eighth, eightsome. See **eight**.

eighty *ā'ti*, *n* and *adj* eight times ten. — *npl* **eight'ies** the numbers eighty to eighty-nine; the years so numbered in life or any century; a range of temperatures from eighty to just less than ninety degrees. — *adj* **eigh'tieth** last of eighty; next after the seventy-ninth; equal to one of eighty equal parts. — *n* an eightieth part; a person or thing in eightieth position. [O.E. *æhtatig*.]

Einsteinian *īn-stī'ni-ən*, *adj* of or relating to Albert *Einstein*, physicist and mathematician (1879–1955), or his theories, esp. that of relativity. — *n* **einstein'ium** the radioactive metallic element (symbol **Es**; atomic no. 99) artificially produced from plutonium and named after Einstein.

eirenic. Same as **irenic**.

EIS *abbrev* for Educational Institute of Scotland.

eisteddfod *ī-sted'fəd* or *ī-stedh'vod*, or in U.S. *ā-stedh'*, *n* orig. a competitive congress of Welsh bards and musicians, now any of several gatherings in Wales for competitions in music, poetry, drama, etc., esp. (with *cap*) the Royal National Eisteddfod: — *pl* **eistedd'fods** or **eisteddfodau** (*-vo-dī*). — *adj* **eisteddfod'ic**. [Welsh, lit. session — *eistedd*, to sit.]

either *ī'dhər* or *ē'dhər*, *adj* the one or the other; each of two, the one and the other. — *pron* the one or the other. — *conj* correlative to *or*. — *adv* (used with a neg.) also, likewise (not), as in *He isn't hungry and she isn't either*; (after a neg.) moreover, besides, as in *She's a golfer, and not a bad one, either*. [O.E. *ǣgther*, contraction of *ǣghwæthEr* — *ā*, aye, pfx. *ge-* and *hwæther*, whether.]

ejaculate *i-jak'ū-lāt*, *vt* to utter with suddenness, to exclaim. — *vi* to utter an ejaculation, to exclaim; to emit semen. — *n* (*-lət*) semen. — *n* **ejacūlā'tion**. — *adj* **ejac'ūlative** (*-lə-* or *-lā-*) or **ejac'ūlatory** (*-lə-* or *-lā-*). [L. *ē*, from, *jaculārī*, *-ātus* — *jacĕre*, to throw.]

eject *i-jekt'*, *vt* to throw out; to dismiss; to turn out; to expel. — *vi* (of a pilot) to cause oneself to be shot out of an aircraft or spacecraft, using an ejector-seat. — *n* **ejec'tion**. — *adj* **ejec'tive**. — *n* **eject'ment** expulsion; dispossession; an action for the recovery of the possession of land (*law*). — *n* **eject'or** any mechanical apparatus for ejecting or discharging; a person who ejects or dispossesses another of his or her land. — **eject'or-seat** or (*US*) **ejection seat** a seat in an aircraft, etc. that can be shot clear with its occupant in an emergency. [L. *ējectāre*, frequentative of *ējicĕre*, *ējectum* — *ē*, from, *jacĕre*, to throw.]

eke *ēk*, *vt* (now only with *out*) to add to, increase, lengthen; to supplement, make up to the required measure. [O.E. *ēcan*.]

ekistics *e-kis'tiks*, *nsing* the science or study of human settlements. — *adj* **ekis'tic**. — *n* **ekistician** (*-tish'ən*). [From a Mod. Gr. coinage, *oikistikē* — Gr. *oikistikos*, of or relating to settlement — *oikos*, a house.]

ekphrasis *ek'frə-sis*, (*art*) *n* a description of a work of art, possibly imaginary, produced as a rhetorical exercise, those of antiquity having provided inspiration for artists of the Renaissance. [Gr., description.]

ekuele *ā-kwā'lā* or **ekpwele** *ek-pwā'lā*, *n* between 1973 and 1985, the name of the standard monetary unit of Equatorial Guinea (100 *céntimos*): — *pl* **ekue'le** or **ekpwe'les**. [Native name.]

el[1] *el*, *n* the twelfth letter of the modern English alphabet (L, l); anything of that shape; a wing giving a building the shape of the letter L (*US*).

el[2] *el*, (*US colloq*) *n* an *el*evated railroad.

elaborate *i-lab'ər-āt*, *vi* (with *on* or *upon*) to add detail, more information, etc. to a bare account. — *vt* to work out in detail; to add detail to; to produce by labour; to convert (e.g. food) into complex substances (*physiol*). — *adj* (*i-lab'ər-ət*) done with fullness and exactness; highly detailed; complicated; wrought with labour. — *adv* **elab'orately**. — *n* **elab'orateness**. — *n* **elaborā'tion** the process of elaborating; a refinement, detail or complication added. — *adj* **elab'orative** (*-rə-* or *-rā*). — *n* **elab'orātor**. [L. *ēlabōrāre*, *-ātum* — *ē*, from, *labōrāre* — *labor*, labour.]

élan *ā-lān'* or *ā-lā*, *n* impetuosity; dash, style. [Fr.]

eland *ē'lənd*, *n* a S. African antelope, resembling the elk in having a protuberance on the larynx. [Du., — Ger. *Elend* (now *Elen*) — Lith. *élnis*, elk.]

elapse *i-laps'*, *vi* (of time, or units of time) to pass silently. [L. *ēlāpsus*, *ēlābī* — *ē*, from, *lābī*, *lāpsus*, to slide.]

elasmobranch *i-laz'mō-brangk* or *-las'*, *n* any member of the class of fishes that includes sharks and skates, having a cartilaginous skeleton and platelike gills. [Gr. *elasmos*, a beaten-metal plate, *branchia*, gills.]

elastic *i-las'tik* or *-läs'*, *adj* having the ability to recover its original form or size after stretching, compression or deformation; springy, resilient; stretchy; flexible; able to recover quickly a former state or condition e.g. after a shock (*fig*); (of terms or expressions) capable of stretching to include much (*fig*). — *n* a stretchable string or ribbon woven with strands of rubber. — *n* **elas'tase** an enzyme found in the pancreatic juice that decomposes elastin. — *adv* **elas'tically.** — *vt* **elas'ticate** to make elastic. — *adj* **elas'ticated.** — *vt* **elas'ticise** or **-ize** (*-ti-sīz*) to make elastic. — *n* **elasticity** (*ē-las-tis'i-ti* or *el-əs-*) the power of returning to original form or size after stretching, compression or deformation; springiness, flexibility, resilience or stretchiness; power to recover from shock, depression, etc. — *n* **elas'ticness.** — *n* **elas'tin** a protein, chief constituent of elastic tissue. — *n* **elas'tomer** any rubberlike substance. — *adj* **elastomeric** (*-mer'*). — **elastic band** a narrow strip of rubber formed into a loop, for holding objects together, etc. (also **rubber band**); **elastic collision** or **scattering** see under **collide; elastic tissue** tissue having fibres with elastic quality, occurring esp. in ligaments and tendons. [Late Gr. *elastikos* — *elaunein*, to drive.]

Elastoplast® *i-last'ə-pläst* or *-plast*, *n* a dressing for a wound, consisting of gauze on a backing of adhesive tape.

elate *i-lāt'*, *vt* to raise the spirits of, cheer, exhilarate; to make exultant or euphoric. — *adv* **elā'tedly.** — *n* **elā'tedness.** — *n* **elā'tion** exaltation, high spirits, euphoria; pride resulting from success. [L. *ēlātus*, used as past p. of *efferre* — *ē*, from, *lātus*, carried.]

elbow *el'bō*, *n* the joint where the arm bends; the corresponding joint in vertebrates; the part of a sleeve which covers the elbow; any sharp turn or bend e.g. in a road. — *vt* to push with the elbow, to jostle. — **el'bow-grease** (*humorously*) vigorous rubbing; hard work; **el'bow-room** room to extend the elbows; space enough for moving or acting; freedom and scope. — **at one's elbow** close at hand, ready for use; **bend** or **lift the elbow** (*facetious*) to drink alcoholic liquor, esp. too much; **out at elbow** (wearing a coat, etc.) ragged or threadbare; **up to the elbows** completely engrossed or involved. [O.E. *elnboga*.]

elder[1] *eld'ər*, *adj* older; having lived a longer time; prior in origin. — *n* a person who is older; an ancestor; esp. in primitive communities, a person advanced to the office of advisor or administrator on account of age; one of a class of office-bearers in the Presbyterian Church (*presbyter* of the New Testament). — *n* **eld'erliness.** — *adj* **eld'erly** old, or somewhat old; bordering on old age. — *n* (with *the*) elderly people. — *adj* **eld'est** oldest. — **elder** or **eldest hand** the player on the dealer's left, who leads in card-playing; **elder statesman** a retired statesman consulted by the government; any administrator of age and experience. [O.E. *eldra*, compar., *eldesta*, superl., of *ald*, old.]

elder[2] *el'dər*, *n* a shrub or tree (*Sambucus*) related to honeysuckle, with small flowers and three-seeded fruits. — **el'derberry** the purple-black fruit of the elder; **elderberry wine.** [O.E. *ellærn*.]

El Dorado or **Eldorado** *el-də-rä'dō*, *n* the golden land (or city) imagined by the Spanish conquerors of America; any place where wealth is easily to be acquired. [Sp. *el*, the, *dorado*, past p. of *dorar*, to gild — the gilded king of the legendary city of Manoa.]

eldritch *el'drich*, (*Scot*) *adj* weird, uncanny.

elecampane *el-i-kam-pān'*, *n* a composite plant (*Inula helenium*) formerly much cultivated for its medicinal root; a sweetmeat flavoured with an extract from the root. [L. *enula campāna*.]

elect *i-lekt'*, *vt* to select by vote; to choose in preference to other options; to select for any office or purpose. — *adj* (placed after the noun) chosen for an office but not yet in it; chosen, e.g. in Christian doctrine chosen for salvation by God. — *npl* (with *the*) those chosen, esp. for God's salvation. — *n* **electabil'ity.** — *adj* **elect'able.** — *n* **elec'tion** (*-shən*) the public choice of a person for office, usually by the votes of a constituent body; the act of electing or choosing; free will; the exercise of God's will in the predetermination of certain people to salvation (*theol*). — *vi* **electioneer'** to work to secure the election of a candidate. — *n* **electioneer'er.** — *n* and *adj* **electioneer'ing.** — *adj* **elect'ive** relating to, dependent on, or exerting the power of choice; optional. — *adv* **elect'ively.** — *n* **electiv'ity** (*ē-* or *el-*). — *n* **elect'or** a person who elects; someone who has a vote at an election; (usu. with *cap*) the title formerly belonging to those princes and archbishops of the German empire who had the right to elect the Emperor: — *fem* **elect'ress.** — *adj* **elect'oral** pertaining to elections or to electors; consisting of electors. — *n* **elect'orate** the body of electors; the dignity or the territory of an elector. — *n* **elect'orship.** — **electoral college** in the U.S., the body of people who elect the President and Vice-President, themselves elected by popular vote; any body of electors with a similar function. [L. *ēligĕre*, *ēlectum* — *ē*, from, *legĕre*, to choose.]

Electra complex *i-lek'trə kom'pleks*, (*psychol*) *n* the attachment of a daughter to her father, with hostility to her mother. [Greek story of *Electra*, who helped to avenge her mother's murder of her father.]

electret *i-lek'trit*, (*electr*) *n* a permanently polarised (piece of) dielectric material. [*electr*icity and mag*net*.]

electric *i-lek'trik*, *adj* relating to electricity; charged with or capable of being charged with electricity; producing or produced by, conveying, operated by, or making use of electricity; thrilling (*fig*); producing a sudden startling effect; full of tension and expectation, as though charged with electricity. — *adj* **elec'trical.** — *adv* **elec'trically.** — *n* **electrician** (*el-ik-trish'ən*) a person whose job is to make, instal or repair electrical apparatus. — *n* **electricity** (*el-ik-tris'i-ti*) the manifestation of a form of energy associated with separation or movement of charged particles, such as electrons and protons; the science that deals with this; an electric charge or current; the attractive power of amber and other substances when rubbed; a feeling of excitement. — **electrical engineer** a specialist in the practical applications of electricity as a branch of engineering; **electrical engineering; electric arc** a luminous space between electrodes when a current passes across; **electric battery** a group of cells connected in series or in parallel for generating an electric current by chemical action; **electric blanket** a blanket incorporating an electric element, used for warming a bed; **electric blue** a steely blue colour; **electric chair** in the U.S., the seat on which a condemned criminal is put to death by electrocution; (with **the**) execution by electrocution in this manner; **electric eel** a S. American fish of the carp genus, shaped like an eel, and able to give powerful electric shocks by means of an electric organ in its long tail; **electric eye** a photoelectric cell; a miniature cathode ray tube; **electric fence** a wire fence electrically charged; **electric guitar** one with an electrical amplifying device; **electric organ** an organ in which the sound is produced by electrical devices instead of wind (*mus*); (in certain fishes) a structure that generates, stores and discharges electricity (*zool*); **electric ray** the torpedo fish; **electric storm** a violent disturbance in the electric condition of the atmosphere. [L. *ēlectrum* — Gr. *ēlektron*, amber, in which electricity was first observed.]

electrify *i-lek'tri-fī*, *vt* to introduce electricity into; to adapt to electricity as the motive power; to excite suddenly; to astonish: — *pr p* **elec'trifying**; *pa t* and *pa p* **elec'trified**. — *adj* **electrifī'able**. — *n* **electrificā'tion**.

electro- *i-lek'trō-* or *el-ik-tro'-*, *combining form* signifying electric or electrolytic. — *n* **elec'tro** (*colloq*) short for **electroplate** and **electrotype**: — *pl* **elec'tros**. — *nsing* **electroacous'tics** the technology of converting sound into electrical energy and vice versa. — *adj* **electroacous'tic**. — *n* **electrobiol'ogist**. — *n* **electrobio'logy** the science of the electrical phenomena in living organisms. — *n* **electrocar'diogram** a photographic record of the electrical variations that occur during contraction of the muscle of the heart. — *n* **electrocar'diograph** a galvanometer used for making such records. — *n* **electrocardiog'raphy**. — *adj* **electrochem'ical**. — *n* **electrochem'ist**. — *n* **electrochem'istry** the study of the relation between electricity and chemical change. — *adj* **electroconvuls'ive** (**electroconvulsive therapy** shock therapy — abbrev. **ECT**). — *n* **electrodeposi'tion** deposition of a layer of metal by electrolysis. — *nsing* **electrodynam'ics** the study of electricity in motion, or of the interaction of currents and currents, or currents and magnets. — *n* **electrodynamom'eter** an instrument for measuring currents by the attraction or repulsion between current-bearing coils. — *n* **electroenceph'alogram** (*-sef'* or *-kef'*) a record made by an **electroenceph'alograph**, an instrument recording small electrical impulses produced by the brain. — *n* **electroencephalog'raphy**. — *n* **electromag'net** a piece of soft iron, etc., rendered magnetic by a current of electricity passing through a coil of wire wound round it. — *adj* **electromagnet'ic** of or relating to an electromagnet or electromagnetism (**electromagnetic theory** Clerk Maxwell's theory explaining light in terms of electromagnetic waves; **electromagnetic unit** any unit, such as the abampere or abvolt, in a centimetre-gram-second system of units based on the magnetic forces exerted by electric currents; **electromagnetic wave** a travelling disturbance in space produced by the acceleration of an electric charge). — *n* **electromag'netism** the science dealing with the relations between, and properties of, magnetism and electric currents. — *n* **electrom'eter** an instrument for measuring difference of electric potential. — *adj* **electromet'ric** or **electromet'rical**. — *n* **electrom'etry** the science of electrical measurements. — *adj* **electromō'tive** pertaining to the motion of electricity or the laws governing it (**electromotive force** difference of potential or the force generated by this, being the force of an electric current — also called **electromō'tance**). — *n* **electromō'tor** an apparatus for applying electricity as a motive power. — *adj* **electroneg'ative** carrying a negative charge; tending to form negative ions. — *n* **electronegativ'ity** an electronegative state; the power of e.g. an atom to attract electrons. — *adj* **electro-op'tic** or **-op'tical**. — *nsing* **electro-op'tics** the study of the effects that an electric field has on light crossing it. — *n* **electro-osmo'sis** movement of liquid, under an applied electric field, through a fine tube or membrane. — *n* **elec'trophile** an electrophilic substance. — *adj* **electrophil'ic** having or involving an affinity for electrons, i.e. negative charge, electron-seeking. — *n* **electrophorē'sis** migration of suspended particles, such as protein macromolecules, under the influence of an electric field. — *adj* **electrophoretic** (*-et'ik*) pertaining to electrophoresis. — *n* **electrophorus** (*-trof'ə-rəs*) an instrument for obtaining static electricity by means of induction. — *vt* **elec'troplate** to plate or cover, esp. with silver, by electrolysis. — *n* electroplated ware. — *n* **elec'troscope** an instrument for detecting the presence of electricity in a body and the nature of it. — *adj* **electroscop'ic**. — *n* **elec'troshock** an electric shock. — *adj* **electrostat'ic** of or relating to electricity at rest (**electrostatic unit** any unit, such as the statvolt, in a centimetre-gram-second system of units based on the forces of repulsion existing between static electric charges). — *nsing* **electrostat'ics** the branch of science concerned with electricity at rest. — *nsing* **electrotech'nics** (also **electrotechnol'ogy**) electric technology. — *nsing* **electrothera-peu'tics** (also **electrother'apy**) treatment of disease by electricity. — *n* **elec'trotype** a printing plate made by electrolytically coating a mould with copper; a facsimile of a coin made by this process. — Also *adj*. — *n* **elec'trotyper**. — *n* **elec'trovalency** union within a chemical compound achieved by transfer of electrons, the resulting ions being held together by electrostatic attraction. — *adj* **elec'trovalent**. [Gr. *ēlektro-*, combining form of *ēlektron*, amber.]

electrocute *il-ek'trə-kūt*, *vt* to kill by electricity; to inflict a death penalty by means of the electric chair. — *n* **electrocū'tion**. [**electro-** and exe*cute*.]

electrode *il-ek'trōd*, *n* a conductor by which a current of electricity enters or leaves an electrolytic cell, discharge-tube, or thermionic valve. [**electro-** and sfx. *-ode* — Gr. *hodos*, way.]

electrolyse or **electrolyze** *il-ek'trə-līz*, *vt* to subject to electrolysis; to break up by electric means. — *n* **electrolysis** (*-trol'i-sis*) decomposition by electric current, with migration of ions shown by changes at the electrodes; removal of hair by applying an electrically charged needle to the follicle. — *n* **elec'trolyte** (*-līt*) a substance that conducts electric current through ionisation. — *adj* **electrolytic** (*-lit'ik*). — *adv* **electrolyt'ically**. [**electro-** and Gr. *lysis*, loosing.]

electron *i-lek'tron*, *n* a minute particle charged with electricity, or a unit charge having inertia, normally forming part of an atom but capable of isolation as in cathode rays. — **electron camera** any device that converts an optical image into a corresponding electric current directly by electronic means; **electron gun** the assembly of electrodes in a cathode ray tube which produces the electron beam; **electron microscope** a microscope that makes use of a beam of electrons instead of light; **electron probe** an X-ray device that bombards the specimen under examination with a very narrow beam of electrons, allowing non-destructive analysis; **electron telescope** an optical instrument with electronic image converter used with a normal telescope; **electron tube** an electronic device in which the electron conduction is in a vacuum or gas inside a gas-tight enclosure — e.g. a thermionic valve; **elec'tron-volt** a unit of energy equal to that acquired by an electron when accelerated by a potential of one volt. [See ety. for **electro-**.]

electronic *el-*, *il-* or *ēl-ik-tron'ik*, *adj* of or pertaining to electronics, or to electrons; worked or produced by devices made according to the principles of electronics; concerned with, or working with, such devices. — *adv* **electron'ically**. — *nsing* **electron'ics** the science and technology of the conduction of electricity in a vacuum, a gas, or a semiconductor; the devices, etc. based on this. — **electronic flash** an extremely intense and brief flash for high-speed photography produced by passing an electric charge through a gas-filled tube; the apparatus for producing it; **electronic mail** the sending and receiving of messages by any electronic means; **electronic mailbox** a section of a central computer's memory reserved for a particular individual, into which messages can be directed;

electronic music music made by arranging sounds previously generated in the laboratory and recorded on tape; **electronic tagging** a monitoring system allowing the supervision of an offender outside prison by means of an **electronic tag** (e.g. a bracelet or anklet fitted with a transmitter) which maintains regular signals to a central computer. — **electronic funds transfer (system)** a method whereby financial credits and debits are transferred electronically (between banks and shops, etc.) by computer network (**at point of sale** signifying such a system in operation at a shop checkout, etc., enabling payment by debit or credit card rather than by cash or cheque); **electronic point of sale** (at shop checkouts) a computerised till system in which a cash till with a bar-code reader is directly linked to a stock control system.

electrophoresis ... to ... electrovalent. See **electro-**.

electuary *i-lek'tū-ər-i*, *n* a medicine mixed with honey or syrup. [L.L. *ēlectuārium*.]

eleemosynary *el-ē* or *el-i-ē-moz'i-nər-i*, or *-mos'*, *adj* relating to charity or almsgiving; dependent on charity; of the nature of alms. [Gr. *eleēmosynē*, alms.]

elegant *el'i-gənt*, *adj* very careful or tasteful in dress; graceful in form and movement; refined and luxurious; (of style) polished; (of apparatus or work in science or mathematics) simple and effective. — *n* **el'egance** or **el'egancy**. — *adv* **el'egantly**. [Fr., — L. *ēlegāns*, *-antis*.]

elegy *el'i-ji*, *n* a song of mourning; a poem of serious, pensive or reflective mood; a poem written in elegiac metre. — *adj* **elegī'ac** belonging to elegy; mournful; used in elegies, esp. applied to classical verse in couplets of hexameter and pentameter lines (**elegiac couplets**), or two stanzas of four iambic pentameters rhyming *abab* (**elegiac stanzas**). — *n* elegiac verse. — *adj* **elegī'acal**. — *adv* **elegī'acally**. — *n* **el'egist** a writer of elegies. — *vi* **el'egise** or **-ize** to write elegiacally. — *vt* to write an elegy on. [L. *elegīa* — Gr. *elegeiā* — *elegos*, a lament.]

element *el'ə-mənt*, *n* a first principle; one of the essential parts of anything; an ingredient; the proper medium, habitat or sphere of any thing or being; any one of the four substances, fire, air, earth and water, supposed by the ancients to be the foundation of everything; (in *pl*) the rudiments of learning; (usu. in *pl*) the bread and wine used in the Eucharist; a substance that cannot be resolved by chemical means into simpler substances (*chem*); a member or unit of a structure; a resistance wire in an electric heater; an electrode; a determining fact or condition in a problem; (in *pl*) the weather, the powers of nature. — *adj* **elemental** (*-ment'l*) pertaining to the elements; belonging to, produced by or inhabiting the elements. — *adj* **element'ary** primary, fundamental; rudimentary, simple; uncompounded; pertaining to the elements or a single element. — **elemental spirits** (*mediaeval hist*) beings believed to preside over the four elements, living in and ruling them; **elementary particle** any of a number of particles, e.g. electron, proton, neutron, neutrino, kaon or pion, so-called because supposed indivisible. — **in one's element** in the surroundings most natural or pleasing to one. [L. *elementum*, pl. *elementa*, first principles.]

elemi *el'im-i*, *n* a fragrant resinous substance obtained from various tropical trees, used esp. in varnishes and inks.

elenchus *i-lengk'əs*, (*logic*) *n* refutation; a sophism: — *pl* **elench'ī**. — *adj* **elenc'tic**. [L., — Gr. *elenchein*, to refute.]

elephant *el'i-fənt*, *n* the largest living land mammal, having a very thick skin, a trunk, and ivory tusks — found in two surviving species (the **African elephant** having larger ears and a flatter head than the **Indian** or **Asian elephant**) and several extinct species. — *n* **elephantī'asis** a disease chiefly of tropical climates, consisting of an overgrowth of the skin and connective tissue usually of the legs and scrotum. — *adj* **elephant'ine** like or pertaining to an elephant; very large or ungainly; (of a memory) capacious and reliable. — *adj* **elephant'oid** elephant-like. — **elephant cord** thick, wide-ribbed corduroy; **elephant seal** the largest of the seals, the male measuring about 6 m. (20 ft.) in length; **el'ephant's-ears** or **-ear** any of various begonias or varieties of ornamental arum with heart-shaped leaves. — **pink elephants** hallucinations caused by overindulgence in alcoholic drink; **white elephant** anything that gives more trouble than it is worth; an unwanted possession, often given away to a jumble sale; something which proves to be useless. [M.E. *olifaunt* — Gr. *elephās*, *-antos*.]

elevate *el'i-vāt*, *vt* to raise to a higher position; to raise in mind and feelings; to exhilarate. — *adj* **el'evated** raised; lofty; exhilarated. — *n* short for elevated railroad. — *n* **elevā'tion** the act of elevating or raising, or the state of being elevated or raised; an elevated place; the external face of a building, or a mathematically accurate drawing of this (*archit*); angular height above the horizon; an angle made by a line with the plane of the horizon; a leap with apparent suspension in the air (*ballet*). — *n* **el'evātor** a person or thing that lifts up; a lift or machine for raising grain, etc., to a higher floor; a lift (*US*); a storehouse for grain; a movable control surface or surfaces at the tail of an aeroplane by which it is made to climb or dive. — *adj* **el'evātory**. — **elevated railroad** (*US*) a raised railway over a roadway, (familiarly **el** or **L**). [L. *ēlevāre*, *-ātum* — *ē*, from, *levāre*, to raise.]

eleven *i-lev'n*, *n* the cardinal number next above ten; a team of eleven (in cricket, association football, etc.); the eleventh hour after noon or midnight. — *adj* of the number eleven. — *n* (usu. *npl*, sometimes *nsing*) **elev'enses** (*colloq*) an eleven o'clock snack; morning coffee or the like. — *adj* **elev'enth** next after the tenth; equal to one of eleven equal parts. — *n* an eleventh part; an octave and a fourth (*mus*). — *adv* **elev'enthly**. — **eleventh hour** the very last moment (*adj* **elev'enth-hour**); **eleven-plus'** or **eleven-plus examination** a school examination taken by pupils about the age of eleven to determine to which type of secondary education (academic, non-academic, or technical) they are to proceed. [O.E. *en(d)le(o)fan*; perh. (ten and) *one left*, from the root of L. *linquĕre*, Gr. *leipein*, to leave.]

elevon *el'ə-vən*, *n* a wing flap on delta-wing or tailless aircraft acting both as an *elev*ator and as an ailer*on*.

ELF *abbrev* for extremely low frequency.

elf *elf*, *n* a supernatural being, generally of human form but diminutive size, sometimes more malignant than a fairy (*European folklore*); a tricky or fairylike being: — *pl* **elves** (*elvz*). — *adj* **elf'in** small, with delicate frame; small, mischievous and charming. — *adj* **elf'ish** or **elv'ish**. — **elf'-child** a changeling, or a child supposed to have been left by elves in place of one stolen by them; **elf'locks** locks of hair tangled together, supposedly by elves. [O.E. *ælf*.]

elicit *i-*, *ē-* or *e-lis'it*, *vt* to draw forth; to evoke. — *n* **elicitā'tion**. — *n* **elic'itor**. [L. *ēlicĕre*, *ēlicitum*.]

elide *ē-* or *i-līd'*, *vt* to cut off (esp. a syllable); to suppress, abridge. — *n* **elision** (*i-lizh'ən*). [L. *ēlīdĕre*, *ēlīsum* — *ē*, from, *laedĕre*, to strike.]

eligible *el'i-ji-bl*, *adj* fit or worthy to be chosen; legally qualified for election or appointment; desirable. — *n* **eligibil'ity**. — *adv* **el'igibly**. [Fr., — L. *ēligĕre*; see ety. for **elect**.]

eliminate *i-*, *ē-* or *e-lim'in-āt*, *vt* to remove, cancel, get rid of; to expel waste matter. — *adj* **elim'inable**. — *adj* **elim'inant** (*med*) causing elimination of waste matter. — *n* an eliminating agent. — *n* **eliminā'tion**.

— *adj* **elim'inative.** — *n* **elim'inātor** someone who or that which eliminates; a device for substituting an electric main for a battery in a wireless receiving set. — *adj* **elim'inatory.** [L. *ēlimināre, -ātum* — *ē*, from, *līmen, -inis*, a threshold.]

ELINT *el'int, abbrev* for *El*ectronic *Int*elligence, that branch of military intelligence concerned with monitoring and recording electronic output (as opp. to intercepting communications. — Cf. **COMINT**.

elision. See **elide.**

élite or **elite** *i-, e-* or *ā-lēt', n* a chosen or select part or group, the pick or flower of anything; a size of typewriter type allowing twelve letters to the inch. — Also *adj.* — *n* **élit'ism** or **elit'ism** (belief in) government by an élite; consciousness of belonging to an élite; the favouring or creation of an élite. — *adj* **élit'ist** or **elit'ist.** — Also *n.* [Fr.]

elixir *i-, ē-* or *e-liks'ər, n* a liquor once supposed to have the power of indefinitely prolonging life (**elixir of life**), or of transmuting metals; the quintessence of anything; a panacea; a clear syrupy, alcoholic or flavoured solution masking the taste of an unpalatable medicine. [L.L., — Ar. *al-iksīr*, the philosopher's stone.]

Elizabethan *i-* or *e-liz-ə-bē'thən, adj* pertaining to a Queen *Elizabeth* or her reign, esp. to Queen Elizabeth I (1533–1603) or her reign (1558–1603) — of dress, manners, literature, etc. — *n* a person, esp. a poet or dramatist, of that age.

elk *elk, n* a deer of northern Europe and Asia, identical or closely related to the moose of N. America, the largest of all living deer; the wapiti (*NAm*). — **elk'hound** a large strong Norwegian breed of dog with a thick coat and curled tail. — **Irish elk** a giant deer now extinct, known from remains found in Ireland. [Poss. O.E. *elh.*]

ell[1] *el, (obs) n* a varying measure of length orig. that of the forearm; a cloth measure equal to $1\frac{1}{4}$ yd. (1.14 m.). [O.E. *eln.*]

ell[2] *el.* Same as **el**[2].

ellipse *i-* or *e-lips', n (geom)* a figure produced by the section of one branch of a right circular cone by a plane passing obliquely and failing to meet the other branch. — *n* **ellip'sis** a figure of syntax by which a word or words are left out and merely implied (*gram*); mark(s) indicating ellipsis (*printing*): — *pl* **ellip'sēs.** — *n* **ellip'soid** (*geom*) a surface of which every plane section is an ellipse or a circle; a solid object of this shape. — *adj* **ellipsoi'dal.** — *adj* **ellip'tic** or **ellip'tical** pertaining to an ellipse or to ellipsis; oval; having a part understood; concise, compendious; obscure, dubious; (*loosely*) circumlocutary. — *adv* **ellip'tically.** — *n* **ellipticity** (*el-ip-tis'i-ti*). [L. *ellipsis* — Gr. *elleipsis* — *elleipein*, to fall short.]

elm *elm, n* a tree (genus *Ulmus*) with serrated leaves unequal at the base, and small flowers in clusters appearing before the leaves; its timber (also called **elm'wood**). — *adj* made of elm. [O.E.]

Elo *el'o, adj* denoting a scale on which the ability of chess-players is assessed, devised by Arpad *Elo*, 20th-cent. U.S. professor of physics. — **Elo ratings; Elo scale.**

elocution *el-ə-kū'shən, n* the art of effective speaking (esp. public speaking) in terms of enunciation or delivery. — *adj* **elocū'tionary.** — *n* **elocū'tionist.** [L. *ēlocūtiō, -ōnis* — *ēloquī, -cūtus* — *ē*, from, *loquī*, to speak.]

Elohist *e-lō'hist, n* the writer or writers of the passages of the Old Testament in which the Hebrew name Elohim (for God) is used instead of Yahweh (Jehovah).

elongate *ē'long-gāt, vt* to make longer; to extend. — *vi* to grow longer. — *adj* **e'longate** or **e'longated.** — *n* **elongā'tion.** [L.L. *ēlongāre, -ātum* — *ē*, from, *longus*, long.]

elope *e-* or *i-lōp', vi* to escape privately, esp. with a lover (usu. to get married); to run away, bolt. — *n* **elope'ment.** — *n* **elō'per.** [Cf. O.Du. *ontlōpen* and Ger. *entlaufen*, to run away.]

eloquent *el'ə-kwənt, adj* having eloquence; persuasive; strongly expressive. — *n* **el'oquence** the power, art or practice of uttering strong emotion in correct, appropriate, expressive and fluent language; the art of such language; persuasive speech. — *adv* **el'oquently.** [L. *ēloquēns, -entis*, pres. p. of *ēloquī*, to speak out.]

Elsan® *el'san, n* a type of portable lavatory in which chemicals are used to kill bacteria and destroy the smell. [*E.L.* Jackson, the manufacturer, and *san*(itation).]

else *els, adj* or *adv* other (in addition or instead). — *adv* otherwise; besides; except that mentioned. — *adv* **elsewhere'** in or to another place. [O.E. *elles*, otherwise, orig. genitive of *el*, other.]

ELT *abbrev* for English Language Teaching.

eluant, eluate. See **elution.**

elucidate *ē-* or *i-lū'si-dāt*, also *-lōō', vt* to make lucid or clear; to throw light upon. — *n* **elucidā'tion.** — *adj* **elu'cidative** or **elu'cidatory.** — *n* **elu'cidator.** [L.L. *ēlūcidāre, -ātum* — *ē-* (intensive) and *lūcidus*, clear.]

elude *ē-* or *i-lūd'*, also *-lōōd', vt* to escape by design or craftiness; to baffle; (of a fact, etc.) to fail to be discovered, remembered, etc. — *n* **elu'der.** — *adj* **elu'dible.** — *n* **elu'sion** (*-zhən*) the act of eluding; evasion. — *adj* **elu'sive** (*-ziv* or *-siv*). — *adv* **elu'sively.** — *n* **elu'soriness.** — *adj* **elu'sory.** [L. *ēlūdere, ēlūsum* — *ē*, from, *lūdere*, to play.]

elution *ē-* or *i-lōō'shən*, also *-lū'shən, (chem) n* purification or separation by washing. — *n* **el'uant** or **el'uent** a liquid used for elution. — *n* **el'uate** liquid obtained by eluting. — *vt* **elute'.** [L. *ēlūtiō, -ōnis*, washing.]

elutriate *ē-* or *i-lōō'tri-āt*, also *-lū'tri-āt, vt* to separate by washing into coarser and finer portions. — *n* **elutriā'tion.** — *n* **elu'triātor** an apparatus for elutriating. [L. *ēlutriāre*, to wash out.]

ELV *abbrev* for expendable launch vehicle (see under **expend**).

elver *el'vər, n* a young eel. [*eelfare*, a young eel.]

elves, elvish. See under **elf.**

Elysium *ē-, i-* or *e-liz'i-əm, n* the abode of the blessed dead (*Gr mythol*); any delightful place. — *adj* **Elys'ian.** [L., — Gr. *elysion* (*pedion*), the Elysian (plain).]

elytrum *el'it-rəm* or **elytron** *el'it-ron, n* a beetle's forewing modified to form a case for the hindwing: — *pl* **el'ytra.** [Gr. *ĕlytron*, a sheath.]

em *em, (printing) n* the unit of measurement (12-point lower-case 'm') used in spacing material and in estimating dimensions of pages.

'em *əm, (colloq) pron* them; to them. [Orig. the unstressed form of *hem*, dat. and accus. pl. of **he.**]

em- *em-, pfx* a form of **en-** used before *b, m* or *p*.

emaciate *i-mā'shi-āt* or *-si-āt, vt* to make meagre or lean; to deprive of flesh; to waste. — *n* **emāciā'tion.** [L. *ēmaciāre* — *ē-* (intensive) and *maciāre*, to make lean.]

e-mail or **E-mail** *ē'-māl, n* short for electronic mail.

emanate *em'ə-nāt, vi* to flow out of or from anything; to proceed from some source; to arise. — *adj* **em'anant.** — *n* **emanā'tion** a flowing out from a source; that which issues or proceeds from some source; a radioactive gas given off by radium, thorium and actinium — radon. — *adj* **em'anative.** [L. *ēmānāre, -ātum* — *ē*, out from, *mānāre*, to flow.]

emancipate *e-* or *i-man'si-pāt, vt* to set free from restraint or bondage or disability of any kind. — *n* **emancipā'tion** the act of setting free from bondage or disability of any kind; the state of being set free. — *n* **emancipā'tionist.** — *n* **eman'cipātor.** — *adj* **emancipa'tory.** [L. *ēmancipāre* — *ē*, away from, *mancipāre*, to transfer property.]

emasculate *i-* or *ē-mas'kū-lāt*, *vt* to deprive of male characteristics; to castrate; to deprive of masculine vigour; to make effeminate; to lessen or take away the power, force or effectiveness of (*fig*). — *n* **emasculā'tion.** — *n* **emas'culātor.** — *adj* **emas'culatory** (*-lə-tər-i*). [L.L. *ēmasculāre* — *ē*, from, *masculus*, dimin. of *mās*, a male.]

embalm *im-* or *em-bäm'*, *vt* to preserve (esp. a dead body) from decay by aromatic drugs; to preserve with fragrance; to preserve unchanged but lifeless; to impregnate with balm, perfume. — *n* **embalm'er.** — *n* **embalm'ing** or **embalm'ment.** [Fr. *embaumer*, from *em-*, in, and *baume*; see **balm.**]

embank *im-* or *em-bangk'*, *vt* to enclose or defend with a bank or dike. — *n* **embank'ment** a bank or mound made to keep water within certain limits; a mound constructed so as to carry a level road or railway over a low-lying place. [**em-** (**en-** (1a)).]

embargo *em-bär'gō*, *n* a temporary order from the Admiralty to prevent the arrival or departure of ships; a stoppage of trade for a short time by authority; a prohibition, ban: — *pl* **embar'goes.** — *vt* to lay an embargo on; to seize: — *pr p* **embar'gōing;** *pa t* and *pa p* **embar'goed** (*-gōd*). [Sp., — *embargar*, to impede, to restrain.]

embark *im-* or *em-bärk'*, *vt* to put on board ship; to engage, or invest, in any affair. — *vi* to go on board ship; to engage in, commence (with *upon* or *in*). — *n* **embarkā'tion** (*em-*) a putting or going on board. [Fr. *embarquer* — *em-*, in, *barque*, bark.]

embarras de richesses *ā-ba-ra də rē-shes*, (Fr.) a perplexing or disconcerting profusion of wealth or abundance of any kind.

embarrass *im-* or *em-bar'əs*, *vt* to put out of countenance, disconcert; to perplex; to involve in difficulty, esp. in money matters. — *vi* to become disconcerted or discomposed. — *adj* **embarr'assed.** — *n* **embarr'assment** the state of feeling embarrassed; something which causes one to feel embarrassed; difficulties in money matters; a perplexing amount. [Fr. *embarrasser* — *em-*, in, *barre*, L.L. *barra*, bar.]

embassy *em'bə-si*, *n* an ambassador's residence or place of business; the charge or function of an ambassador; the person or body of persons sent on an undertaking. [See **ambassador.**]

embattle[1] *im-bat'l*, *vt* to equip with battlements. — *adj* **embatt'led** having battlements; having the outline like a battlement (*heraldry*). [**em-** (**en-** (1c)) and O.Fr. *bataillier*, to embattle.]

embattle[2] *im-bat'l*, *vt* to range in order of battle. — *adj* **embatt'led** arranged for battle; involved in battle (esp. *fig*). [O.Fr. *embataillier* — *em-*, in, *bataille*, battle.]

embay *im-bā'*, *vt* to enclose in a bay. — *n* **embay'ment** a bay. [**em-** (**en-** (1a)).]

embed or sometimes **imbed** *im-bed'*, *vt* to place, set or plant firmly in a mass of matter (also *fig*); to enclose deeply or snugly. — *n* **embed'ment.** [**em-** (**en-** (1a)).]

embellish *im-bel'ish*, *vt* to make beautiful with ornaments; to decorate; to add interesting and possibly untruthful details to (an account, narrative, etc.). — *n* **embell'isher.** — *adv* **embell'ishingly.** — *n* **embell'ishment** the act of embellishing or adorning; a decoration; ornament. [Fr. *embellir*, *embellissant* — *em-*, in, *bel* (*beau*), beautiful.]

ember *em'bər*, *n* a piece of live coal or wood; (the following definitions chiefly in *pl*) red-hot ashes; smouldering remains of a fire, or (*fig*) of love, passion, etc. [O.E. *æmerge.*]

embezzle *im-bez'l*, *vt* to appropriate (money or property that has been entrusted to one) fraudulently. — *n* **embezz'lement.** — *n* **embezz'ler.** [Anglo-Fr. *embesiler*, to make away with.]

embitter *im-bit'ər*, *vt* to make bitter or more bitter; to make more bitterly hostile. — *n* **embitt'erment.** [**em-** (**en-** (1b)).]

emblazon *im-blā'zn*, *vt* to adorn with figures (*heraldry*); to depict heraldically; to celebrate, glorify, praise. — *n* **emblā'zoner.** — *n* **emblā'zonment.** [**em-** (**en-** (1c)).]

emblem *em'bləm*, *n* a symbolic device or badge; a picture representing to the mind something different from itself; a type or symbol. — *adj* **emblemat'ic** or **emblemat'ical** pertaining to or containing emblems; symbolical; representing (with *of*). — *adv* **emblemat'ically.** — *vt* **emblematise** or **-ize** (*-blem'ə-tīz*), **em'blemise** or **-ize** to represent by an emblem. [L., — Gr. *emblēma*, *-atos*, a thing inserted.]

emblements *em'bli-mənts*, (*law*) *npl* crops raised by the cultivator of land, or the profits arising from these. [O.Fr. *emblaer*, to sow with corn — L.L. *imbladāre.*]

embody *im-bod'i*, *vt* to form into a body; to make tangible or material; to express (in words, in tangible form, etc.); to typify, personify; to make part of a body, to incorporate; to organise: — *pr p* **embod'ying;** *pa t* and *pa p* **embod'ied.** — *adj* **embod'ied.** — *n* **embod'iment** the act of embodying; the state of being embodied; that in which something is embodied. [**em-** (**en-** (1a)).]

embolden *im-bōld'n*, *vt* to make bold or courageous; to give the necessary courage for some action; to set in bold type (*typography*). — *n* **embold'ener.** [**em-** (**en-** (1b)).]

embolism *em'bol-izm* or *-bəl-*, *n* the presence of one or more obstructing clots, etc. in the blood-vessels. — *n* **em'bolus** a clot obstructing a blood-vessel. [Late Gr. *embolismos*, intercalation, Gr. *embolē*, insertion, ramming.]

embonpoint *ā-bɔ̃-pwɛ̃'*, *adj* stout, plump, full in figure; well-fed. — *n* stoutness, plumpness, well-fed condition. [Fr., — *en bon point*, in good form.]

embosom *im-bo͝oz'əm*, *vt* to take into or clasp to the bosom; to enclose protectively. [**em-** (**en-** (1a)).]

emboss *im-bos'*, *vt* to raise in relief; to ornament with raised work. — *adj* **embossed'** raised, standing out in relief; having a protuberance in the centre (*bot*). — *n* **emboss'er.** — *n* **emboss'ment.** [**em-** (**en-** (1a)).]

embouchure *ā-bo͞o-shür'*, *n* the mouth of a river; the mouthpiece of a wind instrument; the disposition of the mouth in playing a wind instrument. [Fr., — *emboucher*, to put to the mouth, to discharge — *en*, in, *bouche*, a mouth.]

embrace *im-brās'*, *vt* to take in the arms; to press affectionately to the bosom; to take eagerly or willingly; to comprise; to admit, adopt or receive. — *vi* to join in an embrace: — *pr p* **embrac'ing;** *pa t* and *pa p* **embraced'.** — *n* an act of embracing; a loving hug. — *n* **embrace'ment.** — *n* **embrac'er.** [O.Fr. *embracer* — L. *in*, in, into, *brāchium*, an arm.]

embranchment *im-bränch'mənt* or *-bränsh'*, *n* a branching off, as an arm of a river, a spur of a mountain, etc. [Fr. *embranchement.*]

embrasure *im-brā'zhər*, (*archit*) *n* an internally splayed recess of a door or window; the slant of such a recess; an opening in a wall for cannon. [Fr., — O.Fr. *embraser*, to slope the sides of a window.]

embrittle *im-brit'l*, *vt* and *vi* to make or become brittle. — *n* **embrit'tlement.** [**em-** (**en-** (1b)).]

embrocate *em'brō-kāt*, *vt* to moisten and rub, e.g. with a lotion. — *n* **embrōcā'tion** the act of embrocating; the lotion used. [L.L. *embrocāre*, *-ātum* — Gr. *embrochē*, a lotion — *en-*, in, into, *brechein*, to wet.]

embroider *im-broid'ər*, *vt* to ornament with designs in needlework; to add ornament or fictitious detail to. — *n* **embroid'erer.** — *n* **embroid'ery** the art of producing ornamental designs in needlework on textile fabrics, etc.; ornamental needlework; embellishment; exaggeration or invented detail. [M.E. *embrouderie* — O.Fr. *embroder*; confused with or influenced by O.E. *bregdan*, to weave, braid.]

embroil *im-broil'*, *vt* to involve in a broil, or in perplexity (with); to entangle; to distract; to throw into confusion. — *n* **embroil'ment**. [Fr. *embrouiller* — pfx. *em-* and *brouiller*, to break out.]

embryo *em'bri-ō*, *n* a young animal or plant in its earliest stages of development; the beginning of anything: — *pl* **em'bryos**. — Also *adj*. — *n* **embryogen'esis** or **embryogeny** (*-oj'i-ni*) the formation and development of the embryo. — *n* **em'bryoid** (*bot*) an embryo-like structure produced in tissue culture. — *adj* **embryolog'ic** or **embryolog'ical**. — *n* **embryol'ogist**. — *n* **embryol'ogy** the science of the formation and development of the embryo. — *adj* **em'bryonal** or **embryon'ic** of or relating to anything in an imperfect or incomplete state; rudimentary. — **embryo transfer** (abbrev. **ET**) surgical transfer of the young embryo into the uterus, a technique used in the treatment of infertility. [L.L., — Gr. *embryon* — *en*, in, *bryein*, to swell.]

embus *im-bus'*, *vt* to put (esp. troops) into a bus. — *vi* to board a bus: — *pr p* **embuss'ing**; *pa t* and *pa p* **embussed'**. [**em-** (**en-** (1a)).]

emcee *em-sē'*, (*colloq*) *n* a master of ceremonies, a phonetic representation of the abbrev. **MC**. — *vi* and *vt* to act as a master of ceremonies (for).

emend *ē-mend'*, *vt* to make alterations in with a view to improving (a text). — *adj* **ēmend'able**. — *n* **ēmendā'tion** the removal of an error or fault; correction. — *n* **ē'mendātor**. — *adj* **ēmen'datory**. [L. *ēmendāre, -ātum* — *ē*, from, *mendum*, a fault.]

emerald *em'ər-əld*, *n* a gemstone, a beautiful velvety green variety of beryl; (also **emerald green**) its colour. — **Emerald Isle** Ireland, from its greenness. [O.Fr. *esmeralde* — Gr. *smaragdos*.]

emerge *i-* or *ē-mûrj'*, *vi* to rise out of anything; to issue or come forth; to reappear after being concealed; to come into view; to come into being in the course of evolution; to crop up. — *n* **emer'gence** the act of emerging; a sudden appearance. — *n* **emer'gency** an unexpected occurrence, requiring immediate action; pressing necessity. — Also *adj*. — *adj* **emer'gent** suddenly appearing; coming into being in the course of evolution; (of a state) having recently become independent. — **state of emergency** a situation in which a government suspends the normal constitution in order to deal with an emergency such as a natural disaster or civil disorder. [L. *ēmergĕre, ēmersum* — *ē*, out of, *mergĕre*, to plunge.]

emeritus *i-*, *e-* or *ē-mer'i-təs*, *adj* (often following a noun) honourably discharged from the performance of public duty, esp. denoting a retired professor. [L. *ēmeritus*, having served one's time — *ē-* (signifying completeness) and *merērī*, to deserve.]

emersion *i-* or *ē-mûr'shən*, *n* the act of emerging; the reappearance of a celestial body after eclipse or occultation (*astron*). [See ety. for **emerge**.]

emery *em'ər-i*, *n* a very hard mineral, a variety of corundum, used as powder for polishing, etc. — *vt* to rub or coat with emery. — **em'ery-board** a small flat strip of wood or card coated with emery-powder, used in manicure; **em'ery-cloth** or **-paper** cloth or paper covered with emery-powder for polishing; **em'ery-powder** ground emery. [O.Fr. *esmeril, emeril* — L.L. *smericulum* — Gr. *smēris, smȳris*.]

emetic *i-met'ik*, (*med*) *adj* causing vomiting. — *n* a medicine that causes vomiting. — *n* **emesis** (*em'i-sis*) vomiting. — *adj* **emet'ical**. — *adv* **emet'ically**. — *n* **emetophō'bia** a pathological fear of vomiting. [Gr. *emetikos* — *emeein*, to vomit.]

EMF *abbrev* for: electromotive force (also **emf**); European Monetary Fund, the managing body of the EMS, which issues the ECU.

EMI *abbrev* for: electromagnetic interference (also **emi**); EMI Limited (orig. Electrical and Musical Industries Limited).

emigrate *em'i-grāt*, *vi* and *vt* to move from one country (or state) to another as a place of abode. — *adj* **em'igrant** emigrating or having emigrated. — *n* a person who emigrates or has emigrated. — *n* **emigrā'tion**. — *adj* **em'igrātory**. — *n* **émigré** (*ā-mē-grā'*) an (esp. political) emigrant. [L. *ēmīgrāre, ēmīgrāre, -ātum* — *ē*, from, *migrāre*, to remove.]

éminence grise *ā-mē-nās grēz*, (Fr.) *n* someone exercising power in the background, as did Cardinal Richelieu's private secretary Père Joseph, nicknamed *l'Eminence Grise* ('the Grey Eminence').

eminent *em'i-nənt*, *adj* distinguished; exalted in rank or office; rising above others; conspicuous. — *n* **em'inence** a part eminent or rising above the rest; a rising ground; a ridge or knob; height; distinction; a title given in 1631 to cardinals (previously styled Most Illustrious). — *n* **em'inency**. — *adv* **em'inently**. — **eminent domain** the right by which the supreme authority in a state may appropriate an individual's property for public use. [L. *ēminēns, -entis*, pres. p. of *ēminēre* — *ē*, from, *minēre*, to project.]

emir *ā-mēr'*, *n* a title given in the East and in N. Africa to all independent chieftains, and also (perh. improperly) to all the supposed descendants of Mohammed through his daughter Fatima. — *n* **emir'ate** the office, jurisdiction or state of an emir. — Also **ameer**, **amir** (*a-mēr'* or *ə-mēr'*). [Ar. *amīr*, ruler.]

Emi-scanner® *em'i-skan-ər*, *n* a machine which produces computer-assisted X-ray pictures of the head or body. [**EMI**.]

emit *i-* or *ē-mit'*, *vt* to send out; to throw or give out; to issue; to utter (a declaration): — *pr p* **emitt'ing**; *pa t* and *pa p* **emitt'ed**. — *n* **emissary** (*em'is-ər-i*) someone sent out on a mission, esp. on behalf of a government or state; an agent sent out on a secret mission. — *n* **emission** (*-mish'ən*) the act of emitting; that which is issued at one time; the discharge of semen or other fluid from the body; the release of electrons from parent atoms on absorption of energy exceeding the average (*phys*). — *adj* **emiss'ive** emitting, sending out. — *n* **emissiv'ity** (*ē-*) the property or power of emitting or radiating. [L. *ēmittĕre, ēmissum* — *ē*, out of, *mittĕre*, to send.]

Emmanuel or **Immanuel** *i-man'ū-əl* or *-el*, (*Bible*) *n* the symbolic name of the child announced by Isaiah (Isa. vii. 14), and applied to Jesus as the Messiah in Matt. i. 23. [Gr. *Emmanouēl* — Heb. *'Immānūēl*, God with us.]

Emmental or **Emmenthal** *em'ən-täl*, *n* a hard Swiss cheese, similar to Gruyère. [Name of a Swiss valley.]

emmer *em'ər*, *n* a species of wheat, *Triticum dicoccum*. [Ger. dialect.]

Emmy *em'i*, *n* a television trophy, corresponding to the cinema Oscar, awarded annually by the American Academy of Television Arts and Sciences: — *pl* **Em'mys** or **Em'mies**.

emollient *i-mol'yənt*, *adj* softening; making supple. — *n* (*med*) a softening application such as a poultice, fomentation, etc. [L. *ēmollīre* — *ē* (intensive) and *mollīre*, to soften.]

emolument *i-mol'ū-mənt*, *n* (often in *pl*) profit arising from employment, such as salary or fees. — *adj* **emolumen'tal**. — *adj* **emolumen'tary**. [L. *ēmolimentum, ēmolumentum*, prob. from *ēmŏlĕre*, to grind out.]

emotion *i-mō'shən*, *n* a moving of the feelings; agitation of mind; any of various phenomena of the mind (such as anger, joy, fear, sorrow) associated also with physical symptoms — feeling, distinguished from cognition and will. — *vi* **emote** (*i-mōt'*) to show or express exaggerated emotion. — *adj* **emō'tional**. — *n* **emō'tionalism** a tendency to emotional excitement; the habit of working on the emotions; the indulgence of superficial emotion. — *adv* **emō'tionally.** — *adj* **emō'tive** (-*tiv*) tending to arouse emotion. — *n* **emō'tiveness.** [L. *ēmōtiō, -ōnis* — *ēmovēre, -mōtum*, to stir up.]

Emp. *abbrev* for: Emperor; Empire; Empress.

empanel *im-pan'əl, vt* to enter (the names of a prospective jury) on a list; to select (a jury) from such a list: — *pr p* **empan'elling**; *pa t* and *pa p* **empan'elled.** — *n* **empan'elment.** [**em-** (**en-** (1a)).]

empathy *em'pə-thi, n* the power of entering into another's personality and imaginatively experiencing his or her experiences; the power of entering into the feeling or spirit of something (esp. a work of art) and so appreciating it fully. — *adj* **empathet'ic.** — *adj* **empath'ic.** — *vi* **em'pathise** or **-ize.** [Gr. *en*, in, *pathos*, feeling.]

empennage *em-pen'ij* or *ā-pen-äzh', n* an aeroplane's tail unit, including elevator, rudder and fin. [Fr., feathering of an arrow — L. *penna*, feather, wing.]

emperor *em'pər-ər, n* the head of an empire; a high title of sovereignty; before metrication, a paper size (48 × 72 in.): — *fem* **em'press.** — **emperor moth** the second largest British moth, its wingspan being about three inches; **emperor penguin** the largest of the penguins. [O.Fr. *emperere* — L. *imperātor*, a commander.]

emphasis *em'fə-sis, n* forcible or impressive expression; an insistent or vigorous way of attributing importance or enforcing attention; stress; accent; prominence: — *pl* **em'phases** (-*sēz*). — *vt* **em'phasise** or **-ize** to make emphatic; to lay stress on. — *adj* **emphat'ic** (*im-* or *em-fat'ik*) expressed or expressing with emphasis; stressed forcibly; impressive; strongly marked. — *adv* **emphat'ically.** [Gr. *emphasis*, implied meaning — *en*, in, *phainein*, to show.]

emphysema *em-fis-ē'mə*, (*med*) *n* an unnatural distension of a part of the body with air; distension of the lung, with breathing difficulties, etc. — *adj* **emphysē'matous.** — *n* **emphysē'mic** a sufferer from emphysema. [Gr. *emphȳsēma* — *emphȳsaein*, to inflate.]

empire *em'pīr, n* a dominion, or group of states, peoples, nations, etc., under the same sovereign power (esp. an emperor) spread over an extended area; supreme control or dominion; the government or office of an emperor; the time of its duration; a large industrial organisation embracing many firms. — *adj* (usu. with *cap*) relating to or in the style of, esp. of dress or furniture, the first French Empire (1804–14). — **em'pire-building** the practice or policy of increasing one's power or authority. — Also *adj.* — **em'pire-builder.** [Fr., — L. *imperium.*]

empiric *em-pir'ik, n* a person who makes trials or experiments; someone whose knowledge is got from experience only. — *adj* empirical. — *adj* **empir'ical** resting on trial or experiment; known or knowing only by experience. — *adv* **empir'ically.** — *n* **empir'icism** (-*sizm*) the system which accepts only knowledge based on direct experience (*philos*); the practice of empirical methods; the practice of medicine without a regular education. — *n* **empir'icist** (-*sist*). — **empirical formula** (*chem*) a formula showing in simplest form the ratio of atoms in a molecule, not the absolute number. [Fr., — L. *empīricus* — Gr. *empeirikos* — *en*, in, *peira*, a trial.]

emplacement *im-plās'mənt, n* the act of placing; a gun-platform (*mil*). — *vt* **emplace'** (back-formation) to put in or provide with an emplacement. [Fr. *emplacement.*]

emplane *im-plān', vt* to put or take on an aeroplane. — *vi* to mount an aeroplane. — Also **enplane'.** [**em-** (**en-** (1a)) and **plane**[2].]

employ *im-ploi', vt* to occupy the time or attention of; to use as a means or agent; to give work to. — *n* employment. — *adj* **employ'able.** — *adj* **employed'** having employment, in a job. — *n* **employ'ee** (or *em-ploi-ē'*) a person employed. — *n* **employ'er.** — *n* **employ'ment** the act of employing; that which engages or occupies; occupation. — **employment agency** an agency which finds work for the unemployed and employees for vacant positions; **employment office** a job centre; an office where unemployment benefits are dealt with, paid, etc.; **Employment Service** a government agency run by the Department of Employment, which finds work for the unemployed, pays out unemployment benefit, etc. [Fr. *employer* — L. *implicāre*, to enfold — *in*, in, and *plicāre*, to fold; cf. **imply, implicate.**]

emporium *em-pö'ri-əm, n* a commercial or trading centre or mart; a big shop: — *pl* **empō'ria** or **empō'riums.** [L., — Gr. *empŏrion*, a trading station — *empŏros*, a wayfarer, trader.]

empower *im-pow'ər, vt* to authorise. — *n* **empow'erment.** [**em-** (**en-** (1a)).]

empress. See **emperor.**

empty *emp'ti, adj* having nothing inside; unoccupied; unfurnished; without effect; unsatisfactory; lacking substance; meaningless; hungry (*colloq*); devoid (of). — *vt* to make empty; to deprive of contents; to remove from a receptacle. — *vi* to become empty; to discharge: — *pr p* **emp'tying**; *pa t* and *pa p* **emp'tied.** — *n* an empty bottle, box, sack, etc.: — *pl* **emp'ties.** — *adv* **emp'tily.** — *n* **emp'tiness.** — *adj* **empty-hand'ed** bringing or taking away nothing or no gift. — *adj* **empty-head'ed** frivolous. [O.E. *ǣmetig* — *ǣmetta*, leisure, rest; the *p* is excrescent.]

empyema *em-pī-ē'mə, n* a collection of pus in any cavity, esp. the pleura. [Gr. *empyēma, empyēsis* — *en*, in, *pyon*, pus.]

empyreal *em-pir-ē'əl, adj* formed of pure fire or light; pertaining to the highest and purest region of heaven; sublime. — *adj* **empyre'an** empyreal. — *n* the highest heaven, where the pure element of fire was supposed to subsist; the heavens. [Gr. *empyros*, fiery — *en*, in, *pȳr*, fire.]

empyreuma *em-pir-ū'mə, n* the burned smell and acrid taste that come when vegetable or animal substances are burned: — *pl* **empyreu'mata.** [Gr. *empȳreuma, -atos*, embers — *en*, in, *pȳr*, fire.]

EMS *abbrev* for: Emergency Medical Service; European Monetary System, a system of monetary co-operation between EEC member countries, limiting fluctuations in currency exchange rates between them.

EMU *abbrev* for economic and monetary union.

emu *ē'mū, n* a flightless, fast-running Australian bird, the largest of living birds after the ostrich. [Port. *ema*, an ostrich.]

emulate *em'ū-lāt, vt* to strive to equal or excel (esp. something or someone one admires); to rival successfully; (*loosely*) to imitate. — *n* **emulā'tion.** — *adj* **em'ulātive.** — *n* **em'ulātor.** — *adj* **em'ulous** eager to emulate; keen to achieve the same success or excellence as another; engaged in competition or rivalry. — *adv* **em'ulously.** — *n* **em'ulousness.** [L. *aemulārī, -ātus* — *aemulus*, emulous.]

emulsion *i-mul'shən, n* a colloidal suspension of one liquid in another; a light-sensitive coating on photographic plates; a liquid mixture containing globules of fat (such as milk), or of resinous or bituminous material; emulsion paint. — *n* **emulsificā'tion.** — *n* **emul'sifīer** a chemical which forms or preserves an emulsion, esp. one used as a food additive to prevent the constituents of processed foods separating out; apparatus for preparing emulsions. — *vt* **emul'sify.** — *vt* **emul'sionise** or **-ize.** — *adj* **emul'sive.** — **emulsifying agent** a substance whose presence in small quantities stabilises an emulsion; **emulsion paint** a water-thinnable paint made from a pigmented emulsion of a resin in water. [L. *ēmulgēre*, *ēmulsum*, to milk out — *ē*, from, *mulgēre*, to milk.]

en *en*, *n* half of an em (*printing*; see also **quadrat**).

en- *en-* or *in-*, *pfx* (1) in words derived from L. through Fr., (a) used to form verbs with the sense of *in*, *into*, *upon*; (b) used to form verbs with the sense *cause to be*; (c) used intensively or almost meaninglessly; (2) in words derived from Gr. used to form verbs with the sense of *in*.

enable *in-ā'bl*, *vt* to make able; to give power, strength or authority to; to make possible. — *n* **enab'ler.** — **enabling act, bill** and **resolution** those giving or proposing to give power to act. [**en-** (1b).]

enact *in-akt'*, *vt* to perform; to act the part of; to establish by law. — *adj* **enact'ive.** — *n* **enac'tion** (*-shən*) or **enact'ment** the passing of a bill into law; that which is enacted; a law. — *n* **enact'or.** [**en-** (1b) and **act.**]

enamel *in-am'əl*, *n* vitrified coating applied to a metal or other surface and fired; any glossy enamel-like surface or coating, esp. that of the teeth; a work of art in enamel; a paint giving an enamel-like finish. — *vt* to coat with or paint in enamel; to form a glossy surface on, like enamel: — *pr p* **enam'elling;** *pa t* and *pa p* **enam'elled.** — *n* **enam'eller** or **enam'elist.** [O.Fr. *enameler* — *en*, in, *esmail*, enamel.]

enamour or in U.S. **enamor** *in-am'ər*, *vt* to inflame with love; to charm. — **enamoured of** in love with; keen on. [O.Fr. *enamourer* — *en-*, *amour* — L. *amor*, *-ōris*, love.]

enantiomorph *en-an'ti-ō-mörf*, (*chem*) *n* a shape or object (such as a crystal, a molecule) exactly similar to another except that right and left are interchanged, each being a mirror-image of the other. — *adj* **enantiomorph'ic.** — *n* **enantiomorph'ism.** — *adj* **enantiomorph'ous.** — *n* **enantiomorph'y.** [Gr. *enantios*, opposite, *morphē*, shape.]

enarthrosis *en-är-thrō'sis*, (*anat*) *n* a ball-and-socket joint. [Gr. *enarthrōsis* — *en*, in, *arthron*, a joint.]

en bloc *ã blok*, (Fr.) as one unit, wholesale.

enc. *abbrev* for: enclosed; enclosure.

en cabochon. See **cabochon.**

encage *in-kāj'*, *vt* to shut up in a cage. [**en-** (1a).]

encamp *in-kamp'*, *vi* to pitch tents; to make, or stay in, a camp. — *vt* to form into a camp; to lodge in a camp. — *n* **encamp'ment** the act of encamping; the place where a camper or company is encamped; a camp. [**en-** (1b).]

encapsulate *in-kap'sŭl-āt*, *vt* to enclose in a capsule; to capture the essence of, to describe succinctly but sufficiently. — *n* **encapsulā'tion.** [**en-** (1a).]

encase *in-kās'*, *vt* to enclose in a case; to surround or cover. — *n* **encase'ment.** [**en-** (1a).]

encash *in-kash'*, *vt* to convert into cash. — *n* **encash'ment.** [**en-** (1b).]

encaustic *en-kös'tik*, *adj* having the colours burned in; of or pertaining to encaustic. — *n* an ancient method of painting in melted wax. — **encaustic tile** a decorative glazed and fired tile, having patterns of different coloured clays inlaid in it and burnt with it. [Gr. *enkaustikos* — *enkaiein*, to burn in.]

enceinte *ã-sɛ̃t'*, (*fort*) *n* an enclosure, generally the whole area of a fortified place. [Fr., — *enceindre*, to surround — L. *in*, in, *cingĕre*, *cinctum*, to gird.]

encephalon *en-sef'əl-on* or *-kef'*, (*anat* and *zool*) *n* the brain. — *adj* **encephalic** (*-al'ik*) belonging to the head or brain. — *adj* **encephalit'ic** pertaining to encephalitis. — *n* **encephalī'tis** inflammation of the brain. — *n* **enceph'alogram** or **enceph'alograph** an X-ray photograph of the brain. — *n* **encephalog'raphy** radiography of the brain, its cavities having been filled with air or dye injected into the space around the spinal cord. — *n* **encephalop'athy** a degenerative brain disease. — *adj* **enceph'alous** (*zool*) (of molluscs) having a head. — **encephalitis lethargica** (*-ji-kə*) an acute disease marked by profound physical and mental lethargy — popularly called *sleeping sickness*. [Gr. *enkephalos* — *en*, in, *kephalē*, head.]

enchain *in-chān'*, *vt* to put in chains; to hold fast (*fig*). — *n* **enchain'ment.** [Fr. *enchaîner* — *en*, in, *chaîne*, chain — L. *catēna*.]

enchant *in-chänt'*, *vt* to cast a spell upon; to compel by enchantment; to charm; to delight utterly. — *adj* **enchant'ed** under the power of enchantment; beguiled, captivated; delighted. — *n* **enchant'er,** *fem* **enchant'ress.** — *n* **enchant'ment.** — **enchanter's nightshade** a plant of the evening primrose family, growing in shady places. [Fr. *enchanter* — L. *incantāre*, to sing a magic formula over — *in*, on, *cantāre*, to sing.]

enchase *in-chās'*, *vt* to fix in a border or setting; to set with jewels; to engrave or chase; to adorn with raised or embossed work. [Fr. *enchâsser* — *en*, in, *châsse*, shrine, setting — L. *capsa*, a case.]

enchilada *en-chi-läd'ə*, *n* a Mexican dish consisting of a rolled stuffed tortilla cooked with a chilli-flavoured sauce. [Am. Sp. — Sp. *enchilar*, to season with chilli.]

encierro *en-thye'rō*, (Sp.) *n* in Spanish towns, an event in which bulls are driven through the streets to the bull-ring: — *pl* **encier'ros.** [Lit., enclosure.]

encipher *in-sī'fər*, *vt* to put into cipher. [**en-** (1a).]

encircle *in-sûrk'l*, *vt* to enclose in a circle; to go round. — *n* **encirc'ling.** — *n* **encir'clement.** [**en-** (1a).]

en clair *ã kler*, (Fr.) not in cipher, uncoded.

enclasp *in-kläsp'*, *vt* to clasp. [**en-** (1c).]

enclave *en'klāv*, also *en-klāv'*, or *ã-kläv'*, *n* a piece of territory entirely enclosed within foreign territory; an enclosure. — *vt* to surround. [Fr., — L.L. *inclāvāre* — L. *in*, and *clāvis*, a key.]

enclitic *en-klit'ik*, *adj* (of a word, esp. a particle) without stress, behaving as if not a separate word or, in ancient Greek, transferring its stress to the preceding word (*gram*). — *n* (*gram*) a word or particle which always follows another word and which is enclitic to it. — *adv* **enclit'ically.** [Gr. *enklitikos* — *en*, in, *klīnein*, to lean.]

enclose or **inclose** *in-klōz'*, *vt* to close or shut in; to confine; to surround; to put within, esp. of something sent within a letter or within its envelope; to fence, esp. used of waste land. — *n* **enclos'er** or **inclos'er.** — *n* **enclosure** or **inclosure** (*-klō'zhər*) the act of enclosing; the state of being enclosed; that which is enclosed, esp. in a letter; a space fenced off. — **enclosed order** a Christian religious order leading a contemplative life, not going out into the world to work. [**en-** (1a) and **close²**.]

encode *in-kōd'*, *vt* to encipher; to record in a form other than plain written or printed text; to convert an idea or message into words, or translate (something) into a foreign language (*linguis*). [**en-** (1a).]

encomium *en-kō'mi-əm*, also **encō'mion** *-on*, *n* high commendation; a eulogy: — *pl* **encō'miums** or **encō'mia.** — *n* **encō'miast** a person who utters or writes encomiums; a praiser. — *adj* **encomias'tic** or **encomias'tical** bestowing praise. — *adv* **encomias'tically.** [L., — Gr. *enkōmion*, a song of praise — *en*, in, *kōmos*, festivity.]

encompass *in-kum'pəs*, *vt* to surround or enclose; to include or embrace; to bring about. — *n* **encom'passment.** [**en-** (1a).]

encore *ã'* or *ong'kör*, also *-kör'*, *interj* calling for repetition of a performance, or an additional item. — *n* a call of encore; an item given in response to such a call. — *vt* to call encore to. — *vi* to perform an encore. [Fr., again, still.]

encounter *in-kown'tər*, *vt* to meet face to face, esp. unexpectedly; to meet in a contest; to oppose or confront. — *n* an unexpected or chance meeting; a fight or contentious meeting; an encounter group meeting. — **encounter group** a group which meets with a view to establishing greater self-awareness and greater understanding of others by indulging in unrestrained verbal and physical confrontation and contact. [O.Fr. *encontrer* — L. *in*, in, *contrā*, against.]

encourage *en-kur'ij*, *vt* to put courage in; to inspire with spirit or hope; to incite, spur on; to give patronage to; to cherish, sustain. — *n* **encour'agement** the act of encouraging; something that encourages. — *n* **encour'ager.** — *n* and *adj* **encour'aging.** — *adv* **encour'agingly.** [O.Fr. *encoragier* (Fr. *encourager*) — pfx. *en-*, *corage*, courage.]

encroach *in-krōch'*, *vi* to seize on the rights of others; to intrude beyond boundaries; to extend into the territory, sphere, etc., of others. — *n* **encroach'er.** — *n* **encroach'ment.** [O.Fr. *encrochier*, to seize — *en-* and *croc*, a hook.]

en croûte. See **croûte.**

encrust or **incrust** *in-krust'*, *vt* to cover with a crust or hard coating; to form a crust on the surface of. — *vi* to form a crust. — *n* **encrust'ment.** — *n* **encrustā'tion** or **incrustā'tion**. [L. *incrustāre*, *-ātum* — *in*, on, *crusta*, crust.]

encumber *in-kum'bər*, *vt* to impede the motion of; to hamper; to burden; to load, as with debts, etc. — *n* **encum'brance** something which encumbers or hinders; a legal claim on an estate. [O.Fr. *encombrer* — *en-* and *combrer*; see ety. for **cumbersome.**]

ency., encyc. or **encycl.** *abbrev* for: encyclop(a)edia; encyclop(a)edic.

encyclical *en-sīk'lik-l* or *-sik'*, *adj* (also **encyc'lic**) sent round to many persons or places. — *n* a letter addressed by the Pope to his bishops. [Gr. *enkyklios* — *en*, in, *kyklos*, a circle.]

encyclopaedia or **encyclopedia** *en-sī-klō-pē'di-ə*, *n* a work containing information on every department, or on a particular department, of knowledge, generally alphabetically arranged. — *adj* **encyclopae'dic** or **encyclope'dic** pertaining to an encyclopaedia; all-comprehensive; full of information. — *n* **encyclopae'dism** or **encyclope'dism** comprehensive knowledge. — *n* **encyclopae'dist** or **encyclope'dist** the compiler, or a person who assists in the compilation, of an encyclopaedia. [False Gr. *enkyklopaideiā*, a wrong reading for *enkyklios paideiā*, general education — *en*, in, *kyklos*, circle, *paideiā*, education.]

encyst *en-sist'*, *vt* or *vi* to enclose or become enclosed in a cyst or vesicle. — *n* **encystā'tion.** — *adj* **encyst'ed.** — *n* **encyst'ment.** [**en-** (1a).]

end *end*, *n* the last point or portion; termination or close; death; consequence; an object aimed at; a fragment, odd piece; one of the two sides of a field, court, pitch, etc. defended by a team, player, etc. (*sport*); part of a game played from one end (of the bowling-green, archery-ground, etc.). — *vt* to bring to an end; to destroy. — *vi* to come to an end; to cease; to be at the end. — *adj* **end'ed** brought to an end; having ends. — *n* **end'ing** a termination; a conclusion; that which is at the end; the final syllable or portion of a word, esp. an inflection (*gram*). — *adj* **end'less** without end; returning upon itself; everlasting; incessant. — *adv* **end'lessly.** — *n* **end'lessness.** — *adj* **end'most** farthest. — *adv* **end'ways** or **end'wise** on end; with the end forward. — **end'-game** the final stage of a game of chess or certain other games; one's manner of playing the endgame; **endless chain** a chain whose ends are joined; **endless gearing, screw** or **worm** an arrangement for producing slow motion in machinery, consisting of a screw whose thread gears into a wheel with skew teeth. — *adv* and *adj* **end-on'** in the direction in which the end points. — **end organ** a specialised sensory or motor structure at a nerve-end; **end'-paper** a paper at the beginning or end of a book, pasted to the binding and leaving an additional flyleaf; **end'-product** the final product of a series of operations; **end result** the final result or outcome. — *adj* **end'-stopped** having a pause at the end of each line (of verse). — **end use** the final use to which a manufactured article is put. — *n* **end'-user** the person, company, etc. who will be the recipient of a product being sold; (usu. **end-user certificate**) in international trade, documentation naming the end-user of a product being sold, required e.g. in the exporting of arms. — **all ends up** completely; convincingly; **at a loose end** with nothing to do; **at an end** terminated; discontinued; exhausted; **at one's wits' end** see under **wit**[2]; **at the end of one's tether** utterly exasperated; **be the end of** to cause the death of (often a colloq. exaggeration); **end of story** (*colloq*) that's that; **end up** to arrive or find oneself eventually or finally; to finish (with or by); to become in the end; **get hold of the wrong end of the stick** to misunderstand blunderingly; **get** or **have one's end away** (*slang*) to have sexual intercourse; **in the end** after all; at last; **keep one's end up** to maintain one's part; **loose end** (often in *pl*) an unsettled matter; **make ends meet** to live within one's income; **no end** (*colloq*) very much; **on end** erect; at a stretch; **the end** the last straw; the limit; **the end of the road** the point beyond which one can no longer continue or survive. [O.E. *ende*.]

endamoeba. See **entamoeba.**

endanger *in-dān'jər*, *vt* to place in danger; to expose to loss or injury. — *n* **endan'gerer.** — *n* **endan'germent** hazard, peril. [**en-** (1b).]

endear *in-dēr'*, *vt* to make dear or more dear. — *adj* **endear'ing** arousing affection. — *adv* **endear'ingly.** — *n* **endear'ment** a caress or a spoken expression of love. [**en-** (1b).]

endeavour or in U.S. **endeavor** *in-dev'ər*, *vi* to strive; to attempt. — *n* an attempt or trial. [From such phrases as to *put oneself in devoir*, to do what one can, — Fr. *en*, in, *devoir*, duty.]

endemic *en-dem'ik*, *adj* prevalent or regularly found in a people or a district; confined to a particular area (*biol*). — *n* a disease constantly or generally present in a place. — *adv* **endem'ically.** — *n* **endemicity** (*-is'i-ti*) or **en'demism** the state of being endemic. — *n* **endemiol'ogy** (*-dem-* or *-dēm-*) the scientific study of endemic diseases. [Gr. *endēmios* — *en*, in, *dēmos*, a people, a district.]

endermic *en-dûrm'ik*, *adj* through or applied directly to the skin. [Gr. *en*, in, *derma*, skin.]

endive *en'div* or *-dīv*, *n* a salad plant (*Cichorium endivia*) with crisp, succulent, curly or broad leaves; (*loosely*, esp. in U.S.) chicory. [Fr., — L. *intubus*.]

endo- *en-dō-* or *en-do'-*, *combining form* often interchanging with **ento-** (and opp. to **ecto-**, **exo-**) inside, within. [Gr. *endon* or *endō*, within.]

endoblast *en'dō-blast*, *n* the inner cell-layer of a gastrula, the hypoblast. [**endo-** and **-blast.**]

endocardium *en-dō-kär'di-əm*, *n* the lining membrane of the heart. — *adj* **endocar'diac** or **endocar'dial** within the heart. — *n* **endocardī'tis** inflammation of the endocardium, esp. over the valves. [Gr. *endō*, within, *kardiā*, heart.]

endocarp *en'dō-kärp*, (*bot*) *n* a differentiated innermost layer of the pericarp, usu. hard, such as a plum stone. [Gr. *endō*, within, *karpos*, fruit.]

endocrine *en'dōkrin* or *-krīn*, (*physiol*) *adj* secreting internally; applied esp. to certain glands that pour secretions into the blood (also *n*). — *adj* **endocrī'nal** or **endocrinic** (*-krin'ik*). — *n* **endocrinol'ogy** the science of the discharge of ductless glands. [Gr. *endō*, within, *krīnein*, to separate.]

endoderm *en'do-dûrm*, *n* the inner layer of cells in a gastrula; the tissues derived from that layer. — *adj* **endoderm'al** or **endoderm'ic.** — *n* **endoderm'is** a close-set sheath, one cell thick, enclosing the central cylinder in plants. [Gr. *endō*, within, *derma*, skin.]

endogamy *en-dog'əm-i*, *n* the custom forbidding marriage outside one's own group; inbreeding; pollination between two flowers on the same plant;

the union of female gametes. — *adj* **endogam'ic**. [Gr. *endō*, within, *gamos*, marriage.]

endogenous *en-doj'i-nəs*, *adj* increasing by internal growth; formed within; (of depression) with no external cause. — *n* **endog'eny**. [Gr. *endō*, within, *-genes*, born.]

endolymph *en'dō-limf*, (*zool*) *n* the fluid within the membranous labyrinth of the ear in vertebrates. [**endo-**.]

endometrium *en-dō-mē'tri-əm*, *n* the mucous membrane lining the cavity of the uterus. — *adj* **endomē'trial**. — *n* **endometrī'tis** inflammation of the endometrium. — *n* **endomētriō'sis** (a condition caused by) the presence of active endometrial tissue where it should not be, esp. when affecting other organs of the pelvic cavity. [Gr. *endō*, within, *mētra*, womb.]

endomorph *en'do-mörf*, *n* a mineral enclosed within another mineral, the latter being termed a perimorph; a person of generally heavy or rounded body build. — *adj* **endomorph'ic**. — *n* **endomorph'y**. [*endo*derm (an endomorph having a prevalence of structures formed from this) and Gr. *morphē*, shape.]

endoparasite *en-dō-par'ə-sīt*, *n* a parasite living inside the body of its host. [**endo-**.]

endophyte *en'dō-fīt*, (*bot*) *n* a plant living within another, whether parasitically or not. — *adj* **endophytic** (*-fit'ik*). [Gr. *endō*, within, *phyton*, a plant.]

endoplasm *en'dō-plazm*, (*biol*) *n* the inner portion of the cytoplasm of a cell. — *adj* **endoplas'mic** or **endoplas'tic**. [**endo-**.]

endoradiosonde *en-dō-rā-di-ō-sond'*, (*med*) *n* a miniature battery-powered transmitter designed to be swallowed by the patient to send out information about a bodily function such as digestion. [**endo-**.]

endorphin *en-dör'fin*, *n* any of a group of opiate-like substances produced by the brain and the pituitary gland, with pain-killing and other properties similar to morphine. [**endo-** and m*orphine*.]

endorse or **indorse** *in-dörs'*, *vt* to write (esp. one's signature, a note of contents, a record of an offence) on the back of; to assign by writing on the back of; to give one's sanction to; to express approbation of; to do so as a form of advertising, usu. in return for money. — *adj* **endors'able**. — *n* **endorsee'** (*en-*) the person to whom a bill, etc., is assigned by endorsement. — *n* **endorse'ment** the act of endorsing; that which is written on the back; a sanction; a record of a motoring offence on a driving licence; an additional clause on a policy altering the coverage in some way (*insurance*). — *n* **endors'er**. — **endorse out** (*SAfr*) to order (a person) to leave a place because he or she lacks official permission to be there. [M.E. *endosse* — O.Fr. *endosser* changed under the influence of L.L. *indorsāre* — *in*, on, *dorsum*, the back.]

endoscope *en'də-skōp*, (*med*) *n* an instrument for viewing the cavities of internal organs. — *adj* **endoscopic** (*-skop'ik*). — *n* **endoscopy** (*en-dos'kə-pi*) any technique for viewing internal organs, as by fibre optic apparatus. [**endo-** and **-scope**.]

endoskeleton *en-dō-skel'i-tn*, *n* the internal skeleton or framework of the body. — *adj* **endoskel'etal**. [**endo-**.]

endosperm *en'dō-spûrm*, *n* (in a seed) nutritive tissue formed from the embryo-sac. — *adj* **endosper'mic**. [**endo-**.]

endospore *en'dō-spör*, (*bot*) *n* the innermost layer of a spore wall; a spore formed within a mother-cell. [**endo-**.]

endothelium *en-dō-thē'li-əm*, (*biol*) *n* the layer of cell tissue on the internal surfaces of blood-vessels, lymphatics, etc.: — *pl* **endothē'lia**. — *adj* **endothē'lial**. [N.L., **endo-** and Gr. *thēlē*, nipple.]

endothermic *en-dō-thûr'mik*, *adj* accompanied by, characterised by, or formed with absorption of heat. [**endo-**.]

endotoxin *en'dō-tok-sin*, *n* a toxin (such as those causing typhoid fever and cholera) released only on the death or destruction of the bacterial cells which produced it. [**endo-**.]

endow *in-dow'*, *vt* to give a dowry or marriage portion to; to provide permanent provision or means of support for; to enrich with any gift or faculty. — *adj* **endowed'** having (a gift, ability, etc.) (with *with*). — *n* **endow'er**. — *n* **endow'ment** the act of endowing; that which is settled on any person or institution; a quality, aptitude or skill bestowed on anyone. — **endowment assurance** or **insurance** a form of insurance providing for the payment of a certain sum at a certain date or at death if earlier. [Fr. *en* (— L. *in*), *douer*, to endow — L. *dōtāre* — *dōs*, *dōtis*, a dowry.]

endue or **indue** *in-dū'*, *vt* to invest (with), esp. a quality; to supply, provide with. [O.Fr. *enduire* — L. *indūcĕre* — *in*, into, *dūcĕre*, to lead, influenced by *induĕre*, to put on.]

endure *in-dūr'*, *vt* to bear or put up with without giving in or up; to tolerate. — *vi* to continue to exist; to last. — *adj* **endur'able**. — *n* **endur'ableness**. — *adv* **endur'ably**. — *n* **endur'ance** the state or power of, or capacity for, enduring, bearing or surviving; patient suffering; patience; lasting quality; maximum performance under given conditions. — *n* **endur'er**. — *adj* **endur'ing** lasting. — *adv* **endur'ingly**. [O.Fr. *endurer* — L. *indūrāre* — *in*, in, *dūrus*, hard.]

ENE *abbrev* for east-north-east.

enema *en'i-mə*, (*med*) *n* a fluid injected into the rectum; the process of injecting such a fluid: — *pl* **en'emas** or **ene'mata**. [Gr. *enēma*, *-atos* — *enienai*, to send in.]

enemy *en'i-mi*, *n* a person who hates or dislikes, or who is hated or disliked; a hostile nation or force; something which is harmful to or which acts against (*fig*). — *adj* hostile. [O.Fr. *enemi* (Fr. *ennemi*) — L. *inimīcus* — *in-* (meaning not), *amīcus*, a friend.]

energumen *en-ər-gū'mən*, *n* a person who is possessed; a demoniac. [L.L. *energūmenus* — Gr. *en*, in, *ergon*, work.]

energy *en'ər-ji*, *n* the power required for doing work, for action, etc.; the power exerted in working, etc.; vigorous activity; intensity; the capacity of a material body or of radiation to do work (*phys*). — *adj* **energet'ic** having, requiring or showing energy; active; forcible; effective. — Also **energet'ical**. — *adv* **energet'ically**. — *vt* **en'ergise** or **-ize** to give strength or active force to; to stimulate to activity. — *vi* to release energy, esp. by acting vigorously. — **energy gap** the amount by which energy requirements exceed the energy supply. [Gr. *energeia* — *en*, in, *ergon*, work.]

enervate *en'ər-vāt*, *vt* to weaken by depriving of nerve, strength or vitality. — *adj* weakened; spiritless. — *adj* **en'ervating**. — *n* **enervā'tion**. [L. *ēnervāre*, *-ātum* — *ē*, out of, *nervus*, a nerve.]

en famille *ā fa-mē-y'*, (Fr.) amongst the family, as at a family gathering, at home, informally.

enfant terrible *ā-fā te-rē-bl'*, *n* a precocious child whose sayings and actions cause embarrassment to other (esp. older) people; a person whose behaviour, etc. is indiscreet, embarrassing or (*loosely*) unconventional. [Fr., a dreadful child.]

enfeeble *in-fē'bl*, *vt* to make weak. — *n* **enfee'blement** weakening; weakness. [**en-** (1b).]

en fête *ā fet*, (Fr.) in festivity, in festive mood; keeping, dressed for, etc. a holiday.

enfilade *en-fi-lād'*, *n* a discharge of firearms that sweeps a line or position from end to end (*mil*). — *vt* to discharge firearms along the whole length of a line. [Fr. *enfiler* — *en* (L. *in*), and *fil* — L. *fīlum*, a thread.]

enfold or **infold** *in-fōld'*, *vt* to wrap up; to embrace or enclose. — *n* **enfold'ment**. [**en-** (1a).]

enforce *in-förs'*, *vt* to impose by force; to give effect to; to compel; to emphasise, reinforce. — *adj* **enforce'able**. — *adv* **enforc'edly**. — *n* **enforce'-**

ment. — **enforcement notice** (*law*) an order served on someone who has breached town-planning regulations. [O.Fr. *enforcer* — *en* (L. *in*), and *force*.]

enfranchise or **-ize** *in-fran'chīz* or *-shīz*, *vt* to set free; to give a franchise or political privileges to. — *n* **enfran'chisement** (*-chiz-* or *-shiz-*). [O.Fr. *en-franchir* — *en*, and *franc*, free; see **franchise**.]

ENG *abbrev* for Electronic News Gathering.

Eng. *abbrev* for: England; English.

eng. *abbrev* for: engineer; engineering; engraver; engraving.

engage *in-gāj'*, *vt* to bind by a promise; to secure for service, ensure the services of; to enlist; to win over, attract; to reserve; to hold or occupy; to begin an action against (*mil*); to interlock; to fasten (*archit*). — *vi* to promise; to become bound; to take part; to become occupied or involved; to begin an action (*mil*). — *adj* **engaged'** promised, esp. in marriage; taken or booked; occupied; geared together, interlocked; partly built or sunk into, or appearing so (*archit*); (of literature or a writer) committed (cf. **engagé**). — *n* **engage'ment** the act of engaging; the state of being engaged; something that binds, a promise; betrothal; appointment; employment; a fight or battle; commitment (cf. **engagé**). — *adj* **engāg'ing** charming, winning or attractive. — *adv* **engāg'ingly**. — *n* **engāg'ingness**. — **engagement ring** a ring given, esp. by the man to the woman, as a token of their engagement to marry. [Fr. *engager* — *en gage*, in pledge; see **gage'**.]

engagé *ã-ga-zhā'*, *adj* committed to a point of view, or to social or political action. — *n* **engagement** (*ã-gazh-mã*; sometimes *in-gāj'mənt*) commitment. [Fr.]

en garde *ã gärd*, (Fr.) (in fencing) a warning to assume a defensive position in readiness for an attack.

engender *in-jen'dər*, *vt* to beget, generate, or start the development of; to cause to exist; to produce. — *vi* to be caused or produced. [Fr. *engendrer* — L. *ingenerāre* — *in*, and *generāre*, to generate.]

engine *en'jin*, *n* a mechanical device, esp. a complex piece of machinery in which power is applied to do work; a locomotive; a military machine; a device, contrivance; a source of power (*fig*). — *vt* to equip with an engine or engines. — *n* **engineer'** a person who designs or makes, or puts to practical use, engines or machinery of any type, including electrical; a person who designs or constructs public works, such as roads, railways, sewers, bridges, harbours, canals, etc.; a person who constructs or manages military fortifications, etc. (*hist*); a soldier trained for construction work, such as digging trenches, road-making, etc.; an officer who is responsible for a ship's engines; an engine-driver (esp. *US*); a person who contrives to bring about (with *of*). — *vi* to act as engineer. — *vt* to arrange or contrive; to manoeuvre or guide; to produce by engineering. — *n* **engineer'ing** the art or profession of an engineer; extended to apply to certain techniques or processes not connected with the work of engineers, such as *protein engineering*. — **en'gine-driver** a person who controls an engine, esp. a railway locomotive; **engine management** a system of continuous electronic analysis of the requirements for efficient performance of a car together with continuous electronic control of the necessary responses to these (*autos*); **en'gine-room** the room in a vessel in which the engines are; **en'gine-turning** a kind of ornament made by a rose-engine, as on the backs of watches, etc. [O.Fr. *engin* — L. *ingenium*, skill; see **ingenious**.]

English *ing'glish*, *adj* belonging to *England* or its inhabitants; of or relating to English. — *n* the English people (as *pl*); a Germanic language spoken in the British Isles, U.S., most parts of the British Commonwealth, etc. — *vt* to translate into English; to influence with English characteristics, customs, etc.; to anglicise. — **Eng'lishman**, *fem* **Eng'lishwoman** a native or naturalised inhabitant of England. — **Basic English** see **base**[1]; **Early English** often means Early Middle English; (*archit*) see **early**; **English breakfast** a cooked breakfast, usu. consisting of several dishes or courses (cf. *continental breakfast*); **English disease** the British disease; **English horn** the cor anglais. — **in plain English** in clear, simple language; **Middle English** English as spoken and written from about 1100 or 1150 A.D. till about 1500; **Modern English** English from about 1500 onwards; **Old English** a kind of type — black-letter; the English language down to about 1100 or 1150 A.D. (formerly, and still popularly, *Anglo-Saxon*). [O.E. *Englisc* — *Engle*, Angles.]

engorge *in-görj'*, *vt* to glut. — *adj* **engorged'** congested or excessively full of blood, etc. — *n* **engorge'ment**. [**en-** (1c).]

engraft *in-gräft'*, *vt* to graft or insert; to join on (to something already existing); to fix deeply. — *n* **engraftā'tion** (*en-*). — *n* **engraft'ment**. [**en-** (1a).]

engrain or **ingrain** *in-grān'*, *vt* to fix a dye firmly in; to instil (a habit, attitudes) deeply in. — *adj* **engrained'** or **ingrained'** (or *in'*) deeply coloured or permeated; (e.g. *engrained laziness*) deep-rooted and established; thoroughgoing (*fig*). — *n* **engrain'er**. [Orig. to dye in grain, i.e., with grain; see **grain**.]

engram *en'gram*, sometimes **engramma** *en-gram'ə*, *n* a permanent impression made by a stimulus or experience; a stimulus impression supposed to be inheritable; a memory trace. — *adj* **engrammat'ic**. [Ger. *Engramm* — Gr. *en*, in, *gramma*, that which is written.]

engrave *in-grāv'*, *vt* to cut with a special tool on wood, steel, etc.; to cut into; to impress deeply; to form or represent by engraving: — *pa p* **engraved'** or **engrāv'en**. — *n* **engrāv'er**. — *n* **engrāv'ing** the act or art of cutting or incising designs on metal, wood, etc., in order to print impressions from them — in metal, the lines to be printed are sunk or incised, in wood, they appear in relief, the wood between them being cut away; an impression taken from an engraved plate; a print. [**en-** (1a) and *grave*, an old word meaning to dig.]

engross *in-grōs'*, *vt* to absorb the attention, interest or powers of completely; to monopolise; to copy in large writing or distinct characters; to prepare a legal or an official document. — *adj* **engrossed'**. — *n* **engross'er**. — *adj* **engross'ing** absorbing; monopolising. — *n* **engross'ment** buying up wholesale; something (e.g. a document) which has been engrossed. [Fr. *en gros* — L. *in*, in, *grossus*, large; see **gross**.]

engulf *in-gulf'*, *vt* to swallow up completely; to overwhelm. — *n* **engulf'ment**. [**en-** (1a).]

enhance *in-häns'*, *vt* to raise in value or quality; to add to, increase or improve; to make more important. — *vi* to increase; to rise in value. — *n* **enhance'ment**. — *n* **enhanc'er**. — *adj* **enhanc'ive**. — **enhanced radiation weapon** a neutron bomb. [A.Fr. *enhauncer*.]

enharmonic *en-här-mon'ik* or **enharmonical** (*-kl*), *adj* pertaining to music constructed on a scale containing intervals less than a semitone; of a scale of music current among the Greeks in which an interval of $2\frac{1}{2}$ tones was divided into two quarter tones and a major third; of a minute pitch difference, e.g. between F sharp and G flat, not identifiable in a scale of equal temperament. — *adv* **enharmon'ically**. [Gr. *enharmonikos* — *en*, in, *harmoniā*, harmony.]

enigma *in-ig'mə*, *n* a statement with a hidden meaning to be guessed; anything very obscure; a mysterious person or situation; a riddle. — *adj* **enigmat'ic** or **enigmat'ical** (*en-*) relating to, containing, or resembling an enigma; obscure; puzzling. — *adv* **enigmat'ically**. — *n* **enig'matist** a person who makes up or deals in riddles. [L. *aenigma* — Gr. *ainigma* — *ainissesthai*, to speak obscurely — *ainos*, a fable.]

enjambment or **enjambement** *in-jam'mənt, -jamb'* or *ã-zhãb-mã'*, *n* (in verse) the continuation of the sense without a pause beyond the end of the line. — *vt* and *vi* **enjamb** (*in-jam'*). [Fr. *enjambement* — *enjamber*, to stride, encroach.]

enjoin *in-join'*, *vt* to order or direct, esp. with authority or urgency; to forbid, to prohibit by injunction (*law* and *US*). — *n* **enjoin'er**. — *n* **enjoin'ment**. [Fr. *enjoindre* — L. *injungěre* — *in*, and *jungere*, to join.]

enjoy *in-joi'*, *vt* to take pleasure or delight in; to possess or use with satisfaction or delight; to have the use or benefit of. — *adj* **enjoy'able** capable of being enjoyed; giving pleasure, delightful. — *n* **enjoy'ableness**. — *adv* **enjoy'ably**. — *n* **enjoy'er**. — *n* **enjoy'ment** the state, act or condition of enjoying; the satisfactory possession or use of anything; pleasure; happiness. — **enjoy oneself** to have a pleasant time. [O.Fr. *enjoir*, to enjoy — *en*, and *joir* — L. *gaudēre*, to rejoice.]

enkephalin or **enkephaline** *en-kef'ə-lin*, *n* a chemical found in small quantities in the brain, which relieves pain and can now be produced synthetically. [Gr. *en*, in, *kephalē*, head.]

enkindle *in-kin'dl*, *vt* to kindle or set on fire; to inflame; to excite or rouse. — *adj* **enkin'dled**. [**en-** (1c).]

enlace *in-lās'*, *vt* to encircle; to embrace; to entwine. — *n* **enlace'ment**. [**en-** (1c).]

enlarge *in-lärj'*, *vt* to increase in size or quantity; to expand; to amplify; to reproduce (esp. a photograph) on a larger scale. — *vi* to grow large or larger; to speak or write expansively; to expatiate. — *adj* **enlarged'**. — *adv* **enlar'gedly**. — *n* **enlar'gedness**. — *n* **enlarge'ment** increase; extension; a photograph reproduced on a larger scale. — *n* **enlarg'er** an apparatus with a lens for enlarging photographs. [O.Fr. *enlarger* — *en* (L. *in*), *large*, large.]

enlighten *in-līt'en*, *vt* to impart knowledge or information to; to enlighten or uplift by knowledge or religion; to free from prejudice and superstition. — *n* **enlight'enment** the act of enlightening; the state of being enlightened; (usu. with *cap*) the spirit of the French philosophers of the 18th century, with a belief in reason and human progress and a questioning of tradition and authority. [O.E. *inīhtan* — *in*, in, *līhtan*, to light; or independently formed later.]

enlist *in-list'*, *vt* to enrol; to engage as a soldier, etc.; to obtain the support and help of (for a cause or undertaking). — *vi* to engage in public service, esp. as a soldier; to support a cause with enthusiasm. — *n* **enlist'ment**. — **enlisted man** (*US*) a member of the armed forces below the rank of warrant officer, other than a cadet or midshipman. [**en-** (1a).]

enliven *in-līv'n*, *vt* to put life into; to excite or make active; to make cheerful or bright; to animate. — *n* **enlīv'ener**. — *n* **enlīv'enment**. [**en-** (1b).]

en masse *ã mas*, all together. [Fr., in a body.]

enmesh *in-mesh'*, *vt* to catch in a mesh or net; to entangle. [**en-** (1a).]

enmity *en'mi-ti*, *n* the quality of being an enemy; unfriendliness; ill-will; hostility. [O.Fr. *enemistié* — L. *inimīcus*; see **enemy**.]

ennoble *i-nō'bl*, *vt* to make noble; to elevate or distinguish; to raise to the rank of noble. — *n* **ennō'blement** the act of making noble; conferment of the rank of noble. [Fr. *ennoblir* — Fr. *en* (L. *in*), and *noble*.]

ennui *ã-nwē'*, *on'wē* or *on-wē'*, *n* a feeling of weariness; boredom. — *vt* to weary; to bore: — *pr p* **ennuying**; *pa t* and *pa p* **ennuied** or **ennuyed**. — *adj* **ennuyé** (Fr.; *-yā*) bored. [See ety. for **annoy**.]

ENO *abbrev* for English National Opera.

enoki *ə-nok'ē*, *n* a thin white edible mushroom with a very small cap, native to Japan. [Japanese.]

enormous *i-nör'məs*, *adj* immense; huge; considerable, very much, of large extent (*colloq*); exceedingly good (*colloq*). — *n* **enor'mity** a great crime; great wickedness; outrage; immenseness, vastness. — *adv* **enor'mously**. — *n* **enor'mousness**. [L. *ēnormis* — *ē*, out of, *norma*, rule.]

enosis *en'ō-sis* or *en-ō'sis*, *n* union, the aim and rallying-cry of the Greek Cypriot movement for union with Greece: — *pl* **enoses**. [Gr. *henosis* — *heis*, *henos*, one.]

enough *i-nuf'*, *adj* as much as needed to satisfy (a requirement, lack, demand, etc.); sufficient; satisfying. — *adv* sufficiently; quite; fairly; tolerably. — *n* as much as satisfies a desire or want; a sufficient degree or extent. [O.E. *genōh*.]

ENP *abbrev* for electronic number plate.

en papillote *ã pa-pē-yot*, (Fr.) (of cooking and serving food) in an envelope of oiled paper or foil. [Fr. *papillote*, buttered or oiled paper for cooking in.]

en passant *ã pa-sã*, by the way; applied in chess to the taking of a pawn that has just moved two squares as if it had moved only one. [Fr., in passing.]

en pension *ã pã-syɔ̃*, at a fixed rate for board and lodging. [Fr.]

enplane. See **emplane**.

en plein air *ã plen er*, in the open air. [Fr.]

en plein jour *ã plẽ zhōōr*, in broad daylight. [Fr.]

en primeur *ã prē-mœr*, (of tasting, buying or investing in wine) when the wine is new. [Fr. *en*, in, *primeur* (of wine) youth, newness.]

enquire, etc. See **inquire**.

enrage *in-rāj'*, *vt* to make angry. — *adj* **enraged'** very angry, furious. — *n* **enrage'ment**. [O.Fr. *enrager* — *en* (L. *in*), and *rage*, rage.]

en rappel *ã ra-pel*, (Fr.; *mountaineering*) using a rope which is easily pulled free after descent. [Fr., — *rappel*, recall.]

en rapport *ã ra-pör*, in close touch or sympathy. [Fr.]

enrapture *in-rap'chər*, *vt* to put in rapture or ecstasy; to transport with pleasure or delight. — *adj* **enrap'tured** or **enrapt'** in ecstasy. [**en-** (1a).]

enrich *in-rich'*, *vt* to make rich; to fertilise; to decorate, enhance, improve; to increase the proportion of some valuable substance in; to increase the proportion of one or more particular isotopes in a mixture of the isotopes of an element, e.g. to raise the proportion of fissile nuclei above that for natural uranium in reactor fuel. — *n* **enrich'ment**. [**en-** (1b).]

enrobe *in-rōb'*, (*formal*) *vt* to dress, clothe or invest. [**en-** (1c).]

enrol or in U.S. **enroll** *in-rōl'*, *vt* to insert in a roll, list or register; to enter in a list as pupil, member, etc.; to enlist; to record. — *vi* to enrol oneself: — *pr p* **enroll'ing**; *pa t* and *pa p* **enrōlled'**. — *n* **enroll'er**. — *n* **enrol'ment** or **enroll'ment**. [O.Fr. *enroller* (Fr. *enrôler*) — *en*, and *rolle*, roll.]

en route *ã rōōt*, on the road, on the way; (as *interj*) let us go, march. [Fr.]

ENSA *en'sə*, *abbrev* for Entertainments National Service Association.

ensanguine *in-sang'gwin*, *vt* to stain or cover with blood. — *adj* **ensan'guinated** or (esp. *facetiously*) **ensan'guined** bloody. [Fr. pfx. *en-*, in, L. *sanguis*, *-inis*, blood.]

ensate *en'sāt*, (*bot*) *adj* sword-shaped. [L. *ēnsis*, sword.]

ensconce *in-skons'*, *vt* to settle comfortably; to hide safely. [**en-** (1a).]

ensemble *ã-sã-bl'*, *n* all parts of a thing taken together; a group of musicians playing together; the performance of such a group; the combined effect of the performance; a costume consisting of several (matching) garments; a group of supporting dancers, corps de ballet. — Also *adj*. — **tout ensemble** (*tōō-*

tā-) general appearance or effect. [Fr. *ensemble*, together — L. *in*, in, *simul*, at the same time.]

enshrine *en-shrīn'*, *vt* to enclose in or as if in a shrine; to consider sacred, to cherish. [**en-** (1a).]

enshroud *en-shrowd'*, *vt* to cover up; to cover with a shroud; to cover, hide or envelop as if with a shroud. [**en-** (1a).]

ensiform *en'si-fōrm*, (*bot* and *med*) *adj* sword-shaped. [L. *ēnsis*, a sword, *fōrma*, form.]

ensign *en'sin* or *en'sīn*, *n* a badge, sign or mark; a sign or flag, distinguishing a nation or a regiment (see also under **blue, red, white**); a person who carries the colours; until 1871, the officer of lowest commissioned rank in the British infantry; an officer of lowest commissioned rank (*US navy*). — *n* **en'signcy**. — *n* **en'signship**. [O.Fr. *enseigne* — L. *īnsignia*; see ety. for **insignia**.]

ensilage *en'sil-ij* or *in-sī'lij*, *n* the storing of green fodder in pits or silos. — *vt* **ensile** (*en-sīl'* or *en'sīl*) or **ensilage** to store by ensilage. [Fr., — Sp. *en*, in, and **silo**.]

enslave *in-slāv'*, *vt* to make a slave or slaves of; to subject to a dominating influence. — *adj* **enslaved'**. — *n* **enslave'ment** the act of enslaving; the state of being enslaved; slavery; captivity. — *n* **enslav'er**. [**en-** (1b).]

ensnare *in-snār'*, *vt* to catch in a snare; to entrap; to entangle. [**en-** (1a).]

ensphere *in-sfēr'*, *vt* to enclose or place in a sphere; to give a spherical form to. [**en-** (1a).]

ensue *in-sū'*, *vi* to follow, to come after; to result (with *from*): — *pr p* **ensū'ing**; *pa t* and *pa p* **ensued'**. [O.Fr. *ensuir* (Fr. *ensuivre*) to follow after, to result.]

en suite *ā swēt*, forming a unit or a set. — *n* (*Austr*) an en suite bathroom. [Fr., in sequence, in succession.]

ensure *in-shoor'*, *vt* to make sure; to make safe. — *n* **ensur'er**. [**insure**.]

enswathe *in-swādh'*, *vt* to wrap round. — *n* **enswathe'ment**. [**en-** (1c).]

ENT (*med*) *abbrev* for ear, nose and throat.

ent. or **entom.** *abbrev* for entomology.

ent-. See **ento-**.

entablature *en-tab'lə-chər*, *n* (in classical architecture) that part which surmounts the columns and rests upon the capitals; any similar structure, such as an engine framework upon columns. [It. *intavolatura* — *in*, in, *tavola* — L. *tabula*, a table.]

entablement *in-tā'bl-mənt*, *n* a platform above the dado on a pedestal, on which a statue rests; an entablature. [Fr.]

entail *in-tāl'*, *vt* to bring on or result in as an inevitable consequence; to settle on a series of heirs, so that the immediate possessor may not dispose of the estate (*legal*). — *n* the settlement of an entailed estate; an estate entailed; the transmission, or the rule of descent, of an estate. — *n* **entail'er**. — *n* **entail'ment**. [**en-** (1a), and **tail**[2].]

entamoeba *en-tə-mē'bə*, *n* any amoeba of the genus *Entamoeba*, one of the species of which causes amoebic dysentery in man. — Also **endamoe'ba**. [**ento-, endo-** and **amoeba**.]

entangle *in-tang'gl*, *vt* to twist into a tangle, or so as not to be easily separated; to involve in complications or in an embarrassing or a compromising situation; to perplex or confuse; to ensnare. — *n* **entang'lement** perplexity, confusion; a tangled obstacle; a tangle; an entangling situation or involvement. [**en-** (1c).]

entasis *en'tə-sis*, (*archit*) *n* the slightly swelling outline of the shaft of a column or the like, used to counteract the illusion of concavity that an absolutely straight column would produce. [Gr. *entăsis* — *en*, in, *tasis*, a stretch.]

entelechy *en-tel'ə-ki*, (*philos*) *n* actuality; distinctness of realised existence; a vital principle supposed by vitalists to direct processes in an organism towards realisation of a certain end. [Gr. *entelecheia* — *en*, in, *telos*, perfection, end, *echein*, to have.]

entellus *en-tel'əs*, *n* the hanuman monkey of India. [App. from *Entellus*, the old Sicilian in Virgil's *Aeneid*, from its old-mannish look.]

entente *ā-tāt'*, *n* an understanding; a friendly agreement or relationship between states — as the **entente cordiale** (*kör-dē-äl'*) between Britain and France (1904). [Fr.]

enter *en'tər*, *vi* to go or come in; to penetrate; to come on to the stage; to become a member; to put down one's name (as competitor, candidate, etc.); to join in or become a participator; to take possession. — *vt* to come or go into; to penetrate; to join or engage in; to begin; to put into; to enrol or record; to admit; to inscribe or have inscribed; to register (as a vessel leaving a port, a horse for a race, a pupil for a school, etc.); to insert a record of; to initiate; to become a member of; to take possession of. — *adj* **en'terable**. — *n* **en'terer**. — *n* and *adj* **en'tering**. — **enter into** to become concerned or involved in; to be interested in; to participate actively or heartily in; to understand sympathetically; to take up the discussion of; to be part of; **enter on** or **upon** to begin; to engage in. [Fr. *entrer* — L. *intrāre*, to go into.]

enter- *en-tər-* or **entero-** *-ō-*, *combining form* signifying intestine. — *adj* **en'teral** pertaining to, in, or by way of, the intestine. — *adj* **en'terate** having an alimentary canal. — *n* **enterec'tomy** surgical removal of part of the bowel. — *adj* **enteric** (*en-ter'ik*) pertaining to the intestines; possessing an alimentary canal. — *n* short for **enteric fever**, typhoid fever, an infectious disease due to a bacillus, characterised by fever, rose-red rash, enlargement of the spleen and ulceration of the intestines. — *n* **enterī'tis** inflammation of the intestines, esp. the small intestine. — *n* **en'teron** in coelenterates (animals with only one body-cavity), the body-cavity itself; in higher animals, the gut or alimentary canal: — *pl* **en'tera**. — *n* **enteros'tomy** surgical formation of an opening in the intestine. — *n* **enterot'omy** incision of the intestinal wall. — *n* **enterovī'rus** any of several viruses occurring in and infecting the intestine. [Gr. *enteron*, gut.]

enterprise *en'tər-prīz*, *n* an undertaking or new project, esp. when bold or dangerous; readiness, initiative and daring in undertaking; a business concern. — *adj* **en'terprising** bold and imaginative in undertaking; adventurous; full of initiative. — *adj* **en'terprisingly**. — **enterprise culture** a culture based on an economic policy that encourages commercial initiative and audacious, imaginative planning; **enterprise zone** any of a number of sites in depressed areas in which industrial and commercial renewal is encouraged by the government by financial and other incentives. [O.Fr. *entreprise*, past p. of *entreprendre* — *entre*, between, *prendre*, to seize.]

entertain *en-tər-tān'*, *vt* to provide food or drink as refreshment for; to give hospitality to; to amuse; to give pleasure or amusement to by means of a performance, show, etc.; to take into consideration; to keep in the mind. — *n* **entertain'er** a person who entertains in any sense; a person who gives performances professionally, e.g. a singer or comedian. — *adj* **entertain'ing** giving entertainment; amusing. — Also *n*. — *adv* **entertain'ingly**. — *n* **entertain'ment** the act of entertaining; the reception of and provision (of food and drink) for guests; that which entertains or amuses; a performance or show intended to give pleasure. [Fr. *entretenir* — L. *inter*, among, *tenēre*, to hold.]

enthalpy *en-thal'pi* or *en'thəl-pi*, (*phys*) *n* the heat content of a substance per unit mass. [Gr. *enthalpein*, to warm in.]

enthetic *en-thet'ik*, *adj* (of diseases, etc.) introduced from without. [Gr. *enthetikos* — *entithenai*, to put in.]

enthral or (esp. in U.S.) **enthrall** *in-thröl'*, *vt* to hold spellbound; to hold in bondage or slavery: — *pr p* **enthrall'ing**; *pa t* and *pa p* **enthralled'**. — *adj* **enthrall'ing**. — *n* **enthral'ment** or (esp. in U.S.) **enthrall'ment**. [**en-** (1a).]

enthrone *in-thrōn'*, *vt* to place on a throne; to exalt to the seat of royalty; to install as bishop. — *n* **enthrōne'ment** the act of enthroning or of being enthroned. [**en-** (1a).]

enthusiasm *in-* or *en-thū'zi-azm*, or *-thōō'*, *n* intense and lively interest; passionate zeal. — *vt* and *vi* **enthuse'** (back-formation) to make, be, become or appear enthusiastic. — *n* **enthu'siast** a person filled with enthusiasm; a person deeply interested in a particular subject. — *adj* **enthusias'tic** filled with enthusiasm; zealous; ardent. — *adv* **enthusias'tically**. [Gr. *enthousiasmos*, a god-inspired zeal — *en*, in, *theos*, a god.]

enthymeme *en'thi-mēm*, *n* an argument of probability only (*rhet*); a syllogism in which one premise is suppressed (*logic*). — *adj* **enthymemat'ical**. [Gr. *enthȳmēma*, a consideration — *en*, in, *thȳmos*, the mind.]

entice *in-tīs'*, *vt* to attract by exciting hope or desire; to tempt; to lead astray. — *adj* **entice'able**. — *n* **entice'ment** the act of enticing; something which entices or tempts; allurement. — *n* **entīc'er**. — *n* and *adj* **entīc'ing**. — *adv* **entīc'ingly**. [O.Fr. *enticier*, to provoke.]

entire *in-tīr'*, *adj* whole; complete; intact; unimpaired; (esp. of a horse) not castrated; with untoothed and unlobed margin (*bot*). — *n* a stallion; a stamped, used or unused, envelope (*philat*). — *adv* **entire'ly**. — *n* **entire'ness** or **entī'rety** completeness; the whole. — **in its entirety** (considered, taken, etc.) as a whole. [O.Fr. *entier* — L. *integer*, whole.]

entitle *en-tī'tl*, *vt* to give a title to; to style; to give a right or claim to. — *n* **entī'tlement**. [O.Fr. *entiteler* — L.L. *intitulāre* — *in*, in, *titulus*, title.]

entity *en'ti-ti*, *n* being, existence; something that exists independently; the basic, essential nature of something. [L.L. *entitās*, *-ātis* — *ēns*, pres. p. from L. *esse*, to be.]

ento- *en-tō-* or *en-to'-*, or **ent-** *ent-*, *combining form* denoting inside, often interchanging with **endo-** and opp. to **ecto-**, **exo-**. — *n* **en'toblast** endoderm; a body within a cell nucleus, a nucleolus. — *n* **en'toderm** endoderm. — *adj* **entophytal** (*-fī'tl*). — *n* **en'tophyte** (*-fīt*) an endophyte. — *adj* **entophytic** (*-fit'ik*) or **entophytous** (*en-tof'i-təs* or *en-tō-fī'təs*). — *adj* **entop'ic** developed, etc., in the usual place. — *adj* **entopt'ic** within the eyeball. — *adj* **ento'tic** of the interior of the ear. [Gr. *entos*, within.]

entom. See **ent**.

entomb *in-tōōm'*, *vt* to place in a tomb; to bury. — *n* **entomb'ment** burial. [O.Fr. *entoumber* — *en*, in, *tombe*, a tomb.]

entomic *en-tom'ik*, *adj* pertaining to insects. — *adj* **entomolog'ical** (*-loj'*). — *adv* **entomolog'ically**. — *vi* **entomol'ogise** or **-ize**. — *n* **entomol'ogist** a scientist who specialises in entomology. — *n* **entomol'ogy** (*-ə-ji*) the science of insects. — *adj* **entomophagous** (*-mof'ə-gəs*) living on insects, insectivorous. — *n* **entomoph'agy** (*-ə-ji*) the practice of eating insects. — *adj* **entomoph'ilous** specially adapted for pollination by insects. — *n* **entomoph'ily** pollination by insects; adaptation to pollination by insects. [Gr. *entoma*, insects — *entomos*, cut up.]

entophytal ... to ... **entotic**. See **ento-**.

entourage *ā-tōō-räzh'*, *n* followers, attendants. [Fr., — *entourer*, to surround.]

en tout cas *ā tōō kä*, *n* a parasol that can be used as an umbrella. — *n* **En-Tout-Cas®** a hard tennis court that can be used in all weathers. [Fr., in any case.]

entr'acte *ā-trakt'*, *n* the interval between acts in a play; a piece of music or other performance between acts. [Fr., — *entre*, between, *acte*, act.]

entrails *en'trālz*, *npl* the internal parts of an animal's body, the bowels; the inside of anything. [O.Fr. *entraille* — L.L. *intrālia* — *inter*, within.]

entrain[1] *in-trān'*, *vi* to get into a railway train; to take a train. — *vt* to put into a train. — *n* **entrain'ment**. [**en-** (1a).]

entrain[2] *in-trān'*, (*phys*) *vt* to transport one substance, e.g. small liquid particles, in another, e.g. a vapour; to suspend bubbles or particles in a moving fluid. — *n* **entrain'ment**. [Fr. *entraîner*.]

en train *ā trɛ̃*, (Fr.) in progress.

entrance[1] *en'trəns*, *n* a place of entering; a door; an act of entering; a coming upon the stage; the power or right to enter. — *n* **en'trant** someone who or something which enters. — **entrance fee** the money paid on entering a society, club, etc. [Fr. *entrer* — L. *intrāre*, to enter.]

entrance[2] *in-* or *en-träns'*, *vt* to fill with enthusiastic delight; to put into a trance. — *n* **entrance'ment** a state of trance or of great joy. — *adj* **entranc'ing** charming, delightful. [**en-** (1a).]

entrap *in-trap'*, *vt* to catch in, or as if in, a trap; to entangle. — *n* **entrap'ment** the act of entrapping; the state of being entrapped; the act of luring a person into the commission of a crime so that they may be arrested and prosecuted (*legal*). — *n* **entrapp'er**. [O.Fr. *entraper* — *en*, in, *trappe*, a trap.]

entreat *in-trēt'*, *vt* to ask earnestly; to beseech; to beg for. — *vi* to beseech, ask. — *n* **entreat'y** the act of entreating; earnest prayer. [O.Fr. *entraiter* — *en*, and *traiter*, to treat.]

entrechat *ā-trə-shä'*, (*ballet*) *n* a leap during which a dancer crosses his or her feet and beats his or her heels together. [Fr., — It. (*capriola*) *intrecciata*, plaited, complicated (caper).]

entrecôte *ā'trə-kōt*, *n* a steak cut from between two ribs. — Also *adj*. [Fr.]

entrée *ā'* or *on'trā*, *n* entry, freedom of access, admittance; introduction, means of access; a dish served at dinner between the chief courses, i.e. between fish and roast, or as a substitute, also (esp. *US*) a main course, and (esp. *Austr*) a starter; an introduction or prelude (*mus*); the act of entering, a formal entrance, or music for it. — **entrée dish** a dish, usually silver, with a cover, suitable for an entrée. [Fr.]

entremets *ā'trə-mā* or *-me*, *n* a light dish served at table between the chief courses. [O.Fr. *entremes* — *entre*, between, *mes* (Fr. *mets*), dish.]

entrench or **intrench** *in-trench'* or *-trensh'*, *vt* to dig a trench around; to fortify with a ditch and parapet; to establish in a strong position (esp. *mil*); to establish or fix firmly because of an unwillingness to change or in such a way that change is difficult or impossible. — *n* **entrench'ment** or **intrench'ment** a defensive earthwork of trenches and parapets; any protection. [**en-** (1c).]

entre nous *ā-trə nōō*, (Fr.) between ourselves.

entrepot or **entrepôt** *ā'trə-pō*, *n* a storehouse; a bonded warehouse; a seaport through which exports and imports pass, esp. one from which imports are re-exported without duty being charged on them. [Fr.]

entrepreneur *ā-trə-prə-nœr'*, *n* a person who undertakes an enterprise esp. a commercial one, often at personal financial risk; a contractor or employer; an organiser of musical or other entertainments: — *fem* **entrepreneuse** (*-nœz'*). — *adj* **entrepreneur'ial** (*-nœr'i-əl*, *-nū'* or *-nōō'*). — *n* **entrepreneur'ialism**. — *n* **entrepreneur'ship**. [Fr.]

entresol *en'tər-sol* or *ã'trə-sol*, *n* a low storey between two main storeys of a building, generally between the ground floor and the first floor. [Fr., — *entre*, between, *sol*, the ground.]

entrism, etc. See **entryism** under **entry**.

entropy *en'trə-pi*, (*phys*) *n* a measure of unavailable energy, energy still existing but lost for the purpose of doing work because it exists as the internal motion of molecules; a measure of the disorder of a system; a measure of heat content, regarded as increased in a reversible change by the ratio of heat taken in to absolute temperature. — *adj* **entrop'ic** (often *fig*). [Gr. *en*, in, *tropē*, turning, intended to represent 'transformation content'.]

entrust or **intrust** *in-trust'*, *vt* to give in trust; to commit as a trust; to give responsibility to trustingly. — *n* **entrust'ment**. [**en-** (1c).]

entry *en'tri*, *n* the act of entering in any sense; a coming upon the stage; the coming in of an instrument or performer; entrance; a lobby or vestibule; the act of recording in writing; the thing so written; a list of competitors; a taking possession (*law*). — *n* **en'tryism** or **en'trism** the practice of joining a political body in sufficient numbers to swing its policy, *specif* of Trotskyists, etc. in branches of the Labour Party. — *n* and *adj* **en'tryist** or **en'trist**. — **entry fee** entrance fee. — **card of entry** (*bridge*, etc.) a card to bring in one's hand with; **port of entry** see **port**[1]. [Fr. *entrée* — *entrer* — L. *intrāre*, to go into.]

Entryphone® *en'tri-fōn*, *n* a telephonic device at the entrance to e.g. a block of flats, allowing communication between individual occupiers and visitors.

entwine *in-twīn'*, *vt* to interlace; to weave together. [**en-** (1c).]

enucleate *in-ū'kli-āt*, *adj* without a nucleus. — *vt* (*surg*) to extract, e.g. a tumour, an eyeball or a swelling. — *n* **enucleā'tion**. [L. *ēnucleāre* — *ē*, from, *nucleus*, a kernel.]

enumerate *i-nū'mər-āt*, *vt* to count the number of; to give a list of, one by one. — *n* **enūmerā'tion** the act of numbering; a detailed account. — *adj* **enū'merative**. — *n* **enū'merātor** someone who, or something that, enumerates; a person who collects and deals with population census figures, voters' lists, etc. [L. *ē*, from, *numerāre*, *-ātum*, to number.]

enunciate *i-nun'si-āt* or *-shi-āt*, *vt* to state formally; to pronounce distinctly; to utter. — *adj* **enun'ciable** (*-si-* or *-shi-*). — *n* **enunciation** (*i-nun-si-ā'shən*) the act of enunciating; the manner of uttering or pronouncing; a distinct statement or declaration; the words in which a proposition is expressed. — *adj* **enun'ciative** (*-si-ā-*, *-syā-*, *-shyā-* or *-shə-tiv*) or **enun'ciatory** containing enunciation or utterance; declarative. — *n* **enun'ciātor** a person who or something that enunciates or announces. [L. *ēnuntiāre*, *-ātum* — *ē*, from, *nuntiāre*, to tell — *nuntius*, a messenger.]

enuresis *en-ū-rē'sis*, (*med*) *n* incontinence of urine. — *adj* and *n* **enūret'ic**. [Gr. *en*, in, *ourēsis*, urination.]

envelop *in-* or *en-vel'əp*, *vt* to cover by wrapping; to surround entirely; to hide. — *n* **envelope** (*en'vəl-ōp*) that which envelops, wraps or covers; a cover for a letter (in this sense sometimes pronounced *on'*, *ã'* in imitation of French); one of the coverings of a flower — calyx or corolla (*bot*); the gas-bag of a balloon or airship; the form taken by amplitude peaks of a radio wave (*radio*); the locus of ultimate intersections of a series of curves (*math*). — *n* **envel'opment** a complete wrapping or covering. [O.Fr. *enveloper*.]

envenom *in-ven'əm*, *vt* to put venom into; to poison; to taint with bitterness or malice. — *adj* **enven'omed**. [O.Fr. *envenimer* — *en*, and *venim*, venom.]

environ *in-vī'rən*, *vt* to surround; to encircle. — *npl* **environs** (*in-vī'rənz* or *en'vi-*) the places that environ; the outskirts of a city; neighbourhood. [Fr. *environner* — *environ*, around — *virer*, to turn round.]

environment *in-vī'rən-mənt*, *n* surroundings; external conditions influencing development or growth of people, animals or plants; living or working conditions. — *adj* **environment'al**. — *n* **environment'alism** concern about the environment and its preservation from the effects of pollution, etc.; the belief that environment rather than heredity is the main influence on a person's behaviour and development (*psychol*). — *n* **environment'alist** a person who is concerned with the protection of the environment, esp. from pollution; a person who advocates environmentalism (*psychol*). — *nsing* **environics** (*en-vī-ron'iks*) the study of methods of influencing behaviour by controlling environmental factors. — **environmental health officer** an official whose duty is to enforce regulations regarding e.g. food-handling shops, maintenance of a clean water-supply, waste-disposal, etc. (abbrev. **EHO**). [Ety. as for **environ**.]

envisage *in-viz'ij*, *vt* to consider or contemplate; to picture in one's mind; to visualise; to see, suggest or expect as a possible or likely future target, result, etc. — *n* **envis'agement**. [Fr. *envisager* — *en*, and *visage*, the face.]

envision *in-vizh'ən*, *vt* to visualise; to envisage. [**en-** (1c).]

envoy[1] *en'voi*, *n* a messenger, esp. one sent to transact business with a foreign government; a diplomatic minister. — *n* **en'voyship**. [Fr. *envoyé* — past p. of *envoyer*, to send.]

envoy[2] or **envoi** *en'voi*, *n* the concluding part of a poem or a book; the author's final words, esp. the short stanza concluding a poem written in certain archaic metrical forms. [O.Fr. *envoye* — *envoiier*, to send — *en voie*, on the way.]

envy *en'vi*, *n* a feeling of discontent at the good fortune, qualities, success, etc., of another; an object or person viewed with envy. — *vt* to feel envy towards, or on account of; to wish to have, to covet, someone's property, good fortune, skills, etc.: — *pr p* **en'vying**; *pa t* and *pa p* **en'vied**. — *adj* **en'viable** that is to be envied; causing envy. — *n* **en'viableness**. — *adv* **en'viably**. — *n* **en'vier**. — *adj* **en'vious** feeling envy; directed by envy. — *adv* **en'viously**. — *n* **en'viousness**. [Fr. *envie* — L. *invidia* — *invidēre*, to look askance at.]

enwrap *in-rap'*, *vt* to cover by wrapping; to enfold; to engross. [**en-** (1a).]

enwreathe *in-rēdh'*, *vt* to envelop; to encircle, as if with a wreath. [**en-** (1a).]

Enzed *en-zed'*, (*Austr* and *NZ colloq*) *n* New Zealand; (also **Enzedd'er**) a New Zealander. [The abbrev. **NZ** phonetically represented.]

enzootic *en-zō-ot'ik*, *adj* (of animal diseases) prevalent in a particular district or at a particular season. — *n* a disease of this character. [Gr. *en*, in, *zōion*, animal, in imitation of *endemic*.]

enzyme *en'zīm*, *n* any one of a large class of protein substances produced by living cells which act as catalysts in biochemical reactions. — *adj* **enzymat'ic** or **enzym'ic**. — *n* **enzymol'ogist**. — *n* **enzymol'ogy** the scientific study of enzymes. [Gr. *en*, in, *zȳmē*, leaven.]

EOC *abbrev* for Equal Opportunities Commission.

Eocene *ē'ō-sēn*, (*geol*) *adj* belonging to the oldest division of the Tertiary formation. — *n* the Eocene system, period or strata. [Gr. *ēōs*, daybreak, *kainos*, new — from the very small proportion of living species of molluscs among its fossils; compare **Miocene** and **Pliocene**.]

Eohippus *ē-ō-hip'əs*, *n* the oldest known horselike animal, an Eocene fossil. [Gr. *ēōs*, dawn, *hippos*, horse.]

EOKA *ā-ō'kə*, *abbrev* for *Ethnikē Organōsis Kypriākou Agōnos* (Gr.), National Organisation of the Cypriot Struggle.

eolith *ē'ō-lith*, *n* a very early roughly-broken stone implement, or one naturally formed but assumed to have been used by man. — *adj* **eolith'ic**. [Gr. *ēōs*, dawn, *lithos*, stone.]

eon. See **aeon**.

eonism *ē'ə-nizm*, (*psychiatry*) *n* adoption by a male of female dress and manner. [Chevalier d'*Éon*, Fr. diplomat (d. 1810), who chose female dress as a disguise.]

eosin *ē'ō-sin*, *n* a red dyestuff. — *adj* **eosin'ophil** readily staining with eosin. — *n* a type of white blood cell, so called because it is easily stained by eosin. — *n* **eosinophil'ia** the condition of staining readily with eosin; the condition in which there is an abnormally large number of eosinophils in the blood. — *adj* **eosinophil'ic** or **eosinoph'ilous**. [Gr. *ēōs*, dawn.]

EP *abbrev* for: electroplated; European Parliament; extended play (of records).

Ep. See **Epis**.

ep-. See **epi-**.

EPA *abbrev* for Environmental Protection Agency (U.S.).

Epacris *ep-ak'ris* or *ep'ə-kris*, *n* a chiefly Australian genus of heathlike plants. [Gr. *epi*, upon, *akris*, a summit.]

epact *ē'pakt*, *n* the moon's age at the beginning of the year; the excess of the calendar month or solar year over the lunar. [Fr. *épacte* — Gr. *epaktos*, brought on.]

eparch *ep'ärk*, *n* the governor of a modern Greek province; a metropolitan. — *n* **ep'archate** or **ep'archy** the province, territory or diocese of an eparch. [Gr. *eparchos* — *epi*, upon, *archē*, dominion.]

epaulement *e-pōl'mənt*, (*ballet*) *n* a particular placing of a dancer's shoulders, one forward, one back. [Fr. *épaule*, shoulder — L. *spatula*.]

epaulette or (esp. in U.S.) **epaulet** *ep'əl-et*, *n* an ornament on the shoulder of the uniform of a military or naval officer (now disused in the British Army) or a lady's dress. [Fr. *épaulette* — *épaule*, the shoulder.]

epaxial *ep-aks'i-əl*, (*zool*) *adj* above the axis. [Gr. *epi*, on, over, and **axis**.]

épée *ā-pā'*, *n* a sharp-pointed, narrow-bladed sword, without a cutting edge, used for duelling, and, with a button on the point, for fencing practice. [Fr.]

epeirogenesis *ep-ī-rō-jen'i-sis*, (*geol*) *n* continent-building. — Also **epeirogeny** (*-roj'i-ni*). — *adj* **epeirogen'ic** or **epeirogenetic** (*-jin-et'ik*). [Gr. *ēpeiros*, mainland, *genesis*, formation.]

epergne *i-pûrn'*, *n* a branched ornamental centrepiece for the table. [Fr. *épargne* (saving), as used in phrases *taille* or *gravure d'épargne*, metal or etching with parts left in relief.]

epexegesis *ep-eks-i-jē'sis*, *n* the addition of words to make the sense more clear: — *pl* **epexegē'sēs**. — *adj* **epexeget'ic** (*ep-eks-i-jet'ik*) or **epexeget'ical**. — *adv* **epexeget'ically**. [Gr. *epexēgēsis* — *epi*, in addition, *exēgeesthai*, to explain.]

EPG *abbrev* for Eminent Persons' Group.

Eph. (*Bible*) *abbrev* for (the Letter to the) Ephesians.

epha or **ephah** *ē'fə*, *n* a Hebrew measure for dry goods. [Heb.; prob. of Egyptian origin.]

ephebe *ef-ēb'*, *n* in ancient Greece, a young male citizen from 18 to 20 years of age. — *adj* **ephēb'ic** pertaining to an ephebe; pertaining to the adult period in the life-history of an individual (*biol*). — *n* **ephēbophilia** (*-fil'*) sexual desire for youths or adolescents. [Gr. *ephēbos* — *epi*, upon, *hēbē*, early manhood.]

ephedra *ef'ed-rə*, *ef-ēd'rə* or *ef-ed'rə*, *n* a plant of a genus (*Ephedra*) of jointed, nearly leafless desert plants — the *sea-grape* — *n* **eph'edrine** (or *ef-ed'rin*) an alkaloid obtained from ephedra or produced synthetically, used in treating hay fever, asthma, etc. [Gr. *ephedrā*, horsetail.]

ephelis *e-fē'lis*, (*med*) *n* a freckle; a coloured patch on the skin: — *pl* **ephelides** (*e-fel'i-dēz* or *-fēl'*). [L., — Gr.]

ephemera *ef-em'ər-ə* or *-ēm'ər-ə*, *n* a member of a genus (*Ephemera*) of insects, the mayflies, whose adult life is very short; that which lasts a short time (but see also **ephemeron** below): — *pl* **ephem'eras** or **ephem'erae** (*-ē*). — *adj* **ephem'eral** existing only for a day; short-lived; fleeting. — *n* anything very short-lived. — *n* **ephemeral'ity**. — *n* **ephem'erid** an insect of the mayfly family, **Ephemeridae** (*-mer'i-dē*). — *n* **ephem'eris** an astronomical almanac tabulating the daily positions of the sun, moon, planets and certain stars, etc.: — *pl* **ephemerides** (*ef-e-mer'i-dēz*). — *n* **ephem'erist** someone who studies the daily motions of the planets; a student or collector of ephemera. — *n* **ephem'eron** an insect that lives only for a day; (usu. in *pl*) an object of limited worth or usefulness, having no lasting value; anything ephemeral: — *pl* **ephem'era**. [Gr. *ephēmeros*, living a day — *epi*, for, *hēmerā*, a day.]

Ephesian *ef-ē'zi-ən* or *-ē'zhən*, *adj* of or pertaining to *Ephesus*, ancient Greek city in modern Turkey. — *n* an inhabitant of Ephesus.

ephod *ef'od*, *n* a kind of linen surplice worn by the Jewish priests. [Heb. *ēphōd* — *āphad*, to put on.]

ephor *ef'ör* or *ef'ər*, *n* in ancient Greece, esp. Sparta, a class of powerful senior magistrates elected annually. — *n* **eph'oralty**. [Gr. — *epi*, upon, and root of *horaein*, to see.]

epi- *ep-i-* (or **ep-** *ep-* before a vowel or *h*) *pfx* signifying: above, over, upon, on, as in *epidermis*; in addition, after, as in *epiphenomenon*. [Gr. *epi*, on, over.]

epiblast *ep'i-bläst*, *n* the outer germinal layer of an embryo. — *adj* **epiblast'ic**. [Gr. *epi*, upon, *blastos*, a germ, shoot.]

epic *ep'ik*, *adj* applied to a long narrative poem that relates heroic events in an elevated style; characteristic of an epic poem; impressive; large-scale. — *n* an epic poem; epic poetry as a genre; a story comparable to that of an epic poem, esp. a long adventure novel or film. — *adj* **ep'ical**. — *adv* **ep'ically**. [Gr. *epikos* — *epos*, a word.]

epicalyx *ep-i-kāl'iks* or *-kal'*, (*bot*) *n* an apparent accessory calyx outside the true calyx, composed of bracts or of fused stipules of sepals. [Gr. *epi*, on, and **calyx**.]

epicanthus *ep-i-kan'thəs*, *n* a fold of skin over the inner canthus of the eye, characteristic of the Mongolian race. — *adj* **epican'thic**. [Gr. *epi*, on, and **canthus**.]

epicarp *ep'i-kärp*, (*bot*) *n* the outermost layer of the pericarp or fruit. [Gr. *epi*, upon, *karpos*, fruit.]

epicede *ep'i-sēd* or **epicedium** *ep-i-sē'di-əm* or *-dī'*, *n* a funeral ode: — *pl* **ep'icedes** or **epicē'dia**. — *adj* **epicē'dial** or **epicē'dian** elegiac. [L. *epicēdīum* — Gr. *epikēdeion* — *epi*, upon, *kēdos*, care.]

epicene *ep'i-sēn*, *adj* common to both sexes; having characteristics of both sexes, or neither; effeminate; of common gender (*gram*); sometimes restricted to those words that have one grammatical gender though used for both sexes. — Also *n*. [Gr. *epi*, upon, *koinos*, common.]

epicentre or in U.S. **epicenter** *ep'i-sen-tər*, *n* that point on the earth's surface directly over the point of origin of an earthquake. — Also *fig*. — *adj* **epicen'tral**. [Gr. *epi*, upon, over, *kentron*, a point.]

epiclesis *ep-i-klē'sis*, *n* in the Eastern church, an invocation of the Holy Spirit at the consecration of the elements (bread and wine): — *pl* **epiclē'sēs**. [Gr. *epiklēsis*, invocation — *epikalein*, to summon.]

epicondyle *ep-i-kon'dīl* or *-dil*, (*anat*) *n* the upper or proximal part of the condyle of the humerus or femur. — *n* **epicondylitis** (*-dil-ī'tis*) inflammation of an epicondyle; inflammation of the tissues beside the epicondyle of the humerus. [**epi-**.]

epicotyl *ep-i-kot'il*, (*bot*) *n* the stem of an embryo plant or seedling between the cotyledons and the next leaf. [Gr. *epi*, over, and **cotyledon**.]

epicritic *ep-i-krit'ik*, *adj* (of certain sensory nerve fibres in the skin) able to discriminate accurately between small degrees of sensation. [Gr. *epikritikos*, determining — *epi*, on, *krīnein*, to judge.]

epicure *ep'i-kūr*, *n* a person of refined and fastidious taste, esp. in food, wine, etc. — *adj* **Epicurē'an** pertaining to *Epicurus* (341–270 B.C.), the Greek philosopher, who taught that the real world is a chance composition of atoms or particles and that pleasure, controlled by social conventions, is the greatest good; (without *cap*) given to luxury, esp. refined luxury. — *n* a follower of Epicurus; (without *cap*) a hedonist, an epicure. — *n* **Epicurē'anism** the doctrines of Epicurus; attachment to these doctrines; epicurism. — *n* **ep'icurism** pursuit of pleasure; fastidiousness in luxury. [L. *Epicūrus* — Gr. *Epikouros*.]

epicuticle *ep-i-kū'ti-kəl*, (*biol*) *n* the waxy outermost layer of an insect's cuticle. — *adj* **epicūtic'ular**. [**epi-**.]

epicycle *ep'i-sī-kl*, *n* esp. in Ptolemaic astronomy, a circle whose centre is carried round the circumference of another circle; the circle on whose circumference is the point which describes an epicycloid. — *adj* **epicy'clic**. — *n* **epicy'cloid** a curve described by a point on the circumference of a circle rolling on the outside of the circumference of another circle. — *adj* **epicycloi'dal**. [Gr. *epi*, upon, *kyklos*, a circle.]

epideictic *ep-i-dīk'tik* or **epideictical** *ep-i-dīk'ti-kl*, *adj* done for show or display. [Gr. *epi*, upon, *deiknynai*, to show.]

epidemic *ep-i-dem'ik*, *adj* affecting a community at a certain time; prevalent. — *n* a disease that attacks great numbers in one place, at one time, and itself travels from place to place; a widespread outbreak. — *adj* **epidem'ical**. — *adv* **epidem'ically**. — *n* **epidemic'ity**. — *adj* **epidēmiolog'ical** pertaining to epidemiology. — *n* **epidēmiol'ogy** the science of epidemics, their occurrence, severity, distribution, etc. — *n* **epidēmiol'ogist**. [Gr. *epidēmos*, general — *epi*, among, *dēmos*, the people.]

epidendrum *ep-i-den'drəm*, *n* an orchid of a genus (*Epidendrum*) mainly growing on other plants (also **epiden'drone**). [Gr. *epi*, upon, *dendron*, tree.]

epidermis *ep-i-dûr'mis*, *n* cuticle, forming an external covering of a protective nature for the true skin or corium (*zool*); an outer sheath of close-set cells, usually one deep (*bot*). — *adj* **epider'mal**. — *adj* **epider'mic**. — *adj* **epiderm'oid**. — *n* **Epidermophyton** (*-mof'i-tən*) a genus of parasitic funguses, a cause of athlete's foot. — **epidermolysis bullosa** (*-mol'i-sis bŏŏ-lō'sə*) a mutilating and incapacitating hereditary skin disease in which the skin, on slight contact, readily becomes covered with blisters (abbrev. **EB**). [Gr. *epidermis* — *epi*, upon, *derma*, the skin.]

epidiascope *ep-i-dī'ə-skōp*, *n* an optical device for projecting images of objects whether opaque or transparent. [Gr. *epi*, upon, *dia*, through, *skopeein*, to look at.]

epididymis *ep-i-did'i-mis*, *n* a mass of sperm-carrying tubes at the back of the testis: — *pl* **epididymides** (*ep-i-did'i-mi-dēz* or *ep-i-dī-dim'i-dēz*). [Gr., — *epi*, on, *didymos*, a testicle, twin.]

epidural *ep-i-dūr'əl*, *adj* situated on, or administered outside, the lowest portion of the spinal canal. — *n* short for **epidural anaesthetic**, the epidural injection of an anaesthetic, esp. in childbirth. — **epidural anaesthesia** loss of painful sensation in the lower part of the body produced by injecting an anaesthetic into the lowest portion of the spinal canal. [Gr. *epi*, upon, and **dura (mater)**.]

epifocal *ep-i-fō'kl*, *adj* epicentral.

epigastrium *ep-i-gas'tri-əm*, *n* the part of the abdomen extending from the sternum towards the navel — the pit of the stomach. — *adj* **epigas'tric**. [Gr. *epi*, upon, *gastēr*, the stomach.]

epigeal *ep-i-jē'əl*, **epigeous** *ep-i-jē'əs* or **epigean** *ep-i-jē'ən*, *adj* growing or living close to the ground; with cotyledons above ground. [Gr. *epigaios*, *epigeios* — *epi*, on, *gaia*, *gē*, earth.]

epigene *ep'i-jēn*, (*geol*) *adj* acting or taking place at the earth's surface. [Fr. *épigène* — Gr. *epigenēs*, born after, but understood as meaning born or originating on — Gr. *epi*, on, after.]

epiglottis *ep-i-glot'is*, *n* a cartilaginous flap over the glottis. — *adj* **epiglott'ic**. [Gr. *epiglōttis* — *epi*, over, *glōttis*, glottis.]

epigon *ep'i-gon* or **epigone** *ep'i-gōn*, *n* one of a later generation; (usu. in *pl*) a son or successor; an inferior follower or imitator: — *pl* **ep'igons, ep'igones** (*-gōnz*) or (often with *cap*) **epig'onī**. [Gr. *epi*, after, *gonē*, birth.]

epigram *ep'i-gram*, *n* any concise and pointed or sarcastic saying; a short poem expressing an ingenious thought with point, usually satirical. — *adj* **epigrammatic** (*-grəm-at'ik*) or **epigrammat'ical** relating to or dealing in epigrams; like an epigram; concise and pointed. — *adv* **epigrammat'ically**. — *vt* **epigramm'atise** or **-ize** to make an epigram on. — *n* **epigramm'atist** a writer of epigrams. [Gr. *epigramma* — *epi*, upon, *gramma*, a writing.]

epigraph *ep'i-gräf*, *n* an inscription, esp. on a building; a citation or motto at the beginning of a book or section of a book. — *vt* to provide with an epigraph. — *n* **epigrapher** (*ep-ig'rə-fər*) or **epig'raphist**. — *adj* **epigraphic** (*-graf'ik*). — *n* **epig'raphy**. [Gr. *epigraphē* — *epi*, upon, *graphein*, to write.]

epilate *ep'i-lāt*, *vt* to remove (hair) by any method. — *n* **epilā'tion**. — *n* **ep'ilator**. [Fr. *épiler* — L. *ex*, from, *pilus*, hair.]

epilepsy *ep'i-lep-si*, *n* a chronic functional disease of the nervous system, shown by recurring attacks of sudden insensibility or impairment of consciousness, commonly accompanied by convulsive seizures. — *adj* **epilep'tic**. — *n* an epileptic patient. [Gr. *epilēpsiā* — *epi*, upon, and root of *lambanein*, to seize.]

epilimnion *ep-i-lim'ni-ən*, *n* the upper, warm layer of water in a lake. [Gr. *epi*, upon, *limnion*, dimin. of *limnē*, a lake.]

epilogue, in U.S. also **epilog** *ep'i-log*, *n* the concluding section of a book, etc.; a short poem or speech at the end of a play; the actor giving the epilogue; the conclusion (usu. religious) of a day's radio or TV programmes. — *adj* **epilogic** (*-loj'ik*). — adj **epilogis'tic**. [Fr., — L. *epilogus* — Gr. *epilogos*, conclusion — *epi*, upon, *legein*, to speak.]

epinasty *ep'i-nas-ti*, (*bot*) *n* the curving downwards of an organ, caused by a more active growth on its upper side (opp. to *hyponasty*). — *adj* **epinas'tic**. — *adv* **epinas'tically**. [Gr. *epi*, upon, *nastos*, pressed close.]

epinephrine *ep-i-nef'rin* or *-rēn*, *n* (esp. in U.S.) adrenaline. [Gr. *epi*, upon, *nephros*, kidney.]

epiphany *e-pif'ə-ni*, *n* (with *cap*) a church festival celebrated on 6 January, in commemoration of the manifestation of Christ to the wise men of the East; the manifestation of a god; a usu. sudden revelation or insight into the nature, essence or meaning of something. — *adj* **epiphanic** (*-fan'*). [Gr. *epiphaneia*, appearance.]

epiphenomenon *ep-i-fin-om'ən-ən*, *n* an accompanying phenomenon, a fortuitous, less important, or irrelevant by-product; something appearing after, a secondary symptom of a disease (*pathol*): — *pl* **epiphenom'ena**. — *n* **epiphenom'enalism** interpretation of mind as an epiphenomenon upon the physical. — *n* and *adj* **epiphenom'enalist.** [Gr. *epi*, after, *phainomenon*, neut. pres. p. pass. of *phainein*, to show.]

epiphragm *ep'i-fram*, *n* the disc with which certain molluscs close the aperture of their shell. [Gr. *epiphragma*, covering.]

epiphysis *ep-if'i-sis*, *n* any portion of a bone having its own centre of ossification; the pineal gland (*epiphysis cerebri*): — *pl* **epiph'ysēs.** — *adj* **epiphyseal** (*ep-i-fiz'i-əl*). [Gr., excrescence.]

epiphyte *ep'i-fīt*, *n* a plant growing on another plant, without being parasitic; a vegetable parasite on the surface of an animal (*pathol*). — *adj* **epiphyt'al, epiphytic** (*-fit'ik*) or **epiphyt'ical.** — *n* **ep'i-phytism** (or *-fīt'*). [Gr. *epi*, upon, *phyton*, a plant.]

Epis. *abbrev* for: Episcopal (also **Episc.**); Epistle (also **Ep.**; *Bible*).

episcopacy *e-pis'kə-pəs-i*, *n* church government by bishops; the office of a bishop; a bishop's period of office; the bishops, as a class. — *adj* **epis'copal** governed by bishops; belonging to or vested in bishops. — *adj* **episcopā'lian** pertaining to bishops or to an episcopal church; pertaining to government by bishops. — *n* a person who belongs to an episcopal (especially Anglican) church. — *n* **episcopā'lian-ism** or **epis'copalism** episcopalian government and doctrine. — *adv* **epis'copally.** — *n* **epis'copate** a bishopric; the office of a bishop; a bishop's period of office; the order of bishops. [Gr. *episkopos*, an overseer.]

episcope *ep'i-skōp*, *n* an optical device for projecting images of opaque objects. [Gr. *epi*, on, over, *skopeein*, to look.]

episemon *ep-i-sē'mon*, *n* a badge or characteristic device; one of three obsolete Greek letters. — *adj* **episēmat'ic** (*zool*) serving for recognition. [Gr. *episēmon*, a badge — *epi*, on, *sēma*, a sign.]

episiotomy *ep-iz-i-ot'ə-mi*, (*med*) *n* an incision made in the perineum to facilitate delivery of a foetus. [Gr. *epision*, pubic region, and **-tomy**.]

episode *ep'i-sōd*, *n* a story introduced into a narrative or poem to give variety; an interesting or distinctive incident or occurrence; an occurrence, esp. when one of a series of similar occurrences; a passage affording relief from the principal subject (*mus*); an incident or period detachable from a novel, play, etc.; a part of a radio or television serial which is broadcast at one time. — *adj* **episodic** (*-sod'*) or **episod'ical** pertaining to or contained in an episode; brought in as a digression; having many episodes; sporadic, occurring at intervals. — *adv* **episod'ically** by way of episode; incidentally. [Gr. *epeisodion* — *epi*, upon, *eisodos*, a coming in.]

episome *ep'i-sōm*, (*biol*) *n* a genetically active particle found esp. in bacteria, able to exist and multiply either independently or integrated in a chromosome. [**epi-**, and *-some*, — Gr. *sōma*, body.]

epistaxis *ep-i-stak'sis*, (*med*) *n* bleeding from the nose. [Gr. *epistazein*, to shed in drops.]

epistemology *ep-is-tə-mol'ə-ji*, *n* the theory of knowledge. — *adj* **epistē'mic** relating to knowledge, epistemology or epistemics. — *nsing* **epistē'mics** the scientific study of knowledge, its acquisition and its communication. — *adj* **epistemological** (*-ə-loj'*). — *n* **epistemol'ogist.** [Gr. *epistēmē*, knowledge, *logos*, discourse.]

epistle *i-pis'l*, *n* something written and sent to someone, a letter; esp. a letter to an individual or church from an apostle, such as the N.T. Epistles of Paul; the extract from one of the apostolical epistles read as part of the communion service; a verse composition in letter form. — *n* **epistoler** (*i-pist'ə-lər*) a person who reads the liturgical epistle in the communion service. — *adj* **epis'tolary, epis'to-latory** or **epistolic** (*ep-is-tol'ik*) pertaining to or consisting of epistles or letters; suitable in or for an epistle; contained in letters. [O.Fr., — L. *epistola* — Gr. *epistolē* — *epi*, on the occasion of, *stellein*, to send.]

epistrophe *e-pis'trə-fē*, *n* the ending of successive clauses with the same word; a refrain in music. [Gr. *epistrophē*, a return — *epi*, upon, *strephein*, to turn.]

epistyle *ep'i-stīl*, *n* an architrave. [Gr. *epi*, upon, *stȳlos*, a pillar.]

epitaph *ep'i-täf*, *n* a tombstone inscription; a composition in the form of a tombstone inscription. — *adj* **epitaph'ic.** — *n* **ep'itaphist** a composer of epitaphs. [Gr. *epitaphion* — *epi*, upon, *taphos*, a tomb.]

epitaxy *ep'i-tak-si*, (*crystall*) *n* the growth of a thin layer of crystals on another crystal so that they have the same structure. — *adj* **epitax'ial.** [Gr. *epi*, on, *taxis*, arrangement.]

epithalamium *ep-i-thə-lā'mi-əm* or **epithalamion** *-lā'mi-on*, *n* a song or poem in celebration of a marriage: — *pl* **epithalā'mia.** — *adj* **epithalam'ic.** [L. *epithalamium*, Gr. *epithalamion* — *epi*, upon, *thalamos*, a bride-chamber.]

epithelium *ep-i-thē'li-əm*, *n* the cell-tissue that covers the outer surface of the body and the mucous membranes connected with it, and also the closed cavities of the body. — *adj* **epithē'lial.** — *n* **epithēliō'ma** carcinoma of the skin: — *pl* **epi-thēliō'mas** or **epithelio'mata** (*-mə-tə*). — *adj* **epithēliō'matous.** [N.L., — Gr., *epi*, upon, *thēlē*, nipple.]

epithet *ep'i-thet*, *n* an adjective or adjectival phrase expressing some quality of the person or thing to which it is applied; a descriptive term. — *adj* **epithet'ic** pertaining to an epithet; having or using many epithets. [Gr. *epitheton*, neut. of *epithetos*, added — *epi*, on, *tithenai*, to place.]

epitome *i-pit'ə-mē*, *n* an abridgment or short summary of e.g. a book; a small embodiment; a typical example; a personification. — *adj* **epitomic** (*ep-i-tom'ik*) or **epitom'ical.** — *vt* **epit'omise** or **-ize** to make an epitome of; to shorten; to condense; to typify; to personify. — *n* **epit'omiser** or **-z-**, or **epit'omist** a person who abridges. — **in epitome** on a small scale. [Gr. *epi*, upon, *tomē*, a cut.]

epitrite *ep'i-trīt*, (*prosody*) *n* a foot made up of three long syllables and one short. [Gr. *epitrītos* — *epi*, in addition to, *tritos*, third.]

epizoon *ep-i-zō'on*, *n* an animal that lives on the surface of another animal, whether parasitically or commensally: — *pl* **epizō'a.** — *adj* and *n* **epizō'an.** — *adj* **epizō'ic** dwelling on an animal; having seeds dispersed by animals. — *adj* **epizootic** (*ep-i-zō-ot'ik*) pertaining to epizoa; affecting animals as an epidemic affects humans. — *n* an epizootic disease. — *nsing* **epizōot'ics** the science or study of epidemic animal diseases. [Gr. *epi*, upon, *zōion*, an animal.]

EPNS *abbrev* for electroplated nickel silver.

EPO *abbrev* for European Patent Office.

epoch *ēp'ok* or *ep'ok*, *n* a point of time fixed or made remarkable by some great event from which dates are reckoned; the particular time, used as a point of reference, at which the data had the values in question (*astron*); a planet's heliocentric longitude at the epoch (*astron*); a precise date; a time from which a new state of things dates; an age (geological, historical, etc.). — *adj* **epochal** (*ep'ok-l*). — *adj* **ep'och-māking** important enough to be considered as beginning a new age. — *adj* **ep'och-marking.** [Gr. *epochē* — *epechein*, to stop, take up a position.]

EPOCH *abbrev* for End Physical Punishment of Children.

epode *ep'ōd*, *n* a kind of lyric poem in which a longer verse is followed by a shorter one; the last part of a lyric ode, sung after the strophe and antistrophe. — *adj* **epodic** (*-od'ik*). [Gr. *epōidos* — *epi*, on, *ōidē*, an ode.]

eponychium *ep-o-nik'i-əm*, *n* a narrow band of cuticle over the base of a nail. [Gr. *epi*, on, *onyx*, *onychos*, nail.]

eponym *ep'ə-nim*, *n* a person, real or mythical, from whose name another name, esp. a place name, is derived; the name so derived; a character who gives a play, etc., its title. — *adj* **eponymous** (*i-pon'i-məs*). [Gr. *epōnymos*, eponymous — *epi*, upon, to, *onyma*, *onoma*, a name.]

epopee *ep'o-pē*, *n* epic poetry; an epic poem. [Gr. *epopoiiā* — *epos*, a word, an epic poem, *poieein*, to make.]

EPOS *abbrev* for electronic point of sale.

epoxy *e-pok'si*, *adj* containing oxygen bound to two other atoms, often carbon, which are already attached in some way. — *n* an epoxy resin. — *n* **epox'ide** an epoxy compound. — **epoxy (**or **epoxide) resins** synthetic polymers used as structural plastics, surface coatings, adhesives and for encapsulating and embedding electronic components.

EPP *abbrev* for European People's Party.

EPROM (*comput*) *abbrev* for: electrically programmable read-only memory; erasable programmable read-only memory.

EPS or **eps** (*stock exchange*) *abbrev* for earnings per share.

epsilon *ep-sī'lən* or *ep'si-lon*, *n* the fifth letter (E, ε) of the Greek alphabet, short e. [Gr. *e psīlon*, bare or mere e.]

epsomite *ep'səm-īt*, *n* a mineral, hydrated magnesium sulphate. — **Epsom salt** or **salts** a purgative medicine of similar composition, orig. from the springs at Epsom, in Surrey — used also in dyeing, etc.

Epstein-Barr virus *ep-stīn-bär' vī'rəs*, *n* a virus which causes glandular fever and which is thought to be associated with various human cancers. [M.A. *Epstein* and Y.M. *Barr*, British virologists, who first isolated it in 1964.]

EPT *abbrev* for Environmental Protection Technology.

EPU *abbrev* for European Payments Union.

epyllion *e-pil'i-ən*, *n* a poem with some resemblance to an epic but shorter. [Gr.; dimin. of *epos*, word.]

equable *ek'wə-bl*, *adj* even, uniform; smooth; without great variations or extremes; even-tempered. — *n* **equabil'ity** or **e'quableness**. — *adv* **e'quably**. [L. *aequābilis* — *aequus*, equal.]

equal *ē'kwəl*, *adj* identical in quantity; of the same value; adequate; in just proportion; fit; equable; uniform; equitable; evenly balanced; just; equally developed on each side (*bot*). — *n* one of the same age, rank, etc. — *vt* to be, or to make, equal to; to reach the same level as (*bot*): — *pr p* **e'qualling**; *pa t* and *pa p* **e'qualled**. — *n* **equalisā'tion** or **-z-** the act of making equal; the state of being equalised. — *vt* **e'qualise** or **-ize** to make equal or uniform. — *vi* to become equal; to make one's score equal to one's opponent's. — *n* **equalī'ser** or **-z-** a person or thing that equalises; a score that makes both sides alike; see also **graphic equaliser**. — *adj* **equalitār'ian** (*-kwol-*) of or pertaining to the equality of mankind. — *n* a person who believes in or favours political and social equality of mankind. — *n* **equalitā'rianism**. — *n* **equality** (*ē-kwol'i-ti*) the condition of being equal; sameness; evenness. — *adv* **equally** (*ē'kwə-li*). — *n* **e'qualness**. — **equal opportunities** (in employment, etc.) the avoidance of any discrimination between applicants, etc. on the grounds of sex, race, etc.; **equal (**or **equals) sign** the symbol =, which indicates that two (numerical) values are equal; **equal temperament** see **temperament**. — **equal to the occasion** fit or able to cope with an emergency. [L. *aequālis*, equal, *aequāre*, *-ātum*, to make equal — *aequus*, equal.]

equanimity *e-kwə-nim'i-ti* or *ē-kwə-*, *n* evenness of mind or temper. — *adj* **equanimous** (*i-kwan'i-məs*). — *adv* **equan'imously**. [L. *aequanimitās* — *aequus*, equal, *animus*, the mind.]

equate *ē-kwāt'* or *i-*, *vt* to reduce to an average or to a common standard of comparison; to state as equal; to regard as equal. — *vi* to be, or be regarded, treated, etc. as, equal. — *n* **equation** (*i-kwā'zhən* or *-shən*) the act of making equal; a statement of the equality of two quantities; reduction to a common standard; correction to compensate for an error, irregularity or discrepancy; the quantity added for this purpose; a formula expressing a chemical action and the proportions of the substances involved. — **personal equation** a correction to be applied to the reading of an instrument on account of the observer's tendency to read too high, too low, etc.; any tendency to error or prejudice due to personal characteristics for which allowance must be made. [L. *aequāre*, *-ātum*, to make equal.]

equator *i-kwā'tər*, *n* an imaginary great circle passing round the middle of the globe and equidistant from the North and South poles; the corresponding circle of another body; the imaginary great circle in which the plane of the earth's equator intersects the celestial sphere (so called because day and night are equal when the sun reaches it); the middle belt or line of any globular or nearly globular body that has some sort of polarity. — *adj* **equatorial** (*ek-wə-tö'ri-əl* or *ēk-*) of, pertaining to, of the nature of, or in the neighbourhood of, an equator. — *n* a telescope mounted on an axis, capable of moving parallel to the equator and so following a star in any part of its diurnal course. — *adv* **equato'rially** so as to have motion or direction parallel to the equator. [See **equal**.]

equerry *ek'wə-ri* or *ik-wer'i*, *n* an official in attendance upon a prince or personage. [Fr. *écurie* — L.L. *scūria*, a stable.]

equestrian *i-kwes'tri-ən*, *adj* pertaining to horsemanship; on horseback. — *n* a horse-rider; a performer on horseback: — *fem* (sham Fr.) **equestrienne'**. — *n* **eques'trianism** horsemanship. [L. *equester*, *equestris* — *eques*, a horseman — *equus*, a horse.]

equi- *ē-kwi-* or *ek- wi-*, *pfx* signifying equal. [L. *aequus*.]

equiangular *ē-kwi-ang'gū-lər*, *adj* having equal angles. — *n* **equiangular'ity**. [**equi-**.]

Equidae *ek'wi-dē*, *npl* a family of hoofed mammals consisting of the genus **Eq'uus** (horse, ass, zebra) and various fossil forms. [L. *equus*, horse.]

equidistant *ē-kwi-dis'tənt*, *adj* equally distant. — *n* **equidis'tance**. — *adv* **equidis'tantly**. [**equi-** and **distant**.]

equilateral *ē-kwi-lat'ə-rəl*, *adj* having all sides equal. [**equi-** and L. *latus*, *-eris*, side.]

equilibrium *ēk-* or *ek-wi-lib'ri-əm*, *n* balance; the state of even balance; a state in which opposing forces or tendencies neutralise each other. — *vt* and *vi* **equilibrate** (*ēk-wi-līb'rāt*, *-lib'rāt*, or *ē-kwil'*) to balance; to counterpoise. — *n* **equilibrā'tion**. — *n* **equil'ibrator** (or *ē-kwi-lī'brāt-ər*) a balancing or stability device, esp. an aeroplane fin. — *n* **equil'ibrist** (or *-lib'*, or *-līb'*) someone who does balancing tricks. — *n* **equilib'rity**. [L. *aequilībrium* — *aequus*, equal, *lībra*, balance.]

equine *e'kwin* or *ē'kwīn*, also **equinal** *e-* or *ē-kwīn'əl*, *adj* pertaining to, or of the nature of, a horse or horses. [L. *equīnus* — *equus*, a horse.]

equinox *ek'wi-* or *ēk'wi-noks*, *n* the time when the sun crosses the equator, making the night equal in length to the day, about 21 March and 23 September; an equinoctial point. — *adj* **equinoc'tial** pertaining to the equinoxes, the time of the equinoxes, or to the regions about the equator. — *n* the celestial equator or **equinoctial line**. — *adv* **equinoc'tially** in the direction of the equinox. — **equinoctial gales** high gales popularly supposed to prevail about the times of the equinoxes — the belief is unsupported by observation; **equinoctial point** either of the two points in the heavens where the equinoctial line cuts the ecliptic; **equinoctial year** see **astronomical year** under **year**. [L. *aequus*, equal, *nox*, *noctis*, night.]

equip *i-kwip'*, *vt* to fit out; to furnish with everything needed: — *pr p* **equipp'ing**; *pa t* and *pa p* **equipped'**. — *n* **equipage** (*ek'wi-pāj*) a carriage and attendants; retinue. — *n* **equip'ment** the act of equipping; the state of being equipped; things used in equipping or furnishing; outfit; a set of tools, etc. [Fr. *équiper*, prob. — O.N. *skipa*, to set in order — *skip*, a ship.]

équipe *ā-kēp*, (Fr.) *n* (in motor-racing and other sport) a team.

equipoise *ek'wi-poiz*, *n* a state of balance; a counterpoise. — *vt* to balance; to counterpoise. [L. *aequus*, equal, and **poise**.]

equipollent *ē-kwi-* or *e-kwi-pol'ənt*, *adj* having equal power or force; equivalent. — *n* an equivalent. — *n* **equipoll'ence** or **equipoll'ency**. [L. *aequus*, equal, *pollēns*, *pollentis*, pres. p. of *pollēre*, to be strong, able.]

equiponderate *ē-* or *e-kwi-pon'dər-āt*, *vi* to be equal in weight; to balance. — *adj* (*-ət*) equal in weight. — *n* **equipon'derance**. — *adj* **equipon'derant**. [L. *aequus*, equal, *pondus*, *ponderis*, weight.]

equipotential *ē-kwi-pə-ten'shl*, *adj* of equal power, capability, potential or potentiality.

equisetum *ek-wi-sē'təm*, *n* a plant of the only surviving genus (*Equisetum*) of the family **Equisetā'ceae**, stiff herbaceous plants with almost leafless articulated and whorled stems and branches — also called *horsetail*. [L. *equus*, a horse, *sēta*, a bristle.]

equitation *ek-wi-tā'shən*, *n* the art of riding on horseback. [L. *equitāre*, to ride — *equus*, a horse.]

equity *ek'wi-ti*, *n* right as founded on the laws of nature; moral justice, of which laws are the imperfect expression; the spirit of justice which enables us to interpret laws rightly; fairness; an equitable right; the value of property in excess of any charges upon it (*US*); (in *pl*) ordinary shares; (with *cap*) the trade union for the British acting profession. — *adj* **eq'uitable** possessing or showing or in accordance with equity; held or exercised in equity. — *n* **eq'uitableness**. — *adv* **eq'uitably**. [O.Fr. *equité* — L. *aequitās*, *-ātis* — *aequus*, equal.]

equivalent *i-kwiv'ə-lənt*, *adj* equal in value, power, meaning, etc.; interchangeable; of like combining value (*chem*). — *n* a thing equivalent; an equivalent weight (*chem*). — *n* **equiv'alence** or **equiv'alency**. — *adv* **equiv'alently**. — **equivalent weight** (*chem*) that weight which displaces or combines with or otherwise represents a standard unit — atomic weight, or atomic weight divided by valence. [Fr., — L. *aequus*, equal, *valēns*, *valentis*, pres. p. of *valēre*, to be worth.]

equivocal *i-kwiv'ə-kl*, *adj* capable of meaning two or more things; of doubtful meaning; capable of a double explanation; suspicious; questionable. — *adv* **equiv'ocally**. — *n* **equivocal'ity**. — *n* **equiv'ocalness**. — *vi* **equiv'ocāte** to use equivocal or doubtful words in order to mislead. — *n* **equivocā'tion**. — *n* **equiv'ocātor**. — *adj* **equiv'ocatory** containing or characterised by equivocation. [L. *aequus*, equal, and *vōx*, *vōcis*, the voice, a word.]

Equus. See under **Equidae**.

ER *abbrev* for: *Edwardus Rex* (N.L.), King Edward; *Elizabeth Regina* (N.L.), Queen Elizabeth (**EIIR** Queen Elizabeth II).

Er (*chem*) *symbol* for erbium.

er *ûr*, *interj* expressing hesitation.

-er[1] *-ər*, *sfx* which marks the agent (person or thing), designating persons according to occupation (e.g. writ*er*), or place of abode (e.g. London*er*). [O.E. *-ere*; some similar words, e.g. groc*er*, offic*er*, are from Fr. *-ier* (L. *-arius*).]

-er[2] *-ər*, *sfx* which marks the comparative degree of adjectives (long*er*) and some adverbs (fast*er*). [O.E. *-ra* (*adj*), *-or* (*adv*).]

ERA *abbrev* for Equal Rights Amendment.

era *ē'rə*, *n* a series of years reckoned from a particular point, or that point itself; an important date; an age; a main division of geological time. [L.L. *aera*, a number, orig. counters, pieces of copper used in counting, pl. of *aes*, copper.]

eradiate *i-* or *ē-rā'di-āt*, *vt* and *vi* to shoot out like a ray of light. — *n* **eradiā'tion**. [L. *ē-*, from, *radius*, a ray.]

eradicate *i-rad'i-kāt*, *vt* to destroy, get rid of; to root out; to pull up by the roots. — *adj* **erad'icable**. — *n* **eradicā'tion**. — *adj* **erad'icātive**. — *n* **erad'icātor**. [L. *ērādīcāre*, *-ātum*, to root out — *ē*, from, *rādīx*, *-īcis*, a root.]

erase *i-rāz'*, *vt* to rub or scrape out; to efface; to destroy; to destroy a recording on audio or video tape; to replace the data of a storage area with characters representing zero (*comput*). — *adj* **erā'sable**. — *n* **erā'ser** someone who, or that which, erases (e.g. *ink-eraser*). — *n* **era'sure** (*-zhər*) the act of erasing; a rubbing out; scraping away; the place where something written has been rubbed out. [L. *ērādere* — *ē*, from, *rādere*, *rāsum*, to scrape.]

Erato *er'ə-tō*, (*Gr mythol*) *n* the Muse of amatory lyric poetry. [Gr. *Eratō*.]

erbium *ûr'bi-əm*, *n* a rare metal (atomic no. 68; symbol **Er**), found in gadolinite, at Ytt*erby*, near Stockholm.

ere *ār*, (*literary*) *adv*, *prep* and *conj* before. — **ere long** before long; soon; **ere now** before this time. [O.E. *ǣr*.]

erect *i-rekt'*, *adj* upright; directed upward; right end up, not inverted; not decumbent (*bot*); turgid and raised (*zool*). — *vt* to set upright; to set erect; to set at right angles; to raise; to build. — *n* **erect'er** or **erect'or** someone who, or that which, erects or raises; a muscle which assists in erecting a part or an organ; an attachment to a compound microscope for making the image erect instead of inverted. — *adj* **erect'ile** (*-īl*) that may be erected. — *n* **erectility** (*e-* or *ē-rek-til'i-ti*). — *n* **erec'tion** the act of erecting; the state of being erected; anything erected; a building of any kind; an enlarging and hardening of the penis usu. in response to sexual stimulation. — *adj* **erect'ive** tending to erect. — *adv* **erect'ly**. — *n* **erect'ness**. [L. *ērigĕre*, *ērēctum*, to set upright — *ē*, from, *regĕre*, to direct.]

eremite *er'i-mīt*, *n* a recluse who lives apart, esp. from religious motives; a hermit. — *adj* **eremitic** (*-mit'ik*) or **eremit'ical**. — *n* **er'emītism**. [L.L. *erēmīta* — Gr. *erēmītēs* — *erēmos*, desert.]

erepsin *e-rep'sin*, *n* an enzyme of the small intestine, acting upon casein, gelatine, etc. [L. *ēripĕre*, *ēreptum* — *ē*, from, *rapĕre*, to snatch.]

erethism *er'e-thizm*, *n* excitement or stimulation of an organ; abnormal irritability. — *adj* **erethis'mic**. — *adj* **erethis'tic**. — *adj* **erethit'ic**. [Gr. *erethismos*.]

erf *ûrf*, (*SAfr*) *n* a garden plot or small piece of ground: — *pl* **er'ven**. [Du.]

erg[1] *ûrg*, *n* the unit of work in the centimetre-gram-second system — that is, the quantity of work done when the point of operation of a force of one dyne is allowed to move one centimetre in the direction of the force. [Gr. *ergon*, work.]

erg[2] *ûrg*, *n* a Saharan area of shifting sand dunes: — *pl* **ar'eg** or **ergs**. [Fr. — Ar. *'irj*.]

ergo *ûr'gō*, (*logic*) *adv* therefore (used to introduce the conclusion of a syllogism). [L. *ergō*, therefore.]

ergonomics *ûr-gə-nom'iks*, *nsing* the study of people in relation to their working environment; the adaptation of machines and general conditions to fit individuals so that they may work at maximum efficiency. — *adj* **ergonom'ic**. — *adv* **ergonom'ically**. — *n* **ergon'omist**. [Gr. *ergon*, work.]

ergosterol. See **ergot**.

ergot *ûr'got*, *n* a disease of grasses (esp. rye) and sedges; a seed so diseased. — *n* **ergos'terol** an unsaturated sterol obtained from ergot. — *n* **er'gotism** poisoning caused by eating bread made of rye diseased with ergot. [Fr.]

ERI *abbrev* for *Edwardus Rex Imperator* (N.L.), Edward, King (and) Emperor.

erica *er'i-kə*, *n* any plant of the heath genus (*Erica*). — *adj* **ericaceous** (*er-i-kā'shəs*) pertaining to plants of the genus *Erica*, or its family **Ericā'ceae**; heathlike. [L., — Gr. *ereikē*, heath.]

erigeron *e-rij'ə-ron*, *n* any member of the flea-bane genus (*Erigeron*) of composite plants. [Gr. *ērigerōn*, groundsel — *ēri*, early, *gerōn*, old.]

erio- *er-i-ō-* or *-o-*, *combining form* denoting wool or fibre. — *n* **er'ionite** a mineral which occurs in white wool-like crystals. [Gr. *erion*, wool.]

eristic *er-is'tik* or **eristical** *er-is'ti-kl*, *adj* of or pertaining to controversy or disputatious reasoning. [Gr. *eristikos* — *eris*, strife.]

erk *ûrk*, (*airmen's slang*) *n* an aircraftsman. [From *airk*, for aircraftsman.]

ERM *abbrev* for exchange rate mechanism.

ermine *ûr'min*, *n* the stoat; a white fur, the stoat's winter coat in northern lands, used for the robes of judges and magistrates with the black tail-tip (or an imitation) attached. [O.Fr. *ermine* (Fr. *hermine*).]

erne *ûrn*, *n* an eagle, esp. the sea eagle (*Haliaetus albicilla*). [O.E. *earn*.]

Ernie *ûr'ni*, *n* the computer which picks, by methods that allow full scope for chance, numbers to be used as winning numbers on premium bonds. [Abbrev. of *e*lectronic *r*andom *n*umber *i*ndicator *e*quipment.]

erode *i-* or *e-rōd'*, *vt* to eat away, wear away; to form by wearing away. — Also *vi*. — *adj* and *n* **erō'dent** caustic. [L. *ē*, from, *rōdĕre*, *rōsum*, to gnaw.]

erodium *e-rō'di-əm*, *n* any plant of the stork's-bill genus (*Erodium*) of the geranium family. [Gr. *erōdios*, a heron.]

erogenic *e-rō-jen'ik* or **erogenous** *e-roj'ən-əs*, *adj* producing erotic desire or gratification. [**Eros**.]

Eros *ēr'os* (properly in Gr. *er-ōs*) or *er'os*, *n* the Greek love-god, identified by the Romans with Cupid; a minor planet discovered in 1898, notable for its near approach to the earth. [Gr. *Erōs*, *-ōtos*.]

erotic *e-rot'ik*, *adj* pertaining to sexual love; amatory; amorous. — *npl* **erot'ica** erotic literature or works of art. — *n* **erot'icism** (*-sizm*) or **er'otism** amorous temperament or habit; sexual desire or excitement; the manifestations of sex in its widest application. — *n* **erot'icist**. — *adj* **erotogenic** (*er-ət-ō-jen'ik*) or **erotogenous** (*-oj'*) producing erotic desire or gratification. — *n* **erōtomā'nia** unhealthily strong sexual passion. — *n* **erōtomā'niac**. — *n* **erōtophō'bia** fear of or aversion to any form of sexual involvement. [Gr. *Erōs*, *-ōtos*, the Greek love-god.]

erosion *i-rō'zhən*, *n* eating away, wearing down; the denuding action of weathering, water, ice, wind, etc. (*geol*). — *adj* **erosive** (*i-rō'ziv*). [See **erode**.]

err *ûr*, *vi* to miss the mark; to be inaccurate; to make a mistake; to sin: — *pr p* **erring** (*ûr'ing* or *er'ing*); *pa t* and *pa p* **erred** (*ûrd*). [L. *errāre*, to stray.]

errand *er'ənd*, *n* a commission to say or do something, usually involving a short journey. — **err'and-boy** or **err'and-girl**. — **a fool's errand** a futile journey; **run errands** to be sent to convey messages or perform small pieces of business. [O.E. *ǣrende*, a mission.]

errant *er'ənt*, *adj* wandering; roving; quixotic; erring. — *n* **err'antry** an errant or wandering state; a rambling about like a knight-errant. [M.E. *erraunt* — O.Fr. pres. p. of *errer*, to travel (— L.L. *iterāre*), confused with pres. p. of *errer*, to err (— L. *errāre*).]

erratic *e-ra'tik*, *adj* wandering; having no certain course; not stationary; irregular, capricious, irregular or unpredictable in behaviour. — *n* an erratic block or boulder. — *adv* **errat'ically**. — **erratic block** a mass of rock transported by ice and deposited at a distance. [L. *errāticus* — *errāre*, to stray.]

erratum *e-rä'tum* or *-rā'*, *n* an error in writing or printing, esp. one noted in a list in a book: — *pl* **erra'ta**. [L. — past p. of *errāre*.]

erron. *abbrev* for erroneously.

erroneous *i-rō'ni-əs*, *adj* erring; full of errors; wrong; mistaken. — *adv* **errō'neously**. — *n* **errō'neousness**. [M.E. — L. *errōneus* — *errāre*, to stray.]

error *er'ər*, *n* mistaken opinion; the difference between a quantity obtained by observation and the true value; a blunder or mistake; wrongdoing. [M.E. — L. (see ety. for **err**).]

ersatz *er'zats*, *ûr'-* or *er-zats'*, *n* a substitute. — *adj* substitute; fake. [Ger.]

Erse *ers* or *ûrs*, *n* originally, and still by some, used for Scottish Gaelic; now, by many, used for Irish Gaelic (as opp. to Scottish Gaelic). [Variant of **Irish**.]

erst *ûrst*, *adv* at first; formerly. — *adv* **erst'while** or **erstwhile'** formerly. — *adj* former. [O.E. *ǣrest*, superl. of *ǣr*; see **ere**.]

erubescent *er-ōō-bes'ənt*, *adj* growing red; blushing. — *n* **erubesc'ence** or **erubesc'ency**. [L. *ērubēscĕre*, to grow red.]

Eruca *i-rōō'kə*, *n* a genus of herbs of the family Cruciferae. [L. *ērūca*, rocket (see **rocket**[2]).]

eruciform *e-rōō'si-fōrm*, *adj* like a caterpillar. [L. *ērūca*, caterpillar, *fōrma*, form.]

eruct *i-rukt'* or **eructate** *i-rukt'āt*, *vt* to belch out, as wind from the stomach (also *vi*; also *fig*); (of a volcano) to emit (fumes and ash or lava). — *n* **eructā'tion** (*ē-*). [L. *ēructāre*, *-ātum* — *ē*, from, *ructāre*, to belch forth.]

erudite *er'ōō-dīt* or *-ū-*, *adj* learned. — *n* a learned person. — *adv* **er'uditely**. — *n* **erudi'tion** the state of being learned; knowledge gained by study; learning, esp. in literature. [L. *ērudītus* — *ērudīre*, *ērudītum*, to free from roughness, train, instruct.]

erupt *i-rupt'*, *vi* to break out or through (like a volcano, a tooth from the gum, or a rash on the skin). — *n* **erup'tion** breaking or bursting forth; that which bursts forth; a breaking out of spots on the skin; the action of a volcano. — *adj* **erupt'ive**. — *n* **erupt'iveness**. [L. *ērumpĕre*, *ēruptum* — *ē*, from, *rumpĕre*, to break.]

erven. See **erf**.

eryngo *e-ring'gō*, *n* the candied root of sea-holly; the plant itself, a superficially thistle-like umbellifer: — *pl* **eryn'gos** or **eryn'goes**. — *n* **eryn'gium** (*-ji-əm*) any member of a genus (*Eryngium*) of bristly plants including the sea-holly (family Umbelliferae). [Gr. *ēryngos*.]

erysipelas *er-i-sip'i-ləs*, *n* an inflammatory disease, generally in the face, marked by a bright redness of the skin. [Gr.; prob. — root of *erythros*, red, *pella*, skin.]

erythema *er-i-thē'mə*, *n* redness of the skin. — *adj* **erythemal** (*er-ith'*). — *adj* **erythemat'ic**. — *adj* **erythem'atous**. [Gr. *erythēma* — *erythainein*, to redden.]

erythr- *er-ithr-* or **erythro-** *-rō-*, *combining form* denoting red. — *n* **eryth'roblast** (*-bläst*) a cell in bone marrow that develops into an erythrocyte. — *n* **eryth'rocyte** a red blood corpuscle. — *n* **erythromycin** (*-mī'sin*) an antibiotic similar to penicillin. [Gr. *erythros*, red.]

Es (*chem*) *symbol* for einsteinium.

ESA *abbrev* for: Environmentally Sensitive Area; European Space Agency.

Esc. *abbrev* for escudo (the Portuguese unit of currency).

escalate *es'kə-lāt*, *vi* to increase rapidly in scale or intensity. — Also *vt*. — *n* **escalā'tion**. — *n* **es'calātor** a moving staircase. — *adj* **es'calātory**. — **escalator clause** a clause in an agreement allowing for adjustment up or down according to change in circumstances, as in cost of material in a work contract or in cost of living in a wage agreement. [Orig. a trademark; prob. from *escalade* (to scale walls by ladder — Fr. *escalade* — Sp. *escalada* — *escala*, a ladder) and elev*ator*.]

escallonia *es-kal-ōn'i-ə, n* any plant of a S. American genus (*Escallonia*) of shrubs of the saxifrage family. [Discovered by *Escallon*, an 18th-cent. Spanish traveller.]

escallop *is-kal'əp, n* a variant of **scallop**. — *adj* **escall'oped** (*heraldry*) covered with scallop shells.

escalope *es'ka-lop, n* a boneless slice of meat, cut thin and often beaten out still thinner. [Fr.]

escape *is-kāp', vt* to free oneself from; to pass out of danger from; to evade, elude. — *vi* to come off or come through in safety; to emerge into or gain freedom; to flee; to slip out; to issue; to leak. — *n* the act of escaping; a means of escaping; flight, fleeing; an outlet; a leakage; an accidental or inadvertent emission; an outburst; a person or thing that has escaped, esp. a garden plant maintaining itself wild. — *adj* (of literature) providing escape from reality; (of a clause in an agreement) defining the conditions under which a party is relieved of obligation. — *adj* **escap'able**. — *n* **escapade** (*es-kə-pād'*) a mischievous adventure. — *n* **escapee'** someone who has escaped, e.g. from prison. — *n* **escape'ment** part of a timepiece connecting the wheelwork with the pendulum or balance, and allowing a tooth to escape at each vibration; the clearance in a pianoforte between the string and the hammer after it has struck the string, while the key is held down. — *n* **escāp'er**. — *n* **escāp'ism**. — *n* **escāp'ist** someone who seeks escape, esp. from reality. — Also *adj*. — *n* **escapol'ogist**. — *n* **escapol'ogy** the study of methods of escape from any sort of constraint or confinement and the putting into practice of these methods. — **escape hatch** an emergency exit from a ship, submarine, etc.; **escape mechanism** (*psychol*) a mental process by which one avoids something unpleasant; **escape road** a short track leading off a road on a steep hill, sharp bend, etc., for vehicles going out of control; **escape valve** a valve to let steam, etc., escape when wanted; **escape velocity** (*phys*) the minimum velocity needed to escape from the gravitation field of a body; **escape wheel** the wheel that the pallets act upon in a clock. [O.Fr. *escaper* (Fr. *échapper*) — L.L. *ex cappā*, (lit.) out of one's cape or cloak.]

escargot *es-kar-gō*, (Fr.) *n* an edible snail.

escarp *is-kärp', n* the side of the ditch beside the rampart (*fort*). — *n* **escarp'ment** the precipitous side of a hill or rock; escarp. [Fr. *escarper*, to cut steeply, from root of **scarp**.]

eschatology *es-kə-tol'ə-ji*, (*theol*) *n* the doctrine of the last or final things, such as death, judgment, the state after death. — *adj* **eschatolog'ic** or **eschatolog'ical**. — *n* **eschatol'ogist**. [Gr. *eschatos*, last, *logos*, a discourse.]

escheat *is-chēt', n* property that falls to the feudal lord or to the state for lack of an heir, or by forfeiture. — *vt* to confiscate. — *vi* to fall to the lord of the manor or the state. — *adj* **escheat'able**. — *n* **escheat'age**. — *n* **escheat'ment**. — *n* **escheat'or** (*hist*) an official who watches over escheats. [O.Fr. *eschete* — *escheoir* (Fr. *échoir*) — L. *ex*, from, *cadĕre*, to fall.]

Escherichia *esh-ə-rik'i-ə, n* a genus of rod-shaped, gram-negative bacteria. — **Escherichia coli** (*kō'lī*) the type species of this genus, occurring naturally in the intestines of vertebrates, and sometimes pathogenic (abbrev. **E. coli**). [T. *Escherich* (d. 1911), Ger. physician.]

eschew *is-choo', vt* to shun; to abstain from. [O.Fr. *eschever*.]

eschscholtzia or **eschscholzia** *e-sholt'si-ə, n* any plant of a genus (*Eschschol(t)zia*) of the poppy family, including the Californian poppy, a showy garden annual. [J. F. von *Eschscholtz*, a member of the expedition that discovered the poppy in 1821.]

escort *es'kört, n* a person or persons, ship or ships, etc., accompanying another or others for protection, guidance, or merely courtesy; an armed guard; a police officer accompanying a person under arrest to prevent escape; a man who accompanies a woman on an evening out; a person, usu. of the opposite sex, hired to accompany one to entertainments, etc.; attendance. — Also *adj*. — *vt* **escort'** to accompany or attend as escort. — **escort agency** one which provides people to act as hired escorts. [Fr. *escorte* — It. *scorta* — *scorgere*, to guide.]

escritoire *es-krē-twär', n* a writing-desk. — *adj* **escrito'rial** (*-tör'*). [Fr. *escritoire* — L.L. *scrīptōrium* — L. *scrībĕre, scrīptum*, to write.]

escrow *es-krō'*, (*law*) *n* a deed in the hands of a third party, to take effect when a condition is fulfilled. [A.Fr. *escroele, escroe*; see **scroll**; obs. *scrow*, a scroll, writing.]

escudo *es-koo'dō, n* the Portuguese unit of currency (100 centavos): — *pl* **escu'dos**. [Port. and Sp., shield.]

esculent *es'kū-lənt, adj* eatable; fit to be used for food by human beings. — *n* something that is eatable. [L. *esculentus*, eatable — *esca*, food — *edĕre*, to eat.]

escutcheon *es-kuch'ən, n* a shield on which a coat of arms is represented; a family shield. — **a blot on the escutcheon** a stain on one's good name. [O.Fr. *escuchon* — L. *scūtum*, a shield.]

Esd. (*Bible*) *abbrev* for (the Apocryphal Books of) Esdras.

ESE *abbrev* for east-south-east.

-ese *-ēz, sfx* denoting a relationship with a country or region (e.g. *Japanese, Maltese*) or the literary style, jargon, etc. of a particular group (e.g. in *journalese, officialese*).

esker or **eskar** *esk'ər*, (*geol*) *n* a kame, or ridge of gravel and sand laid down by a subglacial stream or one which issues from a retreating glacier. [Ir. *eiscir*, a ridge.]

Eskimo *es'ki-mō, n* and *adj* one of a people inhabiting arctic America with its islands, Greenland, and the nearest Asiatic coast (the Eskimos themselves prefer to be called *Innuit*); their language: — *pl* **Es'kimo** or **Es'kimos**. — **Eskimo dog** one of a breed of powerful dogs, with a double coat of hair, widely distributed in the Arctic regions, and indispensable for drawing sledges. [Prob. from an Indian word meaning eaters of raw flesh.]

ESL *abbrev* for English as a second language.

ESN *abbrev* for educationally subnormal.

ESOP *abbrev* for employee share ownership plan.

esophagus. A (chiefly *US*) spelling of **oesophagus**.

esoteric *es-ō-ter'ik* or *ē-, adj* inner; secret; mysterious; taught to a select few — opp. to *exoteric* (*philos*). — *npl* **esoter'ica** esoteric objects, etc. — *adv* **esoter'ically**. — *n* **esoter'icism** the holding of esoteric opinions. [Gr. *esōterikos* — *esōterō*, compar. of *esō, eisō*, within.]

ESP *abbrev* for: English for special (or specific) purposes; extrasensory perception.

esp. or **espec.** *abbrev* for especially.

espadrille *es-pə-dril', n* a rope-soled shoe. [Fr., — Prov. *espardillo* — *espart*, esparto.]

espalier *es-pal'yər, n* a lattice-work of wood to train trees on; a fruit-tree trained on stakes. — *vt* to train as an espalier. [Fr., — It. *spalliera*, a support for the shoulders.]

esparto *es-pär'tō, n* a strong grass (*Stipa tenacissima*, and others) grown in Spain, N. Africa, etc., and used for making paper, baskets, cordage, etc.: — *pl* **espar'tos**. [Sp., — L. *spartum* — Gr. *sparton*, a kind of rope.]

espec. See **esp.**

especial *is-pesh'l, adj* special; particular; principal; distinguished. — *adv* **espec'ially**. [O.Fr., — L. *speciālis* — *speciēs*, species.]

Esperanto *es-pər-an'tō, n* an international language devised by Dr Zamenhof, published 1887. — Also *adj*. — *n* **Esperan'tist** a speaker of Esperanto. [The inventor's pseudonym, the hoping one.]

espial *es-pī'əl, n* the act of espying; observation. [**espy**.]

espionage *es-pyon-äzh'* or *es'pi-ə-näzh, n* spying; use of spies. [Fr. *espionner* — *espion*, spy.]

esplanade *es-plə-nād', n* a level space between a citadel and the first houses of the town; any level space for walking or driving in, esp. by the sea. [Fr., — Sp. *esplanada* — L. *explānāre* — *ex*, out, *plānus*, flat.]

espouse *is-powz', vt* to give or take in marriage or betrothal; to take upon oneself or embrace, e.g. a cause. — *n* **espous'al** the taking upon oneself, of e.g. a cause; a formal betrothal. — *n* **espous'er**. [O.Fr. *espouser* (Fr. *épouser*) — L. *spōnsāre*, to betroth.]

espresso *es-pres'ō, n* a form of coffee-making machine giving high extraction under pressure; coffee made in this way: — *pl* **espress'os**. — Also *adj*, esp. of a type of coffee bar or the coffee. [It., pressed.]

esprit *es-prē*, (Fr.) *n* wit, liveliness. — **esprit de corps** (*es-prē də kor*) regard for the honour of the body to which one belongs; loyalty of a member to the whole; **esprit de l'escalier** (*də les-kal-yā*; or sometimes, incorrectly, **d'escalier**) thinking of an apt or witty retort after the opportunity of making it is past. [Fr. *esprit*, spirit, *de*, of, *corps*, body, *escalier*, staircase.]

espumoso *es-pōō-mō'sō*, (Sp.) *n* a sparkling wine: — *pl* **espumo'sos**.

espy *es-pī'*, (*archaic* or *literary*) *vt* to see at a distance; to catch sight of; to observe: — *pr p* **espy'ing**; *pa t* and *pa p* **espied'**; *3rd pers sing* **espies'**. [O.Fr. *espier*; see **spy**.]

Esq. or **Esqr.** *abbrev* for esquire.

-esque *-esk, sfx* denoting in the style or manner of, similar to, e.g. *Kiplingesque*.

esquire *es-kwīr'*, sometimes *es'kwīr, n* a general title of respect for a man, used in addressing letters (usu. abbrev. **esq.**). [Orig. a squire or shield-bearer — O.Fr. *esquier* (Fr. *écuyer*) — L. *scūtārius* — *scūtum*, a shield.]

ESRC *abbrev* for Economic and Social Research Council.

essay *es'ā, n* an attempt; a tentative effort; a written composition less elaborate than a treatise. — *vt* **essay'** to try; to attempt: — *pr p* **essay'ing**; *pa t* and *pa p* **essayed'**. — *n* **essay'er**. — *n* **ess'ayist** a person who essays; a writer of essays. [O.Fr. *essai* — L. *exagium*, weighing — *exagĕre*, to try, examine.]

essence *es'əns, n* the inner distinctive nature of anything; the qualities which make any object what it is; an alcoholic solution of a volatile or essential oil; a perfume of such composition; the extracted virtues of any drug; a liquid having the properties of the substance from which it is obtained. — *adj* **essential** (*is-* or *es-en'shl*) relating to, constituting, or containing the essence; necessary to the existence of a thing; indispensable or important in the highest degree; highly rectified; pure; (of e.g. disease) having no known cause. — *n* something necessary; a leading principle. — *n* **essen'tialism** a philosophical doctrine that distinguishes between the essence of material objects and their existence or appearance. — *n* **essen'tialist**. — *n* **essentiality** (*is-en-shi-al'i-ti*) the quality of being essential; an essential quality or element. — *adv* **essen'tially**. — *n* **essen'tialness**. — **essential oils** oils forming the odorous principles of plants, also called *ethereal oils* or *volatile oils*. — **in essence** basically, fundamentally; **of the essence** of the utmost importance. [Fr., — L. *essentia* — *essēns*, *-entis*, assumed pres. p. of *esse*, to be.]

ESSO *es'ō, abbrev* for Standard Oil. [The initials represented phonetically.]

EST *abbrev* for: Eastern Standard Time; electric shock treatment.

Est. *abbrev* for Estate (in addresses, etc.).

est. *abbrev* for: established; estimated.

-est *-əst, sfx* which marks the superlative degree of adjectives (long*est*) and some adverbs (fast*est*). [O.E. *-est*, *-ost*.]

establish *is-* or *es-tab'lish, vt* to settle or fix; to set up; to place in fixed position, possession or power; to make good; to prove; to ordain; to found; to set up in business; to institute by law as the recognised state church, and to recognise officially. — *adj* **estab'lished**. — *n* **estab'lisher**. — *n* **estab'lishment** the act of establishing; a fixed state; that which is established; a permanent civil or military force; permanent staff; one's residence, household, and style of living; a business; a settlement; the church established by law; (with **the** and *cap*; *derog*) the class in a community, or in a field of activity, who hold power, usu. because they are linked socially, and who are usu. considered to have conservative opinions and conventional values. — *adj* pertaining to an establishment or the Establishment. — *adj* **establishmentār'ian** maintaining the principle of church establishment; favouring or upholding the Establishment. — Also *n*. [O.Fr. *establir* — L. *stabilīre* — *stabilis*, firm — *stāre*, to stand.]

estate *is-* or *es-tāt', n* rank; worldly condition; total possessions; property, esp. a landed property of some size; a piece of land built over either privately or by a local authority, with houses (**housing estate**) or factories (**trading** or **industrial estate**); a piece of land given over to the cultivation of a particular crop; an order or class of people in the body politic; an estate car. — **estate agent** someone who values, buys and sells, and leases and manages property for clients; the manager of landed property; **estate car** a car designed to carry passengers and goods, usu. with a large area behind the seats for luggage, etc., and a rear door; **estate duty** death duty. — **personal estate** see under **personal**; **real estate** see **realty** under **real**[1]; **the estates of the realm** the three divisions of the body politic — Lords Spiritual, Lords Temporal, and Commons; **the fourth estate** (*colloq*) the press. [O.Fr. *estat* (Fr. *état*) — L. *status*, a state.]

esteem *is-* or *es-tēm', vt* to set a high estimate or value on; to regard with respect or friendship; to consider or think. — *n* high estimation or value; favourable regard; estimation of worth. — *adj* **esteemed'** respected; (in commercial correspondence) a colourless complimentary word. [Fr. *estimer* — L. *aestimāre*.]

ester *es'tər, n* a compound formed by the condensation of an alcohol and an acid, with elimination of water. — *n* **esterificā'tion** (*-ter*). — *vt* **ester'ify** (or *es'*). [Named by Leopold Gmelin (1788–1853), prob. — Ger. *Es*sig, vinegar, *Ä*ther, ether.]

Esth. (*Bible*) *abbrev* for (the Book of) Esther.

esthesia, esthesiogen, etc. U.S. spellings of **aesthesia, aesthesiogen**, etc.

Esthonian *es-thō'ni-ən*, or **Estonian** *es-tō'ni-ən, adj* pertaining to *Est(h)onia*, a Baltic republic, till 1918 a province of Russia, incorporated in 1940 as a republic of the U.S.S.R. — *n* a native or citizen of Est(h)onia; its language, related to Finnish.

estimable *es'tim-ə-bl, adj* that can be estimated or valued; worthy of esteem; deserving one's good opinion. — *adv* **es'timably**. [Ety. as for **esteem**.]

estimate *es'ti-māt, vt* to judge the worth of; to ascertain how much is present of; to calculate. — *n* (*-mit*) a valuing in the mind; judgment or opinion of the worth or size of anything; a rough calculation; a preliminary statement of the probable cost of a proposed undertaking; estimation. — *n* **estimā'tion**

an act of estimating; a reckoning of value; esteem, honour; conjecture. — *adj* **es'timātive.** — *n* **es'timātor.** — **hold in estimation** to esteem highly; **the estimates** accounts laid before parliament, etc., showing the probable expenditure for the year. [Ety. as for **esteem.**]

estival, etc. U.S. spelling of **aestival,** etc.

Estonian. See **Esthonian.**

estop *e-stop'*, (*law*) *vt* to hinder, preclude: — *pr p* **estopp'ing;** *pa t* and *pa p* **estopped'.** — *n* **estopp'age** the state of being estopped. — *n* **estopp'el** a conclusive admission, which cannot be denied by the party whom it affects. [O.Fr. *estoper* — *estoupe* — L. *stuppa*, flax; see **stop, stuff.**]

estover *es-tō'vər*, (*law*) *n* a right to necessaries allowed by law, such as wood to a tenant for repairs, etc. — **common of estovers** the right of taking necessary wood from another's estate for household use and the making of implements of industry. [O.Fr. *estover*, to be necessary, necessaries.]

estrange *is-trānj'*, *vt* to cut off, remove; to alienate, esp. from friendship; to divert from original use or possessor. — *adj* **estranged'.** — *n* **estrang'edness.** — *n* **estrange'ment.** — *n* **estrang'er.** [O.Fr. *estranger* (Fr. *étranger*) — L. *extrāneāre* — *extrāneus*; see **strange.**]

estreat *es-trēt'*, (*law*) *n* a true copy of some original record, esp. of fines to be levied. — *vt* to extract from the records of a court, as a forfeited recognisance; to levy, exact. [O.Fr. *estraite* — L. *extrahĕre* — *ex*, from, *trahĕre* to draw; see **extract.**]

estrogen, estrum, etc. Alternative (chiefly *US*) spellings of **oestrogen, oestrum,** etc.

estuary *es'tū-ər-i*, *n* the wide lower tidal part of a river. — *adj* **estūarial** (*-ā'ri-əl*). — *adj* **estūā'rian.** — *adj* **es'tūarine** (*-ə-rīn*). [L. *aestuārium* — *aestus*, burning, boiling, commotion, tide.]

ESU *abbrev* for English-Speaking Union.

ET *abbrev* for: Arab Republic of Egypt (I.V.R.); eastern time; Employment Training (scheme); extraterrestrial.

ETA *abbrev* for: estimated time of arrival; (*et'ə*) *Euzkadi ta Askatasuna*, a militant Basque separatist organisation.

eta *ē'tə* or *ā'tə*, *n* the seventh letter of the Greek alphabet, long e (Η, η). [Gr. *ēta.*]

etaerio *et-ē'ri-ō*, (*bot*) *n* an aggregated fruit, a group of achenes or drupels: — *pl* **etae'rios.** [Fr. *étairion* — Gr. *hetaireiā*, association.]

étagère *ā-ta-zher*, (Fr.) *n* a display stand with open shelves for small objects or ornaments.

et al. *abbrev* for: *et alibi* (L.), and elsewhere; *et alii*, *aliae* or *alia* (L.), and other (people, or things).

etalon *āt'əl-on*, (*phys*) *n* an interferometer used to measure wavelengths, consisting of an air film enclosed between half-silvered plane parallel glass or quartz plates. [Fr., — M.Fr. *estalon*, standard of weights and measures.]

état *ā-ta*, (Fr.) *n* state, rank. — *n* **étatisme** (*ā-ta-tēzm'*) extreme state control over the individual citizen.

etc. See **et cetera.**

et cetera *et set'ər-ə* (usually written as *abbrev* **etc.** or **&c.**) a Latin phrase meaning 'and the rest' — and so on. — *n* something in addition, which can easily be understood from the context.

etch *ech*, *vt* and *vi* to design on metal, glass, etc., by eating out the lines with an acid. — *n* **etch'ant** an acid or corrosive used in etching. — *n* **etch'er.** — *n* **etch'ing** the act or art of etching or engraving; the impression from an etched plate. [Ger. *ätzen*, to corrode by acid; from same root as Ger. *essen.*]

ETD *abbrev* for estimated time of departure.

eternal *i-* or *ē-tûr'nl*, *adj* without beginning or end of existence; everlasting; ceaseless; unchangeable; seemingly endless, occurring again and again (*colloq*). — *vt* **eter'nalise** or **-ize,** also **eter'nise** or **-ize** (or *ē'tər-nīz*), to make eternal; to immortalise with fame. — *adv* **eter'nally.** — *n* **eter'nity** eternal duration; the state or time after death. — **eternal triangle** a sexual relationship, full of tension and conflict, between two men and a woman or two women and a man; **eternity ring** a ring set all round with stones, emblematic of continuity and everlasting love. — **the Eternal** God; **the Eternal City** Rome; **the eternities** the eternal reality or truth. [Fr. *éternel* — L. *aeternus* — *aevum*, an age.]

etesian *e-tē'zhən*, *-zhyən* or *-zyən*, *adj* blowing at stated seasons, as certain winds, esp. the north-west winds of summer in the Aegean. [Gr. *etēsios*, annual — *etos*, a year.]

ethane *eth'ān* or *ēth'*, *n* a colourless, odourless hydrocarbon of the methane series. — *n* **eth'anol** ethyl alcohol. [**ether.**]

ethene. See under **ethyl.**

ether *ē'thər*, *n* the clear, upper air; a medium, not matter, assumed in the 19th cent. to fill all space and transmit electromagnetic waves (in these senses also **aether**); (specif. **ethyl ether** or **diethyl ether**) a colourless, transparent, volatile liquid of great mobility and high refractive power, used as a solvent, an anaesthetic, and in the preparation of explosives; extended to the class of compounds in which two alkyl groups are united with an oxygen atom. — *adj* **ethē'real** or **ethē'rial** consisting of ether; heavenly; airy; spiritlike. — *n* **ethērealisā'tion** or **-z-.** — *vt* **ethē'realise** or **-ize** to convert into ether, or the fluid ether; to make spiritlike. — *n* **ethēreal'ity.** — *adv* **ethē'really.** — *n* **etherisā'tion** or **-z-.** — *vt* **e'therise** or **-ize** to convert into ether; to stupefy with ether. — **ethereal oils** essential oils. [L. *aethēr* — Gr. *aithēr*, the heavens — *aithein*, to light up.]

ethic *eth'ik*, *n* (more commonly *nsing* **eth'ics**) the science of morals, that branch of philosophy which is concerned with human character and conduct; a system of morals, rules of behaviour; a treatise on morals. — *adj* **eth'ical** relating to morals, the science of ethics, professional standards of conduct; relating to, or in accord with, approved moral behaviour; denoting a proprietary pharmaceutical not advertised to the general public (also *n*). — *n* **ethical'ity.** — *n* **eth'icalness.** — *adj* **eth'ically.** — *vt* **eth'icise** or **-ize** (*-sīz*) to make ethical; to treat as ethical. — *n* **eth'icism** the tendency to moralise or ethicise; great interest in ethics or passion for ethical ideals. — *n* **eth'icist** an expert on or student of ethics; someone who detaches ethics from religion. — **eth'ico-** *combining form* denoting something ethical or of ethics. [Gr. *ēthikos* — *ēthos*, custom, character.]

Ethiopian *ē-thi-ō'pi-ən*, *n* a native of Ethiopia. — *adj* **Ēthiopic** (*-op'*) belonging to Ethiopia, to the Ethiopian church, or to a particular group of Semitic languages. [Gr. *Aithiops* — *aithein*, to burn, *ops*, *ōps*, face.]

ethmoid bone *eth'moid bōn*, (*anat*) *n* one of the bones forming the anterior part of the braincase. [Gr. *ēthmos*, a sieve, *eidos*, form, **bone.**]

ethnic *eth'nik* or **ethnical** *eth'nik-əl*, *adj* concerning nations or races; pertaining to the customs, dress, food, etc., of a particular racial group or cult; belonging or pertaining to a particular racial group; foreign; exotic; between or involving different racial groups. — *n* **eth'nic** a member of a racial or cultural minority group. — *adv* **eth'nically.** — *n* **ethni'city** (*-si-ti*). — *adj* **ethnobotan'ical.** — *n* **ethnobot'anist.** — *n* **ethnobot'any** (the study of) traditional plant-lore, plant classification, plant use, etc. — *adj* **ethnocen'tric.** — *adv* **ethnocen'trically.** — *n* **ethnocen'trism** belief in the superiority of one's own cultural group or society and corresponding dislike or misunderstanding of other such groups. — *n* **eth'nocide** (*-sīd*) the extermination of a racial or cultural group. — *n* **ethnog'rapher.** — *adj* **ethnograph'ic** or **ethnograph'ical** pertaining to ethnography; of objects useful in the study of ethnography. — *npl* **ethnograph'ica** (a collection of) ethnographic objects; (*loosely*) exotica. — *n* **ethnog'raphy** the scientific description of the races of the earth. — *n* **eth'nolinguist.** — *adj* **ethnolinguist'ic.** — *nsing* **ethnolinguist'ics** the study of the relationship between language and cultural behaviour. — *adj* **ethnolog'ical.** — *adv* **ethnolog'ically.** — *n* **ethnol'ogist.** — *n* **ethnol'ogy** the science concerned with the varieties of the human race; cultural anthropology. — *n* **ethnomusicol'ogist** a person who makes a study of the music and/or musical instruments of primitive peoples in relation to their cultures. — *n* **ethnomusicol'ogy.** [Gr. *ethnos*, a nation.]

ethos *ē'thos, n* the distinctive habitual character and disposition of an individual, group, race, etc.; moral significance. — *adj* **etholog'ic** or **etholog'ical.** — *n* **ethol'ogist.** — *n* **ethol'ogy** the science of character; bionomics (see under **bio-**); the scientific study of the function and evolution of animal behaviour patterns. [Gr. *ēthos*, custom, character.]

ethyl *eth'il* or *ēth'īl, n* the base (C_2H_5) of common alcohol, ether, etc. — *n* **eth'ylene** (*eth'*; also **eth'ene**) a gas, hydrogen combined with carbon (C_2H_4). — **ethyl alcohol** ordinary alcohol; **ethylene glycol** a thick liquid alcohol used as an antifreeze; **ethyl ether** see **ether.** [**ether,** and Gr. *hȳlē*, matter.]

etiolate *ē'ti-ō-lāt, vt* to cause to grow pale small yellow leaves for lack of light, to blanch (*bot*); to make pale. — *vi* to become pale. — *adj* **e'tiolated.** — *n* **etiolā'tion.** [Fr. *étioler*, to become pale, to grow into stubble.]

etiology. An alternative (esp. *US*) spelling of **aetiology.**

etiquette *et'i-ket, -kət* or *-ket', n* forms of civilised manners or decorum; the conventional laws of courtesy observed between members of the same profession, sport, etc. [Fr. *étiquette*.]

Eton *ē'tn, n* a town opposite Windsor in England with an old-established public school. — *n* **Etonian** (*ē-tōn'i-ən*) a person educated at *Eton* College. — Also *adj.* — **Eton collar** a boy's broad starched turned-down collar; a similar-shaped collar on a woman's jumper, etc.; **Eton crop** a fashion of ladies' hairstyle, short and sleeked flat; **Eton jacket** a boy's black dress-coat, without tails.

étrier *ā-trē-yā', n* a small rope ladder of 1–4 rungs used as a climbing aid by mountaineers. [Fr., stirrup.]

Etruria *i-trōō'ri-ə, n* an ancient state of Italy north of the Tiber. — *n* and *adj* **Etru'rian** Etruscan. — *adj* **Etruscan** (*i-trus'kən*) pertaining to Etruria, or to the language, place, culture, etc. of the Etruscans. — *n* a person inhabiting or from Etruria; the language of the Etruscans. [L. *Etrūria, Etrūscus*.]

et sequens *et se'kwənz* or *sē', (L.)* and what follows (abbrev. **et seq.**); **et sequentes** (*si-kwen'tēz*) or *neuter* **et sequentia** (*se-kwen'ti-a* or *-shi-a*) and those that follow (abbrev. **et seqq.**).

étude *ā-tüd', (mus) n* a composition intended either to train or to test the player's technical skill. [Fr., study.]

étui *ā-twē'* or *et-wē', n* a small case for holding small sewing articles. [Fr. *étui*, a case, sheath.]

ety. or **etym.** *abbrev* for: etymology; etymological.

etymon *et'i-mon, n* the true origin of a word; an original root: — *pl* **et'yma** or **et'ymons.** — *adj* **etymolog'ical.** — *adv* **etymolog'ically.** — *vi* **etymol'ogise** or **-ize** to inquire into or discuss etymology. — *vt* to trace or suggest an etymology for. — *n* **etymol'ogist.** — *n* **etymol'ogy** the science or investigation of the derivation and original meanings of words; an etymon. [Neuter of Gr. *etymos*, true.]

Eu (*chem*) *symbol* for europium.

eucalyptus *ū-kə-lip'təs, n* any tree or shrub of a large characteristically Australian genus (*Eucalyptus*) of the myrtle family, many yielding timber, and some giving oils and gum; eucalyptus oil: — *pl* **eucalyp'tuses** or **eucalyp'tī.** — *n* **eu'calypt** a eucalyptus. [Latinised from Gr. *eu*, well, *kalyptos*, covered.]

eucaryon, eucaryote and **eucaryotic.** Same as **eukaryon,** etc.

eucharis *ū'kər-is* or *ū-kar'is, n* any member of a genus (*Eucharis*) of S. American bulbous plants with fragrant white flowers. [Gr., charming — *eu*, well, *charis*, grace.]

Eucharist *ū'kə-rist*, (*Christian relig*) *n* the sacrament of the Lord's Supper; the elements of the sacrament, bread and wine. — *adj* **Eucharist'ic** or **Eucharist'ical.** [Gr. *eucharistiā*, thanksgiving — *eu*, well, *charizesthai*, to show favour.]

euchre *ū'kər, n* an American card game for two, three, or four people, with the 32, 28, or 24 highest cards of the pack — any player failing to make three tricks is *euchred*, and an adversary scores against them. — *vt* to score over, as above; to outwit.

Euclidean *ū-klid'i-ən, adj* pertaining to *Euclid*, a geometrician of Alexandria *c* 300 B.C., or to space according to his theories and assumptions. — **Euclidean geometry** a geometry based on the theories and assumptions of Euclid.

eudiometer *ū-di-om'i-tər, n* an apparatus for gas analysis, a graduated tube holding the gas over mercury, usually with wires for sparking — previously used for testing the air at different times. [Gr. *eudios*, clear, fine (as weather), *metron*, measure.]

Eugenia *ū-jē'ni-ə, n* the clove genus of the myrtle family. — *n* **eugenol** (*ū'jin-ol*) the chief constituent of oil of cloves — also **eugenic** (*-jen'*) **acid.** [Named after Prince *Eugene* of Savoy (1663–1736).]

eugenic[1] *ū-jen'ik, adj* pertaining to genetic improvement of a race (of animals, etc.) by judicious mating and helping the better stock to prevail. — *adv* **eugen'ically.** — *nsing* **eugen'ics** the science of genetic improvement of a race. — *n* **eu'genism** (*-jin-*). — *n* **eu'genist** or **eugen'icist.** [Gr. *eugenēs*, of good stock.]

eugenic[2]. See **eugenol** under **Eugenia.**

euharmonic *ū-här-mon'ik*, (*mus*) *adj* resulting in perfect harmony. [Gr. *eu*, well, *harmoniā*, harmony.]

Euhemerism *ū-hē'mə-rizm, n* the theory which explains mythology as growing out of real history, its deities as merely larger-than-life people. — *vt* and *vi* **euhē'merise** or **-ize.** — *n* and *adj* **euhē'merist.** — *adj* **euhemeris'tic.** — *adv* **euhemeris'tically.** [From *Euhēmerus*, Gr. *Euēmeros*, a 4th-cent. B.C. Sicilian philosopher.]

eukaryon *ū-kar'i-ən*, (*biol*) *n* the highly organised cell nucleus, surrounded by a membrane, characteristic of higher organisms (cf. *prokaryon*). — *n* **eukar'yote** (*-ōt* or *-ət*) an organism whose cells have such nuclei. — Also *adj.* — *adj* **eukaryot'ic.** — Also **eucaryon,** etc. [Gr. *eu*, well, *karyon*, kernel.]

eulogium *ū-lō'ji-əm* or **eulogy** *ū'lə-ji, n* praise; a speech or writing in praise of a person or thing; a funeral oration: — *pl* **eulō'gia, eulō'giums** or **eu'logies.** — *vt* **eu'logise** or **-ize** to extol, praise. — *n* **eu'logist** a person who extols (esp. a dead friend, etc.). — *adj* **eulogist'ic** full of praise. — *adv* **eulogist'ically.** [L.L. *eulogium* — Gr. *eu*, well, *logos*, a speaking.]

Eumenides *ū-men'i-dēz, npl* another name for the *Erinyes* or Furies (see under **fury**). [Gr. *Eumenidēs*, gracious ones — *eu*, well, *menos*, disposition.]

eunuch *ū'nək, n* a castrated man, esp. one in charge of a harem, or a high-voiced singer; an ineffectual person, lacking in some way in force or power (*fig*). — *vt* **eu'nuchise** or **-ize** (*lit* and *fig*). — *n* **eu'nuchism** the condition of being a eunuch. — *n* **eu'nuchoidism** a condition in which there is some deficiency of sexual development and in which certain female sex characteristics, e.g. high voice, are often present. — *n* and *adj* **eu'nuchoid**. [Gr. *eunouchos* — *eunē*, bed, *echein*, to have (charge of).]

eupatrid *ū-pat'rid*, *n* a member of the aristocracy in ancient Greek states. [Gr. *eupatridēs* — *eu*, well, *patēr*, father.]

eupepsy *ū-pep'si* or **eupepsia**-*pep'si-ə*, *n* good digestion (opp. to *dyspepsia*). — *adj* **eupep'tic** pertaining to good digestion; cheerful. — *n* **eupepticity** (*-tis'i-ti*). [Gr. *eupepsiā*, digestibility — *eu*, well, *pepsis*, digestion.]

euph. *abbrev* for: euphemism; euphemistic; euphemistically.

euphemism *ū'fəm-izm*, *n* a figure of rhetoric by which an unpleasant or offensive thing is described or referred to by a milder term; such a term. — *vt* **eu'phemise** or **-ize** to express by a euphemism. — *vi* to use euphemistic terms. — *adj* **euphemist'ic**. — *adv* **euphemist'ically**. [Gr. *euphēmismos* — *euphēmizein*, to speak words of good omen — *eu*, well, *phanai*, to speak.]

euphenics *ū-fen'iks*, *nsing* the science concerned with the physical improvement of human beings by modifying their development after birth (cf. *eugenics*). [By analogy, from **eugenics** and **phenotype**.]

euphobia *ū-fō'bi-ə*, *n* fear of good news. [Gr. *eu*, well, *phobos*, fear.]

euphony *ū'fə-ni*, *n* an agreeable sound; pleasing, easy pronunciation (often created by modification of the original sounds combined). — *adj* **euphonic**, **euphonical** (*-fon'*) or **euphō'nious** agreeable in sound. — *adv* **euphō'niously**. — *vt* **eu'phonise** or **-ize** to make euphonious. — *n* **euphō'nium** a member of the saxhorn family, the bass tuba. [Gr. *euphōniā* — *eu*, well, *phōnē*, sound.]

euphorbia *ū-för'bi-ə*, *n* any member of the spurge genus (*Euphorbia*) of plants. [*Euphorbos*, Greek physician to Juba, king of Mauritania.]

euphoria *ū-fö'ri-ə*, *n* an exaggerated feeling of well-being, esp. irrational or groundless. — *adj* **euphor'iant** inducing euphoria. — *n* a drug which does this. — *adj* **euphoric** (*-for'*). [Gr. *euphŏriā*.]

euphrasy *ū'frə-si* or *-zi*, (*bot*) *n* eyebright, a plant of the genus *Euphrasia*, once thought good for disorders of the eyes. [Gr. *euphrăsiā*, delight — *euphrainein*, to cheer.]

Euphuism *ū'fū-izm*, *n* the affected and bombastic literary style brought into vogue by John Lyly's romance *Euphues* (1579–80); (without *cap*) a high-flown expression in this style. — *vi* **eu'phuise** or **-ize**. — *n* **eu'phuist**. — *adj* **euphuist'ic**. — *adv* **euphuist'ically**. [Gr. *euphyēs*, graceful, goodly.]

Eur- *ūr-* or **Euro-** *ū'rō-*, *combining form* denoting: European; of or pertaining to the European Community; of or pertaining to Europe. — *adj* **Euraf'rican** pertaining to Europe and Africa, or Europe and North Africa, jointly; of a human race common to Europe and North Africa, the Mediterranean race; of mixed European and African parentage or descent. — *n* a person of Eurafrican race in either sense. — *adj* **Eurā'sian** of mixed European and Asian parentage or descent; of, or pertaining to, Europe and Asia (**Eura'sia**) considered as one continent. — *n* a person of mixed European and Asian parentage. — *n* **Eurat'om** the European Atomic Energy Community (set up 1958), an association for joint peaceful development of nuclear energy. — *n* **Euro-Amer'ican** (also *adj*). — *n* **Eu'robond** a borrowing in Eurocurrency by a company from subscribers, which may or may not be sellable and for which the rate and life may be either fixed or variable. — *adj* **Eurocent'ric** see **Europocentric**. — *n* **Eur'ocheque** a special type of cheque drawn on the user's own bank which may be cashed in banks, and used for making purchases, in any of a number of European, and non-European, countries. — *n* **Eurocomm'unism** the theory of communism professed by Communist parties in Western Europe, more pragmatic than the traditional Soviet theory and asserting independence from it. — *n* **Eurocomm'unist**. — *n* **Eu'rocrat** an official concerned with the administration of any organisation within the European Community, a European bureaucrat. — *n* **Eurocracy** (*ū-rok'rə-si*). — *adj* **Eurocrat'ic**. — *n* **Eu'rocurrency** the currency of any of the countries of the European Community. — *n* **Eu'ro-dollars** U.S. dollars deposited in European banks to facilitate financing of trade between the U.S. and Europe. — *n* **Eu'ro-MP** a member of the European Parliament, an MEP. — *n* **Eu'ronet** an information network linking various European databanks. — *n* **Eur'o-Parliament** the European Parliament. — *n* **Eur'o-passport** a standard form of passport issued to all eligible citizens of the European Community. — *n* **Eu'rovision** the European television network.

eureka *ū-rē'kə*, *interj* announcing a discovery. [Gr. *heurēka*, I have found, perf. tense of *heuriskein*, to find, the cry of Archimedes when he thought of a method of detecting the adulteration of the gold for Hiero's crown.]

eurhythmy or **eurythmy** *ū-rith'mi* or *-ridh'*, *n* rhythmical movement or order; harmony of proportion; (usu. with *cap*) an artistic, therapeutic and educational system based on rhythmic body movement correlated to poetry, music, etc., created by Rudolf Steiner (1861–1925). — *adj* **eurhyth'mic**. — *nsing* **eurhyth'mics** the art or system of rhythmic movement expounded by E. Jaques-Dalcroze (1865–1950). — *n* **eurhyth'mist**. [Gr. *eurythmiā* — *eu*, well, *rhythmos*, rhythm.]

euro *ū'rō*, (*Austr*) *n* a wallaroo, any of several types of large kangaroo: — *pl* **eu'ros**. [Aboriginal.]

Euro-...to...**Euro-Parliament**. See under **Eur-**.

European *ū-rə-pē'ən*, *adj* belonging or pertaining to Europe. — *n* an inhabitant or native of Europe; a member of the white race of man characteristic of Europe; a Europeanist. — *vt* **europē'anise** or **-ize** to assimilate, convert to European character or ways; to integrate into the European Community. — *n* **Europeanisa'tion** or **-z-**. — *n* **Europē'anism**. — *n* **Europē'anist** a person who favours the European Community and seeks to uphold or develop it. — **European Commission** a body composed of members from all the countries of the European Community, which develops and submits policy proposals to the European Parliament; **European currency unit** see **ECU**; **European Economic Community** or **European Community** the common market formed in 1957 by the Treaty of Rome by France, W. Germany, Italy, Belgium, the Netherlands and Luxembourg; joined in 1973 by the United Kingdom, Denmark and the Republic of Ireland, in 1981 by Greece, and in 1986 by Spain and Portugal; **European Parliament** the legislative assembly of the European Community; **European plan** (*US*) in hotels, the system of charging for lodgings and service without including meals. — See also **American plan** at **American**. [Gr. *Eurōpē*.]

europium *ū-rō'pi-əm*, *n* a rare-earth metal (atomic no. 63; symbol **Eu**) discovered spectroscopically by Demarçay in 1896. [**Europe**.]

Europocentric *ū-rōp-ō-sent'rik* or **Eurocentric** *ū-rō-sent'rik*, *adj* centred, or concentrating, on Europe or its civilisation. [**Europe** and **centric** (see **centre**).]

Eustachian *ū-stā'ki-ən* or *-shən*, *adj* pertaining to the Italian physician Bartolommeo *Eustachio* (d. 1574). — **Eustachian tube** the tube leading from the middle ear to the pharynx; **Eustachian valve** the rudimentary valve at the entrance of the lower of the two large veins to the heart.

eustacy or **eustasy** *ū'stə-si*, *n* changes in world shoreline level, prob. caused by rise or fall of the sea-level and not by subsidence or elevation of the land. — *adj* **eustat'ic.** [Gr. *eu*, well, *stasis*, standing, *statikos*, causing to stand.]

eutectic and **eutectoid**. See **eutexia**.

Euterpe *ū-tûr'pē*, (*Gr mythol*) *n* the Muse of music and lyric poetry. — *adj* **Euter'pean**. [Gr. — *eu*, well, *terpein*, to delight.]

eutexia *ū-tek'si-ə*, (*phys*) *n* the property of being easily melted. — *n* **eutec'tic** a mixture in such proportions that the melting-point (or freezing-point) is as low as possible, the constituents melting (or freezing) simultaneously. — *adj* of maximum ease of fusibility; pertaining to a eutectic. — *n* **eutec'toid** an alloy similar to a eutectic but involving formation of two or three constituents from another solid (not melted) constituent. — Also *adj*. — **eutectic point** the temperature at which a eutectic melts or freezes. [Gr. *eutēktos*, easily melted — *eu*, well, *tēkein*, to melt.]

euthanasia *ū-thən-ā'zi-ə*, *n* the act or practice of putting painlessly to death, esp. in cases of incurable suffering. — *n* **euthanā'siast** a supporter of, or believer in, euthanasia. [Gr. *euthanasiā* — *eu*, well, *thanatos*, death.]

euthenics *ū-then'iks*, *nsing* the science concerned with the improvement of living conditions. — *n* **euthen'ist**. [Gr. *euthēneein*, to flourish.]

eutrophy *ū'trə-fi*, *n* healthy nutrition; the state (of a body of water) of being eutrophic. — *adj* **eutrophic** (*ū-trof'ik*) pertaining to healthy nutrition; (of a body of water) over-rich in nutrients, either naturally or as a result of artificial pollutants, and hence having a too-abundant growth of water plants and animals. — *n* **eutrophicā'tion** the process of becoming, or making (a body of water), eutrophic. [Gr. *eutrophiā*.]

eV *abbrev* for electron-volt.

evacuate *i-vak'ū-āt*, *vt* to throw out the contents of; to discharge, empty, void; to withdraw, (re)move, e.g. from a place of danger; to clear out troops, inhabitants, etc., from; to create a vacuum in (*phys*). — *vi* to move away (from a place of danger, usu. temporarily); to void excrement, empty the bowels. — *adj* and *n* **evac'uant** (a) purgative, laxative. — *n* **evacuā'tion** an act of evacuating; withdrawal, removal; the material discharged, excreted, etc. — *adj* **evac'uātive**. — *n* **evac'uātor**. — *n* **evacūee'** a person (re)moved in an evacuation. [L. *ē*, from, *vacuāre*, *-ātum*, to empty.]

evade *i-vād'*, *vt* to escape or avoid by cunning; to shirk; to baffle, elude (*fig*). — *adj* **evā'dable**. [L. *ēvādĕre* — *ē*, from, *vādĕre*, to go.]

evaginate *i-vaj'i-nāt*, (*med*) *vt* to turn outside in. — *n* **evaginā'tion**. [L. *ēvāgīnāre*, *-ātum*, to unsheathe — *ē*, from, *vāgīna*, a sheath.]

evaluate *i-val'ū-āt*, *vt* to determine or estimate the value of. — *n* **evaluā'tion**. — *adj* **eval'uative** tending to evaluate or functioning as an evaluation. [Fr. *évaluer*.]

evanescent *ev-ən-es'ənt*, *adj* fleeting, passing; vanishing. — *vi* **evanesce'** to fade away, vanish. — *n* **evanesc'ence**. — *adv* **evanesc'ently**. [L. *ēvānēscēns*, *-entis* — *ē*, from, *vānēscĕre*, to vanish.]

evangelic *ē-van-jel'ik* or **evangelical** *-jel'i-kəl*, *adj* of or pertaining to the Christian Gospel; according to the doctrine of the Gospel; maintaining or promoting the ideals or teachings of the Gospel; Protestant; of the school of religious belief that insists especially on the total depravity of human nature and the exclusive authority of the Bible; active and ardent in one's advocacy of some principle or cause. — *n* **evangel'ical** a person who belongs to the evangelical school of belief. — *n* **evangel'icalism**. — *adv* **evangel'ically**. — *n* **evangelisā'tion** or **-z-** (*i-van-jəl-*) the act of proclaiming the Gospel; the attempt to persuade others of the rightness of some principle or cause. — *vt* **evan'gelise** or **-ize** to make acquainted with the Gospel; to convert to Christianity. — *vi* to preach the Gospel from place to place; to try to persuade others to support some principle or cause. — *n* **evan'gelism** evangelising; evangelicalism. — *n* **evan'gelist** a person who evangelises, religiously or otherwise; (with *cap*) an author of a Gospel, esp. Matthew, Mark, Luke or John; an assistant of the apostles; a person who is authorised to preach but who is without responsibility for a fixed area; an itinerant preacher. — *adj* **evangelis'tic** tending or intended to evangelise, religiously or otherwise. [L. *evangelicus* — Gr. *euangelikos* — *eu*, well, *angellein*, to bring news.]

evaporate *i-vap'ər-āt*, *vi* to change into vapour form; to pass into an invisible state; to depart, vanish, disappear (*fig*). — *vt* to convert into vapour; to draw moisture off (a metal) in vapour form. — *adj* **evap'orable** able to be evaporated or converted into vapour. — *n* **evaporā'tion** the act of evaporating or drawing off moisture in the form of steam or gas; the process by which a substance changes into vapour. — *adj* **evap'orātive**. — *n* **evap'orātor**. — **evaporated milk** milk thickened by evaporation of some of its water content, unsweetened. [L. *ē*, from, *vapōrāre*, *-ātum* — *vapor*, vapour.]

evapotranspiration *i-vap-ō-tran-spi-rā'shən*, *n* the return of water into the atmosphere as vapour, by evaporation (from soil, water bodies, etc.) and emissions or *transpiration* (from plants); the total amount converted by this process. [**evaporate** and **transpiration**.]

evasion *i-vā'zhən*, *n* the act of evading or eluding; an attempt to escape the point of an argument or accusation; an excuse. — *adj* **evā'sive** (*-siv*) evading or attempting to evade; elusive; not straightforward, devious. — *adv* **evā'sively**. — *n* **evā'siveness**. — **take evasive action** to move or act in such a way as to avoid an object or consequence. [L. *ēvādĕre*, *ēvāsum*; see **evade**.]

eve. See **even**[2].

evection *i-vek'shən*, (*astron*) *n* the combined effect of the irregularity of the point of the moon's orbit at which it is nearest to Earth and the alternate increase and decrease of the eccentricity of the moon's orbit. [L. *ēvectiō*, *-ōnis* — *ē*, from, *vehĕre*, *vectum*, to carry.]

even[1] *ēv'n*, *adj* flat; level; smooth; calm, unexcited; uniform; in a straight line or plane; balanced equally; equal; fair, just; exact; (of people) not owing each other anything; divisible by 2 without a remainder; denoted by such a number. — *vt* to make even or smooth; to put on an equal basis; to make (scores, etc.) equal. — *vi* (often with *up*) to become even. — *adv* exactly (*colloq*); indeed, in fact; still, yet, emphasising a comparative, as in *even better*; used when speaking or writing of something extreme or completely unexpected, as in *even an idiot would know*. — *adv* **ev'enly**. — *n* **ev'enness**. — *adj* **ev'ens** even-money. — **even chance** an equal probability (of success or failure, etc.). — *adj* **even-hand'ed** impartial; just, fair. — *n* **even-hand'edness**. — *adj* **even-mon'ey** in betting odds, considered extremely likely to win or happen, and paying out only the equal of the stake. — *adj* **even-tem'pered** of a placid temperament, calm. — **be** or **get even with** to be revenged on; **even as** at that, or this, very moment when; **even out** to become even, equal; **even so** nevertheless; **on an even keel** balanced, not tilting to one side or the other; (of e.g. business affairs) running smoothly, settled, well-organised. [O.E. *efen*.]

even[2] *ēv'n*, *n* evening (*poetic*). — *n* **eve** (*ēv*) evening (*poetic*); the night, or the whole day, before a festival; the time just preceding an event. — *n* **evening** (*ēv'ning*) the close of the day; the decline or end (of life); an evening party, gathering or entertainment. — *adv* **eve'nings** (esp. *NAm*) in the evening (on a number of occasions). — **evening class** a class held in the evenings, usu. for people who work during the day; **eve'ning-dress** the dress (men's or women's) conventionally appropriate to social functions in the evening; **evening primrose** a N. American plant with pale yellow flowers that open in the evening; **evening-star'** a planet, usu. Venus or Mercury, seen in the western sky, setting soon after the sun; **ev'ensong** evening prayers, the Anglican form being said or sung at evening; the time appropriate to these prayers; **ev'entide** (*poetic*) the time of evening, evening; **eventide home** (*euph*) a home for old people. [O.E. *ǣfen, ǣfnung*.]

event *i-vent'*, *n* anything which happens; result; any incident or occurrence, esp. a memorable one; contingency, possibility of occurrence; an item in a programme (of sports, etc.); a type of horse-riding competition, often over three days (**three-day event**), consisting of three sections — dressage, cross-country riding and show-jumping; an organised activity at a particular venue, e.g. for sales promotion, fund-raising, etc. — *vi* to ride in a horse-riding event. — *n* **event'er** a horse trained to take part in events; the rider of such a horse, e.g. *three-day eventer*. — *adj* **event'ful** full of events, memorable, momentous. — *n* **event'ing** taking part in riding events; the sport of horse-riding in three-day events. — **event horizon** (*astron*) the boundary of a black hole. — **at all events** or **in any event** no matter what happens, anyway; **in the event** as things turned out; if it should turn out (that); **in the event of** in the case of (a given thing happening); if. [L. *ēventus* — *ēvenīre*, to come out, happen.]

eventual *i-vent'ū-əl*, *adj* final, after a time. — *n* **eventūal'ity** an occurrence, happening. — *adv* **event'ūally** finally; at length, in time. — *vi* **event'ū-ate** to turn out. [Ety. as for **event**.]

ever *ev'ər*, *adv* always; eternally; at all times; continually; at any time; on record, in history, in the world (as in *the biggest ever*, the biggest that has at any time been or happened); at all, possibly; very, extremely (*slang*, orig. *NAm*; used as part of an interjection or statement, as in *was I ever hungry*, I was very hungry). — *sfx* giving complete generality to relative adverbs and pronouns, as in *whatever*, etc. — *adj* **ev'ergreen** in leaf throughout the year; always fresh and green; unfading; never failing, retaining one's, or its, vigour, freshness, popularity, interest, etc. for ever. — *n* a tree or shrub that is green throughout the year; a person, piece of music, etc. which retains freshness, popularity, etc. through the years. — *adj* **everlast'ing** endless, perpetual, unceasing; eternal; wearisomely long (*colloq*). — *n* (with *the*) eternity; a flower of a type that may be kept for years without much change of appearance; a very durable type of cloth. — *adv* **everlast'ingly.** — *n* **everlast'ingness.** — *adv* **evermore'** (or *ev'*) for all time to come (also **for evermore**); ever; unceasingly. — **ever so** to a very great extent; **ever such a** (*colloq*) a very; **for ever** for all eternity, always; for a long time (*colloq*). [O.E. *ǣfre*.]

Everest *ev'ə-rəst*, *n* the name of the highest mountain in the world, in the Himalayas; anything extremely difficult to accomplish or conquer, the height of ambition (*fig*).

everglade *ev'ər-glād*, *n* a large shallow lake or marsh; (with *cap*; chiefly in *pl*) such a marsh in southern Florida, enclosing thousands of islets covered with dense thickets.

evert *i-vûrt'*, *vt* to turn inside out; to turn outwards. — *adj* **ever'sible.** — *n* **ever'sion.** [L. *ēvertěre* — *ē*, from, *vertěre*, *versum*, to turn.]

every *ev'ri*, *adj* each one of a number or collection; all taken separately. — *pron* **ev'erybody** or **ev'eryone** every person. — *adj* **ev'eryday** of or happening every day, daily; common, usual; (esp. of clothes) appropriate or pertaining to weekdays, not Sunday. — *n* **everyday'ness.** — *n* **Ev'eryman** the hero of an old morality play, representing (sometimes without *cap*) mankind, everybody, anybody. — *adv* **ev'ery-place** (*US*) everywhere. — *pron* **ev'erything** all things taken singly; all. — *adv* **ev'erywhere** in every place. — **every bit** or **whit** the whole, all of it; quite, entirely; **every last** every (emphatically); **every man Jack** or **every mother's son** everyone, without exception; **every now and then** or **every now and again** at intervals, periodically; **every other** every second or alternate; **every so often** at intervals, periodically; **every which way** (*US*) every direction or method; in disorder; **have everything** (*colloq*) to be well endowed with possessions, attractiveness, etc. [O.E. *ǣfre*, ever, and *ǣlc*, each.]

evict *i-vikt'*, *vt* to dispossess by law; to expel (usu. from a dwelling). — *n* **evic'tion** the act of evicting from house or lands; the dispossession of one person by another having a better title to property or land. — *n* **evic'tor.** — **eviction order** a court order by which a person may be evicted. [L. *ēvictus*, past p. of *ēvincěre*, to overcome.]

evident *ev'i-dənt*, *adj* that can be seen; clear to the mind; obvious. — *n* **ev'idence** that which makes anything evident; means of proving an unknown or disputed fact; support (for a belief); indication; information in a law case; testimony; a witness or witnesses collectively. — *vt* to make evident, apparent, visible; to attest, prove; to indicate. — *adj* **evidential** (*-den'shəl*) or **eviden'tiary** providing evidence; tending to prove. — *adv* **eviden'tially.** — *adv* **ev'idently** obviously; manifestly. — **in evidence** received by the court as competent testimony; plainly visible, conspicuous, present; **turn King's** or **Queen's evidence**, or in U.S. **turn state's evidence** to give evidence for the prosecution against an accomplice in a crime. [L. *ēvidēns*, *-entis* — *ē*, from, *vidēre*, to see.]

evil *ē'vl* or *ē'vil*, *adj* wicked, bad; mischievous; very disagreeable, angry. — *adv* (usu. in compounds) in an evil manner; badly, terribly. — *n* something which produces unhappiness or misfortune; harm; wickedness, depravity, sin. — *adv* **evilly** (*ē'vil-i*) in an evil manner; badly, terribly. — *n* **e'vilness.** — **e'vil-doer** a person who does evil things; **evil eye** a supposed power to cause harm by a look. — *adj* **evil-mind'ed** inclined to evil; malicious; wicked. — *adj* **evil-tem'pered** bad-tempered, unpleasant, spiteful. — **the evil one** the devil; **speak evil of** to slander. [O.E. *yfel*.]

evince *i-vins'*, *vt* to prove beyond doubt; to show clearly, make evident. — *n* **evince'ment.** — *adj* **evinc'ible.** — *adv* **evinc'ibly.** — *adj* **evinc'ive** tending to evince, prove or demonstrate. [L. *ēvincěre*, to vanquish — *ē-* (intensive) and *vincěre*, to overcome.]

eviscerate *i-vis'ər-āt*, *vt* to tear out the viscera or bowels of; to gut (*lit* and *fig*). — *n* **eviscerā'tion.** [L. *ē*, from, *viscera*, the bowels.]

evoke *i-vōk'*, *vt* to call out; to draw out or bring forth; to call up or awaken (esp. memories) in the mind. — *n* **evocā'tion.** — *adj* **evocative** (*i-vok'ə-tiv*). — *n* **evoc'ativeness.** [L. *ēvocāre* — *ē*, from, *vocāre*, to call.]

evolution *ēv-* or *ev-ə-loo'shən*, *n* the doctrine according to which higher forms of life have gradually arisen out of lower; gradual working out or development; a series of things following in sequence; the giving off (of heat, etc.); the calculation of roots (*math*); (usu. in *pl*) orderly movements, as of a body of troops, flock of birds, etc. — *adj* **evolu'tional** or **evolu'tionary** of or pertaining to evolution. — *n* **evolu'tionism** the doctrine of evolution. — *n* and *adj* **evolu'tionist.** — *adj* **ev'olutive.** [L. *ēvolūtiō*, *-ōnis*, — *ēvolvěre*; see **evolve**.]

evolve *i-* or *ē-volv'*, *vt* to develop; to give off (heat, etc.). — *vi* to change gradually, esp. according to the doctrine of evolution; to become apparent gradually; to result (with *into*). — *adj* **evolv'able.** — *n* **evolve'ment.** — *adj* **evolv'ent** evolving. [L. *ēvolvěre* — *ē-*, from, *volvěre*, *volūtum*, to roll.]

ewe *ū*, *n* a female sheep. — **ewe'-lamb** a female lamb. [O.E. *ēowu*.]

ewer *ū'ər*, *n* a large water jug with a wide spout. [Through Fr. from L. *aquārium* (neuter of *aquārius*, of water) — *aqua*, water.]

Ewigkeit *ā'vihh-kīt*, *n* eternity. [Ger.]

Ex. (*Bible*) *abbrev* for (the Book of) Exodus.

ex[1] *eks*, *prep* direct from, as in *ex works*, *ex warehouse* (*commerce*); without, as in *ex dividend*, without the next dividend. [L.]

ex[2]. See under **ex-**.

ex. *abbrev* for: examined; example; exception; excursus; executive; export.

ex- *eks-*, *pfx* denoting: former but still living, e.g. *ex-emperor*; formerly employed, etc. by. — *n* **ex** (*colloq*) a person who is no longer what he or she was, esp. a person's former husband or wife: — *pl* **ex's** or **ex'es.**

exacerbate *igz-as'ər-bāt* or *iks-*, *vt* to make (e.g. an awkward situation or a disease) worse, more violent or more severe. — *n* **exacerbā'tion** increase of irritation or violence, or the increase of a fever or disease. [L. *exacerbāre*, *-ātum* — *ex*, and *acerbāre* — *acerbus*, bitter.]

exact *igz-akt'*, *vt* to force out; to compel payment of; to demand and obtain; to extort; to require as indispensable or prerequisite. — *adj* precise; rigorous; accurate; absolutely correct; strict in correctness of detail. — *adj* **exact'ing** compelling full payment; unreasonable in making demands; demanding much, challenging, difficult. — *n* **exac'tion** the act of exacting or demanding strictly; an oppressive demand; something which is exacted, as (excessive) work or tribute. — *n* **exact'itude** exactness; correctness. — *adv* **exact'ly.** — *n* **exact'ment.** — *n* **exact'ness** the quality of being exact or precise; accuracy. — *n* **exact'or** or **exact'er** a person who exacts; an extortioner. — **exact sciences** the mathematical sciences, whose results are precisely measurable. — **not exactly** not altogether; not at all (*colloq*, *ironic*). [L. *exigěre*, *exāctum*, to demand, to weigh strictly — *ex*, from, *agěre*, to drive.]

exaggerate *igz-aj'ər-āt*, *vt* to magnify unduly; to overstate, to represent too strongly; to intensify. — *vi* to speak hyperbolically, to overstate something. — *n* **exaggerā'tion** extravagant overstatement; a statement displaying this. — *adj* **exagg'erative** or **exagg'eratory** containing exaggeration or tending to exaggerate. — *n* **exagg'erātor.** [L. *exaggerāre*, *-ātum* — *ex-*, *aggerāre*, to heap up — *agger*, a heap.]

exalt *igz-ölt'*, *vt* to place in a high position (of respect, etc.); to elate or fill with the joy of success; to extol, praise. — *n* **exaltā'tion** (*egz-öl-*) elevation in rank or dignity; elation, rejoicing. — *adj* **exalt'ed** elevated, high. — *n* **exalt'edness.** [L. *exaltāre* — *ex-*, *altus*, high.]

exam *eks-am'*, *n*. Short for **examination.**

examine *igz-am'in*, *vt* to test; to inquire into; to question; to look closely at or into, to inspect. — *n* **examinabil'ity.** — *adj* **exam'inable.** — *n* **examinā'tion** careful search or inquiry; close inspection; a test of capacity and knowledge (*colloq* contraction **exam'**); formal interrogation in court of a witness or accused person (*law*). — *n* **examinee'** a person under examination. — *n* **exam'iner** a person who examines. — *n* **exam'inership.** — *adj* **exam'ining.** — **examinātion-in-chief'** (*law*) questioning of one's own witness. — *vt* **examine-in-chief'.** — **need one's head examined** (*slang*) to be crazy, stupid, etc. [Fr. *examiner* — L. *exāmināre* — *exāmen*, the tongue of a balance.]

example *igz-äm'pl*, *n* a specimen, illustration, sample; an instance; a person or thing to be imitated (or not); a warning. — **for example** for instance; as an illustration; **make an example of** to punish severely as a warning to others. [O.Fr., — L. *exemplum* — *eximěre*, to take out — *ex*, out of, *eměre*, *emptum*, to take.]

exanimate *egz-* or *igz-an'i-mit*, *adj* lifeless; spiritless. [L. *exanimātus* — *ex*, from, *anima*, breath.]

exanthem *eks-an'thəm* or **exanthema** *eks-an-thē'mə*, (*med*) *n* a skin eruption, esp. accompanied by fever; a disease characterised by these symptoms: — *pl* **exan'thems** or **exanthē'mata.** — *adj* **exanthemat'ic** or **exanthē'matous.** [Gr. *exanthēma*, *-atos* — *ex-*, out, *antheein*, to blossom.]

exarch *eks'ärk*, *n* a Byzantine provincial governor, esp. of Italy (*hist*); a metropolitan bishop (*Orthodox Ch*); a bishop ranking between a patriarch and a metropolitan bishop (*Orthodox Ch*); the head of the Bulgarian church; a bishop's representative. — *n* **exarch'ate** (or *eks'*) or **ex'archy** the office, jurisdiction or province of an exarch. [Gr. *exarchos*, leader.]

exasperate *igz-äs'pər-āt*, *vt* to make very angry; to irritate to a high degree; to make worse. — *adj* **exas'perāting.** — *n* **exasperā'tion.** — *n* **exas'perātor.** [L. *ex-* (intensive) and *asperāre*, to make rough.]

Exc. *abbrev* for Excellency.

exc. *abbrev* for: excellent; except; exception.

excarnate *eks-kär'nāt*, *vt* to remove the flesh from. — *n* **excarna'tion.** [L.L. *excarnāre*, *-ātum*, — L. *ex*, from, *carō*, *carnis*, flesh.]

ex cathedra *eks kə-thē'drə* or *eks kath'ə-dra*, (L.L.) from the chair of office, esp. the Pope's throne or a professor's chair; authoritatively. — *adj* **ex=cathe'dra** spoken with, or as if with, authority; implying authoritativeness; to be obeyed completely, esp. by Roman Catholics of a papal decree.

excavate *eks'kə-vāt*, *vt* to dig out; to lay open by digging; to hollow or scoop out. — *n* **excavā'tion** the act of excavating; a hollow or cavity made by excavating; an archaeological site, a dig. — *n* **ex'cavātor** a machine used for excavating; a person who excavates. [L. *excavāre* — *ex-*, out, *cavus*, hollow.]

exceed *ik-sēd'*, *vt* to go beyond the limit or measure of; to surpass or excel. — *adv* (*Bible*) **exceed'ing** exceedingly. — *adv* **exceed'ingly** very much; greatly. [L. *ex-*, beyond, *cēděre*, *cēssum*, to go.]

excel *ik-sel'*, *vt* to be superior to, better than; to surpass. — *vi* to have good qualities in large measure; to perform exceptional actions; to be superior, better: — *pr p* **excell'ing**; *pa t* and *pa p* **excelled'.** — *n* **excellence** (*eks'ə-ləns*) great merit; any excellent quality; worth. — *n* **Exc'ellency** a title of honour given to persons high in rank or office. — *adj* **exc'ellent** surpassing others in some good quality; of great virtue, worth, etc.; extremely good. — *adv* **exc'ellently.** — *interj* **excel'sior** (L. *compar adj*, taller, loftier) higher still. — *n* (sometimes with *cap*; orig. *US*) a trade name for wood shavings for packing. [L. *excellěre* — *ex-*, out, up, *celsus*, high.]

excellence[1]. See under **excel.**

excellence[2]. See **par excellence.**

excentric. Same as **eccentric** in mechanical senses.

except *ik-sept'*, *vt* to take out, or leave out; to exclude. — *prep* leaving out; not including; but. — *prep* **except'ing** with the exception of, except. — *n* **excep'tion** the act of excepting; something which is excepted; exclusion; objection, offence. — *adj* **excep'tionable** objectionable. — *adv* **excep'tionably.** — *adj* **excep'tional** unusual (esp. in a good sense). — *adv* **excep'tionally.** — **take exception** to object (to); **the exception proves the rule** the existence of an exception to a supposed rule proves the general truth of the rule (often used in argument when no such conclusion is justified). [L. *excipěre*, *exceptum* — *ex*, from, *capěre*, to take.]

excerpt *ek'sûrpt*, *n* a passage selected from a book, opera, etc., an extract. — *vt* **excerpt'** to select extracts from. — *npl* **excerpta** (*ik-sûrp'tə*; L.) (*nsing* **excerp'tum** *-təm* or *-to͝om*) extracts, selections. — *n* **excerpt'ing** or **excerp'tion.** — *n* **excerp'tor.** [L. *excerptum*, past p. of *excerpĕre* — *ex*, from, *carpĕre*, to pick.]

excess *ik-ses'* or *ek'ses*, *n* a going beyond what is usual or proper; intemperance; something which exceeds; the degree or amount by which one thing exceeds another. — *adj* more than usual, proper, allowed, etc. — *adj* **excess'ive** beyond what is usual or right; immoderate; extreme. — *adv* **excess'ively.** — *n* **excess'iveness.** — **excess fare** payment for distance travelled beyond, or in a class higher than, that allowed by the ticket; **excess baggage** or **luggage** luggage above the weight allowed free; **excess postage** payment due from the addressee when insufficient stamps have been put on a letter or packet. — **carry to excess** to do (something) too much; **excess profits tax** a tax on profits in excess of those for a specified base period or over a rate adopted as a reasonable return on capital; **in excess of** more than. [L. *excēssus* — *excēdĕre, excēssum*, to go beyond.]

exch. *abbrev* for: exchange; exchequer.

exchange *iks-chānj'*, *vt* to give or give up in return for something else; to give and take mutually; to barter. — *vi* to transfer in mutual ownership, position, etc. — *n* the giving and taking of one thing for another; barter; the thing exchanged; the process by which accounts between distant parties are settled by bills instead of money; money-changing business; exchanging currency of one country for that of another — also **foreign exchange**; the difference in the value of money in different places; a stock exchange, etc.; the building where merchants, etc., meet for business; a central office where telephone lines are connected; the taking by both players of an opposing piece in consecutive moves (*chess*). — *n* **exchange-abil'ity.** — *adj* **exchange'able** that may be exchanged. — *n* **exchan'ger** a person who exchanges money, goods, etc., esp. professionally. — **exchange control** the official control of the level of a country's foreign exchange transactions so as to conserve its holding of foreign currency; **exchange rate** (or **rate of exchange**) the ratio at which one currency can be exchanged for another; **exchange rate mechanism** an arrangement set up to regulate exchange rate fluctuations between participating currencies in the EMS by fixing their rates, and limiting fluctuation, against the ECU; **exchange student** or **teacher** a student or teacher spending some time at a school in a foreign country while one from that country attends his or her school, or a school in his or her country. — **exchange words** or **blows** to quarrel verbally or physically. [O.Fr. *eschangier* (Fr. *échanger*) — L.L. *excambiāre* — L. *ex*, from, L.L. *cambiāre*, to barter.]

exchequer *iks-chek'ər*, *n* (also with *cap*) a department of state having charge of revenue, orig. so named from the chequered cloth which covered the table, on which the accounts were reckoned; a national treasury; one's funds, finances, purse (*jocularly*). — **exchequer bill** a bill issued by the Exchequer, as security for money advanced to the government. — **Chancellor of the Exchequer** see under **chancellor**. [See **chequer, check, chess.**]

excise[1] *ek'sīz* or *ek-sīz'*, *n* a tax on certain home commodities, and on licences for certain trades; the department in the civil service concerned with this tax. — Also *adj*. — *vt* to subject to excise duty. — *adj* **excīs'able** liable to excise duty. — **ex'ciseman** (or *-sīz'*) an officer charged with collecting excise duty. [M.Du. *excijs* — O.Fr. *acceis*, tax — L.L. *accensāre*, to tax.]

excise[2] *ek-sīz'*, *vt* to cut off or out. — *n* **excision** (*ik-sizh'ən*) a cutting out or off of any kind; purging. [L. *excīdĕre*, to cut out — *ex*, from, *caedĕre*, to cut.]

excite *ik-sīt'*, *vt* to cause to become active; to stir up (feelings of any kind, people, etc.); to rouse, esp. sexually; to produce electric or magnetic activity in (*phys*); to stir emotionally; to raise (a nucleus, atom, molecule, etc.) to an excited state. — *n* **excitabil'ity.** — *adj* **excit'able** capable of being excited; easily excited; responsive to stimulus (*phys*). — *n* **excit'ableness.** — *n* **excitancy** (*ek'si-tən-si*) excitant property. — *n* **excitant** (*ek'si-* or *ek-sī'*) something which excites or rouses the vital activity of the body; a stimulant (*med*); the electrolyte in an electric cell. — *adj* exciting; stimulating. — *n* **excitā'tion** (*ek-si-* or *-sī-*) the act of exciting; a means of, or reason for, excitement; a state of excitement. — *adj* **excīt'ative** or **excit'atory** tending to excite. — *adj* **excit'ed** agitated; roused emotionally, or sexually; in a state of great activity; having energy higher than that of the ground, or normal, state (*phys*). — *n* **excite'ment** agitation; something which excites emotionally. — *n* **excit'er** a person or thing which excites; an auxiliary machine supplying current for another machine; a sparking apparatus for producing electric waves. — *adj* **excit'ing** tending to excite; stirring, thrilling. — *n* **excīt'on** (or *ek'si-ton*; *phys*) a bound pair comprising an electron and a hole. — *n* **excī'tor** exciter; a nerve bringing impulses to the brain, stimulating a part of the body. [Fr. *exciter* — L. *excitāre, -ātum* — *exciēre* — *ex-*, out, *ciēre*, to set in motion.]

exclaim *iks-klām'*, *vt* and *vi* to cry out (in shock, surprise, indignation or other strong emotion); to utter or speak boldly or sharply. — *n* **exclamation** (*eks-klə-mā'shən*) a sharp cry or other utterance, an uttered expression of surprise or similar; the mark expressing this (!) (also **exclamation mark**); an interjection. — *adj* **exclam'atory** containing or expressing exclamations. [Fr. *exclamer* — L. *exclāmāre, -ātum* — *ex-*, out, *clāmāre*, to shout.]

exclosure *eks-klō'zhər*, *n* an area shut off from intrusion (opp. to *enclosure*). [L. *ex-*, from, and **close**[1].]

exclude *iks-klo͞od'*, *vt* to shut out; to throw out; to prevent from entering; to omit; to prevent from taking part; to except, leave out. — *n* **excludee'** a person who is excluded. — *n* **exclu'sion** (*-zhən*) a shutting or putting out; ejection; prevention from inclusion or entry. — *adj* **exclu'sive** (*-siv*) able or tending to exclude; (mutually) incompatible; preventing participation; of the nature of monopoly; socially inaccessible or aloof; sole, only; not to be had elsewhere or from another source; select, fashionable, only for the lucky few; without taking into account (esp. with *of*). — *n* an exclusive product; a newspaper story published by one paper only. — *adv* **exclu'sively.** — *n* **exclu'siveness** or **exclusiv'ity.** — *adj* **exclu'sory** acting or tending to exclude. — **exclusion order** an order prohibiting the presence in, or entry to, Britain of any person known to be concerned in acts of terrorism; **exclusion principle** a fundamental law of quantum mechanics that no two particles of a group called fermions can exist in identical quantum states; **exclusive zone** or **exclusive economic zone** territorial waters within a certain limit, in which foreign exploitation is totally banned. — **to the exclusion of** so as to exclude. [L. *exclūdĕre, -clūsum* — *ex-*, out, *claudĕre*, to shut.]

excogitate *eks-koj'i-tāt*, *vt* to discover by thinking; to think out earnestly or laboriously. — *n* **excogitā'tion** laborious thinking; invention by thinking out. — *adj* **excog'itātive.** [L. *excōgitāre, -ātum* — *ex-*, out, *cōgitāre*, to think.]

excommunicate *eks-kəm-ūn'i-kāt*, *vt* to forbid or expel from the communion of (any branch of) the church; to deprive of church privileges. — *adj*

excommun'icable. — *adj* **excommun'icate** (*-kit*) excommunicated. — Also *n*. — *n* **excommunicā'tion** the act of expelling from the communion of (any branch of) the church. — *adj* **excommun'icatory** of or pertaining to excommunication. [From L.L. *excommūnicāre* — L. *ex*, *commūnis*, common.]

excoriate *eks-kō'ri-āt*, *vt* to strip the skin from; to criticise severely (*fig*). — *n* **excoriā'tion**. [L. *excoriāre*, *-ātum* — *ex*, from, *corium*, the skin.]

excrement *eks'kri-mənt*, *n* waste matter discharged from the digestive system, dung. — *adj* **excremental** (*-ment'*) or **excrementi'tious**. [L. *excrēmentum* — *excernĕre* — *ex-*, out, *cernĕre*, to sift.]

excrementa *eks-kri-men'tə*, (L. pl. of **excremen'tum** *-təm* or *-tōōm*) *npl* waste matter, rubbish.

excrescence *iks-kres'əns*, *n* an outgrowth or projection, esp. abnormal, grotesque or offensive; a wart or tumour; a superfluous or unattractive part. — *n* **excresc'ency** the state of being excrescent; an excrescence. — *adj* **excresc'ent** growing out; superfluous; (of a sound or letter) added to a word for pleasantness of sound, etc., without etymological justification. — *adj* **excrescential** (*eks-kri-sen'shl*). [L. *excrēscĕre* — *ex-*, out, *crēscĕre*, to grow.]

excrete *eks-krēt'*, *vt* to discharge, esp. from the bowels, bladder, sweat glands, etc.; to eject in a similar or analogous manner. — *npl* **excrē'ta** (esp. waste) products discharged from the body. — *n* **excrē'tion** the excreting of matter from an organism; that which is excreted. — *adj* **excrē'tive** able to excrete; concerned with excretion. — *adj* **excrē'tory** (or *eks'kri-tər-i*) having the quality or power of excreting. [L. *ex*, from, *cernĕre*, *crētum*, to separate.]

excruciate *iks-krōō'shi-āt*, *vt* to torture; to inflict severe pain; to irritate greatly. — *adj* **excru'ciāting** extremely painful; torturing; agonising; intensely irritating (*fig*). — *adv* **excru'ciatingly**. — *n* **excruciā'tion** torture; irritation, annoyance. [L. *excruciāre*, to torture — *ex-*, out, *cruciāre*, *-ātum*, to crucify.]

exculpate *eks'kul-pāt*, also *-kul'*, *vt* to clear from the charge of a fault or crime; to absolve. — *adj* **excul'pable**. — *n* **exculpā'tion**. — *adj* **excul'patory** freeing from the charge of a fault or crime. [L. *ex*, from, *culpa*, a fault.]

excursion *iks-kûr'shən* or *-zhən*, *n* a going out or forth; a pleasure trip, esp. organised by a company; a company or collection of people on a pleasure outing; a deviation from the normal course, a digression. — *n* **excur'sionist** a person who goes on a pleasure trip. — *adj* **excur'sive** rambling; deviating from the main point or topic. — *adv* **excur'sively**. — *n* **excur'siveness**. — *n* **excur'sus** a dissertation or discussion on some particular matter appended to the main body of a book or chapter: — *pl* **excur'suses**. — **excursion fare** a special cheap fare allowed on certain journeys by public transport; **excursion ticket**; **excursion train** a special train, usually with reduced fares, for persons making an excursion, esp. for pleasure. [L. *ex-*, out, *currĕre*, *cursum*, to run.]

excuse *iks-kūz'*, *vt* to free from blame or guilt; to exonerate; to overlook, forgive; to pardon or condone (in small matters); to free (from an obligation); to release, dispense with (temporarily); to allow to go out of one's presence; to seek to explain or justify a person or their actions; to make an apology or ask pardon for. — *n* (*iks-kūs'*) a plea offered in explanation, to avoid punishment; pardon, forgiveness. — *adj* **excūsable** (*iks-kūz'ə-bl*). — *n* **excūs'ableness**. — *adv* **excūs'ably**. — *adj* **excūs'atory** tending to excuse. — **excuse'-me** a dance during which one may change partners. — **be excused** to leave (a room, etc.); to go to the lavatory to relieve oneself (*euph*); **an excuse** (*iks-kūs'*) **for** a very poor example of; **excuse me** an expression used as an apology for any slight or apparent impropriety, esp. as a request to pass, interrupt, or to catch someone's attention, or for contradicting a statement that has been made; **excuse oneself** to ask permission and then leave; to explain and seek pardon (*for* a misdeed). [L. *excūsāre* — *ex*, from, *causa*, a cause, accusation.]

ex-directory *eks-dī-rek'tə-ri* or *-di-*, *adj* (of a telephone number) not listed in a directory; (of a person) having such a number. [**ex**[1] and **directory** (see **direct**).]

ex div. or **ex-div.** *eks-div*, *abbrev* for ex dividend, without the next dividend.

exeat *eks'i-at*, *n* formal leave of absence, esp. for a student to be out of college for more than one night. [L., let him go out.]

exec. *eg-zek'*, *abbrev* for: executive; executor.

execrate *eks'i-krāt*, *vt* to curse; to denounce; to detest. — *adj* **ex'ecrable** deserving execration; detestable; accursed; very bad; of low quality. — *adv* **ex'ecrably**. — *n* **execrā'tion** the act of execrating; a curse pronounced; that which is execrated. — *adj* **ex'ecrātive** of or belonging to execration. — *adv* **ex'ecrātively**. — *adj* **ex'ecrātory**. [L. *exsecrārī*, *-ātus*, to curse — *ex*, from, *sacer*, sacred.]

execute *eks'i-kūt*, *vt* to perform; to give effect to; to carry into effect; to put to use or bring into action; to put to death by law; to run through (a program, etc.) using computer language (*comput*). — *adj* **executable** (*eks'i-kūt-ə-bl* or *ek-sek'ūt-ə-bl*) that can be executed. — *n* **executant** (*eg-zek'*) someone who executes or performs; a technically accomplished performer of music. — *n* **execūter** (*eks'*). — *n* **execū'tion** the carrying into effect of a sentence of death; the act of, or skill in, executing or performing; accomplishment; completion. — *n* **execū'tioner** a person who executes, esp. one who carries out a sentence of death. — *adj* **executive** (*eg-zek'ū-tiv*) concerned with performance, administration or management; qualifying for or pertaining to the execution of the law; administrative; for the use of business executives; hence (*loosely*) expensive, sophisticated. — *n* a person in an executive position in government or business; the people who administer the government or an organisation; the power or authority in government that carries the laws into effect; the head of an executive, e.g. a president, governor, mayor, etc. — *adv* **exec'ūtively**. — *n* **execūtor** (*eg-zek'*) a person who executes or performs; a person appointed by a testator to see a will carried into effect (*law*): — *fem* **exec'ūtrix** (*pl* **exec'utrixes** or **execūtrī'cēs**). — *adj* **execūtō'rial**. — *n* **exec'ūtorship**. — *adj* **exec'ūtory** executing official duties; designed to be carried into effect. — **executive program** (*comput*) a program which controls the use of a computer and of other programs; **executive session** (*US*) a meeting of the Senate for executive business, usu. held in private; any meeting in private. [L. *exsequī*, *exsecūtus* — *ex*, out, *sequī*, to follow.]

exedra *eks'ə-drə*, *n* a columned recess in classical Greek and Roman architecture, containing a continuous semicircular bench, used for holding discussions in; any outdoor bench in a recess. [L. — Gr. *ex*, outside, *hedra*, seat.]

exegesis *eks-i-jē'sis*, *n* a critical interpretation of a text, esp. biblical. — *n* **ex'egēte** or **exegēt'ist** a person who interprets or expounds. — *adj* **exegetic** (*-jet'ik*) or **exeget'ical** (*-əl*) pertaining to exegesis; explanatory. — *adv* **exeget'ically**. — *nsing* **exeget'ics** the science of exegesis. [Gr. *exēgēsis* — *exēgeesthai*, to explain.]

exempla. See **exemplum**.

exemplar *egz-em'plər* or *-plär*, *n* a person or thing to be imitated; the ideal model; a type; an example; a copy of a book or other text. — *adv* **exem'plarily**. — *n* **exem'plariness**. — *n* **exemplarity** (*-plar'*) exemplariness; exemplary conduct. — *adj* **exem'-**

plary worthy of imitation or notice; serving as a model, specimen, illustration or warning. — **exemplary damages** (*law*) damages in excess of the value needed to compensate the plaintiff, awarded as a punishment to the offender. [L. *exemplar* — *exemplum*, example.]

exemplify *igz-em'pli-fī*, *vt* to illustrate by example; to serve as an example; to make an attested copy of: — *pr p* **exem'plifying**; *pa t* and *pa p* **exem'plified**. — *adj* **exem'plifīable**. — *n* **exemplificā'tion** the act of exemplifying; that which exemplifies; an attested copy or transcript. [L. *exemplum*, example, *facĕre*, to make.]

exempli gratia *ig-zem'plī grā'shi-ə* or *eks-em'plē grä'ti-ä*, (L.) by way of example, for instance — often abbreviated **e.g.**

exemplum *ig-zem'pləm*, *n* an example; a short story or anecdote illustrating a moral: — *pl* **exem'pla** (*-plə*). [L., example.]

exempt *igz-empt'* or *-emt'*, *vt* to free, or grant immunity (from). — *adj* not liable (for) or subject (to). — *n* an exempt person or organisation. — *n* **exemp'tion** the act of exempting; the state of being exempt; freedom from any service, duty, burden, etc.; immunity. [Fr., — L. *eximĕre*, *exemptum* — *ex*, from, *emĕre*, to buy.]

exequatur *eks-i-kwā'tər*, *n* an official recognition of a consul or commercial agent given by the government of the country in which he or she is to be based. [L. *exequātur*, let him execute.]

exequy *eks'i-kwi* (usu. in *pl* **ex'equies** *-kwiz*), *n* a funeral procession; funeral rites. — *adj* **exequial** (*eks-ē'kwi-əl*). [L. *exequiae* — *ex*, from, *sequī*, to follow.]

exercise *eks'ər-sīz*, *n* exertion of the body for health or amusement or the acquisition of a skill; a similar exertion of the mind; a task designed or prescribed for these purposes; a putting in practice; a written school task; a study in music; a set of problems, passages for translation, etc., in a text-book; (in *pl*) military drill or manoeuvres; a ceremony or formal proceeding (*NAm*). — *vt* to put in practice; to use; to train by use; to improve by practice; to trouble. — *vi* to take exercise; to drill. — *adj* **ex'ercisable**. — *n* **ex'erciser** someone who, or that which, exercises; a device, usu. with elasticated cords, to help in exercising the muscles. — **ex'ercise-book** a book for writing school exercises in. — **the object of the exercise** the purpose of a particular operation or activity. [O.Fr. *exercice* — L. *exercitium* — L. *exercēre*, *-citum* — *ex-* and *arcēre*, to shut up, restrain.]

exergue *eks'* or *eks-ûrg'*, *n* a part on the reverse of a coin, below the main device, often filled up by the date, etc. — *adj* **exer'gual**. [Fr., — Gr. *ex*, out of, *ergon*, work.]

exert *igz-ûrt'*, *vt* to bring into active operation; to cause (oneself) to make a strenuous (esp. physical) effort. — *n* **exer'tion** a bringing into active operation; striving; strenuous activity. — *adj* **exert'ive** having the power or tendency to exert; using exertion. [L. *exserĕre*, *exsertum* — *ex*, from, *serĕre*, to put together.]

exes *eks'əz*, *npl* a slang abbrev. of **expenses**; see also **ex** under **ex-**.

exeunt *eks'i-unt* or *-ŏŏnt*, (L.) (they) go out, leave the stage. — **exeunt omnes** (*om'nēz* or *-nās*) all go out. [**exit**.]

exfoliate *eks-fō'li-āt*, *vt* (of skin, bark, rocks, etc.) to shed in flakes or layers; to remove in flakes, etc. — *vi* to come off in flakes; to separate into layers. — *n* **exfoliā'tion**. — *adj* **exfō'liative**. [L. *exfoliāre*, *-ātum*, to strip of leaves — *ex*, from, *folium*, a leaf.]

ex gratia *eks grā'shi-ə*, (L.) as an act of grace; given or made as a favour, not out of obligation, and with no acceptance of liability (as *ex gratia payment*).

exhale *eks-hāl'* or *egz-āl'*, *vt* to breathe forth; to emit or send out as vapour, smell, etc. — *vi* to breathe out; to rise or come off as a vapour, smell, or emanation. — *adj* **exhāl'able**. — *n* **exhalation** (*eks-* or *egz-ə-lā'shən*) the act or process of exhaling; that which is exhaled; a breath out; vapour; emanation. [L. *exhālāre* — *ex*, from, *hālāre*, *-ātum*, to breathe.]

exhaust *igz-öst'*, *vt* to draw off; to use the whole strength of; to use up; to empty; to wear or tire out. — *vi* (of exhaust gases in an engine) to be emitted. — *n* the exit of gases or fluids as waste products from the cylinder of an engine, from a turbine, etc.; the gases or fluids so escaping (**exhaust'-gas** or **-steam**). — *adj* **exhaust'ible**. — *n* **exhaustion** (*-öst'yən*) extreme fatigue; the state of being exhausted; the act of exhausting or consuming. — *adj* **exhaust'ive** tending to exhaust; investigating all parts or possibilities; thorough. — **exhaust'-pipe** or **-valve** the pipe or valve through which exhaust gases pass out. [L. *exhaurīre*, *exhaustum* — *ex*, from, *haurīre*, to draw.]

exhibit *igz-ib'it*, *vt* to present or display formally or publicly; to show or manifest (a quality, etc.) — *n* an article at an exhibition; a document or object produced in court to be used as evidence (*law*). — *n* **exhib'iter**. — *n* **exhibition** (*eks-i-bish'ən*) a public show, esp. of works of art, manufactures, etc.; display; showing off; an allowance towards support, esp. to students at a university. — *n* **exhibi'tioner** a university student who is awarded an exhibition. — *n* **exhibi'tionism** extravagant behaviour aimed at drawing attention to self; perversion involving public exposure of one's sexual organs (*psychiatry*). — *n* **exhibi'tionist**. — *adj* **exhibitionist'ic**. — *adv* **exhibitionist'ically**. — *n* **exhibitor** (*igz-ib'i-tər*). — *adj* **exhib'itory**. — **make an exhibition of oneself** to behave foolishly, provoke ridicule. [L. *exhibēre*, *-itum* — *ex-*, out, *habēre*, *-itum*, to have.]

exhilarate *igz-il'ə-rāt*, *vt* to raise the spirits of; to refresh the body and mind of; to enliven; to cheer. — *adj* and *n* **exhil'arant**. — *adj* **exhil'arāting**. — *adv* **exhil'arātingly**. — *n* **exhilarā'tion**. — *adj* **exhil'-arātive** or **exhil'aratory**. [L. *exhilarāre*, *-ātum* — *ex-* (intensive) and *hilaris*, cheerful.]

exhort *ig-zört'*, *vt* to urge strongly and earnestly; to counsel. — *n* **exhortā'tion** (*eks-* or *egz-*) the act of exhorting; speech or writing intended to exhort; counsel; a religious discourse. — *adj* **exhort'ative** or **exhort'atory** (*igz-*) tending to exhort or advise. — *n* **exhort'er**. [L. *exhortārī*, *-ātus* — *ex-* (intensive) and *hortārī*, to urge.]

exhume *eks-hūm'* or *ig-zūm'*, *vt* to take out of the ground or place of burial; to disinter; to bring back into use; to bring up or mention again. — *n* **exhumā'tion** (*eks-*). — *n* **exhum'er**. [L. *ex*, out of, *humus*, the ground.]

ex hypothesi *eks hī-poth'ə-sī*, (L.L.) from the hypothesis stated.

exigent *eks'i-jənt*, *adj* pressing; urgent; exacting; demanding immediate attention or action. — *n* **ex'igence** or **ex'igency** (or *-ij'*) pressing necessity; emergency. [L. *exigēns*, *-entis* — pres. p. of *exigĕre* — pfx. *ex-*, *agĕre*, to drive.]

exigible *eks'i-jib-l*, *adj* liable to be exacted or demanded. [See **exact**.]

exiguous *egz-* or *eks-ig'ū-əs*, *adj* scanty; meagre; slender. — *n* **exigū'ity** (*eks-*) or **exig'ūousness**. [L. *exiguus* — *exigĕre*, to weight strictly; see **exact**.]

exile *eks'īl* or *egz'īl*, *n* enforced or regretted absence from one's country or home; banishment; (with *cap*) the captivity of the Jews in Babylon; someone who is in exile. — *vt* to expel from one's country, to banish. — *adj* **exilic** (*egz-il'ik* or *eks-*) or **exil'ian** pertaining to exile, esp. that of the Jews in Babylon. [O.Fr. *exil* — L. *exsilium*, banishment — *ex*, out of, and root of *salīre*, to leap.]

ex int. (*banking*) *abbrev* for *ex interest*, without interest. [L. *ex*, without.]

exist *igz-ist'*, *vi* to have an actual being; to live; to occur; to continue to live, esp. in unfavourable circumstances. — *n* **exist'ence** the state of existing or being; livelihood; life; anything and everything that exists; being. — *adj* **exist'ent** having being; existing at present. — *adj* **existential** (*eks-is-ten'shəl*) of or relating to (esp. human) existence; of or relating to existentialism. — *n* **existen'tialism** a term covering a number of related philosophical doctrines denying objective universal values and holding that people, as moral free agents, must create values for themselves through actions and must accept the ultimate responsibility for those actions in a seemingly meaningless universe. — *n* and *adj* **existen'tialist.** [L. *existĕre*, *exsistĕre*, to stand forth — *ex-*, out, *sistĕre*, to stand.]

Exit *ek'sit* or *eg'zit*, *n* a British organisation encouraging voluntary euthanasia, and campaigning for its legalisation.

exit *ek'sit* or *eg'zit*, *n* a way of departure; a passage out; any departure; the departure of an actor from the stage; a place on a motorway where vehicles can leave by a slip road; death (*literary*); the last instruction of a subroutine (*comput*): — *pl* **ex'its.** — *vi* to make an exit; to leave or depart; to die (*literary*); to lose the lead deliberately (*cards*): — *pa p* and *pa t* **ex'ited.** — **exit poll** a poll of a sample of voters, taken as they leave the polling-station, used to give an early indication of voting trends in a particular election. [Partly from the L. stage direction *exit*, goes out; partly — L. *exitus*, a way out.]

ex-libris *eks-lī'bris* or *-li'bris*, *n* a name-label pasted into the front of a book; a bookplate. [L. *ex lībrīs*, from the books (of so-and-so).]

ex nihilo *eks nī'hi-lō* or *ni'*, (L.) out of nothing, as in *creation ex nihilo*.

exo- *eks'ō-* or *eks-ō'-*, *combining form* signifying outside (often opp. to **endo-**, **ento-**; see also **ecto-**). [Gr. *exō*, outside.]

exobiology *eks-ō-bī-ol'ə-ji*, *n* the study of (possible) extraterrestrial life. — *adj* **exobiolog'ical.** — *n* **exobiol'ogist.** [**exo-**.]

exocarp *eks'ō-kärp*, (*bot*) *n* the outside layer of the part of a fruit which contains the seeds; the epicarp. [**exo-** and Gr. *karpos*, fruit.]

Exocet® *eks'ə-set*, *n* a subsonic tactical missile, launched from ship, plane or submarine and travelling at low altitude. [Fr., — L. *Exocoetus volitans*, the flying fish.]

exocrine *eks'ō-krin* or *-krīn*, (*physiol*) *adj* (of glands) secreting through a duct. — *n* an exocrine gland. [**exo-** and Gr. *krīnein*, to separate.]

exocytosis *eks-ō-sī-tō'sis*, (*biol*) *n* the discharge from a cell of particles too large to diffuse through the wall. [**exo-**, **cyto-** and **-sis**.]

Exod. (*Bible*) *abbrev* for (the Book of) Exodus.

exoderm *eks'ō-dûrm*, *n* exodermis; ectoderm. — *adj* **exoder'mal.** — *n* **exoder'mis** the outer cortex layer of a root. [**exo-** and Gr. *dermis*, skin.]

exodus *eks'ə-dəs*, *n* a going out, esp. that of the Israelites from Egypt; (with *cap*) the second book of the Old Testament in the Bible. [L., — Gr. *exodos* — *ex-*, out, *hodos*, a way.]

exoenzyme *eks-ō-en'zīm*, *n* an enzyme that functions outside the cell producing it, an ectoenzyme. [**exo-**.]

exoergic *eks-ō-ûr'jik*, (*nuc*) *adj* pertaining to a process in which energy is liberated. [**exo-** and Gr. *ergon*, work.]

ex officio *eks o-fish'i-ō* or *-fik'*, (L.) by virtue of office or position.

exogamy *eks-og'ə-mi*, *n* the practice of marrying only outside of one's own group; the union of gametes not closely related (*biol*). — *adj* **exogam'ic** or **exog'amous.** [**exo-** and Gr. *gamos*, marriage.]

exogenous *eks-oj'ə-nəs*, *adj* growing by successive additions to the outside; developing externally; having an external origin. [**exo-** and Gr. *genēs*, born.]

exon[1] *eks'on*, *n* one of the four commanding officers of the Yeomen of the Guard. [App. intended to express the pronunciation of Fr. *exempt*; see **exempt**.]

exon[2] *eks'on*, (*biol*) *n* any segment of a gene which consists of codons (opp. of *intron*). [L. *ex*, out of, and Gr. neut. sfx. *-on*.]

exonerate *igz-on'ər-āt*, *vt* to free from the burden of blame or obligation; to acquit. — *n* **exonerā'tion** the act of exonerating. — *adj* **exon'erative.** [L. *exonerāre*, *-ātum*, — *ex*, from, *onus*, *oneris*, burden.]

exophthalmia *eks-of-thal'mi-ə*, **exophthalmos** or **exophthalmus** *-thal'məs*, *n* a protrusion of the eyeballs. — *adj* **exophthal'mic.** [Gr. *ex*, out, *ophthalmos*, eye.]

exoplasm *eks'ō-plazm*, *n* ectoplasm. [**exo-** and Gr. *plasma*, mould.]

exor (*law*) *abbrev* for executor.

exorbitant *igz-ör'bi-tənt*, *adj* going beyond the usual limits; excessive. — *n* **exor'bitance.** — *adv* **exor'bitantly.** [L. *exorbitāre* — *ex*, out of, *orbita*, a track — *orbis*, a circle.]

exorcise or **-ize** *eks'ör-sīz*, *vt* to drive away (a spirit); to deliver from the influence of an evil spirit. — *n* **ex'orcism** (*-sizm*) the act of exorcising or expelling evil spirits by certain ceremonies; a formula for exorcising. — *n* **ex'orcist.** [L.L. from Gr. *exorkizein* — *ex-*, out, *horkos*, an oath.]

exordium *egz-ör'di-əm*, *n* an introductory part, esp. of a discourse or composition: — *pl* **exor'diums** or **exor'dia.** — *adj* **exor'dial.** [L., — *ex*, out of, *ordīrī*, to begin.]

exoskeleton *eks-ō-skel'i-tn*, *n* a hard supporting or protective structure secreted externally by the ectoderm. — *adj* **exoskel'etal.** [**exo-**.]

exosphere *eks'ō-sfēr*, *n* the outermost layer of the earth's atmosphere; the boundary of the earth's atmosphere and interplanetary space. — *adj* **exospheric** (*-sfer'*) or **exospher'ical.** [**exo-** and **-sphere** as in **atmosphere**.]

exoteric *eks-ō-ter'ik*, *adj* intelligible to the uninitiated; popular or commonplace (opp. to *esoteric*). — *adj* **exoter'ical.** — *adv* **exoter'ically.** — *n* **exoter'icism** (*-sizm*). [Gr. *exōterikos* — *exōterō*, compar. of *exō*, outside.]

exothermal *eks-ō-thûrm'əl* or **exothermic** *-thûrm'ik*, (*chem*) *adj* involving evolution of heat. — *n* **exothermic'ity.** [**exo-** and Gr. *thermē*, heat.]

exotic *igz-ot'ik*, *adj* introduced from a foreign country; romantically strange, or rich and showy, or glamorous; foreign-looking. — *n* anything of foreign origin; something not native to a country, such as a plant, a word, or a custom. — *npl* **exot'ica** exotic objects; theatrical or musical items with an unusual theme or with a foreign flavour. — *n* **exot'icism** (*-sizm*). — **exotic dancer** a striptease artist or belly dancer. [Gr. *exōtikos* — *exō*, outside.]

exotoxin *eks-ō-tok'sin*, (*biol*) *n* a toxin produced by a micro-organism and secreted into the surrounding medium. — *adj* **exotox'ic.** [**exo-**.]

exp. *abbrev* for: exponential; export; exporter; express.

expand *iks-pand'*, *vt* to enlarge in bulk or surface area; to spread out; to develop, or bring out in fuller detail; to express at length. — *vi* to increase in volume; to enlarge; to spread; to become communicative (*fig*); to speak or write more fully (on). — *adj* **expand'able.** — *n* **expand'er** or **expand'or** an electronic device which increases the range of amplitude variations in a transmission system. — *n* **expanse** (*-pans'*) a wide extent; a stretch; the amount of spread or stretch. — *n* **expansibil'ity.** — *adj* **expans'ible.** — *adv* **expans'ibly.** — *adj* **expans'ile** (*-īl*) capable of expansion. — *n* **expan'sion** enlargement; that which is expanded; amount of expanding; territorial extension; extension. — *adj* **expan'-**

sionary tending to expand. — *n* **expan'sionism** the principle or practice of expanding the territory or the economy of a country. — *n* **expan'sionist.** — Also *adj.* — *adj* **expans'ive** widely extended; causing expansion; worked by expansion; effusive; talkative, communicative; marked by excessive feeling of wellbeing and delusions of self-importance (*psychiatry*). — *adv* **expans'ively.** — *n* **expans'iveness.** — *n* **expansiv'ity.** — **expanded metal** steel, etc., stretched to form a mesh, used for reinforcing concrete, etc.; **expanded plastic** foam plastic; **expanding universe** (*astron*) the theory that the whole universe is constantly expanding and the galaxies moving away from each other; **expansion board** or **card** (*comput*) a printed circuit board which can be inserted into an **expansion slot,** a connector in a computer which allows extra facilities to be added temporarily or permanently; **expansion bolt** a bolt that expands within a hole, crack, etc., thus providing a firm support, e.g. in mountaineering; **expansion joint** (*eng*) a gap left at a joint between e.g. lengths of rail or sections of concrete, to allow for heat expansion. [L. *expandĕre* — *ex-*, out, *pandĕre*, *pānsum*, to spread.]

ex parte *eks pär' tē* or *pär' te*, (*law*) *adj* on one side only, or in the interests of one party only. [L. *ex*, from, *parte*, abl. of *pars*, *partis*, party, side.]

expat *eks'pat*, *n* short for **expatriate.**

expatiate *eks-pā'shi-āt*, *vi* to enlarge in discourse, argument or writing; to wander at large (usu. *fig*). — *n* **expatiā'tion.** — *adj* **expā'tiative** or **expā'tiatory** expansive. — *n* **expā'tiātor.** [L. *exspatiārī*, *-ātus* — *ex*, out of, *spatiārī*, to roam.]

expatriate *eks-pā'tri-āt* or *-pa'*, *vt* to send out of one's country; to banish, exile (oneself or another); to deprive of citizenship. — Also *adj* (*-tri-ət*). — *n* an exile, voluntary or compulsory; a person who lives abroad permanently, for financial or other reasons; someone working abroad for a period. — *n* **expatriā'tion.** [L.L. *expatriāre*, *-ātum* — *ex*, out of, *patria*, fatherland.]

expect *iks-pekt'*, *vt* to look forward to as likely to come or happen, or as due; to suppose. — *adj* **expect'able.** — *adv* **expect'ably.** — *n* **expect'ance** or **expect'ancy** the act or state of expecting; that which is expected; hope. — *adj* **expect'ant** looking or waiting for something; in expectation; not yet but expecting to be; pregnant. — *n* a person who expects; a person who is looking or waiting for some benefit or office. — *adv* **expect'antly.** — *n* **expectā'tion** (*eks-*) the act or state of expecting; the prospect of future good; that which is or may fairly be expected; the degree of probability; the value of something expected; (in *pl*) prospect of fortune or profit by a will. — **be expecting** (*colloq*) to be pregnant; **life expectancy** or **expectation of life** the average length of time that one may expect to live. [L. *expectāre*, *-ātum* — *ex*, out, *spectāre*, to look.]

expectorate *eks-pek'tə-rāt*, *vt* to expel from the chest, air-passages or lungs by coughing, etc.; to spit forth. — *vi* to discharge or eject phlegm from the throat; to spit. — *adj* **expec'torant** tending to promote expectoration. — *n* a medicine that promotes expectoration. — *n* **expectorā'tion** the act of expectorating; that which is expectorated; spittle, phlegm. — *adj* **expec'torātive.** [L. *expectorāre*, *-ātum* — *ex*, from, *pectus*, *pectoris*, breast.]

expedient *iks-pē'di-ənt*, *adj* suitable or appropriate; profitable or convenient rather than fair or just. — *n* means suitable to an end. — *n* **expē'dience** or **expē'diency** appropriateness; desirableness; conduciveness to the need of the moment; that which is opportune; self-interest. — *adv* **expē'diently.** [L. *expediēns*, *-entis*, pres. p. of *expedīre*; see ety. for **expedite.**]

expedite *eks'pi-dīt*, *vt* to free from impediments; to hasten; to despatch with speed and efficiency. — *n* **expedition** (*-di'shən*) speed; promptness; an organised journey to attain some object, such as hunting, warfare, exploration, etc.; the party undertaking such a journey. — *adj* **expedi'tionary** belonging to an expedition; of the nature of an expedition. — *adj* **expedi'tious** characterised by expedition or rapidity; speedy; prompt. — *adv* **expedi'tiously.** — *n* **expedi'tiousness.** [L. *expedīre*, *-ītum* — *ex*, from, *pēs*, *pedis*, a foot.]

expel *iks-pel'*, *vt* to drive out; to eject; to discharge in disgrace (from school, etc.); to banish: — *pr p* **expell'ing**; *pa t* and *pa p* **expelled'.** — *adj* and *n* **expell'ant** or **expell'ent.** — *n* **expellee'** a person who is expelled. [L. *expellĕre*, *expulsum* — *ex*, from, *pellĕre*, to drive.]

expend *iks-pend'*, *vt* to employ or consume in any way; to spend. — *adj* **expend'able** that may be expended, esp. that may be sacrificed to achieve some end. — Also *n.* — *n* **expendabil'ity.** — *n* **expen'der.** — *n* **expend'iture** the act of expending; that which is expended; the process of using up; money spent. — *n* **expense** (*-pens'*) expenditure; outlay; cost; (in *pl*) money from one's own pocket, spent in the performance of one's job, etc.; the money reimbursed by one's company, etc., or an allowance made to cover the amount usually spent. — *adj* **expens'ive** causing or requiring much expense; costly; lavish. — *adv* **expens'ively.** — *n* **expens'iveness.** — **expendable launch vehicle** (*astron*) a launch vehicle made up of throwaway stages with no recoverable parts; **expense (or expenses) account** an arrangement by which expenses incurred during the performance of an employee's duties are reimbursed by the employer; a statement of such incurred expenses. — **at the expense of** to the cost, detriment of (often **at someone's,** etc. **expense**); with the loss or sacrifice of. [L. *expendĕre* — *ex-*, out, *pendĕre*, *pēnsum*, to weigh.]

experience *iks-pē'ri-əns*, *n* practical acquaintance with any matter, gained by trial; long and varied observation, personal or general; wisdom derived in the course of life; the passing through any event or course of events by which one is affected; such an event; anything received by the mind, such as sensation, perception or knowledge. — *vt* to have practical acquaintance with; to prove or know by use; to have experience of; to feel, suffer or undergo. — *adj* **expē'rienced.** — *adj* **expērien'tial** (*-en'shl*; *philos*) pertaining to or derived from experience. — *n* **expērien'tialism** the philosophical doctrine that all knowledge comes from experience. — *n* **expērien'tialist.** — *adv* **expērien'tially.** [Fr. *expérience* and L. *experientia*, from *experīrī* — *ex-* (intensive) and old verb *perīrī*, to try.]

experiment *iks-per'i-mənt*, *n* a trial; something done to test a theory, or to discover something unknown. — *vi* (also *-ment'*) to make an experiment or trial. — *adj* **experiment'al** pertaining to experiment; based on or proceeding by experiment; trying out new styles or techniques; tentative. — *vi* **experiment'alise** or **-ize.** — *n* **experiment'alism** use of or reliance on experiment. — *n* **experiment'alist.** — *n* **exper'imenter** (or *-ment'*). — *adv* **experiment'ally.** — *n* **experimentā'tion.** [L. *experīmentum*, from *experīrī*, to try thoroughly.]

expert *eks'pûrt*, *adj* taught by practice; having a thorough knowledge; having a facility of performance (with *at* or *in*); skilful, adroit (with *at* or *in*). — *n* someone who is skilled in any art or science; a specialist; a scientific or professional witness. — *n* **expertise** (*-ēz'*) expert knowledge; expertness; expert appraisal. — *vi* and *vt* **ex'pertise** or **-ize** (*-īz*) to give an expert opinion (on). — *adv* **ex'pertly.** — *n* **ex'pertness.** — **expert system** (*comput*) a program based on specialist knowledge and using artificial intelligence techniques, which can make decisions or solve problems intelligently. [Fr., — L. *expertus* — *experīrī*, to try thoroughly.]

expiate *eks'pi-āt*, *vt* to make complete atonement for; to make satisfaction or reparation for. — *adj* **ex'piable** capable of being expiated, atoned for or done away with. — *n* **expiā'tion** the act of expiating; the means by which atonement is made; atonement. — *n* **ex'piātor**. — *adj* **ex'piatory** (-*ə*- or -*ā-tər-i*). [L. *expiāre*, -*ātum* — *ex-* (intensive) and *piāre*, to appease, atone for.]

expire *iks-* or *eks-pīr'*, *vt* to breathe out. — *vi* to breathe out; to die; to come to an end; to lapse; to become invalid by lapse of time. — *n* **expirā'tion** (*eks-pi-* or -*pī-*). — *adj* **expī'ratory**. — *n* **expī'ry** the end or termination, esp. by lapse of time; expiration. [Fr. *expirer* — L. *ex*, from, *spīrāre*, -*ātum*, to breathe.]

explain *iks-plān'*, *vt* to make plain or intelligible; to unfold and illustrate the meaning of; to expound; to account for. — *vi* to give an explanation. — *adj* **explain'able**. — *n* **explain'er**. — *n* **explanation** (*eks-plə-nā'shən*) the act of explaining or clearing from obscurity; that which explains or clears up; the meaning or sense given to anything; a reconciliation. — *adv* **explanatorily** (*iks-plan'ə-tər-i-li*). — *adj* **explan'atory** serving to explain or clear up; containing explanations. — **explain away** to modify the force of by explanation, generally in a bad sense. [L. *explānāre* — *ex-*, out, *plānāre*, to level — *plānus*, flat, plain.]

explantation *eks-plän-tā'shən*, *n* the culture in an artificial medium of a part or organ removed from a living individual. — *n* and *vt* **explant'**. [L. *explantāre* — *ex-*, out, *plantāre*, to plant.]

expletive *eks-* or *iks-plē'tiv*, or *eks'pli-tiv*, *adj* filling out; added merely to fill up (a line of verse). — *n* a swear-word of any kind; a meaningless oath; a word or anything present merely to fill a gap. — *adj* **explē'tory** (also *eks'pli-*) serving to fill up; expletive; supplementary. [L. *explētivus* — *ex*, out, *plēre*, to fill.]

explicate *eks'pli-kāt*, *vt* to unfold or develop (a theory, etc.); to lay open or explain the meaning of. — *adj* **explic'able** capable of being explicated or explained. — *n* **explicā'tion** explanation. — *adj* **explic'ative** or **explic'atory** serving to explicate or explain. — *n* **ex'plicātor**. [L. *explicāre* — *ex*, out, *plicāre*, to fold.]

explicit *iks-plis'it*, *adj* not merely implied, but distinctly stated; plain in language; clear; unreserved. — *adv* **explic'itly**. — *n* **explic'itness**. [See ety. for **explicate**.]

explode *iks-plōd'*, *vt* to bring into disrepute, and reject; to cause to blow up. — *vi* to burst with violence; to burst out or break forth suddenly; to increase suddenly and rapidly. — *adj* **explō'ded** blown up; (of a theory, etc.) rejected because proved false; (of a drawing or diagram of a machine, building, organism, etc.) showing the internal structure and separate parts and their relationship. — *n* **explō'der**. — *adj* **explō'sible** liable to explode. — *n* **explō'sion** (-*zhən*) the act of exploding; a sudden violent burst with a loud noise; an outburst; a great and rapid increase or expansion, as in *population explosion*; breaking out of feelings, etc. — *adj* **explō'sive** (-*siv* or -*ziv*) liable to cause or causing an explosion; worked, set in place, etc., by an explosion; bursting out with violence and noise. — *n* something that will explode, esp. a substance specifically created to do so. — *adv* **explō'sively**. — *n* **explō'siveness**. — **exploding star** a star that flares up, such as a nova or supernova; **explosion welding** welding metals with very different melting points by means of pressure produced by an explosion. [L. *explōdĕre*, *explōsum* — *ex*, from, *plaudĕre*, to clap the hands.]

exploit *eks'ploit*, *n* a deed or achievement, esp. a heroic one; a feat. — *vt* (*iks-ploit'*) to make gain out of or at the expense of; to work, make available. — *adj* **exploit'able**. — *n* **exploit'age**. — *n* **exploitā'tion** (*eks-*) the act of using for selfish purposes; the act of successfully applying industry to any object, such as the working of mines, etc.; the setting-up and getting into production of an oilfield, mine, etc. — *adj* **exploit'ative** or **exploit'ive**. — *n* **exploit'er**. [O.Fr. *exploit* — L. *explicitum*, unfolded; see **explicate**.]

explore *iks-plör'*, *vt* and *vi* to search or travel through for the purpose of discovery; to examine thoroughly. — *n* **explorā'tion** (*eks-*) the act of searching, or searching for (something), thoroughly; travel for the sake of discovery; examination of a region's geology, etc., in a search for mineral resources. — *n* **explorā'tionist** a scientist engaged in mineral exploration. — *adj* **explor'ative** or **explor'atory** (-*or-*). — *n* **explor'er** a person who explores, esp. a member of a geological, etc. exploration; (with *cap*) any of the first series of U.S. satellites. [Fr., — L. *explōrāre*, -*ātum*, to search out.]

explosion. See **explode**.

expo *eks'pō*, *n* an exhibition or public showing: — *pl* **ex'pos**. [*expo*sition.]

exponent *eks-pō'nənt*, *n* an interpreter of an art by performance; an example, illustration, type (of); an expounder (of); a symbol showing what power a quantity is raised to, an index (*math*). — *adj* setting forth; expounding. — *adj* **exponential** (*eks-pō-nen'shl*) pertaining to or involving exponents. — *n* an exponential function. — *adv* **exponen'tially**. — **exponential curve** a curve expressed by an exponential equation; **exponential equation** one in which the variable occurs in the exponent of one or more terms; **exponential function** a quantity with a variable exponent, esp. e^x, where e is the base of natural logarithms. [L. *expōnēns*, -*entis*, setting forth — *ex-*, out, *pōnĕre*, to place.]

export *eks-pört'*, *vt* to carry or send out of a country, as goods in commerce. — *n* **ex'port** the act of exporting; that which is exported; a commodity which is or may be sent from one country to another in traffic; a type of strong brown beer. — *adj* **export'able**. — *n* **exportabil'ity**. — *n* **exportā'tion**. — *n* **export'er**. — **export reject** a manufactured article that is flawed in some way and so not passed for export, often sold at a reduced price on the home market. — **invisible exports** such items in a national trade balance as money spent by tourists from abroad, etc. (opp. to **visible exports** goods sold abroad by traders). [L. *exportāre*, -*ātum* — *ex-*, out of, *portāre*, to carry.]

expose *iks-pōz'*, *vt* to lay forth to view; to deprive of cover, protection or shelter; to make bare; to abandon (a child or animal); to submit (to an influence, such as light, weather); to put up (for sale); to disclose; to show up. — *n* **expōs'al** exposure; exposition. — *n* **exposé** (*eks-pō'zā*) an article or programme exposing crime, scandal, etc., to public notice; a formal statement or exposition; an exposing; a shameful showing up. — *n* **exposure** (-*pō'zhər* or -*zhyər*) the act of laying open or bare; subjection to an influence; the act of allowing access of light (*phot*); the duration of such access; the act of showing up an evil; a state of being laid bare; openness to danger; a shelterless state; position with regard to the sun, influence of climate, etc.; appearance in public, esp. on television. — **exposure meter** (*phot*) an instrument, now often incorporated in the camera, for measuring the light falling on or reflected from a subject. — **expose oneself** to expose one's sexual organs in public. [Fr. *exposer* — L. *ex-*, out, and *pausāre*, to rest, confused with *expōnĕre*, to expose.]

exposition *eks-pō-zish'ən*, *n* the act of exposing; a setting out to public view; a public exhibition; explanation; commentary; the enunciation of themes in a composition; that part of a sonata, fugue, etc., in which themes are presented. — *adj* **exposi'tive** (*-poz'*). — *n* **expos'itor** someone who, or that which, expounds. — *adj* **expos'itory** serving to explain; explanatory. [L. *expositiō, -ōnis, expositor, -ōris* — *expōnĕre, expositum*, to expose, set forth; see **expound.**]

ex post facto *eks pōst fak'tō*, (L.; *lit* from what is done or enacted after) retrospective; retrospectively.

expostulate *iks-post'ū-lāt*, *vi* to remonstrate; to discuss or reason (with). — *n* **expostūlā'tion.** — *adj* **expost'ūlātive** (also *-ə-tiv*) or **expost'ūlatory** (*-ā-* or *-ə-tər-i*) containing expostulation. — *n* **expost'ūlator.** [L. *expostulāre, -ātum* — *ex-* (intensive) and *postulāre*, to demand.]

exposure. See under **expose.**

expound *iks-pownd'*, *vt* to expose, or lay open the meaning of; to explain; to interpret; to explain in a certain way. — *vi* to speak, talk informatively or pass comment (on), often at length. — *n* **expound'er.** [O.Fr. *espondre* — L. *expōnĕre* — *ex-*, out, *pōnĕre*, to place.]

express *iks-pres'*, *vt* to put into words; to represent or make known by a likeness, words, signs, symbols, etc.; to state explicitly; to symbolise; to press or force out; to despatch rapidly. — *adj* intended or sent for a particular purpose; directly stated; explicit; clear; clearly brought out; exactly representing; expeditious, esp. of or sent by special messenger service, etc. — *adv* with haste; specially; by express train or messenger. — *n* a regular and quick conveyance; a system for the speedy transmission of messages or goods; an express train; an express messenger. — *n* **express'age** the system of carrying by express; the charge for doing so. — *adj* **express'ible.** — *n* **expression** (*-presh'ən*) representation or revelation by language, art, the features, etc.; the act, or mode, or power, of representing or giving utterance; the manner in which anything is expressed; a word, phrase; a symbol; intonation; due indication of feeling in performance of music, etc.; the act of forcing out by pressure; the effect which a gene produces (*biol*). — *n* **express'ionism** (often with *cap*) in literature and painting, a revolt against impressionism, turning away from the representation of external reality to the expression of the artist's emotions and reactions to experience. — *n* and *adj* **express'ionist.** — *adj* **expressionis'tic.** — *adj* **express'ionless.** — *adj* **express'ive** serving to express or indicate; full of expression; vividly representing (with *of*); emphatic; significant. — *adv* **express'ively.** — *n* **express'iveness.** — *n* **expressiv'ity** the quality of being able to express; the extent to which a gene produces an effect (*biol*). — *adv* **express'ly** explicitly; for the express purpose; definitely. — **express delivery** immediate delivery by special messenger; delivery by express agency; **expression mark** a direction written on a piece of music (usu. in Italian); **expression stop** a stop in a harmonium by which the performer can regulate the air to produce expression; **express letter, packet, parcel,** etc. one sent by special messenger; **express messenger** a special messenger delivering goods faster than the standard service; **express rifle** a rifle for big game at short range, with a heavy charge of powder and a light bullet; **express train** a railway train which travels at high speed and with few stops; **express'way** (*NAm*) a motorway. — **express oneself** to give expression to one's thoughts, ideas and opinions. [L. *exprimĕre, expressum* — *ex*, from, *premĕre, pressum*, to press; partly through Fr. *exprès*, etc.]

expresso *eks-pres'ō*, *n* and *adj*. Same as **espresso.**

expropriate *eks-prō'pri-āt*, *vt* to dispossess (of property), esp. for use by the State. — *adj* **exprō'priable.** — *n* **expropriā'tion.** — *n* **exprō'priator.** [L. *expropriāre, -ātum* — *ex*, from, *proprium*, property.]

expulsion *iks-pul'shən*, *n* the act of expelling; banishment. — *adj* **expul'sive** able or serving to expel. [L. *expulsāre*, frequentative of *expellĕre*; see **expel.**]

expunge *iks-punj'*, *vt* to wipe out; to efface; to mark for deletion. — *n* **expunc'tion** (*-pungk'shən*). — *n* **expun'ger.** [L. *expungĕre*, to mark for deletion by a row of dots.]

expurgate *eks'pûr-gāt* or *-pûr'gāt*, *vt* to purge out or make pure; to revise (a book, etc.) by removing anything supposed to be offensive, noxious or erroneous. — *n* **expurgā'tion** the act of expurgating or purifying. — *n* **expurgator** (*eks'pûr-gā-tər* or *eks-pûr'gə-tər*). — *adj* **expurgatorial** (*-gə-tō'ri-əl*) or **expur'gatory.** [L. *expurgāre, -ātum* — *ex-*, out, *purgāre*, to purge.]

exquisite *eks'kwiz-it* or *-kwiz'*, *adj* delicious; of consummate excellence; of delicate perception or close discrimination; fastidious; (of e.g. pain or pleasure) exceeding or extreme. — *adv* **exquisitely.** — *n* **exquisiteness.** [L. *exquīsītus* — *ex*, out, *quaerĕre*, to seek.]

exscind *ik-sind'*, *vt* to cut off or out. [L. *ex*, from, *scindĕre*, to cut.]

exsert *ik-sûrt'*, *vt* to protrude. — *n* **exser'tion.** [L. *exserĕre, -sertum*; see **exert.**]

ex-service *eks-sûr'vis*, *adj* having formerly served in one of the armed forces. — **ex-ser'viceman** or (*fem*) **ex-ser'vicewoman.**

exsiccate *ek'si-kāt*, *vt* to dry up. [L. *exsiccare* — *ex-*, *siccus*, dry.]

exstrophy or **extrophy** *eks'trə-fi*, (*med*) *n* the turning inside out of a hollow organ, esp. the bladder. [Gr. *ex*, out of, *strophein*, to turn.]

ext. *abbrev* for: extension; external; externally; extinct; extra; extract.

extant *iks-tant'* or *eks'tənt*, *adj* still standing or existing; surviving. [L. *extāns, -antis* — *ex-*, out, *stāre*, to stand.]

extempore *iks-tem'pə-ri*, *adv* on the spur of the moment; without preparation; suddenly. — *adj* sudden; rising at the moment; composed and delivered or performed impromptu. — *adj* **extem'poral.** — *n* **extemporaneity** (*-ə-nē'i-ti*). — *adj* **extemporā'neous** impromptu; temporary or improvised. — *adv* **extemporā'neously.** — *n* **extemporā'neousness.** — *adv* **extem'porarily.** — *n* **extem'porariness.** — *adj* **extem'porary** done on the spur of the moment; hastily prepared; speaking extempore; done without preparation. — *n* **extemporisā'tion** or **-z-.** — *vt* **extem'porise** or **-ize** to speak, or compose and play, extempore or without previous preparation; to speak without notes; to improvise (a solution, etc.). [L. *ex*, out of, and *tempore*, abl. of *tempus*, time.]

extend *iks-tend'*, *vt* to stretch out; to prolong in any direction; to enlarge; to expand; to widen; to unfold; to straighten out; to hold out; to offer, accord; to exert to the full. — *vi* to stretch or reach; to be continued in space or time. — *n* **extendabil'ity, extendibil'ity** or **extensibil'ity.** — *adj* **extend'able, extend'ible** or **extens'ible.** — *adj* **extensile** (*eks-ten'sīl* or *-sil*) that may be extended. — *n* **extension** (*iks-* or *eks-ten'shən*) an act of extending; the condition of being extended; an added piece; a wing or annex of a house; the property of occupying space; the extent of the application of a term or the number of objects included under it (opp. to *intension*) (*logic*); a word or words added to subject, predicate or object (*gram*); an additional telephone using the same line as the main one. — *adj* **exten'sional.** — *adv* **exten'sionally.** — *n* **extensional'ity.** — *adj* **extens'ive** large; widespread; comprehensive; (*eks-*) pertaining to extension; seeking or deriving a comparatively small crop cheaply from a wide area (opp. to *intensive*). — *adv* **extens'ively.** — *n* **extens'iveness.** — *n* **extensom'eter** or **extensim'eter** (*eks-*) an instrument for measuring small changes in length, etc. in metal to which tension has been applied. — *n* **exten'sor** a muscle that extends or straightens any part of the body. — *n* **extent'** the space or degree to which a thing is extended; bulk; compass; scope; degree or amount (as in *to some extent*); a stretch or extended space. — **extended family** a social unit comprising not only a couple and their children but other relatives, e.g. aunts, uncles, grandparents; **extended play** (of a gramophone record) giving longer reproduction because of a closer groove and the use of a larger part of its surface area. — **university extension** the enlargement of the aim of a university, in providing extramural instruction for those unable to become regular students. [L. *extendĕre, extentum*, or *extēnsum* — *ex-*, out, *tendĕre*, to stretch.]

extenuate *iks-ten'ū-āt, vt* to lessen; to weaken the force of; to palliate; to underrate. — *n* and *adj* **exten'ūāting**. — *adv* **exten'ūātingly**. — *n* **extenūā'tion** the act of representing anything as less wrong or criminal than it seems; palliation; mitigation. — *adj* **exten'ūatory** or **exten'ūātive** tending to extenuate; palliative. — *n* **exten'ūātor**. [L. *extenuāre, -ātum* — *ex-* (intensive) and *tenuis*, thin.]

exterior *eks-tē'ri-ər, adj* outer; outward, external; on or from the outside; foreign, or dealing with or involving foreign nations. — *n* the outside, outer surface; an outdoor scene in a cinema film; (esp. in *pl*) an outer part. — *vt* **extē̆r'iorise** or **-ize** to externalise; to bring an internal part temporarily outside the body (*surg*). — *n* **exteriorisā'tion** or **-z-**. — *n* **extē̆riority** (*-or'i-ti*). — *adv* **extē'riorly**. — **exterior angle** (*math*) the angle between any extended side and the adjacent side of a polygon. [L. *exterior*, compar. of *exter, exterus*, outward — *ex*, from.]

exterminate *iks-tûr'mi-nāt, vt* to destroy utterly; to put an end to; to root out. — *adj* **exter'minable**. — *n* **exterminā'tion**. — *adj* **exter'minātive** or **exter'minatory**. — *n* **exter'minātor**. [L. *ex*, out of, *terminus*, boundary.]

external *eks-tûr'nəl, adj* exterior; lying outside; outward; belonging to the world of outward things; that may be seen; not innate or intrinsic; accidental; foreign, or involving foreign nations. — *n* exterior; (in *pl*) the outward parts; (in *pl*) outward or nonessential forms and ceremonies; (in *pl*) outward circumstances or appearances. — *n* **externalīsā'tion** or **-z-**. — *vt* **exter'nalise** or **-ize** to give form or apparent reality to; to give external expression to; to extravert (one's personality); to ascribe to causes outside oneself; to regard as consisting of externals only. — *n* **exter'nalism** undue regard to mere externals or non-essential outward forms, esp. of religion. — *n* **exter'nalist**. — *n* **externality** (*-nal'i-ti*). — *adv* **exter'nally**. — **external examiner** an examiner from another seat of learning who has had no part in teaching the examinees; **external student** one examined (for an **external degree**) by a university in which they have not studied. — **external-combustion engine** one in which the fuel is burned outside the working cylinder. [L. *externus*, outward.]

exteroceptor *eks'tər-ō-sep-tər*, (*zool*) *n* a sensory organ, e.g. the eye, receiving stimuli from outside the body. — *adj* **exterocep'tive**. [L. *exterus*, exterior, and *receptor*.]

exterritorial *eks-ter-i-tö'ri-əl*. Same as **extraterritorial**.

extinct *iks-tingkt', adj* no longer existing; (of a volcano) no longer erupting; quenched or quashed; obsolete; dead. — *n* **extinc'tion** the state of being extinct; extinguishing, quenching or wiping out; destruction; the absorbing by the earth's atmosphere of a planet's or star's light (*astron*). — *adj* **extinct'ive**. [L. *ex(s)tinctum*; see **extinguish**.]

extinguish *iks-ting'gwish, vt* to quench, put out; to put an end to; to destroy, annihilate; to make extinct; to obscure by superior splendour; to pay off (a debt) (*law*). — *adj* **exting'uishable**. — *n* **exting'uisher** a device for putting out fire; someone who, or that which, extinguishes; a small hollow conical instrument for putting out a candle, etc. — *n* **exting'uishment**. [L. *ex(s)tinguĕre, ex(s)tinctum* — *ex-*, out, *stinguĕre*, to quench.]

extirpate *eks'tər-pāt, vt* to destroy totally; to exterminate; to remove surgically; to root out. — *adj* **extirpable** (*eks-tûrp'ə-bl*). — *n* **extirpā'tion** extermination; total destruction. — *n* **ex'tirpātor** someone who extirpates; an implement for weeding. — *adj* **ex'tirpative** or **extirpatory** (*eks-tûrp'ə-tər-i*). [L. *exstirpāre, -ātum* — *ex*, out, *stirps*, a stock, root.]

extol *iks-tōl'* or *-tol', vt* to praise highly: — *pr p* **extoll'ing**; *pa t* and *pa p* **extolled'**. — *n* **extoll'er**. — *n* **extol'ment**. [L. *extollĕre* — *ex-*, up, *tollĕre*, to lift or raise.]

extort *iks-tört', vt* to gain or draw out (money, a promise, etc.) by compulsion or violence. — *n* **extortion** (*-tör'shən*) illegal securing of money by compulsion or violence; that which is extorted. — *adj* **extor'tionary** pertaining to or implying extortion. — *adj* **extor'tionate** (of a price) extremely high; (of a person) using extortion. — *adv* **extor'tionately**. — *n* **extor'tioner** or **extor'tionist** someone who practises extortion. [L. *extorquēre, extortum* — *ex-*, out, *torquēre*, to twist.]

extra *eks'trə, adj* beyond or more than the usual or the necessary; additional. — *adv* unusually or exceptionally. — *n* what is extra or additional; a special edition of a newspaper containing later news; a run scored at cricket from a bye, leg-bye, wide or no-ball (not hit); a film actor temporarily engaged for a minor part, e.g. to be one of a crowd. — **extra cover** (in cricket) a fielding position between cover point and mid-off, or the player in this position; **extra jam** or **marmalade** under EC regulations, jam or marmalade containing a considerably higher percentage (by weight) of fruit than that in ordinary jam or marmalade. — *adj* **extra-spec'ial** very special. — *n* a special late edition of an evening newspaper called for by some news of great importance. — **extra time** additional time allowed at the end of a match because of time lost through injury, etc. [Prob. contracted from **extraordinary**.]

extra- *eks'-tra-* or *-trə-, pfx* signifying outside. — *adj* **extracorpor'eal** outside the body. — *adj* **extra-curric'ular** (of a subject or activity) outside and additional to the regular academic course. — *adj* **extragalac'tic** outside the Milky Way. — *adj* **extrajudi'cial** not made in court, beyond the usual course of legal proceeding. — *adv* **extrajudi'cially**. — *adj* **extramar'ital** (of sexual relations, etc.) outside marriage, though properly confined to marriage. — *adj* **extramū'ral** outside or beyond the walls; connected with a university but not under its direct control. — *adj* **extrasen'sory** outside the ordinary senses, as in clairvoyant and telepathic perception (**extrasensory perception** the ability to perceive without the normal senses (cf. **sixth sense**)). — *adj* **extraterres'trial** outside, or from outside, the earth. — *adj* **extraterrito'rial** outside a territory or territorial jurisdiction — also **exterritor'ial**. — *n* **extraterritorial'ity** the privilege of being outside the jurisdiction of the country one is in — also **exterritorial'ity**. — *adj* **extravehic'ūlar** situated, used or happening outside a spacecraft. [L. *extrā*, outside.]

extract *iks-* or *eks-trakt', vt* to draw out by force or otherwise; to choose out or select; to derive (pleasure, etc.); to find out; to extort; to copy passages from; to publish passages from; to obtain by chemical or physical means from containing or combined matter; to exhaust or treat by extraction. — *n* **extract** (*eks'*) anything drawn from a substance by heat, distillation, solvents, etc., as an essence; a passage taken from a book or writing. — *adj* **extract'able** or **extract'ible**. — *n* **extractabil'ity**. — *n* **extrac'tion** the act of extracting; derivation from a stock or family; birth; lineage; that which is extracted. — *adj* **extract'ive** tending or serving to extract; of the nature of an extract (**extractive matter** the soluble portions of any drug). — *n* an extract. — *n* **extract'or**. — **extractor** or **extractor fan** an electric fan which extracts air, gas, etc., from a room or building. [L. *extrahĕre, extractum* — *ex*, from, *trahĕre*, to draw.]

extradition *eks-trə-dish'ən, n* a delivering up of accused persons by one government to another. — *adj* **extraditable** (*-dīt'ə-bl*). — *vt* **ex'tradite** to hand over for trial or punishment to a foreign government. [L. *ex*, from, *trāditiō, -ōnis* — *trādĕre, trāditum*, to deliver up.]

extrados *eks-trā'dos*, (*archit*) *n* the convex surface of an arch; the external curve of the keystone of an arch. [Fr., — L. *extrā*, outside, Fr. *dos*, back.]

extraneous *eks-trān'yəs, adj* external; foreign; not belonging; not essential; irrelevant. — *n* **extraneity** (*-trə-nē'i-ti*) or **extrān'eousness**. — *adv* **extrān'eously**. [L. *extrāneus*, external, *extrā*, outside.]

extraordinary *eks-trörd'i-nə-ri, -in-ri, eks-trə-örd'* or *iks-trörd', adj* beyond ordinary; not usual or regular; remarkable, wonderful; special or subordinate, as 'physician extraordinary' in a royal household being inferior to the ordinary official. — *adv* **extraord'inarily**. — *n* **extraord'inariness**. [L. *extraordinārius* — *extrā*, outside, *ordō, -inis*, order.]

extrapolate *iks-trap'ō-lāt, -ə-lāt* or *eks', vt* to estimate from observed tendencies the value of (any variable) outside the limits between which values are known; to infer, conjecture from what is known; to project into a new area of experience or activity. — Also *vi*. — *n* **extrapolā'tion**. — *adj* **extrap'olātive** or **extrap'olatory**. — *n* **extrap'olātor**. [**extra**- and inter*polate*.]

extrapose *eks-trə-pōz'*, (*gram*) *vt* to move an item normally positioned within a phrase or sentence to the end, to focus attention on it. — *n* **extraposition** (*-zish'ən*). [L. *extrā*, outside.]

extravagant *iks-trav'ə-gənt, adj* excessive; unrestrained; profuse in expenses; wasteful. — *n* **extrav'agance** excess; lavish expenditure. — *adv* **extrav'agantly**. [L. *extrā*, beyond, *vagāns, -antis*, pres. p. of *vagārī*, to wander.]

extravaganza *iks-trav-ə-gan'zə, n* an extravagant or eccentric musical, dramatic or literary production; extravagant conduct or speech. [It. (*e*)*stravaganza*.]

extravasate *iks-trav'ə-sāt, vt* to let or force (blood or other fluid) out of the proper vessels; to pour out (lava). — *n* **extravasā'tion**. [L. *extrā*, out of, *vās*, a vessel.]

extravert, extraversion. Same as **extrovert**, etc.

extreme *iks-trēm', adj* outermost; most remote; last; highest in degree; greatest; most violent; (of opinions, etc.) not moderate, going to great lengths; stringent. — *n* the utmost point or verge; end; the utmost or highest limit or degree. — *adv* **extreme'ly**. — *n* **extrē'mism**. — *n* **extrē'mist** someone ready to go to extremes; a holder of extreme opinions; an advocate of extreme action. — *n* **extremity** (*-trem'i-ti*) the utmost limit; the highest degree; greatest necessity or distress; extreme condition; an end; a hand or foot. — **extreme unction** see under **unction**. — **extremely high frequency** see **frequency**; **go to extremes** to go too far; to use extreme measures; **in the extreme** in the last, highest degree; extremely; **the last extremity** the utmost pitch of misfortune; death. [O.Fr. *extreme* — L. *extrēmus*, superl. of *exter, exterus*, on the outside.]

extricate *eks'tri-kāt, vt* to free from entanglements or perplexities; to disentangle; to set free. — *adj* **ex'tricable**. — *n* **extricā'tion**. [L. *extricāre, -ātum* — *ex*, from, *trīcae*, hindrances.]

extrinsic *iks-trin'sik, adj* external; not contained in or belonging to a body; foreign; not essential; (of a muscle) running from the trunk to limb or girdle (opp. to *intrinsic*). — *adj* **extrin'sical**. — *n* **extrinsical'ity**. — *adv* **extrin'sically**. [Fr. *extrinsèque* — L. *extrīnsecus* — *exter*, outside, sfx. *-in, secus*, beside.]

extrophy. See **exstrophy**.

extrovert *eks'trə-* or *-trō-vûrt, n* a person concerned more with the outside world than with inner feelings; (*loosely*) a person who mixes well socially, and who is open and unreserved. — *adj* characterised by extroversion. — *n* **extrover'sion** the concentration of thoughts to the world outside, esp. to other people and away from inner feelings. [L. *extrā*, outside, *vertĕre*, to turn.]

extrude *iks-trōōd', vt* to force or urge out; to expel; to make rods, tubes, etc., by forcing material through a die under pressure. — *vi* to protrude. — *n* **extrud'er**. — *n* **extrusion** (*-trōō'zhən*) the act of extruding, thrusting or throwing out; expulsion; a rock formed by the cooling of magma or lava. — *adj* **extrusive** (*-trōō'siv*). [L. *extrūdĕre, extrūsum* — *ex-*, out, *trūdĕre*, to thrust.]

exuberant *eg-, ig-zū'bər-ənt* or *-zōō', adj* in high spirits; lavish; luxuriant. — *n* **exu'berance** the quality of being exuberant; luxuriance, an overflowing quantity. — *adv* **exu'berantly**. [L. *exūberāns, -antis*, pres. p. of *exūberāre* — *ex-* (intensive) and *ūber*, rich.]

exude *igz-* or *iks-ūd', vt* to discharge by sweating; to give off or show. — *vi* to flow out of a body through the pores; to ooze out. — *n* **exudate** (*eks'*) exuded matter. — *n* **exudā'tion** (*eks-*) the act of exuding or discharging through pores; that which is exuded. — *adj* **exūd'ative**. [L. *exūdāre* — *ex*, from, *sūdāre*, to sweat.]

exult *igz-ult', vi* to rejoice exceedingly; to triumph (over). — *n* **exult'ance** or **exult'ancy** exultation; triumph. — *adj* **exult'ant** exulting; triumphant. — *adv* **exult'antly**. — *n* **exultā'tion** (*egz-*) triumphant delight; joyousness, esp. spiritual. — *adv* **exult'ingly**. [L. *ex(s)ultāre, -ātum*, from *ex(s)ilīre* — *ex-*, out or up, *salīre*, to leap.]

exurb *eks'ûrb*, (orig. *US*) *n* a residential area, esp. a prosperous one, outside the suburbs of a town. — *adj* **exur'ban**. — *n* and *adj* **exur'banite**. — *n* **exur'bia** exurbs collectively. [L. *ex-*, outside, and sub*urb*ia.]

exuviae *igz-* or *iks-ū'vi-ē, npl* cast-off skins, shells or other coverings of animals; fossil remains of animals (*geol*). — *adj* **exū'vial**. — *vi* **exū'viate** to shed or cast off (a skin). — *n* **exuviā'tion** the act of exuviating. [L. *exuĕre*, to draw off.]

exvasion *eks-vā'zhən, n* the forcible handing over to a neighbouring nation of hungry, disorganised and rebellious lands. [L. *ex*, out of, and in*vasion*.]

eyas *ī'əs, n* an unfledged hawk. [*An eyas* taken for *a nyas* — Fr. *niais* — L. *nīdus*, nest.]

eye *ī, n* the organ of sight or vision, or *specif* the globe or movable part of it; the power of seeing, sight; aim; keenness of perception; anything resembling an eye; a central spot; the hole of a needle; a round aperture; a wire loop or ring for a hook; the seed-bud of a potato; the central calm area of a cyclone; (in *pl*) the foremost part of a ship's bows, the hawseholes: — *pl* **eyes**. — *vt* to look on; to observe narrowly: — *pr p* **eye'ing** or **ey'ing**; *pa t* and *pa p* **eyed** (*īd*). — *n* **eye'ful** as much as the eye can take in; something worth looking at, e.g. a fascinating sight or an attractive person (*slang*). — *adj* **eye'less**. — *n* **eyelet** see separate entry. — **eye'ball** the ball or globe of the eye. — *vt* (*colloq*) to face someone eyeball to eyeball, to confront; to examine closely. — *adj* (of a measurement) by eye only, not exact. — **eye'-bath** a cup that can be filled with a cleansing solution, etc. and held over the eye to bathe it; **eye'-black** mascara; **eye'bolt** a bolt, with an eye instead of the normal head, used for lifting or fastening; **eye'-bright** a little plant of the genus *Euphrasia* formerly used as a remedy for eye diseases; **eye'brow** the hairy arch above the eye. — *adj* **eye'-catching** striking. — **eye contact** a direct look between two people; **eye'-cup** an eye-bath; **eye'-drops** medicinal drops for the eye; **eye'glass** a glass to assist the sight, esp. a monocle; **eye'-hole** an eyelet; an eye-socket; a peep-hole; **eye'lash** the row, or one, of the hairs that edge the eyelid. — *adj* **eye-leg'ible** (of headings, etc. on microfilm or microprint) able to be read by the naked eye. — *adj* and *n* **eye'-level** (at) the same height above ground as the average person's eyes. — **eye'lid** the portion of movable skin by means of which the eye is opened or closed; **eye'liner** a kind of cosmetic used for drawing a line along the edge of the eyelid in order to emphasise the eye; **eye muscle** a muscle controlling the eye or a part of it; a long muscle running down the back beside the spine; **eye'-opener** something that opens the eyes literally or figuratively, esp. a startling enlightenment; **eye'piece** the lens or combination of lenses at the eye end of an optical instrument; **eye'-rhyme** similarity of words in spelling but not in pronunciation; a would-be rhyme between words that are spelt as if they rhymed but in fact do not; **eye'shade** a piece of stiff, usu. tinted, transparent material, worn like the peak of a cap to protect the eyes from the sun or other bright light; **eye shadow** a coloured cosmetic for the eyelids; **eye'-shot** the reach or range of sight of the eye; **eye'sight** power of seeing; **eye socket** either of the two recesses in the skull in which the eyeballs are situated, the orbit; **eye'sore** anything that is offensive to look at; **eye'stalk** a stalk on the dorsal surface of the head of many Crustacea, bearing an eye; **eye'strain** tiredness or irritation of the eyes; **eye'-tooth** a canine tooth, esp. in the upper jaw, below the eye; **eye'-wash** a lotion for the eye; nonsense (*colloq*); deception (*colloq*); **eye'-witness** someone who sees a thing happening or being done. — **be all eyes** to give all attention; **clap, lay** or **set eyes on** (*colloq*) to see; **cry one's eyes out** see under **cry**; **eyeball to eyeball** of a discussion, confrontation, diplomacy, etc., at close quarters, dealing with matters very frankly and firmly; **electric eye** see under **electric**; **eye for an eye** retaliation; justice enacted in the same way or to the same degree as the crime; **eyes down** the start of a bingo game, or of any non-physical contest; **eye up** (*colloq*) to consider the sexual attractiveness of; **get** or **keep one's eye in** to become or remain proficient; **give an eye to** to attend to; **glad eye, green eyed** see under **glad[1], green**; **have an eye to** to contemplate; to have regard to; to incline towards; **have one's eye on** to keep in mind; to consider acquisitively; **hit one in the eye** to be obvious; **in one's mind's eye** in one's imagination; **in the eyes of** in the estimation or opinion of; **in the wind's eye** against the wind; **keep one's** (or **an**) **eye on** to observe closely; to watch; **keep one's eye(s) skinned** or **peeled (for)** to be keenly watchful (for); **make eyes at** to look at in an amorous way, to ogle; **my eye!** used to express mild disagreement; **naked eye** see under **naked**; **one in the eye** a rebuff; **open a person's eyes** to show them something of which they are ignorant; **private eye** see under **private**; **raise an eyebrow** to be mildly surprised, shocked or doubtful; **see eye to eye** to think alike; **turn a blind eye to** to pretend not to see; **under the eye of** under the observation of; **up to the eyes** deeply involved (in); extremely busy; **with** or **having an eye to** considering. [O.E. *ēage*.]

eyelet *ī'lit*, *n* a small eye or hole to receive a lace or cord, as in garments, sails, etc.; a small hole for seeing through (also **eye'let-hole**); a little eye. [O.Fr. *oillet* — L. *oculus*, influenced by **eye**.]

Eyeti, Eyetie or **Eytie** *ī'tī*, (*slang*) *n* an Italian.

eyra *ī'rə*, *n* a South American wild cat. [Guaraní.]

eyre *ār*, (*hist*) *n* a journey or circuit; a court of itinerant justices in England in the late 12th and 13th cents. [O.Fr. *eire*, journey — L. *iter*, a way, a journey.]

eyrie or **aerie** *ē'ri*, *ī'ri* or *ā'ri*, *n* the nest of a bird of prey, esp. an eagle; a house or stronghold perched on some high or steep place. [O.Fr. *aire* — L. *ārea*, open ground.]

Ez. or **Ezr.** (*Bible*) *abbrev* for (the Book of) Ezra.

Ezek. (*Bible*) *abbrev* for (the Book of) Ezekiel.

F

F or **f** *ef, n* the sixth letter in the modern English and Latin alphabets; the fourth note of the natural diatonic scale of C (*mus*). — **F'-clef** a clef marking F, the fourth line in the bass, the bass-clef; **f'-number** (*phot*) the ratio of the focal length to the true diameter of a lens.

F or **F.** *abbrev* for: Fahrenheit; Fellow (of a society, etc.); fine (on lead pencils); franc(s); France (I.V.R.).

F *symbol* for: farad(s) (*phys*); filial generation, thus $\mathbf{F_1}$ first filial generation (*genetics*); fluorine (*chem*).

F symbol for force.

f or **f.** *abbrev* for: fathom(s); female; feminine; folio; following; foot; forte (*mus*).

f symbol for frequency.

FA *abbrev* for: Faculty of Actuaries; Football Association; see also **Fanny Adams**.

Fa *abbrev* for Florida (U.S. state).

fa or **fah** *fä*, (*mus*) *n* the fourth note in the sol-fa notation.

FAA *abbrev* for Federal Aviation Administration (U.S.).

Fabian *fā'bi-ən, adj* delaying, avoiding battle, cautious; favouring the gradual introduction and spread of Socialism. — *n* a member or supporter of the *Fabian Society* (founded 1884) for this purpose. — *n* **Fā'bianism.** — *n* **Fā'bianist.** [From Q. *Fabius* Maximus, Roman general and consul, surnamed Cunctator (delayer), from the masterly tactics with which he wore out the strength of Hannibal.]

fable *fā'bl, n* a narrative in which things irrational, and sometimes inanimate, are, for the purpose of moral instruction, made to act and speak with human interests and passions; any tale in literary form intended to instruct or amuse; a fiction or myth; a ridiculous story, an old wives' tale; a falsehood; subject of common talk. — *vi* to tell fictitious tales. — *vt* to feign; to invent; to relate as if true. — *adj* **fā'bled** mythical; renowned in story; feigned. — *n* **fā'bler.** — *n* and *adj* **fā'bling.** — *n* **fab'ulist** a person who invents fables. — *n* **fabulos'ity.** — *adj* **fab'ulous** feigned, false; related in fable; celebrated in story; immense, amazing; excellent (*colloq*). — *adv* **fab'ulously.** — *n* **fab'ulousness.** [Fr. *fable*, and L. *fābula* — *fārī*, to speak.]

fabric *fab'rik, n* texture; manufactured cloth; any system of connected parts; buildings, stonework, etc.; anything framed by art and labour; framework (also *fig*). — *vt* **fab'ricate** to put together, manufacture; to produce; to devise falsely. — *n* **fabricā'tion** construction; manufacture; that which is fabricated or invented; a story; a falsehood. — *adj* **fab'ricātive.** — *n* **fab'ricātor.** [L. *fābrica*, fabric — *fāber*, a worker in hard materials.]

fabulist, fabulous, etc. See **fable.**

façade or **facade** *fa-säd', n* the exterior front or face of a building; the appearance presented to the world, esp. if showy and with little behind it (*fig*). [Fr., — *face*, after It. *facciata*, the front of a building — *faccia*, the face.]

face *fās, n* the front part of the head, including forehead and chin; the outside form or appearance; front or surface; a flat surface of a solid geometrical figure, crystal, etc.; the striking surface of a golf club, etc.; the edge of a cutting-tool, etc.; the front or upper surface, or that usually presented; the exposed surface in a cliff, mine or quarry; the dial of a watch, etc.; the printed surface of a playing-card; special appearance or expression; aspect, look, configuration; command of facial expression and bearing; boldness, effrontery; a grimace; presence; anger or favour (*Bible*). — *vt* to meet in the face or in front; to stand opposite to or looking towards; to confront; to stand up to, brave; to resist; to put an additional face or surface on; to cover in front; to trim. — *vi* (often with *on, to* or *towards*) to direct or turn the face; to take or have a direction. — *adj* **faced** having a face; having the outer surface dressed; with the front covered with another material. — *adj* **face'less** without a face; (of person(s) concerned in some action) with identity concealed; robot-like, esp. of bureaucratic officials who allow no degree of personality to intrude on their decision-making processes. — *n* **fac'er** someone who faces something; a tool for smoothing or facing a surface; a severe blow on the face (*slang*); an affront (*colloq*); anything that staggers one (*colloq*). — *adj* **facial** (*fā'shl*) of or relating to the face; for the face. — *n* a beauty treatment to the face (*colloq*). — *adv* **fa'cially.** — *n* **fac'ing** a covering in front for ornament or protection. — **face'-card** a playing-card bearing a face (king, queen or knave); **face'-cloth** or **-flannel** a cloth used in washing the face; **face'-cream** a cosmetic cream for the face; **face'-fungus** (*colloq*) a moustache or beard. — *vt* **face'-harden** to case-harden. — **face'-lift** a renovating process, esp. one applied to the outside of a building (also *fig*); face-lifting; **face'-lifting** an operation aiming at smoothing and firming the face; **face'man** or **face'worker** a miner who works at the coal-face; **face'-off** in ice-hockey, etc., the dropping of the puck between two players to start the game; a confrontation (*fig*); **face pack** a creamy cosmetic mixture put on to the face for a certain time; **face'-powder** a cosmetic powder for the face; **face'-saver** a course of action that saves one's face (see below); **face'-saving** saving one's face (see below). — Also *adj.* — **face value** the value as stated on the face of a coin, etc.; the apparent value of anything, which may not be the same as its real value. — **face down** to abash by stern looks; to confront and make concede; **face out** to carry off by bold looks; to face down; **face the music** (*slang*) to accept the unpleasant consequences at their worst; to brave a trying situation, hostile reception, etc.; **face to face** opposite; in actual presence; in confrontation (*adj* **face-to-face'**); **face up to** to face, stand up to; to recognise (a fact or facts) and prepare to endure or act bravely; **fly in the face of** to set oneself directly against; **in the face of** in defiance of, despite; **look (someone) in the face** to look at without shame or embarrassment; **lose face** to lose prestige; **loss of face** humiliation, loss of dignity; **make** (or **pull) faces at** to distort one's face into exaggerated expressions in order to amuse, annoy, etc.; **on the face of it** on its own showing; as is palpably plain; at first glance; **pull a long face** to look dismal; **put a good** (or **brave) face on (it)** to assume a bold or contented bearing (as regards something); **put one's face on** (*colloq*) to apply cosmetics to one's face; **save one's face** to avoid humiliation or the appearance of climbing down; **set one's face against** to oppose strenuously; **show one's face** to appear; **to one's face** in one's presence, openly. [Fr., — L. *faciēs*, form, face.]

facet *fas'it*, *n* a small surface, as of a crystal; an aspect or view; a small flat area on e.g. a bone (*anat*). — *adj* **fac'eted** having or formed into facets. [Fr. *facette*, dimin. of *face*, face.]

facetious *fə-sē'shəs*, *adj* witty, humorous, jocose; would-be funny. — *adv* **facē'tiously**. — *n* **facē'tiousness**. [L. *facētia* — *facētus*, merry, witty.]

facia *fā'shi-ə*, *n*. Same as **fascia**.

facies *fā'shi-ēz*, *n* general aspect, esp. of plant, animal or geological species or formations; facial appearance or expression, esp. when characteristic of a disease or condition: — *pl* **fā'cies**. [L. *faciēs*, face.]

facile *fas'īl*, *adj* easily persuaded; yielding; easily accomplished; easy; working with ease; fluent (usu. *disparagingly*). — *adv* **fac'ilely**. — *n* **fac'ileness**. — *vt* **facilitāte** (*fə-sil'*) to make easy or easier. — *n* **facilitā'tion**. — *adj* **facil'itātive**. — *n* **facil'itātor**. — *n* **facil'ity** ease in performance or action; fluency; pliancy; (esp. in *pl* **facil'ities**) means or opportunities that render anything readily possible; anything specially arranged or constructed to provide recreation, a service, etc.; an agreed amount of money made available for borrowing (*econ*). [Fr., — L. *facilis*, easy.]

facsimile *fak-sim'i-li*, *n* an exact copy, e.g. of handwriting, a coin, etc.; accurate reproduction: — *pl* **facsim'iles**. — *adj* exactly corresponding. — *vt* to make a facsimile of, to reproduce: — *pr p* **facsim'ileing**; *pa t* and *pa p* **facsim'iled**. — *n* **facsim'ilist**. — **facsimile edition** an edition of a book, etc., that is an exact reproduction of an earlier edition. [L. *fac*, imper. of *facĕre*, to make, *simile*, neut. of *similis*, like.]

fact *fakt*, *n* a truth; truth; reality, or a real state of things, as distinguished from a mere statement or belief; an assertion of fact; a crime committed (*obs* except in **after** and **before the fact**). — *adj* **fact'ūal** pertaining to facts; actual. — *n* **factūal'ity**. — *n* **fact'ūalness**. — *adj* **fact'-finding** appointed to ascertain, or directed towards ascertaining, all the facts of a situation. — **fact sheet** a paper setting out briefly information relevant to a particular subject. — **as a matter of fact** in reality; **facts of life** the details of reproduction, esp. human reproduction; the realities of a situation; **in fact** or **in point of fact** indeed; **the fact of the matter** the plain truth about the subject in question. [L. *factum*, neut. past p. of *facĕre*, to do.]

faction[1] *fak'shən*, *n* a company of persons associated or acting together, mostly used in a bad sense; a contentious party in a state or society; dissension. — *adj* **fac'tional**. — *n* **fac'tionalism**. — *n* **fac'tionalist**. — *adj* **fac'tious** turbulent; given to faction; proceeding from party spirit; seditious. [L. *factiō*, *-ōnis* — *facĕre*, to do.]

faction[2] *fak'shən*, *n* a play, programme, piece of writing, etc., that is a mixture of fact and fiction — also called **drama documentary** or *news fiction*. [*fact* and *fiction*.]

factitious *fak-tish'əs*, *adj* artificial; made; produced by artificial conditions. — *adv* **facti'tiously**. — *n* **facti'tiousness**. — *adj* **fac'titive** causative; (of a verb) which can take both a direct object and a complement. — *adj* **fac'tive** making. [L. *factīcius*, *factitīvus* — *facĕre*, to make.]

factoid *fak'toid*, *n* an unprovable statement which has achieved unquestioning acceptance by frequent repetition. [**fact** and **-oid**.]

factor *fak'tər*, *n* someone who does or transacts business for another person; a person who buys and sells goods for others, on commission; an agent managing heritable estates for another (*Scot*); one of two or more quantities which, when multiplied together, result in the given quantity — e.g. 6 and 4 are factors of 24 (*math*); an element in the composition of anything, or in bringing about a certain result; a fact, etc. which has to be taken into account or which affects the course of events. — *vi* to work, act, etc. as a factor. — *adj* **factō'rial** of or pertaining to a factor. — *n* the product of all whole numbers from a given number down to one. — *n* **fac'toring** the work of a factor; the business of buying up trade debts, or lending money on the security of these. — *n* **factorisā'tion** or **-z-**. — *vt* **fac'torise** or **-ize** to resolve into factors. — *n* **fac'torship**. — *n* **fac'tory** a place where goods are manufactured. — **factor 8** or **factor VIII** one of the proteins which form the clotting agent in blood, absent in haemophiliacs; **factory farm** one carrying out **factory farming**, farming by methods of feeding and housing animals in which everything is subordinated to achieving maximum production, rapid growth, etc.; **fac'tory-ship** a whaling-ship on which whales are processed; a ship which freezes or otherwise processes the catch of a fishing fleet. — **safety factor** see under **safe**. [L. *facĕre*, to do.]

factotum *fak-tō'təm*, *n* a person employed to do all kinds of work for another: — *pl* **facto'tums**. [L.L., — L. *fac*, imper. of *facĕre*, to do, *tōtum*, all.]

factual, factuality, factualness. See **fact**.

faculty *fak'əl-ti*, *n* facility or power to act; any particular ability or aptitude; an original power of the mind; any physical capability or function; personal quality or endowment; right, authority or privilege to act; a department of learning at a university, or the professors and lecturers constituting it; the members of a profession. — *adj* **fac'ultative** optional; incidental; of or pertaining to a faculty; conferring privilege, permission or authority; able to live under different conditions (*zool*). — *adv* **fac'ultatively**. [Fr. *faculté* — L. *facultās*, *-ātis* — *facilis*, easy.]

fad *fad*, *n* a weak or passing hobby or craze; any unimportant belief or practice that is too strongly advocated. — *n* **fadd'iness**. — *adj* **fadd'ish**. — *n* **fadd'ishness**. — *n* **fadd'ism**. — *n* **fadd'ist**. — *adj* **fadd'y**.

fade *fād*, *vi* to lose strength, freshness, loudness, brightness or colour gradually; to die away; to disappear. — *vt* to cause to fade; to cause to change gradually in distinctness (as *fade out* and *fade in*); to impart a fade to (*golf*). — *n* a fading; a slight, delayed (often deliberate) slice (*golf*). — *adj* **fā'ded**. — *adv* **fā'dedly**. — *n* **fā'dedness**. — *n* **fā'der** a sliding control e.g. as used on audio and lighting equipment to set levels of sound and light. — *n* and *adj* **fā'ding**. — **fade down** (of sound or light) to fade out (*n* **fade'-down**); **fade in** (in films, radio, television, etc.) to introduce (sound or a picture) gradually, bringing it up to full volume or clarity (*n* **fade'-in**); **fade out** (in films, radio, television, etc.) to cause (sound or a picture) to disappear gradually (*n* **fade'-out**); **fade up** (of sound or light) to fade in (*n* **fade'-up**). [O.Fr. *fader* — *fade* — L. *vapidum*.]

faeces or in U.S. **feces** *fē'sēz*, *npl* solid excrement. — *adj* **faecal** or in U.S. **fecal** (*fē'kl*). [L., pl. of *faex*, *faecis*, dregs, grounds.]

faff *faf*, (*colloq*) *vi* to dither, fumble (usu. with *about*).

fag[1] *fag*, *vi* to become weary or tired out; to work hard; to be a fag. — *vt* to weary; to use as a fag: — *pr p* **fagg'ing**; *pa t* and *pa p* **fagged**. — *n* a public schoolboy forced to do menial tasks for another; a tiresome piece of work; drudgery; a cigarette (*slang*). — *n* **fagg'ery** drudgery; fagging. — *n* and *adj* **fagg'ing**. — **fag'-end** the stump of a cigar or cigarette (*slang*); the untwisted end of a rope; the end, refuse or inferior part of something. — **fagged out** very tired, exhausted.

fag[2]. See **faggot**.

faggot or **fagot** *fag'ət*, *n* a bundle of sticks for fuel, fascines, etc.; a stick; a bundle of pieces of iron or steel cut off into suitable lengths for welding; a dish made of pig offal, etc. mixed with bread and savoury herbs, shaped into balls or rolls; a male homosexual (also **fag**; *slang*, orig. *US*). — *vt* to tie together. — *n* **fagg'oting** or **fag'oting** a kind of embroidery in which some of the cross threads are drawn together in the middle. [Fr. *fagot*, a bundle of sticks.]

fah. See **fa**.

Fahrenheit *fa'* or *fä'rən-hīt*, *adj* of a thermometer or thermometer scale, having the freezing-point of water marked at 32, and the boiling-point at 212, degrees. [Named from the inventor, Gabriel D. *Fahrenheit* (1686–1736).]

faience or **faïence** *fä-yãs*, *n* glazed coloured earthenware. [Fr.; prob. from *Faenza* in Italy.]

fail *fāl*, *vi* to fall short or be wanting (with *in*); to fall away; to prove deficient under trial, examination, pressure, etc.; to miss achievement; to be disappointed or baffled; to become insolvent or bankrupt. — *vt* not to be sufficient for; to leave undone, omit; to disappoint or desert; to declare deficient after examination. — *n* failure, esp. in an examination. — *adj* **failed**. — *n* **fail'ing** a fault, weakness; a foible; failure. — *adj* that fails. — *prep* in default of, in the absence of. — *n* **fail'ure** a falling short, or cessation; lack of success; omission; bankruptcy; an unsuccessful person. — *adj* **fail'-safe** (of a mechanism) incorporated in a system to ensure that there will be no accident if the system does not operate properly; (of a system) designed to revert to a safe condition in the event of failure. — Also *fig*. — **fail safe** to revert to a safe condition in the event of failure; **without fail** for certain. [O.Fr. *faillir* — L. *fallĕre*, to deceive.]

faille *fāl*, *fīl* or *fä-y'*, *n* a soft, closely-woven silk or rayon fabric with transverse ribs. [Fr.]

failure. See **fail**.

fain *fān*, (*archaic* or *poetic*) *adj* glad or joyful; eager (with *to*). — *adv* gladly. [O.E. *fægen*, joyful.]

faint *fānt*, *adj* dim; lacking distinctness; not bright or forcible; done in a feeble way; inclined to faint. — *vi* to suffer a sudden temporary, loss of consciousness due to inadequate blood flow to the brain. — *n* such a loss of consciousness, a swoon. — *n* and *adj* **faint'ing**. — *adv* **faint'ly**. — *n* **faint'ness** lack of strength; feebleness of colour, light, etc.; dejection. — *adj* **faint'-heart** (also *n*) or **faint-heart'ed** spiritless; timorous. — *adv* **faint-heart'edly**. — *n* **faint-heart'edness**. [O.Fr. *feint*, feigned — L. *fingĕre*, to feign.]

fair[1] *fār*, *adj* bright; clear; clean; free from blemish; pure; pleasing to the eye; beautiful; of a light hue; free from rain, fine, dry; unobstructed, open; smoothly curving; prosperous; impartial; just; good, pleasing; plausible; civil; specious; reasonable; likely; favourable; pretty good; passable. — *adv* in a fair manner (in all senses); full, square, directly (e.g. *hit fair in the centre*). — *n* **fair'ing** adjustment or testing of curves in shipbuilding; streamlined external fittings on an aeroplane, car, etc., to reduce drag. — *adv* **fair'ly** justly; reasonably; plainly; fully, quite; tolerably. — *n* **fair'ness**. — *adj* **fair'-and-square** honest (also *adv*). — **fair copy** a clean copy after correction; **fair-deal'ing**; **fair game** an object for justifiable attack or ridicule. — *adj* **fair'-haired** having light-coloured hair. — **Fair Isle** type of design used in knitwear, named from a Shetland island. — *adj* **fair'-minded** judging fairly. — **fair play** honest dealing; justice. — *adj* **fair-spok'en** bland and civil in language and address. — **fair'way** the navigable channel or usual course of vessels in a river, etc.; the smooth turf between tee and putting-green, distinguished from the uncut rough and from hazards (*golf*). — *adj* **fair'-weather** suitable only for, or found only in, fair weather or (esp. of friends or supporters) favourable circumstances. — **bid fair** see under **bid**[1]; **fair dinkum** (*Austr*) honest(ly); **fair do's** (*dōōz* — *pl* of **do**[1]; *colloq*) an expression appealing for, or agreeing to, fair play, strict honesty, etc.; **fair enough** expressing acceptance, though not necessarily full agreement; **in all fairness** being scrupulously fair; **stand fair with** to be in favour with; **the fair sex** the female sex. [O.E. *fæger*.]

fair[2] *fār*, *n* a large market with or without amusements, held periodically; a collection of shows, rides, etc.; a charity bazaar; a trade show. — *n* **fair'ing** a present given at or from a fair; any complimentary gift. — **fair'ground** (also *adj*). [O.Fr. *feire* — L. *fēria*, holiday.]

fairing. See **fair**[1,2].

fairy *fār'i*, *n* an imaginary being, generally of diminutive and graceful human form, capable of kindly or unkindly acts towards man; a male homosexual (*disparagingly*). — *adj* like a fairy, fanciful, whimsical, delicate. — *adj* and *adv* **fair'ylike**. — **fairy-god'mother** a usu. unknown benefactress, esp. one who appears unexpectedly; **fair'yland** the country of the fairies; **fairy light** (usu. in *pl*) a tiny coloured light used as decoration; **fair'y-ring** a ring of darker-coloured grass due to outward spread of a fungus, traditionally attributed to the dancing of fairies; **fairy tale** a story about fairies or other supernatural beings; a folk-tale; a romantic tale; an incredible tale; a lie (*euph*); a marvel. — *adj* **fair'y-tale** beautiful, fortunate, fanciful, etc., as in a fairy tale. [O.Fr. *faerie*, enchantment.]

fait accompli *fet a-kõ-plē*, (Fr.) *n* an accomplished fact, a thing already done.

faith *fāth*, *n* trust or confidence; belief in the statement of another; belief in the truth of revealed religion; confidence and trust in God; the living reception of religious belief; that which is believed; any system of religious belief, esp. the religion one considers true; fidelity to promises; honesty; word or honour pledged; faithfulness. — *adj* **faith'ful** believing; firm in adherence to promises, duty, friendship, love, etc.; worthy of belief; true; exact. — *adv* **faith'fully** with confidence; with fidelity; with sincerity; with scrupulous exactitude; solemnly (*colloq*). — *n* **faith'fulness**. — *adj* **faith'less** without faith or belief; not believing, esp. in God or Christianity; not adhering to promises, duty, etc.; inconstant; adulterous; untrustworthy; delusive. — *adv* **faith'lessly**. — *n* **faith'lessness**. — **faith'-healer**; **faith'-healing** or **faith'-cure** a system of belief that sickness may be cured without medical advice or appliances, if the prayer of Christians is accompanied in the sufferer by true faith; cure by suggestion. — **bad faith** treachery; the breaking of a promise; **in good faith** with honesty and sincerity; acting honestly; **keep faith** to act honestly, according to one's promise (with); **the Faithful** believers, esp. Muslims; (without *cap*) adherents, supporters, etc. (*colloq*). [M.E. *feith*, *feyth* — O.Fr. *feid* — L. *fīdēs* — *fīdĕre*, to trust.]

fake *fāk*, *vt* to doctor, cook or counterfeit. — *n* a swindle, dodge, sham; a faked article. — *adj* false, counterfeit. — *n* **fak'er**. — *n* **fak'ery**. [Prob. the earlier *feak*, *feague*, Ger. *fegen*, to furbish up.]

fakir *fä-kēr'* or *fā'kər*, *n* a religious (esp. Muslim) mendicant, ascetic, or wonder-worker in India, etc. — *n* **fakir'ism** (or *fā'*). [Ar. *faqīr*, a poor man.]

falafel. See **felafel**.

Falange *fə-lanj'*, also *fä-läng'hhā* (Sp.), *n* a Spanish fascist group. — *n* **Falangism** (*fə-lan'jizm*) (also without *cap*). — *n* **Falan'gist** (also without *cap*). [Sp., — Gr. *phalanx*, phalanx (q.v.).]

Falasha *fə-lä'shə*, *n* one of a community of black Ethiopian Jews. [Amharic, immigrant.]

falcate *fal'kāt* or **falcated** *fal'kāt-id, adj* bent like a sickle. — *adj* **falciform** (*fal'si-förm*) sickle-shaped. — *adj* **fal'cūlate**. [L. *falx, falcis*, a sickle.]

falcon *föl'kən, n* any of the long-winged birds of prey of the genus *Falco* or its kindred; a bird of prey of a kind trained to the pursuit of game; by falconers confined to the female (esp. peregrine) falcon (cf. **tercel**). — *n* **fal'coner** someone who sports with, or who breeds and trains, falcons or hawks for taking wild-fowl. — *n* **fal'conry** the art or practice of training, or hunting with, falcons. [O.Fr. *faucon* — L.L. *falcō, -ōnis.*]

falculate. See **falcate**.

falderal *fal'dər-al* or **folderol** *fol'dər-ol, n* a meaningless refrain in songs; any kind of flimsy trifle.

faldstool *föld'stōōl, n* a folding or camp stool; a coronation stool; a bishop's armless seat; a small desk in churches in England, at which the litany is to be sung or said. [L.L. *faldistolium, faldistorium* — O.H.G. *faldstuol* — *faldan*, to fold, *stuol*, stool.]

fall[1] *föl, vi* to descend, esp. to descend freely and involuntarily by force of gravity; to drop; to drop to the ground; to throw oneself down; to collapse; to become lower literally or figuratively; to die away; to subside; to ebb; to decline; to sink; (of the face) to relax into an expression of dismay; to flow downwards; to slope or incline down; to hang, dangle or trail down; to be cast or shed; to drop dead or as if dead, esp. in a fight; to be overthrown; to come to ruin; to lose power, station, virtue or reputation; to be degraded; to be taken or captured; to become a victim; to yield to temptation; to pass into any state or action, to become, to begin to be (as in *fall asleep, fall in love*); to rush; to become involved; to apply oneself (to); to come to be; to befall; to come about; to come by chance or as if by chance; to come in due course; to occur; to chance, light (on); to issue; to come forth; (esp. of lambs) to be dropped in birth; to appertain; to be apportioned, assigned; to come as one's share, lot, duty, etc.; to take position or arrangement; to find place; to be disposed; to impinge; to lapse; to terminate; to revert: — *pr p* **fall'ing**; *pa t* **fell**; *pa p* **fallen** (*fö'lən*). — *n* the act, manner, occasion, or time of falling or of felling; descent by gravity, a dropping down; that which falls; as much as comes down at one time; onset; overthrow; descent from a better to a worse position; slope or declivity; descent of water; a cascade; length of drop, amount of descent; decrease in value; a sinking of the voice; a cadence; autumn (chiefly *NAm*); a bout of wrestling; the passing of a city or stronghold to the enemy; a lapse into sin, esp. that of Adam and Eve — 'the Fall (of Man)'; a falling band, a hanging fringe, flap or ornament; a lowering or hoisting rope. — *adj* **fall'en** having fallen; killed, esp. in battle; overthrown; seduced; in a degraded state, ruined. — *n* **fall'ing**. — *adj* **fall'-back** used as a retreat, or second alternative. — Also *n*. — **fall-in** see **fall in** below; **falling star** a meteor; **fall'out** by-product, side benefit (*colloq*); a deposit of radioactive dust from a nuclear explosion or plant; the aftermath of any explosive occurrence or situation (*fig*); see **fall out** below. — **fall about** to laugh hysterically, to collapse (with laughter); **fall among** to find oneself in the midst of; **fall apart** to disintegrate; to fail; to collapse, go to pieces; **fall away** to decline gradually; to languish; to grow lean; to revolt or apostatise; **fall back** to retreat, give way; **fall back upon** to have recourse to as an expedient or resource in reserve; **fall behind** to lag; to be outstripped; to get in arrears; **fall between two stools** to be neither one thing nor the other; to succeed in neither of two alternatives; **fall down on** (*colloq*) to fail in; **fall flat** to fail completely, have no effect; **fall flat on one's face** to come to grief, to fail dismally; **fall for** (*colloq*) to become enamoured of; to be taken in by (a trick, etc.); **fall foul of** see under **foul**; **fall in** to (cause to) take places in ranks (*mil*; *n* **fall-in'**); to become hollowed; to revert; to cave in, collapse; **fall in with** to concur or agree with; to comply with; to meet by chance; **fall off** to become detached and drop; to deteriorate; to die away, to perish; to revolt or apostatise; to draw back; **fall on** to begin eagerly; to make an attack; **fall on one's feet** to come well out of a difficulty; to gain any unexpected good fortune; **fall out** to quarrel; to happen or befall; to turn out; to (cause to) quit ranks (*mil*; *n* **fall-out'**); **fall over backwards** see under **back**; **fall over oneself** (*colloq*) to be in great haste or eagerness (to do something); **fall short** to turn out to be short or insufficient; to become used up; to fail to attain or reach what is aimed at (with *of*); **fall through** to fail, come to nothing; **fall to** to begin hastily and eagerly; to apply oneself to; to begin to eat; **fall upon** to attack; to rush against; to devolve upon; to chance upon. [O.E. *fallan*.]

fall[2] *föl, n* a trap. — **fall'-guy** or **fall guy** a dupe, easy victim; a scapegoat. [O.E. *fealle* — *feallan*, to fall.]

fallacy *fal'ə-si, n* something fallacious; deceptive appearance; an apparently genuine but really illogical argument; a wrong but prevalent notion. — *adj* **fallacious** (*fə-lā'shəs*) of the nature of fallacy; deceptive; misleading; not well founded; causing disappointment; delusive. — *adv* **fallā'ciously**. — *n* **fallā'ciousness**. [L. *fallācia* — *fallāx*, deceptive.]

fallible *fal'i-bl, adj* liable to error or mistake. — *n* **fall'ibilism** in philosophy, the doctrine that knowledge gained empirically can never be certain. — *n* **fall'ibilist**. — Also *adj*. — *n* **fallibil'ity** liability to err. — *adv* **fall'ibly**. [L.L. *fallibilis* — *fallĕre*, to deceive.]

Fallopian *fə-lō'pi-ən, adj* relating to the Italian anatomist Gabriele *Fallopio* (1523–62). — **Fallopian tubes** two tubes or ducts through which the ova pass from the ovary to the uterus, perh. discovered by him.

fallow[1] *fal'ō, adj* left untilled or unsown for a time. — *n* land that has lain a year or more untilled or unsown after having been ploughed. — *vt* to plough without seeding. — *n* **fall'owness**. [O.E. *fealgian*, to fallow; *fealh*, fallow land.]

fallow[2] *fal'ō, adj* brownish-yellow. — **fallow deer** a yellowish-brownish deer smaller than the red deer, with broad flat antlers. [O.E. *falu*.]

false *föls, adj* wrong; deceptive or deceiving; untruthful; unfaithful; untrue; not genuine or real; improperly so called; of teeth, etc., artificial (as opp. to natural); incorrect, not according to rule; out of tune. — *adv* incorrectly; untruly; dishonestly; faithlessly. — *n* **false'hood** the state or quality of being false; want of truth; an untrue statement; the act of lying; a lie. — *adv* **false'ly**. — *n* **false'ness**. — *n* **fal'sie** or *npl* **fal'sies** pad(s) of rubber or other material inserted into a brassière to enlarge or improve the shape of the breasts. — *n* **fals'ity** quality of being false; a false assertion. — **false acacia** robinia; **false alarm** a needless warning or panic; **false bottom** a partition cutting off a space between it and the true bottom; **false card** the card played to deceive; **false dawn** deceptive appearance simulating dawn. — Also *fig*. — *adj* **false-heart'ed** treacherous, deceitful. — **false hem** a strip of fabric added to the bottom of a garment, etc. in order to deepen the hem; **false imprisonment** illegal detention by force or influence; **false leg** a proleg; **false pregnancy** pseudocyesis (see under **pseud-**); **false pretences** deception; **false rib** one that does not reach the breastbone; **false start** in a race, a start that is declared invalid (*sport*); an unsuccessful attempt to begin an activity; **false teeth** artificial teeth, dentures. — **play someone false** to act falsely or treacherously to a person; **put in a false position** to bring someone into a position in which they must be misunderstood. [O.Fr. *fals* — L. *falsus*, past p. of *fallĕre*, to deceive.]

falsetto *föl-set'ō*, *n* (usu. in a man) forced voice of a range or register above the natural; someone who uses such a voice; false or strained sentiment: — *pl* **falsett'os**. — *adj* and *adv* in falsetto. [It. *falsetto*, dimin. of *falso*, false.]

falsify *föls'i-fī*, *vt* to forge or counterfeit; to tamper with; to misrepresent; to prove or declare to be false: — *pr p* **fals'ifying**; *pa t* and *pa p* **fals'ified**. — *adj* **fals'ifīable**. — *n* **falsifīabil'ity**. — *n* **falsificā'tion**. — *n* **fals'ifīer**. [Fr. *falsifier* — L.L. *falsificāre* — L. *falsus*, false, *facĕre*, to make.]

falsity. See **false**.

falter *föl'tər*, *vi* to stumble; to go unsteadily; to hesitate in speech as if taken aback; to flinch; to waver; to flag; to fail. — *vt* to utter falteringly. — *n* unsteadiness. — *n* and *adj* **fal'tering**. — *adv* **fal'teringly**. [Prob. a frequentative of M.E. *falden*, to fold.]

fam. *abbrev* for: familiar; family.

fame *fām*, *n* renown or celebrity, chiefly in a good sense. — *adj* **famed** renowned. — **house of ill fame** (*euph*; *archaic* or *literary*) a brothel. [Fr., — L. *fāma*, report, rumour, fame.]

familial *fə-mil'i-əl*, *adj* characteristic of a family.

familiar *fə-mil'yər*, *adj* well acquainted or intimate; in the manner of an intimate friend; unrestrained; unceremonious; having a thorough knowledge; well known or understood; private, domestic; common, everyday. — *n* a close or long-time acquaintance; a spirit or demon supposed to attend a person at call. — *vt* **famil'iarise** or **-ize** to make thoroughly acquainted with; to make easy by practice or study. — *n* **familiarity** (*-i-ar'i-ti*) intimate acquaintanceship; freedom from constraint; any unusual or unwarrantable freedom in act or speech toward another, act of licence (usu. in *pl*). — *adv* **famil'iarly**. [O.Fr. *familier* — L. *familiāris*, from *familia*, a family.]

family *fam'i-li*, *n* the household, or all those who live in one house (such as parents, children, servants); parents and their children; the children alone; the descendants of one common progenitor; race; honourable or noble descent; a group of people related to one another, or otherwise connected; a group of animals, plants, languages, etc., more comprehensive than a genus; a collection of curves in the equations of which different values are given to the parameter(s) (*math*). — *adj* of or concerning the family; belonging to or specially for a family; suitable for the whole family, or for children as well as parents. — **family allowance** an allowance formerly paid by the state for the support of children, now replaced by child benefit; **family Bible** a large Bible for family worship, with a page for recording family events; **family circle** the members of the family taken collectively; one of the galleries at the top of a theatre (esp. *NAm*); **family credit** a payment by the state to a family whose income from employment is below a certain level; **family doctor** a general practitioner; **family man** a man with a family; a domesticated man; a man dedicated to, and who enjoys sharing activities with, his wife and children; **family name** surname; **family planning** regulating the number and spacing of children, e.g. by using contraceptives; **family tree** a diagram showing the branching of a family. — **family income supplement** a payment formerly made by the state to a family whose income from employment is below a certain level, now replaced by family credit; **in the family way** pregnant. [L. *familia* — *famulus*, a servant.]

famine *fam'in*, *n* extreme general scarcity of food; scarcity of anything; hunger; starvation. [Fr., — L. *famēs*, hunger.]

famish *fam'ish*: **be famished** or **be famishing** to feel very hungry. [L. *famēs*, hunger.]

famous *fā'məs*, *adj* renowned; noted; excellent (*colloq*). — *adv* **fā'mously**. — *n* **fā'mousness**. [O.Fr., — L. *fāmōsus* — *fāma*, fame.]

fan[1] *fan*, *n* a broad, flat instrument used esp. by women to cool themselves — typically in or spreading into the shape of a sector of a circle; any fan-shaped structure, such as a deposit of alluvium; anything spreading in a fan shape, e.g. a bird's wing or tail; a propeller screw or propeller blade; a rotating ventilating or blowing apparatus; a basket formerly used for winnowing corn by throwing it in the wind. — *vt* to move by a fan or the like; to direct a current of air upon; to cool or to kindle with, or as with, a fan; to fire (a non-automatic gun) by pulling back and releasing the hammer with the other hand. — *vi* to move like a fan; to flutter; to spread out like a fan: — *pr p* **fann'ing**; *pa t* and *pa p* **fanned**. — *n* **fann'er**. — *npl* **fann'ings** the siftings of tea. — *adv* **fan'-wise**. — **fan belt** (in motor vehicles) a continuous belt that drives the alternator and the cooling fan for the radiator; **fan dance** a solo dance in the nude (or nearly so) in which the performer attempts concealment (or nearly so) by tantalising manipulation of a fan or fans or bunch of ostrich plumes. — *adj* **fan'fold** (of paper) in a continuous strip, scored or perforated so as to fall flat in sections, used for computer print-out. — **fan'-jet** (a plane with) an engine in which air is taken in through a fan and some of it, bypassing compressors, combustion chamber and turbines, mixes with the jet formed by the rest; **fan'light** a window resembling an open fan in shape. — *adj* **fan'-shaped** forming a sector of a circle. — **fan'tail** a tail shaped like a fan; a variety of domestic pigeon with tail feathers spread out like a fan; a member of various other classes of fantailed birds; an artificially bred goldfish with double anal and caudal fins; a feature having parts radiating from a centre (*archit*). — Also *adj* (also **fan'tailed**). — **fan wheel** a wheel with fans on its rim for producing a current of air. — **fan out** to fan, spread as a fan from a centre. [O.E. *fann*, from L. *vannus*, a basket for winnowing.]

fan[2] *fan*, *n* a devotee or enthusiastic follower of some sport or hobby or public favourite. — **fan club** a group united by devotion to a celebrity; **fan mail** letters from devotees to a celebrity. [From **fanatic**.]

Fanagalo *fan'ə-gə-lō*, *n* a South African pidgin language, a mixture of Zulu, Afrikaans and English.

fanatic *fə-nat'ik*, *adj* extravagantly or unreasonably zealous, esp. in religion; excessively enthusiastic. — *n* a person frantically or excessively enthusiastic, esp. on religious subjects. — *adj* **fanat'ical**. — *adv* **fanat'ically**. — *vt* **fanat'icise** or **-ize** (*-i-sīz*) to make fanatical. — *vi* to act as a fanatic. — *n* **fanat'icism** (*-sizm*). [L. *fānāticus*, belonging to a temple, inspired by a god, *fānum*, a temple.]

fancy *fan'si*, *n* that faculty of the mind by which it recalls, represents, or makes to appear past images or impressions — imagination, esp. of a lower, passive, or more trivial kind; an image or representation thus formed in the mind; an unreasonable, lightly-formed or capricious opinion; a whim; capricious inclination or liking; taste. — *adj* pleasing to, or guided by, or originating in fancy or caprice; fantastic; capriciously departing from the ordinary, the simple, or the plain; ornate; (of flowers) parti-coloured; (of gems, esp. diamonds) of a colour other than the normal one. — *vt* to picture in the mind; to imagine; to be inclined to believe; to have a liking for; to be pleased with; to breed or cultivate, with a view to development of conventionally accepted points: — *pr p* **fan'cying**; *pa t* and *pa p* **fan'cied**. — *interj* (also **fancy that!**) an exclamation of surprise. — *adj* **fan'cied** formed or conceived by the fancy; imagined; favoured. — *n* **fan'cier** someone who fancies; a person who has a liking for anything and is supposed to be a judge of it; a breeder for points. — *adj* **fan'ciful** guided or created by fancy; imaginative; whimsical; wild; unreal. — *adv* **fan'cifully**. —

n **fan'cifulness.** — **fancy dress** a costume chosen for fun, esp. for a party, and usu. representing a famous type or character; **fancy dress ball.** — *adj* **fancy-free'** free from the power of love; carefree; free of responsibilities. — **fancy goods** applied generally to articles of show and ornament, esp. small (cheap) gifts; **fancy man** a woman's lover (*derog*); a pimp; **fancy woman** a mistress; a prostitute; **fan'cywork** ornamental needlework. — **fancy oneself** to think too highly of oneself; **tickle (**or **take) someone's fancy** to attract someone mildly in some way. [Contr. from **fantasy.**]

fandangle *fan-dang'gl*, *n* elaborate ornament; nonsense. [Perh. from **fandango.**]

fandango *fan-dang'gō*, *n* an old Spanish dance for two or its music in 3-4 time: — *pl* **fandang'os.** [Sp.]

fanfare *fan'fār*, *n* a flourish of trumpets or bugles. [Fr., perh. from the sound.]

fang *fang*, *n* the tooth of a wolf, dog, etc.; the venom-tooth of a serpent; the embedded part of a tooth, etc.; a tang (of a tool); a prong. — *adj* **fanged** having fangs or anything resembling them. — *adj* **fang'-less.** [O.E. *fang*, from the same root as *fōn*, to seize.]

fanny *fan'i*, (*slang*) *n* buttocks (chiefly *US*); the female genitals (*vulg*).

Fanny Adams *fan'i ad'əmz*: **sweet Fanny Adams** or **sweet FA** (*slang*) *n* nothing at all. [Orig. Services slang for tinned mutton; from a girl murdered and cut up 24 August 1867; now used as a euphemism for *fuck all.*]

fantasia *fan-tā'zi-ə* or *-tə-zē'ə*, *n* a musical or other composition not governed by the ordinary rules of form. [It., — Gr. *phantasiā*; see **fantasy.**]

fantasy or **phantasy** *fan'tə-si* or *-zi*, *n* a story, film, etc., not based on realistic characters or setting; preoccupation with thoughts associated with unobtainable desires; fancy; imagination; mental image; fantasia. — *vt* and *vi* **fan'tasise** or **-ize** to indulge in gratifying fantasies; to have whimsical notions. — *n* **fan'tasist** a person who creates or indulges in fantasies. — *n* **fan'tasm** same as **phantasm.** — *adj* **fantas'tic** incredible; excellent (*slang*). — *adj* **fantas'tic** or **fantas'tical** fanciful; not real; capricious; whimsical; wild. — *adv* **fantas'tically.** — *n* **fantastica'tion.** — *n* **fantas'ticism** (*-sizm*). — *n* **fan'tastry.** [O.Fr. *fantasie* — through L. from Gr. *phantasiā* — *phantazein*, to make visible; cf. **fancy, fantasia.**]

fanzine *fan'zēn*, *n* a magazine produced for fans. [*fan* (**fan**[2]) and maga*zine*.]

FAO *abbrev* for Food and Agriculture Organisation (of the United Nations).

far *fär*, *adj* remote; more distant of two. — *adv* to, at, or over a great distance or advanced stage; remotely; in a great degree; very much. — *adj* **far'most** most distant or remote. — *n* **far'ness.** — *adj* **far'away** distant; abstracted, absent-minded. — **far cry** a long distance; **Far East** China, Korea, Japan, etc.; often also the countries from Myanmar (Burma) to Indonesia and the Philippines and, as used by some, the countries of the Indian subcontinent. — *adj* **far=fetched'** forced, unnatural. — *adj* **far'-flung** thrown far and wide; extensive. — **Far North** the Arctic regions. — *adj* and *adv* **far'-off** in the distance. — *adj* **far-out'** avant-garde; intellectual; satisfying. — *adj* **far-reach'ing** having wide validity, scope or influence. — *adj* **far-sight'ed** seeing far; having defective eyesight for near objects; prescient. — **far-sight'edness; Far South** the Antarctic regions; **Far West** (esp. formerly) the Great Plains, Rocky Mountains and Pacific side of North America; (now usu.) the area between the Rockies and the Pacific. — **as far as** to the extent that; up to (a particular place); **by far** in a very great degree; **far and away** by a great deal; **far and near** or **far and wide** everywhere, all about; **far between** at wide intervals; rare; **far be it** God forbid; **far from it** on the contrary; **go too far** to go beyond reasonable limits, esp. of tact or behaviour; **I'll see you far (**or **farther) first** I will not do it by any means; **in so far as** to the extent that. — See also **farther.** [O.E. *feor(r)*.]

farad *far'əd*, *n* a unit of electrical capacitance, the capacitance of a capacitor between the plates of which appears a difference of potential of one volt when it is charged by one coulomb of electricity. — *n* **far'aday** a unit used in electrolysis, equal to 96 500 coulombs. — *adj* **faradic** (*-ad'ik*) pertaining to Faraday, esp. in connection with induced currents. [From Michael *Faraday* (1791–1867).]

farce *färs*, *n* comedy of extravagant humour, buffoonery and improbability; ridiculous or empty show; a hollow formality. — *n* **farceur** (*fär-sœr'*; Fr.), *fem* **farceuse** (*-sœz'*) a joker, buffoon; a person who writes or acts in farces. — *adj* **far'cical.** — *n* **farcical'ity** farcical quality. — *adv* **far'cically.** [Fr. *farce*, stuffing, from L. *farcīre*, to stuff.]

farcy *fär'si*, (*vet*) *n* chronic glanders. [Fr. *farcin* — L.L. *farcīminum*.]

fardel *fär'dl*, *n* a pack; anything cumbersome or irksome; the manyplies or omasum (*zool*). [O.Fr. *fardel* (Fr. *fardeau*), dimin. of *farde*, a burden.]

fare *fār*, *vi* to get on or succeed; to happen well or badly to; to be in any particular state, to be, to go on. — *n* the price of a journey; a paying passenger (or passengers); food or provisions for the table. — *interj* **farewell'** may you fare well!, a parting wish for safety or success; goodbye. — *n* well-wishing at parting; the act of departure. — *adj* (*fār'wel*) parting; valedictory; final. [O.E. *faran*.]

farina *fə-rī'nə* or *fə-rē'nə*, *n* ground corn; meal; starch; pollen; a mealy powder. — *adj* **farinaceous** (*far-i-nā'shəs*) mealy; consisting of cereals. — *adj* **far'i-nose** (*-i-nōs*) yielding farina. [L. *farīna* — *fār*, corn.]

farm *färm*, *n* a tract of land (orig. one leased or rented) used for cultivation and pasturage, along with a house and other necessary buildings; farmhouse; farmstead; a piece of land or water used for breeding animals, fish, etc. (e.g. *fox-farm, oyster-farm*); a place for treatment and disposal (*sewage-farm*). — *adj* of, belonging to, or appropriate to, a farm. — *vt* to grant or receive the revenues of for a fixed sum; to rent to or from another; to cultivate; to use as a farm; to arrange for maintenance of at fixed price. — *vi* to practise the business of farmer. — *n* **farm'er** a person who farms land; the tenant of a farm; someone who receives taxes, etc., for fixed payment. — *n* **farm'ing** business of cultivating land. — **farm'house** the farmer's house attached to a farm; **farm'-hand** or **-labourer** a person who works on a farm. — *npl* **farm'-offices** outbuildings on a farm. — **farm'-stead** or **farm steading** a farmhouse with buildings belonging to it; **farm'yard** a yard or enclosure surrounded by farm buildings. — **farm out** to board out for fixed payment; to give, e.g. work for which one has made oneself responsible, to others to carry out. [L.L. *firma*, a fixed payment — L. *firmus*, firm.]

farmost. See **far.**

faro *fār'ō*, *n* a game of chance played by betting on the order of appearance of certain cards.

farouche *fə-rōōsh'* or *fa-*, *adj* shy, ill at ease; sullen and unsociable; socially inexperienced and lacking polish. [Fr., wild, shy, savage.]

farrago *fə-rā'gō* or *fä-rä'gō*, *n* a disordered mixture: — *pl* **farrag'oes.** [L. *farrāgō, -inis*, mixed fodder — *fār*, grain.]

farrier *far'i-ər*, *n* someone who shoes horses; someone who cures horses' diseases; someone in charge of cavalry horses. — *n* **farr'iery** the farrier's art; veterinary surgery. [O.Fr. *ferrier* — L. *ferrum*, iron.]

farrow *far'ō*, *n* a litter of pigs. — *vi* or *vt* to bring forth (pigs). [O.E. *fearh*, a pig.]

Farsi *fär'sē*, *n* Modern Persian, an Indo-European language and the official spoken language of Iran. [*Fars* ('Persia'), province of S.W. Iran.]

fart *färt*, (*vulg*) *vi* to break wind from the anus. — *n* an act of breaking wind; a worthless person (*slang*). — **fart about** or **around** (*vulg*) to fool about; to waste time. [O.E. (assumed) *feortan*.]

farther *fär'dhər*, **far'thermore, far'thermost, far'thest.** Same as **further**[1], etc., and sometimes preferred where the notion of distance is more prominent. [A variant (M.E. *ferther*) of **further**[1] that came to be thought a compar. of **far**.]

farthing *fär'dhing*, *n* the fourth of a pre-1971 penny (from January 1961, not legal tender); anything very small. [O.E. *fēorthing*, a fourth part — *fēortha*, fourth, and sfx. *-ing*.]

FAS *abbrev* for: Fellow of the Antiquarian Society; Fellow of the Society of Arts; foetal alcohol syndrome; (also **f a s**) free alongside ship.

fascia *fā'shi-ə*, *n* a broad flat band, as in an architrave, or over a shop front (*archit*); a board in such a position, commonly bearing the shopkeeper's name; the instrument-board of a motor car; any bandlike structure; (*fash'i-ə*) connective tissue enclosing and separating a muscle, etc. (*zool*). — *adj* **fasc'ial.** — *adj* **fasc'iate** or **fasc'iated.** — *n* **fasciā'tion** (*bot*) union of a number of parts side by side in a flat plate. — *n* **fasciola** (*fə-sī'ō-lə*) or **fasciole** (*fas'i-ōl*) (e.g. *zool*) a band of colour. [L. *fascia*, band, bandage.]

fascicle *fas'i-kl*, *n* a bundle or bunch, esp. a bunched tuft of branches, roots, fibres, etc.; a part of a book issued in parts. — Also **fasc'icūle** or **fascic'ūlus**: — *pl* **fascic'ūlī.** — *adj* **fasc'icled.** — *adj* **fascic'ūlar** or **fascic'ūlate.** — *n* **fascicūlā'tion.** [L. *fasciculus*, dimin. of *fascis*, bundle.]

fascinate *fas'i-nāt*, *vt* to interest exceedingly, intrigue; to charm, captivate; to control by the eye like a snake; to hold spellbound. — *adj* **fasc'inating** intriguing, deeply interesting; charming, delightful; compelling, irresistible. — *n* **fascinā'tion** the act of fascinating; ability to allure, charm, captivate, dominate or render helpless; the process or state of being fascinated. — *n* **fasc'inātor.** [L. *fascināre*, *-ātum*.]

fascine *fas-ēn'*, *n* a brushwood faggot, used to fill ditches or trenches, protect a shore, etc. [Fr., — L. *fascīna* — *fascis*, a bundle.]

fasciola, fasciole. See under **fascia.**

Fascism *fash'izm*, *n* the authoritarian form of government in Italy from 1922–43, characterised by extreme nationalism, militarism, anti-communism and restrictions on individual freedom; (also without *cap*) the methods, doctrines, etc. of fascists or the Fascists. — *n* **Fasc'ist** a member of the ruling party in Italy from 1922–43, or a similar party elsewhere; (also without *cap*) an exponent or supporter of Fascism, or (*loosely*) anyone with extreme right-wing, nationalistic, etc. views or methods. — Also *adj.* — *adj* **fascis'tic.** [It. *fascismo* — *fascio*, group.]

fashion *fash'n*, *n* the make or cut of a thing; form or pattern; vogue; a mode or shape of dress, esp. that which prevails or is imposed by those whose lead is accepted; a prevailing custom; manner; sort, type, kind; awareness of, and attention to, the latest trends in dress, behaviour, activities, enthusiasms, etc.; high society. — *vt* to make; to mould according to a pattern; to suit or adapt. — *adj* **fash'ionable** according to prevailing fashion; prevailing or in use at any period; observant of the fashion in dress or living; moving in high society; patronised by people of fashion. — *n* **fash'ionableness.** — *adv* **fash'ionably.** — *n* **fash'ioner.** — **fashion house** an establishment in which fashionable clothes are designed, made and sold; **fashion plate** a picture showing the latest style of (esp. formal) dress; a well-groomed, fashionably dressed person. — **after** or **in a fashion** in a way; to a certain extent; **do something,** etc., **as though it were going out of fashion** (*slang*) to do something with extra vigour or enthusiasm, fast and furiously, as though for the last time; **in fashion** currently favoured; fashionable; **in the fashion** in accordance with the prevailing style of dress, etc.; **out of fashion** old-fashioned; unfashionable. [O.Fr. *fachon* — L. *factiō*, *-ōnis* — *facĕre*, to make.]

fast[1] *fäst*, *adj* quick, rapid; (of a clock) showing a time in advance of the correct time; promoting fast play; for fast-moving traffic, as in *fast lane*; seeking excitement; rash; dissolute; sexually promiscuous. — *adv* swiftly; in rapid succession; in advance of the correct time; extravagantly or dissipatedly. — *adj* **fast'ish.** — *n* **fast'ness.** — **fast'ball** (*baseball*) a high-speed, rising delivery from the pitcher; **fast bowling** (*cricket*) bowling in which the ball is delivered fast, pace-bowling; **fast bowler; fast-breeder reactor** a nuclear reactor using fast neutrons which produces at least as much fissionable material as it uses; **fast food** (or **foods**) kinds of food, e.g. hamburgers, chips, etc., which can be prepared and served quickly; **fast-for'ward** the facility provided in a cassette player for winding a tape quickly forward without playing it. — *vt* to advance (a tape) quickly by this means. — *vi* (*colloq*) to pass or move on without delay. — **fast neutron** a neutron of very high energy; **fast reactor** a nuclear reactor using fast neutrons, and little or no moderator; **fast stream** in e.g. the civil service, a category of personnel who are advanced swiftly into training for administration. — *vt* **fast'-talk** to persuade with rapid, plausible talk. — *adj* **fast'-talking.** — **fast track** (*colloq*) the routine for accelerating the progress of a proposal, etc. through its formalities; the quick but competitive route to advancement. — *vt* **fast'-track** to process or promote speedily. — **a fast buck** (*slang*) money quickly and easily obtained; **fast and furious** (or **furiously**) rapidly and vigorously; **(life) in the fast lane** (a way of life) full of pressure, excitement and glamour; **pull a fast one** or **put a fast one over** (*colloq*) to gain an advantage by trickery (with *on*). [A special use of **fast**[2] derived from Scand. sense of urgent.]

fast[2] *fäst*, *adj* firm; fixed; steadfast; fortified; (of sleep) sound; (of colours) not liable to fade or run. — Also used in combination (esp. *archaic*) to denote firmly fixed, as in *handfast*, an agreement confirmed by handshaking, *lockfast*, firmly locked, and *colourfast*. — *adv* firmly, unflinchingly; soundly or sound (asleep). — *n* **fast'ness** fixedness; a stronghold, fortress, castle. — **hard and fast** (of a rule, etc.) unalterable, inflexible, strict; **play fast and loose** to be unreliable, shifty; to behave without sense of moral obligation; to trifle (with *with*). [O.E. *fæst*.]

fast[3] *fäst*, *vi* to abstain from food altogether, or restrict one's diet, e.g. as a religious duty; to go hungry. — *n* abstinence from food; special abstinence enjoined by the church; the day or time of fasting. — *n* **fast'er.** — *n* **fast'ing.** — **fast'-day.** [O.E. *fæstan*, to fast.]

fasten *fäs'n*, *vt* to make fast or firm; to fix securely; to attach. — *vi* to become fastened; to be capable of being fastened. — *n* **fastener** (*fäs'nər*) a clip, catch, or other means of fastening. — *n* **fas'tening** (*fäs'ning*) a device that fastens. — **fasten on** to focus (one's eyes) on in a fixed or penetrating way; to seize on (e.g. a fact); to fix the blame or responsibility for, on (a person) (*slang*). [**fast**[2].]

fastidious *fas-tid'i-əs*, *adj* easily repelled or disgusted; difficult to please; exacting in taste, highly discriminating; meticulous or over-meticulous; (of bacteria) having complex requirements for growth. — *adv* **fastid'iously.** — *n* **fastid'iousness.** [L. *fastīdiōsus* — *fastīdium*, loathing.]

fastigiate *fas-tij'i-āt*, *adj* pointed, sloping to a point or edge; with branches more or less erect and parallel (*bot*); conical. — *adj* **fastig'iated.** [L. *fastīgium*, a gable-end, roof.]

fat *fat*, *adj* (*compar* **fatt'er**, *superl* **fatt'est**) plump, fleshy; well filled out; thick, full-bodied (as of printing types); corpulent; obese; having much, or of the nature of, adipose tissue or the substance it contains; oily; fruitful or profitable; (of a theatrical role) yielding rich opportunities for displaying one's talent; rich in some important constituent; gross; fulsome. — *n* a substance found in adipose tissue; solid animal or vegetable oil; any member of a group of naturally occurring substances consisting of the glycerides of higher fatty acids, e.g. palmitic acid, stearic acid, oleic acid (*chem*); the richest part of anything; inclination to corpulency. — *vt* to make fat: — *pr p* **fatt'ing**; *pa t* and *pa p* **fatt'ed.** — *n* **fat'ness** quality or state of being fat; fullness of flesh; richness; fertility. — *adj* **fatt'ed.** — *vt* **fatt'en** to make fat or fleshy; to enrich; to make fertile. — *vi* to grow fat. — *n* **fatt'ener.** — *n* **fatt'ening** (also *adj*). — *n* **fatt'iness.** — *adj* **fatt'y** containing fat; having qualities of fat. — *n* (*derog*) a fat person. — **fat cat** (esp. *US slang*) a wealthy, prosperous person; **fat city** (also with *caps*; *US slang*) easy circumstances, prosperous conditions; **fat'-head** a stupid, thick-witted person. — *adj* **fat'-headed.** — **fat stock** or **fat'stock** livestock fattened for market; **fatty acids** acids which with glycerine form fats. — **a fat chance** (*slang*) little or no opportunity; **a fat lot** (*slang*) not much, little or no; **kill the fatted calf** to have an extravagant celebration for someone returning after a long absence; **the fat is in the fire** said in expectation of disastrous consequences from something just said or done. [O.E. *fǣtt*, fatted.]

fatal, fatalism, etc. See **fate.**

fate *fāt*, *n* inevitable destiny or necessity; appointed lot; destined term of life; ill-fortune; doom; final outcome; (in *pl*; with *cap*) the three goddesses of fate, *Clotho*, *Lachesis*, and *Atropos*, who determine the birth, life, and death of men. — *adj* **fāt'al** causing death; mortal; bringing ruin; calamitous; decisive, critical, fateful; destined, unavoidable. — *n* **fāt'alism** the doctrine that all events are subject to fate, and happen by unavoidable necessity; lack of effort in the face of threatened difficulty or disaster. — *n* **fāt'alist.** — *adj* **fātalis'tic.** — *n* **fatality** (*fə-tal'i-ti*) the state of being fatal or unavoidable; the decree of fate; fixed tendency to disaster or death; mortality; a fatal occurrence; a person who has been killed, esp. in an accident, etc. — *adv* **fāt'ally.** — *adj* **fāt'ed** doomed; destined. — *adj* **fate'ful** critical, decisive, having significant consequences; bringing calamity or death; prophetic, portentous; controlled by, or revealing the power of fate. — *adv* **fate'fully.** — *n* **fate'fulness.** [L. *fātum*, a prediction — *fātus*, spoken — *fārī*, to speak.]

father *fä'dhər*, *n* a male parent; an ancestor or forefather; a contriver or originator; a title of respect applied to a venerable man, to confessors, monks, priests, etc.; a member of certain fraternities; (usu. in *pl*) a member of a ruling body, such as *conscript fathers*, *city fathers*; the oldest member, or member of longest standing, of a profession or body; one of a group of ecclesiastical writers of the early centuries, usu. ending with Ambrose, Jerome and Augustine; (with *cap*) the first person of the Trinity (*Christian relig*). — *vt* to be the father of, procreate or beget; to adopt; to acknowledge that one is the father or author of; to ascribe to someone as his offspring or production, foist (with *on*). — *n* **fa'therhood** the state or fact of being a father. — *adj* **fa'therless** without a living father. — *n* **fa'therlessness.** — *adj* **fa'therlike.** — *n* **fa'therliness.** — *adj* **fa'therly** like a father esp. in being benevolent and encouraging; paternal. — **Father Christmas** same as **Santa Claus; fa'ther-figure** a senior person of experience and authority looked on as a trusted leader or protector; **fa'ther-in-law** the father of one's husband or wife: — *pl* **fa'thers-in-law; fa'therland** one's native land; the country of one's ancestors; **Father's Day** a day on which fathers are honoured, the third Sunday in June, the tradition being of U.S. origin, dating from the early 20th cent. — **Holy Father** the Pope; **like father, like son** said on remarking inherited tendencies; **the father and mother (of)** see under **mother.** [O.E. *fæder.*]

fathom *fadh'əm*, *n* a unit of measurement for the depth of water, equal to 6 feet or 1.8 metres: — *pl* **fath'oms** or **fath'om.** — *vt* to measure the depth of, esp. with a sounding-line; to comprehend or get to the bottom of. — *adj* **fath'omable.** — *adj* **fath'omless** unfathomable. — *n* **fathom'eter** a sonic depth measurer. — **fath'om-line** a sailor's line and lead for taking soundings. [O.E. *fæthm.*]

fatigue *fə-tēg'*, *n* weariness from labour of body or of mind; toil; lessened power of response to stimulus, resulting from activity (*physiol*); failure under repeated stress, as in metal; fatigue-duty (sometimes allotted as a punishment); (in *pl*) military overalls. — *vt* to reduce to weariness; to exhaust the strength or power of recovery of: — *pr p* **fatigu'ing**; *pa t* and *pa p* **fatigued'.** — *adv* **fatigu'ingly.** — **fatigue'-dress** working dress; **fatigue'-duty** the part of a soldier's work distinct from the use of arms; **fatigue'-party.** [Fr. *fatigue* — L. *fatīgāre*, to weary.]

Fatimid *fat'i-mid*, *n* a descendant of Mohammed's daughter, *Fatima*, and his cousin, Ali, esp. one of a dynasty ruling parts of northern Africa from 909 to 1171. — Also *adj*.

fatsia *fat'si-ə*, *n* an evergreen spreading shrub of the ivy family, with leathery leaves and clusters of white flowers in the form of umbels. [Perh. Jap. *yatsude*, the name of this plant.]

fatso *fat'sō*, (*derog slang*) *n* a fat person: — *pl* **fat'sos** or **fat'soes. [fat.]**

fatten, fatter, fatty, etc. See under **fat.**

fatuous *fat'ū-əs*, *adj* foolish, inane, asinine, esp. in a cheerfully complacent way. — *n* **fatū'ity** or **fat'ūousness.** [L. *fatuus.*]

fatwa or **fatwah** *fat'wä*, *n* a formal legal opinion or decision issued by a Muslim juridical authority. [Ar.]

faubourg *fō-bo͞or*, (Fr.) *n* a suburb just beyond the walls or a district recently included within a city.

fauces *fö'sēz*, (*anat*) *npl* or *nsing* the upper part of the throat between the back of the mouth and the pharynx. — *adj* **fau'cial** (*-shəl*). [L. *faucēs.*]

faucet *fö'sit*, *n* a pipe inserted in a barrel to draw liquid; another word for **tap²** (*US*). [Fr. *fausset.*]

fault *fölt*, *n* a failing or weakness of character; a blemish, imperfection or flaw; an error; a misdeed or slight offence; culpability for something which has gone wrong; a dislocation of strata or veins where a fracture has occurred in the earth's crust (*geol*); a defect in an electric circuit; a stroke in which the player fails to serve the ball properly or into the proper place (*tennis*); a penalty point for refusing or failing to clear a fence (*showjumping*). — *vi* to develop or show a fault (*geol*); to commit a fault. — *vt* to censure, find fault with; to find flaw(s) in; to cause a fault in (*geol*). — *adv* **fault'ily.** — *n* **fault'iness.** — *adj* **fault'less** without fault or defect, perfect. — *adv* **fault'lessly.** — *n* **fault'lessness.** — *adj* **fault'y** imperfect, defective. — **fault'-finder; fault'-finding** criticism, captiousness; detection and investigation of faults and malfunctions in electronic equipment; **fault plane** (*geol*) a usu. uncurved surface of rock strata where a fault has occurred. — **at fault** culpable, to blame; guilty; (of dogs) unable to find the scent; **find fault** to carp, be critical; (with *with*) to censure for some defect; **to a fault** excessively. [O.Fr. *faute*, *falte* — L. *fallĕre*, to deceive.]

faun *fön*, (*Roman mythol*) *n* a rural deity similar to a satyr, having a man's body, with a goat's horns, ears, tail and hind legs. [L. *Faunus*, a deity of woods and pastures.]

fauna *fö'nə*, *n* the assemblage of animals of a region or period; a list or account of this: — *pl* **fau'nas** or **fau'nae** (*-nē*). — *adj* **fau'nal**. [L. *Fauna*, a rural goddess.]

fauteuil *fō-tœ-y'* or *fō'til*, *n* an armchair, esp. a president's chair; a theatre stall. [Fr.]

Fauvism *fō'vizm*, (*art*) *n* a painting style adopted by a group of expressionists, including Matisse, who regarded a painting as essentially a two-dimensional decoration in colour, not necessarily imitative of nature. [Fr. *fauve*, wild beast.]

faux *fō*, (Fr.) *adj* false. — **faux ami** (*fōz a-mē*) a word in a foreign language that looks similar to one in one's own language, but has a rather different meaning, e.g. Fr. *prétendre*, which means 'claim' or 'assert', not 'pretend'. — *n* and *adj* **faux-naïf** (*fō-na-ēf'*) (a person) seeming or pretending to be simple and unsophisticated. — **faux pas** (*fō pä*) a false step; a mistake, blunder.

favela *fä-vā'lə*, *n* esp. in Brazil, a shanty town. [Port.]

favour or in U.S. **favor** *fā'vər*, *n* approval; esteem; good will; a kind deed; an act of goodwill or clemency; indulgence; partiality; advantage; a concession of amorous indulgence (*literary* or *facetious*); a knot of ribbons indicative of one's allegiance, worn at an election, etc.; a thing given or worn as a token of favour or love (esp. *hist*). — *vt* to regard with good will; to be on the side of; to show partiality to; to treat indulgently; to give support to; to afford advantage to; to resemble (*colloq*); to choose to wear, etc. — *adj* **fā'vourable** or in U.S. **fā'vorable** friendly; propitious; conducive (with *to*); advantageous; satisfactory, promising. — *n* **fā'vourableness** or in U.S. **fā'vorableness**. — *adv* **fā'vourably** or in U.S. **fā'vorably**. — *adj* **fā'voured** or in U.S. **fā'vored** enjoying favour or preference; having a certain appearance, featured — as in *ill-favoured*, *well-favoured*. — *n* **fā'vourer** or in U.S. **fā'vorer**. — *n* **fā'vourite** or in U.S. **fā'vorite** (*-it*) a person or thing regarded with especial preference; a person unduly loved and indulged, e.g. by a king; a runner, contestant, expected to win. — *n* **fā'vouritism** or in U.S. **fā'voritism** inclination to partiality; preference shown to favourites. — **in favour (**or in U.S. **favor) of** for, in support of; on the side of; for the advantage of, to the benefit of; **in favour** (or in U.S. **favor**) approved of; **out of favour** (or in U.S. **favor**) not approved of. [O.Fr. — L. *favor* — *favēre*, to favour, befriend.]

favrile *fəv-rēl'* or *fav'rəl*, *n* a type of iridescent glassware developed in America at the turn of the 20th cent. by L.C. Tiffany. [Orig. trademark, — obs. *fabrile*, relating to a craftsman.]

fawn[1] *fön*, *n* a young (esp. fallow) deer, under a year old; a colour resembling a fawn's, light greyish or yellowish brown. — *adj* having this colour. — *vt* and *vi* (of a deer) to bring forth (young). [O.Fr. *faon*, through L.L. from L. *fētus*, offspring.]

fawn[2] *fön*, *vi* (with *on* or *upon*) to try to please, or flatter, in a servile way; (of an animal, esp. a dog) to lick, rub against, jump up on, etc., in a show of affection. — *n* **fawn'er**. — *n* and *adj* **fawn'ing**. — *adv* **fawn'ingly**. — *n* **fawn'ingness**. [A variant of **fain** — O.E. *fægen*, glad.]

fax *faks*, *n* a shortening of **facsimile** as in **fax machine**, a machine that scans a document, etc. electronically and transmits a photographic image of the contents to a receiving machine by a telephone line; a copy so produced. — *vt* to transmit the contents of (a document, etc.) using a fax machine.

fay *fā*, (*poetic*) *n* a fairy. [O.Fr. *fae* — L.L. *fāta*; see **fate**.]

fayre. An archaic or archaising spelling of **fair**[2].

fazenda *fa-zen'də*, *n* esp. in Brazil, a large estate, plantation or cattle ranch. — *n* **fazendei'ro** (*-dā'ro*) a person who owns or runs such a property: — *pl* **fazendei'ros**. [Port.; cf. **hacienda**.]

FBA *abbrev* for Fellow of the British Academy.

FBI *abbrev* for Federal Bureau of Investigation (U.S.).

FBR *abbrev* for fast-breeder reactor(s).

FC *abbrev* for football club.

FD *abbrev* for *Fidei Defensor* (L.), Defender of the Faith, appearing on coins since decimalisation.

FDA *abbrev* for Food and Drug Administration (U.S.).

fe (*chem*) symbol for *ferrum* (L.), iron.

fealty *fē'əl-ti* or *fēl'ti*, *n* the vassal's obligation of fidelity to his feudal lord (*hist*); loyalty. [O.Fr. *fealte* — L. *fidēlitās*, *-tātis*, — *fidēlis*, faithful.]

fear *fēr*, *n* a painful emotion aroused by danger; apprehension of danger or pain; alarm; solicitude, anxiety; that which causes alarm; risk or possibility; reverence or awe (*relig*); piety towards God (*old relig*). — *vt* to regard with fear, be afraid of; to expect with alarm; to be regretfully inclined to think; to revere (*relig*). — *vi* to be afraid; to suspect some danger to (with *for*); (esp. in *neg*) to be in doubt. — *adj* **fear'ful** timorous; arousing intense fear; terrible; (*loosely*) very great, very bad. — *adv* **fear'fully**. — *n* **fear'fulness**. — *adj* **fear'less** without fear; daring; brave. — *adv* **fear'lessly**. — *n* **fear'lessness**. — *adj* **fear'some** causing fear, frightful. — *adv* **fear'somely**. — **for fear** in case, lest; **for fear of** in order to avoid; **no fear** (*interj*; *slang*) definitely not. [O.E. *fǣr*, fear, *fǣran*, to terrify.]

feasible *fē'zə-bl*, *adj* practicable, possible; (*loosely*) probable, likely. — *n* **feasibil'ity** or **feas'ibleness**. — *adv* **feas'ibly**. — **feasibility study** an investigation to determine whether a particular project, system, etc. is desirable, practicable, etc. [Fr. *faisable*, that can be done — *faire*, *faisant* — L. *facĕre*, to do.]

feast *fēst*, *n* a rich and abundant meal; a regularly occurring religious celebration commemorating a person or event, honouring a deity, etc.; (something that affords) rich gratification of the senses (e.g. a *feast for the eyes*) or stimulation for the mind. — *vi* to partake of a feast; to eat sumptuously (with *on*); to receive intense delight. — *vt* to provide a feast for; to entertain sumptuously; to delight, gratify (e.g. one's eyes; with *on*). — *n* **feast'er**. — *n* **feast'ing**. — **feast'-day** a day on which a religious festival occurs; **movable feast** a festival of variable date, such as Easter. [O.Fr. *feste* (Fr. *fête*) — L. *fēstum*, a holiday, *fēstus*, solemn, festal.]

feat *fēt*, *n* a deed manifesting extraordinary strength, skill or courage, an exploit, achievement. [Fr. *fait* — L. *factum* — *facĕre*, to do: cf. **fact**.]

feather *fedh'ər*, *n* one of the light growths that form the soft covering of a bird; a featherlike appearance, ornament or flaw; the feathered end of an arrow; plumage; condition, spirits; a projecting longitudinal rib or strip; a formation of hair, e.g. on the legs of certain breeds of dog or horse; the action of feathering an oar. — *vt* to fit, furnish, cover or adorn with a feather or feathers; to turn (an oar) so that it lies parallel to the water, to lessen air-resistance, or to make (a propeller-blade, etc.) rotate in such a way as to lessen resistance. — *adj* **feath'ered** covered or fitted with feathers, or anything featherlike. — *n* **feath'eriness**. — *n* **feath'ering** plumage; the addition of a feather or feathers; a featherlike appearance; an arrangement of small arcs separated by cusps, within an arch (*archit*). — *adj* **feath'ery** resembling, or covered with, feathers or an appearance of feathers. — **feather bed** a mattress filled with feathers or down. — *vt* **feath'erbed** to pamper; to protect (an industry, workers, etc.) by such practices as overmanning in order to save jobs. — **feath'erbedding**; **feath'er-brain** a frivolous, feckless person; **feather duster** a brush of feathers, used for dusting; **feath'er-star** see **crinoid; feather stitch** a zigzag stitch in embroidery; **feath'erweight** a weight category applied variously in boxing, wrestling and weightlifting; a sportsman of the specified weight for the category (e.g. in professional boxing above bantamweight, **ju'nior-featherweight** (maximum 55 kg./122 lb.), **feath'erweight** (maximum 57 kg./126 lb.) and **su'per-featherweight** (maximum 59 kg./130 lb.); anyone of little consequence. — **a feather in one's cap** an achievement of which one can be proud; **birds of a feather** people of like character; **feather one's nest** to accumulate wealth for oneself while serving others in a position of trust; **in full (or high) feather** greatly elated or in high spirits; **make the feathers fly** to throw into confusion by a sudden attack; **ruffle someone's feathers** to upset or offend someone; **show the white feather** to show signs of cowardice — a white feather in a gamecock's tail being considered as a sign of degeneracy; **tar and feather** see under **tar**[1]; **you could have knocked me down with a feather** I was astounded. [O.E. *fether*.]

feature *fē'chər*, *n* any of the parts of the face, such as the eyes, nose, mouth, etc.; an element or prominent trait of anything; a characteristic; (in *pl*) the face; a feature film; a non-news article in a newspaper; a feature film; anything offered as a special attraction or distinctive characteristic. — *vt* to have as a feature; to make a feature of; to present prominently. — *vi* to play an important part or role (with *in*), be a feature. — **-fea'tured** (*in combination*) having features of a specified type, as in *sharp-featured*. — *adj* **fea'tureless** destitute of distinctive features. — **feature film** a long film forming the basis of a cinema programme. — *adj* **feat'ure-length** (of films) comparable to a feature film in length. [O.Fr. *faiture* — L. *factura* — *facĕre*, to make.]

Feb. *abbrev* for February.

febrifuge *feb'ri-fūj*, (*med*) *n* a medicine, etc. that reduces fever. — *adj* **febrif'ūgal** (*-gəl*). [Med.L. *febrifugia*, feverfew.]

febrile *fē'brīl* or in U.S. *feb'rəl*, *adj* relating to fever; feverish. — *n* **febril'ity**. [Med.L. *febrīlis*, — L. *febris*, fever.]

February *feb'ro͞o-ər-i*, *n* the second month of the year. [L. *Februārius* (*mēnsis*), the month of expiation, *februa*, the feast of expiation.]

fec. *abbrev* for *fecit* (L.), did it or made it.

feces, fecal. See **faeces, faecal**.

feckless *fek'ləs*, *adj* helpless, shiftless; feeble, ineffectual. — *adv* **feck'lessly**. — *n* **feck'lessness**. [Scot. *feck*, aphetic for **effect**, and **-less**.]

feculent *fek'ū-lənt*, *adj* containing or consisting of faeces or sediment; foul; turbid. — *n* **fec'ulence**. [L. *faeculentus*, full of dregs, thick, impure — *faecula*, dimin. of *faex*, dregs.]

fecund *fē'kənd* or *fek'*, *adj* fruitful; fertile; prolific. — *vt* **fec'undāte** to make fruitful or fertile; to impregnate. — *n* **fecundā'tion**. — *n* **fecundity** (*fi-kun'di-ti*) fruitfulness, fertility; productiveness. [L. *fēcundus*, fruitful.]

Fed *fed*, *abbrev* for Federal Reserve Board (U.S.).

fed *fed*, *pa t* and *pa p* of **feed**[1].

fedayee *fə-dä'yē*, *n* an Arab commando, esp. one involved in the conflict against Israel: — *pl* **feda'yeen**. [Ar. *fidā'ī*.]

federal *fed'ər-əl*, *adj* relating to or consisting of a treaty or covenant; confederated, founded upon mutual agreement; (of a union or government) in which several states, while independent in home affairs, combine for national or general purposes, as in the United States (in the American Civil War, *Federal* was the name applied to the states of the North which defended the Union against the *Confederate* separatists of the South). — *n* a supporter of federation; a Unionist soldier in the American Civil War. — *n* **federalisā'tion** or **-z-**. — *vt* **fed'eralise** or **-ize**. — *n* **fed'eralism**. — *n* **fed'eralist** a supporter of a federal constitution or union. — **Federal Bureau of Investigation** in the U.S., a bureau or subdivision of the Department of Justice that investigates crimes, such as smuggling and espionage, that are the concern of the federal government; **Federal Reserve Board** in the U.S., the board of governors in charge of the **Federal Reserve System**, which, comprising twelve **Federal Reserve Banks**, controls banking activities and supply of money and credit. [L. *foedus*, *foederis*, a treaty.]

federate *fed'ə-rāt*, *vt* and *vi* to join in league or federation. — *adj* (*-rit*) united by league; confederated. — *n* **federā'tion** the act of uniting in league; a federal union. — *adj* **fed'erātive**. [L. *foederāre* — *foedus*, *foedoris*, a treaty.]

fedora *fi-dör'ə*, *n* a brimmed felt hat, dented lengthways. [Said to be from *Fédora*, a play by V. Sardon.]

fee *fē*, *n* the price paid for professional services, as to a lawyer or physician; recompense, wages; the sum exacted for any special privilege; a grant of land for feudal service (*hist*); feudal tenure; fee simple. — *vt* to pay a fee to; to hire (*Scot*): — *pr p* **fee'ing**; *pa t* and *pa p* **feed** or **fee'd**. — **fee simple** unconditional inheritance; **fee tail** an entailed estate, which may descend only to a certain class of heirs. [Partly O.E. *feoh*, cattle, property; partly A.Fr. *fee*.]

feeble *fē'bl*, *adj* very weak, frail, infirm; faint; (of a joke, excuse, etc.) tame, lame, unconvincing or thin; vacillating, lacking resolve. — *n* **fee'bleness**. — *adv* **fee'bly**. — *adj* **feeble-mind'ed** weak-minded to the extent of being unable to compete with others or to manage one's affairs with ordinary prudence; irresolute. — *adv* **feeble-mind'edly**. — *n* **feeble-mind'edness**. [O.Fr. *foible*, for *floible* — L. *flēbilis*, lamentable, from *flēre*, to weep.]

feed[1] *fēd*, *vt* to give, supply, or administer food to; to give as food (with *to*); to nourish; to provide with necessary material; to foster; to give as material to be used progressively; to furnish (an actor) with cues or opportunities of achieving an effect; in football, to pass the ball to. — *vi* to take food; to nourish oneself by eating (with *on*): — *pa t* and *pa p* **fed**. — *n* an allowance of food, given e.g. to babies or to cattle; food for livestock, etc.; a plentiful meal (*colloq*); material supplied progressively for any operation; the means, channel, motion or rate of such supply; rate of progress of a tool; an actor who feeds another, a stooge. — *n* **feed'er** a person, etc. that consumes food (esp. in a specified way, e.g. a *big feeder*) or provides or administers it to another; that which supplies (water, electricity, ore, paper, etc.); any channel of supply to a main system; a transport route linking outlying areas to the trunk line; a tributary; an overhead or underground cable, of large current-carrying capacity, used to transmit electric power between generating stations, substations and feeding points; a feeding-bottle; a bib. — *adj* secondary, subsidiary, tributary. — *n* **feed'ing**. — **feed'back** return of part of the output of an electronic system to the input as a means towards improved quality or self-correction of error (*negative feedback*) or, when in phase with the input signal, resulting in oscillation and instability (*positive feedback*); used also in relation to biological, etc., self-adjusting systems; response or reaction providing useful information or guidelines for further development; in a public address system, etc., the returning of some of the sound output back to the microphone, producing a whistle or howl; **feed'ing-bottle** a bottle for supplying liquid food to an infant; **feed'stock** raw material used in an industrial process. — **fed to the back teeth** or **fed up** (*slang*) jaded; disgruntled; bored; (with *with*) tired of, annoyed by; **feed one's**

face (*slang*) to eat heartily; **off one's feed** without appetite, disinclined to eat. [O.E. *fēdan*, to feed.]

feed[2] *fĕd*, *pa t* and *pa p* of **fee**.

feel *fēl*, *vt* to perceive by the touch; to investigate by touching or handling; to find (one's way) by groping; to be conscious of; to be keenly sensible of; to experience; to be strongly or severely affected by; to have an inward persuasion of; to believe, consider or think; to caress the genitals of (with *up*; *vulg*). — *vi* to be aware that one is (well, ill, happy, etc.); to explore or investigate with one's hand (with *in*, etc.); to impart a particular impression when touched, as in *to feel smooth, sharp*, etc.; to be emotionally affected; to have sympathy or compassion (with *for*): — *pr p* **feel'ing**; *pa t* and *pa p* **felt**. — *n* the sensation of touch; an instinct, touch, knack; an act of feeling something; an impression imparted by something being felt; a general impression or atmosphere associated with something. — *n* **feel'er** a person, etc. that feels; a remark cautiously dropped, or any indirect stratagem, to sound the opinions of others; a tentacle; a jointed organ in the head of insects, etc., possessed of a delicate sense — an antenna. — *n* **feel'ing** the sense of touch; perception of objects by touch; consciousness of pleasure or pain; an impression received physically or mentally; tenderness; an emotion; sensibility, susceptibility, sentimentality; an opinion, sentiment; an instinctive grasp or appreciation (with *for*); mutual or interactive emotion, such as *bad feeling* (resentment), *good feeling* (friendliness), *ill-feeling, fellow-feeling*; (in *pl*) the affections or passions; (in *pl*) one's sensibilities, or amour-propre, as in *hurt someone's feelings*. — *adj* expressive of great sensibility or tenderness; easily or strongly affected by emotion; sympathetic, compassionate. — *adj* **feel'ingless**. — *adv* **feel'ingly**. — **feelings (are) running high** (there is) a general feeling of anger, emotion, etc.; **feel like** to want, have a desire for; **feel oneself** to feel as fit as normal; **feel one's feet** to accustom oneself to a new situation, job, etc.; **feel up to** (with *neg*) to feel fit enough to; **no hard feelings** no offence taken. [O.E. *fēlan*, to feel.]

feet *fēt*, *pl* of **foot**.

feign *fān*, *vt* to invent; to assume fictitiously; to make a show or pretence of, to counterfeit, simulate. — *adj* **feigned**. — *n* **feign'ing**. [Fr. *feindre*, pres. p. *feignant*, to feign — L. *fingĕre, fictum*, to form.]

feint[1] *fānt*, *n* a mock assault; a deceptive movement in fencing, boxing, etc.; a deliberately misleading move, a pretence. — *vi* to make a feint. [Fr. *feinte* — *feindre*, to feign.]

feint[2] *fānt*, *adj* a printers' or stationers' spelling of **faint** — used of stationery printed with pale, fine horizontal lines to guide writing.

feisty *fī'sti*, (*colloq*, orig. *US*) *adj* excitable, irritable, touchy; spirited. — *n* **fei'stiness**. [From old U.S. dialect *fist*, a small aggressive dog — M.E. *fisten*, to break wind.]

felafel or **falafel** *fə-lä'fəl*, *n* a deep-fried ball of ground chick-peas, with onions, peppers, etc. and spices usu. served in a roll or a round of pitta bread. [Ar. *falāfil*.]

feldspar *fel'* or *feld'spär* or **felspar** *fel'spär*, *n* any member of the most important group of rock-forming minerals, anhydrous silicates of aluminium along with potassium, sodium, calcium, or both, or sodium and barium. — *adj* **feldspathic** or **felspathic** (*-spath'ik*). [Sw. *feldtspat*, a name given in 1740 by D. Tilas — Sw. *feldt* or *fält*, field, *spat*, spar.]

felicia *fe-lik'i-ə* or *-lish'ə*, *n* any member of a South African genus of herbs and subshrubs of the daisy family, with blue or lilac flowers. [L. *fēlix, -icis*, happy.]

felicity *fi-lis'i-ti*, *n* happiness; delight; a blessing; a happy event; a happiness of expression. — *vt* **felic'itate** to express joy or pleasure to; to congratulate. — *n* **felicitā'tion** the act of congratulating; (in *pl*) congratulations. — *adj* **felic'itous** happy; prosperous; delightful; pleasingly apposite. — *adv* **felic'itously**. [O.Fr. *felicité* — L. *fēlīcitās, -ātis*, from *fēlix, -icis*, happy.]

felid *fē'lid*, *n* a member of the *Felidae*, the cat family. [N.L. *fēlidae* — L. *fēlēs*, cat.]

feline *fē'līn*, *adj* relating to the cat or the cat family; like a cat, esp. in stealth or elegance. — *n* any animal of the cat tribe. — *n* **felinity** (*fi-lin'i-ti*). [L. *fēlīnus* — *fēlēs*, a cat.]

fell[1] *fel*, *n* a hill; an upland tract of waste, pasture or moorland. — **fell'-walking** (or **-running**) the pastime (or sport) of walking (or running) over fells; **fell'-walker** (or **-runner**). [O.N. *fjall*; Dan. *fjeld*.]

fell[2] *fel*, *pa t* of **fall**[1].

fell[3] *fel*, *vt* to cut down (a tree); to knock down; to bring to the ground, cause to fall; to prostrate; to turn under and stitch down the edges of (a seam; *needlework*). — *n* a quantity of timber felled at a time; a felled seam. — *n* **fell'er**. [O.E. *fælla(n)*, *fella(n)*, causative of *fallan* (*feallan*), to fall.]

fell[4] *fel*, *n* an animal skin; a covering of rough hair. [O.E. *fell*.]

fell[5] *fel*, *adj* cruel; fierce; dire; ruthless; deadly; keen; doughty. — **at one fell swoop** with a single deadly blow; in one quick operation. [O.Fr. *fel*, cruel — L.L. *fellō, -ōnis*; see **felon**[1].]

fellah *fel'ə*, *n* a peasant, esp. in Egypt: — *pl* **fell'ahs, fellaheen** or **fellahin** (*-hēn'*). [Ar. *fellāh*, tiller.]

fellatio *fə-lā'shi-ō*, *n* oral stimulation of the male genitalia. [L. — *fellātus*, past p. of *fellāre*, to suck.]

felloe *fel'ō* or **felly** *fel'i*, *n* a curved piece of the circumference of a wheel; the circular rim of a wheel. [O.E. *felg*.]

fellow *fel'ō*, *n* a man or boy, sometimes used dismissively; a boyfriend (*colloq*); an associate or companion; someone with something in common with one, one's peer or equal in a specified way (often attrib., as in *fellow-worker*); one of a pair, a mate; a counterpart; a senior member of a college; a member of the governing body of a university; a postgraduate student receiving a stipend for a stated period of research; (with *cap*) a member of an academic, scientific or professional society. — *n* **fell'owship** the state of being a fellow or partner; friendly intercourse; communion; an association; an endowment in a college for the support of research fellows; the position and income of a fellow. — **fellow-cit'izen** a person belonging to the same city as oneself; **fellow-coun'tryman** a man of the same country as oneself; **fellow-crea'ture** a creature like oneself; **fellow-feel'ing** feeling of common interest; sympathy; **fellow-man'** a human being like oneself; **fellow-mem'ber** a member of the same body as oneself; **fellow-trav'eller** a person travelling in the same railway carriage, bus, etc., or along the same route as oneself; a term for a person who, though not a party member, takes the same political road, a sympathiser (trans. of Russ. word) (*derog*). [M.E. *felawe* — O.N. *fēlagi*, a partner in goods, from *fē*, cattle, property, and root *lag-*, a laying together, a law.]

felly. See **felloe**.

felon[1] *fel'ən*, *n* a person guilty of felony. — *adj* **felonious** (*fi-lō'ni-əs*) relating to felony. — *adv* **felō'niously**. — *n* **felō'niousness**. — *n* **fel'ony** a grave crime. [O.Fr., — L.L. *fellō, -ōnis*, a traitor.]

felon[2] *fel'ən*, *n* an inflamed sore. [Perh. **felon**[1].]

felspar. See **feldspar**.

felt[1] *felt*, *pa t* and *pa p* of **feel**.

felt[2] *felt*, *n* a fabric formed by matting rather than by weaving, using the natural tendency of the fibres of wool and certain kinds of hair to interlace and cling together. — *vt* to make into felt, to mat; to cover with felt. — *vi* to become felted or matted. — *n* **felt'ing** the art or process of making felt or of matting fibres together; the felt itself. — *adj* **felt'y.** — **felt-tip** (or **felt-tipped) pen,** also **felt'-tip** and **felt pen** a pen with a nib of felt or similar fibrous substance. [O.E.]

felucca *fe-luk'ə*, *n* a small merchant-vessel used in the Mediterranean, with two masts and lateen sails, many such vessels having a rudder at each end. [It. *feluca*.]

fem. *abbrev* for feminine.

female *fē'māl*, *n* a woman or girl (sometimes *derog*); any animal or plant of the same sex as a woman. — *adj* of the sex that produces young or eggs, fructifications or seeds; for, belonging to, characteristic of, or fancifully attributed to that sex; of the sex characterised by relatively large gametes (*biol*); (of parts of mechanism) hollow and adapted to receive a counterpart (*mach*). — *n* **fē'māleness.** — **female circumcision** surgical removal of part or all of the clitoris, clitoridectomy; **female screw** a cylindrical hole with a thread or groove cut on the inward surface. [Fr. *femelle* — L. *fēmella*, a girl, dimin. of *fēmina*, woman; the second syllable infl. by association with **male.**]

feminal *fem'i-nəl*, *adj* (of a man) thinking and acting in a way traditionally held characteristic of women. [L. *fēmina*, woman.]

feminine *fem'in-in*, *adj* female; characteristic of, peculiar or appropriate to, woman or the female sex; womanish; of that gender to which words denoting females, and in some languages various associated classes of words, belong (*gram*). — *n* the female sex or nature; a word of feminine gender. — *adv* **fem'ininely.** — *n* **feminin'ity** the quality of being feminine. — **feminine ending** (*prosody*) in French verse, the ending of a line in mute *e*; the ending of a verse line or musical phrase on an unstressed syllable or note; **feminine rhyme** a two-syllable rhyme, the second syllable being unstressed. [L. *fēminīna*, dimin. of *fēmina*, woman.]

feminise or **-ize** *fem'i-nīz*, *vt* and *vi* to make or become feminine; to (cause a male animal to) develop female characteristics. — *n* **feminisā'tion** or **-z-**. [L. *fēmina*, woman.]

feminism *fem'in-izm*, *n* advocacy of women's rights, of the movement for the advancement and emancipation of women. — *n* **fem'inist** an advocate or favourer of feminism; a student of women. [L. *fēmina*, woman.]

femme *fam*, (Fr.) *n* a woman, wife. — **femme fatale** (*fa-tal*) an irresistibly attractive woman who tends to bring men to despair or disaster; a siren.

femto- *fem-tō-*, *pfx* a thousand million millionth (10^{-15}).

femur *fē'mər*, *n* the thigh-bone in the human skeleton or the corresponding bone in other vertebrates; the third segment of an insect's leg: — *pl* **fē'murs** or **femora** (*fem'ə-rə*). — *adj* **femoral** (*fem'*). [L. *fĕmur*, *-ŏris*, thigh.]

fen *fen*, *n* low marshy land often, or partially, covered with water; a morass or bog. — *adj* **fenn'y.** — **fen'land; fen'man** a dweller in fen country. [O.E. *fenn*.]

fence *fens*, *n* a barrier, esp. of wood or of wood and wire for enclosing, bounding or protecting land; a barrier of varying design for a horse to jump (*showjumping* and *steeplechasing*); a receiver of stolen goods (*thieves' slang*). — *vt* to enclose with a fence (sometimes with *in* or *off*). — *vi* to practise fencing with a sword; to build fences; to be a receiver or purchaser of stolen goods (*thieves' slang*); to answer or dispute evasively. — *adj* **fenced** enclosed with a fence. — *n* **fen'cer** a person who makes or repairs fences; a person who practises fencing with a sword, etc. — *n* **fen'cible** (*hist*) a militiaman or volunteer enlisted in defence of his own country at a time of danger. — *n* **fen'cing** the act, art or sport of attack and defence with a sword, foil, etc.; the act or work of erecting a fence; material for fences; fences collectively; receiving stolen goods (*thieves' slang*). — **fenc'ing-master** a person who teaches fencing. — **mend one's fences** to improve or restore one's relations, reputation, or popularity, esp. in politics (*n* and *adj* **fence'-mending**); **sit on the fence** to avoid committing oneself; to remain neutral; **sunk fence** a ditch or watercourse. [Aphetic from **defence.**]

fend *fend*, *vt* (with *off*) to ward off, parry (blows, questions, etc.). — *vi* (with *for*) to provide. [Aphetic for **defend.**]

fender *fen'dər*, *n* a guard in front of a hearth to confine the ashes; a protection for a ship's side against piers, etc., consisting of a bundle of rope, tyres, etc.; any structure serving as a guard against contact or impact; a mudguard (*US*); a wing of a car (*NAm*). [**fend.**]

fenestra *fi-nes'trə*, *n* a small opening, esp. the *fenestra ovalis* or *fenestra rotunda*, an oval and round window between the middle and inner ear (*biol*); a perforation made surgically; a translucent spot, e.g. that on a moth's wing (*zool*). — *adj* **fenes'tral.** — *adj* **fenestrate** (*fen'is-trāt*) or **fen'estrated** having windows (*archit*); pierced; perforated; having translucent spots. — *n* **fenestrā'tion** the arrangement of windows in a building (*archit*); the fact of being fenestrate; perforation; the operation of making an artificial fenestra in bone, esp. in the ear (*surg*). [L., window.]

feni or **fenny** *fen'i*, *n* an alcoholic spirit produced in Goa from coconuts or cashew nuts.

Fenian *fē'nyən*, *n* a member of an association of Irishmen founded in New York in 1857 for the overthrow of the English government in Ireland; a (esp. Irish) Catholic (*offensive*). — *adj* belonging to the modern Fenians; Catholic (*offensive*). — *n* **Fē'nianism.** [O.Ir. *Féne*, one of the names of the ancient population of Ireland, confused in modern times with *fíann*, the militia of Finn and other ancient Irish kings.]

fennec *fen'ək*, *n* a little African fox with large ears. [Ar. *fenek*.]

fennel *fen'əl*, *n* a yellow-flowered umbelliferous plant of the genus *Foeniculum*, the seeds and leaves being used for seasoning. — **dwarf, Florence, French** or **sweet fennel** see under **finocchio.** [O.E. *finul* — L. *fēniculum*, *fēnuc(u)lum*, fennel — *fēnum*, hay.]

fenny[1]. See **fen.**

fenny[2]. See **feni.**

fenugreek *fen'ū-grēk*, *n* a leguminous plant (*Trigonella foenum-graecum*), with white flowers and aromatic seeds. [L. *fēnum graecum*, Greek hay.]

feoff *fef* or *fēf*, *n* a fief. — *vt* to grant possession of a fief or property in land. — *n* **feoffee'** the person invested with the fief. — *n* **feoff'er** or **feoff'or** the person who grants the fief. — *n* **feoff'ment** the gift of a fief. [O.Fr. *feoffer* or *fiefer* — O.Fr. *fief*.]

feral *fē'rəl* or *fer'əl*, *adj* (of an animal) wild, untamed; (of a plant) uncultivated; having run wild; brutish, savage. — *adj* **fer'alised** or **-z-** run wild from domestication. [L. *fera*, a wild beast.]

fer-de-lance *fer'-də-lãs*, *n* the lance-headed or yellow viper of tropical America. [Fr., lance-head (lit. iron).]

feretory *fer'i-tə-ri*, *n* a shrine for relics carried in processions. [L. *feretrum* — Gr. *pheretron*, bier, litter — *pherein*, to bear.]

ferial *fē'ri-əl*, (*RC*) *adj* relating to any day of the week which is neither a fast nor a festival. [L. *fēria*, a holiday.]

fermata *fûr-mä'tə*, (*mus*) *n* a pause: — *pl* **ferma'tas** or **ferma'te** (*-tī*). [It.]

ferment *fûr'mənt*, *n* a substance that excites fermentation; fermentation; agitation; tumult. — *vt* **ferment** (*-ment'*) to cause fermentation in; to work up, excite. — *vi* to rise and swell by the action of fermentation; (of wine) to work; to be in a state of turmoil or excitement. — *n* **fermentabil'ity.** — *adj* **ferment'able** capable of fermentation. — *n* **fermentā'tion** the act or process of fermenting; a slow decomposition process of organic substances induced by micro-organisms, or by complex nitrogenous organic substances (*enzymes*) of vegetable or animal origin, usu. accompanied by evolution of heat and gas, e.g. alcoholic fermentation of sugar and starch, and lactic fermentation; restless action of the mind or feelings. — *adj* **ferment'ative** causing or consisting in fermentation. — *n* **ferment'ativeness.** — *adj* **ferment'ed.** [Fr., — L. *fermentum*, for *fervimentum* — *fervēre*, to boil.]

fermi *fûr'mi*, (*nuc phys*) *n* a unit of length equal to 10^{-5} angstrom or 10^{-15} metres. [Italian physicist Enrico *Fermi* (1901–54).]

fermion *fûr'mi-on*, (*phys*) *n* one of a group of subatomic particles, such as protons, electrons and neutrons, having half-integral spin and obeying the exclusion principle. [Ety. as for **fermi**.]

fermium *fûr'mi-əm*, *n* an artificially produced metallic, radioactive element (symbol **Fm**; atomic no. 100). [Ety. as for **fermi**.]

fern *fûrn*, *n* one of the class of higher or vascular plants (*Filices*), whose reproduction is by spores formed in clusters on the leaves, many species having feather-like leaves. — *adj* **fern'y.** [O.E. *fearn*.]

ferocious *fə-rō'shəs*, *adj* savage, fierce; cruel. — *adv* **ferō'ciously.** — *n* **ferō'ciousness** or **ferocity** (*-ros'i-ti*). [L. *ferōx*, *ferōcis*, wild.]

ferrate *fer'āt*, *n* a salt of ferric acid. [L. *ferrum*, iron.]

ferret *fer'it*, *n* a half-tamed albino variety of the polecat, employed in unearthing rabbits; a pertinacious searcher or investigator. — *vt* to drive out of a hiding-place; to search out persistently and indefatigably. — *vt* and *vi* to hunt with a ferret: — *pr p* **ferr'eting**; *pa p* **ferr'eted.** — *n* **ferr'eter** a person who ferrets. — *adj* **ferr'ety** like a ferret. [O.Fr. *furet*, a ferret, dimin. — L.L. *fūrō*, *-ōnis*, ferret, robber — L. *fūr*, a thief.]

ferri- *fer-i*, *combining form* signifying the presence of iron, usu. in its trivalent form. — *adj* **ferrimagnet'ic.** — *n* **ferrimag'netism** iron magnetism in which the magnetic moments of neighbouring ions are non-parallel.

ferriage. See under **ferry**.

ferric *fer'ik*, *adj* containing iron in its trivalent form. — **ferric oxide** a red crystalline oxide of iron used as a coating on magnetic tape and as a metal polish (also called *jeweller's rouge*). [L. *ferrum*, iron.]

Ferris wheel *fer'is wēl* or *hwēl*, (orig. *US*) *n* a fairground attraction, a large upright wheel having seats suspended on the circumference which remain horizontal while the wheel rotates. [G.W.G. *Ferris*, American engineer.]

ferrite *fer'īt*, *n* a form of pure iron; any of a number of new magnetic materials (generally mixtures of iron oxide with one or more other metals) which are also electric insulators. — *adj* **ferritic** (*-it'ik*) consisting mainly of ferrite. [L. *ferrum*, iron.]

ferro- *fer-ō-*, *combining form* signifying the presence of iron, usu. in its divalent form; relating to iron. — *n* **ferrocon'crete** reinforced concrete. — *adj* **ferroelec'tric** exhibiting electric polarisation. — *n* **ferroelectric'ity.** — *adj* **ferromagnet'ic.** — *n* **ferromag'netism** the typical form of iron magnetism, with high permeability and hysteresis.

ferrous *fer'əs*, *adj* containing iron; containing iron in its divalent form. — **ferrous sulphate** a salt of iron, usu. used in tanning, etc. [L. *ferrum*, iron.]

ferruginous *fə-rōō'jin-əs*, *adj* of the colour of iron-rust; impregnated with iron. [L. *ferrūgō*, *-inis*, iron-rust — *ferrum*.]

ferrule *fer'ōōl* or *-əl*, *n* a metal band, ring or cap on the tip of a stick, etc. for reinforcing it; a threaded cylindrical fitting for joining two pipes or rods. [O.Fr. *virole* — L. *viriola*, a bracelet.]

ferry *fer'i*, *vt* to carry or convey (often over a water, etc., in a boat, ship or aircraft); to deliver (an aircraft coming from a factory) under its own power. — *vi* to cross by ferry: — *pr p* **ferr'ying**; *pa t* and *pa p* **ferr'ied.** — *n* a boat for the conveyance of passengers and usu. vehicles across a stretch of water (also **ferr'y-boat**); the service thus provided; a place or route of carriage over water; the right of conveying passengers. — *n* **ferr'iage** provision for ferrying; the fare paid for it. — **ferr'yman.** [O.E. *ferian*, to convey.]

fertile *fûr'tīl* or in U.S. *-təl*, *adj* able to bear or produce abundantly; capable of breeding, hatching or germinating; rich in resources; inventive; able to become fissile or fissionable (*phys*). — *adv* **fer'tilely.** — *n* **fertilisation** or **-z-** (*-ti-lī-zā'shən*) the act or process of fertilising. — *vt* **fer'tilise** or **-ize** to make fertile or fruitful; to enrich; to impregnate; to pollinate. — *n* **fer'tiliser** or **-z-** a person who, or that which, fertilises. — *n* **fertility** (*-til'i-ti*) fruitfulness, richness, abundance; the state of being fertile; the ability to produce young. — **Fertile Crescent** a crescent-shaped region stretching from Armenia to Arabia, formerly fertile but now mainly desert, considered to be the cradle of civilisation; **fertility drug** a drug given to apparently infertile women to induce ovulation. [Fr., — L. *fertilis* — *ferre*, to bear.]

ferule *fer'ōōl*, *n* a cane or rod used for punishment. [L. *ferula*, a giant fennel — *ferīre*, to strike.]

fervent *fûr'vənt*, *adj* passionate, ardent. — *n* **fer'vency.** — *adv* **fer'vently.** [Pres. p. of L. *fervēre*, to boil.]

fervid *fûr'vid*, *adj* vehement, impetuous, fiery. — *n* **fervid'ity** or **fer'vidness.** — *adv* **fer'vidly.** [L. *fervidus*, fiery, glowing.]

fervour *fûr'vər*, *n* zeal; vehemence, ardour. [L. *fervor*, violent heat.]

fescue *fes'kū*, *n* any one of the grasses of the genus *Festuca*, which includes many pasture and fodder grasses; a pointer used in teaching. [O.Fr. *festu* — L. *festūca*, a straw.]

fesse or **fess** *fes*, (*heraldry*) *n* a horizontal band over the middle of an escutcheon, usu. one-third of the whole. [Fr. *fasce* — L. *fascia*, a band.]

fest *fest*, *n* (usu. in combination) a festival, party or gathering, esp. for a particular activity, e.g. *songfest*. [Ger. *Fest*, festival.]

festal *fes'tl*, *adj* relating to a feast or holiday; festive; joyous. — *n* a festivity. — *adv* **fes'tally.** [L. *festum*, holiday.]

fester *fes'tər*, *vi* to rot or putrefy; to suppurate; to rankle; to be idle (*colloq*). — *vt* to cause to fester or rankle. — *n* a sore discharging pus. [O.Fr. *festre* — L. *fistula*, an ulcer.]

festival *fes'ti-vəl*, *n* a joyful or honorific celebration; a religious feast; a season or series of performances of music, plays, etc. — Also *adj*. [Med.L. *festīvālis*, relating to a feast — *festīvus*, festive.]

festive *fes'tiv*, *adj* relating to a feast or holiday; celebratory, joyful. — *adv* **fes'tively.** — *n* **festiv'ity** conviviality, rejoicing; joyfulness; (in *pl*) joyful celebrations. [L. *fēstīvus* — *fēstus*, relating to holidays, festive.]

festoon *fes-tōōn'*, *n* a garland suspended between two points; an ornament like a garland (*archit*). — *vt* to adorn, hang or connect with festoons. — *vi* to hang in festoons. — **festoon blind** a window blind ruched to fall in festoon-like folds. [Fr. *feston*, app. conn. with L. *fēstum*, a festival.]

festschrift *fest'shrift*, *n* a celebratory publication, commonly a collection of learned papers, presented by their authors and published in honour of some person. [Ger., festival writing.]

feta *fet'ə*, *n* a white low-fat cheese originating in Greece and the Middle East, traditionally made from goat's or ewe's milk but now sometimes with cow's milk. — Also **fett'a**. [Mod.Gr. *pheta*, a slice (i.e. of cheese) — It. *fetta*.]

fetal. See **foetus**.

fetch *fech*, *vt* to bring; to go and get; to be sold for (a certain price); to cause to come; to call forth; to utter (a sigh or groan); to administer (a blow, etc., usu. with *indirect object*). — *n* the act of bringing; the distance travelled by a wind or wave without obstruction; a stratagem. — *adj* **fetch'ing** fascinating, charming. — **fetch and carry** to perform humble services for another person; **fetch up** to come to a stop. [O.E. *feccan*, app. an altered form of *fetian*, to fetch.]

fête or **fete** *fet* or *fāt*, *n* an outdoor function with entertainments, stalls, refreshments, etc., often in aid of a charity; a festival, a holiday. — *vt* to entertain at a feast; to honour with festivities. — **fête champêtre** (*shã-pe-tr'*) a rural festival or garden party; an early 18th-cent. genre of French painting, typically showing courtly figures in a rural setting (also called **fête galante** *ga-lãt*). [Fr.]

feticide. See under **foetus**.

fetid or **foetid** *fet'id* or *fē'tid*, *adj* stinking; having a strong offensive smell. — *n* **fē'tidness**. [L. *fētidus* — *fētēre*, to stink.]

fetish *fet'ish* or *fē'tish*, *n* an object believed to procure for its owner the services of a spirit lodged within it; an inanimate object to which a pathological sexual attachment is formed; such an attachment; a fixation; something regarded with irrational reverence. — *n* **fet'ishism** the worship of a fetish; a belief in charms; pathological attachment of sexual interest to an inanimate object. — *n* **fet'ishist**. — *adj* **fetishis'tic**. [Fr. *fétiche* — Port. *feiti co*, magic, orig. artificial — L. *factīcius* — *facĕre*, to make.]

fetlock *fet'lok*, *n* a tuft of hair that grows above a horse's hoof; the part where this hair grows.

fetoscopy. See **foetoscopy** under **foetus**.

fetta. See **feta**.

fetter *fet'ər*, *n* (usu. in *pl*) a chain or shackle for the feet; (usu. in *pl*) anything that restrains. — *vt* to put fetters on; to restrain. [O.E. *feter*.]

fettle *fet'l*, *n* condition, trim, form, esp. in *in fine fettle*; lining for a furnace. — *vt* to make ready, set in order, arrange; to line (a furnace). — *n* **fett'ler** a person who fettles, esp. (*Austr*) a maintenance worker on the railway. [Prob. O.E. *fetel*, a belt.]

fettuccine, **fettucine** *fet-ŏŏ-chē'nä* or **fettucini** (*-chē'nē*) *n* tagliatelle. [It.]

fetus. See **foetus**.

fetwa *fat'wä*, *n*. A variant spelling of **fatwa**.

feu *fū*, (*Scot*) *n* a right to the use of land, houses, etc., in perpetuity, for a stipulated annual payment (**feu'=dūty**); a piece of land held in feu. — *vt* to grant land to a person who undertakes to pay the feu-duty. — *adj* **feu'dal** pertaining to a feu. [O.Fr. *feu*; see **fee**.]

feud[1] *fūd*, *n* a war waged by private individuals, families or clans against one another on their own account; a bloody strife; a persistent state of private enmity. — Also *vi*. — *n* and *adj* **feud'ing**. [O.Fr. *faide*, *feide* — L.L. *faida* — O.H.G. *fēhida*.]

feud[2] *fūd*, *n* a fief or land held on condition of service. — *adj* **feu'dal** pertaining to feuds or fiefs; belonging to feudalism. — *n* **feudalīsā'tion** or **-z-**. — *vt* **feu'dalise** or **-ize**. — *n* **feu'dalism** the feudal system or its principles; a class-conscious social or political system resembling the mediaeval feudal system. — *n* **feu'dalist**. — *adj* **feudalis'tic**. — *n* **feudal'ity** the state of being feudal; the feudal system. — *adv* **feu'dally**. — **feudal system** (*hist*) the system by which vassals held lands from lords-superior on condition of military service. [L.L. *feudum*; see **fee**.]

feudal. See under **feu** and **feud**[2].

feuilleton *fœy-tõ*, *n* in French and other newspapers, a part ruled off at the bottom of a page for a critical article or serialised story; a contribution of this kind. [Fr., dimin. of *feuillet*, a leaf.]

fever *fē'vər*, *n* an abnormally high body temperature, associated with a raised pulse rate and hot, dry skin; any of many, usu. infectious, diseases in which this is a marked symptom, such as *scarlet fever*, *yellow fever*; an extreme state of excitement or nervousness. — *vt* to put into a fever. — *adj* **fē'vered** affected with fever; excited. — *adj* **fē'verish** slightly fevered; indicating fever; restlessly excited; morbidly eager, frenzied. — *adv* **fē'verishly**. — *n* **fē'verishness**. — *adj* **fē'verous** feverish; apt to cause fever. — **fever pitch** a state of great excitement, agitation; **fe'ver=tree** a southern African tree of the genus *Acacia* usu. found in swampy, mosquito-infested places, and hence associated, esp. formerly, with the mosquito-borne disease malaria; any of various species of trees, such as the Australian *Eucalyptus globulus* or the American *Pinckneya pubens*, which yield substances useful in the treatment of fevers. [O.E. *fēfor* — L. *febris*.]

feverfew *fē'vər-fū*, *n* a perennial plant of the daisy family, closely related to camomile, formerly believed efficacious in reducing fever. [Med.L. *febrifugia*, this plant, — L. *febris*, fever, *fugare*, to put to flight.]

few *fū*, *adj* small in number; not many, hardly any. — *n* hardly any. — *n* **few'ness** smallness of number. — **a few** a small number (of) — used as a noun, or virtually a compound adjective; **a good few**, **quite a few** (*colloq*) a considerable number; **every few hours, days**, etc. at intervals of a few hours, days, etc.; **few and far between** very rare; **have had a few** (*facetious*) to have consumed a large number of alcoholic drinks; **in few** briefly; **no fewer than** as many as (a stated number); **not a few** a good number; **some few** an inconsiderable number; **the few** the minority. [O.E. *fēa*, pl. *fēawe*.]

fey *fā*, *adj* eccentric, slightly mad; whimsical; fated soon to die — imagined to be marked by extravagantly high spirits (chiefly *Scot*); foreseeing the future, esp. calamity (chiefly *Scot*); fairylike; elfin. [M.E. *fay*, *fey* — O.E. *fǣge*, doomed.]

fez *fez*, *n* a red brimless truncated conical cap of wool or felt, with black tassel, worn in Egypt: — *pl* **fezz'es** or **fez'es**. [From *Fez* in Morocco.]

ff or **ff.** *symbol* for: *fecerunt* (L.), they did it or made it; folios; following pages, lines, etc.; fortissimo (*mus*).

fiacre *fē-ak'r'*, *n* a hackney coach; a cab. [Fr., from the Hôtel de St *Fiacre* in Paris, where first used.]

fiancé, *fem* **fiancée** *fē-ã'sā*, *n* the person one is engaged to, one's betrothed. [Fr.]

fianchetto *fyäng-ket'to*, (*chess*) *n* the early movement of a knight's pawn to develop a bishop on a long diagonal: — *pl* **fianchet'ti** (*-tē*). [It., dimin. of *fianco*, flank.]

fiar *fē'ər*, (*Scots law*) *n* the owner of the fee-simple of a property (in contrast to a *life-renter* of the property). [**fee**.]

fiasco *fē-as'kō*, *n* a ludicrous and humiliating failure, orig. in a musical performance: — *pl* **fias'cos** or **fias'coes**. [It. *fiasco*, a bottle.]

fiat *fī'at*, *n* a formal or solemn command; a short order or warrant of a judge for making out or allowing processes, letters-patent, etc. — **fiat money** or **currency** (esp. *US*) money (paper or coin) made legal tender and assigned a value by government decree, though not convertible into other specie of equivalent value. [L. *fiat*, let it be done, 3rd pers. sing. pres. subjunctive of *fierī*, serving as passive of *facĕre*, to do.]

fib *fib*, *n* a trifling falsehood. — *vi* to tell a fib or lie: — *pr p* **fibb'ing**; *pa t* and *pa p* **fibbed**. — *n* **fibb'er** a person who fibs. [Perh. **fable**.]

fiber. See **fibre**.

Fibonacci numbers *fē-bə-nä'chē num'bərz*, **sequence** (*sē'kwəns*) or **series** (*sē'rēz*), *n* (*pl*) a series of numbers in which each term is the sum of the preceding two terms. [Leonardo (*Fibonacci*) of Pisa (1170–1230).]

fibre or in U.S. **fiber** *fī'bər*, *n* a filament or threadlike cell of animal, vegetable or mineral origin, natural or synthetic; a structure or material composed of fibres; texture; stamina. — *adj* **fī'bred** or in U.S. **fī'bered**. — *adj* **fī'breless** or in U.S. **fī'berless**. — *n* **fī'brin** an insoluble protein precipitated as a network of fibres when blood coagulates. — *n* **fībrinol'ysin** an enzyme in the blood which causes breakdown of fibrin in blood clots; a drug having the same effect. — *adj* **fī'brinous**. — *n* **fī'brō** (*Austr*) short for **fībro-cement'**, a wall-board of a compressed asbestos and cement mixture; a house constructed of such material: — *pl* **fi'bros**. — Also *adj*. — *adj* **fī'broid** of a fibrous character. — *n* a fibrous tumour. — *n* **fībrō'ma** a tumour composed of fibrous tissue: — *pl* **fibrō'mata** or **fibrō'mas**. — *adj* **fibrose** (*fī'brōs*) fibrous. — *n* **fībro'sis** a morbid growth of fibrous tissue. — *n* **fībrosī'tis** inflammation (esp. rheumatic) of fibrous tissue. — *adj* **fībrot'ic** pertaining to fibrosis. — *adj* **fī'brous** composed of or like fibres. — **fī'breboard** or in U.S. **fī'berboard** a material formed from compressed wood fibres; **fī'breglass** or in U.S. **fī'berglass** a synthetic fibre made of extremely fine filaments of molten glass, used in textile manufacture, in heat and sound insulation, and in reinforced plastics; **fibre optics** (as *adj* usu. **fibre optic**) a technique using **fibre optic(s) bundles**, bundles of extremely thin flexible glass fibres used in optical instruments, transmitting maximum light by total internal reflection, and giving images of maximum clarity, their flexibility allowing penetration into otherwise inaccessible places; **fī'brescope** or in U.S. **fī'berscope** a medical instrument using fibre optic bundles that allows examination of internal structures, e.g. the alimentary canal. — **to the very fibre of one's being** deeply, fundamentally. [Fr., — L. *fibra*, thread, fibre.]

fibril *fī'bril*, *n* a small fibre; a root-hair; a minute threadlike structure. — *adj* **fī'brillar**. — *vi* **fī'brillate** to undergo fibrillation. — *n* **fībrillā'tion** the production or formation of fibrils or fibres; a mass of fibrils; a twitching of muscle fibres; uncoordinated contraction of muscle fibres in the heart (*med*). — *adj* **fī'brillose** having, or covered with, small fibres or the appearance of small fibres. [N.L. *fibrilla*, a little fibre.]

fibula *fib'ū-lə*, *n* a brooch formed like a safety pin; the outer and thinner of the two bones from the knee to the ankle in the human skeleton, or a corresponding bone in other animals. — *adj* **fib'ūlar**. [L. *fībula*, brooch.]

fiche *fēsh*, *n* a card or strip of film containing miniaturised data. — Also short for **microfiche**. [Fr., a slip of paper, etc.]

fichu *fish'ōō* or *fē'shü*, *n* a three-cornered cape worn over the shoulders, the ends crossed upon the bosom; a triangular piece of muslin, etc., for the neck. [Fr.]

fickle *fik'l*, *adj* inconstant in affections, loyalties or intentions; changeable. — *n* **fick'leness**. [O.E. *ficol*; *gefic*, fraud.]

fictile *fik'tīl* or *-til*, *adj* moulded by a potter; capable of being moulded, esp. in clay; relating to pottery. [L. *fictilis* — *fingĕre*, to form or fashion.]

fiction *fik'shən*, *n* the novel or story-telling as a branch of literature; an invented or false story; a falsehood; a supposition that a thing is true, which is either certainly not true, or at least is as probably false as true (*law*). — *adj* **fic'tional**. — *vt* **fic'tionalise** or **-ize** to give a fictional character to (a narrative dealing with real facts). — *adj* **fic'tionalised** or **-z-**. [Fr., — L. *fictiō*, *-ōnis* — *fictus*, past p. of *fingĕre*, to form or fashion.]

fictitious *fik-tish'əs*, *adj* of the nature of fiction; imaginary; invented, not authentic. — *adv* **fic-ti'tiously**. [L. *ficticius*, counterfeit, feigned.]

fid *fid*, (*naut*) *n* a conical pin of hard wood, used by sailors to open the strands of rope in splicing; a square bar, with a shoulder, used to support the weight of the topmast or top-gallant mast.

Fid. Def. *abbrev* for *Fidei Defensor* (L.), Defender of the Faith, used on coins before decimalisation.

fiddle *fid'l*, *n* the violin (*colloq*); extended to other instruments of the violin family, such as *bass fiddle*; a violin-player; a raised rim round a table to keep dishes from sliding off it (*naut*); a swindle, esp. petty (*slang*). — *vt* and *vi* to play on a fiddle. — *vt* to falsify (records, accounts, etc.). — *vi* to trifle, idle (with *about* or *around*); to handle things aimlessly (with *with*). — *n* **fidd'ler** a violinist; a trifler; a swindler; (also **fiddler crab**) a small crab of the genus *Uca* or *Gelasimus*, from the movements of its enlarged claw. — *adj* **fidd'ling** trifling; fiddly. — *adj* **fidd'ly** requiring much dexterity; time-consuming; awkward. — **fidd'le-back** (a chair with) a fiddle-shaped back. — *interj* **fiddle-de-dee'** nonsense! — **fidd'le-faddle** trifling talk or behaviour; **fidd'lestick** a violin bow; a mere nothing, a trifle (*derisive*). — *interj* **fidd'lesticks** nonsense! — **as fit as a fiddle** in the best of condition; **play second fiddle** to take a subordinate part in anything. [O.E. *fithele*.]

FIDE *abbrev* for *Fédération Internationale des Echecs* (Fr.), the International Chess Federation.

fidei defensor *fi'dē-ī di-fen'sör* or *fi-dā'ē dā-fen'sör*, *n* defender of the faith (q.v. under **defence**).

fideism *fē'dā-izm*, *n* the doctrine that knowledge depends on faith rather than reason. — *n* **fi'deist**. — *adj* **fideist'ic**. [L. *fīdĕre*, to trust.]

fidelity *fi-del'i-ti*, *n* faithfulness; faithfulness to a husband or wife; firm adherence; exactitude in reproduction. [L. *fidēlitās*, *-ātis* — *fidēlis*, faithful.]

fidget *fij'it*, *vi* to move about restlessly; to touch and handle things aimlessly (with *with*). — *vt* to cause to feel restless and uneasy: — *pr p* **fid'geting**; *pa t* and *pa p* **fid'geted**. — *n* a person who fidgets; restlessness; (in *pl*) general nervous restlessness, an inability to keep still. — *n* **fid'getiness**. — *adj* **fid'gety**.

fiducial *fi-dū'shyəl* or *-shəl*, *adj* (of a point or line) serving as a basis of reckoning (*phys* and *surveying*); showing confidence or reliance; of the nature of trust. — *adv* **fidū'cially**. — *adj* **fidū'ciary** of the nature of a trust; depending upon public confidence; held in trust. — *n* a person who holds anything in trust. [L. *fīdūcia*, confidence — *fīdĕre*, to trust.]

fie *fī*, (*old* or *facetious*) *interj* denoting disapprobation or disgust, real or feigned. [Cf. Fr. *fi*; L. *fī*; O.N. *fȳ*, *fei*; Ger. *pfui*.]

fief *fēf*, *n* land held in fee or on condition of military service. [Fr., — L.L. *feudum*; see **fee, feoff**.]

field *fēld*, *n* country or open country in general; a piece of ground enclosed for tillage or pasture or sport; the range of any series of actions or energies; speciality; an area of knowledge, interest, etc.; a region of space in which forces are at work (*phys*); the locality of a battle; the battle itself; an area of ground reserved and marked out for games-playing, etc.; a place removed from the classroom, office, etc., where practical experience is gained; a wide expanse; area visible to an observer at one time (e.g. in a microscope); one of the two interlaced sets of scanning lines making up the picture (*TV*); one scanning of a field from top to bottom and back (*TV*); a region yielding a mineral, etc.; the surface of a shield (*heraldry*); the background of a coin, flag, etc.; those taking part in a hunt; the entries collectively against which a contestant has to compete; all parties not individually excepted; disposition of fielders (*cricket* or *baseball*); a set of characters comprising a unit of information (*comput*). — *vt* to catch (the ball) or stop and return it to the fixed place (*cricket* or *baseball*); to handle skilfully (esp. questions); to put into the field for play, military action, or (*fig*) other form of contest. — *vi* to stand in position for catching or stopping the ball (*cricket* or *baseball*). — *n* **field'er** a person who fields. — *n* **field'ing.** — **field ambulance** a medical unit on the field of battle; **field artillery** mobile ordnance for active operations in the field; **field battery** a battery of field artillery; **field book** the notebook used by a surveyor in the field; **field day** a day when troops are drawn out for instruction in field exercises; any day of unusual activity or success; **field event** an athletic event other than a race; **field'fare** a species of thrush; **field glass** or **glasses** a binocular telescope for use in the field or open air; **field goal** (*Am football* or *basketball*) a goal scored from normal play; **field gun** a light cannon mounted on a carriage; **field hockey** (*US*) hockey played on grass (as opp. to *ice hockey*); **field hospital** a temporary hospital near the scene of battle; **field ice** ice formed in the polar seas in large surfaces, distinguished from icebergs; **field kitchen** portable cooking equipment for troops, or the place where it is set up; **field marshal** an army officer of highest rank; **field'mouse** a name for various species of mouse and vole that live in the fields; **field notes** data noted in the field, to be worked up later; **field officer** a military officer above the rank of captain, and below that of general. — *adj* **field-sequen'tial** (*TV*) relating to the association of individual primary colours with successive fields. — **fields'man** a fielder. — *npl* **field sports** sports of the field, such as hunting, racing, etc. — **field trial** a test in practice, as distinct from one under laboratory conditions; **field trip** an expedition, esp. by students, to observe and study something at its location; **field'work** work (scientific surveying, etc.) in the field (as opp. to laboratory, office, etc.); (often in *pl*) a temporary fortification thrown up by troops in the field, either for protection or to cover an attack upon a stronghold; **field'-worker** a practical research worker. — **field of view** or **vision** what is visible to one at any particular moment; **play the field** see under **play**; **take the field** to assemble on a playing-field; to begin warlike operations. [O.E. *feld*.]

fiend *fēnd*, *n* a devil; a person actuated by the most intense wickedness or hate; a devotee. — *adj* **fiend'-ish** like a fiend; devilishly cruel. — *n* **fiend'ishness.** [O.E. *fēond*, enemy, orig. pres. p. of *fēon*, to hate.]

fierce *fērs*, *adj* savage, ferocious; (of competition or opposition) strong, intense; violent. — *adv* **fierce'ly.** — *n* **fierce'ness.** [O.Fr. *fers* — L. *ferus*, wild, savage.]

fiery *fīr'i*, *adj* like or consisting of fire; ardent; impetuous; irritable; (of ground in games) dry, hard, fast. — *adv* **fier'ily.** — *n* **fier'iness.** — **fiery cross** a charred cross dipped in blood, formerly carried round in the Scottish Highlands as a call to arms; a burning cross, symbol of the Ku-Klux Klan. [**fire.**]

fiesta *fē-es'tə*, *n* saint's day; holiday; festivity. [Sp.]

FIFA *fē'fə*, *abbrev* for *Fédération Internationale de Football Association* (Fr.), International Association Football Federation.

fife *fīf*, *n* a smaller variety of the flute. — *vi* to play on the fife. — *n* **fif'er** a fife-player. [Ger. *Pfeife*, pipe, or Fr. *fifre*, fifer (both — L. *pīpāre*, to cheep).]

FIFO *fē'fō*, *abbrev* for first in, first out.

fifteen *fif'tēn* or *fif-tēn'*, *adj* and *n* five and ten. — *n* a set, group, or team of fifteen; **(15)** a certificate designating a film passed as suitable only for persons of fifteen and over. — *adj* **fifteenth'** (or *fif'*) last of fifteen; next after the fourteenth; equal to one of fifteen equal parts. — *n* a fifteenth part; a person or thing in fifteenth position; a double octave (*mus*); an organ stop sounding two octaves above the diapason. — *adv* **fifteenth'ly.** [O.E. *fīftēne*; see **five, ten.**]

fifth *fifth*, *adj* last of five; next after the fourth; equal to one of five equal parts. — *n* one of five equal parts; a person or thing in fifth position; an interval of four (conventionally called five) diatonic degrees (*mus*); a tone at that interval from another; a combination of two tones separated by that interval. — *adv* **fifth'ly** in the fifth place. — **Fifth Amendment** an amendment to the U.S. constitution which allows a person on trial not to testify against himself or herself and forbids a second trial if a person has been acquitted in a first; **fifth column** people within a country, etc., who sympathise, and will act, with its enemies (expression used by a Spanish insurgent general when four columns were advancing upon Madrid); **fifth columnist** (*kol'əm-ist*); **fifth generation** (*comput*) the type of computer expected to come into use in the 1990s, incorporating aspects of artificial intelligence (*adj* **fifth'-generation**); **fifth wheel** the spare wheel of a four-wheeled vehicle; a superfluous or useless person or thing. [O.E. *fīfta*.]

fifty *fif'ti*, *adj* and *n* five tens or five times ten. — *npl* **fif'ties** the numbers fifty to fifty-nine; the years so numbered (of a life or century); a range of temperatures from fifty to just less than sixty degrees. — *adj* **fif'tieth** last of fifty; next after the forty-ninth; equal to one of fifty equal parts. — *n* a fiftieth part; a person or thing in fiftieth position. — *adj* **fif'tyish** apparently about fifty years old. — *n*, *adj* and *adv* **fifty-fif'ty** half-and-half; fifty per cent of each of two things; share and share alike. [O.E. *fīftig* — *fīf*, five, and *-tig* (the sfx. *-ty*).]

FIG *abbrev* for *Fédération Internationale de Gymnastique* (Fr.), International Gymnastics Federation.

fig[1] *fig*, *n* the fig-tree (*Ficus*, of the mulberry family), or its fruit, growing in warm climates; a thing of little or no consequence. — **fig'-leaf** the leaf of the fig-tree; a representation of such a leaf for veiling the private parts of a statue or picture; any scanty clothing (from the Bible: Genesis iii. 7); any prudish evasion; a makeshift; something intended to conceal the reality of actions or motives, esp. political or international; **fig'-tree.** [Fr. *figue* — L. *fīcus*, a fig, fig-tree.]

fig[2] *fig*, (*colloq*) *n* figure; dress; form. — **in full fig** in full dress, array. [Perh. **figure.**]

fig. *abbrev* for: figurative; figuratively; figure.

fight *fīt*, *vi* to strive; to contend in war or in single combat. — *vt* to engage in conflict with; to contend against; to maintain or contend for by combat, action at law, etc.; to manipulate in fight; to achieve by struggle; to cause to fight: — *pa t* and *pa p* **fought** (*föt*). — *n* a struggle; a combat; a strong disagreement; a battle or engagement; fighting spirit; inclination to fight. — *adj* **fight'able** able to be fought. — *n* **fight'er** a person, etc. who fights; a boxer; an aircraft engaged in war. — *adj* **fight'ing** engaged in, eager for, or fit for war or strife. — *n* the act of fighting or contending. — **fighting chance** a chance of success given supreme effort; **fighting cock** a gamecock; a pugnacious fellow; **fighting fish** a small freshwater fish of Thailand, kept for its extraordinary readiness for fighting, bets being laid on the outcome. — **fight back** to retaliate; to counter-attack (*n* **fight'back**); **fighting fit** in good condition; **fight it out** to struggle on until the end; **fight off** to resist, repel; **fight shy of** to avoid from mistrust; **fight to the finish** or **to the last ditch** to fight until completely exhausted. [O.E. *fehtan*.]

figment *fig'mənt*, *n* a fabrication or invention. [L. *figmentum* — *fingĕre*, to form.]

figure *fig'ər* or (*US* or *dialect*) *-yər*, also (*old-fashioned*) *fig'ūr*, *n* the form of anything in outline; appearance; a shape; a geometrical form; a diagram; a design; an illustration; bodily shape; a human form or representation of it; a personality, personage, character; an impressive, noticeable, important, ludicrous or grotesque person; a character denoting a number; amount; value or price; a deviation from the ordinary mode of expression (*rhet*); a group of notes felt as a unit (*mus*); a series of steps or movements in a dance or in skating; a type or emblem. — *vt* to make an image of; to represent; to mark with figures or designs; to imagine; to reckon, to work out (often with *out*); to note by figures. — *vi* to make figures; to appear as a figure, make an appearance or show; to follow as a logical consequence, be expected (*colloq*). — *n* **figūrabil'ity** the quality of being figurable. — *adj* **fig'ūrable.** — *adj* **fig'ūral** represented by figure. — *n* **figurant** or **figurante** (*fig'ū-rənt*; It. *fēg-ōō-rän'tā*) a ballet dancer, one of those who form a background for the solo dancers. — *adj* **fig'ūrate** of a certain determinate form; florid (*mus*). — *n* **figūrā'tion** an act of giving figure or form; representation by or in figures or shapes, esp. significant, typical or emblematic, figures; a figure of this kind; ornamentation with a design; florid treatment (*mus*). — *adj* **fig'ūrative** representing by, containing or abounding in figures of speech (*rhet*); metaphorical; representing a figure; emblematic, symbolic; of a style of painting, sculpture, etc. characterised by the realistic depiction of people, objects, etc. (as opp. to *abstract* art). — *adv* **fig'ūratively.** — *n* **fig'ūrativeness.** — *adj* **fig'ured** (*-ərd*) having a figure; marked or adorned with figures; delineated in a figure; in the form of figures. — *n* **fig'ūrine** (*-ēn* or *-ēn'*) a small carved or moulded figure. — **fig'urehead** the figure or bust under the bowsprit of a ship; a nominal head merely. — *adj* nominal, but lacking real power. — **figure skater; figure skating** skating in prescribed patterns on ice; **fig'urework** calculation using numbers. — **cut a figure** to make a conspicuous appearance; **figure of speech** any of various devices (such as simile or metaphor) for using words in such a way as to make a striking effect; **figure on** to count upon or expect; to plan on (*US*). [Fr., — L. *figūra* — *fingěre*, to form.]

filaceous *fil-ā'shəs*, *adj* composed of threads. [L. *fīlum*, a thread.]

filagree. See **filigree.**

filament *fil'ə-mənt*, *n* a slender or threadlike object; a fibre; the stalk of a stamen (*bot*); a chain of cells; a thread of high resistance in an incandescent lamp or thermionic valve (*electr*). — *adj* **filamentary** (*-ment'ə-ri*) like a filament. — *adj* **filament'ous** threadlike. [L. *fīlum*, a thread.]

filar *fī'lər*, *adj* having threads or wires. [L. *fīlum*, a thread.]

Filaria *fi-lā'ri-ə*, *n* a genus of nematode worms introduced into the blood by mosquitoes; (without *cap*) any worm of the genus. — *adj* **filā'rial.** — *n* **filariasis** (*-lə-rī'ə-sis*) a disease due to the presence of filaria in the blood. [L. *fīlum*, a thread.]

filature *fil'ə-chər*, *n* the reeling of silk, or the place where it is done. — *n* **fil'atory** a machine for forming or spinning threads. [Fr., — L. *fīlum*, a thread.]

filbert *fil'bərt*, *n* the nut of the cultivated hazel. [Prob. from St *Philibert*, whose day fell in the nutting season.]

filch *filch*, *vt* to steal; to pilfer. — *n* **filch'er** a thief. — *n* and *adj* **filch'ing.** — *adv* **filch'ingly.**

file[1] *fīl*, *n* any contrivance for keeping papers in order, orig. a line or wire on which papers are strung; a collection of papers arranged for reference; a line of soldiers, etc., ranged one behind another; a small body of soldiers. — *vt* to put in a file; to arrange in an orderly way; to put on record; to bring before a court; to deposit, lodge. — *vi* to march in file. — *adj* **filed.** — *n* **fil'er** someone who, or that which, files; a filing-cabinet (*colloq*). — **file server** (*comput*) a filing store available to all the terminals in a distributed system; **filing cabinet** a cabinet for storing files. — **file off** to wheel off (in file) at right angles to the first direction; **on file** on record, catalogued; **single file** or **Indian file** one behind another. [L. *fīlum*, a thread.]

file[2] *fīl*, *n* an instrument with sharp-edged furrows for smoothing or rasping metals, etc.; a small metal or emery-paper instrument for smoothing fingernails. — *vt* to cut or smooth with, or as with, a file; to polish or improve, esp. of a literary style. — *adj* **filed** polished, smooth. — *n* **fil'er.** — *npl* **fil'ings** particles rubbed off with a file. [O.E. *fȳl*.]

filet *fē-le*, (Fr.) *n* undercut of beef, tenderloin; a kind of lace consisting of embroidery on a square-mesh net.

filet mignon *fē-le mē-nyɔ̃*, (Fr.) *n* a small cut of beef from the thin end of an undercut.

filial *fil'i-əl*, *adj* pertaining to or befitting a son or daughter; bearing the relation of a child. — *adv* **fil'ially.** [Fr., — L.L. *fīliālis* — L. *fīlius*, a son.]

filiate, filiation. Same as **affiliate, affiliation.**

filibeg *fil'i-beg*, *n* the kilt, the dress or petticoat reaching nearly to the knees, worn by the Highlanders of Scotland. [Gael. *feileadhbeag* — *feileadh*, plait, fold, *beag*, little.]

filibuster *fil'i-bus-tər*, *n* a person who obstructs legislation by speeches, motions, etc.; obstruction in a legislative body; a military adventurer, someone who makes unauthorised war. — *vi* to act as a filibuster. — *n* **filibus'terer.** — *n* **filibus'tering.** — *adj* **filibus'terous.** [Sp. *filibustero*, a buccaneer, through Fr. *flibustier*, *fribustier*, from Du. *vrijbuiter* (cf. Eng. **freebooter** under **free**).]

filicide *fil'i-sīd*, *n* the murder of one's own child; someone who murders their own child. [L. *fīlius*, *fīlia*, son, daughter; *caedere*, to kill.]

filiform *fil'i-förm*, *adj* threadlike. [L. *fīlum*, a thread, and **-form.**]

filigree *fil'i-grē*, *n* a kind of ornamental metallic lacework of gold and silver, twisted into convoluted forms, united and partly consolidated by soldering; a delicate structure resembling this. — Also **fil'agree.** — *adj* **fil'igreed** ornamented with filigree. [Fr. *filigrane* — It. *filigrana* — L. *fīlum*, thread, *grānum*, a grain.]

filings. See **file**[2].

Filipino *fil-i-pē'nō*, *fem* **Filipi'na,** *n* a native of the *Philippine* Islands: — *pl* **Filipi'nos,** *fem* **Filipi'nas.** — Also *adj*. [Sp.]

fill *fil*, *vt* to make full; to put into until all the space is occupied; to supply abundantly; to satisfy; to glut; to perform the duties of; to supply (a vacant office); to put amalgam, gold, etc. into (a cavity in a tooth); to fulfil, carry out (esp. *US*); to make up (a prescription) (*US*). — *vi* to become full; to become satiated. — *n* as much as fills or satisfies; a full supply; the fullest extent; anything used to fill. — *n* **fill'er** someone who, or that which, fills; a vessel for conveying a liquid into a bottle; a substance added to various materials to impart desired qualities. — *n* **fill'ing** anything used to fill up, stop a hole, to complete, etc., as amalgam, etc. in a tooth, or the woof in weaving; (in *pl*) the quantity of new whisky spirit that a blender puts into store for maturation in e.g. a year, or the output of a distillery supplied for such purposes. — **filler cap** a device for closing the filling pipe of a petrol tank in a motor vehicle; **fill'-in** something used to fill in (time or space); **filling station** a roadside installation where petrol and oil are sold to motorists. — **fill in** to occupy (time); to add what is necessary to complete, e.g. a form; to act as a temporary substitute (for; *colloq*); **fill out** to make or become more substantial, larger or fuller; to complete (a form, etc.); **fill someone in** (*colloq*) to give someone detailed information about a situation; to thrash or beat up someone (*slang*); **fill the bill** to be adequate; **fill up** to fill, or be filled, by addition of more; **have one's fill of** to have enough of, esp. something unpleasant or tiresome. [O.E. *fyllan* — *full*, full.]

fillet *fil'ət*, *n* a piece of meat without bone, esp. the fleshy part of the thigh or the undercut of the sirloin;

a boned whole, or thick boneless slice of, fish; meat or fish boned and rolled; a narrow piece of wood, metal, etc.; a band for the hair; a small space or band used along with mouldings (*archit*). — *vt* to bone; to make into fillets; to bind or adorn with a fillet: — *pr p* **fill'eting**; *pa t* and *pa p* **fill'eted**. [Fr. *filet*, dimin. of *fil*, from L. *fīlum*, a thread.]

fillip *fil'ip*, *vt* to strike with the fingernail released from the ball of the thumb with a sudden jerk; to incite, stimulate: — *pr p* **fill'iping**; *pa t* and *pa p* **fill'iped**. — *n* a jerk of the finger from the thumb; a stimulus. [A form of **flip**.]

fillister *fil'is-tər*, *n* a kind of rabbeting plane.

filly *fil'i*, *n* a young mare. [Dimin. of **foal**.]

film *film*, *n* a thin skin or membrane; a thin layer or coating; a pellicle; a gauze of very slender threads; a mistiness; a thin sheet of usu. plastic-based material used for wrapping; a coating of a sensitive substance for taking a photograph; a sheet or ribbon of celluloid or similar prepared with such a coating for ordinary photographs or for instantaneous photographs for projection by cinematograph; a motion picture, or connected series of motion pictures; (in *pl*) the cinema. — *vt* to cover with a film; to photograph, record on film; to make a motion picture of; to adapt and enact for the cinema. — *vi* to become covered with a film. — *adj* **film'able** suitable for making a film of. — *n* **filmi'ness**. — *n* **filmog'raphy** a list of the films of a particular actor or director. — *adj* **film'y** composed of or like a film; covered with a film; gauzy; clouded. — **film badge** a badge containing sensitive film worn by those risking exposure to radioactivity, to detect and usu. indicate the amount of exposure; **film'goer**; **film noir** (*nwär*) a bleak or pessimistic film; **film set** the scenery, furniture, etc., arranged for the scene of a film. — *vt* **film'set** to set by a process of typesetting (*printing*). — **film'setting** typesetting by exposing type on to film which is then transferred to printing plates; **film star** a favourite cinema performer; **film'-strip** a film consisting of a series of stills to be shown separately and consecutively. [O.E. *filmen*.]

FILO *fī'lō*, *abbrev* for first in, last out.

filo or **phyllo** *fī'lō*, *n* a type of Greek, etc., pastry, made in thin sheets. [Gr. *phyllon*, a leaf.]

Filofax® *fī'lə-faks*, *n* a small, loose-leaf filing system containing a diary and a selection of information, e.g. addresses, maps, indexes, to assist the user to organise his or her time, business, etc.

filose *fīl'ōs*, *adj* threadlike; having a threadlike end. [L. *fīlum*, a thread.]

filter *fil'tər*, *n* an apparatus for purifying a fluid of solid matter by pouring it through porous material; a device for wholly or partly eliminating undesirable frequencies from light or electric currents; at a road junction, an auxiliary traffic light in the form of a green arrow which allows one lane of traffic to move while the main stream is held up. — *vt* to pass through a filter; to separate by a filter (esp. with *out*). — *vi* to pass through a filter; to percolate; to pass gradually and dispersedly through obstacles; to join gradually a stream of traffic; (of a lane of traffic) to move in the direction specified by the filter; to become known gradually (*fig*). — *n* **filterabil'ity** or **filtrabil'ity**. — *adj* **fil'terable** or **fil'trable** able to pass through a filter; capable of being filtered. — *vt* and *vi* **fil'trate** to filter or percolate. — *n* a filtered liquid. — *n* **filtrā'tion**. — **fil'ter-bed** a bed of sand, gravel, clinker, etc., used for filtering water or sewage; **fil'ter-paper** porous paper for use in filtering; **fil'ter-tip** a cigarette with a filter at the mouth end. [O.Fr. *filtre* — L.L. *filtrum*, felt.]

filth *filth*, *n* foul matter; anything that defiles, physically or morally; obscenity; (with *the*) the police (*derog slang*). — *adv* **filth'ily**. — *n* **filth'iness**. — *adj* **filth'y** foul; unclean; impure. [O.E. *fȳlth* — *fūl*, foul.]

Fimbra *fim'brə*, *abbrev* for Financial Intermediaries, Managers and Brokers Regulatory Association.

fimbria *fim'bri-ə*, *n* a fringing filament. — *adj* **fim'-briate** fringed; having a narrow border (*heraldry*). — *adj* **fim'briated**. — *n* **fimbria'tion**. [L. *fimbriae*, fibres, fringe.]

fin *fin*, *n* an organ by which an aquatic animal steers, balances or swims; a fixed vertical surface on the tail of an aeroplane; a portion of a mechanism like a fish's fin in shape or purpose; a thin projecting edge or plate; hand, arm (*slang*). — *adj* **fin'less**. — *adj* **finned** having fins. — *adj* **finn'y**. — **fin'back** or **fin'-whale** a rorqual. [O.E. *finn*.]

FINA *abbrev* for *Fédération Internationale de Natation Amateur* (Fr.), International Amateur Swimming Federation.

finable. See **fine**[2].

finagle *fi-nā'gəl*, *vt* to wangle; to obtain by guile or swindling; to cheat (a person; usu. with *out of*). — Also *vi* and *n*. [Eng. dialect *fainaigue*, cheat, shirk.]

final *fī'nl*, *adj* last; decisive, conclusive; respecting the end or motive; (of a judgment) ready for execution. — *n* the last of a series (e.g. of games in a contest, examinations in a curriculum, etc.). — *vt* **fī'nalise** or **-ize** to put the finishing touches to; to put an end to completely. — *n* **fī'nalist** someone who reaches the final stage in a competition. — *n* **finality** (*-al'i-ti*) state of being final; completeness or conclusiveness; the principle of final cause; that which is final. — *adv* **fī'nally**. [Fr., — L. *fīnālis* — *fīnis*, an end.]

finale *fi-nä'lā* or *-li*, *n* the end; the last movement in a musical composition; the concluding number of an opera or the like. [It. *finale*, final — L. *fīnālis*.]

finance *fī-* or *fi-nans'*, also *fī'nans*, *n* money affairs or revenue; public money; the art of managing or administering the public money; (in *pl*) money resources. — *vt* to manage financially; to provide with money. — *vi* to engage in money business. — *adj* **finan'cial** (*-shəl*) pertaining to finance. — *n* **finan'cialist** a financier. — *adv* **finan'cially**. — *n* **finan'cier** (*-si-ər* or in U.S. *fin-an-sēr'*) someone skilled in finance; a person who administers the public revenue. — *vi* and *vt* (*-sēr'*) to finance; to swindle. — **finance company** or **house** a company specialising in lending money against collateral, esp. to finance hire-purchase agreements; **financial year** any annual period for which accounts are made up; the annual period ending 5 April, functioning as the income-tax year; the annual period ending, for many public bodies, on 31 March. [Fr., — O.Fr. *finer*, to settle.]

finback. See under **fin**.

finch *finch* or *finsh*, *n* a name applied to many passerine birds, esp. to those of the genus *Fringilla* — bullfinch, chaffinch, goldfinch, etc. [O.E. *finc*.]

find *fīnd*, *vt* to come upon or meet with; to discover or arrive at; to come to perceive; to experience; to determine after judicial inquiry; to supply, succeed in getting; to manage to reach, hit, land on, etc. — *vi* to come upon game: — *pr p* **find'ing**; *pa t* and *pa p* **found**. — *n* an act of finding; something found, esp. of value or interest. — *n* **find'er** a person who finds; a small telescope attached to a larger one, or a lens attached to a camera, to facilitate the directing of it upon the object required. — *n* **find'ing**. — **finders keepers** (*colloq*) those who find something are entitled to keep it; **find one's feet** to become able to cope readily with new conditions; **find oneself** to feel, as regards health, happiness, etc.; to come to terms with oneself; to discover one's true vocation and interests; **find out** to discover, to detect. [O.E. *findan*.]

fin de siècle *fɛ̃ də sye-kl'*, (Fr.) the end of the (19th) century, or of an era; characteristic of the ideas, etc., of that time; decadent.

fine[1] *fīn*, *adj* not coarse or heavy; consisting of small particles; subtle; slender; sharp; keen; exquisite;

nice; delicate; sensitive; over-refined; showy; splendid; striking or remarkable; excellent (often *ironic*); pure; refined; containing so many parts of pure metal out of twenty-four (as 22 carats, or ounces, fine, 22/24 gold or silver), or out of a thousand. — *vt* to refine; to purify; to change by imperceptible degrees (esp. with *away* or *down*). — *adj* and *adv* at a more acute angle with the line of flight of the ball (e.g. *fine leg*); (of a billiards, etc. stroke) making very slight contact. — *adv* well, well enough (*colloq*); narrowly; with little to spare. — *adv* **fine'ly**. — *n* **fine'ness**. — *n* **fin'ery** splendour; showy clothing, etc.; a furnace for making iron malleable. — *npl* **fines** material (ore, coal, etc.) in a fine state of division separated out by screening. — *n* **fīn'ing** the process of refining or purifying; a clarifying agent (often in *pl*). — **fine arts** see under **art**[1]. — *vt* **fine'-draw** to draw or sew up so finely that no seam can be seen; to draw out finely or too finely. — *adj* **fine'-drawn**. — *adj* **fine'-spoken** using fine phrases. — *adj* **fine'-spun** finely spun out; over-subtle. — **fine-tooth (**or **-toothed) comb** a comb with slender teeth set close together. — *vt* **fine-tune'** to make delicate adjustments to. — **fine-tun'ing**. — **cut it fine** to do something with little time or space to spare; **go over** or **through with a fine-tooth (**or **-toothed) comb** to investigate very thoroughly. [Fr. *fin*, prob. a back-formation from L. *fīnītus*, finished.]

fine[2] *fīn*, *n* a fee paid on some particular occasion; a money penalty. — *vt* to impose a fine on; to punish by fine. — *adj* **fīn'able** liable to a fine. — **in fine** in conclusion. [L. *fīnis*, an end.]

fine[3] *fēn*, *n* ordinary French brandy. — **fine Champagne** (*shā-pany'*) brandy distilled from wine made from grapes grown in the Charente region of France. [Fr.]

fines herbes *fēn-zerb*, (Fr.) (*cookery*) *npl* a mixture of herbs used as a garnish or, chopped, as a seasoning.

finesse *fi-nes'*, *n* subtlety of invention or design; sophisticated accomplishment; skill, expertise; an endeavour by a player holding a higher card to take the trick with a lower, risking loss. — *vt* and *vi* to play in finesse. — *vi* to use artifice. — *n* **finess'er**. — *n* **finess'ing**. [Fr.]

finger *fing'gər*, *n* one of the five terminal parts of the hand, or usu. of the four other than the thumb; anything shaped like a finger; the part of a glove that covers a finger; a finger-breadth; share, interest. — *vt* to handle or perform with the fingers; to pilfer; to toy or meddle with; to make or indicate choice of fingering (*mus*); to indicate, identify a guilty person (*slang*). — *vi* to use or move the fingers. — *adj* **fing'ered** having fingers, or anything like fingers, or indication of fingering. — *n* **fing'ering** act or manner of touching with the fingers; the choice of fingers as in playing a musical instrument; the written or printed indication of this. — *adj* **fing'erless**. — *n* **fing'erling** a fish no bigger than a finger, esp. a salmon parr or young trout less than a year old. — **fing'erboard** the part of a violin, etc., against which the strings are stopped by the fingers; **fing'erbowl** a bowl for water to cleanse the fingers at table; **fing'er-breadth** or **fing'er's-breadth** the breadth of a finger, a digit, as a unit of measurement (1.4 cm. or ¾ of an inch); **finger buffet** a buffet consisting of **finger foods**, food (such as sandwiches) which may be eaten with the fingers as opp. to a knife and fork; **fing'erguard** the crosspiece of a sword-handle; **fing'erhold** a grasp by the fingers; something by which the fingers can hold (also *fig*); **fing'erhole** a hole in a wind instrument closed by the finger to modify the pitch; **fing'ermark** a mark, esp. a dirty mark, made by the finger; **fing'ernail**; **fing'erpaint** a rather thick gelatinous paint used esp. by children and applied with the hands and fingers rather than with a brush. — Also *vt*. — **fing'erpainting**; **fing'erplate** a plate to protect a door from dirty fingers; **fing'erprint** an impression of the ridges of the fingertip; an accurate and unique identification feature or profile produced by chemical analysis, genetic analysis, etc. (*fig*); the basic features (*fig*). — *vt* to take the fingerprints of (also *fig*). — **fing'erprinting** (also *fig*); **fing'erstall** a covering for protecting the finger; **fing'ertip**. — **a finger in the pie** a share in the doing of anything (often said of annoying meddling); **get** or **pull one's finger out** (*colloq*) to start working hard or doing one's job properly or efficiently; **have at one's fingertips** to be master of (a subject); **lay** or **put a finger on** to touch; **not lift a finger** to take no action whatever; **point the finger at** to call attention to in reproof; **put** or **lay one's finger on** to indicate, comprehend and express, or recall, precisely; **to one's fingertips** completely; in all respects; **twist, wind** or **wrap someone round one's little finger** habitually to get what one wants from someone (typically older than or senior to oneself) by playing on his or her goodwill towards one. [O.E.]

fingering[1] *fing'gər-ing*, *n* a woollen yarn of two or more strands, used in hand-knitting, orig. esp. for stockings. [Perh. Fr. *fin grain*, fine grain.]

fingering[2]. See **finger**.

fini *fē-nē*, (Fr.) *adj* finished, completed; done for, broken.

finial *fin'i-əl*, *n* a carved bunch of foliage, etc. on the top of a pinnacle, gable, spire, etc. [L. *finis*, end.]

finical *fin'i-kl*, *adj* affectedly or excessively precise in trifles; foppish. — *n* **finicality** (*-kal'i-ti*) the state of being finical; something finical. — *adv* **fin'ically**. — *n* **fin'icalness** fussiness and fastidiousness. — *adj* **finick'ety**, **fin'icking**, **fin'icky** or **fin'ikin** particular about trifles; (of a job) intricate, tricky, fiddly, requiring attention to small details, delicate manipulations, etc. [Prob. conn. with **fine**[1].]

fining. See **fine**[1].

finish *fin'ish*, *vt* to end; to complete the making of; to perfect; to give the last touches to; to complete the education of, esp. for life in society; to complete the course of a race; to put an end to, to destroy. — Also *vi*. — *n* that which finishes or completes; the end of a race, hunt, etc.; the last touch, elaboration, polish; the last coat of plaster or paint; (applied to cattle and sheep) the amount of flesh and fat on an animal. — *adj* **fin'ished** brought to an end or to completion; complete; consummate; perfect. — *n* **fin'isher** someone who finishes; a person who completes or perfects, esp. in crafts. — *n* and *adj* **fin'ishing**. — **finishing school** an establishment where some girls complete their education, with emphasis on social refinements, etc. rather than academic achievement. — **finish up** to finish; to end up, be or become in the end. [Fr. *finir*, *finissant* — L. *fīnīre*, to end.]

finite *fī'nīt*, *adj* having an end or limit; subject to limitations or conditions (opp. to *infinite*). — *adv* **fī'nītely**. — *n* **fī'nīteness** or **finitude** (*fin'i-tūd*). — **finite verb** a verb limited by person, number, tense, mood (opp. to infinitive, gerund, participle). [L. *fīnītus*, past p. of *fīnīre*, to limit.]

fink *fingk*, (*slang*) *n* a strike-breaker; an informer; an unpleasant person. — Also *vi* (often with *on*).

Finn *fin*, *n* a member of a people dwelling in Finland and adjacent regions; more generally, a member of the group of peoples to which the Finns proper belong. — *n* **Fin'lander** a native or citizen of Finland. — *n* **Finlandīsā'tion** or **-z-** in relations with the Soviet Union, a policy of accommodation rather than confrontation. — *adj* **Finn'ic** pertaining to the Finns or the Finno-Ugrians. — *adj* **Finn'ish** pertaining to the Finns, or to Finland, or its language. — *n* the Finno-Ugrian language of Finland. — *adj* **Finno-Ugrian** (*fin-ō-ū'gri-ən* or *-ōō'gri-ən*) or **Finno-U'gric** (*-grik*) belonging to the north-western group of Ural-Altaic languages and peoples — Finnish, Estonian, Lapp, etc. [O.E. *finnas*, Finns.]

Finn. *abbrev* for Finnish.

finnan *fin'ən*, *n* a kind of smoked haddock, prob. named from *Findon*, on the east coast of Scotland. — Also **finnan haddock** or **haddie** (*had'i*).

fino *fē'nō*, *n* a dry sherry: — *pl* **fi'nos**. [Sp., fine, excellent.]

finocchio, finnochio or **finochio** *fin-ok'i-ō*, *n* a dwarf variety of fennel. — Also called **dwarf, Florence, French** or **sweet fennel**. [It., fennel.]

fiord or **fjord** *fyörd*, *n* a long, narrow, rock-bound inlet. [Norw. *fjord*.]

fioritura *fyor-i-tōō'rə*, (*mus*) *n* a florid embellishment: — *pl* **fioriture** (-*rā*). [It., flowering — L. *flōs, flōris*.]

fipple *fip'l*, *n* an arrangement of a block, and a sharp edge against which it directs the wind, in the recorder, etc. — **fipp'le-flute** a flute with a fipple, a recorder or flageolet. [Cf. O.N. *flipi*, a horse's lip.]

fir *fûr*, *n* the name of several coniferous, resinous trees, valuable for their timber. — *adj* **firr'y** abounding in firs; of fir. — **fir'-cone; fir'-tree; fir'-wood**. [O.E. *fyrh*.]

fire *fīr*, *n* the heat and light of burning; a mass of burning matter, as of fuel in a grate; flame or incandescence; a conflagration; firing; fuel; a heating apparatus; heat or light due to other causes than burning; volcanic or subterranean heat; great heat; the heat of fever or inflammation; glowing appearance; a sparkle of light; discharge of firearms (also *fig*); enthusiasm; ardour; spirited vigour or animation; refraction of light in a gemstone. — *vt* to ignite; to cause to explode; to expose to heat; to bake; to cauterise (*farriery*); to fuel; to affect as if by fire; to discharge; to drive out; to dismiss (from employment, etc.); to inflame; to animate; to rouse to passion of any kind. — *vi* to catch fire; to shoot with firearms; to become inflamed; to break out in anger; (of a car, engine, etc.) to start. — *adj* **fired** affected, or having the appearance of having been affected, with fire; baked; ignited; kindled; discharged. — *adj* **fire'less**. — *n* **fir'er** someone who fires, in any sense. — *n* **fir'ing** ignition; discharge of guns, etc.; fuelling; firewood; fuel; cautery; injury by overheating; subjection to heat. — **fire'-alarm** an apparatus for giving warning of fire; a warning of fire; **fire'arm** a weapon discharged by explosion (usu. in *pl*); **fire'-ball** a bolide; ball lightning; an incendiary or illuminating projectile; a flaming ball of burning gases; the luminous sphere of hot gases at the centre of a nuclear explosion; **fire'bomb** an incendiary bomb. — Also vt. — **fire'bombing; fire'brand** a burning piece of wood; an energetic person; someone who stirs up trouble; **fire'-break** a strip of land kept clear to stop the spread of a fire (also *fig*); **fire'brick** a brick refractory to fire, used for furnace-linings, grates, etc.; **fire brigade** a body of firemen; **fire'-bucket** a bucket containing sand or water for putting out fires; **fire'-clay** a clay poor in lime and iron, suitable for making refractory pottery and firebricks; **fire'cracker** a device for making a noise, a cylinder of paper or cardboard containing an explosive and a fuse; **fire'crest** or **fire-crested wren** a bird closely related to the goldcrest; **fire'-damp** a combustible gas given off by coal, etc., chiefly methane; **fire'dog** an andiron; **fire door** a fire-resistant door to prevent the spread of fire within a building; an emergency exit; **fire drill** practice in putting out or escaping from fire; **fire'-eater** a juggler who seems to eat fire; a seeker of quarrels; **fire engine** a vehicle which carries equipment and firemen to fight fires; **fire escape** a fixed or movable way of escape from a burning building; **fire extinguisher** a portable device for spraying water, chemicals, foam, etc. on to a fire to put it out; **fire'-fighter** a fireman; **fire'-fighting** (*fig*) dealing with events as they arise, without long-term planning; **fire'fly** any various nocturnal beetles which emit phosphorescent light; **fire'guard** a protective wire frame or railing in front of a fireplace; **fire hose** a hose for extinguishing fires; **fire insurance** insurance against loss by fire; **fire'-irons** fireside implements — poker, tongs, shovel — not necessarily of iron; **fire'light** the light of a domestic fire; **fire'lighter** a piece of readily inflammable material or other means of lighting a fire; **fire'man** a man whose function is to assist in putting out fires and rescuing those in danger; a stoker; a train driver's assistant (stoker on steam engine); a miner responsible for safety measures; someone who explodes charges; a reporter sent out (esp. abroad) to cover a specific event; **fire'-office** a fire insurance office; **fire'place** the place for a domestic fire, the chimney-opening and surrounding area; **fire'-plug** a hydrant for use against fires; **fire'-power** (*mil*) the weight of missiles that can be fired with effect in a given time. — *adj* **fire'proof** proof against fire; incombustible. — *vt* to make fireproof. — **fire'proofing; fire'-raiser** an incendiary; **fire'-raising** arson. — *adj* **fire'-resistant** or **fire'-resisting** immune to effects of fire up to a required degree. — **fire'-risk; fire'screen** a screen for intercepting the heat of a fire; **fire'ship** a ship carrying combustibles sent among the enemy's ships; **fire'side** the side of the fireplace; the hearth; home. — *adj* domestic; familiar. — **fire station** a place where fire engines, firemen, etc. are kept in readiness to attend a fire; **fire'-stick** a primitive implement for getting fire by friction; **fire'stone** a rock, esp. a sandstone, that stands much heat without damage; **fire'-storm** a huge blaze (esp. a result of heavy bombing) which fans its own flames by creating its own draught (also *fig*); **fire'thorn** pyracantha; **fire'-trap** a building, etc. inadequately provided with fire exits and fire escapes; **fire'-warden** (*NAm*) an official responsible for prevention and extinction of fires; **fire'-water** strong alcoholic spirits; **fire'weed** the rose-bay willow-herb, which springs up on burned ground; **fire'woman** a female fire-fighter; **fire'wood** wood for fuel; **fire'work** a device containing combustible chemicals, for producing coloured sparks, flares, etc. often with loud noises; (in *pl*) a display of these; (in *pl*) a florid technical display in music, talk, etc.; (in *pl*) a display of temper; **firing line** area or troops within range of the enemy for practical purposes (also *fig*); **firing party** a detachment detailed to fire over a grave or shoot a condemned prisoner; **firing pin** a pin that strikes the detonator and explodes the cartridge in a rifle; **firing squad** a firing party to shoot a condemned prisoner. — **catch** or **take fire** to become ignited; to become aroused about something; **fire away** (usu. *imper*; *colloq*) to go ahead; to begin; **fire in one's belly** ardour or passion in speaking, etc.; drive, ambition; **fire off** to discharge; to ask or utter in rapid succession; to expel; **fire up** to start a fire; to fly into a passion; **go through fire and water** see under **go; on fire** in a state of fiery combustion; **play with fire** to expose oneself to unnecessary risk; to treat lightly a situation which could prove dangerous; **St Anthony's fire** see under **Anthony; St Elmo's fire** see under **Saint; set on fire** or **set fire to** to ignite; **under fire** exposed to the enemy's fire; exposed to criticism. [O.E. *fȳr*.]

firkin *fûr'kin*, *n* a measure equal to the fourth part of a barrel (*brewing*); 9 gallons (*brewing*); 56 lb. of butter. [With dimin. sfx. *-kin*, from Old Du. *vierde*, fourth.]

firm[1] *fûrm*, *adj* fixed; compact; strong; not easily moved or disturbed; unshaken; resolute; decided; (of prices, commodities, markets, etc.) steady, stable (*commerce*). — Also *adv*. — *vt* to make firm. — *vi* to become firm; to become stable or rise slightly (*commerce*). — **firm down** to make (ground, etc.) firm or firmer; **firm up** (of prices, etc.) to firm (*commerce*); to make (a promise, etc.) firm or firmer. [O.Fr. *ferme* — L. *firmus*.]

firm² *fûrm*, *n* a business house or partnership. [It. *firma*, a fixed payment — L. *firmus*.]

firmament *fûr'mə-mənt*, *n* the solid sphere in which the stars were thought to be fixed; the sky. — *adj* **firmamental** (*-ment'l*). [L. *firmāmentum* — *firmus*, firm.]

firmer *fûr'mər* or **firmer chisel** (*chiz'l*), *n* a carpenter's or woodworker's wood-cutting chisel. [Fr. *fermoir*, an alteration of *formoir*, — *former*, to form.]

firring. See **furring** under **fur.**

first *fûrst*, *adj* foremost; in front of or before all others; most eminent; chief; referring to the speaker or writer (*gram*). — *n* someone who, or that which, is first or of the first class; a place in the first class; an academic degree of the first class; first gear. — *adv* before anything or anyone else; for the first time. — *n* **first'ling** the first produce or offspring, esp. of animals. — *adv* **first'ly** in the first place. — **first-aid'** treatment of a wounded or sick person before the doctor's arrival; **first-aid'er.** — *adj* **first-attack'** same as **first-strike.** — *adj* **first'-born** born first. — *n* the eldest child. — *adj* **first-class'** of the first class, rank or quality. — **first floor** (*adj* **first'-floor**) see under **floor; first-foot'** (*Scot*) the first person to enter a house after the beginning of the new year. — *vt* to visit as first-foot. — *vi* to go around making visits as first-foot. — **first-foot'er; first-fruit'** or **-fruits'** the fruits first gathered in a season; first products or effects of anything; payment such as annates to a superior; **first gear** see **gear.** — *adj* **first generation** (*comput*) the early type of calculating and computing machine, using thermionic valves. — *adj* **first'-hand** obtained directly, or in order to obtain (information, etc.) directly, without an intermediary. — *adv* **first-hand'.** — **first lady** the wife of the chief executive of a city, state or country, esp. of the president of the U.S.A., or any woman chosen by him to carry out official duties as hostess, etc. (*US*; often with *caps*); a prominent or leading woman in any field, profession, etc.; **first lieutenant** in the Royal Navy, the executive officer, not necessarily a lieutenant, of a ship or naval establishment; **first light** the time when daylight first appears in the morning; **first name** Christian name, or the name that comes first in a full name; **first-night'** the first public performance of a theatrical production; **first-offend'er** someone convicted for the first time. — *adj* **first-past-the-post'** denoting or relating to a system of voting in which each voter casts only one vote, the candidate receiving the most votes being declared the winner. — *adj* **first'-rate** of highest rate or excellence; pre-eminent in quality, size or estimation. — *adv* **first-rate'** excellently. — **first refusal** the chance to buy (esp. property) before it is offered to others; **first school** a school catering for those aged five to eight, nine or ten; **first strike** a pre-emptive disarming attack on an enemy, intended to destroy their nuclear weapons before they can be brought into use (*adj* **first-strike'**). — *adj* **first'-time** immediate; carrying out an action, e.g. the purchase of a house, for the first time. — **at first** at the beginning, in the early stages, etc.; **first-class mail** or **post** mail sent at a higher rate to obtain quicker delivery; **first-day cover** an envelope with stamps postmarked on their first day of issue; **not know the first thing about** to know nothing about; **first thing** before doing anything else. [O.E. *fyrst*, superl.; cf. *fore*, before.]

firth *fûrth*, *n* an arm of the sea, esp. a river-mouth. — Also **frith** (*frith*). [O.N. *fiörthr*; Norw. *fjord*.]

FIS *abbrev* for: Family Income Supplement; *Fédération Internationale de Ski* (Fr.), International Ski Federation.

FISA *fē'sə*, *abbrev* for: *Fédération Internationale du Sport Automobile* (Fr.), International Automobile Sports Federation; Finance Industry Standards Association.

fiscal *fis'kəl*, *adj* pertaining to the public treasury or revenue. — *n* in Scotland, an officer who prosecutes in criminal cases in local and inferior courts — in full, **procurator fiscal.** — **fiscal drag** the means by which the inland revenue automatically benefits from any increase in earned income without any actual increase in taxation rates; **fiscal year** (esp. *US*) financial year. [L. *fiscus*, a basket, a purse.]

fish¹ *fish*, *n* a vertebrate that lives in water and breathes through gills; (*loosely*) any exclusively aquatic animal; the flesh of fish as food; a person, as in *queer fish*; a fish-dive: — *pl* **fish** or **fish'es.** — *vi* to catch or try to catch or obtain fish, or anything that may be likened to a fish (often with *for*); to serve the purpose of fishing. — *vt* to catch and bring out of water; to bring up or out from a deep or hidden place, obscurity or the like; to elicit (with *out*); to practise the fisher's craft in; to ransack. — *n* **fish'er** someone who fishes for sport or gain. — *n* **fish'ery** the business of catching fish; a place for catching fish; right of fishing. — *n* **fish'iness.** — *adj* **fish'ing** used in fishing. — *n* the art or practice of catching fish; a fishing-ground or stretch of water where one fishes. — *adj* **fish'y** consisting of fish; like a fish; abounding in fish; dubious, as of a story; equivocal, unsafe. — **fish'ball** or **fish cake** a ball or cake of chopped fish and mashed potatoes, fried; **fish'burger** a flat cake, similar to a hamburger, made of minced fish; **fish'-dive** (*slang*) a ballerina's leap on to a partner's outstretched arms; **fish eagle** any of various fish-eating eagles of central and southern Africa; **fish'erman** a fisher; **fisheye lens** (*phot*) an ultra-wide-angle lens covering up to 180°; **fish'-farm; fish'-farmer; fish'-farming** rearing fish in ponds or tanks; **fish-fing'er** a fairly small oblong cake of fish coated in batter or breadcrumbs; **fish'-glue** isinglass, or any other glue made from the skins, air-bladders, etc. of fish; **fish'-hawk** osprey; **fish'-hook** a barbed hook for catching fish; **fish'ing-ground** an area of water, esp. of the sea, where fish are caught; **fish'ing-line** a fine strong thread used (e.g. with a rod, hooks, etc.) to catch fish; **fish'ing-rod** a long slender rod to which a line is fastened for angling; **fish'ing-tackle** tackle — nets, lines, etc. — used in fishing; **fish'-kettle** a long oval dish for boiling or poaching fish; **fish'-knife** a knife with a broad, blunt-edged, usu. decorated blade for eating fish with; a broad-bladed knife for cutting and serving fish with; **fish'-ladder** an arrangement of steps and shelters for enabling a fish to ascend a fall, etc.; **fish'-manure** fish used as a fertiliser; **fish'-meal** dried fish ground to meal; **fish'monger** a dealer in fish. — *adj* **fish'-net** woven as a fine net. — **fish'-pond** a pond in which fish are kept; **fish'-slice** a flat implement for carving fish at table; a broad, flat implement for turning fish, etc., in the frying-pan. — *adj* **fish'-tail** shaped like the tail of a fish. — *vi* to swing the tail of an aircraft from side to side to reduce speed while gliding downward; (of the back of a vehicle) to swing or skid from side to side. — **fish'way** (*NAm*) a fish-ladder; **fish'wife** or **fish'-woman** a woman who peddles fish; a coarse loud-mouthed woman. — **a fish out of water** a person in an unaccustomed, unsuitable situation; **big fish** (*slang*) an important or leading person; **drink like a fish** to drink to excess; **fish in troubled waters** to take advantage of disturbed times to further one's own interests; **fishskin disease** ichthyosis; **have other fish to fry** to have something else to do or attend to; **odd fish** or **queer fish** a person of odd habits, or of a nature with which one is not in sympathy; **pretty kettle of fish** see under **kettle.** [O.E. *fisc*; L. *piscis*.]

fish[2] *fish, n* a piece of wood placed alongside another to strengthen it (*naut*); a counter for games. — **fish'= plate** an iron plate used in pairs to join railway rails. [Prob. Fr. *fiche*, peg, mark.]

fishgig. See **fizgig.**

fissile *fis'īl* or *-il, adj* readily split; capable of nuclear fission. — *n* **fissility** (*fis-il'i-ti*) cleavableness. [**fissure.**]

fission *fish'ən, n* a cleaving; reproduction by dividing; the splitting of the nucleus of an atom into two roughly equal parts accompanied by great release of energy. — *adj* **fiss'ionable** capable of nuclear fission. — *adj* **fiss'ive.** — **fission bomb** a bomb deriving its energy from nuclear fission; **fission reactor** a reactor in which nuclear fission takes place. [**fissure.**]

fissiparous *fi-sip'ər-əs,* (*biol*) *adj* reproducing by fission. — *n* **fissip'arism.** — *n* **fissipar'ity** or **fissip'arousness.** — *adv* **fissip'arously.** [L. *fissus*, — *findĕre* (see **fissure**), and L. *parĕre*, to bring forth.]

fissure *fish'ər, n* an act of cleaving; a narrow opening — chasm, cleft, groove; a sulcus, esp. one of the furrows on the surface of the brain, such as the longitudinal fissure separating the hemispheres; a small abnormal crack in the skin or mucous membrane. — *vt* to crack, cleave, divide. — *adj* **fiss'ured** cleft, divided. [L. *findĕre, fissum*, to cleave.]

fist *fist, n* the closed or clenched hand; handwriting (*colloq*); an index (*printing*). — *vt* to strike or grip with the fist. — *n* **fist'ful** a handful. — *adj* **fist'y.** — **fist'icuff** a blow with the fist; (in *pl*) boxing; (in *pl*) a fight with fists. — **make a good, a reasonable, not a bad,** etc. **fist of** to do (something) fairly well, not badly, etc. [O.E. *fȳst*.]

fistula *fist'ū-lə, n* a narrow passage or duct; an artificially made opening (*med*); a long narrow pipe-like ulcer (*pathol*): — *pl* **fist'ulae** (*-lē*) or **fist'ulas.** — *adj* **fist'ūlar, fist'ūlose** or **fist'ūlous.** [L. *fistula*, a pipe.]

fit[1] *fit, adj* suitable; in suitable condition; meeting required standards; convenient; appropriate; in good condition; in good health. — *n* success in fitting; adjustment and correspondence in shape and size; a thing (esp. a garment) that fits. — *vt* to make suitable or able; to alter or make so as to be in adjustment; to adjust; to piece together; to be suitable or becoming for; to be of such size and shape as to adjust closely to; to be in agreement or correspondence with; to furnish, supply. — *vi* to be suitable or becoming; to go into place with accurate adjustment to space; to be of such size and shape as to be able to do so: — *pr p* **fitt'ing;** *pa t* and *pa p* **fitt'ed.** — *adv* **fit'ly.** — *n* **fit'ment** an article of furniture or equipment; a fitting. — *n* **fit'ness.** — *adj* **fitt'ed** (of a cover, clothing, etc.) made, cut, sewn, etc. to fit exactly; (of a cupboard, etc.) constructed to fit a particular space and attached to, or built into, the wall of a room; (of a room) fully furnished with (matching) fitted cupboards, etc. — *n* **fitt'er** a person who or thing which fits or makes fit; a person who fits on garments; someone who assembles the parts of a machine, etc. — *adj* **fitt'ing** fit; appropriate. — *n* anything used in fitting up, esp. (in *pl*) equipment accessories; a fixture; the work of a fitter; the act or time of trying on an article of clothing so that it can be adjusted to fit the wearer. — *adv* **fitt'ingly.** — **fit'-up** temporary, improvised stage and properties (*theat*); a frame-up, esp. by the police (*slang*). — **fit in** to find enough room or time for someone or something; to be, or cause to be, in harmony (with); **fit on** to try on; to try on a garment upon; **fit out** to furnish, equip; **fit up** to provide with fittings; to frame (*slang*); **fitting-out basin** or **dock** a dock where a vessel is completed after launching.

fit[2] *fit, n* an attack of illness, esp. epilepsy; a convulsion or paroxysm; a temporary attack, or outburst of anything, e.g. laughter; a sudden effort or motion; a mood or passing humour. — *adj* **fit'ful** marked by sudden impulses; capriciously intermittent; spasmodic. — *adv* **fit'fully.** — *n* **fit'fulness.** — **fits and starts** spasmodic and irregular bursts of activity. [O.E. *fitt*, a struggle.]

FITA *fē'tə, abbrev* for *Fédération Internationale de Tir a l'Arc* (Fr.), International Archery Federation.

fitch *fich, n* a polecat; polecat fur; a paint-brush of polecat-hair; a small hog's-hair brush. — *n* **fitch'et** or **fitchew** (*fich'o͞o*) the polecat or its fur. [M.Du. *visse* and O.Fr. *fissle, fissau*, from the root of Du. *visse*, nasty.]

five *fīv, n* four and one; a symbol (5, v, etc.) representing that number; a group of five; a score of five points, strokes, etc.; a card with five pips; an article of the size so numbered; the fifth hour after midnight or midday; the age of five years. — *adj* of the number five; five years old. — *adj* and *adv* **five'fold** in five divisions; five times as much; folded in five thicknesses. — *n* **fiv'er** (*colloq*) a five-pound note; a five-dollar note (*US*). — **five'pence.** — *adj* **five'penny.** — **five'pins** a game with five 'pins', resembling ninepins and tenpins. — *adj* **five'pin.** — **five'-stones** the game of dibs or jacks played with five stones. — **bunch of fives** (*slang*) the fist; **five= day week** a week, five days of which are working days; **five-o'clock shadow** (*colloq*) the new growth of hair that becomes noticeable on a man's shaven face in the late afternoon. [O.E. *fīf*.]

fives *fīvz, npl* a ball game played with the (gloved) hand (or a bat) in a walled court.

fix *fiks, vt* to make firm or fast; to establish; to drive in; to settle; to make or keep permanent, solid, rigid, steady or motionless; to fasten or attach; to put to rights, mend; to arrange, attend to (a matter; sometimes by means of trickery); to prepare; to prevent from causing further trouble (*slang*); to get even with (*slang*); to chastise (*slang*). — *vi* to settle or remain permanently; to become firm, stable or permanent. — *n* a difficulty (*colloq*); a dilemma (*colloq*); the position of an aircraft as calculated from instrument readings; the establishment of one's position by any means; a shot of heroin or other drug (*slang*). — *adj* **fix'able** capable of being fixed. — *vt* **fixāte'** to fix, make stable; to direct (the eyes) upon an object; to arrest the emotional development of (*psychol*); to preoccupy. — *n* **fixā'tion** the act of fixing, or state of being fixed; steadiness, firmness; state in which a body does not evaporate; conversion of atmospheric nitrogen into a combined form; emotional arrest of personality, instinctive forces maintaining their earlier channels of gratification; an abnormal attachment, or an obsession. — *n* **fix'ative** a fixing agent. — *adj* **fixed** settled; not apt to evaporate; steadily directed; fast, lasting, permanent; not varying or subject to alteration. — *adv* **fix'edly.** — *n* **fix'edness.** — *n* **fix'er.** — *n* **fix'ing** the act or process of making fixed; arrangement; (in *pl*) adjuncts, trimmings; (in *pl*) equipment. — *n* **fix'ity** fixedness. — *n* **fix'ture** fixing; a movable that has become fastened to land or to a house; a fixed article of furniture; a thing or person permanently established in a place; a fixed or appointed time or event, as a horse-race. — **fixed capital** see **capital**[1]; **fixed charges** overheads such as interest payments, allowance for depreciation, and fixed costs, which do not vary with the volume of business done; **fixed costs** overheads such as rent and rates which do not vary with the volume of business done; **fixed idea** a monomania; **fixed income** one which does not increase or decrease, such as income from a fixed-interest investment. — *adj* **fixed-in'terest** having an invariable rate of interest. — **fixed odds** a betting method whereby a stated amount per unit stake is offered for a certain result or combination of results. — *adj* **fixed-pen'alty** of or relating to an offence, such as illegal parking, the penalty for which is invariable and obligatory, e.g. a fine which may be imposed and paid without the offender appearing in court. — **fixed satellite** a geostationary satellite. — **fixed-wing aircraft** an aircraft in which the wings are attached to the fuselage (as opp. to e.g. a helicopter with rotating 'wings' or propellers); **fix on** to single out, decide for; **fix up** to arrange or make arrangements for; to settle; to put to rights, attend to. [L. *fīgĕre, fīxus*, to fix, prob. through L.L. *fīxāre*.]

fizgig *fiz'gig*, *n* a police informer (*Austr slang*; also **fizz'gig**); a giddy or flirtatious girl; a firework; a harpoon (also **fish'gig**). [Earlier *fisgig*, prob. — obs. *fise*, fart (or **fizz**), *gig*, frivolous girl (cf. gig[1]); Sp. *fisga*, harpoon.]

fizz *fiz*, *vi* to make a hissing or spluttering sound; to produce bubbles; (also **be fizzing**) to be very angry (*colloq*): — *pr p* **fizz'ing**; *pa t* and *pa p* **fizzed**. — *n* a spluttering sound; bubbly quality; a frothy drink, esp. champagne. — *n* **fizz'er** that which fizzes; anything excellent (*colloq*); a very fast ball in cricket. — *n* and *adj* **fizz'ing**. — *vi* **fizz'le** to hiss or splutter; to go out with a spluttering sound (often with *out*); to come to nothing, be a fiasco, fail (often with *out*). — *n* an abortive effort. — *adj* **fizz'y**. [Formed from the sound.]

fjord. See **fiord**.

FL *abbrev* for: Florida (U.S. state); Liechtenstein (i.e. Fürstentum Liechtenstein; I.V.R.).

fl. *abbrev* for: florin; floruit (L.), flourished.

Fla. *abbrev* for Florida (U.S. state).

flabbergast *flab'ər-gäst*, (*colloq*) *vt* to amaze or confound. [Prob. conn. with **flabby** and obs. *gast*, to astonish.]

flabby *flab'i*, *adj* soft, yielding, as of muscles; (of people) having flabby muscles or flesh; overweight; hanging loose. — *n* **flab** (*colloq*) excess body fat. — *n* **flabb'iness**. [**flap**.]

flaccid *fla'sid* or *flak'sid*, *adj* limp; flabby; soft and weak. — *adv* **flac'cidly**. — *n* **flac'cidness** or **flaccid'ity**. [L. *flaccidus* — *flaccus*, flabby.]

flack *flak*, (*NAm slang*) *n* a person who handles publicity and public relations; a press agent. [Poss. from **flak**.]

flag[1] *flag*, *vi* to droop; to flap feebly; to grow languid or spiritless: — *pr p* **flagg'ing**; *pa t* and *pa p* **flagged**. — *n* **flagg'iness**. [Perh. O.Fr. *flac* — L. *flaccus*.]

flag[2] *flag*, *n* a piece of bunting or other cloth with a design, used as an emblem, for signalling, decoration, display, propaganda, etc.; a conspicuous sign to mark a position, e.g. of a golf-hole, or to convey information. — *vi* to indicate or inform by flag-signals. — *vt* to decorate with flags; to inform by flag-signals; to mark (e.g. a passage or item in a book) for attention, by means of a bookmark, pen or pencil mark, etc.; to indicate or code (material on computer tape, etc.) so that particular items or classes of data may be found or extracted. — **flag'-captain** the captain of a flagship; **flag'-day** a day on which collectors levy contributions to a charity in exchange for small flags as badges to secure immunity for the rest of the day; **flag-lieuten'ant** an officer in a flagship, corresponding to an aide-de-camp in the army; **flag'-officer** a naval officer privileged to carry a flag denoting his rank — admiral, vice-admiral, rear-admiral or commodore; **flag'ship** the ship carrying an admiral and flying his flag; anything of a similar level of importance or pre-eminence (*fig*; also *adj*); **flag'pole, flag'staff** or **flag'stick** a pole, etc., for displaying a flag. — *adj* **flag'-waving** serving merely to show (superficial) support for or allegiance to e.g. a nation, or a political party. — Also *n*. — **dip the flag** to lower the flag and then hoist it, as a token of respect; **flag down** to signal (e.g. a car) to stop; **flag of convenience** a foreign flag under which a shipping company registers its tonnage to avoid taxation or other burdens at home; **flag of distress** a flag displayed as a signal of distress — usu. upside down or at half-mast; **flag of truce** a white flag displayed during a battle when some pacific communication is desired; **show, carry** or **fly the flag** or **keep the flag flying** to (continue to) show support for or allegiance to one's own country, company, etc.; to put in an appearance or otherwise ensure that one, or the nation, firm, etc. one represents, is not overlooked; **strike** or **lower the flag** to pull down the flag as a token of relinquishment of command, respect, submission or surrender.

flag[3] *flag* or **flagstone** *flag'stōn*, *n* a flat paving-stone. — *vt* to pave with flagstones. — *n* **flagg'ing** flagstones; a pavement constructed from them. [O.N. *flaga*, a slab.]

flagellum *flə-jel'əm*, *n* a long runner (*bot*); a long cilium or whiplike appendage (*biol*): — *pl* **flagell'a**. — *vt* **flag'ellate** to scourge or flog. — *adj* having a flagellum or flagella. — *adj* **flag'ellated**. — *adj* **flag'ellant** scourging. — *n* someone who scourges, esp. themself in religious discipline. — *n* **flag'ellantism**. — *n* **flagellā'tion**. — *n* **flag'ellātor**. — *adj* **flag'ellatory**. — *adj* **flagellif'erous**. — *adj* **flagell'iform**. — *n* **flagellōmā'nia** enthusiasm for beating and flogging. — *n* and *adj* **flagellōmā'niac**. [L. *flagellum*, dimin. of *flagrum*, a whip.]

flageolet[1] *flaj-ō-let'* or *flaj'*, *n* a small high-pitched flute with two thumb-holes. [Fr., dimin. of O.Fr. *flageol, flajol*, a pipe.]

flageolet[2] *flaj-ō-let'*, *n* a variety of kidney bean. [Corruption of Fr. *fageolet*.]

flagon *flag'ən*, *n* a large, esp. wide, bottle; a liquor-jug. [Fr. *flacon* — *flascon* — L.L. *flascō, -ōnis*; see **flask**.]

flagrant *flā'grənt*, *adj* notorious; outrageous, conspicuous. — *n* **flā'grance** or **flā'grancy**. — *adv* **flā'grantly**. [L. *flagrāns, -antis*, pres. p. of *flagrāre*, to burn.]

flagrante delicto *flə-gran'tē di-lik'tō* or *fla-gran'te dā-lik'tō*, (L.) *adv* in the very act (lit. 'while the crime is blazing').

flail *flāl*, *n* an implement for threshing corn, consisting of a wooden bar (the *swingle*) hinged or tied to a handle; a mediaeval weapon with spiked iron swingle. — *vt* to strike with, or as if with, a flail. — *vi* to move like a flail (often with *about*). [O.E. *fligel*, infl. by O.Fr. *flaiel*, prob. from L. *flagellum*, a scourge.]

flair *flār*, *n* intuitive discernment; faculty for nosing out; a natural aptitude. [Fr., sense of smell — *flairer*, to smell — L.L. *flagrāre* — L. *fragrāre*, to emit a smell.]

flak *flak*, *n* anti-aircraft fire; adverse criticism (*colloq*). — **flak jacket** a heavy protective jacket reinforced with metal. [Initials of Ger. *Flieger-* (or *Flug-*) *abwehrkanone*, anti-aircraft cannon.]

flake[1] *flāk*, *n* a small flat scale or layer; a very small loose mass, as of snow; a spark or detached flame. — *vt* to form into flakes; to sprinkle with, or as if with, flakes. — *vi* to come off in flakes. — *n* **flak'iness**. — *adj* **flak'y** formed of, or tending to form, flakes; (of pastry) formed of thin layers; crazy, eccentric (*US colloq*). — **flake out** to collapse from weariness or illness. [Perh. conn. with O.N. *flōke*, flock of wool.]

flake[2] *flāk*, *n* a frame or rack for storing or drying food. [Cf. O.N. *flake*; Du. *vlaak*.]

flam *flam*, *n* a falsehood; a trick. — *vt* to deceive; to get, manage, etc. by deception. [Perh. **flimflam**.]

flambé *fläm'bā* or *flā-bā*, (*cookery*) *adj* (also **flambéed** *fläm'bād*) prepared or served with a dressing of flaming liquor, usu. brandy. [Fr., past p. of *flamber*, to flame, singe.]

flambeau *flam'bō*, *n* a flaming torch: — *pl* **flam'beaux** or **flam'beaus** (*-bōz*). [Fr., — O.Fr. *flambe* — L. *flamma*.]

flamboyant *flam-boi'ənt*, *adj* gorgeously coloured or decorated; (of a person, style, action, etc.) ostentatious, colourful or extravagant. — *n* **flamboy'ance** or **flamboy'ancy.** — *adv* **flamboy'antly.** [Fr., pres. p. of *flamboyer*, to blaze.]

flame *flām*, *n* the visible flickering luminous streams produced by a gaseous matter undergoing combustion; the gleam or blaze of a fire; rage; ardour of temper; vigour of thought; warmth of affection; love or its object, esp. in the phrase '*an old flame*'. — *vi* to burn as flame; to break out in passion. — *vt* to set aflame. — *adj* **flam'ing** brilliantly red; gaudy; violent; furious; often used intensively or to express irritation, etc. (*colloq*). — *adv* **flam'ingly.** — *n* **flammabil'ity.** — *adj* **flamm'able** inflammable. — *adj* **flam'y** pertaining to or like flame. — *adj* **flame'-coloured** of the colour of flame, bright reddish-yellow. — *adj* **flame'-grilled** cooked on a grill over a direct flame, esp. produced by solid fuel rather than gas. — *n* **flame'-grill.** — **flame'-thrower** an apparatus for throwing jets of flame in warfare; **flame'-tree** a thick-stemmed Australian tree with glossy leaves and scarlet bell-shaped flowers; applied to various other trees, e.g. the yellow-flowered *Acacia farnesiana* of S.W. United States, and the scarlet-flowered *Butea frondosa* of India and Burma. [O.Fr. *flambe* — L. *flamma*.]

flamenco *flä-meng'kō*, *n* a type of emotionally intense gypsy song, or the dance performed to it, originating in Andalusia: — *pl* **flamen'cos.** [Sp., Flem., gypsy.]

flamingo *flə-ming'gō*, *n* a tropical or subtropical wading bird of a pink or bright-red colour, with long legs and neck: — *pl* **flaming'os** or **flaming'oes.** [Sp. *flamengo* (now *flamenco*).]

flammability, flammable. See **flame.**

flan *flan*, *n* a flat open tart filled with a sweet or savoury mixture; the blank metal disc on which a design is stamped to produce a coin. [O.Fr. *flaon*, custard.]

flanch *flanch*, *flänch* or *-sh* or **flaunch** *flönch* or *-sh*, *vi* to widen, esp. outwards or upwards, to flare (often with *out*). — *vt* to cause to slope in towards the top (often with *up*). — *n* **flanch'ing** or **flaunch'ing** the action or state of the verb; (**flaunch'ing**) a sloping piece of cement e.g. round the base of a chimney-pot.

flange *flanj*, *n* a projecting or raised edge or flank, as of a wheel or of a rail, used to give strength or to make a connection or attachment secure. — *vi* to widen out. — *vt* to put a flange on. — *adj* **flanged.** [Perh. conn. with **flank.**]

flank *flangk*, *n* the side of an animal from the ribs to the thigh; a cut of beef from this part of the animal; (*loosely*) the corresponding part of the human body; the side or wing of anything, esp. of an army or fleet; a body of soldiers on the right or left extremity. — *vt* to be on, pass round, attack, threaten or protect the flank of. — *n* **flank'er** a fortification that commands the flank of an assailing force; one of the two outside men of the second row of the scrum (also **flank forward** or **wing forward**; *Rugby football*). — **do, pull** or **work a flanker** (*slang*, orig. *mil*) to trick, deceive, cheat, etc. someone. [Fr. *flanc*.]

flannel *flan'əl*, *n* a light woollen textile used for clothing; a piece of this or other cloth used for washing or rubbing, esp. a piece of towelling for washing the face, a face-cloth; flattery, soft-soap, words intended to hide one's ignorance, true opinions, etc. (*colloq*); (in *pl*) trousers, esp. of flannel or a similar cloth. — *vt* to wrap in flannel; to rub with a flannel; to flatter, to soft-soap, to utter flannel to (*colloq*; also *vi*). — *n* **flannelette'** a cotton imitation of flannel. — *adj* **flann'elled.** — *adj* **flann'elly.** — **flann'elboard** or **flann'elgraph** a board covered with flannel or felt, and letters, pictures, etc., backed with material which will stick when pressed against the board.

flap *flap*, *n* the blow or motion of a broad loose object; anything broad and flexible hanging loose, such as material covering an opening; skin or flesh detached from the underlying part for covering and growing over the end of an amputated limb; a fluster, a panic (*colloq*); any surface attached to the wing of an aircraft which can be adjusted in flight to alter the lift as a whole; an 'r' sound produced by a single light tap of the tongue against the alveolar ridge or uvula (*phon*). — *vt* to beat or move with a flap. — *vi* to move, as wings; to hang like a flap; to get into a panic or fluster: — *pr p* **flapp'ing**; *pa t* and *pa p* **flapped.** — *adj* **flapp'able** easily perturbed, agitated, irritated, flustered, etc.; not unflappable. — *n* **flapp'er** someone who or that which flaps; in the 1920s, a flighty young woman (*slang*). — *adj* **flapp'y** (*colloq*) in a state of nervousness or panic; in a fluster. — **flap'jack** a kind of broad, flat pancake; a biscuit made with rolled oats and syrup; a flat face-powder compact. [Prob. imit.]

flare *flār*, *vi* to spread; to widen out like a bell; to burn with a glaring, unsteady light; to glitter, flash; to blaze up, literally or in anger (with *up*). — *vt* to display glaringly; to dispose of (superfluous gas or oil) by means of a flare (with *off*; *chem eng*). — *n* a widening out, as in the bell of a horn, a bowl, or a skirt; an unshaded flame; a sudden blaze; a torch; a signalling light; (the flame or light produced by) a device composed of combustible material, activated to give warning, illumination, etc.; a device for the safe disposal of superfluous gas, oil, etc. by burning in the open (*chem eng*). — *npl* **flares** trousers that widen (greatly) below the knee, popular in the late 1960s and early 1970s. — *adj* **flār'ing.** — *adv* **flā'ringly.** — *adj* **flā'ry.** — **flare'-path** a path lit up to enable an aircraft to land or take off when natural visibility is insufficient; **flare stack** (*chem eng*) a tall chimney with an automatic igniter at the top, for the safe disposal of superfluous gas, etc.; **flare star** a star, usu. a red dwarf, which has a periodical sudden and unpredictable increase in brightness; **flare'-up.** [Poss. conn. with Norw. *flara*, to blaze.]

flash *flash*, *n* a momentary gleam of light; a sudden, short-lived flare or flame; (the momentary illumination from) a flashbulb or flash-gun (*phot*); a sudden burst, as of merriment; a moment, an instant; a sudden rush of water; a board for deepening or directing a stream of water; a distinctive mark on a uniform; a sticker or overprinted label on a piece of merchandise advertising a reduction in price, etc.; a brief news announcement; a bright garter or ribbon worn on the hose with knickerbockers or kilt, a small portion showing below the knee. — *adj* showy; vulgar; of, like or pertaining to criminals (*slang*). — *vi* to break forth, as a sudden light (*lit* and *fig*); to give forth flashes of light; to sparkle brilliantly; to blaze out; to break out into intellectual brilliancy; to burst out into violence; to move like a flash; to expose oneself indecently (*slang*). — *vt* to cause to flash; to send by some startling or sudden means; to show briefly; to display ostentatiously (often with *about* or *around*). — *n* **flash'er** someone who or that which flashes; a device for turning off and on lights as advertising, warning, etc. signs; the signs themselves; (on a vehicle) a direction indicator; a person given to indecent exposure (*slang*). — *adv* **flash'ily.** — *n* **flash'iness.** — *n* **flash'ing** the act of blazing; a sudden burst, as of water; a thin metal strip put over a junction between roof tiles, slates, etc., to make it watertight; the practice of indecently exposing oneself (*slang*). — *adj* emitting flashes; sparkling. — *adj* **flash'y** dazzling for a moment; showy but empty; gaudy; tawdry. — **flash'back** or **flash'forward** (in a film) a scene of the past or future, inserted as comment or explanation; an echo of the past or vision of the future. — Also *vi.* — **flash blindness** blindness caused by the flash of the explosion of a powerful bomb, etc.; **flash'bulb** an oxygen-filled electric bulb in which aluminium or other foil or filament may be fired to provide a brilliant flash, esp.

for illuminating a photographic subject; **flash burn** one sustained as the result of exposure to a flash of intense heat, e.g. from a nuclear explosion; **flash card** a card on which a picture or word is printed or written, to be shown briefly to a child as an aid to learning; one of a set of large brightly-coloured cards each held up by an individual e.g. in a sports stadium and together forming a picture or message; **flash'-cube** a plastic cube containing four flashbulbs, rotated as the film is wound on; **flash fire** a sudden, extensive (increase in) conflagration; **flash flood** a sudden, severe, brief flood caused by a heavy rainstorm; **flash flooding; flash forward** see **flash-back** above; **flash'-gun** a device holding and firing a flashbulb; **flash'light** a light that flashes periodically; a sudden light used to take photographs; an electric torch (esp. *NAm*); **flash'-over** an electric discharge over the surface of an insulator (*electr eng*); instant combustion of material that has reached a high temperature (in a burning building, etc.) as soon as oxygen reaches it; **flash'-point** the temperature at which a liquid gives off enough inflammable vapour to flash when a light is applied to it; a point in the development of a tense situation when violent action takes place; a place in the world where an outbreak of hostilities may occur at any time as a result of tension. — **flash in the pan** see under **pan**[1]; **news'flash** brief preliminary dispatch about news just becoming known. [Prob. imit.]

flask *fläsk*, *n* a narrow-necked vessel for holding liquids; a bottle; a usu. flat pocket-bottle; a horn or metal vessel for carrying powder. [O.E. *flasce*; prob. from L.L. *flascō* — L. *vasculum*, a flask.]

flat *flat*, *adj* smooth; level; shallow; spread out; monotonous; uniform; fixed, unvarying; exact; vapid, no longer brisk or sparkling; defeated; failing in effect; dejected; downright, out-and-out, sheer; (of drink) having lost all effervescence; (of feet) having little or no arch; (of shoes) not having a raised heel; relatively low (*mus*); below the right pitch (*mus*); having flats in the key-signature (*mus*); (of a battery) dead, unable to generate. — *n* a level part; a plain; (often in *pl*) an area of land covered by shallow water; something broad; a storey or floor of a house, esp. one, or part of one, used as a separate residence; the floor of a particular compartment (*naut*); a flat piece of scenery slid or lowered on to the stage; a character (♭) that lowers a note a semitone (*mus*); a note so lowered (*mus*); a punctured tyre. — *adv* in or to a flat position; evenly; too low in pitch; without qualification; exactly (used in giving time taken for e.g. a race). — *n* **flat'let** a small flat of two or three rooms. — *adv* **flat'ly**. — *n* **flat'ness**. — *vt* **flatt'en** to make flat; to knock to the ground (*colloq*); to knock out (*colloq*); to amaze. — *vi* to become flat. — *adj* **flatt'ish** somewhat flat. — *adj* or *adv* **flat'ways** or **flat'wise** with or on the flat side. — **flat'back** a pottery figure with a flat back, designed to stand on a mantelpiece, etc. and so be viewed only from the front; **flat'bed** or **flatbed truck** (*NAm*) a lorry with a flat sideless platform for its body; **flat'boat** large flat-bottomed boat for transporting goods on a river, canal, etc.; **flat'fish** a marine fish that habitually lies on one side, with unsymmetrical flat body, e.g. flounder, turbot, etc. — *adj* **flat'-footed** having flat feet; ponderous; unimaginative; uninspired; unprepared (*NAm*). — **flat-foot'edness; flat'iron** an old-fashioned iron for pressing clothes, heated on a stove, etc.; **flat'mate** a person with whom one shares a flat; **flat race** a race over a course without jumps; **flat racing; flat rate** a fixed uniform rate; **flat spin** rotation about a horizontal axis; confused excitement (*colloq*). — *adj* **flat'square** (of a television screen) flat and perfectly square, eliminating the distortion produced by convex screens; **flat tyre** a punctured tyre; **flat'worm** a tapeworm or other member of the phylum *Platyhelminthes*. — **flat broke** (*colloq*) having no money at all; **flatten out** to bring an aeroplane into a horizontal position; **flat out** at full speed; using every effort; **that's flat** I tell you plainly; **the flat** flat racing. [O.N. *flatr*, flat.]

flatter *flat'ər*, *vt* to treat with insincere praise and servile attentions, esp. in order to gain some advantage; to please with false hopes or undue praise; to represent over-favourably; to coax; to gratify. — *n* **flatt'erer**. — *adj* **flatt'ering**. — *adv* **flatt'eringly**. — *n* **flatt'ery** exaggerated or insincere praise. [Conn. with O.Fr. *flater*.]

flatulence *flat'ū-ləns* or **flatulency** *flat'ū-lən-si*, *n* distension of stomach or bowels by an excessive amount of gases formed during digestion; emptiness of utterance; pretentiousness. — *adj* **flat'ūlent**. — *adv* **flat'ūlently**. — *n* **flatus** (*flā'təs*) gas generated in the stomach or intestines. [L. *flātus*, *-ūs*, a blowing — *flāre*, to blow.]

flaunch. A variant of **flanch**.

flaunt *flönt*, *vt* to display ostentatiously; to show off. — *vi* to move ostentatiously; to carry a gaudy or saucy appearance. — *n* **flaunt'er**. — *adj* **flaunt'ing**. — *adj* **flaunt'y**. — *adv* **flaunt'ingly**. [Prob. Scand.]

flautist *flöt'ist* or (esp. in U.S.) **flutist** *floo'tist*, *n* a flute player. [It. *flautista*.]

flavour or in U.S. **flavor** *flā'vər*, *n* that quality of anything which affects the taste; a smack or relish; characteristic quality or atmosphere (*fig*); in particle physics, any of the five, or probably six, types of quark. — *vt* to impart flavour to. — *adj* **flā'vorous**. — *n* **flā'vouring** or in U.S. **flā'voring** any substance used to give a flavour to food. — *adj* **flā'vourless** or in U.S. **flā'vorless**. — *adj* **flā'voursome** or in U.S. **flā'vorsome**. — **flavour** (or in U.S. **flavor**) **of the week, month,** etc. the favourite person or thing at a given time. [O.Fr. *flaur*.]

flaw *flö*, *n* a break or crack; a defect. — *vt* to crack or break; to make defective. — *adj* **flawed**. — *adj* **flaw'less**. [O.N. *flaga*, a slab.]

flax *flaks*, *n* the fibres of the plant *Linum*, which are woven into linen cloth; the plant itself. — *adj* **flax'en** made of or resembling flax; light yellow. — *adj* **flax'y** like flax; of a light colour. — **flax'-bush** or **flax'-lily** a New Zealand plant (*Phormium*) of the lily family, yielding a valuable fibre, **New Zealand flax; flax'-dresser** someone who prepares flax for the spinner by the successive processes of rippling, retting, grassing, breaking and scutching; **flax'-seed** linseed. [O.E. *flæx*.]

flay *flā*, *vt* to strip off the skin from; to flog; to subject to savage criticism. — *n* **flay'er**. [O.E. *flēan*.]

flea *flē*, *n* any of an order of wingless, very agile, parasitic, blood-sucking insects. — **flea'-bag** (*slang*) a sleeping-bag; a distasteful place, esp. used of lodgings; **flea'-bane** a name for various composite plants (*Erigeron*, *Pulicaria*, etc.) whose strong smell is said to drive away fleas; **flea'-bite** the bite of a flea; a small mark caused by the bite; a trifle, a slight inconvenience (*fig*). — *adj* **flea'-bitten** bitten by fleas; shabby, badly looked-after; mean (*fig*); having small reddish spots on a lighter background, esp. of horses. — **flea'-circus** a show of performing fleas; **flea market** (*colloq*) a shop, etc. selling second-hand goods, orig. esp. clothes; **flea'pit** a shabby public building, esp. a cinema, supposedly infested with vermin; **flea'wort** any of several European and Eurasian plants, some of which were formerly used to drive away fleas; same as **ploughman's spikenard**. — **a flea in one's ear** a stinging rebuff. [O.E. *flēah*.]

flèche *flesh*, (*archit*) *n* a slender spire rising from the intersection of the nave and transepts in some large churches. [Fr., arrow.]

fléchette or **flechette** *flā-shet'*, *n* a steel dart dropped or thrown from an aeroplane, esp. in World War I; a dart fired from a gun. [Fr., dart, dimin. of *flèche*, arrow.]

fleck *flek, n* a spot or speckle; a little bit of a thing. — *vt* **fleck** or **fleck'er** to spot or speckle. — *adj* **flecked** spotted, dappled. [O.N. *flekkr*, a spot.]

fled *fled, pa t* and *pa p* of **flee**.

fledge *flej, vt* to furnish with feathers or wings; to bring up a young bird until it is ready to fly. — *vi* to acquire feathers for flying. — *adj* **fledged**. — *n* **fledg'ling** or **fledge'ling** a bird just fledged; a very immature or inexperienced person, a recently formed organisation, etc. — Also *adj*. [M.E. *fligge*, *flegge* — an assumed O.E. (Kentish) *flecge*.]

flee *flē, vi* to run away, as from danger; to disappear. — *vt* to run away from, leave hurriedly: — *pr p* **flee'ing**; *pa t* and *pa p* **fled**. — *n* **flē'er**. [O.E. *flēon*.]

fleece *flēs, n* a sheep's coat of wool; the wool shorn from a sheep at one time; anything like a fleece in appearance or texture. — *vt* to shear; to plunder; to charge (a person) exorbitantly; to cover, as with wool. — *adj* **fleeced** having a fleece. — *adj* **fleece'less**. — *n* **fleec'er** someone who strips, plunders or charges exorbitantly. — *adj* **fleec'y** woolly; like a fleece. [O.E. *flēos*.]

fleer[1] *flēr, vi* to make wry faces in contempt; to jeer. — *n* mockery; a gibe. [Cf. Norw. *flira*, Sw. *flissa*, to titter.]

fleer[2]. See **flee**.

fleet[1] *flēt, n* a number of ships, aircraft, motor cars, etc. owned by the same company or otherwise associated; a navy; a division of a navy under an admiral. [O.E. *flēot*, a ship — *flēotan*, to float.]

fleet[2] *flēt, adj* swift; nimble. — *n* **fleet'ness**. [Prob. O.N. *fliōtr*, swift; but ult. cognate with **fleet**[3].]

fleet[3] *flēt, vi* to flit, pass swiftly. — *adj* **fleet'ing** passing quickly; transient; temporary. — *adv* **fleet'ingly**. [O.E. *flēotan*, to float.]

Fleet Street *flēt strēt, n* journalism or its ways and traditions, from the street in London in which many newspaper offices were formerly situated.

Flemish *flem'ish, adj* of or belonging to the Flemings, or Flanders or their language. — *n* the Flemings as a people; one of the two languages of Belgium, virtually identical with Dutch. — *n* **Flem'ing** a native of Flanders; a Flemish-speaking Belgian. [Du. *Vlaamsch*.]

flench *flench*, **flense** *flens* or **flinch** *flinch, vt* to cut up the blubber of, e.g. a whale; to flay. [Dan. *flense*.]

flesh *flesh, n* muscular tissue; all the living substance of the body of similar composition to muscle; the soft substance that covers the bones of animals; the bodies of animals and (sometimes) birds, but not fish, used as food; the body, not the soul or spirit; human bodily nature; mankind; kin; one's own family; bodily appetites; excess weight; the soft substance of fruit, esp. the part fit to be eaten. — *vt* to train to an appetite for flesh, esp. dogs for hunting; (of e.g. a sword) to use upon flesh; to use for the first time. — *adj* **fleshed** (*flesht*) having flesh; fat. — *n* **flesh'er** an instrument for scraping hides; a butcher (esp. *Scot*). — *n* **flesh'iness**. — *npl* **flesh'ings** actors' flesh-coloured tights. — *adj* **flesh'less**. — *n* **flesh'liness**. — *adj* **flesh'ly** corporeal; carnal; not spiritual. — Also *adv*. — *adj* **flesh'y** fat; pulpy; plump. — **flesh'-brush** a brush used for rubbing the skin to excite circulation; **flesh'-colour** the normal colour of the skin of a member of a white-skinned race; **flesh'-fly** a fly (esp. *Sarcophaga*) whose larvae feed on flesh; **flesh'pot** (usu. in *pl*) high living; a place where entertainment of a sexual nature is on offer, e.g. a striptease club; a city known to provide an abundance of this kind of entertainment; **flesh wound** a wound not reaching beyond the flesh. — **flesh and blood** bodily or human nature; **flesh out** to give substance to, elaborate on (an idea, etc.); **in the flesh** in bodily life, alive; incarnate; in person, actually present; **make someone's flesh creep** to arouse a feeling of horror in someone; **one flesh** united in marriage; **press flesh** see under **press**; **one's own flesh and blood** one's own family. [O.E. *flǣsc*.]

fletch *flech, vt* to feather. — *n* **fletch'er** a person who makes arrows. [Fr. *flèche*, an arrow, O.Fr. *flecher*, a fletcher.]

fleur-de-lis or **fleur-de-lys** *flœr-də-lē', n* the iris; an ornament and heraldic bearing of disputed origin (an iris, three lilies, etc.), borne by the kings of France: — *pl* **fleurs-de-lis'** or **fleurs-de-lys'** (*flœr-*). [Fr.; *lis*, being O.Fr. *liz* — L. *lilium*, lily.]

flew[1] *flōō, pa t* of **fly**.

flew[2] *flōō, n* the pendulous upper lip of a bloodhound or similar dog (usu. in *pl*).

flex *fleks, vt* and *vi* to bend; to contract (a muscle). — *n* a bending; a flexible cord or line, esp. of insulated electrical cable. — *combining form* **flex'i-** flexible. — *n* **flexibil'ity**. — *adj* **flex'ible** easily bent; pliant; adaptable; docile. — *n* **flex'ibleness**. — *adv* **flex'ibly**. — *npl* **flex'ihours** hours of working under flexitime. — *adj* **flex'ile** (*-īl* or esp. in N.Am. *-əl*) flexible. — *n* **flexion** (*flek'shən*) a bend; a fold; the action of a flexor muscle; inflexion (*gram*). — *n* **flex'itime** a system of flexible working hours in which an agreed total of hours may be worked at times to suit the worker, often with the proviso that each day certain hours (**core times**) are included. — *n* **flexog'raphy** (printed matter, esp. on plastic, produced by) a method of rotary printing using flexible rubber plates and spirit-based inks. — *n* **flex'or** a muscle that bends a joint, as opp. to an *extensor*. — *adj* **flex'ūose** or **flex'ūous** full of windings and turnings; undulating. — *adj* **flexural** (*flek'shər-əl*). — *n* **flex'ure** a bend or turning; the curving of a line or surface (*math*); the bending of loaded beams. — **flexible disk** (*comput*) a floppy disk. — **flex one's muscles** to cause the muscles of one's arms, shoulders, etc. to contract, in order to display them, test them as a preliminary to a trial of strength, etc. (often *fig*). [L. *flectĕre*, *flexum*, to bend.]

flibbertigibbet *flib'ər-ti-jib-it, n* a flighty, gossipy or mischievous person. [Poss. imit. of meaningless chatter.]

flick[1] *flik, vt* to strike lightly, as with a lash or a fingernail. — *n* a stroke of this kind or the sound made by it. — **flick'-knife** a knife the blade of which springs out when a button in the handle is pressed. — **flick through** to turn the pages of (a book, etc.) idly, or in order to get a rough impression of it. [Echoic.]

flick[2] *flik*, (*slang*) *n* a cinema film; (in *pl*) the cinema. [**flicker**.]

flicker *flik'ər, vi* to flutter or quiver; to burn unsteadily, as a flame. — *n* an act of flickering, a flickering movement or light. — *adv* **flick'eringly**. [O.E. *flicorian*; imit.]

flier, flies. See **fly**.

flight[1] *flīt, n* a passing through the air; a soaring; distance flown; (of a ball in sports) pace or trajectory; a series of steps; a flock of birds flying together; a group of birds born in the same season; the power of flying; the art or the act of flying with wings or in an aeroplane or other machine; a unit of the air force equivalent to a platoon in the army; a regular air journey, numbered and at a fixed time; an aircraft making such a journey; a line of hurdles across a race-track. — *vt* to cause (birds) to fly up; to shoot (wildfowl) in flight; to put a feather in (an arrow); to impart a deceptive trajectory or a deceptively slow speed to (a cricket ball). — *adv* **flight'ily**. — *n* **flight'iness**. — *adj* **flight'less** without power of flying. — *adj* **flight'y** changeable; irresponsible; flirtatious. — **flight attendant** (esp. *NAm*) a member of the cabin crew on an aeroplane; a steward or stewardess; **flight crew** the members of an aircraft crew whose responsibility is operation and navigation; **flight'-deck** the deck of an aircraft-carrier where the planes take off and land; the compartment for the crew in an aircraft; **flight'-feather** a quill of a bird's wing; **flight lieutenant** a Royal Air Force officer of rank corresponding to naval lieutenant or army captain; **flight path** the course (to be) taken by an aircraft, spacecraft, etc.; **flight plan** a statement of the proposed schedule of an aircraft flight; **flight'-recorder** a device which records on tape or wire information about the functioning of an aircraft and its systems, used in determining the cause of an air crash. — **flight of fancy** an instance of rather free speculation or indulgence in imagination; **in the first** or **top flight** in the highest class. [O.E. *flyht* — *flēogan*, to fly.]

flight² *flīt*, *n* an act of fleeing. — **take flight** to flee; to disappear quickly (*fig*). [Assumed O.E. *flyht*; cf. *flēon*, to flee.]

flimflam *flim'flam*, *n* a trick, deception; idle, meaningless talk; nonsense. [Cf. **flam.**]

flimsy *flim'zi*, *adj* thin; light; without solidity, strength or reason; weak. — *n* transfer-paper; a carbon copy on thin paper. — *adv* **flim'sily** in a flimsy manner. — *n* **flim'siness.** [Prob. suggested by **film.**]

flinch¹ *flinch* or *flinsh*, *vi* to shrink back, from pain, fear, etc.; to fail (in a duty, etc.; often with *from*). — *n* **flinch'er.** — *n* and *adj* **flinch'ing.** — *adv* **flinch'ingly.** [Prob. conn. with M.E. *fleechen*, O.Fr. *flechir*, L. *flectěre*, to bend.]

flinch². See **flench.**

flinder *flin'dər*, *n* (usu. in *pl*) a splinter or small fragment. [Norw. *flindra*, a splinter.]

fling *fling*, *vt* to throw, cast, toss; to send forth; to send suddenly; to cause to fall. — *vi* to throw the body about; to dash or rush, throw oneself impetuously: — *pa t* and *pa p* **flung.** — *n* a cast or throw; a try; a period of complete freedom, full enjoyment of pleasure; a brief love affair; a lively Scottish country-dance. — *n* **fling'er.** — **full fling** at the utmost speed, recklessly. [Cf. O.N. *flengja*; Sw. *flänga.*]

flint *flint*, *n* a hard mineral, a variety of quartz, from which fire is readily struck with steel; a concretion of silica; a piece of flint, esp. one used for striking fire, or one manufactured into an implement; a small piece of an iron alloy, used to produce a spark in cigarette lighters; anything proverbially hard. — *adj* made of flint; hard. — *adv* **flint'ily.** — *n* **flint'iness.** — *adj* **flint'y** consisting of, abounding in, or like flint; hard; cruel; obdurate. — **flint glass** a very fine and pure lead glass, orig. made of calcined flints; **flint'lock** a gunlock or gun with a flint. [O.E. *flint.*]

flip *flip*, *vt* and *vi* to fillip; to flick; to spin in the air; to flap. — *vi* to become very excited or enthusiastic (*slang*); to go mad (*slang*). — *n* a fillip; a flick; a hot drink of beer and spirits sweetened, or any similar concoction; a somersault; a trip in an aeroplane, a pleasure-flight (*colloq*). — *adj* flippant; pert, over-smart. — *n* **flipp'er** an animal's limb adapted for swimming; a rubber foot-covering imitating an animal's flipper, worn by swimmers, divers, etc. — *adj* and *adv* **flipp'ing** (*colloq*) nasty, unpleasant; often used intensively or meaninglessly. — **flip'chart** a large blank pad, bound at the top, on which information can be displayed in sequence during a presentation, etc. — *adv* **flip'-flop** with repeated flapping. — Also **flip'-flap.** — *n* a type of flimsy sandal, esp. one held on the foot by a thong between the toes; a form of somersault; orig., and still in U.S. and in computing, a bistable pair of valves, transistors or circuit elements, two stable states being switched by pulses; in Britain, a similar circuit with one stable state temporarily achieved by pulse; **flip side** the side of a gramophone record carrying the song, etc., of lesser importance, the reverse of the side on whose merits the record is expected to sell; a less familiar aspect of anything. — *adj* **flip'-top** having a hinged lid which can be flipped up. — *n* a flip-top pack. — **flip one's lid** (*slang*) to go mad. [Cf. **fillip, flap.**]

flippant *flip'ənt*, *adj* pert and frivolous of speech; showing disrespectful levity. — *n* **flipp'ancy** pert fluency of speech; impertinence; levity. — *adv* **flipp'antly.** [Cf. **flip,** and O.N. *fleipa*, to prattle.]

flirt *flûrt*, *vt* to jerk; to cause to move quickly; to flick or rap. — *vi* to trifle with love; to play at courtship (with *with*); to move briskly about. — *n* a person who behaves in a flirtatious way. — *n* **flirtā'tion** the act of flirting; a light-hearted and short-lived amorous attachment. — *adj* **flirtā'tious** given to flirting; representing a light-hearted sexual invitation. — *n* **flirt'ing.** — *adv* **flirt'ingly.** — *adj* **flirt'y** flirting, flirtatious. — **flirt with** to treat (death, danger, etc.) lightly, by indulging in dare-devil behaviour, etc.; to entertain thoughts of adopting (an idea, etc.) or joining (a movement, etc.). [Perh. conn. with Fr. *fleureter*, to talk sweet nothings.]

flit *flit*, *vi* to move about lightly; to fly silently or quickly; to be unsteady or easily moved; to move house, change one's abode (*colloq*, esp. *Scot*); to do this stealthily in order to avoid creditors, etc.: — *pr p* **flitt'ing**; *pa t* and *pa p* **flitt'ed.** — *n* **flitt'ing.** [O.N. *flytja*; Sw. *flytta.*]

flitch *flich*, *n* a side of pork salted and cured. [O.E. *flicce.*]

flitter *flit'ər*, *vi* to flutter. [**flit.**]

float *flōt*, *vi* to be supported on or suspended in a fluid; to be buoyed up; to move lightly, supported by a fluid; to seem to move in such a way; to be free from the usual attachment; to drift about aimlessly; (in weaving) to pass threads without interweaving with them; to use a float; (of a currency) to be free to fluctuate in value in international exchange (*econ*). — *vt* to cause to float; to convey on floats; to levitate; to separate by flotation; to smooth; to pare off (as turf); to launch (e.g. a scheme); to circulate (e.g. a rumour); to offer for sale (stocks, etc.) to raise capital; to launch (a company) by drawing up various documents and raising cash by selling shares. — *n* a contrivance for floating or for keeping something afloat; a blade in a paddle-wheel or water-wheel; a floating indicator attached to a fishing-line, that moves when a fish takes the bait; a tool for smoothing; a plasterer's trowel; a low cart for carrying cattle, milk, etc., or decorated as an exhibit in a street parade, etc.; a footlight or the footlights collectively; money in hand for a purpose such as to give change to customers, to provide for expenses, etc. — *adj* **float'able.** — *n* **float'age** or **flō'tage** buoyancy; that which floats; flotsam; the part of a ship above the waterline. — *n* **float'ant** an agent that causes something to float. — *n* **floatā'tion** same as **flotation.** — *n* **floatel** see **flotel.** — *n* **float'er** someone who or that which floats; a vagrant, or someone who drifts from job to job or allegiance to allegiance; a dark speck that appears to float before one's eyes, caused by dead cells and fragments of cells in the lens and vitreous humour. — *adj* **float'ing** that floats, in any sense; not fixed; fluctuating; circulating; not clearly committed to one side or the other (*politics*). — *n* action of the verb; the spreading of plaster on the surface of walls. — *adv* **float'ingly.** — *adj* **float'y.** — **float glass** glass hardened while floating on the surface of a liquid; **floating capital** goods, money, etc.; capital not permanently invested; **floating debt** unfunded debt, short-term government loan; **floating dock** a floating structure that can be sunk by admitting water to its air chambers, and raised again carrying a vessel to be repaired; **floating island** a floating aggregation of driftwood, or a mass of vegetation buoyed up from the bottom by marsh gas, or the like; a dessert consisting of egg whites floating in custard; **floating kidney** an abnormally mobile kidney; **floating policy** an insurance policy covering movable property irrespective of its location; **floating rib** see under **rib**; **floating vote** the votes of electors who are not permanently attached to any one political party; **floating voter**; **float'-stone** a porous spongelike variety of silica, so light as to float for a while on water; a bricklayer's smoothing tool. — **floating-point notation** (*comput*) the expressing of numbers in the general form $\pm$ a × bⁿ (e.g. $2{\cdot}3 \times 10^5$); **floating-point number** (*comput*) a number so expressed; **floating-point operation** (*comput*) the addition, subtraction, multiplication, or division of two floating-point numbers. [O.E. *flotian*, to float.]

floccus *flok'əs*, *n* a tuft of woolly hair; a tuft, esp. at the end of a tail; the covering of unfledged birds: — *pl* **flocci** (*flok'sī*). — *adj* **flocc'ose** (or *-ōs'*) woolly. — *adj* **flocc'ūlar.** — *vt* and *vi* **flocc'ūlate** to collect or mass together in tufts, flakes or cloudy masses. — *n* **floccūlā'tion.** — *n* **flocc'ule** a flocculus. — *n* **flocc'ūlence** flocculated condition. — *adj* **flocc'ūlent** woolly; flaky; flocculated. — *n* **flocc'ūlus** a small flock, tuft or flake; a small outgrowth of the cerebellum; a light or dark patch on the sun's surface, usu. near sunspots, caused by calcium or hydrogen vapour: — *pl* **flocculi** (*flok'ū-lī*). [L. *floccus*, a lock, a trifle; dimin. *flocculus*.]

flock¹ *flok*, *n* a company of animals, such as sheep, birds, etc.; a company generally; a church congregation, considered as the charge of a minister. — *vi* to gather or go in flocks or in crowds. — **flock'master** an owner or overseer of a flock; a sheep-farmer or shepherd. [O.E. *flocc*, a flock, a company.]

flock² *flok*, *n* a lock of wool; a tuft; cloth refuse, waste wool (also in *pl*); a woolly-looking precipitate (also in *pl*); fine particles of wool or other fibre applied to cloth to give a raised velvety surface or pattern. — **flock'-bed** a bed stuffed with wool; **flock'-paper** a wallpaper dusted over with flock. [O.Fr. *floc* — L. *floccus*, a lock of wool.]

floe *flō*, *n* a field of floating ice. [Prob. Norw. *flo*, layer — O.N. *flō*.]

flog *flog*, *vt* to beat or strike; to lash; to chastise with blows; to sell (*slang*). — *vi* and *vt* to move or progress toilingly: — *pr p* **flogg'ing**; *pa t* and *pa p* **flogged**. — *n* **flogg'ing.** — **flog a dead horse** (*colloq*) to waste time and energy on a lost or impossible cause; **flog to death** (*colloq*) to talk about, advertise, persuade, etc. too much, often producing the opposite to the desired effect. [Late; prob. an abbrev. of **flagellate.**]

flokati *flə-kä'ti*, *n* a hand-woven Greek rug with a very thick shaggy wool pile. [Gr. *phlokatē*, a peasant's blanket.]

flong *flong*, *n* papier-mâché for making moulds in stereotyping. [Fr. *flan*.]

flood *flud*, *n* a great flow of water; an inundation; a deluge; a condition of abnormally great flow in a river; a river or other water (*poetic*); the rise of the tide; any great inflow or outflow; a floodlight (*colloq*). — *vt* to submerge (land) in water; to overflow; to inundate; to supply in excessive quantity. — *vi* to overflow; to bleed profusely, as after childbirth. — *adj* **flood'ed.** — *n* **flood'ing.** — **flood'gate** a gate for allowing or stopping the flow of water; **flood lamp** a floodlight; **flood'light** lighting of a large area or surface by illumination from lamps situated at some distance (also **flood'-lighting**); one of the lamps providing such lighting. — Also *vt*: — *pa t* and *pa p* **flood'lit.** — **flood'plain** an extensive level area beside a river formed of deposits of sediment brought downstream and spread by the river in flood; **flood'tide** the rising tide; **flood'wall** a wall built as protection against floods; **flood'water**; **flood'way** an artificial passage for floodwater. — **the Flood** the deluge, described in the Old Testament, that covered the whole Earth, and from which Noah and his family and livestock escaped in the ark. [O.E. *flōd*.]

floor *flōr*, *n* the lower supporting surface of a room, etc.; a platform; rooms in a building on the same level; a bottom surface; that on which anything rests or any operation is performed; a levelled area; the ground (*colloq*); the part of a legislative assembly where members sit and speak; the (part of a hall, etc. accommodating) members of the public at a meeting, etc.; the right to speak at a meeting (esp. in the phrases *have* and *be given the floor*); the part of an exchange on which dealers operate; a lower limit of prices, etc. — *vt* to furnish with a floor; to throw or place on the floor; to vanquish, stump (*colloq*). — *adj* **floored.** — *n* **floor'ing** material for floors; a platform. — **floor'board** one of the narrow boards making up a floor; **floor'cloth** a cloth for washing floors; **floor plan** a diagram showing the layout of rooms, etc. on one storey of a building; **floor price** a fixed lowest limit to the possible price of something; **floor show** a performance on the floor of a ballroom, nightclub, etc., not on a platform; **floor'-walker** supervisor of a section of a large store, who attends to customers' complaints, etc. — **cross the floor** (of a member of parliament, etc.) to change one's allegiance from one party to another; **first floor** the floor in a house above the ground floor, the second storey; in U.S. usu. the ground floor (*adj* **first'-floor**); **hold the floor** to dominate a meeting by much speaking; **take the floor** to rise to address a meeting, or begin dancing a dance. [O.E. *flōr*.]

floozie or **floosie** *floo'zi*, (*slang*) *n* a young woman of loose morals; a prostitute, esp. a slovenly one. — Also **floo'zy** or **floo'sy**.

flop¹ *flop*, *n* a limp, heavy, flapping movement, fall or sound; a collapse; a fiasco; a failure; a place to sleep (*NAm slang*). — *adv* with a flop. — *vt* and *vi* to move with a flop; to drop heavily. — *vi* to collapse; to fail dismally. — *adv* **flopp'ily.** — *n* **flopp'iness.** — *adj* **flopp'y.** — *n* (*comput*) a floppy disk. — **floppy disk** (*comput*) a storage device in the form of a thin, bendable disk. [A form of **flap.**]

flop² *flop*, (*comput*) *n* a *floating-point operation* (q.v.).

flor *flōr*, *n* a yeasty growth which is allowed to form on the surface of sherry wines after fermentation and which gives them a nutty taste. [Sp., flower, mould, — L. *flōs*, *flōris*, a flower.]

flor. *abbrev* for floruit.

flora *flō'rə*, *n* the assemblage of plant species of a region, or age; a list or descriptive enumeration of these: — *pl* **flo'ras** or **flo'rae** (*-ē*). — *adj* **flo'ral** pertaining to floras, or to flowers. — *adv* **flo'rally.** — *n* **florescence** (*flor-es'əns*) a bursting into flower; time of flowering (*bot*). — *adj* **floresc'ent** bursting into flowers. — *n* **floret** (*flor'it*) a small flower; one of the single flowers in the head of a composite flower. — *adj* **flo'riated** or **flo'reated** decorated with floral ornament (*archit*). — *n* **floribunda** (*flōr-i-bun'də*) a plant, esp. a rose, whose flowers grow in clusters. — *adj* **flor'id** flowery; bright in colour; (of a complexion) ruddy; characterised by flowers of rhetoric, melodic figures, or other ornament; over-adorned; richly ornamental. — *n* **florid'ity.** — *adv* **flor'idly.** — *n* **flor'idness.** — *adj* **florif'erous** bearing or producing flowers. — *adj* **flo'riform** flower-shaped. — *n* **flor'ist** a cultivator or seller of flowers. — *adj* **florist'ic.** — *adv* **florist'ically.** — *n* **flor'istry** the art of cultivating or selling flowers. [L. *Flōra*, goddess of flowers; *flōs*, *flōris*, a flower.]

Florentine *flor'ən-tīn*, *adj* pertaining to *Florence* in Tuscany. — *n* a native or inhabitant of Florence. [L. *Flōrentīnus* — *Flōrentia*.]

florescent, floret, florid, etc. See under **flora**.

florin *flor'in*, *n* in Holland, the guilder; an English silver or cupro-nickel coin worth one-tenth of a pound, first minted in 1849; orig. a Florentine gold coin with a lily stamped on one side. [Fr., from It. *fiorino* — *fiore*, a lily — L. *flōs*, *flōris*.]

florist, etc. See under **flora**.

floruit *flō'rōō-it, flor'ū-* or *-ōō-*, *n* period during which a person flourished, was most active, produced most works, etc. [L., 3rd pers. sing. perf. indic. of *flōrēre*, to flourish.]

floss *flos*, *n* the rough outside of the silkworm's cocoon, and other waste of silk manufacture; fine silk in spun strands not twisted together, used in embroidery and (**dental floss**) tooth-cleaning; any loose downy or silky plant substance. — *adj* **floss'y** made of, like, or pertaining to floss; showy, overdressed (*slang*). [Prob. O.Fr. *flosche*, down; or from some Gmc. word cogate with **fleece**.]

flotage. See **floatage**.

flotation *flō-tā'shən*, *n* the act of floating; the science of floating bodies; the act of starting a business, esp. a limited liability company, by drawing up various documents and raising capital by selling shares. [**float**.]

flotel or **floatel** *flō-tel'*, *n* a platform or boat containing the sleeping accommodation and eating, leisure, etc. facilities for workers on oil-rigs. [**float** and **hotel**.]

flotilla *flo-til'ə*, *n* a fleet of small ships. [Sp., dimin. of *flota*, a fleet.]

flotsam *flot'səm*, *n* goods lost by shipwreck and found floating on the sea (see also **jetsam**). [A.Fr. *floteson* — O.Fr. *floter*, to float.]

flounce[1] *flowns*, *vi* to move abruptly or impatiently. — *n* an impatient fling, flop or movement. — *adv* with a flounce. [Prob. cognate with Norw. *flunsa*, to hurry, Sw. dialect *flunsa*, to plunge.]

flounce[2] *flowns*, *n* a hanging strip gathered and sewn to the skirt of a dress by its upper edge. — *vt* to furnish with flounces. — *n* **floun'cing** material for flounces. — *adj* **floun'cy** decorated with flounces. [Altered form of old word *frounce*, a plait or wrinkle.]

flounder[1] *flown'dər*, *vi* to struggle with violent and awkward movements; to stumble helplessly in thinking or speaking. — *n* an act of floundering. [Prob. an onomatopoeic blending of the sound and sense of earlier words like **founder** and **blunder**.]

flounder[2] *flown'dər*, *n* a name given to a number of species of flatfish. [A.Fr. *floundre*, O.Fr. *flondre*.]

flour *flowr*, *n* the finely-ground meal of wheat or other grain; the fine soft powder of any substance. — *vt* to reduce into or sprinkle with flour. — *adj* **flour'y** covered with flour; like flour. [M.E. form of **flower**.]

flourish *flur'ish*, *vi* to grow luxuriantly; to thrive; to be prosperous or vigorous; to display ostentatiously; to play or sing ostentatious passages, or ostentatiously (*mus*); to play a fanfare. — *vt* to adorn with flourishes or ornaments; to brandish in show or triumph or exuberance of spirits. — *n* showy splendour; a figure made by a bold stroke of the pen; the waving of a weapon or other object; a parade of words; a showy, fantastic, or highly ornamental passage of music. — *adj* **flour'ished** decorated with flourishes. — *adj* **flour'ishing** thriving; prosperous; making a show. — *adv* **flour'ishingly**. — *adj* **flour'ishy**. — **flourish of trumpets** a fanfare heralding an important person or people; any ostentatious introduction. [O.Fr. *florir*, *floriss-* — L. *flōs*, *flōris*, flower.]

flout *flowt*, *vt* to mock; to treat with contempt; to reject, defy (orders, etc.). — *vi* to jeer (with *at*). — *n* a jeer; a contemptuous act or speech. — *adv* **flout'ingly**. [Prob. a specialised use of *floute*, M.E. form of **flute**, to play on the flute.]

flow *flō*, *vi* to run, as water; to move or change form like a fluid; to rise or come in, as the tide; to move in a stream; to glide smoothly; to abound, run over; to run in smooth lines; to hang, loose and waving. — *vt* to cover with water: — *pa t* and *pa p* **flowed**. — *n* a stream or current; movement of, or like that of, a fluid; that which flows or has flowed; mode of flowing; the setting in of the tide; copious fluency; menstruation (*colloq*). — *adj* **flow'ing** moving, as a fluid; fluent; smooth and continuous; falling or hanging in folds or in waves. — **flow chart** or **sheet** a chart pictorially representing the nature and sequence of operations to be carried out, e.g. in a computer program or an industrial process; **flow'-meter** a device for measuring the rate of flow of a fluid in a pipe. [O.E. *flōwan*.]

flower *flow'ər* or *flowr*, *n* a growth comprising the reproductive organs of seed plants; the blossom of a plant; the flowering state; a flowering plant, esp. one valued for its blossoms; the prime of life; the best of anything; the person or thing most distinguished; the embodiment of perfection; a figure of speech; ornament of style; (in *pl*) a sublimate (e.g. **flowers of sulphur**); (in *pl*) applied to some fungous growths. — *vi* to blossom; to flourish. — *vt* to adorn or decorate with flowers or a floral design. — *n* **flower'er** a plant that flowers. — *n* **flower'iness**. — *n* and *adj* **flower'ing**. — *adj* **flower'less**. — *adj* **flower'y** full of or adorned with flowers; highly embellished, florid. — **flower'-bed** a garden bed for flowers; **flower'-bud** a bud with the unopened flower; **flower child** one of the Flower People; **flower'-garden**; **flower'-girl** a girl or woman who sells flowers in the street; **flower'-head** a close inflorescence in which all the florets grow together at the tip of the stem, rather than on separated stalks; **Flower People** (also without *cap*) colourfully dressed adherents of a cult (**Flower Power**) arising in the mid-1960s which rejected materialism and advocated peace and universal love; **flower'pot** a pot in which a plant is grown; **flower'-show** an exhibition of flowers; **flower'-stalk** the stem that supports the flower. [O.Fr. *flour* (Fr. *fleur*) — L. *flōs*, *flōris*, a flower.]

flown *flōn*, *pa p* of **fly**. — **flown cover** (*philat*) an envelope which has been carried by air over at least part of its delivery route.

fl. oz. *abbrev* for fluid ounce(s).

flu *flōō*, *n* short for **influenza**.

flub *flub*, (*N Am colloq*) *vt* to make a mess of. — Also *vi*. — *n* a gaffe; a mistake; a person given to making mistakes.

fluctuate *fluk'tū-āt*, *vi* to vary this way and that; to go up and down or to and fro; to move like a wave. — *vt* to throw into fluctuation. — *adj* **fluc'tūant**. — *adj* **fluc'tūāting**. — *n* **fluctūā'tion** alternate variation; rise and fall; motion to and fro; wavelike motion. [L. *fluctuāre*, *-ātum* — *fluctus*, a wave — *fluěre*, to flow.]

flue *flōō*, *n* a pipe for conveying hot air, smoke, flame, etc.; a small chimney; a flue pipe (*mus*); the opening by which the air escapes from the foot of a flue pipe. — *vt* **flue'-cure** to cure (tobacco) by heat introduced through flues. — *adj* **flue'-cured**. — **flue pipe** a pipe, esp. in an organ, in which the sound is produced by air impinging upon an edge.

fluent *flōō'ənt*, *adj* able to speak and write a particular language competently and with ease (usu. with *in*); spoken or written competently and with facility; voluble; (of a movement) smooth, easy, graceful. — *n* **flu'ency**. — *adv* **flu'ently**. [L. *fluēns*, *fluentis*, pres. p. of *fluěre*, to flow.]

fluff *fluf*, *n* a soft down from cotton, etc.; anything downy; a fault in performing (a play, piece of music, etc.) (*colloq*); a duffed stroke at golf, etc. (*colloq*). — *vt* to make fluffy (often with *up*). — *vt* and *vi* (*colloq*) to bungle, in sport, musical performance, etc. — *n* **fluff'iness**. — *adj* **fluff'y**. — **a bit of fluff** (*slang*) a sexually attractive woman.

flügelhorn or **flugelhorn** *flü'gəl-hörn* or *flōō'*, *n* a hunting-horn, a kind of keyed bugle. — *n* **flü'gelhornist** or **flu'gelhornist**. [Ger., wing.]

fluid *flōō'id*, *adj* that flows; unsolidified; of, using or pertaining to fluids; likely to, tending to change;

easily changed; (of a movement) smooth and graceful. — *n* a substance whose particles can move about with freedom — a liquid or gas. — *adj* **flu'idal.** — *adj* **fluid'ic.** — *vt* **fluid'ify.** — *vt* **flu'idise** or **-ize** to make fluid; to cause (fine particles) to move as a fluid, e.g. by suspending them in a current of air or gas; to fill with a specified fluid. — *n* **fluidisā'tion** or **-z-.** — *n* **fluid'ity** or **flu'idness.** — **fluid drive** a system of transmitting power smoothly through the medium of the change in momentum of a fluid, usu. oil. [L. *fluidus*, fluid — *fluĕre*, to flow.]

fluke[1] *flōōk*, *n* a flounder; a trematoid worm, esp. that which causes liver-rot in sheep, so called because of its resemblance to a miniature flounder (also **fluke'worm**). [O.E. *flōc*, a plaice.]

fluke[2] *flōōk*, *n* the barb of an anchor; a barb; a lobe of a whale's tail. [Prob. **fluke**[1].]

fluke[3] *flōōk*, *n* an accidental success. — *vt* to make, score, etc. by a fluke. — *adj* **fluk'ey** or **fluk'y.**

flume *flōōm*, *n* an artificial channel for water, for use in industry or as an amusement on which rides usu. in special boats can be taken; a ravine occupied by a stream. [O.Fr. *flum* — L. *flūmen*, a river — *fluĕre*, to flow.]

flummery *flum'ər-i*, *n* an acid jelly made from the husks of oats; blancmange; anything insipid; empty compliment, humbug, pretentiousness. [Welsh *llymru* — *llymrig*, harsh, raw.]

flummox *flum'əks*, (*colloq*) *vt* to perplex.

flump *flump*, (*colloq*) *vt* to throw down heavily. — *vi* to move or fall with a flop or thud. — *n* the dull sound so produced. [Imit.]

flung *flung*, *pa t* and *pa p* of **fling.**

flunk *flungk*, (*slang*) *vi* to fail in an examination; to be dismissed from college, etc. for such failure (with *out*). — Also *vt* and *n*. [Perh. combined **flinch**[1] and **funk**[1].]

flunkey or **flunky** *flung'ki*, *n* orig. a livery servant or footman; any servant; a servile person. [Perh. orig. *flanker*, one who runs alongside.]

fluor *flōō'ər* or *-ör*, *n* fluorite. — *vi* **fluoresce** (*-ər-es'*) to demonstrate fluorescence. — *n* **fluoresc'ence** the property of some substances (e.g. fluor) of emitting, when exposed to radiation, rays of greater wavelength than those received. — *adj* **fluoresc'ent.** — *vt* **flu'oridate, flu'oridise** or **-ize** to add a fluoride to (a water or milk supply). — *n* **fluoridā'tion.** — *n* **flu'oride** a compound of fluorine with another element or radical; (*loosely*) sodium fluoride or sodium monofluorophosphate as the active ingredient in toothpaste. — *n* **flu'orine** (*-ēn*) an element (atomic no. 9; symbol **F**), a pale greenish-yellow gas. — *n* **fluorite** (*flōō'ər-īt*) a mineral, calcium fluoride. — **flu'orocarbon** any of a series of compounds of fluorine and carbon highly resistant to heat and chemical action; **flu'oroscope** an instrument for X-ray examination by means of a fluorescent screen. — *adj* **fluoroscop'ic.** — **fluoros'copy; flu'orspar** fluorite. — **fluorescent lighting** brighter lighting obtained for the same consumption of electricity, by using fluorescent material to convert ultraviolet radiation in the electric lamp into visible light. [L. *fluor*, flow, from its use as a flux.]

flurry *flur'i*, *n* a sudden blast or gust; agitation; a sudden commotion; bustle; a fluttering mass of things, such as snowflakes. — *vt* to agitate, to confuse: — *pr p* **flurr'ying;** *pa t* and *pa p* **flurr'ied.** [Prob. onomatopoeic, suggested by **flaw** and **hurry.**]

flush[1] *flush*, *n* a sudden flow; a flow of blood to the skin, causing redness; a suffusion of colour, esp. red; the device on a lavatory which is operated to release a flow of water to clean the pan; a sudden growth; a renewal of growth; a rush of feeling; bloom, freshness, vigour; abundance. — *vi* to glow; to become red in the face; to flow swiftly, suddenly or copiously. — *vt* to cleanse by a copious flow of water (as a toilet); to clear by a blast of air; to cause to glow; to elate, excite the spirits of. — *adj* overflowing; abounding; well supplied, as with money; flushed. — *adj* **flushed** suffused with ruddy colour; excited. — *n* **flush'ing.** — *n* **flush'ness.** — **in the** (or **one's**) **first flush** young, youthful; **in the first flush of** in the early stages of (esp. youth), when one is at a peak of vigour, excitement, etc. [Prob. **flush**[2] infl. by **flash** and **blush.**]

flush[2] *flush*, *vi* to start up like an alarmed bird. — *vt* to rouse and cause (esp. birds) to move off; to force from concealment (with *out*). — *n* the act of starting. [Prob. onomatopoeic; suggested by **fly, flutter** and **rush**[1].]

flush[3] *flush*, *vt* to make even; to fill up to the level of a surface (often with *up*). — *adj* having the surface in one plane with the adjacent surface (with *with*). — Also *adv*. [Prob. related to **flush**[1].]

flush[4] *flush*, *n* in card-playing, a hand in which all the cards or a specified number are of the same suit. — *adj* (*poker*) consisting of cards all of the same suit. — **busted flush** a flush that is never completed (*poker*); something that has to be abandoned as a failure (*fig*); **straight flush** (*poker*) a sequence of five cards of the same suit (**royal flush,** if headed by ace). [Prob. Fr. *flux* — L. *fluxus*, flow; infl. by **flush**[1].]

fluster *flus'tər*, *n* hurrying; flurry; confused agitation. — *vt* to confuse; to make hot and flurried; to fuddle with drink. — *vi* to bustle; to be agitated or fuddled. — *adj* **flus'tery** confused. [O.N. *flaustr*, hurry.]

flute *flōōt*, *n* a wind instrument, esp. either of two types consisting of a wooden or metal tube with holes stopped by the fingertips or by keys, the one type blown from the end through a fipple, the other (also called *transverse flute*) held horizontally and played by directing the breath across a mouth-hole; in organ-building, a stop with stopped wooden pipes, having a flute-like tone; a longitudinal groove, as on a pillar (*archit*); a tall and narrow wine-glass. — *vi* to play the flute; to make fluty sounds. — *vt* to play or sing in soft flute-like tones; to form flutes or grooves in. — *adj* **flut'ed** ornamented with flutes, channels or grooves. — *n* **flut'er.** — *n* **flut'ing** flute-playing or similar sounds; longitudinal furrowing. — *n* **flut'ist** same as **flautist.** — *adj* **flut'y** like a flute in tone. [Perh. O.Fr. *fleüte*.]

flutter *flut'ər*, *vi* to move about nervously, aimlessly, or with bustle; (of a bird) to flap wings; (of a flag, etc.) to flap in the air; to vibrate, e.g. of a pulse, to beat irregularly; to be in agitation or in uncertainty. — *vt* to throw into disorder; to move in quick motions. — *n* quick, irregular motion; agitation; confusion; a gambling transaction (*colloq*); a small speculation (*colloq*); in wind-instrument playing, rapid movement of the tongue as for a rolled 'r' (also **flutt'er-tonguing**); in sound reproduction, undesirable variation in pitch or loudness; abnormal oscillation of a part of an aircraft. [O.E. *flotorian*, to float about.]

fluvial *flōō'vi-əl*, *adj* of, belonging to, found in or occurring in rivers. [L. *fluviālis* — *fluvius*, a river, *fluĕre*, to flow.]

flux *fluks*, *n* the act of flowing; a flow of matter; a state of flow or continuous change; matter discharged; excrement; an easily fused substance, esp. one added to another to make it more fusible; the rate of flow of mass, volume or energy (*phys*). — *vt* to melt; to apply flux to when soldering. — *vi* to flow; to fuse. — *n* **fluxion** (*fluk'shən*) a flowing or discharge; excessive flow of blood or fluid to any organ (*med*); a difference or variation; the rate of change of a continuously varying quantity (*math*). — **in a state of flux** in an unsettled, undetermined state. [O.Fr., — L. *fluxus* — *fluĕre*, to flow.]

fly *flī*, *vi* to move through the air, esp. on wings or in an aircraft; to operate an aircraft; to move swiftly; to hurry; to pass quickly; to flee; to flutter. — *vt* to cause to fly, e.g. a kite, aircraft, etc.; to conduct or transport by air; to cross or pass by flying; to avoid, flee from: — *pa t* **flew** (*flōō*); *pa p* **flown** (*flōn*); *3rd pers sing present indicative* **flies**. — *n* any insect of the *Diptera*; often so widely used, esp. in combination — e.g. *butterfly, dragonfly, mayfly* — as to be virtually equivalent to insect; a fish-hook dressed in imitation of a fly; a flap, esp. a tent-door; a flap of material covering, e.g. trouser opening; the trouser fastener, e.g. zip; the free end of a flag, or the like; a flywheel; (in *pl*) the large space above the proscenium in a theatre, from which the scenes, etc., are controlled: — *pl* **flies**. — *adj* (*slang*) wide-awake, knowing; surreptitious, sly. — *n* **flier** or **flyer** (*flī'ər*) a person who flies or flees; an airman; an object, e.g. a train, moving at top speed; an ambitious person, esp. one for whom fast promotion in the workplace is assured; a financial speculation (*slang*); a rectangu lar step in stairs; a flying leap (*colloq*); a handbill. — *n* **fly'ing**. — *adj* that flies or can fly; moving or passing very rapidly; organised for speedy action or transfer to any location as the need arises; (of a visit) very brief. — **fly agaric** a poisonous type of toadstool, *Amanita muscaria*, used in the production of flypaper and having hallucinogenic properties; **fly ash** fine particles of ash released into the air during e.g. the burning of fossil fuels in power stations; **fly'blow** the egg of a fly, esp. when found in meat. — *adj* **fly'-blown** tainted with flies' eggs or maggots (also *fig*). — **fly'boat** a long, narrow, swift boat used on canals; **fly'book** a case like a book for holding fishing-flies; **fly'-by** a flight, at low altitude or close range, past a place, target, etc., for observation; **fly'-by-night** someone who gads about at night; an absconding debtor; an irresponsible person. — *adj* irresponsible, esp. in business matters; unreliable; transitory. — *adj* **fly-by-wire'** (of the control systems of an aircraft) operated electronically, not mechanically. — **fly'catcher** a name for various birds that catch flies on the wing; **fly'-dressing** fly-tying; **fly'-drive** a package holiday in which the rental of a car, etc. is included and the vehicle collected at the destination airport. — Also *adj*. — **fly'-dumping** unauthorised disposal of waste materials. — *vi* **fly'-fish** to fish using artificial flies as lure. — **fly'-fisher**; **fly'-fishing**; **fly front** a concealed fastening on a jacket, coat, etc. — *adj* **fly'-fronted**. — **flying boat** a seaplane with a boat's body; **flying bomb** a bomb in the form of a jet-propelled aeroplane. — *npl* **flying colours** flags unfurled; triumphant success. — **Flying Corps** the precursor (1912–18) of the Royal Air Force; **flying doctor** a doctor, esp. orig. in the remote parts of Australia, who can be called by radio, etc., and who flies to visit patients; **flying fish** a fish that can leap from the water and sustain itself in the air for a short time by its long pectoral fins, as if flying; **flying fox** a large fruit-eating bat; **flying jib** in a vessel with more than one jib, the one set furthest forward; **flying leap** one made from a running start; **flying lemur** an animal (not in fact a lemur) of the islands of SE Asia, whose fore- and hindlimbs are connected by a fold of skin; **flying lizard** a dragon lizard; **flying machine** a power-driven aircraft; **flying officer** an officer in the Royal Air Force of rank corresponding to sub-lieutenant in the navy and lieutenant in the army; **flying pickets** mobile pickets available for reinforcing the body of local pickets during a strike; **flying saucer** any of several disc-like flying objects reported to have been seen by various people and alleged to be craft from outer space; **flying squad** a body of police, etc. with special training, available for duty where the need arises, or one organised for fast action or movement; **flying squirrel** a name for several kinds of squirrels with a parachute of skin between the fore and hind legs; also applied to a flying phalanger; **flying start** (in a race) a start given with the competitors already in motion; an initial advantage; a promising start; **flying suit** a pilot's one-piece suit; a similar fashion garment, worn esp. by women; **fly'-kick** a kick made while running; **fly'leaf** a blank leaf at the beginning or end of a book; **fly'-man** one who works the ropes in theatre flies; **fly'over** a road or railway-line carried over the top of another one at an intersection; a processional flight of aircraft, a fly-past (*US*); **fly'paper** a sticky or poisonous paper for destroying flies; **fly'-past** a ceremonial flight analogous to a march past; **fly'pitch** (*colloq*) a market-stall for which the operator has no licence; **fly'pitcher**; **flypost'ing** the practice of affixing political, etc. bills illegally; **fly'-sheet** a piece of canvas that can be fitted to the roof of a tent to give additional protection; a handbill; **fly'-spray** (an aerosol containing) an insecticide; **fly'-tipping** fly dumping; **fly'trap** a trap to catch flies; a plant that traps flies (*bot*); **fly'-tying** making artificial flies for angling; **fly'-under** a road or railway-line carried under another one at an intersection; **fly'way** a migration route used by birds; **fly'weight** a weight category applied variously in boxing, wrestling and weight-lifting; a sportsman of the specified weight for the category (e.g. in professional boxing the lowest weight — **min'i-flyweight** (under 48 kg./105 lb.), **light'-** or **ju'nior-flyweight** (maximum 49 kg./108 lb.), **fly'weight** (maximum 51 kg./112 lb.) and **su'per-flyweight** (maximum 52 kg./115 lb.); **fly'-wheel** a large wheel with a heavy rim applied to machinery to equalise the effect of the driving effort. — **a fly in the ointment** some slight flaw which corrupts something of value; a minor disadvantage in otherwise favourable circumstances; **a fly on the wall** the invisible observer that one would like to be on certain occasions; **fly a kite** see **kite-flying**; **fly at** or **upon** to attack suddenly; **fly high** to aim high, be ambitious; **fly in the face of** to oppose, defy; to be at variance with; **fly off the handle** (*slang*) to lose one's temper; **fly open** to open suddenly or violently; **let fly** to attack (also *fig*); to throw or send off; **like flies** (dying, etc.) in vast numbers with little resistance like insects; **no flies on** no lack of alertness or shrewdness in. [O.E. *flēogan*, to fly, past t. *flēah*; *flēoge*, fly, insect.]

FM *abbrev* for: Field Marshal; frequency modulation.

Fm (*chem*) *symbol* for fermium.

Fmk *abbrev* for Finnish mark (unit of currency).

FMS *abbrev* for flexible manufacturing system.

FO *abbrev* for: Field Officer; Flying Officer; Foreign Office; Full Organ.

fo. or **fol.** *abbrev* for folio.

foal *fōl*, *n* the young of the horse family. — *vi* and *vt* to give birth to (a foal). — **in foal** or **with foal** (of a mare) pregnant. [O.E. *fola*.]

foam *fōm*, *n* bubbles on surface of liquid; a suspension of gas in a liquid; frothy saliva or perspiration; any of many light, cellular materials, rigid or flexible, produced by aerating a liquid, then solidifying it; the sea (*poetic*). — *vi* to gather or produce foam; to come in foam; to be furious (*colloq*). — *vt* to pour out in foam; to fill or cover with foam. — *adv* **foam'ily**. — *n* **foam'iness**. — *n* and *adj* **foam'ing**. — *adv* **foam'ingly**. — *adj* **foam'less**. — *adj* **foam'y** frothy. — **foam at the mouth** to be extremely angry (*colloq*); to produce frothy saliva. [O.E. *fām*.]

fob[1] *fob*, *vt* (*archaic* except as **fob off**) to cheat, trick; to put off (with excuses, prevarication, etc.); to foist, palm. [Cf. Ger. *foppen*, to jeer.]

fob[2] *fob*, *n* a small watch pocket in a waistcoat or the waistband of trousers; a chain attaching a watch to a waistcoat, etc.; a decoration hanging from such a chain; a decorative tab on a key-ring. — **fob'-watch**. [Perh. conn. with L.Ger. *fobke*, little pocket.]

f o b *abbrev* for free on board.
FOC *abbrev* for father of the chapel (in a trade union).
f o c *abbrev* for free of charge.
focal, foci, focimeter. See **focus.**
fo'c'sle *fōk'sl, n* a contracted form of **forecastle.**
focus *fō'kəs, n* any central point; the point or region of greatest activity; the point of origin (as of an earthquake); a fixed point such that the distances of a point on a conic section from it and from the directrix have a constant ratio (*geom*); a point in which rays converge after reflection or refraction, or from which (*virtual focus*) they seem to diverge (*optics*); the position, or condition, of sharp definition of an image: — *pl* **foci** (*fō'sī*) or **fo'cuses.** — *vt* to bring or adjust to a focus; to adjust so as to get a sharp image of; to concentrate: — *pr p* **fo'cusing;** *pa t* and *pa p* **fo'cused;** also (by some) **fo'cussing** and **fo'cussed.** — *adj* **fō'cal** of or belonging to a focus. — *n* **focalisā'tion** or **-z-.** — *vt* **fō'calise** or **-ize** to focus. — *adv* **fō'cally.** — *n* **focimeter** (*fō-sim'ə-tər*) an instrument for measuring the focal length of a lens. — **in focus** placed or adjusted so as to secure distinct vision, or a sharp, definite image. [L. *fŏcus*, a hearth.]
fodder *fod'ər, n* food supplied to cattle; people seen, callously, as a plentiful and consumable commodity (as in *cannon fodder*). — *vt* to supply with fodder. — *n* **fodd'erer.** — *n* **fodd'ering.** [O.E. *fōdor*.]
FOE or **FoE** *abbrev* for Friends of the Earth.
foe *fō*, (*literary* or *archaic*) *n* an enemy: — *pl* **foes.** [M.E. *foo* — O.E. *fāh, fā* (adj.) and *gefā* (noun).]
foehn. See **föhn.**
foetid. See **fetid**.
foetus or **fetus** *fē'təs, n* the young animal in the egg or in the womb, after its parts are distinctly formed. — *adj* **foe'tal** or **fē'tal.** — *n* **foe'ticide** or **fē'ticide** destruction of a foetus. — *adj* **foeticī'dal** or **fēticī'dal.** — *n* **foetos'copy** or **fetos'copy** a procedure for viewing the foetus directly, within the uterus, or for taking a sample of foetal blood from the placenta, by inserting a hollow needle through the abdomen into the uterus, for ascertaining any disorder. — **foetal alcohol syndrome** the *in vitro* alcohol abuse of a baby by the mother. [L. *fētus*, offspring.]
fog[1] *fog, n* a thick mist; watery vapour condensed about dust particles in drops; cloudy obscurity; confusion, bewilderment; a blurred patch on a negative, print or transparency (*phot*). — *vt* to shroud in fog; to obscure; to confuse; to produce fog on (*phot*). — *vi* (esp. with *up* or *over*) to become coated, clouded, blurred or confused; to be affected by fog (*phot*). — *adj* **fogged** (*fogd*) clouded, obscured; bewildered. — *adv* **fogg'ily.** — *n* **fogg'iness.** — *adj* **fogg'y** misty; damp; fogged; clouded in mind; stupid. — *adj* **fog'less.** — **fog'-bank** a dense mass of fog like a bank of land. — *adj* **fog'bound** impeded or brought to a standstill by fog. — **fog'horn** a horn used as a warning signal by or to ships in foggy weather; a big bellowing voice; **fog'-lamp** a lamp, esp. on a vehicle, used to improve visibility in fog; **fog'-signal** a detonating cap or other audible warning used in fog. — **not have the foggiest** (*colloq*) not to have the least idea.
fog[2] *fog* or **foggage** *fog'ij, n* grass that grows after the hay is cut.
fogy or **fogey** *fō'gi, n* a dull old fellow (also **old fog(e)y**); someone with antiquated notions. — *adj* **fo'gyish** or **fo'geyish.** — *n* **fo'gyism** or **fo'geyism.** [Prob. from *foggy*, moss-grown.]
föhn or **foehn** *fœn, n* a hot dry wind which blows to the lee of a mountain range, esp. the Alps. [Ger., — Romansch *favugn* — L. *Favōnius*, the west wind.]
foible *foi'bl, n* a weakness; a penchant; a failing. [O.Fr. *foible*, weak; see ety. for **feeble.**]
foie gras *fwä grä*, (Fr.) *n* fat liver (of goose) made into **pâté de foie gras** (*pä-tā də*).
foil[1] *foil, vt* to defeat; to baffle; to frustrate. — *n* an incomplete fall in wrestling; a blunt fencing sword with a button on the point. [O.Fr. *fuler*, to stamp or crush — L. *fullō*, a fuller of cloth.]
foil[2] *foil, n* a leaf or thin plate of metal, such as tinfoil; a mercury coating on a mirror; metal-coated paper; a thin leaf of metal put under a precious stone to show it to advantage; anything that serves to set off something else; a small arc in tracery; an aerofoil or hydrofoil. — *adj* **foil'borne** (of a craft) lifted up from, or travelling along, the water on hydrofoils. [O.Fr. *foil* (Fr. *feuille*) — L. *folium*, a leaf.]
foist *foist, vt* to pass off (*on* or *upon* the person affected); to insert wrongfully (*in* or *into* the thing affected); to bring in by stealth. — *n* **foist'er.** [Prob. Du. dialect *vuisten*, to take in hand.]
fol. *abbrev* for: followed; following.
folate. See **folic acid.**
fold[1] *fōld, n* a doubling of anything upon itself; a crease; the concavity of anything folded; a part laid over on another. — *vt* to lay in folds, double over; to enclose in a fold or folds, to wrap up. — *vi* to become folded; to be capable of folding; (of a business, etc.) to collapse, cease functioning (also with *up*; *colloq*). — *adj* **fold'able.** — *n* **fold'er** the person or thing that folds; a folding case for loose papers. — *adj* **fold'ing** that folds, or that can be folded. — *n* a fold or plait; the bending of strata, usu. as the result of compression (*geol*). — *adj* **fold'away** which can be folded and put away. — **folding-door'** a door consisting of two parts hung on opposite jambs; **folding money** (*colloq*) paper money. — *adj* and *n* **fold'-out** (a large page, e.g. containing a diagram) folded to fit into a book, and to be unfolded for inspection (also called **gate'fold**). — **fold in** to mix in carefully and gradually (*cookery*). [O.E. *faldan*, to fold.]
fold[2] *fōld, n* an enclosure for protecting domestic animals, esp. sheep; a church or its congregation (*fig*). [O.E. *falod, fald*, a fold, stall.]
-fold *-fōld, sfx* (with numerals) times, as in *tenfold.* [M.E. *-fold, -fald* — O.E. *-feald, -fald.*]
folderol. See **falderal.**
foliaceous *fō-li-ā'shəs, adj* leaflike; like a foliage leaf; leaf-bearing; laminated. **[foliage.]**
foliage *fō'li-ij, n* leaves collectively; a mass of leaves; plant forms in art. — *adj* **fō'liaged** having foliage; worked like foliage. — *adj* **fō'liar** pertaining to leaves; resembling leaves. — *vt* **fō'liate** to cover with leaf-metal; to number the leaves (not pages) of. — *vi* to split into laminae; (of a plant) to grow leaves. — *adj* **fō'liated** decorated with leaf ornaments or foils; consisting of layers or laminae. — *n* **fōliā'tion** or **fō'liature.** — *n* **fō'liole** a leaflet of a compound leaf (*bot*); a small leaflike structure. — **foliage plant** one grown for the beauty of its foliage; **foliar feed** a plant food applied in solution to the leaves. [L. *folium*, a leaf.]
folic acid *fō'lik as'id, n* an acid in the vitamin B complex (*tetrahydrofolate*), deficiency of which causes anaemia, etc. (see also **pteroic acid** under **pterin**). — *adj* **fo'late** of or pertaining to folic acid. — *n* (a salt of) folic acid. [L. *folium*, a leaf (because occurring in green leaves).]
folie *fo-lē*, (Fr.) *n* madness, insanity; folly. — **folie de grandeur** (*grā-dœr*) delusions of grandeur.
folio *fō'li-ō, n* a leaf (two pages) of a book; a sheet of paper once folded; a large-format book of such sheets; a leaf of paper in a manuscript, numbered only on the front; a page in an account-book, or two opposite pages numbered as one (*bookkeeping*); a page number in a book (*printing*); a wrapper for loose papers: — *pl* **fō'lios.** — *adj* consisting of paper folded only once; of the size of a folio. — *vt* to number the leaves or the pages of: — *pr p* **fō'lioing;** *pa t* and *pa p* **fō'lioed.** — **in folio** in sheets folded once; in the form of a folio. [L. *in foliō*, on leaf (so-

and-so), used in references; L. *folium*, a leaf, a sheet of paper.]

folk *fōk*, *n* people, collectively or distributively; a nation or people; those of one's own family, relations (*colloq*); now generally used as a *pl* (either **folk** or **folks**) to denote ordinary people in general; folk music. — *adj* handed down by tradition of the people. — *adj* **folk'ie** (*colloq*) a lover of folk music; a folk musician. — *adj* **folk'sy** (chiefly *US*) everyday; friendly; sociable; of ordinary people; (artificially) traditional in style. — *n* **folk'siness**. — **folk'-dance** a dance handed down by tradition of the people; **folk'-etymology** popular unscientific attempts at etymology; **folk hero** a hero in the eyes of the ordinary people, or in the tradition of a people; **folk'lore** the ancient observances and customs, the notions, beliefs, traditions, superstitions and prejudices of the common people. — *adj* **folk'lōric**. — **folk'lōrist** a person who studies folklore; **folk-mem'ory** a memory of an event that survives in a community through many generations; **folk music** the music (esp. song) handed down in the popular tradition of the people, or contemporary music of a similar style; **folk'-singer**; **folk'-song** any song or ballad (frequently anonymous) originating among the people and traditionally handed down by them; a modern song composed and performed in the same idiom (esp. by a singer-songwriter); **folk'-tale** a popular story handed down by oral tradition from a more or less remote antiquity; **folk'-weave** a loosely woven fabric. [O.E. *folc*.]

follicle *fol'i-kl*, *n* a fruit formed from a single carpel containing several seeds, splitting along the ventral suture only (*bot*); any small saclike structure, such as the pit surrounding a hair-root (*zool*). — *adj* **follic'ūlar** or **follic'ūlose**. — **follicle-stimulating hormone** (abbrev. **FSH**) a hormone which stimulates growth of the Graafian follicles of the ovary, and sperm production. [L. *folliculus*, dimin. of *follis*, a wind-bag.]

follow *fol'ō*, *vt* to go after or behind; to keep along the line of; to come after, succeed; to pursue; to attend; to imitate; to obey; to adopt, e.g. an opinion; to keep the eye or mind fixed on; to grasp or understand the whole course or sequence of; to result from, as an effect from a cause. — *vi* to come after; to result; to be the logical conclusion. — *n* **foll'ower** someone who follows; a disciple, supporter or devotee; an attendant; a part of a machine driven by another part. — *n* **foll'owing** a body of supporters. — *adj* coming next after; to be next mentioned; (of a wind) blowing in the same direction as a boat, aircraft, etc., is travelling. — *prep* after. — **follow-my-lead'er** a game in which all have to mimic whatever the leader does; **follow-on'** an act of following on; **follow-through'** an act of following through; a stroke that causes the ball to follow the one it has struck (*billiards*). — **follow on** to take a second innings immediately after the first, as compulsory result of being short in number of runs (*cricket*); to follow immediately (*colloq*); to start where another left off (*colloq*); **follow out** to carry out (e.g. instructions); to follow to the end or conclusion; **follow suit** to play a card of the same suit as the one which was led (*cards*); to do what another has done; **follow through** to complete the swing of a stroke after hitting the ball (*sports*); to carry any course of action to its conclusion; **follow up** to pursue an advantage closely; to pursue a question that has been started (*n* **foll'ow-up**). [O.E. *folgian, fylgan*.]

folly *fol'i*, *n* silliness or weakness of mind; a foolish thing; a monument of folly, such as a great useless structure, or one left unfinished because it was begun without establishing the cost. [O.Fr. *folie* — *fol*, foolish.]

foment *fō-ment'*, *vt* to apply a warm lotion to; to foster or instigate (usu. evil). — *n* **fomentā'tion** the application of a warm lotion, or a warm, moist preparation such as a poultice, to reduce inflammation and pain; the lotion, etc. so applied; instigation. — *n* **fomen'ter**. [L. *fōmentum* for *fovimentum* — *fovēre*, to warm.]

fond *fond*, *adj* kindly disposed; prizing highly (with *of*); very affectionate; weakly indulgent. — *vt* **fond'le** to handle with fondness; to caress. — *n* **fond'ler**. — *n* **fond'ling**. — *adv* **fond'ly**. — *n* **fond'ness**. [Orig. sense foolish, past p. of *fon* — M.E. *fonnen*, to act foolishly, and *fon*, a fool.]

fondant *fon'dənt*, *n* a soft sweet made with flavoured sugar and water, that melts in the mouth. [Fr., — *fondre*, to melt.]

fondie, etc. See **fond**.

fondue *fon'do͞o* or *fɔ̃-dü*, *n* a sauce made from melted cheese and wine, etc., and which is eaten by dipping pieces of bread, etc., in the mixture (also called **Swiss fondue**); a dish consisting of small cubes of meat cooked at the table on forks in hot oil and served with piquant sauces (also called **fondue bourguignonne**, *bo͞or-gē-nyon*); a soufflé with bread or biscuit crumbs. [Fr., — fem. past p. of *fondre*, to melt.]

font[1] *font*, (*eccles*) *n* a vessel for baptismal water. — *adj* **font'al**. [O.E. *font* — L. *fōns, fontis*, a fountain.]

font[2] *font*. See **fount**[1].

fontanelle or **fontanel** *fon-tə-nel'*, *n* a gap between the bones of the skull of a young animal. [Fr. dimin., — L. *fōns, fontis*, fountain.]

food *fo͞od*, *n* a substance that a living thing feeds on; a substance that, when digested, nourishes the body; whatever sustains or promotes growth (also *fig*); substances produced by the plant from raw materials taken in (*bot*). — *n* **food'ie** (*colloq*) someone greatly (even excessively) interested in the preparation and consumption of good food. — *n* **food'ism** great interest in or concern over food. — **food canal** the alimentary canal; **food chain** a series of organisms connected by the fact that each forms food for the next higher organism in the series; **food court** an area in a shopping precinct containing a variety of (fast-)food booths and an area with communal seating and tables for the customers; **food'-fish** an edible fish; **food poisoning** a gastrointestinal disorder caused by the ingestion of foods naturally toxic to the system or of foods made toxic by contamination with bacteria or chemicals; **food processor** an electrical appliance for cutting, blending, mincing, etc. food; **food'stuff** a substance used as food; **food values** the relative nourishing power of foods. [O.E. *fōda*.]

fool[1] *fo͞ol*, *n* someone without wisdom, judgment or sense; a weak-minded person; a jester, buffoon; a dupe, sucker, victim; a person with a weakness for (with *for*). — *vt* to deceive; to make to appear foolish; to obtain by fooling. — *vi* to play the fool; to trifle. — *adj* (*Scot* and *US*) foolish. — *n* **fool'ery**. — *n* **fool'ing**. — *adj* **fool'ish** simple-minded; unwise, ill-considered; indiscreet; ridiculous; idiotic, silly. — *adv* **fool'ishly**. — *n* **fool'ishness**. — *n* **fool'-hardiness**. — *adj* **fool'hardy** foolishly bold; rash or incautious. — *adj* **fool'proof** infallible; guaranteed not to cause injury or damage if misused. — **fool's cap** a jester's hat, usu. a coxcomb hood with bells; **fool's errand** a silly or fruitless enterprise; **fool's gold** iron pyrites; **fool's mate** (*chess*) the simplest of the mates (in two moves each); **fool's paradise** a state of happiness based on fictitious hopes or expectations. — **fool around** to waste time; to mess about; to trifle with someone's affections, or to be unfaithful to them with a reckless attitude; **fool with** to meddle with irresponsibly or thoughtlessly; **make a fool of** to cause (someone) to look ridiculous or stupid; to humiliate, dupe; **nobody's fool** an astute person; **play** or **act the fool** to behave like a fool; to be reckless or foolish; to be exuberantly comical or high-spirited. [O.Fr. *fol* — L. *follis*, a wind-bag.]

fool[2] *fōōl*, *n* a purée of fruit, mixed with cream or custard and sugar, such as *gooseberry fool*. [Prob. a use of **fool**[1] suggested by *trifle*.]

foolscap *fōōl'skap*, *n* a superseded size of long folio writing- or printing-paper, generally $17 \times 13\frac{1}{2}$ in., which orig. had the watermark of a *fool's cap* and bells.

foot *fŏŏt*, *n* the part of its body on which an animal stands or walks; the part on which a thing stands; the base; the lower or less dignified end; a measure = 12 in. (0.3048 m.), taken originally as the length of a man's foot; the corresponding square or cubic unit; foot-soldiers; a division of a line of poetry; a manner of walking; a part of a sewing machine that holds the fabric still under the needle; a muscular development of the ventral surface in molluscs: — *pl* **feet**, also (as a measure) **foot**; in some compounds and in sense of dregs, or footlights, **foots**. — *vt* and *vi* (esp. with *it*) to dance; to walk. — *vt* to kick; to pay (the bill); to add a foot to; to grasp with the foot. — *n* **foot'age** measurement or payment by the foot; an amount (i.e. length) of cinema or TV film. — *adj* **foot'ed** provided with a foot or feet. — In combination **-foot'ed** having a specified number of feet; having a specified manner of walking. — *n* **foot'er** (*slang*) football. — In combination **-foot'er** something of a specified length in feet. — *n* **foot'ie** or **foot'y** football (*colloq*, esp. *Austr* and *NZ*); footsie. — *n* **foot'ing** a place for the feet to rest on, esp. a secure or stable one; standing; terms; foundation or basis; lower part of a column or wall, immediately above the foundation; position or rank; a surface or track. — *adj* **foot'less.** — **foot'ball** a large ball for kicking about in sport; a game played with this ball, esp. soccer (see under **association football**); a bargaining-point, point of controversy, etc. that is tossed around (*fig*); **foot'baller** a football player. — *adj* **foot'balling** of or relating to football. — **foot'bar** the bar controlled by the pilot's feet, for operating the rudder in aircraft; **foot'board** a support for the feet in a carriage, etc.; the footplate of a locomotive engine; an upright board at the foot of a bed; **foot brake** a brake operated by the foot; **foot'bridge** a bridge for pedestrians; **foot'fall** the sound of setting the foot down; **foot'fault** (*lawn tennis*) a fault made by stepping over the baseline when serving. — Also *vt* and *vi*. — **foot'hill** a minor elevation below a higher mountain or range (usu. in *pl*); **foot'hold** a place to fix the foot in; a grip; a firm starting position; **foot'light** one of a row of lights along the front of the stage; (in *pl*) the theatre as a profession. — *adj* **foot'loose** free, unhampered. — **foot'man** a servant or attendant in livery: — *pl* **foot'men**; **foot'mark** see **foot'print**; **foot'note** a note of reference or comment at the foot of a page; **foot'path** a way for walkers only; a side pavement; **foot'-patrol** a patrol on foot; **foot'plate** a platform for **foot'platemen** or **foot'platewomen** (*nsing* **foot'plateman** or **foot'platewoman**), the train driver and assistant (on steam locomotive, the stoker); **foot'-pound** or **foot-pound force** the energy needed to raise a mass of one pound through the height of one foot; **foot'print** the mark left on the ground or floor by a person's or animal's foot (also **foot'mark**); **foot'-pump** a pump held or operated by the foot; **foot'rest** a support for the foot; **foot'rot** an infection of the feet in sheep or cattle; **foot'rule** a rule or measure a foot in length or measured off in feet. — *vi* **foot'slog** to march, tramp. — **foot'slogger**; **foot'slogging**; **foot'-soldier** a soldier serving on foot. — *adj* **foot'sore** having sore or tender feet, usu. after much walking. — **foot'-stalk** (*bot*) the stalk or petiole of a leaf; **foot'step** a tread; a footfall; a footprint; (in *pl*; *fig*) path, example; **foot'stool** a stool for placing one's feet on when sitting. — *adj* **foot'-tapping** (of music) that makes one tap, or want to tap, one's feet in time with it. — **foot'-ton** or **foot-ton force** a unit of work or energy equal to the work done in raising one ton one foot against normal gravity, 2240 foot-pounds; **foot'warmer** a device which keeps the feet warm; **foot'way** a footpath; **foot'wear** boots, shoes, socks, etc.; **foot'work** the use or management of the feet, as in sport. — *adj* **foot'worn** footsore; showing signs of much wear by feet. — **a foot in the door** a first step towards a usu. difficult desired end; **at the feet of** under the spell of, in a position of submission, homage, supplication or devotion to; **catch on the wrong foot** to catch unprepared; **drag one's feet** see under **drag**; **foot-and-mouth disease** a contagious disease of cloven-hoofed animals, characterised by vesicular eruption, esp. in the mouth and in the clefts of the feet; **get off on the wrong foot** to make a bad beginning; **have one foot in the grave** to be not far from death; **have one's feet on the ground** to act habitually with practical good sense; **have the ball at one's feet** to have nothing to do but seize one's opportunity; **my foot!** *interj* expressing disbelief, usu. contemptuous; **on foot** walking or running; **play footsie (with)** (*colloq*) to rub one's foot or leg against (another person's), usu. with amorous intentions; to make furtively flirtatious advances towards (someone) (*fig*); **put a** (or **one's) foot wrong** (usu. in *neg*) to make a mistake or blunder; **put one's best foot forward** to make one's best effort; **put one's foot down** to take a firm decision, usu. against something; **put one's foot in it** to make a tactless blunder or remark. [O.E. *fōt*, pl. *fēt*.]

footle *fōōt'l*, *vi* to trifle, waste time, potter (with *about* or *around*). — *n* silly nonsense. — *n* and *adj* **foot'ling.**

Footsie *fŏŏt'si*. See **FTSE**.

footsie. See **play footsie (with)** under **foot**.

foo yung, fu yong. See **fu yung**.

fop *fop*, *n* an affected dandy. — *adj* **fopp'ish** vain and showy in dress; affectedly refined in manners. — *adv* **fopp'ishly.** — *n* **fopp'ishness.** [Cf. Ger. *foppen*, to hoax.]

for *fōr* or *fər*, *prep* in the place of; in favour of; wanting, wishing for; on account of; in the direction of; having as goal or intention; with respect to; in respect of; by reason of; appropriate or adapted to, or in reference to; beneficial to; in spite of; in recompense of; during; in the character of; to the extent of. — *conj* because. — **as for** as far as concerns; **for all that** notwithstanding; **there is nothing for it but (to)** there is no other possible course but (to); **be for it** or **be in for it** to have something unpleasant about to happen. [O.E. *for*.]

f o r *abbrev* for free on rail.

for- *fōr-* or *fər-*, *pfx* (1) in words derived from O.E., used to form verbs with the senses: (a) away, off; (b) against; (c) thoroughly, utterly (intensive); (d) exhaustion; (e) destruction. (2) used in words derived from O.E. to form adjs. with superlative force. (3) a contraction of *fore-*. (4) in words derived from L. *forīs*, outside, *forās*, forth, out.

fora. See **forum**.

forage *for'ij*, *n* fodder, or food for horses and cattle; provisions; the act of foraging. — *vi* to go about and forcibly carry off food for horses and cattle; to rummage about for what one wants. — *vt* to plunder. — *n* **for'ager.** — **for'age-cap** the undress cap worn by infantry soldiers. [Fr. *fourrage*, O.Fr. *feurre*, fodder.]

foramen *fō-rā'mən*, *n* (*zool* or *anat*) a small opening: — *pl* **foramina** (*-ram'i-nə*). — *adj* **foram'inal.** — *adj* **foram'inated** or **foram'inous** pierced with small holes; porous. [L. *forāmen* — *forāre*, to pierce.]

forasmuch *fōr-* or *fər-əz-much'*, (*archaic* or *formal*) *conj* because, since (with *as*).

foray *for'ā*, *n* a raid; a venture, attempt. — *vt* and *vi* to raid; to forage. — *n* **for'ayer.** [**forage.**]

forbad, forbade. See **forbid.**

forbear[1] *för-* or *fər-bār'*, *vi* to keep oneself in check; to abstain, refrain. — *vt* to abstain, refrain from; to avoid voluntarily; to spare, to withhold: — *pa t* **forbore'**; *pa p* **forborne'**. — *n* **forbear'ance** exercise of patience; command of temper; clemency. — *adj* **forbear'ing** long-suffering; patient. — *adv* **forbear'ingly.** [O.E. *forberan*; see **for-** (1a) and **bear**[1].]

forbear[2] *för'bār*. Same as **forebear** (see under **fore-**).

forbid *fər-* or *för-bid'*, *vt* to prohibit; to command not to: — *pa t* **forbade** (*-bad'*, or sometimes *-bād'*) or **forbad'**; *pa p* **forbidd'en.** — *adj* **forbidd'en** prohibited; unlawful; not permitted, esp. in certain scientific rules; (of a combination of symbols) not in an operating code, i.e., revealing a fault (*comput*). — *n* **forbidd'ing.** — *adj* uninviting; sinister; unprepossessing; threatening or formidable in look. — *adv* **forbidd'ingly.** — *n* **forbidd'ingness.** — **forbidden degrees** see under **degree; forbidden fruit** (*Bible*) that forbidden to Adam (Genesis ii. 17); anything tempting and prohibited. [O.E. *forbēodan*; see **for-** (1a) and **bid**[2].]

forbore, forborne. See **forbear**[1].

force[1] *förs*, *n* strength, power, energy; efficacy; validity; influence; vehemence; violence; coercion; a group of people assembled for collective action (e.g. *police force*); (in *pl*; sometimes with *cap*) navy, army and air force; any cause which changes the direction or speed of the motion of a portion of matter. — *vt* to draw or push by main strength; to thrust; to compel; to overcome the resistance of by force; to achieve or bring about by force; to break or break open by force; to take by violence; to cause to grow or ripen rapidly (*hort*); to strain or work up to a high pitch; to induce or cause someone to play in a particular way (*cards*). — *adj* **forced** accomplished by great effort, e.g. *forced march*; strained, excessive, unnatural; artificially produced. — *adv* **forc'edly.** — *n* **forc'edness.** — *adj* **force'ful** full of force or strength; energetic; driven or acting with power. — *adv* **force'fully.** — *n* **force'fulness.** — *adj* **force'less.** — *n* **forc'er.** — *adj* **forc'ible** having force; done by force. — *n* **forc'ibleness** or **forcibil'ity.** — *adv* **forc'ibly.** — **forced labour** compulsory hard labour. — *vt* **force'-feed** to feed (a person or animal) forcibly, usu. by the mouth: — *pa t* and *pa p* **force'-fed.** — **force-feed'ing.** — *vi* **force'-land** to make a forced landing. — **forced landing** (*aeronautics*) a necessary or emergency landing at a place where no landing was orig. planned; **force'-pump** a pump that delivers liquid under pressure greater than its suction pressure; **forc'ing-house** a hothouse for forcing plants, or a place for hastening the growth of animals. — **in force** operative, legally binding; in great numbers. [Fr., — L.L. *fortia* — L. *fortis*, strong.]

force[2] *förs*, *n* a waterfall. [O.N. *fors*.]

force[3] *förs*, (*cookery*) *vt* to stuff, esp. fowl. — **force'meat** finely-chopped and highly seasoned meat, used as a stuffing or alone. [For **farce.**]

force majeure *fors mä-zhœr*, *n* superior power; an unforeseeable or uncontrollable course of events, excusing one from fulfilling a contract (*legal*).

forceps *för'seps*, *n* a pincerlike instrument with two blades, for holding, lifting or removing (e.g in surgery): — *pl* **for'ceps.** [L., — *formus*, hot, *capere*, to hold.]

forcible, etc. See under **force**[1].

ford *förd*, *n* a place where water may be crossed by wading. — *vt* to wade across. — *adj* **ford'able.** [O.E. *ford-faran*, to go.]

fore *för*, *adj* in front. — *adv* at or towards the front; previously. — *n* the front; the foremast. — *interj* (*golf*) a warning cry to anybody in the way of the ball. — *adj* and *adv* **fore-and-aft'** lengthwise of a ship; without square sails. — *n* **fore-and-aft'er** a schooner, etc., with a fore-and-aft rig. — **fore-and-aft sail** any sail not set on yards and lying fore-and-aft when untrimmed. — **to the fore** at hand; prominent, towards the front. [O.E. *fore*, from the same root as **for** (prep.).]

fore- *för-*, *pfx* denoting: before; beforehand; in front. — *n* **fore'arm** the part of the arm between the elbow and the wrist. — *vt* **forearm'** to arm or prepare beforehand. — *n* **forebear** or **forbear** (*för'bār*) an ancestor (from **be** and sfx. **-er**[1]). — *vt* **forebode'** to prognosticate; to have a premonition of (esp. of evil). — *n* **forebod'ing** a perception beforehand; apprehension of approaching evil. — *adv* **forebod'ingly.** — *n* **fore'brain** the front part of the brain. — *vt* **fore'cast** to assess or calculate beforehand; to foresee; to predict. — *vi* to devise beforehand: — *pa t* and *pa p* **fore'cast,** sometimes **fore'casted.** — *n* **fore'cast** a prediction; a weather forecast (q.v.); an assessment or calculation beforehand. — *n* **fore'caster.** — *n* **forecastle** or **fo'c'sle** (*fōk'sl*, or sometimes *för'käs-l*) a short raised deck at the fore-end of a vessel; the forepart of the ship under the main-deck, the quarters of the crew. — *n* **fore'court** a court in front of a building; an outer court; the front area of a garage or filling-station, where the petrol pumps are situated; the part of a tennis court between the net and the service line. — *vt* **foredate'** to date before the true time. — *n* **fore'deck** the forepart of a deck or ship. — *n* **fore'-end.** — *n* **fore'father** an ancestor. — *n* **fore'finger** the finger next to the thumb. — *n* **fore'foot** one of the front feet of a quadruped: — *pl* **fore'feet.** — *n* **fore'front** the front or foremost part. — *adj* **fore'gone** (**foregone conclusion** a conclusion come to before examination of the evidence; an obvious or inevitable conclusion or result). — *n* **fore'ground** the part of a picture or field of view nearest the observer's eye (as opp. to the *background*; also *fig*). — *vt* (*US*; *fig*) to spotlight, emphasise. — *n* **fore'gut** the front section of the digestive tract of an embryo, from which the forepart of the alimentary canal develops. — *n* **fore'hand** the upper hand, advantage, preference; the part of the court to the right of a right-handed player or to the left of a left-handed player (*tennis*); a stroke played forehand (*tennis*); the part of a horse that is in front of its rider. — *adj* with the palm in front (opp. to *backhand*); done beforehand. — *adv* with hand in forehand position. — *adj* **fore'handed** (*US*) planning ahead, with thought or provision for the future; well-off; forehand (*tennis*). — *n* **forehead** (*för'hed*, also *for'id* or *-ed*) the front of the head above the eyes, the brow. — *vt* **forejudge'** to judge before hearing the facts and proof; (or **forjudge'**) to deprive of a right, etc., by a judgment (*law*). — *vt* **foreknow'** to know beforehand; to foresee. — *adj* **foreknow'able.** — *n* **foreknowledge** (*-nol'ij*). — *adj* **foreknown'.** — *n* **fore'land** a point of land running forward into the sea, a headland; a front region. — *n* **fore'leg** a front leg. — *n* **fore'limb.** — *n* **fore'lock** the lock of hair on the forehead (**pull, touch** or **tug the forelock** to raise one's hand to the forehead in sign of respect, subservience, etc.). — *n* **fore'man** the first or chief man, one appointed to preside over, or act as spokesman for, others; an overseer: — *pl* **fore'men.** — *n* **fore'mast** the mast that is forward, or next to the bow of a ship. — *adj* **foremen'tioned** mentioned before in writing or discussion. — *n* **fore'name** the first or Christian name. — *adj* **fore'named** mentioned before. — *n* **forenoon** (*för-nōōn'* or *för'nōōn*; chiefly *Scot* and *Ir*) the morning, esp. the part of the day before midday (as opp. to early morning). — *adj* (*för'*) pertaining to this time. — *vt* **foreordain'** to arrange or determine beforehand. — *n* **fore'part** the front; the early part.

— *n* **fore'paw** a front paw. — *n* **forepay'ment** payment beforehand. — *n* **fore'play** sexual stimulation before intercourse. — *n* **fore'quarter** the front portion of a side of meat, incl. the leg; (in *pl*; of an animal, esp. a horse) the forelegs and shoulders, and the body areas adjoining them. — *vt* **forerun'** to run or come before; to precede. — *n* **fore'runner** a runner or messenger sent before, a precursor; a forewarning, an omen. — *adj* **fore'said** already mentioned. — *n* **foresail** (*för'sl* or *-sāl*) the chief and lowest square sail on the foremast; a triangular sail on the forestay. — *vt* and *vi* **foresee'** to see or know beforehand: — *pa t* **foresaw'**; *pa p* **foreseen'**. — *n* **foreseeabil'ity**. — *adj* **foresee'able**. — *adj* **foresee'ing**. — *adv* **foresee'ingly**. — *vt* **foreshad'ow** to give, or have, some indication of in advance; to shadow or typify beforehand. — *n* **fore'shore** the space between high and low water marks. — *vt* **foreshort'en** to draw or cause to appear as if shortened, by perspective. — *n* **foreshort'ening**. — *n* **fore'sight** the act or power of foreseeing; wise forethought, prudence. — *adj* **fore'sighted**. — *adj* **fore'sightful**. — *adj* **fore'sightless**. — *n* **fore'skin** the retractable skin that covers the glans penis, the prepuce. — **forestall** see separate entry. — *n* **fore'stay** a rope reaching from the foremast-head to the bowsprit end to support the mast. — *n* **fore'taste** a taste beforehand; anticipation. — *vt* **foretell'** to tell before; to prophesy: — *pa t* and *pa p* **foretold'**. — *n* **fore'thought** thought or care for the future; anticipation; thinking beforehand. — *n* **fore'token** a token or sign beforehand. — *vt* **foretō'ken** to signify beforehand. — *n* **fore'top** (*naut*) the platform at the head of the foremast. — *n* **foretop'mast** the mast erected at the head of the foremast, at the top of which is the **foretop-gall'ant-mast**. — *vt* **forewarn'** to warn beforehand; to give previous notice. — *n* **forewarn'ing**. — *n* **fore'wing** either of an insect's front pair of wings. — *n* **fore'woman** a woman overseer, a headwoman, a spokeswoman for a group (e.g. for a jury): — *pl* **fore'women**. — *n* **fore'word** a preface. [O.E. *fore*.]

foreclose *för-klōz'*, *vt* to close beforehand; to prevent; to stop; to bar the right of redeeming (a mortgage, etc.). — *adj* **foreclos'able**. — *n* **foreclosure** (*-klō'zhər*) the act, or an instance, of foreclosing; the process by which a mortgagor, failing to repay the money lent on the security of a property, is compelled to forfeit the right to redeem it (*law*). [O.Fr. *forclos*, past p. of *forclore*, to exclude — L. *forīs*, outside, and *claudĕre*, *clausum*, to shut.]

forecourt ... to ... **forefront**. See under **fore-**.

foregather. See **forgather**.

forego. See **forgo**.

foregone ... to ... **forehead**. See under **fore-**.

foreign *for'in*, *adj* belonging to another country; from abroad; pertaining to, characteristic of or situated in another country; alien; extraneous; not belonging; unconnected; not appropriate. — *n* **for'eigner** a person belonging to, or from, another country; a stranger or outsider. — *n* **for'eignism** a mannerism, turn of phrase, etc., typical of a foreigner. — *n* **for'eignness**. — **foreign correspondent** a newspaper correspondent in a foreign country in order to report its news, etc.; **foreign exchange** the exchange, conversion, etc. of foreign currencies; **Foreign Legion** a former French army unit, consisting of soldiers of all nationalities, serving outside France; **Foreign Office** government department dealing with foreign affairs. [O.Fr. *forain* — L.L. *forāneus* — L. *forās*, out of doors.]

forejudge ... to ... **forementioned**. See under **fore-**.

foremost *för'mōst*, *adj* first in place; most advanced; first in rank and dignity. [O.E. *forma*, first (superl. of *fore*) and superl. sfx. *-st*.]

forename, forenoon. See under **fore-**.

forensic *fə-ren'sik*, *adj* belonging to courts of law; of or pertaining to sciences or scientists connected with legal investigations. — *n* **forensical'ity**. — *adv* **foren'sically**. — **forensic medicine** medical jurisprudence, the application of medical knowledge to the elucidation of doubtful questions in a court of justice. [L. *forēnsis*, of the forum (and hence of the law courts held there by the Romans) — *forum*, market-place, forum.]

foreordain ... to ... **foreskin**. See under **fore-**.

forest *for'ist*, *n* a large uncultivated stretch of land covered with trees and underwood; woody ground and rough pasture; a royal preserve for hunting; any area resembling a forest because thickly covered with tall, upright objects. — *adj* of, pertaining to, or consisting of a forest; rustic. — *vt* to cover with trees; to cover thickly with tall, upright objects. — *adj* **for'estal** or **forestial** (*fər-est'i-əl*). — *n* **forestā'tion** afforestation. — *adj* **for'ested**. — *n* **for'ester** a person who has charge of a forest; someone who has care of growing trees; (with *cap*) a member of the Ancient Order of Foresters; an inhabitant of a forest. — *n* **for'estry** the science, and art, of planting, tending and managing forests. [O.Fr. *forest* (Fr. *forêt*) — L.L. *forestis* (*silva*), the outside wood, as opp. to the *parcus* (park) or walled-in wood.]

forestall *för-stäl'*, *vt* to buy up before reaching the market, so as to sell again at higher prices; to anticipate; to hinder by anticipating; to bar. — *n* **forestall'er**. — *n* **forestall'ing**. — *n* **forestal'ment**. [O.E. *foresteall*, ambush, lit. a place taken beforehand — *steall*, stand, station.]

forestay ... to ... **foretopmast**. See under **fore-**.

forever *fər-ev'ər*, *adv* for ever, for all time to come; eternally; continually. — *n* an endless or indefinite length of time. — *adv* **forev'ermore** for ever hereafter.

forewarn ... to ... **foreword**. See under **fore-**.

forfaiting *för'fā-ting*, *n* a method of export finance whereby debts on exported goods are bought and then sold on to banks, etc. — *n* **for'faiter** a person who, or company which, buys and sells such debts. [Fr. *forfait*, forfeit, contract.]

forfeit *för'fit*, *n* something to which a right is lost; a penalty or fine for a crime, or breach of some condition; (esp. in *pl*) a game in which a player surrenders some item (a **forfeit**) which can be redeemed only by performing a task, or fulfilling a challenge, set for them. — *adj* forfeited. — *vt* to lose the right to by some fault or crime; to penalise by forfeiting; (*loosely*) to give up voluntarily. — *adj* **for'feitable**. — *n* **for'feiture** an act of forfeiting; the state of being forfeited; the thing forfeited. [O.Fr. *forfait* — L.L. *forisfactum*.]

forgather or **foregather** *fər-gadh'ər*, *vi* (of people) to gather, assemble; to fraternise. [**for-** (1c).]

forgave. See **forgive**.

forge[1] *förj*, *n* a place where iron, etc., is worked, a smithy; a furnace, esp. one in which iron is heated. — *vt* to form by heating and hammering, by heating and pressure, or by pressure alone; to form or fashion (an object); to counterfeit for purposes of fraud; to form by great pressure, electricity or explosion. — *vi* to commit forgery. — *adj* **forge'able**. — *n* **forg'er**. — *n* **forg'ery** fraudulently making or altering anything, esp. a writing; something which is forged or counterfeited. — *n* **forg'ing**. [O.Fr. *forge* — L. *fabrica* — *faber*, a workman.]

forge[2] *förj*, *vi* to move steadily on (usu. with *ahead*).

forget *fər-get'*, *vt* to lose or drop from the memory; to fail to remember or think of; to leave behind accidentally; to neglect: — *pr p* **forgett'ing**; *pa t* **forgot'**; *pa p* **forgott'en** (also, in *US*, but otherwise *archaic* **forgot'**). — *adj* **forget'ful** apt to forget; inattentive. — *adv* **forget'fully**. — *n* **forget'fulness**. — *adj* **forgett'able**. — *n* **forgett'er**. — *n* and *adj* **forgett'ing.** — *adj* **forgott'en.** — *n* **forgott'enness.** — **forget'-me-not** a plant with clusters of small, blue flowers (genus *Myosotis*) of loving remembrance. — **forget it** (*colloq*; esp. in *imper*) used to state that there is no need to offer apologies, thanks, etc., or to say or do anything further about a particular matter; **forget oneself** to lose one's self-control or dignity. [O.E. *forgetan* — pfx. *for-*, away, *getan*, to get.]

forgive *fər-giv'*, *vt* to pardon; to overlook. — *vi* to be merciful or forgiving: — *pa t* **forgave'**; *pa p* **forgiv'en.** — *adj* **forgiv'able.** — *n* **forgive'ness** pardon; a readiness to forgive. — *adj* **forgiv'ing** ready to pardon; merciful; compassionate. [O.E. *forgiefan* — *for-*, away, *giefan*, to give.]

forgo or **forego** *för-* or *fər-gō'*, *vt* to give up, to relinquish; to do without; to refrain from using or benefiting from: — *pr p* **forgo'ing** or **forego'ing**; *pa p* **forgone'** or **foregone'**; *pa t* **forwent'** or **forewent'**. [O.E. *forgān*, to pass by, abstain from — *for-*, away, *gān*, to go.]

forgot, forgotten. See **forget.**

forint *for'int*, *n* the monetary unit of Hungary since 1946 (100 *fillér*). [Hung., — It. *fiorino*, florin.]

forjudge. See **forejudge** under **fore-**.

fork *förk*, *n* a pronged instrument (such as an eating implement or garden tool) for spiking and lifting, etc.; anything that divides into prongs or branches; a branch or prong; the space or angle between branches; a confluent, tributary or branch of a river; one of the branches into which a road divides; a place where something divides into two branches; a simultaneous attack on two pieces by one piece (*chess*). — *vi* to branch; to take a branch road. — *vt* to form as a fork; to move or lift with a fork; to stab or dig with a fork; to menace (two pieces) simultaneously (*chess*). — *adj* **forked** shaped like a fork; (as in *with forked tongue*) insincere, deceitful. — *adv* **fork'edly.** — *n* **fork'er.** — *n* **fork'ful** as much as a fork will hold: — *pl* **fork'fuls.** — *adj* **fork'y.** — **fork lunch** or **luncheon, fork supper,** etc., a buffet-type meal eaten with a fork. — **fork-lift truck** (or in short **fork'-lift**) a power-driven truck with an arrangement of steel prongs which can lift, raise up high, and carry heavy packages and stack them where required (often used with a pallet); **fork out, over** or **up** (*slang*) to hand or pay over, esp. unwillingly. [O.E. *forca* — L. *furca*.]

forlorn *fər-lörn'*, *adj* forsaken; neglected; wretched. — *adv* **forlorn'ly.** — *n* **forlorn'ness.** [O.E. *forloren*, past p. of *forlēosan*, to lose — *for-*, away, *lēosan*, to lose.]

forlorn hope *fər-lörn' hōp*, *n* a desperate enterprise of last resort; a vain or faint hope (from association with hope = expectation). [Formerly, a body of soldiers selected for a very dangerous mission — Du. *verloren hoop*, lost troop.]

form *förm*, *n* shape; a mould; something that holds or shapes; a species or kind; a pattern or type; a way of being; a manner of arrangement; order; regularity; system; structural unity in music, literature, etc.; a prescribed set of words or course of action; behaviour; condition of fitness or efficiency; a schedule to be filled in with details; a specimen document; the inherent nature of an object (*philos*); a forme (*US*, etc.); a long seat, a bench; a school class; a criminal record (*slang*); the condition of fitness of e.g. a horse or an athlete; a record of past performance of an athlete, horse, etc.; (*colloq*; with **the**) the situation, position. — *vt* to give form or shape to; to bring into being; to make; to contrive; to conceive in the mind; to go to make up; to establish. — *vi* to assume a form. — *adj* **form'able.** — *adj* **form'ative** giving form, determining, moulding; capable of development; growing; serving to form words by derivation or inflection, not radical (*gram*). — *n* (*gram*) a formative element; any grammatical element from which words and sentences are constructed. — *adj* **formed.** — *n* **form'er.** — *n* **form'ing.** — *adj* **form'less.** — *adv* **form'lessly.** — *n* **form'lessness.** — **form horse** the favourite, the expected winner (*horse-racing*; also *fig*); **form letter** a letter with a fixed form and contents, used esp. when writing to a number of people about the same or essentially similar matters; **form master, mistress** or **teacher** esp. in a secondary school, the teacher who is responsible for the administration, welfare, etc. of a form. — **good** (or **bad**) **form** according to good or accepted (or bad or unaccepted) social use. [L. *fōrma*, shape.]

-form *-förm* or **-iform** *-i-förm*, *combining form* used to mean having a specified form or number of forms. [L. *fōrma*, form.]

formal *för'məl*, *adj* relating to form; according to form or established style; ceremonious, punctilious, methodical; proper; having the outward form only. — *n* **formalīsā'tion** or **-z-**. — *vt* **form'alise** or **-ize** to make formal; to make official or valid; to make precise, give a clear statement of. — *n* **form'alism** excessive observance of form or conventional usage; stiffness of manner; concentration on form or technique at the expense of social or moral content (*art*). — *n* **form'alist** a person who has exaggerated regard to rules or established usages; someone who practises formalism (*art*). — Also *adj*. — *adj* **formalis'tic.** — *n* **formal'ity** the precise observance of forms or ceremonies; a matter of form; stiffness, conventionality; mere convention at the expense of substance. — *adv* **form'ally.** — **formal verdict** (*law*) one in which the jury follows the judge's directions; in a fatal accident inquiry, a finding of death by misadventure with no apportioning of blame (*Scot*). [**form.**]

formaldehyde *fər-mal'də-hīd*, *n* a formic aldehyde, formalin.

formalin *för'mə-lin* or **formol** *för'mol* or *för'mōl*, *n* a formic aldehyde used as an antiseptic, germicide or preservative.

formant *för'mənt*, (*acoustics*) *n* a component of a speech sound determining its particular quality. [Ger. *Formant* — L. *formant-*, *formans*, pres. p. of *formāre*, to form.]

format *för'mat*, *n* (of books, etc.) the size, form, shape in which they are issued; the style, arrangement and contents of e.g. a radio or television programme; (the description of) the way data is, or is to be, arranged in a file, on a card, disk, tape, etc. (*comput*). — *vt* to arrange a book, etc., into a specific format; to arrange data for use on a disk, tape, etc. (*comput*); to prepare a disk, etc., for use by dividing it into sectors: — *pr p* **for'matting**; *pa t* and *pa p* **for'matted.** — *n* **for'matter** a program for formatting a disk, tape, etc. [Fr.]

formation *för-mā'shən*, *n* a making or producing; something formed or made, a structure; an arrangement (of e.g. troops, aircraft, players); a group of rock strata used as a basis for rock mapping (*geol*). [**form.**]

forme *förm*, (*printing*) *n* the type and blocks assembled in a chase and ready for printing. [**form.**]

former *förm'ər*, *adj* (*compar* of **fore**) before in time; past. — *adv* **form'erly** in former times; before this time. [Formed late on analogy of M.E. *formest*, foremost, by adding compar. sfx. *-er* to base of O.E. *forma*, first, itself superlative.]

formic *för'mik*, *adj* pertaining to ants. — *n* **formicā'tion** a sensation like that of ants creeping on the skin. — **formic acid** a fatty acid, H·CO·OH, found in ants and nettles. [L. *formīca*, an ant.]

Formica® *för-mī'kə*, *n* a brand of plastic laminates used to provide hard, heat-resistant, easily-cleaned surfaces.

formidable *för'mid-ə-bl* or *för-mid'ə-bl*, *adj* causing fear; inspiring awe; redoubtable. — *n* **formida-**

bil'ity. — *n* **for'midableness.** — *adv* **for'midably** (or *-mid'*). [Fr., — L. *formīdābilis* — *formīdō*, fear.]

formol. See **formalin.**

formula *förm'ū-lə*, *n* a prescribed form; a formal statement of doctrines; a recipe; a milk mixture used as baby food; a statement of joint aims or principles worked out for practical purposes by diplomats of divergent interests; a solution or answer worked out by different sides in a dispute, etc.; a technical specification governing orig. cars entered for certain motor-racing events, now also applied to other racing vehicles or craft; a general expression for solving problems (*math*); a set of symbols expressing the composition of a body (*chem*); a list of ingredients of a patent medicine: — *pl* **formulae** (*förm'ū-lē*) or **form'ūlas.** — *adj* **formulaic** (*-lā'ik*). — *adj* **form'ūlar** or **formūlaris'tic.** — *vt* **form'ūlarise** or **-ize.** — *n* **formūlarīsā'tion** or **-z-**, or **formūlā'-tion.** — *n* **form'ūlary** a formula; a book of formulae or precedents. — *adj* prescribed; ritual. — *vt* **form'ūlate** or **form'ūlise** or **-ize** to reduce to or express in a formula; to state or express in a clear or definite form. — *n* **form'ūlism** excessive use of, or dependence on, formulae. — *n* **form'ūlist.** [L. *fōrmula*, dimin. of *fōrma.*]

fornicate *för'ni-kāt*, *vi* to commit fornication. — *n* **fornicā'tion** voluntary sexual intercourse of the unmarried, sometimes extended to cases where only one of the pair concerned is unmarried; adultery (*Bible*); idolatry (*fig*). — *n* **for'nicātor,** *fem* **for'ni-cātress.** [L. *fornīcārī*, *-ātus* — *fornix*, a vault, brothel.]

forsake *fər-sāk'* or *för-*, *vt* to desert; to abandon: — *pr p* **forsāk'ing;** *pa t* **forsook';** *pa p* **forsāk'en.** — *adj* **forsāk'en.** — *adv* **forsāk'enly.** — *n* **forsāk'en-ness.** — *n* **forsāk'ing** abandonment. [O.E. *forsacan* — *for-*, away, *sacan*, to strive.]

forswear *fər-swār'* or *för-*, *vt* to deny or renounce upon oath. — *vi* to swear falsely: — *pa t* **forswore';** *pa p* **forsworn'.** — *adj* **forsworn'** perjured, having forsworn oneself. — *n* **forsworn'ness.** — **forswear oneself** to swear falsely. [**for-** (1b).]

forsythia *för-sī'thi-ə* or *-si'dhi-ə*, *n* a plant of the *Forsythia* genus of shrubs with flowers like jasmine. [After William *Forsyth* (1737–1804), botanist.]

fort *fört*, *n* a small fortress; (in N. America) an outlying trading-station. — *vt* to fortify. — **hold the fort** to take temporary charge. [Fr., — L. *fortis*, strong.]

forte[1] *för'ti*, *n* that in which one excels. [Fr. *fort*, strong.]

forte[2] *för'ti*, (*mus*) *adj* and *adv* loud: — *superl* **fortis'simo,** *double superl* **fortissis'simo** as loud as possible. — *n* a loud passage in music. — *adj* and *adv* loud with immediate relapse into softness. [It.]

forth *förth*, *adv* forward; onward; out; into the open; in continuation; abroad. — *adj* **forthcom'ing** just coming forth; about to appear; approaching; at hand, ready to be produced; (of a person) friendly, communicative. — *adv* **forth'right** (or *-rīt'*) straightforward; at once. — *adj* straightforward; downright. — *adv* **forth'rightly.** — *n* **forth'-rightness.** — *adv* **forthwith** (*-with'* or *-widh'*, or *förth'*) immediately. — **and so forth** and so on. [O.E. *forth* — *fore*, before.]

forties, fortieth. See **forty.**

fortify *för'ti-fī*, *vt* to strengthen with forts, etc., against attack; to invigorate; to confirm; to strengthen (esp. certain wines) by adding alcohol; to enrich (a food) by adding e.g. vitamins. — *vi* to put up fortifications: — *pr p* **for'tifying;** *pa t* and *pa p* **for'tified.** — *adj* **for'tifīable.** — *n* **fortificā'tion** the art of strengthening a military position by means of defensive works; (often in *pl*) the work so constructed; that which fortifies. — *n* **for'tifīer.** [Fr. *fortifier* — L.L. *fortificāre* — *fortis*, strong, *facĕre*, to make.]

fortissimo, fortississimo. See **forte**[2].

fortitude *för'ti-tūd* or in U.S. *-tōōd*, *n* courage in endurance. [L. *fortitūdō*, *-inis* — *fortis*, strong.]

fortnight *fört'nīt*, *n* two weeks or fourteen days. — *adj* and *adv* **fort'nightly** once a fortnight. — *n* a magazine, etc. appearing fortnightly. [O.E. *fēowertȳne niht*, fourteen nights.]

Fortran *för'tran*, *n* computer language widely used in scientific work. [*For*mula *tran*slation.]

fortress *för'trəs*, *n* a fortified place. [O.Fr. *forteresse*, another form of *fortelesce.*]

fortuitous *för-tū'i-təs* or in U.S. *-tōō'i-təs*, *adj* happening by chance; fortunate. — *n* **fortū'itism** belief in evolution by fortuitous variation. — *n* **fortū'itist.** — *adv* **fortū'itously.** — *n* **fortū'itous-ness.** — *n* **fortū'ity.** [L. *fortuītus.*]

fortune *för'chən*, *n* whatever comes by lot or chance; luck; the arbitrary ordering of events; a prediction of one's future; success; a great accumulation of wealth; a large amount of money. — *adj* **for'tunate** happening by good fortune; lucky; auspicious; felicitous. — *adv* **for'tunately** in a fortunate way, by good luck; I'm glad to say, happy to report. — **fortune cookie** (*US*) dough wrapped and cooked around a piece of paper which has a (supposed) fortune or a maxim on it, served esp. in Chinese homes and restaurants; **for'tune-hunter** a person who hunts for a wealthy marriage; **for'tune-teller** someone who professes to foretell one's fortune; **for'tune-telling.** — **a small fortune** quite a large fortune, a considerable amount of money. [Fr., — L. *fortūna.*]

forty *för'ti*, *adj* and *n* four times ten. — *npl* **for'ties** the numbers forty to forty-nine; the years so numbered (of life or a century); a range of temperature from forty to just less than fifty degrees; (with *cap* and **the**) the sea area lying between N.E. Scotland and S.W. Norway, with a minimum depth of 40 fathoms. — *adj* **for'tieth** the last of forty; next after the thirty-ninth; equal to one of forty equal parts. — *n* one of forty equal parts; a person or thing in fortieth position. — *adj* **for'tyish** apparently about forty years old. — **forty-five'** a record played at a speed of 45 revolutions per minute; (with *cap* and **the**) Jacobite rebellion of 1745; **forty winks** a short nap, esp. after dinner. — **roaring forties** the tract of stormy west winds south of 40°S latitude (occasionally also in the Atlantic north of 40°N). [O.E. *fēowertig* — *fēower*, four, *-tig*, ten (as sfx.).]

forum *fö'rəm*, *n* orig. a market-place, esp. that in Rome where public business was transacted and justice dispensed; a meeting to discuss topics of public concern; a publication, regular meeting, etc., serving as a medium for debate: — *pl* **fo'rums** or **fo'ra.** [L. *forum.*]

forward *för'wərd*, *adj* near or at the forepart; in advance; well advanced; ready; too ready; presumptuous; officious; early ripe. — *vt* to help on; to send on. — *adv* **for'ward** or **for'wards** towards what is in front; onward; progressively. — *adv* **forward** (*for'əd*) towards, or in, the front part of a ship. — *n* **for'ward** (in football, etc.) a player in the front line. — *n* **for'warder.** — *n* **for'warding** the act of sending forward merchandise, etc. — *adv* **for'-wardly.** — *n* **for'wardness.** — **forward delivery** delivery of goods at a future date. — *adj* **for'ward-looking** having regard to the future; progressive. — **forward market** a market in which commodities, etc., are contracted to be bought and sold at a future date at an agreed price (**forward price**); **forward pass** (*Rugby football*) an illegal pass in which the ball is thrown forward towards the opponents' goal-line. [O.E. *foreward* — *fore*, and *-ward* signifying direction; the *s* of *forwards* is a genitive ending.]

forwent *fər-* or *för-went'*. See **forgo.**

Fosbury flop *foz'bə-ri flop*, *n* a method of high-jumping in which the athlete goes over the bar horizontally on his or her back. [R. *Fosbury* (b. 1947), U.S. athlete.]

foss or **fosse** *fos*, *n* a ditch, moat, trench or canal. [Fr. *fosse* — L. *fossa* — *fodĕre*, *fossum*, to dig.]

fossa *fos'ə*, (*anat*) *n* a pit or depression: — *pl* **foss'ae** (-*ē*). [L., a ditch.]

fosse. See **foss.**

fossil *fos'l*, or *-il*, *n* a relic or trace of a former living thing preserved in the rocks (*geol*); an antiquated, out-of-date, or unchanging person or thing (*fig*). — *adj* dug out of the earth; in the condition of a fossil; antiquated. — *adj* **fossilif'erous** bearing or containing fossils. — *n* **fossilisā'tion** or **-z-**. — *vt* **foss'ilise** or **-ize** to convert into a fossil (also *fig*). — *vi* to become fossil; to look for fossils (*colloq*). — *adj* **foss'il-fired** (of a power station, etc.) burning fossil fuel. — **fossil fuel** coal, oil, etc., produced in the earth by process of fossilisation; **fossil water** water which has been trapped in an underground reservoir since a previous geological age. [Fr. *fossile* — L. *fossilis* — *fodĕre*, to dig.]

fossorial *fos-ö'ri-əl*, (*zool*) *n* adapted for digging. [L. *fossor* — *fodĕre*, to dig.]

foster *fos'tər*, *vt* to bring up or nurse, esp. a child not one's own; to put a child into the care of someone not its parent; to encourage; to promote; to cherish. — *vi* to care for a child in a foster-home. — *adj* of or concerned with fostering. — *n* **fos'terage** the act or custom of fostering or nursing; the condition or relation of foster-child; the care of a foster-child; the act of encouraging or cultivating. — *n* **fos'terer.** — *n* **fos'tering.** — *n* **fos'terling** a foster-child. — **fos'ter-brother** a male child nursed or brought up with a child or children of different parents; **fos'ter-child** a child nursed or brought up by someone who is not its parent; **fos'ter-daughter; fos'ter-father** a man who brings up a child in place of its father; **fos'ter-home; fos'ter-mother** a woman who brings up a child not her own; **fos'ter-nurse; fos'ter-parent; fos'ter-sister; fos'ter-son.** [O.E. *fōstrian*, to nourish, *fōster*, food.]

Foucault current. Same as **eddy current.**

fouetté *fwe'tā*, *n* ballet-step in which the foot makes a whip-like movement. [Fr.]

fought *föt*, *pa t* and *pa p* of **fight.**

foul *fowl*, *adj* filthy; dirty; disfigured; untidy; loathsome; obscene; impure; shameful; gross; in bad condition; stormy; unfavourable; unfair; of little worth; choked up; entangled; bad (*colloq*). — *vt* to make foul; to collide with, come in accidental contact with; to obstruct. — *vi* to collide. — *n* the act of fouling; any breach of the rules in games or contests. — *adv* in a foul manner; unfairly. — *adv* **foul'ly.** — *n* **foul'ness.** — *adj* **foul'-mouthed** or **foul'-spoken** addicted to the use of foul or profane language. — **foul'-mouthedness; foul play** unfair action in any game or contest; dishonest dealing generally; violence or murder; **foul'-up** see **foul up.** — **claim a foul** to assert that a rule has been broken, and claim the penalty; **fall foul of** to come against; to clash with; to assail; **foul up** to make dirty; to (cause to) be or become blocked or entangled; to spoil (*colloq*); to cause to fail or break down (*colloq*); to bungle, make a mistake in (*colloq*; *n* **foul'-up**); **make foul water** (*naut*) to come into such shallow water that the keel raises the mud. [O.E. *fūl*.]

foulard *fōō-lärd'* or *-lär'*, *n* a soft untwilled silk fabric. [Fr.]

found[1] *fownd*, *pa t* and *pa p* of **find.** — **all found** see under **all**; **found money** money gain got for nothing.

found[2] *fownd*, *vt* to lay the bottom or foundation of; to establish on a basis; to originate; to endow. — *vi* to rely (with *on*). — *n* **foundā'tion** the act of founding; (often in *pl*) the base of a building; the groundwork or basis; a permanent fund for a benevolent purpose or for some special object; a cosmetic preparation used as a base for facial make-up; a priming substance applied to a canvas or board as a base for oil-painting. — *adj* **foundā'tional.** — *n* **foundā'tioner** someone supported from the funds or foundation of an institution. — *n* **found'er**, *fem* **found'ress**, someone who founds, establishes or originates; an endower. — **foundation course** an introductory course of study; **foundation garment** a woman's undergarment for supporting or controlling the figure; **foundā'tion-stone** one of the stones forming the foundation of a building, esp. a stone laid with public ceremony; **foundā'tion-stop** any organ stop whose sounds are those belonging to the keys, or differing by whole octaves only; a fundamental flue stop; **found'er-member** one of those members of a society who were instrumental in its foundation; **founding father** someone who forms or establishes an institution, organisation, etc. [Fr. *fonder* — L. *fundāre*, *-ātum*, to found — *fundus*, the bottom.]

found[3] *fownd*, *vt* to make by melting and allowing to harden in a mould (esp. metals); to cast. — *n* **found'er.** — *n* **found'ing.** — *n* **found'ry** the art of founding or casting; a place where founding is carried on; articles produced by founding. [Fr. *fondre* — L. *fundĕre*, *fūsum*, to pour.]

founder *fownd'ər*, *vi* (of a building) to subside; to collapse in ruins (also *fig*); to go to the bottom; (of a ship) to fill with water and sink; (of a horse) to stumble, go lame; to stick in mud. — *vt* to cause to founder. — *n* a collapse. [O.Fr. *fondrer*, to fall in — *fond* — L. *fundus*, bottom.]

foundling *fownd'ling*, *n* a little child found deserted.

fount[1] *fownt* or (esp. in U.S.) **font** *font*, (*printing*) *n* a complete assortment of types of one sort, with all that is necessary for printing in that kind of letter. [Fr. *fonte* — *fondre* — L. *fundĕre*, to cast.]

fount[2] *fownt*, *n* a spring of water; a source. [L. *fōns*, *fontis*.]

fountain *fownt'in*, *n* a spring of water, a jet; a structure for supplying drinking water or other liquid; an ornamental structure with jets, spouts, and basins of water; a reservoir from which oil, ink, etc., flows, as in a lamp or a pen; the source. — *vi* to spring up or gush, as from a fountain. — **fount'ain-head** the head or source; the beginning; **fount'ain-pen** a pen with a reservoir for ink. [Fr. *fontaine* — L.L. *fontāna* — L. *fōns*, *fontis*, a spring.]

four *för*, *n* the cardinal number next above three; a symbol representing that number; a set of four things or persons (leaves, oarsmen, etc.); a four-oar boat; a four-cylinder engine or car; a shoe or other article of a size denoted by 4; a card with four pips; a score of four points, tricks, strokes, etc.; the fourth hour after midday or midnight; having four dimensions, esp. length, breadth and depth, with the addition of time; the age of four years. — *adj* of the number four; four years old. — *adj* and *adv* **four'fold** in four divisions; four times as much. — *n* **four'foldness.** — *n* **four'some** a group of four; anything in which four act together, esp. a game of golf (two against two, partners playing the same ball) or a reel — also *adj*. — *adj* (*golf*) played two against two with four balls, best balls counting. — *adj* **four'-figure** running into four figures; to four places of decimals. — *adj* **four'-foot** measuring four feet. — *adj* **four'-footed** having four feet. — *adj* **four'-handed** having four hands; played by four players (*cards*). — **four'-in-hand** a coach drawn by four horses. — *adj* **four'-leaved**, **four'-leafed** or **four'-leaf.** — *adj* **four'-legged.** — **four'-pack** (*colloq*) four cans of drink packaged together and sold as a single item. — *adj* **four'-part** in four parts. — **four'pence** the value of four pennies. — *adj* **four'penny** sold or offered for fourpence. — **four-post'er** a large bed with four curtain posts; **four-pound'er** a gun that throws a four-pound shot. — *adj* **four'score** eighty. — **four-**

seat'er a vehicle seated for four. — *adj* **four'-square** (also *adv*) square; presenting a firm bold front; frank, honest, forthright. — *adj* **four'-wheel** acting on or by means of four wheels. — *adj* **four'-wheeled**. — **four-letter word** any of a number of vulgar short words, esp. of four letters, referring to sex or excrement; **fourpenny one** (*slang*) a blow, punch; **four-stroke cycle** in an internal-combustion engine, a recurring series of four strokes of the piston — an out-stroke drawing the mixed gases into the cylinder, an in-stroke compressing them, an out-stroke impelled by their explosion and working the engine, and an in-stroke driving out the burnt gas; **on all fours** on four feet, or hands and feet or hands and knees; analogous, strictly comparable. [O.E. *fēower*.]

fourchette *fōōr-shet'*, *n* a forked piece between glove fingers, uniting the front and back parts; the furcula, or wishbone, of a bird; an animal's web foot; part of the external female genitals, a membrane at the posterior junction of the labia minora. [Fr., dimin. of *fourche* — L. *furca*, fork.]

fourteen *fōr-tēn'* or *fōr'tēn*, *n* and *adj* four and ten. — *adj* **four'teenth** (or *-tēnth'*) last of fourteen; next after the thirteenth; equal to one of fourteen equal parts. — *n* a fourteenth part; a person or thing in fourteenth position. — *adv* **fourteenth'ly**. [O.E. *fēowertēne* (*-tīene*); see **four** and **ten**.]

fourth *fōrth*, *adj* last of four; next after the third; equal to one of four equal parts. — *n* one of four equal parts; a person or thing in fourth position; an interval of three (conventionally called four) diatonic degrees (*mus*); a tone at that interval from another; a combination of two tones separated by that interval. — *adv* **fourth'ly**. — **fourth dimension** that of time, as opp. to the three spatial dimensions; that which is beyond ordinary experience. — *adj* **fourth-dimen'sional**. — *adj* **fourth'-rate** of the fourth order; inferior. — **fourth gear** see **gear**; **Fourth World** the poorest and least developed of the poor countries of the world; the poorest people in the developed countries. [O.E. *fēowertha*, *fēortha*.]

fousty *fōō'sti*, (*Scot*) *adj* mouldy or damp; having a musty smell; fusty.

fovea *fō'vi-ə*, (*anat*) *n* a depression or pit: — *pl* **fō'veae** (*-vi-ē*). — *adj* **fō'veal** of or like a fovea; of the fovea centralis. — *adj* **fō'veate** pitted. — **fovea centralis** (*sen-trä'lis* or *-trā'*) a fovea in the centre of the back of the retina, the place where vision is sharpest. [L. *fŏvea*.]

fowl *fowl*, *n* a bird; a bird of the poultry kind, a cock or hen; the flesh of fowl: — *pl* **fowls** or **fowl**. — *vi* to kill or try to kill wildfowl. — *n* **fowl'er** a person who takes wildfowl. — *n* **fowl'ing**. — **fowl'ing-net** a net for catching birds; **fowl'ing-piece** a light gun for small-shot, used in fowling; **fowl'-pest** an acute contagious virus disease of birds (**fowl'-plague**); another similar disease, Newcastle disease. [O.E. *fugol*.]

fox *foks*, *n* an animal related to the dog having upright ears and a long bushy tail (*fem* **vix'en**); extended to other animals, such as flying-fox; anyone notorious for cunning. — *vt* (*colloq*) to baffle, deceive, cheat. — *vi* (*colloq*) to act cunningly; to cheat. — *vi* and *vt* (of paper) to discolour, showing brownish marks. — *adj* **foxed** (of books) discoloured; drunk; baffled. — *n* **fox'iness** craftiness; decay; a harsh, sour taste; spotted state as in books. — *n* **fox'ing** the act of one who foxes; discoloration (as of paper). — *adj* **fox'y** of foxes; fox-like; cunning; reddish brown; (esp. *US*; *slang*) sexually attractive. — **fox'-bat** a flying-fox, a fruit-bat; **fox'-earth** a fox's burrow; **fox'glove** a plant (digitalis) with flowers like glove-fingers; **fox'-hole** a fox's earth; a small entrenchment (*mil*); **fox'hound** a hound used for chasing foxes; **fox'-hunt**; **fox'-hunter**; **fox'-hunting**; **fox'-mark** a brownish mark on paper that has foxed; **fox'-tail** a fox's brush; a genus (*Alopecurus*) of grasses, with head like a fox's tail; **fox'-terrier** a kind of terrier trained to unearth foxes; **fox'-trot** a ballroom dance to syncopated music. [O.E.]

foyer *foi'ā* or *foi'ər* (Fr. *fwä-yā*), *n* in theatres, a public room, an anteroom; the entrance hallway of a hotel, etc. [Fr., — L. *focus*, hearth.]

FP *abbrev* for: fireplug; former pupil; Free Presbyterian.

fp *abbrev* for: forte-piano; freezing-point.

FPA *abbrev* for Family Planning Association.

FPS or **fps** *abbrev* for foot-pound-second.

Fr. *abbrev* for: Father; franc; France; French; Friar; Friday.

Fr (*chem*) *symbol* for francium.

fr. *abbrev* for: fragment; franc; frequently.

fra *frä*, (It.) *n* brother, friar.

frabjous *frab'jəs*, *adj* perh. joyous; surpassing. — *adv* **frab'jously**. [Invented by Lewis Carroll.]

fracas *frak'ä* or *frä-kä'*, *n* uproar; a noisy quarrel: — *pl* **fracas** (*-käz*). [Fr., — It. *fracasso* — *fracassare*, to make an uproar.]

fractal *frak'təl*, *n* a geometrical entity characterised by a basic pattern that is repeated at ever decreasing sizes. — Also *adj*. — *n* **fractal'ity**. [Fr. — L. *fractūs*, past p. of *frangĕre*, to break.]

fraction *frak'shən*, *n* a fragment or small piece; any part of a unit (*arith*); a portion separated by fractionation; the breaking of the bread in the Eucharist (*Christian relig*); a group of Communists acting as a unit within a larger non-Communist body; a faction or schismatic group within the Communist party. — *adj* **frac'tional**. — *n* **fractionalīsā'tion** or **-z-**. — *vt* **frac'tionalise** or **-ize** to break up into parts. — *n* **frac'tionalism** the state of consisting of discrete units; the action of forming a fraction within the Communist party. — *n* **frac'tionalist** a breaker-up of political unity. — *adv* **frac'tionally**. — *adj* **frac'tionary** fractional; fragmentary. — *vt* **frac'tionate** to break up into smaller units; to separate the components of by distillation or otherwise. — *n* **fractionā'tion**. — *n* **frac'tionātor** a plant for carrying out fractional distillation. — *n* **fractionīsā'tion** or **-z-**. — *vt* **frac'tionise** or **-ize** to break up into fractions. — **fractional distillation** a distillation process for the separation of the various constituents of liquid mixtures by means of their different boiling-points. [L. *frangĕre*, *fractum*, to break.]

fractious *frak'shəs*, *adj* ready to quarrel; cross. — *adv* **frac'tiously**. — *n* **frac'tiousness**. [L. *frangĕre*, to break.]

fractography *frak-tog'rə-fi*, *n* the microscopic study of fractures in metal surfaces.

fracture *frak'chər*, *n* breaking; the breach or part broken; the surface of breaking, other than cleavage; the breaking of a bone. — *vt* and *vi* to break through; to crack. — **Colles' fracture** see **Colles'**; **comminuted fracture** a fracture in which the bone is splintered; **compound fracture** the breaking of a bone, communicating with a co-existing skin wound; **greenstick fracture** a fracture where the bone is partly broken, partly bent, occurring esp. in limbs of children; **impacted fracture** a fracture in which the ends of bone are driven into each other; **simple fracture** a fracture of bone without wound in the skin. [L. *frangĕre*, *frāctum*, to break.]

fraena, fraenum. See **frenum**.

fragile *fraj'īl* or in U.S. *-əl*, *adj* easily broken; frail; delicate. — *adv* **fra'gilely**. — *n* **fragility** (*frə-jil'i-ti*) or **fra'gileness**. [Fr., — L. *fragilis* — *frangĕre*, *frāctum*, to break.]

fragment *frag'mənt*, *n* a piece broken off; a usu. small piece of something broken or smashed; an unfinished portion. — *vt* and *vi* (*frag-ment'*) to break into fragments. — *adj* **fragmental** (*-ment'*; also *frag'mən-təl*) composed of fragments of older rocks;

in fragments. — *adv* **frag'mentarily**. — *n* **frag'mentariness**. — *adj* **frag'mentary** or **fragment'ed** consisting of fragments; broken; in fragments; existing or operating in separate parts, not forming a harmonious unity. — *n* **fragmentā'tion** division into fragments; cell division without mitosis (*biol*). — **fragmentation bomb** or **grenade** one which shatters into small destructive fragments on explosion. [L. *fragmentum* — *frangĕre*, *frāctum*, to break.]

fragrant *frā'grənt*, *adj* sweet-scented. — *n* **fra'grance** or **fra'grancy**. — *vt* **frag'rance** to perfume, give a fragrance to. — *adv* **fra'grantly**. — *n* **fra'grantness**. [L. *frāgrāns*, *-antis*, pres. p. of *frāgrāre*, to smell.]

frail *frāl*, *adj* very easily shattered; feeble and infirm (esp. *Scot*); decrepit; morally weak. — *adv* **frail'ly**. — *n* **frail'ness**. — *n* **frail'ty**. [O.Fr. *fraile* — L. *fragilis*, fragile.]

fraise *frāz*, *n* a tool for enlarging a drillhole. [Fr.]

framboesia *fram-bē'zi-ə*, *n* yaws. [Fr. *framboise*, raspberry.]

frame *frām*, *vt* to form; to put together; to plan, adjust or adapt; to contrive or concoct; to bring about; to articulate; to set about; to enclose in a frame or border; to make victim of a frame-up. — *n* the body; a putting together of parts; a structure; a case made to enclose, border or support anything; the skeleton of anything; the rigid part of a bicycle; a structure on which embroidery is worked; a stocking-making machine; a structure for cultivation or sheltering of plants; state (of mind), mood; the individual unit picture in cinema film or in a photographic film, cartoon strip, etc.; the total TV picture; a triangular support in which the balls are grouped for the break (*snooker*, etc.); the balls so grouped (*snooker*, etc.); in the jargon of certain games, a definite part of a game, a game, or a definite number of games. — *n* **fram'er** a person who forms or constructs; a person who makes frames for pictures, etc.; someone who devises or formulates. — *n* **fram'ing** the act of constructing; a frame or setting. — **frame'-maker** a maker of picture-frames; **frame'-saw** a thin saw stretched in a frame; **frame'-up** a trumped-up affair, esp. a false criminal charge against an innocent person; **frame'-work** the work that forms the frame; the skeleton or outline of anything. — **frame of reference** a set of axes with reference to which the position of a point, etc., is described (*lit*); the structure of standards, arising from the individual's experience, and continually developing, to which they refer, in all cases from the simplest to the most complicated, when judging or evaluating (*fig*). [O.E. *framian*, to be helpful, *fram*, forward.]

franc *frangk*, *n* a coin forming since 1795 the unit of the French monetary system (100 centimes); the unit also in Belgium, Switzerland, etc. [O.Fr. *franc*, from the legend *Francorum rex* on the first coins.]

franchise *fran'chīz* or *fran'shīz*, *n* liberty; a privilege or exemption by prescription or grant; the right of voting, esp. for an M.P.; voting qualification; a commercial concession by which a retailer is granted by a company the generally exclusive right of retailing its goods or providing its services in a specified area, with use of the company's expertise, marketing, trademark, etc.; a similar concession granted by a public authority to a broadcasting company. — *n* **franchīsee'** someone to whom a franchise is granted. — *n* **fran'chīser** a voter; a firm, etc. which grants a commercial concession. [O.Fr., — *franc*, free.]

Franciscan *fran-sis'kən*, *adj* belonging to the order of mendicant friars in the R.C. Church, founded by St *Francis* of Assisi (1182–1226). — *n* a friar of this order. [L. *Franciscus*, Francis.]

francium *fran'si-əm*, *n* the chemical element (symbol **Fr**; atomic no. 87) discovered by a Frenchwoman, Mlle Perey. [*France*.]

Franco- *frangk-ō-*, *combining form* signifying: French; French and, as in **Franco-Ger'man** or **Franco-Russ'ian**, etc. — *adj* **Franc'ophone** (also without *cap*) French-speaking (used e.g. of Africans for whom French is a second mother-tongue or French-speaking Canadians).

francolin *frang'kō-lin*, *n* a bird of the *Francolinus* genus of partridges. [Fr.]

frangible *fran'ji-bl*, *adj* easily broken. — *n* **frangibil'ity**. [L. *frangĕre*, to break.]

frangipani *fran-ji-pä'nē*, *n* the red jasmine or other species of *Plumeria*, tropical American shrubs with scented flowers; a perfume from or in imitation of red jasmine; (also **frangipane** *fran'ji-pān*) a pastry-cake filled with cream, almonds and sugar. [From the name of the inventor of the perfume *Frangipani*.]

Frank *frangk*, *n* a German of a confederation in Franconia of which a branch conquered Gaul in the 5th century, and founded France; (in the East) a Western European. — *adj* **Frank'ish**. [See **frank**.]

frank *frangk*, *adj* free, open; open or candid in expression. — *vt* to sign or mark so as to ensure free carriage; to send thus signed or marked; to mark by means of a **frank'ing-machine** to show that postage has been paid. — *n* the signature of a person who had the right to frank a letter; the mark left by a franking machine; a franked cover. — *adv* **frank'ly** to be frank; in a frank manner. — *n* **frank'ness**. [O.Fr. *franc* — L.L. *francus*.]

Frankenstein *frangk'ən-stīn*, *n* the hero of Mrs Shelley's Gothic novel so named, who creates an animate creature like a man, only to his own torment; by confusion, any creation that brings disaster to its author.

frankfurter *frangk'fûr-tər* or *-fo͝or-tər*, *n* a small smoked sausage. [Short for Ger. *Frankfurter Wurst*, Frankfurt sausage.]

frankincense *frangk'in-sens*, *n* olibanum, a sweet-smelling resin from Arabia, used as incense; spruce resin. [O.Fr. *franc encens*, pure incense.]

frantic *fran'tik*, *adj* mad, furious; wild. — *adv* **fran'tically**. — *n* **fran'ticness**. [O.Fr. *frenetique* — L. *phrenēticus* — Gr. *phrenētikos*, mad — *phrēn*, the mind.]

frappé *fra'pā*, *adj* (*fem* **frapp'ée**) iced; artificially cooled. — *n* an iced drink. [Fr., past p. of *frapper*, to strike.]

frat. *abbrev* for: fraternise; fraternity.

fraternal *frə-tûr'nl*, *adj* belonging to a brother or brethren; brotherly; (of twins) dizygotic, not identical. — *adv* **frater'nally**. [L. *frāter*, a brother.]

fraternise or **-ize** *frat'ər-nīz*, *vi* to associate as brothers; to seek brotherly fellowship; to come into friendly association (with). — *n* **fraternīsā'tion** or **-z-**. — *n* **frat'erniser** or **-z-**. — *n* **frater'nity** the state of being brothers; a brotherhood; a society formed on a principle of brotherhood; an American college association; any set of people with something in common. [L. *frāter*, a brother.]

fratricide *frat'ri-sīd* or *frāt'*, *n* someone who kills his brother; the murder of a brother. — *adj* **fratricī'dal**. [Fr., — L. *frāter*, *frātris*, a brother, *caedĕre*, to kill.]

Frau or **frau** *frow*, *n* a woman; a wife; Mrs. — *n* **Fräulein** or **fräulein** (*froi'līn*) an unmarried woman; often applied to a German governess; Miss. [Ger.]

fraud *fröd*, *n* deceit; imposture; criminal deception done with the intention of gaining an advantage; a deceptive trick; a cheat, swindler (*colloq*); a fraudulent production. — *n* **frauds'man** a person involved in criminal fraud. — *n* **fraud'ster** a swindler. — *n* **fraud'ūlence** or **fraud'ūlency**. — *adj* **fraud'ūlent** using fraud. — *adv* **fraud'ūlently**. [O.Fr. *fraude* — L. *fraus*, fraud.]

fraught *fröt*, *adj* filled (with); having or causing (esp. something bad or undesirable, e.g. danger; with *with*); feeling or making anxious or distressed, tension-filled. [Prob. Old Du. *vracht*.]

Fräulein. See **Frau.**

fray[1] *frā*, *n* an affray; a brawl. [Aphetic from **affray.**]

fray[2] *frā*, *vt* to wear off by rubbing; to ravel out the end or edge of; to cause a strain on (e.g. nerves, temper, etc.). — *vi* to become frayed. — *n* **fray'ing** the action of the verb; frayed-off material. [Fr. *frayer* — L. *fricāre*, to rub.]

frazil *fraz'il* or *frā'zil*, *n* ice formed in small spikes and plates in rapid streams. [Can. Fr. *frasil*; prob. Fr. *fraisil*, cinders.]

frazzle *fraz'l*, *vt* to fray, wear out. — *n* the state of being worn out; a shred. — **burnt** or **worn to a frazzle** completely burnt, or worn out.

FRCP *abbrev* for Fellow of the Royal College of Physicians (**-Edin.**, of Edinburgh; **-Lond.**, of London; **-Irel.**, of Ireland).

FRCPSGlasg. *abbrev* for Fellow of the Royal College of Physicians and Surgeons of Glasgow.

FRCS *abbrev* for Fellow of the Royal College of Surgeons (**-Ed.**, of Edinburgh; **-Eng.**, of England; **-Irel.**, of Ireland).

freak *frēk*, *n* an abnormal production of nature, a monstrosity; an eccentric; a weirdly unconventional person; someone who is wildly enthusiastic about something (esp. in combination as in *film-freak*). — *adj* capricious; unusual. — *n* **freak'iness** or **freak'ishness.** — *adj* **freak'ish, freak'ful** or **freak'y** apt to change the mind suddenly; unusual, odd. — *adv* **freak'ishly.** — **freak'-out** (*slang*) a (drug-induced) hallucinatory or (*loosely*) wildly exciting, unconventional experience or occurrence (*vi* **freak** or **freak out**). — **phone freak(ing)** see under **phone.** [Orig., a caprice; cf. O.E. *frīcian*, to dance.]

freckle *frek'l*, *vt* to spot; to colour with spots. — *n* a yellowish or brownish-yellow spot on the skin, esp. of fair-haired persons; any small spot. — *n* **freck'ling** a little spot. — *adj* **freck'ly** or **freck'led** full of freckles. [O.N. *freknur* (pl.), Dan. *fregne*.]

free *frē*, *adj* (*compar* **freer** *frē'ər*, *superl* **freest** *frē'əst*) not bound; not under arbitrary government; not strict, or bound by rules; not literal; unimpeded; unconstrained; readily cut, separated or wrought; frank; lavish; uncombined; unattached; exempt (with *from*); not suffering from or encumbered with (with *of* or *from*); having a franchise (with *of*); without payment; bold; indecent. — *adv* freely; without payment; without obstruction. — *vt* to set at liberty; to deliver from what confines; to rid (with *from* or *of*): — *pr p* **free'ing;** *pa t* and *pa p* **freed.** — In combination denoting free from, as in *trouble-free*. — *n* **free'bie** (orig. *US*; *slang*) something supplied free of charge. — Also *adj*. — *n* **free'dom** liberty; frankness; outspokenness; unhampered boldness; separation; privileges connected with a city (often granted as an honour merely); improper familiarity; licence. — *adv* **free'ly.** — *n* **free'ness.** — *n* **freer** (*frē'ər*) a liberator. — **free agency** the state or power of acting freely, or without necessity or constraint upon the will; **free agent.** — *adj* **free'-arm** with unsupported arm. — **free association** a technique in psychoanalysis based either on the first association called forth by each of a series of words or on a train of thought suggested by a single word; **free'-board** the distance between waterline and deck (*naut*); a strip of land outside a fence, or a right thereto; **free'booter** someone who roves about freely in search of booty (Du. *vrijbuiter*). — *adj* **free'born** born free. — **Free Church** that branch of the Presbyterians in Scotland which left the Established Church in the Disruption of 1843; the small minority of that group who refused to combine with the United Presbyterians in the United Free Church; in England, a Nonconformist church; **freed'man** or **freed'woman** a man or woman who has been a slave and has been freed: — *pl* **freed'men** or **freed'women; freedom fighter** someone who fights in an armed movement for the liberation of a nation, etc. from a government considered unjust, tyrannical, etc.; **free enterprise** the conduct of business without interference from the state; **free'-fall** the motion of an unpropelled body in a gravitational field, as that of a spacecraft in orbit; the part of a parachute jump before the parachute opens. — *adj* of or pertaining to freefall or to a parachute jump which is partly a freefall. — *vi* to fall with one's parachute kept closed. — **free-fall'ing; free fight** a confused or promiscuous fight; **free flight** the flight of a rocket, etc. when its motor is no longer producing thrust; **Free'fone®** a British Telecom service allowing callers e.g. to a business or organisation to make their calls free of charge, the charges being paid by the business or organisation concerned; **free'-for-all** a contest open to anybody; a free fight. — Also *adj*. — *adj* **free gift** something given free with a product as an incentive to buy. — *adj* **free'-hand** executed by the unguided hand. — **free hand** complete freedom of action. — *adj* **free-hand'ed** open-handed; liberal. — **free-hand'edness.** — *adj* **free'hold** a property held by fee simple, fee tail, or for life; the holding of property in any of such ways. — Also *adj*. — **free'holder** a person who possesses a freehold; **free house** a public house that is not tied to a particular supplier; **free kick** (*football*) a kick allowed without interference, as a penalty against the opposing side for infringing the rules; **free'lance** anyone who works for himself or herself, employed or paid by others only for particular, usu. short-term, assignments (also **free'lancer**). — Also *adj*, *adv* and *vi*. — *vi* **free'load** (esp. *US*; *colloq*) to eat at someone else's expense; to sponge; to gain from others' efforts. — *n* a free meal. — **free'loader.** — *n* and *adj* **free'-loading.** — **free love** the claim to freedom in sexual relations, unshackled by marriage; **free'-lover** someone who advocates free love; **free'man** or **free'-woman** a man or woman who is free or enjoys liberty; someone who holds a particular franchise or privilege: — *pl* **free'men** or **free'women; free'-māson** (often with *cap*) a member of a secret fraternity, united in lodges for social enjoyment and mutual assistance. — *adj* **freemason'ic.** — **free-mā'sonry** (also with *cap*) the institutions, practices, etc. of freemasons; instinctive understanding and sympathy; **free'-port** a port open on equal terms to all traders; a free-trade zone adjacent to a port, allowing duty-free import and re-export of goods; **Free'post®** a Royal Mail service which allows inquirers or potential customers to write to a business or organisation free of charge, the postage costs being paid by the business or organisation concerned; **free radical** a group of atoms containing at least one unpaired electron existing briefly during certain chemical reactions. — *adj* **free'-range** (of poultry) allowed some freedom to move about; (of eggs) laid by free-range hens. — **free'-school** a school where no tuition fees are exacted; **free'sheet** a newspaper distributed free; **free skating** competitive figure skating in which the skater selects movements from an officially approved list of jumps, spins, etc.; **free speech** the right to express one's opinions freely in public. — *adj* **free'-spōken** accustomed to speak without reserve. — **free'-spōkenness.** — *adj* **free'-standing** not supported by or attached to anything else. — **free'stone** any easily wrought building stone without tendency to split in layers; a freestone fruit. — *adj* (of a type of peach, etc.) having a stone from which the pulp easily separates (opp. to *clingstone*). — *adj* **free'style** of a (e.g. swimming or skiing) race or competition, in which a competitor is free to choose which style or method to use or which movements to perform; (of wrestling) all-in; (of a competitor) taking part in freestyle competitions, etc. — *n* freestyle competitions; **free'styler** a competitor in such competitions. — *adj* **free'-swimming** swimming about, not attached. — **free'thinker** a person who rejects authority in religion; a rationalist. — *n* and *adj* **free'-thinking.** — **free'-thought; free'-trade** free or unrestricted trade; free interchange of commodities without protective duties; **free'-trader** someone who practises or advocates this; a smuggler; a smuggling vessel; **free verse** verse defying the usual conventions as to regularity of metre, rhyme, length of lines, etc.; rhythmic prose arranged as irregular verses; **free vote** a vote left to individual choice, free from party discipline; **free'way** a toll-free road for high-speed traffic (*US*); a motorway (*SAfr*); **free'wheel** the mechanism of a bicycle by which the hind-wheel may be temporarily disconnected and set free from the driving-gear. — *vi* to cycle with wheel so disconnected; (of motor vehicle or its driver) to coast; to move, act, live, without restraint or concern (*fig*). — **free'wheeling; free-will'** freedom of the will from restraint; liberty of choice; the power of self-determination. — *adj* **free'-will** spontaneous; voluntary. — **freewoman** see **freeman; Free World** the collective name used of themselves by non-communist countries. — **free collective bargaining** collective bargaining (q.v.) without government-imposed or other restrictions; **for free** (*colloq*) given without desire for payment or other return; **free and easy** informal in manner, unceremonious; easy-going; **free on board** (abbrev **f o b**) delivered on a vessel or other conveyance without charge; **it's a free country** (*colloq*) there is no objection to or law against the carrying-out of whatever action has been proposed; **make free with** to be familiar with, to take liberties with; to help oneself liberally to; **make so free as to** to venture to. [O.E. *frēo*.]

freebie, Freefone®. See under **free**.

freesia *frē'zi-ə*, *n* a plant of the South African genus (*Freesia*) of the iris family, scented greenhouse plants. [After F.H.T. *Freese*, or H.Th. *Frees*, German physicians, or according to some, E.M. *Fries*, Swedish botanist.]

freeze *frēz*, *vi* to become ice; to become solid by fall of temperature; to be at a temperature at which water would freeze; to be very cold; to become motionless, stiff, attached, or stopped by, or as if by, cold. — *vt* to cause to freeze; to fix; to stabilise; to prevent the use of or dealings in; to stop at, not develop beyond, a particular state or stage; to put a temporary stop to; to stop (a moving film) at a particular frame; to preserve (esp. food) by freezing and storing below freezing-point; to anaesthetise (a part of the body): — *pr p* **freez'ing;** *pa t* **frōze;** *pa p* **frōz'en.** — *n* a frost; a stoppage. — *adj* **freez'able.** — *n* **freez'er** a freezing apparatus; anything that freezes; a special compartment in a refrigerator designed to freeze fresh foods; a deep-freeze. — *adj* **freez'ing** very cold. — *vt* **freeze'-dry.** — **freeze'-drying** rapid freezing and evaporation to dryness in a vacuum for preservation or storage of a substance, e.g. an antibiotic; **freeze'-frame** a frame of a cinematographic film repeated, or a frame of a video film held, to give a still picture; **freeze'-out** see **freeze out** below; **freeze'-up** in U.S. and Canada, the period when ice forms on lakes, etc., at onset of winter; **freez'ing-down** lowering of the body temperature; **freez'ing-point** the temperature at which a liquid solidifies. — **freeze down** to lower the body temperature in preparation for heart and other operations; **freeze out** (*colloq*) to oblige to leave; to exclude (*n* **freeze'-out**). [O.E. *frēosan*, past p. *froren*.]

freight *frāt*, *n* the lading or cargo, esp. of a ship; the charge for transporting goods by water or land. — *vt* to load (esp. a ship). — *n* **freight'age** money paid for freight. — *n* **freight'er** a person who freights a vessel; a cargo-carrying boat, etc.; a transporting agent (*US*). — **freight'liner** a train having specially designed containers and rolling-stock and used for rapid transport of goods. — Also *adj*. — **freight'-train** a goods train. [Prob. Old Du. *vrecht*, a form of *vracht*.]

frena. See **frenum**.

French *french* or *-sh*, *adj* belonging to *France* or its people; originating in France (sometimes without *cap*). — *n* the people of France; the language of France, also an official language in Belgium, Switzerland, Canada and other countries. — *n* **Frenchificā'tion.** — *vt* **French'ify** to make French or Frenchlike. — *n* **French'y** a contemptuous name for a Frenchman. — **French bean** (sometimes without *cap*) the common kidney-bean eaten, pods and all, as a vegetable. — *adj* **French'-Canādian** of the French-speaking part of Canada. — *n* a French-Canadian person; the French language of Canada; **French chalk** soapstone; **French cricket** an esp. children's game resembling cricket, in which the batsman's legs serve as the wicket; **French curve** a thin plate with the outlines of various curves on it, used for drawing curves; **French dressing** a salad dressing consisting of oil and vinegar or lemon juice, and usu. seasoning; **French fry** (*pl* **French fries**) or **French fried potato** a potato-chip; **French horn** the orchestral horn; **French kiss** a kiss in which the tongue is inserted into one's partner's mouth; **French letter** (*slang*) a condom; **French loaf** crusty bread baked in long narrow shape with tapered ends; **French'man**: — *pl* **French'men; French polish** a varnish for furniture, consisting chiefly of shellac dissolved in spirit. — *vt* **French-pol'ish** to treat with French polish. — **French-pol'isher; French-pol'ishing; French seam** a seam stitched on right side then on wrong side to enclose raw edges; **French stick** a very narrow French loaf; **French toast** bread dipped in egg (and milk) and fried; **French window** a doorlike window; **French'woman**: — *pl* **French'women.** — **pardon** (or **excuse**) **my French** (*colloq*) pardon my bad language; **take French leave** to depart without notice or permission; to disappear suspiciously. [O.E. *Frencisc* — L. *Francus* — O.H.G. *Franko*.]

frenetic *fri-net'ik*, *adj* delirious; frantic; frenzied; mad; distracted. — *adj* **frenet'ical.** — *adv* **frenet'ically.** [O.Fr. *frénétique* — L. *phrenēticus* — late Gr. *phrenētikos* — Gr. *phrenītis*, delirium — *phrēn*, heart, mind.]

frenum or **fraenum** *frē'nəm*, *n* a ligament restraining the motion of a part of the body: — *pl* **fre'na** or **frae'na.** [L. *frēnum*, a bridle.]

frenzy *fren'zi*, *n* a violent excitement; a paroxysm of madness. — *vt* to drive to frenzy. — *adj* **fren'zical.** — *adj* **fren'zied.** [O.Fr. *frenesie* — L. and late Gr. *phrenēsis* — Gr. *phrenītis*.]

Freon® *frē'on*, *n* any of the family of chemicals containing fluorine, used as refrigerants, etc. (also without *cap*). — **Frē'on-12** dichlorodifluoromethane (CF_2Cl_2), widely used in household refrigerators.

frequent *frē'kwənt*, *adj* coming or occurring often. — *vt* (*fri-kwent'*) to visit often; to associate with; to resort to; to crowd. — *n* **frē'quency** or **frē'quence** commonness of recurrence; the number of vibrations, cycles, or other recurrences in unit time (in ascending order, *high, very high, ultra-high, extremely high, super-high frequency*). — *n* **frēquentā'tion** the act of visiting often. — *adj* **frequentative** (*fri-kwent'ə-tiv*; *gram*) denoting the frequent repetition of an action. — *n* (*gram*) a verb expressing this repetition. — *n* **frequent'er.** — *adv* **frē'-**

quently. — *n* **frē'quentness**. — **frequency modulation** modulation in radio transmission by varying the frequency of the carrier wave, giving greater fidelity than amplitude modulation and almost freedom from atmospherics; **high frequency** a radio frequency of between 3 and 30 megahertz; **low frequency** a radio frequency of between 30 and 300 kilohertz. [L. *frequēns*, *frequentis*; conn. with *farcīre*, to stuff.]

frère *frer*, (Fr.) *n* a brother.

fresco *fres'kō*, *n* a mode of painting upon walls covered with damp plaster; a picture so painted: — *pl* **fres'coes** or **fres'cos**. — *vt* to paint in fresco. — *adj* **fres'coed** (*-kōd*). — *n* **frescoer** (*fres'kō-ər*). — *n* **fres'coing**. — *n* **fres'coist**. [It. *fresco*, fresh.]

fresh *fresh*, *adj* in new condition; not stale, faded or soiled; new, recently added; raw, inexperienced; in youthful bloom; cool, invigorating; brisk; amorously over-free (*slang*); without salt; not preserved by pickling, drying, salting, etc.; cheeky, pert. — *adv* freshly; afresh; newly. — *vt* **fresh'en** to make fresh; to take the saltness from. — *vi* to grow fresh. — *vt* and *vi* to make (oneself) fresh by washing, etc. (often with *up*). — *n* **fresh'er** a student in their first year. — *adj* **fresh'ish**. — *adv* **fresh'ly** with freshness, newly; anew. — *n* **fresh'ness**. — **fresh'man** a newcomer; a student in his or her first year. — *adj* **fresh'water** of or pertaining to, or living in, fresh water not salt; accustomed to sail only on fresh water. [O.E. *fersc*.]

fret[1] *fret*, *vt* to eat into; to corrode; to wear away by rubbing; to rub, chafe; to vex, irritate. — *vi* to wear away; to vex oneself; to worry; to chafe: — *pr p* **frett'ing**; *pa t* and *pa p* **frett'ed**. — *n* irritation; worry; a worn or eroded spot; sea fret. — *adj* **fret'ful** peevish. — *adv* **fret'fully**. — *n* **fret'fulness**. — *adj* **frett'ing** vexing. — *n* peevishness. [O.E. *fretan*, to gnaw — *for-* (intensive) and *etan*, to eat.]

fret[2] *fret*, *vt* to ornament with interlaced work; to variegate: — *pr p* **frett'ing**; *pa t* and *pa p* **frett'ed**. — *n* ornamental network; a type of decoration for a cornice, border, etc., consisting of lines meeting usu. at right angles, the pattern being repeated to form a continuous band. — *adj* **frett'ed** or **frett'y** ornamented with frets. — **fret'saw** a saw with a narrow blade and fine teeth, used for fretwork, scrollwork, etc.; **fret'work** ornamental work consisting of frets; perforated woodwork. [O.Fr. *freter*, to adorn with interlaced work, *frete*, trellis-work; prob. infl. by or confused with O.E. *frætwa*, ornament.]

fret[3] *fret*, *n* any of the wooden or metal ridges on the fingerboard of a guitar or other instrument on to which the strings are pressed in producing the various notes. — *vt* to furnish with frets: — *pr p* **frett'ing**; *pa t* and *pa p* **frett'ed**. [Prob. same as **fret**[2].]

Freudian *froid'i-ən*, *adj* pertaining to Sigmund *Freud* (1856–1939), his theory of the libido, or his method of psychoanalysis. — *n* a follower of Freud. — **Freudian slip** an error or unintentional action, esp. a slip of the tongue, supposed to reveal an unconscious thought.

FRG *abbrev* for Federal Republic of Germany.

Fri. *abbrev* for Friday.

friable *frī'ə-bl*, *adj* apt to crumble; easily reduced to powder. — *n* **frīabil'ity**. — *n* **frī'ableness**. [Fr., — L. *friābilis* — *friāre*, *friātum*, to crumble.]

friar *frī'ər*, *n* a member of one of the mendicant religious orders in the R.C. Church — the Franciscans (*Friars Minor* or *Grey Friars*), Dominicans (*Friars Preachers* or *Black Friars*), Carmelites (*White Friars*), Augustinians (*Austin Friars*), and others. — *n* **fri'ary** a convent of friars. — **fri'arbird** an Australian honey-eater with featherless head; **friar's balsam** a tincture of benzoin, storax, tolu and aloes used as an inhalant. [O.Fr. *frere* — L. *frāter*, a brother.]

fricadel. See **frikkadel**.

fricandeau *frik-ən-dō'* or *frik'*, *n* a thick slice of veal, etc., larded: — *pl* **fricandeaux** (*-dōz*). [Fr.]

fricassee *frik'ə-sē* or *-sē'*, *n* a dish of fowl, rabbit, etc. cut into pieces served in sauce. — *vt* to dress as a fricassee: — *pr p* **fricasseeing**; *pa t* and *pa p* **fricasseed**. [Fr.]

friction *frik'shən*, *n*, rubbing; a force acting in the tangent plane of two bodies, when one slides or rolls upon another, in direction opposite to that of the movement (*statics*); disagreement, jarring. — *adj* **fric'ative** produced by friction; pertaining to, or being, a fricative. — *n* a consonant produced by the breath being forced through a narrow opening. — *adj* **fric'tional**. — *adj* **fric'tionless**. [L. *fricāre*, *frictum*, to rub.]

Friday *frī'di*, *n* the sixth day of the week. — **Black Friday** Good Friday, from the black vestments of the clergy and altar in the Western Church; any Friday marked by a great calamity; **Good Friday** the Friday before Easter, kept in commemoration of the Crucifixion; **Holy Friday** one of the three Fast-days in each church quarter, sometimes used for Good Friday itself. [O.E. *Frīgedæg*, day of (the goddess) *Frīg*.]

fridge *frij*, (*colloq*) *n* short for **refrigerator**. — **fridge-freez'er** a refrigerator and a deep-freeze constructed as a single unit of furniture.

fried. See **fry**[1].

friend *frend*, *n* a close or intimate acquaintance; a favourer, well-wisher, supporter; a member of a society so named; a lover (*euph*). — *adj* **friend'less**. — *n* **friend'lessness**. — *adv* **friend'lily**. — *n* **friend'liness**. — *adj* **friend'ly** like a friend; having the disposition of a friend; favourable; amicable; (of a football match, etc.) played for amusement rather than competitively (also *n*); able to handle small variations in the input format and/or enabling the easy correction of input errors (*comput*). — **-friendly** (in combination) denoting compatible with, helpful to, in sympathy with. — *n* **friend'ship** attachment from mutual esteem; friendly assistance. — **friendly society** a benefit society, an association for relief in sickness, old age, widowhood, by provident insurance. — **be friends with** to be on good terms with, well disposed towards; **Friends of the Earth** an organisation of conservationists and environmentalists; **have a friend at court** to have a friend in a position where his or her influence is likely to prove useful; **Religious Society of Friends** the proper designation of a sect of Christians better known as Quakers. [O.E. *frēond*.]

frier, fries. See **fry**[1].

Friesian. See **Frisian**.

frieze[1] *frēz*, *n* a rough, heavy woollen cloth. [Fr. *frise*.]

frieze[2] *frēz*, *n* the part of the entablature between the architrave and cornice, often ornamented with figures (*classical archit*); a decorated band along the top of a room wall (*archit*). [O.Fr. *frise*.]

frig[1] *frig*, (*vulg*) *vi* and *vt* to masturbate; (*loosely*) to have sexual intercourse with; (often with *about*) to potter about: — *pr p* **frigg'ing**; *pa t* and *pa p* **frigged**. — *n* masturbation. — *n* **frigg'ing** masturbation; pottering about. — *adj* and *adv* (as an intensive) to a great extent, very; often used as a colourless descriptive. [Late M.E. *friggen* — L. *fricāre*, to rub.]

frig[2] *frij*, (*colloq*) *n* short for **refrigerator**.

frigate *frig'it*, (*naval*) *n* formerly a vessel in the class next to ships of the line; now denoting a small escort vessel. — **frigate bird** a large tropical seabird (*Fregata*) with very long wings. [O.Fr. *fregate* — It. *fregata*.]

fright *frīt*, *n* sudden fear; terror; a figure of grotesque or ridiculous appearance (*colloq*). — *vt* **fright'en** to make afraid; to alarm; to drive by fear. — *adj* **fright'ened**. — *npl* **fright'eners** (*slang*; also in *sing*) something intended to frighten, esp. for criminal purposes. — *adj* **fright'ening.** — *adv* **fright'eningly.** — *adj* **fright'ful** terrible; horrible; unpleasant (*colloq*); great (*colloq*). — *adv* **fright'fully** dreadfully; very (*colloq*). — *n* **fright'fulness.** — **put the frighteners on someone** (*slang*) to frighten someone into (not) doing something, esp. for criminal purposes; **take fright** to become afraid. [O.E. *fyrhto*.]

frigid *frij'id, adj* frozen or stiffened with cold; cold; chillingly stiff; without spirit or feeling; unanimated; leaving the imagination untouched; (usu. of a woman) sexually unresponsive. — *n* **frigid'ity** coldness; coldness of affection; lack of animation; sexual unresponsiveness. — *adv* **frig'idly.** — *n* **frig'idness.** — **frigid zones** the parts of the earth's surface within the polar circles. [L. *frīgidus* — *frīgēre*, to be cold — *frīgus*, cold.]

frijol or **frijole** *frē'hhōl* or *frē-hhōl', n* the kidney-bean, or any species of *Phaseolus*: — *pl* **frijoles** (*-les*). [Sp. *fríjol, frijol, fréjol*.]

frikkadel or **fricadel** *frik'ə-del,* (*S Afr*) *n* a fried ball of minced meat. [Afrik. — Fr.; cf. **fricandeau.**]

frill *fril, vt* to furnish with a frill. — *n* a ruffle; a ruffled or crimped edging; superfluous ornament; (in *pl*) affected airs. — *npl* **frill'ies** light and pretty women's underwear. — *n* **frill'ing.** — *adj* **frill'y.** — **frilled lizard** a large Australian lizard (*Chlamydosaurus*) with an erectile frill about its neck. — **without frills** (in a manner, form, etc. which is) straightforward, clear, without posturing, with no superfluous additions, etc.

fringe *frinj, n* a border of loose threads; hair falling over the brow; a border; anything bordering on or additional to an activity. — *vt* to adorn with a fringe; to border. — *adj* bordering, or just outside, the recognised or orthodox form, group, etc., as in *fringe medicine, fringe banks*; unofficial, not part of the main event, as in *fringe meeting*; less important or popular, as in *fringe sports.* — *adj* **fringed.** — *adj* **fringe'less.** — *adj* **fring'y** ornamented with fringes. — **fringe benefit** something in addition to wages or salary that forms part of the regular remuneration from one's employment; **fringe'-dweller** (*Austr*) someone, esp. an Aborigine, who lives, usu. in poverty and squalor, on the edge of a town or community. — **lunatic fringe** any, usu. small, group of fanatics or extremists within a political party, pressure group, etc. [O.Fr. *frenge* — L. *fimbriae*, threads.]

frippery *frip'ər-i, n* tawdry finery; useless trifles. — *adj* useless; trifling. [O.Fr. *freperie* — *frepe*, a rag.]

Frisbee® *friz'bi, n* a plastic saucer-shaped disc which can be made to skim through the air, used in various catching-games, etc.

Frisian *friz'i-ən, n* a native of *Friesland*; the Low German language of Friesland. — *adj* of Friesland, its people, or their language. — *adj* **Friesian** (*frēz'*) Frisian, esp. of a heavy breed of dairy cattle. — *n* a Frisian; a Friesian bull or cow.

frisk *frisk, vi* to gambol; to leap playfully. — *vt* to search (a person or pockets) (*slang*); to search for radioactive radiation by contamination meter. — *n* a frolicsome movement. — *n* **frisk'er.** — *adv* **frisk'ily.** — *n* **frisk'iness.** — *adv* **frisk'ingly.** — *adj* **frisk'y** lively; jumping with gaiety; frolicsome. [O.Fr. *frisque*.]

frisson *frē-sɔ̃, n* a shiver; a shudder; a thrill. [Fr.]

frit[1] *frit, n* the mixed materials for making glass, pottery glazes, etc. — *vt* to fuse partially: — *pr p* **fritt'ing**; *pa t* and *pa p* **fritt'ed.** [Fr. *fritte* — It. *fritta* — L. *frīgĕre, frīctum*, to roast.]

frit[2] *frit* or **fritfly** *frit'flī, n* a small fly destructive to wheat and other cereal crops.

frith. See **firth.**

fritillary *frit'il-ər-i* or *-il', n* a member of the genus (*Fritillaria*) of the lily family, the best-known species with chequered purple flowers; a name for several butterflies of similar pattern. [L. *fritillus*, a dice-box.]

fritter[1] *frit'ər, n* a piece of fruit, etc., fried in batter. [O.Fr. *friture* — L. *frīgĕre, frīctum*, to fry.]

fritter[2] *frit'ər, vt* to squander piecemeal. — *n* **fritt'erer** someone who wastes time.

fritto misto *frē'tō mēs'tō,* (It.) *n* a mixed dish of fried food.

fritz *frits*: **on the fritz** (*US colloq*) *adj* out of order.

frivolous *friv'ə-ləs, adj* trifling; silly. — *n* **frivolity** (*-ol'*) a trifling habit or nature; levity. — *adv* **friv'olously.** — *n* **friv'olousness.** [L. *frīvolus*.]

frizz *friz, vt* to curl tightly. — *n* a curl; frizzed hair. — *adj* **frizzed** having the hair crisped into frizzes. — *adj* **frizz'y.** [O.Fr. *friser*, to curl.]

frizzante *frē-dzan'tā,* (It.) *adj* (of wine) sparkling.

frizzle[1] *friz'l, vt* to form in small short curls. — *vi* to go into curls. — *n* a curl; frizzled hair. — *adj* **frizz'ly.** [Related to **frizz** and **frieze[1]**.]

frizzle[2] *friz'l, vt* and *vi* to fry; to scorch. [Perh. onomatopoeic adaptation of **fry[1]**.]

fro *frō*. See **to and fro** under **to.**

frock *frok, n* a monk's wide-sleeved garment; a woman's or child's dress; an undress regimental coat. — *adj* **frocked** clothed in a frock. — **frock'-coat** a double-breasted full-skirted coat for men. [O.Fr. *froc*, a monk's frock.]

Froebelian *frœ-bēl'i-ən, adj* pertaining to Friedrich *Froebel*, German educationist (1782–1852), or to his system (**Froebel system**) of kindergarten schools. — *n* **Froe'belism.**

frog[1] *frog, n* a tailless web-footed amphibian, esp. one of the genus *Rana*, more agile than a toad; a swelling in the throat; (with *cap*) a contemptuous name for a Frenchman; on a railway, a structure in the rails allowing passage across or to another track; a depression made in the face(s) of a brick; the block by which the hair is attached to the heel of e.g. a violin bow. — *adj* **frogg'y.** — *n* (with *cap*) a contemptuous name for a Frenchman. — **frog'bit** a small aquatic plant with floating leaves; **frog'-fish** a name for various fishes, esp. the angler; **frog'-hopper** a froth-fly; **frog'man** an underwater swimmer fitted with webbed froglike feet. — *vt* **frog'-march** to carry face downwards between four men, each holding a limb; now usually, to seize from behind and force forwards while holding firmly by the arms or clothing; sometimes, to propel backwards between two people, each holding an arm. — *n* the act or process of frog-marching. — **frog'-spit** cuckoo-spit. — **a frog in the** (or **one's**) **throat** hoarseness. [O.E. *frogga*; also *frox*.]

frog[2] *frog, n* a V-shaped band of horn on the underside of a horse's hoof.

frog[3] *frog, n* an ornamental fastening or tasselled or braided button; an attachment to a belt for carrying a weapon. — *adj* **frogged** having ornamental stripes or workings of braid or lace, mostly on the breast of a coat. — *n* **frogg'ing.** [Perh. Port. *froco* — L. *floccus*, a flock, lock.]

frolic *frol'ik, n* gaiety; a prank; a gambol; a merry-making. — *vi* to play wild pranks or merry tricks; to gambol: — *pr p* **frol'icking**; *pa t* and *pa p* **frol'icked.** — *adj* **frol'icsome** merry; sportive. [Du. *vrolijk*, merry.]

from *from* or *frəm, prep* out of; away, to or at a greater distance relatively to; springing out of; beginning at; apart relatively to; by reason of. [O.E. *fram, from*.]

frond *frond, n* a leaf, esp. of a palm or fern; a leaflike thallus, or a leaflike organ of obscure morphological nature. [L. *frōns, frondis*, a leaf.]

front *frunt, n* the face, appearance; the forepart of anything; the side presented to view; the face of a building, esp. the principal face; the part facing the sea or other water; a seaside promenade; the foremost line; the scene of hostilities; the direction in which troops are facing when lined up (*mil*); a combined face presented against opponents; a group of people, organisations or parties having the same or broadly similar (esp. political or revolutionary) outlook and aims, who act together against opponents, as in *popular front* (q.v.); the breast of a man's shirt, a dickey; the bounding surface between two masses of air of different density and temperature (*meteorol*); the apparent or nominal leader behind whom the really powerful person works anonymously (also **front man**); something acting as a cover or disguise for secret or disreputable activities; boldness; impudence. — *adj* of, relating to, or in, the front; articulated with the front of the tongue. — *vt* to stand in front of or opposite; to face towards; to meet, or to oppose, face to face; to add a front to; to serve as a front to; to change into or towards a front sound; to act as the front man of; to act as the compère or frontman of; to stand, perform, etc. in front of or at the front of, as e.g. the singer with a band. — *vi* to face; to act as a front for someone else or as a cover for something secret or illicit. — *n* **front'age** the front part of a building; extent of front; ground in front. — *n* **front'ager** (*law*) a person who owns or occupies property along a road, river or shore. — *adj* **frontal** (*frunt'l*, also *front'l*) of or belonging to the front, or the forehead; pertaining to a front (*meteorol*). — *n* the façade of a building; something worn on the forehead or face; a hanging of silk, satin, etc., embroidered for an altar — now usu. covering only the top. — *adj* **front'ed** formed with a front; changed into or towards a front sound. — *n* **front'let** a band worn on the forehead. — *n* **frontogen'esis** (*meteorol*) the formation or intensification of a front. — *n* **frontol'ysis** (*-is-is*; *meteorol*) the weakening or disappearance of a front. — *adv* **front'ward** or **front'wards** towards the front. — *adv* **front'ways** or **front'wise** with face or front forward. — *adj* **front'-bench** (in the House of Commons) sitting on a front bench, as a minister, or an opposition member of similar standing. — **front=bench'er; front door; front line** the battle positions closest to the enemy; the most active, exposed or dangerous position or rôle in any activity or situation, esp. a conflict (*fig*). — *adj* **front'-line** of or relating to the front line; of or relating to a state bordering on another state in which there is an armed conflict, and often involved in that conflict. — *adj* **front-loaded** see **front-end loaded** below. — **front-loading** see **front-end loading; front'man** the person who appears on television as presenter of a programme, esp. a documentary programme; **front man** see **front** *n* above. — *adj* **front-of=house** see **front of the house** below. — *adj* **front'=page** suitable for the front page of a newspaper; important. — *adj* **front'-rank** of foremost importance. — **front'-ranker; front'-runner** in a race, a person who runs best while leading the field or one who sets the pace for the rest of the runners; someone who or that which is most popular, most likely to succeed, etc., esp. in some kind of competition. — **front-end computer** or **processor** a subsidiary computer which receives and processes data before passing it to a more powerful computer for further processing; **front-end load** an initial charge made to a person taking on a long-term savings or investment plan; **front-end loaded** or **front'=loaded; front-end loading** or **front'-loading** the taking of a large part of the total costs and commission of an investment or insurance policy out of the early payments or profits made; any similar weighting of borrowing, deduction, etc., towards the early stages of a financial transaction or accounting period; **front-end system** that part of a computerised printing system which receives the matter to be printed and provides the input to the typesetter; **front of the house** in a theatre, the collective activities such as box-office and programme selling carried on in direct contact with the public (*adj* **front'-of-house**); **front-wheel drive** a system in which the driving power is transmitted to the front wheels of a vehicle as opp. to the rear wheels; **in front** or **in front of** before. [L. *frōns*, *frontis*, the forehead.]

frontier *frunt'* or *front'ēr*, *-yər* or *-ēr'*, *n* the border of a country; the border of settled country, esp. in U.S. the advancing limit of the West pioneered in the 19th cent.; (in *pl*) the extreme limit of knowledge and attainment in a particular discipline or line of inquiry. — *adj* belonging to a frontier; bordering. — **front'iersman** (or *-tērz'*) a dweller on a frontier. [O.Fr. *frontier* — L. *frōns*, *frontis*.]

frontispiece *frunt'is-pēs* or *front'*, *n* the principal face of a building (*archit*); an illustration at the front of a book facing the title-page. [Fr. *frontispice* — L.L. *frontispicium* — *frōns*, *frontis*, forehead, and *specĕre*, *spicĕre*, to see.]

fronton *frun'tən*, (*archit*) *n* a pediment. [Fr., — It. *frontone*.]

frost *frost*, *n* a state of freezing; temperature at or below the freezing-point of water; frozen dew, or *hoar-frost*; coldness of manner or relations. — *vt* to affect with frost; to cover with hoar-frost; to make like hoar-frost. — *vi* to assume a frostlike appearance. — *adj* **frost'ed** covered by frost; having a frostlike appearance; damaged by frost. — *adv* **frost'ily**. — *n* **frost'iness**. — *n* **frost'ing** coating with hoar-frost; material or treatment to give appearance of hoar-frost; icing (esp. *US*). — *adj* **frost'less**. — *adj* **frost'like**. — *adj* **frost'y** producing, characterised by, or covered with, frost; chill (*lit* and *fig*); frostlike. — **frost'bite** inflammation, sometimes leading to gangrene, in a part of the body, caused by exposure to cold. — *adj* **frost'bitten** affected by frost (*lit* or *fig*); suffering from frostbite. — *adj* **frost'bound** bound or confined by frost. — **frost'work** tracery made by frost, as on windows; work resembling frost tracery, etc. [O.E. *frost*, *forst*.]

froth *froth*, *n* foam; chatter (*fig*); something frivolous or trivial. — *vt* to cause froth on. — *vi* to make froth. — *n* **froth'ery** mere froth. — *adv* **froth'ily**. — *n* **froth'iness**. — *adj* **froth'less**. — *adj* **froth'y** full of or like froth or foam; empty; unsubstantial. — **froth'-fly** or **froth'-hopper** any insect of the family *Cercopidae*, whose larvae live surrounded by froth (cuckoo-spit) on plants, a frog-hopper. [O.N. *frotha*.]

frottage *fro-täzh'*, *n* rubbing; the use of rubbing or rubbings to obtain texture effects in a work of art; a work of art made by this means. [Fr.]

frown *frown*, *vi* to wrinkle the brow as in anger; to look angry, gloomy, threatening; to show disapprobation. — *vt* to express, send or force by a frown. — *n* a wrinkling or contraction of the brow in displeasure, etc.; a stern look. — *adj* **frown'ing** gloomy; disapproving; threatening. — *adv* **frown'ingly**. — **frown on** or **upon** to disapprove of. [From O.Fr. *froignier*, to knit the brow.]

frowst *frowst*, *n* hot stuffy fustiness. — *n* **frowst'iness**. — *adj* **frowst'y** fusty; close-smelling; bad-smelling.

frowzy or **frowsy** *frow'zi*, *adj* fusty; stuffy, offensive; unkempt.

frozen *frōz'n*, *pa p* of **freeze**. — *adj* preserved by keeping at a low temperature; very cold; stiff and unfriendly. — **frozen shoulder** a shoulder joint which has become stiff owing to injury or enforced immobilisation.

FRS *abbrev* for Fellow of the Royal Society (**FRSE**, of Edinburgh).

fructans *fruk'tanz*, *n* a polymer of fructose, found in grasses and some vegetables. [L. *frūctus*, fruit.]

fructiferous *fruk-tif'ər-əs, adj* bearing fruit. — *n* **fructificā'tion** fruit-production; a structure that contains spores or seeds (*bot*). — *vt* **fruc'tify** to make fruitful; to fertilise. — *vi* to bear fruit. — *adj* **fruc'tive** productive, fruitful. [L. *frūctus*, fruit, *ferre*, to bear.]

fructose *fruk'tōz, n* a water-soluble simple sugar found in honey and fruit. [L. *frūctus*, fruit, and sfx. *-ose* denoting sugar (— gluc*ose*).]

fructuous *fruk'tū-əs, adj* fruitful. [L. *frūctuosus*.]

frugal *froō'gl, adj* economical in the use of means; sparing; meagre; thrifty. — *n* **frugality** (*-gal'*) economy; thrift. — *adv* **fru'gally**. [L. *frūgālis* — *frūx, frūgis*, fruit.]

frugiferous *froō-jif'ə-rəs, adj* (L. *ferre*, to bear) fruit-bearing. — *adj* **frugiv'orous** (L. *vorāre*, to eat) feeding on fruits or seeds. [L. *frūx, frūgis*, fruit.]

fruit *froōt, n* an edible part of a plant, generally sweet, acid, and juicy, esp. a part that contains the seed; a fructification, esp. the structure that develops from the ovary and its contents after fertilisation, sometimes including also structures formed from other parts of the flower or axis (*bot*); produce; (often in *pl*) product, effect, advantage; a male homosexual (*slang*, esp. *US*). — *vi* to produce fruit. — *adj* **fruit'ed** having produced fruit. — *n* **fruit'er** a tree, etc. as a producer of fruit, as in *good fruiter*; a fruit-grower. — *n* **fruit'erer** a person who deals in fruit. — *adj* **fruit'ful** productive. — *adv* **fruit'fully**. — *n* **fruit'fulness**. — *adj* **fruit'less** barren; without profit; useless; in vain. — *adv* **fruit'lessly**. — *n* **fruit'lessness**. — *n* **fruit'let** a small fruit; one of the small fruit-like parts that forms an aggregate or multiple fruit. — *adj* **fruit'y** like, or tasting like, fruit; rich; (of a voice) mellow, resonant; salacious, saucy, smutty; crazy (*US slang*); male homosexual (*slang*, esp. *US*). — **fruit'-bat** any bat of the suborder *Megacheiroptera*, large fruit-eating bats of the Old World; **fruit'-cage** an enclosure with mesh sides and roof to protect growing fruit and vegetables from birds, etc.; **fruit'-cake** a cake containing dried fruit; a slightly mad person (*colloq*); **fruit cocktail** a fruit salad, esp. one of small, usu. diced, pieces of fruit; **fruit'-fly** an insect of genus *Drosophila*; **fruit'-knife** a knife with a blade of silver, etc., for cutting fruit; **fruit'-machine** a coin-operated gaming machine in which chance must bring pictures of different fruits, etc. together in a certain combination to give a win; **fruit salad** a mixture of pieces of fruit, fresh or preserved; **fruit'wood** the wood of a fruit-tree. — Also *adj*. — **bush fruits** small fruits growing on woody bushes; **first-fruits** see **first** and **annates**; **small** or **soft fruit** or **fruits** strawberries, currants, etc. [O.Fr. *fruit, fruict* — L. *frūctus* — *fruī, frūctus*, to enjoy.]

fruition *froō-ish'ən, n* enjoyment; maturation, fulfilment, completion; use or possession, esp. accompanied with pleasure; bearing fruit. — *adj* **fru'itive**. [O.Fr. *fruition* — L. *fruī*, to enjoy.]

frump *frump, n* a dowdy woman. — *adj* **frump'ish** or **frump'y** ill-dressed, dowdy.

frustrate *frus-trāt'* or *frus'trāt, vt* to bring to nothing; to balk; to thwart. — *adj* **frustra'ted** thwarted; having a sense of discouragement and dissatisfaction; sexually unfulfilled. — *adj* **frustrat'ing**. — *adv* **frustrat'ingly**. — *n* **frustrā'tion**. [L. *frustrārī*.]

frustule *frust'yoōl, n* the siliceous two-valved shell of a diatom, with its contents. [See **frustum**.]

frustum *frust'um, n* a slice of a solid body; the part of a cone or pyramid between the base and a parallel plane, or between two planes: — *pl* **frust'ums** or **frust'a**. [L., a bit.]

frutex *froō'teks, n* a shrub: — *pl* **fru'tices** (*-ti-sēz*). — *adj* **frutesc'ent** or **fru'ticose** shrubby. [L. *frutex, -icis*, shrub.]

fry[1] *frī, vt* to cook in oil or fat in a pan; to burn or scorch (*fig*). — *vi* to undergo frying: — *pr p* **fry'ing**; *pa t* and *pa p* **fried**; *3rd pers present indicative* **fries**. — *n* a dish of anything fried, esp. the offal of a pig, lamb, etc.; (in *pl*) fried potato-chips. — *n* **fri'er** or **fry'er** someone who fries (esp. fish); a vessel for frying; a fish suitable for frying. — *n* and *adj* **fry'ing**. — **fry'ing-pan** a broad, shallow pan for frying food in; **fry'-up** (*colloq*) mixed fried foods, or the frying of these. — **out of the frying-pan into the fire** out of one difficult situation into a greater. [Fr. *frire* — L. *frīgĕre*.]

fry[2] *frī, n* young, collectively; a swarm of young, esp. of fishes just spawned; young salmon in their second year. — **small fry** small things collectively, persons or things of little importance; children. [O.N. *friō*, seed.]

FSH *abbrev* for follicle-stimulating hormone.

FT *abbrev* for the Financial Times (newspaper).

ft *abbrev* for: feet; foot.

FTA *abbrev* for Freight Transport Association.

fth. or **fthm** *abbrev* for fathom.

FT Index *abbrev* for Financial Times (Industrial Ordinary Share) Index.

FTSE, FT-SE 100 or **FT-SE** (often *foōt'si*) *abbrev* for Financial Times Stock Exchange 100-Share Index, which records the share prices of the top 100 UK public companies (also *colloq* **Foot'sie**).

fuchsia *fū'shə, n* any plant of a S. American genus (*Fuchsia*) of the evening primrose family, with long pendulous flowers; a reddish-purple colour. — Also *adj*. — *n* **fuchsine** (*fooks'ēn*) the dyestuff magenta, a green solid, purplish-red in solution (from its colour, similar to that of the flower). [Named after Leonard *Fuchs*, a German botanist (1501–66).]

fuck *fuk*, (all words and meanings *vulg*) *vi* to have sexual intercourse; (with *about* or *around*) to play around, act foolishly; (with *off*) to go away (often *imper*). — *vt* to have sexual intercourse with (usu. of a male); (with *about* or *around*) to deal inconsiderately with; (with *up*) to botch, damage or break (*n* **fuck'-up**). — *n* an act of sexual intercourse; a person, esp. female, considered as a (good, poor, etc.) partner in sexual intercourse; used in various phrases expressing displeasure, emphasis, etc. — *interj* an expression of displeasure, etc. (often with an object, as in *fuck him!*). — *adj* **fucked** exhausted. — *n* **fuck'er** a person who fucks; a term of abuse; a person. — *n* **fuck'ing** sexual intercourse. — *adj* expressing scorn or disapprobation; often used as a meaningless qualification. — *adv* very, to a great extent. — **fuck all** or **sweet fuck all** nothing at all. [Ety. uncertain; cf. Ger. *ficken*, to strike, to copulate with.]

fuddle *fud'l, vt* to stupefy, esp. with drink; to confuse. — *vi* to drink to excess or habitually: — *pr p* **fudd'ling**; *pa t* and *pa p* **fudd'led**. — *n* intoxication; a drinking bout; confusion. — *n* **fudd'ler** a drunkard. — *n* and *adj* **fudd'ling** tippling.

fuddy-duddy *fud'i-dud-i, n* an old fogy, a stick-in-the-mud. — *adj* old-fogyish; old-fashioned; stuffy; prim; censorious.

fudge[1] *fuj, n* a type of soft confectionery made from sugar, butter and flavouring, etc.; nonsense. — *interj* bosh.

fudge[2] *fuj, vi* to cheat; to fail; to dodge. — *vt* to patch up; to fake; to distort; to dodge; to obscure, cover up. — *n* the action of fudging; distortion; evasion. [Variant of old word *fadge*, to agree, to succeed.]

fuel *fū'əl, n* material for burning as a source of heat or power; something that maintains or intensifies emotion, etc. (*fig*); food, as maintaining bodily processes; fissile material for a nuclear reactor. — *vt* to furnish with fuel; to incite, encourage or stimulate (esp. anger, hate, violence, etc.). — *vi* to take or get fuel: — *pr p* **fū'elling**; *pa t* and *pa p* **fū'elled**. — *n* **fū'eller**. — **fu'el-cell** a cell generating electricity as part of a chemical reaction between an electrolyte and a combustible gas or vapour. — *adj* **fuel-injec'ted** having **fuel-injec'tion**, a system of operating an internal-combustion engine in which vaporised liquid fuel is introduced under pressure directly into the combustion chamber, so dispensing with a carburettor. — **add fuel to the fire** to make an angry person angrier, a heated discussion more heated, etc. [O.Fr. *fowaille* — L.L. *focāle* — L. *focus*, a fireplace.]

fug *fug*, *n* a very hot, close, often smoky, state of atmosphere. — *adj* **fugg'y**.

fugacious *fū-gā'shəs*, *adj* apt to flee away; fleeting; readily shed. — *n* **fugā'ciousness** or **fugacity** (*-gas'*). [L. *fugāx*, *-ācis* — *fugĕre*, to flee.]

fugal, fugato. See under **fugue**.

fugitive *fū'ji-tiv*, *adj* apt to flee away; fleeing; fleeting; evanescent. — *n* a person who flees or has fled; someone hard to catch; an exile. — *adv* **fū'gitively**. — *n* **fū'gitiveness**. [L. *fugitīvus* — *fugĕre*, to flee.]

fugue *fūg*, *n* a form of composition in which the subject is given out by one part and immediately taken up by a second (in *answer*), during which the first part supplies an accompaniment or counter-subject, and so on (*mus*); a form of amnesia which is a flight from reality. — *adj* **fū'gal**. — *adv* **fū'gally**. — *adj* and *adv* **fugato** (*fū-gä'tō* or It. *fōō-gä'tō*) in the manner of a fugue without being strictly a fugue. — Also *n*: — *pl* **fuga'tos**. [Fr., — It. *fuga* — L. *fuga*, flight.]

Führer *fū'rər* or Ger. *fü'rər*, *n* the title taken by Hitler as dictator of Nazi Germany. [Ger., leader, guide.]

fulcrum *ful'krəm* or *fōōl'krəm*, *n* the prop or fixed point on which a lever moves (*mech*); a support; a means to an end (*fig*): — *pl* **ful'crums** or **ful'cra**. [L. *fulcrum*, a prop — *fulcīre*, to prop.]

fulfil or in U.S. **fulfill** *fōōl-fil'*, *vt* to complete; to accomplish; to carry into effect; to bring to consummation; to develop and realise the potential of: — *pr p* **fulfill'ing**; *pa t* and *pa p* **fulfilled'**. — *n* **fulfill'er**. — *n* **fulfill'ing** or **fulfil'ment** full performance; completion; accomplishment. [O.E. *fullfyllan* — *full*, full, *fyllan*, to fill.]

fulgent *ful'jənt*, *adj* shining; bright. — *n* **ful'gency**. [L. *fulgēns*, *-entis*, pres. p. of *fulgēre*, to shine.]

fuliginous *fū-lij'i-nəs*, *adj* sooty; dusky. — *n* **fūliginos'ity**. [L. *fūlīgō*, *-īnis*, soot.]

full[1] *fōōl*, *adj* (*compar* **full'er**, *superl* **full'est**) holding all that can be contained; having no empty space; abundantly supplied or furnished; copious; filling; containing the whole matter; complete; perfect; maximum; strong; clear; intense; swollen or rounded; protuberant; having excess of material; at the height of development or end of course; (with *of*) unable to think or talk of anything but; drunk (*colloq*). — *n* the completest extent, as of the moon; the highest degree; the whole; the time of full moon. — *vt* to make with gathers or puckers. — *vi* to become full. — *adv* quite; thoroughly, veritably; directly. — *n* **full'ness** or **ful'ness** the state of being full; the moment of fulfilment. — *adv* **full'y** completely; entirely; quite. — **full back** see **back**; **full blast** full operation. — *adv* **full-blast'** with maximum energy and fluency. — **full'-blood** an individual of pure blood. — *adj* **full-blood'ed** having a full supply of blood; vigorous; thoroughbred, of unmixed descent; related through both parents. — *adj* **full'-blown** fully expanded, as a flower; beyond the first freshness of youth; fully qualified or admitted. — *adj* **full-bod'ied** with much body or substance. — *adj* **full'-bore** (of a firearm) of larger calibre than small-bore. — **full brother** son of the same parents. — *adv* **full-cir'cle** round in a complete revolution. — **full cousin** the son or daughter of an uncle or aunt, a first cousin. — *adj* **full'-cream** (of milk) not skimmed; made with unskimmed milk. — *adj* **full'-face** or **full'-faced** facing straight towards the viewer; having a full or broad face. — *adj* **full-front'al** of the front view of a completely naked man or woman; with no detail left unrevealed (*fig*). — *adj* **full'-grown** grown to full size. — **full hand** see **full house**; **full house** a performance at which every seat is taken (*theat*); three cards of a kind and a pair (*poker*; also **full hand**); (in bingo) all the numbers needed to win; a complete set (of anything). — *adj* **full'-length** extending the whole length. — *n* a portrait showing the whole length. — *adv* stretched to the full extent. — **full marks** the maximum marks possible in an examination (also used as an expression of approval); **full moon** the moon with its whole disc illuminated, when opposite the sun; the time when the moon is full; **full nelson** a type of wrestling hold, a nelson. — *adj* **full'-out** at full power; total. — *adj* **full'-page** occupying a whole page. — *adv* **full-pelt'**, **full-speed'** or **full-tilt'** with highest speed and impetus. — *adj* **full'-rigged** having three or more masts square-rigged. — *adv* **full-sail'**. — *adj* **full'-sailed** having all sails set; having sails filled with wind; advancing with speed and momentum. — *adj* **full'-scale** of the same size as the original; involving full power or maximum effort. — **full sister** a daughter of the same parents. — *adv* **full-speed** see **full-pelt**. — **full stop** a point marking the end of a sentence; an end, a halt. — *adj* **full'-throated** or **full'-voiced** singing with the whole power of the voice. — *adv* **full-tilt** see **full-pelt**. — **full time** the end of a football, rugby, etc. match. — *adj* **full'-time** occupied during or extending over the whole working day, week, etc. — **full'-timer**. — *adj* **full-voiced** see **full-throated**. — *adj* **full'y-fashioned** (of garments, esp. stockings) shaped to fit closely. — *adj* **full'y-fledged** completely fledged; having attained full rank or membership. — **full of oneself** having a high or exaggerated opinion of one's own importance, etc. (also **full of one's own importance**), too much the subject of one's own conversation; **full of years** old, aged; at a good old age; **full up** full to the limit; sated, wearied (*slang*); **in full** without reduction; **in full cry** (esp. of hounds) in hot pursuit; **in full rig** with maximum number of masts and sails; **in full swing** at the height of activity; **in the fullness of time** at the due or destined time; **to the full** in full measure, completely. [O.E. *full*.]

full[2] *fōōl*, *vt* to scour and beat, as a means of finishing, thickening, or cleansing woollens. — *n* **full'er** a person who fulls cloth. — **fuller's earth** an earthy hydrous aluminium silicate, capable of absorbing grease. [O.Fr. *fuler* (see **foil**[1]) and O.E. *fullere*, fuller, both — L. *fullō*, a cloth-fuller.]

fulmar *fōōl'mär* or *-mər*, *n* a gull-like bird of the petrel family. [Perh. O.N. *fūll*, foul, *mār*, gull.]

fulminate *ful'min-āt*, *vi* to detonate; to issue decrees with violence or threats; to inveigh; to flash. — *vt* to cause to explode; to utter or publish, e.g. a denunciation; to denounce. — *adj* **ful'minant** fulminating; developing suddenly or rapidly (*pathol*). — *adj* **ful'mināting** detonating. — *n* **fulminā'tion** an act of denouncing or detonating; a denunciation. — *adj* **ful'minatory**. [L. *fulmināre*, *-ātum* — *fulmen*, *-inis*, lightning.]

fulness. See **full**[1].

fulsome *fōōl'səm*, *adj* cloying or causing surfeit, excessive; disgustingly fawning. — *adv* **ful'somely**. — *n* **ful'someness**. [**full**[1] and sfx. **-some**[1].]

fulvous *ful'vəs*, *adj* dull yellow; tawny. — *adj* **ful'vid**. [L. *fulvus*, tawny.]

fumarole *fūm'ə-rōl*, *n* a hole emitting gases in a volcano or volcanic region. [Fr. *fumerolle* or It. *fumaruola* — L. *fūmus*, smoke.]

fumble *fum'bl*, *vi* to grope about awkwardly; to make bungling or unsuccessful attempts. — *vt* to handle, manage or effect awkwardly or bunglingly. — *n* an act of fumbling; a dropped or fumbled ball, e.g. in Am. football. — *n* **fum'bler**. — *adv* **fum'blingly**. [Cf. Du. *fommelen*, to fumble; O.N. *fālma*, to grope about.]

fume *fūm*, *n* smoke or vapour, often odorous (often in *pl*); rage or fretful excitement. — *vi* to smoke; to throw off vapour; to come off in fumes; to be in a rage. — *vt* to treat with fumes; to give off; to offer incense to. — *adj* **fūm'ous** or **fūm'y**. — **fume'=chamber** or **-cupboard** a case for laboratory operations that give off fumes; **fumed oak** oak darkened by ammonia fumes. — **fuming sulphuric acid** see **oleum** under **oleate**. [L. *fūmus*, smoke.]

fumigate *fūm'i-gāt*, *vt* to expose to fumes, esp. for purposes of disinfecting, or destroying pests. — *n* **fūm'igant** a source of fumes, esp. a substance used for fumigation. — *n* **fūmigā'tion**. — *n* **fūm'igator** a fumigating apparatus. — *adj* **fūm'igatory**. [L. *fūmigāre*, *-ātum*.]

fumitory *fūm'i-tər-i*, *n* a plant of the genus *Fumaria*. [O.Fr. *fume-terre*, lit. earth-smoke so called because its rapid growth was thought to resemble the dispersal of smoke.]

fun *fun*, *n* merriment; jest or sport; a source of merriment or amusement. — *adj* providing amusement; enjoyable, full of fun. — **fun'fair** a fair with side-shows, rides and other amusements; **fun park** an outdoor place of entertainment with various amusements; **fun run** a long-distance race undertaken for amusement rather than serious athletic competition. — **in fun** as a joke, not seriously; **like fun** (*colloq*) rapidly; not at all; **make fun of** or **poke fun at** to ridicule. [Prob. a form of obs. *fon*, to befool.]

funambulist *fū-nam'bū-list*, *n* a rope-walker or rope-dancer. [L. *fūnambulus*, a rope walker — *fūnis*, rope, *ambulāre*, to walk.]

function *fung'shən* or *fungk'shən*, *n* an activity appropriate to any person or thing; duty peculiar to any office; faculty or the exercise of faculty; a solemn service; a ceremony; a social gathering; a variable so connected with another that for any value of the one there is a corresponding value for the other (*math*); a correspondence between two sets of variables such that each member of one set can be related to one particular member of the other set (*math* and *logic*); an event, etc. dependent on some other factor or factors; the technical term in physiology for the vital activity of an organ, tissue or cell; the part played by a linguistic form in a construction (*linguis*). — *vi* to perform a function; to act; to operate; to work. — *adj* **func'tional** pertaining to or performed by functions; (of disease) characterised by impairment of function, not of organs; designed with special regard to purpose and practical use; serving a function. — *n* **func'tionalism** the theory or practice of adapting method, form, materials, etc., primarily with regard to the purpose in hand. — *n* **func'tionalist**. — *adv* **func'tionally**. — *n* **func'tionary** a person who discharges any duty; someone who holds an office. — *adj* **func'tionless**. — **function word** (*linguis*) a word, such as an article or auxiliary, which has little or no meaning apart from the grammatical concept it expresses. [O.Fr., — L. *functiō*, *-ōnis* — *fungī*, *functus*, to perform.]

fund *fund*, *n* a sum of money on which some enterprise is founded or expense supported; a supply or source of money; a store laid up; a supply; (in *pl*) permanent government debts paying interest; (in *pl*) money available to an organisation, for a project, etc., or (*colloq*; usu. *facetious*) available to an individual. — *vt* to form into a stock charged with interest; to place in a fund; to provide (an organisation, project, etc.) with money. — *adj* **fund'ed** invested in public funds; existing in the form of bonds. — *n* **fund'er** a financial backer. — *n* **fund'ing** the action of providing money for a project, etc.; financial backing, funds. — *n* **fund'-raising** the raising of money for an organisation, project, etc. — Also *adj*. [L. *fundus*, the bottom.]

fundamental *fun-də-men'tl*, *adj* serving as foundation; essential; primary; important. — *n* that which serves as a groundwork; an essential; the root of a chord or of a system of harmonics (*mus*). — *n* **fund'ament** (*-mənt*; *facetious*) the buttocks or anus. — *n* **fundamen'talism** belief in the literal truth of the Bible, against evolution, etc.; adherence to strictly orthodox religious or (*fig*) other, e.g. political, doctrines. — *n* and *adj* **fundamen'talist**. — *n* **fundamental'ity**. — *adv* **fundamen'tally**. — **fundamental particle** same as **elementary particle**; **fundamental unit** any of a number of arbitrarily defined units in a system of measurement, such as metre, second, candela, etc., from which the other quantities in the system are derived. [L. *fundāmentum*, foundation, *fundāre*, to found.]

fundi *fōōn'dē*, (*SAfr*) *n* an expert. [Nguni (S.Afr. language) *umfundisi*, a teacher.]

fundus *fun'dəs*, *n* bottom; the rounded bottom of a hollow organ (*anat*): — *pl* **fun'di** (*-ī*). [L.]

funeral *fū'nər-əl*, *n* disposal of the dead, with any ceremonies or observances connected therewith; a procession to the place of burial or cremation, etc. — *adj* pertaining to the disposal of the dead. — *adj* **fū'nerary** pertaining to or suiting a funeral. — *adj* **fūnē'real** pertaining to a funeral; dismal; mournful. — **funeral director** an undertaker; **funeral home** (*US*) an undertaker's place of business with facilities for funerals; **funeral parlour** a room that can be hired for funeral ceremonies; a funeral home. — **your, my,** etc. **funeral** your, my, etc. affair, or lookout. [L.L. *fūnerālis* and L. *fūnerārius*, *fūnebris*, *fūnĕreus* — L. *fūnus*, *fūnĕris*, a funeral procession.]

fungibles *fun'ji-blz*, (*law*) *npl* movable effects which are consumed by use, and which are estimated by weight, number and measure. [L.L. *fungibilis* — L. *fungī*, to perform; see **function**.]

fungus *fung'gəs*, *n* a plant of a group lacking chlorophyll and reproducing by spores, including mushrooms, toadstools, mould, yeasts, etc.; a soft, morbid growth (*pathol*): — *pl* **fungi** (*fun'jī*, *-ji* or *fung'gī*) or **fung'uses**. — *adj* **fung'al** pertaining to or resembling fungus. — *adj* **fungicīd'al** fungi-destroying; pertaining to a fungicide. — *n* **fungicide** (*fun'ji-sīd*) a substance which kills fungi. — *adj* **fung'oid** (*-goid*) fungus-like; of the nature of a fungus. — *n* **fungos'ity**. — *adj* **fung'ous** of or like fungus; spongy; growing suddenly. — **fung'us-gall** a malformation in a plant caused by a fungal attack. [L. *fungus*, a mushroom.]

funicle *fū'ni-kl*, *n* a small cord or ligature; a fibre; the stalk of an ovule (*bot*). [L. *fūniculus*, dimin. of *fūnis*, a rope.]

funicular *fūn-ik'ū-lər*, *adj* relating to a funicle; relating to a string or cable. — *n* (also **funicular railway**) a cable railway. [**funicle**.]

funk[1] *fungk*, (*colloq*) *n* a state of fear; panic; shrinking or shirking from loss of courage; a person who funks. — *vi* to flinch; to draw back or hold back in fear. — *vt* to balk at or shirk from fear. — *n* **funk'iness**. — *adj* **funk'y**. — **funk'hole** (*slang*, orig. *mil*) a place of refuge, dug-out; a place to which one can retreat for shelter, etc. (*fig*); a job that enables one to avoid military service. — **blue funk** see under **blue**[1]. [Poss. Flem. *fonck*.]

funk[2] *fungk*, (*slang*, chiefly *US*) *n* a strong, unpleasant smell, esp. of smoke; funky music. — *adj* **funk'y** with a strong, musty, or bad smell; (of jazz, pop music, etc.) unsophisticated, earthy and soulful, like early blues music in style, emotion, etc.; in the latest fashion, trendy; kinky; odd, quaint.

funnel *fun'l*, *n* a utensil, usu. a cone ending in a tube, for pouring fluids into narrow-necked vessels; a passage for the escape of smoke, etc. — *vt* to pour, pass, transfer, etc. through, or as if through, a funnel. — *adj* **funn'elled** with a funnel; funnel-shaped. — **funn'el-web** or **funnel-web spider** a venomous spider (genus *Atrax*) of eastern Australia which constructs a tube-shaped or funnel-shaped lair. [Prob. through Fr. or Port. from L. *infundibulum* — *fundĕre*, to pour.]

funny *fun'i, adj* full of fun; droll; amusing; queer, odd. — *n* a joke (*colloq*); (in *pl*) comic strips, or the comic section of a newspaper (*NAm*). — *adv* **funn'ily**. — *n* **funn'iness**. — **funny bone** the bone at the elbow with the comparatively unprotected ulnar nerve which, when struck, shoots a tingling sensation down the forearm to the fingers (a pun on *humerus*); **funny business** tricks, deception (*slang*); amusing behaviour, joke-telling, etc. (*colloq*); **funny farm** (*slang*) a mental hospital or institution; **funny man** (*colloq*) a comedian; **funny money** (*colloq*) any currency or unit of account considered in some way less real or solid than 'ordinary' money, or a sum of money similarly regarded as in some way unreal; **funny paper** (*NAm*) the comic section of a newspaper. [**fun**.]

funster *fun'stər, n* a person who causes merriment; a joker or prankster. [**fun**.]

fur *fûr, n* the thick, soft, fine hair of certain animals; the skin with this hair attached; a garment of fur; furred animals (opp. to *feather*); a coating on the tongue; a crust formed by hard water in boilers, etc.; a strengthening piece nailed to a rafter. — *vt* to clothe, cover, coat, trim or line with fur; to coat. — *vi* to become coated: — *pr p* **furr'ing**; *pa t* and *pa p* **furred**. — *adj* **furred**. — *n* **furr'ier** a dealer or worker in furs. — *n* **furr'ing** fur trimmings; a coating on the tongue; (also **firr'ing**) strips of wood fastened to joists, etc.; a lining to a wall to carry lath, provide an airspace, etc. — *adj* **furr'y** consisting of, like, covered with, or dressed in fur. — **fur fabric** a fabric with a fur-like pile; **fur'-seal** an eared seal with dense fur under its long hairs. [O.Fr. *forrer*, to line, encase — *forre*, *fuerre*, sheath.]

fur. *abbrev* for furlong.

furbelow *fûr'bi-lō, n* a plaited border or flounce; a superfluous ornament. — *vt* to decorate with a furbelow. [Fr., It., and Sp. *falbala*.]

furbish *fûr'bish, vt* to purify or polish; to rub up until bright; to renovate. — *n* **fur'bisher**. [O.Fr. *fourbir*, *fourbiss-*, from O.H.G. *furban*, to purify.]

furcate *fûr'kāt* or *-kit* or **furcated** *-kā'tid, adj* forked. — *adj* **fur'cal**. — *n* **furcā'tion**. — *adj* **furciferous** (*-sif'*) bearing a forked appendage. — *n* **fur'cūla** the united clavicles of a bird — the wishbone. — *adj* **fur'cūlar** furcate; shaped like a fork. [L. *furca*, fork.]

furfur *fûr'fûr* or *-fər, n* dandruff, scurf. — *adj* **furfuraceous** (*fûr-fū-rā'shəs*) branny; scaly; scurfy. [L. *furfur*, bran.]

furioso *fōō-ri-ō'sō* or *fū-, adj* and *adv* (*mus*) with fury. [It.; cf. **furious**.]

furious *fū'ri-əs, adj* extremely angry; violent, raging. — *adv* **fū'riously** violently, angrily; with great energy, enthusiasm, etc. — *n* **fu'riousness**. — **fast and furious** see under **fast**[1]. [M.E. — L. *furiōsus* — L. *furĕre*, to be angry.]

furl *fûrl, vt* to roll up. [Perh. **fardel**.]

furlong *fûr'long, n* 220 yards (201.168 metres), one-eighth of a mile. [O.E. *furlang* — *furh*, furrow, *lang*, long.]

furlough *fûr'lō, n* leave of absence. — *vt* to grant furlough to. [Du. *verlof*.]

furnace *fûr'nis, n* an enclosed structure in which great heat is produced. [O.Fr. *fornais* — L. *fornāx*, *-ācis* — *fornus*, an oven.]

furnish *fûr'nish, vt* to equip (a house, etc.) with furniture, carpets, curtains, etc.; to fit up or supply completely, or with what is necessary; to supply, provide; to equip. — *adj* **fur'nished** equipped; stocked with furniture. — *n* **fur'nisher**. — *npl* **fur'nishings** fittings of any kind, esp. articles of furniture, etc., within a house. — *n* **fur'nishment**. [O.Fr. *furnir*, *furniss-*; of Gmc. origin.]

furniture *fûr'ni-chər, n* movables, either for use or ornament, with which a house is equipped; the necessary equipment in some arts or trades; accessories; metal fittings for doors and windows; the piece of wood or metal put round pages of type to make margins and fasten the matter in the chase (*printing*). — **furniture van** a long, high-sided van for transporting furniture, etc., e.g. when moving house. [Fr. *fourniture*.]

furor *fū'rör, n* fury; excitement, enthusiasm. [L.]

furore *fū'rör* or *fōō-rör'ā, n* a craze; wild enthusiasm; wild excitement. [It.]

furrier, furring. See **fur**.

furrow *fur'ō, n* the trench made by a plough; a groove; a wrinkle. — *vt* to form furrows in; to groove; to wrinkle. — *adj* **furr'owy**. [O.E. *furh*.]

furry. See **fur**.

further[1] *fûr'dhər, adv* at or to a greater distance or degree; in addition. — *adj* more distant; additional, more, other. — *adv* **fur'thermore** in addition to what has been said, moreover, besides. — *adj* **fur'thermost** most remote. — *adv* **fur'thest** at or to the greatest distance. — *adj* most distant. — **further education** post-school education other than at university, polytechnic, etc.; **further outlook** (*meteorol*) a general forecast given for a longer or more distant period than that covered by a more detailed forecast. [O.E. *furthor* (adv.), *furthra* (adj.) — *fore* or *forth* with compar. sfx. *-ther*.]

further[2] *fûr'dhər, vt* to help forward, promote. — *n* **fur'therance** a helping forward. — *n* **fur'therer** a promoter, advancer. [O.E. *fyrthran*.]

furtive *fûr'tiv, adj* stealthy; secret. — *adv* **fur'tively**. — *n* **fur'tiveness**. [L. *fūrtīvus* — *fūr*, a thief.]

furuncle *fū'rung-kl*, (*pathol*) *n* a boil. — *adj* **fūrun'cūlar** or **fūrun'cūlous**. [L. *fūrunculus*, lit. a little thief.]

fury *fū'ri, n* rage; violent passion; madness; (with *cap*) any one of the three goddesses of vengeance (*Gr mythol*); a passionate, violent woman. — **like fury** (*colloq*) furiously. [Fr. *furie* — L. *furia* — *furĕre*, to be angry.]

furze *fûrz, n* gorse or whin. [O.E. *fyrs*.]

fusain *fū-zān', n* an important constituent of coal, resembling charcoal (also *fū'zān*); artists' fine charcoal; a drawing done with this. [Fr., the spindle-tree, or charcoal made from it.]

fuse[1] *fūz, vt* to melt; to liquefy by heat; to join by, or as if by, melting together; to cause to fail by melting of a fuse (*electr*). — *vi* to be melted; to be reduced to a liquid; to melt together; to blend, unite; (of an electric appliance) to fail by melting of a fuse. — *n* a bit of fusible metal, with its mounting, inserted as a safeguard in an electric circuit. — **fuse box** a box containing the switches and fuses for the leads of an electrical system. [L. *fundĕre*, *fūsum*, to melt.]

fuse[2] or (esp. in U.S.) **fuze** *fūz, n* a train of combustible material in waterproof covering, used with a detonator to initiate an explosion; any device used to explode a bomb, mine, etc. under specified circumstances or at a specified time. — **have** or **burn on a short fuse** to be quick-tempered. [It. *fuso* — L. *fūsus*, a spindle.]

fusee or **fuzee** *fū-zē', n* the spindle in a watch or clock on which the chain is wound; a match with long, oval head for outdoor use; a fuse for firing explosives. [O.Fr. *fusée*, a spindleful — L. *fūsus*, a spindle.]

fuselage *fū'zil-ij* or *fū-zə-läzh', n* the body of an aeroplane. [Fr. *fuseler*, to shape like a spindle — L. *fūsus*, spindle.]

fusel-oil *fū'zl-oil, n* a nauseous mixture of alcohols in spirits distilled from potatoes, grain, etc. [Ger. *Fusel*, bad spirits.]

fusible *fūz'ible, adj* able to be fused; easily fused. — *n* **fūsibil'ity**. [**fuse**[1].]

fusidic acid *fū-sid'ik a'sid*, *n* an antibiotic steroid, $C_{31}H_{48}O_6$. [From the fungus *Fusidium coccineum*, from which it was first isolated.]

fusileer or **fusilier** *fū-zil-ēr'*, *n* (in *pl*) a historical title borne by a few regiments which were formerly armed with muskets; a member of such a regiment. [O.Fr. *fuisil*, a flint-musket — L.L. *focile*, steel (to strike fire with), dimin. of L. *focus*, a fireplace.]

fusillade *fū-zil-ād'*, *n* a simultaneous or continuous discharge of firearms; a barrage (*lit* or *fig*). [Ety. as for **fusileer**.]

fusilli *fū-zi'li*, *n* pasta in the form of short, thick spirals. [It.]

fusion *fū'zhən*, *n* fusing; melting; a close union of things, as if melted together; nuclear fusion (q.v.). — **fusion bomb** one deriving its energy from fusion of atomic nuclei, such as the hydrogen bomb; **fusion reactor** a nuclear reactor operating by nuclear fusion. [Ety. as for **fuse**[1].]

fuss *fus*, *n* a bustle; flurry; commotion, esp. over trifling matters; petty ostentatious activity or attentions. — *vi* to be in a fuss, or agitate over things of little importance. — *vt* to agitate, flurry. — *n* **fuss'er**. — *adv* **fuss'ily**. — *n* **fuss'iness**. — *adj* **fuss'y** given to making a fuss; finicky; requiring careful attention; overtrimmed. — **fuss'-pot** a person who fusses. — **make a fuss of** to give much (genuinely or apparently) affectionate or amicable attention to.

fustanella *fus-tə-nel'ə*, *n* a white kilt worn by Greek and Albanian men. [Mod.Gr. *phoustanella*, dimin. of *phoustani*, Albanian *fustan* — It. *fustagno*, fustian.]

fustian *fus'chən*, *n* a kind of coarse, twilled cotton fabric including moleskin, velveteen, corduroy, etc.; a pompous and unnatural style of writing or speaking; bombast. — *adj* made of fustian; bombastic. [O.Fr. *fustaigne* — It. *fustagno* — L.L. *fustāneum*, prob. from *El-Fustāt* (Old Cairo) where it may have been made.]

fustic *fus'tik*, *n* the wood of a tropical American tree (*Chlorophora tinctoria*) also called **old fustic**; the yellow dye obtained from this, or from **young fustic**, the Venetian sumach or its wood. [Fr. *fustoc* — Sp. — Ar. *fustuq* — Gr. *pistakē*, pistachio.]

fusty *fust'i*, *adj* musty; stale; stuffy; old-fashioned. — *adv* **fust'ily**. — *n* **fust'iness**. [O.Fr. *fusté*, smelling of the cask — *fust*, cask.]

fut. *abbrev* for future.

futhork, futhorc *fōō'thörk* or **futhark** *fōō'thärk*, *n* the Runic alphabet. [From the first six letters, *f*, *u*, *þ*(*th*), *o* or *a*, *r*, *k*.]

futile *fū'tīl* or in U.S. *-təl*, *adj* ineffectual; trifling. — *adv* **fu'tilely**. — *n* **futility** (*-til'*) uselessness. [L. *fūtilis*, leaky, futile — *fundĕre*, to pour.]

futon *fōō'ton*, *n* a Japanese floor-mattress used as a bed. [Jap.]

futtock *fut'ək*, *n* one of the crooked timbers of a wooden ship.

future *fū'chər*, *adj* about to be; that is to come; expressive of time to come (*gram*). — *n* time to come; life, fate or condition in time to come; prospects, likelihood of future success; the future tense (*gram*); (in *pl*) commodities or securities traded at an agreed price, to be delivered and paid for at a specified future time. — *adj* **fut'ureless** without prospects. — *n* **fut'urism** (*art*) a movement claiming to anticipate or point the way for the future, esp. a 20th-century revolt against tradition. — *n* **fut'urist** someone whose chief interests are in what is to come; a believer in futurism. — *adj* **futurist'ic**. — *n* **futurity** (*fū-tū'ri-ti*) time to come; an event, or state of being, yet to come. — *adj* **futurological** (*-loj'-*). — *n* **futurol'ogist**. — *n* **futurol'ogy** the science and study of sociological and technological developments, values and trends, with a view to planning for the future. — *adj* **future-per'fect** (*gram*) expressive of action viewed as past in reference to an assumed future time. — *n* the future-perfect tense; a verb in that tense. — **future studies** futurology. [Fr. *futur* — L. *futūrus*, used as fut. p. of *esse*, to be.]

fu yung or **fu yong** *fōō yōōng*, *n* a Chinese omelette-like dish with bean sprouts, onion, meat, etc. — Also **foo yung** or **yong**. [Chin., hibiscus.]

fuze. See **fuse**[2].

fuzee. See **fusee**.

fuzz *fuz*, *n* light fine particles or fibres, like dust; fluff; blurr; police (*slang*). — *adv* **fuzz'ily**. — *n* **fuzz'iness**. — *adj* **fuzz'y** covered with fuzz; fluffy; with many small tight curls; blurred.

fwd *abbrev* for: forward; four-wheel drive; front-wheel drive.

fz. *abbrev* for sforzando.

G

G or **g** *jē*, *n* the seventh letter of the modern English alphabet; the fifth note of the diatonic scale of C major — also called *sol* (*mus*); the scale or key having that note for its tonic (*mus*). — **G'-clef** a clef, the treble clef, on the second line of the treble stave, marking G; **G'-string** same as **gee-string**.

G or **G**. *abbrev* for: Gauss; German; giga- (10^9); good; gourde (Haitian currency); Government. — **G'-man** (*US*) an agent of the Federal Bureau of Investigation (for Government-man).

G *symbol* for: the constant of gravitation, the factor linking force with mass and distance; conductor (*phys*).

g or **g**. *abbrev* for gram or gramme.

g *symbol* for acceleration due to gravity. — ***g*'-suit** a close-fitting suit with cells that inflate to prevent flow of blood away from the head, worn by airmen as a defence against blackout due to high acceleration and resultant great increase in weight.

G5, G7, G10, etc. or in U.S. **G-5, G-7, G-10**. etc. *abbrev* for Group of Five, Seven, Ten, etc. (q.v. under **group**).

GA *abbrev* for: General Assembly; general average; Georgia (U.S. state; also **Ga**).

Ga (*chem*) *symbol* for gallium.

gab *gab*, (*colloq*) *vi* to chatter, prate: — *pr p* **gabb'ing**; *pa t* and *pa p* *gabbed*. — *n* idle or fluent talk. — *n* **gabb'er** a chatterer. — *adj* **gabb'y** garrulous. — **gab'fest** (*slang*; chiefly *US*) a gathering characterised by much talk or gossip; a prolonged conversation, discussion, etc. — **gift of the gab** a talent (or propensity) for talking.

gabardine. See **gaberdine**.

gabble *gab'l*, *vi* to talk inarticulately; to chatter; to cackle like geese. — *n* a noise as of unintelligible chatter. — *n* **gabb'ler**. — *n* **gabb'ling**.

gabbro *gab'rō*, *n* a coarsely crystalline igneous rock composed of a plagioclase feldspar and pyroxene: — *pl* **gabb'ros**. — *adj* **gabbro'ic** or **gabbroitic** (*-it'ik*). — *adj* **gabb'roid** resembling gabbro. [It.]

gaberdine or **gabardine** *gab'ər-dēn*, *n* a closely woven twill fabric, esp. of cotton and wool; a coat of this material; a loose cloak, esp. a Jew's (*hist*). [O.Fr. *gauvardine*; perh. M.H.G. *wallevart*, pilgrimage.]

gabfest. See **gab**.

gabion *gā'bi-ən*, (*civ eng*) *n* a wire basket of stones used for embankment work, etc. [Fr., — It. *gabbione*, a large cage — *gabbia* — L. *cavea*, a cage.]

gable *gā'bl*, (*archit*) *n* the triangular part of an exterior wall of a building between the top of the side walls and the slopes on the roof; a gable-shaped structure over a window or door. — *adj* **gā'bled**. — **gable end** the end wall of a building on the side where there is a gable; **gable window** a window in a gable end or one surmounted by a gable. [Prob. through O.Fr. *gable*, from O.N. *gafl*.]

gad *gad*, *vi* to wander about, often restlessly, idly or in pursuit of pleasure (often with *about*): — *pr p* **gadd'ing**; *pa t* and *pa p* **gadd'ed**. — *n* wandering, gadding about. — *n* **gadd'er**. — **gad'about** a person who goes about idly looking for amusement, etc. [Back-formation from O.E. *gædeling*, companion, later vagabond.]

Gadarene *gad'ə-rēn*, *adj* indicative of mass panic and headlong flight towards disaster. [From the swine of *Gadara*, in the Bible: Matt. viii. 28.]

gadfly *gad'flī*, *n* a blood-sucking fly that distresses cattle; sometimes applied to a botfly; a mischievous gadabout; someone who provokes and irritates, esp. deliberately. [O.E. *gād* (see **goad**) and **fly**.]

gadget *gaj'it*, *n* any small ingenious device. — *n* **gad'getry** gadgets; the making of gadgets.

Gadhelic *gə-del'ik*, *adj* relating to the Gaels (the Celts of Ireland, the Highlands of Scotland, and the Isle of Man) or their languages. — *n* the Celtic language group to which Irish, Scottish Gaelic and Manx belong. — See also **Gael** and **Goidelic**. [Ir. *Gaedheal*, a Gael.]

gado-gado *gad-ō-gad'ō*, *n* a Malaysian dish of mixed vegetables, hard-boiled egg and peanut sauce.

gadoid *gā'doid*, *n* a fish of the genus *Gadus*, to which the cod and hake belong. — *adj* belonging to, or resembling, this genus. [Gr. *gados*, cod.]

gadolinite *gad'ə-lin-īt*, *n* a silicate of yttrium, beryllium and iron. — *n* **gadolin'ium** a metallic element, one of the rare earths (symbol **Gd**; atomic no. 64). [From the Finnish chemist *Gadolin* (1760–1852).]

gadroon or **godroon** *gə-drōōn'*, *n* an embossed, cable-like decoration used as an edging on silverware, etc. — *adj* **gadrooned'**. — *n* **gadroon'ing**. [Fr. *godron*.]

gadwall *gad'wöl*, *n* a northern freshwater duck.

Gaea *gī'ə* or *jē'ə*, **Gaia** *gī'ə* or *gā'ə* or **Ge** *gā* or *jē*, *n* in Greek mythology the goddess or personification of Earth, mother of Uranus and (by him) of Oceanus, Cronus and the Titans; (**Gaia**) Earth apprehended as a living entity within the solar system. [Gr.]

Gael *gāl*, *n* a Celt of the Scottish Highlands, Ireland or the Isle of Man, esp. one who speaks Gaelic. — *n* **Gael'dom**. — *adj* **Gaelic** (*gā'lik* or *gal'ik*) relating to the Gaels or their languages; relating to sports, such as shinty and hurling, played especially in, or originating in, Ireland and the Scottish Highlands. — *n* any of the Celtic languages of Ireland, the Scottish Highlands and the Isle of Man, esp. (usu. *gal'ik*) that of the Scottish Highlands. — **Gaelic coffee** same as **Irish coffee**; **Gaelic football** a form of football, played mainly in Ireland, between teams of 15 players, using a round ball which may be kicked, bounced or punched, but not thrown or run with. — See also **Goidelic**. [Scottish Gael. *Gaidheal*.]

Gael. *abbrev* for Gaelic.

Gaeltacht *gāl'tähht*, *n* the Irish-speaking districts of Ireland. [Ir. *gaedhealtacht*.]

gaff[1] *gaf*, *n* a hook used esp. for landing large fish; the spar to which the head of a fore-and-aft sail is bent (*naut*). — *vt* to hook or bind by means of a gaff. — *adj* **gaff'-rigged** (of a vessel) having a gaff. — **gaff sail** a sail attached to the gaff. [Fr. *gaffe*, a boat-hook.]

gaff[2] *gaf*, (*slang*) *n* humbug, nonsense. — **blow the gaff** to disclose a secret, to blab.

gaff[3] *gaf*, (*slang*) *n* a house or other building, orig. as the site of a burglary; one's private accommodation, apartment, flat, room, pad, etc.

gaffe *gaf*, *n* a social blunder. [Fr. *gaffe*.]

gaffer *gaf'ər*, *n* an old man (*derog*); the foreman of a squad of workmen; the senior electrician responsible for the lighting in a television or film studio (orig. *US*). [**grandfather**, or **godfather**.]

gag[1] *gag*, *vt* to stop the mouth of, forcibly; to silence; to prevent free expression by (the press, etc.). — *vi* to choke; to retch: — *pr p* **gagg'ing**; *pa t* and *pa p* **gagged**. — *n* something put into the mouth or over it to enforce silence, or to distend jaws during an operation; the closure applied in a debate. — *n* **gagg'er**. [Prob. imitative of sound made in choking.]

gag[2] *gag*, (*colloq*) *n* a joke; a hoax. — *vi* to make gags, joke: — *pr p* **gagg'ing**; *pa t* and *pa p* **gagged**. [Possibly **gag**[1].]

gaga *gä'gä*, (*slang*) *adj* in senile dotage. [Fr.]

gagaku *gä-gä'ko͞o* or *gä'gä-*, *n* a type of Japanese classical music played mainly on ceremonial occasions at the Japanese court. [Jap. — *ga*, graceful, noble, *gaku*, music.]

gage[1] *gāj*, *n* a pledge; something thrown down as a challenge, esp. a glove (*hist*). [O.Fr. *guage*; Gmc.]

gage[2] *gāj*, (*drug-taking slang*) *n* marijuana.

gage[3]. See **gauge**.

gage[4] *gāj*, *n*. Same as **greengage**.

gaggle *gag'l*, *n* a flock of geese on water, in contrast to a *skein* in the air; a group or knot of people. — *vi* to cackle. — *n* a cackling noise. [Prob. imit.]

Gaia. See **Gaea**.

gaiety, gaily. See **gay**.

gain *gān*, *vt* to obtain to one's advantage; to earn; to win; to increase (speed, weight, height, momentum); to draw to one's own party; to reach. — *vi* to profit; to become or appear better, to progress; (of a clock, etc.) to go fast by so much in a given time. — *n* that which is gained; profit; an instance of gaining, a win; ratio of output and input voltages (*telecomm*); (or **gain control**) a means of volume control in an amplifier or receiving set (*telecomm*). — *adj* **gain'able**. — *n* **gain'er**. — *adj* **gain'ful** lucrative; profitable; engaged in for pay, paid. — *adv* **gain'fully**. — *n* **gain'fulness**. — *npl* **gain'ings**. — **gain ground** to grow in influence, become more widely accepted; **gain on** or **upon** to get closer to, catch up on; to overtake by degrees; to increase one's advantage against; **gain time** to contrive a delay by temporising, etc. [O.Fr. *gaaignier*, to graze or forage.]

gainsay *gān'sā*, *vt* to contradict; to deny; to dispute: — *pr p* **gainsay'ing**; *pa t* and *pa p* **gainsaid** (*gān-sād'* or *-sed'*); *3rd pers sing present indicative* **gainsays** (*-sāz'*). — *n* **gainsay'er**. — *n* **gainsay'ing**. [O.E. *gegn*, against, and **say**.]

gait *gāt*, *n* way of walking; the pattern of leg-movements used by a horse in trotting, cantering, galloping, etc. — *vt* to teach (a horse) its gaits. — *combining form* **-gait'ed** having a particular gait, e.g. *slow-gaited*. [**gate**[2].]

gaiter *gā'tər*, *n* a covering for the (lower leg and) ankle, fitting over the upper of one's shoe. [Fr. *guêtre*.]

Gal. (*Bible*) *abbrev* for (the Letter to the) Galatians.

gal[1] *gal*, old colloq. for **girl**.

gal[2] *gal*, (*phys*) *n* a unit of acceleration, one centimetre per second per second. [*Gal*ileo, Italian astronomer and physicist (1564–1642).]

gal. *abbrev* for gallon(s).

gala *gä'lə* or *gā'lə*, *n* a festivity; a sporting occasion, with competitions, etc. — *adj* of the nature of, or suitable for, a great occasion or festivity. — **ga'la-dress** festive costume for a gala day. [Fr. *gala*, show — It. *gala*, finery.]

galactic *gə-lak'tik*, *adj* relating to or obtained from milk (*med*); relating to a galaxy or the Galaxy. — *n* **galac'tagogue** (*-tə-gog*) a medicine that promotes secretion of milk. — **galactic plane** the plane that passes through the centre of the bulging disc formed by the spiral arms of the Galaxy. [Gr. *gala*, *galaktos*, milk.]

galago *gə-lā'gō* or *-lä'gō*, *n* a bushbaby: — *pl* **gala'gos**. [Perh. Wolof *golokh*, monkey.]

galah *gə-lä'*, *n* an Australian cockatoo with a grey back and pink underparts; a fool (*Austr slang*). [Aboriginal.]

Galahad *gal'ə-had*, *n* a person notable for nobility and integrity of character. [From Sir *Galahad* in Arthurian legend, the noblest knight of the Round Table.]

galantine *gal'ən-tēn*, *n* a dish of poultry, veal, etc., served cold in jelly. [Fr., — Med. L. *galatina*, poss. — L. *gelātus*, frozen.]

Galaxy *gal'ək-si*, *n* the disc-shaped system, composed of spiralling arms of stars, that contains our solar system near its edge; (without *cap*) any similar system; (without *cap*) a splendid assemblage. [Gr. *galaxias*, the Milky Way, orig. also the meaning of *galaxy* — *gala*, *-aktos*, milk.]

galbanum *gal'bə-nəm*, *n* an aromatic gum resin obtained from several umbelliferous Asian plants. [L., — Gr. *chalbanē*, prob. an Eastern word.]

gale *gāl*, *n* a strong wind of between about 30 and 60 mph, force 8 on the Beaufort scale; an outburst.

galea *gal'i-ə* or *gā'li-ə*, (*biol*) *n* a helmet-shaped structure. — *adj* **gal'eate** or **gal'eated**. [L. *galea*, a skin helmet.]

galena *gə-lē'nə*, *n* lead sulphide, the commonest ore of lead, occurring as grey cubic crystals. — Also **galē'nite**. — *adj* **galē'noid**. [L. *galēna*, lead ore.]

Galenic *gə-len'ik*, *adj* relating to *Galen*, the 2nd-cent. Greek physician, or to his methods and theories.

Galilean[1] *gal-i-lē'ən*, *adj* of or relating to *Galileo*, the great Italian mathematician (1564–1642).

Galilean[2] *gal-i-lē'ən*, *adj* of or relating to *Galilee*, one of the Roman divisions of Palestine. — *n* a native of Galilee.

galingale *gal'ing-gāl*, *n* the aromatic rootstock of certain E. Indian plants of the ginger family, formerly much used like ginger; a sedge of the genus *Cyperus*, or its rootstock, of ancient medicinal repute. [O.Fr. *galingal* — Ar. *khalanjān* — Chin. *ko-liang-kiang* — *Ko*, a district near Canton, *liang*, mild, *kiang*, ginger.]

galiot. See **galliot**.

galipot *gal'i-pot*, *n* the turpentine that exudes from the cluster pine. [Fr.]

gall[1] *göl*, *n* bile, the greenish-yellow fluid secreted from the liver (*old*); bitterness; malignity; impudence, presumption. — **gall bladder** the bile-storing sac attached to the liver; **gall'stone** a concretion in the gall bladder or biliary ducts. [O.E. *galla*, *gealla*, gall.]

gall[2] *göl*, *n* an abnormal growth on a plant caused by a parasite such as an insect or fungus, or by bacteria. — **gall'fly** or **gall wasp** an insect that causes galls by depositing its eggs in plants; **gall midge** a gall-making midge; **gall'nut** a nutlike gall produced on an oak by a gall wasp, used esp. formerly for making ink. [Fr. *galle* — L. *galla*, oak-apple.]

gall[3] *göl*, *n* a painful swelling, esp. in a horse; a sore due to chafing; a state or cause of irritation. — *vt* to fret or hurt by rubbing; to irritate. — *adj* **gall'ing** irritating. — *adv* **gall'ingly**. [O.E. *galla*, *gealla*, a sore place.]

gall. *abbrev* for gallon(s).

gallant *gal'ənt*, *adj* brave; noble; attentive to ladies, chivalrous; amorous (sometimes *gə-lant'* in the last two senses). — *n* a dashing, debonair young man; a lover (also *gə-lant'* in this sense). — *adv* **gall'antly**. — *n* **gall'antness**. — *n* **gall'antry** bravery in battle, etc.; attention or devotion to ladies; a chivalrous attention or remark. [Fr. *galant* — O.Fr. *gale*, a merrymaking.]

galleon *gal'i-ən*, *n* a large vessel with lofty stem and stern, mostly used formerly by Spaniards for carrying treasure. [Sp. *galeón* — O.Fr. *galie*, galley.]

galleria *gal-ə-rē'ə*, *n* a shopping-arcade. [It., arcade.]

gallery *gal'ə-ri, n* a covered walk; a long balcony; a long passage; a long narrow room; an upper floor of seats in a theatre, usu. the highest; the occupants of the gallery; a body of spectators; a room or building for the exhibition of works of art; a photographer's studio; in a television studio, a soundproof room overlooking the action, for the director or lighting engineer; an underground passage, drift or level. — *vt* to tunnel. — *adj* **gall'eried** furnished with, or made in the form of, a gallery or arcade. — **play to the gallery** to play for the applause of the least cultured. [O.Fr. *galerie*.]

galley *gal'i, n* a long, low-built ship with one deck, propelled by oars and sails; a Greek or Roman warship; the cooking-place on board ship; a flat oblong tray for type that has been set up (*printing*); a galley proof (*printing*). — **galley proof** an impression taken from type on a galley; in photocomposition, an early proof before make-up; **galley slave** a person condemned to work as a slave at the oar of a galley; a drudge. [O.Fr. *galie, galee* — L.L. *galea*.]

galley-west *gal-i-west', (US slang) adv* into confusion or unconsciousness. [Eng. dialect *collywest*, perh. from Northamptonshire village *Collyweston*.]

galliard *gal'yərd, n* a spirited dance for two, in triple time, common in the 16th and 17th centuries. [O.Fr. *gaillard*.]

Gallic *gal'ik, adj* relating to France or the French; relating to Gaul or the ancient Gauls. — (All the following also without *cap*) *vt* and *vi* **Gall'icise** or **-ize** to assimilate or conform to French habits, etc. — *n* **Gall'icism** an expression or idiom peculiar to French occurring as a use in another language. — **Gallo-** *gal-ō-, combining form* signifying France or Gaul, as in *Gallo-Roman*. — *n* **Gallomā'nia** a mania for French ways. — *n* **Gall'ophil** or **Gall'ophile** a person who is friendly to France. — *n* **Gall'ophobe** a person who dislikes or fears France or what is French. — *n* **Gallophō'bia**. [L. *Gallus*, a Gaul; *Gallicus*, Gaulish.]

gallic acid *gal'ik as'id, n* a crystalline substance present in gallnuts, tea, and various plants, and obtained by hydrolysis from tannin, used as a tanning agent, and for making inks and dyes. [Fr. *gallique* — *galle*, **gall**[2].]

galligaskins *gal-i-gas'kinz, npl* wide hose or breeches worn in the 16th and 17th centuries. [O.Fr. *garguesque* — It. *grechesco*, Greekish — L. *graecus*, Greek.]

gallinaceous *gal-i-nā'shəs, adj* of or relating to the order of birds that includes grouse, pheasants and the domestic fowl. [L. *gallīna*, a hen — *gallus*, a cock.]

galling. See **gall**[3].

gallinule *gal'i-nūl, n* a moorhen. [L. *gallīnula*, a chicken — *gallīna*, a hen.]

galliot or **galiot** *gal'i-ət, n* a small galley; an old Dutch cargo-boat. [Fr. *galiote* — L.L. *galea*, galley.]

gallipot *gal'i-pot, n* a small glazed pot, esp. for medicine. [Prob. a **pot** brought in **galleys**.]

gallium *gal'i-əm, n* a metallic element (symbol **Ga**; atomic no. 31), as gallium arsenide an important semiconductor. [L. *gallus*, a cock, from the discoverer's name, *Lecoq* de Boisbaudran, or *Gallia*, Gaul, France, his country.]

gallivant *gal'i-vant, vi* to spend time frivolously; to gad about. [Perh. **gallant**.]

galliwasp *gal'i-wosp, n* a W. Indian lizard.

gallnut. See **gall**[2].

Gallo-, etc. See under *Gallic*.

gallon *gal'ən, n* a unit of capacity, in Britain equal to 4·546 litres (277·4 cubic inches), also called **imperial gallon**, in the U.S. equal to 3·785 litres (231 cubic inches). — *n* **gall'onage** an amount in gallons; the rate of use in gallons. [O.N.Fr. *galun, galon*.]

galloon *gə-lōōn', n* a kind of lace; a narrow tape-like trimming or binding material. [Fr. *galon, galonner*.]

gallop *gal'əp, vi* to go at a gallop; to ride a galloping animal; to move very fast. — *vt* to cause to gallop. — *n* the fastest pace of a horse, etc., at each stride of which all four feet are off the ground; a ride at a gallop; a fast pace (*fig*). — *n* **gall'oper** one who, or that which, gallops; an aide-de-camp (*mil*); (esp. in *pl*) a fairground merry-go-round wth wooden horses that rise and fall in imitation of galloping. — *adj* **gall'oping** proceeding at a gallop; advancing rapidly, as in *galloping inflation*. [O.Fr. *galoper, galop*.]

Gallophil, Gallophile, Gallophobe, etc. See under **Gallic**.

Galloway *gal'ə-wā, n* a small strong horse, 13–15 hands high; a breed of large black hornless cattle, orig. from *Galloway* in Scotland.

gallows *gal'ōz, nsing* (orig. *pl*) a wooden frame for hanging criminals; any contrivance with posts and crossbeam for suspending things. — **gallows humour** grim, sardonic humour; **gallows tree** a gallows. — **cheat the gallows** to deserve but escape hanging. [M.E. *galwes* (pl.) — O.E. *galga*.]

gallstone. See **gall**[1].

gallumph. See **galumph**.

Gallup poll *gal'əp pōl, n* a method of gauging public opinion by questioning suitably distributed sample individuals, devised by George Horace *Gallup* (1901–84).

galoot *gə-lōōt', (slang) n* a clumsy fellow. [Orig. naut. slang.]

galop *gal'əp, n* a lively dance or dance tune in double time; a lively sideways slipping step used in dancing. — *vi* to dance a galop; to perform a lively sideways slipping step. [Fr.; cf. **gallop**.]

galore *gə-lōr', adv* in abundance. [Ir. *go*, an adverbialising participle, *leōr*, sufficient.]

galosh or **golosh** *gə-losh', n* a waterproof overshoe. [Fr. *galoche* — prob. L.L. *gallicula*, small Gaulish shoe.]

galtonia *gōl-tō'ni-ə* or *gal-, n* any of several bulbous plants of the lily family (genus *Galtonia*) native to Southern Africa, esp. the Cape hyacinth. [Named after Sir Francis *Galton* (1822–1911), British scientist.]

galumph or **gallumph** *gə-lumf', vi* to stride along exultantly; to bound about in a noisy, ungainly way. — *n* **galum'pher**. [A coinage of Lewis Carroll.]

galvanic *gal-van'ik, adj* relating to the production of an electric current by chemical means, esp. the action of an acid on a metal; (of a response, behaviour, etc.) sudden, startling or convulsive, as though produced by an electric shock. — *adv* **galvan'ically**. — *n* **galvanisā'tion** or **-z-** (*gal-və-nī-zā'shən*). — *vt* **gal'vanise** or **-ize** to subject to the action of an electric current; to stimulate to spasmodic action by, or as if by, an electric shock; to confer a false vitality upon; to coat with metal by an electric current; to coat with zinc without using a current. — *n* **gal'vanism** the production of an electric current by chemical means, as in a battery. — *n* **galvanom'eter** an instrument for measuring electric currents. — *adj* **galvanomet'ric**. — *n* **galvanom'etry**. — *n* **galvan'oscope** an instrument for detecting electric currents. [From Luigi *Galvani*, of Bologna (1737–98), the discoverer of galvanism.]

gam[1] *gam, n* a collective noun for whales, a school.

gam[2] *gam, (slang)* a leg, esp. female. [Perh. Fr. dialect *gambe*, leg.]

gam[3] *gam, (vulg) n* and *vi* (to practise) oral sex. [Fr. *gam*ahuche or *gam*aruche, term popularised through the Services.]

gamba *gam'bə, (mus) n* an organ stop of stringlike quality. [From viola da *gamba*, a cello-like instrument.]

gambado *gam-bā'dō, (dressage) n* a bound or spring performed by a horse, a curvet: — *pl* **gambā'does** or **gambā'dos**. [Sp. *gambada*.]

gambier or **gambir** *gam'bēr, n* an astringent substance prepared from the leaves of a climbing shrub

(*Uncaria gambir*) of S.E. Asia, used in tanning and dyeing. [Malay.]

gambit *gam'bit*, *n* an initial move in a conversation, discussion, etc., esp. one with an element of trickery; the (offer of a) sacrifice of a piece for the sake of an advantage in timing or position in the opening stages of a game (*chess*). [Sp. *gambito* — It. *gambetto*, a tripping up — *gamba*, leg.]

gamble *gam'bl*, *vi* to play for money, esp. for high stakes; to take a chance (with *on*); to engage in wild financial speculations; to take great risks for the sake of possible advantage. — *vt* to squander or lose by staking. — *n* a transaction depending on chance. — *n* **gam'bler** a person who gambles, esp. one who makes it his or her business. — *n* **gam'bling.** [Frequentative of **game**[1].]

gamboge *gam-bōōzh'*, *-bōj'* or *-bōōj'*, *n* a yellow gum resin, obtained from any of a number of Asian trees, used as a pigment and in medicine. — *adj* **gambogian** (*-bō'* or *-bōō'*) or **gambogic** (*-bō'*). [From *Cambodia*, whence it was brought about 1600.]

gambol *gam'bl*, *vi* to leap; to frisk playfully: — *pr p* **gam'bolling;** *pa t* and *pa p* **gam'bolled.** — *n* a playful frisk or frolic. [Formerly *gambold* — O.Fr. *gambade* — It. *gambata*, a kick — L.L. *gamba*, leg.]

gambrel *gam'brəl*, *n* the hock of a horse; gambrel roof. — **gambrel roof** in the U.K., a hipped roof in which the upper parts of the hipped ends take the form of a small vertical gable end; in the U.S., a roof with the lower part at a steeper pitch than the upper (called a *mansard* roof in the U.K.). [O.Fr. *gamberel*.]

game[1] *gām*, *n* a sport of any kind; (in *pl*) (an event consisting of competitions in) athletic sports; a contest for recreation; a competitive amusement according to a system of rules; the state of a game; manner of playing a game; form in playing; the requisite number of points to be gained to win a game; a bout or contest in a series; a spell or set period of playing a game; a bit of fun, a jest; any object of pursuit; a scheme or method of seeking an end, or the policy that would be most likely to attain it; business, activity, operation; (usu. **the game**) prostitution (*slang*); the spoil of the chase; wild animals hunted by sportsmen; the flesh of such animals. — *adj* of or belonging to animals hunted as game; full of fight (*colloq*); plucky, courageous (*colloq*); having the necessary spirit and willingness for some act (*colloq*). — *vi* to gamble. — *adv* **game'ly.** — *n* **game'ness.** — *adj* **game'some** playful. — *n* **game'ster** a gambler. — *adj* **gamesy** (*gām'zi*) keen on sports. — *n* **ga'ming** gambling. — *adj* **gā'my** or **gā'mey** having the flavour of game, esp. that kept till tainted; savouring of scandal, sensational; spirited, plucky, lively (*colloq*). — *n* **gā'miness** or **gā'meyness.** — **game bag** a bag for holding a sportsman's game; **game ball** see **game point; game bird** a bird hunted for sport; **game call** (*bridge*) a bid (and contract) which, if successful, will win a game; **game chips** thinly-cut (usu. disc-shaped) potato chips served with game; **game'cock** a cock of a breed trained to fight, a fighting cock; **game'-dealer; game fish** any freshwater fish of the salmon family except the grayling (opp. to *coarse fish*); **game fishing; game'keeper** a person who has the care of game on an estate, etc; **game laws** laws relating to the protection of game; **game licence** a licence to kill, or to sell, game; **game plan** the strategy or tactics used by a football team, etc.; any carefully devised strategy; **game point** or **game ball** the stage at which the next point wins the game; **game preserve** a tract of land stocked with game preserved for sport or with protected wild animals; **games'manship** (*facetious*, coined by Stephen Potter) the art of winning games or, generally, of scoring points, by talk or conduct aimed at putting one's opponent off; **games theory** (*math*) the theory concerned with analysing the choices and strategies available in a game or other conflict in order to choose the optimum course of action; **game warden** a person who looks after game, esp. in a game preserve; **ga'ming-house** a gambling-house; **ga'ming-table** a table used for gambling. — **big game** the larger animals hunted; **give the game away** to disclose a secret; **have a game with** or **make game of** to make sport of, to ridicule; **off one's game** playing badly; **on one's game** playing well; **on the game** (*colloq*) earning one's living as a prostitute; **play the game** to act in a fair, sportsmanlike, straightforward manner; **red game** grouse; **round game** a game, e.g. at cards, in which the number of players is not fixed; **the game is up** the plot has failed, all is revealed. [O.E. *gamen*, play.]

game[2] *gām*, *adj* lame.

gamelan *gam'ə-lan*, *n* an instrument resembling a xylophone; an orchestra of S.E. Asia consisting of percussion (chiefly), wind instruments and stringed instruments. [Jav.]

gamete *gam'ēt* or *ga-mēt'*, *n* a sexual reproductive cell; an egg cell or sperm cell. — *adj* **gam'etal** (or *gə-mē'təl*) or **gametic** (*gə-met'ik* or *gə-mē'tik*). — *n* **gametangium** (*gam-i-tan'ji-əm*) a cell or organ in which gametes are formed: — *pl* **gametan'gia.** — *n* **gametogen'esis** the formation of gametes. — *n* **gamē'tophyte** (or *gam'*) in alternation of generations, a plant of the sexual generation, producing gametes. [Gr. *gametēs*, husband, *gametē*, wife — *gameein*, to marry.]

gamin *gam'in* or *ga-mẽ*, *n* a precocious and mischievous street urchin: — *fem* **gamine** (*-mēn'*) a girl of a pert, boyish, impish appearance and disposition. — *adj* boyish or impish. [Fr.]

gamma *gam'ə*, *n* the third letter of the Greek alphabet (Γ or γ = G or g); in classification, the third, or someone or something of the third grade, the grade below beta. — **gamma camera** a device which detects gamma radiation and which is used to produce images of parts of the body into which radioactive material has been introduced; **gamma globulin** any of a group of globulins occurring in blood plasma which contain antibodies that protect against various diseases; **gamma rays** a penetrating radiation given off by radium and other radioactive substances. [Gr.]

gammadion *gə-mā'di-ən*, *n* a figure composed of Greek capital gammas, esp. a swastika: — *pl* **gammā'dia.** [Late Gr., little gamma.]

gammon[1] *gam'ən*, *n* the cured meat from the hindquarters and leg of a pig; the back part of a side of bacon. [O.N.Fr. *gambon*, *gambe*, leg.]

gammon[2] *gam'ən*, *n* a double game at backgammon, won by removing all one's men before one's opponent removes any; patter, chatter; nonsense, humbug. — *vt* to defeat by a gammon at backgammon; to hoax, impose upon. — *vi* to talk gammon; to feign. [Prob. O.E. *gamen*, a game.]

gammy *gam'i*, *adj* lame, injured. [Cf. **game**[2].]

gamo- *gam-ō-*, *gam-ə-* or *ga-mo'-*, *combining form* signifying: marriage; union; reproduction or fertilisation. — *n* **gamogen'esis** sexual reproduction. — *adj* **gamopet'alous** with petals united. — *adj* **gamophyll'ous** with perianth leaves united. — *adj* **gamosep'alous** with sepals united.

-gamous *-gə-məs*, *combining form* denoting: having a stated number of spouses, as in *bigamous*; relating to a stated means of fertilisation or reproduction, as in *allogamous*. — **-gamy** (*-gə-mi*) *combining form* denoting marriage, or supposed marriage, to a stated number of spouses; a stated means of fertilisation or reproduction. [Gr. *gamos*, marriage.]

gamp *gamp*, (*colloq*) *n* a large, untidily furled umbrella; an umbrella. [From Mrs Sarah *Gamp*, in Dickens's *Martin Chuzzlewit*.]

gamut *gam'ət*, *n* the full range or compass of anything, e.g. the emotions; any recognised scale or range of notes; the whole compass of a voice or instrument. [From *gamma*, the Gr. letter G, adopted when it was required to name a note added below the A with which the old scale began, and *ut*, which became do in sol-fa notation.]

gamy. See **game**[1].

-gamy. See **-gamous**.

gander *gan'dər*, *n* the male of the goose. — **take a gander at** (*slang*) to take a look at. [O.E. *ganra*, *gandra*.]

gandy dancer *gan'di dän'sər*, (*US colloq*) *n* a railway labourer; any manual labourer; an itinerant or seasonal labourer. [Prob. from the *Gandy* Manufacturing Company, which made tools used by railway workmen.]

gang[1] *gang*, *n* a band of roughs or criminals; a number of people or animals (esp. elk) associating together; a number of labourers working together; a set of children who habitually play together; a set of tools, etc., used together. — *vt* and *vi* to associate in a gang or gangs. — *vt* to adjust in co-ordination. — *n* **ganger** (*gang'ər*) the foreman of a gang of labourers. — *n* **gang'ing**. — *n* **gang'ster** a member of a gang of roughs or criminals. — *n* **gang'sterdom**. — *n* **gang'sterism**. — **gang'-bang** (*slang*) successive sexual intercourse with one, usu. unwilling, female by a group of males; **gang'land** or **gang'sterland** the domain of gangsters, the world of (esp. organised) crime; **gang mill** a sawmill with gang saws; **gang plug** an electrical adaptor with a row of sockets. — *vt* **gang'-punch** (*comput*) to punch (the same information) in a number of cards, or to punch (a number of cards) with the same information. — **gang rape** a number of successive rapes committed by members of a group on one victim on one occasion. — *vt* **gang'-rape**. — **gang saw** a saw fitted in a frame with others; **gangs'man** the foreman of a gang. — **gang switches** a number of electrical switches connected so that they can be operated simultaneously. — **gang up on** to make a concerted attack on; **gang up with** to join in the (doubtful) activities of. [O.E. *gang* — *gangan*, to go.]

gang[2]. See **gangue**.

gangling *gang'gling* or **gangly** *gang'gli*, *adj* loosely-built, lanky. [Orig. Scot. and Eng. dialect; O.E. *gangan*, to go.]

ganglion *gang'gli-ən*, *n* a tumour in a tendon sheath (*med*); a nerve centre: — *pl* **gan'glia** or **gan'glions**. — *adj* **gan'gliar** or **ganglion'ic** relating to a ganglion. — *adj* **gan'gliate** or **gan'gliated** having a ganglion or ganglia. — *adj* **gan'gliform**. [Gr.]

gangplank *gang'plangk*, *n* a wooden board used to form a bridge to give access on to or out of a ship, or on to another ship. [O.E. *gangan*, go, and **plank**.]

gangrene *gang'grēn*, *n* necrosis of part of the body, with decay of body tissue, resulting from a failure in the blood supply to the part. — *adj* **gangrenous** (*gang'gri-nəs*) mortified. [Gr. *gangraina*, gangrene.]

gangster. See under **gang**[1].

gangue or **gang** *gang*, *n* rock in which ores are embedded. [Fr., — Ger. *Gang*, a vein.]

gangway *gang'wā*, *n* a gangplank, usu. with sides for the protection of users, giving access on to or out of a ship; an opening in a ship's side to take a gangway; any passageway on a ship; an aisle between rows of seats; the cross-passage halfway down the House of Commons. — *interj* make way, make room to pass. [O.E. *gangan*, to go, and **way**.]

ganister or **gannister** *gan'is-tər*, *n* a hard, close-grained siliceous stone, found in N. England. [Perh. from quarry at *Gannister*, Cheshire.]

ganja *gän'jə*, *n* an intoxicating preparation, the female flowering tops of Indian hemp, i.e. marijuana. [Hind. *gājā*.]

gannet *gan'ət*, *n* a large white sea-bird of the family *Sulidae*, with black-tipped wings; a greedy person (*colloq*). — *n* **gann'etry** a breeding-place of gannets. [O.E. *ganot*, a sea-fowl.]

gannister. See **ganister**.

ganoid *gan'oid*, *adj* (of fish scales) having a glistening outer layer over bone; (of fishes) belonging to an order that commonly have such scales. — *n* a ganoid fish. — *n* **ganoin** (*gan'ō-in*) a calcareous substance, forming an enamel-like layer on ganoid scales. [Gr. *ganos*, brightness, *eidos*, appearance.]

gansey *gan'zi*, *n* a woollen sweater, a jersey. [From the island of *Guernsey*.]

gantry *gan'tri*, *n* a stand for barrels; the shelving, racks, etc. in which drinks are displayed in a bar; a platform or bridge for a travelling crane, railway signals, etc.; the servicing tower beside a rocket on its launching pad. — **gantry crane** a crane in bridge form with vertical members running on parallel tracks. [Perh. O.Fr. *gantier* — L. *cantērius*, a trellis — Gr. *kanthēlios*, a pack ass.]

Ganymede *gan'i-mēd*, *n* a catamite. [From *Ganymēdēs*, the beautiful youth who served Zeus as cup-bearer.]

gaol, etc. See **jail**, etc.

gap *gap*, *n* an opening or breach; a cleft; a passage; a notch or pass in a mountain ridge; a gorge (*US*); a breach of continuity; an unfilled space, a lack; a divergence, disparity; the space between discharge electrodes, over which a spark can jump (also **spark gap**; *electr eng*); a break in the magnetic circuit of the recording or erasing head of a tape-recorder, which allows the signal to interact with the oxide film (*electronics*). — *vt* to make a gap in. — *adj* **gapp'y**. — **gap site** a piece of land in a built-up area lying empty because the building which once stood on it has been demolished. — *adj* **gap'-toothed** with teeth set wide apart. — **bridge, close, fill** or **stop the gap** to supply the deficiency. [O.N. *gap*.]

gape *gāp*, *vi* to open the mouth wide; to yawn; to stare with open mouth; to be wide open. — *n* an act of gaping; the extent to which the mouth can be opened; the angle of the mouth; a wide opening, parting, fissure, chasm or failure to meet; (in *pl*) a yawning fit; (in *pl*) a disease of birds of which gaping is a symptom, caused by a threadworm (**gape'worm**) in the windpipe and bronchial tubes. — *n* **gā'per** a person, etc. that gapes; a mollusc (*Mya*) with shell open at each end; a sea-perch (*Serranus*); an easy catch (*cricket*). — *n* and *adj* **gā'ping**. — *adv* **gā'pingly**. [O.N. *gapa*, to open the mouth.]

gar. See **garfish**.

garage *gar'äzh*, *gar'ij* or in U.S. *gə-räzh'*, *n* a building for housing motor vehicles; an establishment where motor vehicles are tended, repaired, bought and sold. — *adj* (of music) of the kind played by a garage band. — *vt* to put into or keep in a garage. — *n* **gar'aging** accommodation for cars, etc. — **garage band** an unsophisticated rock group; **garage sale** a sale of various items held on the seller's premises, esp. in the garage. [Fr., — *garer*, to secure.]

garam masala *gar'əm mə-sä'lə*, *n* a spice mixture used in making curry.

garb *gärb*, *n* fashion of dress; dress; semblance, appearance. — *vt* to clothe, array. [It. *garbo*, grace.]

garbage *gär'bij*, *n* any worthless matter; household food and other refuse; extraneous matter or invalid data (*comput*). — **gar'bageman** (*US*) a dustman; **garbage can** (*US*) a bin for food waste, etc.; a dustbin.

garbanzo *gär-ban'zō*, *n* a chick-pea: — *pl* **garban'zos**. [Sp.]

garble *gär'bl*, *vt* to misrepresent or falsify by suppression and selection; to mangle, mutilate. — *adj* **gar'bled**. — *n* **gar'bler**. [It. *garbellare* — Ar.

ghirbāl, a sieve, perh. — L.L. *crībellum*, dimin. of *crībrum*, a sieve.]

garbo *gär'bō*, (*Austr colloq*) *n* a dustman, garbage-collector; rubbish. [*garb*age.]

garboard *gär'bōrd*, (*naut*) *n* the first range of planks or plates laid on a ship's bottom next to the keel. — Also **garboard strake.** [Du. *gaarboord.*]

garbologist *gär-bol'ə-jist*, (*US facetious*) *n* a dustman, garbage-collector. — *n* **garbol'ogy.** [**garb**age.]

garçon *gär-sɔ̃*, *n* a male servant, esp. a waiter in a restaurant. [Fr., a boy.]

garda *gör'də* or *gär'*, *n* an Irish policeman or guard: — *pl* **gardaí** (*gör'də-ē* or *gär'*). — **Garda Siochana** (*shē'hhə-nə*) the Irish police force. [Ir. *gárda.*]

garden *gär'dən*, *n* a piece of ground on which flowers, etc., are cultivated, adjoining a house; (often in *pl*) a usu. public area laid out with walks, flowerbeds, lawns, trees, etc.; a pleasant spot; a fertile region; (in *pl*, with *cap*) used in street names. — *adj* of, used in or grown in a garden or gardens. — *vi* to cultivate or work in a garden. — *n* **gar'dener** a person who gardens, or is skilled in gardening; a person employed to tend a garden. — *n* **gar'dening** the laying out and cultivation of gardens. — **garden centre** an establishment where plants, gardening equipment, etc. are sold; **garden city** or **suburb** a model town or suburb laid out with broad roads, trees, and much garden ground between the houses; **garden party** a social gathering held in a garden. — **everything in the garden is lovely** all is, or appears to be, well; **hanging garden** a garden formed in terraces rising one above another; **lead someone up the garden path** to draw someone on insensibly, to mislead someone; **market garden** a garden in which vegetables, fruits, etc., are raised for sale; **market gardener.** [O.Fr. *gardin* (Fr. *jardin*).]

gardenia *gär-dē'ni-ə*, *n* any of several evergreen shrubs or trees of the genus *Gardenia*, with fragrant, usu. white flowers of a waxy appearance; one of these flowers. [American botanist Dr Alex. *Garden* (*c* 1730–91).]

garfish *gär'fish*, *n* a pike-like fish (*Belone*) with long slender beaked head; the bony pike, an American ganoid river fish (*Lepidosteus* or *Lepisosteus*); any of various similar Australian fish. — Also **gar** or **gar'pike.** [O.E. *gār*, spear.]

garganey *gär'gə-ni*, *n* a small duck of Europe and Asia, the male having a curved white stripe over the eye. [It. *garganello.*]

Gargantuan *gär-gan'tū-ən*, *adj* like or worthy of Rabelais's hero *Gargantua*, a giant of vast appetite; (without *cap*) enormous, prodigious.

garget *gär'git*, *n* inflammation of the throat or udder in cows, swine, etc. (*vet*); (also **garget plant**) pokeweed (*US*).

gargle *gär'gl*, *vt* and *vi* to swill a liquid round the back of one's throat, usu. for medicinal purposes, avoiding swallowing it by breathing out through it. — *n* a liquid for gargling; an act of gargling. [O.Fr. *gargouiller* — *gargouille*, the throat.]

gargoyle *gär'goil*, *n* a spout, usu. in the form of a grotesquely carved face or figure, projecting from a roof gutter. [O.Fr. *gargouille* — L.L. *gurguliō*, throat.]

garial. See **gavial.**

garibaldi *gar-i-böl'di*, *n* (also **Garibaldi biscuit**) a biscuit with a layer of currants. [After G. *Garibaldi*, Italian patriot (1807–82), app. arbitrarily.]

garigue. See **garrigue.**

garish *gār'ish*, *adj* gaudy, showy; (of colours) glaring. — *adv* **gar'ishly.** — *n* **gar'ishness.**

garland *gär'lənd*, *n* a wreath of flowers or leaves; a book of selections in prose or poetry. — *vt* to deck with a garland. [O.Fr. *garlande.*]

garlic *gär'lik*, *n* a bulbous liliaceous plant of the genus *Allium*, having a pungent taste and very strong smell; extended to others of the genus, such as **wild garlic** (ramsons). — *adj* **gar'licky.** [O.E. *gārlēac* — *gār*, a spear, *lēac*, a leek.]

garment *gär'mənt*, *n* any article of clothing; a covering. — *vt* to clothe or cover. — *adj* **gar'mented.** [O.Fr. *garniment* — *garnir*, to furnish.]

garner *gär'nər*, (*literary*) *vt* to (gather up and) store. — *n* (*old* or *poetic*) a granary or store. [O.Fr. *gernier* (Fr. *grenier*) — L. *grānārium* (usu. in pl.), a granary.]

garnet *gär'nit*, *n* a mineral, in some varieties a precious stone, generally red, crystallising in dodecahedra and icositetrahedra, a silicate of di- and trivalent metals. [O.Fr. *grenat* — L.L. *grānātum*, pomegranate; or L.L. *grānum*, grain, cochineal, red dye.]

garni *gär-nē*, (Fr.; *cookery*) *adj* trimmed, garnished.

garnish *gär'nish*, *vt* to adorn, decorate, trim; to add herbs, etc., to (a dish) for flavour or decoration; to garnishee (*law*). — *n* something placed round a principal dish at table, whether for embellishment or relish; decoration, embellishment. — *n* **gar'nishee** (*law*) a person warned not to pay money owed to another, because the latter is indebted to the garnisher who gives the warning. — *vt* to attach in this way; to serve with a garnishment. — *n* **garnishee'ment.** — *n* **gar'nisher.** — *n* **gar'nishing.** — *n* **gar'nishment** that which garnishes or embellishes; a garnisheement (*law*). [O.Fr. *garniss-*, stem of *garnir*, to furnish.]

garniture *gär'ni-chər*, *n* embellishments, trimmings, decorations or accessories. [Fr., — *garnir*, to trim, decorate.]

garotte. See **garrotte.**

garpike. See **garfish.**

garran. Same as **garron.**

garret *gar'it*, *n* a room just under the roof of a house, an attic. — *adj* **garr'eted.** [O.Fr. *garite*, a place of safety — *guarir*, *warir*, to preserve.]

garrigue or **garigue** *gə-rēg'*, *n* uncultivated open scrubland of the Mediterranean region; the scrub growing on it. [Fr. — Prov. *garriga*, stony ground.]

garrison *gar'i-sn*, *n* a body of troops stationed in a town, fortress, etc., to defend it; a fortified place. — *vt* to furnish (a town, etc.) with a garrison; to station (troops) as a garrison. — **garrison town** a town in which a garrison is stationed. [O.Fr. *garison* — *garir*, to furnish.]

garron or **garran** *gar'ən*, *n* a small horse. [Ir. *gearran.*]

garrotte, garotte or in U.S. **garrote** *gə-rot'*, *n* a Spanish mode of putting criminals to death; the apparatus for the purpose — originally a string round the throat tightened by twisting a stick, later a metal collar tightened by a screw, whose point enters the spinal marrow. — *vt* to execute by the garrotte; suddenly to make unconscious by semi-strangulation in order to rob: — *pr p* **garrott'ing** or **garott'ing**; *pa t* and *pa p* **garrott'ed** or **garott'ed.** — *n* **garrott'er** or **garott'er.** — *n* **garrott'ing** or **garott'ing.** [Sp. *garotte*; cf. Fr. *garrot*, a stick.]

garrulous *gar'ōō-ləs*, *adj* talkative, loquacious; wordy, voluble. — *n* **garrulity** (*-ōō'li-ti*). — *adv* **garr'ulously.** — *n* **garr'ulousness.** [L. *garrulus* — *garrīre*, to chatter.]

garryowen *ga-ri-ō'ən*, (*Rugby football*) *n* a high kick forward together with a rush towards the landing-place of the ball. [*Garryowen* Rugby Club in Limerick.]

garter *gär'tər*, *n* a band used to support a stocking; a suspender (*NAm*); (with *cap*) (the badge of) the highest order of knighthood in Great Britain. — *vt* to put a garter on; to support, bind, decorate or surround with a garter. — **garter snake** in N. America, any snake of the genus *Eutaenia*, non-venomous, longitudinally striped; **garter stitch** a plain stitch in knitting; horizontally ribbed knitting made by using plain stitches only. — **Garter King-of-Arms** the chief herald of the Order of the Garter. [O.Fr. *gartier* — O.Fr. *garet*, ham of the leg, prob. Celt.]

garth *gärth*, *n* a courtyard within a cloister. [O.N. *garthr*, a court.]

gas *gas*, *n* a substance in a condition in which it has no definite boundaries or fixed volume, but will fill any space; often restricted to such a substance above its critical temperature; a substance or mixture which is in this state in ordinary terrestrial conditions; esp. coal-gas, or other gas for lighting or heating, or one used for attack in warfare; gaslight; empty, boastful, garrulous talk (*colloq*); something delightful, impressive or exciting (*colloq*); petrol (short for *gasoline*; *NAm*, *Austr* and *NZ*): — *pl* **gas'es**. — *vt* to supply or fill with gas; to poison or asphyxiate with gas. — *vi* to chatter, esp. vapidly: — *pr p* **gass'ing**; *pa t* and *pa p* **gassed**. — *adj* **gaseous** (*gas'i-əs*, *gā'shəs* or *gash'əs*) in the form of gas; of, or relating to, gas. — *n* **gas'eousness**. — *n* **gasificā'tion**. — *vt* **gas'ify** to convert into gas. — *n* **gas'ohol** or **gas'ahol** a mixture of 8 or 9 parts petrol and 1 or 2 parts alcohol, used as a fuel. — *n* **gasom'eter** a gasholder. — *n* **gasom'etry** the measurement of amounts of gas. — *n* **gassi'ness**. — *adj* **gass'y** full of gas; abounding in or emitting gas; gaseous. — **gas'bag** (*colloq*) a talkative person; **gas centrifuge** a centrifuge for separating gases; **gas chamber** an enclosed place designed for killing by means of gas (also **gas oven**); **gas chromatography** a widely used form of chromatography in which a gas is passed down the column which contains the mixture to be separated and a solvent; **gas cooker** a cooking-stove using gas as fuel. — *adj* **gas'-cooled** cooled by a flow of gas. — **gas engine** an engine worked by the explosion of gas; **gas escape** a leakage of gas; **gas'field** a region in which natural gas occurs. — *adj* **gas'-filled**. — **gas fire** a room-heating apparatus in which gas is burned. — *adj* **gas'-fired** fuelled by gas. — **gas'-fitter** a person whose job is to fit up the pipes, etc. for gas appliances; **gas gangrene** gangrene resulting from infection of a wound by certain bacteria which form gases in the flesh; **gas'-guzzler** (*US colloq*) a car that consumes large amounts of petrol; **gas heater** any heating apparatus in which gas is used; **gas'holder** a storage tank for gas; **gas jar** a tall, narrow, cylindrical glass vessel for collecting and holding a gas in chemical experiments; **gas jet** the perforated part of a gas fitting where the gas issues and is burnt, a burner; **gas lamp** a lamp that burns gas; **gas'light** light produced by a gas lamp. — *adj* **gas'lit**. — **gas main** a principal gas pipe from the gasworks; **gas mantle** a gauze covering, chemically prepared, enclosing a gas jet, and becoming incandescent when heated; **gas mask** a respiratory device (covering nose, mouth and eyes) as a protection against poisonous gases; **gas meter** an instrument for measuring gas consumed; **gas oil** a petroleum distillate, intermediate between kerosine and lubricating oil, used as (esp. heating) fuel; **gas oven** the oven of a gas cooker; a gas chamber. — *adj* **gas-per'meable** (of hard contact lenses) allowing oxygen to penetrate through to the eye. — *n* **gas pipe** a pipe for conveying gas; **gas poker** a poker-shaped gas appliance with gas jets, that can be inserted into fuel to kindle a fire; **gas ring** a hollow ring with perforations serving as gas jets; **gas stove** a gas cooker; **gas tap** a tap by which to turn the gas supply on or off; **gas turbine** a machine consisting of a combustion chamber, to which air is supplied by a compressor and in which the air is heated at constant pressure, and a turbine driven by the hot expanding gases; **gasworks** a factory where gas is made. — **gas and gaiters** nonsense; **step on the gas** (*colloq*) to press the accelerator pedal of a motor car; to speed up, hurry. [A word invented by J.B. van Helmont (1577–1644); suggested by Gr. *chaos*.]

gasahol, gaseous. See under **gas**.

gash *gash*, *vt* to cut deeply into. — *n* a deep, open cut. [Formerly *garse* — O.Fr. *garser*, to scarify — L.L. *garsa*, scarification.]

gasification, gasify. See under **gas**.

gasket *gas'kit*, *n* a canvas band used to bind the sails to the yards when furled (*naut*); a strip of tow, etc., for packing a piston, etc.; a layer of packing material, esp. a flat sheet of asbestos compound, sometimes between thin copper sheets, used for making gas-tight joints between engine cylinders and heads, etc.

gasohol. See under **gas**.

gasoline or **gasolene** *gas'ə-lēn*, *n* petrol (*NAm*); a low-boiling petroleum distillate. [**gas** with *-ol-* and *-ine* or *-ene*.]

gasometer, etc. See **gas**.

gasp *gäsp*, *vi* to pant, or breathe in a distressed manner (often *gasp for breath*); to breathe in sharply, in astonishment, horror, etc.; to desire eagerly (with *for*). — *vt* to utter with gasps. — *n* a sharp, noisy intake of breath. — *n* **gasp'er** a person who gasps; a cheap cigarette (*slang*). — *adj* **gasp'y**. — **the last gasp** the point of death. [O.N. *geispa*, to yawn.]

Gastarbeiter *gast'är-bī-tər*, *n* a migrant worker, esp. one who does menial work. [Ger., lit. guest-worker.]

gasteropod. See **gastropod** under **gastro-**.

gastrectomy. See under **gastro-**.

gastric *gas'trik*, *adj* of, or relating to the stomach. — **gastric juice** a thin clear acid fluid secreted by the stomach to effect digestion. [Gr. *gastēr*, belly.]

gastrin *gas'trin*, (*biol*) *n* a hormone that stimulates production of gastric juice. [Gr. *gastēr*, belly.]

gastritis *gas-trī'tis*, (*med*) *n* inflammation of the stomach. [Gr. *gastēr*, belly, sfx. *-itis*, inflammation.]

gastro- *gas-trō-*, *gas-trə-* or *gas-tro'-*, or **gastr-** *combining form* denoting stomach or belly. — *n* **gastrectomy** (*gas-trek'tə-mi*) surgical removal of the stomach, or part of it. — *adj* **gastroenteric** (*gas-trō-en-ter'ik*) gastrointestinal. — *n* **gastroenterī'tis** inflammation of the lining of the stomach and intestines. — *n* **gastroenterol'ogist**. — *n* **gastroenterol'ogy** the study of the stomach and intestines. — *adj* **gastrointestinal** *gas-trō-in-tes'ti-nl* (or *-īn'l*) of, relating to, or consisting of, the stomach and intestines. — *n* **gastronome** (*gas'trə-nōm*), **gastronomer** (*-tron'ə-mər*) or **gastron'omist** an epicure. — *adj* **gastronomic** (*-nom'ik*). — *n* **gastron'omy** the art or science of good eating. — *n* **gastropod** (*gas'trə-pod*) or **gas'teropod** any of a class of asymmetrical molluscs, including the limpets, whelks, snails and slugs, in which the foot is broad and flat, and the shell, if any, in one piece and conical. — *n* **gas'troscope** an instrument for inspecting the interior of the stomach. [Gr. *gastēr*, belly.]

gastrula *gas'trŏŏ-lə*, (*zool*) *n* an embryo at the stage in which it forms a two-layered cup by the invagination of its wall. — *n* **gastrulā'tion**. [N.L., a little stomach.]

gat[1] *gat*, (*slang*, chiefly *US*) *n* a gun, a revolver. [**gatling-gun**.]

gat[2] *gat*, (*Bible*) *pa t* of **get**.

gat[3] *gät*, *n* in Indian music, the second and usu. final section of a raga. [Sans. *gāth*.]

gate[1] *gāt*, *n* a passage into a city, enclosure, or any large building; a narrow opening or defile; a frame for closing an entrance; an entrance, passage or channel; an obstacle consisting of two posts, markers, etc. between which competitors in a slalom, etc. must pass; (at an airport) any of the numbered exits from which to board an aircraft; the people who pay to see a game, hence, the number attending; the total amount of money paid for entrance (also **gate money**); an electronic circuit which passes impressed signals when permitted by another independent source of similar signals; the part of a film projector which holds the film in front of the lens; an H-shaped series of slots for controlling the movement of a gear lever in a gearbox. — *vt* to supply with a gate; to punish (students or schoolchildren) by imposing a curfew on them or by confining to school precincts for a time. — *adj* **gā'ted** having a gate or gates; punished by gating. — *adj* **gate'less.** — *n* **gā'ting.** — *vi* and *vt* **gate'crash** to enter without paying or invitation. — **gate'crasher; gate'fold** an oversize folded leaf in a book, etc., a fold-out; **gate'house** (*archit*) a building over or at a gate; **gate'keeper** a person who watches over a gate and supervises the traffic through it (also **gate'man**); any of several large butterflies with brown or orange wings. — *adj* **gate'-legged** or **gate'leg** (of a table) having a hinged and framed leg that can swing in to let down a leaf. — **gate'post** a post from which a gate is hung or against which it shuts; **gate'way** the way through a gate; a structure at a gate; a connection between computer networks, or between a computer network and a telephone line; any entrance. [O.E. *geat*, a way.]

gateau or **gâteau** *gat'ō*, *n* a rich cake, filled with cream, decorated with icing, etc.: — *pl* **gateaus** (*gat'ō*) or **gâteaux** (*gat'ōz* or *gä-tō*). [Fr.]

gather *gadh'ər*, *vt* to collect; to assemble; to amass; to cull; to pick up; to draw together; (in sewing) to draw into puckers by passing a thread through and pulling it tight; to learn by inference; to have increase in (e.g. speed). — *vi* to assemble or muster; to increase; to suppurate; to arrange signatures of a book in correct sequence for binding. — *n* a plait or fold in cloth, made by drawing threads through; (in *pl*) that part of the dress which is gathered or drawn in. — *n* **gath'erer** a person who collects, amasses, assembles or culls. — *n* **gath'ering** a crowd or assembly; a narrowing; the assembling of the sheets of a book; a suppurating swelling. — **gather oneself together** to collect all one's powers, like someone about to leap; **gather to a head** to ripen; to come into a state of preparation for action or effect. [O.E. *gaderian*, to gather, assemble.]

gatling gun *gat'ling gun*, *n* a machine gun invented by R.J. *Gatling* about 1861.

GATT *gat*, *abbrev* for General Agreement on Tariffs and Trade, an international treaty to promote trade and economic benefits, signed in 1947.

gauche *gōsh*, *adj* clumsy; tactless. — *n* **gaucherie** (*gō'shə-rē*) clumsiness; social awkwardness; an instance of this. [Fr., left.]

gaucho *gow'chō*, *n* a cowboy of the pampas, usually of mixed Spanish and Indian descent: — *pl* **gau'chos.** [Sp.]

gaud *göd*, *n* an ornament; a piece of finery. [In part app. — O.Fr. *gaudir* — L. *gaudēre*, to be glad, or *gaudium*, joy.]

gaudy *gö'di*, *adj* showy; gay; vulgarly bright. — *n* an entertainment or feast in some schools and colleges. — *adv* **gaud'ily.** — *n* **gaud'iness.** [**gaud.**]

gauge or **gage** *gāj*, *n* a measuring apparatus; a standard of measure; a means of limitation or adjustment to a standard; a measurement, such as the diameter of a wire, calibre of a tube, etc.; the distance between a pair of wheels or rails; a means of estimate; relative position of a ship to another vessel and the wind (in this sense usu. **gage**). — *vt* to measure; to estimate; to adjust to a standard. — *vi* to measure the contents of casks. — *adj* **gauge'able.** — *n* **gaug'er** a person who gauges; an excise man. — **gauge glass** a tube to show height of water; **gaug'ing-rod** an instrument for measuring the contents of casks. — *adj* **broad'-gauge** and **narr'ow-gauge** in railway construction respectively greater or less than **standard gauge**, in Britain 56½ in. (1·435 m.). [O.Fr. *gauge* (Fr. *jauge*).]

Gaul *göl*, (*hist*) *n* a name of ancient France; an inhabitant of Gaul. — *adj* **Gaul'ish.** — *n* the Celtic language of the Gauls. [Fr. *Gaule* — L. *Gallia*, *Gallus*.]

gauleiter *gow'lī-tər*, *n* a chief official of a district under the Nazi régime; an overbearing wielder of petty authority. [Ger., — *Gau*, district, *Leiter*, leader.]

Gaullist *gōl'ist*, *n* a follower of the French soldier and statesman General Charles A.J.M. de *Gaulle* (President of the Fifth Republic 1958–69). — Also *adj*. — *n* **Gaull'ism** principles and policies of Gaullists.

gaultheria *göl-thē'ri-ə*, *n* a plant belonging to the *Gaultheria* genus of evergreen aromatic plants of the heath family, including the American wintergreen and salal, an American ericaceous plant. [From the Swedish–Canadian botanist Hugues *Gaulthier*.]

gaunt *gönt*, *adj* thin; of a pinched appearance; haggard; grim. — *adv* **gaunt'ly.** — *n* **gaunt'ness.**

gauntlet[1] *gönt'lit*, *n* the iron glove of armour, formerly thrown down in challenge and taken up in acceptance; a heavy glove with a long, wide cuff; the cuff of such a glove. — *adj* **gaunt'leted** wearing a gauntlet or gauntlets. — **throw down** and **take up the gauntlet** respectively to give and to accept a challenge. [Fr. *gantelet*, dimin. of *gant*, glove, of Gmc. origin.]

gauntlet[2] *gönt'lit*, *n* the punishment (formerly military or naval) of having to run through a lane of men who strike as one passes. — **run the gauntlet** to undergo the punishment of the gauntlet; to expose oneself to hostile treatment. [Sw. *gatlopp* — *gata*, lane, *lopp*, course (cf. **leap**); confused with **gauntlet**[1].]

gaup, gauper. See **gawp.**

gaur *gowr*, *n* a species of large wild ox inhabiting parts of India. [Hindustani.]

gauss *gows*, *n* the CGS unit of magnetic flux density. — *adj* **Gauss'ian** (also without *cap*) of or due to Johann Karl Friedrich *Gauss* (1777–1855), German mathematician and physicist.

gauze *göz*, *n* a thin, transparent fabric; an openwork fabric or fine mesh. — *n* **gauz'iness.** — *adj* **gauz'y.** [Fr. *gaze*.]

gave *gāv*, *pa t* of **give.**

gavel *gav'l*, *n* a mallet; a chairman's, auctioneer's or judge's hammer.

gavial *gā'vi-əl*, **garial** or **gharial** *gur'i-əl*, *n* an Indian crocodile with very long slender muzzle. [Hindi *ghariyāl*, crocodile.]

gavotte *gə-vot'*, *n* a dance, somewhat like a country-dance, originally a dance of the *Gavots*, people of the French Upper Alps; the music for such a dance in common time, often occurring in suites.

gawk *gök*, *n* an awkward or ungainly person, esp. from tallness, shyness or simplicity; a person who stares and gapes. — *vi* to stare and gape. — *n* **gawk'er.** — *n* **gawk'iness.** — *adj* **gawk'y** awkward; ungainly. — *n* a tall awkward person; a gawk.

gawp or **gaup** *göp*, (*colloq*) *vi* to gape in astonishment. — *n* **gawp'er** or **gaup'er.** [From obs. *galp*.]

gay *gā*, *adj* (*compar* **gay'er**, *superl* **gay'est**) lively; bright; playful, merry; pleasure-loving; showy; in modern use, homosexual (*orig prison slang*); pertaining to or frequented by homosexuals (as in *gay bar*). — *n* a homosexual. — *n* **gai'ety** gayness (but not used in sense of homosexuality). — *adv* **gai'ly.** — *n* **gay'ness.** — **gay liberation** the freeing of homosexuals from social disadvantages and prejudice. [O.Fr. *gai*, perh. — O.H.G. *wâhi*, pretty.]

gaz. *abbrev* for: gazette; gazetteer.

gazania *gə-zā'ni-ə*, *n* a plant of the southern hemisphere with bright yellow or orange composite flowers. [Theodore of *Gaza* (1398–1478), who translated the botanical works of Theophrastus.]

gaze *gāz*, *vi* to look fixedly. — *n* a fixed look. — *n* **gā'zer.** [Prob. cognate with obs. *gaw*, to stare.]

gazebo *gə-zē'bō*, *n* a summerhouse or other small structure giving a commanding view of the landscape, a belvedere: — *pl* **gazē'bos** or **gazē'boes.**

gazelle *gə-zel'*, *n* any of various small, large-eyed antelopes of Africa and Asia, esp of the genus *Gazella*. [Fr., — Ar. *ghazāl*, a wild goat.]

gazette *gə-zet'*, *n* (with *cap*) an official newspaper containing lists of government appointments, legal notices, despatches, etc.; a title used for some newspapers. — *vt* to publish or mention in a gazette; to announce or confirm a person's appointment or promotion, esp. in an official gazette: — *pr p* **gazett'ing**; *pa t* and *pa p* **gazett'ed.** — *n* **gazetteer** (*gaz-ə-tēr'*) a geographical dictionary. — *vt* to describe in a gazetteer. [It. *gazzetta*, dimin. of *gazza*, magpie.]

gazpacho *gas-päch'ō* or *gəz-*, *n* a spicy Spanish vegetable soup, served cold: — *pl* **gazpach'os.** [Sp.]

gazump *gə-zump'*, (*colloq*) *vt* and *vi* (of a seller) to raise the price of property, etc., after accepting an offer from (a buyer), but before the contract has been signed. [Prob. Yiddish *gezumph*, to swindle.]

gazunder *gə-zun'dər*, (*colloq*) *vt* and *vi* to lower the sum offered to (the seller of a property) just before contracts are due to be signed. [*gaz*ump and **under**.]

GB *abbrev* for Great Britain (also I.V.R.).

Gb (*phys*) *abbrev* for gilbert.

GBA *abbrev* for Alderney, Channel Islands (I.V.R.).

GBE *abbrev* for (Knight or Dame) Grand Cross of the British Empire.

GBG *abbrev* for Guernsey, Channel Islands (I.V.R.).

GBH or **gbh** *abbrev* for grievous bodily harm.

GBJ *abbrev* for Jersey, Channel Islands (I.V.R.).

GBM *abbrev* for Isle of Man (I.V.R.).

GBZ *abbrev* for Gibraltar (I.V.R.).

GC *abbrev* for George Cross (q.v.).

GCA *abbrev* for: ground control (or controlled) approach system, or ground control apparatus (*aeronautics*); Guatemala, Central America (I.V.R.).

GCB *abbrev* for (Knight or Dame) Grand Cross of the (Order of the) Bath.

GCE *abbrev* for General Certificate of Education (q.v.). — *n* a subject studied or certificate gained for a GCE examination.

GCHQ *abbrev* for Government Communications Headquarters.

G-clef. See under **G** (noun).

GCM *abbrev* for: General Court-martial; (or **gcm**) greatest common measure.

GCMG *abbrev* for (Knight or Dame) Grand Cross of (the Order of) St Michael and St George.

GCSE *abbrev* for General Certificate of Secondary Education (q.v.).

GCVO *abbrev* for (Knight or Dame) Grand Cross of the (Royal) Victorian Order.

Gd (*chem*) *symbol* for gadolinium.

Gde *abbrev* for gourde (Haitian currency).

Gdns *abbrev* for Gardens (in street names, etc.).

GDP *abbrev* for gross domestic product.

GDR *abbrev* for German Democratic Republic (the former East Germany).

Ge. See **Gaea**.

Ge (*chem*) *symbol* for germanium.

gean *gēn*, *n* the European wild cherry. [O.Fr. *guigne*.]

geanticline *jē-an'ti-klīn*, *n* an anticline on a great scale. — *adj* **geanticlī'nal.** [Gr. *gē*, earth, and **anticline**.]

gear *gēr*, *n* equipment; accoutrements; tackle; clothes, esp. (*colloq*) young people's fashion clothes; armour; harness; apparatus; a set of tools or a mechanism for some particular purpose; personal belongings; stuff; illicit drugs (*slang*); any moving part or system of parts for transmitting motion, e.g. levers, gearwheels; connection by means of such parts; the actual gear ratio in use, or the gearwheels involved in transmitting that ratio, in an automobile gearbox, e.g. **first gear** (low gear), **fourth gear** (high gear); working connection; working order. — *vt* to put (e.g. machinery) in gear; to connect in gear; to adjust in accordance with requirements of a particular plan, need, etc. (with *to*). — *vi* to be in gear. — *adj* **geared.** — *n* **gear'ing** harness; working implements; a means of transmission of motion, esp. a series of toothed wheels and pinions; (in a company's capital) the ratio of ordinary shares to shares with fixed interest, or (*loosely*) the ratio of equity to loans (*econ*). — *adj* **gear'less.** — **gear'box** the box containing the apparatus for changing gear; (in a motor vehicle) the apparatus itself; **gear lever** or **gear'shift** a device for selecting or engaging and disengaging gears; **gear ratio** the ratio of the driving to the driven members of a gear mechanism; **gear'-wheel** a wheel with teeth or cogs which impart or transmit motion by acting on a similar wheel or a chain. — *adj* **high'-gear** and **low'-gear** geared to give a high and a low number respectively of revolutions of the driven part relative to the driving part. — **change gear** to select a higher or lower gear; **gear down** to make the speed of the driven part lower than that of the driving part; **gear up** to make the speed of the driven part higher than that of the driving part; to prepare for increased production, new demands, etc.; to raise the gearing of (a company); **highly geared** (of a company or its capital) having a high ratio of fixed-interest shares to ordinary shares, or of loans to equity. [M.E. *gere*, prob. O.N. *gervi*.]

GEC *abbrev* for General Electric Company.

gecko *gek'ō*, *n* any lizard of the genus **Gecko** or the subclass **Geckō'nēs**, mostly thick-bodied, dull-coloured animals with adhesive toes: — *pl* **geck'os** or **geck'oes.** [Malay *gēkoq*; imit. of its cry.]

gee[1] *jē*, *n* the seventh letter of the modern English alphabet (G or g).

gee[2] *jē*, (*NAm*) *interj* expressing surprise, sarcasm, enthusiasm, etc.; sometimes used only for emphasis. — **gee whiz** *interj* expressing surprise, admiration, etc. [Perh. **Jesus.**]

geebung *jē'bung*, *n* an Australian proteaceous tree (*Persoonia*) or its fruit. [Aboriginal.]

gee-gee *jē'jē*, *n* a childish or humorous word for horse.

geek[1] *gēk*, (*US slang*) *n* a strange or eccentric person, a creep or misfit. — *adj* **geek'y.** [Br. dialect *geck*, a fool.]

geek[2] *gēk*, (*Austr colloq*) *n* a look, esp. a good long look. [Br. dialect, to peep or peer.]

geep *gēp*, *n* a creature produced by artificially combining DNA from a *g*oat and a sh*eep*.

geese *gēs*, *pl* of **goose**.

gee-string or **G-string** *jē'-string*, *n* a string or strip worn round the waist supporting a strip worn between the legs, or this strip itself, or both, or any similar covering for the genitals.

gee up *jē up*, *interj* a command to a horse to move on or go faster. — *vt* to encourage, stimulate, or buck up.

geezer *gē'zər*, (*slang*) *n* a strange elderly person; a man. [A form of **guiser**, a mummer.]

gefilte fish or **gefüllte fish** *gə-fil'tə fish*, *n* a cooked mixture of fish, eggs, breadcrumbs or matzo meal, and seasoning served as balls or cakes or stuffed into a fish. [Yiddish, lit. filled fish.]

Gehenna *gi-hen'ə*, *n* the valley of Hinnom, near Jerusalem, in which the Israelites sacrificed their children to Moloch, and to which, at a later time, the refuse of the city was conveyed to be slowly burned; hell (*NT*); a place of torment. [Heb. *Ge-hinnōm*, valley of Hinnom.]

Geiger counter *gī'gər kown'tər*, *n* an instrument for detecting and measuring radioactivity by registering electrical output pulses caused by ionisation of particles in a gas-filled tube. [Hans *Geiger*, German physicist.]

geisha *gā'shə, n* a Japanese girl trained to provide entertainment (such as conversation, performance of dances, etc.) for men: — *pl* **gei'sha** or **gei'shas**. [Jap.]

Geissler tube *gīs'lər tūb, (chem) n* a gas-filled discharge tube, characterised by a capillary section for concentrated illumination. [Heinrich *Geissler* (1814–79), the inventor.]

gel *jel, n* a jelly-like apparently solid colloidal solution; a transparent substance, or a sheet of this, used in theatre and photographic lighting to produce light of different colours (short for **gelatine**). — *vi* to form a gel; to come together, to begin to work, take shape (*colloq*; also **jell**): — *pr p* **gell'ing**; *pa t* and *pa p* **gelled**. [**gelatine**.]

gelati. See **gelato**.

gelatine *jel'ə-tēn*, or **gelatin** *jel'a-tin, n* a colourless, odourless, and tasteless substance, prepared from albuminous matter, e.g. bones and hides, used for foodstuffs, photographic films, glues, etc. — *vt* **gelatinate** (*ji-lat'i-nāt*) or **gelat'inise** or **-ize** to make into gelatine or jelly; to coat with gelatine or jelly. — *vi* to be converted into gelatine or jelly. — *n* **gelatinā'tion**, **gelatinisā'tion** or **-z-**. — *n* **gelat'iniser** or **-z-**. — *n* **gelat'inoid** a substance resembling gelatine. — Also *adj*. — *adj* **gelat'inous** resembling or formed into jelly. [Fr., — It. *gelatina*, *gelata*, jelly — L. *gelāre*, to freeze.]

gelation *jə-lā'shən, n* a solidification by cooling; formation of a gel from a sol. [Partly L. *gelātiō*, *-ōnis* — *gelāre*, to freeze; partly **gel**.]

gelato *je-lä'tō, (Austr) n* a type of whipped ice-cream made from cream, milk and/or water and flavoured with fruit or nuts: — *pl* **gelati** (*-tē*). [It.]

geld *geld, vt* to emasculate, castrate; to spay; to deprive of anything essential, to enfeeble, to weaken. — *n* **geld'er**. — *n* **geld'ing** act of castrating; a castrated animal, esp. a horse. [O.N. *gelda*.]

gelid *jel'id, adj* icy cold; chilly. — *adv* **gel'idly**. — *n* **gel'idness** or **gelid'ity**. [L. *gelidus* — *gelū*, frost.]

gelignite *jel'ig-nīt, n* a powerful explosive used in mining, made from nitroglycerine, nitrocotton, potassium nitrate, and wood-pulp. [**gelatine** and L. *ignis*, fire.]

gem *jem, n* any precious stone, esp. when cut (also **gem'stone**); a person or thing regarded as extremely admirable or flawless. — *adj* **gemolog'ical** or **gemmolog'ical**. — *n* **gemol'ogist** or **gemmol'ogist** a person with special knowledge of gems. — **gemol'ogy** or **gemmol'ogy** the science of gems. — *adj* **gemm'y**. — **gem'-cutting** the art of cutting and polishing precious stones; **gem'-engraving** the art of engraving figures on gems. [O.E. *gim*; O.H.G. *gimma* — L. *gemma*, a bud.]

Gemara *gə-mä'rə, (Judaism) n* the second part of the Talmud, consisting of commentary and complement to the first part, the Mishnah. [Aramaic, completion.]

geminate *jem'in-āt, vt* to double; to arrange in pairs. — *adj* (*bot*) in pairs. — *n* **geminā'tion** a doubling. [L. *gemināre*, to double — *geminus*, twin.]

Gemini *jem'i-nī, n* (as *pl*) the twins, a constellation containing the two bright stars Castor and Pollux; the sign of the zodiac associated with this; a person born between 22 May and 22 June, under the sign of Gemini. [L. *geminus*, twin.]

gemma *jem'ə, n* a small multicellular body produced vegetatively, capable of separating and becoming a new individual (*bot*); a bud or protuberance from the body that becomes a new individual (*zool*): — *pl* **gemm'ae** (*-ē*). — *adj* **gemmā'ceous** bud-like; relating to gemmae. — *adj* **gemm'ate** having or reproducing by buds or gemmae. — *vi* to reproduce by gemmae. — *n* **gemmā'tion** budding or gemma-formation. — *adj* **gemm'ative** pertaining to gemmation. — *adj* **gemmif'erous** bearing gemmae. — *adj* **gemmip'arous** reproducing by gemmae. [L. *gemma*, a bud.]

gemmologist, gemologist, gemmy, etc. See **gem**.

Gems *jemz, abbrev* for Global Environment Monitoring System (set up by the United Nations Environment Programme).

gemsbok *hhemz'bok* (in S. Africa) or *gemz'bok, n* a large S. African antelope (*Oryx gazella*) with long straight horns and distinctive markings on its face and underparts. [Du., male chamois — Ger. *Gemsbock*.]

gemütlich *gə-müt'lēhh*, (Ger.) *adj* amiable; congenial; comfortable; cosy. — *n* **Gemüt'lichkeit** (*-kīt*) kindness; comfort; cosiness.

Gen. *abbrev* for: General; (the Book of) Genesis (*Bible*).

gen *jen, (slang) n* general information; the low-down or inside information. — **gen up** to learn (with *on*): — *pr p* **genn'ing up**; *pa t* and *pa p* **genned up**.

gen. *abbrev* for: gender; genitive; genus.

-gen *-jən*, or **-gene** *-jēn, combining form* used to denote: (1) producing or produced, as in *oxygen*, *phosgene* (*chem*); (2) growth, as in *endogen* (*bot*). [Gr. *-genēs*, born.]

gendarme *zhã'därm, n* since the French Revolution one of a corps of French military police; a similar policeman elsewhere: — *pl* **gen'darmes**. — *n* **gendarm'erie** (*-ə-rē*) an armed police force; a police station or barracks. [Fr. *gendarme*, sing. from pl. *gens d'armes*, men-at-arms — *gens*, people, *de*, of, *armes*, arms.]

gender *jen'dər, n* the classification of words roughly answering to sex (*gram*); any of the four classes so distinguished — masculine, feminine, neuter or common gender; a person's sex (*colloq*); the members of a sex collectively. — *adj* **gen'derless** not having or indicating gender; not indicating differences in sex, suitable for either sex. — **gen'der-bender** (*colloq*) a sexually ambiguous, or bisexual person; **gen'der-bending** (*colloq*) the blurring of the distinctions between the sexes through sexual ambiguity or bisexuality in behaviour or dress. [Fr. *genre* — L. *genus*, kind.]

gene *jēn, (biol) n* one of the units of DNA, arranged in linear fashion on the chromosomes, responsible for passing on specific characteristics from parents to offspring. — *adj* **gen'ic** of or relating to a gene. — **gene flow** the passing of genes to succeeding generations; **gene splicing** the artificial introduction of DNA from one organism into the genetic material of another, in order to produce a desired characteristic in the recipient; **gene therapist**; **gene therapy** the treatment or prevention of (esp. heritable) diseases by genetic engineering. [Ger. *Gen* — Gr. *-genēs*, born.]

-gene. See **-gen**.

genealogy *jē-ni-al'ə-ji* or *jen-i-, n* history of the descent of families; the pedigree of a particular person or family. — *adj* **genealogical** (*-ə-loj'i-kl*) or **genealog'ic**. — *adv* **genealog'ically**. — *vi* **geneal'ogise** or **-ize** to investigate or discuss genealogy. — *n* **geneal'ogist** a person who studies or traces genealogies or descents. — **genealogical tree** a table of descent in the form of a tree with branches. [Gr. *geneālogiā* — *geneā*, race, *logos*, discourse.]

genera *jen'ə-rə, pl* of **genus**.

generable. See **generate**.

general *jen'ə-rəl, adj* relating to the whole or to all or most; not special; not restricted or specialised; universal; nearly universal; common; prevalent; widespread; public; vague; relating to a genus or whole class; including various species; (after an official title, etc.) chief, of highest rank, at the head of a department (such as *director-general*, *postmaster-general*). — *n* an army officer between a field marshal and lieutenant-general in rank; the chief commander of an army in service; a person acting as leader, planning tactics or management; the head of a religious order, such as the Jesuits; the universal as opposed to the particular. — *vt* to act as general of: — *pr p* **gen'eralling**; *pa t* and *pa p* **gen'eralled**. — *n* **generalīsā'tion** or **-z-**. — *vt* **gen'eralise** or **-ize** to make general; to include under a general term; to reduce to a general form; to comprehend as a particular case within a wider concept, proposition, definition, etc.; to represent or endow with the common characters of a group without the special characters of any one member; to bring to general use or knowledge; to infer inductively. — *vi* to make general statements; to form general concepts; to depict general character; to reason inductively. — *n* **generaliss'imo** supreme commander of a great or combined force: — *pl* **generaliss'imos**. — *n* **gen'eralist** a person whose knowledge and skills are not restricted to one particular field (opp. of *specialist*). — *n* **general'ity** a statement having general application; the state of being general; broadness or vagueness; the majority; the general public. — *adv* **gen'erally** in a general or collective manner or sense; in most cases; on the whole. — *n* **gen'eralship** the position of a military commander; the art of manipulating armies; tactical management and leadership. — **general election** an election of all the members of a body at once; **general practice** the work of a **general practitioner** (abbrev. **GP**), a doctor who treats patients for most illnesses or complaints, referring other cases to specialists; **general principle** a principle to which there are no exceptions within its range of application. — *adj* **general-pur'pose** generally useful, not restricted to a particular function. — **general staff** military officers who advise senior officers on policy, administration, etc. — **General Certificate of Education** in secondary education in England and Wales, a certificate obtainable at Ordinary (*formerly*), Advanced, and Scholarship levels for proficiency in one or more subjects; **General Certificate of Secondary Education** in England and Wales, a certificate based on coursework as well as examinations, designed to suit a wide range of academic ability; **general post office** the head post office of a town or district; **in general** as a generalisation; mostly, as a general rule. [O.Fr. — L. *generālis* — *genus*.]

generate *jen'ə-rāt*, *vt* to produce; to bring into life or being; to evolve; to originate; to trace out (*geom*). — *adj* **gen'erable** that may be generated or produced. — *n* **gen'erant** (*geom*) a line, point or figure that traces out another figure by its motion. — *n* **gen'erātor** a begetter or producer; an apparatus for producing gases, etc.; an apparatus for turning mechanical into electrical energy. — **generating station** a plant where electricity is generated. [L. *generāre*, *-ātum* — *genus*, a kind.]

generation *jen-ə-rā'shən*, *n* production or originating; a single stage in natural descent; the people of the same age or period; descendants removed by the same number of steps from a common ancestor; the ordinary time interval between the births of successive generations — usu. reckoned at 30 or 33 years; offspring or progeny; any series of files, each one an amended and updated version of the previous one (*comput*); any of a number of stages, levels or series, generally in which each stage, etc. is seen as a development of or improvement on the preceding one; (see also **first generation**, **fifth generation**). — **generation gap** lack of communication and understanding between one generation and the next. [**generate**.]

generative *jen'ə-rə-tiv*, *adj* having the power of, or concerned with, generating or producing. — **generative grammar** (*linguis*) a description of the language as a finite set of grammatical rules able to generate an infinite number of grammatical sentences. [**generate**.]

generic *ji-ner'ik*, *adj* general, applicable to any member of a group or class; (of a drug, etc.) not patented or sold as a proprietary brand (also *n*). — *adv* **gener'ically**. — **generic name** the name of the genus, placed first in naming the species (*biol*); the name of a generic drug, etc. [Ety. as for **genus**.]

generous *jen'ə-rəs*, *adj* of a noble, magnanimous nature; liberal; bountiful; ample. — *adv* **gen'erously**. — *n* **gen'erousness** or **generos'ity** nobleness, magnanimity or liberality of nature. [L. *generōsus*, of noble birth — *genus*, birth.]

Genesis *jen'i-sis*, *n* the first book of the Bible, telling of the Creation.

genesis *jen'i-sis*, *n* generation, creation, development or production: — *pl* **gen'esēs**. — **-gen'esis** *combining form*, as in *pathogenesis*, development of disease, *parthenogenesis*, virgin birth. [Gr.]

genet[1]. See **jennet**.

genet[2] or **genette** *jen'it* or *ji-net'*, *n* a carnivorous animal (genus *Genetta*) related to the civet; its fur, or an imitation. [Fr. *genette* — Sp. *gineta* — Ar. *jarnait*.]

genetic *ji-net'ik* or **genetical** *-et'ik-kəl*, *adj* of or relating to genes or genetics; causal, relating to origin. —**-genetic** *combining form* as in *pathogenetic*, productive of disease. — *adv* **genet'ically**. — *n* **genet'icist** (*-i-sist*) a student of genetics. — *nsing* **genet'ics** the branch of biology dealing with heredity and variation; inherited characteristics of an organism; origin; development. — **genetic code** the system by which genes pass on instructions that ensure transmission of hereditary characters; **genetic counselling** advice given to prospective parents on possible heritable defects in their children; **genetic engineering** a biological science whose aims include the control of hereditary defects by the modification or elimination of certain genes, and the mass production of useful biological substances (e.g. insulin) by the transplanting of genes; **genetic fingerprint** the particular DNA configuration exclusive to an individual human or animal or its offspring; **genetic fingerprinting** the identification of genetic fingerprints (e.g. in forensic science, to identify or eliminate a specific individual); **genetic manipulation** the alteration of natural genetic processes, usu. for the purposes of research; **genetic parents** the 'natural' parents, those whose genes the child carries. [**genesis**.]

genetotrophic *ji-net-ə-trof'ik*, *adj* denoting deficiency diseases which have an underlying genetic, and a direct nutritional, cause and which are treatable by dietary means. [**genus** and **troph-**.]

Genevan *ji-nē'vən* or **Genevese** *jen-ə-vēz'*, *adj* pertaining to *Geneva*. — *n* an inhabitant of Geneva; an adherent of Genevan or Calvinistic theology. — **Geneva bands** the two strips of white linen hanging down from the neck of some clerical robes; **Geneva Bible** a version of the Bible in English produced by English Protestant exiles at Geneva in 1560; **Geneva Convention** an international agreement of 1864, with subsequent revisions, concerning the status and treatment in wartime of the sick and wounded, prisoners of war, etc.; **Geneva cross** a red cross on a white ground displayed for protection in war of persons serving in hospitals, etc.

genial[1] *jē'ni-əl*, *adj* (of a climate) mild, pleasant, favouring growth; cheering; kindly; sympathetic; healthful. — *n* **gēniality** (*-al'i-ti*) or **gē'nialness**. — *adv* **gē'nially**. [L. *geniālis* — *genius*, the tutelary spirit.]

genial[2] *jə-nī'əl*, *adj* of or pertaining to the chin. [Gr. *geneion*, chin — *genys*, jaw.]

genic. See **gene**.

-genic *combining form* signifying: (1) productive of, generating, as in *pathogenic*, *carcinogenic*; (2) ideal or suitable for, as in *photogenic*; (3) caused by, as in *iatrogenic*. [**-gen** and sfx. *-ic*.]

genie *jē'ni*, *n* a jinnee (see **jinn**); a magical being who carries out a person's wishes. [Fr. *génie* — L. *genius*, adopted because of its similarity to the Arabic word.]

genii. See **genius**.

genista *jə-nis'tə*, *n* a plant belonging to the *Genista* genus of shrubby, papilionaceous plants, with simple leaves and yellow flowers. [L. *genista*, broom.]

genital *jen'i-təl*, *adj* belonging to generation or the act of producing. — *npl* **gen'itals** or **genitā'lia** the sexual organs esp. external. [L. *genitālis* — *gignĕre*, *genitum*, to beget.]

genitive *jen'-i-tiv*, (*gram*) *adj* of or belonging to a case expressing origin, possession, or similar relation. — *n* the genitive case; a word in the genitive case. — *adj* **genitī'val**. — *adv* **genitī'vally**. [L. *genitīvus* — *gignĕre*, *genitum*, to beget.]

genito-urinary *jen-i-tō-ū'rin-ə-ri*, *adj* pertaining to genital and urinary organs and functions.

genius *jēn'yəs* or *jē'ni-əs*, *n* the special inborn faculty of any individual; special taste or natural disposition; consummate intellectual, creative, or other power, more exalted than talent; a person so endowed; a good or evil spirit, supposed to preside over every person, place and thing, and esp. to preside over a person's destiny from their birth; a person who exerts a power or influence (whether good or bad) over another; a prevailing spirit or tendency: — *pl* **ge'niuses**; in sense of spirit, **genii** (*jē'ni-ī*). [L. *genius* — *gignĕre*, *genitum*, to beget.]

Genl *abbrev* for General.

gennet. See **jennet**.

genoa or **Genoa** *jen'ō-ə* or *jə-nō'ə*, *n* (*naut*) a large jib which overlaps the mainsail. — **Genoa cake** a rich cake containing fruit, with almonds on the top. [*Genoa* in Italy.]

genocide *jen'ə-sīd*, *n* the deliberate extermination of a race or other group. — *adj* **genocī'dal**. [Gr. *genos*, race, and L. *caedĕre*, to kill.]

genom or **genome** *jē'nōm*, *n* the full set of chromosomes of an individual; the total number of genes in such a set. [*gene* and chromo*some*.]

genotype *jen'ə-tīp*, *n* genetic or factorial constitution of an individual; a group of individuals all of which possess the same genetic constitution. — *adj* **genotypic** (*-tip'ik*). — *adv* **genotyp'ically**. — *n* **genotypic'ity**. [**gene** and **type**.]

genre *zhã-r'*, *n* kind; a literary or artistic type or style; a style of painting scenes from familiar or rustic life. — Also *adj*. [Fr., — L. *genus*.]

gent *jent*, *n* short for **gentleman**: — *pl* **gents**. — *n* **gents'** a men's public lavatory.

genteel *jen-tēl'*, *adj* well-bred; graceful in manners or in form; now used mainly with mocking reference to a standard of obsolete snobbery or false refinement. — *n* **genteel'ism** a word or phrase used in place of an accustomed one, where this is felt to be coarse or vulgar. — *vt* **genteel'ise** or **-ize** make genteel or falsely refined. — *adv* **genteel'ly**. — *n* **genteel'ness**. [Fr. *gentil* — L. *gentīlis*; see **gentle**.]

gentian *jen'shən*, *n* any plant of the genus *Gentiana*, herbs, usu. blue-flowered, abounding chiefly in alpine regions; the root and rhizome of the yellow gentian used as a tonic and stomachic. — **gentian violet** in the British pharmacopoeia, crystal violet; sometimes, methyl violet; sometimes, a mixture of the two. [L. *gentiāna*, accus.]

Gentile or **gentile** *jen'tīl*, *n* anyone not a Jew, or not a Mormon; a heathen or pagan. — *adj* belonging to the Gentiles. [L. *gentīlis* — *gēns*, a nation, clan.]

gentility *jen-til'i-ti*, *n* good birth or ancestry; respectability; courtesy; genteel people. [O.Fr. *gentilite* — L. *gentīlitās* — *gentīlis*; see **gentle**.]

gentle *jen'tl*, *adj* mild and refined in manners; mild in disposition or action; amiable; soothing; moderate; gradual. — *n* **gen'tleness**. — *adv* **gent'ly**. — *npl* **gen'tlefolk** people of good family. — *adj* **gentle-heart'ed** having a gentle or kind disposition. [O.Fr. *gentil* — L. *gentīlis*, belonging to the same *gens* or clan, later, well-bred.]

gentleman *jen'tl-mən*, *n* a man of good birth or high social standing; a man of refined manners; a man of good feeling and instincts, courteous and honourable; a polite term used for a man in general: — *pl* **gen'tlemen** — also a word of address. — *adj* **gen'tlemanlike** like or characteristic of a gentleman. — *adj* **gen'tlemanly** befitting a gentleman; well-bred, refined, generous. — *n* **gen'tlemanliness**. — **gentleman farmer** a landowner who lives on his estate superintending the cultivation of his own soil; a farmer who delegates the work of his farm to a farm manager and other staff; **gentleman's (**or **gentlemen's) agreement** an agreement resting on honour, not on a formal contract; **gentleman's gentleman** a valet. [**gentle** and **man**.]

gentlewoman *jen'tl-wŏŏ-mən*, (*archaic*) a woman of good breeding and refinement; a woman in attendance on a lady of standing: — *pl* **gen'tlewomen**.

Gentoo *jen'tōō* or *jen-tōō'*, *n* a Falkland Island penguin. [Port. *gentio*, a Gentile.]

gentry *jen'tri*, *n* the class of people next below the rank of nobility; people of a particular, esp. an inferior, sort (*colloq*). — *n* **gentrificā'tion** the move of middle-class people into a formerly working-class area with the consequent change in the character of the area; the modernising of old, badly-equipped property, usu. with a view to increasing its value. — *vt* **gen'trify**. [O.Fr. *genterise*, *gentelise*, formed from adj. *gentil*, gentle.]

genuflect *jen'ū-flekt*, *vi* to bend the knee in worship or respect. — *n* **genūflex'ion** or **genūflec'tion**. [L. *genū*, the knee, *flectĕre*, *flexum*, to bend.]

genuine *jen'ū-in*, *adj* natural; native; not spurious; real; pure; sincere. — *adv* **gen'uinely**. — *n* **gen'uineness**. [L. *genuīnus* — *gignĕre*, to beget.]

genus *jē'nəs*, *n* a taxonomic group of lower rank than a family, consisting of closely related species, in some cases of one species only (*biol*); a class of objects comprehending several subordinate species (*logic*): — *pl* **genera** (*jen'ə-rə*) or **gē'nuses**. [L. *gĕnus*, *generis*, birth.]

Geo. *abbrev* for George.

geo- *jē-ō-*, *combining form* denoting the earth. [Gr. *gē*, the earth.]

geocentric *jē-ō-sen'trik*, *adj* having the earth for centre; as viewed or reckoned from the centre of the earth (*astron*); taking life on earth as the basis for evaluation. — *adv* **geocen'trically**. — *n* **geocen'tricism** (*-sizm*) belief that the earth is the centre of the universe. [Gr. *gē*, the earth, *kentron*, point, centre.]

geochemistry *jē-ō-kem'is-tri*, *n* the chemistry of the crust of the earth. — *adj* **geochem'ical**. — *adv* **geochem'ically**. — *n* **geochem'ist**. [**geo-**.]

geochronology *jē-ō-krə-nol'ə-ji*, *n* the science of measuring geological time. — *adj* **geochronolog'ical**. — *n* **geochronol'ogist**. [**geo-**.]

geode *jē'ōd*, *n* a cavity in a rock lined with crystals that have grown inwards; a rock or stone having this. — *adj* **geod'ic**. [Fr. *géode* — Gr. *geōdēs*, earthy.]

geodesy *jē-od'i-si*, *n* earth measurement on a large scale; surveying with allowance for the earth's curvature. — *adj* **geodesic** (*jē-ō-des'ik* or *-dē'sik*) pertaining to or determined by geodesy. — *n* a geodesic line. — *n* **geod'esist** someone skilled in geodesy. — **geodesic dome** a light strong dome made by combining a grid of triangular or other straightline elements with a section of a sphere; **geodesic line** the shortest line on a surface between two points on it. [Gr. *geōdaisiā* — *gē*, the earth, *daisis*, division.]

geodetics *jē-ō-det'iks, nsing* geodesy. — *adj* **geodet'ic** or **geodet'ical**. — *adv* **geodet'ically**. — **geodetic line** see **geodesic line** under **geodesy**; **geodetic surveying** geodesy.

geodimeter *jē-ō-dim'i-tər, n* an instrument which measures distances by means of a beam of light, calculating on the basis of the speed of light. [Orig. trademark.]

geodynamics *jē-ō-dī-nam'iks, nsing* the study of the dynamic processes and forces within the earth. — *adj* **geodynam'ic**. [**geo-**.]

geog. *abbrev* for geography.

geogony *jē-og'ə-ni* or **geogeny** (*-oj'*), *n* the science or theory of the formation of the earth. — *adj* **geogonic** (*jē-ō-gon'ik*). [Gr. *gē*, the earth, *gonē*, generation.]

geography *jē-og'rə-fi, n* the science of the surface of the earth and its inhabitants; the features or the arrangement of a place. — *n* **geog'rapher**. — *adj* **geographic** (*jē-ō-graf'ik*) or **geograph'ical**. — *adv* **geograph'ically**. [Gr. *geōgraphiā* — *gē*, earth, *graphein*, to write.]

geoid *jē'oid, n* the figure of the earth's mean sea-level surface assumed to be continued under the land. — *adj* **geoid'al**. [Gr. *geōdēs*, *geoeidēs*, earth-like — *gē*, earth, *eidos*, form.]

geol. *abbrev* for geology.

geology *jē-ol'ə-ji, n* the science relating to the history and development of the earth's crust, with its successive floras and faunas. — *n* **geol'ogist**. — *adj* **geologic** (*-loj'ik*) or **geolog'ical**. — *adv* **geolog'ically**. — *vi* **geol'ogise** or **-ize** to work at geology in the field. — *vt* to investigate the geology of. — **geological time** time before written history, divided into epochs each of which saw the formation of one of the great rock systems. — **dynamical** or **dynamic geology** the study of the work of natural agents in shaping the earth's crust — wind, frost, rivers, volcanic action, etc.; **structural geology** the study of the arrangement and structure of rock masses. [Fr. *géologie* — Gr. *gē*, earth, *logos*, a discourse.]

geom. *abbrev* for geometry.

geomagnetism *jē-ō-mag'nə-tizm, n* terrestrial magnetism; the study of this. — *adj* **geomagnet'ic**. — *n* **geomag'netist**. [**geo-**.]

geomedicine *jē-ō-med'sin, n* the study of diseases as influenced by geographical environment. — *adj* **geomed'ical**. [**geo-**.]

geometry *jē-om'i-tri, n* that part of mathematics which deals with the properties of points, lines, surfaces and solids, either under classical Euclidean assumptions, or (in the case of *elliptic*, *hyperbolic*, etc., *geometry*) involving postulates not all of which are identical with Euclid's; any study of a mathematical system in which figures undergo transformations, concerned with discussion of those properties of the figures which remain constant; a textbook of geometry. — *n* **geom'eter** or **geometrician** (*-me-trish'ən*) a person skilled in geometry. — *adj* **geometric** (*-met'*) or **geomet'rical** relating to or according to geometry; consisting of or using simple figures such as geometry deals with. — *adv* **geomet'rically**. — *n* **geometrīsā'tion** or **-z-**. — *vt* and *vi* **geom'etrise** or **-ize** to work geometrically; to show in geometric form. — *n* **geom'etrist**. — **geometrical progression** a series of quantities each of which has the same ratio to its predecessor. [Gr. *geōmetriā* — *gē*, earth, *metron*, a measure.]

geomorphogeny *jē-ō-mör-foj'ə-ni, n* the scientific study of the origins and development of land forms. — *adj* **geomorphogen'ic**. — *n* **geomorphog'enist**. [**geo-**.]

geomorphology *jē-ō-mör-fol'ə-ji, n* the morphology and development of land forms, including those under the sea; the study of this. — *adj* **geomorpholog'ic** or **geomorpholog'ical**. — *adv* **geomorpholog'ically**. — *n* **geomorphol'ogist**. [**geo-**.]

geophilous *jē-of'il-əs, adj* living in or on the ground; having a short stem with leaves at ground-level. — *adj* **geophil'ic**. [Gr. *gē*, earth, *phileein*, to love.]

geophysics *gē-ō-fiz'iks, nsing* the physics of the earth. — *adj* **geophys'ical**. — *n* **geophys'icist** (*-i-sist*). [**geo-**.]

geopolitics *jē-ō-pol'it-iks, nsing* a science concerned with problems of states, such as frontiers, as affected by their geographical environment; the special combination of geographical and political considerations in a particular state. — *adj* **geopolit'ical**. — *adv* **geopolit'ically**. — *n* **geopoliti'cian**. [Ger. *Geopolitik*; see **geo-**.]

geoponic *jē-ō-pon'ik* or **geoponical** *-pon'i-kəl, adj* agricultural. — *nsing* **geopon'ics** the science of agriculture. [Gr. *geōponikos* — *gē*, earth, *ponos*, labour.]

Geordie *jör'di, n* a native of Tyneside; the dialect of Tyneside. — *adj* pertaining to Tyneside, its people or dialect.

George *jörj, n* a jewelled figure of St *George* slaying the dragon, worn by Knights of the Garter; the automatic pilot of an aircraft. — **George Cross** an award for outstanding courage or heroism given in cases where a purely military honour is not applicable — instituted during World War II; **George Medal** an award for gallantry given to civilians and members of the armed forces. — **St George's cross** the Greek cross of England, red on a white ground.

georgette *jör-jet', n* a thin silk material. [From *Georgette* de la Plante, French dressmaker.]

Georgian *jör'ji-ən, adj* relating to or contemporary with any of the various *Georges*, kings of Great Britain or other of the name; belonging to *Georgia* in the Caucasus, its people, language, etc.; of or pertaining to the U.S. state of *Georgia*. — Also *n*.

geoscience *jē'ō-sī-əns, n* any of the scientific disciplines, such as geology or geomorphology, which deal with the earth, or all of these collectively. — *adj* **geoscientif'ic**. [**geo-**.]

geosphere *jē'ō-sfēr, n* the solid part of the earth, distinguished from *atmosphere* and *hydrosphere*. [Gr. *gē*, earth, *sphaira*, sphere.]

geostatic *jē-ō-stat'ik, adj* capable of sustaining the pressure of earth from all sides. — *nsing* **geostat'ics** the statics of rigid bodies. [Gr. *gē*, the earth, *statikos*, causing to stand.]

geostationary *jē-ō-stā'shə-nə-ri, adj* (of a satellite, etc.) orbiting the earth in time with the earth's own rotation, i.e. circling it once every 24 hours, so remaining above the same spot on the earth's surface. [**geo-**.]

geostrophic *jē-ō-strof'ik, adj* of a virtual force used to account for the change in direction of the wind relative to the surface of the earth arising from the earth's rotation; of a wind whose direction and force are partly determined by the earth's rotation. [Gr. *gē*, earth, *strophē*, a turn.]

geosynchronous *jē-ō-sing'krə-nəs, adj* (of a satellite, etc.) geostationary. [**geo-**.]

geosyncline *jē-ō-sin'klīn, n* a syncline on a great scale. — *adj* **geosynclī'nal**. [**geo-**.]

geotaxis *jē-ō-taks'is, n* response of an organism to the stimulus of gravity. — *adj* **geotact'ic** or **geotact'ical**. — *adv* **geotact'ically**. [Gr. *gē*, earth, *taxis*, arrangement.]

geotechnics *jē-ō-tek'niks, nsing* the application of scientific and engineering principles to the solution of civil engineering and other problems created by the nature and constitution of the earth's crust. — *adj* **geotech'nic** or **geotech'nical**. — *n* **geotechnol'ogy** the application of science and technology to the extraction and use of the earth's natural resources. — *adj* **geotechnolog'ical**. [**geo-**.]

geothermic *jē-ō-thûr'mik*, or **geothermal** *-thûr'məl, adj* pertaining to or heated by the internal heat of the earth. — **geothermal energy** energy extracted from the earth's natural heat, i.e. from hot springs and certain kinds of rock. [Gr. *gē*, earth, *thermē*, heat.]

geotropism *jē-ot'ro-pizm*, (*bot*) *n* geotaxis. — *adj* **geotrop'ic.** — *adv* **geotrop'ically.** — **positive** and **negative geotropism** the tendency respectively to grow towards and away from the centre of the earth. [Gr. *gē*, earth, *tropos*, a turning.]

Ger. *abbrev* for German.

ger. *abbrev* for: gerund; gerundive.

geranium *ji-rān'i-əm*, *n* a plant of the genus *Geranium* with seed-vessels like a crane's bill, typical of the family **Geraniaceae** (*-i-ā'si-ē*); (*loosely*) any cultivated plant of the genus *Pelargonium*. [L., — Gr. *geranion* — *geranos*, a crane.]

gerbera *gûr'bə-rə* or *jûr'*, *n* a plant belonging to the *Gerbera* genus of composite plants of S. Africa, etc. [T. *Gerber*, German naturalist.]

gerbil *jûr'bil*, *n* a small desert-dwelling rodent capable of causing great damage to crops but often kept as a pet. — Also **jer'bil.** [Fr. *gerbille*.]

gerenuk *ge'rə-nōōk*, *n* a long-legged, long-necked antelope of East Africa. [From the Somali name.]

gerfalcon. See **gyrfalcon.**

geriatrics *jer-i-at'riks*, *nsing* medical care of the old. — *adj* **geriat'ric.** — *n* (*colloq*) an old person. — *n* **geriatrician** (*-ə-trish'ən*) or **geriatrist** (*-at'rist*). — *n* **geriatry** (*jə-rī'ə-tri*) care of the old or old people's welfare. [Gr. *gēras*, old age, *iātros*, physician.]

germ *jûrm*, *n* a rudimentary form of a living thing, whether plant or animal; a shoot; that from which anything springs, the origin or beginning; a first principle; that from which a disease springs; a micro-organism, esp. a harmful one. — *vi* to put forth buds, sprout. — *n* **germ'icide** a substance which kills germs. — *adj* **germicī'dal.** — *adj* **germ'inable** that can be germinated. — *adj* **germ'inal** pertaining to a germ or rudiment; in germ, or earliest stage of development; seminal. — *adj* **germ'inant** sprouting; budding; capable of developing. — *vi* **germ'inate** to begin to grow (esp. of a seed or spore). — *vt* to cause to sprout. — *n* **germinā'tion.** — *adj* **germ'inative.** — **germ cell** a sperm or ovum, a gamete or cell from which it springs; **germ plasm** that part of the nuclear protoplasmic material which is the vehicle of heredity, and maintains its continuity from generation to generation; **germ warfare** warfare in which bacteria are used as weapons. [Partly through Fr. *germe*, from L. *germen*, *-inis*, a sprout, bud, germ.]

German *jûr'mən*, *n* a native or citizen of *Germany*, or one of the same linguistic or ethnological stock (*pl* **Ger'mans**); the German language, esp. High German. — *adj* of or from Germany, or the Germans; German-speaking. — *adj* **Germanic** (*-man'ik*) of Germany; of the linguistic family to which German, English, Norwegian, etc., belong — Teutonic. — *n* an extinct Indo-European language which differentiated into **East Germanic** (Gothic and other extinct languages), **North Germanic** or Scandinavian (Norwegian, Danish, Swedish, Icelandic) and **West Germanic** (English, Frisian, Dutch, Low German, High German). — *adv* **German'ically.** — *vt* **Ger'manise** or **-ize** to make German. — *vi* to become German; to adopt German ways. — *n* **Germanisā'tion** or **-z-.** — *n* **Ger'manism** a German idiom; German ideas and ways. — *n* **Ger'manist** an expert in German philology or other matters relating to Germany. — *adj* **Germanis'tic** pertaining to the study of German. — *n* **German'ophile** a lover of the Germans and things German. — *n* **Germanophil'ia.** — *n* **German'ophobe** a person who fears or hates the Germans and things German. — **German measles** rubella; **German shepherd** or **German shepherd dog** the Alsatian dog; **High German** the literary language throughout Germany (orig. that of High or Southern Germany); **Low German** *Platt-Deutsch*, the language of Low or Northern Germany; (*formerly*) all the West Germanic dialects except High German. [L. *Germānus*, German.]

german *jûr'mən*, *adj* full (see **cousin**). [O.Fr. *germain* — L. *germānus*, having the same parents.]

germander *jər-man'dər*, *n* a bitter, aromatic herb with two-lipped flowers. [L.L. *germandra* — Late Gr. *chamandrya* — Gr. — *chamai*, on the ground, *drȳs*, oak.]

germane *jûr-mān'*, *adj* relevant, appropriate (to); closely related (to). [Ety. as for **german.**]

germanium *jər-mā'ni-əm*, *n* a metallic element (symbol **Ge**; atomic no. 32), much used in diodes, transistors and rectifiers for its properties as a semiconductor. [Discovered and named by a German chemist, C.A. Winkler (1838–1904).]

germicide, germinal, germinate, etc. See under **germ.**

gerontocracy *jer-on-tok'rə-si*, *n* government by old men. — *adj* **gerontocrat'ic.** [Gr. *gerōn*, *-ontos*, old man, *-kratia* (— *kratos*, power).]

gerontology *jer-on-tol'ə-ji*, *n* scientific study of the processes of growing old. — *adj* **gerontolog'ical.** — *n* **gerontol'ogist.** [Gr. *gerōn*, *-ontos*, old man.]

Gerry. See **Jerry.**

gerrymander *jer'i-man-dər*, also *ger'*, *vt* to rearrange (voting districts) in the interests of a particular party or candidate; to manipulate (facts, arguments, etc.) so as to reach undue conclusions. — *n* an arrangement of the above nature. [Formed from the name of Governor Elbridge *Gerry* (1744–1814) and sala*mander*, from the similarity of the gerrymandered map of Massachusetts in 1811 to that animal.]

gerund *jer'ənd*, *n* in English, a noun with the ending *-ing* formed from a verb and having some of the qualities of a verb, such as the possibility of governing an object, etc.; often preceded by a possessive (e.g. *My leaving her was unwise*); a part of a Latin verb with the value of a verbal noun, such as *amandum*, loving. — *adj* **gerundial** (*ji-rund'i-əl*), **gerundival** (*jer-ən-dī'vl*) or **gerundive** (*ji-rund'iv*). — *n* **gerund'ive** a Latin verbal adjective expressing necessity, such as *amandus*, *-a*, *-um*, deserving or requiring to be loved. [L. *gerundium* — *gerĕre*, to bear.]

gesso *jes'ō*, *n* plaster of Paris; a plaster surface prepared as a ground for painting: — *pl* **gess'oes.** [It., — L. *gypsum*; see **gypsum.**]

gestalt *gə-shtält'*, *n* (also with *cap*) form, shape, pattern; organised whole or unit. — **gestalt'ism** or **Gestalt psychology** the outlook or theory based on the concept of the organised whole being something more than the sum of the parts into which it can be logically analysed. [Ger.]

Gestapo *gə-stä'pō*, *n* the secret police in Nazi Germany; (without *cap*) any such secret police organisation associated with harsh and unscrupulous methods: — *pl* **gesta'pos.** — Also *adj*. [From Ger. *Ge*heime *Sta*ats*po*lizei, secret state police.]

gestate *jes-tāt'*, *vt* to carry in the womb during the period from conception to birth; to conceive and develop slowly in the mind. — *vi* to be in the process of gestating. — *n* **gestation** (*jes-tā'shən*). — *adj* **gestā'tional** or **gest'ative** of carriage, esp. in the womb. [L. *gestāre*, *-ātum*, to carry.]

gesticulate *jes-tik'ū-lāt*, *vi* to make vigorous gestures. — *n* **gesticulā'tion.** — *n* **gestic'ulātor.** — *adj* **gestic'ulative** or **gestic'ulatory.** [L. *gesticulāri*, *-ātus* — *gesticulus*, dimin. of *gestus*, gesture.]

gestodene *jest'ə-dēn*, *n* a progestogen used in certain low-dose oral contraceptive pills.

gesture *jes'chər*, *n* an action, esp. of the hands, which expresses an emotion or is intended to show inclination or disposition; the use of such movements; an action dictated by courtesy or diplomacy, or by a desire to impress or create an impression e.g. of willingness (also *adj*). — *vi* to make a gesture or gestures. — *vt* to express by gesture(s). — *adj* **ges'tural**. [L.L. *gestūra* — L. *gestus*, from L. *gerĕre*, to carry, behave.]

Gesundheit *gə-zōōnt'hīt*, (Ger.) *interj* your health (said to someone who has just sneezed).

get *get*, *vt* to obtain; to acquire; to procure; to receive; to attain; to come to have; to catch; to grasp or take the meaning of; to learn; to hit; to descry; to make out; to succeed in making contact with (e.g. a radio station); to have the better of, gain a decisive advantage over; to irritate; to grip emotionally, take, captivate; to induce; to cause to be, go, or become; to attack or injure, esp. in revenge (*colloq*). — *vi* to arrive, to bring or put oneself (in any place, position or state); to become; to clear off, go (*colloq*; used in *imperative*): — *pr p* **gett'ing**; *pa t* **got**; *pa p* **got**, or (*US*) **gott'en**. — *n* **gett'er** someone who, or something which, evacuates; a material used, when evaporated by high-frequency induction currents, for evacuation of gas left in vacuum valves after sealing during manufacture. — *vt* to evacuate (a valve) using a getter. — *vi* to use a getter. — *n* **gett'ering** evacuation using a getter. — *n* **gett'ing**. — *adj* **get-at'-able** easily accessible. — **get'away** an escape; a start. — *adj* used in a getaway. — **get'-out** (*colloq*) a way of escape or avoidance. — Also *adj*. — *adj* **get-rich-quick'** (*colloq*) wanting, or leading to, easy prosperity. — **get'-together** a social gathering; an informal conference; **get'-up** (style of) equipment, outfit, make-up; **get-up-and-go'** (*colloq*) energy. — **get about** or **around** to travel, go visiting; to be mobile and active; **get across** (*colloq*) to communicate (something) successfully; **get ahead** to make progress, advance; **get along** to get on (see below); **get at** to reach, attain; to poke fun at (*slang*); to mean; to attack verbally; to influence by underhand or unlawful means; **get away with (something)** to carry (something) through successfully, without punishment or consequences; **get back at** to have one's revenge on; **get by** to succeed in passing; to elude notice and come off with impunity, manage satisfactorily, be sufficiently good (*colloq*); **get down** to alight; to depress (*colloq*); **get down to** set to work on, tackle seriously; **get in** to (manage to) enter; to gather; to send for; to manage; to be elected; **get in on** (*colloq*) to join in, become a participant in; **get it on** or **off (with)** to have sexual intercourse (with); **get off** to escape; to learn; to get high (on a drug) (*slang*); **get off on** to get excitement from; **get off (with)** to gain the affection of or have a sexual encounter (with); **get on** to proceed, advance, fare; to prosper; to agree, associate harmoniously; **get one's own back** (*colloq*) to have one's revenge (on); **get out** to produce; to extricate oneself (with *of*); to take oneself off; **get over** to surmount; to recover from; to make an impression on an audience; **get (something) over with** to accomplish (an unpleasant task, etc.) as quickly as possible; **get round** to circumvent; to persuade, talk over; **get round to** to bring oneself to do (something); **get there** (*slang*) to achieve one's object, succeed; **get through** to finish; to reach a destination; to receive approval, or to obtain it for (something); to obtain a connection by telephone; to communicate with, reach the comprehension of (with *to*); **get together** to meet socially or for discussion; **get up** to rise, esp. from bed; to ascend; to arrange, dress, prepare (oneself); to learn up for an occasion; **have got** to have; **have got to** to be obliged to; **tell someone where they get off** (*colloq*) to deal summarily or dismissively with someone; **you've got me there** (*colloq*) I don't know the answer to your question. [O.N. *geta*.]

geta *gā'tə*, *n* a Japanese wooden sandal with a thong between the big toe and the other toes: — *pl* **ge'ta** or **ge'tas**. [Jap.]

geum *jē'əm*, *n* an avens, a plant of the genus *Geum* of the rose family. [L.]

GeV (*phys*) *abbrev* for giga-electron-volt, a unit of particle energy (in U.S. sometimes **BeV**).

gewgaw *gū'gö*, *n* a toy; a bauble. — *adj* showy without value.

geyser *gē'zər*, *gā'zər* or *gī'zər*, *n* a spring that spouts hot water into the air; (usu. *gē'zər*) an apparatus for heating water as it is drawn. — *n* **gey'serite** sinter. [*Geysir*, a geyser in Iceland — Icel. *geysa*, O.N. *göysa*, to gush.]

GH *abbrev* for Ghana (I.V.R.).

Ghanaian *gä-nā'yən*, *adj* of or pertaining to Ghana, a W. African republic. — *n* a native or citizen of Ghana.

gharial. Same as **gavial**, **garial**.

gharri or **gharry** *ga'ri*, *n* in India, a wheeled vehicle, esp. one for hire. [Hind. *gārī*, a cart.]

ghastly *gäst'li*, *adj* deathlike; hideous; deplorable (*colloq*). — *n* **ghast'liness**. [O.E. *gǣstan*.]

ghat or **ghaut** *göt*, *n* in India, a mountain pass; a landing-stair on a riverside; a place of cremation (*burning ghat*). [Hindi *ghāt*, descent.]

ghazi *gä'zē*, *n* a veteran Muslim warrior, slayer of infidels; a high Turkish title. [Ar. *ghāzi*, fighting.]

ghee *gē*, *n* in Indian cookery, clarified butter, esp. buffalo butter. [Hind. *ghī*.]

gherao *ge-row'*, *n* in India, the surrounding or trapping of a person (e.g. an employer) in a room, building, etc. until he or she meets one's demands: — *pl* **gheraos'**. — Also *vt*. [Hindi, siege.]

gherkin *gûr'kin*, *n* a small cucumber used for pickling. [From an earlier form of Du. *augurk(je)*, a gherkin.]

ghetto *get'ō*, *n* a quarter, esp. poor, underprivileged or socially inferior, inhabited by any racial, or other identifiable group; the Jews' quarter in an Italian or other city, to which they used to be confined: — *pl* **ghett'oes** or **ghett'os**. — *vt* **ghett'oise** or **-ize** (*get'ō-īz*) to make or put into a ghetto. — **ghett'oblaster** (*colloq*) a usu. fairly large portable radio and cassette-recorder unit with built-in speakers. [It. *ghetto*, foundry, after one which previously occupied the site of the Venetian Jewish ghetto.]

ghilgai. See **gilgai**.

ghillie. Same as **gillie**.

ghost *gōst*, *n* a spirit appearing after death; a spirit or soul; a person who does another's work, in writing their speeches, etc.; a faint or false appearance; a duplicated image (*TV*). — *vi* and *vt* to do another's work, esp. to write (their speeches, memoirs, etc.); to haunt; to disappear, vanish like a ghost; to transfer (a prisoner) quickly and secretly overnight; to progress by sail despite very little wind (*naut*). — *adj* **ghost'like**. — *n* **ghost'liness**. — *adj* **ghost'ly** spiritual; pertaining to apparitions; ghostlike; faint. — **ghost gum** an Australian tree, *Eucalyptus papuana*, with smooth white bark; **ghost story** a story in which ghosts figure; **ghost town** one which once flourished owing to some natural resource in the vicinity but which is now deserted since the natural resource has been exhausted (also *fig*); **ghost word** a word that originated in a copyist's or printer's error. — *vi* and *vt* **ghost'-write** to write for someone else, as a ghost. — **ghost'-writer**. — **give up the ghost** to die; **Holy Ghost** the Holy Spirit, the third person in the Christian Trinity; **not to have a ghost (of a chance)** not to have the least chance of success. [O.E. *gāst*.]

ghoul *gōōl* or *gowl*, *n* an Eastern demon that preys on the dead; a gruesome fiend; a person of gruesome or revolting habits or tastes. — *adj* **ghoul'ish**. — *adv* **ghoul'ishly**. — *n* **ghoul'ishness**. [Ar. *ghūl*.]

GHQ *abbrev* for General Headquarters.

ghyll *gil*. See **gill**[3].

GHz *abbrev* for gigahertz.

GI *jē-ī'*, *n* a regular soldier in the U.S. Army. [Abbrev. for government (or general) issue.]

giant *jī'ənt*, *n* a huge mythical being of more or less human form; a person of abnormally great stature; anything much above the usual size of its kind; someone with much greater powers than the average person: — *fem* **gī'antess.** — *adj* **gī'ant** gigantic. — *n* **gī'antism** the occurrence of giants; gigantism. — *adj* **gī'antly** giantlike. — *n* **gī'antry** giants collectively; giant stories or mythology. — **gi'ant-killer** someone who defeats a far superior opponent. — *n* and *adj* **gi'ant-killing.** — **giant star** (*astron*) a star of great brightness and low mean density. [O.Fr. *geant* (Fr. *géant*) — Gr. *gigās, gigantos.*]

giaour *jowr*, *n* an infidel, a term applied by the Turks to all who are not of their own religion. [Through Turk. — Pers. *gaur.*]

Giardia *jē-är'di-ə*, *n* a genus of parasitic protozoa which commonly infect the small intestine of mammals including man. — *n* **giardī'asis** intestinal infection with protozoa of the Giardia genus. [Fr. biologist, A. *Giard* (1846–1908).]

Gib. *jib*, (*colloq*) *n* for Gibraltar.

gib *jib* or *gib*, *n* a wedge-shaped piece of metal holding another in place, etc. — *vt* to fasten with a gib: — *pr p* **gibb'ing**; *pa t* and *pa p* **gibbed.**

gibber *jib'ər*, *vi* to utter senseless or inarticulate sounds. [Imit.]

Gibberella *jib-ə-rel'ə*, *n* a genus of fungi found esp. on grasses — e.g. wheat scab. — *n* **gibberell'in** any of several plant-growth regulators produced by a fungus of the genus.

gibberish *jib'ə-rish* or *gib'*, *n* rapid, gabbling talk; meaningless words. — *adj* meaningless, nonsensical. [Imit.]

gibbet *jib'it*, *n* a gallows on which criminals were hung after execution; the projecting beam of a crane. — *vt* to expose on, or as on, a gibbet. [O.Fr. *gibet*, a stick.]

gibbon *gib'ən*, *n* an E. Indian anthropoid ape (of several species) with very long arms.

gibbous *gib'əs*, *adj* hump-backed; humped; swollen or pouched; (of the moon or planet) between half and full. — *n* **gibbos'ity** or **gibb'ousness.** — *adv* **gibb'ously.** [L. *gibbōsus* — *gibbus*, a hump.]

gibe or **jibe** *jīb*, *vi* to scoff; to jeer. — *vt* to scoff at; to taunt. — *n* a jeer; a taunt. — *n* **gī'ber** or **jī'ber.** — *adv* **gī'bingly.**

giblets *jib'lits*, *npl* the internal eatable parts of a fowl, etc.; entrails. [O.Fr. *gibelet.*]

giddy *gid'i*, *adj* unsteady, dizzy; causing giddiness; whirling; light-headed; flighty. — *vi* and *vt* to make or become giddy. — *adv* **gidd'ily.** — *n* **gidd'iness.** [O.E. *gidig, gydig*, insane, possessed by a god.]

Gideon *gid'i-ən*, *n* a member of an organisation of Christian businessmen, founded in the U.S. in 1899, best known for putting Bibles (**Gideon Bibles**) in hotel rooms, etc. [Named after *Gideon*, the judge of Israel (Judges vi. ff.).]

gidgee or **gidjee** *gi'jē*, (*Austr*) *n* a small acacia tree, the foliage of which at times emits an unpleasant odour. [Aboriginal.]

GIFT *abbrev* for gamete intra-Fallopian transfer, an infertility treatment involving direct transfer of eggs and sperm into the woman's Fallopian tubes, where conception may occur.

gift *gift*, *n* a thing given; a quality bestowed by nature; the act of giving; something easily obtained, understood, etc. — *vt* to endow; to present. — *adj* **gift'ed** highly endowed by nature with talents, abilities, etc.; (esp. of a child) exceptionally clever. — *adv* **gift'edly.** — *n* **gift'edness.** — **gift book** a book suitable or intended for presentation; **gift'shop** a shop selling articles suitable for presents. — *vt* **gift'-wrap** to wrap (a present) in coloured paper, with ribbons, etc. — **look a gift horse in the mouth** to criticise, delay or niggle over a gift or lucky opportunity. [See **give.**]

gig¹ *gig*, *n* a light, two-wheeled carriage; a long, light boat. [M.E. *gigge*, a whirling thing.]

gig² *gig*, *n* a pronged spear for fishing, a fishgig. [**fizgig.**]

gig³ *gig*, (*slang*) *n* an engagement, esp. of a band or pop group for one performance only. — *vt* to play a gig: — *pr p* **gigg'ing**; *pa t* and *pa p* **gigged.**

giga. See **gigue.**

giga- *gī-gə-, gig-ə-, jī-gə-* or *jig-ə-*, *pfx* meaning ten to the ninth power (10^9), a thousand million or in U.S. a billion. — *n* **giga-elec'tron-volt** a unit equal to a thousand million electron-volts. — *n* **gi'gahertz.** — *n* **gi'gawatt.** [Gr. *gigas*, giant.]

gigantic *jī-gan'tik*, *adj* of, like or characteristic of a giant; huge. — *adj* **gigantesque'** befitting or suggestive of a giant. — *adv* **gigan'tically.** — *n* **gigan'ticide** the act of killing a giant. — *n* **gigan'tism** (of a business concern, etc.) hugeness; excessive overgrowth, usually owing to overactivity of the pituitary gland. [L. *gīgās, gigantis*, Gr. *gīgās, -antos*, a giant.]

giggle *gig'l*, *vi* to laugh with short catches of the breath, or in a silly manner. — *n* (*slang*) a laugh of this kind; something unimportant, amusing and silly. — *n* **gigg'ler.** — *n* **gigg'ling.** — *adj* **gigg'ly.** [Echoic.]

GIGO *gig'ō, gī'gō* or *gē'gō*, (*comput*, etc.) *abbrev* for garbage in, garbage out, i.e. bad input results in bad output.

gigolo *jig'ə-lō*, *n* a professional male dancing partner; a young man living at the expense of an older woman: — *pl* **gig'olos.** [Fr.]

gigot *jig'ət*, *n* a leg of mutton, etc.; a leg-of-mutton sleeve. [Fr.]

gigue *zhēg* or (It.) **giga** *jē'gə*, (*mus*) *n* a lively dance form, usu. in 6/8 or 12/8 time, often used to complete 18th-cent. dance suites. [Fr.; cf. **jig.**]

gila *hhē'lə*, (in full **gila monster**) *n* either of the two *Heloderma* species, the only venomous lizards known. [*Gila* River, Arizona.]

gilbert *gil'bərt*, *n* the CGS unit of magnetomotive force. [From the English physician and physicist William *Gilbert* (1540–1603).]

gild¹ *gild*, *vt* to cover or overlay with gold or with any goldlike substance; to gloss over, give a specious appearance to; to adorn with lustre: — *pr p* **gild'ing**; *pa t* and *pa p* **gild'ed** or **gilt.** — *n* **gild'er** someone who coats articles with gold. — *n* **gild'ing** the task or trade of a gilder; gold or imitation gold laid on a surface. — **gilded youth** rich young people of fashion. — **gild the lily** to embellish to an unnecessary extent. [O.E. *gyldan* — *gold*; see **gold.**]

gild². See **guild.**

gilet *zhē-lā*, *n* a waistcoat; in a woman's dress, a front part shaped like a waistcoat; in ballet dress, a bodice shaped like a waistcoat. [Fr.]

gilgai or **ghilgai** *gil'gī*, (*Austr*) *n* a saucer-shaped depression forming a natural reservoir. [Aboriginal.]

gilgie or **jilgie** *jil'gi*, (*Austr*) *n* a yabby. [Aboriginal.]

gill¹ *gil*, *n* an organ for breathing in water; one of the radiating plates on the underside of the cap of a mushroom or toadstool; a projecting rib of a heating surface; the flesh round a person's jaw, as in *green* or *white round the gills* (i.e. sickly-looking). — *vt* to gut (fish); to catch (fish) by the gills in a net. — **gill cover** a fold of skin, usu. with bony plates, protecting the gills; **gill net** a type of fishing-net in which fish are caught by their gills. [Cf. Dan. *gjælle*; Sw. *gäl.*]

gill² *jil*, *n* a small liquid measure, in recent times = $\frac{1}{4}$ pint. [O.Fr. *gelle.*]

gill³ or **ghyll** *gil*, *n* a small ravine, a wooded glen; a brook. [O.N. *gil.*]

gillie, ghillie or **gilly** *gil'i*, *n* (esp. in Scotland) an attendant on or guide of hunting and fishing sportsmen. — *vi* to act as gillie. [Gael. *gille*, a lad.]

gillyflower *jil'i-flowr, n* a flower that smells like cloves, esp. *clove gillyflower* and *stock gillyflower*. [O.Fr. *girofle* — Gr. *karyophyllon*, the clove-tree.]

gilt *gilt, pa t* and *pa p* of **gild**[1]. — *adj* gilded; gold-coloured. — *adj* **gilt'-edged** having the edges gilt; of the highest quality (**gilt-edged securities** also called **gilts** those stocks whose interest is considered perfectly safe).

gimbals *jim'blz* or *gim'*, *npl* a contrivance with self-aligning bearings for keeping e.g. hanging objects, nautical instruments, etc. horizontal. [O.Fr. *gemel* — L. *gemellus*, dimin. of *geminus*, twin.]

gimcrack *jim'krak, n* a dodge, trick; a knick-knack; a poorly made flimsy article. — Also **jim'crack.** — *adj* shoddy. — *n* **gimcrack'ery.** [M.E. *gibecrake*.]

gimlet *gim'lit, n* a small tool for boring holes by turning it by hand; a cocktail of gin or vodka, with lime juice. — *vt* to pierce as with a gimlet; to turn like a gimlet. — *adj* **gim'let-eyed** very sharp-sighted. [O.Fr. *guimbelet*, from Gmc.]

gimmal *jim'l, n* a ring (also **gimmal ring**) that can be divided into two (or three) rings.

gimme *gim'i, (slang)* contracted form of **give me.** — *n* a short putt that one is willing to accept as played by one's opponent (*colloq*); (usu. in *pl*, as **the gimmes**) avarice (*US slang*).

gimmick *gim'ik, n* a secret device for performing a trick; a device (often peculiar to the person adopting it) to catch attention or publicity; an ingenious mechanical device. — *vt* to provide, use or devise gimmick(s) for or in, to accomplish by means of gimmick(s). — *n* **gimm'ickry** gimmicks collectively; use of gimmick(s). — *adj* **gimm'icky.**

gimp *gimp, n* a yarn with a hard core; a trimming made of this; a fishing-line bound with wire; a coarse thread in lace-making. — *vt* to make or furnish with gimp. [Fr. *guimpe*.]

gin[1] *jin, n* a spirit distilled from grain or malt and flavoured with juniper berries or other aromatic substances, made chiefly in Britain and the U.S. — **gin fizz** a drink of gin, lemon juice, effervescing water, etc.; **gin palace** (*derog*) a showily pretentious public house; **gin sling** a cold gin and water, sweetened and flavoured. — **gin and it** gin and *It*alian vermouth. [Contr. from *geneva*, altered from O.Du. *genever* — L. *juniperus*, juniper.]

gin[2] *jin, n* a snare or trap; a machine, esp. one for hoisting; a cotton gin. — *vt* to trap or snare; to clear of seeds by a cotton gin: — *pr p* **ginn'ing**; *pa t* and *pa p* **ginned.** — *n* **ginn'er** someone who gins cotton. — *n* **ginn'ery** a place where cotton is ginned. — **gin'house** a ginnery; **gin trap** a powerful spring trap fitted with teeth. [**engine.**]

gin[3] *jin, n* an Australian Aboriginal woman. [Aboriginal.]

gin[4] *jin* or **gin rummy** *jin rum'i, n* a type of rummy in which a player whose unmatched cards count ten or less is out.

ginger *jin'jər, n* the rootstock of *Zingiber officinale*, or other species of the genus (family *Zingiberaceae*) with a hot taste, used as a condiment, etc.; ginger beer; stimulation; mettle. — *adj* sandy, reddish. — *vt* to put ginger into; to make spirited, to enliven (often with *up*). — *n* **gingerade'** ginger ale. — *adj* **gin'gery** of or like ginger; sandy in colour. — **ginger ale** an aerated drink flavoured with ginger; **ginger beer** an effervescent drink made with fermenting ginger; **ginger cordial** a cordial made of ginger, lemon peel, raisins, water, and sometimes spirits; **ginger group** a group within e.g. a political party seeking to inspire the rest with its own enthusiasm and activity; **ginger nut** a small thick gingersnap; **gin'gersnap** a gingerbread biscuit; **ginger wine** an alcoholic drink made by fermenting sugar and water, and flavoured with various spices, chiefly ginger. [M.E. *gingivere* — O.Fr. *gengibre* — L.L. *gingiber* — L. *zingiber*, ult. — Sans. *śṛnga*, horn, *vera*, body.]

gingerbread *jin'jər-bred, n* a cake flavoured with treacle and usually ginger; (with *cap*) a self-help support group for single parents. — *adj* (of ornamental work) cheap and tawdry. — **take the gilt off the gingerbread** to destroy the glamour. [O.Fr. *gingimbrat* — L.L. *gingiber* (see ety. for **ginger**); confused with **bread.**]

gingerly *jin'jər-li, adv* with soft steps; with extreme wariness and delicate gentleness. — Also *adj*.

gingham *ging'əm, n* a kind of cotton cloth, woven from coloured yarns into stripes or checks. [Fr. *guingan*, orig. from Malay *ginggang*, striped.]

gingili *jin'ji-li, n* a species of sesame; an oil obtained from its seeds. [Hind. *jinjalī*.]

gingival *jin-jī'vl, adj* pertaining to the gums. — *n* **gingivī'tis** inflammation of the gums. [L. *gingīva*, gum.]

gingko. See **ginkgo.**

ginglymus *jing'gli-məs* or *ging'*, *n* a joint that permits movement in one plane only, a hinge joint: — *pl* **ging'lymī.** — *adj* **ging'limoid.** [N.L. — Gr. *ginglymos*.]

gink *gingk, (slang) n* a fellow.

ginkgo *gingk'gō* or **gingko** *ging'kō, n* the maidenhair tree, an ornamental Chinese fan-leaved tree, the only species in the **Ginkgoā'les** order of gymnosperms: — *pl* **gink'goes** or **ging'koes.** [Jap. *ginkyo* — Chin. *yin*, silver, *hing*, apricot.]

ginn. See **jinn.**

ginormous *jī-nör'məs, (colloq) adj* huge, altogether enormous. [*gi*gantic and *enormous*.]

ginseng *jin'seng, n* a plant (genus *Panax*), cultivated esp. in the Far East; its root, believed to have important restorative and curative properties. [Chin. *jên-shên*, perh. image of man.]

giocoso *jo-kō'sō, (mus) adj* played in a lively or humorous manner. [It.]

gip *jip, n.* Same as **gyp**[2].

gippy (or **gyppy**) **tummy** *jip'i tum'i, (colloq) n* diarrhoea, severe stomach upset, thought of as a hazard of holidaying in hot countries. [Short for *Egyptian* tummy.]

gipsy. See **gypsy.**

giraffe *ji-räf', n* an African ruminant mammal with a remarkably long neck and forelegs and a brown-patched gingery coat. — *adj* **giraff'id, giraff'īne** or **giraff'oid.** [Ar. *zarāfah*.]

girandole *jir'ən-dōl, n* a branched chandelier; a pendant, etc., with small jewels attached around it; a rotating firework; a number of linked mines (*mil*). [Fr., — It. *girandola* — *girare*, to turn round.]

girasol *jir'ə-sol* or **girasole** *jir'ə-sōl, n* an opal or other stone that seems to send a firelike glow from within in certain lights. [It., — *girare*, to turn, *sole*, the sun.]

gird *gûrd, vt* to bind round; to secure by a belt or girdle; to encompass; to surround; to clothe: — *pa t* and *pa p* **gird'ed** or **girt.** — *n* **gird'er** a large beam of wood, iron or steel, to take a lateral stress, e.g. to support a floor, wall, roadway of a bridge; a strip of strengthening tissue (*bot*). — *n* **gird'ing.** — **girder bridge** a bridge whose load is sustained by girders resting on supports. — **gird oneself** (literally) to tuck up loose garments under one's girdle; to brace oneself for any trial or effort. [O.E. *gyrdan*.]

girdle[1] *gûr'dl, n* a waistbelt; a cord worn about the waist by a monk, etc.; anything that encloses like a belt; a woman's lightweight, close-fitting undergarment, a form of corset, reaching from waist to thigh; a bony arch to which a limb is attached (*anat*); a ring-shaped cut around a tree; the rim of a brilliant-cut gem. — *vt* to bind or enclose, like a girdle; to cut a ring round (a tree, etc.); to cut a circular outline around (a gemstone). — *adj* **gird'led.** [O.E. *gyrdel* — *gyrdan*, to gird.]

girdle[2]. See **griddle.**

girl *gûrl, n* a female child; a daughter; a young unmarried woman; a woman irrespective of age (*colloq*); a girlfriend (*colloq*); a maid. — *n* **girl'hood** the state or time of being a girl. — *adj* **girl'ie** or **girl'y** (of magazines, photographs etc.) showing nude or scantily clad young women. — *adj* **girl'ish** of or like a girl. — *adv* **girl'ishly.** — *n* **girl'ishness.** — **Girl Friday** a young female general office worker; **girl'-friend** one's sweetheart, or girl who is one's regular companion; **Girl Guide** see **guide; Girl Scout** a member of an American organisation similar to the Guides. — **old girl** a female former pupil; an amiably disrespectful term for a female of any age or species. [M.E. *gerle, girle, gurle*, boy or girl.]

giro *jī'rō, n* (also with *cap*) a banking system by which money can be transferred direct from the account of one holder to that of another person (or to those of others); a social security payment by giro cheque (*colloq*): — *pl* **gī'ros.** — **giro cheque, order**, etc. one issued through the giro system. [Ger., transfer — Gr. *gyros*, ring.]

girt *gûrt, pa t* and *pa p* of **gird.** — *vt* to gird; to girth. — *vi* to girth.

girth *gûrth, n* the belly-band of a saddle; a circumferential measure of thickness. — *vt* to put a girth on; to measure the girth of. — *vi* to measure in girth. [O.N. *gjörth*.]

gism. See **jism.**

gismo or **gizmo** *giz'mō*, (*colloq*) *n* gadget, thingumajig: — *pl* **gis'mos** or **giz'mos.**

gist *jist, n* the main point or pith of a matter. [O.Fr. *gist* (Fr. *gît*) — O.Fr. *gesir*, to lie.]

git *git*, (*slang*) *n* a person (used contemptuously); a fool. [Dialect *get*, offspring, brat.]

give *giv, vt* to bestow; to impart; to yield; to grant; to donate; to permit; to provide; to pay or render (thanks, etc.); to pronounce (a judgment or decision); to show (a result); to apply (oneself); to allow or admit. — *vi* to yield to pressure; to begin to melt or soften; to open, or give an opening or view, to lead (with *upon, on* or *into*): — *pr p* **giv'ing;** *pa t* **gāve;** *pa p* **given** (*giv'n*). — *n* a yielding quality; elasticity. — *adj* **giv'en** bestowed; specified; addicted, disposed; granted; admitted. — *n* something that is granted, assumed or accepted as true. — *n* **giv'er.** — *n* **giv'ing** the act of bestowing; the thing given. — *adj* that gives; generous, liberal. — **give'-away** a betrayal, revelation, esp. if unintentional; something given free with the aim of increasing sales; **given name** the first or Christian name, distinguished from the *surname*. — **give and take** reciprocity in concession; mutually compensatory variations; fair exchange of repartee; **give away** to give free; to betray; to bestow ceremonially (as a bride); **give birth to** to bring forth; to originate; **give chase** to pursue; **give ground** or **place** to give way, yield; **give in to** to yield to; **give it to (someone)** (*colloq*) to scold or beat someone severely; **give line, head, rein** etc., to give more liberty or scope; **give me** I would choose if I had the choice; **give off** to emit (e.g. a smell); **give oneself away** to betray one's secret unawares; **give out** to report; to emit; to distribute to individuals; **give over** to transfer; to cease (*colloq*); **give the lie to** to accuse openly of falsehood; to prove wrong; **give up** to abandon; to surrender; to desist from; **give way** to fall back, yield, withdraw; to break, snap, collapse, under strain; to allow traffic in a direction crossing one's path to proceed first; **give way to,** to yield to, submit to; to allow to take precedence, give priority to; to succumb to (e.g. grief). [O.E. *gefan*.]

gizmo. See **gismo.**

gizzard *giz'ərd, n* a muscular stomach, esp. the second stomach of a bird. — **stick in someone's gizzard** to be more than someone can accept or tolerate. [M.E. *giser* — O.Fr. *guiser* (supposed to be — L. *gigeria* (pl.), cooked entrails of poultry).]

Gk *abbrev* for Greek.

glabella *glə-bel'ə*, (*anat*) *n* the part of the forehead between the eyebrows and just above their level: — *pl* **glabell'ae** (*-bel'ē*). — *adj* **glabell'ar.** [L. *glaber*, bald, smooth.]

glabrous *glā'brəs, adj* hairless, bald. [L. *glaber*, bald.]

glacé *gla'sā, adj* frozen, or with ice; iced with sugar; candied; glossy, lustrous, esp. of thin silk or kid leather. — *vt* to ice with sugar; to candy: — *pr p* **glac'éing;** *pa t* and *pa p* **glac'éed.** [Fr.]

glacial *glā'si-əl* or *glā'-shəl, adj* icy; frozen; readily or ordinarily solidified (*chem*); pertaining to ice or its action; of progress, ponderously slow, like that of a glacier. — *n* a glacial period, an ice age. — *n* **glā'cialist** or **glaciol'ogist** someone who studies the geological action of ice. — *vt* **glaciate** (*glā'si-āt* or *glā'shi-āt*) to polish by ice action; to subject to the action of land ice; to freeze. — *n* **glaciā'tion.** — *adj* **glaciolog'ical.** — *n* **glaciol'ogy** the study of the geological nature, distribution and action of ice. — **Glacial Period** the Ice Age, or any ice age. [L. *glaciālis*, icy, *glaciāre, -ātum*, to freeze.]

glacier *glas'i-ər, glā'si-ər* or *glā'shər, n* a mass of ice, fed by snow on a mountain, slowly creeping downhill to where it melts or breaks up into icebergs. [Fr., — *glace*, ice — L. *glaciēs*, ice.]

glaciology. See **glacial.**

glacis *gläs-ē, glas'is* or *glās'is, n* a gentle slope, esp. in fortification: — *pl* **glacis** (*gläs-ē, glas'iz* or *glās'iz*), or **glac'ises.** [Fr., orig. a slippery place — L. *glaciēs*, ice.]

glad *glad, adj* pleased; cheerful; giving pleasure. — *vt* **gladd'en** to make glad; to cheer. — *adv* **glad'ly.** — *n* **glad'ness.** — **glad eye** (*slang*) an ogle; **glad hand** (*US*) the hand of welcome or of effusive greeting. — *vi* and *vt* **glad-hand'** to extend the glad hand (to); to proceed in this manner. — **glad-hand'er** (*US*) a person who is out to make up to all and sundry (esp. of a vote-seeking politician); **glad rags** (*colloq*) best clothes, party attire. — **glad of** glad to have; glad because of. [O.E. *glæd*.]

gladdie *glad'i*, (*colloq*) *n* a gladiolus.

glade *glād, n* an open space in a wood.

gladiate *glad'i-āt* or *glā'di-āt, adj* sword-shaped. [L. *glādius*, sword.]

gladiator *glad'i-ā-tər, n* in ancient Rome, a professional combatant with men or wild animals in the arena. — *adj* **gladiatorial** (*-ə-tö'ri-əl*). [L.]

gladiolus *glad-i-ō'ləs, n* any plant of a genus (*Gladiolus*) of the iris family, with sword-shaped leaves: — *pl* **gladiō'lī** or **gladiō'luses.** — Also **gladiole** (*glad'i-ōl*). [Dimin. of L. *glādius*, sword.]

Gladstone bag *glad'stən bag, n* a travelling bag or small portmanteau, opening out flat, named after W.E. *Gladstone* (1809–98), four times prime minister.

Glagolitic *glag-ə-lit'ik, adj* of or pertaining to Glagol, an ancient Slavonic alphabet. [Old Slav. *glagolu*, a word.]

glair *glār, n* the clear part of an egg used as varnish; any viscous, transparent substance. — *vt* to varnish with white of eggs. [Fr. *glaire*, perh. — L. *clārus*, clear.]

glamour or in U.S. **glamor** *glam'ər, n* allure, magnetism; an excitingly or fascinatingly attractive quality; groomed beauty and studied charm. — *adj* **glam** (*slang*) glamorous. — *adj* **glam'orous** full of glamour; bewitching, alluring. — *n* **glamorīsā'tion** or **-z-.** — *vt* **glamor'ise** or **-ize** to make glamorous; to romanticise. — *adv* **glam'orously.** — **glamour boy** or **girl** (*colloq*) a man or woman considered to be very glamorous (often *derog*); **glam'ourpuss** (*colloq*) a glamorous person, esp. female. — *adj* and *n* **glam'-rock** (of or relating to) the glamorised side of the rock music scene or industry.

glance[1] *gläns, vi* to fly (off) obliquely on striking; to make a passing allusion, esp. unfavourable (with *at*);

to snatch a momentary view (with *at*); to dart a reflected ray, to flash. — *vt* to cause to glance; to deflect. — *n* an oblique impact or movement; a stroke by which the ball is allowed to glance off an upright bat to fine leg (*cricket*); a sudden shoot of reflected light; a darting of the eye; a momentary look. — *n* and *adj* **glanc'ing.** — *adv* **glanc'ingly.** — **at a glance** immediately, at a first look. [M.E. *glenten.*]

glance[2] *gläns, n* a black or grey mineral with metallic lustre. [Ger. *Glanz*, glance, lustre.]

gland[1] *gland, n* a secreting structure in plant or animal. — *adj* **glandif'erous** bearing acorns or nuts. — *adj* **glan'diform** resembling a gland; acorn-shaped. — *adj* **gland'ūlar** or **gland'ūlous** containing, consisting of, or pertaining to glands. — *adv* **gland'ūlarly** or **gland'ulously.** — *n* **glan'dūle** a small gland. — *adj* **glandūlif'erous.** — **glandular fever** a disease characterised by slight fever, enlargement of glands, and increase in the white cells of the blood. [L. *glāns, glandis*, an acorn.]

gland[2] *gland*, (*eng*) *n* a device for preventing leakage at a point where a rotating or reciprocating shaft emerges from a vessel containing fluid under pressure.

glanders *glan'dərz, nsing* a malignant, contagious and fatal disease, esp. of the horse, affecting the mucous membrane of the nose, the lungs, and the lymphatic system. — *adj* **glan'dered** or **glan'derous.** [O.Fr. *glandre*, a gland.]

glandiferous, glandular, etc. See **gland**[1].

glans *glanz, n* an acorn or similar fruit; a glandular structure, of similar shape (*anat*): — *pl* **glan'des** (*-dēz*). — **glans clitoris** and **glans penis** respectively the extremity of the clitoris and of the penis. [L.]

glare *glār, n* an oppressive or unrelieved dazzling light; cheap or showy brilliance; a fierce stare. — *vi* to emit a hard, fierce, dazzling light; to be obtrusively noticeable, intense or strong, to shine dazzlingly; to stare fiercely. — *vt* to send out or express with a glare. — *adj* **glar'ing** bright and dazzling; flagrant. — *adv* **glar'ingly.** — *n* **glar'ingness.**

glasnost *glaz'* or *glas'nost, n* the policy of openness and forthrightness followed by the Soviet government, initiated by Premier Mikhail Gorbachev. — *adj* **glasnos'tian** or **glasnos'tic** of, relating to, or in the spirit of, glasnost. [Russ., speaking aloud.]

glass *gläs, n* a hard, amorphous, brittle substance, usually transparent, made by fusing together one or more of the oxides of silicon, boron, or phosphorus with certain basic oxides, and cooling the product rapidly to prevent crystallisation; an article made of or with glass, esp. a drinking-vessel, a mirror, a lens, a telescope, etc.; the quantity of liquid a glass holds; (in *pl*) spectacles. — *adj* made of glass. — *vt* to put in, under, or behind glass. — *n* **glass'ful** as much as a glass will hold: — *pl* **glass'fuls.** — *adv* **glass'ily.** — *n* **glassine** (*-ēn'*) a transparent paper, used for book-covers. — *n* **glass'iness.** — *adj* **glass'y** like glass; (of eyes) expressionless. — **glass'-blower; glass'-blowing** the process of making glassware by inflating a viscid mass; **glass ceiling** an indistinct yet unmistakable barrier on the career ladder, through which certain categories of employees (usu. women) find they can see but not progress; **glass cloth** a cloth for drying glasses; a material woven from glass threads; a polishing cloth covered with powdered glass; **glass'-cutter** a tool for cutting sheets of glass; someone who does cut-glass work; **glass'-cutting** the act or process of cutting, shaping and ornamenting the surface of glass; **glass eye** an artificial eye made of glass; **glass fibre** glass melted and then drawn out into extremely fine fibres, which are later to be spun, woven, etc. (also **fibreglass**); **glass'house** a house made of glass or largely of glass, esp. a greenhouse; military detention barracks; a glass factory. — *adj* **glass'like.** — **glass paper** paper coated with finely pounded glass, used like sandpaper; **glass snake** a legless lizard (*Ophisaurus*) with brittle tail; **glass soap** manganese dioxide or other substance used by glass-makers to remove colouring from glass; **glass'ware** articles made of glass; **glass wool** glass spun into woolly fibres; **glass'work** furnishings or articles made of glass; (usu. in *pl*) a glass factory; **glass'worker.** — **live in a glass house** to be open to attack or retort; **water** (or **soluble**) **glass** sodium or potassium silicate. [O.E. *glæs.*]

Glaswegian *glas-* or *gläs-wē'j(y)ən, n* a native or citizen of *Glasgow.* — Also *adj.* [Modelled on *Norwegian.*]

glauberite *glö'bə-rīt, n* a greyish-white mineral, sodium calcium sulphate, found chiefly in rock salt, named after the German chemist Johann Rudolf *Glauber* (1604–68). — **Glauber** (or **Glauber's**) **salt** hydrated sodium sulphate, discovered by him.

glaucescence, etc. See **glaucous.**

glaucoma *glö-kō'mə, n* an insidious disease of the eye, marked by increased pressure within the eyeball and growing dimness of vision. — *adj* **glaucomatous** (*-kō'mə-təs*). [Gr. *glaukōma*, cataract; see **glaucous.**]

glaucous *glö'kəs, adj* greyish- or bluish-green; covered with a fine greenish or bluish bloom (*bot*). — *n* **glaucescence** (*-ses'əns*). — *adj* **glaucesc'ent** somewhat glaucous. [L. *glaucus* — Gr. *glaukos*, bluish-green or grey (orig. gleaming).]

glaze *glāz, vt* to furnish or set with glass; to cover with a thin surface of glass or something glassy; to cover with a layer of thin semitransparent colour; to give a glassy surface to; to apply a thin wash containing e.g. milk, eggs, or sugar to (e.g. pastry) to give a shiny appearance. — *n* the glassy coating put upon pottery; a thin coat of semitransparent colour; any shining exterior; a thin wash of eggs, milk, sugar, etc. for glazing food. — *vi* to become glassy. — *adj* **glazed.** — *n* **glā'zer** a workman who glazes pottery, paper, etc. — *n* **glā'zier** (*-zyər*) a person who sets glass in window-frames, etc. — *n* **glā'zing** the act or art of setting glass; the art of covering with a vitreous substance. [M.E. *glasen* — *glas*, glass; see **glass.**]

GLC *abbrev* for the Greater London Council (abolished in 1986, the residue of its responsibilities being wound up by the London Residuary Body).

Gld. *abbrev* for guilder (the Dutch unit of currency).

gleam *glēm, vi* to glow or shine, usu. not very brightly. — *vt* to flash. — *n* a faint or moderate glow; a small stream of light; a beam; brightness; often used fig. as *a gleam of hope, a gleam of understanding.* — *n* and *adj* **gleam'ing.** — *adj* **gleam'y.** [O.E. *glǣm*, gleam, brightness; see **glimmer.**]

glean *glēn, vt* to follow the harvester(s) gathering any residue; to collect (what is thinly scattered, neglected or overlooked); to pick up (facts or information); to find out by laboriously scraping together pieces of information. — *vi* to gather the corn left by a reaper or anything that has been left by others; to gather facts bit by bit. — *n* **glean'er.** — *n* **glean'ing.** [O.Fr. *glener* (Fr. *glaner*), through L.L. *glenāre.*]

glebe *glēb, n* the land attached to a parish church. — **glebe house** a manse. [L. *glēba*, a clod.]

glee *glē, n* joy; mirth and gaiety; impish enjoyment; a form of short unaccompanied part-song, popular from the mid-17th to the 19th century. — *adj* **glee'ful** merry. — **glee club** (chiefly *NAm*) a choir for singing part-songs, etc. [O.E. *glēo, glīw*, mirth.]

gleet *glēt, n* a viscous, transparent discharge from a mucous surface. — *vt* to discharge gleet. — *adj* **gleet'y.** [O.Fr. *glette, glecte*, a flux.]

glei. See **gley.**

glen *glen, n* a narrow valley with a stream, often with trees; a depression, usu. of some extent, between hills. [Gael. *gleann.*]

glengarry *glen-gar'i*, (*Scot*) *n* a Highlander's cap of thick-milled woollen cloth, usu. with a point in front, and ribbons hanging down behind. [*Glengarry* in Inverness-shire.]

glenoid *glē'noid*, (*anat*) *adj* socket-shaped; slightly cupped. — Also *n*. [Gr. *glēnoeidēs* — *glēnē*, a socket.]

gley or **glei** *glā*, *n* a bluish-grey sticky clay found under some types of very damp soil. [Russ. *gley*, clay.]

glia *glī'ə* or *glē'ə*, *n* the supporting tissue of the brain and spinal cord, neuroglia. — *adj* **gli'al**. — *n* **gli'adin** or **gli'adine** a protein in gluten. — *n* **gliō'ma** a tumour of the neuroglia in the brain and spinal cord: — *pl* **gliō'mata** or **gliō'mas**. — *adj* **gliō'matous**. — *n* **gliomatō'sis** diffuse overgrowth of neuroglia in the brain or spinal chord. — *n* **gliō'sis** excessive growth of fibrous tissue in the neuroglia. [Gr. *gliā*, glue.]

glib *glib*, *adj* easy; facile; fluent and plausible. — *adv* **glib'ly**. — *n* **glib'ness**. [Cf. Du. *glibberig*, slippery.]

glide *glīd*, *vi* to slide smoothly and easily; to flow gently; to pass smoothly or stealthily; to travel through the air without expending power; to travel by glider; to play a glide stroke. — *n* an act of gliding; a transitional sound produced in passing from one position to another (*phon*); a smooth and sliding dance-step; an inclined plane or slide; a stretch of shallow gliding water. — *n* **glī'der** someone who, or that which, glides; an aircraft like an aeroplane without engine (a *powered glider* has a small engine); a hydroplane. — *n* **glī'ding** the action of the verb in any sense; the sport of flying in a glider. — *adv* **glī'dingly**. — **glide slope** or **path** the slope along which aircraft are assumed to come in for landing, marked out, e.g. by a radio beam. [O.E. *glīdan*, to slip.]

glimmer *glim'ər*, *vi* to burn or appear faintly. — *n* a faint light; feeble rays of light; an inkling, faint perception. — *n* **glimm'ering** a glimmer; an inkling. — *adv* **glimm'eringly**. — *adj* **glimm'ery**. [M.E. *glemern*, frequentative from root of **gleam**.]

glimpse *glimps*, *n* a passing appearance; a momentary view. — *vt* to get a glimpse of. [M.E. *glymsen*, to glimpse.]

glint *glint*, *vi* to flash with a glittering light. — *vt* to reflect. — *n* a gleam; a momentary flash. [Earlier *glent*; prob. Scand.]

glioblastoma *gli-ō-blas-tō'mə*, (*pathol*) *n* a very malignant tumour of the central nervous system. [**glia** and **blastoma**.]

glioma, etc. See **glia**.

glissade *glēs-äd'*, *n* act of sliding down a slope in a standing or squatting position, often with the aid of an ice axe; a gliding movement in ballet. — *vi* to slide or glide down. [Fr.]

glissando *glē-san'dō*, (*mus*) *n* the effect produced by sliding the finger along keyboard or strings; a similar effect on the trombone, etc.: — *pl* **glissan'dos** or **glissan'di**. — Also *adj* and *adv*. [19th-cent. It., formed from Fr. *glissant*, sliding.]

glisten *glis'n*, *vi* to gleam or shimmer as a wet or oily surface does. — *n* gleam. [M.E. *glistnen* — O.E. *glisnian*, to shine.]

glitch *glich*, *n* an instance of imperfect functioning in equipment, esp. an electronic circuit.

glitter *glit'ər*, *vi* to sparkle with light; to be splendid (usu. with *with*); to be showy. — *n* sparkle; showiness. — *n* and *adj* **glitt'ering**. — *adv* **glitt'eringly**. — *adj* **glitt'ery**. [M.E. *gliteren*.]

glitterati *glit-ə-rä'tē*, (*colloq*) *npl* the society lions of the day — famous, fashionable and beautiful people.

glittery. See **glitter**.

glitzy *glits'i*, (*NAm colloq*) *adj* showy, garish or gaudy; glittering. — *n* **glitz** (a back-formation) showiness, garishness. [Perh. from Ger. *glitzern*, to glitter.]

gloaming *glō'ming*, (*poetic*) *n* twilight, dusk. [App. from a derivative of O.E. *glōmung* — *glōm*, twilight.]

gloat *glōt*, *vi* to eye with intense, usu. malicious, satisfaction (esp. with *over*); generally, to exult (over). — *n* an act of gloating. — *n* **gloat'er**. — *adv* **gloat'ingly**. [Perh. O.N. *glotta*, to grin.]

glob *glob*, (*colloq*) *n* a roundish drop, dollop, etc. of a (semi-)liquid substance. — *adj* **globb'y**.

globe *glōb*, *n* a ball; a round body, a sphere; the earth; a sphere representing the earth (terrestrial globe), or one representing the heavens (celestial globe); an orb, emblem of sovereignty; a light bulb (esp. *Austr* and *NZ*); a nearly spherical glass vessel. — *vt* and *vi* to form into a globe. — *adj* **glō'bal** spherical; worldwide; affecting, or taking into consideration, the whole world or all peoples; comprehensive. — *n* **glōbalisā'tion** or **-z-**. — *vt* **glō'balise** or **-ize** to make global. — *adv* **glō'bally**. — *adj* **glō'bate** or **glō'bated** globe-shaped. — *adj* **glōbed** globe-shaped; having a globe. — *n* **glō'bin** the protein constituent of haemoglobin. — *adj* **glō'boid** or **glōbose'** (or *glō'*) globate. — *n* **glōbos'ity** (something having) the quality of being globate. — *adj* **glō'bous**. — *adj* **globular** (*glob'ū-lər*) spherical. — *n* **globularity** (*glob-ū-lar'i-ti*). — *adv* **glob'ūlarly**. — *n* **glob'ūle** a little globe or round particle; a drop; a small pill. — *n* **glob'ūlet**. — *n* **glob'ūlin** any one of a class of proteins soluble in dilute salt solutions but not in pure water. — *n* **glob'ūlite** a minute spheroidal crystallite occurring esp. in glassy rocks. — *adj* **globulif'erous** producing or having globules. — *adj* **glob'ūlous**. — **global village** the world, in reference to its apparent smallness due to improved communications, and the way in which changes in one area are likely to affect the rest of the world; **global warming** the slow increase in the earth's surface air temperature caused by man-made carbon dioxide in the atmosphere trapping excessive amounts of solar radiation which would otherwise be reflected back into space (also called the **greenhouse effect**); **globe fish** any fish of the families *Diodontidae* and *Tetrodontidae*, capable of blowing itself up into a globe; **globe'flower** any plant of the genus *Trollius*, with a globe of large showy sepals enclosing the small inconspicuous petals; **globe'-trotter** a person who goes sightseeing about the world; **globe'trotting**. [L. *globus*.]

globigerina *glob-i-jə-rī'nə*, *n* a minute marine invertebrate of the genus *Globigerina* with calcareous shell of globose chambers in a spiral; a shell of this type: — *pl* **globigerinae** (*-ī'nē*). — **globigerina ooze** a deep-sea deposit of globigerina shells. [L. *globus*, globe, *gerĕre*, to carry.]

globin, globoid, globule, globulin, etc. See under **globe**.

glockenspiel *glok'ən-shpēl*, *n* an orchestral instrument consisting of a set of bells or bars struck by hammers, with or (more usually) without a keyboard. [Ger. *Glocke*, bell, *Spiel*, play.]

glom[1] *glom*, (*US slang*) *vt* to snatch; to steal: — *pr p* **glomm'ing**; *pa t* and *pa p* **glommed**. — **glom on to** to appropriate; to catch on to. [Variant of esp. Scot. dialect *glaum*, to grab, — Gael. *glàm*, to seize, devour.]

glom[2] *glom*, (*US slang*) *vt* to look at, to eye: — *pr p* **glomm'ing**; *pa t* and *pa p* **glommed**.

glomerate *glom'ər-āt*, (*bot* and *anat*) *adj* balled; clustered in heads. — *n* **glomerā'tion**. — *adj* **glomer'ūlate** of a glomerule. — *n* **glom'erule** (*-ōōl*) a little ball of spores; a cluster of short-stalked flowers. [L. *glomerāre*, *-ātum* — *glomus*, *glomeris*, a ball of yarn.]

glonoin *glo-nō'in*, (*chem*) *n* a name for nitroglycerine, as used in medicine. [*glycerine*, *O* (oxygen), NO_3 (nitric anhydride).]

gloom *glōōm*, *n* partial darkness; cloudiness; heaviness of mind; sullenness; a dark place (*poetic*). — *vi* to be or look sullen or dejected; to be or become cloudy, dark or obscure; to scowl. — *adj* **gloom'ful**.

— *adv* **gloom'ily**. — *n* **gloom'iness**. — *adj* **gloom'y** dim or obscure; dimly lit; depressed in spirits; dismal. [M.E. *gloumbe*; see **glum**.]

glop *glop*, (*slang*, esp. *NAm*) *n* a mushy mess of something, esp. unappetising food.

gloria[1] *glö'ri-ə*, *n* an aureole; a halo. [L.]

gloria[2] *glö'ri-ə*, (L.) *n* glory; any doxology beginning with the word 'Gloria'. — **gloria in excelsis** (*in eks-chel'sis* or *-sēs*) glory (to God) on high; **gloria Patri** (*pat'ri* or *pä'trē*) glory (be) to the Father.

glorify *glö'ri-fī*, *vt* to make glorious; to cast glory upon; to worship; to exalt to glory; to ascribe great charm, beauty, etc., to, usually to a markedly exaggerated extent; to add undeserved prestige to, esp. under a euphemistic or overblown title: — *pr p* **glō'rifying**; *pa t* and *pa p* **glō'rified**. — *n* **glorificā'tion** an act of glorifying. [L. *glōria*, glory, *facěre*, to make.]

glory *glö'ri*, *n* renown; exalted or triumphant honour; widespread praise; an object of supreme pride; splendour, beauty; resplendent brightness; summit of attainment, prosperity or gratification; (in religious symbolism) a combination of the nimbus and the aureola, but often erroneously used for the nimbus; the presence of God; the manifestation of God to the blessed in heaven; a representation of the heavens opened; heaven. — *vi* to exult proudly; to rejoice (with *in*): — *pr p* **glō'rying**; *pa t* and *pa p* **glō'ried**. — *interj* expressing surprise. — *adj* **glō'rious** noble; splendid; conferring renown. — *adv* **glō'riously**. — *n* **glō'riousness**. — **glo'rybox** (*Austr* and *NZ*) a box in which a young woman keeps her trousseau, etc., — a bottom drawer. — **glory be** a devout ascription of glory to God; a shout of exultation, also used to express surprise; **Old Glory** the Stars and Stripes. [O.Fr. *glorie* and L. *glōria*.]

glory hole *glö'ri hōl*, *n* a hole for viewing the inside of a furnace; a room, cupboard or receptacle for miscellaneous odds and ends (*colloq*); a steward's room on a ship; an excavation. [Perh. M.E. *glory*, to defile, or Scot. *glaury*, miry, or **glory**, and **hole**.]

Glos. *glos*, *abbrev* for Gloucestershire.

gloss[1] *glos*, *n* brightness or lustre, as from a polished surface; external show; superficial appearance. — *vt* to make glossy; to give a superficial lustre to; to render plausible; to palliate. — *n* **gloss'er**. — *adv* **gloss'ily**. — *n* **gloss'iness**. — *adj* **gloss'y** smooth and shining; highly polished. — *n* (*colloq*) a glossy magazine. — **gloss paint** paint containing varnish, giving a hard, shiny finish; **glossy magazine** a magazine printed on glossy paper, with many illustrations and advertisements. — **gloss over** to explain away, make more acceptable. [Cf. O.N. *glossi*, blaze, *glōa*, to glow.]

gloss[2] *glos*, *n* a marginal or interlinear explanation, e.g. of an obscure or unusual word; a deceptive or intentionally misleading explanation; a collection of explanations of words, a glossary. — *vt* to give a gloss on; to explain away. — *vi* to comment or make explanatory remarks. — *n* **glossā'tor** or **gloss'er** a writer of glosses or comments, a commentator. — *n* **glossog'rapher**. — *adj* **glossograph'ical**. — *n* **glossog'raphy** the writing of glosses or comments. [Gr. *glōssa*, *glōtta*, tongue, a word requiring explanation.]

gloss- *glos-* or **glosso-** *glos-ō-*, *glos-ə-* or *glə-so'-*, *combining form* denoting the tongue or a gloss (see **gloss**[2]). — *n* **glossec'tomy** surgical removal of the tongue. — *n* **glossī'tis** inflammation of the tongue. — *n* **glossolā'lia** the 'gift of tongues', the speaking of wholly or partly unintelligible utterances thought to form part of an unknown language or languages and considered by (esp. Early) Christians to be a manifestation of the Holy Spirit. [Gr. *glōssa*, tongue.]

glossal *glos'əl*, (*anat*) *adj* of, or relating to, the tongue. [Gr. *glōssa*, tongue.]

glossary *glos'ə-ri*, *n* a collection or list of explanations of words; a dictionary of terms used in a specialised subject area. — *adj* **glossā'rial**. — *adv* **glossā'rially**. — *n* **gloss'arist** the compiler of a glossary. [L. *glossārium*, glossary, — Gr. *glōssa*, tongue.]

glossator. See **gloss**[2].

glosseme *glos'ēm*, (*linguis*) *n* a unit or feature of a language that in itself carries significance and cannot be further analysed into meaningful units. [**gloss-** and sfx. *-eme*, rather than Gr. *glossēma*, a word needing explanation.]

glosser. See **gloss**[1,2].

-glot *-glot*, *combining form* denoting speaking, or written in, a language or languages, as in *monoglot*, *polyglot*. [Gr. *glōtta*, tongue, language.]

glottal. See **glottis**.

glottis *glot'is*, *n* the opening of the larynx or entrance to the windpipe: — *pl* **glott'ises** or **glott'ides** (*-i-dēz*). — *adj* **glott'al** of the glottis. — *adj* **glott'ic** pertaining to the glottis or to the tongue; linguistic. — *adj* **glottid'ean**. — **glottal stop** a consonant sound produced by closing and suddenly opening the glottis, occurring as a phoneme in some languages, e.g. Arabic, and as a feature of others, and sometimes heard as a substitute for *t* in English. [Gr. *glōttis* — *glōtta*, the tongue.]

glottochronology *glot-ə-krə-nol'ə-ji*, *n* a statistical study of vocabulary to determine the degree of relationship between particular languages and the chronology of their independent development. [Gr. *glōtta*, tongue, language, and **chronology**.]

glove *gluv*, *n* a covering for the hand, with a sheath for each finger; a boxing-glove. — *vt* to cover with, or as if with, a glove. — *adj* **gloved**. — *n* **glov'er** a person who makes or sells gloves. — **glove box** a closed compartment in which radioactive or toxic material may be manipulated by the use of gloves attached to the walls; a glove compartment; **glove compartment** a small compartment in the front of a car, usu. part of the dashboard, in which gloves, etc. can be kept; **glove puppet** a puppet worn on the hand like a glove and manipulated by the fingers. — **fit like a glove** to fit exactly; **the gloves are off** (*colloq*) now the fight, argument, etc. is about to begin in earnest, without qualification or reservation (*adj* **gloves'-off**). [O.E. *glōf*.]

glow *glō*, *vi* to shine with an intense heat; to burn without flame; to emit a steady light; (esp. of the complexion) to flush; to tingle with bodily warmth or with emotion; to be ardent. — *n* a shining with heat; a luminous appearance; a redness of complexion; a feeling of warmth; brightness of colour; warmth of feeling. — *adj* **glow'ing**. — *adv* **glow'ingly**. — **glow discharge** a luminous electrical discharge in gas at low pressure; **glow plug** an electric plug fitted in a diesel engine to make starting easier in cold weather; a similar device that can be switched on to re-ignite the flame in a gas turbine automatically; **glow'-worm** a beetle, esp. *Lampyris noctiluca*, whose larvae and wingless females are luminous. [O.E. *glōwan*, to glow.]

glower *glow'ər* or *glowr*, *vi* to stare fiercely, scowl. — *n* a fierce or threatening stare.

gloxinia *glok-sin'i-ə*, *n* a plant of the tropical American *Gloxinia* genus, with bright bell-shaped flowers. [*Gloxin*, a German botanist.]

glucagon *gloo͞'kə-gon*, *n* a polypeptide hormone secreted by the pancreas which accelerates glycogen breakdown in the liver, so increasing blood glucose levels. [Gr. *glykys*, sweet.]

glucocorticoid *gloo͞-kō-kör'ti-koid*, *n* any of a group of steroid hormones which affect glucose metabolism, having an anti-inflammatory effect. [Gr. *glykys*, sweet, and **corticoid**.]

gluconeogenesis *gloo͞-kō-nē-ō-jen'ə-sis*, *n* the conversion of non-carbohydrate substances, e.g. amino-acids, into glucose. — *adj* **gluconeogen'ic**. [Gr. *glykys*, sweet, **neo-** and **genesis**.]

glucoprotein. See **glycoprotein**.

glucose *glōō'kōs*, *n* any of several forms of naturally occurring sugar, esp. dextrose; a yellowish syrup containing glucose, produced by the incomplete hydrolysis of starch, used in confectionery, etc. — *adj* **glucos'ic** (*-kos'*). — *n* **glu'coside** any of the vegetable products making up a large group of the glycosides, which, on treatment with acids or alkalis, yield glucose or a similar substance. — *n* **glucosū'ria** sugar in the urine, glycosuria. — *adj* **glucosū'ric**. [Gr. *glykys*, sweet.]

glue *glōō*, *n* an impure gelatine produced by boiling animal products, used as an adhesive; any of several synthetic substances used as adhesives. — *vt* to join with, or as if with, glue or any other adhesive: — *pr p* **glu'ing**; *pa t* and *pa p* **glued**. — *n* **glu'er**. — *adj* **glu'ey** containing glue; sticky; viscous. — *n* **glu'ey-ness**. — **glue ear** a condition of the ear where middle ear fluid fails to drain down the Eustachian tube, collecting instead behind the eardrum and causing deafness, infection and discharge; **glue'-sniffer** a person who inhales the fumes of certain types of glue to achieve hallucinatory effects, etc.; **glue'-sniffing** the practice (sometimes fatal) of doing this. — **marine glue** not a glue, but a composition of rubber, shellac and oil that resists seawater. [Fr. *glu* — L.L. *glus*, *glūtis*.]

glug *glug*, *n* a word representing the sound of liquid being poured from a bottle, down someone's throat, etc. — *vi* to flow making this sound. — *vt* to drink in large draughts: — *pr p* **glugg'ing**; *pa t* and *pa p* **glugged**. [Imit.]

glühwein or **Glühwein** *glü'vīn*, *n* hot, sweetened, spiced red wine; mulled wine as prepared in Germany, Austria, etc. [Ger., — *glühen*, to glow, *Wein*, wine.]

glum *glum*, *adj* sullen; gloomy. — *adv* **glum'ly**. — *n* **glum'ness**. [M.E. *glombe*, *glome*, to frown.]

glume *glōōm*, (*bot*) *n* an outer sterile bract which, alone or with others, encloses the spikelet in grasses and sedges. — *adj* **glumā'ceous** like a glume, in being thin, brownish and papery. [L. *glūma*, husk — *glūbĕre*, to peel.]

gluon *glōō'on*, *n* the name given to a hypothetical particle thought of as passing between quarks and so signifying the force that holds them together. [**glue**.]

glut *glut*, *vt* to gorge; to feed beyond capacity; to saturate; to block or choke up: — *pr p* **glutt'ing**; *pa t* and *pa p* **glutt'ed**. — *n* a glutting; a surfeit; an oversupply. [L. *gluttīre*, to swallow.]

glutamate *glōō'tə-māt*, *n* a salt of glutamic acid.

glutamic acid *glōō-tam'ik as'id*, *n* an important amino-acid, found in many proteins. [**gluten** and **amine**.]

gluten *glōō'tən*, *n* the nitrogenous part of the flour of wheat and other grains, insoluble in water. — *adj* **glu'tenous** containing, made from, etc. gluten. [L. *glūten*, *-inis*, glue.]

gluteus *glōō-tē'əs*, (*anat*) *n* any of three muscles of the buttock and hip: — *pl* **glutē'ī**. — *adj* **glutē'al**. [Gr. *gloutos*, the rump.]

glutinous *glōō'ti-nəs*, *adj* gluey; tenacious, sticky. [L. *glūten*, *glūtinis*, glue.]

glutton[1] *glut'n*, *n* someone who eats to excess; someone who is extremely eager (for something, e.g. hard work). — *vi* **glutt'onise** or **-ize** to eat to excess. — *adj* **glutt'onous** or **glutt'onish** given to, or consisting in, gluttony. — *adv* **glutt'onously**. — *n* **glutt'ony** excess in eating. — **glutton for punishment** a person who seems indefatigable in seeking and performing strenuous or unpleasant work, etc. [Fr. *glouton* — L. *glūtō*, *-ōnis*, glutton, — *glūtīre*, *gluttīre*, to devour.]

glutton[2] *glut'n*, *n* a N. European carnivore (*Gulo gulo*), 60–90cm. (2–3ft.) long, having dark shaggy fur; a related animal (*Gulo luscus*) of N. America, the wolverine. [Trans. of Ger. *Vielfrass*, lit. large feeder.]

glycerine *glis'ə-rēn*, **glycerin** *glis'ə-rin* or **glycerol** *glis'ə-rol*, *n* a trihydric alcohol, a colourless, viscous, neutral inodorous fluid, of a sweet taste, soluble in water and alcohol. — *adj* **glycer'ic**. — *n* **glyc'eride** an ester of glycerol. — *n* **gly'ceryl** a radical of which glycerine is the hydroxide. [Gr. *glykeros*, sweet — *glykys*, sweet.]

glycin *glī'sin*, **glycine** *glī'sin* or *glī'sēn*, or **glycocoll** *glīk'ō-kol*, *n* amino-acetic acid, present in proteins. [Gr. *glykys*, sweet.]

glycogen *glik'ə-jən* or *glī'kə-jən*, *n* animal starch, a starch found in the liver, yielding glycose on hydrolysis. — *n* **glycogen'esis** the synthesis of glycogen; the synthesis of sugar from glycogen. — *adj* **glycogenet'ic**. — *adj* **glycogen'ic**. [Gr. *glykys*, sweet, and the root of *gennaein*, to produce.]

glycol *glik'ol* or *glī'kol*, *n* the type of a class of compounds with two hydroxyl groups on adjacent carbon atoms, and so intermediate between alcohol and glycerine. — *adj* **glycol'ic** or **glycoll'ic**. [From *glyc*erine and alco*hol*.]

glycolysis *glī-kol'i-sis*, *n* the breaking down of glucose into acids, with the release of energy. — *adj* **glycolyt'ic**. [*glyco*se and **-lysis**.]

glycoprotein *glī-kō-prō'tēn* or **glucoprotein** *glōō-kō-*, *n* any of the compounds formed by the conjugation of a protein with a substance containing a carbohydrate group other than a nucleic acid. [Gr. *glykys*, sweet, and **protein**.]

glycose *glī'kōs*, *n* glucose. — *n* **gly'coside** any of a group of compounds derived from monosaccharides, yielding, on hydrolysis, a sugar and usu. a non-carbohydrate. — *adj* **glycosid'ic**. — *n* **glycosū'ria** the presence of sugar in the urine. — *adj* **glycosū'ric**. [Gr. *glykys*, sweet.]

glycosyl *glī'kə-sil*, (*biochem*) *n* a radical derived from glucose. — *vt* **glycos'ylate**. — *n* **glycosylā'tion** the process that attaches sugar to proteins to make glycoproteins.

glyph *glif*, (*archit*) *n* an ornamental channel or fluting, usually vertical; a sculptured mark. — *adj* **glyph'ic** carved. [Gr. *glyphē* — *glyphein*, to carve.]

glyptic *glip'tik*, *adj* pertaining to carving, esp. gem-carving. — *nsing* **glyp'tics** the art of gem-engraving. — *adj* **glyptograph'ic**. — *n* **glyptog'raphy** the art of engraving on precious stones. [Gr. *glyptos*, carved.]

GM *abbrev* for: general manager; General Motors; George Medal.

gm *abbrev* for gram or gramme.

G-man. See under **G** (abbrev.).

GMBATU *abbrev* for General, Municipal, Boilermakers and Allied Trades Union.

Gmbh *abbrev* for *Gesellschaft mit beschränkter Haftung* (Ger.), a limited company.

Gmc *abbrev* for Germanic.

GMC *abbrev* for General Medical Council.

GMT *abbrev* for Greenwich Mean Time.

GMWU *abbrev* for General and Municipal Workers Union.

gnarl *närl*, *n* a lump or knot in a tree. — *adj* **gnarled** or **gnarl'y** knotty; contorted; rugged, weatherbeaten; ill-natured, bad-tempered. [After Shakespeare's *gnarled* for *knurled*, knobby.]

gnash *nash*, *vt* and *vi* to strike (the teeth) together in rage or pain; to bite with a snap or clash of the teeth. — *n* a snap of the teeth. — *n* **gnash'er** someone who, or that which gnashes; (usu. in *pl*) a tooth (*facetious*). — *adv* **gnash'ingly**. [M.E. *gnasten*; ultimately onomatopoeic.]

gnat *nat*, *n* any small fly of the family *Culicidae*, of which the females are commonly bloodsuckers; a mosquito; extended to other small insects. —

gnat'catcher any of the insectivorous American songbirds of the genus *Polioptila*. [O.E. *gnæt*.]

gnathic *nath'ik* or **gnathal** *nath'* or *nā'thəl*, *adj* of, or relating to, the jaws. [Gr. *gnathos*, jaw.]

gnaw *nö*, *vt* and *vi* (with *at*) to bite with a scraping or mumbling movement; to wear away; to bite in agony or rage; to distress persistently: — *pa t* **gnawed**; *pa p* **gnawed** or **gnawn**. [O.E. *gnagan*.]

gneiss *nīs*, *n* coarse-grained foliated metamorphic rock, usually composed of quartz, feldspar and mica. — *adj* **gneiss'ic** of the nature of gneiss. — *adj* **gneiss'oid** like gneiss. — *adj* **gneiss'ose** having the structure of gneiss. [Ger. *Gneis*.]

gnocchi *no'kē* or *nyok'ē*, *n* a dish of small dumplings made from flour, semolina or potatoes, sometimes served with a sauce. [It.]

gnome[1] *nōm*, *n* a sprite guarding the inner parts of the earth and its treasures; a dwarf or goblin; a statue of a gnome, esp. in a garden as an ornament; an obscure but powerful international financier or banker (*facetious*). — *adj* **gnōm'ish**. — **the gnomes of Europe** or **Zürich**, etc., the big bankers. [N.L. *gnomus*, dwarf, pigmy, coined by Paracelsus, 16th-cent. scientist.]

gnome[2] *nōm* or *nō'mē*, *n* a pithy and sententious saying, generally in verse, embodying some moral sentiment or precept: — *pl* **gnomes** (*nōmz* or *nō'mēz*) or **gnomae** (*nō'mē*). — *adj* **gnō'mic** relating to or characterised by gnomes; (of writers) expressing themselves in gnomes. — *n* **gnō'mist** a writer of gnomes. [Gr. *gnōmē*, an opinion, maxim.]

gnomon *nō'mon*, *n* the pin of a dial, whose shadow points to the hour; an upright rod for taking the sun's altitude by its shadow; an index or indicator; that which remains of a parallelogram when a similar parallelogram within one of its angles is taken away (*geom*). — *adj* **gnomon'ic** or **gnomon'ical** pertaining to a gnomon or to the art of gnomonics. — *adv* **gnomon'ically**. — *nsing* **gnomon'ics** the art of measuring time by the sundial. [Gr. *gnōmōn*, a gnomon, a carpenter's square — *gnōnai* (aorist), to know.]

gnosis *nō'sis*, *n* knowledge, esp. spiritual: — *pl* **gnō'sēs**. — *combining form* **-gnō'sis** (*-nō'sis* or *-gnō'sis*) used to denote knowledge, recognition: — *pl* **-gnō'sēs**. — *adj* and *adv combining forms* **-gnos'tic** and **-gnos'tically**. — *n* **gnōseol'ogy** or **gnōsiol'ogy** the philosophy of knowledge. — *adj* **gnostic** (*nos'tik*) having knowledge; (with *cap*) pertaining to Gnosticism. — *n* (with *cap*) an adherent of Gnosticism. — *adj* **gnos'tical**. — *adv* **gnos'tically**. — *n* **Gnos'ticism** the eclectic doctrines of the Gnostics, whose philosophy, esp. in early Christian times, taught the redemption of the spirit from matter by spiritual knowledge, and believed creation to be a process of emanation from the original essence or Godhead. [Gr. *gnōsis*, knowledge, adj. *gnōstikos* — *gignōskein*, to know.]

GNP *abbrev* for gross national product.

gnu *nōō* or *nū*, *n* a large African antelope, superficially like a horse or buffalo: — *pl* **gnu** or **gnus**. — Also called **wildebeest**. [From Hottentot.]

go[1] *gō*, *vi* to pass from one place to another; to be in motion; (of a path, etc.) to lead or give access (to); to proceed; to run (in words or notes); to depart; to work, to be in operation; (of e.g. a bell or gun) to sound; to take a direction; to extend; (with *to*) to attend habitually (school, church, etc.); (of a rumour, etc.) to be current; to be valid, hold true; to be reckoned, to be regarded (as); to be known (*by* or *under* a name); to be on the whole or ordinarily; to tend, serve as a means; to be or continue in a particular state; to elapse; to be sold; to be spent, consumed; to move or act in a way shown or specified; to be assigned or awarded (to); (of colours, shapes, etc.) to harmonise; to die; (with *by*, *on* or *upon*) to be directed by, to act according to; (with *to*) to subject oneself (to expense, trouble, etc.); to become, or become as if; to be considered generally as a concept; to be compared or ranked with others; to change to a new system, e.g. *go decimal*, *go metric*; to happen in a particular way; to be accepted as ultimately authoritative; to turn out; to fare; to contribute (to or towards a whole, purpose or result); to be contained; to be able to pass; to be finished or done away with; to give way; (with an infinitive without *to*) to move off with the intention of doing something, as in *go see* (*NAm*; see also **go and** below). — *vt* to stake, bet; to call, bid or declare (*cards*); (used when reporting speech; *dialect*) to say: — *pr p* **gō'ing**, *pa p* **gone** (*gon*) (see separate article for *adj* senses); *pa t* **went** (supplied from **wend**); *3rd pers sing present indicative* **goes**. — *n* a going; energy, activity (*colloq*); a bargain, deal (*colloq*); a spell, turn or bout (*colloq*); a portion supplied at one time (*colloq*); an attempt (*colloq*): — *pl* **goes**. — *interj* (called to start race, etc.) begin! — *n* (*colloq*) **gō'er** a lively, energetic person; a sexually promiscuous person, esp. a woman; used in combination, denoting a person who regularly goes to or attends a particular place, institution, etc., as in *cinema-goer*. — *n* and *adj* **gō'ing** see separate article. — *adj* **go'-ahead** dashing, energetic; enterprisingly progressive. — *n* permission to proceed. — *adj* **go-as-you-please'** not limited by rules; informal. — **go'-between** an intermediary; **go'-by** any intentional disregard, as in *give (someone) the go-by*; **go'-cart** same as **go-kart**; **go'-getter** (*colloq*) a forceful aggressive person who sets about getting what he or she wants. — *adj* **go'-getting** forcefully ambitious. — **go'-kart** a low racing vehicle consisting of a frame with wheels, engine, and steering gear (often simply **kart**). — **all systems go** everything in the spacecraft is operating as it should; everything is in readiness; **at one go** in a single attempt or effort, simultaneously; **from the word go** from the very beginning; **give it a go** (*colloq*) to try, make an attempt at something; **go about** to pass from place to place; to busy oneself with; to seek, endeavour to do something (with gerund); (of a rumour, etc.) to circulate; (of a ship) to change course; **go about one's business** to attend to one's own affairs; to leave or depart; **go abroad** to go to a foreign country or (*old-fashioned*) out of doors; (of a rumour, etc.) to circulate; **go against** to turn out unfavourably for; to be repugnant to; to be in conflict with; **go ahead** to proceed at once; **go along with** to agree with, support; **go and** to be so stupid or unfortunate as to (e.g. hurt oneself) (*colloq*); to go in order to (do something), as in *go and see*; **go at** to attack vigorously; **go back on** to betray, fail to keep (a promise, etc.); **go bail** to give security (for); **go down** to sink, decline; to deteriorate; to be swallowed, believed or accepted; (of a computer or other electronic system) to break down; to fail to fulfil one's contract (*bridge*); to leave a university; to happen (*US slang*); **go down on** (*vulg*) to perform fellatio or cunnilingus on; **go down the drain** (*colloq*) to be wasted; to become valueless; **go down with** (*colloq*) to contract (an illness); **go far** to go a long way; to achieve success; **go for** to assail; to set out to secure; to go to get or fetch; to be attracted by (*colloq*); to be true of; **go for nothing** to have no value; **go halves** to share (the substance or the expense of something) equally between two; **go hard (with)** to prove difficult or unfortunate (for); **go in** to enter; (of the sun or moon) to become concealed behind cloud; to take the batting (*cricket*); **go in and out** to come and go freely; **go in for** to make a practice of; to take up as a career or special interest; to take part in (a competition, etc.); **go into** to enter; to examine thoroughly, investigate; to adopt as a profession, etc.; **go in with** to enter into partnership with; to join, combine with; **go it** to act in a striking or dashing manner — often in *imper* by way of encouragement; **go it alone** to undertake a usu. difficult or dangerous task alone; to manage by oneself; **go live** (*līv*) (*colloq*) of a radio station, automation equipment, etc., to go into operation; **go native** to assimilate oneself to an alien culture or to the way of life of a foreign country (usu. considered less advanced than one's own); **go off** to leave; to explode; to deteriorate; (of food) to become rotten and inedible; to proceed to an expected conclusion; to cease to like or be fond of (a person, etc.) (*colloq*); to cease to operate; **go off with** to go away with; to remove, take away (*colloq*); **go on** to continue, to proceed; an exclamation expressing disbelief (*colloq*); to behave, conduct oneself (*colloq*); to talk at length (*colloq*); to be capable of being fitted on to; to appear on stage; to fare; to begin to function; to proceed from (as in *nothing to go on*); **go one better** to excel; to cap a performance; **go one's own way** to act independently; **go one's way** to depart; **go out** to become extinguished; to become unfashionable; to mingle in society (*old-fashioned*); **go over** to pass in review; to recall; to revise; **go over to** to transfer allegiance to; **go places** to travel widely; to go far in personal advancement; **go round** to be enough for all; **go slow** (of workers) deliberately to restrict output or effort in order to obtain concessions from employers (*adj* and *n* **go-slow'**); **go steady** to court romantically (with *with*); **go through** to perform to the end, often perfunctorily; to examine in order; to undergo; **go through fire and water** to undertake any trouble or risks (from the usage in ancient ordeals); **go through with** to carry out; **go under** to become submerged, overwhelmed or ruined; **go up** to ascend; to be erected; to be destroyed by fire or explosion; (of costs, prices, etc.) to increase; to enter a university; **go with** to accompany; to agree with, accord with; to court romantically; **go without** to suffer the want of; **go without saying** to be self-evident; **have a go** (*colloq*) to make an attempt; **have a go at** (*colloq*) to criticise severely; to attack physically; to tease or pick on; **have something going for one** (*colloq*) to enjoy the advantage of something; **I could go** (*colloq*) I could do with, I wouldn't mind (a drink, rest, etc.); **no go** not possible; futile; in vain; **no-go area** a part of a city, etc. to which normal access is prevented by the erection of barricades, esp. by local militants, a paramilitary group, etc.; **on the go** very active; **to be going on with** (*colloq*) for the moment, in the meantime. [O.E. *gān*, to go.]

go[2] *gō*, *n* a Japanese game for two, played with black and white stones (or counters) on a board, the object being to capture one's opponent's stones and be in control of the larger part of the board. [Jap.]

goa *gō'ə*, *n* a grey-brown gazelle of Tibet, with backward-curving horns. [Tibetan *dgoba*.]

goad *gōd*, *n* a sharp-pointed stick, often tipped with iron, for driving oxen; a stimulus. — *vt* to drive with a goad; to urge forward; to incite; to provoke (with *into*). [O.E. *gād*.]

goal *gōl*, *n* the structure or station into which the ball is driven in some games; the sending of the ball between the goalposts or over the crossbar in some games; a score for doing so; an end or aim; the finishing point of a race; the winning-post or a similar marker; a pillar marking the turning-point in a Roman chariot race. — *adj* **goal'less** with no goals scored; without goals in life, unambitious. — **goal'-keeper** a player charged with defence of the goal; **goal kick** (*soccer*) a free kick awarded to a defending player when an opponent has sent the ball over the goal line but not between the posts; **goal'kicker** a player who kicks a goal, or takes a goal kick; **goal'kicking; goal line** the boundary marking each end of the field, on which the goals are situated; **goal'mouth** the space between the goalposts and immediately in front of the goal; **goal'post** one of the upright posts at the goal; **goal'-tender** (in ice hockey) a goalkeeper; **goal'-tending.** — **change, move** or **shift the goalposts** to alter the rules of a game, conditions of an agreement, etc. after proceedings have begun, or the agreement has been entered into; **own goal** a goal scored against one's own side by a player from one's own team; any self-inflicted disadvantage.

goalie *gō'li*, (*colloq*) *n* a goalkeeper.

goanna *gō-an'ə*, *n* in Australia, any large monitor lizard. [**iguana.**]

goat *gōt*, *n* a horned ruminant of Europe, Asia and N. Africa, allied to the sheep; a lecher; a foolish person; (in *pl*) the wicked (*Bible*); (with *cap*) the zodiacal sign or the constellation Capricorn. — *adj* **goat'ish** resembling a goat, esp. in smell; lustful; foolish. — *n* **goat'ishness.** — *n* **goat'ling** a young goat in its second year. — *adj* **goat'y.** — **goat fig** the wild fig; **goat'fish** (*NAm*) the red mullet; **goat'herd** someone who tends goats; **goat's'-beard** a composite plant of the genus *Tragopogon*, which closes early in the day, also called *John-go-to-bed-at-noon*; a herbaceous perennial of the genus *Aruncus*; **goat'skin** the skin of the goat; leather, or a container for wine, made from it; **goat'sucker** the nightjar, a bird similar to the swift, falsely thought to suck goats. — **get someone's goat** to enrage someone. [O.E. *gāt*.]

goatee *gō-tē'*, *n* a tuft on the chin, resembling a goat's beard. — *adj* **goateed'**. [**goat** and sfx. *-ee*.]

gob *gob*, *n* the mouth (*slang*); a mouthful, lump; spittle (*slang*). — *vi* (*slang*) to spit. — *adj* **gob'smacked** (*slang*) shocked; taken aback; astounded. — **gob'-stopper** a very large hard round sweet for prolonged sucking. [O.Fr. *gobe*, mouthful, lump; cf. Gael. *gob*, mouth.]

gobang *gō-bang'*, *n* a game played on a board of 256 squares, with fifty counters, the object being to get five in a row. [Jap. *goban*.]

gobbet *gob'it*, *n* a mouthful; a lump to be swallowed; an extract, esp. for translation or comment. [O.Fr. *gobet*, dimin. of *gobe*, mouthful.]

gobble *gob'l*, *vt* to swallow in lumps; to swallow hastily (often with *up*). — *vi* to eat greedily; (of a turkey) to make a noise in the throat. — *n* **gobb'ler** a turkey cock. [O.Fr. *gober*, to devour.]

gobbledegook or **gobbledygook** *gob'əl-di-go͞ok*, *n* unintelligible official jargon; rubbish, nonsense. [Imit.]

gobbo *gob'bō*, (It.) *n* a hunchback; a hunchbacked figure: — *pl* **gob'bi** (*-bē*).

Gobelin *gō'bə-lin*, *gob'ə-* or *go-blɛ̃*, or **Gobelins** (also *-linz*) *n* a rich French pictorial tapestry. — Also *adj.* [From the *Gobelins*, a famous family of French dyers.]

gobioid. See **goby**.

goblet *gob'lit*, *n* a large drinking-cup, properly one without a handle. [O.Fr. *gobelet*, dimin. of *gobel*.]

goblin *gob'lin*, *n* an unpleasant sprite; a bogy. [O.Fr. *gobelin* — L.L. *gobelīnus*, perh. — *cobālus* — Gr. *kobālos*, a mischievous spirit.]

gobo *gō'bō*, (chiefly *US*) *n* a device used to protect a camera lens from light; a device for preventing unwanted sound from reaching a microphone: — *pl* **gō'boes** or **gō'bos**.

goby *gō'bi*, *n* any fish of the family **Gobī'idae**, small fishes with ventral fins forming a sucker. — *adj* **gō'bioid**. [L. *gōbius* — Gr. *kōbios*, a fish of the gudgeon kind.]

GOC *abbrev* for General Officer Commanding.

god *god*, *n* a superhuman being, an object of worship (*fem* **godd'ess**); (with *cap*) the Supreme Being of monotheist religions, the Creator; an idol (*fem* **godd'ess**); an object of excessive devotion (*fem* **godd'ess**); a man of outstandingly fine physique; an extremely influential or greatly admired man (*fem*

godd'ess); (in *pl*) the gallery (*theat*). — *n* **god'head** the state of being a god; divine nature; (with *cap* and **the**) God. — *n* **god'hood** the position or state of being divine. — *adj* **god'less** without a god; living without God. — *adv* **god'lessly.** — *n* **god'lessness.** — *adj* **god'like.** — *n* **god'liness.** — *adj* **god'ly** like God in character; pious; according to God's laws. — *adj* and *adv* **god'ward** towards God. — *adv* **god'-wards.** — *adj* **god-aw'ful** (*colloq*) very bad; unpleasant, distasteful. — **god'child** a person to whom one is a godparent. — *adj* **godd'am, godd'-amn** or **god'damned** (*colloq*) damned, accursed, hateful; utter, out-and-out. — Also *adv*. — **god'-daughter** a female godchild; **god'father** a male godparent; the head of a criminal organisation, esp. the Mafia (*colloq*). — *adj* **God'-fearing** reverencing God. — *adj* **god'forsaken** or **god'forgotten** (or with *cap*) remote, miserable, behind the times. — *adj* **God'-gifted** or **God'-given.** — **god'mother** a female godparent; **god'parent** a person who, at a baptism, guarantees a child's religious education or who (*loosely*) undertakes to bring up the child in the event of the death of its parents; **god'send** a very welcome piece of good fortune; **God slot** (*colloq*) a regular spot during the week's, day's, etc. broadcasting reserved for religious exhortation, exposition or discussion; **god'son** a male godchild; **god'speed** (also with *cap*) a wish for good fortune, expressed at parting; **God's truth** the absolute truth, used as an emphatic asseveration. — **for God's sake** an expression of urgent entreaty; (as *interj*) expressing e.g. annoyance, disgust; **God knows** God is my, his, etc. witness that; it is beyond human understanding (*flippantly*); **God's own country** a particularly well-favoured (esp. scenically beautiful) region; **God willing** if circumstances permit; **household gods** (among the Romans) the special gods presiding over the family. [O.E. *god*.]

Gödel's theorem *gø'dəlz thē'ə-rəm*, *n* the theorem first demonstrated by Kurt *Gödel*, Austrian mathematician, in 1931, that in logic and mathematics there must be true statements that cannot be proved or disproved within the system, also that there can be no proof of the consistency of such a system from within itself.

godetia *gō-dē'sh(y)ə* or *gə-*, *n* a plant of an American genus (*Godetia*) closely related to the evening primrose. [C.H. *Godet*, Swiss botanist.]

godown *gō-down'*, *n* a warehouse or storeroom in Eastern countries. [Malay *gudang*.]

godroon. See **gadroon**.

godwit *god'wit*, *n* a bird of the plover family, with a long slightly up-curved bill and long slender legs, with a great part of the tibia bare.

goer, goes, etc. See **go**[1].

gofer *gō'fər*, (*NAm slang*) *n* a junior office worker who is given errands to run by other members of staff. [Alteration of **go for**.]

goffer *gof'ər* or *gō'fər*, *vt* to plait or crimp. — *n* **goff'ering** plaits or ruffles, or the process of making them; indented tooling on the edge of a book. [O.Fr. *gauffrer* — *goffre*, a wafer.]

goggle *gog'l*, *vi* to strain or roll the eyes; to stare wide-eyed, in amazement, etc.; (of the eyes) to protrude. — *vt* to turn about (the eyes). — *adj* (of the eyes) rolling; staring; prominent. — *n* a stare or affected rolling of the eyes; (in *pl*) spectacles with projecting eye tubes; (in *pl*) protective spectacles. — *adj* **gogg'led** wearing goggles. — *n* **gogg'ler** a person with goggle eyes (*colloq*); an assiduous television-viewer (*colloq*). — *n* **gogg'ling.** — Also *adj*. — *adj* **gogg'ly.** — **gogg'le-box** (*colloq*) a television set. — *adj* **gogg'le-eyed** having bulging, staring or rolling eyes. — Also *adv*.

go-go *gō'-gō*, used loosely as *adj* active, alert to seize opportunities. — **go-go dancer** or **girl** a girl, usu. scantily dressed, employed to dance (usu. erotically) to a musical accompaniment in nightclubs or discothèques. [Fr. *à gogo*, galore.]

Goidelic *goi-del'ik*, *adj* relating to the Gadhelic peoples or their language-group. — *n* the Gadhelic language-group. [O.Ir. *Góidel*, Gael.]

going[1] *gō'ing*, *n* the act of moving; departure; condition of the ground for e.g. walking, racing; progress. — *adj* in motion or activity; about, to be had; in existence; current. — **going concern** a business in actual activity (esp. successfully); **going-o'ver** a thorough check, examination; a complete treatment; a beating; **goings-on'** behaviour, activities, esp. if open to censure. — **be hard, heavy, tough,** etc. **going** to prove difficult to do, etc.; **going-away dress** that worn by a bride when leaving for the honeymoon. [**go**[1].]

going[2] *gō'ing*, *pr p* of **go**[1], in any sense; about or intending (to). — **-gōing** (used in combination) meaning regularly attending, as in *the cinema-going public*. — **going on (for)** approaching (an age or time); **going strong** in full activity, flourishing.

goitre *goi'tər*, *n* enlargement of the thyroid gland, producing a swelling at the front of the throat, sometimes accompanied by exophthalmus. — *adj* **goi'tred.** — *adj* **goi'trous.** [Fr. *goître* — L. *guttur*, the throat.]

go-kart. See under **go**[1].

gold *gōld*, *n* a heavy yellow element (symbol **Au**; atomic no. 79), one of the precious metals, used for coin, etc.; articles made of it; money in the form of gold coins; a standard of money value which varies with the price of the metal; the gold standard; riches; anything very precious or noble; the centre of an archery target; a gold medal; yellow, the colour of gold. — *adj* made of or like gold; golden in colour. — *adj* **gold'en** of gold; of the colour of gold; bright, shining like gold; most valuable; happy; most favourable; of outstanding excellence. — *adv* **gold'enly.** — *adj* **gold'less.** — *adj* **gold'y** somewhat like gold. — **gold'-beater** a person whose trade is to beat gold into gold leaf; **gold-beater's skin** the outer coat of the caecum of an ox, used for separating sheets of gold being beaten into gold leaf; **gold'-beating; gold brick** a block of gold or (orig. *US slang*) of pretended gold, hence a sham or swindle; a person who shirks duties or responsibilities. — Also *vt* **gold-brick'.** — **gold'crest** a golden-crested bird of the genus *Regulus* (also **golden-crested wren**); **gold'-digger** a person who digs for gold; a person who treats an intimate relationship chiefly as a source of material gain; **gold'-digging; gold disc** a long-playing gramophone record that has sold 250 000 copies (500 000 in the U.S.) or a single that has sold 500 000 (one million in the U.S.); **gold dust** gold in fine particles, as found in some rivers; **golden age** an imaginary past time of innocence and happiness; any time of highest achievement; **golden boy** or **girl** a young man or woman of outstanding talents, good looks, etc. likely to win renown; **Golden Delicious** a kind of sweet eating-apple; **golden eagle** a large eagle found in mountainous regions in Northern countries, so called from a slight golden gleam about the head and neck; **golden fleece** (*Gr mythol*) the fleece of the ram Chrysomallus, the recovery of which was the object of the famous expedition of the Argonauts; **golden goose** the fabled layer of golden eggs, killed by its over-greedy owner; a source of profit (also **the goose that lays the golden eggs**); **golden handshake** (*colloq*) a large sum given to an employee on retirement or as compensation for dismissal; **golden hello** (*colloq*) a large sum given to a new employee as an inducement to join a firm; **golden jubilee** a fiftieth anniversary; **golden mean** the middle way between extremes; moderation; **golden oldie** (*colloq*) a song, recording, motion picture, etc. issued some considerable time ago and still popular;

golden opportunity a very favourable one; **golden parachute** (*colloq*) an unusually lavish cash payment to a senior member of a firm on his or her dismissal; **golden pheasant** a golden-crested Chinese pheasant; **golden plover** a plover with yellow-speckled feathers; **gold'enrod** any plant of the composite genus *Solidago*, with rodlike stems and yellow heads crowded along the branches; **golden rule** the precept that one should do as one would be done by; a rule of the first importance, a guiding principle; **golden section** division of a line so that one segment is to the other as that to the whole; **golden share** a large share in a company etc., held by an institution or (often) a government, which prevents take-over by another company; **golden wattle** any of various kinds of yellow-flowered Australian acacia, esp. *Acacia pycnantha*; **gold-exchange standard** a monetary system by which a country whose government is not on the gold standard is linked in its exchange rate to another's which is; **gold fever** a mania for seeking gold; **gold'field** a gold-producing region; **gold'finch** a European finch of the genus *Carduelis*, black, red, yellow and white, fond of eating thistle seeds; any of several American finches of the genus *Spinus*, the male being yellow with black wings, tail and crown; **gold'fish** a Chinese and Japanese freshwater fish closely allied to the carp, golden or (*silverfish*) pale in its domesticated state, brownish when wild; **goldfish bowl** a glass aquarium for goldfish; a situation entirely lacking in privacy; **gold foil** gold beaten into thin sheets, but not as thin as gold leaf; **gold'ilocks** a golden-haired person; **gold lace** lace made from gold thread. — *adj* **gold'-laced.** — **gold leaf** gold beaten extremely thin; **gold medal** (in athletics competitions, etc.) the medal awarded as first prize; **gold'mine** a mine producing gold; a source of great profit; **gold'miner; gold plate** vessels and utensils of gold collectively; metal, esp. silver, plated with gold. — *vt* **gold-plate'** to coat (another metal) with gold (also *fig*). — **gold point** in international transactions, an exchange rate at which it is advisable to export (**gold export point**) or import (**gold import point**) gold bullion rather than settle by bills of exchange (*finance*); **gold record** a gold disc (q.v. above); **gold reserve** the gold held by a central bank, etc., to cover and support all its dealings; **gold rush** a rush of prospectors to a new goldfield; **gold'smith** a worker in gold and silver; **goldsmith beetle** a beetle with wing-covers of a gold colour; **gold'smithry** or **-smithery; gold standard** a monetary standard or system according to which the unit of currency has a precise value in gold; **gold'stone** see **aventurine; gold thread** gold wire used in weaving; silk wound with gilded wire; **gold'washer** someone who obtains gold from sand and gravel by washing; a cradle or other implement for washing gold; **gold wasp** any wasp of the family *Chrysididae*, with brilliant metallic colouring and telescopic abdomen, whose larvae feed on those of wasps and bees — cuckoo-fly, ruby-tail or ruby-wasp; **gold wire** wire made of or covered with gold. — **as good as gold** behaving in an exemplary manner (usu. of children). [O.E. *gold*.]

goldarn *gol'därn*, (*NAm slang*) *adj* and *adv* a euphemistic alteration of **goddamn**.

golf *golf*, *n* a game played with a club or set of clubs over a prepared stretch of land, the aim being to propel a small ball into a series of holes. — *vi* to play golf. — *n* **golf'er.** — *n* **golfiana** (*-i-ä'nə*) a collector's or dealer's term for items of golfing interest. — *n* **golf'ing.** — **golf bag** a bag for carrying golf clubs; **golf ball** a small ball used in golf; in certain typewriters, etc. a small detachable metal sphere or hemisphere with the type characters moulded on to its surface; **golf club** a club used in golf; a golfing society or its premises; **golf course** the ground on which golf is played; **golf links** a golf course, esp. by the sea, typically open and undulating.

Goliath *gə-lī'əth*, *n* a giant; a person or organisation of enormous stature or power. [From *Goliath*, the reputedly invincible Philistine giant killed by David with a stone from a sling, in 1 Samuel xvii.]

golliwog. Same as **gollywog**.

gollop *gol'əp*, *vt* and *vi* to gulp greedily or hastily. [Perh. **gulp**.]

golly[1] *gol'i*, *interj* expressing surprise. [A modification of **God**.]

golly[2] *gol'i*, *n* a short form of **gollywog**.

gollywog or **golliwog** *gol'i-wog*, *n* a fantastical rag doll with black face, staring eyes, and bristling hair; a person who has fuzzy hair or is in some way grotesque. [*Golliwogg*, a doll in certain U.S. children's books, the first of which, by Florence Upton, was published in 1895.]

gompa *gom'pə*, *n* a Buddhist temple or monastery in Tibet. [Tibetan *gömpa*, a place of seclusion, a hermitage.]

gomphosis *gom-fō'sis*, *n* an immovable articulation, as of the teeth in the jaw. [Gr. *gomphōsis* — *gomphos*, a bolt.]

gon *gon*, (*geom*) *n* a grade. [Gr. *gonia*, angle.]

-gon *-gon* or *-gən*, *combining form* used of something having a certain number of angles as in *hexagon*, *polygon*. [Gr. *gōniā*, angle.]

gonad *gon'ad*, (*biol*) *n* an animal organ that produces sex-cells. — *adj* **gonadial** (*-ā'di-əl*) or **gonadic** (*-ad'*). — *adj* **gonadotroph'ic** or **gonadotrop'ic** stimulating the gonads. — *n* **gonadotroph'in** or **gonadotrop'in** a substance that does this, used as a drug to promote fertility. [Gr. *gonē*, generation.]

gondola *gon'də-lə*, *n* a long, narrow boat used chiefly on the canals of Venice; the car suspended from an airship or balloon; a car resembling this suspended from an earth-supported structure, esp. on a ski-lift or aerial tramway, etc.; a (free-standing) shelved unit for displaying goods in a supermarket, etc. — *n* **gondolier** (*-lēr'*) a man who rows a gondola. [Venetian dialect.]

gone *gon*, *adj* in an advanced stage; lost, passed beyond help; departed; dead; weak, faint, feeling a sinking sensation; pregnant (with specified time, e.g. *six months gone*); (of the time) past, as in *gone six*; (of an arrow) wide of the mark; enamoured of (with *on*; *slang*); in an exalted state (*slang*). — *n* **gone'ness** a sinking sensation. — *n* **gon'er** (*slang*) a person or animal dead or ruined beyond recovery; a thing beyond hope of recovery. — **gone under** ruined beyond recovery. [Past p. of **go**[1].]

gonfalon *gon'fə-lon* or **gonfanon** *gon'fə-non*, *n* an ensign or standard with streamers, hung from a horizontal bar, used esp. in certain mediaeval Italian republics. — *n* **gonfalonier** (*-ēr'*) someone who carries a gonfalon. [It. *gonfalone* and O.Fr. *gonfanon* — O.H.G. *gund*, battle, *fano*, a flag.]

gong *gong*, *n* a metal disc, usu. rimmed, that sounds when struck with a drumstick; an instrument of call, esp. to meals; a steel spiral for striking in a clock; a flat bell sounded by a hammer; a medal (*slang*). — *vt* to call by sounding a gong. — **gong stick**. [Malay.]

gonidium *gon-id'i-əm*, *n* an algal cell in a lichen: — *pl* **gonid'ia**. — *adj* **gonid'ial** or **gonid'ic**. [Gr. *gonē*, generation, seed.]

goniometer *gō-ni-om'i-tər*, *n* an instrument for measuring angles, esp. between crystal faces; a direction-finding apparatus, used esp. to trace radio signals. — *adj* **goniometric** (*-ə-met'rik*) or **goniomet'rical** (*-kəl*). — *adv* **goniomet'rically**. — *n* **goniom'etry**. [Gr. *gōniā*, an angle, *metron*, measure.]

gonk® *gongk*, *n* a small cushion-like soft toy, usu. with arms and legs. [Nonsense word.]

gonna *gon'ə*, (esp. *NAm*) a colloq. contraction of **going to**.

gonococcus *gon-ə-kok'əs, n* the bacterium that causes gonorrhoea: — *pl* **gonococci** (*-kok'sī*). — *adj* **gonococc'al** or **gonococcic** (*-kok'sik*). — *adj* **gonococc'oid**. [Gr. *gonos*, seed, *kokkos*, a berry.]

gonocyte *gon'ə-sīt, n* an oocyte or spermatocyte. [Gr. *gonos*, seed.]

gonorrhoea or in N.Am. **gonorrhea** *gon-ə-rē'ə, n* a contagious infection of the mucous membrane of the genital tract. — *adj* **gonorrhoe'al, gonorrhoe'ic** or in N.Am. **gonorrhē'al** or **gonorrhē'ic**. [Gr. *gonorroiā* — *gonos*, seed, *rheein*, to flow, from a mistaken notion of its nature.]

gonzo *gon'zō* or *gon'zö*, (*slang*, esp. *NAm*) *adj* bizarre; weird. [Perh. It. *gonzo*, a simpleton.]

goo *gōō*, (*slang*) *n* a sticky substance; sentimentality. — *adj* **goo'ey**.

goober *gōō'bər, n* a peanut. — Also **goober pea**. [African.]

good *good, adj* (*compar* **bett'er**, *superl* **best**) having suitable or desirable qualities; promoting health, welfare or happiness; virtuous; pious; kind; benevolent; well-behaved; not troublesome; of repute; worthy; commendable; suitable; adequate; thorough; competent; sufficient; valid; sound; serviceable; beneficial; genuine; pleasing; favourable; ample, moderately estimated; considerable, as in *a good deal, a good mind*; able to be counted on; financially or commercially safe or advisable; (from a range) of the better or best quality; (used in patronising address or reference, as in *my good man, your good lady* (i.e. wife). — *n* that which is morally or ethically right; prosperity; welfare; advantage, temporal or spiritual; benefit; avail; virtue; (usu. in *pl*) movable property, chattels, merchandise, freight. — *interj* well; right; be it so. — *adv* well. — *n* **good'iness** weak, priggish or canting goodness. — *adj* **good'ish**. — *n* **good'liness**. — *adj* **good'ly** (*compar* **good'lier**, *superl* **good'liest**) excellent; ample. — *n* **good'ness** virtue; excellence; benevolence; substituted for God in certain expressions, as *for goodness sake*, and as *interj*. — *n* **good'y** (usu. in *pl*) a delicacy; (usu. in *pl*) something pleasant or desirable (usu. *facetious*); the hero of a book, motion picture, etc. (*colloq*); a goody-goody. — *interj* expressing pleasure. — *adj* goody-goody. — *n* and *interj* **good afternoon** a salutation on meeting or parting in the afternoon. — *n* or *interj* **goodbye'** farewell, a form of address at parting (formed from *God be with you*). — *n* or *interj* **good day** a traditional salutation at meeting or parting, now rather *formal* or *archaic*, but in Australia a common greeting; **good evening** a salutation on meeting or parting in the evening. — *adj* **good'-for-nothing** worthless, useless. — *n* an idle or worthless person. — **Good Friday** see **Friday**. — *interj* **good grief!** an exclamation of surprise, dismay or exasperation. — *interj* **good heavens!** an exclamation of surprise. — **good humour** cheerful, tolerant mood or disposition. — *adj* **good-hu'moured**. — *adv* **good-hu'mouredly**. — **good-hu'mouredness**. — *adj* **good-look'ing** handsome, attractive. — **good-look'er** (*colloq*); **good looks** attractive appearance. — *n* and *interj* **good morning** a salutation at meeting or parting early in the day. — **good nature** natural goodness and mildness of disposition. — *adj* **good-na'tured**. — *adv* **good-na'turedly**. — **good-na'turedness**. — *n* and *interj* **goodnight'** a common salutation on parting at night or well on in the day. — *interj* **good'-o** or **good'-oh** expressing pleasure. — *adv* (*Austr*) well; thoroughly. — **good offices** mediation; instrumentality; **good sailor** a person who tends not to suffer from seasickness; **goods engine** an engine used for drawing goods trains; **good sense** sound judgment. — *adj* **good'-sized** (fairly) large. — **goods train** a train of goods wagons. — *adj* **good-tem'pered** of a kindly disposition; not easily made angry. — *adj* **good'time** pleasure-seeking. — **good turn** something done for someone in a kind and helpful spirit or manner; **goodwill'** benevolence; well-wishing; the established custom or popularity of any business or trade — often appearing as one of its assets, with a marketable money value. — *adj* **good'will** well-wishing; expressive of goodwill. — **good works** acts of charity. — *adj* **good'y-goody** mawkishly good; weakly benevolent or pious. — Also *n*. — **as good as** the same as, no less than; virtually; **be as good as one's word** to fulfil one's promise; **for good** or **for good and all** permanently; irrevocably; **good and** (*colloq*) very; **goodies and baddies** characters in a drama regarded respectively as definitely good and definitely bad; **good for anything** ready for any kind of work; **good for you** *interj* well done, congratulations (*Austr colloq* **good on you**); **in someone's good books** in favour with someone; **make good** to fulfil, perform; to compensate; to come to success, esp. unexpectedly; to do well, redeeming an unpromising start; to repair; to justify; **no good** useless; unavailing; worthless; **not, hardly,** etc. **good enough** not sufficiently good; mean, unfair, very different from what was expected or promised; **stand good** to be lastingly good; to remain; **the Good Book** the Bible; **the goods** (*slang*) the real thing; that which is required, promised, etc.; **to the good** for the best; on the credit or advantage side. [O.E. *gōd*.]

gooey. See **goo**.

goof *gōōf*, (*colloq*) *n* a stupid or awkward person; a blunder. — *vi* to make a blunder; to mess (about or around); to waste time, behave idly, etc. (*NAm*; with *off*). — *vt* to make a mess of (often with *up*). — *adv* **goof'ily**. — *n* **goof'iness**. — *adj* **goof'y** foolish or stupid; (of teeth) protruding. — **goof'ball** (*slang*) a barbiturate sleeping pill; a goofy person. [Perh. Fr. *goffe*.]

googly *gōōg'li*, (*cricket*) *n* an off-breaking ball with an apparent leg-break action on the part of a right-arm bowler to a right-handed batsman, or conversely for a left-arm bowler. — Also *adj*. — *vi* **goog'le** to behave or bowl in such a manner.

gook *gōōk*, (*offensive slang*) *n* a person of Asiatic race, esp. a Japanese, Korean or Vietnamese soldier.

gooly, gooley or **goolie** *gōō'li, n* (usu. in *pl*) testicles (*humorous*); a small stone (*Austr colloq*). [Perh. Hind. *goli*, a bullet, ball.]

goon *gōōn, n* a hired thug (*NAm slang*); a stupid person. [After 'Alice the *Goon*', a character created by American cartoonist E.C. Segar (1894–1938).]

goonda *gōōn'da* or *gōōn'də, n* (in India and Pakistan) a hired thug esp. one in the pay of a political party. [Hindi *goonda*, a scoundrel.]

gooneybird *gōō'nē-bûrd, n* an (esp. black-footed) albatross. [Prob. dialect, simpleton — obs. *gony*.]

goop *gōōp, n* a fool; a fatuous person; a rude, ill-mannered person (*NAm*). — *adj* **goop'y**. [Cf. **goof**.]

goosander *gōōs-an'dər, n* a large duck of the merganser genus. [Perh. **goose**, and O.N. *önd*, pl. *ander*, duck.]

goose *gōōs, n* any one of a group of birds of the duck family, intermediate between ducks and swans; a domesticated member of the group, descended mainly from the greylag; the female of such a bird (*masc* **gan'der**); a tailor's smoothing-iron, from the likeness of the handle to the neck of a goose; a stupid, silly person: — *pl* **geese** (*gēs*), or, of a tailor's goose, **goos'es**. — *vt* (*slang*) to hiss off the stage; to grab the buttocks of; to goad into action. — *n* **goos'ery** a place for keeping geese; stupidity. — *n* **goos'ey** or **goos'y** a goose; a blockhead. — *adj* like a goose; affected with gooseflesh. — **goose'flesh** a condition of the skin, like that of a plucked goose or other fowl; the bristling feeling in the skin due to erection of hairs through cold, horror, etc.; **goose'foot** any plant of the genus *Chenopodium* of the beet family, from the shape of the leaf; also applied to any member of the family *Chenopodiaceae*: — *pl* **goose'foots; goosegog** and **goosegob** see under **gooseberry; goose'grass** cleavers; silverweed; **goose'herd** a person who herds geese; **goose'neck** a hook, bracket, pipe, etc., bent like a goose's neck; **goose pimples** gooseflesh; **goose quill** one of the quills or large wing feathers of a goose, esp. one formerly used as a pen; **goose skin** gooseflesh, horripilation; **goose step** (*mil*) a method of marching (resembling a goose's walk) with knees stiff and soles brought flat on the ground. — Also *vi*. [O.E. *gōs* (pl. *gēs*).]

gooseberry *go͞oz'bə-ri* or *go͞os'-*, *n* the fruit of the **gooseberry bush**, a prickly shrub of the saxifrage family. — *n* **goose'gog** or **goose'gob** (*colloq* and *dialect*) a gooseberry. — **Chinese gooseberry** a subtropical vine with brown, hairy, edible fruit. [Perh. **goose** and **berry**[1].]

gopak *gō'pak*, *n* a high-leaping folk-dance from the Ukraine. [From Russ.]

gopher *gō'fər*, *n* a name in America applied to various burrowing animals incl. the pouched rat, the ground squirrel, the land tortoise of the Southern States, and a burrowing snake. — *vi* to burrow; to mine in a small way. [Perh. Fr. *gaufre*, honeycomb.]

gorblimey or **gorblimy** *gör-blī'mi*, (*Cockney*) *interj* for *God blind me*.

Gordian *gör'di-ən*, *adj* pertaining to *Gordium* the capital, or *Gordius* the king, of ancient Phrygia, or to the intricate knot he tied; intricate; difficult. — **cut the Gordian knot** to overcome a difficulty by violent measures, as Alexander cut the knot with his sword.

Gordon Bennett *gör'dən ben'it*, *interj* expressing mild surprise, annoyance, etc.

Gordon setter *gör'dən set'ər*, *n* an orig. Scottish breed of setter with a black and tan coat. [Alexander *Gordon*, 19th cent. Scottish nobleman.]

gore[1] *gör*, *n* clotted blood; blood. — *adv* **gor'ily**. — *n* **go'riness**. — *adj* **gor'y** like gore; covered with gore; bloody. [O.E. *gor*, filth, dung.]

gore[2] *gör*, *n* a triangular piece of land; a triangular piece let into a garment to widen it; a sector of a curved surface such as a parachute or umbrella. — *vt* to shape like or furnish with gores; to pierce with anything pointed, such as a spear or horns. [O.E. *gāra*, a pointed triangular piece of land, *gār*, a spear.]

gorge *görj*, *n* the throat; a ravine; the entrance to an outwork (*fort*); the contents of the stomach; a gluttonous feed. — *vt* to swallow greedily; to glut. — *vi* to feed gluttonously. — *adj* **gorged** having a gorge or throat; glutted. — **one's gorge rises** one is filled with loathing or revulsion (with *at*). [O.Fr.]

gorgeous *gör'jəs*, *adj* showy; splendid; magnificent; (*loosely*) pleasant, good, beautiful, etc. — *adv* **gor'geously**. — *n* **gor'geousness**. [O.Fr. *gorgias*, gaudy.]

gorget *gör'jət*, *n* a piece of armour for the throat; a wimple; a neck ornament. [O.Fr., — *gorge*, a throat.]

gorgio *gör'jō* or *gör'ji-ō*, *n* a gypsy word for a non-gypsy: — *pl* **gor'gios**. [Romany.]

Gorgon *gör'gən*, *n* one of three female monsters (Stheno, Euryale and Medusa), of horrible and petrifying aspect, winged and with hissing serpents for hair (*Gr mythol*); (usu. without *cap*) anybody, esp. a woman, very ugly or formidable. — Also *adj*. — *vt* **gor'gonise** or **-ize** to turn to stone. [Gr. *Gorgō*, pl. *-ŏnĕs* — *gorgos*, grim.]

Gorgonia *gör-gō'ni-ə*, *n* a genus of sea-fans or horny corals. — *adj* **gorgo'nian**. — *n* a horny coral. [L. *gorgŏnia*, coral — *Gorgō*, Gorgon (from hardening in the air).]

Gorgonzola *gör-gən-zō'lə*, *n* a blue cheese of cow's milk. [*Gorgonzola*, Italian town near Milan.]

gorilla *gə-ril'ə*, *n* a great African ape, the largest anthropoid; a thug (*slang*). — *adj* **gorill'ian** or **gorill'ine**. [Gr. *Gorillai* (pl.), a tribe of hairy women.]

gormandise or **-ize** *gör'mən-dīz*, *vi* to eat hastily or voraciously. — *n* **gor'mandise** (*-dēz*) gluttony; gormandising, a less common form of **gourmandise**. — *n* **gor'mandīser** or **-z-**. — *n* **gor'mandising** or **-z-**. — *n* **gor'mandism** gluttony. [**gourmand**.]

gorse *görs*, *n* any prickly papilionaceous shrub of the genus *Ulex*, with yellow flowers. — *adj* **gors'y**. [O.E. *gorst*.]

gory. See **gore**[1].

gosh *gosh*, (*colloq*) *interj* for **God**.

goshawk *gos'hök*, *n* a short-winged hawk, once used for hunting wild geese and other fowl. [O.E. *gōshafoc* — *gōs*, goose, *hafoc*, hawk.]

gosling *goz'ling*, *n* a young goose. [O.E. *gōs*, goose, double dimin. *-l-ing*.]

gospel *gos'pəl*, *n* the teaching of Christ; a narrative of the life of Christ, esp. one of those included in the New Testament, Matthew, Mark, Luke and John; the principles set forth therein; the stated portion of these read at service; any strongly advocated principle or system; absolute truth (*colloq*); a type of ardently religious jazz music (esp. songs) originating amongst the black population of the southern U.S. — *n* **gos'peller** a preacher; an evangelist; a person who reads the gospel in church. [O.E. *godspel(l)*, — *gōd*, good (understood as *God*, God) and *spel(l)*, story.]

gossamer *gos'ə-mər*, *n* very fine spider-threads that float in the air or form webs on bushes in fine weather; any very thin material. — *adj* light, flimsy. — *adj* **goss'amery** like gossamer; flimsy. [M.E. *gossomer*.]

gossip *gos'ip*, *n* scandalous rumours; tittle-tattle; idle talk; a person who goes about telling and hearing news, or idle, malicious, and scandalous tales; easy familiar writing. — *vi* to run about telling idle or malicious tales; to talk a lot; to chat: — *pa t* **goss'iped**. — *n* and *adj* **goss'iping**. — *adj* **goss'ipy**. — **gossip column** the newspaper column written by a gossip-writer; **gossip columnist; goss'ip-monger** a person who spreads gossip and rumours; **goss'ip-writer** a journalist who writes articles about the lives and loves of well-known people. [O.E. *godsibb*, godparent, later a female friend, orig. one present at a birth.]

got. See under **get**.

Goth *goth*, *n* one of an ancient Germanic nation, originally settled on the southern coasts of the Baltic, and later founding kingdoms in Italy, southern France, and Spain; a rude or uncivilised person, a barbarian. — *adj* **Goth'ic** of the Goths or their language; (also without *cap*) barbarous; romantic; denoting the 12th–16th-cent. style of architecture in churches, etc., with high-pointed arches, clustered columns, etc.; generally, the style, related to this, favoured in all the fine arts during this time; black-letter (*printing*); orig. applied to 18th-cent. tales, novels etc. of mystery with gloomy sinister backgrounds, now denoting psychological horror tales (also **Goth'ick** or **goth'ic**); lurid, extravagantly macabre, grotesque (*slang*). — *n* the language of the Goths, an East Germanic tongue; Gothic architecture (also, when imitated in the 18th and 19th cents., **Goth'ick**). [O.E. *Gotan* (sing. *Gota*).]

Goth. *abbrev* for Gothic.

Gothamite *gō'tə-mīt* or *got'ə-mīt*, *n* a simpleton; (*goth'ə-mīt* or *gō'thə-mīt*) a New Yorker (*US*). [From *Gotham*, a village in Nottinghamshire, with which name are connected many simpleton stories.]

Gothic, Gothick, etc. See **Goth** (noun).

gotta *got'ə*, a colloq. contraction of **got to**.

gotten. See under **get**.

Götterdämmerung *gœ-tər-dem'ə-rōōng*, (*Ger mythol*) *n* lit. the twilight of the gods, the ultimate defeat of the gods by evil.

gouache *gōō-äsh'*, *gōō'ash* or (chiefly *NAm*) *gäsh*, *n* watercolour painting with opaque colours, mixed with water, honey and gum, producing a matt surface; work painted according to this method. [Fr.]

Gouda *gow'də*, *n* a kind of mild cheese from *Gouda* in the Netherlands.

gouge *gowj*, *n* a chisel with a hollow blade for cutting grooves or holes. — *vt* to scoop out, as with a gouge; to force out, as the eye with the thumb. [O.Fr., — L.L. *gubia*, a kind of chisel.]

gougère *gōō-jer'*, *n* a kind of choux pastry, the dough of which has been mixed with grated cheese prior to baking. [Fr.]

goujons *gōō-zhɔ̃*, *npl* small strips of fish or meat coated in flour and deep-fried. [Fr.]

goulash *gōō'lash*, *n* a stew of beef, vegetables, esp. onions, and paprika; a re-deal of cards, so many (as e.g. 5) cards at a time (*bridge*). [Hung. *gulyás* (*hús*) herdsman (meat).]

gourami *gōō'rə-mi* or *-rä'mi*, *n* a large freshwater food-fish of S.E. Asia. [Malay *gurāmī*.]

gourd *gōōrd*, *n* a large hard-rinded fleshy fruit of the cucumber family; the rind of one used as a bottle, cup, etc.; a gourd-bearing plant. [O.Fr. *gourde*, contraction from *cougourde* — L. *cucurbita*, a gourd.]

gourde *gōōrd*, *n* the standard monetary unit of Haiti (100 centimes).

gourmand *gōōr'mənd* or *-mã*, *n* someone who eats greedily; a glutton; a lover of good food. — *adj* voracious; gluttonous. — *n* **gourmandise** (*gōōr-mã-dēz*) indulgence in good eating. — *n* **gour'mandism**. [Fr.]

gourmet *gōōr'mā* or *-me*, *n* a connoisseur of good food and wines. [Fr., a wine-merchant's assistant.]

gout *gowt*, *n* a disease in which excess of uric acid in the blood is deposited as urates in the joints, etc., with swelling esp. of the big toe. — *n* **gout'iness**. — *adj* **gout'y**. [Orig. a drop, spot — O.Fr. *goutte* — L. *gutta*, a drop.]

gov. *abbrev* for governor.

govern *guv'ərn*, *vt* to direct; to control; to rule with authority; to determine; to determine the case of (*gram*); to require as the case of a noun or pronoun (*gram*). — *vi* to exercise authority; to administer the laws. — *adj* **gov'ernable**. — *n* **gov'ernance**. — *n* **gov'erness** a woman entrusted with the care and education of a child or children, esp. one employed in a private household. — *adj* **gov'ernessy** like a governess, esp. prim. — *adj* **gov'erning** having control. — *n* **government** (*guv'ərn-mənt* or *guv'ər-ment*) a ruling or managing; control; system of governing; the body of people authorised to administer the laws, or to govern a state; tenure of office of someone who governs; the power of one word in determining the case of another (*gram*). — *adj* of or pursued by government. — *adj* **governmental** (*-ment'l*) pertaining to government. — *n* **gov'ernor** a real or titular ruler, esp. of a state, province or colony; the head of an institution or a member of its ruling body; (usu. *guv'nər*) a father, chief or master, applied more generally in kindly, usually ironically respectful, address (sometimes shortened to **guv** or **gov** *guv*) (*slang*); a regulator or other contrivance for maintaining uniform velocity with a varying resistance (*mach*). — *n* **gov'ernorship**. — **governor-gen'eral** the representative of the British crown in Commonwealth countries which recognise the monarchy as their head of state; orig. the supreme governor of a country, etc., with deputy governors under him: — *pl* **governors-gen'eral**; **governor-gen'eralship**. [O.Fr. *governer* — L. *gubernāre* — Gr. *kybernaein*, to steer.]

gown *gown*, *n* a loose flowing outer garment; a woman's dress; an academic, clerical or official robe; the members of a university as opposed to the townspeople (see under **town**). — *vt* and *vi* to dress in a gown. — *vt* to invest or furnish with a gown. — *adj* **gowned**. [O.Fr. *goune* — L.L. *gunna*.]

goy *goi*, *n* a non-Jew, a Gentile: — *pl* **goyim** (*goi'im*) or **goys**. — *adj* **goy'ish** or **goyisch** (*goi'ish*). [Heb., (non-Jewish) nation.]

GP *abbrev* for: Gallup Poll; General Practitioner; Grand Prix.

GPI *abbrev* for general paralysis of the insane, same as **general paresis** (see under **paresis**).

GPO *abbrev* for General Post Office.

GR *abbrev* for Greece (I.V.R.).

Gr. *abbrev* for Greek.

gr. *abbrev* for: grain; gram or gramme; gross.

Graafian *grä'fi-ən*, *adj* relating to the Dutch anatomist Regnier de *Graaf* (1641–73) who discovered the **Graafian follicles** in which the ova are contained in the ovary of higher vertebrates.

grab *grab*, *vt* to seize or grasp suddenly; to lay hands on; to impress or interest (*slang*). — *vi* to clutch: — *pr p* **grabb'ing**; *pa t* and *pa p* **grabbed**. — *n* a sudden grasp or clutch; unscrupulous seizure; a mechanical double scoop hinged like a pair of jaws, used in excavating, etc.; anything similar. — *n* **grabb'er** someone who grabs; an avaricious person. — **how does that grab you?** (*slang*) what's your reaction to that?; **up for grabs** (*slang*) (ready) for the taking, for sale, etc. [Cf. Sw. *grabba*, to grasp.]

grace *grās*, *n* easy elegance in form or manner; favour; kindness; the undeserved mercy of God; divine influence; eternal life or salvation; a short prayer of thanks before or after a meal; a ceremonious title in addressing a duke, an archbishop, or formerly a king; a short period of time in hand before a deadline is reached. — *vt* to mark with favour; to adorn. — *adj* **grace'ful** elegant and easy; marked by propriety or fitness, becoming; having or conferring grace, in any sense. — *adv* **grace'fully**. — *n* **grace'fulness**. — *adj* **grace'less**. — *adv* **grace'lessly**. — *n* **grace'lessness**. — *adj* **grace-and-fa'vour** (of a residence) belonging to the British sovereign and granted rent-free to a person of importance (also with *caps*). — **grace note** (*mus*) a note introduced as an embellishment, not being essential to the harmony or melody; **days of grace** days allowed for the payment of a note or bill of exchange after it falls due; **fall from grace** to backslide, to lapse from the state of grace and salvation or from favour; **saving grace** divine grace so bestowed as to lead to salvation; a compensating virtue or quality; **with a good** or **bad, grace** in an amiable (or ungracious) fashion; **year of grace** year of the Christian era, A.D. [Fr. *grâce* — L. *grātia*, favour — *grātus*, agreeable.]

gracious *grā'shəs*, *adj* full of, or characterised by, grace and kindness; affable; of becoming demeanour; used as an epithet of royal acts or inclinations; elegant, tasteful, esp. classically so. — *n* used as a substitute for God. — *adv* **grā'ciously**. — *n* **grā'ciousness**. — **gracious living** (living in) conditions of ease, plenty, and good taste. — **good gracious** or **gracious me** exclamations of surprise. [L. *grātiōsus* — *grātia*, favour.]

grackle *grak'l*, *n* a myna (hill myna) or similar bird; an American 'blackbird' of the family *Icteridae*. [L. *grāculus*, jackdaw.]

grad *grad*, (*colloq*) *n* a graduate.

grade *grād*, *n* a degree or step in quality, rank or dignity; a stage of advancement; rank; a yearly stage in education (*NAm*); a pupil's mark of proficiency (*NAm*); position in a scale; a class, or position in a class, according to value; gradient or slope; a class of animals produced by crossing a breed with one purer. — *vt* to arrange according to grade; to assign a grade to; to adjust the gradients of. — *vi* to change gradually from one grade, level, value, etc. to another. — *adj* of improved stock. — *adj* **grā'dable**. — *vt* and *vi* **gradate** (*grə-dāt'*) to change grade, values, etc. imperceptibly. — *vt* to arrange according to grades. — *n* **gradā'tion** a degree or step; a rising step by step; progress from one degree or state to another; position attained; state of being arranged in ranks; a gradual shift in grade, etc.; ablaut (*philol*). — *adj* **gradā'tional**. — *adv* **gradā'tionally**. — *adj* **gradā'tioned** formed by gradations or stages. — *adj* **gradatory** (*grad'ət-ə-ri*) proceeding step by step; adapted for walking. — *n* **grād'er** someone who or that which grades; a machine used to create a flat surface for road-building. — **grade crossing** (*NAm*) a level crossing; **graded post** (in British schools) a post with some special responsibility, and so extra payment; **grade school** (*NAm*) elementary school, a primary school. — **make the grade** to overcome obstacles; to succeed; to be up to standard. [L. *gradus*, a step — *gradī*, to step.]

gradient *grā'di-ənt* or *grā'-dyənt*, *n* the degree of slope as compared with the horizontal; rate of change in any quantity with distance (e.g. in barometer readings); an incline. — *adj* rising or falling by degrees; sloping uniformly. [L. *gradiens*, *-entis*, pres. p. of *gradī*, to step.]

gradin *grā'din* or **gradine** *grə-dēn'*, *n* a rising tier of seats, as in a theatre; a raised step or ledge behind an altar. [It. *gradino*, dimin. of *grado*, step.]

gradual *grad'ū-əl*, *adj* happening by grades or degrees; (of a slope) gentle and slow. — *n* (in the R.C. church) the portion of the mass between the epistle and the gospel, formerly always sung from the steps of the altar; a book containing the sung parts of the Mass. — *n* **grad'ualism** the principle, policy or phenomenon of proceeding by degrees. — *n* **grad'ūalist**. — *adj* **grad'ūalist** or **gradūalis'tic**. — *n* **gradūal'ity**. — *adv* **grad'ūally**. [Med.L. *graduālis* — L. *gradus*, a step.]

graduate *grad'ū-āt*, *vt* to divide into regular intervals; to mark by degrees; to proportion. — *vi* to pass by grades; to receive a degree from a higher-education institution. — *n* (*grad'ū-ət*) a person who has obtained a degree from a university, college or polytechnic. — *n* **graduand** (*grad'ū-ənd* or *-and*) a person about to receive a degree from a higher-education institution. — *adj* **grad'ūated** (of a thermometer, etc.) marked with degrees. — *n* **gradū-ā'tion** division into proportionate or regular sections, for measurement, etc.; a mark or all the marks made for this purpose; the gaining of a degree from a higher-education institution; the ceremony marking this. [Med.L. *graduāri*, *-ātus*, to take a degree — L. *gradus*, step.]

Graeae or **Graiae** *grī'ī*, (*Gr mythol*) *npl* three sea-goddesses, sisters of the Gorgons, having the form of old women who shared between them a single eye and a single tooth. [Gr. *graia*, old woman.]

Graecise or **-ize** or (esp. in N.Am.) **Grecize** *grē'sīz*, *vt* to make Greek; to hellenise. — *n* **Grae'cism** or (esp. in N.Am.) **Gre'cism** a Greek idiom; the Greek spirit. — *adj* **Graeco-Ro'man** or in N.Am. **Greco-** (*grē-kō-*) of or pertaining to both Greece and Rome, esp. the art of Greece under Roman domination; applied to a mode of wrestling imagined to be that of the Greeks and Romans. [L. *Graecus* — Gr. *Graikos*, Greek; *graikizein*, to speak Greek.]

graffito *grə-fē'tō*, *n* a mural scribbling or drawing, as at Pompeii, Rome, and other ancient cities. — *npl* or (*loosely*) *nsing* **graffi'ti** (*-tē*) scribblings or drawings, often indecent, found on public buildings, in lavatories, etc. — *n* **graffi'tist**. [It., — Gr. *graphein*, to write.]

graft[1] *gräft*, *n* a small piece of a plant or animal inserted in another individual or another part so as to come into organic union; the act of inserting a part in this way; the place of junction of stock and scion (*bot*); the double plant composed of stock and scion. — *vt* to insert a graft in; to insert as a graft. — *vi* to insert grafts. — *n* **graft'er**. — *n* **graft'ing**. [From older *graff* — Gr. *graphion*, a pencil or stylus.]

graft[2] *gräft*, *n* hard work (*colloq*); a criminal's special branch of practice (*slang*); illicit profit by corrupt means, esp. in public life (*slang*); corruption in official life (*slang*). — *vi* to work hard (*colloq*); to engage in graft or corrupt practices (*slang*). — *n* **graft'er**.

Graiae. See **Graeae**.

grail *grāl*, *n* (often **holy grail** or **Holy Grail**) in mediaeval legend, the platter (sometimes supposed to be a cup) used by Christ at the Last Supper, in which Joseph of Arimathaea caught his blood — said to have been brought by Joseph to Glastonbury, and the object of quests by King Arthur's Knights; a cherished ambition or goal. [O.Fr. *graal* or *grael*, a flat dish — L.L. *gradālis*, a flat dish.]

grain *grān*, *n* a single small hard seed; corn, in general; a hard particle; a very small quantity; the smallest British weight (the average weight of a seed of corn) = 1/7000 of a pound avoirdupois; the arrangement, size and direction of the particles, fibres, or plates of stone, wood, etc.; texture; a granular surface; innate quality or character; the particles in a photographic emulsion which go to compose the photograph. — *vt* to form into grains, cause to granulate; to paint in imitation of grain; to dye in grain; (in tanning) to take the hair off. — *n* **grain'age** duties on grain. — *adj* **grained** granulated; subjected to graining; having a grain. — *n* **grain'er** someone who grains; a paint-brush for graining. — *n* **grain'-ing** (*specif*) painting to imitate the grain of wood; a process in tanning in which the grain of the leather is raised. — *adj* **grain'y** having grains or kernels; having large grains, and so indistinct (*phot*). — **grain alcohol** alcohol made by the fermentation of grain; **grain amaranth** see **amarant**. — **against the grain** against the fibre of the wood; against one's natural inclination. [Fr. *grain*, collective *graine* — L. *grānum*, seed and *grāna*, orig. pl.]

gram[1] *gram*, *n* chick-pea; a pulse generally. [Port. *grão* (sometimes *gram*) — L. *grānum*, a grain.]

gram[2] or **gramme** *gram*, *n* a unit of mass in the metric system — a thousandth part of the International Prototype Kilogram (see **kilogram**). — **gram-at'om** or **gram-atomic weight** and **gram-mol'-ecule** or **gram-molecular weight** the quantity of an element whose mass in grams is equal to its atomic weight and molecular weight respectively; **gram-equiv'alent** or **gram-equivalent weight** the quantity of a substance whose mass in grams is equal to its equivalent weight. [Fr. *gramme* — L. *gramma* — Gr. *gramma*, a letter, a small weight.]

-gram *-gram*, *combining form* denoting something written or drawn to form a record. [Gr. *gramma*, letter.]

graminaceous *gram-i-nā'shəs* or **gramineous** *grə-min'i-əs*, *adj* of, or relating to, the grass family; grasslike, grassy. — *adj* **graminiv'orous** feeding on grass or cereals. [L. *grāmen*, *-inis*, grass.]

grammalogue *gram'ə-log*, *n* a word represented by a single sign; a sign for a word in shorthand. [Gr. *gramma*, a letter, *logos*, a word.]

grammar *gram'ər*, *n* the science of language, from the points of view of pronunciation, inflexion, syntax and historic development; the art of the right use of language by grammatical rules; a book that teaches these subjects; any elementary work; a grammar school (*colloq*). — *n* **grammā'rian** a person who has made a study of grammar, a teacher of or writer on grammar. — *adj* **grammat'ical** belonging to, or according to the rules of, grammar. — *adv* **grammat'ically**. — **grammar school** a secondary school in which academic subjects predominate (orig. one in which grammar, esp. Latin grammar, was taught); **grammatical meaning** the functional significance of a word, etc. within the grammatical framework of a particular sentence, etc. [Gr. *gramma*, *-atos*, a letter.]

gramme. See **gram²**.

Grammy *gram'i*, (*US*) *n* an award (corresponding to the cinema Oscar) in the form of a gold-plated disc, awarded by the National Academy of Recording Arts and Sciences. [From *gramophone*.]

Gram-negative *gram-neg'ə-tiv*, *adj* (of bacteria) that lose a stain of methyl violet and iodine on treatment with alcohol. — *adj* **Gram-pos'itive** retaining the stain. [H.J.C. *Gram*, deviser of this microbiological staining method.]

gramophone *gram'ə-fōn*, *n* (with *cap*, ® in U.S.) an instrument (invented by E. Berliner, 1887) for reproducing sounds by means of a needle moving along the grooves of a revolving disc, a record-player; any record-player (now used *facetiously* or *archaically*). — *adj* **gramophonic** (*-fon'ik*). — *adv* **gramophon'ically**. [Improperly formed from Gr. *gramma*, letter, record, *phōnē*, sound.]

Gram-positive. See **Gram-negative**.

grampus *gram'pəs*, *n* Risso's dolphin (*Grampus griseus*); a popular name for many whales, esp. the killer. [O.Fr. *graspeis* — L. *crassus*, fat, *piscis*, fish.]

gran² *gran*, (*colloq*) *n* short for **granny**.

granadilla *gran-ə-dil'ə*, *n* the edible, oblong, fleshy fruit of the tropical American passion-flower; the edible fruit of various other passion-flowers. [Sp.]

granary *gran'ə-ri*, *n* a storehouse for grain or threshed corn; a rich grain-growing region; (**Granary®**) a make of bread with a special nutty flavour, made with malted wheat flour (also *adj*). — *adj* (loosely, of bread) containing whole grains of wheat. [L. *grānārium* — *grānum*, a grain.]

grand¹ *grand*, *adj* exalted; magnificent; dignified; sublime; imposing; would-be-imposing; on a great scale; in complete form; in full proportions; very good (*colloq*); pre-eminent; chief. — *n* a grand piano; a thousand dollars or pounds (*slang*). — *adv* **grand'ly**. — *n* **grand'ness**. — *adj* **grand-dū'cal** relating to a grand duke. — **grand duke** a title of sovereignty over a **grand duchy** orig. created for the rulers of Florence and Tuscany, later assumed by certain German and Russian imperial princes (*fem* **grand duchess**); **grand juror** a member of a **grand jury**, a special U.S. jury which decides whether there is sufficient evidence to put an accused person on trial; **grand'master** (*chess*) the title given to an unusually skilled player, orig. only to the winner of a major international tournament; **grand Mufti** the head of the Muslim community in Jerusalem; the former head of the Turkish state religion; **Grand National** a steeplechase held annually at Aintree in Liverpool; **grand piano** a large, harp-shaped piano with horizontal strings; **grand slam** the winning of every trick at bridge; the winning of all major championships in a season (*sport* e.g. *tennis*, *golf*); **grand'stand** an elevated structure on a race-course, etc. affording a good view; **grandstand finish** a close and exhilarating finish to a sporting contest; a supreme effort to win in the closing stages of such a contest; **grand total** the sum of all subordinate totals. [Fr. *grand* — L. *grandis*, great.]

grand² *grã*, (Fr.) *adj* great. — **grand cru** (*krü*) (of a wine) from a famous vineyard or group of vineyards; **grand mal** (*mal*) a violently convulsive form of epilepsy (see **petit mal**); **grand prix** (*prē*) (with *cap*) any of several international motor races; any competition of similar importance in other sports: — *pl* **grands prix**.

grand- *grand-*, *combining form* (signifying a person) of the second degree of parentage or descent. — *n* **grand'-aunt** a great-aunt. — *n* **grand'child** a son's or daughter's child. — *n* **grand'dad** (*colloq*) old man; a grandfather; (**granddad collar** a round collar, not folded over (orig. intended to take a detachable stud-fastened collar); **granddad shirt** one with such a collar). — *n* **grand'daddy** (*colloq*) a person or thing considered the oldest, biggest, first, etc. of its kind. — *n* **grand'daughter** a son's or daughter's daughter. — *n* **grand'father** a father's or mother's father. — *adj* **grand'fatherly** like a grandfather, kindly. — *n* **grand'mamma** or **grand'ma** (*colloq*) a grandmother. — *n* **grand'mother** a father's or mother's mother. — *n* **grand'-nephew** a great-nephew. — *n* **grand'-niece** a great-niece. — *n* **grand'papa** or **grand'pa** (*colloq*) a grandfather. — *n* **grand'parent** a grandfather or grandmother. — *n* **grand'son** a son's or daughter's son. — *n* **grand'-uncle** a great-uncle. — *n* **grandfather clock** an old-fashioned clock (longcase clock) standing on the ground — larger than a **grandmother clock**. [**grand¹**.]

grande *grãd*, (Fr.) *adj fem* of **grand²**. — **grande dame** (*däm*) a great and aristocratic lady, or a socially important and very dignified one.

grandee *gran-dē'*, *n* (in Spain or Portugal) a noble of the highest rank; a man of high rank or station. — *n* **grandee'ship**. [Sp. *grande*.]

grandeur *gran'dyər*, *n* vastness; splendour, magnificence; loftiness of thought or deportment. [Fr. — *grand*, great.]

grandiloquent *gran-dil'ə-kwənt*, *adj* speaking, or expressed, bombastically. — *n* **grandil'oquence**. — *adv* **grandil'oquently**. [*L. grandiloquus* — *grandis*, great, *loqui*, to speak.]

grandiose *gran'di-ōs*, *adj* grand or imposing; bombastic. — *adv* **gran'diosely**. — *n* **grandios'ity**. [It. *grandioso* — *grande*, great.]

grange *grānj*, *n* a farmhouse with its stables and other buildings. — *n* **gran'ger** the keeper of a grange. [O.Fr. *grange*, barn.]

granite *gran'it*, *n* a coarse-grained igneous crystalline rock, composed of quartz, feldspar and mica. — *adj* made of granite; hard like granite; unyielding, resolute. — *adj* **granit'ic** pertaining to, consisting of, or like granite. — *n* **granitificā'tion**. — *adj* **granit'iform**. — *n* **granitisā'tion** or **-z-**. — *vt* **gran'itise** or **-ize**. — *adj* **gran'itoid** of the form of or resembling granite. — *adj* **granolith'ic** composed of cement and granite chips. — **graniteware** (*gran'it-wār*) a kind of speckled pottery resembling granite; a type of enamelled ironware. [It. *granito*, granite, lit. grained.]

granivorous *grə-niv'ər-əs*, *adj* grain-eating; feeding on seeds. — *n* **gran'ivore**. [L. *grānum*, grain, *vorāre*, to devour.]

granny or **grannie** *gran'i*, *n* a grandmother (*colloq*); an old-womanish person (*colloq*); a revolving cap on a chimney-pot. — **granny bonds** a former name of index-linked National Savings certificates, before 1981 only available to people over 50 years old; **granny flat** or **annexe** a self-contained flat, bungalow, etc., built on to, as part of, or close to, a house, for a grandmother or other elderly relative; **granny glasses** small, round, gold or steel-rimmed spectacles; **granny knot** a knot like a reef knot, but unsymmetrical, apt to slip or jam; **Granny Smith** a crisp, green, flavoursome, Australasian variety of apple.

granola *grə-nō'lə*, (*NAm*) *n* a type of crunchy breakfast cereal made with mixed grain, oats, dried fruit, nuts, etc., and honey or brown sugar. [Orig. a trademark.]

granolithic. See under **granite**.

grant *gränt*, *vt* to bestow; to admit as true; to concede. — *n* something bestowed, an allowance; a gift; conveyance of property by deed; a granting. — *adj* **grant'able**. — *pa p* or *conj* **grant'ed** (often with *that*) (it is) admitted, accepted. — *n* **grantee'** (*law*) the person to whom a grant, gift or conveyance is made. — *n* **grant'er** or **grant'or** (*law*) the person by whom a grant or conveyance is made. — **grant-in-aid'** an official money grant for a particular purpose, esp. from the government; **grant of arms** (*heraldry*) provision of an achievement to a petitioner by a king-of-arms, in exchange for a fee. — **take for granted** to presuppose or assume, esp. tacitly or unconsciously; to treat casually, without respect. [O.Fr. *graanter*, *craanter*, *creanter*, to promise — L. *crēdĕre*, to believe.]

Granth *grunt* or **Granth Sahib** *grunt sä'ib*, *n* the holy book of the Sikhs (also **Adi'-Grant**). — *n* **Gran'thi** (-*ē*) the guardian of the Granth Sahib and of the gurdwara. [Hindi *granth*, a book.]

gran turismo *gran too-rēz'mō*, (It.) *n* and *adj* a motor car designed for touring in luxury and at high speed (abbrev. **GT**).

granule *gran'ūl*, *n* a little grain; a fine particle. — *adj* **gran'ūlar**, **gran'ūlose** or **gran'ūlous** consisting of or like grains or granules; containing or marked by the presence of grains or granules. — *n* **granūlar'ity**. — *adv* **gran'ūlarly**. — *vt* **gran'ūlate** to form or break into grains or small masses; to make rough on the surface. — *vi* to be formed into grains. — *adj* granular; having the surface covered with small elevations. — *n* **granūlā'tion** the act of forming into grains, esp. of metals by pouring them through a sieve into water while hot; a granulated texture; applied decoration made up of grains of metal (esp. gold). — *adj* **gran'ūlative**. — *n* **gran'ūlātor** or **gran'ulāter**. — *adj* **granūlif'erous**. — *adj* **gran'ūliform**. — *n* **gran'ūlōcyte** a blood cell of the leucocyte division. — *adj* **granūlocyt'ic**. — *n* **granulō'ma** (*pathol*) a small localised tumour composed of growing connective tissue, caused by infection or invasion by a foreign body. — **granulated sugar** white sugar in fairly coarse grains. [L. *grānulum*, dimin. of *grānum*, grain.]

grape *grāp*, *n* the small, green or dark purple-skinned fruit of the grapevine, growing in bunches, used to make wine, dried to make raisins, or eaten raw. — *adj* **grape'less** (of wine) without the flavour of the grape. — *n* **grā'pery** a building or place where grapes are grown. — *adj* **grā'pey** or **grā'py** made of or like grapes. — **grape'fruit** a large, round, yellow-skinned citrus fruit, so called because it grows in large bunches like grapes; **grape hyacinth** a plant (*Muscari*) closely related to the hyacinths, with clusters of small grapelike flowers; **grape'seed** the seed of the vine; **grape'seed-oil** an oil pressed from it; **grape'shot** clustered iron shot that scatters when fired; **grape'stone** the pip of the grape; **grape sugar** glucose or dextrose; **grape'vine** *Vitis vinifera* or other species of Vitis; the bush telegraph, rumour (*colloq*). — **sour grapes** saying or pretending that something is not worth having because one cannot have it oneself; **the grape** (usu. *facetious*) wine. [O.Fr. *grape*, *grappe*, a cluster of grapes — *grape*, a hook.]

graph *gräf*, *n* a symbolic diagram; a drawing depicting the relationship between two or more variables. — *vt* to plot on a graph. — *combining form* **-graph** used as an ending in many compounds to denote an agent that writes, records, etc. (e.g. *telegraph*, *seismograph*) or the thing written (e.g. in *autograph*, etc.). — *adj* **graphic** (*graf'ik*) or **graph'ical** pertaining to writing, describing, delineating or diagrammatic representation; picturesquely described or describing; vivid. — *n* **graph'ic** a painting, print; illustration or diagram. — *n* **graph'icacy** accurate understanding of and use of visual information. — *adv* **graph'ically**. — *n* **graph'icness**. — *nsing* **graph'ics** graphic means of presenting, or means of reproducing, informational material; the art or science of mathematical drawing, and of calculating stresses, etc., by geometrical methods. — *combining form* **-graphy** used as an ending in compounds to denote either a particular style of writing, drawing, etc. (e.g. *photography*, *lithography*) or a method of arranging and recording data within a particular discipline (e.g. *seismography*, *biography*). — *n* **graphomā'nia** obsession with writing. — *n* **graphopho'bia** fear of writing. — **graphic arts** painting, drawing, engraving (as opp. to music, sculpture, etc.); **graphic equaliser** a device for boosting or cutting frequencies of an audio signal, using faders; **graphic formula** a chemical formula in which the symbols for single atoms are joined by lines representing valency bonds; **graphic novel** a novel in comic-book picture form, aimed mainly at adults; **graphics tablet** (*comput*) a peripheral input device which digitises the movements of a pen over the sensitive pad (tablet), so that a traced pattern will appear on the screen; **graph paper** squared paper suitable for drawing graphs. [Gr. *graphē*, a writing — *graphein*, to write.]

grapheme *graf'ēm*, *n* a letter of an alphabet; all the letters or combinations of letters together that may be used to express one phoneme. — *adj* **graphē'mic**. — *adv* **graphē'mically**. — *nsing* **graphē'mics** the study of systems of representing speech sounds in writing. [Gr. *graphēma*, a letter.]

graphite *graf'īt*, *n* a soft black or grey mineral composed of carbon, with many commercial and industrial uses, and formerly esp. used in lead pencils. — *adj* **graphit'ic**. — *n* **graphitisā'tion** or **-z-**. — *vt* **graph'itise** or **-ize** to convert wholly or partly into graphite. [Ger. *Graphit* — Gr. *graphein*, to write, and **-ite** (3).]

graphology *grə-fol'ə-ji*, *n* the art of estimating and analysing character from handwriting. — *adj* **grapholog'ic** or **graphologʼical**. — *n* **graph-ol'ogist** a person skilled in, or who practises, graphology. [Gr. *graphē*, writing, and **-logy**.]

graphomania, graphophobia. See under **graph**.

grapnel *grap'nəl*, *n* a small anchor with several claws or arms; a grappling-iron; a hooking or grasping instrument. [Dimin. of O.Fr. *grapin* — *grape*, a hook.]

GRAPO or **Grapo** *grä'pō*, *abbrev* (Sp.) for First of October Anti-Fascist Resistance Groups, a left-wing terrorist organisation.

grappa *grap'ə*, *n* a brandy (orig. Italian) made from the residue from a wine-press. [It., grape stalk.]

grapple *grap'l*, *n* an instrument for hooking or holding; a grasp, grip, hold or clutch; a state of being held or clutched. — *vt* to seize; to grasp or grip. — *vi* to contend in close fight; to wrestle mentally (with). — **grapp'ling-iron** or **-hook** an instrument for grappling; a large grapnel for seizing hostile ships in naval engagements. [Cf. O.Fr. *grappil* — *grape*, a hook.]

graptolite *grap'tə-līt*, *n* one of an extinct group of Hydrozoa which occur as fossils in Palaeozoic rocks, and appear like writing on shales. — *adj* **grapto-lit'ic**. [Gr. *graptos*, written — *graphein*, to write, *lithos*, stone.]

GRAS *gras*, (*US*) *abbrev* for generally recognised as safe (used to designate an officially approved food additive).

grasp *gräsp*, *vt* to seize and hold; to take eagerly; to comprehend. — *vi* to endeavour to seize (with *at* or *after*); to seize or accept eagerly (with *at*). — *n* grip; power of seizing; mental power of apprehension. — *adj* **grasp'able**. — *n* **grasp'er**. — *adj* **grasp'ing** seizing; avaricious. — *adj* **grasp'ingly**. — *n* **grasp'ingness**. [M.E. *graspen*, *grapsen*, from the root of *grāpian*, to grope.]

grass *gräs*, *n* any plant of the monocotyledonous family *Gramineae*, the most important to man in the vegetable kingdom, with long, narrow leaves and tubular stems, including wheat and other cereals, reeds (but not sedges), bamboo, sugar-cane; pasture grasses; an area planted with or growing such grasses, e.g. a lawn or meadow; pasturage; an informer (*slang*); marijuana (*slang*). — *vt* to cover, sow or turf with grass; to feed with grass; to bring on or down to the grass or ground (e.g. a fish or game bird); to inform (on) (*slang*). — *vi* to inform (on) (*slang*). — *n* **grass'iness.** — *n* **grass'ing** bleaching by exposure on grass. — *adj* **grass'y** covered with or resembling grass; green. — **grass box** a receptacle attached to some lawnmowers to catch the grass cuttings; **grass court** a grass-covered tennis court; **grass'-cutter** a mowing machine. — *adj* **grass'-green** green with grass; green as grass. — **grass'-hopper** a name for various jumping insects of the *Orthoptera* order, related to locusts and crickets, that chirp by rubbing their wing-covers; **grasshopper mind** a mind that jumps about and is unable to concentrate on any one subject for long; **grass'land** permanent pasture; **grass roots** (orig. *US*) the ordinary people, the rank and file in a country, political party, etc., thought of as voters; foundation, basis, origin, primary aim or meaning. — *adj* **grass'-roots.** — **grass snake** the harmless common ringed snake; **grass style** a form of Chinese calligraphy in which the shapes of the characters are greatly simplified for artistic effect; **grass tree** an Australian plant (*Xanthorrhoea*) of the lily family, with shrubby stems, tufts of long wiry foliage at the summit, and a tall flower-stalk, with a dense cylindrical spike of small flowers; **grass widow** a wife temporarily separated from or deserted by her husband: — *masc* **grass widower; grass'wrack** eelgrass. — **go (**or **be put out) to grass** to be turned out to pasture, esp. of a horse too old to work; to go into retirement or to live in the country; **let the grass grow under one's feet** to loiter or linger, and so lose one's opportunity. [O.E. *gærs*, *græs*.]

grate[1] *grāt*, *n* a framework of bars, esp. one for holding coal, etc. in a fire, or for looking through a door, etc.; a cage; a grid. — *adj* **grāt'ed** having a grating. — *n* **grāt'ing** the bars of a grate; a perforated cover for a drain or the like; a partition or frame of bars; a surface ruled closely with fine lines to give a diffraction spectrum. [L.L. *grāta*, a grate — L. *crātis*, a hurdle; see **crate.**]

grate[2] *grāt*, *vt* to rub hard, scrape or wear away with anything rough; to grind (the teeth); to emit or utter jarringly. — *vi* to make a harsh sound; to jar or rasp. — *n* **grāt'er** an instrument with a rough surface for rubbing (e.g. cheese) down to small particles. — *adj* **grāt'ing** rubbing harshly; harsh; irritating. — *adv* **grāt'ingly.** [O.Fr. *grater*, through L.L., from O.H.G. *chrazzōn* (Ger. *kratzen*), to scratch.]

grateful *grāt'fo͝ol* or *-fl*, *adj* thankful; expressing gratitude; having a due sense of benefits one has received; causing pleasure. — *adv* **grate'fully.** — *n* **grate'fulness.** — *n* **gratificā'tion** (*grat-*) an act of pleasing or indulging; that which gratifies; delight, feeling of satisfaction. — *n* **grat'ifier.** — *vt* **grat'ify** to please; to satisfy; to indulge; to do what is agreeable to: — *pr p* **grat'ifying;** *pa t* and *pa p* **grat'ified.** — *adj* **grat'ifying.** — *adv* **grat'ifyingly.** [O.Fr. *grat* — L. *grātus*, pleasing, thankful.]

graticule *grat'i-kūl*, *n* a ruled grating for the identification of points on a map, the field of a telescope, etc. — *n* **graticulā'tion** the division of a design into squares for convenience in making an enlarged or diminished copy. [L. *crātīcula*, dimin. of *crātis*, wickerwork.]

gratin. See **au gratin.**

gratiné *grat-ē-nā*, (Fr.) *adj* cooked or served au gratin: — *fem* **gratinée** (*-nā*).

gratis *grā'tis* or *grä'tis*, *adv* for nothing; without payment or recompense. [L. *grātis* — *grātia*, favour — *grātus*, thankful.]

gratitude *grat'i-tūd*, *n* thankfulness; warm and friendly feeling towards a benefactor. [Fr., — L.L. *grātitūdō* — L. *grātus*.]

gratuity *grə-tū'i-ti*, *n* a tip, or present (usu. in the form of money); a payment to a soldier, etc., on discharge. — *adj* **gratū'itous** done or given for nothing; voluntary; without reason, ground or proof; uncalled for. — *adv* **gratū'itously.** [Fr. *gratuité* — L.L. *grātuitās*, *-ātis* — L. *grātus*.]

graunch *grönch*, *vt* to grind or crunch (a mechanism). [Imit.]

gravadlax. See **gravlax.**

gravamen *grə-vā'men*, (*law*) *n* the substantial or chief ground of complaint or accusation: — *pl* **gravā'mina.** [L. *gravāmen* — *gravis*, heavy.]

grave[1] *grāv*, *n* a pit dug out to bury the dead in; any place of burial; death, destruction; a deadly place. — *npl* **grave clothes** the clothes in which the dead are buried. — **grave'-digger; grave'stone** a stone placed as a memorial at a grave; **grave'yard** a burial-ground. — **turn in one's grave** (of a dead person) to be disturbed from one's rest by an occurrence that would have been particularly distressing to one's living self; **with one foot in the grave** on the brink of death. [O.E. *grafan*, to dig, *græf*, a cave, grave, trench.]

grave[2] *grāv*, *adj* of importance; serious; sedate; solemn; weighty; calling for anxiety; low in pitch. — *n* (usu. *gräv*) grave accent. — *adv* **grave'ly.** — *n* **grave'ness.** — **grave accent** (in the U.K. *gräv*) a mark (`), originally indicating a pitch falling somewhat, or failing to rise, now used for various special purposes (as in French). [Fr., — L. *gravis*.]

gravel *grav'l*, *n* a mass of small rounded stones; small collections of gravelly matter in the kidneys or bladder. — *vt* to cover with gravel; to puzzle, perplex; to irritate (*colloq*): — *pr p* **grav'elling;** *pa t* and *pa p* **grav'elled.** — *adj* **grav'elly** of, full, or like, gravel; (of sound, esp. a voice) harsh, rough. — **gravel pit** a pit from which gravel is dug. [O.Fr. *gravele* (Fr. *gravier*); prob. Celt.]

graven *grā'vn*, *adj* engraved; deeply fixed (e.g. on the mind). — **graven image** an engraved idol. [Old verb *grave*, to engrave — O.E. *grafan*, to dig.]

graver *grā'vər*, *n* an engraving tool, e.g. a burin. [Ety. as for **graven.**]

Graves *gräv*, *n* a white (or red) table wine from the *Graves* district in the Gironde department of France.

gravid *grav'id*, *adj* pregnant. — *n* **gravid'ity.** [L. *gravidus* — *gravis*, heavy.]

gravimeter *grə-vim'i-tər*, *n* an instrument for measuring variations in gravity at points on the earth's surface. — *adj* **gravimetric** (*grav-i-met'rik*) or **gravimet'rical** pertaining to measurement by weight. — *n* **gravim'etry.** — **gravimetric analysis** the chemical analysis of materials by the separation of the constituents and their estimation by weight. [L. *gravis*, heavy, Gr. *metron*, measure.]

gravitas *grav'i-täs*, *n* seriousness; weight, importance. [L.; see next ety.]

gravity *grav'i-ti*, *n* weightiness; gravitational attraction or acceleration; graveness, solemnity; lowness of pitch. — *vi* **grav'itāte** to tend towards the earth or other body; to be attracted, or move, by force of gravitation; to sink or settle down; to be strongly attracted or move (towards). — *n* **gravitā'tion** the act of gravitating; the force of attraction between bodies (*phys*). — *adj* **gravitā'tional** of, pertaining to, etc. gravity; of the weakest type of interaction between nuclear particles (*phys*). — *adv* **gravitā'tionally.** — *adj* **grav'itātive.** — *n* **gravitom'eter** an instrument for measuring specific gravities. — *n* **grav'iton** a hypothetical quantum of gravitational field energy. — **gravitational field** that region of space in which appreciable gravitational force exists; **gravity platform** a drilling platform, used in the oil industry, made from concrete and steel, the weight of which enables it to hold its position on the sea bed; **gravity wave** liquid surface waves controlled by gravity and not by surface tension. — **acceleration due to gravity** (symbol *g*) the acceleration of a body falling freely under the action of gravity in a vacuum, about 9·8 metres (32.174 feet) per second. [L. *gravitās, -ātis* — *gravis*, heavy.]

gravlax *gräv'läks* or *grav'laks*, also **gravadlax** *grav'ad-laks*, *n* a Scandinavian dish of salmon dry-cured with spice (usu. dill), sugar, salt and pepper, sliced on the slant to serve. [Sw. *gravlax*, Norw. *gravlaks*, lit. buried salmon.]

gravure *grə-vūr'*, *n* any process of making an intaglio printing plate, including photogravure; the plate, or an impression from it. [Fr., engraving.]

gravy *grā'vi*, *n* the juices from meat while cooking; a sauce made by thickening and seasoning these juices; money, profit or pleasure, unexpected or in excess of what one might expect (*colloq*); graft (*slang*). — **gravy boat** a container for serving and pouring gravy; **gravy train** (*colloq*) a position in which one can have excessive profits or advantages in contrast to other people. [Perh. *gravé*, a copyist's mistake for O.Fr. *grané* — *grain*, a seasoning or cookery ingredient.]

gray[1]. Same as **grey**.

gray[2] *grā*, *n* the SI unit (symbol **Gy**) of absorbed dose of ionising radiation, equivalent to one joule per kilogram (or 100 rads). [Louis H. *Gray* (1905–65), British radiobiologist.]

grayling *grā'ling*, *n* a silvery-grey fish (*Thymallus*) of the salmon family, with larger scales; a grey satyrid butterfly. [**gray**[1].]

graze[1] *grāz*, *vt* to eat or feed on (growing grass or pasture); to feed or supply with grass. — *vi* to eat grass; to supply grass; to eat on one's feet and on the move, e.g. without stopping work, or (straight from the shelves) in a supermarket (*slang*); to browse, skim along or through (reading matter, TV or radio programmes, etc.) (*slang*). — *n* **grā'zer** an animal that grazes; a person who eats on his or her feet and on the move (*slang*). — *n* **grā'zier** someone who pastures cattle and rears them for the market. — *n* **grā'zing** the act or practice of grazing; the feeding or raising of cattle. [O.E. *grasian* — *græs*, grass.]

graze[2] *grāz*, *vt* to pass lightly along the surface of; to damage or scrape the top surface of (the skin). — *n* a passing touch or scratch.

grazioso *grä-tsē-ō'sō*, (*mus*) *adj* and *adv* graceful, gracefully. [It.]

grease *grēs*, *n* a soft thick animal fat; oily matter of any kind; condition of fatness. — *vt* to smear with grease; to lubricate; to bribe (*slang*); to facilitate. — *n* **greaser** (*grē'zər* or *grē'sər*) a person who greases; a member of a gang of motorcyclists; a ship's engineer. — *adv* **greas'ily**. — *n* **greas'iness**. — *adj* **greas'y** (or *grē'zi*) of or like grease or oil; smeared with grease; having a slippery coating; fatty; oily; unctuous or ingratiating. — **grease cup** a lubricating device which stores grease and feeds it into a bearing; **grease gun** a lubricating pump; **grease monkey** (*slang*) a mechanic; **grease paint** a tallowy substance used by actors in making up. — *adj* **grease'-proof** resistant or impermeable to grease. — **grease the wheels** to make things go smoothly; **like greased lightning** quickly. [O.Fr. *gresse*, fatness, *gras*, fat — L. *crassus*.]

great *grāt*, *adj* big; large; of a high degree of magnitude of any kind; elevated in power, rank, station, etc.; pre-eminent in genius; highly gifted; chief; sublime; weighty; outstanding; devoted to or obsessed by a certain thing; in a high degree; on a large scale; excellent (*colloq*, often *ironic*); used in combination to indicate one degree more remote in the direct line of descent (as in **great-grand'father, great-grand'son** and similarly **great-great-grand'father** and so indefinitely). — *n* someone who has achieved lasting fame; used collectively for such people. — *adv* (*colloq*) very well. — *vt* **great'en** to make great or greater. — *vi* to become great. — *adj* **great'er** compar. of great; (with geographical names) in an extended sense (as *Greater London*). — *adv* **great'ly**. — *n* **great'ness**. — *npl* **Greats** the final honours School of Classics and Philosophy (*Classical Greats*) or of Modern Philosophy (*Modern Greats*) at Oxford University. — **great ape** any of the larger anthropoid apes — the chimpanzee, gibbon, gorilla, orang-utan; **great auk** a large, flightless auk once common in the N. Atlantic areas, now extinct; **great'-aunt** a grandparent's sister; **Great Britain** England, Scotland and Wales; **great circle** see under **circle**; **great'coat** an overcoat; **Great Dane** one of a breed of very large smooth- (and short-) haired dogs; **great-grand'child** the child of a grandchild; **great-grand'father** (and **-grand'mother**) the father (and mother) of a grandparent; **great-neph'ew** (and **-niece'**) a brother's or sister's grandson (and granddaughter); **great Scot** or **Scott** an exclamation of surprise; **great tit** a kind of tit with yellow, black and white markings; **great'-uncle** a grandparent's brother; **Great War** the war of 1914–18. — **the greatest** (*slang*) a wonderful, marvellous person or thing; **the great unwashed** a contemptuous term for the common people. [O.E. *great*.]

greave *grēv*, *n* a piece of armour for the leg below the knee. [O.Fr. *greve*, shin, greave.]

grebe *grēb*, *n* a short-winged almost tailless freshwater diving bird. [Fr. *grèbe*.]

Grecian *grē'shən* or *grē'shyən*, *adj* Greek. — *n* a Greek; a scholar of Greek language and literature. — **Grecian nose** a straight nose which forms a continuous line with the forehead. [L. *Graecia*, Greece — Gr. *Graikos*, Greek.]

Grecise or **-ize, Grecism, Greco-Roman.** See **Graecise** or **-ize**, etc.

greedy *grē'di*, *adj* having a voracious appetite; craving or longing eagerly, esp. too eagerly; eager to increase, or to obtain or keep more than, one's own share. — *n* **greed** an eager desire or longing; covetousness, esp. excessive. — *adv* **greed'ily**. — *n* **greed'iness**. — **greedy guts** (*slang*) a glutton. [O.E. *grǣdig*.]

greegree. See **grisgris**.

Greek *grēk*, *adj* of Greece, its people, or its language. — *n* a native or citizen of Greece, of a Greek state, or of a colony elsewhere of a Greek state; the language of Greece; any language of which one is ignorant, jargon or anything unintelligible (*colloq*). — **Greek architecture** that developed in ancient Greece (Corinthian, Doric and Ionic); **Greek Church** or **Greek Orthodox Church** see **Eastern Church** under **east**; **Greek cross** an upright cross with arms of equal length; **Greek gift** a treacherous gift (from Virgil's *Aeneid*, ii, 49); **Greek nose** a Grecian nose. — **Greek-letter society** (*US*) a fraternity or sorority, using a combination of Greek letters as a title. [O.E. *Grēcas*, *Crēcas*, Greeks, or L. *Graecus* — Gr. *Graikos*, Greek.]

green *grēn*, *adj* of the colour usual in leaves, between blue and yellow in the spectrum; growing; vigorous; new; young; unripe; fresh; undried; raw; incompletely prepared; immature; inexperienced; jealous or envious; easily imposed on; relating to currency values expressing EEC farm prices (e.g. *green pound*, *green franc*, *green rate*, etc.); concerned with care of the environment or conservation of natural resources, esp. as a political issue; (of goods etc.) environment-friendly; (of people) environment-conscious. — *n* the colour of green things; a grassy plot, esp. that common to a village or town, or for bowling, or drying of clothes; the prepared ground (*putting-green*) round a golf hole; a member of the Green Party, or an environmentalist; a green pigment; (in *pl*) green vegetables for food, esp. of the cabbage kind. — *vt* and *vi* to make or become green; to introduce trees and parks into urban areas. — *vi* to become environmentally conscious. — *n* **green'ery** green plants or boughs; fresh, green growth. — *n* **green'ie** (*Austr*) an environmentalist. — Also *adj*. —

n **green'ing** a becoming or making green; a kind of apple, green when ripe. — *adj* **green'ish**. — *adv* **green'ly**. — *n* **green'ness**. — *adj* **green'y**. — **green audit** an assessment of and investigation into a company's green, i.e. environment-conscious, claims, methods, policies, etc.; **green'back** (*colloq*) a note of US currency, a dollar bill; **green ban** (*Austr*) the refusal of trade unions to work on environmentally and socially objectionable projects; **green belt** a strip of open land surrounding a town; **Green Beret** (*colloq*) a British or American commando. — *adj* **green'-eyed** jealous (**the green-eyed monster** jealousy). — **greenfield site** a site, separate from existing developments, which is to be developed for the first time; **green'finch** or **green linnet** a finch of a green colour, with some grey; **green fingers** a knack of making plants grow well; **green'fly** a plant louse or aphis; **green'grocer** a dealer in fresh vegetables; **green'grocery** the produce sold by a greengrocer; **green'heart** a S. American tree of the laurel family with very hard wood; **green'horn** a raw, inexperienced youth; **green'house** a glasshouse for plants, esp. one with little or no artificial heating; **greenhouse effect** global warming, the progressive warming-up of the earth's surface due to the blanketing effect of man-made carbon dioxide, etc. in the atmosphere; **greenhouse gas** a gas (esp. carbon dioxide, also ozone, methane, nitrous oxide and chlorofluorocarbons) that contributes to the greenhouse effect; **Green** or **Emerald Isle** Ireland; **green'-keeper** a person who has the care of a golf course or bowling-green; **Greenland spar** see **cryolite**; **green light** a traffic signal indicating that vehicles may advance; permission to go ahead; **green'mail** a form of business blackmail whereby a company buys a strategically significant block of shares in another company, sufficient to threaten takeover and thus to force the parent company to buy back the shares at a premium; **green manuring** growing one crop (**green manure**) and digging it under to fertilise its successor; **green monkey** a West African long-tailed monkey; **green monkey disease** a sometimes fatal virus disease with fever and haemorrhaging, orig. identified among technicians handling green monkeys in Marburg, Germany; **green paper** a statement of proposed government policy, intended as a basis for parliamentary discussion; **Green Party** a party principally concerned with resource conservation and the decentralisation of political and economic power; **Green'peace** an environmental pressure group which campaigns esp. against nuclear power and dumping, and also whaling; **green plover** the lapwing; **green pound** the agreed value of the pound used to express EEC farm prices in sterling; **green room** in a theatre, a room for the actors to relax or entertain guests in, etc. backstage; **green'shank** a large sandpiper with long, greenish legs; **green sickness** chlorosis; **greenstick fracture** see **fracture**; **green stocks** (*commerce*) those of any organisation engaged in combating pollution, or professing to avoid it in the manufacture of its products; **green'stone** nephrite; any basic or intermediate igneous rock; **green'stuff** green vegetables, esp. of the cabbage kind; **green tea** tea made from leaves that have been dried without fermentation and retain a light colour; **green turtle** a tropical and subtropical sea turtle with a greenish shell; **green'wash** (*facetious*) a specious overlay, or ineffectual display, of concern for the environment. — Also *vt*. — *adj* **green-well'ie** of, belonging to or relating to the British upper-class country-dwelling set (represented stereotypically as wearing a certain kind of heavy green wellingtons). — **Green Cross Code** a code of road-safety rules for children issued in 1971. [O.E. *grēne*.]

greengage *grēn'gāj*, *n* a green and very sweet variety of plum. [Said to be named from Sir W. *Gage* of Hengrave Hall, near Bury St Edmunds, before 1725.]

Greenwich Mean Time *grin'ij* or *gren'* (or *-ich*) *mēn tīm*, *n* mean solar time for the meridian of *Greenwich*. — Also called **Greenwich Time**.

greet[1] *grēt*, *vt* to acknowledge upon meeting, with formal, familiar or customary words, or a customary or friendly gesture; to meet, receive; to send kind wishes to; to become evident to: — *pr p* **greet'ing**; *pa t* and *pa p* **greet'ed**. — *n* **greet'er**. — *n* **greet'ing** an expression of acknowledgment or good wishes; salutation. [O.E. *grētan*.]

greet[2] *grēt*, (*Scot*) *vi* to weep. — *n* weeping; a spell of weeping. [Northern M.E. *grete* — O.E. *grētan*.]

gregarious *gri-gā'ri-əs*, *adj* associating in flocks and herds; fond of the company of others; growing together but not matted (*bot*). — *adv* **gregā'riously**. — *n* **gregā'riousness**. [L. *gregārius* — *grex*, *gregis*, a flock.]

Gregorian *gri-gö'ri-ən*, *adj* belonging to or established by *Gregory* — such as the **Gregorian chant** introduced by Pope Gregory I (6th cent.), plainsong, the **Gregorian calendar**, that now generally in use, being the Julian calendar as reformed by Gregory XIII (1582), and the **Gregorian telescope**, a type of reflecting telescope devised by James Gregory (1638–75).

gremial *grē'mi-əl*, *n* a cloth laid on a bishop's knees to keep his vestments clean from oil at ordinations. [L. *gremium*, the lap.]

gremlin *grem'lin*, *n* an imaginary mischievous agency; orig. a goblin accused of vexing airmen, causing mechanical trouble to aircraft.

grenade *gri-nād'*, *n* a small bomb thrown by the hand or shot from a rifle; a glass projectile containing chemicals for putting out fires, testing drains, dispensing poison gas or tear gas, etc. — *n* **grenadier** (*gren-ə-dēr'*) now used as the title (Grenadier Guards) of part of the Guards Division of infantry; orig. a soldier who threw grenades, and later a member of the first company of every battalion of foot. [Fr., — Sp. *granada*, pomegranate — L. *grānātus*, full of seeds.]

grenadine[1] *gren'ə-dēn*, *n* a pomegranate syrup, or similar, used in certain drinks. [Ety. as for **grenade**.]

grenadine[2] *gren'ə-dēn*, *n* a thin silk or mixed fabric. [Fr., perh. *Granada*.]

gressorial *grə-sö'ri-əl*, (*zool*) *adj* adapted for walking. — Also **gresso'rious**. [L. *gressus*, past p. of *gradī*, to walk.]

grew *groo*, *pa t* of **grow**.

grey or **gray** *grā*, *adj* of a mixture of black and white with little or no hue; dull, miserable; grey-haired, old, mature; neutral, anonymous; intermediate in character, condition, etc. — *n* a grey colour; a grey or greyish animal, esp. a horse; grey clothing. — *n* **grey'ing** the process of becoming grey; (of a population) the process or phenomenon of having a growing elderly or retired sector. — *vt* to make grey or dull. — *vi* to become grey or dull. — *adj* **grey'ish**. — *adv* **grey'ly**. — *n* **grey'ness**. — **grey area** an area between two extremes, having (mingled) characteristics of both of them; a situation in which there are no clear-cut distinctions; **Grey Friar** a Franciscan; **grey goose** the common wild goose (*Anser anser*). — *adj* **grey'-haired**. — **grey'hen** the female of the blackcock; **grey'lag** or **greylag goose** the grey goose (perhaps from its lateness in migrating); **grey literature** material published non-commercially, e.g. government reports; **grey market** the unofficial and often secret, but not necessarily illegal, selling of goods, etc. alongside or in addition to an official or open market; a financial market trading in shares not yet officially listed; **grey matter** the ashen-grey active part of the brain and spinal cord; **grey'-out** a mild or less severe blackout; **grey seal** a type of seal that populates N. Atlantic coastal waters; **grey squirrel** a N. American squirrel naturalised in Britain; **grey wolf** the N. American timber wolf. [O.E. *græg*.]

greyhound *grā'hownd*, *n* a tall and slender dog with great speed and keen sight. [O.E. *grīghund*, prob. bitch-dog.]

greywacke *grā-wak'i*, *n* a sandstone composed of grains (round or angular) and splinters of quartz, feldspar, slate, etc., in a hard matrix. [Ger. *Grauwacke*, partly translated, partly adopted.]

gribble *grib'l*, *n* a small marine crustacean (genus *Limnoria*) that bores into timber under water.

gricer *grī'sər*, *n* a train-spotter or railway enthusiast. — *n* **grī'cing.**

Grid *grid*, *abbrev* for the Global Resource Information Database (of the United Nations).

grid *grid*, *n* a grating; a gridiron; a framework; a network; a network of power transmission lines; a network of lines for finding places on a map, or for other purpose; a framework above a theatre stage from which scenery and lights may be suspended. — *n* **gridd'er** (*US*) an American football player. — **grid'lock** (*US*) a traffic jam. [**gridiron**.]

griddle *grid'l*, or (*Scot*) **girdle** *gûr'dl*, *n* a flat iron plate placed over heat for making e.g. drop-scones; a flat, heated, metal cooking surface. [A.Fr. *gridil*, from a dimin. of L. *crātis*, a hurdle.]

gridiron *grid'ī-ərn*, *n* a frame of iron bars for broiling over a fire; a frame to support a ship during repairs; a network; an American football field (*US*). — *vt* to cover with parallel bars or lines. [M.E. *gredire*, a griddle; from the same source as **griddle**, but *-ire* confused with M.E. *ire*, iron.]

gridlock. See under **grid**.

grief *grēf*, *n* sorrow; distress; great mourning; affliction; a cause of sorrow; trouble, bother (*slang*). — *adj* **grief'-stricken** crushed with sorrow. — **come to grief** to meet with a setback, disaster or mishap. [O.Fr., — L. *gravis*, heavy.]

grieve *grēv*, *vt* to cause grief or distress to; to make sorrowful; to vex. — *vi* to feel grief; to mourn. — *n* **griev'ance** a ground of complaint; a condition felt to be oppressive or wrongful; hardship. — *n* **griev'er.** — *adv* **griev'ingly.** — *adj* **griev'ous** causing grief; burdensome; painful; severe. — *adv* **griev'ously.** — *n* **griev'ousness.** [O.Fr. *grever* — L. *gravāre* — *gravis*, heavy.]

griffin, gryfon or **gryphon** *grif'ən*, *n* an imaginary animal with lion's body and eagle's beak and wings. — *adj* **griff'inish.** [Fr. *griffon* — L. *grȳphus* — Gr. *gryps*, a bird, probably the lämmergeier, a griffin — *grȳpos*, hook-nosed.]

griffon[1] *grif'ən*, *n* a dog like a coarse-haired terrier. — **Brussels griffon** a toy dog with a rather snub nose. [Fr.; related to **griffin**.]

griffon[2] *grif'ən*, *n* a European vulture (*Gyps fulvus*), or any vulture of the Gyps genus. [**griffin**.]

grift *grift*, (*US*) *vi* to swindle. — *n* **grif'ter** a con man, swindler. [Perh. **graft**[2].]

grigri. See **grisgris**.

grill[1] *gril*, *vt* to cook on a gridiron, under a grill, etc. by radiant heat; to cross-examine harassingly; to brand or mark with a gridiron. — *vi* to undergo grilling. — *n* a grating; a gridiron; the part of a cooker on which meat, etc. is grilled; a grill room; a grilled dish; an act of grilling. — *n* **grillade'** a grilled dish. — *adj* **grilled.** — *n* **grill'ing.** — **grill room** part of a restaurant where beefsteaks, etc., are served grilled to order; **grill'steak** a large steak-shaped burger of seasoned minced beef, lamb, etc., usu. stored frozen and grilled without preliminary defrosting. — **mixed grill** a dish of several grilled meats usu. with mushrooms, tomatoes, etc. [Fr. *griller* — *gril*, a gridiron, from a dimin. of L. *crātis*, a grate.]

grill[2] or **grille** *gril*, *n* a lattice, grating or screen, or openwork of metal, generally used to enclose or protect a window, car radiator, etc.; a grating in a convent or jail door, etc. [Fr.; see ety. for **grill**[1].]

grilse *grils*, *n* a young salmon on its first return from salt water.

grim *grim*, *adj* forbidding; ferocious; ghastly; sullen; stern; unyielding; unpleasant. — *adv* **grim'ly.** — *n* **grim'ness.** [O.E. *grimm*.]

grimace *gri-mās'*, *n* a distortion of the face, in fun or disgust, etc.; a smirk. — *vi* to make grimaces. [Fr.]

grimalkin *gri-mal'kin* or *-möl'kin*, *n* an old (esp. female) cat; a cat generally. [**grey** and **Malkin**, a dimin. of *Maud*.]

grime *grīm*, *n* ingrained dirt; sooty or coaly dirt. — *vt* to soil deeply. — *adv* **grīm'ily.** — *n* **grīm'iness.** — *adj* **grīm'y.** [M.E. — M.Du. *grīme*.]

grin *grin*, *vi* to give a broad smile; to set the teeth together and draw back the lips, e.g. in pain or derision. — *vt* to express by grinning: — *pr p* **grinn'ing**; *pa t* and *pa p* **grinned.** — *n* an act of grinning. — *n* **grinn'er.** [O.E. *grennian*.]

grind *grīnd*, *vt* to reduce to powder by friction or crushing; to wear down, sharpen, smooth or roughen by friction; to rub together; to force (in or into); to produce by great effort (with *out*); to oppress or harass (usu. with *down*); to work by a crank. — *vi* to be moved or rubbed together; to jar or grate; to drudge at any tedious task; to study hard: — *pr p* **grīnd'ing**; *pa t* and *pa p* **ground** (*grownd*). — *n* the act, sound or jar of grinding; drudgery; laborious study for a special examination, etc. — *n* **grind'er.** — *n* **grind'ery** a place where knives, etc. are ground. — *adj* **grind'ing** for grinding; wearing down; very severe; extortionate; (of sound) harsh. — **grind'-stone** a circular revolving stone for grinding or sharpening tools; **ground glass** glass fogged by grinding, sandblasting or etching. — **grind to a halt** to move more and more slowly until finally coming to a standstill; **keep one's** (or **someone's**) **nose to the grindstone** to subject oneself (or someone) to severe continuous toil. [O.E. *grindan*.]

gringo *gring'gō*, *n* in Spanish-speaking America, someone whose language is not Spanish, esp. an English-speaker: — *pl* **grin'gos.** [Sp., gibberish, perh. — *Griego*, Greek.]

grip *grip*, *n* a grasp or firm hold, esp. with the hand or the mind; strength of grasp; the handle or part by which anything is grasped; a method or style of grasping; a travelling-bag; a holding or clutching device, e.g. a clasp for the hair, or a cable-car braking device; mastery; power of holding the mind or commanding the emotions; a small channel to carry away surface water; a stagehand who moves scenery, etc., or a member of a camera crew responsible for manoeuvring the camera. — *vt* to take or keep a firm hold of; to hold fast the attention, interest or emotions of. — Also *vi*: — *pr p* **gripp'ing**; *pa t* and *pa p* **gripped** (*gript*). — *n* **gripp'er** someone who, or that which, grips; a clutch; a claw. — **grip'sack** a grip, travelling-bag. — **come** or **get to grips (with)** to tackle at close quarters, or (*fig*) seriously and energetically. [O.E. *gripe*, grasp, *gripa*, handful.]

gripe *grīp*, *vt* to cause a painful stomach spasm in. — *vi* to cause, or to suffer, a painful stomach spasm; to keep on complaining (*colloq*). — *n* a grumble (*colloq*); (esp. in *pl*) severe spasmodic pain in the intestines. — *n* **grīp'er.** — *adj* **grīp'ing** (of a person) constantly complaining; (of a pain) seizing acutely. — *adv* **grīp'ingly.** — **gripe water** or specif. **Gripe Water**® a carminative solution given to infants to relieve colic and minor stomach ailments. [O.E. *grīpan* (*grāp*, *gripen*).]

grippe *grēp*, *n* (an old term for) influenza. [Fr., — *gripper*, to seize.]

grisaille *grē-zāl'* or *-zä'ē*, *n* a style of painting on walls or ceilings, in greyish tints in imitation of bas-reliefs; a similar style of painting on pottery, enamel or glass; a work in this style. — Also *adj*. [Fr., — *gris*, grey.]

griseofulvin *griz-i-ō-fo͞ol'vin*, (*med*) *n* an oral antibiotic used as a treatment for fungus infections of the skin and hair. [Isolated from the fungus *Penicillium griseofulvum* — Med.L. *griseus*, grey, L. *fulvus*, reddish yellow.]

grisette *gri-zet'*, *n* (esp. formerly) a young French working girl; a name given to varieties of e.g. birds, moths, fungi. [Fr., the grey fabric in which French working girls dressed, — *gris*, grey.]

grisgris, gris-gris, or **greegree** *grē'grē*, *n* an African charm, amulet or spell: — *pl* **gris'gris, gris'-gris** (*grēz*) or **gree'-grees**. [Fr.; prob. of African origin.]

grisly *griz'li*, *adj* frightful, ghastly. — *n* **gris'liness**. [O.E. *grislic*.]

grist *grist*, *n* corn for grinding, or ground; corn for grinding, or ground, at one time; malt for one brewing. — **grist mill** a mill for grinding grain. — **grist to the mill** raw material for feeding a process; matter that can be turned to profit or advantage. [O.E. *grīst*; related to **grind**.]

gristle *gris'l*, *n* cartilage, esp. when present in meat. — *n* **grist'liness**. — *adj* **grist'ly**. [O.E. *gristle*.]

grit[1] *grit*, *n* small hard particles of sand, stone, etc.; a coarse sandstone, often with angular grains (also **grit'stone**); texture of stone; strength of character, toughness, indomitability. — *vt* to grind or clench (one's teeth); to spread (e.g. icy roads, to prevent skidding) with grit. — *n* **gritt'er** a person who, or apparatus or a vehicle that, applies grit. — *n* **gritt'iness**. — *adj* **gritt'y** having or containing hard particles; of the nature of grit; determined, plucky. — **grit blasting** a process used in preparation for metal spraying which cleans the surface and gives it the roughness required to retain the sprayed metal particles. [O.E. *grēot*.]

grit[2] *grit*, (*agri*) *adj* (of a ewe) in lamb.

grits *grits*, *npl* coarsely ground grain, esp. oats or (in U.S.) hominy; a boiled dish of this. [O.E. *grytta*.]

grizzle *griz'l*, *vi* to grumble; to whimper; to fret. — *n* a bout of grizzling. — *n* **grizz'ler**.

grizzled *griz'ld*, *adj* (of hair or beard) grey, or mixed with grey. [M.E. *grisel* — Fr. *gris*, grey.]

grizzly bear *griz'li bār*, *n* a fierce brown bear of the Rocky Mountains, whose white-tipped fur gives it a grizzled appearance (often shortened to **grizz'ly**). [Ety. as for **grizzled**.]

Gro. *abbrev* for Grove (in street names).

groan *grōn*, *vi* to utter a sustained, deep-toned sound expressive of distress, disapprobation, etc.; to creak loudly; to be weighed down (with *under*, *beneath* or *with*; esp. of a table *with* food); to be oppressed, suffer (with *under* or *beneath*). — *vt* to utter or express through a groan. — *n* the sound, or an act, of groaning. — *n* **groan'er**. — *n* and *adj* **groan'ing**. [O.E. *grānian*.]

groat *grōt*, *n* an obsolete English silver coin, worth fourpence (4d). [O.L.G. *grote*, or Du. *groot*, lit. great, i.e. thick.]

groats *grōts*, *npl* hulled (and crushed) grain, esp. oats. [O.E. *grotan* (pl.).]

grocer *grō'sər*, *n* a dealer in staple foods and general household supplies. — *n* **grō'cery** the trade or business of a grocer; (usu. in *pl*) articles sold by grocers. [Earlier *grosser*, a wholesale dealer; O.Fr. *grossier*.]

grockle *grok'l*, (*colloq derog*) *n* a tourist or incomer in an (esp. holiday) area.

grog *grog*, *n* (*formerly*) a mixture of spirits and water; any alcoholic drink (esp. *Austr* and *NZ colloq*). — *vi* (*Austr colloq*; with *on*) to drink steadily. — *n* **grogg'iness**. — *adj* **grogg'y** dazed, unsteady from illness or exhaustion; weak and staggering from blows (*boxing*); somewhat drunk (*old*). — **grog'-on** or **grog'-up** (*Austr*) a drinking party or drinking session. [From Old *Grog*, the nickname (app. from his *grogram* cloak) of Admiral Vernon, who in 1740 ordered that rum (until 1970 officially issued to sailors) should be mixed with water.]

grogram *grog'rəm*, *n* a kind of coarse cloth of silk and mohair. [O.Fr. *gros grain*, coarse grain.]

groin[1] *groin*, *n* the fold between the belly and the thigh; the genitals, esp. the testicles (*euph*); the line of intersection of two vaults, also a rib along the intersection (*archit*). — *vt* to form into groins, to build in groins. — *adj* **groined**. — *n* **groin'ing**. [Early forms *grind*, *grine*, perh. — O.E. *grynde*, abyss.]

groin[2]. U.S. spelling of **groyne**.

grommet. Same as **grummet**.

groom *gro͞om* or *gro͝om*, *n* a person who has the charge of horses; a title of several officers in a noble or royal household; a bridegroom. — *vt* to tend (esp. a horse); to smarten; to prepare for political office, stardom, or success in any sphere. — **grooms'man** the attendant on a bridegroom.

groove *gro͞ov*, *n* a furrow, or long hollow, usu. one cut with a tool; the track cut into the surface of a record along which the needle of the record-player moves; a set routine; an exalted mood, one's highest form (*old slang*). — *vt* to cut a groove or furrow in. — *vi* (*old slang*) to experience great pleasure; to be groovy. — *n* **groov'er**. — *adj* **groov'y** in top form, up to date in style, or, generally, pleasant or delightful (*old slang*); passé, outmoded (*mod slang*). — **in the groove** (*old slang*) in excellent form; up to date, fashionable. [Prob. Du. *groef*, *groeve*, a furrow.]

grope *grōp*, *vi* to search, feel about, as if blind or in the dark (often with *for*). — *vt* to find (one's way) by feeling; to fondle (someone) lasciviously (*colloq*). — *adv* **gro'pingly**. [O.E. *grāpian*; related to **grab** and **gripe**.]

groper. Same as **grouper**.

grosbeak *grōs'bēk*, *n* any of several finches, esp. the hawfinch, with thick, heavy, seed-crushing bill. [Fr. *grosbec* — *gros*, thick, *bec*, beak.]

groschen *grō'shən*, *n* an Austrian coin, a 100th part of a schilling; in Germany, a ten-pfennig piece. [Ger.]

grosgrain *grō'grān*, *n* a heavy corded silk used especially for ribbons and hat bands. [Fr.]

gros point *grō pwẽ*, *n* a large cross-stitch; embroidery composed of this stitch. [Fr.]

gross *grōs*, *adj* total, including everything, without deductions; extremely fat, obese; enormous, bulky; stupid, dull, slow; coarse, sensual; obscene; flagrant, glaring, palpable; crass, boorish; dense in growth, rank; solid, earthbound, not ethereal. — *n* the main bulk; the whole taken together, sum total; twelve dozen, 144: — *pl* **gross**. — *vt* to make as total income or revenue. — *adv* **gross'ly**. — *n* **gross'ness**. — **gross domestic product** the gross national product less income from foreign investments; **gross national product** the total value of all goods and services produced by a country in a specified period (usu. annually); **gross up** to convert a net figure into a gross one for the purpose of tax calculation, etc.; **in gross** in bulk, wholesale. [Fr. *gros* — L. *grossus*, thick.]

grotesque *grō-tesk'*, *adj* extravagantly formed; fantastic; bizarre; ludicrous, absurd. — *n* extravagant ornament, containing animals, plants, etc., in fantastic or incongruous forms (*art*); a bizarre figure or object. — *adv* **grotesque'ly**. — *n* **grotesque'ness**. — *n* **grotesqu'ery** or **grotesqu'erie**. [Fr. *grotesque* — It. (*pittura*) *grottesca*, cave painting — *grotta*, a cave.]

grotto *grot'ō*, *n* a cave; an imitation cave, usu. fantastic: — *pl* **grott'oes** or **grott'os**. [It. *grotta* — L. *crypta* — Gr. *kryptē*, a crypt, vault.]

grotty *grot'i*, (*slang*) *adj* ugly, in bad condition, or useless. [**grotesque**.]

grouch *growch*, *vi* to grumble. — *n* a spell of grumbling; a grumbler. — *adv* **grouch'ily**. — *n* **grouch'iness**. — *adj* **grouch'y**.

ground[1]. See **grind**.

ground[2] *grownd, n* the solid surface of the earth; land; soil; the floor, etc.; earth (*electr*; *NAm*); position; an area associated with some activity (such as *football ground, playground, battleground*); distance to be covered; matter to be dealt with; foundation; sufficient reason; the surface on which the work is represented (*art*); surrounding rock (*mining*); the space with which the batsman must be in touch if he is not to be stumped or run out (*cricket*); (in *pl*) an area of land attached to or surrounding a building; (in *pl*) dregs or sediment; (in *pl*) basis or justification. — *vt* to base on a foundation or principle; to put or rest on the ground; to cause to run aground; to instruct in first principles; to cover with a preparatory layer or coating, as a basis for painting, etching, etc.; to earth (*electr*; *NAm*); to keep on the ground, prevent from flying; to suspend from usual activity (e.g. as a punishment). — *vi* to come to the ground; to strike the sea-bottom, etc. and remain fixed. — *n* **ground'age** a charge on a ship in port. — *adj* **ground'ed**. — *n* **ground'ing** foundation; sound general knowledge of a subject. — *adj* **ground'less** without ground, foundation, or reason. — *adv* **ground'lessly**. — *n* **ground'lessness**. — *n* **ground'ling** a fish that keeps near the bottom of the water; a person on the ground in contrast to one in an aircraft, etc. — **ground'bait** bait dropped to the bottom to bring fish to the neighbourhood; **ground bass** a bass part constantly repeated with varying melody and harmony (*mus*); **ground'breaking** (esp. *US*) the breaking of ground at the beginning of a construction project. — *adj* innovative, breaking new ground. — **ground'burst** the explosion of a bomb on the ground (as opposed to in the air); **ground cherry** any of the European dwarf cherries; any of several plants of the genus *Physalis*; the fruit of these plants; **ground control** control, by information radioed from a ground installation, of aircraft observed by radar; **ground cover** low plants and shrubs growing among the trees in a forest; various low herbaceous plants used to cover an area instead of grass; **ground crew** see **ground staff**; **ground effect** the extra aerodynamic lift, exploited by hovercraft, etc. and affecting aircraft flying near the ground, caused by the cushion of trapped air beneath the vehicle; **ground floor** the floor on or near a level with the ground; **ground frost** frost on the surface of the ground; a temperature of 0°C or less registered on a horizontal thermometer in contact with the shorn grass tips of a turf surface; **ground'hog** the woodchuck; the aardvark; **ground ivy** a British labiate creeping plant (*Nepeta*) whose leaves when the edges curl become ivy-like; **ground'-mass** (*geol*) the fine-grained part of an igneous rock, glassy or minutely crystalline, in which the larger crystals are embedded; **ground'nut** the peanut or monkey-nut; **ground plan** a plan of the horizontal section of the lowest or ground floor of a building; first plan, general outline; **ground'prox** a device, fitted to large passenger aircraft, which warns the pilot when altitude falls below a given level (*ground prox*imity warning system); **ground rent** rent paid to a landlord for the use of the ground for a specified term, usually in England ninety-nine years; **ground rule** a basic rule of procedure; a modifying (sports) rule for a particular place or circumstance; **ground'sheet** a waterproof sheet spread on the ground by campers, etc.; **grounds'man** a man whose job is to take care of a cricket ground or a sportsfield; **ground'speed** (*aeronautics*) speed of an aircraft relative to the ground; **ground squirrel** the chipmunk or any of several burrowing rodents; **ground staff** aircraft mechanics, etc. whose work is on the ground (also **ground crew**); people employed to look after a sportsfield; **ground stroke** a return played after the ball has bounced (*tennis*); **ground'swell** a broad, deep undulation of the ocean caused by a distant gale or earthquake; a gathering wave of public or political feeling; **ground'work** essential preparatory work; the ground of a painting (*art*); **ground zero** the point on the ground directly under the explosion of a nuclear weapon in the air. — **break ground** to begin working untouched ground; to take the first step in any project; **break new** (or **fresh**) **ground** to be innovative; **cover a lot of ground** to make good progress; **cover the ground** to treat a topic, etc. adequately; **cut** or **take the ground from under someone** or **from under someone's feet** to anticipate someone's arguments or actions and destroy their force; **fall to the ground** to come to nothing; **forbidden ground** an unmentionable topic; **gain ground** to advance; to become more widely influential; to spread; **give ground** to fall back, retreat; **hold** or **stand one's ground** to stand firm; **home ground** familiar territory; **into the ground** to the point of exhaustion; **(let in) on the ground floor** (to admit) on the same terms as the original promoters, or at the start (of a business venture, etc.); **lose ground** to fall back; to decline in influence, etc.; **off the ground** started, under way; **on firm ground** in a strong position; **on one's own** (or **home**) **ground** in circumstances with which one is familiar; **prepare the ground** to ease the way for, facilitate the progress of, something (with *for*); **run to ground** to hunt out, track down; **shift one's ground** to change one's standpoint in a situation or argument; **to ground** into hiding. [O.E. *grund*.]

groundsel *grownd'sl* or *grown'sl, n* a very common yellow-flowered composite weed of waste ground, of the genus *Senecio*. [O.E. *gundeswilge*, app. — *gund*, pus, *swelgan*, to swallow, from its use in poultices.]

group *grōōp, n* a number of people or things together; a number of individual things or people related in some definite way differentiating them from others; a clique, school or section of a party; a number of commercial companies combined under single ownership and central control; a division of an air force subordinate to a wing; a scientific classification; a combination of figures forming a harmonious whole (*art*); a system of elements having a binary operation that is associative, an identity element for the operation, and an inverse for every element (*math*); a vertical column of the periodic table containing elements with similar properties, etc. (*chem*); a number of atoms that occur together in several compounds (also **radical**; *chem*); a pop group. — *vt* to form into a group or groups. — *vi* to fall into harmonious combination. — *adj* **group'able**. — *n* **group'age** the collection of objects or people into a group or groups. — *n* **group'ie** (*slang*) a (usu. female) fan who follows pop groups, or other celebrities, wherever they appear, often in the hope of having sexual relations with them. — *n* **group'ing** (*art*) the act of disposing and arranging figures in a group. — **group captain** an airforce officer the equivalent of a colonel or naval captain; **group dynamics** (*psychol*) the interaction of human behaviour within a small social group; **group insurance** insurance issued on a number of people under a single policy; **group practice** a medical practice in which several doctors work together as partners; **group sex** sexual activity in which several people take part simultaneously; **group theory** (*math*) the investigation of the properties of groups; **group therapy** therapy in which a small group of people with the same psychological or physical problems discuss their difficulties under the chairmanship of, e.g., a doctor. — **Group of Five, Seven, Ten,** etc. (also **G5, G7, G10** or **G-5, G-7, G-10,** etc.) (*econ*) during the 1960s, '70s and '80s (committees representing) groups of countries with common economic interests, the *Five* comprising the major

Western-style economies — United States, Japan, West Germany, Britain and France, the *Seven* these with the addition of Italy and Canada, and the *Ten* the main industrial members of the International Monetary Fund. [Fr. *groupe* — It. *groppo*, a bunch, knot — Gmc.]

grouper *grōō'pər* or **groper** *grō'pər*, *n* names given to many fishes, esp. various kinds resembling bass. [Port. *garoupa*.]

grouse[1] *grows*, *n* a plump reddish game bird (*Lagopus scoticus*) of the family *Tetraonidae*, with feathered legs, found on Scottish moors and hills and in certain other parts of Britain (also **red grouse**): — *pl* **grouse**. — **grouse moor** a tract of moorland on which grouse live, breed, and are shot for sport.

grouse[2] *grows*, *vi* to grumble. — *n* a spell of grumbling. — *n* **grous'er**.

grouse[3] *grows*, (*Austr colloq*) *adj* very good.

grout[1] *growt*, *n* coarse meal; sediment, lees; a thin coarse mortar; a fine plaster for finishing ceilings. — *vt* to fill and finish with grout. — *n* **grout'er**. — *n* **grout'ing** filling up or finishing with grout; the material so used.

grout[2] *growt*, *vi* to root or grub with the snout. [Perh. connected with O.E. *grēot*, grit.]

grove *grōv*, *n* a wood of small size, generally of a pleasant or ornamental character; an avenue of trees; (with *cap*) used in street names. [O.E. *grāf*, possibly tamarisk.]

grovel *grov'l*, *vi* to humble oneself, behave abjectly, e.g. in apologising; to behave obsequiously or sycophantically; to lie face downwards, or crawl, in abject fear, etc.: — *pr p* **grov'elling** or in U.S. **grov'eling**; *pa t* and *pa p* **grov'elled** or in U.S. **grov'eled**. — *n* **grov'eller**. — *adj* **grov'elling** abject, cringing, servile. [Back-formation from M.E. *groveling*, *grofling*, prone.]

grow *grō*, *vi* to have life; to become enlarged by a natural process; to advance towards maturity; to increase in size; to tend in a certain direction while growing; to develop; to become greater in any way; to become; to come by degrees (to love, like, hate, etc.). — *vt* to cause or allow to grow; to produce or cultivate; (in *passive*) to cover with growth: — *pa t* **grew** (*grōō*); *pa p* **grown** (*grōn*). — *adj* **grow'able**. — *n* **grow'er**. — *n* and *adj* **grow'ing**. — *adj* (sometimes in combination) **grown** having reached full, or a certain degree of, growth, as in *full-grown*, *half-grown*. — *n* **growth** a growing; gradual increase; progress, development; that which has grown; a morbid formation; increase in value. — Also *adj*. — **grow bag** a large plastic bag containing compost in which seeds can be germinated and plants grown to full size; **growing pains** neuralgic pains sometimes experienced by growing children; initial problems in the establishment and running of an enterprise, etc.; **growing point** (*bot*) the formative tissue or meristem at the apex of an axis, where active cell-division occurs and differentiation of tissues begins; **grown'-up** an adult. — Also *adj*. — **growth hormone** a hormone secreted by the anterior lobe of the pituitary gland, that promotes growth in vertebrates; any of several natural or artificial substances that promote growth in plants; **growth industry** an industry or branch of industry which is developing and expanding. — **grow into** to grow big enough to fill comfortably; **grow on** to gain in the estimation of, become ever more acceptable to; (of seedlings) to (be stimulated to) develop into mature plants by suitable positioning, treatment, etc.; **grow out of** to issue from, result from; to pass beyond in development; to become too big for; **grow together** to become united by growth; **grow up** to advance in growth, become full-grown, mature or adult; to spring up. [O.E. *grōwan*.]

growl *growl*, *vi* (of a dog) to make a deep rough murmuring sound in the throat, expressive of hostility; (of thunder, etc.) to make a sound similar to this; to speak in a surly fashion, snarl. — *vt* to utter or express by growling. — *n* a murmuring, snarling sound, as of an angry dog; a surly grumble. — *n* **growl'er**. — *n* and *adj* **growl'ing**. — *adv* **growl'ingly**. — *adj* **growl'y**.

grown, growth. See **grow**.

groyne *groin*, *n* a breakwater, of wood or other material, to check erosion and sand-drifting. [Prob. O.Fr. *groign*, snout.]

grub *grub*, *vi* to dig, work, or search in the dirt (with *about* or *around*); to be occupied meanly, toil, slog; (of a horse) to take its feed. — *vt* to dig or root out of the ground (with *up* or *out*); to dig up the surface of (ground) to clear it for agriculture, etc. — *n* an insect larva, esp. one thick and soft; food (*colloq*). — *n* **grubb'er** a person who, or that which, grubs; an implement for grubbing or stirring the soil; a grub kick. — *adj* **grubb'y** dirty; infested with grubs. — **grub kick** (*Rugby football*) a kick where the ball moves along the ground; **grub screw** a small headless screw; **grub shop** (*colloq*) a restaurant; **grub'stake** (*NAm*) outfit, provisions, etc., given to a prospector for a share in finds. — *vt* to provide with such. — **Grub Street** a former name of Milton Street, London, once inhabited by hacks and shabby writers generally; the milieu of hack writers or activity of hack writing. — Also (usu. **Grub'street**) *adj*. [M.E. *grobe*.]

grudge *gruj*, *vt* to envy (someone something); to give or allow (someone something) only unwillingly; to resent (doing something). — *n* an old cause of resentment; a feeling of enmity or envy. — *n* and *adj* **grudg'ing**. — *adv* **grudg'ingly**. [O.Fr. *groucher*, to grumble.]

gruel *grōō'əl*, *n* a thin food made by boiling oatmeal in water. [O.Fr., groats — L.L. *grūtellum*, dimin. of *grūtum*, meal.]

gruelling or in U.S. **grueling** *grōō'ə-ling*, *adj* punishing, backbreaking, exhausting. [Ety. as for **gruel**.]

gruesome *grōō'səm*, *adj* horrible; grisly; macabre. — *n* **grue'someness**. [Cf. Ger. *grausam*.]

gruff *gruf*, *adj* rough, or abrupt in manner or sound. — *adv* **gruff'ly**. — *n* **gruff'ness**. [Du. *grof*, coarse.]

grumble *grum'bl*, *vi* to express discontent, complain; to mutter, mumble, murmur; to rumble. — *n* a spell of grumbling; a cause or occasion for grumbling. — *n* **grum'bler**. — *n* and *adj* **grum'bling**. — *adv* **grum'blingly**. — *adj* **grum'bly** inclined to grumble. [Cf. Du. *grommelen*, frequentative of *grommen*, to mutter.]

grummet or **grommet** *grum'it*, *n* a ring of rope or metal; a metal ring lining an eyelet; an eyelet; a washer to protect or insulate electrical wire passing through a hole; (usu. **grommet**) a small tube passed through the eardrum to drain the middle ear (*med*). [Perh. 15th-cent. Fr. *grom(m)ette*, curb of a bridle.]

grump *grump*, (*colloq*) *n* an ill-tempered, surly person; (in *pl*) a fit of ill temper, the sulks. — *vi* to grumble, complain. — *adv* **grum'pily**. — *n* **grum'piness**. — *adj* **grum'py** surly. [Obs. *grump*, snub, sulkiness.]

grungy *grun'ji*, (*slang*) *adj* dirty, messy; unattractive, unappealing. [Prob. imit. coinage.]

grunion *grun'yən*, *n* a small Californian sea-fish which spawns on shore. [Prob. Sp. *gruñon*, grunter.]

grunt *grunt*, *vi* (of a pig) to make a gruff snorting noise; to produce a short gruff noise in the throat. — *vt* to utter with a grunt. — *n* a sound made by a pig; any similar sound made by a person or animal; a tropical spiny-finned fish that grunts when taken from the sea; an infantryman (*US slang*). — *n* **grunt'er** a person who grunts; a pig; any of several kinds of grunting fish. — *n* and *adj* **grunt'ing**. [O.E. *grunnettan*, frequentative of *grunian*.]

Gruyère *grü'yer*, *groo'* or *-yer'*, *n* a whole-milk cheese, made at *Gruyère* (Switzerland) and elsewhere.

gr. wt. *abbrev* for gross weight.
gryfon, gryphon. See **griffin**.
grysbok *grīs'bok*, *n* a small S. African antelope, ruddy chestnut with white hairs. [Du., greybuck.]
GS *abbrev* for General Staff.
gs *abbrev* for gauss.
GSO *abbrev* for General Staff Officer.
G-string. Same as **gee-string**.
g*-suit.** See under ***g.
GT *abbrev* for *gran turismo* (It.), a designation of fast touring cars.
Gt or **gt** *abbrev* for Great or great.
gtd *abbrev* for guaranteed.
guacamole *gwa-kə-mō'li*, *n* a dish of mashed avocado with tomatoes, onions and seasoning. [Am. Sp. — Nahuatl *ahuacamolli* — *ahuacatl*, avocado, *molli*, sauce.]
guaiacum *gwī'ə-kəm*, *n* any of a family of tropical American trees of the genus *Guaiacum*, some yielding lignum vitae; their greenish resin, used in medicine. [Sp. *guayaco*, from a Haitian word.]
guanaco *gwä-nä'kō*, *n* a wild llama: — *pl* **guana'co** or **guana'cos**. [Quechua *huanaco*.]
guango *gwang'gō*, *n* the rain tree or saman: — *pl* **guan'gos**. [Sp., prob. from Quechua.]
guanin or **guanine** *gwä'nēn*, *n* a yellowish-white, amorphous substance, found in guano, liver, other organs of animals, germ cells of plants — a constituent of nucleic acids. [**guano** and sfx. *-in(e)*.]
guano *gwä'nō*, *n* the dung of sea-fowl, used as manure; artificially produced fertiliser, esp. made from fish: — *pl* **gua'nos**. — *adj* **guanif'erous**. [Sp. *guano*, *huano* — Quechua *huanu*, dung.]
guarani *gwä-rä-nē'*, *n* the standard monetary unit of Paraguay (100 *céntimos*): — *pl* **guaranis', gwarani'** or **guaranies'**. [*Guaraní*, name of a people of southern Brazil and Paraguay.]
guarantee *gar-ən-tē'*, *n* a formal promise that something will be done, esp. one in writing by the maker of a product to replace or repair it if it proves faulty within a stated period; generally, a promise or assurance; an agreement to take responsibility for another person's obligation or undertaking; a pledge or surety; someone to whom a guarantee is given, who gives a guarantee, or who acts as guarantor. — *vt* to issue a guarantee in respect of (e.g. an article or product); to secure (with *against* or *from*); to ensure, make certain or definite; to engage or undertake; to undertake as surety for another person: — *pr p* **guarantee'ing**; *pa t* and *pa p* **guaranteed'**. — *n* **guar'antor** (or *-tör'*) a person who gives a guarantee or stands surety for another. — *n* **guar'anty** a securing, guaranteeing; a written undertaking to be responsible; a person who guarantees; a security. — *vt* to guarantee. [A.Fr. *garantie* — *garant*, warrant and prob. Sp. *garante*.]
guard *gärd*, *vt* to keep, watch over; to take care of; to protect from danger or attack; to control passage through (a doorway, etc.); to escort; to provide, or fit, with guards; in any of several games, to make a move to protect (a piece, etc.). — *vi* to watch; to be wary; to take precautions. — *n* custody, keeping; protection; watch; that which guards from danger; a person or contingent stationed to watch, protect, or keep in custody; a person in charge of a railway train; state of caution; posture of defence; a device on machinery for protecting the user; part of a sword hilt; a watch chain; a cricketer's pad; (in *pl* with *cap*) household troops (Foot, Horse, and Life Guards). — *adj* **guard'able**. — *adj* **guard'ant** (*heraldry*) having the face turned towards the viewer. — *adj* **guard'ed** wary; cautious; uttered with caution. — *adv* **guard'edly**. — *n* **guard'edness**. — *n* **guardee'** (*colloq*) a guardsman. — *adj* **guard'less**. — **guard dog** a watchdog; **guard hair** one of the long coarse hairs which form the outer fur of certain mammals; **guard'house** a building for the accommodation of a military guard, where prisoners are confined; **guard'rail** a rail (on a ship, train, etc., or beside a road) acting as a safety barrier; an additional rail fitted to a railway track to improve a train's stability; **guard ring** a keeper ring, a finger ring that keeps another from slipping off; **guard'room** a room having the same function as a guardhouse; **guards'man** a soldier of the Guards, or in the U.S., National Guard; **guard's van** (on a railway train) the van in which the guard travels. — **guard of honour** see **honour; mount guard** to go on guard; **on (or off) one's guard** on (or not on) the alert for possible danger; wary (or unwary) about what one says or does; **stand guard** to keep watch, act as sentry. [O.Fr. *garder* — O.H.G. *warten* (Mod. Eng. **ward**).]
guardian *gär'di-ən*, *n* a person who guards or takes care of something; someone who has charge of the person, property and rights of another, e.g. a minor (*law*). — *adj* protecting. — *n* **guard'ianship**. — **guardian angel** an angel supposed to watch over a particular person; a person specially devoted to the interests of another; (in *pl*, with *caps*) vigilantes patrolling New York's subway (and active elsewhere) to prevent crimes of violence. [A.Fr. *gardein*.]
guava *gwä'və*, *n* a small tropical American myrtaceous tree of the genus *Psidium*; its yellow pear-shaped fruit. [Sp. *guayaba*, guava fruit; of S. Am. origin.]
guayule *gwä-ū'lā*, *n* a silvery-leaved shrub of the daisy family, native to Mexico and south-west U.S.; the rubber yielded by it. [Sp.; of Nahuatl origin.]
gubbins *gub'inz*, (*colloq*) *nsing* a trivial object; a device, gadget. — *nsing* or *npl* rubbish. [From obs. *gobbon*, portion.]
gubernatorial *gū-bər-nə-tō'ri-əl*, (*US*) *adj* of, or relating to, a governor. [L. *gubernātor*, a steersman.]
guck *guk*, (esp. *US*, *slang*) *n* slimy, gooey muck; anything unpleasant or unappealing. — *adj* **guck'y** slimy, gooey, mucky; slushy, sloppy, sentimental. [Prob. **goo** or **gunk** and **muck**.]
gudgeon¹ *guj'ən*, *n* an easily caught small carp-like freshwater fish (*Gobio*); a person easily cheated. — *vt* to impose on, cheat. [O.Fr. *goujon* — L. *gōbiō, -ōnis*, a kind of fish — Gr. *kōbios*.]
gudgeon² *guj'ən*, *n* the bearing of a shaft, esp. when made of a separate piece; a piece let into the end of a wooden shaft; a pin. — **gudgeon pin** in an internal combustion engine, a pin fastening the piston to the connecting rod. [O.Fr. *goujon*, pin of a pulley.]
guelder rose *gel'dər rōz*, *n* a shrub of the genus *Viburnum*, with large white balls of flowers. [From *Geldern* or *Gelderland*, a province of the Netherlands.]
guenon *gen'ən* or *gə-nɔ̃*, *n* any species of the genus *Cercopithecus*, long-tailed African monkeys. [Fr.]
guerilla. See **guerrilla**.
guernsey *gûrn'zi*, *n* a close-fitting knitted woollen jersey, esp. worn by sailors; a usu. sleeveless football shirt (*Austr*); (with *cap*) a breed of dairy cattle from *Guernsey*, in the Channel Islands. — **get a guernsey** (*Austr*) to be selected for a team; to win approval.
guerrilla or **guerilla** *gə-ril'ə*, *n* a member of an irregular force engaging in petty warfare or in the harassment of an army, usu. operating in small bands. — **guerrilla tactics; guerrilla warfare**. [Sp. *guerrilla*, dimin. of *guerra*, war.]
guess *ges*, *vt* to judge upon inadequate knowledge or none at all; to conjecture; to hit on or solve by conjecture; to think, believe, suppose (esp. *NAm*). — *vi* to make a conjecture or conjectures. — *n* a judgment made or opinion formed without sufficient evidence or grounds; a random surmise. — *adj* **guess'able**. — *n* **guess'er**. — *n* and *adj* **guess'ing**. — **guess'work** the process or result of guessing. — **anybody's guess** purely a matter for individual

conjecture, impossible for anyone to know. [M.E. *gessen*.]

guesstimate *ges'ti-mət*, *n* a *guessed estimate*, or one based on very little knowledge. — *vt* to estimate using a rough guess.

guest *gest*, *n* a person visiting one's home by invitation, to stay, for a meal, etc.; a person invited out and paid for at a restaurant, club, theatre, etc.; a person paying for accommodation in a hotel, etc.; a person honoured with hospitality by a government, organisation etc. — *adj* and *n* (an artist, conductor, etc.) not a regular member of a company, etc., or not regularly appearing on a programme, but taking part on a special occasion. — *vi* to be a guest artist, etc. — *vt* to have as a guest artist on a show. — **guest'house** a small boarding-house; **guest room** a room for the accommodation of a guest; **guest rope** a rope hanging over the side of a vessel to help other vessels drawing alongside, etc.; **guest worker** a foreign worker employed temporarily in a country, a Gastarbeiter (q.v.). [O.E. (Anglian) *gest*.]

guff *guf*, *n* nonsense, humbug (*colloq*); a smell, stink (*Scot*). [Perh. imit.]

guffaw *gə-fö'*, *vi* to laugh vociferously. — *n* a loud, boisterous laugh. [From the sound.]

guichet *gē'shā*, *n* a hatch or other small opening in a wall, door, etc.; a ticket-office window. [Fr.]

guide *gīd*, *vt* to lead, conduct or direct; to regulate, steer, control; to influence. — *n* a person who, or that which, guides; a person who conducts travellers, tourists, mountaineers, etc.; (with *cap*) a member of an organisation for girls, analogous to the Scout Association (also *formerly* **Girl Guide**); a guidebook; anything serving to direct, show the way, determine direction of motion or course of conduct. — *adj* **gui'dable**. — *n* **gui'dance** direction; leadership. — *n* **Gui'der** a captain or lieutenant in the Guides. — *adj* **gui'ding**. — *n* (usu. with *cap*) the activities of a Guide. — **guide'book** a book of information for tourists; **guided missile** a jet- or rocket-propelled projectile carrying a warhead and electronically directed to its target for the whole or part of the way by remote control; **guide dog** a dog trained to lead a blind person; **guide'line** a line drawn, or a rope, etc., fixed, to act as a guide; an indication of the course that should be followed, or of what future policy will be; **guide'post** a post to guide the traveller; **guiding light** or **star** a person or thing adopted as a guide or model. [O.Fr. *guider*.]

guild or **gild** *gild*, *n* an association for mutual aid; a corporation; a mediaeval association providing mutual support and protection (*hist*). — **guild'hall** the hall of a guild; a town hall. [O.E. *gield*, influenced by O.N. *gildi*.]

guilder or **gilder** *gild'ər*, *n* a modern Dutch gulden; an old Dutch and German gold coin. [Du. *gulden*.]

guile *gīl*, *n* cunning; deceit. — *adj* **guile'ful** crafty; deceitful. — *adv* **guile'fully**. — *n* **guile'fulness**. — *adj* **guile'less** without deceit; artless. — *adv* **guile'lessly**. — *n* **guile'lessness**. [O.Fr. *guile*, deceit.]

Guillain-Barré syndrome *gē-yẽ-ba-rā' sin'drōm*, (*med*) *n* an acute polyneuritis causing weakness or paralysis of the limbs. [Georges *Guillain* and Jean *Barré*, French neurologists.]

guillemot *gil'i-mot*, *n* a diving bird of the genus *Uria*, belonging to the auk family. [Fr., dimin. of *Guillaume*, William, perh. suggested by Breton *gwelan*, gull.]

guilloche *gi-lōsh'*, (*art* or *archit*) *n* an ornamental border or moulding formed of interlacing bands enclosing roundels. [Fr.]

guillotine *gil'ə-tēn*, *n* an instrument for beheading by descent of a heavy oblique blade — adopted during the French Revolution, and named after Joseph Ignace *Guillotin* (1738–1814), a physician, who first proposed its adoption; a machine for cutting paper, straw, etc.; a surgical instrument for excising the tonsils; a specially drastic rule or closure for shortening discussion. — *vt* to behead, crop, excise or cut short by guillotine.

guilt *gilt*, *n* the state of having done wrong; sin, sinfulness or consciousness of it; the state of having broken a law; liability to a penalty. — *adv* **guilt'ily**. — *n* **guilt'iness**. — *adj* **guilt'less** free from crime; innocent. — *adv* **guilt'lessly**. — *n* **guilt'lessness**. — *adj* **guilt'y** justly chargeable; wicked; involving, indicating, burdened with, or relating to guilt. — **guilt complex** a mental preoccupation with one's (real or imagined) guilt; **guilty party** a person, organisation, etc. that is guilty. — **guilty of** having committed (an evil or injudicious act). [Orig. a payment or fine for an offence; O.E. *gylt*.]

guinea *gin'i*, *n* an obsolete English gold coin first made of gold brought from *Guinea*, in Africa; its value, 21 shillings (now 1.05), a unit still favoured by certain professionals in charging fees. — **guinea fowl** an African bird (*Numida*) of the pheasant family, dark-grey with white spots, known formerly as a turkey; **guinea hen** a (esp. female) guinea fowl; **guinea pig** a small S. American rodent, the cavy; (also **human guinea pig**) a person used as the subject of an experiment — as the cavy commonly is in the laboratory.

guipure *gē-pōōr'*, *n* a kind of lace having no ground or mesh, the pattern sections fixed by interlacing threads; a species of gimp. [Fr. *guipure* — O.Fr. *guiper*.]

guiro *gwē'rō*, *n* a notched gourd used as a percussion instrument in Latin America: — *pl* **gui'ros**. [Sp., gourd.]

guise *gīz*, *n* semblance, pretence or mask; external appearance, shape, likeness; dress (*archaic*). — *n* **gui'ser** someone who goes guising. — *n* **gui'sing** esp. in Scotland, a survival of mumming, whereby children dress up and go from house to house collecting cash in return for some musical performance, etc. [O.Fr. *guise*.]

guitar *gi-tär'*, *n* a fretted musical instrument, now six-stringed — like the lute, but flat-backed. — *n* **guitar'ist**. [Fr. *guitare* — L. *cithara* — Gr. *kitharā*.]

gulag *gōō'lag*, *n* (*formerly*) (one of) the system of esp. political prisons and forced labour camps in the Soviet Union; any camp or system for the detention and silencing of political prisoners. [Russ. acronym of the title of the body administering the system, familiarised by A. Solzhenitsyn (1918–) in *The Gulag Archipelago*.]

gulch *gulch*, (*NAm*) *n* a ravine or narrow rocky valley, a gully.

gulden *gōōl'dən*, *n* a Dutch coin, the guilder or florin; a gold or silver coin in Germany in the Middle Ages. [Ger., lit. golden.]

gules *gūlz*, (*heraldry*) *n* a red colour. [O.Fr. *gueules*, perh. — L. *gūla*, the throat.]

gulf *gulf*, *n* an indentation in the coast; a deep place; an abyss; a whirlpool; a wide separation, e.g. between opponents' viewpoints; (with *cap* and **the**) the Arabian or Persian Gulf, or (*loosely*) the region of and surrounding this, or the Gulf States. — *vt* to engulf. — *vi* to flow like a gulf. — *adj* (with *cap*) of or relating to the Gulf. — **Gulf States** the small Arab states, rich in oil, bordering the Arabian Gulf, i.e. Bahrain, Kuwait, Qatar and the United Arab Emirates; **Gulf Stream** the warm ocean current which flows north from the Gulf of Mexico, eventually to merge into the North Atlantic Drift; **gulf'weed** a large olive-brown seaweed that floats unattached in great 'meadows' at the branching of the Gulf Stream and elsewhere in tropical oceans. [O.Fr. *golfe* — Late Gr. *kolphos* — Gr. *kolpos*, the bosom.]

gull[1] *gul*, *n* a sea-bird of the family *Laridae*, esp. of the genus *Larus*, usu. with predominantly white plumage. — *n* **gull'ery** a place where gulls breed. — *adj*

gull'-wing (of a motor car door) opening upwards; (of an aircraft wing) having an upward-sloping short inner section and a long horizontal outer section. [Prob. Welsh *gwylan*.]

gull[2] *gul*, *n* a dupe or fool. — *vt* to beguile or hoax.

gullet *gul'it*, *n* the passage in the neck by which food is taken into the stomach; the throat. [O.Fr. *goulet*, dimin. of *goule* — L. *gŭla*, the throat.]

gullible *gul'i-bl*, *adj* easily deceived or tricked, credulous. — *n* **gullibil'ity.** [**gull**[2].]

gully or **gulley** *gul'i*, *n* a channel worn by running water, as on a mountainside; a ravine; a ditch; the fielding position between point and slips, or a fielder in this position (*cricket*): — *pl* **gull'ies** or **gull'eys.** — *vt* to wear a gully or channel in. [Prob. **gullet.**]

gulp *gulp*, *vt* to swallow spasmodically, in large draughts or with effort; to stifle or suppress (with *back* or *down*). — *vi* to make a swallowing movement. — *n* a spasmodic or copious swallow; a movement as if of swallowing; a quantity swallowed at once; capacity for gulping. — *n* **gulp'er.** [Cf. Du. *gulpen*, *gulp*.]

gum[1] *gum*, *n* the firm fleshy tissue that surrounds the bases of the teeth. — *vt* (*NAm*) to deepen and widen the gaps between the teeth of (a saw) to make it last longer. — *adj* **gumm'y** toothless. — **gum'boil** a small abscess on the gum; **gum'shield** a soft pad worn by boxers to protect the teeth and gums. [O.E. *gōma*, palate.]

gum[2] *gum*, *n* a substance that collects in or exudes from certain plants, and hardens on the surface, dissolves or swells in water, but does not dissolve in alcohol or ether; a plant gum or similar substance used as an adhesive or stiffener, or for other purposes; any gumlike or sticky substance; chewing-gum; a gumdrop (q.v.). — *vt* to smear, coat, treat or unite with gum. — *vi* to become gummy; to exude gum: — *pr p* **gumm'ing**; *pa t* and *pa p* **gummed.** — *adj* **gummif'erous** producing gum. — *n* **gumm'iness.** — *n* **gumm'ing.** — *adj* **gumm'ous** or **gumm'y** consisting of or resembling gum; producing or covered with gum. — **gum ammoniac** or **ammoniacum** a gum resin used in medicine; **gum arabic** a gum obtained from various acacias, used in the production of inks and food-thickeners; **gum'boot** a rubber boot; **gum'-digger** (*NZ*) someone who digs up fossilised kauri-gum; **gum'drop** a gelatinous type of sweet containing gum arabic; **gum elastic** rubber; **gum'nut** the woody fruit of the eucalyptus; **gum resin** a resin mixed with gum; **gum'shoe** (*NAm*) a rubber overshoe; a shoe with a rubber sole; a detective or policeman (*slang*). — Also *vi* (*slang*) to snoop or pry. — **gum tree** a tree that exudes gum, or gum resin, etc., esp. a eucalyptus tree. — **gum up the works** (*colloq*) to make a machine, a scheme, etc. unworkable; **up a gum tree** in a difficult situation (from the opossum's refuge). [O.Fr. *gomme* — L. *gummi* — Gr. *kommi*.]

gumbo *gum'bō*, *n* the okra or its mucilaginous pods; a soup of which okra is an ingredient; a dish of okra pods seasoned; (in central U.S.) a fine soil which becomes sticky when wet; (with *cap*) a patois spoken by Creoles in Louisiana: — *pl* **gum'bos.** [Angolan Negro (*ki*)*ngombo*.]

gumption *gump'shən* or *gum'shən*, *n* common sense; shrewdness; courage. — *adj* **gump'tious.**

gun *gun*, *n* a tubular weapon from which projectiles are discharged, usually by explosion; a cannon, rifle, revolver, etc.; a device for spraying, squirting, or otherwise propelling material; a signal by gun; someone who carries a gun, e.g. a member of a shooting-party; a professional killer (*NAm slang*); the throttle of an aircraft; the accelerator of a car; an expert or champion, esp. in shearing (*Austr* and *NZ colloq*). — *vt* to shoot; to shoot at; to provide with guns; to open the throttle of, to increase speed (*colloq*; also **give the gun**); to rev up (the engine of a stationary car) noisily (*colloq*). — *vi* to shoot; to go shooting. — *adj* (*Austr* and *NZ*) expert, pre-eminent. — *n* **gunn'er** someone who works a gun; a private in the artillery. — *n* **gunn'ery** the art of managing guns, or the science of artillery. — *n* **gunn'ing.** — **gun barrel** the tube of a gun; **gun'boat** a small vessel of light draught, fitted to carry one or more guns; **gunboat diplomacy** a show or threat of (orig. naval) force in international negotiation; **gun carriage** a carriage on which a cannon is mounted; **gun'cotton** an explosive prepared by saturating cotton with nitric and sulphuric acids; **gun dog** a dog trained to work with a shooting-party; **gun'fight** a fight involving two or more people with guns, esp. formerly in the American West. — Also *vi.* — **gun'fighter; gun'fire; gun'lock** the mechanism in some guns by which the charge is exploded; **gun'man** a man who carries a gun, esp. an armed criminal; **gun'metal** an alloy of copper and tin or zinc in the proportion of about 9 to 1, once used in making cannon; any of various metals used in imitation of this; any of various colours with a metallic sheen; **gun'play** the use of guns, esp. in a fight or display of skill; **gun'powder** an explosive mixture of saltpetre, sulphur, and charcoal; **gun'-room** a room where guns are kept; on board ship, a mess-room for junior officers; **gun'runner; gun'-running** smuggling guns into a country; **gun'ship** an armed ship, helicopter, etc.; **gun'shot** the shot fired from a gun; the range of a gun. — *adj* caused by the shot of a gun. — *adj* **gun'-shy** frightened of the sound of guns. — **gun'slinger** (*colloq*) a gunfighter; **gun'smith** a smith or workman who makes or repairs guns or small arms. — **at gunpoint** under or using the threat of injury from a gun; **go great guns** (*colloq*) to function, be carried out, etc. with great success, speed, efficiency, etc.; **great gun** a person of great importance (*colloq*; also **big gun**); **gun for** to seek, try to obtain; to seek to ruin; **son of a gun** a rogue or rascal (*slang*); used as an affectionate greeting. — Also *interj* (*NAm*). — **stick to one's guns** to maintain one's position staunchly. [M.E. *gonne*, poss. from the woman's name *Gunhild*.]

gunge *gunj*, (*colloq*) *n* any dirty, messy or sticky substance. — *adj* **gun'gy.** [Perh. a combination of **goo** and **sponge.**]

gung-ho *gung-hō'*, (*NAm colloq*) *adj* (excessively or irrationally) enthusiastic, eager or zealous. [Chin. *kung*, work, *ho*, together.]

gunk *gungk*, (*colloq*) *n* unpleasant, dirty or sticky material, or semi-solid usu. valueless residue from a chemical process. [Orig. trademark of a grease-solvent.]

gunnel[1] *n.* See **gunwale.**

gunnel[2] *gun'l*, *n* a small eel-like coast fish of the blenny family.

gunnery. See **gun.**

gunny *gun'i*, *n* a strong coarse jute fabric. [Hindi *ganī*, *gonī*, sacking — Sans. *gonī*, a sack.]

gunter *gun'tər*, *n* a Gunter's scale; a rig with topmast sliding on rings. — **Gunter's chain** a surveyor's chain of 100 links, 66 feet long; this distance used as a unit; **Gunter's scale** a rule graduated in several lines for numbers, logarithmic sines, etc., so arranged that trigonometrical problems can be roughly solved by use of a pair of compasses, or in another form by sliding. [From the inventor, Edmund *Gunter* (1581–1626), astronomer.]

gunwale or **gunnel** *gun'l*, *n* the *wale* or upper edge of a ship's side next to the bulwarks, so called because the upper *guns* were pointed from it. — **full** or **packed to the gunwales** absolutely full; **gunwales to** or **under** with gunwales at or below the surface of the water.

gunyah *gun'yə*, (*Austr*) *n* an Australian Aborigine's hut; a roughly made shelter in the bush. [Aboriginal.]

guppy *gup'i*, *n* a small West Indian fish that multiplies very rapidly and feeds on mosquito larvae; also called *millions*: — *pl* **gupp'ies**. [From R.J.L. *Guppy*, who sent it to the British Museum.]

gurdwara *gûr'dwä-rə*, *n* a Sikh place of worship. [Punjabi *gurduārā* — Sans. *guru*, teacher, *dvāra*, door.]

gurgle *gûr'gl*, *vi* to flow in an irregular noisy current; to make a bubbling sound. — *n* the sound of gurgling. [Cf. It. *gorgogliare*.]

gurjun *gûr'jun*, *n* an East Indian tree of the genus *Dipterocarpus*, yielding timber and a balsamic liquid used against leprosy. — Also **gar'jan**. [Hind. *garjan*.]

Gurkha *gōōr'kə* or *gûr'kə*, *n* one of the dominant people of Nepal, a broad-chested fighting race claiming Hindu origin, but Mongolised, from whom regiments in the British and Indian armies were formed. — *n* **Gurkhali** (*gōōr-kä'lē* or *gûr-kä'lē*) the Indo-European language spoken by Gurkhas.

gurnard *gûr'nərd* or **gurnet** *gûr'-nit*, *n* a fish with a large angular head and three fingerlike walking rays in front of the pectoral fin. [O.Fr. *gornard*, related to Fr. *grogner*, to grunt; from the sound they emit when caught.]

gurney *gûr'ni*, (*NAm*) *n* a wheeled stretcher or cart. [Perh. from the personal name.]

guru *gōō'rōō*, *n* a spiritual teacher; (often *facetious*) a revered instructor, mentor or pundit. — *n* **gu'rudom**, **gu'ruism** or **gu'ruship** the state of being a guru. [Hind. *gurū* — Sans. *guru*, venerable.]

gush *gush*, *vi* to flow out with violence or copiously; to be over-effusive or highly sentimental. — *vt* to pour forth copiously. — *n* that which flows out; a violent issue of a fluid; sentimentality, effusiveness. — *n* **gush'er** someone who gushes; an oil well that does not have to be pumped. — *adj* **gush'ing**. — *adv* **gush'ingly**. — *adj* **gush'y** effusively sentimental. [M.E. *gosshe*, *gusche*.]

gusset *gus'it*, *n* an angular piece inserted in a garment to strengthen or enlarge some part of it or give freedom of movement; the piece of chainmail covering a join in armour, as at the armpit. — *vt* to make with a gusset; to insert a gusset into. [O.Fr. *gousset* — *gousse*, pod, husk.]

gussy up *gus'i up*, (*NAm colloq*) *vi* to put one's best clothes on; to smarten up.

gust *gust*, *n* a sudden blast of wind; a burst of smoke, fire, etc.; a violent burst of passion. — *vi* to blow in gusts. — *adj* **gust'y** stormy; irritable or temperamental. — *n* **gust'iness**. — **gust lock** a mechanism on an aeroplane which prevents damage to the elevators by gusts of wind when the aeroplane is stationary. [O.N. *gustr*, blast.]

gustation *gus-tā'shən*, *n* the act of tasting; the sense of taste. — *adj* **gust'ative** or **gust'atory** of or pertaining to the sense of taste. [L. *gustus*, taste.]

gusto *gus'tō*, *n* exuberant enjoyment, zest. [It. — L. *gustus*, taste.]

gut *gut*, *n* the alimentary canal, esp. the lower part; sheep's or other intestines or silkworm's glands prepared for violin-strings, etc.; a narrow passage; the belly, paunch (*slang*); (in *pl*) the viscera; (in *pl*) the inner or essential parts; (in *pl*) stamina, toughness of character, tenacity, staying power, endurance, forcefulness (*colloq*). — *adj* (*colloq*) (of feelings or reactions) strong, deeply personal; (of issues, etc.) having immediate impact, arousing strong feelings. — *vt* to take out the guts of; to remove the contents of; to reduce to a shell (by burning, dismantling, plundering, etc.); to extract what is essential from: — *pr p* **gutt'ing**; *pa t* and *pa p* **gutt'ed**. — *adj* **gut'less** cowardly, lacking strength of character. — *vi* and *vt* **guts** (*colloq*) to eat greedily. — *n* **guts'iness**. — *adj* (*colloq*) **guts'y** having pluck or nerve; lusty, passionate; gluttonous. — *adj* **gutt'ed** (*colloq*) extremely shocked, upset or disappointed. — *n* **gutt'er**. — **gut'rot** (*colloq*) rough, cheap alcohol. — **hate someone's guts** (*colloq*) to have a violent dislike for someone; **have had a gutful (of)** (*slang*) to be thoroughly fed up with, have had as much as, or more than, one is prepared to tolerate; **have someone's guts (for garters)** (*slang*; esp. as a threat) to make a thorough job of slaughtering someone; **work, sweat, slog**, etc. **one's guts out** (*slang*) to work oneself into a state of exhaustion. [O.E. *guttas* (pl.).]

gutta *gut'ə*, *n* a drop (*med*); a small droplike ornament (*archit*); a small round colour-spot (*zool*): — *pl* **gutt'ae** (*-ē*). — *adj* **gutt'ate** or **gutt'ated** containing drops; spotted. [L. *gutta*, drop.]

gutta-percha *gut-ə-pûr'chə*, *n* a substance like rubber, but harder and not extensible, obtained chiefly from the latex of Malaysian trees of the genera *Palaquium*, *Payena*, etc. [Malay *getah*, gum, *percha*, a tree producing it.]

guttate, etc. See **gutta**.

gutter[1] *gut'ər*, *n* a channel for conveying away water, esp. at the roadside or at the eaves of a roof; a furrow, groove; the space comprising the fore-edges of pages lying together internally in a forme (*printing*); according to some, the inner margins between two facing pages (*printing*); the slums, slum life, social degradation or sordidness (with **the**). — *vt* to cut or form into small hollows. — *vi* to become hollowed; to trickle; to run down in drops, as a candle does; (of flame) to be blown downwards, or threaten to go out. — *n* **gutt'ering** gutters collectively; material for gutters. — **gutter press** that part of the press which specialises in sordid, sensationalistic journalism; **gutt'ersnipe** a street urchin. [O.Fr. *goutiere* — *goute* — L. *gutta*, a drop.]

gutter[2]. See **gut**.

guttural *gut'ər-əl*, *adj* pertaining to the throat; formed in the throat; throaty in sound. — *n* a sound pronounced in the throat or (*loosely*) by the back part of the tongue (*phon*); a letter representing such a sound. — *vt* **gutt'uralise** or **-ize** to sound gutturally; to make guttural. — *adv* **gutt'urally**. [L. *guttur*, the throat.]

GUY *abbrev* for Guyana (I.V.R.).

guy[1] *gī*, *n* a rope, rod, etc., used to steady anything, or hold it in position. — *vt* to keep in position by a guy. — **guy rope**. [O.Fr. *guis*, *guie*; Sp. *guia*, a guide.]

guy[2] *gī*, *n* an effigy of *Guy* Fawkes, dressed up grotesquely on the anniversary of the Gunpowder Plot (5 Nov.); a man or boy (*colloq*); a person (*NAm colloq*). — *vt* to turn to ridicule, make fun of.

guzzle *guz'l*, *vt* and *vi* to swallow greedily. — *n* a bout of guzzling. — *n* **guzz'ler**. [Perh. connected with Fr. *gosier*, throat.]

gwyniad or **gwiniad** *gwin'i-ad*, *n* a whitefish found in Bala Lake in Wales. [Welsh *gwyniad* — *gwyn*, white.]

gybe or **jibe** *jīb*, *vi* (of a sail) to swing over from one side to the other; to alter course in this way. — *vt* to cause to gybe. — *n* an act of gybing. — **gybe mark** a marker on a yacht-race course indicating a turning-point at which yachts must gybe. [See **jib**.]

gym *jim*, *n* and *adj* a familiar shortening of **gymnasium**, **gymnastic** and **gymnastics**. — **gym shoe** a plimsoll; **gym slip** or **tunic** a belted pinafore dress worn (esp. formerly) by schoolgirls.

gymkhana *jim-kä'nə*, *n* a public meeting in which (esp. amateur) riders compete against each other in various equestrian sports; (*formerly* in Anglo-India) a public place providing athletics facilities, etc.; a meeting for such sports. [Hindi *gend-khāna* (ball-house), racket-court, remodelled on *gym*nastics.]

gymnasium *jim-nā'zi-əm*, *n* a place, hall, building or school for gymnastics; orig. a public place or building where the Greek youths exercised themselves; a top-grade secondary school in many European countries, esp. Germany: — *pl* **gymnā'siums** or **gymnā'sia**. — *adj* **gymnā'sial**. — *n*

gym'nast (*-nast*) a person skilled in gymnastics. — *adj* **gymnas'tic** pertaining to athletic exercises; athletic, vigorous. — *adv* **gymnas'tically**. — *nsing* **gymnas'tics** exercises and activities devised to strengthen the body and improve agility and co-ordination. — *npl* feats or tricks of agility. [Latinised from Gr. *gymnasion* — *gymnos*, naked.]

gymno- *gim-nō-*, *gim-nə-*, *gim-no'-*, or *jim-*, *combining form* denoting (esp. in *biol* terms) naked. — *adj* **gym'nosperm** any of the lower or primitive group of seed-plants whose seeds are not enclosed in any ovary. — *adj* **gymnosper'mous**. [Gr. *gymnos*, naked.]

gyn-. See **gyno-**.

gynaecium. See **gynoecium**.

gynaeco- or in U.S. **gyneco-** *gī-ni-kō-*, *gī-ni-kə-* or *gī-ni-ko'-*, *combining form* denoting female, woman. — *n* **gynaecoc'racy** female rule. — *adj* **gynaeco-crat'ic**. — *adj* **gynaecolog'ical** or **gynaeco-log'ic**. — *n* **gynaecol'ogist**. — *n* **gynaecol'ogy** the science of, or branch of medicine dealing with, women's physiology and diseases. — *n* **gynaeco-mas'tia** (*pathol*) the abnormal enlargement of a man's breasts. [Gr. *gynē*, *gynaikos*, woman.]

gyno- *gī-nō-*, *gī-nə-*, *gī-no'-*, *jī-* or *ji-* or **gyn-**, *combining form* denoting female, woman or (*bot*) the female reproductive organ. — *n* **gynan'dromorph** an organism that combines male and female physical characteristics. — *adj* **gynandromor'phic** or **gynandromor'phous**. — *n* **gynandromor'phism** or **gynandromor'phy**. — *adj* **gynan'drous** with stamen concrescent with the carpel, as in orchids (*bot*); hermaphroditic. — *n* **gynan'dry** or **gynan'-drism**. — *n* **gynoc'racy** female rule. — *adj* **gyno-crat'ic**. — *n* **gynophō'bia** the fear or dislike of women. — *adj* and *n* **gynophō'bic**. — *n* **gy'no-phore** (*bot*) an elongation of the receptacle of a flower carrying carpels only. [Gr. *gynē*, woman.]

gynoecium, gynaeceum or in U.S. **gyneceum** *gī-nē'si-əm* or *jī-*, *n* the female organs of a flower (*bot*); the women's quarters in an ancient Greek or Roman house. [Gr. *gynaikeion*, women's apartments.]

-gyny *-ji-ni*, *combining form* denoting: female, woman, as in *misogyny*; the female organs (*bot*). — *adj combining form* **-gynous**. [Gr. *gynē*, woman.]

gyp[1] *jip*, (*slang*) *n* a swindle; a cheat. — *vt* to swindle: — *pr p* **gypp'ing**; *pa t* and *pa p* **gypped**.

gyp[2] *jip*, (*slang*) *n* pain, torture. — **give someone gyp** to cause someone pain. **[gee up.]**

gyppie, gyppo, gyppy. See **gippy**.

gypseous, gypsiferous. See **gypsum**.

gypsophila *jip-sof'i-lə*, *n* any plant of the genus *Gypsophila*, hardy perennials with chickweed-like appearance. [Gr. *gypsos*, chalk, *phileein*, to love.]

gypsum *jip'səm*, *n* a soft mineral, hydrated calcium sulphate, source of plaster of Paris and other plasters. — *adj* **gyp'seous**. — *adj* **gypsif'erous** producing or containing gypsum. — **gypsum block** a building block (usu. hollow) made of a gypsum plaster; **gypsum plasterboard** a building board consisting of a core of gypsum or anhydrous gypsum plaster between two sheets of paper. [L., — Gr. *gypsos*, chalk.]

gypsy or **gipsy** *jip'si*, *n* a Romany, a member of a wandering dark-skinned people of Indian origin, living mainly in Europe and the U.S.; a person who looks or behaves like a gypsy. — *adj* of the gypsies; unconventional; operating independently or illegally (*NAm colloq*). — **gypsy moth** a moth of the family *Lymantriidae*. [**Egyptian**, because once thought to have come from Egypt.]

gyre *jīr*, *n* (*literary*) a ring, circle; a circular or spiral turn or movement. — *adj* **gy'ral** or **gy'rant**. — *adv* **gy'rally**. — *vi* **gyrate'** to revolve, spin, whirl. — *adj* **gy'rate** curved round in a coil. — *n* **gyrā'tion** a whirling motion; a whirl or twist; a whorl. — *adj* **gyrā'tional**. — *adj* **gy'ratory** revolving; spinning round; (of traffic) revolving in one-way lines. — *n* **gy'rō** a gyrocompass; a gyroscope: — *pl* **gy'ros**. — *adj* **gyroid'al** spiral; rotatory. — *adj* **gy'rose** having a folded surface; marked with wavy lines or ridges. — *adj* **gy'rous**. — *n* **gy'rus** a convoluted ridge between two grooves; a convolution of the brain. — *n* **gyrocom'pass** a compass which indicates direction by the freely moving axis of a rapidly spinning wheel, owing to the earth's rotation, the axis assuming and maintaining a north and south direction. — *adj* **gyromagnet'ic** pertaining to magnetic properties of rotating electric charges. — *n* **gyromag'netism**. — *n* **gy'roscope** an apparatus in which a heavy flywheel or top rotates at high speed, the turning movement resisting change of direction of axis, used as a toy, an educational device, a compass, etc. — *adj* **gyroscop'ic**. — *n* **gyrostabilisā'tion** or **-z-**. — *n* **gyrostā'biliser** or **-z-** a gyroscopic device for countering the roll of a ship, etc. — *n* **gy'rostat** a gyroscope fixed in a rigid case. — *adj* **gyrostat'ic**. — *nsing* **gyrostat'ics** the science of rotating bodies. — **gyromagnetic compass** a compass used in aircraft in which, in order to eliminate errors caused by changes of course and speed (greater in an aircraft than in a ship), a gyroscope is combined with a magnet system. [L. *gȳrus* — Gr. *gȳros*, a circle, ring.]

gyrfalcon or **gerfalcon** *jûr'fōl-kn*, *n* a large northern and arctic falcon. [O.Fr. *gerfaucon*.]

gyrose, gyrous, gyrus. See under **gyre**.

H

H or **h** *āch*, sometimes spelt out **aitch**, *n* the eighth letter of the modern English alphabet, representing in Old English a guttural sound, gradually softened down to a spirant, and now often silent. — **H'-beam** a metal girder H-shaped in section.

H or **H.** *abbrev* for: height; heroin (*slang*); hospital; Hungary (I.V.R.); hydrant.

H *symbol* for: hard (on lead pencils); hydrogen (*chem*). — **H'-bomb** a hydrogen bomb.

h or **h.** *abbrev* for: hecto-; hot; hour.

h *symbol* for Planck('s) constant.

Ha (*chem*) *symbol* for hahnium.

ha *hä, interj* denoting various emotions or responses, e.g. surprise, joy, exultation, dismay, enquiry, scepticism, encouragement, hesitation, and when repeated, laughter. [Spontaneous utterance.]

ha. *abbrev* for hectare.

haar *här*, (*dialect*) *n* a cold sea mist. [O.N. *hārr*, hoary.]

Hab. (*Bible*) *abbrev* for (the Book of) Habakkuk.

habanera *hä-bä-nā'rə*, *n* a Cuban dance or dance tune in 2-4 time. [*Habana* or Havana, in Cuba.]

habdabs *hab'dabz*, (*colloq*) *npl* a state of extreme nervousness. — Also **ab'dabs.**

habeas corpus *hā'bi-əs kör'pəs*, *n* a writ to a jailer to produce a prisoner in person, and to state the reasons of detention. [L., lit. have the body (*ad subjiciendum*, to be brought up before the judge).]

haberdasher *hab'ər-dash-ər*, *n* a seller of small sewing articles, e.g. ribbons, tape, etc.; a men's outfitter (*NAm*). — *n* **hab'erdashery** (or *-dash'*) a haberdasher's goods, business or shop. [O.Fr. *hapertas*.]

habergeon *hab'ər-jən*, (*hist*) *n* a sleeveless mail-coat, orig. lighter than a hauberk. [O.Fr. *haubergeon*, dimin. of *hauberc*.]

habilitate *hə-bil'i-tāt*, *vt* to equip or finance (e.g. a mine). — *vi* to qualify, esp. as a German university lecturer. — *n* **habilitā'tion.** — *n* **habil'itātor.** [L.L. *habilitāre*, to enable — L. *habilis*, able.]

habit *hab'it*, *n* ordinary course of behaviour; tendency to perform certain actions; custom; familiarity; bodily constitution; characteristic mode of development; the geometric form taken by a crystal (*crystall*); official or customary dress, esp. the costume of a nun or monk; a garment, esp. a riding-habit; an addiction to a drug, etc. — *vt* to dress. — *adj* **hab'ited** clothed. — *adj* **habit'ūal** customary; usual; confirmed by habit. — *n* someone who has a habit; a habitual drunkard, drug-taker, frequenter, etc. — *adv* **habit'ūally.** — *n* **habit'ūalness.** — *vt* **habit'ūate** to accustom. — *n* **habitūā'tion** the act of accustoming; the process of becoming accustomed; acquired tolerance for a drug, which thereby loses its effect; development of psychological, without physical, dependence on a drug. — *n* **hab'itūde** habit. — *adj* **habitū'dinal.** — *n* **habitué** (*hab-it'ū-ā*) a habitual frequenter. — *n* **hab'itus** physical type, esp. as predisposing to disease (*med*); characteristic appearance, manner of growth, etc., of a plant or animal. — *adj* **hab'it-forming** (of a drug) such that a taker will find it difficult or impossible to give up using. [L. *habitus*, state, dress — *habitāre*, to dwell.]

habitable *hab'i-tə-bl*, *adj* able to be lived in; fit to live in. — *n* **habitabil'ity** or **hab'itableness.** — *adv* **hab'itably.** — *n* **hab'itant** an inhabitant; (*ab-ē-tã*; Fr.) a native of esp. Canada or Louisiana of French descent (*pl* in this sense sometimes **habitans**). — *n* **hab'itat** the normal abode or locality of an animal or plant (*biol*); the physical environment of any community; the place where a person or thing can usually be found (*facetious* or *colloq*). — *n* **habita'tion** the act of inhabiting; a dwelling or residence. — *adj* **habita'tional.** [L. *habitāre*, to dwell.]

habitation, etc. See **habitable.**

habitual, etc. See **habit.**

haček *hä'chek*, *n* in Slavonic languages, the diacritic mark (ˇ) placed over a letter to modify its sound. [Czech.]

hachure *hash'ūr* or *ä-shür*, *n* a hill-shading line on a map. — *vt* to shade with hachures. [Fr.]

hacienda *as-i-en'də*, (*SpAm*) *n* a landed estate; a ranch or farm; a main dwelling-house on an estate; a country house; a stock-rearing, manufacturing or mining establishment in the country. [Sp., — L. *facienda*, things to be done.]

hack[1] *hak*, *vt* to cut with rough blows; to notch; to kick the shins of (in some sports, illicitly); to put up with or bear (*slang*). — *vi* to slash or chop; to cough; to use a computer with great skill; to gain unauthorised access to other computers (often with *into*). — *n* an act of hacking; a gash; a notch; a chap in the skin; a kick on the shin; a mattock or pick. — *n* **hack'er** a skilled and enthusiastic computer operator, esp. an amateur (*colloq*); an operator who uses his or her skill to break into commercial or government computer systems. — *n* **hack'ing.** — *adj* short and interrupted, used e.g. of a broken, troublesome cough. — **hack'saw** a saw for metals. [Assumed O.E. *haccian*, found in composition *tō-haccian*.]

hack[2] *hak*, *n* a horse (or formerly, and still in U.S., a vehicle) kept for hire, esp. a poor one; an ordinary riding-horse; any person overworked on hire; a literary or journalistic drudge. — *adj* hired; hackneyed. — *vt* to make a hack of; to use as a hack; to hackney. — *vi* to work as a hack; to journey on horseback. — *n* **hackette'** (*slang*) a woman journalist. — **hack'ing jacket** or **coat** a waisted jacket with slits in the skirt and flapped pockets on a slant; **hack'work** literary drudgery for publishers. [**hackney.**]

hack[3] *hak*, *n* a grating or rack, e.g. for feeding cattle; a rack on which food is placed for a hawk; a bank for drying bricks. [O.E. *hæce*, *hæc*, grating, hatch.]

hackamore *hak'ə-mör*, *n* a halter used esp. in breaking in foals, consisting of a single length of rope with a loop to serve instead of a bridle; a bridle without a bit, exerting pressure on the horse's muzzle, not its mouth. [Sp. *jáquima*.]

hackberry *hak'ber-i*, *n* the hagberry; an American tree allied to the elm; its wood. [See **hagberry.**]

hackette. See **hack**[2].

hackle *hak'l*, *n* a comb for flax or hemp; a cock's neck feather; this worn as a decoration in a cap, etc.; (in *pl*) the hair of a dog's neck; an angler's fly made of a cock's hackle, or its frayed-out part. — *vt* to dress with a hackle. — *n* **hack'ler.** — *adj* **hack'ly** rough and broken, as if hacked or chopped; jagged and rough (*mining*). — **make someone's hackles rise** to make someone angry. [Perh. partly from O.E. *hacele*, *hæcele*, cloak, vestment.]

hackmatack *hak'mə-tak*, *n* an American larch; its wood. [Indian word.]

hackney *hak'ni*, *n* a horse for general use, esp. for hire; a horse with a high-stepping action, bred to draw light carriages. — *vt* to use to excess; to make commonplace. — *adj* **hack'neyed** trite; dulled by excessive use. — **hackney cab, carriage** or **coach** a vehicle let out for hire. [O.Fr. *haquenée*, an ambling nag; poss. — *Hackney* in East London, where horses were pastured.]

had *had*, *pa t* and *pa p* of **have**.

hadal *hā'dəl*, *adj* forming, or belonging to, the levels of the ocean deeper than 6000 metres. [**Hades.**]

haddock *had'ək*, *n* a N. Atlantic sea fish of the cod family. [M.E. *haddok.*]

hade *hād*, (*mining*) *n* the angle between the plane of a fault, etc., and a vertical plane. — *vi* to incline from the vertical.

Hades *hā'dēz*, *n* the underworld, roamed by the souls of the dead (*Gr mythol*); the abode of the dead; hell (*NT*). [Gr. *Aidēs*, *Haidēs*, the god of the underworld; the abode of the dead.]

Hadith *had'ith* or *hä-dēth'*, *n* the body of traditions about Mohammed, supplementary to the Koran. [Ar. *hadīth.*]

hadj, haj or **hajj** *häj*, *n* a Muslim pilgrimage to Mecca. — *n* **hadj'i, haj'i** or **hajj'i** (*-i*) someone who has performed a hadj; a Christian who has visited Jerusalem. [Ar. *hajj*, effort, pilgrimage.]

hadn't *had'ənt*, contracted form of **had not.**

hadron *had'ron*, *n* one of a class of subatomic particles, including baryons and mesons. — *adj* **hadron'ic.** [Gr. *hadros*, heavy, *-on* as in **proton**, etc.]

haecceity *hek-sē'i-ti* or *hēk-*, (*philos*) *n* that element of existence on which individuality depends, hereness-and-nowness. [Med. L. *haeccēitas*, lit. thisness — L. *haec.*]

haem- *hēm-* or *hem-*, **haemat-** *-ət-* or **haemo-** *-ō-* or *-o-* or in U.S. **hem-, hemat-** and **hemo-** *combining form* denoting blood. — *n* **haem** (also **hem** and **heme**) the pigment combined with the protein (globin) in haemoglobin. — *adj* **haemal** or **hemal** (*hē'məl*) of the blood or blood-vessels; ventral (opp. to *dorsal* or *neural*) (*old*). — *n* **haematem'esis** (Gr. *emesis*, vomiting) vomiting of blood from the stomach. — *adj* **haemat'ic** pertaining to blood. — *n* **hae'matin** brown substance containing ferric iron obtainable from oxyhaemoglobin or from dried blood. — *n* **hae'matite** a valuable iron ore, often blood-red, with red streak. — *n* **hae'matocrit** a graduated capillary tube in which the blood is centrifuged, to determine the ratio, by volume, of blood cells to plasma. — *adj* **haematogenous** (*-toj'i-nəs*) producing blood; produced by, or arising in, the blood; spread through the bloodstream. — *n* **haematol'ogist.** — *n* **haematol'ogy** the study of blood, diseases of blood, and blood-forming tissues. — *n* **haematol'ysis** haemolysis. — *n* **haematō'ma** a swelling composed of blood effused into connective tissue. — *n* **haematopoiesis** (*-poi-ē'sis*) the formation of blood. — *n* **haematū'ria** presence of blood in the urine. — *adj* **haem'ic** haematic. — *n* **haemocy'anin** a blue respiratory pigment with functions similar to haemoglobin, in the blood of crustaceans and molluscs. — *n* **hae'mocyte** a blood cell, esp. a red one. — *n* **haemodial'ysis** the purifying of the blood (in e.g. cases of kidney failure) by circulating it through an apparatus containing a semi-permeable membrane that blocks the passage of waste products. — *n* **haemoglō'bin** the red oxygen-carrying pigment in the red blood corpuscles. — *n* **haemol'ysis** breaking up of red blood corpuscles. — *adj* **haemolyt'ic.** — *n* **haemophil'ia** a constitutional tendency to excessive bleeding when any blood-vessel is even slightly injured. — *n* **haemophil'iac** someone who suffers from haemophilia. — *n* **haemop'tysis** the spitting or coughing up of blood. — *n* **haemorrhage** (*hem'ə-rij*) a discharge of blood from the blood-vessels; a steady and persistent draining away (*fig*). — Also *vi.* — *adj* **haemorrhagic** (*-raj'*). — *n* **haemorrhoid** (*hem'ər-oid*; usu. in *pl*) dilatation of a vein about the anus, piles. — *adj* **haemorrhoid'al.** — *n* **haemo'stasis** stoppage of bleeding or the flow of the blood. — *n* **hae'mostat** an instrument for stopping bleeding. — *n* and *adj* **haemostat'ic** styptic. [Gr. *haima*, *-atos*, blood.]

haeremai *hī'rə-mī*, (*NZ*) *interj* welcome. [Maori, come hither.]

hafnium *haf'ni-əm*, *n* an element (symbol **Hf**; atomic no. 72) discovered in 1922 by Profs. Coster and Hevesy of Copenhagen. [L. *Hafnia*, Copenhagen.]

haft *häft*, *n* a handle, esp. of an axe or knife. — *vt* to set in a haft. [O.E. *hæft.*]

Hag. (*Bible*) *abbrev* for (the Book of) Haggai.

hag[1] *hag*, *n* an ugly old woman, orig. a witch; one of the round-mouths, of the same type as the lamprey (also **hag'fish**). — *adj* **hagg'ish.** — *adv* **hagg'ishly.** — *adj* **hag'-ridden** tormented by nightmares or driven by obsessions, as though possessed by a witch. [Perh. O.E. *hægtesse*, a witch.]

hag[2] *hag*, (*Scot* and *NEng*) *n* any broken ground in a moss or bog; a relatively high and firm place in a bog. [O.N. *högg*, a gash, ravine, a cutting of trees.]

hagberry *hag'ber-i*, *n* the bird-cherry, a small Eurasian tree with white flowers; the American hackberry tree or its cherry-like fruit. [Cf. O.N. *heggr*, bird-cherry.]

Haggadah *hä-gä'də*, *n* the homiletical and illustrative part of the authoritative book of Jewish civil and religious law and tradition, the Talmud, recited at a ceremonial meal, the Seder, on the first two nights of the Passover. — *adj* **Haggad'ic.** [Heb.]

haggard *hag'ərd*, *adj* hollow-eyed, gaunt, from weariness, hunger, etc.; intractable; (of a hawk) untamed. — *n* an untamed hawk, or one caught when adult, esp. a female. — *adv* **hagg'ardly.** — *n* **hagg'ardness.** [O.Fr. *hagard.*]

haggis *hag'is*, *n* a Scottish dish made of the heart, lungs and liver of a sheep, calf, etc., chopped up with suet, onions, oatmeal, etc., seasoned and boiled in a sheep's stomach-bag or a substitute.

haggle *hag'l*, *vi* to bargain contentiously or wranglingly; to quibble; to raise trifling objections. — *n* **hagg'ler.** [O.N. *heggra*, to hew.]

hagio- *hag-i-ō-*, *hag-i-ə-* or *hag-i-o'-*, *combining form* signifying holy or denoting saint. — *n* **hagioc'racy** government by holy men. — *npl* **Hagiog'rapha** those books which with the Law and the Prophets make up the Old Testament. — *n* **hagiog'rapher** a writer of the Hagiographa; a writer of saints' lives. — *adj* **hagiograph'ic** or **hagiograph'ical.** — *n* **hagiog'raphist.** — *n* **hagiog'raphy** a biography of a saint; a biography which overpraises its subject. — *n* **hagiol'ater** a worshipper of saints. — *n* **hagiol'atry.** — *adj* **hagiolog'ic** or **hagiolog'ical.** — *n* **hagiol'ogist** a writer of, or someone versed in, saints' legends. — *n* **hagiol'ogy.** — *n* **hag'ioscope** a squint in a church, giving a view of the high altar. — *adj* **hagioscop'ic.** [Gr. *hagios*, holy.]

hah *hä*, *interj.* Same as **ha.**

ha-ha[1] *hä'-hä'*, *interj* in representation of a laugh. — *interj* **ha-ha'** an expression of triumph, e.g. on discovering something. [Imit.]

ha-ha[2] *hä'-hä* or **haw-haw** *hö'-hö*, *n* a ditch or vertical drop, often containing a fence, forming a barrier without interrupting the view. [Fr. *haha.*]

hahnium *hä'ni-əm*, *n* an artificially-produced transuranic element (symbol **Ha**; atomic no. 105). [Otto *Hahn* (1879–1968), Ger. physicist.]

haik or **haick** *hīk*, *n* an oblong cloth worn by Arabs on the head and body. [Ar. *hayk.*]

haiku *hī'koo*, *n* a Japanese poem in three lines of 5, 7, 5 syllables, usu. comical. [From Jap.]

hail[1] *hāl*, *n* a call from a distance; a greeting; earshot (esp. in the phrase '*within hail*'). — *vt* to greet; to address; to call to; to summon. — *interj* of greeting or salutation. — *n* **hail'er**. — *adj* **hail-fellow-well-met'** readily or overly friendly and familiar; **hail Mary** (a recital of) the English version of the ave Maria. — **hail from** to belong to, come from (a particular place). [O.N. *heill*, health, (*adj*) sound; cf. **hale**[1] and **heal**[1].]

hail[2] *hāl*, *n* frozen rain or grains of ice falling from the clouds; a shower or bombardment, of missiles, abuse, etc. — *vi* and *vt* to shower hail; to shower vigorously or abundantly. — **hail'stone** a ball of hail; **hail'-storm**. [O.E. *hægl* (*hagol*).]

hair *hār*, *n* a filament growing from the skin of an animal; an outgrowth of the epidermis of a plant; a fibre; a mass or aggregate of hairs, esp. that covering the human head; anything very small and fine; a hair's-breadth; a locking spring or other safety contrivance on a firearm. — *n* **hair'iness**. — *adj* **hair'less** having no hair; very angry (*slang*); desperate (*slang*). — *n* **hair'lessness**. — *adj* **hair'like**. — *adj* **hair'y** of or like hair; covered with hair; dangerous, risky (*colloq*). — **hair'-ball** a concretion of hair in the stomach, e.g. in cats as a result of swallowing fur, etc. during cleaning; **hair'-band** a band, usu. of or incorporating elastic material, worn over the hair. — *adj* **hair'-brained** same as **hare-brained**. — **hair'brush** a brush for the hair; **hair'cloth** coarse cloth made from horsehair, used in upholstery, etc.; **hair'cut** a cutting of the hair or the style in which this is done; **hair'do** (*colloq*) the process, or a style of hairdressing: — *pl* **hair'dos**. — **hair'dresser** someone whose occupation is the cutting, colouring, arranging, etc. of hair; a barber; **hair'dressing**; **hair'dryer** or **hair'drier** any of various types of hand-held or other apparatus producing a stream of warm air for drying the hair; **hair'-grass** a genus of narrow-stemmed coarse grasses; **hair'-grip** a short, narrow band of metal, bent double, worn in the hair to keep it in place; **hair'line** a very fine line in writing, type, etc.; a finely striped cloth; the edge of the hair on the forehead. — *adj* (of e.g. a crack) very thin. — **hair'net** a net for keeping (usu. a woman's) hair in place; **hair oil** a scented oil for dressing the hair; **hair'piece** a length of false hair, or a wig covering only part of the head; **hair'pin** a U-shaped pin for fastening up the hair. — *adj* narrowly U-shaped, as a bend on a road. — *adj* **hair'-raising** very exciting; terrifying. — **hair'-restorer** a preparation claiming to make hair grow on bald places; **hair shirt** a penitent's garment of haircloth; **hair's'-breadth** the breadth of a hair; a minute distance. — *adj* (of an escape, etc.) extremely narrow. — **hair slide** a hinged clasp, often decorative, worn in the hair esp. by young girls; **hair space** (*printing*) the thinnest metal space used by compositors, or its equivalent in photocomposition; **hair'-splitter** a maker of over-fine distinctions. — *n* and *adj* **hair'-splitting**. — **hair'spray** lacquer sprayed on the hair to hold it in place; **hair'spring** a slender spring regulating a watch balance; **hair'-streak** any butterfly of several genera with a fine white band under the wing; **hair'-stroke** a hairline in handwriting; **hair'style** a particular way of cutting and arranging the hair; **hair'stylist**; **hair trigger** a trigger, responding to very light pressure, that releases the hair of a gun. — *adj* having a hair trigger; responding to the slightest stimulus. — **a hair of the dog (that bit him, her,** etc.) a smaller dose of that which caused the trouble; a morning drink of the alcohol that caused the hangover, as a cure for it; **by the short hairs** or (*colloq*) **by the short and curlies** in a powerless position, at someone's mercy; **get in someone's hair** (*colloq*) to become a source of irritation to someone; **keep one's hair on** (*colloq*) to keep calm; **let one's hair down** to forget reserve and speak or behave freely; **make someone's hair curl** to shock someone; **make someone's hair stand on end** to terrify or astonish someone; **not turn a hair** not to be ruffled or disturbed; **split hairs** to make superfine distinctions; **tear one's hair (out)** to display frenzied grief or (*colloq*) great irritation; **to a hair** exactly. [O.E. *hǣr*.]

Haitian *ha-ē'shən* or *hā'shən*, *n* a native or citizen of Haiti; the creolised form of French spoken in Haiti. — *adj* of or from Haiti, or the Haitians; Haitian-speaking.

haj, haji, hajj and **hajji**. See **hadj**.

hake *hāk*, *n* a gadoid fish resembling the cod. [Prob. Scand.; cf. Norw. *hake-fisk*, lit. hook-fish.]

Hakenkreuz *hä'kən-kroits*, *n* the swastika. [Ger., hook-cross.]

hakim[1] *hä-kēm'*, *n* a Muslim physician. [Ar. *hakīm*.]

hakim[2] *hä'kim*, *n* a judge, governor or official in Pakistan. [Ar. *hakim*.]

Halachah, Halakah or **Halacha** *hä-lä'hhä* or *-kä*, *n* the legal element in the Jewish book of civil and religious obedience, the Talmud. — *adj* **Halach'ic**. [Heb., — *hālak*, to walk.]

halal or **hallal** *hä-läl'*, *vt* to slaughter according to Muslim law: — *pr p* **halall'ing** or **hallall'ing**; *pa t* and *pa p* **halalled'** or **hallalled'**. — *n* meat that may lawfully be eaten from animals that have been so slaughtered. — Also *adj*. [Ar. *halāl*, lawful.]

halation *hə-lā'shən*, *n* blurring in a photograph by reflection and dispersion of light; a bright area around a bright spot on a fluorescent screen. **[halo.]**

halberd *hal'bərd*, *n* an axe-like weapon with a hook or pick on its back, and a long shaft, used in the 15th and 16th centuries, in the 18th century denoting the rank of sergeant. — Also **hal'bert**. — *n* **halberdier** (*-dēr'*) a person armed with a halberd. [O.Fr. *halebard* — M.H.G. *helmbarde* — *Halm*, stalk, or *Helm*, helmet, O.H.G. *barta*, axe.]

halcyon *hal'si-ən*, *n* the kingfisher, once believed to make a floating nest on the sea, which remained calm during hatching. — *adj* calm; peaceful; happy and carefree. — **halcyon days** a time of peace and happiness. [Gr. *alkyōn*, fancifully changed to *halkyōn* as if from *hals*, sea, *kyōn*, conceiving.]

hale[1] *hāl*, *adj* healthy; robust; sound of body. — *n* **hale'ness**. — **hale and hearty** in good health. [Northern, from O.E. *hāl*.]

hale[2] *hāl*, *vt* to drag. [O.Fr. *haler*; Germanic in origin.]

half *häf*, *n* one of two equal parts; a half-year or term; half-fare, on a bus, train, etc.; a halfback; a halved hole in golf; half a pint, usu. of beer (*colloq*); a measure of an alcoholic spirit, esp. whisky (*Scot*): — *pl* **halves** (*hävz*) or **halfs** (except first definition). — *adj* having or consisting of one of two equal parts; partial; incomplete, as measures. — *adv* to the extent of one-half; in part; imperfectly. — **half'-adder** (*comput*) a circuit having two inputs and outputs, which can add two binary digits and give the sum and the carry digit; **half-and-half'** a mixture of two things in equal proportions. — *adj* and *adv* in the proportion of one to one, or approximately; in part one thing, in part another. — **half back** in football, a player or position directly behind the forwards — in Rugby (*scrum* half and *fly* half), a link between forwards and three-quarters. — *adj* **half-baked'** underdone; incomplete; crude; immature; half-witted. — **half'-beak** a fish with spearlike under-jaw; **half-bind'ing** a bookbinding with only backs and corners of leather or some similar material; **half'-blood** relation between those who have only one parent in common; a half-breed. — *adj* **half-blood'ed**. — **half-blue'** at university, a substitute for a full blue, or the colours awarded him or her; **half board** (in hotels, etc.) the providing of bed, breakfast and one main meal per day, demi-pension;

half'-boot a boot reaching halfway to the knee; **half'-breed** (*offensive*) someone of mixed breed (esp. a mixture of white and coloured races); **half'-brother** and **half'-sister** a brother or sister by one parent only. — *adj* **half-calf** see under **calf**[1]. — **half'-caste** a person whose parents are from different races, esp. a Eurasian; **half-cen'tury** a score of fifty in several sports; **half-cock'** the position of the cock of a gun drawn back halfway and retained by the first notch (**at half-cock** only partially prepared). — *adj* **half-cocked'**. — **half-crown'** a coin worth **half'-a-crown** or two shillings and sixpence, from 1970 no longer legal tender. — *adj* **half-cut'** (*colloq*) drunk. — **half-day'** a holiday of half a working day. — *adj* **half-dead'** (*colloq*) very weary, exhausted. — *n* and *adj* **half-doz'en** six. — *adj* **half-dū'plex** (*comput*, *teleg*, etc.) allowing communication or transmission in both directions, but not simultaneously. — *adj* **half'-frame** (of a photograph) taking up half the normal area of a frame. — *adj* **half-hard'y** able to grow in the open air except in winter. — *adj* **half-heart'ed** lacking in zeal. — *adv* **half-heart'edly**. — **half-heart'edness**; **half'-hitch** a simple knot tied round an object; **half-hol'iday** half of a working day for recreation; **half-hour'** a period of 30 minutes. — Also *adj*. — *adj* and *adv* **half-hour'ly** (done, occurring, etc.) at intervals of 30 minutes. — **half-hunter** see **hunter** at **hunt**; **half-in'teger** a number formed by the division of an odd integer by two. — *adj* **half-in'tegral**. — **half'-landing** small landing at the bend of a staircase; **half'-leather** a half-binding for a book, with leather on back and corners; **half'-length** a portrait showing the upper part of the body. — *adj* of half the whole or ordinary length. — **half'-life** the period of time in which the activity of a radioactive substance falls to half its original value; **half'-light** dim light; twilight; **half-mar'athon** a foot-race half the length of a marathon (21·1 km., 13 miles 192 $\frac{1}{2}$ yards); **half-mast'** the position of a flag partly lowered, in respect for the dead. — Also *adv*. — **half-meas'ure** (often in *pl*) any means inadequate for the end proposed; **half-mi'ler** a runner specialising in races of half a mile; **half-moon'** the moon at the quarters when half the disc is illuminated; anything semicircular; **half-mourn'ing** mourning attire less than deep or full mourning; **half nelson** see under **nelson**; **half'-note** (*mus*; *NAm*) a minim; **half-pay'** reduced pay, as of an officer not on active service. — *adj* **half'-pay** on half-pay. — **halfpenny** (*hāp'ni*) a coin worth half a penny, withdrawn from circulation in 1985; its value: — *pl* **halfpence** (*hā'pəns*) or **halfpennies** (*hāp'niz*). — *adj* valued at a halfpenny. — **half-pennyworth** (*hāp'ni-wûrth* — also **hap'orth** *hā'pərth*) as much as is sold for or is worth a halfpenny; **half'-pint** (*slang*) a very small person; **half-plate** see **plate**; **half-price'** a charge reduced to half. — *adj* and *adv* (sold) at half the usual price. — *adj* and *adv* **half-seas-o'ver** (*colloq*) half-drunk. — **half-size'** any size in clothes halfway between two full sizes; **half'-sole** the part of a shoe-sole from the instep to the toe; **half-sov'ereign** a gold coin worth **half a sovereign** or ten shillings; **half'-step** (*mus*; *NAm*) a semitone; **half-term'** (a holiday taken at) the mid point of an academic term. — *adj* **half-tim'bered** built of a timber frame, with spaces filled in. — **half-time'** a short break halfway through a game (*sport*); in industry, half the time usually worked; **half-ti'mer** someone who works half the full time; **half'-title** a short title preceding the title page or before a section of a book. — *adj* **half'-tone** representing light and shade photographically by dots of different sizes. — *n* an illustration of this type; a semitone (*mus*); **half'-track** a motor vehicle with wheels in front and caterpillar tracks behind. — Also *adj*. — **half-truth'** a belief containing an element of truth; a statement conveying only part of the truth; **half volley** see **volley**. — *adv* **halfway'** (sometimes *häf'wā*) midway; at half the distance; imperfectly; slightly, barely (*colloq*). — *adj* **half'way** equidistant from two points. — **halfway house** an inn, etc. situated midway between two towns, points on a journey, etc.; a midway point or state; a centre offering accommodation and rehabilitation; **half'-wit** an idiot. — *adj* **halfwitt'ed**. — **half-year'** a period of six months. — *adj* **half-year'ly** occurring or appearing every half-year. — *adv* twice a year. — *n* a half-yearly publication. — **by half** by a long way; **by halves** incompletely; half-heartedly; **go halves** to share equally; **half past one, two,** etc., **half after one, two,** etc. (*NAm*) or **half one, two,** etc. (*colloq*) thirty minutes after one o'clock, two o'clock, etc.; **how the other half lives** (*facetious*) other (esp. richer or poorer) people's way of life; **not half** (*slang*) very much, exceedingly; **one's other** (or **better) half** (*facetious*) one's spouse. [O.E. (Anglian) *half* (W. Sax. *healf*), side, half.]

halibut *hal'i-bət*, *n* a large flatfish, more elongated than flounder or turbot. [App. *holy butt* as much eaten on holy days (*butt* being a flatfish of various kinds).]

halide *hā'līd* or *hal'īd*, *n* a compound of a halogen with a metal or radical — a chloride, bromide, etc. [Gr. *hals*, salt.]

halieutic *hal-i-ū'tik*, *adj* pertaining to fishing. [Gr. *halieutikos* — *halieus*, fisher — *hals*, sea.]

haliotis *hal-i-ō'tis*, *n* a gasteropod with a perforated ear-shaped shell lined with mother-of-pearl: — *pl* **haliō'tis**. [Gr. *hals*, sea, *ous*, *ōtos*, ear.]

halite *hal'īt*, *n* rock salt. [Gr. *hals*, salt.]

halitus *hal'i-təs*, *n* a vapour. — *n* **halitō'sis** foul breath. — *adj* **halitō'tic**. [L.]

hall *höl*, *n* the main room in a great house; a building or large chamber for meetings, concerts, exhibitions, etc.; a passage or lobby at the entrance of a house; a large room entered immediately by the front door of a house; a manor-house; a place for special professional education, or the conferring of diplomas, licences, etc.; the headquarters of a guild, society, etc.; the main building of a college; in some cases the college itself; a residence for students; a large dining-room. — **hall'mark** the authorised stamp impressed on gold, silver or platinum articles at Goldsmiths' Hall or some other place of assaying, indicating date, maker, fineness of metal, etc.; any mark of authenticity or good quality. — *vt* to stamp with such a mark. — **hall'stand** a tall piece of furniture fitted with hooks, etc., on which hats, coats and umbrellas can be left; **hall'way** an entrance hall. — **hall of fame** a gallery of busts, portraits, etc. of celebrated people; the ranks of the great and famous; **hall of residence** a building providing residential accommodation for students at a university, etc.; **Liberty Hall** a place where everyone may do as they please; **the halls** music halls. [O.E. *hall* (*heall*).]

hallal. See **halal**.

hallelujah or **halleluiah** *hal-ə-lōō'yə*, *n* and *interj* the exclamation 'Praise Jehovah'; a musical composition based on the word. — Also **allelu'ia**. [Heb. *hallelū*, praise ye, and *Jāh*, Jehovah.]

halliard. See **halyard**.

hallo *hə-lō'* or *ha-*, **hello** *hə-lō'* or *he-*, or **hullo** *hə-lō'*, or *hu-*, *interj* expressing surprise, discovery, becoming aware; used also in greeting, calling attention, etc. — *n* a call of hallo: — *pl* **hallōs'**, **hellos'** or **hullos'**. [Imit.]

halloo *hə-lōō'* or **halloa** *hə-lō'*, *n* a cry to urge on a chase or to call attention. — *vi* to raise an outcry. — *vt* to encourage with halloos; to hunt with halloos. — **don't halloo till you're out of the wood** keep quiet till you are sure you are safe. [Imit.]

halloumi *hal'ōō-mi*, *n* a Greek dish of fried goat's cheese, eaten as a starter.

hallow *hal'ō, vt* to make holy; to reverence. — *n* (*archaic*) a saint. — *adj* **hall'owed** holy, revered. — *n* **Hallowe'en'** the eve of, or the evening before, All Saints' Day, celebrated by masquerading and the playing of pranks by children; **Hall'owmas** the feast of All Hallows or All Saints, 1 November. [O.E. *hālgian*, to hallow, *hālga*, a saint — *hālig*, holy.]

Hallstatt *häl'shtät, adj* relating to a European culture transitional between Bronze Age and Iron Age. [From finds at *Hallstatt* in upper Austria.]

hallucinate *hə-lo͞o'si-nāt* or *hə-lū', vt* to affect with hallucination. — *vi* to experience hallucination. — *n* **hallucinā'tion** a perception without objective reality; (*loosely*) delusion. — *adj* **hallu'cinative** or **hallu'cinatory**. — *n* **hallu'cinogen** (*-nə-jen*) a drug producing hallucinatory sensations. — *adj* **hallucinogen'ic** causing hallucinations. [L. *hallūcinārī, -ātus*, to wander in the mind.]

hallux *hal'əks*, (*zool*) *n* the innermost digit of the hind-limb of a bird, mammal, reptile or amphibian; the human big toe; a bird's hind-toe: — *pl* **halluces** (*-ū'sēz*). [Wrong form of L. (*h*)*allex, -ĭcis*.]

halma *hal'mə, n* in the Greek pentathlon, a long jump with weights in the hands (*hist*); a game played on a board of 256 squares, in which the pieces are moved by jumps. [Gr., a jump.]

halo *hā'lō, n* a ring of light or colour, esp. one round the sun or moon caused by refraction by ice crystals; (in paintings, etc.) such a ring round the head of a holy person; an ideal or sentimental glory or glamour attaching to anything: — *pl* **hā'loes** or **hā'los**. — *vt* to surround with a halo: — *pa p* **hā'loed** or **hā'lo'd**. — **halo effect** (*psychol*) the tendency to judge a person favourably on the basis of one or only a few positive characteristics. [Gr. *halōs*, a threshing-floor, disc, halo.]

halocarbon *hal'ō-kär-bən*, (*chem*) *n* a compound consisting of carbon and one or more halogens.

halogen *hal'ə-jen, n* any one of certain elements in the seventh group of the periodic table, fluorine, chlorine, bromine, iodine, and astatine (the first four defined in the 19th cent. as forming salts by direct union with metals; astatine discovered in 1940). — *vt* **halogenate** (*-oj'*) to combine with a halogen. — *adj* **halog'enous**. [Gr. *hals*, salt, and **-gen[1]**.]

haloid *hal'oid, n* a halide. — *adj* having the composition of a halide. — **hal'ophile** an organism that thrives in very salty conditions, e.g. the Dead Sea. [Gr. *hals*, salt.]

halt[1] *hölt, vi* to come to a standstill; to make a temporary stop. — *vt* to cause to stop. — *n* a standstill; a stopping-place; a railway station not fully equipped. — **call a halt (to)** to stop, put an end (to). [Ger. *Halt*, stoppage.]

halt[2] *hölt, vi* to proceed lamely or imperfectly, as in logic, rhythm, etc. — *adj* (*Bible, archaic*) lame, crippled. — *n* and *adj* **halt'ing**. — *adv* **halt'ingly**. [O.E. *halt* (*healt*), lame.]

halter *höl'tər, n* a rope for holding and leading an animal, or for hanging criminals; a woman's backless bodice held in place by straps round the neck and across the back. — *vt* to put a halter on. [O.E. *hælftre*.]

halteres *hal-tēr'ēz*, (*entom*) *npl* the rudimentary hindwings of flies, used to maintain balance in flight. [Gr. *haltērēs*, dumb-bells held by jumpers — *hallesthai*, to jump.]

halva or **halvah** *häl'və, n* a sweetmeat, orig. Turkish, containing sesame seeds, honey, nuts and saffron. [Yiddish *halva*; ult. from Ar.]

halve *häv, vt* to divide in half; to reduce by half; (in golf) to draw, be equal in; (in carpentry) to join by cutting away half the thickness of each. [**half**.]

halyard or **halliard** *hal'yərd, n* a rope or purchase for hoisting or lowering a sail, yard or flag. [For *halier* — **hale[2]**; associated with **yard[1]**.]

ham[1] *ham, n* the thigh of an animal, esp. of a pig salted and dried; the meat from this part; the back of the thigh or hock. — *adj* **hamm'y**. — *adj* **ham-fist'ed** or **ham-hand'ed** clumsy. [O.E. *hamm*.]

ham[2] *ham*, (*colloq*) *n* an actor who rants and overacts; an amateur, esp. an amateur radio operator. — *adj* given to overacting or ranting; amateur; clumsy, coarse, inexpert. — *vi* and *vt* to overact. — *adj* **hamm'y**. — *adv* **hamm'ily**. [Prob. *hamfatter*, a third-rate minstrel.]

hamadryad *ham-ə-drī'ad, n* a wood nymph who died with the tree in which she dwelt (*classical mythol*); a large poisonous Indian snake, *Naja hamadryas*; a large baboon of Abyssinia: — *pl* **hamadry'ads** or **hamadry'ades** (*-ēz*). [Gr. *hamadryas* — *hama*, together, *drȳs*, (oak) tree.]

hamamelis *ham-ə-mē'lis, n* a shrub of the American witch-hazel genus. [Gr. *hamamēlis*, medlar — *hama*, together with, *mēlon*, an apple.]

Hamburg *ham-bûrg, n* a black variety of grape; a small blue-legged domestic fowl. — *n* **ham'burger** (a bread roll containing) a flat round cake of finely chopped meat, fried; a large sausage. [*Hamburg* in Germany.]

hame *hām, n* one of the two curved bars of a draught-horse's collar. [Cf. Du. *haam*, L.G. *ham*.]

Hamite *ham'īt, n* a descendant or supposed descendant of *Ham*, son of Noah; a member of a dark-skinned race of N.E. Africa (*Galla, Hadendoa*, etc.); a speaker of any language of a N. African family distantly related to Semitic (ancient Egyptian, Berber, etc.). — *adj* **Hamitic** (*-mit'ik*).

hamlet *ham'lit, n* a cluster of houses in the country; a small village. [O.Fr. *hamelet*, dimin. of *hamel* (Fr. *hameau*), from Gmc.]

hammam *hə-mäm', hum'um* or *ham'am, n* an Oriental bathing establishment, a Turkish bath. [Ar. *hammām*.]

hammer *ham'ər, n* a tool for beating metal, breaking rock, driving nails, etc.; a striking-piece in the mechanism of a clock, piano, etc.; the apparatus that causes explosion of the charge in a firearm; the mallet with which an auctioneer announces that an article is sold; a small bone of the ear, the malleus; a metal ball weighing about 7 kg., attached to a long handle of flexible wire, for throwing in competition (*athletics*). — *vt* to beat, drive, shape, or fashion with or as with a hammer; to contrive or think out by intellectual labour (with *out*); to arrive at (a conclusion) or settle (differences) after much argument (with *out*); to trounce or criticise severely (*colloq*); to teach by frequent and energetic reiteration (with *in* or *into*); to declare a defaulter on the Stock Exchange; to beat down the price of (a stock), to depress (a market). — *vi* to use a hammer; to make a noise as of a hammer; to persevere doggedly (with *away*). — *n* **hamm'erer**. — *n* **hamm'ering** a severe beating or defeat (esp. in the phrases *give* and *take a hammering*). — **hammer beam** a horizontal piece of timber at or near the feet of a pair of principal rafters; **hamm'erhead** a shark with a hammer-shaped head; a crested, thick-billed African wading bird (*Scopus umbretta*); **hamm'erlock** a hold in wrestling in which one's opponent's arm is twisted upwards behind their back; **hammer-toe'** a condition in which a toe is permanently bent upwards at the base and doubled down upon itself. — **(come) under the hammer** (to come up for sale) by auction; **hammer and sickle** crossed hammer-and-sickle emblem of the Soviet Union, or of Communism; **hammer and tongs** with great noise and violence; **hammer home** to impress (a fact) strongly and effectively on someone. [O.E. *hamor*.]

hammock *ham'ək, n* a cloth or netting hung by the ends, for use as a bed or couch. [Sp. *hamaca*, from Caribb.]

Hammond organ® *ham'ənd ör'gən, n* orig., a two-keyboard organ, with tones electromagnetically generated by means of rotating wheels controlled by the keys; (*loosely*) any two-keyboard digital organ. [Invented by L. *Hammond*, 20th-cent. U.S. mechanical engineer.]

hamper[1] *ham'pər, vt* to impede the progress or movement of. — *n* (*naut*) essential but somewhat cumbrous equipment on a vessel. [First, in Northern writers; cf. Icel. *hemja*, to restrain.]

hamper[2] *ham'pər, n* a large basket, usu. with a cover; the basket and its contents, usu. food; a laundry basket (*NAm*). [O.Fr. *hanapier* — *hanap*, drinking-cup.]

hamster *ham'stər, n* a small Eurasian rodent with cheek-pouches reaching almost to the shoulders. [Ger.]

hamstring *ham'string, n* (in humans) one of the five tendons at the back of the knee; (in a horse, etc.) the large tendon at the back of the knee or hock of the hindleg. — *vt* to lame by cutting the hamstring; to make powerless: — *pa t* and *pa p* **ham'stringed** or **ham'strung.** [**ham[1]** and **string[1]**.]

hamza or **hamzah** *häm'zä* or *ham'zə, n* in Arabic, the sign used to represent the glottal stop. [Ar. *hamzah*, a compression.]

Han *han, n* and *npl* (a member of) the native Chinese people, as opposed to Mongols, Manchus, etc. [Chin.]

hand *hand, n* (in humans) the extremity of the arm below the wrist; any corresponding member in the higher vertebrates; the forefoot of a quadruped; the extremity of the hind-limb when it is prehensile; a pointer or index; a measure of four inches; a division of a bunch of bananas; side, direction, quarter; a worker, esp. in a factory or a ship; a doer, author, or producer; instrumentality; influence; share in performance; power or manner of performing; skill; touch; control; (often in *pl*) keeping, custody; possession; assistance; style of handwriting; a signature, esp. of a sovereign; pledge; consent to or promise of marriage, or fulfilment of such promise; the set of cards held by a player at one deal; the play of a single deal of cards; (*loosely*) a game of cards; a round of applause; (in *pl*) skill in handling a horse's reins. — *vt* to pass with the hand; to lead, escort or help (e.g. *into* a vehicle) with the hands; to transfer or deliver (often with *over*); to lower (a sail) (*naut*). — **hand-** (in combination) denoting: by hand, or direct bodily operation (*hand-knitted, handmade*); for the hands (*hand lotion, handtowel*); operated by hand (*hand punch*); held in the hand (*hand basket*). — **-hand'ed** used in combination to signify: using one hand in preference to the other, as in *left-handed*; having a hand or hands as stated, as in *one-handed*. — *n* **hand'edness** the tendency to use one hand rather than the other; inherent asymmetry in particles, etc., e.g. causing twisting in one direction (*phys*). — **-hander** used in combination to denote: a blow, etc. with the hand or hands as stated, e.g. *right-hander, back-hander*; a play with a specified number of characters, e.g. *two-hander*. — *n* **hand'ful** enough to fill the hand; a small number or quantity; a charge that taxes one's powers: — *pl* **hand'fuls.** — *adv* **hand'ily.** — *n* **hand'iness.** — *adj* **hand'less** awkward; incompetent. — *adj* **hand'y** dexterous; ready to the hand; convenient; near. — **hand'bag** a bag for small articles, carried by women; **hand'ball** a game between goals in which the ball is struck with the palm of the hand; a game in which a ball is struck with the gloved hand against a wall or walls (usu. four); **hand'-barrow** a wheelless barrow, carried by handles; **hand'bell** a small bell with a handle, rung by hand; **hand'bill** a bill or loose sheet bearing an announcement; **hand'book** a manual; **hand'brake** a brake applied by hand-operated lever; **hand'-breadth** or **hand's breadth** the breadth of a hand; **hand'cart** a light cart drawn by hand; **hand'clap** a clap of the hands; **hand'craft** handicraft; **hand'-cuff** (esp. in *pl*) a shackle locked upon the wrist; **hand'-gallop** an easy gallop, restrained by the bridle-hand; **hand'glass** a mirror or a magnifying-glass with a handle; **hand grenade** a grenade to be thrown by hand; **hand'grip** something for the hand to grasp; **hand'gun** a gun which can be held and fired in one hand. — *adj* **hand'-held** held in the hands rather than mounted on some support. — **hand'hold** a hold by the hand; a place or part that can be held by the hand. — *n* and *adj* **hand'-knit** (a garment) knitted by hand. — *vt* **hand-knit'.** — **hand line** a fishing-line without a rod. — *vi* **hand'-line** to fish with such a line. — **hand'list** a list without detail, for handy reference. — *adj* **hand'made.** — **hand'-maid** or **hand'maiden** (*archaic*) a female servant or attendant. — *adj* **hand'-me-down** second-hand, esp. formerly belonging to a member of one's own family. — *n* a second-hand garment. — **hand organ** a barrel-organ; **hand'out** a portion handed out, esp. to the needy; an issue; a prepared statement issued to the press; a usu. free leaflet containing information, propaganda, etc.; **hand'over** a transfer, handing over. — *vt* **hand-pick'** to pick by hand; to select carefully for a particular purpose. — **hand puppet** a glove puppet; **hand'rail** a rail to hold for safety, support, etc., as on stairs; **hand'saw** a saw worked by hand, specif. with a handle at one end; **hand'set** on a telephone, the part held by the hand, containing the mouthpiece and earpiece; **hand'shake** a shaking of hands in greeting, etc. (also **hand'shaking**); an exchange of signals (on a separate line) between two or more devices which synchronises them in readiness for the transfer of data (*comput*); **hand'shaking** (*comput*) the process of performing a handshake. — *adj* **hands-off'** not touching with the hands; operated by remote control; that cannot be touched; not interfering. — *adj* **hands-on'** operated by hand; involving practical rather than theoretical knowledge, experience, method of working, etc.; (of museums, etc.) with exhibits that can be handled. — **hand'spike** a bar used as a lever; **hand'spring** a cartwheel or somersault with hands on the ground; **hand'stand** an act of balancing one's body on the palms of one's hands with one's trunk and legs in the air; **hands'turn** or **hand's turn** (usu. with a negative) the least bit of work, the smallest task; **hand'writing** writing, script; style of writing; individual style discernible in one's actions. — *adj* **hand'written** written by hand, not typed or printed. — **hand'yman** a man employed to carry out, or skilled in doing, odd jobs. — **at first hand** directly from the source; **at hand** conveniently near; within easy reach; near in time; **at the hand (or hands) of** by the act of; **by hand** by use of the hands, or tools worked by the hand, not by machinery or other indirect means; by personal delivery, not by post; **change hands** to pass to other ownership or keeping; **come to hand** to arrive; to be received; **for one's own hand** to one's own account; **get one's hand in** to get control of the play so as to turn one's cards to good use; to get into the way or knack; **good hands** good keeping; care of those who may be trusted to treat one well; **hand and foot** with assiduous attention; **hand and (or in) glove** on very intimate terms; in close co-operation; **hand down** or **on** to transmit in succession or by tradition; **hand in hand** with hands mutually clasped; with one person holding the hand of another; in close association; conjointly (*adj* **hand-in-hand'**); **hand it to someone** (*colloq*) to admit someone's superiority, esp. as shown by their success in a difficult matter; **hand of God** unforeseen and unavoidable accident, such as lightning or storm; **hand out** to distribute, pass by hand to individuals (see also **handout**); **hand over** to transfer; to relinquish possession of; **hand over fist** with steady and rapid gain; **hand over hand** by passing the hands alternately one before or above another, as in climbing a rope;

hands down with utter ease (as in winning a race); **hands off** (as a command) keep off; do not touch or strike; **hands up** (as a command) hold the hands above the head in surrender; **hand to hand** at close quarters (*adj* **hand-to-hand'**); **hand to mouth** with provision for immediate needs only (*adj* **hand-to-mouth'**); **have one's hands full** to be preoccupied, very busy; **hold hands** see **hold; in hand** in preparation; under control; **keep one's hand in** see under **keep; lay hands on** to seize; to obtain or find; to subject physically to rough treatment; to bless or to ordain by touching with the hand or hands — also to **lay on hands; laying on of hands** the touch of a bishop or presbyters in ordination; **lend a hand** to give assistance; **lift a hand** (usu. with a negative) to make the least effort (to help, etc.); **off one's hands** no longer under one's responsible charge; **old hand** see under **old; on all hands** or **on every hand** on all sides, by everybody; **on hand** ready, available; in one's possession; **on one's hands** under one's care or responsibility; remaining as a burden or encumbrance; **on the one hand . . . on the other hand** phrases used to introduce opposing points in an argument, etc.; **out of hand** at once, without premeditation; out of control; **poor hand** an unskilful person or way of handling; **raise one's hand to** (often with a negative) to strike, behave violently towards; **set** or **put one's hand to** to engage in, undertake; to sign; **shake hands with** see under **shake; show of hands** a vote by holding up hands; **show one's hand** to expose one's purpose; **sit on one's hands** to take no action; **slow handclap** slow rhythmic clapping showing disapproval; **stand one's hand** (*colloq*) to buy someone else a drink; **take in hand** to undertake; to take charge of in order to educate, discipline, etc.; **take off someone's hands** to relieve someone of; **throw in one's hand** to give up a venture or plan; to concede defeat; **tie someone's hands** to render someone powerless; **try one's hand at** to attempt; to test one's prowess at; **under one's hand** with one's proper signature attached; **upper hand** mastery; advantage; **wash one's hands (of)** to disclaim responsibility (for). [O.E. *hand*.]

h and c *abbrev* for hot and cold (water laid on).

handicap *han'di-kap*, *vt* to impose special disadvantages or impediments upon, in order to offset advantages and make a better contest; to place at a disadvantage. — *n* any contest so adjusted, or the condition imposed; an amount added to or subtracted from one's score in stroke competitions (*golf*); a disadvantage. — *adj* **hand'icapped** suffering from some physical or mental disability; disadvantaged in some way. — *n* **hand'icapper** an official in some sports who fixes the handicaps of competitors. [App. *hand i' cap*, from the drawing from a cap in an old lottery game.]

handicraft *han'di-kräft*, *n* a manual craft or art; objects produced by such craft. — *n* **hand'icraftsman** or *fem* **hand'icraftswoman** a man or woman skilled in a manual art. [O.E. *handcræft* — *hand*, *cræft*, craft, assimilated to **handiwork**.]

handiwork *hand'i-wûrk*, *n* work done by the hands, performance generally; work of skill or wisdom; creation; doing. [O.E. *handgewerc* — *hand* and *gewerc* (*geweorc*), work.]

handkerchief *hang'kər-chif* or *-chēf*, *n* a cloth or paper for wiping the nose, etc.: — *pl* **hand'kerchiefs.** [**hand** and **kerchief**.]

handle *hand'l*, *vt* to hold, move about, feel freely, etc. with the hand; to make familiar by frequent touching; to manage (esp. successfully); to deal with, treat; to cope with, take in one's stride (*colloq*, esp. *NAm*); to trade or do business in. — *vi* to respond to control (in a specified way). — *n* a part by which a thing is held, opened or picked up; anything affording an advantage or pretext to an opponent. — *n* **hand'ler** someone who handles; a boxer's trainer or second; someone who trains, holds, controls, incites or shows off an animal at a show, fight, etc.; someone who trains and uses a dog or other animal which works for the police or an armed service. — **hand'lebar** the steering-bar of a cycle, or one half of it; **handlebar moustache** a wide, thick moustache with curved ends thought to resemble handlebars. — **a handle to one's name** a title; **fly off the handle** see **fly**. [O.E. *handle*, *handlian* — *hand*.]

hand of glory *hand əv glö'ri*, *n* a charm made orig. of mandrake root, afterwards of a murderer's hand from the gallows. [A translation of Fr. *main de gloire* — O.Fr. *mandegloire*, mandrake.]

handsel or **hansel** *han'səl*, *n* an inaugural gift; something thought of as an inauguration, such as the first money taken, earnest money, a first instalment, the first use of anything. — *vt* to give a handsel to; to inaugurate; to begin: — *pr p* **hand'selling** or **han'selling;** *pa p* and *pa t* **hand'selled** or **han'selled.** [O.E. *handselen*, hand-gift, giving; or O.N. *handsal*.]

handsome *han'səm*, *adj* good-looking; well-proportioned; dignified; liberal or noble; generous; ample. — *adv* **hand'somely.** — *n* **hand'someness.** [**hand** and **-some**[1].]

handy. See **hand.**

hanepoot *hä'nə-pōōt*, (*SAfr*) *n* a kind of grape. — Also **hon'eypot.** [Du. *haane-poot* — *haan*, cock, *poot*, foot.]

hang *hang*, *vt* to support from above against gravity; to suspend; to put to death by suspending by the neck, usu. with a rope; to suspend (meat and game) until mature; to fix, fit (a door, etc.); to fasten, stick (wallpaper, etc.); to decorate (a wall) with pictures, tapestries, etc.; to exhibit (pictures); to prevent (a jury) from coming to a decision; (in the *imper* and *passive*) a euphemism for *damn*. — *vi* to be suspended, so as to allow free sideways motion; to be put to death by suspending by the neck; to cling (with *on* or *on to*); (of clothes) to drape (well, badly, etc.); (of a jury) to be undecided; to hover; to impend; to linger; to depend for outcome (on): — *pa t* and *pa p* **hung** (in all senses) or **hanged** (by the neck). — *n* the action or mode of hanging; knack; meaning; a euphemism for *damn*. — *n* **hangabil'ity.** — *adj* **hang'able.** — *n* **hang'er** that on which anything is hung; someone who hangs something; (in place names) a wood on a hillside; a short sword. — *adj* **hang'ing** suspending; suspended; drooping; deserving or involving death by hanging. — *n* death by the noose; (esp. in *pl*) something which is hung, e.g. drapery or decorations. — *adj* **hung** (of an election, etc.) not decisive, producing no (viable) majority for any one party; (of a parliament) resulting from such an election; (of a man) genitally endowed in a specified way, as in *well-hung* (*colloq*). — *adj* **hang'dog** with a sneaking or cowed, dejected look. — **hanger-on'** a person who hangs around or sticks to a person or place for personal gain. — *vi* **hang'-glide.** — **hang'-glider** an apparatus for hang-gliding, or the person using it; **hang'-gliding** a sport in which one glides from a cliff-top, etc. hanging in a harness from a large kite; **hanging committee** a committee which chooses the works of art to be shown in an exhibition; **hanging garden** see under **garden; hanging matter** a crime leading to capital punishment; **hanging valley** a tributary valley falling steeply to the main valley, a product of large-scale glaciation (*geog*); **hang'man** a public executioner; **hang'out** a haunt (*colloq*); **hang'over** a survival (from another time); after-effects, esp. of drinking alcohol (see also **hung over** below); **hang'-up** (*slang*) a problem about which one is obsessed or preoccupied; an inhibition (see also **hung up** below); **hung beef** beef cured and dried; **hung jury** a jury that cannot agree. — **get the hang of** (*colloq*) to grasp the principle or meaning of; **hang about** or **around** to loiter; to stay, remain, persist; **hang a left** or **right** (*US colloq*) to turn left or right (esp. when driving); **hang back** to show reluctance; to lag behind; **hang by a thread** to depend upon very precarious conditions, a most slender chance, etc.; **hang, draw, and quarter** to hang (a person), cut them down while still alive, disembowel and cut them into pieces for display at different places; **hang fire** to be a long time in exploding or discharging; to delay; **hang in** (*slang*) to persist (also **hang in there**); **hang in the balance** to be in doubt or suspense; **hang loose** (*slang*) to do nothing; to be relaxed; **hang on** (*colloq*) to wait; **hang one's head** to look ashamed or sheepish; **hang on someone's lips** or **words** to give close, admiring attention to someone; **hang out** to hang up outside; to stay, reside or spend one's time (at) (*slang*); **hang out for** to insist on, and wait until one gets (something); **hang over** to project over or lean out from; (of an unresolved problem, decision, etc.) to overshadow, threaten; **hang together** to keep united; to be consistent; **hang up** to suspend; to replace a telephone receiver and so break off communication; **hung over** suffering from a hangover; **hung up** (*colloq*) in a state of anxiety, obsessed (with *about* or *on*); **let it all hang out** (*colloq*) to be completely uninhibited, relaxed. [O.E. *hangian*.]

hangar *hang'ər*, *n* a large shed or building for aircraft, etc. [Fr.]

hangnail *hang'nāl*, *n* a torn shred of skin beside the fingernail. — Also **ag'nail**. [O.E. *angnægl*, corn — *ange*, *enge*, compressed, painful, *nægl*, nail (for driving in), confused with *hang* and (finger-)*nail*.]

Hang Seng index *hang seng in'deks*, *n* the indicator of relative prices of stocks and shares on the Hong Kong stock exchange.

hank *hangk*, *n* a coil or skein of a specified length, varying with the type of yarn or wool; a tuft or handful e.g. of hair; a ring for attaching a luff to a sail (*naut*). [O.N. *hanki*, a hasp.]

hanker *hang'kər*, *vi* to yearn (with *after*, *for*). — *n* a yearning. — *n* **hank'ering**.

hankie or **hanky** *hang'ki*, (*colloq*) *n* dimin. of **handkerchief**.

hanky-panky *hang-ki-pang'ki*, *n* funny business, underhand trickery, goings on; faintly improper (esp. sexual) behaviour. [Arbitrary coinage.]

Hanoverian *han-ə-vē'ri-ən*, *adj* pertaining to *Hanover*; pertaining to the dynasty that came from Hanover to the British throne in 1714. — *n* a native of Hanover; a supporter of the royal house of Hanover, opp. to a *Jacobite*.

Hansa. See **Hanseatic league**.

Hansard *han'särd*, *n* the printed reports of debates in parliament, from Luke *Hansard* (1752–1828), whose descendants continued to print them down to 1889.

Hanseatic league *han-si-at'ik lēg*, **Hanse** *hans* or **Hansa** *han'sə* or *-zə*, *n* a league of German commercial cities, operating in the 14th and 15th centuries. [O.H.G. *hansa*, a band of men (M.H.G. *hanse*, merchants' guild).]

hansel. See **handsel**.

hansom *han'səm*, or **han'som-cab** *n* a light two-wheeled horse-drawn cab with the driver's seat raised behind. [From the inventor, Joseph A. *Hansom* (1803–82).]

Hants. *hants*, *abbrev* for Hampshire. [*Hantsharing*, orig. name of county.]

Hanukkah, Chanukah or **Chanukkah** *hä'nə-kə*, *hä'nōō-kä* or *hhä'nōō-kä*, *n* the Jewish festival of lights commemorating the re-dedication of the temple in 165 B.C. [Heb., consecration.]

hanuman *han-ōō-män'*, *n* a long-tailed sacred monkey of India — the entellus monkey. [*Hanumān*, Hindu monkey god.]

hapax legomenon *hap'aks lə-gom'ə-non*, (Gr.) *n* lit. said once; a word or phrase that is found once only (shortened to **hap'ax**).

ha'pence *hā'pəns*, short for **halfpence**.

ha'penny *hāp'ni*, short for **halfpenny**.

haphazard *hap-haz'ərd*, *adj* random; chance. — *adv* at random. — *adv* **haphaz'ardly**. — *n* **haphaz'ardness**. [*hap*, chance, and **hazard**.]

hapless *hap'lis*, *adj* unlucky; unhappy. — *adv* **hap'lessly**. [O.N. *happ*, good luck.]

haplo- *hap-lō-*, *hap-lə-* or *hap-lo'-*, *combining form* denoting single. — *n* **haplog'raphy** the inadvertent writing once of what should have been written twice. — *adj* **hap'loid** (*biol*) having the reduced number of chromosomes characteristic of the species in question, as in germ-cells (opp. to *diploid*). — *n* **haploid'y**. — *n* **haplol'ogy** omission in an utterance of a word of a sound resembling a neighbouring sound (as *idolatry* for *idololatry*, or indeed, '*haplogy*' for *haplology*). [Gr. *haploos*, single, simple.]

hap'orth *hā'pərth*, short for **halfpennyworth**.

happen *hap'ən*, *vi* to come to pass; to take place, occur; to chance. — *n* **happ'ening** an event, occurrence; a performance in which elements from everyday life are put together in a non-realistic way (*theatre*). —*adv* fashionable, up to the minute. — *n* **happ'enstance** chance; a chance circumstance. — **happen on** or **upon** to meet or come across by chance. [O.N. *happ*, good luck.]

happy *hap'i*, *adj* lucky, fortunate; expressing, full of, or characterised by, content, well-being, pleasure, or good; apt, felicitous; carefree; mildly drunk (*colloq*); used in combination signifying drunk with, as in *power-happy*, *bomb-happy*, usu. implying irresponsibility. — *adv* **happ'ily** in a happy manner; contentedly; by chance; I'm glad to say, luckily. — *n* **happ'iness**. — *adj* **happy-go-luck'y** easy-going, carefree; taking things as they come. — **happy event** (usu. *facetious* or *jocular*) the birth of a baby; **happy hour** (in a club, bar, etc.) a time, usu. in the early evening, when drinks are sold at reduced prices; **happy hunting-ground** the Paradise of the American Indian; **happy medium** a prudent or sensible middle course. — **happy as Larry** (*colloq*) completely happy. [Ety. as for **happen**.]

haptic *hap'tik*, *adj* pertaining to the sense of touch. — *nsing* **hap'tics** the science of studying data obtained by means of touch. [Gr. *haptein*, to fasten.]

hara-kiri *ha-rə-ki'ri*, *n* ceremonial Japanese suicide by ripping the belly with the sword. [Jap. *hara*, belly, *kiri*, cut.]

harambee *hä-räm-bē'*, *n* and *interj* a rallying cry used in Kenya, meaning 'let's organise together'. [Swahili.]

harangue *hə-rang'*, *n* a loud, aggressive speech addressed to a crowd; a pompous or wordy address. — *vi* to deliver a harangue. — *vt* to address by a harangue. — *n* **harangu'er**. [O.Fr. *arenge*, *harangue* — O.H.G. *hring* (Ger. *Ring*), ring (of listeners).]

harass *har'əs* or *hə-ras'*, *vt* to beset or trouble constantly; to annoy, pester. — *adj* **harassed**. — *adv* **harassedly**. — *n* **harasser**. — *n* and *adj* **harassing**. — *adv* **harassingly**. — *n* **harassment**. [O.Fr. *harasser*.]

harbinger *här'bin-jər*, *n* a forerunner, a thing which tells of the onset or coming (of something). — Also *vt*. [M.E. *herbergeour*.]

harbour or in N.Am. **harbor** *här'bər*, *n* a shelter, natural or artificial, for ships; a haven. — *vt* to lodge, shelter, or give asylum to; to have, keep in the mind (feelings, esp. unfriendly ones); to put (a ship) into a harbour. — *vi* to take shelter. — *n* **har'bourage** or in N.Am. **har'borage** a place of shelter; the act of harbouring. — *n* **har'bourer** or in N.Am. **har'borer**; **harbour dues** charges for the use of a harbour. **harbour light** a guiding light into a harbour; **har'bourmaster** an officer who has charge of a harbour; **harbour seal** a small seal found in Atlantic waters. [O.E. *herebeorg* — *here*, army, *beorg*, protection.]

hard *härd*, *adj* not easily penetrated or broken; unyielding to pressure; firm, solid; difficult; strenuous; laborious; vigorous; difficult to bear or endure; difficult to please; unfeeling; severe; rigorous, stiff; intractable; obdurate; troublesome; (of water) lathering with difficulty, owing to its content of calcium or magnesium salt; harsh; glaring; over-sharply defined; used as a classification of pencil-leads to indicate durable quality and faintness in use; (of drink) alcoholic or extremely so; (of a drug) habit-forming; (of news) definite, substantiated; (of consonants) representing a guttural, not a sibilant, sound (*phon*); (of photographic paper) giving a high degree of image contrast; (of a person) tough; (of spaces or hyphens in typesetting or word-processing) orthographically necessary, not merely the chance requirement of a particular piece of text-setting, as, for instance, is the hyphen used to break a word at the end of a justified line — opp. to *soft*; (of radiation) penetrating. — *n* a firm beach or foreshore; hard labour (*colloq*). — *adv* with urgency, vigour, etc.; earnestly, forcibly; to the full extent, as in *turn hard right*; with difficulty; close, near, as in *hard by*. — *vt* **hard'en** to make hard or harder, or hardy; to make firm; to strengthen; to make insensitive. — *vi* to become hard or harder. — *adj* **hard'ened**. — *n* **hard'ener**. — *n* **hard'ening** the act or fact of making or becoming hard; a substance added to harden anything; sclerosis of the arteries. — *adv* **hard'ly** with difficulty; scarcely, not quite; severely, harshly. — *interj* I shouldn't think so, it seems unlikely. — *n* **hard'ness**. — *n* **hard'ship** a thing, or conditions, hard to endure. — *adj* **hard-and-fast'** (of a rule, etc.) rigidly laid down and adhered to. — **hard-and-fast'ness**; **hard'back** a book with rigid covers. — Also *adj*. — *adj* **hard'backed**. — **hard'-ball** no-nonsense, tough tactics used for (esp. political) gain. — *adj* **hard-bitt'en** ruthless, callous. — **hard'board** compressed board made from wood fibre. — *adj* **hard-boiled'** (of eggs) boiled until solid; (of a person) callous, brazen or cynical (*colloq*). — **hard case** a person difficult to deal with or reform (*slang*); **hard cash** ready money, paper or coins; **hard cheese** (chiefly as *interj*, often insincere; *slang*) bad luck; **hard copy** (*comput*) output on paper legible to the human reader, as distinct from material which is coded or stored on disk. — *adj* **hard'-copy**. — **hard core** a durable, central part; (usu. **hard'-core**) the rubble and other material used in the foundation of roadways; something resistant to change, as, e.g. the most loyal members of a group. — *adj* **hard'-core** (of pornography) explicit, very obscene. — **hard court** a tennis court laid with asphalt, concrete, etc., not a grass court; **hard currency** a currency with a high exchange value, not easily subject to depreciation; a currency backed by the value of gold; **hard disk** (*comput*) a metal disc with a magnetic coating, in a sealed, rigid container, usually having a higher recording density than a floppy disc; **hard drinker** a person who drinks persistently and excessively. — *adj* **hard-earned'** earned through hard work or with difficulty. — **hard ECU, Ecu** or **ecu** see **ECU**. — *adj* **hard'-edge** of a style of abstract painting using bright areas of colour with sharply defined edges. — **hard facts** undeniable facts. — *adj* **hard-fa'voured** or **-feat'ured** having coarse features. — *adj* **hard-fought'** strongly contested. — **hard hat** a protective helmet worn by building workers. — *adj* **hard-head'ed** shrewd. — *adj* **hard-heart'ed** unfeeling; cruel. — *adv* **hard-heart'edly**. — **hard-heart'edness**. — *adj* **hard-hit'** seriously hurt, as by a loss of money, the death of a loved one, etc.; deeply smitten with love. — *adj* **hard-hitt'ing** frankly critical, pulling no punches. — **hard labour** physical labour as an additional punishment to imprisonment, abolished in 1948; **hard landing** one made by a spacecraft, etc. in which the craft is destroyed on impact; **hard left**, or **hard right** the extremes of political thought, allegiance, etc., favouring the left (socialist) or right (conservative) views. — *adj* **hard'line** (of an attitude or policy) definite and unyielding; having such an attitude or policy. — **hardli'ner**; **hard lines** bad luck (usu. as *interj*); **hard man** (*colloq*) a criminal specialising in acts of violence; generally, a tough person. — *adj* **hard'-nosed** (*colloq*) tough, unsentimental. — **hard'-on** (*vulg slang*) an erection of the penis; **hard'-pad** once considered a viral disease of dogs, now recognised as a symptom of distemper causing hardness of the pads of the feet. — *adj* **hard-pressed'** or **-pushed'** in difficulties. — **hard sauce** sauce made with butter and sugar, and flavoured with rum or other liquor; **hard science** any of the physical or natural sciences. — *adj* **hard-sec'tored** (*comput*) (of a floppy disk) formatted by a set of holes punched near the hub of the disk, each hole marking the start of a sector. — **hard sell** aggressive and insistent method of promoting, advertising or selling; **hard shoulder** a surfaced strip forming the outer edge of a motorway, used when stopping in an emergency; **hard-stand'ing** a hard (concrete, etc.) surface on which cars, aircraft, etc., may be parked; **hard stuff** (*slang*) strong alcohol, spirits; important information; **hard'tack** ship's biscuit, a hard biscuit formerly used as food on sailing ships; **hard'top** a rigid roof on a motor car; a motor car with such a roof. — *adj* **hard-up'** short of money, or of anything else (with *for*). — **hard'ware** domestic goods (esp. tools, etc.) made of the baser metals, such as iron or copper; mechanical equipment including war equipment; mechanical, electrical or electronic components of a computer — opp. to *software*; **hard'wareman**. — *adj* **hard-wear'ing** lasting well in use, durable. — **hard wheat** wheat having a hard kernel with a high gluten content. — *adj* **hard'-wired** (*comput*) having or being a circuit built in, whose function therefore cannot be altered. — *adj* **hard-won'** won with hard work and difficulty. — **hard'wood** timber of deciduous trees, whose comparatively slow growth produces compact hard wood; **hard words** harsh or angry words. — *adj* **hard-work'ing** diligent, industrious. — **be hard going** see under **going**[1]; **go hard with** turn out badly for; **hard as nails** very hard; callous, very tough; **hard at it** working hard, very busy; **hard by** close by; **hard done by** badly treated; **harden off** to accustom (a plant) to outdoor conditions by gradually increasing its periods outside; **hard-luck story** a person's (esp. false or exaggerated) account of his or her own bad luck and suffering, usu. intended to gain sympathy; **hard of hearing** somewhat deaf; **hard on the heels of** following immediately after; **hard put to it** in great difficulty; **no hard feelings** no offence taken, no animosity (as a result of a defeat, etc.); **the hard way** through personal endeavours or difficulties. [O.E. *hard* (*heard*); allied to Gr. *kratys*, strong.]

hardy *här'di*, *adj* brave; confident; able to bear cold, exposure or fatigue. — *n* **hard'ihood** boldness, courage; audacity. — *adv* **hard'ily**. — *n* **hard'iness**. — **hardy annual** an annual plant which can survive frosts; a story or topic of conversation which comes up regularly (*facetious*). [O.Fr. *hardi* — O.H.G. *hartjan*, to make hard.]

hare *hār*, *n* a common, very timid and very swift mammal, in appearance like, but larger than, a rabbit. — *vi* (*colloq*) to run like a hare, hasten (with *along*, etc.). — **hare-and-hounds'** a paper-chase; **hare'bell** a slender-stemmed plant with a hanging blue bell-shaped flower, the Scottish bluebell. — *adj* **hare'-brained** or sometimes **hair'-brained** giddy, silly, stupid. — **harelip**' a cleft upper lip like that of a hare. — *adj* **harelipped**'. — **hare's'-foot** or **hare's'-foot tre'foil** a variety of clover with long soft fluffy heads. — **first catch your hare** make sure you have a thing first before you decide what to do with it; **raise** or **start a hare** to introduce a topic of conversation, line of inquiry, etc. **run with the hare and hunt with the hounds** to play a double game, to support both sides at once. [O.E. *hara*.]

harem *hä'rēm* or *hā'rəm*, *n* women's quarters in a Muslim house; a set of wives and concubines; the equivalent in the society of certain animals. [Ar. *harīm*, *haram*, anything forbidden — *harama*, to forbid.]

harewood *här'wŏŏd*, *n* stained sycamore wood, used for making furniture. [Ger. dialect *Ehre* — L. *acer*, maple.]

haricot *har'i-kō* or *-kot*, *n* a kind of ragout or stew of mutton and beans or other vegetables; (usu. **haricot bean**) the kidney bean or French bean (plant or seed). [Fr. *haricot*.]

hark *härk*, *vi* to listen; to listen (to; also with *at*). — **hark back to** to revert to or be reminiscent of (an earlier topic, etc.). [Ety. as for **hearken**.]

harken *här'kən*, *vi*. Same as **hearken**.

harl[1] *härl* or **herl** *hûrl*, *n* a fibre of flax, etc.; a barb of a feather, esp. one used in making an artificial fly for angling. [M.E. *herle* — L.G.]

harl[2] *härl*, (*Scot*) *vt* and *n* roughcast. — *n* **har'ling**.

harlequin *här'li-kwin*, *n* a pantomime character wearing a close-fitting, multicoloured, diamond-patterned outfit and a black mask. — *adj* brightly-coloured; multicoloured. — *n* **harlequināde**' part of a pantomime in which the harlequin plays a chief part. — **harlequin duck** a multicoloured northern sea-duck. [Fr. *harlequin*, *arlequin* (It. *arlecchino*).]

harlot *här'lət*, *n* a whore, a prostitute. — *n* **har'lotry** prostitution; lack of chastity. [O.Fr. *herlot*, *arlot*, vile fellow.]

harm *härm*, *n* injury, physical, mental or moral. — *vt* to injure. — *adj* **harm'ful**. — *adv* **harm'fully**. — *n* **harm'fulness**. — *adj* **harm'less** not harmful or objectionable, innocent. — *adv* **harm'lessly**. — *n* **harm'lessness**. — **out of harm's way** in a safe place. [O.E. *herm* (*hearm*).]

harmattan *här-mat'ən*, *n* a dry, dusty N.E. wind from the desert in W. Africa. [Fanti *harmata*.]

harmonic *här-mon'ik*, *adj* in aesthetically pleasing proportion; pertaining to (good) harmony (*mus*); in accordance with the physical relations of sounds in harmony or bodies emitting such sounds (*math*). — *n* a component of a sound whose frequency is an integral multiple of the basic frequency; a flutelike sound produced on a violin, etc., by lightly touching a string at a node and bowing; one of the components of what the ear hears as a single sound; (in television broadcasting) a reflected signal received on a different channel from that on which the main signal is received. — *n* **harmon'ica** the musical glasses, an instrument consisting of drinking-glasses (or revolving glass basins in Benjamin Franklin's mechanised version) filled to different levels with water, and touched on the rim with a wet finger to produce sounds of different pitch; a mouth-organ. — *adv* **harmon'ically**. — *nsing* **harmon'ics** the science or study of musical acoustics. — *adj* **harmonious** (*-mō'ni-əs*) in, having, or producing harmony; in agreement; aesthetically pleasing to the ear or eye. — *adv* **harmō'niously**. — *n* **harmō'niousness**. — *n* **harmonisation** or **-z-** (*här-mə-nī-zā'shən*). — *vi* **har'monise** or **-ize** to be or get in harmony; to sing in harmony; to be compatible (orally, visually, or *fig*). — *vt* to bring into harmony; to reconcile (e.g. points of view); to provide non-unison parts to (e.g. a song or tune) (*mus*). — *n* **har'moniser** or **-z-**. — *n* **har'monist** a person skilled in harmony (in theory or composition); a person who seeks to reconcile apparent inconsistencies. — *adj* **harmonist'ic**. — *n* **harmōn'ium** a reed-organ, esp. one in which the air is forced (not drawn) through the reeds. — *n* **harmony** (*här'mə-ni*) a fitting together of parts so as to form a connected whole; in any art, a normal and satisfying state of completeness and order in the relations of things to each other; a simultaneous and successive combination of aesthetically agreeable sounds (*mus*); the whole chordal structure of a piece, as distinguished from its melody or its rhythm (*mus*); concord, agreement; a collation of parallel passages to demonstrate agreement — e.g. of Gospels. — **harmonic mean** the middle term of three in harmonic progression; **harmonic minor** a minor musical scale with minor sixth and major seventh, ascending and descending; **harmonic motion** (*math*) the motion along a diameter of a circle of the foot of a perpendicular from a point moving uniformly round the circumference; **harmonic progression** a series of numbers whose reciprocals are in arithmetical progression, such numbers being proportional to the lengths of strings that sound harmonics. [Gr. *harmoniā* — *harmos*, a joint fitting.]

harmony. See under **harmonic**.

harness *här'nis*, *n* equipment, esp. now the reins, etc. of a draught animal; an arrangement of straps, etc., for attaching a piece of equipment to the body, such as a parachute harness, a child's walking reins, a seat belt, etc.; the wiring system of a car, etc. when built separately for installing as a unit. — *vt* to put (a) harness on; to attach by harness; to control and make use of. — **harness racing** trotting races between horses harnessed to a type of two-wheeled, one-person light carriage. — **in harness** occupied in the routine of one's daily work, not on holiday or retired. [O.Fr. *harneis*, armour.]

haroseth, **haroset**, **charoseth** or **charoset** *ha-rō'set*, *-seth* or *hha-*, *n* in Judaism, a mixture of finely chopped apples, nuts, spices, etc. mixed with wine, and eaten with bitter herbs at the Passover meal, symbolising the clay from which the Israelites made bricks in Egypt. [Heb. — *charsit*, clay.]

harp *härp*, *n* a musical instrument played by plucking strings stretched from a curved neck to a sloping sound board. — *vi* to play on the harp. — *n* **harp'ist** a player on the harp. — Also **harp'er**. — **harp seal** the Greenland seal, a grey animal with dark bands. — **harp on about** (*colloq*) to dwell tediously or repeatedly on in speech or writing. [O.E. *hearpe*.]

harpoon *här-pōōn'*, *n* a barbed dart, esp. for killing whales. — *vt* to strike with a harpoon. — *n* **harpoon'er**. — *n* **harpoon gun**. [Fr. *harpon*, a clamp — L. *harpa* — Gr. *harpē*, sickle.]

harpsichord *härp'si-körd*, *n* a keyboard instrument in which the strings are twitched by quills or leather points. [O.Fr. *harpechorde*; see **harp**, **chord**.]

harpy *här'pi*, *n* a rapacious and filthy monster, part woman, part bird (*mythol*); a large South American eagle (also **harpy eagle**); a grasping, greedy woman. [Gr. *harpyia*, lit. snatcher — *harpazein*, to seize.]

harquebus *här'kwi-bəs*, *n*. Same as **arquebus**.

harridan *har'i-dən*, *n* a sharp-tongued scolding or bullying woman.

harrier[1] *har'i-ər*, *n* a medium-sized keen-scented dog for hunting hares; a cross-country runner.

harrier[2]. See **harry**.

Harrovian *hə-rō'vi-ən*, *adj* pertaining to *Harrow* town or school. — *n* a pupil of Harrow school.

harrow *har'ō*, *n* a spiked frame or other device for smoothing and pulverising land and covering seeds. — *vt* to draw a harrow over; to distress or harass. — *adj* **harr'owing** acutely distressing. — *adv* **harr'owingly**. [M.E. *harwe*.]

harrumph *hə-rumf'*, *vi* to make a noise as of clearing the throat, esp. self-importantly. [Imit.]

harry *har'i*, *vt* to plunder, ravage, destroy; to harass: — *pr p* **harr'ying**; *pa t* and *pa p* **harr'ied**. — *n*

harr'ier a person who, or thing which, harries; a kind of hawk that preys on small animals (also **hen'-harrier**). [O.E. *hergian* — *here*, army.]

harsh *härsh*, *adj* rough; jarring on the senses or feelings; rigorous, severe. — *adv* **harsh'ly**. — *n* **harsh'ness**. [M.E. *harsk*, a Northern word.]

hart *härt*, *n* a male deer (esp. red deer), esp. over five years old, when the uppermost antler begins to appear: — *fem* **hind** (*hīnd*). — **harts'horn** a solution of ammonia in water, orig. a solution of the shavings of hart's horn; **hart's'-tongue** a fern with strap-shaped leaves. [O.E. *heort*.]

hartal *här'tal* or *hûr'täl*, (*Ind*) *n* a stoppage of work in protest or boycott. [Hindi *hartāl*.]

hartebeest *här'ti-bēst* or (*Afrik*) **hartbees** *härt'bēs*, *n* a large South African antelope. [S.Afr. Du., hart-beast.]

harum-scarum *hā-rəm-skā'rəm*, *adj* scatty, disorganised; rash. — *n* a giddy, rash person.

haruspex *ha-rus'peks*, (*hist*) *n* a person (among the Etruscans) who foretold events from inspection of entrails of animals: — *pl* **harus'pices** (*-pi-sēz*). [L.]

harvest *har'vist*, *n* the time of gathering in crops; crops gathered in; the product or result of any labour or act. — *vt* to reap and gather in. — *vi* to gather a crop. — *n* **har'vester** a person who harvests; a reaping-machine; any member of a class of *Arachnida* with very long legs (also **har'vestman** or **harvest spider**). — **harvest bug, louse, mite** or **tick** a minute larval form of mite of species abundant in late summer, a very troublesome biter; **harvest festival** a church service of thanksgiving for the harvest; **har'vest-home** (a celebration of) the bringing home of the harvest; **harvest moon** the full moon nearest the autumnal equinox; **harvest mouse** a very small mouse that nests in the stalks of corn. [O.E. *hærfest*.]

has *haz*. See **have**. — **has'-been** a person or thing no longer as popular, influential, useful, etc. as before: — *pl* **has'-beens**.

hash[1] *hash*, *vt* to mince; to chop small. — *n* something which is hashed; a mixed dish of meat and vegetables in small pieces; a mixture and preparation of old matter. — **hash browns** or **hash brown potatoes** shredded potatoes, mixed with onion and fried. — **make a hash of** (*colloq*) make a mess of; **settle someone's hash** (*slang*) to silence or subdue someone. [Fr. *hacher* — *hache*, hatchet.]

hash[2] *hash*, (*slang*) *n* short for **hashish**.

hash[3] *hash* or **hashmark** *hash'märk*, *n* the symbol #, used to mean: (1) number, e.g. apartment number (esp. *NAm*); (2) space, e.g. in proofreading and marking up copy for printing. [Cf. **hatch**[3] and **hachure**.]

hashish *hash'ish* or *-ēsh*, *n* leaves, shoots, or resin of hemp, smoked, or swallowed, as an intoxicant. [Ar. *hashīsh*.]

Hasid *has'id* or *hhä'sid*, *n* a member of any of a number of extremely devout and in many cases mystical Jewish sects existing at various times throughout history: — *pl* **Hasidim** (*has'i-dim* or *hhä-sē'dim*). — Also **Hass'id, Chass'id** or **Chas'id**. — *adj* **Hasid'ic, Hassid'ic, Chasid'ic** or **Chassid'ic**. [Heb. *hāsid*, (someone who is) pious.]

haslet *haz'lit*, *n* edible entrails, esp. of a pig, shaped into a loaf and cooked. [O.Fr. *hastelet*, roast meat — *haste*, spit — L. *hasta*, a spear.]

hasn't *haz'ənt*, contracted form of **has not**.

hasp *häsp*, *n* a clasp; a slotted part that receives a staple, e.g. for a padlock. — *vt* to fasten with a hasp. [O.E. *hæpse*.]

Hassid, Hassidic, etc. See **Hasid**.

hassle *has'l*, (*colloq*) *vi* to be involved in a struggle or argument. — *vt* to argue with, bother, make trouble with. — *n* bother; (a) difficulty; something requiring trouble; an argument.

hassock *has'ək*, *n* a tussock of grass, etc.; a firmly stuffed cushion for kneeling on in church. — *adj* **hass'ocky**. [O.E. *hassuc*.]

hastate *hast'āt*, *adj* spear-shaped; with basal lobes turned outward (*bot*). [L. *hastātus* — *hasta*, spear.]

haste *hāst*, *n* urgency calling for speed; hurry; inconsiderate or undue speed. — *vt* **haste** or **hasten** (*hās'n*) to hurry on; to drive forward. — *vi* to move with speed; to hurry; (**hasten**) to be quick to, make an immediate move to (do something), as in *I hasten to say that ....* — *adv* **hastily** (*hās'ti-li*). — *n* **hast'iness**. — *adj* **hast'y** speedy, quick; rash, over-eager; irritable. — **hasty pudding** flour and milk or water made into a porridge. — **make haste** to hurry. [O.Fr. *haste* (Fr. *hâte*), from Gmc.]

hat *hat*, *n* a covering for the head, often with crown and brim. — *vt* to provide with or cover with a hat: — *pa t* and *pa p* **hatt'ed**. — *adj* **hat'less**. — *n* **hat'lessness**. — *n* **hatt'er** a maker or seller of hats. — **hat'band** a ribbon round a hat; **hat'box; hat'-brush; hat'peg** a peg on which to hang a hat; **hat'pin** a long pin for fastening a hat to the hair; **hat'stand** a piece of furniture with hatpegs; **hat'-trick** the taking of three wickets by consecutive balls in cricket, or a corresponding feat (as three goals) in other games; three successes in any activity. — **a bad hat** (*slang*) an unscrupulous person; **hats off to** (give) all honour to; **keep something under one's hat** to keep something confidential or secret; **mad as a hatter** completely mad (poss. from the odd behaviour of some hatters due to mental and physical disorders caused by the mercury in the chemicals used in the making of felt hats); **my hat!** an exclamation of surprise or disbelief; **pass** or **send round the hat** to take up a collection, solicit contributions; **take off one's hat to** to acknowledge in admiration; to praise; **talk through one's hat** to talk wildly or nonsensically; **throw one's hat into the ring** see under **ring**[1]; **wear several hats, another hat**, etc., to act in several capacities. [O.E. *hæt*.]

hatch[1] *hach*, *n* a half-door; the covering of a hatchway; a hatchway. — **hatch'back** (a car with) a sloping rear door which opens upwards; **hatch'way** an opening with a hinged or sliding door in a deck, floor, wall, or roof. — **down the hatch** (*colloq*) your health, cheers — said when about to drink something, esp. alcohol. [O.E. *hæcc*, *hæc*, grating, half-gate, hatch.]

hatch[2] *hach*, *vt* to bring out from an egg; to breed; to originate, develop or concoct (e.g. a plan). — *vi* to bring young from the egg: to come from the egg. — *n* an act of hatching; the brood hatched. — *n* **hatch'ery** a place for artificial hatching, esp. of fish eggs. — **count one's chickens before they are hatched** to rely too much on some uncertain future event. [Early M.E. *hacchen*.]

hatch[3] *hach*, *vt* to mark with fine (usu. diagonal) lines, incisions, or inlaid or applied strips. — *n* **hatch'ing** shading in fine lines. [O.Fr. *hacher*, to chop.]

hatchet *hach'it*, *n* a small axe for use in one hand. — *adj* **hatch'et-faced** having a narrow face with a sharp profile like a hatchet. — **hatchet job** (*colloq*) the (attempted) destruction of a person's reputation or standing; a severely critical attack; a severe reduction, a cutting of e.g. resources; **hatchet man** (*colloq*) a severely critical journalist; a person who does illegal, unpleasant or destructive work for a politician, political party, or other boss or company. — **bury the hatchet** to end a war or dispute (from a North American Indian custom). [Fr. *hachette* — *hacher*, to chop.]

hate *hāt*, *vt* to dislike intensely. — *n* extreme dislike, hatred; an object of hatred. — *adj* **hāt'able** or **hate'able**. — *adj* **hate'ful** provoking hate; detestable. — *adv* **hate'fully**. — *n* **hate'fulness**. — *n* **hā'tred** extreme dislike; enmity; ill will. — **hate mail** correspondence containing anything from insults to death threats, etc.; **hate'-monger** a person who stirs up hatred. [O.E. *hete*, hate, *hatian*, to hate.]

hatha yoga. See **yoga.**

hatred. See **hate.**

hatter. See **hat.**

hauberk *hö'bərk*, *n* a long coat of chain-mail. [O.Fr. *hauberc* — O.H.G. *halsberg* — *hals*, neck, *bergan*, to protect.]

haughty *hö'ti*, *adj* proud; arrogant, contemptuous. — *adv* **haught'ily.** — *n* **haught'iness.** [O.Fr. *halt*, *haut*, high — L. *altus*, high.]

haul *höl*, *vt* to drag; to pull with violence or effort; to transport by road. — *vi* to tug, to try to draw something; to alter a ship's course; (of a ship) to change direction. — *n* an act of pulling, or of pulling in; the contents of a hauled-in net or nets; the gain, winnings, or proceeds from a robbery; a distance (to be) covered in hauling or travelling. — *n* **haul'age** the act of hauling; the business of transporting goods, esp. by heavy road transport; the charge for, or cost of, this transportation. — *n* **haul'er.** — *n* **haulier** (*höl'yər*) a person or firm employed in transporting goods, esp. by road. — **long haul** a long distance to travel; a difficult objective gained only after a lengthy process. — **haul over the coals** see under **coal; haul up** to call to account (before a court, judge, etc.). [A variant of **hale²**.]

haunch *hönch* or *hönsh*, *n* the hip and buttock taken together; the leg and loin (of venison, etc.); the side or flank of an arch between the top and the start of its curve. — **haunch bone** the hip bone. [O.Fr. *hanche*; cf. O.H.G. *anchâ*, leg.]

haunt *hönt*, *vt* to visit frequently; to associate a great deal with; to intrude upon continually; (of a ghost, etc.) to inhabit or visit; to keep coming back into the memory of. — *n* a place frequently visited. — *adj* **haunt'ed** frequented or infested, esp. by ghosts or apparitions; obsessed; greatly worried. [O.Fr. *hanter*.]

Hausa *how'zə* or *-sə*, *n* a Negroid people living mainly in N. Nigeria; a member of this people; their language.

hausfrau *hows'frow*, *n* a housewife, esp. a woman exclusively interested in domestic matters. [Ger.]

hautboy *hō'boi* or *ō'boi*, *n* an *archaic* name for **oboe;** a large kind of strawberry (also **haut'bois**). [Fr. *hautbois* — *haut*, high, *bois*, wood.]

haute couture *ōt ko͞o-tür'*, (Fr.) *n* fashionable, expensive dress-designing and dressmaking.

haute cuisine *ōt kwē-zēn'*, (Fr.) *n* cookery of a very high standard.

haute école *ōt ā-kol'*, (Fr.) *n* horsemanship of the most difficult kind.

haute vulgarisation *ōt vül-gar-ēz-as-yɔ̃*, (Fr.) *n* popularisation of scholarly subjects.

hauteur *ō-tœr*, *n* haughtiness; arrogance. [Fr.]

haut monde *ō mɔ̃d*, (Fr.) *n* high society.

Havana *hə-van'ə*, *n* a fine quality of cigar, made in *Havana* or Cuba generally.

have *hav*, *vt* to hold; to keep; to possess; to own; to hold in control; to bear; to be in a special relation to (analogous to, if not quite, ownership; e.g. *to have a son, an assistant, a government*); to be characterised by; to be given the use or enjoyment of; to experience; to know; to entertain in the mind; to grasp the meaning or point of; to receive as information; to put, assert or express; to suffer, endure, tolerate; to cause or allow to (do something; esp. *NAm*); to accept, take; to remove (with *off* or *out*); to cause to be removed; to get; to give birth to; to get the better of, hold at a disadvantage or in one's power in a dilemma; to take in, deceive (usu. in passive); to entertain in one's home (with *back*, *in*, *round*, etc.); *colloq*); to ask to do a job in one's house, etc. (with *in*, *round*, etc.); as an auxiliary verb, used with the *pa p* in forming the perfect tenses: — *3rd pers sing* **has**, *pl* **have;** *pres subjunctive* **have;** *pa t* and *pa p* **had;** *past subjunctive* **had;** *pr p* **hav'ing.** — *n* a person who has possessions: — *pl* **haves.** — *n* **hav'ing** the fact of possessing. — *adj* **have-a-go'** willing to attempt something, esp. to stop a criminal in the act. — *n* **have'-not** a person who lacks possessions: — *pl* **have'-nots.** — **had better** or **best** would do best to; **had rather** would prefer to; **have at** (let me) attack; **have away** (*slang*) to steal; **have done** see under **do¹; have had it** (*colloq*) to be ruined; to have missed one's opportunities; to be doomed, beyond hope; to have been killed; **have had that** (*colloq*) not to be going to get or do that; **have it away** (*slang*) to escape; to have it off; **have it coming (to one)** (*colloq*) to deserve the bad luck, punishment, etc. that one is getting or will get; **have it in for (someone)** (*colloq*) to have a grudge against (someone); **have it in one** to have the courage or ability within oneself (to do something); **have it off** or **away** (*vulg slang*) to have sexual intercourse (with *with*); **have it out** to discuss a point of contention, etc. explicitly and exhaustively; **have on** to wear; to take in, hoax, deceive; to have as an engagement or appointment; **have to** to be obliged to; **have to be** (*colloq*) to surely be; **have to do with** see under **do¹; have up** to call to account (before a court of justice, etc.); **have what it takes** to have the necessary qualities or capabilities (to do something); **I have it!** I have found the answer (to a problem, etc.); **let (someone) have it** to attack (someone) with words, blows, etc.; **not be having any (of that)** to be unwilling to accept, tolerate, etc. the thing proposed or mentioned. [O.E. *habban*, past tense *hæfde*, past p. *gehæfd*.]

havelock *hav'lək*, *n* a white cover for a military cap, with a flap over the neck. [From Gen. Henry *Havelock*, 1795–1857.]

haven *hā'vn*, *n* an inlet affording shelter to ships; a harbour; any place of retreat, protection, peace or asylum. [O.E. *hæfen*.]

haven't *hav'ənt*, contracted form of **have not.**

haver *hā'vər*, *vi* to talk nonsense, or foolishly (esp. *Scot* and *Northern*); to waver, to be slow or hesitant in making a decision. — *n* (usu. in *pl*; esp. *Scot* and *Northern*) foolish talk, nonsense.

haversack *hav'ər-sak*, *n* a bag carried over one shoulder for holding provisions, etc. (orig. horse's oats) on a journey. [O.N. (pl.) *hafrar*; cf. Ger. *Hafer*, *Haber*, oats.]

havildar *hav'il-där*, *n* an Indian sergeant. [Pers. *hawāl-dār*.]

havoc *hav'ək*, *n* general destruction; devastation; chaos. — **play havoc with** see under **play.** [A.Fr. *havok* — O.Fr. *havot*, plunder.]

haw¹ *hö*, *n* the fruit of the hawthorn. — **haw'thorn** a small tree of the rose family, much used for hedges. [O.E. *haga*, a yard or enclosure, a haw.]

haw² *hö*, *vi* to make indecisive noises, as in *hum and haw* (q.v.). — **haw-haw'** *vi* to guffaw, to laugh boisterously. [Imit.]

Hawaiian *hə-wī'ən*, *adj* pertaining to *Hawaii*, to its citizens, or its language. — *n* a citizen or native of Hawaii. — **Hawaiian guitar** a guitar, usu. held horizontally, on which the required notes and esp. glissandos are produced by sliding a metal bar or similar object along the strings while plucking.

haw-haw. See **ha-ha²** and **haw².**

hawk¹ *hök*, *n* a name given to many birds of prey, esp. to those of the sparrow-hawk and goshawk genus; a predatory or a keen-sighted person; (in politics, industrial relations, etc.) a person who advocates aggressiveness rather than conciliation (opp. to *dove*). — *vt* and *vi* to hunt with trained hawks; to hunt on the wing. — *n* **hawk'er.** — *n* **hawk'ing** falconry. — *adj* **hawk'ish.** — *adv* **hawk'ishly.** — *n* **hawk'-ishness.** — *adj* **hawk'-eyed** sharp-sighted. — **hawk'-moth** any member of the *Sphinx* family, heavy moths with hovering flight. — *adj* **hawk-nosed'** having a hooked beak or nose. — **hawk'-weed** a genus of yellow-headed Compositae (*bot*). — **know a hawk from a handsaw** to be able to judge between things pretty well. [O.E. *hafoc*.]

hawk[2] *hök*, *vt* to force up (phlegm, etc.) from the throat. — *vi* to clear the throat noisily. — *n* the act of doing so.

hawk[3] *hök*, *n* a plasterer's slab with handle below.

hawk[4] *hök*, *vt* to convey about for sale; to cry one's wares while doing this. — *n* **hawk'er** a person who goes round houses or streets offering goods for sale. [Cf. L.G. and Ger. *Höker*, Du. *heuker*.]

hawse *höz*, *n* part of a vessel's bow in which the hawseholes are cut. — **hawse'hole** a hole for a ship's cable; **hawse'pipe** a tubular casting, fitted to a ship's bows, through which the anchor chain or cable passes. [O.N. *hāls*, neck.]

hawser *hö'zər*, *n* a small cable or large rope used in tying a ship to a quayside, etc. [O.Fr. *haucier*, *haulser*, to raise — L.L. *altiāre*.]

hawthorn. See **haw**[1].

hay *hā*, *n* grass, etc., cut down and dried for fodder or destined for that purpose. — *vt* and *vi* to make hay. — **hay'box** an airtight box of hay used to continue the cooking of dishes already begun; **hay'cock** a conical pile of hay in the field; **hay fever** irritation by pollen of the nose, throat, etc., with sneezing and headache; **hay'field**; **hay'fork** a long-handled fork used in turning and lifting hay; **hay'loft**; **hay'-maker** a person who makes hay; a wild swinging blow with the fist (*slang*); **hay'making**; **hay'mow** a rick of hay; a mass of hay stored in a barn; **hay'rick** a haystack; **hay'ride** a pleasure ride in a hay wagon; **hay'seed** seed from hay; a rustic, traditionally stupid person (*colloq*); **hay'stack**. — *adj* **hay'wire** (*slang*) crazy; all awry. — Also *adv*. — **hit the hay** (*slang*) to go to bed; **make hay** to throw (things) into confusion (with *of*); **make hay while the sun shines** to seize an opportunity while it lasts. [O.E. *hīeg*, *hīg*, *hēg*.]

hazard *haz'ərd*, *n* an old dice game; chance; risk; the pocketing of the object ball (*winning* hazard), or of the player's own ball after contact (*losing* hazard; *billiards*); the side of the court into which the ball is served (*real tennis*); any difficulty on a golf course — bunker, water, etc.; anything which might create danger, etc. — *vt* to risk; to venture; to venture to say or utter; to jeopardise. — *adj* **haz'ardable**. — *adj* **haz'ardous** dangerous; uncertain. — *adv* **haz'ard-ously**. — *n* **haz'ardousness**. [O.Fr. *hasard*.]

haze[1] *hāz*, *n* vapour, mist or shimmer due to heat, often obscuring vision; lack of definition or precision. — *vt* to make hazy. — *vi* to form a haze. — *adv* **hā'zily**. — *n* **hā'ziness**. — *adj* **hā'zy**.

haze[2] *hāz*, *vt* to vex with needless or excessive tasks, rough treatment, practical jokes. — *n* **hā'zer**. — *n* **hā'zing**. [O.Fr. *haser*, to annoy.]

hazel *hā'zl*, *n* a tree of the birch family; its wood. — *adj* made or consisting of hazel; light-brown, like a hazelnut. — **hā'zelnut** the edible nut of the hazel tree. [O.E. *hæsel*.]

HB *abbrev* for hard black (on lead pencils).

HBM *abbrev* for His (or Her) Britannic Majesty.

H-bomb. See under **H** (symbol).

HC *abbrev* for: Heralds' College; Holy Communion; House of Commons.

HCF *abbrev* for: highest common factor (also **hcf**); Honorary Chaplain to the Forces.

HCM *abbrev* for His (or Her) Catholic Majesty.

HDTV *abbrev* for high definition television, an advanced TV system in which the image is formed by a much greater number of scanning lines than in standard TV, giving much improved picture quality.

HE *abbrev* for: High Explosive; His Eminence; His Excellency.

He (*chem*) *symbol* for helium.

he *hē* (or when unemphatic *hi*, *ē* or *i*), *nominative* (irregularly, in dialect, or ungrammatically, *accusative* or *dative*) *masc pron* of the *3rd pers sing* the male (or thing spoken of as male) named before, indicated, or understood (*pl* **they**). — *n* (*nominative*, *accusative* and *dative*) a male (*pl* **hēs**). — *adj* and *combining form* signifying male, as in *he-goat*, *he-pigeon*. — **he'-man** a man of exaggerated or extreme virility, or what some women consider to be virility. [O.E. *hē*, *he*.]

HEA *abbrev* for Health Education Authority.

head *hed*, *n* the uppermost or foremost part of an animal's body; the brain; the understanding; a chief or leader; a headmaster, principal; the place of honour or command; the front or top of anything; a rounded or enlarged end or top; a mass (of leaves, flowers, hair, etc.); used when counting animals or people as a group, e.g. 100 *head of cattle*; a title, heading; energy of a fluid or gas owing to height, velocity, or pressure; the highest point of anything; a headland; culmination; the length or height of an animal's or person's head; a froth on liquor, esp. beer, poured out; a point where pus gathers at the surface of the skin; (in *pl*) the obverse of a coin; (often in *pl*) a ship's toilet (*naut slang*); an electromagnetic device in tape recorders, etc. for converting electrical signals into the recorded form or vice versa, or erasing recorded material. — *adj* of, or pertaining to, the head; for the head; chief, principal; at, or coming from, the front. — *vt* to supply with a head, top, or heading; to be the head, or at the head of (also **head up**); to cause to face or front; to strike with the head; to be ahead of. — *vi* to direct one's course, make (for). — *n* **head'er** a dive head foremost; a brick or stone with the short side showing on the wall surface; a heading for a chapter, article, etc.; the act of heading a ball; an optional piece of coded information preceding a collection of data, giving certain details about the data (*comput*); a card attached to the top of a dumpbin giving information such as the name(s) and author(s) of the book(s) displayed; a person who or a machine which removes heads from or supplies heads for casks, etc. — *adv* **head'ily**. — *n* **head'iness**. — *n* **head'ing** a part forming a head; words placed at the head of a chapter, paragraph, etc. — *adj* **head'less**. — *adv* **head'long** with the head foremost or first; without thought; precipitately, at full speed. — *adj* precipitate, at full speed. — *adj* **head'most** furthest ahead or forward. — *n* **head'ship** the position or office of head or chief. — *adj* **head'y** affecting the brain, intoxicating; exciting. — **head'-ache** (a) pain in the head; a source of worry (*colloq*). — *adj* **head'achy**. — **head'band** a decorative band for the head; **head'-banger** (*slang*) a person who is crazy, foolish, fanatical, etc.; **head'board** an often ornamental board or panel at the head of a bed; **head boy** the senior boy in a school; **head-bummer** see under **bum**[2]. — *vt* **head'-butt** to strike (a person) violently with the head. — Also *n*. — **head'case** (*colloq*) a person who is mad, crazy, etc.; **head cold** a cold which affects mainly the head, e.g. the nasal passages and eyes; **head count** (*colloq*) a count of people, bodies, etc.; **head'-crash** (*comput*) the accidental contact of a computer head with the surface of a hard disk in a disk drive, damaging the disk and wiping out the data stored on it; **head'dress** a (sometimes ceremonial) covering for the head; **head'fast** a mooring rope at the bows of a ship; **head'gear** anything worn on the head; **head girl** the senior girl in a school. — *vi* **head'hunt** to (attempt to) deprive a political opponent of power and influence (*US*). — *vi* and *vt* to seek out and recruit (executives, etc.) for a business or organisation, esp. to do so professionally e.g. as a management consultant. — **head'hunter**; **head'hunting** the practice of collecting human heads; the practice of trying to undermine one's opponent's power (*US*);

the seeking out of senior staff for one's organisation; **headlamp** see **headlight** below; **head'land** a point of land running out into the sea; a cape; the border of a field where the plough turns, ploughed separately afterwards; **head'lease** a main or original lease, which can be divided into subleases; **head'light** or **head'lamp** a strong light on the front of a vehicle; **head'line** a line at the top of a page containing title, folio, etc. (*printing*); the title of an article, esp. a main article, in a newspaper; a news item given very briefly (*radio* and *TV*). — *vt* to add a headline to. — *vi* to be a headliner. — **head'liner** a person whose name is made most prominent in a playbill or programme; **head'lock** a wrestling hold made by putting one's arm round one's opponent's head and tightening the grip by interlocking the fingers of both hands; **head'man** a chief, a leader (in primitive societies); **headmas'ter** the principal master of a school; **headmis'tress** the principal mistress of a school; **head'note** a note placed at the head of a chapter or page (*printing*). — *adj* and *adv* **head-on'** head to head, esp. (of a collision) with the front of one vehicle, etc. hitting the front of another; with the head pointing directly forward; directly opposed, confronting each other. — **head'phone** (usu. in *pl*) a telephone receiver worn in pairs over the ears, esp. for listening to radios or cassette players; **head'-piece** a top part; a decorative engraving at the beginning of a book, chapter, etc. (*printing*). — *npl* and *nsing* **headquar'ters** the quarters or residence of a commander-in-chief or general; a central or chief office of a company, etc. — **head'race** the channel leading to a waterwheel; **head'rest** a support for the head; (also **head restraint**) a cushioned frame fitted to the top of a seat in a car, etc. to prevent the head jerking back in a collision; **head'room** space below a ceiling, bridge, etc.; space overhead, below an obstacle, etc.; **head'scarf** a scarf worn over the head, a headsquare: — *pl* **head'scarves; head sea** (*naut*) a sea running directly against a ship's course; **head'set** a set of headphones, often with a microphone attached; **head'shot** a photograph or television picture of someone's head (and shoulders) only; **head'shrinker** a headhunter who shrinks the heads of his victims; a psychiatrist (*colloq*); **heads'-man** an executioner who cuts off heads; **head'-square** a square of material worn as a covering for the head; **head'stall** the part of a horse's bridle round the head; **head'stock** (*mach*) a device for supporting the end or head of a member or part; **head'stone** the principal stone of a building; the main principle, the cornerstone; a gravestone; **head'-stream** a head-water; the stream forming the highest or remotest source (of a river). — *adj* **head'strong** obstinately self-willed. — **head-teach'er** a headmaster or headmistress; **head waiter** the most senior waiter of a restaurant or hotel; **head'-water** the highest part of a stream or river, before receiving tributaries; **head'way** motion ahead, esp. of a ship; progress; the time interval or distance between buses, trains, etc. travelling on the same route in the same direction; **head'wind** a wind blowing directly against one's course; **head-wom'an** a female leader or chief; **head'word** a word forming a heading e.g. of an entry in a dictionary or encyclopaedia; a word under which other related words are grouped, e.g. in a dictionary; **head'work** mental work; **head'worker**. — **above** or **over one's head** beyond one's capacity for understanding; **against the head** (of the ball in a rugby scrum, or the scrum itself) won by the team not putting the ball in; **bring** or **come to a head** to (cause to) reach a climax or crisis; **get** or **take it into one's head** to conceive the (esp. wrong or foolish) notion (with *that*); **give a horse his head** to let it go where, and as quickly as it chooses; **give head** (*vulg*) to perform oral sex; **give someone his** or **her head** to increase someone's scope for initiative; **go over someone's head** to take a complaint, etc. directly to a person more senior than someone; **go to someone's head** to make someone vain or conceited; to make someone drunk; **have a good,** etc. **head on one's shoulders** to have ability; **have one's head screwed on (the right way)** to be sensible, bright, etc.; **head and shoulders** very much, as if taller by a head and shoulders; **head first** or **foremost** with the head in front; **head off** to get ahead of so as to turn back; to deflect from a path or intention; **head over heels** as in a somersault; completely; **heads or tails** an invitation to guess how a coin will fall; **head to head** in direct competition (*adj* **head-to-head'**); **hit the headlines** to get prominent attention in the press or other media; **hold up one's head** see **hold**[1]; **keep (**or **lose) one's head** to keep (or lose) one's self-possession, calmness, control; **keep one's head above water** see under **water; off one's head** (*colloq*) crazy; **on your (own) head be it** you must accept responsibility for any unpleasant or undesirable consequences of your actions; **out of one's head** crazy, mad (*colloq*); of one's own invention; **over one's head** beyond one's control; beyond one's understanding; **put heads together** to confer and co-operate; **put one's head on the block** to stick one's neck out, run the risk of censure, etc.; **take it into one's head to (do something)** to conceive the (esp. misguided) intention of (doing something). [O.E. *hēafod*.]

heal *hēl*, *vt* to make healthy; to cure; to restore to health, good condition (physical or mental); to remedy, amend. — *vi* to grow sound or healthy again. — *adj* **heal'able**. — *n* **heal'er**. — *n* and *adj* **heal'ing**. — *adv* **heal'ingly**. [O.E. *hǣlan* — *hāl*, whole.]

health *helth*, *n* sound physical or mental condition; well-being; degree of soundness. — *adj* **health'ful** conducive to health. — *adv* **health'fully**. — *n* **health'fulness**. — *adv* **health'ily**. — *n* **health'i-ness**. — *adj* **health'y** in good health; morally, spiritually, economically, etc. wholesome; conducive to or indicative of good health. — **health camp** (*NZ*) a camp intended to improve the physical and emotional condition of children who attend it; **health'care** the care of one's own or others' health; **health centre** a centre for clinical and administrative health welfare work; **health farm** a place, usu. in the country, where people go to improve their health by dieting, exercise, etc.; **health food** a food thought to be particularly good for one's health, esp. that grown, prepared, etc. without artificial fertilisers, chemical additives, etc.; **health stamp** (*NZ*) a stamp, part of the cost of which goes to supporting health camps; **health visitor** a nurse concerned mainly with health education or advice, and preventive medicine rather than the treatment of disease, who visits esp. mothers with young children, and the elderly, in their own homes. [O.E. *hǣlth* — *hāl*, whole.]

heap *hēp*, *n* a mass of things placed one above another; a mound; a great number, a great deal (often in *pl*), a collection (*colloq*); an old dilapidated motor car. — *vt* to throw into a heap; to amass; to load with a heap or heaps; to pile high (also *vi*). — *adj* **heap'ing** (*NAm*; of a spoonful, etc.) heaped. — *adv* **heaps** (*colloq*) very much. [O.E. *hēap*.]

hear *hēr*, *vt* to perceive by the ear; to listen to; to try in a court of law; to be informed. — *vi* to have or exercise the sense of hearing; to listen; to have news (of or from): — *pa t* and *pa p* **heard** (*hûrd*). — *n* **hear'er**. — *n* **hear'ing** power or act of perceiving sound; an opportunity to be heard; a judicial investigation and listening to evidence and arguments, esp. without a jury; earshot. — **hear'ing-aid** any device, electrical or other, for enabling the deaf to hear or to hear better; **hear'say** rumour; common talk. — *adj* of the nature of, or based on, reports given by others. — **hear, hear!** an exclamation of approval from the hearers of a speech or statement; **hear out** to listen to (someone) until they have said all they wish to say; **hear tell of** to hear someone speak of; **hear things** see under **thing; will** or **would not hear of** will or would not allow or tolerate. [O.E. *hēran, hīeran, hȳran*.]

hearken *här'kn*, (*archaic* or *literary*) *vi* to hear attentively; to listen. — *n* **heark'ener**. [O.E. *heorcnian*.]

hearse *hûrs*, *n* a vehicle for carrying the dead to a funeral. [O.Fr. *herse* — L. *hirpex, -icis*, a harrow.]

heart *härt*, *n* the organ that circulates the blood through the body; the innermost part; the core; the chief or vital part; the breast, bosom; the (imagined) place of origin of the affections, understanding, and thought, as opposed to the head as the place of reason; courage; vigour; inmost feelings or convictions; a term of endearment or encouragement; a heart-shaped figure or object; a playing-card with heart-shaped pips; the centre of a cabbage, lettuce, etc. — *vi* (of a lettuce, etc.) to form a compact head or inner mass. — **-heart'ed** used in combination to signify having a heart, esp. of a specified kind (*hard-hearted*, etc.). — *vt* **heart'en** to encourage, stimulate; to give courage or strength to. — *vi* to take courage. — *adv* **heart'ily** lustily, vigorously; completely (sick, tired, etc.). — *n* **heart'iness**. — *adj* **heart'less** without heart, courage, consideration or feeling; callous. — *adv* **heart'lessly**. — *n* **heart'lessness**. — *adj* **heart'y** heartfelt; cordial; robust; enthusiastic; in, or indicating, good spirits, appetite or condition; sound. — *n* a hearty person, esp. one who goes in for sports, outdoor pursuits, etc.; (in *pl*) an old form of address to fellow sailors. — **heart'ache** sorrow; anguish; **heart attack** an occurrence of coronary thrombosis, with the death of part of the heart muscle, or some other sudden malfunction of the heart; **heart'beat** a pulse of the heart; **heart'break** a crushing sorrow or grief. — *adj* **heart'breaking**. — *adj* **heart'broken**. — **heart'burn** a burning, acrid feeling in throat or breast, severe indigestion; **heart disease** any morbid condition of the heart; **heart'-failure** stoppage or inadequate functioning of the heart. — *adj* **heart'felt** felt deeply; sincere. — **heart'land** an area of a country that is centrally situated and/or vitally important; **heart murmur** an abnormal sound from the heart indicating a structural or functional abnormality. — *adj* **heart'-rending** agonising. — **heart's'-blood** blood of the heart; life, essence; **heart'-searching** examination of one's deepest feelings; **heart's'-ease** the pansy. — *adj* **heart'-shaped** shaped like the conventional representation of the human heart. — *adj* **heart'-sick** greatly depressed, despondent. — **heart'-sickness**. — *adj* **heart'-sore** greatly distressed, very sad. — **heart'-string** (in *pl*) affections; **heart'-throb** (*colloq*) a person who is the object of great romantic affection from afar. — *adj* **heart-to-heart'** candid, intimate and unreserved. — *n* a conversation of this sort. — *adj* **heart'warming** emotionally moving; very gratifying, pleasing. — **heart'water** a fatal tick-borne viral disease of cattle, sheep and goats, with accumulation of fluid in the area of the heart and lungs; **heart'wood** the hard inner wood of a tree. — **after one's own heart** exactly to one's own liking; **at heart** in one's real character; **break one's heart** to die of, or be broken down by, grief or disappointment; **break someone's heart** to cause deep grief to someone; (*loosely*) to disappoint someone romantically; **by heart** by memory, rote; **change of heart** see under **change; cross one's heart** to emphasise the truth of a statement (often literally, by making the sign of the cross over one's heart); **dear** or **near to one's heart** whom or which one feels a warm interest in, concern or liking for; **find it in one's heart** to be able to bring oneself; **from the bottom of one's heart** most sincerely; **have a change of heart** to alter one's former opinion or viewpoint; **have a heart** (usu. in *imper*) to show pity or kindness; **have at heart** to cherish as a matter of deep interest; **have one's heart in it** (often in *neg*) to have enthusiasm for what one is doing; **have one's heart in one's boots** to feel a sinking of the spirit; **have one's heart in one's mouth** to be in great fear or anxiety; **have one's heart in the right place** to be basically decent, generous; **have one's heart set on** to desire earnestly; **have the heart** (usu. in *neg*) to have the courage or resolution (to do something unpleasant); **heart and soul** with complete sincerity; with complete devotion to a cause; **heart-lung machine** a machine used in chest surgery to take over for a time the functions of the heart and lungs; **heart of hearts** inmost feelings or convictions; deepest affections; **heart of oak** a brave, resolute person; **in good heart** in sound or fertile condition; in good spirits or courage; **lose heart** to become discouraged; **lose one's heart to** to fall in love with; **near to one's heart** see **dear to one's heart** above; **set one's heart on** or **upon** to come to desire earnestly; **set someone's heart at rest** to render someone reassured, easy in mind; **take heart** to be encouraged; **take to heart** to come to believe (esp. advice) earnestly; **take to one's heart** to form an affection for; **to one's heart's content** as much as one wishes; **wear one's heart on one's sleeve** to show one's feelings openly; **with all one's heart** most willingly. [O.E. *heorte*.]

hearth *härth*, *n* the floor of a fireplace, or the area of floor surrounding it; the fireside; the house itself; the home circle; the lowest part of a blast-furnace. — **hearth money** or **hearth tax** a former tax based on the number of hearths in a house; **hearth'rug** a rug laid over the hearthstone or in front of the hearth or fireplace; **hearth'stone** a stone forming a hearth; a soft stone used for whitening hearths, doorsteps, etc. [O.E. *heorth*.]

heartily, heartiness, etc. See **heart**.

heat *hēt*, *n* that which excites the sensation of warmth; sensation of warmth, esp. in a high degree; degree of hotness; a high temperature; the hottest time; redness of the skin, esp. when irritated; vehemence, passion; sexual excitement in animals, or its period, esp. in the female, corresponding to *rut* in the male; a single eliminating round in a race; a division of a contest from which the winner goes on to a further or final test; animation; pressure intended to coerce (*colloq*); period of intensive search, esp. by the police; trouble (*colloq*). — *vt* to make hot; to agitate. — *vi* to become hot. — *adj* **heat'ed** having become, or been made, hot; angry, agitated or impassioned. — *n* **heat'er** someone who, or that which, heats; an apparatus for heating a room or building; a gun, pistol (esp. *US*; *slang*). — *n* and *adj* **heat'ing**. — **heat barrier** difficulties caused by a thin envelope of hot air which develops round aircraft at high speeds and occasions structural and other problems; **heat death** the final state of the universe (if it is a closed system) predicted by the Second Law of Thermodynamics, in which heat and energy are uniformly distributed throughout the substance of the universe; **heat engine** an engine that transforms heat into mechanical work; **heat'-exchanger** a device for transferring heat from one fluid to another; **heat pump** a device (on the refrigerator principle) for drawing heat from water, air, or the earth, and giving it out to warm e.g. a room. — *adj* **heat'-resistant**. — **heat shield** an object or substance designed to protect against excessive heat, esp. that which protects a spacecraft re-entering the earth's atmosphere; **heat sink** something into which unwanted heat can be shot; **heat'spot** a spot or blotch on the skin caused by heat; **heat'stroke** exhaustion or illness due to exposure to heat; sunstroke; **heat wave** a heated state of atmosphere passing from one locality to another; a hot spell. — **in heat** or **on heat** (of a female animal) ready to mate; **latent heat** the heat required to change solid to liquid, or liquid to gas, without change of temperature; **specific heat** see under **specify; take the heat out of** to lessen the vehemence or acrimony of (a situation, etc.); **turn on the heat** (*slang*) to use brutal treatment in order to coerce. [O.E. *hǣtu*, heat; *hāt*, hot.]

heath *hēth, n* barren open country, esp. covered with low shrubs; any shrub of genus *Erica*, sometimes extended to heather. — *adj* **heath'y.** [O.E. *hǣth.*]

heathen *hē'dhən, n* someone who is not a Christian, Jew, or Muslim but follows another form of religion, esp. polytheistic; a pagan; someone who has no religion; someone who is ignorant or unmindful of religion; an uncivilised person (*colloq*): — *pl* **hea'then** (collectively) or **hea'thens** (individually). — *adj* pagan; irreligious. — *n* **hea'thendom.** — *vt* **hea'thenise** or **-ize** to make heathen or heathenish. — *adj* **hea'thenism** relating to the heathen; uncivilised; cruel. — *adv* **hea'thenishly.** — *n* **hea'thenishness.** — *n* **hea'thenism.** — *n* **hea'thenry.** [O.E. *hǣthen.*]

heather *hedh'ər, n* ling, a common low shrub of the heath family; sometimes extended to the heaths (*Erica*). — *adj* of the purple colour of (red) heather; composed of or from heather. — *adj* **heath'ery.** — **heath'er-mixture** a woollen fabric speckled in colours like heather. [Older Scots *hadder.*]

Heath-Robinson *hēth-rob'in-sən, adj* used to describe an over-ingenious mechanical contrivance. [*William Heath Robinson* (1872–1944), who drew such contraptions.]

heave *hēv, vt* to lift up, esp. with great effort; to throw; to haul; to force (a sigh) from the chest. — *vi* to rise like waves; to retch; to strive to lift or move something; to move, orig. of a ship: — *pa t* and *pa p* **heaved** or (*naut*) **hōve.** — *n* an effort upward; a throw; an effort to vomit. — **give (**or **get) the heave** or **heave-ho** (*colloq*) to dismiss, reject (or be dismissed, rejected); **heave ho!** an orig. sailors' call to exertion, as in heaving the anchor; **heave in sight** to come into view; **heave to** to bring a vessel to a standstill. [O.E. *hebban*, past t. *hōf*, past p. *hafen.*]

heaven *hev'n, n* the vault of sky overhanging the earth (commonly in *pl*); the upper regions of the air; a great and indefinite height; (often *cap*) the dwelling-place of God or the gods, and the blessed; supreme happiness. — *interj* (in *pl*) expressing surprise, dismay, etc. — *n* **heav'enliness.** — *adj* **heav'enly** of or inhabiting heaven; of or from God or the angels or saints; celestial; pure; supremely blessed; excellent (*colloq*). — *adj* **heav'enward.** — *adv* **heav'enward** or **heav'enwards.** — *adj* **heav'en-born** descended from heaven. — **heavenly bodies** the sun, moon, planets, comets, stars, etc.; **heavenly host** a multitude of angels. — *adj* **heav'en-sent** sent by heaven; very timely. — **good heavens** or **heavens above** expressing surprise, dismay, etc.; **heaven forbid** may it not happen (that); **heaven knows** God knows; it is beyond human knowledge; it is anyone's guess; **in (the) seventh heaven** in a state of the most exalted happiness; **move heaven and earth** to do everything possible; **the heavens opened** there was a sudden downpour of rain. [O.E. *heofon.*]

heavy *hev'i, adj* (*compar* **heav'ier**, *superl* **heavi'est**) weighty; laden; abounding; of high specific gravity; not easy to bear; oppressive; grave; dull, lacking interest; pompous; laborious; in low spirits; drowsy; with great momentum; deep-toned; massive; not easily digested; doughy; impeding the feet in walking; (of the ground) very wet and soft; heavy-armed (*mil*); (of liquor) strong; dark with clouds; pertaining to grave or serious roles (*theat*); (of newspapers) serious, highbrow; tense, emotional, strained (*slang*); serious, important (*slang*); (of a market) with falling prices (*commerce*). — *adv* heavily. — *n* the villain on stage or screen; a large, strong man employed for purposes of a violent nature (*slang*); in Scotland, a type of beer similar to, but not as strong as, export. — *adv* **heav'ily.** — *n* **heav'iness.** — *adj* **heavier-than-air'** of greater specific gravity than air, not sustained by a gasbag. — *adj* **heav'y-armed** bearing heavy armour or arms. — **heavy breather; heavy breathing** loud and laboured breathing due to exertion, excitement, etc., sometimes associated with anonymous obscene telephone calls. — *adj* **heavy-du'ty** made to withstand very hard wear or use. — *adj* **heavy-hand'ed** clumsy, awkward; oppressive. — *adj* **heavy-heart'ed** weighted down with grief. — **heavy hydrogen** deuterium; also tritium; **heavy industry** see **industry.** — *adj* **heavy-lad'en** with a heavy burden. — **heavy metal** a metal of high specific gravity; guns or shot of large size; a person to be reckoned with; a particularly loud, simple and repetitive form of rock (*mus*); **heavy particle** a baryon; **heavy spar** barytes; **heavy water** water in which deuterium takes the place of ordinary hydrogen, or a mixture of this and ordinary water; **heav'yweight** a person or thing well above the average weight; someone important or very influential (*colloq*); a competitor in the heaviest class (*sport*); a weight category variously applied in boxing and wrestling; a sportsman of the specified weight for the category (e.g. in professional boxing above middleweight, **light'-heavyweight** (maximum 79 kg. 175 lb.), **jun'ior-heavyweight** or **cruis'erweight** (maximum 88 kg. 195 lb.) and **heav'yweight** any weight above these). — **be heavily into** (*colloq*) to be keen on or an enthusiastic practitioner of; **be heavy going** see under **going**[1]; **the heavies** the more serious newspapers, journals, etc. (*colloq*); (shares in) the heavy industries. [O.E. *hefig* — *hebban*, to heave.]

Heb. or **Hebr.** *abbrev* for: Hebrew; (the Letter to the) Hebrews (*Bible*).

hebdomad *heb'də-mad, n* a week. — *adj* **hebdomadal** (*-dom'ə-dl*) weekly. — *adv* **hebdom'adally.** [Gr. *hebdomas, -ados*, a set of seven, a week — *hepta*, seven.]

hebetate *heb'i-tāt, adj* dull; blunt; soft-pointed. [L. *hebes, -etis*, blunt.]

Hebrew *hē'broo͞, n* a Jew; the Semitic language of the Hebrews. — *adj* of the Hebrews or their language. — *adj* **Hebraic** (*hē-brā'ik*) or **Hebrā'ical** relating to the Hebrews or to their language. — *adv* **Hebrā'ically.** — *n* **Hē'brāism** a Hebrew idiom. — *n* **Hē'brāist** a person skilled in Hebrew. [O.Fr. *Ebreu* — Aramaic *'ebrai*, lit. one from the other side (of the Euphrates).]

Hebridean *heb-ri-dē'ən, adj* of the **Hebrides** (*heb'ri-dēz*). — *n* a native of the Hebrides. [Due to a misprint of L. *Hebŭdēs.*]

hecatomb *hek'ə-too͞m* or *-tōm, n* a great public sacrifice; any large number of victims. [Gr. *hekatombē* — *hekaton*, a hundred, *bous*, an ox.]

heck *hek, n* and *interj* euphemism for **hell.**

heckelphone *hek'l-fōn, n* an instrument of the oboe family, invented by W. *Heckel* (1856–1909), between the cor anglais and the bassoon in pitch.

heckle *hek'l, vt* to ply with embarrassing questions, or shout or jeer abusively or disruptively at (as at an election hustings or public lecture); to comb out (flax or hemp fibres). — *n* **heck'ler.** — *n* **heck'ling.** [Cf. **hackle.**]

hectare *hek'tär* or *-tār, n* 100 ares or 10 000 sq. metres.

hectic *hek'tik, adj* feverish, agitated, rushed; relating to hectic fever (*old*). — *n* a hectic fever or flush. — *adv* **hec'tically.** — **hectic fever** (*old*) fever occurring in connection with certain wasting diseases, esp. tuberculosis, typically producing a flush in the cheeks. [Gr. *hektikos*, habitual — *hexis*, habit.]

hecto- *hek-tō-* or *hek-tə-*, or **hect-** *combining form* denoting (esp. in the metric system) 100 times. — *n* **hec'togram** or **hec'togramme** 100 grammes. — *n* **hec'tograph** a gelatine pad for printing multiple copies. — *vt* to reproduce in this way. — *adj* **hectograph'ic.** — *n* **hec'tolitre** 100 litres. — *n* **hec'tometre** 100 metres. [Fr. contraction of Gr. *hekaton*, a hundred.]

hector *hek'tər*, *n* a bully, a blusterer. — *vt* to treat insolently; to annoy. — *vi* to play the bully; to bluster. — *n* **hec'torer.** — *n* **hec'toring** (also *adj*). [Gr. *Hektōr*, the Trojan hero.]

he'd *hēd*, a contraction of **he had** or **he would**.

heddle *hed'l*, (*weaving*) *n* a series of vertical cords or wires, each having in the middle a loop to receive a warp-thread, and passing round and between parallel bars. [An assumed O.E. *hefedl*.]

hedge *hej*, *n* a close row of bushes or small trees serving as a fence; a barrier, protection (*fig*); an act of hedging; something bought as, or which acts as, a protection against financial loss. — *vt* to enclose with a hedge; to obstruct; to surround; to protect oneself from loss on, by compensatory transactions, e.g. bets on the other side. — *vi* to make hedges; to shuffle, be evasive, e.g. in an argument; to buy or sell something as a financial hedge. — *adj* living in or frequenting hedges; wayside; low; debased. — *n* **hedg'er.** — **hedge'hog** a small prickly-backed insectivorous animal that lives in hedges and bushes, and has a snout like a hog; a small, strongly fortified, defensive position. — *vi* **hedge'-hop** (*airmen's slang*) to fly low as if hopping over hedges. — **hedge'row** a line of hedge, often with trees; **hedge'-sparrow** the dunnock (*Prunella modularis*), superficially like a sparrow but with a slenderer bill. [O.E. *hecg*.]

hedonism *hē'də-nizm* or *hed'*, *n* (in ethics) the doctrine that pleasure is the highest good; the pursuit of pleasure; a lifestyle devoted to pleasure-seeking. — *adj* **hedon'ic** or **hedonis'tic.** — *nsing* **hedon'ics** that part of ethics or of psychology that deals with pleasure. — *n* **he'donist.** [Gr. *hēdonē*, pleasure.]

heebie-jeebies *hē-bi-jē'biz*, *npl* (with **the**; *slang*) a fit of nerves; the creeps. [A coinage.]

heed *hēd*, *vt* to observe; to look after; to attend to. — *vi* to mind, care. — *n* notice; caution; attention. — *adj* **heed'ful** attentive; cautious. — *adv* **heed'fully.** — *n* **heed'fulness.** — *adj* **heed'less.** — *adv* **heed'lessly.** — *n* **heed'lessness.** [O.E. *hēdan*.]

heehaw *hē'hö*, *vi* (of a donkey) to bray. — *n* a bray. [Imit.]

heel¹ *hēl*, *n* the hind part of the foot below the ankle; the whole foot (esp. of beasts); the covering or support of the heel; the hinder part of anything, such as a violin bow; a heel-like bend, as on a golf club; the end of a loaf; a despicable person, often someone who lets others down (*slang*). — *vt* to execute or perform with the heel; to strike with the heel; to provide with a heel; to supply with a weapon, money, etc. — *vi* to move one's heels to a dance rhythm; to kick the ball backwards out of the scrum with the heel (*Rugby football*). — **-heeled** in combination signifying (of shoes) having a heel of a specified type, as in *high-heeled*, and used (*fig*) in *well-heeled*, comfortably off. — *adj* **down-at-heel'** having the heels of one's shoes trodden down; slovenly; in poor circumstances. — **heel'-ball** a black waxy composition for blacking the heels and soles of shoes and for taking brass-rubbings, etc.; **heel'-tap** a layer of material in a shoe-heel; a small quantity of liquor left in the glass after drinking. — **Achilles' heel** see under **Achillean; at** (or **on** or **upon**) **the heels of** following close behind; **bring to heel** to persuade to come to heel; **come to heel** to obey or follow like a dog; to submit to authority; **cool** (or **kick**) **one's heels** to be kept waiting for some time; **dig in one's heels** to behave stubbornly; **heel and toe** with strict walking pace, as opposed to running; **heel in** see **heel³**; **kick up one's heels** to frisk; **show a clean pair of heels** to run off; **take to one's heels** to flee; **turn on** (or **upon**) **one's heel** to turn sharply round, to turn back or away; **under the heel** crushed, tyrannised over; **walk to heel** (of a dog) to walk obediently at the heels of the person in charge of it. [O.E. *hēla*.]

heel² *hēl*, *vi* to incline, slope; (of a ship) to lean on one side. — *vt* to tilt. [Earlier *heeld*, *hield*; O.E. *hieldan*, to slope.]

heel³ *hēl*, *vt*: **heel in** to cover the roots, etc. of (a plant) with soil temporarily to keep them moist. [O.E. *helian* — *hellan* blended with *helan*, both meaning to hide.]

heft *heft*, (*US*) *n* weight. — *vt* to lift; to try the weight of. — *adv* **hef'tily.** — *n* **hef'tiness.** — *adj* **hef'ty** rather heavy; muscular; sizeable; vigorous. [**heave.**]

Hegelian *hā-gēl'i-ən*, *adj* of or pertaining to Wilhelm Friedrich *Hegel* (1770–1831) or his philosophy. — *n* a follower of Hegel. — *n* **Hegel'ianism.**

hegemony *hi-gem'ən-i*, *n* leadership; preponderant influence, esp. of one state over others. [Gr. *hēgemoniā* — *hēgemōn*, leader — *hēgeesthai*, to lead.]

hegira *hej'rə*, *hej'i-rə* or *hi-jī'rə*, *n* the flight of Mohammed from Mecca, A.D. 622, from which is dated the Muslim era; any flight. [Ar. *hijrah*, flight, *hajara*, to leave.]

he-he *hē-hē*, *interj* representing a high-pitched or gleeful laugh. — *n* such a laugh. — *vi* to laugh thus. [Imit.]

heifer *hef'ər*, *n* a young cow. [O.E. *hēahfore*, *hēahfru*, *-fre*; lit. prob. high-goer — *faran* to go.]

heigh *hā*, *interj* a cry of enquiry, encouragement, or exultation. — *interj* **heigh'-ho** an exclamation expressive of weariness. [Imit.]

height *hīt*, *n* the condition of being high; degree of highness; distance upwards; angle of elevation; that which is elevated; a hill; a high place; elevation in rank or excellence; utmost degree. — *vt* and *vi* **height'en** to make or become higher; to make or become brighter or more conspicuous, or (*fig*) stronger or more intense. — **height of land** a watershed, esp. if not a range of hills; **height to paper** (*printing*) the standard height of type, blocks, etc., from foot to face (approx. 0·918 in.) [O.E. *hīehtho*, *hēahthu* — *hēah*, high.]

heil! *hīl*, (Ger.) *interj* hail!

heinous *hā'nəs* or *hē'nəs*, *adj* outrageously wicked, odious, atrocious. — *adv* **hei'nously.** — *n* **hei'nousness.** [O.Fr. *haïnos* — *haïr*, to hate.]

heir *ār*, *n* (in law) a person who actually succeeds to property, title, etc., on the death of its previous holder; popularly, someone entitled to succeed when the present possessor dies; a child, esp. a first-born son; a successor to a position, e.g. of leadership; inheritor of qualities, or of social conditions, or the past generally. — *n* **heir'dom.** — *n* **heir'ess** a female heir; a woman who has succeeded or is likely to succeed to a considerable fortune. — *adj* **heir'less.** — *n* **heir'ship.** — **heir-appa'rent** the one by law acknowledged to be heir, no matter who may subsequently be born; a person expected to succeed the leader of a party, etc.; **heir'loom** any piece of furniture or personal property which descends to the heir by special custom; any object which is passed down through a family from generation to generation; **heir-presump'tive** a person who will be heir if no nearer relative should be born (also *fig*). — **fall heir to** to inherit (also *fig*). [O.Fr. *heir* — L. *hērēs*, an heir.]

heist *hīst*, (*slang*) *vt* to steal or rob in a heist. — *n* a robbing or theft, esp. an armed hold-up, or a particularly clever or spectacular theft. — *n* **heist'er.** [Variant of **hoist.**]

hejab *hi-jab'* or *he-jäb'*, *n* a covering for a Muslim woman's head and face, sometimes reaching the ground. [Ar. and Pers.]

hejira. See **hegira.**

held *held, pa t* and *pa p* of **hold**[1].

heli- *hel-i-*, *combining form* denoting helicopter. — *n* **hel'ideck** a landing-deck for a helicopter on a ship. — *n* **hel'ipad** a landing-place for a helicopter. — *n* **hel'iport** the equivalent of an aerodrome for helicopters, usu. for commercial services. [Gr. *helix*, *-ikos*, screw.]

heliacal *hē-lī'ə-kəl, adj* solar; coincident with that of the sun, or as nearly as could be observed. — *adv* **helī'acally.** — **heliacal rising** the emergence of a star from the light of the sun; **heliacal setting** its disappearance in it. [Gr. *hēliakos* — *hēlios*, the sun.]

helianthus *hē-li-an'thəs, n* the plant of the sunflower genus *Helianthus*. [Gr. *hēlios*, sun, *anthos*, flower.]

helical, etc. See under **helix.**

helicopter *hel'i-kop-tər, n* a flying-machine sustained by rotating blades revolving on a vertical axis above the machine. [Gr. *helix*, screw, *pteron*, wing.]

helio- *hē-li-ō-, hē-li-ə-* or *hē-li-o'-*, *combining form* denoting sun. — *adj* **heliocentric** (*-sen'trik*; *astron*) referred to the sun as centre. — *adv* **heliocen'trically.** — *n* **he'liograph** an apparatus for signalling by flashing the sun's rays; an engraving obtained photographically; an apparatus for photographing the sun; an instrument for measuring intensity of sunlight. — *vt* and *vi* to communicate by heliograph. — *adj* **heliograph'ic** or **heliograph'ical.** — *adv* **heliograph'ically.** — *n* **heliog'raphy.** — *n* **heliogravure** (*-grə-vūr'*) photo-engraving. — *n* **heliom'eter** an instrument for measuring angular distances, e.g. the sun's diameter. — *n* **he'liostat** an instrument by means of which a beam of sunlight is reflected in an invariable direction, for study of the sun or for signalling. — *n* **heliother'apy** medical treatment by exposure to the sun's rays. — *n* **he'liotrope** (*-trōp*) a plant of the borage family, with small fragrant lilac-blue flowers; the colour of its flowers; a kind of perfume imitating that of the flower; a bloodstone (*mineralogy*). — *adj* **heliotropic** (*-trop'ik*) or **heliotrop'ical.** — *adv* **heliotrop'ically.** — *n* **heliotropism** (*-ot'rə-pizm*) or **heliot'ropy** the tendency of stem and leaves to bend towards (*positive heliotropism*), and of roots from (*negative heliotropism*), the light. — *n* **he'liotype** a photograph by heliotypy. — *adj* **heliotypic** (*-tip'ik*). — *n* **he'liotypy** (*-tī-pi*) a photo-mechanical process in which the gelatine relief is itself used to print from. [Gr. *hēlios*, the sun.]

helium *hē'li-əm, n* an element (symbol **He**; atomic no. 2); a very light inert gas, discovered (1868) by Lockyer in the sun's atmosphere, isolated (1895) by Ramsay from *cleveite*, a pitchblende formed in octahedral crystals, and found in certain natural gases. [Gr. *hēlios*, sun.]

helix *hē'liks, n* a screw-shaped coil; a small volute or twist in the capital of a Corinthian column (*archit*); any mollusc of the genus *Helix*, including the best-known land-snails: — *pl* **hē'lixes** or **helices** (*hel'i-sēz* or *hē'*). — *adj* **helical** (*hel'i-kəl*). — *adv* **hel'ically.** — *adj* **hel'icoid** or **hel'icoidal** like a helix, screw-shaped. [Gr. *hĕlix*, a spiral — *helissein*, to turn round.]

Hell *hel, n* the place of the dead in general; the place or state of punishment of the wicked after death; the abode of evil spirits; (the following meanings without *cap*) any place of vice or misery; (a state of) supreme misery or discomfort; anything causing misery, pain or destruction; ruin, havoc; commotion, uproar; severe censure or chastisement; used in various colloq. phrases indicating annoyance (as in *what in hell?*, *get the hell out of here*, *I wish to hell he'd go away*) or inserted merely for emphasis. — *interj* (*colloq*) expressing annoyance or used for mildly shocking effect. — *adj* **hell'ish.** — *adv* **hell'ish** or **hell'ishly.** — *n* **hell'ishness.** — *adj* (*colloq*) **hell'uva** or **hell'ova** hell of a (see below). — **hell'bender** a large American salamander; a reckless or debauched person. — *adj* **hell'-bent** (with *on*) recklessly determined. — *adv* with reckless determination. — **hell'-cat** a violent-tempered woman; **hell'-fire** the fire of hell; punishment in hell; **hell'-hole** the pit of hell; **hell'hound** a hound of hell; an agent of hell; **hell's angel** (often with *cap*) a member of any gang of young motorcyclists who indulge in violent or antisocial behaviour. — *interj* (*colloq*) **hell's bells, hell's teeth,** etc. expressions of irritation, surprise, etc. — (the following phrases all *colloq*) **all hell breaks (**or **is let) loose** there is chaos or uproar; **as hell** absolutely; very; **beat, kick, knock,** etc. **(the) hell out of** to beat, etc. severely; **come hell or high water** no matter what difficulties may be encountered; **for the hell of it** for fun or adventure; **give someone hell** to punish, rebuke someone severely; to cause someone pain or misery; **hell for leather** at a furious pace; **hell of a** great, terrific, as in *at a hell of a speed*, *a hell of a row*; **hell to pay** serious trouble, unpleasant consequences; **like hell** very much, very hard, very fast, etc.; (also **the hell** or **hell**) used to express strong disagreement or refusal, as in *like hell I will!*, *the hell I will!*, *will I hell!*); **not have a cat in hell's chance** see under **cat**[1]; **not have a hope in hell** to have no hope at all; **play hell with** see under **play; raise hell** see under **raise; to hell with** an expression of angry disagreement with, intention to ignore, etc. (someone or something); **what the hell** what does it matter, who cares? [O.E. *hel, hell.*]

he'll *hēl*, a contraction of **he will** or **he shall.**

Helladic *hə-lad'ik, adj* Greek; of the Greek mainland Bronze Age. [Gr. *Helladikos*, Greek — *Hellas*, Greece.]

hellbender. See under **Hell.**

hellebore *hel'i-bör, n* any of several plants of the buttercup family (e.g. *black hellebore* or Christmas rose, *stinking hellebore, green hellebore*); a plant of the lily family (*American, false* or *white hellebore*, known also as Indian poke or itchweed); the winter aconite (*winter hellebore*); the rhizome and roots of these prepared as a drug. [Gr. *helleboros.*]

Hellene *hel'ēn, n* a Greek. — *adj* **Hellē'nic** (or *hə-len'*) Greek. — *vi* **hell'enise** or **-ize** (*-i-nīz*; often with *cap*) to conform, or tend to conform, to Greek usages. — *vt* to make Greek. — *n* **Hell'enism** a Greek idiom; the Greek spirit; Greek nationality; conformity to Greek ways, esp. in language. — *n* **Hell'enist** someone skilled in the Greek language; a person who adopted Greek ways and language, esp. a Jew. — *adj* **Hellenist'ic** or **Hellenist'ical** pertaining to the Hellenists; pertaining to Greek culture, affected by foreign influences after the time of Alexander. — *adv* **Hellenist'ically.** [Gr. *Hellēn*, a Greek.]

hellion *hel'yen*, (esp. *US*; *colloq*) *n* a mischievous child or other troublesome person. [Poss. dialect *hallion*, a rascal.]

hello. See **hallo.**

helm *helm, n* steering apparatus. — **helms'man** a steersman. [O.E. *helma*; O.N. *hjālm*, a rudder, Ger. *Helm*, a handle.]

helmet *hel'mit, n* an armoured or protective covering for the head; any similar covering for the head; anything resembling a helmet, e.g. a cloud on a mountain top, the top of a guinea fowl's head, the hooded upper lip of certain flowers. — *adj* **hel'meted.** [O.E. *helm*; Ger. *Helm.*]

helminth *hel'minth, n* a worm. — *n* **helminthī'asis** infestation with worms. — *adj* **helmin'thic.** — *adj* **helmin'thoid** worm-shaped. — *adj* **helmintholog'ic** or **helmintholog'ical.** — *n* **helminthol'ogist.** — *n* **helminthol'ogy** the study of worms, esp. parasitic ones. [Gr. *helmins*, *-inthos*, a worm.]

help *help*, *vt* to contribute towards the success of, to aid or assist; to give means for doing anything; to relieve the wants of; to provide or supply with a portion; to deal out; to remedy; to mitigate; to prevent, to keep from. — *vi* to give assistance; to contribute. — *n* means or strength given to another for a purpose; assistance; relief; someone who assists; a hired servant, esp. domestic. — *adj* **help'able**. — *n* **help'er** someone who helps; an assistant. — *adj* **help'ful** giving help; useful. — *n* **help'fulness**. — *adj* **help'ing** giving help or support. — *n* a portion served at a meal. — *adj* **help'less** without ability to do things for oneself; wanting assistance. — *adv* **help'lessly**. — *n* **help'lessness**. — **helping hand** assistance; a long-handled device used for reaching and gripping objects that one cannot reach by hand; **help'line** an often free telephone line by means of which people with some problem or other may contact advisers who will help them deal with it; **help'mate** a helper, esp. a wife. — **cannot help** (or **be helped**) cannot avoid (or be avoided); **help off with** to aid in taking off, disposing of or getting rid of; **help oneself (to)** to take for oneself without waiting for offer or authority; **help on with** to help to put on; **help out** to supplement; to assist; **more than one can help** more than is necessary; **so help me (God)** a form of solemn oath; on my word. [O.E. *helpan*, past t. *healp* (pl. *hulpon*), past p. *holpen*.]

helter-skelter *hel-tər-skel'tər*, *adv* in a confused hurry; tumultuously. — *n* disorderly motion; a fairground or playground spiral slide. — *adj* confused. [Imit.]

helve *helv*, *n* the handle of an axe or similar tool. — *vt* to furnish with a helve. — **helve'-hammer** a trip-hammer. [O.E. *helfe*, a handle.]

Helvetic *hel-vet'ik*, or **Helvetian** *hel-vē'shən*, *adj* Swiss. [L. *Helvētia*, Switzerland.]

hem[1] *hem*, *n* an edge or border; a border doubled down and sewed. — *vt* to form a hem on; to edge: — *pr p* **hemm'ing**; *pa t* and *pa p* **hemmed**. — **hem'line** the height or level of the hem of a dress, skirt, etc.; **hem'stitch** the ornamental finishing of the inner side of a hem, made by pulling out several threads adjoining it and drawing together in groups the cross-threads by successive stitches. — **hem in** to surround. [O.E. *hemm*, a border.]

hem[2] *hem* or *hm*, *n* and *interj* a sort of half-cough to draw attention. — *vi* to utter this kind of cough: — *pr p* **hemm'ing**; *pa t* and *pa p* **hemmed**. [Sound of clearing the throat.]

hem[3], **hem-**. See under **haem-**.

he-man. See under **he**.

hematite, etc. See **haematite**, etc. under **haem-**.

hemato-. See **haemato-** under **haem-**.

heme. See **haem** under **haem-**.

hemeralopia *hem-ə-rə-lō'pi-ə*, *n* day-blindness; vision requiring dim light. [Gr. *hēmerā*, day, *alaos*, blind, *ōps*, eye.]

Hemerocallis *hem-ə-rə-kal'is*, *n* a day-lily. [Gr. *hēmerokalles* — *hēmerā*, day, *kallos*, beauty.]

hemi- *hem-i-*, *combining form* used to denote half. — *n* **hemial'gia** pain confined to one side of the body. — *n* **hemianops'ia** blindness in half of the field of vision. — *adj* **hemianop'tic**. — *n* **hemicellulose** (*-sel'ū-lōs*) a type of polysaccharide, found in plant cell walls, which can be more easily broken down than cellulose. — *n* **hemidemisem'iquaver** (*mus*) a note equal in time to half a demisemiquaver. — *n* **hemiplegia** (*-plē'ji-ə*) paralysis of one side only. — *adj* **hemiplē'gic**. — Also *n*. — *npl* **Hemip'tera** an order of insects, variously defined, with wings (when present) often half leathery, half membranous — the bugs, cicadas, greenfly, etc. — *adj* **hemip'terous**. — *n* **hem'isphere** a half-sphere divided by a plane through the centre; half of the globe or a map of it; one of the two divisions of the cerebrum (*anat*). — *adj* **hemispher'ic** or **hemispher'ical**. — *n* **hemistich** (*hem'i-stik*) one of the two divisions of a line of verse. — *adj* **hem'istichal**. — **Eastern and Western hemispheres** the eastern and western halves of the terrestrial globe, the former including Europe, Asia and Africa, the latter, the Americas; **Northern and Southern hemispheres** the northern and southern halves of the terrestrial globe divided by the equator. [Gr. *hēmi-*, half.]

hemlock *hem'lok*, *n* a poisonous spotted umbelliferous plant (*Conium maculatum*); the poison obtained from it; extended to other umbelliferous plants, e.g. water hemlock; a N. American tree (hemlock spruce) whose branches are fancied to resemble hemlock leaves. [O.E. *hymlīce*.]

hemo-. See **haemo-** under **haem-**.

hemp *hemp*, *n* a plant (*Cannabis sativa*) yielding a coarse fibre, a narcotic drug, and an oil; the fibre itself; the drug; a similar fibre got from various other plants. — *adj* **hemp'en** made of hemp. — **hemp agrimony** a composite plant with hemp-like leaves; **hemp nettle** a coarse bristly labiate weed. [O.E. *henep*, *hænep*.]

hen *hen*, *n* a female bird; a female domestic fowl; applied loosely to any domestic fowl; the female of certain fishes and crustaceans. — **hen'bane** a poisonous plant of the nightshade family; **hen'coop** a coop for a hen; **hen'-harrier** a bird of prey, the common harrier; **hen'house** a house for fowls; **hen party** (*colloq*) a gathering of women only. — *vt* **hen'peck** (of a wife) to domineer over (one's husband). — *adj* **hen'pecked**. — **hen roost** a roosting-place for fowls; **hen run** an enclosure for fowls. — *adj* **hen-toed'** with toes turned in. [O.E. *henn*, fem. of *hana*, a cock.]

hence *hens*, (*formal* or *archaic*) *adv* from this place or origin; from this time onward; in the future; from this cause or reason. — *adv* **hence'forth** or **hence-for'ward** from this time forth or forward. [M.E. *hennes*, formed with genitive ending from *henne* — O.E. *heonan*, from the base of **he**.]

henchman *hench'mən* or *hensh'mən*, *n* a servant; a page; a right-hand man; an active partisan; a thick-and-thin supporter: — *fem* **hench'woman**; *pl* **hench'men** or **hench'women**. [O.E. *hengest*, a horse and *man*.]

hendecagon *hen-dek'ə-gon*, *n* a plane figure of eleven angles and eleven sides. — *adj* **hendecag'onal**. [Gr. *hendeka*, eleven, *gōniā*, an angle.]

hendecasyllable *hen'dek-ə-sil-ə-bl*, *n* a metrical line of eleven syllables. — *adj* **hendecasyllab'ic**. [Gr. *hendeka*, eleven, *syllabē*, a syllable.]

hendiadys *hen-dī'ə-dis*, *n* a rhetorical figure in which a notion, normally expressible by an adjective and a noun, is expressed by two nouns joined by *and* or another conjunction, as in *clad in cloth and green* for *clad in green cloth*. [Med. L. — Gr. *hen dia dyoin*, lit. one by means of two.]

henequen, **henequin** or **heniquin** *hen'ə-kən*, *n* a Mexican agave; its leaf-fibre, sisal-hemp used for cordage. [Sp. *henequén*, *jeniquén*.]

henge *henj*, *n* a circular or oval area enclosed by a bank and internal ditch, often containing burial chambers, or a circular, oval or horseshoe-shaped construction of large upright stones or wooden posts. [Back-formation from *Stonehenge*, a famous example.]

heniquin. See **henequen**.

henna *hen'ə*, *n* a small Oriental shrub (*Lawsonia*) of the loosestrife family, with fragrant white flowers; a red or reddish-orange pigment made from its leaves for dyeing hair and for skin decoration. — *adj* **hennaed** (*hen'əd*) dyed with henna. [Ar. *hinnā'*.]

henotheism *hen'ō-thē-izm*, *n* in polytheistic religions, the cultivation of a particular god as the god of one's tribe, household, etc. — *n* **henothē'ist.** — *adj* **henothēist'ic.** [Gr. *heis, henos*, one, *theos*, god.]

henpeck. See under **hen.**

henry *hen'ri*, (*electr*) *n* the unit of inductance, such that an electromotive force of one volt is induced in a circuit by current variation of one ampere per second: — *pl* **hen'ries** or **hen'rys.** [Joseph *Henry*, American physicist (1797–1878).]

hep *hep*. Same as **hip**[4].

heparin *hep'ə-rin*, *n* complex substance formed in tissues of liver, lung, etc., that delays clotting of blood, used in medicine and surgery. [Gr. *hepar*, liver.]

hepatic *hi-pat'ik*, *adj* pertaining to, or acting on, the liver; liver-coloured. — *n* a liverwort; a hepatic medicine. — *n* **hepat'ica** a plant with a slightly liverlike leaf and white, pink or purple flowers. — *n* **hepatī'tis** inflammation of the liver. — *n* **hepatol'ogist** a specialist in liver diseases. — *n* **hepatol'ogy.** [Gr. *hēpar, hēpătos*, liver.]

Hepplewhite *hep'l-wīt*, *adj* belonging to a graceful school of furniture design typified by George *Hepplewhite* (d. 1786).

hepta- *hep-tə-* or *hep-ta'-*, *combining form* signifying seven. — *n* **hep'tachord** (in Greek music) a diatonic series of seven tones, containing five whole steps and one half-step; an instrument with seven strings. — *n* **hep'tad** a group of seven. — *adj* **hep'taglot** in seven languages. — *n* a book in seven languages. — *n* **hep'tagon** a plane figure with seven angles and seven sides. — *adj* **heptag'onal.** — *n* **heptam'eter** a verse of seven measures or feet. — *n* **hep'tane** a hydrocarbon (C_7H_{16}), seventh of the methane series. — *n* **hep'tarch** ruler in a heptarchy. — *adj* **heptar'chic.** — *n* **heptarchy** (*hep'tär-ki*) a government by seven persons; a country governed by seven; a misleading term for a once supposed system of seven English kingdoms — Wessex, Sussex, Kent, Essex, East Anglia, Mercia and Northumbria. — *adj* **heptasyllab'ic** seven-syllabled. — *n* **Hep'tateuch** (*-tūk*) the first seven books of the Old Testament. — *n* **heptath'lon** since 1984, a seven-event contest consisting of 100 metres hurdles, shot-put, javelin, high jump, long jump, 200 metres sprint and 800 metres race at the Olympic games. [Gr. *hepta*, seven.]

her *hûr*, *pron*, *genitive* (or *possessive adj*), *dative* and *accus* of the *pron* **she;** herself (*reflexive*; *poetic* or *dialect*); she (*colloq nominative*). [O.E. *hire*, genitive and dative sing. of *hēo*, she.]

her. *abbrev* for: heraldry; *heres* (L.), heir.

herald *her'əld*, *n* (in ancient times) an officer who made public proclamations and arranged ceremonies; (in mediaeval times) an officer who had charge of all the etiquette of chivalry, keeping a register of the genealogies and armorial bearings of the nobles; an officer whose duty is to read proclamations, blazon the arms of the nobility, etc.; a proclaimer; a forerunner; a name given to many newspapers. — *vt* to usher in; to proclaim. — *adj* **heraldic** (*hə-ral'dik*). — *adv* **heral'dically.** — *n* **her'aldry** the art or office of a herald; the science of recording genealogies and blazoning coats of arms. [O.Fr. *herault*; of Gmc. origin.]

herb *hûrb*, *n* a plant with no woody stem above ground, distinguished from a tree or shrub; a plant used in medicine; an aromatic plant used in cookery. — *adj* **herbā'ceous** pertaining to, composed of, containing, or of the nature of, herbs; usu. understood as of tall herbs that die down in winter and survive in underground parts (*hort*). — *n* **herb'age** herbs collectively; herbaceous vegetation covering the ground; right of pasture. — *adj* **herb'al** composed of or relating to herbs; pertaining to the use of plants, e.g. medicinally. — *n* a book containing descriptions of plants with medicinal properties. — *n* **herb'alism** herbal medicine, the use of (extracts of) roots, seeds, etc. for medicinal purposes. — *n* **herb'alist** a person who studies, collects or sells herbs or plants; someone who practises herbalism; an early botanist. — *n* **herbā'rium** (a room, building, etc. for) a classified collection of preserved plants: — *pl* **herbā'riums** or **herbā'ria.** — *adj* **herb'icīdal.** — *n* **herb'icide** (*-i-sīd*) a substance for killing weeds, etc., esp. a selective weedkiller. — *n* **herb'ist** a herbalist. — *npl* **herbiv'ora** (*-ə-rə*) grass-eating animals, esp. ungulates. — *n* **herb'ivore** (*-vör*). — *adj* **herbiv'orous** eating or living on grass or herbage. — *n* **herbiv'ory.** — **herb bennet** (L. *herba benedicta*, blessed herb) avens; **herb garden; herb Paris** a plant (*Paris quadrifolia*) of the lily family; **herb Robert** stinking cranesbill (*Geranium robertianum*), a plant with small reddish-purple flowers; **herb tea** a drink made from aromatic herbs. [Fr. *herbe* — L. *herba*.]

Herculean *hûr-kū-lē'ən*, *adj* of or pertaining to *Hercules* (*hûr'kū-lēz*); (without *cap*) extremely difficult or dangerous, or requiring enormous effort, from the twelve labours of Hercules. — **Hercules beetle** a gigantic S. American beetle. — **Pillars of Hercules** two rocks flanking the entrance to the Mediterranean at the Strait of Gibraltar.

herd[1] *hûrd*, *n* a company of animals, esp. large animals, that habitually keep together; a group of domestic animals, esp. cows or swine, with or without a guardian; a stock of cattle; the people regarded as a mass, as acting from contagious impulse, or merely in contempt. — *vi* to associate (as if) in herds; to live like an animal in a herd. — *vt* to put in a herd; to drive together. — **herd book** a pedigree book of cattle or pigs; **herd instinct** the instinct that urges people or animals to act upon contagious impulses or to follow the herd; **herds'man** keeper of a herd. [O.E. *heord*.]

herd[2] *hûrd*, *n* (esp. in combination) a keeper of a herd or flock (of a particular animal, as in *goatherd*, *swineherd*, etc.). [O.E. *hirde*, *hierde*.]

here *hēr*, *adv* in, at, or to this place; in the present life or state; at this point or time. — *interj* calling attention to one's presence, or to what one is going to say. — *adv* **here'about** or **here'abouts** around or near this place; in this area. — *adv* **hereaf'ter** after this, in some future time, life, or state. — *n* a future state; the after-life. — *adv* **hereat'** (*archaic*) at or by reason of this. — *adv* **hereby'** not far off; by this. — *adv* **herein'** (*formal*) contained in this letter, document, etc.; in this respect. — *adv* **hereinaf'ter** (*formal*) afterward in this (document, etc.) (opp. to **hereinbefore'**). — *adv* **hereof'** (*formal*) of or concerning this. — *adv* **hereon'** (*formal*) on or upon this. — *adv* **hereto'** (*formal*) to this; for this object. — *adv* **heretofore'** (*formal*) before this time; formerly. — *adv* **hereund'er** (*formal*) under this; below; following; by the authority of this (document, etc.). — *adv* **here'unto** (*formal*) (also *-un'*) to this point or time. — *adv* **hereupon'** on this; immediately after this. — *adv* **herewith'** with this; enclosed with this letter, etc. — **here and now** at this present moment, straight away; **here and there** in various places; thinly; irregularly; **here goes!** an exclamation indicating that the speaker is about to proceed with some proposed act, narration, etc.; **here's to** I drink the health of; **here today, gone tomorrow** a comment on the transient, ephemeral nature of things; **here we are** (*colloq*) this is what we are looking for; we have now arrived (at); **here we go again** (*colloq*) the same undesirable situation is recurring; **here you are** (*colloq*) this is what you want; this is something for you; this way; **neither here nor there** of no special importance; not relevant; **the here and now** the present time. [O.E. *hēr*, from base of *hē*, he.]

heredity *hi-red'i-ti*, *n* the transmission of recognisable characteristics to descendants; the sum of such characteristics transmitted. — *n* **hereditabil'ity.** —

adj **hered'itable** that may be inherited. — *n* **hereditament** (*her-i-dit'*; *law*) any property that may pass to an heir. — *n* **hereditā'rian** (also **hereditā'rianist**) an adherent of **hereditā'rianism**, the view that heredity is the major factor in determining human and animal behaviour. — *adv* **hered'itarily**. — *n* **hered'itariness**. — *adj* **hered'itary** descending or coming by inheritance; transmitted to offspring; succeeding by inheritance; according to inheritance. — *n* **hered'itist** a hereditarian. [L. *hērēditās, -ātis* — *hērēs, -ēdis*, an heir.]

Hereford *her'i-fərd, adj* of a breed of white-faced red cattle, originating in *Hereford*shire. — Also *n*.

heresy *her'i-si, n* belief contrary to the authorised teaching of the religious community to which one ostensibly belongs; an opinion opposed to the usual or conventional belief; heterodoxy. — *n* **heresiarch** (*he-rē'zi-ärk*) a leader of a heretical movement. — *n* **heresiol'ogist** a student of, or writer on, heresies. — *n* **heresiol'ogy**. — *n* **heretic** (*her'ə-tik*) the upholder of a heresy; a person whose views are at variance with those of the majority. — *adj* **heretical** (*hi-ret'i-kl*). — *adv* **heret'ically**. [O.Fr. *heresie* — L. *haeresis* — Gr. *hairesis*, the act of taking, choice, set of principles, school of thought — *haireein*, to take.]

heriot *her'i-ət*, (*hist*) *n* a fine due to the lord of a manor on the death of a tenant — originally their best beast or chattel. — *adj* **her'iotable**. [O.E. *heregeatu*, a military preparation — *here*, an army, *geatwe*, equipment.]

heritable *her'i-tə-bl, adj* that may be inherited. — *n* **heritabil'ity**. — *adv* **her'itably**. — *n* **her'itor** a person who inherits. — *n* **heritage** (*her'i-tij*) that which is inherited; all inherited characteristics, the condition of one's birth; anything transmitted from ancestors or past ages, esp. historical buildings and the natural environment. [O.Fr. (*h*)*eritable*, (*h*)*eritage* — L.L. *hērēditāre*, to inherit — *hērēditas*, heredity.]

herl *hûrl, n*. Same as **harl**[1].

herm *hûrm, n* a head or bust (originally of *Hermes*) on a square base, often double-faced.

hermaphrodite *hûr-maf'rə-dīt, n* a human being, animal or plant with the organs of both sexes, whether normally or abnormally; a compound of opposite qualities. — *adj* uniting the characteristics of both sexes; combining opposite qualities. — *n* **hermaph'rodītism** the union of the two sexes in one body. — *adj* **hermaphrodit'ic** or **hermaphrodit'ical**. — *adv* **hermaphrodit'ically**. — **hermaphrodite brig** a sailing vessel which is square-rigged forward and schooner-rigged aft. [Gr. *Hermaphrodītos*, the son of *Hermēs* and *Aphrodītē*, who grew together with the nymph Salmacis into one person.]

hermeneutic *hûr-mə-nū'tik* or **hermeneutical** *-nū'ti-kəl, adj* interpreting; concerned with interpretation, esp. of Scripture. — *adv* **hermeneu'tically**. — *nsing* **hermeneu'tics** the science of interpretation, esp. of Scriptural exegesis; the study of human beings in society (*philos*). — *n* **hermeneu'tist**. [Gr. *hermēneutikos* — *hermēneus*, an interpreter, from *Hermēs*.]

hermetic *hûr-met'ik* or **hermetical** *-met'i-kəl, adj* (usu. with *cap*) belonging to magic or alchemy, magical; perfectly closed, completely sealed; obscure, abstruse. — *adv* **hermet'ically**. — *n* **hermetic'ity**. — *nsing* **hermet'ics** esoteric science; alchemy. — **hermetically sealed** closed completely; made airtight by melting the glass. [Med. L. *hermēticus* — *Hermēs Trismegistos*, Hermes the thrice-greatest, the Greek name for the Egyptian Thoth, god of science, esp. alchemy.]

hermit *hûr'mit, n* a solitary religious ascetic; a person who lives a solitary life. — *n* **her'mitage** a hermit's cell; a retreat; a secluded place. — **hermit crab** a soft-bodied crustacean that inhabits a mollusc shell. [M.E. *eremite*, through Fr. and L. from Gr. *erēmītēs* — *erēmos*, solitary.]

hernia *hûr'ni-ə, n* a protrusion of an organ through the wall of the cavity containing it, esp. of part of the viscera through the abdominal cavity; a rupture. — *adj* **her'nial**. — *adj* **her'niated**. — *n* **hernior'rhaphy** the surgical repair of a hernia by an operation involving suturing. [L.]

hernshaw *hûrn'shö, n*. See **heronshaw**.

hero *hē'rō, n* a man of distinguished bravery; any illustrious person; a person reverenced and idealised; the principal male figure, or the one whose career is the thread of the story, in a history, work of fiction, play, film, etc.; orig. a man of superhuman powers, a demigod: — *pl* **hē'roes**. — *adj* **heroic** (*hi-rō'ik*) befitting a hero; of or pertaining to heroes; epic; supremely courageous; using extreme or elaborate means to obtain a desired result, as the preserving of life; on a superhuman scale, larger-than-life. — *n* a heroic verse; (in *pl*) extravagant phrases, bombast; (in *pl*) unduly bold behaviour. — *adv* **herō'ically**. — *vt* **hē'rōise** or **-ize** to treat as a hero, make a hero of; to glorify. — *n* **heroism** (*her'ō-izm*) the qualities of a hero; courage; boldness. — **heroic age** any semi-mythical period when heroes or demigods were represented as living among men; **heroic couplet** a pair of rhyming lines of heroic verse. — *adj* **herōi-com'ic** or **herōi-com'ical** consisting of a mixture of heroic and comic; high burlesque. — **heroic poem** an epic; **heroic remedy** one that may kill or cure; **heroic verse** the form of verse in which the exploits of heroes are celebrated (in classical poetry, the hexameter; in English, the iambic pentameter, esp. in couplets; in French, the alexandrine); **he'ro-worship** the worship of heroes; excessive admiration of great men, or of anybody. — Also *vt*. [Through O.Fr. and L. from Gr. *hērōs*.]

heroin *her'ō-in, n* a derivative of morphine used in medicine and by drug-addicts. [Said to be from Gr. *hērōs*, a hero, from its effect.]

heroine *her'ō-in, n* a woman of heroic character, a female hero; a woman admired and idealised; the central female character in a story, play, film, etc. [Fr. *héroïne* — Gr. *herōinē*, fem. of *hērōs*, hero.]

heron *her'ən, n* a large long-legged, long-necked wading bird, commonly grey or white in colour. — *n* **her'onry** a place where herons breed. [O.Fr. *hairon* — O.H.G. *heigir*.]

heronshaw *her'ən-shö* or **hernshaw** *hûrn'shö, n* a young heron; (esp. *dialect*) a heron. [O.Fr. *heroun cel*, confounded with *shaw* (wood).]

herpes *hûr'pēz, n* a skin disease of various kinds, with spreading clusters of watery blisters on an inflamed base — esp. *herpes simplex* a sexually transmitted disease, and *herpes zoster* or shingles. — *adj* **herpetic** (*-pet'ik*). [Gr. *herpēs* — *herpein*, to creep.]

herpetology *hûr-pi-tol'ə-ji, n* the study of reptiles and amphibians. — *adj* **herpetolog'ic** or **herpetolog'ical**. — *adv* **herpetolog'ically**. — *n* **herpetol'ogist**. [Ger. *herpeton*, a reptile — *herpein*, to creep.]

Herr *her, n* lord, master, the German term of address equivalent to sir, or (prefixed) Mr: — *pl* **Herr'en**. — **Herrenvolk** (*her'ən-folk*) lit. 'master race', who believe themselves fitted and entitled by their superior qualities to rule the world. [Ger.]

herring *her'ing, n* a common small sea-fish of great commercial value, found moving in great shoals or multitudes in northern waters. — *adj* **herr'ing-bone** like the spine of a herring, applied to a kind of masonry in which the stones slope in different directions in alternate rows, and to a zigzag stitch crossed at the corners, etc.; in skiing, of a method of climbing a slope, the skis being placed at an angle and leaving a herring-bone-like pattern in the snow. — *vt* to make or mark with herring-bone pattern. — *vt* and *vi* to climb (a slope) on skis by herring-bone steps. — **herr'ing-gull** a large white gull with black-tipped wings. — **red herring** see under **red**. [O.E. *hǣring*, *hēring*.]

hers *hûrz*, *pron* possessive of **she** (used without a noun).

herself *hûr-self'*, *pron* an emphatic form for **she** or **her**; in her real character; the reflexive form of **her**; predicatively (or *n*) a woman when in command of her faculties, sane, in good form or normal condition. [See **her** and **self**.]

Herts. *härts*, *abbrev* for Hertfordshire.

hertz *hûrts*, *n* the unit of frequency, that of a periodic phenomenon of which the periodic time is one second — sometimes called **cycle per second** in U.K. — **Hertzian waves** electromagnetic waves used in communicating information through space. [After Heinrich *Hertz* (1857–94), German physicist.]

hesitate *hez'i-tāt*, *vi* to hold back or delay in acting, speaking or making a decision; to be in doubt. — *n* **hes'itance, hes'itancy** or **hesitā'tion**. — *n* wavering; doubt; stammering; delay. — *adj* **hes'itant** hesitating. — *adv* **hes'itātingly**. — *adj* **hes'itātive**. — *n* **hes'itātor**. — *adj* **hes'itātory**. [L. *haesitāre*, *-ātum*, frequentative of *haerēre*, *haesum*, to stick.]

Hesperus *hes'pə-rəs*, *n* Venus as the evening star. — *adj* **Hesperian** (*-pē'ri-ən*) western (*poetic*); of the Hesperides. — *npl* **Hesperides** (*-per'i-dēz*; *Gr mythol*) the sisters who guarded in their gardens in the west the golden apples which Hera had received from Gaea. — *n* **hesperid'ium** (*bot*) a fruit of the orange type. [Gr. *hesperos*, evening, western.]

Hessian *hes'i-ən*, *adj* of or pertaining to Hesse; mercenary (from the use of Hessian mercenaries by the British against the Revolutionaries) (*US*). — *n* a native or citizen of Hesse; (without *cap*) a cloth made of jute. — **Hessian fly** a midge whose larva attacks wheat stems in America, once believed to have been introduced in straw for the Hessian troops. [*Hesse*, Ger. *Hessen*, in Germany.]

het[1] *het*, (*Br* and *NAm dialect*) *pa p* for **heated**. — **het up** agitated.

het[2] *het*, (*slang*) *n* a heterosexual. — Also *adj*.

hetaera *hi-tē'rə* or **hetaira** *hi-tī'rə*, *n* in ancient Greece, a prostitute or courtesan, esp. of a superior class: — *pl* **hetae'rae** (*-rē*), **hetai'rai** (*-rī*) or **hetai'ras** — *n* **hetae'rism** or **hetai'rism** concubinage; the system of society that admitted hetairai; a supposed primitive communal marriage. — *adj* **hetaeris'mic** or **hetairis'mic**. [Gr. *hetairā*, fem. of *hetairos*, companion.]

heter- *het-ər-* or **hetero-** *het-ə-rō-*, *het-ə-rə-* or *-ro'-*, *combining form* signifying: other, different; one or other (often opposed to *homo-*, *auto-*). — *adj* **heterochromat'ic** or **heterochromous** (*-krō'məs*) having different or varying colours. — *adj* **het'eroclite** (*-klīt*; *gram*) irregularly inflected; irregular; having forms belonging to different declensions. — *n* a word irregularly inflected; anything irregular. — *adj* **heterocyclic** (*-sī'klik*) having a closed chain in which the atoms are not all alike (*chem*). — *adj* **het'erodox** holding an opinion other than or different from the one generally received, esp. in theology; heretical. — *n* **het'erodoxy** heresy. — *adj* **het'erodyne** (*-ō-dīn*) in radio communication, applied to a method of imposing on a continuous wave another of slightly different length to produce beats. — *adj* **heteroecious** (*-ē'shəs*). — *n* **heteroecism** (*-ē'sizm*; *biol*) parasitism upon different hosts at different stages of the life-cycle. — *adj* **heterog'amous**. — *n* **heterog'amy** alternation of generations (*biol*); reproduction by unlike gametes (*biol*); presence of different kinds of flower (male, female, hermaphrodite, neuter, in any combination) in the same inflorescence (*bot*); indirect pollination (*bot*). — *n* **heterogenē'ity**. — *adj* **heterogeneous** (*-jē'ni-əs*) different in kind; composed of parts of different kinds (opp. to *homogeneous*). — *adv* **heteroge'neously**. — *n* **heteroge'neousness**. — *n* **heterogenesis** (*-jen'i-sis*; *biol*) spontaneous generation; alternate generation. — *adj* **heterogenetic** (*-ji-net'ik*). — *n* **heterogeny** (*-oj'ə-ni*) a heterogeneous assemblage; heterogenesis. — *adj* **heterogonous** (*-og'ə-*) having flowers differing in length of stamens (*bot*); having alternation of generations (*biol*). — *n* **heterog'ony**. — *n* **het'erograft** a graft of tissue from a member of one species to a member of another species. — *n* **heterologous** (*-ol'ə-gəs*) not homologous; different; of different origin; abnormal. — *n* **heterol'ogy** lack of correspondence between apparently similar structures due to different origin. — *adj* **heterom'erous** having different numbers of parts in different whorls (*bot*); (of lichens) having the algal cells in a layer (*bot*); having unlike segments (*zool*). — *adj* **heteromor'phic** deviating in form from a given type; of different forms — also **heteromor'phous**. — *n* **heteromor'phism** or **het'eromorphy**. — *adj* **heteron'omous** subject to different laws; subject to outside rule or law (opp. to *autonomous*). — *n* **heteron'omy**. — *n* **het'eronym** a word of the same spelling as another but of different pronunciation and meaning. — *adj* **heterophyllous** (*-fil'əs*) having different kinds of foliage leaf. — *n* **het'erophylly**. — *n* **heteroplasia** (*-plā'zi-ə* or *-si-ə*) development of abnormal tissue or tissue in an abnormal place. — *adj* **heteroplastic** (*-plas'tik*). — *n* **het'eroplasty** heteroplasia; grafting of tissue from another person. — *npl* **Heterop'tera** a suborder of insects, the bugs, Hemiptera with fore and hind wings (when present) markedly different. — *adj* **heterop'terous**. — *n* **heterosex'ism** the belief that homosexuality is a perversion, used as grounds for discrimination against homosexuals. — *n* **heterosex'ist** someone who discriminates against homosexuals. — Also *adj*. — *adj* **heterosex'ūal** having, or pertaining to, sexual attraction towards the opposite sex. — Also *n*. — *n* **heterosexual'ity**. — *n* **heterō'sis** (*biol*) cross-fertilisation; the increased size and vigour (relative to its parents) often found in a hybrid. — *adj* **heteros'porous** (or *het-ə-rə-spö'rəs*) having different kinds of asexually produced spores. — *adj* **heterotac'tic**. — *n* **heterotax'is** or **het'erotaxy** anomalous arrangement of, e.g. parts of the body, etc. — *n* **het'erotroph** a heterotrophic organism. — *adj* **heterotroph'ic**. — *n* **heterot'rophy** (*bot*) dependence (immediate or ultimate) upon green plants for carbon (as in most animals, fungi, etc.). — *n* **heterozygote** (*-zī'gōt*) a zygote or individual formed from gametes differing with respect to some pair of alternative characters (one dominant and one recessive). — *adj* **heterozy'gous**. [Gr. *heteros*, other, one or other.]

hetero *het'ə-rō*, (*colloq*) *n* and *adj* short for (a) heterosexual: — *pl* **het'eros**.

hetman *het'man*, (*hist*) *n* a Polish or Cossack military commander: — *pl* **het'mans**. [Pol., — Ger. *Hauptmann*, captain.]

heuristic *hū-ris'tik*, *adj* serving or leading to find out; encouraging desire to find out; (of method, argument, etc.) depending on assumptions based on past experience; consisting of guided trial and error. — *n* (in *pl*) principles used in making decisions when all possibilities cannot be fully explored. — *adv* **heuris'tically**. [Irreg. formed from Gr. *heuriskein*, to find.]

hevea rubber *hē'vē-ə rub'ər*, *n* rubber from the S. American tree **he'vea**, *Hevea brasiliensis*, used in electrical insulators for its good electrical and mechanical properties.

hew *hū*, *vt* to cut, shape, fell or sever with blows of a cutting instrument. — *vi* to deal blows with a cutting instrument: — *pa t* **hewed**; *pa p* **hewed** or **hewn**. — *n* **hew'er**. [O.E. *hēawan*.]

hex *heks*, *n* a witch; a wizard; a spell; something which brings bad luck. — *vt* to bring misfortune, etc. to by a hex; to bewitch. — *n* **hex'ing.** [Pennsylvania Dutch — Ger. *Hexe* (fem.), *Hexer* (masc.).]

hex- *heks-* or **hexa-** *heks-ə-* or *heks-a'-*, *combining form* denoting six. — *n* **hex'achord** (*-körd*) a diatonic series of six notes having a semitone between the third and fourth. — *n* **hexachlo'rophene** a bactericide, used in antiseptic soaps, deodorants, etc. — *n* **hexad** (*hek'sad*; Gr. *hexas*, *-ados*) a series of six numbers; a set of six things; an atom, element or radical with a combining power of six units (*chem*). — *n* and *adj* **hexadec'imal** (of) a number system with 126 as its base. — *n* **hex'afoil** a pattern with six leaflike lobes or sections. — Also *adj*. — *n* **hex'agon** a figure with six sides and six angles. — *adj* **hexagonal** (*-ag'ə-nl*). — *n* **hex'agram** a figure of six lines, esp. a stellate hexagon. — *adj* **hexahē'dral.** — *n* **hexahē'dron** a solid with six sides or faces, esp. a cube: — *pl* **hexahē'drons** or **hexahē'dra**. — *adj* **hexam'erous** having six parts, or parts in sixes. — *n* **hexam'eter** a verse of six measures or feet; (in Greek and Latin verse) such a line where the fifth is almost always a dactyl and the sixth a spondee or trochee, the others dactyls or spondees. — *n* **hexane** (*hek'sān*) a hydrocarbon, sixth member of the methane series. — *n* **hex'apla** (Gr. — *hexaploos*, sixfold) an edition (esp. of the Bible) in six versions. — *adj* **hex'aplar**. — *n* **hex'apod** an animal with six feet; an insect. — *n* **hexap'ody** a line or verse of six feet. — *adj* **hexastyle** (*hek'sə-stīl*) having six columns. — *n* a building or portico having six columns in front. — *n* **Hexateuch** (*hek'sə-tūk*; Gr. *teuchos*, tool, later a book) the first six books of the Old Testament. — *adj* **hexateuch'al.** — *n* **hex'ose** a sugar (of various kinds) with six carbon atoms to the molecule. [Gr. *hex*, six.]

hey *hā*, *interj* expressing joy or interrogation, or calling attention. — *interj* **hey presto** a conjuror's command in performing tricks, etc. [Imit.]

heyday *hā'dā*, *n* culmination or climax of vigour, prosperity, gaiety, etc.; flush or full bloom.

HF *abbrev* for high frequency.

Hf (*chem*) *symbol* for hafnium.

hf *abbrev* for half.

HG *abbrev* for: High German; His or Her Grace.

HGH *abbrev* for human growth hormone.

HGV *abbrev* for heavy goods vehicle.

HH *abbrev* for: His or Her Highness; His Holiness.

HH *symbol* for very hard (on lead pencils).

HI *abbrev* for: Hawaii (U.S. state); Hawaiian Islands.

hi *hī*, *interj* calling attention; hello; hey. [**hey**.]

hiatus *hī-ā'təs*, *n* a gap; an opening; a break in continuity, a defect; a concurrence of vowel sounds in two successive syllables (*gram*): — *pl* **hiā'tuses.** — **hiatus hernia** a hernia in which a part protrudes through opening in the diaphragm intended for the oesophagus. [L. *hiātus*, *-ūs* — *hiāre*, *hiātum*, to gape.]

hibachi *hi-bä'chi*, *n* a portable barbecue for cooking food out of doors: — *pl* **hiba'chi** or **hiba'chis**. [Japanese *hi*, fire, *bachi*, bowl.]

hibakusha *hib-ä'ko͞o-shə*, *n* a survivor of the 1945 atomic bombings of Hiroshima and Nagasaki: — *pl* **hiba'kusha**. [Jap.]

hibernate *hī'bər-nāt*, *vi* to pass the winter in a dormant state; to be inactive. — *adj* **hīber'nal** belonging to winter; wintry. — *n* **hībernā'tion.** [L. *hībernāre*, *-ātum* — *hībernus*, wintry.]

Hibernian *hī-bûr'ni-ən*, *adj* relating to Hibernia or Ireland; Irish; characteristic of Ireland. — *n* an Irishman. — *n* **Hiber'nicism** (*-sizm*) an Irish idiom or peculiarity. [L. *Hībernia*, Ireland.]

hibiscus *hi-bis'kəs*, *n* a plant of the *Hibiscus* genus, mostly tropical shrubs or trees with large colourful flowers. [L., — Gr. *ibiskos*, marsh-mallow.]

hiccup *hik'up*, *n* the involuntary contraction of the diaphragm while the glottis is spasmodically closed; the sound caused by this; a temporary, and usu. minor, difficulty or setback (*colloq*). — *vi* to produce a hiccup; to falter or malfunction (*colloq*). — *vt* to say with a hiccup: — *pr p* **hicc'uping**; *pa t* and *pa p* **hicc'uped.** — Also spelt **hiccough**. [Imit. The spelling *hiccough* is due to a confusion with *cough*.]

hic iacet *hēk yak'et*, (L.) here lies, frequently preceding the dead person's name on older grave monuments.

hick *hik*, (*derog*) *n* a person from the country; any unsophisticated or unintelligent person. [A familiar form of *Richard*.]

hickey *hik'i*, (*NAm colloq*) *n* a gadget; a doodah; a thingummy; a love-bite.

hickory *hik'ər-i*, *n* a North American genus of trees of the walnut family, yielding edible nuts and heavy strong tenacious wood. [Earlier *pohickery*; of Indian origin.]

hic sepultus *hēk sə-po͝ol'təs*, (L.) here (lies) buried, frequently preceding the dead person's name on older grave monuments.

hid, hidden. See **hide**[1].

hidalgo *hi-dal'gō*, *n* a Spanish gentleman or nobleman of the lowest class: — *pl* **hidal'gōs.** [Sp. *hijo de algo*, son of something.]

hide[1] *hīd*, *vt* to conceal; to keep in concealment; to keep secret or out of sight. — *vi* to go into, or to stay in, concealment: — *pa t* **hid** (*hid*); *pa p* **hidden** (*hid'n*) or **hid**. — *n* a hiding-place; a concealed place from which to observe wild animals, etc. — *adj* **hidd'en** concealed; kept secret. — *n* **hidd'enness.** — *n* **hi'ding** concealment; a place of concealment. — **hidden economy** see **black economy** under **black**; **hide-and-seek'** or **hide-and-go-seek'** a game in which one person seeks the others, who have hidden themselves; **hide'away** a place of concealment; a refuge; **hide'out** a retreat; **hi'ding-place**; **hi'dy-hole** or **hi'dey-hole** a hiding-place. — **hide one's head** (*colloq*) to hide, keep out of sight, from shame, etc. (usu. (*fig*). [O.E. *hȳdan*.]

hide[2] *hīd*, *n* the skin of an animal, esp. the larger animals, sometimes used derogatorily or facetiously for human skin. — *vt* to flog or whip (*colloq*); to skin. — *n* **hī'ding** (*colloq*) a thrashing. — *adj* **hide'bound** (of animals) having the hide attached so closely to the back and ribs that it is taut, not easily moved, as a result of incorrect feeding; (of trees) having the bark so close that it impedes the growth; stubborn, bigoted, obstinate (*derog*). — **hide nor hair of** the slightest trace of (something or someone). — **on a hiding to nothing** (*colloq*) in a situation in which one is bound to lose, in spite of all one's efforts; **tan someone's hide** (*colloq*) to whip or beat someone. [O.E. *hȳd*.]

hide[3] *hīd*, *n* (in old English law) a variable unit of area of land, enough for a household. [O.E. *hīd*, contracted from *hīgid*; cf. *hīwan*, *hīgan*, household.]

hideous *hid'i-əs*, *adj* frightful; horrible; ghastly; extremely ugly. — *n* **hid'eousness.** — *adv* **hid'eously.** [O.Fr. *hideus*, *hisdos* — *hide*, *hisde*, dread.]

hiding. See **hide**[1] and **hide**[2].

hidrosis *hi-drō'sis*, (*med*) *n* sweating, esp. in excess. — *n* and *adj* **hidrotic** (*-drot'ik*). [Gr. *hidrōs*, *-ōtos*, sweat.]

hie *hī*, (*archaic* or *poetic*) *vi* to hasten. — *vt* to urge (on); to pass quickly over (one's way): — *pr p* **hie'ing** or **hy'ing**; *pa t* and *pa p* **hied**. [O.E. *hīgian*.]

hieracium *hī-ə-rā'shi-əm*, *n* any plant of the hawkweed genus of Compositae. [Latinised from Gr. *hierākion*, hawkweed — *hierāx*, hawk.]

hierarch *hī'ə-rärk*, *n* a ruler in holy things; a chief priest; a prelate; any senior person in a hierarchy. — *adj* **hīerarch'ic** or **hierarch'ical.** — *adv* **hierarch'ically.** — *n* **hī'erarchism.** — *n* **hī'erarchy** a body or organisation classified in successively subordinate grades; (*loosely*) in an organisation so classified, the group of people who control that organisation; classification in graded subdivisions; graded government amongst priests or other religious ministers; the collective body of angels, grouped in three divisions and nine orders of different power and glory; each of the three main classes of angels. [Gr. *hierarchēs* — *hieros*, sacred, *archein*, to rule.]

hieratic *hī-ə-rat'ik, adj* priestly; applying to a certain kind of ancient Egyptian writing which consisted of abridged forms of hieroglyphics; also to certain styles in art bound by religious convention. [L. *hierāticus* — Gr. *hierātikos* — *hieros*, sacred.]

hierocracy *hī-ə-rok'rə-si, n* government by priests or other religious ministers. [Gr. *hieros*, sacred, *krateein*, to rule.]

hieroglyph *hī'ə-rə-glif, n* a sacred character used in ancient Egyptian picture-writing or in picture-writing in general. — *adj* **hīeroglyph'ic** or **hieroglyph'ical**. — *n* **hīeroglyph'ic** a hieroglyph; (in *pl*) hieroglyphic writing; (in *pl*) writing that is difficult to read. — *adv* **hīeroglyph'ically**. [Gr. *hieroglyphikon* — *hieros*, sacred, *glyphein*, to carve.]

hierogram *hī'ə-rə-gram, n* a sacred or hieroglyphic symbol. — *n* **hī'erograph** a sacred symbol. [Gr. *hieros*, sacred, *gramma*, a character, *graphein*, to write.]

hierolatry *hī-ə-rol'ə-tri, n* the worship of saints or sacred things. [Gr. *hieros*, sacred, *latreiā*, worship.]

hierology *hī-ə-rol'ə-ji, n* the science of sacred matters, esp. ancient writing and Egyptian inscriptions. — *adj* **hīerologic** (*-ə-loj'ik*) or **hierolog'ical** (*-kəl*). — *n* **hīerol'ogist**. [Gr. *hieros*, sacred, *logos*, discourse.]

hierophant *hī'ə-rə-fant, n* a revealer of sacred mysteries; a priest; an expounder. — *adj* **hīerophant'ic**. [Gr. *hierophantēs* — *hieros*, sacred, *phainein*, to show.]

hierophobia *hī-ə-rə-fō'bi-ə, n* fear of sacred objects. — *adj* **hierophō'bic**. [Gr. *hieros*, sacred, *phobos*, fear.]

hi-fi *hī'-fī, n high-fi*delity sound reproduction; equipment for this, e.g. tape-recorder, record-player, etc.; the use of such equipment, esp. as a hobby. — Also *adj*.

higgledy-piggledy *hig-l-di-pig'l-di*, (*colloq*) *adv* and *adj* haphazard; in confusion.

high *hī, adj* elevated; lofty; tall; far up from a base, such as the ground, sea-level, the zero of a scale, etc.; advanced in a scale; reaching far up; expressible by a large number; of a height specified or to be specified; of advanced degree of intensity; advanced, full (in time, e.g. *high season, high summer*); (of a period) at its peak of development, as in *High Renaissance, high drama*, etc.; of grave importance; advanced; exalted; eminent; chief, as in *high priestess*; noble; haughty; extreme in opinion; powerful; loud; violent; acute in pitch; luxurious, as in *the high life*; elated; drunk; over-excited; under the influence of a drug; (of a price) dear; for heavy stakes; (of meat, etc.) slightly tainted or decomposed or, in the case of game, ready to cook; (of facial colouring) florid. — *adv* at or to a height; in or into a raised position. — *n* that which is high; a high level; the maximum, highest level; a euphoric or exhilarated frame of mind (esp. *drug-taking slang*). — *adj* **high'er** *compar* of **high**. — *n* **High'er** (in Scotland, a pass in) an examination generally taken at the end of the 5th year of secondary education, more advanced than Ordinary grade. — Also *adj*. — *adj* **high'est** *superl* of **high**. — *adv* **high'ly** in or to a high degree; in a high position. — *n* **high'ness** the state of being high; dignity of rank; (with *cap*) a title of honour given to princes, princesses, royal dukes, etc. — **high admiral** a high or chief admiral of a fleet; **high altar** see under **altar**; **high bailiff** an officer who serves writs, etc.; **high'ball** (*NAm*) an alcoholic spirit and soda with ice in a tall glass. — *vi* to go at great speed. — *vt* to drive very fast. — *adj* **high'-born** of noble birth. — **high'boy** (*NAm*) a tallboy; **high'brow** an intellectual. — Also *adj*. — **high'browism**; **high camp** see under **camp²**; **high'chair** a baby's or young child's tall chair, used esp. at mealtimes. — *adj* **High Church** of a section within the Church of England that exalts the authority of the episcopate and the priesthood, the saving grace of sacraments, etc.; of similar views in other churches. — **High-Church'man**. — *adj* **high-class'** superior; typical of or belonging to an upper social class. — *adj* **high-col'oured** having a strong or glaring colour; (of a complexion) ruddy. — **high comedy** comedy set in refined sophisticated society, characterised more by witty dialogue, complex plot and good characterisation than by comical actions or situations; **high command** the commander-in-chief of the army together with his staff, or the equivalent senior officers of any similar force; **High Commission** and **High Commissioner** see under **commission**; **high court** a supreme court; **high day** a holiday or festival; **high definition television** see **HDTV**. — *adj* **high-den'sity** (*comput*) of a disk having very compact data-storage capacity. — **higher education** education beyond the level of secondary education, e.g. at a university or college; **Higher grade** a Higher; **high'er-up** (*colloq*) someone occupying an upper position; **high explosive** a detonating explosive (e.g. dynamite, T.N.T.) of great power and exceedingly rapid action. — Also *adj*. — **highfalutin** or **highfaluting** (*-lōōt'*) bombastic discourse. — *adj* affected; pompous. — **high fidelity** good reproduction of sound. — *adj* **high-fidel'ity**. — See also **hi-fi**. — *n* **high five** or **high-five'-sign** a sign of greeting or celebration, esp. popular in N.Am., consisting of the slapping of raised right palms. — *vi* and *vt* **high-five'**. — **high-flī'er** or **-fly'er** an ambitious person, or one naturally equipped to reach prominence. — *adj* **high-fly'ing**. — *adj* **high'-flown** extravagant or pretentious; elevated; turgid. — **high frequency** see under **frequent**. — *adj* **high'-gear** see under **gear**. — **High German** the standard form of the German language, as it is written and spoken amongst educated people. — *adj* **high'-grade** superior. — *adj* **high-hand'ed** overbearing. — **high-hand'edness**; **high'-hat** (*colloq*) orig. a wearer of a top-hat; a snob or aristocrat; someone who puts on airs; a pair of cymbals on a stand, the upper one operated by a pedal so as to strike the lower one (also **hi'-hat**). — *adj* affectedly superior. — *vi* to put on airs. — *vt* to adopt a superior attitude towards or to ignore socially. — *adj* **high'-heeled** having or wearing high heels. — **High Holidays** or **High Holy Days** the Jewish festivals of Rosh Hashanah and Yom Kippur; **high'jack** and **high'jacker** see **hijack**; **high jinks** boisterous play, jollity; **high jump** (a field event consisting of) a jump over a high bar; punishment, a severe reproof, esp. in the phrase '*be for the high jump*'. — *adj* **high'-key** (of paintings and photographs) having pale tones and very little contrast. — **high kick** a dancer's kick high in the air, usu. with a straight leg; **high'land** a mountainous district; (with *cap*; in *pl*) the north-west of Scotland, from Dumbarton to Stonehaven, or the narrower area in which Gaelic is, or was till recently, spoken. — *adj* belonging to or characteristic of a highland, esp. (usu. with *cap*) the Highlands of Scotland. — **high'lander** an inhabitant or native of a mountainous region, esp. (with *cap*) the Highlands of Scotland; **Highland cattle** a shaggy breed with very long horns; **Highland dress** kilt, plaid and sporran; **Highland fling** a lively solo dance of the Scottish Highlands. — *adj* **high-lev'el** at a high level, esp. involving very important people. — **high life** the life of fashionable society; the people of this society; a blend of traditional West African music and North American jazz, popular in West Africa; **high'light** an outstanding feature; (in *pl*) the most brightly lighted spots; the most memorable moments; (usu. in *pl*) a portion or patch of the hair which reflects the light or which is artificially made lighter in colour than the rest of the hair. — *vt* to throw into relief by strong light; to draw attention to or point out; to overlay (parts of a text) with a bright colour, for special attention: — *pa t* and *pa p* **high'lighted**. — **high'lighter** a broad-tipped felt pen for highlighting parts of a text, etc.; **high living** luxurious living. — *adj* **highly-strung'** nervously sensitive, excitable. — **high mass** a mass celebrated with music, ceremonies and incense. — *adj* **high-mind'ed** having lofty principles and thoughts. — **high-mind'edness; high-muck-a-muck** see separate entry; **high noon** exactly noon; the peak (*fig*). — *adj* **high-oc'tane** (of petrol) of high octane number and so of high efficiency. — *adj* **high-pitched'** acute in sound, tending towards treble; steep (as a roof). — **high places** positions of importance and usu. influence; **high point** the most memorable, pleasurable, successful, etc. moment or occasion; a high spot; **high polymer** a polymer of high molecular weight. — *adj* **high-pow'ered** very powerful; very forceful and efficient. — *adj* **high-press'ure** making or allowing use of steam or other gas at a pressure much above that of the atmosphere; involving intense activity. — **high priest** a chief priest; **high priestess; high-priest'hood; high'-ranker**. — *adj* **high'-ranking** senior; eminent. — **high relief** bold relief, standing out well from the surface. — *adj* **high'-rise** containing a large number of storeys. — *n* such a building. — *adj* **high'-risk** vulnerable to some sort of danger; potentially dangerous. — **high'road** one of the public or chief roads; a road for general traffic; **high school** a secondary school, in U.K. formerly, often a grammar school; **high seas** the open ocean; **high season** the peak tourist period; **high society** fashionable, wealthy society. — *adj* **high-sound'ing** pompous; imposing. — *adj* **high'-speed** working, or suitable for working, at a great speed. — *adj* **high-spir'ited** having a high spirit or natural fire; bold; daring. — **high spirits** a happy, exhilarated frame of mind; **high spot** an outstanding feature, place, etc.; **high-stepp'er** a horse that lifts its feet high from the ground; a person of imposing bearing or fashionable pretensions; **high street** (sometimes with *caps*) the main shopping street of a town; **(with the)** shops generally, the everyday marketplace. — *adj* **high'-street** typical of or readily found in high streets. — *adj* **high'-strung** (esp. *NAm*) highly-strung. — **high table** the dons' table in a college dining-hall. — *vi* **high'tail** to hightail it (see below). — **high tea** an early-evening meal comprising a hot dish followed by cakes, etc. and tea; **high tech** or **hi tech** a style or design of furnishing, etc. imitative of or using industrial equipment. — *adj* **high'-tech** or **hi'-tec**. — **high technology** advanced, sophisticated technology in specialist fields, e.g. electronics, involving high investment in research and development. — *adj* **high-ten'sion** high-voltage. — **high tide** high water; a tide higher than usual; **high time** quite time (that something were done). — *adj* **high'-toned** high in pitch; morally elevated; superior, fashionable. — **high treason** treason against the sovereign or state; **high'-up** (*colloq*) a person in a high position (also *adj*). — *adj* **high-vol'tage** of or concerning a voltage great enough to cause injury or damage. — **high water** the time at which the tide or other water is highest; the greatest elevation of the tide; **high-water mark** the highest line so reached; a tide-mark; **high'way** a public road on which all have the right to go; the main or usual way or course; a road, path or navigable river (*law*); see **bus** (*comput*); **Highway Code** (the booklet containing) official rules and guidance on correct procedure for road-users; **high'wayman** a robber who attacks people on the public way; **high wire** a tightrope high above the ground; **high words** angry altercation. — **for the high jump** (*colloq*) about to be reprimanded or chastised; **from on high** from a high place, heaven, or (*facetious*) a position of authority; **high and dry** up out of the water, stranded, helpless; **high and low** rich and poor; up and down; everywhere; **high and mighty** (*ironic*) exalted; arrogant; **high as a kite** (*colloq*) over-excited, drunk, or very much under the influence of drugs; **high-level language** a computer-programming language, in which statements are written in a form similar to the user's normal language and which can be used in conjunction with a variety of computers (opp. to *low-level language*); **high old time** (*colloq*) a time of special jollity or enthusiasm; **high-speed steel** an alloy that remains hard when red-hot, suitable for metal-cutting tools; **hightail it** (*colloq*, esp. *NAm*) to hurry away; **hit the high spots** to go to excess; to reach a high level; **on high** aloft; in heaven; **on one's high horse** in an attitude of imagined superiority; very much on one's dignity. [O.E. *hēah*.]

high-muck-a-muck *hī-muk-ə-muk'*, (*NAm colloq*) *n* an important, pompous person. [Chinook Jargon *hiu*, plenty, *muckamuck*, food.]

HIH *abbrev* for His or Her Imperial Highness.

hijack or **highjack** *hī'jak*, *vt* to force a pilot to fly (an aeroplane) to an unscheduled destination; to force the driver to take (a vehicle or train) to a destination of the hijacker's choice; to stop and rob (a vehicle); to steal in transit. — Also *fig*. — *n* **hi'jacker** or **high'jacker**.

hike *hīk*, *vi* to go walking, esp. wearing boots and carrying camping equipment, etc.; to tramp; (of shirts, etc.) to move up out of place (with *up*). — *vt* (usually with *up*; *colloq*) to raise up with a jerk; to increase (e.g. prices), esp. sharply and suddenly (*NAm*). — *n* a walking tour, outing or march; an increase (in prices, etc.; *NAm*). — *n* **hi'ker**. [Perh. **hitch**.]

hila, hilar. See **hilum**.

hilarious *hi-lā'ri-əs*, *adj* extravagantly merry; very funny. — *adv* **hilā'riously**. — *n* **hilarity** (*hi-lar'i-ti*) gaiety; pleasurable excitement. [L. *hilaris* — Gr. *hilaros*, cheerful.]

Hilary term *hil'ə-ri tûrm*, *n* the Spring term or session of the High Court of Justice in England; also the Spring term at Oxford and Dublin universities — from St *Hilary* of Poitiers (d. *c* 367; festival, Jan. 13).

hill *hil*, *n* a high mass of land, smaller than a mountain; a mound; an incline on a road. — *n* **hill'iness**. — *n* **hill'ock** a small hill. — *adj* **hill'ocky**. — *adj* **hill'y**. — **hill'billy** (*NAm*) a rustic of the hill country; any unsophisticated person; country-and-Western music. — Also *adj*. — **hill fort** a prehistoric stronghold on a hill; **hill'side** the slope of a hill; **hill station** a government station in the hills esp. of Northern India; **hill'top** the summit of a hill; **hill'walker; hill'walking**. — **old as the hills** (*colloq*) immeasurably old; **over the hill** (*colloq*) past one's highest point of efficiency, success, etc.; on the downgrade; past the greatest difficulty; **up hill and down dale** vigorously and persistently. [O.E. *hyll*.]

hilt *hilt*, *n* the handle, esp. of a sword or dagger. — *vt* to provide with a hilt. — **up to the hilt** completely, thoroughly, to the full. [O.E. *hilt*.]

hilum *hī'ləm*, *n* the scar on a seed where it joined its stalk (*bot*); the depression or opening where ducts, vessels, etc., enter an organ (*anat*): — *pl* **hī'la**. — *adj* **hi'lar**. — *n* **hī'lus** a hilum (*anat*): — *pl* **hī'lī**. [L. *hīlum*, a trifle, 'that which adheres to a bean'.]

HIM *abbrev* for His or Her Imperial Majesty.

him *him*, *pron* the dative and accusative (objective) case of **he**; the proper character of a person (as in *that's not like him*). [O.E. *him*, dat. sing. of *hē*, *he*, he, *hit*, it.]

Himalayan *him-ə-lā'ən* or *hi-mäl'yən, adj* pertaining to the Himalayas, the mountain range along the border of India and Tibet.

himself *him-self', pron* the emphatic form for **he** or **him**; the reflexive form of **him**; predicatively (or *n*) a man when in command of his faculties, sane, in good form or normal condition. [See **him** and **self**.]

Hinayana *hin-ə-yä'nə, n* Theravada, one of the two main systems of practice and belief into which Buddhism split; the form of Buddhism found in Ceylon and S.E. Asia, holding more conservatively than Mahayana Buddhism to the original teachings of the Buddha and the practices of the original Buddhist communities. — Also *adj.* [Sans. *hīna*, little, lesser, *yāna*, vehicle.]

Hind. *abbrev* for Hindustani.

hind[1] *hīnd, adj* placed in the rear; pertaining to the part behind; backward (opp. to *fore*). — *adj* **hinder** (*hīn'dər*) hind. — *adj* **hīnd'ermost** or **hīnd'most** farthest behind. — *adv* **hīndfore'most** with the back part in the front place. — **hīnd'leg; hind'-limb.** — *npl* **hīnd'quarters** the rear parts of an animal. — **hīnd'sight** wisdom after the event; the rear sight on a gun, etc; **hind'wing.** [O.E. *hinder*, backwards.]

hind[2] *hīnd, n* the female of the red deer. [O.E. *hind.*]

hind[3] *hīnd*, (now *Scot*) *n* a farm servant, with a cottage on the farm; a rustic. [O.E. *hīna, hīwna*, genitive pl. of *hīwan*, members of a household.]

hinder[1] *hin'dər, vt* to keep back; to stop or prevent progress of. — *vi* to be an obstacle. — *n* **hin'derer.** — *adv* **hin'deringly.** — *n* **hin'drance** an act of hindering; that which hinders; prevention; obstacle. [O.E. *hindrian.*]

hinder[2]. See **hind**[1].

Hindi *hin'dē, n* a group of Indo-European languages of Northern India, including Hindustani; a recent literary form of Hindustani, with terms from Sanskrit, one of the official languages of India. — Also *adj.* [Hindi *Hindī* — *Hind*, India.]

hindmost. See **hind**[1].

hindrance. See **hinder**[1].

Hindu *hin-dōō'* or *hin'dōō, n* a native or citizen of Hindustan or India; specif. an adherent of Hinduism. — Also *adj.* — *n* **Hindu'ism** (or *hin'*) the aggregation of religious values and beliefs and social customs dominant in India, including the belief in reincarnation, the worship of several gods and the arrangement of society in a caste system. [Pers. *Hindū* — *Hind*, India.]

Hindustani *hin-dōō-stä'nē, n* a form of Hindi containing elements from other languages, used as a lingua franca in much of India and Pakistan. — Also *adj.*

hinge *hinj, n* the hook or joint on which a door or lid turns; a joint as of a bivalve shell; a small piece of gummed paper used to attach a postage-stamp to the page of an album (also **stamp hinge**); a cardinal point; a principle or fact on which anything depends or turns. — *vt* to furnish with hinges; to bend. — *vi* to hang or turn as on a hinge; to depend (with *on*): — *pr p* **hinging** (*hinj'ing*); *pa t* and *pa p* **hinged** (*hinjd*). — **hinge'-joint** (*anat*) a joint (e.g. the knee) that allows movement in one plane only. [Related to **hang.**]

hinny *hin'i, n* the offspring of a stallion and female donkey or ass. [L. *hinnus* — Gr. *ginnos*, later *hinnos*, a mule.]

hint *hint, n* a distant or indirect indication or allusion; slight mention; insinuation; a helpful suggestion, tip. — *vt* to intimate or indicate indirectly. — *vi* to give hints. — **hint at** to give a hint, suggestion or indication of. [O.E. *hentan*, to seize.]

hinterland *hin'tər-land, n* a region lying inland from a port or centre of influence. [Ger.]

hip[1] *hip, n* the haunch or fleshy part of the thigh; the hip-joint; the external angle formed by the sides of a roof when the end slopes backwards instead of terminating in a gable (*archit*). — *adj* **hipped** having a hip or hips; (of a roof) having gables that slope back towards the ridge. — *adj* **hipp'y** having large hips. — *npl* **hip'sters** trousers from the hips, not the waist. — **hip bath** a bath to sit in; **hip'bone** the innominate bone; **hip flask** a flask carried in a hip pocket; **hip joint** the articulation of the head of the thighbone with the ilium; **hip pocket** a trouser pocket behind the hip. — **have** or **catch on the hip** to get an advantage over someone (from wrestling); **shoot** or **fire from the hip** to speak bluntly or deal with assertively. [O.E. *hype.*]

hip[2] *hip, n* the fruit of the dog-rose or other rose. [O.E. *hēope.*]

hip[3] *hip, interj* an exclamation to invoke a united cheer. — **hip-hip-hurrah'** or **-hooray'.**

hip[4] *hip*, (*colloq*) *adj* knowing, informed or following the latest trends in music, fashion, political ideas, etc. — *n* **hipp'ie** or **hipp'y** one of the hippies, successors of the beatniks as rebels against the values of middle-class society, who stress the importance of love, organise to some extent their own communities, and wear colourful clothes. — *n* **hipp'iedom** or **hipp'ydom** the lifestyle or community of hippies. — *n* **hipster** (*hip'stər*) a person who knows and appreciates up-to-date jazz; a member of the beat generation (1950s and early 1960s). — **hip'-hop** a popular culture movement developed in the U.S. in the early 1980s and comprising rap music, break-dancing and graffiti, and whose adherents typically wear baggy clothes and loosely tied or untied training shoes or boots. — Also *adj.* [Earlier form *hep.*]

hipp- *hip-* or **hippo-** *hip-ō-, hip-ə-* or *hi-po'-, combining form* denoting a horse. [Gr. *hippos*, a horse.]

hippeastrum *hip-i-as'trəm, n* any plant of the S. American genus *Hippeastrum*, bulbous, with white or red flowers. [Gr. *hippeus*, horseman, *astron*, star.]

hippie, hippiedom. See **hip**[4].

hippo *hip'ō, n* a shortened form of **hippopotamus**: — *pl* **hipp'os.**

hippocampus *hip-ō-kam'pəs, n* a fish-tailed horselike sea-monster (*mythol*); a genus of small fishes with horselike head and neck, the sea-horse; a raised curved trace on the floor of the lateral ventricle of the brain (*anat*): — *pl* **hippocamp'ī.** [Gr. *hippokampos* — *hippos*, a horse, *kampos*, a sea-monster.]

hippocras *hip'ō-kras, n* an old English drink of spiced wine, formerly much used as a cordial. [M.E. *ypocras*, Hippocrates.]

Hippocratic *hip-ə-krat'ik, adj* pertaining to the Greek physician *Hippocrates* (born about 460 B.C.). — **Hippocratic oath** an oath taken by a doctor binding him or her to observe the code of medical ethics contained in it — first drawn up (perhaps by Hippocrates) in the 4th or 5th century B.C.

hippodrome *hip'ə-drōm, n* a racecourse for horses and chariots (in ancient Greece and Rome); a circus; a variety theatre. [Gr. *hippodromos* — *hippos*, a horse, *dromos*, a course.]

hippogriff or **hippogryph** *hip'ō-grif, n* a fabulous mediaeval animal, a griffin-headed winged horse. [Fr. *hippogriffe* — Gr. *hippos*, a horse, *gryps*, a griffin.]

hippophagy *hip-of'ə-ji* or *-gi, n* feeding on horse-flesh. [**hippo-**, and Gr. *phagein* (aorist), to eat.]

hippopotamus *hip-ō-pot'ə-məs, n* a large African hoofed mammal of aquatic habits, with very thick skin, short legs, and a large head and muzzle: — *pl* **hippopot'amus, hippopot'amuses** or **hippopot'ami** (*-mī*). [L., — Gr. *hippopotamos* — *hippos*, a horse, *potamos*, a river.]

hippy. See **hip**[1,4].

hippydom, hipster, hipsters. See **hip**[4].

hircine *hûr'sīn, adj* goatlike. [L. *hīrcus*, a he-goat.]

hire *hīr, n* wages for service; the price paid for the use of anything; an arrangement by which use or service is granted for payment. — *vt* to procure the use or service of, at a price; to engage for wages; to grant temporary use of for payment (often with *out*). — *adj* **hir'able** or **hire'able.** — *n* **hire'ling** (*derog*) a hired servant; a person activated solely by material considerations. — **hire car** a rented car, usu. one rented for a short period; **hire-pur'chase** a system by which a hired article becomes the hirer's property after a stipulated number of payments. — Also *adj.* — **on hire** for hiring. [O.E. *hȳr*, wages, *hȳrian*, to hire.]

hirsute *hûr'sūt* or *hər-sūt'*, *adj* hairy; rough; shaggy; having long, stiffish hairs (*bot*). — *n* **hirsute'ness.** [L. *hirsūtus* — *hirsus*, *hirtus*, shaggy.]

his *hiz*, *pron*, genitive (or *possessive adj*) of **he**. [O.E. *his*, genitive of *hē*, *he*, he, and of *hit*, it.]

Hispanic *hi-span'ik*, *adj* Spanish; of Spanish origin, e.g. Mexican. — Also *n.* — *vt* **hispan'icise** or **-ize** (*-i-sīz*). — *n* **hispan'icism** a Spanish phrase. [L. *Hispānia*, Spain.]

Hispano- *his-pan-ō-*, *combining form* Spanish, as *Hispano-American*, Spanish-American. [L. *hispānus*.]

hispid *his'pid*, (*bot* and *zool*) *adj* covered with strong hairs or bristles. — *n* **hispid'ity**. [L. *hīspidus*.]

hiss *his*, *vi* to make a sibilant sound like that represented by the letter *s*, the sound made by a goose, snake, gas escaping from a narrow hole, a disapproving audience, etc. — *vt* to condemn by hissing; to drive by hissing. — *n* a hissing sound. [Imit.]

hist *hist* or *st*, *interj* demanding silence and attention; hush; silence. [Imit.]

hist. *abbrev* for: histology; historian; history.

hist- *hist-* or **histo-** *hist-ō-*, *hist-ə-* or *hi-sto'-*, *combining form* denoting animal or plant tissue. — *n* **hist'amine** (*-ə-mēn*) a base present in all tissues of the body, being liberated into the blood, e.g. when the skin is cut or burnt. — *n* **histogenesis** (*-jen'i-sis*) the formation or differentiation of tissues (*biol*). — *adj* **histogenetic** (*-ji-net'ik*). — *adv* **histogenet'ically** or **histogen'ically**. — *adj* **histogen'ic**. — *n* **histogeny** (*hi-stoj'i-ni*) histogenesis. — *adj* **histolog'ic** or **histolog'ical**. — *adv* **histolog'ically**. — *n* **histologist** (*hi-stol'*). — *n* **histol'ogy** the study of the minute structure of the tissues of organisms. — *n* **histol'ysis** the breakdown of organic tissues. — *adj* **histolytic** (*-ō-lit'ik*). — *adv* **histolyt'ically**. — *adj* **histopatholog'ical**. — *n* **histopathol'ogist** a pathologist who studies the effects of disease on the tissues of the body. — *n* **histopathol'ogy**. — *n* **histoplasmō'sis** a disease of animals and man due to infection by the fungal organism *Histoplasma capsulatum*. [Gr. *histos*, a web.]

history *hist'ə-ri*, *n* an account of an event; a systematic account of the origin and progress of the world, a nation, an institution, etc.; the knowledge of past events; the academic discipline of understanding or interpreting past events; a course of events; a life story; an eventful life, a past of more than common interest; a drama representing historical events. — *n* **historian** (*hi-stö'ri-ən*) a writer of history (usu. in the sense of an expert or an authority on it). — *adj* **histo'riāted** decorated with elaborate ornamental designs and figures (also **sto'riated**). — *adj* **historic** (*hi-stor'ik*) famous or important in history. — *adj* **histor'ical** pertaining to history; containing history; derived from history; associated with history; according to history; authentic. — *adv* **histor'ically**. — *n* **histor'icism** a theory that all sociological phenomena are historically determined; a strong or excessive concern with, and respect for, the institutions of the past. — *n* and *adj* **histor'icist**. — *n* **historicity** (*his-tə-ris'i-ti*) historical truth or actuality. — *vt* **histor'ify** to record in history. — *n* **historiog'rapher** a writer of history (esp. an official historian). — *adj* **historiograph'ic** or **historiograph'ical**. — *adv* **historiograph'ically**. — *n* **historiog'raphy** the art or employment of writing history. — **historical novel** a novel having as its setting a period in history and involving historical characters and events; **historical present** the present tense used for the past, to add life and reality to the narrative; **historical school** those, esp. in the fields of economics, legal philosophy and ethnology, who emphasise historical circumstance and evolutionary development in their researches and conclusions. — **be history** (*colloq*) to be finished, gone, dead, etc., as in *he's history*; **make history** to do that which will mould the future or will have to be recognised by future historians; to do something never previously accomplished. [L. *historia* — Gr. *historiā*, enquiry, account — *histōr*, knowing.]

histrionic *his-tri-on'ik*, *adj* orig. relating to the stage or actors; stagy, theatrical; affected; melodramatic. — *adv* **histrion'ically**. — *npl* **histrion'ics** insincere exhibition of emotion; stagy action or speech; play-acting. [L. *histriōnicus* — *histriō*, an actor.]

hit *hit*, *vt* to strike; to reach with a blow or missile; to come into forceful contact with; to knock (e.g. oneself, one's head); to inflict (a blow); to drive by a stroke; to move on to (a road), reach (a place); (of news) to be published in (*colloq*); to light upon, or attain, by chance; to imitate exactly; to suit, fit, conform to; to hurt, affect painfully; to ask or demand (*NAm colloq*). — *vi* to strike; to make a movement of striking; to come in contact; to arrive suddenly and destructively; to come, by effort or chance, luckily (upon): — *pr p* **hitt'ing**; *pa t* and *pa p* **hit.** — *n* an act or occasion of striking; a successful stroke or shot; a lucky chance; an overwhelming success; an effective remark, e.g. a sarcasm, witticism; something that pleases the public or an audience; a murder (*slang*); a dose of a hard drug (*slang*). — *adj* **hit-and-miss'** hitting or missing, according to circumstances. — *adj* **hit-and-run'** (e.g. of an air raid) lasting only a very short time; (of a driver) causing injury and running away without reporting the incident. — Also *n.* — **hit list** (*slang*) a list of people to be killed by gangsters or terrorists; generally, a list of targeted victims; **hit'-man** (*slang*) someone employed to kill or attack others (also *fig*). — *adj* **hit-or-miss'** random. — **hit parade** a list of currently popular songs (*old*); a list of the most popular things of any kind. — **hard hit** gravely affected by some trouble, or by love; **hit at** to aim a blow, sarcasm, jibe, etc., at; **hit below the belt** see under **belt**; **hit it** to find, often by chance, the right answer; **hit it off** to agree, be compatible and friendly (sometimes with *with*); **hit it up** (*slang*) to inject a drug; **hit off** to imitate or describe aptly (someone, something); **hit on** or **upon** to come upon, discover, devise; to single out; **hit out** to strike out, esp. with the fist; to attack strongly (absolute or with *at*); **hit the bottle** (*slang*) to drink excessively; **hit the ceiling** or **roof** to be seized with, or express, violent anger; **hit the hay** or **sack** (*slang*) to go to bed; **hit the nail on the head** see under **nail**; **hit the road** (*slang*) to leave, go away; **hit wicket** the act, or an instance, of striking the wicket with the bat or part of the body (and thus being out) (*cricket*); **make** or **score a hit with** to become popular with; to make a good impression on. [O.E. *hyttan*, app. O.N. *hitta*, to light on, to find.]

hitch *hich*, *vi* to move jerkily; to hobble or limp; to catch on an obstacle; to connect with a moving vehicle so as to be towed (orig. *NAm*); to travel by getting lifts. — *vt* to jerk; to hook; to catch; to fasten; to tether; to harness to a vehicle; to make fast; to throw into place; to obtain (a lift) in a passing vehicle. — *n* a jerk; a stoppage owing to a small or passing difficulty; a type of knot by which one rope is connected with another, or to some object (*naut*); a lift in a vehicle. — *n* **hitch'er**. — *vi* **hitch'-hike** to hike with the help of lifts in vehicles. — Also *n*. — *n* **hitch'-hiker; hitching post** a post, etc. to which a horse's reins can be tied. — **get hitched** (*slang*) to get married; **hitch up** to harness a horse to a vehicle; to jerk up; to marry (*slang*).

hi tech. See **high tec** under **high.**

hither *hidh'ər, adv* to this place. — *adj* on this side or in this direction; nearer. — *adj* **hith'ermost** nearest on this side. — *adv* **hitherto'** up to this time. — **hither and thither** to and fro; this way and that. [O.E. *hider*.]

Hitler *hit'lər, n* a person similar, in having an overbearing or despotic character, to Adolf *Hitler* (1889–1945), German Nazi dictator (also, *contemptuously*, **little Hitler**). — *n* **Hit'lerism** the principles, policy and methods of Hitler. — *n* and *adj* **Hit'lerist** or **Hit'lerite.**

Hittite *hit'īt, n* one of the Khatti or Heth, an ancient people of Syria and Asia Minor; an extinct language belonging to the Anatolian group of languages and discovered from documents in cuneiform writing. — Also *adj*. [Heb. *Hitti*.]

HIV *abbrev* for human immunodeficiency virus.

hive *hīv, n* a box or basket in which bees live and store up honey; a colony of bees; a scene of great industry; a teeming multitude or breeding-place. — *vt* to collect into a hive; to lay up in store (often with *away* or *up*). — *vi* (of bees) to enter or take possession of a hive; to take shelter together; to reside in a body. — **hive off** to withdraw as if in a swarm; to assign (work) to a subsidiary company; to divert (assets or sections of an industrial concern) to other concerns (*n* **hive'-off**). [O.E. *hȳf*.]

hives *hīvz, n* a popular term for nettle-rash and similar diseases, or for laryngitis.

hiya *hī'yə,* (*slang*) *interj* a greeting developed from **how are you.**

Hizbollah or **Hizbullah** *hiz-bə-lä', n* an organisation of militant Shiite Muslims. [Ar., party of God.]

Hizen *hē-zen',* (also without *cap*) *adj* of a type of richly decorated Japanese porcelain. — Also *n*. [*Hizen* province in Kyushu, Japan.]

HK *abbrev* for: Hong Kong (I.V.R.); House of Keys, the Manx parliament.

HKJ *abbrev* for Hashemite Kingdom of Jordan (I.V.R.).

hl *abbrev* for hectolitres.

HM *abbrev* for (His or) Her Majesty.

hm *abbrev* for hectometre.

HMG *abbrev* for (His or) Her Majesty's Government.

HMI *abbrev* for (His or) Her Majesty's Inspector or Inspectorate.

HMS *abbrev* for (His or) Her Majesty's Service or Ship.

HMSO *abbrev* for (His or) Her Majesty's Stationery Office.

HNC *abbrev* for Higher National Certificate (a qualification awarded by BTEC).

HND *abbrev* for Higher National Diploma.

Ho (*chem*) *symbol* for holmium.

ho or **hoh** *hō, interj* a call to excite attention, to announce destination or direction, to express exultation, surprise, or (repeated) derision or laughter. [Cf. O.N. *hō*, Fr. *ho*.]

ho. *abbrev* for house.

hoactzin. See **hoatzin.**

hoar *hör, adj* white or greyish-white, esp. with age or frost (*poetic*). — *n* hoariness; age. — *n* **hoar'iness.** — *adj* **hoar'y** white or grey with age; ancient; covered with short, dense, whitish hairs (*bot* and *entom*). — **hoar'frost** rime or white frost, the white particles formed by the freezing of the dew. [O.E. *hār*, hoary, grey.]

hoard *hörd, n* a store; a hidden stock; a treasure. — *vt* to store, esp. in excess; to treasure up; to amass and deposit in secret. — *vi* to store up; to collect and form a hoard. — *n* **hoard'er.** [O.E. *hord*.]

hoarding *hör'ding, n* a screen of boards, esp. for enclosing a place where builders are at work, or for the display of bills, advertisements, etc. [O.Fr. *hurdis* — *hurt, hourt, hourd*, a palisade.]

hoarse *hörs, adj* rough and husky; having a rough husky voice; harsh. — *adv* **hoarse'ly.** — *vt* and *vi* **hoars'en.** — *n* **hoarse'ness.** [M.E. *hors, hoors* — O.E. *hās*, inferred *hārs*.]

hoatzin *hō-at'sin* or **hoactzin** *-akt', n* a S. American crested bird with a large crop, and, in the tree-climbing and swimming young, clawed wings. — Also **stink'-bird.** [Nahuatl *uatsin*.]

hoax *hōks, n* a deceptive trick played as a practical joke or maliciously. — Also *adj*. — *vt* to trick, by a practical joke or fabricated tale. — *n* **hoax'er.** [App. **hocus.**]

hob¹ *hob, n* a surface beside a fireplace, on which anything may be laid to keep hot; the flat framework or surface on top of a gas, etc. cooker on which pots are placed to be heated; a gear-cutting tool. — **hob'nail** a nail with a thick strong head, used in horseshoes, heavy workshoes, etc. — *adj* **hob'-nailed.** [Cf. **hub.**]

hob² *hob, n* a fairy, elf; a male ferret. — **hob'goblin** a mischievous fairy; a frightful apparition. [From *Rob*, short for *Robert*.]

hobbit *hob'it, n* one of a race of imaginary beings, half human size, hole-dwelling and hairy-footed, invented by J.R.R. Tolkien in his novel *The Hobbit* (1937). — *n* **hobb'itry.**

hobble *hob'l, vi* to walk with short unsteady steps; to walk awkwardly; to move irregularly. — *vt* to fasten the legs of (a horse) loosely together; to hamper. — *n* an awkward hobbling gait; anything used to hamper the feet of an animal. — **hobble skirt** a narrow skirt that hampers walking. [Cf. Du. *hobbelen, hobben*, to toss.]

hobbledehoy *hob'l-di-hoi, n* an awkward youth, a stripling, neither man nor boy. — *n* **hobbledehoy'hood.** — *adj* **hobbledehoy'ish.**

hobby¹ *hob'i, n* a favourite pursuit followed as an amusement; a subject on which one is constantly setting off; a small or smallish, strong, active horse; a hobby-horse. — **hobb'y-horse** a stick or figure of a horse straddled by children; one of the chief parts played in the ancient morris dance; the wooden horse of a merry-go-round; a rocking-horse; a favourite topic or obsession, esp. in the phrase *be on one's hobby-horse*. [M.E. *hobyn, hoby*, prob. *Hob*, a by-form of *Rob*.]

hobby² *hob'i, n* a small species of falcon. [O.Fr. *hobe*.]

hobgoblin. See **hob².**

hobnail. See **hob¹.**

hobnob *hob'nob, vi* to associate or drink together familiarly; to talk informally (with): — *pr p* **hob'-nobbing.** [Prob. *hab nab*, have or have not, give and take.]

hobo *hō'bō, n* a tramp; an itinerant workman, esp. unskilled (*NAm*): — *pl* **ho'boes** or **ho'bos.**

Hobson's choice. See under **choice.**

hock¹ *hok, n* a joint on the hindleg of a quadruped, between the knee and the fetlock, corresponding to the ankle-joint in man; a piece of meat extending from the hock-joint upward. — *vt* to hamstring. [O.E. *hōh*, the heel.]

hock² *hok,* (*slang*) *vt* to pawn. — *n* the state of being in pawn. — **in hock** in debt; in prison; having been pawned, in pawn (*colloq*). [Du. *hok*, prison, hovel.]

hock³ *hok, n* properly, the wine made at *Hochheim*, on the Main, in Germany; now applied to all white Rhine wines. [Obs. *Hockamore* — Ger. *Hochheimer*.]

hockey *hok'i, n* a ball game played by two teams of eleven players, each with a club or stick curved at one end; a hockey stick (*NAm*); ice hockey. [Prob. O.Fr. *hoquet*, a crook.]

hocus-pocus *hō-kəs-pō'kəs, n* skill in conjuring; deception; mumbo-jumbo. — *vt* **ho'cus** to cheat; to stupefy with drink; to drug (drink): — *pr p* **hō'cusing** or **hō'cussing**; *pa t* and *pa p* **hō'cused** or **hō'cussed**. [Conjuror's sham Latin, once conjectured to be a corruption of *hoc est corpus*, this is my body, Christ's words used in the communion service at the consecration of the bread.]

hod *hod*, *n* a V-shaped stemmed trough with a pole for carrying bricks or mortar on the shoulder; a coal-scuttle. [Cf. dialect *hot*, *hott*, M.H.G. *hotte*, obs. Du. *hodde*, Fr. *hotte*, a basket.]

hodden *hod'n*, (*Scot*) *n* coarse, undyed homespun woollen cloth.

hodgepodge. See **hotchpotch**.

Hodgkin's disease *hoj'kinz di-zēz'*, *n* a disease in which the spleen, liver and lymph nodes become enlarged, and progressive anaemia occurs. [After Thomas *Hodgkin*, 19th cent. British physician.]

hodiernal *hō-di-ûr'nəl*, *adj* of or pertaining to the present day. [L. *hodiernus* — *hodiē*, today.]

hodograph *hod'ə-gräf*, (*math*) *n* a curve whose radius vector represents the velocity of a moving point. [Gr. *hodos*, a way, *graphein*, to write.]

hodometer, hodometry. See **odometer**.

hoe *hō*, *n* a long-handled instrument with a narrow blade for scraping or digging up weeds and loosening the earth. — *vt* to scrape, remove or clean with a hoe; to weed. — *vi* to use a hoe: — *pr p* **hoe'ing**; *pa t* and *pa p* **hoed**. — **hoe'-cake** (*US*) a thin cake of maize flour (originally baked on a hoe-blade); **hoe'down** (esp. *US*) a country-dance, esp. a square dance; a gathering to perform such dances. [O.Fr. *houe* — O.H.G. *houwâ* (Ger. *Haue*), a hoe.]

hog *hog*, *n* a general name for swine; a castrated boar; a pig reared for slaughter; a yearling sheep not yet shorn (also **hogg**); a greedy person; an inconsiderate boor; a person of coarse manners. — *vt* and *vi* to eat hoggishly; to arch or hump like a hog's back, esp. of the hull of a ship. — *vt* to cut like a hog's mane; to take or use selfishly: — *pr p* **hogg'ing**; *pa t* and *pa p* **hogged**. — *adj* **hogged** (*hogd*). — *n* **hogg'et** a yearling sheep or colt. — *adj* **hogg'ish**. — *adv* **hogg'ishly**. — *n* **hogg'ishness**. — **hog'back** or **hog's'-back** a hill-ridge, or other object, shaped like a hog's back, i.e. curving down towards the ends; **hog'-cholera** swine-fever; **hog'fish** a fish having bristles on the head; **hog'nose** any of various species of short-bodied, harmless American snakes; **hog'-skin** leather made of the skin of swine. — *vt* **hog'tie** to tie (a person) up so they are unable to move their arms or legs; to thwart, stymie, frustrate, impede. — **hog'wash** the refuse of a kitchen, brewery, etc., given to pigs; thin worthless stuff; insincere nonsense; **hog'weed** the cow-parsnip; applied also to many other coarse plants. — **go the whole hog** see under **whole**; **hog it** (*slang*) to eat greedily; to live in a slovenly fashion. [O.E. *hogg*.]

hogan *hō'gən*, *n* a log hut, usu. covered with earth, built by the Navaho tribe of North American Indians. [Navaho.]

hogg, hogget, etc. See under **hog**.

Hogmanay *hog-mə-nā'*, (*Scot*) *n* the last day of the year; New Year's Eve. [Prob. from North Fr. dialect *hoginane* — 16th cent. *aguillanneuf* (*-l'an neuf*) a gift at the New Year.]

hogshead *hogz'hed*, *n* a large cask; a measure of capacity = $52\frac{1}{2}$ imperial gallons, or 63 old wine gallons (238 litres); *of beer* = 54 gallons (245 litres); *of claret* = 46 gallons (309 litres); *of tobacco* (*NAm*) = 750 to 1200 lb. (337 to 540 kilos). [App. **hog's**, and **head**.]

hogtie, hogwash, hogweed. See **hog**.

hoh. See **ho**.

hoi *hoi*, (*colloq*) *interj* used to attract attention.

hoick or **hoik** *hoik*, *n* a jerk. — *vt* and *vi* to hitch up; (esp. of aeroplanes) to jerk upwards. [Poss. a variant of **hike**.]

hoi polloi *hoi pə-loi'*, (*derog*) *n* the many; the masses; the rabble. [Gr.]

hoist *hoist*, *vt* to lift; to heave upwards; to raise or move with tackle. — *n* act of lifting; the height of a sail; that part of a flag next to the mast; tackle for lifting heavy goods. — *n* **hoist'er** someone who or that which lifts. — **hoist with one's own petard** caught in one's own trap. [Past t. and past p. of archaic verb *hoise*, to hoist.]

hoity-toity *hoi-ti-toi'ti*, *interj* an exclamation of surprise or disapprobation. — *adj* superciliously haughty. [From *hoit* (obs.), to romp.]

hoke, hokey. See **hokum**.

hokey cokey *hō'ki kō'ki*, *n* a Cockney song whose lyrics dictate a pattern of accompanying movements, usu. performed by several people in a circle; these dance-type movements.

hokum *hō'kəm*, (*NAm slang*) *n* something done for the sake of applause; claptrap; pretentious or over-sentimental rubbish. — Also **hoke**. — *vt* **hoke** (*hōk*) to overact (a part in a play); to give an impressive facade or appearance to (usu. with *up*). — *adj* **hokey** (*hō'ki*) overdone, contrived; phoney. [App. **hocus-pocus** combined with **bunkum**.]

hoky-poky or **hokey-pokey** *hō-ki-pō'ki*, *n* hocus-pocus; a kind of ice cream sold on the streets.

Holarctic *hə-lärk'tik*, *adj* of the north temperate and Arctic biological region. [Gr. *holos*, whole, *arktikos*, northern — *arktos*, a bear, the Great Bear constellation.]

hold[1] *hōld*, *vt* to keep; to have; to grasp; to have in one's possession, keeping, or power; to sustain; to defend successfully; to maintain; to assert authoritatively; to think, believe; to occupy; to bind; to contain; to have a capacity of; to enclose; to confine; to restrain; to detain; to retain; to reserve; to keep the attention of; to catch; to stop; to continue; to persist in; to celebrate, observe; to conduct; to carry on; to convoke and carry on; to esteem or consider; to aim, direct. — *vi* to grasp; to remain fixed; to be true or unfailing; to continue unbroken or unsubdued; to remain valid; to continue, to persist; to adhere; when making a telephone call, to wait, without replacing the receiver, e.g. to be connected to a person one wants to speak to (also **hold the line**): — *pr p* **hōld'ing**; *pa t* and *pa p* **held**. — *n* an act or manner of holding; grip; power of gripping; tenacity; a place of confinement; custody; stronghold; (a sign for) a pause (*mus*); an order to keep in reserve (a room etc.) or to suspend (operations) (*NAm*); a means of influencing or controlling. — *n* **hold'er**. — *n* **hold'ing** anything held, esp. (in *pl*) land, shares, etc.; a farm managed for its owner; intensive embracing and prolonged eye-contact as a technique for developing intimacy between parent (esp. mother) and child, claimed by some to be a cure for autism (*psychiatry*). — **hold'all** an accommodating receptacle for clothes, etc., esp. a canvas bag; **hold'fast** that which holds fast; a long nail; a catch; a plant's fixing organ other than a root; **holding company** an industrial company that owns and controls part or all of one or more other companies, usu. without having a direct hand in production; **holding operation** a course of action designed to preserve the status quo; **holding pattern** a specific course which aircraft are instructed to follow when waiting to land; **hold'over** (*NAm*) something or someone held over; a leftover, relic; **hold'-up** an attack with a view to robbery; an act or state of holding up; a stoppage. — **get hold of** to obtain; to get in touch with; **hold against** (*colloq*) to remember as a failing or as a misdemeanour on the part of; **hold back** to restrain; to hesitate; to keep in reserve; **hold by** to believe in; to act in accordance with; **hold down** to restrain; to keep (a job) by carrying out its duties efficiently, esp. in spite of difficulties; **hold forth** to put forward; to show; to speak in public, to declaim; **hold good** to remain the case; **hold hands** (of two people) to be hand in hand or clasping both of each other's hands; (of several people) each to clasp the hand of the person on either side, thus forming a line, circle, etc.; **hold hard!** stop!; **hold in** to restrain, check; to restrain oneself; **hold it!** keep the position exactly!; stop!; **hold off** to keep at a distance; to refrain (from); **hold on** to persist in something; to continue; to cling; to keep (with *to*); stop (*imper*); to wait a bit; **hold one's own** to maintain one's position; (in the course of an illness) not to fail or lose strength; **hold one's peace** or **tongue** to keep silence; **hold out** to endure, last; to continue resistance; to offer; **hold out for** to wait determinedly for something one wants or has asked for; **hold out on** (*colloq*) to keep information from; **hold over** to postpone; **hold the line** see **hold** (*vi*) above; **hold the road** (of a vehicle) to remain stable and under the driver's control e.g. in wet weather, at high speeds or on bends; **hold to** or **hold someone to** to keep or make someone keep (a promise), adhere to (a decision), etc.; **hold together** to remain united; to cohere; **hold up** to raise; to keep back; to endure; to bring to, or keep at, a standstill; to stop and rob; to rob by threatening assault; **hold up one's head** to face the world with self-respect; **hold water** see under **water**; **hold with** to take sides with, support; to approve of; **no holds barred** not observing any rules of fair play (*adj* **no-holds-barred'**); **on hold** postponed; in abeyance. [O.E. *haldan*.]

hold[2] *hōld*, *n* the interior cavity of a ship used for the cargo. [**hole** with excrescent *d*.]

hole *hōl*, *n* a hollow place; a cavity; an aperture; a gap; a breach; a pit; a difficult situation; a scrape; an animal's excavation or place of refuge; a miserable or contemptible place; a cavity into which golf balls are played; the distance, or the part of the game, between tee and hole (*golf*); the score for playing a hole in fewest strokes; a vacancy in an energy band, caused by removal of an electron, which moves and is equivalent to a positive charge (*electronics*). — *vt* to form holes in; to put, send or play into a hole. — *vi* to go, play, into a hole. — *adj* **holey** (*hō'li*) full of holes. — *adj* **hole-and-cor'ner** secret; underhand; in obscure places. — **hole card** (in stud poker) the card dealt face down in the first round. — *adj* **hole-in-the-wall'** (*colloq*) small, insignificant, difficult to find. — **hole in one** (*golf*) a shot from the tee that goes into the hole, and so completes the hole with a single stroke; **hole in the heart** imperfect separation of the left and right sides of the heart; **hole out** (*golf*) to play the ball into the hole; **hole up** (*colloq*) to go to earth, hide; **in holes** full of holes; **make a hole in** (e.g. **one's pocket**) to use up a large amount of (e.g. money); **toad in the hole** meat, esp. sausages, baked in batter. [O.E. *hol*, a hole, cavern.]

holiday *hol'i-dā*, *n* orig., a religious festival; a day or (esp. in *pl*) a season of rest and recreation; (often in *pl*) a period of time spent away from home, for recreation. — *vi* to go away from home for a holiday. — *adj* befitting a holiday; cheerful. — **holiday camp** an area, esp. at the seaside, with chalets, hotels, entertainments, etc., for holidaymakers; **hol'iday-maker** someone on holiday away from home; a tourist. [**holy** and **day**.]

holism *hol'izm* or *hō'lizm*, *n* the theory that the fundamental principle of the universe is the creation of wholes, i.e. complete and self-contained systems from the atom and the cell by evolution to the most complex forms of life and mind; the theory that a complex entity, system, etc., is more than merely the sum of its parts. — *n* **hol'ist**. — *adj* **holist'ic**. — *adv* **holist'ically**. — **holistic medicine** a form of medicine which considers the whole person, physically and psychologically, rather than treating merely the diseased part. [Gr. *holos*, whole; coined by General Smuts.]

holland *hol'ənd*, *n* a coarse linen fabric, unbleached or dyed brown, which is used for covering furniture, etc.; orig. a fine kind of linen first made in *Holland*. — *n* **Holl'ander** a native or citizen of Holland; a Dutch ship. — *adj* **Holl'andish**. — *n* **Holl'ands** gin made in Holland. — **sauce hollandaise** (*sōs ol-ã-dez*; Fr.) or **hollandaise sauce** (*hol-ən-dāz'* or *hol'ən-dāz sös*) a sauce made of the yolk of an egg with melted butter and lemon juice or vinegar.

holler *hol'ər*, (*NAm* and *dialect*) *n*, *vi* and *vt*. Same as **hollo**.

Hollerith code *hol'ə-rith kōd*, (*comput*) *n* a code for transforming letters and numerals into a pattern of holes, for use in punched cards. [H. *Hollerith* (1860–1929), U.S. inventor.]

hollo *hol'ō*, *n* and *interj* a shout of encouragement or to call attention; a loud shout: — *pl* **holl'oes** or **holl'os**. — *vt* and *vi* to shout. [Cf. **hallo**.]

hollow *hol'ō*, *n* a hole, cavity; a depression; an emptiness; a groove or channel. — *adj* having an empty space within or below, not solid; concave; sunken; unsound, insincere, worthless; echoing, as if coming from a hollow place. — *vt* (often with *out*) to make a hole or cavity in; to make hollow; to excavate. — *adv* completely, as in *beat* (i.e. defeat) *someone hollow*. — *adv* **holl'owly**. — *n* **holl'owness**. — *adj* **hollow-eyed'** having sunken eyes. — *adj* **holl'ow-ground** ground so as to have a concave surface or surfaces. — **holl'ow-ware** or **holl'oware** hollow articles of iron, china, etc., e.g. pots and kettles. [O.E. *holh*, a hollow place — *hol*; see **hole**[1].]

holly *hol'i*, *n* an evergreen shrub having leathery, shining spiny leaves and scarlet or yellow berries, much used for Christmas decorations. — **holl'y-fern** a spiny-leaved fern; **holl'y-oak** the holm-oak. [O.E. *holegn*.]

hollyhock *hol'i-hok*, *n* a plant of the mallow family, with flowers of many colours, brought into Europe from the Holy Land. [M.E. *holihoc* — *holi*, holy, and O.E. *hoc*, mallow.]

Hollywood *hol'i-wŭd*, *adj* of or belonging to *Hollywood*, a suburb of Los Angeles in California, a centre of the U.S. cinema industry; typical of or resembling films made there, brash and romantic, presenting the image of an affluent and often artificial society. — *vt* **Holl'ywoodise** or **-ize** to refurbish or trivialise in the Hollywood manner.

holm[1] *hōm*, *n* (in place names) an islet, esp. in a river; rich flat land beside a river. [O.E. *holm*; Ger. *Holm*, etc.]

holm[2] *hōm*, *n* the holm-oak. — **holm'-oak** the evergreen oak, not unlike holly. [M.E. *holin*; see **holly**.]

holmium *hol'mi-əm*, *n* a metallic element (symbol **Ho**; atomic no. 67). [N.L. *Holmia*, Stockholm.]

holo- *hol-ō-*, *hol-ə-* or *hə-lo'-* or **hol-** *hol-*, *combining form* denoting: whole; wholly. — *adj* **holobenth'ic** (*zool*) passing the whole life-cycle in the depths of the sea. — *adj* **holohē'dral**. — *n* **holohē'drism** (*math*) the property of having the maximum number of symmetrically arranged planes crystallographically possible. — *n* **holohē'dron** a geometrical form possessing this property. — *adj* **holometabol'ic**. — *n* **holometab'olism** (of an insect) complete metamorphosis. — *adj* **holometab'olous**. — *adj* **holophōt'al**. — *n* **hol'ophote** an apparatus by which all the light from a lighthouse is thrown in the required direction. — *n* **hol'ophyte** (*-fīt*). — *adj* **holophytic** (*-fit'ik*) obtaining nutrient wholly in the manner of a green plant. — *n* **holophytism** (*-fī'tizm*). [Gr. *holos*, whole.]

holocaust *hol'ə-kōst*, *n* a huge slaughter or destruction of life; (with *cap*) the mass murder of Jews by the Nazis during World War II. [Gr. *holokauston* — *kaustos*, burnt.]

Holocene *hol'ə-sēn*, (*geol*) *n* the most recent period of geological time, approximating to the period since the last glaciation. [**holo-** and Gr. *kainos*, new.]

hologram *hol'ə-gram*, *n* a photograph made without use of a lens by means of interference between two parts of a split laser beam, the result appearing as a meaningless pattern until suitably illuminated, when it shows as a 3-D image. — *n* **hol'ograph** (*-gräf*) a document wholly written by the person from whom it comes. — Also *adj*. — *vt* to make a hologram of. — *adj* **holographic** (*-graf'ik*). — *n* **holog'raphy** (the technique or process of) making or using holograms. [**holo-** and **-graph**.]

holohedron, holometabolism, holophote, etc. See under **holo-**.

holothurian *hol-ō-thū'ri-ən*, *n* any member of a class of wormlike unarmoured echinoderms — the sea cucumbers. — Also *adj*. [Gr. *holothourion*, a kind of sea animal.]

hols *holz*, (*schoolchildren's slang*) *npl* short for holidays.

holster *hōl'stər*, *n* a pistol-case slung on a saddle or belt. — *adj* **hol'stered.**

holt[1] *hōlt*, *n* (in place names) a wood or woody hill; an orchard. [O.E. *holt*, a wood.]

holt[2] *hōlt*, *n* an otter's den. [Ety. as for **hold**[1].]

holus-bolus *hō-ləs-bō'ləs*, *adv* altogether, all at once. [Sham Latin.]

holy *hō'li*, *adj* religious, associated with God or gods; set apart for a sacred use; perfect in a moral sense; pure in heart; regarded with awe (often *ironic*); saintly; sanctimonious, simulating holiness. — *adv* **ho'lily.** — *n* **ho'liness** sanctity. — *adj* **holier-than-thou'** offensively sanctimonious and patronising. — **holy city** Jerusalem; Rome; Mecca; Benares; Allahabad, etc., depending on the religion; **holy day** a religious festival (see also **holiday**); **Holy Family** the infant Christ with Joseph, Mary, etc.; **Holy Ghost** or **Spirit** the third person of the Christian Trinity; **holy grail** see under **grail**; **holy Joe** (*slang*) a parson; an offensively sanctimonious person; **Holy Land** Palestine; **holy orders** see under **order**; **holy rood** a cross, esp. in R.C. churches over the entrance to the chancel; **Holy Roller** (*derog slang*) a preacher or follower of an extravagantly emotional religious sect; **Holy Saturday** the Saturday before Easter Sunday; **Holy See** the Roman Catholic bishopric of Rome, i.e. the Pope's see; **ho'lystone** a sandstone used by seamen for cleansing the decks, said to be named from cleaning the decks for Sunday, or from kneeling in using it; **holy terror** (*colloq*, esp. *jocular*) a formidable person, or one given to causing commotion or agitation; **Holy Thursday** Maundy Thursday; **holy war** a war waged for the eradication of heresy or a rival religion; a Crusade; **holy water** water blessed for religious uses; **Holy Week** the week before Easter; **holy writ** the Scriptures. — **holy of holies** the inner chamber of the Jewish tabernacle; **Holy Roman Empire** the unification of Europe with papal blessing, under a Christian emperor, 800–814 and 962–1806. [O.E. *hālig*, lit. whole — *hāl*, sound.]

homage *hom'ij*, *n* anything done or rendered as an acknowledgment of superiority; reverence, esp. as shown by outward action; a vassal's acknowledgment that he is the servant of his feudal superior (*hist*). [O.Fr. *homage* — L.L. *hominātícum* — L. *homō*, a man.]

Homburg *hom'bûrg*, *n* a man's hat, of felt, with narrow brim and crown, with a depression in the top. [First worn at *Homburg*.]

home *hōm*, *n* a habitual dwelling-place, or the place felt to be such; the residence of one's family; the scene of domestic life, with its emotional associations; a building occupied by a family, a house; one's own country; habitat; natural or usual place of anything; the den or base in certain games; an institution providing refuge or residence; a private hospital; (in football pools) a match won by a team playing on their own ground; a home signal. — *adj* pertaining or belonging to or being in one's own dwelling, country, playing-ground, etc.; domestic; coming or reaching home; made or done at home, not in a factory, abroad, etc. — *adv* to one's home; at one's home; to the innermost, most significant or final place; effectively. — *vi* to go home; to find the way home; to be guided to a target or destination (usu. with *in*). — *vt* to guide to a target or destination (usu. with *in on*); to send home; to provide with a home. — *adj* **home'less** of or pertaining to people who, having no permanent place of residence, live and sleep rough in public places, or in squats or doss-houses. — Also *n* (with **the**; *collectively*). — *n* **home'lessness.** — *n* **home'liness.** — *adj* **home'ly** pertaining to home; familiar; plain, unpretentious; (of people) ugly (*NAm*). — *n* **ho'mer** a pigeon of a breed that can readily be trained to find its way home from a distance; a home run (*baseball*). — *adv* **home'ward** or **home'wards.** — *adj* **home'ward** in the direction of home. — *adj* **home'y** or **ho'my** homelike; homely. — *adj* **ho'ming** (esp. of pigeons) trained to return home; (of a navigational device on a missile, etc.) guiding to the target; guiding home. — **home banking** the facility offered by some banks to their private customers of paying bills, ordering statements, etc. by telephone rather than in person. — *adj* **home-brewed'** brewed at home or for home use (*n* **home'-brew**). — **home'buyer** a person in the process of arranging to buy their own home; **home'coming** arrival at home; return home; **home counties** the counties over and into which London has extended — Middlesex, Essex, Kent, Surrey (and sometimes also Herts, Sussex); **home'craft** household arts; arts practised at home or concerned with domestic life; **Home Department** that part of government which is concerned with the maintenance of the internal peace of England — its headquarters the **Home Office,** its official head the **Home Secretary; home economics** domestic science, household skills and management; **home economist; home farm** the farm belonging to and near a great house. — *adj* **home-grown'** produced in one's own country, or garden. — **home guard** a member of a volunteer force for defence of a country; (with *caps*) a force of this kind (first formed in Britain in the war of 1939–45; **home help** a person employed by a local authority to help the sick, handicapped or the aged with domestic work; **home'land** native land, mother-country; in South Africa, an area reserved for Black African peoples; **home loan** a mortgage. — *adj* **home-made'** made at home; made in one's own country; plain. — **home'maker** a housewife or house-husband; **home market** the market for goods in the country that produces them; **home movie** a motion picture made by an amateur, usu. on a portable camcorder; **home'owner; home plate** (*baseball*) the final point which a batter must reach in order to score a run; **home port** the port at which a boat is registered. — *adj* **home-produced'** produced within the country in question, not imported. — **Home Rule** self-government, as that claimed by Irish, Scottish and Welsh Nationalists, including a separate parliament to manage internal affairs; **home run** (*baseball*) a hit which goes far enough to allow the batter to run to all four bases in turn; the score made in this way. — *adj* **home'sick** pining for home. — **home'sickness; home signal** a signal at the beginning of a section of railway line showing whether or not the section is clear. — *adj* **home'spun** spun or made at home; plain, unadorned; simple, artless, rustic; inelegant. — *n* cloth made at home. — **home'stead** a dwelling-house with outhouses and enclosures immediately connected with it; **home'steading** (orig. *US*) a scheme by which people are permitted to live rent-free in or buy semi-derelict buildings and improve them with the help of Government grants, etc.; **home straight** or **stretch** the last stretch of a racecourse; the final or winning stage of anything; **home town** the town where one's home is or was; **home truth** a pointed, usually unanswerable, typically wounding, statement that strikes home; **home unit** (*Austr*) a flat or apartment; **home video** a home movie made with a video camera. — *adj* **homeward-bound'** bound homeward or to one's native land. — **home'work** work or preparation to be done at home, esp. for school; paid work, esp. work paid for according to quantity completed, done at home; **home'worker** a person who works from home, but linked to an office by computer, and under terms and conditions similar to conventional office-workers; **home'working**. — **at home** in one's own house; ready to receive a visitor; feeling the ease of familiarity with a place or situation (*n* **at-home'** a reception); **bring home to** to prove to, in such a way that there is no way of escaping the conclusion; to impress upon; **do one's homework** (*colloq*) to prepare oneself, e.g. for a discussion, by acquainting oneself with the relevant facts; **eat out of house and home** (*colloq*) to eat huge amounts at the expense of (another person); **go** or **strike home** (of a remark, etc.) to impress itself duly on the mind of the person addressed; **home and dry** having arrived, achieved one's aim, etc.; **home from home** a place where one feels totally comfortable and at ease; **make oneself at home** to be as free and unrestrained as in one's own house; **not at home** out of one's house or not accepting visitors; **nothing to write home about** (*colloq*) not very exciting or attractive. [O.E. *hām*.]

homeopathy, etc. Same as **homoeopathy**, etc., under **homo-**.

Homeric *hō-mer'ik*, *adj* pertaining to *Homer*, the great poet of Greece (who flourished *c* 850 B.C.); attributed to Homer; resembling Homer or his poetry; in the heroic or epic manner. [Gr. *hŏmērikos* — *Hŏmēros*, Homer.]

homicide *hom'i-sīd*, *n* manslaughter or murder; a person who kills someone. — *adj* **homicī'dal** pertaining to homicide; inclined to murder. — *adv* **homicī'dally**. [L. *homicīdium*, manslaughter, and *homicīda*, a man-slayer — *homō*, a man, *caedĕre*, to kill.]

homily *hom'i-li*, *n* a plain explanatory sermon, practical rather than based on religious teachings; a talk giving advice and encouragement. — *adj* **homilet'ic** or **homilet'ical**. — *nsing* **homilet'ics** the art of preaching. [Gr. *homīliā*, an assembly, a lecture or sermon — *homos*, the same, *īlē*, a company.]

hominid *hom'in-id*, (*zool*) *n* an animal of the family comprising man and his ancestors (also *adj*). — *n* and *adj* **hom'inoid**. [L. *homō*, *-inis*, man.]

hominy *hom'i-ni*, *n* maize hulled, or hulled and crushed; a kind of porridge made by boiling this. [Am. Ind. origin.]

homo *hō'mō*, *n* man generically; (with *cap*; *zool*) the human genus. — **Homo sapiens** the one existing species of man. [L. *homō*, *-inis*, man, human being.]

homo- *hom-ō-*, *hom-ə-*, *hə-mo'-* or *hō-*, *combining form* denoting same. — **homoeo-**, **homeo-** *hom-i-ō-*, *hom-i-ə-*, *hom-i-o'-* or *hō-*, or **homoio-** *-moi-*, *combining form* denoting like or similar. — *n* and *adj* **homo** (*hō'mō*; usu. *derog*, now *old slang*) a homosexual: — *pl* **ho'mos**. — *adj* **homocentric** (*-sen'trik*) concentric; proceeding from or diverging to the same point; (of rays) either parallel or passing through one focus (*phys*). — *adj* **homocyclic** (*-sī'klik*; *chem*) having a closed chain of similar atoms. — *n* **homeopath** or **homoeopath** (*hom'i-ə-path* or *hō'*), **homeopathist** or **homoeopathist** (*-op'ə-thist*) a person who believes in or practises homoeopathy. — *adj* **homeopathic** or **homoeopathic** (*-path'ik*). — *adv* **homeopath'ically** or **homoeopath'ically**. — *n* **homeopathy** or **homoeopathy** (*-op'ə-thi*) the system of treating diseases by small quantities of drugs that produce symptoms similar to those of the disease. — *n* **homeostasis** or **homoeostasis** (*-os'tə-sis*) the tendency for the internal environment of the body to remain constant in spite of varying external conditions; a tendency towards health, stable physical condition. — *adj* **homeostat'ic** or **homoeostat'ic**. — *adj* **homeotherm'al**, **homoeotherm'al**, **homeotherm'ic**, **homoeotherm'ic**, **homeotherm'ous** or **homoeotherm'ous** homothermal. — Also **homoiotherm'al**, etc. — *n* **homoerot'icism** or **homoerot'ism** orientation of the libido towards a person of the same sex. — *adj* **homoerot'ic**. — *adj* **homogamic** (*-gam'ik*), or **homogamous** (*hə-mog'ə-məs*). — *n* **homogamy** (*hə-mog'ə-mi*) the condition of having all the flowers on an axis sexually alike (*bot*); simultaneous ripening of stamens and stigmas (*bot*). — *n* **homogenate** (*-oj'ə-nāt*) a substance produced by homogenising. — *n* **homogeneity** (*hom-ə-ji-nē'i-ti* or *-nā'*) the state or fact of being homogeneous. — *adj* **homogeneous** (*hom-ə-jē'ni-əs*; also *hō-*) of the same kind or nature; having the constituent elements similar throughout; of the same degree or dimensions in every term (*math*). — *n* **homogē'neousness**. — *n* **homogenesis** (*-jen'i-sis*; *biol*) a mode of reproduction in which the offspring is like the parent, and passes through the same cycle of existence. — *adj* **homogenet'ic** or **homogenet'ical** homogenous. — *vt* **homog'enise** or **-ize** to make homogeneous; to make (milk) more digestible by breaking up fat globules, etc. — *n* **homogenisa'tion** or **-z-**. — *n* **homog'eniser** or **-z-**. — *adj* **homogenous** (*hə-moj'ən-əs*) similar owing to common descent or origin. — *n* **homog'eny** similarity owing to common descent or origin. — *n* **homograft** (*hom'ə-gräft*) a graft from one individual to an unrelated member of the same species (*med*). — *n* **homograph** (*hom'ə-gräf*) a word of the same spelling as another, but of different meaning, pronunciation or origin. — *adj* **homoiousian** (*hom-oi-ōō'si-ən* or *-ow'*; Gr. *ousiā*, being) of similar (as opp. to identical) essence; believing God the Father and God the Son to be of similar (not identical) essence. — *n* a holder of such belief. — *vt* **homol'ogate** (L.L. *homologāre*, *-ātum* — Gr. *homologeein*, to agree) to confirm; to approve; to consent to; to ratify. — *n* **homologā'tion**. — *adj* **homological** (*-loj'*). — *adv* **homolog'ically**. — *vt* and *vi* **homol'ogise** or **-ize** (*-jīz*). — *adj* **homologous** (*hə-mol'ə-gəs*) agreeing; of the same essential nature, corresponding in relative position, general structure, and descent (*med* or *biol*). — *n* **hom'ologue** or in U.S. **hom'olog** (*-ə-log*) anything which is homologous to something else, as a man's arm, a whale's flipper, a bird's wing. — *n* **homol'ogy** (*-ə-ji*) the quality of being homologous; sameness of structure and origin, apart from form or use. — *n* **hom'omorph** a thing having the same form as another. — *adj* **homomorph'ic** or **homomorph'ous** alike in form, esp. if essentially different otherwise; uniform. — *n* **homomorph'ism**. — *n* **hom'onym** a word having the same sound and perhaps the same spelling as another, but a different meaning and origin; a name rejected as already used by another genus or species (*biol*); a namesake. — *adj* **homonym'ic** pertaining to homonyms. — *adj* **homon'ymous** having the same name; having different meanings and origins but the same sound. — *adv* **homon'ymously**. — *n* **homon'ymy** or **homonym'ity**. — *adj* **homoousian** or **homousian** (*hom-ō-ōō'si-ən*, *ho-mōō'* or *-ow'*; Gr. *ousiā*, being) of the same essence; believing God the Son to be of the same essence as God the Father. — *n* a holder of such belief. — *n* **hom'ophobe** (*-fōb*) a person with a strong aversion to homosexuals. — *n* **homophō'bia**.

— *adj* **homophō'bic.** — *n* **homophone** (*hom'ə-fōn*) a character representing the same sound as another; a word pronounced the same as another but different in spelling and meaning. — *adj* **homophonic** (*-fon'*) sounding alike; in the monodic style of music, where one voice only carries the melody. — *adj* **homophonous** (*hə-mof'*). — *n* **homoph'ony.** — *n* **homophyly** (*hə-mof'i-li*; Gr. *phȳlon*, a race; *biol*) resemblance due to common ancestry. — *n* **hom'oplasmy** (*-plaz-mi*) or **homop'lasy** the quality or fact of being homoplastic. — *adj* **homoplast'ic** (*biol*) similar in structure and development owing to parallel or convergent evolution but not descended from a common source. — *adj* **homopō'lar** (*chem*) having an equal distribution of charge, as in a covalent bond. — *n* **homopolar'ity.** — *npl* **Homoptera** (*-op'*) an order of insects having wings of a uniform texture — cicadas, greenfly etc. — *adj* **homop'terous.** — *adj* **homosex'ūal** having, or pertaining to, sexual attraction to one's own sex. — *n* a person sexually attracted only to their own sex. — *n* **homosex'ualism.** — *n* **homosexual'ity.** — *adj* **homotherm'al, homotherm'ic** or **homotherm'ous** keeping the same temperature, warm-blooded. — *n* **homozygō'sis** the condition of having inherited a given genetic factor from both parents, so producing gametes (reproductive cells) of only one kind as regards that factor; genetical stability as regards a given factor. — *n* **homozy'gote** a zygote, or product of the union of two gametes, which is formed as a result of homozygosis. — *adj* **homozygot'ic.** — *adj* **homozy'gous.** [Gr. *homos*, same, *homoios*, like, similar.]

homunculus *hə-mung'kū-ləs*, *n* a tiny man, dwarf, manikin: — *pl* **homun'culī.** — Also **homun'cūle.** [L., dimin. of *homō*.]

homy. See **home.**

hon *hun*, (*colloq*) *n* short for **honey** as a term of endearment.

hone *hōn*, *n* a smooth stone used for sharpening instruments. — *vt* to sharpen on or as on a hone. — *n* **ho'ner.** [O.E. *hān*.]

honest *on'ist* or *-əst*, *adj* truthful; full of honour; just; fair-dealing; upstanding; the opposite of thieving; free from fraud or trickery; candid, frank; respectable (*patronising*). — *adv* **hon'estly** in an honest way; in truth. — *interj* expressing annoyance, disbelief, etc. — *n* **hon'esty** the state of being honest; integrity; candour, frankness, truthfulness; a common garden plant with shining silver or satiny white leaflike pods. — **honest broker** an impartial mediator in a dispute. — *adj* **honest-to-God'** or **honest-to-good'ness** genuine, out-and-out, complete. — Also *adv*. — **honest Injun** (*colloq*) upon my honour; **make an honest woman of** (now usu. *facetious*) to marry, where the woman has first been seduced. [O.Fr. *honeste* — L. *honestus* — *honor*.]

honey *hun'i*, *n* a sweet, thick fluid made by bees from the nectar of flowers; its colour, golden brown; nectar of flowers; anything sweet like honey; a term of endearment; a thing which is pleasant or delightful (*colloq*). — *vt* to sweeten; to make agreeable: — *pr p* **hon'eying;** *pa t* and *pa p* **hon'eyed.** — *adj* **hon'eyed** or **hon'ied** (often falsely) sweet; seductive. — *adj* **hon'eyless.** — **hon'ey-badger** the ratel, a badger-like animal from India and Africa; **hon'ey-bee** any of the varieties of bee living in hives and producing honey; **hon'eybun** or **hon'eybunch** terms of endearment; **honey buzzard** a hawk that feeds on the larvae and honey of bees, wasps, etc.; **hon'eycomb** (*-kōm*) a comb or mass of waxy cells formed by bees, in which they store their honey; anything like a honeycomb; a bewildering maze (of rooms, cavities, etc.). — *vt* to make like a honeycomb; to spread into all parts of. — **honey creeper** any of several kinds of small, brightly-coloured S. American birds which feed on nectar; **hon'eydew** a sugar secretion from aphids or plants; **honeydew melon** a sweet-flavoured melon with smooth green or orange rind; **hon'ey-eater** any bird of a large Australian family, which feeds on nectar; **honey fungus** a kind of honey-coloured edible mushroom, a parasite on the roots of trees and shrubs, which it can kill; **hon'ey-guide** a species of bird of a mainly African family which guides people and honey-badgers to honey-bees' nests by hopping from tree to tree with a peculiar cry; a marking on a flower said to show the way to the nectaries; **hon'eymoon** the first weeks after marriage, commonly spent on holiday, before settling down to the business of life; a period of (unusual or merely temporary) harmony at the start of a new business relationship, etc. — *vi* to spend one's honeymoon (with *in*). — **hon'eymooner; hon'eypot** a container for honey; anything that attracts people in great numbers. — See also **hanepoot; hon'ey-sac** the sac in the body of a bee where it carries nectar; **hon'ey-sucker** a honey-eater; **hon'eysuckle** a climbing shrub with cream-coloured flowers, so named because honey is readily sucked from the flower (by long-tongued insects only); the rewarewa (*NZ*). [O.E. *hunig*.]

honied. See **honeyed** under **honey.**

Honiton lace *hon'i-tən lās* or (*locally*) *hun'*, *n* a kind of pillow lace with a pattern of sprigs, made at *Honiton*, Devon.

honk *hongk*, *n* the cry of the wild goose; the noise of a motor horn. — *vi* to make such a sound; to smell unpleasantly (*slang*); to vomit (*slang*). — *n* **honk'er.** [Imit.]

honky or **honkie** *hong'ki*, (*derog slang*, orig. *US*) *n* a white man. — Also *adj*.

honky-tonk *hong'ki-tongk*, (*slang*) *n* a low drinking haunt (*NAm*); a style of jangly piano music (also *adj*, as in *honky-tonk music* or *piano*).

honor. See **honour.**

honorand *on'ə-rand*, *n* a person receiving an honour, esp. an honorary degree. [L. *honōrandus*, gerundive of *honōrāre*, to honour.]

honorarium *on-ə-rā'ri-əm*, *n* a voluntary fee paid, esp. to a professional person for their services: — *pl* **honorā'ria** or **honorā'riums.** [L. *honōrārius*, *honōrārium* (*dōnum*), honorary (gift) — *honor*, *-ōris*, honour.]

honorary *on'ə-rə-ri*, *adj* conferring honour; (holding a title or office) without performing services or without reward. — *n* an honorarium. [Ety. as for **honorarium.**]

honorific *on-ə-rif'ik*, *adj* attributing or giving honour or respect. — *n* an honorific form of title, address or mention. — *adv* **honorif'ically.** [L. *honōrificus* — *honor*, *-ōris*, honour, and *facĕre*, to do, make.]

honoris causa *hon-ör'is kow'zə* or *kö'zə*, (L.L.) as an honour or token of respect.

honour or in U.S. **honor** *on'ər*, *n* the esteem due or paid to a worthy person; respect; high estimation; that which confers distinction or does credit; integrity; a scrupulous sense of what is right; chastity, virginity; distinction; exalted rank; any mark of esteem; a title or decoration; a title of respect in addressing or referring to judges, etc.; a prize or distinction; (in *pl*) privileges of rank or birth; (in *pl*) civilities, respects paid; (in *pl*) in universities, etc., a higher grade of distinction for meritorious, advanced, or specialised work; the right to play first from the tee (*golf*); any one of four (in whist) or five (in bridge) best trumps, or an ace in a no-trump hand; (in *pl*) a score for holding these. — *vt* to hold in high esteem; to respect; to exalt; to do honour to; to confer honour(s) upon; to grace (e.g. with one's presence); to accept and pay (a debt, etc.) when due. — *adj* **hon'ourable** worthy of honour; governed by principles of honour, good, honest, etc.; conferring honour; befitting people of exalted rank; (with *cap*; written **Hon.**) prefixed to the names of various people as a courtesy title. — *n* **hon'ourableness**. — *adv* **hon'ourably**. — **hon'or-guard** (*US*) a guard of honour. — **honour-bound** see **in honour bound** below. — **honours list** a list of people who have received or are to receive a knighthood, order, etc. from the monarch. — **affair of honour** a duel; **birthday honours** honours granted to mark the monarch's birthday; **Companions of Honour** an order instituted in 1917 for those who have rendered conspicuous service of national importance; **debt of honour** see under **debt**; **do the honours** (*colloq*) to perform a task, esp. as host; **guard of honour** a body of soldiers serving as a ceremonial escort; **guest of honour** the most important or distinguished guest (at a party, etc.); **honour bright** (*schoolchildren's slang*) an oath or appeal to honour; **honours of war** the privileges granted to a surrendering force of marching out with their arms, flags, etc.; **in honour bound** (or *adj* **honour-bound**') obliged by duty, conscience, etc. (to); **in honour of** out of respect for; celebrating; **last honours** funeral rites; **maid of honour** a lady in the service of a queen or princess; a bridesmaid (*NAm*); a type of small cake flavoured with almonds; **matron of honour** a married woman in the service of a queen or princess; a married woman performing the duties of a bridesmaid; **military honours** ceremonial tokens of respect paid by troops to royalty, or at the burial of an officer, etc.; **point of honour** any scruple caused by a sense of duty, honour, self-respect, etc.; the obligation to demand and receive satisfaction for an insult, esp. by duelling; **word of honour** a solemn promise which cannot be broken without disgrace. [A.Fr. (*h*)*onour* — L. *honor*, *-ōris*.]

hooch. See **hootch**.

hood[1] *hŏŏd*, *n* a flexible covering for the head and back of the neck; a covering for a hawk's head; a distinctively coloured ornamental loop of material, derived from a hood, worn on the back over an academic gown; a folding roof for a car, carriage, etc.; an overhanging or protective cover; the expansion of a cobra's neck; a motor car bonnet (*NAm*). — *vt* to cover with a hood; to blind. — *adj* **hood'ed**. [O.E. *hōd*.]

hood[2] *hŏŏd*, (*slang*) *n* a hoodlum, a violent criminal.

-hood *-hŏŏd*, *n sfx* indicating: state or nature, as in *hardihood*, *manhood*; a group of people, as in *priesthood*, *sisterhood*. [O.E. *hād*, Ger. *-heit*, state.]

hoodlum *hŏŏd'ləm*, *n* a small-time criminal or gangster.

hoodoo *hoo'doo*, *n* voodoo; a jinx; bad luck. — *vt* to bring bad luck to: — *pr p* **hoo'dooing**; *pa t* and *pa p* **hoo'dooed**.

hoodwink *hŏŏd'wingk*, *vt* to deceive, cheat. [**hood**[1] and **wink**.]

hooey *hoo'i*, (*slang*) *n* nonsense.

hoof *hoof*, *n* the horny part of the feet of certain animals, e.g. horses, etc.; a hoofed animal; a foot (*colloq*): — *pl* **hooves** or **hoofs**. — *vt* to strike with the hoof, to kick; (with *it*) to walk (*slang*); (with *it*) to dance (*slang*). — *adj* **hoofed** having hooves. — *n* **hoof'er** (*slang*) a dancer. — **on the hoof** alive (of e.g. cattle). [O.E. *hōf*.]

hoo-ha or **hoo-hah** *hoo'-hä*, (*slang*) *n* a noisy fuss. [Imit.]

hook *hŏŏk*, *n* a bent object, such as would catch on or hold anything; a snare, trap, attraction, etc.; a curved instrument for cutting grain, branches, etc.; a boxer's blow made with the elbow bent; the curve of a ball in flight (*sport*); a particular way of striking the ball which makes it curve in a convex shape (*golf*) or in the direction of the swing (*cricket*); in pop music, a catchy, easily memorised phrase. — *vt* to catch, fasten, or hold with or as if with a hook; to form into or with a hook; to ensnare, trap, attract; to pull (the ball) abruptly to one's left if right-handed, or right if left-handed (*golf* and *cricket*); to obtain possession of (the ball) in the scrum (*Rugby football*). — *vi* to bend; to be curved; to pull abruptly; to curve in a particular direction (*golf*). — *pa p* or *adj* **hooked** (*hŏŏkt*) physically dependent (on drugs); (with *on*, *by*) addicted (to a drug, activity, or indulgence); enthralled. — *n* **hook'er** a person who hooks; a person whose job it is to hook the ball out of a scrum (*Rugby football*); a prostitute (*slang*). — *adj* **hook'y**. — *adj* **hook'-nosed**. — **hook'-up** a connection; a temporary linking up of separate broadcasting stations, etc., for a special transmission; **hook'worm** a parasitic round worm with hooks in the mouth; the disease it causes, ankylostomiasis or miner's anaemia. — **by hook or by crook** by one method or another; **hook and eye** a way of fastening garments by means of a hook that catches in a loop or eye; **hook, line and sinker** complete or completely; **off the hook** out of difficulty or trouble; of a telephone handset, not on its rest, so that incoming calls cannot be received. [O.E. *hōc*; Du. *hoek*.]

hookah or **hooka** *hŏŏk'ə*, *n* the tobacco-pipe of Arabs, Turks, etc., where the smoke is inhaled through water. [Ar. *huqqah*, bowl, casket.]

hooker[1] *hŏŏk'ər*, *n* a two-masted Dutch or Irish fishing vessel; a small fishing-smack. [Du. *hoeker*.]

hooker[2]. See **hook**.

hookey or **hooky** *hŏŏk'i*, (*US*) *n* truant (in the phrase *play hookey*).

hooligan *hoo'li-gən*, *n* a street tough, vandal; a (young) violent, rude person. — *n* **hoo'liganism**.

hoop[1] *hoop*, *n* a ring or circular band, esp. for holding together the staves of casks, etc.; a large ring of metal, etc., for a child to trundle, for leaping through, for holding wide a skirt, or other purposes; a (usu. small) ring; a croquet arch. — *vt* to bind with hoops; to encircle. — **hoop'-la** a fairground game in which small hoops are thrown over prizes; pointless activity, nuisance, nonsense (*US slang*). — **go through the hoop** to suffer an ordeal, undergo punishment. [O.E. *hōp*.]

hoop[2], **hooper** and **hooping-cough**. See under **whoop**.

hoopoe *hoop'oo*, *n* a crested bird with salmon-coloured plumage, an occasional visitor to Britain. [Earlier *hoop* — O.Fr. *huppe*, partly remodelled on L. *ŭpŭpa*.]

hooray or **hoorah**. Same as **hurrah**. — **Hooray** (or **Hoorah**) **Henry** a young middle- or upper-class man with loudly philistine manner.

hoosegow *hoos'gow*, (*US slang*) *n* a prison, jail. [Sp. *juzgado*, tribunal, courtroom.]

hoot *hoot*, *vi* (of an owl) to give a hollow cry; to make a sound like an owl, usually expressing hostility or scorn; to laugh loudly; to sound a motor horn, siren, or the like (also *vi*). — *n* the sound of hooting; the note of an owl, motor horn, etc.; a whit, a care (often *two hoots*); a hilarious performance, escapade, situation, etc. (*colloq*). — *n* **hoot'er** a siren or steam whistle at a factory or mine; a nose, esp. a large or ugly one (*slang*). [Imit.]

hootch or **hooch** *hooch*, *n* whisky or any strong liquor, esp. if illicitly got or made; (orig.) a drink made by the *Hooch*inoo Indians of Alaska from fermented dough and sugar.

hootenany *hoot'ə-nan-i*, (*US colloq*) *n* an informal concert with folk music.

Hoover® *hoo'vər*, *n* a vacuum-cleaner (also without *cap*). — *vt* and *vi* (usu. without *cap*) to clean with, or as if with, a vacuum-cleaner.

hooves. See **hoof**.

hop[1] *hop*, *vi* to leap on one leg; to move in jumps like a bird or frog; to walk lame, limp; to move smartly (in or out); to fly (in aircraft) (*colloq*). — *vt* to jump or fly over: — *pr p* **hopp'ing**; *pa t* and *pa p* **hopped**. — *n* a leap on one leg; a jump; a dance, dancing-party (*slang*); (one stage in) a journey by aeroplane. — *n* **hopp'er** a hopping or leaping animal, esp. (*US*) a grasshopper; a shaking or moving receiver, funnel, or trough (originally a shaking one) in which something is placed to be conveyed or fed, e.g. to a mill; a barge with an opening in its bottom for discharging refuse; a railway wagon with an opening in the bottom for discharging its cargo; a container in which seed-corn is carried for sowing; a device which holds and passes on punched cards to a feed mechanism (*comput*). — **hop'scotch** a game in which children hop over lines scotched or scored on the ground. — **hop it** (*slang*) to take oneself off, go away; **hopping mad** (*colloq*) extremely angry; **hop, skip (**or **step) and jump** a leap on one leg, a step, and a jump with both legs, (as an athletic event) the triple jump; **on the hop** in a state of restless activity; unawares. [O.E. *hoppian*, to dance.]

hop[2] *hop*, *n* a plant of the mulberry family with a long twining stalk; (in *pl*) its bitter catkin-like fruit-clusters used for flavouring beer and in medicine; opium (*US slang*). — *vi* to gather hops: — *pr p* **hopp'ing**; *pa t* and *pa p* **hopped**. — *n* **hopp'er** a person or machine that picks hops. — *n* **hopp'ing** the time of the hop harvest. — *adj* **hopp'y** tasting of hops. — **hop'bind** or **hop'bine** the stalk of the hop; **hop'-fly** a greenfly harmful to hops; **hop garden** a field of hops; **hop'-head** (*derog slang*) a drug addict. — *adj* **hopped-up'** (*US slang*) drugged; artificially stimulated. — **hop'-picker** a hopper; **hop'sack** or **hop'-sacking** sacking for hops; a coarse fabric of hemp and jute, or a woollen or cotton fabric with roughened surface. [Du. *hop*.]

hope[1] *hōp*, *vi* to desire (that something good will happen), with some expectation of success or fulfilment; to be hopeful. — *n* a desire for something good, with a certain expectation of obtaining it; confidence; anticipation; reason for belief that the thing hoped for will happen, etc.; the event, object, etc. which is hoped for. — *adj* **hope'ful** full of hope; having qualities which excite hope; promising good or success. — *n* a (usu. young) person of ambition. — *adv* **hope'fully** in a hopeful manner; if all goes well (*colloq*). — *n* **hope'fulness**. — *adj* **hope'less** without hope; giving no reason to expect good or success; incurable. — *adv* **hope'lessly**. — *n* **hope'lessness**. — **hope chest** (*NAm*) a place, often a trunk or chest, for things stored by a woman for her marriage. — **hope against hope** to continue to hope when there is no (longer any) reason for hope; **no-ho'per** (*slang*) a racehorse that is not nearly good enough to have a chance of winning; any thing or person that has absolutely no chance of success (*adj* **no-hope'**); **some hope, what a hope** or **not a hope** (*ironic*) that will never happen. [O.E. *hopian* — *hopa*, hope.]

hope[2]. See **forlorn hope**.

hopper. See hop[1,2].

hopsack. See **hop**[2].

hopscotch. See **hop**[1].

Horatian *hə-rā'shən*, *adj* of or pertaining to *Horace*, the Latin poet(65–8 B.C.), or to his manner or verse.

horde *hörd*, *n* a migratory or wandering tribe or clan; a multitude, huge crowd. — *vi* to live together as a horde; to come together to form a horde. [Fr., — Turk. *ordu*, camp.]

horizon *hə-rī'zən*, *n* the line at which earth and sky seem to meet (called the *sensible*, *apparent*, or *visible horizon*); a plane through the earth's centre parallel to the sensible horizon (called the *rational horizon*), or the great circle in which it meets the heavens (*astron*); a horizontal reflecting surface used as a substitute for the horizon in taking an observation (an *artificial horizon*); a level of strata, characterised generally by some particular fossil or fossils (*geol*), by a different physical property of the soil (*soil science*) or by artefacts characteristic of a particular culture or period (*archaeol*); the limit of one's experience or mental vision. — *adj* **horizontal** (*hor-i-zon'tl*) pertaining to the horizon; parallel to the horizon; level; measured in the plane of the horizon; applying equally to all members of a group, aspects of an activity, etc.; of relationships between separate groups of equal status or stage of development. — *n* a horizontal line, position, or object. — *n* **horizontal'ity**. — *adv* **horizon'tally**. — **horizontal bar** (*gymnastics*) a steel bar used for swinging and vaulting exercises. [Fr., — L., — Gr. *horīzōn* (*kyklos*), bounding (circle) — *horos*, a limit.]

hormone *hör'mōn*, *n* an internal secretion which on reaching some part of a plant or animal body has a specific physiological action. — *adj* **hormō'nal**. — **hormone replacement therapy** a treatment for post-menopausal women involving the artificial provision of a hormone which is no longer produced naturally after the menopause, thereby reducing the risk of brittle bones in later life. [Gr. *hormōn*, contracted pres. p. of *hormaein*, to stir up.]

horn *hörn*, *n* a hard outgrowth on the head of an animal, the hollow structure on an ox, sheep, goat, etc., a deer's antler, the growth on a rhinoceros's snout, etc.; a beetle's antenna; a snail's tentacle; any projection resembling a horn; a crescent tip, e.g. that of the moon; either of the pair of outgrowths supposed to spring from a cuckold's forehead; the material of which horns are composed, keratin; an object made of horn or like a horn, e.g. a drinking vessel; a wind musical instrument of several designs, orig. made from a horn, now of brass, etc.; an apparatus for making a noise warning of approach, on motor vehicles; an erection of the penis (*vulg slang*); the telephone (*US slang*). — *adj* made of horn. — *vt* to furnish with horns (real or cuckold's); to dehorn; to gore, to butt or push with a horn or horns. — *adj* **horned** having a horn or horns. — *adj* **horn'y** of or like horn; hard, calloused; sexually aroused (*slang*); lecherous, lustful (*slang*). — **horn'beam** a tree resembling a beech, with hard, tough wood; **horn'bill** a type of bird with a horny growth on its bill; **horn'book** (*hist*) a first book for children, which consisted of a single leaf set in a frame, with a thin plate of semitransparent horn in front to preserve it; **horned toad** a spiny American lizard; a S. American toad with a bony shield on the back. — *adj* **horn'-rimmed** (esp. of spectacles) having rims of horn, or material resembling horn. — **horn'-rims** spectacles with rims of dark horn; **horn'stone** (*mineralogy*) a flinty chalcedony; hornfels; **horn'wort** a rootless water plant with much-divided submerged leaves that turn translucent and horny. — **horn in** (*slang*) to interpose, butt in (on); **horn of plenty** see **cornucopia**; a trumpet-shaped edible fungus; **horns of a dilemma** see **dilemma**; **pull** or **draw in one's horns** to control one's strong emotions; to curtail or restrict one's activities, esp. spending, etc. [O.E. *horn*.]

hornblende *hörn'blend*, *n* a rock-forming mineral, essentially silicate of calcium, magnesium and iron, generally green to black. — *adj* **hornblend'ic**. [Ger.; cf. **horn**, and **blende**.]

hornet *hör'nit*, *n* a large kind of wasp. — **stir up a hornet's (**or **hornets') nest** to do something which causes a violent reaction. [O.E. *hyrnet*.]

hornfels *hörn'fels*, (*mineralogy*) *n* a compact type of rock composed of lime silicates. [Ger., — *Horn*, horn, *Fels*, rock.]

hornpipe *hörn'pīp*, *n* an old Welsh musical instrument like a clarinet, prob. sometimes with a horn mouthpiece or bell; a lively English dance, usually by one person, popular amongst sailors; a tune for the dance. [**horn** and **pipe**[1].]

hornswoggle *hörn'swog-l*, (*slang*; orig. and esp. *US*) *vt* to trick, deceive or cheat.

horologer *hə-rol'ə-jər* or **horologist**, *-rol'ə-jist n* a maker of clocks, etc. — *adj* **horolog'ic** or **horolog'ical**. — *n* **horol'ogy** the science of the measurement of time; the art of clock-making. [L. *hōrologium* — Gr. *hōrologion* — *hōrā*, an hour, *legein*, to tell.]

horoscope *hor'ə-skōp*, *n* a prediction by an astrologer of the events of a person's life, based on a map of the heavens at the hour or on the day of their birth; a map of the heavens for this purpose; any similar prediction about the future. — *adj* **horoscopic** (*-skop'*). — *n* **horos'copy** the art of predicting the events of a person's life from his or her horoscope; the aspect of the stars at the time of birth. [Gr. *hōroskopos* — *hōrā*, an hour, *skopeein*, to observe.]

horrendous *hə-ren'dəs*, (*colloq*) *adj* dreadful; frightful; horrible. — *adv* **horrend'ously**. — *n* **horrend'ousness**. [L. *horrendus*, gerundive of *horrēre*, to bristle.]

horrible *hor'i-bl*, *adj* producing horror; dreadful; detestable, foul (*colloq*). — *n* **horr'ibleness**. — *adv* **horr'ibly**. [L. *horribilis* — *horrēre*, to shudder.]

horrid *hor'id*, (*colloq*) *adj* nasty, repellent, detestable. — *adv* **horr'idly**. — *n* **horr'idness**. [L. *horridus* — *horrēre*, to bristle.]

horrify *hor'i-fī*, *vt* to produce a reaction of horror: — *pr p* **horr'ifying**; *pa t* and *pa p* **horr'ified**. — *adj* **horrif'ic** producing horror; frightful, awful. — *adv* **horrif'ically**. — *adv* **horr'ifyingly**. [L. *horrificus* — root of *horrēre*, to shudder, *facĕre*, to make.]

horripilation *hor-i-pi-lā'shən*, *n* a contraction of the skin muscles causing erection of the hairs and goose-flesh. — *adj* **horrip'ilant**. [L. *horripilātiō*, *-ōnis* — root of *horrēre*, to bristle, *pilus*, a hair.]

horrisonant *hə-ris'ə-nənt*, *adj* dreadful-sounding. [From root of L. *horrēre*, to bristle, *sonāns*, *-antis*, sounding.]

horror *hor'ər*, *n* intense repugnance or fear; the power of producing such feelings; a source of such feelings; any thing or person that is mildly objectionable, ridiculous, grotesque, or distasteful (*colloq*). — **horror comic, film, novel,** etc., one having gruesome, violent, horrifying, or bloodcurdling themes; **horror story** a story (often true) of one disaster after another; such a sequence of events, a chapter of accidents. — *adj* **horr'or-stricken** or **horr'or-struck** shocked, horrified, dismayed. — **the horrors** extreme depression, frightening thoughts, etc. [L. *horror*, a shudder, bristling, etc.]

hors *or*, (Fr.) *prep* out of, outside. — **hors concours** (*kɔ̃-kōōr*) not in competition; **hors de combat** (*də kɔ̃-ba*) unfit to fight, disabled; **hors d'œuvre** (*pl* **d'œuvre** or **d'œuvres**; *dœ-vr'*) a savoury snack, e.g. olives, sardines, etc., to whet the appetite before a meal.

horse *hörs*, *n* a four-legged, solid-hoofed animal (with flowing tail and mane); any member of the genus *Equus* (horse, ass, zebra, etc.) or the family *Equidae*; a male adult of the species; cavalry (*collectively*); a gymnastic apparatus for vaulting over, etc.; a horse-like apparatus or support of various kinds (such as *saw-horse*, *clothes-horse*); a mass of barren country interrupting a lode (*mining*); heroin (*slang*): — *pl* **hor'ses**, sometimes **horse**. — *vt* to mount or put on or as if on a horse; to provide with a horse. — *vi* to get on horseback; to travel on horseback. — *adj* **horse'less** without a horse; mechanically driven, motorised. — *n* **hors'iness**. — *adj* **hors'ey** or **hors'y** of or pertaining to horses; horselike, esp. in appearance (*derog* of people); devoted to horses, horse-racing, or breeding. — **horse'back** the back of a horse; **horse block** a block or stage for mounting and dismounting horses by; **horse'-box** a road trailer or railway car designed to carry horses; a high-sided church pew (*facetious*); **horse brass** a usu. brass ornament orig. for hanging on the harness of a horse; **horse'-breaker** or **-tamer** a person who breaks or tames horses, or teaches them to pull or carry loads; **horse chestnut** a smooth, brown, bitter seed or nut, perh. so called from its coarseness contrasted with the edible chestnut; the tree that produces it; **horse'cloth** a cloth for covering a horse; **horse collar** a stuffed collar for a draught-horse; **horse'-coper** a person who deals in horses; **horse'-dealing** horse-trading; **horse'-doctor** a veterinary surgeon; **horse'flesh** the flesh of a horse, esp. when eaten as meat, or traded on the hoof; horses collectively; **horse'fly** any of several large flies that sting horses; **horse guards** cavalry soldiers employed as guards; (with *cap*) the cavalry brigade of the British household troops; **horse'hair** a hair from a horse's mane or tail; a mass of such hairs; a fabric woven from horsehair. — *adj* made of or stuffed with horsehair. — **horse'hide**; **horse latitudes** two zones of the Atlantic Ocean (about 30°N and 30°S, esp. the former) noted for long calm periods; **horse laugh** a harsh, boisterous laugh; **horse leech** a large species of leech, supposed to fasten on horses; **horse mackerel** the scad or allied fish; the tunny; applied to various other fishes; **horse'man** a rider; a person skilled in managing a horse; a mounted soldier; a person who has charge of horses; **horse'manship**; **horse mushroom** a type of large coarse mushroom; **horse opera** a Wild West film (*facetious*); **horse'-play** rough, boisterous play; **horse'power** the power a horse can exert, or its conventional equivalent (taken as 745.7 watts); **horse race** a race by horses; **horse'-racing**; **horse'radish** a plant with a pungent root, used to make a savoury sauce; **horse'-rider**; **horse'-riding**; **horse sense** (*colloq*) plain common sense; **horse'shoe** a metal plate for horses' feet, consisting of a curved piece of iron; a representation of this, esp. as a symbol of good luck; anything of similar shape. — *adj* shaped like a horseshoe. — **horse'-trading** hard bargaining; **horse'-trainer** a person who trains horses for racing, etc.; **horse'whip** a whip for driving horses. — *vt* to thrash with a horsewhip. — **horse'woman** a woman who rides on horseback, or who rides well. — **dark horse** see under **dark**; **flog a dead horse** to try to work up excitement about a subject in which others have lost interest; **gift horse** see under **gift**; **high horse** see **on one's high horse** (under **high**[1]); **hold your horses** not so fast; wait a moment; **horse around** (*slang*) to fool about, play boisterously; **horse of a different colour** another matter altogether; **horses for courses** a phrase expressing the view that each racehorse will do best on a certain course which peculiarly suits it (also *fig* of people); **put the cart before the horse** see under **cart**; **(straight) from the horse's mouth** from a very trustworthy source (of information); **white horse** see under **white**; **willing horse** a willing, obliging worker. [O.E. *hors*.]

horst *hörst*, (*geol*) *n* a block of the earth's crust that has remained in position while the ground around it has subsided. [Ger.]

horsy. See **horse**.

hort. *abbrev* for horticulture.

hortative *hör'tə-tiv*, *adj* inciting; encouraging; giving advice. — Also **hort'atory**. — *adv* **hort'atively** or **hort'atorily**. — *n* **hortā'tion**. [L. *hortārī*, *-ātus*, to incite.]

horticulture *hör'ti-kul-chər*, *n* the art of gardening. — *adj* **horticul'tural**. — *n* **horticul'turist** a person expert in the art of cultivating gardens. [L. *hortus*, a garden, *cultūra* — *colĕre*, to cultivate.]

Horus *hör'əs*, *n* the Egyptian sun-god, son of Isis and Osiris, usu. depicted with a falcon's head. [Egyp. *hur*, hawk.]

Hos. (*Bible*) *abbrev* for (the Book of) Hosea.

hosanna *hō-zan'ə*, *n* an exclamation of praise to God. [Gr. *hōsanna* — Heb. *hōshī'āh nnā*, save, I pray.]

hose[1] *hōz*, *n* an old-style covering for the legs or feet; stockings; socks: — *pl* **hose**. — *n* **hosier** (*hōzh'ər*, *-yər* or *hōz'yər*) a dealer in or a maker of hosiery. —

n **hō'siery** stockings, etc. collectively; knitted underwear. [O.E. *hosa*, pl. *hosan*.]

hose² *hōz*, *n* a flexible pipe for conveying water, etc.: — *pl* **hos'es** — *vt* to direct a hose at when washing (often with *down*). — **hose'pipe; hose reel** a large revolving drum for carrying a hose. [Ety. as for **hose¹**.]

hospice *hos'pis*, *n* a home for the care of the terminally ill; a hostel, esp. one maintained by monks, etc. [Fr., — L. *hospitium* — *hospes*, *-itis*, a stranger, guest.]

hospitable *hos'pi-tə-bl* or *hos-pit'*, *adj* kind to strangers; welcoming and generous towards guests. — *n* **hos'pitableness** (or *-pit'*). — *adv* **hos'pitably** (or *-pit'*). — *n* **hospitality** (*-al'i-ti*) (friendly welcome and) entertainment of guests. [L.L. *hospitāgium* — L. *hospes*, *-itis*, stranger, guest.]

hospital *hos'pi-tl*, *n* formerly, a charitable institution for the old or destitute, or for the reception (and education) of the needy young; an institution for the treatment of the sick or injured; a building for any of these purposes. — *n* **hospitalisā'tion** or **-z-**. — *vt* **hos'pitalise** or **-ize** to send to hospital; to injure so badly that hospital treatment is needed. — *n* **hos'pitaller** or in U.S. **hos'pitaler** one of a charitable brotherhood for the care of the sick in hospitals; one of the Knights of St John (otherwise called Knights of Rhodes, and afterwards of Malta), an order which built a hospital for pilgrims at Jerusalem. — **hospital ship** a ship fitted out exclusively for the treatment and transport of the sick and wounded. [O.Fr. *hospital* — L.L. *hospitāle* — *hospes*, *-itis*, a guest.]

host¹ *hōst*, *n* a person who entertains a stranger or guest at his or her house; an innkeeper or publican; a person who introduces performers or participants, chairs discussions, etc. on a programme or show; a place acting as venue for an event, usu. implying some involvement in the organisation of the event and the welcoming of the participants; an organism on which another lives as a parasite; a person or animal that has received transplanted tissue or a transplanted organ; a host computer. — *vt* to receive and entertain as one's guest; to act as the chairperson, compère, etc. of (a show, programme, event, etc.). — *n* **hōst'ess** a female host; a paid female partner at a dance-hall, nightclub, etc.; a prostitute (*euph*). — **host computer** a computer attached to and in control of a multi-terminal computer system, or one attached to a multi-computer network and able e.g. to provide access to a number of databases. — **air'-hōstess** see under **air**. [O.Fr. *hoste* — L. *hospes*, *hospitis*.]

host² *hōst*, *n* a great multitude; an army (*Bible* or *archaic*). — **heavenly host** (*Bible*) the angels and archangels; **Lord of hosts** a favourite Hebrew term for Jehovah, considered as head of the hosts of angels, etc. [O.Fr. *host* — L. *hostis*, an enemy.]

host³ *hōst*, *n* (often with *cap*) in the R.C. Church, the consecrated wafer of the eucharist. [L. *hostia*, a victim.]

hosta *hos'tə*, *n* any plant of the *Hosta* genus of decorative perennial herbaceous plants from Asia with ribbed leaves and blue, white, and lilac flowers. [After Austrian botanist N.T. *Host*.]

hostage *hos'tij*, *n* a person kept prisoner by an enemy as security. — **hostages to fortune** the people and things one values most, of which the loss would be particularly painful. [O.Fr. *hostage* (Fr. *ôtage*) — L. *obses*, *obsidis*, a hostage.]

hostel *hos'təl*, *n* an inn; in some universities, a hall outside the college confines for students; a residence for students or for some class or society of people, esp. one run charitably or not for profit; a youth hostel. — *n* **hos'teller** or **hos'teler** the keeper of a hostel; a person who lives in, or uses, a hostel, esp. a youth hostel. — *n* **hos'telling** holidaying in youth hostels. — *n* **hos'telry** (esp. *jocularly*) an inn. [O.Fr. *hostel*, *hostellerie* — L. *hospitāle*.]

hostess. See **host¹**.

hostile *hos'tīl* or in U.S. *-təl*, *adj* pertaining to an enemy; showing enmity or unfriendliness, or angry opposition; (with *to*) resistant to (esp. new ideas, changes, etc.); (of a place or conditions) inhospitable, harsh; engaged in hostilities; pertaining to hostilities. — *adv* **hos'tilely**. — *n* **hostility** (*-til'*) enmity, unfriendliness: — *pl* **hostil'ities** (acts of) warfare. — **hostile bid** (*commerce*) one not welcomed by the company whose shares are to be bought; **hostile witness** (*legal*) a witness who gives evidence against the party he or she was called by. [L. *hostīlis* — *hostis*.]

hot *hot*, *adj* (*compar* **hott'er**, *superl* **hott'est**) having a high temperature; very warm; fiery; pungent; giving a feeling suggestive of heat; animated; ardent, passionate; violent; sexually excited (*slang*); dangerously charged with electricity; dangerous; (in e.g. hide-and-seek) near the object sought; (of news) fresh, exciting; (of jazz, etc.) intensely played with complex rhythms and exciting improvisations; skilful (*slang*); recently stolen (*slang*); highly radioactive (*colloq*). — *adv* hotly. — *vt* (*colloq*) to heat: — *pr p* **hott'ing**; *pa t* and *pa p* **hott'ed**. — *adv* **hot'ly**. — *n* **hot'ness**. — *n* **hott'ie** (*colloq*) a hot-water bottle. — *adj* **hott'ish**. — **hot air** empty talk. — *adj* **hot'-air** making use of heated air. — **hot-air balloon** one containing air which is heated by a flame to maintain or increase altitude; **hot'bed** a glass-covered bed heated by a layer of fermenting manure for bringing plants on rapidly; a place or conditions favourable to rapid growth or development, usu. of a bad kind. — *adj* **hot-blood'ed** having relatively hot blood, which stays at a constant temperature; passionate; high-spirited. — **hot cross bun** a bun bearing a pastry cross, customarily eaten on Good Friday; **hot dog** a hot-sausage sandwich; (**hot-dog'**) a person who performs clever manoeuvres, such as spins and turns, while skiing, surfing or skate-boarding (*colloq*; esp. *US*). — *vi* **hot-dog'** (*colloq*; esp. *US*). — **hot-dogg'er; hot-dogg'ing; hot favourite** in sports, races, etc., the one (considered) most likely to win. — *adv* **hot'foot** in haste (**hotfoot it** (*colloq*) to rush). — **hot gospeller** a loud, forceful proclaimer of a vigorously interactive kind of religious faith; a fanatical propagandist; **hot-gos'pelling; hot'-head** an impetuous, headstrong person. — *adj* **hot'headed.** — **hot'house** a greenhouse kept hot for the rearing of tropical or tender plants; any heated chamber or drying-room, esp. that where pottery is placed before going into the kiln; any establishment promoting the development of skills, etc. — *adj* (of a plant) suitable for rearing only in a greenhouse; (too) delicate, unable to exist in tough, or even normal, conditions. — **hot line** a special telephone and teleprinter link with the Kremlin, White House, etc., giving speedy communication ready for an emergency; **hot melt**, or **hot-melt glue** or **adhesive** an adhesive that is applied hot and which sets as it cools; **hot metal** machines or methods using printing type made from molten metal. — Also *adj*. — **hot money** funds transferred suddenly from one country to another because conditions make transfer financially advantageous; **hot'plate** the flat top surface of a stove for cooking; a similar plate, not part of a cooker, for keeping things hot; **hot'pot** a dish of chopped mutton or beef, etc. seasoned and stewed in a pot, with sliced potatoes, or a similar mixture; **hot potato** see under **potato**; **hot-rod** a motor car converted for speed by stripping off non-essentials and heightening in power; **hot seat** any uncomfortable, tricky situation; the electric chair (*US slang*); **hot'shot** a person who is (esp. boastfully or showily) successful, skilful, etc.; **hot spot** an area of (too) high temperature in an engine, etc.; a region of the earth where there is evidence of isolated volcanic activity due to hot material rising through the earth's mantle; a popular nightclub (*colloq*); an area of potential trouble, esp. political or military; a place of very high local radioactivity; **hot spring** a spring of water which has been heated underground, occurring esp. in volcanic regions; **hot stuff** (*slang*) any person, thing, or performance that is outstandingly remarkable, excellent, vigorous or attractive. — *adj* **hotted-up** see **hot up** below. — *adj* **hot-tem'pered** quick to become angry. — **hot water** (*colloq*) trouble, problems; **hot-water bottle** a (usu. rubber) container of hot water, used to warm a bed. — **go** or **sell like hot cakes** to sell or disappear promptly; **have the hots for** (*vulg slang*) to be sexually attracted to, desire sexually; **hot on** (*colloq*) very fond of, interested in; good at, well-informed about; **hot on the heels of** (*colloq*) following or pursuing closely; **hot under the collar** (*colloq*) indignant; embarrassed; **hot up** (*colloq*) to increase in excitement, energy, performance, etc. (*adj* **hotted-up'**); **in hot pursuit** pursuing at full speed; **make it hot for** (*colloq*) to make it unpleasant or impossible for. [O.E. *hāt*.]

hotchpotch *hoch'poch* or **hodgepodge** *hoj'poj*, *n* a confused mass of ingredients shaken or mixed together; a kind of mutton broth with vegetables of many kinds. [Fr. *hochepot* — *hocher*, to shake, *pot*, a pot.]

hotel *hō-tel'*, *n* a commercial building with rooms for the accommodation of the paying public. — *n* **hotelier** (*hō-tel'i-ā* or *-i-ər*) a person who owns or runs a hotel. — *n* **hotel'-keeper**. [Fr. *hôtel* — L. *hospitālia*, guest-chambers — *hospes*.]

HOTOL *hō'tol*, (*aeronautics*) *abbrev* for horizontal take-off and landing, a proposed single-stage-to-orbit launch vehicle burning oxygen and hydrogen propellants. Cf. VTOL.

Hotspur *hot'spər*, *n* a violent, rash man like Henry Percy (1364–1403), so nicknamed.

Hottentot *hot'n-tot*, *n* one of a dwindling, nomad, pastoral, pale-brown-skinned race in S.W. Africa; their language. — Also *adj*. [Du. imit.; the language was unintelligible to them and sounded staccato.]

hottie. See under **hot**.

houdah. See **howdah**.

hound *hownd*, *n* a dog (*colloq*); a dog of a kind used in hunting; a contemptible scoundrel; a hunter, tracker or assiduous seeker of anything; an addict or devotee — often as a combining form. — *vt* to set on in chase; to drive by harassing. — **hound's'-tongue** a plant of the borage family (from its leaf); **hound's'-tooth** a textile pattern of broken checks. — Also *adj*. — **master of hounds** the person responsible for looking after a pack of hunting hounds, associated hunting equipment, etc.; **ride to hounds** to hunt foxes (on horseback). [O.E. *hund*.]

hour *owr*, *n* 60 minutes, or the 24th part of the day; the time as indicated by a clock, etc.; an hour's journey; a time or occasion; (in *pl*) set times of prayer, the *canonical hours*, the offices or services prescribed for these, or a book containing them, often illustrated (also **book of hours**); (in *pl*) the prescribed times for doing business. — *adj* **hour'ly** happening or done every hour. — *adv* every hour. — **hour'-circle** (*astron*) a great circle passing through the celestial poles; the equivalent of a meridian; **hour'glass** an instrument for measuring the hours by the running of sand through a narrow neck. — *adj* having the form of an hourglass; slim-waisted. — **hour hand** the hand which shows the hour on a clock, etc. — *adj* and *adv* **hour'long** lasting an hour. — **at all hours** at irregular hours, esp. late hours; **at the eleventh hour** at the last moment; **keep good hours** to go to bed and to rise early; to lead a quiet and regular life; **on the hour** at exactly one, two, etc. o'clock. [O.Fr. *hore* (Fr. *heure*) — L. *hora* — Gr. *hōrā*.]

houri *hōō'ri* or *how'ri*, *n* a nymph of the Muslim paradise; a voluptuously alluring woman. [Pers. *hūrī* — Ar. *hūriya*, a black-eyed girl.]

house *hows*, *n* a building for living in; a building in general; a dwelling-place; an inn; a public house; a household; a family in line of descent; kindred; a trading establishment; one of the twelve divisions of the heavens in astrology; a legislative or deliberative body or its meeting-place; a convent; a school boarding-house; the pupils belonging to it (*collectively*); a section of a school; an audience, auditorium or performance; (**the House**) at Oxford — Christ Church, in London — the Stock Exchange, the Houses of Parliament; bingo, esp. when played for money (esp. *army slang*): — *pl* **houses** (*howz'iz*). — *adj* domestic; of a restaurant, hotel, etc. or its management, as in *house rules*; (of wine) unnamed and cheaper than those listed on a menu, etc. by name or region. — *vt* **house** (*howz*) to protect by covering; to shelter; to store; to provide houses for. — *n* **house'ful**: — *pl* **house'fuls**. — *n* **housing** (*how'zing*) houses, accommodation, or shelter, or the provision of any of these; a cavity into which a timber fits; anything designed to cover, protect, contain, etc. machinery, etc. — Also *adj*. — **house agent** a person who arranges the buying, selling and letting of houses; **house arrest** confinement, under guard, to one's house, or to a hospital, etc., instead of imprisonment; **house'boat** a barge with a deck-cabin that may serve as a dwelling-place; **house'bote** a tenant's right to wood to repair his or her house (*law*). — *adj* **house'bound** confined to one's house because of illness, etc. — **house'boy** a male domestic servant, esp. in Africa or India; **house'-breaker** someone who breaks into and enters a house for the purpose of stealing; someone whose work is demolishing old houses; **house'breaking**; **house'coat** a woman's usu. long coatlike dressing-gown, worn at home; **house'craft** skill in domestic activities; **house'-dog** a watchdog; **house'-father** the male head of a household or community; a man in charge of children in an institution; **house flag** the distinguishing flag of a shipowner or shipping company; **house fly** the common fly universally distributed; **house guest** a guest in a private house; **house'hold** those who are held together in the same house, and compose a family. — *adj* pertaining to the house and family; well known to the general public, as in *household name, household word*. — **house'-holder** the holder or tenant of a house; **household gods** see **god**; **household troops** Guards regiments whose peculiar duty is to attend the sovereign; **household word** a familiar saying or name. — *vi* **house'-hunt** to look for a house to live in. — **house'-hunter**; **house'-hunting**; **house'-husband** a married man who looks after the house and family and does not have a paid job; **house'keeper** a person employed to run a household; **house'-keeping** the keeping or management of a house or of domestic affairs; the money used for this; operations carried out on or within a computer program or system to ensure the efficient functioning of the program or system (*comput*). — *adj* domestic. — **house'leek** a plant of the stonecrop family with succulent leaves, often growing on roofs; **house lights** (*theat*) the lights illuminating the auditorium; **house'maid** a maid employed to keep a house clean, etc.; **housemaid's knee** an inflammation of the sac between the knee-cap and the skin, to which those whose work involves frequent kneeling are especially liable; **house'man** a recent graduate in medicine holding a junior resident post in a hospital; **house'martin** a kind of black and white swallow with a slightly forked tail; **house'master** or **house'-mistress** (in schools) respectively the male or female head of a (boarding-)house, esp. in connection with a public school; **house'-mother** a woman in charge of children in an institution; **house'-parent** a man or woman in charge of children in an institution; **house party** a company of guests spending some days in a private house, esp. one in the country; **house'plant** a plant that can be grown indoors as decoration. — *adj* **house'-proud** taking a pride (often an excessive and fussy pride) in the condition of one's house. — **house'room** room for accommodating something in one's house (also *fig*); **house'-sitting** looking after a person's house by living in it while they are away, on holiday, etc. — *vi* **house'-sit.** — **house sparrow** see **sparrow**; **house surgeon** a resident surgeon in a hospital — so also **house physician.** — *adj* **house-to-house'** performed or conducted by calling at house after house. — **house'top** the top or roof of a house. — *adj* **house'-trained** (of animals) taught to urinate and defecate outdoors. — **house'-warming** a party given after moving into a new house; **housewife** (*hows'wīf*) a married woman who looks after the house and family and does not have a paid job; (*huz'if*) a pocket sewing-outfit. — *adj* **house'wifely.** — **housewifery** (*hows'wif-ri*); **house'work** domestic work; **housey-house'y** a game in which numbers are drawn at random and marked off on players' boards until one is clear — now usu. called **bingo; housing estate** a planned residential area, esp. one built by a local authority; **housing joint** a joint where the end of one board fits into a groove cut across another board; **housing scheme** a plan for the designing, building and provision of houses, esp. by a local authority; sometimes applied to an area coming under such a plan. — **bring the house down** to evoke very loud applause in a place of entertainment; **full house** see under **full**[1]**; house of cards** an unstable situation, etc.; **House of Commons, Lords,** and **Representatives** see under **common, lord** and **represent; house of correction** a jail; **house of God, prayer** or **worship** a place of worship; **house of ill repute** a brothel; **House of Keys** the Manx parliament; **keep a good house** to keep up a plentifully supplied table; **keep house** to maintain or manage an establishment; **keep open house** to give entertainment to all comers; **like a house on fire** with astonishing rapidity; very well or successfully; **on the house** (of drinks) at the publican's expense; free, with no charge; **put** or **set one's house in order** to settle one's affairs; **set up house** to start a domestic life of one's own; **the Household** the royal domestic establishment. [O.E. *hūs*; Goth, *hūs*, Ger. *Haus*.]

housing[1] *how'zing*, *n* an ornamental covering for a horse; a saddle-cloth; (in *pl*) the trappings of a horse. [O.Fr. *houce*, a mantle, of Gmc. origin.]

housing[2]. See **house.**

hove. See **heave.**

hovel *hov'əl* or *huv'əl*, *n* a small or wretched dwelling; a shed.

hover *hov'ər*, *vi* to remain aloft flapping the wings; to remain suspended; to remain undecided (with *between*); to linger, esp. nervously or solicitously; to move about near. — *n* an act or state of hovering. — Used in combination to describe vessels, vehicles or stationary objects which move or rest on a cushion of air, e.g. **hov'ercraft** (a craft able to move at a short distance above the surface of sea or land supported by a down-driven blast of air); **hov'erfly** a wasplike fly that hovers and darts; **hov'erport** a port for hovercraft; **hov'ertrain** one which moves supported by a cushion of air, like a hovercraft.

how *how*, *adv* and *conj* in what manner; to what extent; by what means; in what condition; for what reason; to what extent, in what degree; that. — *n* manner, method. — **and how!** (*NAm colloq*) yes, certainly; very much indeed; I should think so indeed; **how about** what do you think of; would you like (something); are you interested in (doing something); **how are you?** a conventional greeting to an acquaintance; sometimes specifically referring to his or her state of health; **how come?** (*colloq*) how does that come about?; **how do you do?** see **do**[1]; **how now** what is this?; why is this so?; **how's that** (*howzat'*; sometimes written **howzat**; *cricket*) the appeal of the fielding side to the umpire to give the batsman out; **how's your father** (*facetious*) amorous frolicking; sexual intercourse; nonsense, foolish activity; **the how and the why** the manner and the cause. [O.E. *hū*, prob. an adverbial form from *hwā*, who.]

howbeit *how-bē'it*, (*archaic* or *formal*) *conj* be it how it may; notwithstanding; yet; however. [**how, be,** and **it**[1].]

howdah or **houdah** *how'dä*, *n* a pavilion or seat fixed on an elephant's back. [Ar. *haudaj*.]

howdy *how'di*, *interj* a colloquial form of the common greeting, *How do you do*? — **how-d'ye-do'** or **howdy-do'** a troublesome state of matters: — *pl* **how-d'ye-dos'** or **howdy-dos'.**

however *how-ev'ər*, *adv* and *conj* in whatever manner or degree; nevertheless; at all events. [**how** and **ever.**]

howitzer *how'it-sər*, *n* a short squat gun used for shelling at a steep angle, esp. in siege and trench warfare. [Ger. *Haubitze* — Czech *houfnice*, a sling.]

howl *howl*, *vi* to yell or cry, like a wolf or dog; to utter a long, loud, whining sound; to wail; to roar; to laugh or cry (*colloq*). — *vt* to utter through a shriek or wail. — *n* a loud, prolonged cry of distress; a mournful cry; a loud sound like a yell, made by the wind, a wireless receiver, etc. — *n* **howl'er** someone who howls; a S. American monkey, with prodigious power of voice; a glaring and amusing blunder (*colloq*). — *adj* **howl'ing** tremendous (*colloq*). — *n* a howl. — **howl down** to drown out (a speaker) with angry cries. [O.Fr. *huller* — L. *ululāre*, to shriek or howl — *ulula*, an owl.]

howsoever *how-sō-ev'ər*, *adv* in whatever way; although; however. [**how, so**[1] and **ever**; and M.E. *sum*, as.]

howzat. See **how's that** at **how.**

hoy[1] *hoi*, *n* a large one-decked boat, commonly rigged as a sloop. [M.Du. *hoei*; Du. *heu*, Flem. *hui*.]

hoy[2] *hoi*, *interj* ho! stop!

hoya *hoi'ə*, *n* any plant of the Australasian *Hoya* genus of the *Asclepiadaceae*. [Thomas *Hoy*, d. 1821, English gardener.]

hoyden *hoi'dən*, *n* a tomboy. — *n* **hoy'denism.** — *adj* **hoy'denish.** [Perh. Du. *heiden*, a heathen, a gypsy, *heide*, heath.]

HP *abbrev* for: half-pay; high pressure; High Priest; hire purchase; Houses of Parliament.

hp *abbrev* for horsepower.

HQ or **hq** *abbrev* for headquarters.

HR *abbrev* for: Home Rule; House of Representatives (*US*).

hr *abbrev* for hour.

HRE *abbrev* for Holy Roman Emperor or Empire.

HRH *abbrev* for His or Her Royal Highness.

HRT *abbrev* for hormone replacement therapy.

HS *abbrev* for: High School; Home Secretary.

hs *abbrev* for *hoc sensu* (L.), in this sense.

Hse *abbrev* for House (in addresses, place names).

HSH *abbrev* for His or Her Serene Highness.

HSM *abbrev* for His or Her Serene Majesty.

HT *abbrev* for high tension.

ht *abbrev* for height.

HTLV *abbrev* for human T-cell lymphotrophic virus.

hub *hub*, *n* the centre of a wheel, the nave; the focal point (of a discussion, problem, etc.). — **hub'cap** a metal covering over the hub of a wheel. [Prob. a form of **hob**[1].]

hubble-bubble *hub-l-bub'l*, *n* a bubbling sound; tattle; confusion; a crude kind of hookah. [Reduplication from **bubble.**]

hubbub *hub'ub*, *n* a confused sound of many voices; riot; uproar. [App. of Irish origin.]

hubby *hub'i*, (*colloq*) *n* a husband.

hubris *hū'bris*, *n* insolence; over-confidence; arrogance, such as invites disaster or ruin (*classical Gr theat*). — *adj* **hubris'tic**. — *adv* **hubris'tically**. [Gr. *hybris*.]

huckaback *huk'ə-bak*, *n* a coarse linen or cotton with raised surface, used for towels, etc.

huckle *huk'l*, *n* the haunch; the hip. — *adj* **huck'le-backed** having the back round; humpbacked. — **huckle'-bone** the hip-bone; the talus or ankle-bone of a quadruped. [Poss. connected with **hook**.]

huckleberry *huk'l-bə-ri* or *-ber-i*, *n* a N. American shrub related to whortleberry; its fruit. [App. for *hurtleberry*, whortleberry.]

huckster *huk'stər*, *n* a hawker or pedlar; an aggressive seller; a mercenary person. — *vi* to hawk or peddle; to haggle meanly or sell aggressively.

huddle *hud'l*, *vt* to jumble; to hustle, bundle; to drive, draw, throw or crowd together in disorder. — *vi* to crowd closely together, e.g. because of cold (sometimes with *up*); to form or gather into a huddle (*Am football*). — *n* a confused mass; a jumble; confusion; a secret conference (*colloq*); a gathering together of the team members to receive instructions, etc. before the next play (*Am football*). — *adj* **hudd'led** jumbled; crowded closely together; crouching. [Poss. connected with **hide**[1].]

Hudibrastic *hū-di-bras'tik*, *adj* similar in style to *Hudibras*, a metrical burlesque on the Puritans by Samuel Butler (1612–80); mock-heroic.

hue[1] *hū*, *n* appearance; colour; tint; dye. — *adj* **hued** having a hue, often in combination, as in *dark-hued*. — *adj* **hue'less**. [O.E. *hīow*, *hēow*.]

hue[2] *hū*, *n* a shouting, clamour. — **hue and cry** a loud clamour about something; an outcry calling upon all to pursue someone who is to be made prisoner (*hist*); a proclamation or publication to the same effect (*hist*); the pursuit itself. [Imit.]

huff *huf*, *n* a fit of anger, sulks or offended dignity, esp. in the phrase *in a huff* (*colloq*); an act of huffing (*draughts*). — *vt* to give offence; to remove from the board for omitting capture (*draughts*). — *vi* to take offence. — *adj* **huff'ish** or **huff'y** touchy; ready to take offence. — *adv* **huff'ishly** or **huff'ily**. — *n* **huff'ishness** or **huff'iness**. — **huffing and puffing** loud talk, noisy objections. [Imit.]

hug *hug*, *vt* to clasp close with the arms; to embrace; to cherish; to keep close to or skirt: — *pr p* **hugg'ing**; *pa t* and *pa p* **hugged**. — *n* a close embrace; a particular grip in wrestling. — *adj* **hugg'able**.

huge *hūj*, *adj* vast; enormous. — *adv* **huge'ly**. — *n* **huge'ness**. [O.Fr. *ahuge*.]

hugger-mugger *hug-ər-mug'ər*, *n* secrecy; confusion. — *adj* secret; disorderly. — *adv* in secrecy or disorder.

Huguenot *hū'gə-nō* or *-not*, (*hist*) *n* a French Protestant. — Also *adj*. [Fr., — earlier *eiguenot* — Ger. *Eidgenoss*, confederate.]

huh *hu*, *interj* expressing disgust, disbelief, enquiry, etc. [Imit.]

hula-hula *hōō-lə-hōō'lə*, *n* a Hawaiian women's dance. — Also **hu'la**. — **hu'la-hoop** a light hoop used in the diversion of keeping the hoop in motion about the waist by a swinging movement of the hips; **hula skirt** a grass skirt worn by hula dancers. [Hawaiian.]

hulk *hulk*, *n* an unwieldy ship; a dismantled ship; a big ungainly or awkward person (*derog slang*); anything unwieldy; (in *pl* with **the**) old ships formerly used as prisons. — *adj* **hulk'ing** big and clumsy. [O.E. *hulc*.]

hull[1] *hull*, *n* a husk or outer covering. — *vt* to separate from the hull; to husk. [O.E. *hulu*, a husk, as of corn — *helan*, to cover.]

hull[2] *hul*, *n* the frame or body of a ship; part of a flying-boat in contact with the water; the heavily armoured body of a tank, missile, rocket, etc. — *vt* to pierce the hull of. — *adv* and *adj* **hull-down'** so far away that the hull is below the horizon. [Perh. same word as above.]

hullabaloo *hul-ə-bə-lōō'*, *n* an uproar. [Perh. **halloo**.]

hullo. See **hallo**.

hum[1] *hum*, *vi* to make a sound like bees or that represented by *m*; to sing with closed lips without words or articulation; to pause in speaking and utter an inarticulate sound; to stammer through embarrassment; to be audibly astir; to have a strong, unpleasant smell (*slang*); to be busily active. — *vt* to render by humming: — *pr p* **humm'ing**; *pa t* and *pa p* **hummed**. — *n* the noise of bees; a murmurous sound; an inarticulate murmur; the sound of humming. — *adj* **humm'able**. — **humm'ing-bird** any member of the tropical family *Trochilidae*, very small birds of brilliant plumage and rapid flight (from the humming sound of the wings); **humm'ing-top** a top that produces a humming sound as it spins. — **hum and haw** or **ha** to make inarticulate sounds when at a loss; to hesitate; **make things hum** to set things going briskly. [Imit.]

hum[2] *hum*, *interj* expressing doubt or reluctance to agree.

human *hū'mən*, *adj* belonging or pertaining to or of the nature of man or mankind; having the qualities of a person or the limitations of people; humane; not invidiously superior; genial or kind. — *n* a human being. — *adj* **humane** (*hū-mān'*) having the feelings proper to man; kind; tender; merciful; humanising; classical, elegant, polite. — *adv* **humane'ly**. — *n* **humane'ness**. — *vt* **humanise** or **-ize** (*hū'mə-nīz*) to render human or humane; to soften; to impart human qualities to, to make like that which is human or of mankind. — *n* **humanīsā'tion** or **-z-**. — *n* **hū'manism** literary culture; classical studies; any system which puts human interests and the mind of man paramount, rejecting the supernatural, belief in a god, etc. — *n* **hū'manist** at the Renaissance, a student of Greek and Roman literature; a student of human nature; an advocate of any system of humanism. — Also *adj*. — *adj* **hūmanist'ic** of or pertaining to humanism; emphasising observation of one's own feelings and reactions to others as a basis for a greater understanding of the self (*psychol* and *psychiatry*). — *n* **hū'mankind** the human species. — *adj* **hū'manlike**. — *adv* **hū'manly** in a human manner; by human agency; having regard to human limitations; humanely. — *n* **hū'manness**. — *n* **hū'manoid** one of the immediate kindred of man (closer than *anthropoid*); resembling, with the characteristics of, a human being. — Also *adj*. — **human being** any member of the human race; a person; **humane society** a society promoting humane behaviour, usu. to animals; **human immunodeficiency virus** (abbrev. **HIV**) a virus which breaks down the human body's natural immune system, often causing Aids; **human interest** (in newspaper articles, broadcasts, etc.) reference to people's lives and emotions; **human nature** the nature of man; the qualities of character common to all human beings that differentiate them from other species; irrational or less than saintly behaviour (often *facetious*); **human rights** the right each human being has to personal freedom, justice, etc.; **human shield** a person or people (civilian, P.O.W., etc.) deliberately deployed in strategic sites (during hostilities) to deter enemy attack upon them; this use of people, as a tactic in war. [Fr. *humain* — L. *hūmānus* — *homō*, a human being.]

humanity *hū-man'i-ti*, *n* the nature peculiar to a human being; humanness; humaneness; the kind feelings of man; mankind collectively; (in Scottish universities) Latin language and literature; (in *pl*) grammar, rhetoric, Latin, Greek and poetry, so called from their humanising effects. — *n* **humanitarian** (*hū-man-i-tā'ri-ən*) a philanthropist. — *adj* of or belonging to humanity, benevolent. — *n* **humanitā'rianism**. [Fr. *humanité* — L. *hūmānitās* — *hūmānus* — *homō*, a man.]

humble *hum'bl*, *adj* low; lowly; modest; unpretentious; having a low opinion of oneself or of one's claims; abased. — *vt* to bring down to the ground; to lower; to abase; to degrade. — *n* **hum'bleness**. — *adj* **hum'bling**. — *adv* **hum'bly**. — **your humble servant** an old formula used in subscribing a letter. [Fr., — L. *humilis*, low — *humus*, the ground.]

humble-bee *hum'bl-bē*, *n* the bumble-bee (*Bombus*). [Perh. from *humble*, frequentative of **hum**[1].]

humbles *npl*. Same as **umbles**. — **humble-pie'** a pie made from the umbles of a deer. — **eat humble-pie** (punningly) to humble or abase oneself, to eat one's words, etc.

humbug *hum'bug*, *n* hollowness, pretence, fraud, deception; an impostor; a lump of toffee, esp. a peppermint drop. — *vt* to deceive; to hoax; to cajole: — *pr p* **hum'bugging**; *pa t* and *pa p* **hum'bugged**. — *n* **hum'buggery**.

humdinger *hum-ding'ər*, (*slang*) *n* an exceptionally excellent person or thing. [Prob. **hum**[1] and **ding**.]

humdrum *hum'drum*, *adj* dull; monotonous; commonplace. — *n* a stupid fellow; monotony; tedious talk. [**hum**[1] and perh. **drum**[1].]

humect *hū-mekt'*, *vt* and *vi* to make or become moist. — *adj* and *n* **humect'ant**. [L. (*h*)*ūmectāre* — *ūmēre*, to be moist.]

humerus *hū'mə-rəs*, (*anat*) *n* the bone of the upper arm: — *pl* **hū'merī**. — *adj* **hū'meral** belonging to the shoulder or the humerus. [L. (*h*)*umerus*, shoulder.]

humic. See **humus**.

humid *hū'mid*, *adj* moist; damp; rather wet. — *n* **humidificā'tion**. — *n* **humid'ifier** a device for increasing or maintaining humidity. — *vt* **humid'ify** to make humid. — *n* **humid'istat** a device for controlling humidity. — *n* **humid'ity** moisture, esp. in the air; a moderate degree of wetness. — *adv* **hu'midly**. — *n* **hu'midness**. — *n* **hu'midor** a box or chamber for keeping cigars or tobacco moist. [L. (*h*)*ūmidus* — (*h*)*ūmēre*, to be moist.]

humify *hū'mi-fī*, *vt* and *vi* to make or turn into humus. — *n* **humificā'tion**. [**humus**.]

humiliate *hū-mil'i-āt*, *vt* to humble; to injure the self-respect or pride of. — *n* **humiliā'tion**. [L. *humiliāre*, *-ātum*.]

humility *hū-mil'i-ti*, *n* the state or quality of being humble; lowliness of mind; modesty. [O.Fr. *humilite* — L. *humilitās* — *humilis*, low.]

hummock *hum'ək*, *n* a hillock; a pile or ridge of ice. — *adj* **humm'ocked** or **humm'ocky**. [At first nautical.]

hummus *hum'əs* or *hōō'məs*, *n* a Middle Eastern hors d'oeuvre of puréed chick-peas and sesame oil with garlic and lemon. [Turk.]

humour or in U.S. **humor** *hū'mər* or *ū'mər*, *n* a mental quality which apprehends and delights in the ludicrous and mirthful; that which causes mirth and amusement; the quality of being funny; temperament or disposition of mind; state of mind (as in *good humour*, *ill humour*); disposition; caprice; a fluid (*med*); a fluid of the animal body, esp. formerly any one of the four that in old physiology were held to determine temperament. — *vt* to go along with the humour of; to gratify by compliance. — *adj* **hū'moral** pertaining to a body fluid. — *n* **hūmoresque'** a musical caprice. — *n* **hū'morist** a writer of comic stories; someone possessed of a sense of humour. — *adj* **hūmoris'tic** humorous. — *adj* **hū'morous** full of humour; exciting laughter. — *adv* **hū'morously**. — *n* **hū'morousness**. — *adj* **hū'mourless** or in U.S. **hu'morless**. — **out of humour** displeased, in a bad mood. [O.Fr. *humor* (Fr. *humeur*) — L. (*h*)*ūmor* — (*h*)*ūmēre*, to be moist.]

humous. See **humus**.

hump *hump*, *n* a rounded projection in the back due to spinal deformity; a protuberance; a rounded mass, e.g. of earth; despondency or annoyance, esp. in the phrase *have* or *give* (*someone*) *the hump* (*slang*). — *vt* to bend in a hump; to hunch; to shoulder, to carry on the back. — *vi* to put forth effort; to have sexual intercourse (also *vt*) (*slang*). — *adj* **hump'y** having a hump or humps; sulky, irritable (*colloq*). — **hump'back** a back with a hump or hunch; a person with a humpback; a whale with a humplike dorsal fin. — *adj* (also **hump'backed**) having a humpback. — **humpback bridge** a bridge with a sharp rise in the middle. — **over the hump** (*colloq*) past the crisis or difficulty.

humph *həmf*, *interj* expressive of reserved doubt or dissatisfaction.

humpty *hump'ti* or *hum'ti*, *n* a low padded seat, a pouffe.

Humpty-dumpty *hump-ti-dump'ti* or *hum-ti-dum'ti*, *n* a short, squat, egg-like character of nursery folklore.

humpy[1] *hum'pi*, (*Austr*) *n* an Aboriginal hut. [Aboriginal *oompi*.]

humpy[2]. See **hump**.

humus *hū'məs*, *n* decomposed organic matter in the soil. — *adj* **hū'mic** or **hū'mous**. [L. *humus*.]

Hun *hun*, *n* one of a powerful and savage nomad race of Asia who moved westwards, and under Attila (433–453) overran Europe; a barbarian; a German (*derog slang*). — *adj* **Hunn'ish**. [O.E. (pl.) *Hūne*, *Hūnas*.]

hunch *hunch* or *hunsh*, *n* a premonition; an intuitive feeling; a hump. — *vt* to hump or bend. — **hunch'back** a person whose spine is convexly curved to an abnormal degree. — *adj* **hunch'-backed**.

hundred *hun'drəd*, *n* the number of ten times ten; a set of a hundred things; a hundred pounds, dollars, etc.; (in *pl*) an unspecified large number; a division of a county in England orig. supposed to contain a hundred families (chiefly *hist*): — *pl* **hundreds** or, if preceded by a numeral, **hundred**. — *adj* to the number of a hundred; also used indefinitely, very many (*colloq*). — *adj*, *adv* and *n* **hun'dredfold** a hundred times as much. — *adj* **hun'dredth** last of a hundred; next after the ninety-ninth; equal to one of a hundred equal parts. — *n* one of a hundred equal parts; a person or thing in hundredth position. — *adj* **hundred-per-cent'** out-and-out; thoroughgoing. — **hundreds-and-thou'sands** little sweets used as an ornamental dressing; **hun'dredweight** 1/20 of a ton, or 112 lb. avoirdupois (50·80 kg.; also called **long hundredweight**); orig. and still in U.S., 100 lb. (45·3 kg.; also called **short hundredweight**); 50 kg. (also called **metric hundredweight**) — abbrev. **cwt** (*c* standing for L. *centum*, *wt* for weight). — **great** or **long hundred** usually six score; sometimes some other number greater than ten tens (e.g. of herrings, 132 or 126); **not a hundred miles from** (*colloq*) at, very near; **not a hundred per cent** not in perfect health; **one, two,** etc. **hundred hours** one, two, etc., o'clock, from the method of writing hours and minutes 1.00, 2.00, etc. [O.E. *hundred* — old form *hund*, a hundred, with the sfx. *-red*, a reckoning.]

Hung. *abbrev* for: Hungarian; Hungary.

hung *hung*, *pa t* and *pa p* of **hang**.

Hungarian *hung-gā'ri-ən*, *adj* pertaining to *Hungary* or its inhabitants. — *n* a person of Hungarian birth, descent, or citizenship; the Magyar or Hungarian language.

hunger *hung'gər*, *n* craving for food; need or lack of food; strong desire for anything. — *vi* to crave food; to long. — *adj* **hung'rily**. — *adj* **hung'ry** having an eager desire for food; greedy, desirous, longing (with *for*); lean; poor; used in combination to signify eager for, in need of, as in *land-hungry*. — **hunger march** a procession of unemployed or others in need, as a demonstration; **hung'er-marcher; hunger strike** prolonged refusal of all food by a prisoner, etc. as a form of protest, or a means to ensure release. — *vi* **hung'er-strike**. — **hung'er-striker**. — **go hungry** to remain without food. [O.E. *hungor* (n.), *hyngran* (vb.).]

hung over, hung up. See under **hang**.

hunk *hungk*, *n* a lump; a strong or sexually attractive man (*colloq*). — *adj* **hunk'y** (*colloq*) strong or sexually attractive. [Ety. as for **hunch**.]

hunky-dory *hung-ki-dō'ri*, (*colloq*) *adj* in good position or condition; excellent; all right.

hunker *hung'kər*, *vi* to squat (often with *down*). — *npl* **hunk'ers** the hams or haunches. [Perh. connected with O.N. *hūka*, to squat.]

hunky[1] *hung'ki*, (*NAm*) *n* a derogatory name for a person of East European descent, esp. an unskilled workman. [For **Hungarian**.]

hunky[2]. See **hunk**.

hunt *hunt*, *vt* to chase or go in quest of for prey or sport; to search for; to pursue; to hound or drive; to seek or pursue game over; to use in the hunt. — *vi* to go out in pursuit of game; to search; to oscillate or vary in speed (*mech*); (of a bell) to move its order of ringing through a set of changes (**hunt up** to be rung progressively earlier; **hunt down** to be rung progressively later). — *n* a chase of wild animals; a search; a pack of hunting hounds; an association of huntsmen; the district hunted by a pack. — *n* **hunt'er** a person or animal that hunts (*fem* **hunt'ress**); a horse used in hunting, esp. fox-hunting; a watch whose face is protected with a metal case (a **half'-hunter** if that case has a small circle of glass let in). — **hunt ball** a ball given by the members of a hunt; **hunter-gath'erer** (*anthrop*) a member of a society which lives by hunting and gathering fruit, etc., as opposed e.g. to cultivating crops; **hunter-kill'er** a surface craft or submarine designed to hunt down and destroy enemy vessels; **hunter's moon** full moon following harvest moon; **hunt'ing-box, -lodge** or **-seat** temporary accommodation for hunters; **hunt'ing-cog** an extra cog in one of two geared wheels, by means of which the order of contact of cogs is changed at every revolution; **hunt'ing-horn** a horn used in hunting, a bugle; **hunt'ing-spider** a wolf-spider; **hunt saboteur** a person opposed to all blood sports, esp. fox-hunting, who usu. as part of an organised group, takes action to thwart the activities of hunters; **hunts'man** a person who hunts; a person who manages the hounds during a fox-hunt; **hunt-the-slipp'er** a game in which a person in the middle of a ring tries to catch a shoe passed around by the others. — **good hunting!** (*colloq*) good luck!; **hunt after** or **for** to search for; **hunt down** to pursue to extremities; to persecute out of existence; see also at **hunt** above; **hunt out** or **up** to seek out; **hunt up** see **hunt** above. [O.E. *huntian*.]

Huon pine *hū'on pīn*, *n* a Tasmanian conifer found first on the *Huon* river.

hurdle *hûr'dl*, *n* (in certain races) a portable barrier over which runners jump; an obstacle to be surmounted, difficulty to be overcome; a frame of twigs or sticks interlaced; a movable frame of timber or iron for gates, etc.; a rude sledge on which criminals were drawn to the gallows (*hist*). — *vt* to jump over (a hurdle, an obstacle, etc.); to enclose with hurdles. — *n* **hurd'ler** an athlete who takes part in hurdles events; a maker of hurdles. [O.E. *hyrdel*.]

hurdy-gurdy *hûr-di-gûr'di*, *n* a stringed musical instrument, whose strings are sounded by the turning of a wheel; a barrel-organ. [Imit.]

hurl *hûrl*, *vt* to fling with violence. — *vi* to play hurley. — *n* an act of hurling. — *n* **hurl'ey** or **hurl'ing** a game similar to hockey, of Irish origin, played by teams of 15, with broad-bladed sticks (**hurl'eys**) and a hide-covered cork ball. [Cf. L.G. *hurreln*, to hurl, precipitate; influenced by **hurtle** and **whirl**.]

hurly-burly *hûr-li-bûr'li*, *n* tumult; confusion. [Perh. from **hurl**.]

hurrah, hoorah *hōō-rä'* or **hurray, hooray** *hōō-rā'*, *interj* an exclamation of approbation or joy. — Also *n* and *vi*. [Cf. Norw., Sw., Dan. *hurra*, Ger. *hurrah*, Du. *hoera*.]

hurricane *hur'i-kən* or *-kān*, *n* a West Indian cyclonic storm of great violence; a wind of extreme violence; a tumult, commotion; (with *cap*) a type of fighting aeroplane used in World War II. — **hurricane lamp** an oil lamp encased so as to defy strong wind; a protected electric lamp. [Sp. *huracán*, from Carib.]

hurry *hur'i*, *vt* to urge forward; to hasten. — *vi* to move or act with haste, esp. perturbed or impatient haste: — *pr p* **hurr'ying**; *pa t* and *pa p* **hurr'ied**. — *n* a driving forward; haste; flurried or undue haste; commotion; a rush; need for haste. — *adj* **hurr'ied**. — *adv* **hurr'iedly**. — *n* **hurr'iedness**. — **hurry-scurr'y** confusion and bustle. — *adv* confusedly. — **in a hurry** in haste, speedily; soon; easily; willingly; **hurry up** to make haste. [Prob. imit.]

hurt *hûrt*, *vt* to cause pain to; to damage; to injure; to wound (someone's feelings, etc.). — *vi* to give pain; to be the seat or source of pain; to be injured (*colloq*; esp. *NAm*): — *pa t* and *pa p* **hurt**. — *n* a wound; injury. — *adj* injured; pained in body or mind. — *adj* **hurt'ful** causing hurt or loss; harmful, esp. emotionally. — *adv* **hurt'fully**. — *n* **hurt'fulness**. [O.Fr. *hurter*, to knock, to run against.]

hurtle *hûr'tl*, *vt* to dash; to hurl. — *vi* to move rapidly with a clattering sound. [Frequentative of **hurt** in its original sense of strike or knock.]

husband *huz'bənd*, *n* a man to whom a woman is married. — *vt* to manage with economy; to conserve. — *n* **hus'bandry** the business of a farmer; tillage; economical management; thrift. [O.E. *hūsbonda*, O.N. *hūsbōndi* — *hūs*, a house, *būandi*, inhabiting, pres. p. of O.N. *būa*, to dwell.]

hush *hush*, *interj* or *imper* silence; be still. — *n* a silence, esp. after noise. — *adj* (*colloq*) for the purpose of concealing information (e.g. *hush money*). — *vi* to become silent or quiet. — *vt* to make quiet; to calm; to procure silence or secrecy about (sometimes with *up*). — *n* **hush'aby** (-ə-bī) a lullaby used to soothe babies to sleep. — Also *vt* and *interj*. — *adj* **hush-hush'** (*colloq*) secret. — **hush kit** (*colloq*) a device fitted to the jet engine of an aeroplane to reduce noise; **hush puppy** (*US*; usu. in *pl*) a ball or balls of maize dough, deep-fried (from its occasional use as dog food); a light soft esp. suede shoe for men. — **hush up** to stifle, suppress; to be silent. [Imit.]

husk *husk*, *n* the dry, thin covering of certain fruits and seeds; a case, shell or covering, esp. one that is worthless or coarse; (in *pl*) refuse, waste. — *vt* to remove the husk or outer integument from. — *adv* **husk'ily**. — *n* **husk'iness**. — *adj* **husk'y** of the nature of husks; like a husk; dry; sturdy like a corn-husk; (of a voice) dry and almost whispering; (of words) spoken in a husky voice. — *n* (*NAm*) a big strong man. [Perh. connected with **house**.]

husky[1] *hus'ki*, *n* an Eskimo sledge-dog. [App. — *Eskimo*.]

husky[2]. See **husk**.

huss *hus*, *n* dogfish when used as food. [M.E. *huske*.]

hussar *hōō-zär'* or *hə-*, *n* a soldier of a light cavalry regiment; orig. a soldier of the national cavalry of Hungary in the 15th century. [Hung. *huszar*, through Old Serb. — It. *corsaro*, a freebooter.]

Hussite *hus'īt* or *hōōs'īt*, *n* a follower of the Bohemian reformer John *Hus*, martyred in 1415.

hussy *hus'i* or *huz'i*, (*derog*) *n* a promiscuous or worthless girl or woman. [**housewife**.]

hustings *hus'tingz*, *nsing* formerly the booths where the votes were taken at an election of an M.P., or the platform from which the candidates gave their addresses; electioneering (esp. in the phrase *on the hustings*). [O.E. *hūsting*, a council — O.N. *hūsthing* — *hūs*, a house, *thing*, an assembly.]

hustle *hus'l*, *vt* to shake or push together; to crowd with violence; to jostle; to thrust hastily; to exert pressure on; to obtain (money) illicitly (*slang*). — *vi* to act strenuously or aggressively; (of e.g. a prostitute) to earn money illicitly (*slang*). — *n* frenzied activity; a type of lively disco dance with a variety of steps. — *n* **hus'tler** a lively or energetic person; a swindler (*slang*); a prostitute (*slang*). [Du. *hutselen*, to shake to and fro.]

hut *hut*, *n* a small or crudely built house; a small temporary dwelling or similar structure. — *vt* to quarter (troops) in or furnish with a hut or huts. — *vi* to dwell in a hut or huts: — *pr p* **hutt'ing**; *pa t* and *pa p* **hutt'ed**. — *n* **hut'ment** an encampment of huts (*mil*). — **hut'-circle** (*antiq*) the remains of a prehistoric circular hut, a pit lined with stones, etc. [Fr. *hutte* — O.H.G. *hutta*.]

hutch *huch*, *n* a cage for small animals, esp. rabbits; a small, cramped house (*colloq*); a trough used with some ore-dressing machines; a low wagon in which coal is drawn up out of the pit. [Fr. *huche*, a chest — L.L. *hūtica*, a box.]

HV or **hv** *abbrev* for high voltage.

HWM *abbrev* for high water mark.

hyacinth *hī'ə-sinth*, *n* a bulbous genus (*Hyacinthus*) of the lily family, much cultivated; extended to others of the family, as **wild hyacinth** (the English bluebell), **grape hyacinth** (*Muscari*), **Cape hyacinth** a species of Galtonia, *G. candicans*, with white flowers; a purple colour, of various hues; a red, brown, or yellow zircon; a blue stone of the ancients (perh. aquamarine). — *adj* **hyacin'thine**. [Gr. *hyakinthos*, a flower (the bluebell or blue larkspur) that sprang from the head of *Hyakinthos*, a youth killed by Apollo, or a blue stone.]

Hyades *hī'ə-dēz* or **Hyads** *hī'adz*, *npl* a cluster of five stars in the constellation of the Bull, supposed by the ancients to bring rain when they rose with the sun. [Gr. *Hўădĕs*, *Hўădĕs*, explained by the ancients as from *hyein*, to rain; more prob. little pigs, *hўs*, a pig.]

hyaena. See **hyena.**

hyaline *hī'ə-lin* or *-līn*, *adj* of or like glass; clear; transparent. — *n* **hyalinisā'tion** or **-z-**. — *vt* and *vi* **hy'alinise** or **-ize** (*med*) (of tissue) to change to a firm, glassy consistency. — *n* **hy'alite** transparent colourless opal. — *adj* **hy'aloid** (*anat*) hyaline, transparent. — **hyaline cartilage** a translucent bluish-white cartilage, e.g. covering bones at points of articulation; **hyaline degeneration** hyalinisation; **hyaloid membrane** the transparent membrane which encloses the vitreous humour of the eye. [Gr. *hyalos*, glass.]

hybrid *hī'brid*, *n* an organism which is the offspring of a union between different races, species, genera or varieties; a mongrel; a word formed of elements from different languages. — *adj* produced from different species, etc.; mongrel. — *adj* **hy'bridīsable** or **-z-**. — *n* **hy'bridīsātion** or **-z-**. — *vt* **hy'bridise** or **-ize** to cause to interbreed. — *vi* to interbreed. — *n* **hy'bridīser** or **-z-**. — *n* **hy'bridism**. — *n* **hybridō'ma** a hybrid cell produced from a cancer cell and an antibody-producing cell. — **hybrid bill** (*politics*) a parliamentary public bill which affects certain private interests; **hybrid computer** one which combines features of digital and analog computers; **hybrid vigour** heterosis. [L. *hibrida*, offspring of a tame sow and wild boar; with associations of Gr. *hybris*, insolence, overweening.]

hydatid *hī'də-tid*, *n* a water cyst or vesicle in an animal body, esp. one containing a tapeworm larva; the larva itself; hydatid disease. — *adj* **hydatid'iform** resembling a hydatid. — **hydatid disease** an infection, esp. of the liver, caused by tapeworm larvae, giving rise to expanding cysts. [Gr. *hydatis*, *-idos*, a watery vesicle — *hydōr*, *hydatos*, water.]

hydr-. See **hydro-**.

Hydra *hī'drə*, *n* a water-monster with many heads, which when cut off were succeeded by others (*mythol*); a large southern constellation; (without *cap*) any manifold evil; (without *cap*) a freshwater hydrozoon, remarkable for power of multiplication on being cut or divided. [Gr. *hydrā* — *hydōr*, water.]

hydrangea *hī-drān'jə* or *-jyə*, *n* any plant of a genus (*Hydrangea*) of shrubby plants with large globular clusters of showy flowers, native to China and Japan. [**hydr-** and Gr. *angeion*, vessel.]

hydrant *hī'drənt*, *n* a connection for attaching a hose to a water main or a fire-plug. [**hydr-** and sfx. *-ant*.]

hydrate, hydraulic, etc. See under **hydro-**.

hydrazine *hī'drə-zēn*, *n* a fuming corrosive liquid used as a rocket fuel; any of a class of organic bases derived from it. — **hydrazoic** (*-zō'ik*) **acid** a colourless, foul-smelling liquid that combines with lead and other heavy metals to produce explosive salts (azides). [From **hydr-** and **azo-**.]

hydric. See **hydro-, hydrogen.**

hydride, hydriodic. See **hydrogen**.

hydro *hī'drō*, *n* short form of **hydroelectric** or **hydropathic establishment** (see under **hydro-**): — *pl* **hy'dros**.

hydro- *hī-drō-*, *hī-drə-* or *hī-dro'-*, or **hydr-** *combining form* denoting of, like or by means of, water (see also **hydrogen**). — *n* **hydrarthrō'sis** (*med*) swelling of a joint caused by the accumulation in it of watery fluid. — *n* **hy'drate** a compound containing water which is chemically combined and which can be expelled without affecting the composition of the other substance. — *vt* to combine with water; to cause to absorb water. — *n* **hydrā'tion**. — *adj* **hydraulic** (*hī-drö'lik* or *-drol'*; Gr. *aulos*, a pipe) relating to hydraulics; conveying water; worked by water or other liquid in pipes; setting in water. — *adv* **hydraul'ically**. — *nsing* **hydraul'ics** the science of hydrodynamics in general, or its practical application to water pipes, etc. — *adj* **hy'dric** pertaining to an abundance of moisture; see also under **hydrogen**. — *n* **hy'drocele** (*-sēl*; Gr. *kēlē*, swelling; *med*) a swelling containing serous fluid, esp. in the scrotum. — *adj* **hydrocephal'ic** or **hydroceph'alous**. — *n* **hydrocephalus** (*-sef'ə-ləs*, or *-kef'*) an accumulation of serous fluid within the cranial cavity. — *adj* **hydrodynamic** (*-dī-nam'ik*) or **hydrodynam'ical**. — *n* **hydrodynam'icist**. — *nsing* **hydrodynam'ics** the science of the motions and equilibrium of a material system partly or wholly fluid (called *hydrostatics* when the system is in equilibrium, *hydrokinetics* when it is not). — *adj* **hydroelastic** see **hydroelastic suspension** below. — *adj* **hydroelec'tric**. — *n* **hydroelectric'ity** electricity produced by means of water, esp. by water-power. — *n* **hy'drofoil** a device on a boat for raising it from the water as its speed increases; a boat fitted with this device. — *n* **hydrog'rapher**. — *adj* **hydrographic** (*-graf'ik*) or **hydrograph'ical**. — *adv* **hydrograph'ically**. — *n* **hydrog'raphy** the investigation of seas and other bodies of water, including charting, sounding, study of tides, currents, etc. — *adj* **hy'droid** like a Hydra; polypoid. — *n* a hydrozoan; a hydrozoan in its asexual generation. — *adj* **hydrokinet'ic** pertaining to hydrokinetics; pertaining to the motion of fluids; pertaining to fluids in motion; operated or operating by the movement of fluids. — *nsing* **hydrokinet'ics** a branch of hydrodynamics (q.v.). — *adj* **hydrolog'ic** or **hydrolog'ical**. — *adv* **hydrolog'ically**. — *n* **hydrol'ogist**. — *n* **hydrol'ogy** the study of the water resources of the world. — *vt* **hydrolyse** or **-yze** (*hī'drə-līz*) to subject to hydrolysis. — Also *vi*. — *n*

hydrolysis (*hī-drol'i-sis*) chemical decomposition or ionic dissociation caused by water. — *n* **hy'drolyte** (*-līt*) a body subjected to hydrolysis. — *adj* **hydrolytic** (*-lit'ik*). — *adj* **hydromagnet'ic**. — *nsing* **hydromagnet'ics** magnetohydrodynamics. — *n* **hydromā'nia** a craving for water. — *nsing* **hydromechan'ics** hydrodynamics. — *n* **hy'dromel** (Gr. *hydromeli* — *meli*, honey) a beverage made of honey and water; mead. — *n* **hydrom'eter** a float for measuring specific gravity. — *adj* **hydrometric** (*-met'*) or **hydromet'rical**. — *n* **hydrom'etry**. — *n* **hy'dronaut** a person trained to work in an underwater vessel, e.g. a submarine. — *adj* **hydropathic** (*hī-drə-path'ik*) of, for, relating to or practising hydropathy. — *n* (in full **hydropathic establishment**; *colloq* **hy'dro**, *pl* **hy'dros**) a hotel (with special baths, etc., and often situated near a spa) where guests can have hydropathic treatment. — *adv* **hydropath'ically**. — *n* **hydrop'athist** a person who practises hydropathy. — *n* **hydrop'athy** the treatment of disease by water, externally and internally. — *n* **hydrophane** (*hī'drə-fān*; Gr. *phānos*, bright) a translucent opal transparent in water. — *adj* **hydrophil'ic** (*chem*) attracting water. — *n* **hydrophō'bia** horror of water; inability to swallow water owing to a contraction in the throat, a symptom of rabies; rabies itself. — *adj* **hydrophō'bic** pertaining to hydrophobia; repelling water (*chem*). — *n* **hydrophobic'ity**. — *n* **hy'drophone** (*-fōn*) an apparatus for listening to sounds conveyed by water. — *n* **hy'drophyte** (*-fīt*) a plant growing in water or in very moist conditions. — *adj* **hydrophytic** (*-fit'ik*). — *n* **hy'droplane** a light, flat-bottomed motorboat which, at high speed, skims along the surface of the water; a seaplane. — *vi* (of a boat) to skim like a hydroplane; (of a vehicle) to skid on a wet road. — *adj* **hydropneumat'ic** using water and air acting together. — *n* **hydropol'yp** a hydrozoan polyp. — *adj* **hydropon'ic**. — *adv* **hydropon'ically**. — *nsing* **hydroponics** (*hī-drə-pon'iks*; Gr. *ponos*, toil) the art or practice of growing plants in (sand or gravel containing) a chemical solution without soil. — *n* **hy'dropower** hydroelectric power. — *n* **hydroquinone** (*-kwin-ōn'*, *-kwin'*, or *-kwī'*) quinol. — *n* **hydrosphere** (*hī'drə-sfēr*) the water on the surface of the earth — the seas and oceans. — *adj* **hydrostat'ic** or **hydrostat'ical**. — *adv* **hydrostat'ically**. — *nsing* **hydrostat'ics** a branch of hydrodynamics (q.v.). — *adj* **hydrotherapeu'tic**. — *n* **hydrother'apy** or **hydrotherapeu'tics** treatment of disease by the external use of water, e.g. treatment of disability by developing movement in water. — *adj* **hydrotrop'ic**. — *n* **hydrot'ropism** the turning of a plant root towards (*positive*) or away from (*negative*) moisture. — *adj* **hydrous** (*hī'drəs*; *chem* and *mineralogy*) containing water. — *npl* **Hydrozō'a** a class of Coelenterata, chiefly marine organisms in which alternation of generations typically occurs, the hy droid phase colonial, giving rise to the medusoid phase by budding — e.g. the zoophytes, etc.; sometimes extended to include the true jellyfishes; (without *cap*) hydrozoans. — *n* and *adj* **hydrozō'an**. — *n* **hydrozō'on** a coelenterate of the Hydrozoa: — *pl* **hydrozō'a**. — **hydraulic brake** a brake in which the force is transmitted by means of a compressed fluid; **hydraulic press** a press operated by forcing water into a cylinder in which a ram or plunger works; **hydraulic ram** a device whereby the pressure head produced when a moving column of water is brought to rest is caused to deliver some of the water under pressure; **hydraulic suspension** a system of car suspension using hydraulic units; **hydroelastic suspension** a system of car suspension in which a fluid provides interconnection between the front and rear suspension units; **hydrostatic paradox** the principle that, disregarding molecular forces, any quantity of fluid, however small, may balance any weight, however great; **hydrostatic press** a hydraulic press. [Gr. *hydōr*, water.]

hydrobromic ... to ... **hydrofluoric**. See under **hydrogen**.

hydrogen *hī'drə-jən*, *n* a gas (symbol **H**; atomic no. 1) which in combination with oxygen produces water, is the lightest of all known substances and very inflammable, and is of great importance in the moderation (slowing down) of neutrons. — *adj* **hy'dric** of or containing hydrogen. — *n* **hy'dride** a compound of hydrogen with an element or radical. — *adj* **hydriodic** (*hī-dri-od'ik*) of an acid composed of hydrogen and iodine, hydrogen iodide. — **hydro-** (*hī-drō-*, *hī-drə-*, or *hī-dro'-*) *combining form* denoting hydrogen in a chemical compound. — *adj* **hydrobrō'mic** applied to an acid composed of hydrogen and bromine, hydrogen bromide. — *n* **hy'drocarbon** a compound of hydrogen and carbon with nothing else, occurring notably in oil, natural gas and coal. — *adj* **hydrochloric** (*-klor'ik* or *-klōr'*) applied to an acid composed of hydrogen and chlorine, hydrogen chloride, still sometimes called *muriatic acid*. — *n* **hydrochlor'ide** a compound of hydrochloric acid with an organic base. — *n* **hydrocor'tisone** one of the corticosteroids, a synthesised form of which is used to treat rheumatoid arthritis, etc. — *adj* **hydrocyanic** (*-sī-an'ik*) denoting an acid (*prussic acid*) composed of hydrogen and cyanogen. — *adj* **hydrofluor'ic** applied to an acid composed of fluorine and hydrogen, hydrogen fluoride. — *vt* and *vi* **hydrogenate** (*hī'drə-jə-nāt* or *hī-droj'ə-nāt*) to combine with hydrogen. — *n* **hydrogenā'tion**. — *adj* **hydrog'enous**. — *n* **hydrosul'phide** a compound formed by action of hydrogen sulphide on a hydroxide. — *n* **hydrosul'phite** a hyposulphite (esp. sodium hyposulphite). — *adj* **hydrosulphū'ric** formed by a combination of hydrogen and sulphur. — *n* **hydrox'ide** a chemical compound which contains one or more hydroxyl groups. — *adj* **hydrox'y** (of a compound) containing one or more hydroxyl groups (also *combining form* **hydroxy-**). — *n* **hydrox'yl** a compound radical consisting of one atom of oxygen and one of hydrogen. — **hydrogen bomb** or **H'-bomb** a bomb in which an enormous release of energy is achieved by converting hydrogen nuclei into helium nuclei — a fusion, not fission, process started by great heat; **hydrogen ion** an atom or molecule of hydrogen having a positive charge, esp. an atom formed in a solution of acid in water — strong acids being highly ionised and weak acids only slightly; **hydrogen peroxide** see under **peroxide**; **hydrogen sulphide** a compound of hydrogen and sulphur. — **heavy hydrogen** see under **heavy**. [Coined by Cavendish (1766) from Gr. *hydōr*, water, and *gennaein*, to produce.]

hyena or **hyaena** *hī-ē'nə*, *n* a carrion-feeding carnivore (genus *Hyaena*, constituting a family *Hyaenidae* with long thick neck, coarse mane and sloping body. — **hyena dog** an African wild dog, with markings like those of a hyena. — **spotted hyena** an animal (*Crocuta*) resembling a hyena, with a hysterical-sounding laugh. [L. *hyaena* — Gr. *hyaina* — *hȳs*, a pig.]

hyetal *hī'i-tl*, *adj* pertaining to rain or rainfall. [Gr. *hȳetos*, rain.]

hygiene *hī'jēn*, *n* the science or art of preserving health; sanitary principles and practices. — *adj* **hygienic** (*hī-jēn'ik*). — *adv* **hygien'ically**. — *nsing* **hygien'ics** principles of hygiene. — *n* **hygien'ist** (or *hī'ji-nist*) a person skilled in hygiene. [Fr. *hygiène* — Gr. *hygieinē* (*technē*), hygienic (art) — *hygieiă*, health.]

hygro- *hī-grō-*, *hī-grə-* or *-gro'-*, *combining form* signifying wet, moist. — *n* **hygrol'ogy** the study of the humidity of the air or other gases. — *n* **hygrom'eter** an instrument for measuring the humidity of the air or of other gases. — *adj* **hygro-**

metric (*-met'rik*) or **hygromet'rical** belonging to hygrometry; hygroscopic. — *n* **hygrom'etry** measurement of the humidity of the air or of other gases. — *adj* **hy'grophil** or **hygrophilous** (*-grof'*) moisture-loving; living where there is much moisture. — *n* **hy'grophyte** (*-fīt*) a plant adapted to plentiful water-supply. — *adj* **hygrophytic** (*-fit'ik*). — *n* **hy'groscope** an instrument that shows, without measuring, changes in the humidity of the air. — *adj* **hygroscopic** (*-skop'ik*) or **hygroscop'ical** relating to the hygroscope; readily absorbing moisture from the air; (of e.g. some movements of plants) indicating or caused by absorption or loss of moisture. — *n* **hygroscopicity** (*-sko-pis'i-ti*). [Gr. *hygros*, wet.]

hying *hī'ing, pr p* of **hie**.

hymen *hī'men, n* a thin membrane partially closing the vagina of a virgin. — *adj* **hy'menal** pertaining to the hymen. [Gr. *hymen*, membrane.]

Hymenoptera *hī-mə-nop'tə-rə, npl* an order of insects with four transparent wings — ants, bees, wasps, etc. — *n* and *adj* **hymenop'teran**. — *adj* **hymenop'terous**. [N.L. — Gr. *hȳmenopteros*, membrane-winged.]

hymn *him, n* a song of praise, esp. to God, but also to a nation, etc. — *vt* to celebrate in song; to worship by hymns. — *vi* to sing in adoration: — *pr p* **hymning** (*him'ing*); *pa t* and *pa p* **hymned** (*himd*). — *n* **hym'nal** or **hym'nary** a hymn-book. — Also *adj*. — *adj* **hym'nic**. — *n* **hym'nist** or **hym'nodist** a person who composes hymns. — *n* **hym'nody** hymns collectively; hymn-singing; hymnology. — *n* **hymnographer** (*him-nog'*). — *n* **hymnog'raphy** the art of writing hymns; the study of hymns. — *n* **hymnol'ogist** (*him-nol'*). — *n* **hymnol'ogy** the study or composition of hymns. — **hymn'-book** a book of hymns. [Gr. *hymnos*.]

hyoid *hī'oid, adj* having the form of the Greek letter upsilon (*υ*), applied to a bone at the base of the tongue. [Gr. *hȳoeidēs* — *hȳ*, the letter upsilon, and *eidos*, form.]

Hyoscyamus *hī-ō-sī'ə-məs, n* the henbane genus. — *n* **hy'oscine** (*-sēn, -sən*; also called **scopolamine**; used as a truth drug, for travel sickness, etc.) and **hyoscy'amine** two poisonous alkaloids similar to atropine, obtained from henbane. [Gr. *hyoskyamos*.]

hyp. *abbrev* for: hypotenuse; hypothesis; hypothetical.

hypaethral *hi-pē'thrəl* or (esp. in N.Am.) *hī-, adj* roofless, open to the sky. — *n* **hypae'thron** an open court. [Gr. *hypo*, beneath, *aithēr*, upper air, sky.]

hypallage *hi-pal'ə-jē* or *hī-*, (*rhet*) *n* a figure of speech in which the customary relations of words in a sentence are mutually interchanged. — *adj* **hypallact'ic**. [Gr. *hypo*, under, *allassein*, to exchange.]

hype *hīp*, (*slang*) *n* a hypodermic needle; a drug addict; something which stimulates artificially; intensive or artificially induced excitement about or enthusiasm for something or someone; a sales gimmick, etc.; a publicity stunt; the person or thing promoted by such a stunt; a deception. — *vi* (esp. with *up*) to inject oneself with a drug. — *vt* (often with *up*) to stimulate artificially; to promote or to advertise extravagantly. — **hyped up** (or **hyped'-up** when attributive) artificially stimulated; highly excited; artificial, fake. [Abbrev. of **hypodermic**.]

hyper- *hī-pər-* or *hī-pûr'-, combining form* signifying: over; excessive; more than normal. — *n* **hyperacid'ity** excessive acidity, esp. in the stomach. — *adj* **hyperact'ive** abnormally or pathologically active. — *n* **hyperactiv'ity**. — *n* **hyperaemia** or in N.Am. **hyperemia** (*-ē'mi-ə*) congestion or excess of blood in any part of the body. — *adj* **hyperae'mic** or in N.Am. **hypere'mic**. — *n* **hyperaesthesia** (*-ēs-thē'zi-ə*) or in N.Am. **hyperesthesia** (*-is-thē'*) excessive sensitivity to stimuli; an abnormal extension of the bodily senses assumed to explain telepathy and clairvoyance. — *adj* **hyperaesthetic** or in N.Am. **hyperesthetic** (*-thet'ik*) abnormally or morbidly sensitive. — *n* **hyper'baton** (*rhet*) a figure of speech in which the customary order of words is reversed. — *n* **hyper'bola** (Gr. *hyperbolē*, over-shooting; *pl* usu. **hyper'bolas**; *geom*) one of the conic sections, the intersection of a plane with a cone when the plane cuts both branches of the cone. — *n* **hyperbole** (*hī-pûr'bə-li*) a rhetorical figure of speech which produces a vivid impression by extravagant and obvious exaggeration. — *adj* **hyperbol'ic** or **hyperbol'ical** of a hyperbola or hyperbole. — *adv* **hyperbol'ically**. — *vt* **hyper'bolise** or **-ize** to represent hyperbolically. — *vi* to speak hyperbolically or with exaggeration. — *n* **hyper'bolism**. — *n* **hyper'boloid** a solid figure certain of whose plane sections are hyperbolas. — *adj* **hyperborean** (*-bö'*; Gr. *Hyperboreoi*, a people supposed to live in sunshine beyond the north wind — *Boreas*, the north wind) belonging to the extreme north. — *n* an inhabitant of the extreme north. — *n* **hypercrit'ic**. — *adj* **hypercrit'ical** excessively critical, esp. of very small faults. — *adv* **hypercrit'ically**. — *vt* **hypercrit'icise** or **-ize** (*-sīz*). — *n* **hypercrit'icism**. — *n* **hyperdulia** (*-dōō-lī'ə*) see **dulia**. — **hyperemia, hyperesthesia** see **hyperaemia, hyperaesthesia** above. — *adj* **hypereutec'tic** (of a compound) containing more of the minor component than a eutectic compound. — *adj* **hyperfō'cal** (*phot*) referring to the minimum distance from a lens to the point from which all objects can be focused clearly. — *adj* **hyper'gamous** pertaining to hypergamy. — *n* **hypergamy** (*hī-pûr'gə-mi*) a custom that allows a man but forbids a woman to marry a person of lower social standing; now sometimes more generally marriage of one person with another of higher social rank. — *n* **hyperglycaemia** or in N.Am. **hyperglycemia** (*-glī-sē'mi-ə*) abnormal rise in the sugar content of the blood. — *adj* **hypergolic** (*-gol'ik*) (of two or more liquids) spontaneously explosive on mixing. — *n* **hyperinflā'tion** rapid inflation uncontrollable by normal means. — *n* **hy'permarket** a very large self-service store with a wide range of goods. — *adj* **hypermet'rical** (*prosody*) beyond or exceeding the ordinary metre of a line; having or being an additional syllable. — *n* **hypermetrō'pia** long-sightedness. — Also **hyperō'pia**. — *adj* **hypermetrop'ic**. — *n* **hy'pernym** (Gr. *onyma*, name) a superordinate word representing a class or family of which several other words can be members, as *flower* is a hypernym of *rose* and *daisy*. — *n* **hyper'nymy**. — *n* **hy'peron** any baryon that is not a nucleon. — *n* **hyperpar'asite** a parasite living on another parasite. — *adj* **hyperphys'ical** beyond physical laws; supernatural. — *n* **hyperpyrex'ia** abnormally high body temperature. — *adj* **hypersens'itive** excessively sensitive. — *n* **hypersens'itiveness** or **hypersensitiv'ity**. — *n* **hypersom'nia** a pathological tendency to sleep excessively. — *adj* **hyperson'ic** (of speeds) greater than Mach 5; (of aircraft) able to fly at such speeds; (of sound waves) having a frequency greater than 1000 million Hz. — *npl* **hyperson'ics**. — *n* **hy'perspace** (*math*) space having more than three dimensions; (in science fiction) a theoretical fourth dimension. — *n* **hypersthene** (*hī'pər-sthēn*; Gr. *sthenos*, strength) rock-forming orthorhombic pyroxene, anhydrous silicate of magnesium and iron, generally dark green, brown, or raven-black with metallic lustre. — *n* **hyperten'sion** blood pressure higher than normal; a state of great emotional tension. — *adj* **hyperten'sive**. — *n* a victim of hypertension. — *adj* **hypertherm'al**. — *n* **hypertherm'ia** (dangerous) overheating of the body. — *n* **hyperthyroidism** (*-thī'roi-dizm*) overproduction of thyroid hormone by the thyroid gland, and the resulting condition. — *adj* **hyperton'ic** (of muscles) having excessive tone;

tensed to an abnormally high degree; (of a solution) having a higher osmotic pressure than a specified solution. — *adj* **hypertroph'ic** or **hyper'trophied.** — *n* **hyper'trophy** overnourishment (of an organ, etc.) causing abnormal enlargement. — *n* **hyperventilā'tion** abnormally increased speed and depth of breathing. — **hyperbolic functions** (*math*) a set of six functions (sinh, cosh, tanh, etc.) analogous to the trigonometrical functions; **hyperbolic geometry** that involving the axiom that through any point in a given plane there can be drawn more than one line that does not intersect a given line; **hyperbolic logarithms** natural logarithms; **hyperfine structure** (*phys*) the splitting of spectrum lines into two or more very closely spaced components. [Gr. *hyper*, over.]

hyperb. *abbrev* for hyperbolically.

hypericum *hī-per'i-kəm*, *n* any shrub of the genus *Hypericum*, with yellow five-petalled flowers, the St John's wort. [Gr. *hyperikon* — *hypo*, under, *ereikē*, heath.]

hypha *hī'fə*, *n* a thread of fungus mycelium: — *pl* **hy'phae** (*-fē*). — *adj* **hy'phal.** [Gr. *hyphē*, web.]

hyphen *hī'fən*, *n* a short stroke (-) joining two syllables or words. — *vt* to hyphenate. — *vt* **hy'phenate** to join or separate by a hyphen. — *adj* **hy'phenated** containing a hyphen; of mixed nationality, expressed by a hyphenated word, e.g. Irish-American (*NAm*). — *n* **hyphena'tion.** [Gr. *hyphĕn* — *hypo*, under, *hen*, one.]

hypno- *hip-nō-*, *hip-nə-* or *hip-no'-*, or **hypn-** *combining form* denoting: sleep; hypnosis. — *n* **hypnoanal'ysis** psychoanalysis of a hypnotised patient. — *n* **hypnogen'esis** production of the hypnotic state. — *adj* **hypnogenet'ic** or **hypnogen'ic.** — *adj* **hyp'noid** or **hypnoid'al** like sleep; like hypnosis; esp. of a state between hypnosis and waking. — *n* **hypnol'ogy** the scientific study of sleep. — *n* **hypnopae'dia** learning or conditioning, by repetition of recorded sound during sleep (or semi-wakefulness). — *adj* **hypnopomp'ic** (Gr. *pompē*, a sending) dispelling sleep; pertaining to a state between sleep and wakefulness. — *n* **hypnō'sis** a sleeplike state in which the mind responds to external suggestion and can recover forgotten memories. — *n* **hypnotee'** a person who has been hypnotised. — *n* **hypnother'apy** the treatment of illness by hypnotism. — *adj* **hypnot'ic** of or relating to hypnosis; soporific. — *n* a soporific; a person subject to hypnotism or in a state of hypnosis. — *adv* **hypnot'ically.** — *adj* **hyp'notīsable** or **-z-.** — *n* **hypnotisabil'ity** or **-z-.** — *n* **hypnotīsā'tion** or **-z-.** — *vt* **hyp'notise** or **-ize** to put in a state of hypnosis; to fascinate, dazzle, overpower the mind of. — *n* **hyp'notism** the science of hypnosis; the art or practice of inducing hypnosis; hypnosis. — *n* **hyp'notist** a person skilled in hypnotism. [Gr. *hypnos*, sleep.]

hypo *hī'po*, (*colloq*) *n* short for **hyposulphite**, in the sense of sodium thiosulphate, used as a fixing agent (*phot*); short for **hypodermic syringe** or **injection** (see also **hype**): — *pl* **hy'pos.** — *adj* short for **hypodermic**; short for **hypoglycaemic.**

hypo- *hī-pō-*, *hī-pə-* or *hī-po'-* or occasionally *hip-ō-* or *hi-po'-*, *combining form* signifying: under; defective; inadequate. — *n* **hy'poblast** (*-bläst*; *zool*) the inner germ-layer of a gastrula. — *adj* **hypoblast'ic.** — *n* **hy'pocaust** (*-köst*; Gr. *hypokauston* — *hypo*, under, *kaiein*, to burn) a space under a floor for heating by hot air or furnace gases, esp. in ancient Roman villas. — *n* **hypochlorite** (*-klö'rīt*) a salt of **hypochlo'rous acid,** an acid (HClO) with less oxygen than chlorous acid. — *n* **hypochondria** (*-kon'dri-ə*) originally the *pl* of **hypochondrium** (see below); morbid anxiety about health; imaginary illness. — *adj* **hypochon'driac** relating to or affected with hypochondria; melancholy. — *n* a sufferer from hypochondria. — *adj* **hypochondrī'acal.** — *n* **hypochondrī'asis** hypochondria. — *n* **hypochon'drium** (Gr. *hypochondrion* — *chondros*, cartilage; *anat*) the region of the abdomen on either side, under the costal cartilages and short ribs. — *n* **hypocorism** (*hī-pok'ə-rizm*; Gr. *hypokorisma* — *hypokorizesthai*, to use child-talk) a pet-name; a diminutive or abbreviated name. — *adj* **hypocorist'ic** or **hypocorist'ical.** — *adv* **hypocorist'ically.** — *n* **hypocotyl** (*-kot'il*) that part of the axis of a plant which is between the cotyledons and the primary root. — *adj* **hypocotylē'donary.** — *n* **hypocrisy** (*hi-pok'ri-si*; Gr. *hypokrisiā*, acting, playing a part) a feigning to be better than one is, or to be what one is not; concealment of true character or belief (not necessarily conscious); an instance or act of hypocrisy. — *n* **hypocrite** (*hip'ə-krit*; Gr. *hypokritēs*, actor) a person who practises hypocrisy. — *adj* **hypocrit'ical** practising hypocrisy; of the nature of hypocrisy. — *adv* **hypocrit'ically.** — *n* **hypocycloid** (*-sī'kloid*) a curve generated by a point on the circumference of a circle which rolls on the inside of another circle. — *adj* **hypocycloid'al.** — *n* **hy'poderm** (*-dûrm*), **hypoder'ma** or **hypoder'mis** (*bot* and *anat*) the tissue beneath the epidermis. — *adj* **hypoder'mic** pertaining to the hypodermis; under the epidermis; under the skin, subcutaneous, esp. of a method of injecting a drug in solution under the skin by means of a fine hollow needle to which a small syringe is attached. — *n* a hypodermic injection; a drug so injected; a syringe for the purpose. — *adv* **hypoder'mically.** — *adj* **hypogastric** (*-gas'trik*) belonging to the lower median part of the abdomen. — *n* **hypogas'trium** the hypogastric region. — *adj* **hypogeal** (*-jē'əl*), **hypogean** (*-jē'ən*) or **hypogeous** (*-jē'əs*; Gr. *hypogeios*, *-gaios* — *gē* or *gaia*, the ground; *bot*) underground; germinating with cotyledons underground. — *adj* **hy'pogene** (*-jēn*; *geol*) of or pertaining to rocks formed, or agencies at work, under the earth's surface; plutonic (opp. to *epigene*). — *n* **hypogeum** (*-jē'əm*) an underground chamber; a subterranean tomb: — *pl* **hypoge'a.** — *adj* **hy'poid** of a type of bevel gear in which the axes of the driving and driven shafts are at right angles but not in the same plane. — *n* **hypolim'nion** (Gr. *limnion*, dimin. of *limnē*, lake) a lower and colder layer of water in a lake. — *n* **hypomania** (*-mā'ni-ə*; *pathol*) a milder form of mania, a condition marked by overexcitability. — *adj* **hypomanic** (*-man'*). — *n* **hy'ponasty** (*-nas-ti*; Gr. *nastos*, pressed close; *bot*) increased growth on the lower side causing an upward bend (opp. to *epinasty*). — *n* **hyponī'trite** a salt or ester of **hyponī'trous acid,** crystalline acid, an oxidising or reducing agent. — *n* **hy'ponym** (Gr. *onyma*, a name) one of a group of terms whose meanings are included in the meaning of a more general term, e.g. *spaniel* and *puppy* in the meaning of *dog*. — *n* **hypon'ymy.** — *n* **hypophosphite** (*-fos'fīt*) a salt of **hypophos'phorous acid,** an acid with less oxygen than phosphorous acid. — *adj* **hypophyseal** or **hypophysial** (*-fiz'i-əl*). — *n* **hypophysis** (*hī-pof'i-sis*; Gr. *hypophysis*, an attachment underneath — *phyein*, to grow; *pl* **hypoph'ysēs**) the pituitary gland. — *n* **hypostasis** (*hī-pos'tə-sis*; Gr. *hypostasis* — *stasis*, setting; *pl* **hypos'tasēs**) orig. basis, foundation; substance, essence (*metaphys*); the essence or real personal subsistence or substance of each of the three divisions of the Trinity; Christ as the union of human and divine qualities (*theol*). — *adj* **hypostatic** (*-stat'ik*) or **hypostat'ical.** — *adv* **hypostat'ically.** — *vt* **hypos'tatise** or **-ize** to treat as hypostasis; to personify. — *adj* **hypostyle** (*hī'pə-stīl*; Gr. *stȳlos*, pillar; *archit*) having the roof supported by pillars. — Also *n*. — *adj* **hypotac'tic.** — *n* **hypotaxis** (*-tak'sis*; Gr. *taxis*, arrangement; *gram*) dependent construction; subordination of one clause to another (opp. to *parataxis*). — *n* **hypo-**

ten'sion low blood-pressure. — *adj* **hypoten'sive.** — *n* a person with low blood-pressure. — *n* **hypotenuse** (*hī-pot'ə-nūz*; Fr. *hypoténuse* — L. *hypotēnūsa* — Gr. *hypoteinousa,* — *teinein,* to stretch) the side of a right-angled triangle opposite to the right angle. — *n* **hypothalamus** (*-thal'ə-məs*; L.L.; *med*) the part of the brain which makes up the floor and part of the lateral walls of the third ventricle. — *adj* **hypothalam'ic.** — *n* **hypothec** (*hī-poth'ik*; Gr. *hypothēkē,* a pledge) (in Scots law) a lien or security over goods in respect of a debt due by the owner of the goods. — *vt* **hypoth'ecate** to place or assign as security under an arrangement; to mortgage; to hypothesise (*NAm*). — *adj* **hypotherm'al.** — *n* **hypothermia** (*-thûr'mi-ə*) subnormal body temperature, caused by exposure to cold or induced for purposes of heart and other surgery (see **freeze down**). — *n* **hypothesis** (*hī-poth'i-sis*; Gr. *thesis,* placing) a supposition; a proposition assumed for the sake of argument; a theory to be proved or disproved by reference to facts; a provisional explanation of anything: — *pl* **hypoth'esēs.** — *vt* and *vi* **hypoth'esise** or **-ize.** — *adj* **hypothet'ic** or **hypothet'ical.** — *adv* **hypothet'ically.** — *adj* **hypothy'roid** pertaining to, or affected by, hypothyroidism. — *n* **hypothy'roidism** insufficient activity of the thyroid gland; a condition resulting from this, cretinism, etc. — *n* **hypotō'nia** a hypnotic condition. — *adj* **hypoton'ic** (of muscles) lacking normal tone; (of a solution) having lower osmotic pressure than a specified solution. — *n* **hypox'ia** deficiency of oxygen reaching the body tissues. — *adj* **hypox'ic.** [Gr. *hypo,* under.]

hypso- *hip-sō-, hip-sə-* or *hip-so'-*, *combining form* denoting height. — *n* **hypsog'raphy** the branch of geography dealing with the measurement and mapping of heights above sea-level; a map showing topographic relief; a method of making such a map. — *n* **hypsom'etry** the art of measuring the heights of places on the earth's surface. — *n* **hypsom'eter** an instrument for doing this by taking the boiling point of water. — *adj* **hypsomet'ric.** [Gr. *hypsos,* height.]

Hyrax *hī'raks, n* a genus of mammals like marmots but really closer to the ungulates, living among rocks in Africa and Syria — the dassie or rock-rabbit; (without *cap*) any animal of this genus: — *pl* **hy'raxes** or **hy'races** (*-sēz*). — *adj* **hy'racoid.** [Gr. *hȳrax,* a shrew.]

hyson *hī'son, n* a very fine sort of green Chinese tea. [From Chin.]

hyssop *his'əp, n* an aromatic herb used in perfumery and folk medicine; an unknown wall-plant used as a ceremonial sprinkler (*Bible*); a holy-water sprinkler. [L. *hyssōpus, -um* — Gr. *hyssōpos, -on.*]

hyster- *his-tər-* or **hystero-** *his-tə-rō-, his-tə-rə-* or *his-tə-ro'-*, *combining form* signifying womb. — *n* **hysterec'tomy** (Gr. *ektomē,* cutting out) surgical removal of the uterus. [Gr. *hysterā,* the womb.]

hysteresis *his-tə-rē'sis, n* the retardation or lagging of an effect behind the cause of the effect; the influence of earlier treatment of a body on its subsequent reaction. — *adj* **hysteret'ic.** [Gr. *hysterēsis,* a deficiency, coming late — *hysteros,* later.]

hysteria *hi-stē'ri-ə, n* a psychoneurosis in which repressed complexes become split off or dissociated from the personality, forming independent units, giving rise to hypnoidal states and manifested by various physical symptoms (such as tics, paralysis, blindness, deafness, etc.), general features being an extreme degree of emotional instability and an intense craving for affection; an outbreak of wild emotionalism. — *adj* **hysteric** (*hi-ster'ik*) or **hyster'ical** pertaining to, of the nature of, or affected with hysterics or hysteria; like hysterics; fitfully and violently emotional; (**hyster'ical**) extremely funny (*colloq*). — *n* **hyster'ic** a hysterical person. — *adv* **hyster'ically.** — *npl* **hyster'ics** hysteric fits; popularly, fits of uncontrollable laughter or crying, or of both alternately. — **hysterical pregnancy** pseudocyesis; **hysteroid dysphoria** pathological depression esp. of women. [Gr. *hysterā,* the womb, with which hysteria was formerly thought to be connected.]

hysteron-proteron *his-tə-ron-prot'ə-ron, n* a figure of speech in which what would ordinarily follow comes first; an inversion. [Gr., lit. latter-former.]

Hz *symbol* for hertz.

I

I[1] or **i** *ī*, *n* the ninth letter of the modern English alphabet. — **I'-beam** a metal girder I-shaped in section.

I[2] *ī*, *pron* the nominative singular of the first person pronoun. — *n* the object of self-consciousness, the ego. — *pron* **I-and-I'** Rastafarian for **we, us.** [M.E. *ich* — O.E. *ic*.]

I or **I.** *abbrev* for: independence; independent; institute; island or isle; Italy (I.V.R.).

I *symbol* for: iodine (*chem*); (Roman numeral) the number one, 1.

I (*phys*) *symbol* for electric current.

i (*math*) *symbol* for the imaginary square root of −1.

IA or **Ia** *abbrev* for Iowa (U.S. state).

-ia *-ē'ə* or *-yə*, *sfx* used in naming: (1) a pathological condition; (2) a genus of plants or animals; (3) (as L. or Gr. *neut pl*) a taxonomic division; (4) (as *pl*) things pertaining to (something specified).

IAEA *abbrev* for International Atomic Energy Agency.

iambus *ī-am'bəs*, (*prosody*) *n* a foot of two syllables, a short followed by a long, or an unstressed by a stressed: — *pl* **iam'buses** or **iam'bī**. — Also **i'amb**. — *adj* **iam'bic** consisting of iambuses; of the nature of an iambus; using iambic verse. — *n* an iambus; (in *pl*) iambic verse. — **iambic pentameter** a verse form comprising lines each of five feet, each foot containing two syllables — heroic verse. [L. *īambus* — Gr. *iambos* — *iaptein*, to assail, this metre being first used by satirists.]

-iana. See **-ana**.

-iasis *-ī'ə-sis*, (*med*) *sfx* denoting a diseased condition, as in *pityriasis*, *psoriasis*. [Gr. sfx. meaning state or condition.]

IATA *ī-ä'tə*, *abbrev* for International Air Transport Association.

-iatric *-i-at'rik*, (*med*) *adj combining form* relating to care or treatment within a particular specialty, as in *paediatric*, *psychiatric*. — *nsing combining form* **-iat'rics**. — *n combining form* **-ī'atry**. [Gr. *iātros*, physician.]

iatrogenic *ī-at-rə-jen'ik*, *adj* (of a disease or symptoms) induced in a patient by the treatment or comments of a physician. — *n* **iatrogenic'ity**. [Gr. *iātros*, a physician, *-genēs*, born.]

IB *abbrev* for International Baccalaureate.

ib. *abbrev* for *ibidem* (L.), in the same place.

IBA *abbrev* for Independent Broadcasting Authority, to be replaced by **ITC**.

Iberian *ī-bē'ri-ən*, *adj* of Spain and Portugal; of the ancient inhabitants of these, or their later representatives; of a Mediterranean people of Neolithic culture in Britain, etc. — *n* a member of any of these peoples. [L. *Ībēria* — Gr. *Ībēriā*.]

ibex *ī'beks*, *n* a wild mountain goat with large, ridged, backward-curving horns: — *pl* **i'bex, i'bexes** or **ibices** (*ī'bi-sēz*). [L. *ibex*, *-icis*.]

ibidem *ib-ī'dəm*, *ib'i-dəm* or *i-bē'dem*, (L.) *adv* (used in referring to a book already cited) in the same place (abbrev. **ib.** or **ibid.**).

ibis *ī'bis*, *n* a wading bird of the genus *Threskiornis*, with curved bill, similar to the spoonbills. — See also **stork.** [L. and Gr. *ībis*, prob. Egyptian.]

-ible *-ə-bl*, *adj sfx* having similar uses to those of **-able** (q.v.), esp. the passive 'capable of being'. — *n sfx* **-ibility.** — *adv sfx* **-ibly.** [L. *-ibilis* — *-bilis* as used with a 2nd-, 3rd- or 4th-conjugation verb.]

Ibo *ē'bō*, *n* a Negro people of S.E. Nigeria; a member of this people; their language, widely used in southern Nigeria: — *pl* **I'bo** or **I'bos.** — Also *adj.* — Also **Igbo** (*ē'bō*).

IBRD *abbrev* for International Bank for Reconstruction and Development (i.e. the World Bank, q.v.).

ibuprofen *ī-bū-prō'fən*, *n* a non-steroidal anti-inflammatory drug used for relieving rheumatic pain, headaches, etc. [From its full name, *iso*butyl*phen*yl *pro*pionic acid.]

i/c *abbrev* for in charge.

ICAO *abbrev* for International Civil Aviation Organisation.

ICBM *abbrev* for intercontinental ballistic missile.

ICE *abbrev* for: Institution of Civil Engineers; internal-combustion engine.

ice *īs*, *n* frozen water; any substance resembling this; a portion of ice cream or water ice; reserve, formality, coldness of manner; diamond(s) (*slang*). — *vt* to cool with ice; to cover with icing. — *vi* to freeze; to become covered with ice (with *up* or *over*): — *pr p* **i'cing;** *pa t* and *pa p* **iced.** — *adj* **iced** (*īst*) covered with or cooled with ice; coated or topped with icing. — *n* **i'cer** a person who makes and applies icing. — *adv* **i'cily.** — *n* **i'ciness.** — *n* **i'cing** a coating of concreted sugar; the formation of ice, e.g. on roads, aircraft, ships, etc. — *adj* **i'cy** composed of, abounding in, or like ice; frosty; cold; chilling; (of manner) distant, hostile. — **ice age** (*geol*) any time when a great part of the earth's surface has been covered with ice, esp. in the Pleistocene; **ice axe** an axe used by mountain-climbers to cut steps in ice; **ice'berg** (from Scand. or Du.) a huge mass of floating ice; a cold and unemotional person (esp. *US colloq*); a type of crisp light-green lettuce (also **iceberg lettuce**); **ice'blink** a gleam reflected from distant masses of ice. — *adj* and *n* **ice'-blue** (a) very pale blue. — **ice boat** a boat for forcing a way through ice, an ice-breaker; a craft mounted on runners for moving over ice (also **ice yacht**). — *adj* **ice'-bound** covered, surrounded or immobilised by ice. — **ice'box** the freezing compartment of a refrigerator; a refrigerator (*old US*); a portable insulated box filled with ice, used for storing cold food and drink; **ice'-breaker** a ship for breaking channels through ice; anything for breaking ice; something or someone that breaks the ice (q.v. below) or breaks down reserve. — *n* and *adj* **ice'-breaking.** — **ice bucket** a receptacle with ice for cooling bottles of wine; **ice'cap** a covering of ice over a convexity, such as a mountain top, the polar regions of a planet. — *adj* **ice-cold'** cold as, or like, ice. — **ice cream** a sweet frozen food containing cream or a substitute, and flavouring (**ice-cream soda** soda-water with ice cream added); **ice cube** a small cube of ice used for cooling drinks, etc.; **ice dance** or **dancing** a form of ice-skating based on the movements of ballroom dancing; **ice'field** a large area covered with ice, esp. floating ice; **ice floe** a large sheet of floating ice; **ice hockey** a form of hockey played on ice with a puck by skaters; **ice'house** (esp. *formerly*) a building for keeping ice in; **ice lolly** a lollipop consisting of water-ice on a stick; **ice machine** a machine for making ice in large quantities; **ice'man** a dealer in ice; **ice'pack** drifting ice packed together, pack ice; an ice-filled bag for applying to a part of the body to reduce swelling (*med*); a gel-filled pack that remains frozen for long periods, for use in a cool box, etc.; **ice pick** a tool with a pointed end used by climbers for splitting ice; **ice'plant** a plant (*Mesembrianthemum*) whose leaves glisten like ice in the sun; **ice rink** a skating rink of ice; **ice sheet** a layer of ice covering a whole region; **ice skate** a skate for moving on ice (see **skate**[1]). — *vi* **ice'-skate.** — **ice'-skater; ice'-skating; ice-store** see **cryolite; ice track** a track composed of ice for use in the sport of speedskating; **ice water** water from melted ice; iced water; **ice yacht** see **ice boat; icing sugar** sugar in the form of a very fine powder, for icing cakes, etc. — **break the ice** to break through the barrier of reserve and inhibition on first meeting; to move to restore friendly relations after a period of hostility; **cut no ice** to count for nothing; **dry ice** solid carbon dioxide, which changes directly into vapour at −78·5° Celsius, and is chiefly used for refrigeration, but is also exploited in the theatre, the dense, swirling, floor-level white cloud it produces on evaporation creating a spectacular stage-effect. — *adj* **dry'-iced.** — **ice out** (*slang*) to exclude (someone) from one's company by ignoring them; **icing on the cake** (*colloq*) anything that is a desirable addition to something already satisfactory; **on ice** kept, or waiting in readiness; postponed; certain of achievement; **put on ice** to put into abeyance, to suspend; **(skate) on thin ice** (to be) in a delicate, difficult or potentially embarrassing situation; **tip of the iceberg** the small obvious part of a much larger problem, etc. [O.E. *īs*.]

Icelander *īs'lən-dər* or *īs-lan'dər*, *n* a native or citizen of Iceland. — *adj* **Iceland'ic** of Iceland. — *n* the modern language of the Icelanders; Old Norse. — **Iceland moss** a lichen of northern regions, used as a medicine and for food; **Iceland poppy** a dwarf poppy with flowers varying from white to orange-scarlet; **Iceland spar** a transparent calcite with strong double refraction.

I Ching *ē ching*, *n* an ancient Chinese system of divination, consisting of a set of symbols made up of solid and broken horizontal lines in varying combinations, and the text, the *I Ching*, used to interpret them. [Chin., book of changes.]

ichneumon *ik-nū'mən*, *n* any animal of the mongoose genus, esp. the Egyptian species that destroys crocodiles' eggs; (in full **ichneumon fly**) any insect of a large family of Hymenoptera whose larvae are parasitic in or on other insects. [Gr. *ichneumōn*, lit. tracker.]

ichnite *ik'nīt* or **ichnolite** *ik'nə-līt*, *n* a fossil footprint. [Gr. *ichnos*, a footprint, track.]

ichnography *ik-nog'rə-fi*, *n* a ground plan; the art of drawing ground plans. — *adj* **ichnographic** (*-nō-graf'ik*) or **ichnograph'ical** (*-kəl*). — *adv* **ichnograph'ically.** [Gr. *ichnos*, a track, footprint, *graphein*, to write.]

ichor *ī'kör*, *n* the ethereal juice in the veins of the gods (*mythol*); colourless matter from an ulcer or wound (*med*). — *adj* **ī'chorous.** [Gr. *īchōr*.]

ichthyo- *ik-thi-ō-* or *-ə-*, or **ichthy-** *ik-thi-*, *combining form* signifying fish. — *n* **ichthyog'raphy** a description of fishes. — *n* **ich'thyoid** a vertebrate of the fish type. — *adj* **ich'thyoid** or **ich'thyoidal** fishlike. — *adj* **ichthyolog'ical.** — *n* **ichthyol'ogist.** — *n* **ichthyol'ogy** the branch of natural history that deals with fishes. — *n* **ichthyosaur** (*ik'thi-ə-sör*) gigantic Mesozoic fossil sharklike marine reptile, with a long snout and four paddle-like limbs. — Also **ichthyosaur'us**: — *pl* **icthyosaur'uses** or **icthyosaur'i** (*-ī*). — *n* **ichthyō'sis** a disease in which the skin becomes hardened, thickened and rough. — *adj* **ichthyot'ic.** [Gr. *ichthȳs*, fish.]

ICI *abbrev* for Imperial Chemical Industries.

icicle *īs'i-kl*, *n* a hanging, tapering piece of ice formed by the freezing of dropping water. [O.E. *īsesgicel* — *īses*, genitive of *īs*, ice, *gicel*, icicle.]

icing. See **ice.**

-icism. See **-ism.**

ICL *abbrev* for International Computers Ltd.

icon or **ikon** *ī'kon*, *n* in the Eastern Churches a figure representing Christ, or a saint, in painting, mosaic, etc. (not sculpture); a symbol, representation; anybody or anything uncritically admired; a visual symbol in a graphic display, representing a particular operation, usu. activated by means of a mouse (*comput*). — *adj* **icon'ic.** — *adv* **icon'ically.** — *n* **icon'oclasm** (Gr. *klaein*, to break) the act of breaking images; opposition to image-worship. — *n* **icon'oclast** a breaker of images; a person opposed to image-worship, esp. those in the Eastern Church, from the 8th century; a person who assails old cherished errors and superstitions. — *adj* **iconoclast'ic.** — *n* **iconog'raphy** the study of the subjects depicted in paintings, etc.; pictorial representation of subjects; the symbols used in paintings, etc. and their conventional significance; a description, catalogue or collective representation of portraits. — *n* **iconol'ogist.** — *n* **iconol'ogy** the study of icons; symbolism. — *n* **iconom'eter** an instrument for inferring distance from size or size from distance of an object, by measuring its image; a direct photographic viewfinder. — *n* **iconom'etry.** — *n* **icon'oscope** a form of electron camera. — *n* **iconos'tasis** or **icon'ostas** (Gr. *eikonostasis* — *stasis*, placing) in Eastern churches, a screen shutting off the sanctuary, on which the icons are placed. — **iconic memory** the persistence of a sense impression after the disappearance of the stimulus. [L. *īcōn* — Gr. *eikōn*, an image.]

icosahedron *ī-kos-ə-hē'drən*, (*geom*) *n* a solid with twenty plane faces: — *pl* **icosahē'dra.** — *adj* **icosahē'dral.** — *n* **icositetrahē'dron** (*geom*; Gr. *tetra-*, four) a solid figure with twenty-four plane faces: — *pl* **icositetrahē'dra.** [Gr. *eikosi*, twenty, *hedrā*, a seat.]

ICR (*comput*) *abbrev* for intelligent character recognition.

-ics *-iks*, *nsing* or *npl sfx* denoting specialties in the arts and sciences, special types of activity, etc., as in *aeronautics, paediatrics, politics, graphics, gymnastics.* [Gr. *-ika*, neuter pl. adj. ending.]

icterus *ik'tə-rəs*, *n* jaundice. — *adj* **icteric** (*-ter'ik*) or **icter'ical.** [Gr. *ikteros*, jaundice.]

ictus *ik'təs*, *n* rhythmical or metrical stress in contradistinction to the usual stress of a word in prose, etc. (*prosody*); a stroke (*med*): — *pl* **ic'tuses** (or L. *pl* **ic'tus** *-tōōs*). — *adj* **ic'tal** or **ic'tic.** [L., a blow.]

ICU (*med*) *abbrev* for intensive care unit.

ID *abbrev* for: Idaho (U.S. state); identification; infectious diseases (*med*).

I'd *īd*, contracted from *I would* or *I had*; also used for *I should.*

id[1] *id* or **ide** *īd*, *n* a fish of the same family as the carp, inhabiting fresh water in Northern Europe. [Sw. *id*.]

id[2] *id*, (*psychol*) *n* the sum total of the primitive instinctive forces in an individual, representing a major part of the subconscious mind and concerned with the obtaining of pleasure and avoidance of pain. [L. *id*, it.]

id. *abbrev* for *idem* (L.), the same.

-id[1] *-id*, *adj sfx*, as in *fluid, stupid, solid, tepid, turgid, gelid*, etc. [L. *-idus*.]

-id[2] *-id*, *n* and *adj sfx* used in the names of a particular zoological or racial group, or dynastic line, as in *arachnid, hominid, Fatimid.* [Gr. *-idēs*, son of.]

-id[3] *-id*, *n sfx* used: (1) in names of bodies, formations, particles, etc., as *hydatid*; (2) in the names of meteors coming from a particular constellation, as in *Perseid, Orionid.* [Gr. *-is, -idos*, daughter of.]

IDA *abbrev* for International Development Association.

Ida. *abbrev* for Idaho (U.S. state).

Id al-Adha *ēd əl-äd'hä*, *n* the Muslim 'Feast of Sacrifice', celebrating Abraham's sacrifice of his son. [*'Id al-Adha.*]

Id al-Fitr *ēd əl-fē'tər*, *n* the Muslim 'Feast of Breaking Fast', celebrated on the first day after Ramadan. [*'Id al-Fitr*].

IDD (*telecomm*) *abbrev* for International Direct Dialling.

ide. See **id**[1].

idea *ī-dē'ə*, *n* an image of an external object formed by the mind; a notion, thought, impression, conception, any product of intellectual action, of memory and imagination; a plan; in Plato, an archetype of the manifold varieties of existence in the universe, belonging to the supersensible world, in Kant, one of the three products of the reason (the Soul, the Universe, and God) transcending the conceptions of the understanding, and in Hegel, the ideal realised, the absolute truth of which everything that exists is the expression (*philos*). — **get** or **have ideas** (*slang*) to become or be overambitious; to have undesirable ideas; **have no idea** to be unaware of what is happening; to be ignorant or naive; **not my idea of** (*colloq*) the opposite of my (or the accepted and familiar) conception of; **put ideas into someone's head** to fill someone with unsuitable or over-exalted aspirations; **that's an idea** that plan is worth considering; **the very idea** the mere thought; (as an ejaculation) that's absurd, outrageous; **what an idea!** that's preposterous; **what's the big idea?** (*slang*, usu. *ironic*) what's the intention, purpose? [Gr. *idĕā*; cf. *idein*, to see.]

ideal *ī-dē'əl*, *adj* conceptual; existing in imagination only; highest and best conceivable; perfect, as opposed to the real, the imperfect; theoretical, conforming absolutely to theory. — *n* the highest conception of anything, or its embodiment; a standard of perfection; that which exists in the imagination only. — *n* **idēalisā'tion** or **-z-**. — *vt* **idē'alise** or **-ize** to regard or represent as ideal. — *vi* to form ideals; to think or work idealistically. — *n* **idē'alīser** or **-z-**. — *n* **idē'alism** a tendency towards the highest conceivable perfection, love for or the search after the best and highest; the habit or practice of idealising; impracticality; the doctrine that in external perceptions the objects immediately known are ideas, that all reality is in its nature psychical (*philos*). — *n* **idē'alist** a person who strives after the ideal; an impractical person; a person who holds the doctrine of idealism. — *adj* **idēalist'ic**. — *adv* **idēalist'ically**. — *adv* **idē'ally** in an ideal manner; in ideal circumstances; mentally. [L.L. *idealis*, — Gr. *idea* — *idein*, to see.]

idée *ē-dā*, (Fr.) *n* an idea. — **idée fixe** (*fēks*) a fixed idea, an obsession or monomania.

idem *ī'dem* or *id'em*, (L.) *pron* the same (abbrev. **id.**).

identic *ī-den'tik*, *adj* identical, as in **identic note** or **action** (*diplomacy*) an identical note sent by, or identical action taken by, two or more governments in dealing with another, or others. [Med. L. *identicus*, — L. *idem*, the same.]

identical *ī-den'ti-kəl*, *adj* the very same; not different, exactly alike; expressing or resulting in identity (*logic* or *math*). — *adv* **iden'tically**. — *n* **iden'ticalness**. — **identical twins** twins who are the same sex and look very alike, having developed from one zygote. [Med. L. *identicus*, — L. *idem*, the same.]

identify *ī-den'ti-fī*, *vt* to ascertain or establish the identity of; to assign (a plant, animal, etc.) to a species; to associate closely (e.g. one concept with another, a person with a group, movement, etc.); to regard (oneself) as in sympathy (with a group, movement, etc.); to see clearly, pinpoint (a problem, etc.). — *vi* to be emotionally in sympathy (with e.g. a character, esp. the hero or heroine, of a book, play, etc.): — *pr p* **iden'tifying**; *pa t* and *pa p* **iden'tified**. — *adj* **iden'tifīable**. — *n* **identificā'tion** (*-fi-*) the act of identifying; the process of being identified; something that proves one's identity; a process by which a person assumes the behaviour, ideas, etc. of someone else, particularly someone whom he or she admires (*psychol*). — **identification card, disc,** etc. a card, disc, etc. carried on one's person, with one's name, etc. on it; **identification parade** a group of people assembled by the police, from among whom a witness tries to identify a suspect. [L.L. *identificāre* — *idem*, the same, *facĕre*, to make.]

identikit (orig. *US* **Identi-Kit**) *ī-den'ti-kit*, *n* a device for building up a composite portrait from a stack of differing features shown on transparent slips, by means of which a witness can be helped to produce a likeness of someone sought by the police. [*identi*ty and **kit**.]

identity *ī-den'ti-ti*, *n* state of being the same; sameness; individuality; personality; who or what a person or thing is; an equation true for all values of the symbols involved (*math*). — **identity card, disc,** etc. a card, disc, etc. bearing the owner's or wearer's name, etc., used to establish his or her identity; **identity crisis** psychological confusion caused by inability to reconcile differing elements in one's personality. [L.L. *identitās*, *-ātis* — L. *idem*, the same.]

ideogram *id'i-ə-gram* or **ideograph** *id'i-ə-gräf*, *n* a written character or symbol that stands not for a word or sound but for the thing itself directly. — *adj* **ideographic** (*-graf'ik*) or **ideograph'ical** (*-kəl*). — *adv* **ideograph'ically**. — *n* **ideography** (*-og'rə-fi*). [Gr. *idĕā*, idea, *gramma*, a drawing, *graphein*, to write.]

ideology *ī-di-ol'ə-ji*, *n* the science of ideas, metaphysics; abstract speculation; visionary speculation; a body of ideas, usu. political and/or economic, forming the basis of a national or sectarian policy; way of thinking. — *adj* **ideological** (*-loj'*) of or relating to an ideology; arising from, concerned with, rival ideologies. — *n* **ideol'ogist** a person occupied with ideas or an idea; a mere theorist or visionary; a supporter of a particular ideology. — *n* **ideologue** (*ī-dē'ə-log*; usu. *derog*) a doctrinaire adherent of an ideology. [Gr. *idĕā*, idea, *logos*, discourse.]

ideophone *id'i-ə-fōn*, *n* a word or phrase that is spoken but not written, usu. one that is only fully comprehensible in the context in which it is spoken. [Gr. *idĕā*, idea, *phōnē*, *sound*.]

Ides *īdz*, *npl* in ancient Rome, the 15th day of March, May, July, October, and the 13th of the other months. [Fr. *ides* — L. *īdūs* (pl.).]

id est *id est*, (L.) that is, that is to say (abbrev. **i.e.**).

idiocy. See **idiot**.

idiolect *id'i-ə-lekt*, *n* an individual's own distinctive form of speech. — *adj* **idiolec'tal** or **idiolec'tic**. [Gr. *idios*, own, and dia*lect*.]

idiom *id'i-əm*, *n* a mode of expression peculiar to a language; a distinctive expression whose meaning is not determinable from the meanings of the individual words; a form or variety of language; a dialect; a characteristic mode of artistic expression of a person, school, etc. — *adj* **idiomat'ic**. — *adv* **idiomat'ically**. [Gr. *idiōma*, *idiōtikon* — *idios*, own.]

idiomorphic *id-i-ə-mör'fik*, *adj* having the faces belonging to its crystalline form, as a mineral that has had free room to crystallise out. [Gr. *idios*, own, *morphē*, form.]

idiopathic *id-i-ə-path'ik*, *adj* (of a state of experience) peculiar to the individual; (of a disease, etc.) primary, not occasioned by a disease already present in the patient (*med*). — *adv* **idiopath'ically**. [Gr. *idios*, own, *pathos*, suffering.]

idiosyncrasy *id-i-ō-sing'krə-si*, *n* peculiarity of temperament or mental constitution; any characteristic of a person; hypersensitivity of an individual to a particular food, drug, etc. (*med*). — *adj* **idiosyncratic** (*id-i-ō-sing-krat'ik*). — *adv* **idiosyncrat'ically**. [Gr. *idios*, own, *synkrāsis*, a mixing together — *syn*, together, *krāsis*, a mixing.]

idiot *id'i-ət*, *n* a person suffering from the worst degree of feeble-mindedness or mental retardation; a foolish or unwise person. — *adj* afflicted with idiocy; idiotic. — *n* **id'iocy** (*-ə-si*) the state of being an idiot; imbecility; folly. — *adj* **idiotic** (*-ot'ik*) relating to or like an idiot; foolish. — *adv* **idiot'ically**. — **idiot board** (*colloq*) an autocue. — *adj* **id'iot-proof** (of a tool, method of working, etc.) so simple that even an idiot cannot make a mistake. — **idiot tape** (*comput*) a tape that prints out in a continuous flow of characters, without breaks. [Fr., — Gr. *idiōtēs*, a private person, ordinary person, lacking public office or professional knowledge — *idios*, own, private.]

idiot savant *ē-dyō sa-vã*, (Fr.) *n* a mentally retarded individual who demonstrates remarkable talent in some restricted area such as memorising or rapid calculation.

idle *ī'dl*, *adj* vain; baseless; trifling; unemployed; averse to labour; not occupied; not in use; useless; unimportant; unedifying. — *vt* to spend in idleness. — *vi* to be idle or unoccupied; (of machinery) to run without doing work; (of an engine) to run slowly when disengaged from the transmission. — *n* **i'dleness**. — *n* **i'dler** a person who wastes time or is reluctant to work; an idle pulley. — *adv* **i'dly**. — **idle pulley** a pulley which rotates freely and guides, or controls the tension of, a belt (also **ī'dler**); **idle time** a period or periods when a computer is able to function properly but is not being used for productive work or program testing; **idle wheel** a wheel placed between two others for transferring the motion from one to the other without changing the direction.

idol *ī'dl*, *n* an image of a god; an object of worship; an object of love, admiration, or honour in an extreme degree. — *vt* **i'dolise** or **-ize** to make an idol of, worship, venerate, love or admire excessively. — *n* **i'doliser** or **-z-**. [Gr. *eidōlon* — *eidos*, form.]

idolater *ī-dol'ə-tər*, *n*, *fem* **idol'atress**, a worshipper of idols; a besotted admirer. — *adj* **idol'atrous**. — *adv* **idol'atrously**. — *n* **idol'atry** the worship of an image held to be the abode of a superhuman personality; excessive love. [Fr. *idolâtre* — Gr. *eidōlolatrēs* — *eidōlon*, idol, *latreuein*, to worship.]

idolise. See **idol**.

idolum *ī-dō'ləm*, *n* a mental image; a fallacy (*logic*). [L., — Gr. *eidolon*, phantom.]

IDP (*comput*) *abbrev* for integrated data processing.

idyll or sometimes in U.S. **idyl** *id'il*, *n* a short pictorial poem, chiefly on pastoral subjects; a story, episode, or scene of happy innocence or rusticity; a work of art of this character in any medium. — *adj* **idyll'ic**. — *adv* **idyll'ically**. — *n* **id'yllist**. [Gr. *eidyllion*, dimin. of *eidos*, image.]

IE (*linguis*) *abbrev* for Indo-European.

i.e. *abbrev* for *id est* (L.), that is, that is to say.

-ie *-i*, (esp. *Austr*) *sfx* variant of, and forming nouns in the same way as, **-y**, as in *nightie*, *hippie*, *movie*.

if *if*, *conj* on condition that; provided that; supposing that; whether; though; whenever; in surprise or irritation, as in *if it isn't John!*, *if that isn't the doorbell again!* — *n* a condition; a supposition; an uncertainty. — *adj* **iff'y** (*colloq*) dubious, uncertain, risky. — *n* **iff'iness**. — **as if** as it would be if; **even if** even supposing that, although, accepting that; **if only** see under **only**; **if only to** if for no other reason than to; **ifs and buts** objections; **if you like** if you want, if you approve; to use another expression, to put it a different way. [O.E. *gif*.]

iff *if*, (*logic*) *conj* used to express *if and only if*.

iffy. See **if**.

-iform *-i-fôrm*, *pfx*. See **-form**.

Igbo. See **Ibo**.

igloo *ig'loo*, *n* orig. a dome-shaped hut of snow; now usu. a dwelling of other materials; a dome-shaped place of storage or container for goods. [Eskimo.]

igneous *ig'ni-əs*, *adj* of or like fire; produced by solidification of the earth's internal molten magma (*geol*). [L. *igneus*, fiery — *ignis*, fire.]

ignimbrite *ig'nim-brīt*, *n* a hard rock formed by fusion of the volcanic fragments and dust emitted in cloud form from a volcano. [L. *ignis*, fire, *imber*, *imbris*, a shower of rain, and **-ite**.]

ignis fatuus *ig'nis fat'ū-əs* or *fat'oo-oos*, *n* will-o'-the-wisp — the light of combustion of marsh-gas, apt to lead travellers into danger; any delusive ideal that leads one astray: — *pl* **ignes fatui** (*ig'nēz fat'ū-ī* or *ig'nās fat'oo-ē*). [L. *ignis*, fire, *fatuus*, foolish.]

ignite *ig-nīt'*, *vt* to set on fire; to heat to the point at which combustion occurs. — *vi* to catch fire. — *adj* **ignī'table** (or **ignī'tible**). — *n* **ignītabil'ity** or **ignītibil'ity**. — *n* **ignī'ter**. — *n* **ignition** (*-nish'ən*) an act of igniting; a means of igniting; the process of being ignited; the firing system of an internal-combustion engine. — **ignition key** in a motor vehicle, the key which is turned to operate the ignition system. [L. *ignīre*, *ignītum*, to set on fire, to make red-hot — *ignis*, fire.]

ignoble *ig-nō'bl*, *adj* of low birth; mean or worthless; unworthy; dishonourable. — *n* **ignōbil'ity** or **ignō'bleness**. — *adv* **ignō'bly**. [Fr., — L. *ignōbilis* — *in-*, not, (*g*)*nōbilis*, noble.]

ignominy *ig'nə-min-i*, *n* public disgrace; humiliation; dishonour, infamy. — *adj* **ignomin'ious** disgraceful; humiliating. — *adv* **ignomin'iously**. [L. *ignōminia*, *in-*, not, (*g*)*nōmen*, *-inis*, name.]

ignoramus *ig-nə-rā'məs*, *n* an ignorant person: — *pl* **ignorā'muses**. [L. *ignōrāmus*, we are ignorant, in legal use, we ignore.]

ignorant *ig'nə-rənt*, *adj* lacking knowledge, ill-educated; having no understanding or awareness (with *of*); showing or arising from lack of knowledge; discourteous, rude, ill-bred. — *n* **ig'norance** lack of knowledge, awareness, education or enlightenment. — *adv* **ig'norantly**. [Fr., — L. *ignōrāns*, *-antis*, pres. p. of *ignōrāre*; see **ignore**.]

ignoratio elenchi *ig-nə-rā'shō i-leng'kī*, *ig-nō-rä'ti-ō el-eng'kē*, (L.) *n* a fallacy in arguing whereby one refutes a point that is not in question.

ignore *ig-nör'*, *vt* wilfully to disregard; to pay no heed or attention to; to waive or set aside. — *adj* **ignor'able**. — *n* **ignor'er**. [L. *ignōrāre*, not to know — *in-*, not, and the root of (*g*)*nōscĕre*, to know.]

iguana *i-gwä'nə*, *n* a large thick-tongued grey-green arboreal lizard of tropical America, having a row of spines along the back; in South Africa, a monitor lizard. [Sp., from Caribb.]

iguanid *i-gwä'nid*, *n* a lizard of the family *Iguanidae*, to which the iguana belongs. [**iguana** and **-id**[2].]

Iguanodon *i-gwä'nə-don*, *n* a large, bipedal, bird-hipped, Jurassic and Cretaceous herbivorous dinosaur, with teeth like those of the iguana. [**iguana**, and Gr. *odous*, *odontos*, tooth.]

IHC or **IHS** (Gr.) *abbrev* for *Iesous*, Jesus, using Greek capital iota, capital eta, and capital sigma (**C** or **S**), the first two and the last letters of the name.

ikat *ik'at*, *n* a technique of dyeing yarn and tying it prior to weaving, resulting in a fabric with a geometric pattern of colours. [Malay-Indonesian *mengikat*, to tie.]

ikebana *ē-ke-bä'nə*, *n* the Japanese art of flower arrangement. [Jap., living flowers, arranged flowers.]

ikon. Another spelling of **icon**.

IL *abbrev* for: Illinois (U.S. state); Israel (I.V.R.).

il- *il-*, *pfx* same as **in-**, but the form used with words beginning with *l*, as in *illegible*.

Ilchester cheese *il'chəs-tər chēz, n* Cheddar cheese flavoured with beer, spices, etc. [*Ilchester*, in Somerset, where it was first made.]

ileac. See **ileum**.

ileum *il'i-əm* or *ī'li-əm, (anat) n* the posterior part of the small intestine: — *pl* **il'ea** (or *ī'li-ə*). — *adj* **il'eac** (or *ī'li-ak*). — *n* **ileitis** (*il-i-ī'tis* or *ī-li-ī'tis*) inflammation of the ileum. [L.L. *īleum*, L. *īlia* (pl.), the groin, flank, intestines.]

ileus *il'i-əs* or *ī'li-əs, (med) n* obstruction of the intestine accompanied by severe pain, vomiting, etc. [Gr. *īleos* or *eileos*, colic.]

ilex *ī'leks, n* the holm-oak; a shrub or tree of the genus *Ilex*, to which the holly belongs. [L. *īlex*, holm-oak.]

ilium *il'i-əm* or *ī'li-əm, (anat) n* the bone that unites with the ischium and pubis to form the innominate bone: — *pl* **il'ia** (or *ī'li-ə*). — *adj* **il'iac** (or *ī'li-ak*). [L. *īlium* (in classical L. only in pl. *īlia*); see **ileum**.]

ilk *ilk, n* type, kind. — *adj* (*Scot*) same. — **of that ilk** of that type; of that same, i.e. of the estate of the same name as the family (*Scot*). [O.E. *ilca*, same.]

I'll *īl*, a contraction of **I will** or **I shall**.

Ill. *abbrev* for Illinois (U.S. state).

ill *il, adj* (*compar* **worse**, *superl* **worst**) ailing, sick; evil, bad, wicked; producing evil; hurtful; unfortunate; unfavourable; difficult; reprehensible; incorrect; incompetent; (of temper, etc.) peevish. — *adv* (*compar* **worse**, *superl* **worst**) badly; not well; not rightly; wrongfully; unfavourably; amiss; with hardship; with difficulty. — *n* evil; wickedness; misfortune; harm; ailment. — *n* **ill'ness** sickness; disease. — *adj* **ill-advised'** imprudent; ill-judged. — *adj* **ill-assort'ed** incompatible; not matching. — *adj* **ill-behaved'** behaving badly, ill-mannered. — **ill blood** or **ill feeling** resentment, enmity. — *adj* **ill-bred'** badly brought up or educated; uncivil. — **ill breeding**. — *adj* **ill-consid'ered** badly thought out; misconceived. — *adj* **ill-defined'** having no clear outline; vague, imprecise, hazy. — *adj* **ill-disposed'** unfriendly. — **ill fame** disrepute. — *adj* **ill-fa'ted** unlucky. — *adj* **ill-fā'voured** deformed; unattractive, ugly. — **ill-fā'vouredness**; **ill-feel'ing** bad feeling, resentment, animosity; **ill fortune** bad luck. — *adj* **ill-found'ed** without foundation, baseless. — *adj* **ill'-gotten** procured by dishonest or unworthy means. — **ill health** poor health; **ill humour**. — *adj* **ill-hu'moured** bad-tempered. — *adj* **ill-informed'** ignorant. — *adj* **ill-judged'** foolish, unwise, ill-timed. — **ill luck** bad luck. — *adj* **ill-mann'ered** rude, discourteous; boorish, uncouth. — *adj* **ill-matched'** not suited to one another; not matching well. — **ill nature**. — *adj* **ill-na'tured** bad-tempered; spiteful, malevolent, mean. — *adv* **ill-na'turedly**. — **ill-na'turedness**. — *adj* **ill-o'mened** unfortunate, unlucky; inauspicious, doomed. — *adj* **ill-spent'** misspent, wasted, squandered. — *adj* **ill-starred'** unlucky, ill-fated. — **ill success** lack of success, failure; **ill temper**. — *adj* **ill-tem'pered** bad tempered; morose. — *adj* **ill-timed'** said or done at an unsuitable time; inappropriate, ill-judged. — *vt* **ill-treat'** to treat badly or cruelly; to abuse. — **ill-treat'ment**; **ill turn** an act of unkindness or enmity; **ill-u'sage** or **ill-use'**. — *vt* **ill-use'** to ill-treat. — *adj* **ill-used'** badly treated. — **ill-will'** unkind feeling; enmity, hostility. — **go ill with** to result in danger or misfortune to; **ill at ease** uneasy; embarrassed; **take it ill** to be offended; **with an ill grace** ungraciously. [O.N. *illr*.]

illation *il-ā'shən, n* the act of inferring from premises; inference; conclusion. — *adj* **illative** (*il'ə-tiv* or *i-lā'tiv*) relating to, of the nature of, expressing, or introducing an inference; denoting a case in some Finno-Ugric languages expressing direction into or towards (*gram*). — *n* the illative case; a word in this case. — *adv* **ill'atively** (or *i-lā'*). [L. *illātiō, -ōnis* — *illātus*, used as past p. of *inferre*, to infer.]

illegal *i-lē'gl, adj* prohibited by law, unlawful. — *n* **illegality** (*-gal'i-ti*). — *adv* **ille'gally**. [**il-** (**in-** (2)).]

illegible *i-lej'i-bl, adj* impossible, or very difficult, to read. — *n* **illegibil'ity** or **illeg'ibleness**. — *adv* **illeg'ibly**. [**il-** (**in-** (2)).]

illegitimate *il-i-jit'i-mit, adj* born of parents not married to each other at the time; (of a birth) happening outside marriage; unlawful, improper; not properly inferred or reasoned (*logic*); (of the use of a word, etc.) not recognised by authority or good usage. — *n* a person born outside marriage. — *n* **illegit'imacy** (*-mə-si*) or **illegit'imateness**. — *adv* **illegit'imately**. [**il-** (**in-** (2)).]

illiberal *i-lib'ə-rəl, adj* narrow-minded, intolerant or prejudiced; niggardly, ungenerous; narrow in culture, unenlightened. — *n* **illiberality** (*-al'i-ti*). — *adv* **illib'erally**. [**il-** (**in-** (2)).]

illicit *i-lis'it, adj* not allowable; unlawful; unlicensed. — *adv* **illic'itly**. — *n* **illic'itness**. [L. *illicitus* — *il-* (*in-*), not, *licitus*, past p. of *licēre*, to be allowed.]

illimitable *i-lim'it-ə-bl, adj* limitlessly infinite. — *n* **illim'itableness**. — *adv* **illim'itably**. [**il-** (**in-** (2)).]

illiquid *i-lik'wid, adj* (of assets, etc.) not readily converted into cash. — *n* **illiquid'ity**. [**il-** (**in-** (2)).]

illit. *abbrev* for illiterate.

illite *il'īt, (mineralogy) n* a white or pale clay mineral found in shales and sediments, having a similar structure to the micas. [U.S. state of *Ill*inois, and **-ite** (3).]

illiterate *i-lit'ər-it, adj* unable to read and write; ignorant, uneducated; betraying ignorance or lack of education; ignorant in a particular field or subject, as in *mathematically illiterate*. — *n* an illiterate person. — *adv* **illit'erately**. — *n* **illit'eracy** (*-ə-si*) or **illit'erateness**. [**il-** (**in-** (2)).]

illocution *il-ə-kū'shən, (philos) n* an act which is performed by a speaker in actually speaking the words, such as an order or a promise (cf. **perlocution**). — *adj* **illocū'tionary**. [**il-** (**in-** (1)).]

illogical *i-loj'i-kəl, adj* contrary to the rules of logic; regardless or incapable of logic; crazy, senseless, unreasonable. — *n* **illogicality** (*-kal'i-ti*) or **illog'icalness**. — *adv* **illog'ically**. [**il-** (**in-** (2)).]

illuminable. See **illumine**.

illuminate *i-lōō'mi-nāt* or *i-lū'mi-, vt* to light up; to make bright, fill with light; to enlighten; to illustrate; to adorn with coloured lettering or illustrations. — *n* **illuminā'tion** lighting up; strength of light; source of light; intellectual enlightenment; spiritual inspiration; splendour; brightness; (in *pl*) a decorative display of lights; adorning of books with coloured lettering or illustrations; illuminance (*phys*). — *adj* **illu'minating**. — *adj* **illu'minative** (*-ə-tiv* or *-ā-tiv*). — *n* **illu'minātor** a decorator of manuscripts, etc.; a person who provides clarification or enlightenment. [L. *illūmināre, -ātum*, — *lumen*, light.]

illumine *i-lōō'min* or *i-lū'min, vt* (*literary*) to illuminate. — *adj* **illu'minable**. [L. *illūmināre, in*, in, upon, *lūmināre*, to cast light.]

illusion *i-lōō'zhən* or *i-lū'zhən, n* deceptive appearance; an apparition; false conception; delusion; a false sense-impression of something actually present (*psychol*). — *n* **illu'sionism** the doctrine that the external world is illusory; the production of illusion, esp. the use of artistic techniques, such as perspective, etc., to produce an illusion of reality. — *n* **illu'sionist** a believer in or practitioner of illusionism; a person who produces illusions, a conjurer. — *adj* **illu'sive** (*-siv*) or **illu'sory** (*-sə-ri*) misleading by false appearances; false, deceptive, unreal. — *adv* **illu'sively**. — *n* **illu'siveness**. [L. *illūsio, -ōnis* — *illūdere*, to mock, make sport of.]

illustrate *il'əs-trāt, vt* to execute pictures for (a book, etc.); to elucidate and amplify by pictures; to exemplify. — *n* **illustrā'tion** a picture or diagram elucidating, or at least accompanying, text; the act of illustrating or process of being illustrated; exemplification; an example. — *adj* **ill'ustrated** having pictorial illustrations. — *n* an illustrated periodical. — *adj* **illustrative** (*il'əs-trā-tiv*, *-trə-tiv* or *i-lus'trə-tiv*) or **illus'tratory** serving to clarify, explain or adorn. — *adv* **ill'ustratively** (or *i-lus'*). — *n* **ill'ustrātor.** [L. *illūstrāre*, to light up, prob. — *lūx*, light.]

illustrious *i-lus'tri-əs*, *adj* distinguished, renowned; noble, glorious. [L. *illūstris*, lustrous, or renowned.]

illywhacker *il'i-wak-ər*, (*Austr slang*) *n* a con-man, a trickster.

IM *abbrev* for intramuscular(ly).

im- *im*, *pfx* same as **in-**, but the form used with words beginning with *b*, *m*, or *p*, as in *imbalance*, *immodest*.

I'm *īm*, a contraction of **I am.**

image *im'ij*, *n* likeness; a statue; an idol; a representation in the mind, an idea; a picture or representation (not necessarily visual) in the imagination or memory; an appearance; that which very closely resembles anything; (a person who is) the epitome or personification of a quality; the figure of any object formed by rays of light reflected or refracted (*optics*); an analogous figure formed by other rays (*optics*); the element of a set which is associated with an element in a different set when one set is a function or transformation of the other (*math*); a metaphor or simile (*rhetoric*); (**public image**) the character or attributes of a person, institution, etc., as perceived by the general public. — *vt* to form an image of; to form a likeness of in the mind; to mirror; to imagine; to portray; to typify; to produce a pictorial representation of (a part of the body) for diagnostic medical purposes. — *adj* **im'ageable.** — *n* **imagery** (*im'ij-ri* or *-ə-ri*) the work of the imagination; mental pictures; figures of speech; images in general or collectively. — *n* **im'aging** image formation. — *n* **im'agism.** — *n* **im'agist** an exponent of a twentieth-century school of poetry aiming at concentration, exact and simple language, and freedom of form and subject. — Also *adj.* — *adj* **imagist'ic.** — **image intensifier** an electronic device for increasing the brightness of an optical image, such as the fluoroscopic image in X-ray examinations; **image orthicon** a television camera tube which converts the images it receives into electronic impulses which are transmitted as television signals. [O.Fr., — L. *imāgō*, image.]

imaginal. See **imago.**

imagine *im-aj'in*, *vt* to form an image of in the mind; to conceive; to think; to think vainly or falsely; to conjecture. — *vi* to form mental images; to exercise imagination. — *adj* **imag'inable.** — *n* **imag'inableness.** — *adv* **imag'inably.** — *adj* **imag'inary** existing only in the imagination; not real, illusory. — *n* **imaginā'tion** the act of imagining; the faculty of forming images in the mind; the creative power of the mind; resourcefulness, contrivance. — *adj* **imag'inative** (*-ə-tiv* or *-ā-tiv*) full of imagination; done or created with, or showing, imagination. — *n* **imag'inativeness.** — *n* **imag'iner.** — *n* **imag'ining** (in *pl*) things imagined. — **imaginary numbers** or **quantities** non-existent quantities involving the square roots of negative quantities. [O.Fr. *imaginer* — L. *imāginārī* — *imāgō*, an image.]

imagism, imagist. See under **image.**

imago *i-mā'gō* or *i-mä'go*, *n* the last or perfect stage of an insect's development; an elaborated type, founded esp. on a parent, persisting in the unconscious as an influence (*psychol*): — *pl* **imagines** (*i-mā'ji-nēz*, *i-mā'gi-nēz* or *-mä'*), **ima'gos** or **ima'goes.** [L. *imāgō*, *-inis*, image.]

imam *i-mäm'* or **imaum** *i-möm'*, *n* the officer who leads the devotions in a mosque; (with *cap*) a title for various Muslim potentates, founders and leaders. — *n* **imam'ate** (the period of) office of an imam; the territory under the jurisdiction of an imam. [Ar. *imām*, chief.]

imbalance *im-bal'əns*, *n* a lack of balance or proportion. [**im-** (**in-** (2)).]

imbecile *im'bi-sēl* or *-sil*, *n* a person of very defective intelligence, but not as severely retarded as an idiot; a foolish, unwise or stupid person. — *adj* extremely feeble-minded; foolish, fatuous. — *adj* **imbecilic** (*im-bi-sil'ik*). — *n* **imbecil'ity.** [Fr. *imbécille* (now *imbécile*) — L. *imbēcillus*, weak, feeble.]

imbed. See **embed.**

imbibe *im-bīb'*, *vt* to drink; to absorb, drink in, receive into the mind. — *vi* to drink. — *n* **imbī'ber.** [L. *imbĭbĕre* — *in*, in, into, *bibĕre*, to drink.]

imbosom. See **embosom.**

imbricate *im'bri-kāt*, *vt* to lay one overlapping another, as tiles on a roof. — *vi* to be so placed. — *adj* (*-kit* or *-kāt*) (of fish-scales, bird-scales, layers of tissue, teeth) overlapping like roof-tiles. — *n* **imbricā'tion.** [L. *imbrex*, a tile, *imbricāre*, *-ātum*, to tile — *imber*, a shower of rain.]

imbroglio *im-brōl'yō*, *n* a confused mass; a tangle; an embroilment; an ordered confusion (*mus*): — *pl* **imbro'glios.** [It., confusion — *imbrogliare*, to confuse, embroil.]

imbrue *im-brōō'*, *vt* to wet or moisten; to soak; to drench; to stain or dye. — *n* **imbrue'ment.** [O.Fr. *embreuver* — *bevre* (Fr. *boire*) — L. *bibĕre*, to drink.]

imbue *im-bū'*, *vt* to fill, permeate (e.g. the mind) (with *with*); to moisten; to tinge deeply. [O.Fr. *imbuer* — L. *imbuĕre* — *in*, and root of *bibĕre*, to drink.]

IMF *abbrev* for International Monetary Fund.

imide *im'īd*, (*chem*) *n* any of a class of organic compounds formed from ammonia or a primary amine by replacing two hydrogen atoms by a metal or acid radical. [Alteration of **amide.**]

imine *im'īn* or *i-mīn'*, *n* a highly reactive nitrogen-containing organic substance having a carbon-to-nitrogen double bond. [Alteration of **amine.**]

imipramine *i-mip'rə-mēn*, *n* an antidepressant drug also used in the treatment of enuresis. [From d*i*methyl*pr*opyl*amine*.]

imit. *abbrev* for imitative.

imitate *im'i-tāt*, *vt* to strive to be like or produce something like; to copy or take as a model; to mimic. — *n* **imitability** (*-ə-bil'i-ti*). — *adj* **im'itable.** — *n* **imitā'tion** the act of imitating; that which is produced as a copy or counterfeit; a performance in mimicry; the repeating of the same passage, or the following of a passage with a similar one in one or more of the other parts (*mus*). — *adj* sham, counterfeit; produced as a substitute, by a cheaper method in cheaper materials, etc. — *adj* **im'itātive** (or *im'i-tə-tiv*) inclined to imitate; formed after a model; mimicking; (of words) onomatopoeic — imitating a sound or representative of a physical movement or impression. — *adv* **im'itatively.** — *n* **im'itativeness.** — *n* **im'itātor.** [L. *imitārī*, *-ātus*.]

immaculate *i-mak'ū-lit*, *adj* clean, spotless; perfectly groomed; flawless; unstained; pure. — *adv* **immac'ulately.** — *n* **immac'ulateness.** — **Immaculate Conception** the R.C. dogma that the Virgin Mary was conceived without original sin — first proclaimed as article of faith in 1854 — not the same as the Virgin Birth. [L. *immaculātus* — *in-*, not, *maculāre*, to spot.]

immanent *im'ə-nənt*, *adj* indwelling; pervading; inherent. — *n* **imm'anence** or **imm'anency** the pervasion of the universe by the intelligent and creative principle — a fundamental conception of pantheism. — *n* **imm'anentism** belief in an immanent God. — *n* **imm'anentist.** [L. *in*, in, *manēre*, to remain.]

Immanuel. See **Emmanuel.**

immaterial *im-ə-tē'ri-əl*, *adj* not consisting of matter; incorporeal; unimportant. — *vt n* **immatē'rialism** (*philos*) the doctrine that there is no material substance, that material things do not exist outside the mind. — *n* **immatē'rialist.** — *n* **immatēriality** (*-al'i-ti*). — *adv* **immatē'rially.** [**im-** (**in-** (2)).]

immature *im-ə-tyōōr'* or *-chōōr'*, *adj* not fully grown; not yet ripe; not fully developed (mentally, physically, etc.); (of behaviour, attitudes, etc.) childish. — *adv* **immature'ly.** — *n* **immature'ness** or **immatur'ity.** [**im-** (**in-** (2)).]

immeasurable *i-mezh'ər-ə-bl*, *adj* too great to be measured. — *n* **immeas'urableness.** — *adv* **immeas'urably.** [**im-** (**in-** (2)).]

immediate *i-mē'di-it*, *-dyət*, *-dyit* or *-jət*, *adj* done or happening without delay; direct, with nothing intervening; next, nearest or closest; involving, or resulting from, nothing other than direct knowledge or intuitive understanding (*philos*). — *n* **immē'diacy** the state of being immediate; directness or freshness of appeal. — *adv* **immē'diately.** — *conj* as soon as. — *n* **immē'diateness.** [**im-** (**in-** (2)).]

immedicable *i-med'i-kə-bl*, *adj* incurable. [**im-** (**in-** (2)).]

Immelmann turn *im'əl-mən tûrn*, (*aeronautics*) *n* a manoeuvre involving a half loop and a half roll carried out to achieve greater height and reverse the direction of flight. [Named after the pilot who invented it.]

immemorial *im-i-mö'ri-əl*, *adj* ancient beyond the reach of memory. — *adv* **immemo'rially.** [**im-** (**in-** (2)).]

immense *i-mens'*, *adj* vast in extent; very large, enormous; fine, very good (*slang*). — *adv* **immense'ly.** — *n* **immense'ness** or **immens'ity** a measureless expanse; vastness. [Fr., — L. *immēnsus* — *in-*, not, *mēnsus*, past p. of *metīrī*, to measure.]

immerse *i-mûrs'*, *vt* to dip under the surface of a liquid; to baptise by submerging the whole body in water; to engage or involve deeply. — *adj* **immersed'** embedded in another part (*bot* or *zool*); growing entirely submerged in water (*bot*). — *n* **immer'sion** the act of immersing; the process or state of being immersed; deep absorption or involvement; baptism by immersing; entry into a position of invisibility as in eclipse or occultation (*astron*); a method of teaching a foreign language by giving the learner intensive practice in a situation in which all communication is in the language concerned. — *n* **immer'sionism.** — *n* **immer'sionist** a person who favours or practises baptism by immersion. — **immersion heater** an electrical apparatus directly immersed in the liquid, used for heating water. [L. *immergere*, *-mersum*, to dip, submerge.]

immigrate *im'i-grāt*, *vi* to migrate or remove into a country with intention of settling in it. — *n* **imm'igrant** a person who immigrates. — *n* **immigrā'tion.** [L. *immigrāre* — *in*, into, *migrāre*, *-ātum*, to remove.]

imminent *im'i-nənt*, *adj* impending, approaching, forthcoming; looming, threatening. — *n* **imm'inence** or **imm'inency.** — *adv* **imm'inently.** [L. *imminēns*, *-entis* — *in*, upon, *minēre*, to project, jut.]

immiscible *i-mis'i-bl*, *adj* not capable of being mixed. — *n* **immiscibil'ity.** [**im-** (**in-** (2)).]

immobile *i-mō'bīl* or in U.S. *-bil*, *adj* immovable; not readily moved; unable to move; motionless; stationary. — *n* **immobilīsā'tion** or **-z-.** — *vt* **immo'bilise** or **-ize** to render immobile; to put or keep out of action or circulation. — *n* **immobil'ity.** [**im-** (**in-** (2)).]

immoderate *i-mod'ər-it*, *adj* excessive; extravagant; unrestrained. — *adv* **immod'erately.** — *n* **immoderā'tion, immod'erateness** or **immod'eracy.** [**im-** (**in-** (2)).]

immodest *i-mod'ist*, *adj* shameless; indecent, improper; too self-assertive, boastful. — *adv* **immod'estly.** — *n* **immod'esty.** [**im-** (**in-** (2)).]

immolate *im'ə-lāt*, *vt* to offer in sacrifice. — *n* **immolā'tion.** — *n* **imm'olātor.** [L. *immolāre*, *-ātum*, to sprinkle meal (on a victim), hence to sacrifice — *in*, upon, *mola*, meal.]

immoral *i-mor'əl*, *adj* inconsistent with accepted moral principles or standards, wrong; evil, unscrupulous; sexually improper; promiscuous, licentious, dissolute. — *n* **immorality** (*im-ə-ral'i-ti*) the quality of being immoral; an immoral act or practice. — *adv* **immor'ally.** [**im-** (**in-** (2)).]

immortal *i-mör'tl*, *adj* exempt from death; living in perpetuity without fading or decaying; imperishable; never to be forgotten. — *n* a being who will never cease to exist; (often with *cap*) a god, esp. of the ancient Greeks and Romans; a person whose greatness will never fade, whose genius will always be revered. — *n* **immortalīsā'tion** or **-z-.** — *vt* **immor'talise** or **-ize** to make immortal. — *n* **immortality** (*im-ör-tal'i-ti*). — *adv* **immor'tally.** — **the Immortal Memory** a toast in memory of the Scottish poet, Robert Burns, usu. made on the anniversary of his birth, 25 January. [**im-** (**in-** (2)).]

immortelle *im-ör-tel'*, *n* an everlasting flower; a china replica of flowers, as a graveyard monument. [Fr. (*fleur*) *immortelle*, immortal (flower).]

immovable *i-mōō'və-bl*, *adj* impossible to move; steadfast; unyielding; impassive; motionless; unalterable; not liable to be removed (*law*; commonly **immove'able**); real, not personal (*law*). — *n* (*law*; usu. in *pl* **immove'ables**) immoveable property. — *n* **immo'vableness** or **immovabil'ity.** — *adv* **immo'vably.** [**im-** (**in-** (2)).]

immune *i-mūn'*, *adj* exempt (with *from*); free from obligation (with *from*); not liable to danger, protected (with *to*); having a high resistance to a disease due to the formation of humoral antibodies or cellular cytotoxins in response to the presence of antigens (with *to*); unaffected, not susceptible (with *to*). — *adj* **immunifā'cient** producing immunity. — *n* **immunīsā'tion** or **-z-.** — *vt* **imm'unise** or **-ize** to render immune, esp. to make immune from a disease by injecting disease germs, or their poisons (either active or rendered harmless). — *n* **immu'nity** the condition of being immune. — **immuno-** (*i-mū-nō-*, *i-mū-nə-* or *im'ū-*) *combining form* denoting immune, immunity. — *n* **immunoass'ay** (or *-ə-sā'*) a bioassay by immunological methods. — *adj* **immunochem'ical.** — *adv* **immunochem'ically.** — *n* **immunochem'istry** the chemistry of antibodies, antibody reactions, etc. — *adj* **immunocom'promised** (*med*) having an impaired immune system. — *n* **immunocytochem'istry** the study of the chemical aspects of cellular immunity. — *adj* **immunocytochem'ical.** — *adv* **immunocytochem'ically.** — *n* **immunodefi'ciency** deficiency in immune response due to depletion or inactivity of lymphoid cells. — *n* **immū'nogen** same as **antigen.** — *nsing* **immunogenet'ics** the study of inherited characteristics of immunity. — *n* **immunoglob'ulin** a protein (antibody) found in body fluids, capable of combining with and neutralising antigens. — *adj* **immunolog'ical.** — *adv* **immunolog'ically.** — *n* **immunol'ogist.** — *n* **immunol'ogy** the scientific study of immunity. — *adj* **immunopatholog'ical.** — *adv* **immunopatholog'ically.** — *n* **immunopathol'ogy** the study of immune factors associated with disease. — *n* **immunosuppress'ant** a drug which inhibits the body's rejection of e.g. transplanted organs. — *n* **immunosuppress'ion.** — *adj* **immunosuppress'ive.** — *n* **immunother'apy** the treatment of disease, now esp. cancer, by antigens which stimulate the patient's own natural immunity. — *n* **immunotransfū'sion** the transfusion of blood or plasma containing in high concentration the appropriate antibodies for the infection from which the patient is suffering. — **immune body** an antibody; **immune response** the production of antibodies in the body as a defensive response to the presence of antigens; **immune system** the process within an organism whereby antigenic or foreign matter is distinguished and neutralised through antibody or cytotoxic action. [L. *immūnis* — *in-*, not, *mūnis*, serving.]

immure *im-ūr'*, *vt* to wall in; to shut up; to imprison; to confine. — *n* **immure'ment.** [L. *in*, in, *mūrus*, a wall.]

immutable *i-mū'tə-bl*, *adj* unchangeable; changeless. — *n* **immūtabil'ity** or **immū'tableness.** — *adv* **immū'tably.** [**im-** (**in-** (2)).]

Imp. *abbrev* for *Imperator* (L.), Emperor; Imperial.

imp *imp*, *n* a mischievous child; a little devil or wicked spirit. — *adj* **imp'ish** like or characteristic of an imp, teasingly mischievous. — *adv* **imp'ishly.** — *n* **imp'ishness.** [O.E. *impa* — L.L. *impotus*, a graft — Gr. *emphytos*, engrafted.]

impact *im'pakt*, *n* the blow of a body in motion impinging on another body; the impulse resulting from collision; the impulse resulting from a new idea or theory; strong effect, influence. — *vt* (*im-pakt'*) to drive (an object) with force into something else; to drive or press (two objects) together with force; to have an impact or effect on. — *vi* (*im'pakt*) to make an impact. — *n* **impac'tion** the act of pressing together, or of fixing a substance tightly in a body cavity; the condition so produced. — **impacted fracture** a fracture in which the broken ends of the bone are driven into each other; **impacted tooth** one wedged between the jawbone and another tooth and therefore unable to come through the gum; **impact parameter** (*nuc*) the distance at which two particles which collide would have passed if no interaction had occurred between them. [L. *impactus*, past p. of *impingĕre*; see **impinge.**]

impair *im-pār'*, *vt* to diminish; to injure, damage or spoil; to weaken. — *n* **impair'ment.** [O.Fr. *empeirer*, from L. *im-* (intensive) and *pējōrāre*, to make worse — *pējor*, worse.]

impala *im-pä'lə*, *n* an African antelope with horns curved in the shape of a lyre, capable of prodigious leaps: — *pl* **impa'la** or **impa'las.** [Zulu *i-mpālaj.*]

impale *im-pāl'*, *vt* to put to death by piercing with a stake; to transfix; to juxtapose (two coats of arms) on a single vertically divided shield (*heraldry*). — *n* **impale'ment** the act or punishment of impaling; the marshalling side by side of two escutcheons combined in one (*heraldry*). [Fr. *empaler* — L. *in*, in, *pālus*, a stake.]

impalpable *im-pal'pə-bl*, *adj* not perceivable by touch; not capable of being comprehended or grasped; extremely fine-grained. — *n* **impalpabil'ity.** — *adv* **impal'pably.** [**im-** (**in-** (2)).]

impar- *im-par-* or **impari-** *im-par-i-*, *combining form* signifying unequal. — *n* **imparity** (*im-par'i-ti*) inequality. [L. *impār* — *in-*, not, *pār*, equal.]

impart *im-pärt'*, *vt* to give (something abstract); to communicate, make known. — *vi* to give a part (of). — *n* **impartā'tion.** — *n* **impart'er.** [O.Fr. *empartir* — L. *impartīre* — *in*, on, *pars*, *partis*, a part.]

impartial *im-pär'shl*, *adj* not favouring one more than another; just. — *n* **impartiality** (*-shi-al'i-ti*). — *adv* **impar'tially.** — *n* **impar'tialness.** [**im-** (**in-** (2)).]

impartible *im-pärt'i-bl*, (*law*) *adj* not partible; indivisible. — *n* **impartibil'ity.** [**im-** (**in-** (2)).]

impassable *im-päs'ə-bl*, *adj* not capable of being passed or travelled through. — *n* **impassabil'ity** or **impass'ableness.** — *adv* **impass'ably.** — *n* **impasse** (*am-pas'* or *ē-pas*) a situation from which there is no outlet; a deadlock. [**im-** (**in-** (2)).]

impassion *im-pash'ən*, *vt* to move with passion; to make passionate. — *adj* **impass'ionate** impassioned; dispassionate. — *adj* **impass'ioned** moved by or charged with passion; animated. [It. *impassionare* — L. *in*, in, *passiō*, *-ōnis*, passion.]

impassive *im-pas'iv*, *adj* not susceptible of feeling; not showing feeling; imperturbable. — *adv* **impass'ively.** — *n* **impass'iveness** or **impassiv'ity.** [**im-** (**in-** (2)).]

impaste *im-pāst'*, *vt* to lay colours thick on. — *n* **impasto** (*im-päs'tō*) in painting and pottery, the thick laying on of pigments; the paint laid on this way: — *pl* **impast'os.** — *adj* **impast'oed, impast'o'd** or **impāst'ed.** [L.L. *impastāre* — *in*, into, *pasta*, paste.]

impatient *im-pā'shənt*, *adj* not able to endure or to wait; fretful; restless; intolerant (of). — *n* **impā'tience.** — *adv* **impā'tiently.** [L. *impatiēns*, *-entis*, impatient — *in*, not, *patiēns*, patient.]

impeach *im-pēch'*, *vt* to disparage; to find fault with; to call in question; to arraign (esp. when a lower legislative house charges a high officer with grave offences before the upper house as judges); to turn king's evidence against (*law*). — *adj* **impeach'able.** — *n* **impeach'er.** — *n* **impeach'ment.** [O.Fr. *empech(i)er*, to hinder (Fr. *empêcher*) — L. *impedicāre*, to fetter.]

impeccable *im-pek'ə-bl*, *adj* faultless; not liable to sin. — *n* **impeccabil'ity.** — *adv* **impecc'ably.** — *adj* **impecc'ant** without sin. [**im-** (**in-** (2)).]

impecunious *im-pi-kū'ni-əs* or *-nyəs*, *adj* without money; short of money. — *n* **impecunios'ity.** [**im-** (**in-** (2)).]

impede *im-pēd'*, *vt* to hinder or obstruct. — *n* **impē'dance** hindrance; an apparent increase of resistance to an alternating current owing to induction in a circuit (*electr*). — *n* **impediment** (*-ped'*) obstacle; a defect preventing fluent speech. — *npl* **impediment'a** (L. *impedīmenta*) military baggage; baggage generally; encumbrances. — *adj* **impedimen'tal** or **imped'itive** hindering. [L. *impedīre* — *in*, in, *pēs*, *pedis*, a foot.]

impel *im-pel'*, *vt* to urge forward; to excite to action; to instigate: — *pr p* **impell'ing;** *pa t* and *pa p* **impelled'.** — *adj* **impell'ent** impelling or driving on. — *n* an impelling agent or power. — *n* **impell'er** someone who, or something which, impels; a rotor for transmitting motion. [L. *impellĕre*, *impulsum* — *in*, on, *pellĕre*, to drive.]

impend *im-pend'*, *vi* to threaten; to be about to happen. — *adj* **impend'ing.** [L. *impendēre* — *in*, on, *pendēre*, to hang.]

impenetrable *im-pen'i-trə-bl*, *adj* not to be penetrated; impervious; inscrutable; occupying space exclusively (*phys*). — *n* **impenetrabil'ity.** — *adv* **impen'etrably.** [**im-** (**in-** (2)).]

impenitent *im-pen'i-tənt*, *adj* not repenting. — *n* someone who does not repent; a hardened sinner. — *n* **impen'itence.** — *n* **impen'itency.** — *adv* **impen'itently.** [**im-** (**in-** (2)).]

imper. *abbrev* for imperative.

imperative *im-per'ə-tiv*, *adj* expressive of command, advice or request; urgently necessary; calling out for action; obligatory; authoritative, peremptory. — *n* that which is imperative; the imperative mood; a verb in the imperative mood. — *adv* **imper'atively.** — **categorical imperative** see under **category.** [L. *imperātīvus* — *imperāre*, to command.]

imperceptible *im-pər-sep'ti-bl*, *adj* not discernible by the senses; very small, slight or gradual. — *n* **imperceptibil'ity.** — *n* **impercep'tibleness.** — *adv* **impercep'tibly.** — *adj* **impercep'tive** or **impercip'ient** not perceiving; having no power to perceive. [**im-** (**in-** (2)).]

imperf. *abbrev* for imperfect.

imperfect *im-pûr'fikt*, *adj* incomplete; defective; falling short of perfection; lacking any normal part, or the full normal number of parts; expressing continued or habitual action in past time (*gram*); diminished, less by a semitone (*mus*). — *n* (*gram*) the imperfect tense; a verb in the imperfect tense. — *n* **imperfectibil'ity.** — *adj* **imperfect'ible.** — *n* **imperfection** (*-fek'shən*) the state of being imperfect; a defect. — *adj* **imperfec'tive** (*gram*) denoting the aspect of the verb which indicates that the action described is in progress. — *adv* **imperfec'tively** (*gram*). — *adv* **imper'fectly**. — *n* **imper'fectness**. — **imperfect cadence** (*mus*) a cadence which is not resolved to the tonic key, esp. one passing from tonic to dominant chord; **imperfect fungus** a fungus of the order *Fungi Imperfecti* of which no sexual stage is known. [**im-** (**in-** (2)).]

imperforate *im-pûr'fə-rit* or **imperforated** *-pûr'fə-rā-tid*, *adj* not pierced through or perforated; having no opening; abnormally closed (*med*); without perforations for tearing apart, as in a sheet of postage stamps. [**im-** (**in-** (2)).]

imperial *im-pē'ri-əl*, *adj* pertaining to, or of the nature of, an empire or emperor; sovereign, supreme; commanding, august; (of products, etc.) of superior quality or size. — *n* a tuft of hair beneath the lower lip; the top of a carriage, or a trunk for carrying on it (*old*); a size of paper, (British) 22 × 30 in. (56 × 76 cm.), (U.S.) 23 × 33 in. (58 × 84 cm.). — *vt* **impē'rialise** or **-ize** to make imperial. — *n* **impē'rialism** the power or authority of an emperor; the policy of making or maintaining an empire; the spirit of empire. — *n* **impē'rialist**. — *adj* **impērialist'ic**. — *n* **impēriality** (*-al'i-ti*) imperial power, right or privilege. — *adv* **impē'rially**. — *adj* **impē'rious** assuming command; haughty; tyrannical; domineering; peremptory; authoritative. — *adv* **impē'riously**. — *n* **impē'riousness**. — **imperial city** Rome; **imperial measure** or **weight** non-metric standard of measure or weight (**imperial gallon, yard** and **pound**) as fixed by parliament for the United Kingdom (final act 1963). [L. *impĕrium*, sovereignty.]

imperil *im-per'il*, *vt* to endanger: — *pa p* **imper'illed**. — *n* **imper'ilment**. [**im-** (**in-** (1)).]

imperious, etc. See under **imperial**.

imperishable *im-per'ish-ə-bl*, *adj* indestructible; everlasting. — *n* **imperishabil'ity**. — *n* **imper'ishableness**. — *adv* **imper'ishably**. [**im-** (**in-** (2)).]

impermanence *im-pûr'mə-nəns*, *n* lack of permanence. — *n* **imper'manency**. — *adj* **imper'manent**. [**im-** (**in-** (2)).]

impermeable *im-pûr'mi-ə-bl*, *adj* not permitting passage, esp. of fluids; impervious. — *n* **impermeabil'ity**. — *n* **imper'meableness**. — *adv* **imper'meably**. [**im-** (**in-** (2)).]

impermissible *im-pər-mis'i-bl*, *adj* not permissible. — *n* **impermissibil'ity**. — *adv* **impermiss'ibly**. [**im-** (**in-** (2)).]

impers. *abbrev* for impersonal.

impersonal *im-pûr'sə-nəl*, *adj* not having personality; used only in the third person singular (in English usu. with *it* as subject; *gram*); without reference to any particular person; objective, uncoloured by personal feeling, cold. — *vt* **imper'sonalise** or **-ize**. — *n* **impersonality** (*-al'i-ti*). — *adv* **imper'sonally**. [**im-** (**in-** (2)).]

impersonate *im-pûr'sə-nāt*, *vt* to assume the person or character of, esp. on the stage. — *n* **impersonā'tion**. — *n* **imper'sonātor**. [L. *in*, in, *persōna*, person; see **personate**.]

impertinent *im-pûr'ti-nənt*, *adj* saucy, impudent; intrusive, presumptuous; not pertinent (*archaic* or *legal*). — *n* **imper'tinence** or **imper'tinency** that which is impertinent; intrusion; impudence, overforwardness; matter introduced into an affidavit, etc., not pertinent to the matter (*law*). — *adv* **imper'tinently**. [**im-** (**in-** (2)).]

imperturbable *im-pər-tûr'bə-bl*, *adj* that cannot be disturbed or agitated; permanently quiet. — *n* **imperturbabil'ity**. — *adv* **impertur'bably**. — *n* **imperturbā'tion**. [L. *imperturbābilis* — *in-*, not, *perturbāre*, to disturb; see **perturb**.]

impervious *im-pûr'vi-əs* or **imperviable** *im-pûr'vi-ə-bl*, *adj* not to be penetrated; not easily influenced by ideas, arguments, etc., or moved or upset (with *to*). — *n* **imperviabil'ity**. — *n* **imper'viableness**. — *adv* **imper'viously**. — *n* **imper'viousness**. [**im-** (**in-** (2)).]

impetigo *im-pi-tī'gō*, *n* a skin disease characterised by thickly-set clusters of pustules: — *pl* **impetigines** (*-tij'i-nēz*) or **impetī'gos**. — *adj* **impetiginous** (*-tij'*). [L. *impetīgō* — *impetĕre*, to rush upon, attack.]

impetus *im'pi-təs*, *n* momentum; impulse; incentive: — *pl* **im'petuses**. [Ety. as for **impetuous**.]

impetuous *im-pet'ū-əs*, *adj* rushing on with impetus or violence; vehement; acting with headlong energy. — *n* **impetuosity** (*-os'i-ti*). — *adv* **impet'uously**. — *n* **impet'uousness**. [L. *impetus* (pl. *impetūs*) — *in*, into, on, *petĕre*, to seek.]

impi *im'pi*, *n* a group of southern African native warriors. [Zulu.]

impiety *im-pī'ə-ti*, *n* lack of piety or veneration. [L. *impietās, -ātis* — *in*, not; cf. **piety**.]

impinge *im-pinj'*, *vi* (with *on*, *upon* or *against*) to strike; to encroach. — *vt* to drive, strike: — *pr p* **imping'ing**. — *n* **impinge'ment**. — *adj* **imping'ent**. [L. *impingĕre* — *in*, against, *pangĕre*, to fix, drive in.]

impious *im'pi-əs* (also, esp. in U.S., *im-pī'əs*), *adj* irreverent; lacking veneration, as for gods, parents, etc. — *adv* **im'piously** (or *im-pī'*). [L. *impĭus* — *im-* (*in-*), not, *pĭus*; cf. **pious**.]

impish. See **imp**.

implacable *im-plak'ə-bl*, *adj* not to be appeased; inexorable; irreconcilable. — *n* **implacabil'ity** or **implac'ableness**. — *adv* **implac'ably**. [**im-** (**in-** (2)).]

implant *im-plänt'*, *vt* to engraft; to plant firmly; to fix in; to insert; to instil or inculcate; to plant (ground, etc., with). — *n* (*im'plänt*) something implanted in body tissue, e.g. a graft or a pellet containing a hormone. — *n* **implantā'tion**. [**im-** (**in-** (1)).]

implausible *im-plöz'i-bl*, *adj* not plausible. — *n* **implausibil'ity**. [**im-** (**in-** (2)).]

implement *im'pli-mənt*, *n* a piece of equipment, a requisite; a tool or instrument of labour. — *vt* (often *-ment'*) to give effect to; to fulfil or perform. — *adj* **implemen'tal** instrumental; effective. — *n* **implementā'tion** performance, fulfilment; the various steps involved in installing and operating a computer data-processing or control system (*comput*). [L.L. *implēmentum* — L. *in*, in, *plēre*, to fill.]

implicate *im'pli-kāt*, *vt* to involve; to entangle; to imply; to show to be, or to have been, a participator. — *n* a thing implied. — *adj* (*-kit*) involved; intertwined. — *n* **implicā'tion**. — *adj* **im'plicātive** (or *im-plik'ə-tiv*) tending to implicate. — *adv* **im'plicatively** (or *-plik'*). — *adj* **implicit** (*im-plis'it*) implied; relying entirely, unquestioning. — *adv* **implic'itly**. — *n* **implic'itness**. [L. *implicāre, -ātum*, also *-ĭtum* — *in*, in, *plicāre, -ātum* or *-itum*, to fold.]

implied, etc. See **imply**.

implode *im-plōd'*, *vt* and *vi* to burst inwards; to sound by implosion. — *n* **implō'dent** an implosive sound. — *n* **implo'sion** (*-zhən*) a bursting inward; in the formation of voiceless stops, compression of enclosed air by simultaneous stoppage of the mouth parts and the glottis (*phon*); inrush of air in a suction stop (*phon*). — *adj* **implo'sive** (*-siv* or *-ziv*). — *n* an implosive consonant; a suction stop or (sometimes) a click. [L. *in*, in, *plōdĕre* (*plaudĕre*), to clap.]

implore *im-plōr'*, *vt* to ask earnestly; to entreat. — Also *vi*. — *n* **implorā'tion**. — *adj* **imploratory** (*-plor'ə-tə-ri*). — *n* **implor'er**. — *adv* **implor'ingly** in an imploring manner. [L. *implōrāre*, to invoke with tears — *in*, in, *plōrāre*, to weep.]

implosion, implosive. See under **implode**.

imply *im-plī'*, *vt* to express indirectly; to insinuate; to signify; to involve the truth or reality of: — *pr p*

imply'ing: *pa t* and *pa p* **implied'**. — *adv* **im-plī'edly**. [O.Fr. *emplier* — L. *implicāre*.]

impolite *im-pə-līt'*, *adj* having rough manners; bad-mannered, rude. — *adv* **impolite'ly**. — *n* **impolite'-ness**. [**im-** (**in-** (2)).]

impolitic *im-pol'i-tik*, *adj* not politic; inexpedient. — *adv* **impol'iticly**. [**im-** (**in-** (2)).]

imponderable *im-pon'də-rə-bl*, *adj* not able to be weighed or estimated; without weight, immaterial; without sensible weight. — Also *n*. — *n* **impon-derabil'ity** or **impon'derableness**. — *npl* **im-pon'derables** factors in a situation whose influence cannot be gauged. — *adj* **impon'derous** weightless; very light. [**im-** (**in-** (2)).]

import *im-pört'*, *vt* to bring in; to bring from abroad; to convey, as a word; to signify; to portend. — Also *vi*. — *n* (*im'pört*) something which is brought from abroad; meaning; importance; tendency. — *adj* **import'able**. — *n* **import'ance** the fact of being important; extent of value or significance; weight, consequence; appearance of dignity. — *adj* **import'-ant** of great import or consequence; momentous, significant; pompous. — *adv* **import'antly**. — *n* **importā'tion** the act of importing; a commodity imported. — *n* **import'er**. — **invisible imports** such items in a national trade balance as money spent by tourists abroad, etc.; **visible imports** goods bought from foreign countries by traders. [L. *importāre*, *-ātum* — *in*, in, *portāre*, to carry.]

importune *im-pör-tūn'* or *im-pör'tūn*, *vt* to urge or crave repeatedly and often with harassment; to solicit for immoral purposes, make improper advances to. — *vi* to be importunate. — *n* **impor'-tunacy** or **impor'tunateness**. — *adj* **impor'tu-nate** (*-it* or *-āt*) troublesomely urgent; pressing; pertinacious. — *vi* to solicit pertinaciously. — *adv* **impor'tunately**. — *adv* **importune'ly** (or *-pör'*). — *n* **importun'er**. — *n* **importun'ing**. — *n* **impor-tun'ity**. [L. *importūnus*, inconvenient — *im-* (*in-*), not, *portus*, a harbour.]

impose *im-pōz'*, *vt* to place upon something; to lay on; to enjoin; to set as a burden or task; to set up in, or by, authority; to pass off unfairly. — *vi* (with *on* or *upon*) to mislead, deceive; to burden by taking undue advantage of someone's good nature; to act with constraining effect. — *adj* **impos'able**. — *n* **im-pos'er**. — *adj* **impos'ing** commanding, impressive; adapted to impress forcibly; specious; deceptive. — *adv* **impos'ingly**. — *n* **impos'ingness**. [Fr. *im-poser*.]

imposition *im-pə-zish'ən*, *n* an act or instance of imposing or laying on; something imposed, a burden; a punishment task; the assembling of pages and locking them into a chase (*printing*). [L. *impositiō*, *-ōnis* — *in*, on, *pōnĕre*, *pŏsitum*, to place.]

impossible *im-pos'i-bl*, *adj* that cannot be; that cannot be done or dealt with; that cannot be true; out of the question; hopelessly unsuitable or difficult to deal with (*colloq*); beyond doing anything with. — *n* a person or thing that is impossible. — *n* **impossi-bil'ity**. [**im-** (**in-** (2)).]

impost[1] *im'pōst*, *n* a tax, esp. on imports; the weight carried by a horse in a handicap race (*colloq*). [O.Fr. *impost* (Fr. *impôt*) — L. *impōnĕre*, *impŏsitum*, to lay on.]

impost[2] *im'pōst*, (*archit*) *n* the upper part of a pillar in vaults and arches, on which the weight of the building is laid; a horizontal block resting on uprights. [Fr. *imposte* — It. *imposta* — L. *impōnĕre*, *impŏsitum*.]

impostor or **imposter** *im-pos'tər*, *n* someone who assumes a false character or impersonates another. — *n* **impos'ture** (*-chər*) an imposition, fraud. [L.L., — L. *impōnĕre*, *impŏsitum*, to impose.]

impotent *im'pə-tənt*, *adj* powerless; helpless; (of a male) unable to perform sexual intercourse, owing to inability to achieve or maintain an erection. — *n* **im'potence** or **im'potency**. — *adv* **im'potently**. [**im-** (**in-** (2)).]

impound *im-pownd'*, *vt* to confine, as within in a pound; to restrain within limits; to take legal possession of; to hold up in a reservoir. — *adj* **impound'able**. — *n* **impound'age**. — *n* **im-pound'er**. — *n* **impound'ment**. [**im-** (**in-** (1)), and **pound**[2].]

impoverish *im-pov'ə-rish*, *vt* to make poor (*lit* or *fig*). — *n* **impov'erishment**. [From O.Fr. *empovrir*, *-iss*, — L. *in*, in, *pauper*, poor.]

impracticable *im-prak'ti-kə-bl*, *adj* not able to be done or put into practice; not able to be used. — *n* **impracticabil'ity**. — *n* **imprac'ticableness**. — *adv* **imprac'ticably**. [**im-** (**in-** (2)).]

impractical *im-prak'ti-kl*, *adj* not practical. — *n* **impracticality** (*-kal'*). — *n* **imprac'ticalness**. [**im-** (**in-** (2)).]

imprecate *im'pri-kāt*, *vt* to call down by prayer (esp. something evil); to invoke evil upon. — *vi* to curse. — *n* **imprecā'tion**. — *adj* **im'precatory** (*-kə-tə-ri* or *-kā-*). [L. *imprecāri* — *in*, upon, *precāri*, *-ātus*, to pray.]

imprecise *im-pri-sīs'*, *adj* not precise. — *n* **impre-cision** (*-si'zhən*). [**im-** (**in-** (2)).]

impregnable *im-preg'nə-bl*, *adj* that cannot be captured; proof against attack. — *n* **impregna-bil'ity**. — *adv* **impreg'nably**. [Fr. *imprenable* — L. *in-*, not, *prendĕre*, *prehendĕre*, to take; *g*, a freak of spelling, has come to be pronounced.]

impregnate *im'preg-nāt* or *-preg'*, *vt* to make pregnant; to fecundate; to fill or imbue (with the particles or qualities of another thing); to saturate (also *fig*). — *n* **impregnā'tion**. [L.L. *impraegnāre*, *-ātum* — *in*, in, *praegnāns*, pregnant.]

impresario *im-pri-sä'ri-ō*, *n* the manager of an opera company, etc.; a producer or organiser of entertainments; a showman: — *pl* **impresa'rios** or **im-presa'ri** (*-rē*). [It., — *impresa*, enterprise.]

imprescriptible *im-pri-skrip'ti-bl*, *adj* not liable to be lost by prescription, or lapse of time; inalienable. — *n* **imprescriptibil'ity**. [**im-** (**in-** (2)).]

impress[1] *im-pres'*, *vt* to press; to apply with pressure, esp. so as to leave a mark; to mark by pressure; to produce by pressure; to stamp or print; to fix deeply in the mind; to affect the mind; to produce a profound effect upon, or upon the mind of. — *vi* to be impressive, make a good impression. — *n* (*im'*) that which is made by pressure; stamp; distinctive mark. — *n* **impressibil'ity**. — *adj* **impress'ible** susceptible. — *n* **impression** (*im-presh'ən*) the act or result of impressing; pressure; a difference produced in a thing by action upon it; a single printing of a book; the effect of anything on the mind; a profound effect on the emotions; a vague uncertain memory or inclination to believe; belief, generally ill-founded; an impersonation. — *n* **impressionabil'ity**. — *adj* **impress'ionable** able to receive an impression; very susceptible to impressions. — *n* **impress'ionism** a 19th-century movement in painting, originating in France, aiming at the realistic representation of the play of light in nature, purporting to render faithfully what the artist actually saw, dispensing with the academic rules of composition and colouring (often with *cap*); any similar tendency in other arts. — *n* and *adj* **impress'ionist** an exponent of impressionism (often with *cap*); an entertainer who impersonates people. — *adj* **impressionis'tic**. — *adv* **impres-sionis'tically**. — *adj* **impressive** (*-pres'*) exerting or tending to exert pressure; capable of making a deep impression on the mind; solemn. — *adv* **impress'ively**. — *n* **impress'iveness**. — **be under the impression** to think or believe without certainty. [L. *imprimĕre*, *-pressum* — *in*, *premĕre*.]

impress[2] *im-pres'*, *vt* to force into service. — *n* **impress'ment** the act of impressing for service, esp. in the navy. [**im-** (**in-** (1)), and cf. **press**[2].]

imprest *im'prest*, *n* earnest money; money advanced. [**im-** (**in-** (1)) and cf. **press**[2].]

imprimatur *im-pri-mā'tər*, *n* a licence or permission to print a book, etc. [L. *imprĭmātur*, let it be printed.]

imprint *im-print'*, *vt* to print; to stamp; to impress; to fix in the mind; to cause (a young animal) to undergo imprinting (usu. with *on*). — *n* (*im'print*) that which is imprinted; the name of the publisher, time and place of publication of a book, etc., printed usu. on or on the back of the title-page; the printer's name on the back of the title-page or at the end of the book. — *n* **imprint'ing** a learning process in young animals in which their social preferences become restricted to their own species, or a substitute for this. [**im-** (**in-** (1)).]

imprison *im-priz'n*, *vt* to put in prison; to shut up; to confine or restrain. — *adj* **impris'onable** liable to be, or capable of being, imprisoned; (of an offence) likely to lead to imprisonment. — *n* **impris'onment.** [**im-** (**in-** (1)).]

improbable *im-prob'ə-bl*, *adj* unlikely. — *n* **improbabil'ity.** — *adv* **improb'ably.** [**im-** (**in-** (2)).]

improbity *im-prō'bi-ti* or *-prob'*, *n* lack of probity. [**im-** (**in-** (2)).]

impromptu *im-promp'tū*, *adj* improvised; offhand. — *adv* without preparation; on the spur of the moment. — *n* an extempore witticism or speech; an improvised composition; a musical composition with the character of an extemporisation. [L. *impromptū* for *in promptū* (abl.), *in*, in, *promptus*, readiness.]

improper *im-prop'ər*, *adj* not strictly belonging; not properly so called; not suitable; unfit; unbecoming; unseemly; indecent. — *adv* **improp'erly.** — *n* **imprōprī'ety.** — **improper fraction** a fraction that has a numerator of higher value than the denominator. [L. *im-* (*in-*), not, *proprius*, own.]

improve *im-prōōv'*, *vt* to make better. — *vi* to grow better; to make progress; to make improvements; to follow up with something better (with *on*). — *n* **improvabil'ity** or **improv'ableness.** — *adj* **improv'able.** — *adv* **improv'ably.** — *n* **improve'ment** the act of improving; a change for the better; a thing changed, or introduced in changing, for the better; a better thing substituted for or following one not so good (often with *on*). — *n* **improv'er.** — *pr p* and *adj* **improv'ing** tending to cause improvement; instructive; edifying; uplifting. — *adv* **improv'ingly.** [A.Fr. *emprower* — O.Fr. *en prou*, *preu*, into profit.]

improvident *im-prov'i-dənt*, *adj* not provident or prudent; lacking foresight; thoughtless. — *n* **improv'idence.** — *adv* **improv'idently.** [**im-** (**in-** (2)).]

improvise *im'prə-vīz* or *-vīz'*, *vt* to compose and recite, or perform, without preparation; to bring about suddenly; to make or contrive without preparation or in emergency. — *vi* to perform extempore; to do anything without proper materials or preparation. — *n* **improvīsā'tion** the act of improvising; that which is improvised. — *adj* **improvisatō'rial** (*-iz-ə-*). — *adj* **improvisatory** (*-iz'* or *-īz'*). — *n* **im'provīser.** [Fr. *improviser* — L. *in-*, not, *prōvīsus*, foreseen; see **provide.**]

imprudent *im-prōō'dənt*, *adj* lacking foresight or discretion; incautious; inconsiderate. — *n* **impru'dence.** — *adv* **impru'dently.** [**im-** (**in-** (2)).]

impudent *im'pū-dənt*, *adj* shamelessly bold; pert; insolent; mischievous. — *n* **im'pudence.** — *adv* **im'pudently.** [L. *im-* (*in-*), not, *pudēns*, *-entis*, pres. p. of *pudēre*, to be ashamed.]

impugn *im-pūn'*, *vt* to oppose; to attack by words or arguments; to call in question. — *adj* **impugnable** (*-pūn'*). — *n* **impugn'er.** — *n* **impugn'ment.** [L. *impugnāre* — *in*, against, *pugnāre*, to fight.]

impulse *im'puls*, *n* the act of impelling; the effect of an impelling force; force suddenly and momentarily communicated; a beat; a single blow, thrust or wave; a disturbance travelling along a nerve (**nerve impulse**) or a muscle; an outside influence on the mind; a sudden inclination to act. — *n* **impul'sion** (*-shən*) impelling force; instigation. — *adj* **impuls'ive** having the power of impelling; acting or actuated by impulse; not continuous; tending or likely to act upon impulse. — *adv* **impuls'ively.** — *n* **impuls'iveness.** — **impulse buyer; impulse buying** the buying of goods on a whim rather than because of previous intent. [L. *impulsus*, pressure — *impellĕre*.]

impunity *im-pū'ni-ti*, *n* freedom or safety from punishment or ill consequences. [L. *impūnitās*, *-ātis* — *in*, not, *poena*, punishment.]

impure *im-pūr'*, *adj* mixed with something else; unclean materially, morally or ceremonially. — *adv* **impure'ly.** — *n* **impure'ness.** — *n* **impur'ity** an impure or unclean thing or constituent; the quality or state of being impure. [**im-** (**in-** (2)).]

impute *im-pūt'*, *vt* to ascribe (usually evil); to charge; to attribute vicariously (*theol*). — *adj* **imput'able** capable of being imputed or charged; open to accusation; attributable. — *n* **imputabil'ity.** — *n* **imput'ableness.** — *adv* **imput'ably.** — *n* **imputā'tion** the act of imputing or charging; censure; reproach; the reckoning as belonging. [Fr. *imputer* — L. *imputāre*, *-ātum* — *in*, in, *putāre*, to reckon.]

IMRO *abbrev* for Investment Management Regulatory Organisation.

IN *abbrev* for Indiana (U.S. state).

In (*chem*) *symbol* for indium.

in *in*, *prep* expressing the relation of a thing to that which surrounds, encloses, includes or conditions it, or to that which is assumed, held, maintained, or the relation of a right or possession to the person who holds or enjoys it; at; among; into; within; during; consisting of; by way of; because of; by or through; by the medium or method of; among the characteristics or possibilities of; wearing; belonging to. — *adv* within; not out; at home; on the spot; in or to a position within or inward; in or into office, parliament, etc.; in favour; in mutual favour; in intimacy; in fashion; in the market; in season; having innings (*cricket*); as an addition; alight; in pocket. — *n* a member of the party in office or the side that is having its innings. — *adj* inward; proceeding inwards; that is fashionable, much in use, as **in'=word** or **in-thing'**; within a small group. — **-in** used in combination indicating a (public) gathering of a group of people in one room, building, etc., orig. as a form of protest (as in *sit-in*, *work-in*), now for any joint purpose (as in *teach-in*). — *adj* **in'-built** built in. — *adj* **in'-depth** (of a survey, research, etc.) detailed or penetrating; thorough, comprehensive, not superficial. — **in'-fighting** fighting or bitter rivalry, between individuals or within a group, that goes on more or less secretly (see also **infighting** — separate article). — *adj* **in'-flight** provided during an aeroplane flight. — **Ingathering, Feast of.** See under **tabernacle**; **in'group** a social group of people having the same interests and attitudes. — *adj* and *adv* **in'-house** within a particular company, establishment, etc. — **in-joke'** a joke to be fully appreciated only by members of a particular limited group; **in-off'** (*billiards*) a losing hazard; **in'=patient** a patient living and being treated in a hospital. — *adj* **in'-service** carried out while continuing with one's ordinary employment, e.g. *in-service training*. — *adj* **in'shore** close to the shore; moving towards the shore. — *adj* **in'-store** provided within a shop. — **in'-tray** a shallow container for letters, etc., still to be dealt with. — **in as far as, in so far as,** or **insofar as** to the extent that; **in as much as** or **inasmuch as** considering that; **in for** doomed to receive (esp. unpleasant consequences); involved to the extent of; entered for; (see also **go in for** under **go**[1]); **in for it** in for trouble; committed to a certain course; **in itself** intrinsically, apart from relations; **in on** (*slang*) participating in or aware of; **ins and outs** (or **outs and ins**) turnings this way and that; nooks and corners; the whole details of any matter; those who repeatedly enter and leave; **in that** for the reason that; **in with** friendly with, associating much with; enjoying the favour of; **nothing in it** no truth, no importance, no difficulty in the matter; no important difference. [O.E. *in*.]

in. *abbrev* for inch(es).

-in *-in*, (*chem*, etc.) noun-forming *sfx* usu. indicating: (1) a neutral substance such as a protein, fat or glycoside, such as *albumin*, *insulin*; (2) certain enzymes, as *pepsin*; (3) an antibiotic or other pharmaceutical production, such as *penicillin*, *aspirin*. [Variant of **-ine**[1].]

in- *in-*, *pfx* (1) in words derived from L. and O.E., used to form verbs with the sense in, into; sometimes used to form other parts of speech with this sense; sometimes used as an intensive or almost meaningless pfx.; (2) in words derived from L., used to form negatives.

inability *in-ə-bil'i-ti*, *n* lack of sufficient power; incapacity. [**in-** (2).]

in absentia *in ab-sen'shyə*, (L.) in (his, her, their, etc.) absence.

inaccessible *in-ak-* or *in-ək-ses'i-bl*, *adj* not able to be reached, obtained, or approached. — *n* **inaccessibil'ity** or **inaccess'ibleness**. — *adv* **inaccess'ibly**. [**in-** (2).]

inaccurate *in-ak'ū-rit*, *adj* not accurate; incorrect. — *n* **inacc'uracy** (*-rə-si*). — *adv* **inacc'urately**. [**in-** (2).]

inactive *in-ak'tiv*, *adj* not active; inert; having no power to move; sluggish; idle; lazy; having no effect; not showing any action (*chem*). — *n* **inac'tion**. — *adv* **inac'tively**. — *n* **inactiv'ity** inaction; inertness; idleness. [**in-** (2).]

inadaptable *in-ə-dap'tə-bl*, *adj* that cannot be adapted. — *n* **inadaptā'tion** (*-ad-*). [**in-** (2).]

inadequate *in-ad'i-kwit*, *adj* insufficient; short of what is required; incompetent. — Also *n*. — *n* **inad'equacy** (*-kwə-si*) or **inad'equateness** insufficiency. — *adv* **inad'equately**. [**in-** (2).]

inadmissible *in-əd-mis'i-bl*, *adj* not allowable. — *n* **inadmissibil'ity**. — *adv* **inadmiss'ibly**. [**in-** (2).]

inadvertent *in-əd-vûrt'ənt*, *adj* unintentional; inattentive. — *n* **inadvert'ence** or **inadvert'ency** negligence; oversight. — *adv* **inadvert'ently**. [**in-** (2).]

inadvisable *in-ad-vī'zə-bl*, *adj* not advisable, unwise. — *n* **inadvisabil'ity** or **inadvi'sableness**. [**in-** (2).]

inalienable *in-āl'yən-ə-bl* or *in-ā'li-ən-ə-bl*, *adj* not capable of being transferred or removed. — *n* **inalienabil'ity**. — *adv* **ina'lienably**. [**in-** (2).]

inalterable *in-öl'tə-rəbl*, *adj* not alterable. — *n* **inalterabil'ity**. — *n* **inal'terableness**. — *adv* **inal'terably**. [**in-** (2).]

inane *in-ān'*, *adj* empty, void; vacuous; senseless; characterless. — *adv* **inane'ly**. — *n* **inane'ness**. — *n* **inanition** (*in-ə-nish'ən*) exhaustion from want of food. — *n* **inanity** (*in-an'i-ti*) senselessness; mental vacuity; emptiness; an insipid frivolous utterance. [L. *inānis*.]

inanimate *in-an'i-mit*, *adj* without animation; without life; dead; spiritless; dull. — *n* **inan'imateness**. — *n* **inanimā'tion**. [**in-** (2).]

inapplicable *in-ap'li-kə-bl* or *in-ə-plik'ə-bl*, *adj* not applicable. — *n* **inapplicabil'ity**. [**in-** (2).]

inapposite *in-ap'ə-zit*, *adj* not apposite, suitable or pertinent. — *adv* **inapp'ositely**. — *n* **inapp'ositeness**. [**in-** (2).]

inappreciable *in-ə-prē'shə-bl* or *-shyə-bl*, *adj* too small or slight to be noticed, or to be important. — *n* **inappreciation** (*-shi-ā'shən*). — *adj* **inapprē'ciative** (*-shi-ə-tiv*) not valuing justly or at all. [**in-** (2).]

inappropriate *in-ə-prō'pri-it*, *adj* not appropriate, not suitable. — *adv* **inappro'priately**. — *n* **inappro'priateness**. [**in-** (2).]

inapt *in-apt'*, *adj* not apt; unfit or unqualified. — *n* **inapt'itude** or **inapt'ness** unfitness, awkwardness. — *adv* **inapt'ly**. [**in-** (2).]

inarticulate *in-är-tik'ū-lit*, *adj* not jointed or hinged; indistinctly uttered or uttering; incapable of clear and fluent expression. — *n* **inartic'ulacy**. — *adv* **inartic'ulately**. — *n* **inartic'ulateness** or **inarticulā'tion** indistinctness of sounds in speaking. [**in-** (2).]

inartistic *in-är-tis'tik*, *adj* not artistic; deficient in appreciation of art. — *adv* **inartis'tically**. [**in-** (2).]

inasmuch *in-az-much'* or *in-əz-*. See under **in**.

inattentive *in-ə-ten'tiv*, *adj* careless; not paying attention; neglectful. — *n* **inatten'tion**. — *adv* **inatten'tively**. — *n* **inatten'tiveness**. [**in-** (2).]

inaudible *in-öd'i-bl*, *adj* not able to be heard. — *n* **inaudibil'ity**. — *n* **inaud'ibleness**. — *adv* **inaud'ibly**. [**in-** (2).]

inaugurate *in-ö'gū-rāt*, *vt* to induct formally into an office; to cause to begin; to make a public exhibition of for the first time. — *adj* **inau'gural** pertaining to, or done at, an inauguration. — *n* an inaugural address. — *n* **inaugurā'tion**. — *n* **inau'gurātor**. — *adj* **inau'guratory** (*-ə-tə-ri*). [L. *inaugurāre*, *-ātum*, to inaugurate with taking of the auspices; see **augur**.]

inauspicious *in-ö-spish'əs*, *adj* not auspicious; ill-omened; unlucky. — *adv* **inauspic'iously**. — *n* **inauspic'iousness**. [**in-** (2).]

inauthentic *in-ö-then'tik*, *adj* not authentic; not genuine; untrue. [**in-** (2).]

in-between *in-bi-twēn'*, *adj* intervening; intermediate. — *n* an interval; an intermediary; any thing or person that is intermediate.

inboard *in'bōrd*, *adv* and *adj* within the hull or interior of a ship. [**in-** (1).]

inborn *in'börn*, *adj* born in or with one; innate; implanted by nature. [**in-** (1).]

inbreed *in'brēd* or *in-brēd'*, *vt* to breed or generate within; to breed from closely related parents: — *pa p* and *adj* **in'bred** innate; bred from closely related parents. — *n* **in'breeding**. [**in-** (1).]

inc. *abbrev* for: including; inclusive; incorporated.

Inca *ing'kə*, *n* an Indian of Peru before the Spanish conquest; a member of the old royal family of Peru; a Peruvian king or emperor. — Also *adj*. [Quechua, prince.]

incalculable *in-kal'kū-lə-bl*, *adj* not calculable or able to be reckoned; too great to calculate; unpredictable. — *n* **incalculabil'ity**. — *n* **incal'culableness**. — *adv* **incal'culably**. [**in-** (2).]

in camera. See under **camera**.

incandesce *in-kan-des'*, *vi* to be luminous by heat. — *n* **incandesc'ence** a white heat. — *adj* **incandesc'ent** white-hot. — **incandescent lamp** one whose light is produced by heating something to white heat. [L. *in*, in, *candēscere* — *candēre*, to glow.]

incantation *in-kan-tā'shən*, *n* a formula of words said or sung for purposes of enchantment; the use of spells. [L. *incantāre*, to sing a magical formula over.]

incapable *in-kā'pə-bl*, *adj* not capable; unable (with *of*); incompetent; helplessly drunk; disqualified. — *n* **incapabil'ity**. — *adv* **incā'pably**. [**in-** (2).]

incapacious *in-kə-pā'shəs*, *adj* not large, narrow; of small capacity. — *n* **incapā'ciousness**. — *vt* **incapacitate** (*-pas'*) to disable; to make unfit (for); to disqualify legally. — *n* **incapacitā'tion** (a) disqualifying. — *n* **incapac'ity** lack of capacity; inability; disability; legal disqualification. [L. *incapāx*, *-ācis*.]

incapsulate *in-kap'sū-lāt*, *vt* to enclose as in a capsule. [**in-** (1).]

incarcerate *in-kär'sə-rāt*, *vt* to imprison; to confine. — *n* **incarcerā'tion** imprisonment; obstinate constriction or strangulation (*surg*). [L. *in*, in, *carcer*, a prison.]

incarnadine *in-kär'nə-dīn* or *-din*, *vt* to dye red. — *adj* carnation-coloured; flesh-coloured; blood-red. [Fr. *incarnadin* — It. *incarnadino*, carnation, flesh-colour.]

incarnate *in-kär'nāt* or *in'*, *vt* to embody in flesh, give human form to; to personify (*fig*). — *vi* to form flesh, heal. — *adj* (*-kär'nit* or *-nāt*) invested with flesh; personified. — *n* **incarnā'tion** the act of embodying in flesh, esp. of Christ (often with *cap*); an incarnate form; manifestation, visible embodiment; the process of healing, or forming new flesh (*surg*). [L.L. *incarnāre, -ātum* — L. *in*, in, *carō, carnis*, flesh.]

incautious *in-kö'shəs*, *adj* not cautious or careful. — *n* **incau'tion**. — *adv* **incau'tiously**. — *n* **incau'tiousness**. [**in-** (2).]

incendiary *in-sen'di-ər-i*, *n* a person who maliciously sets fire to property; a person who inflames passions or promotes strife; an incendiary bomb. — *adj* relating to incendiarism; adapted or used for setting buildings, etc., on fire; tending to excite strife. — *n* **incen'diarism**. — **incendiary bomb** a bomb containing a highly inflammable substance and designed to burst into flames on striking its objective. [L. *incendiārius* — *incendium* — *incendĕre*, to kindle.]

incense[1] *in-sens'*, *vt* to inflame with anger; to incite, urge. [O.Fr. *incenser* — L. *incendĕre, incēnsum*, to kindle.]

incense[2] *in'sens*, *n* material burned or volatilised to give fragrant fumes, esp. in religious rites — usu. a mixture of resins and gums, etc.; the fumes so obtained; any pleasant smell. — *vt* to perfume or fumigate with incense; to offer incense to. [O.Fr. *encens* — L. *incēnsum* — *incendĕre*, to set on fire.]

incentive *in-sen'tiv*, *adj* inciting, encouraging. — *n* something that incites to action. [L. *incentīvus*, striking up a tune — *incinĕre* — *in*, in, *canĕre*, to sing.]

inception *in-sep'shən*, *n* beginning. — *adj* **incep'tive** beginning or marking the beginning; inchoative (*gram*). — *n* (*gram*) an inchoative verb. [L. *incipĕre*, *inceptum*, to begin — *in*, in, on, *capĕre*, to take.]

incessant *in-ses'ənt*, *adj* uninterrupted; continual. — *n* **incess'ancy**. — *adv* **incess'antly** unceasingly. — *n* **incess'antness**. [L. *incessāns, -antis* — *in-*, not, *cessāre*, to cease.]

incest *in'sest*, *n* sexual intercourse between people who are so closely related that marriage is prohibited. — *adj* **incest'ūous** pertaining to, or characterised by, incest; turned inward on itself, or of or within a small closely-knit group (*fig*). — *adv* **incest'uously**. — *n* **incest'uousness**. [L. *incestum* — *in-*, not, *castus*, chaste.]

inch[1] *inch* or *insh*, *n* the twelfth part of a foot, equal to 2·54 cm.; the amount of e.g. rainfall that will cover a surface to the depth of one inch (now measured in millimetres); the amount of atmospheric pressure needed to balance the weight of a column of mercury one inch high (now measured in millibars); proverbially, a small distance or degree; (in *pl*) stature. — *vt* and *vi* to move by slow degrees. — **inch'-tape** a measuring tape divided into inches; **inch'-worm** a looper caterpillar. — **by inches** or **inch by inch** by small degrees; **every inch** entirely, thoroughly; **within an inch of** very close to; **within an inch of someone's life** to the point where there is danger of death. [O.E. *ynce*, an inch — L. *uncia*, a twelfth part; cf. **ounce**[1].]

inch[2] *insh*, (*Scot*) *n* an island. [Gael. *innis*, island.]

inchoate *in-kō'āt* or *in'kō-āt*, *adj* only begun; unfinished, rudimentary; not established. — *adj* **inchoative** (*in-kō'ə-tiv* or *in-kō-ā'tiv*) incipient; denoting the beginning of an action (*gram*). — *n* (*gram*) an inchoative verb. [L. *inchoāre* (for *incohāre*), *-ātum*, to begin.]

incident *in'si-dənt*, *adj* falling (on something); liable to occur; naturally belonging (to); consequent. — *n* an event; a subordinate action; that which naturally belongs to or is consequent on something else; a minor event showing hostility and threatening more serious trouble; a brief violent action, e.g. a bomb explosion. — *n* **in'cidence** the frequency or range of occurrence; the fact or manner of falling; the falling of a ray on a surface; the falling of a point on a line, or a line on a plane (*geom*). — *adj* **incidental** (*-dent'l*) incident; striking or impinging; liable to occur; naturally attached; accompanying; concomitant; occasional, casual. — *n* anything that occurs incidentally. — *adv* **incident'ally** in an incidental way; by the way, parenthetically, as a digression. — *n* **incident'alness**. — **incidental music** music accompanying the action of a play, film, etc. [L. *incidēns, -entis* — *in*, on, *cadĕre*, to fall.]

incinerate *in-sin'ər-āt*, *vt* to reduce to ashes. — *n* **incinerā'tion**. — *n* **incin'erātor** a furnace for burning anything to ashes. [L. *incinerāre, -ātum* — *in*, in, *cinis, cineris*, ashes.]

incipient *in-sip'i-ənt*, *adj* beginning; nascent. — *n* **incip'ience**. — *n* **incip'iency**. — *adv* **incip'iently**. [L. *incipiēns, -entis*, pres. p. of *incipĕre*, to begin.]

incise *in-sīz'*, *vt* to cut into; to cut or gash; to engrave. — *adj* **incised'** cut; engraved; cut to about the middle (*bot*). — *n* **incision** (*in-sizh'ən*) the act of cutting in, esp. (*surg*) into the body; a cut; a notch; trenchancy. — *adj* **incisive** (*in-sī'*) having the quality of cutting in; trenchant; acute; sarcastic. — *adv* **inci'sively**. — *n* **inci'siveness**. — *n* **incisor** (*-sī'zər*) a tooth in the front of the mouth, a cutting tooth. [Fr. *inciser* — L. *incīdĕre, incīsum* — *in*, into, *caedĕre*, to cut.]

incite *in-sīt'*, *vt* to move to action; to instigate. — *n* **incitā'tion** (*-si-* or *-sī-*) the act of inciting or rousing; an incentive. — *n* **incite'ment**. — *n* **incit'er**. — *adv* **incit'ingly**. [Fr., — L. *incitāre* — *in*, in, *citāre*, to rouse — *ciēre*, to put in motion.]

incivility *in-si-vil'i-ti*, *n* lack of civility or courtesy; impoliteness; an act of discourtesy (often in *pl*). [**in-** (2).]

incl. *abbrev* for: included; including; inclusive.

inclasp *in-kläsp'*, *vt*. Same as **enclasp**.

inclement *in-klem'ənt*, *adj* severe; stormy; harsh. — *n* **inclem'ency**. — *adv* **inclem'ently**. [**in-** (2).]

inclinable *in-klīn'ə-bl*, *adj* capable of being tilted or sloped; tending; favourably disposed. — *n* **inclīn'ableness**. [**incline**.]

inclination *in-klin-ā'shən*, *n* the act of inclining; a slope or tilt; a deviation; an angle with the horizon or with any plane or line; tendency; disposition, esp. favourable; preference, affection. — *adj* **inclina'tional**. [**incline**.]

incline *in-klīn'*, *vi* to lean forward or downward; to bow or bend; to deviate or slant; to slope; to tend; to be disposed. — *vt* to cause to bend downwards; to turn; to cause to deviate; to slope; to tilt; to direct; to dispose. — *n* (*in'klīn* or *in-klīn'*) a slope; a sloping tunnel or shaft (*mining*). — *adj* **inclined'** bent; sloping; oblique; having a tendency; disposed. — *n* **inclīn'ing** inclination. — *n* **inclinom'eter** (*-klin-*) an instrument for measuring slopes or inclination. [L. *inclīnāre*, to bend towards — *in*, into, *clīnāre*, to lean.]

inclose, inclosure. See **enclose**.

include *in-klood'*, *vt* to comprise as a part; to classify, or reckon as part; to take in. — *adj* **includ'ed** comprised; not protruding (*bot*). — *adj* **includ'ible**. — *prep* (or *pr p* merging into *prep*) **includ'ing** with the inclusion of. — *n* **inclusion** (*-kloo'zhən*) the act of including; that which is included; a foreign body enclosed in a crystal, or the like; a pocket of liquid or gas in a rock or mineral. — *adj* **inclusive** (*-kloo'siv*) comprehensive; including everything; comprehending the stated limit or extremes, including (with *of*); included. — *adv* **inclu'sively**. — **inclusion body** (*med*) a particulate body found in the cells of tissue infected with a virus. [L. *inclūdĕre, inclūsum* — *in*, in, *claudĕre*, to shut.]

incog. *abbrev* for incognito.

incognisable or **-z-** *in-kog'niz-ə-bl* or *in-kon'iz-ə-bl*, *adj* that cannot be known or distinguished. — *adj* **incog'nisant** or **-z-** not cognisant; unaware (with *of*). — *n* **incog'nisance** or **-z-** failure to recognise. [See **cognition** and **recognise**.]

incognito *in-kog'ni-tō*, *adv* or *in-kog-nē'tō*, *adj* unknown, unidentified; disguised; under an assumed name or title. — *n* a person concealing his or her identity; an assumed identity: — *pl* **incognitos**. [It., — L. *incognitus* — *in-*, not, *cognitus*, known — *cognōscĕre*, to recognise, come to know.]

incognizable, etc. See **incognisable**.

incoherent *in-kō-hē'rənt*, *adj* not coherent; loose; rambling. — *n* **incohē'rence** or **incohē'rency**. — *adv* **incohē'rently**. [**in-** (2).]

incombustible *in-kəm-bust'i-bl*, *adj* incapable of combustion. [**in-** (2).]

income *in'kum*, *in'kəm* or *ing'kəm*, *n* profit, or interest from anything; revenue. — *n* **incomer** (*in'kum-ər*) a person who comes to live in a place, not having been born there. — *adj* **in'coming** coming in; accruing; ensuing, next to follow. — *n* the act of coming in; (usu. in *pl*) revenue. — **incomes policy** a government policy of curbing inflation by controlling wages; **income support** a state benefit paid to those on low incomes, to bring them up to a certain level; **income tax** a tax directly levied on income or on income over a certain amount. [**in-** (1).]

incommensurable *in-kə-men'shə-rə-bl*, *adj* having no common standard or measure; not reaching the same standard; disproportionate. — *n* a quantity that has no common measure with another, esp. with rational numbers. — *n* **incommensurabil'ity** or **incommen'surableness**. — *adv* **incommen'surably**. [**in-** (2).]

incommensurate *in-kə-men'shə-rət*, *adj* incommensurable; inadequate. — *adv* **incommen'surateness**. [**in-** (2).]

incommode *in-kə-mōd'*, *vt* to cause trouble or inconvenience to. — *adj* **incommō'dious** inconvenient; (of e.g. a house) cramped, poky. — *adv* **incommō'diously**. — *n* **incommō'diousness**. [Fr. *incommoder* — L. *incommodāre* — *in-*, not, *commodus*, commodious.]

incommunicable *in-kə-mū'ni-kə-bl*, *adj* that cannot be communicated or passed on to others. — *n* **incommunicabil'ity** or **incommu'nicableness**. — *adv* **incommu'nicably**. [**in-** (2).]

incommunicado *in-kə-mū-ni-kä'dō*, *adj* and *adv* without means of communication; in solitary confinement. [Sp. *incomunicado*.]

incommutable *in-kə-mū'tə-bl*, *adj* that cannot be commuted or exchanged. — *n* **incommutabil'ity** or **incommu'tableness**. — *adv* **incommu'tably**. [**in-** (2).]

incomparable *in-kom'pər-ə-bl*, *adj* not admitting comparison; matchless. — *n* **incomparabil'ity** or **incom'parableness**. — *adv* **incom'parably**. [**in-** (2).]

incompatible *in-kəm-pat'i-bl*, *adj* not consistent; contradictory; incapable of existing together in harmony, or at all; incapable of combination, co-operation, or functioning together; mutually intolerant or exclusive; irreconcilable. — *n* a thing incompatible with another; (in *pl*) things which cannot co-exist. — *n* **incompatibil'ity** the state of being incompatible; an incompatible feature, element, etc. — *n* **incompat'ibleness**. — *adv* **incompat'ibly**. [**in-** (2).]

incompetent *in-kom'pi-tənt*, *adj* without the proper legal qualifications; lacking ability or skill, esp. for one's work. — *n* an incompetent person. — *n* **incom'petence** or **incom'petency**. — *adv* **incom'petently**. [**in-** (2).]

incomplete *in-kəm-plēt'*, *adj* imperfect; unfinished; without calyx, corolla, or both (*bot*). — *adv* **incomplete'ly**. — *n* **incomplete'ness**. — *n* **incomplē'tion**. [**in-** (2).]

incomprehensible *in-kom-pri-hens'i-bl*, *adj* not capable of being understood; not to be contained within limits (*theol*). — *n* **incomprehensibil'ity** or **incomprehens'ibleness**. — *adv* **incomprehens'ibly**. — *n* **incomprehen'sion** lack of comprehension. — *adj* **incomprehens'ive** not comprehensive. — *n* **incomprehens'iveness**. [**in-** (2).]

incompressible *in-kəm-pres'i-bl*, *adj* not to be compressed into smaller bulk. — *n* **incompressibil'ity** or **incompress'ibleness**. [**in-** (2).]

inconceivable *in-kən-sēv'ə-bl*, *adj* that cannot be conceived by the mind; incomprehensible; involving a contradiction in terms; physically impossible; taxing belief or imagination (*colloq*). — *n* **inconceivabil'ity** or **inconceiv'ableness**. — *adv* **inconceiv'ably**. [**in-** (2).]

inconclusive *in-kən-klōōs'iv*, *adj* not settling a point in debate, indeterminate, indecisive. — *adv* **inconclus'ively**. — *n* **inconclus'iveness**. [**in-** (2).]

incongruous *in-kong'grōō-əs*, *adj* inconsistent; out of keeping; unsuitable. — *n* **incongruity** (*-kong-* or *-kən-grōō'*) the fact of being incongruous; an incongruous thing. — *n* **incon'gruousness**. — *adv* **incon'gruously**. [**in-** (2).]

inconsequent *in-kon'si-kwənt*, *adj* not following from the premises; illogical; irrelevant; disconnected; unrelated; unimportant. — *n* **incon'sequence**. — *adj* **inconsequential** (*-kwen'shl*) not following from the premises; of no consequence or value. — *adv* **inconsequen'tially**. — *adv* **incon'sequently**. [**in-** (2).]

inconsiderable *in-kən-sid'ər-ə-bl*, *adj* not worthy of notice; unimportant; of no great size. — *n* **inconsid'erableness**. — *adv* **inconsid'erably**. [**in-** (2).]

inconsiderate *in-kən-sid'ər-it*, *adj* without care or regard for others; thoughtless; rash, imprudent. — *adv* **inconsid'erately**. — *n* **inconsid'erateness** or **inconsiderā'tion**. [**in-** (2).]

inconsistent *in-kən-sist'ənt*, *adj* not consistent; not suitable or agreeing; intrinsically incompatible; self-contradictory; changeable, fickle. — *n* **inconsist'ence** or **inconsist'ency**. — *adv* **inconsist'ently**. [**in-** (2).]

inconsolable *in-kən-sōl'ə-bl*, *adj* not able to be comforted. — *n* **inconsol'ableness**. — *adv* **inconsol'ably**. [**in-** (2).]

inconsonant *in-kon'sən-ənt*, *adj* not agreeing or in harmony with. — *n* **incon'sonance**. — *adv* **incon'sonantly**. [**in-** (2).]

inconspicuous *in-kən-spik'ū-əs*, *adj* not conspicuous. — *adv* **inconspic'uously**. — *n* **inconspic'uousness**. [**in-** (2).]

inconstant *in-kon'stənt*, *adj* subject to change; fickle. — *n* **incon'stancy**. — *adv* **incon'stantly**. [**in-** (2).]

incontestable *in-kən-test'ə-bl*, *adj* too clear to be called in question; undeniable. — *n* **incontestabil'ity**. — *adv* **incontest'ably**. [**in-** (2).]

incontinent *in-kon'ti-nənt*, *adj* unable to control urination or defecation; lacking self-restraint, esp. in sexual matters; lacking control over (with *of*) (*med*). — *n* **incon'tinence** or **incon'tinency**. — *adv* **incon'tinently**. [L. *incontinēns*, *-entis* — *in*, not, *continēns*; see **continent**.]

incontrovertible *in-kon-trə-vûrt'i-bl*, *adj* incontestible. — *n* **incontrovertibil'ity**. — *adv* **incontrovert'ibly**. [**in-** (2).]

inconvenient *in-kən-vēn'yənt*, *adj* unsuitable; causing trouble or uneasiness; increasing difficulty. — *vt* **inconvēn'ience** to trouble or incommode. — *n* the state of being inconvenient; something causing difficulty or giving trouble. — *adv* **inconvēn'iently**. [**in-** (2).]

inconvertible *in-kən-vûrt'i-bl*, *adj* that cannot be changed or exchanged. — *n* **inconvertibil'ity**. — *adv* **inconvert'ibly**. [in- (2).]

inco-ordinate (also **incoor-** in both words) *in-kō-ör'di-nit* or *-dnit*, *adj* not co-ordinate. — *n* **inco-ordination** (*-di-nā'shən*) lack or failure of co-ordination. [in- (2).]

incorporate *in-kör'pər-āt*, *vt* to form into a body; to combine into one mass; to merge; to absorb; to form into a corporation; to admit to a corporation. — *vi* to unite into one mass; to form a corporation. — *adj* (*-it*) united in one body; constituted as an incorporation. — *adj* **incor'porāting** (*philol*) polysynthetic. — *n* **incorporā'tion** the act of incorporating; the state of being incorporated; the formation of a legal or political body; an association; an incorporated society. — *adj* **incor'porative** (*-ə-tiv* or *-ā-tiv*). — *n* **incor'porātor**. [L. *incorporāre*, *-ātum* — *in*, in, into, *corpus*, *-oris*, body.]

incorporeal *in-kör'pö-ri-əl*, *adj* not having a body; spiritual; intangible. [L. *incorporātus*, *incorporālis*, bodiless — *in-*, not, *corpus*, *-oris*, body.]

incorrect *in-kə-rekt'*, *adj* containing faults; not accurate; not correct in manner or character. — *adv* **incorrect'ly**. — *n* **incorrect'ness**. [in- (2).]

incorrigible *in-kor'i-ji-bl*, *adj* beyond correction or reform. — Also *n*. — *n* **incorrigibil'ity** or **incorr'igibleness**. — *adv* **incorr'igibly**. [in- (2).]

incorrupt *in-kə-rupt'*, *adj* sound; pure; not decayed; not depraved; not to be influenced by bribes. — *adj* **incorrupt'ible** not capable of decay; that cannot be bribed; inflexibly just. — *n* **incorruptibil'ity** or **incorrupt'ibleness**. — *adv* **incorrupt'ibly**. — *n* **incorrup'tion** or **incorrupt'ness**. — *adj* **incorrupt'ive**. — *adv* **incorrupt'ly**. [in- (2).]

increase *in-krēs'*, *vi* to grow in size or number. — *vt* to make greater in size or number. — *n* (*in'*) growth; increment; addition to the original stock; profit; produce. — *adj* **increas'able**. — *n* **increas'er**. — *n* and *adj* **increas'ing**. — *adv* **increas'ingly**. [M.E. *encressen* — A.Fr. *encresser* — L. *incrēscĕre* — *in*, *crēscĕre*, to grow.]

incredible *in-kred'i-bl*, *adj* unbelievable; difficult to believe in; very great; unusually good (*colloq*). — *n* **incredibil'ity**. — *n* **incred'ibleness**. — *adv* **incred'ibly**. [in- (2).]

incredulous *in-kred'ū-ləs*, *adj* unwilling to believe, sceptical; not believing. — *n* **incredū'lity** (*-kri-*) or **incred'ūlousness**. — *adv* **incred'ūlously**. [in- (2).]

increment *ing'* or *in'kri-mənt*, *n* increase; amount of increase; an amount or thing added; the finite increase of a variable quantity (*math*); an adding of particulars towards a climax (*rhet*). — *adj* **incremental** (*-ment'l*). — **incremental plotter** (*comput*) a device presenting computer output on paper in the form of line images, e.g. graphs; **unearned increment** any exceptional increase in the value of land, houses, etc., not due to the owner's labour or outlay. [L. *incrēmentum* — *incrēscĕre*, to increase.]

incriminate *in-krim'in-āt*, *vt* to charge with a crime or fault; to implicate, involve in a charge. — *adj* **incrim'inatory**. [in- (1).]

incross *in'kros*, *n* a plant or animal produced by crossing two inbred individuals of different lineage but of the same breed. — Also *vt*. — *n* **incross'bred** a plant or animal produced by crossing two inbred individuals of different breeds. — *vt* **incross'breed**. [in- (1).]

incrust, incrustation. See **encrust, encrustation**.

incubate *in'* or *ing'kū-bāt*, *vi* to brood eggs; to hatch; to undergo incubation. — *vt* to hatch; to foster the development of (e.g. bacteria, etc.). — *n* **incubā'tion** the act of sitting on eggs to hatch them; hatching (natural or artificial); fostering (as of bacteria, etc.); the period between infection and appearance of symptoms (*med*). — *adj* **in'cubātive** or **in'cubātory**. — *n* **in'cubātor** an apparatus for hatching eggs by artificial heat, for rearing prematurely born babies, or for developing bacteria; a brooding hen. [L. *incubāre*, *-ātum* (usu. *-ĭtum*) — *in*, on, *cubāre*, to lie, recline.]

incubus *in'* or *ing'kū-bəs*, *n* the nightmare; a devil supposed to assume a male body and have sexual intercourse with women in their sleep; any oppressive person, thing or influence: — *pl* **in'cubuses** or **in'cubi** (*-bī*). [L. *incŭbus*, nightmare — *in*, on, *cubāre*, to lie.]

incudes. See **incus**.

inculcate *in'kul-kāt* or *-kul'*, *vt* to instil by frequent admonitions or repetitions. — *n* **inculcā'tion**. — *adj* **incul'cative** (*-kə-tiv*). — *n* **in'culcātor**. — *adj* **incul'catory**. [L. *inculcāre*, *-ātum* — *in*, into, *calcāre*, to tread — *calx*, heel.]

inculpate *in'kul-* or *in-kul'pāt*, *vt* to blame; to incriminate; to charge. — *n* **inculpā'tion**. — *adj* **incul'patory** (*-pə-tə-ri*). [L.L. *inculpāre*, *-ātum* — L. *in*, in, *culpa*, a fault.]

incumbent *in-kum'bənt*, *adj* lying, resting or weighing on something; overlying (*geol*); laid on or upon someone as a duty; lying along a surface, as a moth's wings at rest. — *n* a person who holds an ecclesiastical benefice, or any office. — *n* **incum'bency** the state or fact of being incumbent or an incumbent; a duty or obligation; the holding of an office; an ecclesiastical benefice. — *adv* **incum'bently**. [L. *incumbēns*, *-entis*, pres. p. of *incumbĕre*, to lie upon.]

incunabula *in-kū-nab'ū-lə*, *npl* early printed books esp. before the year 1501; the cradle, birthplace, origin of a thing: — *nsing* **incūnab'ūlum**. [L. *incūnābŭla*, swaddling-clothes, infancy, earliest stage — *in*, in, *cūnābula*, dimin. of *cūnae*, a cradle.]

incur *in-kûr'*, *vt* to become liable to; to bring upon oneself; to suffer: — *pr p* **incurr'ing**; *pa t* and *pa p* **incurred'**. — *adj* **incurr'able**. — *n* **incurr'ence**. [L. *incurrĕre*, *incursum* — *in*, into, *currĕre*, to run.]

incurable *in-kūr'ə-bl*, *adj* unable to be cured or corrected. — *n* someone beyond cure or correction. — *n* **incur'ableness** or **incurabil'ity**. — *adv* **incur'ably**. [in- (2).]

incurious *in-kū'ri-əs*, *adj* not curious or inquisitive; inattentive; indifferent. — *adv* **incū'riously**. — *n* **incū'riousness** or **incūrios'ity**. [in- (2).]

incursion *in-kûr'shən* or *-zhən*, *n* a hostile inroad; the action of leaking or running in; a sudden attack, invasion. — *adj* **incur'sive** making inroads; aggressive; invading. [L. *incursiō*, *-ōnis* — *incurrĕre*.]

incurve *in-kûrv'*, *vt* and *vi* to curve; to curve inward. — *n* **in'curve** a curve inwards. [L. *incurvāre*, to bend in, *incurvus*, bent.]

incus *ing'kəs*, *n* one of the bones in the middle ear, considered to resemble an anvil in shape: — *pl* **incudes** (*ing-kū'dēz* or *ing'*). — *adj* anvil-shaped. [L. *incūs*, *incūdis*, an anvil; see ety. for **incuse**.]

incuse *in-kūz'*, *vt* to impress (e.g. a coin) with a design, or a design on a coin etc., by stamping. — *adj* hammered. — *n* an impression, a stamp. [L. *incūsus*, past p. of *incūdĕre* — *in*, on, *cūdĕre*, to strike; to work on the anvil.]

IND *abbrev* for: *in Dei nomine* (L.), in the name of God; India (I.V.R.).

Ind. *abbrev* for: Independent; India; Indian; Indiana (U.S. state).

indaba *in-dä'bə*, *n* an important tribal conference; an international Scout conference. [Zulu.]

indebted *in-det'id*, *adj* being in debt; obliged by something received. — *n* **indebt'edness**. [in- (1).]

indecent *in-dē'sənt*, *adj* offensive to common modesty; unbecoming; gross, obscene. — *n* **indē'cency** the quality of being indecent; anything violating modesty or seemliness. — *adv* **indē'cently**. — **indecent assault** a sexual assault not involving rape; **indecent exposure** the offence of indecently exposing part of one's body (esp. the genitals) in public. [**in-** (2).]

indecipherable *in-di-sī'fər-ə-bl, adj* incapable of being deciphered; illegible. [**in-** (2).]

indecision *in-di-si'zhən, n* lack of decision or resolution; hesitation; wavering. — *adj* **indecisive** (*-sī'siv*) inconclusive; undecided; vacillating; hesitant. — *adv* **indecī'sively**. — *n* **indecī'siveness**. [**in-** (2).]

indeclinable *in-di-klīn'ə-bl,* (*gram*) *adj* not varied by inflection. — *adv* **indeclin'ably**. [**in-** (2).]

indecorous *in-dek'ə-rəs, adj* unseemly; violating good manners. — *adv* **indec'orously**. — *n* **indec'orousness** or **indecō'rum** improper or impolite behaviour; a breach of decorum. [L. *indĕcōrus*.]

indeed *in-dēd', adv* in fact; in truth; in reality. It emphasises an affirmation, marks a qualifying word or clause, a concession or admission, or, used as an *interj*, expresses surprise or interrogation, disbelief, or mere acknowledgment. [**in** and **deed**.]

indef. *abbrev* for indefinite.

indefatigable *in-di-fat'i-gə-bl, adj* untiring; unflagging; unremitting in effort. — *n* **indefat'igableness**. — *adv* **indefat'igably**. [Fr. (obs.), — L. *indēfatīgābilis* — *in-*, not, *dē*, from, *fatīgāre*, to tire.]

indefeasible *in-di-fēz'i-bl, adj* not to be annulled or forfeited. — *n* **indefeasibil'ity**. — *adv* **indefeas'ibly**. [**in-** (2).]

indefensible *in-di-fens'i-bl, adj* untenable, that cannot be defended (*lit* or *fig*); that cannot be excused or justified. — *n* **indefensibil'ity**. — *adv* **indefens'ibly**. [**in-** (2).]

indefinable *in-di-fīn'ə-bl, adj* that cannot be defined; hard to identify or describe. — *adv* **indefin'ably**. [**in-** (2).]

indefinite *in-def'i-nit, adj* without clearly marked outlines or limits; of a character, not clearly distinguished; not precise; undetermined; not referring to a particular person or thing (*gram*; see also **article**). — *adv* **indef'initely**. — *n* **indef'initeness**. [**in-** (2).]

indehiscent *in-di-his'ənt,* (*bot*) *adj* not dehiscent; (of fruits) not opening when mature. — *n* **indehisc'ence**. [**in-** (2).]

indelible *in-del'i-bl, adj* unable to be erased or blotted out; making an indelible mark. — *n* **indelibil'ity** or **indel'ibleness**. — *adv* **indel'ibly**. [L. *indēlēbilis* — *in-*, not, *dēlēre*, to destroy.]

indelicate *in-del'i-kit, adj* immodest or verging on the immodest; tactless; in poor taste; coarse. — *n* **indel'icacy**. — *adv* **indel'icately**. [**in-** (2).]

indemnify *in-dem'ni-fī, vt* to secure (with *against*); to compensate; to free, exempt (with *from*): — *pr p* **indem'nifying**; *pa t* and *pa p* **indem'nified**. — *n* **indemnification** (*-fi-kā'shən*). [L. *indemnis*, unhurt (— *in-*, not, *damnum*, loss), and *facĕre*, to make.]

indemnity *in-dem'ni-ti, n* security from damage or loss; compensation for loss or injury; legal exemption from incurred liabilities or penalties. [Fr. *indemnité* — L. *indemnis*, unharmed — *damnum*, loss.]

indemonstrable *in-dem'ən-strə-bl* or *in-di-mon', adj* that cannot be demonstrated or proved. — *n* **indemonstrabil'ity**. [**in-** (2).]

indent *in-dent', vt* to cut into zigzags; to divide along a zigzag line; to notch; to indenture, apprentice; to draw up (as a deed, contract, etc.) in exact duplicate; to begin farther in from the margin than the rest of a paragraph; to make a dent in. — *vt* and *vi* to make out a written order with counterfoil or duplicate; to order (esp. from abroad); to requisition; (of a coastline, etc.) to penetrate, form recesses. — *n* (*in'dent* or *in-dent'*) a cut or notch; a recess like a notch; an indenture; an order for goods (esp. from abroad); an official requisition for goods; a dint. — *n* **indentā'tion** a hollow or depression; the act of indenting or notching; notch; recess. — *adj* **indent'ed** having indentations; serrated; zigzag. — *n* **indent'er**. — *n* **inden'tion** indentation; blank space at the beginning of a line. [Two different words fused together: (1) — L.L. *indentāre* — L. *in*, in, *dēns*, *dentis*, a tooth; (2) — English **in** and **dint**, **dent**.]

indenture *in-den'chər, n* the act of indenting, indentation; a written agreement between two or more parties, esp. (in *pl*) between an apprentice and his master; a contract. — *vt* to bind by indentures; to indent. [A.Fr. *endenture* — L.L. *indentāre*; see **indent**.]

independent *in-di-pend'ənt, adj* not dependent or relying on others (with *of*); not subordinate; completely self-governing; (of a business, etc.) not affiliated or merged with a larger organisation; thinking or acting for oneself; too self-respecting to accept help; not subject to bias; having or affording a comfortable livelihood without necessity of working or help from others; not depending on another for its value, said of a quantity or function (*math*); (with *cap*) belonging to the Independents. — *n* (with *cap*) a person who in ecclesiastical affairs holds that every congregation should be independent of every other and subject to no superior authority — a Congregationalist; a politician or other not committed to any party. — *n* **independ'ence** the state of being independent; a competency. — *n* **independ'ency** independence; a sovereign state; (with *cap*) Congregationalism. — *adv* **independ'ently**. — **Independence Day** (see **Declaration of Independence** below) a day when a country becomes self-governing or the anniversary of this event; **independent school** one not part of the state education system. — **Declaration of Independence** the document (1776) proclaiming with reasons the secession of the thirteen colonies of America from the United Kingdom, reported to the Continental Congress, 4 July 1776 — observed in the U.S. as a national holiday, **Independence Day**. [**in-** (2).]

indescribable *in-di-skrīb'ə-bl, adj* that cannot be described. — *n* **indescribabil'ity**. — *adv* **indescrib'ably**. [**in-** (2).]

indestructible *in-di-struk'ti-bl, adj* that cannot be destroyed. — *n* **indestructibil'ity** or **indestruc'tibleness**. — *adv* **indestruc'tibly**. [**in-** (2).]

indeterminable *in-di-tûr'min-ə-bl, adj* not to be ascertained or fixed; of argument, etc., that cannot be settled. — *n* **indeter'minableness**. — *adv* **indeter'minably**. — *n* **indeter'minacy**. — *adj* **indeter'minate** not determinate or fixed; uncertain; having no defined or fixed value. — *adv* **indeter'minately**. — *n* **indeter'minateness** or **indeterminā'tion** lack of determination; absence of fixed direction. [**in-** (2).]

index *in'deks, n* the forefinger (also **in'dex-finger**), or the digit corresponding; a pointer or hand on a dial or scale, etc.; a moving arm, as on a surveying instrument; the gnomon of a sundial; the finger of a fingerpost; a figure of a pointing hand, used to draw attention (*printing*); an alphabetical register of subjects dealt with, usu. at the end of a book, with page or folio references; a similar list of other things; a list of prohibited books; a symbol denoting a power (*math*); a number, commonly a ratio, expressing some relation (as *cranial index*, the breadth of skull as a percentage of its length); a numerical scale showing the relative changes in the cost of living, wages, etc., with reference to some predetermined base level: — *pl* of a book usu. **in'dexes**; other senses **indices** (*in'di-sēz*). — *vt* to provide with or place in an index; to link to an index, index-link. — *n* **indexā'tion** or **in'dexing** a system by which wages, rates of interest, etc., are directly linked (**index-linked'**) to changes in the cost of living index. — *n* **in'dexer**. — *adj* **index'ical**. — *adj* **in'dexless**. — *vt* **index-link'**. —

index-link'ing indexation; **index number** a figure showing periodic movement up or down of a variable compared with another figure (usu. 100) taken as a standard. [L. *index, indicis* — *indicāre*, to show.]

Indian *in'di-ən, adj* of or belonging to India (with various boundaries) or its native population, or to the Indies, East or West, or to the aborigines of America, or to the Indians of South Africa. — *n* a member of one of the races of India; an aboriginal of America; in South Africa, a person belonging to the Asian racial group; someone who carries out orders, a worker, etc., as opposed to a leader or organiser, as in *chiefs and Indians*. — *n* **Indianisā'tion** or **-z-**. — *vt* **In'dianise** or **-ize** to make Indian; to assimilate to what is Indian; to cause to be done, controlled, etc., by Indians. — *vi* to become Indian or like an Indian. — **Indian club** a bottle-shaped block of wood, swung in various motions by the arms to develop the muscles; **Indian corn** maize, so called because brought from the West Indies; **Indian fig** the bania tree; the prickly pear; **Indian file** see under **file**[1]; **Indian gift** (*US colloq*) a gift that is asked back or for which a return gift is expected; **Indian giver; Indian hemp** *Cannabis sativa* (*Cannabis indica* is a variety), source of the drug variously known as hashish, marihuana, etc.; **Indian ink** see under **ink; Indian meal** ground maize; **Indian millet** durra; **Indian red** red ochre, or native ferric oxide, formerly imported from the East as a red pigment, also made artificially; **Indian rice** see **zizania; Indian rope-trick** the supposed Indian trick of climbing an unsupported rope; **Indian runner** a breed of domestic duck; **Indian sign** a magic spell which brings a person bad luck or puts him or her in the power of another; **Indian summer** (orig. in America) a period of warm, dry, calm weather in late autumn; a time of particular happiness, success, etc., towards the end of a life, era, etc. (*fig*); **Indian wrestling** a trial of strength in which two people sitting with elbows touching a table clasp hands, each trying to force the other's arm backwards; **India paper** a thin soft absorbent paper, of Chinese or Japanese origin, used in taking the finest proofs (**India proofs**) from engraved plates; a thin tough opaque paper used for printing Bibles; **india-rubb'er** or **India rubber** an elastic gummy substance, the inspissated juice of various tropical plants; a piece of this material, esp. one used for rubbing out pencil marks. — **East Indian** an inhabitant or native of the East Indies, usually applied to a Eurasian; **East Indies** the Indian subcontinent, south-east Asia, and the Malay archipelago (*hist*); Sumatra, Borneo, Java and the other islands of Indonesia, by some, but not generally, taken to include the Philippines and New Guinea; **Red Indian** (now considered *offensive*) one of the aborigines of America (from the coppery-brown colour of some tribes); **West Indian** a native or an inhabitant of the West Indies; **West Indies** an archipelago stretching from Florida to Venezuela. [L. *India* — *Indus* (Gr. *Indos*), the Indus.]

Indic *in'dik, adj* originating or existing in India; of the Indian branch of the Indo-European languages.

indic. *abbrev* for indicative.

indicate *in'di-kāt, vt* to point out; to show; to give some notion of; to be a mark or token of; to give grounds for inferring; to point to as suitable treatment (*med*), also (usu. in *passive*) as a desirable course of action in any sphere. — *n* **indicā'tion** the act of indicating; mark; token; suggestion of treatment; symptom. — *adj* **indicative** (*in-dik'ə-tiv*) pointing out; giving intimation; applied to the mood of the verb that expresses matter of fact (*gram*). — *n* the indicative mood; a verb in the indicative mood. — *adv* **indic'atively**. — *n* **in'dicātor** someone who or that which indicates; a pointer; a diagram showing names and directions of visible objects, as on a mountain top; a substance showing chemical condition by change of colour; a measuring contrivance with a pointer or something similar; any device for exhibiting condition for the time being. — *adj* **in'dicatory** (or *-dik'*). [L. *indicāre, -ātum* — *in*, in, *dicāre*, to proclaim.]

indices. See **index**.

indict *in-dīt'*, (*law*) *vt* to charge with a crime formally or in writing. — *adj* **indict'able.** — *n* **indictee'** a person who is indicted. — *n* **indict'ment** a formal accusation; the written accusation against one who is to be tried by jury; the form under which one is put to trial at the instance of the Lord Advocate (*Scot*). [With Latinised spelling (but not pronunciation) from A.Fr. *enditer* — L. *in*, in, *dictāre*, to declare.]

indie *in'di*, (*colloq*) *adj* (of films or (now usu.) pop music) produced by small independent companies, not mainstream or commercial. [**independent**.]

indifferent *in-dif'ər-ənt, adj* without importance; uninteresting; of a middle quality; not very good, inferior; neutral; unconcerned. — *n* **indiff'erence** or **indiff'erency**. — *n* **indiff'erentism** indifference; the doctrine that religious differences are of no importance (*theol*). — *n* **indiff'erentist.** — *adv* **indiff'erently** in an indifferent manner; tolerably; passably; without distinction, impartially. [**in-** (2).]

indigenous *in-dij'in-əs, adj* native born; originating or produced naturally in a country (opp. to *exotic*). — *n* **in'digene** (*-jēn*) native, aborigine. — *n* **indigenisā'tion** or **-z-**. — *vt* **indi'genise** or **-ize** to adapt or subject to native culture or influence; to increase the proportion of indigenous people in administration, employment, etc. — *adv* **indig'enously.** [L. *indigena*, a native — *indu-*, in, and *gen-*, root of *gignĕre*, to produce.]

indigent *in'di-jənt, adj* in need, esp. of means of subsistence. — *n* **in'digence** or **in'digency.** — *adv* **in'digently.** [Fr., — L. *indigēns, -entis*, pres. p. of *indigēre* — *indu-*, in, *egēre*, to need.]

indigestible *in-di-jes'ti-bl, adj* not digestible; not easily digested (*lit* or *fig*). — *n* **indigestibil'ity.** — *adv* **indigest'ibly.** — *n* **indigestion** (*in-di-jes'chən*) difficulty in digesting food; pain, flatulence, etc. caused by this. — *adj* **indigest'ive** dyspeptic. [L. *indīgestus*, unarranged — *in*, not, *dīgerĕre*, to arrange, digest.]

indignant *in-dig'nənt, adj* feeling or showing justifiable anger (often mixed with scorn). — *adv* **indig'nantly.** — *n* **indignā'tion** righteous anger at injustice, etc.; feeling caused by an unjustified slight, etc., to oneself. — *n* **indig'nity** disgrace; dishonour; unmerited contemptuous treatment; incivility with contempt or insult. [L. *indīgnus*, unworthy — *in-*, not, *dīgnus*, worthy.]

indigo *in'di-gō, n* a violet-blue dye obtained from the leaves of the indigo plant, from woad, or synthetically; the colour of this dye; the indigo plant, any of various species of a tropical leguminous genus of the *Papilionaceae*: — *pl* **in'digos** or **in'digoes.** — *adj* deep blue. — **indigo bird** an American finch, of which the male is blue. [Sp. *índico, índigo* — L. *indicum* — Gr. *Indikon*, Indian.]

indirect *in-di-rekt'* or *in-dī-rekt', adj* not direct or straight; not lineal or in direct succession; not related in the natural way, oblique; not straightforward or honest. — *adv* **indirect'ly.** — *n* **indirect'ness.** — **indirect object** (*gram*) a noun, pronoun or noun-phrase dependent on a verb less immediately than an accusative governed by it; **indirect speech** speech reported with adjustment of the speaker's words to change persons and time; **indirect tax** one collected not directly from the taxpayer but through an intermediate agent, as e.g. a customs duty or sales tax; **indirect taxation.** [**in-** (2).]

indiscernible *in-di-sûrn'i-bl* or *-zûrn'i-bl, adj* not discernible. — *adv* **indiscern'ibly.** [**in-** (2).]

indiscipline *in-dis'i-plin, n* lack of discipline. — *adj* **indisc'iplinable.** [**in-** (2).]

indiscreet *in-dis-krēt'*, *adj* not discreet; imprudent; injudicious. — *adv* **indiscreet'ly**. — *n* **indiscreet'ness**. [**in-** (2).]

indiscrete *in-dis-krēt'*, *adj* not separated into parts; indivisible; homogeneous. — *adv* **indiscrete'ly**. — *n* **indiscrete'ness**. [**in-** (2).]

indiscretion *in-dis-kresh'ən*, *n* lack of discretion; rashness; an indiscreet act, or one apparently so; (esp. formerly) an imprudent and immoral action. [**indiscreet**.]

indiscriminate *in-dis-krim'i-nit*, *adj* not making distinctions; choosing or chosen at random; promiscuous. — *adv* **indiscrim'inately**. — *adj* **indiscrim'ināting** undiscriminating. — *n* **indiscriminā'tion**. — *adj* **indiscrim'inative** (*-ə-tiv*) not discriminative. [**in-** (2).]

indispensable *in-dis-pens'ə-bl*, *adj* that cannot be dispensed with; absolutely necessary; (of a law, etc.) that cannot be set aside. — *n* **indispensabil'ity** or **indispens'ableness**. — *adv* **indispens'ably**. [**in-** (2).]

indispose *in-dis-pōz'*, *vt* to make indisposed, averse or unfit. — *pa p* and *adj* **indisposed'** averse; slightly unwell. — *n* **indispos'edness**. — *n* **indisposition** (*-pə-zish'ən*) the state of being indisposed; disinclination; slight illness. [**in-** (2).]

indisputable *in-dis-pū'tə-bl*, *adj* beyond doubt or question. — *n* **indisput'ableness**. — *adv* **indisput'ably**. [**in-** (2).]

indissoluble *in-dis-ol'ū-bl*, *adj* that cannot be broken or dissolved; inseparable; binding for ever. — *n* **indissolubil'ity** or **indissol'ubleness**. — *adv* **indissol'ubly**. [**in-** (2).]

indistinct *in-dis-tingkt'*, *adj* not plainly marked; confused; not clear to the mind; dim. — *adj* **indistinct'ive** not constituting a distinction; not discriminating. — *adv* **indistinct'ively** indiscriminately. — *n* **indistinct'iveness**. — *adv* **indistinct'ly**. — *n* **indistinct'ness**. [**in-** (2).]

indistinguishable *in-dis-ting'gwish-ə-bl*, *adj* that cannot be told apart; indiscernible. — *n* **indistin'guishableness**. — *adv* **indistin'guishably**. [**in-** (2).]

indium *in'di-əm*, *n* a soft malleable silver-white metallic element (symbol **In**; atomic no. 49). [From two *ind*igo-coloured lines in the spectrum.]

indiv. *abbrev* for individual.

individual *in-di-vid'ū-əl*, *adj* not divisible without loss of identity; subsisting as one; pertaining to one only or to each one separately of a group; single, separate. — *n* a single person, animal, plant, or thing considered as a separate member of its species or as having an independent existence; a person (*colloq*). — *n* **individualīsā'tion** or **-z-**. — *vt* **individ'ualise** or **-ize** to stamp with individual character; to particularise. — *n* **individ'ualism** individual character; independent action as opposed to co-operation; the political theory which opposes interference of the state in the affairs of individuals (opp. to *socialism* or *collectivism*); the theory that looks to the rights of individuals, not to the advantage of an abstraction such as the state. — *n* **individ'ualist** a person who thinks and acts with independence; someone who advocates individualism. — Also *adj*. — *adj* **individualist'ic**. — *n* **individuality** (*-al'i-ti*) separate and distinct existence; distinctive character. — *adv* **individ'ually**. — *vt* **individ'uate** to individualise; to give individuality to. — *n* **individuā'tion**. [L. *indīviduus* — *in-*, not, *dīviduus*, divisible.]

indivisible *in-di-viz'i-bl*, *adj* not divisible. — *n* (*math*) an indefinitely small quantity. — *n* **indivisibil'ity** or **indivis'ibleness**. — *adv* **indivis'ibly**. [**in-** (2).]

Indo- *in'dō-*, *combining form* denoting Indian.

Indo-Chinese *in-dō-chī-nēz'*, *adj* of or pertaining to Indo-China, the south-eastern peninsula of Asia.

Indocid® *in'do-sid*, *n* proprietary name for indomethacin.

indoctrinate *in-dok'trin-āt*, *vt* to instruct in any doctrine; to imbue with any opinion. — *n* **indoctrinā'tion**. — *n* **indoc'trinātor**. [**in-** (1).]

Indo-European *in-dō-ū-rō-pē'ən*, (*philol*) *adj* of the family of languages, also called **Indo-German'ic** and sometimes Aryan, whose great branches are Aryan proper or Indian, Iranian, Armenian, Greek or Hellenic, Italic, Celtic, Tocharian, Balto-Slavonic, Albanian, Germanic, and probably Anatolian. — *n* the hypothetical parent-language of this family.

indolent *in'dəl-ənt*, *adj* disliking activity; lazy; not painful (*med*). — *n* **in'dolence**. — *adv* **in'dolently**. [L. *in-*, not, *dolēns*, *-entis*, pres. p. of *dolēre*, to suffer pain.]

indomethacin *in-dō-meth'ə-sin*, *n* an anti-inflammatory, anti-pyretic and analgesic drug, used in the treatment of arthritis.

indomitable *in-dom'it-ə-bl*, *adj* not to be overcome. — *n* **indomitabil'ity** or **indom'itableness**. — *adv* **indom'itably**. [**in-** (2).]

Indonesian *in-də-nē'zi-ən*, *adj* of the East Indian or Malay Archipelago, *specif* of the Republic of Indonesia, covering much of this territory; of a short, mesocephalic black-haired, light-brown race distinguishable in the population of the East Indian Islands; of a branch of the Austronesian family of languages chiefly found in the Malay Archipelago and Islands (Malay, etc.). — *n* an Indonesian national, a member of the race or speaker of one of the languages; the official language of the Republic of Indonesia. [Gr. *Indos*, Indian, *nēsos*, island.]

indoor *in'dör*, *adj* practised, used, or being within a building; (of a game or sport) adapted for playing indoors. — *adv* **indoors'** inside a building. [**in-** (1).]

indorse. See **endorse**.

indraught or **indraft** *in'dräft*, *n* a drawing in; an inward flow of current or air. [**in** and **draught**.]

indrawn *in'drön* or *in-drön'*, *adj* drawn in. [**in** and **drawn**.]

Indri *in'drē* or **Indris** *-in'drēs*, *n* a genus of lemurs found in Madagascar; (without *cap*) a member of a species of these.

indubitable *in-dū'bit-ə-bl*, *adj* that cannot be doubted; certain. — *n* **indūbitabil'ity** or **indū'bitableness**. — *adv* **indū'bitably** without doubt, certainly. [**in-** (2).]

induce *in-dūs'*, *vt* to prevail on, make, cause, encourage (to do something); to bring into being; to initiate or speed up (labour of childbirth) artificially, as by administering drugs (also *vi*) (*med*); to cause, as an electric state, by mere proximity (*phys*); to infer inductively (*logic*). — *vi* to reason or draw inferences inductively. — *n* **induce'ment** that which induces; incentive, motive; a statement of facts introducing other important facts (*law*). — *n* **induc'er**. — *adj* **indu'cible**. — **induced current** (*electr*) a current set in action by the influence of the surrounding magnetic field, or by the variation of an adjacent current. — See also **induct, induction** below. [L. *indūcere*, *inductum* — *in*, into, *dūcere*, to lead.]

induct *in-dukt'*, *vt* to introduce; to put in possession, as of a benefice, to install. — *n* **induct'ance** the property of inducing an electromotive force by variation of current in a circuit; a device having inductance. — *n* **induc'tion** a bringing or drawing in; installation in office, benefice, etc.; a prelude; an introductory section or scene; magnetising by proximity without contact; the production by one body of an opposite electric state in another by proximity; production of an electric current by magnetic changes in the neighbourhood; reasoning from particular cases to general conclusions (*logic*). — *adj* **induc'tional**. — *adj* **induct'ive**. — *adv* **induct'ively**. — *n* **inductiv'ity**. — *n* **induct'or**. — **induction coil** an electrical machine consisting of two coils of wire, in which every variation of the current in one induces a current in the other; **induction course** formal instruction given to a new employee or appointee; **induction heating** the heating of a conductive material by means of an induced current passing through it; **induction loop system** a method of sound distribution in which signals fed into a wire loop are received via headphones or hearing-aids by those inside the area enclosed by the loop; **induction motor** an electric motor in which currents in the primary winding set up an electromagnetic flux which induces currents in the secondary winding, interaction of these currents with the flux producing rotation. [See ety. for **induce**.]

indue. See **endue**.

indulge *in-dulj'*, *vt* to yield to the wishes of; to favour or gratify; to treat with favour or undue favour; not to restrain; to grant an indulgence to or on. — *vi* to gratify one's appetites freely, or permit oneself any action or expression (with *in*); to partake, esp. of alcohol (*colloq*). — *n* **indulg'ence** gratification; excessive gratification; favourable or unduly favourable treatment; (in the R.C. Church) a remission, to a repentant sinner, of the temporal punishment which remains due after the sin and its eternal punishment have been remitted; exemption of an individual from an ecclesiastical law. — *adj* **indulg'ent** ready to gratify the wishes of others; compliant; not severe. — *adv* **indulg'ently**. — *n* **indulg'er**. [L. *indulgēre*, to be kind to, indulge — *in*, in and prob. *dulcis*, sweet.]

indult *in-dult'*, *n* a licence granted by the Pope, authorising something to be done which the common law of the Church does not sanction. [Ety. as for **indulge**.]

indurate *in'dū-rāt*, *vt* and *vi* to harden. — Also *adj*. — *n* **indurā'tion**. — *adj* **in'durative**. [L. *indūrāre*, *-ātum* — *in*, in, *dūrāre*, to harden.]

indusium *in-dū'zi-əm*, *n* a protective membrane or scale, esp. that covering the spores of a fern; an insect larva-case: — *pl* **indu'sia**. [L. *indūsium*, an undergarment.]

industry *in'dəs-tri*, *n* the quality of being diligent; assiduity; steady application; habitual diligence; any branch of manufacture and trade, *heavy industry* relating to industries involving heavy equipment, *light industry* to smaller factory-processed goods, e.g. knitwear, glass, electronics components, etc.; all branches of manufacture and trade collectively. — *adj* **industrial** (*-dus'*) relating to, characteristic of, or used in industry. — *n* (in *pl*) stocks and shares in industrial concerns. — *n* **industrialīsā'tion** or **-z-**. — *vt* **indus'trialise** or **-ize** to give an industrial character, or character of industrialism, to. — *n* **indus'trialism** devotion to labour or industrial pursuits; that system or condition of society in which industrial labour is the chief and most characteristic feature. — *n* **indus'trialist** a person who owns, or holds a powerful position in, an industrial concern or concerns. — *adj* of or characterised by industry. — *adv* **indus'trially**. — *adj* **indus'trious** diligent or active in one's labour or in a particular pursuit. — *adv* **indus'triously**. — **industrial action** a strike or go-slow; **industrial archaeology** the study of industrial machines and buildings of the past; **industrial disease** a disease or condition caused by one's occupation, e.g. pneumoconiosis; **industrial estate** a planned industrial area, with factories organised to provide varied employment; **industrial relations** relations between management and workers; **industrial revolution** the economic and social changes arising out of the change from industries carried on in the home with simple machines to industries in factories with power-driven machinery — esp. such changes (from about 1760) in Britain, the first country to be industrialised; **industrial tribunal** a tribunal set up to hear complaints and make judgments in disputes between employers and employees on matters such as industrial relations and alleged unfair dismissal. — **Industrial Injuries Disablement Benefit** in Britain, a National Insurance weekly payment for injury sustained while at work. — Also **injury benefit**. [L. *industria*.]

indwell *in-dwel'*, (*literary*) *vi* and *vt* to dwell or abide in: — *pa t* and *pa p* **indwelt'**. — *adj* **in'dwelling** dwelling within, abiding permanently in the mind or soul. — *n* residence within, or in the heart or soul. [**in-** (1).]

-ine[1] *-īn*, *-ēn* or *-in*, (*chem*) noun-forming *sfx* indicating: (1) a basic organic compound containing nitrogen, such as an amino-acid or alkaloid; (2) a halogen, such as *chlorine* and *fluorine*; (3) a mixture of compounds, such as *kerosine*, *benzine*. [L. fem. adjectival ending *-īna*.]

-ine[2] *-īn*, adjectival *sfx* meaning: (1) belonging to or characteristic of, as in *elephantine*; (2) like, similar to, or being, as in *adamantine*, *crystalline*. [L. adjectival ending *-īnus*.]

inebriate *in-ē'bri-āt*, *vt* to make drunk, to intoxicate; to exhilarate greatly. — *adj* (*-it* or *-ət*) drunk; intoxicated. — *n* a drunk person; a drunkard. — *adj* **inē'briant** intoxicating. — Also *n*. — *n* **inēbriā'tion** or **inebriety** (*in-ē-brī'i-ti* or *in-i-*) drunkenness; intoxication. — *adj* **inē'brious** drunk. [L. *inēbriāre*, *-ātum* — *in* (intensive) and *ēbriāre*, to make drunk — *ēbrius*, drunk.]

inedible *in-ed'i-bl*, *adj* not good to eat; not suitable for eating (e.g. because poisonous or indigestible). — *n* **inedibil'ity**. [**in-** (2).]

ineducable *in-ed'ū-kə-bl*, *adj* not capable of being educated or of learning. — *n* **ineducabil'ity**. [**in-** (2).]

ineffable *in-ef'ə-bl*, *adj* not able to be described, inexpressible. — *n* **ineff'ableness**. — *adv* **ineff'ably**. [L. *ineffābilis* — *in-*, not, *effābilis*, expressible.]

ineffective *in-i-fek'tiv*, *adj* not effective; useless. — *adv* **ineffec'tively**. — *n* **ineffec'tiveness**. — *adj* **ineffec'tual** fruitless; ineffective, weak. — *n* **ineffectual'ity** or **ineffec'tualness**. — *adv* **ineffect'ually**. [**in-** (2).]

inefficacious *in-ef-i-kā'shəs*, *adj* not having power to produce an effect, or the desired effect. — *adv* **inefficā'ciously**. — *n* **inefficacy** (*-ef'i-kə-si*) lack of efficacy. [**in-** (2).]

inefficiency *in-i-fi'shən-si*, *n* lack of the power or skill to do or produce something in the best, most economical, etc. way. — *adj* **ineffi'cient** not efficient. — *adv* **ineffi'ciently**. [**in-** (2).]

inelastic *in-i-las'tik*, *adj* not elastic; incompressible. — *n* **inelasticity** (*in-el-əs-tis'i-ti*). — **inelastic collision** or **scattering** see under **collide**. [**in-** (2).]

inelegance *in-el'i-gəns*, *n* lack of grace or refinement. — Also **inel'egancy**. — *adj* **inel'egant**. — *adv* **inel'egantly**. [**in-** (2).]

ineligible *in-el'i-ji-bl*, *adj* not qualified to stand for election; not suitable to be available for choice or to be chosen; unsuitable. — Also *n*. — *n* **ineligibil'ity**. — *adv* **inel'igibly**. [**in-** (2).]

ineluctable *in-i-luk'tə-bl*, *adj* not to be escaped from or avoided. [L. *inēluctābilis* — *in-*, not, *ē*, from, *luctārī*, to struggle.]

inept *in-ept'*, *adj* foolish, silly; awkward, clumsy; unsuitable; irrelevant and futile; void (*law*). — *n* **inept'itude** or **inept'ness**. — *adv* **inept'ly**. [L. *ineptus* — *in-*, not, *aptus*, apt.]

inequable *in-ek'wə-bl* or *-ēk'*, *adj* not equable, changeable. [**in-** (2).]

inequality *in-i-* or *in-ē-kwol'i-ti*, *n* lack of equality; difference; inadequacy; incompetency; unevenness; dissimilarity; an uneven place; a statement that two quantities or expressions are not equal (*math*). [**in-** (2).]

inequitable *in-ek'wi-tə-bl, adj* unfair, unjust. — *adv* **ineq'uitably**. — *n* **ineq'uity** lack of equity or fairness; an unjust action. [**in-** (2).]

ineradicable *in-i-rad'i-kə-bl, adj* not able to be got rid of, removed completely, or rooted out. — *adv* **inerad'icably**. [**in-** (2).]

inert *in-ûrt', adj* without inherent power of moving, or of active resistance to motion; passive; chemically inactive; sluggish; disinclined to move or act. — *n* **inertia** (*in-ûr'shi-ə, -shyə* or *-shə*) inertness; the inherent property of matter by which it continues, unless constrained, in its state of rest or uniform motion in a straight line. — *adj* **iner'tial** of or pertaining to inertia. — *adv* **inert'ly**. — *n* **inert'ness**. — **inert gas** one of a group of elements whose outer electron orbits are complete, rendering them inert to all the usual chemical reactions; **inertia-reel seat-belt** a type of self-retracting seat-belt in which the wearer is constrained only when violent deceleration of the vehicle causes the belt to lock; **inertia selling** sending unrequested goods to householders and attempting to charge for them if they are not returned. [L. *iners, inertis*, unskilled, idle — *in-*, not, *ars, artis*, art.]

inescapable *in-is-kā'pə-bl, adj* unescapable; inevitable. [**in-** (2).]

inessential *in-is-en'shl, adj* not essential; not necessary; immaterial. [**in-** (2).]

inestimable *in-es'tim-ə-bl, adj* not able to be estimated or valued; priceless. — *adv* **ines'timably**. [**in-** (2).]

inevitable *in-ev'it-ə-bl, adj* not to be evaded or avoided; certain to happen; exactly right, giving the feeling that the thing could not have been any other way than it is. — *n* **inevitabil'ity**. — *n* **inev'itableness**. — *adv* **inev'itably**. [L. *inēvītābilis* — *in-*, not, *ē*, from, *vītāre*, to avoid.]

inexact *in-ig-zakt', adj* not precisely correct or true; lax. — *n* **inexact'itude** lack of exactitude; an example of inexactitude. — *n* **inexact'ness**. — *adv* **inexact'ly**. [**in-** (2).]

in excelsis *in eks-chel'sis* or *-sēs*, (L.) on high; in the highest degree.

inexcusable *in-ik-skūz'ə-bl, adj* not justifiable; unpardonable. — *n* **inexcusabil'ity**. — *n* **inexcus'ableness**. — *adv* **inexcus'ably**. [**in-** (2).]

inexhaustible *in-ig-zös'tə-bl, adj* not able to be exhausted or spent; unfailing. — *n* **inexhaustibil'ity**. — *adv* **inexhaust'ibly**. — *adj* **inexhaust'ive** not exhaustive. [**in-** (2).]

inexorable *in-eks'ər-ə-bl, adj* not to be moved by entreaty or persuasion; unrelenting; unyielding. — *n* **inexorabil'ity** or **inex'orableness**. — *adv* **inex'orably**. [L.L. *inexōrābilis* — *in-*, not, *exōrāre* — *ex*, out of, *ōrāre*, to entreat.]

inexpedient *in-ik-spē'di-ənt, adj* contrary to expediency; not in accordance with good policy, impolitic. — *n* **inexpe'dience** or **inexpe'diency**. — *adv* **inexpe'diently**. [**in-** (2).]

inexpensive *in-ik-spens'iv, adj* not costing much, cheap in price. — *adv* **inexpens'ively**. — *n* **inexpens'iveness**. [**in-** (2).]

inexperience *in-ik-spē'ri-əns, n* lack of experience. — *adj* **inexpe'rienced** not having experience; unskilled or unpractised. [**in-** (2).]

inexpert *in-eks'pûrt, adj* unskilled. — *n* **inex'pertness**. [**in-** (2).]

inexplicable *in-eks'pli-kə-bl* or *-ik-splik'ə-bl, adj* incapable of being explained or accounted for. — *n* **inexplicabil'ity** or **inexplic'ableness**. — *adv* **inex'plicably** (or *-plik'*). [**in-** (2).]

inexplicit *in-ik-splis'it, adj* not explicit; not clear. [**in-** (2).]

inexpressible *in-ik-spres'i-bl, adj* that cannot be expressed; indescribable. — *adv* **inexpress'ibly**. — *adj* **inexpress'ive** unexpressive. — *n* **inexpress'iveness**. [**in-** (2).]

inexpungible *in-ik-spun'ji-bl, adj* incapable of being wiped out or effaced. [**in-** (2).]

inextinguishable *in-ik-sting'gwish-ə-bl, adj* that cannot be extinguished, quenched or destroyed. — *adv* **inextin'guishably**. [**in-** (2).]

in extremis *in ik-strē'mis* or *ek-strā'mēs*, (L.) at the point of death; in desperate circumstances.

inextricable *in-eks'tri-kə-bl* or *-ik-strik'ə-bl, adj* not able to be extricated or disentangled. — *adv* **inex'tricably** (or *-strik'*). [L. *inextrīcābilis*.]

INF *abbrev* for intermediate-range nuclear forces.

inf. *abbrev* for: infantry; informal; *infra* (L.), below.

infall *in'föl, n* falling in. [**in** and **fall**[1].]

infallible *in-fal'i-bl, adj* incapable of error; incapable of making a mistake. — *n* **infall'ibilism** the doctrine of the Pope's infallibility. — *n* **infall'ibilist**. — *n* **infallibil'ity**. — *adv* **infall'ibly**. — **the doctrine of infallibility** (*RC*) the doctrine (defined in 1870) that the Pope, when speaking *ex cathedra*, is kept from error in faith and morals. [**in-** (2).]

infamous *in'fə-məs, adj* having a very bad reputation; publicly branded guilty; notoriously vile; disgraceful. — *adv* **in'famously**. — *n* **in'famy** ill repute; public disgrace; an infamous act or happening; extreme vileness. [L. *īnfāmāre* — *in-*, not, *fāma*, fame.]

infant *in'fənt, n* a baby; a person under the age of legal maturity (*Eng law*). — *adj* of or belonging to infants; of or in infancy; at an early stage of development. — *n* **in'fancy** the state or time of being an infant; childhood; the beginning or an early stage of anything. — *adj* **infantile** (*in'fən-tīl* or in U.S. *-til*, also *in-fant'īl*) pertaining to infancy or to an infant; having characteristics of infancy; no better than that of an infant, childish; undeveloped. — *n* **infan'tilism** persistence of infantile characteristics; a childish utterance or characteristic. — **infantile paralysis** poliomyelitis; **infant mortality (rate)** (the rate of) deaths in the first year of life; **infant school** a school for children up to about the age of seven. [L. *infāns, infantis* — *in-*, not, *fāns*, pres. p. of *fārī*, to speak.]

infante *in-fan'tā*, (*hist*) *n* a prince of the blood royal of Spain or Portugal, esp. a son of the king other than the heir-apparent: — *fem* **infan'ta** a princess similarly defined; the wife of an infante. [Sp. and Port. from the root of **infant**.]

infanticide *in-fan'ti-sīd, n* the killing of a child by its mother, within twelve months of its birth; loosely, the murder of an infant; a mother who kills, or someone who murders, an infant. — *adj* **infanticī'dal** (or *-fant'*). [L. *īnfanticīdium*, child-killing — *infāns*, an infant, *caedĕre*, to kill.]

infantry *in'fənt-ri, n* foot-soldiers; a part of an army made up of such soldiers. — Also *adj*. — *n* **in'fantryman**. [Fr. *infanterie* — It. *infanteria* — *infante*, youth, servant, foot-soldier — L. *īnfāns*, *-antis*, a youth.]

infarct *in-färkt', n* a portion of tissue that is dying because the blood supply to it has been cut off. — *n* **infarc'tion**. [Med. L. *īnfarctus* — *in*, in, *far(c)tus* — *farcīre*, to cram, stuff.]

infatuate *in-fat'ū-āt, vt* to inspire with foolish and unreasoning passion; to cause to behave foolishly or unreasonably; to deprive of judgment. — *adj* infatuated. — *pa p* and *adj* **infat'uated**. — *n* **infatuā'tion**. [L. *īnfatuāre, -ātum* — *in*, in, *fatuus*, foolish.]

infeasible *in-fēz'i-bl, adj* not feasible. — *n* **infeasibil'ity**. [**in-** (2).]

infect *in-fekt', vt* to taint, especially with disease; to corrupt; to spread to. — *n* **infec'tion** (*-shən*) the act of infecting; something that infects or taints; an infectious disease. — *adj* **infec'tious** (*-shəs*) or **infec'tive** (*-tiv*) (of a disease) able to be transmitted by infection; caused by infection; corrupting; apt or likely to spread to others. — *adv* **infec'tiously**. — *n* **infec'tiousness**. — *n* **infec'tiveness**. — *n* **infec'tor**. [L. *inficĕre, īnfectum* — *in*, into, *facĕre*, to make.]

infelicitous *in-fi-lis'i-təs, adj* not felicitous or happy; inappropriate, inapt. — *n* **infelic'ity** something that is inappropriate or inapt. [**in-** (2).]

infer *in-fûr', vt* to derive from what has gone before; to arrive at as a logical conclusion; to conclude; (usu. of a thing or statement) to entail or involve as a consequence, to imply — a use now often condemned, but generally accepted for over four centuries: — *pr p* **inferr'ing**; *pa t* and *pa p* **inferred'**. — *adj* **in'ferable** (or *-fûr'*; also **inferr'able** or **inferr'ible**). — *n* **in'ference** something that is inferred or deduced; the act of drawing a conclusion from statements of fact; consequence; conclusion. — *adj* **inferential** (*-en'shl*) relating to inference; deduced or able to be deduced by inference. — *adv* **inferen'tially**. [L. *īnferre* — *in*, into, *ferre*, to bring.]

inferior *in-fē'ri-ər, adj* lower in any respect; subordinate; poor or poorer in quality; set slightly below the line (*printing*); (of an ovary) having the other parts above it (*bot*); (of the other parts) below the ovary (*bot*); (of a planet) revolving within the earth's orbit (*astron*). — *n* a person who is lower in rank or station. — *n* **inferiority** (*-or'*). — *adv* **infe'riorly** in an inferior manner. — **inferiority complex** a complex involving a suppressed sense of personal inferiority (*psychol*); popularly, a feeling of inferiority. [L. *īnferior*, compar. of *īnferus*, low.]

infernal *in-fûr'nəl, adj* belonging to the regions below the earth, the underworld; resembling or suitable to hell; outrageous, very unpleasant (*colloq*); extremely annoying (*colloq*). — *adv* **infer'nally**. — *n* **infer'no** (also with *cap*) hell (*It*); a place or situation of horror and confusion, esp. a conflagration. [L. *īnfernus* — *īnferus*, low.]

infertile *in-fûr'tīl* or in U.S. *-til, adj* not productive; barren. — *n* **infertility** (*-til'*). [**in-** (2).]

infest *in-fest', vt* to swarm over, cover or fill, in a troublesome, unpleasant or harmful way; to disturb or harass. — *n* **infestā'tion** attack, or the condition of being attacked, esp. by parasites. [L. *īnfestāre*, from *īnfestus*, hostile.]

infibulate *in-fib'ū-lāt, vt* to fasten with a clasp. — *n* **infibulā'tion** the act of confining or fastening, esp. the fastening or partial closing-up of the prepuce or the labia majora by clasps or stitches. [**in-** (1) and *fibula*, a clasp.]

infidel *in'fi-dl, n* someone who rejects a religion, esp. Christianity or Islam; (*loosely*) someone who disbelieves in any theory, etc. — *adj* unbelieving; sceptical. — *n* **infidelity** (*-del'*) lack of faith or belief; disbelief in a specific religion; unfaithfulness, esp. in marriage; treachery. [O.Fr. *infidèle* — L. *īnfidēlis* — *in*, not, *fidēlis*, faithful.]

infield *in'fēld, n* the space enclosed within the baselines (*baseball*); the part of the field near the wicket (*cricket*); the players stationed in the infield. — *n* **in'fielder** a player on the infield. [**in** and **field**.]

infighting *in'fīt-ing, n* boxing at close quarters. — See also under **in**. [**in** and **fighting**.]

infilling *in'fil-ing, n* filling up or in; something used to fill up or in; material used to fill up or level (*building*); infill development. — *vt* **in'fill** to fill in. — *n* material for infilling. — **infill housing** or **development** new houses built between or among older ones. [**in** and **fill**.]

infiltrate *in'fil-trāt* or *in-fil'trāt, vt* to cause to filter; to cause to filter into; to sift into; to permeate. — *vi* to permeate gradually; to sift or filter in. — *vt* and *vi* of troops, agents, to enter (a hostile area) secretly and for subversive purposes. [**in-** (1).]

infin. *abbrev* for infinitive.

infinite *in'fin-it, adj* without end or limit; greater than any quantity that can be assigned or quantified (*math*); extending to infinity; vast; in vast numbers; inexhaustible. — *n* something that has no determinate bounds, and for which there is no possible bound or limit; the Absolute, or God. — *adv* **in'finitely**. — *n* **in'finiteness**. — *adj* **infinitesimal** (*-es'*) infinitely small; (*loosely*) extremely small. — *n* an infinitely small quantity. — *adv* **infinites'imally**. — *n* **infin'ity** the state or quality of having no limits or bounds; an infinite quantity or distance; vastness, immensity; a countless or indefinite number. [**in-** (2).]

infinitive *in-fin'it-iv*, (*gram*) *adj* expressing, or in the mood that expresses, the idea without person or number. — *n* the infinitive mood; a verb in the infinitive mood. — *adj* **infinitī'val**. — *adv* **infin'itively**. [L. *īnfīnītīvus* — *in-*, not, *fīnīre*, to limit.]

infinity. See under **infinite**.

infirm *in-fûrm', adj* sickly; weak; frail; unstable. — *n* **infirm'ity**. — *adv* **infirm'ly**. — *n* **infirm'ness**. [L. *īnfirmus* — *in-*, not, *firmus*, strong.]

infirmary *in-fûrm'ə-ri, n* a hospital or place for the treatment of the sick or injured. [**infirm**.]

infix *in-fiks', vt* to fix in; to set in by piercing; to insert an element within (a root) (*philol*). — *n* **in'fix** (*philol*) an element or affix inserted within a root or word. [L. *īnfīxus* — *in*, in, *fīgĕre*, *fīxum*, to fix.]

infl. *abbrev* for influenced.

in flagrante delicto *in flə-gran'ti di-lik'tō* or *flä-gran'te dā-lik'tō*, (L.) in the very act of committing the crime.

inflame *in-flām', vt* to cause to burn; to make hot; to cause inflammation in; to arouse strong emotion in; to anger; to exacerbate. — *vi* to burst into flames; to become hot, painful, red, excited or angry; to suffer inflammation. — *adj* **inflamed'**. — *n* **inflām'er**. [O.Fr. *enflammer* — L. *īnflammāre*; see ety. for **inflammable**.]

inflammable *in-flam'ə-bl, adj* capable of being set on fire (see **flammable**); easily kindled or excited. — *n* an inflammable substance. — *n* **inflammabil'ity**. — *n* **inflamm'ableness**. — *adv* **inflamm'ably**. — *n* **inflammation** (*-flə-mā'shən*) the state of being in flames or inflamed; heat of a part of the body, with pain, redness and swelling. — *adj* **inflamm'atory** tending to inflame; inflaming; exciting, tending to stir up trouble. [L. *īnflammāre* — *in*, into, *flamma*, a flame.]

inflate *in-flāt', vt* to cause to swell up with air or gas; to puff up; to expand unduly; to increase excessively; to elate. — *vi* to become full of air or gas; to distend. — *adj* and *n* **inflat'able** (any object) that can be inflated. — *adj* **inflat'ed** swollen or blown out; turgid; pompous; excessive, exaggerated; hollow, filled with air (*bot*). — *n* **inflation** (*in-flā'shən*) the act of inflating; the condition of being inflated; undue increase in quantity of money in proportion to buying power; a progressive increase in the general level of prices; turgidity of style. — *adj* **infla'tionary**. — *n* **infla'tionism** the policy of inflating currency. — *n* **infla'tionist**. [L. *īnflāre*, *-ātum* — *in*, into, *flāre*, to blow.]

inflect *in-flekt', vt* to modulate (e.g. the voice); to vary the terminations of (*gram*). — *n* **inflec'tion** or **inflex'ion** modulation of the voice; the varying of terminations to express the relations of case, number, tense, etc. (*gram*). — *adj* **inflec'tional** or **inflex'ional**. — *adj* **inflect'ive**. [L. *īnflectĕre* — *in*, in, *flectĕre*, *flexum*, to bend.]

inflexible *in-flek'si-bl, adj* incapable of being bent; unyielding; rigid; unbending. — *n* **inflexibil'ity** or **inflex'ibleness**. — *adv* **inflex'ibly**. [**in-** (2).]

inflexion, inflexional. See **inflect**.

inflict *in-flikt', vt* to lay on; to impose (as punishment or pain). — *n* **inflic'tion** the act of inflicting or imposing; something inflicted. [L. *īnflīgĕre*, *īnflīctum* — *in*, against, *flīgĕre*, to strike.]

inflorescence *in-flor-es'əns* or *-flər-*, (*bot*) *n* mode of branching of a flower-bearing axis; aggregate of flowers on an axis. [L. *īnflōrēscĕre*, to begin to blossom.]

inflow *in'flō*, *n* the act of flowing in, influx; something that flows in. — *adj* **in'flowing**. [**in-** (1).]

influence *in'flŏŏ-əns*, *n* the power of producing an effect, esp. unobtrusively; the effect of power exerted; something having such power; someone exercising such power; domination, often hidden or inexplicable; exertions of friends who have useful connections and are able to secure advantages for one. — *vt* to have or exert influence upon; to affect. — *adj* **in'fluent** flowing in; exerting influence. — *n* a tributary stream. — *adj* **influential** (*-en'shl*) of the nature of influence; having a great deal of influence; effectively active (in bringing something about). — *adv* **influen'tially**. [O.Fr., — L.L. *īnfluentia* — L. *in*, into, *fluĕre*, to flow.]

influenza *in-flŏŏ-en'zə*, *n* an epidemic virus disease attacking esp. the upper respiratory tract. — *adj* **influen'zal**. [It., influence, influenza (as a supposed astral visitation) — L.L. *īnfluentia*; see ety. for **influence**.]

influx *in'fluks*, *n* a flowing in; accession; that which flows in. — *n* **influxion** (*in-fluk'shən*). [L. *īnfluxus* — *īnfluĕre*.]

info *in'fō*, *n* colloq. short form of **information**. — *n* **infomercial** (*-mûr'shl*) a short television film which is in fact an advertising medium. — *n* **infotain'ment** the presentation of serious news or current affairs as entertainment.

infold. See **enfold**.

infomercial. See **info**.

inforce. Same as **enforce**.

inform *in-fŏrm'*, *vt* to pass on knowledge to; to tell; to animate or give life to; to give a quality to. — *vi* to give information, make an accusation (with *against* or *on*). — *n* **inform'ant** someone who informs or communicates information. — *nsing* **informa'tics** information science; information technology. — *n* **information** (*in-fər-mā'shən*) intelligence given; knowledge; an accusation made before a magistrate or court. — *adj* **informā'tional**. — *adj* **inform'ative** having power to form; instructive. — *adj* **informed'** knowing, intelligent, educated. — *n* **inform'er** a person who gives information; a person who informs against another; an animator. — **information retrieval** the storage, classification, and subsequent tracing of (esp. computerised) information; **information science** (the study of) the processing and communication of data, esp. by means of computerised systems; **information scientist**; **information technology** the (esp. computerised or electronic) technology related to the gathering, recording and communicating of information. [O.Fr. *enformer* — L. *īnfōrmāre* — *in*, into, *fōrmāre*, to form, *fōrma*, form.]

informal *in-fŏr'məl*, *adj* not according to form or convention; relaxed, friendly, unceremonious; (esp. of clothes) everyday, casual; (of a vote) invalid (*Austr*). — *n* **informal'ity**. — *adv* **inform'ally**. [L. *in-*, not, *fōrma*, form.]

infotainment. See **info**.

infra *in'frə* or *ēn'frä*, (L.) below; lower down on the page, or further on in the book. — **infra dignitatem** (*dig-ni-tā'təm* or *-tä'tem*) beneath one's dignity (colloq. abbrev. **infra dig.**).

infraction *in-frak'shən*, *n* violation, esp. of law; a breach. — *vt* **infract'** to infringe. — *adj* **infract'ed** broken; interrupted; bent in. — *n* **infrac'tor** a person who infracts. [L. *īnfringĕre*, *īnfrāctum* — *in*, in, *frangĕre*, *frāctum*, to break.]

infra dig. See **infra**.

infrangible *in-fran'ji-bl*, *adj* not able to be broken; not to be violated. — *n* **infrangibil'ity** or **infran'gibleness**. [L. *in-*, not, *frangĕre*, to break.]

infrared *in-frə-red'*, *adj* beyond the red end of the visible spectrum; using infrared radiation; sensitive to this radiation. [L. *īnfrā*, below.]

infrasonic *in-frə-son'ik*, (*acoustics*) *adj* (of frequencies) below the usual audible limit. — *n* **in'frasound**. [L. *infrā*, below.]

infrastructure *in'frə-struk-chər*, *n* inner structure, structure of component parts; a system of communications and services as backing for military, commercial, etc., operations. — *adj* **infrastruc'tural**. [L. *īnfrā*, below.]

infrequent *in-frē'kwənt*, *adj* seldom occurring; rare; uncommon. — *n* **infrē'quence** or **infrē'quency**. — *adv* **infrē'quently**. [**in-** (2).]

infringe *in-frinj'*, *vt* to violate, esp. law; to neglect to obey. — *n* **infringe'ment**. [L. *īnfringĕre* — *in*, into, *frangĕre*, to break.]

infundibular *in-fun-dib'ū-lər*, *adj* funnel-shaped. [L. *īnfundibulum*, a funnel — *in*, in, *fundĕre*, to pour.]

infuriate *in-fū'ri-āt*, *vt* to enrage; to madden. [L. *in*, in, *furiāre*, *-ātum*, to madden — *furĕre*, to rave.]

infuse *in-fūz'*, *vt* to pour in; to instil; to steep in liquor without boiling; to imbue. — *vi* to undergo infusion. — *n* **infus'er** device for making an infusion, esp. of tea. — *adj* **infus'ible**. — *n* **infusion** (*in-fū'zhən*) pouring in; something poured in or introduced; the pouring of water over any substance in order to extract its active qualities; a solution in water of an organic, esp. a vegetable, substance. — *adj* **infusive** (*-fū'siv*) having the power of infusion or of being infused. [L. *īnfundĕre*, *īnfūsum* — *in*, into, *fundĕre*, *fūsum*, to pour.]

infusible *in-fūz'i-bl*, *adj* that cannot be fused; having a high melting-point. — *n* **infusibili'ity**. [**in-** (2).]

ingathering *in'gadh-ər-ing*, *n* collection; securing of the fruits of the earth; harvest. — **Feast of Ingathering** see **Feast of Tabernacles** under **tabernacle**. [**in-** (1).]

ingenious *in-jē'nyəs* or *-ni-əs*, *adj* skilful in invention or contriving; skilfully contrived. — *adv* **ingē'niously**. — *n* **ingē'niousness** power of ready invention; facility in combining ideas; cleverly contrived or unconventional design. [L. *ingenium*, common sense.]

ingénue *ẽ-zhā-nü*, (Fr.) *n* a naive young woman, esp. on the stage: — *masc* **ingénu**.

ingenuity *in-ji-nū'i-ti*, *n* orig., ingenuousness; now (by confusion with **ingenious**) ingeniousness. [L. *ingenuitās*, *-ātis*; see ety. for **ingenuous**.]

ingenuous *in-jen'ū-əs*, *adj* frank; honourable; free from deception. — *adv* **ingen'uously**. — *n* **ingen'uousness**. — *n* **ingenu'ity** (see previous entry). [L. *ingenuus*, free-born, ingenuous.]

ingest *in-jest'*, *vt* to take (e.g. food) into the body. — *adj* **ingest'ible**. — *n* **ingestion** (*in-jes'chən*). — *adj* **ingest'ive**. [L. *ingerĕre*, *ingestum*, to carry in — *in*, in, *gerĕre*, to carry.]

ingle *ing'gl* or in Scot. *ing'l*, *n* a fire; fireplace. — **ing'lenook** a chimney-corner; **ing'le-side** a fireside. [Possibly Gael. *aingeal*; or L. *igniculus*, dimin. of *ignis*, fire.]

inglorious *in-glō'ri-əs*, *adj* not glorious; unhonoured; shameful. — *adv* **inglō'riously**. — *n* **inglō'riousness**. [**in-** (2).]

ingoing *in'gō-ing*, *n* a going in; entrance. — *adj* going in; thorough, penetrating. [**in** and **go**[1].]

ingot *ing'gət* or *-got*, *n* a mass of unwrought metal, esp. gold or silver, cast in a mould. [Perh. O.E. *in*, in, and the root *got*, as in *goten*, past p. of *gēotan*, to pour.]

ingraft. Same as **engraft**.

ingrain *in-grān'*, *vt* see **engrain**. — *adj* (pronounced *in'grān* when *attrib*) dyed in the yarn or thread before manufacture; deeply fixed; through and through. — *adj* **ingrained'** (*attrib in'grānd*). [**in-** (1).]

ingrate *in-grāt'* or *in'grāt*, *n* an ungrateful person. — *adj* (*archaic* or *formal*) ungrateful. [L. *ingrātus* — *in-*, not, *grātus*, pleasing, grateful.]

ingratiate *in-grā'shi-āt*, *vt* to commend (usu. oneself) persuasively to someone's favour (followed by *with*). — *adj* **ingra'tiating**. [L. *in*, into, *grātia*, favour.]

ingratitude *in-grat'i-tūd*, *n* lack of gratitude or thankfulness. [L.L. *ingrātitūdō* — L. *ingrātus*, unthankful.]

ingredient *in-grē'di-ənt*, *n* something that is put into a mixture or compound; a component. [L. *ingrediēns*, *-entis*, pres. p. of *ingredī* — *in*, into, *gradī*, to walk.]

ingress *in'gres*, *n* entrance; power, right or means of entrance. — *n* **ingression** (*in-gresh'ən*). — *adj* **ingress'ive** (*phon*) (of speech sounds) pronounced with inhalation rather than exhalation of breath. [L. *ingressus* — *ingredī*; see ety. for **ingredient**.]

ingroup. See under **in**.

ingrowing *in'grō-ing*, *adj* growing inwards; growing into the flesh; growing in or into. — *adj* **in'grown**. — *n* **in'growth** growth within or inwards; a structure formed in this way. [**in-** (1).]

inguinal *ing'gwin-əl*, *adj* relating to, in or of the groin. [L. *inguinālis* — *inguen*, *inguinis*, the groin.]

inhabit *in-hab'it*, *vt* to dwell in; to occupy. — *adj* **inhab'itable** capable of being inhabited. — *n* **inhab'itance** or **inhab'itancy** the act of inhabiting; abode or residence. — *n* **inhab'itant** a person who or an animal which inhabits; a resident. — *n* **inhabitā'tion** the act of inhabiting; abode or residence. [L. *inhabitāre* — *in*, in, *habitāre*, to dwell.]

inhale *in-hāl'*, *vt* and *vi* to breathe in; to draw in. — *adj* **inhā'lant** inhaling; drawing in. — *n* a medicinal preparation to be inhaled; an inhaling organ, structure or apparatus. — *n* **inhalation** (*in-hə-lā'shən*) the act of drawing into the lungs; something to be inhaled. — *n* **inhalator** (*in'hə-lā-tər* or *-lā'*) an apparatus for enabling someone to inhale a gas, etc. — *n* **inhā'ler** a person who inhales; a person who habitually inhales tobacco smoke; an inhalator; a respirator or gas mask. [L. *in*, upon, *hālāre*, to breathe.]

inharmonious *in-här-mō'ni-əs*, *adj* discordant, unmusical; disagreeing; marked by disagreement and discord. — *adj* **inharmonic** (*in-här-mon'ik*) or **inharmon'ical** lacking harmony; inharmonious. — *adv* **inharmō'niously**. — *n* **inharmō'niousness**. — *n* **inharmony** (*in-här'mən-i*). [**in-** (2).]

inhere *in-hēr'*, *vi* (with *in*) to stick, remain firm in something; to be inherent. — *adj* **inhēr'ent** (or *-her'*) existing in and inseparable from something else; innate; natural. — *adv* **inher'ently**. [L. *inhaerēre*, *inhaesum* — *in*, in, *haerēre*, to stick.]

inherit *in-her'it*, *vt* to get possession of as heir; to possess by transmission from past generations; to have at secondhand from anyone (*colloq*); to have by genetic transmission from ancestors. — *vi* to succeed. — *adj* **inher'itable** same as **heritable**. — *n* **inher'itance** that which is or may be inherited; hereditary descent. — *n* **inher'itor** someone who inherits or may inherit; an heir: — *fem* **inher'itress** or **inher'itrix**. — **inheritance tax** a tax (replacing **death duty**) levied on inheritors according to their relationship to the testator. [O.Fr. *enhériter*, — L.L. *inhērēditāre*, to inherit.]

inhibit *in-hib'it*, *vt* to hold in or back; to keep back; to restrain or check. — *n* **inhibi'tion** the act of inhibiting or restraining; the state of being inhibited; a restraining action of the unconscious will; the blocking of a mental process by another set up at the same time by the same stimulus; stoppage, complete or partial, of a physical process by some nervous influence. — *adj* **inhib'itive**. — *n* **inhib'itor** something which inhibits; a substance that interferes with a chemical or biological process. — *adj* **inhib'itory** prohibitory. [L. *inhibēre*, *-hibitum* — *in*, in, *habēre*, to have.]

inhospitable *in-hos'pit-ə-bl* or *-pit'*, *adj* not kind or welcoming to strangers; (of a place) barren, not offering shelter, food, etc. — *n* **inhospitableness** or **inhospital'ity**. — *adv* **inhospitably**. [**in-** (2).]

inhuman *in-hū'mən*, *adj* barbarous; cruel; without human feeling. — *n* **inhumanity** (*in-hū-man'i-ti*). — *adv* **inhū'manly**. [**in-** (2).]

inhumane *in-hū-mān'*, *adj* not humane, cruel. — *adv* **inhūmane'ly**. [**in-** (2).]

inimical *in-im'i-kl*, *adj* unfriendly; hostile; unfavourable; opposed. — *adv* **inim'ically**. — *n* **inim'icalness** or **inimical'ity**. [L. *inimīcālis* — *inimīcus*, enemy — *in-*, not, *amīcus*, friend.]

inimitable *in-im'it-ə-bl*, *adj* that cannot be imitated; exceptionally good or remarkable. — *n* **inimitabil'ity** or **inim'itableness**. — *adv* **inim'itably**. [**in-** (2).]

iniquity *in-ik'wi-ti*, *n* injustice; wickedness; a crime. — *adj* **iniq'uitous** unjust; scandalously unreasonable; wicked. — *adv* **iniq'uitously**. [Fr. *iniquité* — L. *inīquitās*, *-ātis* — *in-*, not, *aequus*, equal.]

init. *abbrev* for *initio* (L.), in or at the beginning.

initial *in-ish'l*, *adj* beginning; of, at, or serving as the beginning; original. — *n* the letter beginning a word, esp. a name. — *vt* to put the initials of one's name to, esp. when acknowledging or agreeing to something: — *pr p* **ini'tialling**; *pa t* and *pa p* **ini'tialled**. — *vt* **ini'tialise** or **-ize** (*comput*) to assign initial values to variables, e.g. in a computer program; to return a device (e.g. a computer or a printer) to its initial state. — *adv* **ini'tially**. — **Initial Teaching Alphabet** a 44-character alphabet in which each character corresponds to a single sound of English, sometimes used for the teaching of reading. [L. *initiālis* — *initium*, a beginning, *inīre*, *initum* — *in*, into, *īre*, *itum*, to go.]

initiate *in-i'shi-āt*, *vt* to begin, start; to introduce (to) (e.g. knowledge); to admit (into) esp. with rites (e.g. to a secret society, a mystery). — *vi* to perform the first act or rite. — *n* (*-it*) someone who is initiated. — *adj* initiated; belonging to someone newly initiated. — *n* **initiā'tion**. — *adj* **ini'tiative** (*-shə-tiv*) serving to initiate; introductory. — *n* the lead, first step, often considered as determining the conditions for oneself or others; the right or power of beginning; energy and resourcefulness enabling one to act without prompting from others; the right to originate legislation. — *n* **ini'tiātor** a person who or something which initiates. — *adj* **ini'tiatory** (*-shə-tə-ri*) tending or serving to initiate; introductory. — *n* introductory rite. [L. *initiāre*, to originate or initiate — *initium*, a beginning; see ety. for **initial**.]

inject *in-jekt'*, *vt* to force in; to inspire or instil; to fill by injection. — *adj* **injec'table** able to be injected. — Also *n*. — *n* **injec'tion** (*-shən*) the act of injecting or forcing in, esp. a liquid; a liquid injected into the body with a syringe or similar instrument; the spraying of oil-fuel into the cylinder of a compression-ignition engine by an injection pump (*autos*); an amount of money added to an economy in order to stimulate production, expansion, etc.; a mapping function in which each element in a set corresponds to only one element in another set (*math*). — *n* **injec'tor** a person who injects; something used for injecting, especially an apparatus for forcing water into a boiler. — **injection moulding** moulding of thermoplastics by squirting the material from a heated cylinder into a water-chilled mould. [L. *injicĕre*, *injectum* — *in*, into, *jacĕre*, to throw.]

injudicious *in-jōō-di'shəs*, *adj* not judicious; ill-judged. — *adv* **injudi'cial** not according to legal forms. — *adv* **injudi'cially**. — *n* **injudi'ciously**. — *n* **injudi'ciousness**. [**in-** (2).]

Injun *in'jən*, (*US colloq*) *n* an American Indian. — Also *adj*. — **honest Injun** see under **honest**.

injunction *in-jungk'shən, n* the act of enjoining or commanding; an order; a precept; an exhortation; an inhibitory writ by which a superior court stops or prevents some inequitable or illegal act being done (*law*). [L.L. *injunctiō, -ōnis — in*, in, *jungĕre, junctum*, to join.]

injure *in'jər, vt* to wrong; to harm; to damage; to hurt. — *n* **in'jurer.** — *adj* **injurious** (*in-jōō'ri-əs*) tending to injure; wrongful; hurtful; damaging to reputation. — *adv* **inju'riously.** — *n* **inju'riousness.** — *n* **injury** (*in'jə-ri*) that which injures; wrong; physical damage, a wound; hurt; impairment; annoyance. — **injury benefit** see **Industrial Injuries Disablement Benefit; injury time** (in ball games) extra time allowed for play to compensate for time lost as a result of injury stoppages during the game. [L. *injūria*, injury — *in-*, not, *jūs, jūris*, law.]

injustice *in-jus'tis, n* the violation or withholding of another's rights or dues; the fact or an act of being unjust; wrong; iniquity. [**in-** (2).]

ink *ingk, n* a black or coloured liquid used in writing, printing, etc.; a dark liquid ejected by cuttlefishes, etc. — *vt* to daub, cover, blacken or colour with ink. — *n* **ink'er** someone who inks; a pad or roller for inking type, etc. — *n* **ink'iness.** — *adj* **ink'y** consisting of or resembling ink; very black; blackened with ink. — **ink'berry** (the fruit of) any of various N. American shrubs, esp. *Ilex glabra* of the holly family and *Phytolacca americana*, pokeweed; **ink'-cap** any mushroom of the genus *Coprinus*; **ink'spot** a small ink stain. — *adj* **ink'-stained.** — **ink'stand** a stand or tray for bottles of ink and (usually) pens; **ink'stone** a kind of stone containing sulphate of iron, used in making ink; **ink'well** a container for ink in or on a desk, etc. — **China ink, Chinese ink** or **Indian ink,** in U.S. **India ink** (sometimes without *caps*) a mixture of lamp-black and size or glue, usu. kept in solid form and used in water; a liquid suspension of the solid ink; **ink-blot test** see **Rorschach test; ink in** to fill in in ink; **invisible ink** a kind of ink that remains invisible on the paper until it is heated. [O.Fr. *enque* — L.L. encaustum, the purple-red ink used by the later Roman emperors — Gr. *enkauston — enkaiein*, to burn in; see **encaustic.**]

Inkatha *in-kä'tə, n* a Zulu cultural and liberation movement.

inkling *ingk'ling, n* a slight hint; intimation; a dim notion or suspicion. [M.E. *inclen*, to hint at.]

INLA *abbrev* for Irish National Liberation Army.

inlaid. See **inlay.**

inland *in'land* or *in'lənd, n* the interior part of a country. — *adj* remote from the sea; carried on, or produced, within a country; confined to a country. — *adv* (also *in-land'*) landward; away from the sea; in an inland place. — **inland navigation** passage of boats or vessels on rivers, lakes or canals within a country; **inland revenue** internal revenue, derived from direct taxes such as income tax and stamp duty; (with *caps*) the government department responsible for collecting such taxes. [O.E. *inland*, a domain — *in* and *land*.]

in-law *in'-lö*, (*colloq*) *n* a relative by marriage, e.g. mother-in-law, brother-in-law: — *pl* **in'-laws.**

inlay *in'lā* or *in-lā', vt* to insert, embed; to ornament by laying in or inserting pieces of metal, ivory, etc.; on television, to mix images electronically, using masks: — *pr p* **inlaying;** *pa t* and *pa p* **inlaid.** — *n* (*in'*) inlaying; inlaid work; material inlaid. — *adj* **inlaid'** (or *in'lād*) inserted by inlaying; decorated with inlay; consisting of inlay; having a pattern set into the surface. — *n* **inlayer.** — *n* **inlaying.** [**in-** (1).]

inlet *in'let* or *-lət, n* a small bay or opening in the land; a piece let in or inserted; an entrance; a passage by which anything is let in; a place of entry. [**in** and **let**[1].]

inlier *in'lī-ər*, (*geol*) *n* an outcrop of older rock surrounded by younger. [**in** and **lie**[2].]

in loc. *in lok, abbrev* for *in loco* (L.), in its place.

in loc. cit. *in lok sit, abbrev* for *in loco citato* (L.), in the place cited.

in loco parentis *in lō'kō pə-ren'tis*, (L.) in the place of a parent.

inly *in'li, adv* inwardly; in the heart; thoroughly, entirely. [**in.**]

INMARSAT *in'mär-sat, abbrev* for International Maritime Satellite.

inmate *in'māt, n* one of the people who live in a house; a person confined in an institution esp. a prison. [**in** or **inn** and **mate**[1].]

in memoriam. See under **memory.**

inmost. See **innermost** under **inner.**

inn *in, n* a small hotel open to the public for food, drink and accommodation; (*loosely*) a public house. — *n* **inn'keeper** a person in charge of an inn. — **Inns of Court** the buildings of four voluntary societies that have the exclusive right of calling to the English bar (Inner Temple, Middle Temple, Lincoln's Inn and Gray's Inn); the societies themselves. [O.E. *inn*, an inn, house — *in, inn*, within (adv.), from the prep. *in*, in.]

innards *in'ərdz*, (*colloq*) *npl* entrails; internal parts of a mechanism; interior. [**inwards.**]

innate *in-āt'* or *in'āt, adj* inborn; instinctive; inherent. — *adv* **innate'ly** (or *in'*). — *n* **innate'ness** (or *in'*). [L. *innātus — in-*, in, *nāscī, nātus*, to be born.]

inner *in'ər, adj* (*compar* of **in**) farther in; interior. — *n* (a hit on) that part of a target next to the bull's-eye. — *adj* **inn'ermost** or **in'most** (*superl* of **in**) farthest in; most remote from the outside. — **inner city** the central part of a city, esp. with regard to its special social problems, e.g. poor housing, poverty; **inner man** mind or soul; stomach (*facetious*); **inner space** the undersea region regarded as an environment; **inner tube** the rubber tube inside a tyre, which is inflated. [O.E. *in*, comp. *innera*, superl. *innemest*.]

innervate *in'ər-vāt* or *in-ûr'vāt, vt* to supply with nerves or a nervous stimulus. — Also **innerve'.** — *n* **innervā'tion.** [**in-** (1).]

inning *in'ing, n* (in *pl*, in U.S. sometimes in *sing*) a team's turn of batting in cricket, etc., or a turn of batting for both teams in baseball, etc.; the time during which a person, group or team is in possession of anything, a spell or turn. — **a good innings** (*colloq*) a long life. [**in** or **inn.**]

innocent *in'ə-sənt, adj* not hurtful; inoffensive; blameless, pure; harmless; guileless; simple-minded; ignorant of evil; not legally guilty; devoid (with *of*); not malignant or cancerous (*med*). — *n* someone having no fault; someone having no knowledge of evil; a child; a foolish, simple-minded person; an idiot. — *n* **inn'ocence** harmlessness; blamelessness; guilelessness; simplicity; freedom from legal guilt. — *adv* **inn'ocently.** — **Innocents' Day** see **Childermas.** [O.Fr., — L. *innocēns, -entis — in-*, not, *nocēre*, to hurt.]

innocuous *in-ok'ū-əs, adj* harmless. — *adv* **innoc'uously.** — *n* **innocū'ity** or **innoc'uousness.** [L. *innocuus — in-*, not, *nocuus*, hurtful — *nocēre*, to hurt.]

innominate *i-nom'i-nāt* or *-nit, adj* having no name. — **innominate bone** (*anat*) the hip-bone formed by fusion in the adult of the ilium, ischium and pubis. [L. *in-*, not, *nōmināre, -ātum*, to name.]

innovate *in'ə-vāt, vt* to introduce as something new. — *vi* to introduce novelties; to make changes. — *n* **innovā'tion** the act of innovating; a thing introduced as a novelty. — *n* **innovā'tionist.** — *adj* **inn'ovative.** — *n* **inn'ovātor.** — *adj* **inn'ovatory.** [L. *innovāre, -ātum — in*, in, *novus*, new.]

innoxious *in-ok'shəs, adj* not noxious. — *adv* **innox'iously.** — *n* **innox'iousness.** [**in-** (2).]

innuendo *in-ū-en'dō, n* insinuation; an indirect reference or intimation: — *pl* **innuen'dos.** [L. *innuendō*, by nodding at (i.e. indicating).]

Innuit or **Inuit** *in'ū-it* or *in'ōō-it, n* the Eskimo people, esp. those of Greenland, Canada and Northern Alaska; a member of this people; their language. [Eskimo, people, *pl.* of *inuk*, a person.]

innumerable *i-nū'mə-rə-bl, adj* that cannot be numbered; countless. — *n* **innūmerabil'ity.** — *n* **innū'merableness.** — *adv* **innū'merably.** [in- (2).]

innumerate *i-nū'mə-rit, adj* having little or no knowledge or understanding of mathematics or science. — Also *n.* — *n* **innu'meracy.** [Coined 1959 by Sir Geoffrey Crowther (on analogy of *illiterate*) — L. *numerus*, number.]

inobservant *in-əb-zûr'vənt, adj* unobservant; heedless. — *adj* **inobser'vable** incapable of being observed. — *n* **inobser'vance** lack of observance. — *n* **inobservā'tion** (*-ob-*). [in- (2).]

inoculate *i-nok'ū-lāt, vt* to introduce (e.g. bacteria, a virus) into an organism; to give a mild form of (a disease) in this way; to make an inoculation in, esp. for the purpose of safeguarding against subsequent infection; to insert as a bud or graft; to graft; to imbue. — *vi* to practise inoculation. — *n* **inoculā'tion** the act or practice of inoculating; the communication of disease by the introduction of a germ or virus, esp. that of a mild form of the disease to produce immunity; the analogous introduction of anything, e.g. nitrogen-fixing bacteria into soil, seed, a crystal into a supersaturated solution to start crystallisation; the insertion of the buds of one plant into another. — *adj* **inoc'ulative** (*-ə-tiv* or *-ā-tiv*). — *n* **inoc'ulātor.** — *adj* **inoc'ulatory** (*-ə-tə-ri*). — *n* **inoc'ulum** material used for inoculating. [L. *inoculāre, -ātum* — *in*, into, *oculus*, an eye, a bud.]

inodorous *in-ō'də-rəs, adj* having no smell. — *adv* **ino'dorously.** — *n* **ino'dorousness.** [in- (2).]

inoffensive *in-ə-fen'siv, adj* giving no offence; harmless. — *adv* **inoffen'sively.** — *n* **inoffen'siveness.** [in- (2).]

inofficious *in-ə-fish'əs, adj* regardless of duty (*law*); inoperative. [in- (2).]

inoperable *in-op'ə-rə-bl, adj* that cannot be operated on successfully, or without undue risk (*med*); not workable. — *n* **inoperabil'ity** or **inop'erableness.** — *adv* **inop'erably.** — *adj* **inop'erative** not in action; producing no effect. — *n* **inop'erativeness.** [in- (2).]

inopportune *in-op'ər-tūn* or *-tūn', adj* badly timed, inconvenient. — *adv* **inopp'ortūnely** (or *-tūn'*). — *n* **inopp'ortuneness** (or *-tūn'*) or **inopportūn'ity.** [in- (2).]

inordinate *in-ör'di-nit, adj* unrestrained; excessive; immoderate. — *n* **inor'dinacy** or **inor'dinateness.** — *adv* **inor'dinately.** — *n* **inordinā'tion** deviation from rule; irregularity. [L. *inordinātus* — *in-*, not, *ordināre, -ātum*, to arrange, regulate.]

inorganic *in-ör-gan'ik, adj* not organic; not belonging to an organism; of accidental origin, not normally developed. — *adv* **inorgan'ically.** — *adj* **inor'ganised** or **-ized** unorganised. — **inorganic chemistry** the chemistry of all substances but carbon compounds, generally admitting a few of these also (as oxides of carbon, carbonates). [in- (2).]

inosculate *in-os'kū-lāt*, (*physiol*) *vt* and *vi* to unite by mouths or ducts, as two vessels in a body; to anastomose. — *n* **inosculā'tion.** [L. *in*, in, *osculārī, -ātus*, to kiss.]

inositol *in-os'i-tol, n* a member of the vitamin B complex, occurring in practically all plant and animal tissues. [Gr. *īs, īnos*, a sinew, muscle, and suffixes *-ite* and *-ol.*]

inotropic *in-ə-trop'ik*, (*med*) *adj* affecting or controlling muscular contraction, esp. in the heart. [Gr. *īs, īnos*, tendon, *tropos*, a turn.]

in pace *in pā'sē, pä'chā* or *pä-ke*, (L.) in peace.

inpayment *in'pā-mənt, n* the payment of money into a bank account; the amount paid in. [**in** and **payment.**]

in personam *in pər-sō'nam*, (*legal*) against a person — used of a proceeding, etc., against a specific person (see also **in rem**).

input *in'pŏŏt, n* amount, material or energy that is put in; power, or energy, or coded information, stored or for storage; information available in a computer for dealing with a problem; process of feeding in data. — *adj* relating to computer input. — *vt* to feed (data, etc.) into e.g. a computer: — *pr p* **in'putting;** *pa t* and *pa p* **in'put.** — *n* **in'putter.** — **input-output analysis** (*econ*) a method of studying an economy as a whole by analysing the relationship between the input and output of each industry. [**in** and **put**[1].]

inquest *in'kwest, n* a judicial inquiry before a jury into any matter, esp. any case of violent or sudden death; the body of men appointed to hold such an inquiry; an inquiry or investigation. [O.Fr. *enqueste* — L. *inquīsīta* (*rēs*) — *inquīrĕre*, to inquire.]

inquietude *in-kwī'i-tūd, n* uneasiness; disturbance. — *adj* **inquī'et** unquiet. — *adv* **inquī'etly.** [in- (2).]

inquire or **enquire** *in-kwīr', vi* to ask a question; to make an investigation. — *vt* to ask. — *n* **inquir'er** or **enquir'er.** — *adj* **inquir'ing** tending to inquire; eager to acquire information; (of e.g. a look) expressing inquiry. — *adv* **inquir'ingly.** — *n* **inquir'y** or **enquir'y** (or *ing'kwi-ri*, esp. in U.S.) the act of inquiring; a search for knowledge; (an) investigation; a question. [O.Fr. *enquerre* — L. *inquīrĕre* — *in*, in, *quaerĕre, quaesītum*, to seek.]

inquisition *in-kwi-zish'ən, n* a searching examination; an investigation; a judicial inquiry; (with *cap*) a tribunal in the R.C. church for discovery, repression, and punishment of heresy, unbelief, etc., 'the Holy Office', now the 'Congregation for the Doctrine of the Faith'. — *adj* **inquisi'tional** searching, often unduly vexatiously, in inquiring; relating to inquisition or the Inquisition. — *adj* **inquisitive** (*-kwiz'i-tiv*) eager to know; apt to ask questions, esp. about other people's affairs; curious. — *adv* **inquis'itively.** — *n* **inquis'itiveness.** — *n* **inquis'itor** a person who inquires, esp. with undue pertinacity or searchingness; an official inquirer; a member of the Inquisition tribunal. — *adj* **inquisito'rial** pertaining to an inquisitor or inquisition; unduly pertinacious in interrogation; used of criminal proceedings in which the prosecutor is also judge, or in which the trial is held in secret (*law*). — *adv* **inquisito'rially.** — *n* **inquisito'rialness.** — **Grand Inquisitor** the chief in a court of Inquisition. [L. *inquīsītiō, -ōnis*; see ety. for **inquire.**]

inquorate *in-kwör'it, adj* not making up a quorum. [in- (2) and **quorum.**]

in re *in rē* or *rā*, (L.) in the matter (of).

in rem *in rem*, (L.) against a thing, property — used of a proceeding, etc., against property, as the arrest of a ship.

INRI *abbrev* for *Jesus Nazarenus Rex Judaeorum* (L.), Jesus of Nazareth King of the Jews.

inro *in'rō, n* a small Japanese container for pills and medicines, once part of traditional Japanese dress: — *pl* **in'rō.** [Jap., seal-box.]

inroad *in'rōd, n* an incursion into an enemy's country; a raid; encroachment. — **make inroads into** to make progress with; to use up large quantities of. [**in** and **road** in sense of riding; cf. **raid.**]

inrush *in'rush, n* an inward rush. — *n* and *adj* **in'rushing.** [**in** and **rush**[1].]

insalubrious *in-sə-lōō'bri-əs* or *-lū', adj* unhealthy. — *adv* **insalu'briously.** — *n* **insalu'brity.** [in- (2).]

insane *in-sān', adj* not sane or of sound mind; crazy; mad; utterly unwise; senseless. — *adv* **insane'ly.** — *n* **insane'ness** insanity; madness. — *n* **insanity** (*in-san'i-ti*) lack of sanity; mental disorder causing a person to act against the social or legal demands of society; madness. [L. *īnsānus*.]

insanitary *in-san'i-tə-ri, adj* not sanitary; dirty and unhealthy. — *n* **insan'itariness**. — *n* **insanitā'tion**. [**in-** (2).]

insatiable *in-sā'shyə-bl* or *-shə-bl, adj* not capable of being satiated or satisfied. — *n* **insātiabil'ity** or **insā'tiableness**. — *adv* **insā'tiably**. — *adj* **insā'tiate** not sated; insatiable. — *adv* **insā'tiately**. — *n* **insā'tiateness**. — *n* **insatiety** (*in-sə-tī'i-ti*) the state of not being or of being incapable of being sated. [**in-** (2).]

inscribe *in-skrīb', vt* to engrave or mark in some other way; to engrave or mark on; to enter in a book or roll; to dedicate; to describe within another figure so as either to touch all sides or faces of the bounding figure or to have all angular points on it (*geom*). — *adj* **inscrī'bable**. — *n* **inscrī'ber**. — *n* **inscription** (*in-skrip'shən*) the act of inscribing; that which is inscribed; a dedication; a record inscribed on stone, metal, clay, etc. — *adj* **inscrip'tional** or **inscrip'tive**. — *adv* **inscrip'tively**. [L. *īnscrībĕre, īnscrīptum* — *in*, upon, *scrībĕre*, to write.]

inscrutable *in-skrōō'tə-bl, adj* that cannot be scrutinised or searched into and understood; mysterious, enigmatic, inexplicable. — *n* **inscrutabil'ity** or **inscrut'ableness**. — *adv* **inscrut'ably**. [L. *īnscrūtābilis* — *in-*, not, *scrūtārī*, to search into.]

insect *in'sekt, n* a word loosely used for a small invertebrate creature, esp. one with a body apparently cut or divided into sections; a member of the Insecta (*zool*). — *npl* **Insec'ta** a division of arthropods having a distinct head, thorax and abdomen, with three pairs of legs attached to the thorax, usually winged in adult life, and commonly having a metamorphosis in the life-history. — *n* **insec'ticide** (*-ti-sīd*) an insect-killing substance. — *n* **insec'tifuge** a substance that drives away insects. — *npl* **Insectiv'ora** an order of mammals, mostly terrestrial, insect-eating, nocturnal in habit, and small in size — shrews, moles, hedgehogs, etc. — *n* **insec'tivore** a member of the Insectivora. — *adj* **insectiv'orous** living on insects. — *n* **insectol'ogist**. — *n* **insectol'ogy** the study of insects. — **in'sect-powder** powder for stupefying and killing insects; an insecticide or insectifuge. [L. *īnsectum*, past p. of *īnsecāre* — *in*, into, *secāre*, to cut.]

insecure *in-si-kūr', adj* apprehensive of danger or loss; anxious because not well-adjusted to life; exposed to danger or loss; unsafe; uncertain; not fixed or firm. — *adv* **insecure'ly**. — *n* **insecur'ity**. [**in-** (2).]

inselberg *in'zəl-bûrg* or *in'səl-berg*, (*geol*) *n* a steep-sided hill arising from a plain, often found in the semi-arid regions of tropical countries: — *pl* **in'selberge** (*-gə*). [Ger., island-hill.]

inseminate *in-sem'in-āt, vt* to sow; to implant; to introduce (ideas, philosophies, attitudes, etc.) into people's minds; to impregnate (a female) esp. artificially. — *n* **inseminā'tion**. — *n* **insem'inator**. [L. *īnsēmināre* — *in*, in, *sēmen, -inis*, seed.]

insensate *in-sen'sāt* or *-sit, adj* without sensation, inanimate; having little or no sensibility or moral feeling; having little or no good sense. — *adv* **insen'sately**. — *n* **insen'sateness**. [L. *īnsēnsātus* — *in-*, not, *sēnsātus*, intelligent — *sēnsus*, feeling.]

insensible *in-sen'si-bl, adj* not having feeling; not capable of emotion; callous; dull; unconscious; not capable of being sensed. — *n* **insensibil'ity**. — *adv* **insen'sibly**. [**in-** (2).]

insensitive *in-sen'si-tiv, adj* not sensitive; unfeeling, inconsiderate, crass. — *adv* **insen'sitively**. — *n* **insen'sitiveness** or **insensitiv'ity**. [**in-** (2).]

insentient *in-sen'shyənt* or *-shənt, adj* not having perception. — *n* **insen'tience**. [**in-** (2).]

inseparable *in-sep'ə-rə-bl, adj* incapable of being separated; (of e.g. friends or siblings) unwilling to be separated; (of e.g. a prefix) not existing as a separate word (*gram*). — *n* **insep'arableness** or **inseparabil'ity**. — *adv* **insep'arably**. [**in-** (2).]

insert *in-sûrt', vt* to put in; to introduce (into). — *n* **in'sert** something inserted; a paper placed within the folds of a periodical or leaves of a book. — *n* **insert'er**. — *n* **insertion** (*in-sûr'shən*) the act of inserting; something inserted; a piece of embroidery inserted in a dress, etc. — *adj* **inser'tional**. [L. *īnserĕre, īnsertum* — *in*, in, *serĕre*, to join.]

in-service. See under **in**.

insessorial *in-ses-ö'ri-əl, adj* (of e.g. birds' claws) adapted for perching. [L. *īnsessor*, percher.]

inset *in'set, n* something set in, an insertion or insert, a leaf or leaves inserted between the folds of other leaves; a small map or figure inserted in a spare corner of another; a piece let in; the setting in of a current. — *vt* **inset'** to set in, to infix or implant: — *pa t* and *pa p* **inset'**. [**in** and **set**.]

inshore *in-shör', adv* near or toward the shore. — *adj* (*in'shör*) near the shore.

inside *in-sīd'* or *in'sīd, n* the side, space or part within; (often in *pl*) the entrails; inner nature; that which is not visible at first sight. — *adj* being within; interior; indoor; from within; from a secret or confidential source; (of a criminal 'job') carried out by, or with the help of, someone trusted and/or employed by the victim (*colloq*). — *adv* in, to or near the interior; indoors; on the inner side; in or into prison (*colloq*). — *prep* within; into; on the inner side of. — *n* **insi'der** a person who is inside; someone within a certain organisation, etc.; someone possessing some particular advantage. — **inside left** and **inside right** in some games, a forward between the centre and outside; **insider dealing** or **trading** using information not publicly available to deal on the Stock Exchange, a criminal offence. — **inside of** (esp. *US*) in less than, within; **inside out** with the inner side turned outwards; **know (something) inside out** (*colloq*) to know (something) thoroughly. [**in** and **side**.]

insidious *in-sid'i-əs, adj* deceptively attractive; advancing or encroaching imperceptibly; cunning and treacherous. — *adv* **insid'iously**. — *n* **insid'iousness**. [L. *īnsidiōsus* — *īnsidiae*, an ambush.]

insight *in'sīt, n* power of discerning and understanding things; imaginative penetration; practical knowledge; a view into anything; awareness, often of one's own mental condition (*psychol*); the apprehension of the principle of a task, puzzle, etc. (*psychol*). — *adj* **insight'ful**. [**in** and **sight**.]

insignia *in-sig'ni-ə, npl* (in U.S. treated as *sing*) signs or badges of office, honour, membership, occupation, etc.; marks by which anything is known. [L., neut. pl. of *īnsignis* — *in*, in, *signum*, a mark.]

insignificant *in-sig-nif'i-kənt, adj* having no meaning; unimportant; small in size, amount, etc.; petty. — *n* **insignif'icance** or **insignif'icancy**. — *adv* **insignif'icantly**. [**in-** (2).]

insincere *in-sin-sēr', adj* not sincere, hypocritical. — *adv* **insincere'ly**. — *n* **insincerity** (*-ser'i-ti*). [**in-** (2).]

insinuate *in-sin'ū-āt, vt* to hint or indirectly suggest (usu. something unpleasant); to introduce or insert gently or artfully (with *into*); (with *into*) to work (esp. oneself) into (someone's favour). — *adj* **insin'uating**. — *adv* **insin'uatingly**. — *n* **insinuā'tion**. — *adj* **insin'uative** insinuating or stealing on the confidence; using insinuation. — *n* **insin'uator**. — *adj* **insin'uatory** (*-ə-tə-ri*). [L. *īnsinuāre, -ātum* — *in*, in, *sinus*, a curve.]

insipid *in-sip'id, adj* without satisfying or definite flavour, tasteless; lacking spirit or interest; dull. — *adv* **insip'idly**. — *n* **insip'idness** or **insipid'ity**. [L.L. *īnsipidus* — L. *in-*, not, *sapidus*, well-tasted — *sapĕre*, to taste.]

insist *in-sist'*, *vi* (often with *on*) to maintain very firmly; to persist in demanding; to take no refusal. — *vt* to maintain persistently. — *n* **insist'ence** or **insist'ency**. — *adj* **insist'ent** urgent; compelling attention; insisting. — *adv* **insist'ently**. [L. *īnsistĕre* — *in*, upon, *sistĕre*, to stand.]

in situ *in sī'tū* or *si'tōō*, (L.) in the original situation.

insobriety *in-sō-brī'ə-ti*, *n* lack of sobriety, drunkenness. [**in-** (2).]

insofar. See under **in**.

insolation *in-sə-lā'shən*, *n* solar radiation falling upon a given surface. [L. *insolatus*, past p. of *insolare*, to expose to the sunlight.]

insole *in'sōl*, *n* the inner sole of a boot or shoe; a sole of some material placed inside a shoe for warmth, dryness or comfort. [**in** and **sole**[1].]

insolent *in'sə-lənt*, *adj* disrespectful and rude; impudent. — *n* **in'solence**. — *adv* **in'solently**. [L. *īnsolēns*, *-entis* — *in-*, not, *solēns*, past p. of *solēre*, to be wont.]

insoluble *in-sol'ū-bl*, *adj* not capable of being dissolved; not capable of being solved or explained. — *n* **insolubil'ity** or **insol'ubleness**. — *adv* **insol'ubly**. [**in-** (2).]

insolvable *in-sol'və-bl*, *adj* not solvable. — *n* **insolvabil'ity**. — *adv* **insol'vably**. [**in-** (2).]

insolvent *in-sol'vənt*, *adj* not able to pay one's debts, bankrupt; concerning insolvent persons. — *n* a person unable to pay their debts. — *n* **insolv'ency** bankruptcy. [**in-** (2).]

insomnia *in-som'ni-ə*, *n* sleeplessness; prolonged inability to sleep. — *n* **insom'niac** a person who suffers from insomnia. — *adj* suffering from, causing, or caused by, insomnia. [L. *īnsomnis*, sleepless.]

insomuch *in-sō-much'*, *adv* to such a degree (with *as* or *that*); inasmuch (with *as*).

insouciant *in-sōō'si-ənt* or *ẽ-sōō-sē-ã*, *adj* indifferent, unconcerned; heedless. — *n* **insouciance** (*in-sōō'si-əns* or *ẽ-sōō-sē-ãs*). — *adv* **insouciantly** (*in-sōō'si-ənt-li* or *ẽ-sōō-sē-ãt'li*). [Fr.]

inspect *in-spekt'*, *vt* to look into; to examine; to look at closely, officially or ceremonially. — *n* **inspec'tion** the act of inspecting or looking into; careful or official examination. — *adj* **inspec'tive**. — *n* **inspec'tor**, *fem* **inspec'tress**, a person who inspects; an examining officer; a police officer ranking below a superintendent; an officer in any of several humane societies. — *n* **inspec'torate** a district under charge of an inspector; the office of inspector; a body of inspectors. — *adj* **inspectō'rial**. — *n* **inspec'torship** the office of inspector. — **inspector general** the head of an inspectorate; a military officer who conducts investigations. [L. *īnspectāre*, frequentative of *īnspicĕre*, *īnspectum* — *in*, into, *specĕre*, to look.]

inspire *in-spīr'*, *vt* to breathe in or blow in (air, etc.); to draw or inhale into the lungs; to infuse into (the mind), esp. with an encouraging or exalting influence; (of divine influence, etc.) to instruct or guide; to instruct or affect with a particular emotion; to bring about; to animate. — *vi* to draw in the breath. — *n* **inspirā'tion** (*in-spə-*, *-spi-* or *-spī-*) the act of inspiring or breathing in; a breath; instruction, dictation or stimulation by a divinity, a genius, an idea or a passion; an inspired condition; an object or person that inspires; an inspired thought or idea. — *adj* **inspirā'tional**. — *adv* **inspirā'tionally**. — *n* **inspirator** (*in'spi-rā-tər*) an inspirer; an apparatus for injecting or drawing in vapour, liquid, etc. — *adj* **inspiratory** (*in-spir'ə-tər-i* or *in-spīr'*) belonging to or aiding inspiration or inhalation. — *adj* **inspīred'** actuated or directed by divine influence; influenced by elevated feeling; prompted by superior, but not openly declared, knowledge or authority; actually authoritative; (of a guess, etc.) unexpectedly accurate. — *n* **inspīr'er**. — *adv* **inspīr'ingly**. [L. *īnspīrāre* — *in*, in, into, *spīrāre*, to breathe.]

inspirit *in-spir'it*, *vt* to infuse spirit into, encourage. — *adj* **inspir'iting**. — *adv* **inspir'itingly**. [**in-** (1).]

inspissate *in-spis'āt*, *vt* to thicken, condense. [L. *in*, in, *spissāre* — *spissus*, thick.]

Inst. *abbrev* for: Institute; Institution.

inst. *abbrev* for instant — the present month (used in formal correspondence).

instability *in-stə-bil'i-ti*, *n* lack of stability, physical or mental. — *adj* **instā'ble** unstable. [**in-** (2).]

install (also **instal**) *in-stöl'*, *vt* to set up and put in use; to place in an office or order; to place in a certain position; to invest with any charge or office with the customary ceremonies: — *pr p* **install'ing**; *pa t* and *pa p* **installed'**. — *n* **installā'tion** the act of installing; a placing in position for use; apparatus placed in position for use; the complete apparatus for electric lighting, or the like; a military base, etc. [L.L. *īnstallāre* — *in*, in, *stallum*, a stall.]

instalment or in U.S. **installment** *in-stöl'mənt*, *n* one of a series of partial payments; a portion (e.g. of a serial story) supplied or completed at one time. [A.Fr. *estaler*, to fix, set; prob. influenced by **install**.]

instance *in'stəns*, *n* an example; an occurrence; an occasion; solicitation, urging; process, suit (*law*). — *vt* to mention as an example. — *n* **in'stancy** insistency; urgency; imminence. — *adj* **in'stant** immediate; without delay; present, current; of the current month (used in formal correspondence); (esp. of food, drink) pre-prepared so that little has to be done to it before use. — *n* the present moment of time; a very brief period of time, moment; any moment or point of time; the present month. — *n* **instantaneity** (*in-stan-tə-nē'i-ti*). — *adj* **instantaneous** (*in-stən-tā'ni-əs*) done in an instant; momentary; occurring or acting at once or very quickly; for the instant; at a particular instant. — *adv* **instantā'neously**. — *n* **instantā'neousness**. — *vt* **instan'tiate** (*-shi-āt*) to be or provide an example of. — *n* **instantiā'tion**. — *adv* **in'stantly** at once. — **at the instance of** at the urging or request of; **court of first instance** a lower court in which a legal case is first heard, from which it may be referred to a higher court; **for instance** as an example; **in the first instance** firstly, originally; **on the instant** immediately; **this instant** immediately. [L. *īnstāns*, *īnstantis*, pres. p. of *īnstāre*, to be near, press upon, urge.]

instar *in'stär*, *n* the form of an insect between moult and moult. [L. *īnstar*, image.]

instate *in-stāt'*, *vt* to put in possession; to install. — *n* **instate'ment**. [**in-** (1) and **state**.]

in statu quo *in stā'tū* (or *stat'ōō*) *kwō*, (L.) in the former state.

instead *in-sted'*, *adv* in the stead, place, or room (of); as an alternative or substitute. [**in** and **stead**.]

instep *in'step*, *n* the prominent arched part of the human foot near its junction with the leg; the corresponding part of a shoe, stocking, etc.; (in horses) the hindleg from the ham to the pastern joint.

instigate *in'sti-gāt*, *vt* to urge on, incite; to initiate, bring about. — *n* **instigā'tion** the act of inciting; impulse, esp. to evil. — *adj* **in'stigātive**. — *n* **in'stigātor** an inciter, generally in a bad sense. [L. *īnstīgāre*, *-ātum*.]

instil *in-stil'*, *vt* to drop in; to infuse slowly into the mind: — *pr p* **instill'ing**; *pa t* and *pa p* **instilled'**. — Also **instill'**. — *n* **instillā'tion** or **instil'ment** the act of instilling or pouring in by drops; that which is instilled or infused. [L. *īnstillāre* — *in*, in, *stillāre*, to drop.]

instinct *in'stingkt*, *n* impulse; an involuntary prompting to action; intuition; the natural impulse by which animals are guided apparently independently of reason or experience. — *adj* **instinc'tive** prompted by instinct; involuntary; acting according to or determined by natural impulse. — *adv* **instinc'-**

tively. — *adj* **instinc'tual** concerning instincts. [L. *īnstinctus* — *īnstinguĕre*, instigate.]

institute *in'sti-tūt*, *vt* to set up, establish; to originate, inaugurate. — *n* anything instituted or formally established; an institution; a literary and philosophical society or organisation for education, research, etc.; the building in which such an organisation is housed; a foundation for further education, esp. in technical subjects; established law; precept or principle; (in *pl*) a book of precepts, principles, or rules. — *n* **institution** (*-tū'shən*) the act of instituting or establishing; that which is instituted or established; foundation; established order; enactment; a society or organisation established for some object, esp. cultural, charitable or beneficent, or the building housing it; a custom or usage, esp. one familiar or characteristic; the act by which a bishop commits a cure of souls to a priest. — *adj* **institū'tional** concerning an institution, institutions or institutes; being, or of the nature of, an institution; depending on or originating in institution; associated with, or typical of, institutions, routine, uninspiring. — *n* **institutionalisa'tion** or **-z-**. — *vt* **institu'tionalise** or **-ize** to make an institution of; to confine to an institution; (usu. in *passive*) as a result of such confinement, to cause to become apathetic and dependent on routine. — *n* **institū'tionalism** the system or characteristics of institutions or institution life; belief in the nature of institutions. — *n* **institu'tionalist** a writer on institutes; a person who sets a high value on institutionalism. — *adv* **institu'tionally.** — *adj* **institū'tionary** institutional. — *n* **in'stitūtor** or **in'stitūter** a person who institutes. [L. *īnstituĕre*, *-ūtum* — *in*, in, *statuĕre*, to cause to stand — *stāre*, to stand.]

instruct *in-strukt'*, *vt* to inform; to teach; to direct; (of a judge) to give (a jury) guidance concerning the legal issues of a case; to give (a lawyer) the facts concerning a case; to order or command. — *adj* **instruc'tible.** — *n* **instruc'tion** (the art of) instructing or teaching; information; direction; command; an element in a computer program or language that activates a particular operation; (in *pl*) special directions, commands. — *adj* **instruc'tional** relating to instruction; educational. — *adj* **instruc'tive** affording instruction; conveying knowledge. — *adv* **instruc'tively.** — *n* **instruc'tiveness.** — *n* **instruc'tor,** *fem* **instructress,** a teacher; a college or university lecturer, below assistant professor in rank (*US*). — *n* **instruc'torship.** [L. *īnstruĕre*, *īnstructum* — *in*, in, *struĕre*, to pile up.]

instrument *in'strə-mənt*, *n* a tool or utensil; a device for producing musical sounds; a writing containing a contract; a formal record; a person or thing used as a means or agency; a term generally employed to denote an indicating device but also other pieces of small electrical apparatus. — *vt* (*-ment'*) to score for instruments; to equip with indicating, measuring, or control, etc. apparatus. — *adj* for instruments; by means of instruments (as *instrument flight*). — *adj* **instrumental** (*-ment'l*) acting as an instrument or means; serving to promote an object; helpful; of, for, belonging to, or produced by, musical instruments; denoting a type of learning process in which a particular response is always associated with a reinforcement, the response then intensifying (*psychol*); serving to indicate the instrument or means (*gram*). — *n* the instrumental case (*gram*); a piece of music for instruments only, i.e. without a vocal part. — *n* **instrument'alist** a person who plays on a musical instrument. — *n* **instrumentality** (*-men-tal'i-ti*) agency. — *adv* **instrument'ally.** — *n* **instrumentā'tion** the use or provision of instruments; the arrangement of a composition for performance by different instruments (*mus*). — **instrument flying** and **landing** navigation of aircraft by means of instruments only, landing of aircraft by means of instruments and ground radio devices only, when visibility is poor. [L. *instrūmentum* — *īnstruĕre*, to instruct; see **instruct.**]

insubordinate *in-sə-börd'i-nit*, *adj* refusing to submit to authority; disobedient, rebellious. — *adv* **insubord'inately.** — *n* **insubordinā'tion.** [**in-** (2).]

insubstantial *in-səb-stan'shəl*, *adj* not substantial; tenuous, flimsy; not real. — *n* **insubstantiality** (*-shi-al'i-ti*). — *adv* **insubstan'tially.** [**in-** (2).]

insufferable *in-suf'ə-rə-bl*, *adj* not able to be endured, intolerable; detestable. — *adv* **insuff'erably.** [**in-** (2).]

insufficient *in-sə-fish'ənt*, *adj* not sufficient; inadequate. — *n* **insuffic'iency.** — *adv* **insuffic'iently.** [**in-** (2).]

insular *in'sū-lər*, *adj* belonging to an island; surrounded by water; standing or situated alone; narrow, prejudiced. — *n* **in'sūlarism** or **insūlarity** (*-lar'i-ti*) the state of being insular. — *adv* **in'sūlarly.** [**insulate.**]

insulate *in'sū-lāt*, *vt* to cut off from connection or communication; to prevent the passing of heat, sound, electricity, etc. from (a body, area, etc.) to another; to separate, esp. from the earth, by a non-conductor (*electr*). — *n* **insula'tion** material which insulates or is a non-conductor of electricity; the process of insulating. — *n* **in'sulator** a device for insulating a conductor. — **insulating tape** a usu. adhesive tape made from, or impregnated with, water-resistant insulating material, used for covering joins in electrical wires, etc. [L. *īnsula*, island.]

insulin *in'sū-lin*, *n* an extract obtained from the islands or islets of Langerhans in the pancreas of animals, used for treating diabetes and also mental diseases. — **insulin shock** or **reaction** a state of collapse produced by an overdose of insulin. [**insulate.**]

insult *in-sult'*, *vt* to treat with indignity or contempt; to affront. — *n* **in'sult** an offensive remark or action, an affront; injury, damage (*med*, esp. *US*). — *adj* **insult'able.** — *adj* **insult'ing.** — *adv* **insult'ingly.** [L. *īnsultāre* — *insilīre*, to spring at.]

insuperable *in-sū'pə-rə-bl* or *-sōō'*, *adj* not capable of being overcome or surmounted. — *n* **insuperabil'ity** or **insu'perableness.** — *adv* **insu'perably.** [L. *īnsuperābilis* — *in-*, not, *superāre*, to pass over — *super*, above.]

insupportable *in-sə-pört'əbl*, *adj* unbearable; not sustainable or defensible. — *adv* **insupport'ably.** [**in-** (2).]

insuppressible *in-sə-pres'i-bl*, *adj* not capable of being suppressed or concealed. — *adv* **insuppress'ibly.** [**in-** (2).]

insure *in-shōōr'*, *vt* to make an arrangement for the payment of a sum of money in the event of loss or injury to; to guarantee; to make sure or secure. — *vi* to effect or undertake insurance. — *n* **insurabil'ity.** — *adj* **insur'able** capable of being insured. — *n* **insur'ance** the act, or business system, of insuring; a contract of insurance, a policy; the premium paid for insuring; means of avoiding risk, loss, damage, etc.; the sum to be received. — *n* **insur'ant** an insurance policy holder. — *n* **insured'** an insured person or organisation. — *n* **insur'er** either party to a contract of insurance (now, strictly the insurance company). [O.Fr. *enseurer* — *en*, and *seur*, sure; see **ensure** and **sure.**]

insurgent *in-sûr'jənt*, *adj* rising in revolt; rising; rushing in. — *n* a person who rises in opposition to established authority; a rebel. — *n* **insur'gence** or **insur'gency.** [L. *īnsurgēns*, *-entis* — *in*, upon, *surgĕre*, to rise.]

insurmountable *in-sər-mown'tə-bl*, *adj* not surmountable; not capable of being overcome. — *n* **insurmountabil'ity.** — *adv* **insurmoun'tably.** [**in-** (2).]

insurrection *in-sə-rek'shən*, *n* a rising or revolt. — *adj* **insurrec'tional** or **insurrec'tionary.** — *n* **insur-**

rec'tionary or **insurrec'tionist.** — *n* **insurrec'tionism.** [L. *īnsurrēctiō, -ōnis* — *īnsurgĕre*; see **insurgent.**]

inswing *in'swing, n* an inward swing or swerve. — *n* **inswinger** (*in'swing-ər*) a ball bowled so as to swerve to leg (*cricket*); a ball kicked so as to swing in towards the goal or the centre of the pitch (*football*). [**in** and **swing.**]

Int. *abbrev* for International.

int. *abbrev* for: interest; interior.

intact *in-takt', adj* untouched; unimpaired; whole; undiminished. — *n* **intact'ness.** [L. *intactus* — *in-*, not, *tangĕre, tactum*, to touch.]

intaglio *in-täl'yō, n* a figure cut into any substance; a stone or gem in which the design is hollowed out (opp. to *cameo*); the production of such figures, stones or gems; a countersunk die: — *pl* **intagl'ios.** — Also *vt.* — *adj* **intagl'iated** incised, engraved. [It., — *in*, into, *tagliare*, to cut.]

intake *in'tāk, n* amount, quantity, etc. taken in; an airway in a mine; a place where water, gas, etc. is taken in; a narrowing in a pipe; decrease by knitting two stitches together; the place where contraction occurs; a body of people taken into an organisation, such as new recruits, or new pupils at a school; the point at which fuel mixture enters the cylinder of an internal-combustion engine. [**in** and **take.**]

Intal® *in'tal, n* a drug (*sodium cromoglycate*) used to control asthma.

intangible *in-tan'ji-bl, adj* not tangible or perceptible to touch; insubstantial; eluding the grasp of the mind. — *n* something intangible. — *n* **intangibil'ity** or **intan'gibleness.** — *adv* **intan'gibly.** [See **intact.**]

intarsia *in-tär'si-ə, n* decorative wood inlay work; coloured geometrical patterning in knitting. [It. *intarsio.*]

integer *in'ti-jər, n* a whole; any positive whole number, any negative whole number, or zero (*arith*). [L. — *in*, not, and root of *tangere*, to touch.]

integral *in'tə-grəl, adj* entire or whole; not involving fractions; relating to integrals; unimpaired, intact; intrinsic, belonging as a part to the whole. — *n* a whole; the whole as made up of its parts; the value of the function of a variable whose differential coefficient is known (*math*). — *n* **integral'ity.** — *adv* **in'tegrally.** — **integral calculus** calculus. [L.L. *integralis*; see ety. for **integer.**]

integrand *in'ti-grənd,* (*math*) *n* a function to be integrated. [L. *integrandus*, gerundive of *integrare.*]

integrant *in'ti-grənt, adj* making part of a whole; necessary to form an integer or an entire thing. [Fr. *intégrant.*]

integrate *in'ti-grāt, vt* to make up as a whole; to make entire; to combine, amalgamate; to incorporate (one person or thing) into another; to desegregate; to find the integral of (*math*); to find the total value of. — *vi* to become integral; to perform integration. — *adj* made up of parts; complete; whole. — *adj* **in'tegrable** (*-grə-bl*) capable of being integrated. — *n* **integrā'tion** the act or process of integrating (*math*); unification into a whole, e.g. of diverse elements (such as racial variety) in a community; the state of being integrated; the formation of a unified personality (*psychol*). — *n* **integrā'tionist** someone who favours integration of a community. — Also *adj.* — *adj* **in'tegrātive** integrating; tending to integrate. — *n* **in'tegrātor** a person who integrates; an instrument for finding the results of integrations. — **integrated circuit** a circuit consisting of an assembly of electronic elements in a single structure which cannot be subdivided without destroying its intended function. [L. *integrare*, to make whole.]

integrity *in-teg'ri-ti, n* entireness, wholeness; the unimpaired state of anything; uprightness; honesty; purity. [**integer.**]

integument *in-teg'ū-mənt, n* an external covering, such as the skin, exoskeleton, etc. — *adj* **integumentary** (*-men'tər-i*). [L. *integumentum* — *in*, upon, *tegĕre*, to cover.]

intellect *in'ti-lekt, n* the mind, in reference to its rational powers; the thinking principle. — *adj* **intellectual** (*-lekt'ū-əl*) of or relating to the intellect; perceived or performed by the intellect; having the power of understanding; endowed with a superior intellect; appealing to, or (thought to be) intended for, intellectuals; intelligible only to a person with a superior intellect. — *n* a person of superior intellect or enlightenment. — *vi* **intellect'ualise** or **-ize** to reason intellectually. — *vt* to endow with intellect; to give an intellectual character to. — *n* **intellect'ualism** the doctrine that derives all knowledge from pure reason. — *n* **intellect'ualist.** — *n* **intellectuality** (*-al'i-ti*) intellectual power. — *adv* **intellect'ually.** [L. *intellēctus, -ūs* — *intelligĕre, intellēctum*, to understand.]

intelligent *in-tel'i-jənt, adj* endowed with the faculty of reason; having or showing highly developed mental faculties; well-informed; knowing, aware (*of*); capable of performing some of the functions of a computer (*automation*). — *n* **intell'igence** intellectual skill or knowledge; mental brightness; information communicated; news; intelligence department. — *adv* **intell'igently.** — **intelligence department** or **service** a department of state or armed service for securing and interpreting information, especially about an enemy; **intelligence quotient** the ratio, commonly expressed as a percentage, of a person's mental age to his or her actual age (abbrev. **IQ**); **intelligence test** a test by questions and tasks to determine a person's mental capacity, or the age at which his or her capacity would be normal. [L. *intelligēns, -entis*, pres. p. of *intelligĕre.*]

intelligentsia or **intelligentzia** *in-tel-i-jent'si-ə* or *-gent'si-ə, n* the intellectual or cultured classes, originally esp. in Russia. [Russ., — L. *intelligentia.*]

intelligible *in-tel'i-jə-bl, adj* capable of being understood; easy to understand, clear. — *n* **intelligibil'ity** or **intell'igibleness.** — *adv* **intell'igibly.** [L. *intelligibilis.*]

intemperance *in-tem'pə-rəns, n* lack of due restraint; excess of any kind; habitual overindulgence in alcoholic liquor. — *adj* **intem'perate** indulging to excess in any appetite or passion; given to an immoderate use of alcoholic liquors; exceeding the usual degree; immoderate. — *adv* **intem'perately.** — *n* **intem'perateness.** [L. *intemperans*, intemperate.]

intend *in-tend', vt* to have as a purpose, plan; to mean; to design or destine. — *adj* **intend'ed** planned. — *n* (*colloq*) a fiancé or fiancée. [O.Fr. *entendre* — L. *intendĕre, intentum* and *intēnsum* — *in*, towards, *tendĕre*, to stretch.]

intense *in-tens', adj* strained; concentrated, dense; extreme in degree; (of a person, manner, etc.) earnestly or deeply emotional, or affecting to have deep feeling; (of a photographic negative) opaque. — *adv* **intense'ly.** — *n* **intense'ness** or **intens'ity.** — *n* **intensificā'tion.** — *n* **intens'ifier** an utterance that lends force or emphasis. — *vt* **intens'ify** to make more intense. — *vi* to become intense: — *pr p* **intens'ifying**; *pa t* and *pa p* **intens'ified.** [O.Fr. *intens* — L. *intensus.*]

intension *in-ten'shən, n* straining; intentness; intensity; the sum of the qualities implied by a general name (*logic*). — *adj* **inten'sional.** [See ety. for **intend.**]

intensive *in-ten'siv, adj* concentrated, intense; strained; unremitting; relating to intensity or to intension; using large amounts of capital or labour to increase production; intensifying; intensified; giving force or emphasis (*gram*). — *n* an intensifier. — used in combination to signify having, using or requiring, a great deal of something, as in *labour-intensive, capital-intensive*. — *adv* **inten'sively.** — *n* **inten'siveness.** — **intensive culture** getting the very most out of the soil of a limited area. — **intensive care unit** an area in a hospital where a patient's condition is carefully monitored. [See ety. for **intend.**]

intent *in-tent'*, *adj* fixed with close attention; concentrating on a particular end or purpose. — *n* the thing aimed at or intended; purpose, intention; meaning or connotation. — *adv* **intent'ly** earnestly; diligently. — *n* **intent'ness.** — **to all intents (and purposes)** in every important respect; virtually; **well- (or ill-) intentioned** having good (or bad) designs; meaning well (or ill); **with intent** (*law*) deliberately, with the intention of doing the harm, etc., that is or was done. [See ety. for **intend.**]

intention *in-ten'shən*, *n* design; purpose, aim; application of thought to an object; a concept; (in *pl*) purpose with respect to marriage (*colloq*). — *adj* **inten'tional** with intention; intended; designed; directed towards, or pertaining to the mind's capacity to direct itself towards, objects and states of affairs (*philos*). — *n* **intentional'ity.** — *adv* **inten'tionally** with intention; on purpose. [See ety. for **intend.**]

inter *in-tûr'*, *vt* to bury: — *pr p* **interr'ing**; *pa t* and *pa p* **interred'.** — *n* **inter'ment** burial. [Fr. *enterrer* — L.L. *interrāre* — L. *in*, into, *terra*, the earth.]

inter- *in-tər-*, *pfx* between, among, in the midst of; mutual, reciprocal; together. [L. *inter*.]

interact *in-tər-akt'*, *vi* to act on one another. — *n* **interac'tant** a substance, etc., which interacts. — *n* **interaction** (*-ak'shən*) mutual action. — *adj* **interac'tive** allowing, or capable of, mutual action; allowing continuous two-way communication between a computer and its user; (of television) denoting a facility whereby the viewer can choose between options within a channel, call up action replay during a match, etc. [**inter-.**]

inter alia *in'tər ā'li-ə* or *a'li-a*, (L.) among other things; **inter alios** (*-ōs*) among other persons.

interatomic *in-tə-rə-tom'ik*, *adj* existing, happening, etc., between atoms. [**inter-.**]

interbreed *in-tər-brēd'*, *vt* and *vi* to breed together, esp. of different races: — *pa t* and *pa p* **interbred'.** — *n* **interbreed'ing.** [**inter-.**]

intercalate *in-tûr'kə-lāt*, *vt* to insert between others (e.g. a day in a calendar); to interpolate. — *adj* **inter'calary** inserted between others. — *n* **intercalā'tion.** — *adj* **inter'calative** (*-lā-tiv* or *-lə-tiv*). [L. *intercalāre*, *-ātum* — *inter*, between, *calāre*, to proclaim; see **calends.**]

intercede *in-tər-sēd'*, *vi* to act as peacemaker between two parties, mediate; to plead (for). — *adj* **intercēd'ent.** — *n* **intercēd'er.** [L. *intercēděre*, *-cēssum* — *inter*, between, *cēděre*, to go.]

intercept *in-tər-sept'*, *vt* to stop and seize on the way from one place to another; to cut off; to stop, alter or interrupt the progress of; to take or comprehend between (*math*). — *n* (*in'*) (*math*) that part of a line that is intercepted. — *n* **intercep'ter** or **intercep'tor** a person or thing which intercepts; a light, swift aeroplane for pursuit. — *n* **intercep'tion.** — *adj* **intercep'tive.** [L. *intercipěre*, *-ceptum* — *inter*, between, *capěre*, to seize.]

intercession *in-tər-sesh'ən*, *n* the act of interceding or pleading for another. — *adj* **intercess'ional.** — *n* **intercessor** (*-ses'ər*) a person who intercedes; a bishop who acts during a vacancy in a see. — *adj* **intercessorial** (*-ör'*) or **intercess'ory** interceding. — **intercession of saints** prayer offered on behalf of Christians on earth by saints. [See **intercede.**]

interchange *in-tər-chānj'*, *vt* to give and take mutually; to exchange. — *vi* to succeed alternately. — *n* (*in'*) mutual exchange; alternate succession; a road junction or series of junctions designed to prevent streams of traffic crossing one another. — *adj* **interchange'able** capable of being interchanged. — *n* **interchangeabil'ity** or **interchange'ableness.** — *adv* **interchange'ably.** [**inter-.**]

intercity *in-tər-sit'i*, *adj* between cities. [**inter-.**]

intercollegiate *in-tər-kə-lē'jət*, *adj* between colleges. [**inter-.**]

intercom *in'tər-kom*, *n* a telephone system within a building, aeroplane, tank, etc. [*Inter*nal *com*munication.]

intercommunicate *in-tər-kə-mū'ni-kāt*, *vt* to communicate mutually or together; to have free passage from one to another. — *n* **intercommunicā'tion** or **intercommu'nion** mutual communion or relation, esp. between churches; the permitting of members of one denomination to receive Holy Communion in the churches of another denomination (*Christian relig*). [**inter-.**]

interconnect *in-tər-kə-nekt'*, *vt* to connect (things) with each other. — *vi* to be mutually connected. — *n* **interconnec'tedness, interconnec'tion** or **interconnex'ion.** — *n* **interconnec'tor** in the electricity industry, a feeder that interconnects two substances or generating stations. [**inter-.**]

intercontinental *in-tər-kon-ti-nen'tal*, *adj* between or connecting different continents. [**inter-.**]

interconversion *in-tər-kən-ver'shən*, *n* the conversion of two things or more into one another, mutual conversion. — *vt* **interconvert'** to convert (two or more things) into one another. — *adj* **interconvert'ible** mutually convertible; interchangeable; exactly equivalent. [**inter-.**]

intercostal *in-tər-kos'təl*, *adj* between the ribs or the leaf-veins. [L. *inter*, between, *costa*, a rib.]

intercourse *in'tər-körs*, *n* connection or dealings between people; communication; commerce; communion; coition. [O.Fr. *entrecours* — L. *intercursus*, a running between — *inter*, between, *currěre*, *cursum*, to run.]

intercurrent *in-tər-kur'ənt*, *adj* occurring between or during. [**inter-.**]

intercut *in-tər-kut'*, (*cinema*) *vt* to alternate (contrasting shots) within a sequence by cutting. [**inter-.**]

interdenominational *in-tər-di-nom-i-nā'shə-nl*, *adj* common to, with participation of, various religious denominations; independent of denomination. [**inter-.**]

interdental *in-tər-den'tl*, *adj* between the teeth; pertaining to the surfaces of the teeth where they adjoin (*dentistry*); pronounced with the tip of the tongue between upper and lower teeth. — *adv* **interden'tally.** [**inter-.**]

interdepartmental *in-tər-dē-pärt-men'tl*, *adj* between departments. — *adv* **interdepartmen'tally.** [**inter-.**]

interdepend *in-tər-di-pend'*, *vi* to depend on one another. — *n* **interdepend'ence.** — *adj* **interdepend'ent.** [**inter-.**]

interdict *in-tər-dikt'*, *vt* to prohibit; to forbid; to forbid (someone) to take communion (*RC*). — *n* (*in'*) prohibition; a prohibitory decree. — *n* **interdic'tion** (*-shən*). — *adj* **interdic'tive** or **interdic'tory.** [L. *interdīcěre*, *-dictum* — *inter*, between, *dīcěre*, to say.]

interdigital *in-tər-dij'i-tl*, *adj* between digits. — *vt* and *vi* **interdig'itate** to interlock by finger-like processes, or in the manner of the fingers of clasped hands. — *n* **interdigitā'tion.** [**inter-.**]

interdisciplinary *in-tər-di-si-plin'ə-ri*, *adj* involving two or more fields of study. [**inter-.**]

interest *in'trəst*, *in'trist*, *in'tə-rəst* or *in'tə-rist*, *n* premium paid for the use of money; benefit, advantage; concern, importance; a right to some advantage; claim to participate or be concerned in some way; stake, share; partisanship or side; the body of persons whose advantage is bound up in anything; regard to advantage; a state of engaged attention and curiosity; disposition towards such a state; the power of arousing it; something in which one has interest or is interested. — *vt* to concern deeply; to cause to have an interest; to engage the attention of; to awaken concern in; to excite (on behalf of another). — *adj* **in'terested** having an interest or concern; affected or biased by personal considerations, self-interest, etc. — *adv* **in'terestedly.** — *adj* **in'teresting** engaging or apt to engage the attention or regard; exciting emotion or passion. — *adv* **in'terestingly.** — **interest group** a number of people grouped together to further or protect a common interest. — **in the interest(s) of** with a view to furthering or to helping. [From old word *interess*, influenced by O.Fr. *interest*, L. *interest*, it concerns.]

interface *in'tər-fās*, *n* a surface forming a common boundary; a meeting-point or area of contact between objects, systems, subjects, etc.; the connection or junction between two systems or two parts of the same system (*comput*). — *vt* to connect by means of an interface. — *vi* (*comput*) to interact or operate compatibly (with). — *adj* **interfacial** (*-fā'shl*) between plane faces; of an interface. [**inter-**.]

interfacing *in'tər-fās-ing*, *n* firm material sewn between layers of fabric to shape and stiffen a garment. [**inter-**.]

interfemoral *in-tər-fem'ə-rəl*, *adj* situated, occurring or relating to the area between the thighs. [**inter-**.]

interfere *in-tər-fēr'*, *vi* to intervene; to come in the way, obstruct; to interpose; (of a horse) to strike a foot against the opposite leg in walking; (of waves, rays of light, etc.) to act reciprocally. — *n* **interfēr'ence** the act of interfering; the effect of combining similar rays of light, etc. (*phys*); the spoiling of a wireless or television signal by other signals or by natural disturbances. — *adj* **interferential** (*-fə-ren'shl*). — *n* **interfēr'er.** — *adv* **interfēr'ingly.** — *n* **interfēr'ogram** (*phys*) a photographic or diagrammatic record of interference. — *n* **interfērom'eter** an instrument which, by observing interference fringes, makes precision measurements of wavelengths, wave speeds, angles, distances, etc; a radio telescope (**radio interferometer**) using two or more antennas spaced at known intervals and linked to a common receiver, one of its applications being the precise determination of the position of sources of radio waves in space. — *n* **interfērom'etry.** — *n* **interfēr'on** any of several proteins produced naturally in the body, active against many viruses. — **interfere with** to meddle in; to get in the way of, hinder; to assault sexually. [O.Fr. *entreférir* — L. *inter*, between, *ferīre*, to strike.]

interfuse *in-tər-fūz'*, *vt* to cause to mix or fuse. — *vi* to mix or fuse, mingle. [**inter-**.]

intergalactic *in-tər-gə-lak'tik*, *adj* between or among galaxies. [**inter-**.]

interglacial *in-tər-glā'shəl* or *-shyəl*, (*geol*) *adj* occurring between two periods of glacial action. — *n* a retreat of ice between glaciations. [**inter-**.]

interim *in'tə-rim*, *n* the time between or intervening; the meantime; (with *cap*) in the history of the Reformation, the name given to certain edicts of the German emperor for the regulation of religious and ecclesiastical matters, till they could be decided by a general council. — *adj* temporary, provisional. — **interim dividend** (*finance*) a dividend distributed part of the way through a company's financial year. [L.]

interior *in-tē'ri-ər*, *adj* inner; remote from the frontier or coast; inland; domestic rather than foreign; situated within or further in (sometimes with *to*); devoted to mental or spiritual life. — *n* the inside of anything; the inland part of a country; a picture of a scene within a house; home affairs of a country; inner nature or character. — *n* **interiority** (*-or'i-ti*). — *adv* **inte'riorly.** — **interior angle** an angle between two sides of a polygon. — **interior decoration** or **design** the construction and furnishing of the interior of a building. — *adj* **interior-sprung'** (of a mattress, etc.) containing springs. [L., compar. of assumed *interus*, inward.]

interj. *abbrev* for interjection.

interject *in-tər-jekt'*, *vt* to throw between; to interpose; to exclaim in interruption or parenthesis; to insert. — *vi* to throw oneself between. — *n* **interjec'tion** (*-shən*) an act of interjecting; a syntactically independent word or phrase of an exclamatory nature, an ejaculation or exclamation (*gram*). — *adj* **interjec'tional, interjec'tionary** or **interjec'tural.** — *adv* **interjec'tionally.** — *n* **interjec'tor.** [L. *inter(j)icěre, interjectum* — *inter*, between, *jacěre*, to throw.]

interlace *in-tər-lās'*, *vt* to lace, weave or entangle together. — *vi* to intermix. — *n* **interlace'ment.** — **interlaced scanning** in television, the alternate scanning of an image in two sets of alternate lines. [**inter-**.]

interlard *in-tər-lärd'*, *vt* to mix in, as fat with lean; to diversify by mixture, to intersperse. [**inter-**.]

interlay *in-tər-lā'*, *vt* to lay between; to interpose. [**inter-**.]

interleave *in-tər-lēv'*, *vt* to put a leaf between; to insert blank leaves in. — *n* **in'terleaf** a leaf so inserted: — *pl* **in'terleaves.** [**inter-**.]

interleukin *in-tər-lū'kin*, *n* a protein produced by white blood cells that plays an important part in the combating of infection.

interline[1] *in-tər-līn'*, *vt* to write in alternate lines; to insert between lines; to write between the lines of. — *adj* **interlinear** (*-lin'i-ər*) written between lines. — *n* **interlinea'tion.** [**inter-**.]

interline[2] *in-tər-līn'*, *vt* to supply (a part of a garment, e.g. the collar) with an additional lining to reinforce or stiffen it. — *n* **interlin'ing.**

interline[3] *in-tər-līn'*, *vi* to join an airline route at a point other than its starting-point. [**inter-**.]

interlinear, interlineation. See **interline**[1].

interlink *in-tər-lingk'*, *vt* and *vi* to link together. [**inter-**.]

interlock *in-tər-lok'*, *vt* to lock or clasp together; to connect so as to work together. — *vi* to be locked together. — *n* **in'terlock** an interlocked condition; synchronising mechanism. [**inter-**.]

interlocution *in-tər-lə-kū'shən*, *n* conference; an intermediate decree before final decision. — *n* **interlocutor** (*-lok'ū-tər*) a person who speaks in dialogue (*fem* **interloc'utrix**); a judge's decree (*Scots law*). — *adj* **interloc'utory.** [L. *interlocūtiō, -ōnis* — *inter*, between, *loquī, locūtus*, to speak.]

interloper *in'tər-lō-pər*, *n* an intruder; a person who meddles in another's affairs, esp. for profit. — *vi* and *vt* **interlope'** (or *in'*) to intrude into any matter in which one has no fair concern. [Prob. L. *inter*, between, and **lope.**]

interlude *in'tər-lo͞od* or *-lūd*, *n* an interval between acts of a play, etc.; a short dramatic or comic piece, formerly often performed during this interval; a short piece of music played between the parts of a drama, opera, hymn, etc.; an interval, any period of time or any happening different in character from what comes before or after. [L. *inter*, between, *lūdus*, play.]

interlunar *in-tər-lo͞o'nər* or *-lū'*, *adj* belonging to the moon's monthly time of invisibility. — *n* **interlunā'tion** the dark time between old moon and new. [L. *inter*, between, *lūna*, the moon.]

intermarry *in-tər-mar'i*, *vi* to marry within one's own group or kin; (of groups, races etc.) to mingle by repeated marriage. — *n* **intermarr'iage.** [**inter-**.]

intermediate *in-tər-mē'dyit* or *-di-it*, *adj* placed, occurring, or classified between others, or between extremes, limits, or stages; (of igneous rocks) between acid and basic in composition; intervening. —

n that which is intermediate; any compound manufactured from a primary that serves as a starting material for the synthesis of some other product (*chem*). — *vi* (*-di-āt*) to mediate; to act as an agent or go-between. — *n* **intermē'diacy** (*-ə-si*) the state of being intermediate. — *adj* **intermē'diary** acting as an intermediate; intermediate. — *n* an intermediate agent. — *adv* **intermē'diately**. — *n* **intermēdiā'tion**. — *n* **intermē'diātor**. — *adj* **intermē'diatory** (*-ə-tə-ri*). — **intermediate technology** technology which combines simple, basic materials with modern sophisticated tools and methods. [**inter-**.]

interment. See **inter**.

intermetallic *in-tər-mə-tal'ik*, *adj* (of an alloy) formed from two or more metallic elements. [**inter-**.]

intermezzo *in-tər-met'sō*, *n* a short dramatic or musical entertainment as entr'acte; a short intermediate movement or the like (*mus*): — *pl* **intermez'zi** (*-sē*) or **intermezz'os**. [It., — L. *intermedius*, intermediate.]

interminable *in-tûr'min-ə-bl*, *adj* without termination or limit; boundless; endless; tediously long. — *n* **inter'minableness**. — *adv* **inter'minably**. [**in-** (2).]

intermingle *in-tər-ming'gl*, *vt* and *vi* to mingle or mix together. [**inter-**.]

intermit *in-tər-mit'*, *vt* and *vi* to stop for a time. — *n* **intermission** (*-mish'ən*) an act of intermitting; an interval; music played during the interval at a theatre, etc.; pause; a respite. — *adj* **intermissive** (*-mis'iv*) coming and going; intermittent. — *n* **intermitt'ence** or **intermitt'ency**. — *adj* **intermitt'ent** intermitting or ceasing at intervals. — *adv* **intermitt'ently**. [L. *intermittĕre*, *-missum* — *inter*, between, *mittĕre*, to cause to go.]

intermix *in-tər-miks'*, *vt* and *vi* to mix together. — *n* **intermix'ture** a mass formed by mixture; something added and intermixed. [L. *intermiscēre*, *-mixtum* — *inter*, among, *miscēre*, to mix.]

intermodulation *in-tər-mod-ū-lā'shən*, (*electronics*) *n* unwanted mutual interference between electronic signals, affecting the amplitude of each. [**inter-**.]

intermolecular *in-tər-mə-lek'ū-lər*, *adj* between molecules. [**inter-**.]

intern *in'tûrn*, *n* an inmate, e.g. of a boarding-school; a resident assistant surgeon or physician in a hospital (also **in'terne**; *US*). — *vt* (*in-tûrn'*) to confine to a prescribed area or imprison (e.g. an enemy ship or alien, a suspected terrorist) as a precautionary measure. — *n* **internee'** a person interned. — *n* **intern'ment** confinement of this kind. [Fr. *interne* — L. *internus*, inward.]

internal *in-tûr'nəl*, *adj* in the interior; domestic as opposed to foreign; intrinsic; pertaining to the inner nature or feelings; inner. — *n* (in *pl*) inner parts. — *vt* **inter'nalise** or **-ize** to assimilate (an idea, etc.) into one's personality; to withdraw (an emotion, etc.) into oneself (rather than express it). — *participial adj* **inter'nalised** or **-z-**. — *n* **internality** (*-nal'i-ti*). — *adv* **inter'nally**. — **internal evidence** evidence derived from the thing itself. — **internal-combustion engine** an engine in which the fuel is burned within the working cylinder. [L. *internus* — *inter*, within.]

international *in-tər-nash'ə-nl* or *-nash'nl*, *adj* between nations or their representatives; transcending national limits; extending to several nations; pertaining to the relations between nations. — *n* (with *cap*) an international socialist organisation — the **First International** set up in London in 1864, the **Second International** formed in Paris in 1889 as a successor to it, the **Third International** founded by the Bolsheviks in 1919 to encourage World revolution, the **Fourth International** formed in 1938 as a rival to the Third, by that time dominated by Stalin; a game or contest between players chosen to represent different nations (*colloq*); a player who takes (or has taken) part in an international match. — *n* **Internationale** (*ɛ̃-ter-na-syō-näl'*) an international communist song, composed in France in 1871; the Second International. — *vt* **interna'tionalise** or **-ize** to make international; to put under international control. — *n* **interna'tionalism**. — *n* **interna'tionalist** someone who favours the common interests, or action, of all nations; someone who favours the principles of an International; a specialist in international law. — *adj* **internationalis'tic**. — *adv* **interna'tionally**. — **International Baccalaureate** (a school-leaving examination giving) an international qualification for higher education; **International Date Line** the line east and west of which the date differs — the 180th meridian with deviations; **international law** the law regulating the relations of states (**public international law**) or that determining what nation's law shall in any case govern the relations of private persons (**private international law**); **international master** (also with *caps*) (a person holding) the second highest international chess title; **international modern** or **style** a 20th-cent. architectural style characterised by the use of modern building materials and techniques, lack of ornament and simple geometric shapes; **International Monetary Fund** an organisation, established in 1945 to promote international trade through increased stabilisation of currencies, which maintains a pool of money on which member countries can draw; **International Phonetic Alphabet** the alphabet of the International Phonetic Association, a series of symbols representing human speech sounds; **international standard book number** see under **standard**; **international system of units** see **SI units**. [**inter-**.]

interne. See **intern**.

internecine *in-tər-nē'sīn*, *adj* mutually destructive; involving conflict within a group. [L. *internecīnus* — *internecāre* — *inter*, between (used intensively), *necāre*, to kill.]

internee. See **intern**.

interneural *in-tər-nū'rəl*, (*anat*) *adj* situated between the neural spines or spinous processes of successive vertebrae. [**inter-**.]

internist *in-tûr'nist*, *n* a specialist in internal diseases; a physician, in contrast to a surgeon. [*intern*al and **-ist**.]

internment. See **intern**.

internuncio *in-tər-nun'shi-ō*, *n* a messenger between two parties; the Pope's representative at minor courts: — *pl* **internun'cios**. — *adj* **internun'cial** relating to an internuncio. [It. *internunzio*, Sp. *internuncio*, L. *internuntius* — *inter*, between, *nuntius*, a messenger.]

interoceptor *in-tə-rō-sep'tər*, (*physiol*) *n* a sensory receptor of the viscera. — *adj* **interocep'tive**. [*Inter*ior and *receptor*.]

interoperate *in-tər-op'ə-rāt*, *vi* (of a machine or system) to operate in conjunction with another; to use the same parts, commands, etc. as another. — *n* **interoperabil'ity**. [**inter-**.]

interparietal *in-tər-pə-rī'ə-təl*, (*zool*) *adj* situated between the right and left parietal bones of the skull. [**inter-**.]

inter partes *in'tər pär'tāz*, (L.) between parties.

interpellation *in-tər-pə-lā'shən*, *n* a question raised during the course of a debate. — *vt* **inter'pellate** (or *-pel'*) to question by interpellation. [Fr., — L. *interpellāre*, *-ātum*, to disturb by speaking — *inter*, between, *pellĕre*, to drive.]

interpersonal *in-tər-pûr'sə-nəl*, *adj* between persons. — *adv* **interper'sonally**. [**inter-**.]

interphone *in'tər-fōn*, *n* intercom. [Gr. *phōnē*, voice.]

interplanetary *in-tər-plan'i-tə-ri*, *adj* between planets. [**inter-**.]

interplay *in'tər-plā*, *n* mutual action; interchange of action and reaction. **[inter-.]**

interplead *in-tər-plēd'*, (*law*) *vi* to discuss adverse claims to property by bill of interpleader. — *n* **interplead'er** a person who interpleads; a form of process in the English courts, intended to protect a defendant who claims no interest in the subject matter of a suit, but has reason to know that the plaintiff's title is disputed by some other claimant. **[inter-.]**

interpleural *in-tər-plōō'rəl*, (*med*) *adj* situated between the right and left pleural cavities. **[inter-.]**

Interpol *in'tər-pol*, *n* the *Inter*national Criminal *Pol*ice Commission, directed to international co-operation in the suppression of crime.

interpolable. See **interpolate.**

interpolar *in-tər-pō'lər*, *adj* between or connecting the poles. **[inter-.]**

interpolate *in-tûr'pə-lāt*, *vt* to insert a word or passage in a book or manuscript esp. in order to mislead; to tamper with, to corrupt by spurious insertions; to insert, interpose, interject; to fill in as an intermediate term of a series (*math*). — *adj* **inter'polable.** — *n* **interpolā'tion.** — *adj* **inter'polātive.** — *n* **inter'polātor.** [L. *interpolāre, -ātum* — *inter*, between, *polīre*, to polish.]

interpose *in-tər-pōz'*, *vt* to place between; to thrust in; to offer (e.g. aid or services); to put in by way of interruption. — *vi* to come between; to mediate; to interfere. — *n* **interpō'sal.** — *n* **interpō'ser.** — *n* **interposition** (*in-tər-pə-zish'ən*) the act of interposing; intervention; mediation; (in U.S.) the right of a state to oppose the federal government for encroachment on the prerogatives of the state; anything interposed. [Fr. *interposer* — L. *inter*, between, Fr. *poser*, to place; see **pose**[1].]

interpret *in-tûr'prit*, *vt* to explain the meaning of, to elucidate, unfold, show the significance of; to translate into intelligible or familiar terms. — *vi* to practise interpretation. — *adj* **inter'pretable** capable of being explained. — *n* **interpretā'tion** the act of interpreting; the sense given by an interpreter; the representation of a dramatic part, performance of a piece of music, etc., according to one's conception of it. — *adj* **inter'pretative** (*-tā-tiv* or *-tə-tiv*) or **inter'pretive** inferred by or containing interpretation. — *adv* **inter'pretatively** or **inter'pretively.** — *n* **inter'preter** a person who translates orally for the benefit of two or more parties speaking different languages; an expounder; a machine which prints out on punched cards fed into it the data contained in the patterns of holes in the cards (*comput*); a program which executes other programs (*comput*; cf. **compiler** under **compile**). — *n* **inter'pretership.** [L. *interpretārī, -ātus.*]

interproximal *in-tər-prok'si-məl*, (*dentistry*) *adj* pertaining to the surfaces of teeth where they adjoin. **[inter-.]**

interracial *in-tə-rā'shəl*, *adj* between races. **[inter-.]**

interregnum *in-tə-reg'nəm*, *n* the time between two reigns; the time between the cessation of one and the establishment of another government; any breach of continuity in order, etc.: — *pl* **interreg'na** (*-nə*) or **interreg'nums.** [L. *inter*, between, *regnum*, rule.]

interrelation *in-tə-ri-lā'shən*, *n* reciprocal relation. — *n* **interrelā'tionship.** **[inter-.]**

interrogate *in-ter'ə-gāt*, *vt* to question; to examine by asking questions; (of a radar set, etc.) to send out signals to (a radio-beacon) in order to ascertain position. — *vi* to ask questions. — *adj* **interr'ogable.** — *n* **interrogatee'** a person who is interrogated. — *n* **interrogā'tion** the act of interrogating; a question put; the mark placed after a question (?) (also **interrogation mark**). — *adj* **interrogative** (*in-tə-rog'ə-tiv*) denoting a question; expressed as a question. — *n* a word used in asking a question. — *adv* **interrog'atively.** — *n* **interr'ogator.** — *n* **interrog'atory** a question or inquiry. — *adj* expressing a question. [L. *interrogāre, -ātum* — *inter*, between, *rogāre*, to ask.]

interrog. *abbrev* for: interrogation; interrogative; interrogatively.

interrupt *in-tə-rupt'*, *vt* to break in between; to stop or hinder by breaking in upon; to break continuity in. — *vi* to make an interruption. — *adj* **interrup'ted** broken in continuity; irregular in spacing or size of parts (*biol*). — *adv* **interrup'tedly** with interruptions; irregularly. — *n* **interrup'ter** or **interrup'tor** a person who interrupts; an apparatus for interrupting, e.g. for breaking an electric circuit. — *n* **interrup'tible** (of a process, supply, etc.) which may be interrupted without harm. — **interrup'tion** the act of interrupting; hindrance; temporary cessation. — *adj* **interrup'tive** tending to interrupt. — *adv* **interrup'tively.** — **interrupted cadence** (*mus*) a cadence in which some other chord (often the submediant) replaces the expected tonic. [L. *interrumpĕre, -ruptum* — *inter*, between, *rumpĕre*, to break.]

interscapular *in-tər-skap'ū-lər*, (*anat*) *adj* between the shoulder blades. **[inter-.]**

interscholastic *in-tər-skə-las'tik*, *adj* between schools. **[inter-.]**

inter se *in'tər sā*, (L.) between or among themselves.

intersect *in-tər-sekt'*, *vt* to cut across; to cut or cross mutually; to divide into parts. — *vi* to cross each other. — *n* (*in'*) a point of intersection. — *n* **intersec'tion** intersecting; the point or line in which lines or surfaces cut each other (*geom*); the set of elements which two or more sets have in common (*math*); a crossroads. — *adj* **intersec'tional.** [L. *inter*, between, *secāre, sectum*, to cut.]

intersex *in'tər-seks*, (*biol*) *n* an individual developing some characteristic of the other sex; the condition of being intersexual. — *adj* **intersex'ūal** between the sexes; intermediate between the sexes. — *n* **intersexūal'ity.** **[inter-.]**

interspace *in'tər-spās*, *n* an interval. — *vt* (*-spās'*) to put intervals between. **[inter-.]**

interspecific *in-tər-spə-sif'ik*, *adj* between species. **[inter-.]**

intersperse *in-tər-spûrs'*, *vt* to scatter or set here and there; to diversify. — *n* **interspersion** (*-spûr'shən*). [L. *interspergĕre, -spersum* — *inter*, among, *spargĕre*, to scatter.]

interstadial *in-tər-stā'di-əl*, (*geol*) *n* a retreat of ice during a glacial period, less extensive than an interglacial. — *adj* belonging to an interstadial.

interstate *in'tər-stāt* or *-stāt'*, *adj* pertaining to relations, esp. political and commercial, between states; between states. — *adv* into or to another state. — *n* (*US*) (*in'*) an interstate highway. **[inter-.]**

interstellar *in-tər-stel'ər*, *adj* beyond the solar system or among the stars; in the intervals between the stars. [L. *inter*, between, *stella*, a star.]

interstice *in-tûr'stis*, *n* a small space between things closely set, or between the parts which compose a body; the time interval required by canon law before receiving higher orders (*RC*); a space between atoms in a lattice where other atoms can be located. — *adj* **interstitial** (*-stish'l*) occurring in interstices; pertaining to the surfaces of teeth where they adjoin (*dentistry*). [L. *interstitium* — *inter*, between, *sistĕre*, *stătum*, to stand, set.]

interstratification *in-tər-strat-i-fi-kā'shən*, *n* the state of lying between, or alternating with, other strata. — *adj* **interstrat'ified.** — *vt* and *vi* **interstrat'ify.** **[inter-.]**

intertarsal *in-tər-tär'sl*, (*anat*) *adj* between tarsal bones. **[inter-.]**

interterritorial *in-tər-ter-i-tö'ri-əl*, *adj* between territories. **[inter-.]**

intertidal *in-tər-tī'dl*, *adj* between low-water and high-water mark. **[inter-.]**

intertie *in'tər-tī*, *n* (in roofing, etc.) a short timber binding together upright posts.

intertribal *in-tər-trī'bl*, *adj* between tribes. [**inter-**.]

intertrigo *in-tər-trī'gō*, (*med*) *n* an inflammation of the skin from chafing or rubbing: — *pl* **intertri'gos**. [L. *intertrīgō* — *inter*, between, *terĕre*, *trītum*, to rub.]

intertwine *in-tər-twīn'*, *vt* and *vi* to twine or twist together. — *n* **intertwine'ment**. — *n* and *adj* **intertwīn'ing**. [**inter-**.]

interunion *in-tər-ūn'yən*, *n* a blending together. [**inter-**.]

interurban *in-tər-ûr'bən*, *adj* between cities. [L. *inter*, between, *urbs*, *urbis*, a city.]

interval *in'tər-vəl*, *n* time or space between; a break between lessons, acts of a play, etc.; difference of pitch between any two musical tones (*mus*). [L. *intervallum* — *inter*, between, *vallum*, a rampart.]

intervene *in-tər-vēn'*, *vi* to come or be between; to occur between points of time; to interrupt; to step in so as to affect the outcome of a situation, etc.; to interpose in an action to which one was not at first a party (*law*). — *n* **interve'ner** a person who intervenes. — Also (*law*) **interve'nor**. — *adj* **interve'ning** coming in between. — *n* **intervention** (*-ven'shən*) intervening; interference; mediation; interposition; a system of removing surplus produce from the market and storing it until prices rise. — *n* **interven'tionism**. — *n* **interven'tionist** someone who advocates interference (also *adj*). — **intervening sequence** (*biol*) an intron; **intervention price** the market price at which intervention occurs. [L. *inter*, between, *venīre*, to come.]

interview *in'tər-vū*, *n* a formal meeting; a meeting between employer, board of directors, etc., and a candidate to ascertain by questioning and discussion the latter's suitability for a post, etc.; a meeting between a journalist, or radio or TV broadcaster, and a notable person to discuss the latter's views, etc. for publication or broadcasting; an article or programme based on such a meeting. — *vt* to conduct an interview with. — *n* **interviewee'** a person who is interviewed. — *n* **in'terviewer**. [O.Fr. *entrevue* — *entre*, between, *voir*, to see.]

inter vivos *in'tər vē'vōs*, (L.; *law*) from one living person to another.

interwar *in-tər-wör'*, *adj* between wars. [**inter-**.]

interweave *in-tər-wēv'*, *vt* and *vi* to weave together; to intermingle. [**inter-**.]

intestate *in-tes'tāt* or *-tit*, *adj* dying without having made a valid will; not disposed of by will. — *n* a person who dies without making a valid will. — *n* **intes'tacy** (*-tə-si*). [L. *intestātus* — *in-*, not, *testārī*, *-ātus*, to make a will.]

intestine *in-tes'tin*, *n* (commonly in *pl*) a part of the digestive system, divided into the small intestine (comprising the duodenum, jejunum, and ileum) and the large intestine. — *adj* **intes'tinal** (or *-tī'nl*) pertaining to the intestines. [L. *intestīnus* — *intus*, within.]

inti *in'ti*, *n* the standard unit of currency of Peru (100 centavos). [Quechua.]

intifada *in-ti-fä'də*, *n* the uprising in 1987 and continuing resistance by Palestinians to Israeli occupation of the Gaza Strip and West Bank of the Jordan. [Ar., shaking off.]

intimate *in'ti-mət*, *adj* innermost; internal; close; deep-seated; private; personal; closely acquainted; familiar; in illicit sexual connection; encouraging informality and closer personal relations through smallness, exclusiveness. — *n* a familiar friend; an associate. — *vt* (*-māt*) to hint; to announce. — *n* **in'timacy** (*-mə-si*) the state of being intimate; close familiarity; illicit sexual intercourse. — *adv* **in'timately**. — *n* **intimā'tion** indication; hint; announcement. [L. *intimāre*, *-ātum* — *intimus*, innermost — *intus*, within.]

intimidate *in-tim'i-dāt*, *vt* to strike fear into; to influence by threats or violence. — *n* **intimidā'tion** the act of intimidating; the use of violence or threats to influence the conduct or compel the consent of another; the state of being intimidated. — *n* **intim'idator**. — *adj* **intim'idatory**. [L. *in*, into, *timidus*, fearful.]

into *in'too*, *prep* to a position within; to a state of; used to indicate the dividend in dividing (*math*); in contact or collision with; interested in or enthusiastic about (*slang*); to part of (*math*). — *adj* (*math*) describing a mapping of one set to a second set, involving only some of the elements of the latter. [**in** and **to**.]

intolerable *in-tol'ə-rə-bl*, *adj* not to be endured. — *n* **intolerabil'ity** or **intol'erableness**. — *adv* **intol'erably**. — *n* **intol'erance** the state of being intolerant. — *adj* **intol'erant** not able or willing to endure; not tolerating difference of opinion; persecuting. — *adv* **intol'erantly**. [**in-** (2).]

intonate *in'tə-nāt*, *vt* and *vi* to intone. — *n* **intonā'tion** modulation or rise and fall in pitch of the voice; the opening phrase of any plainsong melody, sung usually either by the officiating priest alone, or by one or more selected choristers; pitching of musical notes; intoning. — *vt* and *vi* **intone** (*in-tōn'*) to chant, read or utter in musical tones, singsong or monotone; to begin by singing the opening phrase; to utter with a particular intonation. [L.L. *intonāre*, *-ātum* — L. *in*, in, *tonus*, tone.]

in toto *in tō'tō*, (L.) entirely.

intoxicate *in-tok'si-kāt*, *vt* to make drunk; to excite to enthusiasm or madness; to elate excessively. — *adj* **intox'icant** intoxicating. — *n* an intoxicating agent. — *adj* **intox'icāting**. — *n* **intoxicā'tion** the state of being drunk; high excitement or elation. [L.L. *intoxicāre*, *-ātum* — *in*, in, *toxicum* — Gr. *toxikon*, arrow-poison — *toxon*, a bow.]

Intoximeter® *in-tok'si-mē-tər*, *n* a device for assessing the amount of alcohol in the blood of a person who breathes into it, and showing this on a printout. — Also without *cap*.

intra *in'trə* or *in'trä*, (L.) within. — **intra muros** (*mū'rōs*) within the wall; **intra vires** (*vē'rāz*) within the legal power of.

intra- *in'trä-* or *-trə-*, *pfx* signifying within, as in **intra-abdom'inal** situated within the cavity of the abdomen. — *adj* **intramū'ral** within walls; included within the college. — *adj* **intramus'cular** within, or introduced into, a muscle. — *adv* **intramus'cularly**. — *adj* **intravē'nous** within, or introduced into, a vein. [L. *intrā*, within.]

intractable *in-trak'tə-bl*, *adj* unmanageable; obstinate. — *n* **intractabil'ity** or **intract'ableness**. — *adv* **intract'ably**. [**in-** (2).]

intrados *in-trā'dos*, (*archit*) *n* the under surface of an arch or vault: — *pl* **intra'dos** or **intra'doses**. [Fr., — L. *intrā*, within, *dorsum*, the back.]

intramural, intramuscular. See under **intra-**.

in trans. *abbrev* for *in transitu* (L.), in transit.

intrans. *abbrev* for intransitive.

intransigent *in-tran'si-jənt*, *adj* refusing to come to any understanding, irreconcilable; obstinate. — *n* an intransigent person. — *n* **intran'sigence** or **intran'sigency**. [Fr. *intransigeant* — Sp. *intransigente* — L. *in-*, not, *transigēns*, *-entis*, pres. p. of *transigĕre*, to transact; see **transact**.]

intransitive *in-tran'si-tiv*, *adj* representing action confined to the agent, i.e. having no object (*gram*). — *adv* **intran'sitively**. [**in-** (2).]

intransmissible *in-trans-mis'i-bl*, *adj* that cannot be transmitted. [**in-** (2).]

intransmutable *in-trans-mū'tə-bl*, *adj* that cannot be changed into another substance. — *n* **intransmutabil'ity**. [**in-** (2).]

intrapreneur *in-trə-prə-nœr'*, *n* a person who initiates commercial ventures within a large organisation. — *adj* **intrapreneu'rial**. [**intra-** and **entrepreneur**.]

intrauterine *in-trə-ū'tə-rīn, adj* within the uterus. — **intrauterine device** a contraceptive device fitted in the uterus. [**intra-**.]

intravenous. See under **intra-**.

intrench, intrenchment. See **entrench**.

intrepid *in-trep'id, adj* without trepidation or fear; bold; brave. — *n* **intrepid'ity** firm, unshaken courage; daring. — *adv* **intrep'idly**. [L. *intrepidus* — *in-*, not, *trepidus*, alarmed.]

intricate *in'tri-kit, adj* involved; entangled; complex. — *n* **in'tricacy** (*-kə-si*) or **in'tricateness**. — *adv* **in'tricately**. [L. *intrīcātus* — *in-*, in, *trīcāre*, to make difficulties — *trīcae*, hindrances.]

intrigue *in-trēg'* or *in'trēg, n* indirect or underhand scheming or plot; a private scheme; the plot of a play or romance; a secret illicit love affair. — *vi* (*in-trēg'*) to engage in intrigue. — *vt* to puzzle, to fascinate. — *n* **intrigu'er**. — *adj* **intrigu'ing**. — *adv* **intrigu'ingly**. [Fr.; see **intricate**.]

intrinsic *in-trin'sik* or **intrin'sical** *-kəl, adj* inward; genuine; inherent; essential, belonging to the point at issue; (of muscles) entirely contained within the limb and girdle. — *adv* **intrin'sically**. [Fr. *intrinsèque* — L. *intrīnsecus* — *intrā*, within, sfx. *-in*, *secus*, following.]

intro *in'trō*, (*colloq*) *n* an introduction, esp. the opening passage of a jazz or popular music piece: — *pl* **in'tros**.

intro- *in-trō-* or *in-tro'-*, *pfx* within, into. [L. *intrō*.]

introd. *abbrev* for introduction.

introduce *in-trə-dūs', vt* to lead or bring in; to conduct into a place; formally to make known or acquainted; to bring into notice or practice; to preface. — *n* **introduc'er**. — *adj* **introduc'ible**. — *n* **introduction** (*-duk'shən*) the act of introducing; formal presentation; preliminary matter to a book; a preliminary passage or section leading up to a movement (*mus*); a treatise introductory to a science or course of study; something introduced. — *adv* **introduc'torily**. — *adj* **introduc'tory** serving to introduce; preliminary; prefatory. [L. *intrōdūcěre*, to bring in.]

introit *in'troit, n* the anthem sung at the beginning of Mass, immediately after the *Confiteor*, and when the priest has ascended to the altar (*RC*); in other churches, an introductory hymn, psalm or anthem. [L. *introïtus* — *introīre*, to go in.]

introjection *in-trə-jek'shən, n* the taking into the self of persons or things from the outer world so as to experience a oneness with them and to feel personally touched by their fate. — *vt* and *vi* **introject'**. [L. *intrō*, within, *jacěre*, to throw.]

intromit *in-trə-mit', vt* to admit; to insert. — *vi* to have dealings (*Scots law*); to interfere, esp. with the effects of another (esp. *Scots law*): — *pr p* **intromitt'ing**; *pa t* and *pa p* **intromitt'ed**. — *n* **intromission** (*-mish'ən*). — *adj* **intromiss'ive** pertaining to intromission; intromitting. — *adj* **intromitt'ent** intromitting; adapted for insertion, esp. (*zool*) in copulation. — *n* **intromitt'er**. [L. *intrō*, inward, *mittěre*, *missum*, to send.]

intron *in'tron*, (*biol*) *n* any of the segments of a eukaryotic gene that do not carry coded information for the synthesis of proteins (compare **exon²**). — Also known as **intervening sequence**. [Perh. *intervening sequence and -on* as in **codon** and **exon**.]

introrse *in-trörs', adj* turned or facing inward; (of an anther) opening towards the centre of the flower. — *adv* **introrse'ly**. [L. *introrsus*, toward the middle, inward — *intrō*, inward, *versus* — *vertěre*, to turn.]

introspection *in-trə-spek'shən, n* the observation and analysis of the processes of one's own mind. — *vi* **intrōspect'** to practise introspection. — *n* **introspec'tionist**. — *adj* **introspec'tive**. [L. *intrō*, within, *specěre*, to look at.]

introvert *in-trə-vûrt', vt* to turn inwards; to turn in upon itself; to turn inside out; to withdraw part within the rest of. — *n* (*in'*) anything introverted; a person interested mainly in his or her own inner states and processes (opp. to *extrovert* (*extravert*); *psychol*). — *adj* **introver'sible**. — *n* **introver'sion** (*-shən*). — *adj* **introver'sive** or **introver'tive**. [L. *intrō*, inwards, *vertěre*, *versus*, to turn.]

intrude *in-trood', vi* to thrust oneself in; to enter uninvited or unwelcome. — *vt* to force in. — *n* **intru'der** a person who or thing which intrudes; a military aircraft which raids enemy territory alone; a person who enters premises secretly or by force, with criminal intentions. — *n* **intrusion** (*-troo'zhən*) (an) act of intruding; encroachment; an injection of rock in a molten state among and through existing rocks; a mass so injected. — *adj* **intru'sive** (*-siv*) tending or apt to intrude; intruded; (of a speech element) inserted without etymological justification; entering without welcome or right; (of a rock) which has been forced while molten into cracks and fissures in other rocks. — *n* an intrusive rock. — *adv* **intru'sively**. — *n* **intru'siveness**. [L. *in*, in, *trūdere*, *trūsum*, to thrust.]

intrust. A variant of **entrust**.

intubate *in'tū-bāt, vt* to insert a tube in; to treat by insertion of a tube into, e.g. the larynx (*med*). — *n* **intūbā'tion** insertion of a tube. [L. *in*, in, *tubus*, a tube.]

intuition *in-tū-i'shən, n* the power of the mind by which it immediately perceives the truth of things without reasoning or analysis; immediate, instinctive knowledge or belief. — *vt* and *vi* **intuit** (*in-tū'it*) to know intuitively. — *adj* **intu'ited**. — *adj* **intuitional** (*-i'shə-nəl*). — *n* **intui'tionalism** or **intui'tionism** the doctrine that the perception of truth is by intuition; a philosophical system which stresses intuition and mysticism as opposed to the idea of a logical universe. — *n* **intui'tionalist** or **intui'tionist**. — *adj* **intu'itive** perceived or perceiving by intuition; received or known by simple inspection and direct apprehension. — *adv* **intu'itively**. — *n* **intu'itivism**. [L. *in*, into or upon, *tuērī*, *tuitus*, to look.]

intumesce *in-tū-mes', vi* to swell up. — *n* **intumesc'ence**. — *adj* **intumesc'ent**. [L. *in*, in, *tumēscěre*, to swell.]

intussusception *in-təs-sə-sep'shən, n* the passing of part of a tube (esp. the intestine) within the adjacent part (*med*); growth by intercalation of particles. [L. *intus*, within, *susceptiō*, *-ōnis* — *suscipěre*, to take up.]

Inuit. See **Innuit**.

Inuktitut *i-nook'ti-toot, n* the Innuit language. [See **Innuit**.]

inunction *in-ungk'shən, n* anointing; smearing or rubbing with an ointment or liniment. [L. *inunctiō*, *-ōnis* — *inunguěre*, to anoint.]

inundate *in'ən-dāt, vt* (of water) to flow upon or over in waves; to flood; to overwhelm, swamp. — *n* **inundā'tion**. [L. *inundāre*, to flow over — *unda*, a wave.]

inure *in-ūr', vt* to accustom; to habituate; to harden. — *vi* (*law*) to come into use or effect. — *n* **inure'ment**. [**in-** (1) and *ure*, an old word for use, operation.]

in utero *in ū'tə-rō*, (L.) in the womb.

inv. *abbrev* for: *invenit* (L.), designed it; invented; invoice.

in vacuo *in vak'ū-ō*, (L.) in a vacuum; unrelated to a context, without specific application.

invade *in-vād', vt* to enter by military force; to attack; to encroach upon; to violate; to overrun; to enter; to penetrate; to rush into. — *n* **inva'der**. [L. *invāděre* — *in*, in, *vāděre*, to go.]

invaginate *in-vaj'i-nāt, vt* to ensheath; to push or withdraw within, introvert. — *vi* to be introverted; to form a hollow ingrowth. — *n* **invaginā'tion**. [**in-** (1) and L. *vāgīna*, a sheath.]

invalid *in-val'id, adj* without validity, efficacy, weight or cogency; having no effect; void; null; (*in'və-lid* or *-lēd*) disabled through injury or chronic sickness; (*in'*) suitable for invalids. — *n* (*in'və-lid* or *-lēd*) a feeble, sickly or disabled person; someone disabled for active service, esp. a soldier or sailor. — *vt* (*in'və-lid* or *-lēd*) to disable or affect with disease; to enrol or discharge as an invalid. — *vt* **invalidate** (*in-val'i-dāt*) to make not valid or ineffective. — *n* **invalidā'tion**. — *n* **in'validing** the sending or return home, or to a more healthy climate, of those rendered incapable of active duty by wounds, sickness, etc. — *n* **invalid'ity** the state of being an invalid; lack of validity. — *adv* **inval'idly**. — *n* **inval'idness** lack of cogency or force. — **invalidity benefit** an allowance paid by the government to someone who has been unable to work through illness for more than 28 weeks. [**in-** (2).]

invaluable *in-val'ū-ə-bl, adj* that cannot have a value set upon it; priceless. — *adv* **inval'uably**. [**in-** (2).]

Invar® *in'vär* or *in-vär', n* an alloy of iron, nickel and carbon, very slightly expanded by heat, used in the making of scientific instruments. [From **invariable**.]

invariable *in-vā'ri-ə-bl, adj* not variable; without alteration or change; unalterable; constantly in the same state. — *n* **invāriabil'ity** or **invā'riableness**. — *adv* **invā'riably**. — *n* **invar'iance** invariableness; the theory of the constancy of physical laws. — *n* **invā'riant** that which does not change; an expression or quantity that is unaltered by a particular procedure (*math*). — Also *adj*. [**in-** (2).]

invasion *in-vā'zhən, n* the act of invading; an attack; incursion; an attack on the rights of another; encroachment; penetration; a violation. — *adj* **invasive** (*-vā'siv*) invading; aggressive; encroaching; infringing another's rights; entering, penetrating. [Ety. as for **invade**.]

invective *in-vek'tiv, n* severe or reproachful accusation or denunciation; an attack with words; abusive language; sarcasm or satire. — *adj* sarcastic; abusive; satirical. [L. *invectīvus*, attacking — *invehi*, to assail; see **inveigh**.]

inveigh *in-vā', vi* to attack in speech or writing; to rail; to revile. [L. *invehi*, to assail, launch oneself at.]

inveigle *in-vē'gl* or *in-vā'gl, vt* to entice; to persuade by cajolery; to wheedle. — *n* **invei'glement**. — *n* **invei'gler**. [Prob. altered from A.Fr. *enveogler* (Fr. *aveugler*), to blind — L. *ab*, from, *oculus*, the eye.]

invent *in-vent', vt* to devise or contrive; to design for the first time, originate; to form or compose by imagination; to fabricate (something false). — *adj* **inven'tible**. — *n* **inven'tion** that which is invented; contrivance; a deceit; faculty or power of inventing; ability displayed by any invention or effort of the imagination; a short piece working out a single idea (*mus*). — *adj* **inven'tive** able to invent, devise or contrive; showing imaginative skill. — *adv* **inven'tively**. — *n* **inven'tiveness**. — *n* **inven'tor**, *fem* **inven'tress**. [L. *invenīre*, *inventum* — *in*, upon, *venīre*, to come.]

inventory *in'vən-tər-i, n* a list of articles comprised in an estate, etc.; a catalogue; stock, equipment; the total quantity of material in a nuclear reactor. — *vt* to make an inventory of; to amount to. — *adj* **inventō'rial**. [L.L. *inventōrium*, a list of things found — *invenīre*, to find.]

inverse *in'vûrs* or *in-vûrs', adj* inverted; upside down; in the reverse or contrary order; opposite; related by inversion. — *n* an inverted state; the result of inversion; a direct opposite. — *adv* **inversely**. — *n* **inver'sion** (*-shən*) the act of inverting; the state of being inverted; a change or reversal of order or position; that which is got by inverting. — *adj* **inver'sive**. — **inverse proportion** (*math*) a process by which one quantity decreases while another increases, their product remaining constant; **inverse ratio** the ratio of reciprocals. [L. *inversus*, past p. of *invertěre*, *inversum* — *in*, in, *vertěre*, to turn.]

invert *in-vûrt', vt* to turn in or about; to turn upside down; to reverse; to change the customary order or position of; to form the inverse of; to change by placing the lowest note an octave higher (*mus*); to modify by reversing the direction of motion; to break up (cane-sugar) into dextrose and laevulose. — *n* (*in'*) inverted sugar; a homosexual. — *n* **in'vertase** (or *-vûr'*) an enzyme that inverts cane-sugar. — *adj* **inver'ted** turned inwards; upside down; reversed; pronounced with tip of tongue turned up and back. — *adv* **inver'tedly**. — *n* **inver'ter** or **inver'tor**. [L. *invertěre* — *in*, in, *vertěre*, to turn.]

invertebrate *in-vûr'ti-brit* or *-brāt, adj* without a vertebral column or backbone. — *n* a member of the Invertebrata. — *npl* **Invertebrā'ta** all animals other than vertebrates. [**in-** (2).]

invest *in-vest', vt* to clothe with the insignia of office; to place in office or authority (with *with* or *in*); to give rights, privileges or duties to; to adorn; to lay out for profit, e.g. by buying property, shares, etc.; to expend time and effort in doing something. — *vi* (*colloq*) to make a purchase (with *in*). — *adj* **inves'titive**. — *n* **inves'titure** the ceremony of investing. — *n* **invest'ment** the act of investing; investiture; any placing of money to secure income or profit; that in which money is invested. — *n* **inves'tor** a person who invests, esp. money. — **investment trust** see under **trust**. [L. *investīre*, *-ītum* — *in*, on, *vestīre*, to clothe.]

investigate *in-ves'ti-gāt, vt* to search or inquire into with care and accuracy. — *vi* to make investigation. — *adj* **inves'tigable** able to be investigated. — *n* **investigā'tion** the act of examining; research. — *adj* **inves'tigātive** or **inves'tigātory**. — *n* **inves'tigātor**. — **investigative journalism** journalism involving the investigation and exposure of corruption, crime, inefficiency, etc. [L. *investīgāre*, *-ātum* — *in*, in, *vestīgāre*, to track.]

inveterate *in-vet'ə-rit, adj* firmly established by long continuance; deep-rooted, confirmed in any habit; stubborn; rootedly hostile. — *adv* **invet'erately**. — *n* **invet'erateness** or **invet'eracy** (*-rə-si*). [L. *inveterātus*, stored up, long continued — *in*, in, *vetus*, *veteris*, old.]

invidious *in-vid'i-əs, adj* likely to incur or provoke ill-will; likely to excite envy, enviable; offensively discriminating. — *adv* **invid'iously**. — *n* **invid'iousness**. [L. *invidiōsus* — *invidia*, envy.]

invigilate *in-vij'i-lāt, vt* and *vi* to supervise, esp. at examinations. — *n* **invigilā'tion**. — *n* **invig'ilātor**. [L. *in*, on, *vigilāre*, *-ātum*, to watch.]

invigorate *in-vig'ə-rāt, vt* to give vigour to; to strengthen; to animate. — *n* **invig'orant** an invigorating agent. — *n* **invigorā'tion**. — *n* **invig'orātor**. [**in-** (1).]

invincible *in-vin'si-bl, adj* that cannot be overcome; insuperable. — *n* **invin'cibleness** or **invincibil'ity**. — *adv* **invin'cibly**. [**in-** (2).]

inviolable *in-vī'ə-lə-bl, adj* that must not be profaned; that cannot be injured. — *n* **invīolabil'ity** or **invī'olableness** the quality of being inviolable. — *adv* **invī'olably**. — *adj* **invī'olate** (*-lit* or *-lāt*) not violated; unprofaned; uninjured. — *adv* **invī'olately**. — *n* **invī'olateness**. [**in-** (2).]

invisible *in-viz'i-bl, adj* incapable of being seen; unseen; relating to services rather than goods (*econ*); not shown in regular statements, as in *invisible assets* (see under **export** and **import**; *finance*). — *n* an invisible export, etc.; (in *pl*) invisible imports and exports collectively. — *n* **invisibil'ity** or **invis'ibleness**. — *adv* **invis'ibly**. — **invisible earnings** profits from invisibles, esp. invisible exports. [**in-** (2).]

invite *in-vīt', vt* to ask hospitably or politely to come; to express affable willingness to receive or to have done; to request formally or publicly; to encourage or tend to bring on; to offer inducement; to attract. — *n* (*in'*) (*colloq*) an invitation. — *n* **invitation** (*in-vi-tā'shən*) the act of inviting; a request or solicitation; the written or verbal form with which a person is invited; an enticement; the brief exhortation introducing the confession in the Anglican communion office. — *adj* **invī'ting** alluring; attractive. — *adv* **invī'tingly**. — *n* **invī'tingness** attractiveness. [L. *invītāre*, to invite.]

in vitro *in vē'trō*, (L.) in glass; in the test tube (opp. to **in vivo**).

in vivo *in vē'vō*, (L.) in the living organism.

invocation *in-və-kā'shən*, *n* the act or the form of invoking or addressing in prayer or supplication; an appellation under which a divinity, etc. is invoked; any formal invoking of the blessing or help of a god, a saint, etc.; an opening prayer in a public religious service or in the Litany (*eccles*); a call for inspiration from a Muse or other deity as at the beginning of a poem; an incantation or calling up of a spirit; a call or summons, esp. for evidence from another case (*law*). — *adj* **invocatory** (*in-vok'ə-tə-ri*) making invocation. [L. *invocātio* — *invocāre*, to invoke.]

invoice *in'vois*, *n* a letter of advice of the despatch of goods, with particulars of their price and quantity. — *vt* to list (goods) on an invoice; to send an invoice to (a customer). [Prob. pl. of Fr. *envoi*.]

invoke *in-vōk'*, *vt* to call upon earnestly or solemnly; to implore the assistance of; to address in prayer; to conjure up; to resort to. [Fr. *invoquer* — L. *invocāre* — *in*, on, *vocāre*, to call.]

involucre *in'və-lū-kər* or **involucrum** *-lū'krəm*, *n* an envelope (*anat*); a ring or crowd of bracts around a capitulum, umbel, etc. (*bot*). — *adj* **involu'cral** of the nature of, pertaining to, an involucre. — *adj* **involu'crate** having an involucre. [L. *involūcrum* — *involvĕre*, to involve.]

involuntary *in-vol'ən-tə-ri*, *adj* not voluntary; not having the power of will or choice; not under control of the will; not done voluntarily. — *adv* **invol'untarily**. — **invol'untariness**. [**in-** (2).]

involution *in-və-lū'shən* or *-lo͞o'*, *n* the state of being involved or entangled; complicated grammatical construction; raising to a power (*math*); degeneration; shrinking or return to normal size (*physiol*). — *adj* **involu'tional**. [See ety. for **involve**.]

involve *in-volv'*, *vt* to entangle; to complicate; to implicate; to comprehend; to entail or imply, bring as a consequence; to be bound up with; to concern; to raise to a power (*math*); to make (oneself) emotionally concerned (in, with); to engage the emotional interest of. — *n* **involve'ment**. [L. *involvĕre* — *in*, in, *volvĕre*, *volūtum*, to roll.]

invulnerable *in-vul'nə-rə-bl*, *adj* that cannot be wounded; not vulnerable. — *n* **invulnerabil'ity** or **invul'nerableness**. — *adv* **invul'nerably**. [**in-** (2).]

inward *in'wərd*, *adj* placed or being within; internal; seated in the mind or soul, not perceptible to the senses. — *adv* toward the interior; into the mind or thoughts. — *adv* **in'wardly** within; in the heart; privately; toward the centre. — *adv* **in'wards** same as **inward**. [O.E. *inneweard* (adv.).]

IOB *abbrev* for Institute of Building.

IOC *abbrev* for International Olympic Committee.

iodine *ī'ə-dēn*, *n* a halogen element (symbol **I**; atomic no. 53) giving a violet-coloured vapour. — *n* **i'odate** a salt of iodic acid. — *adj* **iodic** (*ī-od'ik*) pertaining to or caused by iodine. — *n* **i'odīde** a salt of hydriodic acid. — *vt* **i'odise** or **-ize** to treat with iodine. — *n* **iodoform** (*ī-od'* or *-ō'də-fōrm*) a lemon-yellow crystalline compound of iodine with a saffron-like odour, used as an antiseptic. [Gr. *ĭoeidēs*, violet-coloured — *ion*, a violet, *eidos*, form.]

IoJ *abbrev* for Institute of Journalists.

IOM *abbrev* for Isle of Man.

ion *ī'ən* or *ī'on*, *n* an electrically charged particle formed by the loss or gain of electrons by an atom, effecting by its migration the transport of electricity. — **ion exchange** transfer of ions from a solution to a solid or another liquid, used in water-softening and many industrial processes; **ion implantation** the introduction of ions into a crystalline material by subjecting the material to bombardment with a stream of ions — an important element in the production of integrated circuits. [Gr. *ĭōn*, neut. pres. p. of *ienai*, to go.]

Ionian *ī-ō'ni-ən*, *adj* Ionic; of or relating to an area off the west coast of Greece, as in *Ionian Islands*, *Ionian Sea*. — *n* an Ionic Greek. [Gr. *Iōnios*.]

Ionic *ī-on'ik*, *adj* relating to the Ionians, one of the main divisions of the ancient Greeks, to their dialect, to Ionia, the coastal district of Asia Minor settled by them, or to a style of Greek architecture characterised by the volute of its capital. — *n* the **Ionic dialect**, the most important of the three main branches of the ancient Greek language (Ionic, Doric, Aeolic), the language of Homer and Herodotus, of which Attic is a development. [Gr. *Iōnikos*.]

ionic *ī-on'ik*, *adj* of or relating to ions. — **ionic bond** a bond within a chemical compound achieved by transfer of electrons, the resulting ions being held together by electrostatic attraction.

ionise or **ionize** *ī'ə-nīz*, *vt* to produce ions in; to turn into ions. — *n* **ionīsā'tion** or **-z-**. — **ionisation chamber** an instrument used to detect and measure ionising radiation, consisting of an enclosure containing electrodes between which ionised gas is formed. [**ion**.]

iono- *ī-on-ə-*, *combining form* denoting ion. — *n* **ion'omer** the product of ionic bonding action between long-chain molecules, characterised by toughness and high degree of transparency. — *n* **ion'opause** the region of the earth's atmosphere at the outer limit of the ionosphere. — *n* **ionophore** (*ī'ə-nə-fōr*) a chemical compound able to combine with an ion and enable it to pass through a cell membrane, etc. — *n* **ionophorē'sis** electrophoresis, esp. of small ions. — *n* **ion'osphere** the region of the upper atmosphere that includes the highly ionised Appleton and Kennelly-Heaviside layers. — *adj* **ionospher'ic**. [**ion**.]

iota *ī-ō'tə*, *n* the Greek letter *I*, *ι*, corresponding to I; a tiny amount, a jot. [Gr. *iōta*, the smallest letter in the alphabet, *I*, *ι*.]

IOU *ī-ō-ū'*, *n* a memorandum of debt given by a borrower, requiring no stamp, but a holograph, usually dated, and addressed to the lender; any similar document. [Pronunciation of *I owe you*.]

IOW *abbrev* for Isle of Wight.

IPA *abbrev* for: Institute of Practitioners in Advertising; International Phonetic Alphabet; International Phonetic Association; International Publishers' Association.

IPC *abbrev* for International Publishing Corporation.

IPCC *abbrev* for Intergovernmental Panel on Climate Change.

IPCS *abbrev* for Institution of Professional Civil Servants.

ipecacuanha *ip-i-kak-ū-an'ə* or **ipecac** *ip-i-kak'*, *n* the dried root of various South American plants, used as a purgative or emetic; a plant from which this is obtained, chiefly *Cephaelis* or *Uragoga* (family *Rubiaceae*). [Port. — Tupí.]

IPM *abbrev* for Institute of Personnel Management.

IPPF *abbrev* for International Planned Parenthood Federation.

ipse dixit *ip'sē dik'sit*, (L.) he himself said it; his unsupported word; a dogmatic pronouncement.

ipsissima verba *ip-sis'i-mə vûr'bə*, (L.) the very words used.

ipso facto *ip'sō fak'tō*, (L.) by that very fact; thereby.

IQ *abbrev* for Intelligence Quotient.
iq *abbrev* for *idem quod* (L.), the same as.
IQS *abbrev* for Institute of Quantity Surveyors.
IR *abbrev* for: Inland Revenue; Iran (I.V.R.); Irish.
Ir. *abbrev* for Irish.
Ir (*chem*) *symbol* for iridium.
ir *abbrev* for infrared.
ir- *ir-*, *pfx* same as **in-**, the form used with words beginning with *r*, as in *irradiate*.
IRA *abbrev* for Irish Republican Army.
Iranian *i-rā'ni-ən, ī-* or *i-rä'ni-ən, n* a native or inhabitant of Iran; the modern Persian language; the branch of Indo-European which includes Persian. — *adj* of or relating to Iran, its people or language; of or relating to this branch of Indo-European. [Pers. *Īrān.*]
Iraqi *i-rä'ki, n* a native of Iraq; the form of Arabic spoken in Iraq. — *adj* pertaining to the country of Iraq, its inhabitants or language. [Ar. *'Irāqī.*]
irascible *i-ras'i-bl, adj* quick-tempered; irritable. — *n* **irascibil'ity**. — *adv* **irasc'ibly**. [Fr., — L. *īrāscibilis* — *īrāscī*, to be angry — *īra*, anger.]
irate *ī-rāt'*, *adj* enraged, angry. — *adv* **irate'ly**. [**ire**.]
IRBM *abbrev* for intermediate range ballistic missile.
ire *īr, n* anger; rage; keen resentment. [L. *īra*, anger.]
irenic *ī-rē'nik* or *-ren'*, or **irenical** *ī-ren'i-kəl, adj* tending to create peace; pacific. — *adv* **iren'ically**. — *n* **iren'icism**. — *nsing* **iren'ics** irenical theology (promoting peace between Christian churches; opp. to *polemics*). [Gr. *eirēnē*, peace.]
irid- *i-rid-* or **irido-** *-dō-, -də-* or *-do'*, also *ī-*, *combining form* denoting the iris (of the eye). — *n* **iridec'tomy** surgical removal of part of the iris. — *n* **iriditis** (*-ī'tis*) inflammation of the iris. — *n* **iridodiagnos'tics** or **iridol'ogy** diagnosis by examination of the iris. — *n* **iridol'ogist**. — *n* **irido-t'omy** surgical incision into the iris. [See **iris**.]
iridescence *ir-i-des'əns, n* play of rainbow colours, e.g. on bubbles, mother-of-pearl, etc. — *adj* **iridesc'ent** glittering with changing colours. — *adv* **iridesc'ently**. [Ety. as for **iris**.]
iridic *ī-rid'ik* or *i-, adj* containing or consisting of iridium; of or relating to the iris of the eye. [Ety. as for **iris**.]
iridium *ī-rid'i-əm* or *i-, n* a very heavy steel-grey metallic element (symbol **Ir**; atomic no. 77) with a very high melting-point and resistance to corrosion. [Ety. as for **iris**.]
iridosmine *ir-i-doz'min* or *ī-*, or **iridosmium** *-doz'mi-əm, n* a native alloy of iridium and osmium used for pen-points, also called *osmiridium*.
iris *ī'ris, n* the coloured diaphragm surrounding the pupil of the eye; a plant of the genus *Iris* with tuberous roots, long tapering leaves and large showy flowers: — *pl* **irides** (*ī'ri-dēz* or *ir'-*) or **ī'rises**. — **iris diaphragm** an adjustable stop for a lens, giving a continuously variable hole. [Gr. *īris, -dos*, the rainbow goddess.]
Irish *ī'rish, adj* relating to, produced in, derived from, or characteristic of, Ireland; self-contradictory, ludicrously inconsistent (as Irish thought and speech is traditionally supposed to be; *facetious*, rather *derog*). — *n* the Celtic language of Ireland; an Irish commodity, esp. whiskey; (as *pl*) the natives or people of Ireland. — *n* **I'rishism** an Irish phrase, idiom or characteristic, esp. an apparently nonsensical one. — *n* **I'rishman**, *fem* **I'rishwoman**. — **Irish coffee** a beverage made of sweetened coffee and Irish whiskey and topped with cream; **Irish elk** see under **elk**; **Irish Guards** a regiment formed in 1900 to represent Ireland in the Foot Guards; **Irish moss** carrageen; **Irish Republican Army** a militant organisation seeking to bring about union between the Republic of Ireland and Northern Ireland, and independence from Britain; **Irish stew** mutton, onions and potatoes stewed with flour; **Irish terrier** a breed of dog with a rough, wiry, reddish-brown coat.
irk *ûrk, vt* (now usu. used impersonally) to weary; to disgust; to distress; to annoy, gall. — *adj* **irk'some** tedious; burdensome. — *adv* **irk'somely**. — *n* **irk'someness**. [M.E. *irken*.]
IRL *abbrev* for Ireland (I.V.R.).
IRO *abbrev* for Inland Revenue Office.
iroko *i-rō'kō, n* either of the two timber trees of the genus *Chlorophora* of central and western Africa; the hard wood of these trees, often used as a substitute for teak: — *pl* **irō'kos**. [Yoruba.]
iron *ī'ərn, n* an element (symbol **Fe**; atomic no. 26), the most widely used of all the metals; a weapon, instrument or utensil made of iron; an appliance for smoothing cloth; a pistol or revolver (*slang*); a golf club with an iron head; strength; a medicinal preparation of iron; (in *pl*) fetters, chains; a stirrup. — *adj* formed of iron; resembling iron; not to be broken; robust; insensitive; inflexible. — *vt* to smooth with an iron; to arm with iron; to fetter; to smooth, clear up (with *out*). — *n* **i'roner** a person who irons; an iron for pressing clothes. — *n* **i'roning** the act or process of smoothing with hot irons; clothes etc. that are to be, or have been, ironed. — *adj* **i'rony** (*ī'ər-ni*) made, consisting of, or rich in iron; like iron; hard. — **Iron Age** the stage of culture of a people using iron as the material for their tools and weapons (*archaeol*). — *adj* **i'ron-clad** clad in iron; covered or protected with iron. — **i'ron-clay** clay ironstone; **Iron Cross** a Prussian war medal instituted in 1813, revived in 1870 and 1914 and reinstated by Hitler as a German war medal in 1939; **iron curtain** an impenetrable barrier to observation or communication, esp. (with *caps*), in the mid to late 20th cent., between communist Russia with its satellites and the West; **i'ron-founder** a person who founds or makes castings in iron; **i'ron-foundry**. — *adj* **iron-gray'** or **-grey'** of a grey colour like that of iron freshly cut or broken. — *n* this colour. — **iron hand** strict, despotic control (the iron hand is sometimes hidden in the *velvet glove*, q.v.). — *adj* **iron-hand'ed**. — **i'roning-board** a smooth board covered with cloth, usu. on a stand, on which clothes, etc. are ironed; **iron lung** an apparatus consisting of a chamber that encloses a patient's chest, the air pressure within the chamber being varied rhythmically so that air is forced into and out of the lungs; **iron man** a man of extraordinary strength (esp. *Austr*); (the winner of) a test of endurance at a surf carnival, comprising swimming, surfing and running events (*Austr*); **i'ronmaster** a proprietor of ironworks; **i'ronmonger** a dealer in ironmongery or (*loosely*) in household goods and equipment generally; **i'ronmongery** articles made of iron; domestic hardware; **iron ore**; **iron pyrites** common pyrites, sulphide of iron; **iron ration** a ration of concentrated food, esp. for an extreme emergency; **I'ronside** or **I'ronsides** a nickname for a man of iron resolution (e.g. Oliver Cromwell); a Puritan; (in *pl*) a name given to Cromwell's cavalry; **i'ronstone** any iron ore, esp. carbonate; **i'ronware** wares or goods of iron. — *adj* **iron-willed'** firmly determined. — **i'ronwood** timber of great hardness, and many kinds of trees producing it; **i'ronwork** the parts of a building, etc., made of iron; anything of iron, esp. artistic work; (often in *pl*) an establishment where iron is smelted or made into heavy goods. — **rule with a rod of iron** to rule with stern severity; **strike while the iron is hot** to seize one's opportunity while the circumstances are favourable to one; **too many irons in the fire** too many things on hand at once. [O.E. *īren, īsern* or *īsen*.]
irony[1] *ī'rə-ni, n* conveyance of meaning (generally satirical) by words whose literal meaning is the opposite, esp. words of praise used as a criticism or condemnation; a situation or utterance (e.g. in a

tragedy) that has a significance unperceived at the time, or by the persons involved (cf. **dramatic irony** at **drama**); a condition in which one seems to be mocked by fate or the facts; orig. the Socratic method of discussion by professing ignorance. — *adj* **ironic** (*ī-ron'ik*) or **iron'ical.** — *adv* **iron'ically.** — *vt* and *vi* **i'ronise** or **-ize.** — *n* **i'ronist.** [L. *īrōnīa* — Gr. *eirōneiā*, dissimulation.]

irony[2]. See under **iron.**

Iroquoian *ir-ə-kwoi'ən, adj* of, or belonging to, the *Iroquois*, a confederation of American Indian tribes; of the group of languages spoken by these tribes. — Also *n.*

IRQ *abbrev* for Iraq (I.V.R.).

irradiate *i-rā'di-āt, vt* to shed light or other rays upon or into; to treat by exposure to rays; to light up; to brighten; to radiate. — *vi* to radiate; to shine. — *adj* adorned with rays of light or with lustre. — *n* **irra'diance** or **irra'diancy.** — *adj* **irra'diant.** — *n* **irradiā'tion** the act of irradiating; exposure to rays; that which is irradiated; brightness; apparent enlargement of a bright object by spreading of the excitation of the retina, or in a photograph by reflections within the emulsion; spread of a nervous impulse beyond the usual area affected; intellectual light. — *adj* **irra'diative.** [**ir-** (**in-** (1)).]

irrational *i-ra'shə-nəl, adj* not rational; not commensurable with natural numbers. — *n* an irrational being or number. — *vt* **irra'tionalise** or **-ize** to make irrational. — *n* **irra'tionalism** an irrational system; irrationality. — *n* **irra'tionalist.** — *adj* **irrationalist'ic.** — *n* **irrational'ity.** — *adv* **irra'tionally.** [**ir-** (**in-** (2)).]

irreclaimable *ir-i-klā'mə-bl, adj* that cannot be claimed back, brought into cultivation, or reformed; incorrigible. — *n* **irreclaimabil'ity** or **irreclaim'ableness.** — *adv* **irreclaim'ably.** [**ir-** (**in-** (2)).]

irreconcilable *i-rek-ən-sī'lə-bl* or *i-rek', adj* incapable of being brought back to a state of friendship or agreement; inconsistent. — *n* an irreconcilable opponent; an intransigent; any of two or more opinions, desires, etc. that cannot be reconciled. — *n* **irreconcīlabil'ity** or **irreconcī'lableness.** — *adv* **irreconcī'lably.** — *adj* **irrec'onciled** not reconciled; not brought into harmony. — *n* **irreconcile'ment.** [**ir-** (**in-** (2)).]

irrecoverable *ir-i-kuv'ə-rə-bl, adj* irretrievable; not reclaimable; beyond recovery. — *n* **irrecov'erableness.** — *adv* **irrecov'erably.** [**ir-** (**in-** (2)).]

irrecusable *ir-i-kū'zə-bl, adj* that cannot be rejected. — *adv* **irrecūs'ably.** [Fr. — L.L. *irrecūsābilis*.]

irredeemable *ir-i-dē'mə-bl, adj* not redeemable; not subject to be paid at the nominal value. — *n* **irredeemabil'ity** or **irredeem'ableness.** — *npl* **irredeem'ables** undated government or debenture stock. — *adv* **irredeem'ably.** [**ir-** (**in-** (2)).]

Irredentist *ir-i-den'tist, n* a member of an Italian party formed in 1878, its aims to gain or regain for Italy various regions claimed on language and other grounds; a person who makes similar claims for any nation (often without *cap*). — Also *adj.* — *n* **Irredent'ism** or **irredent'ism.** [It. (*Italia*) *irredenta*, unredeemed (Italy) — L. *in-*, not, *redemptus*, past p. of *redimĕre*, to redeem.]

irreducible *ir-i-dū'si-bl, adj* that cannot be reduced or brought from one degree, form, or state to another; not to be lessened; not to be overcome. — *n* **irredu'cibleness.** — *adv* **irredu'cibly.** — *n* **irreducibil'ity** or **irreductibility** (*-duk-ti-bil'i-ti*). [**ir-** (**in-** (2)).]

irrefragable *i-ref'rə-gə-bl, adj* that cannot be refuted; unanswerable. — *n* **irrefragabil'ity** or **irref'ragableness.** — *adv* **irref'ragably.** [L. *irrefrāgābilis* — *in-*, not, *re-*, backwards, *frangĕre*, to break.]

irrefutable *i-ref'ū-tə-bl*, also *ir-ə-fū'tə-bl, adj* that cannot be refuted. — *n* **irrefutabil'ity** or **irref'utableness** (or *-fū'*). — *adv* **irref'utably** (also *-fū'*). [**ir-** (**in-** (2)).]

irreg. *abbrev* for: irregular; irregularly.

irregular *i-reg'ū-lər, adj* not regular; not conforming to rule or to the ordinary rules; disorderly; uneven; unsymmetrical; variable; (of troops) not trained under the authority of a government; (of a marriage) not celebrated by a minister after proclamation of banns or of intention to marry. — *n* an irregular soldier. — *n* **irregularity** (*-lar'i-ti*) a rough place or bump on an even surface; an instance of action, behaviour, etc. not conforming to rules or regulations. — *adv* **irreg'ularly.** [**ir-** (**in-** (2)).]

irrelevant *i-rel'ə-vənt, adj* not relevant. — *n* **irrel'evance** or **irrel'evancy.** — *adv* **irrel'evantly.** [**ir-** (**in-** (2)).]

irreligious *ir-i-lij'əs, adj* destitute of religion; regardless of religion; opposed to religion; ungodly. — *n* **irrelig'ion** lack of religion; hostility to or disregard of religion. — *n* **irrelig'ionist.** — *adv* **irrelig'iously.** — *n* **irrelig'iousness.** [**ir-** (**in-** (2)).]

irremediable *ir-i-mē'di-ə-bl, adj* beyond remedy or redress. — *n* **irremē'diableness.** — *adv* **irremē'diably.** [**ir-** (**in-** (2)).]

irremissible *ir-i-mis'i-bl, adj* not to be remitted or forgiven. — *n* **irremissibil'ity** or **irremiss'ibleness.** — *n* **irremission** (*-mish'ən*). — *adj* **irremiss'ive** unremitting. [**ir-** (**in-** (2)).]

irreparable *i-rep'ə-rə-bl, adj* that cannot be made good or rectified; beyond repair. — *n* **irreparabil'ity** or **irrep'arableness.** — *adv* **irrep'arably.** [**ir-** (**in-** (2)).]

irreplaceable *ir-i-plās'ə-bl, adj* whose loss cannot be made good; without possible substitute. — *adv* **irreplace'ably.** [**ir-** (**in-** (2)).]

irrepressible *ir-i-pres'i-bl, adj* not to be put down or kept under. — *n* **irrepressibil'ity** or **irrepress'ibleness.** — *adv* **irrepress'ibly.** [**ir-** (**in-** (2)).]

irreproachable *ir-i-prōch'ə-bl, adj* free from blame; faultless. — *n* **irreproachabil'ity** or **irreproach'ableness.** — *adv* **irreproach'ably.** [**ir-** (**in-** (2)).]

irreprovable *ir-i-prōō'və-bl, adj* blameless. — *adv* **irreprov'ably.** [**ir-** (**in-** (2)).]

irresistance *ir-i-zis'təns, n* lack of resistance; passive submission. — *adj* **irresist'ible** not to be opposed with success; resistless; overpowering; overmastering; fascinating, enticing. — *n* **irresistibil'ity** or **irresist'ibleness.** — *adv* **irresist'ibly.** [**ir-** (**in-** (2)).]

irresoluble *i-rez'ə-lū-bl* or *-lə-bl, adj* that cannot be resolved into parts; that cannot be solved. — *n* **irresolubil'ity.** — *adv* **irres'olubly.** [**ir-** (**in-** (2)).]

irresolute *i-rez'ə-lūt* or *-lōōt, adj* not firm in purpose. — *adv* **irres'olutely.** — *n* **irres'oluteness** or **irresolution** (*-lū'shən* or *-lōō'shən*) lack of resolution. [**ir-** (**in-** (2)).]

irrespective *ir-i-spek'tiv, adj* not having regard (with *of*). — Also *adv.* — *adv* **irrespec'tively.** [**ir-** (**in-** (2)).]

irresponsible *ir-i-spon'si-bl, adj* not responsible; without sense of responsibility; free from feeling of responsibility, light-hearted, carefree; reprehensibly careless; done without feeling of responsibility. — *n* **irresponsibil'ity** or **irrespon'sibleness.** — *adv* **irrespon'sibly.** — *adj* **irrespon'sive** not responding; not readily responding. — *adv* **irrespon'sively.** — *n* **irrespon'siveness.** [**ir-** (**in-** (2)).]

irretrievable *ir-i-trē'və-bl, adj* not to be recovered; irreparable. — *n* **irretrievabil'ity** or **irretriev'ableness.** — *adv* **irretriev'ably.** [**ir-** (**in-** (2)).]

irreverent *i-rev'ə-rənt, adj* not reverent; proceeding from irreverence. — *n* **irrev'erence.** — *adj* **irreverential** (*-ren'shəl*). — *adv* **irrev'erently.** [**ir-** (**in-** (2)).]

irreversible *ir-i-vûr'si-bl, adj* not reversible; that cannot proceed in the opposite direction or in both directions; incapable of changing back; not alike both ways; that cannot be recalled or annulled; (involving damage which is) permanent (*med*). — *n* **irreversibil'ity** or **irrever'sibleness**. — *adv* **irrever'sibly**. [**ir-** (**in-** (2)).]

irrevocable *i-rev'ə-kə-bl, adj* that cannot be recalled or revoked. — *n* **irrevocabil'ity** or **irrev'ocableness**. — *adv* **irrev'ocably**. [**ir-** (**in-** (2)).]

irrigate *ir'i-gāt, vt* to wet or moisten; to water by means of canals or watercourses; to cause a stream of liquid to flow upon. — *n* **irrigā'tion**. — *adj* **irrigā'tional**. — *adj* **irr'igative**. — *n* **irr'igātor** someone who, or something which, irrigates; an appliance for washing a wound, etc. [L. *irrigāre, -ātum*, to water — *in*, upon, *rigāre*, to wet.]

irritate *ir'i-tāt, vt* to excite or stimulate; to rouse; to provoke; to make angry or fretful; to excite a painful, uncomfortable or unhealthy condition (e.g. heat and redness) in. — *n* **irritabil'ity** the quality of being easily irritated; the peculiar susceptibility to stimuli possessed by living matter. — *adj* **irr'itable** that may be irritated; easily annoyed; susceptible to excitement or irritation. — *n* **irr'itableness**. — *adv* **irr'itably**. — *n* **irr'itancy**. — *adj* **irr'itant** irritating. — *n* a person or thing which causes irritation. — *n* **irritā'tion** the act of irritating or exciting; anger, annoyance; stimulation; the term applied to any morbid excitement of the vital actions not amounting to inflammation, often, but not always, leading to that condition (*med*). — *adj* **irr'itātive** tending to irritate or excite; accompanied with or caused by irritation. — *n* **ir'ritātor**. [L. *irrītāre, -ātum*, to annoy, vex.]

irrupt *i-rupt', vi* to break in; to make irruption. — *n* **irruption** (*i-rup'shən*) a breaking or bursting in; a sudden invasion or incursion. — *adj* **irrup'tive** rushing suddenly in. — *adv* **irrup'tively**. [L. *irrumpĕre, irruptum* — *in*, in, *rumpĕre*, to break.]

IRS *abbrev* for the Internal Revenue Service (U.S.).

IS *abbrev* for: Iceland (I.V.R.); independent suspension (*mech*).

Is.[1] or **Isa.** (*Bible*) *abbrev* for (the Book of) Isaiah.

Is.[2] *abbrev* for Island(s) or Isle(s).

is *iz*, used as 3rd pers. sing. pres. indic. of **be**. [O.E. *is*.]

is-. See **iso-**.

isagogic *ī-sə-goj'ik* or *-gog'ik, adj* introductory. — *n* **isagoge** (*ī'sə-gō-ji* or *-gō'*) an academic introduction to a subject. — *nsing* **isagog'ics** that part of theological study introductory to exegesis. [Gr. *eisagōgē*, an introduction — *eis*, into, *agein*, to lead.]

ISBN *abbrev* for International Standard Book Number.

ISCh. *abbrev* for Incorporated Society of Chiropodists.

ischaemia or **ischemia** *i-skē'mi-ə, n* deficiency of blood in a part of the body. — *adj* **ischaem'ic** or **ischem'ic**. [Gr. *ischein*, to restrain, *haima*, blood.]

ischium *is'ki-əm, n* a posterior bone of the pelvic girdle: — *pl* **is'chia**. — *adj* **ischiad'ic, is'chial** or **ischiat'ic**. [Latinised from Gr. *ischion*, the hip-joint.]

ISD *abbrev* for international subscriber dialling.

ISDN *abbrev* for integrated services digital network, an advanced telecommunications network.

-ise or **-ize** *-īz, sfx* forming verbs from adjs., meaning to make, as in equal*ise*, or from nouns, as in botan*ise* or satir*ise*. [L. *-izāre*, from Gr. *-izein*; Fr. *-iser*.]

isenergic *ī-sə-nûr'jik*, (*phys*) *adj* denoting equal energy. [Gr. *isos*, equal, *energeia*, energy.]

isentropic *ī-sen-trop'ik*, (*phys*) *adj* of equal entropy. [Gr. *isos*, equal, *entropē*, a turning about — *en*, in, *trepein*, to turn.]

-ish *-ish, sfx* signifying: somewhat (as in brown*ish*, old*ish*), like or similar to; sometimes implying deprecation (as in outland*ish*, child*ish*); roughly, approximately, as in six*ish*. [O.E. *-isc*.]

isinglass *ī'zing-gläs, n* a material, mainly gelatine, obtained from sturgeons' air-bladders and other sources. [App. from obs. Du. *huizenblas* — *huizen*, a kind of sturgeon, *blas*, a bladder.]

ISIS *ī'sis, abbrev* for Independent Schools Information Service.

Isl. *abbrev* for Island.

Islam *iz'läm, is'* or *-läm'*, also **Is'lamism** (*-izm*) *n* the Muslim religion; the whole Muslim world. — *adj* **Islamic** (*-lam'ik*). — *adj* **Islamitic** (*-lə-mit'ik*). — *vt* **Islam'icise** or **-ize** to Islamise. — *n* **Islam'icist** a person who studies Islam, Islamic law, Islamic culture, etc. — *n* **Islamīsā'tion** or **-z-**. — *vt* and *vi* **Is'lamise** or **-ize** to convert or (cause to) conform to Islam. [Ar. *islām*, surrender (to God).]

island *ī'lənd, n* a mass of land (not a continent) surrounded with water; anything isolated, detached or surrounded by something of a different nature; a small raised traffic-free area in a street esp. for pedestrians; tissue or cells detached and differing from their surroundings. — *adj* of an island; forming an island. — *n* **islander** (*ī'lən-dər*) an inhabitant of an island. — **island universe** a spiral nebula regarded as forming a separate stellar system. — **islands of Langerhans** same as **islets of Langerhans**; **Islands of the Blest** in Greek mythology, the abode of the blessed dead, situated somewhere in the far west. [M.E. *iland* — O.E. *īegland, īgland, ēgland* — *īeg, īg, ēg*, island, and *land*; the *s* is due to confusion with *isle*.]

isle *īl, n* an island. — *n* **islet** (*ī'lit*) a little isle. — **isles'man** or **isle'man** an islander, esp. an inhabitant of the Hebrides. — **islets of Langerhans** (*läng'ər-häns*) groups of epithelial cells discovered by Paul *Langerhans*, a German anatomist (1847–88), in the pancreas, producing a secretion the lack of which causes diabetes. [M.E. *ile, yle* — O.Fr. *isle* (Fr. *île*) — L. *īnsula*.]

ism *izm, n* any distinctive doctrine, theory or practice — usually in disparagement. [From the sfx. **-ism**.]

-ism *-izm*, **-asm** *-azm*, or (with **-ic**) **-icism** *-i-sizm, sfx* forming abstract nouns signifying condition or system (as in ego*ism*, de*ism*, Calvin*ism*, pleon*asm*, Angl*icism*, witt*icism*). [L. *-ismus, -asmus* — Gr. *-ismos, -asmos*.]

Ismaili *is-mä-ē'lē*, or *is-mā'i-li, n* a member of a sect of Shiite Muslims whose imam or spiritual head is the Aga Khan. — Also *adj*. — *n* and *adj* **Ismailian** (*is-mā-il'i-ən* or *-mä-*). — *n* **Is'mailism**. — *adj* **Ismailit'ic**.

isn't *iz'ənt*, contraction for **is not**.

ISO *abbrev* for: Imperial Service Order; International Standards Organisation.

iso- *ī-sō-, ī-sə-* or *ī-so'-*, also **is-** *īs-, combining form* signifying equal; denoting an isomeric substance — e.g. **iso-oc'tane** one of the isomers of normal octane (*chem*). [Gr. *isos*, equal.]

isobar *ī'sō-bär, n* a curve running through places of equal pressure; esp. one connecting places, or their representations on a map, of equal barometric pressure (*meteorol*); (see **isobare**; *chem*). — *adj* **isobaric** (*-bar'ik*). — *adj* **isobaromet'ric**. [**iso-** and Gr. *baros*, weight.]

isobare *ī'sō-bār* or **isobar** *ī'sō-bär*, (*chem*) *n* either of two atoms of different chemical elements but of identical atomic mass (e.g. an isotope of titanium and an isotope of chromium both of atomic mass 50). [Same as **isobar** above.]

isobase *ī'sō-bās*, (*geol*) *n* a contour line of equal upheaval of the land. [**iso-** and Gr. *basis*, step.]

isocheim or **isochime** *ī'sō-kīm, n* a contour line of mean winter temperature. [**iso-** and Gr. *cheima*, winter weather.]

isochor or **isochore** *ī'sō-kör, n* a curve representing variation of some quantity under conditions of constant volume. — *adj* **isochoric** (*-kor'ik*). [**iso-** and Gr. *chōrā*, space.]

isochromatic *ī-sō-krō-mat'ik*, *adj* having the same colour (*optics*); orthochromatic (*phot*). [**iso-** and Gr. *chrōma*, *-atos*, colour.]

isochronal *ī-sok'rə-nəl* or **isochronous** *-sok'rə-nəs*, *adj* of equal time; performed in equal times; in regular periodicity. — *adv* **isoch'ronally** or **isoch'ronously**. — *n* **i'sochrone** a line on a chart or map joining points associated with a constant time difference, e.g. in reception of radio signals. — *vt* **isoch'ronise** or **-ize**. — *n* **isoch'ronism**. [**iso-** and Gr. *chronos*, time.]

isoclinal *ī-sō-klī'nəl*, *adj* folded with nearly the same dip in each limb (*geol*); in terrestrial magnetism, having the same magnetic dip. — *n* a contour line of magnetic dip. — *n* **ī'socline** an area of rock strata with isoclinal folds; an isoclinal. — *adj* and *n* **isoclinic** (*-klin'ik*) isoclinal. [**iso-** and Gr. *klīnein*, to bend.]

isocracy *ī-sok'rə-si*, *n* (a system of government in which all people have) equal political power. — *adj* **isocrat'ic**. [**iso-** and Gr. *krateein*, to rule.]

isocyclic *ī'sō-sī-klik*, *adj* homocyclic. [**iso-** and **cyclic**.]

isodiametric *ī-sō-dī-ə-met'rik* or **isodiametrical** *-met'ri-kəl*, *adj* of equal diameters; about as broad as long. [**iso-**.]

isodimorphism *ī-sō-dī-mör'fizm*, (*crystall*) *n* isomorphism between each of the two forms of a dimorphous substance and the corresponding forms of another dimorphous substance. — *adj* **isodimorph'ic**. — *adj* **isodimorph'ous**. [**iso-**.]

isodont *ī'sō-dont* or **isodontal** *-don'təl*, (*zool*) *adj* having all the teeth similar in size and form. — *n* an isodontal animal. [Gr. *isos*, equal, *odous*, *odontos*, tooth.]

isodynamic *ī-sō-dī-nam'ik* or *-di-*, *adj* of equal strength, esp. of magnetic intensity. — *n* an isodynamic line on the earth or the map, a contour line of magnetic intensity. [**iso-** and Gr. *dynamis*, strength.]

isoelectric *ī-sō-i-lek'trik*, *adj* having the same potential. [**iso-**.]

isoelectronic *ī-sō-el-ik-tron'ik*, *adj* having an equal number of electrons, or similar electron patterns. [**iso-**.]

isogeny *ī-soj'ə-ni*, *n* likeness of origin. — *adj* **isogenetic** (*ī-sō-ji-net'ik*). — *adj* **isog'enous**. [**iso-** and Gr. *genos*, kind.]

isogeotherm *ī-sō-jē'ō-thûrm*, *n* a subterranean contour of equal temperature. — *adj* **isogeotherm'al** or **isogeotherm'ic**. — *n* an isogeotherm. [**iso-** and Gr. *gē*, the earth, *thermē*, heat — *thermos*, hot.]

isogloss *ī'sō-glos*, *n* a line separating one region from another region which differs from it in a particular feature of dialect. — *adj* **isogloss'al**, **isoglott'al** or **isoglott'ic**. [**iso-** and Gr. *glōssa*, tongue.]

isogonic *ī-sō-gon'ik* or **isogonal** *ī-sog'ə-nəl*, *adj* of equal angles, esp. of magnetic declination. — *n* an isogonic line or contour line of magnetic declination. — *n* **i'sogon** an equiangular polygon. [**iso-** and Gr. *gōniā*, an angle.]

isogram *ī'sō-gram*, *n* a line drawn on a map or diagram showing all points which have an equal numerical value with respect to a given climatic or other variable. — See also **isopleth**. [**iso-** and Gr. *gramma*, a letter.]

isohel *ī'sō-hel*, *n* a contour line of equal amounts of sunshine. [**iso-** and Gr. *hēlios*, sun.]

isohyet *ī-sō-hī'ət*, *n* a contour line of equal rainfall. — *adj* **isohy'etal**. — *n* an isohyet. [**iso-** and Gr. *hyetos*, rain — *hyein*, to rain.]

isokinetic *ī-sō-ki-net'ik*, *adj* (of the withdrawal of a fluid sample) accomplished without disturbance to the speed and direction of flow. [**iso-** and Gr. *kīneein*, to move.]

isolate *ī'sə-lāt*, *vt* to place in a detached situation, like an island; to detach; to insulate; to separate (esp. those who might be infected) (*med*); to seclude; to segregate; to obtain in a pure, uncombined state; to establish a pure culture of (a micro-organism). — *n* (*-lit* or *-lāt*) something isolated, esp. for individual study or experiment. — Also *adj*. — *n* **isolabil'ity**. — *adj* **i'solable**. — *n* **isolā'tion**. — *n* **isolā'tionism** the policy of avoiding political entanglements with other countries. — *n* **isolā'tionist**. — *adj* **i'solātive**. — *n* **i'solātor**. — **isolating languages** those in which each word is a bare root, not inflected or compounded. [It. *isolare* — *isola* — L. *īnsula*, an island.]

isoleucine *ī-sō-lū'sīn*, *n* an essential amino acid. [**iso-**.]

isoline *ī'sō-līn*. Same as **isopleth**.

isomagnetic *ī-sō-mag-net'ik*, *adj* having equal magnetic induction or force. — *n* (also **isomagnetic line**) an imaginary line joining places at which the force of the earth's magnetic field is constant. [**iso-**.]

isomer *ī'sə-mər*, (*chem*) *n* a substance, radical, or ion isomeric with another; an atomic nucleus having the same atomic number and mass as another or others but a different energy state. — *n* **i'somēre** (*zool*) an organ or segment corresponding to or homologous with another. — *adj* **isomeric** (*-mer'ik*; *chem*) identical in percentage composition and molecular weight but different in constitution or the mode in which the atoms are arranged; (of nuclei) differing only in energy state and half-life. — *vt* and *vi* **isomerise** or **-ize** (*ī-som'ə-rīz*) to change into an isomer. — *n* **isomerīsā'tion** or **-z-**. — *n* **isom'erism** the property of being isomeric; the existence of isomers. — *adj* **isom'erous** (*bot*) having the same number of parts (esp. in floral whorls). [**iso-** and Gr. *meros*, part.]

isometric *ī-sō-met'rik*, or **isometrical** *-met'ri-kəl*, *adj* having equality of measure; pertaining to isometrics; having the plane of projection equally inclined to three perpendicular axes; of the cubic system, or referable to three equal axes at right angles to one another (*crystall*). — *n* **isomet'ric** (also **isometric line**) a line on a graph showing variations of pressure and temperature at a constant volume. — *adv* **isomet'rically**. — *nsing* **isomet'rics** a system of strengthening the muscles and tuning up the body by opposing one muscle to another or to a resistant object. — *n* **isom'etry** equality of measure. [**iso-** and Gr. *metron*, measure.]

isomorph *ī'sō-mörf*, *n* that which shows isomorphism. — *adj* **isomorph'ic** showing isomorphism. — *n* **isomorph'ism** similarity in unrelated forms (*biol*); close similarity in crystalline form combined with similar chemical constitution (*crystall*); a one-to-one correspondence between the elements of two or more sets and between the sums or products of the elements of one set and those of the equivalent elements of the other set or sets (*math*). — *adj* **isomorph'ous**. [**iso-** and Gr. *morphē*, form.]

isonomy *ī-son'ə-mi*, *n* equal law, rights or privileges. — *adj* **isonom'ic** or **ison'omous**. [Gr. *isonomiā* — *isos*, equal, *nomos*, law.]

isopleth *ī'sō-pleth*, *n* an isogram, esp. one on a graph showing variations of a climatic element as a function of two variables; cf. **nomogram**. [**iso-** and Gr. *plēthos*, great number.]

isopolity *ī-sō-pol'i-ti*, *n* reciprocity of rights of citizenship in different communities. [**iso-** and Gr. *polīteiā*, citizenship.]

isoprene *ī'sō-prēn*, (*chem*) *n* a hydrocarbon of the terpene group, which may be polymerised into synthetic rubber.

isosceles *ī-sos'i-lēz*, (*geom*) *adj* (of a triangle) having two equal sides. [Gr. *isoskelēs* — *isos*, equal, *skelos*, a leg.]

isoseismal *ī-sō-sīz'məl*, *n* a curve or line connecting points at which an earthquake shock is felt with equal intensity. — *adj* **isoseis'mal** or **isoseis'mic**. [**iso-** and Gr. *seismos*, a shaking.]

isospin *ī'sō-spin*, *n* (in particle physics) a quantum number applied to members of closely related groups of particles to express and explain the theory that such particles (e.g. protons and neutrons) are in fact states of the same particle differing with regard to electric charge. — Also called **isotopic spin**. [*isotopic spin*.]

isosporous *ī-sos'pə-rəs* or *ī-sō-spö'rəs*, (*bot*) *adj* having spores of one kind only (opp. to *heterosporous*). — *n* **isos'pory**. [**iso-** and Gr. *sporos*, seed.]

isostasy *ī-sos'tə-si*, (*geol*) *n* a condition of equilibrium held to exist in the earth's crust, equal masses of matter underlying equal areas, whether of sea or land down to an assumed level of compensation. — *adj* **isostatic** (*ī-sō-stat'ik*) in hydrostatic equilibrium from equality of pressure; in a state of isostasy; pertaining to isostasy. — *adv* **isostat'ically**. [Gr. *isos*, equal, *stasis*, setting, weighing, *statikos*, pertaining to weighing.]

isothere *ī'sō-thēr*, *n* a contour line of equal mean summer temperature. — *adj* **isotheral** (*ī-soth'ə-rəl* or *ī-sō-thē'rəl*). — *n* an isothere. [Gr. *theros*, summer — *therein*, to make warm.]

isotherm *ī'sō-thûrm*, *n* a contour line of equal temperature. — *adj* **isotherm'al** at constant temperature; pertaining to isotherms. — *n* an isothermal line, isotherm. — *adv* **isotherm'ally**. [**iso-** and Gr. *thermē*, heat — *thermos*, hot.]

isotone *ī'sō-tōn*, (*phys*) *n* one of a number of nuclides having the same number of neutrons in the nucleus with differing numbers of protons. [**iso-** and prob. Gr. *tonos*, tension.]

isotonic *ī-sō-ton'ik*, *adj* having the same tone, tension, or osmotic pressure. — *n* **isotonicity** (*-nis'*). [**iso-** and Gr. *tonos*, tension, tone.]

isotope *ī'sə-tōp*, (*phys*) *n* one of a set of chemically identical species of atom which have the same atomic number but different mass numbers (a natural element is made up of isotopes, always present in the same proportions). — *adj* **isotopic** (*-top'ik*). — *n* **isotopy** (*ī-sot'ə-pi*) the fact or condition of being isotopic. [**iso-** and Gr. *topos*, place (i.e. in the periodic table).]

isotype *ī'sō-tīp*, *n* a presentation of statistical information by a row of diagrammatic pictures each representing a particular number of instances. [**iso-** and Gr. *typos*, form.]

I-spy *ī-spī'*, *n* a word game, in which one guesses objects in view, whose names begin with a certain letter of the alphabet; a children's game of hide-and-seek, so called from the cry when someone is spied. [**I** and **spy**.]

Israeli *iz-rā'li*, *n* a citizen of the modern state of Israel. — Also *adj*. [See **Israelite**.]

Israelite *iz'ri-ə-līt* or *-rə-līt*, *n* a descendant of Israel or Jacob (*Bible*); a Jew (*Bible*); one of the elect (*fig*). — *adj* **Israelit'ic** or **Is'raelītish**. [Gr. *Israēlītēs* — *Israēl*, Heb. *Yisrāēl*, perh. contender with God — *sara*, to fight, *El*, God.]

ISS *abbrev* for International Social Service.

issei *ē-sā'*, *n* a Japanese immigrant to the U.S., orig. one to U.S. or Canada after 1907, who did not qualify for citizenship till 1952: — *pl* **issei'**. [Jap., first generation.]

ISSN *abbrev* for International Standard Serial Number.

issue *ish'ū*, *-o͞o* or *is'ū*, *n* a going or flowing out; an outlet; (an) act of sending out; that which flows or passes out; children; produce, profits; a putting into circulation, giving out for use; a set of things put forth at one time; a single thing given out or supplied (chiefly *mil*); ultimate result, outcome; upshot; critical determination; a point in dispute; a point on which a question depends; a question awaiting decision or ripe for decision; a discharge or flux (*archaic med*). — *vi* to go, flow, or come out; to proceed from a source; to spring; to be produced; to come to a point in fact or law (*law*); to turn out, result, terminate. — *vt* to send out; to put forth; to put into circulation; to publish; to give out for use; to supply (*mil jargon*). — *adj* **iss'uable** capable of issuing, admitting of an issue. — *n* **iss'uance** the act of giving out, promulgation. — *adj* **iss'ueless** without issue; childless. — *n* **iss'uer**. — **at issue** in dispute; in disagreement; **force the issue** to hasten or compel a final decision on a matter; **join (**or **take) issue** to take an opposite position, or opposite positions, in dispute; to enter into dispute; to take up a point as basis of dispute; **side issue** a subordinate issue arising from the main business. [O.Fr. *issue* — *issir*, to go or flow out, — L. *exīre* — *ex*, out, *īre*, to go.]

-ist *-ist*, *sfx* denoting the person who holds a doctrine or practises an art (as in Calvin*ist*, chem*ist*, novel*ist*, art*ist*, royal*ist*). [L. *-ista* — Gr. *-istēs*.]

ISTC *abbrev* for Iron and Steel Trades Confederation.

isthmus *isth'məs* or *is'məs*, *n* a narrow neck of land connecting two larger portions; a narrow part of a structure connecting two larger parts (*anat*); a constriction. — *adj* **isth'mian** pertaining to an isthmus, esp. the Isthmus of Corinth. [L., — Gr. *isthmos*.]

istle *ist'li* or **ixtle** *ikst'li*, *n* a valuable fibre obtained from Agave, *Bromelia*, and other plants. [Mexican Sp. *ixtle* — Nahuatl *ichtli*.]

IT *abbrev* for Information Technology.

It. *abbrev* for: Italian; Italian vermouth.

it[1] *it*, *pron* the neut. of **he** and **him** applied to a thing without life, a lower animal, a young child, rarely (except as an antecedent, as in *it's a man*, or in contempt) to a man or woman; used as an impersonal, indefinite, or anticipatory or provisional subject or object, as the object of a transitive verb that is normally an intransitive, or a noun; (in children's games) the player chosen to oppose all others; that which answers exactly to what one is looking for (*colloq*); an indefinable crowning quality by which one carries it off — personal magnetism; sex-appeal (*slang*): — *genitive* **its**; *pl* **they** and **them**. [O.E. *hit*, neut. (nom. and accus.) of *hē*.]

it[2] *it*, (*colloq*) *n* Italian vermouth.

i.t.a. or **ITA** *abbrev* for initial teaching alphabet.

itaconic acid *it-ə-kon'ik as'id* or *ī-tə-kon'ik*, *n* a white crystalline solid got by fermentation of sugar with Aspergillus mould, used in plastics manufacture. [Anagram of *aconitic*.]

Ital. *abbrev* for Italian.

ital. *abbrev* for italic.

Italian *i-tal'yən*, *adj* of or relating to *Italy* or its people or language. — *n* a native or citizen of Italy, or person of the same race; the language of Italy. — *adj* **Ital'ianate** Italianised. — *vt* **Ital'ianise** or **-ize** to make Italian; to give an Italian character to. — *vi* to become Italian; to play the Italian; to speak Italian; to use Italian idioms; to adopt Italian ways. — *n* **Italianīsā'tion** or **-z-**. — *n* **Ital'ianism** or **Ital'icism** (*-sizm*) an Italian idiom or habit; Italian sympathies. — *n* **Ital'ianist** a person who has a scholarly knowledge of Italian; a person of Italian sympathies. — *adj* **Ital'ic** pertaining to Italy, esp. ancient Italy; of or pertaining to Italic; (without *cap*) of a sloping type introduced by the Italian printer Aldo Manuzio in 1501, used esp. for emphasis or other distinctive purposes. — *n* a branch of Indo-European usu. considered to comprise Umbrian, Latin, and related languages; (without *cap*, usu. in *pl*) an italic letter. — *n* **italicīsā'tion** or **-z-**. — *vt* **ital'icise** (*-sīz*) or **-ize** to print in, or mark for, italics. — **Italian garden** a formal garden with statues. [L. *Ītaliānus* and Gr. *Ītalikos* — L. *Ītalia*, Gr. *Ītaliā*, Italy.]

Italo- *i-tal'ō-* or *it'ə-lō-*, *combining form* denoting Italian.

ITC *abbrev* for Independent Television Commission (replacing **IBA**).

itch *ich, n* an irritating sensation in the skin; scabies, an eruptive disease in the skin, caused by a parasitic mite; a constant teasing desire. — *vi* to have an uneasy, irritating sensation in the skin; to have a constant, teasing desire. — *n* **itch'iness**. — *adj* **itch'y** pertaining to or affected with itch or itching. [O.E. *giccan*, to itch.]

-ite *-īt*, *sfx* used to form: (1) names of persons, indicating their origin, place of origin, affiliations, loyalties, etc. (e.g. *Semite*, *Durhamite*, *Jacobite*, *Thatcherite*); (2) names of fossil organisms (e.g. *ammonite*); (3) names of minerals (e.g. *calcite*); (4) names of salts of acids with sfx. *-ous* (e.g. *sulphite*, salt of sulphurous acid); (5) names of bodily parts (e.g. *somite*). The nouns may be used also as adjs.

item *ī'təm, n* a separate article or particular in an enumeration; a piece of news or other matter in a newspaper, magazine, etc. — *vt* to set down in enumeration; to make a note of. — *adv* (*archaic*) likewise; also. — *vt* **i'temise** or **-ize** to give or list by items. [L. *ĭtem*, likewise.]

iterate *it'ə-rāt, vt* to do again; to say again, repeat. — *n* **it'erance** or **iterā'tion** repetition. — *adj* **it'erant** or **it'erative** (*-ə-tiv* or *-ā-tiv*) repeating. — *adv* **it'erātively**. [L. *iterāre*, *-ātum* — *iterum*, again.]

itinerant *i-* or *ī-tin'ər-ənt, adj* making journeys from place to place; travelling. — *n* someone who travels from place to place, esp. a judge, a preacher, a strolling musician, or a peddler; a wanderer. — *n* **itin'eracy** (*-ə-si*) or **itin'erancy**. — *adv* **itin'erantly**. — *adj* **itin'erary** travelling; relating to roads or journeys. — *n* a plan or record of a journey; a road-book; a route; an itinerant. — *vi* **itin'erate** to travel from place to place, esp. for the purpose of judging, preaching or lecturing. [L. *iter*, *itineris*, a journey.]

-itis *-ī'tis, combining form* denoting: an inflammatory disease, as in bronch*itis*; jocularly extended to conditions considered disease-like, as in jazz*itis*. [Gr. *-ītis*.]

it'll *it'l*, a contraction of **it will**.

ITN *abbrev* for Independent Television News.

ITO *abbrev* for International Trade Organisation.

its *its, pron, genitive* (or *possessive adj*) of **it**. — *pron* **itself** *it-self'*, the emphatic and reflexive form of **it**. — **by itself** alone, apart; **in itself** by its own nature.

it's *its*, a contraction of **it is** or **it has**.

itsy-bitsy *it-si-bit'si*, (*colloq*) *adj* tiny. [Prob. a childish reduplicated form of **little** influenced by **bit**[1].]

ITT *abbrev* for International Telephone and Telegraph Corporation.

ITU *abbrev* for International Telecommunication Union.

ITV *abbrev* for Independent Television.

IU *abbrev* for international unit.

IUCD or **IUD** *abbrev* for intrauterine (contraceptive) device.

IUCN *abbrev* for International Union for Conservation of Nature and Natural Resources.

IUD. See **IUCD**.

IUPAC *abbrev* for International Union of Pure and Applied Chemistry.

IUPAP *abbrev* for International Union of Pure and Applied Physics.

I've *īv*, a contraction of **I have**.

IVF *abbrev* for in-vitro fertilisation.

Ivorian *ī-vö'ri-ən, adj* of or relating to the Ivory Coast, now officially Côte d'Ivoire, a W. African republic. — *n* a native or citizen of the Ivory Coast.

ivory *ī'və-ri, n* dentine, esp. the hard white substance composing the tusks of the elephant, walrus, hippopotamus and narwhal; (in *pl*) objects of, or resembling, ivory, e.g. billiard-balls, piano-keys, dice, teeth (*slang*). — *adj* made of, resembling, or of the colour of, ivory. — *adj* **i'voried** made like ivory; furnished with teeth (*slang*). — *n* **i'vorist** a worker in ivory. — **i'vory-nut** the nut of the S. Am. palm *Phytelephas* or other palm, yielding **vegetable ivory**, a substance like ivory; **i'vory-palm**; **ivory-por'celain** a fine ware with an ivory-white glaze; **ivory tower** a place of retreat from the world and one's fellows; a lifestyle remote from that of most ordinary people, leading to ignorance of practical concerns, problems, etc. [O.Fr. *ivurie* (Fr. *ivoire*) — L. *ebur*, *eboris*, ivory.]

IVR *abbrev* for International Vehicle Registration.

ivy *ī'vi, n* an evergreen plant that climbs by roots on trees and walls. — *adj* **i'vied** (also **i'vy'd**) overgrown with ivy. — **Ivy League** a name given to eight eastern U.S. universities of particular academic and social prestige. — *adj* **i'vy-leaved** having five-lobed leaves like ivy. [O.E. *īfig*.]

IW *abbrev* for Isle of Wight.

IWC *abbrev* for International Whaling Commission.

ixia *ik'si-ə, n* any plant of the iridaceous genus *Ixia*, found in Southern Africa. [N.L., from Gr. *ixos*, mistletoe, birdlime.]

ixtle. See **istle**.

-ize. See **-ise**.

J

J or **j** *jā* or (*Scot*) *jī*, *n* the tenth letter in the modern English alphabet, developed from I, specialised to denote a consonantal sound (*dzh* in English, *y* in German and other languages, *zh* in French, an open guttural in Spanish), I being retained for the vowel sound — a differentiation not general in English books till about 1630. — **J'-curve** (*econ*) a small initial deterioration, decrease, etc., followed by a larger sustained improvement, increase, etc., appearing on a graph as a J-shaped curve.

J or **J.** *abbrev* for: Japan (I.V.R.); joule; Journal; Judge; Justice.

JA *abbrev* for Jamaica (I.V.R.).

jab *jab*, *vt* and *vi* to poke, stab. — *n* a sudden thrust or stab; a short straight punch; an injection (*colloq*). [App. imit.]

jabber *jab'ər*, *vi* to gabble or talk rapidly. — *vt* to speak indistinctly. — *n* rapid indistinct speaking. — *n* **jabb'erer**. — *n* and *adj* **jabb'ering**. — *adv* **jabb'eringly**. [Imit.]

jabberwock *jab'ər-wok*, *n* a fabulous monster created by Lewis Carroll in his poem *Jabberwocky*. — *n* **jabb'erwocky** nonsense, gibberish.

jabiru *jab'i-ro͞o* or *-ro͞o'*, *n* a large Brazilian stork; extended to other kinds of stork. [Tupí *jabirú*.]

jabot *zha'bō*, *n* a frill of lace, etc., worn in front of a woman's dress or on a man's shirt front, esp. (now) as part of full Highland dress. [Fr.]

jaçana *zhä-sə-nä'* or **jacana** *jak'ə-nə*, *n* a long-toed swamp bird of the tropics. [Port., from Tupí.]

jacaranda *jak-ə-ran'də*, *n* a tropical American, etc. tree of the *Bignoniaceae*, with lilac-coloured flowers, fernlike leaves and hard, heavy, brown wood. [Port. and Tupí *jacarandá*.]

jacinth *jas'inth* or *jās'*, *n* orig. a blue gemstone, perhaps sapphire; a reddish-orange variety of transparent zircon — hyacinth (*mineralogy*); a variety of garnet, topaz, quartz or other stone (*jewellery*); a reddish-orange colour; a slaty-blue fancy pigeon. [**hyacinth**.]

jack *jak*, *n* (with *cap*) a familiar form or diminutive of John; (sometimes with *cap*) an attendant, servant or labourer; (often with *cap*) a sailor; a machine or device which orig. took the place of a servant, such as a *boot-jack* for taking off boots; an apparatus for raising heavy weights such as a motor car; a winch; a socket whose switching arrangements are such that the switch turns only when a jack plug is inserted (*telecomm*, etc.); the male of some animals; a jackass (also **jack donkey**); a jack-rabbit; a jackdaw; a young pike; (in keyboard instruments) part of the action that moves the hammer or carries the quill or tangent; a small flag indicating nationality, flown by a ship, usu. at the bow or the bowsprit; a knave in cards; (in *pl*) the game of dibs; a piece used in this game; the small white ball aimed at in bowls. — *vt* to raise with, or as if with, a jack (with *up*); to act upon with a jack; to throw up or abandon (usu. with *in*; *slang*); to increase (e.g. prices) (with *up*). — *vi* (with *off*) to masturbate (*slang*); (with *up*) to inject oneself, take a fix (*drug-taking slang*); (with *up*) to refuse, resist (*Austr slang*). — *adj* (*Austr*) tired, fed up. — **Jack-a-lan'tern** a Jack-o'-lantern; **jack'boot** a large boot reaching above the knee, to protect the leg, orig. covered with iron plates and worn by cavalry; military rule, esp. when brutal (*fig*). — *vi* (with *around*; also *vt* with *it*) to behave in an oppressive or brutally authoritarian way, to domineer, throw one's weight around. — **Jack Frost** frost personified; **jack'hammer** a hand-held compressed-air hammer drill for rock-drilling. — *adj* and *adv* **jack-high'** (in bowls) as far as the jack. — **Jack'-in-the-box** a figure that springs up from a box when the lid is released; a public hangman — from one so named under James II; **jack'knife** a large clasp-knife; a dive in which the performer doubles up in the air and straightens out again. — *vi* and *vt* to double up as a jackknife does; (of articulated vehicles or parts) through faulty control, to form, or cause to form, an angle of 90° or less. — **Jack-of-all'-trades** someone who can turn a hand to any job; **jack-o'-lan'tern** a lantern made from a hollowed-out pumpkin, turnip, etc., with holes cut to resemble eyes, mouth and nose; **jack'-plane** a large strong plane used by joiners; **jack plug** (*telecomm*, etc.) a one-pronged plug used to introduce an apparatus quickly into a circuit; **jack'pot** a poker game, played for the pot or pool (consisting of equal stakes from all the players), which must be opened by a player holding two jacks or better; a money pool in card games, competitions, etc. that can be won only on certain conditions being fulfilled and accumulates till such time as they are (see also **hit the jackpot** below); a prize-money fund; **jack'-rabbit** a long-eared American hare; **Jack Russell** or **Jack Russell terrier** a breed of small terrier, introduced by *John Russell*, 19th-cent. parson; **jack'-staff** the staff on which the jack (flag) is hoisted; **jack'-stays** ropes or strips of wood or iron stretched along the yards of a ship to bind the sails to; **Jack tar** (also without *cap*) a sailor; **jack towel** a continuous towel passing over a roller; **jack'-up** an offshore oil rig or accommodation platform, etc. secured by legs that are lowered from the platform to the sea bed; an act of non-co-operation or resistance (*Austr slang*). — **before you can say Jack Robinson** very quickly; **every man Jack** one and all; **hit the jackpot** to win a jackpot; to have a big success or stroke of good fortune; **I'm all right, Jack** an expression of selfish or indifferent complacency at the misfortunes or difficulties of others; **Jack the lad** a flashy, cocksure young man. [App. Fr. *Jacques*, the most common name in France, hence used as a substitute for *John*, the most common name in England; really = *James* or *Jacob* — L. *Jacōbus*.]

jackal *jak'l*, *n* a wild, carnivorous, gregarious animal closely related to the dog — erroneously supposed to act as a lion's provider or hunting scout; someone who does another's dirty work; someone who wants to share the spoil without sharing the danger. [Pers. *shaghāl*.]

jackaroo or **jackeroo** *jak-ə-ro͞o'*, (*Austr*) *n* a newcomer, or other person, gaining experience on a sheep- or cattle-station: — *fem* **jillaroo'**. — *vi* to be a jackaroo. [Aboriginal.]

jackass *jak'as*, *n* a male ass; a blockhead, fool. — **laughing jackass** the kookaburra. [**jack** and **ass**.]

jackdaw *jak'dö*, *n* a daw, a small species of crow with greyish neck. [**jack** and **daw**.]

jackeroo. See **jackaroo**.

jacket *jak'it, n* a short coat; an animal's coat; skin (of potatoes); a loose paper cover; outer casing of a boiler, pipe, etc.; the aluminium or zirconium alloy covering of the fissile elements in a reactor. — *vt* to provide or cover with a jacket. — *adj* **jack'eted.** — **jacket potato** a potato cooked in its skin. [O.Fr. *jaquet*, dimin. of *jaque*.]

jacksie or **jacksy** *jak'si,* (*slang*) *n* the buttocks, bottom; the anus. [Perh. **jack.**]

Jacob *jā'kəb, n* (also **Jacob sheep**) a kind of sheep, piebald in colour, with 2 or 4 horns, orig. imported to Britain from Spain. [From the Bible: Gen. xxx, 40.]

Jacobean *jak-ə-bē'ən, adj* of or characteristic of the period of James I of England (1603–25). [L. *Jacōbus*, James.]

Jacobin *jak'ə-bin, n* a French Dominican monk, of the order originally established at St *Jacques*, Paris; one of a society of revolutionists in France; an extremist or radical, esp. in politics. — *adj* **Jacobin'ic** or **Jacobin'ical.** [Fr., — L. *Jacōbus*, James.]

Jacobite *jak'ə-bīt, n* an adherent of James II of England and his descendants. — Also *adj.* — *adj* **Jacobitic** (*-bit'*) or **Jacobit'ical** (*-kəl*). — *n* **Jac'obītism.** [L. *Jacōbus*, James.]

Jacob's-ladder *jā-kəbz-lad'ər, n* a ladder made of ropes with wooden steps (*naut*); a wild or garden plant (*Polemonium*) with ladderlike leaves. [From the *ladder* reaching to heaven, seen by *Jacob* in his dream, Gen. xxviii, 12.]

Jacob's-staff *jā-kəbz-stäf',* (*hist*) *n* (in surveying) a cross-staff. [From its likeness to a pilgrim's staff, prob. — the pilgrimage to St James (L. *Jacōbus*) of Compostela.]

jaconet *jak'ə-net, n* a cotton fabric, rather stouter than muslin — different from the fabric orig. so named which was imported from *Jagannāth* (Puri) in India; a thin material with waterproof backing used for medical dressings.

jacquard *jak'ärd* or *jak-ärd', n* (often with *cap*) an apparatus with perforated cards for controlling the movement of the warp threads in weaving intricate designs; a fabric woven by this method. — **Jacq'uard-loom** a loom with jacquard, producing jacquard. [Joseph Marie *Jacquard* (1752–1834), the inventor.]

jactation *jak-tā'shən, n* the act of throwing; jactitation (*pathol*); boasting. [L. *jactātiō, -ōnis*, tossing, boasting — *jactāre*, to throw.]

jactitation *jak-ti-tā'shən, n* restless tossing in illness (*pathol*); bodily agitation, twitching, jerking, etc. (*pathol*); bragging; public assertion, esp. ostentatious and false. — **jactitation of marriage** pretence of being married to another. [L.L. *jactitātiō, -ōnis* — L. *jactitāre, -ātum*, frequentative of *jactāre*, to throw.]

Jacuzzi® *jə-koo'zi, n* a type of bath or small pool equipped with a mechanism that agitates the water to provide extra invigoration; (usu. without *cap*) a bathe in such a bath or pool.

jade¹ *jād, n* a pitiful, worn-out horse; a worthless nag; a woman, esp. perverse, ill-natured or not to be trusted (often *ironically*). — *vt* to weary, dull, cloy or cause to flag from excess or over-exposure; to make a jade of. — *vi* to become weary. — *adj* **jā'ded.** — *adv* **jā'dedly.**

jade² *jād, n* a hard ornamental stone of varying shades of green and sometimes almost white — esp. *nephrite* (silicate of calcium and magnesium) and **jade'ite** (silicate of aluminium and sodium) — once believed to cure side pains. — *adj* **jade** made of jade; of the colour of jade. [Fr., — Sp. *ijada*, the flank — L. *ilia*.]

j'adoube *zha-doob,* (Fr.) I adjust (*chess*; a warning that only an adjustment is intended, not a move).

Jaeger® *yā'gər, n* woollen material used in making clothes, orig. containing no vegetable fibre. [Dr Gustav *Jaeger*, the original manufacturer.]

Jaffa *jaf'ə, n* (also **Jaffa orange**) an orange from *Jaffa* in Israel.

jag¹ *jag, n* a notch or slash in a garment, etc.; a ragged protrusion; a cleft or division (*bot*); a prick (*Scot*); an inoculation, injection (chiefly *colloq*; *Scot*). — *vt* to cut into notches; to prick or pierce: — *pr p* **jagg'ing**; *pa p* **jagged** (*jagd*). — *adj* **jagg'ed** notched, rough-edged, uneven. — *adv* **jagg'edly.** — *n* **jagg'edness.** — *adj* **jagg'y** notched; slashed; prickly (*Scot*).

jag² *jag, n* a spree, bout of indulgence; one's fill of liquor or narcotics; a spell, fit.

jaggery *jag'ə-ri, n* a coarse, dark sugar made from palm-sap. [Hindi *jāgrī*, Sans. *śarkarā*; cf. **sugar, Saccharum.**]

jaguar *jag'wär, jag'ū-är* or *-ər, n* a powerful feline beast of prey, related to the leopard, native to S. America. [Tupí *jaguāra*.]

jaguarundi *jä-gwə-run'dē* or **jaguarondi** *-ron'dē, n* a S. American wild cat. [Tupí, — Guaraní.]

Jah *yä* or *jä, n* Jehovah, the Hebrew God. — *n* **Jah'veh** same as **Yahweh.** [Heb. *Yah*.]

jai alai *hī* (*ə-*)*lī'*, a game resembling handball but played with a long curved basket strapped to the wrist, a type of pelota. [Sp., — Basque — *jai*, festival, *alai*, merry.]

jail or **gaol** *jāl, n* a prison. — *vt* to imprison. — *n* **jail'er, jail'or** or **gaol'er** a person in charge of a jail or of prisoners; a turnkey. — **jail'-bait** (*slang*) a girl who has not reached the legal age of consent (also *adj*); **jail'-bird** or **gaol'-bird** (*colloq*) someone who often is, has been, or should be in jail; **jail'house** (*US*) a prison. — **break jail** (or **gaol**) to force one's way out of prison (*n* **jail'-break** or **gaol'-break**). [O.Fr. *gaole* (Fr. *geôle*) — L.L. *gabiola*, a cage — L. *cavea*, a cage — *cavus*, hollow.]

Jain *jīn* or *jān*, also **Jaina** *jī'na, n* an adherent of an Indian religion related to Brahmanism and Buddhism. — Also *adj.* — *n* **Jain'ism.** [Hind. *jina*, a deified saint.]

jake *jāk,* (*colloq*, orig. *US*, now also *Austr* in sense of 'fine') *adj* honest; correct; fine, OK, first-rate.

JAL *abbrev* for Japan Air Lines.

jalap *jal'ap, n* the purgative root of an *Ipomoea* or *Exogonium*, first brought from *Jalapa* (or Xalapa), in Mexico.

jalapeño *hä-lə-pān'yō* or **jalapeño pepper** (*pep'ər*) (chiefly *US*) *n* an especially hot type of Capsicum pepper, used in Mexican cooking. [Mexican Sp.]

jalopy or **jaloppy** *jə-lop'i, n* an old motor car or aeroplane.

jalousie *zhal-oo-zē'* or *zhal', n* an outside shutter with slats. — *adj* **jal'ousied.** [Fr., — *jalousie*, jealousy.]

jam¹ *jam, n* a conserve of fruit boiled with sugar. — *vt* to spread with jam; to make into jam. — *adj* **jamm'y** smeared or sticky with jam; like jam; lucky, excellent (*colloq*). — **jam'pot** a jar for jam (also **jam'jar**). — **jam tomorrow** better things promised for the future that always remain in the future; **want jam on it** (*colloq*) to expect or want too much. [Perh. from **jam².**]

jam² *jam, vt* to press or squeeze tight; to crowd full; to block by crowding; to bring to a standstill by crowding or interlocking; to interfere with by emitting signals of similar wavelength (*radio*); to interfere or block (signals generally). — *vi* to become stuck, wedged, etc.; to become unworkable; to press or push (as into a confined space); (in jazz) to play enthusiastically, interpolating and improvising freely: — *pr p* **jamm'ing**; *pa t* and *pa p* **jammed.** — *n* a crush, squeeze; a block or stoppage due to crowding or squeezing together; a jammed mass (as of logs in a river); a jamming of radio messages; a difficult or embarrassing situation (*colloq*). — *n* **jamm'er** someone who, or that which, jams something. — *adj* **jam-packed'** completely full, crowded, etc. — **jam session** a gathering of jazz musicians (orig. an informal one) at which jazz (as described at *vi*) is played. [Poss. onomatopoeic; connected with **champ**[1].]

jamahiriya or **jamahiriyah** *ja-mä-hē-rē'ya*, *n* people's state, state of proletariat. [Ar., connected with *jumhūrīya*, republic — *jumhūr*, people.]

Jamaica *jə-mā'kə* or **Jamaican** *-mā'kən*, *adj* of the island of Jamaica. — *n* **Jamai'can** a native or inhabitant of Jamaica. — **Jamaica pepper** allspice; **Jamaica rum** a slowly-fermented, full-bodied pungent rum.

jamb *jam*, *n* the sidepiece or post of a door, fireplace, etc.; leg-armour (in this sense also **jambe** (*jam*)). [Fr. *jambe*, leg.]

jambalaya *jum-bə-lī'ə*, (*US*) *n* a Creole or Cajun dish made with rice mixed with seafood or chicken, seasonings, etc.; a mixture generally. [Prov. *jambalaia*.]

jambiya or **jambiyah** *jam-bē'yä*, *n* a type of Middle Eastern curved, double-edged dagger. [Ar.]

jamboree *jam-bə-rē'*, *n* a boisterous frolic, a spree; a large Scout rally.

jammy. See **jam**[1].

jampan *jam'pan*, *n* an Indian sedan chair. — *n* **jampanee'** or **jampani** (*-ē'*) its bearer. [Beng. *jhāmpān*.]

Jan. *abbrev* for January.

jandal *jan'dəl*, (*NZ*) *n* a thong, a type of sandal.

JANET *jan'ət*, *abbrev* for Joint Academic Network, a computer network linking universities, research councils, etc.

jangle *jang'gl*, *vt* and *vi* to sound with an unpleasant irritating tone, such as a harsh, dissonant metallic or ringing noise. — *vt* to upset, irritate. — *vi* to wrangle or quarrel. — *n* dissonant clanging; contention. — *n* **jang'ler**. — *n* **jang'ling**. — *adj* **jang'ly**. [O.Fr. *jangler*.]

janitor *jan'i-tər*, *n* a doorkeeper; attendant or caretaker: — *fem* **jan'itrix** or **jan'itress**. — *adj* **janitorial** (*-tö'*). — *n* **jan'itorship**. [L. — *jānua*, a door.]

jankers *jang'kərz*, (*mil slang*) *nsing* punishment, detention, etc. for defaulting.

Jansenism *jan'sən-izm*, (*Christian relig*) *n* a system of evangelical doctrine deduced from Augustine by Cornelius *Jansen* (1585–1638), maintaining that human nature is corrupt, and that Christ died only for the elect, all others being irretrievably condemned to hell. — *n* **Jan'senist** a believer in Jansenism. — Also *adj*.

jansky *jan'ski*, (*astron*) *n* the unit of strength of radio-wave emission, 10^{-26} $W^{-2}Hz^{-1}$. [Named after Karl G. *Jansky*, the American radio engineer who first discovered radio interference coming from the stars.]

January *jan'ū-ər-i*, *n* the first month of the year, dedicated by the Romans to Janus, the ancient Italian two-faced god of doors. [L. *Jānuārius*.]

Jap *jap*, (*derog*) *n* and *adj* Japanese. — **Jap.** *abbrev* for Japanese.

japan *jə-pan'*, *adj* of Japan; japanned. — *n* Japanese ware or work; a glossy black varnish of lacquer; japanned work. — *vt* to varnish with japan, esp. in imitation of Japanese work; to make black: — *pr p* **japann'ing**; *pa t* and *pa p* **japanned'**. — *adj* **Japanese** (*jap-ə-nēz'* or *jap'*) of Japan, of its people, or of its language. — *n* a native or citizen of Japan; the language of Japan: — *pl* **Japanese**. — *adj* **Japanesque'** or **Japanēs'y** savouring of the Japanese. — *n* **japann'er**. — **Japanese cedar** a very tall Japanese conifer; **Japan laurel** a shrub of the dogwood family, with spotted yellow leaves; **Japan varnish** a varnish derived from a species of sumach, extended to various other similar varnishes.

jape *jāp*, *vi* to jest, joke. — *vt* to mock. — *n* a jest, joke, trick. [O.Fr. *japer*, to yelp.]

Japonic *jə-pon'ik*, *adj* Japanese. — *n* **japon'ica** the Japanese quince (*Chaenomeles japonica*), camellia, or other Japanese plant. [N.L. *japonicus*, fem. *japonica*, Japanese.]

jar[1] *jär*, *vi* to make a harsh discordant sound or unpleasant vibration; to give an unpleasant shock; to grate (on); to be discordant or distasteful; to be inconsistent. — *vt* to shake, as by a blow; to cause to vibrate unpleasantly; to grate on; to make dissonant: — *pr p* **jarr'ing**; *pa t* and *pa p* **jarred**. — *n* a harsh sudden vibration; a dissonance; a grating sound or feeling; clash of interests or opinions; conflict. — *n* **jarr'ing** the act of jarring; severe reproof. — Also *adj*. — *adv* **jarr'ingly**. [Imit.]

jar[2] *jär*, *n* a wide-mouthed wide vessel; as much as a jar will hold; a drink (of an alcoholic beverage) (*colloq*). — *vt* to put in jars. — *n* **jar'ful**: — *pl* **jar'fuls**. [Fr. *jarre* or Sp. *jarra* — Ar. *jarrah*.]

jardinière *zhär-dēn-yer'*, *n* a container for the display of flowers, growing or cut; a dish including a mixture of diced or sliced cooked vegetables. [Fr., gardener (fem.).]

jargon[1] *jär'gən*, *n* chatter, twittering; confused talk; slang; artificial or barbarous language; the terminology of a profession, art, group, etc. — *n* **jargoneer'** or **jar'gonist** a person who uses jargon. — *n* **jargonīsā'tion** or **-z-**. — *vt* **jar'gonise** or **-ize** to express in jargon. — *vi* to speak jargon. [Fr. *jargon*.]

jargon[2] *jär'gən* or **jargoon** *jär'gōōn*, (*mineralogy*) *n* a brilliant colourless or pale zircon. [Fr. *jargon*; prob. connected with **zircon**.]

jarrah *jar'ə*, *n* a Western Australian timber tree, *Eucalyptus marginata*. [Aboriginal.]

Jas. *abbrev* for: James; (the Letter of) James (*Bible*).

jasmine *jaz'-* or *jas'min*, also **jessamine** *jes'ə-min*, *n* a genus (*Jasminum*) of oleaceous shrubs, many with very fragrant flowers. — **red jasmine** frangipani, a tropical American shrub related to periwinkle. [Fr. *jasmin*, *jasemin* — Ar. *yāsmin*, *yāsamīn* — Pers. *yāsmīn*.]

jasper *jas'pər*, *n* an opaque quartz containing clay or iron compounds, used in jewellery or ornamentation and red, yellow, brown or green in colour; a fine hard porcelain (also **jas'perware**). — *adj* made of jasper. — *adj* **jaspe** (*jasp*) or **jaspé** (*jas'pā*) mottled, variegated or veined. — *n* cotton or rayon cloth with a shaded effect used for bedspreads, curtains, etc. — *vt* **jasp'erise** or **-ize** to turn into jasper. — *adj* **jasp'erous** or **jasp'ery**. [O.Fr. *jaspe*, *jaspre* — L. *iaspis*, *-idis*; and directly from Gr. *iaspis*, *-idos*, of Eastern origin.]

jataka *jä'tə-kə*, *n* a nativity, the birth-story of Buddha. [Sans. *jātaka* — *jāta*, born.]

jato *jā'tō*, (*aeronautics*) *n* a jet-assisted take-off, using a **jato unit** consisting of one or more rocket motors, usu. jettisoned after use: — *pl* **jā'tos**.

jaundice *jön'dis*, *n* a disease in which there is yellowing of the eyes, skin, etc., by excess of bile pigment, the patient in rare cases seeing objects as yellow; a disease showing this condition; state of taking an unfavourable, prejudiced view. — *vt* to affect with jaundice, in any sense. — *adj* **jaun'diced** affected with jaundice; feeling, or showing, prejudice, distaste or jealousy. [Fr. *jaunisse* — *jaune*, yellow.]

jaunt *jönt*, *vi* to go from place to place, esp. for pleasure; to make an excursion. — *n* an excursion; a ramble. — *adj* **jaunt'ing** strolling; making an excursion.

jaunty *jön'ti*, *adj* having an airy or sprightly manner approaching a swagger. — *adv* **jaun'tily**. — *n* **jaun'tiness**. [Fr. *gentil*.]

Java *jä'və*, *adj* of the island of Java. — *adj* and *n* **Ja'van** or **Javanese'**. — **Java man** the early man formerly known as Pithecanthropus erectus, later re-designated Homo erectus.

Javel (or Javelle) water *zha-* or *zhə-vel' wö'tər*, also **eau de** (*ō də*) **Javel** or **Javelle** *n* a solution of potassium chloride and hypochlorite used for bleaching, disinfecting, etc. [After *Javel*, former town, now part of the city of Paris.]

javelin *jav'ə-lin* or *jav'lin*, *n* a throwing-spear. [Fr. *javeline*; prob. Celt.]

jaw *jö*, *n* a mouth-structure for biting or chewing; one of the bones of a jaw; one of a pair of parts for gripping, crushing, cutting, grinding, etc.; (in *pl*) a narrow entrance; talkativeness, scolding (*slang*). — *vt* (*slang*) to scold. — *vi* to talk, esp. in excess. — *adj* **jawed** having jaws. — *n* **jaw'ing** (*slang*) talk, esp. unrestrained, abusive or reproving. — **jaw'bone** the bone of the jaw; **jaw'-breaker** a heavy-duty rock-breaking machine with hinged jaws (also **jaw'-crusher**); a word hard to pronounce (*slang*); **jaw lever** an instrument for opening the mouth of a horse or cow to admit medicine. — **hold one's jaw** (*colloq*) to stop talking or scolding.

ja wohl *ya vōl'*, (Ger.) yes indeed.

jay[1] *jā*, *n* a bird of the crow family with colourful plumage; a stupid, awkward or easily duped person (*US slang*). — *adj* (*US slang*) stupid, unsophisticated. — *vi* **jay'walk**. — **jay'walker** a careless pedestrian whom motorists are expected to avoid running down; **jay'walking**. [O.Fr. *jay*.]

jay[2] *jā*, *n* the tenth letter of the modern English alphabet (J, j); an object or mark of that shape.

jazz *jaz*, *n* any of various styles of music with a strong rhythm, syncopation, improvisation, etc., originating in American Negro folk music; a musical art form and also various types of popular dance music derived from it; garish colouring, lively manner, vivid quality; insincere or lying talk (*slang*, esp. *US*). — Also *adj*. — *vt* to impart a jazz character to (often with *up*). — *adv* **jazz'ily**. — *n* **jazz'iness**. — *adj* **jazz'y**. — **jazz age** the decade following World War I, esp. in America; **jazz band** one that plays jazz; **jazz-funk'**, **-pop'** and **-rock'** music which is a blend of jazz and funky, pop and rock music respectively; **jazz'man** a jazz musician.

JCB *jā-sē-bē'*, *n* a type of mobile excavator used in the construction industry. [Abbrev. for *J.C. B*amford, the manufacturer's name.]

JCR *abbrev* for junior common room (see under **junior**).

jealous *jel'əs*, *adj* suspicious of, upset or angered by rivalry; envious; solicitous, anxiously heedful; mistrustfully vigilant; unable to tolerate unfaithfulness, or the thought of it. — *adv* **jeal'ously**. — *n* **jeal'ousy**. [O.Fr. *jalous* — L. *zēlus* — Gr. *zēlos*, emulation.]

jean *jēn*, or (esp. formerly) *jān*, *n* a twilled-cotton cloth; (in *pl*) trousers or overalls made originally of jean; (in *pl*) casual trousers made esp. of denim, and also of corduroy or other similar material. [O.Fr. *Janne* — L. *Genua*, Genoa.]

Jeep *jēp*, *n* (®) a light, strong, four-wheel-drive, military vehicle suitable for rough terrain; (often without *cap*) any similar model of car. [From G.P., for general *purpose*.]

jeepers *jē'pərz* or **jeepers creepers** *krē'pərz*, (*US slang*) *interj* expressing surprise. [Euphemism for *Jesus Christ*.].

jeer *jēr*, *vi* (usu. with *at*) to scoff; to deride; to mock. — *vt* to mock; to treat with derision. — *n* invective; sarcastic or satirical jest; mockery. — *n* **jeer'er**. — *n* and *adj* **jeer'ing**. — *adv* **jeer'ingly**.

jehad. See **jihad**.

Jehovah *ji-hō'və*, *n* Yahweh, the Hebrew God, a name used by Christians. — **Jehovah's Witnesses** a Christian fundamentalist sect which rejects all other religions and denominations, believes in the imminent end of the world, and refuses to accept civil authority where it clashes with its own principles — orig. called the International Bible Students' Association. [Heb.; for *Yĕhōwāh*, i.e. *Yahweh* with the vowels of *Adōnāi*.]

Jehu *jē'hū*, (*colloq*) *n* a king of Israel renowned for his furious chariot-driving; any fast and furious coachman or driver. [From the Bible: 2 Kings ix. 20.]

jejune *ji-jōōn'*, *adj* naive, immature, callow; showing lack of information or experience; spiritless, meagre, arid. — *adv* **jejune'ly**. — *n* **jejune'ness** or **jeju'nity**. [L. *jejūnus*, hungry, empty.]

jejunum *ji-jōō'nəm*, (*anat*) *n* the part of the small intestine between the duodenum and the ileum. [Med. L. *jejunum intestinum*, empty intestine (thought always to be empty after death).]

Jekyll and Hyde *jēk'il* (or *jek'il*) *ənd hīd*, the good side and the bad side of a human being — from R.L. Stevenson, *The Strange Case of Dr Jekyll and Mr Hyde* (1886).

jell. See under **jelly**[1], **gel**.

jellaba, jellabah. See **djellaba**.

jelly[1] *jel'i*, *n* anything gelatinous; the juice of fruit boiled with sugar; a conserve of fruit, jam (*US* and formerly *Scot*); a clear, gelatinous fruit-flavoured dessert. — *vi* to set as a jelly; to congeal. — *vt* to make into a jelly. — *vi* and *vt* **jell** to jelly; to take distinct shape (*colloq*). — *adj* **jell'ied** in a state of jelly; enclosed in jelly. — *adj* **jell'iform**. — *vt* **jell'ify** to make into a jelly. — *vi* to become gelatinous. — **jelly baby** a kind of gelatinous sweet in the shape of a baby; **jelly bag** a bag through which fruit juice is strained for jelly; **jell'ybean** a kind of sweet in the shape of a bean with a sugar coating and jelly filling; **jell'yfish** a marine coelenterate with jelly-like body; a person who lacks firmness of purpose. [Fr. *gelée*, from *geler* — L. *gelāre*, to freeze; cf. **gelatine**.]

jelly[2] *jel'i*, *n* a colloq. shortening of **gelignite**.

jemmy *jem'i*, *n* a burglar's short crow-bar. — *vt* (usu. with *open*) to force open with a jemmy or similar: — *pr p* **jemm'ying**; *pa t* and *pa p* **jemm'ied**. [A form of the name *James*.]

je ne sais quoi *zhə nə se kwa*, *n* an indefinable something; a special unknown ingredient or quality. [Fr., I don't know what.]

jennet *jen'it*, *n* a small Spanish horse; a jenny donkey. — Also **genn'et** or **gen'et**. [O.Fr. *genet* — Sp. *jinete*, a light horseman.]

Jenny *jen'i*, *n* a wren or owl regarded as female; a female ass (also **jenny donkey**); a travelling crane; a spinning-jenny. [From the name *Jenny*.]

jeopardy *jep'ər-di*, *n* hazard, danger (of loss or damage); the danger of trial and punishment faced by the accused on a criminal charge (*US law*). — *vt* **jeop'ardise** or **-ize** to put in jeopardy, risk losing or damaging. [Fr. *jeu parti*, a divided or even game — L.L. *jocus partītus* — L. *jocus*, a game, *partītus*, divided.]

jequirity *jə-kwi'ri-ti*, *n* the tropical shrub Indian liquorice, the seeds of which are used ornamentally and medicinally, and its root for a liquorice substitute. — **jequirity bean** its seed.

Jer. (*Bible*) *abbrev* for (the Book of) Jeremiah.

jerbil. Same as **gerbil**.

jerboa *jûr-bō'ə*, *n* a desert rodent (family *Dipodidae*) that jumps on long hind legs like a kangaroo. [Ar. *yarbū'*.]

jerfalcon. Same as **gyrfalcon**.

jerk *jûrk*, *n* a short movement begun and ended suddenly; a twitch; an involuntary spasmodic contraction of a muscle; a movement in physical exercises; a useless or idiotic person (*slang*); (in weight-lifting) a movement lifting the barbell from shoulder height to a position on outstretched arms above the head; (also **clean and jerk**) a weight-lifting competition involving such a lift (cf. **clean**). — *vt* to throw or move with a jerk. — *vi* to move with a jerk. — *n* **jerk'er**. — *n* **jerk'iness**. — *adj* **jerk'y** moving or coming by jerks or starts, spasmodic. — **jerk off** (*vulg*) to masturbate.

jerkin *jûr'kin*, *n* a sleeveless jacket, short coat or close-fitting waistcoat.

jeroboam *jer-ō-bō'əm, n* a large bottle, esp. one for wine holding the equivalent of 6 normal bottles, or for champagne, the equivalent of 4 normal bottles. [Allusion to 1 Kings xi. 28.]

Jerry or **Gerry** *jer'i, n* (*war slang*) a German. — *n* **jerr'ycan** a kind of petrol-can, orig. German.

jerry[1] *jer'i,* (*slang*) *n* a chamber-pot. [**jeroboam**.]

jerry[2] *jer'i, n* (*colloq*) a jerry-builder. — *adj* hastily made and with bad materials. — **jerr'y-builder** someone who builds flimsy houses cheaply and hastily; **jerr'y-building**. — *adj* **jerr'y-built**. [Prob. the personal name.]

jersey *jûr'zi, n* the finest part of wool; combed wool; a knitted (usu. woollen) garment for the upper body; a fine knitted fabric in cotton, nylon, etc.; (with *cap*) a cow of Jersey breed. [From the island of *Jersey*.]

Jerusalem artichoke *jər-ōō'sə-ləm är'ti-chōk, n.* See **artichoke**.

jess *jes, n* a short strap round the leg of a hawk. — *adj* **jessed** having jesses on. [O.Fr. *ges* — L. *jactus*, a cast — *jacĕre*, to throw.]

jessamine. See **jasmine**.

jest *jest, n* something spoken in fun; fun; joke; object of laughter; something ludicrous. — *vi* to make a jest; to joke. — *vt* to jeer at, ridicule; to say as a jest. — *n* **jest'er** a person who jests; a buffoon; a court fool. — *adj* **jest'ful** given to jesting. — *n* and *adj* **jest'ing**. — *adv* **jest'ingly**. [Orig. a deed, a story, M.E. *geste* — O.Fr. *geste* — L. *gesta*, things done, doings — *gerĕre*, to do.]

Jesuit *jez'ū-it, n* a member of the Society of *Jesus*, a famous religious order, founded in 1534 by Ignatius Loyola; (*offensively*) a crafty person, an intriguer, a prevaricator. — *adj* **Jesuit'ic** or **Jesuit'ical**. — *adv* **Jesuit'ically**. — *n* **Jes'uitism** or **Jes'uitry** the principles and practices of, or ascribed to, the Jesuits.

Jesus *jē'zəs, n* the founder of Christianity, acknowledged by Christians as the Son of God and Saviour of mankind. — Also **Jesus Christ, Jesus of Nazareth** and (in hymns, etc., esp. in the vocative) **Jesu** (*jē'zū*). — *interj* a loose profanity expressing anger, surprise, etc. [Gr. *Iēsous* (voc. and oblique cases *Iēsou*) — Heb. *Yēshūa'*, contr. of *Yehōshūa'*, Joshua.]

jet[1] *jet, n* a rich black variety of lignite, very hard and compact, taking a high polish, used for ornaments; jet-black. — *adj* made of jet; jet-black. — *n* **jett'iness**. — *adj* **jett'y** of the nature of jet, or black as jet. — *adj* **jet-black'** black as jet. — Also *n.* [O.Fr. *jaiet* — L. and Gr. *gagātēs* — *Gagas* or *Gangai*, a town and river in Lycia, where it was obtained.]

jet[2] *jet, n* a narrow spouting stream; a spout, nozzle or pipe emitting a stream or spray of fluid; a jetplane. — *vt* and *vi* to spout. — *vi* to travel by jetplane: — *pr p* **jett'ing**; *pa t* and *pa p* **jett'ed**. — **jet'-drive**. — *adj* **jet'-driven** driven by the backward emission of a jet of gas, etc. — **jet'foil** a hydrofoil powered by a jet of water; **jet'-lag** exhaustion, discomfort, etc., resulting from the body's inability to adjust to the rapid changes of time zone necessitated by high-speed long-distance air travel. — *adj* **jet'-lagged**. — **jet'liner** an airliner powered by a jet engine; **jet'plane** or **jet'-plane** a jet-driven aeroplane. — *adj* **jet-propell'ed**. — **jet-propul'sion**; **jet'-setter** a member of the jet set (see below). — *adj* **jet'-setting** living in the style of the jet set. — **jet'-ski** a powered craft comparable to a motorbike adapted to plane across water on a ski-like keel. — *vi* to ride a jet-ski (as a water sport or recreation). — **jet'stream** or **jet'-stream** very high winds more than 20 000 feet above the earth; the exhaust of a rocket engine. — **the jet set** a wealthy social set able to spend much of their time travelling to fashionable resorts around the world. [O.Fr. *jetter* — L. *jactāre*, to fling.]

jeté *zhə-tā,* (*ballet*) *n* a leap from one foot to the other in which the free leg usu. finishes extended forward, backward or sideways. [Fr., thrown.]

jeton. See **jetton**.

jetsam *jet'səm, n* goods jettisoned from a ship and washed up on shore; according to some, goods from a wreck that remain under water (cf. **flotsam**). — **flotsam and jetsam** (*fig*) unclaimed odds and ends, unwanted debris. [Contraction of **jettison**.]

jettison *jet'i-sən, vt* to throw overboard (from a craft), esp. goods in time of danger; to abandon, reject (*fig*). — *n* the act of throwing goods overboard. [A.Fr. *jetteson* — L. *jactātiō* — *jactāre*, frequentative of *jacĕre*, to throw.]

jetton or **jeton** *jet'ən, n* a piece of stamped metal used as a counter in card-playing, casting accounts, etc.; a (usu. metal) token for operating a machine, esp. a pay telephone. [Fr. *jeton* — *jeter*, to throw — L. *jactāre*, frequentative of *jacĕre*, to throw.]

jetty *jet'i, n* a pier, or similar projection structure. [O.Fr. *jettee*, thrown out; see **jet**[2].]

jeu *zhœ,* (Fr.) *n* a game. — **jeu de mots** a play on words, a pun: — *pl* **jeux de mots** (*də mō*); **jeu d'esprit** a witticism: — *pl* **jeux d'esprit** (*des-prē*).

jeunesse dorée *zhœ-nes do-rā,* (Fr.) *n* literally, gilded youth; luxurious, stylish, sophisticated young people.

Jew *jōō, n* a person of Hebrew descent or religion; an Israelite; (*offensively*) a usurer, miser, etc.: — *fem* **Jew'ess**. — *vt* (*offensively*) to cheat or get the better of in a bargain. — *adj* **Jew'ish** of the Jews or their religion. — *adv* **Jew'ishly**. — *n* **Jew'ishness**. — **jew'fish** a name for several very large American and Australian fishes; **Jew's'-ear** an ear-like fungus (*Auricularia*) parasitic on elder and other trees; **Jew's-harp'** or **Jews'-harp'** (also without *cap*) a small lyre-shaped instrument played against the teeth by twitching a metal tongue with the finger. [O.Fr. *Jueu* — L. *Jūdaeus* — Gr. *Ioudaios* — Heb. *Yehūdāh*, Judah.]

jewel *jōō'əl, n* a precious stone; a personal ornament of precious stones, gold, etc.; a hard stone (ruby, etc.) used for pivot bearings in a watch; an imitation of a gemstone; an ornamental glass boss; anything or anyone highly valued. — *vt* to adorn with jewels; to fit with a jewel: — *pr p* **jew'elling**; *pa t* and *pa p* **jew'elled**. — *n* **jew'eller** a person who deals in, or makes, jewels. — *n* **jewellery** (*jōō'əl-ri*) or **jew'elry** jewels in general. — **jew'el-case** a casket for holding jewels; **jew'elfish** an African cichlid popular in aquaria for its bright colours; **jew'el-house** a room in the Tower of London where the crown jewels are kept. — **jewel in the crown** orig. (in *pl*) any or all of the countries of the (former) British Empire, esp. (in *sing*) India; the best, most highly prized, most successful, etc. of a number or collection (*fig*). [O.Fr. *jouel* (Fr. *joyau*).]

Jewry *jōō'ri, n* Judaea; a district inhabited by *Jews*; the Jewish world, community or religion.

Jezebel *jez'ə-bel, n* a shamelessly immoral woman. [From Ahab's wife (in the Bible): 2 Kings ix. 30.]

jiao *jow, n* a unit of Chinese currency, equal to 10 *fen* or $\frac{1}{10}$ of a yuan. [Chin.]

jib *jib, n* a triangular sail stretched in front of the foremast of a ship; the boom of a crane or derrick; an act of jibbing. — *vt* to cause to gybe. — *vi* (usu. with *at*) to gybe; (of a horse) to balk or shy; to refuse, show objection, boggle: — *pr p* **jibb'ing**; *pa t* and *pa p* **jibbed**. — **jib'-boom** a boom or extension of the bowsprit, on which the jib is spread; **jib'-crane** a crane with an inclined arm fixed to the foot of a rotating vertical post, the upper ends connected; **jib'-sail**; **jib'-sheet** a rope for trimming the jib. — **the cut of one's jib** (*colloq*) one's appearance.

jibe[1], **jiber**. See **gibe**.

jibe[2] *jīb,* (chiefly *US*) *vi* to agree, accord (with).

jibe[3]. See **gybe**.

jiffy *jif'i*, (*colloq*) *n* an instant (sometimes shortened to **jiff**).

jiffy bag® *jif'i bag*, *n* a stout padded envelope.

jig *jig*, *n* a jerky movement; a lively dance usu. in 6–8 time; a dance-tune for such a dance; a lure which moves jerkily when drawn through the water (*angling*); an appliance for guiding or positioning a tool; an appliance of various kinds in mechanical processes, e.g. a jigger in mining. — *vt* and *vi* to jerk; to perform as a jig. — *vt* to work upon with a jig: — *pr p* **jigg'ing**; *pa t* and *pa p* **jigged**. — *n* **jigg'er** a person who jigs in any sense; anything that jigs; one of many kinds of subsidiary appliances, esp. with reciprocating motion, such as an oscillation transformer, an apparatus for separating ores by jolting them in sieves in water, and a type of warehouse crane; a light hoisting tackle (*naut*); a small aft sail on a ketch, etc. (*naut*); a boat with such a sail (*naut*); a jiggermast (*naut*); a sail on a jiggermast (*naut*); a small measure for alcoholic drinks. — *vt* to jerk or shake; to form with a jigger; to ruin (sometimes with *up*). — *vi* to tug or move with jerks. — *adj* **jigg'ered** (*colloq*) exhausted; surprised; bewildered. — *n* **jigg'ing**. — *vt* and *vi* **jigg'le** to move with vibratory jerks. — *n* a jiggling movement. — **jig borer** an adjustable precision machine-tool for drilling holes; **jigg'ermast** a four-masted ship's aftermost mast; a small mast astern; **jig'saw** a narrow reciprocating saw; a jigsaw puzzle. — *vt* and *vi* to cut with a jigsaw. — **jigsaw puzzle** a picture cut up into pieces (as by a jigsaw) to be fitted together.

jigajig, etc. See **jig-jog**.

jigger[1] *jig'ər*, *n* a form of **chigoe**.

jigger[2], **jiggered**. See **jig**.

jiggery-pokery *jig-ə-ri-pō'kə-ri*, (*colloq*) *n* trickery; deception.

jiggety-jog. See **jig-jog**.

jiggle. See **jig**.

jig-jog *jig'-jog*, *adv* with a jolting, jogging motion. — *n* a jolting motion; a jog. — Also **jick'ajog**, **jig'jig**, **jig'ajig**, **jig'ajog** and **jiggety-jog'**. — **jig'-a-jig** or **jig'-jig** (*slang*, used esp. in pidgins) sexual intercourse. [**jig** and **jog**.]

jigot. Same as **gigot**.

jihad or **jehad** *jē-had'*, *n* a holy war (for the Muslim faith); a fervent crusade. [Ar. *jihād*, struggle.]

jilgie. See **gilgie**.

jillaroo. See **jackaroo**.

jilt *jilt*, *n* a person (orig. a woman) who encourages and then rejects a lover. — *vt* to discard abruptly a lover one had previously encouraged.

jimcrack. See **gimcrack**.

Jim Crow *jim krō*, (*US derog slang*) *n* a generic name for the Negro; racial discrimination against Negroes. — **Jim Crow car, school** etc., one for Negroes only. [From a Negro minstrel song with the refrain 'Wheel about and turn about and jump *Jim Crow*'.]

jimjams *jim'jamz*, (*slang*) *npl* delirium tremens; the fidgets; pyjamas (*colloq*).

jimmy *jim'i*, (chiefly *US*) *n* a burglar's jemmy. — *vt* to force open, esp. with a jimmy. [From the personal name *James*.]

Jimmy *jim'i*, (*slang*) *n* an act of urinating. — Also **Jimmy Riddle**. [Rhyming slang for *piddle*.]

jingle *jing'gl*, *n* a succession of clinking sounds; something which makes a tinkling sound, esp. a metal disc on a tambourine; a short, simple verse, usu. with music, used to advertise a product, etc. — *vt* and *vi* to sound with a jingle. — *n* **jing'ler**. — *adj* **jing'ly**. — **jing'le-jangle** a dissonant continued jingling. [Imit.]

jingo or **Jingo** *jing'gō*, *n* used in the mild oath 'By jingo!' (*Scot* 'By jings!') expressing surprise; a chauvinistic, sabre-rattling patriot: — *pl* **jing'oes**. — *adj* **jing'o** or **jing'oish** chauvinist, sabre-rattling. — *n* **jing'oism**. — *n* **jing'oist**. — *adj* **jingois'tic** characteristic of jingoism. — *adv* **jingois'tically**.

jinjili. See **gingili**.

jink *jingk*, (orig. *Scot*) *vi* to dodge nimbly; to make a sudden evasive turn (*aeronautics*). — *vt* to elude; to cheat. — *n* (esp. *aeronautics* and *Rugby football*) a quick, deceptive turn. — **high jinks** see under **high**.

jinker *jing'kər*, (Austr) *n* a sulky or other light horse-drawn passenger conveyance; a two-wheeled trailer for carrying logs.

jinn *jin*, *npl* (*nsing* **jinnee, jinni, djinni** or **genie** (*jin-ē'* or *jē'ni*)) a class of spirits in Muslim mythology, assuming various shapes, sometimes as enormous monstrous men with supernatural powers. — Also **djinn** or **ginn**. The *jinn* are often called *genii* by a confusion and **jinns** is sometimes erroneously used as a plural. [Ar. *jinn*, sing. *jinnī*.]

jinricksha, jinrickshaw. See **ricksha**.

jinx *jingks*, *n* a bringer of bad luck; an unlucky influence. — *vt* to bring bad luck to, or put an unlucky spell on. — *adj* **jinxed** beset with bad luck. [App. from *Jynx*, the bird being used in spells, and the name itself coming to mean 'a spell or charm'.]

jism, gism *jiz'əm* or **jissom** *jis'əm*, *n* energy, force (*colloq*, chiefly *US*); semen (*vulg*).

JIT (*business*) *abbrev* for just-in-time (q.v.).

jitter *jit'ər*, (orig. *US*) *vi* to behave in a flustered way. — *npl* **jitt'ers** a flustered state. — *adj* **jitt'ery**. — **jitt'erbug** (*US*) a type of two-step to jazz music, the standard movements allowing for energetic improvisation; someone who performs this dance; (in Britain, by misunderstanding or extension) a scaremonger, alarmist. — *vi* to dance a jitterbug.

jiu-jitsu. Same as **ju-jitsu**.

jive *jīv*, *n* a lively style of jazz music, swing; the style of fast dancing done to this music; jargon, *specif* of Harlem and of jazz musicians (*slang*). — *vi* to play or dance jive; to talk jive (also **jive talk**; *slang*). — *n* **jī'ver**.

Jnr or **jnr** *abbrev* for Junior or junior.

joanna *jō-an'ə*, (*slang*) *n* a piano. [Rhyming slang.]

Job *jōb*, *n* a person of great patience — from the biblical figure *Job* in the Book of Job. — **Job's comforter** someone who aggravates the distress of the unfortunate person they have come to comfort.

job *job*, *n* any definite piece of work; any undertaking or employment with a view to profit; an appointment or situation; a criminal enterprise, esp. theft (*colloq*). — *adj* employed, hired, or used by the job or for jobs; bought or sold lumped together. — *vi* to work at jobs; to buy and sell, as a broker; to practise jobbery. — *vt* to perform as a job; to put or carry through by jobbery; to deal in, as a broker. — *n* **jobb'er** a person who jobs; a person who buys and sells, as a broker; in combination with *first*, *second*, etc., someone in, or seeking, their first, second, etc. job. — *n* **jobb'ery** jobbing; unfair means employed to secure some private end. — *n* **jobb'ie** (*colloq*) a lump of excrement. — *adj* **jobb'ing** working by the job. — *n* the doing of jobs; miscellaneous printing-work; buying and selling as a broker; stock-jobbing; jobbery. — *adj* and *npl* **job'less** (people) having no job. — **job centre** or **Job'centre** (also without *cap*) a government-run employment office, esp. one where information about available jobs is displayed; **job club** or **Job'club** an association directed towards helping the jobless to find employment for themselves through learning and using the required skills, motivation, etc.; **job-lot'** a collection of odds and ends, esp. for sale as one lot; any collection of inferior quality; **job share** or **job sharing** the practice of dividing one job between two part-time workers. — **a bad** (or **good**) **job** a piece of work badly (or well) done; an unlucky (or lucky) fact; **have a job to** (*colloq*) to have difficulty in; **job off** to sell (goods) cheaply to get rid of them; **job of work** a task, bit of work; **job out** to divide (work) among contractors, etc.; **jobs for the boys** jobs given to or created for friends or supporters; **just the job** (*colloq*) exactly what is wanted; **odd jobs** see under **odd**; **on the job** at work, in action.

jobsworth *jobz'wûrth*, (*derog slang*) *n* a minor official, esp. one who adheres rigidly and unco-operatively to petty rules. [From 'It's more than my *job's worth* to let you . . .'.]

Jock *jok*, (*slang*) *n* a Scottish soldier; a Scotsman. [**Jack**.]

jock *jok*, *n* a jockstrap (*colloq*); a male athlete or sportsman (*US slang*); a disc-jockey (*slang*).

jockey *jok'i*, *n* a person who rides (esp. professionally) in horse-races; someone who takes undue advantage in business. — *vt* to jostle by riding against; to manoeuvre; to trick by manoeuvring. — *vi* (often with *for*) to seek advantage by manoeuvring. — *n* **jockette'** (*facetious*) a female jockey. — *n* **jock'eyism**. — *n* **jock'eyship** the art or practice of a jockey. — **Jockey Club** an association for the promotion and ordering of horse-racing. [Dimin. of **Jock**, i.e. a lad (jockeys orig. being boys).]

jockstrap *jok'strap*, *n* a genital support worn by men participating in athletics. [Dialect *jock*, the penis, and **strap**.]

jocose *jō-kōs'*, *adj* full of jokes; facetious; merry. — *adv* **jocose'ly**. — *n* **jocose'ness** or **jocosity** (*-kos'i-ti*) the quality of being jocose. [L. *jocōsus* — *jocus*, a joke.]

jocular *jok'ū-lər*, *adj* given to or inclined to joking; of the nature of, or intended as, a joke. — *n* **jocularity** (*-lar'i-ti*). — *adj* **joc'ularly**. [L. *joculāris* — *jocus*.]

jocund *jō'kund*, *jok'und* or *-ənd*, *adj* merry, cheerful. — *n* **jocundity** (*-kund'i-ti*). — *adv* **joc'undly**. [O.Fr., — L.L. *jocundus* for L. *jūcundus*, pleasant, modified by association with *jocus*.]

jodhpurs *jod'pûrz*, *npl* riding-breeches, loose round the hip and tight-fitting from the knee to the ankle. — Also **jodhpur breeches**. — **jodhpur boots** ankle-high boots worn with jodhpurs for riding. [*Jodhpur* in India.]

Joe *jō*, *n* a man, ordinary fellow. — **Joe Bloggs** or (*US* and *Austr*) **Joe Blow** the average man in the street. — Also **Joe Public**.

joey *jō'i*, (*Austr*) *n* a young animal, esp. a kangaroo; an opossum (*NZ*). [Aboriginal.]

jog *jog*, *vt* to shake; to push with the elbow or hand; to stimulate or stir up, e.g. the memory. — *vi* to move by jogs; (with *on* or *along*) to move along or progress slowly, steadily, unremarkably; to run at a slow, steady pace, as a form of exercise: — *pr p* **jogg'ing**; *pa t* and *pa p* **jogged**. — *n* a slight shake; a push or nudge; a spell of jogging. — *n* **jogg'er** a person who jogs for exercise; a piece of mechanical equipment which shakes sheets of paper into alignment ready for stapling, binding, etc. — *n* **jogg'ing** running at a slow, steady pace, esp. for exercise. — **jog'trot** a slow jogging trot; humdrum routine. [M.E., app. imit.]

joggle[1] *jog'l*, *n* a tooth, notch or pin to prevent contacting surfaces from sliding; a joint made in this way. — *vt* to join with a joggle. [Perh. connected with **jag**[1].]

joggle[2] *jog'l*, *vt* to jog or shake slightly; to jostle. — *vi* to shake: — *pr p* **jogg'ling**; *pa t* and *pa p* **jogg'led**. [App. dimin. or frequentative of **jog**.]

John *jon*, *n* a proper name, a diminutive of which, **Johnn'y** (also **Johnn'ie**), is sometimes used in slang for a simpleton, an empty-headed man-about-town or fellow generally; (without *cap*) a lavatory (*slang*, esp. *US*); a prostitute's client (*slang*). — *n* **johnn'ie** or **johnn'y** (*slang*) a condom. — **John Bull** an Englishman; **John Bullism** the typical English character, or any act or word expressive of it; **John Canoe** see separate entry; **John Collins** an alcoholic drink based on gin; **John Dory** see **dory**; **Johnny-come-late'ly** a newcomer; **John Thomas** (*slang*) the penis. [L. *Jōhannēs*.]

John Canoe *jon kə-nōō'*, (*WIndies*) *n* a boisterous rhythmic dance performed esp. as part of Christmas celebrations; the celebrations themselves; any of, esp. the leader of, the dancers; the mask or headdress of such a dancer. [From a W. African language.]

joie de vivre *zhwa də vē-vr'*, (Fr.) *n* joy of living; exuberance.

join *join*, *vt* to connect; to unite; to associate; to add or annex; to become a member of; to come into association with or the company of; to go to and remain with, in, or on; to draw a straight line between (*geom*). — *vi* to be connected; to combine, unite; to run into one; to grow together; to be in, or come into, close contact. — *n* a joining; a place where things have been joined; a mode of joining. — *n* **join'der** (esp. *law*) joining, uniting. — *n* **join'er** a worker in wood, esp. one who makes smaller structures than a carpenter; a person who joins or unites. — *n* **join'ery** the art of the joiner; a joiner's work. — *n* **join'ing** the act of joining; a seam; a joint. — *n* **joint** a joining; the place where, or mode in which, two or more things join; a place where two things (esp. bones) meet allowing a hingelike movement; a node, or place where a stem bears leaves, esp. if swollen; a segment; a piece of an animal's body as cut up for serving at the table; a crack intersecting a mass of rock (*geol*); the place where adjacent surfaces meet; the condition of adjustment at a joint (in the phrase *out of joint*); a place generally, esp. a meeting place such as a public house or hotel (*colloq*); a cigarette containing marijuana (*colloq*); see also **the joint** below. — *adj* joined, united or combined; shared among more than one; sharing with another or others. — *vt* to unite by joints; to provide with joints or an appearance of joints; to divide into joints. — *adj* **joint'ed** having joints; composed of segments; constricted at intervals. — *n* **joint'er** the largest kind of plane used by a joiner; a bricklayer's tool for putting mortar in joints. — *adj* **joint'less**. — *adv* **joint'ly** in a joint manner; unitedly or in combination; together. — *n* **joint'ness**. — **joint account** a bank account held in the name of two or more people, any of whom can deposit or withdraw money; **joint heir** a person who inherits jointly with another or others; **joint'ing-rule** a long straight-edged rule used by bricklayers; **joint-stock'** stock held jointly or in company (**joint-stock company** one in which each shareholder can transfer shares without consent of the rest); **joint-ten'ancy**; **joint-ten'ant** a person who is owner of land or goods along with others; **joint venture** a business activity undertaken by two or more companies acting together, sharing costs, risks and profits. — **join issue** to begin to dispute; to take up the contrary view or side; **join up** to enlist, esp. as part of a general movement; **out of joint** dislocated; disordered, awry (*fig*); **put someone's nose out of joint** to disconcert, rebuff or offend (someone); **the joint** (*slang*, esp. *US*) jail; **universal joint** a device, one part of which is able to move freely in all directions, as in the ball-and-socket joint. [O.Fr. *joindre* — L. *jungěre*, to join.]

jointure *joyn'tyər*, *n* property settled on a woman at her marriage to be enjoyed after her husband's death. — *vt* to settle a jointure upon, arrange a jointure for. — *n* **joint'uress** or **joint'ress** a woman on whom a jointure is settled. [O.E., — O.Fr. — L. *junctūra*, a joining.]

joist *joist*, *n* a beam supporting the boards of a floor or the laths of a ceiling. — *vt* to fit with joists. [O.Fr. *giste* — *gesir* — L. *jacēre*, to lie.]

jojoba *hō-hō'bə*, *n* a desert shrub of the box family, native to Mexico, Arizona and California, whose edible seeds yield a waxy oil chemically similar to spermaceti. [Mex. Sp.]

joke *jōk*, *n* an amusing quip or story; a witticism; anything said or done to provoke a laugh; anything provocative of laughter; an absurdity. — *vi* to jest; to be humorous; to tell jokes; to make fun. — *n* **jok'er** a person who jokes or jests; an additional card in the pack, used at poker, etc.; an unforeseen factor affecting a situation; a fellow, often one viewed with mild, usu. amicable, amusement (*slang*). — *adj* **jō'key** or **jō'ky**. — *adv* **jok'ingly**. — **joking apart** if I may be serious, seriously; **no joke** a serious or difficult matter. [L. *jocus*.]

jolly *jol'i*, *adj* merry; expressing or provoking fun and gaiety, jovial. — *vt* (esp. with *along*) to put or keep in good humour, amuse. — *adv* (*colloq*) very. — *n* (*colloq*) a jollification. — *n* **jollificā'tion** an occasion of merrymaking or being jolly; noisy festivity and merriment. — *vi* **joll'ify**. — *adv* **joll'ily**. — *n* **joll'iness** or **joll'ity**. — **Jolly Roger** a black flag with white skull and crossbones, flown by pirate ships. [O.Fr. *jolif*, *joli*.]

jollyboat *jol'i-bōt*, *n* a small boat kept hoisted at the stern of a ship.

jolt *jōlt*, *vi* to shake or proceed with sudden jerks. — *vt* to shake with a sudden shock. — *n* a sudden jerk; a shock; a surprising or activating shock. — *n* **jolt'er**. — *adv* **jolt'ingly** in a jolting manner. — *adj* **jolt'y**.

Jonah *jō'nə*, *n* a person thought to bring bad luck, esp. to a ship. [From the biblical prophet *Jonah*, whose disobedience to God provoked a storm at sea in which he was washed overboard.]

jonquil *jong'kwil*, *n* a name given to certain species of narcissus with rushlike leaves. [Fr. *jonquille* — L. *juncus*, a rush.]

josephinite *jo'zə-fēn-īt*, *n* a mineral found only in *Josephine* Creek, in Oregon, U.S.A., and believed to have originated at the outer edge of the earth's core and been carried up nearly 2 000 miles to the surface.

Josephson junction *jō'zif-sən jungk'shən*, (*electronics*) *n* a junction formed from two superconducting metals separated by a thin insulating layer, allowing the unimpeded passage of a current and generating microwaves when subjected to a certain voltage. [B.D. *Josephson* (1940–), English physicist.]

Josh. (*Bible*) *abbrev* for (the Book of) Joshua.

josh *josh*, *vt* to ridicule; to tease. — *n* a hoax; a derisive jest. — *n* **josh'er**.

joss *jos*, *n* a Chinese idol; luck or fate. — *n* **joss'er** a clergyman (*Austr*). — **joss'-house** a temple; **joss'-stick** a stick of gum which gives off a perfume when burned, used as incense esp. in India, China, etc. [Port. *deos*, god — L. *deus*.]

jostle *jos'l* or **justle** *jus'l*, *vt* and *vi* to shake or jar by collision; to hustle; to elbow. — *n* an act of jostling. — *n* **jos'tling**. [Frequentative of **joust**.]

jot *jot*, *n* an iota, a whit, a tittle. — *vt* to set down briefly; to make a memorandum of: — *pr p* **jott'ing**; *pa t* and *pa p* **jott'ed**. — *n* **jott'er** someone who jots; a book or pad for rough notes. — *n* **jott'ing** a memorandum; a rough note. [L. *iōta* (read as *jōta*) — Gr. *iōta*, the smallest letter in the alphabet, equivalent to *i*.]

jota *hhō'tä*, *n* a Spanish dance in triple time. [Sp.]

joule *jōōl*, *n* a unit of energy, work and heat in the MKS and SI systems, equal to work done when a force of 1 newton advances its point of application 1 metre (1 joule = 10^7 ergs). [After the physicist J.P. *Joule* (1818–89).]

jounce *jowns*, *vt* and *vi* to jolt, shake.

journal[1] *jûr'nəl*, *n* a daily register or diary; a book containing a record of each day's transactions; a newspaper published daily (or otherwise); a magazine; the transactions of any society. — *n* **journalese'** the jargon of bad journalism. — *vi* **jour'nalise** or **-ize** to write for or in a journal. — *vt* to enter in a journal. — *n* **journ'alism** the profession of collecting, writing, publishing, etc. news reports and other articles for newspapers, journals, television, radio and related media; the style of writing associated with the reporting of news, current affairs and popular interest subjects via a transitory medium. — *n* **jour'nalist** a person who writes for or manages a newspaper, magazine or other news-related medium; a person who keeps a journal. — *adj* **journalist'ic**. — *n* **jour'no** (*Austr colloq*) a journalist: — *pl* **jour'nos**. [Fr., — L. *diurnālis*; see **diurnal**.]

journal[2] *jûr'nəl*, (*mech*) *n* that part of a shaft or axle which is in contact with and supported by a bearing. — *vt* to provide with or fix as a journal. — **jour'nal-box** a box or bearing for a journal.

journey *jûr'ni*, *n* any travel from one place to another; a tour or excursion; movement from end to end of a fixed course: — *pl* **jour'neys**. — *vi* to travel: — *pr p* **jour'neying**; *pa t* and *pa p* **jour'neyed** (*-nid*). — *n* **jour'neyer**. — **jour'neyman** a hired workman, orig. one hired by the day; a worker whose apprenticeship is completed. [Fr. *journée* — *jour*, a day — L. *diurnus*.]

joust *jowst* (less commonly *jōōst* or *just*), *n* an encounter between two lance-bearing knights on horseback at a tournament. — *vi* to tilt. — *n* **joust'er**. [O.Fr. *juste*, *jouste*, *joste* — L. *juxtā*, near to.]

Jove *jōv*, *n* another name for the god Jupiter. — *adj* **Jō'vian** of the god, or the planet, Jupiter. — **by Jove** an exclamation of surprise, admiration, etc. [L. *Jovis* (in the nominative usu. *Juppiter*, *Jupiter*), the god Jove or Jupiter, or the planet Jupiter, an auspicious star.]

jovial *jō'vi-əl*, *adj* full of jollity and geniality; (with *cap*) of or influenced by Jupiter. — *n* **joviality** (*-al'i-ti*) or **jō'vialness**. — *adv* **jō'vially**. [**Jove**.]

Jovian. See **Jove**.

jowl *jowl*, *n* the jaw; the cheek; a pendulous double chin; (in animals) a dewlap. — *adj* **jowled**. — *adj* **jow'ly** having noticeably heavy or droopy jaws.

joy *joi*, *n* intense gladness; rapture, delight; a cause of joy, e.g. a beloved person, thing or event. — *adj* **joy'ful** full of joy; feeling, expressing, or giving joy. — *adv* **joy'fully**. — *n* **joy'fulness**. — *adj* **joy'less** without joy; not giving joy. — *adv* **joy'lessly**. — *n* **joy'lessness**. — *adj* **joy'ous** joyful. — *adv* **joy'ously**. — *n* **joy'ousness**. — *vi* **joy'-pop** (*slang*) to take addictive drugs from time to time without forming an addiction. — **joy'-ride** (*slang*) a pleasure-drive, esp. reckless or surreptitious and in a stolen car. — Also *vi*. — **joy'-rider**; **joy'-riding**; **joy'stick** the control-lever of an aeroplane, invalid car, video game, etc.; a lever controlling the movement of the cursor on a VDU screen (*comput*). — **(get** or **have) any joy** (*colloq*) (to achieve) satisfaction, success (in an attempt, etc.); **no joy** (*colloq*) no news, reply, information, luck or success. [Fr. *joie* (cf. It. *gioja*) — L. *gaudium*.]

JP *abbrev* for Justice of the Peace.

Jr or **jr** *abbrev* for Junior or junior.

jubate *jōō'bāt*, (*zool*, etc.) *adj* maned. [L. *jubātus* — *juba*, mane.]

jubbah *jōōb'ə* or *jub'ə*, *n* a long loose outer garment worn by Muslims. [Ar. *jubbah*.]

jube[1] *jōō'bē*, *n* a rood-loft. [L. imper. of *jubēre*, to command.]

jube[2] *jōōb*, *n* an Austr. colloq shortening of **jujube** (the sweet).

jubilant *jōō'bi-lənt*, *adj* rejoicing, feeling or expressing great joy; singing or shouting in joy or triumph. — *n* **ju'bilance** or **ju'bilancy** exultation. — *adv* **ju'bilantly**. — *vi* **ju'bilate** to exult, rejoice. — *n* (*jōō-bi-lä'tē* or *yōō-bi-lä'te*) the third Sunday after Easter; (usu. with *cap*) the 100th Psalm which begins in Latin with *Jubilate* (rejoice). — *n* **jubilā'tion** rejoicing, the expression of joy; joyful or triumphal shouting or singing. [L. *jūbilāre*, to shout for joy.]

jubilee *jōō'bi-lē*, *n* a time, season or circumstance of great joy and festivity; the celebration of a 50th or

25th anniversary — e.g. of a king's accession; a year (every 25th year — *ordinary jubilee*) of indulgence for pilgrims and others, an *extraordinary jubilee* being specially appointed by the Pope (*RC*); among the Jews, every 50th year, a year of release of slaves, cancelling of debts, return of property to its former owners, proclaimed by the sound of a trumpet; jubilation. — **jubilee clip** a metal loop with a screw fitting, placed round a tube, hose, etc., and tightened to form a watertight connection. — **silver, golden** or **diamond jubilee** respectively a 25th, 50th and 60th anniversary. [Fr. *jubilé* — L. *jūbilaeus* — Heb. *yōbēl*, a ram, ram's horn.]

JUD *abbrev* for *Juris Utriusque Doctor* (L.), Doctor of both laws (i.e. Canon and Civil).

Jud. (*Bible*) *abbrev* for: (the Book of) Judges (also **Judg.**); (the Apocryphal Book of) Judith.

Judaean or **Judean** *jōō-dē'ən, adj* of Judaea or the Jews. — *n* a native of Judaea; a Jew. [L. *Judaea.*]

Judaeo- *jōō-dā-ō-* or in U.S. **Judeo** *jōō-dē-ō-, combining form* denoting Jewish, as in *Judaeo-Spanish*, Jewish-Spanish, Ladino. [L. *Judaea.*]

Judaic *jōō-dā'ik, adj* pertaining to the Jews. — *npl* **Judā'ica** the culture of the Jews — their literature, customs, etc., esp. as described in books, articles, etc. — *adj* **Judā'ical** Judaic. — *adv* **Judā'ically.** — *n* **Judāīsā'tion** or **-z-**. — *vt* **Ju'dāīse** or **-īze** to conform to, adopt or practise Jewish customs or Judaism. — *n* **Ju'dāīser** or **-z-**. — *n* **Ju'dāism** the doctrines and rites of the Jews; conformity to the Jewish rites. — *n* **Ju'dāist** someone who holds the doctrines of Judaism. — *adj* **Judāist'ic.** — *adv* **Judāist'ically.** [L. *Jūdaicus* — *Jūda*, Judah, a son of Israel.]

Judas *jōō'dəs, n* a traitor; (also without *cap*) a Judas-hole; used attributively, as in *Judas goat*, denoting an animal or bird used to lure others. — **Ju'das-hole** or **-window** (also without *cap*) a spy-hole in a door, etc.; **Ju'das-kiss** any act of treachery under the guise of kindness, as specif. that of Judas related in the Bible (Matt. xxvi. 48, 49). [*Judas* Iscariot.]

judder *jud'ər, n* a strong vibration in an aircraft or other mechanical apparatus; an intense, jerking motion; in singing, a vibratory effect produced by alternations of greater or less intensity of sound. — Also *vi.* [Prob. **jar**[1] and **shudder.**]

Judg. See **Jud.**

Judeo-. See **Judaeo-.**

judge *juj, vi* to point out or declare what is just or law; to try to decide questions of law, guiltiness, etc.; to pass sentence; to act in the capacity of a judge; to compare facts to determine the truth; to form or pass an opinion; to distinguish. — *vt* to hear and determine authoritatively; to sit in judgment on; to pronounce on the guilt or innocence of; to sentence; to decide the merits of; to find fault in, to censure; to decide; to award; to estimate; to form an opinion on; to conclude; to consider (to be). — *n* a person who judges; a person appointed to hear and settle causes, and to try accused persons; someone chosen to award prizes, to decide doubtful or disputed points in a competition, etc.; an arbitrator; someone who can decide upon the merit of anything; someone capable of discriminating well; (with *cap*; in *pl*) the title of the 7th book of the Old Testament. — *n* **judge'ship** the office of a judge. — *n* **judg'ment** or **judge'ment** the act of judging; the comparing of ideas to find out the truth; the faculty by which this is done, the reason; an opinion formed; discrimination; good taste; a legal sentence; a misfortune thought to be sent as a punishment from God. — *adj* **judgment'al** or **judgement'al** involving judgment; apt to pass judgment. — **judge-ad'vocate** the crown-prosecutor at a court-martial; **Judges' Rules** (*formerly*) in English law, a system of rules governing the behaviour of the police towards suspects; **judg'-ment-day** (also **Judgment Day**) the day of God's final judgment on mankind. — **judgment of Solomon** a judgment intended to call the bluff of the false claimant — like that of Solomon in the Bible (1 Kings iii. 16–28); **judgment reserved** a decision delayed after the close of a trial. [A.Fr. *juger* — L. *jūdicāre* — *jūs*, law, *dīcĕre*, to say, to declare.]

judicature *jōō'di-kə-chər, n* power of dispensing justice by legal trial; jurisdiction; the office of judge; the body of judges; a court or system of courts. — *n* **ju'dicatory** (*-kə-tər-i*) judicature; a court. — *adj* pertaining to a judge; distributing justice. [L. *jūdicāre, -ātum*, to judge.]

judicial *jōō-di'shəl, adj* pertaining to a judge or a court of justice; established by statute; arising from process of law; of the nature of judgment; judgelike, impartial. — *adj* **judi'cially.** — **judicial separation** the separation of two married people by a Divorce Court order. [L. *jūdiciālis* — *jūdicium*, a court, judgment.]

judiciary *jōō-di'shər-i* or *-shi-ər-i, adj* pertaining to judgment, judges or courts of law. — *n* a body of judges; a system of courts. [L. *jūdiciārius.*]

judicious *jōō-di'shəs, adj* according to sound judgment; possessing sound judgment; discreet. — *adv* **judi'ciously.** — *n* **judi'ciousness.** [Fr. *judicieux* — L. *jūdicium*, a judgment.]

judo *jōō'dō, n* a sport and physical discipline based upon unarmed self-defence techniques, a modern variety of ju-jitsu. — *n* **judogi** (*jōō'dō-gi* or *-dō'gi*) the costume (jacket and trousers) worn by a **ju'dōist** or **judoka** (*jōō'dō-kə* or *-dō'kə*), a person who practises, or is expert in, judo. [Jap. *jiu*, gentleness, *do*, way.]

Judy *jōō'di, n* Punch's wife in the street puppet-show 'Punch and Judy'; (without *cap*) a girl (*Austr* or *Br slang*). [From the personal name, *Judith.*]

jug[1] *jug, n* a vessel with a handle and a spout or lip, for holding and pouring liquids; a jugful. — *vt* to boil or stew as in a closed jar: — *pr p* **jugg'ing**; *pa t* and *pa p* **jugged.** — *n* **jug'ful** as much as a jug will hold: — *pl* **jug'fuls.** — *n* **jug'let** (*archaeol*) a small juglike vessel. — **jug band** a band using jugs and other utensils as musical instruments; **jugged hare** hare cut in pieces and stewed with wine and other seasoning.

jug[2] *jug*, (*slang*) *n* prison.

jugate *jōō'gāt, adj* paired (*bot*); having the leaflets in pairs (*bot*); joined side by side or overlapping. [L. *jugāre, -ātum*, to join.]

juggernaut *jug'ər-nöt, n* a very large lorry; any relentless destroying force or object of devotion and sacrifice; (with *cap*) an incarnation of Vishnu, whose idol at Puri is traditionally drawn on a processional chariot, beneath which devotees were once believed to throw and crush themselves. [Sans. *Jagannātha*, lord of the world.]

juggins *jug'inz*, (*slang*) *n* a simpleton.

juggle *jug'l, vi* to throw and manipulate balls or other objects in the air with great dexterity (also *fig*); to conjure, practise sleight-of-hand; to trick or deceive; to tamper or manipulate. — *vt* to keep (several different items, activities, etc.) in motion, progress or operation simultaneously, esp. with dexterity. — *n* an act of juggling; a fraudulent trick. — *n* **jugg'ler.** — *n* **jugg'lery** (*-lə-ri*) the art or an act of a juggler; legerdemain; trickery. — *n* and *adj* **jugg'ling.** — *adv* **jugg'lingly.** [O.Fr. *jogler* — L. *joculārī*, to jest.]

jughead *jug'hed*, (*US slang*) *n* an idiot, fool, mindless person. [**jug**[1] and **head.**]

Jugoslav. Same as **Yugoslav.**

jugular *jug'* or *jōōg'ū-lər, adj* pertaining to the neck or throat. — *n* one of the large veins on each side of the neck. — *vt* **jug'ūlate** to cut the throat of; to strangle, check by drastic means (*fig*). — **go for the jugular** to attack someone at the place at which they are most vulnerable and liable to greatest harm. [L. *jugulum*, the collar-bone — *jungĕre*, to join.]

juice *jo͞os*, *n* the sap of plants; the fluid part of animal bodies; vitality, piquancy (*fig*); electric current, petrol vapour, or other source of power (*slang*). — *vt* to squeeze juice from (a fruit); (with *up*) to enliven (*US*). — *adj* **juice'less.** — *n* **juic'er** (esp. *US*) a juice extractor. — *n* **juic'iness.** — *adj* **juic'y** full of juice; of popular interest, esp. of a scandalous or sensational kind; profitable. — **juice extractor** a kitchen device for extracting the juice from fruit, etc. — **step on the juice** (*slang*) to accelerate a motor car. [Fr. *jus*, broth, lit. mixture.]

ju-jitsu or **jiu-jitsu** *jo͞o-jit'so͝o*, *n* a system of fighting without weapons developed by the samurai in Japan; a sport founded on it. [Jap. *jū-jutsu*.]

ju-ju or **juju** *jo͞o'jo͞o*, *n* an object of superstitious worship in West Africa; a fetish or charm. [App. Fr. *joujou*, a toy.]

jujube *jo͞o'jo͞ob*, *n* a spiny shrub or small tree (*Zizyphus*) of the buckthorn family; its dark red fruit, which is dried and eaten as a sweetmeat; a chewy, fruit-flavoured lozenge, sweet or lolly made with sugar and gum or gelatine (*Austr*; also shortened to **jube**). [Fr. *jujube* or L.L. *jujuba* — Gr. *zizyphon*.]

juke-box *jo͝ok'-boks*, (orig. *US*) *n* a slot machine that plays gramophone records. — **juke'-joint** a place for dancing and drinking. [Gullah *juke*, disorderly — W. African *dzug*, to lead a careless life.]

jukskei *yo͝ok'skā*, (*SAfr*) *n* an outdoor game similar to quoits, in which bottle-shaped pegs are thrown at stakes fixed in the ground; one of these pegs. [Afrik. *yuk*, yoke, *skei*, pin (orig. yoke pins were thrown).]

Jul. *abbrev* for July.

julep *jo͞o'ləp*, *n* a sweet drink, often medicated; an American drink of spirits, sugar, ice and mint (also **mint-ju'lep**). [Fr., — Sp. *julepe* — Ar. *julāb* — Pers. *gulāb* — *gul*, rose, *āb*, water.]

Julian *jo͞ol'yən*, *adj* pertaining to *Julius* Caesar (100–44 B.C.). — **Julian calendar** that in which a year was set at 365 days with a leap year every 4 years (from which the Gregorian calendar later evolved), instituted by Julius Caesar in 46 B.C.

julienne *jo͞o-li-en'* or *zhü-lyen*, *n* a clear soup, with shredded vegetables; any foodstuff which has been shredded. [Fr. personal name.]

juliet cap *jo͞o'li-et kap*, *n* a round close-fitting skullcap worn by women. [Prob. *Juliet*, in Shakespeare's *Romeo and Juliet*.]

July *jo͞o-lī'* or *jo͞o'lī*, *n* the seventh month of the year. [L. *Jūlius*, from Gaius Julius Caesar, who was born in it.]

jumble *jum'bl*, *vt* to mix confusedly; to throw together without order. — *vi* to be mixed together confusedly; to be agitated. — *n* a confused mixture; confusion; things sold at a jumble sale. — *n* **jum'bler.** — *adv* **jum'blingly** in a confused or jumbled manner. — *adj* **jum'bly.** — **jumble sale** a sale of miscellaneous articles, secondhand or home-made, etc. to raise money for a charity or other body.

jumbo *jum'bō*, *n* anything very big of its kind; an elephant (after a famous large one so named); a jumbo jet: — *pl* **jum'bos.** — *adj* huge; colossal; extra-large. — **jumbo jet** a large jet airliner. [Prob. mumbo-*jumbo*.]

jumbuck *jum'buk*, (*Austr colloq*) *n* a sheep.

jump *jump*, *vi* to spring or bound; to move suddenly; to bounce; to rise suddenly. — *vt* to leap over, from, or on to; to skip over; to cause or help to leap; to appropriate (a claim), as when the owner has failed to satisfy conditions or has abandoned it; to attack (*slang*); (of a male) to have sexual intercourse with (*vulg*). — *n* an act of jumping; a bound; an obstacle to be jumped over; a height or distance jumped; a sudden rise or movement; a start; (in *pl*) convulsive movements, chorea, delirium tremens, or the like (*slang*); a bounce; a discontinuity; a jump-cut. — *n* **jump'er.** — *adv* **jump'ily.** — *n* **jump'iness.** — *adj* **jump'y** nervy, on edge, always liable to jump or start. — **jump'-cut** in filming, an abrupt change from one scene or subject to another, across an interval of time. — *adj* **jumped'-up** (*colloq*) upstart. — **jump'ing-bean** the seed of a Mexican plant (esp. *Sebastiania*), containing a moth larva which causes it to move or jump; **jump'ing-deer** the black-tailed American deer; **jump'ing-jack** a toy figure whose limbs jump up when a string is pulled; **jump'ing-spider** any spider of the family *Salticidae* that leap upon their prey; **jump'-jet** a fighter plane able to land and take off vertically; **jump leads** two electrical cables for supplying power to start a car from another battery; **jump'-off** (*US*) the start; starting-place; see **jump off** below; **jump'-seat** a movable seat in a car or aircraft; a folding seat; **jump suit** a one-piece garment for either sex, combining trousers and jacket or blouse; **jump'-up** (*Caribb*) a social dance. — **jump at** to accept eagerly; **jump down someone's throat** to berate or snap at someone angrily and suddenly; **jumping-off place** the terminus of a route, destination; a place from which one sets out into the wilds, the unknown, etc.; somewhere very remote (*US*); **jump off** (*showjumping*) to compete in another, more difficult round, when two or more competitors have an equal score after the first round (*n* **jump'-off**); **jump on** to jump so as to come down heavily upon; to censure promptly and vigorously; **jump (one's) bail** to abscond, forfeiting (one's) bail; **jump ship** (*colloq*) (of a sailor) to leave one's ship while still officially employed, in service, etc.; **jump start** to start a car by using jump leads; to bump start a car. — Also *n* **jump'-start.** — **jump the gun** (i.e. the starting-gun in a race) to get off one's mark too soon, act prematurely, take an unfair advantage; **jump the queue** to get ahead of one's turn (*lit* and *fig*); **jump to conclusions** to make assumptions prematurely, based upon insufficient facts or consideration; **jump to it!** hurry!; **one jump ahead of** in a position of advantage over. [Prob. onomatopoeic.]

jumper[1] *jum'pər*, *n* a knitted upper garment, a jersey or sweater; a pinafore dress (*US*). [Obs. or dialect *jump*, a short coat, perh. from Fr. *juppe*, now *jupe*, a petticoat.]

jumper[2]. See **jump.**

Jun. *abbrev* for: June; Junior.

junco *jung'kō*, *n* a N. American snow-bird: — *pl* **jun'coes** or **jun'cos.** [Sp. *junco* — L. *juncus*, rush.]

junction *jungk'shən* or *jung'shən*, *n* a joining, a union or combination; place or point of union, esp. of railway lines. — **junction box** a casing for a junction of electrical wires. [L. *junctiō*, *-ōnis*; see ety. for **join.**]

juncture *jungk'chər*, *n* a joining, a union; a critical or important point of time. [L. *junctūra*; see ety. for **join.**]

June *jo͞on*, *n* the sixth month of the year. — **June'-berry** the fruit of the shadbush; **June drop** a falling of immature fruit through a variety of causes, at its height around June. [L. *Jūnius*.]

Jungian *yo͝ong'i-ən*, *adj* of or according to the theories of the Swiss psychologist, Carl Gustav *Jung* (1875–1961).

jungle *jung'gl*, *n* a dense tropical growth of thickets, brushwood, etc.; dense tropical forest; a jumbled assemblage of large objects; a confusing mass of, e.g. regulations; a place or situation where there is ruthless competition, or cruel struggle for survival. — *adj* **jung'ly.** — **jungle fever** a severe malarial fever; **jungle fowl** any of several Asiatic fowl of the genus *Gallus gallus*, thought to be the wild ancestor of the domestic fowl; the mound-bird (*Austr*); **jungle juice** (*slang*) alcoholic liquor, esp. of poor quality, or home-made. — *adj* **jun'gle-green** very dark green. [Orig. waste ground — Sans. *jāngala*, desert.]

junior *jo͞on'yər*, *adj* younger; less advanced; of lower standing. — *n* someone younger, less advanced, or of lower standing; a young person (*colloq*). — *n* **juniority** (*-i-or'i-ti*). — **junior common room** (abbrev. **JCR**) in some universities, a common room for the use of students, as opposed to a *senior common room*, for the use of staff. [L. *jūnior*, compar. of *juvenis*, young.]

juniper *jōō'ni-pər*, *n* an evergreen coniferous shrub whose berries are used in making gin. [L. *jūniperus*.]

junk[1] *jungk*, *n* a Chinese flat-bottomed sailing vessel, with high forecastle and poop, sometimes large and three-masted. [Port. *junco*, app. — Javanese *djong*.]

junk[2] *jungk*, *n* rubbish generally; nonsense (*fig*); a narcotic, esp. heroin (*slang*). — *vt* to treat as junk; to discard or abandon as useless. — *n* **junk'ie** or **junk'y** a narcotics, esp. heroin, addict; (*loosely*) someone hooked on something, an addict (*colloq* usu. in combination, as in *art junkie*, *coffee junkie*). — *adj* **junk'y** rubbishy; worthless. — **junk bond** a bond offering a high yield but with low security; **junk'-dealer** or **junk'man** a dealer in junk; **junk fax** unsolicited material (as **junk mail**) sent by fax; **junk food** food of little nutritional value, usu. easily available and quick to prepare; **junk mail** unsolicited mail such as advertising circulars, etc.; **junk'-shop** a shop where assorted secondhand bric-à-brac is sold; **junk'-yard** a yard in which junk is stored or collected for sale.

Junker *yōōng'kər*, (*hist*) *n* a young German noble or squire; an overbearing, narrow-minded, reactionary aristocrat or official. — *n* **Jun'kerdom**. — *n* **Jun'kerism**. [Ger., — *jung*, young, *Herr*, lord.]

junket *junk'it*, *n* curds mixed with cream, sweetened and flavoured; a feast or merrymaking, a picnic, an outing, a spree, now (esp. *NAm*) one enjoyed by officials using public funds. — *vi* to feast, banquet or take part in a convivial entertainment or spree; to go on a junket (chiefly *NAm*). — *vt* to feast, regale or entertain: — *pr p* **junk'eting**; *pa p* **junk'eted**. — *n* **junketeer'**. — *n* (often in *pl*) **junk'eting** merry feast or entertainment, picnicking. [Orig. dialect, a rush basket (in which it was made and served) — A.Fr. *jonquette*, rush basket — L. *juncus*, a rush.]

junkie, junky. See **junk[2]**.

Juno *jōō'nō*, (*Roman mythol*) *n* the wife of Jupiter, identified with the Greek Hera, protectress of marriage and guardian of woman. [L. *Jūnō*, *-ōnis*.]

junta *jun'tə* or *hōōn'ta*, *n* a government formed by a usu. small group of military officers following a coup d'état; (also **junto** *jun'tō*: — *pl* **jun'tos**) a body of men joined or united for some secret intrigue. [Sp., council — L. *jungĕre*, *junctum*, to join.]

Jupiter *jōō'pi-tər*, *n* the chief god among the Romans, the parallel of the Greek Zeus (also **Jove**); the largest and, next to Venus, the brightest of the planets, fifth in outward order from the sun. [L. *Jūpiter*, *Juppiter*, Father (*pater*) Jove.]

Jurassic *jōō-ras'ik*, (*geol*) *adj* of the middle division of the Mesozoic rocks, well-developed in the *Jura* Mountains. — *n* the Jurassic period or system. — Also **Ju'ra**.

jurat[1] *jōō'rat*, (*law*) *n* the official memorandum at the end of an affidavit, showing the time when and the person before whom it was sworn. [L. *jūrātum*, sworn — *jūrāre*, to swear.]

jurat[2] *jōō'rat*, *n* a sworn officer, esp. (*Fr* and *Channel Is*) a magistrate. [Fr., — L. *jūrāre*, *-ātum*, to swear.]

juridical *jōō-rid'ik-əl* or **juridic** *-rid'ik*, *adj* relating to the distribution of justice; pertaining to a judge; used in courts of law. — *adv* **jurid'ically**. [L. *jūridicus* — *jūs*, *jūris*, law, *dīcĕre*, to declare.]

jurisconsult *jōō-ris-kon-sult'*, *n* someone who is consulted on the law; a lawyer who gives opinions on cases put to him or her; a person knowledgeable in law. [L. *jūris cōnsultus* — *jūs*, *jūris*, law, *cōnsulĕre*, *cōnsultus*, to consult.]

jurisdiction *jōō-ris-dik'shən*, *n* the distribution of justice; legal authority; extent of power; district over which any authority extends. — *adj* **jurisdic'tional** or **jurisdic'tive**. [L. *jūrisdictiō*, *-ōnis*.]

jurisprudence *jōō-ris-prōō'dəns*, *n* the science or knowledge of law. — *adj* **jurispru'dent** learned in law. — *n* a person who is knowledgeable in law. [L. *jūrisprūdentia* — *jūs*, *jūris*, law, *prūdentia*, knowledge.]

jurist *jōō'rist*, *n* a person versed in the science of law, esp. Roman or civil law; a student of law; a graduate in law; a lawyer (*US*). — *adj* **jurist'ic** or **jurist'ical**. — *adv* **jurist'ically**. [Fr. *juriste*.]

jury *jōō'ri*, *n* a group of people sworn to declare the truth on evidence before them; a committee of adjudicators or examiners. — *n* **ju'ror** a person who serves on a jury (also **ju'ryman** and **ju'rywoman**: — *pl* **ju'rymen** and **ju'rywomen**). — **ju'ry-box** the place in court in which the jury sits during a trial; **jury duty**; **jury service**. [A.Fr. *juree* — *jurer* — L. *jūrāre*, to swear.]

jury-rigged *jōō'ri-rigd*, (*naut*) *adj* rigged in a temporary way. — *n* **jury rig** a temporary, makeshift rig. [Perh. O.Fr. *ajurie*, aid, and **rig[1]**.]

just *just*, *adj* righteous (*Bible*); fair; impartial; according to justice; due; in accordance with facts; well-grounded; accurately true; exact. — *adv* precisely; exactly; so much and no more; barely; only; merely; quite (*colloq*). — *adv* **just'ly** in a just manner; equitably; accurately; by right. — *n* **just'ness** equity; fittingness; exactness. — **just about** nearly; more or less; **just about to** see **about to** at **about**; **just now** at this moment; a little while ago, or very soon; **just so** exactly, I agree; in a precise, neat manner. [Fr. *juste*, or L. *jūstus* — *jūs*, law.]

justice *jus'tis*, *n* the quality of being just; integrity; impartiality; rightness; the awarding of what is due; a judge. — *n* **jus'ticeship** the office or dignity of a justice or judge. — *n* **justiciary** (*-tish'i-ə-ri*) a judge or administrator of justice; jurisdiction of a (*Scot*) justiciary. — *adj* pertaining to the administration of justice. — **chief justice** in the Commonwealth, a judge presiding over a supreme court; in the U.S., a judge who is chairman of a group of judges in a court. — **do justice to** to give full advantage to; to treat fairly; to appreciate (a meal, etc.) fully (*colloq*); **European Court of Justice** an EEC institution whose function is to ensure that the laws embodied in the EEC treaties are observed, and to rule on alleged infringements; **High Court of Justiciary** the supreme criminal court in Scotland; **Justice of the Peace** (abbrev. **JP**) in England and Wales, a local lay magistrate commissioned to keep the peace with power to try minor cases, etc. [Fr., — L. *jūstitia*.]

justify *jus'ti-fī*, *vt* to prove or show to be just or right; to vindicate; to absolve; to adjust by spacing to fill the required line length and form an even margin (*printing*): — *pr p* **jus'tifying**; *pa t* and *pa p* **jus'tified**. — *adj* **jus'tifiable** (or *-fī'*) that may be justified or defended. — *n* **jus'tifīableness** (or *-fī'*). — *adv* **jus'tifīably** (or *-fī'*). — *n* **justification** (*jus-ti-fi-kā'shən*) an act of justifying; something which justifies; vindication; absolution; a plea showing sufficient reason for an action (*law*). — *adj* **jus'tificātive** or **justificatory** (*jus-tif'i-kə-tə-ri* or *jus'ti-fi-kā-tə-ri*, or *-kā'*) having power to justify. — *n* **jus'tificātor** or **jus'tifīer** a person who defends or vindicates; a person who pardons and absolves from guilt and punishment. — **justifiable homicide** the killing of a person in self-defence, or to prevent an atrocious crime. — **justification by faith** the doctrine that mankind is absolved from sin by faith in Christ. [Fr. *justifier* and L. *jūstificāre* — *jūstus*, just, *facĕre*, to make.]

just-in-time *just-in-tīm'*, (*business*) *n* a method of stock control in which little or no warehoused stock is kept at the production site, supplies being delivered just in time for use. — Also *adj*.

justle. See **jostle.**

jut *jut*, *vi* to project or protrude from the main body, esp. sharply: — *pr p* **jutt'ing**; *pa t* and *pa p* **jutt'ed.** — *adj* **jutt'ing.** — *adv* **jutt'ingly.** [A form of **jet**[2].]

Jute *jōōt*, *n* a member of a Germanic people originally from Jutland, who with the Angles and Saxons invaded Britain in the 5th century. [M.E. — L.L. *Jutae*, Jutes.]

jute *jōōt*, *n* the fibre of two Asian plants, *Corchorus capsularis* and *C. olitorius*, used for making sacks, mats, etc.; the plants themselves. — Also *adj.* [Bengali *jhuto* — Sans. *jūta*, matted hair.]

juv. *abbrev* for juvenile.

juvenescent *jōō-vən-es'ənt*, *adj* becoming youthful. — *n* **juvenesc'ence.** [L. *juvenēscĕre*, to grow young.]

juvenile *jōō'və-nīl*, *adj* young; pertaining or suited to youth or young people; having or retaining characteristics of youth; childish. — *n* a young person; a book written for the young; an actor who plays youthful parts. — *n* **ju'venileness.** — *npl* **juvenilia** (*-il'yə*) writings or works of one's childhood or youth. — *n* **juvenility** (*-il'i-ti*) juvenile character. — **juvenile court** a special court for the trial of children and young persons aged under seventeen; **juvenile delinquent** or **juvenile offender** a young lawbreaker, in Britain under the age of seventeen. [L. *juvenīlis* — *juvenis*, young.]

juxtaposition *juks-tə-pə-zish'ən*, *n* a placing or being placed close together. — *vt* **jux'tapose** (or *-pōz'*) to place side by side. — *adj* **juxtaposi'tional.** [L. *juxtā*, near, and **position, pose**[1].]

ā face; ä far; û fur; ū fume; ī fire; ō foam; ö form; ōō fool; ŏŏ foot; ē feet; ə former

K

K or **k** *kā*, *n* the eleventh letter in the modern English alphabet, derived from Greek kappa, representing a back voiceless stop, formed by raising the back of the tongue to the soft palate. — **the five Ks** the symbols of a Sikh's spiritual and cultural allegiance to Sikhism, worn by baptised Sikhs — **kaccha, kangha, kara, kesh,** and **kirpan** (qq.v.).

K or **K.** *abbrev* for: Kampuchea (I.V.R.); kaon (*phys*); kelvin, (a degree on) the Kelvin scale; kina (Papua New Guinea currency); king (*cards* and *chess*); Kirkpatrick (catalogue of Domenico Scarlatti's works); knight; Köchel (catalogue of Mozart's works); krona (Swedish currency); króna (Icelandic currency); krone (Danish and Norwegian currency); kwacha (Zambian currency).

K *symbol* for: *kalium* (L.), potassium (*chem*); a thousand; a unit of 1024 words, bytes or bits (*comput*).

k or **k.** *abbrev* for: karat or carat; kilo or kilo-.

k *symbol* for: Boltzmann constant (*phys*); velocity constant (*chem*).

Kaaba *kä'bə*, *n* the cube-shaped holy building at Mecca into which the Black Stone is built. [Ar. *ka'bah* — *ka'b*, cube.]

kabala, kabbala, kabbalah, etc. Same as **cabbala.**

kabuki *kä-bōō-kē'* or *-bōō'*, *n* a popular Japanese dramatic form, historical, classical, eclectic, with music, in which traditionally men played both male and female roles.

Kabyle *ka-bīl'*, *n* one of a branch of the great Berber people of North Africa; a dialect of Berber. [Fr., — Ar. *qabā'il*, pl. of *qabīlah*, a tribe.]

kaccha *kuch'ə*, *n* the short trousers traditionally worn by Sikhs. [Punjabi.]

kack-handed. Same as **cack-handed.**

Kaddish *kad'ish*, *n* a Jewish form of thanksgiving and prayer, used at funerals, etc. [Aramaic *qaddīsh*.]

kade. See **ked.**

kadi *kä'di*, *n*. Same as **cadi.**

Kaffir or **Kaffer** *kaf'ər* or *kuf'ər*, *n* a black African (*SAfr*; offensive); a name applied to certain indigenous peoples of South Africa including the Xhosa, and to the languages spoken by them (*hist*); (in *pl*) South African mining shares (*stock exchange slang*). — *Also adj.* — **kaffir corn** sorghum. [**Kafir.**]

kaffiyeh *käf-ē'ye*, **keffiyeh** or **kufiyah** *kə-fē'yə*, *n* an Arab headdress of cloth, folded and held by a cord around the head. [Ar. *kaffīyah*.]

Kafir *käf'ər*, *n* an infidel (*offensive*); a native of Kafiristan (in Afghanistan); a Kaffir. [Ar. *kāfir*, unbeliever.]

Kafkaesque *kaf-kə-esk'*, *adj* in the style of, or reminiscent of, the ideas, work, etc. of the Czech novelist Franz *Kafka* (1883–1924), esp. in his vision of man's isolated existence in a dehumanised world.

kaftan. Same as **caftan.**

kagool, kagoul, kagoule. See **cagoul.**

kai *kä'ē* or *kī*, (*NZ*) *n* food; a meal. — Also **kai'kai.** — *vt* to eat. [Maori.]

kail. See **kale.**

kainite *kī'nīt*, *kā'nīt* or *kā'in-īt*, *n* hydrous magnesium sulphate with potassium chloride, found in salt deposits, used as a fertiliser. [Ger. *Kainit* — Gr. *kainos*, new, recent.]

kaiser *kī'zər*, *n* an emperor, esp. a German Emperor. — *n* **kai'serdom.** — *n* **kai'serin** the wife of a kaiser. — *n* **kai'sership.** [Ger., — L. *Caesar*.]

kaka *kä'kə*, *n* a green New Zealand parrot. — *n* **ka'kapō** the rare New Zealand owl-parrot, nocturnal and flightless: — *pl* **ka'kapōs.** [Maori *kaka*, parrot, *po*, night.]

kakemono *kak-i-mō'nō*, *n* a Japanese wall-picture or calligraphic inscription on a roller: — *pl* **kakemō'nos.** [Jap. *kake*, to hang, *mono*, thing.]

kakiemon *kä-ki-ā'mon*, *n* a Japanese porcelain, first made by Sakaida *Kakiemon* in the 17th century, recognisable from its characteristic use of iron-red.

kala-azar *kä-lä-ä-zär'*, *n* an often fatal tropical fever, characterised by acute anaemia, etc., caused by a protozoan parasite and usu. transmitted by sandfly bites. [Assamese *kālā*, black, *āzār*, disease.]

kalanchoe *kal-ən-kō'ē*, *n* a succulent plant which bears red, yellow or pink flower clusters on long stems. [Fr., — Mandarin.]

kalashnikov *kə-lash'ni-kof*, *n* a submachine-gun made in the U.S.S.R. [Russ.]

kale or **kail** *kāl*, *n* a cabbage with open curled leaves; cabbage generally (*Scot*); broth of which kale is a chief ingredient (*Scot*); money (*US slang*). — *n* **kail'yard** a cabbage-patch, kitchen-garden. — **Kailyard school** a late 19th- to early 20th-century group of Scottish writers of sentimental stories. [Northern form of **cole.**]

kaleidoscope *kə-lī'də-skōp*, *n* an optical toy in which one sees an ever-changing variety of beautiful colours and patterns; a delightfully diverse and unpredictable sequence of sights, events, etc. (*fig*). — *adj* **kaleidoscopic** (*-skop'ik*) pertaining to a kaleidoscope; showing constant change. [Gr. *kalos*, beautiful, *eidos*, form, *skopeein*, to look.]

kalendar, kalends. Same as **calendar, calends.**

Kalevala *kä'le-vä-lə*, *n* the great Finnish epic, pieced together from oral tradition by Dr. Elias Lönnrot in 1835–49, telling the exploits of the hero Kaleva. [Finnish *kaleva*, a hero, *-la*, denoting place.]

kali *kal'i* or *kā'lī*, *n* the prickly saltwort. [Ar. *qili* as in root of **alkali.**]

Kalmia *kal'mi-ə*, *n* a genus of North American evergreen shrubs of the heath family; (without *cap*) a shrub of the genus. [From Peter *Kalm*, pupil of Linnaeus.]

Kalmuck *kal'muk*, *n* a member of a Mongolian race in China and Russia; their language. — Also *adj*. [Turk. and Russ.]

kalong *kä'long*, *n* a large fruit-bat. [Malay *kālong*.]

Kamasutra or **Kama Sutra** *kä-mə-sōō'trə*, *n* an ancient Sanskrit text on sexual love. [Sans. — *kama*, love, *sūtra*, a string, rule.]

kame *kām*, *n* a low irregular ridge; an esker, a bank or ridge of gravel, sand, etc., associated with the glacial deposits of Scotland (*geol*). [Northern form of **comb**[1] (from its shape like a cock's comb).]

kameez *kə-mēz'*, *n* in S. Asia, a loose tunic with tight sleeves, worn by women. — See also **shalwar-kameez** under **shalwar.** [Urdu *kamis* — Arab. *qamīs*.]

kamik *kä'mik*, *n* a knee-length sealskin boot. [Eskimo.]

kamikaze *kä-mi-kä'zē*, *n* (a Japanese airman, or plane, making) a suicidal attack. — *adj* of, or pertaining to, a kamikaze attack or someone who carries it out; of, or of someone or something engaged upon, an act of certain or deliberate self-destruction in pursuit of a particular cause (*fig*); reckless, foolhardy (*colloq*). [Jap., divine wind.]

kampong *kam'pong* or *kam-pong'*, *n* in Malaysia, a compound or a village. [Malay.]

Kan. *abbrev* for Kansas (U.S. state).

Kanak *kan-ak'*, *n* a Melanesian; one of the Melanesian population of New Caledonia seeking its independence from France. [Hawaiian, *kanaka*, a man.]

Kanaka *kən-ak'ä* or *kan'ə-kä*, *n* a Hawaiian; (also without *cap*) a South Sea Islander, esp. an indentured or forced labourer in Australia (*derog*). [Hawaiian, a man.]

Kanarese or **Canarese** *kan-ər-ēz'*, *adj* of *Kanara* in western India. — *n* one of the people of Kanara; their Dravidian language, now called *Kannada*, akin to Telugu.

kanga or **khanga** *kang'gə*, *n* in East Africa, a piece of cotton cloth, usually brightly decorated, wound around the body as a woman's dress. [Swahili.]

kangaroo *kang-gə-rōō'*, *n* a large Australian herbivorous marsupial (family *Macropodidae*), with short forelimbs, very long hind-legs and great leaping power; (in *pl*; with *cap*) the Australian national Rugby league team. — **kangaroo closure** the method of allowing the chairman to decide which clauses shall be discussed and which passed or leaped over; **kangaroo court** a court operated by a mob, by prisoners in jail, or by any improperly constituted body; a tribunal before which a fair trial is impossible; a comic burlesque court; **kangaroo'-rat** a North American rodent related to the jerboa. [Supposed to be a native Aboriginal name].

kangha *kung'hə*, *n* the comb traditionally worn by Sikhs in their hair. [Punjabi.]

kanji *kan'ji*, *n* in the Japanese writing system, the set of characters derived from Chinese ideographs; one of these characters: — *pl* **kan'ji** or **kan'jis**. [Jap., — Chin., a Chinese word.]

Kannada *kun'ə-də*, *n* an important Dravidian language. [Kanarese.]

Kans. *abbrev* for Kansas (U.S. state).

Kantian *kan'ti-ən*, *adj* pertaining to the German philosopher Immanuel *Kant* (1724–1804) or his philosophy. — *n* **Kan'tianism** or **Kan'tism** the doctrines or philosophy of Kant. — *n* **Kan'tist** a person who is a disciple or follower of Kant.

kaolin or **kaoline** *kā'ō-lin*, *n* China clay, esp. that composed of kaolinite. — *vt* and *vi* **ka'olinise** or **-ize** to turn into kaolin. — *n* **ka'olinite** a hydrated aluminium silicate occurring in minute monoclinic flakes, a decomposition product of feldspar, etc. — *adj* **kaolinit'ic.** — *n* **kaolinō'sis** a disease caused by inhaling kaolin dust. [From the mountain *Kao-ling* (high ridge) in China.]

kaon *kā'on*, (*phys*) *n* one of several types of subatomic particle of smaller mass than a proton. [*K* (pronounced *kā*) and mes*on*.]

kapellmeister *kə-pel'mīs-tər*, *n* the director of an orchestra or choir. [Ger. *Kapelle*, chapel, orchestra, *Meister*, master.]

kapok *kā'pok*, *n* very light, waterproof, oily fibre covering the seeds of a species of silk-cotton tree, used for stuffing pillows, lifebelts, etc. [Malay *kāpoq*.]

Kaposi's sarcoma *kap'ə-sēz* (or *ka-pō'sēz*) *sär-kō'mə*, *n* a form of cancer characterised by multiple malignant tumours, esp. of the skin of the feet and legs, first described by Hungarian-born dermatologist Moritz *Kaposi* (1837–1902) — now a common feature of AIDS.

kappa *kap'ə*, *n* the tenth letter of the Greek alphabet (Κ, κ); as a numeral κ' = 20, $_{,}\kappa$ = 20 000.

kaput *kə-pōōt'*, (*slang*) *adj* ruined; broken; smashed. [Ger.]

kara *kur'ə*, *n* the steel bangle, signifying the unity of God, traditionally worn by Sikhs. [Punjabi.]

karabiner *ka-rə-bēn'ər*, (*mountaineering*) *n* a steel link with a spring clip in one side. [Ger.]

karakul or **caracul** *kär'ə-kōōl* or *-kōōl'*, *n* (often with *cap*) an Asiatic breed of sheep; a fur prepared from the skin of very young lambs of the Karakul or Bukhara breed, or of kids; a cloth imitating it. [Russ. *Kara Kul*, a lake near Bukhara, U.S.S.R.]

karaoke *kar-i-ō'kē*, *n* the (orig. and esp. Japanese) practice and entertainment, popular at public venues and parties, of singing personally-selected hit pop songs to accompanying backing music provided (from a large pre-recorded selection similar to a jukebox system) by a **karaoke machine**, which also enables the singer, using a microphone, to follow the words on a screen. — **karaoke bar** a bar equipped with a karaoke machine, providing karaoke entertainment. [Jap., lit. empty orchestra.]

karat. N.Am. spelling of **carat**.

karate *ka-rä'ti*, *n* a Japanese combative sport using blows and kicks. — *n* **kara'teka** an expert in karate. — **karate chop** a sharp downward blow with the side of the hand.

karma *kur'mə* or *kär'mə*, *n* the conception (Buddhist, etc.) of the quality of actions, including both merit and demerit, determining the future condition of all sentient beings; the theory of inevitable consequence generally; the result of the actions of a life. — *adj* **kar'mic.** [Sans. *karma*, act.]

Karoo or **Karroo** *kä-rōō'*, *n* a high inland pastoral tableland (*SAfr*); a series of strata in South Africa of Permian and Trias age (*geol*). [Believed to be of Hottentot origin.]

kaross *kä-ros'*, *n* a S. African skin blanket. [Perh. a Hottentot modification of Du. *kuras*, cuirass.]

karri *kar'ē*, *n* a Western Australian gum-tree; its red timber. [Aboriginal.]

Karroo. See **Karoo.**

karsey. See **kazi.**

karst *kärst*, *n* rough limestone country with underground drainage. [From the *Karst* district, east of the Adriatic.]

karsy. See **kazi.**

kart *kärt*, *n* a go-kart. — *n* **kart'er.** — *n* **kart'ing** go-kart racing.

kary- *ka-ri-* or **karyo-** *ka-ri-ō-*, *pfx* denoting nucleus. — *n* **karyokinesis** (*-kin-ē'sis*; Gr. *kinēsis*, movement; *biol*) mitosis. — *n* **karyol'ogy** the study of cell-nuclei, esp. of chromosomes. — *n* **kar'yolymph** a colourless, watery fluid, occupying most of the space inside the nuclear membrane; nuclear sap. — *n* **karyol'ysis** dissolution of the nucleus by disintegration of the chromatin; gradual disappearance of the nucleus in a dead cell; liquefaction of the nuclear membrane in mitosis. — *n* **kar'yoplasm** the protoplasm of a cell-nucleus. — *n* **kar'yosome** an aggregation of chromatin. [Gr. *karyon*, kernel.]

karzy. See **kazi.**

kasbah or **casbah** *kaz'bä*, *n* a castle or fortress in a N. African town or the area round it.

kasha *kash'ə*, *n* a porridge or gruel-like dish made from crushed cereal, usu. buckwheat. [Russ.]

Kashmiri *kash-mē'ri*, *adj* belonging to Kashmir, a region in the north-west of the Indian subcontinent.

kat. See **khat.**

kata *kat'a*, (*karate*) *n* a formal sequence of practice exercises and movements. [Jap.]

katabatic *kat-ə-bat'ik*, *adj* (of a wind) blowing down a slope, because of air density differences resulting from overnight cooling, etc. [Gr. *katabatikos* — *katabainein*, to go down.]

katabolism or **catabolism** *kat-ab'ə-lizm*, (*biol*) *n* the disruptive processes of chemical change in organisms — destructive metabolism (opposed to *anabolism*). — *adj* **katabolic** (*kat-ə-bol'ik*). [Gr. *katabolē* —

KL M

kataballein, to throw down.]

katakana *kat-ə-kä'nä*, *n* a Japanese syllabary. [Jap.]

katana *kä-tä'nä*, *n* a long single-edged samurai sword, slightly curved towards the tip. [Jap.]

katathermometer *ka-tə-thər-mom'i-tər*, *n* an alcohol thermometer for measuring the cooling power of the air. [Gr. *kata*, down, and **thermometer**.]

kathak *kəth-äk'*, *n* a classical dance of Northern India in which brief passages of mime alternate with rapid, rhythmic dance. [Sans., a professional storyteller — *katha*, story.]

kation. Same as **cation**.

katydid *kā'ti-did*, *n* an American insect related to the grasshopper. [Imit. of its distinctive sound.]

katzenjammer *kat'sən-jam-ər* or *-jam'ər*, (*US*) *n* a hangover; a similar state of emotional distress (*fig*); an uproar, clamour. [Ger., meaning 'cats' misery'.]

kauri *kow'ri* or **kauri-pine** (*-pīn'*), *n* a tall coniferous forest-tree of New Zealand, source of **kau'ri-gum**, a resin used in making varnish. [Maori.]

kava *kä'və*, *n* an aromatic plant of the pepper family; a narcotic drink prepared from its root and stem. [Polynesian.]

kay *kā*, *n* the eleventh letter of the modern English alphabet (K, k).

kayak *kī'ak*, *n* an Eskimo sealskin canoe; a canvas, fibreglass, etc. canoe built in this style. [Eskimo.]

kayoe *kā-ō'* (*slang*). Stands for **KO** (knockout) *n* and *vt*: — *pl* **kayos'**; *pr p* **kayo'ing**; *pa t* and *pa p* **kayoed'**.

Kazak or **Kazakh** *kaz-äk'*, *n* a member of a Turko-Tatar people of the S.W. Asian part of the Soviet Union; the Turkic dialect spoken by Kazaks. [Russ.]

kazi, karzy, karsey or **karsy** *kä-zi*, (*slang*) *n* a lavatory. [Said to be from It. *casa*, house.]

kazoo *kə-zoo'*, *n* a would-be musical instrument, a tube with a strip of catgut, plastic, etc., that resonates to the voice. [Prob. imit.]

KB *abbrev* for: kilobyte (*comput*); King's Bench; king's bishop (*chess*); knight bachelor.

KBE *abbrev* for Knight Commander of the (Order of the) British Empire.

kbyte (*comput*) *abbrev* for kilobyte.

KC *abbrev* for: Kennel Club; King's Counsel.

kcal *abbrev* for kilocalorie.

KCB *abbrev* for Knight Commander of the (Order of the) Bath.

KCMG *abbrev* for Knight Commander of (the Order of) St. Michael and St. George.

Kčs *abbrev* for *koruna československá* (Czech), koruna (Czechoslovakian currency).

KCVO *abbrev* for Knight Commander of the (Royal) Victorian Empire.

KD *abbrev* for: knocked down (*finance*); Kuwaiti dinar (unit of currency, = 1000 *fils*).

kea *kē'ə*, *n* a large New Zealand parrot that has been known to kill sheep. [Maori.]

kebab *kə-bab'*, *n* (also used in *pl*) a dish of small pieces of meat cooked with vegetables, etc., esp. (from Turkish **shish kebab**) when cooked and served on a skewer. — *vt* (*lit* and *fig*) to skewer. — **doner kebab** (*dō'nər* or *don'ər*) a Middle Eastern dish, thin slices cut from a block of minced and seasoned lamb grilled on a spit, eaten in a split piece of unleavened bread. [Ar. *kabab*.]

keck *kek*, *vi* to retch, feel sick or loathing. — *n* a retching. [Imit.]

ked *ked* or **kade** *kād*, *n* a wingless fly that infests sheep.

kedge *kej*, (*naut*) *n* a small anchor for keeping a ship steady, and for warping (q.v.) the ship. — *vt* to move by means of a kedge, to warp. — *n* **kedg'er** a kedge.

kedgeree *kej'ə-rē*, *n* an Indian dish of rice, cooked with butter and dal, flavoured with spice, shredded onion, etc.; a similar European dish made with fish, rice, etc. [Hind. *khichrī*.]

keek *kēk*, (*Scot*) *vi* to peep. — *n* a peep. [M.E. *kyke*.]

keel[1] *kēl*, *n* the part of a ship extending along the bottom from stem to stern, and supporting the whole frame; a longitudinal member running along the underside of an airship's hull, or any similar structure functioning like a ship's keel (*biol*); any narrow prominent ridge. — *vt* or *vi* to turn keel upwards. — *adj* **keeled** having a ridge on the back. — **keel'boat** a type of yacht with a heavy external keel providing weight to offset that of the sails; see also under **keel**[2]. — *vt* **keel'haul** to punish by hauling under the keel of a ship by ropes from the one side to the other; to rebuke severely. — **keel'hauling.** — **keel over** to stagger or fall over; **on an even keel** calm, or calmly. [O.N. *kjölr*.]

keel[2] *kel*, *n* a low flat-bottomed boat, a barge. — Also **keel'boat.** — *n* **keel'man** a man who works on a barge. [Du. *kiel*, ship.]

keelson *kel'sən* or *kēl'* or **kelson** *kel'sən*, *n* a ship's inner keel, which binds the floor-timbers to the outer keel. [**keel**[1].]

keen[1] *kēn*, *adj* eager; sharp, having a fine edge; with an acute or penetrating mind; intense; competitive, low (as of prices). — *vt* to sharpen. — *adv* **keen'ly.** — *n* **keen'ness.** — **keen on** (*colloq*) devoted to; fond of; very interested in, esp. romantically or sexually. [O.E. *cēne*, bold, fierce, keen.]

keen[2] *kēn*, *n* a lamentation over the dead. — *vi* to wail over the dead. — *n* **keen'er** a professional mourner. — *n* **keen'ing** wailing, lamentation. [Ir. *caoine*.]

keep *kēp*, *vt* to tend; to have the care of; to guard; to maintain; to manage, conduct, run; to attend to the making of records in; to retain; to retain as one's own; to have in one's custody; to have habitually in stock for sale; to support financially, or otherwise supply with necessaries; to have in one's service; to remain in or on; to continue to follow or hold to; to continue to make; to maintain hold upon; to restrain from leaving, to hold back; to prevent; to reserve; to preserve in a certain state; to observe, celebrate; to conform to the requirements of, to fulfil. — *vi* (usu. with *on*) to continue to be or go; to be or remain in a specified condition; to remain fresh or good; to last or endure: — *pr p* **keep'ing**; *pa t* and *pa p* **kept** (*kept*). — *n* food, means of subsistence, board; the innermost and strongest part of a mediaeval castle, the central tower; a stronghold. — *n* **keep'er** a person who or something that keeps, in any sense; an attendant in charge of animals in captivity; a custodian of a museum or gallery; a prison guard; a gamekeeper; the title of certain officials; a wicket-keeper; the socket that receives the bolt of a lock; the armature of a magnet; a guard ring. — *n* **keep'ing** care, custody, charge; preservation, retention; reservation; observance, compliance; just proportion; harmonious consistency. — **keep fit** a programme of physical exercises designed to keep the muscles, circulation and respiratory system in good condition; **keep'net** a cone-shaped net suspended in a river, etc., in which fish caught by anglers can be kept alive; **keep'sake** something given, or kept, as a reminder of the giver, or a certain event, time, etc.; **kept woman** a woman maintained financially by a man as his mistress. — **for keeps** (*colloq*) for good; permanently; **how are you keeping?** how are you?; **in keeping with** in accord with, suitable to; **keep at it** to persist in anything; **keep back** to withhold; to keep down, repress; **keep body and soul together** to stay alive; **keep down** to restrain, to repress; to remain low; to retain (food) in the stomach, not to vomit; **keep from** to abstain from; to remain away from; **keep in** to prevent from escaping; to confine in school after school hours; to conceal; to restrain; **keep in with** to maintain the confidence or friendship of someone; **keep off** to hinder or prevent from approaching or making an attack, etc.; to stay away or refrain from; **keep on** to continue; **keep on about** to continue talking about; **keep on at** to nag, badger (*colloq*); **keep one's hand in** to retain one's skill by practice; **keep one's head down** to avoid attracting attention to oneself; **keep one's mind on** to concentrate on; **keep tabs on** to keep a check on, to keep account of; **keep time** to observe rhythm accurately, or along with others; (of a clock or watch) to go accurately; **keep to** to stick closely to; to confine oneself to; **keep under** to hold down in restraint; **keep up** to support, to prevent from falling; to continue, to prevent from ceasing; to maintain in good condition; to continue to be in touch (with); to keep pace (with; also *fig*, as in **keep up with the Joneses,** to keep on an equal social footing with one's neighbours, e.g. by having possessions of the same quality in the same quantity); **keep wicket** to act as a wicket-keeper. [O.E. *cēpan*.]

kef *kāf* or **kif** *kif* or *kēf*, *n* a state of dreamy repose; a drug, such as marijuana, smoked to produce this state. [Ar. *kaif*, pleasure.]

keffiyeh. See **kaffiyeh**.

kefuffle. Same as **kerfuffle**.

keg *keg*, *n* a small cask; a metal cask in which beer is kept under gas pressure. — **keg beer** any of various types of beer kept in and served from pressurised kegs. [Earlier *cag* — O.N. *kaggi*.]

keister *kē'stər*, (*US slang*) *n* the buttocks, arse; a safe or strong-box; a case or box. [Prob. Ger. *Kiste*, chest, case.]

kelim. See **kilim**.

kelly *kel'i*, *n* in drilling processes, the top pipe of a rotary string of drill pipes, with which is incorporated a flexibly attached swivel through which mud is pumped to the bottom of the hole.

keloid or **cheloid** *kē'loid*, *n* a hard growth of scar tissue in skin that has been injured. — *adj* **keloid'al** or **cheloid'al**. [Gr. *chēlē*, claw.]

kelp *kelp*, *n* any large brown seaweed, wrack; the calcined ashes of seaweed, a source of soda, iodine, etc. — *n* **Kel'per** (also without *cap*) an inhabitant of the Falkland Islands. — *adj* of or pertaining to the Falkland Islands. [M.E. *culp*.]

kelpie or **kelpy** *kel'pi*, *n* a malignant water sprite that haunts fords (*Scot*; *folklore*); an Australian breed of sheepdog.

kelson. See **keelson**.

kelt *kelt*, *n* a salmon, etc., that has just spawned.

Kelvin *kel'vin*, *adj* applied to a thermometer scale with absolute zero for zero and centigrade degrees. — *n* **kel'vin** (in SI units) the unit of temperature (formerly known as 'degree Kelvin'). [Sir William Thomson, Lord *Kelvin* (1824–1907), physicist.]

Ken. *abbrev* for Kentucky (U.S. state).

ken *ken*, *vt* to know (mainly *Scot*): — *pa t* and *pa p* **kenned** or **kent**. — *n* range of sight or knowledge. — *adj* **kent** known. — **beyond one's ken** outside the limits of one's knowledge. [O.E. *cennan*, causative of *cunnan*.]

kenaf *kə-naf'*, *n* a herbaceous plant, the fibres of which can be used as a substitute for wood-pulp in paper-making. [Persian.]

kendo *ken'dō* or *-dō'*, *n* the Japanese art of swordsmanship practised with bamboo staves, in 18th-century-style armour, and observing strict ritual. [Jap. *kendō*.]

kennel *ken'l*, *n* a house for dogs; a pack of hounds; (in *pl*) an establishment where dogs are boarded. — *vt* to put or keep in a kennel. — *vi* to live in a kennel: — *pr p* **kenn'elling**; *pa t* and *pa p* **kenn'elled**. — **kenn'el-maid** or **kenn'el-man** a female or male attendant who looks after dogs. [From an O.N.Fr. form answering to Fr. *chenil* — L. *canīle* — *canis*, a dog.]

Kennelly-Heaviside layer *ken-ə-li-hev'i-sīd lā'ər*, *n* a strongly ionised region of the upper atmosphere about 60 miles up, in which wireless waves are deflected. — Also **E'-layer.**

kenophobia *ken-ō-fō'bi-ə*, *n* a morbid fear of empty spaces. [Gr. *kenos*, empty, and **phobia**.]

kenspeckle *ken'spek-l*, (*Scot*) *adj* easily recognised; conspicuous. — Also **ken'speck.** [App. O.N. *kennispeki*, power of recognition.]

kent. See **ken**.

Kentish *kent'ish*, *adj* of *Kent*, a county in south-east England. — *n* the dialect of Kent, Essex, etc.

kentledge *kent'lij*, *n* pig-iron in a ship's hold for ballast.

Kenyapithecus *kēn-yə-pith'ə-kəs* or *ken-yə-*, *n* a lower Pliocene genus of fossil anthropoid ape; an example of this genus, first discovered by L.S.B. Leakey in Kenya in 1961. [*Kenya* and Gr. *pithēkos*, ape.]

kepi *kā'pē*, *n* a flat-topped military cap with a straight peak. [Fr. *képi*.]

kept *kept*, *pa t* and *pa p* of **keep**.

keratin *ker'ə-tin*, *n* a nitrogenous compound, the essential ingredient of horny tissue, as of horns, nails, etc. — *vt* and *vi* **ker'atinise** or **-ize** to make or become horny. — *n* **keratinisā'tion** or **-z-** formation of keratin; becoming horny. — *adj* **keratinous** (*kə-rat'i-nəs*) horny. — *n* **keratī'tis** inflammation of the cornea. — *adj* **keratogenous** (*-oj'i-nəs*) producing horn or keratin. — *adj* **ker'atoid** resembling horn or keratin. — *n* **keratom'eter** an instrument for measuring power and curvature of the cornea. — *n* **ker'atōplasty** grafting of part of a healthy cornea to replace a piece made opaque by disease, etc. — *adj* **ker'atose** (esp. of certain sponges) having a horny skeleton. — *n* **keratō'sis** a horny growth on or over the skin, e.g. a wart; a skin condition producing this: — *pl* **kerato'ses** (*-sēz*). — *n* **keratotomy** (*-tot'*) surgery of the cornea. [Gr. *keras*, *-atos*, a horn.]

kerb or (esp. in N. Am). **curb** (q.v.) *kûrb*, *n* a kerbstone, pavement edge; an edging or margin of various kinds. — *adj* (of a market, of dealing, etc.) unofficial, outside official trading hours. — **kerb'-crawler** someone who drives along slowly with the intention of enticing people into the car, usu. for sexual motives; **kerb'-crawling; kerb drill** the safe procedure for crossing a road recommended for pedestrians; **kerb'-merchant, -trader** or **-vendor** a person who sells on or beside the pavement; **kerb'side** (also *adj*); **kerb'stone** a stone placed edgeways as an edging to a path or pavement; **kerb weight** the weight (of a car) without passengers and luggage. [Fr. *courbe* — L. *curvus*, bent.]

kerchief *kûr'chif*, *n* a square piece of cloth worn to cover the head, neck, etc. [O.Fr. *cuevrechief* (Fr. *couvrechef*) — *covrir*, to cover, *chef*, the head.]

kerf *kûrf*, *n* a cut, a notch, groove, etc., made by a saw; the place where a cut is made. [O.E. *cyrf*, a cut.]

kerfuffle *kər-fuf'l*, *n* commotion, agitation. [Gael. pfx. *car-*, Scot. *fuffle*, to disorder.]

kermes *kûr'mēz*, *n* the female bodies of a coccus insect used as a red dyestuff; the oak (**kermes oak**) on which they breed. [Pers. and Ar. *qirmiz*.]

kermesse *kûr'mis*, *n* a cycle-race held in an urban area. [Flem. *kermesse*, kermis.]

kermis or **kirmess** *kûr'məs*, *n* a fair in the Low Countries; an indoor fair. usu. for charity (*US*). [Du. *kermis* — *kerk*, church, *mis*, mass.]

kern *kûrn*, (*printing*) *n* part of a type that projects beyond the body and rests on an adjoining letter. — *vt* to give (a typeface) a kern; to adjust (esp. by reduction) the kerning of (a typeface or piece of printing). — *n* **kern'ing** the adjustment, esp. reduction, of space between characters in type. [Fr. *carne*, a projecting angle — L. *cardō*, *-inis*.]

kernel *kûr'nl*, *n* a seed within a hard shell; the edible part of a nut; the important, central part of anything. [O.E. *cyrnel* — *corn*, grain, and dimin. suffix *-el*.]

kernicterus *kûr-nik'tər-əs*, (*pathol*) *n* a condition of acute neural dysfunction linked with high levels of reddish bile pigment (*bilirubin*) in the blood. [Ger. *Kern*, nucleus, and Gr. *ikteros*, jaundice.]

kerosine or **kerosene** *ker'ə-sēn*, *n* paraffin-oil obtained from shale or by distillation of petroleum, esp. that used to fuel jet aircraft; paraffin (*US*). [Gr. *kēros*, wax.]

kerria *ker'i-ə*, *n* any plant of the *Kerria* genus of deciduous yellow-flowering shrub, the Jew's mallow. [From William *Kerr*, late 18th–early 19th-cent. English gardener.]

kersey *kûr'zi*, *n* a coarse woollen cloth. [Perh. from *Kersey* in Suffolk.]

kerseymere *kûr'zi-mēr* or *-mēr'*, *n* a twilled cloth of very fine wool. [For **cashmere**.]

kerygma *kə-rig'mə*, (*theol*) *n* (preaching of) the Christian gospel, esp. in the way of the early Church. — *adj* **kerygmat'ic**. [Gr. *kērygma*, proclamation, preaching.]

kesh *kāsh*, *n* the uncut hair and beard traditionally worn by Sikhs. [Punjabi.]

kestrel *kes'trəl*, *n* a small species of falcon. [O.Fr. *cresserelle*.]

ket-. See **keto-**.

keta *kē'tə*, *n* a Pacific salmon. [Russ. *keta*.]

ketch *kech*, *n* a small two-masted sailing vessel, the foremast being the taller. [Earlier *catch*, perh. from the verb **catch**.]

ketchup *kech'əp*, *n* a smooth, thick sauce made from tomatoes, mushrooms, etc. — Also **catch'up** or **cat'sup**. [Malay *kēchap*, perh. from Chinese.]

keto- *kē-tō-* or **ket-** *kēt-*, *pfx* denoting a ketone compound or derivative.

ketone *kē'tōn*, *n* an organic compound consisting of a carbonyl group united to two like or unlike alkyl radicals. — *n* **kē'tose** any of a class of monosaccharide sugars which contain a ketone group. — *n* **ketō'sis** the excessive formation in the body of ketone or acetone bodies, due to incomplete oxidation of fats—occurs in e.g. diabetes. [Ger. *Keton*, from *Aketon*, acetone.]

kettle *ket'l*, *n* a vessel for heating or boiling liquids, esp. one with a spout and a lid for domestic use. — *n* **kett'leful**. — **kett'ledrum** (*mus*) a percussion instrument, consisting of a hollow metal hemisphere with a parchment head, tuned by screws which adjust the tension; **kett'ledrummer**; **kett'lestitch** (*bookbinding*) the stitch which is made at the head and tail of each section of a book to interlock the sections. — **a kettle of fish** (*ironically* — often **a pretty kettle of fish**) an awkward mess. [O.E. *cetel*.]

Ketubah *ke-tōō-vä'*, *n* a formal Jewish marriage contract which couples sign before their wedding. [Heb. *kethūbhāh*, document.]

Kevlar® *kev'lär*, *n* a lightweight synthetic fibre of exceptionally high strength and heat resistance, used in aerospace, fire-fighting equipment, etc.

key[1] *kē*, *n* an instrument for locking or unlocking, winding up, turning, tuning, tightening or loosening; in musical instruments, a lever or piston-end pressed to produce the sound required; a similar part in other instruments for other purposes, as in a typewriter or calculating machine; a system of tones definitely related to one another in a scale (*mus*); something which gives command of anything or upon which success turns; a scheme or diagram of explanation or identification; a set of answers to problems; that which leads to the solution of a problem; a leading principle; general tone of voice, emotion, morals, etc.; a piece inserted to prevent relative motion; a tapered piece of metal for fixing the boss of a wheel, etc. to a shaft; a spanner; the middle stone of an arch; a piece of wood let into another piece crosswise to prevent warping; a lever to close or break an electrical circuit; a fret pattern; preparation of a surface to take plaster, glue, or the like; an artificial system for distinguishing similar species (*biol*). — *vt* to provide with a key; to mark the position on the layout of (something to be printed), using symbols (*printing*); to use a keyboard to type; to stimulate (to a state of nervous tension and excitement), raise (in pitch or standard), or increase (with *up*); to attune (with *to*); to prepare (a surface) e.g. for plastering; to give (an advertisement) a feature that will enable replies to it to be identified; to lock or fasten with a key. — Also *vi*. — *adj* vital; essential; crucial. — *adj* **keyed** equipped with a key or keys; set to a particular key (*mus*); in a state of tension or readiness. — *adj* **key'less**. — **key'board** a range of keys or levers in a musical instrument, computer, etc.; (in *pl*) usu. in pop groups, musical instruments, esp. electronic, incorporating keyboards. — *vi* and *vt* to operate a device by means of a keyboard. — **key'hole** the hole in which a key of a lock is inserted; **keyhole saw** a pad-saw (q.v. under **pad**[2]); **key'line** (*printing*) an outline drawing showing the shape, size, position, etc. of an illustration; **key man** an indispensable worker, essential to the continued conduct of a business, etc.; **key money** a premium, fine, or sum additional to rent, demanded for the grant, renewal or continuance of a tenancy; **key'note** the fundamental note or tonic; any central principle or controlling thought. — *adj* of fundamental importance. — *vt* and *vi* to give the keynote; to put forward the central principle in an opening address at a convention. — **key pad** a device incorporating push-button controls by which a television, etc. can be operated; **key punch** (*comput*) a device operated by a keyboard, which transfers data onto punch-cards, etc.; **key'-ring** a ring for holding a bunch of keys; **key signature** (*mus*) the indication of key by marking sharps, flats or naturals where the key changes or at the beginning of a line; **key'stone** the stone at the apex of an arch; the chief element, or something on which everything else depends. — *vt* and *vi* to produce a **keystone effect** i.e. the distortion of a television picture in which a rectangular pattern is transformed into a trapezoidal pattern. — **key'stroke** the operation of a key on a typewriter or other machine using keys; **key'-stroking**; **key word** a headword; a word that encapsulates the passage in which it appears. — **key in** or **into** (*comput*) to transfer, store, etc. (data) by operating a keyboard. [O.E. *cǣg*.]

key[2] or **cay** *kē*, *n* a low island or reef. [Sp. *cayo*.]

KG *abbrev* for Knight of the (Order of the) Garter.

kg *abbrev* for: keg(s); kilogram(s), kilogramme(s).

KGB *abbrev* for *Komitet Gosudarstvennoi Bezopasnosti* (Russ.), Committee of State Security — the Soviet secret police.

kgy *abbrev* for kilogray(s).

khaddar *kud'ər* or **khaddi** *kud'i*, *n* in India, hand-spun, hand-woven cotton cloth. [Hind. *khādar*, *khādī*.]

khaki *kä'ki*, *adj* dust-coloured, dull brownish or greenish yellow. — *n* a light drab cloth used for military uniforms. [Urdu and Pers. *khākī*, dusty.]

khalif. See **caliph**.

khamsin *kam'sin* or *-sēn'*, *n* a hot south or south-east wind in Egypt, which blows for about fifty days from mid-March. [Ar. *khamsīn* — *khamsūn*, fifty.]

khan[1] *kän*, *n* an Eastern inn, a caravanserai. [Ar. *khān*.]

khan[2] *kän*, *n* in central Asia, a prince or chief; in ancient Persia, a governor. — *n* **khan'ate** a region governed by a khan. [Turk. *khān*, lord or prince.]

khanga. See **kanga**.

khat, kat or **qat** *kat*, *n* a shrub of East Africa, Arabia, etc., or *specif* its leaves, chewed or taken as tea for their stimulant effect.

khedive *ke-dēv'*, *n* the title (1867–1914) of the viceroy of Egypt. — *n* **khedi'va** his wife. — *n* **khedi'vate** or **khedi'viate** the khedive's office or territory. — *adj*

khedi'val or **khedi'vial**. [Fr. *khédive* — Turk. *khidīv*, *hudîv* — Pers. *khidīw*, prince.]

khilim. See **kilim**.

Khmer *kmûr* or *kmer*, *n* a member of a people inhabiting Cambodia (formerly (1975–89) Kampuchea); their language, the official language of Cambodia. — Also *adj*. — **Khmer Rouge** (*ro͞ozh*) the Communist guerrilla movement in Cambodia.

khutbah *ko͞ot'bä*, *n* a Muslim prayer and sermon delivered in the mosques on Fridays. [Ar.]

kiang *kyang* or *ki-ang'*, *n* the Tibetan wild ass. [Tibetan *rkyang*.]

kibble[1] *kib'l*, *n* the bucket of a well. — **kibb'le-chain** the chain for drawing up a bucket. [Cf. Ger. *Kübel*, bucket.]

kibble[2] *kib'l*, *vt* to grind cereal, etc. fairly coarsely.

kibbutz *ki-bo͞ots'*, *n* a Jewish communal agricultural settlement in Israel: — *pl* **kibbutzim** (*ki-bo͞ots-ēm'*). — *n* **kibbutz'nik** a person who lives and works on a kibbutz. [Heb.]

kibe *kīb*, *n* a chilblain, esp. on the heel. [Prob. Welsh *cibi*.]

kibitzer *kib'it-sər*, (*US slang*) *n* an onlooker (at cards, etc.) who gives unwanted advice; an interferer. — *vi* **kib'itz** to give unwanted advice, to meddle, comment out of turn. [Yiddish.]

kiblah *kib'lä*, *n* the point toward which Muslims turn in prayer, the direction of Mecca. [Ar. *qiblah*.]

kibosh or **kybosh** *kī'bosh* or *ki-bosh'*, (*colloq*) *n* nonsense, rot. — *vt* to dispose of finally. — **put the kibosh on** to kibosh, destroy, finish off completely.

kick *kik*, *vt* to hit with the foot; to put or drive by blows with the foot; to start or work by foot on a pedal; to achieve by a kick or kicking; to free oneself from (e.g. a habit; *slang*). — *vi* to thrust out the foot with violence; to show opposition or resistance; to recoil or jerk violently (esp. with *back*); to move suddenly as if kicked; to make an extra spurt of speed (in running, etc.); to be exposed to kicking, lie around (often with *about*). — *n* a blow or fling with the foot; the recoil of a gun; a jerk; kicking power; resistance; resilience; stimulus, pungency (*colloq*); a thrill (*colloq*); dismissal (esp. with *the*; *slang*); an enthusiastic but short-lived interest; a phase of such interest. — *adj* **kick'able**. — *n* **kick'er** someone or something that kicks, e.g. a horse; (in some sports) a player whose function is to take (esp. set-piece) kicks. — **kick'back** part of a sum received paid to another by confidential agreement for favours past or to come; money paid in return for protection; loose material thrown up from the track by a galloping horse (*horse-racing*); a strong reaction (*fig*); **kick boxing** a martial art in which the combatants kick with bare feet and punch with gloved fists; **kick'down** a method of changing gear in a car with automatic gear transmission, by pressing the accelerator pedal right down; **kick'-off** the first kick in a game of football; **kick pleat** a pleat at the back of a narrow skirt from knee-level to hem, which allows one to walk easily; **kick'stand** a piece of metal attached to a motorcycle, etc., which is kicked into position to hold the machine upright when parked; **kick'-start** the starting of an engine by a pedal. — *vt* to start an engine thus; to give a sudden (advantageous) impulse to (*fig*). — **kick turn** a skiing turn through 180°. — **for kicks** for thrills; **kick about** or **around** (*colloq*) to consider; to provisionally discuss; (of a person) to wander around doing nothing in particular; (of an object) to lie about serving no useful purpose; **kick oneself** to reproach oneself; **kick out** (*colloq*) to eject with force; to dismiss; **kick over the traces** to throw off control; **kick the bucket** (*slang*) to die; **kick upstairs** (*colloq*) to promote (usu. to a less active or less powerful position). [M.E. *kiken*.]

kickshaws *kik'shöz* or **kickshaw** *kik'shö*, *n* a trinket, a cheap, worthless article. [Fr. *quelque chose*, something.]

kid[1] *kid*, *n* a young goat; extended to young antelope, etc.; a child or young person (*colloq*); leather made of kidskin, or a substitute. — *adj* made of kid leather or imitation kid leather. — *vt* and *vi* (of a goat) to give birth to a kid or kids: — *pr p* **kidd'ing**; *pa t* and *pa p* **kidd'ed**. — *n* **kidd'y** diminutive of kid, a little child: — *pl* **kidd'ies**. — *n* **kiddy'wink**, **kidd'iewink** or **kidd'iewinkie** (*facetiously*) extended forms of **kiddy**, a child. — **kid-glove'** a glove made of kid leather. — *adj* as if done by someone wearing kid-gloves; overnice, delicate. — **kid'skin** kid leather, typically soft and smooth; **kids' stuff** (*colloq*) something very easy. — **handle with kid gloves** to treat carefully and gently; to deal with very tactfully. [O.N. *kith*.]

kid[2] *kid*, (*colloq*) *vt* and *vi* to hoax; to pretend, esp. banteringly; to tease. — *n* a deception. — *n* **kidd'er**. — *n* **kidol'ogist** (*-jist*). — *n* **kidology** (*kid-ol'ə-ji*; *colloq*) the art of kidding, sometimes to gain a psychological advantage. — **kid on** to pretend (*n* **kid'-on**). [Perh. connected with **kid**[1], a child.]

Kidderminster *kid'ər-min-stər*, *n* a two-ply or ingrain carpet formerly made at *Kidderminster*. — Also *adj*.

kiddy, etc. See **kid**[1].

kidnap *kid'nap*, *vt* to steal (a human being), esp. for ransom: — *pr p* **kid'napping**; *pa t* and *pa p* **kid'-napped**. — *n* an instance of this. — *n* **kid'napper**. [**kid**[1], a child, and obsolete *nap*, to seize, steal.]

kidney *kid'ni*, *n* one of two flattened glands that secrete urine. — **kid'ney-bean** the French bean; any kidney-shaped variety of bean, esp. the red variety of runner bean; **kidney machine** an apparatus used, in cases where the kidney functions badly, to remove harmful substances from the blood by dialysis; **kid'ney-stone** a hard deposit formed in the kidney. [M.E. *kidenei*.]

kidology. See under **kid**[2].

kie-kie *kē'-kē*, *n* a New Zealand climbing plant (*Freycinetia banksii*). [Maori.]

kif. See **kef**.

kike *kīk*, (*offensive slang*; esp. *NAm*) *n* and *adj* Jew. [Possibly from the *-ki* ending of many E. European Jewish immigrants' names in U.S. at the end of the 19th cent.]

kilerg *kil'ûrg*, *n* a thousand ergs. [Gr. *chīlioi*, thousand, and **erg**.]

kiley. See **kylie**.

kilim *ki-lēm'*, *n* a pileless woven rug traditionally made in the Middle East. — Also **kelim'** or **khilim'**. [Turk. — Pers. *kilīm*.]

kill *kil*, *vt* to put to death, to murder or execute; to deprive of life; to destroy; to nullify or neutralise, to make inactive, to weaken or dilute; to reject, discard, defeat; to overwhelm, stun, dazzle (*colloq*); to spoil; to muffle or still; to exhaust (*colloq*); to cause severe pain (*colloq*). — *vi* to murder, slaughter. — *n* an act or instance of killing, destroying, etc.; prey or game killed. — *n* **kill'er** a person or creature that kills; someone who murders readily or habitually; the grampus or the killer whale, a ferocious black-and-white toothed marine whale. — *adj* **kill'ing** depriving of life; destructive; deadly, irresistible; exhausting; irresistibly funny (*colloq*). — *n* slaughter; a large financial gain, esp. sudden. — **kill'joy** a spoil-sport. — **dressed to kill** dressed so as to dazzle, attract and impress others; **in at the kill** (*fig*) present at the culminating moment; **kill off** to exterminate; **kill the fatted calf** to prepare an elaborate feast, etc., for a homecoming or welcome (also *fig*); **kill time** to occupy oneself with amusements, etc., in order to pass spare time or to relieve boredom; **kill two birds with one stone** to accomplish one thing by the same means as, or by accomplishing, another; **make a killing** (*colloq*) to make a lot of money, a large profit. [M.E. *killen* or *cullen*.]

killdeer *kil'dēr*, *n* the largest North American ring-necked plover: — *pl* **kill'deer** or **kill'deers**. [Imit.]

killick *kil'ik* or **killock** *kil'ək*, *n* a small anchor; its fluke or barb.

killifish *kil'i-fish*, *n* any of several small freshwater fish used as bait and to control mosquitoes. [U.S. dialect *kill*, a stream, river.]

kiln *kiln*, *n* a large oven for drying, baking or calcining corn, hops, bricks, pottery, limestone, etc. — *vt* to dry, fire, etc. in a kiln. — *vt* **kiln'-dry** to dry in a kiln: — *pa p* and *adj* **kiln'-dried**. — **kiln'-hole** the mouth of a kiln. [O.E. *cyln*, *cylen* — L. *culīna*, a kitchen.]

Kilner jar® *kil'nər jär*, *n* a glass jar with an airtight lid, used for preserving fruit and vegetables.

kilo *kēl'ō*, *n* a shortened form of **kilogram**, **kilogramme** or sometimes of other words with the prefix **kilo-**: — *pl* **kil'os**.

kilo- *kil'ə-* or *kil'ō-*, *pfx* denoting 1000 times the unit to which it is attached, e.g. **kil'obar** = 1000 bars. — *n* **kil'obit** (*comput*) 1024 bits. — *n* **kil'obyte** (*comput*) 1000 bytes; 2^{10} (1024) bytes. — *n* **kil'ocalorie** 1000 calories, used to measure energy content of food. — *n* **kil'ogram** or **kil'ogramme** the SI base unit of mass, the mass of a platinum-iridium cylinder kept as the standard (International Prototype Kilogram) at Paris, 2·205 lb. — *n* **kil'ogram-calorie** same as **kilocalorie**. — *n* **kil'ogray** 1000 grays (see **gray²**), used to measure the absorbed dose of radiation, e.g. in food irradiation. — *n* **kil'ohertz** 1000 cycles of oscillation per second, used to measure frequency of sound and radio waves. — *n* **kil'ojoule** 1000 joules, used to measure energy, work and heat. — *n* **kil'ometre** (also *-om'-*) 1000 metres, 0·6214 or about $\frac{5}{8}$ mile. — *n* **kil'oton** or **kil'otonne** a measure of explosive force equivalent to that of 1000 tons (or tonnes) of TNT. — *n* **kil'ovolt** 1000 volts. — *n* **kil'owatt** 1000 watts, the power dissipated by one bar of the average electric fire. — **kilowatt hour** the energy consumed by a load of one kilowatt in one hour of use (3·6 megajoules), the unit by which electricity is charged to the consumer. [Gr. *chīlioi*, a thousand.]

kilt *kilt*, *n* a man's short pleated skirt, usu. of tartan, forming part of Highland dress; any similar garment. — *vt* to tuck up (skirts); to pleat vertically. — *adj* **kilt'ed** dressed in a kilt; tucked up; vertically pleated. — *n* **kilt'y** or **kilt'ie** (*colloq*) a wearer of a kilt. [Scand.]

kilter *kil'tər*, *n* (esp. *US*) good condition. — **off-kil'ter** or **out of kilter** out of order, not functioning properly; out of correct condition or shape.

kimberlite *kim'bər-līt*, *n* a mica peridotite, an igneous rock in which the diamonds at *Kimberley* and elsewhere in South Africa were found.

kimchi *kim'chi*, *n* a very spicy Korean dish made with a variety of raw vegetables, esp. cabbage, radish, cucumber, garlic, ginger, etc. [Korean.]

kimono *ki-mō'nō*, *n* a loose robe with wide sleeves, fastened with a sash, an outer garment in Japan; a dressing-gown of similar form: — *pl* **kimō'nos**. [Jap.]

kin *kin*, *n* people belonging to the same family; relatives. — *adj* related. — *n* **kinsfolk** (*kinz'fōk*) people related to one another (also, chiefly in U.S., **kin'folk** or **kin'folks**). — *n* **kin'ship** relationship. — *n* **kins'man** a man of the same kin or race as another: — *fem* **kins'woman**. — **next of kin** the relatives of a deceased person, among whom that person's property is distributed if they die intestate; the person or persons most closely related to an individual by blood or marriage, or a legal ruling. [O.E. *cynn*.]

-kin *-kin*, *sfx* denoting a diminutive in nouns, including proper names, such as Jen*kin* (for *John*) and Wil*kin* (for *William*). [Prob. Du. or L.G.; cf. Ger. *-chen*.]

kina *kē'nə*, *n* the standard monetary unit of Papua New Guinea (100 *toea*).

kinaesthesis or in U.S. **kinesthesis** *kīn-ēs-thē'sis*, also *kin-* and *-es-*, *n* sense of movement or of muscular effort. — Also **kinaesthē'sia**, (*US*) **kinesthesia** (*-zi-ə* or *-zyə*). — *adj* **kinaesthetic**, (*US*) **kinesthetic** (*-thet'ik*) pertaining to kinaesthesis. [Gr. *kīneein*, to move, *aisthēsis*, sensation.]

kind *kīnd*, *n* related people, a race; sort or species, a particular variety; fundamental qualities (of a thing); produce, as distinguished from money. — *adj* disposed to do good to others; benevolent; having or springing from the feelings natural for people of the same family. — *adv* **kind'a** (*colloq*) shortening of **kind of** (somewhat, sort of). — *adv* **kind'ly** in a kind manner; a (rather peremptory) substitute for 'please' (for the *adj* see separate entry). — *n* **kind'ness** the quality or fact of being kind; a kind act. — *adj* **kind-heart'ed**. — *n* **kind-heart'edness**. — **after its kind** according to its nature; **in kind** in goods instead of money; tit for tat; **kind of** (*colloq*) of a kind, somewhat, sort of, to some extent, as it were — used adjectivally and adverbially. [O.E. (*ge*)*cynde* — *cynn*, kin.]

kindergarten *kin'dər-gär-tn*, *n* an infant school, in which object-lessons and games figure largely. [Ger., — *Kinder*, children, *Garten*, garden.]

kindle *kin'dl*, *vt* to set fire to, to light; to inflame, e.g. the passions; to provoke, incite. — *vi* to catch fire; to begin to be excited; to be roused. — *n* **kin'dler**. — *n* **kin'dling** the act of causing to burn; materials for starting a fire, such as twigs, dry wood. [Cf. O.N. *kyndill*, a torch — L. *candēla*, candle.]

kindly *kīnd'li*, *adj* inclined to kindness, benign; genial, pleasant. — *adv* in a kind or kindly manner (see also under **kind**). — *n* **kind'liness**. — **take kindly to** (often with *neg*) to take a favourable view of. [O.E. *gecyndelic*.]

kindred *kin'drid*, *n* relationship by blood, or, less properly, by marriage; relatives; a group of relatives, family, clan. — *adj* related; cognate; congenial. [M.E. *kinrede* — O.E. *cynn*, kin, and the suffix *-rǣden*, expressing mode or state.]

kindy *kin'di*, (*Austr*) *n* a short form of **kindergarten**.

kine *kīn*, (*Bible*) *npl* cows. [M.E. *kyen*.]

kinematics *kin-i-mat'iks* or *kīn-*, *nsing* the science of motion without reference to force. — *adj* **kinemat'ic** or **kinemat'ical**. [Gr. *kīnēma*, motion.]

kinesis *kī-nē'sis* or *ki-*, *n* movement, change of position, *specif* under stimulus and with direction not precisely determined. — *nsing* **kinē'sics** (study of) body movements which convey information in the absence of speech. — *n* **kinesiol'ogist**. — *n* **kinesiol'ogy** scientific study of human movement and posture, relating body mechanics and anatomy. [Gr. *kīnēsis*, movement.]

kinesthesis, etc. See **kinaesthesis**.

kinetics *kī-net'iks* or *ki-*, *nsing* the science of the action of force in producing or changing motion. — *adj* **kinet'ic** or **kinet'ical** pertaining to motion or to kinetics; due to motion. — **kinetic art** or **sculpture** art or sculpture in which movement (produced by air currents, or electricity, or sound, etc.) plays an essential part; **kinetic energy** energy possessed by a body by virtue of its motion. [Gr. *kīnetikos* — *kīneein*, to move.]

kinfolk. See **kinsfolk** (q.v. under **kin**).

king *king*, *n* a male hereditary chief ruler or titular head of a nation; a male monarch; a playing-card having the picture of a king; the most important piece in chess; a piece that has been crowned (*draughts*); a man or other male animal who is pre-eminent among his fellows: — *fem* **queen**. — *vt* to make king. — *n* **king'dom** the state or attributes of a king; a monarchical state; a region that was once a monarchical state; one of the three major divisions of natural history (animal, vegetable, mineral). — *adj* **king'less**. — *n* **king'liness**. — *adj* **king'ly** belonging or suitable to a king; royal; king-like. — Also *adv*. — *n* **Kings** the title of two historical books of the Old Testament. — *n* **king'ship** the state, office or dignity of a king. — **king'-bird** an American flycatcher; **king-co'bra** a large Asiatic species of cobra; **king'-crab** a large marine arachnid, with convex horseshoe-shaped armoured body; **king'-cup** the buttercup; the marsh-marigold; **king'fish** the opah; any of various fish notable for their size or value (*Austr*); **king'fisher** a European fish-eating bird with very brilliant blue-green and chestnut plumage; any bird of the same family, most species of which are not fish-eating; a brilliant blue colour (also *adj*); **king'maker** a person who has the power to create kings or other high officials; **king-of-arms'** (sometimes **king-at-arms'**) a principal herald; **king penguin** a large penguin, smaller than the emperor; **king'-pin** a tall pin, or one prominently placed; a pin on which the axle of an automobile front-wheel swivels; the most important person of a group engaged in an undertaking; the key issue; **king'post** a perpendicular beam in the frame of a roof rising from the tie-beam to the ridge; **king prawn** a large prawn, esp. of the genus *Penaeus*, found around Australia; **King's Bench** see **Queen's Bench**; **King's Counsel** see **Queen's Counsel**; **King's English** (or **Queen's English**) correct standard English speech; **king's evidence** see **queen's evidence**; **king's-e'vil** a scrofulous disease formerly supposed to be healed by the touch of the monarch. — *adj* **king'-size** or **king'-sized** of large size. — **King's Regulations** see **Queen's Regulations**; **king's speech** see **queen's speech**. — **kingdom come** (*slang*) the state after death; some inconceivably far-off time; **king hit** (*Austr*) to hit very hard, or knock out; **king it** to play king, act as though superior to or in authority over others; **King James Bible** (or **Version**) the Authorised Version; **king of the castle** (orig. from a children's game) the most important, powerful person in a group. [O.E. *cyning* — *cynn*, a tribe.]

kinin *kī'nin*, (*biol*) *n* a plant hormone which promotes cell-division and is used commercially as a preservative for cut flowers; any of a group of polypeptides in the blood, causing dilation of the blood vessels and contraction of smooth muscles. [Gr. *kīn(ēsis)*, movement.]

kink *kingk*, *n* a twisted loop in a string, rope, etc.; a mental twist or quirk; a crick; a whim; an imperfection; an unusual sexual preference, or a person who has one (*colloq*). — *vi* to form a kink. — *vt* to cause a kink in. — *n* **kink'le** a slight kink. — *adj* **kink'y** twisted; curly; eccentric (*colloq*); crazy (*colloq*); out of the ordinary in an attractive (esp. provocative) way (*colloq*); with unusual or perverted sexual tastes (*colloq*).

kinkajou *king'kə-jōō*, *n* a South American tree-dwelling animal related to the raccoon. [App. from a N.Am. Indian word misapplied.]

kinkle, kinky. See **kink**.

kino *kē'nō*, *n* an astringent exudation from various tropical trees: — *pl* **kin'os**. [App. of W. African origin.]

kinsfolk, kinship, etc. See **kin**.

kiosk *kē'osk*, *n* orig., an Eastern garden pavilion; a small roofed stall for sale of papers, sweets, etc., either out-of-doors or inside a public building; a bandstand; a public telephone box. [Turk. *köşk*, *keushk* — Pers. *kūshk*.]

kip[1] *kip*, *n* the skin of a young animal. — **kip'-skin** leather made from the skin of young cattle, intermediate between calfskin and cowhide.

kip[2] *kip*, (*slang*) *n* a nap; a bed; a lodging-house. — *vi* to lie, sleep, nap; to go to bed. — **kip down** to go to bed. [Cf. Dan. *kippe*, a low alehouse.]

kip[3] *kip*, (*Austr*) *n* a short flat stick used to throw up pennies in the game of two-up.

kip[4] *kip*, *n* a unit of weight equal to 1000 pounds. [*kilo*, *pound*.]

kip[5] *kip*, *n* the standard unit of currency in Laos (100 *at*).

kipper *kip'ər*, *n* a male salmon during the spawning season after spawning; a salmon or (*esp*) herring split open, seasoned, and dried. — *vt* to cure or preserve, as a salmon or herring. — *n* **kipp'erer**. — **kipper tie** (*colloq*) a very wide, and often garish, necktie.

kir *kēr*, *n* a drink made of white wine and blackcurrant syrup or liqueur. [F. *Kir* (1876–1968), the Frenchman who is said to have invented it.]

Kirbigrip®, kirby-grip or **kirbigrip** *kûr'bi-grip*, *n* a kind of hairgrip. [From *Kirby*, the name of one of the original manufacturers.]

kirk *kûrk*, (*Scot*) *n* church, in any sense; sometimes specially applied to the Church of Scotland. [A Northern Eng. form of **church** — O.N. *kirkja* — O.E. *cirice*.]

kirmess. See **kermis**.

kirpan *kər-pän'*, *n* a small sword or dagger, worn by Sikh men as a symbol of religious loyalty. [Punjabi.]

kirsch *kērsh* or **kirschwasser** *kērsh'väs-ər*, *n* a liqueur made from the wild cherry. [Ger., cherry water.]

kismet *kiz'met* or *kis'mət*, *n* fate, destiny. [Turk. *qismet* — Ar. *qisma*.]

kiss *kis*, *vt* to caress or greet by touching with the lips; (of an inanimate object) to touch gently. — *vi* to greet by touching with the lips; (of two people) to press their lips together, esp. as an expression of affection; (of billiard balls) to touch gently while moving. — *n* a caress, greeting, etc. by touching with the lips. — *adj* **kiss'able**. — *n* **kiss'er** a person who, or object that, kisses; the mouth (*slang*). — *n* **kiss'ogram** or **kiss'agram** a service whereby a kiss is delivered to a specific person (e.g. on their birthday) by a **kissogram girl** (or **man**), usu. in glamorous or unusual costume. — **kiss'-curl** a flat, circular curl at the side of the forehead; **kissing cousin** a more or less distant relation with whom one is on familiar enough terms to kiss on meeting; **kissing gate** a gate set in a V- or U-shaped frame; **kiss'-off** (*slang*) a sudden, usu. offensive dismissal. — **kiss and tell** (*colloq*) to give an exposé of one's sexual adventures (*adj* **kiss'-and-tell**); **kiss hands** to kiss the sovereign's hands on acceptance of office; **kiss of death** (*colloq*) something that causes failure, destruction, etc.; **kiss of life** in first-aid, a mouth-to-mouth method of restoring breathing; a means of restoring vitality or vigour (*fig*). [O.E. *cyssan*.]

kit *kit*, *n* an outfit; equipment; material, tools, instructions, assembled in a container for some specific purpose; the container itself; a small wooden tub, for carrying fish, etc. — *vt* (sometimes with *out*) to provide with kit. — **kit'-bag** a strong canvas bag for holding one's kit or outfit (*mil*); a knapsack; a strong canvas grip; **kit'-boat** or **-car** a boat or car put together, from standard components, by an amateur builder.

kitchen *kich'ən*, *n* a place where food is cooked; cooking department or equipment. — *n* **kitchenette'** a very small kitchen, or part of a room modified as such. — **kitchen cabinet** an informal, unelected group of advisers to a political office-holder; **kitchen-gar'den** a garden where vegetables are cultivated for the kitchen; **kitchen-gar'dener**; **kitch'en-maid** a maid or servant whose work is in the kitchen. — *adj* **kitchen-sink'** (of plays, etc.) dealing with sordid real-life situations. — **kitchen tea** (*Austr*) a bride's shower, the gifts being kitchen utensils, etc.; **kitchen unit** one of a set of up-to-date kitchen fitments. [O.E. *cycene* — L. *coquěre*, to cook.]

kite *kīt*, *n* a long-tailed bird of prey of the hawk family; a light frame covered with paper or cloth for flying in the air; a more complicated structure built of boxes (*box-kite*), often for carrying recording instruments or a man in the air; a rumour or suggestion given out to see how the wind blows, test public opinion, etc. —

vt to cause to fly like a kite; to write (a cheque) before one has sufficient money in one's bank to cover it (*slang*). — *vi* to fly like a kite; to rise sharply. — **kite'-balloon** an observation-balloon designed on the principle of the kite to prevent revolving, etc.; **kite'-flying** sending up and controlling a kite; dealing in fictitious accommodation papers to raise money; testing public opinion by circulating rumours, etc. (**fly a kite** to take part in kite-flying); **Kite mark, Kite'mark** or **kite'-mark** a kite-shaped mark on goods indicating conformity in quality, size, etc., with the specifications of the British Standards Institution. — *adj* **kite'-marked** bearing this mark. [O.E. *cyta*.]

kith *kith*, *n* friends (orig. home-country friends) and relatives, as in the phrase **kith and kin**. [O.E. *cȳth*, knowledge, native land — *cunnan*, to know.]

kitsch *kich*, *n* work in any of the arts that is pretentious and inferior or in bad taste. — *adj* **kitsch'y**. — *adv* **kitsch'ily**. [Ger.]

kitten *kit'n*, *n* a young cat (*dimin* **kitt'y**); sometimes the young of another animal. — *vt* and *vi* (of a cat) to give birth. — *adj* **kitt'enish** or **kitt'eny** frolicsome; skittish; affectedly playful. — **have kittens** to be in a state of great excitement or anger. [M.E. *kitoun* — O.N.Fr. *caton*, dimin. of *cat* — L.L. *cattus*, cat.]

kittiwake *kit'i-wāk*, *n* a species of gull with long wings and rudimentary hind-toe. [Imit.]

kittle *kit'l*, (*Scot*) *adj* ticklish, intractable. — *vt* to tickle; to puzzle. — *adj* **kitt'ly** easily tickled, sensitive.

kitty[1] *kit'i*, *n* a pool or fund of money held in common; the jack (*bowls*).

kitty[2]. See **kitten**.

kitty-cornered *kit'i-kör-nərd*, (*NAm*) *adj* and *adv*. Same as **cater-cornered**.

kiwi *kē'wē*, *n* the Apteryx, a stocky, flightless, nocturnal bird of New Zealand, with a long beak and hairlike feathers; a New Zealander (*colloq*); a kiwi fruit. — **kiwi fruit** the edible green fruit of the Chinese gooseberry (q.v.). [Maori, from its cry.]

KKK *abbrev* for Ku-Klux Klan.

KL *abbrev* for Kuala Lumpur, the capital of Malaysia.

klaxon *klaks'ən*, *n* orig., a mechanical horn with rasping sound; an electric horn.

klebsiella *kleb'zi-el-ə*, *n* a genus of gram-negative rodlike bacteria, which cause various diseases in man and animals, incl. pneumonia. [E. *Klebs* (d. 1913), Ger. pathologist.]

Kleenex® *klē'neks*, *n* a kind of soft paper tissue used as a handkerchief.

Klein bottle *klīn bot'l*, (*math*) *n* a one-sided four-dimensional surface, which in three dimensions can be represented as a surface obtained by pulling the narrow end of a tapering tube over the wall of the tube and then stretching the narrow end and joining it to the larger end. [Felix *Klein*, German mathematician.]

kleptocracy *klep-tok'rə-si*, *n* government by thieves, a thieves' régime; a country with such a government. — *adj* **kleptocrat'ic**. [Gr. *kleptēs*, thief, and **-cracy**.]

kleptomania *klep-tō-mā'ni-ə*, *n* a mania for stealing; a morbid impulse to hide things away. — *n* **kleptomā'niac**. [Gr. *kleptein*, to steal, *maniā*, madness.]

Klieg light *klēg līt*, *n* a type of incandescent flood-lighting lamp for film studio use. [From *Kliegl* brothers, the inventors.]

klinker or **clinker** *klingk'ər*, *n* a very hard paving-brick. [Du.]

klipspringer *klip'spring-ər*, *n* a small South African antelope. [Du. *klip*, rock, *springer*, jumper.]

KLM *abbrev* for *Koninklijke Luchtvaart Maatschappij* (Du.), Royal Dutch Airlines.

Klondike *klon'dīk*, (also without *cap*) *n* a very rich source of wealth. [From the gold rush to *Klondike* in the Yukon, in 1896, etc.]

kloof *kloof*, (*SAfr*) *n* a mountain ravine. [Du., cleft.]

kludge *kluj*, (*comput*; *colloq*) *n* a botched or makeshift device or program which is unreliable or inadequate in function.

klutz *kluts*, (*US slang*) *n* an idiot; an awkward, stupid person. [Ger. *Klotz*, idiot.]

klystron *klis'* or *klīs'tron*, *n* any of a number of electron tubes (amplifiers, oscillators, etc.) in which the velocity of the electron beam is modulated by an ultra-high-frequency field and subsequently imparts energy to it or other UHF fields. [Gr. *klystēr*, syringe.]

KM *abbrev* for Knight of Malta.

km. *abbrev* for kilometre(s). — **km/h** *abbrev* for kilometres per hour.

kn. *abbrev* for knot(s) (the nautical, etc. measure).

knack *nak*, *n* a clever trick or skill; dexterity, adroitness. — *n* **knack'iness**. — *adj* **knack'ish** or **knack'y** cunning, crafty. [Orig. imit.]

knacker *nak'ər*, *n* a horse-slaughterer; someone who buys and breaks up old houses, ships, etc.; a worn-out horse; (in *pl*) testicles (*slang*). — *vt* to wear out, exhaust. — *adj* **knack'ered** (*slang*) exhausted, worn out.

knackwurst *nak'wōōrst*, *-wûrst* or (Ger.) *-vōōrst*, *n* a kind of highly seasoned sausage. — Also **knock'-wurst**. [Ger.]

knag *nag*, *n* a knot in wood; a peg. — *adj* **knagg'y** knotty; rugged. [Cf. Dan. *knag*, Ger. *Knagge*.]

knapsack *nap'sak*, *n* a bag made of strong material, with straps for carrying on the back, e.g. when hiking; a rucksack. [Du. *knappen*, to crack, eat.]

knapweed *nap'wēd*, *n* a composite plant of the genus *Centaurea*, like a spineless thistle.

knar *när*, *n* a knot on a tree. — *adj* **knarred** gnarled, knotty. [Cf. L.G. *knarre*, Du. *knar*; also **knur**.]

knave *nāv*, *n* orig., a boy or serving-boy; a false, deceitful fellow; a playing-card bearing the picture of a servant or soldier. — *n* **knav'ery** dishonesty. — *adj* **knav'ish** fraudulent; rascally. — *adv* **knav'ishly**. — *n* **knav'ishness**. [O.E. *cnafa*, *cnapa*, a boy, a youth.]

knead *nēd*, *vt* to work and press together into a mass, as flour into dough; to massage. — *n* **knead'er**. [O.E. *cnedan*.]

knee *nē*, *n* the joint between the thigh and shin bones; in a horse's foreleg, the joint corresponding to the wrist; in a bird the joint corresponding to the ankle; part of a garment covering the knee; a root upgrowth by which swamp-growing trees breathe; a piece of timber or metal like a bent knee. — *vt* to provide with a knee; to press, strike or nudge with the knee; to make baggy at the knee. — *adj* **kneed** or **knee'd** having knees or angular joints; (of trousers) baggy at the knees. — **knee'-breeches** breeches extending to just below the knee; **knee'-cap** the knee-pan. — *vt* to subject to knee-capping. — **knee'-capping** a form of torture or (terrorist) punishment in which the victim is shot or otherwise injured in the knee-cap. — *adj* **knee-deep'** rising to the knees. — *adj* **knee-high'** rising or reaching to the knees. — **knee'hole** the space beneath a desk or bureau for the knees when sitting; **knee'-jerk** a reflex throwing forward of the leg when tapped below the knee-cap. — *adj* (of a reaction) automatic, unthinking, predictable. — **knee'-joint** the joint of the knee; a joint with two pieces at an angle, so as to be very tight when pressed into a straight line. — *adj* **knee'-length** reaching down to the knee. — **knee'-pad** a protective cover for the knee; **knee'-pan** the patella, a flat round bone on the front of the knee-joint; **knee sock** a sock reaching to just below the knee; **knees'-up** (*colloq*) a riotous dance or party; **knee'-trembler** (*slang*) an act of sexual intercourse in a standing position. [O.E. *cnēow*, *cnēo*.]

kneel *nēl*, *vi* to rest or fall on the bended knee: — *pa t* and *pa p* **knelt** (*nelt*) or **kneeled**. — *n* **kneel'er** a person who kneels; a flat cushion to rest the knees on while kneeling; a hassock. [O.E. *cnēowlian*.]

knell *nel*, *n* the stroke of a bell; the sound of a bell at a death or funeral. — *vi* to sound as a bell; to toll. — *vt* to summon, etc. as by a tolling bell. [O.E. *cnyllan*, to beat noisily.]

knelt *nelt*, *pa t* and *pa p* of **kneel**.

knickerbocker *nik'ər-bok-ər*, *n* (in *pl*) loose breeches gathered in at the knee; (with *cap*) a descendant of one of the original Dutch settlers of New York. — Also *npl* **knick'ers** (*colloq*). — **knickerbocker glory** a large and opulent ice-cream sundae. [From the wide-breeched Dutchmen in Knickerbocker's (Washington Irving's) humorous *History of New York*.]

knickers *nik'ərz*, *npl* women's or girls' underpants (*colloq*); a woman's undergarment covering (and sometimes gathered in at) the thigh; knickerbockers. — *interj* (*slang*) now usu. a mild expression of exasperation, etc. — **get one's knickers in a twist** (*colloq*) to become harassed, anxious or agitated. [**knickerbocker**.]

knick-knack *nik'-nak*, *n* a small, trifling ornamental or would-be ornamental article. — *n* **knick-knack'ery** knick-knacks collectively. — *adj* **knick'-knacky**. [A doubling of **knack**.]

knife *nīf*, *n* an instrument for cutting: — *pl* **knives** (*nīvz*). — *vt* to cut; to stab; to convey or apply with a knife; to try to defeat by treachery. — *vi* to cut (with *through*) or penetrate (with *into*) as if with a knife. — **knife'-edge** a sharp-edged ridge; a sharp piece of steel like a knife's edge serving as the axis of a balance, etc. (also *fig*, esp. as *adj*); **knife'-man** a man wielding or using a knife; **knife pleat** a narrow, flat pleat; **knife'-point** the sharp tip of a knife (**at knife-point** under threat of injury by a knife); **knife'-switch** a switch in an electric circuit, in which the moving element consists of a flat blade which engages with fixed contacts. — **have one's knife in** to be persistently hostile or vindictive towards; **under the knife** undergoing a surgical operation. [M.E. *knif* — O.E. *cnīf*.]

knight *nīt*, *n* a man of the rank immediately below baronet with the title 'Sir'; a chessman, usu. with a horse's head, that moves one square forward, backward, or to either side, and one diagonally, at each move; (in feudal times) a gentleman, bred to arms, admitted to a certain honourable military rank; a man devoted to the service of a lady, her champion. — *vt* to make a knight. — *n* **knight'age** knights collectively. — *n* **knight'hood** the rank, title or status of knight; the order or fraternity of knights. — *adj* **knight'ly** like or befitting a knight; chivalrous; of a knight or knights. — **knight bachelor** a knight belonging to no special order of knighthood (the lowest form in rank and earliest in origin); **knight-err'ant** a knight who travelled in search of adventures; a man or boy who behaves in a quixotic fashion: — *pl* **knights-err'ant**; **knight-err'antry**; **knight's progress** a series of moves in which a knight may visit every square on the chess-board; **Knights Templars** see under **Templar**. [O.E. *cniht*, youth, servant, warrior.]

kniphofia *nip-hō'fi-ə* or *nī-fō'fi-ə*, *n* any plant of the African *Kniphofia* genus of the lily family, otherwise called *Tritoma*, the red-hot poker. [After J.H. *Kniphof* (1704–65), German botanist.]

knish *knish*, *n* in Jewish cookery, dough with a potato, meat, etc. filling, baked or fried. [Yiddish, — Russ.]

knit *nit*, *vt* to intertwine; to make by means of knitting-needles or knitting-machine; to unite closely, to draw together; to contract. — *vi* to interweave with needles; to grow together: — *pr p* **knitt'ing**; *pa t* and *pa p* **knitt'ed** or **knit**. — *n* a knitted fabric or article. — *n* **knitt'er**. — *n* **knitt'ing** the work of a knitter; union, junction; the network formed by knitting. — Also *adj*. — **knitt'ing-machine** a machine for knitting; **knitt'ing-needle** a long needle or wire, without an eye, used for knitting; **knit'wear** knitted clothing. — **knit one's brows** to frown. [O.E. *cnyttan* — *cnotta*, a knot.]

knives *nīvz*, pl. of **knife**.

knob *nob*, *n* a hard protuberance; a hard swelling; a round ornament or handle; the penis (*slang*). — *adj* **knobbed** containing or set with knobs. — *n* **knobb'iness**. — *n* **knobb'le** a little knob. — *adj* **knobb'ly** or **knobb'y** having, full of knobs; knotty. — **with knobs on** (*colloq*) with interest, more so. [Cf. Low Ger. *knobbe*.]

knobkerrie *nob'ker-i*, *n* a round-headed stick used as a club and a missile by tribal South Africans. [Afrik. *knopkierie*.]

knock *nok*, *vi* to strike with something hard or heavy; to drive or be driven against something; to strike (esp. a door) for admittance; to make a noise by, or as if by, striking; (of machinery) to rattle; (of internal-combustion engine) to give noise of detonation. — *vt* to strike; to drive against; to render, put, make or achieve by blows; to disparage, criticise in a carping way (*colloq*). — *n* a sudden stroke; a rap; the noise of detonation in an internal-combustion engine; a reversal, shock, setback (*colloq*); a criticism (*colloq*). — *n* **knock'er** someone who knocks or doorknocks; a device suspended on a door for making a knock; a carper or critic (*colloq*); (in *pl*) breasts (*slang*). — *n* **knock'ing** a beating on a door; a rap; a noise as if of something that knocks; knock in an internal-combustion engine. — **knock'about** a boisterous performance with horseplay; a performer of such turns; a rough-and-tumble; a doer of odd jobs, esp. on a station (*Austr*). — *adj* of the nature of knockabout; suitable for rough use. — **knock'-back** a setback; a refusal of parole from prison (*slang*). — *adj* **knock'-down** adapted for being taken to pieces; (of prices) very low. — **knocker-up'** a person employed to rouse workers in the morning; **knocking copy** advertising material which denigrates competing products; **knock'ing-shop** (*slang*) a brothel; **knock'-knee** state of being knock-kneed. — *adj* **knock-kneed'** having knees that knock or touch in walking. — **knock-on** see **knock on** and **knock-on effect** below. — *adj* (*colloq*) causing a series of effects. — **knock'out** the act of knocking out; a blow that knocks out; any person or thing of outstanding attraction or excellence (*colloq*). — *adj* (of a competition) eliminating losers at each round; stunningly attractive or excellent (*colloq*). — **knock-out drops** a drug put in a drink to make the drinker unconscious; **knock'-rating** the measurement of freedom from detonation (or knocking) of a fuel in an internal-combustion engine, as compared with a standard fuel; **knock'-up** (in tennis, etc.) practice immediately before a match. — **knock about** or **around** to mistreat physically; to saunter, loaf about; to travel about, roughing it and having varied experiences; to be a casual friend of, associate with (with *with*); **knock back** (*slang*) to drink, eat, esp. swiftly; to cost; to shock; to rebuff, reject, turn down; **knock copy** to disparage a rival's products; **knock down** to fell with a blow; to demolish; to assign (a sale) with a tap of the auctioneer's hammer (to); to reduce in price (*adj* **knock'-down** see above); **knock-for-knock agreement, policy**, etc., an arrangement between motor insurance companies by which, after an accident involving two cars, each company settles the damage to the car it insures without considering which driver was to blame; **knock into a cocked hat** see under **cock**[1]; **knock off** to stop work; to accomplish hastily; to deduct; to steal (*slang*); to copy illegally, to pirate (*slang*); to kill (*slang*); to have sexual intercourse with (*slang*); **knock on** (*Rugby football*) to knock forward with the hand or arm (an infringement of the rules; *n* **knock-on'**); **knock-on effect** the effect one action or occurrence has on one or more indirectly related matters or circumstances; **knock on the head** (*colloq*) to suppress, put an end to; **knock out** to strike unconscious or incapable of recovering in time (*boxing*); to overcome, demolish; to produce, esp. quickly or roughly (*colloq*); to tire (oneself) out (*slang*); to overwhelm with admiration, etc. (*slang*); **knock sideways** to put off one's usual course; **knock the bottom out of** to make, or show to be, invalid; to make ineffectual, bring to nothing; **knock the living daylights out of** see under **day; knock together** to get together or construct hastily; **knock up** to rouse by knocking; to be worn out; to construct or arrange hastily; to score (so many runs) (*cricket*); to make pregnant (*slang*). [O.E. *cnocian.*]

knockwurst. See **knackwurst.**

knoll *nōl*, *n* a round hillock. [O.E. *cnol.*]

knot[1] *not*, *n* a snipelike shore bird of the sandpiper family.

knot[2] *not*, *n* an interlacement of parts of a cord or cords, etc., by twisting the ends around each other, and then drawing tight the loops thus formed; a piece of ribbon, lace, etc., folded or tied upon itself; anything like a knot in form; a bond of union; a tangle (in string, hair, etc.); a difficulty; the main point or central part of a tangle, intricacy, problem or difficulty; the base of a branch buried in a later growth of wood; a nautical mile per hour, used in navigation and meteorology; (*loosely*) a nautical mile; a node or joint in a stem, esp. of a grass; a solidified lump; a swelling; a knob; a clump or cluster; a measured quantity of yarn. — *vt* to tie in a knot; to unite closely; to make knotty or by knotting; to cover knots in (before painting wood). — *vi* to form a knot or knots: — *pr p* **knott'ing;** *pa t* and *pa p* **knott'ed.** — *adj* **knot'less.** — *adj* **knott'ed** full of, or having, knots. — *n* **knott'er.** — *n* **knott'iness.** — *n* **knott'ing** formation or removal of knots. — *adj* **knott'y** containing knots; hard, rugged; difficult; intricate. — **knot garden** a garden with intricate formal designs of shrubs, flower-beds, etc.; **knot'-grass** a much-jointed species of *Polygonum*, a common weed; applied also to various grasses; **knot'-hole** a hole in wood where a knot has fallen out. — **at a rate of knots** (*colloq*) very fast; **get knotted!** (*slang*) *interj* expressing anger, defiance, etc.; **tie someone in knots** to confuse or bewilder someone completely. [O.E. *cnotta.*]

know *nō*, *vt* to be informed or assured of; to be acquainted with; to recognise. — *vi* to possess knowledge: — *pr p* **know'ing;** *pa t* **knew** (*nū*, or in U.S. *no͞o*); *pa p* **known** (*nōn*). — *n* possession of the relevant facts. — *adj* **know'able** capable of being known, discovered or understood. — *n* **know'er.** — *adj* **know'ing** intelligent; skilful; cunning. — *adv* **know'ingly** in a knowing manner; consciously; intentionally. — *n* **know'ingness** the quality of being knowing or intelligent; shrewdness. — *adj* **known** widely recognised. — **know'-all** someone who thinks they know everything; **know'-how** the faculty of knowing the right thing to do in any contingency; specialised skill. — **in the know** in possession of private information; initiated; **I wouldn't know** I am not in a position to know; **know all the answers** to be completely informed on everything, or to think one is; **know better** to be wiser, better-instructed (than to do this or that); **know how many beans make five** to be sensible, aware, have one's wits about one; **known as** going by name of; **know the ropes** to understand the detail or procedure; **know what's what** to be able to judge what is important, to be well-informed or sensible; **know which side one's bread is buttered (on)** to be fully aware of one's own best interests; **what do you know?** a greeting or expression of incredulity; **you never know** (*colloq*) perhaps. [O.E. *cnāwan.*]

knowledge *nol'ij*, *n* that which is known; information, instruction; enlightenment, learning; practical skill; assured belief; acquaintance. — *adj* **knowl'edgeable** possessing knowledge; intelligent. — *adv* **knowl'edgeably.** — **knowledge base** (*comput*) a collection of specialist knowledge formulated for use esp. in expert systems. — **to one's knowledge** so far as one knows. [M.E. *knowleche.*]

knuckle *nuk'l*, *n* projecting joint of a finger; the knee-joint of a calf or pig (*cookery*). — *vi* to yield (usu. with *down* or *under*); to bend the knuckles or knee. — *vt* to touch with the knuckle. — **knuck'le-bone** any bone with a rounded end; (in *pl*) the game of dibs; **knuck'leduster** a metal covering for the knuckles, worn on the hand as a weapon in fist-fighting; **knuck'le-head** (*colloq*) idiot. — *adj* **knuck'le-headed.** — **knuckle-head'edness; knuck'le-joint** a joint where the forked end of a connecting-rod is joined by a bolt to another piece of the machinery; **knuckle sandwich** (*slang*) a blow with the fist. — **knuckle down (to)** to set oneself to hard work — see also at **knuckle** above; **knuckle under** to yield to authority, pressure, etc.; **near the knuckle** on the verge of the indecent; **rap someone's knuckles** to reprimand someone. [M.E. *knokel.*]

knur or **knurr** *nûr*, *n* an excrescence on a tree; a hard ball or knot of wood.

knurl or **nurl** *nûrl*, *n* a ridge or bead, esp. in series. — *vt* to make knurls on, to mill. — *adj* **knurled** covered with knurls. — *n* **knurl'ing** mouldings or other woodwork elaborated into a series of knobs. — *adj* **knurl'y** gnarled. [Prob. a dimin. of **knur.**]

KO or **ko** *abbrev* for: kick-off; knockout; knock out. — *vt* (*kā-ō'*; *colloq*) to knock out: — *pr p* **KO''ing** or **ko''ing;** *pa t* and *pa p* **KO'd'** or **ko'd'.** — *n* a knockout: — *pl* **KO's'** or **ko's'.**

koa *kō'ə*, *n* a Hawaiian acacia. [Hawaiian.]

koala *kō-ä'lə*, *n* an Australian tailless marsupial, like a small bear, which feeds on eucalyptus leaves. — Also called **Koala bear** or **native bear.** [Australian *kūlā.*]

koan *kō'än*, *n* (in Zen Buddhism) a nonsensical question given to students as a subject for meditation. [Jap., a public proposal or plan.]

kobold *kō'bold*, *n* (in German folklore) a spirit of the mines; a domestic brownie. [Ger.]

Kodiak *kō'di-ak* or **Kodiak bear** (*bār*), *n* the largest variety of brown bear, *Ursus arctos*, found in Alaska and the Aleutian Islands. [From *Kodiak* Island, Alaska.]

kofta *kof'tə*, *n* (in Indian cookery) minced and seasoned meat or vegetables, shaped into a ball and fried.

kohl *kōl*, *n* a fine black powder of native stibnite (formerly known as antimony), used (orig. in the East) to shade the area around the eyes. [Ar. *koh'l.*]

kohlrabi *kōl-rä'bi*, *n* a cabbage with a turnip-shaped stem. [Ger., — It. *cavolo rapa* — L. *caulis*, cabbage, *rapa*, turnip.]

Koine *koi'nē*, *n* a Greek dialect developed from Attic, used in the Eastern Mediterranean in Hellenistic and Byzantine times; (often without *cap*) any dialect which has spread and become the common language of a larger area. [Gr. *koinē* (*dialektos*) common (dialect).]

kola. See **cola.**

kolinsky *ko-lin'ski*, *n* (the fur of) a species of mink found in eastern Asia. [Russ. *kolinski*, of the Kola Peninsula.]

kolkhoz *kol-hhoz'*, *n* a collective or co-operative farm. [Russ. abbrev. of *kollektivnoe khozyaistvo.*]

Kol Nidre *kōl* or (esp. *US*) *kōl nid'rā*, *n* in Judaism, the opening prayer said on the eve of Yom Kippur; its traditional musical setting. [Aramaic, all vows (the first words of the prayer).]

komatik *kom'ə-tik*, *n* an Eskimo sled with wooden runners. [Eskimo.]

Komodo dragon or **lizard** *kə-mō'dō drag'ən* or *liz'ərd*, *n* a very large monitor lizard of some Indonesian islands. [From *Komodo* Island, Indonesia.]

Komsomol *kom'sō-mol*, *n* the Communist youth organisation of Russia. [Russ. abbrev. of *Kommunisticheskii Soyuz Molodezhi*.]

konimeter *kon-im'i-tər*, *n* an instrument for measuring dust in air. — *n* **koniol'ogy** the study of dust in the air and its effects. — *n* **kon'iscope** an instrument for estimating the dustiness of air. [Gr. *konis*, dust, *metron*, measure, *skopeein*, to look at.]

koodoo. See **kudu.**

kook *ko͝ok*, (*slang*) *n* a person who is mad, foolish, or eccentric and amoral. — *adj* **kook'ie** or **kook'y** with the qualities of a kook; (of clothes) smart and eccentric. [Prob. from **cuckoo.**]

kookaburra *ko͝ok'ə-bur-ə*, *n* an Australian kingfisher which has a discordant laughing call, the laughing jackass. [Aboriginal.]

kookie, kooky. See **kook.**

kopeck or **copeck** *kō'pek*, *n* a Russian coin, the hundredth part of a rouble. [Russ. *kopeika*.]

koori *ko͞o'ri*, (*Austr*) *n* an Aboriginal; a young Aboriginal woman. [Aboriginal.]

kop *kop*, *n* a hill (*SAfr*); (with *cap*) a bank of terracing at a football ground, esp. (and orig.) that at Liverpool's Anfield ground. — *n* **koppie** or **kopje** (*kop'i*; *SAfr*) a low hill. [Cape Du. *kopje* — *kop*, head.]

Koran *kö-rän'*, sometimes *kō'* or *kö'rən*, *n* the Muslim Scriptures in Arabic, believed by the faithful to be the true word of God as spoken by Mohammed. — Also **Qoran, Qur'an.** — *adj* **Koranic** (*-rän'ik*). [Ar. *qurān*, reading.]

korfball *körf'böl*, *n* a game of Dutch origin resembling basketball played by teams of six men and six women a side. [Du. *korfbal* — *korf*, basket, *bal*, ball.]

korma *kör'mə*, *n* a mild-flavoured Indian dish, meat or vegetables braised in water, stock, yoghurt or cream.

koruna *kör'ə-nä*, *n* the standard unit of currency of Czechoslovakia (100 *haler*). [Czech. — L. *corona*, crown.]

kosher *kō'shər*, *adj* pure, clean, according to Jewish law — as of meat killed and prepared by Jews; legitimate, proper, genuine (*colloq*). — *n* kosher food. [Heb. *kāshēr*, right.]

kosmos. Same as **cosmos.**

koto *kō'tō*, *n* a Japanese musical instrument consisting of a long box with thirteen silk strings: — *pl* **kō'tos.** [Jap.]

koulan, koumiss, kourbash, kouskous. See **kulan, kumiss, kurbash, couscous.**

kouprey *ko͞o'prā*, *n* the very rare Indo-Chinese wild cow, believed to be closely related to the ancestors of modern domestic cattle. [Kampuchean native name.]

kowhai *kō'hī* or *-wī*, *n* New Zealand tree or shrub of the genus *Sophora*, with golden flowers. [Maori.]

kowtow *kow-tow'*, *n* the old Chinese ceremony of touching the forehead to the ground. — *vi* to perform that ceremony; to abase oneself before (with *to*); to grovel or fawn. [Chin. *k'o*, knock, *t'ou*, head.]

KP *abbrev* for Knight of (the Order of) St Patrick.

kpg *abbrev* for kilometres per gallon.

kph *abbrev* for kilometres per hour.

Kr (*chem*) *symbol* for krypton.

kr *abbrev* for: krona (Swedish currency); króna (Icelandic currency); krone (Danish and Norwegian currency).

kraal *kräl*, *n* a South African village of huts surrounded by a fence; a corral. — *vt* to pen. [Afrik., — Port. *curral*.]

kraft *kräft*, *n* a type of strong brown wrapping paper made from pulp treated with a sulphate solution. [Ger. *Kraft*, strength.]

krait *krīt*, *n* a deadly Indian rock snake. [Hind. *karait*.]

kraken *krä'kən*, *n* a fabled sea-monster. [Norw.]

krans *kräns* or **krantz** *kränts*, (*SAfr*) *n* a crown of rock on a mountain-top; a precipice. [Afrik.]

kraut *krowt*, (often with *cap*; *slang*) *n* a German. [From **sauerkraut.**]

kremlin *krem'lin*, *n* a citadel, esp. (with *cap*) that of Moscow; (with *cap*) the central government of the U.S.S.R. [Russ. *kreml'*.]

kriegspiel *krēg'spēl*, *n* a war-game played on a map to train officers; a form of chess in which the players use separate boards and are allowed only limited communication through an umpire. [Ger. *Kriegsspiel* — *Krieg*, war, *Spiel*, game.]

krill *kril*, *n* a species of minute shrimplike animals eaten by whales, etc. [Norw. *kril*.]

krimmer *krim'ər*, *n* tightly curled grey or black fur from a Crimean type of lamb. [Ger. *Krim*, Crimea.]

kris *krēs*, *n* a Malay dagger with a wavy blade: — *pl* **kris'es.** [Malay.]

Krishna *krish'nə*, (*Hinduism*) *n* a deity, a form of Vishnu. — *n* **Krish'naism** belief in, and worship of, Krishna. [Sans.]

krone *krō'nə*, *n* (*pl* **kro'ne**) in Denmark and Norway, **krona** *kro͞o'nə* (*pl* **kro'nor**) in Sweden, and in Iceland **króna** *krō'nə* (*pl* **kró'nur**) a silver coin and monetary unit equal to 100 *öre*, or in Iceland 100 *aurar*. [Cf. **crown.**]

Kronos *kron'os*, *n* a supreme god of the Greeks, son of Ouranos and Gaia, dethroned by his son Zeus.

krónur. See under **krone.**

Krugerrand *kro͞o'gər-rand*, *n* a South African coin containing one troy ounce of fine gold and bearing a portrait of President *Kruger*. — Also **rand** or **kru'gerrand. [rand.]**

krummhorn or **crumhorn** *kro͞om'hörn*, *n* an old double-reed wind instrument with curved end. [Ger., curved horn.]

krypton *krip'ton*, *n* an inert gas present in the air in extremely small quantity, used in fluorescent lights and lasers (symbol **Kr**; atomic no. 36). [Gr. *kryptein*, to hide.]

krytron *krī'tron*, (*tech*) *n* a sophisticated electronic timing device used for detonating nuclear and other explosive charges, and for varied industrial and scientific purposes.

KS *abbrev* for: Kansas (U.S. state); Kaposi's sarcoma.

KT *abbrev* for Knight of the Thistle.

Kt *abbrev* for Knight.

kt *abbrev* for: karat (carat); knot (*naut*).

Ku (*chem*) *symbol* for kurchatovium.

kudos *kū'dos*, *n* credit, fame, renown, prestige. [Gr. *kȳdos*, glory.]

kudu or **koodoo** *ko͞o'do͞o*, *n* an African antelope with long spiral horns. [From Hottentot.]

kudzu *ko͝od'zo͞o*, *n* an ornamental climbing plant with edible root tubers and a stem yielding a fibre. [Jap.]

kufiyah. See **kaffiyeh.**

Ku-Klux Klan *ko͞o'-kluks klan*, *n* a secret organisation in several Southern U.S. states after Civil War of 1861–65, to oppose Northern influence, and prevent Negroes from enjoying their rights as freemen — revived in 1916 to deal drastically with Jews, Catholics, Negroes, etc., and to preserve white Protestant supremacy. — *n* **Klan'sman** or **Ku-Klux Klansman** a member of this organisation. [Gr. *kyklos*, a circle, and **clan.**]

kukri *ko͝ok'rē*, *n* a sharp, curved Gurkha knife or short sword. [Hindi *kukrī*.]

kulak *ko͞o-lak'*, *n* in Tsarist times, a rich peasant; later, an exploiter. [Russ., fist.]

kulan or **koulan** *ko͞o'län*, *n* the onager, or a related wild Asian ass. [Tartar.]

kumara *kōō'mə-rə*, *n* sweet potato. [Maori.]

kumiss or **koumiss** *kōō'mis*, *n* fermented mares' milk. [Russ. *kumis* — Tartar *kumiz*.]

kümmel *küm'l*, *kim'l* or *kōōm'l*, *n* a liqueur flavoured with cumin and caraway seeds. [Ger., — L. *cumīnum*, cumin.]

kumquat *kum'kwot*, *n* a small kind of orange with a sweet rind. [Cantonese, gold orange.]

kung fu *kung fōō*, *n* an all-embracing martial art (of both armed and unarmed combat and self-defence) developed in ancient China. [Chin., combat skill.]

Kuo-yü *kwō'-yü* or *gwö'-yü*, *n* lit. 'national language', a form of Mandarin taught all over China.

kurbash or **kourbash** *kōōr'bash*, *n* a hide whip used in the East. — *vt* to whip with a kurbash. [Ar. *qurbāsh*.]

kurchatovium *kûr-chə-tō'vi-əm*, *n* the element (symbol **Ku**; atomic no. 104) named by Russians (who claimed its discovery in 1966) after a Russian physicist (American name **rutherfordium**).

Kurd *kōōrd* or *kûrd*, *n* one of the Islamic people of Kurdistan, a mountainous region of Turkey, Iran and Iraq. — *adj* and *n* **Kurd'ish**.

kurrajong or **currajong** *kur'ə-jong*, *n* a name for various Australian trees with fibrous bark. [Aboriginal.]

kurta *kōōr'tä*, *n* a loose-fitting collarless shirt or tunic worn in India. [Hindi.]

kurtosis *kər-tō'sis*, (*statistics*) *n* the relative degree of sharpness of the peak on a frequency-distribution curve. [Gr. *kurtōsis*, bulging, swelling.]

Kushitic. Same as **Cushitic**.

kV *abbrev* for kilovolt.

kvass *kväs*, *n* rye beer. [Russ. *kvas*.]

kvetch *kvech*, *vi* to complain, whine, esp. incessantly. — *n* **kvetch** or **kvetch'er** a complainer, fault-finder. [Yiddish.]

kW *abbrev* for kilowatt. — **kWh** *abbrev* for kilowatt-hour.

KWAC *kwak*, *abbrev* for keyword and context.

kwacha *kwäch'ə*, *n* the standard unit of currency in Zambia (100 *ngwee*) and Malawi (100 *tambala*). [Native name, meaning 'dawn'.]

kwanza *kwän'zə*, *n* the standard unit of currency of Angola (100 *lweis*).

kwashiorkor *kwä-*, *kwo-* or *kwa-shi-ör'kör*, *n* a widespread nutritional disease of children in tropical and subtropical regions due to deficiency of protein. [Ghanaian name.]

kwela *kwā'la*, *n* Zulu folk-music of jazz type. [Bantu, lift (from leaping upward in dancing to the music).]

KWIC *kwik*, *abbrev* for keyword in context.

KWOC *kwok*, *abbrev* for keyword out of context.

KWT *abbrev* for Kuwait (I.V.R.).

KY or **Ky** *abbrev* for Kentucky (U.S. state).

kyanise or **-ize** *kī'ə-nīz*, *vt* to preserve from dry rot by injecting corrosive sublimate into the pores of (wood). [From John H. *Kyan* (1774–1830).]

kyanite *kī'ə-nīt*, *n* a mineral, an aluminium silicate, generally sky-blue. [Gr. *kyanos*, blue.]

kyat *kyät*, *n* the standard unit of currency of Burma (100 *pyas*).

kybosh. See **kibosh**.

kyle *kīl*, *n* a narrow strait. [Gael. *caol*.]

kylie or **kiley** *kī'li*, *n* a boomerang. [Aboriginal.]

kyllosis *kil-ō'sis*, *n* club-foot. [Gr. *kyllōsis*.]

kyloe *kī'lō*, *n* one of the long-haired cattle of the Hebrides.

kymograph *kī'mō-gräf*, *n* an instrument for recording the pressure of fluids, esp. of blood in a blood-vessel. — *n* **ky'mogram** such a record. — *adj* **kymographic** (*-graf'ik*). — *n* **kymog'raphy**. [Gr. *kȳma*, a wave, *graphein*, to write.]

kyphosis *kī-fō'sis*, (*pathol*) *n* a hunchbacked condition. — *adj* **kyphotic** (*-fot'ik*). [Gr. — *kȳphos*, a hump.]

Kyrie eleison *kēr'i-e el-ā'i-son*, also *kir'*, and *el-ā'son*, (in short **Kyrie**) *n* a form of prayer in all the ancient Greek liturgies, retained in the R.C. mass, following immediately after the introit (including both words and music); one of the responses to the commandments in the Anglican ante-communion service. [Gr. *Kȳrie*, *eleēson*, Lord, have mercy.]

ā face; *ä* far; *û* fur; *ū* fume; *ī* fire; *ō* foam; *ö* form; *ōō* fool; *ŏŏ* foot; *ē* feet; *ə* former

L

L[1] or **l** *el*, *n* the twelfth letter in the modern English alphabet, representing a lateral liquid sound, the breath passing the side or sides of the tongue; anything shaped like the letter L.

L[2] *el*, (*US colloq*) *n* an elevated railroad.

L or **L.** *abbrev* for: Lake; lambert; Latin; learner (driver); left; Liberal; *libra* (L.), pound sterling (usu. written **£**); licenciate; lira or (pl.) lire; litre; Luxembourg (I.V.R.).

L *symbol* for (Roman numeral) 50.

L *symbol* for: angular momentum (*phys*); inductance (*electr*); luminance (*phys*); molar latent heat (*chem*).

L- *el-*, *pfx* denoting: laevo (or levo-); laevorotatory. — ***L*-dopa** see **dopa**.

l or **l.** *abbrev* for: laevorotatory (*chem*); latitude; league; left; length; *libra* (L.), pound weight (usu. written **lb.**); line; lira or (pl.) lire; litre.

l (*chem*) *symbol* for specific latent heat per gramme.

LA *abbrev* for: Legislative Assembly; Library Association; Literate in Arts; Los Angeles; Louisiana (U.S. state; also **La**).

La *abbrev* for Lane (in street names, etc.).

La (*chem*) *symbol* for lanthanum.

la *lä*, (*mus*) *n* the sixth note of the scale in sol-fa notation — also spelt **lah**.

laager *lä'gər*, *n* in South Africa, a defensive ring of ox-wagons; any extemporised fortification; an encampment; a defensive group of people drawn together by a similar opinion, etc. (*fig*). — *vt* and *vi* to arrange or camp in a laager. [Cape Du. *lager* — Ger. *Lager*, a camp.]

Lab. *abbrev* for: Labour; Labrador.

lab *lab*, *n* a familiar contraction of **laboratory**.

labarum *lab'ə-rəm*, *n* the imperial standard after Constantine's conversion — with a monogram of the Greek letters XP (ChR), for Christ; a similar ecclesiastical banner carried in processions; any moral standard or guide. [L., — Late Gr. *labaron*.]

label *lā'bl*, *n* a small slip of paper or other material placed on or near anything to denote its nature, contents, ownership, destination, etc.; a characterising or classificatory designation (*fig*); a manufacturer's or retailer's tradename attached to goods to identify them; a strip of material with this or other information on it; the piece of paper on a record, cassette, compact disc, etc. giving the maker's production company's tradename and identifying the recorded material; the tradename itself (*colloq*); a character or set of characters indicating the start of an instruction in a program and used elsewhere in the program to refer to that instruction (*comput*); a paper appended to a will, such as a codicil (*law*); a dripstone (*archit*). — *vt* to fix a label to; to describe by or on a label; to replace an atom in (a molecule or compound) by a radioactive isotope, for the purpose of identification (*phys*): — *pr p* **lā'belling**; *pa t* and *pa p* **lā'belled**. [O.Fr. *label*.]

labellum *lə-bel'əm*, (*bot*) *n* the lower petal of an orchid; applied also to other liplike structures in flowers: — *pl* **labell'a**. [L., dimin. of *labrum*, lip.]

labial *lā'bi-əl*, *adj* of or formed by the lips; sounded by the impact of air on a liplike projection, as an organ flue-pipe (*mus*). — *n* a sound formed by the lips. — *vt* **lā'bialise** or **-ize** to make labial; to pronounce with rounded lips. — *adv* **lā'bially**. — *adj* **lā'biate** lipped; having a lipped corolla (*bot*). — *n* **lā'bium** a lip or liplike part: — *pl* **lā'bia**. — *adj* and *n* **lābiodent'al** (a sound) produced by the lips and teeth together, such as *f* and *v*. — **labia majora** and **labia minora** the two outer and inner folds of skin surrounding the vaginal orifice in human females. [L. *lăbium*, lip.]

labile *lā'bīl* or (esp. in U.S.) *lā'bəl*, *adj* unstable; apt to slip or change. — *n* **lability** (*lə-bil'i-ti*). [L. *lābilis* — *lābī*, to slip.]

labium. See under **labial**.

laboratory *lə-bor'ə-tə-ri* or (esp. in U.S.) *lab'ə-rə-tə-ri*, *n* a place for experimental work or research; orig. a chemist's workroom. [L. *labōrāre* — *labor*, work.]

laborious, etc. See under **labour**.

labour or (esp. in N.Am.) **labor** *lā'bər*, *n* physical or mental toil, work; duties; a task requiring hard work; effort made toward the satisfaction of needs; workers collectively; supply or services of workers, esp. physical workers; (with *cap*) the Labour Party or its cause, principles or interest (*politics*); the pains and physical efforts of childbirth; heavy pitching or rolling of a ship. — *adj* of labour or (with *cap*) the Labour Party. — *vi* to experience labour; to work; to take pains; to be oppressed or burdened; to move slowly and with difficulty; to undergo childbirth; to pitch and roll heavily (*naut*). — *vt* to over-elaborate, repeat unnecessarily. — *adj* **laborious** (*lə-bö'ri-əs*) involving or devoted to labour; strenuous; arduous. — *adv* **labo'riously**. — *n* **labo'riousness**. — *adj* **lā'boured** showing signs of effort in execution; over-elaborated, repeated unnecessarily. — *n* **lā'bourer** a person who labours; a person who does physical rather than skilled work. — **labour camp** a penal institution where the inmates are forced to work; temporary accommodation for workers; **Labour Day** a public holiday held in many countries on 1 May, in celebration of labour and workers; in U.S. and Canada (**Labor Day**), a holiday held on the first Monday in September; **Labour Exchange** a former name for an **employment office; labour force** the workers collectively employed in an industry, factory, etc. — *adj* **labour-intens'ive** requiring a relatively large number of workers for the capital invested (opp. of *capital-intensive*). — **Labour Party** in Britain, a political party formed in 1900 by trade unions, etc. to represent the working community and its interests; a similar party in various countries, esp. (as **Labor Party**) Australia. — *adj* **la'bour-saving** intended to supersede or lessen labour. — **labor union** (*US*) a trade union. — **hard labour** compulsory work imposed in addition to imprisonment, abolished in U.K. in 1948; **labour of love** work undertaken for its own sake and without hope of any tangible reward. [O.Fr. *labour*, *labeur* — L. *labor*.]

Labrador *lab'rə-dör* or *lab-rə-dör'*, *n* a mainland region of Newfoundland and Quebec; a Labrador dog. — Also *adj*. — **Labrador dog** or **Labrador retriever** a sporting dog about 56 cm. in height, either black or (**yellow** or **golden Labrador**) from red to fawn in colour.

labrum *lā'brəm*, (*zool*) *n* a lip; a liplike part, esp. in insects: — *pl* **lā'bra**. [L. *lăbrum*, a lip.]

laburnum *lə-bûr'nəm*, *n* a small poisonous tree or shrub, which bears slim seed-pods and hanging clusters of yellow flowers. [L.]

labyrinth *lab'i-rinth, n* orig. a building with intricate passages; a maze or any tangle of intricate ways and connections; the cavities of the internal ear (*anat*). — *adj* **labyrinth'ian** or **labyrinth'ine** (*-īn* or *-in*). — *n* **labyrinthī'tis** (*med*) inflammation of the inner ear. [Gr. *labyrinthos*.]

LAC *abbrev* for leading aircraft(s)man.

lac[1] *lak, n* a dark-red transparent resin used in making shellac, secreted on the twigs of trees in Asia by certain coccid insects (**lac insects**). [Hind. *lākh* — Sans. *lākṣā*, 100 000, hence the (teeming) lac insect.]

lac[2]. See **lakh**.

laccolith *lak'ō-lith, (geol) n* a mass of igneous rock that has risen in a molten condition and bulged up the overlying strata to form a dome. — *adj* **laccolith'ic**. [Gr. *lakkos*, a reservoir, *lithos*, a stone.]

lace *lās, n* a string or cord for passing through holes, e.g. to tie up a shoe or garment, etc.; a delicate ornamental fabric made by looping, knotting, plaiting or twisting threads into definite patterns. — *vt* to fasten with a lace (often with *up*); to compress or pinch in by lacing; to trim or decorate with lace; to streak with colour (*fig*); to thrash; to intermingle, e.g. coffee with brandy, etc.; to intertwine. — *vi* to have lacing as the means of fastening. — *adj* **laced**. — *n* and *adj* **lac'ing**. — *adj* **lac'y** of or like lace; decorated with lace. — **lace'-ups** boots or shoes tied with laces; **lace'wing** a type of green or brown insect with two pairs of gauzy wings which feeds on aphids, etc. [O.Fr. *las*, a noose — L. *laqueus*.]

lacerate *las'ə-rāt, vt* to tear or rip; to wound; to distress severely. — *n* **lacerā'tion**. — *adj* **lac'erative** tearing; having power to tear. [L. *lacerāre*, *-ātum*, to tear.]

laches *lach'iz, (law) n* negligence or undue delay in carrying out a legal duty, esp. until the entitlement period (for a claim, remedy, etc.) has expired. [A.Fr. *lachesse*.]

lachrymal *lak'ri-məl, adj* of or for tears. — *n* a bone near the tear gland; (in *pl*) lachrymal glands. — *n* **lachrymā'tion** the secretion of tears. — *n* **lach'rymātor** a substance that causes tears to flow, such as tear-gas. — *adj* **lach'rymatory** lachrymal; causing tears to flow. — *adj* **lach'rymose** shedding tears; tearful, given to weeping; lugubrious. — *adv* **lach'rymosely**. — **lachrymal duct** (*anat*) a duct that conveys tear-water from the inner corner of the eye to the nose; **lachrymal gland** (*anat*) a gland at the outer angle of the eye that secretes tears. [From *lachryma*, a mediaeval spelling of L. *lacrima*, tear.]

lacinia *lə-sin'i-ə, (bot) n* a long narrow lobe in a leaf, etc.: — *pl* **lacin'iae** (*-ē*). — *adj* **lacin'iate** or **lacin'iated** cut into narrow lobes, slashed. — *n* **laciniā'tion**. [L., a little flap, tag.]

lack *lak, n* want, deficiency; something absent or in short supply. — *vt* to be without; to be short of or deficient in; to need. — *vi* (now usu. in *pr p*; with *in* or *for*) to be deficient. — *adj* **lack'ing**. — *adj* **lack'-lustre** or in U.S. **lack'luster** dull, without brightness, sheen or vitality. — Also *n*. [Cf. M.L.G. and Du. *lak*, blemish.]

lackadaisical *lak-ə-dā'zi-kl, adj* affectedly pensive; vapidly sentimental; listless; languid and ineffectual. [Prob. **lack** and **day**.]

lackey *lak'i, n* a footman or valet; a servile follower: — *pl* **lack'eys**. — *vt* and *vi* to serve or attend as or like a footman or slavish servant. [O.Fr. *laquay* (Fr. *laquais*) — Sp. *lacayo*.]

laconic *lə-kon'ik, adj* expressing or expressed in few words; sententiously brief. — *adv* **lacon'ically**. [Gr. *lakōnikos*, of Laconia, i.e. Spartan (in reference to the succinct style of Spartan speech).]

lacquer *lak'ər, n* a solution of film-forming substances in a volatile solvent, esp. a varnish of lac and alcohol; a similar substance sprayed on the hair to hold it in place; a covering of one of these. — *vt* to cover with lacquer; to varnish. — *n* **lacqu'erer**. — *n* **lacqu'ering** varnishing with lacquer; a coat of lacquer varnish. [Fr. *lacre* — Port. *lacre*, *laca*, lac.]

lacrimal, lacrimation, lacrimator, lacrimose, lacrimosely. Variants of **lachrymal, lachrymation,** etc.

lacrimoso *läk-ri-mō'sō, (mus) adj* and *adv* plaintive or plaintively. [It., — L. *lacrimōsus*, tearful — *lacrima*, a tear.]

lacrosse *lə-* or *lä-kros', n* a team sport (orig. American Indian) in which a long-handled, netted stick (**lacrosse stick** or **crosse**) is used to throw, catch and cradle (q.v.) the ball, etc. — **min'i-lacrosse** and **pop'-lacrosse** simplified versions of lacrosse. [Can. Fr.]

lacteal *lak'ti-əl, adj* of milk; conveying chyle. — *n* a lymph vessel conveying chyle from the intestines to the thoracic ducts. — *n* **lactase** (*lak'tās*) an enzyme that acts on lactose. — *n* **lac'tate** a salt of lactic acid. — *vi* (also *lak-tāt'*) to secrete milk. — *n* **lactā'tion** secretion or yielding of milk; the period of suckling. — *adj* **lac'teous** milky. — *n* **lactesc'ence**. — *adj* **lactesc'ent** turning to milk; producing milky juice. — *adj* **lac'tic** derived from or pertaining to milk. — *adj* **lactif'ic** producing milk or milky juice. — *adj* **lactogen'ic** inducing lactation. — *n* **lac'tone** (*chem*) an organic compound which can be formed by the reaction between the hydroxyl group and the carboxyl group in a molecule. — *n* **lac'tose** milk-sugar, a crystalline sugar obtained by evaporating whey. — **lactic acid** an acid obtained from milk, used as a preservative. [L. *lac*, *lactis*, milk.]

lacuna *lə-* or *la-kū'nə, n* a gap or hiatus; an intercellular space (*biol*); a cavity; a depression in a pitted surface: — *pl* **lacū'nae** (*-nē*). — *adj* **lacū'nal** or **lacū'nary** pertaining to, or including, lacunae. — *adj* **lacū'nose** having lacunae; pitted. [L. *lacūna*, a hollow, gap.]

lacustrine *lə-kus'trīn, adj* pertaining to lakes; dwelling in or on lakes; formed in lakes. [L. *lacus*, a lake.]

lacy. See **lace**.

lad *lad, n* a boy; a youth; a stable-man or -woman; a dashing, high-spirited or extrovert man (*colloq*). — *n* **ladd'ie** a little lad; a boy (*Northern Br*). [M.E. *ladde*, youth, servant.]

ladanum *lad'ə-nəm, n* a fragrant resin exuded from rock rose leaves in Mediterranean countries. [L. — Gr. *lādanon*, *lēdanon* — *lēdon*, the rock rose plant.]

ladder *lad'ər, n* a piece of equipment, generally portable, with horizontal rungs between two vertical supports, used for going up or down; anything of a similar form or pattern, such as a run in knitwear where the breaking of a thread gives an appearance of rungs; an arrangement which enables fish to ascend a waterfall (*fish-ladder*, *salmon-ladder*); a means of climbing to a higher status (*fig*). — *vi* (of knitwear, fabric, etc.) to develop a ladder. — *adj* **ladd'ered** or **ladd'ery**. — **ladder-back chair** a chair with a back consisting of several horizontal bars between two long uprights. [O.E. *hlǣder*.]

laddie. See **lad**.

lade *lād, vt* to load; to put on board; to ladle or scoop (now usu. *tech*). — *vi* to take cargo aboard: — *pa t* **lād'ed**; *pa p* **lād'en** or **lād'ed**. — *n* **lād'ing** the act of loading; that which is loaded; cargo; freight. [O.E. *hladan*, to load, draw water.]

laden *lā'dən, adj* loaded; burdened, weighed down. [**lade**.]

la-di-da or **lah-di-dah** *lä-di-dä', (slang) adj* affectedly elegant or superior, esp. in speech or manner.

ladle *lād'l, n* a large, esp. deep spoon for lifting liquid; a long-handled pan or bucket for holding and conveying molten metal. — *vt* to transfer or distribute with a ladle. — *n* **lad'leful** as much as a ladle will hold: — *pl* **lad'lefuls**. — **ladle out** (*colloq*) to distribute generously. [O.E. *hlædel* — *hladan*, to lade.]

lady *lā'di*, (with *cap* when used as a prefix) *n* the mistress of a house; used as the feminine of **lord** and of **gentleman**, and ordinarily as a less formal substitute for **dame**; any woman with refined manners and instincts; a lady-love or object of chivalric devotion; a girlfriend, mistress, etc.; a feminine prefix with various formal uses, e.g. for the wife of a knight, baron or baronet; (in combination) denoting a woman who performs a certain job, etc., such as *tea-lady*: — *pl* **ladies** (*lā'diz*). — *n* **ladies'** a ladies' lavatory. — *n* **la'dyhood** the condition or character of a lady. — *adj* **la'dylike** like a lady in manners; refined; soft, delicate; genteel. — *n* **la'dyship** the title of a lady. — **ladies' fingers** see **lady's finger(s)** below; **ladies' man** or **lady's man** a man who enjoys the company of women and being attentive to them; **la'dieswear** clothing for women; **la'dybird** any member of the family *Coccinellidae*, of little round beetles, often brightly spotted, which prey on greenfly, etc. — also called **la'dybug, la'dycow** or **la'dyfly; Lady Bountiful** (also without *caps*; often *derog*) a rich and generous woman, often applied to one who is ostentatiously or offensively so; **lady chapel** a chapel dedicated to the Virgin Mary, usually behind the high altar, at the end of the apse; **Lady Day** 25 March, the day of the annunciation of the Virgin; **lady-in-wait'ing** a female attendant to a lady of royal status; **la'dy-killer** a man who is, or fancies himself, irresistible to women; **la'dy-love** a beloved lady or woman; a sweetheart; **lady's finger** or **fingers** a name for many plants, esp. the kidney vetch; gumbo or okra; a finger-shaped cake; **la'dy's-maid** a lady's female attendant, responsible for her clothes, etc.; **la'dy's-mantle** a genus of plants of the rose family with small, yellowish-green flowers and leaves like folded drapery; **lady's-slipp'er** a genus of orchids with large slipperlike lip; **lady's-smock'** the cuckoo-flower, a meadow-plant, with pale lilac-coloured flowers. — **find the lady** see **three-card trick** under **three; our Lady** the Virgin Mary. [O.E. *hlǣfdige*, lit. app. the bread-kneader.]

laevo- or **levo-** *lē-vō-*, *combining form* signifying on or to the left. [L. *laevus*, left.]

laevorotatory or **levorotatory** *lē-vō-rō'tə-tə-ri* or *-rō-tā'*, *adj* counterclockwise; rotating the plane of polarisation of light to the left (*optics*). — *n* **laevorotā'tion.** [L. *laevus*, left, *rotāre*, to rotate.]

lag[1] *lag*, *n* a retardation or falling behind; the amount by which one phenomenon is delayed behind another; delay; someone who, or that which, comes behind. — *vi* to fall behind; to move or walk slowly; to loiter: — *pr p* **lagg'ing**; *pa t* and *pa p* **lagged**. — *adj* **lagg'ard** lagging behind. — *n* **lagg'ard** or **lagg'er** a person who lags behind. — *n* and *adj* **lagg'ing**. — *adv* **lagg'ingly**. — **lag of the tides** the progressive lengthening of the interval between tides as neap tide is approached (opp. to *priming*).

lag[2] *lag*, *n* an insulating wooden or other lining; a non-conducting covering for pipes, etc.; boarding; a wooden stave or lath. — *vt* to provide with a lag or lagging. — *n* **lagg'er** a person who insulates pipes, machinery, etc. against heat loss. — *n* **lagg'ing** a non-conducting covering for pipes, etc. to minimise loss of heat; boarding, as across the framework of a centre for an arch, or in a mine to prevent ore falling into a passage. [Prob. O.N. *lögg*, barrel-rim.]

lag[3] *lag*, (*slang*) *vt* to arrest; to imprison. — *n* a convict or former convict; a term in prison.

lagan *lag'ən*, *n* wreckage or goods at the bottom of the sea, now esp. such goods attached to a buoy with a view to recovery. [O.Fr.]

lager *lä'gər*, *n* (in full **lager beer**) a light beer traditionally matured for up to six months before use. — **lager lout** a youth noted for his boorish, aggressive and unruly behaviour brought on by an excess of lager, beer, etc.; **lager loutery** (*colloq*) the phenomenon or behaviour of lager louts. [Ger. *Lager-bier* — *Lager*, a storehouse.]

lagomorph *lag'o-mörf*, *n* an animal of the order *Lagomorpha*, gnawing mammals with two pairs of upper incisors, e.g. hares, rabbits. — *adj* **lagomor'phic**. [Gr. *lagōs*, hare, *morphē*, form.]

lagoon *lə-gōōn'*, *n* a shallow lake, esp. one near or communicating with the sea or a river. — *adj* **lagoon'al**. [It. *laguna* — L. *lacūna*.]

lah. Same as **la** (noun).

lahar *lā'här*, (*geol*) *n* a mud-lava or other mud-flow on the slopes of a volcano. [Jav.]

lah-di-dah. See **la-di-da**.

laic, laical, laicise, etc., **laicity**. See **lay**[4].

laid *lād*, *pa t* and *pa p* of **lay**[2]. — *adj* put down, prostrate; pressed down; spread or set out. — *adj* **laid-back'** or **laid back** (*slang*) relaxed; easy-going; unhurried. — **laid paper** paper that shows the marks of the close parallel wires on which the pulp was laid (opp. to *wove*); **laid work** in embroidery, the simplest type of couching.

laika *lī'kə*, *n* any of several similar breeds of small, reddish-brown working dog, originating in Finland.

lain *lān*, *pa p* of **lie**[2].

Laingian *lang'i-ən*, *adj* of or pertaining to the theories or practices of R.D. *Laing* (1927–89), British psychiatrist, esp. his view that mental illness is a response to stress caused by a person's family life or by social pressures. — *n* a supporter of Laing's theories and practices.

lair[1] *lār*, *n* the den or retreat of a wild animal; an enclosure for beasts; the ground for one grave in a graveyard (*Scot*). — *vt* to put in a lair. — *vi* to lie in a lair; to go to a lair. — *n* **lair'age** a place, or accommodation, where cattle are housed or laired, esp. at markets and docks. [O.E. *leger*, a couch — *licgan*, to lie down.]

lair[2] *lār*, (*Austr slang*) *n* a flashily dressed man. — *vi* **lair'ise** or **-ize** to act the lair. — *adj* **lair'y**. — **laired up** dressed flashily.

laird *lārd*, (*Scot*) *n* an estate landowner. — *n* **laird'-ship**. [Northern form of **lord**.]

lairy. See **lair**[2].

laissez-aller *les-ā-al'ā*, *n* lack of constraint; relaxed freedom. — Also **laisser-all'er**. [Fr., let go.]

laissez-faire *les-ā-fer'*, *n* a general principle of non-interference in the concerns of other people or parties. — Also **laisser-faire'**. [Fr., let do.]

laissez-passer *les-ā-päs'ā*, *n* a pass, special passport or similar, to allow one to travel in a restricted area, etc. [Fr., let pass.]

laitance *lā'təns*, *n* a milky accumulation of fine particles which forms on the surface of newly-laid concrete if the concrete is too wet, etc. [Fr., — *lait*, milk.]

laity. See under **lay**[4].

lake[1] *lāk*, *n* a reddish pigment originally derived from lac; a coloured substance derived by combining a dye with a metallic hydroxide; its colour; carmine. — *adj* **lak'y**. [**lac**[1].]

lake[2] *lāk*, *n* a large or considerable body of water within land; a large quantity, an excess, e.g. of wine, etc. (*econ*). — *n* **lake'let** a little lake. — **lake'-basin** a hollow now or once containing a lake; the area drained by a lake; **Lake District** a picturesque and mountainous region in Cumbria, with many lakes. [M.E. *lac*.]

lakh or **lac** *läk* or *lak*, (*Ind* and *Pak*) *n* the number 100 000, esp. in referring to rupees; an indefinitely vast number. [Hindi, — Sans. *laksha*.]

Lalique glass *lal-ēk' gläs*, *n* ornamental glassware, esp. with bas-relief decoration of figures, flowers, etc. [Named after René *Lalique* (d. 1945), Fr. designer of jewellery and glassware.]

Lallans *lal'ənz*, *n* the Broad Scots language or dialect; a form of Scots developed by modern Scottish writers. [Scot. *lallan*, lowland.]

lallation *lal-ā'shən, n* (in speech) pronouncing *r* like *l*. [Orig. childish speech — L. *lallare*, to sing lullaby.]

lallygag *lal'i-gag* or **lollygag** *lol'i-gag*, (*US colloq*) *vi* to idle, mess about, loiter.

Lam. (*Bible*) *abbrev* for (the Book of) Lamentations.

lam *lam, vt* to beat. — *n* **lamm'ing.** [Cf. O.E. *lemian*, to subdue, lame, O.N. *lemja*, to beat, lit. lame.]

lama *lä'mə, n* a Buddhist priest in Tibet. — *n* **Lamaism** (*lä'mə-izm*) the religion prevailing in Tibet and Mongolia, being Buddhism influenced by Tantrism, and by Shamanism or spirit-worship. — *n* **La'maist.** — *adj* **lamaist'ic.** — *n* **la'masery** (also *lä-mä'sə-ri*) or **lamaserai (**-*rī*) a Tibetan monastery. [Tibetan, *blama*, the *b* silent.]

Lamarckism *lä-märk'izm, n* the theory of the French naturalist J.B.P.A. de Monet de *Lamarck* (1744–1829) that species have developed by the efforts of organisms to adapt themselves to new conditions. — *adj* and *n* **Lamarck'ian.**

lamaserai, lamasery. See under **lama.**

lamb *lam, n* the young of a sheep; its meat as a food; lambskin; someone simple, innocent, sweet or gentle like a lamb (*fig*); a dear (*colloq*). — *vt* and *vi* to give birth to a lamb or lambs; to tend at lambing. — *adj* **lamb'like** like a lamb; gentle. — **lamb's ears** or **lamb's tongue** a labiate plant with silver woolly leaves; **lamb'skin** the skin of a lamb dressed with the wool on; the skin of a lamb dressed as leather; **lamb's'-lettuce** corn-salad; **lamb's'-tails** hazel catkins; **lamb's tongue** see **lamb's ears; lamb's'-wool** fine wool, *specif* wool obtained from the first shearing of a (yearling) lamb. — *adj* and *n* **lambs'-wool** (made of) lamb's-wool. — **like a lamb to the slaughter** meekly, innocently, without resistance; **the Lamb** or **Lamb of God** applied to Christ, in allusion to the paschal lamb and John i. 29. [O.E. *lamb*.]

lambada *lam-bä'də, n* a rhythmic, energetic (Latin-American) dance.

lambast *lam-bast'* or **lambaste** *lam-bāst', vt* to thrash; to reprimand severely. [Perh. **lam** and **baste**[1].]

lambda *lam'də, n* the Greek letter (Λ, λ) corresponding to Roman *l*; used as a symbol for the lambda particle (*phys*). — *adj* **lamb'doid** or **lamb'doidal** shaped like, or pertaining to, the Greek letter Λ. — **lambda particle** (*phys*) a subatomic particle, the lightest of the hyperons. [Gr. *lambda*, properly *labda* — Heb. *lāmedh*.]

lambent *lam'bənt, adj* moving about as if touching lightly like a flame; gliding or playing over; flickering; softly radiant, glowing; (esp. of wit) light and brilliant. — *n* **lam'bency** the quality of being lambent; a flicker. — *adv* **lam'bently.** [L. *lambĕre*, to lick.]

lambert *lam'bərt*, (*phys*) *n* a unit of brightness, one lumen per square centimetre. [After J.H. *Lambert* (1728–77), German scientist.]

lambrequin *lam'bər-kin* or *-bri-kin, n* a veil over a helmet; a stylised representation of such drapery in a coat-of-arms (*heraldry*); a strip of drapery over a window, doorway, from a mantelpiece, etc. [Fr.]

LAMDA *lam'də, abbrev* for the London Academy of Music and Dramatic Art.

lame *lām, adj* disabled, *specif* in the use of a leg; hobbling; unsatisfactory, imperfect; weak, implausible; conventional, unfashionable (*US slang*). — *n* (*US slang*) an old-fashioned person. — *vt* to make lame; to cripple. — *adv* **lame'ly.** — *n* **lame'ness.** [O.E. *lama*, lame.]

lamé *lä'mā, n* and *adj* (of) a fabric in which metallic (usu. gold or silver) threads are interwoven. [Fr.,— L. *lāmina*, a thin plate.]

lamella *lə-mel'ə, n* a thin plate or layer: — *pl* **lamell'ae** (*-ē*). — *adj* **lamell'ar** (also *lam'i-lər*). — *adj* **lam'ellate** (also *-el'*) or **lam'ellated.** — *adj* **lamell'iform.** — *adj* **lamell'oid.** — *adj* **lamell'ose.** [L. *lāmella*, dimin. of *lāmina*.]

lamellibranch *lə-mel'i-brangk, n* a bivalve mollusc (e.g. the mussel, oyster, clam) with platelike gills. — *adj* **lamellibranch'iate.** [N.L. — L. *lāmella*, a thin plate, *branchia*, a gill.]

lamellicorn *lə-mel'i-körn, n* any of a group of beetles (e.g. the cockchafer) with flattened plates on the end of their antennae. [N.L. — L. *lāmella*, a thin plate, *cornū*, a horn.]

lament *lə-ment', vi* to cry out in grief; to wail; to mourn. — *vt* to mourn for; to deplore. — *n* sorrow expressed by crying out; an elegy or dirge; a musical composition of a similar character. — *adj* **lamentable** (*lam'ənt-ə-bl*) deserving or expressing sorrow; sad; pitiful; worthless (*colloq*). — *adv* **lam'entably.** — *n* **lamentā'tion** the act of lamenting; the audible expression of grief; wailing. — *n* **Lamenta'tions** a book of the Old Testament traditionally attributed to Jeremiah. — *adj* **lament'ed.** — *n* and *adj* **lament'ing.** — *adv* **lament'ingly.** [L. *lāmentārī*.]

lamina *lam'i-nə, n* a thin plate or layer; a leaf blade; a thin plate of bone; a plate of sensitive tissue within a hoof: — *pl* **lam'inae** (*-nē*). — *adj* **lam'inable** suitable for making into thin plates. — *adj* **lam'inar** or **lam'inary** consisting of or like thin plates or layers; of or relating to a fluid, streamlined flow. — *vt* **lam'inarise** or **-ize** to make (a surface, etc.) such that a flow over it will be laminar. — *adj* **lam'inate** or **lam'inated** in laminae or thin plates; consisting of scales or layers, over one another; made by laminating; covered by a thin layer (e.g. of protective material). — *vt* **lam'inate** to make into a thin plate; to separate into layers; to make by bonding thin layers together; to cover with a thin layer (e.g. of protective material). — *n* a laminated plastic, or other material similarly made. — *n* **laminā'tion.** — *n* **lam'inator.** — *n* **laminī'tis** (*vet*) inflammation of a horse's lamina. — **laminar flow** viscous flow; a fluid flow in which the particles move smoothly without turbulence, esp., as in aircraft, such a non-impeding flow over a streamlined surface (*phys*); **laminated plastic** sheets of paper, canvas, linen or silk, impregnated with a resin and bonded together, usu. by means of heat and pressure. [L. *lāmina*, a thin plate.]

Lammas *lam'əs, n* 1 August, an old feast day celebrating the first fruits of the harvest; that time of year. [O.E. *hlāf-mæsse*, *hlāmmæsse* — *hlāf*, loaf, *mæsse*, feast.]

lammergeier or **lammergeyer** *lam'ər-gī-ər, n* the great bearded vulture of southern Europe, etc. [Ger. *Lämmergeier* — *Lämmer*, lambs, *Geier*, vulture.]

lamp *lamp, n* any appliance or device containing a source of artificial light, usu. an electric light bulb; a vessel with a wick for burning oil, paraffin, etc. to give light. — **lamp'black** soot obtained from a fuel-burning lamp, or from burning substances rich in carbon (mineral oil, turpentine, tar, etc.) in a limited supply of air; a pigment made from it and used in chemical and industrial processes, etc. — *vt* to blacken with lampblack. — **lamp'-burner** the part of a lamp from which the flame rises; **lamp'-chimney** or **lamp'-glass** a glass funnel placed round the flame of a lamp; **lamp'holder** a socket for an electric bulb; **lamp'light** the light shed by a lamp or lamps; **lamp'post** or **lamp'-standard** the pillar supporting a street-lamp; **lamp'shade** a decorative or protective cover designed to moderate or direct the light of a lamp or light bulb; **lamp'-shell** a brachiopod, a marine invertebrate, the shell of which resembles an antique lamp. [Fr. *lampe*, and Gr. *lampas, -ados* — *lampein*, to shine.]

lampas[1] *lam'pas, n* a flowered material of silk and wool used in upholstery. [Fr.]

lampas² *lam'pas*, (*vet*) *n* swelling of the roof of the mouth in horses. [Fr.]

lampern *lam'pərn*, *n* the European river lamprey. [O.Fr. *lamprion*.]

lampoon *lam-pōōn'*, *n* a personal satire. — *vt* to attack or ridicule by personal satire. — *n* **lampoon'er** or **lampoon'ist**. — *n* **lampoon'ery**. [O.Fr. *lampon*, perh. from a drinking-song with the refrain *lampons*, let us drink.]

lamprey *lam'pri*, *n* a type of primitive fishlike vertebrate which fixes itself to the fish it preys on and to stones, etc. by its sucking mouth: — *pl* **lam'preys**. [O.Fr. *lamproie*.]

lampuki *lam'pōō-kē*, *n* an edible Mediterranean fish, the dolphin-fish.

LAN (*comput*) *abbrev* for local area network.

Lancashire *lang'kə-shər* or *-shēr*, *n* a crumbly, white cheese made originally in the county of *Lancashire*.

Lancastrian *lang-kas'tri-ən*, *adj* of or pertaining to Lancaster or Lancashire, or to the dukes or (*hist*) house of Lancaster. — *n* a native of Lancaster or Lancashire; a supporter of the house of Lancaster (*hist*).

lance *läns*, *n* a cavalry weapon with a long shaft, a spearhead, and a small flag; a similar weapon for other purposes, such as hunting; a surgeon's lancet; a blade in a cutting tool to sever the grain in advance of the main blade (*carpentry*); a lancer. — *vt* to pierce, as with a lance; to open or incise with a lancet in order to allow drainage (*med*). — *n* **lan'cer** a light cavalry soldier armed with a lance, or belonging to a regiment formerly so armed. — *nsing* **lan'cers** a set of quadrilles, first popular in England about 1820, or its music. — *adj* **lan'ciform** shaped like a lance. — **lance'-corporal** acting corporal; the military rank between private and corporal, the lowest rank of non-commissioned officer in the British Army; **lance'-sergeant** a corporal acting as a sergeant; **lance'-wood** any of various West Indian, Australian and New Zealand trees with strong, elastic, durable wood. [Fr., — L. *lancea*.]

lanceolate *län'si-ə-lāt* or **lan'ceolated** *-id*, *adj* shaped like a lance head; lancet-shaped; tapering toward both ends and two or three times as long as broad (*bot*). [L. *lanceolātus* — *lanceola*, dimin. of *lancea*, lance.]

lancet *län'sit*, *n* a surgical instrument used for opening veins, abscesses, etc.; a lancet window; a lancet arch. — *adj* shaped like a lancet, narrow and pointed. — *adj* **lan'ceted**. — **lancet arch** high and narrow pointed arch; **lancet window** a tall, narrow, acutely arched window. [O.Fr. *lancette*, dimin. of **lance**.]

lancinating *län'sin-āt-ing*, *adj* (of pain) shooting, darting. — *n* **lancinā'tion** sharp, shooting pain. [L. *lancināre*, *-ātum*, to tear.]

Lancs. *langks*, *abbrev* for Lancashire.

Land *länt*, *n* a state or province in Germany and Austria functioning as a unit of local government: — *pl* **Länder** (*len'dər*). [Ger. *Land*, land.]

land *land*, *n* the solid portion of the surface of the globe; a country; a district; a nation or people; real estate; ground; soil; a group of dwellings or tenements under one roof and having a common entry (*Scot*); (in combination) denoting a domain or district frequented or dominated by, as in *gangland*. — *vt* to set on land or on shore; to set down; to deposit, drop or plant; to cause to arrive; to bring ashore; to capture; to secure; to attach to one's interest. — *vi* to come on land or on shore; to alight; to arrive, find oneself or end up being. — *adj* of or on the land; land-dwelling; terrestrial. — *adj* **land'ed** possessing land or estates; consisting in or derived from land or real estate. — *n* **land'ing** disembarkation; a coming to ground; alighting; putting ashore; setting down; a place for getting on shore or onto the ground; the level part of a staircase between flights of steps or at the top. — *adj* relating to the unloading of a vessel's cargo, or to disembarking, or to alighting from the air. — *adj* **land'less**. — *adj* **land'ward** lying towards the land; inland. — *adv* **land'ward** or **land'wards** towards the land. — **land'-agent** a person employed to let farms, collect rents, etc.; an agent or broker for buying and selling of land; **land bank** a bank which finances real estate transactions using the land as security; **land'-bridge** a connection by land allowing terrestrial plants and animals to pass from one region to another (*geol*); a route by land allowing passage between countries or regions previously unconnected; **landed interest** the combined interest of the land-owning class in a community; **land'fall** an approach to land, or the land approached, after a journey by sea or air; **land'fill** the disposal of refuse by burying it under the soil; refuse disposed of in this way; a place where landfill is practised; **land'filling**; **land'-girl** a girl who does (esp. wartime) farm-work; **land'-grabbing**; **land grant** a grant of public land (to a college, etc.). — *vt* **land'-haul** to haul (e.g. a boat) overland. — **land'holder** a tenant or proprietor of land. — *adj* **land'holding**. — **land'ing-beam** a radio beam by which an aircraft is guided in to land; **land'ing-carriage** the wheeled structure on which an aeroplane runs when starting or landing; **land'ing-craft** a small, low, open vessel (or vessels) for landing troops and equipment on beaches; **land'ing-field** a field that allows aircraft to land and take off safely; **land'ing-gear** wheels, floats, etc., of an aircraft used in alighting; **land'ing-ground** a piece of ground prepared for landing aircraft as required; **land'ing-net** a kind of scoop-net for landing a fish that has been hooked; **land'ing-place** a place for landing; **land'ing-ship** a ship whose forward part can be let down in order to put vehicles ashore; **land'ing-speed** the minimum speed at which an aircraft normally lands; **land'ing-stage** a platform (fixed or floating) for landing passengers or goods; **land'ing-strip** a narrow hard-surfaced runway; **land'lady** a woman who has tenants or lodgers; the manageress or proprietress of a public house or hotel; **land'-line** an overland line of communication or transport. — *adj* **land'-locked** almost or quite shut in by land; cut off from the sea. — **land'lord** a man who has tenants or lodgers; the manager or proprietor of a public house or hotel; **land'lordism** the authority, policy, behaviour or united action of the land-owning class; the system of land-ownership; **land'-lubber** (*naut*; in contempt) a landsman. — *adj* **land'-lubberly**. — **land'mark** any land-boundary mark; any conspicuous object on land marking a locality or serving as a guide; an event of outstanding significance in history, thought, etc.; **land'mass** a large area of land unbroken by seas; **land'-mine** a type of bomb laid on or near the surface of the ground which explodes when trodden on or driven over; — *vt* to lay land- mines. — **land'-mining**; **land'owner** a person who owns land; **land'-ownership**. — *adj* **land'-owning**. — **land'-rail** the corncrake; **Land Registry** in England and Wales, the official body which registers title to land; **Land'-Rover®** a sturdy motor vehicle used for driving on rough ground; **land set-aside** (also **set-aside**) the practice of taking arable land out of production, e.g. for environmental and national economic reasons; **land'slide** a landslip (orig. *US*); an overwhelming victory in a political election; **land'slip** a fall of land or rock from a hillside or cliff; a portion of land fallen in this way; **lands'man** a man who lives or works on land; a man with no seafaring experience; **land'-spring** a shallow intermittent spring; **land'-steward** the manager of a landed estate; **land'-surveying** measurement and mapping of land; **land'-surveyor**; **land'- tax** a tax upon land; **land'-value** (usu. in *pl*) the economic value of land as a basis of taxation; **land'-yacht** and

land'-yachting see **yacht**. — **land of milk and honey** a land of great fertility promised to the Israelites by God; any region of great fertility, abundance, contentment, etc.; **land of Nod** sleep (*colloq*); **land with** to encumber with (a burden, difficult situation, etc.); **see how the land lies** to find out in advance how matters stand. [O.E. *land*.]

landau *lan'dö*, *n* a horse-drawn carriage with a folding top. — *n* **landaulet'** or **laundaulette'** a motor car with a folding top; a small landau. [*Landau* in Germany, where it is said to have been first made.]

ländler *lent'lər*, *n* a South German and Austrian dance, or the music for it, similar to a slow waltz. [Ger., — *Landl*, a nickname for Upper Austria.]

landloper *land'lōp-ər* or **land louper** *lowp'ər*, (now *dialect*, esp. *Scot*) *n* a vagabond or vagrant. [M.Du. *landlooper* — *land*, land, *loopen*, to ramble.]

landscape *land'skāp*, *n* the appearance of the area of land which the eye can view at once; the aspect of a country, or a picture or photograph representing it; the painting of such pictures. — *vt* to improve by landscape-gardening or interior landscaping. — Also *vi*. — *adj* of a page, illustration, etc., wider than it is deep (*printing*). — **landscape-gar'dening** the art of laying out grounds so as to produce the effect of a picturesque landscape; **land'scape-painter** or **land'scapist** a painter of landscapes; **land'scape-painting**. — **interior landscaping** the supply and display of plants in order to landscape (esp. office) interiors. [Du. *landschap*.]

Landseer *land'sēr* or **Landseer Newfoundland** (*nū'fənd-lənd* or *nū-fownd'lənd*), *n* a type of black and white Newfoundland dog, as painted by Sir Edwin *Landseer* (1802–73).

Landtag *länt'tähh*, *n* the legislative assembly of a German state or land; the Diet of the Holy Roman Empire, or of the German Federation. [Ger., — *Land*, country, *Tag*, diet, day.]

lane *lān*, *n* a narrow passage or road; a passage through a crowd or between obstructions; a division of a road for a single stream of traffic; a channel; a prescribed course. [O.E. *lane*, *lone*.]

lang *lang*, *adj* a Scottish form of **long**. — *adv* **lang syne** (*sīn*) long since, long ago. — *n* time long past.

lang. *abbrev* for language.

Langerhans. See **islets of Langerhans** under **isle**.

langlauf *läng'lowf*, *n* cross-country skiing. [Ger. *lang*, long and *Lauf*, race, run, leap.]

langouste *lã-go͞ost'*, *n* the spiny lobster. — *n* **langoustine** (-*ēn'*) the *Norway lobster*, *spiny* or *rock lobster* (*Nephrops*), larger than a prawn but smaller than a lobster. [Fr.]

langrage or **langridge** *lang'grij*, (*naval warfare*) *n* shot consisting of a canister containing irregular pieces of iron, formerly used to damage sails and rigging.

language *lang'gwij*, *n* human speech; a variety of speech or body of words and idioms, esp. that of a nation; mode of expression; diction; any manner of expressing thought or feeling; an artificial system of signs and symbols, with rules for forming intelligible communications, for use in e.g. a computer; a national branch of one of the religious and military orders, e.g. the Hospitallers. — **language laboratory** a room in a school or college, etc. in which pupils sit in separate cubicles and are taught a language by means of material recorded on tapes. — **bad language** swearing; **dead language** a language no longer spoken; **speak the same language** to have the same tastes, understanding, background or way of thinking. [Fr. *langage* — *langue* — L. *lingua*, the tongue.]

langue *lãg*, *n* language viewed as a general or abstract system, as opposed to *parole* (*linguis*); a language (q.v.) of a religious or military order. [Fr., — L. *lingua*, tongue.]

langue de chat *lãg də sha*, *n* a very thin finger-shaped biscuit or piece of chocolate. [Fr., cat's tongue.]

Langue d'oc *lãg dok*, *n* a collective name for the Romance dialects of southern France, often used as synonymous with Provençal, one of its chief branches. The name itself survives in the province *Languedoc*. — *adj* **Languedocian** (*lang-gə-dō'shi-ən*). — **Langue d'oil** (*lãg do-ēl* or *doil*) the Romance dialect of northern France, the main element in modern French. [O.Fr. *langue* — L. *lingua*, tongue; *de*, of; Prov. *oc*, yes; O.Fr. *oil*, *oui*, yes.]

languid *lang'gwid*, *adj* slack; flagging; inert; listless; faint; relaxed; spiritless. — *adv* **lan'guidly**. — *n* **lan'guidness**. [L. *languidus* — *languēre*, to be weak.]

languish *lang'gwish*, *vi* to become or be languid, inert or depressed; to lose strength and animation; to pine; to flag or droop; to look languishingly. — *n* **lan'guisher**. — *n* **lan'guishing**. — *adj* expressive of languor, or merely sentimental emotion; lingering. — *adv* **lan'guishingly**. — *n* **lan'guishment**. [M.E. *languishen* — Fr. *languiss-* (stem of *languir*) — *languēre*, to be faint.]

languor *lang'gər*, *n* languidness, listlessness; weariness, weakness; dreamy inertia; tender softness. — *adj* **lan'guorous** full of or expressing languor; languishing. [L. *languor*, *-ōris*.]

langur *lung-go͞or'*, *n* the entellus monkey or another of its genus. [Hindi *lāgūr*.]

laniard. See **lanyard**.

laniferous *lan-if'ər-əs*, *adj* wool-bearing. — Also **lanigerous** (-*ij'*). [L. *lānifer*, *lāniger* — *lāna*, wool, *ferre*, *gerĕre*, to bear.]

lank *langk*, *adj* long and thin; flaccid; limp, drooping; (of hair) long, straight and lifeless. — *n* **lank'iness**. — *adv* **lank'ly**. — *n* **lank'ness**. — *adj* **lank'y** lean, tall and ungainly; long and limp. [O.E. *hlanc*.]

lanner *lan'ər*, *n* a kind of falcon native to regions of Africa, S.E. Asia and the Mediterranean; the female of this species (*falconry*). — *n* **lann'eret** the male lanner. [Fr. *lanier*, possibly — L. *laniārius*, tearing.]

lanolin *lan'ō-lin* or **lanoline** *lan'ə-lin* or *-lēn*, *n* fat from wool, a mixture of palmitate, oleate and stearate of cholesterol, used as a base for certain ointments. [L. *lāna*, wool, *oleum*, oil.]

lant *lant*, *n*. Same as **launce**.

lantern *lan'tərn*, *n* a case for holding or carrying a light; the light-chamber of a lighthouse; an open structure like a lantern, esp. one surmounting a building, giving light and air. — *adj* **lan'tern-jawed** hollow-faced. — **lantern jaws** thin long jaws. [Fr. *lanterne* — L. *lanterna*.]

lanthanum *lan'thə-nəm*, *n* a metallic element (symbol **La**; atomic no. 57). — *npl* **lan'thanides** the rare-earth elements. [Gr. *lanthanein*, to escape notice, because it lay hidden in rare minerals till 1839.]

lanugo *lan-ū'gō*, *n* down, fine hair; an embryonic woolly coat of hair: — *pl* **lanū'gos**. — *adj* **lanū'ginose** (-*jin-*) or **lanū'ginous** downy; covered with fine soft hair. [L. *lānūgō*, *-inis*, down — *lāna*, wool.]

lanyard or **laniard** *lan'yərd*, *n* a short rope used as a fastening or handle (*naut*); a cord for hanging a knife, whistle, etc. around the neck. [Fr. *lanière*.]

LAO *abbrev* for Laos (I.V.R.).

Laodicean *lā-od-i-sē'ən*, *adj* lukewarm, half-hearted, esp. in religion, like the Christians of *Laodicea* (Rev. iii. 14–16). — *n* **Laodicē'anism**.

Laotian *la-ō'shən*, *adj* of Laos in S.E. Asia or of its people. — *n* a native of Laos.

lap[1] *lap*, *vt* to scoop up with the tongue (often with *up*); to take in greedily or readily (usu. with *up*; *fig*); to wash or flow against. — *vi* to drink by licking up; to make a sound or movement as of lapping: — *pr p* **lapp'ing**; *pa t* and *pa p* **lapped**. — *n* a motion or sound of lapping; that which may be lapped; thin liquid food for animals. — *n* and *adj* **lapp'ing**. [O.E. *lapian*.]

lap² *lap, n* the fold of the clothes and body from waist to knees of a person sitting down; the part of a garment covering this area; part of a garment for holding or catching something; a fold; a round of a race-course, track or of anything coiled; an overlap or amount of overlap; a hollow; place where one is nurtured or where one can rest secure (*fig*; in phrases); a flap; a lobe (of the ear); a polishing disc, cylinder, or similar; the length of material needed to go round a drum, etc.; a layer or sheet of (cotton, etc.) fibres. — *vt* to wrap, enfold or surround; to lay overlappingly; to get or be a lap ahead of; to traverse as a lap or in laps; to polish with a lap. — *vi* to lie with an overlap; to overlap; to extend beyond some limit. — *n* and *adj* **lapp'ing.** — **lap'-board** a flat wide board resting on the lap, used by tailors and seamstresses; **lap'dog** a dog small enough to be petted in the lap; a devoted, docile, dependent person (also *fig*; *derog*); **lap joint.** — *adj* **lap'-jointed** having joints formed by overlapping edges. — *adj* **lap'top** (of a computer) somewhat smaller than a desktop computer, able to be carried in a briefcase, etc. and set on one's lap. — *n* a laptop computer. — **in the lap of luxury** in luxurious conditions; **in the lap of the gods** of a situation, such that the result cannot be predicted; **lap of honour** a ceremonial circuit of field, track, show ring, made by the victor(s) in a contest. [O.E. *læppa*, a loosely hanging part.]

laparoscopy *lap-ə-ros'kə-pi, n* surgical examination by means of a **laparoscope** (*lap'ə-rə-skōp*), a tube-shaped optical instrument which permits examination of the internal organs from outside, also used in female sterilisation procedures. [Gr. *laparā*, flank, *skopeein*, to see.]

lapel *la-* or *lə-pel'*, *n* part of a coat, jacket, etc. folded back as a continuation of the collar. — *adj* **lapelled'**. [Dimin. of **lap²**.]

lapis *lap'is, n* a stone (the Latin word, used in certain phrases only). — *adj* **lapidār'ian** pertaining to stones; inscribed on stones; knowledgeable about stones. — *n* **lap'idarist** (*-ə-rist*) an expert in gems. — *n* **lap'idary** (*-ə-ri*) a cutter of stones, esp. gemstones. — *adj* pertaining to stones; (of a bee) dwelling in stone-heaps; inscribed on stone; suitable for an inscription, e.g. on a monument; written in such a style, i.e. pithy, polished, impressive. — *adj* **lapid'-eous** stony. — *adj* **lapidic'olous** (L. *colĕre*, to inhabit) living under or among stones. — *npl* **lapilli** (*lä-pil'lē*) small fragments (in size from a pea to a walnut) of lava ejected from a volcano (pl. of It. *lapillo*; also of L. *lapillus*). — *adj* **lapill'iform.** — **lapis laz'ūlī** a beautiful stone consisting of calcite and other minerals coloured ultramarine by lazurite, etc., commonly spangled with iron pyrites (see **azure, lazulite, lazurite**). — **lapis lazuli blue** a deep blue, sometimes veined with gold, used in decoration and in porcelain. [L. *lapis*, *-idis*, a stone.]

Lapp *lap* or **Laplander** *lap'lən-dər, n* a native or inhabitant of Lapland; a person of the race or people inhabiting Lapland. — *adj* **Lapp** or **Lap'landish.** — *n* **Lapp** or **Lapp'ish** the language of the Lapps. — *adj* **Lapp'ish.**

lappet *lap'it, n* a little lap or flap. — *adj* **lapp'eted.** — **lappet moth** a moth whose caterpillar has lappets on its sides. [Dimin. of **lap²**.]

lapsang *lap'sang* or **lapsang souchong** (*soō'shong*, *-chong*, *soō-shong'* or *-chong'*) (also with *caps*) *n* a variety of souchong tea with a smoky flavour. [Chin.]

lapse *laps, vi* to slip or glide; to pass by degrees; to fall away by ceasing or relaxing effort or cause; to fall from the faith; to fail in virtue or duty; to pass into disuse; to pass or fail owing to some omission or non-fulfilment; to become void. — *n* a slip; passage (of time); a falling away; a failure (in virtue, attention, memory, etc.); a vertical gradient as of atmospheric temperature. — *adj* **laps'able** liable to lapse. — *adj* **lapsed** having slipped or passed or been let slip; (esp. in the Christian Church) fallen away from the faith. — **lapse rate** (*meteorol*) rate of change in temperature in relation to height in the atmosphere. [L. *lāpsāre*, to slip, *lāpsus*, a slip.]

lapwing *lap'wing, n* a bird of the plover family, the peewit. [M.E. *lappewinke*.]

LAR *abbrev* for Libya (I.V.R.; Libyan Arab Jamahiriya).

larceny *lär'sə-ni, n* the legal term in England and Ireland for stealing; theft. — *n* **lar'cener** or **lar'-cenist** a thief. — *adj* **lar'cenous.** — *adv* **lar'cen-ously.** [O.Fr. *larrecin* (Fr. *larcin*) — L. *latrōcinium* — *latrō*, a robber.]

larch *lärch, n* any tree of the coniferous genus *Larix*, distinguished from cedar by the deciduous leaves. [Ger. *Lärche* — L. *larix*, *-ĭcis*.]

lard *lärd, n* the rendered fat of the pig; a usu. modified form of this, produced esp. in a solid, white form for use in cookery. — *vt* to smear or enrich with lard; to stuff with bacon or pork; to fatten; to stuff or load; to garnish, strew. — *n* **lar'don** or **lardoon'** a strip of bacon used for larding. — *adj* **lar'dy.** — **lar'dy-cake** (esp. in S. England) a rich sweet cake made of bread dough, with lard, dried fruit, etc. [O.Fr., — L. *lāridum*, *lārdum*.]

larder *lärd'ər, n* a place where food is kept; a stock of provisions. — *n* **lard'erer** a person in charge of a larder. — **larder fridge** a type of refrigerator without a freezer compartment. [O.Fr. *lardier*, bacon-tub; see **lard.**]

lardon, lardoon, lardy. See under **lard.**

large *lärj, adj* great in size; extensive; bulky; broad; copious; abundant; generous; magnanimous; in a great way. — *adv* ostentatiously; prominently, importantly. — *adv* **large'ly** in a large manner; in great measure; mainly, especially. — *n* **large'ness.** — *adj* **larg'ish** fairly large, rather big. — *adj* **large-heart'ed** having a large heart; of liberal disposition or comprehensive sympathies; generous. — *adj* **large-mind'ed** magnanimous; characterised by breadth of view. — *adj* **large'-scale** (of maps, models, etc.) made in accordance with a series of larger measurements; (of enterprises, etc.) extensive. — **as large as life** actually, really; **at large** at liberty; at random; in general. [Fr., — L. *largus*, abounding.]

largess or **largesse** *lär-jes', n* a bestowal or distribution of gifts; generosity, magnanimous spirit or manner. [Fr. *largesse*.]

largo *lär'gō*, (*mus*) *adj* broad and slow. — Also *adv.* — *n* a movement to be performed in this manner: — *pl* **lar'gos.** — *adj* **larghet'to** (*-get'*) somewhat slow; not so slow as largo. — Also *adv.* — *n* a somewhat slow movement: — *pl* **larghet'tos.** [It., — L. *largus*.]

lariat *lar'i-ət, n* a lasso, a picketing rope. [Sp. *la*, the, *reata*, picketing rope.]

lark¹ *lärk, n* a bird of the genus *Alauda*, well known for flying high as it sings; extended to various similar birds. — *vi* to catch larks. — *adj* **lark'-heeled** having a long hind-claw. — **lark's'-heel** the larkspur. — **get up with the lark** to rise very early in the morning. [M.E. *laverock* — O.E. *lǣwerce*, *lāwerce*.]

lark² *lärk, n* a frolic; a piece of mischief. — *vi* to frolic, play about, have fun (now usu. with *about*). — *n* **lark'er.** — *n* **lark'iness.** — *adj* **lark'ish.** — *adj* **lark'y** (*colloq*). [Perh. from the preceding (cf. **skylarking**).]

larkspur *lärk'spûr, n* any plant of the genus *Delphinium*, from the spurred flowers.

larn *lärn*, (*dialect* or *facetious*) *vt* and *vi* to learn; to teach. [**learn.**]

larrigan *lar'i-gən, n* a long boot made of oiled leather worn by lumbermen, etc.

larrikin *lar'i-kin*, (*Austr*) *n* a rough or hooligan. — Also *adj.* — *n* **larr'ikinism.** [Br. dialect — *Larry*, personal name, and **-kin.**]

larrup *lar'əp*, (*colloq*) *vt* to flog, thrash. [Cf. Du. *larpen*, thresh with flails.]

larva *lär'və*, *n* an animal in an immature but active state markedly different from the adult, e.g. a caterpillar: — *pl* **larvae** (*lär'vē*; L. *-vī*). — *adj* **lar'val**. — *adj* **larvicī'dal** destroying larvae. — *n* **lar'vicide**. — *adj* **lar'viform**. [L. *lārva*, *lārua*, a spectre, a mask.]

larynx *lar'ingks*, *n* the upper part of the windpipe: — *pl* **larynges** (*lar'in-jēz* or *lar-in'jēz*) or **lar'ynxes**. — *adj* **laryngal** (*lar-ing'gl*) or **laryngeal** (*lar-in'ji-əl*). — *n* **laryngectomee** (*-jek'*) a person who has undergone a laryngectomy. — *n* **laryngectomy** (*-jek'*) surgical removal of the larynx. — *adj* **laryngitic** (*-jit'ik*). — *n* **laryngitis** (*-jī'tis*) inflammation of the larynx. — *adj* **laryngological** (*-ing-gə-loj'*). — *n* **laryngol'ogist**. — *n* **laryngology** (*-gol'ə-ji*) the science of the larynx. — *n* **laryng'oscope** a mirror for examining the larynx and trachea. — *adj* **laryngoscop'ic**. — *n* **laryngos'copist**. — *n* **laryngos'copy**. — *n* **laryngot'omy** the operation of cutting into the larynx. [Gr. *larynx*, *-yngos*.]

lasagne *lə-zän'yə* or *-sän'*, *npl* flat pieces of pasta; (*nsing*) a baked dish of this with tomatoes, cheese, meat. — Also **lasa'gna**. [It.]

lascar *las'kər*, *-kär* or *las-kär'*, *n* an Oriental (orig. Indian) sailor or camp-follower. [Hind. and Pers. *lashkar*, army, or *lashkarī*, a soldier.]

lascivious *lə-siv'i-əs*, *adj* wanton; lustful; inclining or tending to lechery. — *adv* **lasciv'iously**. — *n* **lasciv'iousness**. [L.L. *lascīviōsus* — L. *lascīvus*, playful.]

laser *lā'zər*, *n* a device which amplifies an input of light, producing an extremely narrow and intense monochromatic beam. — Also *adj*. — *vi* **lase** (of a crystal, etc.) to be, or become, suitable for use as a laser. — *adj* and *n* **lā'sing**. — **laser disc** a disc on which digitally recorded data, audio or video material is registered as a series of pits that are readable by laser beam, a compact disc; **laser disc player**; **laser printer** a fast, high quality printer using a laser beam to form characters on paper; **Laser Vision®** a video disc system for playing digitally-recorded audio-visual material through a TV or hi-fi; (without *caps*) a similar video disc system. [*L*ight *a*mplification by *s*timulated *e*mission of *r*adiation.]

lash *lash*, *n* the flexible part of a whip; a scourge; an eyelash; a stroke with a whip or anything pliant; a sweep or flick; a stroke of satire. — *vt* to strike with, or as if with, a lash; to dash against; to drive, urge or work by blows of anything flexible (or figuratively); to whisk or flick with a sweeping movement; to secure with a rope or cord; to scourge with sarcasm or satire. — *vi* to dash, rush; to make a rapid sweeping or flicking movement; to use the whip. — *n* **lash'er** a person who lashes or whips; a rope for binding one thing to another. — *n* **lash'ing** an act of whipping; a rope for making things secure; (*colloq*, esp. in *pl*) an abundance of anything. — **lash'-up** an improvisation. — **lash out** to kick out, fling out or hit out without restraint; to spend extravagantly.

lasket *las'kit*, *n* a loop at the foot of a sail, to fasten an extra sail.

lass *las*, *n* a girl, young woman. — *n* (*dimin*) **lassie** (*las'i*) the Scots word for a girl.

Lassa fever *la'sə fē'vər*, *n* an infectious tropical virus disease, often fatal, transmitted by rodents. [From *Lassa*, in Nigeria, where it was first recognised.]

lassi *las'i* or *lus'i*, (*Ind*) *n* a (sweet or savoury) flavoured cold drink made with yoghourt or buttermilk. [Hindi.]

lassitude *las'i-tūd*, *n* faintness; weakness; weariness; languor. [L. *lassitūdō* — *lassus*, faint.]

lasso *la-soo'* or *la'sō*, *n* a long rope with a running noose for catching wild horses, etc.: — *pl* **lassoes'** or **lassos'** (also *las'*). — *vt* to catch with the lasso: — *pr p* **lasso'ing** (also *las'*); *pa p* **lassoed** (*las-ood'* or *las'*). [S.Am. pronunciation of Sp. *lazo* — L. *laqueus*, a noose.]

last[1] *läst*, *n* a shoemaker's model of the foot on which boots and shoes are made or repaired. [O.E. *lǣste*, last, *lāst*, footprint.]

last[2] *läst*, *vi* to continue, endure; to remain fresh, unimpaired; to hold out; to survive. — *n* **last'er** a person who has staying power; a thing that keeps well. — *adj* **last'ing** enduring; durable. — *adv* **last'ingly**. — *n* **last'ingness**. — **last out** to last as long as or longer than; to last to the end or as long as is required. [O.E. *lǣstan*, to follow a track, keep on, suffice, last; see **last**[1].]

last[3] *läst*, *n* a varying weight, generally about 4000 lb. — *n* **last'age** the lading of a ship. [M.E., a load, burden — O.E. *hlæst*.]

last[4] *läst*, *adj* latest; coming or remaining after all the others; final; immediately before the present; utmost; ending a series; most unlikely, least to be preferred. — Also *adv*. — *adv* **last'ly** finally. — *adj* **last'-ditch** (of an attempt, etc.) made at the last moment or in the last resort. — *adj* **last'-gasp** made, etc. when almost at the point of death, defeat, etc. — *adj* **last-min'ute** made, done or given at the latest possible time. — **last post** (*mil*) the second of two bugle-calls denoting the time for retiring for the night; the farewell bugle-call at military funerals; **last rites** religious rites performed for a person close to death; **last straw** (the straw that breaks the camel's back) that small event or factor which, following a series of others, finally makes the situation intolerable or irreparable; **last word** the final remark in an argument; the final decision; the most up-to-date of its kind (*colloq*). — **at last** in the end; **at long last** after long delay; **breathe one's last** to die; **first and last** altogether; **last thing** after doing everything else; **on one's last legs** on the verge of utter failure or exhaustion; **see (or hear) the last of** to see (or hear) for the last time; **the Last Day** the Day of Judgment; **the Last Supper** the supper taken by Christ and his disciples on the eve of the crucifixion; **to the last** to the end; till death. [O.E. *latost*, superl. of *læt*, slow, late.]

Lat. *abbrev* for Latin.

lat *lat*, (*colloq*) *n* short for *latrine*.

lat. *abbrev* for: lateral; latitude.

latch *lach*, *n* a door catch lifted from the outside by a lever or string; a light door-lock, opened from the outside by a key. — *vt* and *vi* to fasten with a latch. — *n* **latch'key** or **latch'-string** a key or string, for opening a latched door. — **latchkey child** a child who regularly returns home to an empty house; **latch on to** (*colloq*) to attach oneself to; to gain comprehension of; **on the latch** not locked, but able to be opened by a latch. [O.E. *læccan*, to catch.]

late *lāt*, *adj* (*compar* **lāt'er**, *superl* **lāt'est**) tardy; behindhand; coming, remaining, flowering, ripening, producing, etc., after the due, expected or usual time; long delayed; nearly at the end; deceased, departed; out of office; former; not long past; most recent. — Also *adv*. — *adv* **late'ly** recently. — *n* **late'ness**. — *n* **lāt'est** (*colloq*; with *the*) the latest news. — *adj* and *adv* **lāt'ish**. — **late'-comer** a person who arrives late. — **at the latest** not later than (a stated time); **late in the day** (*fig*) at an unreasonably late stage of development, etc.; **of late** recently. [O.E. *læt*, slow.]

lateen *lə-tēn'*, *adj* (*naut*) applied to a triangular sail, common in the Mediterranean, the Lake of Geneva, etc.; rigged with such a sail. — *n* a lateen sail; a boat with a lateen rig. [Fr. (*voile*) *latine* — L. *Latīnus*, Latin.]

La Tène *la ten*, of a division of the Iron Age exemplified at *La Tène* near Neuchâtel in Switzerland, later than Hallstatt.

latent *lā'tənt*, *adj* hidden, concealed; not visible or apparent; dormant; undeveloped, but capable of development. — *n* **lā'tence** or **lā'tency**. — *adv* **lā'tently**. — **latent image** (*phot*) the invisible image produced by the action of light on the sensitive chemicals on a film, etc., which becomes visible after development; **latent period** the time between stimulus and reaction; that between contracting a disease and appearance of symptoms. [L. *latēns, -entis*, pres. p. of *latēre*, to lie hidden.]

lateral *lat'ə-rəl, adj* belonging to the side; (of a consonant) produced by air passing over one or both sides of the tongue (*phon*). — *n* a lateral part, movement, consonant, etc. — *n* **lateralīsā'tion** or **-z-** the specialised development in one or other hemisphere of the brain of the mechanisms controlling some activity or ability. — *n* **laterality** (*-ral'i-ti*) the state of belonging to the side; physical one-sidedness, either right or left. — *adv* **lat'erally**. — **lateral thinking** thinking which seeks new ways of looking at a problem and does not merely proceed by logical steps from the starting-point of what is known or believed. [L. *laterālis* — *latus, latĕris*, a side.]

Lateran *lat'ə-rən, adj* pertaining to the Church of St John *Lateran* at Rome, the Pope's cathedral church. — **Lateran Councils** five general councils of the Western Church, held in the Lateran basilica (1123, 1139, 1179, 1215, and 1512–17), regarded by Roman Catholics as ecumenical; **Lateran Treaty** the treaty that restored the independent papal state (Vatican City) in 1929.

laterigrade *lat'ə-ri-grād, adj* running sideways, like a crab. [L. *latus, -ĕris*, side, *gradus*, step.]

laterite *lat'ə-rīt, n* a clay formed by weathering of rocks in a tropical climate, composed chiefly of iron and aluminium hydroxides. — *adj* **lateritic** (*-it'*) of laterite; similar to laterite in composition. [L. *later, latĕris*, a brick.]

latex *lā'teks*, (*bot*) *n* the milky juice of some plants, e.g. rubber trees: — *pl* **lā'texes** or **lā'ticēs**. [L. *lătex, lăticis*.]

lath *läth, n* a thin slip of wood; a substitute for such a slip, used in slating, plastering, etc.: — *pl* **laths** (*lädhz* or *läths*). — *vt* to cover with laths. — *n* **lath'ing** the act or process of covering with laths; a covering of laths. — *adj* **lath'y** like a lath. [O.E. *lætt*.]

lathe *lādh, n* a machine for turning and shaping articles of wood, metal, etc.; the part of a loom carrying the reed for separating the warp threads and beating up the weft. — **capstan lathe** and **turret lathe** see under **capstan** and **turret**.

lather *ladh'ər* or *lädh'ər, n* a foam made with water and soap; froth from sweat; a state of agitation (*colloq*). — *vt* to spread over with lather; to thrash (*colloq*). — *vi* to form a lather. — *adj* **lath'ery**. [O.E. *lēathor*.]

lathi or **lathee** *lä-tē'*, (*Ind*) *n* a long heavy stick, used as a weapon. [Hind. *lāthī*.]

Latin *lat'in, adj* pertaining to ancient Latium (esp. Rome) or its inhabitants, or its language, or to those languages that are descended from Latin, or to the peoples speaking them, esp. (*popularly*) the Spanish, Portuguese and Italians or the inhabitants of Central and South America of Spanish, etc. extraction; of or denoting the temperament considered characteristic of the Latin peoples, passionate, excitable, volatile; written or spoken in Latin; Roman Catholic. — *n* an inhabitant of ancient Latium; the language of ancient Latium, and esp. of Rome; a person belonging to a Latin people; a Roman Catholic. — *adj* **Lat'inate** imitating Latin style; (of vocabulary) borrowed from Latin. — *n* **Lat'inism** a Latin idiom; the use or inclination towards use of Latin idioms, words or ways. — *n* **Lat'inist** a person skilled in Latin. — *n* **Latin'ity** the quality of one's Latin. — **Latin America** those parts of America where Spanish, Portuguese and French are the official languages, with the exception of French-speaking Canada. — *adj* and *n* **Latin-Amer'ican**. — **Latin Church** the Roman Catholic Church; **Latin cross** an upright cross with the lowest limb longest; **Latin Kingdom** the Christian kingdom of Jerusalem ruled by French or Latin kings, and lasting from 1099 to 1187; **Latin Quarter** the educational and students' quarter of Paris around the Sorbonne (where Latin was spoken in the Middle Ages; Fr. *quartier latin*), famous for its unconventional way of life. — **classical Latin** the Latin of the writers who flourished from about 75 B.C. to about A.D. 200; **dog-Latin** see **dog**; **Late Latin** the Latin written by authors between A.D. 200 and *c* 600; **Low Latin** Mediaeval, or Late and Mediaeval, Latin; **New** or **Modern Latin** Latin as written between 1500 and the present time, mostly used as a scientific medium; **Vulgar Latin** colloquial Latin, esp. that of the period under the emperors. [L. *Latīnus*, belonging to *Latium*, the district round Rome.]

latitude *lat'i-tūd, n* angular distance from the equator (*geog*); a place of specified angular distance from the equator (*geog*); angular distance from the ecliptic (*celestial latitude*) (*astron*); a wide extent; range; scope; allowance; breadth in interpretation; extent of signification; freedom from restraint; laxity; width (chiefly *humorous*). — *adj* **latitūd'inal** pertaining to latitude; in the direction of latitude. — *adj* **latitūdinā'rian** broad or liberal, esp. in religious belief; lax. — *n* a member of a school of liberal and philosophical theologians within the English Church in the later half of the 17th century; a person who regards specific creeds, methods of church government, etc., with indifference. — *n* **latitūdinā'rianism**. — *adj* **latitūd'inous** broad, wide, esp. in interpretation. [L. *lātitūdō, -inis* — *lātus*, broad.]

latke *lät'kə, n* a traditional Jewish pancake, esp. one made with grated potato. [Yiddish, — Russ. *latka*, a pastry.]

latria *lä-trī'ə*. See **dulia**. [Gr. *latreiā* — *latreuein*, to serve.]

latrine *lə-trēn', n* a lavatory, esp. in barracks, camps, etc. [L. *lātrīna* — *lavātrīna* — *lavāre*, to wash.]

-latry *-lə-tri, combining form* signifying worship. [Gr. *latreiā* — *latreuein*, to serve.]

latten *lat'ən, n* brass or similar alloy in former use; tinplate; metal in thin plates. [O.Fr. *laton*, prob. — O. Prov. — Ar. *lātūn*, copper.]

latter *lat'ər, adj* later; coming or existing after; second-mentioned of two; modern; recent. — *adv* **latt'erly** towards the latter end; of late. — *adj* **latt'ermost** last. — *adj* **latt'er-day** modern; recent. — **latter end** the final part; the end of life. — **Latter-day Saint** a Mormon. [O.E. *lætra*, slower, later.]

lattice *lat'is, n* a network of crossed laths or bars, called also **latt'ice-work**; anything of a similar pattern; a window with small esp. diamond-shaped panes set in lead, called also **lattice window**; the geometrically regular, three-dimensional arrangement of fissionable and non-fissionable material in an atomic pile; the regular arrangement of atoms in crystalline material; a system of lines for position-fixing overprinted on a navigational chart. — *vt* to form into open work; to furnish with a lattice. — **latt'ice-bridge** a bridge of lattice-girders; **latt'ice-girder** a girder composed of upper and lower members joined by a web of crossing diagonal bars; **latt'ice-leaf** a plant of Madagascar that grows in water, having leaves like open lattice-work. [Fr. *lattis* — *latte*, a lath.]

Latvian *lat'vi-ən, adj* of or relating to Latvia, Lettish. — *n* a native or citizen of Latvia; the language of Latvia, Lettish. [Latvian *Latvija*, Latvia.]

laud *löd, vt* to praise; to celebrate. — *n* praise; (in *pl*) in the R.C. Church, the prayers immediately following matins. — *adj* **laud'able** praiseworthy. — *n* **laud'ableness**. — *adv* **laud'ably**. — *n* **laudā'tion** praise; honour paid. — *adj* **laud'ative** or **laud'atory**

containing praise; expressing praise. [L. *laudāre* — *laus, laudis*, praise.]

laudanum *löd'ə-nəm* or *löd'nəm*, *n* tincture of opium. [Coined by Paracelsus.]

lauf *lowf*, *n* a run in a bobsleigh contest. [Ger.]

laugh *läf*, *vi* to express by inarticulate sounds of the voice, amusement, joy, scorn, etc. or a reaction to tickling, etc.; to be entertained or amused by (with *at*); to make fun of (with *at*); to express scorn for (with *at*). — *vt* to have an effect on, affect or force into by laughing; to express by laughter. — *n* an act or sound of laughing. — *adj* **laugh'able** ludicrous. — *n* **laugh'ableness.** — *adv* **laugh'ably.** — *n* **laugh'er.** — *adj* **laugh'ful** mirthful. — *n* and *adj* **laugh'ing.** — *adv* **laugh'ingly.** — *n* **laugh'ter** the act or sound of laughing. — **laugh'ing-gas** nitrous oxide, which may excite laughter when breathed, used as an anaesthetic, esp. in dentistry; **laughing hyena** the spotted hyena (see under **hyena**); **laughing jackass** the kookaburra; **laugh'ing-stock** an object of ridicule. — **be laughing** (*colloq*) to have no (further) problems, worries, etc.; to be in a favourable or advantageous position; **don't make me laugh** (*colloq*) an expression of scornful disbelief; **have the last laugh** to triumph finally after one or more setbacks or defeats; to have one's actions, etc. finally vindicated after being scorned; **laugh in someone's face** to scorn or mock a person openly; **laugh off** to treat (injuries, etc.) as of no importance; **laugh on the other side of one's face** to be made to feel disappointment or sorrow, esp. after boasting, etc.; **laugh someone out of court** to prevent someone getting a hearing by ridicule; **laugh up one's sleeve** to laugh inwardly; **no laughing matter** a very serious matter. [O.E. *hlæhhan*.]

launce *löns* or **lance** *läns*, *n* a sand eel (*Ammodytes*), an eel-like fish that buries itself in wet sand when the tide is ebbing. — Also known as **lant.**

launch[1] *lönch* or *lönsh*, *vt* to throw or hurl; to dart; to send forth; to set going; to initiate; to cause or allow to slide into water or to take off from land; to put (a book or other product) on the market, esp. with attendant publicity, etc.; to throw (oneself) freely, venturesomely, or enthusiastically (into some activity) (with *into*). — *vi* to rush, dart, plunge, fling oneself; to be launched; to take off; to throw oneself freely, enthusiastically, or in a spirit of adventure (into some activity) (with *out* or *into*); to begin a usu. long story, speech, etc. (with *into*). — *n* the act or occasion of launching. — *n* **launch'er** a device for launching, esp. for sending off a rocket. — **launch'ing-pad** a platform from which a rocket can be launched; a place, event, etc. which gives a good start to a career, etc., or at which a project, campaign, etc. is launched (*fig*); **launch'ing-site.** — *npl* **launch'ing-ways** the timbers on which a ship is launched. — **launch pad** or **site** same as **launching-pad** or **-site; launch vehicle** see under **vehicle; launch window** the period of time during which the launching of a spacecraft must take place if the flight is to be successful. [O.Fr. *lanchier, lancier* — Gr. *lonchē*, a lance.]

launch[2] *lönch* or *lönsh*, *n* a large power-driven boat for pleasure or short runs; the largest boat carried by a man-of-war. [Sp. *lancha*.]

launder *lön'dər*, *vt* to wash and iron clothes, etc.; to handle the transfer of money, goods, etc. or the movement of people in such a way that the identity or illegality of the source, the illegality of the transfer, or the identity or criminality of the people remains undetected (*colloq*). — *vi* to wash and iron clothes, etc.; to be capable of being laundered. — *n* **laun'derer.** — *n* **laun'dress** a woman who washes and irons clothes. — *n* **laun'dry** a place where clothes, etc. are washed and ironed; clothes, etc. for or from the laundry; a collection of articles for washing or that have been washed. — **laundry list** a list of items to be laundered; a list of matters to be dealt with, etc. (*fig*); **laun'dry-maid; laun'dry-man** or **laun'dry-woman** a worker in a laundry; a person who collects and delivers laundry. [L. *lavandārius*, from *lavāre*, to wash.]

launderette *lön-dər-et'* or **laundrette** *-dret'*, *n* a shop where customers wash clothes in washing-machines. [Orig. trademark.]

Laundromat® *lön'drō-mat*, *n* a launderette.

laureate *lö'ri-it*, *adj* crowned with laurel; honoured by a distinction. — *n* a person crowned with laurel; a person honoured by a distinction; a poet laureate. — *n* **lau'reateship.** — **Poet Laureate** see under **poet.** [L. *laureātus*, laurelled.]

laurel *lo'rəl*, *n* the sweet bay tree (*Laurus nobilis*), used in ancient time for making wreaths of honour; extended to various trees and shrubs; a crown of laurel; honours gained (often in *pl*). — *adj* **lau'rel.** — *adj* **lau'relled** crowned, adorned or covered with laurel. — **lauryl alcohol** (*lo'ril* or *lö'*) a liquid made from coconut oil or its fatty acids, used in the manufacture of detergents. — **look to one's laurels** to take care in case one loses one's pre-eminent position; **rest on one's laurels** (sometimes said as a criticism) to be content with one's past successes and the honour they bring, without attempting any further achievements. [Fr. *laurier* — L. *laurus*.]

Laurentian *lö-ren'shən* or *-shyən*, *adj* of or pertaining to the river St *Lawrence*; applied to a series of Pre-Cambrian rocks covering a large area in the region of the Upper Lakes of North America.

laurustine *lö'rəs-tīn* or **laurustinus** *lö-rəs-tī'nus*, *n* a winter-flowering shrub (*Viburnum tinus*). [L. *laurus*, laurel, *tīnus*, laurustine.]

lauryl alcohol. See under **laurel.**

LAUTRO *low'trō*, *abbrev* for Life Assurance and Unit Trust Regulatory Organisation.

lav *lav*, (*colloq*) *n* short for **lavatory.**

lava *lä'və*, *n* molten material discharged in a stream from a volcano or fissure; such material subsequently solidified: — *pl* **la'vas.** — *adj* **la'vaform** in the form of lava. [It., poss. — L. *lavāre*, to wash, or from L. *lābes*, a falling down — *lābī*, to slide, fall.]

lavabo *lav-ā'bō*, *n* in the mass, the ritual act of washing the celebrant's fingers (*RC*); a monastic lavatory; a fixed basin or washstand: — *pl* **lavā'bo** or **lavā'boes.** [L., I shall wash (from Psalm xxvi. 6).]

lavage. See **lave.**

lavatera *la-və-tē'rə* or *lə-vä'tə-rə*, *n* any plant of the genus *Lavatera* of herbs and shrubs with large pink, white, or purple mallowlike flowers. [The brothers *Lavater*, 17th- and 18th-century Swiss physicians and naturalists.]

lavatory *lav'ə-tər-i*, *n* a bowl, usu. with a wooden or plastic seat and flushed by water, used for urination and defecation; a room containing a lavatory and often a washbasin; orig. a place, room, fixture or vessel for washing; a ritual washing. — *adj* **lavator'ial.** — **lavatory paper** toilet paper. [L.L. *lavatorium* — *lavare, -atum*, to wash.]

lave *lāv*, *vt* and *vi* to wash; to bathe. — *n* **lavage** (*lav'ij* or *läv-äzh'*; *med*) irrigation or washing out. — *n* **lavation** (*lav-ā'shən*) washing. — *n* **lāv'er** a large vessel for washing, esp. ritual washing. [L. *lavāre*, *-ātum*.]

lavender *lav'ən-dər*, *n* a labiate plant with fragrant pale-lilac flowers, yielding an essential oil; sprigs of it used for perfuming clothes, linen, etc.; the colour of its blossoms. — *adj* of the colour of lavender flowers. — **lav'ender-water** a perfume composed of spirits of wine, essential oil of lavender, and ambergris. [A.Fr. *lavendre* — L.L. *lavendula*.]

laver[1]. See **lave.**

laver[2] *lāv'ər*, *n* edible seaweed of various kinds, esp. porphyra (*purple laver*) and Ulva (*green laver*). — **laver bread** or **laverbread** (*lä'vər* or *lā'vər bred*) the fronds of porphyra boiled, dipped in oatmeal and fried. [L. *laver*, a kind of plant growing in water.]

lavish *lav'ish*, *vt* to expend or give profusely or generously; to waste. — *adj* generous or profuse in giving; prodigal, wasteful; extravagant; unrestrained. — *adv* **lav'ishly**. — *n* **lav'ishment** or **lav'ishness**. [O.Fr. *lavasse*, *lavache*, deluge of rain — L. *lavāre*, to wash.]

law[1] *lö*, *n* a rule of action established by authority; a statute; the rules of a community or state; jurisprudence; established usage; that which is lawful; the whole body of persons connected professionally with the law; litigation; a rule or code in any department of action, such as morality, art, honour, arms (including heraldry), a game; a theoretical principle extracted from practice or observation; a statement or formula expressing the constant order of certain phenomena; the Mosaic code or the books containing it (*theol*). — *adj* **law'ful** allowed by law; rightful. — *adv* **law'fully**. — *n* **law'fulness**. — *adj* **law'less** not subject to or controlled by law; unruly. — *adv* **law'lessly**. — *n* **law'lessness**. — *n* **law'yer** a practitioner in the law, esp. a solicitor; a person learned or skilled in law; an interpreter of the Mosaic law (*NT*). — *adj* **law'-abiding** having respect for and obedient to the law. — **law agent** (*Scots law*; *old*) a solicitor; **law'-book** a book dealing with the law or law cases; **law'-breaker** a person who does not observe or who abuses a law; **law centre** an office, usu. in a socially deprived area, where free legal advice and assistance are given (also **neighbourhood law centre**); **law'-court** a court of justice; **law'-day** a day when court proceedings may be held in public, a day of open court; **lawful day** a day on which particular kinds of business may be legally done; **law'-giver** a person who enacts or imposes laws. — *adj* **law'-giving**. — **law Latin** Latin as used in law and legal documents; **law'-list** an annual book of information about lawyers, courts, etc.; **Law Lord** a peer in parliament who holds or has held high legal office; in Scotland, a judge of the Court of Session; **law'-maker** a legislator; **law'man** a sheriff or policeman (*US*; now *archaic* or *facetious* except in Texas); **law'-merchant** the customs that have grown up among merchants with reference to mercantile documents and business, commercial law; **law'-officer** a legal official and adviser of the government, esp. Attorney-General, Solicitor-General, or Lord Advocate; **law'-stātioner** a person who sells parchment, documents and other articles needed by lawyers; **law'suit** a suit or process in law; **law'-writer** a writer on law; a copier or engrosser of legal papers. — **be a law unto oneself** or **itself** to act in a way that does not follow established rules or conventions; **Bode's law** (*astron*) a rule popularised by Johann *Bode* (1747–1826, German astronomer), which states that the distances of the planets from the sun in astronomical units is found by adding 4 to the series 0, 3, 6, 12, 24, . . . and dividing the number so obtained by 10; **Boyle's (or Mariotte's) law** the law that, for a gas at a given temperature, pressure varies inversely as volume — announced by Robert *Boyle* in 1662, and confirmed by Mariotte (1620–84, French physicist); **Charles's law** the law that all gases have the same value for the coefficient of expansion at constant pressure, stated by J.A.C. *Charles* (1746–1823, Fr. physicist) — also called **Gay-Lussac's law** after J.L. Gay-Lussac (1778–1850, French chemist and physicist); **go to law with** to resort to litigation against; **have** or **get the law on** (*colloq*) to enforce the law against; **Kepler's laws** three laws of planetary motion discovered by Johann *Kepler* (1571–1630); **law of averages** see under **average**; **law of nations**, now **international law** (q.v.) originally applied to those ethical principles regarded as obligatory on all communities; **law of nature** the invariable order of nature; natural law; **law of the jungle** the rules for surviving, succeeding, etc. in a competitive or hostile situation by the use of force, etc.; **law of the land** the established law of a country; **lay down the law** to state authoritatively or dictatorially; **Murphy's law** (*facetious*) the law which states that if anything can go wrong, it will; **Parkinson's law** see separate entry; **Snell's law** the law of refraction discovered by Willebrod *Snell* (1591–1626), a Dutch mathematician, which states that the sine of the angle of incidence divided by the sine of the angle of refraction is a constant, known as the refractive index; **Sod's law** see under **sod**[2]; **take the law into one's own hands** to obtain justice, or what one considers to be justice, by one's own actions, without recourse to the law, the police, etc.; **the law** (*colloq*) the police; a policeman. [M.E. *lawe*, from the same root as **lie**[2], **lay**.]

law[2] *lö*, (*Scot*) *n* a hill, esp. rounded or conical. [Northern *low*, — O.E. *hlāw*.]

lawn[1] *lön*, *n* a sort of fine linen or cotton. — *adj* made of lawn. [Prob. from *Laon*, near Rheims.]

lawn[2] *lön*, *n* a smooth space of ground covered with grass, generally beside a house. — **lawn'mower** a machine for cutting grass on a lawn; **lawn'-sprinkler** a machine for watering a lawn by sprinkling; **lawn tennis** a game derived from tennis, played by one or two a side on an unwalled court (hard or of turf), the aim being to hit the ball over the net and within the court, if possible in such a way as to prevent its return. [Old word *laund* — O.Fr. *launde*.]

lawrencium *lö-ren'si-əm*, *n* the name given to the element (symbol **Lr**; atomic no. 103) first produced at Berkeley, California. [Ernest O. *Lawrence* (1901–58), American physicist.]

lax[1] *laks*, *adj* slack; loose; soft, flabby; not strict in discipline or morals; careless, negligent. — *adj* **lax'ative** stimulating loosening of the bowels. — *n* a purgative or aperient medicine. — *n* **lax'ativeness**. — *n* **laxā'tor** a muscle that relaxes an organ or part. — *n* **lax'ity** or **lax'ness**. — *adv* **lax'ly**. [L. *laxus*, loose.]

lax[2] *laks*, *n* a salmon (usu. one caught in Swedish or Norwegian waters). [Revived use — O.E. *leax*; cf. **lox**[2].]

lay[1] *lā*, *pa t* of **lie**[2].

lay[2] *lā*, *vt* to cause to lie; to place, set or beat down; to spread on a surface; to spread or set something on; to cover; to apply; to cause to subside; to exorcise; to deposit; to make (a bet); to put forward; to cause to be; to set; to produce and deposit; to locate; to put in (a particular) position; to waylay; to attribute, impute; to set material in position for making; to form by setting in position and twisting (as a rope); to design, plan; to layer (*hort*); to have sexual intercourse with (*slang*). — *vi* to produce eggs; to wager, bet; to deal blows; to lie (*archaic*, *naut*, and *illit*): — *pr p* **lay'ing**; *pa t* and *pa p* **laid**. — *n* a place for lying; an oyster-bed; a way of lying; a disposition, arrangement or plan; a layer; a mode of twisting; laying activity; an act of sexual intercourse (*slang*); a partner, usually female, in sexual intercourse (*slang*). — *n* **layer** (*lā'ər* or *lār*) someone who or that which lays — e.g. a hen, a bricklayer; (*lār*) a course, bed or stratum; a distinctively coloured space between contour-lines on a map; a shoot bent down to earth in order to take root. — *vt* and *vi* to propagate by layers. — *vt* to put in layers. — *vi* to be laid flat, lodge. — *adj* **lay'ered** in or with layers. — *n* **lay'ering**. — *n* **lay'ing** the first coat of plaster; the act or time of laying eggs; the eggs laid. — **lay'about** a lazy, idle person, a loafer; **lay'away** goods on which a deposit has been paid, kept for a customer until payment is completed (as *vt* **lay away**); **lay'-by** an expansion of a roadway to allow vehicles to draw up out of the stream of traffic: — *pl* **lay'-bys**; **lay'er-cake** a cake made up of different layers; **lay'-off** the act of laying off or the period of time during which someone lays off or is laid off; **lay'out** that which is laid out; a display; an outfit; the disposition, arrangement, plan, esp. of buildings or ground; the general appearance of a printed page; a set, unit, organisation; **lay'-shaft** an auxiliary geared shaft in a machine, esp. the secondary shaft in an automobile gearbox. — **lay about one** to deliver blows vigorously or on all sides; **lay a course** to succeed in sailing to the place required without tacking; **lay aside** or **away** to discard; to put on one side for future use (see also **layaway** above); **lay bare** to show clearly, disclose; **lay before** to submit (e.g. plans) to; **lay by** to keep for future use; **lay down** to give up; to deposit, as a pledge; to formulate; to assert (law, rule); to store; to plant; to record; to lay on (*printing*); **lay hold of** or **on** to seize; **lay in** to get in a supply of; **lay into** to beat thoroughly; **lay it on** to charge exorbitantly; to do anything, e.g. to exaggerate, or to flatter, excessively; **lay off** to dismiss from employment temporarily; to cease (*colloq*); **lay on** to install a supply of; to provide; **lay oneself open to** to make oneself vulnerable to or exposed to (criticism, etc.); **lay open** to make bare, to show, expose; to cut open; **lay out** to display; to spend money; to plan; to arrange according to a plan; to prepare for burial; to knock unconscious; **lay siege to** to besiege; **lay the table** to put dishes, etc. on the table in preparation for a meal; **lay to** to bring a ship to rest; **lay under** to subject to; **lay up** to store up, preserve; (usu. in *passive*) to confine to bed or one's room; to put in dock for cleaning, repairs, etc. or because no longer wanted for or fit for service; **lay wait** to lie in wait, or ready to ambush; **lay waste** to devastate. [O.E. *lecgan*, to lay.]

lay[3] *lā*, *n* a short narrative poem; a lyric; a song. [O.Fr. *lai.*]

lay[4] *lā*, *adj* pertaining to the people; not clerical; non-professional; not trumps (*cards*). — *n* the laity. — *adj* **laic** (*lā'ik*) lay. — *n* a layman. — *adj* **lā'ical**. — *n* **lāicisā'tion** or **-z-**. — *vt* **laicise** or **-ize** (*lā'i-sīz*) to make laical; to open to the laity. — *n* **lāic'ity** the state of being lay; the nature of the laity; the influence of the laity. — *n* **lā'ity** the people as distinguished from some particular profession, usu. the clerical. — **lay brother** or **sister** a person under vows of celibacy and obedience, who serves a religious house, but is exempt from the studies and choir duties of monks or nuns; **lay'man** one of the laity; a non-professional man; someone who is not an expert; **lay'person**; **lay reader** (in some branches of the Anglican communion **reader**) a man or woman who is not ordained but is licensed by a bishop to undertake a range of ecclesiastical duties. [O.Fr. *lai* — *Gr. lāos*, the people.]

lay-day *lā'-dā*, *n* one of a number of days allowed for loading and unloading of cargo (*commerce*); a day a vessel is delayed in port (*naut*). — **lay'time** the total time allowed. [Perh. formed from **delay** and **day**, combined with **time**.]

layer. See **lay**[2].

layette *lā-et'*, *n* a baby's complete outfit. [Fr.]

lay-figure *lā'-fig-ər*, *n* a jointed model used by painters; a living person or a fictitious character lacking in individuality. [Earlier *layman*, — Du. *leeman* — *led* (now *lid*), joint, *man*, man.]

layman. See **lay**[4].

lazar *laz'ər*, *n* a leper; a person with a pestilential disease such as leprosy. — *n* **lazar house** a lazaretto. [From *Lazarus* the beggar with leprosy, in the Bible (Luke xvi. 20).]

lazaretto *laz-ə-ret'ō*, *n* a hospital for infectious diseases, esp. leprosy; a place of quarantine; a place for keeping stores on a ship: — *pl* **lazarett'os**. [It. *lazzaretto.*]

lazulite *laz'ū-līt*, *n* a blue mineral. [L.L. *lazulum* — Pers. *lājward*; cf. **azure, lapis lazuli, lazurite.**]

lazurite *laz'ū-rīt*, *n* a blue mineral, a constituent of lapis lazuli. [L.L. *lazur* — Pers. *lājward*; cf. **azure, lapis lazuli, lazulite.**]

lazy *lā'zi*, *adj* reluctant to exert oneself; averse to work; sluggish. — *vi* **laze** to be idle (back-formation). — *adv* **la'zily**. — *n* **la'ziness**. — **la'zy-bones** (*colloq*) a lazy or idle person; **lazy eye** an apparently healthy eye having, nevertheless, impaired vision; amblyopia; **lazy Susan** a revolving tray, often with a number of separate dishes or sections for foods, intended to be placed on a dining-table, etc.; **la'zy-tongs** a series of diagonal levers pivoted together at the middle and ends, capable of being extended by a movement of the scissors-like handles so as to pick up objects at a distance. — *adj* constructed on the model of lazy-tongs.

LB *abbrev* for Liberia (I.V.R.).

lb *abbrev* for: leg before (wicket) (*cricket*); *libra* (L.), pound weight.

LBC *abbrev* for London Broadcasting Company.

lbf *abbrev* for pound force.

lbw (*cricket*) *abbrev* for leg before wicket.

lc *abbrev* for: left centre; letter of credit; *loco citato* (L.), in the place cited; lower case (*printing*).

LCD *abbrev* for: liquid crystal display; lowest common denominator.

LCDT *abbrev* for London Contemporary Dance Theatre.

***L*-dopa**. See **dopa**.

LEA *abbrev* for local education authority.

lea[1] *lē*, *n* open country — meadow, pasture or arable. [O.E. *lēah.*]

lea[2] *lē*, *adj* and *n* fallow; (of) arable land under grass or pasture. — **lea'-rig** an unploughed rig or grass field. [O.E. *lǣge.*]

leach *lēch*, *vt* to allow (a liquid) to percolate through something; to subject (something) to percolation so as to separate soluble constituent(s); to drain away by percolation. — *vi* to percolate through or out of; to pass out of by the action of a percolating liquid; to lose soluble elements by the action of a percolating liquid. — *n* **leach'ate** a liquid that has percolated through or out of some substance; a liquid that has been polluted or made toxic by percolating through rubbish; a solution obtained by leaching. — *n* **leach'ing**. — *adj* **leach'y** liable to be leached. — **bacterial leaching** the use of selected strains of bacteria to accelerate the acid leach of sulphide minerals. [O.E. *leccan*, to water, irrigate, moisten.]

lead[1] *lēd*, *vt* to show the way by going first; to precede; to guide by the hand; to direct; to guide; to conduct; to convey; to induce; to live; to cause to live or experience; to adduce (*Scots law*); to have a principal or guiding part or place in; to play as the first card of a round (*cards*). — *vi* to be first or among the first; to be guide or chief; to act or play (a card) first; to cart crops to the farmyard (often with *in*); to afford a passage (to), or (*fig*) tend towards; (of a newspaper, etc.) to have as its main story, feature, etc. (with *with*): — *pa t* and *pa p* **led**. — *n* first place; precedence; the amount by which one is ahead; direction; guidance; an indication; a precedent or example; a chief rôle; the player of a chief rôle; leadership; initiative; the act or right of playing first, or the play of whoever plays first; the first player of a side (*curling*, etc.); a leash; a watercourse leading to a mill; a channel among ice; a main conductor in electrical distribution. — *adj* chief; main; leading. — *n* **lead'er** a person who leads or goes first; a chief; the principal first violin; the head of a party, expedition, etc.; the leading editorial article in a newspaper (also **leading article**); a horse in a front place in a team; a tendon; a translucent connection between a fishing-line and bait; a line of dots to guide the eye (*printing*); the principal wheel in any machinery; an alternative name for conductor (of an orchestra, etc.) (*US*). — *n* **lead'ership** the office of leader or conductor; those acting as leaders of a particular organisation or group; ability to lead. — *n* **lead'ing** guidance; spiritual guidance; leadership; carting (crops, etc.). — *adj* acting as leader; directing, controlling; principal; preceding. — **lead'-in** the cable connecting the transmitter or receiver to the elevated part of an aerial; the introduction to, or introductory passage of, a commercial, discussion, newspaper article, piece of music, etc. — Also *adj*. — **leading aircraftman** or **aircraftsman**, or **aircraftwoman** or **aircraftswoman** the rank above aircraft(s)man or aircraft(s)-woman; **leading business** the acting of the principal parts or rôles in plays (by the **leading lady** and the **leading man**); **leading case** (*law*) a case serving as a precedent; **leading edge** the edge first met; the foremost edge of an aerofoil or propeller blade; rising amplitude portion of a pulse signal (*telecomm*). — *adj* **leading-edge'** at the forefront, most up-to-date (of technology, etc.). — **leading lady** and **leading man** see **leading business; leading light** a very influential member; **leading question** a question put in such a way as to suggest the desired answer; **lead'ing-strings** (*US*) children's walking reins; vexatious care or custody; **lead time** (orig. *US*) the time between the conception or design of a product, factory, alteration, etc. and its production, completion, implementation, etc. — **lead astray** to draw into a wrong course; to seduce from right conduct; **lead by the nose** to make (someone) follow submissively; **Leader of the House of Commons** or **Lords** a senior member of the government in whom rests the primary authority for initiating the business of the House; **lead off** to begin or take the start in anything; **lead on** to persuade to go on, to draw on; to persuade to do something foolish; to trick or deceive in fun; **lead out** to bring out by preceding; to begin to play (*cards*); **leads and lags** (*commerce*) in international trade, the early payment of bills, etc. to concerns abroad, and the delayed invoicing of foreign customers in order to take advantage of expected changes in the rate of exchange; **lead the way** to go first and guide others; **lead up to** to bring about by degrees, to prepare for by steps or stages. [O.E. *lǣdan*, to lead, *lād*, a way.]

lead[2] *led*, *n* a heavy soft bluish-grey metal (symbol **Pb**; atomic no. 82); a plummet for sounding; a thin plate of lead separating lines of type; a lead frame for a window-pane; blacklead, graphite; the core of coloured material in a coloured pencil; a stick of graphite for a pencil; (in *pl*) sheets of lead for covering roofs, or a flat roof so covered. — *adj* made of lead. — *vt* to cover, weight, or fit with lead; to set (e.g. window-panes) in lead; to separate the lines of with leads (*printing*). — *adj* **lead'ed** fitted or weighted with or set in lead; separated by leads (*printing*). — *n* **lead'en** made of lead; lead-coloured; oppressive; depressing; heavy; dull. — *vt* and *vi* to make or become leaden. — *adv* **lead'enly**. — *n* **lead'enness**. — *adj* **lead'less**. — *adj* **lead'y** like lead. — *adj* **lead-free** see **unleaded**. — **lead'-glance** galena; **lead'-line** a sounding-line; **lead-paint'** paint with red lead or white lead as base; **lead-pen'cil** a blacklead pencil for writing or drawing; **lead poisoning** poisoning by the absorption of lead into the system; death by shooting (*slang*); **leads'man** a seaman who heaves the lead or plummet for sounding. — **swing the lead** (*naut* and *mil slang*) to invent specious excuses to evade duties. [O.E. *lēad*.]

leaf *lēf*, *n* one of the lateral organs developed from the stem or axis of a plant below its growing-point, esp. one of those flat green structures that transpire and assimilate carbon; any similar structure, as a scale or a petal; the condition of having leaves; leaves collectively; anything beaten thin like a leaf; two pages of a book on opposite sides of the same paper; a broad thin part, structure or extension, hinged or sliding for a table, folding doors, etc.: — *pl* **leaves** (*lēvz*). — *vt* and *vi* (with *through*) to turn the pages of (a book, etc.). — *vi* (also **leave**) to produce leaves: — *pr p* **leaf'ing**; *pa p* **leafed**. — *adj* in the form of leaves. — *n* **leaf'age** foliage. — *adj* **leafed** (*lēft*) having leaves (also **leaved** *lēvd*). — *n* **leaf'ery** leafage. — *n* **leaf'iness**. — *adj* **leaf'less** having no leaves. — *n* **leaf'let** a single sheet of printed political, religious, advertising, etc. matter, flat or folded, or several sheets folded together; a little leaf; a division of a compound leaf. — *vt* to distribute leaflets to. — *vi* to distribute leaflets: — *pr p* **leaf'leting**, or, less correctly, **leaf'letting**; *pa t* and *pa p* **leaf'leted** or, less correctly, **leaf'letted**. — *adj* **leaf'like**. — *adj* **leaf'y** or **leav'y** covered with or having many leaves; leaflike. — **leaf'-base** the base of a leaf-stalk, where it joins the stem; **leaf'-curl** a plant disease of various kinds characterised by curling of the leaves; **leaf'-cutter** an insect (ant or bee) that cuts pieces out of leaves; **leaf'-cutting** leaf used as a cutting for propagation; **leaf'-hopper** a name for various hopping insects that suck plant juices; **leaf'-insect** an insect with wing-covers like leaves; **leaf'-metal** metal, especially alloys imitating gold and silver, in very thin leaves, for decoration; **leaf'-mosaic** a name for various virus diseases of potato, tobacco, etc., in which the leaf is mottled; **leaf'-mould** or **leaf'-soil** earth formed from decayed leaves, used with soil as a compost for plants. — *adj* **leaf'-nosed** having a leaflike structure on the nose, as certain bats. — **leaf'-roll** a potato disease; **leaf'-stalk** a petiole (*bot*). — **take a leaf out of someone's book** see under **book; turn over a new leaf** to begin a new and better course of conduct. [O.E. *lēaf*.]

league[1] *lēg*, *n* a nautical measure, 1/20 of a degree, 3 international nautical miles, 5·556 km. (3·456 statute miles); an old measure of length, varying in extent, in general, e.g. in poetry, taken to be about 4·828 km. (3 miles). [L.L. *leuga*, *leuca*, Gallic mile of 1500 Roman paces.]

league[2] *lēg*, *n* a bond or alliance; a union for mutual advantage; an association or confederacy; an association of clubs for games; a class or group. — *vt* and *vi* to join in league. — *n* **lea'guer** a member of a league. — **league match** a match between two clubs in the same league; **league table** a table in which clubs in a league are placed according to their performances, or (*fig*) any grouping made to reflect relative success, importance, etc. — **in league with** having made an alliance with, usu. for a bad purpose; **in the big league** (*colloq*) among the most important, powerful, etc. people, organisations, etc.; **League of Nations** an international body, formed under a covenant drawn up in 1919, to secure peace, justice, scrupulous observance of treaties, and international co-operation generally — superseded in 1945 by the United Nations; **not in the same league as** not of the same calibre, ability, importance, etc. as; **top (or bottom) of the league** (*fig*) highest (or lowest) in a particular field of achievement, or in quality. [Fr. *ligue* — L.L. *liga* — L. *ligāre*, to bind.]

leak *lēk*, *n* a crack or hole in a vessel through which fluid may pass; passage through such an opening; urination (*slang*); a place, means, instance, of unintended or undesirable admission or escape (*lit* and *fig*); the usu. unauthorised, but sometimes only apparently unauthorised, divulgation of secret information; a high resistance, esp. serving as a discharging path for a condenser (*electr*). — *vi* to have a leak; to pass through a leak. — *vt* to cause to leak; to let out or in by, or (*fig*) as if by, a leak; to divulge (secret information) without, or apparently without, authorisation, or to cause this to be done. — *n* **leak'age** a leaking; that which enters, escapes, or is divulged by leaking; an allowance for leaking. — *n*

leak'er. — *n* **leak'iness.** — *adj* **leak'y.** — **leak out** (of air) to escape; (of secret information) to be divulged to the public without, or apparently without, authorisation; **spring a leak** to become leaky; to urinate (*colloq*). [O.E. *hlec*, leaky.]

lean[1] *lēn, vi* to incline; to be or become inclined to the vertical; to rest sideways against something; to bend over; to swerve; to abut; to have an inclination; to rely. — *vt* to cause to lean: — *pa t* and *pa p* **leaned** (*lĕnd*) or **leant** (*lent*). — *n* an act or condition of leaning; a slope. — *n* and *adj* **lean'ing.** — **lean'-to** a shed or penthouse propped against another building or wall: — *pl* **lean'-tos.** — **lean on** (*slang*) to put pressure on, to use force on (a person). [O.E. *hlēonian, hlinian.*]

lean[2] *lēn, adj* thin, without (much) flesh; not fat; without fat; unproductive. — *n* flesh without fat. — *adv* **lean'ly.** — *n* **lean'ness.** [O.E. *hlǣne.*]

leap *lēp, vi* to move with bounds; to spring upward or forward; to rush with vehemence; to pass abruptly or over a wide interval. — *vt* to bound over; to cause to take a leap: — *pr p* **leap'ing;** *pa t* and *pa p* **leaped** (*lĕpt*) or **leapt** (*lept*). — *n* an act of leaping; a bound; the space passed by leaping; a place of leaping; an abrupt transition; a wide gap or interval. — *n* **leap'er** a steeplechaser; someone who or something that leaps. — **leap day** an intercalary day in the calendar (29 February); **leap'-frog** a sport in which each person in turn vaults over the back of the person stooping in front; a jump as in the sport (also *fig*). — *vt* and *vi* to jump (over) as in leap-frog (also *fig*); to go in advance of each other alternately: — *pr p* **leap'-frogging;** *pa t* and *pa p* **leap'-frogged.** — *adj* and *n* **leap'-frogging.** — **leap year** a year with an intercalary or inserted day (perh. because any anniversary after that day misses or leaps over a day of the week). — **by leaps and bounds** by a large amount or extent; very quickly; **leap in the dark** an act of which the consequences cannot be foreseen. [O.E. *hlēapan.*]

learn *lûrn, vt* to be informed; to get to know; to gain knowledge, skill or ability in; to teach (now *illit*). — *vi* to gain knowledge or skill: — *pa t* and *pa p* **learned** (*lûrnd*) or **learnt** (*lûrnt*). — *adj* **learn'able.** — *adj* **learned** (*lûrn'id*) having learning; knowledgeable about literature, etc.; skilful. — *adv* **learn'edly.** — *n* **learn'edness.** — *n* **learn'er** a person who learns; a person who is still in the early stages of learning. — *n* **learn'ing** what is learned; knowledge; scholarship; skill in languages or science. — **learning curve** a graph used in education and research to represent progress in learning. [O.E. *leornian.*]

leary. Same as **leery** under **leer.**

lease *lēs, n* a contract letting or renting a house, farm, etc. for a term; tenure or rights under such a contract; duration of such tenure; a hold upon, or prospect of continuance of, life, enjoyment, health, etc. — *vt* to grant or take under lease. — *adj* **leas'able.** — *n* **leas'er** a lessee. — **lease'back** the selling of a building, etc. to a person or organisation from whom the seller then leases it — also called *sale and leaseback*; **lease'hold** a tenure by lease; land, etc. so held. — *adj* held by lease. — **lease'holder.** — *n* and *adj* **lease'-lend** same as **lend-lease** (see under **lend**). [Fr. *laisser*, to leave — L. *laxāre*, to loose, *laxus*, loose.]

leash *lēsh, n* a line for holding a hawk or hound; control by a leash, or as if by a leash; a set of three, especially animals. — *vt* to hold by a leash; to bind. [O.Fr. *lesse*, a thong to hold a dog by — L. *laxus*, loose.]

least *lēst, adj* (used as superl. of **little**) little beyond all others; smallest. — *adv* in the smallest or lowest degree. — *n* the smallest amount; the lowest degree. — *adv* **least'aways** or **least'ways** (*dialect*) or **least'wise** (*rare* or *US*) at least; however — used to tone down a preceding statement. — **at least** or **at the least** at the lowest estimate; at any rate. [O.E. *lǣst* (adj. and adv.).]

leather *ledh'ər, n* a tanned, tawed, or otherwise treated skin; a strap or other piece of leather; the ball in certain games; (in *pl*) riding breeches made from leather; (in *pl*) clothes made of leather. — *adj* of leather; — *vt* to apply leather to; to thrash (*colloq*). — *n* **leatherette'** cloth or paper made to look like leather. — *n* **leath'ering** (*colloq*) a thrashing. — *adj* **leath'ern** of or like leather. — *adj* **leath'ery** resembling leather; tough. — **leath'er-back** a large variety of sea-turtle; **leath'er-cloth** a fabric coated on one surface so as to resemble leather — called also *American cloth*; **leath'ergoods** objects and utensils made from leather; **leath'er-jacket** one of various fishes; a grub of the crane-fly. — *adj* **leath'er-mouthed** (*-mowdhd*) of certain fish, having a mouth like leather, smooth and toothless. — **leath'er-neck** a sailors' name for a soldier or marine (from the leather stock he once wore), esp. now a U.S. marine. — **artificial leather** any of certain plastic materials treated so as to simulate leather. [O.E. *lether*, leather.]

leave[1] *lēv, n* permission; a formal parting; a farewell; permission to depart or be absent; permitted absence from duty; the time of this; holidays. — **leave'-taking** bidding farewell. — **leave of absence** permission to be absent, or the (time of) permitted absence; **take leave** to assume permission; **take leave of one's senses** to become irrational; **take one's leave (of)** or **take leave (of)** to depart (from), say farewell (to). [O.E. *lēaf*, permission.]

leave[2] *lēv, vt* to abandon, resign; to quit or depart from; to have remaining at death; to bequeath; to refer for decision, action, etc. — *vi* to desist; to cease; to depart: — *pr p* **leav'ing;** *pa t* and *pa p* **left.** — *n* **leav'er.** — *npl* **leav'ings** things left; relics; refuse. — **be left with** to have remaining; **leave a little** (or **much) to be desired** to be slightly (or very) inadequate or unsatisfactory; **leave alone** to let remain undisturbed; **leave be** to leave undisturbed; **leave behind** to forget to bring, or leave intentionally or accidentally; to go away from (also *fig*); **leave go** (*colloq*) to let go; **leave it at that** to take no further action, make no further comment, etc.; **leave off** to desist, to terminate; to give up using; **leave out** to omit; **leave unsaid** to refrain from saying. [O.E. *lǣfan.*]

leave[3]**, leaved, leaves, leavy.** See **leaf.**

leaven *lev'n, n* the ferment, e.g. yeast, that makes dough rise; anything that makes a general change. — *vt* to raise with leaven; to permeate with an influence. — *n* **leav'ening.** [Fr. *levain* — L. *levāmen* — *levāre*, to raise.]

Lebensraum *lāb'ənz-rowm*, (Ger.) *n* room to live (and, if necessary, expand); *specif* territory claimed as necessary for economic growth (as by the Nazis).

lecher *lech'ər, n* an obsessively lewd man. — *n* **lech** (*lech*; *slang*; back-formation) lust, a lewd desire; a lecher. — *vi* to lust. — *adj* **lech'erous** lustful; provoking lust. — *adv* **lech'erously.** — *n* **lech'erousness.** — *n* **lech'ery.** [O.Fr. *lecheor* — *lechier*, to lick.]

lechwe *lēch'wē* or *lech'wā, n* an African antelope, smaller than the water buck to which it is related. [Bantu.]

lecithin *les'i-thin, n* a very complex substance containing phosphorus, found in yolk of egg, brain, blood, etc. [Gr. *lekithos*, egg-yolk.]

lectern *lek'tərn, n* a reading-desk (usu. one from which the lessons are read in a church). [L.L. *lectrīnum* — *lectrum*, a pulpit — Gr. *lektron*, a couch.]

lectin *lek'tin, n* any of a number of naturally occurring substances, usu. proteins derived from plants, which act like antibodies but are not formed in response to an antigen. [L. *lectus*, past p. of *legĕre*, to choose, select.]

lection *lek'shən, n* a reading; a lesson read in church. — *n* **lec'tionary** a book of church lessons for each day. [L. *lectiō, -ōnis — legĕre, lectum,* to read.]

lector *lek'tör* or *lek'tər, n* a reader, esp. in a college; someone who has the duty of reading the Scripture lesson in a church service; an ecclesiastic in one of the minor orders, lowest in the Orthodox, second-lowest in the Roman Catholic. — *n* **lec'torate.** — *n* **lec'torship.** [L. *lector, -ōris — legĕre, lectum,* to read.]

lecture *lek'chər, n* a lesson or period of instruction; a discourse on any subject, esp. a professorial or tutorial discourse; a long, formal, stern reproof. — *vt* to instruct by lectures; to instruct authoritatively; to scold lengthily and sternly. — *vi* to give a lecture or lectures. — *n* **lec'turer** a person who lectures; a college or university instructor of lower rank than a professor. — *n* **lec'tureship** the post, job of a lecturer; the foundation of a course of lectures. [L. *lectūra — legĕre, lectum,* to read.]

LED *abbrev* for light-emitting diode (q.v. under **light**[1]).

led *led, pa t* and *pa p* of **lead**[1]. — *adj* under leading or control.

lederhosen *lā'dər-hōz-ən, npl* short leather trousers with braces. [Ger., leather trousers.]

ledge *lej, n* a shelflike projection; a ridge or shelf of rocks; a lode or vein (of ore or rock); an attached strip. — *adj* **ledg'y.** [M.E. *legge,* prob. from the root of **lay**[2].]

ledger *lej'ər, n* the principal account-book of a company, in which details of all transactions, assets, etc. are entered; ledger-bait, -tackle or -line (*angling*); a horizontal timber in scaffolding; a flat grave-slab. — *adj* resident, stationary. — *vi* to fish with a ledger-line. — **ledg'er-bait** fishing bait that lies on the bottom, the **ledg'er-tackle** being weighted; **ledg'er-line** a line fixed in one place (*angling*); (often **leg'er-line**) a short line added above or below the stave where required (*mus*). [App. from O.E. *licgan,* to lie, *lecgan,* to lay.]

lee *lē, n* shelter; the sheltered side; the quarter toward which the wind blows. — *adj* (opp. to *windward* or *weather*) sheltered; on or towards the sheltered side. — *adj* **lee'ward** (also (*naut*) *lū'ərd* or *lōō'ərd*) pertaining to, or in, the direction towards which the wind blows. — *adv* towards the lee. — Also *n.* — **lee'-board** a board lowered on the lee side of a vessel, to lessen drift to leeward; **lee'-gage** or **-gauge** position to leeward (opp. to *weather-gage*); **lee side** the sheltered side; **lee tide** a tide in the same direction as the wind; **lee'way** leeward drift; room to manoeuvre, latitude. — **make up leeway** to make up for lost time, ground, etc. [O.E. *hlēo(w),* genitive *hlēowes,* shelter.]

leech[1] *lēch, n* the side edge of a sail. [Cf. O.N. *līk*; Dan. *lig*; Sw. *lik,* a bolt-rope.]

leech[2] *lēch, n* a blood-sucking annelid worm, usu. aquatic; a person who attaches him- or herself to another for personal gain; a physician (*archaic*). — *vt* to apply leeches to (in order to draw blood from a patient — a former medical treatment); to cling to like a leech; to drain. — *vi* (usu. with *on*) to cling (to). [O.E. *lǣce.*]

leek *lēk, n* a vegetable of the onion genus, with broad flat leaves and a slim white bulb which extends into a long stem — taken as national emblem of Wales. [O.E. *lēac,* leek, plant.]

leer *lēr, n* a sly, sidelong or lecherous look. — *vi* to look lecherously; to glance sideways. — *n* and *adj* **leer'ing.** — *adv* **leer'ingly.** — *adj* **leer'y** cunning; wary (with *of*). [O.E. *hlēor,* face, cheek.]

lees *lēz, npl* sediment or dregs of liquor. [Fr. *lie.*]

leet *lēt,* (*Scot*) *n* a selected list of candidates for an office. — **short leet** a select list for the final choice.

leeward, leeway. See **lee.**

left[1] *left, pa t* and *pa p* of **leave**[2]. — *adj* **left'-off** laid aside, discarded. — *adj* **left'over** remaining over from a previous occasion. — *n* something left over; a survival; food uneaten at a meal (usu. in *pl*). — **left-luggage office** a room at an airport or a railway station where for a small fee one can safely leave one's luggage for a time.

left[2] *left, adj* on, for, or belonging to that side (or part of the body, etc. on that side) which in human beings has normally the weaker and less skilful hand; on the west side from the point of view of a person looking north; relatively democratic, progressive, innovating (as opp. to conservative) in politics; inclined towards socialism or communism. — *n* the left side; the region to the left side; the left hand; a blow with the left hand; a glove, shoe, etc. for the left hand or foot, etc.; the more progressive, democratic, socialist, radical or actively innovating party or wing (from its sitting in some legislatures to the president's left). — *adv* on or towards the left. — *adj* and *n* **left'ie** or **left'y** (often *derog*) (a) leftist. — *adj* **left'ish.** — *adj* and *n* **left'ist.** — *adj* and *adv* **left'ward** towards the left; on the left side; more left-wing. — *adv* **left'wardly** or **left'wards.** — **Left Bank** the artistic quarter of Paris on the south bank of the Seine. — *adj* **left'-bank.** — *adj* **left-foot'ed** performed with the left foot; having more skill or strength in the left foot. — *adj* **left'-hand** on the left side; towards the left; performed with the left hand. — *adj* **left-hand'ed** having the left hand stronger and readier than the right; for the left hand; counter-clockwise; forming a mirror-image of the right-handed form; awkward; dubious (as in *a left-handed compliment*); (of a marriage) morganatic. — *adv* **left-hand'edly.** — **left-hand'edness; left-hand'er** a blow with the left hand; a left-handed person; **left wing** the political left; the wing on the left side of an army, football pitch, etc. — *adj* **left-wing'** playing on the left wing; belonging to the more leftwardly inclined section; (having opinions which are) progressive, radical, socialist, etc. — **left-wing'er** a person with left-wing views or who supports the left wing of a party, etc.; a player on the left wing. — **have two left feet** to be clumsy or awkward, esp. in dancing; **left-hand drive** a driving mechanism on the left side of a vehicle which is intended to be driven on the right-hand side of the road; **left, right and centre** in, from, etc. all directions; everywhere. [M.E. *lift, left* — O.E. *left,* weak, worthless.]

leg *leg, n* a limb for walking by; the human lower limb; a long, slender support of e.g. a table; a branch or limb of anything forked or jointed, like a pair of compasses; the part of a garment that covers the leg; a distinct part or stage of a course or journey; in sports, one event or part in a contest consisting of two or more parts or events; in cricket, that part of the field, or that fielder, on or behind a line straight out from the batsman on the on side (also *adj*). — *vt* and *vi* to walk briskly, run, or dash away (*vt* with *it*); to propel through a canal tunnel by pushing with the feet on wall or roof. — *adj* **legged** (*legd* or *leg'id*; usu. in combination) having (a certain type, number, etc. of) legs. — *n* **legg'iness.** — *n* **legg'ing** a covering for the leg, e.g. (in *pl*) thick, footless tights, usu. of wool or knitted fabric, or fashion varieties made in other, thinner materials; an outer and extra protective covering for the lower leg. — *adj* **legg'y** having noticeably long slim legs. — *adj* **leg'less** having no legs; very drunk (*colloq*). — *n* **leg'lessness.** — **leg before** see **leg before wicket** below; **leg break** (*cricket*) a ball that breaks from the leg side towards the off side on pitching; a ball bowled to have this deviation; spin imparted to a ball to cause such a deviation; **leg bye** (*cricket*) a run made when the ball touches any part of the batsman's person except his or her hand; **leg'-guard** a cricketer's pad; **leg'-iron** a fetter for the leg; **leg'-man** (or **-woman**) a man (or woman) who travels on errands, or gathers information, etc. outside the office; a newspaper reporter. — *adj* **leg-of-mutt'on** shaped like a leg of mutton; (of a sleeve) tight on the lower arm and full above. — **leg'-pull** a good-humoured hoax, bluff or practical joke; **leg'-puller; leg'-pulling; leg'-rest** a support for the legs; **leg'room** space for one's legs, as in a car; **leg side** (or **the leg;** *cricket*) that half of the field nearest the batsman's legs (opp. to *off side*). — *adj* **leg'-side.** — **leg slip** (*cricket*) a fielder or position on the leg side somewhat behind the batsman; **leg spin** (*cricket*) a leg break. — *adj* **leg'-spin.** — **leg spinner** (*cricket*) someone who bowls leg breaks; **leg theory** (*cricket*) the policy of bowling on the striker's legs with a trap of leg-side fielders; bodyline; **leg'warmers** long footless socks; **leg-woman** see **leg-man; leg'work** (*colloq*) work involving much travelling, searching, etc. — **a leg up** a help or hoist in mounting, climbing, etc.; **find one's legs** to become familiar or accustomed; **fine, long, short** and **square leg** (*cricket*) fielding positions respectively fine from, far from, near to and square to, the batsman on the leg side; **get one's leg over** (*vulg slang*; of a man) to copulate with a woman; **leg before wicket** or **leg before** (*cricket*) a way of being given out as penalty for stopping with the leg (or any part of the body except the hands) a straight or off-break ball that would have hit the wicket (abbrev. **lbw**); **not have a leg to stand on** to have no case at all; **pull someone's leg** to make a playful attempt to hoax or deceive someone; **shake a leg** (*colloq*) to hurry up; **show a leg** to make an appearance; to get up. [O.N. *leggr*, a leg.]

leg. *abbrev* for: legal; legate; legislature.

legacy *leg'ə-si, n* that which is left to one by will; a bequest of personal property. — *n* **legatee'** a person to whom a legacy is left. — *n* **legator** (*li-gā'tər*) a person who leaves a legacy. [L. *lēgāre*, *-ātum*, to leave by will.]

legal *lē'gl, adj* pertaining to, or according to, law; lawful; created by law. — *n* **lēgalese'** complicated legal jargon. — *n* **lēgalisā'tion** or **-z-** a process whereby something previously unlawful is made lawful. — *vt* **lē'galise** or **-ize** to make lawful. — *n* **lē'galism** strict adherence to law; the doctrine that salvation depends on strict adherence to the law (*theol*); the tendency to observe letter or form rather than spirit, or to regard things from the point of view of law. — *n* **lē'galist.** — *adj* **lēgalis'tic.** — *adv* **lēgalis'tically.** — *n* **lēgality** (*-gal'i-ti*). — *adv* **lē'gally.** — **legal aid** financial assistance given to those unable to pay the full costs of legal proceedings; **legal eagle** (*colloq*) a bright, discerning lawyer; **legal holiday** (*US*) a public holiday, bank holiday; **legal tender** that which a creditor cannot refuse in payment of a debt; **legal year** see **year.** [L. *lēgālis* — *lēx, lēgis*, law.]

legate *leg'it, n* an ambassador, esp. from the Pope; a delegate, deputy, esp. orig. a Roman general's lieutenant; the governor of a Papal province (*hist*). — *n* **leg'ateship.** — *n* **legation** (*li-gā'shən*) a diplomatic mission, body of delegates, or its official quarters; the office or status of legate; a Papal province (*hist*). [L. *lēgātus* — *lēgāre*, to send with a commission.]

legatee. See **legacy.**

legato *le-gä'tō*, (*mus*) *adj* and *adv* smooth, smoothly, the notes running into each other without a break (*superl* **legatis'simo**). — *n* a legato passage or manner: — *pl* **lega'tos.** [It., bound, tied — L. *ligāre*, *-ātum*, to tie.]

legend *lej'ənd, n* a traditional story (orig. a saint's life); an untrue or unhistorical story; a collection of such stories; a body of tradition; a person having a special place in popular opinion for their striking qualities or deeds, real or fictitious; the body of fact and fiction gathered round such a person; a motto, inscription or explanatory words (with e.g. a picture). — *adj* **leg'endary** pertaining to, of the nature of, consisting of, or described in, legend; romantic; fabulous. [Fr. *légende* — L.L. *legenda*, to be read.]

legerdemain *lej-ər-də-mān', n* dexterous trickery or conjuring, sleight-of-hand; jugglery. [Lit. light of hand — Fr. *léger*, light, *de*, of, *main*, hand.]

leger-line. See **ledger-line.**

legged, legginess, legging, leggy. See **leg.**

leghorn *leg'hörn* or *li-görn', n* fine straw plait made in Tuscany; a hat made of it; (*li-görn'*) a small breed of domestic fowl. [*Leghorn* (It. *Legorno*, now *Livorno*) in Italy.]

legible *lej'i-bl, adj* clear enough to be deciphered; easy to read. — *n* **legibil'ity.** — *adv* **leg'ibly.** [L. *legibilis* — *legĕre*, to read.]

legion *lē'jən, n* in ancient Rome, a body of three to six thousand soldiers; a military force, esp. applied to several in French history; a very great number. — *adj* **le'gionary** of, or consisting of, a legion or legions; containing a very great number. — *n* a member of a legion. — *n* **lēgionnaire** (*-nār'*; Fr. *légionnaire*) a member of the British, Foreign, etc. Legion. — **American Legion** an association of U.S. war veterans; **British Legion** (in full **Royal British Legion**) an ex-servicemen's and -women's association; **Foreign Legion** a legion composed of foreigners, esp. that in the French army organised in 1831; **Legionnaire's (**or **Legionnaires') Disease** a severe, sometimes fatal, pneumonia-like disease caused by the bacterium *Legionella pneumophilia* (so named after an outbreak of the disease at an American Legion convention in Philadelphia in 1976); **Legion of Honour** a French order instituted in 1802 by Napoleon I; **their name is Legion** they are beyond numbering (from the Bible: Mark v. 9). [L. *legiō, -ōnis* — *legĕre*, to levy.]

legislate *lej'is-lāt, vi* to make laws. — *n* **legislā'tion.** — *adj* **leg'islātive** (or *-lə-tiv*) law-making; having power to make laws; pertaining to legislation. — *n* law-making power; the law-making body. — *adv* **leg'islatively.** — *n* **leg'islator** a lawgiver; a member of a legislative body. — *adj* **legislatorial** (*-lə-tö'ri-əl*) of or pertaining to, or of the nature of, a legislator, legislature or legislation. — *n* **leg'islatorship.** — *n* **leg'islature** a law-making body. [L. *lēx, lēgis*, law, *latum*, serving as supine to *ferre*, to bear.]

legit *li-jit', adj* a colloq. shortening of **legitimate.**

legitimate *li-jit'i-mit* or *-māt, adj* lawful; lawfully begotten, born in wedlock, or having the legal status of those born in wedlock; related, derived, or transmitted by birth in wedlock or subsequently legitimated; according to strict rule of heredity and primogeniture; logically inferred; following by natural sequence; genuine; conforming to an accepted standard. — *vt* (*-māt*) to make lawful; to give the rights of a legitimate child to. — *n* **legit'imacy** (*-mə-si*) the fact or state of being legitimate. — *adv* **legit'imately.** — *n* **legit'imateness.** — *n* **legitimā'tion** the act of making legitimate, esp. of conferring the privileges of legitimate birth. — *vt* **legit'imise** or **-ize** to legitimate. — *n* **legit'imist** a person who believes in the right of royal succession according to the principle of heredity and primogeniture. [L.L. *lēgitimāre*, *-ātum* — L. *lēgitimus*, lawful — *lēx*, law.]

Lego® *leg'ō, n* a toy consisting of small interlocking plastic pieces, principally bricks for constructing model buildings, etc.

legume *leg'ūm* or *li-gūm', n* a pod of one carpel (as in pea, bean, lentil, etc.); a vegetable used as food. — *npl* **Legūminō'sae** (*-sē*) an order of angiosperms characterised by the legume or seed pod. — *adj* **legū'minous** pertaining to pulse vegetables; of or pertaining to the Leguminosae; bearing legumes. [L. *legūmen*, pulse.]

lei[1]. See **leu**.

lei[2] *lä'ē*, *n* a garland, wreath, esp. of flowers, shells or feathers. [Hawaiian.]

Leibnitzian or **Leibnizian** *līb-nit'si-ən*, *adj* pertaining to the great German philosopher and mathematician Gottfried Wilhelm *Leibniz* (1646–1716), esp. his doctrine of primordial monads, pre-established harmony and fundamental optimism on the principle of sufficient reason.

Leicester *les'tər*, *adj* of a long-woolled breed of sheep that originated in *Leicestershire*. — *n* a sheep of that breed.

Leics. *abbrev* for Leicestershire.

leish *lēsh*, (*Scot*) *adj* active, supple, athletic.

leishmaniasis *lēsh-mən-ī'ə-sis* or **leishmaniosis** *-mən-i-ō'sis*, *n* any of various diseases, such as kala-azar, due to infection with any protozoon of the genus *Leishmania*: — *pl* **leishmani'asēs** or **leishmaniō'sēs**. [Named after Sir William *Leishman* (1865–1926), who discovered the cause of kala-azar.]

leisure *lezh'ər* or (*US* and *old-fashioned*) *lēzh'ər*, *n* time away from work; freedom from occupation, free time; convenient opportunity. — *adj* free from necessary business; for casual wear; for or relating to leisure, recreational time or pursuits. — *adj* **leis'ured** having much leisure. — *adj* and *adv* **leis'urely** not hasty or hastily. — **leisure centre** a centre providing a variety of recreational facilities; **leisure suit** a loose-fitting garment comprising matching top and trousers made from a soft fabric; **leisure wear** comfortable, casual clothing worn on informal or recreational occasions. — **at leisure** or **at one's leisure** free from occupation; at one's ease or convenience. [O.Fr. *leisir* — L. *licēre*, to be permitted.]

leitmotiv or **leitmotif** *līt'mō-tēf*, (*mus*) *n* a theme associated with a person or a thought, recurring when the person appears on the stage or the thought becomes prominent in the action; a recurring theme (*fig*). [Ger., — *leiten*, to lead, and *Motiv*, a motif.]

lek[1] *lek*, *n* the standard monetary unit of Albania (100 *qintars*).

lek[2] *lek*, *n* the piece of ground on which the blackcocks and cock capercailzies gather to display. — *vt* to gather and display at a lek: — *pr p* **lekk'ing**; *pa t* and *pa p* **lekked**. [App. from Sw. *leka*, to play.]

lekythos *lē'ki-thos*, (*antiq*) *n* a narrow-necked Greek flask. [Gr. *lēkythos*.]

LEM or **lem** *lem*, *abbrev* for Lunar Excursion Module.

lemel or **limail** *lē'mel*, *n* the dust and filings of metal. [M.E. *lemaille* — M.Fr. — O.Fr. *limer*, to file.]

lemma *lem'ə*, *n* a preliminary proposition, or a premise taken for granted (*math*); a theme, argument, heading or headword: — *pl* **lemm'as** or **lemm'ata**. — *vt* **lemm'atise** or **-ize** to organise (words in a text) so that inflected and variant forms are grouped under the appropriate lemma. [Gr. *lēmma*, *-atos*, from the root of *lambanein*, to take.]

lemming *lem'ing*, *n* a northern rodent (of the genus *Lemmus* and others) closely related to voles. [Norw.]

lemon[1] *lem'ən*, *n* a pale yellow oval citrus fruit with acid pulp; the tree that bears it; a pale yellow colour; something or someone disappointing, worthless, unattractive or defective (*slang*) — *adj* flavoured with lemon; (coloured) pale yellow. — *vt* to flavour with lemon. — *n* **lemonade'** a drink (still or aerated) made with lemon juice or more or less flavoured with lemon. — *adj* **lem'ony**. — **lemon balm** same as **balm**; **lemon cheese** or **curd** a soft paste of lemons, eggs and butter; **lemon drop** a hard lemon-flavoured sweet; **lemon peel** the skin of lemons (sometimes candied); **lemon squash** a concentrated lemon drink; **lemon squeezer** a small hand-press for extracting the juice of lemons. — *n* and *adj* **lemon-yell'ow**. — **the answer is a lemon** (*colloq*) one is given an unsatisfactory answer or no answer at all. [Fr. *limon* (now the lime).]

lemon[2] *lem'ən*, *n* a species of sole; a kind of dab resembling a sole (**lemon-dab'** or **lemon-sole'**, also called **smear'-dab** or **smooth dab**). [Fr. *limande*.]

lempira *lem-pē'rə*, *n* the standard monetary unit of Honduras (100 centavos). [*Lempira*, a department of Honduras named after a native chief.]

lemur *lē'mər*, *n* any member of a group of forest-dwelling, long-tailed mammals akin to the monkeys, mainly nocturnal, common in Madagascar. — *n* and *adj* **lemurian** (*li-mū'ri-ən*) or **lem'ūroid**. [L. *lĕmŭrēs*, ghosts.]

lend *lend*, *vt* to give the use of for a time; to provide, grant or supply, in general; to supply (money) at interest. — *vi* to make a loan: — *pr p* **lend'ing**; *pa t* and *pa p* **lent**. — *n* **lend'er**. — *n* **lend'ing** the act of giving in loan. — **lend'-lease** in World War II, an arrangement by which the President could supply war materials to other countries whose defence he deemed vital to the United States. — Also *adj*. — **lend an ear** (*colloq*) to listen; **lend itself to** to be able to be used for. [O.E. *lǣnan* — *lǣn*, *lān*, a loan.]

lenes. See **lenis**.

length *length*, *n* quality of being long; extent from end to end; the longest measure of anything; long duration; time occupied in uttering a vowel or syllable (*phon*); any definite portion of a known extent; a stretch or extent; distance (chiefly *Scot*); a suitable distance for pitching a cricket ball; the lengthwise measurement of a horse, boat, etc. (*racing*); used in combination to denote stretching downwards, or sometimes along, as far as, e.g. *knee-length*, *arm's-length*. — *vt* and *vi* **length'en** to increase (in length). — *adv* **length'ily**. — *n* **length'iness**. — *adv* **length'ways** or **length'wise** in the direction of the length. — *adj* **length'y** of great or tedious length; rather long. — **lengths'man** someone responsible for the upkeep of a particular stretch of road or railway. — **at length** in full; fully extended; at last; **go to great lengths, all lengths, any length** or **any lengths** to do everything possible (sometimes more than is ethical) to achieve a purpose. [O.E. *lengthu* — *lang*, long.]

lenient *lēn'yənt* or *-ni-ənt*, *adj* mild; tolerant; merciful. — *n* **lēn'ience** or **lēn'iency**. — *adv* **lēn'iently**. — *adj* **lenitive** (*len'*) soothing; laxative. — *n* any palliative; an application for easing pain (*med*). — *n* **len'ity** mildness; clemency. [L. *lēniēns*, *-entis*, pres. p. of *lēnīre*, to soften.]

Leninism *len'in-izm*, *n* the political, economic and social principles and practices of the Russian revolutionary leader Vladimir Ilyich Ulyanov *Lenin* (1870–1924), esp. his theory of government by the proletariat. — *n* and *adj* **Len'inist** or **Len'inite**.

lenis *lē'nis*, (*phon*) *adj* (of a consonant) articulated with relatively little muscular effort and pressure of breath (opp. to *fortis*). — Also *n*: — *pl* **lē'nes** (*-ēz*). — *n* **lenition** (*li-nish'ən*) a softening of articulation, common in Celtic languages. [L., soft.]

lenitive, lenity. See **lenient**.

leno *lē'nō*, *n* a thin muslin-like fabric: — *pl* **lē'nos**. [Perh. Fr. *linon*.]

lens *lenz*, *n* a piece of transparent matter (glass, plastic, etc.) with one or both surfaces curved to cause regular convergence or divergence of rays passing through it; the refracting structure (*crystalline lens*) between the crystalline and vitreous humours of the eye; a mechanical equivalent of the human lens on a camera, allowing the subject image to fall on the eye or (on the opening of the shutter) the film plane (see also **fisheye lens** at **fish**, **telephoto lens** at **telephoto**, **wide-angle** at **wide**); a contact lens: — *pl* **lens'es**. — *n* **lens'man** (*colloq*) a cameraman. [L. *lens*, *lentis*, a lentil (from the shape).]

Lent *lent*, (*Christianity*) *n* the time from Ash Wednesday to Easter as a time of fasting in commemoration of Christ's fast in the wilderness (Matt. iv. 2). — *adj* **Lent'en** (also without *cap*) of Lent; meagre. — **lenten rose** a herbaceous perennial (*Helleborus orientalis*) which flowers from February to April; **lent'-lily** the daffodil. [O.E. *lencten*, the spring.]

lent *lent*, *pa t* and *pa p* of **lend**.

lentamente, lentando, lenti. See **lento.**

Lenten, lenten. See **Lent.**

lentic *len'tik*, (*ecol*) *adj* associated with standing water; inhabiting ponds, swamps, etc. [L. *lentus*, slow.]

lenticle *len'ti-kl*, (*geol*) *n* a lenticular mass. — *adj* **lenti'cūlar** shaped like a lens or lentil seed; double-convex. — *n* a three-dimensional picture made up of photographs of a scene which have been taken from several different angles, split into strips, juxtaposed and laminated with corrugated plastic, the corrugations acting as lenses to create an illusion of depth. — *adv* **lentic'ūlarly.** — *adj* **lent'iform** or **lent'oid** lenticular. [L. *lēns*, *lentis*, lentil.]

lentigo *len-tī'gō*, *n* a freckle; (usu.) freckles: — *pl* **lentigines** (*len-tij'i-nēz*). — *adj* **lentig'inose** or **lentig'inous** (*bot*) minutely dotted. [L. *lentīgō*, *-inis*, a freckle.]

lentil *len'til*, *n* a leguminous annual plant common near the Mediterranean; its small, flattish, round seed, orange or brown, used for food. [O.Fr. *lentille* — L. *lēns*, *lentis*.]

lentivirus *len'ti-vī-rəs*, *n* a slow virus. [N.L., — L. *lentus*, slow, and **virus.**]

lento *len'tō*, (*mus*) *adj* slow. — *adv* slowly. — *n* a slow passage or movement: — *pl* **len'tos** or **len'ti** (*-tē*). — *adv* **lentamen'te** (*-tā*). — *adj* and *adv* **lentan'do** slowing. — *adj* and *adv* **lentiss'imo** very slow(ly). [It., — L. *lentus*, slow.]

lentoid. See under **lenticle.**

Leo *lē'ō*, *n* the Lion, a constellation between Cancer and Virgo; the 5th sign of the zodiac, in which it used to be (the constellation is now in the sign Virgo); a person born between 24 July and 23 August, under the sign of Leo. [L. *leō*, *-ōnis*, lion.]

leone *lē-ō'nē*, *n* the standard monetary unit of Sierra Leone (100 Sierra Leone cents).

leonine *lē'ə-nīn*, *adj* lionlike. [L. *leoninus*.]

leopard *lep'ərd*, *fem* **leopardess** *lep'ərd-es*, *n* a large spotted animal of the cat family found in Africa and Asia (also called the panther); in N.Am. any similar large cat. — **leop'ard-cat** a spotted wild cat of India; **leop'ard-moth** a white moth with black spots on wings and body. — **snow leopard** a Central Asian relative of the leopard, with pale fur and dark markings; **the leopard cannot change its spots** personality traits cannot be changed. [O.Fr., — L. *leopardus* — Gr. *leopardos* — *leōn*, lion, *pardos*, pard (an old word for leopard).]

leotard *lē'ə-tärd*, *n* a skin-tight garment worn by dancers, acrobats, etc., sleeveless or long-sleeved, legs varying from none at all to ankle-length. [Jules *Léotard*, 19th-century French trapeze artist.]

leper *lep'ər*, *n* a person affected with leprosy; a spurned person (*fig*); an outcast. [O.Fr. *lepre*, Gr. *leprā*, fem. of *lepros*, scaly — *lepos*, a scale, *lepein*, to peel.]

lepid- *lep-id-* or **lepido-** *-ō-* or *-o'-*, *combining form* denoting scales. — *npl* **Lepidop'tera** an order of insects, with four wings covered with fine scales — butterflies and moths. — *n* **lepidop'terist** a person who studies butterflies and moths. — *n* **lepidopterol'ogy.** — *adj* **lepidop'terous.** [Gr. *lepis*, *-idos*, a scale.]

leporine *lep'ə-rīn*, *adj* of or resembling the hare. [L. *leporīnus* — *lepus*, *lepŏris*, the hare.]

LEPRA *lep'rə*, *abbrev* for Leprosy Relief Association.

lepra *lep'rə*, *n* leprosy (*med*); a scurfy, mealy substance on some plants (*bot*). [See ety. for **leper.**]

leprechaun *lep'rə-hhön* or *-kön*, (*folklore*) *n* a little brownie, who helps Irish housewives, mends shoes, grinds meal, etc. [Prob. Old Ir. *luchorpán*, *lu*, small, *corpan*, *corp*, a body.]

leprosy *lep'rə-si*, *n* a chronic skin disease caused by a bacillus and occurring in two forms — tubercular, beginning with spots and thickenings of the skin, and anaesthetic, attacking the nerves, with loss of sensation in areas of skin. — *adj* **lep'rous** of or affected with leprosy; scaly; scurfy. [See ety. for **leper.**]

-lepsy *-lep-si*, (*med*) *combining form* denoting a seizing or seizure, as in *catalepsy*. — **-leptic** adjectival combining form. [Gr. *lēpsis* — *lambanein*, to seize, take.]

lepton *lep'ton*, *n* any of a group of subatomic particles with weak interactions, electrons, negative muons, tau particles and neutrinos (opp. to *baryon*; *pl* **lep'tons**); a modern Greek coin, 1/100th of a drachma (*pl* **lep'ta**); the smallest ancient Greek coin, translated 'mite' in the N.T. (*pl* **lep'ta**). — *adj* **leptocephal'ic** narrow-skulled. — *adj* **lepton'ic** of or pertaining to leptons. — *n* **lep'tosome** a person with a slight, slender physical build; an asthenic. — *adj* **leptosō'mic** or **leptosomatic** (*-sə-mat'ik*). — *n* **leptospīrō'sis** a disease of animals or man caused by bacteria of the genus **Leptospī'ra.** [Gr. *leptos* (neut. *lepton*), slender.]

lerp *lûrp*, *n* in Australia, a scalelike, waxy, protective, edible secretion produced on leaves of certain psyllid larvae. [Aboriginal.]

les. See **lez.**

lesbian *lez'bi-ən*, *adj* (of women) homosexual; (with *cap*) of the Aegean island of Lesbos. — *n* a woman homosexual. — *n* **les'bianism.**

lese-majesty or **leze-majesty** *lēz-maj'is-ti*, *n* an offence against the sovereign power, treason. [Fr. *lèse majesté*, transl. of L. *laesa mājestās*, injured majesty — *laedĕre*, to hurt.]

lesion *lē'zhən*, *n* a morbid change in the structure of body tissue caused by disease or injury, esp. an injury or wound (*med*); an injury, hurt. [Fr. *lésion* — L. *laesiō*, *-ōnis* — *laedĕre*, *laesum*, to hurt.]

less *les*, *adj* (used as *compar* of **little**) smaller (not now used of material things); in smaller quantity (not number); inferior, lower in estimation; fewer (*colloq*); younger. — *adv* not so much; in a lower degree. — *n* a smaller portion or quantity. — *prep* without; with diminution of, minus. — **much less** often used by confusion for much more; not to mention; **no less** (usu. *ironically*) a phrase used to express admiration; **nothing less than** quite as much as; tantamount to. [O.E. *lǣssa*, less, *lǣs* (adv.); apparently not connected with **little.**]

-less *-les* or *-lis*, *adj sfx* meaning free from or lacking (as in guilt*less*, god*less*). [O.E. *-lēas*.]

lessee *les-ē'* or *les'ē*, *n* a person to whom a lease is granted. [**lease.**]

lessen *les'n*, *vt* to make less, in any sense; to lower in estimation; to disparage; to belittle. — *vi* to become less, shrink. [**less.**]

lesser *les'ər*, *adj* less; smaller; inferior; minor. [Double compar. from **less.**]

lesson *les'n*, *n* a portion of Scripture read in divine service; a period, division, or prescribed portion of instruction; a set exercise; an instructive or warning experience or example; a severe reproof. [Fr. *leçon* — L. *lectiō*, *-ōnis* — *legĕre*, to read.]

lessor *les'ör*, *n* a person who grants a lease. [**lease.**]

lest *lest*, *conj* that not; for fear that. [M.E. *leste* — O.E. *thȳ lǣs the*, the less that; see ety. for **the**[2].]

let[1] *let*, *vt* to allow to go or come; to give leave or power to, to allow, permit, suffer (usu. with infin. without *to*); to grant to a tenant or hirer; in the imper. with accus. and infin. without *to*, often used virtually as an auxiliary with imperative or optative effect: — *pr p* **lett'ing**; *pa t* and *pa p* **let.** — *n* a letting for hire. — *adj* **lett'able** able to be hired out, suitable for letting.

— *n* **lett'er** a person who lets, esp. on hire. — *n* **lett'ing.** — **let'-down** an act or occasion of letting down; a disappointment; **let'-out** a chance to escape, avoid keeping an agreement, contract, etc.; **let'-up** end, ceasing; respite, relief; abatement. — **let alone** not to mention, much less; to refrain from interference with; **let be** to leave undisturbed; **let down** to allow to fall; to lower; to leave in the lurch, betray trust, fail, disappoint; **let fall** to drop; to mention or hint; **let fly** to fling, discharge, shoot; **let go** to cease holding; to slacken (*naut*); **let in** to allow to enter; (with *for*) to involve in or betray into (anything unpleasant or troublesome); to insert; to leak inwards; **let in on** (*colloq*) to allow to take part in; **let loose** to set free; to let go of restraint. to indulge in unrestrained talk or conduct; **let off** to allow to go free or without exacting all; to fire off, discharge; **let on** (*colloq*) to allow to be believed, to pretend; to disclose awareness; to reveal, divulge; **let oneself go** (*colloq*) to allow one's appearance, lifestyle, etc. to deteriorate; to act without restraint; **let out** to allow to get free, or to become known; to widen, slacken, enlarge; to put out to hire; to leak outwards; **let someone know** to inform someone; **let up** (*colloq*) to become less; to abate; **let well alone** to let things remain as they are from fear of making them worse; **to let** available for hire. [O.E. *lǣtan*, to permit, past t. *lēt*; past p. *lǣten*.]

let² *let*, *n* obstruction by the net, or some other reason for cancelling a service (*lawn tennis*, etc.); a service affected in such a way. [O.E. *lettan*, to hinder — *læt*, slow.]

-let *-lit* or *-lət*, *n sfx* used to form diminutives (as in brace*let*, leaf*let*, stream*let*).

lethal *lē'thəl*, *adj* deadly; mortal. [L. *lēt(h)ālis* — *let(h)um*, death.]

lethargy *leth'ər-ji*, *n* heavy unnatural slumber; torpor. — *adj* **lethargic** or **lethargical** (*-är'*) pertaining to lethargy; unnaturally sleepy; torpid. — *adv* **lethar'gically.** — *adj* **leth'argied.** — *vt* **leth'argise** or **-ize.** [Gr. *lēthārgiā*, drowsy forgetfulness — *lēthē*, forgetfulness, *ārgos*, idle.]

Lethe *lē'thē*, *n* a river of the underworld causing forgetfulness of the past to all who drank of it (*Gr mythol*); oblivion. — *adj* **lethē'an.** [Gr. *lēthē*, forgetfulness.]

Letraset® *let'rə-set*, *n* a transfer lettering system of alphabets, symbols, etc. which can be stripped into position on paper, film, etc.

letter¹ *let'ər*, *n* a conventional mark primarily used to express a sound of speech; a written or printed message; literal meaning; printing-type; (in *pl*) learning, literary culture. — *vt* to stamp letters upon; to mark with a letter or letters. — *adj* **lett'ered** marked with letters; educated; literary. — *n* **lett'erer.** — *n* **lett'ering** act of impressing or marking with letters; the letters impressed or marked; their style or mode of formation. — **lett'er-bomb** a device inside an envelope which explodes when the envelope is opened; **lett'er-box** a box or slot for receiving mail; **lett'er-card** a card folded and gummed like a letter, with perforated margin for opening; **lett'erhead** a printed heading on notepaper, etc.; a piece of notepaper with such heading; **lett'erpress** printed reading matter; a copying-press; a method of printing in which ink on raised surfaces is pressed on to paper. — *npl* **letters patent** a document conferring a patent or privilege, so called because written on open sheets of parchment. — **lett'er-stamp** an instrument for cancelling postage-stamps; a stamp for imprinting dates, etc. — **letter of credit** a letter authorising credit or cash to a certain sum to be given to the bearer; **letter of the law** literal interpretation of the law; **letters of credence** or **letters credential** a diplomat's formal document accrediting him or her to a foreign government; **to the letter** exactly, in every detail. [Fr. *lettre* — L. *littera*, *lītera*.]

letter², letting. See **let¹**.

lettuce *let'is*, *n* a composite plant (*Lactuca sativa*) or one of many varieties, whose leaves are used for salad; extended to other (inedible) plants of the genus. [App. from some form of A.Fr. *letue* — L. *lactūca* — *lac*, milk (from the milky juice of the leaves).]

leu *le'ōō*, *n* the standard monetary unit of Romania (100 *bani*): — *pl* **lei** (*lā*). [Rom., lion.]

leuc- or **leuk-** *lūk-*, *lōōk-*, *lūs-* or *lōōs-*, also **leuco-** or **leuko-** *lū-kō-*, *lōō-kō-* or *-ko'-*, *combining form* denoting white. [Gr. *leukos*, white.]

leucaemia, leukaemia or (esp. in U.S.) **leukemia** *lōō-kē'mi-ə*, *n* a sometimes fatal cancerous disease in which too many leucocytes are accumulated in the body, associated with changes in the lymphatic system and enlargement of the spleen. — *adj* **leucae'mic, leukae'mic** or **leuke'mic.** — *n* **leucae'mogen, leukae'mogen** or **leuke'mogen** a substance that encourages the development of leucaemia. — *adj* **leucaemogen'ic, leukaemogen'ic** or **leukemogen'ic.** [**leuc-** and Gr. *haima*, blood.]

leucin or **leucine** *lū'*, *lōō'sin* or *-sēn*, *n* an essential amino-acid, a product of protein hydrolysis. [Gr. *leukos*, white.]

leuco-. See **leuc-**.

leucoblast or **leukoblast** *lōō'kō-blast*, *n* an immature cell which will develop into a leucocyte. [**leuco-** and **-blast.**]

leucocyte or **leukocyte** *lōō'kō-sīt*, *n* a white corpuscle of the blood or lymph. [**leuco-** and Gr. *kytos*, container, used as if cell.]

leucoma or in U.S. **leukoma** *lū-* or *lōō-kō'mə*, *n* a white opacity of the cornea. [Gr. *leukōma* — *leukos*.]

leucotomy or **leukotomy** *lū-* or *lōō-kot'ə-mi*, *n* a surgical scission of the white nerve fibres between the frontal lobes of the brain and the thalamus to relieve cases of severe schizophrenia and manic-depressive psychosis. [**leuco-** and Gr. *tomē*, a cutting.]

leuk- or **leuko-**. See **leuc-**.

leukaemia, leukemia, etc., **leukoblast, leukocyte, leukoma, leukotomy**. See **leucaemia**, etc., **leucoblast, leucocyte, leucoma, leucotomy**.

Lev. or **Levit.** (*Bible*) *abbrev* for (the Book of) Leviticus.

lev *lef*, *n* the standard monetary unit of Bulgaria (100 *stotinki*): — *pl* **leva** (*lev'ä*). [Bulg., lion.]

Levant *li-vant'*, *n* the eastern Mediterranean and its shores. — *n* **Levant'er** an inhabitant of the Levant. — *adj* **Levant'ine** (or *lev'ən-tīn*) of the Levant. [Fr. *levant* or It. *levante*, east, lit. rising — L. *levāre*, to raise.]

levant *li-vant'*, *n* a kind of morocco leather; the levanter wind. — *adj* (*lev'ənt*) eastern. — *n* **levant'er** a boisterous easterly wind in the Levant. — *n* **lev'antine** a closely-woven twilled silk cloth. [Levant.]

levator *le-vā'tər* or *-tör*, (*anat*) *n* a muscle that raises (opp. to *depressor*). [L. *levātor*, a lifter.]

levee¹ *lev'i* or *li-vē'*, (*hist* or *archaic*) *n* a morning (or comparatively early) reception of visitors, esp. by a person of distinction. [Fr. *levée*, *lever* — L. *levāre*, to raise.]

levee² *lev'i* or *li-vē'*, (*US*) *n* a natural or artificial riverside embankment; a quay. [Fr. *levée*, raised.]

level *lev'l*, *n* a horizontal position; a horizontal plane or line; a nearly horizontal surface, or a region with no considerable inequalities; the horizontal plane, literal or figurative, that anything occupies or reaches up to; height; an instrument for testing horizontality; a horizontal mine gallery; an ascertainment of relative elevation; natural or appropriate position or rank; a condition of equality; a ditch or channel for drainage, esp. in flat country. — *adj* horizontal; even, smooth; even with anything else; uniform; well-balanced, sound of judgment; in the same line or plane; filled to a level with the brim; equal in position or dignity. — *adv* in a level manner; point-blank. — *vt* to make horizontal; to make flat or smooth; to raze; to aim; to make equal; to direct; to survey by taking levels. — *vi* to make things level; to aim; to speak honestly, to be frank (usu. with *with*; *colloq*). — *vt* and *vi* to change in spelling or pronunciation, making one word or form the same as another: — *pr p* **lev'elling**; *pa t* and *pa p* **lev'elled**. — *n* **lev'eller** someone who levels in any sense; a person who would like to remove all social or political inequalities, esp. (with *cap*) one of an ultra-republican party in the parliamentary army, crushed by Cromwell in 1649. — *n* **lev'elling**. — **level best** (*colloq*) one's utmost; **level-cross'ing** a place at which a road crosses a railway at the same level. — *adj* **level-head'ed** having sound common sense. — **level-pegg'ing** equal state of two rivals, contestants, etc. (often in the form **be level-pegging with**). — *adj* at the same level, equal. — **find one's level** to settle in one's natural position or rank; **level down** (or **up**) to lower (or raise) to the same level or status; **level off** to make flat or even; to reach and maintain equilibrium; **level with** (*slang*) to tell the truth; **on the level** fair; honestly speaking. [O.Fr. *livel*, *liveau* — L. *lībella*, a plummet, dimin. of *lībra*, a balance.]

lever *lē'vər* or in U.S. *lev'ər*, *n* a bar turning on a support or fulcrum for imparting pressure or motion from a source of power to a resistance. — *vt* to move with a lever. — *n* **le'verage** the mechanical power gained by the use of the lever; advantage gained for any purpose, e.g. (in *finance*) power gained over a resource greater than that one actually owns. — *vi* and *vt* (*finance*) to borrow necessary capital (esp. for a management buy-out) counting on the profits from the deal to cover interest repayments. — *adj* **le'veraged** financed by borrowed capital. — **le'ver-watch** one with a vibrating lever in the escapement mechanism. [O.Fr. *leveor* — *lever* — L. *levāre*, to raise.]

leveret *lev'ə-rit*, *n* a hare in its first year. [O.Fr. *levrette* — L. *lepus*, *lepŏris*, a hare.]

leviable. See **levy**.

leviathan *le-vī'ə-thən*, *n* a biblical sea-monster; anything of huge size, esp. a ship or a man. — *adj* gigantic, formidable. [Heb. *livyāthān*.]

levigate *lev'i-gāt*, *vt* to smooth; to grind to fine powder, esp. with a liquid. — *n* **levigā'tion**. [L. *lēvigāre*, *-ātum* — *lēvis*, smooth.]

Levis® *lē'vīz*, *npl* heavy, close-fitting denim, etc. trousers, reinforced at points of strain with copper rivets.

Levit. See **Lev**.

levitation *lev-i-tā'shən*, *n* the act of rising by virtue of lightness; the act of making light; the floating of heavy bodies in the air, according to spiritualists; raising and floating on a cushion of air. — *vi* and *vt* **lev'itate** to float, or cause to float. [On the model of *gravitate* — L. *levis*, light.]

Levite *lē'vīt*, *n* a descendant of *Levi*; a subordinate priest of the ancient Jewish Church. — *adj* **levitic** (*li-vit'ik*) or **levit'ical**. — *adv* **levit'ically**. — *n* **Levit'icus** the third book of the Old Testament.

levity *lev'it-i*, *n* lightness of temper or conduct; thoughtlessness; a trifling or frivolous tendency. [L. *levitās*, *-ātis* — *levis*, light.]

levo-. See **laevo-**.

levy *lev'i*, *vt* to raise or collect, e.g. an army or tax; to call for; to impose; to begin to wage: — *pr p* **lev'ying**; *pa t* and *pa p* **lev'ied**. — *n* the act of levying; a contribution called for from members of an association; a tax; the amount collected; troops levied. — *adj* **leviable** (*lev'i-ə-bl*). [Fr. *levée* — *lever* — L. *levāre*, to raise.]

lewd *lōōd* or *lūd*, *adj* obscene; sensual. — *adv* **lewd'ly**. — *n* **lewd'ness**. [O.E. *lǣwede*, ignorant.]

lewis *lōō'is*, *n* a dovetail iron tenon for lifting blocks of stone.

Lewis gun *lōō'is gun*, *n* a light machine-gun designed by the American Samuel McLean and perfected by Col. Isaac Newton *Lewis* (1858–1931).

lewisia *lōō-is'i-ə*, *n* a perennial herb with pink or white flowers, of the genus *Lewisia*. [American explorer Meriwether *Lewis* (1774–1909)].

lewisite *lōō'is-īt*, *n* an arsine derivative that causes blistering and other irritation, used in chemical warfare as a poison gas. [Named after W.L. *Lewis*, American chemist.]

lexeme *lek'sēm*, (*linguis*) *n* a word or other essential unit of vocabulary in its most abstract sense. [*lexicon*, and *-eme*.]

lexicon *lek'si-kən*, *n* a wordbook or dictionary; a vocabulary of terms used in connection with a particular subject. — *adj* **lex'ical** belonging to a lexicon; pertaining to the words of a language as distinct from its grammar and constructions. — *adv* **lex'ically**. — *n* **lexicographer** (*-kog'rə-fər*). — *adj* **lexicographic** (*-kə-graf'ik*) or **lexicograph'ical**. — *n* **lexicog'raphist**. — *n* **lexicog'raphy** the writing and compiling of dictionaries. — *n* **lexicol'ogist**. — *n* **lexicol'ogy** the study of the history and meaning of words. [Gr. *lexikon*, a dictionary — *lexis*, a word, *legein*, to speak.]

lexigram *lek'si-gram*, *n* a sign which represents a word. [Gr. *lexis*, a word, and **-gram**.]

lexigraphy *lek-sig'rə-fi*, *n* a system of writing in which each sign represents a word. — *adj* **lexigraphic** (*-graf'ik*) or **lexigraph'ical**. [Gr. *lexis*, word, *graphein*, to write.]

lexis *lek'sis*, *n* the way in which a piece of writing is expressed in words, diction; the total stock of words in a language. [Gr., word.]

ley *lā*, *n* (also **ley line**) one of the straight lines between features of the landscape, possibly pathways, or perhaps having scientific or magical significance in prehistoric times. [Variant of **lea**[1].]

Leyden jar *lā'dən jär*, *n* a condenser for electricity, a glass jar coated inside and outside with tinfoil or other conducting material. [*Leyden* in Holland, where it was invented.]

lez, **lezz** or **les** *lez*, also **lezzy** *lez'i*, (*colloq*; often *offensive*) *n* short forms of **lesbian**.

leze-majesty. See **lese-majesty**.

LF *abbrev* for low frequency.

LGU *abbrev* for Ladies' Golf Union.

LH *abbrev* for luteinising hormone.

lh *abbrev* for left hand. — **lhd** *abbrev* for left-hand drive.

lhasa apso *lä'sə ap'sō*, *n* a Tibetan (breed of) small, long-haired terrier: — *pl* **lhasa apsos**. [*Lhasa*, the capital of Tibet.]

LHD *abbrev* for: *Litterarum Humaniorum Doctor* (L.), lit. Doctor of the Humaner Letters, Doctor of Humanities.

lhd. See **lh**.

LI *abbrev* for: Light Infantry; Long Island (U.S.).

Li (*chem*) *symbol* for lithium.

liable *lī'ə-bl*, *adj* subject to an obligation; exposed to a possibility or risk; responsible (for); tending (usu. with *to*); apt; likely (to). — *n* **liabil'ity** the state of being liable; that for which one is liable, a debt, etc. — **limited liability** a principle of modern statute law which limits the responsibilities of shareholders in a partnership, joint-stock company, etc., by the extent of their personal interest therein. [App. — Fr. *lier* — L. *ligāre*, to bind.]

liaison *lē-ā'zon*, *n* union, or bond of union; connection; an illicit union between the sexes; effective conjunction with another unit or force (*mil*); in French, the linking in pronunciation of a final (and otherwise silent) consonant to a vowel beginning the next word. — *vi* **liaise** (*lē-āz'*; back-formation) to form a link (with); to be or get in touch (with). — **liaison officer** an officer forming a link with another unit or force. [Fr., — L. *ligātiō, -ōnis* — *ligāre*, to bind.]

liana *lē-ä'nə* or **liane** *lē-än'*, *n* any climbing plant, esp. a twisted woody kind of the tropical forest. — *adj* **lian'oid**. [Fr. *liane*, app. from *lier* — L. *ligāre*, to bind.]

liar. See under **lie**[1].

Lias *lī'əs*, (*geol*) *n* and *adj* Lower Jurassic. — *adj* **Liassic** (*lī-as'ik*). [A Somerset quarryman's word, app. from O.Fr. *liois*, a kind of limestone.]

Lib. *lib*, *abbrev* for Liberal.

lib *lib*, *n* a colloq. shortening of **liberation** (q.v. at **liberate**).

lib. *abbrev* for *liber* (L.), book.

libation *lī-bā'shən* or *li-*, *n* the pouring of wine or other liquid in honour of a god, or (*facetiously*) for some other purpose; the liquid poured. [L. *lībāre, -ātum*, to pour, sip, touch.]

libber *lib'ər*, *n* a colloq. shortening of **liberationist** (q.v. at **liberate**).

libel *lī'bl*, *n* any malicious defamatory publication or statement; written defamation (*English law*; distinguished from *slander* or spoken defamation; in Scots law both are slander); the statement of a plaintiff's grounds of complaint. — *vt* to defame by libel; to satirise unfairly; to proceed against by producing a written complaint (*law*): — *pr p* **lī'belling**; *pa t* and *pa p* **lī'belled**. — *n* **lī'bellant** a person who brings a libel. — *n* **libellee'** a person against whom a libel is brought. — *n* **lī'beller**. — *n* **lī'belling**. — *adj* **lī'bellous** containing a libel; defamatory. — *adv* **lī'bellously**. [L. *libellus*, dimin. of *liber*, a book.]

liberal *lib'ə-rəl*, *adj* generous; noble-minded; broad-minded; not bound by authority or traditional orthodoxy; looking to the general or broad sense rather than the literal; candid; free; free from restraint; generous; ample; (with *cap*) of the Liberal Party (see below); (of studies or education) directed towards the cultivation of the mind for its own sake, disinterested (opp. to *technical* and *professional*). — *n* a person who advocates greater freedom in political institutions; (with *cap*) a member of the Liberal Party; someone whose views are liberal. — *n* **liberalīsā'tion** or **-z-**. — *vt* and *vi* **lib'eralise** or **-ize** to make or become liberal, or enlightened. — *n* **lib'eralism** the principles of a liberal in politics or religion. — *n* **lib'eralist**. — *adj* **liberalist'ic**. — *n* **liberality** (*-al'i-ti*) the quality of being liberal; generosity; magnanimity, broad-mindedness; freedom from prejudice. — *adv* **lib'erally**. — **liberal arts** the studies that make up a liberal (q.v.) education; **liberal democracy** (*politics*) a state or system which combines the right to individual freedom with the right to representative government; **Liberal Democrat** a member of the **Liberal Democrats** (formerly called Social and Liberal Democrats), a UK party formed in 1988 from the Liberal Party and the Social Democratic Party; **Liberal Party** in the UK, a former political party which emerged, as successors to the Whigs, in the mid 19th cent.; in Australia, one of the major political parties; generally, a party advocating democratic reform and individual liberty. [L. *līberālis*, relating to freedom — *līber*, free.]

liberate *lib'ə-rāt*, *vt* to set free; to release from restraint, confinement or slavery; to give off (*chem*). — *n* **liberā'tion** setting free, releasing; freeing, or seeking to free (a group) from social disadvantages, prejudices, injustice or abuse. — *n* **liberā'tionism**. — *n* **liberā'tionist** a person who supports the cause of social freedom and equality for sections of society believed to be underprivileged or discriminated against. — *n* **lib'erātor**. [L. *līberāre, -ātum* — *līber*, free.]

libero *lē'bə-rō*, (*football*) *n* a footballer who plays behind the backs, acting as the last line in the defence but able to move freely throughout the field, a sweeper: — *pl* **li'beros**. [It., free.]

libertine *lib'ər-tēn* or *-tīn*, *n* a person who leads a licentious life, a rake or debauchee. — *adj* unrestrained; licentious. — *n* **lib'ertinism**. [L. *libertīnus*, a freedman.]

liberty *lib'ər-ti*, *n* freedom from constraint, captivity, slavery or tyranny; freedom to do as one pleases; the unrestrained enjoyment of natural rights; permission; free range; leisure; presumptuous, improper or undue freedom of speech or action. — *n* **libertā'rian** a believer in free-will; someone who believes in the maximum amount of freedom of thought, behaviour, etc. — Also *adj*. — *n* **libertā'rianism**. — **liberty bodice** an undergarment like a vest formerly worn by children. — **at liberty** free; unoccupied; available; **civil liberty** freedom of an individual within the law; individual freedom as guaranteed by a country's laws; **liberty of the press** freedom to print and publish without government permission; **take liberties with** to treat with undue freedom or familiarity, or indecently; to falsify; **take the liberty** to venture, presume. [Fr. *liberté* — L. *lībertās, -ātis*, liberty.]

libido *li-bē'dō* or *li-bī'dō*, *n* sexual impulse; vital urge, either in general or as of sexual origin (*psychol*): — *pl* **libi'dos**. — *adj* **libidinal** (*-bid'i-nəl*). — *n* **libidinos'ity** or **libid'inousness**. — *adj* **libid'inous** lustful, lascivious, lewd. — *adv* **libid'inously**. [L. *libīdō, -inis*, desire — *libet*, *lubet*, it pleases.]

LIBOR or **Libor** *lī'bör*, (*finance*) *abbrev* for London Inter-Bank Offered Rate.

Libra *lē'brə*, *n* the Balance, a constellation between the Virgin and the Scorpion; the seventh sign of the zodiac, in which it used to be (it is now in Scorpio); a person born between 24 Sept. and 23 Oct., under the sign of Libra. [L. *lībra*.]

libra *lī'brə* or *lē'brə*, *n* a Roman pound (*antiq*; used contracted to **lb**, for the British pound in weight, and to **£** for a pound in money).

library *lī'brə-ri*, *n* a collection of books; a building or room containing it; a publisher's series; a collection of gramophone records, films, etc.; a collection of computer programs. — *n* **librā'rian** the keeper of a library. — *n* **librā'rianship**. — **library edition** an edition of a book with high-quality binding, etc. — **lending library** one from which people may take books away on loan. [L. *librārium*, a bookcase — *liber*, a book.]

librate *lī'brāt*, *vi* to oscillate; to be poised. — *n* **lībrā'tion**. — **libration of the moon** a slight turning of the moon to each side alternately so that more than half of its surface is visible at one time or other. [L. *lībrāre, -ātum* — *lībra*, balance.]

libretto *li-bret'ō*, *n* the text or book of words of an opera, oratorio, etc.: — *pl* **librett'i** (*-ē*) or **librett'os**. — *n* **librett'ist** a writer of libretti. [It., dimin. of *libro* — L. *liber*, a book.]

Libyan *lib'i-ən*, *adj* of *Libya* in North Africa. — *n* a native or citizen of Libya. [Gr. *Libyē*, Libya.]

lice *līs*, *npl*. See **louse**.

licence or in U.S. **license** *lī'səns*, *n* being allowed; leave; grant of permission; the document by which authority is conferred; excess or abuse of freedom; licentiousness, libertinage, debauchery; a departure from a rule or standard for artistic or literary effect; tolerated freedom. — *vt* **li'cense** to grant licence to; to issue with a licence; to permit to depart, dismiss; to authorise or permit. — *adj* **li'censable**. — *adj* **li'censed** holding a (valid) licence; permitted, tolerated. — *n* **licensee'** a person to whom a licence is granted, esp. to sell alcoholic drink. — *n* **li'censer** or (chiefly *US*) **li'censor** a person who grants licence or permission; someone authorised to license. — *n* **licentiate** (*lī-sen'shi-ət*) a holder of an academic diploma of various kinds; in some European universities, a graduate ranking between bachelor and doctor; among Presbyterians, a person authorised by a Presbytery to preach. — *adj* **licentious** (*-sen'shəs*) indulging in excessive freedom, esp. of animal passions; dissolute. — *adv* **licen'tiously.** — *n* **licen'tiousness.** — **licence block** see **block; licensed victualler** a person licensed to sell food and esp. drink, for consumption on the premises, a publican; **license plate** (*US*) a vehicle number plate. — **special licence** (a) licence given by the Archbishop of Canterbury permitting the marriage of two specified people without banns, and at a place and time other than those prescribed by law — loosely used in Scotland in speaking of marriage by consent registered by warrant of the sheriff. [Fr. *licence* — L. *licentia* — *licēre*, to be allowed.]

lichee. See **lychee.**

lichen *lī'kən* or *lich'ən*, *n* a compound plant consisting of a fungus and an alga living symbiotically, forming crusts and tufts on stones, trees, and soil; an eruption on the skin. — *n* **li'chenist** or **lichenol'ogist** a specialist in **lichenol'ogy,** the study of lichens. — *adj* **li'chenoid.** — *adj* **li'chenose** or **li'chenous** abounding in, pertaining to, or of the nature of, lichens or lichen. [Gr. *leichēn*, lichen.]

lichgate or **lychgate** *lich'gāt*, *n* a roofed churchyard gate (orig. to rest a bier under). [M.E. *lich*, *liche*, a body — O.E. *līc*.]

licit *lis'it*, *adj* lawful, allowable. — *adv* **lic'itly.** [L. *licitus*.]

lick *lik*, *vt* to pass the tongue over (e.g. to moisten or taste); to take into the mouth using the tongue; to lap; to pass over or play upon in the manner of a tongue; to flicker over or around; to beat (*slang*); to smoke crack (*drug-taking slang*). — *vi* (*slang*) to go at full speed. — *n* an act of licking; a quantity licked up, or such (a small amount) as might be imagined to be licked up; a place where animals lick salt; vigorous speed (*colloq*); a short instrumental passage (*US slang*). — *n* **lick'er.** — *n* **lick'ing** a thrashing. — **a lick and a promise** a perfunctory wash; **lick into shape** to mould into satisfactory form; **lick one's lips** to look forward with pleasure; **lick one's wounds** to retire from a defeat, failure, etc., esp. in order to try to recover one's strength, pride, etc.; **lick the dust** to be killed, finished off (*colloq*). [O.E. *liccian*.]

licorice. Another spelling (chiefly *US*) for **liquorice.**

lictor *lik'tör* or *-tər*, (*hist*) *n* an officer who attended a Roman magistrate, bearing the fasces. [L.]

lid *lid*, *n* a cover, hinged or separate, for the opening of a receptacle; an eyelid; an effective restraint (*colloq*). — *adj* **lidd'ed** having a lid or lids. — *adj* **lid'less.** — **put the lid on it** (*colloq*) to end the matter; to be a culminating injustice, misfortune, etc.; **take, lift** or **blow the lid off** (*colloq*) to uncover, reveal (a scandal, etc.). [O.E. *hlid* — *hlīdan*, to cover.]

lido *lē'dō*, *n* a bathing beach; an open-air swimming-pool: — *pl* **lid'os.** [From the *Lido* at Venice — L. *lītus*, shore.]

lidocaine *lī'də-kān*, *n* U.S. name for **lignocaine.** [Acetani*lid* and *co*caine.]

lie[1] *lī*, *n* a false statement made with the intention of deceiving; anything misleading or of the nature of imposture; (with *the*) an accusation of lying. — *vi* to make a false statement with an intention to deceive; to give a false impression: — *pr p* **ly'ing;** *pa t* and *pa p* **lied.** — *n* **lī'ar** a person who lies, esp. habitually. — *adj* **ly'ing** addicted to telling lies. — *n* the habit of telling lies. — *adv* **ly'ingly.** — **lie detector** an instrument claimed to detect lying by recording abnormal involuntary bodily reactions in a person not telling the truth. — **give someone the lie** to accuse someone directly of lying; **give the lie to** to charge with lying; to prove false; **lie in one's throat** or **through one's teeth** (usu. *facetious*) to lie shamelessly; **white lie** a minor falsehood, esp. one told for reasons of tact, etc. [O.E. *lyge* (noun), *lēogan* (verb).]

lie[2] *lī*, *vi* to be in a horizontal or nearly horizontal posture; to assume such a posture; to lean; to press; to be situated; to have a position or extent; to be or remain passively; to be still; to be incumbent; to depend; to consist; to be sustainable (*law*): — *pr p* **ly'ing;** *pa t* **lay;** *pa p* **lain.** — *n* mode or direction of lying; slope and disposition; relative position; general situation; a spell of lying; an animal's lair or resting-place; the position from which a golf ball is to be played. — *n* **lī'er.** — **lie-down** see **lie down** below; **lie-in'** a longer than usual stay in bed in the morning; **lying-in'** confinement during childbirth: — *pl* **lyings-in'.** — Also *adj.* — **lie at someone's door** (of something untoward) to be directly attributable to someone; **lie back** to lean back on a support; to rest after a period of hard work; **lie down** to place oneself in a horizontal position, esp. in order to sleep or rest (*n* **lie'-down**); **lie hard (**or **heavy) on, upon** or **to** to oppress, burden; **lie in** to be in childbed; to stay in bed later than usual; **lie in wait** to lie in ambush (often with *for*); **lie low** to keep quiet or hidden; to conceal one's actions or intentions; **lie of the land** (*fig*) the current situation; **lie on** or **upon** to be incumbent on; **lie on one's hands** to remain unwanted, unclaimed or unused; **lie over** to be deferred to a future occasion; **lie to** (*naut*) to be or become nearly stationary with head to wind; **lie up** to abstain from work; to take to or remain in bed; (of a ship) to go into or be in dock; **lie with** to rest with as a choice, duty, etc.; to have sexual intercourse with (*Bible* or *archaic*); **take it lying down** (*colloq*) to endure without resistance or protest. [O.E. *licgan*.]

Liebfraumilch *lēb'frow-milk* or *-milhh*, *n* a German white wine made with grapes from the Rhine region. [Ger. *Liebfrau*, the Virgin Mary (after the convent where originally made), *Milch*, milk.]

lied *lēt*, *n* a German lyric or song: — *pl* **lieder** (*lē'dər*). [Ger.]

liege *lēj*, (*hist*) *adj* free except as within the relations of vassal and feudal lord; under a feudal tenure. — *n* a person under a feudal tenure; a vassal; a loyal vassal, a subject; a lord or superior (also in this sense, **liege'-lord**). — **liege'man** a vassal; a subject. [O.Fr. *lige*.]

lien *lē'ən* or *lēn*, (*law*) *n* a right to retain possession of another's property until the owner pays a debt. [Fr., — L. *ligāmen*, tie, band.]

lier. See **lie**[2].

lierne *li-ûrn'*, (*archit*) *n* a cross-rib in vaulting. [Fr.]

lieu *lū* or *lōō*, *n* place, stead, used chiefly in the phrase *in lieu of.* — *adj* in place of, substitute, as in *lieu day* or *lieu holiday*. [Fr., — L. *locus*, place.]

Lieut. *abbrev* for Lieutenant.

lieutenant *ləf-ten'ənt* or *lef-*, also (esp. *navy*) *lōō-ten'-* or *lə-*, and in U.S. *lōō-*, *n* a person representing, or performing the work of, a superior; a commissioned officer in the army next below a captain, or in the navy next below a lieutenant-commander and ranking with captain in the army; an officer in the police or fire departments next below a captain (*US*); a person holding a place next in rank to a superior, as in the compounds **lieutenant-col'onel, lieutenant-command'er** and **lieutenant-gen'eral.** — *n* **lieuten'ancy** or **lieuten'antship** the post or commission of a lieutenant. — **lieutenant-gov'ernor** a State governor's deputy (*US* and *Austr*); a governor subordinate to a governor-general; a governor in the Isle of Man, Jersey and Guernsey; **lieutenant-gov'ernorship.** — **Lord Lieutenant** a permanent governor of a county, head of the magistracy and the chief executive authority: — *pl* **Lords Lieutenant,**

Lord Lieutenants or **Lords Lieutenants**. [Fr.; see **lieu** and **tenant**.]

life *līf*, *n* the state of being alive; conscious existence; existence; continued existence, activity, vitality or validity of anything; the period of usefulness (of machinery, etc.); the period between birth and death; any of a number of opportunities of remaining in a game; career; current state of existence; manner of living; animation; liveliness, vivacity; appearance of being alive; a living being, esp. human; living things (*collectively*); social vitality; human affairs; a narrative of a life, a biography; that on which continued existence depends; (in wines) sparkle; (in cut gems) reflection, sparkle; imprisonment for life (*colloq*); a person insured against death: — *pl* **lives** (*līvz*). — *adj* (and in combination) for the duration of life; of life. — *adj* **life'less** dead; unconscious; without vigour or vivacity; (of food or drink) insipid; sluggish. — *adv* **life'lessly**. — *n* **life'lessness**. — *adj* **life'like** (of something inanimate) like a living person or the copied original. — *n* **lī'fer** a person sentenced to imprisonment for life. — *adj* **life-and-death'** critical; determining or affecting whether someone lives or dies. — **life annuity** a sum paid to a person yearly during their life; **life assurance** or **insurance** insurance providing a sum of money for a specified beneficiary in the event of the policy-holder's death, and sometimes for the policy-holder if he or she reaches a specified age; **life'belt** a buoyant circular belt for keeping a person afloat in water; any aid to survival; **life'-blood** the blood necessary to life; anything which gives essential strength or life; **life'boat** a boat for saving shipwrecked people; **life'buoy** a float for supporting a person in the water till he or she can be rescued; **life class** an art class in which the students draw or paint the human body from a live model; **life'-cycle** (*biol*) the round of changes in the life and generations of an organism, from zygote to zygote; **life'-force** a directing principle supposed to be inherent in living things. — *adj* **life'-giving** imparting life; invigorating. — **life'guard** a person employed to rescue bathers in difficulties; **Life Guards** two troops of cavalry, first so called in 1685, amalgamated in 1922 and forming, with the Royal Horse Guards, the Household Cavalry; **life-his'tory** the history of a (person's, plant's, animal's) life; the succession of changes from zygote to maturity and death, the life-cycle; **life'-jacket** a buoyant jacket for keeping a person afloat in water; **life'line** a rope for saving or safeguarding life; a vital means of communication. — *adj* **life'long** lasting throughout one's life. — **life peer** a peer whose title is not hereditary; **life peerage**; **life peeress**; **life'-raft** a raft kept on board a ship for use in an emergency; **life'-saver** a person who saves another from death, esp. from drowning; a lifeguard; something, or someone, that comes to one's aid at a critical moment (*colloq*); **life'-saving**. — *adj* designed to save life, esp. from drowning. — **life school** a school where artists work from living models; **life sciences** those sciences (biology, medicine, etc.) concerned with living organisms; **life sentence** a prison sentence to last for the rest of the prisoner's natural life (usu. now lasting approx. 15 years). — *adj* **life'-size** or **life'-sized** of the size of the object represented. — **life'span** the length of time for which a person or animal normally lives, or a machine, etc., functions; **life story** a biography or autobiography, esp. as recounted in the media or book form; **life'style** manner of living, i.e. one's material surroundings, attitudes, behaviour, etc.; the characteristic way of life of a group or individual; **life-support machine** or **system** a device or system of devices designed to maintain human life in adverse conditions, e.g. in space, during grave illness, etc.; **life'time** time during which one is alive; **life'-work** or **life's work** the work to which one's life is, has been, or is to be devoted. — **bring to life** to give life to, make alive; to animate; **come to life** to become alive; to become animated; **for life** for the whole period of one's existence; **for the life of me, him**, etc. (usu. with *can* and a *neg*) try as I, he, etc. might; **high life** fashionable society or its (exciting) manner of living; **not on your life** (*colloq*) on no account, absolutely not; **see life** to see how other people live, esp. the less well off or respectable; **the life and soul** the person who is the chief source of fun, etc., esp. at a party; **the life of Riley** (*rī'li*; *colloq*) an easy, carefree (and often irresponsible) life; **to the life** very closely like the original. [O.E. *līf*.]

LIFFE *abbrev* for London International Financial Futures Exchange.

LIFO *abbrev* for last in, first out (a rough guide to likely order of redundancies).

lift *lift*, *vt* to bring or take to a higher or (with *down*) lower position; to elate, encourage; to take and carry away; to hold up, support; to arrest (*slang*); to steal (*colloq*); to plagiarise; to remove or revoke. — *vi* to rise. — *n* an act of lifting; lifting power; vertical distance of lifting; the component of the aerodynamic force on an aircraft acting upwards at right angles to the drag; an enclosed platform or cagelike structure moving in a vertical shaft to carry people or goods up and down; one of the layers of material in a shoe heel, esp. an extra one to increase the wearer's height; a mechanism for raising or lowering a vessel to another level of a canal; a step in advancement, promotion, etc.; a boost to one's spirits, a feeling of elation; a (usu. free) journey in someone else's vehicle. — *adj* **lift'able**. — *n* **lift'er**. — **lift'back** a motor car with a sloping rear door lifting up from the bottom, a hatchback; **lift'-off** the take-off of an aircraft or rocket; the moment when this occurs; **lift'-pump** any pump that is not a force-pump. — **have one's face lifted** to undergo an operation for smoothing and firming the skin of one's face; **lift a finger** or **hand (to)** to make the smallest effort (to help, etc.); **lift off** (of a rocket, etc.) to take off, be launched. [O.N. *lypta* — *lopt*, the air.]

lig *lig*, (*slang*) *vi* to lie about, to idle; to be a freeloader, esp. in the entertainment industry. — *n* **ligg'er**. — *n* **ligg'ing**. [Orig. dialect for **lie²**.]

ligament *lig'ə-mənt*, *n* anything that binds; the bundle of fibrous tissue joining bones or cartilages (*anat*); a bond or tie. — *adj* **ligamental** (*-men'tl*), **ligamen'tary** or **ligamen'tous**. — *n* **ligand** (*lig'ənd* or *lī'gənd*) an atom, molecule, radical or ion which forms a complex with a central atom. — *n* **ligature** (*lig'ə-chər*) anything that binds; a bandage; a tie or slur (*mus*); a character formed from two or more letters (e.g. *æ*, *ff*; *printing*); a cord for tying the blood-vessels, etc. (*med*). — *vt* to bind with a ligature. [L. *ligāre*, to bind.]

ligan *lī'gən*, *n*. Same as **lagan**.

ligand, ligature. See under **ligament**.

liger *lī'gər*, *n* the offspring of a lion and a tigress. [*li*on and *tiger*.]

ligger, ligging. See **lig**.

light¹ *līt*, *n* the agency by which objects are rendered visible; electromagnetic radiation capable of producing visual sensation; anything from which it originates, such as the sun, or a lamp; a high degree of illumination; day; a gleam or shining from a bright source; a gleam or glow in the eye or on the face; means of igniting or illuminating; a lighthouse; mental or spiritual illumination; enlightenment; a hint, clue, help towards understanding; an aperture for admitting light; a vertical division of a window. — *adj* not dark; bright; whitish; well lit. — *vt* to shine light on, provide light in; to set fire to; to follow or proceed (someone, or their path) with a light: — *pr p* **light'ing**; *pa t* and *pa p* **light'ed** or **lit**. — *n* **light'er** a person who sets alight; a means of igniting, esp. a small device for igniting cigarettes. — *n*

light'ing illumination; ignition; arrangement or quality of lights. — Also *adj*. — *adj* **light'ish**. — *n* **light'ness**. — **light'-box** a box-shaped device with an internal lamp to facilitate viewing through paper, negatives, etc. placed on its translucent surface; **light bulb** a glass bulb containing a metal filament which glows when an electric current is passed through it, one of the most common methods of electric lighting; **light-emitting diode** a semiconducting device that emits light when an electric current passes through it, as used for alphanumeric displays in digital clocks, electronic calculators, etc. (abbrev. **LED**). — *adj* **light'-fast** (of colour in fabric, or coloured fabric) not liable to fade from prolonged exposure to light. — **light'house** a building with a powerful light to guide or warn off ships or aircraft; **light'houseman** or **light'house-keeper** the person in charge of a lighthouse; **lighting-up time** the time of day from which vehicles must show lights; **light meter** (*phot*) a meter for measuring the level of light present, an exposure meter; **light pen** (*comput*) a pen-shaped photoelectric device that can enter or alter data on a visual display unit; a light-sensitive fibre-optic device shaped like a pen, used for reading bar-coded labels; **light'ship** a ship serving the purpose of a lighthouse; **light'-table** (*printing*) (a table incorporating) a ground-glass surface, illuminated from below, for use when working on (esp. overlaid) translucent materials; **light'-year** the distance light travels in a year (about 6 000 000 000 000 miles). — **according to one's lights** as far as one's knowledge, spiritual illumination, etc., enable one to judge; **bring to light** to reveal; **come to light** to be revealed; **inner light** spiritual illumination; **in one's (or the) light** between the stated person or speaker and the source of illumination; **in the light of** considering, taking into account; **leading light** see under **lead**[1]; **light at the end of the tunnel** an indication that success, completion, etc. is approaching; **lights out** (*mil*) a bugle call or trumpet call for extinction of lights; the time at which lights are turned out for the night in a boarding-school, barracks, etc.; **light up** to light one's lamp, pipe, cigarette, etc.; to make or become light, bright, happy, etc.; **northern** and **southern lights** the aurora borealis and australis respectively; **see the light** to come into view or being; to realise a fact, mistake, etc.; to be religiously converted; **shed** or **throw light on** to clarify, help to explain. [M.E. *liht* — O.E. *leht*, *lēht*.]

light[2] *līt*, *adj* not heavy; of incorrectly short weight; (of work) easily suffered or performed; easily digested; (of bread) well risen; containing little alcohol; not heavily armed; not heavily burdened or equipped; unimportant; not dense or copious or intense; slight; gentle, delicate; nimble; frivolous; unheeding; gay, lively; amusing; (of soil) loose, sandy; falling short in the number of tricks one has contracted to make (*bridge*). — *adv* lightly. — *vt* **light'en** to make lighter. — *vi* to become lighter. — *n* **light'er** a large open boat used in unloading and loading ships. — *n* **light'erage** loading, unloading and ferrying by lighters; the payment for such service. — *adj* **light'ish**. — *adv* **light'ly** in a light manner; slightly. — *n* **light'ness**. — *npl* **lights** the lungs of an animal. — *adj* **light-armed'** (*mil*) armed in a manner suitable for activity. — **light'erman** a person employed in lighterage. — *adj* **lighter-than-air'** (of aircraft) kept aloft by gas which is lighter than air. — *adj* **light-fing'ered** light or active with one's fingers; inclined to steal. — *adj* **light-foot'ed** nimble, active. — *adj* **light-hand'ed** with a light, delicate or dexterous touch; insufficiently manned. — *adj* **light-head'ed** giddy in the head; delirious; thoughtless; unsteady, esp. through slight drunkenness. — **light-head'edness**. — *adj* **light-heart'ed** free from anxiety; cheerful. — *adv* **light-heart'edly**. — **light-heart'edness**; **light-heavyweight** see under **heavy**; **light horse** light-armed cavalry; **light industry** see **industry**; **light infantry** light-armed infantry; **light-middleweight** see **middleweight**; **light'weight** a weight category applied in boxing and wrestling; a sportsman of the specified weight for the category (e.g., in professional boxing above featherweight, **jun'ior-lightweight** (maximum 59 kg./130 lb.) and **light'weight** (maximum 61 kg./135 lb.)); a person of little importance or authority; a light article of any kind, e.g. a motorcycle. — *adj* light in weight; lacking substance, earnestness, solemnity, etc. — **lighten up** (*slang*; esp. *US*) to become less serious, angry, or otherwise emotional; **make light of** to treat as being of little consequence. [O.E. *līht*.]

light[3] *līt*, *vi* to dismount, alight; to come down e.g. from a horse or vehicle or from a fall or flight; to settle; to rest; to come upon by chance: — *pr p* **light'ing**; *pa t* and *pa p* **light'ed** or **lit**. — **light into** (*colloq*) to attack, with blows or words; **light out** (*colloq*) to decamp, run away. [O.E. *līhtan*, to dismount, lit. make light; see **light**[1].]

lighten[1] *lī'tn*, *vt* to make light or lighter, or brighter. — to illuminate. — *vi* to become light, lighter or brighter. — *n* **light'ening** a making or becoming lighter or brighter. [Ety. as for **light**[1].]

lighten[2]. See **light**[2].

lightning *līt'ning*, *n* flashes of light in the sky, caused by electricity being discharged from thunderclouds. — *adj* characterised by speed and suddenness. — **light'ning-conductor** or **-rod** a metallic rod for protecting buildings from lightning; **lightning strike** an industrial or military strike done without warning. [Ety. as for **light**[1].]

lignocaine *lig'nə-kān*, *n* a local anaesthetic used e.g. in dentistry and also to regulate an unsteady heartbeat. [L. *lignum*, wood, and *cocaine*.]

lignum *lig'nəm*, *n* wood. — *adj* **lig'neous** woody; wooden. — *n* **lignificā'tion**. — *adj* **lig'niform** resembling wood. — *vt* and *vi* **lig'nify** to turn into wood or make woody: — *pr p* **lig'nifying**; *pa t* and *pa p* **lig'nified**. — *n* **lig'nin** a complicated mixture of substances deposited in the thickened cell-walls of plants, making them rigid. — *n* **lig'nite** (*-nīt*) brown coal, a stage in the conversion of vegetable matter into coal. — *adj* **lignitic** (*-nit'ik*). — *n* **ligno-cell'ulose** any of several compounds of lignin and cellulose occurring in woody tissue. — **lignum vitae** (*vī'tē* or *vē'tī*; L., wood of life) the wood of a tropical American genus of trees, *Guaiacum*. [L. *lignum*, wood.]

likable. See **likeable** under **like**[2].

like[1] *līk*, *adj* identical, equal, or nearly equal in any respect; similar, resembling; suiting, befitting; characteristic of; used in requesting a description, as in *what is it like*?; used in combination to form adjs. from nouns, with the force 'resembling', 'suitable to', 'typical of', e.g. *catlike*, *ladylike*; used in combination to form adjs. and advs. from adjs. with the force 'somewhat', 'kind of', e.g. *stupid-like* (*colloq*). — *n* one of the same kind; the same thing; an exact resemblance. — *adv* in the same manner. — *conj* (*colloq*) as; as if. — *prep* in the same manner as; to the same extent as. — *n* **like'lihood** probability. — *n* **like'liness** likelihood. — *adj* **like'ly** promising; probable; credible. — *adv* (*colloq*) probably. — *vt* **li'ken** to represent as like or similar; to compare. — *n* **like'ness** a resemblance; semblance, guise; a person who or thing which has a resemblance; a portrait. — *adv* **like'wise** in the same or similar manner; moreover; too. — *adj* **like-mind'ed** having similar opinions, values, etc. — **compare like with like** to compare only such things as are genuinely comparable; **feel like** to be disposed or inclined towards; used in requesting a description, as in *what does it feel like*?; **look like** to show a probability of; to appear similar to; used in requesting a description, as in *what does it look like?*; **something like (a)** a fine specimen, a model of what the thing should be; around, approximately; **such like** of that kind, similar; **the like** (*colloq*) similar things; **the likes of** people such as. [O.E. *līc*, seen in *gelīc*.]

like[2] *līk*, *vt* to be fond of; to be pleased with; to approve; to enjoy. — *n* a liking, chiefly in the phrase 'likes and dislikes'. — *adj* **lī'kable** or **like'able** lovable; amiable, pleasant. — *n* **lī'ker.** — *n* **lī'king** affection, fondness; taste, preference; satisfaction. [Orig. impersonal — O.E. *līcian*, to please, to be suitable — *līc*, like, suitable, likely.]

lilac *lī'lək*, *n* a European tree of the olive family, with light-purple or white flowers, or other species of the genus; a light purple colour (also *adj*). [Fr. (obs.; now *lilas*) and Sp.]

lilangeni *lil-ən-gen'i*, *n* the standard unit of currency of Swaziland (100 cents): — *pl* **emalangeni** (*em-ə-lən-gen'i*).

liliaceous, lilied, etc. See **lily.**

Lilliputian *lil-i-pū'shən*, *n* an inhabitant of **Lill'iput** (*-po͝ot*), an imaginary country described by Swift in *Gulliver's Travels*, inhabited by pygmies; a midget, pygmy. — *adj* (also without *cap*) diminutive.

LILO *abbrev* for last in, last out (a rough guide to likely order of redundancies).

Lilo® *lī'lō*, *n* (also without *cap*) an inflatable mattress, used in camping, etc.

lilt *lilt*, *vi* and *vt* to sing or play, esp. merrily, or vaguely and absent-mindedly, giving the swing or cadence rather than the structure of the melody. — *n* a cheerful song or air; cadence, movement of a tune or the like; a springy quality in gait, etc. [M.E. *lulte*.]

lily *lil'i*, *n* any plant or flower of the genus **Lil'ium,** typical genus of **Liliā'ceae**; extended to other plants; the fleur-de-lis; a person or thing of great purity or whiteness. — *adj* white; pale. — *adj* **liliā'ceous.** — *adj* **lil'ied** adorned with lilies; resembling lilies. — *adj* **lil'y-livered** cowardly. — **lily pad** a leaf of a waterlily. — *adj* **lil'y-white.** — **lily of the valley** *Convallaria*, a plant related to the lilies, with two long oval leaves and spikes of white bell-shaped flowers. [O.E. *lilie* — L. *līlium* — Gr. *leirion*, lily.]

lima *lī'mə* or *lē'mə*, *n* (in full **Lima bean**) a flattened, whitish, edible bean, the seed of a tropical American plant related to the French bean — also called **butter bean.** [*Lima* in Peru.]

limail. See **lemel.**

limb[1] *lim*, *n* an arm, leg or wing; a projecting part; a main branch of a tree, spur of a mountain, etc.; a member of a body of people, as in *a limb of the law*; an imp, mischievous child, as in *a limb of Satan*. — *adj* **limbed** having limbs, esp. in combination, as in *long-limbed*. — *adj* **limb'less.** — **out on a limb** in a hazardous position on one's own. [O.E. *lim*.]

limb[2] *lim*, *n* an edge or border, e.g. of the sun, etc.; the edge of a sextant, etc.; the free or expanded part of a floral or other leaf (*bot*). — *adj* **lim'bate** bordered. — *adj* **lim'bous** overlapping. [L. *limbus*, a border.]

limber[1] *lim'bər*, (*mil*) *n* the detachable forepart of a gun carriage. — *vt* to attach to the limber.

limber[2] *lim'bər*, *adj* pliant, flexible, supple. — *vt* to make limber. — **limber up** to loosen up the muscles in preparation for physical effort of some sort.

limber[3] *lim'bər*, (*naut*) *n* (usu. in *pl*) a channel or hole on either side of the inner keel for drainage. [Fr. *lumière* — L. *lumināria*, windows.]

limbic *lim'bik*, *adj* of, or relating to, the **limbic system** in the brain, the hypothalamus, etc., concerned with basic emotions. [L. *limbicus* — *limbus*, border.]

Limbo or **limbo** *lim'bō*, *n* the borderland of Hell, reserved for the unbaptised; any unsatisfactory place of consignment or oblivion; an uncertain or intermediate state; prison: — *pl* **Lim'bos** or **lim'bos.** [From the Latin phrase *in limbo*, *in*, in, *limbus*, border.]

limbo *lim'bō*, *n* a West Indian dance in which the dancer bends backwards and passes under a bar which is progressively lowered: — *pl* **lim'bos.**

Limburger *lim'bûrg-ər*, *n* a white cheese from *Limburg* in Belgium, with a strong taste and smell. — Also **Limburger cheese.**

lime[1] *līm*, *n* bird-lime, a sticky substance for catching birds; the white caustic earth (calcium oxide, quicklime, caustic lime) obtained by driving off water and carbon dioxide from calcium carbonate (as limestone); calcium hydroxide (slaked lime) obtained by adding water to quicklime; (*loosely*) limestone or calcium carbonate. — *adj* of lime. — *vt* to cover with lime; to treat with lime; to manure with lime; to ensnare, trap. — *n* **lī'miness.** — *n* **lī'ming** the soaking of skins in limewater to remove hair; application of lime. — *adj* **lī'my** smeared with, containing, like, or of the nature of, lime. — **lime'kiln** a kiln or furnace in which calcium carbonate is reduced to lime; **lime'light** light produced by a blowpipe-flame directed against a block of quicklime; the glare of publicity (from a type of lamp formerly used in theatre stage lighting, which used heated lime to provide light). — *vt* to illuminate by limelight, to subject to the glare of limelight: — *pa t* and *pa p* **lime'lit** or **lime'lighted.** — **lime'pit** a lime-filled pit in which hides are steeped to remove hair; **lime'stone** a sedimentary rock of calcium carbonate; **lime'wash** a milky mixture of slaked lime and water, used for coating walls, etc.; **lime'-water** a suspension of calcium hydroxide in water, sometimes used as an antacid. [O.E. *līm*.]

lime[2] *līm*, *n* a tropical citrus tree; its small nearly globular fruit, with acid-tasting pulp; the colour of the fruit, a yellowish green. — *n* **lime'y** (*NAm slang*) a British sailor or ship (from the use of lime-juice on British ships to prevent scurvy); any British person. — **lime'-juice.** [Fr., — Sp. *lima*; cf. **lemon**[1].]

lime[3] *līm*, *n* the linden tree (of the genus *Tilia*), or other tree of the genus, with heart-shaped leaves and small yellowish flowers. — **lime'-tree; lime'-wood.** [Ety. as for **linden.**]

limen *lī'men*, (*psychol*) *n* the threshold of consciousness; the limit below which a stimulus is not perceived. — *adj* **liminal** (*lim'i-nəl*). [L. *līmen*, *-inis*, threshold.]

limerick *lim'ə-rik*, *n* a form of humorous verse with five lines. [Said to be from a refrain formerly used, referring to *Limerick* in Ireland.]

limey. See **lime**[2].

limit *lim'it*, *n* a boundary, esp. one which may not be passed; a restriction; a predetermined price at which a broker is instructed to buy or sell (*stock exchange*); a value, position or figure that can be approached indefinitely (*math*); that which is bounded, a region or division; (with *the*) the unspeakable extreme of what may be endured (*colloq*). — *vt* to confine within bounds; to restrict. — *adj* **lim'itable.** — *adj* **lim'itary** (*-ə-ri*) of a boundary; placed at the boundary; confined within limits. — *n* **limitā'tion** a limiting; a lack of physical ability, talent, etc.; a specified period within which an action must be brought, etc. (*law*). — *adj* **lim'itātive** tending to limit. — *adj* **lim'ited** within limits; narrow; restricted. — *adv* **lim'itedly.** — *n* **lim'itedness.** — *n* **lim'iter** a person, device or circumstance that limits or confines. — *n* and *adj* **lim'iting.** — *adj* **lim'itless** having no limits; boundless; immense; infinite. — *adv* **lim'itlessly.** — *n* **lim'itlessness.** — **limited edition** an edition, esp. of a book, of which only a certain number of copies is printed or made; **limited liability** see under **liable; limited (-liability) company** one whose owners have liability for its debts, etc. only according to their financial stake in it. — **off limits** out of bounds; **statute of limitations** an act specifying the period within which a certain action must be taken; **within limits** to a limited extent. [L. *līmes*, *-itis*, boundary.]

limnetic *lim-net'ik*, *adj* living in fresh water. — *adj* **limnolog'ical**. — *n* **limnol'ogist**. — *n* **limnol'ogy** the scientific study (embracing physical, geographical, biological, etc. characteristics) of lakes and other freshwater bodies. — *adj* **limnoph'ilous** living in ponds or marshes. [Gr. *limnē*, a pool or marsh.]

limo *lim'ō*, (*colloq*; esp. *US*) short for **limousine**.

limonite *lī'mə-nīt*, *n* brown iron ore, hydrated ferric oxide, a deposit in bogs and lakes (*bog-iron*) or a decomposition product in rocks. — *adj* **limonitic** (*-it'ik*). [Gr. *leimōn*, a meadow.]

Limousin *lē-mōō-zē̃*, *n* a breed of cattle. [*Limousin*, a district in France.]

limousine *lim'ə-zēn*, *n* a large closed motor car which has a partition separating driver and passengers; (*loosely*) any large motor car (sometimes used *ironically*). [Fr., after a type of long cloak once worn in the *Limousin* district (see above).]

limp[1] *limp*, *adj* lacking stiffness; flaccid; drooping; (of a cloth binding for books) not stiffened by boards. — *n* **limp'ness**.

limp[2] *limp*, *vi* to walk unevenly, esp. when one leg is injured; (of a damaged ship or aircraft) to proceed with difficulty. — *n* a limping gait. — *n* and *adj* **limp'ing**. — *adv* **limp'ingly**. [O.E. *lemp-healt*, halting.]

limpet *lim'pit*, *n* a gasteropod with a conical shell, that clings to rocks; a person not easily got rid of. — **limpet mine** an explosive device designed to cling to a surface, esp. one attached to a ship's hull by a magnet, etc. [O.E. *lempedu*, lamprey.]

limpid *lim'pid*, *adj* clear; transparent. — *n* **limpid'ity**. — *adv* **lim'pidly**. — *n* **lim'pidness**. [L. *limpidus*.]

limpkin *limp'kin*, *n* an American wading bird like a rail. [From its limping gait.]

limy. See **lime**[1].

lin. See **linn**.

lin. *abbrev* for: lineal; linear.

linchpin *linch'pin* or *linsh'pin*, *n* a pin used to keep a wheel on its axle; a person or thing essential to a plan, organisation, etc. [O.E. *lynis*, axle, and **pin**.]

Lincoln-green *ling'kən-grēn*, *n* a bright green cloth once made at *Lincoln*; its colour.

lincomycin *ling-kō-mī'sin*, *n* an antibiotic used against streptococcal and staphylococcal infections, produced from the bacterium *Streptomyces lincolnensis*. [L. *linco*lnensis and *-mycin*.]

lincrusta *lin-krus'tə*, *n* a thick, embossed type of wallpaper. [L. *līnum*, flax, *crusta*, rind, on analogy of **linoleum**.]

Lincs. *lingks*, *abbrev* for Lincolnshire.

linctus *lingk'təs*, *n* a syruplike medicine for coughing and sore throats: — *pl* **linc'tuses**. [L. *linctus*, *-ūs*, a licking.]

linden *lin'dən*, *n*. Same as **lime**[3]. [O.E. *lind*.]

line[1] *līn*, *vt* to cover on the inside; to fill, stuff; to reinforce, strengthen (esp. books); to be placed all along the side of; to serve as lining for. — *adj* **lined** having a lining. — *n* **lin'er** a person who lines things; something which serves as a lining; a sleeve of metal, resistant to wear and corrosion, etc., fitted inside or outside a cylinder, tube, etc. (*eng*); a sleeve for a gramophone record, or an insert inside it, or the text printed on either (usu. **liner notes**). — *n* **līn'ing** the action of a person who lines; material applied to a surface, esp. material on the inner surface of a garment, etc.; contents. — **line one's pockets** to make a profit, esp. dishonestly. [O.E. *līn*, flax; cf. ety. for **line**[2].]

line[2] *līn*, *n* a thread, string, cord or rope, esp. one for fishing, sounding, hanging clothes on, or guidance; something which has length without breadth or thickness (*math*); a long narrow mark, a streak, stroke, or narrow stripe; a row; a row of printed or written characters, ships, soldiers, etc.; a series or succession, e.g. of descendants; a service of ships, buses, etc. or a company running them; a course, route or system; a railway or tramway track or route; a stretch or route of telegraph, telephone, or power wires or cables; a connection by telephone; an order given to an agent for goods; such goods received; (trade in, or the stock on hand of) any particular product; a rank, column of figures, etc.; a short letter or note; a wrinkle, esp. on the face; a trench or other military position; a limit; method; policy; a rule or canon; (with **the**; often with *cap*) the equator; lineage, ancestry; direction; occupation; course; province or sphere of life, interest or taste; the regular army; glib talk, not always honest (*slang*); in a TV, the path traversed by the electron beam or scanning spot in moving once from side to side (horizontal scanning) or from top to bottom (vertical scanning) of the picture; (in *pl*) a certificate of marriage or of church membership; (in *pl*) the words of an actor's part; (in *pl*) a school punishment of writing out a phrase or sentence a wearisome number of times. — *vt* to mark out with lines; to cover with lines; to put in line; to form a line along. — *vi* to take a place in line. — *n* **linage** or **lineage** (*lī'nij*) measurement or payment by the line, as in newspapers; number of lines. — *n* **lineage** (*lin'i-ij*) ancestry. — *adj* **lineal** (*lin'i-əl*) of or belonging to a line or lines or one dimension; composed of lines; in the direction of a line; in, of, or transmitted by, direct line of descent, or legitimate descent. — *n* **lineality** (*-al'i-ti*). — *adv* **lin'eally**. — *n* **lineament** (*lin'i-ə-mənt*) a feature; a distinguishing mark in the form esp. of the face. — *adj* **linear** (*lin'i-ər*) of or belonging to a line; in or of one dimension; consisting of, or having the form of, lines; long and very narrow, with parallel sides; capable of being represented on a graph by a straight line; of a system in which doubling the cause doubles the effect. — *n* **linearity** (*lin-i-ar'i-ti*). — *adv* **lin'early**. — *adj* **lin'eate** or **lin'eated** marked with lines. — *n* **lineā'tion** marking with lines; arrangement of or in lines. — *adj* **lined** (*līnd*) marked with lines; having a line. — *adj* **lineolate** (*lin'i-ə-lāt*) marked with fine lines. — *n* **lī'ner** a person who makes, marks, draws, paints or writes lines; a paint-brush for making lines; a line-fisherman; a line-fishing boat; any large passenger-carrying vessel or aircraft of a particular company; colouring matter used to outline the eyes. — *n* **lī'ning** alignment; the making of a line; use of a line; marking with lines. — *adj* **lī'ny** or **lī'ney**. — **linear accelerator** an apparatus in which electrons are accelerated while travelling down a metal tube or tubes, e.g. by means of electromagnetic waves; **linear equation** an equation with more than two terms, of which none is raised above the power one; **linear motor** an electric motor which produces direct thrust, without the use of gears; **linear programming** programming which enables a computer to give an optimum result when fed with a number of unrelated variables, used in determining the most efficient arrangement of e.g. an industrial process; **line'backer** (*Am football*) a defensive player whose position is just behind the line of scrimmage; **line block** a printing block consisting of black and white only, without gradations of tone; **line drawing** a drawing in pen or pencil using lines only, without gradations of tone; **line'-engraver**; **line'-engraving** the process of engraving in lines, steel or copperplate engraving; an engraving so done; **line'-fish** one taken with a line rather than a net; **line'-fisher** or **line'-fisherman**; **line'-fishing**; **line judge** an official whose job is to watch a line to see which side of it the ball falls (*lawn tennis*); **line'man** a person who attends to the lines of a railway, telegraph, telephone, or electric-light wires, etc.; a player in the forward line (*Am football*); **line'-out** (*Rugby football*) a method of restarting play when the ball has gone into touch, the forwards of each team lining up behind each other facing the touch-line and trying to catch or deflect the ball when it is thrown in; **linesman** (*līnz'mən*) a lineman; (in Association football) an official who marks the spot at which the ball goes into touch; a line judge; **line'-up** arrangement in line; putting or coming into line; a queue; an identification parade; the bill of artists appearing in a show; a list of team members. — **above the line** (of advertising) through the media and by poster; **all along the line** at every point; **below the line** (of advertising) by such means as free gifts, direct mailings to households, etc.; **bring into line** to cause to conform; **down the line** of a shot, travelling parallel to and close to the side of the court (*tennis*); in the future (*colloq*); **end of the line** a point beyond which it is useless or impossible to proceed; **fall into line** to conform; **get a line on** (*slang*) to get information about; **in line** in a straight line; in agreement or harmony (with *with*); in contention (with *for*); in a line of succession (with *to*); **lay it on the line** (*colloq*) to speak out firmly and frankly; **lay** or **put on the line** to risk, stake (a reputation, etc.); **line of country** one's field of study or interest; **line of sight** the straight line between the eye and the object on which it is focused, or between two objects along which they are visible from each other (also **line of vision**); the straight line along which the eye looks, in any direction; the straight line between a transmitter and the receiving antenna (*telecomm*); **line up** to bring into alignment; to make a stand (*in support of*, or *against*); to gather together in readiness; to arrange (for a person); **on** or **along the lines of** in a (specified) manner or direction; **read between the lines** to infer what is not explicitly stated. [Partly from O.E. *līne*, cord (from or cognate with L. *līnum*, flax), partly through Fr. *ligne*, and partly directly from L. *līnea*; cf. **line**[1].]

lineage, lineal, linear, etc. See under **line**[2].

lined. See **line**[1] and **line**[2].

linen *lin'ən*, *n* cloth made of lint or flax; underclothing, orig. of linen; articles of linen, or of other materials generally, such as cotton, rayon, etc., as in *table-linen, bed-linen*. — *adj* of or like linen. — **wash one's dirty linen in public** to expose sordid private affairs. [O.E. *līnen* (adj.) — *līn*, flax; see **line**[1].]

lineolate. See under **line**[2].

ling[1] *ling*, *n* a fish of the cod family.

ling[2] *ling*, *n* heather. — *adj* **ling'y**. [O.N. *lyng*.]

-ling *-ling*, *sfx* forming nouns and denoting a diminutive, such as duck*ling*; hence expressing affection, as in dar*ling* (O.E. *dēorling*); sometimes implying deprecation, as in under*ling*.

lingam *ling'gam*, *n* the Hindu phallus, a symbol of Siva. — Also **ling'a**. [Sans.]

linger *ling'gər*, *vi* to remain for long; to be left, remain behind; to delay, in reluctance to leave; to loiter; to be protracted; to remain alive, although gradually dying. — *n* **ling'erer**. — *n* and *adj* **ling'ering**. — *adv* **ling'eringly**. [Frequentative from O.E. *lengan*, to protract — *lang*, long.]

lingerie *lẽzh'ə-rē*, *n* women's underclothing. [Fr., — *linge*, linen — L. *līnum*, flax, thread, linen.]

lingo *ling'gō*, *n* a language, esp. one poorly regarded or not understood; the jargon of a profession or class: — *pl* **ling'oes**. [Prov. *lengo, lingo*, or some other form of L. *lingua*, language.]

lingua *ling'gwə*, *n* (*anat*) the tongue; a tonguelike structure. — *adj* **ling'ual** relating to the tongue; pronounced using the tongue (*phon*); (of a tooth-surface) facing towards the tongue (*dentistry*). — *adv* **ling'ually**. — *adj* **ling'uiform** tongue-shaped. — *n* **ling'uist** a person who has a good knowledge of languages; a person who studies linguistics; in West Africa, an intermediary between chief or priest, and the people. — *adj* **linguist'ic** or **linguist'ical** pertaining to languages or knowledge or the study of languages. — *adv* **linguist'ically**. — *n* **linguisti'cian** a student of linguistics. — *nsing* **linguist'ics** the scientific study of language in its widest sense, in every aspect and in all its varieties. — *n* **lingula** (*ling'gū-lə*) a little tonguelike part. — *adj* **ling'ular** pertaining to a lingula. — *adj* **ling'ulate** tongue-shaped. — **lingua franca** (*ling'gwə frang'kə*; It., Frankish language) a mixed Italian trade jargon used in the Levant; a language chosen as a medium of communication among speakers of different languages; any hybrid language used for the same purpose; the familiar conventions of any style (esp. in music or the arts) readily recognised and understood by devotees. [L. *lingua* (for *dingua*), the tongue.]

linguini *ling-gwē'nē* or **linguine** *-gwē'nā*, *npl* a style of pasta made in long thin flat pieces. [It., pl. of *linguino, linguina*, dimins. of *lingua*, tongue.]

lingula, lingular, lingulate. See under **lingua**.

liniment *lin'i-mənt*, *n* a thin ointment; an embrocation for relieving muscular stiffness. [L. *linīmentum* — *linīre, linĕre*, to smear.]

lining. See under **line**[1] and **line**[2].

link *lingk*, *n* a ring of a chain, chain-mail, etc.; anything that connects; a unit in a communications system; the 1/100th part of the surveyor's chain, 7·92 in. (approx. 20 cm.); a segment or unit in a connected series; a cuff-link. — *vt* to connect, join up. — *vi* to be or become connected; to go arm-in-arm. — *n* **link'age** an act or mode of linking; the fact of being linked; a system of links, a connection; a chemical bond. — **link man** a person who provides a connection, e.g. by passing on information, or by holding together separate items of e.g. a broadcast programme; **link'-motion** reversing gear of a steam engine; a system of pieces moving as a linkage; **link'-up** a connection, union. — **missing link** any point or fact needed to complete a series or a chain of thought or argument; an intermediate form in the evolution of man from his ape ancestors.

links *lingks*, *npl* (often treated as *nsing*) a stretch of flat or gently undulating ground along a seashore; a golf course orig. by the sea. [O.E. *hlinc*, a ridge of land, a bank.]

linn or **lin** *lin*, *n* a waterfall; a pool at the foot of a waterfall; a deep ravine. [O.E. *hlynn*, a torrent, combined with Gael. *linne*, Ir. *linn*, Welsh *llyn*, pool.]

Linnaean or **Linnean** *li-nē'ən* or *-nā'ən*, *adj* pertaining to *Linnaeus* or *Linné*, the Swedish botanist (1707–78), or to his artificial system of classification.

linnet *lin'it*, *n* a common finch, feeding on flax seed. — **green linnet** the greenfinch. [O.Fr. *linette, linot* — *lin*, flax — L. *līnum*.]

linoleic *lin-ə-lē'ik* (or **linolenic** *lin-ə-lē'nik*) **acid** *as'id*, *n* highly unsaturated fatty acids obtained from the glycerides of certain fats and oils, such as linseed oil, and constituting Vitamin F.

linoleum *lin-ō'li-əm*, *n* stiff hard-wearing floor-covering made by impregnating a fabric with a mixture of oxidised linseed-oil, resins and fillers (esp. cork). — Also *adj*. — Also **lino** (*lī'nō*; *colloq*): — *pl* **lī'nos**. — **linocut** (*lī'nō-kut*) a design cut in relief in linoleum; a print from such a block; **lino tile** a floor tile made of linoleum or a similar material. [L. *līnum*, flax, *oleum*, oil.]

Linotype® *lī'nō-tīp*, *n* a machine for producing stereotyped lines of printer's type; a slug or line of printing-type cast in one piece by this method.

linseed *lin'sēd*, *n* flax seed. — **lin'seed-cake** the cake remaining when the oil is pressed out of lint or flax seed, used as a food for sheep and cattle; **linseed-oil'** oil extracted from flax seed, having many industrial applications. [O.E. *līn*, flax, *saed*, seed.]

linsey *lin'zi*, *n* cloth made from linen and wool. — Also *adj*. — **linsey-woolsey** (*-wŏŏl'zi*) a thin coarse material of linen and wool mixed, or inferior wool with cotton. — *adj* made of linen and wool; neither one thing nor another, presenting a confusing mixture.

lint *lint*, *n* scraped linen, or a cotton substitute, for dressing wounds; cotton fibre (esp. *US*); raw cotton. — *adj* **lint'y**. [M.E. *lynt*, *lynet*.]

lintel *lin'tl*, *n* a timber or stone over a doorway or window. — *adj* **lin'telled**. [O.Fr. *lintel* (Fr. *linteau*) — a dimin. of L. *līmes*, *-itis*, border.]

lion *lī'ən*, *n* a large, fierce, tawny, loud-roaring animal of the cat family, the male having a shaggy mane (*fem* **li'oness**); a person of unusual courage; (with *cap*) the constellation or the sign Leo (*astron* and *astrol*). — *vt* **li'onise** or **-ize** to treat as a hero or celebrity. — *n* **li'onism** lionising; a lionlike appearance occurring in leprosy. — *adj* **li'onlike** or **li'only**. — **li'on-cub** a young lion; **li'on-heart** a person of great courage. — *adj* **li'on-hearted**. — **li'on-hunter; lion's mouth** a dangerous position; **lion's share** the whole or greater part; **li'on-tāmer**. [A.Fr. *liun* — L. *leō*, *-ōnis* — Gr. *leōn*, *-ontos*.]

lip *lip*, *n* either of the muscular flaps in front of the teeth, forming the opening to the mouth; any similar feature, such as either of the two divisions of a liplike flower corolla; the edge or rim of an orifice, cavity, deep geographical depression, vessel, etc.; part of such a rim bent outwards like a spout; insolence, cheek (*slang*); used in combination signifying from the lips only, not sincere. — *vt* to touch with the lips; to kiss; to wash, overflow, or overrun the edge of; to form a lip on; (of a golfer or shot) to get the ball to the very edge of (the hole). — *vi* to use the lips in playing a wind-instrument; to lap at the brim; to have water lapping over: — *pr p* **lipp'ing**; *pa t* and *pa p* **lipped**. — *adj* of the lip; formed or sounded by the lips. — *adj* **lip'less**. — *adj* **lipped** (*lipt*) having a lip or lips; labiate. — *adj* **lipp'y** having a hanging lip; saucy, cheeky (*slang*). — **lip'gloss** a substance applied to the lips to give them a glossy appearance. — *vi* **lip'=read**. — **lip'-reader; lip'-reading** gathering what a person says by watching the movement of their lips; **lip'-rounding** rounding of the lips, as in pronouncing *o* (*phon*); **lip'-salve** ointment for the lips; **lip'=service** insincere praise or worship; professed, not real, belief, respect or loyalty. — *adj* **lip'-smacking** (*colloq*) delicious, appetising. — **lip'stick** (a short stick of) colouring for the lips. — *vt* and *vi* to paint with (a) lipstick. — **lip-sync** or **lip-synch** (*lip'-singk*) the synchronisation of lip movements with already recorded sound, esp. by singers making television appearances; the synchronisation of the voice with already filmed lip-movements (in dubbing; also *vt* and *vi*). — **bite one's lip** to do this in manifesting annoyance or in attempting to repress laughter, tears, an angry retort, etc.; **hang on someone's lips** to listen eagerly to all that someone has to say; **(keep) a stiff upper lip** (to show) resolution, with no yielding to emotion; **smack one's lips** to bring the lips together and part them with a smacking noise, as an indication of relish. [O.E. *lippa*.]

lip- *lip-* or **lipo-** *lip-ō-*, *lip-ə-* or *li-po'-*, also *lī-*, *combining form* denoting fat. — *n* **lip'ase** (*-ās* or *-āz*) an enzyme that breaks up fats. — *n* **lip'id**, sometimes **lip'ide** (*-īd*), any of a group of chemicals found in bodily tissues, including fats, oils and waxes (esters of fatty acids), derivatives of these, and other substances such as steroids and terpenes. — *adj* **lip'oid** fatlike. — *n* a fatlike substance; a lipid. — *n* **lipō'ma** a fatty tumour: — *pl* **lipō'mata**. — *n* **lipomatō'sis** the excessive growth of fat. — *adj* **lipō'matous**. — *n* **lipoprō'tein** a water-soluble protein found in the blood, which carries cholesterol. — *adj* **liposō'mal**. — *n* **lip'ōsome** a naturally occurring lipid globule in the cytoplasm of a cell; an artificial droplet of an aqueous substance surrounded by a lipid, used in the treatment of various diseases. — *n* **lip'ōsuction** a surgical process for the removal of excess, unwanted fat from the body. [Gr. *lipos*, fat.]

Lipizzaner *lip-it-sä'nər*, *n* (an example of) a breed of horses (usu. grey or white in colour) particularly suited and trained for displays of dressage. — Also **Lippiza'ner, Lippizza'ner, Lippiza'na** (*-nə*) or **Lippizza'na**. [*Lipizza* (*Lippiza* or *Lippizza*), near Trieste, where orig. bred.]

lipo-, etc. See **lip-**.

liq. *abbrev* for liquid.

liquate *lik'wāt*, *vt* to melt; to subject to liquation. — *adj* **liq'uable**. — *n* **liquā'tion** melting; separation of metals with different melting-points. [L. *liquāre*, *-ātum*, to liquefy.]

liquefy *lik'wi-fī*, *vt* and *vi* to make or become liquid: — *pr p* **liq'uefying**; *pa t* and *pa p* **liq'uefied**. — *n* and *adj* **liquefacient** (*-fā'shənt*). — *n* **liquefaction** (*-fak'shən*). — *adj* **liq'uefiable**. — *n* **liq'uefier**. — **liquefied petroleum gas** propane or butane under moderate pressure, used in some vehicles in place of petrol or diesel fuel. [L. *liquefacĕre* — *liquēre*, to be liquid, *facĕre*, to make.]

liquesce *li-kwes'*, *vi* to become liquid. — *n* **liquesc'ence** or **liquesc'ency**. — *adj* **liquesc'ent**. [L. *liquēscĕre* — *liquēre*, to be liquid.]

liqueur *li-kūr'* or *li-kœr'*, *n* an alcoholic preparation flavoured or perfumed and sweetened, e.g. chartreuse, cherry brandy. — *adj* (of brandy or whisky) that may be drunk as a liqueur. — **liqueur'-glass** a very small drinking-glass. [Fr., — L. *liquor*; see **liquor**.]

liquid *lik'wid*, *adj* flowing, fluid; watery; in a state between solid and gas, in which the molecules move freely about one another but do not fly apart (*phys*); clear; (of sound, etc.) free from harshness; unfixed; readily converted into cash. — *n* a fluid substance; a flowing consonant sound such as *l* or *r*. — *vt* **liq'uidate** to bring the trading of (a commercial firm, etc.) to an end; to turn (assets) into cash; to dispose of; to wipe out, do away with, kill (*slang*). — *vi* to go into liquidation. — *n* **liquidā'tion**. — *n* **liq'uidator**. — *vt* **liq'uidise** or **-ize** to render liquid; to purée (food). — *n* **liq'uidiser** or **-z-** a machine which purées foodstuffs. — *n* **liquid'ity** the state of being liquid; the condition of having liquid assets. — *adv* **liq'uidly**. — *n* **liq'uidness**. — **liquid crystal** a liquid which, like a crystal, has different optical properties depending on its polarity, over a definite range of temperature above its freezing point. — **go into liquidation** (of a commercial firm, etc.) to be wound up, become bankrupt; **liquid crystal display** a display, esp. in electronic instruments, based on the changes in reflectivity of a liquid crystal cell when an electric field is applied. [L. *liquidus*, liquid, clear — *liquēre*, to be clear.]

liquor *lik'ər*, *n* anything liquid, esp. the product of cooking or a similar operation; strong alcoholic drink; any prepared solution, esp. a strong one (*chem*). — *vt* to apply liquor or a solution to. [O.Fr. *licur*, *licour* (Fr. *liqueur*) — L. *liquor*.]

liquorice or **licorice** *lik'ə-ris* (in U.S. also *-rish*), *n* a butterfly-like plant of Europe and Asia; its long sweet root used in medicine; an extract from the root; confectionery having a laxative effect, made from it. — **liquorice allsorts** an assortment of sweets flavoured with liquorice. [A.Fr. *lycorys* — L.L. *liquirītia*, a corruption of Gr. *glykyrrīza* — *glykys*, sweet, *rhīza*, root.]

lira *lē'rə*, *n* the standard Italian monetary unit (100 *centesimi*); the standard monetary unit of Turkey (100 *kurus*): — *pl* **lire** (*lē'rā*) or **li'ras**. [It., — L. *lībra*, a pound.]

lisle *līl*, *n* a long-stapled, hard-twisted cotton yarn. — Also *adj*. [Old spelling of *Lille*, France.]

lisp *lisp*, *vi* to speak with the tongue against the upper teeth or gums, as in pronouncing *th* for *s* or *z*; to articulate childishly; to utter imperfectly. — *vt* to utter with a lisp. — *n* the act or habit of lisping; a defect of speech by which one lisps. — *n* **lisp'er**. — *adj* and *n* **lisp'ing**. — *adv* **lisp'ingly**. [O.E. *wlisp* (adj.), stammering.]

lissome or **lissom** *lis'əm*, *adj* lithe, nimble, flexible. — *n* **liss'omeness** or **liss'omness**.

list[1] *list*, *n* the selvage on woven textile fabrics; a border; a strip, esp. one cut from an edge; (in *pl*; in knightly combat) the boundary of a tilting-ground, hence the ground itself, combat. — *vt* to border; to put list on; to remove the edge from. — *adj* **list'ed** enclosed for tilting, etc.; fought in lists. — **enter the lists** to come forward for a contest, to do battle. [O.E. *līste*.]

list[2] *list*, *n* a catalogue, roll or enumeration (of items). — *vt* to place in a list or catalogue; to make a list of; to enrol (e.g. soldiers). — *vi* to enlist (also, **list**, as if for **enlist**). — *n* **list'ing** a list; a position in a list; a printout of all the data stored in a file or the commands in a program (*comput*); an official quotation for stock so that it can be traded on the Stock Exchange; (in *pl*) a guide to currently-running theatrical or other entertainments. — **listed building** one officially listed as being of special architectural or historic interest, which cannot be demolished or altered without (local) government consent; **list price** the recommended price of an article as shown in a manufacturer's catalogue or advertisement. — **active list** the roll of those liable for active military service; **List D schools** since 1969 the name given in Scotland to community homes for young offenders (formerly approved schools). [O.F. *liste*, of Gmc. origin, ultimately the same word as **list**[1], from the sense of a strip of paper.]

list[3] *list*, (*naut*) *vt* to cause to heel or lean over. — *vi* to heel over. — *n* the action or degree of heeling over.

listen *lis'n*, *vi* to attempt to hear something or pay attention (to what is being said or to the person saying it); to follow advice. — *n* an act or period of listening. — *adj* **list'enable** pleasant to listen to. — *n* **listener** (*lis'nər*) a person who listens. — *n* **list'enership** the estimated number of listeners to a radio broadcast. — **listening-in'**. — **listen in** to listen (to a wireless broadcast); to overhear intentionally a message intended for another person; **listen up** (*US colloq*) pay attention, listen hard. [O.E. *hlysnan*, recorded in the Northumbrian form *lysna*.]

listeria *lis-tē'riə*, *n* a bacterium frequently found in certain foods (esp. chicken, soft cheeses, etc.), which if not killed in cooking can affect the central nervous system, causing meningitis, encephalitis, miscarriage and even death in the very young and elderly. — *n* **listeriō'sis** the disease caused by listeria bacteria. [From Joseph *Lister* (1872–1912), surgeon and pioneer of antiseptics.]

listless *list'lis*, *adj* uninterested; languid. — *adv* **list'lessly**. — *n* **list'lessness**. [O.E. *lystan*, impers., to please — *lust*, pleasure.]

lit *lit*, *pa t* and *pa p* of **light**[1] and **light**[3].

lit. *abbrev* for: literal; literally; (*lit*) literature.

litany *lit'ə-ni*, *n* a prayer of supplication, esp. in processions; an appointed form of responsive prayer in public worship in which the same thing is repeated several times; a long list or catalogue, evocative or merely boring. [L.L. *litanīa* — Gr. *litaneiā* — *litesthai*, to pray.]

litchi. See **lychee**.

liter. U.S. spelling of **litre**.

literacy. See under **literate**.

literal *lit'ə-rəl*, *adj* pertaining to, or consisting of, letters of the alphabet; according to the letter, following word for word; not figurative or metaphorical; inclined to use or understand words in a matter-of-fact sense. — *n* a misprint of a letter in a word (*printing*). — *vt* **lit'eralise** or **-ize**. — *n* **lit'eraliser** or **-z-**. — *n* **lit'eralism** strict adherence to the literal form; interpretation that is not figurative or metaphorical; exact and unimaginative rendering (*art*). — *n* **li'teralist**. — *n* **literality** (*-al'i-ti*). — *adv* **lit'erally** (often used by no means literally, merely to reinforce a metaphor). — *n* **lit'eralness**. [L. *litterālis* — *littera* (*lītera*), a letter.]

literary *lit'ə-rə-ri*, *adj* pertaining to, of the nature of, versed in, or practising literature or the writing of books; bookish; (of language) formal, such as found in (esp. older) literature. — *adv* **lit'erarily**. — *n* **lit'erariness**. — *n* **lit'eraryism** a bookish expression. — **literary agent** a person who deals with the business affairs of an author; **literary criticism** (the art of making) qualitative judgments on literary works; **literary executor** a person appointed to deal with unpublished material after an author's death. [L. *līterārius* — *lītera* (*littera*), a letter.]

literate *lit'ə-rit*, *adj* able to read and write; learned, scholarly; having a competence in or with (often used in combination, as in *computer-literate*). — *n* a person who is literate; an educated person without a university degree, esp. a candidate for priestly orders. — *n* **lit'eracy** the condition of being literate. — *npl* **literati** (*-ä'tē*) men and women of letters, the learned. [L. *līterātus* — *lītera* (*littera*), letter.]

literature *lit'rə-chər* or *lit'ə-rə-chər*, *n* the art of composition in prose and verse; the whole body of literary composition universally, or in any language, or on a given subject, etc.; literary matter; printed matter; humane learning; literary culture or knowledge. [L. *līterātūra* — *lītera* (*littera*), a letter.]

lith- *lith-* or **litho-** *lith-ō-*, *lith-ə-* or *li-tho'-*, *combining form* denoting stone or (*med*) calculus. [Gr. *lithos*, stone.]

litharge *lith'ärj*, *n* lead monoxide, obtained for instance in the process of refining silver. [Fr., — Gr. *lithargyros* — *lithos*, a stone, *argyros*, silver.]

lithe *līdh*, *adj* supple, limber. — *adv* **lithe'ly**. — *n* **lithe'ness**. [O.E. *līthe*, soft, mild.]

lithia *lith'i-ə*, *n* lithium oxide, a white crystalline substance that absorbs carbon dioxide and water vapour; lithium in the form of salts, found in mineral waters. — *adj* **lith'ic** relating to or got from lithium. — *n* **lith'ium** (*-i-əm*) the lightest metallic element (symbol **Li**; atomic no. 3), whose salts, esp. lithium carbonate, are used to treat manic depression and other psychiatric illnesses. [Gr. *lithos*, stone.]

litho *lī'thō*, *n* (*pl* **lī'thos**) and *adj* short for **lithograph**, **lithographic**, **lithography**.

litho- *combining form*. See **lith-**.

lithograph *lith'ə-gräf*, (*printing*) *n* a print produced by lithography. — *vt* and *vi* to print by lithography. — *n* **lithographer** (*li-thog'rə-fər*). — *adj* **lithographic** (*lith-ə-graf'ik*). — *adv* **lithograph'ically**. — *n* **lithog'raphy** a method of printing from a stone or metal plate that makes use of the immiscibility of oil and water, the image to be printed being receptive to the oil-based ink, and the rest of the plate to moisture, so that when ink comes into contact with the dampened plate, only the image prints. [Gr. *lithos*, stone, *graphein*, to write.]

lithology *li-thol'ə-ji*, *n* the science of rocks as mineral masses. — *adj* **litholog'ical** (*lith-ə-loj'i-kəl*). — *n* **lithol'ogist**. [Gr. *lithos*, stone, and *-logy*.]

lithophyte *lith'ə-fīt*, *n* a plant that grows on rocks or stones; a stony organism, such as coral. — *adj* **lithophytic** (*-fit'ik*). [Gr. *lithos*, stone, *phyton*, plant.]

lithosphere *lith'ə-sfēr*, (*geol*) *n* the rocky crust of the earth. — *adj* **lithospheric** (*-sfer'ik*). [Gr. *lithos*, stone, *sphaira*, sphere.]

lithotomy *li-thot'ə-mi*, *n* the surgical operation of removing a stone from a bodily organ, esp. the bladder. [Gr. *lithos*, stone, *-tomia*, the operation of cutting.]

lithotripsy *lith'ō-trip-si* or **lithotrity** *li-thot'ri-ti*, *n* the surgical operation of crushing a stone in the bladder, kidney or gall bladder, so that its fragments may be passed naturally from the body. — *n* **litho'tripter** or **lith'otriptor** a device using ultrasound to crush stones in the bladder, etc. [Gr. *lithōn* (genitive pl.) *thryptika*, breakers of stones.]

Lithuanian *li-thū-ā'ni-ən, adj* relating to the republic of *Lithuania* on the Baltic Sea, or its people, or their language. — *n* the Lithuanian language; a native or inhabitant of Lithuania.

lit. hum. *abbrev* for *lit(t)erae humaniores* (L.), lit. the humaner letters, i.e. the humanities, Latin and Greek language and literature.

litigate *lit'i-gāt, vt* and *vi* to dispute, esp. by a lawsuit. — *adj* **lit'igable.** — *adj* **lit'igant** contending at law; engaged in a lawsuit. — *n* a person engaged in a lawsuit. — *n* **litigā'tion.** [L. *litigāre, -ātum* — *lis, litis*, strife, *agĕre*, to do.]

litigious *li-tij'əs, adj* relating to litigation; inclined to engage in lawsuits; open to contention. — *adv* **litig'iously.** — *n* **litig'iousness.** [L. *litigiōsus* — *litigium*, quarrel, dispute.]

litmus *lit'məs, n* a substance obtained from certain lichens, turned red by acids, blue by alkalis. — **litmus paper** a test paper dipped in litmus solution; **litmus test** the using of litmus paper to establish acidity or alkalinity. [O.N. *litmosi*, herbs used in dyeing — *litr*, colour, *mosi*, moss.]

litotes *lit'ō-tēz* or *lī'tə-tēz*, (*rhet*) *n* meiosis or understatement; esp. affirmation by negation of the contrary, as in *not a little angry* (= furious). [Gr. *lītotēs*, simplicity — *lītos*, plain.]

litre *lē'tər, n* the metric unit of capacity, now one cubic decimetre, formerly the volume of a kilogram of water at 4°C, under standard atmospheric pressure (1·000 028 cu. dm.). — **-litre** (used in combination) denoting the capacity of the cylinders of a motor vehicle engine (e.g. *three-litre*). [Fr., — L.L. *lītra* — Gr. *lītrā*, a pound.]

litter *lit'ər, n* rubbish, esp. rejected food-containers, wrappings, etc. carelessly dropped in a public place; any scattered or confused collection of objects, esp. of little value; a brood of young born to e.g. a bitch or sow; a stretcher, or bed supported on poles, for transporting a sick person; straw, hay, etc. provided as bedding for animals (see also **cat litter**). — *vt* to scatter carelessly about; (of animals) to give birth to; to supply (animals) with litter. — *vi* to produce a litter or brood; to strew rubbish, etc. untidily. — *adj* **litt'ered.** — **litter basket** or **bin** a receptacle for rubbish; **litter lout** or in N. Am. **litt'erbug** a person who wilfully drops litter. [O.Fr. *litiere* — L.L. *lectāria* — L. *lectus*, a bed.]

little *lit'l, adj* small in size, extent, quantity or significance; petty; small-minded; young; resembling or reminiscent of something else, but on a small(er) scale. — *n* (or *adj* with a noun understood) that which is small in quantity or extent; a small quantity; a small thing; not much. — *adv* in a small quantity or degree; not much; not at all. — **less** and **least** serve as compar. and superl. to the adv. and to some extent, along with **lesser,** to the adj. — *n* **litt'leness.** — **Little Bear** or in U.S. **Little Dipper** Ursa Minor; **little people** the fairies, or other race of small supernatural beings; **little woman** (*facetious*, mainly *old*) one's wife. — **little by little** gradually, by degrees; **make little of** to treat as of little consequence, belittle; to comprehend only slightly; **twist, wind** or **wrap someone round one's little finger** see under **finger**. [O.E. *lȳtel*.]

littoral *lit'ə-rəl, adj* belonging, or relating, to the seashore or to the shore of a lake; inhabiting the shore or shallow water in a lake or sea. — *n* the shore or coastal strip of land. [L. *littorālis* — *lītus, lītoris*, shore.]

liturgy *lit'ər-ji, n* the form of service or regular ritual of a church; the form of service used in the Eastern Orthodox Church in the celebration of the Eucharist. — *adj* **liturgical** (*li-tûr'ji-kəl*). — *adv* **litur'gically.** [Gr. *leitourgiā*.]

live[1] *liv, vi* to have life, be alive; to enjoy life; to lead one's life in a certain way, e.g. *live well, loosely*, etc.; to be supported, subsist, get a living; to survive, remain alive, escape death; to continue, last, escape oblivion or destruction; to reside, dwell. — *vt* to spend or pass; to act in conformity to; to express (e.g. a set of principles, a creed, etc.) by one's life: — *pr p* **liv'ing**; *pa t* and *pa p* **lived** (*livd*). — *adj* **liv'able** or **live'able** worth living, supportable, bearable; (usu. followed by *in*) habitable; (usu. followed by *with*) such as one could endure to live with, bearable. — *n* **livabil'ity** or **liveabil'ity.** — *n* **liv'er.** — *adj* **lived'-in** (of a room, etc.) homely with the signs of habitation; (of a face) marked by life's experiences. — *adj* **live'-in** (of an employee) living at the place of work; (of a sexual partner) sharing the same dwelling. — **live and breathe** to be passionately enthusiastic about; **live and learn** to keep learning new and surprising things; **live and let live** to give and expect toleration or forbearance; **live by** to order one's life according to (a principle, etc.); **live down** eventually to rehabilitate oneself in people's eyes after (a failure, mistake, etc.); **live for** to make (something) the chief concern of one's life; to look forward longingly to; **live in** to reside at one's place of employment; **live it up** to go on the spree; to cram one's life with excitement and pleasure; **live off** to be financially supported by; to feed oneself exclusively on (particular foods); **live on** to live by feeding upon, or with expenditure limited to; **live on air** (*facetious*) to have no apparent means of sustenance; **live out** to live (one's life) entirely in a particular way or place; to fulfil (e.g. the destiny reserved for one); (of e.g. a hotel worker, hospital doctor, etc.) to live away from one's place of employment; (of a student) to have accommodation outside the college or university campus; **live out of** (*colloq*) to depend on the limited range of e.g. food offered by (tins) or clothes contained in (a suitcase); **live through** to experience at first hand and survive (esp. an unpleasant event); **live to** to live long enough to, come at last to; **live together** to cohabit; **live up to** to rule one's life in a manner worthy of; to spend up to the scale of; **live well** to live luxuriously; **live with** to cohabit with; to accept and adapt to as an inescapable part of one's life. [O.E. *lifian*.]

live[2] *līv, adj* having life; alive, not dead; (of a volcano) active, not extinct; stirring; in operation or motion; current, applicable, relevant; charged with energy (e.g. from electricity, chemicals, etc.) and still capable of discharge; burning; vivid; (of the theatre, etc.) concerned with living performance as distinct from filming, broadcasting or televising; (of a broadcast) made directly from the actual event, not from a recording; fully operational (*comput*). — **-lived** (*-livd*) used in combination to mean having life (as in *long-lived*). — **live birth** birth in a living condition (opp. to *stillbirth*); **live load** a moving weight or variable force on a structure; **live'stock** domestic animals, esp. horses, cattle, sheep, and pigs; **live'-ware** (*colloq*) all the people working with a computer system, personnel as distinct from hardware or software; **live weight** weight of living animals; **live wire** a wire charged with an electric current; a person of intense energy or alertness. — **liven up** to enliven or become lively. [**alive.**]

livelihood *līv'li-ho͝od, n* occupation or employment as a means of support. [O.E. *līflād* — *līf*, life, *lād*, course.]

livelong[1] *liv'long*, (*poetic*) *adj* (of the day or night) complete, entire, in all its pleasant or tedious length. [M.E. *lief*, dear, **long**.]

livelong[2] *liv'long, n* the orpine, a plant difficult to kill. [**live[1]** and **long.**]

lively *līv'li, adj* brisk; active; sprightly; spirited; vivid. — *adv* **live'lily.** — *n* **live'liness.** — **look lively!** make haste. [O.E. *līflic* — *līf*, life.]

liven up. See under **live²**.

liver¹ *liv'ər, n* a large gland that secretes bile, stores and filters blood, converts sugar into glycogen and performs other metabolic functions; this organ taken from an animal's body, used as food. — *adj* of the colour of liver, dark reddish-brown. — **-livered** used in combination, e.g. in *lil'y-livered* (literally having a pallid, blood-starved liver), cowardly. — *adj* **liv'erish** (*old*) suffering from a disordered liver; irritable. — **liver fluke** a trematode worm that infects the bile-ducts of sheep and other animals; **liver salts** mineral salts taken to cure indigestion; **liver sausage** a rich sausage made of liver; **liver spot** a deep brown mark on the skin appearing in old age; **liv'erwort** (*-wûrt*) a plant similar to a moss, growing in damp places and having leaves of a liverlike shape, some varieties having formerly been used medicinally in diseases of the liver; **liv'erwurst** (*-wûrst*) liver sausage. [O.E. *lifer*.]

liver². See under **live¹**.

Liverpudlian *liv-ər-pud'li-ən, adj* belonging to Liverpool. — *n* a native of Liverpool. [*Liverpool*, with *-puddle* facetiously substituted for *-pool*.]

livery *liv'ə-ri, n* the feeding, care and stabling of a horse at a certain rate; the distinctive garb of the menservants attached to a particular household, etc., or of a body, e.g. a trade guild; any characteristic garb; the distinctive decoration used for all its aircraft, etc. by an airline, etc. — *adj* **liv'eried** clothed in livery. — **livery company** any of the trade guilds of the city of London which assumed a distinctive dress in the 14th century; **liv'eryman** a freeman of the city of London entitled to wear the livery and enjoy other privileges of his company; a man who keeps or works at a livery stable; **livery servant** a servant who wears a livery; **livery stable** a stable where horses are kept at livery and for hire. — **at livery** (of a horse) kept at the owner's expense at a livery stable. [A.Fr. *liveré*, lit. handed over — *livrer* — L. *līberāre*, to free.]

lives *līvz, n* pl. of **life.**

livid *liv'id, adj* black and blue; of a lead colour; discoloured; pale, ashen; extremely angry (*colloq*). — *n* **livid'ity** lividness of hue. — *n* **liv'idness.** [L. *līvidus* — *līvēre*, to be of a lead colour.]

living *liv'ing, adj* live; alive; having vitality; lively; (of a likeness) strikingly exact; currently in existence, activity or use. — *n* means of subsistence; manner of life; a property; a benefice. — **living death** a life of unrelieved misery; **living fossil** an animal or a plant of a group of which most are extinct; **living memory** the memory of anybody or somebody still alive; **living rock** rock still forming part of the bedrock, not detached; **liv'ing-room** a sitting-room for the general use of a family, etc.; **living wage** a wage that is adequate to support wage-earner and family. — **the living** those alive at present. [Pres. p. of **live¹**.]

Livingstone daisy *liv'ing-stən dā'zi, n* a South African annual succulent plant, with daisylike flowers.

lizard *liz'ərd, n* any member of the *Lacertilia*, an order of scaly reptiles, usually differing from snakes in having four legs, movable eyelids, and non-expansible mouths. — *adj* **liz'ard-hipped** (of dinosaurs) saurischian, i.e. having a pelvis slightly similar to a lizard's, the pubis extending forwards and downwards from the limb socket. [O.Fr. *lesard* (Fr. *lézard*) — L. *lacerta*.]

L.L. *abbrev* for Late Latin or Low Latin.

ll *abbrev* for lines.

'll *l.* Shortened form of **will** and **shall.**

llama *lä'mə, n* a South American transport animal of the camel family, a domesticated guanaco; its wool; cloth made of this. [Sp., from Quechua.]

llano *lyä'nō* or *lä'nō, n* one of the vast steppes or plains in the northern part of South America: — *pl* **lla'nos.** [Sp., — L. *plānus*, plain.]

LL.B. and **LL.D.** *abbrev* for, respectively, *legum baccalaureus* and *legum doctor* (L.), Bachelor of Laws and Doctor of Laws.

lm *abbrev* for lumen, the SI unit of luminous flux.

LMS *abbrev* for local management of schools (in which a school's board of governors is responsible for managing its allocated budget).

lo *lō*, (*archaic*) *interj* look; behold. — **lo and behold** (often *facetious*) used to signal a startling revelation. [O.E. *lā*.]

loach *lōch, n* a small river fish of a family related to carp, having a long narrow body and spines round its mouth. [Fr. *loche*.]

load *lōd, n* that which is carried; that which may or can be carried at one time or journey; a burden; a freight or cargo; a definite quantity, varying according to the goods; weight carried; power output of an engine, etc.; work imposed or expected; power carried by an electric circuit; a large quantity borne; that which burdens or grieves; a weight or encumbrance. — *vt* to burden; to charge; to put a load on or in; to put on or in anything as a load; to put film in (a camera); to weigh down; to overburden; to supply, present or assail overwhelmingly or lavishly; to weight or bias; to give weight or body to, by adding something; to lay (colour) on in masses (*painting*); to add charges to (*insurance*); to doctor, drug, adulterate, or fortify (wine); to transfer (data or a program) to the main memory (*comput*). — *vi* to put or take on a load; to charge a gun; to become loaded or burdened. — **-load** (in combination) denoting the goods or people conveyed in a vehicle (as in *busload, coachload, lorryload*). — *adj* **load'ed** rich, wealthy; under the influence of drink or drugs (*slang*); weighted in discussion in a certain direction; charged with contentious material. — *n* **load'er.** — *n* **load'ing** the act of lading; that with which anything is loaded. — *npl* **loads** (*colloq*) a lot, heaps. — *adv* (*colloq*) very much, as in *loads nicer*. — *adj* **load'-bearing** (of a wall, etc.) supporting a structure, carrying weight. — **loaded question** a question designed to make an unwilling answerer commit himself or herself to some opinion, action or course; **loading bay** see under **bay³**; **loading gauge** a suspended bar that marks how high a railway truck may be loaded; the maximum horizontal and vertical space that rolling-stock may safely occupy above the track; **load line** a line on a ship's side to mark the depth to which her cargo may be allowed to sink her; **load'master** a member of an aircrew who is in charge of the cargo; **load'-shedding** temporarily reducing the amount of electricity sent out by a power station. — **a load of** a quantity of (something distasteful or senseless, e.g. *a load of rubbish, a load of tripe*); **a load off one's mind** relief from anxiety; **get a load of** (*slang*) to listen to, look at, pay attention to; **have a load on** (*NAm*) to be drunk; **load the dice** to make one side heavier than the other so as to influence their fall for purposes of cheating; **load the dice against someone** to deprive someone of a fair chance of success. [O.E. *lād*, course, journey, conveyance; meaning affected by the unrelated **lade.**]

loadsa- *lōd-zə-*, (*slang combining form*) representing *loads of*, chiefly in (and originating as a back-formation from) **load'samoney,** (a person loaded with) wealth accumulated as a result of the Thatcherite economics of the 1980s. [*Loadsamoney*, grotesque character invented by comedian H. Enright, 1988.]

loadstar, loadstone. Same as **lodestar, lodestone** (see under **lode**).

loaf¹ *lōf, n* a portion of bread baked in one mass; a moulded portion of food, esp. bread or meat; a conical mass of sugar; the head, or brains (*slang*): — *pl* **loaves** (*lōvz*). — **loaf sugar** refined sugar moulded into a large cone. [O.E. *hlāf*, bread.]

loaf[2] *lōf*, *vi* to loiter or stand idly about, pass time idly. — *n* **loaf'er** a person who loafs; a casual shoe, esp. one resembling a moccasin. — *n* **loaf'ing**. [Poss. — Ger. *Landläufer*, tramp, vagabond.]

loam *lōm*, *n* a soil consisting of a natural mixture of clay and sand, with animal and vegetable matter; a composition basically of moist clay and sand used in making bricks. — *vt* to cover with loam. — *n* **loam'iness**. — *adj* **loam'y**. — **Loam'shire** an imaginary rural county in the novels of George Eliot, the name more recently being used to convey the idea of exaggerated stage rusticity. [O.E. *lām*.]

loan *lōn*, *n* anything lent, esp. money at interest; the act of lending; the condition of being lent; an arrangement for lending; permission to use. — *vt* to lend. — *adj* **loan'able**. — **loan shark** (*colloq*) a person who lends money at exorbitant rates of interest, a usurer; **loan'-sharking**; **loan translation** a compound, phrase, etc. that is a literal translation of a foreign expression (also called a **calque** (see under **calk**[3])); **loan word** a word taken into one's own language from another language, generally with slight adaptation. [O.N. *lān*.]

loath. See **loth**.

loathe *lōdh*, *vt* to dislike intensely; to feel disgust at. — *adj* **loathed**. — *n* **loath'er**. — *n* **loath'ing** extreme hate or disgust; abhorrence. — *adj* **loathsome** (*lōdh'səm*) abhorrent, detestable. — *adv* **loath'somely**. — *n* **loath'someness**. [O.E. *lāthian*; cf. **loth**.]

loaves *lōvz*, pl. of **loaf**[1].

lob *lob*, *n* a slow, high, underhand ball (*cricket*); a ball high overhead, dropping near the back of the court (*lawn tennis*). — *vt* to bowl or strike as a lob: — *pr p* **lobb'ing**; *pa t* and *pa p* **lobbed**. [Cf. Fris. and Du. *lob*.]

lobar, lobate, etc. See **lobe**.

lobby *lob'i*, *n* a small hall or waiting-room; a passage serving as a common entrance to several apartments; the antechamber of a legislative hall; a corridor into which members of parliament pass as they vote (also **division lobby**); a group of people who campaign to persuade legislators to make regulations favouring their particular interests. — *vt* to seek to influence (public officials) (esp. in the lobby). — *vi* to frequent the lobby in order to influence members or to collect political intelligence; to conduct a campaign in order to influence public officials. — *n* **lobb'yer**. — *n* **lobb'ying**. — *n* **lobb'yist**. [L.L. *lobia* — M.H.G. *loube*, a portico, arbour.]

lobe *lōb*, *n* a broad, esp. rounded, segmental division, branch or projection; the soft lower part of the ear; a division of the lungs, brain, etc.; a division of a leaf. — *adj* **lō'bar** relating to or affecting a lobe. — *adj* **lō'bate** having lobe(s). — *n* **lōbā'tion**. — *adj* **lobed**. — *adj* **lobe'less**. — *n* **lō'bing**. — *adj* **lobular** (*lob'ū-lər*). — *n* **lobule** (*lob'*) a small lobe. [Gr. *lobos*, lobe.]

lobectomy *lə-bek'tə-mi*, (*med*) *n* the excision of a lobe from any organ or gland of the body. [Gr. *lobos*, lobe, *ektomē*, cutting out.]

lobelia *lō-bēl'yə*, *n* a garden plant (genus *Lobelia*) having red, white, blue, purple or yellow flowers. [Named after the botanist Matthias de *Lobel* (1538–1616).]

lobo *lō'bō*, (*US*) *n* a timber-wolf. [Sp., wolf — L. *lupus*.]

lobotomy *lə-bot'ə-mi*, (*med*) *n* surgical incision into a lobe of an organ or gland; (*loosely*) leucotomy, a surgical operation on the frontal lobes of the brain, to treat severe psychiatric illness. [Gr. *lobos*, lobe, *tomia*, cutting.]

lobster *lob'stər*, *n* a large strong-clawed edible crustacean (genus *Homarus*), red when boiled; any of several crustaceans resembling it; the flesh of these as food. — **lobster pot** a basket for trapping lobsters. [O.E. *loppestre* — L. *locusta*, a lobster; cf. **locust**.]

lobular, lobule. See under **lobe**.

lobworm *lob'wûrm*, *n* a lugworm; an earthworm, used as fishing bait. [**lob** (in archaic sense), a lump, something thick and heavy, and **worm**.]

local *lō'kl*, *adj* relating to position in space; of or belonging to a place; confined to a place or places; (of a bus or train) serving the community of a particular area, stopping at every stop. — *n* a person belonging to a particular place, an inhabitant; one's nearest public house; a local anaesthetic (q.v. below); a local train; a news item of local interest (*N Am journalism*). — *n* **localīsa'tion** or **-z-**. — *vt* **lo'calise** or **-ize** to assign or limit to a place. — *n* **lo'caliser** or **-z-** something that localises, esp. a radio transmitter used in effecting a blind landing. — Also *adj*. — *n* **locality** (*lō-kal'i-ti*) place; position; district. — *adv* **lo'cally**. — **local action** (*law*) a legal action that relates to a specific place and must be brought there; **local anaesthesia** anaesthesia affecting only a restricted area of the body; **local anaesthetic** a solution for injecting into part of the body to anaesthetise it, or an injection of this; **local authority** the elected body for local government; **local call** a telephone call made to another number on the same exchange or group of exchanges; **local colour** faithful, characteristic details of particular scenery, manners, etc., giving verisimilitude in works of art and fiction; **local government** self-administration (in local affairs) by towns, counties, etc., as distinct from *national* or *central government*; a local authority (*US*); **local radio** radio (programmes) broadcast from a local station to a relatively small area, often on local themes; **local time** the time of a place as measured by the passage of the sun over the meridian passing through that place. — **local area network** (*comput*) a computer network operating over a small area such as an office or group of offices, in which a high rate of data transfer is possible (abbrev. **LAN**); **local education authority** the department of a local authority which administers state education (abbrev. **LEA**). [L. *locālis* — *locus*, a place.]

locale *lō-käl'*, *n* the scene of some event, etc. [Fr. *local*, with *e* to show stress.]

locate *lō-kāt'*, *vt* to place; (*often passive*) to set in a particular position, situate; to designate or find the position of; to find, pinpoint. — *vi* (*N Am*) to establish oneself in residence or business in an area. — *adj* **locāt'able** or **locate'able**. — *n* **locā'tion** the act of locating or process of being located; a farm (*Austr*); in South Africa, under apartheid, any of the townships or other areas in which the Black or Coloured population are obliged to live; position, site; site for filming outside the studio (*cinema*); a leasing on rent (*law*); a position in a memory which can hold a unit of information, e.g. a word (*comput*). — *adj* **locative** (*lok'ə-tiv*; *gram*) denoting a case representing 'place where'. — *n* the locative case; a word in the locative case. — **on location** (*cinema*; of filming, etc.) at a site outside the studio. [L. *locāre*, to place.]

loc. cit. *lok sit*, *abbrev* for *loco citato* (L.), in the passage just quoted.

loch *lohh*, (*Scot*) *n* a lake or (also **sea loch**) an arm of the sea. — *n* **loch'an** (*lohh'ən*; Gael.) a little loch. [Gael. *loch*.]

lochia *lok'i-ə*, (*med*) *n* a discharge from the uterus after childbirth. — *adj* **loch'ial**. [Gr. *lochia* (pl.).]

loci *lō'sī* or *lō'kē*, pl. of **locus**.

lock[1] *lok*, *n* a fastening device, esp. one in which a bolt is moved by mechanism, with or without a key; an immobilising device that can be operated on machinery, etc.; an enclosure on a canal in which water can be adjusted to allow boats to be raised or lowered; the part of a firearm by which it is discharged; a grapple in wrestling or a disabling hold generally; (in Rugby football) one of the two inside men in the second row of a scrum (also **lock forward**); a state of being jammed or immovable; a state of being firmly interlocked or engaged; (usu. **air'-lock**) a bubble blocking the flow of fluid through a pipe, etc.; the full extent of the turning arc of the front wheels of a motor vehicle. — *vt* to fasten (a door, chest, etc.) with a lock; to fasten so as to impede motion; to engage; to jam; to shut up, secure; to hold closely, e.g. in an embrace; to construct locks on (a canal). — *vi* to become fixed, to jam; to unite or engage firmly; to become, or have the means of becoming, locked. — *adj* **lock'able.** — *n* **lock'age** the locks of a canal; the difference in the levels of locks; materials used for locks; water lost by use of a lock; tolls paid for passing through locks. — **lock gate** a gate for opening or closing a lock in a canal, river or dock-entrance; **lock'jaw** a popular name for trismus, a disorder that puts the masticatory muscles into spasm and is an early symptom of tetanus, or for tetanus itself; **lock'-keeper** the attendant at a lock; **lock'nut** or **locking nut** a nut screwed on top of another one to prevent it loosening; a nut designed never to work loose once screwed tight; **lock'out** the act of locking out, esp. of employees by the employer during an industrial dispute; **lock'smith** a person who makes and mends locks; **lock'step** a method of marching in tight formation, with minimum space between one marcher and the one behind; **lock'-stitch** a sewing-machine stitch formed by the locking of two threads together; **lock'-up** a cell for locking up prisoners; a lockable shelter for a motor car; a small shop; a locking up. — *adj* capable of being locked up. — **lock away** to hide, usu. by locking up out of sight; **lock horns** to engage in combat, physical or otherwise; **lock in** to confine by locking doors; **lock on (to)** (of a radar beam) to track (an object) automatically; **lock out** to keep out by locking doors; to exclude (employees) from a factory, etc.; to prevent other users from accessing (a file) while one user is reading or updating it (*comput*); **lock, stock and barrel** altogether, entirely; **lock up** to confine; to lock securely; to lock whatever is to be locked; to make inaccessible or unavailable; to invest (capital) so that it cannot be readily realised; **under lock and key** locked up; imprisoned. [O.E. *loc.*]

lock² *lok*, *n* a piece, strand, tuft or ringlet (of hair); a wisp of wool or cotton; (in *pl*) hair. [O.E. *locc.*]

locker *lok'ər*, *n* a small cupboard that can be locked. — **locker room** a room for changing clothes and storing belongings in lockers.

locket *lok'it*, *n* a little ornamented case containing a miniature portrait, photograph or memento, worn on a chain, etc. round the neck. [Fr. *loquet*, latch.]

loco¹ *lō'kō*, (*US*) *adj* (of cattle) suffering from loco disease; mad, crazy (*slang*). — *n* (also **lo'coweed**) *Astragalus* or other leguminous plant: — *pl* **lō'cos** or **lō'coes.** — **loco disease** a disease of farm animals caused by eating locoweed, with disordered vision and paralysis. [Sp. *loco*, mad.]

loco² *lō'kō*, (*colloq*) *n* a locomotive: — *pl* **lō'cos.**

locomotion *lō-kə-mō'shən*, *n* power of moving from place to place. [L. *locus*, place, *motio*, *motiōnis*, motion.]

locomotive *lō-kə-mō'tiv*, *n* a railway engine, a self-propelled engine running on rails, used for pulling trains, and driven by steam, electricity or diesel power. — *adj* relating to, capable of, or causing locomotion. [L. *locus*, place, *movēre*, *mōtum*, to move, and sfx. *-ive.*]

locomotor *lō-kə-mō'tər*, *adj* relating to locomotion. — *adj* **locomo'tory.** — **locomotor ataxia** (*pathol*) failure of muscle co-ordination in the late stages of syphilis, caused by degeneration of the nerve fibres. [L. *lŏcus*, place, *mōtor*, that which propels.]

loculus *lok'ū-ləs*, *n* a small compartment or chamber (*bot*, *anat* or *zool*): — *pl* **loc'uli** (*-lī*). — Also **loc'ule** (*-ūl*). — *adj* **loc'ular.** [L. *loculus*, dimin. of *locus*, a place.]

locum *lō'kəm*, *n* a locum tenens or a locum-tenency: — *pl* **lō'cums.** — **locum tenens** (*lō'kəm tē'nenz* or *ten'enz*) a deputy or substitute, esp. for a doctor or clergyman: — *pl* **lō'cum tenen'tes** (*-tēz*). — **lōcum-ten'ency.** [L. *lŏcum*, accus. of *lŏcus*, a place, *tĕnēns*, pres. p. of *tenēre*, to hold.]

locus *lō'kəs*, *n* a place, locality, location; a passage in a book, piece of writing, etc.; the line or surface constituted by all positions of a point or line satisfying a given condition (*math*); the position of a gene on a chromosome (*genetics*): — *pl* **loci** (*lō'sī* or *lō'kē*). — **locus classicus** (*klas'i-kəs*) the classical passage, the stock quotation; **locus standi** (*stan'dī* or *-dē*) a place for standing; a right to interfere. [L. *lŏcus*, place.]

locust *lō'kəst*, *n* a name for several kinds of migratory winged insects related to grasshoppers, highly destructive to vegetation; extended to various similar insects; a devourer or devastator; a locust bean; a locust tree. — **locust bean** the carob bean; **locust bird** any of several pratincoles that feed on locusts; **locust tree** the carob; the false acacia (genus *Robinia*) or its wood. [L. *locusta*, lobster, locust.]

locution *lə-kū'shən*, *n* an act or mode of speaking; an expression, word, or phrase. — *adj* **locū'tionary.** [L. *locūtio*, *-ionis*, an utterance, an idiom.]

lode *lōd*, *n* a vein containing metallic ore. — **lode'star** or **load'star** the star that guides, the Pole Star — often used figuratively; **lode'stone** or **load'stone** a form of magnetite which exhibits polarity, behaving, when freely suspended, as a magnet; a magnet (often *fig*). [O.E. *lād*, a course, the original form also of **load.**]

loden *lō'dən*, *n* a thick waterproof woollen cloth with a short pile; (also **loden coat**) a coat made of this cloth. [Ger.]

lodge *loj*, *n* a house in the wilds for sportsmen; a gatekeeper's cottage; a college head's residence; a porter's room; the meeting-place of a branch of some societies, e.g. freemasons; the branch itself; an American Indian's tent; the dwelling-place of a beaver, otter, etc.; a frequently used element in the name of a house or hotel. — *vt* to supply with temporary accommodation; to deposit for safety, etc.; to bring (a charge or accusation) against someone; to make (a complaint or objection) officially; to vest (a power, talent, etc.) in someone; to settle, fix firmly. — *vi* to stay temporarily, rent accommodation as a lodger; to come to rest in a fixed position. — *n* **lodg'er** a person who lodges; a person who lives in a hired room or rooms. — *n* **lodg'ing** temporary accommodation; (often in *pl*) a room or rooms rented in another person's house. — *n* **lodg'ment** or **lodge'ment** the act of lodging, or state of being lodged; an accumulation of something or a blockage caused by it; a position gained and held within enemy territory (*mil*). — **lodge'-keeper**; **lodge'pole** a pole used by American Indians in making a lodge; **lodging house** a house where lodgings are let; a house where vagrants may lodge. [O.Fr. *loge* — O.H.G. *lauba*, shelter.]

loess *lœs*, *n* a wind-blown loamy deposit found in river valleys. [Ger. *Löss.*]

loft *loft*, *n* a room or space immediately under a roof; a gallery in a hall or church; an upper room; an attic or upper floor, usu. unfurnished, for storage, etc. e.g. in a warehouse (*US*); a room for pigeons; a stroke that causes a golf ball to rise; a backward slope on a golf-club head for the purpose of lofting; a lifting action. — *vt* to strike (the ball) so that it rises (*golf*); to toss; to propel high into the air or into space. — *adj* **loft'ed.** — *n* **loft'er** a golf iron for lofting. — *adv* **loft'ily.** — *n* **loft'iness.** — *adj* **loft'y** very high in position, character, sentiment, manner or diction;

stately; haughty. [Late O.E. *loft* — O.N. *lopt*, sky, an upper room.]

log[1] *log*, *n* short for **logarithm.** — **log tables** a book of tables setting out logarithmic values.

log[2] *log*, *n* a fallen tree trunk; a bulky piece of wood, used e.g. as firewood; an apparatus (orig. a block of wood) for ascertaining a ship's speed; a record of a ship's, or other, performance and experiences, a logbook. — *adj* consisting or constructed of logs. — *vt* to cut or haul in the form of logs; to enter in a logbook, or record otherwise; to cover a distance of, according to the log; to record the name and punishment of; to punish or fine. — *vi* to fell timber: — *pr p* **logg'ing;** *pa t* and *pa p* **logged.** — **-logged** (*logd*) used in combination to denote saturated, permeated, impregnated, entirely filled, as in *water-logged, smoke-logged.* — *n* **logg'er** a lumberman; (also **data logger**) a device which automatically records data. — *n* **logg'ing.** — **log'book** a book containing an official record of a ship's progress and proceedings on board, or of a journey made by an aircraft or car, or of any progress; the registration documents of a motor vehicle; **log cabin** a hut built of hewn or unhewn logs; **log jam** jamming that brings floating logs to a standstill; a deadlock or impasse; **log'line** the line fastened to the log, and marked for finding the speed of a vessel. — *vt* and *vi* **log'-roll.** — **log'-roller; log'-rolling** a gathering of people to facilitate the collection of logs after the clearing of a piece of land, or for rolling logs into a stream; the sport of trying to dislodge another person standing on the same floating log; mutual aid among politicians, etc., esp. the trading in of votes to secure passage of legislation; **log'-saw** a bow-saw, a saw with a narrow blade stretched like a bowstring in a bowlike frame; **log'wood** a tropical American tree of the *Caesalpinia* family, exported in logs; its dark-red heartwood; an extract from it used in dyeing. — **log in** or **on** (*comput*) to gain access to a mainframe system, usually by means of a code; **log out** or **off** (*comput*) to exit from a mainframe system; **sleep like a log** to sleep very soundly.

-log *-log.* U.S. variant of **-logue.**

loganberry *lō'gən-bə-ri* or *-ber-i*, *n* a supposed hybrid between a raspberry and a Pacific coast blackberry, obtained by Judge J.H. *Logan* (d. 1928).

logarithm *log'ə-ridhm*, *n* the power of a fixed number (called the base of the system, usu. 10 or *e*) that equals the number in question, used, esp. before electronic computing, to simplify multiplication and division (abbrev. **log**). — *adj* **logarith'mic.** — *adv* **logarith'mically.** [Gr. *logos*, ratio, reckoning, *arithmos*, number.]

logger. See under **log**[2].

loggerhead *log'ər-hed*, *n* (also **loggerhead turtle**) a large-headed type of turtle; an implement consisting of a large metal ball attached to a shaft, heated for melting tar, etc. — **at loggerheads** at variance, engaged in a quarrel (with *with*). [Poss. from *logger*, a block of wood used for hobbling a horse.]

loggia *loj'ə* or *loj'yə*, *n* a covered open arcade: — *pl* **loggie** (*loj'ā*) or **logg'ias.** [It.; cf. **lodge.**]

logic *loj'ik*, *n* the science and art of reasoning correctly; the science of the necessary laws of thought; the principles of any branch of knowledge; sound reasoning; individual method of reasoning; convincing and compelling force (e.g. of facts or events); basis of operation as designed and effected in a computer, comprising **logical elements** which perform specified elementary arithmetical functions. — *adj* **log'ical** of or according to logic; reasoning correctly; following necessarily from facts or events; of, or used in, logic circuits (*comput*). — *n* **logical'ity** or **log'icalness.** — *adv* **log'ically.** — *n* **logician** (*lo-jish'ən*) a person skilled in logic. — *n* **log'icism** (*log'i-sizm*) Frege's theory that underlying mathematics is a purely logical set of axioms, mathematics being thus a part of logic. — *n* **log'icist.** — **logic circuit** (*comput*) an electronic circuit with usu. two or more inputs and one output, which performs a logical operation, e.g. *and, not*; **logic diagram** (*comput*) a diagram showing logical elements and interconnections without engineering details. [Gr. *logikē* (*technē*), logical (art) — *logos*, speech, reason.]

logistic *lə-jis'tik* or **logistical** *-jis'ti-kəl*, *adj* relating to reasoning, to calculation, or to logistic(s); proportional. — *n* **logistician** (*-tish'ən*) a person skilled in logistics. — *nsing* or *npl* **logis'tics** the art of movement and supply of troops; the handling of the practical detail of any large-scale enterprise or operation. [Gr. *logistikos* — *logizesthai*, to compute; influenced by Fr. *loger*, to lodge.]

loglog *log'log*, *n* the *log*arithm of a *log*arithm.

LOGO *lō'gō*, (*comput*) *n* a simple programming language with list-processing features and distinctive graphics.

logo *lō'gō* or *log'ō*, *n* a small design used as the symbol of an organisation, etc.: — *pl* **lō'gos** (or *log'ōz*). [Short for **logotype.**]

logogram *log'ə-gram*, (*shorthand*) *n* a single sign standing for a word, phrase or morpheme. [Gr. *logos*, word, *gramma*, letter, *graphein*, to write.]

logophile *log'ə-fīl*, *n* a lover of words. [Gr. *logos*, word, and **-phile.**]

Logos *log'os*, *n* in the Stoic philosophy, the active principle living in and determining the world; the Word of God incarnate (*Christian theol*). [Gr. *logos*, word.]

logotype *log'ō-tīp*, (*printing*) *n* a piece of type representing a word or several letters, cast in one piece; a single piece of type comprising a name and/or address, trademark or design; (usu. **logo**) an identifying symbol consisting of a simple picture or design and/or letters. [Gr. *logos*, word, *typos*, an impression.]

-logue or in U.S. **-log** *-log*, *combining form* denoting: speech or discourse, as in *monologue, dialogue, travelogue*; compilation, as in *catalogue*; student, enthusiast, as in *ideologue*.

-logy *-lə-ji*, *combining form* indicating: science, theory; discourse, treatise. [Gr. *logos*, word, reason.]

loin *loin*, *n* meat from the lower part of an animal's back; (usu. in *pl*) the waist and lower part of the back, or the hips and top of the legs; (in *pl*) the genital area, esp. (*poetic*) as a source of new life. — **loin'cloth** a piece of cloth for wearing round the loins. — **gird up one's loins** to prepare for energetic action. [O.Fr. *loigne* — L. *lumbus*, loin.]

loipe *loi'pə*, *n* a track used for cross-country skiing: — *pl* **loi'pen.** [Dan. *løjpe.*]

loir *loir*, *n* a large European species of dormouse. [Fr. — L.L. *lis, liris.*]

loiter *loi'tər*, *vi* to dawdle; to linger or lurk. — *n* **loi'terer.** — *n* and *adj* **loi'tering.** — *adv* **loi'teringly.** [Du. *leuteren*, to dawdle.]

lokshen *lok'shən*, *npl* noodles. — **lokshen pudding** a traditional Jewish pudding made with noodles, egg, sugar, dried fruit and cinnamon; **lokshen soup** a traditional Jewish noodle soup. [Yiddish, pl. of *loksh*, a noodle — Russ. *loksha.*]

loll *lol*, *vi* to lie lazily about, to lounge, sprawl; (of the tongue) to dangle, hang. — *n* **loll'er.** — *adv* **loll'ingly.** [Perh. imit.; cf. Du. *lollen*, to sit over the fire.]

Lollard *lol'ərd*, (*hist*) *n* a follower of John Wycliffe, the 14th-cent. English religious reformer; an idler. — *n* **Loll'ardism.** [M.Du. *lollaerd*, mutterer, droner.]

lollipop *lol'i-pop*, *n* a large boiled sweet which has been allowed to solidify around a stick. — **lollipop man, woman** or **lady** a person appointed to conduct children across a busy street, distinguished by carrying a pole with a disc on the end. [Perh. Northern dialect *lolly*, tongue.]

lollop *lol'əp, vi* to bound about in an unco-ordinated, puppylike manner: — *pr p* **loll'oping**; *pa t* and *pa p* **loll'oped.** [Poss. from **loll**.]

lolly *lol'i, (colloq) n* a lollipop; money.

lollygag. See **lallygag.**

loma *lō'mə, (US) n* in the south-western states, a hill with a broad, flat top. [Sp., back, ridge.]

Lombard *lom'bərd* or *-bärd, n* an inhabitant of *Lombardy* in N. Italy; one of a Germanic tribe, the *Langobardi*, which founded a kingdom in Lombardy (568), overthrown by Charlemagne (774). — Also *adj.* — *adj* **Lombar'dic.** — **Lombard Street** the chief centre of the banking interest in London; **Lombardy poplar** a variety of black poplar with erect branches. [O.Fr., — L. *Langobardus, Longobardus.*]

lomentum *lō-men'təm, n* a pod that breaks in pieces at constrictions between the seeds: — *pl* **lomen'ta.** — Also **lō'ment** *(-mənt).* — *adj* **lomentā'ceous.** [L. *lōmentum*, bean-meal (used as a cosmetic) — *lavāre, lōtum*, to wash.]

Londoner *lun'də-nər, n* a native or citizen of *London.* — **London clay** a Lower Eocene formation in south-eastern England; **London pride** a hardy perennial saxifrage — also *none-so-pretty* and *St Patrick's cabbage.* — **London Inter-Bank Offered Rate** (abbrev. **LIBOR**) the rate of interest at which the major clearing banks lend money amongst themselves.

lone *lōn, adj* isolated; solitary; unfrequented, uninhabited. — *n* **lone'ness.** — **lone wolf** a loner. [**alone.**]

lonely *lōn'li, adj* unaccompanied; isolated; uninhabited, unfrequented; uncomfortably conscious of being alone. — *n* **lone'liness.** — **lonely heart** a usu. unmarried person, esp. one in search of a happy relationship. — *adj* **lone'ly-heart.** [**alone.**]

loner *lōn'ər, n* a person who prefers to be or to act alone, and avoids close relationships. [**lone.**]

lonesome *lōn'səm*, (esp. *NAm*) *adj* solitary; lonely. — *adv* **lone'somely.** — *n* **lone'someness.** — **by** or **on one's lonesome** alone. [**lone** and sfx. **-some**[1].]

long *long, adj* (*compar* **longer** *long'gər, superl* **longest** *long'gist*) not short; of a specified length; extended in space in the direction of greatest extension; far-extending; extended in time; of extended continuance; taking a considerable time to utter or do; (of a speech sound) of extended duration (*phon*); (of a syllable; *loosely*) accented; (of a vowel; *loosely*) in a long syllable; (of a dress, etc.) coming down to the ankles, full-length; (of the memory) retentive; (of a word) abstruse or grandiose; numerically extensive; (of e.g. a suit of cards) of more than average number; exceeding the standard value, as in *long dozen, long hundred*; having a large holding in a commodity or security, in expectation of a rise in prices (*finance*); (of a chance) remote; tedious. — *n* a long time; a long syllable (*prosody*); (in *pl*) long trousers; (in *pl*) long-dated securities. — *adv* for, during, or by, a great extent of time; throughout the whole time: — *compar* and *superl* as for *adj.* — *vi* to yearn (with *for*). — *n* **long'ing** an eager desire, craving. — *adj* yearning. — *adv* **long'ingly.** — *adj* **longish** (*long'ish*). — *adv* **long'ways** or in N. Am. **long'wise** lengthways. — *adj* **long'-ago** of the far past. — *n* the far past. — **long arm** far-reaching power; **long'boat** the largest and strongest boat of a ship; a longship; **long'bow** a bow drawn by hand as distinct from the crossbow; **longcase clock** a grandfather clock. — *adj* **long'-dated** (of securities) due for redemption in more than fifteen years. — *adj* **long-dis'tance** covering big distances, as in *long-distance runner, lorry-driver.* — **long division** division in which the working is shown in full; **long dozen** thirteen. — *adj* **long-drawn-out'** prolonged; unduly protracted. — **long drink** a large thirst-quenching drink in a tall glass. — *adj* **long-eared'** with long ears or earlike feather-tufts. — **long face** a dismal expression. — *adj* **long-faced'** dismal-looking. — **long field** (*cricket*) a fielder or station near the boundary on the bowler's side, long off or long on. — *adj* **long-haired'** unconventional, hippy; highbrow. — **long'hand** ordinary writing as distinct from *shorthand*; **long haul** a journey over a great distance; any activity requiring lengthy effort. — *adj* **long'-haul.** — *adj* **long-head'ed** dolichocephalous; shrewd; sagacious. — **long-head'edness; long'horn** an animal belonging to a breed of cattle with long horns; a longicorn beetle, with long antennae; **long'house** a long communal house, e.g. in South-East Asia or among the American Indians; a large oblong hall or dwelling built by the Vikings (*archaeol*); **long hundred** see under **hundred; long johns** long underpants; **long jump** an athletic contest in which competitors jump as far as possible along the ground from a running start; **long leg** (*cricket*) a fielder or a fielder's station, far out behind, and a little to the on side of, the batsman. — *adj* **long-legged'** (or *-leg'id*) having long legs. — *adj* **long'-life** (of foodstuffs) treated so as to prolong freshness. — **long'-line** a long fishing line with many hooks attached. — *adj* (of clothing) long or lengthened in shape, as of a brassiere or top extending over the ribcage. — *adj* **long-lived** (*-livd'*) having a long life. — **long mark** a macron; **long odds** (in betting) a remote chance, unfavourable odds in terms of risk, favourable in terms of potential gain; **long off** and **long on** (*cricket*) the fielders in the long field to the off and on of the batsman respectively; their positions; **long paddock** (*Austr*) the grass verge of a road, sometimes used for grazing animals on; **long pig** (from cannibal term) human flesh as food. — *adj* **long'-playing** (of a gramophone record) giving length in reproduction because of the extremely fine groove. — *adj* **long'-range** (of weapons) long in range, designed to reach remote targets; (of aircraft, etc.) covering long distances without having to refuel; (of a forecast) extending well into the future. — **long'-ship** (*hist*) a distinctive type of long vessel built by the Vikings; **long shot** (a bet, entry, venture, etc. with) a remote chance of success; a shot taken at a distance from the object filmed. — *adj* **long-sight'ed** able to see far but not close at hand; hypermetropic; presbyopic; having foresight; sagacious. — **long-sight'edness; long slip** (*cricket*) a fielder some distance behind the batsman on the off side. — *adj* **long'-standing** of long existence or continuance. — *adj* **long'-stay** (of e.g. patients in a hospital) staying permanently or semi-permanently. — **long stop** a fielder who stands to the rear of the wicket to stop balls missed by the wicket-keeper (*cricket*); a person or thing that acts as a final safeguard or check. — *adj* **longsuff'ering** enduring long and patiently. — *n* long endurance or patience. — **long suit** the suit with most cards in a player's hand; a particular talent, good quality, or advantage that one has. — *adj* **long-term'** extending over a long time; (of a policy) concerned with time ahead as distinct from the immediate present. — *adj* **long'-time** enduring for a long time. — **long-track (skating** or) **speedskating** speedskating in which contestants race against the clock; **long vacation** a long holiday during the summer, when schools, etc. are closed; **long view** the taking into consideration of events, etc. in the distant future. — *adj* **long-waist'ed** (of a garment) having a deep or dropped waist; (of a person) long from the armpits to the hips. — **longwall system** or **working** a mining technique in which a seam is exposed along its length and then removed layer by layer. — *adj* **long'-wave** (*radio*) of, or using, wavelengths over 1000 metres. — *adj* **long-winded** (*-win'did*) tediously wordy and circumlocutory. — **long-wind'edness.** — **as long as** provided only that; **before long** or (*poetic* or *facetious*) **ere long** soon; **go long** (*finance*) to acquire more holdings in commodities or securities in expectation of a rise in prices; **long on** well supplied with; **long since** a long time ago; **make a long nose** to cock a snook or put a thumb to the nose; **no longer** not now as formerly; **not long for this world** near death; **so long!** (*colloq*) goodbye; **so long as** provided only that; **the long and the short of it** the sum of the matter in a few words. [O.E. *lang, long* (adj.), *lange, longe* (adv.).]

longan *long'gan, n* a tropical Asian tree (genus *Nephelium*) related to the lychee; its fruit. [Chin. *lung-yen*, dragon's eye.]

longe. Same as **lunge²**.

longevity *lon-jev'i-ti, n* great length of life. [L. *longaevitās, -ātis* — *longus*, long, *aevum*, age.]

longicorn *lon'ji-körn, n* a longhorn beetle, any of several beetles of the family *Cerambycidae*, with very long antennae. — *adj* denoting, or having, long antennae. [L. *longus*, long, *cornū*, horn.]

longitude *lon'ji-tūd* or *long'gi-, n* the arc of the equator between the meridian of a place and a standard meridian (usually that of Greenwich) expressed in degrees E. or W.; the arc of the ecliptic between a star's circle of latitude and the first point of Aries or vernal equinox (21 March), measured eastwards (*astron*); length. — *adj* **longitū'dinal** relating to longitude; lengthways. — *adv* **longitū'dinally**. — **longitudinal wave** (*acoustics*) a wave in which the particles are displaced in the direction of advance of the wave. [L. *longitūdō, -inis*, length — *longus*, long.]

longshore *long'shör, adj* existing or employed along the shore. — **long'shoreman** a stevedore; a person who makes a living along the shore by fishing, etc. [**alongshore**.]

lonicera *lon-is'ə-rə, n* the honeysuckle, a shrub of the genus *Lonicera*. [A. *Lonicerus* (d. 1586), German botanist.]

loo¹ *lōō*, (*Br colloq*) *n* a lavatory. — **loo roll** a roll of lavatory paper.

loo² *lōō, n* a card game. [From *lanterloo*, name of another game.]

loof. See **luff**.

loofah, loofa *lōō'fə* or **luffa** *luf'ə, n* a tropical plant (genus *Luffa*) of the gourd family; the fibrous network of its fruit, used as a hard rough sponge. [Ar. *lūfah*.]

look *lŏŏk, vi* to direct one's eyes and attention; to give attention; to face; to seem or appear; to seem to be; to have an appearance. — *vt* to ascertain by a look; to look at; to express by a look. — *n* an act of looking; view; air; appearance; (in *pl*) beauty, comeliness (also *good looks*). — *imper* or *interj* see; behold. — *n* **look'er** a person who looks; an observer; a person who has good looks (*colloq*). — **-looking** (in combination) having a specified appearance or expression, as in *sad-looking*. — **look'-alike** a person who closely resembles one in personal appearance, a double; **look'-in** a chance of doing anything effectively or of sharing; a short casual call; **look'ing-glass** a mirror; **look'out** a careful watch; a place to observe from; a person set to watch; prospect; concern; **look-see'** (*slang*) a look around. — **look after** to take care of; **look alive** (*colloq*) to rouse oneself for action; **look and say** (*educ*) a method of teaching reading, whereby the pupil is trained to recognise words at a glance, and say them, rather than articulate the letters of the word one by one; **look down on** to despise; **look down one's nose at** to regard with contempt; **look for** to search for; to expect; **look forward to** to anticipate with pleasure; **look here!** used to draw attention to something, or as an angry response; **look in** to make a short call; to watch television (*colloq*); **look into** to inspect closely; to investigate; **look like** to resemble; to promise or threaten (e.g. rain); used in requesting a description, as in *what does it look like*?; **look on** to regard, view, think; to be a spectator; **look out** to be watchful; to be on one's guard; to look for and select; **look over** to examine cursorily; **look sharp** (*colloq*) be quick about it; **look small** to appear or feel foolish and ashamed; **look the part** to have, or assume, an appearance in keeping with one's rôle; **look to** to look at or towards; to watch; to take care of; to depend on (with *for*); to expect (to do); **look to be** (*colloq*) to seem to be; **look up** to search for, refer to; to take courage; to improve, take a turn for the better; to seek out and call upon, visit (*colloq*); **look up to** to feel respect or veneration for; **not much to look at** (*colloq*) unattractive. [O.E. *lōcian*, to look.]

loom¹ *lōōm, n* a machine for weaving; the shaft of an oar; an electrical wiring assembly complete with insulating covering. [O.E. *gelōma*, a tool.]

loom² *lōōm, vi* to appear indistinctly, esp. in an alarmingly exaggerated or magnified form; (of an event) to impend, be imminent; to overhang threateningly (with *over*). — *n* an indistinct or miragelike appearance.

loon¹ *lōōn*, (*colloq*) *n* a simple-minded or eccentric person.

loon² *lōōn*, (esp. *NAm*) *n* the diver, a sleek-bodied sharp-beaked bird of northern waters, of the genus *Gavia*. [O.N. *lōmr*.]

loony *lōō'ni*, (*slang*) *adj* crazy, insane, lunatic. — *n* a mad person, a lunatic. — *n* **loo'niness**. — **loony bin** (*slang*) a lunatic asylum. [Shortening of **lunatic**.]

loop¹ *lōōp, n* the oval-shaped coil made in a piece of string, chain, etc. as it crosses back over itself; any similar doubling in the shape or structure of anything; a branch of anything that returns to the main part; a closed circuit sound which a signal can pass (*electronics*); a set of instructions used more than once in a program (*comput*); an aerobatic manoeuvre in which an aircraft climbs, from level flight, to describe a circle in the sky; any loop-shaped movement or manoeuvre; an intrauterine contraceptive device shaped like a loop (also called *Lippes loop*). — *vt* to fasten in or with a loop; to adorn with loops; to make a loop of. — *vi* to travel in loops. — *adj* **looped**. — *n* **loop'er** a caterpillar of the *Geometridae*, so called from its mode of walking. — *n* and *adj* **loop'ing**. — *adj* **loop'y** having loops; slightly crazed (*slang*). — **loop the loop** to move in a complete vertical loop or circle, head downwards at the top of the curve.

loop² *lōōp* or **loophole** *lōōp'hōl, n* a vertical slit in a wall e.g. of a castle, for peering through, firing through or receiving light and air through; a means of escape or evasion. — *vt* **loop'hole** to make loopholes in. [Perh. M.Du. *lûpen*, to peer.]

loose *lōōs, adj* slack; free; unbound; not confined; not compact; unattached; untied; not close-fitting; not tight; relaxed; (of the joints) freely mobile; (of the bowels) affected by diarrhoea; inexact; indefinite; vague; not strict; unrestrained; lax; licentious; dispersedly or openly disposed; (of the ball) not in the possession of any player (*football*); denoting all play except for the set scrums and line-outs (*Rugby football*). — *adv* loosely. — *n* (*Rugby football*) loose play. — *vt* to make loose; to set free; to unfasten; to untie; to disconnect; to relax; to slacken; to discharge. — *vi* to shoot. — *adv* **loose'ly**. — *vt* **loos'en** to make loose; to relax; to make less dense; to open or relieve (the bowels). — *vi* to become loose; to become less tight. — *n* **loose'ness** the state of being loose; diarrhoea. — *adj* **loose-bod'ied** (of clothes) flowing, loose-fitting. — **loose box** a part of a stable where horses are kept untied; **loose change** coins kept about one's person for small expenditures; **loose cover** a detachable cover, e.g. for an armchair; **loose forward** in Rugby union football, either of the two wing forwards or the no. 8, at the back of the scrum; in Rugby league, the player at the back of the scrum; **loosehead prop** the prop forward on the left of the front row in the scrum. — *adj* **loose'-leaf** (of a folder, binder, etc.) designed so as to allow leaves to be inserted or removed. — *adj* **loose-limbed'** or **-joint'ed** supple. — **be at a loose end** to be disengaged, have nothing to do; **break loose** to escape from confinement; **let loose** to set at liberty; **loosen up** to become less shy or taciturn; to exercise gently, e.g. in preparation for athletic effort; **on the loose** indulging in a bout of unrestraint; freed from confinement; **stay loose** (*slang*) keep cool, keep relaxed. [O.N. *lauss*; O.E. *lēas*; see **less**.]

loosestrife *lōōs'strīf*, *n* a plant (genus *Lysimachia*) of the primrose family, or other member of the genus; a tall waterside plant (*Lythrum salicaria*, purple loosestrife). [Gr. *lȳsimacheion*, common loosestrife (as if from *lyein*, to loose, *machē*, strife), but possibly from the personal name *Lȳsimachos*.]

loot *lōōt*, *n* plunder; stolen goods; money (*slang*). — *vt* or *vi* to plunder. — *n* **loot'er**. [Hindi *lūt*.]

lop[1] *lop*, *vi* to hang down loosely. — *adj* **lop'-eared** (of animals) having drooping ears. — *adj* **lopsid'ed** leaning to one side, off balance; heavier, bigger, on one side than the other.

lop[2] *lop*, *vt* to cut off the top or ends of, esp. of a tree; to cut away (e.g. superfluous parts): — *pr p* **lopp'ing**; *pa t* and *pa p* **lopped**. — *n* twigs or branches of trees cut off; an act of lopping. — *n* **lopp'er**. — *n* **lopp'ing** a cutting off; the part or parts cut off. [O.E. *loppian*.]

lope *lōp*, *vi* to run with a long stride. [O.N. *hlaupa*; cf. **leap**.]

lopho- *lōf-ō-* or *lof-ō-*, *combining form* signifying crested or tufted. — *n* **loph'ophore** (*-fōr*; Gr. *phoros*, bearing) a ring of ciliated tentacles round the mouth of some sedentary marine animals. [Gr. *lophos*, a crest.]

loq. *abbrev* for *loquitur* (L.), he or she speaks (used with a name as a stage direction).

loquacious *lō-kwā'shəs*, *adj* talkative. — *adv* **loquā'ciously**. — *n* **loquā'ciousness** or **loquacity** (*-kwas'i-ti*). [L. *loquāx*, *-ācis* — *loquī*, to speak.]

loquat *lō'kwot* or *-kwat*, *n* a Chinese and Japanese ornamental tree of the rose family; its small, yellow edible fruit. [Chin. *luh kwat*.]

lor or **lor'**. See **lord**.

loran *lö'rän*, *n* a long-range radio-navigation system. [For *long-range navigation*.]

lord *lörd*, (with *cap*, when used as a prefix) *n* a master; a feudal superior (also **lord-supe'rior**; *hist*); a ruler; the proprietor of a manor (*hist*); a titled nobleman; a bishop, esp. if a member of the House of Lords; a judge of the Court of Session; used in various official titles, such as *Lord Chief Justice*; (with *cap*) God; (with *cap*) Christ. — *vt* (with *it*) to act like a lord, tyrannise. — *interj* expressing surprise (*colloq* **lor**, **lor'**, **law** or **lord'y**). — *adj* **lord'ly** like, befitting or in the manner of a lord, haughty, proud; magnificent; lavish; lofty; tyrannical. — Also *adv*. — *n* **lord'ship** state or condition of being a lord; dominion; authority; used in referring to or addressing a lord (with *his* or *your*), or a woman sheriff or judge (with *her* or *your*). — **Lord's Day** Sunday; **Lord's Prayer** the prayer that Christ taught his disciples (Matt. vi. 9–13); **lords spiritual** the archbishops and bishops in the House of Lords; **Lord's Supper** holy communion; **Lord's table** the communion table; **lord-superior** see **lord**; **lords temporal** the lay peers. — **drunk as a lord** extremely drunk; **House of Lords** the upper house of British parliament; **live like a lord** to live in luxury; **Lord knows (who, what,** etc.) I don't know, and I doubt if anybody knows; **Lord of Session** a judge of the Court of Session; **lords and ladies** (*bot*) common arum. [M.E. *lovered*, *laverd* — O.E. *hlāford* — *hlāf*, bread, *ward*, keeper, guardian.]

lordosis *lör-dō'sis*, *n* abnormal curvature of the spinal column, the convexity towards the front. — *adj* **lordot'ic**. [Gr. *lordōsis* — *lordos*, bent back.]

lore[1] *lör*, *n* learning, esp. of a special, traditional, or out-of-the-way miscellaneous kind, as in *folklore*, *plant-lore*. [O.E. *lār*.]

lore[2] *lör*, (*zool*) *n* the side of the head between the eye and bill of a bird; the corresponding area of a reptile or fish. [L. *lōrum*, thong.]

Lorelei *lor'ə-lī*, *n* in German legend, a siren of the Rhine who lured sailors to their death. [Ger. *Lurlei*, the name of the rock she was believed to inhabit.]

lorgnette *lörn-yet'*, *n* eyeglasses with a handle; an opera-glass. [Fr. *lorgner*, to look sidelong at, to ogle.]

lorica *lö-* or *lə-rī'kə*, *n* a leather corslet (*hist*); the case of a protozoan, rotifer, etc. (*zool*): — *pl* **lori'cae** (*-sē*). — *adj* and *n* **lor'icate**. [L. *lōrīca*, a leather corslet — *lōrum*, a thong.]

lorikeet *lor-i-kēt'*, *n* a small lory. [From **lory**, on analogy of para*keet*.]

loris *lö'ris*, *n* the slender lemur of Sri Lanka; an East Indian lemur (the *slow loris*). [Fr. *loris*.]

lorry *lor'i*, *n* a heavily-built motor vehicle for transporting heavy loads by road; a long (esp. railway) wagon without, or with low, sides.

lory *lö'ri*, *n* any parrot of a family with brushlike tongues, natives of New Guinea, Australia, etc.; in South Africa, a touraco. [Malay *lūrī*.]

lose *lōōz*, *vt* to fail to keep or obtain; to be deprived or bereaved of; to cease to have; to cease to hear, see or understand; to mislay; to waste, (e.g. time); to miss; to be defeated in; to cause the loss or ruin of; to cause to perish. — *vi* to fail, to be unsuccessful; to suffer waste or loss; (of a clock or watch) to go slow: — *pr p* **los'ing**; *pa t* and *pa p* **lost** (*lost*). — *adj* **los'able**. — *n* **los'er**. — *n* and *adj* **los'ing**. — *adv* **los'ingly**. — *adj* **lost** (*lost*) parted with; no longer possessed; not able to be found; missing; thrown away; squandered, wasted; ruined; confused, unable to find the way (*lit* and *fig*). — **losing game** a game played with the aim of losing; **lost cause** a hopeless ideal or endeavour; **lost soul** a soul that is damned, an irredeemably evil person. — **get lost!** (*slang*) go away and stay away!; stop annoying or interfering!; **lose oneself** to lose one's way; to become totally engrossed; **lose out** (*colloq*) to suffer loss or be at a disadvantage; (also with *on*) to fail to acquire something desired; **lost to** insensible to. [O.E. *losian*, to be a loss.]

loss *los*, *n* losing; diminution; bereavement; destruction; defeat; deprivation; detriment; something lost. — **loss adjuster** an assessor employed by an insurance company, usu. in fire damage claims; **loss'-leader** something sold at a loss to attract other custom. — **at a loss** in, or resulting in, deficit; off the scent; at fault; nonplussed; perplexed. [O.E. *los*, influenced by **lost**.]

lost. See **lose**.

lot *lot*, *n* an object, such as a slip of wood or a straw, drawn or thrown out from among a number in order to reach a decision by chance; decision by this method; divination; a prize won through divination; destiny; that which falls to anyone as their fortune; a separate portion; a parcel of ground; a set; a set of things offered together for sale; the whole; a plot of ground allotted or assigned to any person or purpose, esp. for building; a large quantity or number; a batch of horses grouped for daily exercise (*horse-racing*). — *vt* to allot; to separate into lots; to divide (a property) into lots, esp. for selling purposes: — *pr p* **lott'ing**; *pa t* and *pa p* **lott'ed**. — **bad lot** an unscrupulous person with a bad reputation; **cast** or **throw in one's lot with** to share the fortunes of; **cast** or **draw lots** to draw from a set alike in appearance in order to reach a decision; **lots of** (*colloq*) many; **the lot** the entire number or amount. [O.E. *hlot*, lot — *hlēotan*, to cast lots.]

loth or **loath** *lōth, adj* reluctant, unwilling. — **nothing loth** not at all unwilling. [O.E. *lāth*, hateful; cf. **loathe**.]

loti *lō'tē, n* the standard monetary unit of Lesotho (100 *lisente*): — *pl* **maloti** (*mä-lō'tē*).

lotion *lō'shən, n* a liquid preparation for applying to the skin, medicinally or cosmetically. [L. *lōtiō, -ōnis*, a washing — *lavāre, lōtum*, to wash.]

lottery *lot'ər-i, n* an arrangement for distributing prizes by lot; a matter of chance; a card game of chance. — *n* **lott'o** a game played by covering on a card each number drawn till a line of numbers is completed: — *pl* **lott'os**. [It. *lotteria, lotto*; cf. **lot**.]

lotus *lō'təs, n* an Egyptian or Indian waterlily of various species; a North African tree (possibly the jujube) whose fruit induced in the eater a state of blissful indolence and forgetfulness (*Gr mythol*); an architectural ornament like a waterlily. — **lo'tus-eater** an indolent person who enjoys the luxuries of life. — *adj* **lo'tus-eating**. — **lotus position** a seated position, cross-legged, with each foot resting on the opposite thigh (*yoga*). [Latinised Gr. *lōtos*.]

louche *lōōsh, adj* squinting; ambiguous, shady, shifty, disreputable. — *adv* **louche'ly**. [Fr.]

loud *lowd, adj* making a great sound; noisy; obtrusive; flashy or showy in a vulgar way. — *adv* **loud** or **loud'ly**. — *vt* and *vi* **loud'en** to make or grow louder. — *adj* **loud'ish**. — *n* **loud'ness**. — **loud-hail'er** a portable megaphone with microphone and amplifier; **loud'mouth** (*colloq*) someone who talks too much or too offensively; a boaster. — *adj* **loud'mouthed**. — **loudspeak'er** an electro-acoustic device which amplifies sound. — *adj* **loud-voiced'**. [O.E. *hlūd*.]

lough *lohh, n* the Irish form of **loch**.

lounge *lownj, vi* to lie in a relaxed way; to idle. — *vt* to idle (away). — *n* a sitting-room in a private house; a room in a public building for sitting or waiting, often providing refreshment facilities; (also **lounge-bar'**) a more expensive and luxurious bar in a public house; an act, spell or state of lounging; an idle stroll; a kind of sofa, esp. with back and one raised end. — *n* **loung'er** a person who lounges; a woman's long loose dress for wearing indoors; an extending chair or light couch for relaxing on. — *n* and *adj* **loung'ing**. — *adv* **loung'ingly**. — **lounge chair** an easy chair suitable for lounging or relaxing in; **lounge lizard** a person who indolently spends time at social events and gatherings; **lounge suit** a man's matching jacket and trousers for (formal) everyday wear.

loupe *lōōp, n* a small jeweller's and watchmaker's magnifying glass, worn in the eye-socket. [Fr.]

lour or **lower** *lowr* or *low'ər, vi* to look sullen or threatening; to scowl. — *n* a scowl, glare; a gloomy threatening appearance. — *n* and *adj* **lour'ing** or **lower'ing**. — *adv* **lour'ingly** or **lower'ingly**. — *adj* **lour'y** or **lower'y**. [M.E. *louren*.]

louse *lows, n* a wingless insect (Pediculus) that lives on other creatures, with a flat body, and short legs; extended to similar animals, related and unrelated: — *pl* **lice** (*līs*); a person worthy of contempt (*slang*; *pl* **lous'es**). — *vt* to remove lice from; to spoil, make a mess of (with *up*; *slang*). — *adv* **lou'sily** (*-zi-li*). — *n* **lou'siness**. — *adj* **lousy** (*low'zi*) infested with lice; swarming or full (with *with*; *slang*); inferior, bad, unsatisfactory (*slang*). [O.E. *lūs*, pl. *lȳs*.]

lout *lowt, n* an ill-mannered, aggressive or awkward man or youth. — *adj* **lout'ish** awkward, ill-mannered and coarse. — *adv* **lout'ishly**. — *n* **lout'ishness**.

louvre or **louver** *lōō'vər, n* a louvre-board; a turretlike structure on a roof for the escape of smoke or for ventilation; an opening or shutter with louvre-boards. — *adj* **lou'vred** or **lou'vered**. — **lou'vre-** (or **lou'ver-**)**board** a sloping slat placed horizontally or vertically across an opening; **louvre-** (or **louver-**)**door'** or **louvre-** (or **louver-**)**win'dow** a door or open window crossed by a series of sloping boards. [O.Fr. *lover, lovier*.]

lovage *luv'ij, n* an umbelliferous salad plant (*Levisticum officinale*) of southern Europe similar to Angelica; any plant of the related genus *Ligusticum*, including *Scottish lovage*. [O.Fr. *luvesche* — L.L. *levisticum*, L. *ligusticum*, lit. Ligurian.]

lovat *luv'ət, n* a greyish- or bluish-green colour, usu. in tweed or woollen cloth; cloth or wool of this colour (also **lovat-green'**). — Also *adj*. [From *Lovat*, near Inverness.]

love *luv, n* charity; an affection for something that gives pleasure; strong liking; devoted attachment to one of the opposite sex; sexual attachment; a love affair; the object of affection; a term of address indicating endearment or affection (often spelled **luv** to represent *dialect* or *colloq* use); in some games, no score. — *vt* to be fond of; to regard with pleasure and affection; to delight in with exclusive affection; to regard with benevolence. — *vi* to feel love and affection. — *adj* **lovable** or **loveable** (*luv'ə-bl*) worthy of love; attracting affection. — *adj* **love'less**. — *n* **love'liness**. — *adj* **love'ly** exciting admiration; attractive; extremely beautiful; delightful (*colloq*). — *adv* delightfully, very well (*dialect*). — *n* (*colloq*) a beautiful woman, esp. a model or showgirl. — *n* **lov'er** a person who loves, esp. someone in love with a person of the opposite sex (in the singular usually used of the man); one of the partners in a love affair; a person who is fond of anything. — *n* **lov'ey** (*colloq*) a term of endearment. — *n* and *adj* **lov'ing**. — *adv* **lov'ingly**. — *n* **lov'ingness**. — **love affair** a romantic sexual relationship, esp. a temporary one; **love'-apple** the tomato; **love'bird** a small African parrot (*Agapornis*), strongly attached to its mate; extended to other kinds of bird; **love'bite** a temporary red patch left on the skin after sucking and biting during lovemaking; **love'-child** an illegitimate child; **love game** (*lawn tennis*) a game in which the loser has not scored (poss. from Fr. *l'œuf*, egg — cf. **duck**[3] in cricket); **love-in-a-mist'** a flower of the *Nigella* genus (*Nigella damascena*); a West Indian passion-flower; **love'-knot** or **lover's-knot'** an intricate knot, used as a token of love; **love'-letter** a letter written during the period of courtship; **love-lies-bleed'ing** a kind of amaranth with drooping red spike; **love life** state of events in, or area of life concerning, romance or sexual attachments. — *adj* **love'lorn** forsaken by or pining for one's love. — **love'making** amorous courtship; sexual play and often intercourse; **love'-match** a marriage for love, not money, status, etc.; **love'-nest** a place where lovers, often illicit, meet or live; **love'-potion** a philtre; **lovers' lane** a quiet path or road frequented by lovers. — *adj* **love'sick** sad, pining for love. — **love'-song** a song expressing or relating to love; **love'-story** a story with romantic love as its subject; **love'-token** a gift in evidence of love. — *adj* **lovey-dovey** (*luv-i-duv'i*; *colloq*) sentimentally and obviously affectionate. — **lov'ing-cup** a cup passed round at the end of a feast for all to drink from; **loving-kind'ness** (*Bible*) kindness together with love; mercy. — **fall in love** to become in love (with); **for love or money** in any way or for any reason whatever; **for the love of it** for the sake of it; for the pleasure of it; **for the love of Mike** (*slang*) for any sake; **in love (with)** romantically and sexually attracted, devoted (to); **make love to** to try to gain the affections of; to have sexual intercourse with; **there's no love lost between them** they have no liking for each other. [O.E. *lufu*, love.]

low[1] *lō, vi* to make the noise of cattle. — *n* sound made by oxen. — Also **low'ing**. [O.E. *hlōwan*.]

low[2] *lō, adj* (*compar* **lower** *lō'ə*, *superl* **lowest** *lō'ist* or **low'ermost**) occupying a position that is far down or not much raised; not reaching a high level; not tall; reaching far down; of clothes, cut so as to expose the neck and chest; quiet and soft, not loud; of deep pitch, as sounds produced by slow vibrations are; produced with part of the tongue low in the mouth (*phon*); nearly level, not much raised; expressed in measurement by a small number; (of numbers) small; of small value, intensity, quantity or rank; having little vitality, badly nourished; scanty, deficient; unfavourable; debased; humble; socially depressed; backward in organisation or culture; of latitude, near the equator. — *n* that which is low or lowest; an area of low barometrical pressure; a low or minimum level; low gear. — *adv* in or to a low position, state or manner; humbly; with a low voice or sound; at low pitch; at a low price; in small quantity or to small degree. — *vt* **low'er** to make lower; to let or put down; to lessen. — *vi* to become lower or less. — *n* **low'ering** the act of bringing low or reducing. — *adj* letting down; sinking; degrading. — *adj* **low'ermost** lowest. — *adv* **low'lily** (*-li-li*). — *n* **low'liness.** — *adj* **low'ly** humble; modest; low in stature or in organisation. — *n* **low'ness.** — *adj* **low'-born** of humble birth. — *adj* **low-bred'** ill-bred; unmannerly. — **low'-brow** a person who is not intellectual or makes no pretensions to intellect (also *adj*). — *adj* **low'-cal** low in calories. — *adj* **Low Church** of a party within the Church of England setting little value on sacerdotal claims, ecclesiastical constitutions, ordinances and forms, holding evangelical views of theology (opp. to *High Church*). — **Low-Church'ism; Low-Church'man; low comedy** comedy of farcical situation, slapstick, low life. — *adj* **low-cost'** cheap. — *adj* **low'-country** lowland (**the Low Countries** Holland and Belgium). — *adj* **low-cut'** (of a garment) with a low neckline, revealing much of the chest. — *adj* **low'-down** (*colloq*) base; dishonourable. — *n* (*slang*) information, esp. of a confidential or damaging nature. — *adj* **lower-case'** (*printing*) small as distinguished from capital (orig. because kept in a lower case) (also *n*). — *adj* **lower-class'** pertaining to people of low social class. — **low'er-deck** the deck immediately above the hold; ship's crew (as opposed to officers) (also *adj*). — **lower house** or **chamber** the larger and more representative of two legislative chambers; **lower regions** Hades, hell. — *adj* **low-fat'** containing only a small proportion of fat. — *adj* **low-key'** (in painting or photography) in mostly dark tones or colours, with few, if any, highlights; undramatic, understated, restrained; (of a person) not easily excited, showing no visible reaction. — **low'land** land low in relation to higher land (also *adj*); **low'lander** (also with *cap*) a native of lowlands, esp. the **Lowlands** of Scotland; **low life** sordid social circumstances; people of low social class; **low'light** (usu. in *pl*) a portion of hair artificially brightened to enhance the natural colour of the hair. — Also *vt*. — **low'-loader** a low wagon without sides, used for very heavy loads; **low mass** mass celebrated without music and incense. — *adj* **low-mind'ed** having crude or vulgar motives or interests. — *adj* **low'-necked** (of a dress, blouse, etc.) cut low in the neck and away from the shoulders, décolleté. — *adj* **low-paid'** (of a worker) receiving or (of a job) rewarded by low wages. — *adj* **low'-pitched** (of sound) low in pitch; (of a roof) gentle in slope; having a low ceiling. — *adj* **low-press'ure** employing or exerting a low degree of pressure, said of steam and steam-engines; having low barometric pressure. — **low profile** a manner or attitude revealing very little of one's feelings, intentions, activities, etc. — *adj* **low-pro'file** (of people) having such a manner or attitude; (of a tyre) wide in proportion to its height (*autos*). — **low relief** same as **bas-relief.** — *adj* **low'-rise** (of buildings) having only a few storeys, in contrast to *high-rise* (q.v.). — *adj* **low-spir'ited** downcast or depressed; not lively, sad. — **low-spir'itedness; Low Sunday** the first Sunday after Easter; **low technology** or (*colloq*) **low tech** simple, unsophisticated technology used in the production of basic commodities (also (with hyphen) *adj*). — *adj* **low-ten'sion** using, generating or operating at a low voltage. — **low tide** or **low water** the lowest point of the ebbing tide; **Lowveld** (*lō'felt* or *-velt*; also without *cap*) the lower altitude areas of the eastern Transvaal; **low-wat'ermark** the lowest line reached by the tide; anything marking the point of greatest degradation, decline, etc. (*fig*). — **an all-time low** the lowest recorded level; **lay low** to overthrow, fell or kill; **low-level language** any computer-programming language that is designed as a machine code rather than as a language comprehensible to the user (opp. to *high-level language*); **low-noise converter** (*TV*) an aerial component that receives, magnifies and transmits by wire a satellite signal. [O.N. *lāgr*, Du. *laag*, low.]

lowan *lō'ən*, *n*. Same as **mallee-bird** or **mound'-bird**.

lower[1] *lowr*, **lowering** and **lowery**. See **lour**.

lower[2] *lō'ər*. See **low**[2].

lox[1] *loks*, *n l*iquid *ox*ygen, used as a rocket propellant.

lox[2] *loks*, *n* a kind of smoked salmon. [Yiddish *laks*, from M.H.G. *lahs*, salmon.]

loxodrome *loks'ə-drōm*, *n* a line on the surface of a sphere which makes equal oblique angles with all meridians, a rhumb-line. — Also called **loxodromic curve, line** or **spiral**. [Gr. *loxos*, oblique, *dromos*, a course.]

loyal *loi'əl*, *adj* faithful, true; firm in allegiance; personally devoted to a sovereign, government, leader, etc.; expressing or manifesting loyalty. — *n* **loy'alist** a loyal adherent, esp. of a king or of an established government; (also with *cap*) in Northern Ireland, a supporter of the British government; (also with *cap*) in English history, a partisan of the Stuarts; (also with *cap*) in the American War of Independence, a person siding with the British. — *adv* **loy'ally.** — *n* **loy'alty.** — **loyal toast** a toast to the sovereign, drunk at a formal dinner. [Fr., — L. *lēgālis* — *lēx*, *lēgis*, law.]

lozenge *loz'inj*, *n* a diamond-shaped parallelogram or rhombus; a small sweet, sometimes medicated, originally diamond-shaped. — *adj* **loz'enge-shaped**. [Fr. *losange*.]

LP *el-pē'*, (*colloq*) *n* a *l*ong-*p*laying record.

LP *abbrev* for: Labour Party; Lord or Lady Provost; low pressure.

LPG *abbrev* for liquefied petroleum gas.

LPO *abbrev* for London Philharmonic Orchestra.

Lr *abbrev* for lira (the Italian unit of currency).

Lr (*chem*) *symbol* for lawrencium.

LRAM *abbrev* for Licentiate of the Royal Academy of Music.

LRB *abbrev* for London Residuary Body (see **GLC**).

LRCP *abbrev* for Licentiate of the Royal College of Physicians (**Edin.**, of Edinburgh; **Lond.**, of London; **Irel.**, of Ireland).

LRCS *abbrev* for Licentiate of the Royal College of Surgeons (**Ed.**, of Edinburgh; **Eng.**, of England; **Irel.**, of Ireland).

LS *abbrev* for: Lesotho (I.V.R.); Linnaean Society; *loco sigilli* (L.), in the place of the seal.

LSD *abbrev* for lysergic acid diethylamide (see under **lysis**).

L.S.D. *abbrev* for *librae, solidae, denarii* (L.), pounds, shillings, pence.

LSE *abbrev* for London School of Economics.

LSO *abbrev* for London Symphony Orchestra.

LTOM *abbrev* for London Traded Options Market.

Lu (*chem*) *symbol* for lutetium.

luau *loō-ow'*, *n* a Hawaiian dish made of coconut, taro, octopus, etc.; a Hawaiian feast or party. [Hawaiian *lu'au*.]

lubber *lub'ər* or **lubbard** *lub'ərd*, *n* an awkward, big, clumsy fellow. — *adj* lubberly. — *adj* and *adv* **lubb'erly**. — **lubb'er-line** (*naut*) a line on a ship's compass marking the ship's forward direction.

lubricate *lōō'* or *lū'bri-kāt*, *vt* to make smooth or slippery; to cover or supply with oil or other material to overcome friction; to supply with alcoholic drink (*colloq*); to bribe. — *adj* **lu'bricant** lubricating. — *n* a substance used to reduce friction. — *n* **lubricā'tion**. — *adj* **lu'bricātive**. — *n* **lu'bricātor**. — *n* **lubritō'rium** (*chiefly US*) a place in a garage or service station where motor vehicles are lubricated. [L. *lūbricus*, slippery.]

lubricity *lōō-* or *lū-bris'i-ti* , *n* slipperiness, smoothness (*rare*); instability; lewdness (*literary*). [Ety. as for **lubricate**.]

lucarne *lōō-* or *lū-kärn'*, *n* a dormer window, esp. in a church spire. [Fr.]

lucent *lōō'* or *lū'sənt*, *adj* shining; bright. — *n* **lu'cency**. [L. *lūcēns*, *-entis*, — *lūx*, *lūcis*, light.]

lucerne *lōō-* or *lū-sûrn'*, *n* purple medick, a plant resembling clover, also called alfalfa (esp. *US*), valuable as fodder for cattle, etc. [Fr. *luzerne*.]

luces. See **lux**.

lucid *lōō'* or *lū'sid*, *adj* shining; transparent; easily understood; not confused, sane. — *n* **lucid'ity** or **lu'cidness**. — *adv* **lu'cidly**. [L. *lūcidus* — *lūx*, *lūcis*, light.]

Lucifer *lōō'* or *lū'si-fər*, *n* the planet Venus as morning-star; Satan; (without *cap*; *archaic*) a match of wood tipped to be ignited by friction. [L. *lūcifer*, light-bringer — *lūx*, *lūcis*, light, *ferre*, to bring.]

luck *luk*, *n* fortune; good fortune; an object with which a family's fortune is supposed to be bound up. — *adv* **luck'ily** in a lucky way; I'm glad to say, fortunately. — *n* **luck'iness**. — *adj* **luck'less** without good luck; unhappy. — *adv* **luck'lessly**. — *n* **luck'lessness**. — *adj* **luck'y** having, attended by, portending or bringing good luck. — **luck'y-bag** a bag sold without its contents being disclosed; a bag in which to dip and draw a prize; **lucky charm** an object which is supposed to ensure good fortune; **lucky dip** a tub or container in which to dip and draw a prize; **lucky strike** a stroke of luck. — **luck out** (*US*) to have a run or instance of good luck; **push one's luck** (*colloq*) to try to make too much of an advantage, risking total failure; **tough luck** an expression of real or affected sympathy for someone's predicament; **try one's luck (at)** to attempt something; **worse luck** unfortunately. [Prob. L.G. or Du. *luk*.]

lucre *lōō'* or *lū'kər*, *n* sordid gain; riches. — *adj* **lu'crative** (*-krə-tiv*) profitable. — *adv* **lu'cratively**. [L. *lucrum*, gain.]

lucubration *lōō-* or *lū-kə-brā'shən*, *n* study or composition protracted late into the night; a product of such study.

luculent *lōō'* or *lū'kū-lənt*, *adj* bright; clear; convincing. — *adv* **lu'culently**. [L. *lūculentus* — *lūx*, light.]

Lucy Stoner *lōō'si stō'ner*, (*US*) *n* a woman who keeps her maiden name after marriage. [From *Lucy Stone*, an American suffragist (1818–93).]

Luddite *lud'īt*, *n* one of a band of protesters against unemployment who destroyed machinery in northern England about 1812–18; hence, any opponent of technological innovation, etc. — Also *adj*. — *n* **Ludd'ism**. [Said to be from Ned *Ludd*, who had smashed stocking-frames (machines on which stockings were knitted) at a slightly earlier date.]

ludic *lōō'dik*, *adj* playful, esp. spontaneously and aimlessly. — *adj* **lu'dically**. [Fr. *ludique* — L. *ludus*, play.]

ludicrous *lōō'* or *lū'di-krəs*, *adj* intended to excite, or exciting laughter; ridiculous, absurd; laughable. — *adv* **lu'dicrously**. — *n* **lu'dicrousness**. [L. *lūdicrus* — *lūděre*, to play.]

ludo *lōō'* or *lū'dō*, *n* a game in which counters are moved on a board according to the numbers shown on thrown dice: — *pl* **lud'os**. [L. *lūdō*, I play.]

lues *lōō'* or *lū'ēz*, *n* syphilis (**lues venerea**). — *adj* **luetic** (*-et'ik*). [L. *lŭēs*, a pestilence.]

luff *luf*, *n* the windward side of a ship; the act of sailing a ship close to the wind; the part of a ship's bow where the planks begin to curve in towards the cut-water (also **loof**). — *vi* to turn a ship towards the wind. — *vt* to turn nearer to the wind; to move (the jib of a crane) in and out. [M.E. *luff*, *lof(f)* — O.Fr. *lof*.]

luffa. See **loofah**.

Luftwaffe *lōōft'vä-fə*, (Ger.) *n* air force.

lug[1] *lug*, *vt* to pull; to drag heavily; to carry (something heavy); (of sailing-ships) to carry (too much sail). — *vi* to pull: — *pr p* **lugg'ing**; *pa t* and *pa p* **lugged**. — *adj* **lugg'able** (esp. of computers) portable, but with some difficulty. — Also *n*. — **lug in** to introduce without any apparent connection or relevance. [Cf. Sw. *lugga*, to pull by the hair; perh. connected with **lug**[3].]

lug[2] *lug* or **lugsail** *lug'sāl* or *lug'sl*, *n* a square sail bent upon a yard that hangs obliquely to the mast. — *n* **lugg'er** a small vessel with lugsails.

lug[3] *lug*, *n* a side flap of a cap; the ear (*colloq*; chiefly *Scot*); an earlike projection or appendage; a handle; a loop. — *adj* **lugged** (*lugd*) having lugs or a lug. — **lug'hole** (*slang*) (the hole in) the ear.

lug[4] *lug* or **lugworm** *lug'wûrm*, *n* a sluggish worm found in the sand on the seashore, often used for bait.

luge *lōōzh* or *lüzh*, *n* a light toboggan. — *vi* to glide on such a sledge: — *pr p* **lug'ing** or **luge'ing**. — *n* **lu'ger**. — *n* **lug'ing** or **luge'ing**. [Swiss Fr.]

Luger® *lōō'gər*, (Ger.) *n* a type of pistol.

luggage *lug'ij*, *n* the suitcases and other baggage of a traveller. — **lugg'age-van** a railway wagon for luggage. [Ety. as for **lug**[1].]

lugger, lugsail. See **lug**[2].

lugubrious *lōō-gōō'bri-əs* or *-gū'*, *adj* mournful; dismal. — *adv* **lugu'briously**. — *n* **lugu'briousness**. [L. *lūgubris* — *lūgēre*, to mourn.]

lugworm. See **lug**[4].

lukewarm *lōōk'wörm*, *adj* moderately warm, tepid; half-hearted. — *adj* **luke'warmish**. — *adv* **luke'warmly**. — *n* **luke'warmness** or **luke'warmth**. [M.E. *luek*, *luke*, moderately warm.]

lull *lul*, *vt* to soothe; to compose; to quiet. — *vi* to become calm; to subside. — *n* an interval of calm; a calming influence. [Imit.]

lullaby *lul'ə-bī*, *n* a song to lull children to sleep, a cradle-song. — *vt* to lull to sleep. [Ety. as for **lull** and **bye**[2].]

lulu *lōō'lōō*, (*slang*) *n* a thing or person that is outstandingly bad or impressive.

lumbago *lum-bā'gō*, *n* rheumatic pain in the muscles or fibrous tissues in the lumbar region: — *pl* **lumbā'gos**. — *adj* **lumbaginous** (*-baj'i-nəs*). [L. *lumbāgō*, lumbago — *lumbus*, loin.]

lumbar *lum'bər*, *adj* (*anat*) of or relating to the section of the spine between the lowest rib and the pelvis. — **lumbar puncture** (*med*) the process of inserting a needle into the lower part of the spinal cord to take a specimen of cerebrospinal fluid, inject drugs, etc. [L. *lumbus*, loin.]

lumber[1] *lum'bər*, *n* furniture stored away out of use; anything cumbersome or useless; timber, esp. sawn or split for use (*NAm*). — *vt* to fill with lumber; to heap together in confusion; to burden with something, e.g. a task or responsibility, that is unwanted or troublesome (*colloq*); to cut the timber from. — *vi* to work as a lumberjack. — *n* **lum'berer** a lumberjack. — *n* **lum'bering** felling, sawing and removal of timber. — **lum'ber-camp** a lumberjack's camp; **lum'berjack** or **lum'berman** someone employed in the felling, sawing, etc. of timber; **lum'ber-jacket** a man's longish, loose-fitting, sometimes belted jacket fastened right up to the neck and usu. in bold-patterned heavy material; a woman's cardigan similarly fastened; **lum'ber-mill** a sawmill; **lum'ber-yard** a timber-yard. [Perhaps from **lumber²**.]

lumber² *lum'bər, vi* to move heavily and clumsily; to rumble. — *n* **lum'berer.** [M.E. *lomeren.*]

lumen *lōō'* or *lū'men, n* a unit of luminous flux — the light emitted in one second in a solid angle of one steradian from a point that is a radiation source of uniform intensity of one candela; the cavity of a tubular organ (*anat*); the space within the cell-wall (*bot*): — *pl* **lu'mina** or **lu'mens.** — *adj* **lu'menal** or **lu'minal** of a lumen. — *n* **lu'minance** luminousness; the measure of brightness of a surface, measured in candela/cm² of the surface radiating normally. — *adj* **lu'minant** giving light. — *n* a means of lighting. — *n* **lu'minarism.** — *n* **lu'minarist** a person who paints luminously, or with skill in lights; an impressionist. — *n* **lu'minary** a source of light, esp. one of the heavenly bodies; someone who illustrates any subject or instructs mankind. — Also *adj.* — *n* **luminā'tion** a lighting up. — *vi* **luminesce'** to show luminescence. — *n* **luminescence** (*-es'əns*) emission of light otherwise than by incandescence and so at a relatively cool temperature; the light so emitted. — *adj* **luminesc'ent.** — *n* **lu'minist** a luminarist. — *n* **luminosity** (*-os'i-ti*) luminousness; the measure of the quantity of light actually emitted by a star, irrespective of its distance. — *adj* **lu'minous** giving light; shining; lighted; clear; lucid. — *adv* **lu'minously.** — *n* **lu'minousness.** [L. *lūmen, -inis*, light — *lūcēre*, to shine.]

lumme or **lummy** *lum'i*, (*colloq*) *interj* expressing surprise or concern. [(Lord) love me.]

lump *lump, n* a shapeless mass; a bulge or swelling; a feeling of a swelling or tightening in the throat; a considerable quantity; the total as a whole; an inert, dull, good-natured or substantial person; a lumpfish. — *vt* to throw into a confused mass; to consider everything together; to include regardless; to endure willy-nilly; to put up with regardless; to dislike. — *vi* to collect into a lump; to walk or move heavily. — *n* **lumpec'tomy** the surgical removal of a lump, caused by cancer, in the breast, esp. as opposed to removal of the entire breast. — *n* **lump'er** someone who works on the lump (see **the lump** below). — *adv* **lump'ily.** — *n* **lump'iness.** — *adj* **lump'ing** heavy, bulky. — *adj* **lump'ish** like a lump; heavy, gross; dull, sullen. — *adv* **lump'ishly.** — *n* **lump'ishness.** — *adj* **lump'y** full of lumps; like a lump. — **lump'fish** or **lump'sucker** a sea-fish (*Cyclopterus*), clumsy and with excrescences on its skin, with pectoral fins transformed into a sucker; **lump-su'gar** loaf-sugar broken in small pieces or cut in cubes; **lump sum** a single sum of money in lieu of several. — **lump it** (*colloq*) to put up with it; **the lump** system of using self-employed workmen for a particular job, esp. in order to evade tax and national insurance payments.

lumpen *lum'pən, adj* pertaining to a dispossessed and/or degraded section of a social class, as in **lumpen proletariat** (also as one word), the poorest down-and-outs; stupid, boorish. [From Ger. *Lumpen*, a rag.]

lunacy *lōō'nə-si, n* a form of insanity once believed to come with changes of the moon; insanity generally; extreme folly. — *adj* **lunatic** (*lōō'nə-tik*) affected with lunacy. — *n* a person so affected; a madman. — **lunatic asylum** a former, now offensive, name for a mental hospital; **lunatic fringe** the more nonsensical, extreme-minded, or eccentric members of a community or movement. [Ety. as for **lunar**.]

lunar *lōō'nər, adj* belonging to the moon; measured by the moon's revolutions; caused by the moon; like the moon. — *adj* **lu'nate** or **lu'nated** crescent-shaped. — *n* **lunā'tion** a synodic month. — *n* **lunette'** a crescent-shaped ornament; a semicircular or crescent-shaped space where a vault intersects a wall or another vault, often occupied by a window or by decoration; an arched opening in a vault; a detached bastion (*fort*); a small horseshoe; a moon-shaped case for the consecrated host (*RC*). — *adj* **lunisō'lar** pertaining to the moon and sun jointly (**lunisolar calendar, lunisolar year** one divided according to the changes of the moon, but made to agree in average length with the solar year). — *adj* **lunitī'dal** pertaining to the moon and its influence on the tide (**lunitidal interval** the time interval between the moon's transit and the next high tide at a particular place). — *n* **lu'nūla** a lunule; a crescentlike appearance, esp. the whitish area at the base of a nail; a Bronze Age crescent-shaped gold ornament forming part of a necklace. — *adj* **lu'nūlar.** — *adj* **lu'nūlate** or **lu'nulated** shaped like a small crescent (*bot*); having crescent-shaped markings. — *n* **lu'nule** anything shaped like a small crescent; a geometrical figure bounded by two arcs of circles. — **lunar cycle** a **metonic cycle; Lunar Excursion Module** (abbrev. **LEM** or **lem**) a module for use in the last stage of the journey to land on the moon. [L. *lūna*, the moon — *lūcēre*, to shine.]

lunch *lunch* or *lunsh, n* midday meal; formerly a snack at any time of day, now a light midday meal (*US*). — *vi* to take lunch. — *vt* to provide lunch for. — *n* **lunch'eon** (esp. a formal) lunch. — *n* **luncheonette'** (orig. *US*) a restaurant serving snacks and light meals. — **lunch box** a box or container for carrying, esp. to work, sandwiches, etc. for lunch; **lunch'eon-meat** a type of precooked meat containing preservatives, usually served cold; **luncheon voucher** a ticket or voucher given by employer to employee to be used to pay for the latter's lunch; **lunch'-hour** or **lunch'-time** the time of, or allotted to, lunch; an interval allowed for lunch. [Shortened form of **luncheon** — M.E. *none(s)chench*, noon drink.]

lung *lung, n* a respiratory organ in animals that breathe atmospheric air; an open space in a town (*fig*). — *adj* **lunged.** — *n* **lung'ful.** — **lung'-fish** a fish that has lungs as well as gills. [O.E. *lungen.*]

lunge¹ *lunj, n* a sudden thrust as in fencing; a forward plunge. — *vi* to make a lunge; to plunge forward. — *vt* to thrust with a lunge: — *pr p* **lunge'ing** or **lung'ing.** [Fr. *allonger*, to lengthen — L. *ad*, to, *longus*, long.]

lunge² or **longe** *lunj, n* a long rope used in horse-training; training with a lunge; a training-ground for horses. — *vt* to train or cause to go with a lunge. [Fr. *longe* — L. *longus*, long.]

lungi *lōōn'gē, n* a long cloth used as loin-cloth, sash, turban, etc. [Hind. and Pers. *lungī.*]

lunisolar to **lunule.** See under **lunar**.

lupin or (esp. in U.S.) **lupine** *lōō'* or *lū'pin, n* a plant of the papilionaceous genus (*Lupinus*), with flowers on long spikes; its seed. [L. *lupīnus.*]

lupine *lōō'* or *lū'pīn, adj* of a wolf; like a wolf; wolfish. [L. *lupīnus* — *lupus*, a wolf.]

lupus *lōō'* or *lū'pəs, n* a chronic tuberculosis of the skin, often affecting the nose (*med*); (with *cap*) a constellation in the southern hemisphere (*astron*). [L. *lupus*, a wolf.]

lur. See **lure²**.

lurch¹ *lûrch, n* (in various games) a situation in which one side fails to score at all, or is left far behind. — **leave someone in the lurch** to leave someone in a difficult situation without help. [O.Fr. *lourche.*]

lurch² *lûrch, vi* to roll or pitch suddenly forward or to one side. — *n* a sudden roll or pitch.

lurcher *lûrch'ər, n* a dog that is a cross between a greyhound and esp. a collie.

lure¹ *lōōr* or *lūr, n* any enticement; bait; a decoy; a bunch of feathers used to recall a hawk (*falconry*). — *vt* to entice; decoy. [O.Fr. *loerre* — M.H.G. *luoder*, bait.]

lure² or **lur** *lōōr*, *n* a long curved Bronze Age trumpet still used in Scandinavian countries for calling cattle, etc. [O.N. *lūthr*; Dan. and Norw. *lur*.]

Lurex® *loo'* or *lū'reks*, *n* (fabric made from) a plastic-coated aluminium thread.

lurgy or **lurgi** *lûr'gi*, (esp. *facetious*) *n* a fictitious disease. [Invented and popularised by the cast of BBC Radio's *The Goon Show* (1949–60).]

lurid *lōō'* or *lū'rid*, *adj* glaringly bright; pale or wan; melodramatically sensational; gloomily threatening; dingily reddish-yellow or yellowish-brown (*bot*). — *adv* **lu'ridly.** — *n* **lu'ridness.** [L. *lūridus*.]

lurk *lûrk*, *vi* to lie in wait; to be concealed; to linger around furtively. — *n* a prowl; a lurking-place; a dodge or swindle (esp. *Austr slang*). — *n* **lurk'er.** — *n* and *adj* **lurk'ing.** — **lurk'ing-place.**

luscious *lush'əs*, *adj* exceedingly sweet; delightful, pleasurable; (esp. of musical sound or literary style) too rich, cloying; attractive and voluptuous. — *adv* **lusc'iously.** — *n* **lusc'iousness.** [**delicious**, influenced by **lush¹**, has been suggested.]

lush¹ *lush*, *adj* rich, juicy and succulent; luxuriant; luxurious. — *adv* **lush'ly.** — *n* **lush'ness.** [Perh. a form of *lash* (archaic slang) liquor, drink.]

lush² *lush*, (*slang*, esp. *NAm*) *n* a drinker or drunkard; alcohol. — *vi* to overindulge in alcohol. [Perh. from **lush¹**.]

lust *lust*, *n* strong sexual desire; passionate desire; eagerness to possess; longing. — *vi* to have strong sexual desire; to desire eagerly (with *after* or *for*). — *n* **lust'er.** — *adj* **lust'ful** having lust; inciting to lust; sensual. — *adv* **lust'fully.** — *n* **lust'fulness.** [O.E. *lust*, pleasure.]

lustrate *lus'trāt*, *vt* to purify by sacrifice. — *n* **lustrā'tion.** [L. *lūstrum*, prob. — *luĕre*, to wash, to purify.]

lustre or in U.S. **luster** *lus'tər*, *n* characteristic surface appearance in reflected light; sheen, gloss, brightness; splendour; renown, distinction (*fig*); a candlestick, vase, etc., ornamented with pendants of cut-glass; a dress material with cotton warp and woollen weft, and highly finished surface; a metallic pottery glaze. — *vt* to impart a lustre to. — *vi* to become lustrous. — *adj* **lus'treless.** — *n* **lus'tring.** — *adj* **lus'trous** bright; shining; luminous. — *adv* **lus'trously.** — **lus'treware** pottery, etc. with a metallic glaze. [Fr., — L. *lūstrāre*, to shine on.]

lusty *lus'ti*, *adj* vigorous; healthy and strong; stout, bulky. — *adv* **lust'ily.** — *n* **lust'iness.** [Ety. as for **lust.**]

lute¹ *lōōt* or *lūt*, *n* an old stringed instrument shaped like half a pear. — *n* **lut'anist, lut'enist, lut'er** or **lut'ist** a player on the lute. — *n* **luthier** (*lūt'i-ər*) a maker of lutes, guitars, and other stringed instruments. [O.Fr. *lut*, from Ar. *al*, the, *'ūd*, wood, the lute.]

lute² *lōōt* or *lūt*, *n* clay, cement or other material used as a protective covering, an airtight stopping, a waterproof seal, etc. — *vt* to coat or close with lute. — *n* **lut'ing.** [L. *lutum*, mud — *luĕre*, to wash.]

luteal. See **lutein.**

lutecium *lōō-* or *lū-tē'shi-əm*, *n.* Same as **lutetium.**

lutein *lōō'tē-in* or *lū'*, *n* a yellow pigment found in yolk of egg. — *adj* **luteal** (*lōō'ti-əl*) pertaining to (the formation of) the corpus luteum. — *n* **luteinīsā'tion** or **-z-** the process of stimulation to the ovary, whereby ovulation occurs and a corpus luteum is formed. — *vt* and *vi* **lu'teinise** or **-ize.** — **luteinising hormone** a hormone that, in females, stimulates ovulation and the formation of the corpus luteum (q.v. under **corpus**), and in males, the production of androgen. [L. *lūteus*, yellow, *lūteum*, yolk of egg.]

lutenist. See under **lute¹.**

lutetium *lōō-* or *lūtē'shi-əm*, *n* metallic element (symbol **Lu**; atomic no. 71) first separated from ytterbium by Georges Urbain, a Parisian. [L. *Lutetia*, Paris.]

Lutheran *lōō'thər-ən*, *adj* pertaining to Martin *Luther*, the German Protestant reformer (1483–1546), or to his doctrines. — *n* a follower of Luther. — *n* **Lu'theranism** or **Lu'therism.** — *n* **Lu'therist.**

luthern *lōō'* or *lū'thərn*, *n* a dormer window. [Prob. a variant of **lucarne.**]

luthier. See under **lute¹.**

Lutine bell *lōō-tēn'* (or *lōō'tēn*) *bel*, *n* a bell recovered from the frigate *Lutine*, and rung at Lloyd's of London before certain important announcements.

lutz *lŏŏts*, *n* in figure-skating, a jump (with rotation) from the back outer edge of one skate to the back outer edge of the other. [Poss. Gustave *Lussi* of Switzerland, born 1898, the first exponent.]

luv. See **love.**

lux *luks*, *n* a unit of illumination, one lumen per square metre: — *pl* **lux, lux'es** or **luces** (*lōō'sēz*). — **lux'meter** an instrument for measuring illumination. [L. *lūx*, light.]

luxate *luks'āt*, (*med*) *vt* to put out of joint; to displace. — *n* **luxā'tion** a dislocation. [L. *luxāre*, *-ātum* — *luxus* — Gr. *loxos*, slanting.]

luxe *lŏŏks* or *luks* or (Fr.) *lüks*, *n* luxury. — See also **de luxe.** [Fr., — L. *luxus*, a dislocation, extravagance, luxury.]

luxmeter. See under **lux.**

luxury *luk'shə-ri* or *lug'zhə-ri*, *n* abundant provision of means of comfort, ease and pleasure; indulgence, esp. in costly pleasures; anything delightful, often expensive, but not necessary; a dainty. — *adj* relating to or providing luxury. — *n* **luxuriance** (*lug-zhōō'ri-əns*, *-zū'*, *-zhū'*, or *luk-*, etc.) growth in rich abundance or excess; exuberance; overgrowth; rankness. — *adj* **luxu'riant** exuberant in growth; overabundant; profuse; erroneously, luxurious. — *adv* **luxu'riantly.** — *vi* **luxu'riate** to be luxuriant, grow profusely; to live luxuriously; to enjoy luxury; to enjoy or revel in indulgence. — *n* **luxuriā'tion.** — *adj* **luxu'rious** of luxury; enjoying or indulging in luxury; aiming to provide luxury; furnished with luxuries. — *adv* **luxu'riously.** — *n* **luxu'riousness.** [O.Fr. *luxurie* — L. *luxuria*, luxury — *luxus*, excess.]

lycanthropy *lī-* or *li-kan'thrə-pi*, *n* power of changing oneself into a wolf; a kind of madness, in which the patient has fantasies of being a wolf. — *n* **lycanthrope** (*lī'kan-thrōp* or *-kan'*) or **lycan'thropist** a werewolf; a person suffering from lycanthropy. — *adj* **lycanthropic** (*-throp'*). [Gr. *lykos*, a wolf, *anthrōpos*, a man.]

lycée *lē'sā*, *n* a state secondary school in France. [Fr., lyceum.]

Lyceum *lī-sē'əm*, *n* a gymnasium and grove beside the temple of Apollo at Athens, in whose walks Aristotle taught; (without *cap*) a college; (without *cap*) a place or building devoted to literary studies, lectures, etc.: — *pl* **lyce'ums.** [L. *Lȳcēum* — Gr. *Lykeion* — *Lykeios*, an epithet of Apollo (perh. wolf-slayer, perhaps the Lycian).]

lychee, litchi, lichee or **lichi** *lī'chē*, *lē'chē* or *-chē'*, or **leechee** *lē'chē*, *n* a Chinese fruit, a nut or berry with a pale fleshy aril; the tree (*Litchi chineasis*) that bears it. [Chin. *li-chi*.]

lychgate. See **lichgate.**

Lycra® *lī'krə*, *n* (a fabric made from) a lightweight, synthetic, elastomeric fibre.

Lydian *lid'i-ən*, *adj* pertaining to *Lydia* in Asia Minor; (of music) soft and slow, luxurious and effeminate. — *n* a native of Lydia; the language of ancient Lydia, apparently related to Hittite. [Gr. *Lȳdiā*, Lydia.]

lye *lī*, *n* a strong alkaline solution; a liquid used for washing; a solution got by leaching. [O.E. *lēah*, *lēag*.]

lying. See **lie¹·².**

lykewake *līk'wāk*, **likewalk** or **lykewalk** *līk'wök*, (*Scot*; *Eng* **lichwake** *lich'*) *n* watch over the dead, often involving festivities. [O.E. *līc*.]

Lyme disease *līm di-zēz'*, *n* a viral disease transmitted to humans by ticks, affecting the joints, heart and nervous system. [First discovered in *Lyme*, Connecticut, U.S.]

Lymeswold® *līmz'wōld*, *n* a kind of mild blue full-fat soft cheese.

lymph *limf*, *n* a colourless or faintly yellowish fluid collected into the lymphatic vessels from the tissues in animal bodies, of a rather saltish taste, and with an alkaline reaction; a vaccine. — *n* **lymphadenop'athy** (Gr. *adēn*, a gland, *pathos*, suffering) a disease of the lymph nodes. — *adj* **lymphangial** (*-an'jəl*; Gr. *angeion*, vessel) pertaining to the lymphatic vessels. — *n* **lymphangitis** (*-an-jī'tis*) inflammation of a lymphatic vessel. — *adj* **lymphat'ic** pertaining to lymph; inclined to be sluggish and flabby, orig. considered as the result of excess of lymph. — *n* a vessel that conveys lymph. — *adv* **lymphat'ically**. — *n* **lymph'ocyte** (*-ō-sīt*) a kind of leucocyte formed in the lymph nodes and spleen. — *n* **lymphog'raphy** radiography of the lymph glands and lymphatic system, recorded on a **lymph'ogram**. — *adj* **lymph'oid** of, carrying, or like lymph; pertaining to the lymphatic system. — *n* **lymphō'ma** a tumour consisting of lymphoid tissue. — *adj* **lymphotroph'ic** (of a virus) preferentially infecting lymphocytes. — **lymphatic system** the network of vessels that conveys lymph to the venous system; **lymph gland** or **node** any of the small masses of tissue sited along the lymphatic vessels, in which lymph is purified, and lymphocytes are formed. [L. *lympha*, water; *lymphāticus*, mad.]

lynch *linch* or *linsh*, *vt* to judge and put to death without the usual forms of law. — **lynch'-law**. [Thought to be after Captain William *Lynch* (1742–1820) of Virginia who set up and presided over tribunals outside the regular law.]

lynchpin. A variant of **linchpin**.

lynx *lingks*, *n* an animal of the cat family, with long legs, a short tail, and tufted ears (*pl* **lynx'es**); (with *cap*) the genus to which this cat belongs. — *adj* **lynx'-eyed** sharp-sighted. [L., — Gr. *lynx*, *lynkos*.]

Lyon *lī'ən*, *n* the chief herald of Scotland. — Also **Lord Lyon** or **Lyon King-of-arms** (or **Lyon-at-arms**). — **Lyon Court** the court over which he presides, having jurisdiction in questions of coat-armour and precedency. [From the heraldic *lion* of Scotland.]

lyophil *lī'ō-fil* or **lyophile** *lī'ō-fīl*, also **lyophilic** *-fil'ik*, *adj* (of a colloid) readily dispersed in a suitable medium. — *n* **lyophilisā'tion** or **-z-** freeze-drying. — *vt* **lyoph'ilise** or **-ize** to dry by freezing. — *adj* **ly'ophobe** (*-fōb*) or **lyophobic** (*-fob'*) of a colloid, not readily dispersed. [Gr. *lўē*, separation, *phileein*, to love, *phobeein*, to fear.]

lyre *līr*, *n* a musical instrument like the harp, used esp. in ancient Greece as an accompaniment to poetry — a convex resonating box with a pair of curved arms connected by a cross-bar, from which the strings were stretched over a bridge to a tailpiece. — *adj* **ly'rate** or **ly'rated** lyre-shaped; having the terminal lobe much larger than the lateral ones (*bot*). — *adj* **lyric** (*lir'ik*) of poems or their authors, expressing individual or private emotions; pertaining or to be sung to the lyre. — *n* a lyric poem; a song; (in *pl*) the words of a popular song. — *adj* **lyrical** (*lir'*) lyric; songlike; expressive, imaginative; effusive. — *adv* **lyr'ically**. — *n* **lyricism** (*lir'i-sizm*) a lyrical expression; lyrical quality. — *n* **lyr'icist** the writer of the words of a song, musical, opera, etc.; a lyric poet. — *adj* **lyriform** (*lī'*) shaped like a lyre. — *n* **lyr'ism** (*līr'* or *lir'*) lyricism; singing. — *n* **lyrist** (*līr'* or *lir'*) a player on the lyre or harp; (*lir'*) a lyric poet. — **lyre'-bird** either of two Australian ground-dwelling birds of the genus *Menura*, which are about the size of a pheasant, the tail-feathers of the male arranged, in display, in the form of a lyre; **lyriform organs** (*zool*) patches of chitin on the legs and other parts of spiders, believed to be olfactory in function. — **wax lyrical** to become increasingly expressive or effusive in praise of something. [L. *lyra* — Gr. *lyrā*.]

lysis *lī'sis*, *n* the gradual abatement of a disease, as distinguished from *crisis*; breaking down as of a cell (*biol*). — *vt* **lyse** (*līz*) to cause to undergo lysis. — *combining form* **-lysis** (*-lis-is*) denoting the action of breaking down or dividing into parts. — *verb combining form* **-lyse** or **-lyze** (*-līz*) to break down or divide into parts. — *n* **lysine** (*lī'sēn*) an essential amino acid, a product of protein hydrolysis. — *adj combining form* **-lyst** (*-list*) or **-lyte** (*-līt*) denoting something that can be broken down or divided into parts. — *adj combining form* **-lytic** or **-lytical** (*-lit'*) used of something that can be broken down or divided into parts. — **lysergic acid** (*lī-sûr'jik*) a substance, $C_{16}H_{16}O_2N_2$, derived from ergot, causing (in the form of lysergic acid diethylamide — **LSD** or **ly'sergide**) a schizophrenic condition, with hallucinations and thought processes outside the normal range. [Gr. *lysis*, dissolution — *lyein*, to loose.]

lyssa *lis'ə*, (*pathol*) *n* rabies. [Gr., madness, rabies.]

-lytic, -lytical, -lyte. See under **lysis**.

M

M or **m** *em*, *n* the twelfth letter of the Roman alphabet, and the thirteenth of the modern English alphabet, representing a labial nasal consonant; an object or figure shaped like the letter. — See also **em**.

M or **M.** *abbrev* for: Malta (I.V.R.); *Monsieur* (Fr.), Mr (*pl* **MM.**); Motorway (followed by a number).

M *symbol* for: (Roman numeral) 1000; followed by a number (as M0, M1, M2, M3), used to designate categories within the money supply, the lower the number, the more liquid the money (*econ*).

M'. See **Mac**.

M-1 *em-wun'*, *n* a Garand rifle (q.v.).

'm *m*, a shortened form of **am**; a contraction of **madam**.

m' *m* or *mə*, a shortened form of **my** as in **m'lord**.

m or **m.** *abbrev* for: male; mark(s) (German currency); married; masculine; medium; *meridiem* (L.), noon; metre(s); mile(s); million(s).

MA *abbrev* for: Massachusetts (U.S. state); Master of Arts; Morocco (I.V.R.).

ma *mä*, *n* a childish contraction for **mamma**; (*colloq*) mother (esp. *Scot*).

ma'am *mäm*, *mam* or *məm*, *n* a contraction of **madam**, the pronunciation *mäm* being used as a form of address to female royalty. — Also (*colloq*) **marm** (*mäm*) and **mum**.

Mac *mak* or *mək*, a Gaelic prefix in names, meaning son (of). — Also written **Mc** and **M'**. [Gael. and Ir. *mac*, son; Welsh *mab*, O.Welsh *map*.]

mac. See **mackintosh**.

macabre *ma-* or *mə-kä'br'*, or *ma-* or *mə-kä'bər*, *adj* gruesome; of or like the Dance of Death. — *adj* **macaberesque** (*-bər-esk'*). [Fr. *macabre*, formerly also *macabré*, perh. a corruption of *Maccabee* in reference to 2 Macc. xii. 43–6, or from Heb. *meqabēr*, gravedigger.]

Macadamia *mak-ə-dā'mi-ə*, *n* an orig. Australian genus of evergreen trees (family *Proteaceae*); (without *cap*) a tree of this genus. — **macadamia nut** (also **Queensland nut**) the edible nut of two species of macadamia, *M. ternifolia* and *M. integrifolia*; the tree bearing this nut. [John *Macadam* (1827–65), Scottish-born Australian chemist.]

macadamise or **-ize** *mək-ad'əm-īz*, *vt* to cover with small broken stones, usu. bound together with tar or asphalt, so as to form a smooth, hard surface. — *n* **macad'am** macadamised road surface; material for macadamising. — *n* **macadamīsā'tion** or **-z-**. [From John Loudon *McAdam* (1756–1836).]

macaque *mə-käk'*, *n* a monkey of genus *Macacus* or *Macaca*, to which belong the rhesus and the Barbary ape. [Fr., — Port. *macaco*, a monkey.]

macaroni *mak-ə-rō'ni*, *n* pasta in the form of long thin tubes; in the 18th century, a dandy: — *pl* **macarō'nies** or **macaro'nis**. — **macaroni cheese** macaroni served with a cheese sauce. [It. *maccaroni* (now *maccheroni*), pl. of *maccarone*, prob. — *maccare*, to crush.]

macaroon *mak-ə-ro͞on'*, *n* a sweet biscuit made of almonds. [Fr. *macaron* — It. *maccarone* (see ety. above).]

macassar oil *mə-kas'ər oil*, *n* an oil once used for the hair. [*Macassar* or Mangkasara in Celebes.]

macaw *mə-kö'*, *n* any of the large, long-tailed, brightly coloured tropical American parrots of the genus *Ara*. [Port. *macao*.]

Macc. *abbrev* for (the Apocryphal Books of) Maccabees.

Maccabean *mak-ə-bē'ən*, *adj* pertaining to Judas *Maccabaeus*, or to his family the Hasmonaeans or **Macc'abees**, who freed the Jewish nation from the persecutions of Antiochus Epiphanes, king of Syria, about 166 B.C. (1 Macc., 2 Macc.).

Mace® *mās*, *n* a type of tear gas (also called *Chemical Mace*). — *vt* (also without *cap*) to spray, attack or disable with Mace.

mace[1] *mās*, *n* a metal or metal-headed war-club, often spiked; a somewhat similar staff carried as a ceremonial mark of authority by some officials; a mace-bearer; a light, flat-headed stick formerly used in billiards. — **mace'-bearer** a person who carries the mace in a procession. [O.Fr. *mace* (Fr. *masse*) — hypothetical L. *matea*, whence L. dimin. *mateola*, a kind of tool.]

mace[2] *mās*, *n* a spice which is ground from the dried layer immediately within the shell and kernel of a nutmeg. [M.E. *macis* — Fr.]

macédoine *ma-sā-dwän'* or *-sə-*, *n* a mixture of diced vegetables or of fruit, sometimes diced, in syrup or jelly; a mixture or medley. [Fr., lit. Macedonia.]

macerate *mas'ər-āt*, *vt* to soak; to soften, or remove the soft parts of, by soaking; to wear down, esp. by fasting; to mortify. — *vi* to undergo maceration; to waste away, esp. as a result of fasting. — *n* **macerā'tion**. — *n* **mac'erātor** someone who macerates; a paper-pulping apparatus. [L. *mācerāre*, *-ātum*, to soak.]

mach. *abbrev* for machinery.

machete *ma-shet'i* or *ma-chā'tā*, *n* a heavy knife or cutlass used in Central and South America as a tool and a weapon. [Sp.]

Machiavellian *mak-i-ə-vel'yən*, *adj* destitute of political morality, ruled by expediency only; crafty, perfidious and amoral in conduct and activity. — *n* a person who imitates Niccolo *Machiavelli*, statesman and writer, of Florence (1469–1527); any cunning and unprincipled person, esp. a politician. — *n* **Machiavell'ianism** or **Machiavell'ism** the principles taught by Machiavelli, or the conduct regulated by them; cunning statesmanship.

machicolation *ma-chik-ō-lā'shən*, (*archit*) *n* a space between the corbels supporting a parapet, or an opening in the floor of a projecting gallery, for dropping missiles on an attacking enemy; a structure with such openings; the provision of such openings or structures. — *adj* **machic'olated**. [Fr. *mâchicoulis*.]

machinate *mak'i-nāt* or *mash'*, *vi* to form a plot or scheme esp. for doing harm. — *n* **machinā'tion** act of machinating; (often in *pl*) an intrigue or plot. — *n* **mach'inātor** someone who machinates. [L. *māchinārī*, *-ātus* — *māchina* — Gr. *mēchanē*, contrivance.]

machine *mə-shēn'*, *n* any artificial means or contrivance; any instrument for the conversion of motion; an engine; a vehicle, esp. a motorcycle; a person who can do only what they are told; an organised system of people or institutions, esp. political. — *vt* to use machinery for; to print, sew or make by machinery. — *n* **machin'ery** machines in general; the working parts of a machine; combined means for keeping anything in action, or for producing a desired result. — *n* **machin'ist** a person who works a machine; a constructor of machines. — **machine code** or **language** instructions for processing data, put into a form that can be directly understood and obeyed by a (specific) computer; **machine'-gun** an automatic quick-firing gun on a stable but portable mounting. — *vt* to shoot at with a machine-gun. — *adj* with the speed or rhythm of a machine-gun. — **machine'-gunner; machine intelligence** artificial intelligence. — *adj* **machine-made'** made by machinery. — **machine-pis'tol** a small submachine-gun. — *adj* **machine-read'able** (of data) in a form that can be directly processed by a computer. — **machine'-shop** a workshop where metal, etc. is machined to shape; **machine tool** a power-driven machine, as a lathe, milling machine, drill, press, etc. for shaping metal, wood or plastic material. [Fr., — L. *māchina* — Gr. *mēchanē*, akin to *mēchos*, contrivance.]

machismo. See **macho.**

Mach number *mähh* or *mahh num'bər*, *n* the ratio of the air speed (i.e. speed in relation to the air) of an aircraft to the velocity of sound under the given conditions; (loosely) the speed of sound. [Ernst *Mach*, Austrian physicist and philosopher (1838–1916).]

macho *mach'ō*, *adj* aggressively male; ostentatiously virile. — *n* a man of this type (*pl* **mach'os**); machismo. — *n* **machismo** (*ma-chiz'mō*, *-chēz'*, *-kiz'* or *-kēz'*) the cult of male virility and masculine pride. [Sp. *macho*, male — L. *masculus*.]

macintosh. See **mackintosh.**

mack. Shortened form of **mackintosh.**

mackerel *mak'ər-əl*, *n* an edible bluish-green N. Atlantic fish with a silvery underside and wavy cross-streaks on its back. — **mackerel breeze** a strong breeze that ruffles the surface of the sea and so favours mackerel fishing; **mackerel shark** the porbeagle; **mackerel sky** a sky with clouds broken into long, thin, white, parallel masses. [O.Fr. *makerel* (Fr. *maquereau*).]

mackintosh or **macintosh** *mak'in-tosh*, *n* a waterproof overcoat (often shortened to **mack** or **mac**); waterproof cloth. [From Charles *Macintosh* (1766–1843), a Scottish chemist, the patentee.]

mackle *mak'l*, *n* a blemish in printing. [See **macle.**]

macle *mak'l*, *n* a dark spot in a crystal. — *adj* **macled** (*mak'ld*) spotted. [Fr. *macle* — L. *macula*, spot.]

macramé or **macrami** *mə-krä'mi*, *n* knotted thread-work or the art of producing it; a fringe or trimming of knotted thread. [App. Turk. *maqrama*, towel.]

macro- *mak-rō-* or *-ro-*, *combining form* denoting long, great, sometimes interchanging with *mega-*. — *n* **mac'rō** (*comput*) a macroinstruction: — *pl* **mac'ros.** — *adj* (*phot*) close-up. — *adj* **macrobiotic** (*-bī-ot'ik*) prolonging life; long-lived; relating to longevity, or to macrobiotics. — *nsing* **macrobiot'ics** the art or science of prolonging life; a cult partly concerned with diet, foods regarded as pure being vegetable substances grown and prepared without chemicals or processing. — *n* **macrocar'pa** an evergreen conifer of New Zealand planted esp. for ornamentation and as a windbreak. — *adj* **macrocephalic** (*-si-fal'ik*) or **macrocephalous** (*-sef'ə-ləs*). — *n* **macrocephaly** (*-sef'ə-li*) abnormal largeness of the head. — *n* **mac'rocode** (*comput*) a macroinstruction. — *n* **mac'rocosm** (*-kozm*) a large and complex structure considered a whole, of which smaller similar structures contained within it are microcosms; the whole universe. — *adj* **macrocos'mic.** — *adv* **macrocos'mically.** — *n* **mac'rocycle** a macrocyclic organic molecule or compound. — *adj* **macrocy'clic** being or having a ring structure with a large number of atoms. — *adj* **macroeconom'ic.** — *nsing* **macroeconomics** (*-ēk-ə-nom'iks* or *-ek-*) the study of economics on a large scale or of large units. — *n* **macroevolu'tion** major evolutionary developments over a long period of time, such as have given rise to the taxonomic groups above the species level. — *n* **mac'rofauna** and **mac'roflora** animals and plants (respectively) that are visible to the naked eye. — *n* **mac'rofossil** a fossil large enough to be seen with the naked eye. — *n* **mac'roinstruction** (*comput*) an instruction written in a programming language, usu. in assembly language, which generates and is replaced by a series of microinstructions. — *adj* **macromolec'ular.** — *n* **macromol'ecule** a large molecule, esp. one formed from a number of simpler molecules. — *n* **mac'ropod** an animal of the **Macropod'idae** (*-ē*), the family of marsupials comprising the kangaroos and related animals. — *adj* **macroscop'ic** visible to the naked eye (opp. to *microscopic*). — *adv* **macroscop'ically.** [Gr. *makros*, long, great.]

macron *mak'ron*, *n* a straight line placed over a vowel to show it is long (as in *ē*) (opp. to *breve*, the mark of a short vowel (*ĕ*)).

macropod, macroscopic, etc. See under **macro-.**

macula *mak'ū-lə*, *n* a spot, as on the skin, the sun, a mineral, etc.: — *pl* **mac'ulae** (*-lē*). — *adj* **mac'ular** spotted; patchy; of or pertaining to the macula lutea. — *vt* **mac'ulate** to spot, to defile. — *adj* (*-lit*) spotted; soiled. — *n* **maculā'tion** a spot, a pattern of spots or the act of spotting or marking. — *n* **mac'ule** a macula; a mackle. — *adj* **mac'ulose** spotted. — **macula lutea** (*lōō'ti-ə*) the yellow-spot (q.v.). [L. *macula*, a spot.]

MAD *mad*, *abbrev* for mutual assured destruction, a theory of nuclear deterrence.

mad *mad*, *adj* (*compar* **madd'er**, *superl* **madd'est**) disordered in intellect; insane; proceeding from madness; extremely and recklessly foolish; extremely enthusiastic; infatuated; frantic with pain, violent passion or appetite; furious with anger (*colloq*, orig. *NAm*); extravagantly playful or exuberant; rabid. — *vt* **madd'en** to make mad; to enrage. — *adj* **madd'ening** driving to madness; making very angry; extremely annoying. — *adv* **madd'eningly.** — *adj* **madd'ing** (*archaic*) distracted, acting madly. — *adv* **madd'ingly.** — *adv* **mad'ly** insanely; frantically; extremely (*colloq*). — *n* **mad'ness.** — **mad'-cap** a person who acts madly; a wild, rash, hot-headed person; an exuberantly frolicsome person. — *adj* fond of wild and reckless or extravagantly merry action. — **mad'house** (*formerly*) a house for mad people, an asylum; a place where there is noise, confusion and unpredictable behaviour; **mad'man,** *fem* **mad'woman,** a man or woman who is mad; a foolish and reckless man or woman. — **go mad** to become demented; to become very angry (*colloq*); **like mad** madly, furiously; **mad as a hatter** see under **hat; mad cow disease** bovine spongiform encephalopathy (see under **bovine**). [O.E. *gemǣd(e)d*.]

madam *mad'əm*, *n* a courteous form of address to a woman, esp. an elderly or married one, or any female customer in a shop, restaurant, etc.; (with *cap*) the word of address to a woman in a formal letter (*pl* **Mesdames** (*mā-däm*)); a woman of rank or station, esp. prefixed to an official title, e.g. *Madam Chairman*; a general term of reproach for a woman, esp. an arrogant young one; the woman in charge of a brothel (*pl* **mad'ams**). — *n* **madame** (*ma-däm'* or *mad'əm*; usu. with *cap*) prefixed instead of Mrs to a French or other foreign woman's name: — *pl* **mesdames** (*mā-däm*). [Fr. *ma*, my, *dame*, lady — L. *mea domina*.]

madder *mad'ər*, *n* a plant of the *Rubia* genus whose root yields a red dye; one of other plants of the genus. — **field madder** a minute lilac-flowered plant of the same family. [O.E. *mæddre*, *mædere*.]

made *mād*, *pa t* and *pa p* of **make**, and *adj*. — **made dish** a dish of various ingredients, often recooked; **made ground** ground formed by artificial filling in; **made man** or **woman** someone whose prosperity is assured; **made road** one with a deliberately made surface, not merely formed by traffic; a road with a metalled surface as opposed to a gravel surface. — **be made** (*colloq*) to have one's prosperity assured; **have it made** (*colloq*) to have one's happiness assured; **made to measure** or **order** made to individual requirements; **made up** put together, finished; parcelled up; dressed for a part, disguised; painted and powdered; meretricious; artificial, invented.

Madeira *mə-dē'rə* or *ma-dā'ra*, *n* a rich wine of the sherry class produced in *Madeira*. — **Madeira cake** a variety of rich sponge-cake.

madeleine *mad-len'*, *n* a small, shell-shaped rich cake. [Fr., prob. named after *Madeleine* Paulmier, 19th-cent. French cook.]

mademoiselle *mad-mwə-zel'*, *n* (a form of address for) an unmarried French or other foreign woman; (with *cap* when used as a prefix) Miss (*pl* **Mesdemoiselles'** *mād-*); a French governess. — Contracted to **mamselle** (*mam-zel'*), *pl* **mamselles** (*-zelz'*). [Fr. *ma*, my, and *demoiselle*; see **damsel**.]

maderise or **-ize** *mad'ə-rīz*, *vi* (of a white wine) to become rusty in colour and flat in taste, as a result of absorbing too much oxygen during maturation. — *n* **maderisā'tion** or **-z-**. [Fr. *maderiser*, from the colour of the wine Madeira.]

Madonna *mə-don'ə*, *n* the Virgin Mary, esp. as seen in works of art. [It., lit. my lady — L. *mea domina*.]

madras *mə-dräs'*, *n* a fine cotton fabric, often with a woven stripe.

madrepore *mad'ri-pör*, *n* a coral of the common reef-building type. — *adj* **madreporic** (*-por'ik*). [It. *madrepora* — *madre*, mother — L. *māter*, and Gr. *pōros*, a soft stone, stalactite, etc., or L. *porus*, a pore.]

madrigal *mad'ri-gəl*, *n* an unaccompanied song in several parts in counterpoint, popular in the 16th and 17th cents. (*mus*); a lyrical poem suitable for such treatment. — *adj* **madrigā'lian**. — *n* **mad'rigalist**. [It. *madrigale*, prob. from L.L. *mātricālis*, primitive, simple (— L. *mātrix*, see **matrix**), altered under the influence of It. *mandria*, a herd.]

Maecenas *mē-sē'nas*, *n* a rich patron of art or literature. [*Maecēnās*, a Roman knight who befriended Virgil and Horace.]

maelstrom *māl'strom*, *n* a particularly powerful whirlpool; a confused and disordered state of affairs; an overpowering, irresistible influence for destruction. [Du. (now *maalstroom*), a whirlpool.]

maenad *mē'nad*, *n* a female follower of Bacchus (*Gr mythol*); a woman beside herself with frenzy. — *adj* **maenad'ic** bacchanalian; furious. [Gr. *mainas*, *-ados*, raving — *mainesthai*, to be mad.]

maestoso *mī-stō'sō* or *mä-es-tō'sō*, (*mus*) *adj* and *adv* (to be performed) with dignity or majesty. [It.]

maestro *mī'strō* or *mä-es'trō*, *n* a master, esp. an eminent musical composer or conductor: — *pl* **maestros** (*mī'strōz*) or **maestri** (*mä-es'trē*). [It.]

Mae West *mā west*, *n* an airman's inflatable life-jacket. [From its supposed resemblance, when inflated, to the figure of an American actress of that name.]

MAFF *maf*, *abbrev* for Ministry of Agriculture, Fisheries and Food.

Mafia *mä'fē-ə*, *n* a spirit of opposition to the law in Sicily, hence a preference for private and unofficial rather than legal justice; a secret criminal society originating in Sicily, controlling many illegal activities, e.g. gambling, narcotics, etc., in many parts of the world, and particularly active in the U.S. (also called **Cosa Nostra**); (also without *cap*) any group considered to be like the Mafia, e.g. with regard to its criminal and unscrupulous use of power, fear, etc. to gain its ends. — *n* **Mafioso** (*-fē-ō'sō* or *-zō*) a member of the Mafia (also without *cap*): — *pl* **Mafio'si** (*-sē* or *-zē*). [Sicilian Italian *mafia*.]

ma foi *ma fwa*, (Fr.) my goodness (lit., (upon) my faith).

mag *mag*, (*colloq*) *n* short for **magazine** (periodical publication).

magazine *mag-ə-zēn'* or *mag'ə-*, *n* a periodical publication or broadcast containing articles, stories, etc. by various people; a container for holding cartridges that attaches on to a rifle; a place for military stores; any storehouse. [Fr. *magasin* — It. *magazzino* — Ar. *makhāzin*, pl. of *makhzan*, a storehouse.]

Magdalen *mag'də-lən* or **magdalene** *mag'də-lēn* (or, in the names of Oxford and Cambridge colleges, *möd'lin*), *n* (without *cap*) a repentant prostitute; an institution for receiving such people (abbrev. for *Magdalene hospital* or *asylum*). [From Mary *Magdalene*, i.e. (Gr.) *Magdalēnē*, of Magdala (Luke viii. 2), on the assumption that she was the woman of Luke vii. 37–50.]

mage. See under **magus**.

Magellanic clouds *mag-el-an'ik* or *maj-el-an'ik klowdz*, *n pl* two galaxies in the southern hemisphere, appearing to the naked eye like detached portions of the Milky Way, the nearest galaxies to the earth.

magenta *mə-jen'tə*, *n* the dyestuff fuchsine; its colour, a reddish purple. — *adj* reddish purple. [From its discovery about the time of the battle of *Magenta* in North Italy, 1859.]

maggot *mag'ət*, *n* a legless grub, esp. of a fly. — *adj* **magg'oty** full of maggots. — *n* **maggotorium** (*-tö'*) a place where maggots are bred for sale to fishermen. [Poss. a modification of M.E. *maddok*, *mathek*, dimin. see **mawkish**.]

Maghreb or **Maghrib** *mag'rəb*, *n* the countries of N.W. Africa collectively, sometimes including Libya. — Also *adj*. [Ar., the West.]

magi, magian. See **magus**.

magic *maj'ik*, *n* the art of producing marvellous results by compelling the aid of spirits, or by using the secret forces of nature, such as the power supposed to reside in certain objects as 'givers of life'; enchantment; sorcery; art of producing illusions by sleight of hand; a secret or mysterious power over the imagination or will. — *vt* to affect by, or as if by, magic; to produce by, or as if by, magic: — *pr p* **mag'icking**; *pa t* and *pa p* **mag'icked**. — *adj* pertaining to, used in, or done by magic; causing wonderful or startling results; marvellous, exciting (*colloq*). — *adj* **mag'ical** pertaining to magic; wonderful, enchanting. — *adv* **mag'ically**. — *n* **magician** (*mə-jish'ən*) a person skilled in magic; a wizard; an enchanter; a wonder-worker. — **magic carpet** one that, in fairy stories, can transport people magically through the air; **magic eye** a miniature cathode ray tube in a radio receiver which helps in tuning the receiver by indicating, by means of varying areas of luminescence and shadow, the accuracy of the tuning; **magic lantern** an apparatus for projecting pictures on slides on to a screen; **magic mushroom** any of various mushrooms, e.g. *Psilocybe mexicana*, which contain a hallucinogen; **magic (or magical) realism** a style of art, literature or cinema in which fantastical or surreal events or images are presented in a realistic or everyday context; **magic square** a square filled with rows of figures so arranged that the sums of all the rows will be the same, perpendicularly, horizontally or diagonally — as the square formed from the three rows 2, 7, 6; 9, 5, 1; 4, 3, 8 — **magic circles, cubes, cylinders** and **spheres** are similarly arranged. — **black magic** the black art, magic by means of evil spirits; **natural magic** the art of working wonders by a superior knowledge of the powers of nature; the power of investing a work of art with an atmosphere of imagination; sleight of hand; **sympathetic magic** magic aiming at the production of effects by mimicry, as bringing rain by libations, injuring a person by melting their image or sticking pins in it; **white magic** magic without the aid of the devil. [Gr. *magikē* (*technē*), magic (art). See **magus.**]

magilp. See **megilp.**

magisterial *maj-is-tē'ri-əl, adj* authoritative; dictatorial; pertaining or suitable to, or in the manner of, a teacher, master artist, or magistrate; of the rank of a magistrate. — *adv* **magistē'rially.** — *n* **magistē'rialness.** — *n* **mag'istracy** (*-trə-si*) the office or dignity of a magistrate; magistrates in general; a body of magistrates. — *adj* **magistral** (*mə-jis'trəl* or *maj'is-*) of or pertaining to a master; masterly; authoritative; specially prescribed for a particular case as a medicine; effectual. — *n* **mag'istrate** a person who has power of putting the law in force, esp. a justice of the peace, a provost or a bailie. — *adj* **magistratic** (*-trat'ik*) or **magistrat'ical.** — *n* **mag'istrature.** — **Magister Artium** (*mə-jis'tər är'shi-əm*) Master of Arts. [L. *magister*, master.]

Maglemosian *mag-li-mō'zi-ən*, (*archaeol*) *adj* of a culture represented by finds at *Maglemose* in Denmark, transitional between Palaeolithic and Neolithic.

maglev *mag'lev, adj* of or pertaining to a railway, train, carriage, etc. operating by *mag*netic *lev*itation (q.v.).

magma *mag'mə, n* molten or pasty rock material formed beneath the earth's solid crust, from which igneous rock is formed; any pasty or doughy mass: — *pl* **mag'mata** (*-mə-tə*) or **mag'mas.** — *adj* **magmatic** (*-mat'ik*). [Gr. *magma, -atos*, a thick unguent.]

Magna Carta (or **Charta**) *mag'nə kär'tə, n* the Great Charter obtained from King John in 1215, the basis of English political and personal liberty; any document establishing rights. [L.]

magna cum laude *mag'nə kum lö'dē* or *mag'nä ko͝om low'de*, (L.) with great distinction; used as the mark of the second level of excellence in N.Am. universities (*laus, laudis*, praise).

magnanimity *mag-nə-nim'i-ti, n* generosity; greatness of soul; that quality of mind which raises a person above all that is mean or unjust. — *adj* **magnanimous** (*-nan'*). — *adv* **magnan'imously.** [L. *magnanimitās* — *magnus*, great, *animus*, mind.]

magnate *mag'nāt* or *-nit, n* a noble; a person of rank, wealth or power, esp. in industry. [L. *magnās, -ātis* — *magnus*, great.]

magnesium *mag-nē'zi-əm, -zhi-əm, -zyəm, -zhyəm, -shi-əm* or *-shyəm, n* a metallic element (symbol **Mg**; atomic no. 12) of a bright, silver-white colour, burning with a dazzling white light. — *n* **magnē'sia** a light white powder, magnesium oxide; basic magnesium carbonate, used as a medicine. — *adj* **magnē'sian** belonging to, containing, or resembling magnesia. — *n* **magnesite** (*mag'nəs-īt*) native magnesium carbonate. [From *Magnesia*, in Thessaly, E. Greece.]

magnet *mag'nit, n* a bar or piece of metal, esp. iron, to which the property of attracting other substances containing iron or some other metals has been imparted and which, when suspended, will point approximately north to south; anything or anyone that attracts (*fig*). — *adj* **magnetic** (*mag-net'ik*) pertaining to a magnet or magnetism; having, or capable of acquiring, the properties of a magnet; attractive; strongly affecting others by personality; hypnotic. — *adv* **magnet'ically.** — *n* **magnetician** (*-ish'ən*) someone knowledgeable about magnetism. — *nsing* **magnet'ics** the science of magnetism. — *adj* **mag'netīsable** or **-z-.** — *n* **magnetīsā'tion** or **-z-.** — *vt* **mag'netise** or **-ize** to render magnetic; to attract as if by a magnet; to hypnotise. — *n* **mag'netīser** or **-z-.** — *n* **mag'netism** the cause of the attractive power of the magnet; the phenomena connected with magnets; the science which deals with the properties of magnets; attraction; influence of personality. — *n* **mag'netite** magnetic iron ore, called lodestone when polar. — *n* **magneto** (*mag-nē'tō*; short for magneto-electric machine) a small generator with a permanent magnet, used for ignition in an internal-combustion engine, etc.: — *pl* **magnē'tos.** — *combining form* **magneto-** magnetic; pertaining to magnetism; magneto-electric. — *adj* **magnēto-elec'tric** or **-elec'trical** pertaining to magneto-electricity. — *n* **magnēto-electric'ity** electricity produced by the action of magnets; the science of this. — *n* **magnē'tograph** an instrument for recording the variations of the magnetic elements. — *n* **magnetometer** (*mag-ni-tom'i-tər*) an instrument for measuring the strength or direction of a magnetic field, esp. the earth's. — *n* **magnetom'etry.** — *adj* **magnētomō'tive** producing a magnetic flux. — *n* **magnetosphere** (*-net'*) the region surrounding the earth or other body corresponding to its magnetic field. — *n* **mag'netron** a vacuum tube combined with a magnetic field to deflect electrons. — **animal magnetism** Mesmer's name for hypnotism; the power to hypnotise; sexual power of attraction due entirely to physical attributes; **artificial magnet** a magnet made by rubbing with other magnets; **bar magnet** a magnet in the form of a bar; **horse-shoe magnet** a magnet bent like a horse-shoe; **magnet high school** or **magnet school** (in the U.S.) a school which in addition to providing a general education specialises in teaching in one particular subject area such as science, languages or performing arts; **magnetic battery** several magnets placed with their like poles together, so as to act with great force; **magnetic dip** or **inclination** the angle between the horizontal and the line of the earth's magnetic field; **magnetic disk** (*comput*) a disk or disk file; **magnetic drum** (*comput*) a storage device consisting of a rotating cylinder with a magnetic coating; **magnetic equator** the line round the earth where the magnetic needle remains horizontal; **magnetic field** the space over which magnetic force is felt; **magnetic flux** the surface integral of the product of the permeability of the medium and the magnetic field intensity perpendicular to the surface; **magnetic flux density** the product of the field intensity and the permeability of the medium; **magnetic inclination** see **magnetic dip; magnetic ink** ink with magnetic quality used e.g. in printing cheques that are to be sorted by machine; **magnetic ink character recognition** (*comput*) computer recognition or reading of stylised characters printed in magnetic ink; **magnetic levitation** suspension of e.g. a train above a track by means of a magnetic field; **magnetic mine** a mine sunk to the sea-bottom, detonated by a pivoted magnetic needle when a ship approaches; **magnetic monopole** see **monopole; magnetic needle** the light bar in a mariner's compass which, because it is magnetised, points always to the north; **magnetic north** the direction indicated by the magnetic needle; **magnetic poles** two nearly opposite points on the earth's surface, where the dip of the needle is 90°; **magnetic resonance imaging** the use of nuclear magnetic resonance of protons to produce images of the human body, etc.; **magnetic storm** a disturbance in the magnetism of the earth; **magnetic tape** flexible plastic tape, coated on one side with magnetic material, used to register for later reproduction television images, or sound, or computer data; **magnet school** see **magnet high school** above; **permanent magnet** a magnet that keeps its magnetism after the force which magnetised it has been removed; **personal magnetism** power of a personality to make itself felt and to exercise influence; **terrestrial magnetism** the magnetic properties possessed by the earth as a whole.

[Through O.Fr. or L., from Gr. *magnētis* (*lithos*), Magnesian (stone), from *Magnēsiā*, in Thessaly, E. Greece.]

magnifiable. See **magnify**.

Magnificat *mag-nif'i-kat, n* the song of the Virgin Mary (Luke i. 46–55) beginning in the Vulgate with this word. [L. *magnificat* '(my soul) doth magnify', 3rd pers. sing. pres. indic. of *magnificāre*.]

magnification. See **magnify**.

magnificence *mag-nif'i-səns, n* the quality of being magnificent. — *adj* **magnif'icent** great in deeds or in appearance; noble; displaying greatness of size or extent; excellent (*colloq*). — *adv* **magnif'icently**. [L. *magnificēns, -entis*, lit. doing great things.]

magnify *mag'ni-fī, vt* to cause to appear greater; to exaggerate: — *pr p* **mag'nifying**; *pa t* and *pa p* **mag'nified**. — *adj* **mag'nifīable**. — *n* **magnification** (*-fi-kā'shən*) the act or power of magnifying; the state of being magnified; enlarged appearance or state or copy; extolling. — *n* **mag'nifier** (*-fī-ər*) someone who or that which magnifies or enlarges, esp. a pocket lens (**magnifying glass**). [L. *magnificāre — magnus*, great, *facĕre*, to make.]

magniloquent *mag-nil'ə-kwənt, adj* speaking in a grand or pompous style; bombastic. — *n* **magnil'oquence**. — *adv* **magnil'oquently**. [L. *magnus*, great, *loquēns, -entis*, pres. p. of *loquī*, to speak.]

magnitude *mag'ni-tūd, n* greatness; size; extent; importance; a measure of the intensity of a star's brightness. — **of the first magnitude** (of a star) of the first degree of brightness (*astron*); of a very important, significant or catastrophic kind (*fig*). [L. *magnitūdō — magnus*.]

magnolia *mag-nōl'i-ə* or *-yə, n* any tree of the American and Asiatic genus *Magnolia*, with beautiful foliage and large solitary flowers; a light pinkish-white or purplish-white colour. — *adj* **magnoliā'ceous**. [From Pierre *Magnol* (1638–1715), a Montpellier botanist.]

magnum *mag'nəm, n* a two-quart bottle or vessel; as a bottle-size of champagne or other wine, the equivalent of two ordinary bottles, containing usu. $1\frac{1}{2}$ litres: — *pl* **mag'nums**. [L. *magnum* (neut.), big.]

magnum opus *mag'nəm ō'pəs* or *mag'nŏŏm op'ŏŏs*, (L.) *n* a great work, esp. of literature or learning, esp. a writer's greatest achievement or culmination of efforts.

Magnus effect *mag'nəs i-fekt'* or **Magnus force** *förs*, (*phys*) *n* the force which acts on a cylinder rotating in a stream of fluid flowing in a direction perpendicular to the cylinder's axis, the force thrusting in a direction perpendicular to both the axis and the direction of the flow. [H.G. *Magnus* (1802–70), German scientist.]

magpie *mag'pī, n* the pie (*Pica rustica*), a black-and-white chattering bird of the same type as the crow; extended to other black-and-white or pied birds (in Australia, a piping crow); a chattering person; a person who hoards or steals small objects (*fig*). [*Mag*, shortened form of *Margaret*, and **pie**[1].]

maguey *mag'wā* or *mä-gā'i, n* an agave. [Sp.]

magus *mā'gəs, n* an ancient Persian priest; an Eastern magician; any magician; (with *cap*) one of the three wise men from the East who brought gifts to the infant Christ: — *pl* **mā'gi** (*-jī*). — *n* **mage** (*māj*) a magus or sorcerer. — *adj* **mā'gian** pertaining to the magi or to a sorcerer. — *n* a magus; a sorcerer. [L., — Gr. *magos* — O.Pers. *magus*.]

Magyar *mag'yär, n* one of the prevailing people of Hungary; the language spoken in Hungary. — *adj* of the Magyars or their language; (without *cap*) (of a garment) cut with the sleeves in a piece with the rest. [Magyar.]

maharaja or **maharajah** *mä-hə-rä'jä* or *mə-hä-rä'jə, n* formerly, a great Indian prince, esp. a ruler of a state. — *n* **maharani** or **maharanee** (*-rä'nē*) the wife of a maharaja; a woman with the rank of a maharaja in her own right. [Hind., from Sans. *mahat*, great, *rājan*, king, *rānī*, queen.]

maharishi *mä-hə-rē'shi, n* a leading instructor in the Hindu faith. [Sans. *mahat*, great, *rishi*, sage.]

mahatma *mə-hät'mä* or *-hat'mə, n* a person skilled in mysteries or religious secrets; an adept; a wise and holy Hindu leader. [Sans. *mahātman*, high-souled.]

Mahayana *mä-hə-yä'nə, n* the branch of Buddhism practised esp. in China, Japan, Tibet and the Himalayas, that seeks enlightenment for all humanity, embraces many methods for attaining it, and recognises many texts as scripture. — Also *adj*. — *n* **Mahaya'nist**. [Sans., lit. great vehicle.]

Mahdi *mä'dē, n* the great leader of the faithful Muslims, who is to appear in the last days to convert all mankind to Islam; a title of various insurrectionary leaders, esp. in the Sudan. [Ar. *mahdīy*.]

mah-jong or **mah-jongg** *mä-jong', n* an old Chinese table game for four, played with small painted bricks or 'tiles'. [Chin., lit. sparrows — perh. an allusion evoked by the chattering sound of the tiles during play.]

mahlstick. See **maulstick**.

mahogany *mə-hog'ə-ni, n* a tropical American tree (*Swietenia mahogoni*); its timber, valued for furniture-making; the colour of the timber, a dark reddish brown; a dining-table (*colloq*).

Mahometan. See **Mohammedan**.

mahout *mä-howt', n* the keeper and driver of an elephant. [Hind. *mahāut, mahāwat*.]

mahseer or **mahsir** *mä'sēr, n* a large fish found in the rivers of Northern India. [Hind. *mahāsir*.]

maid *mād, n* a female servant; a spinster; an unmarried woman, esp. one who is young (*archaic* or *poetic*). — *n* **maid'servant** a female servant. — **maid of all work** or **maid-of-all'-work** a maid who does general housework; **maid of honour** see under **honour**; **old maid** a woman left unmarried; a card game played with an odd number of cards, the loser being the player left with the unpaired card at the end of the game. [Shortened from **maiden**.]

maiden *mād'n, n* a maid; a horse that has never won a race. — *adj* unmarried; virgin; female; fresh; new; unused; in the original or initial state; that has never been captured, climbed, trodden, penetrated, pruned, etc.; that has never won a race (of a horse); first. — *n* **maid'enhead** virginity; the hymen. — *n* **maid'enhood** the state or time of being a maiden; maidenhead. — *adj* **maid'enish** (*derog*) like a maiden. — *adj* **maid'enlike**. — Also *adv*. — *n* **maid'enliness**. — *adj* **maid'enly** maidenlike; suiting or suitable for a maiden; gentle; modest. — Also *adv*. — **maid'enhair** a fern with fine footstalks; **maiden name** the family name of a married woman before her marriage; **maiden over** (in cricket) an over in which no runs are made; **maiden speech** one's first speech, esp. in Parliament; **maiden stakes** (in horse-racing) the prize in a race (**maiden race**) between horses that have not won before the date of entry; **maiden voyage** a first voyage. [O.E. *mægden*.]

maieutic *mī-* or *mā-ūt'ik, adj* (of the Socratic method of inquiry) bringing out latent thoughts and ideas. — *nsing* **maieut'ics** the Socratic art. [Gr. *maieutikos — maia*, good woman, a midwife.]

maigre *mā'gər* or *meg'r', adj* (*RC*) (of food) made without flesh; of, belonging to or suitable for a fast-day or fast. — *n* (also **meagre** *mē'gər*) a large Mediterranean fish noted for the sound it emits. [Fr. *maigre*, lean — L. *macer*.]

maiko *mī'kō, n* an apprentice geisha: — *pl* **mai'ko** or **mai'kos**. [Jap.]

mail[1] *māl, n* defensive armour for the body, formed of steel rings or network; armour generally; the protective covering of an animal. — *vt* to clothe in mail. — *adj* **mailed** protected by mail. — **mailed fist** (*fig*) physical force. [Fr. *maille* — L. *macula*, a spot or a mesh.]

mail[2] *māl, n* post; correspondence; a batch of letters, etc.; the person, train or vehicle by which the mail is conveyed. — *vt* to post; to send by post. — *adj* **mail'able** capable of being sent by mail. — **mail'-bag** a bag in which letters are carried; **mail'boat** a boat that carries the public mail; **mail'box** (*NAm*) a letter-box; **mail drop** (*NAm*) a receptacle for mail; **mailing list** a list of the names and addresses of those to whom advertising material, information, etc. is to be posted; **mail'man** a postman (also **mail'=carrier**); **mail'merge** (a computer program for) the producing of a series of letters addressed to individuals by merging a file of names with a file containing the text of the letter. — Also *vi.* — **mail order** an order for goods to be sent by post (*adj* **mail'-order**); **mail shot** an item of unsolicited, usu. advertising, material sent by post. [O.Fr. *male*, a trunk, a mail — O.H.G. *malha, malaha*, a sack.]

maillot *mä-yō, n* tights worn by a ballet-dancer, etc.; a one-piece close-fitting swimsuit; a jersey. [Fr., swaddling-clothes.]

maim *mām, vt* to disable; to mutilate; to lame or cripple; to render defective. — *adj* **maimed.** — *n* **maimedness** (*māmd'* or *mām'id-nis*). — *n* **maim'-ing.** [O.Fr. *mahaing*.]

main *mān, n* a principal pipe or conductor in a branching system distributing water, gas, electricity, etc.; the principal part; (*pl*) the water, gas or electricity supply available through such a system; that which is essential; the most part; strength, esp. in the phrase *might and main*; the mainland; the high sea. — *adj* chief, principal; first in importance or extent; leading; important; extensive; general; sheer (as in *main force*); great. — *adv* **main'ly** chiefly, principally. — **main'brace** the brace attached to the mainyard (see **splice**); **main clause** (*gram*) a principal clause; **main'-deck** the principal deck of a ship; **main'frame** the central processing unit and storage unit of a computer; a large computer. — *adj* (of a computer) of the large, powerful type rather than the small-scale kind. — **main'land** (*-lənd* or *-land*) the principal or larger land, as opposed to neighbouring islands; **main'lander; main line** a railway line between important centres; an important vein (*drug-taking slang*). — *adj* **main'line.** — *vi* (*drug-taking slang*) to take narcotics intravenously. — **main'liner; main'lining; main'mast** (*-məst* or *-mäst*) the principal mast, usually second from the prow; **main'sail** (*-sl* or *-sāl*) the principal sail, generally attached to the mainmast; **main'spring** the spring that gives motion to any piece of machinery, esp. that of a watch or a clock; principal motive, motivating influence (*fig*); **main'stay** a rope stretching forward and down from the top of the mainmast; chief support (also *fig*); **main store** the memory or store (q.v.) of a computer; **main stream** a river with tributaries; (usu. **main'stream**) the chief direction or trend in any historical development, including that of an art. — *adj* **main'stream** pertaining to the main stream (*lit* and *fig*); (of swing) coming in the line of development between early and modern (*jazz*); in accordance with what is normal or standard. — *vt* (esp. *NAm*) to make mainstream; to integrate (e.g. handicapped children into classes of able-bodied children) (*education*). — **main'yard** the lower yard on the mainmast. — **in the main** for the most part; on the whole; **might and main** utmost strength. [Partly O.E. *mægen*, strength, partly O.N. *meginn*, strong.]

maintain *mān-tān', mən-* or *men-, vt* to keep in existence or in any state; to preserve from capture, loss or deterioration; to uphold; to carry on; to keep up; to support; to make good; to support by argument; to affirm; to defend; to support in an action in which one is not oneself concerned (*law*). — *n* **maintainabil'ity.** — *adj* **maintain'able.** — *adj* **maintained'** financially supported, e.g. (of a school, etc.) from public funds. — *n* **maintain'er.** — *n* **maintenance** (*mān'tən-əns*) the act of maintaining, supporting or defending; continuance; the means of (esp. financial) support; defence, protection. — **main'tenance-man** a man who keeps machines, etc. in working order. [Fr. *maintenir* — L. *manū* (abl.) *tenēre*, to hold in the hand.]

maiolica. See **majolica.**

maisonette or **maisonnette** *māz-on-et'* or *mez-, n* a small house or a flat within a larger house, esp. one occupying more than one floor. [Fr. *maisonnette*.]

maître d'hôtel *metr' dō-tel, n* a house-steward, major-domo; the manager or head-waiter of a hotel (also (*colloq*) **maître d' dē**). — See also **à la maître d'hôtel.**

maize *māz, n* a staple cereal in America, etc., with large ears (corncobs) — called also *Indian corn*, or *mealies*; the yellow colour of maize. — Also *adj.* [Sp. *maíz* — from Haitian.]

Maj. *abbrev* for Major.

majesty *maj'is-ti, n* grandeur; dignity; elevation of manner or style; royal state; a title of monarchs (*His, Her* or *Your Majesty*; *Their* or *Your Majesties*); a representation of God (sometimes Christ) enthroned. — *adj* **majestic** (*mə-jes'tik*) or **majes'tical** (*-kl*) having or exhibiting majesty; stately; sublime. — *adv* **majes'tically** in a majestic manner. [Fr. *majesté* — L. *mājestās, -ātis* — *mājor, mājus*, compar. of *magnus*, great.]

Majlis *mäj-lis', n* the Iranian parliament; (also without *cap*) an assembly or council in various N. African and Middle Eastern countries. [Pers. *majlis*.]

majolica *mə-jol'i-kə, -yol'* or **maiolica** *-yol', n* glazed or enamelled earthenware, esp. that made in Italy during the Renaissance. — **majol'icaware.** [Perh. from *Majorca*.]

major *mā'jər, adj* greater or great in number, quantity, size, value, importance, dignity, etc.; greater (than minor) by a semitone (*mus*); involving a major third (see below; *mus*). — *n* a person of full legal age (in U.K., before 1970, 21 years; from 1970, 18 years); an officer in rank between a captain and lieutenant-colonel; anything that is major as opposed to minor; a student's special subject (esp. *NAm*). — *vi* to specialise in a particular subject at college (with *in*; esp. *US*); to specialise in a particular product, etc. (with *in* or *on*). — *n* **mājorette'** a member of a group of girls who march in parades, etc., wearing a decorative approximation to military uniform, sometimes twirling batons, playing instruments, etc. — *n* **majority** (*mə-jor'i-ti*) pre-eminence; the greater number; the greater part, the bulk; the difference between the greater and the lesser number; full age (see **major** above). — Also *adj.* — *n* **mā'jorship.** — **major-dō'mō** an official in charge of the general management of a large household; a general steward; **major-gen'eral** an officer in the army next in rank below a lieutenant-general; **majority rule** government by members, or by a body including members, of the largest ethnic group(s) in a country, as opp. to a political system which excludes them; **majority verdict** the verdict reached by the majority in a jury, as distinct from a unanimous verdict; **major key, mode** and **scale** one with its third a major third above the tonic; **major orders** (in the R.C. Church) the higher degrees of holy orders, i.e. bishop, priest and deacon; **major premise** (*logic*) that in which the major term occurs; **major suit** (*bridge*) spades or hearts, valued more highly than diamonds or clubs; **major term** (*logic*) the term which is the predicate of the conclusion; **major third** (*mus*) an interval of four semitones. — **go over to** or **join the majority** to die. [L. *mājor*, compar. of *magnus*.]

majuscule *mə-jus'kūl* or *maj'əs-kūl*, (*palaeog*) *n* a large letter whether capital or uncial. — Also *adj*. — *adj* **majus'cūlar**. [L. (*littera*) *mājuscula*, somewhat larger (letter).]

make *māk*, *vt* to fashion, frame, construct, compose or form; to create; to bring into being; to produce; to conclude, contract; to bring about; to perform; to force; to cause; to result in; to cause to be; to convert or turn; to appoint; to render; to represent as doing or being; to reckon; to get as result or solution; to bring into any state or condition; to establish; to prepare; to obtain, gain or earn; to score; to constitute; to amount to; to count for; to turn out; to be capable of turning or developing into or serving as; to reach, succeed in reaching; to accomplish, achieve; to attempt, offer or start; to do; to cause or assure the success of; to persuade (esp. a woman) to have sexual intercourse with one (*slang*); to have sexual intercourse with (*slang*). — *vi* to behave (as if), esp. in order to deceive; to proceed; to tend, to result: — *pr p* **māk'ing**; *pa t* and *pa p* **māde**. — *n* form or shape; structure, texture; build; formation; manufacture; brand; type; making; character or disposition; quantity made. — *adj* **mak'able**. — *n* **māk'er** someone who makes; (with *cap*) the Creator, God. — *n* **māk'ing** the act of forming (often in combination, as in *bread-making*, *cabinet-making*); structure; form; (in *pl*) gains; (in *pl*) that from which something can be made (*lit* and *fig*). — **make'-believe** feigning (also **make'-belief**). — *adj* feigned or pretended. — *vi* see **make believe** below. — *adj* **make-do'** makeshift. — **make'-ready** preparation of a letterpress sheet for printing, so as to obtain evenness of impression; **make'shift** a temporary expedient or substitute. — *adj* of the nature of or characterised by temporary expedient. — **make'-up** the way anything is arranged, composed or constituted, or the ingredients in its constitution; one's character, temperament, mental qualities, etc.; cosmetics for self-beautification, worn esp. by women, and by actors as an aid to impersonation; the effect produced by the application of cosmetics; **make'-weight** that which is thrown into a scale to make up the weight; a person or thing of little value added to supply a deficiency. — **in the making** in the process of being formed, developed, etc., or of becoming; **make a face** to grimace, contort the features; **make after** to follow or pursue; **make amends** to render compensation or satisfaction; **make an ass of oneself** to behave like a fool; **make a night (or day) of it** to extend an (esp. enjoyable) activity through the whole night (or day); **make as if** or in N.Am. **make like** or **make as though** to act as if, to pretend that; **make believe** (also **make'-believe**) to pretend, feign; to play at believing; **make certain (of)** to find out; to put beyond doubt; to secure; **make do (with)** to manage (with the means available — usually inferior or inadequate); **make for** to set out for, seek to reach; **make free with** see under **free**; **make friends** to become friendly with; to acquire friends; **make head or tail of** to find any sense in; **make it** to reach an objective; to succeed in a purpose; to become a success (*colloq*); to have one's way sexually (with) (*vulg*); **make much of** to treat with fondness, to cherish or to foster; to turn to great account; to find much sense in or succeed in understanding; **make nothing of** to think it of little importance or to have no hesitation or difficulty; to be totally unable to understand; **make of** to construct from (as material); to understand by; **make off** to decamp; **make off with** to run away with; **make one's way** to proceed; to succeed; **make or break** or **make or mar** to be the crucial test that brings success or failure to (*adj* **make-or-break'**); **make out** to descry, to see; to discern; to decipher; to comprehend, understand; to prove; to seek to make it appear; to draw up; to succeed; to engage in lovemaking (with) (*slang*); **make over** to remake or reconstruct; to transfer (*n* **make'-over**); **make sail** to increase the quantity of sail on a ship or boat; to set sail; **make someone's day** see under **day**; **make sure (of)** to ascertain; to put beyond doubt or risk; to secure; to feel certain; **make the best of** to turn to the best advantage; to take in the best spirit; **make the most of** to use to the best advantage; **make up** to fabricate; to feign; to collect; to put together; to parcel; to put into shape; to arrange; to become friends again (after a quarrel, etc.); to constitute; to repair; to complete or supplement; to adjust one's appearance (as an actor for a part); to apply paint and powder, etc. to the face; to make good; to compensate (for); **make up one's mind** to come to a decision; **make up to** to make friendly, adulatory or amorous approaches to; to compensate; **make with** (*colloq*, orig. *NAm*) to start using, doing, etc. (something); to bring on or into operation; **on the make** (*colloq*) bent on self-advancement or promotion, or on finding a sexual partner. [O.E. *macian*.]

mako[1] *mä'kō*, *n* any of several sharks of the genus *Isurus*: — *pl* **ma'kos**. — Also **mako shark**. [Maori.]

mako[2] *mä'kō*, *n* a small tree of New Zealand with red berries that turn purple as they ripen: — *pl* **ma'kos**. [Maori.]

MAL *abbrev* for Malaysia (I.V.R.).

Mal. (*Bible*) *abbrev* for (the Book of) Malachi.

mal *mal*, (Fr.) *n* pain, sickness. — **grand mal** see under **grand**; **mal de mer** (*də mer*) seasickness; **mal du pays** (*dü pā-ē*) homesickness; **petit mal** see under **petit**.

mal- *mal-*, *pfx* signifying bad or badly. [Fr., — L. *male*, badly.]

Malacca cane *məl-ak'ə kān*, *n* a brown walking-stick made from a rattan. [*Malacca*, a centre of the trade.]

malachite *mal'ə-kīt*, *n* a green mineral, basic copper carbonate. [Gr. *malachē*, mallow, as of the colour of a mallow leaf.]

maladaptation *mal-ad-ap-tā'shən*, *n* faulty or poor adaptation. — *adj* **maladap'ted**. — *adj* **maladap'tive**. [**mal-**.]

maladjusted *mal-ə-just'id*, *adj* poorly or inadequately adjusted, esp. to one's environment or circumstances; psychologically incapable of dealing with day-to-day situations. — *n* **maladjust'ment**. [**mal-**.]

maladministration *mal-əd-min-is-trā'shən*, *n* bad management, esp. of public affairs. — *vt* **malad-min'ister**. [**mal-**.]

maladroit *mal'ə-droit* or *-droit'*, *adj* not dexterous; unskilful; clumsy; tactless. — *adv* **maladroit'ly**. — *n* **maladroit'ness**. [Fr.]

malady *mal'ə-di*, *n* illness; disease, either of the body or of the mind; a faulty condition. [Fr. *maladie* — *malade*, sick — L. *male habitus*, in bad condition — *male*, badly, *habitus*, past p. of *habēre*, to have, hold.]

Malagasy *mal-ə-gas'i*, *adj* of or pertaining to Madagascar, its inhabitants or their language. — *n* a native of Madagascar; the language of Madagascar.

malaise *mal-āz'*, *n* uneasiness; a feeling of discomfort or of sickness. [Fr.]

malamute. See **malemute**.

malapportionment *mal-ə-pör'shən-mənt*, (*NAm*) *n* unequal or unfair apportioning of members to a legislative body. [**mal-**.]

malapropism *mal'ə-prop-izm*, *n* (an example of) the misapplication of words without mispronunciation, from Mrs *Malaprop* in Sheridan's play, *The Rivals*, who uses words *malapropos*.

malapropos *mal'a-prō-pō* or *mal-ə-prō-pō'*, *adj* out of place; unsuitable; inapt. — *adv* inappropriately; unseasonably. [**mal-**.]

malar *mā'lər*, *adj* pertaining to the cheek. — *n* the cheekbone. [L. *māla*, the cheek — *mandĕre*, to chew.]

malaria *mə-lā'ri-ə*, *n* poisonous air arising from marshes, once believed to produce fever; the fever once attributed to bad air, actually due to a protozoan parasite transmitted by mosquitoes (*med*). — *adj* **malā'rial**, **malā'rian** or **malā'rious**. — *n* **malāriol'ogist**. — *n* **malāriol'ogy** the study of malaria. [It. *mal' aria* — L. *malus*, bad, *āēr*, *āĕris*, air.]

malarkey or **malarky** *mə-lär'ki*, (*colloq*) *n* absurd talk; nonsense.

Malathion® *mal-ə-thī'on*, *n* a phosphorus-containing insecticide used chiefly in the house and garden.

Malay *mə-lā'* or **Malayan** *mə-lā'ən*, *n* a member of a race inhabiting Malaysia, Singapore and Indonesia (formerly known as the Malay Archipelago); the language of the Malays. — *adj* of the Malays, their language or their countries. — *adj* **Malay'sian** (*-si-ən*, *-zhən* or *-shən*) relating to the Malay Archipelago or esp. to Malaysia. — Also *n*. [Malay *malāyu*.]

Malayalam or **Malayalaam** *ma-lə-yä'ləm*, *n* the Dravidian language of Kerala, a state in S.W. India. — Also *adj*.

malcontent *mal'kən-tent*, *adj* discontented, dissatisfied, esp. in political matters. — *n* a discontented person. — *adj* **malcontent'ed**. — *adv* **malcontent'edly**. — *n* **malcontent'edness**. [O.Fr.]

mal de mer. See under **mal**.

male *māl*, *adj* masculine; of or pertaining to the sex that begets (not bears) young, or produces relatively small gametes; staminate (*bot*); adapted to fit into a corresponding hollow part (*mach*). — *n* a person of the male sex. — **male chauvinist** or **male chauvinist pig** (*colloq derog*) a man who believes in the superiority of men over women and acts accordingly (abbrev. **MCP**); **male menopause** a critical period of change affecting late middle-aged men, often marked by decline in sexual power, loss of energy and decisiveness, etc.; **male rhymes** those in which stressed final syllables correspond. [O.Fr. *male* — L. *masculus*, male — *mās*, a male.]

malediction *mal-i-dik'shən*, *n* cursing; a calling down of evil. — *adj* **maledic'tive** or **maledic'tory**. [L. *maledīcĕre*, *-dictum* — *male*, ill, *dīcĕre*, to speak.]

malefactor *mal'i-fak-tər*, *n* an evil-doer; a criminal. — *adj* **malefac'tory**. — *adj* **malefic** (*məl-ef'ik*) doing mischief; producing evil. — *adv* **malef'ically**. — *n* **maleficence** (*-ef'i-səns*). — *adj* **malef'icent** hurtful; wrongdoing. [L. *malefacĕre*, to do evil.]

maleic. See under **malic**.

malemute or **malamute** *mäl'ə-mūt*, *n* an Eskimo dog. [From a tribe on the Alaskan coast.]

malevolent *mal-ev'ə-lənt*, *adj* wishing evil; ill disposed towards others; rejoicing in another's misfortune. — *n* **malev'olence**. — *adv* **malev'olently**. [L. *malevolēns*, *-entis*, ill disposed, wishing evil.]

malfeasance *mal-fē'zəns*, (*law*) *n* an illegal deed, esp. of an official. — *adj* **malfea'sant**. [Fr. *malfaisance* — L. *male*, ill, *facĕre*, to do.]

malformation *mal-för-mā'shən*, *n* faulty structure; deformity. — *adj* **malformed'**. [**mal-**.]

malfunction *mal-fungk'shən*, *n* the act or fact of working imperfectly. — *vi* to work or function imperfectly. — *n* **malfunc'tioning**. [**mal-**.]

malic *mā'lik* or *mal'ik*, *adj* obtained from apple juice — applied to an acid found in unripe fruits. — *adj* **maleic** (*mə-lē'ik*). — *n* **malonate** (*mal'ə-nāt*) a salt or ester of malonic acid. — **maleic acid** an acid obtained from malic acid; **malonic acid** a white crystalline acid. [L. *mālum*, an apple.]

malice *mal'is*, *n* ill-will; spite; disposition or intention to harm another or others; a playfully mischievous attitude of mind. — *adj* **malicious** (*mə-li'shəs*) bearing ill-will or spite; moved by hatred or ill-will; mischievous. — *adv* **mali'ciously**. — *n* **mali'ciousness**. — **malice aforethought** (*law*) the predetermination to commit a crime esp. against a person, i.e. serious injury or murder. [Fr., — L. *malitia* — *malus*, bad.]

malign *mə-līn'*, *adj* evil; injurious; malignant. — *vt* to speak evil of, especially falsely and rancorously; to defame. — *n* **malign'er**. — *n* **malignity** (*mə-lig'ni-ti*) state or quality of being malign; a malicious act; great hatred or virulence; deadly quality. — *adv* **malign'ly**. [Fr. *malin*, fem. *maligne* — L. *malignus* for *maligenus*, of evil disposition — *malus*, bad, and *gen-*, root of *genus*.]

malignant *mə-lig'nənt*, *adj* disposed to do harm; baleful; actuated by great hatred; tending to cause death, or to go from bad to worse, esp. cancerous (*med*). — *n* **malig'nancy**. — *adv* **malig'nantly**. [L. *malignāns*, *-antis*, pres. p. of *malignāre*, to act maliciously.]

malinger *mə-ling'gər*, *vi* to feign sickness in order to avoid work. — *n* **maling'erer**. — *n* **maling'ery** feigned sickness. [Fr. *malingre*, sickly.]

mall *möl* or *mal*, *n* a street, area, etc. of shops, along which vehicles are not permitted; (from a former alley of the kind in London) a level shaded walk; a public walk. [See **maul**.]

mallam *mal'əm*, *n* an African scribe, teacher or learned man. [Hausa.]

mallard *mal'ərd*, *n* a kind of wild duck, common in the northern hemisphere, of which the male has a shiny green head. [O.Fr. *mallart*, *malart*.]

malleable *mal'i-ə-bəl*, *adj* able to be beaten, rolled, etc. into a new shape (also *fig*). — *n* **malleabil'ity** or **mall'eableness**. [L. *malleus*, a hammer.]

mallee *mal'ē*, *n* any of many small trees of the genus *Eucalyptus*, esp. *E. dumosa*; a vegetation community of such trees (also **mallee scrub**); an arid area where mallee forms the predominant vegetation. — **mall'ee-bird**, **-fowl** or **-hen** an Australian mound-bird; **mallee gate** a makeshift gate. [Aboriginal.]

malleolus *mə-lē'ə-ləs*, (*anat*) *n* a bony protuberance on either side of the ankle. — *adj* **mallē'olar** (or *mal'i-*). [L. *malleolus*, dimin. of *malleus*, hammer.]

mallet *mal'it*, *n* a hammer with a large head, e.g. of wood; a long-handled hammer for playing croquet or polo. [Fr. *maillet*, dimin. of *mail*, a mall.]

malleus *mal'i-əs*, (*zool*) *n* one of the small bones of the middle ear in mammals. [L. *malleus*, a hammer.]

mallow *mal'ō*, *n* any plant of the genus *Malva*, from its emollient properties or its soft downy leaves; extended to other genera of Malvaceae; a mauve colour. [O.E. *m(e)alwe* — L. *malva*; Gr. *malachē* — *malassein*, to soften.]

malm *mäm*, *n* calcareous loam; earth of this kind, formerly used for making brick; an artificial mixture of clay and chalk. [O.E. *m(e)alm(-stān)*, a soft (stone).]

malmsey *mäm'zi*, *n* a sort of grape; a strong and sweet wine, first made in Greece. [L.L. *malmasia*.]

malnutrition *mal-nū-trish'ən*, *n* imperfect or faulty nutrition. [**mal-**.]

malodour *mal-ō'dər*, *n* a bad smell. — *adj* **malo'dorous**. — *n* **malo'dorousness**. [**mal-**.]

malo-lactic *māl-ə-lak'tik* or *mal-*, *adj* concerning or involving the conversion of malic acid to lactic acid in the fermentation of wine.

malonate. See under **malic**.

maloti. See **loti**.

malpractice *mal-prak'tis*, *n* an evil or improper practice; professional misconduct; treatment falling short of reasonable skill or care; illegal attempt of a person in a position of trust to benefit themselves at others' cost. — *n* **malpractitioner** (*-tish'ən-ər*). [**mal-**.]

malt *mölt*, *n* barley or other grain steeped in water, allowed to sprout, and dried in a kiln, used in brewing ale, etc.; malt whisky; malt liquor. — *vt* to make into malt; to treat or combine with malt. — *adj* containing or made with malt. — *n* **malt'ase** an enzyme that produces grape sugar from maltose. — *adj* **malt'ed** containing or made with malt. — *n* **malt'ing** a building where malt is made. — *n* **malt'ose** a hard, white crystalline sugar, formed by the action of malt or diastase on starch. — *n* **malt'ster** a person who makes or deals in malt. — *adj* **malt'y**. — **malt extract** a fluid medicinal food made from malt; **malt'-floor** a perforated floor in the chamber of a malt-kiln, through which heat rises; **malt'house; malt'-kiln; malt liquor** a liquor, such as ale or porter, formed from malt; **malt whisky** a whisky which is the product of one distillate of malted barley, etc., not a blend of several. [O.E. *m(e)alt*.]

Malta *mol'* or *möl'tə*, *adj* of the island of Malta. — *adj* **Maltese** (*-tēz'*) of Malta, its people or their language. — *n* one of the people of Malta (*pl* **Maltese'**); an official language of Malta — Semitic with a strong Italian infusion. — **Maltese cross** the badge of the knights of Malta, a cross with two-pointed expanding limbs. [L. *Melita*, Gr. *Melitē*.]

Malthusian *mal-thūz'i-ən*, *adj* relating to Thomas Robert *Malthus* (1766–1834), or to his teaching that the increase of population tends to outstrip that of the means of living. — *n* a disciple of Malthus. — *n* **Malthūs'ianism**.

maltreat *mal-trēt'*, *vt* to treat roughly or unkindly. — *n* **maltreat'ment**. [Fr. *maltraiter* — L. *male*, badly, *tractāre*, to treat.]

Malva *mal'və*, *n* the mallow genus, giving name to the family **Malvā'ceae**, including hollyhock, cotton, etc. — *adj* **malvā'ceous**. [L.; cf. **mallow**.]

malversation *mal-vər-sā'shən*, *n* misbehaviour in office e.g. by bribery, extortion, embezzlement; corrupt administration (of funds). [Fr., — L. *male*, badly, *versārī*, *-ātus*, to occupy oneself.]

Mam *mam*, *n* a Mayan language. [Sp. *mame*, from Amerindian.]

mam *mam*, (*dialect*) *n* mother.

mama. See **mamma**[1].

mamba *mam'bə*, *n* a large, deadly African snake, black or green. [Kaffir *im mamba*, large snake.]

mambo *mam'bō*, *n* a voodoo priestess; a West Indian dance, or dance-tune, like the rumba: — *pl* **mam'bos**. — *vi* to dance the mambo. [Am. Sp., prob. from Haitian.]

mamelon *mam'ə-lən*, *n* a rounded hill or protuberance. [Fr., nipple.]

Mameluke *mam'ə-lo͞ok*, *n* a member of a military force originally of Circassian slaves — afterwards the ruling class and sultans of Egypt; (in Muslim countries) a slave, esp. white. [Ar. *mamlûk*, a purchased slave — *malaka*, to possess.]

mamilla or in N.Am. **mammilla** *mam-il'ə*, *n* the nipple of the mammary gland (*anat*); a nipple-shaped protuberance: — *pl* **mamill'ae** or in N.Am. **mammill'ae** (*-ē*). — *adj* **mam'illary** pertaining to the breast; nipple-shaped; studded with rounded projections. [L. *mam(m)illa*, dimin. of *mamma*.]

mamma[1] or **mama** *mə-mä'*, *n* mother — used chiefly by young children. — *n* **mammy** (*mam'i*) a child's word for mother; a black nurse or housemaid (*NAm*; *offensive* or *derog*). [Repetition of *ma*, a child's natural utterance.]

mamma[2] *mam'ə*, *n* (*zool*) the milk gland; the breast: — *pl* **mamm'ae** (*-ē*). — *adj* **mamm'ary** of the nature of or relating to the mammae or breasts. — *adj* **mamm'ate** having breasts. — *adj* **mammif'erous** having mammae. — *adj* **mamm'iform** having the form of a breast. — *n* **mamm'ogram** or **mamm'ograph** X-ray photograph of the breast. — *n* **mammog'raphy** radiological examination of the breast. [L. *mamma*.]

mammal *mam'əl*, *n* a member of the **Mammalia** (*mə-mā'li-ə*), the class of animals that suckle their young. — *adj* **mammā'lian**. [L. *mammālis*, of the breast — *mamma*, the breast.]

mammary, mammate. See **mamma**[2].

mammilla. See **mamilla**.

mammography. See under **mamma**[2].

mammon *mam'ən*, *n* riches regarded as the root of evil; (with *cap*) the god of riches. — *adj* **mamm'onish** devoted to money-getting. — *n* **mamm'onism** devotion to gain. — *n* **mamm'onist** or **mamm'onite** a person devoted to riches. — *adj* **mammonist'ic**. [L.L. *mam(m)ōna* — Gr. *mam(m)ōnās* — Aramaic *māmōn*, riches.]

mammoth *mam'əth*, *n* an extinct species of elephant. — *adj* resembling the mammoth in size; gigantic. [Former Russ. *mammot* (now *mamant* or *mamont*).]

mammy. See **mamma**[1].

mamselle. See **mademoiselle**.

man *man*, *n* a grown-up human male; mankind; a workman, employee; a husband, or man living as a husband with a woman; a piece used in playing chess or draughts or similar game; a male adult possessing a distinctively manly character; a word of familiar address: — *pl* **men**. — *adj* and *combining form* male. — *vt* to furnish with a man or men; to provide with a (human) worker, operator, etc.: — *pr p* **mann'ing**; *pa t* and *pa p* **manned** (*mand*). — *adj* **man'ful** manly. — *adv* **man'fully**. — *n* **man'fulness**. — *n* **man'hood** the state of being a man; manly quality; human nature. — *n* **mankind'** the human race, the mass of human beings; (*man'kīnd*) human males collectively. — *adj* **man'like** having the appearance or qualities of a human being or of an adult human male. — *adv* in the manner of a man; in a way that might be expected of a male person; manfully. — *n* **man'liness**. — *adj* **man'ly** befitting a man, esp. strong and brave; dignified; noble; pertaining to manhood; not childish or womanish. — *adj* **manned** (*mand*). — *adj* **mann'ish** (of a child or woman) like or savouring of a male or grown-up man (usu. *derog*); masculine. — *n* **mann'ishness**. — **man-about-town'** a fashionable, sophisticated man; **man-at-arms'** a soldier, esp. mounted and heavily-armed; **man'-day** a day's work of one person: — *pl* **man'-days**; **man'-eater** a cannibal; a tiger or other animal that has acquired the habit of eating humans; a woman given to chasing, catching and devouring men (*colloq*); **Man Friday** a factotum or servile attendant — from Robinson Crusoe's man. — *vt* **man'handle** to move by manpower; to handle or treat roughly (orig. *slang*). — **man'hole** a hole large enough to admit a man, esp. to a sewer, cable-duct, or similar place; **man'-hour** an hour's work of one person: — *pl* **man'-hours**; **man'hunt** an organised search for a person, esp. one mounted by police, etc. for a criminal; **man-jack'** or **man jack** individual person (as in *every man-jack*). — *adj* **man-made'** made by man; humanly made or originated; (of fibre, fabric, etc.) artificial, synthetic. — **man-man'agement** the organisation of the work of subordinates; **man-of-war'** or **man-o'-war'** a warship: — *pl* **men-of-war'** or **men-o'-war'**. — See also **Portuguese man-of-war**. — **man'power** the agency or energy of man in doing work; the rate at which a person can work; available resources in population or in able-bodied people; **man'servant** a male servant: — *pl* **men'-servants**; **man'shift** the work done by one person in one shift or work period. — *adj* **man'-sized** or **-size** suitable for, or requiring, a man; very big (*colloq*). — **man'slaughter** the slaying of a man; unlawful homicide without malice aforethought (*law*); **man'trap** a trap for catching trespassers; any source of potential danger; **men'folk** or **men'folks** male people, esp. a woman's male relatives; **mens'wear** clothing for men. — **as one man** all together; unanimously; **be one's own man** to be independent, not answerable to anyone else; **be someone's man** to be exactly the person someone is seeking for a particular purpose; **man alive!** an exclamation of surprise; **man in the**

moon the likeness of a man's face which can be seen on the surface of the moon; the fanciful character of children's rhymes, etc. derived from this; **man in the street** the ordinary, everyday man — Tom, Dick or Harry; **man of God** a holy man; a clergyman; **man of letters** a scholar; a writer; **man of straw** a person of no substance (esp. financially); someone nominally, but not really, responsible; a sham opponent or argument set up for the sake of disputation; **man of the match** the most outstanding player in a cricket, football, etc. match (also *fig*); **man of the moment** the man (most capable of) dealing with the present situation; **man of the world** a man with experience of the pains and (esp. sexual) pleasures of life; **man to man** one man to another as individuals in fight or talk; frank and confidential; **to a man** without exception. [O.E. *mann*.]

mana *mä'nä*, *n* a mysterious power associated with persons and things. [Maori.]

manacle *man'ə-kl*, *n* a handcuff. — *vt* to handcuff; to shackle. [O.Fr. *manicle* — L. *manicula*, dimin. of *manica*, sleeve, glove, handcuff — *manus*, hand.]

manage *man'ij*, *vt* to administer, be at the head of; to be able to cope with; to deal tactfully with; to train by exercise, as a horse; to handle; to conduct; to control; to manipulate; to contrive; to have time for; to bring about. — *vi* to conduct affairs; to get on, contrive to succeed. — *n* **manageabil'ity** the quality of being manageable. — *adj* **man'ageable** that can be managed; governable. — *n* **man'ageableness**. — *adv* **man'ageably**. — *n* **man'agement** the art or act of managing; manner of directing or of using anything; administration; skilful treatment; a body of managers. — *n* **man'ager** a person who manages; in an industrial firm or business, a person who deals with administration and with the design and marketing, etc. of the product, as opposed to its actual construction; someone who organises other people's activities; a person legally appointed to manage a business, property, etc. as receiver. — *n* **manageress'** a female manager (not usu. used in official titles). — *adj* **managē'rial** of or pertaining to a manager, or to management. — *n* **man'agership**. — *adj* **man'aging** handling; controlling; administering; contriving; domineering. — **management buyout** the purchase, by its management, of the majority of the shares in a company, esp. when an outside takeover is imminent; **management consultant** a person, usu. employed on a freelance basis, who advises firms on the most efficient procedures applicable to particular businesses or industries. [It. *maneggio* — L. *manus*, the hand.]

mañana *man-yä'nə* or *män-yä'nä*, (Sp.) *n* tomorrow; an unspecified time in the future. — Also *adv*.

manatee *man-ə-tē'*, *n* a large aquatic herbivorous mammal of the warm parts of the Atlantic and the rivers of Brazil. [Sp. *manatí* — Carib *manatoui*.]

Manchester *man'chis-tər*, *adj* belonging to or made in *Manchester*, or similar to goods made in Manchester, applied esp. to cotton cloths.

manchineel *manch-i-nēl'*, *n* a tropical American tree of the spurge family, with poisonous latex. [Sp. *manzanilla*, dimin. of *manzana*, apple.]

Manchu *man-cho͞o'* or *man'cho͞o*, *n* a member of the Mongoloid race from which Manchuria took its name, and which governed China from the 17th to the 20th century; their language. — *adj* of or pertaining to Manchuria or to its inhabitants. — *n* **Manchu'ria**. — *adj* **Manchu'rian**. [Manchu, pure.]

manciple *man'si-pl*, *n* a steward; a purveyor, particularly of a college or an inn of court. [O.Fr., — L. *manceps*, *-cipis*, a purchaser.]

Mancunian *man-* or *mang-kūn'i-ən*, *adj* belonging to Manchester. — *n* a Manchester person. [Doubtful L. *Mancunium*, a Roman station in Manchester. *Mamucium* is probably right.]

-mancy *-man-si* or *-mən-si*, *combining form* signifying divination. — *adj combining form* **-mantic**. [Gr. *manteiā*.]

mandala *mun'də-lə*, *n* (in Buddhism and Hinduism) a symbol of the universe, varying a little but having an enclosing circle and usu. images of deities, used as an aid to religious meditation; (in the psychology of Jung) symbol of the wholeness of the self (in imperfect form shows lack of harmony in the self). [Sans. *maṇḍala*.]

mandamus *man-dā'məs*, (*law*) *n* a writ or command issued by a higher court to a lower: — *pl* **mandā'muses**. [L. *mandāmus*, we command.]

mandarin *man'də-rin* or *-rēn*, *n* a member of any of nine ranks of officials under the Chinese Empire (*hist*); a statuette of a seated Chinese figure, often with a movable head (a *nodding mandarin*); (with *cap*) the most important form of the Chinese language; a high-ranking official or bureaucrat; a person of standing in the literary world, often one who tends to be reactionary or pedantic; (also **man'darine**) a small kind of orange (of Chinese origin); its colour. — *adj* pertaining to a mandarin. — *n* **man'darinate** the office of mandarin; mandarins as a group. — **mandarin collar** or **neck** a high, narrow, stand-up collar the front ends of which do not quite meet; **mandarin duck** a crested Asiatic duck. [Port. *mandarim* — Malay (from Hind.) *mantrī*, counsellor — Sans. *mantra*, counsel.]

mandate *man'dāt*, *n* a charge; a command from a superior official or judge to an inferior, ordering them how to act; a right given to a person to act in name of another; the sanction held to be given by the electors to an elected body, to act according to its declared policies, election manifesto, etc.; the power conferred upon a state by the League of Nations in 1919 to govern a region elsewhere; (also with *cap*) any of the regions governed in this way (also **mandated territory**). — *vt* **mandate'** to assign by mandate; to invest with authority. — *n* **man'datary** or **man'datory** (*-də-tə-ri*) the holder of a mandate; a mandate. — *n* **mandā'tor** the giver of a mandate. — *adj* **man'datory** containing a mandate or command; of the nature of a mandate; bestowed by mandate; compulsory; allowing no option. [L. *mandātum* — *mandāre* — *manus*, hand, *dăre*, give.]

mandible *man'di-bl*, (*zool*) *n* a jaw or jaw-bone, esp. the lower; either part of a bird's bill; an organ performing the functions of a jaw in the lower animals. — *adj* **mandib'ular** relating to the jaw. — *adj* **mandib'ulate** or **mandib'ulated**. [L. *mandibula* — *mandĕre*, to chew.]

mandilion. See **mandylion**.

mandolin or **mandoline** *man'də-lin* or *-lēn*, *n* a round-backed instrument like a lute, sustained notes being played by repeated plucking. — *n* **mandō'la** or **mandō'ra** a large mandoline. [It. *mandola*, *mandora*, dimin. *mandolino*.]

mandrake *man'drāk*, *n* a poisonous plant of the potato family, subject of many strange fancies. [L. *mandragora* — Gr. *mandragorās*.]

mandrel or **mandril** *man'drəl*, *n* a bar of iron fitted to a turning-lathe on which articles to be turned are fixed; the axle of a circular saw. [Fr. *mandrin*.]

mandrill *man'dril*, *n* a large West African baboon with a red and blue muzzle. [Prob. **man** and **drill**[2].]

mandylion *man-dil'i-ən*, *n* a loose outer garment worn e.g. by soldiers over their armour (also **mandil'ion**) (*hist*); (with *cap*) the name of a cloth supposed to bear the imprint of the face of Jesus. [M.Fr. *mandillon*, cloak, and Late Gr. *mandylion*, cloth.]

mane *mān*, *n* long hair on the back of the neck and neighbouring parts, as in the horse and the lion; a long bushy head of hair. — *adj* **maned**. — *adj* **mane'less**. [O.E. *manu*.]

-mane *-mān, combining form* denoting a person who is very enthusiastic about a specified thing. [Gr. *maniā*.]

manège *man-ezh'*, *n* the managing of horses; the art of horsemanship or of training horses; a horse's actions and paces as taught it; a riding-school. — *vt* to train (a horse). [Fr.; cf. **manage**.]

manes *mā'nēz*, (*Roman mythol*; sometimes with *cap*) *npl* the spirits of the dead. [L. *mānēs*.]

maneuver, etc. N.Am. spelling of **manoeuvre**, etc.

mangabey *mang'gə-bā*, *n* the white-eyelid monkey, any species of the mainly West African genus *Cercocebus*, esp. the sooty mangabey. [From a district in Madagascar, where, however, they are not found.]

manganese *mang-gə-nēz'* or *mang'gə-*, *n* a hard brittle greyish-white metallic element (symbol **Mn**; atomic no. 25); (originally and commercially) its dioxide (*black manganese*) or other ore. — *n* **mang'anate** a salt of manganic acid. — **manganese steel** a very hard, shock-resistant steel containing a higher than usual percentage of manganese; **manganic acid** a hypothetical acid existing only in solution. [Fr. *manganèse* — It. *manganese* — L. *magnēsia*.]

mange. See **mangy**.

mangel-wurzel *mang'gl-wûr-zl* or **mangold-wurzel** *man'gōld-*, *n* a variety of beet cultivated as cattle food. — Also **mang'el** or **mang'old**. [Ger. *Mangold*, beet, *Wurzel*, root.]

manger *mān'jər*, *n* a trough in which food is laid for horses and cattle. [O.Fr. *mangeoire* — L. *mandūcāre*, to chew, eat.]

mangetout *mãzh-tōō*, *n* a type of pea, the pod of which is also eaten. — Also **mangetout pea** or **sugar pea**. [Fr., lit., eat-all.]

mangey. See **mangy**.

mangle[1] *mang'gl*, *vt* to mutilate; to bungle (*fig*); to distort; to spoil; to hack or tear into a ragged state. — *n* **man'gler**. [A.Fr. *mangler*, *mahangler*, prob. — O.Fr. *mahaigner*, to maim — *mahaing*, a hurt.]

mangle[2] *mang'gl*, *n* a rolling-press for drying wet clothes. — *vt* to wring (clothes) with a mangle. — *n* **man'gler**. [Du. *mangel* — Gr. *manganon*.]

mango *mang'gō*, *n* a tropical, orig. East Indian, tree of the cashew-nut family; its yellowish-red fleshy fruit: — *pl* **man'goes**. [Port. *manga* — Malay *manggā* — Tamil *mān-kāy*, mango-fruit.]

mangold, mangold-wurzel. See **mangel-wurzel**.

mangrove *mang'grōv*, *n* a tree that grows in muddy swamps covered at high tide or on tropical coasts and estuary shores.

mangy or **mangey** *mānj'i*, *adj* scabby; affected with mange; shabby, seedy. — *n* **mange** (*mānj*; a back-formation) inflammation of the skin of animals caused by mites. — *n* **mang'iness**. [Fr. *mangé*, eaten, past p. of *manger* — L. *mandūcāre*, to chew.]

manhandle. See under **man**.

Manhattan *man-hat'ən*, *n* a cocktail containing vermouth, whisky, bitters, etc. [*Manhattan*, New York.]

manhole, manhood, manhunt. See under **man**.

mania *mā'ni-ə*, *n* a mental illness characterised by an exaggerated feeling of wellbeing, excessively rapid speech and violent, destructive actions (*psychiatry*); the elated phase of manic-depressive disorders (*psychiatry*); excessive or unreasonable desire; (*loosely*) a craze. — *combining form* **-mānia** denoting an abnormal and obsessive desire or inclination, or, more loosely, an extreme enthusiasm, for a specified thing. — *combining form* **-māniac** forming nouns and adjectives. — *n* **mā'niac** a person affected with (a) mania; a madman. — *adj* affected by, or relating to, (a) mania; raving mad. — *adj* **maniacal** (*mə-nī'ə-kl*). — *adv* **manī'acally**. — *adj* **manic** (*man'ik*) of or affected by mania. — *adv* **man'ically**. — **manic-depress'ive** a person suffering from manic-depressive psychosis. — Also *adj*. — **manic-depressive psychosis** a form of mental illness characterised by phases of extreme depression and elation, either alone or alternately, with lucid intervals. [L., — Gr. *maniā*.]

manicure *man'i-kūr*, *n* the care of hands and nails; a professional treatment for the hands and nails; a person who practises this professionally. — *vt* to apply manicure to. — *n* **man'icurist**. [L. *manus*, hand, *cūra*, care.]

manifest *man'i-fest*, *adj* easily seen by the eye or perceived by the mind. — *vt* to make clear or easily seen; to put beyond doubt; to reveal or declare. — *n* a list or invoice of the cargo of a ship or aeroplane to be exhibited at a custom-house; a list of passengers carried by an aeroplane. — *adj* **man'ifestable** that can be manifested or clearly shown. — *n* **manifestā'tion** act of showing something publicly; act of disclosing what is dark or secret; (the form of) an apparition, ghost, etc. — *adv* **man'ifestly** obviously, undoubtedly. [L. *manifestus*.]

manifesto *man-i-fest'ō*, *n* a public written declaration of the intentions, opinions or motives of a sovereign, or of a leader, political party, or body: — *pl* **manifest'os** or **manifest'oes**. [It.; see **manifest**.]

manifold *man'i-fōld*, *adj* various in kind or quality; many in number; having many features; performing several functions. — *n* a pipe with several lateral outlets to others, as in the exhaust system of the internal-combustion engine. [**many** and sfx. **-fold**.]

manikin or **mannikin** *man'i-kin*, *n* a dwarf; an anatomical model of a human body used for teaching purposes, as in art and medicine. [Du. *manneken*, a double dimin. of *man*.]

manila or **manilla** *mə-nil'ə*, *n* small cigar made in *Manila*; the fibre of the abaca plant; strong brownish paper orig. made from abaca plant fibre. — **Manila (or Manilla) hemp** abaca plant fibre.

manioc *man'i-ok*, *n* a plant of the *Manihot* genus, cassava; meal made from this plant. [Tupí *mandioca*.]

maniple *man'i-pl*, *n* in the Western Church, a clerical vestment used during the sacrament, a narrow strip worn on the left arm. [L. *manipulus* — *manus*, the hand, *plēre*, to fill.]

manipulate *mə-nip'ū-lāt*, *vt* to work with the hands, esp. in changing the position, etc. of; to handle or manage, esp. in a way harmful to the person, etc. managed; to give a false appearance to, change the character, etc. of; to turn to one's own purpose or advantage. — *adj* **manip'ulable** or **manip'ulatable** capable of being manipulated. — *adj* **manip'ular**, **manip'ulative** or **manip'ulatory** tending or attempting to manipulate. — *n* **manipulā'tion**. — *n* **manip'ulātor** a person who manipulates; a mechanical device for handling very small, remote or radioactive objects. [L.L. *manipulāre*, *-ātum*; see **maniple**.]

manitou *man'i-tōō*, *n* a spirit or object of reverence among some American Indians: — *pl* **man'itous**. — Also **man'ito** (*-tō*). [Algonquin.]

man-jack, mankind. See under **man**.

manky *mang'ki*, (*slang*) *adj* filthy, dirty, rotten. [Obs. Scot. *mank*, defective — O.Fr. *manc*.]

manly. See under **man**.

manna *man'ə*, *n* the food miraculously provided for the Israelites in the wilderness (*Bible*); acceptable nourishment for body or mind; anything advantageous happening to one as by divine intervention or fate; a sugary substance exuded from the **mann'a-ash** and other trees. [Heb. *mān hū*, what is it?, or from *man*, a gift.]

mannequin *man'i-kin*, *n* a dummy figure, e.g. as used in shop windows; a person, usu. a woman, employed to wear and display clothes. [Fr., manikin.]

manner *man'ər*, *n* the way in which anything is done; method; fashion; personal style of acting or bearing;

custom; style of writing or of thought; sort (of); (in *pl*) social conduct; (in *pl*) good behaviour. — *adj* **mann'ered** having manners (esp. in combination, as in *well-* or *ill-mannered*); affected with mannerisms; artificial, stilted. — *n* **mann'erism** a constant sameness of manner; stiltedness, artificiality; a marked peculiarity or trick of style or manner, esp. in literary composition. — *n* **mann'erist** a writer, painter, etc. addicted to mannerism. — *adj* **manneris'tic.** — *adv* **manneris'tically.** — *n* **mann'erliness.** — *adj* **mann'erly** showing good manners; well-behaved; not rude. — *adv* with good manners; civilly, respectfully, without rudeness. — **all manner of** all kinds of; **by no manner of means** under no circumstances, in no way whatever; **in a manner** in a certain way; **to the manner born** accustomed from birth. [Fr. *manière* — *main* — L. *manus*, the hand.]

mannikin. See **manikin.**

manning, mannish. See under **man.**

manoeuvre or in N.Am. **maneuver** *ma-nōō'vər* or *-nū'*, *n* a piece of skilful management; a stratagem; a skilful and clever movement in military or naval tactics; (usu. in *pl*) a large-scale battle-training exercise of armed forces. — *vi* and *vt* to perform a manoeuvre; to manage skilfully; to change the position of troops or ships; to effect or gain by manoeuvres. — *n* **manoeuvrabil'ity.** — *adj* **manoeu'vrable.** — *n* **manoeu'vrer.** — In U.S. **maneuverabil'ity,** etc. [Fr. *manœuvre* — L. *manū*, by hand, *opera*, work.]

manometer *man-om'i-tər*, *n* an instrument for measuring and comparing the pressure of fluids. — *adj* **manometric** (*man-ō-met'rik*) or **manōmet'rical.** — *n* **manom'etry.** [Gr. *manos*, rare, thin, *metron*, measure.]

ma non troppo *ma non trop'ō*, (*mus*) but not too much. — See **troppo.** [It.]

manor *man'ər*, *n* the land belonging to a nobleman, or that part he formerly kept for his own use, including the manor-house. — *adj* **manorial** (*ma-nö'ri-əl*) pertaining to a manor. — **man'or-house** or **man'or-seat** the house belonging to a manor. [O.Fr. *manoir* — L. *manēre*, *mānsum*, to stay.]

manqué *mā-kā*, (Fr.) *adj* having had ambition or potential, but without it being fulfilled — placed after the noun.

mansard-roof *man-särd-rōōf'*, *n* a roof with four sides, having the lower part steeper than the upper. — Also **man'sard.** [Employed by François *Mansard* or *Mansart* (1598–1666), French architect.]

manse *mans*, *n* an ecclesiastical residence, esp. that of a parish minister of the Church of Scotland. — **son of the manse** a minister's son. [L.L. *mansus*, *mansa*, a dwelling — *manēre*, *mānsum*, to remain.]

mansion *man'shən*, *n* a large house; a manor-house; a house (*astrol*); (in *pl*) a large block of flats. — **man'sion-house** a mansion, a large house. — **the Mansion House** the official residence of the Lord Mayor of London. [O.Fr., — L. *mānsiō*, *-ōnis* — *manēre*, *mānsum*, to remain, to stay.]

manslaughter. See under **man.**

manta *man'tə*, *n* a blanket; a cloak; (with *cap*) a type of gigantic fish with winglike fins and whiplike tail — also called **manta ray.** [Sp.]

mantel *man'tl*, *n* a mantelpiece; a mantelshelf. — **man'telpiece** the ornamental structure over and in front of a fireplace; a mantelshelf; **man'telshelf** the ornamental shelf over a fireplace. [Ety. as for **mantle.**]

mantelet or **mantlet** *man'tlət*, *n* a small cloak for women. [Dimin. of O.Fr. *mantel*, a mantle.]

mantilla *man-til'ə*, *n* a cloak; a kind of veil covering the head and falling down upon the shoulders. [Sp.; dimin. of *manta*.]

mantis *man'tis*, *n* an insect of the genus (*Mantis*) of the cockroach family, which carry their large spiny forelegs in the attitude of prayer, or one of a related genus. — Also called **praying insect** or **praying mantis.** [Gr. *mantis*, *-eōs*, prophet.]

mantissa *man-tis'ə*, (*math*) *n* the fractional part of a logarithm. [L., make-weight.]

mantle *man'tl*, *n* a cloak or loose outer garment, esp. (*fig*) as a symbol of authority, etc.; a covering (esp. *poetic*); a fold of the external skin of a mollusc, etc., secreting the substance forming the shell; a hood or network of fire-resistant material that becomes incandescent when exposed to a flame; the part of the earth immediately beneath the crust, constituting the greater part of the earth's bulk, and presumed to consist of solid heavy rock. — *vt* (esp. *poetic*) to cover; to obscure; to disguise. — *vi* to spread like a cloak. — *n* **man'tlet** see **man'telet.** — *n* **man'tling** cloth suitable for mantles; the drapery of a coat-of-arms (*heraldry*). [L. *mantel(l)um.*]

mantra *man'trə*, *n* a Vedic hymn; a sacred text used as an incantation; a word, phrase, etc. chanted or repeated inwardly in meditation. [Sans., instrument of thought.]

mantrap. See under **man.**

manual *man'ū-əl*, *adj* of the hand or hands; done, worked, or used by the hand(s), as opposed to automatic, computer-operated, etc.; working with the hands. — *n* drill in the use of weapons, etc. (*mil*); a handbook or handy compendium on a large subject or treatise; an instruction book for a piece of machinery, etc.; an organ keyboard played by hand. — *adv* **man'ually.** — **manual alphabet** the signs for letters made by the deaf and dumb; **manual exercise** drill in handling arms (*mil*). [L. *manuālis* — *manus*, the hand.]

manufacture *man-ū-fak'chər*, *vt* to make, originally by hand, now usu. by machinery and on a large scale; to fabricate, concoct, invent. — *vi* to be occupied in manufacture. — *n* the practice, act or process of manufacturing; anything manufactured. — *n* **manufac'turer** a person or business engaged in manufacturing; a director or manager of a firm that manufactures goods; a person who makes, concocts or invents. — *adj* **manufac'turing** pertaining to manufacture. [Fr., — L. *manū* (abl.) by hand, *factūra*, a making, from *facĕre*, *factum*, to make.]

manuka *mä'nōō-kä*, *n* an Australian and New Zealand tree of the myrtle family, with hard wood, its leaves formerly a substitute for tea. [Maori.]

manumit *man-ū-mit'*, *vt* to release from slavery; to set free: — *pr p* **manumitt'ing**; *pa t* and *pa p* **manumitt'ed.** — *n* **manumission** (*-mish'ən*). [L. *manus*, the hand, *mittĕre*, *missum*, to send.]

manure *mən-ūr'*, *vt* to cover, or enrich, with any fertilising substance. — *n* any substance, esp. dung, applied to land to make it more fertile. — *n* **manūr'er.** — *n* **manūr'ing.** [A.Fr. *maynoverer* (Fr. *manœuvrer*); see **manoeuvre.**]

manus *mā'nəs* or *mä'nōōs*, *n* the hand or corresponding part of a vertebrate. [L. *mănus*, pl. *-ūs*.]

manuscript *man'ū-skript*, *adj* written by hand or typed, not printed. — *n* a book or document written by hand before the invention of printing; copy for a printer, handwritten or typed; handwritten form. — Abbrev. **MS.** [L. *manū* (abl.), by hand, *scrībĕre*, *scrīptum*, to write.]

Manx *mangks*, *n* the language of the Isle of *Man*, belonging to the Gaelic branch of Celtic. — *adj* pertaining to the Isle of Man or to its inhabitants. — **Manx cat** a breed of cat with only a rudimentary tail; **Manx'man,** *fem* **Manx'woman.**

many *men'i*, *adj* (*compar* **more** *mör*, *superl* **most** *mōst*) a great number of; numerous. — *n* and *pron* many people; a great number (usu. with omission of *of*). — *adj* **many-col'oured, many-eyed',** etc., having many colours, eyes, etc. — *adj* **man'yfold** (compare **manifold**) many in number. — *adj* **many-sid'ed** having many qualities or aspects; having wide interests or varied abilities. — **many-sid'edness.** — **many a** many (with singular noun and verb); **the many** the crowd, ordinary people in general. [O.E. *manig*.]

manyplies *men'i-plīz*, *nsing* and *npl* the third stomach of a ruminant. [**many** and **ply**[1].]

manzanilla *man-zə-nil'ə* or *-nē'yə*, *n* a very dry, light sherry. [Sp.]

manzello *man-zel'ō*, *n* a musical instrument like the soprano saxophone.

Maoist *mow'ist* or *mä'ō-ist*, *n* a person who adheres to the Chinese type of communism as expounded by *Mao* Tse-tung. — Also *adj*. — *n* **Mao'ism.** — **Mao'-jacket** or **-suit** a jacket or suit in the style of those worn by Mao Tse-tung and his followers — common dress in modern China.

Maori *mow'ri* or *mä'ō-ri*, *n* a member of the aboriginal people of New Zealand; the language of this people: — *pl* **Mao'ris.** — Also *adj*. — **Maoritanga** (*mow-ri-tän'gə*) Maori traditions and culture. [Maori.]

map *map*, *n* a representation in outline of the surface features of the earth, the moon, etc., or of part of it, usu. on a plane surface; a similar plan of the stars in the sky; a representation, scheme, or example of the layout or state of anything; see **function** (*math*). — *vt* to make a map of; to place (the elements of a set) in one-to-one correspondence with the elements of another set (*math*): — *pr p* **mapp'ing**; *pa t* and *pa p* **mapped.** — *n* **mapp'er** or **mapp'ist.** — **map'-reading** the interpretation of what one sees on a geographical map. — **map out** to plan, lay out a plan of; **off the map** out of existence; (of a location) remote from main thoroughfares, etc.; **on the map** into public notice. [L. *mappa*, a napkin, a painted cloth.]

maple *mā'pl*, *n* any tree of the genus *Acer*, from the sap of some species of which sugar and syrup can be made; its timber. — *adj* of maple. — **maple leaf** the emblem of Canada. [O.E. *mapul*, maple.]

maquette *ma-ket'*, *n* a small model of something to be made on a larger scale, esp. a model in clay or wax of a piece of sculpture. [Fr.]

maquillage *ma-kē-yäzh*, *n* (the art of using) cosmetics, make-up. [Fr.]

maquis *mä-kē'*, *nsing* and *npl* a thicket formation of shrubs, as in Corsica and on Mediterranean shores (*bot*); (often with *cap*) French guerrilla resistance forces (1940–45), or a member of them. [Fr., — It. *macchia* — L. *macula*, mesh.]

Mar. *abbrev* for March.

mar *mär*, *vt* to spoil, impair; to injure, damage; to disfigure: — *pr p* **marr'ing**; *pa t* and *pa p* **marred.** [O.E. *merran*.]

marabou *mar'ə-bōō* or **marabout** *mar'ə-bōōt*, *n* an adjutant bird, esp. an African species; its feathers; a plume or trimming of its feathers. [Ety. as for **marabout**.]

marabout *mar'ə-bōōt*, *n* a Muslim hermit, esp. in N. Africa; a practitioner of the occult, a type of witch-doctor; a Muslim shrine. [Fr., — Ar. *murābit*, hermit.]

maraca *mə-rak'ə*, *n* (usu. in *pl*) a dance-band instrument, a gourd or substitute, containing beans, beads, shot, or the like. [Caribb.]

maraschino *mar-ə-skē'nō* or *-shē'nō*, *n* a liqueur distilled from a cherry grown in Dalmatia, Yugoslavia: — *pl* **maraschi'nos.** — **maraschino cherry** a cherry preserved in real or imitation maraschino and used for decorating cocktails, etc. [It., — *marasca*, *amarasca*, a sour cherry — L. *amārus*, bitter.]

marasmus *mə-raz'məs*, *n* a wasting away of the body. — *adj* **maras'mic.** [Latinised — Gr. *marasmos* — *marainein*, to decay.]

marathon *mar'ə-thon* or *-thən*, *n* (with *cap*) scene of the Greek victory over the Persians, 490 B.C., about 22 miles from Athens; a marathon race; a long, severe test of endurance. — *adj* pertaining to marathon races or running; of great length in time, distance, etc.; displaying powers of endurance and stamina. — *n* **mar'athoner.** — **marathon race** a long-distance foot-race (usually 26 miles 385 yards — 42·195 kilometres), commemorating the tradition that a Greek ran from Marathon to Athens with news of the victory; a long-distance race in other sports, e.g. swimming. [Gr. *Marathōn*.]

maraud *mə-röd'*, *vi* to rove in search of plunder. — *n* **maraud'er.** — *adj* **maraud'ing.** [Fr. *maraud*, rogue.]

marble *mär'bl*, *n* a hard granular crystalline limestone taking a high polish and smooth finish; (*loosely*) any rock of similar appearance taking a high polish; a slab, work of art, tombstone, tomb, or other object made of marble; a little hard ball (originally of marble) used in children's games; marbling; anything hard, cold, polished, white, or otherwise like marble (*fig*); (in *pl*) any of several games played with little (now usu. glass) marbles. — *adj* composed or made of marble; shining like marble; unyielding; hard; insensible; marbled. — *vt* to stain, vein or print like marble. — *adj* **mar'bled** irregularly mottled and streaked like some kinds of marble; made from marble. — *n* **mar'bler.** — *n* **mar'bling** a marbled appearance or colouring; the act of veining or painting in imitation of marble, esp. as on book endpapers. — *adj* **mar'bly** like marble. — *adj* **marble-edged'** (e.g. of a book) having the edges marbled. — *adj* **marble-heart'ed** hard-hearted, uncaring, insensible. — **Elgin marbles** a collection of marbles obtained chiefly from the Parthenon by Lord *Elgin* and purchased by the British Museum in 1816. — **have** or **lose (all) one's marbles** to have or lose one's wits (*slang*). [O.Fr. *marbre* — L. *marmor*; cf. Gr. *marmaros* — *marmairein*, to sparkle.]

marc *märk*, *n* fruit-refuse in wine- or oil-making; brandy made from this (also **marc brand**). [Fr.]

marcasite *mär'kə-sīt*, *n* sulphide of iron in orthorhombic white or yellowish crystals (in the gem trade can be pyrite, polished steel, etc.). [L.L. *marcasīta* — Ar. *marqashīt(h)ā*.]

marcato *mär-kä'tō*, (*mus*) *adj* marked; emphatic; strongly accented: — *superl* **marcatis'simo.** — Also *adv*. [It., — *marcare*, to mark.]

March *märch*, *n* the third month of the year. — **March hare** a hare gambolling in the breeding season, proverbially mad because of its antics. [L. *Martius* (*mēnsis*), (the month) of Mars.]

march[1] *märch*, *n* a boundary; a border; a border district, esp. in Scotland — used chiefly in *pl* **march'es.** — *vi* to have a common boundary (usu. with *with*). — *n* **march'er** an inhabitant or lord of a border district. — Also *adj*. — **march'man** a person living on or near a border; **march'-stone** a boundary stone. — **riding the marches** the old ceremony of riding round the bounds of a town, etc. [Fr. *marche*; of Gmc. origin.]

march[2] *märch*, *vi* to walk in a markedly rhythmical military manner, or in a grave, stately or resolute manner; to advance steadily or irresistibly. — *vt* to cause to march; to force to go. — *n* a marching movement; an act of marching; distance travelled at a stretch by marching; steady advance; a piece of music written for marching to, or similar in character and rhythm; a move made by a chess piece. — **marching orders** orders to march; (as from employment, etc.) dismissal (*colloq*); **march past** the march of a body of troops, etc. in front of the person who reviews it. — **forced march** a march necessarily carried out at great speed; **on the march** marching; advancing; **steal a march on** to gain an advantage over, esp. in a cunning or secret manner. [Fr. *marcher*, to walk.]

marchioness *mär'shən-es* or *-is*, *n* the wife of a marquis or marquess; a woman who holds a mar-quisate in her own right. [L.L. *marchiōnissa*, fem. of *marchiō*, *-ōnis*, a lord of the marches.]

Marco Polo sheep *mär'kō pōl'ō shēp*, *n* a type of Asiatic wild sheep with large horns. [After the Venetian explorer.]

Mardi Gras *mär-dē grä*, (Fr.) *n* Shrove Tuesday, celebrated with a carnival in many places, famously Rio de Janeiro.

mare[1] *mār*, *n* the female of the horse. — **mare's-nest'** a supposedly worthwhile discovery that turns out to have no reality; **mare's-tail'** a tall marsh plant of the genus *Hippuris*; (in *pl*) long straight stands of grey cirrus cloud. [O.E. *mere*, fem. of *mearh*, a horse.]

mare[2] *mä'rā* or *-ri*, *n* any of various darkish level areas on (*a*) the moon, (*b*) Mars: — *pl* **maria** (*mä'ri-ə*). [L., sea.]

Marek's disease *mā'reks diz-ēz'*, (*vet*) *n* a viral cancerous disease causing paralysis in poultry. [After a German veterinary surgeon.]

maremma *mə-rem'ə*, *n* seaside marshland; an Italian sheepdog. [It., — L. *maritima*, seaside.]

marg. See **margarine.**

marg. *abbrev* for margin; marginal.

margarine *mär'jər-ēn* or *-gər-* (contr. **marg** or **marge** *märj*), *n* a butterlike substance made from vegetable oils and fats, etc. [Ety. as for **margarite.**]

margarita *mär-gə-rē'tə*, *n* a cocktail of tequila, lemon or lime juice, and orange-flavoured liqueur. [From the Sp. name *Margarita*.]

margarite *mär'gə-rīt*, *n* a pearly-lustred mineral, a mica formed from calcium and aluminium. — *adj* **margaric** (*-gar'ik*) or **margarit'ic** pearl-like. [Gr. *margarītēs*, a pearl.]

margay *mär'gā*, *n* a spotted S. American tiger-cat. [Fr. (or Sp.), — Tupí *mbaracaïa*.]

marge[1] *märj*, (*poetic*) *n* margin, brink. [Fr., — L. *margō*, *-inis*.]

marge[2]. See **margarine.**

margin *mär'jin*, *n* an edge, border, fringe, limit; the blank edge on the page of a book or sheet of paper, or the rule (if any) separating it from the rest of the page; something allowed for safety's sake more than is needed; a deposit to protect a broker against loss; difference between selling and buying price, profit. — *vt* to provide with a margin or margins. — *adj* **mar'ginal** pertaining to a margin; in or on a margin; barely sufficient; not very relevant. — *n* anything on or in a margin, esp. a marginal constituency, etc. — *npl* **marginā'lia** notes written in a margin. — *n* **marginalisa'tion** or **-z-**. — *vt* **mar'ginalise** or **-ize** to write notes in the margin of; to push to the edges of anything, esp. of consciousness, society, etc. in order to reduce effectiveness. — *n* **mar'ginalism** an economic theory that the value of a product depends on its value to the final consumer. — *n* **mar'ginalist.** — *n* **marginal'ity.** — *adv* **mar'ginally.** — *adj* **mar'ginate** or **mar'ginated** having a well-marked border (*bot* or *biol*). — *adj* **mar'gined.** — **marginal constituency, seat** or **ward** a constituency or ward with a small majority at the last election, not providing a safe seat for any of the political parties; **marginal land** less fertile land which will be brought under cultivation only if economic conditions justify it. [L. *margō*, *marginis*.]

margrave *mär'grāv*, (*hist*) *n* a German nobleman of rank equivalent to an English marquis: — *fem* **margravine** (*mär'grə-vēn*). [M.Du. *markgrave* — *mark*, a border, *grave* (mod. *graaf*), a count.]

marguerite *mär-gə-rēt'*, *n* the ox-eye daisy or other single chrysanthemum. [Fr., daisy — Gr. *margarītēs*, pearl.]

maria. See **mare**[2].

Marian *mā'ri-ən*, *adj* relating to the Virgin *Mary* or to Queen Mary (Tudor or Stewart). — *n* a devotee, follower, or defender of (either) Mary. — *n* **Mariol'atry** (excessive) worship of the Virgin Mary. [L. *Marīa*.]

mariculture *mar'i-kul-chər*, *n* the cultivation of plants and animals of the sea in their own environment. [L. *mare*, sea.]

marigold *mar'i-gōld*, *n* a composite plant (*Calendula*) or its orange-yellow flower; extended to other yellow flowers. [From the Virgin *Mary* and **gold.**]

marijuana or **marihuana** *ma-ri-wä'nə*, *n* hemp; its dried flowers and leaves smoked as an intoxicant. [Am. Sp.]

marimba *mə-rim'bə*, *n* an African xylophone, adopted by Central Americans and jazz musicians (also **marim'baphon**). [African origin.]

marinade *mar-i-nād'*, *n* a liquor or pickle in which fish or meat is soaked before cooking, to improve the flavour, tenderise it, etc. — *vt* **mar'inade** or **mar'inate** to steep in wine, oil, herbs, etc. [Ety. as for **marine.**]

marine *mə-rēn'*, *adj* of, in, near, concerned with, or belonging to, the sea; done or used at sea; inhabiting, found in or got from the sea. — *n* a soldier serving on board ship; naval or mercantile shipping fleet. — *n* **marina** (*mə-rē'nə*) a berthing area for yachts, etc., prepared with every kind of facility for a sailing holiday. — *n* **mar'iner** (esp. *literary*) a sailor. — **marine engine** a ship's engine; **marine insurance** insurance of ships or cargoes. — **tell that to the marines** (*colloq*) a phrase expressing disbelief and ridicule. [Fr., — L. *marīnus* — *mare*, sea.]

marinière *ma-rin-yer'*, *adj* (esp. of mussels) cooked in white wine with onions and herbs. [Fr. *à la marinière*, in the manner of the bargeman's wife.]

Mariolatry. See under **Marian.**

marionette *mar-i-ə-net'*, *n* a puppet with jointed limbs moved by strings. [Fr., dimin. of the name *Marion*, itself a dimin. of *Marie*, Mary.]

marital *mar'i-təl*, *adj* pertaining to a husband, or to a marriage; of the nature of a marriage. — *adv* **mar'itally.** [L. *marītālis* — *marītus*, a husband.]

maritime *mar'i-tīm*, *adj* pertaining to the sea; relating to sea-going or sea-trade; having a sea-coast; situated near the sea; (of plants, etc.) living on the shore; having a navy and sea-trade. [L. *maritimus* — *mare*, sea.]

marjoram *mär'jə-rəm*, *n* an aromatic plant whose leaves are used as a seasoning. [O.Fr. *majorane*.]

mark[1] *märk*, *n* a visible indication or sign; a symbol; an object indicating position or serving as a guide; an object to be aimed at, striven for, or attained, such as a target or a goal; a distinctive design; a brand; a set, group or class, marked with the same brand; a type, model, issue, etc. (usu. numbered, as in *mark* 1); a rubber stamp; a substitute for a signature, e.g. an X; a distinguishing characteristic; an impression or trace; a discoloured spot, streak, smear, or other local (usu. small) modification of appearance; noteworthiness, distinction; a point awarded for merit; a footprint; a suitable victim (of trickery, theft, etc.) (*slang*); the impression of a Rugby football player's heel on the ground on making a fair catch. — *vt* to make a mark on; to indicate; to record; to put marks on, award marks to (a child's, student's, etc., written work) to show where it is correct or incorrect; to make emphatic, distinct or prominent; to characterise in a specified, distinct way; to stamp with a sign, etc.; to take note of; (in football, hockey, etc.) to remain close to (one's opponent) in order to try and prevent him or her from obtaining or passing the ball (also *vi*). — *vi* to take particular notice. — *adj* **marked** having visible marks; indicated; noticeable, prominent, emphatic; watched and suspected; destined (with *for*); doomed. — *adv* **mark'edly** (*mär'kid-li*) noticeably. — *n* **mark'er** a person or tool that marks; something that marks a position, such as a stationary light, a flare; a person who marks the score at games; a counter or other device for scoring; a bookmark; the soldier who forms the pivot round which a body of soldiers wheels when marching. — *n*

mark'ing the act of making a mark or marks; (esp. in *pl*) disposition, pattern of marks. — Also *adj*. — **marking gauge** a carpenter's tool for scoring a line parallel to the edge of a piece of wood; **mark'ing-ink** indelible ink, used for marking clothes; **marks'man** or **marks'woman** a person who is good at hitting a target; a person who shoots well; **marks'manship** skill as a marksman or markswoman. — **make one's mark** to make a notable impression; **mark down** to set down in writing; to label at a lower price or to lower the price of (*n* **mark'-down**); to destine; **mark off** to lay out the boundaries of; to mark graduations on; to mark (on a list) as attended to, disposed of; **mark out** to lay out the plan or outlines of; to destine; **mark someone's card** to give someone the information he or she wants; **mark time** to move the feet alternately in the same manner as in marching, but without moving forward; to merely keep things going without progressing; **mark up** to raise the price of, profit on (*n* **mark'-up**); **off the mark** off target; away from the start in a race, etc.; **on your marks (**or **mark)** said before a race begins, to prepare the runners for the starting command or signal; **soft mark** (*colloq*) an easy victim; a person who is easy to cope with or manoeuvre; **up to the mark** satisfactory, of a good standard; fit and well. [O.E. (Mercian) *merc* (W. Saxon *mearc*), a boundary, a limit.]

mark[2] *märk*, *n* a coin of Germany (in 1924 officially named the Reichsmark; in 1948 the Deutsche mark, also Deutschmark), of Finland (the *markka*: — *pl. markkaa*, originally equivalent to a franc), and formerly of various countries. [O.E. *marc*.]

market *mär'kit*, *n* a periodic gathering of people for the purposes of buying and selling; a building, square or other public place used for such meetings; a shop; a region or type of clientele in which there is a demand for certain goods; buying and selling; opportunity for buying and selling; demand; rate of sale. — *adj* relating to buying and selling; relating to a market or markets. — *vi* to buy and sell, esp. at a market. — *vt* to put on the market, sell: — *pr p* **mar'keting**; *pa t* and *pa p* **mar'keted**. — *adj* **mar'ketable** fit for the market; saleable. — *n* **marketabil'ity** or **mar'ketableness**. — *n* **marketeer'** a person who buys or sells, esp. at a market; (esp. with *cap*) a supporter of Britain's entry into the Common Market. — See also **black-marketeer** under **black**. — *n* **mar'keter** a person who goes to market, buys or sells at a market. — *n* **mar'keting** the act or practice of buying and selling in the commercial market-place. — **market-cross'** a cross or similar structure set up where a market was originally held; **mar'ket-day** the fixed day of the week on which a market is held; **market-gar'den** a garden in which fruit and vegetables are grown for public sale; **market-gar'dener**; **market-gar'dening**; **mar'ket-hall** or **mar'ket-house** a building in which a market is held; **market leader** a company that sells more goods of a specified type than any other company; a brand of goods selling more than any other of its kind; **mar'ket-maker** since the changes of 27 October 1986, a broker-dealer on the Stock Exchange; **mar'ket-making**; **mar'ket-place** the market-square of a town, etc.; broadly, the world of commercial transactions; **mar'ket-price** or **market-val'ue** the current price a commodity, etc. will fetch at sale; **market research** research to determine consumers' preferences and what they can afford to buy; **market-square'** the open space in a town where markets are or were held; **mar'ket-town** a town having the privilege of holding a public market. — **in the market for** wanting to buy; **on the market** available for buying; on sale. [Late O.E. *market* — O.N.Fr. *market* — L. *mercātus*, trade, a market.]

markka *mär-kä'*, *n* the standard monetary unit of Finland (100 *penni*): — *pl* **markkaa'** or **markkas'**. [See **mark[2]**.]

Markov chain *mär'kof chān*, *n* a series of events, in which the probability of each event depends on the probability of the event immediately preceding it.

marksman, markswoman. See under **mark[1]**.

marl *märl*, *n* a limy clay often used as manure. — *vt* to cover with marl. — *adj* **marl'y** like marl; containing large amounts of marl. [O.Fr. *marle* (Fr. *marne*) — L.L. *margila*, a dimin. of L. *marga*, marl.]

marlin *mär'lin*, *n* a large oceanic fish of the genus *Makaira* similar to the swordfishes. [From **marline-spike**, because of the shape of its snout.]

marline *mär'lin*, *n* a small rope for winding round a larger one to keep it from wearing. — Also **mar'lin**. — **mar'line-spike** a spike for separating the strands of a rope in splicing. — Also **mar'linspike**. [Du. *marling*, verbal n. from *marlen*, or *marlijn* — *marren*, and *lijn*, rope.]

marly. See **marl**.

marm. See **ma'am**.

marmalade *mär'mə-lād*, *n* a jam or preserve generally made of the pulp (and rind) of oranges, originally of quinces. [Fr. *marmelade* — Port. *marmelada* — *marmelo*, a quince — L. *melimēlum* — Gr. *melimēlon*, a sweet apple — *meli*, honey, *mēlon*, an apple.]

marmelise or **-ize** *mär'mə-līz*, (*jocular slang*) *vt* to thrash, defeat heavily, destroy, etc.

marmem alloy *mär'məm al'oi*, *n* an alloy which, under the influence of temperature changes, can be changed from one condition to another and back again. [*mar*tensite and *mem*ory, because the alloy 'remembers' its former condition.]

marmite *mär'mīt* or *mär-mēt'*, *n* a metal or earthenware cooking pot, esp. for soup. [Fr., pot or kettle.]

marmoreal *mär-mör'i-əl*, *adj* of or like marble. [L. *marmor*, marble.]

marmoset *mär'mə-zet*, *n* a very small American monkey. [Fr. *marmouset*, grotesque figure.]

marmot *mär'mət*, *n* a genus of stout burrowing rodents, in America called woodchuck. [It. *marmotto*.]

marocain *mar'ə-kān*, *n* a dress material finished with a grain surface like morocco-leather. [Fr. *maroquin*, morocco-leather.]

maroon[1] *mə-ro͞on'*, *n* a brownish crimson; a detonating firework, esp. one used as a distress signal. — *adj* of the colour maroon. [Fr. *marron*, a chestnut.]

maroon[2] *mə-ro͞on'*, *n* a fugitive slave, or a descendant of the same; a marooned person. — *vt* to put and leave ashore on a desolate island; to isolate uncomfortably (*lit* or *fig*). — *n* **maroon'er**. — *n* **maroon'ing**. [Fr. *marron* — Sp. *cimarrón*, wild.]

Marq. *abbrev* for Marquis.

marque[1] *märk*, *n* a privateer. — **letter-of-marque'** or **letters-of-marque'** a privateer's licence to commit acts of hostility. [Fr.]

marque[2] *märk*, *n* a brand or make, esp. of car. [Fr.]

marquee *mär-kē'*, *n* a large tent, used for parties, exhibitions, etc. [*marquise*, old word for tent.]

marquess, etc. See **marquis**.

marquetry or **marqueterie** *märk'i-tri*, *n* work, esp. in furniture, inlaid with pieces of varicoloured wood, ivory, metal, etc. [Fr. *marqueterie* — *marqueter*, to inlay — *marque*, a mark.]

marquis or (spelling used by some holders of the title) **marquess** *mär'kwis*, *n* a title of nobility next below that of a duke: — *fem* **marchioness** (*mär'shən-es* or *-nes'*). — *n* **mar'quisate** or **mar'quessate** the lordship of a marquis. — *n* **marquise** (*mär-kēz'*) in France, a marchioness; a ring set with gems arranged to form a pointed oval; a gem cut into the shape of a pointed oval. — *n* **marquisette'** a woven clothing fabric, used also for curtains and mosquito nets. [O.Fr. *marchis*, assimilated later to Fr. *marquis* — L.L. *marchēnsis*, a prefect of the marches.]

marram *mar'əm, n* a coarse seaside grass frequently used to counter sand-erosion. [O.N. *marr*, sea, *halmr*, haulm, stem.]

marriage *mar'ij, n* (an instance of) the ceremony, act or contract by which a man and woman become husband and wife; a similar ceremony, etc. between homosexuals; a close union (*fig*). — *adj* **marr'iage-able** suitable for marriage. — *n* **marr'iageable-ness.** — **marr'iage-bed** the bed of a married couple; sexual intercourse within marriage (*euph*); the rights and obligations of marriage; **marr'iage-broker** a person who, in certain cultures, arranges a marriage contract for a fee; **marr'iage-contract** a formal agreement to be married; an agreement concerning property rights by persons about to marry; **marriage guidance** help and advice given to married people with problems in their personal relationships; **marr'iage-licence** a licence to marry; **marr'iage-settlement** an arrangement of property, etc. before marriage, by which something is guaranteed to the wife and sometimes also to her children if the husband dies. — **marriage of convenience** a marriage (or *fig*, a close business union, etc.) for reasons of expediency rather than affection. [O.Fr. *mariage*; see **marry**.]

marrons glacés *ma-rɔ̃ gla-sā*, (Fr.) chestnuts coated with glacé icing.

marrow *mar'ō, n* the soft tissue in the hollow parts of the bones; a vegetable marrow (see under **veg-etable**); the essence or best part of anything; the inner meaning or purpose. — *adj* **marr'owless** having no marrow. — *adj* **marr'owy** full of marrow; strong; pithy. — **marr'ow-bone** a bone containing marrow; **marr'owfat** a rich kind of pea. [O.E. (Anglian) *merg*, *mærh*.]

marry *mar'i, vt* to take as a husband or wife; to give in marriage; to unite in matrimony; to unite, join, put together (sometimes with *up*; *fig*). — *vi* to take a husband or wife: — *pr p* **marr'ying**; *pa t* and *pa p* **marr'ied.** — *adj* **marr'ied.** — *n* **marr'ier** a person who marries; the sort of person likely to take a husband or wife. — **marry into** to become a member of (a family) by marriage; **marry off** to find a spouse for (e.g. one's son or daughter). [Fr. *marier* — L. *marītāre*, to marry.]

Mars *märz, n* the Roman god of war; the planet next after the Earth in order of distance from the sun. [L. *Mārs*.]

Marsala *mär-sä'lə, n* a sweet wine resembling sherry, from *Marsala* in Sicily.

Marseillaise *mär-sə-lāz'* or *-sā-ez', n* the French national anthem, in origin a revolutionary hymn composed in 1792. [Orig. sung by the volunteer soldiers of *Marseilles*.]

marsh *märsh, n* a tract of wet land; a morass, swamp or fen. — *adj* inhabiting or found in marshes. — *n* **marsh'iness.** — *adj* **marsh'y** like marsh; covered with marsh. — **marsh'-fever** malaria; **marsh'-gas** methane; **marsh harrier** a marsh-inhabiting harrier hawk; **marsh hawk** a common N. American hawk with a white patch on its rump (also **hen harrier**); **marsh'land** marshy country; **marsh'lander** a person who inhabits marshland; **marsh-mall'ow** a maritime marsh-growing plant very similar to hollyhock; **marshmall'ow** a jellylike sweet, orig. made from the root of the marsh-mallow; a person or thing excessively soft, sweet or sentimental; **marsh marigold** a marsh plant of the buttercup family with flowers like large buttercups. [O.E. *mersc*, *merisc*, orig. adj.]

marshal *mär'shl, n* an officer in a royal household, originally the king's farrier, later having responsibility for military arrangements, the regulation of ceremonies, preservation of order, points of etiquette, etc.; any official with similar functions; a law-court officer with charge of prisoners; in France, etc., an officer of the highest military rank; a civil officer appointed to carry out the process of the courts (*US*); a police or fire-brigade chief officer (*US*). — *vt* to arrange in order; to usher; to combine in or with one coat of arms. — *vi* to come together in order: — *pr p* **mar'shalling**; *pa t* and *pa p* **mar'shalled.** — *n* **mar'shalcy** the rank, office or department of a marshal. — *n* **mar'shaller.** — *n* **mar'shalling.** — *n* **mar'shalship.** — **marshalling yard** a place where railway wagons are sorted out and arranged into trains. [O.Fr. *mareschal*; from O.H.G. *marah*, a horse, *schalh*, a servant.]

marsupium *mär-sū'pi-əm*, (*zool*) *n* a pouch. — *adj* **marsū'pial** pertaining to a pouch or to the Marsupialia; of the nature of a pouch; of the Marsupialia. — *n* a member of the Marsupialia. — *npl* **Marsupiā'lia** an order of mammals whose young are born in a very imperfect state and then complete their development carried in an external pouch by the female. [L. *marsūpium* — Gr. *marsip(p)ion*, *marsyp(p)ion*, a pouch.]

mart *märt, n* a place of trade, market. [Du. *markt*.]

martello *mär-tel'ō, n* (in full **martello tower**) a circular fort for coastal defence: — *pl* **martell'os.** [From Cape *Mortella* in Corsica, where one resisted a British cannonade for some time in 1794.]

marten *mär'tən, n* an animal (e.g. the pine marten) closely related to the weasels, or other species of *Mustela*. [Fr. *martre*, from the Gmc. root seen in Ger. *Marder*, and O.E. *mearth*, marten.]

martensite *mär'tən-zīt, n* a constituent of rapidly cooled steel consisting of a solid solution of carbon in iron. [After Adolph *Martens* (d. 1914), German metallurgist.]

martial *mär'shl, adj* belonging or pertaining to Mars, the god of war, or to the planet Mars; of or belonging to war, or to the army and navy; warlike. — *n* **mar'tialism.** — *n* **mar'tialist** a soldier. — *adv* **mar'tially.** — **martial art** (usu. in *pl*) any of various combative sports or methods of self-defence (usu. of oriental origin) including karate, kung fu, etc.; **martial law** exercise of military power by the supreme authority in time of emergency (war, riot, etc.), ordinary administration and policing ceasing to operate. [Fr. *martial* — L. *mārtiālis* — *Mārs*.]

Martian *mär'shən, adj* of Mars (god or planet). — *n* an inhabitant of Mars (*science fiction*). [L. *Mārtius* — *Mārs*.]

martin *mar'tin, n* a bird of the swallow genus. [The name *Martin*.]

martinet *mär-ti-net'* or *mär', n* a strict disciplinarian. — *n* **martinet'ism.** [*Martinet*, an officer of Louis XIV.]

martingale *mär'tin-gāl, n* a strap passing between a horse's forelegs, fastened to the girth and to the bit, noseband, or reins, to keep its head down; a short spar under the bowsprit (*naut*); in gambling, the policy of doubling the stake on losing. [Fr.]

Martini® *mär-tē'nē, n* a type of vermouth made by the firm of *Martini* and Rossi; (without *cap*) a cocktail of vermouth, gin, bitters, etc.

Martinmas *mär'tin-məs, n* the *mass* or feast of St *Martin*, 11 November.

martlet *märt'lit*, (*heraldry*) *n* a martin or swallow without feet. [From Fr. *martinet*, dimin. of *martin*, martin.]

martyr *mär'tər, n* a person who by their death bears witness to their (esp. religious) belief; a person who suffers for their belief; a person who suffers greatly for any reason, a victim (*loosely*). — *vt* to put to death as a martyr. — *n* **mar'tyrdom** the state of being a martyr; the sufferings or death of a martyr; torment generally. — *vt* **mar'tyrise** or **-ize** to offer as a sacrifice; to cause to suffer martyrdom, to martyr. — *adj* **martyrolog'ical.** — *n* **martyrol'ogist.** — *n* **martyrol'ogy** a history of martyrs; an official list of martyrs. — *n* **mar'tyry** a shrine, chapel or monument erected in memory of a martyr or martyrs. [O.E., — L., — Gr., a witness.]

marvel *mär'vl*, *n* a wonder; something astonishing or wonderful. — *vi* to wonder; to feel astonishment: — *pr p* **mar'velling**; *pa t* and *pa p* **mar'velled**. — *adj* **mar'vellous** very good, extremely pleasing; astonishing; almost or altogether beyond belief. — *adv* **mar'vellously**. — *n* **mar'vellousness**. — **marvel of Peru** (*pə-ro͞o'*) a showy garden flower from Mexico, open and scented in the evening. [Fr. *merveille* — L. *mīrābilis*, wonderful — *mīrārī*, to wonder.]

Marxian *märks'i-ən*, *adj* pertaining to Karl *Marx* (1818–83) or his socialism, esp. as interpreted in Russia. — *n* a follower of Marx. — *n* **Marx'ianism** or **Marx'ism**. — *n* and *adj* **Marx'ist**.

marzipan *mär-zi-pan'*, *n* a sweet almond paste, used in sweetmeats, cakes, etc. [Ger., — It. *marzapane*.]

mas. or **masc.** *abbrev* for masculine.

-mas *-məs*, *combining form* denoting a church festival or feast day, as in *Candlemas*, *Christmas*, *Martinmas*, etc. [Ety. as for **mass²**.]

Masai *ma-sī'* or *mä'sī*, *n* an African people of the highlands of Kenya and Tanzania. — Also *adj*.

masc. See **mas**.

mascara *mas-kä'rə*, *n* colouring for the eyelashes, a cosmetic. [See ety. for **mask**.]

mascaron *mas'kə-ron*, (*archit*) *n* a grotesque face on a keystone, door-knocker, etc. [See ety. for **mask**.]

mascle *mas'kl*, (*heraldry*) *n* a design, lozenge-shaped and perforated.

mascon *mas'kon*, *n* any of several mass concentrations of dense material, of uncertain origin, lying beneath the moon's surface. [*mas*s *con*centration.]

mascot *mas'kət*, *n* a talisman, a supposed bringer of good luck. [Fr. *mascotte*.]

masculine *mas'kū-lin*, *adj* characteristic of, peculiar to, or appropriate to, a man or the male sex; mannish; of that gender to which belong words denoting males and, in some languages, various other words (*gram*). — *n* the male sex or nature; a word of masculine gender. — *adv* **mas'culinely**. — *n* **mas'culineness**. — *vt* **mas'culinise** or **-ize** to cause to develop masculine character or appearance. — *vi* to develop such character or appearance. — *n* **masculin'ity**. — **masculine ending** a stressed syllable at the end of a line (*prosody*); **masculine rhyme** a rhyme on a final stressed syllable; in French, one without a final mute *e*. [Fr., — L. *masculīnus* — *masculus*, male — *mās*, a male.]

maser *māz'ər*, *n* a device used to amplify long range radar and radio astronomy signals. [*m*icrowave *a*mplification by *s*timulated *e*mission of *r*adiation.]

mash *mash*, *n* in brewing, a mixture of crushed malt and hot water; a mixture, as of bran with meal or turnips, beaten and stirred as a food for animals; any material beaten or crushed into a soft or pulpy state; mashed potatoes (*colloq*); crushed condition. — *vt* to make into a mash; to pound down or crush. — *n* **mash'er**. — *n* **mash'ing**. — **mash'man** a worker, e.g. in a distillery, who helps to make the mash; **mash'-tub, -tun, -vat** or **mash'ing-tub** a vessel in which the mash in breweries is mixed. [O.E. *masc*(*-wyrt*), mash(-wort).]

mashie or **mashy** *mash'i*, *n* an old-fashioned iron golf club for lofting, a number five iron. — **mashie-nib'lick** an old-fashioned club between mashie and niblick, a number six iron. [Perh. Fr. *massue*, club.]

masjid *mus'jid*, *n* a mosque. [Ar.]

mask *mäsk*, *n* a covering for the face, or the upper part of it, for concealment, disguise, protection, amusement or ceremonial purposes; a grotesque representation of a face worn in ancient or Japanese, etc. drama, or used as an architectural ornament, etc.; a fox's (or other animal's) face or head; a mould of a face; a masque; a disguise, pretence or concealment (*fig*); any means of screening or disguising; a screen to cover part of a light-sensitive surface (*phot*); a screen used to cover parts of a surface onto the exposed parts of which an integrated circuit is to be etched. — *vt* to cover the face of with a mask; to hide, cloak, screen or disguise. — *adj* **masked** wearing, screened, etc. by a mask; concealed. — *n* **mask'er** a person who wears a mask; a person attending a masque; a device that produces a noise to mask another noise, used e.g. by tinnitus sufferers. — **masked ball** a ball at which the dancers wear masks. [Fr. *masque* — Sp. *máscara* or It. *maschera*.]

masochism *mas'ə-kizm*, *n* pleasure, esp. sexual, in being dominated or treated cruelly; (*loosely*) unwholesome gratification in suffering pain, physical or mental. — *n* **mas'ochist**. — *adj* **masochist'ic**. [From the novelist Sacher-*Masoch*, who described it.]

mason *mā'sn*, *n* a person who cuts, prepares, and lays stones; a builder in stone; a member of the society of freemasons. — *vt* to build or repair in stonework. — *adj* **masonic** (*mə-son'ik*) relating to freemasonry. — *adj* **mā'sonried** constructed of masonry. — *n* **mā'sonry** the art, skill or work of a stonemason; stonework; freemasonry. — *adj* consisting of stone. [O.Fr. *masson* (Fr. *maçon*) — L.L. *maciō*, *-ōnis*.]

Mason-Dixon Line *mā-sn-dik'sn līn*, *n* the boundary between Pennsylvania and Maryland following a line surveyed between 1763 and 1767 by Charles *Mason* and Jeremiah *Dixon*, later thought of as separating the free Northern states from the slave states of the South.

masque *mäsk*, *n* a masked person; a masquerade or masked ball; a form of courtly spectacle in vogue in the 16th and 17th centuries, in which masked performers danced and acted, developing into a form of drama with scenery and music; a literary composition for the purpose. [Ety. as for **mask**.]

masquerade *mäsk-ər-ād'*, *n* an assembly of people wearing masks, generally at a ball; a disguise or pretence. — *vi* to wear a mask; to take part in a masquerade; to go in disguise; to pretend to be (with *as*). — *n* **masquerā'der**. [Fr. *mascarade*.]

Mass. *abbrev* for Massachusetts (U.S. state).

mass¹ *mas*, *n* a lump of matter; a quantity; a collected or coherent body of matter; an unbroken expanse; the aggregate, total; the main body; the greater or principal part; the quantity of matter in any body, measured by its resistance to change of motion and the force of gravity exerted upon it; (in *pl*) the ordinary people, the people as a whole. — *adj* pertaining to a mass, or to large numbers or quantities, or to ordinary people as a whole. — *vt* to form into a mass; to bring together in masses. — *vi* to assemble, come together in a mass or masses. — *adj* **massive** (*mas'iv*) bulky; weighty; giving an impression of weight; not separated into parts or elements; without crystalline form; (*loosely*) great in quantity; on a very large scale, or of great size or power (*fig*). — *adv* **mass'ively**. — *n* **mass'iveness**. — *adj* **mass'y** massive, made up of masses. — **mass defect** the difference between the sum of the masses of the neutrons and protons in a nucleus and the mass of the nucleus itself; **mass market** the market for mass-produced goods. — *vt* **mass-mar'ket**. — **mass-mar'keting**; **mass media, mass medium** see **medium**; **mass meeting** a large meeting for a public protest or discussion; **mass number** the atomic weight of an isotope, the number of neutrons and protons in the nucleus; **mass observation** study of the habits, opinions, etc. of the general body of a community. — *vt* **mass-produce'** to produce in great quantity by a standardised process. — *adj* **mass-produced'**. — **mass-produc'tion**; **mass radiography** X-raying large numbers of people by means of mobile units; **mass spectrograph** an instrument by means of which a positive ray spectrum can be obtained, the images corresponding to particles of different masses being spaced according to the masses, so that the atomic weights of the particles can be deduced; **mass spectrometer** an instrument like the mass spectrograph but measuring not the masses of particles but the relative number of particles of each mass present; **mass spectrometry**. [Fr. *masse* — L. *massa*, a lump.]

mass[2] (often with *cap*) *mas* or *mäs*, *n* the celebration of the Lord's Supper or Eucharist in R.C. and some Protestant churches; the religious service for it; a musical setting of certain parts of the R.C. liturgy. [O.E. *mæsse* — L.L. *missa* — L. *mittĕre*, to send away.]

massacre *mas'ə-kər*, *n* indiscriminate slaughter, esp. of large numbers; carnage. — *vt* to kill with violence and cruelty; to slaughter, usu. in large numbers. [Fr.]

massage *ma'säzh* or *mə-säzh'*, *n* a (system of) treatment for painful muscles, etc. by pressing, tapping, kneading, friction, etc.; manipulation, alteration of the appearance of something (esp. data of any kind) to show it in a more favourable light. — *vt* to subject to massage; to present in a favourable light by devious means. — *n* **massa'gist** or **masseur** (*-sœr'* or *-sûr'*), *fem* **masseuse** (*-sœz'*). [Fr., from Gr. *massein*, to knead.]

massé *mas'ā*, (*billiards*) *n* a sharp stroke made with the cue vertical or nearly so. [Fr.]

masseur, masseuse. See under **massage**.

massif *ma-sēf'* or *mas'if*, *n* a central mountain mass. [Fr.]

massive, massy, etc. See **mass**[1].

mast[1] *mäst*, *n* a long upright pole, esp. one for carrying the sails of a ship. — *vt* to supply with a mast or masts. — *adj* **mast'ed**. — *adj* **mast'less**. — **mast'head** the top of a mast; the name of a newspaper or periodical in the typographical form in which it normally appears at the top of the front page, or a similar block of information regularly used as a heading. — **before the mast** as a common sailor (whose quarters are in the forecastle, forward of the mast). [O.E. *mæst*.]

mast[2] *mäst*, *n* the fruit of the oak, beech, chestnut, and other trees, on which pigs feed. — *adj* **mast'y** of the nature of mast; as if well fed on mast. — **mast cell** a cell in connective tissue thought to produce histamine and other agents controlling the release of acid in the stomach. — *adj* **mast'-fed**. [O.E. *mæst*.]

mastaba *mas'tə-bə*, *n* an ancient Egyptian tomb with sloping sides and flat roof, in an outer chamber of which offerings were made, and with a shaft descending to the actual grave. [Ar. *mastabah*, a bench.]

mastectomy *mas-tek'tə-mi*, (*med*) *n* surgical removal of a breast. — **radical mastectomy** the surgical removal of a breast together with some pectoral muscles and lymph nodes in the armpit. [Gr. *mastos*, breast, *ektomeē*, excision.]

master *mäs'tər*, *n* a person (esp. male) who commands or controls; a lord or owner; a leader or ruler; a teacher; an employer; the commander of a ship; a person eminently skilled in anything, esp. art; a person who has complete knowledge of an art, science, etc.; (with *cap*) formerly prefixed to a name or designation as Mr is now, now only of a boy in this use; (usu. with *cap*) a title of dignity or office, e.g. a degree conferred by universities, such as *Master of Arts*, etc., an official of the Supreme Court, the head of some corporations, of a lodge of freemasons, etc.; an original (film, record, etc.) from which copies are made; a master-card. — *adj* chief; controlling; predominant; of a master; of the rank or skill level of a master; original. — *vt* to become master of; to overcome; to gain control over; to acquire a thorough knowledge of; to become skilful in; to rule as master. — *adj* **mas'terful** exercising the authority, skill or power of a master; imperious. — *adv* **mas'terfully**. — *n* **mas'terfulness**. — *adj* **mas'terless** without a master or owner; ungoverned; beyond control. — *n* **mas'terliness**. — *adj* **mas'terly** like a master; with the skill of a master. — *n* **mas'tership** the condition, authority, status, office, or term of office of master; rule or dominion; superiority. — *n* **mas'tery** the power or authority of a master; upper hand; control; complete, supreme skill or knowledge. — **master-build'er** a chief builder; a builder who directs or employs others; **mas'ter-card** the card that commands a suit or is the highest of all those remaining to be played; **mas'ter-class** the dominant class in a society; a lesson, esp. in music, given to talented students by a renowned expert; **mas'ter-key** a key that opens many (different) locks, esp. all the locks in a certain building; a clue able to guide one out of many difficulties (*fig*); **master-mar'iner** the captain of a merchant-vessel or fishing-vessel; **master-ma'son** a freemason who has attained the third degree; **mas'termind** a mind, or a person having a mind, of very great ability; the person conceiving or directing a project, esp. a criminal enterprise. — *vt* to originate, think out, and direct. — **mas'terpiece** a piece of work worthy of a master; one's greatest achievement. — Also **mas'terwork**; **mas'terstroke** an action or performance worthy of a master; an effective, well-timed act; **mas'ter-switch** a switch for controlling the effect of a number of other switches or contacts. — **old masters** a term applied collectively to the great painters around the time of the Renaissance, esp. the Italians; **past master** see under **past**. [Partly O.E. *mægester*, partly O.Fr. *maistre* (Fr. *maître*), both from L. *magister*, from root of *magnus*, great.]

mastic *mas'tik*, *n* a pale yellow gum resin from certain Mediterranean trees, used for varnish or cement; a tree exuding mastic; a bituminous or oily cement of various kinds used as a sealant or filler. [Fr. *mastic* — L.L. *mastichum* — Gr. *mastichē*.]

masticate *mas'ti-kāt*, *vt* to chew; to knead mechanically, as in rubber manufacture. — *adj* **mas'ticable** able to be chewed. — *n* **masticā'tion**. — *n* **mas'ticātor** a person who masticates; a machine for grinding; a machine for kneading india-rubber. — *adj* **mas'ticatory** (*-kə-tə-ri*) chewing; adapted for chewing. — *n* a substance chewed to increase the saliva. [L. *masticāre*, *-ātum*, to chew.]

mastiff *mas'tif*, *n* a thick-set, powerful breed of dog used as a watchdog. [O.Fr. *mastin*, app. — L. *mansuētus*, tame.]

mastitis *mas-ti'tis*, *n* inflammation of the breast or udder. [Gr. *mastos*, breast, and **-itis**.]

mastodon *mas'tə-don*, *n* an extinct mammal similar to an elephant, so named from the teatlike prominences of its molar teeth. [Gr. *mastos*, breast, *odous*, *odontos*, a tooth.]

mastoid *mas'toid*, *adj* like a nipple or breast. — *n* a prominence on the temporal bone behind the ear (also **mastoid bone** or **process**). — *adj* **mastoid'al**. — *n* **mastoidī'tis** inflammation of the air cells of the mastoid process. [Gr. *mastoeidēs*, like a breast.]

masturbation *mas-tər-bā'shən*, *n* stimulation, usually by oneself, of the sexual organs by manipulation, etc., so as to produce orgasm. — *vi* and *vt* **mas'turbate**. — *n* **mas'turbātor**. — *adj* **masturbā'tory**. [L. *masturbārī*, to masturbate.]

masty. See **mast**[2].

mat[1] *mat*, *n* a piece of fabric or material of any of various types and thicknesses, laid on the ground for any of various purposes, e.g. covering part of the floor, standing or lying on, wiping one's shoes on at a threshold, absorbing shock on landing or falling in gymnastics, wrestling, etc.; a smaller piece of cloth, cork or other material for placing under a vase, dish, or other object to prevent damage to the surface it stands on; a closely interwoven or tangled mass, esp. of hair or vegetation. — *vt* to cover with mats; to interweave or tangle into a compact mass. — *vi* to become tangled into a compact mass: — *pr p* **matt'ing**; *pa t* and *pa p* **matt'ed**. — *n* **matt'ing** mat-making; becoming matted; mats, or material used as, or for making, mats. — **mat'grass** or **mat'weed** a small, tufted, rushlike moorland grass (genus *Nardus*); marram. — **on the mat** being scolded, on the carpet. [O.E. *matt(e)* — L. *matta*, a mat.]

mat[2], **matt** or **matte** *mat*, *adj* (of a surface) dull, lustreless, or roughened to eliminate gloss. — *vt* to produce a dull surface on; to frost (glass). [Fr. *mat*.]

mat. *abbrev* for matinée.

matador *mat'ə-dör*, *n* the man who kills the bull in bullfights. [Sp. *matador* — *matar*, to kill — L. *mactāre*, to kill.]

match[1] *mach*, *n* a short stick of wood or other material tipped with an easily ignited material; a piece of treated cord, readily inflammable but slow-burning, for firing cannon, etc. — **match'box** a box for holding matches; **match'-maker**; **match'stick** the wooden shaft of a match. — *adj* very thin, like a matchstick; (of figures in a drawing, etc.) having limbs suggested by single lines. — **match'wood** touchwood; wood suitable for matches; splinters. [O.Fr. *mesche*.]

match[2] *mach*, *n* that which tallies or exactly agrees with another thing; an equal; a person who can stand up to or get the better of someone else; a condition of exact agreement, compatibility or close resemblance, esp. in colours; equality in contest; a formal contest or game; a pairing; a marriage; a person to be gained in marriage. — *vi* to be exactly or nearly alike; to correspond; to compete or encounter (esp. on equal terms). — *vt* to be equal to; to be a counterpart to; to be compatible with, or exactly like, in colour, etc.; to be able to compete with; to find an equal or counterpart to; to pit or set against another in contest or as equal; to treat as equal; to fit in with; to suit; to join in marriage; to make the impedances of (two circuits) equal, so as to produce maximum transfer of energy (*electronics*). — *adj* **match'able.** — *adj* **matched.** — *n* **match'er.** — *adj* **match'ing.** — *adj* **match'less** having no match or equal; superior to all. — *adv* **match'lessly.** — *n* **match'lessness.** — **match'board** one of a number of boards with a tongue cut along one edge and a groove in the opposite edge, fitted one into the next to make wall facing, etc.; **match'maker** a person who attempts to arrange marriages by bringing suitable partners together; **match'making**; **match'-play** scoring in golf according to holes won and lost rather than the number of strokes taken; **match point** the stage at which another point wins the match; the point that wins the match; a unit of scoring in bridge tournaments. — **to match** in accordance or co-ordination, esp. in colour. [O.E. *gemæcca*.]

match-maker. See under **match**[1].

matchmaker. See under **match**[2].

mate[1] *māt*, *n* a companion; an equal; a fellow workman; a friendly or ironic form of address; a husband or wife; an animal with which another is paired to produce young; one of a pair; a ship's officer under the captain or master; an assistant, deputy (as in *plumber's mate*). — *vt* to marry; to cause (esp. animals) to copulate; to couple, link up or fit. — *vi* to marry; (usu. of animals) to copulate. — *adj* **mate'less.** — *n* **mate'ship** (esp. *Austr*) the bond between close friends. — *adj* **mate'y** or **māt'y** (*colloq*) friendly and familiar, esp. in a studied or overdone manner. — *adv* **mā'tily.** — *n* **mā'tiness** or **mā'teyness.** [Prob. M.L.G. *mate* or earlier Du. *maet*.]

mate[2] *māt*, *vt* to checkmate. — *n* and *interj* checkmate. [O.Fr. *mat*, checkmated; see **checkmate** under **check.**]

mate[3] or **maté** *ma'tā*, *n* a South American species of holly; an infusion of its leaves and green shoots, Paraguay tea. [Sp. *mate* — Quechua *mati*, a gourd (in which it is made).]

mater *mā'tər*, *n* mother (*slang*, esp. *public school*). [L. *māter*.]

material *mə-tē'ri-əl*, *adj* relating to matter; consisting of matter; corporeal, not spiritual; bodily; physical; gross, lacking spirituality; relating to subject-matter; relevant; of serious importance, esp. of legal importance. — *n* that out of which anything is or may be made; a fabric; that which may be made use of for any purpose; a person who is suitable for a specified occupation, training, etc.; (in *pl*) equipment, implements, etc. needed for a task or activity. — *adv* **matē'rially** to a considerable or important degree; in respect of matter or material conditions, or material cause. — *n* **matē'rialness** or **materiality** (*-al'i-ti*). [L. *matēriālis* — *matēria*, matter.]

materialise or **-ize** *mə-tē'ri-ə-līz*, *vi* to take bodily form; to become actual; to take shape, develop; to turn up, put in an appearance, arrive (*colloq*). — *vt* to cause to assume bodily form; to render material; to reduce to or regard as matter. [**material** and sfx. *-ise*.]

materialism *mə-tē'ri-ə-lizm*, *n* the doctrine that denies the independent existence of spirit, and maintains that there is but one substance — matter; the explanation of history as the working out of economic conditions; blindness to, or denial of, the spiritual; excessive devotion to bodily wants or financial success. — *n* **matē'rialist.** — Also *adj*. — *adj* **materialist'ic.** — *adv* **materialist'ically.** — **dialectical materialism** Karl Marx's view of history as a conflict between two opposing forces, *thesis* and *antithesis*, which is resolved by the forming of a new force, *synthesis*; present conditions are due to a class struggle between the capitalists, whose aim is private profit, and the workers, who resist exploitation. [**material** and **-ism**.]

matériel *ma-tā-ri-el'* or *-ryel'*, *n* material; equipment, esp. the munitions, hardware and supplies, etc. of an army. [Fr.]

maternal *mə-tûr'nəl*, *adj* of a mother; motherly; on the mother's side; of the nature, or in the person, of a mother. — *adv* **mater'nally.** [Fr. *maternel* — L. *maternus* — *mater*, mother.]

maternity *mə-tûr'ni-ti*, *n* the fact of being in the relation of mother; motherhood; motherliness. — *adj* of or for women at or near the time of childbirth. [Fr. *maternité* — L. *māternus* — *māter*, mother.]

matey. See under **mate**[1].

matgrass. See under **mat**[1].

math. *abbrev* for mathematics.

mathematics *math-i-mat'iks*, *nsing* the science of magnitude and number, the relations of figures and forms, and of quantities expressed as symbols (colloq. short form **maths**, (*US*) **math**). — *adj* **mathemat'ical** relating to, or done by, mathematics; very accurate. — *adv* **mathemat'ically.** — *n* **mathematician** (*-mə-tish'ən*) a person specialising in, or expert at, mathematics. [Gr. *mathēmatikē* (*epistēmē*, skill, knowledge) relating to learning, — *manthanein*, to learn.]

matily. See under **mate**[1].

Matilda *mə-til'də*, (*Austr*) *n* a tramp's bundle or swag. — **waltz Matilda** to travel around carrying one's swag.

matin or **mattin** *mat'in*, *n* (in *pl*; often with *cap*) one of the seven canonical hours of the R.C. Church, usually sung between midnight and daybreak, or now by anticipation the afternoon or evening before; (in *pl*) the daily morning service of the Church of England. — *adj* **mat'inal.** [Fr. *matines* (fem. pl.) — L. *mātūtīnus*, belonging to the morning.]

matinée or **matinee** *mat'i-nā, mat'nā* or *mat'ə-nā, n* a performance of a play or showing of a film in the daytime, usu. the afternoon. — **matinée coat** or **jacket** a usu. knitted jacket for a baby; **matinée idol** a handsome male filmstar or actor, popular esp. among women. [Fr., a pre-dinner gathering or entertainment — *matin*, morning.]

matiness. See under **mate**[1].

matlo, matlow or **matelot** *mat'lō*, (*slang*) *n* a seaman, sailor: — *pl* **mat'los, mat'lows** or **matelots** (*-lōz*). [Fr. *matelot.*]

matriarch *mā'tri-ärk, n* the female head of a family, tribe or community; an elderly woman who dominates her family or associates; an elderly and much respected woman of great dignity. — *adj* **matriar'chal.** — *n* **mā'triarchy** an order of society in which descent is reckoned through the female line, or in which a woman is head of the family or the community. [Formed on the analogy of **patriarch** — L. *māter*, mother.]

matric. See under **matriculate**.

matrices. See **matrix**.

matricide *mat'ri-sīd* or *mā'tri-sīd, n* a murderer of his or her own mother; the murder of one's own mother. — *adj* **matricī'dal.** [L. *mātricīda, mātricīdium* — *māter*, mother, *caedĕre*, to kill.]

matriculate *mə-trik'ū-lāt, vt* and *vi* to admit or be admitted to membership of a university or college. — *n* **matriculā'tion** the act of matriculating; the process of being matriculated; an entrance examination, or one by which one qualifies for a course at a university or college (familiarly **matric'**). [L.L. *mātrīculāre*, to register, — *mātrīcula*, a register, dimin. of L. *mātrīx*.]

matrilineal *mat-ri-lin'i-əl, adj* (of descent or kinship) reckoned through the mother or through females alone. — *adv* **matrilin'eally.** [L. *māter*, a mother, *līnea*, a line.]

matrimony *mat'ri-mə-ni, n* the state of being married, wedlock; the marriage ceremony; a card game of chance in which one of the winning combinations is that of king and queen; the combination of king and queen in that and in various other games. — *adj* **matrimonial** (*-mō'ni-əl*) relating to marriage. [L. *mātrimōnium* — *māter, mātris*, mother.]

matrix *mā'triks* or *mat'riks, n* the place in which anything is developed or formed; the rock in which a fossil, gemstone, etc. is embedded; a mould, e.g. for casting printing type; a rectangular array of quantities or symbols (*math*); any rectangular array in rows and columns: — *pl* **ma'trices** (*-tri-sēz*) or **ma'trixes.** [L. *mātrīx, -īcis*, a breeding animal, later, the womb — *māter*, mother.]

matron *mā'trən, n* a person in charge of nursing and domestic arrangements in a school or other institution; the senior nursing officer in charge of the nursing staff in a hospital; a prison wardress (*US*); a usu. married, and middle-aged to elderly, woman of dignified appearance and dependable personality. — *n* **mā'tronhood.** — *adj* **mā'tronly** (of a woman) plump or portly with the onset of middle age, or dignified and imposing; belonging, or suitable, to a matron. — *n* **mā'tronship.** — **matron of honour** see **honour**. [Fr. *matrone* — L. *mātrōna* — *māter*, mother.]

Matt. (*Bible*) *abbrev* for (the Gospel according to St) Matthew.

matt. See **mat**[2].

mattamore *mat'ə-mōr, n* a subterranean chamber. [Fr. *matamore* — Ar. *matmūrah.*]

matte. See **mat**[2].

matted. See **mat**[1].

matter *mat'ər, n* that which occupies space, and with which we become acquainted by our bodily senses; that out of which anything is composed, material; subject or material of thought, speech, writing, dispute, etc.; substance as distinct from form (*philos*); whatever has physical existence, as distinct from mind (*philos*); anything engaging the attention; an affair, thing, concern, subject or question; a thing or substance of the kind specified, such as *printed matter, vegetable matter*; cause or ground (e.g. *of concern*); (with *neg*) importance, significance or consequence; an approximate amount e.g. of money, as in *a matter of a few pounds*; pus (*med*). — *vi* to be of importance, to signify; to form or discharge pus. — *adj* **matt'ery** containing, discharging, or covered with pus. — *adj* **matter-of-fact'** adhering to literal, actual or pedestrian fact; not fanciful; prosaic. — **as a matter of fact** really; **for that matter** as for that; indeed; **matter of course** a thing occurring routinely, in natural time and order; **matter of form** a (mere) official procedure or conventional etiquette; **no matter** it does not matter; it makes no difference; **the matter** (the thing that is) amiss (with *with*). [O.Fr. *matiere* — L. *māteria*, matter.]

matting. See under **mat**[1].

mattock *mat'ək, n* a kind of pickaxe with a cutting end instead of a point. [O.E. *mattuc.*]

mattress *mat'ris, n* a more or less resilient large oblong pad for sleeping or lying on, usu. forming part of a bed, composed of a strong cotton or linen outer case containing any of various types of stuffing, and sometimes also metal springs, or else made of a piece of foam rubber or plastic; a mass of brushwood, etc., used to form a foundation for roads, etc. or for the walls of embankments, etc. [O.Fr. *materas* (Fr. *matelas*) — Ar. *matrah*, a place where anything is thrown.]

maturate *mat'ū-rāt, vt* and *vi* to make or become mature; to (cause to) suppurate (*med*). — *n* **maturā'tion** a bringing or a coming to maturity; the process of suppurating fully; the final stage in the production of a germ-cell. — *adj* **maturā'tional.** — *adj* **matur'ative** promoting ripening; promoting suppuration. [L. *matūrāre, -ātum*, to bring to ripeness or maturity.]

mature *mə-tūr', adj* fully developed; having the mental, emotional and social development appropriate to an adult; perfected; ripe; well thought out; (of a bill, bond, or insurance policy) due for payment or conversion. — *vt* to bring to ripeness, full development or perfection. — *vi* to come to or approach ripeness, full development, or perfection; to become due for payment or conversion (*finance*). — *adj* **matur'able.** — *adv* **mature'ly.** — *n* **mature'ness.** — *n* **matur'ity** ripeness; full development; the time of becoming due or convertible (*finance*). [L. *mātūrus*, ripe.]

matutinal *mat-ū-tī'nl* (or *mə-tū'ti-nl*), *adj* relating to the morning; happening early in the day. [L. *mātūtīnālis* — *mātūtīnus*, relating to the morning.]

matweed. See under **mat**[1].

maty. See under **mate**[1].

matzo *mat'sō, n* unleavened bread; a wafer of it: — *pl* (sometimes with *sing* verb) **mat'zoth** (*-sōt* or *-sōth*) or **mat'zos.** [Yiddish *matse*; from Heb.]

maudlin *möd'lin, adj* foolishly lachrymose, esp. when in a fuddled, half-drunk state; weakly sentimental. [M.E. *Maudelein* — Gr. *Magdalēnē*, from the assumption that Mary Magdalene was the penitent woman of Luke vii. 38.]

maul *möl, n* a heavy wooden hammer; a loose scrum (*Rugby football*). — *vt* to injure by pawing or clawing; to handle roughly, maltreat. — *npl* **maul'ers** (*slang*) hands. [Fr. *mail* — L. *malleus*, hammer.]

maulstick or **mahlstick** *möl'stik, n* a stick used by painters as a rest for the hand. [Du. *maalstok* — *malen*, to paint, *stok*, stick, assimilated to **stick**.]

maulvi *möl'vi, n* a teacher of Islamic law, a learned man. [Urdu *mulvī* — Arab. *maulawiyy*.]

maunder *mön'dər, vi* to talk in a rambling, inconclusive way, drivel; to wander about or behave in a listless, aimless way. — *n* **maun'derer.** — *n* **maun'dering.** [Perh. *maunder* (obs.), to beg — L. *mendicāre*, to beg.]

maundy *mön'di, n* the religious ceremony of washing the feet of the poor, in commemoration of Christ's washing the disciples' feet (John xiii) — long practised by some monarchs. — **maundy money** the dole given away on **Maundy Thursday**, the day before Good Friday, by the royal almoner, usu. a silver penny for each year of sovereign's age — the small silver coins specially minted since 1662. [Fr. *mandé* — L. *mandātum*, command (John xiii. 34).]

mausoleum *mö-sə-lē'əm, n* a magnificent tomb or monument: — *pl* **mausolē'a** or **mausolē'ums.** — *adj* **mausolē'an.** [L. *mausōlēum*, the magnificent tomb of *Mausōlos* (d. 353 B.C.) at Halicarnassus.]

mauve *mōv, n* a purple aniline dye; its colour, that of mallow flowers. — *adj* of this colour. [Fr., — L. *malva*, mallow.]

maverick *mav'ə-rik, n* a stray animal without an owner's brand, esp. a calf; a person who does not conform, a determined individualist. [From Samuel *Maverick*, a Texas cattle-raiser.]

mavin or **maven** *mā'vən*, (*US slang*) *n* an expert, a pundit. [Yiddish — Hebrew *mevin*, understanding.]

mavis *mā'vis, n* the song-thrush (see **thrush**[1]). [Fr. *mauvis.*]

maw *mö, n* the stomach of an animal, esp. the last stomach of a ruminant; the jaws or gullet of a voracious animal or (*facetious*) person; an insatiable gulf or ever-open mouth (*fig*). [O.E. *maga.*]

mawkish *mö'kish, adj* insipid; sickly; sentimental, maudlin. — *adv* **maw'kishly.** — *n* **maw'kishness.** [O.N. *mathkr*, maggot.]

max. *abbrev* for maximum.

maxi *mak'si, adj* (*colloq*) or *combining form* signifying very, or extra, large or long, as in *maxi-coat, skirt* or *dress*, an ankle-length coat, skirt, etc. — *n* a maxi garment; a large size of racing yacht. — **max'i-single** a gramophone record longer than an ordinary single. [*maxi*mum.]

maxilla *mak-sil'ə*, (*zool*) *n* a jawbone, esp. the upper; in arthropods, e.g. insects, an appendage with masticatory function, just behind the mouth: — *pl* **maxill'ae** (*-ē*). — *adj* **maxill'ary** (or *maks'*) relating to a jaw or maxilla. — *n* a bone forming the posterior part of the upper jaw. [L. *maxilla*, jawbone.]

maxim *mak'sim, n* a general principle, serving as a rule or guide; a pithy saying; a proverb. [Fr. *maxime* — L. *maxima* (elliptical for *maxima prōpositiō*, axiom) fem., superl. of *magnus*, great.]

maxima, maximal, maximise. See **maximum.**

maximin *mak'si-min, n* the highest value in a set of minimum values (*math*); in games theory, the strategy of making all decisions in such a way as to maximise the chances of incurring the minimum potential loss. [*maxi*mum and *min*imum.]

maximum *mak'si-məm, adj* greatest possible. — *n* the greatest possible number, quantity or degree; the highest point reached; the value of a variable when it ceases to increase and begins to decrease (*math*): — *pl* **max'ima**; opp. to *minimum.* — *adj* **max'imal** of the highest or maximum value. — *adv* **max'imally.** — *vt* **max'imise** or **-ize** to raise to the highest degree. — **maximum and minimum thermometer** a thermometer that shows the highest and lowest temperatures that have occurred since last adjustment. [L., superl. neut. of *magnus*, great.]

maxixe *mä-shē'shā, n* a Brazilian dance; a tune for it. [Port.]

maxwell *maks'wəl, n* the cgs unit of magnetic flux, equal to 10^{-8} weber. [James Clerk-*Maxwell* (1831–79), Scottish physicist.]

May *mā, n* the fifth month of the year; (without *cap*) may-blossom. — *n* **may'ing** the observance of May day customs. — **may apple** an American plant bearing a yellow egg-shaped fruit; **may beetle** or **may bug** the cockchafer; **may blossom** the hawthorn flower; **May day** the first day of May, given to sports and to socialist and labour demonstrations (see also **mayday**); **may'flower** the hawthorn or other flower that blooms in May; **may'fly** a short-lived insect (*Ephemera*) that appears in May; the caddis-fly; **may'pole** a pole traditionally erected for dancing round on May day; **May queen** a young woman crowned with flowers as queen on Mayday; **May'time** the season of May; **may tree** the hawthorn. [O.Fr. *Mai* — L. *Māius* (*mēnsis*), prob. (month) sacred to *Māia*, mother of Mercury.]

may *mā, auxiliary verb* expressing ability, possibility or contingency, permission or competence, probability, concession, purpose or result, a wish, or uncertainty (used with infinitive without *to*): — *infin* and *participles* obsolete; *3rd pers* **may**; *pa t* **might** (also used instead of *may* to make a possibility more remote, a question more tentative, or to make requests or administer rebukes). — **be that as it may** in spite of that; **may (or might) as well** used to make suggestions or to indicate frustration or despair; **may I add** or **it may be added** used to introduce an additional point; **may I ask** (usu. *ironic*) used before or after a question; **that's as may be** that may be so. [O.E. *mæg*, pres. t. (old past t.) of *magan*, to be able, past t. *mihte.*]

Maya *mä'yə, n* one of an Indian people of Central America and Southern Mexico who developed a remarkable civilisation. — *adj* **Ma'ya** or **Ma'yan.**

maybe *mā'bē* or *-bi, adv* perhaps, possibly. [*may be* — **may.**]

mayday *mā'dā, n* the international radiotelephonic distress signal for ships and aircraft. [Fr. (infin.) *m'aider*, pronounced *mā-dā*, help me.]

mayflower, mayfly. See under **May.**

mayhem *mā'hem, n* maiming; malicious damage (*legal* and *US*); (loosely) havoc, chaos. [Ety. as for **maim.**]

mayonnaise *mā-ə-nāz', n* a sauce composed of the yolk of eggs, salad oil, and vinegar or lemon juice, seasoned; any cold dish of which it is an ingredient, such as *shrimp mayonnaise.* [Fr.]

mayor *mā'ər* or *mār, n* the chief magistrate of a city or borough in England, Ireland, etc., whether man or woman; the head of a municipal corporation. — *adj* **may'oral.** — *n* **may'oralty** or **may'orship** the office of a mayor. — *n* **may'oress** a mayor's wife, or other lady who performs her social and ceremonial functions. [Fr. *maire* — L. *mājor*, compar. of *magnus*, great.]

maypole. See under **May.**

mayweed *mā'wēd, n* stinking camomile (genus *Anthemis*); corn feverfew (genus *Matricaria*; a scentless mayweed); applied to various similar plants. [O.E. *mægtha*, mayweed, and **weed.**]

mazarine *maz-ə-rēn', n* a rich blue colour; a blue gown or fabric. [Perh. Cardinal *Mazarin* or Duchesse de *Mazarin.*]

maze *māz, n* a labyrinth; a set of intricate windings; any confusingly elaborate and complicated system, etc. — *adv* **mā'zily.** — *adj* **mā'zy.**

mazhbi *maz'bi, n* a Sikh of low caste. [Hindi — Ar. *mazhab*, religion or sect.]

mazurka *mə-zo͞or'kə* or *-zûr'kə, n* a lively Polish dance; music for it, in triple time. [Pol., Masurian woman.]

MB *abbrev* for *Medicinae Baccalaureus* (L.), Bachelor of Medicine.

mb *abbrev* for millibar.

MBE *abbrev* for Member of (the Order of) the British Empire.

MC *em-sē', n* a master of ceremonies (see under **ceremony**).

MC *abbrev* for: Member of Congress; Military Cross; Monaco (I.V.R.).

Mc. See **Mac**.

MCC *abbrev* for Marylebone Cricket Club.

McCarthyism *mə-kär'thi-izm*, *n* the hunting down and removal from public employment of all those suspected of Communism. — *adj* **McCar'thyite** of, or relating to, this kind of purge or any manic purge of dissident factions in a party, etc. — Also *n*. [From Joseph *McCarthy* (1909–57), U.S. politician.]

McCoy: the real McCoy. See under **real**[1].

McNaghten rules *mək-nö'tən rōōlz*, (*law*) *npl* the rules under which mental abnormality relieves from criminal responsibility only if the person did not know what they were doing, or did not know that what they were doing was wrong.

MCP *abbrev* for male chauvinist pig (see under **male**).

Mc/s *abbrev* for megacycles per second.

MD *abbrev* for: Managing Director; Maryland (U.S. state; also **Md**); *Medicinae Doctor* (L.), Doctor of Medicine; mentally deficient.

Md (*chem*) *symbol* for mendelevium.

ME *abbrev* for: Maine (U.S. state; also **Me**); Middle English; myalgic encephalomyelitis (see under **my-algia**).

me[1] *mē* or *mi*, *pers pron* the form of **I** used for the objective (accusative and dative) case. — **me generation** the generation either of the 1970s, typically self-absorbed, or of the 1980s, typically greedy and materialistic. — See also **me-too**. [O.E. *mē*.]

me[2]. An anglicised spelling of **mi**.

mea culpa *mā'ä kōōl'pä*, (L.) (by) my own fault, I am to blame — an acknowledgement of one's guilt or mistake.

mead[1] *mēd*, *n* an alcoholic drink made by fermenting honey and water, usu. with the addition of spices, etc. [O.E. *meodu*.]

mead[2] *mēd*, (*poetic*) *n* a meadow. [O.E. *mæd*; see **meadow**.]

meadow *med'ō*, *n* a tract of grassland, esp. used for hay; a rich pasture-ground, esp. beside a stream. — *adj* **mead'owy**. — **meadow foxtail** a perennial grass (genus *Alopecurus*), common in Europe and N. Asia, and introduced into N. America; **meadow grass** any grass of the genus *Poa*; **meadow lark** (*US*) a name for various species of birds of the genus *Sturnella*; **meadow pipit** a common brown and white European songbird (genus *Anthus*); **meadow saffron** the autumn crocus (genus *Colchicum*); **mead'owsweet** a tall fragrant rosaceous plant (genus *Spiraea*) of watery meadows. [O.E. *mǣdwe* (the oblique-case form of *mæd*, *mead*) — *māwan*, to mow.]

meagre *mē'gər*, *adj* scanty, insubstantial, inadequate; poor in quality, lacking richness or fertility; lean, thin, weak; jejune, lacking fullness or imagination. — *adv* **mea'grely**. — *n* **mea'greness**. [Fr. *maigre* — L. *macer*, lean.]

meal[1] *mēl*, *n* the food taken at one time; the act or occasion of taking food, as a breakfast, dinner, or supper. — **meals-on-wheels'** a welfare service taking cooked, usu. hot, meals to old people in need of such help; **meal ticket** a ticket that can be exchanged for a meal (esp. at reduced price); a person or thing that one depends on for one's income (*colloq*); **meal'time** the time at which a meal is regularly taken. — **make a meal of** to consume as a meal; to enjoy to the full; to treat or perform in an unnecessarily laborious or meticulous way. [O.E. *mæl*, measure, time, portion of time.]

meal[2] *mēl*, *n* grain ground to powder; other material in ground or powdered form, such as *bone meal*. — *n* **meal'iness**. — *adj* **meal'y** like meal, powdery; covered with meal or with something like meal; pale, whitish. — **meal'worm** the larva of a beetle (genus *Tenebrio*) abounding in granaries and flour-stores; **mealy bug** a hothouse pest, an insect with a white powdery appearance. — *adj* **mealy-mouthed** (*-mowdhd'*) over-squeamish in one's choice of words, afraid to use straightforward language. — **mealy-mouth'edness**. [O.E. *melu*, *melo*.]

mealie *mē'li*, (*SAfr*) *n* an ear of maize; (esp. in *pl*) maize. — **mealie meal** finely ground maize. [S.Afr. Du. *milie*, millet.]

mean[1] *mēn*, *adj* low in rank or birth; low in worth or estimation; of little value or importance; poor, humble; inconsiderable; despicable; ungenerous; malicious, bad-tempered; skilful, excellent (*slang*). — *n* **mean'ie** or **mean'y** (*colloq*) an ungenerous, ungracious, small-minded, or malicious person. — *adv* **mean'ly**. — *n* **mean'ness**. — *adj* **mean-spir'ited**. — **mean-spir'itedness**. [O.E. *gemǣne*; L. *commūnis*, common.]

mean[2] *mēn*, *adj* intermediate; average. — *n* that which is between or intermediate; an average amount or value; a middle state or position; an intermediate term in a progression. — *nsing* or *npl* **means** that by whose instrumentality anything is caused or brought to pass; a way to an end; (*npl*) pecuniary resources; (*npl*) what is required for (comfortable) living. — *n* **mean'time** or **mean'while** the intervening time. — *adv* in the intervening time. — **means test** the test of private resources, determining or limiting claim to concession or allowance. — *vt* **means'-test**. — **mean sun** an imaginary sun moving uniformly in the equator, its position giving **mean time** or **mean solar time** (coinciding with true sun time four times a year). — **arithmetic** (or **arithmetical**) **mean** the sum of a number of quantities divided by their number; **by all means** certainly; **by any means** in any way; **by means of** with the help or use of; **by no means** certainly not; **geometric** (or **geometrical**) **mean** the *n*th root of the product of *n* quantities; **golden mean** the middle course between two extremes; a wise moderation. [O.Fr. *meien* (Fr. *moyen*) — L. *mediānus* — *medius*, middle.]

mean[3] *mēn*, *vt* to have in mind as signification; to intend, to purpose; to destine, design; to signify. — *vi* (with *well* or *ill*) to have good, or bad, intentions or disposition; (with *much*, *little*, etc.) to be of much, little, etc. importance (with *to*): — *pr p* **mean'ing**; *pa t* and *pa p* **meant** (*ment*). — *n* **mean'ing** that which is in the mind or thoughts; signification; the sense intended; purpose. — *adj* significant. — *adj* **mean'ingful** having a valid meaning; full of significance, expressive. — *adj* **mean'ingless** senseless; pointless, futile; without significance. — *adv* **mean'ingly** significantly, expressively. [O.E. *mǣnan*.]

meander *mi-an'dər*, *vi* to wind about in a circuitous course; to wander randomly. — *n* a winding course; an intricate fret pattern (*art*). — *adj* **mean'dering** winding. [L. *Maeander* — Gr. *Maiandros*, a winding river in Asia Minor.]

means. See **mean**[2].

meant *ment*, *pa t* and *pa p* of **mean**[3].

measles *mē'zlz*, *nsing* an infectious fever accompanied by eruptions of small red spots upon the skin; a disease of swine and cattle, caused by larval tapeworms. — *n* **mea'sliness**. — *adj* **mea'sly** infected with measles, or (of meat) with tapeworm larvae; spotty; paltry, miserable (*colloq*). — **German measles** rubella. [M.E. *maseles*.]

measure *mezh'ər*, *n* the ascertainment of extent by comparison with a standard; a system of expressing the result of such ascertainment; the amount ascertained by comparison with a standard; that by which extent is ascertained or expressed; size; a standard or unit; a quantity by which another can be divided without remainder; an instrument for finding the extent of anything, esp. a graduated rod or tape for length, or a vessel of known content for capacity; the quantity contained in a vessel of known capacity; adequacy or due amount; some amount or degree, a portion; proportion; moderation; extent; a means to an end; an enactment or bill; rhythm; a unit of verse — one foot or two feet; metre; strict time; a bar of music; the width of a page or column, usually in *ems* (*printing*); (in *pl*) a series of beds or strata (*geol*). — *vt* to ascertain or show the dimensions or amount of (sometimes with *out* or *up*); to mark out or divide off (often with *off* or *out*); to be a unit of measurement of; to mete out, distribute (with *out*); to proportion; to pit; to traverse. — *vi* to be of the stated size; to take measurements. — *adj* **meas'urable** substantial enough, or not too large, to be measured or computed. — *n* **meas'urableness.** — *adv* **meas'urably.** — *adj* **meas'ured** determined by measure; with slow, steady rhythm; considered, calculated, deliberate; restrained. — *adv* **meas'uredly.** — *adj* **meas'ureless** boundless. — *n* **meas'urement** the act of measuring. — *n* the quantity found by measuring. — *n* **meas'urer.** — *n* and *adj* **meas'uring.** — **meas'uring-rod** or **-tape** a rod or tape graduated for measuring with. — **above** or **beyond measure** to an exceedingly great degree; **be the (**or **a) measure of** to be the (or a) standard by which to judge the quality, etc. of; **for good measure** as something extra or above the minimum necessary; **get** or **have someone's measure** to realise or know what someone's character and abilities really are; **in a (or some) measure** to some degree; **made to measure** see under **made; measure one's length** to fall or be thrown down at full length; **measure up** (sometimes with *to*) to reach a certain or required standard, to be adequate; **short measure** less than the due and professed amount; **take measures** to adopt means (to gain an end); **take someone's measure** to estimate someone's character and abilities; **tread a measure** to go through a dance; **within measurable distance of** getting dangerously close to (something usu. calamitous); **within measure** moderately; **without measure** immoderately. [O.Fr. *mesure* — L. *mēnsūra*, a measure — *mētīrī*, *mēnsum*, to measure.]

meat *mēt*, *n* the flesh of animals used as food, as distinct from fish; the edible part of anything, such as *lobster meat*, *crab meat*, etc.; food in general; a meal (*old*); substance or content in something said or written. — *adv* **meat'ily.** — *n* **meat'iness.** — *adj* **meat'less.** — *adj* **meat'y** full of meat; full of useful content or substance. — **meat'ball** a ball of minced meat; **meat'-eater** a person who eats meat; a carnivore; **meat'head** (*US slang*) a stupid person; **meat jelly** jelly formed from the solidified juices of cooked meat; **meat loaf** a loaf-shaped mass of chopped or minced meat, cooked and usually eaten cold; **meat paste** a spread made of ground meat; **meat pie** a pie containing meat, esp. a small one for individual consumption; **meat plate** a large, esp. oval, plate on which meat is served; **meat safe** a ventilated cupboard for storing meat. — **meat and drink** a required source of sustenance or invigoration. [O.E. *mete*.]

meatus *mi-ā'təs*, (*anat*) *n* an opening of a passage or canal: — *pl* **mea'tuses.** — *adj* **mea'tal.** [L. *meātus* (pl. *-ūs*) — *meāre*, to go.]

Mecca *mek'ə*, *n* the birthplace of Mohammed, a place of pilgrimage for Muslims; any outstanding place reverenced or resorted to — as, e.g. St. Andrews, *Mecca of golf*.

Meccano® *mi-kä'nō*, *n* (a set of) small metal plates, rods, nuts and bolts, etc., with which models can be constructed.

mech. *abbrev* for: mechanics; mechanical.

mechanic *mi-kan'ik*, *n* a skilled worker specialising in making and repairing machinery; (also **card mechanic**) a card-sharper (*US* and *Austr slang*). — *adj* **mechan'ical** relating to machines or mechanics; relating to dynamics; dynamical; worked or done by machinery or by mechanism; acting or done by physical, not chemical, means; machinelike; of the nature of a machine or mechanism; without intelligence or conscious will; performed simply by force of habit; reflex; mechanistic (*philos*). — *adv* **mechan'ically.** — *n* **mechanician** (*mek-ə-nish'ən*) a person skilled in constructing machines and tools. — *nsing* **mechan'ics** dynamics, the science of the action of forces on bodies, including kinetics and statics; the art or science of machine-construction; the details of making or creating by manual or other process (also *npl*); the system on which something works (also *npl*). — *npl* routine procedure(s). — **mechanical drawing** instrument-aided drawing, e.g. of a machine, architectural construction, etc.; **mechanical engineer; mechanical engineering** the branch of engineering concerned with the design and construction of machines or mechanical contrivances; **mechanical tissue** any tissue that gives a plant power of resisting stresses. [Gr. *mēchanikos* — *mēchanē*, a contrivance.]

mechanise or **-ize** *mek'ə-nīz*, *vt* to make mechanical; to adapt to mechanical working; to provide (troops, etc.) with armoured armed vehicles. — *n* **mechanisā'tion** or **-z-**. [*mechanic* and *-ise*.]

mechanism *mek'ə-nizm*, *n* a group of moving parts that interact to perform a function in a machine, etc.; the arrangement and action by which a result is produced; a philosophy that regards the phenomena of life as explainable by mechanical forces; the means adopted unconsciously towards a subconscious end (*psychol*). — *n* **mech'anist** a mechanician; a believer in philosophical mechanism. — *adj* **mechanist'ic.** — *adv* **mechanist'ically.** [*mechanic* and *-ism*, etc.]

Mechlin *mek'lin*, *n* (also **Mechlin lace**) lace made at *Mechlin* or *Malines* in Belgium.

meconium *mi-cō'ni-əm*, (*med*) *n* the first faeces of a newborn child. [L., poppy juice, — Gr. *mēkōn*, poppy.]

meconopsis *mē-kə-nop'sis*, *n* an Asiatic type of poppy. — *pl* **meconop'sēs.** [Gr. *mēkōn*, the poppy.]

med. *abbrev* for: mediaeval; medical; medicine.

medal *med'l*, *n* a piece of metal usu. in the form of a coin bearing some device or inscription, struck or cast usually in commemoration of an event or as a reward of merit. — *n* **med'allist** a person with expert knowledge of medals, or a collector of medals; a designer or maker of medals; a person who has gained a medal, e.g. as a prize in sports. — **medal play** golf scored by strokes for the round, not by holes. [Fr. *médaille* — It. *medaglia*; through L.L. from L. *metallum*, metal.]

medallion *mi-dal'yən*, *n* a large medal; a circular architectural ornament, sometimes containing a bas-relief. [Fr. *médaillon*.]

meddle *med'l*, *vi* to interfere unnecessarily and ill-advisedly (with *with* or *in*); to tamper (with *with*). — *n* **medd'ler.** — *adj* **medd'lesome** given to meddling. — *n* **medd'lesomeness.** — *n* and *adj* **medd'ling.** [O.Fr. *medler*, a variant of *mesler* — L. *miscēre*, to mix.]

media[1] *mē'di-ə*, *n* a voiced consonantal stop, as *p*, *b* or *d* (*phon*); the middle coat of a blood-vessel layer in the wall of a blood vessel (*biol*): — *pl* **mē'diae** (*mē'di-ē*). [L. *media*, fem. of *medius*, middle.]

media[2]. See **medium**.

mediaeval or **medieval** *med-i-ē'vl*, *adj* of the Middle Ages. — *n* **mediae'valism** or **medie'valism** the spirit of the Middle Ages; devotion to mediaeval ideals; a practice, etc. revived or surviving from the Middle Ages. — *n* **mediae'valist** or **medie'valist** a person versed in the history, art, etc. of the Middle Ages; a devotee of mediaeval practices. — *adv* **mediae'vally** or **medie'vally.** [L. *medius*, middle, *aevum*, age.]

medial *mē'di-əl*, *adj* intermediate; (of a consonant) occurring between two vowels; median; relating to a mean or average. — *adv* **me'dially.** [L.L. *mediālis* — L. *medius*, middle.]

median *mē'di-ən, adj* in the middle, running through the middle; situated in the straight line or plane (*median line* or *plane*) that divides anything longitudinally into symmetrical halves. — *n* a straight line joining an angular point of a triangle with the middle point of the opposite side; in a series of values, the value middle in position (*statistics*). [L. *mediānus* — *medius*, middle.]

mediant *mē'di-ənt, (mus) n* the third tone of a scale, about midway between tonic and dominant. [L.L. *mediāns, -antis*, pres. p. of *mediāre*, to be in the middle.]

mediastinum *mē-di-ə-stī'nəm, (anat) n* a membranous septum, or a cavity, between two principal portions of an organ, esp. the folds of the pleura and the space between the right and left lungs: — *pl* **mediastī'na.** — *adj* **mediastī'nal.** [Neut. of L.L. *mediastīnus*, median (in classical L. *mediastinus* is a drudge) — *medius*.]

mediate *mē'di-āt, vi* to interpose between parties as a friend of each; to act as intermediary; to intercede; to be or act as a medium; to hold a mediate position. — *vt* to bring about, end, promote, obtain or communicate by friendly intervention, or by intercession, or through an intermediary; to be the medium or intermediary of; to transmit, convey, pass on. — *adj* (*mē'di-it*) intervening; indirect; related, or acting through something intervening. — *adv* **mē'diately.** — *n* **mediā'tion** the act of mediating or coming between; an intercession. — *n* **mē'diātor** a person who mediates between parties in dispute. — *adj* **mē'diatory.** [L.L. *mědiāre, -ātum*, to be in the middle — L. *mědius*.]

medic[1] *med'ik, (colloq) n* a medical student or medical practitioner.

medic[2]. See **medick.**

Medicaid *med'i-kād*, (also without *cap*) *n* in the U.S., a scheme providing assistance with medical expenses for people with low incomes. [*Medical aid.*]

medical *med'i-kl, adj* relating to the art of healing; relating to medicine as the art of the physician, as distinct from surgery. — *n* a medical examination to ascertain the state of a person's physical health. — *adv* **med'ically.** — **medical certificate** a certificate from a doctor stating that a person is, or has been, unfit for work, etc., or that a person has, or has not, passed a medical examination; **medical jurisprudence** forensic medicine; **medical officer** a doctor in charge of medical treatment, etc., in an armed service or other organisation; **medical practitioner** a doctor or surgeon. [L.L. *medicālis* — L. *medicus*, a physician — *medērī*, to heal.]

medicament *mə-dik'ə-mənt* or *med'*, *n* a substance used in curative treatment, esp. externally. [L. *medicāmentum* — *medicāre.*]

Medicare *med'i-kār*, (also without *cap*) *n* in N.Am., a scheme providing medical insurance for people aged 65 and over; in Australia, the system providing universal medical insurance. [*Medical care.*]

medicate *med'i-kāt, vt* to treat with medicine; to impregnate with anything medicinal; to drug, doctor, tamper with. — *adj* **med'icable** that may be healed. — *adj* **med'icated.** — *n* **medicā'tion** medical treatment; a medicine, drug, etc. — *adj* **med'icative.** [L. *medicāre, -ātum*, to heal — *medicus.*]

medicine *med'sin* or *-sn*, also (esp. *US*) *med'i-sin* or *-sn, n* any substance used (esp. internally) for the treatment or prevention of disease; a drug; the art or science of prevention, diagnosis, and cure (esp. non-surgically) of disease; the practice or profession of a physician; remedial punishment; in primitive societies, something regarded as magical or curative, a charm. — *adj* **medicinal** (*mə-dis'i-nl*) used in medicine; curative; relating to medicine; like medicine. — *adv* **medic'inally.** — **medicine ball** a heavy ball tossed and caught for exercise; **medicine bottle; medicine chest** a chest for keeping a selected set of medicines; **medicine man** in primitive or tribal societies, a witch-doctor or magician. — **a dose** or **taste of one's own medicine** harsh or unpleasant treatment given, often in revenge, to someone used to giving such treatment to others. [L. *medicīna* — *medicus.*]

medick or in U.S. **medic** *med'ik, n* any species of *Medicago*, a genus distinguished from clover by its spiral or sickle-shaped pods and short racemes — including lucerne. [L. *mēdica* — Gr. *Mēdikē* (*poā*), Median (herb), i.e. lucerne.]

medico *med'ik-ō, (slang) n* a medical practitioner or student: — *pl* **med'icos.** [It. *medico*, or Sp. *médico* — L. *medicus*, a physician.]

medico- *med-i-kō, combining form* relating to medicine or medical matters, as in **medico-le'gal,** concerned with the application of medicine to questions of law.

medieval. See **mediaeval.**

medio- *mē-di-ō-, combining form* denoting middle. [L. *medius*, middle.]

mediocre *mē-di-ō'kər, adj* only middling or average; rather inferior. — *n* **medioc'rity** (*-ok'*) average or inferior quality; a mediocre person. [Fr. *médiocre* — L. *mediocris* — *medius*, middle.]

meditate *med'i-tāt, vi* to reflect deeply (with *on* or *upon*); to engage in contemplation, esp. religious. — *vt* to consider deeply, reflect upon; to revolve in the mind; to intend. — *adj* **med'itated.** — *n* **meditā'tion** the act of meditating; deep thought; serious continuous contemplation, esp. on a religious or spiritual theme; a meditative discourse; a meditative treatment of a literary or musical theme. — *adj* **med'itātive.** — *adv* **med'itātively.** — *n* **med'itātiveness.** [L. *meditārī.*]

Mediterranean *med-i-tə-rā'ni-ən, adj* relating to or belonging to the *Mediterranean* Sea and the area surrounding it; (of physical type) slight in build, and of dark complexion. — **Mediterranean race** a long-headed dark race of white men, of medium stature, inhabiting south Europe and north Africa. [L. *mediterrāneus* — *medius*, middle, *terra*, earth.]

medium *mē'di-əm, adj* intermediate or moderate, coming midway between two opposing degrees or extremes. — *n* an intermediate of middle position, condition or course; any intervening means, instrument or agency; instrumentality; a substance through which any effect is transmitted; that through which communication is maintained; (*pl* **me'dia**) a channel (e.g. newspapers, radio, television) through which information, etc. is transmitted to the public (also **mass medium,** *pl* **mass media**); (*pl* usu. **me'dia**) any material, e.g. magnetic disk, magnetic tape, paper, etc. on which data is recorded (*comput*); an enveloping substance or element in which a thing exists or lives; environment; a vehicle for paint, etc.; a nutritive substance on which a culture (as of bacteria, tissue, etc.) may be fed; (*pl* **me'diums**) in spiritualism, the person through whom spirits are said to communicate with the material world; (*pl* **me'diums**) a person of supernormal sensibility: — *pl* **mē'dia** or **mē'diums.** — *adj* **me'dium-dated** (of securities) redeemable in five to fifteen years' time. — *adj* **me'dium-term** intermediate between short-term and long-term. — **medium waves** (*radio*) an electromagnetic wave of between 200 and 1000 metres, used in short- and medium-range broadcasting. — *adj* **me'dium-wave.** [L. *medium*, neut. of *medius*, middle.]

medlar *med'lər, n* a small tree (genus *Mespilus*) related to the apple; its fruit. [O.Fr. *medler, mesler* — L. *mespilum* — Gr. *mespilon.*]

medley *med'li, n* a mingled and confused mass; a miscellany; a song or piece of music made up of bits from various sources. — **medley relay** a race in which each team member runs a different distance or (in swimming) uses a different stroke. [O.Fr. *medler*, *mesler*, to mix.]

medulla *me-dul'ə*, *n* the inner portion of an organ, hair, or tissue; bone-marrow; pith; a loose or spongy mass of hyphae: — *pl* **medull'ae** (*-ē*) or **medull'as**. — *adj* **medull'ar** or **medull'ary** consisting of, or resembling, marrow or pith. — **medulla oblongata** (*ob-long-gä'tə*) that part of the brain that tapers off into the spinal cord; **medullary sheath** a thin layer surrounding the pith (*bot*); a whitish fatty membrane covering the core of a nerve fibre (*anat*). [L. *medulla*, marrow.]

Medusa *mə-dū'zə*, *n* one of the three Gorgons, whose head, with snakes for hair, turned beholders into stone, but was cut off by Perseus (*Gr mythol*); (without *cap*) a jellyfish: — *pl* **medū'sae** (*-zē*) or **medū'sas**. — *adj* and *n* **medū'san**. — *adj* and *n* **medū'soid**. [L. *Medūsa* — Gr. *Medousa*, the Gorgon *Medusa* (lit. ruler).]

meek *mēk*, *adj* having a mild and gentle temper; submissive. — *adv* **meek'ly**. — *n* **meek'ness**. [O.N. *mjūkr*.]

meerkat *mēr'kat*, *n* any of sevaral South African carnivores related to the mongoose. [Du. *meerkat*, monkey, as if 'overseas cat', from *meer*, sea, *kat*, cat.]

meerschaum *mēr'shəm*, *n* a fine light whitish clay; a tobacco-pipe made of it. [Ger., — *Meer*, sea, *Schaum*, foam.]

meet[1] *mēt*, (*archaic* or *formal*) *adj* fitting; qualified. — *adv* **meet'ly**. — *n* **meet'ness**.

meet[2] *mēt*, *vt* to come face to face with; to come into the company of; to become acquainted with, be introduced to; to come into contact with, join; to encounter in conflict; to find or experience; to be suitable to; to satisfy, as by payment; to receive, as a welcome; to cause to meet, bring into contact; to await the arrival of; to keep an appointment with. — *vi* to come together from different points; to assemble; to come into contact; to have an encounter; to balance, come out correct: — *pa t* and *pa p* **met**. — *n* a meeting of huntsmen; a sporting gathering for competition, etc. — *n* **meet'ing** a coming face to face for friendly or hostile ends; an interview; an assembly; an organised assembly for transaction of business; an assembly for religious worship; a place of meeting; a junction. — **meet'ing-house** a house or building where people, esp. Quakers, meet for public worship. — **meet halfway** to make concessions to, or come to a compromise with; **meet the ear** or **eye** to be readily apparent; **meet up (with)** to meet, by chance or arrangement; **meet with** to come to or upon, esp. unexpectedly; to meet, come together with, usu. for a purpose (*US*); to undergo, chance to experience; **race meeting** a stated occasion for horse-racing; **well met** an old complimentary greeting. [O.E. *mētan*, to meet — *mōt*, *gemōt*, a meeting.]

mega *meg'ə*, (*slang*) *adj* enormous, huge; very good or great. [From combining form **mega-**.]

mega- *meg-ə-*, **megal-** *meg-əl-* or **megalo-** *-ō-*, *-o-* or *-ə-*, *combining form* meaning very big, unusually large, on a very large scale; in names of units, denoting a million. — *n* **meg'abar**. — *n* **meg'abit**. — *n* **meg'abuck** (*NAm slang*) a million dollars. — Also *adj*. — *n* **meg'abyte**. — *adj* **megacephalous** (*-sef'ə-ləs*) large-headed. — *n* **meg'acurie**. — *n* **meg'acycle** a million cycles; a million cycles per second. — *n* **meg'adeath** death of a million people, a unit in estimating casualties in nuclear war. — *n* **meg'adyne**. — *n* **meg'afarad**. — *n* **meg'afauna** (or *-fö'nə*) and **meg'aflora** (or *-flö'rə*) large animals and plants respectively, visible to the naked eye. — *n* **meg'agauss**. — *n* **meg'ahertz**. — *n* **meg'ajoule**. — *n* **meg'alith** a huge stone, as in prehistoric monuments (*archaeol*). — *adj* **megalith'ic** constructed with, or characterised by the use of, huge stones (*archaeol*). — *n* **megalomā'nia** the delusion that one is great or powerful; (*loosely*) a lust for power; a passion for possessions on a grandiose scale. — *n* and *adj* **megalomā'niac**. — *adj* **megalomaniacal** (*-mə-nī'ə-kl*). — *n* **megalop'olis** an enormous city; a wide-spreading, thickly-populated urban area. — *n* and *adj* **megalopol'itan**. — *n* **meg'alosaur** or **megalosau'rus** any gigantic bipedal carnivorous Jurassic or Cretaceous dinosaur. — *adj* **megalosau'rian**. — *n* **meg'anewton**. — *n* **meg'aparsec**. — *n* **meg'aphone** a funnel-shaped device for directing or magnifying the voice. — *n* **meg'apode** a gallinaceous Australasian bird that incubates its eggs in mounds of sand, the mound-bird. — *n* **meg'arad**. — *n* **meg'astore** (*colloq*) any of the very large chain stores. — *n* **megatechnol'ogy** rapidly advancing high technology in e.g. microelectronics. — *n* **meg'aton** (*-tun*) one million tons; a unit of explosive power equalling a million tons of TNT (**megaton bomb** a bomb of this force). — *n* **meg'atonnage** the total explosive capacity in megatons. — *n* **meg'avolt**. — *n* **meg'awatt** (**megawatt day** the unit of energy used in connection with nuclear power reactors (day = 24 hours)). — *n* **meg'ohm** a million ohms. [Gr. *megas*, fem. *megalē*, neut., *mega*, big.]

megilp or **magilp** *mə-gilp'*, *n* a medium used by oil-painters, consisting of linseed oil and mastic varnish.

megohm. See under **mega-**.

megrim *mē'grim*. Same as **migraine**.

meiofauna *mī'ə-fö-nə* or *-fö'nə*, *n* animals less than 1 mm. and more than 0·1 mm. across. [Gr. *meion*, less, and **fauna**.]

meiosis *mī-ō'sis*, *n* understatement as a figure of speech (*rhet*); litotes; cell-division with reduction of the number of chromosomes towards the development of a reproductive cell (*biol*): — *pl* **meiō'sēs**. — *adj* **meiotic** (*-ot'ik*). [Gr. *meiōsis*, diminution.]

Meissen (china, porcelain, ware). Same as **Dresden**.

Meistersinger *mīs'tər-zing-ər*, *n* one of the burgher poets and musicians of Germany in the 14th–16th centuries: — *pl* **Meis'tersinger** or **Meis'tersingers**. [Ger., master-singer.]

melamine *mel'ə-mēn*, *n* a white crystalline organic substance used in forming **melamine resins**, thermosetting plastics used as adhesives, coatings, etc. [Ger. *Melamin*.]

melancholy *mel'ən-kə-li*, *n* prolonged depression of spirits; indulgence in thoughts of pleasing sadness, wistful pensiveness. — *adj* prone to, affected by, expressive of, or causing, melancholy; depressed; pensive; deplorable. — *n* **melanchō'lia** a mental state characterised by dejection and misery. — *n* and *adj* **melanchō'liac**. — *adj* and n **melancholic** (*-kol'ik*). [Gr. *melancholiā* — *melās*, *-ănos*, black, *cholē*, bile.]

Melanesian *mel-ə-nē'zi-ən*, *-nē'zyən* or *-nē'zhən*, *adj* relating to *Melanesia*, a group of islands lying N.E. of Australia, in which the dominant race is dark-skinned. — *n* a native, or a language, of these islands. [Gr. *melās*, *-ănos*, black, *nēsos*, an island.]

mélange or **melange** *mā-lãzh'*, *n* a mixture; a medley. [Fr.]

melanin *mel'ə-nin*, *n* the dark pigment in skin, hair, etc. — *n* **mel'anism** the biological condition of having dark skin, plumage, etc.; more than normal development of dark colouring matter, melanosis. — *adj* **melanist'ic**. — *n* **mel'anocyte** (*-sīt*) an epidermal cell that can produce melanin. — *n* **melanō'ma** a skin tumour consisting of melanin-pigmented cells. — *n* **melanō'sis** a condition of skin or body characterised by abnormally large deposits of melanin. [Gr. *melās*, *-ănos*, black.]

melatonin *mel-ə-tō'nin*, *n* a hormone secreted by the pineal gland during the hours of darkness that induces sleepiness and is thought to have useful applications e.g. in the treatment of jet lag. [Gr. *melas*, black, and sero*tonin*.]

melba toast *mel'bə tōst*, *n* very thin crisp toast. — **melba sauce** a sauce for puddings, made from raspberries. — **peach Melba** see under **peach**. [Named after Dame Nellie *Melba* (1861–1931), Australian operatic singer.]

meld[1] *meld*, *vt* and *vi* to merge, blend, combine. — Also *n*. [Poss. **melt** and **weld**[2].]

meld[2] *meld*, (*cards*) *vt* and *vi* to declare, lay down (cards) in order to score points. — Also *n*. [O.E. *meldan*.]

mêlée *mel'ā*, *n* a noisy fight in which the participants become intermingled; a confused conflict. [Fr., — *mêler*, to mix.]

meliorate *mē'li-ə-rāt*, *vt* and *vi* to improve. — *n* **meliorā'tion**. — *adj* **mē'liorātive** causing improvement. — *n* **mē'liorātor**. — *n* **mē'liorism** the doctrine that the world is capable of improvement, as opposed to *optimism* and *pessimism*. — *n* **mē'liorist**. [L.L. *meliōrāre*, *-ātum* — L. *melior*, better.]

meliphagous *mel-if'ə-gəs*, *adj* feeding upon honey. [Gr. *meli*, honey, *phagein*, to eat.]

melisma *mel-iz'mə*, *n* a melodic unit of several notes, sung to one syllable; an embellished vocal melody: — *pl* **melis'mata** or **melis'mas**. [Gr. *melisma*, *-matos*, a song, tune.]

melliferous *mel-if'ə-rəs*, *adj* producing or forming honey. — *n* **mellificā'tion** honey-making. — *n* **mellif'luence** a flow of sweetness; a smooth sweet flow. — *adj* **mellif'luent** or **mellif'luous** flowing with honey or sweetness; sweetly smooth. — *adv* **mellif'luently** or **mellif'luously**. — *adj* **melliv'orous** eating honey. [L. *mel*, *mellis*, honey.]

mellow *mel'ō*, *adj* soft and ripe; well matured; soft to the touch, palate, ear, etc.; genial; slightly, but genially, drunk. — *vt* to soften by ripeness or age; to mature. — *vi* to become soft; to be matured, ripened; to become gentler and more tolerant. — *adv* **mell'owly**. — *n* **mell'owness**. — *adj* **mell'owy** mellow. — **mellow out** (*slang*) to become relaxed or calm (esp. under the influence of drugs). [Prob. O.E. *melu*, meal, influenced by *mearu*, soft, tender.]

melodeon or **melodion** *mi-lō'di-ən*, *n* a small reed-organ, a harmonium or kind of accordion. [Ety. as for **melody**.]

melodica *mi-lod'i-kə*, *n* a small wind instrument with a mouthpiece at one end and a keyboard. [From *melod*eon and harmon*ica*.]

melodrama *mel'ō-drä-mə* or *-drä'mə*, *n* a kind of romantic and sensational drama, crude, sentimental and conventional, involving poetic justice and happy endings; a film or play that is excessively sensational, emotional, etc. — *adj* **melodramatic** (*-drə-mat'ik*) characteristic of melodrama, overstrained and sensational; expressing excessive emotion, sensation, etc. — *vt* **melodram'atise** or **-ize** to make melodramatic. — *n* **melodramatist** (*-dram'ə-tist*) a writer of melodramas. [Gr. *melos*, a song, *drāma*, action.]

melody *mel'ə-di*, *n* an air or tune; music; a tuneful succession of single musical sounds, as distinguished from *harmony*. — *adj* **melodic** (*mi-lod'ik*) tuneful; relating to or involving a succession of single musical sounds. — *nsing* **melod'ics** the branch of music concerned with melody. — *adj* **melō'dious** full of melody; pleasant to listen to. — *adv* **melō'diously**. — *n* **melō'diousness**. — *vi* **mel'odise** or **-ize** to make melody; to perform a melody. — *vt* to add a melody to; to make melodious. — *n* **mel'odist**. [Fr., — Gr. *melōidiā*.]

melon *mel'ən*, *n* any of several juicy, edible gourds; the plant bearing it. — **mel'on-pear** a fruit, the pepino. [Fr., — L. *mēlō*, *-ōnis* — Gr. *mēlon*, an apple.]

Melpomene *mel-pom'i-nē*, (*Gr mythol*) *n* the Muse of tragedy. [Gr. *Melpomĕnē*, lit. songstress.]

melt *melt*, *vi* to become liquid from the solid state, esp. by heat; to fuse; to dissolve; to lose distinct form, to blend; to shade off, to become imperceptible; to disperse, be dissipated, disappear (sometimes with *away*); to soften emotionally. — *vt* to cause to melt. — *n* the act of melting; the state of being melted; molten material; the quantity melted. — *n* and *adj* **melt'ing**. — *adv* **melt'ingly**. — *n* **melt'ingness**. — **melt'down** the process in which, due to a failure of the cooling system, the radioactive fuel in a nuclear reactor overheats, melts through its insulation, and is released into the environment; an unforeseen and disastrous failure, with possible wide-reaching effects, as a crash on the stock-market; **melt'ing-point** the temperature at which a given solid begins to become liquid; **melt'ing-pot** a container for melting things in (see **in the melting-pot** below); **melt'-water** water running off melting ice or snow. — **in the melting-pot** in the process of changing and forming something new. [O.E. *meltan* (intrans. strong verb), and *mæltan*, *meltan* (causative weak verb).]

melton *mel'tən*, *n* a strong, smooth, woollen cloth for overcoats. [*Melton* Mowbray, in Leicestershire.]

Mem. *abbrev* for Member.

mem. *abbrev* for: *memento* (L.), remember; memorandum.

member *mem'bər*, *n* a distinct part of a whole, esp. a limb of an animal; a person who belongs to a society, club, political party, etc.; a representative in a legislative body; an animal or plant that is part of a group. — *adj* **mem'bered** having limbs. — *n* **mem'bership** the state of being a member of or belonging to a society, etc.; the members of a body, organisation, etc. regarded as a whole. — *adj* **mem'bral** pertaining to the limbs rather than the trunk. — **member of parliament** a member of the House of Commons (abbrev. **MP**). [Fr. *membre* — L. *membrum*.]

membrane *mem'brān* or *-brin*, *n* a thin flexible solid sheet or film; a thin sheetlike structure, usually fibrous, connecting other structures or covering or lining a part or organ (*biol*); a skin of parchment. — *adj* **membranaceous** (*-brə-nā'shəs*) or **mem'branous** (*-brə-nəs*) like or of the nature of a membrane; thin, translucent and papery (*bot*). [L. *membrāna* — *membrum*.]

memento *mi-men'tō*, *n* something kept or given as a reminder: — *pl* **memen'tos** or **memen'toes**. — **memento mori** (*mō'rī* or *mo'rē*) (L.) remember that you must die; anything (e.g. a skull) to remind one of mortality. [L., imper. of *meminisse*, to remember.]

memo *mem'ō*, *n* a contraction for **memorandum**: — *pl* **mem'os**. — *vt* to make a memorandum of; to send a memorandum to: — *pr p* **mem'oing**; *pa p* and *pa t* **mem'oed**.

memoir *mem'wär* or *-wör*, *n* (usu. in *pl*) a written record set down as material for history or biography; a biographical sketch; a record of a study of some subject investigated by the writer; (in *pl*) the transactions of a society. — *n* **mem'oirism** the act or art of writing memoirs. — *n* **mem'oirist** a writer of memoirs. [Fr. *mémoire* — L. *memoria*, memory — *memor*, mindful.]

memorabilia, memorable, etc. See **memory**.

memorandum *mem-ə-ran'dəm*, *n* something to be remembered; a note to assist the memory; a brief note of some transaction (*law*); a summary of the state of a question (*diplomacy*): — *pl* **memoran'dums** or **memoran'da**. — *n* **memoran'dum-book** a book for keeping notes or memoranda. [L., a thing to be remembered, neut. gerundive of *memorāre*, to remember.]

memory *mem'ə-ri*, *n* the power of retaining and reproducing mental or sensory impressions; an impression so reproduced; the mind's store of remembered things; time within which past things can be remembered; commemoration; remembrance; a store (q.v.) (*comput*). — *npl* **memorabil'ia** (from L.) things worth remembering and preserving; noteworthy points. — *n* **memorabil'ity**. — *adj* **mem'orable** deserving to be remembered; remarkable; easily remembered. — *n* **mem'orableness**. — *adv* **mem'orably**. — *adj* **memorial** (-*ör'*) serving or intended to preserve the memory of anything; done in remembrance of a person, event, etc.; pertaining to memory. — *n* something which serves to keep in remembrance; a donation to charity in memory of someone who has died (*US*); a monument; a written statement of facts; a record; (in *pl*) historical or biographical notices. — *vt* **memor'ialise** or **-ize** to present a memorial to; to commemorate. — *n* **memor'ialist** someone who writes, signs or presents a memorial. — *n* **memorīsā'tion** or **-z-**. — *vt* **mem'orise** or **-ize** to commit to memory. — **memory bank** (*comput*) a memory or store (q.v.); **memory trace** (*psychol*) a hypothetical change in the cells of the brain caused by the taking-in of information, etc. — **in living memory** within the memory of people still alive; **in memoriam** (L.) to the memory of; in memory. [L. *memoria*, memory.]

mem-sahib *mem'-sä-ib*, *n* in India, a married European lady. [**ma'am** and **sahib**.]

men *men*, plural of **man**. — **menfolk(s)** and **menswear** see under **man**.

menace *men'əs* or *-is*, *n* a threat or threatening; a show of an intention to do harm; a threatening danger. — *vt* to threaten. — *vi* to act in a threatening manner. — *n* **men'acer**. — *adj* **men'acing**. — *adv* **men'acingly**. [Fr., — L. *mināciae* (pl.), threats.]

ménage *mā-näzh'*, *n* a household; the management of a house. — **ménage à trois** (*a trwä*; Fr. *colloq*, a household of three) a household composed of a husband and wife and the lover of one of them. [Fr., — L. *mānsiō*, dwelling.]

menagerie *mi-naj'ə-ri*, *n* a collection of wild animals in cages for exhibition; the place where these are kept. [Fr. *ménagerie* — *ménage*.]

menarche *mə-när'kē*, (*med*) *n* the first menstruation. [Gr. *mēn*, month, *archē*, beginning.]

mend *mend*, *vt* to remove a fault from; to repair; to make better; to correct; to improve; to improve upon. — *vi* to grow better; to reform. — *n* a repair; a repaired place; an act of mending. — *n* **mend'er**. — *n* **mend'ing** the act of repairing; a repair; things requiring to be mended, esp. clothes by sewing. — **mend one's ways** to reform one's behaviour; **on the mend** improving, recovering. [**amend**.]

mendacious *men-dā'shəs*, *adj* lying. — *adv* **mendā'ciously**. — *n* **mendacity** (*-das'i-ti*) lying; a falsehood. [L. *mendāx*, *-ācis*, conn. with *mentīrī*, to lie.]

mendelevium *men-de-lē'vi-əm* or *-lā'vi-əm*, *n* the element (symbol **Md**; atomic no. 101), artificially produced in 1955 and named after the Russian D.I. *Mendeleev* (1834–1907), who developed the periodic table of elements.

Mendelian *men-dēl'i-ən*, *adj* pertaining to the Austrian-German Gregor *Mendel* (1822–84), or his teaching on heredity. — *n* a believer in Mendel's theory. — *n* **Men'delism** (*-də-lizm*).

mendicant *men'di-kənt*, *adj* (of a friar) depending on alms; begging. — *n* a friar who depends on alms; a beggar. — *n* **men'dicancy** or **mendicity** (*-dis'i-ti*) the condition of a beggar; begging. [L. *mendīcāns*, *-antis*, pres. p. of *mendīcāre*, to beg.]

menfolk(s). See under **man**.

menhaden *men-hā'dn*, *n* an oily fish of the herring family, found off the east coast of the United States. [From an Ind. name.]

menhir *men'hēr*, *n* an ancient monumental standing stone. [Breton *men*, stone, *hir*, long.]

menial *mē'ni-əl*, *adj* of or pertaining to servants or work of a humiliating or servile nature; servile. — *n* a servant; a person performing servile work; a naturally servile person. [A.Fr. *menial*.]

meninx *mē'ningks*, (*anat*) *n* (usu. in *pl*) any of three membranes that envelop the brain and spinal cord: — *pl* **meninges** (*men-in'jēz*). — *adj* **mening'eal**. — *n* **meningitis** (*-jī'*) inflammation of the meninges. — *n* **meningocele** (*men-ing'gō-sēl*) protrusion of the meninges through the skull. [Gr. *mēninx*, *-ingos*, a membrane.]

meniscus *men-is'kəs*, *n* a crescent-shaped figure; a convexo-concave lens; a liquid surface curved by capillarity: — *pl* **menis'ci** (*-kī* or *-sī*) or **menis'cuses**. — *adj* and *n* **menis'coid**. [Gr. *mēniskos*, dimin. of *mēnē*, the moon.]

Mennonite *men'ən-īt*, (*Christian relig*) *n* one of a Protestant sect combining some of the distinctive characteristics of the Baptists and Friends. [From *Menno* Simons (d. 1559), their chief founder.]

menopause *men'ō-pöz*, *n* the ending of menstruation, change of life. — *adj* **menopaus'al** of, relating to, or experiencing, the menopause; suffering from strange moods or behaviour in middle age (*colloq*). — **male menopause** see under **male**. [Gr. *mēn*, month, *pausis*, cessation.]

menorah *mə-nö'rə*, *n* (also with *cap*) a candelabrum with a varying number of branches, usu. seven, used in Jewish religious ceremony. [Heb. *menōrāh*.]

menorrhagia *men-ə-rā'ji-ə*, *n* excessive flow of blood during menstruation. [Gr. *mēn*, month, and *-rragia* — *rhēgnynai*, to break, burst.]

menorrhoea or in U.S. **menorrhea** *men-ə-rē'ə*, *n* the normal flow of the menses. [Gr. *mēn*, month, *roiā*, flow.]

mensch *mensh*, (*US slang*) *n* an honest, decent, morally-principled person. [Yiddish *mensch*, a person.]

menses *men'sēz*, *npl* the monthly discharge from the uterus, period. [L. *mēnsēs*, pl. of *mēnsis*, month.]

mensh *mensh*, (*colloq*) *n* and *vt* short for **mention**.

Menshevik *men'shə-vik*, (*hist*) *n* a moderate or minority socialist in Russia (as opp. to *Bolshevik*). [Russ. *menshye*, smaller, *-(v)ik*, agent sfx.]

mens rea *menz rē'ə*, (*law*) *n* knowledge of the unlawfulness of an act, criminal intent. [L.]

menstruum *men'stroo-əm*, *n* a solvent, esp. one used in the preparation of drugs: — *pl* **men'strua** or **men'struums** (**menstrua** also the menses). — *adj* **men'strual** monthly; pertaining to the menses or period. — *vi* **men'struate** to discharge the menses, have a period. — *n* **menstruā'tion**. — *adj* **men'struous**. [L. neut. of *mēnstruus*, monthly — *mēnsis*.]

mensurable *men'shər-ə-bl* or *-sūr-ə-bl*, *adj* measurable; having a fixed relative time-value for each note (*mus*). — *n* **mensurabil'ity**. — *adj* **mens'ural** pertaining to measure; measurable (*mus*). — *n* **mensurā'tion** the act or art of finding by measurement and calculation the length, area, volume, etc., of bodies. — *adj* **men'surātive**. [L. *mēnsūrāre*, to measure.]

menswear. See under **man**.

mental *men'tl*, *adj* of, in or relating to the mind; done in the mind, esp. in the mind alone, without outward expression; suffering from, or provided for, or involved in the care of, disease or disturbance of the mind; mentally unbalanced (*slang*). — *n* **men'talism** the process of mental action; the theory that the physical world exists and is explicable only as an aspect of the mind, idealism (*philos*). — *n* **men'talist**. — *n* **mentality** (*-tal'i-ti*) mind; mental endowment; a type of mind; a way of thinking. — *adv* **men'tally**. — **mental age** the age in years, etc., at which an average child would have reached the same stage of mental development as the individual under consideration; **mental cruelty** conduct in marriage, not involving physical cruelty or violence, that wounds feelings or personal dignity; **mental de-**

ficiency mental retardation; **mental home** or **hospital; mental patient; mental retardation** retarded development of learning ability, whether arising from innate defect or from some other cause. [Fr., — L. *mēns, mentis*, the mind.]

menthol *men'thol, n* a camphor obtained from oil of peppermint, used as a decongestant and a local analgesic. — *adj* **men'tholated** containing menthol. [L. *mentha*, mint.]

mention *men'shən, n* a brief notice; the occurrence or introduction of a name or reference. — *vt* to notice briefly; to remark; to name. — *adj* **men'tionable** fit to be mentioned; worth mentioning. — **honourable mention** an award of distinction not entitling to a prize; **not to mention** to say nothing of — a rhetorical pretence of refraining from saying all one might say. [L. *mentiō, -ōnis*.]

mentor *ment'ər* or *-tör, n* a wise counsellor; a tutor; a trainer. — *n* **men'toring.** — *n* **men'torship.** [Gr. *Mentōr*, the tutor by whom Telemachus, son of Odysseus, was guided.]

menu *men'ū, n* (in a restaurant, etc.) a list of dishes that may be ordered; the card listing these; a list of subjects, options, etc. (*comput* or *fig*). — *adj* **men'u-driven** (of computer software) offering the user lists of options for movement through the system. [Fr., — L. *minūtus*, small.]

meow *mi-ow'* or *myow*. A form of **miaow**.

MEP *abbrev* for Member of the European Parliament.

mepacrine *mep'ə-krēn, n* a bitter yellow powder derived from acridine dye compounds, formerly used against malaria. — Also called **atabrin** or **atebrin**.

meperidine *me-per'i-dēn* or *-din, n* pethidine.

Mephistopheles *mef-is-tof'i-lēz, n* the devil in the *Faust* story. — Also **Mephistoph'ilis, Mephostoph'ilus**, etc. — Also short form **Mephis'tō.** — *adj* **Mephistophelē'an, Mephistophē'lian** or **Mephistophelic** (*-fel'*) cynical, scoffing, fiendish.

mephitis *me-fī'tis, n* a poisonous exhalation; a foul stink. — *adj* **mephitic** or **mephitical** (*-fit'*). [L. *mephītis*.]

meprobamate *mep-rō-bam'āt, n* a drug used as a muscle relaxant and as a sedative.

mercantile *mûr'kən-tīl, adj* having to do with trade; pertaining to merchants; commercial; mercenary. — *n* **mer'cantilism.** — *n* **mer'cantilist.** — **mercantile law** the law relating to the dealings of merchants with each other; **mercantile marine** the ships and crews of any country employed in commerce. [Fr., — It. *mercantile* — L. *mercārī*.]

mercaptan *mər-kap'tan, n* thiol, a substance analogous to an alcohol, with sulphur instead of oxygen. [L. *mercūrium captāns*, seizing of mercury.]

Mercator *mər-kā'tər* or *mer-kä'tör, n* a Latin translation of the name of the Flemish-born German cartographer Gerhard Kremer (lit. shopkeeper; 1512–94). — **Mercator's projection** a representation of the surface of the globe in which the meridians are parallel straight lines, the parallels straight lines at right angles to these, their distances such that everywhere degrees of latitude and longitude have the same ratio to each other as on the globe itself.

mercenary *mûr'sin-ər-i, adj* hired for money; actuated by the hope of reward; too strongly influenced by desire of gain; sold or done for money. — *n* a person who is hired; a soldier hired into foreign service. — *adv* **mer'cenarily.** — *n* **mer'cenarism** the state of being a mercenary. [L. *mercēnārius* — *mercēs*, hire.]

mercer *mûr'sər, n* a dealer in (esp. expensive) textiles. [Fr. *mercier*.]

mercerise or **-ize** *mûr'sər-īz, vt* to treat (cotton) so as to make it appear like silk. — *n* **mercerīsā'tion** or **-z-.** — *adj* **mer'cerised** or **-z-.** — *n* **mer'ceriser** or **-z-.** [From John *Mercer* (1791–1866), the inventor of the process.]

merchandise *mûr'chən-dīz, n* goods bought and sold for gain; dealing. — *vt* (also **-ize**) to buy and sell; to plan the advertising of, the supplying of, or the selling campaign for (a product). — Also *vi* (also **-ize**). — *n* **mer'chandiser** or **-z-** a person who is responsible for supplying a product. — *n* **mer'chandising** or **-z-.** [Ety. as for **merchant**.]

merchant *mûr'chənt, n* a trader, esp. wholesale; a shopkeeper; a person who specialises or indulges in a particular, usu. undesirable, activity, e.g. *a speed merchant* (*colloq*). — *adj* commercial. — *vi* to trade. — *vt* to trade in. — *adj* **mer'chantable** fit or ready for sale; marketable. — *n* **mer'chanting.** — **mer'chantman** a trading ship: — *pl* **mer'chantmen; merchant navy** or **service** the mercantile marine; **merchant ship** a ship that carries merchandise. [Fr. *marchand*.]

mercury *mûr'kū-ri, n* a silvery metallic element (symbol **Hg**; atomic no. 80), liquid at ordinary temperatures, also called *quicksilver*; the column of mercury in a thermometer or barometer; a plant of the spurge family; a messenger; a common title for newspapers; (with *cap*) the Roman god of merchandise, theft and eloquence, messenger of the gods, identified with the Greek Hermes; (with *cap*) the planet nearest the sun. — *vt* **mer'curate** to mercurialise; to convert into a compound with mercury. — *n* **mercurā'tion.** — *adj* **mercū'rial** containing mercury; of or like mercury; caused by mercury; active, sprightly, often changing; (with *cap*) of or pertaining to Mercury the god or the planet; (sometimes with *cap*) having the qualities attributed to people born under the planet — eloquent, etc. — *n* a drug containing mercury. — *vt* **mercū'rialise** or **-ize** to treat with mercury or a drug containing mercury (*med*); to make mercurial. — *adv* **mercū'rially.** — *adj* **mercū'ric** containing bivalent mercury. — *adj* **mer'curous** containing univalent mercury. — **mercury (or mercury tilt) switch** a quiet electric switch activated by the movement of mercury in a phial over the contacts; **mercury vapour light** or **lamp** a bright greenish-blue light, high in ultraviolet rays, produced by an electric discharge through mercury vapour. [L. *Mercūrius*, prob. — *merx, mercis*, merchandise.]

mercy *mûr'si, n* forbearance towards someone who is in one's power; a good thing regarded as derived from God; a happy chance (*colloq*); a forgiving disposition; clemency; compassion for the unfortunate. — *interj* an expression of surprise (for *God have mercy*). — Also **mercy on us.** — *adj* **mer'ciful** full of, or exercising, mercy. — *adv* **mer'cifully.** — *n* **mer'cifulness.** — *adj* **mer'ciless** without mercy; unfeeling, cruel. — *adv* **mer'cilessly.** — *n* **mer'cilessness.** — **mercy flight** an aircraft flight taking a seriously ill or injured person to hospital when other means of transport are impracticable or unavailable; **mercy killing** killing, esp. painlessly, to prevent incurable suffering, euthanasia; **mer'cy-seat** (*relig*) the covering of the Jewish Ark of the Covenant; the throne of God. — **at the mercy of** wholly in the power of; **for mercy's sake!** an exclamation in the form of an appeal to pity; **leave (a person) to someone's tender mercies** or **mercy** (*ironic*) to leave (a person) exposed to doubtful or unpleasant treatment at someone's hands; **sisters of mercy** members of female religious communities who tend the sick, etc. [Fr. *merci*, grace — L. *mercēs, -ēdis*, the price paid, wages, and (later) favour.]

mere[1] *mēr, n* a pool or lake. [O.E. *mere*, sea, lake, pool.]

mere[2] *mēr, adj* only what is said and nothing else, nothing more, nothing better. — *adv* **mere'ly** simply; only; without being more or better. [L. *merus*, unmixed.]

mere[3] or **meri** *mer'i, n* a war-club. [Maori.]

meretricious *mer-i-trish'əs, adj* characteristic of harlotry; characteristic or worthy of a harlot; flashy, gaudy. — *adv* **meretri'ciously.** — *n* **meretri'ciousness.** [L. *meretrīx, -īcis*, a harlot — *merēre*, to earn.]

merganser *mûr-gan'sər, n* any bird of the genus *Mergus* (goosander, smew, etc.). [L. *mergus*, a diving bird, *ānser*, a goose.]

merge *mûrj, vt* to cause to be swallowed up or absorbed in something greater or superior; to cause to coalesce, combine or amalgamate. — *vi* to be swallowed up, or lost; to coalesce; to lose identity in something else; to combine or amalgamate. — *n* **mer'gence.** — *n* **mer'ger** a sinking of an estate, title, etc., in one of larger extent or of higher value (*law*); the combining of commercial companies into one. [L. *mergĕre, mersum.*]

meri. See **mere**[3].

meridian *mə-rid'i-ən, adj* of or at midday; on the meridian; pertaining to a meridian or to the sun or other body on the meridian; at culmination or highest point. — *n* midday; an imaginary great circle through the poles of the earth, the heavens, or any spherical body or figure, or its representation on a map; in particular, that cutting the observer's horizon at the north and south points, which the sun crosses at local noon; culmination or highest point, as of success, splendour, power, etc. — *adj* **merid'ional** pertaining to the meridian; in the direction of a meridian; midday; culminating; southern; characteristic of the south. — *adv* **merid'ionally.** — **prime (or first) meridian** the meridian from which longitudes are measured east or west, *specif* that through Greenwich. [L. *merīdiānus, merīdiōnālis* — *merīdiēs* (for *medīdiēs*), midday — *medius*, middle, *diēs*, day.]

meringue *mə-rang', n* a crisp cake or covering made of a mixture of sugar and white of eggs. [Fr.]

merino *mə-rē'nō, n* a sheep of a fine-woolled Spanish breed; a fine dress fabric, orig. of merino wool; a fine woollen yarn, now mixed with cotton; knitted goods made of this: — *pl* **meri'nos.** — *adj* belonging to the merino sheep or its wool; made of merino. [Sp., a merino sheep, also a governor — L. *mājōrīnus*, greater, also (L.L.) a headman — L. *mājor*, greater.]

meristem *mer'is-tem, (bot) n* the formative tissue of plants, distinguished from the permanent tissues by the power its cells have of dividing and forming new cells. — *adj* **meristematic** (*-sti-mat'ik*). [Gr. *meristos*, divisible, *merizein*, to divide — *meros*, a part.]

merit *mer'it, n* excellence that deserves honour or reward; worth; value; desert; (in *pl*, esp. in *law*) the intrinsic right or wrong. — *vt* to earn; to have a right to claim as a reward; to deserve. — *n* **meritoc'racy** the class of persons who are in prominent positions because of their ability, real or apparent; government by this class. — *n* **mer'itōcrat.** — *adj* **meritō-crat'ic.** — *adj* **meritorious** (*-tör'*) possessing merit or desert; deserving of reward, honour or praise. — *adv* **meritor'iously.** — *n* **meritor'iousness.** — **order of merit** arrangement in which the best is placed first, the next best second, and so on; (with *caps*) a strictly limited British order (abbrev. **OM**), instituted in 1902, for eminence in any field. [L. *meritum* — *merēre, -ĭtum*, to obtain as a lot, to deserve.]

merlin *mûr'lin, n* a species of small falcon, *Falco columbarius*. [A.Fr. *merilun* — O.Fr. *esmerillon.*]

mermaid *mûr'mād, n* a mythical sea-woman, a woman to the waist, with a fish's tail. — *n* **mer'man.** — **mermaid's purse** the egg-case of skate, etc. [O.E. *mere*, lake, sea, *mægden*, maid.]

merome *mer'ōm* or **merosome** *mer'ō-sōm, n* one of the serial segments of which a body is composed, such as the ring of a worm. [Gr. *meros*, part, *sōma*, body.]

Merovingian *mer-ō-vin'ji-ən, (hist) adj* pertaining to the first dynasty of Frankish kings in Gaul, founded by Clovis. — *n* a member of this family. [L. *Merovingi* — *Merovaeus* or *Merovech*, king of the Salian Franks (448–457), grandfather of Clovis.]

merry *mer'i, adj* sportive; cheerful; noisily gay; causing laughter; enlivened by drink; lively; used as an intensifier of *hell*, as in *play merry hell with*. — *adv* **merr'ily.** — *n* **merr'iment** gaiety with laughter and noise; mirth; hilarity. — *n* **merr'iness.** — **merry-an'drew** a quack's zany; a buffoon; a clown; **merry England** an idealistically jovial picture of life in England in the past, esp. in Elizabethan times; **merr'y-go-round** a fairground roundabout; a whirl of activity, etc. (*fig*); any activity inclined to circularity (*fig*); **merr'ymaker; merr'ymaking** a merry entertainment; festivity, revelry; **merry men** an outlaw's companions; followers, assistants (*facetious*). — **make merry** to be festive; to indulge in lively enjoyment; to turn to ridicule (with *with* or *over*); **the merry monarch** Charles II. [O.E. *myr(i)ge.*]

merse *mûrs, n* low flat marshland. [Scots form of **marsh.**]

mesa *mā'sə, n* a table-shaped hill. [Sp., — L. *mēnsa*, table.]

mésalliance *mā-zal-yās*, (Fr.) *n* an unsuitable marriage, esp. with someone of lower social status.

mescal *mes-kal', n* the peyote cactus, chewed or drunk in infusion as an intoxicant in Mexico; an intoxicant distilled from the agave plant. — *n* **mescalin** or **mescaline** (*mes'kəl-in*) the principal alkaloid in mescal, producing hallucinations and symptoms of schizophrenia. — *n* **mescal'ism** addiction to mescal. [Sp. *mescal, mezcal* — Nahuatl *mexcalli.*]

mesdames, Mesdemoiselles. See **madam, mademoiselle.**

mesembrianthemum, conventionally **Mesembryanthemum** *mi-zem-bri-an'thi-məm, n* any plant of a genus (*Mesembrianthemum*) of succulent plants (family *Aizoaceae*), mostly South African (also called *Hottentot fig*, iceplant, Livingstone daisy). [Gr. *mesēmbriā*, midday — *mesos*, middle, *hēmerā*, day, and *anthemon*, a flower: some are open only about midday.]

mesencephalon *mes-en-sef'ə-lon, (anat) n* the midbrain. — *adj* **mesencephalic** (*-si-fal'ik*). [Gr. *mesos*, middle, and **encephalon.**]

mesentery *mes'ən-tər-i* or *mez', n* a fold of the peritoneum, keeping the intestines in place (*anat*); in coelenterates, a vertical inward fold of the body wall (*zool*). — *adj* **mesenterial** (*-tē'ri-əl*) or **mesenteric** (*-ter'ik*). — *n* **mesenteron** (*-en'tər-on*) the mid-gut. [Gr. *mesos*, middle, *enteron*, intestines.]

mesh *mesh, n* the opening between the threads of a net; the threads and knots surrounding the opening; a network; a trap; the engagement of geared wheels or the like. — *vt* to provide or make with meshes; to entwine. — *vi* to become engaged, as gear-teeth do; to work in conjunction with; to become entangled. — *n* **mesh'ing.** — *adj* **mesh'y** formed like network. [Perh. M.Du. *maesche.*]

mesial *mē'zi-əl, adj* middle; in or towards the median plane or line. — *adv* **mē'sially.** [Gr. *mesos*, middle.]

mesic. See **meson.**

mesmerise or **-ize** *mez'mər-īz, vt* to hypnotise; (*loosely*) to fascinate, dominate the will or fix the attention of. — *adj* **mesmeric** (*-mer'ik*) or **mesmer'ical.** — *n* **mesmerīsā'tion** or **-z-.** — *n* **mes'meriser** or **-z-,** or **mes'merist.** — *n* **mes'merism** hypnotism as expounded, with some fanciful notions, from 1775 by Friedrich Anton or Franz *Mesmer*, a German physician (1734–1815); hypnotic influence.

mesne *mēn, (law) adj* intermediate. [Law Fr. *mesne*, middle; cf. **mean**[2].]

meso- *mes-ō-, -o-, mez-* or *mē-*, also **mes-** *combining form* denoting middle. — *n* **Mesoamer'ica** central

America, between Northern Mexico and Panama. — *adj* **Mesoamer'ican** (also without *cap*). — *n* **mes'oblast** the middle germinal layer. — *adj* **mesoblas'tic**. — *n* **mes'ocarp** the middle layer of a pericarp. — *adj* **mesocephalic** (*-si-fal'ik*) or **mesocephalous** (*-sef'ə-ləs*) having a medium skull, with a breadth of approx. 75 to 80 per cent of its length. — *n* **mesoceph'alism** or **mesoceph'aly**. — *n* **mes'oderm** the mesoblast or tissues derived from it. — *adj* **Mesolith'ic** intermediate between Palaeolithic and Neolithic. — *n* **mes'omorph** (*-mörf*) a person of muscular body build. — *adj* **mesomor'phic** or **mesomor'phous** relating to a mesomorph; relating to an intermediate state of matter between solid and liquid (*chem*). — *n* **mes'omorphy**. — *n* **mes'ophyll** the spongy tissue within a leaf. — *n* **mes'ophyte** (*-fīt*; Gr. *phyton*, plant) a plant intermediate between a xerophyte and a hydrophyte. — *adj* **mesophytic** (*-fit'ik*). — *n* **mes'osphere** the region of the earth's atmosphere above the stratosphere. — *adj* **mesothē'lial**. — *n* **mesothēliō'ma** a rare malignant tumour of the lining of the chest or abdomen, sometimes caused by blue asbestos dust. — *n* **mesothē'lium** the cell tissue that forms the lining of the chest and abdomen in vertebrates and lines the body cavity in vertebrate embryos. — *adj* **Mesozō'ic** of the Secondary geological period, including the Triassic, Jurassic and Cretaceous systems. [Gr. *mesos*, middle.]

meson *mēz'on* or *mes'on*, (*phys*) *n* a short-lived subatomic particle of smaller mass than a proton. — *adj* **mes'ic** or **meson'ic**. [Gr. *meson*, neut. of *mesos*, middle.]

mesophyll ... to ... **Mesozoic**. See under **meso-**.

mesquite or **mesquit** *mes-kēt'* or *mes'kēt*, *n* a leguminous tree or shrub (*Prosopis*) of America, with nutritious pods. [Mex. Sp. *mezquite*.]

mess *mes*, *n* a number of persons who take their meals together, esp. in the fighting services; a place where such a group take their meals together; a quantity of a specified food (*archaic* or *dialect US*); liquid, pulpy or smeary dirt; a mixture disagreeable to the sight or taste; a medley; disorder; confusion; embarrassment; a bungle. — *vt* to supply with a mess; to make a mess of (usu. with *up*); to muddle; to make dirty or messy. — *vi* to eat at a common table; to belong to a mess; to make a mess; to meddle, involve oneself (with, or in) (*colloq*, esp. *US*); to tangle (with) (*colloq*, esp. *US*). — *adv* **mess'ily**. — *n* **mess'iness**. — *adj* **mess'y** confused, untidy (also *fig*); involving, or causing, dirt or mess; bungling. — **mess'mate**; **mess'-tin** a soldier's utensil serving as plate, cup and cooking-vessel; **mess'-up** a mess, muddle, bungle or confusion. — **mess about** or **around** (*colloq*) to potter about; to behave in a foolish or annoying way; to meddle or interfere (with); to upset, put into a state of disorder or confusion; **mess of pottage** a material advantage accepted in exchange for something more valuable, as by Esau (from the Bible: Genesis xxv. 29 ff.). [O.Fr. *mes* (Fr. *mets*), a dish — L. *mittĕre*, *missum*, to send, in L.L. to place.]

message *mes'ij*, *n* any communication sent from one person to another; an errand; an official communication of a president, governor, etc., to a legislature or council; the teaching that a poet, sage or prophet has to communicate to the world. — *vt* to send as a message; to transmit as by signalling. — *n* **mess'enger** (*-ən-jər*) a person who brings a message; someone employed to carry messages and perform errands; a forerunner. — **mess'age-boy** or **-girl** an errand boy or girl; **mess'age-stick** (*Austr*) a carved stick carried as identification by an aboriginal messenger; **messenger RNA** (*biochem*) a short-lived, transient form of RNA which serves to carry genetic information from the DNA of the genes to the ribosomes where the requisite proteins are made (abbrev. **mRNA**); **mess'enger-wire** a wire supporting an overhead cable. — **get the message** (*slang*) to understand. [Fr., — L.L. *missāticum* — L. *mittĕre*, *missum*, to send.]

Messiah *mə-sī'ə*, *n* the expected deliverer of the Jews; by Christians, applied to Jesus; (also without *cap*) a hoped-for deliverer, saviour or champion generally. — *adj* **Messianic** (*mes-i-an'ik*) of or relating to a Messiah; (also without *cap*) inspired, or as though inspired, by a Messiah. — *n* **Messī'anism** belief in a Messiah. — *n* **Messī'anist**. [Gr. *Messīās* — Heb. *māshīah*, anointed — *māshah*, to anoint.]

Messrs. *mes'ərs*, *abbrev* for *Messieurs* (Fr.), Sirs, Gentlemen; used as pl. of **Mr.**

mestizo *mes-tē'zō*, *n* a half-caste, esp. of Spanish and American Indian parentage: — *pl* **mesti'zos**; *fem* **mesti'za**: — *pl* **mesti'zas**. [Sp. *mestizo* — a L.L. deriv. of L. *mixtus*, mixed.]

Met *met*: **the Met** (*colloq*) Metropolitan Opera, New York; (London) Metropolitan police; Metropolitan Railway; the Met Office (see **met²**).

met¹ *pa t* and *pa p* of **meet²**.

met² *met*, *n* short for meteorology. — **met'cast** a weather forecast; **met man** a weather forecaster; **Met Office** the Meteorological Office.

meta- *met-ə-*, or before a vowel often **met-** *combining form* signifying: among or with; after, later; often implies change, as in *metamorphose*; beyond, above, as in *metamathematics*. In *chem* **meta-** indicates (1) a derivative of, or an isomer or polymer of, the substance named, or (2) an acid or hydroxide derived from the **ortho-** form of the substance by loss of water molecules, or (3) a benzene substitution product in which the substituted atoms or groups are attached to two carbon atoms which are themselves separated by one carbon atom. — *adj* **metacarp'al** (also *n*). — *n* **metacarp'us** the part of the hand (or its bones) between the wrist and the fingers, or its corresponding part, e.g. the foreleg of a horse between 'knee' and fetlock. — *n* **met'acentre** the point of intersection of a vertical line through the centre of gravity of a body floating in equilibrium and that through the centre of gravity of the displaced liquid when the body is slightly displaced. — *adj* **metacen'tric**. — *n* **met'alanguage** a language or a system of symbols used to discuss another language or symbolic system. — *n* **metamathemat'ics** the logical analysis of formal mathematics, its concepts, terminology, use of symbols, etc. — *n* **met'amer** (*chem*) a compound metameric with another. — *n* **met'amere** (*-mēr*; *zool*) a segment, merosome or somite. — *adj* **metamer'ic**. — *n* **metam'erism** a particular form of isomerism in which different groups are attached to the same central atom (*chem*); segmentation of the body along the primary axis, producing a series of homologous parts (*zool*). — *adj* **metapsycholog'ical**. — *n* **metapsychol'ogy** theories and theorising on psychological matters, such as the nature of the mind, which cannot be proved or disproved by experiment or reasoning. — *adj* **metatarsal** (*-tär'sl*; also *n*). — *n* **metatar'sus** that part of the foot (or its bones) between the tarsus and the toes, or its corresponding part — cf. **metacarpus**. [Gr. *meta*, among, with, beside, after.]

metabolism *met-ab'əl-izm*, *n* the sum total of chemical changes of living matter; metamorphosis. — *adj* **metabolic** (*-bol'ik*) exhibiting or relating to metabolism. — *vt* and *vi* **metab'olise** or **-ize** to subject to, or be changed by, metabolism. — *n* **metab'olite** a product of metabolism. [Gr. *metabolē*, change.]

metacarpal, metacarpus, metacentre, metacentric. See under **meta-**.

metal *met'l*, *n* an opaque elementary substance, possessing a peculiar lustre, fusibility, conductivity for heat and electricity, readiness to form positive ions, etc., such as gold, etc.; an alloy; that which behaves chemically like a true metal; molten material for glass-making; broken stones used for macadamised roads or as ballast for railways; (in *pl*) the rails of a railroad. — *adj* made of metal. — *vt* to fit or cover with metal: — *pr p* **met'alling** (or in U.S. **met'aling**); *pa t* and *pa p* **met'alled** (or in U.S. **met'aled**). — *adj* **met'alled** covered with metal, as a road. — *adj* **metallic** (*mi-tal'ik*) pertaining to, or like, a metal; consisting of metal; (of a colour, etc.) having the lustre characteristic of metals; (of a sound) like the sound produced by metal when struck. — *adv* **metall'ically**. — *adj* **metallif'erous** bearing or yielding metal. — *adj* **met'alline** of, like, consisting of, or mixed with, metal. — *n* **met'alling** road-metal, broken stones. — *n* **metallīsā'tion** or **-z-**. — *vt* **met'allise** or **-ize** to make metallic; to deposit thin metal films on glass or plastic. — *n* **met'allist** a worker in metals. — *adj* **metallogenet'ic** (*geol*) relating to metallogeny. — *adj* **metallogēn'ic** (or *-jen'ik*; *geol*) (of an element) occurring as an ore or a naturally occurring metal, as opposed to in rocks; metallogenetic (*US*). — *n* **metallog'eny** (*geol*) the origin and distribution of mineral deposits, esp. with regard to petrological, etc., features; the study of this. — *n* **metallog'rapher**. — *adj* **metallograph'ic**. — *n* **metallog'raphy** the study of the structure and constitution of metals. — *n* **met'alloid** a non-metal resembling a metal in some respects, such as selenium and tellurium. — *adj* **met'alloid** or **metalloid'al** pertaining to, or of the nature of, the metalloids. — **met'alwork** the craft of working in metal; the products of this; **met'alworker**. [O.Fr., — L. *metallum* — Gr. *metallon*, a mine.]

metalanguage. See under **meta-**.

metall. *abbrev* for metallurgy.

metallic. See **metal**.

metallurgy *met-al'ər-ji* or *met'əl-ûr-ji*, *n* art and science applied to metals, including extraction from ores, refining, alloying, shaping, treating, and the study of structure, constitution and properties. — *adj* **metallur'gic** or **metallur'gical** pertaining to metallurgy. — *n* **metal'lurgist**. [Gr. *metallourgein*, to mine — *metallon*, a mine, *ergon*, work.]

metamathematics ... to ... **metamerism**. See under **meta-**.

metamorphosis *met-ə-mör'fəs-is* or *-fōs'is*, *n* change of shape, transformation; transformation of a human being to a beast, stone, tree, etc. (*folklore*); the marked change which some living beings undergo in the course of growth, such as caterpillar to butterfly, tadpole to frog: — *pl* **metamor'phoses** (*-sēz* or *-fō'sēz*). — *adj* **metamor'phic** showing or relating to change of form; formed by alteration of existing rocks by heat, pressure, or other processes in the earth's crust (*geol*). — *n* **metamor'phism** transformation of rocks in the earth's crust. — *vt* **metamor'phose** (*-fōz*) to transform; to subject to metamorphism or metamorphosis; to develop in another form. — *vi* to undergo metamorphosis. [Gr. *metamorphōsīs* — *meta* (see **meta-**) and *morphē*, form.]

metaphor *met'ə-fər*, *n* a figure of speech by which a thing is spoken of as being that which it only resembles, as when a ferocious person is called a tiger. — *adj* **metaphoric** (*-for'ik*) or **metaphor'ical**. — *adv* **metaphor'ically**. — *n* **met'aphorist**. — **mixed metaphor** an expression in which two or more metaphors are incongruously joined, such as *to take arms against a sea of troubles*. [Gr. *metaphorā* — *meta* (see **meta-**) and *pherein*, to carry.]

metaphrase *met'ə-frāz*, *n* a turning of prose into verse or verse into prose; a rendering in a different style or form; an altered wording; a word-for-word translation. [Gr. *metaphrasis* — *meta* (see **meta-**) and *phrasis*, a speaking.]

metaphysics *met-ə-fiz'iks*, *nsing* the branch of philosophy which investigates the first principles of nature and thought; ontology or the science of being; loosely and vaguely applied to anything abstruse, abstract, philosophical, subtle, transcendental, occult, supernatural or magical. — *adj* **metaphys'ical** pertaining to metaphysics; abstract; beyond nature or the physical; supernatural; fanciful; addicted to far-fetched ideas. — *adv* **metaphys'ically**. — *n* **metaphysician** (*-ish'ən*) a person versed in metaphysics. [Orig. applied to those writings of Aristotle which in the accepted order came after (Gr. *meta*) those dealing with natural science (*ta physika* — *physis*, nature).]

metapsychological, metapsychology. See under **meta-**.

metastable *met'ə-stā-bl*, *adj* having metastability. — *n* **metastabil'ity** a state which appears to be chemically stable, often because of the slowness with which equilibrium is attained — said of e.g. a supersaturated solution. — **metastable state** an excited state, esp. of an atom which has, however, insufficient energy to emit radiation. [**meta-**.]

metastasis *met-as'tə-sis*, *n* removal from one place to another; transition; transformation; transfer of disease from its original site to another part of the body; a secondary tumour distant from the original site of disease: — *pl* **metas'tasēs**. — *vi* **metas'tasise** or **-ize** to pass to another part of the body, as a tumour. — *adj* **metastatic** (*-stat'ik*). [Gr. *metastasis*, change of place — *meta* (see **meta-**) and *stasis*, a standing.]

metatarsal, metatarsus. See under **meta-**.

metathesis *met-ath'ə-sis*, *n* transposition or exchange of places, esp. between the sounds or letters of a word: — *pl* **metath'esēs**. — *vt* **metath'esise** or **-ize** to transpose by metathesis. — *adj* **metathetic** (*met-ə-thet'ik*) or **metathet'ical**. [Gr., — *metatithenai*, to transpose — *meta* (see **meta-**) and *tithenai*, to place.]

Metazoa *met-ə-zō'ə*, *npl* (also without *cap*) many-celled animals (opp. to single-celled *Protozoa*): — *nsing* **Metazō'on**. — *adj* and *n* **metazō'an**. — *adj* **metazō'ic**. [**meta-** and Gr. *zōion*, animal.]

metcast. See **met²**.

mete *mēt*, *vt* to apportion. [O.E. *metan*, measure.]

metempsychosis *met-emp-sī-kō'sis*, *n* the passing of the soul after death into some other body: — *pl* **metempsychō'sēs**. [Gr. *metempsȳchōsis* — *meta* (see **meta-**), *en*, in, *psȳchē*, soul.]

meteor *mē'tyər* or *mē'ti-ər*, *n* one of numberless small bodies travelling through space, revealed to observation when they enter the earth's atmosphere as aerolites, fireballs or shooting stars; anything brilliant or dazzling but short-lived. — *adj* **meteoric** (*mē-ti-or'ik*) of or pertaining to meteors in any sense; of the nature of a meteor; transiently flashing like a meteor; rapid (*fig*). — *adv* **meteor'ically**. — *n* **me'teorite** a meteor that has fallen to earth as a lump of stone or metal. — *adj* **meteorit'ic**. — *n* **meteorit'icist**. — *n* **me'teoroid** a meteor that has not reached the earth's atmosphere. — **meteor (**or **meteoric) shower** the profusion of meteors visible as the earth passes through a meteor swarm; **meteor swarm** a number of meteoroids travelling on parallel courses. [Gr. *ta meteōra*, things on high — *meta* and the root of *aeirein*, to lift.]

meteorology *mē-ti-ər-ol'ə-ji*, *n* the study of weather and climate. — *adj* **meteorolog'ic** or **meteorolog'ical**. — *adv* **meteorolog'ically**. — *n* **meteorol'ogist**. — **Meteorological Office** a government department issuing weather forecasts, etc. [Ety. as for **meteor**; and see **-ology**.]

meter¹ *mē'tər*, *n* an apparatus for measuring, esp. the quantity of a fluid, or of electricity, used; a gauge or indicator; a parking meter. — *vt* to measure by a meter. [**mete**.]

meter². U.S. spelling of **metre¹·²**.

-meter *-mi-tər* or *-mē-tər, combining form* denoting an instrument for measuring. — *adj combining form* **-metric** (*-met'rik*) or **-met'rical.** — *adv combining form* **-met'rically.** [Gr. *metron*, measure.]

methadone *meth'ə-dōn*, (*pharm*) *n* a synthetic addictive drug similar to morphine. [di*meth*yl*a*mino-, *d*iphenyl, heptan*one*.]

methamphetamine *meth-am-fet'ə-mēn* or **methylamphetamine** *mēth-il-am-fet'ə-*, (*pharm*) *n* a methyl derivative of amphetamine with rapid and long-lasting action, used as a stimulant to the central nervous system.

methanal *meth'ə-nal*, *n* formaldehyde.

methane *mē'thān* or *meth'ān*, *n* an odourless, colourless, inflammable gas, the simplest hydrocarbon, produced by decomposition of vegetable matter in wet conditions. — **mēthanom'eter** (*mining*) an instrument for detecting the presence of methane in mines. [**methyl.**]

methanol *meth'ə-nol*, *n* methyl alcohol, wood spirit. [**methane**, and *-ol* sfx. — L. *oleum*, oil.]

methaqualone *meth-ə-kwā'lōn*, *n* a hypnotic sedative drug.

Methedrine® *meth'ə-drēn*, *n* a former proprietary name for a form of methamphetamine, used by drug addicts.

methinks *mi-thingks'*, (*archaic* or *jocular*) *impersonal verb* it seems to me; I think: — *pa t* **methought** (*mi-thöt'*). [O.E. *mē thyncth*, it seems to me; *thyncan*, to seem, has been confused with *thencan*, to think.]

methionine *meth-ī'o-nēn*, (*chem*) *n* an essential sulphur-bearing amino-acid.

method *meth'əd*, *n* the mode or rule used in carrying out a task or accomplishing an aim; orderly procedure; manner; orderly arrangement; methodicalness; classification; a system, rule; manner of performance. — *adj* **methodic** (*mi-thod'ik*) or **methodical** arranged with method; disposed in a just and natural manner; observing method; formal. — *adv* **method'ically.** — *n* **method'icalness.** — *vt* **meth'odise** or **-ize** to reduce to method; to dispose in due order. — *n* **Meth'odism** (*Christian relig*) the principles and practice of the Methodists. — *n* **meth'odist** a person who observes method; (with *cap*) a follower of John and Charles Wesley — a name given first to a group of students at Oxford 'for the regularity of their lives as well as studies'; a member of the Methodist Church, a nonconformist denomination founded on John Wesley's doctrines. — *adj* **Methodist'ic** or **Methodist'ical** resembling the Methodists (esp. as viewed by opponents); strict in religious matters. — *adj* **methodolog'ical.** — *n* **methodol'ogist.** — *n* **methodol'ogy** a system of methods and rules applicable to research or work in a given science or art; evaluation of subjects taught and principles and techniques of teaching them. — **method acting** acting as a personal living of a part, contrasted with mere technical performance (also called **the method**). [Gr. *methodos* — *meta*, after, *hodos*, a way.]

methotrexate *meth-ō-treks'āt*, *n* a drug used in cancer treatment.

methought. See **methinks.**

meths *meths*, *nsing* short for **methylated spirits.**

Methuselah *mi-thū'zə-lə* or *-thōō'*, *n* a biblical patriarch said to have lived 969 years (Genesis v. 27); any very aged person.

methyl *meth'il* or *mē'thīl*, (*chem*) *n* the radical (CH_3) of wood (or methyl) alcohol ($CH_3 \cdot OH$). — *n* **methylamphetamine** see **methamphetamine.** — *vt* **meth'ylate** to mix or impregnate with methyl alcohol; to introduce the radical CH_3 into. — *n* a methyl alcohol derivative; a compound with a methyl group. — *n* **methylā'tion.** — *n* **methyldō'pa** an antihypertensive drug. — *n* **meth'ylene** the hypothetical compound CH_2, found only in compounds. — *adj* **methyl'ic.** — **methyl alcohol** see **methyl** above; **methylated spirit** or **spirits** alcohol made unpalatable with methyl alcohol, and usu. other things; **methyl chloride** a refrigerant and local anaesthetic; **methyltestos'terone** (*-ōn*) a synthetic androgen with similar actions and functions to those of testosterone; **methyl violet** an antiseptic dye used as a stain in microscopy and formerly used as a disinfectant; crystal violet. [Gr. *methu*, wine, *hȳlē*, wood.]

metical *met'i-kəl*, *n* the monetary unit of Mozambique (100 centavos). [Port. *metical*, — Ar. *mithqāl*, a measure of weight.]

meticulous *me-tik'ū-ləs*, *adj* scrupulously careful; (*popularly*) overcareful. — *adv* **metic'ulously.** — *n* **metic'ulousness.** [L. *meticulōsus*, frightened — *metus*, fear.]

métier *mā'tyā*, *n* one's calling or business; that in which one is specially skilled. [Fr., — L. *ministerium*.]

métis *mā-tēs'*, *n* (sometimes with *cap*) a person of mixed descent, esp., in Canada, a half-breed of French and Indian parentage: — *pl* **métis** (*-tēs'* or *-tēz'*); *fem* **métisse'** (sometimes with *cap*): — *pl* **métisses'.** [Fr.; cf. **mestizo.**]

metol *mē'tol*, *n* a water-soluble, colourless substance, used esp. as the basis of a rapid developer for photographic negatives. [From *Metol*, a trademark.]

Metonic *mi-ton'ik*, *adj* pertaining to the Athenian astronomer *Mětōn* or his cycle (**Metonic cycle** beginning on 27 June, 432 B.C.) of 19 years, after which the moon's phases recur on the same days of the year.

metonym *met'ə-nim*, *n* a word used in a transferred sense. — *adj* **metonym'ic** or **metonym'ical.** — *adv* **metonym'ically.** — *n* **metonymy** (*mi-ton'i-mi*) a trope in which the name of one thing is put for that of another related to it, the effect for the cause, etc., such as 'the bottle' for 'drink'. [Gr. *metōnymiā* — *meta*, indicating change, and *onyma* = *onoma*, a name.]

me-too *mē-tōō'*, *adj* imitative. — *n* a product resulting from me-tooism. — *n* **me-too'er** a person who imitates or adopts the policy or activity of another, for his or her own advantage. — *n* **me-too'ism** imitating the policy or activity which is proving successful for a rival. [Colloq. interj. *me too!*]

metope *met'o-pē*, (*archit*) *n* the slab, plain or sculptured, between the triglyphs of a Doric frieze. [Gr. *metŏpē* — *meta* and *ŏpē*, an opening for a beam-end.]

metre[1] or in U.S. **meter** *mē'tər*, *n* that regulated succession of certain groups of syllables (long and short, stressed and unstressed) in which poetry is usu. written; a scheme of versification, the character of a stanza as consisting of a given number of lines composed of feet of a given number, arrangement and kind; musical time. — *vt* and *vi* to versify. — *adj* **metred** (*mē'tərd*) rhythmical. — *adj* **metric** (*met'rik*) or **met'rical** pertaining to metre; in metre; consisting of verses. — *adv* **met'rically.** — *n* **metrician** (*me-trish'ən*) a metricist. — *vt* **met'ricise** or **-ize** (*-sīz*) to analyse the metre of. — *n* **met'ricist** (*-sist*) a person skilled in the use of metres; someone who writes in metre. — *nsing* **met'rics** the art or science of versification. — *n* **metrificā'tion** metrical structure; the act of making verses. — *n* **met'rifier** a versifier. — *n* **met'rist** a person skilled in the use of metres; a student of metre. [O.E. *mēter* and O.Fr. *metre*, both — L. *metrum* — Gr. *metron*, measurement, metre.]

metre[2] or in U.S. **meter** *mē'tər*, *n* the fundamental unit of length in the metric or SI system — orig. intended to be one ten-millionth of distance from pole to equator; later defined in terms of the distance between two marks on a platinum-iridium bar kept in Paris; defined more recently in terms of the wavelength of the orange radiation of the krypton-86 atom; 1 yard equals 0·9144 metre. — *adj* **metric** (*met'rik*) pertaining to the metre, or to the metric system. — *vt* and *vi* **met'ricate** to convert or change to the metric system. — *n* **metricā'tion.** — **metre-kilogram-second** (or **-kilogramme-**) (abbrev. **mks** or **MKS**) **system** a system of scientific measurement having the metre, etc., as units of length, mass, time; **metric system** the SI or any decimal system of weights and measures. [Fr. *mètre* — Gr. *metron*, measure.]

metric[1] *met'rik*, *adj* quantitative. — *adj* **met'rical** pertaining to measurement. — *nsing* **met'rics** the theory of measurement. — *adj* **metrologic** (*-loj'ik*) or **metrolog'ical.** — *n* **metrol'ogist.** — *n* **metrol'ogy** the science of weights and measures, or of weighing and measuring. [Gr. *metron*, measure.]

metric[2]. See **metre**[1].

metric[3], **metricate.** See **metre**[2].

-metric, -metrically. See **-meter.**

metrician, etc., **metrifier, metrist.** See **metre**[1].

métro *mā'trō* or **metro** *me'tro*, *n* (often with *cap*) an urban railway system, running wholly or partly underground, orig. the Paris subway: — *pl* **mét'ros.** [Fr. *métro.* Abbrev. for *chemin de fer métropolitain*, metropolitan railway.]

metrology. See **metric**[1].

metronome *met'rə-nōm*, *n* an instrument with an inverted pendulum that can be set to beat so many times a minute, the loud ticking giving the right speed of performance for a piece of music. — *adj* **metronomic** (*-nom'ik*). [Gr. *metron*, measure, *nomos*, law.]

metronymic *met-rə-nim'ik*, *adj* derived from the name of one's mother or other female ancestor; indicating the mother; using such a system of naming. — *n* an appellation so derived (cf. *patronymic*). [Gr. *mētēr*, *-tros*, mother, *onyma* = *onoma*, name.]

metropolis *mi-trop'ə-lis*, *n* the capital of a country, county, etc.; the chief cathedral city, such as Canterbury of England, or chief see of a province; a chief centre, seat or focus: — *pl* **metrop'olises.** — *adj* **metropolitan** (*met-rə-pol'i-tən*) of a metropolis; of or comprising a city and its suburbs; of the mother church. — *n* the bishop of a metropolis, presiding over the other bishops of a province, in the R.C. Church and the Church of England, an archbishop; an inhabitant of a metropolis. — *n* **metropol'itanate.** — *vt* **metropol'itanise** or **-ize** to make into or like a metropolis. — *adj* **metropolit'ical.** — **metropolitan county** or **district** a county or district in a heavily-populated industrial area of England, the district running more, and the county fewer, public services than other districts or counties. [Gr. *mētropolis* — *mētēr*, mother, *polis*, city.]

-metry *-mə-tri*, *combining form* signifying: measuring; the science of measuring. [Gr. — *etron*, measure.]

mettle *met'l*, *n* temperament; fervent temperament; spirit; sprightliness; courage. — *adj* **mett'led** or **mett'lesome** high-spirited; ardent. — *n* **mett'lesomeness.** — **put (someone) on his** (or **her**) **mettle** to rouse (a person) to do his (or her) best. [**metal.**]

MeV *abbrev* for mega-electron-volt(s).

mew[1] *mū*, *n* a gull. [O.E. *mǣw*.]

mew[2] *mū*, *vi* to cry as a cat. — *n* the cry of a cat. [Imit.]

mew[3] *mū*, *vt* to shed, moult or cast; to confine, as in a cage. — *vi* to moult. — *n* a cage for hawks, esp. while mewing. — *n* **mews** (*mūz*; orig. *pl* of **mew**, now commonly as *nsing* with new *pl* **mews'es**) a street or yard of stabling (often converted into residential houses or garages) — from the king's mews at Charing Cross when hawks were succeeded by horses. [O.Fr. *muer* — L. *mūtāre*, to change.]

mewl *mūl*, *vi* to mew; to cry feebly, as a child. [Imit.]

mews. See **mew**[3].

MEX *abbrev* for Mexico (I.V.R.).

Mex. *abbrev* for: Mexican; Mexico.

Mexican *meks'i-kən*, *adj* of Mexico and its people. — *n* a native or citizen of Mexico; an Aztec; the Nahuatl language. [Sp. *Mexicano*, now *Mejicano*.]

MEZ *abbrev* for *mitteleuropäische Zeit* (Ger.), Central European Time.

mezuza or **mezuzah** *mə-zōōz'ə*, *n* a parchment scroll containing scriptural texts which is placed in a case and fixed to the doorpost by some Jewish families as a sign of their faith: — *pl* **mezu'zahs** or **mezuzoth** (*-zōō-zōt'*). [Heb., doorpost.]

mezzanine *mez'ə-nēn*, *n* an entresol (*archit*; also **mezzanine floor**); a room below the stage; the first balcony in a theatre, the circle (*NAm*). — **mezzanine finance** finance usu. for the takeover of a large company, consisting of an unsecured, high-interest loan, sometimes with a share option for the lender. [Fr., — It. *mezzanino* — *mezzano* — L. *mediānus* — *medius*, middle.]

mezzo-forte *met-sō-* or *med-zō-fōr'tā*, (*mus*) *adj* and *adv* rather loud. [It.]

mezzo-relievo or **-rilievo** *met-sō-ri-lyä'vō*, (*art*) *n* a degree of relief in figures halfway between high and low relief. [It.]

mezzo-piano *met-sō-* or *med-zō-pyä'nō* or *-pē-ä'nō*, (*mus*) *adj* and *adv* rather soft. [It.]

mezzo-soprano *met-sō-* or *med-zō-sə-prä'nō*, *n* a voice between soprano and contralto; a part for such a voice; a person possessing it: — *pl* **mezzo-sopra'nos.** [It. *mezzo*, middle, and *soprano*.]

mezzotint *met'sō-* or *med'zō-tint*, *n* a method of copperplate engraving giving an even gradation of tones by roughening a plate and removing the bur for lights; an impression from a plate produced in this way. [It. *mezzotinto* — *mezzo*, middle, half, *tinto*, tint — L. *tingĕre*, *tinctum*, to dye.]

MF *abbrev* for: machine finished; medium frequency; multi-frequency.

mf *abbrev* for mezzo-forte.

mfd *abbrev* for manufactured.

MFH *abbrev* for Master of Foxhounds.

mfrs *abbrev* for manufacturers.

MG *abbrev* for: machine-gun; Morris Garages.

Mg (*chem*) *symbol* for magnesium.

mg *abbrev* for milligram(s).

mganga *m-gang'gə*, *n* in East Africa, a native doctor, a witch doctor. [Swahili.]

Mgr *abbrev* for: Manager; Monseigneur; Monsignor.

MHG *abbrev* for Middle High German.

MHR *abbrev* for Member of the House of Representatives.

MHz *abbrev* for megahertz.

MI *abbrev* for: Michigan (U.S. state; also **Mich.**); Military Intelligence. — **MI5** Security Services; MI6 Secret Intelligence Services (initials based on wartime Military Intelligence departments).

mi *mē*, (*mus*) *n* the third note of the scale in sol-fa notation — also anglicised in spelling as **me.**

miaow *mi-ow'* or *myow'*. Same as **mew**[2].

miasma *mi-* or *mī-az'mə*, *n* an unwholesome exhalation: — *pl* **mias'mata** or **mias'mas.** — *adj* **miasmat'ic** or **mias'mic.** [Gr. *miasma*, *-atos*, pollution — *miainein*, to stain, pollute.]

miaul *mi-öl'* or *mi-owl'*. Same as **mew**[2].

Mic. (*Bible*) *abbrev* for (the Book of) Micah.

mica *mī'kə*, *n* a rock-forming mineral with perfect basal cleavage, the laminae flexible and elastic, and usu. transparent, of various colours, used as an electric insulator and as a substitute for glass: — *pl* **mi'cas.** — *adj* **micaceous** (*-kā'shəs*). — **mica-schist'** or **-slate'** a metamorphic rock consisting of alternate laminae of mica and quartz. [L. *mīca*, a crumb.]

mice *mīs*, plural of **mouse.**

micelle *mī-sel'* or **micella** *mī-sel'ə*, (*chem*) *n* a group of molecular chains, a structural unit found in colloids. — *adj* **micell'ar.** [Dimin. of L. *mīca*, crumb, grain.]

Mich. *abbrev* for Michigan (U.S. state).

Michaelmas *mik'əl-məs*, *n* the Christian festival of St *Michael*, 29 September. — **Michaelmas-dai'sy** a wild aster; any of several garden plants of genus *Aster* with clusters of small purple, pink, blue, etc., flowers; **Michaelmas term** the autumn term at Oxford, Cambridge and some other universities. [**mass**[2].]

mick, *mik*, **mickey** or **micky** *mik'i*, *n* an Irishman (rather *offensive*); a flask for alcohol (mainly *Can*). — *n* **mickey, Mickey** or **Mickey Finn** (*slang*) a doped drink; that which is added to the drink, usu. a stupefying drug or a strong laxative. — **Mickey Mouse** an animated cartoon character created by Walt Disney in 1928. — *adj* (*slang*) simple, easy, often derisively so; unimportant, insignificant; (of music, a band, etc.) trite, corny. — **mick'ey-taking** (*slang*). — **take the mick, mickey** or **micky out of** (*slang*; perh. with different origin) to annoy; to make fun of. [*Michael*.]

mickle *mik'l* or **muckle** *muk'l*, (*archaic* or *Scot*) *adj* much; great. — *n* a great quantity. — *adv* much. — Also (*Scot*) **muck'le.** — **many a mickle makes a muckle** every little helps. [O.E. *micel, mycel*.]

micky. See **mick.**

MICR *abbrev* for magnetic ink character recognition.

micro *mī'krō*, (*colloq*) *n* short for **microprocessor, microcomputer** or **microwave:** — *pl* **mi'cros.**

micro- *mī-krō-* or *mī-krə-*, or before a vowel sometimes **micr-**, *combining form* denoting: (1) (a) abnormally or extremely small; (b) using, or used in, or prepared for, microscopy; (c) dealing with minute quantities, objects or values; (d) dealing with a small area; (e) magnifying, amplifying; (f) reducing, or reduced, to minute size; (2) a millionth part, as in **mī'croampere** a millionth part of an ampere, **mi'crobar** one-millionth of a bar of pressure, **mī'crofarad, mī'crogram,** and many others. [Gr. *mikros*, little.]

microanalysis *mī-krō-ə-nal'i-sis*, *n* chemical analysis of minute quantities. — *adj* **microanalyt'ical.** [**micro-** (1c).]

microanatomy *mī-krō-ə-nat'ə-mi*, *n* the study of the anatomical structures of microscopic tissues. [**micro-** (1c).]

microbalance *mī'krō-bal-əns*, *n* a balance for measuring very small weights. [**micro-** (1c).]

microbarograph *mī-krō-bar'ō-gräf*, *n* a barograph that records minute variations of atmospheric pressure. [**micro-** (1c).]

microbe *mī'krōb*, *n* a microscopic organism, esp. a disease-causing bacterium. — *adj* **micrō'bial, micrō'bian** or **micrō'bic.** — *n* **mīcrobiol'ogist.** — *n* **mīcrobiol'ogy** the biology of microscopic or ultramicroscopic organisms, such as bacteria, viruses, fungi. [Fr., — Gr. *mikros*, little, *bios*, life.]

microburst *mī'krō-bûrst*, *n* a sudden, violent downward rush of air usu. associated with thunderstorms. [**micro-** (1d).]

microcassette *mī'krō-kə-set*, *n* a tiny cassette using very thin recording tape to give a similar recording time to standard cassettes. [**micro-** (1f).]

microcephalous *mī-krō-sef'ə-ləs* or **microcephalic** *-si-fal'ik*, *adj* abnormally small-headed. — *n* **microceph'aly** abnormal smallness of head. [Gr. *mikros*, little, *kephalē*, head.]

microchemistry *mī-krō-kem'is-tri*, *n* chemistry dealing with very small quantities. [**micro-** (1c).]

microchip *mī'krō-chip*, *n* a chip (q.v.) of silicon, etc. [**micro-** (1f).]

microcircuit *mī'krō-sûr-kit*, *n* an electronic circuit with components formed in one unit of semiconductor crystal. [**micro-** (1f).]

microcirculation *mī-krō-sûr-kū-lā'shən*, *n* the circulation of blood or lymph in the finest blood-vessels or capillaries of the circulatory and lymphatic systems. [**micro-** (1a).]

microclimate *mī'krō-klī-māt* or *-klī-mit*, *n* the climate of a small or very small area, esp. if different from that of the surrounding area. [**micro-** (1d).]

microcode *mī'krō-kōd*, (*comput*) *n* a microinstruction or a sequence of microinstructions. [**micro-** (1c).]

microcomponent *mī-krō-kəm-pō'nənt*, *n* a minute component of e.g. a microcircuit. [**micro-** (1a).]

microcomputer *mī-krō-kəm-pū'ter*, *n* a small computer containing a microprocessor, often used as the control unit for some instrument, tool, etc., or as a personal computer; the microprocessor itself. [**micro-** (1f).]

microcopying *mī-krō-kop'i-ing*, *n* copying on microfilm. — *n* and *vt* **mī'crocopy.** [**micro-** (1f).]

microcosm *mī'krō-kozm*, *n* a little universe or world; man, who was regarded by ancient philosophers as a model or epitome of the universe. — *adj* **microcos'mic** or **microcos'mical** pertaining to the microcosm. — **in microcosm** on a small scale, as an exact copy or representative model of a larger group, etc. [Gr. *mikros*, small, *kosmos*, world.]

microdot *mī'krə-dot*, *n* a photograph of usu. secret material reduced to the size of a large dot; a small pill containing concentrated LSD (*slang*). [**micro-** (1f).]

microeconomics *mī-krō-ēk-ə-nom'iks* or *-ek-ə-nom'iks*, *nsing* that branch of economics dealing with individual households, firms, industries, commodities, etc. — *npl* economic methods, principles, etc., applicable to an individual firm, etc. — *adj* **micro-econom'ic.** [**micro-** (1d).]

microelectronics *mī-krō-el-ik-tron'iks* or *-ē-lik-tron'iks*, *nsing* the technology of electronic systems involving microminiaturisation, microcircuits or other very small electronic devices. — *adj* **micro-electron'ic.** [**micro-** (1f).]

microevolution *mī-krō-ē-və-lōō'shən* or *-ev-ə-lōō'shən*, *n* evolutionary change taking place over a relatively short period within a species or subspecies as a result of the repeated selection of certain characteristics. [**micro-** (1c).]

microfauna *mī'krō-fö-nə* or *-fö'nə*, *n* extremely small animals, usu. those invisible to the naked eye. [**micro-** (1a, b).]

microfiche *mī'krə-fēsh*, *n* a sheet of microfilm suitable for filing: — *pl* **mī'crofiche** or **mī'crofiches.** [**micro-** (1f), and Fr. *fiche*, slip of paper, etc.]

microfilm *mī'krə-film*, *n* a photographic film for preserving a microscopic record of a document, which can be enlarged in projection. — *vt* to record on microfilm. [**micro-** (1f).]

microfloppy *mī'krō-flop-i*, *n* a small (usu. 3.5 in.) magnetic floppy disk. [**micro-** (1f).]

microflora *mī'krō-flö-rə*, *n* extremely small plants, usu. those invisible to the naked eye. [**micro-** (1a, b).]

microform *mī'krə-förm*, *n* any of the media of reproduction by microphotography, such as microfiche, microfilm, videotape, etc. [**micro-** (1f).]

microfossil *mī'krō-fos-l* or *-fos-il*, *n* a fossil that may only be examined by means of a microscope. [**micro-** (1a, b).]

microgram *mī'krə-gram*, *n* a micrograph — a photograph or drawing of an object under the microscope; a message typed and photographically reduced for sending by air, enlarged on receipt and printed on a card; the card concerned. [**micro-** (1f).]

micrograph *mī'krə-gräf*, *n* a pantograph instrument for minute writing or drawing; a minute picture; a drawing or photograph of a minute object as seen through a microscope. — *n* **micrographer** (*mī-krog'rə-fər*) a person who draws or describes microscopic objects. — *adj* **micrographic** (*mī-krə-graf'ik*) pertaining to micrography; minutely written or delineated. — *n* **microg'raphy** study with the microscope; the description of microscopic objects. [**micro-** (1f) and Gr. *graphein*, to write.]

microgravity *mī-krō-grav'i-ti*, *n* the state or condition of having little or no gravity. — Also *adj*. [**micro-** (1c).]

microgroove *mī'krə-grōōv*, *n* the fine groove of long-playing gramophone records. [**micro-** (1a).]

microhabitat *mī-krō-hab'i-tat*, (*biol*) *n* a small area having environmental conditions differing from those of the surrounding area. [**micro-** (1d).]

microinstruction *mī'krō-in-struk-shən*, (*comput*) *n* a single, simple command encoding any of the individual steps, (e.g. add, compare) to be carried out by a computer. [**micro-** (1a).]

microlight *mī'krə-līt*, *n* a very light miniature aircraft having either fixed or flexible wings. [**micro-** (1a).]

microlite *mī'krə-līt*, *n* a mineral composed of calcium, tantalum, and oxygen, occurring in very small crystals; an incipient crystal, detected under the microscope by polarised light. — *n* **mī'crolith** a microlite; a very small stone implement of the Stone Age, usu. used with a haft. — *adj* **microlith'ic**. — *adj* **microlitic** (*-lit'ik*). [**micro-** (1a) and Gr. *lithos*, a stone.]

micrology *mī-krol'ə-ji*, *n* the study of microscopic objects. — *adj* **micrologic** (*-loj'*) or **microlog'ical**. — *adv* **microlog'ically**. — *n* **microl'ogist**. [Gr. *mikros*, little, *logos*, discourse.]

micromanipulation *mī-krō-mə-nip-ū-lā'shən*, *n* the technique of using delicate instruments, such as **microneedles** and **micropipettes**, to work on cells, bacteria, etc., under high magnifications; the technique of working with extremely small quantities in microchemistry. [**micro-** (1b, c).]

micromesh *mī'krō-mesh*, *adj* and *n* (having or made of) a very fine mesh, e.g. of hosiery. [**micro-** (1a).]

micrometer[1] *mī-krom'i-tər*, *n* an instrument, often attached to a microscope or telescope, for measuring very small distances or angles; (also **micrometer gauge** or **micrometer calliper(s)**) an instrument which measures small widths, lengths, etc., to a high degree of accuracy; micrometre (*US*). — *adj* **micrometric** (*mī-krə-met'rik*) or **micromet'rical**. — *n* **microm'etry** measuring with a micrometer. [**micro-** (1c).]

micrometer[2]. See **micrometre**.

micrometre or in U.S. **micrometer** *mī'krə-mē-tər*, *n* one millionth of a metre (denoted by μ). [**micro-** (2).]

microminiature *mī-krō-min'i-chər* or *-min'i-ə-chər*, *adj* made on an extremely small scale. — *n* **mīcrominiaturisā'tion** or **-z-** reduction to extremely small size of scientific or technical equipment or any part of it. — *vt* **mīcromin'iaturise** or **-ize**. [**micro-** (1f).]

micron *mī'kron*, *n* a micrometre. [Gr. *mikron*, neut. of *mikros*, little.]

microneedle *mī'krō-nēd-l*, *n*. See under **micromanipulation**.

Micronesian *mī-krə-nē'zhən*, *-zyən* or *-zi-ən*, *adj* pertaining to *Micronesia*, a group of small islands in the Pacific, north of New Guinea. — *n* a native of the group. [Gr. *mikros*, little, *nēsos*, an island.]

micro-organism *mī-krō-ör'gən-izm*, *n* a microscopic or ultramicroscopic organism. [**micro-** (1a).]

microphone *mī'krə-fōn*, *n* an instrument for intensifying sounds; a sensitive instrument (popularly contracted to **mike** *mīk*), similar to a telephone transmitter, for picking up sound waves to be broadcast or amplified and translating them into a fluctuating electric current. — *adj* **microphonic** (*-fon'ik*). [Gr. *mikros*, small, *phōnē*, voice.]

microphotograph *mī-krə-fōt'ə-gräf*, *n* strictly, a photograph reduced to microscopic size; (*loosely*) a photomicrograph, or photograph of an object as magnified by the microscope. — *n* **microphotographer** (*-tog'rə-fər*). — *adj* **microphotographic** (*-ə-graf'ik*). — *n* **microphotog'raphy**. [**micro-** (1f).]

micropipette *mī-krō-pip-et'*, *n*. See under **micromanipulation**.

microprint *mī'krō-print*, *n* a microphotograph of e.g. printed text, reproduced on paper, card, etc. — *adj* **mī'croprinted**. — *n* **mī'croprinting**. [**micro-** (1f).]

microprobe *mī'krō-prōb*, *n* a device that produces a very thin electron beam by means of which the chemical make-up of various compounds may be examined. [**micro-** (1b).]

microprocessor *mī-krō-prō'ses-ər*, *n* an integrated circuit on a silicon chip, or a number of these, acting as the central processing unit of a computer. [**micro-** (1f).]

micropropagation *mī-krō-pro-pə-gā'shən*, *n* propagation by growing new plants from single cells of the parent plant. [**micro-** (1c).]

micropyle *mī'krə-pīl*, *n* the orifice in the ovule through which the pollen-tube carrying the gametes commonly enters (*bot*); an opening by which a spermatozoon may enter an ovum (*zool*). — *adj* **micropy'lar**. [Gr. *mikros*, little, *pylē*, gate.]

microscope *mī'krə-skōp*, *n* an instrument for magnifying minute objects. — *adj* **microscopic** (*-skop'ik*) or **microscop'ical** pertaining to a microscope or to microscopy; magnifying; invisible or hardly visible without the aid of a microscope; minute. — *adv* **microscop'ically**. — *n* **microscopist** (*mī-kros'kop-ist* or *mī-krə-skō'pist*). — *n* **micros'copy**. — **acoustic microscope** one in which ultrasonic waves passed through the specimen are scanned by a laser beam; **come under the microscope** to be subjected to minute examination; **compound microscope** and **simple microscope** microscopes with respectively two lenses and a single lens; **electron, proton** and **ultraviolet microscope** one using a beam of electrons, protons, or ultraviolet rays respectively. [Gr. *mikros*, little, *skopeein*, to look at.]

microstructure *mī-krō-struk'chər* or *mī'*, *n* structure, esp. of metals and alloys, as revealed by the microscope. [**micro-** (1a, b).]

microsurgery *mī-krō-sûr'jə-ri*, *n* surgery performed on cells or other very small plant or body structures, requiring the use of a microscope. — *n* **microsur'geon**. [**micro-** (1b).]

microtechnology *mī-krō-tek-nol'əj-i*, *n* microelectronic technology. [**micro-** (1f).]

microtome *mī'krə-tōm*, *n* an instrument for cutting thin sections of objects for microscopic examination. — *adj* **microtomic** (*-tom'ik*) or **microtom'ical**. — *n* **microtomist** (*-krot'ə-mist*). — *n* **microt'omy**. [Gr. *mikros*, little, *tomē*, a cut.]

microtone *mī'krə-tōn*, (*mus*) *n* an interval less than a semitone. — *n* **microtonal'ity**. [**micro-** (1a).]

microwave *mī'krō-wāv*, *n* in radio communication, a wave having a very short wavelength; now usu. a wave in the radiation spectrum between normal radio waves and infrared; a microwave oven. — *vt* to cook by microwaves. — *adj* **microwav'able** or **microwave'able** suitable for cooking or use in a microwave oven. — **microwave oven** an oven in which food is cooked by the heat produced by microwaves passing through it. [**micro-** (1a).]

microwriter *mī'krō-rīt-ə*, *n* a hand-held five- or six-key device by means of which text can be generated on a printer or VDU. [**micro-** (1a).]

micturition *mik-tū-rish'ən*, (*med*) *n* the frequent desire to pass urine; the act of urinating. — *vi* **mic'turate** to urinate. [L. *micturīre*, *-ītum* — *mingĕre*, *mi(n)ctum*, to pass urine.]

mid- *mid-*, used in combination to denote: the middle part of; of or in the middle of. [From **mid**, adj.; not always hyphenated.]

mid *mid*, *adj* middle; situated between extremes; uttered with the tongue in a position between high and low (*phon*). — *n* the middle. — **mid-air'** a region somewhat above the ground; the midst of a course through the air. — Also *adj*. — *adj* **mid-Atlan'tic** evincing both British and American characteristics. — **mid'brain** the part of the brain derived from the second brain vesicle of the embryo; **mid'day** noon. — *adj* of, at, or pertaining to, noon. — **mid'field** the middle area of a football, etc. pitch, not close to either team's goal; the players who operate in this area, acting as links between a team's defending and attacking players; **mid'fielder; mid'-gut** (*biol*) that part of the alimentary canal formed from the original gastrula cavity and lined with endoderm; also, the small intestine; **mid'iron** a heavy golf club used for long approach shots. — *adj* **mid'land** in the middle of, or surrounded by, land; distant from the coast; inland. — *n* the interior of a country; (in *pl*; esp. with *cap*) the central parts of England. — **midlife crisis** the feeling of panic, pointlessness, etc., experienced at middle age by those who are concerned that they are no longer young; **midlitt'oral** that part of the seashore that lies between high and low neap tidemarks. — Also *adj*. — **mid-mor'ning; mid'-night** the middle of the night; twelve o'clock at night. — *adj* of or at midnight; dark as midnight. — **midnight sun** the sun visible at midnight in the polar regions; **mid-o'cean; mid-off'** and **mid-on'** (*cricket*) a fielder on the *off* or *on* side respectively, nearly in line with the bowler; his or her position; **mid'-point** a point lying halfway between two other points (whether in time or space); a point lying at the centre of an area; **mid'rib** the rib along the middle of a leaf; **mid-seas'on** (also *adj*). — *adj* **mid'ship** in the middle of a ship. — **mid'shipman** formerly the title of a young officer (orig. quartered *amidships*) entering the navy; now only a shore ranking during training; **midstream'** the middle of the stream. — *adv* in the middle of the stream. — **mid'summer** (also *-sum'*) the middle of the summer; the summer solstice, about June 21; **Midsummer day** June 24, a quarter-day; **midsummer madness** madness attributed to the hot sun of midsummer; **mid'term** the middle of an academic term, term of office, etc. — Also *adj*. — **mid'way** the middle of the way or distance; a middle course. — *adj* in the middle of the way or distance. — *adv* halfway. — *prep* halfway along or across. — *adj* **mid'week** in the middle of the week. — **Mid'west** Middle West; **mid-wick'et** a fielder on the on side, about midway between mid-on and square leg; his or her position; **midwin'ter** the middle of winter; the winter solstice (December 21 or 22), or the time near it. [O.E. *midd*.]

'mid, mid, short for **amid.**

MIDAS *mī'dəs*, *abbrev* for Missile Defence Alarm System.

Midas *mī'das*, (*Gr mythol*) *n* a king of Phrygia whose touch turned all to gold, and on whom Apollo bestowed ass's ears. — **Midas touch** the ability to make money easily.

midbrain, midday. See under **mid.**

midden *mid'ən*, *n* a dunghill; a refuse-heap. [Scand., as Dan. *mødding* — *møg*, dung; cf. **muck.**]

middle *mid'l*, *adj* equally distant (in measurement or in number of steps) from the extremes; avoiding extremes, done as a compromise; intermediate; intervening; (with *cap*; of languages) between Old and Modern (as *Middle English*, *Middle High German*). — *vt* to place in the middle; to fold in the middle (*naut*); to hit (the ball) with the middle of the bat (*cricket*). — *n* the middle point, part or position; midst; the central portion, waist; the middle term (*logic*); a middle article. — **middle-age'**. — *adj* **middle-aged** (*-ājd'*) between youth and old age, usu. considered as between 40 and 60. — **middle-age (or -aged) spread** a thickening of the body attributable to the onset of middle-age; **Middle Ages** the time between the fall of the Western Roman empire and the Renaissance (5th–15th cent.); **Middle America** the countries lying between the United States of America and Colombia, sometimes including the West Indies; the American middle class, esp. the conservative elements of it. — *n* and *adj* **Middle-Amer'ican.** — *adj* **midd'le-bracket** in a midway grouping in a list. — *adj* **midd'lebrow** midway between highbrow and lowbrow. — Also *n*. — **middle C** the C in the middle of the piano keyboard; the first line below the treble or above the bass stave; **middle class** the section of society which comes between the aristocracy and the working-class. — *adj* **midd'le-class.** — **middle distance** (in a picture) the middle ground. — *adj* **midd'le-distance** (in athletics) of or denoting a race of 400, 800 or 1500 metres, or an athlete who takes part in such a race. — **middle ear** the part of the ear containing the malleus, incus and stapes; **midd'le-earth** the earth, considered as placed between the upper and lower regions; **Middle East** now generally used of an area including the Arabic-speaking countries around the eastern end of the Mediterranean Sea and in the Arabian Peninsula, along with Greece, Turkey, Cyprus, Iran and the greater part of N. Africa; formerly the countries from Iran to Burma (now Myanma). — *adj* **Middle-East'ern.** — **middle eight** an eight-bar section occurring two-thirds of the way through a conventionally structured pop song and acting as a foil to the rest of the piece; **Middle English** see under **English; middle game** the part of a chess game between the opening and the end game; **middle ground** the part of a picture between the foreground and background; a compromise position. — *adj* **midd'le-income** having, or relating to those who have, an average income which makes them neither rich nor poor. — **midd'leman** someone occupying a middle position; an intermediary, esp. between producer and consumer; **middle management** the junior managerial executives and senior supervisory personnel in a firm. — *adj* **midd'lemost** nearest the middle. — **middle name** any name between a person's first name and surname; the notable quality or characteristic of a specified thing or person (*facetious*). — *adj* **midd'le-of-the-road** midway between extremes; unexciting, mediocre. — **middle price** (of a stock market share) a price midway between the buying (offer) price and the selling (bid) price, as often shown in newspapers; **middle school** a school for children between the ages of about 9 to 13; in some secondary schools, an administrative unit usu. comprising the third and fourth forms. — *adj* **midd'le-sized** of average size. — **middle term** (*logic*) that term of a syllogism which appears in both premises but not in the conclusion; **middle watch** that from midnight to 4 a.m.; **midd'leweight** a weight category applied variously in boxing, wrestling and weightlifting; a sportsman of the specified weight for the category (e.g. in professional boxing above welterweight, **light'-middleweight** (maximum 70 kg./154 lb.), **midd'leweight** (maximum 73 kg./160 lb.), **su'per-middleweight** (maximum 77 kg./170 lb.)); **Middle West** the region between the Appalachians and the Rockies, the Mississippi basin as far south as Kansas, Missouri, and the Ohio River. — **in the middle of** occupied with, engaged in (doing something); during; while. [O.E. *middel* (adj.); see **mid.**]

middling *mid'ling*, *adj* moderate (*colloq*); indifferent; mediocre; fairly good. — *adv* (*colloq*) fairly; fairly well. [Orig. Scots — **mid** and **-ling.**]

Middx *abbrev* for Middlesex.

middy *mid'i*, (*Austr colloq*) *n* a measure of beer, varying in amount from one place to another; the glass containing it.

midfield, etc. See under **mid**.

midge *mij*, *n* a small gnat-like fly. — *n* **midg'et** something very small of its kind; a very small person. [O.E. *mycg*, *mycge*.]

midi *mid'i*, *n* short for **midi-skirt** or **midi-system**.

midi- *mid'i-*, *combining form* used to denote something of middle size, length, etc., such as **mid'i-skirt**, one reaching to about mid-calf, **mid'i-system** a (usu. one-piece) music system, resembling a medium-sized stack system, i.e. with CD, tape deck, etc. stacked vertically. [**mid**; cf. **mini-**.]

midinette *mi-di-net'*, *n* a Paris shop-girl in the millinery or fashion trade. [Fr. *midi*, midday, *dînette*, snack (as the girls are noticeable at lunch-hour).]

midland ... to ... **midnight**. See under **mid**.

midmost *mid'mōst*, *adj* middlemost. — *n* the very middle. — *adv* in the very middle. — *prep* in the very middle of. [**mid**.]

mid-ocean ... to ... **midrib**. See under **mid**.

midriff *mid'rif*, *n* the diaphragm, the division in the middle of the body between the abdomen and the thorax, or stomach and chest; (*loosely*) the area of the body, or of clothing, from below the breast down to the waist. [O.E. *midd*, middle, *hrif*, belly.]

mid-season, midship, midshipman. See under **mid**.

midst *midst*, *n* middle. — *adv* in the middle. — *prep* (also **'midst** as if for **amidst**) amidst. [O.E. *in middes* amidst.]

midstream ... to ... **mid-wicket**. See under **mid**.

midwife *mid'wīf*, *n* a woman, or occasionally a man, who assists women in childbirth: — *pl* **midwives** (*mid'wīvz*). — *n* **midwifery** (*mid-wif'ə-ri* or *-wif'ri*) the art, practice or training of a midwife; assistance at childbirth; obstetrics. — **midwife toad** either of two species of small European toad, *Alytes obstetricians* and *Alytes cisternasi*, so called because the males bear the fertilised eggs on their backs until they hatch. [O.E. *mid*, with, *wīf*, woman.]

midwinter. See under **mid**.

mien *mēn*, (*literary*) *n* an air or look, manner, bearing. [Perh. **demean**[1], infl. by Fr. *mine*.]

miff *mif*, (*colloq*) *n* a slight feeling or fit of resentment. — *vt* to put out of humour, annoy or offend. — *vi* to take offence. — *adj* **miffed**. — *n* **miff'iness**. — *adj* **miff'y** ready to take offence; touchy. [Cf. Ger. *muffen*, to sulk.]

MiG or **Mig** *mig*, (*aeronautics*) *abbrev* for *Mi*koyan and *G*urevich (Soviet aircraft designers).

might[1] *mīt*, *pa t* of **may** (q.v.). — **might'-have-been** someone who, or that which, might have been, or might have come to something.

might[2] *mīt*, *n* power; ability; strength; energy or intensity of purpose or feeling. — *adv* **might'ily**. — *n* **might'iness**. — *adj* **might'y** having great power; strong; valiant; very great; important; exhibiting might; wonderful. — *adv* (*colloq*, usu. with a tinge of irony except in *US*) very. — **might and main** utmost strength.

mignon *mē-nyɔ̃*, (Fr.) *adj* small and dainty: — *fem* **mignonne** (*mē-nyon*).

mignonette *min-yə-net'*, *n* a sweet-scented plant of the *Reseda* genus; a fine kind of lace. [Fr., fem. dimin. of *mignon*, daintily small, a darling.]

migraine *mē'grān* or *mī'grān*, *n* a pain affecting only one half of the head or face and usu. accompanied by nausea and disturbances of vision; a condition marked by recurring migraines. — *n* **migraineur** (*-œr'*) a person who suffers migraines. — *adj* **mi'grainous**. [Fr., — Gr. *hēmikrāniā* — *hēmi*, half, *krānion*, skull.]

migrate *mī-grāt'*, *vi* to pass from one place to another; to change one's place of abode to another country, etc.; to change habitat according to the season; to move (as parasites, etc.) to another part of the body; to pass in a stream (as ions, or particles). — *n* **mi'grant** a person or animal that migrates or is migrating. — Also *adj*. — *n* **migrā'tion** a change of habitation from one country or climate to another, esp. in a large number; a number moving together in this way. — *n* **mi'grātor**. — *adj* **mi'gratory** (*-grə-tə-ri*) migrating or accustomed to migrate; wandering. [L. *migrāre*, *-ātum*; cf. *meāre*, to go.]

mihrab *mē-räb'* or *mēhh'räb*, *n* a niche or slab in a mosque marking the direction of Mecca. [Ar. *mihrāb*.]

mikado *mi-kä'dō*, (*hist*) *n* a title given by foreigners to the Emperor of Japan: — *pl* **mika'dos**. [Jap., exalted gate.]

mike *mīk*, *n* a contraction of **microphone** and **microscope**.

mil *mil*, *n* a unit (1/1000 in.) in measuring the diameter of wire; a millilitre (*pharm*); a unit of angular measurement, used esp. with artillery, equal to 1/6400 of a circle or 0.05625°. [L. *mīlle*, a thousand.]

mil. or **milit.** *abbrev* for military.

milady *mi-lād'i*, *n* a term of address used for an aristocratic or rich English lady e.g. by household staff. [Fr. modification of **my lady**.]

milage. See **mile**.

milch *milch* or *milsh*, *adj* giving milk. — **milch'-cow** a cow yielding milk or kept for milking; a ready source of gain or money (*fig*). [O.E. *milce*; cf. ety. for **milk**.]

mild *mīld*, *adj* gentle in temper and disposition; not sharp or bitter; acting gently; gently and pleasantly affecting the senses; soft; calm. — *n* mild ale. — *vt* **mild'en** to make mild. — *vi* to become mild. — *adv* **mild'ly**. — *n* **mild'ness**. — **mild ale** ale with less hop flavouring than pale ale; **mild steel** steel containing very little carbon. — **put it mildly** to understate the case. [O.E. *milde*, mild.]

mildew *mil'dū*, *n* a disease on plants, caused by the growth of minute fungi; a similar appearance on other things or of another kind, as on paper or cloth, etc. kept in damp conditions; a fungus causing the disease. — *vt* to taint with mildew. — *adj* **mil'dewy**. [O.E. *meledēaw*, *mildēaw*.]

mile *mīl*, *n* in Britain and U.S., a unit of length, 1760 yards or 5280 feet (1.61 km.) — a *statute mile*; orig. a Roman unit of length, 1000 (double) paces (*mīlle passūs* or *passuum*; about 1618 English yards); applied to various later units; a great distance or length (*colloq*). — *n* **mile'age** or **mīl'age** the total number of miles covered by a motor vehicle, etc.; travelling allowance at so much a mile; miles travelled per gallon of fuel; use, benefit (*fig*, *colloq*). — *n* **mī'ler** a runner of a mile race. — **mileom'eter** or **mīlom'eter** an instrument that records the number of miles that a vehicle, etc. has travelled; **mile'stone** a stone or mark showing distance in miles; an important event, stage, etc. (*fig*). — **geographical** or **nautical mile** one-sixtieth of a degree of latitude, a distance varying with latitude; *UK nautical mile*, 6080 feet (1.8532 km.); *international nautical mile*, 6076.1033 feet (or 1.852 km.). [O.E. *mīl* — L. *mīlia*, pl. of *mīlle* (*passuum*) a thousand (paces).]

milfoil *mil'foil*, *n* yarrow or other species of *Achillea*; extended to other plants with finely divided leaves, such as **wat'er-milfoil**. [O.Fr., — L. *mīllefolium* — *mīlle*, a thousand, *folium*, a leaf.]

miliary *mil'i-ər-i*, *adj* like a millet-seed; characterised by an eruption like millet-seeds. — *n* **miliaria** (*mil-i-ā'ri-ə*; *med*) prickly-heat. [L. *miliārius* — *milium*, millet.]

milieu *mēl-yø'*, *n* environment, setting, medium, element: — *pl* **milieus'** or **milieux** (*-yø'*). [Fr., middle.]

milit. *abbrev* for military.

militant *mil'it-ənt*, *adj* fighting; engaged in warfare; combative; using violence; militaristic. — *n* a person who takes active part in a struggle; someone who seeks to advance a cause by violence. — *n* **mil'itancy.** — *adv* **mil'itantly.** — *adv* **mil'itarily.** — *n* **militarīsā'tion** or **-z-.** — *vt* **mil'itarise** or **-ize** to reduce or convert to a military model or method; to make militaristic; to subject to military domination. — *n* **mil'itarism** an excess of the military spirit; domination by an army, or military class or ideals; belief in such domination; a tendency to overvalue military power or to view things from the soldier's point of view. — *n* **mil'itarist** a student of military science; someone imbued with militarism. — *adj* **militarist'ic.** — *adj* **mil'itary** pertaining to soldiers, armies or warfare; warlike. — *n* soldiery; the army. — *vi* **mil'itate** to contend; to have weight, tell (esp. with *against*); to fight for a cause. — **military academy** a training-college for army officer cadets; **military band** a band of brasses, woodwinds and percussion; **military cross** a decoration (abbrev. **MC**) awarded since 1914 to army officers (below major) and warrant officers; **military honours** see under **honour; military medal** a medal awarded since 1916 to non-commissioned and warrant officers and serving men; **military police** a body of men and women functioning as a police force within the army; **military policeman** or **-woman.** [L. *mīles, -itis*, a soldier, *mīlitāris*, military, *mīlitāre, -ātum*, to serve as a soldier.]

militaria *mil-i-tā'ri-ə, npl* weapons, uniforms, and other things connected with wars past and present. [*military*, and noun sfx. *-ia*; or L., things military, neut. pl. of *militāris*, military.]

militarise, military, etc. See under **militant.**

militia *mi-li'shə, n* a body of men or women enrolled and drilled as soldiers; the National Guard and its reserve (*US*); a territorial force; troops of the second line. — **mili'tiaman** or **-woman.** [L. *mīlitia*, military service or force.]

milk *milk, n* a white liquid secreted by female mammals for the nourishment of their young; a milklike juice or preparation; lactation. — *vt* to squeeze or draw milk from; to supply with milk; to extract money, venom, etc., from; to extract; to manipulate as if milking a cow. — *vi* to yield milk. — *n* **milk'er** a person who milks cows, etc.; a machine for milking cows; a cow that gives milk. — *adv* **milk'ily.** — *n* **milk'iness** cloudiness; mildness. — *n* **milk'ing** the act or art of milking (*lit* or *fig*); the amount of milk drawn at one time. — Also *adj.* — *adj* **milk'less.** — *adj* **milk'like.** — *adj* **milk'y** made of, full of, like, or yielding, milk; clouded; soft; gentle. — *adj* **milk'-and-water** insipid; wishy-washy. — **milk'-bar** a shop where milk, milk shakes, etc. are sold for drinking on the spot; **milk cap** any fungus of the large and mainly inedible genus *Lactarius*, so called because of a milky fluid that it exudes when bruised; **milk chocolate** eating chocolate made from cocoa, cocoa-butter, sugar, and condensed or dried milk; **milk'-cow** a milch-cow; **milk-denti'tion** the first set of teeth; **milk float** a small, usu. electrically-powered vehicle in which milk is carried for delivery to houses; **milking machine** a machine for milking cows; **milking stool** a stool on which the milker sits; **milk'maid** a woman who milks; **milk'man** a man who sells or delivers milk; **milk-pudd'ing** rice, tapioca, etc., cooked with milk; **milk round** a milkman's normal morning route; the periodic recruitment of undergraduates by large companies; **milk run** a milkman's morning round; a routine flight (*airmen's slang*); **milk shake** milk shaken up with a flavouring; **milk sickness** the acute trembling, vomiting and weakness occurring in humans as a result of the consumption of meat or dairy products of cattle afflicted with trembles; **milk snake** a non-venomous, North American snake of the *Colubridae* family, popularly believed to milk cattle; **milk'sop** a piece of bread sopped or soaked in milk; a soft, unadventurous, effeminate young man; **milk stout** stout sweetened with lactose; **milk'-sugar** lactose; **milk tooth** one of the first set of teeth. — *adj* **milk'-white.** — **milk'wood** any of various trees with latex; **milk'wort** a plant (*Polygala*) supposed by some to promote production of milk; **Milky Way** the Galaxy. — **milk and honey** abundance, plenty; luxury; **milk of magnesia** an antacid and laxative, a suspension of magnesium hydroxide in water. [O.E. (Mercian) *milc* (W. Saxon *meolc*), milk.]

mill *mil, n* a machine for grinding by crushing between hard, rough surfaces, or for more or less similar operations; a building or factory where corn, wheat, etc. is ground, or manufacture of some kind is carried on. — *vt* to grind; to press, stamp, roll, cut into bars, full, furrow the edges of, or otherwise treat in a mill. — *vi* to move round in a curve; to practise the business of a miller; (often with *about* or *around*; of a crowd) to move in an aimless or confused manner. — *adj* **milled** prepared by a grinding-mill or a coining-press; transversely grooved on the edge (as a coin or screw-head); treated by machinery, esp. smoothed by calendering rollers in a paper-mill. — *n* **mill'er** a person who owns or works a mill. — *n* **mill'ing** the business of a miller; the act of passing anything through a mill; the act of fulling cloth; the process of turning and ridging the edge of a screw-head or coin; aimless and confused movement of a crowd. — **mill'board** stout pasteboard, used esp. in binding books; **miller's-thumb'** a river fish, the bullhead; **mill'-hand** a factory worker; **milling machine** a machine-tool for shaping metal, with rotating cutters; **mill'pond** a pond to hold water for driving a mill (proverbially smooth and calm); **mill'race** the current of water that turns a millwheel, or the channel in which it runs; **mill'run** a millrace; a test of the quality or mineral content of ore or rock by milling it; **mill'stone** one of the two stones used in a mill for grinding corn; a very heavy burden (*fig*); **millstone-grit'** a hard, gritty sandstone suitable for millstones; (with *cap*) a series of grits, sandstones, shales, underlying the British Coal Measures; **mill'-stream** the stream of water that turns a mill-wheel; **mill'-wheel** a waterwheel used for driving a mill; **mill'wright** a wright or mechanic who builds and repairs mills. — **go** or **put through the mill** to undergo or subject to probationary hardships, suffering or experience, or severe handling. [O.E. *myln* — L.L. *molīna* — L. *mola*, a mill — *molĕre*, to grind.]

millefeuille *mēl-fœy', n* a type of layered cake made with puff-pastry. [Fr. — *mille*, a thousand, *feuille*, a leaf.]

millenary *mil'in-ər-i, n* a thousand years; a thousandth anniversary; a believer in the millennium. — *adj* consisting of, or relating to, a millenary. — *adj* **millenā'rian** pertaining to the millennium. — *n* a believer in the millennium. — *n* **millenā'rianism** or **mill'enarism.** [L. *mīllēnārius*, of a thousand — *mīlle*.]

millennium *mil-en'i-əm, n* a thousand years; a thousandth anniversary, millenary; the thousand years after the second coming of Christ; (usu. *ironical*) a coming golden age: — *pl* **millenn'ia** or **millenn'iums.** — *adj* **millenn'ial.** — *n* **millenn'ialist** a believer in the millennium. — *n* **millenn'ianism** or **millenn'iarism.** [L. *mīlle*, a thousand, *annus*, a year.]

millepede. See **millipede.**

miller. See **mill.**

millesimal *mil-es'im-əl, adj* thousandth; consisting of thousandth parts. — *adv* **milles'imally.** [L. *mīllēsimus* — *mīlle*, a thousand.]

millet *mil'it, n* a food-grain (*Panicum miliaceum*); extended to other species and genera. — **mill'et-seed.** — *adj* of the size or appearance of seeds of millet; miliary. [Fr. *millet* — L. *milium*.]

milli- *mil'i-, combining form* (in names of units) used to denote a thousandth part. [L. *mīlle*, a thousand.]
milliard *mil'yärd, n* a thousand million. [Fr., — L. *mīlle*, a thousand.]
millibar *mil'i-bär, n* a thousandth of a bar (**bar²**). [**milli-**.]
millilitre *mil'i-lē-tər, n* a unit of volume, a thousandth of a litre (abbrev. **ml**). [**milli-**.]
millimetre *mil'i-mē-tər, n* a unit of length, a thousandth of a metre (abbrev. **mm**). [**milli-**.]
millimole *mil'i-mōl, (chem) n* a thousandth of a mole (abbrev. **mmol**). [**milli-** and **mole¹**.]
milliner *mil'in-ər, n* a person who makes or sells women's headgear, trimmings, etc. — *n* **mill'inery** the articles made or sold by milliners; the industry of making them. [*Milaner*, a trader in Milan wares or 'fancy goods'.]
million *mil'yən, n* a thousand thousands (1 000 000); a very great number; a million pounds, dollars, etc. — Also *adj.* — *n* **millionaire** (*-ār'*), *fem* **millionair'ess** someone worth a million pounds, dollars, etc. (more or less). — *adj* and *n* **mill'ionth** the ten hundred thousandth. [Fr., — L.L. *mīlliō, -ōnis* — L. *mīlle*, a thousand.]
millipede or **millepede** *mil'i-pēd, n* any many-legged creature of the class *Chilognatha*, vegetarian cylindrical animals with many joints, most of which bear two pairs of legs. [L. *mīllepeda*, a woodlouse — *mīlle*, a thousand, *pēs, pēdis*, a foot.]
millirem *mil'i-rem, n* a unit of radiation dosage, a thousandth of a rem. [**milli-**.]
millisecond *mil'i-sek-ənd, n* a thousandth of a second (abbrev. **ms**). [**milli-**.]
millisievert *mil'i-sē-vert, n* a unit of radiation dosage a thousandth of a sievert (abbrev. **msv**). [**milli-**.]
milometer. See **mileometer.**
milord *mi-lörd', n* a term of address for an aristocratic or rich Englishman e.g. by household staff. [Fr. modification of **my lord**.]
milt *milt, n* the spleen (also, in Jewish cookery, **miltz** *milts*); the semen, or soft roe, of male fishes. — *vt* (of fishes) to impregnate. — *n* **milt'er** a male fish, esp. in the breeding season. [O.E. *milte*, spleen.]
Miltonic *mil-ton'ik, adj* relating to *Milton* (1608–74), or relating to his poetry, or (written) in his manner.
miltz. See **milt.**
mimbar *mim'bär* or **minbar** *min', n* a mosque pulpit. [Ar. *minbar*.]
mime *mīm, n* a play without dialogue, relying solely on movement, expression, etc.; (or **mime artist**) an actor in such a play; mimicry without words; an ancient farcical play of real life, with mimicry (esp. in its Latin form); an actor in such a farce. — *vt* and *vi* to act as a mime; to mimic. — *n* **mīm'er.** [Gr. *mīmos*.]
mimeograph *mim'i-ō-gräf, n* an apparatus on which handwritten or typescript sheets can be reproduced from a stencil; a copy so produced. — *vt* to produce a copy or copies of (something) in this way. [*Mimeograph*, formerly a trademark.]
mimesis *mim-* or *mīm-ē'sis, n* imitation or representation in art; the rhetorical use of a person's supposed or imaginable words; simulation of one disease by another (*med*); mimicry (*biol*). — *adj* **mimet'ic** or **mimet'ical** (*mim-* or *mīm-*) imitative; pertaining to, showing mimicry, mimesis or miming. — *adv* **mimet'ically.** [Gr. *mīmēsis*, imitation.]
mimic *mim'ik, n* someone who imitates, esp. someone who performs in ludicrous imitation of others' speech and gestures; an unsuccessful imitator or imitation; a plant or animal exemplifying mimicry. — *adj* imitative; mock or sham. — *vt* to imitate, esp. in ridicule or so as to incur ridicule; to produce an imitation of; to resemble deceptively: — *pr p* **mim'icking**; *pa t* and *pa p* **mim'icked.** — *n* **mim'icker.** — *n* **mim'icry** an act of mimicking; an advantageous superficial resemblance to some other species or object (*biol*). [L. *mīmicus*, imitative — Gr. *mīmikos* — *mīmos*, a mime.]
miminy-piminy *mim'i-ni-pim-i-ni.* Same as **niminy-piminy.**
mimosa *mim-ō'zə, n* a plant of the sensitive plant genus *Mimosa*, as esp. with clusters of yellow flowers; popularly extended to *Acacia* and other genera of the **Mimosā'ceae** (*mim-* or *mīm-*) a regular-flowered leguminous family. — *adj* **mimosā'ceous** (*mim-* or *mīm-*). [Gr. *mīmos*, a mimic.]
mimulus *mim'ū-ləs, n* a plant of the musk and monkey-flower genus of the figwort family *Mimulus.* [Gr. *mīmos*, a mime, with L. dimin. sfx. *-ulus*.]
Min. *abbrev* for: Minister; Ministry.
min. *abbrev* for: minimum; minute(s).
mina. See **myna.**
minaret *min'ə-ret* or *-ret', n* a mosque tower, from which the call to prayer is given. [Ar. *manār, manārat*, lighthouse — *nār*, fire.]
minatory *min'-* or *mīn'ə-tə-ri, adj* threatening. [L. *mināri, -ātus*, to threaten.]
minbar. See **mimbar.**
mince *mins, vt* to cut into small pieces; to chop finely; to diminish or suppress a part of in speaking; to pronounce affectedly. — *vi* to walk with affected nicety; to speak affectedly: — *pr p* **minc'ing**; *pa t* and *pa p* **minced** (*minst*). — *n* minced meat; mincemeat. — *n* **minc'er.** — *adj* **minc'ing** speaking or walking or behaving with affected nicety. — Also *n.* — *adv* **minc'ingly.** — **mince'meat** a chopped mixture of raisins, peel, and other ingredients; anything thoroughly broken or cut to pieces; **mince-pie'** a pie made with mincemeat. — **make mincemeat of** to destroy utterly (esp. *fig*); **mince matters** or **words** to speak of things with affected delicacy, or to soften an account, or one's stated opinion, etc. unduly. [O.Fr. *mincier, minchier* — L. *minūtus*; cf. **minute¹**.]
MIND *mīnd, n* the name of the National Association of Mental Health.
mind *mīnd, n* the state of thought and feeling; wits, right senses, sanity; consciousness; intellect; that which thinks, knows, feels and wills; memory; thought; judgment; opinion; inclination; attention; direction of the will; personality; a thinking or directing person. — *vt* to attend to; to tend, have care or oversight of; to be careful about; to be troubled by, object to, dislike. — *vi* to attend; to care; to look out, take heed; to be troubled, object. — *interj* be careful, watch out! — *adj* **mind'ed** inclined; disposed. — (In combination) **-mind'ed** used to denote having a mind of such-and-such a kind or inclined towards this or that. — (In combination) **-mind'edness** denoting inclination. — *n* **mind'er** a person who minds a machine, child, etc.; a bodyguard, usu. of a criminal (*slang*). — *adj* **mind'ful** bearing in mind; taking thought or care; attentive; observant. — *adv* **mind'fully.** — **mind'fulness.** — *adj* **mind'less** without mind; stupid; unmindful. — *adv* **mind'lessly.** — **mind'lessness**; **mind'-bender** a brain-teaser, a puzzle. — *adj* **mind'-bending** forcing the mind to unwonted effort, teasing the brain. — *adj* **mind'-blowing** (of a drug) producing a state of ecstasy; (of an exhilarating experience, etc.) producing a similar state. — *adj* **mind'-boggling** astonishing; incomprehensible. — **mind'-reader** a thought reader; **mind'-reading**; **mind'set** (a fixed) attitude of habit of mind; **mind's eye** visual imagination, mental view, contemplation. — **absence of mind** inattention to what is going on owing to absorption of the mind in other things; **cast one's mind back** to think about, try to recall past events, etc.; **change one's mind** to come to a new decision or opinion; **cross someone's mind** see under **cross**; **do you mind?** an interjection usu. expressing annoyance or disagreement; **do (or would) you mind?** please do; do you object?; **have**

a good mind (to) to wish or to be inclined strongly (to); **have a mind of one's own** to be strong-willed and independent, unwilling to be persuaded or dissuaded by others; **have half a mind (to)** to be somewhat inclined (to); **if you don't mind** if you have no objection; **in two minds** wavering; **know one's own mind** to be sure of one's intentions and opinions; **make up one's mind** to come to a decision; **mind one's p's and q's** to be carefully accurate and punctilious; **mind out** (often with *for*) to beware (of) or look out (for); **mind you** an expression used to introduce a qualification added to something already said; **mind your own business** this is not your concern; **never mind** do not concern yourself; it does not matter; **of one** (or **a**, or **the same**) **mind** agreed; **of two minds** uncertain what to think or do; **on one's mind** in one's thoughts, esp. as a cause of concern; **out of mind** forgotten; out of one's thoughts; **out of one's mind** mad; **presence of mind** a state of mental calmness when one is on the alert and ready for action; **put in mind** to remind (of); **put out of one's mind** to think no more about, forget about; **set one's mind on** to be determined to have or attain; **set** or **put one's mind to** to focus one's attention on; **speak one's mind** to say plainly what one thinks; **take someone's mind off** to distract someone from; **time out of mind** from time immemorial; **to my,** etc. **mind** in my, etc. opinion. [O.E. *gemynd* — *munan*, to think.]

mine[1] *mīn, pron*, genitive of **I**, used predicatively or absolutely, belonging to me; that which belongs to me; my people. [O.E. *mīn*.]

mine[2] *mīn, n* a place from which minerals, esp. coal or precious metals, are dug; a rich source (*colloq*); a submerged or floating charge of explosives in a metal case to destroy ships; a land-mine; an excavation dug under a position to enter it secretly, subvert it, or to blow it up (*mil*); an explosive charge for this; a burrowing animal's gallery, such as an insect's in a leaf. — *vt* to excavate, tunnel, make passages in or under; to obtain by excavation; to work as a mine; to bring down or blow up by a mine; to lay mines in or under. — *vi* to dig or work a mine or mines; to tunnel; to burrow; to lay mines; to proceed secretly, insidiously (*fig*). — *n* **min'er** someone who works in a mine; a soldier who lays mines. — *n* and *adj* **min'ing**. — **mine'-detector** an apparatus for detecting explosive mines; **mine'field** an area laid with mines; a dangerous or potentially explosive situation, matter, item, etc.; **mine'-hunter** a ship for locating mines; **mine'-layer** a ship for laying mines; **miner's lamp** a lamp carried by a miner, commonly on his cap; **mine'sweeper** a ship for removing mines from the sea. [Fr. *mine* (noun), *miner* (verb).]

mineola. See **minneola**.

mineral *min'ər-əl, n* a substance produced by processes of inorganic nature; a substance obtained by mining; ore; a substance neither animal nor vegetable; a mineral water (in a wide sense). — *adj* relating to minerals; having the nature of minerals; impregnated with minerals, as water; of inorganic substance or nature. — *n* **mineralisā'tion** or **-z-**. — *vt* **min'eralise** or **-ize** to give the properties of a mineral to; to make into a mineral. — *n* **min'eralīser** or **-z-** someone who, or that which, mineralises; an element that combines with a metal to form an ore, as sulphur. — *adj* **mineralog'ical** pertaining to mineralogy. — *adv* **mineralog'ically**. — *vi* **mineralogise** or **-ize** (*-al'*) to collect or study minerals. — *n* **mineral'ogist** a person skilled or trained in mineralogy. — *n* **mineral'ogy** the science of minerals. — **mineral oil** any oil of mineral origin; **mineral spring** or **well** a spring of mineral water; **mineral water** spring water impregnated with minerals, or an artificial imitation of this; (*loosely*) an effervescent non-alcoholic beverage; **mineral wool** a mass of fibres made by blowing steam through molten slag, used for insulating, etc. [Fr. *minéral* — *miner*, to mine; cf. **mine**[2].]

minestrone *min-i-strōn'i, n* a thick vegetable soup with pieces of pasta, etc. [It.]

Ming *ming, n* a Chinese dynasty (1368–1643). — *adj* of the dynasty, its time, or esp. its pottery and other art.

mingle *ming'gl, vt* and *vi* to mix. — *n* a mixture; a medley. — *n* **ming'lement**. — *n* **ming'ler**. — *n* **ming'ling**. — *adv* **ming'lingly**. [O.E. *mengan*.]

mingy *min'ji,* (*colloq*) *adj* meagre, ungenerous, stingy. — *n* **min'giness**. [Perh. **mangy** or **mean**[1] and **stingy**[1].]

mini *min'i, n* short for **mini-car, minicomputer, miniskirt**; something small of its type. — *adj* (*colloq*) small, miniature.

mini- *min'i-, combining form* used to signify small (abbrev. of **miniature**) as in the following: — **min'ibike** a lightweight motorcycle, esp. for use off the public road; **min'ibreak** a short holiday, e.g. a weekend or long weekend break; **min'ibus** a small motor bus; **min'icab** a small motor vehicle plying for hire; **min'icabbing**; **min'icam** a portable, shoulder-held TV camera, as used in news reporting; **min'i-car**; **min'icomputer** a computer, which may have several terminals, lying in capability between a mainframe and a microcomputer; **min'idisk** a very compact magnetic disk storage medium for microcomputers; **mini-lacrosse** see under **lacrosse**; **min'ipill** a low-dose oral contraceptive containing no oestrogen; **min'i-series** a short series of television programmes broadcast usu. over consecutive days; **min'iskirt** a skirt whose hemline is well above the knees; **min'i-sub** or **-sub'marine**.

miniature *min'i-chər, min'yə-tūr* or *-tyər, n* a small or reduced copy, type or breed of anything; a small-scale version of anything; manuscript illumination; a painting on a very small scale, on ivory, vellum, etc.; the art of painting in this manner. — *adj* on a small scale; minute. — *n* **miniaturisā'tion** or **-z-**. — *vt* **min'iaturise** or **-ize** to make very small; to make something on a small scale. — *n* **min'iaturist** a person who paints or makes miniatures. — **in miniature** on a small scale. [It. *miniatura* — L. *minium*, red lead; infl. by L. *minor*, *minimus*, etc., and their derivatives.]

minibike . . . to . . . **minidisk**. See under **mini-**.

minim *min'im, n* a note, formerly the shortest, equal to two crotchets (*mus*); an apothecaries' measure, one-sixtieth of a fluid dram or drachm; an apothecaries' weight, a grain; a short down-stroke in handwriting. — **minim rest** a rest for the duration of a minim. [L. *minimus*, smallest.]

minimal *min'i-məl, adj* very small indeed; of the nature of a minimum; negligible. — *n* **min'imalism**. — *n* **min'imalist** a person advocating a policy of the least possible action, intervention, etc.; a practitioner or advocate of minimal art. — Also *adj*. — **minimal art**, etc. art, etc. whose practitioners reject such traditional elements as composition and interrelationship between parts of the whole; **minimal invasive therapy** (*surg*) operating procedure that does not necessitate stitching or scarring, e.g. gall-stone removal by endoscopy and laser treatment. [L. *minimus*, smallest.]

minimax *min'i-maks,* (*math*) *n* (in game theory, e.g. *chess*) a strategy designed to minimise one's maximum possible loss; the theory (in a game for two players) that minimising one's maximum loss equates with maximising one's minimum gain. [*mini*mum and *max*imum.]

minimise or **-ize** *min'i-mīz, vt* to reduce to the smallest possible amount; to make as light or insignificant as possible; to estimate at the lowest possible; to diminish or belittle. — *n* **minimisā'tion** or **-z-**. [L. *minimus*, smallest.]

minimum *min'i-məm, n* the least quantity or degree, or the smallest possible; the lowest point or value reached; a value of a variable at which it ceases to diminish and begins to increase (*math*; opp. of *maximum*): — *pl* **min'ima**. — *adj* (*attrib*) smallest or lowest (possible obtained, recorded, etc.). — **minimum wage** the lowest wage permitted by law or regulation for certain work; a fixed bottom limit to workers' wages in various industries; **minimum lending rate** the minimum rate of interest charged by the Bank of England to the discount market. [L. *minimus, -a, -um*, smallest.]

minion *min'yən, n* a servile dependant, flunky; a flatterer. [Fr. *mignon, mignonne*.]

minipill. See **mini-**.

miniscule. An alternative, less acceptable spelling of **minuscule**.

minister *min'is-tər, n* someone who administers or proffers, in service or kindness; a clergyman; the head, or assistant to the head, of several religious orders; the responsible head of a department of state affairs; the representative of a government at a foreign court; a person transacting business for another. — *vi* to give attentive service (to); to perform duties; to supply or do things that are necessary. — *adj* **ministē'rial** pertaining to a minister or ministry (in any sense); on the government side; administrative; executive; instrumental. — *adj* **ministē'rialist**. — *adv* **ministē'rially**. — *adj* **min'istering** attending and serving. — *adj* **min'istrant** administering; attendant. — Also *n*. — *n* **ministrā'tion**. — *adj* **ministrative** (*min'is-trə-tiv*) serving to aid or assist; ministering. — *n* **min'istry** the act of ministering; service; the office or duties of a minister; the clergy; the clerical profession; the body of ministers who manage the business of the country; a department of government, or the building it occupies; a term of office as minister. — **minister of state** an additional, usu. non-Cabinet, minister in (but ranking below the head of) a large government department; **Minister of the Crown** a government minister in the Cabinet; **Minister without Portfolio** a government minister, a member of the cabinet having no specific department. [L. *minister* — *minor*, less.]

miniver *min'i-vər, n* white fur, orig. a mixed or variegated fur; the ermine in winter coat. [O.Fr. *menu*, small — L. *minūtus*, and *vair*, fur.]

mink *mingk, n* a small animal (of several species) of the weasel kind; its fur; a coat or jacket made from its fur. [Perh. from Sw. *mänk*.]

minke *mink'ə, n* a type of whale, the lesser rorqual. [From a Norwegian whaler, *Meincke*, who harpooned one by accident.]

Minn. *abbrev* for Minnesota (U.S. state).

minneola or **mineola** *min-i-ō'lə, n* a variety of citrus fruit developed from a tangerine and a grapefruit and resembling an orange, grown in the U.S. and elsewhere. [Poss. *Mineola* in Texas.]

Minnesinger *min'i-sing-ər* or Ger. *-zing-ər, n* one of a 12th–13th cent. school of German amatory lyric poets, mostly of noble birth. [Ger. *Minne*, love, *Singer*, singer.]

minnow *min'ō, n* a very small freshwater fish (*Phoxinus phoxinus*) closely related to chub and dace; loosely extended to other small fish; a small, unimportant person or thing (*fig*).

Minoan *min-ō'ən* or *mīn-ō'ən, adj* pertaining to prehistoric Crete and its culture. — *n* a prehistoric Cretan. [Gr. *Mīnōs*, a legendary king of Crete.]

minor *mī'nər, adj* lesser; inferior in importance, degree, bulk, etc.; inconsiderable; lower; smaller (than major) by a semitone (*mus*); (in boys' schools) junior. — *n* a person under age; the minor term, or minor premise (*logic*); anything that is minor opposed to major. — *vi* (*NAm*; with *in*) to study as a minor, subsidiary subject at college or university. — *n* **minority** (*min-* or *mīn-or'i-ti*) the condition or fact of being little or less; the state or time of being under age (also **mī'norship**); the smaller number; less than half; the party, social group, section of the population, etc., of smaller numbers; the number by which it falls short of the other party (opp. to *majority*). — *adj* of the minority. — **minority carrier** (*electronics*) in a semiconductor, the electrons or holes which carry the lesser degree of measured current; **minority group** a section of the population with a common interest, characteristic, etc., which is not common to most people; **minor key, mode** and **scale** one with its third a minor third above the tonic; **minor orders** the lower degrees of holy orders, e.g. lector or acolyte; **minor planet** a small planet, any one of many hundreds with orbits between those of Mars and Jupiter, an asteroid; **minor poet** a genuine but not great poet; **minor prophets** the twelve from Hosea to Malachi in the Old Testament; **minor suit** (in bridge) clubs or diamonds; **minor third** (*mus*) an interval of three semitones. [L. *minor*, less; cf. **minus**.]

Minotaur *min'* or *mīn'ə-tör*, (*Gr mythol*) *n* the bull-headed monster in the Cretan Labyrinth, offspring of Pasiphae, wife of Minos. [Gr. *Mīnōtauros* — *Mīnōs*, a legendary king of Crete, *tauros*, bull.]

minster *min'stər, n* an abbey church or priory church; often applied to a cathedral or other great church without any monastic connection. [O.E. *mynster* — L. *monastērium*, a monastery.]

minstrel *min'strəl, n* a mediaeval harper who sang or recited his own or others' poems; one of a troupe of entertainers with blackened faces. — *n* **min'strelsy** (*-si*) the art or occupation of a minstrel; a company of minstrels; a collection of minstrels' poems or songs. [O.Fr. *menestrel* — L.L. *ministeriālis* — L. *minister*, attendant.]

mint[1] *mint, n* a place where money is coined, esp. legally; a vast sum of money. — *vt* to coin; to invent; to stamp. — *adj* in mint condition. — *n* **mint'age** coining; coinage; stamp; duty for coining. — *n* **mint'er**. — **mint condition** the condition of a new-minted coin; perfect condition, as if unused; **mint'mark** a mark showing where a coin was minted. [O.E. *mynet*, money — L. *monēta*; see **money**.]

mint[2] *mint, n* any plant of the aromatic genus *Mentha*, such as spearmint and peppermint; any sweet flavoured with mint. — *adj* **mint'y**. — **mint-ju'lep** see **julep**; **mint-sauce'** chopped spearmint or other mint mixed with vinegar and sugar, used esp. as a sauce for roast lamb. [O.E. *minte* — L. *mentha* — Gr. *minthē*.]

minuend *min'ū-end*, (*math*) *n* the number from which another is to be subtracted. [L. *minuendus* (*numerus*) — *minuĕre*, to lessen.]

minuet *min-ū-et', n* a slow, graceful dance in triple measure, invented in the 17th cent. and fashionable in the 18th cent.; the music for, or as for, such a dance; the standard third movement in the classical sonata, symphony, etc. [Fr. *menuet* — *menu*, small — L. *minūtus*, small.]

minus *mī'nəs, prep* diminished by (*math*); deficient in respect of, deprived of, without (*colloq*). — *adj* negative. — *n* a deficiency or subtraction; a negative quantity or term; the sign (also **minus sign**) of subtraction or negativity (−), opp. to *plus*. [L. *minus*, neut. of *minor*, less.]

minuscule *min'əs-kūl, adj* very small, very unimportant. — *n* a small cursive script, originated by the monks in the 7th–9th centuries (*palaeog*; opp. to **majuscule**); a lower-case letter (*printing*). — *adj* **minus'cūlar**. [L. (*littera*) *minuscula*, smallish (letter).]

minute[1] *mīn-ūt', adj* extremely small; relating to the very small; exact, detailed. — *adv* **minute'ly**. — *n* **minute'ness**. [L. *minūtus*, past p. of *minuĕre*, to lessen.]

minute[2] *min'it, n* the sixtieth part of an hour; the sixtieth part of an angular degree; an indefinitely small space of time; a moment; a brief jotting or note; (in *pl*) a brief summary of the proceedings of a meeting; a distance traversed in a minute. — *vt* to make a brief jotting or note of; to record in the minutes. — **min'ute-book** a book of minutes or short notes; **min'ute-gun** a gun discharged every minute, as a signal of distress or mourning; **min'ute-hand** the hand that indicates the minutes on a clock or watch; **min'uteman** (often with *cap*) a man ready to turn out at a minute's warning, as in the American war of independence (*hist*); a member of an armed right-wing organisation in the U.S., formed to take prompt action against Communist activities; a three-stage intercontinental ballistic missile; **minute steak** a small thin piece of steak which can be cooked quickly. — **up to the minute** right up to date. [Same word as **minute**[1].]

minutia *mi-nū'shi-ə, n* a minute particular or detail: — usu. in *pl* **minū'tiae** (*-ē*). [L. *minūtia*, smallness.]

minx *mingks, n* a pert young girl.

Miocene *mī'ō-sēn*, (*geol*) *adj* of the Tertiary period preceding the Pliocene and having a smaller proportion of molluscan fossils of species now living. — *n* the Miocene system, period or strata. [Gr. *meiōn*, smaller, *kainos*, recent.]

miosis or **myosis** *mī-ō'sis, n* abnormal contraction of the pupil of the eye. — *adj* **miot'ic**. [Gr. *mȳein*, to close, blink.]

MIPS or **mips** (*comput*) *abbrev* for millions of instructions per second.

MIR *abbrev* for mortgage interest relief.

miracle *mir'ə-kl, n* an event or act which breaks a law of nature; a marvel, a wonder. — *adj* **miraculous** (*-ak'ū-ləs*) of the nature of a miracle; done by supernatural power; very wonderful or remarkable. — *adv* **mirac'ulously**. — *n* **mirac'ulousness**. — **miracle play** a mediaeval form of drama founded on Old or New Testament history, or the legends of the saints. [Fr., — L. *mīrāculum* — *mīrārī*, *-ātus*, to wonder at.]

mirage *mi-räzh', n* an optical illusion, appearing as a floating and shimmering image, like water, on the horizon, caused by the varying refractive index of surface layers of hot and cold air; something illusory (*fig*). [Fr. *mirer*, to look at — L. *mīrārī*, to wonder at.]

MIRAS *mī'ras, abbrev* for mortgage interest relief at source.

mire *mīr, n* deep mud. — *vt* to plunge and fix in mire; to soil with mud; to swamp, bog down. — *vi* to sink in mud. — *n* **mir'iness**. — *adj* **mir'y** consisting of mire; covered with mire. [O.N. *mȳrr*, bog.]

mirepoix *mēr-pwa', n* sautéed vegetables used for making sauces, etc. [Prob. after the Duc de *Mirepoix*, 18th-cent. French general.]

mirk, etc. Same as **murk**, etc.

mirror *mir'ər, n* a looking-glass; a reflecting surface; a faithful representation of something else (*fig*). — *vt* to reflect an image of, as in a mirror; to furnish with a mirror or mirrors: — *pr p* **mirr'oring**; *pa p* **mirr'ored**. — **mirr'or-image** an image with right and left reversed as in a mirror; **mirror symmetry** the symmetry of an object and its reflected image; **mirr'or-writing** writing which is like ordinary writing as seen in a mirror, i.e. in reverse. [O.Fr. *mireor*, *mirour* — L. *mīrārī*, *-ātus*, to wonder at.]

mirth *mûrth, n* jollity; laughter; merriness. — *adj* **mirth'ful** full of or causing mirth. — *adv* **mirth'fully**. — *n* **mirth'fulness**. — *adj* **mirth'less**. — *adv* **mirth'lessly**. — *n* **mirth'lessness**. [O.E. *myrgth* — *myrige*, merry.]

MIRV *mûrv, n* a missile containing many thermonuclear warheads, able to attack separate targets. [Acronym from *M*ultiple *I*ndependently Targeted *R*e-entry *V*ehicle.]

miry. See **mire**.

mis- *mis, pfx* denoting: wrongly, badly, as in *misbehave*; wrong, bad, as in *misdeed*. [O.E.; cf. **miss**[1].]

misadventure *mis-əd-ven'chər, n* bad luck; mishap; accidental killing. [M.E. — O.Fr., *mesaventure*.]

misadvise *mis-əd-vīz', vt* to advise wrongly or badly. — *adj* **misadvised'**. — *adv* **misadvīs'edly**. — *n* **misadvīs'edness**. [**mis-**.]

misalign *mis-ə-līn', vt* to align wrongly. [**mis-**.]

misalliance *mis-ə-lī'əns, n* an unsuitable alliance, esp. in marriage. — *adj* **misallied'**. — *vt* **misally** (*mis-ə-lī'*): — *pr p* **misally'ing**; *pa t* and *pa p* **misallied'**. [Fr. *mésalliance*.]

misandry *mis'ən-dri, n* hatred of men. — *n* **mis'andrist**. [Gr. *misandria* — *misandros*, hating men.]

misanthrope *mis'ən-thrōp* or **misanthropist** *-an'thrə-pist, n* a hater of mankind, someone who distrusts everyone else. — *adj* **misanthropic** (*mis-ən-throp'ik*) or **misanthrop'ical** hating or distrusting mankind. — *adv* **misanthrop'ically**. — *n* **misan'thropy** hatred or distrust of mankind. [Gr. *mīsanthrōpos* — *mīseein*, to hate, *anthrōpos*, a man.]

misapply *mis-ə-plī', vt* to apply wrongly; to use for a wrong purpose. — *n* **misapplicā'tion** (*-ap-li-*). [**mis-**.]

misapprehend *mis-ap-ri-hend', vt* to apprehend wrongly; to take or understand in a wrong sense. — *n* **misapprehen'sion**. — *adj* **misapprehen'sive**. — *adv* **misapprehen'sively** by or with misapprehension or mistake. — *n* **misapprehen'siveness**. [**mis-**.]

misappropriate *mis-ə-prō'pri-āt, vt* to put to a wrong use; to take dishonestly for oneself. — *n* **misappropriā'tion**. [**mis-**.]

misarrange *mis-ə-rānj', vt* to arrange wrongly; to put in wrong order. — *n* **misarrange'ment**. [**mis-**.]

misbegotten *mis-bi-got'n, adj* badly or unlawfully obtained; ill-conceived. [**mis-**, and past p. of **beget**.]

misbehave *mis-bi-hāv', vt* (*reflexive*) and *vi* to behave badly or improperly. — *n* **misbehav'iour**. [**mis-**.]

misbelief *mis-bə-lēf'* or *mis', n* belief in a false doctrine or notion. — *n* **misbeliev'er**. — *adj* **misbeliev'ing**. [**mis-**.]

misc. *abbrev* for miscellaneous.

miscalculate *mis-kal'kū-lāt, vt* and *vi* to calculate wrongly. — *n* **miscalculā'tion**. [**mis-**.]

miscall *mis-köl', vt* to call by a wrong name; (in games) to make a bad or inaccurate call; to abuse or revile (*archaic*). [**mis-**.]

miscarriage *mis-kar'ij, n* an act or instance of miscarrying; the act of giving birth prematurely, esp. of expelling a foetus between the third and seventh months; failure to reach the intended result or destination. — *vi* **miscarr'y** to give birth prematurely; to be unsuccessful; to fail to attain the intended or complete effect. — **miscarriage of justice** failure of the courts to do justice. [**mis-**.]

miscast *mis-käst', vt* and *vi* to cast (in any sense) wrongly or in any way resulting in blame or reproach. [**mis-**.]

miscegenation *mis-i-jin-ā'shən, n* interbreeding, intermarriage or sexual intercourse between different races. [L. *miscēre*, to mix, *genus*, race.]

miscellaneous *mis-əl-ān'i-əs, adj* consisting of several kinds; mixed or mingled. — *adv* **miscellān'eously**. — *n* **miscellān'eousness**. — *n* **miscellanist** (*mis-el'ən-ist* or, esp. in N.Am. *mis'əl-*) a writer of miscellanies. — *n* **miscellany** (*mis-el'* or, esp. in N.Am. *mis'əl-*) a mixture of various kinds; a collection of writings on different subjects or by different authors. [L. *miscellāneus* — *miscēre*, to mix.]

mischance *mis-chäns', n* bad luck; mishap. [M.E. — O.Fr. *meschance*.]

mischief *mis'chif, n* petty misdeeds or annoyance; pestering playfulness; a mischievous person; the troublesome fact; a source of harm; damage, hurt;

evil. — *adj* **mischievous** (*mis'chiv-əs*) causing mischief; prone to mischief; injurious. — *adv* **mis'chievously**. — *n* **mis'chievousness**. — **mis'chief-maker** someone who stirs up trouble. — *n* and *adj* **mis'chief-making**. [O.Fr. *meschef*, from *mes-* (as **mis-**) and *chef* — L. *caput*, the head.]

miscible *mis'i-bl*, *adj* that may be mixed. — *n* **miscibil'ity**. [L. *miscēre*, to mix.]

misclassify *mis-klas'i-fī*, *vt* to classify wrongly. — *n* **misclassificā'tion**. [**mis-**.]

misconceive *mis-kən-sēv'*, *vt* and *vi* to conceive wrongly; to mistake. — *adj* **misconceived'**. — *n* **misconcep'tion**. [**mis-**.]

misconduct *mis-kon'dukt*, *n* bad conduct; wrong management; improper behaviour, such as would lead any reasonable employer to dismiss an employee (*legal*). — *vt* **misconduct** (*-kən-dukt'*). [**mis-**.]

misconstrue *mis-kən-stroo'*, *vt* to construe or to interpret wrongly. [**mis-**.]

miscount *mis-kownt'*, *vt* to count wrongly; to miscalculate. — *n* a wrong counting. [**mis-**.]

miscreant *mis'kri-ənt*, *n* a wrongdoer; a rogue, scoundrel; orig. a misbeliever, a heretic or infidel. — *adj* depraved, scoundrelly, wicked. [O.Fr. *mescreant* — *mes-* (as **mis-**) and L. *crēdēns*, *-entis*, pres. p. of *crēdĕre*, to believe.]

miscue *mis-kū'*, *n* (in billiards, etc.) a stroke spoiled by the slipping off of the cue; a mistake; a wrong cue (in any sense). — *vt* to hit (a billiard ball) wrongly. — *vi* to make a faulty stroke (*billiards*, etc.); to answer the wrong cue, or to miss one's cue (*theat*); to make a mistake. [**mis-**.]

misdate *mis-dāt'*, *vt* to date wrongly. — *n* a wrong date. [**mis-**.]

misdeal *mis-dēl'*, *n* a wrong deal, as at cards. — *vt* and *vi* to deal wrongly; to divide improperly: — *pa t* and *pa p* **misdealt** (*-delt'*). [**mis-**.]

misdeed *mis-dēd'*, *n* a wrongdoing, a bad or wicked deed. [O.E. *misdǣd*.]

misdemeanour or in U.S. **misdemeanor** *mis-də-mē'nər*, *n* a misdeed; bad conduct; (in U.K. formerly) a legal offence of less gravity than a felony. — *n* **misdemean'ant** a person guilty of petty crime or misconduct. [Archaic *misdemean*, to misbehave — **mis-**, **demean**[1].]

misdiagnose *mis-dī'əg-nōz* or *-nōz'*, *vt* to diagnose wrongly. — *n* **misdiagnō'sis**. [**mis-**.]

misdial *mis-dī'əl* or *-dīl'*, *vi* and *vt* to dial (a telephone number) incorrectly. [**mis-**.]

misdid. See **misdo**.

misdirect *mis-di-rekt'* or *-dī-*, *vt* to direct wrongly. — *n* **misdirec'tion**. [**mis-**.]

misdo *mis-doo'*, *vt* to do wrongly or badly: — *pa t* **misdid'**; *pa p* **misdone'**. — *n* **misdo'er**. [**mis-**.]

misdraw *mis-drö'*, *vt* to draw or draft badly. — *n* **misdraw'ing**. [**mis-**.]

miseducation *mis-ed-ū-kā'shən*, *n* improper or harmful education. [**mis-**.]

mise en scène *mēz ã sen*, (Fr.) *n* the act, result, or art, of setting a stage scene or arranging a pictorial representation; setting, physical surroundings.

misemploy *mis-im-ploi'*, *vt* to employ wrongly or badly; to misuse. — *n* **misemploy'ment**. [**mis-**.]

miser *mī'zər*, *n* a person who lives miserably in order to hoard wealth; someone tight-fisted, niggardly. — *n* **mi'serliness**. — *adj* **mi'serly**. [L. *miser*, wretched.]

miserable *miz'ə-rə-bl*, *adj* wretched; exceedingly unhappy; causing misery; extremely poor or mean; contemptible. — *n* **mis'erableness**. — *adv* **mis'erably**. [Fr. *misérable* — L. *miserābilis* — *miser*.]

misère *mē-zer'* or *miz-ār'*, (*cards*) *n* an undertaking to take no tricks. [Fr., misery.]

Miserere *miz-e-rē'ri* or *mis-e-rā're*, *n* the 51st Psalm (from its first word in the Vulgate, where it is 50th Psalm); a musical setting of it. [L. imper. of *miserērī*, to have mercy, to pity.]

misericord *miz-ār'i-körd* or *-körd'*, *n* a bracket on a turn-up seat in a choir-stall, allowing the user some support when standing, often intricately carved; a room in a monastery where some relaxation of rule was allowed; a narrow-bladed dagger for killing a wounded enemy. [O.Fr. *misericorde* — L. *misericordia* — *misericors*, *-cordis*, tender-hearted.]

miserliness, miserly. See **miser**.

misery *miz'ər-i*, *n* wretchedness; extreme pain; miserable conditions; very unhappy experience; a doleful person (*colloq*). [O.Fr., — L. *miseria*.]

misfeasance *mis-fēz'əns*, (*law*) *n* the doing of a lawful act in a wrongful manner, as distinguished from *malfeasance*. — *n* **misfeas'or**. [O.Fr. *mesfaisance* — *mes-* (as **mis-**) and *faisance* — *faire* to do.]

misfeed *mis-fēd'*, *vt* to feed (e.g. a machine) incorrectly (with paper, materials or the like): — *pa t* and *pa p* **misfed'**. [**mis-**.]

misfile *mis-fīl'*, *vt* to file (information) under the wrong headings, etc. [**mis-**.]

misfire *mis-fīr'*, *vi* to fail to go off, explode or ignite, at all or at the right time; to fail to have the effect intended (*fig*). — *n* a failure to fire, or to achieve effect. [**miss**[1] and **fire**.]

misfit *mis'fit*, *n* a bad fit; a thing that fits badly; a person who does not adjust to his or her social environment, job, etc. — *vt* and *vi* (*mis-fit'*) to fit badly. [**mis-**.]

misfortune *mis-för'tūn*, *n* bad luck; an unfortunate accident; calamity. [**mis-**.]

misgive *mis-giv'*, *vt* to suggest apprehensions to, fill with forebodings; to distrust. — *vi* to have apprehensive forebodings: — *pa t* **misgave'**; *pa p* **misgiv'en**. — *n* **misgiv'ing** distrust; a feeling that all is not well. [**mis-**.]

misgovern *mis-guv'ərn*, *vt* to govern badly or unjustly. — *n* **misgov'ernment**. — *n* **misgov'ernor**. [**mis-**.]

misguide *mis-gīd'*, *vt* to guide wrongly; to lead into error. — *n* **misguid'ance**. — *adj* **misguid'ed** erring; misdirected; ill-judged. — *adv* **misguid'edly**. — *n* **misguid'er**. [**mis-**.]

mishandle *mis-han'dl*, *vt* to handle wrongly or unskilfully; to maltreat. [**mis-**.]

mishap *mis-hap'* or *mis'hap*, *n* ill chance; unlucky accident; misfortune. [**mis-**.]

mishear *mis-hēr'*, *vt* and *vi* to hear wrongly. [**mis-**.]

mishit *mis-hit'*, (*sport*) *vt* to hit (a ball) faultily. — *n* (*mis'hit*) a faulty hit. [**mis-**.]

mishmash *mish'mash*, *n* a hotchpotch, medley. [Reduplication of **mash**.]

Mishnah or **Mishna** *mish'nä*, *n* the Jewish oral law, finally redacted A.D. 220 and forming the first section of the Talmud: — *pl* **Mishnayōth'**. — *adj* **Mishnā'ic** or **Mish'nic**. [Heb. *mishnāh* — *shānāh*, to repeat, teach, learn.]

misidentify *mis-ī-den'ti-fī*, *vt* to identify incorrectly. — *n* **misidentificā'tion**. [**mis-**.]

misinform *mis-in-förm'*, *vt* to inform or tell incorrectly, or misleadingly. — *n* **misinform'ant**. — *n* **misinformā'tion**. — *n* **misinform'er**. [**mis-**.]

misinterpret *mis-in-tûr'prit*, *vt* to interpret wrongly; to explain wrongly. — *n* **misinterpretā'tion**. — *n* **misinter'preter**. [**mis-**.]

misjudge *mis-juj'*, *vt* and *vi* to judge wrongly. — *n* **misjudg'ment** — also **misjudge'ment**. [**mis-**.]

miskey *mis-kē'*, *vt* to key (data on a computer, etc. keyboard) incorrectly: — *pa p* and *pa t* **miskeyed'**. [**mis-**.]

mislay *mis-lā'*, *vt* to lay or place wrongly; to lay in a place not remembered; to lose: — *pa t* and *pa p* **mislaid'**. [**mis-** and **lay**[2].]

mislead *mis-lēd'*, *vt* to lead into error; to direct, inform or advise wrongly; to cause to go wrong: — *pa t* and *pa p* **misled'**. — *n* **mislead'er**. — *adj* **mislead'ing** deceptive, confusing. — *adv* **mislead'ingly**. [**mis-**.]

mismanage *mis-man'ij, vt* to conduct or manage badly, carelessly or wrongly. — *n* **misman'agement.** [**mis-**.]

mismatch *mis-mach', vt* to match unsuitably or badly. — *n* a bad match. [**mis-**.]

misnomer *mis-nō'mər, n* a misnaming; a wrong or unsuitable name. [O.Fr. from *mes-* (as **mis-**) and *nommer* — L. *nōmināre*, to name.]

miso *mē'sō, n* a paste, used for flavouring, prepared from soy beans and fermented in brine: — *pl* **mi'sos.** [Jap.]

miso- *mis-ō-* or *mīs-ō-, combining form* signifying a hater of, or hating. — *n* **misogamist** (*-og'ə-mist*) a hater of marriage. — *n* **misog'amy.** — *n* **misogynist** (*-oj'i-nist* or *-og'i-nist*) a woman-hater. — *adj* **misogynist'ical** or **misog'ynous.** — *n* **misog'yny.** — *n* **misology** (*-ol'ə-ji*) hatred of reason, reasoning or knowledge. — *n* **misol'ogist.** [Gr. *mīseein*, to hate.]

mispickel *mis'pik-əl, n* arsenical pyrites, a mineral composed of iron, arsenic and sulphur. [Ger.]

misplace *mis-plās', vt* to put in a wrong place; to mislay; to set on, or attach to, the wrong or an inappropriate object; to indulge in in unsuitable circumstances. — *n* **misplace'ment.** [**mis-**.]

misplay *mis-plā', n* a wrong play, as in sport or games. — Also *vt* and *vi.* [**mis-**.]

misprint *mis-print', vt* to print wrongly. — *n* (*mis'-print*) a mistake in printing, such as an incorrect or damaged character. [**mis-**.]

misprise or **misprize** *mis-prīz', vt* to scorn; to slight; to undervalue. — *n* scorn; failure to value. [O.Fr. *mespriser* — *mes-*, **mis-**, *prisier*, to **prize**[3].]

misprision[1] *mis-prizh'ən, n* criminal oversight or neglect in respect to the crime of another (*law*); any serious offence or failure of duty — *positive* or *negative*, according to whether it is maladministration or mere neglect. — **misprision of heresy, treason,** etc., knowledge of and failure to give information about heresy, treason, etc. [O.Fr. *mes-* (as **mis-**), L.L. *prēnsiō, -ōnis* — L. *praehendere*, to take.]

misprision[2] *mis-prizh'ən, n* failure to appreciate. [**misprise,** after the model of **misprision**[1].]

mispronounce *mis-prə-nowns', vt* to pronounce incorrectly. — *n* **mispronunciation** (*-nun-si-ā'shən*) wrong or improper pronunciation. [**mis-**.]

misquote *mis-kwōt', vt* to quote wrongly. — *n* **misquotā'tion.** [**mis-**.]

misread *mis-rēd', vt* to read wrongly; to misconstrue. — *n* **misread'ing.** [**mis-**.]

misrelate *mis-ri-lāt', vt* to relate incorrectly. — *n* **misrelā'tion.** — **misrelated participle** a participle which the grammatical structure of the sentence insists on attaching to a word it is not intended to qualify (e.g. *Lost in thought, the bus passed me without stopping*). [**mis-**.]

misremember *mis-ri-mem'bər, vt* and *vi* to remember wrongly or imperfectly; to forget (*dialect*). [**mis-**.]

misreport *mis-ri-pört', vt* to report falsely, misleadingly, or wrongly. — *n* false reporting or report. [**mis-**.]

misrepresent *mis-rep-ri-zent', vt* to represent falsely; to give a misleading interpretation to the words or deeds of; to be an unrepresentative representative of. — *n* **misrepresentā'tion.** [**mis-**.]

misroute *mis-rōōt', vt* to route (e.g. a telephone call, traffic) wrongly. [**mis-**.]

misrule *mis-rōōl', n* disorder; bad or disorderly government. — *vt* and *vi* to govern badly. [**mis-**.]

Miss *mis, n* a title prefixed to the name of an unmarried woman or girl; also prefixed to a representational title, esp. in beauty contests, e.g. *Miss World*; vocatively used alone in (usu. mock) severity, or to address a waitress, female teacher, etc.; (without *cap*) a schoolgirl, or girl or woman with the faults attributed to schoolgirls; a person between a child and a woman, esp. in reference to clothing size: — *pl* **miss'es** — either 'the Miss Hepburns' or (more formally) 'the Misses Hepburn' may be said. — *n* **miss'y** (usu. subservient) the little girl. [Shortened form of **mistress.**]

Miss. *abbrev* for Mississippi (U.S. state).

miss[1] *mis, vt* to fail to hit, reach, find, meet, touch, catch, get, have, take advantage of, observe or see; to avoid (a specified danger); to omit; to discover the absence of; to feel the loss or absence of; to think of (an absent person or thing) longingly, or (a former time) nostalgically. — *vi* to fail to hit or obtain; to fail. — *n* the fact or condition or an act or occasion of missing; failure to hit the mark. — *adj* **miss'able.** — *adj* **miss'ing** not to be found; not in the expected place; lacking, absent; of unascertained fate (*mil*). — **missing link** a hypothetical extinct creature thought to be intermediate between man and the anthropoid apes; any one thing required to complete a series. — **go missing** to disappear, esp. unexpectedly and inexplicably; to be mislaid; **miss out** to omit; (with *on*) to fail to experience or benefit from; **miss the bus** or **boat** (*colloq*) to lose one's opportunity. [O.E. *missan.*]

miss[2]**.** See under **Miss.**

missa (also with *cap*) *mis'ə* or *mis'a*, (L.) *n* the Mass (*RC*). — **missa (or Missa) solemnis** (*sol-em'nis*) high mass.

missal *mis'l*, (*RC*) *n* a book containing the complete service for mass throughout the year. [L.L. *missāle*, from *missa*, mass.]

missel. Same as **mistle.**

misshape *mis-shāp', vt* to shape badly or wrongly; to deform. — *n* deformity. — *adj* **misshap'en** badly-shaped; deformed. — *n* **misshap'enness.** [**mis-**.]

missile *mis'īl* or in U.S. *mis'l, n* a weapon or object for throwing by hand or shooting from a bow, gun, or other instrument, now esp. a rocket-launched weapon, often nuclear (see **guided missile** and **ballistic missile**). — *adj* capable of being thrown or projected; pertaining to a missile. — *n* **miss'ilery** or **miss'ilry** (*-īl-ri* or *-l-ri*) missiles collectively; their design, manufacture and use. [L. *missilis* — *mittěre, missum*, to throw.]

missing. See **miss**[1].

mission *mish'ən, n* an act of sending, esp. to perform some function; a flight with a specific purpose, such as a bombing raid or a task assigned to an astronaut or astronauts; the errand or purpose for which one is sent; vocation, life's purpose; a sending out of persons on a political or diplomatic errand, for the spread of a religion, etc.; an organisation that sends out missionaries; its activities; a station or establishment of missionaries; any particular field of missionary enterprise; the body of persons sent on a mission; an embassy; a settlement for religious, charitable, medical or philanthropic work in a district. — *adj* of a mission or missions. — *n* **miss'ionary** a person sent upon a mission, esp. religious. — *adj* pertaining to missions. — **missionary position** in sexual intercourse, the face-to-face position with the male on top. [L. *missiō, -ōnis* — *mittěre*, to send.]

missis or **missus** *mis'is* or *-iz*, (*illit* or *colloq*) *n* lady of the house; wife; a term of address to a woman (usu. by an unacquainted man). [**mistress.**]

missive *mis'iv, n* a document which is sent, such as an official letter. [L.L. *missīvus* — L. *mittěre, missum*, to send.]

misspell *mis-spel', vt* and *vi* to spell wrongly: — *pa t* and *pa p* **misspelt'** or **misspelled'.** — *n* **misspell'ing** a wrong spelling. [**mis-**.]

misspend *mis-spend', vt* to spend wrongly; to waste or squander: — *pa t* and *pa p* **misspent'.** [**mis-**.]

misstate *mis-stāt', vt* to state wrongly or falsely. — *n* **misstate'ment.** [**mis-**.]

misstep *mis-step'*, *vi* to make a false step; to make a mistake. — *n* a mistake in conduct, etc. [**mis-**.]

missus. See **missis.**

mist *mist*, *n* watery vapour seen in the atmosphere; cloud in contact with the ground; thin fog; rain in very fine drops; a suspension of liquid in a gas; condensed vapour on a surface; a dimness or anything that dims or darkens the sight or judgment. — *vt* to obscure or veil with mist or as with mist. — *vi* to become misty or veiled; to form a mist or vapour-cloud. — *adj* **mist'ful.** — *adv* **mist'ily.** — *n* **mist'iness.** — *n* **mist'ing** mist; the action of the verb *mist*. — *adj* misty; hazy; dimming. — *adj* **mist'y** full of, covered with, or obscured by, mist; like mist; obscure; vague; unclear. [O.E. *mist*, darkness, dimness.]

mistake *mis-tāk'*, *vt* to think or understand wrongly; to take for another thing or person; to be wrong about. — *vi* to err: — *pa t* **mistook'**; *pa p* **mistak'en.** — *n* something understood or taken wrongly; an error; (*mis'tāk*) a faulty shot (*cinematography*). — *adj* **mistak'able.** — *n* **mistak'en** understood wrongly; guilty of or under a mistake; erroneous; incorrect; ill-judged. — *adv* **mistak'enly.** — *n* **mistak'enness.** — **mistaken identity** an error in identifying someone. — **and no mistake** (*colloq*) assuredly. [M.E. *mistaken* — O.N. *mistaka*, to take wrongly — *mis-*, wrongly, *taka*, to take.]

Mister *mis'tər*, *n* a title prefixed to a man's name, and to certain designations (such as Mr Justice, Mr Speaker), written **Mr**; (without *cap*) sir (*colloq* or *illit*). [**master.**]

mistime *mis-tīm'*, *vt* to time wrongly. [**mis-**.]

mistle or **mistle-thrush** *mis'l* or *miz'l* (*thrush*), *n* a large thrush with spotted breast, fond of mistletoe berries. [O.E. *mistel*, *mistil*, mistletoe.]

mistletoe *mis'* or *miz'l-tō*, *n* an evergreen shrubby plant, a partial parasite (*Viscum album*) with white viscous fruits, growing on the apple, apricot, etc. (very rarely on the oak); extended to other species of its genus or family (*Loranthaceae*). [O.E. *misteltān* — *mistel*, *mistil*, mistletoe, *tān*, twig.]

mistook *mis-tŏŏk'*, *pa t* of **mistake.**

mistral *mis'tral* or *-träl*, *n* a strong cold dry north-east wind which blows down the Rhône valley toward the coast of southern France. [Fr., — Prov. — L. *magistrālis*, masterful.]

mistranslate *mis-trans-lāt'*, *vt* and *vi* to translate incorrectly. — *n* **mistranslā'tion.** [**mis-**.]

mistreat *mis-trēt'*, *vt* to treat badly. — *n* **mistreat'ment.** [**mis-**.]

mistress *mis'tris*, *n* (*fem* of **master**) a woman employer of servants or head of a house or family; a woman (or anything personified as a woman) having power of ownership; a woman involved in an established sexual relationship with a married man, sometimes supported by him financially; a woman loved and courted by a man (*archaic*); a woman teacher, esp. in a school; a woman well skilled in anything; (with *cap*) a title corresponding to the modern form **Mrs**, once prefixed to the name of any woman or girl (*archaic* or *dialect*). [O.Fr. *maistresse* — L.L. *magistrissa*, fem. from L. *magister*, master.]

mistrial *mis-trī'əl*, *n* a trial void because of error; an inconclusive trial (*US*). [**mis-**.]

mistrust *mis-trust'*, *n* distrust. — *vt* to distrust; to suspect. — *vi* to have suspicion. — *adj* **mistrust'ful.** — *adv* **mistrust'fully.** — *n* **mistrust'fulness.** — *adv* **mistrust'ingly.** — *adj* **mistrust'less.** [**mis-**.]

misty. See **mist.**

misunderstand *mis-und-ər-stand'*, *vt* to take in a wrong sense; to fail to appreciate the true nature, motives, etc. of: — *pa t* and *pa p* **misunderstood'.** — *n* **misunderstand'ing** a mistake as to meaning; a slight disagreement. — *adj* **misunderstood'.** [**mis-**.]

misuse *mis-ūs'*, *n* improper use; application to a bad purpose. — *vt* **misuse** (*mis-ūz'*) to use for a wrong purpose or in a wrong way; to treat badly or wrongly. — *n* **misus'age** ill-usage; wrong use. — *n* **misus'er.** [**mis-**.]

MIT *abbrev* for the Massachusetts Institute of Technology.

mite[1] *mīt*, *n* a very small usu. parasitic arachnid of the large and varied Acarida order. — *adj* **miticidal** (*mī-ti-sī'dəl*). — *n* **mīt'icide** a poison or other agent that destroys mites. — *adj* **mīt'y** infested with mites. [O.E. *mīte*.]

mite[2] *mīt*, *n* a very small amount, a jot; a small child; orig. an old Flemish coin of very small value. [M.Du. *mīte* (Du. *mijt*).]

miter. See **mitre**[1,2].

Mithras *mith'ras* or **Mithra** *mith'rä*, *n* the ancient Persian god of light, whose worship became popular in the Roman Empire. — *adj* **Mithrā'ic.** — *n* **Mithrā'icism** or **Mith'raism** (*-rä-izm*). — *n* **Mith'raist.** [L. and Gr. *Mithrās* — O.Pers. *Mithra*.]

mithridate *mith'ri-dāt*, *n* an antidote to poison. — *adj* **mithridat'ic.** — *vt* **mithrid'atise** or **-ize.** — *n* **mith'ridatism** (*-dāt-izm*) immunity to a poison acquired by taking gradually increased doses of it. [After *Mithridates*, king of Pontus (reigned *c* 120–63 B.C.), who was said to have acquired immunity to poisons in this way.]

MITI or **Miti** *abbrev* for the Ministry of International Trade and Industry (Japan).

miticidal, miticide. See **mite**[1].

mitigate *mit'i-gāt*, *vt* to lessen the severity, violence or evil of; to temper; to mollify, appease. — *adj* **mit'igable.** — *adj* **mit'igant** mitigating. — *n* **mitigā'tion.** — *n* and *adj* **mit'igātive.** — *n* **mit'igātor.** — *adj* **mit'igātory.** [L. *mītigāre*, *-ātum* — *mītis*, mild.]

mitochondrion *mīt-* or *mit-ō-kon'dri-ən*, (*biol*) *n* an energy-producing body, threadlike to spherical in shape, present in cytoplasm: — *pl* **mitochon'dria.** — *adj* **mitochon'drial.** [Gr. *mitos*, thread, *chondros*, granule.]

mitogen *mīt'-* or *mit'ō-jen*, (*immun*) *n* a substance that causes cells to divide. — *adj* **mitogenet'ic** or **mitogen'ic.** [Gr. *mitos*, fibre, *gennaein*, to engender.]

mitosis *mī-* or *mi-tō'sis*, (*biol*) *n* an elaborate process of cell-division involving the arrangement of protoplasmic fibres in definite figures: — *pl* **mitō'ses** (*-sēz*). — *adj* **mitotic** (*-tot'ik*). — *adv* **mitot'ically.** [Gr. *mitos*, fibre.]

mitre[1] or in U.S. **miter** *mī'tər*, *n* a high headdress, split deeply from the top, worn by archbishops and bishops, and by some abbots; an eastern hat or turban. — *adj* **mī'tral** of or like a mitre; of the mitral valve. — *adj* **mit'riform** (*mīt'* or *mit'*) mitre-shaped. — **mitral** (or in U.S. **miter**) **valve** a mitre-shaped valve of the heart. [Fr., — Gr. *mitrā*, fillet.]

mitre[2] or in U.S. **miter** *mī'tər*, *n* a joint (also **mi'tre-joint**) in which each piece is cut at an angle of 45° to its side, giving a right angle between the pieces; sometimes applied to any joint where the plane of junction bisects the angle; an angle of 45°; a gusset, a tapered insertion. — *vt* to join with a mitre; to turn a corner in, by cutting out a triangular piece and joining (*needlework*). [Prob. same as **mitre**[1].]

mitt *mit*, *n* a mitten; a hand (*slang*); a padded leather glove worn in baseball. [Abbrev. of **mitten.**]

mitten *mit'n*, *n* a kind of glove, without a separate cover for each finger; a glove for the hand and wrist, but not the fingers. [Fr. *mitaine*.]

mittimus *mit'i-məs*, (*law*) *n* a warrant granted for sending to prison a person charged with a crime. [L., we send — *mittĕre*, to send.]

mity. See **mite**[1].

mix *miks*, *vt* to combine so that the parts of one thing, or the things of one sort, are diffused among those of another; to prepare or compound in such a way; to blend; to mingle; to join, combine; to combine in one film (*cinematography*); to combine and adjust (separate sound elements) for one recording (*mus*, *broadcasting*, etc.); to interbreed, cross. — *vi* to become, or to be capable of becoming, mixed; to be joined or combined; to associate. — *n* a mixing, mingling; a mixture, esp. a standard mixture; a formula giving constituents and proportions; a jumble, a mess. — *adj* **mix'able.** — *adj* **mixed** (*mikst*) mingled; of or for both sexes; miscellaneous; confused; not select; combining characters of two or more kinds. — *adv* **mix'edly** (or *mikst'li*). — *n* **mix'edness** (or *mikst'*). — *n* **mix'er** a person who mixes; something by which or in which things are mixed; a person who is easily sociable in all sorts of company (*colloq*); a soft drink for adding to an alcoholic one; a troublemaker (*slang*); a device by means of which two or more input signals are combined to give a single output signal (*electronics*). — *n* **mix'ture** (*-chər*) an act of mixing; a state of being mixed; the product of mixing; a product of mixing in which the ingredients retain their properties — distinguished from *compound* (*chem*); a mixture of petrol vapour and air (*autos*). — *adj* **mixed-abil'ity** (of classes, etc.) accommodating members who differ in (esp. academic) ability. — **mixed bag** any assortment of diverse people, things, characteristics, etc.; **mixed blessing** something which has both advantages and disadvantages; **mixed crystal** a crystal formed from two or more distinct compounds; **mixed doubles** a type of tennis match with a male and a female player as partners on each side; **mixed economy** a national economy of which parts are state-owned and other parts privately-owned; **mixed farming** farming of both crops and livestock; **mixed foursome** a golf match with a male and female player as partners on each side; **mixed language** one which contains elements (e.g. vocabulary, syntax) from two or more separate languages; **mixed marriage** one between persons of different religions or races. — *adj* **mixed-mē'dia** (of a work in the arts) combining traditional forms, e.g. acting, dance, painting, and electronic media, e.g. tape recording. — **mixed metaphor** see under **metaphor; mixed number** one consisting of an integer and a fraction, e.g. $2\frac{1}{2}$. — *adj* **mixed'-up** socially confused, bewildered and badly-adjusted. — **mixing valve** one which mixes hot and cold water (as in a **mixer tap**); **mix'-up** confusion; a confused jumble. — **mix it** (*slang*) to fight; to cause trouble. [L. *miscēre*, *mixtus*, to mix.]

miz or **mizz** *miz*, (*colloq*) *n* and *adj* short for **misery** or **miserable.**

mizzen or **mizen** *miz'n*, *n* in a three-masted vessel, the hindmost of the fore-and-aft sails. — *adj* belonging to the mizzen; nearest the stern. — **mizz'en-course; mizz'en-mast; mizz'en-sail.** [Fr. *misaine*, foresail, foremast — It. *mezzana*, mizzen-sail — L. *mediānus*, middle.]

mizzle[1] *miz'l*, *vi* to rain in small drops. — *n* fine rain. — *n* **mizz'ling.** — *adj* **mizz'ly.** [Cf. L.Ger. *miseln*, mist.]

mizzle[2] *miz'l*, (*slang*) *vi* to decamp.

MK *abbrev* for mark (of cars).

Mk *abbrev* for: Mark (German currency); markka (Finnish currency).

MKS or **mks** *abbrev* for metre-kilogram-second (unit or system). — **MKSA** *abbrev* for metre-kilogram-second-ampere (unit or system).

ml. *abbrev* for millilitre(s).

MLA *abbrev* for: Member of the Legislative Assembly; Modern Language Association (U.S.).

MLC *abbrev* for Member of the Legislative Council.

MLD *abbrev* for: mean lethal dose (*radiol*); minimum lethal dose.

MLF *abbrev* for multilateral (nuclear) force.

MLitt. *abbrev* for *Magister Litterarum* (L.), Master of Letters, or of Literature.

Mlle *abbrev* for *Mademoiselle* (Fr.), Miss: — *pl* **Mlles** Mesdemoiselles.

MLR *abbrev* for minimum lending rate.

MLRS *abbrev* for multiple launch rocket system.

MLSO *abbrev* for Medical Laboratory Scientific Officer.

MM *abbrev* for: *Messieurs* (Fr.), Gentlemen, Sirs; Military Medal.

mm. *abbrev* for millimetre(s).

MMC *abbrev* for Monopolies and Mergers Commission.

Mme *abbrev* for *Madame* (Fr.), Mrs: — *pl* **Mmes** Mesdames.

mmf *abbrev* for magnetomotive force.

MMR *abbrev* for measles, mumps and rubella (vaccine).

MN *abbrev* for: Merchant Navy; Minnesota (U.S. state).

Mn (*chem*) *symbol* for manganese.

MND *abbrev* for motor neurone disease.

mneme *nē'mē*, (*psychol*) *n* a memorylike capacity of living matter for after-effect of stimulation of the individual or an ancestor. — *adj* **mnē'mic** pertaining to the mneme. — *n* **mne'mon** a hypothetical unit of memory. — *n* **mnemonic** (*ni-mon'ik*) a device, e.g. verse, to help memory; (in *pl*, treated as *sing*) the art of assisting memory. — *adj* pertaining to the mneme. — *adj* **mnemon'ical.** — *n* **mnē'monist** a teacher or practitioner of mnemonics; someone from whose memory nothing is erased. [Gr. *mnēmē*, memory, *mnēmōn*, mindful, *Mnēmosynē*, Mnemosyne, the Greek goddess of memory.]

MO *abbrev* for: Medical Officer; Missouri (U.S. state; also **Mo.**); modus operandi; money order.

Mo (*chem*) *symbol* for molybdenum.

mo *n*. See **moment.**

mo. *abbrev* for month.

-mo *-mō*, *sfx* the final syllable of certain Latin ordinal numbers, used in composition with English cardinal numbers to denote the number of leaves in a gathering of a book; see **twelvemo, sixteenmo** under **twelve, sixteen.**

moa *mō'ə*, *n* a gigantic extinct bird of New Zealand. [Maori.]

moan *mōn*, *n* a complaint; a grumble (*colloq*); a low murmur of pain; a sound like a murmur of pain; a lament. — *vt* to bemoan, lament; to utter with moans. — *vi* to make or utter a moan; to grumble (*colloq*). — *n* **moan'er.** — *adj* **moan'ful.** — *adv* **moan'fully.** — **moaning minnie** an air-raid siren (*war slang*); a person given to complaining (*colloq*). [Unrecorded O.E. *mān* (noun) answering to the verb *mǣnan*.]

moat *mōt*, *n* a deep trench round a castle or fortified place, sometimes filled with water. — *vt* to surround with a moat. — *adj* **moat'ed.** [O.Fr. *mote*, mound.]

mob *mob*, *n* the rabble; a disorderly crowd; a riotous gathering; a gang; a large herd or flock (*Austr* and *NZ*). — *adj* of or relating to the mob or a mob. — *vt* to attack in a disorderly crowd; to crowd around agitatedly, curiously, excitedly, or attentively; to drive by mob action. — *vt* and *vi* to form into a mob: — *pr p* **mobb'ing**; *pa t* and *pa p* **mobbed.** — *adj* **mobbed** (*colloq*) densely crowded. — *adj* **mobb'ish.** — *n* **moboc'racy** (*slang*) rule or ascendency exercised by the mob. — *n* **mob'ocrat.** — *adj* **mobocrat'ic.** — *n* **mob'ster** (*US*) a gangster. — **the mob** or **the Mob** (*US slang*) the Mafia; organised crime in general. [L. *mōbile* (*vulgus*), fickle (multitude); *movere*, to move.]

mob-cap *mob'-kap*, (*hist*) *n* a woman's indoor morning cap with puffy crown, a broad band, and frills. [Obs. *mob*, a loose-living woman, and **cap.**]

mobile *mō'bīl*, *-bēl* or *-bil*, *adj* movable; able to move about; easily, speedily moved; not fixed; changing rapidly; (of a liquid) characterised by great fluidity. — *n* a moving or movable body or part; an artistic structure, orig. consisting of dangling forms, now sometimes having a base, in which movement is caused by air currents; short for mobile police, library, etc. — *n* **mobilisation** or **-z-** (*mō-* or *mo-bil-i-zā'shən* or *-ī-*). — *vt* **mō'bilise** or **-ize** to make movable, mobile or readily available; to put in readiness for service in war; to call (e.g. troops) into active service. — *vi* to make armed forces ready for war; to undergo mobilisation. — *n* **mo'biliser** or **-z-**. — *n* **mobility** (*mō-bil'i-ti*) quality or power of being mobile; freedom or ease of movement. — **mobile home** a caravan or other vehicle with sleeping, cooking, etc. facilities; **mobile shop, library,** etc. one set up in a motor vehicle, driven to customers' homes or neighbourhoods; **mobility allowance** money paid by the government to disabled people to compensate for their travel costs. [Fr., — L. *mōbilis* — *movēre*, to move.]

Möbius strip *mœ'bē-əs strip*, (*math*) *n* the one-sided surface formed by joining together the two ends of a long rectangular strip, one end being twisted through 180 degrees before the join is made. [August F. *Möbius* (1790–1868), German mathematician.]

mobocracy, mobster, etc. See under **mob**.

moccasin *mok'ə-sin*, *n* a North American Indian's shoe of deerskin or other soft leather; a shoe or slipper more or less resembling it; a venomous North American pit viper. — **mocc'asin-flower** a lady's-slipper orchid. [Am. Ind.]

mocha *mok'ə* or *mō'kə*, *n* a fine coffee; a coffee, or coffee and chocolate, flavour; a deep brown colour; a soft leather used for gloves, made from sheepskin or goatskin. [*Mocha*, on the Red Sea.]

mock *mok*, *vt* to deride; to scoff at derisively; to make fun of; to mimic in ridicule; to simulate; to defy, tantalise, disappoint, deceive, disparage, or make a fool of, as if in mockery (*fig*). — *vi* to jeer; to scoff; to speak or behave insincerely or disparagingly. — *n* a mockery; a thing mocked; (esp. in *pl*) a practice examination taken at school as a preparation for a public examination. — *adj* sham; false; resembling, or accepted as a substitute for, the true or real. — *adj* **mock'able**. — *n* **mock'er**. — *n* **mock'ery** derision; ridicule; a subject of ridicule; imitation, esp. a contemptible or insulting imitation; insulting or ludicrous futility. — *n* and *adj* **mock'ing**. — *adv* **mock'ingly**. — *adj* **mock-hero'ic** imitating the heroic style exaggeratedly. — *n* a mock-heroic composition; (in *pl*) mock-heroic verses; (in *pl*) sham heroic utterances or behaviour. — *adj* **mock-hero'ical**. — *adv* **mock-hero'ically**. — **mock'ingbird** an American bird (*Mimus*) of the thrush family, that mimics other birds' songs and other sounds; **mock moon** a paraselene, or bright spot in the moon's halo, 22° to right or left of the moon, due to refraction from ice crystals floating vertically; **mock-or'ange** a tall shrub (*Philadelphus*, commonly called syringa) of the saxifrage family with strong-scented flowers; **mock sun** a spot in the sun's halo, a parhelion; **mock'-up** a full-size dummy model; a rough layout of a printed text, package, etc. showing size, colour, etc. — Also *adj*. — **mock turtle soup** an imitation of turtle soup, made of calf's head or veal; **put the mockers on** (*slang*) to put an end to, put paid to. [O.Fr. *mocquer*.]

MOD *abbrev* for Ministry of Defence.

Mod *mod*, *n* a member of a teenage faction in (orig.) the 1960s distinguished by special dress (typically neat), etc., from their rivals, the Rockers (see under **rock²**).

mod *mod* or *mōd*, *n* a Highland Gaelic literary and musical festival. [Gael. *mòd* — O.N. *mōt*; cf. **moot**.]

mod. *abbrev* for: moderate; modern.

mod. con. *mod kon*, *abbrev* for *mod*ern *con*venience, any item of up-to-date plumbing, heating, etc.

mode *mōd*, *n* way or manner of acting, doing, happening or existing; kind; form; state of being; a method of operation as provided by the software (*comput*); modality; fashion; that which is fashionable; style; a mood (*gram*); character as necessary, contingent, possible or impossible (*logic*); a mood (*logic*); the value of greatest frequency (*statistics*); the method of dividing the octave according to the position of its steps and half-steps (*mus*); (in old music) the method of time-division of notes. — *adj* **modal** (*mōd'l*) relating to mode. — *n* **modality** (*mōd-al'i-ti*) the fact or condition of being modal; mode; method, terms, style; any of the primary methods of sensation; classification of propositions as to whether true, false, necessary, possible or impossible (*logic*). — *adv* **mod'ally**. — *adj* **modish** (*mōd'ish*) fashionable. — *adv* **mod'ishly**. — *n* **mod'ishness**. — *n* **modiste** (*mō-dēst*; Fr.) a professedly fashionable dressmaker or milliner. [L. *modus*; partly through Fr. *mode*.]

model *mod'l*, *n* a preliminary solid representation, generally small, or in mouldable material, to be followed in construction; something to be copied; a pattern; an imitation of something on a smaller scale; a person or thing closely resembling another; a person who poses for an artist, photographer, etc.; a person who exhibits clothes, etc. for a shop, company, designer, etc. by wearing them; a pattern of excellence; an article of standard design or a copy of one; structural type. — *adj* of the nature of a model; set up for imitation; completely suitable for imitation, exemplary. — *vt* to form after a model; to shape; to make a model or copy of; to form in some mouldable material; (of a mannequin) to display (a garment) by wearing it. — *vi* to practise modelling: — *pr p* **mod'elling** (or in U.S. **mod'elling**); *pa t* and *pa p* **mod'elled** (or in U.S. **mod'eled**). — *n* **mod'eller** (or in U.S. **mod'eler**). — *n* **mod'elling** the act or art of making a model of something, a branch of sculpture; rendering of solid form; working as a model. [O.Fr. *modelle* — It. *modello*, dimin. of *modo* — L. *modus*, a measure.]

modem *mō'dəm* or *-dem*, (*comput*) *n* an electronic device which converts digital data from a computer into analogue signals that are transmissible to another computer over a telephone system. [*mod*ulator, *dem*odulator.]

moderate *mod'ə-rāt*, *vt* to keep within measure or bounds; to regulate; to reduce in intensity; to make temperate or reasonable; to pacify; to preside as moderator over or at. — *vi* to become less violent or intense; to preside or act as a moderator. — *adj* (*-rit*) kept within measure or bounds; not excessive or extreme; temperate; of middle rate, average. — *n* someone whose views are far from extreme. — *adv* **mod'erately**. — *n* **mod'erateness**. — *n* **moderā'tion** the act of moderating; the state of being moderated or moderate; freedom from excess; self-restraint; the process of slowing down neutrons in an atomic pile; (in *pl*, usu. with *cap*) the first public examination for B.A. at Oxford (*colloq* **Mods** or **mods**). — *n* **mod'eratism** moderate opinions in religion or politics. — *n* **mod'erātor** a person who, or that which, moderates; a president, esp. in Presbyterian church courts; an officer at Oxford and Cambridge who superintended degree examinations; a moderations examiner at Oxford; a person appointed to standardise the marking, etc., of school public examinations; the material in which neutrons are slowed down in an atomic pile. — *n* **mod'erātorship**. [L. *moderārī*, *-ātus* — *modus*, a measure.]

moderato *mod-ə-rä'tō*, (*mus*) *adj* and *adv* at a moderate speed. — *n* a movement or passage to be played at this speed. [It.]

modern *mod'ərn*, *adj* of or characteristic of present or recent time; not ancient or mediaeval; (in education) mainly or wholly concerned with subjects other than

Greek and Latin; (with *cap*) (of a language) of or near the form now spoken and written, distinguished from *Old* and *Middle*. — *n* a person living in modern times, esp. distinguished from the ancient Greeks and Romans; a modernist. — *n* **modernīsā'tion** or **-z-**. — *vt* **mod'ernise** or **-ize** to adapt to the present time, conditions, needs, language or spelling; to make modern. — *vi* to adopt modern ways. — *n* **mod'erniser** or **-z-**. — *n* **mod'ernism** modern usage, expression or trait; modern spirit or character; a tendency to adjust Christian dogma to the results of science and criticism. — *n* **mod'ernist** an admirer of modern ideas, ways, literature, studies, etc.; someone who favours modernism. — *adj* **mod'ernist** or **modernis'tic**. — *n* **modern'ity**. — *adv* **mod'ernly**. — *n* **mod'ernness**. — **modern dance** a style of dance more expressive and less stylised than classical ballet; **modern jazz** a style of jazz which evolved in the early 1940s, characterised by greater rhythmic and harmonic complexity than previously. [L.L. *modernus* — *modo*, just now, orig. abl. of *modus*.]

modest *mod'ist*, *adj* unobtrusive; unpretentious; unassuming; diffident; restrained by a sense of propriety; decent; chaste; pure and delicate; not excessive or extreme; moderate. — *adv* **mod'estly**. — *n* **mod'esty** the quality or fact of being modest; a slight covering for a low neck. [L. *modestus* — *modus*, a measure.]

modi. See **modus**.

modicum *mod'i-kəm*, *n* a small quantity: — *pl* **mod'icums**. [L. neut. of *modicus*, moderate — *modus*.]

modify *mod'i-fī*, *vt* to moderate; to change the form or quality of; to alter slightly; to vary; to differentiate; (of a word or phrase) to limit or qualify the sense of (*gram*): — *pr p* **mod'ifying**; *pa t* and *pa p* **mod'ified**. — *adj* **mod'ifiable**. — *n* **modification** (*-fi-kā'shən*) the act of modifying or state of being modified; the result of alteration or change; changed shape or condition. — *adj* **mod'ificātive** or **mod'ificātory** tending to modify; causing change of form or condition. — *adj* **mod'ified** (*-fīd*) altered by modification. — *n* **mod'ifier** (*-fī-ər*). [Fr. *modifier* — L. *modificāre*, *-ātum* — *modus*, a measure, *facĕre*, to make.]

modish, etc. **modiste**. See **mode**.

Mods, mods. See under **moderate**.

modulate *mod'ū-lāt*, *vt* to regulate, adjust; to inflect; to soften; to vary the pitch or frequency of; to impress characteristics of signal wave on (carrier wave) (*radio*); to vary velocity of electrons in electron beam. — *vi* to pass from one state to another; to pass from one key into another using a logical progression of chords that links the two keys (*mus*). — *n* **modulabil'ity** the capability of being modulated. — *adj* **mod'ular** of or pertaining to mode or modulation, or to a module. — *adj* **mod'ularised** or **-ized** consisting of modules; produced in the form of modules; divided into modules. — *n* **modular'ity**. — *n* **modulā'tion**. — *n* **mod'ulātor** someone who, or that which, modulates; any device for effecting modulation (*radio*); a chart used in the tonic sol-fa notation on which modulations are shown (*mus*). [L. *modulārī*, *-ātus*, to regulate.]

module *mod'ūl*, *n* a small measure or quantity; a unit of size, used in standardised planning of buildings and design of components; a self-contained unit forming part of a spacecraft or other structure; a standard unit or part of machinery, etc. in a system; a set course forming a unit in an educational scheme; an assembly within a geometrical framework of electronic units functioning as a system; a component part of a program, complete in itself and with its own function (*comput*); a measure, often the semi-diameter of a column, for regulating proportions of other parts (*archit*). [L. *modulus*, a small measure.]

modulus *mod'ū-ləs*, *n* a constant multiplier or coefficient (*math*); a quantity used as a divisor to produce classes of quantities, each class distinguished by its members yielding the same remainders (*math*); the positive square root of the sum of the squares of the real and imaginary parts of a complex number (*math*); a quantity expressing the relation between a force and the effect produced: — *pl* **moduli** (*mod'ū-lī*). [L. *modulus*, dimin. of *modus*, a measure.]

modus *mō'dəs* or *mo'dōōs*, *n* manner, mode; the way in which anything works: — *pl* **mō'dī**. — **modus operandi** (*op-ər-an'dī* or *-an'dē*) mode of operation, way of working; **modus vivendi** (*vi-ven'dī* or *-dē*) way of life or living; an arrangement or compromise by means of which those who differ may get on together for a time. [L. *mŏdus*, manner.]

Mogadon® *mog'ə-don*, *n* proprietary name for nitrazepam, a drug used to treat insomnia.

moggy, moggie *mog'i* or **mog** *mog*, (*slang*) *n* a cat, esp. an ordinary mongrel cat. [Perh. *Maggie*.]

mogul[1] *mō'gul*, *n* (without *cap*) an influential person, a magnate; (with *cap*) a Mongol or Mongolian, esp. one of the followers of Baber, the conqueror of India (1483–1530). — *adj* pertaining to the Mogul Empire, architecture, etc. [Pers. *Mughul*, properly a Mongol.]

mogul[2] *mō'gəl*, *n* a mound of hard snow forming an obstacle on a ski-slope; (in *pl*) a skiing discipline or event that involves skiing down a run which includes moguls. — *adj* **moguled** (*mō'gəld*) (of a ski-run) having moguls. [Poss. — Norw. dialect *muge*, heap.]

MOH *abbrev* for Medical Officer of Health.

mohair *mō'hār*, *n* the long, white, fine silky hair of the Angora goat; other hair as a substitute for it; cloth made of it. [Ar. *mukhayyar*; influenced by **hair**.]

Mohammedan *mō-ham'i-dən*, **Mahometan** *mə-hom'it-ən* or **Muhammadan** *mōō-ham'a-dən*, *adj* pertaining to the prophet Mohammed (formerly popularly written Mahomet) or to his religion, Islam. — *n* a follower of Mohammed, a Muslim; a person who professes Mohammedanism, Islam. — *vt* and *vi* **Mohamm'edanise** or **-ize**, etc., to convert to, or conform to, Mohammedanism, Islam. — *n* **Mohamm'edanism, Mohamm'edism**, etc., Islam, the religion of Mohammed, contained in the Koran. These terms are felt to be offensive by many Muslims, who prefer **Muslim, Islam, Islamic**, etc. [Ar. *Muhammad*, the great prophet of Arabia (*c* 570–632); lit. praised.]

Mohawk *mō'hök*, *n* an Indian of an Iroquois tribe of New York State; (often without *cap*) a skating movement consisting of a stroke on the edge of one skate followed by a stroke in the opposite direction on the same edge of the other skate. [From an Algonquian name.]

mohel *mō'(h)el*, *moi'(h)el* or *-hel'*, also Heb. *mō-hel'*, *n* an official Jewish circumciser. [Heb.]

Mohican *mō-hē'kən* or **Mahican** *mə-hē'kən*, *n* a N. American Indian of a former tribe chiefly in the upper Hudson valley; a hairstyle in which the head is shaved except for a central strip from the nape to the brow, based on a Mohican style but now esp. associated with punk fashion, in which the hair is spiked into a (usu. brightly-coloured) crest. [Algonquian.]

Mohs scale *mōz skāl'*, *n* a scale of numbers from 1 to 10 (1 representing talc, 10 representing diamond) in terms of which the relative hardness of minerals is measured. [F. *Mohs* (1773–1839), German mineralogist.]

moi *mwu*, *pers pron* me, often used *facetiously* in mock affectation, e.g. in the form of a question to express surprise at an allegation against the speaker. [Fr.]

moiety *moi'ə-ti*, *n* half; one of two parts or divisions. [O.Fr. *moité* — L. *medietās*, *-tātis*, middle point, later half — *medius*, middle.]

moire *mwär*, *n* orig. watered mohair; now watered silk or other fabric with watered appearance (also called **moire antique**). — *adj* **moiré** (*mwär'ā*) watered. — *n* a watered appearance on cloth or metal surface; sometimes for moire, the material. — **moiré effect** or **pattern** an optical effect, a shifting wavy pattern seen when two surfaces covered with regular lines are superimposed. [Fr., from Eng. **mohair**.]

moist *moist*, *adj* damp; humid; rainy; watery. — *vt* **moisten** (*mois'n*) to make moist; to wet slightly. — *adv* **moist'ly**. — *n* **moist'ness**. — *n* **moist'ure** moistness; that which makes slightly wet; liquid, esp. in small quantity. — *adj* **moist'ureless**. — *vt* **moist'urise** or **-ize** to add or restore moisture to. — *vi* to apply moisturiser. — *n* **moist'uriser** or **-z-** something which moisturises, esp. a cosmetic cream which restores moisture to the skin. [O.Fr. *moiste*, perh. — L. *mustum*, juice of grapes, new wine.]

moke *mōk*, (*slang*) *n* a donkey; a worn-out or inferior horse.

moki *mō'ki*, *n* a New Zealand sea-fish belonging either to the species *Latridopsis ciliaris* or *Chironemus spectabilis* (**red moki**). [Maori.]

mol, **molal**, etc. See **mole**[1].

molar[1] *mō'lər*, *adj* used for grinding; pertaining to a grinding tooth. — *n* a grinding tooth, or back tooth. [L. *molāris* — *mola*, a millstone — *molĕre*, to grind.]

molar[2], **molarity**. See **mole**[1].

molasses *mo-las'iz*, *nsing* a thick, usu. dark, treacle that is drained from sugar during refining. [Port. *melaço* — L.L. *mellāceum* — *mel*, *mellis*, honey.]

mold. See **mould**[1,2,3].

mole[1] *mōl*, (*chem*) *n* the amount of substance that contains as many (specified) entities (e.g. atoms, molecules, ions, photons) as there are atoms in 12 grams of carbon-12 (abbrev. **mol** *mōl*). — *adj* **mol'al** of, relating to, or containing, a mole. — *n* **molal'ity** the concentration of a solution expressed as the number of moles of dissolved substance per thousand grams of solvent. — *adj* **mol'ar** of, or relating to, a mole; per mole; per unit amount of substance. — *n* **molar'ity** the concentration of a solution expressed as the number of moles of dissolved substance per litre of solution. [Ger., — *Molekül*, molecule; both words (Ger. and Eng.) ult. from L. *mōlēs*, mass.]

mole[2] *mōl*, *n* a small spot or raised mark on the skin, often pigmented and hairy. [O.E. *māl*.]

mole[3] *mōl*, *n* a small insectivorous animal (genus *Talpa*) with very small eyes and soft fur, which burrows in the ground and casts up little heaps of loose earth; a person who works in darkness or underground; a spy who successfully infiltrates a rival organisation, esp. one who does not begin to engage in espionage until firmly established and trusted; a boring machine which makes a tunnel, e.g. for a pipeline. — **mole'cast** a molehill; **mole'-catcher** a person whose business it is to catch moles; **mole'-cricket** a burrowing insect of the cricket family; **mole'hill** a little hill or heap of earth cast up by a mole; **mole'hunt**; **mole'hunter**; **mole'rat** a name for several burrowing rodents (*Spalax*, *Bathyergus*, etc.); **mole'skin** the skin or fur of a mole; a heavy kind of fustian fabric used to make working clothes, having a smooth face and a twill back; (in *pl*) clothes, esp. trousers, made of this. — **make a mountain out of a molehill** to magnify, over-dramatise, etc. a trifling matter. [M.E. *molle*, *mulle*.]

mole[4] *mōl*, *n* a massive breakwater, causeway or masonry pier. [Fr. *môle* — L. *mōlēs*, mass.]

mole[5] *mō'li*, *n* in Mexican cooking, a sauce made mainly with chilli and chocolate, served with meat dishes. [Am. Sp.; see **guacamole**.]

molecule *mol'i-kūl*, *n* the smallest particle of any substance that retains the properties of that substance, usu. consisting of a limited group of atoms; a gram-molecule. — *adj* **molecular** (*mol-ek'ū-lər*). — *n* **molecularity** (*mol-ek-ū-lar'i-ti*). — *adv* **molec'ularly**. — **molecular biology** study of the molecules of the substances involved in the processes of life; **molecular formula** a formula showing the number of atoms of each element in a molecule, e.g. benzene, C_6H_6; **molecular genetics** (*biol*) the study and manipulation of the molecular basis of heredity; **molecular weight** a former term for relative molecular mass (q.v.). [Fr. *molécule*, — L. *mōlēs*, mass.]

molehill ... to ... **moleskin**. See under **mole**[3].

molest *mə-* or *mō-lest'*, *vt* to interfere with in a troublesome or hostile way; to annoy or vex. — *n* annoyance. — *n* **molestā'tion** (*mo-* or *mō-*). — *n* **molest'er**. [Fr. *molester* — L. *molestāre* — *molestus*, troublesome.]

moline *mō'līn* or *mō-līn'*, (*heraldry*) *adj* like the rind of a millstone — applied to a cross with each arm ending in two outward curving branches. — *n* a moline cross. [L. *mola*, a mill.]

moll *mol*, *n* a gangster's girlfriend; a prostitute. [*Moll*, an old familiar form of *Mary*.]

mollify *mol'i-fī*, *vt* to soften; to assuage; to cause to abate; to appease. — *vi* to become soft; to relax in severity or opposition: — *pr p* **moll'ifying**; *pa t* and *pa p* **moll'ified**. — *n* **mollification** (*-fi-kā'shən*). — *n* **moll'ifier**. [Fr. *mollifier* — L. *mollificāre* — *mollis*, soft, *facĕre*, to make.]

mollusc or in U.S. also **mollusk** *mol'əsk*, *n* an animal of the large phylum of invertebrates **Mollusca** (*-us'kə*), having no segments or limbs, and usu. a mantle or fold of skin that secretes a shell (e.g. lamellibranchs, gasteropods, cephalopods, and some smaller groups). — *adj* **mollus'can** or **mollus'cous** of or belonging to the Mollusca; like a mollusc. [L. *molluscus*, softish — *mollis*, soft.]

mollycoddle *mol'i-kod-l*, *vt* to coddle. — *n* an effeminate fellow. [*Molly*, dimin. of the personal name *Mary*, and **coddle**.]

Moloch *mō'lok*, *n* a Semitic god to whom children were sacrificed; (without *cap*) any cause to which dreadful sacrifice is made; (without *cap*) a spiny Australian lizard. — *vt* **mol'ochise** or **-ize** to sacrifice (as to Moloch). [Gr. and L. — Heb. *Mōlek*.]

Molotov cocktail *mol'ə-tof kok'tāl*, *n* a crude form of hand grenade consisting of a bottle containing inflammable liquid, and a wick to be ignited just before the missile is thrown, a petrol bomb. [V.M. *Molotov* (1890–1986), Russian statesman.]

molt. See **moult**.

molten *mōl'tən*, *adj* melted; made of melted metal. — *adv* **mōlt'enly**. [Past p. of **melt**.]

molto *mol'tō*, (*mus*) *adv* very; much. [It.]

mol. wt. *abbrev* for molecular weight.

molybdenum *mol-ib'din-əm*, also *mol-ib-dē'nəm*, *n* a silvery-white metallic element (symbol **Mo**; atomic no. 42). — *n* **molyb'date** a salt of molybdic acid. — *n* **molybdēn'ite** (or *-ib'dən-īt*) a lustrous lead-grey crystalline mineral, molybdenum disulphide. — *adj* **molyb'dic**. — *n* **molybdō'sis** lead-poisoning. — *adj* **molyb'dous**. — **molybdic acid** H_2MoO_4. [Latinised neut. — Gr. *molybdaina*, a lump of lead, a leadlike substance — *molybdos*, lead.]

mom *mom*, (*NAm colloq*) *n* mother. — Also **momm'a** and **momm'y**. [See **mamma**[1].]

moment *mō'mənt*, *n* a point of time; a time so short that it may be considered as a point; a very short time (*slang* abbrev. **mo**); a second; a precise instant; the present, or the right, instant; a stage or turning-point; an element or factor; a measure of turning effect — the *moment of a force* about a point is the product of the force and the perpendicular distance of the point from its line of action. — *adv* **mo'mentarily** for a moment; at any moment (*NAm*). — *n* **mo'mentariness**. — *adj* **mo'mentary** lasting for a moment; short-lived. — *adv* **mo'mently** every moment; for a moment. — *adj* occurring every moment; of a moment. — *adj* **momentous** (*-ment'*) of great consequence. — *adv* **moment'ously.** — *n* **moment'ousness.** — **moment of truth** a moment when, suddenly and dramatically, one is face to face with stark reality — often a testing moment; orig. the climax of the bullfight. [L. *mōmentum*, for *movimentum* — *movēre*, *mōtum*, to move.]

momentum *mō-men'təm*, *n* the quantity of motion in a body measured by the product of mass and velocity; force of motion gained in movement, impetus (*colloq*): — *pl* **moment'a.** [Ety. as for **moment.**]

MOMI *abbrev* for Museum of the Moving Image (London).

momma, mommy. See **mom.**

Mon. *abbrev* for: Monday; Monmouthshire (a former county, now mostly incorporated into modern Gwent).

mon-. See **mono-.**

monacid *mon-as'id* or **monoacid** *mon-ō-as'id*, *adj* having one replaceable hydrogen atom; capable of replacing one hydrogen atom of an acid. [**mono-.**]

monad *mon'ad*, *n* an ultimate unit of being, material and psychical; the number one, a unit (*hist*); a hypothetical primitive living organism or unit of organic life (*biol*); a flagellated unicellular organism, esp. of the genus *Monas*; a univalent element, atom or radical. — *adj* **monad'ic** or **monad'ical.** — *adj* **monad'iform** like a monad. [Gr. *monas*, *-ados*, a unit — *monos*, single, alone.]

monadelphous *mon-ə-del'fəs*, (*bot*) *adj* (of stamens) united by the filaments in one bundle; (of a flower or plant) having all the stamens so united. [Gr. *monos*, single, alone, *adelphos*, brother.]

monadic, monadical, monadiform. See **monad.**

monandrous *mon-an'drəs*, *adj* having or allowing one husband or male mate (at a time); having one stamen or one antheridium (*bot*). — *n* **monan'dry** the condition or practice of being monandrous. [Gr. *monos*, single, alone, *anēr*, *andros*, a man, male.]

monarch *mon'ərk*, *n* a sole hereditary head of a state, whether titular or ruling; a large butterfly (*Danaus plexippus*) with orange and black wings. — *adj* **monarchal** (*-ärk'əl*), **monarch'ial, monarch'ic** or **monarch'ical.** — *vt* **mon'archise** or **-ize** to rule over as a monarch; to convert into a monarchy. — *n* **mon'archism** the principles of monarchy; love of monarchy. — *n* **mon'archist** an advocate of monarchy; a believer in monarchy. — Also *adj*. — *adj* **monarchist'ic.** — *n* **mon'archy** a kind of government of which there is a monarch; a state with such a government; the territory of a monarch. [Gr. *monarchēs* — *monos*, single, alone, *archein*, to rule.]

monarda *mən-är'də*, *n* a plant of the *Monarda* genus of North American aromatic herbs of the mint (*Labiatae*) family. [N. *Monardes* (d. 1588), Spanish botanist.]

monastery *mon'əs-tər-i* or *-tri*, *n* a house for a community of monks, or (sometimes) nuns. — *adj* **monastē'rial, monastic** (*-as'tik*) or **monas'tical** pertaining to monasteries, monks, or nuns; recluse; solitary. — *n* **monas'tic** a monk. — *adv* **monas'tically.** — *n* **monas'ticism** (*-sizm*) the corporate monastic life or system of living. [Late Gr. *monastērion* — *monastēs*, a monk — *monos*, single, alone.]

monatomic *mon-ə-tom'ik*, (*chem*) *adj* consisting of one atom; having one replaceable atom or group; univalent. [**mono-.**]

monaural *mon-ö'rəl*, *adj* having or using only one ear; pertaining to one ear; (of a gramophone record, etc.) giving the effect of sound from a single direction — not stereophonic. [**mono-.**]

monazite *mon'əz-īt*, (*mineralogy*) *n* a phosphate of cerium, lanthanum, neodymium, praseodymium, and usu. thorium, a source of thorium. [Gr. *monazein*, to be solitary — on account of its rarity.]

mondain *mɔ̃-dɛ̃*, *fem* **mondaine** *mɔ̃-den*, *adj* worldly, fashionable. — *n* a man, or woman, living in fashionable society. [Fr., — L. *mundānus* — *mundus*, world.]

Monday *mun'di* or *-dā*, *n* the second day of the week. — **Monday Club** a right-wing group of Conservatives; **Monday morning feeling** the feeling of tiredness and disinclination to work felt at the prospect, after the weekend, of another week's work ahead. [O.E. *mōnandæg*, *mōnan*, genitive of *mōna*, moon, *dæg*, day.]

mondial *mon'di-əl*, *adj* of the whole world, worldwide. [Fr. — L. *mundus*, world.]

monecious. Same as **monoecious.**

Monel metal® *mō-nel' met'l*, *n* a nickel-base alloy with high strength and resistance to corrosion.

monetary *mon'* or *mun'i-tər-i*, *adj* of or relating to money; consisting of money. — *n* **mon'etarism.** — *n* **mon'etarist** a person who advocates an economic policy based chiefly on the control of a country's money supply. — *n* **monetīsā'tion** or **-z-.** — *vt* **mon'etise** or **-ize** to give the character of money to, to coin as money. — **monetary unit** the principal unit of currency of a state. [L. *monēta* (see ety. for **money**).]

money *mun'i*, *n* coin; pieces of stamped metal used in commerce; any currency used in the same way; wealth: — *pl* **mon'eys** or **mon'ies** sums of money; money. — *adj* **mon'eyed** or **mon'ied** having money; rich in money; consisting in money. — *adj* **mon'eyless.** — **money'-bag** a bag for or of money; **mon'eybags** (*colloq*) a rich person; **money belt** a belt with a pocket in it for holding money; **money'-box** a box for collecting or saving money in, usu. with a slit for insertion; **mon'ey-broker** a person who carries out transactions in money for others; **mon'ey-changer** a person who exchanges one currency for another; **mon'ey-grubber** a sordid accumulator of wealth. — *n* and *adj* **mon'ey-grubb'ing.** — **mon'eylender** a professional lender of money at interest; **mon'eylending; mon'ey-maker** a person who acquires wealth; anything that brings profit; a person who earns money; **mon'ey-making** the act of gaining wealth. — *adj* lucrative, profitable. — **mon'ey-market** (the dealers in) the market for short-term loans for business, etc.; **mon'ey-order** an order for money deposited at one post-office, and payable at another; **mon'ey-spider** a very small spider supposed to bring luck in money; **mon'ey-spinner** anything that brings much money; a successful speculator; **mon'ey's-worth** something as good as money; full value. — **for my money** if I were to choose, express an opinion, etc.; **hard money** coin; **in the money** among the prize-winners (*racing*, etc.); well-off; **make money** to acquire wealth; to make a profit; **money down** money paid on the spot; **money for jam, old rope,** etc., money obtained without effort; **money of account** a monetary unit (not represented by current coins) used in keeping accounts; **money talks** the wealthy have much influence; **on the money** (*US slang*) spot-on, exact, just right; **pots of money** a large amount of money; **put money into** to invest in; **put money on** to place a bet on; **put one's money where one's mouth is** to support one's stated opinion by betting money; to give practical (esp. financial) rather than merely hypothetical support; **ready money** money paid for a thing at the time at which it is bought; money ready for immediate payment. [O.Fr. *moneie* — L. *monēta*, money, a mint, *Monēta* (the reminder) being a surname of Juno, in whose temple at Rome money was coined.]

monger *mung'gər*, *n* (chiefly as a *combining form*) a dealer (except in a few instances, such as *ironmonger*), someone who trafficks in a petty, or discreditable way, or in unpleasant subjects. — *n* **mong'ering** or **mong'ery**. [O.E. *mangere* — L. *mangō*, *-ōnis*, a furbisher, slave-dealer — Gr. *manganeuein*, to use trickery.]

Mongol *mong'gol*, *n* a member of Genghis Khan's clan, or of the various populations under him (*hist*); one of the people of Mongolia; their language; a member of a broad-headed, yellow-skinned, straight-haired, small-nosed human race; (esp. without *cap*) the old term for a person affected by Down's syndrome (no longer preferred, by some considered *offensive*). — *adj* of the Mongols, Mongolia, or Mongolian. — *adj* **Mongolian** (*mong-gō'li-ən*) of Mongolia, the Mongols, or their language. — *n* the language of Mongolia. — *adj* **Mongolic** (*-gol'ik*) Mongolian; of Mongolian type. — *n* **Mong'olism** (often without *cap*) an old term for Down's syndrome. — *adj* **Mong'oloid** of Mongolian race or type. — *n* a person of Mongolian type; (often without *cap*) an old term for a person affected by Down's syndrome (also *adj*; no longer preferred). [Said to be from Mongol *mong*, brave.]

mongoose *mong'gōōs* or *mung'gōōs*, *n* an Indian animal of the civet family, which preys on snakes and rats; any other species of the genus, including the ichneumon; a Madagascan lemur: — *pl* **mon'gooses**. [Marathi *mangūs*.]

mongrel *mung'grəl*, *n* an animal, esp. a dog, of a mixed breed; a person, thing or word of mixed or indefinite origin or nature; that which is neither one thing nor another. — *adj* mixed in breed; ill-defined. — *vt* **mong'relise** or **-ize**. — *n* **mong'relism**. — *adj* **mong'relly**. [Prob. from root of O.E. *mengan*, to mix.]

monicker or **moniker** *mon'i-kər*, (*slang*; orig. *tramps' slang*) *n* an alias, nickname or real name.

monied, monies. See **money**.

monism *mon'izm*, *n* a philosophical theory that all being may ultimately be referred to one category; thus *idealism*, *pantheism*, *materialism* are monisms — as opp. to the dualism of matter and spirit. — *n* **mon'ist**. — *adj* **monist'ic** or **monist'ical**. [Gr. *monos*, single, alone.]

monition *mon-ish'ən*, *n* a reminding or admonishing; warning; notice. — *adj* **mon'itive** conveying admonition. — *n* **mon'itor** a senior pupil who assists in school discipline or other pupil with a special responsibility; a person employed to monitor; a genus (*Varanus*) of very large lizards of Africa, Asia and Australia (from the idea that they give warning of the presence of a crocodile); an apparatus for testing transmission in electrical communication; a video display screen, as in a television studio showing the picture being transmitted; an instrument used in a production process to keep a variable quantity within prescribed limits by transmitting a controlling signal; a detector for radioactivity; a person who admonishes: — *fem* **mon'itress**. — *vt* to act as monitor to; to check (as the body and clothing of persons working with radioactive materials) for radioactivity; to track, or to control (an aeroplane, guided missile, etc.); to watch, check, supervise. — *vi* (*radio*) to listen to foreign broadcasts in order to obtain news, code messages, etc.; to tap on to a communication circuit, usu. in order to ascertain that the transmission is that desired. — *adj* **monitorial** (*-ör'*) relating to a monitor. — *adv* **monitor'ially**. — *n* **mon'itorship**. — *adj* **mon'itory** giving admonition or warning. [L. *monēre*, *-itum*, to remind.]

monk *mungk*, *n* a man (other than a friar, but loosely often applied to a friar also) of a religious community living together under vows; (*formerly*) a hermit. — *adj* **monk'ish** (*disparagingly*) pertaining to a monk; like a monk; monastic. — **monk'fish** the angel fish (shark); any of several types of angler fish; **monk's cloth** a type of heavy cotton cloth; **monks'hood** a poisonous plant (*Aconitum*) with a large hoodlike posterior sepal. [O.E. *munuc* — L. *monachus* — Gr. *monachos* — *monos*, alone.]

monkey *mungk'i*, *n* any mammal of the Primates except man and (usu.) the anthropoid apes; an ape; a mischievous or badly-behaved child or person; the falling weight of a pile-driver; a large hammer; £500 or $500 (*slang*); an oppressive burden or habit, *specif* a drug addiction (*US slang*); a liquor-vessel or other container of various kinds: — *pl* **monk'eys**. — *vi* (often with *around*) to meddle with anything, to fool. — *vt* to mimic. — *adj* **monk'eyish**. — **monk'ey-bread** the baobab tree or its fruit; **monkey business** underhand dealings; mischievous behaviour; **monk'ey-engine** a pile-driving engine; **monk'ey-flower** a species of mimulus; **monk'ey-gland** ape's testicle, grafted experimentally on man (1920–30s) to effect rejuvenescence; **monk'ey-jacket** a short, close-fitting jacket; **monk'ey-nut** the peanut or ground-nut (*Arachis*); **monkey pod** the rain-tree; **monk'ey-puzzle** a coniferous tree, also called Chile pine (*Araucaria imbricata*), with close-set prickly leaves; **monk'ey-shine** (*US slang*) a monkeyish trick; **monk'ey-suit** (*slang*) a man's evening suit; **monk'ey-tricks** mischief, pranks; **monk'ey-wrench** a wrench with a movable jaw. — **have a monkey on one's back** (*US slang*) to be addicted to drugs; **have** or **get one's monkey up** (*slang*) to be angry; **make a monkey (out) of** to make a fool of; **not to give a monkey's** (*vulg slang*) not to care, or be interested, at all. [Perh. from M.L.G. *moneke*, connected with Sp., Port. *mono*, monkey.]

monkfish, monkshood. See under **monk**.

mono- *mon-ō-* or **mon-** *mon-*, *combining form* denoting single. [Gr. *monos*, single, alone.]

mono *mon'ō*, (*colloq*) *n* a monaural gramophone record; monaural reproduction: — *pl* **mon'os**. — Also *adj*.

monoacid. See **monacid.**

monoamine *mon-ō-am'īn* or *-ēn*, *n* an amine containing only one amino-group. [**mono-**.]

monobasic *mon-ō-bā'sik*, (*chem*) *adj* capable of reacting with one equivalent of an acid; (of an acid) having one replaceable hydrogen atom. [**mono-**.]

monocarpellary *mon-ō-kär'pəl-ə-ri* or *-pel'ə-ri*, (*bot*) *adj* of or with only one carpel. [**mono-**.]

monocarpic *mon-ō-kär'pik*, (*bot*) *adj* fruiting once only. — *n* **mon'ocarp** a monocarpic plant. — *adj* **monocar'pous** monocarpic; having only one ovary; producing one fruit. [Gr. *monos*, single, alone, *karpos*, fruit.]

monochlamydeous *mon-ō-klə-mid'i-əs*, (*bot*) *adj* having a one-whorled perianth. [**mono-**.]

monochord *mon'ō-körd*, *n* an acoustical instrument with one string, sound board and bridge. [**mono-**.]

monochroic *mon-ō-krō'ik*, *adj* of one colour. [Gr. *monochroos* — *monos*, *chrōs*, colour.]

monochromatic *mon-ō-krō-mat'ik*, *adj* of one colour or wavelength only; completely colour-blind; done in monochrome. — *n* **monochro'masy** complete colour-blindness. — *n* **monochro'mat** a person who sees all colours as differing in brilliance only. — *n* **monochro'matism** monochromatic vision. — *n* **monochro'mator** a device capable of isolating and transmitting monochromatic or nearly monochromatic light. — *n* **mon'ochrome** representation in one colour; a picture in one colour; black and white; monochromy. — *n* **monochro'mist** a person who practises monochrome. — *adj* done, reproduced, etc. in a single colour or hue; black and white. — *n* **mon'ochromy** the art of monochrome. [Gr. *monochrōmatos* — *monos*, single, alone, *chrōma*, *-atos*, colour.]

monocle *mon'ə-kl*, *n* a single eyeglass. — *adj* **mon'ocled** wearing a monocle. [Fr. *monocle* — Gr. *monos*, L. *oculus*, eye.]

monocline *mon'ō-klīn*, (*geol*) *n* a fold in strata followed by resumption of the original direction. — *adj* **monoclīn'al**. [Gr. *monos*, single, alone, *klīnein*, to cause to slope.]

monoclinic *mon'ō-klin-ik*, (*crystall*) *adj* referable to three unequal axes, two intersecting each other obliquely and at right angles to the third. [Gr. *monos*, single, alone, *klīnein*, to incline.]

monoclinous *mon'ō-klī-nəs* or *mon-ō-klī'nəs*, (*bot*) *adj* hermaphrodite. [Gr. *monos*, single, alone, *klīnē*, bed.]

monoclonal *mon-ō-klō'nəl*, *adj* (of an antibody) derived from a single cell clone that can reproduce itself in vast quantities in the laboratory, having applications in the diagnosis and treatment of infections, etc. **[mono-.]**

mono-compound *mon-ō-kom'pownd*, (*chem*) *n* a compound containing one atom or group of that which is indicated. **[mono-.]**

monocoque *mon-ō-kok'* or *-kōk'*, *n* a fuselage or nacelle in which all structural loads are carried by the skin (*aeronautics*); a motor vehicle structure in which body and chassis are in one and share stresses (*autos*); the hull of a boat made in one piece (*naut*). [Fr., lit. single shell.]

monocotyledon *mon-ō-kot-i-lē'dən*, *n* (often shortened to **monocot**) a plant of the **Monocotylē'dones** (*-ēz*), or **Monocot'ylae**, one of the two great divisions of angiosperms, the embryos with one cotyledon, leaves commonly parallel-veined, the parts of the flower usu. in threes, and the vascular bundles scattered. — *adj* **monocotylē'donous**. **[mono-.]**

monocracy *mon-ok'rə-si*, *n* government by one person. — *n* **mon'ocrat** (*-ō-krat*). — *adj* **monocrat'ic**. [Gr. *monos*, single, alone, *kratos*, power.]

monocrystal *mon'ō-kris-təl*, *n* a single crystal. — *adj* **monocrys'talline**. **[mono-.]**

monocular *mon-ok'ū-lər*, *adj* one-eyed; of, for, or with, one eye. [Gr. *monos*, single, alone, L. *oculus*, an eye.]

monoculture *mon'ō-kul-chər*, *n* the growing of one kind of crop only, or a large area, over which it is grown. — *adj* **monocul'tural** of or relating to monoculture; of or relating to a single, shared culture (e.g. ethnic, social, religious). **[mono-.]**

monocyte *mon'ō-sīt*, *n* a large phagocytic leucocyte with a single oval or kidney-shaped nucleus and clear cytoplasm. [Gr. *monos*, single, *kytos*, vessel.]

monodic, monodist. See **monody**.

monodrama *mon'ō-drä-mə*, *n* a dramatic piece for a single performer. — *adj* **monodramatic** (*-drə-mat'ik*). **[mono-.]**

monody *mon'ə-di*, *n* a composition in which one part or voice carries the melody, the others accompanying (*mus*); a song for one voice; a mournful ode or poem performed by a single mourner. — *adj* **monodic** (*mə-nod'ik*). — *n* **mon'odist** a person who writes monodies. [Gr. *monōidiā* — *monos*, single, *ōidē*, song.]

monoecious *mon-ē'shəs*, (*biol*) *adj* hermaphrodite; having separate male and female flowers on the same plant. — *n* **monoecism** (*-ē'sizm*). [Gr. *monos*, single, *oikos*, a house.]

monofilament *mon-ō-fil'ə-mənt*, *n* a single strand of synthetic fibre. [Gr. *monos*, single, L. *fīlum*, a thread.]

monogamy *mo-nog'ə-mi*, *n* the rule, custom or condition of marriage to one wife or husband at a time; the practice, custom or condition of having no more than one mate (*zool*), or (*loosely*) one sexual partner, at a time. — *n* **monog'amist**. — *adj* **monogamous** (*mo-nog'ə-məs*). [Gr. *monos*, single, *gamos*, marriage.]

monogenesis *mon-ō-jen'i-sis*, *n* development of offspring from a parent like itself; asexual reproduction; community of origin. — *adj* **monogenet'ic**. — *adj* **monogen'ic** of or relating to monogenism; of or determined by a single gene. — *n* **monogenism** (*-oj'ən-izm*) the doctrine of the common descent of all living things, or of any particular group (esp. mankind) from one ancestor or pair. — *n* **monog'enist**. — *adj* **monogenist'ic**. — *adj* **monog'enous**. — *n* **monog'eny** descent from one common ancestor or pair; asexual reproduction. **[mono-.]**

monoglot *mon'ō-glot*, *n* a person who knows only one language. — Also *adj*. [Gr. *monos*, single, *glōtta*, tongue.]

monogony *mon-og'ən-i*, *n* asexual reproduction. [Gr. *monos*, single, alone, *gonos*, begetting.]

monogram *mon'ə-gram*, *n* a figure consisting of several letters interwoven or written into one. — *adj* **monogrammatic** (*-grə-mat'ik*). [Gr. *monos*, single, *gramma*, *grammatos*, a letter.]

monograph *mon'ə-gräf*, *n* a treatise, book or paper written on one particular subject or any branch of it. — *vt* to write a monograph upon. — *n* **monographer** (*mon-og'rə-fər*) or **monog'raphist** a writer of monographs. — *adj* **monographic** (*-graf'*) or **monograph'ical** pertaining to a monograph or a monogram. [Gr. *monos*, single, *graphein*, to write.]

monogyny *mon-oj'i-ni* or *-og'i-ni*, *n* the custom, practice or condition of having only one wife; the habit of mating with one female. — *adj* **monog'ynous** having one wife; practising monogyny. [Gr. *monos*, single, *gynē*, woman.]

monohull *mon'ō-hul*, *n* a vessel with one hull (as opp. to catamaran or trimaran). **[mono-.]**

monolingual *mon-ō-ling'gwəl*, *adj* expressed or written in one language; speaking only one language. — *n* **monoling'ualism**. — *n* **monoling'uist**. [Gr. *monos*, single, L. *lingua*, tongue.]

monolith *mon'ō-lith*, *n* a single block of stone; anything resembling a monolith in uniformity, massiveness or intractability. — *adj* **monolith'ic** pertaining to or resembling a monolith; (of a state, an organisation, etc.) massive, and difficult to deal with. [Gr. *monos*, single, *lithos*, a stone.]

monologue *mon'ə-log*, *n* a soliloquy or speech by one person, or a composition intended to be spoken by one person; a tedious, loud or opinionated speech that blocks conversation (*colloq*). — *adj* **monologic** (*-loj'ik*) or **monolog'ical**. — *vi* **monologise** or **-ize** (*mon-ol'ə-jīz*) to indulge in this. — *n* **monol'ogist** a person who talks in, or performs a monologue. — *n* **monol'ogy**. [Gr. *monos*, single, alone, *logos*, speech.]

monomania *mon-ō-mā'ni-ə*, *n* madness confined to one subject; an unreasonable interest in any particular thing. — *n* **monomā'niac** a person affected with monomania. — *adj* **monomā'niac** or **monomaniacal** (*-mə-nī'ə-kl*). [Gr. *monos*, single, *maniā*, madness.]

monomark *mon'ō-märk*, *n* a particular combination of letters, figures, etc. as a mark of identification. **[mono-.]**

monomer *mon'* or *mōn'ə-mər*, (*chem*) *n* the simplest of any series of compounds having the same empirical formula (opp. to *polymer*). — *adj* **monomer'ic**. [Gr. *monos*, single, *meros*, part.]

monometallic *mon-ō-mi-tal'ik*, *adj* involving or using only one metal as a standard of currency. — *n* **monometallism** (*-met'əl-izm*). — *n* **monomet'allist**. **[mono-.]**

monomial *mon-ō'mi-əl*, *n* an algebraic expression of one term only. — *adj* **monō'mial**. [Gr. *monos*, single, L. *nōmen*, name.]

monomode *mon'ō-mōd*, *adj* designating a very fine optical fibre (less than 10 micrometres in diameter) used in telecommunications. **[mono-]**

monomorphic *mon-ō-mör'fik*, (*biol*) *adj* existing in one form only. — *adj* **monomor'phous**. [Gr. *monos*, single, *morphē*, form.]

mononuclear *mon-ō-nū'kli-ər, adj* having a single nucleus. — *n* (*med*) **mononucleosis** (*mon-ō-nūk-li-ō'sis*) the presence in the blood of an abnormally large number of a type of leucocytes. [**mono-**.]

monophasic *mon-ō-fāz'ik, adj* (of electric current) single-phase (also called **mon'ophase**); having one period of rest and one of activity during the 24 hours (*biol*). [**mono-**.]

monophobia *mon-ō-fō'bi-ə, n* morbid fear of being alone. — *adj* **monophō'bic**. — *n* a person affected by monophobia. [**mono-**.]

monophonic *mon-ō-fon'ik, adj* homophonic; monaural (opp. to *stereophonic*). — *n* **monoph'ony**. [Gr. *monos*, single, *phōnē*, voice, sound.]

monophthong *mon'of-thong, n* a simple vowel sound. — *adj* **monophthongal** (*-thong'gəl*). [Gr. *monophthongos* — *monos*, single, *phthongos*, sound, vowel.]

Monophysite *mō-nof'i-zīt* or *-sīt*, (*Christian relig*) *n* a person who holds that Christ had only one composite nature. — *adj* **Monophysitic** (*-sit'ik* or *-zit'ik*). — *n* **Monoph'ysitism**. — All words also without *cap*. [Gr. *monos*, single, *physis*, nature.]

monopitch *mon'ō-pich*, (*archit*) *adj* (of a roof) forming a single, uniform slope. [**mono-**.]

monoplane *mon'ə-plān, n* an aeroplane or glider with one set of planes or wings. [**mono-**.]

monoplegia *mon-ō-plē'ji-ə*, (*med*) *n* paralysis limited to a single part of the body, or to one limb or muscle. [Gr. *monos*, single, *plēgē*, stroke.]

monopode *mon'ə-pōd*, now also **monopod** *mon'ə-pod, n* a one-footed support, platform, stand, etc., e.g. for a camera. — *adj* one-footed. — *adj* **monopod'ial** of or relating to a monopodium. — *adv* **monopo'dially**. — *n* **monopo'dium** (*bot*) an axis that continues to grow without being supplanted by a lateral branch. [L. *monopodius, -um* — Gr. *monos*, single, *pous, podos*, foot.]

monopole *mon'ō-pōl*, (*phys*) *n* (usu. **magnetic monopole**) a particle, thought to exist, that has a single magnetic charge. [**mono-**.]

monopoly *mon-op'ə-li, n* sole power, or privilege, of dealing in anything; that of which one has exclusive command or possession; (with *cap*; ®) a board-game for two or more players, the aim being to acquire property. — *vt* **monop'olise** or **-ize** to have a monopoly of; to keep to oneself; to engross. — *n* **monop'oliser, -z-** or **monop'olist**. — *adj* **monopolis'tic**. — **Monopoly money** (*colloq*) large sums of money treated lightly as though of no real consequence or value, like the sham notes exchanged in Monopoly®. — **Monopolies and Mergers Commission** a body set up by the government to investigate monopolies, etc., where a monopoly is defined as 25 per cent of the market. [L. *monopōlium* — Gr. *monopōlion* — *monos*, single, alone, *pōleein*, to sell.]

monopsony *mon-op'sə-ni, n* a situation where only one buyer exists for the product of several sellers, or where one of several buyers is large enough to exert undue influence over the price of a product. — *n* **monop'sonist**. — *adj* **monopsonis'tic**. [Gr. *monos*, single, *opsonia*, a purchase — *opsonein*, to buy.]

monopulse *mon'ō-puls, n* a type of radar system used in many gun-control and missile guidance systems, involving the transmission of a single pulse. [**mono-**.]

monorail *mon'ō-rāl, n* a railway with carriages running astride of, or suspended from, one rail. — Also *adj*. [**mono-**.]

monosaccharide *mon-ō-sak'ə-rīd*, (*chem*) *n* a simple sugar that cannot be hydrolysed. [**mono-**.]

monosepalous *mon-ō-sep'ə-ləs*, (*bot*) *adj* having the sepals all united. [**mono-**.]

mono-ski *mon'ō-skē, n* a ski on which both feet are placed. — *vi* to use a mono-ski. — *n* **mon'o-skier**. [**mono-**.]

monosodium glutamate *mon-ō-sō'di-əm glōō'tə-māt, n* a white crystalline salt which brings out the flavour of meat (*glutamate*, a salt of glutamic acid).

monosyllable *mon-ə-sil'ə-bl, n* a word of one syllable. — *adj* **monosyllabic** (*-ab'ik*). — *n* **monosyll'abism**. [**mono-**.]

monotheism *mon'ō-thē-izm, n* the belief in only one God. — *n* **mon'otheist**. — *adj* **monotheist'ic** or **monotheist'ical**. [Gr. *monos*, single, *theos*, God.]

monotint *mon'ə-tint, n* drawing or painting in a single tint. [**mono-**.]

monotone *mon'ə-tōn, n* a single, unvaried tone or utterance; a succession of sounds having the same pitch; continued or extended sameness; sameness in colour. — *adj* in monotone; monotonic (*math*). — *adj* **monotonic** (*-ton'ik*) in monotone; (of a function or sequence) having the property of either never increasing or never decreasing. — *adj* **monotonous** (*mon-ot'ə-nəs*) uttered in one unvaried tone; marked by dull uniformity. — *adv* **monot'onously**. — *n* **monot'onousness**. — *n* **monot'ony** dull uniformity of tone or sound; absence of modulation in speaking or reading; tedious sameness or lack of variety (*fig*). [Gr. *monos*, single, *tonos*, a tone.]

Monotremata *mon-ō-trē'mə-tə, npl* the lowest order of mammals, having a single opening for the genital and digestive organs. — *adj* **monotre'matous**. — *n* **mon'otreme** a member of the Monotremata. [Gr. *monos*, single, *trēma, -atos*, a hole.]

monotype *mon'ə-tīp, n* a sole type, a species forming a genus by itself (*biol*); a single print made from a picture painted on a metal or glass plate (*graphic art*); (with *cap*; ®) the name of a machine that casts and sets type, letter by letter (*printing*). — Also *adj*. — *adj* **monotypic** (*-tip'ik*). [**mono-**.]

monovalent *mon-ō-vā'lənt* or *mon-ov'əl-ənt*, (*chem*) *adj* having a valency of one, capable of combining with one atom of hydrogen or its equivalent. — *n* **monova'lence** or **monova'lency**. [**mono-**.]

monoxide *mon-ok'sīd*, (*chem*) *n* an oxide with one oxygen atom in the molecule. [**mono-**.]

monozygotic *mon-ō-zī-got'ik*, (*biol*) *adj* developed from one zygote. — **monozygotic twins** twins developed from a single zygote, identical twins. [**mono-**.]

Monroe doctrine *mən-rō' dok'trin, n* the principle of non-intervention of European powers in the affairs of independent countries in the American continents. [President *Monroe's* Message to the U.S. Congress, December 1823.]

Monseigneur *mɔ̄-sen-yœr, n* my lord; a title in France given to a person of high birth or rank, esp. to bishops, etc. (written abbrev. **Mgr**): — *pl* **Messeigneurs** (*me-sen-yœr*). [Fr. *mon seigneur*, *sieur*, my lord — L. *meum seniōrem* (accus.), my elder.]

Monsieur *mə-syø, n* sir; a title of courtesy in France = *Mr* in English (printed **M** or in full); a Frenchman generally: — *pl* **Messieurs** (Fr. *mes-yø*, written **MM**; Eng. *mes'ərz*, written **Messrs**) and (of **monsieur**) **messieurs**. [Fr. *mon sieur*, my lord.]

Monsignor *mon-sēn'yər* or It. *mon-sēn-yōr'*, or **Monsignore** (*-yō'rā*), *n* a title conferred on prelates and on dignitaries of the papal household (written abbrev. **Monsig.** or **Mgr**): — *pl* **Monsignors** (*-sēn'*) or **Monsigno'ri** (*-rē*). [It. — Fr.]

monsoon *mon-sōōn', n* a periodical wind of the Indian Ocean, the **wet monsoon** from the S.W. between April and October, and the **dry monsoon** from the N.E. the rest of the year; a wind which blows in opposite directions at different seasons of the year; in N. and W. India, the rains accompanying the S.W. monsoon. — *adj* **monsoon'al**. [Port. *monção* — Malay *mūsim* — Ar. *mausim*, a time, a season.]

mons pubis *monz pū'bis.* Same as **mons veneris**: — *pl* **montes pubis** (*mon'tēz*). [L., hill of the pubis.]

monster *mon'stər, n* an extraordinary, grotesque or gigantic animal, as told of in fables and folklore; anything out of the usual course of nature; an abnormally formed animal or plant; anything gigantic; anything horribly ugly or wicked. — *adj* gigantic, huge. — *n* **monstrosity** (*-stros'i-ti*) the state or fact of being monstrous; marked abnormality; an abnormally formed animal, plant, part or object; anything outrageously constructed. — *adj* **mon'strous** out of the common course of nature; enormous; horrible; outrageous; preposterous. — *adv* **mon'strously**. — *n* **mon'strousness**. [Fr. *monstre* — L. *mōnstrum*, an evil omen, a monster — *monēre, monitum*, to warn.]

monstera *mon-stē'rə, n* any plant of the genus of tropical American evergreen plants **Monstera**, that have shiny green perforated leaves and can be grown to a height of 20 feet as hothouse or indoor plants, esp. the Swiss cheese plant. [N.L., perh. because the leaves seem freakish.]

monstrance *mon'strəns, n* the ornamental receptacle in which the consecrated host is exposed in R.C. churches for the adoration of the people. [O.Fr., — L. *mōnstrāre*, to show.]

monstrosity, monstrous, etc. See under **monster**.

mons veneris *monz ven'ə-ris, n* the mound of flesh over the pubis on the female human body: — *pl* **montes veneris** (*mon'tēz*). [L., hill of Venus.]

Mont. *abbrev* for: Montana (U.S. state); Montgomeryshire (former county, now part of Powys).

montage *mɔ̃-täzh', n* selection, piecing together and editing of film material to produce an integrated visual effect; (the act or process of making) a composite photograph; setting-up, assemblage, superimposition; a picture made partly by sticking objects on the canvas. — *vt* to make into, or set in, a montage. [Fr., — *monter*, to mount.]

montane *mon'tān, adj* mountainous; mountain-dwelling. [L. *montānus* — *mōns, montis*, a mountain.]

montbretia *mont-* or *mon-brēsh'yə, n* a plant of the *Montbretia* genus of S. African iridaceous plants; a plant (*Crocosmia*) of the iris family bearing bright orange-coloured flowers; a plant of the genus *Tritonia*. [After a French botanist, Coquebert de *Montbret* (1780–1801).]

monte *mon'tā* or *-ti, n* a Spanish-American gambling card-game. — **three-card monte** a Mexican three-card trick. [Sp., mountain, scrub, cards remaining after a deal — L. *mōns, montis*, a mountain.]

montelimar *mon-tel'i-mär* or Fr. *mɔ̃-tā-lē-mär, n* a type of nougat, orig. made in *Montélimar*, S.E. France.

Montessori *mon-tes-ör'i, n* a method of education developed by Dr Maria Montessori (*c* 1900), insisting on spontaneity and freedom from restraint. — *adj* **Montessor'ian**.

Montezuma's revenge *mon-tə-zōō'məz ri-venj'*, (*colloq*) *n* diarrhoea, esp. caused by travelling in Mexico and/or eating Mexican food. [*Montezuma II*, a 15th-cent. Mexican ruler.]

month *munth, n* one of the twelve conventional divisions of the year, or its length — a **calendar month**; such a length of time; the length of time taken by the moon to revolve once around the earth (29.53 days) — a **lunar month**. — *adj* **month'ly** performed in a month; done, recurring, or appearing once a month. — *n* a monthly publication; (as *pl* **month'lies**) a monthly period, the menses (*colloq*). — *adv* once a month; in every month. — **a month of Sundays** see under **Sunday**. [O.E. *mōnath* — *mōna*, moon.]

monticule *mon'ti-kūl, n* a little elevation, hill, mound; a secondary volcanic cone. [L. *monticulus*, dimin. of *mōns*, mountain.]

montmorillonite *mont-mə-ril'ə-nīt*, (*mineralogy*) *n* a hydrated silicate of aluminium, one of the important clay minerals and the chief constituent of bentonite and fuller's earth. [From *Montmorillon*, in France.]

monture *mon'tūr, n* a mounting, setting, frame. [Fr.]

monument *mon'ū-mənt, n* anything that preserves the memory of a person or an event, a building, pillar, tomb, tablet, statue, etc.; any structure, natural or artificial, considered as an object of beauty or of interest as a relic of the past; a historic document or record; a stone, post, river, etc. marking a boundary (*US*); a relic, indication or trace; a notable or enduring example. — *adj* **monumental** (*-ment'əl*) of, relating to or of the nature of a monument, tomb, memento or token; memorial; massive and lasting; vast, impressive or amazing. — *adv* **monument'ally**. [L. *monumentum, monimentum* — *monēre*, to remind.]

moo *mōō, vi* to low. — *n* a cow's low. [Imit.]

mooch *mōōch, vi* to loiter, wander (about); to skulk; to sponge, cadge. — *vt* to pilfer; to beg, cadge. — *n* the act of mooching. — *n* **mooch'er**. [Perh. O.Fr. *muchier*, to hide.]

mood[1] *mōōd, n* a form of the verb to express the mode or manner of an action or of a state of being (*gram*); the form of the syllogism as determined by the quantity and quality of its three constituent propositions (*logic*). [**mode**.]

mood[2] *mōōd, n* temporary state of the emotions or of attitude; state of gloom or sullenness. — *adv* **mood'ily**. — *n* **mood'iness** sullenness. — *adj* **mood'y** indulging in moods; sullen; faked, pretended (*prison slang*). — *n* (*slang*) insidious, flattering talk; lies, deception. — *vt* (*slang*) to persuade by flattery and cajolery. [O.E. *mōd*, mind.]

Moog synthesizer® *mōōg* or *mōg sin'thi-sīz-ər, n* an electronic musical instrument with a keyboard, that can produce a wide range of sounds. [Developed by Robert *Moog*, an American engineer.]

mooi *mo'i*, (*Afrik*) *adj* fine — a general word of commendation. [From Du.]

mooli *mōō'li, n* a long white carrot-shaped root vegetable from East Africa, tasting similar to a radish. [Native word.]

Moon *mōōn, n* a system of writing for the blind. [British inventor William *Moon* (1818–94).]

moon *mōōn, n* (often with *cap*) the earth's satellite; a satellite; a month; anything in the shape of a moon or crescent. — *vi* to wander about or gaze vacantly at anything (usu. with *around, about*); to present one's bare buttocks to public view, esp. through a vehicle window (*slang*). — *adj* **mooned** marked with the figure of a moon. — *n* **moon'er** a person who moons about. — *adj* **moon'less** without moonlight. — *n* **moon'let** a small earth-satellite, whether natural or man-made. — *adj* **moon'y** of or relating to the moon; inclined to moon, dreamy. — **moon'beam** a beam of light from the moon; **moon boot** a bulky padded boot with a quilted fabric covering, for wearing in snow, reminiscent of a spaceman's boot; **moon'calf** a false conception or fleshy mass formed in the womb; a dolt; **moon daisy** the ox-eye daisy; **moon'face** a full, round face. — *adj* **moon'-faced**. — **moon'-fish** the opah or other silvery disc-shaped fish; **moon'-flower** the ox-eye daisy; a night-blooming twining plant; **moon'light** the light of the moon — sunlight reflected from the moon's surface. — *adj* lit by the moon; occurring in moonlight. — *vi* to work outside one's normal working hours, esp. when the income from this is not declared for tax assessment. — **moon'lighter** a person who moonlights; **moonlight flit** a removal by night, with rent unpaid; **moon'lighting**. — *adj* **moon'lit** lit by the moon. — **moon pool** (*oil industry*) the open shaft let through the hull of a deep-sea drilling vessel to accommodate the vertical pipeline connected to the oil-well; **moon'quake** a tremor of the moon's surface; **moon'rise** the rising of the moon; **moon'-scape** the physical appearance of the surface of the moon, or a representation of it; **moon'set** the setting of the moon; **moon'shine** moonlight; nonsense (*colloq*); spirits illicitly distilled or smuggled; **moon'-shiner** a smuggler or illicit distiller of spirits; **moon'shot** an act or process of launching an object or vehicle to orbit, or land on, the moon; **moon'-stone** an opalescent orthoclase feldspar, perh. sometimes selenite. — *adj* **moon'struck** or **moon'-stricken** affected by the moon, lunatic, crazed. — **over the moon** (*colloq*) delighted. [O.E. *mōna*.]

moong bean. Same as **mung bean**.

Moonie *mōōn'i*, *n* a colloquial (often *derog*) term for a member of the Unification Church, a sect founded in 1954 by Sun Myung *Moon*, a S. Korean.

Moor *mōōr*, *n*, *fem* **Moor'ess**, a member of the mixed Arab and Berber people of Morocco and the Barbary coast; one of the Arab and Berber conquerors and occupants of Spain from 711 to 1492. — *adj* **Moor'ish**. [Fr. *More*, *Maure* — L. *Maurus*.]

moor[1] *mōōr*, *n* a wide tract of uncultivated ground, often covered with heath, and having a poor, peaty soil; a heath. — *adj* **moor'y** resembling a moor; marshy, boggy. — **moor'cock** and **moor'fowl** red, or black, grouse; **moor'hen** waterhen; female moorfowl; **moor'land** a tract of moor. — *adj* of moorland. — **moor'log** a deposit of decayed woody material under a marsh, etc. [O.E. *mōr*.]

moor[2] *mōōr*, *vt* to fasten by cable or anchor. — *vi* to make fast a ship, boat, etc.; to be made fast. — *n* **moor'age** condition of being moored; act of mooring; a due paid for mooring; a place for mooring. — *n* **moor'ing** the act of mooring; that which serves to moor or confine a ship; (in *pl*) the place or condition of a ship thus moored; anything providing security or stability. [Prob. from an unrecorded O.E. word answering to M.Du. *mâren*.]

moose *mōōs*, *n* the American elk: — *pl* **moose**. [Algonquian *mus*, *moos*.]

moot *mōōt*, *n* orig. a meeting; a deliberative or administrative assembly or court (*hist*); its meeting-place; discussion; a law student's discussion of a hypothetical case. — *vt* to argue, dispute; to propose for discussion. — *vi* to dispute, plead. — *adj* debatable. — *adj* **moot'able**. — *n* **moot'er**. — *n* **moot'ing**. — **moot case** a case for discussion; a case about which there may be difference of opinion; **moot'-court** a meeting for discussion of hypothetical cases; **moot'-hall** or **-house** a town hall or council chamber; a hall for moot-courts; **moot point** an undecided or disputed point. [O.E. (*ge*)*mōt* (noun), *mōtian* (verb).]

mop *mop*, *n* a bunch of rags, yarn, or the like, on the end of a stick, for washing, removing dust, soaking up liquid, etc.; any similar instrument, as for cleansing a wound, polishing, etc.; a thick or bushy head of hair; an act of mopping. — *vt* to wipe, dab, soak up, or remove, with a mop or as if with a mop; to clear away or dispose of as residue: — *pr p* **mopp'ing**; *pa t* and *pa p* **mopped**. — *n* **mopp'er**. — **mop'head** (a person with) a shaggy unkempt head of hair. — *adj* **mop'-headed** having such a head of hair. — **mop'stick** the handle of a mop; a handrail nearly circular in section; a rod for raising a piano damper; **mop'-up** an action of mopping up. — **mop up** to clear away or clean up with a mop; to clear away, dispose of; to absorb (e.g. surplus credit); to capture or kill (enemy stragglers) after a victory, etc.; **Mrs Mop** a cleaner, charwoman. [Poss. O.Fr. *mappe* — L. *mappa*, a napkin.]

mope *mōp*, *vi* to go aimlessly and listlessly; to be listless or depressed. — *n* a listless person; (esp. in *pl*) a state of moping. — *n* **mop'er**. — *adv* **mop'ingly**. — *adj* **mop'ish** dull, spiritless. — *adv* **mop'ishly**. — *n* **mop'ishness**. — *adj* **mop'y**.

moped *mō'ped*, *n* a motor-assisted pedal cycle, under 50 c.c.

mopoke *mō'pōk*, *n* the owl *Ninox novaeseelandiae*, of Australia and New Zealand; (*Austr*) the tawny *frogmouth*, a nocturnal bird of the *Podargus* genus (to which the call is wrongly attributed); a silly person. [From the cry of the owl.]

mopper, etc. See **mop**.

moppet *mop'it*, *n* a rag doll; a doll-like woman; (a term of endearment or contempt for) a little girl or child. [**mop**.]

mopy. See under **mope**.

moquette *mō-ket'*, *n* a carpet and soft furnishing material with a loose velvety pile, the back made of thick canvas, etc. [Fr.]

MOR *abbrev* for middle-of-the road (music), esp. in broadcasting.

mora[1] *mō'rə*, (*law*) *n* delay, esp. unjustifiable. [L., delay.]

mora[2] or **morra** *mor'ə*, *n* the game of guessing how many fingers are held up. [It. *mora*.]

moraine *mo-rān'*, *n* a continuous marginal line of débris borne on or left by a glacier; a garden imitation of this. — *adj* **morain'al** or **morain'ic**. [Fr.]

moral *mor'əl*, *adj* of or relating to character or conduct considered as good or evil; ethical; adhering to or directed towards what is right, virtuous, esp. in matters of sex; capable of knowing right and wrong; subject to the moral law; having an effect on the mind or will; supported by evidence of reason or probability. — *n* (in *pl*) writings on ethics; the doctrine or practice of the duties of life; moral philosophy or ethics; principles and conduct, esp. sexual; (in *sing*) the practical lesson that can be drawn from anything; an exposition of such a lesson by way of conclusion; a symbol; a certainty (*slang*). — *n* **moralisā'tion** or **-z-** act of moralising, explanation in a moral sense. — *vt* **mor'alise** or **-ize** to apply to a moral purpose; to explain in a moral sense; to make moral. — *vi* to speak or write on moral subjects; to make moral reflections. — *n* **mor'aliser** or **-z-**. — *n* **mor'alism** a moral maxim; moral counsel; morality as distinct from religion. — *n* **mor'alist** a person who teaches morals, or who practises moral duties; a moral as distinguished from a religious man; someone who prides themselves on their morality. — *adj* **moralist'ic**. — *adv* **moralist'ically**. — *n* **morality** (*mor-al'i-ti*) quality of being moral; that which renders an action right or wrong; the practice of moral duties apart from religion; virtue; the doctrine of actions as right or wrong; ethics; a mediaeval allegorical drama in which virtues and vices appear as characters (also **morality play**). — *adv* **mor'ally** in a moral manner; in respect of morals; to all intents and purposes, practically. — **moral agent** a person who acts under a knowledge of right and wrong; **moral certainty** a likelihood great enough to be acted on, although not capable of being certainly proved; **moral courage** power of facing disapprobation and ridicule; **moral defeat** a success so qualified as to count as a defeat, or to point towards defeat; **moral faculty** moral sense; **moral law** a law or rules for life and conduct, founded on what is right and wrong; the law of conscience; that part of the Old Testament which relates to moral principles, esp. the ten commandments; **moral majority** the majority of a society that is presumed to favour a strict moral code; **moral philosophy** ethics; **Moral Rearmament** a movement for spiritual renewal, originally (1921–38) known as the *Oxford Group*, advocating absolute private and public morality; **moral sense** that power of the mind which knows or judges actions to be right or wrong, and determines conduct accordingly; **moral support** encouragement shown by approval rather than by active help; **moral theology** ethics treated with reference to a divine source; **moral victory** a defeat in appearance, but in some important sense a real victory. [L. *mōrālis* — *mōs, mōris*, manner, custom, (esp. in pl.) morals.]

morale *mor-äl'*, *n* degree of confidence or optimism in a person or group. [**moral**.]

moralise, etc., **morality, morally**. See under **moral**.

morass *mə-ras'*, *n* a tract of soft, wet ground, a marsh; a situation of confusion, etc., esp. one that prevents progress. — *adj* **morass'y**. [Du. *moeras* — O.Fr. *maresc*, infl. by Du. *moer*, moor.]

moratorium *mor-ə-tō'ri-əm*, *n* an emergency measure authorising the suspension of payments of debts for a given time; the period thus declared; a temporary ban on, or cessation of, an activity: — *pl* **morato'ria** or **morato'riums**. — *adj* **moratory** (*mor'ə-tə-ri*) delaying; deferring. [Neut. of L.L. *morātōrius*, adj. from *mora*, delay.]

Moravian *mo-rā'vi-ən*, *adj* relating to *Moravia* or the Moravians. — *n* one of the people of Moravia; one of a small body of Protestants of extraordinary missionary energy, founded in the 15th cent. — *n* **Morā'vianism**. [L. *Moravia*, Moravia — *Morava*, the river March.]

moray *mō'rā*, *n* an eel of the family *Muraenidae*. [Port. *moreia* — L. *mūraena* — Gr. *(s)mȳraina*, fem. of *(s)mȳros*, eel.]

morbid *mör'bid*, *adj* sickly; unwholesome; inclined to dwell on unwholesome or horrible thoughts; relating to, or of the nature of, disease. — *n* **morbid'ity** the state of being morbid; ratio of incidence of an illness. — *adv* **mor'bidly**. — *n* **mor'bidness**. — **morbid anatomy** the science or study of diseased organs and tissues. [L. *morbidus* — *morbus*, disease.]

morbiferous *mör-bif'ər-əs*, *adj* disease-bringing. — *adj* **morbif'ic** disease-causing. [L. *morbus*, disease, *ferre*, to carry.]

morbilli *mör-bil'ī*, *npl* measles. — *adj* **morbill'iform** or **morbill'ous**. [L.L. dimin. of L. *morbus*, disease.]

morceau *mör'sō*, *n* a morsel, a fragment; a piece of music; a short literary composition: — *pl* **mor'ceaux** (*-sō*). [Fr.; see **morsel**.]

mordacious *mör-dā'shəs*, *adj* given to biting; biting in quality (*lit* or *fig*). — *adv* **mordā'ciously**. — *n* **mordacity** (*-das'i-ti*). [**mordant**.]

mordant *mör'dənt*, *adj* biting; incisive; serving to fix dyes, paints, gold leaf. — *n* a corroding substance; any substance that combines with and fixes a dyestuff in material that cannot be dyed direct; a substance used to cause paint or gold leaf to adhere. — *vt* to treat with a mordant. — *n* **mor'dancy**. — *adv* **mor'dantly**. [L. *mordēre*, to bite.]

mordent *mör'dənt*, (*mus*) *n* a grace note in which the principal note is preceded in performance by itself and the note below, or itself and the note above. [Ger., — It. *mordente*.]

more *mör*, *adj* (serving as *compar* of **many** and **much**) in greater number or quantity; additional; other besides. — *adv* to a greater degree; rather; again; longer; further; moreover. — *n* a greater thing; something further or in addition: — *superl* (*adj* and *adv*) **most** (*mōst*). — *adj* **mo'rish** or **more'ish** such that one wants more. — **any more** anything additional; further; **more and more** continually increasing; **more or less** about; in round numbers; **no more** nothing in addition; never again; no longer in existence; dead. [O.E. *māra*, greater.]

morel *mor-el'*, *n* any edible fungus of the genus *Morchella*. [Fr. *morille*.]

morello *mə-rel'ō*, *n* a dark-red cherry, much used in cooking and for cherry brandy: — *pl* **morell'os**. [Poss. — It. *morello*, dark-coloured.]

moreover *mör-ō'vər*, *adv* more over or beyond what has been said; further, besides. [**more** and **over**.]

mores *mō'rēz* or *mō'rās*, *npl* customs, manners. [L. *mōs, mōris*, custom.]

Morgan *mör'gən*, *n* any horse of an American breed developed in Vermont by Justin *Morgan* in the late 18th century — light and sturdy for farm work, they are also bred for trotting races.

morganatic *mör-gən-at'ik*, *adj* of or relating to a marriage between persons of unequal rank, the marriage being valid, the children legitimate, but unable to inherit the higher rank, the lower-born spouse not being granted the higher-born spouse's title. — *adv* **morganat'ically**. [L.L. *morganātica*, a gift from a bridegroom to his bride.]

morgen *mör'gən*, *n* a unit of land-measurement — in Holland, S. Africa, and parts of the U.S., a little over two acres; formerly in Norway, Denmark and Prussia, about two-thirds of an acre. [Du. and Ger.; perh. *morgen*, morning, hence a morning's ploughing.]

morgue *mörg*, *n* a place where dead bodies are laid out for identification, or kept prior to burial or cremation; a gloomy or depressing place (*fig*); a place, as in a newspaper office, where miscellaneous material for reference is kept. [Fr.]

MORI *mor'i*, *abbrev* for Market and Opinion Research Institute.

moribund *mor'i-bund*, *adj* about to die; lacking in strength or vitality. — *n* **moribund'ity**. [L. *moribundus* — *morī*, to die.]

morish. See **more**.

Mormon *mör'mən*, *n* one of a religious sect with headquarters since 1847 in Salt Lake City, polygamous till 1890, calling itself *The Church of Jesus Christ of Latter-day Saints*, founded in 1830 by Joseph Smith, whose *Book of Mormon* was given out as translated from the golden plates of *Mormon*, a prophet. — *n* **Mor'monism**. — *n* **Mor'monite**.

morn *mörn*, (*poetic* or *dialect*) *n* the first part of the day; morning. — **the morn** (*Scot*) tomorrow. [M.E. *morwen* — O.E. *morgen*.]

mornay *mör'nā* or **mornay sauce** (*sös*), *n* a cream sauce with cheese flavouring. — *adj* (placed after noun) served with this sauce. [Perh. Philippe de *Mornay*, Fr. Huguenot leader.]

morning *mörn'ing*, *n* the first part of the day, until noon or the time of the midday meal; the early part of anything. — *adj* of the morning; taking place or being in the morning. — *adv* **morn'ings** (*colloq* or *dialect*) in the morning. — **morning coat** cutaway coat worn as part of morning dress; **morning dress** dress, esp. formal dress, worn in the early part of day, as opp. to *evening dress*; **morning-glo'ry** a plant of the genus *Ipomoea* (esp. *Ipomoea purpurea*) or *Convolvulus*, with showy flowers of various colours; **morn'ing-prayer** prayer in the morning; matins; **morn'ing-room** a sitting-room for use in the morning; **morning sickness** nausea and vomiting in the morning, common in the early stages of pregnancy; **morning star** a planet, esp. Venus, when it rises before the sun; a precursor; a mediaeval weapon, a spiky ball attached directly or by a chain to a handle; **morning watch** the watch between 4 and 8 a.m. — **morning-after pill** a contraceptive pill taken within a specified time after intercourse; **the morning after** (*colloq*) the unpleasant after-effects of a night of excessive drinking, etc. [Contr. of M.E. *morwening*; cf. **morn**.]

Moro *mör'ō*, *n* a member of any of the tribes of Muslim Malays in the Philippine Islands: — *pl* **Moro** or **Mor'os**. [Sp., lit. moor, L. *Maurus*.]

morocco *mə-rok'ō*, *n* a fine goatskin leather tanned with sumac, first brought from *Morocco* (also **morocco leather**); a sheepskin leather imitation of it: — *pl* **morocc'os**. — *adj* consisting of morocco. — **French morocco** an inferior kind of Levant morocco, with small grain; **Levant morocco** a fine quality of morocco, with large grain; **Persian morocco** a morocco finished on the grain side.

moron *mör'on*, *n* a feeble-minded person; a former category of mental retardation, describing a person with an I.Q. of 50–69, i.e. someone who remains throughout life at the mental age of eight to twelve. — *adj* **moron'ic**. — *adv* **moron'ically**. [Gr. *mōros*, foolish.]

morose *mə-rōs'*, *adj* ill-tempered, gloomy. — *adv* **morose'ly**. — *n* **morose'ness**. [L. *mōrōsus*, peevish — *mōs*, *mōris*, manner.]

morph[1] *morf*, (*zool*, etc.) *n* a variant form of an animal, etc. [Gr. *morphē*, form.]

morph[2]. See under **morpheme**.

-morph, **morph-** *-mörf-* or **morpho-** *mör-fō-*, *combining form* denoting something of a specified form, shape or structure. — *adj combining form* **-morph'ic**. — *n combining form* **-morph'ism**. — *n combining form* **-morphy**. [Gr. *morphē*, form.]

morpheme *mör'fēm*, (*linguis*) *n* a linguistic unit that has meaning. — *n* **morph** (back-formation from **morpheme**) the whole or a part of a spoken or written word corresponding to or representing one or more morphemes. — *adj* **morphēm'ic**. — *nsing* **morphēm'ics** the study of morphemes. [Gr. *morphē*, form.]

morphia. See **morphine**.

morphic *mör'fik*, *adj* relating to form, morphological.

morphine *mör'fēn* or **morphia** *mör'fi-ə*, *n* the principal alkaloid in opium, a hypnotic drug used extensively for pain-relief. — *n* **mor'phinism** the effect of morphine on the system; the habit of taking morphine. [Gr. *Morpheus*, the god of dreams.]

morpho-. See **morph-**.

morphogenesis *mör-fə-jen'i-sis*, *n* the origin and development of a part, organ or organism. — *adj* **morphogenet'ic**. — *n* **morphogeny** (*-foj'i-ni*) morphogenesis. [**morpho-**.]

morphography *mör-fog'rə-fi*, *n* descriptive morphology. — *n* **morphog'rapher**.

morphology *mör-fol'ə-ji*, *n* the science of form, esp. that of the outer form, inner structure, and development of living organisms and their parts; the science of the external forms of rocks and land-features; the study of the forms of words. — *adj* **morpholog'ic** or **morpholog'ical**. — *n* **morphol'ogist**. [Gr. *morphē*, form, *logos*, word.]

morra. See **mora**[2].

Morris chair *mor'is chār*, *n* a kind of armchair with an adjustable back. [From William *Morris*, 19th-cent. English designer and architect.]

morris dance *mor'is däns*, *n* a type of English folk-dance, perh. of Moorish origin, which came to be associated with May games, with (latterly) Maid Marian, Robin Hood, and other characters, who had bells attached to their dress; a tune for such dancing. — Also **morr'is**. — *vi* **morr'is** to perform by dancing. — *n* **morr'is-dancer**. [**Moorish**.]

morro *mor'ō*, *n* a rounded hill or headland: — *pl* **morr'os**. [Sp.]

morrow *mor'ō*, (*archaic* or *poetic*) *n* the day following the present; the next following day; the time immediately after any event. [**morn**.]

Morse *mörs*, *n* (a method of) signalling by a code in which each letter is represented by a combination of dashes and dots or long and short light-flashes, sound signals, etc., invented by Sam F. B. *Morse* (1791–1872).

morsel *mör'səl*, *n* a bite or mouthful; a small or choice piece of food; a small piece of anything. [O.Fr. *morsel* (Fr. *morceau*, It. *morsello*), dimin. from L. *morsus* — *mordēre*, *morsum*, to bite.]

mortal *mör'tl*, *adj* liable to death; causing death, deadly, fatal; punishable with death; (of a sin) involving the penalty of spiritual death, as opp. to *venial*; to the death; implacable; human; very great (*colloq*); tediously long (*colloq*). — *n* a human being. — *vt* **mor'talise** or **-ize** to make mortal. — *n* **mortality** (*-tal'i-ti*) the condition of being mortal; death; frequency or number of deaths, esp. in proportion to population; the human race, nature or estate. — *adv* **mor'tally**. [L. *mortālis* — *morī*, to die.]

mortar *mör'tər*, *n* a vessel in which substances are pounded with a pestle; a short piece of artillery for throwing a heavy shell, a bomb, a lifeline, etc.; a mixture of cement, sand and water. — *vt* to join or plaster with mortar; to bombard with a mortar. — **mor'tarboard** a square board, with a handle beneath, for holding mortar; a square-topped college cap. [O.E. *mortere* — L. *mortārium*, a mortar, matter pounded.]

mortgage *mör'gij*, *n* a conditional conveyance of, or lien upon, land or other property as security for the performance of some condition (as the payment of money), becoming void on the performance of the condition; the act of conveying, or the deed effecting it; the amount of money advanced by a building society, bank, etc., on the security of one's property. — *vt* to subject (a property) to a mortgage; to pledge. — *n* **mortgagee'** a person to whom a mortgage is made or given; someone who gives or grants a mortgage. — *n* **mort'gagor** or **mort'gager** (*-jər*) someone who mortgages his or her property. [O.Fr., — *mort*, dead, *gage*, a pledge.]

mortice. See **mortise**.

mortician *mör-tish'ən*, (*US*) *n* an undertaker. [L. *mors*, *mortis*, death.]

mortify *mör'ti-fī*, *vt* to cause to feel humiliated or ashamed; to subdue (physical desires, etc.) by severities and penance. — *vi* to lose vitality; to become gangrenous; to practise asceticism: — *pr p* **mor'tifying**; *pa t* and *pa p* **mor'tified**. — *n* **mortification** (*mör-ti-fi-kā'shən*) the act of mortifying or state of being mortified; the death of part of the body; subduing the passions and appetites by a severe or strict manner of living; something which mortifies or vexes. — *adj* **mor'tified**. — *n* **mor'tifier**. — *adj* and *n* **mor'tifying**. [Fr. *mortifier* — L.L. *mortificāre*, to cause death to — *mors*, *mortis*, death, *facĕre*, to make.]

mortise or **mortice** *mör'tis*, *n* a hole made in wood, stone, etc. to receive a tenon; a recess cut into a printing-plate for the insertion of type, etc. (*printing*). — *vt* to cut a mortise in; to join by a mortise and tenon. — *n* **mor'tiser** or **mor'ticer**. — **mor'tise-lock** or **mor'tice-lock** a lock whose mechanism is covered by being sunk into the edge of a door, etc. [Fr. *mortaise*.]

mortuary *mört'ū-ər-i*, *n* a place where the dead are kept temporarily. — *adj* connected with death or burial. [L. *mortuārius* — *mortuus*, dead, *morī*, to die.]

morula *mör'ū-lə*, (*zool*) *n* a solid spherical mass of cells resulting from the cleavage of an ovum: — *pl* **mor'ulae** (*-lē*) or **mor'ulas**. — *adj* **mor'ular**. [L. *mōrum*, a mulberry.]

morwong *mör'wong*, *n* an Australian and New Zealand food fish. [Aboriginal.]

MOS *abbrev* for metal oxide semiconductor.

Mosaic *mō-zā'ik*, *adj* of or relating to *Moses*, the great Jewish lawgiver. — *n* **Mō'saism**. — **Mosaic Law** the law of the Jews given by Moses at Mount Sinai.

mosaic *mō-zā'ik*, *n* the fitting together in a design of small pieces of coloured marble, glass, etc.; a piece of work of this kind; anything of similar appearance, or composed by the piecing together of different things; a leaf-mosaic; leaf-mosaic disease (or **mosaic disease**); a hybrid with the parental characters side by side and not blended. — *adj* relating to, or composed of, mosaic. — *adv* **mosā'ically**. — *n* **mosā'icism** (*-i-sizm*) presence side by side of patches of tissue of unlike constitution. — *n* **mosaicist** (*mō-zā'i-sist*) a worker in mosaic. [Fr. *mosaïque* — L.L. *mosaicum*, *mūsaicum* — *mūsa* — Gr. *mousa*, a muse.]

moschatel *mos-kə-tel'*, *n* a small plant with pale-green flowers and a supposed musky smell. [Fr. *moscatelle* — It. *moschatella* — *moscato*, musk.]

Moselle or **Mosel** *mō-zel'*, *n* white wine from the district of the river *Moselle*, with an aromatic flavour.

Moses basket *mō'zəz bäs'kit*, *n* a portable cot for babies. [Story of Moses in the bulrushes, from the Bible: Exodus ii. 3.]

mosey *mō'zi*, (*slang*) *vi* to move along slowly, saunter.

moshav *mō-shäv'*, *n* an agricultural settlement in Israel: — *pl* **moshavim** (*-shə-vēm'*). [Heb., dwelling.]

Moslem *moz'lem* or *-ləm*, *n* and *adj*. Same as **Muslim**.

mosque *mosk*, *n* a Muslim place of worship. [Fr. *mosquée* — It. *moschea* — Ar. *masjid*.]

mosquito *mos-kē'tō*, *n* (*loosely*) any small biting or stinging insect; any of several long-legged insects of the family *Culicidae*, the females of which have their mouthparts adapted for bloodsucking and can therefore transmit diseases including malaria: — *pl* **mosqui'toes** or **mosqui'tos**. — **mosquito canopy, curtain** or **net** an arrangement of netting to keep out mosquitoes; **mosquito fish** the topminnow; **mosquito hawk** the nighthawk or goatsucker. [Sp. dimin. of *mosca*, a fly — L. *musca*.]

moss *mos*, *n* any of the *Musci*, a class of *Bryophyta*, small plants with simply constructed leaves, and no woody material, attached by rhizoids, the zygote growing into a small spore-bearing capsule that grows parasitically on the parent plant; a mass of such plants; a mosslike growth, covering or excrescence; loosely extended to plants of similar appearance to true mosses; boggy ground or soil. — *vt* to cover with moss; to clear of moss. — *vi* to gather moss. — *n* **moss'iness**. — *adj* **moss'like**. — *adj* **moss'y** overgrown or abounding with moss; like moss; boggy. — **moss agate** chalcedony with mosslike inclusions of chlorite, manganese oxide, etc.; **moss'back** a person of antiquated views (*NAm*); **moss green** a muted yellowy-green. — *adj* **moss'-grown** covered with moss. — **moss'land** wet, peaty land; **moss'plant** a plant of moss; the sexual generation in the life history of a moss, on which the asexual generation is parasitic; **moss'rose** a variety of rose having a mosslike growth on and below the calyx; **moss stitch** a knitting stitch — alternate plain and purl stitches along each row and in succeeding rows; **moss'-trooper** one of the freebooters that used to frequent the borders of England and Scotland. [O.E. *mōs*, bog.]

mossbunker *mos'bung-kər*, *n* the menhaden. [Du. *mars-banker*, the scad or horse mackerel.]

mossie[1] *mos'i* or **mozzie** *moz'i*, (*colloq*) *n* short for **mosquito**.

mossie[2] *mos'i*, (*SAfr*) *n* (also called **Cape sparrow**) a common South African sparrow, the male of which has a black head and curved white mark at the eye. [Afrik., from Du. *mosje*, dimin. of *mos*, sparrow.]

most *mōst*, *adj* the majority of; greatest in amount or number. — *adv* used to form the superlative of adjectives and adverbs; used as an intensifier; almost (*US colloq*). — *n* the greatest number or quantity. — *adv* **most'ly** for the most part; usually. — **at most** or **at the most** at the maximum; **for the most part** chiefly; in the main. [The Northumbrian form *māst* may have occurred in O.E. beside the ordinary form *mǣst*; or the vowel may come from analogy with the comparative.]

-most *-mōst*, *sfx* indicating superlative, e.g. *hindmost*, *farthermost*. [O.E. superl. sfx. *-mæst*, *-mest*.]

MOT *em-ō-tē'*, *n* a compulsory annual check made by order of the *M*inistry *o*f *T*ransport on vehicles of more than a certain age. — Also **MOT test**.

mot *mō*, (Fr.) *n* a word; a pithy or witty saying. — **le mot juste** (*lə mō zhüst*) the word which fits the context exactly.

mote *mōt*, *n* a particle of dust; a speck; a seed or other foreign particle in wool or cotton; a stain or blemish; anything very small. [O.E. *mot*.]

motel *mō-tel'*, *n* a hotel for motorists with rooms that are usu. accessible from a parking area. — *n* **motel'ier** the owner or manager of a motel. [*mo*tor ho*tel*.]

motet *mō-tet'*, (*mus*) *n* a polyphonic choral composition, usu. unaccompanied, with biblical or similar prose text; (*loosely*) an anthem or church cantata. — *n* **motett'ist**. [M.E. — O.Fr. dimin. of *mot*, word.]

moth *moth*, *n* the cloth-eating larvae of the clothes-moth; the imago of the same kind; any member of the *Heterocera*, broadly distinguished from butterflies by duller colouring, thicker body, antennae not clubbed, wings not tilted over the back in rest, and by the habit of flying by night. — *adj* **moth'y** full of moths; moth-eaten. — **moth'ball** a ball of naphthalene or other substance for keeping away clothes-moths. — *vt* to lay up in mothballs; to spray with a plastic and lay up (a ship, etc.); to lay aside temporarily, postpone work on, keep in readiness for eventual use. — *adj* **moth'-eaten** eaten or cut by the larvae of moths (also *fig*). — *adj* **moth'proof** (of clothes, etc.) chemically rendered resistant to moths. — *vt* to put in mothballs. [O.E. *moththe*, *mohthe*.]

mother[1] *mudh'ər*, *n* a female parent; that which has produced anything; the female head of a religious house or other establishment; a familiar term of address to, or prefix to the name of, an old woman; extended to an ancestress, a stepmother, mother-in-law, foster-mother. — *adj* received by birth, as it were from one's mother; being a mother; acting the part of a mother; originating; used to produce others from. — *vt* to give birth to; to acknowledge, to adopt, to treat as a son or daughter; to foster; to attribute the maternity or authorship of (with *on* or *upon*); to find a mother for. — *n* **moth'erhood** state of being a mother. — *n* **moth'ering** a rural English custom of visiting the mother church or one's parents on Mid-Lent Sunday **(Mothering Sunday)**. — *adj* **moth'erless** without a mother. — *n* **moth'erliness**. — *adj* **moth'erly** pertaining to, or becoming, a mother; like a mother. — **moth'erboard** a printed circuit board that can be plugged into the back of a computer and into which can be slotted other boards so that the computer can operate various peripherals; **moth'er-cell** (*biol*) a cell that gives rise to others by division; **mother church** the church from which others have sprung; a principal church; **moth'er-city** one from which another was founded as a colony; **mother country** or **moth'erland** the country of one's birth; the country from which a colony has gone out; **moth'ercraft** knowledge and skill required for care of child; **mother figure** an older woman who symbolises for one the qualities and authority of one's mother; **moth'erfucker** an unpleasant person or thing (*US vulg slang*); **moth'er-in-law** the mother of one's husband or wife: — *pl* **moth'ers-in-law**; **mother-in-law's tongue** a houseplant with swordlike leaves; **motherland** see **mother country**; **mother lode** (*mining*) the main lode of any system; **mother-of-pearl'** the nacreous internal layer of the shells in some molluscs (also *adj*); **moth'er-of-thousands** a perennial creeping plant with ivy-shaped leaves; **Mother's Day** a day for honouring mothers, as, in U.S., second Sunday in May; also used for Mothering Sunday; **mother's help** a person employed to help a mother with domestic duties, esp. the supervision of children; **mother ship** a ship having charge of torpedo-boats or small craft; a ship which provides a number of other, usu. smaller, ships with services, supplies, etc.; **mother superior** the head of a convent or any community of nuns; **mother-to-be'** a woman who is pregnant, esp. with her first child; **mother tongue** native language; a language from which another has its origin; **moth'er-water** residual liquid, still containing certain chemical substances, left after others have been crystallised or precipitated from it; **mother wit** native wit; common sense. — **be mother** (*colloq, facetious*) to pour the tea or dish out the food; **every mother's son** every man without exception; **Mother Carey's chicken** or **goose** the storm petrel, or similar bird; **the mother and father (**or **father and mother) of** (*colloq*) the biggest, greatest (usu. *fig*), as in *the mother and father of an argument* (or *of all arguments*). [O.E. *mōdor*.]

mother² *mudh'ər, n* a slimy mass of bacteria that oxidises alcohol into acetic acid (also **mother of vinegar**). — *adj* **moth'ery** like or containing mother. [Poss. the same as **mother¹**; or poss. — Du. *modder*, mud; cf. **mud**.]

mothering, motherly. See under **mother¹**.

mothproof. See under **moth**.

motif *mō-tēf', n* a theme or subject; an element in a composition, esp. a dominant element; a figure, subject or leitmotif (*mus*); an ornament added to a garment, often symbolic. [Fr. *motif*; see **motive**.]

motile *mō'tīl* or in U.S. *-til, adj* capable of moving spontaneously as a whole; characterised by motion. — *n* **motility** (*-til'i-ti*). [L. *mōtus*, movement.]

motion *mō'shən, n* the act, state or manner of changing place; a single movement; change of posture; power of moving or of being moved; agitation; a working in the mind; a formal proposal put before a meeting; an application to a court, during a case before it, for an order or rule that something be done, esp. something incidental to the progress of the cause rather than its issue; evacuation of the intestine; a piece of mechanism; faeces. — *vt* to direct or indicate by a gesture; to move, propose; to give motion to. — *vi* to offer a proposal. — *adj* **mō'tional.** — *adj* **mō'tionless.** — **mōtion picture** a cinema film; **motion sickness** same as **travel sickness; motion study** same as **time and motion study.** — **go through the motions** to make a half-hearted attempt; to pretend; **laws of motion** Newton's three laws: (1) Every body continues in its state of rest, or of uniform motion in a straight line, except so far as it may be compelled by force to change that state; (2) Change of motion is proportional to force applied, and takes place in the direction of the straight line in which the force acts; (3) To every action there is always an equal and contrary reaction. [Fr. *motion* — L. *mōtiō, -ōnis* — *movēre, mōtum*, to move.]

motive *mō'tiv, adj* causing motion; having power to cause motion; concerned with the initiation of action. — *n* an incitement of the will; a consideration or emotion that excites to action; a motif. — *vt* **mo'tivate** to provide with a motive; to induce; to give an incentive. — *n* **motivā'tion** motivating force, incentive. — *adj* **motivā'tional** relating to motivation. — *adv* **motiva'tionally.** — *n* **mo'tivator.** — *adj* **mo'tiveless.** — *n* **mo'tivelessness.** — *n* **motiv'ity** power of moving or of producing motion. — **motivation (**or **motivational) research** research into motivation, esp. into consumer reaction, carried out scientifically; **motive power** the energy or source of the energy by which anything is operated. [L.L. *mōtīvus* — L. *movēre, mōtum*, to move.]

motley *mot'li, adj* multicoloured, variegated; made of, or dressed in, motley; heterogeneous. — *n* a particoloured garb, such as a jester wore. [Poss. from O.E. *mot*, a speck.]

motocross *mō'tō-kros, n* a form of scrambling, motorcycle racing round a very rough circuit. [**motor**.]

motor *mō'tər, n* a mover; that which gives motion; a machine whereby some source of energy is used to give motion or perform work, esp. an internal-combustion engine or a machine for converting electrical into mechanical energy; a motor car; a muscle or nerve, concerned in bodily movement. — *adj* giving or transmitting motion; driven by a motor; of, for, with, or relating to, motor vehicles; concerned with the transmission of impulses; initiating bodily movement; pertaining to muscular movement or the sense of muscular movement. — *vt* and *vi* to convey, traverse or travel by a motor vehicle; to put on speed, to move fast (*colloq*). — *adj* **mo'torable** (of roads) able to be used by motor vehicles. — *n* **motorisā'tion** or **-z-**. — *vt* **mo'torise** or **-ize** to provide with, or adapt to the use of, a motor or motors; to interpret or imagine in terms of motor sensation. — *n* **mo'torist** a person who drives a motor car, esp. for pleasure. — **mo'torbike, mo'torboat, motor car, mo'torcycle** various types of vehicle driven by a motor; **motorcade** (*mō'tər-kād*) a procession of cars; **motor caravan** a motor vehicle with living, sleeping, etc. facilities, like a caravan; **mo'torcycling; mo'torcyclist.** — *adj* **mo'tor-driven** driven by a motor. — **motor generator** an electrical generator driven by an electric motor, whereby one voltage, frequency or number of phases, i.e. those of the motor, can be used to produce a different voltage, frequency or number of phases, i.e. those of the generator; **mo'torman** a man who controls a motor, esp. that of a tram-car or electric train; **mo'tormouth** a non-stop talker (*US slang*); **motor neurone** (*anat*) a neurone conveying a voluntary or motor impulse (**motor neurone disease** a disease in which progressive damage to motor neurones leads to muscle weakness and degeneration); **mo'tor-scooter** a small motorcycle, usu. with an engine of under 225 c.c.; **mo'tor-tractor** an internal-combustion engine for hauling loads, esp. for drawing agricultural implements; **mo'torway** a trunk road for fast-moving motor vehicles, with separate carriageways for vehicles travelling in opposite directions, and limited access and exit points. — **motorway madness** (*colloq*) reckless driving in bad conditions on motorways, esp. in fog. [L. *mōtor* — *movēre*, to move.]

motorail *mō'tō-rāl, n* a system of carrying cars and passengers by train on certain routes. [**motor**.]

motorbike ... to ... **motorway.** See under **motor**.

Motown *mō'town, n* a type of music that blends rhythm and blues and pop with gospel rhythms. [*Motor Town*, i.e. Detroit, Michigan, where it originated.]

mottle *mot'l, vt* to variegate blotchily. — *n* a blotched appearance, condition or surface. — *adj* **mott'led.** — *n* **mott'ling.** [Prob. from **motley**.]

motto *mot'ō, n* a short sentence or phrase adopted as representative of a person, family, etc., or accompanying a coat of arms; a passage prefixed to a book or chapter anticipating its subject; a scrap of verse or prose enclosed in a cracker or accompanying a sweetmeat: — *pl* **mott'oes** or **mott'os** (*-ōz*). [It., — L. *muttum*, a murmur.]

Motu *mō'too, n* a member of a group of aboriginal people of Papua New Guinea; their language, of the Malayo-Polynesian family: — *pl* **Mo'tu** or **Mo'tus.**

moue *moo*, (Fr.) *n* a grimace of discontent, pout.

moufflon or **mouflon** *moof'lon, n* a wild sheep of the mountains of Corsica, etc.; extended to large big-horned wild sheep of other kinds: — *pl* **mouff'lon** or **mouff'lons.** [Fr. *mouflon* — L.L. *mufrō, -ōnis*.]

mouillé *moo'yā*, (*phon*) *adj* (of *l* and *n*) sounded in a liquid manner, palatalised — as *gl* in 'seraglio', *ñ* in 'señor'. [Fr., moistened.]

moujik. See **muzhik**.

moulage *moo-läzh', n* the making of moulds (esp. of objects of interest in criminal investigation). [Fr. — M.Fr. *mollage* — O.Fr. *mouler*, to model.]

mould¹ or in U.S. **mold** *mōld, n* loose soft earth; earth, considered as the material of which the body is formed or to which it turns; the earth of the grave; soil rich in decayed matter. — *vt* to cover with soil. — *vi* **mould'er** to crumble to mould; to turn to dust; to waste away gradually. — *vt* to turn to dust. — *adj* **mould'y** like, or of the nature of, mould. —

mould'board the curved plate in a plough which turns over the soil. [O.E. *molde*.]

mould[2] or in U.S. **mold** *mōld*, *n* a woolly growth on bread, cheese, or other vegetable or animal matter; any one of various small fungi of different classes, forming such growths. — *vi* to become mouldy. — *vt* to cause or allow to become mouldy. — *n* **mould'iness**. — *adj* **mould'y** overgrown with mould; like mould; stale; bad, nasty (*colloq*). [M.E. *mowle*.]

mould[3] or in U.S. **mold** *mōld*, *n* template; the matrix in which a cast is made; a formed surface from which an impression is taken; the foundation up on which certain manufactured articles are built up; a thing formed in a mould, esp. a jelly or blancmange; nature; a form, model or pattern; that which is or may be moulded; a wire tray used to make paper by hand. — *vt* to knead; to shape; to model; to form in a mould. — *adj* **mould'able**. — *n* **mould'er**. — *n* **mould'ing** the process of shaping, esp. any soft substance; anything formed by or in a mould; an ornamental edging or band projecting from a wall or other surface, such as a fillet, astragal, bead, etc.; a strip of wood that can be applied for the purpose. — **mould'ing-board** a baker's board for kneading dough. — *adj* **mould'-made** (of paper) made on a machine, but having a deckle-edge like that of handmade paper. [O.Fr. *modle*, *molle* (Fr. *moule*) — L. *modulus*, a measure.]

moulin *moo͞'lɛ̃*, *n* a shaft in a glacier worn by water running down a crack. [Fr. mill.]

moult or in U.S. **molt** *mōlt*, *vi* to cast feathers or other covering; to be shed. — *vt* to shed. — *n* the act, process, condition or time of moulting. — *n* **moult'ing**. [O.E. (*bi*)*mūtian*, to exchange — L. *mūtāre*; the *l*, first a freak of spelling, afterwards sounded.]

mound[1] *mownd*, *n* a bank of earth or stone raised as a protection; a hillock; a heap. — *vt* to fortify with an embankment; to heap in a mound. — **mound'-bird** a megapode, or bird of the Australian family *Megapodidae*, gallinaceous birds that build large mounds as incubators; **mound'-builder** one of the Indians who in early times built great mounds in the eastern United States; a mound-bird.

mound[2] *mownd*, *n* a king's orb, as in *heraldry*. [Fr. *monde* — L. *mundus*, the world.]

mount[1] *mownt*, *n* a mountain (*archaic* except as **Mount**, as prefix to a name); a small hill or mound, natural or artificial; a fleshy protuberance on the hand (*palmistry*). [O.E. *munt* — L. *mōns*, *montis*, mountain.]

mount[2] *mownt*, *vi* to go up; to climb; to get up on horseback, bicycle, or the like; to rise in level or amount. — *vt* to climb, ascend; to get up on; to cover or copulate with; to place upon anything high; to put on horseback, or the like; to provide with an animal, bicycle, etc., to ride on; to fix in a setting, on a support, stand, or mount; to put in position and state of readiness for use or exhibition; to stage; to put into operation, carry out. — *n* manner of mounting; a step to mount by; a riding animal or cycle; that upon which a thing is placed or in which it is set for fixing, strengthening, embellishing, esp. the card surrounding a picture; the slide, etc., used in mounting an object for the microscope. — *adj* **mount'ed** on horseback; equipped with horses; set on high; set up; set. — **-moun'ted** (used in combination) set in or with a specified material, e.g. *silver-mounted*. — *n* **mount'er**. — *n* **mount'ing**. — **mount'ing-block** a block or stone to enable one to mount a horse. — **have the mount on** to ride (a particular horse) in a race; **mount guard** see under **guard**. [Fr. *monter*, to go up — L. *mōns*, *montis*, mountain.]

mountain *mownt'in*, *n* a high hill; a large quantity, excess, esp. of agricultural, dairy, etc. products bought up by an economic community to prevent a fall in prices. — *adj* of a mountain; growing, dwelling, etc. on or among mountains. — *n* **mountaineer'** a climber of mountains. — *vi* to climb mountains. — *n* **mountaineer'ing** mountain-climbing. — *adj* **mount'ainous** full of, or characterised by, mountains; large as a mountain; huge. — **mountain ash** the rowan tree; **mountain bicycle** a bicycle with a strong, heavy frame and wide tyres designed for use over rough terrain; **mountain cat** a catamount, a wildcat; **mountain chain** a range of mountains forming a long line; **mountain dew** (*colloq*) whisky; **mountain goat** a white goatlike animal of the Rocky Mountains (genus *Oreamnus*); any of various wild goats of mountainous regions; **mountain hare** a small species of hare, grey in summer, usu. white in winter. — *adv* and *adj* **mount'ain-high** overwhelmingly high. — **mountain laurel** an ericaceous shrub of N. America (genus *Kalmia*); **mountain lion** the puma or cougar; **mountain railway** a light narrow-gauge railway for mountainous regions, usually a rack-railway (see under **rack**[1]); **mountain ringlet** a rare alpine butterfly (genus *Erebia*); **mountain sheep** the bighorn, a large wild sheep of the Rocky Mountains in N. America, with large horns; **mountain sickness** sickness brought on by breathing rarefied air; **mount'ainside** the slope of a mountain; **mount'ain-top**. [O.Fr. *montaigne* — L. *mōns*, *montis*, mountain.]

mountant *mownt'ənt*, *n* an adhesive paste for mounting photographs, etc.; any substance in which specimens are suspended on a microscope slide. [Fr. *montant*, pres. p. of *monter*, to mount.]

mountebank *mown'ti-bangk*, *n* a charlatan; (*formerly*) a quack seller of remedies, etc. — *n* **moun'tebankery**. [It. *montimbanco* — *montare in banco*, to mount a bench, so as to harangue a crowd.]

Mounty or **Mountie** *mown'ti*, (*colloq*) *n* a member of the Royal Canadian *Mount*ed Police.

mourn *mörn*, *vi* to grieve for a death or other loss; to be sorrowful; to wear mourning. — *vt* to grieve for; to utter in a sorrowful manner. — *n* **mourn'er** a person who mourns a death, etc.; a person who attends a funeral, esp. a relative of the deceased. — *adj* **mourn'ful** causing, suggesting, or expressing sorrow; feeling grief. — *adv* **mourn'fully**. — *n* **mourn'fulness**. — *n* **mourn'ing** the act of expressing grief; the dress of mourners, or other tokens of mourning; the period during which one is officially mourning a death. — *adj* suitable for, or concerned with, mourning. — *adv* **mourn'ingly**. — **mourn'ing-band** a band of black material worn round the sleeve to signify that one is in mourning; **mourning dove** an American pigeon with plaintive note. — **in mourning** wearing black in token of mourning. [O.E. *murnan*.]

mousaka. See **moussaka**.

mouse *mows*, *n* a little rodent animal found in houses and in the fields; extended to various voles and other animals more or less like the mouse; a device which is moved by hand over a flat surface thereby causing the cursor to move correspondingly on screen (*comput*); a timid, shy, colourless person; a black eye, or discoloured swelling (*slang*): — *pl* **mice** (*mīs*). — *vi* (*mowz* or *mows*) to hunt for mice; to prowl. — *n* **mouser** (*mow'zər* or *mow'sər*) a cat that catches mice. — *n* and *adj* **mousing** (*mow'zing* or *mow'sing*). — *adj* **mousey** or **mousy** (*mow'si*) like a mouse in colour or smell; (of hair) limp and dull greyish-brown; (of a person) uninteresting, too unassertive. — **mouse colour** the grey colour of a mouse. — *adj* **mouse'-colour** or **-coloured**. — **mouse deer** a chevrotain; **mouse-eared bat** a kind of bat, *Myotis myotis*, found chiefly in continental Europe and Western Asia; **mouse'hole** a hole made or used by mice; a small hole or opening; **mouse'trap** a trap for mice; any cheese of indifferent quality; Cheddar cheese. [O.E. *mūs*, pl. *mȳs*.]

moussaka or **mousaka** *mōō-sä'kə*, *n* a Greek dish consisting of minced meat, aubergines, tomatoes and cheese sauce.

mousse *mōōs*, *n* a a frothy dish made with whipped cream, eggs, etc., flavoured and usu. eaten cold; a cosmetic preparation of similar consistency, esp. an application for shaping the hair into a style. [Fr., moss, froth.]

mousseline *mōōs-lēn'*, *n* fine French muslin; a very thin glassware; a claret glass made of it; a dish made with mousseline sauce. — **mousseline-de-laine** (*-də-len'*) an all-wool muslin; **mousseline-de-soie** (*-də-swä'*) a silk muslin. — **mousseline sauce** a kind of sauce hollandaise made light by adding whipped cream or egg-white. [Fr.]

moustache or in U.S. **mustache** *məs-*, *mus-* or *mōōs-täsh'*, *n* the hair upon the upper lip. — Also in *pl*. — *adj* **moustached'**. — **moustache cup** a cup with the top partly covered, formerly used to keep the moustache from getting wet. — See also **mustachio**. [Fr. *moustache* — It. *mostaccio* — Doric Gr. *mystax*, *-ăkos*, the upper lip, moustache.]

mouth *mowth*, *n* the opening in the head of an animal or human by which it eats and utters sound; an opening or entrance, as of a bottle, river, cave, etc.; a person thought of as a consumer of food; a wry face, a grimace; backchat, insolence or boastful talk; the responsiveness of a horse to the bit: — *pl* **mouths** (*mowdhz*). — *vt* (*mowdh*) to utter with exaggerated, affectedly pompous, or self-conscious action of the mouth; to form (words) silently by moving the lips. — *vi* to declaim, rant; to grimace. — *combining form* **-mouthed** (*mowdhd*) having a mouth of specified type, as *wide-mouthed*. — *n* **mouther** (*mowdh'ər*). — *n* **mouthful** (*mowth'fəl*) as much food etc. as fills the mouth; a small quantity of food or drink; a big word; a momentous utterance (*slang*); an outburst of strong language: — *pl* **mouth'fuls**. — *adj* **mouth'-less**. — **mouth'breather** a person who habitually breathes through the mouth; **mouth'-breeder** a fish that carries its young in its mouth for protection; **mouth music** music (usu. accompanying dance) sung, not played on instrument(s); **mouth organ** a small musical instrument encasing metallic reeds, played by the mouth — a harmonica; **mouth'parts** any of the limblike parts adapted for feeding that surround the mouth of an anthropod; **mouth'piece** the piece of a musical instrument, tobacco pipe, mask, etc., held to or in the mouth; a spokesman. — *adj* **mouth-to-mouth'** denoting a method of artificial respiration in which one breathes air directly into the patient's mouth to inflate the lungs. — **mouth'wash** an antiseptic solution for cleansing the mouth and for gargling with. — *adj* **mouth'-watering** causing the release of saliva in the mouth, highly appetising. — **be all mouth** (*slang*) to be unable to support one's boastful talk with action; **have a big mouth** (*colloq*) to (habitually) talk indiscreetly, loudly, or too much; **keep one's mouth shut** (*colloq*) not to divulge a secret etc.; **shoot one's mouth off** (*slang*) to talk freely, inaccurately, tactlessly, etc.; **shut** or **stop the mouth of** to silence. [O.E. *mūth*.]

mouton *mōō'tən*, *n* a sheepskin which has been processed, sheared and dyed to resemble the fur of another animal. [Fr. *mouton*, a sheep.]

mouvementé *mōōv-mā-tā*, (Fr.) *adj* full of movement, lively.

move *mōōv*, *vt* to cause to change place or posture; to set in motion; to impel; to excite to action; to cause (the bowels) to be evacuated; to persuade; to instigate; to arouse; to provoke; to touch the feelings of; to propose formally before those present at a meeting; to recommend. — *vi* to go from one place to another; to change place or posture; to walk, to carry oneself; to change residence; to make a motion as in an assembly; to begin to act; to take action; to become active or exciting (*colloq*); to hurry up (*colloq*); to go about one's activities, live one's life, pass one's time; (in chess, draughts, etc.) to transfer a piece in one's turn to another square: — *pr p* **mov'ing**; *pa t* and *pa p* **moved**. — *n* an act of moving; a proceeding or step, a manoeuvre; the changing of one's residence or business premises; (in chess, draughts, etc.) one's turn to play; the manner in which a chessman or other playing-piece is or can be moved. — *adj* **movable** or (esp. *law*) **moveable** (*mōōv'ə-bl*) mobile; changeable; not fixed. — *n* (esp. in *pl*) a portable piece of furniture; a piece of movable or moveable property. — *n* **mov'ableness, move'-ableness, movabil'ity** or **moveabil'ity**. — *adv* **mov'ably** or **move'ably**. — *n* **move'ment** an act or manner of moving; change of position; an action or gesture; activity; impulse; the moving parts in a mechanism, esp. the wheel assembly of a clock or watch; tempo or pace; a main division of an extended musical composition, with its own more or less independent structure; the suggestion of motion conveyed by a work of art; a general tendency or current of thought, opinion, taste or action, whether organised and consciously propagated or a mere drift. — *n* **mov'er**. — *adj* **mov'ing** causing motion; changing position; affecting the feelings; pathetic. — *adv* **mov'ingly**. — **movable feast** a church feast, such as Easter, whose date varies from year to year; **moving average** a sequence of values derived from an earlier sequence from which a mean was taken of each successive group of values with a constant number of members. — *adj* **mov'ing-coil** of, or pertaining to, electrical equipment that incorporates a coil of wire so placed within a magnetic field as either to vibrate when current is passed through it, or to generate a current when vibrated. — **moving map** a map used on board a ship or aircraft that adjusts to keep the position of the moving vessel always in correspondence with a fixed centre point on the map; **moving pavement** (in an airport, etc.) a moving strip set into the floor that carries pedestrians along as though on a conveyor belt; **moving pictures** motion pictures, cinematograph films; **moving staircase** an escalator. — **get a move on** to hurry up; to make progress; **make a move** to take a step, perform a manoeuvre; to prepare to depart; **move heaven and earth** see under **heaven**; **move house** to move to a new place of residence; to move one's possessions to one's new home; **move in** to occupy new premises, etc.; **move out** to vacate premises; **move over** or **up** to move so as to make room for someone, etc.; **movers and shakers** (esp. *US*) the people with power and influence; **on the move** travelling about; progressing. [A.Fr. *mover*, O.Fr. *movoir* (Fr. *mouvoir*) — L. *movēre*, to move.]

movie *mōō'vi*, (*colloq*) *n* a motion picture, a cinematograph film; (in *pl* with **the**) motion pictures in general or the industry producing them. — **mov'iegoer**; **mov'ieland** the world of film-making; **mov'ie-maker**. [*Mov*ing picture and *-ie*.]

Moviola® *mōō-vē-ō'lə*, *n* a machine reproducing both the sound and picture, used to facilitate film-editing. [**movie** and **Pianola**.]

mow *mō*, *vt* to cut (grass, hay, etc.) or cut the hay etc. in (a field) or grass on (a lawn) with a machine or scythe; to cut down in great numbers (with *down*): — *pr p* **mow'ing**; *pa t* **mowed** (*mōd*); *pa p* **mowed** or **mown** (*mōn*). — *adj* **mowed** or **mown**. — *n* **mow'er** a person who mows grass, etc.; a machine with revolving blades for mowing grass. — *n* **mow'ing** the act of cutting. — **mow'ing-machine**. [O.E. *māwan*.]

moxie *mok'si*, (*US slang*) *n* courage, daring, energy. [*Moxie*®, a soft drink.]

moya *moi'ä*, *n* volcanic mud. [Prob. Am. Sp.]

Moygashel® *moi'gə-shel, n* (also without *cap*) a type of linen manufactured in Northern Ireland. [Place name.]

moz or **mozz** *moz*, (*Austr slang*) *n* a curse or jinx. — *n* **mozz'le** luck, esp. bad luck. [Heb. *mazzāl*, luck.]

Mozartian or **Mozartean** *mō-tsär'ti-ən, adj* of or like (the style, etc. of) Wolfgang Amadeus *Mozart* (1756–91), Austrian composer.

mozz. See **moz.**

mozzarella *mot-sə-rel'ə, n* a soft Italian curd cheese. [It.]

mozzie. See **mossie**[1].

mozzle. See **moz.**

mpg and **mph** *abbrev* respectively for miles per gallon and miles per hour.

MPhil. *abbrev* for Master of Philosophy.

MR *abbrev* for: Master of the Rolls; Mauritian rupee; motivation(al) research (investigative study of consumer reaction).

Mr *mis'tər, n* the normal form of title prefixed to a man's name, whether full name or surname only, or sometimes to an office held by a man: — *pl* sometimes **Messrs** (*mes'ərz*). — **Mr Right** (*colloq*) the ideal mate or marriage partner sought by a woman. [Abbrev. of **Mister.**]

MRC *abbrev* for Medical Research Council.

MRCGP *abbrev* for Member of the Royal College of General Practitioners.

MRCP *abbrev* for Member of the Royal College of Physicians.

MRI *abbrev* for magnetic resonance imaging.

mridangam or **mridamgam** *mri-däng'gəm*, **mridang** *mri-däng'* or **mridanga** *mri-däng'gə, n* a two-headed Indian drum, one of the heads being larger than the other. [Sans. *mridaṁga.*]

mRNA (*genetics*) *abbrev* for messenger RNA.

MRRP *abbrev* for manufacturer's recommended retail price.

Mrs *mis'iz, n* the normal form of title prefixed to a married woman's name, whether her full name with her own or her husband's given name, or her surname only. [Abbrev. of **Mistress.**]

MS *abbrev* for: manuscript; Mauritius (I.V.R.); Mississippi (U.S. state); multiple sclerosis.

Ms *miz* or *məz, n* a title substituted for **Mrs** or **Miss** before the name of a woman, to avoid distinguishing between the married and the unmarried.

ms *abbrev* for: manuscript; millisecond(s).

MSc *abbrev* for Master of Science.

MSDOS *em-es-dos'*, (*comput*) *abbrev* for Microsoft® disk-operating system.

MSF *abbrev* for Manufacturing, Science and Finance (Union).

MSS or **mss** *abbrev* for manuscripts.

msv *abbrev* for millisievert(s).

MT *abbrev* for Montana (U.S. state).

Mt *abbrev* for: metical (currency of Mozambique); Mount.

mth *abbrev* for month.

Mts *abbrev* for Mountains.

mu *mū, n* the Greek letter M, μ, equivalent to M; used as a symbol for **micron** and **micro-** (2). — **mu-** (or μ-) **meson** a subatomic particle, classed formerly as the lightest type of meson, now as the heaviest type of lepton, and largely superseded by **muon** (*mū'*) (q.v.). [Gr. *mȳ.*]

much *much, adj* (*compar* **more;** *superl* **most**) a great quantity of. — *adv* in a great degree; to a great extent; in nearly the same way; by far. — *n* a great deal; anything of importance or worth. — **a bit much** too much to put up with, unreasonable; **as much as** or **much as** although, even though; **make much of** see **make; much of a muchness** just about the same value or amount; **not much of a** a rather poor specimen of a; **not up to much** (*colloq*) not very good; **too much for** more than a match for; **too much of a good thing** or **too much** more than can be tolerated. [M.E. *muche, muchel* — O.E. *micel, mycel.*]

muciferous, mucigen. See under **mucus.**

mucilage *mū'si-lij, n* a gluey mixture of carbohydrates in plants; any sticky substance; gum used as an adhesive. — *adj* **mucilaginous** (*-laj'*). — *n* **mucilag'inousness.** [L.L. *mucilago*, mouldy juice, — *mucēre*, to be mouldy.]

mucin. See under **mucus.**

muck *muk*, (*colloq*) *n* dung; manure; wet or clinging filth; anything contemptible or worthless; dirt, debris, rubble; rubbishy reading matter; a mess. — *vt* to clear of muck (with *out*); to manure with muck; to make dirty (with *up*); to make a mess of, to bungle (with *up*; *n* **muck'-up**); to treat inconsiderately (with *about* or *around*). — *vi* (usu. with *about* or *around*) to potter; to act the fool. — *n* **muck'er** a coarse, unrefined person; a best friend, mate, sidekick. — *n* **muck'iness.** — *adj* **muck'y** nasty, filthy; like muck. — **muck'heap** a dunghill. — *vi* **muck'-rake** to seek out and expose scandals, esp. concerning those in the public eye. — **muck'-raker; muck'-raking.** — *vi* **muck'spread** to spread manure. — **muck'-spreader** an agricultural machine for spreading manure; **muck'sweat** (*Brit*) profuse sweat. — **make a muck of** (*colloq*) to mismanage; **muck in (with)** (*colloq*) to share with; to help, participate (in). [Prob. Scand.]

muckluck or **mukluk** *muk'luk, n* an Eskimo sealskin boot. [Eskimo.]

mucus *mū'kəs, n* the slimy fluid secreted by the mucous membrane of the nose or other parts. — *adj* **muciferous** (*-sif'*) secreting or conveying mucus. — *n* **mu'cigen** (*-si-jen*) a substance secreted by the cells of mucous membrane, converted into mucin. — *n* **mucin** (*mū'sin*) any one of a class of albuminous substances in mucus. — *adj* **mucoid** (*mū'koid*) like mucus. — *adj* **mucopū'rulent** of mucus and pus. — *n* **mucosa** (*mū-kō'sə*) the mucous membrane: — *pl* **mucō'sae** (*-sē*). — *adj* **mucosanguin'eous** consisting of mucus and blood. — *n* **mucos'ity.** — *adj* **mu'cous** like mucus; slimy; viscous; producing mucus. — *adj* **mu'cūlent** like mucus. — **mucous membrane** the lining of various tubular cavities of the body, with glands secreting mucus. [L. *mūcus*, nose mucus; cf. *mungĕre*, to wipe away.]

mud *mud, n* wet soft earth; a mixture of earthy or clayey particles with water; a similar mixture with certain added chemicals used as a lubricant in drilling oil-wells; vilification, abuse, slander, thought of as sticking or clinging like mud. — *adv* **mudd'ily.** — *n* **mudd'iness.** — *adj* **mudd'y** foul with mud; containing mud; covered with mud; like mud; mud-coloured; cloudy, murky; confused; stupid. — *vt* and *vi* to make or become muddy: — *pr p* **mudd'ying;** *pa t* and *pa p* **mudd'ied.** — **mud'bath** a bath in mud, esp. as a remedy; an outdoor event taking place in muddy conditions (*colloq*); **mud'-dauber** a wasp that deposits its eggs in individual cells constructed of mud; **mud'fish** a fish that burrows in mud, esp. a lung-fish; **mud'flap** a flap fixed behind the wheels of a vehicle to prevent mud, etc. being thrown up behind; **mud'flat** a muddy stretch submerged at high water; **mud'guard** a curved hood fixed over a wheel to catch mud splashes thrown up by it; **mud hen** any of a variety of water-birds, such as rails, coots, gallinules, that live in marshy places; **mud'-lark** a name for various birds that frequent mud; a person who picks up a living along the banks of tidal rivers; a street urchin; a racehorse that responds well to muddy conditions (*Austr*). — *vi* to work or play in mud. — **mud'pack** a cosmetic paste for cleansing the skin, containing fuller's earth; **mud pie** a small moulded mass of mud to play with made by children; an insult or calumny hurled at someone; **mud puppy** an aquatic salamander (genus *Necturus*) of N. America that retains certain larval features, including external gills; **mud skipper** a goby that can skip about on bare mud; **mud'slide** a slippage of a mass of mud down a hillside, etc.; **mud'-slinger; mud'-slinging** vilification; **mud turtle** a freshwater turtle of the genus *Kinosternon*. — **clear as mud** not at all clear; **his, her,** etc., **name is mud** he, she, etc., is very much out of favour; **muddy the waters** to confuse the issue; **mud in your eye** a facetious drinking-toast; **throw, fling** or **sling mud at** to insult, to slander. [Cf. Old Low Ger. *mudde*, Du. *modder*.]

muddle *mud'l, vt* to confuse; to mix up, fail to distinguish between (with *up*); to mix, stir (drinks, etc.; *US*). — *n* confusion, mess; mental confusion, bewilderment. — *n* **mudd'lehead** a vague, easily confused person. — *adj* **muddlehead'ed.** — *adv* **muddlehead'edly.** — *n* **muddlehead'edness.** — *n* **mudd'ler.** — **muddle through** (*Brit*) to get through difficulties more by good luck than good organisation. [Frequentative of **mud**.]

mudéjar *mōō-dhā'hhar*, (Sp.) *n* a Spanish Moor, esp. one permitted to remain in Spain after the Christian reconquest: — *pl* **mudé'jares** (*-rās*). — *adj* of a style of architecture characteristic of the mudéjares. — Also with *cap*. [Ar. *mudajjan*, person allowed to remain.]

mudge *muj*, (*colloq*) *vt* to blur, confuse. — *vi* to equivocate, prevaricate. — *n* **mudg'er.** [Orig. used in *fudge and mudge*, poss. from **muddle** and **fudge**[2].]

mudra *mə-drä'*, *n* any of the symbolic hand gestures in Hindu religious ceremonies and Indian dance. [Sans., lit. sign, token.]

muesli *mü'zli*, *n* a dish of rolled oats, nuts, fruit, etc. eaten esp. as a breakfast cereal. [Swiss Ger.]

muezzin *mōō-ez'in*, *n* the Muslim official who calls the faithful to prayer. [Ar. *mu'adhdhin*.]

muff[1] *muf*, *n* a cylinder of fur or thick fabric for keeping the hands warm; a contrivance of fur, etc. for keeping the feet, ears, etc. warm. [Prob. from Du. *mof*.]

muff[2] *muf*, *n* (*colloq*) a bungler, esp. in sport; an unpractical person; a man lacking male vigour and heartiness (*derog*); a failure, esp. to hold a ball. — *vt* to perform awkwardly; to bungle; to miss. — *adj* **muff'ish.** [Poss. **muff**[1].]

muffin *muf'in*, *n* a soft, breadlike cake, eaten hot, with butter; a cup-shaped cake made with batter (*US*). — **muffin man** an itinerant muffin-seller.

muffle[1] *muf'l*, *vt* to envelop, for warmth, concealment, stifling of sound, etc.; to deaden or dull the sound of. — *n* a means of muffling; a receptacle, oven or compartment in which things can be heated in a furnace without contact with the fuel and its products; (a kiln containing) an inner chamber in which to fire painted porcelain, enamel, etc. — *adj* **muff'led.** — *n* **muff'ler** a scarf for the throat; a person or thing that muffles; a silencer (*US*). [App. Fr. *mouffle*, mitten.]

muffle[2] *muf'l*, *n* the thick naked upper lip and nose, as of a ruminant. [Fr. *mufle*.]

Mufti *muf'ti*, *n* an expounder of Muslim law: — *pl* **Muf'tis.** [Ar. *muftī* — *'aftā*, to make a legal decision.]

mufti *muf'ti*, *n* the civilian dress of someone who wears a uniform when on duty. [Prob. from **Mufti**.]

mug[1] *mug*, *n* a cup with more or less vertical sides; its contents. — *n* **mug'ful** (*-fəl*): — *pl* **mug'fuls.** [Poss. Scand.]

mug[2] *mug*, (*colloq*) *n* the face; the mouth. — **mug'shot** (*colloq*) a photograph of a person's face, esp. one taken for police records. [Poss. from the grotesque face on a drinking-mug.]

mug[3] *mug*, (*colloq*) *n* a simpleton; an easy dupe. — **a mug's game** something only fools would do. [Poss. from **mug**[2].]

mug[4] *mug*, (*colloq*) *vt* and *vi* (often with *up*) to study hard, to swot up.

mug[5] *mug*, (*slang*) *vt* and *vi* to attack suddenly with the intention of robbing. — *n* **mugg'er.** — *n* **mugg'ing.** [Perh. **mug**[2] or **mug**[3].]

muggins *mug'inz*, *n* a fool, sucker, esp. used *facetiously* to refer to oneself as such.

muggy *mug'i*, *adj* foggy; close and damp, as weather. [Perh. O.N. *mugga*, mist.]

mugwort *mug'wûrt*, *n* a common British wormwood. [O.E. *mucgwyrt*, lit. midge-wort.]

mugwump *mug'wump*, (*NAm*) *n* someone who keeps politically aloof. — *n* **mug'wumpery.** [Old slang, important person, bigwig, — Algonquian *mugquomp*, a great chief.]

Muhammedan. See **Mohammedan.**

mujahedin or **mujaheddin** *mōō'jə-hə-dēn'*, *npl* Islamic fundamentalist freedom fighters. [Ar. *mujāhidīn*, fighters.]

mukluk. See **muckluck.**

mulatto *mū-lat'ō*, *n* the offspring of a Negro and a person of European stock (also *adj*): — *pl* **mulatt'os** or **mulatt'oes.** [Sp. *mulato*, dimin. of *mulo*, mule; Fr. *mulâtre*.]

mulberry *mul'bə-ri*, *n* the edible blackberry-like fruit of any tree of the genus *Morus*; the tree bearing it, with leaves on which silkworms feed; a dark purple colour (also *adj*). [Prob. O.H.G. *mulberi* (Mod. Ger. *Maulbeere*) — L. *mōrum*.]

mulch *mulch*, *n* loose material, strawy dung, etc., laid round the roots of plants to protect them and promote growth. — *vt* to cover with mulch. [Cf. Ger. dialect *molsch*, soft, beginning to decay; O.E. *melsc*.]

mulct *mulkt*, *n* a fine; a penalty. — *vt* to fine; to swindle; to deprive (with *of*). [L. *mulcta*, a fine.]

mule[1] *mūl*, *n* the offspring of the ass and horse (esp. a male donkey and mare) used as a beast of burden; a hybrid, e.g. a cross between a canary and another finch; a cotton-spinning machine; an obstinate person; a person employed to smuggle drugs into a country (*slang*); a coin with obverse and reverse designs struck from dies of two different issues. — *n* **muleteer** (*mū-li-tēr'*) a mule-driver. — *adj* **mu'lish** obstinate. [O.E. *mūl* — L. *mūlus*, *mūla*.]

mule[2] *mūl*, *n* a backless slipper. [Fr. *mule*.]

mulga *mul'gə*, *n* an acacia found in arid regions of Australia; (with **the**) the outback. — **mulga wire** (*Austr*) bush telegraph. [Native word.]

muliebrity *mū-li-eb'ri-ti*, *n* womanhood. [L. *muliebritās*, *-tātis* — *mulier*, a woman.]

mull[1] *mul*, (*Scot*) *n* a promontory. [Prob. Gael. *maol* or O.N. *mūli*, snout.]

mull[2] *mul*, *n* a soft muslin. — Also **mul'mul** or **mul'mull.** [Hind. *malmal*.]

mull[3] *mul*, *vi* and *vt* (with *over*) to cogitate, ponder or turn over in the mind.

mull[4] *mul*, *vt* to warm, spice and sweeten (wine, ale, etc.). — *adj* **mulled.** — *n* **mull'er.**

mullah *mul'ə* or *mōōl'ə*, *n* a Muslim learned in theology and law; a title of respect for a person whose work lies in advising on, expounding the law, etc. [Pers., Turk., Hind. *mullā* — Ar. *maulā*.]

mullein *mul'in*, *n* a tall, stiff, yellow-flowered woolly plant (genus *Verbascum*) of the Mediterranean area, also known as *Aaron's rod*. [A.Fr. *moleine*.]

muller[1]. See **mull**[4].

muller[2] *mul'ər*, *n* a pulverising tool for medicinal powders, painters' colours, etc. [Perh. O.Fr. *moloir* — *moldre* (Fr. *moudre*), to grind.]

mullet *mul'it*, *n* a nearly cylindrical fish of the genus *Mugil* (the *grey mullet*) or a slightly compressed fish of the genus *Mullus* (the *red mullet*), both palatable. [O.Fr. *mulet*, dimin. — L. *mullus*, red mullet.]

mulligan *mul'i-gən*, (*US colloq*) *n* a stew made from various scraps of food. [Perh. from the surname.]

mulligatawny *mul-i-gə-tö'ni*, *n* an East Indian curry soup. [Tamil *milagu-tannīr*, pepper-water.]

mullion *mul'yən*, (*archit*) *n* an upright division between the panes or casements of a window, etc. — *adj*

mull'ioned. [Poss. by metathesis from older, synonymous *monial*, — O.Fr.]

mullock *mul'ək*, (*Austr*) *n* rubbish, esp. mining refuse. — **poke mullock at** to mock, ridicule. [From obs. or dialect *mull*, dust.]

mulloway *mul'ə-wā*, *n* a large Australian food-fish, (genus *Sciaena*).

mulmul or **mulmull**. See **mull**[2].

multi- *mul-ti-*, or sometimes before a vowel **mult-** *combining form* denoting much or many. — *adj* **multi-acc'ess** (*comput*) denoting a system which permits several operators working at different terminals to have access to its facilities at the same time. — *adj* **multi-auth'or** (or **-auth'ored**) denoting a text which has been written by several individuals. — *adj* **multicell'ular** having or made up of many cells. — *adj* **multichann'el** having or employing several communications channels. — *adj* **mul'ticoloured** many-coloured. — *adj* **multicul'tural** (of a society) made up of many distinct cultural groups. — *n* **multicul'turalism** the policy of accommodating any number of distinct cultures within the one society without prejudice or discrimination. — *n* and *adj* **multicul'turalist**. — *adj* **multidimen'sional** having several aspects or dimensions; of more than three dimensions (*math*). — *adj* **multidirec'tional** extending in a number of directions. — *adj* **multidisciplin'ary** involving a combination of several (academic) disciplines, methods, etc. — *adj* **multifac'eted** (of a gem) having many facets; having many aspects, characteristics, etc. — *adj* **multifactor'ial** involving or caused by many different factors. — *adj* **mul'tiform** having many forms. — *n* **multiform'ity**. — *adj* **mul'ti-grade** denoting a motor oil with a viscosity such as to match the properties of several grades of motor oil. — *n* **multigrav'ida** (L. *gravida*, pregnant) a pregnant woman who has had one or more previous pregnancies: — *pl* **multigrav'idae** (*-dē*) or **multigrav'idas**. — *n* **mul'tigym** an apparatus incorporating weights and levers in a variety of arrangements, enabling one to exercise and tone up one set of muscles at a time. — *n* **mul'tihull** a sailing vessel with more than one hull. — *adj* **multilat'eral** many-sided; with several parties or participants. — *n* **multilat'eralism**. — *n* and *adj* **multilat'eralist** (a person) favouring multilateral action, esp. in abandoning or reducing production of nuclear weapons. — *adj* **multilingual** (*-ling'gwəl*) in many languages; speaking several languages; (of a country, state or society) in which several languages are spoken. — *n* **multilin'gualism** the ability to speak several languages. — *n* **multilin'guist** a person who is multilingual. — *n* **multimē'dia** the use of a combination of different media of communication (in e.g. entertainment, education); simultaneous presentation of several visual and/or sound entertainments. — Also *adj*. — *n* **multimillionaire'** a person who is a millionaire several times over. — *n* **multina'tional** a large business company which operates in several countries. — *adj* relating to this type of company. — *n* **multi-own'ership** ownership of property on the principle of time-sharing (q.v.). — *n* **multipa'ra** (L. *parēre*, to bring forth) a woman who has given birth for the second or subsequent time, or is about to do so as distinct from a *primipara*. — *n* **multipar'ity** the condition of being a multipara or multiparous. — *adj* **multip'arous** giving birth for the second or subsequent time; producing several young at one birth (*zool*); giving rise to several lateral axes (*bot*). — *adj* **multipar'tite** divided into many parts. — *n* **mul'tiplex** (*telecomm*) a system enabling two or more signals to be sent simultaneously on one communications channel. — *vt* to incorporate in a multiplex system. — Also *adj*. — *n* **mul'tiplexer**. — *n* **multipro'gramming** (*comput*) a technique of handling several programs simultaneously by interleaving their execution through time-sharing. — *adj* **multipur'pose**. — *adj* **multirā'cial** embracing, or consisting of, many races. — *n* **multirā'cialism** the policy of recognising the rights of all in a multiracial society. — *n* **multiskill'ing** in technologically advanced industries, the training of employees in a variety of skills. — *adj* **mul'ti-stage** in a series of distinct parts; (of a rocket) consisting of a number of parts that fall off in series at predetermined places on its course. — *adj* **mul'tistorey** having a (large) number of levels or storeys. — *adj* **mul'ti-track** (of a recording) made up of several different tracks blended together. — *adj* **multi-u'ser** (*comput*; of a computer) able to be used by several people at once. — *n* **multivā'lence** (or *-tiv'ə-*) or **multivā'lency** (or *-tiv'ə-*). — *adj* **multivā'lent** (or *-tiv'ə-*; *chem*) having a valency greater than one. [L. *multus*, much.]

multi-access ... to ... **multifactorial**. See under **multi-**.

multifarious *mul-ti-fā'ri-əs*, *adj* having great diversity; made up of many parts; manifold. — *adv* **multifā'riously**. — *n* **multifā'riousness**. [L. *multifārius*.]

multiform ... to ... **multipartite**. See under **multi-**.

multiple *mul'ti-pl*, *adj* consisting of many elements or components, esp. of the same kind; manifold; compound; multiplied or repeated; allowing many messages to be sent over the same wire (*teleg*). — *n* a quantity which contains another an exact number of times. — *adv* **multiply** (*mul'ti-pli*). — *adj* **multiple-choice'** (of an examination question) accompanied by several possible answers from which the correct answer is to be chosen. — **multiple cinema** a cinema which has been converted into two or more separate cinemas; **multiple fruit** a single fruit formed from several flowers in combination, such as a pineapple, fig, or mulberry; **multiple personality** (*psychiatry*) a disorder in which the subject's personality fragments into a number of distinct personalities; **multiple sclerosis** a chronic progressive disease in which there is patchy deterioration of the myelia forming a sheath for the nerve fibres, resulting in various forms of paralysis throughout the body; **multiple shop** or **store** one of many shops belonging to the same firm, often dispersed about the country; **multiple star** a group of stars so close as to seem one. — **common multiple** a number or quantity that can be divided by each of several others without a remainder; **lowest** or **least common multiple** the smallest number that forms a common multiple. [Fr., — L.L. *multiplus* — root of L. *plēre*, to fill.]

multiplex[1] *mul'ti-pleks*, *adj* multiple. — *n* a cinema divided up into several small cinemas, a multiple cinema. [L. *multiplex* — *plicāre*, to fold.]

multiplex[2], **multiplexer**. See under **multi-**.

multiply[1] *mul'ti-plī*, *vt* to increase the number of; to accumulate; to reproduce; to obtain the product of (*math*). — *vi* to become more numerous; to be augmented; to reproduce; to perform the mathematical process of multiplication: — *pr p* **mul'tiplying**; *pa t* and *pa p* **mul'tiplied**. — *adj* **mul'tipliable** or **mul'tiplicable**. — *n* **multiplicand'** a quantity to be multiplied by another (the multiplier). — *n* **multiplicā'tion** the act of multiplying or increasing in number; the rule or operation by which quantities are multiplied. — *n* **multiplicity** (*-plis'i-ti*) the state of being manifold; a great number. — *n* **mul'tiplier** a person or thing that multiplies; a quantity by which another (the multiplicand) is multiplied; a device or instrument for intensifying some effect (*phys*); the ratio of the change in national income to the change in the level of investment or spending that causes the income change (*econ*). — **multiplication table** a tabular arrangement giving the products of pairs of numbers usu. up to 12. [Fr. *multiplier* — L. *multiplicāre* — *plicāre*, to fold.]

multiply[2] *mul'ti-plī*. See under **multiple**.
multiprogramming ... to ... **multi-track**. See under **multi-**.
multitude *mul'ti-tūd*, *n* a great number; a crowd; the mob; the state of being many, numerousness. — *adj* **multitu'dinous**. — *adv* **multitu'dinously**. — *n* **multitu'dinousness**. [L. *multitūdō*, *-inis* — *multus*.]
multi-user ... to ... **multivalent**. See under **multi-**.
mum[1] *mum* or **mummy** *mum'i*, (*colloq*) *n* mother, used esp. by a child to address or refer to its mother.
mum[2] *mum*, *adj* silent. — *n* silence. — *interj* not a word. — *vi* (also **mumm**) to act in dumb show; to act in a mummers' play; to masquerade: — *pr p* **mumm'ing**; *pa t* and *pa p* **mummed**. — *n* **mumm'er** (*formerly*) an actor in a folk-play, usu. at Christmas; an actor (*facetious*). — *n* **mumm'ery** mumming; foolish or phoney ceremonial. — *n* **mumm'ing**. — **mum's the word** not a word. [An inarticulate sound with closing of the lips; partly O.Fr. *momer*, to mum, *momeur*, mummer.]
mum[3] *mum*. See **ma'am**.
mumble *mum'bl*, *vt* and *vi* to say, utter or speak indistinctly, softly or perfunctorily; to mouth with the lips, or as with toothless gums. — *n* **mum'bler**. — *n* and *adj* **mum'bling**. — *adv* **mum'blingly**. [Frequentative from **mum**[2].]
mumbo-jumbo *mum-bō-jum'bō*, *n* baffling jargon, professional gobbledegook; mummery, foolish ritual; an object of foolish worship or fear. [Said to be from *Mama Dyanbo*, a Mandingo god.]
mumm, mummer, mummery. See **mum**[2].
mummify. See **mummy**[1].
mummy[1] *mum'i*, *n* an embalmed or otherwise preserved dead body; anything pounded to a formless mass; a bituminous drug or pigment. — *n* **mummificā'tion**. — *vt* **mumm'ify** to make into a mummy: — *pr p* **mumm'ifying**; *pa t* and *pa p* **mumm'ified**. [O.Fr. *mumie* — L.L. *mumia* — Ar. and Pers. *mūmiyā* — Pers. *mūm*, wax.]
mummy[2]. See **mum**[1].
mumps *mumps*, *nsing* an acute infectious disease characterised by a painful swelling of the parotid glands. — *npl* the swellings thus caused, protruding on either side of the face. [From earlier *mump*, a grimace.]
munch *munch* or *munsh*, *vt* and *vi* to chew with a steady, deliberate action of the jaws, and often with a crunching noise. — *n* **munch'er**. — **the munchies** (*slang*) an alcohol- or drug-induced craving for food. [Prob. imit.]
mundane *mun-dān'*, *adj* worldly; earthly; ordinary, banal. — *adv* **mundane'ly**. — *n* **mundanity** (*-dan'i-ti*). [L. *mundānus* — *mundus*, the world.]
mung bean *mo͝ong* (or *mung*) *bēn*, *n* a leguminous Asian plant (genus *Phaseolus*) or its seeds, grown for forage and as a source of bean sprouts. [Hindi *mūng*.]
mungo *mung'gō*, *n* the waste produced in a woollen-mill from hard spun or felted cloth, used in making cheap cloth: — *pl* **mun'gos**.
municipal *mū-nis'i-pl*, *adj* pertaining to (the government of) a borough, town or city. — *n* **municipalisā'tion** or **-z-**. — *vt* **munic'ipalise** or **-ize** to make into a municipality; to bring under municipal control or ownership. — *n* **municipality** (*-pal'i-ti*) a self-governing town or district; its governing body. — *adv* **munic'ipally**. [L. *mūnicipālis* — *mūniceps*, *-ipis*, an inhabitant of a *mūnicipium*, a free town — *mūnia*, official duties, *capĕre*, to take.]
munificence *mū-nif'i-səns*, *n* magnificent liberality in giving; bountifulness. — *adj* **munif'icent**. — *adv* **munif'icently**. [L. *mūnificentia* — *mūnus*, a present, *facĕre*, to make.]
muniment *mū'ni-mənt*, *n* (usu. in *pl*) a record fortifying or making good a claim, esp. a title deed to land. [L. *mūnīmentum*, fortification, later, title deed.]
munition *mū-ni'shən*, *vt* to supply with munitions. — *n* (commonly in *pl*) material used in war; weapons; military stores. — **muni'tion-worker** a worker engaged in making munitions. [L. *mūnīre*, *-ītum*, to fortify.]
Munro *mun-rō'*, *n* a designation orig. of Scottish (now also English, Irish and Welsh) mountains over 3000 feet: — *pl* **Munros'**. [Orig. list made by H.T. *Munro*.]
munster *mo͞on'stər*, *n* a semi-soft cheese of *Munster* in N.E. France, often flavoured with caraway or aniseed.
muntjak or **muntjac** *munt'jak*, *n* a small S.E. Asian deer, the male having tusks and small antlers. [From the Malay name.]
muon *mū'on*, (*phys*) *n* a lepton formerly classified as a **mu-** (or *μ*) **meson**. See **mu**. — *adj* **mūon'ic**. — *n* **muonium** (*mū-ōn'i-əm*) an isotope of hydrogen. — **muonic atom** (*mū-on'ik*) a hydrogen-like atom, formed by the slowing down of an energetic muon by ionisation as it traverses matter.
mural *mū'rəl*, *adj* of, on, attached to, or of the nature of, a wall. — *n* a mural decoration, esp. a painting. — *n* **mu'ralist** a person who paints or designs murals. — **mural painting** a painting executed, esp. in distemper colours, upon the wall of a building. [L. *mūrālis* — *mūrus*, a wall.]
murder *mûr'dər*, *n* the act of putting a person to death intentionally and unlawfully; excessive or reprehensible slaughter that is not legally murder; (*hyperb*) torture, excessive toil or hardship. — *vt* to kill (a person) unlawfully with malice aforethought; to slaughter; (*hyperb*) to torture; to beat, defeat utterly (*colloq*); to destroy (*colloq*); to mangle in performance (*colloq*). — *n* **mur'derer**, *fem* **mur'deress**. — *adj* **mur'derous**. — *adv* **mur'derously**. — **cry** or **scream blue murder** see under **blue**[1]; **get away with murder** to do as one pleases yet escape punishment or censure; **murder will out** murder cannot remain hidden; the truth will come to light. [O.E. *morthor* — *morth*, death.]
murex *mū'reks*, *n* a gasteropod mollusc yielding a purple dye: — *pl* **mu'rexes** or **mu'rices** (*-ri-sēz*). [L. *mūrex*, *-icis*.]
murine *mūr'īn*, *adj* mouselike; belonging to the mouse family or subfamily. [L. *mūrīnus* — *mūs*, *mūris*, mouse.]
murk *mûrk*, *n* darkness. — *adv* **murk'ily**. — *n* **murk'iness**. — *adj* **murk'y** dark; obscure; gloomy. [O.E. *mirce* (n. and adj.).]
murmur *mûr'mər*, *n* a low, indistinct sound, like that of running water; an abnormal rustling sound from the heart, lungs, etc.; a muttered or subdued grumble or complaint. — *vi* to utter a murmur; to grumble. — *vt* to say or utter in a murmur. — *n* **mur'murer**. — *n* and *adj* **mur'muring**. — *adv* **mur'muringly**. — *adj* **mur'murous**. — *adv* **mur'murously**. [Fr. *murmure* — L. *murmur*.]
murphy *mûr'fi*, (*colloq*) *n* a potato: — *pl* **mur'phies**. — **Murphy's law** that one of Sod's laws by which if something can go wrong, it will. [From the common Ir. name *Murphy*.]
murrain *mur'in*, *n* a cattle-plague, esp. foot-and-mouth disease. [O.Fr. *morine*, pestilence, carcass.]
murram *mur'əm*, *n* a tough, clayey gravel used as road metal in tropical Africa. [Native name.]
mus. *abbrev* for: music; musical.
Musak. See **Muzak**.
MusB *abbrev* for Bachelor of Music.
muscadel. See **muscatel**.
Muscadet *mus'kə-dā* or (Fr.) *müs-kä-de*, *n* a variety of white grape grown esp. in the lower Loire valley region of France; a typically light dry white wine made from this grape. [Fr.; cf. **muscatel**.]

muscae volitantes *mus'ē vol-i-tan'tēz*, (L.) *npl* lit. fluttering flies, — ocular spectra like floating black spots before the eyes.

muscat *mus'kat, n* muscatel wine; a musky grape or its vine. [Prov. *muscat*.]

muscatel *mus-kə-tel'* or **muscadel** *mus-kə-del'*, *n* a rich spicy wine, of various kinds; a grape of musky smell or taste; the vine producing it; a raisin from the muscatel grape. [O.Fr. — Prov. *muscat*, musky.]

muscle *mus'l, n* a contractile structure by which bodily movement is effected; the tissue forming it; bodily strength; power, strength of other kinds (financial, political, etc.) (*colloq*). — *vi* to force one's way, thrust. — *adj* **musc'ly** muscular. — *adj* **muscular** (*mus'kū-lər*) relating to a muscle; consisting of muscles; having strong muscles; brawny; strong; vigorous. — *n* **muscularity** (*-lar'i-ti*). — *adv* **mus'cularly**. — *n* **mus'culature** the disposition and system of muscles. — *adj* **musc'le-bound** having the muscles stiff and enlarged by over-exercise. — **musc'leman** a man of extravagant physical development, esp. one employed as an intimidator. — *adj* **musculo-skel'etal** relating to muscles and skeleton. — **muscular dystrophy** (*dis'trə-fi*) any of the forms of a hereditary disease in which muscles progressively deteriorate. — **muscle in** (*colloq*) to push in; to grab a share. [L. *mūsculus*, dimin. of *mūs*, a mouse, muscle.]

muscology *mus-kol'ə-ji, n* the study of mosses, bryology. [L. *muscus*, moss.]

muscone. See **muskone** under **musk**.

muscovado *mus-kō-vä'dō, n* sugar in its unrefined state after evaporating the cane-juice and draining off the molasses: — *pl* **muscova'dos**. [Sp. *mascabado*.]

Muscovite *mus'kə-vīt*, (*old*) *n* a citizen of Moscow, or, generally, a Russian. — **muscovy duck** see **musk duck** under **musk**. [*Moscovia*, Latinised from Russ. *Moskva*, Moscow, and *-ite*.]

muscular, etc., **musculature**. See **muscle**.

MusD *abbrev* for Doctor of Music.

Muse *mūz*, (*Gr mythol*) *n* one of the nine goddesses of the liberal arts — daughters of Zeus and Mnemosyne (**Calliope** of epic poetry; **Clio** of history; **Erato** of love poetry; **Euterpe** of music and lyric poetry; **Melpomene** of tragedy; **Polyhymnia** of sacred lyrics; **Terpsichore** of dancing; **Thalia** of comedy; **Urania** of astronomy); an inspiring goddess more vaguely imagined; poetic genius or inspiration; poetry or art. [Fr., — L. *Mūsa* — Gr. *Mousa*.]

muse *mūz, vi* to reflect in silence; to meditate or ponder (with *on*); to look or gaze in contemplation (with *on*). — *vt* to say musingly. — *n* **mu'ser**. — *n* and *adj* **mu'sing**. — *adv* **mu'singly**. [Fr. *muser*, to loiter, in O.Fr. to muse.]

musette *mū-zet'*, *n* an old French bagpipe; a small knapsack (*US*). [Fr., dimin. of *muse*, a bagpipe.]

museum *mū-zē'əm, n* an institution or repository for the collection, exhibition and study of objects of artistic, scientific, historic or educational interest; a collection of curiosities. — **museum piece** a specimen so fine as to be suitable for exhibition in a museum, or so old-fashioned as to be unsuitable for anything else. [L. *mūsēum* — Gr. *mouseion*, temple of the Muses, place dedicated to study.]

mush[1] *mush, n* anything pulpy; sloppy sentimentality (*colloq*). — *vt* to reduce to mush. — *adv* **mush'ily**. — *n* **mush'iness**. — *adj* **mush'y**. [Prob. **mash**.]

mush[2] *mush*, (*NAm*) *vi* to travel on foot with dogs over snow. — *n* a journey of this kind. — *interj* and *imper* a command to dogs to start moving or move faster. — *n* **mush'er**. [Prob. Fr. *marcher*, to walk.]

mushroom *mush'ro͝om, n* an edible fungus of rapid growth, with a stem and umbrella-shaped cap, esp. the *Agaricus campestris* or *field mushroom*; any edible fungus; any fungus of umbrella shape whether edible or not; any fungus; an object shaped like a mushroom, e.g. a wooden one for use in darning; a pinkish-brown colour, like that of the field mushroom. — *adj* of or like a mushroom in appearance, rapidity of growth, etc.; of a pinkish-brown colour. — *vi* to expand like a mushroom cap; to gather mushrooms; to increase, spread with disconcerting rapidity. — **mushroom cloud** a mushroom-shaped cloud, esp. one resulting from a nuclear explosion; **mushroom pink** a dusky brownish pink. [O.Fr. *mousseron*, perh. *mousse*, moss.]

music *mū'zik, n* the art of expression in sound, in melody, and harmony, including both composition and execution; (the art of) instrumental performance, as distinct from singing; the science underlying it; the performance of musical compositions; compositions collectively; a connected series of (sweet) sounds; melody or harmony; pleasing sound; sound of definite pitch, not mere noise; written or printed representation of what is to be played or sung; sheets or books of parts or scores collectively; harmonious character. — *adj* of or for music. — *adj* **mu'sical** relating to, of, with, or producing, music; pleasing to the ear; of definite pitch (unlike mere noise); melodious; having skill in, or aptitude or taste for, music. — *n* a theatrical performance or film in which singing and usu. dancing play an important part. — *n* **musicality** (*-kal'i-ti*) or **mu'sicalness**. — *adv* **mu'sically**. — *n* **musician** (*mū-zish'ən*) a person skilled in music; a performer or composer of music, esp. professional. — *adj* **musi'cianly** characteristic of, or suitable to, a musician. — *n* **musi'cianship**. — *adj* **musicolog'ical**. — *n* **musicol'ogist**. — *n* **musicol'ogy** academic study of music in its historical, scientific, and other aspects. — **musical box** or **music box** a toy that plays tunes automatically, by means of projections from a revolving barrel twitching a comb; **musical chairs** the game of prancing round a diminishing row of chairs and securing one when the music stops; a series of interrelated shifts and changes involving a number of people (*facetious*); **musical comedy** a light dramatic entertainment with sentimental songs and situations held together by a minimum of plot; **musical director** the conductor of an orchestra in a theatre, etc.; **music case** a portfolio or case for carrying sheet music; **music centre** a unit consisting of a record player, cassette-player and radio, with loudspeakers; **music drama** that form of opera introduced by Wagner in which the relations of music and drama are reformed; **music hall** variety entertainment or vaudeville, consisting of a series of turns by different artists, interspersed with interludes of song, dance, etc. (also *adj*); a theatre for this kind of entertainment; **music master, mistress** or **teacher** a teacher of music; **music paper** paper ruled for writing music; **music pen** a five-channelled pen for drawing the stave; **music roll** a roll of perforated paper for mechanical piano-playing; **music room** a room in which music is performed; **mu'sic-seller** a dealer in printed music; **music stand** a light adjustable desk for holding music during performance; **music stool** a piano stool. — **music of the spheres** see under **spheres**; **music to one's ears** anything that one is very glad to hear. [Fr. *musique* — L. *mūsica* — Gr. *mousikē* (*technē*) musical (art) — *Mousa*, a Muse.]

musique concrète *mü-zēk kɔ̃-kret*, (Fr.) *n* a kind of mid-20th-century music, made up of odds and ends of recorded sound variously handled.

musk *musk, n* a strong-smelling substance, used in perfumery, obtained chiefly from the male musk deer; the odour thereof; the musk deer; a species of *Mimulus*, said once to have smelt of musk. — *adj* (used attributively with the names of many animals and plants) supposed to smell of musk. — *adv* **musk'ily**. — *n* **musk'iness**. — *n* **mus'kone** or **mus'cone** a macrocyclic ketone that gives musk its distinctive smell and is synthesised for use as an ingredient in perfumes. — *adj* **musk'y** having the odour of musk. — **musk deer** a hornless deer (genus *Moschus*) of Asia, chief source of musk; **musk duck** (also by confusion **muscovy duck**) a large musky-smelling South American duck (genus *Cairina*); **musk gland** a skin pit in some animals producing musk; **musk melon** any of various common varieties of melon, including the honeydew (the name apparently transferred from a musky-scented kind); **musk orchid** a small musk-scented European orchid (genus *Herminium*); **musk ox** a long-haired ruminant (genus *Ovibos*) of northern Canada and Greenland, exhaling a strong musky smell; **musk'rat** the musquash; its fur; **musk rose** a fragrant species of rose; **musk turtle** any of a group of small American turtles of the genus *Sternotherus*, that have a musky smell. [Fr. *musc* — L. *muscus* perh. — Sans. *muska*, a testicle (for which the gland has been mistaken).]

muskeg *mus'keg*, (*Can*) *n* swamp, bog or marsh. [Cree Ind. word.]

muskellunge *mus'kə-lunj*, *n* a large North American freshwater fish of the pike family. [Algonquian.]

musket *mus'kit*, *n* a military hand firearm, esp. of an old-fashioned smooth-bore kind. — *n* **musketeer'** a soldier armed with a musket. — *n* **mus'ketry** muskets collectively; practice with, or the art of using, small arms; a body of troops armed with muskets. [O.Fr. *mousquet*, musket, formerly a hawk — It. *moschetto*, perh. — L. *musca*, a fly.]

muskone, muskrat, musky. See under **musk**.

Muslim *mŏŏz'lim* or *muz'lim* or **Moslem** *moz'ləm*, *n* a follower of the Islamic religion, a Mohammedan. — *adj* of, or belonging to, the followers of Islam, Mohammedans. — *n* **Mus'limism** or **Mos'lemism**. [Ar. *muslim* — *salma*, to submit (to God); cf. **Islam**.]

muslin *muz'lin*, *n* a fine soft plain-woven cotton fabric of gauzy appearance. — *adj* made of muslin. [Fr. *mousseline* — It. *mussolino*, from It. *Mussolo*, the town of Mosul in Mesopotamia.]

musquash *mus'kwosh*, *n* a large aquatic American animal related to the vole, very destructive to dams and waterways (also **muskrat**); its fur. [From an Am. Ind. word.]

muss *mus*, (*NAm*) *n* disturbance; confusion, disorder; a mess. — *vt* and *vi* to disarrange; to mess. — *n* **muss'iness**. — *adj* **muss'y** disordered.

mussel *mus'l*, *n* a marine lamellibranch shellfish of the family *Mytilidae*; a freshwater lamellibranch shellfish of the *Unionidae*; the shell of any of these. — **muss'el-shell**. [O.E. *mūs(c)le*; from L. *mūsculus*, dimin. of *mūs*, mouse.]

mussy. See **muss**.

must¹ *must*, *auxiliary verb* (taking *infinitive* without *to*) used to express compulsion, necessity or obligation, with ellipsis of verb (as in *I must away*), resolute intention, likelihood or conviction, or inevitability: — *3rd pers sing* **must**; *pa t* **must** (often replaced by **had to**). — *n* an essential, a necessity; a thing that should not be missed or neglected. — **must needs** see under **need**. [O.E. *mōste*, past tense of *mōt*.]

must² *must*, *n* new wine; unfermented, or only partially fermented, grape juice or other juice or pulp for fermentation; process of fermentation. — *adj* **must'y**. [O.E. *must* — L. *mustum* (*vīnum*) new (wine).]

must³ *must*, *n* mustiness; mould. [App. a back-formation — **musty²**.]

must⁴ or **musth** *must*, *n* dangerous frenzy in some male animals, such as elephants. — *adj* in such a state. [Pers. and Hind. *mast*, intoxicated.]

mustache. The U.S. spelling of **moustache**.

mustachio *mə-stä'shi-ō*, *n* (often in *pl*) a large, elegantly curling moustache: — *pl* **musta'chios**. — *adj* **musta'chioed**. [Sp. *mostacho*, It. *mostaccio*.]

mustang *mus'tang*, *n* the feralised horse of the American prairies. [Sp. *mestengo*, now *mesteño*, belonging to the *mesta* or graziers' union, combined with *mostrenco*, homeless, stray.]

mustard *mus'tərd*, *n* any of various species of the *Sinapis* section of the genus *Brassica*; their (powdered) seeds; a pungent condiment prepared from the seeds; the brownish-yellow colour of the condiment. — **mustard gas** the vapour from a poisonous blistering liquid derived from ethylene and sulphur chloride; **mustard plaster** a counter-irritant skin application made from mustard flour. — **French mustard** mustard prepared for the table by adding salt, sugar, vinegar, etc.; **mustard and cress** a salad of seedlings of mustard and garden cress; **wild mustard** charlock, a common cornfield weed with yellow flowers. — **keen as mustard** (*colloq*) intensely enthusiastic. [O.Fr. *mo(u)starde* (Fr. *moutarde*) — L. *mustum*, **must²** (because the condiment was prepared with must).]

muster *mus'tər*, *vt* and *vi* to assemble (e.g. for inspection or duties); to enroll; to number. — *vt* to summon, gather (arguments, courage, etc.; sometimes with *up*); to round up (livestock) (*Austr* and *NZ*). — *n* an assembly or gathering e.g. of troops for inspection or duties; a gathering together, round-up; a round-up of livestock (*Austr* and *NZ*). — *n* **must'erer** (*Austr* and *NZ*) a person who musters (livestock). — **muster in** (*US*) to enroll, receive as recruits; **muster out** (*US*) to discharge from service; **pass muster** to bear examination, appear adequate. [O.Fr. *mostre*, *moustre*, *monstre* — L. *mōnstrum* — *monēre*, to warn.]

musth. See **must⁴**.

musty¹. See **must²**.

musty² *mus'ti*, *adj* mouldy; spoiled by damp; stale in smell or taste; deteriorated from disuse. — *adv* **mus'tily**. — *n* **mus'tiness**.

mutable *mū'tə-bl*, *adj* that may be changed; subject to change; variable; inconstant, fickle. — *n* **mutabil'ity** or **mū'tableness**. — *adv* **mū'tably**. [L. *mūtābilis*, changeable.]

mutagen *mū'tə-jən*, (*biol*) *n* a substance that produces mutations. — *adj* **mutagenic** (*-jen'ik*). — *n* **mutagen'esis** the origin or induction of a mutation. — *n* **mutagenic'ity** the condition of being mutagenic. [*muta*tion and **-gen**.]

mutant *mū'tənt*, (*biol*) *adj* (of a gene, animal or organism) suffering, or resulting from, mutation. — *n* a form resulting from mutation. [L. *mūtans*, *-antis*, pres. p. of *mūtāre*, to change.]

mutate *mū-tāt'*, *vt* and *vi* to cause or undergo mutation. — *n* **mutā'tion** change; a genetic change that can be transmitted to offspring as an inheritable divergence from ancestral type (*biol*); in German orthography, another name for the umlaut; in Celtic languages, an alteration to the sound of an initial consonant caused by a preceding word. — *adj* **mutā'tional**. — *adv* **mutā'tionally**. [L. *mūtātio* — *mūtāre*, to change, **mutate** being a back-formation from **mutation**.]

mutatis mutandis *mŏŏ-tä'tēs mŏŏ-tan'dēs*, (L.) with the necessary changes.

mutch *much*, (*Scot*) *n* a woman's close-fitting linen cap. [M.Du. *mutse*; Du. *muts*, Ger. *Mütze*.]

mute *mūt*, *adj* dumb; silent; refusing to plead (*law*); without vocal utterance, unspoken; (of a letter) unpronounced or only faintly pronounced; pronounced by stoppage of the breath-passage, plosive (*phon*). — *n* a dumb person; a person who refuses to plead (*law*); a hired funeral attendant; a dumb servant in an Eastern house; an actor with no words to speak; a stop-consonant, a plosive; a clip, pad, or other device for subduing the sound of a musical instrument. — *vt* to deaden or muffle the sound of (e.g. a musical instrument) with a mute. — *adj* **mu'ted** (of e.g. sound, colour) softened, not loud, harsh or bright. — *adv* **mute'ly**. — *n* **mute'ness**. —

n **mu'tism** dumbness. — **mute swan** the common swan, from its habitual silence. [L. *mūtus*.]

muti *mōō'ti*, (*SAfr*) *n* traditional medicine, esp. associated with witchcraft or witch doctors. [Zulu *umuthi*, tree.]

mutilate *mū'ti-lāt*, *vt* to maim; to remove a material part of; to deform by slitting, boring, or removing a part. — *n* **mutilā'tion**. — *n* **mu'tilātor**. [L. *mutilāre*, *-ātum* — *mutilus*, maimed.]

mutiny *mū'ti-ni*, *n* insurrection against constituted authority, esp. naval or military; revolt, tumult, strife. — *vi* to rise against authority, esp. in military or naval service: — *pr p* **mu'tinying**; *pa t* and *pa p* **mu'tinied**. — *n* **mutineer'** a person who mutinies or takes part in a mutiny. — *adj* **mu'tinous** disposed to mutiny; of the nature of, or expressing, mutiny. — *adv* **mu'tinously**. — *n* **mu'tinousness**. [Fr. *mutin*, riotous — L. *movēre*, *mōtum*, to move.]

mutt *mut*, (*slang*, orig. *US*) *n* a stupid, clumsy person; a dog, esp. a mongrel. [Perh. for **muttonhead**.]

mutter *mut'ər*, *vi* to utter words in a low, indistinct voice; to murmur, esp. in hostility, mutiny or menace; to grumble; (of thunder) to rumble faintly. — *vt* to utter indistinctly. — *n* indistinct utterance; faint rumbling; subdued grumbling. — *n* **mutt'erer**. — *n* and *adj* **mutt'ering**. — *adv* **mutt'eringly**. [Prob. imit.]

mutton *mut'n*, *n* sheep's flesh as food; an em (*printing*). — *adj* **mutt'ony**. — **mutton bird** an Australasian shearwater; **mutton chop** a piece of mutton cut from the rib. — *adj* (of whiskers) shaped like a mutton chop, i.e. broad and rounded on the cheek, tapering to meet the hairline. — **mutton cloth** a plain-knitted cloth (usu. cotton) of loose texture; **mutt'onhead** a stupid person. — *adj* **mutt'on-headed**. — **leg-of-mutton** see under **leg**; **mutton dressed as lamb** (*colloq*) an elderly woman who dresses or makes herself up in style suitable to a young one. [O.Fr. *moton* (Fr. *mouton*), a sheep — L.L. *multō*, *-ōnis*.]

mutual *mū'tū-əl*, *adj* interchanged; reciprocal; given and received; common, joint, shared by two. — *n* **mutuality** (*-al'i-ti*). — *adv* **mu'tually**. — **mutual funds** (*US*) unit trusts (see under **trust**); **mutual inductance** (*electr*) the generation of electromotile force in one system of conductors by a variation of current in another system linked to the first by magnetic flux; **mutual inductor** (*electr*) a component consisting of two coils designed to have a definite mutual inductance; **mutual insurance** the system of a company in which the policy-holders are the shareholders. [Fr. *mutuel* — L. *mūtuus* — *mūtāre*, to change.]

muu-muu *mōō'-mōō*, *n* a simple loose dress worn chiefly in Hawaii. [Hawaiian *mu'u mu'u*.]

Muzak® or (*erron*) **Musak** *mū'zak*, *n* piped music (q.v.).

muzhik or **moujik** *mōō'zhik*, (*hist*) *n* a Russian peasant. [Russ. *muzhik*.]

muzzle *muz'l*, *n* the projecting jaws and nose of an animal; a strap or a cage for the mouth to prevent biting; the extreme end of a gun, etc. — *vt* to put a muzzle on; to keep from hurting; to gag or silence. — *n* **muzz'ler** a person who applies a muzzle; a blow on the mouth; a muzzle-loader. — **muzz'le-loader** a firearm loaded through the muzzle, as distinct from a *breech-loader*. — *adj* **muzz'le-loading**. — **muzzle velocity** the velocity with which a projectile leaves the muzzle of a gun. [O.Fr. *musel* — L.L. *mūsellum*, dimin. of *mūsum* or *mūsus*, beak.]

muzzy *muz'i*, *adj* dazed, bewildered; befuddled; blurred; hazy. — *adv* **muzz'ily**. — *n* **muzz'iness**.

mv *abbrev* for merchant vessel.

MVO *abbrev* for Member of the (Royal) Victorian Order.

MW *abbrev* for: Malawi (I.V.R.); medium wave; megawatt.

M-way *abbrev* for motorway.

mx *abbrev* for **maxwell** (unit measuring magnetic flux).

my *mī*, *possessive adj* (in *attributive* use only) of or belonging to me; sometimes used in addressing others, as, formerly, *my lord*, *my lady* or affectionately, patronisingly, etc. as *my dear*, *my friend*; used in interjection, as *my God!* — *interj* expressing surprise (perh. for **my word** or **my God**). [**mine**[1] — O.E. *mīn* (genitive), of me.]

myalgia *mī-al'jə*, *n* pain in a muscle. — *adj* **myal'gic**. — **myalgic encephalomyelitis** (*en-sef-ə-lō-mī-ə-lī'tis*; Gr. *encephalos*, brain, *myelos*, spinal cord) a long-term post-viral syndrome with chronic fatigue and muscle pain on exercise (abbrev. **ME**). [Gr. *mȳs*, muscle, *algos*, pain.]

myalism *mī'ə-lizm*, *n* West Indian witchcraft. [Prob. of W. Afr. origin.]

myall[1] *mī'əl*, *n* an Australian aboriginal living traditionally. — *adj* wild; unaccustomed to white society. [Aboriginal *mayal*, stranger.]

myall[2] *mī'əl*, *n* an Australian acacia of various species with hard, scented wood; the wood of such a tree. [Transformed use of **myall**[1].]

myasthenia *mī-əs-thē'ni-ə*, *n* muscular weakness or debility. — *adj* **myasthenic** (*-then'*). [Gr. *mys*, muscle, *astheneia*, weakness.]

mycelium *mī-sē'li-əm*, *n* the white mass of filaments forming the vegetative part of a fungus: — *pl* **mycē'lia**. — *adj* **mycē'lial**. [Gr. *mȳkēs*, a mushroom.]

Mycenaean *mī-si-nē'ən*, *adj* of the ancient city state of *Mycenae* in Argolis, Agamemnon's kingdom, or its culture culminating in the Bronze Age.

mycetes *mī-sē'tēz*, *npl* fungi. — *combining form* **mycet-** or **myceto-** (*mī-sē-tō-* or *-o-*). — *n* **mycetol'ogy** mycology. [Gr. *mȳkēs*, *-ētos*, pl. *mȳkētēs*, a mushroom.]

myco- *mī-kō-*, *-kə-* or *-ko-*, or **myc-** *mīk-*, *combining form* denoting fungus or mushroom. — *adj* **mycologic** (*mī-kə-loj'ik*) or **mycolog'ical** (*-kəl*). — *n* **mycologist** (*-kol'*). — *n* **mycol'ogy** the study of fungi. — *n* **mycophagist** (*mī-kof'ə-jist*; Gr. *phagein*, to eat) a fungus-eater. — *n* **mycoph'agy**. — *n* **mycosis** (*-kō'sis*) a disease due to growth of a fungus. — *adj* **mycotic** (*-kot'ik*). — *n* **mycotoxicosis** (*-tok-si-kō'sis*) poisoning caused by a mycotoxin. — *n* **mycotoxin** (*-tok'sin*) any poisonous substance produced by a fungus. — *adj* **mycotrophic** (*-trof'ik*) (of a plant) living in symbiosis with a fungus. [Gr. *mȳkēs*, a mushroom.]

myel- *mī-əl-* or **myelo-** *mī-ə-lō*, *-lo-* or *-lə-*, *combining form* denoting bone marrow or the spinal cord. — *n* **my'elin** the substance forming the medullary sheath of nerve-fibres. — *n* **myelī'tis** inflammation of the spinal cord; inflammation of the bone marrow. — *n* **my'eloblast** an immature cell of bone marrow, found in the circulating blood only in diseased conditions. — *adj* **my'eloid** like, pertaining to, or of the nature of, marrow. — *n* **myeloma** (*-lō'mə*) a tumour of the bone marrow, or one composed of cells normally present in bone marrow. [Gr. *myelos*, marrow.]

myna, mynah or **mina** *mī'nə*, *n* any of various Asiatic birds of the starling family, some of which can be taught to imitate human speech. [Hind. *mainā*.]

mynheer *mīn-hār'* or (Du.) *mə-nār'*, *n* Dutch for *Mr* or *sir*; a Dutchman. [Du. *mijn*, my, *heer*, lord.]

myo- *mī-ō-*, *mī-ə-* or *mī-o-*, *combining form* meaning muscle. — *n* **my'oblast** a cell producing muscle-tissue. — *adj* **myoblast'ic**. — *adj* **myocar'dial** (**myocardial infarction** destruction of the myocardium due to interruption of blood supply to the area). — *n* **myocardī'tis** inflammation of the myocardium. — *n* **myocar'dium** the muscular substance of the heart. — *n* **my'ogram** a myographic record. — *n* **my'ograph** an instrument for recording muscular contractions. — *adj* **myograph'ic** or **myograph'ical.** — *n* **myog'raphy.** — *adj* **my'oid** like muscle. — *adj* **myolog'ical.** — *n* **myol'ogist.** — *n* **myol'ogy** the study of muscles. — *n* **myō'ma** a tumour composed of muscular tissue. — *n* **my'osin** a protein that contributes to contraction in muscles. — *n* **myosī'tis** inflammation of a muscle. [Gr. *mȳs*, *mȳos*, muscle.]

myopia *mī-ō'pi-ə*, *n* short-sightedness. — *n* **my'ope** (*-ōp*) a short-sighted person. — *adj* **myopic** (*-op'ik*) short-sighted. [Gr. *myōps*, short-sighted — *mȳein*, to shut, *ōps*, the eye.]

myosin, myositis. See under **myo-**.

myosis. See **miosis.**

myosotis *mī-ə-sō'tis*, *n* a plant of the genus *Myosotis*, the forget-me-not genus. [Gr. *myosōtis*, mouse-ear, from its furry leaves, — *mȳs*, *mȳos*, a mouse, *ous*, *ōtos*, an ear.]

myriad *mir'i-əd*, *n* any immense number. — *adj* numberless. [Gr. *mȳrias*, *-ados*, ten thousand.]

myriapod *mir'i-ə-pod*, *n* any member of a class of crawling arthropods with many legs, such as the centipedes and millipedes. [Gr. *mȳriopous*, *-podos*, many-footed — *mȳrios*, numberless, *pous*, *podos*, a foot.]

myrmecoid *mûr'mi-koid*, *adj* ant-like. [Gr. *myrmēkoeidēs*, like an ant.]

myrmecology *mûr-mi-kol'ə-ji*, *n* the study of ants. — *adj* **myrmecolog'ical.** — *n* **myrmecol'ogist.** [Gr. *myrmēx*, *-ēkos*, ant.]

Myrmidon *mûr'mi-dən*, *n* one of a tribe of warriors who accompanied Achilles to Troy (*Gr mythol*); a ruffianly follower or henchman. [Gr. *Myrmidŏnĕs* (pl.).]

myrobalan *mī-rob'ə-lən* or *mi-*, *n* the astringent fruit of certain Indian mountain species of the genus *Terminalia* used medicinally, and in ink, dyeing and tanning. [Gr. *mȳrobalanos*, — *myron*, an unguent, *balanos*, an acorn.]

myrrh *mûr*, *n* a bitter, aromatic, transparent gum, exuded from the bark of a tree of the genus *Commiphora*, used medicinally and in perfume and incense. [O.E. *myrra* — L. *myrrha* — Gr. *myrrā*.]

myrtle *mûr'tl*, *n* an evergreen shrub with beautiful fragrant leaves; extended to various other plants. [O.Fr. *myrtil*, dimin. of *myrte* — L. *myrtus* — Gr. *myrtos*.]

myself *mī-self'*, *pron* (used in apposition with **I** or **me**, for emphasis or clarification) in person; (used reflexively) me. [**me**[1] and **self.**]

mystery *mis'tə-ri*, *n* a phenomenon, circumstance or happening that cannot be explained; someone or something inscrutable, an enigma; enigmatic quality; something obscure, abstruse or arcane; a tale of suspense that baffles and intrigues; a truth divinely imparted (*relig*); a sacrament (*relig*); (also **mystery play**) a play depicting the life of Christ (*hist*); (in *pl*) in ancient religious, etc. rites, known only to the initiated. — *adj* **mystē'rious** containing mystery; having an air of mystery; obscure; secret; incomprehensible. — *adv* **mystē'riously.** — *n* **mystē'riousness.** — **mystery tour** an excursion to a destination which remains secret until the journey's end. [L. *mystērium* — Gr. *mystērion* — *mystēs*, an initiate — *mўeein*, to initiate — *mȳein*, to close the eyes.]

mystic *mis'tik* or **mystical** *mis'ti-kəl*, *adj* relating to mystery, the mysteries, or mysticism; mysterious; sacredly obscure or secret; involving a sacred or a secret meaning hidden from the eyes of the ordinary person, only revealed to a spiritually enlightened mind; allegorical. — *n* **mys'tic** a person who seeks or attains direct intercourse with God in elevated religious feeling or ecstasy. — *adv* **mys'tically.** — *n* **mys'ticism** (*-sizm*) the habit or tendency of religious thought and feeling of those who seek direct communion with God or the divine; fogginess and unreality of thought. [Gr. *mystikos* — *mystēs*, an initiate.]

mystify *mis'ti-fī*, *vt* to make mysterious, obscure or secret; to involve in mystery; to bewilder; to puzzle: — *pr p* **mys'tifying**; *pa t* and *pa p* **mys'tified.** — *n* **mystificā'tion.** — *adj* **mys'tifying.** [Fr. *mystifier*.]

mystique *mi-stēk'*, *n* incommunicable spirit, gift or quality; the secret of an art, known to its inspired practitioners; sense of mystery, remoteness from the ordinary, and power or skill surrounding a person, activity, etc. [Fr.]

myth *mith*, *n* an ancient traditional story of gods or heroes, esp. one offering an explanation of some fact or phenomenon; a story with a veiled meaning; mythical matter; a figment; a commonly-held belief that is without foundation. — *adj* **myth'ical** or **myth'ic** relating to myths; fabulous; fictitious, untrue. — *adv* **myth'ically.** — *vt* **myth'icise** or **-ize** (*-i-sīz*) to make the subject of myth; to explain as myth. — *n* **myth'iciser** or **-z-**, or **myth'icist.** — *n* **myth'icism** (*-sizm*). — *adj* **mytholog'ical** or **mytholog'ic** relating to mythology, fabulous. — *adv* **mytholog'ically.** — *vt* **mythol'ogise** or **-ize** to interpret or explain the mythological character of; to turn into myth; to create myths. — *n* **mythol'ogiser** or **-z-.** — *n* **mythol'ogist.** — *n* **mythol'ogy** a body of myths; the scientific study of myths. — *n* and *adj* **myth'omane** mythomaniac. — *n* **mythomā'nia** (*psychiatry*) lying or exaggerating to an abnormal extent. — *n* and *adj* **mythomā'niac.** — *n* **mythopoeia** (*mith-ə-pē'ə*) the creation or formation of myths. — *adj* **mythopoe'ic.** [Gr. *mythos*, myth.]

mythos *mīth'os*, *n* myth; mythology; theme, scheme of events; the characteristic or current attitudes of a culture or group, expressed symbolically (through poetry, art, drama, etc.). [Gr. *mȳthos*, talk, story, myth.]

myxoedema or in U.S. **myxedema** *mik-si-dē'mə*, *n* a diseased condition due to deficiency of thyroid secretion, characterised by loss of hair, increased thickness and dryness of the skin, increase in weight, slowing of mental processes, and diminution of metabolism. [Gr. *myxa*, mucus, *oidēma*, swelling.]

myxoma *mik-sō'mə*, *n* a tumour of jellylike or mucous substance: — *pl* **myxō'mata.** — *n* **myxomatō'sis** a contagious virus disease of rabbits. — *adj* **myxō'matous.** [Gr. *myxa*, mucus.]

myxomycete *mik-sō-mī'sēt*, *n* any of the slime fungi, a class of very simple plants, creeping on wet soil, rotten wood, etc. [Gr. *myxa*, mucus, *mykētēs*, pl. of *mykēs*, a mushroom.]

myxovirus *mik'sō-vī-rəs*, *n* any of a group of related viruses causing influenza, mumps, etc. [Gr. *myxa*, mucus, and **virus.**]

MZM *abbrev* for (Mozambique) metical.

mzungu *əm-zŏŏng'gōō*, *n* in E. Africa, a white person. [Swahili.]

N

N or **n** *en, n* the fourteenth letter of the modern English alphabet, thirteenth of the Greek, representing a point nasal consonant sound, or before *g* or *k* a back nasal (as in *sing, sink*); an indefinite number, esp. in a series (*math*); a unit of measurement (**en**) = half an em (*printing*). — *adj* **n^{th}** or **nth**. — **to the nth** or **nth** to any power; hence to an unlimited degree (*colloq*).
N or **N.** *abbrev* for: naira (Nigerian currency); navy; newton; ngultrum (Bhutanese currency); Norse; North or Northern; Norway (I.V.R.).
N (*chem*) *symbol* for nitrogen.
n or **n.** *abbrev* for: name; nano-; neuter; new; nominative; noon; note; noun; number.
'n' a colloq. shortening of **and**.
NA *abbrev* for: Netherlands Antilles (I.V.R.); New Age; North America.
Na (*chem*) *symbol* for sodium.
n/a *abbrev* for not applicable.
Naafi *nä'fi, n* an organisation for providing canteens for servicemen and servicewomen; one of the canteens. — Also **NAAFI**. [From the initials of *N*avy, *A*rmy, and *A*ir-*F*orce *I*nstitute(s).]
naartje. See **nartjie.**
nab *nab, vt* to seize or snatch; to arrest (*colloq*): — *pr p* **nabb'ing**; *pa t* and *pa p* **nabbed.** — *n* **nabb'er**.
nabla *nab'lə, (math) n* (in Cartesian co-ordinates) the symbol ∇, an inverted delta, also called *del*, representing the vector operator $\mathbf{i}\partial/\partial x + \mathbf{j}\partial/\partial y + \mathbf{k}\partial/\partial z$. [Gr. *nabla*, a Hebrew instrument, the *nebel* (app. a harp) from the shape.]
nabob *nā'bob, n* a European who has amassed a fortune in the East (*archaic*; used in Europe only); (in Europe) any person of great wealth, an important person. [Hind. *nawwāb*; see **nawab.**]
NACAB *abbrev* for National Association of Citizens' Advice Bureaux.
nacarat *nak'ə-rat, n* a bright orange-red colour; a fabric so coloured. [Fr.]
nacelle *nä-sel', n* the car of a balloon, airship, etc.; a body on an aircraft housing engine(s), etc. [Fr., — L.L. *nāvicella*, — L. *nāvis*, ship.]
nacre *nā'kər, n* mother-of-pearl or a shellfish yielding it. — *adj* **nā'creous** or **nā'crous.** [Fr.]
NACRO *nak'rō, abbrev* for National Association for the Care and Resettlement of Offenders.
nada *nä'də, n* nothing; nothingness. [Sp.]
nadir *nā'dēr* or *-dər, n* the point of the heavens diametrically opposite to the zenith; the lowest point of anything, esp. an emotional state. [Fr., — Ar. *nadīr* (*nazīr*), opposite to.]
naevus *nē'vəs* or (L.) *nī'vŏŏs, n* a birthmark; a pigmented spot or an overgrowth of small blood-vessels in the skin: — *pl* **naevi** (*nē'vī* or *nī'vē*). — *adj* **nae'void.** [L.]
naff *naf, (slang) adj* inferior, worthless; vulgar, socially crass. — *n* an incompetent. — *adj* and *adv* **naff'ing** used as an offensive qualification. — **naff all** nothing at all; **naff off** an offensive injunction to go away. [Origin disputed; suggested derivations are: *naf*, back-slang for *fan*(*ny*), the female genitalia; *naff*, navel, or nothing; *naffy* (**Naafi**) generally contemptuous, specif. 'shirking'.]
nag[1] *nag, n* a horse, esp. a small one; a riding-horse, or an inferior horse (*colloq*). [M.E. *nagge*.]
nag[2] *nag, vt* or *vi* to find fault with, urge (to do something), cause pain to, or worry, constantly; (with *at*) to worry or annoy continually: — *pr p* **nagg'ing**; *pa t* and *pa p* **nagged.** — *n* **nag** or **nagg'er** a person, esp. a woman, who nags. [Cf. Norw. *nage*, to grow, rankle, Sw. *nagga*, to gnaw.]
naga *nä'gə, n* a snake, esp. the cobra (*Ind*); a divine snake (*Hindu mythol*). [Sans. *nāga*.]
nagana *nä-gä'nə, n* a disease of horses and cattle in central and southern Africa caused by a trypanosome transmitted by tsetse flies. [Zulu *nakane*.]
nagapie *nahh'ə-pi, (SAfr) n* the bush-baby or nocturnal lemur. [Afrik., lit. 'night-ape' (see **bush-baby**) — Du. *nacht*, night, *aap*, monkey.]
nagari *nä'gə-rē, n* devanagari, the script in which Sanskrit, Hindi and other Indian languages are written; the group of alphabets to which devanagari belongs. [Sans. *nāgarī*, town-script — *nāgaran*, town; addition of *deva-* to form *devanagari* was a later development.]
nagor *nā'gör, n* a West African antelope. [Fr., arbitrarily formed by Buffon from earlier *nanguer*.]
NAHT *abbrev* for National Association of Head Teachers.
Nahuatl *nä'wät-l, n* the language of the Aztecs. — Also *adj*.
naiad *nī'ad* or *nā'əd, n* a river or spring nymph; the aquatic larva of the dragonfly, mayfly, stone-fly or damselfly: — *pl* **nai'adēs** or **nai'ads.** — *n* **Nai'as** a genus of water plants, giving name to a family **Naiadā'ceae** related to or including the pondweeds. [Gr. *nāias*, *-ados*, pl. *-adĕs*, from *naein*, to flow.]
naïf *nä-ēf, adj* naive.
nail *nāl, n* a horny plate at the end of a finger or toe, usu. distinguished from a claw by being flattened; a claw; a small usu. metal spike with a head, used for fastening wood, etc.; a nail-shaped excrescence, esp. one at the tip of a bird's bill; a measure of length (5.5 cm. or $2\frac{1}{4}$ in.). — *vt* to fix with a nail; to pin down or hold fast; to expose, as a lie; to cause the downfall of (*colloq*); to catch or secure (*colloq*). — *n* **nail'er** a maker of nails. — *n* **nail'ery** a place where nails are made. — **nail'-bed** that portion of the true skin on which a fingernail or toenail rests; **nail'-biting** chewing off the ends of one's fingernails. — *adj* (of an event or experience — a **nail-biter**) which induces nail-biting (as a sign of anxiety, excitement or tension). — **nail'-bomb** an explosive device containing gelignite and packed with long metal nails; **nail'-brush** a brush for cleaning the nails; **nail'-file** a file for trimming fingernails or toenails; **nail gun** an implement used to put in nails; **nail'-head** the head of a nail; an ornament shaped like it; **nail polish** nail varnish; **nail'-scissors** small scissors designed for trimming the fingernails and toenails; **nail varnish** varnish for fingernails or toenails. — **a nail in one's (or the) coffin** any event, experience, etc. which has the effect of shortening one's life; a contributory factor in the downfall of anything; **hard as nails** callous, unsympathetic, unsentimental; **hit the nail on the head** to touch the exact point; **nail one's colours to the mast** see under **colour; on the nail** on the spot, without delay, as payment. [O.E. *nægel*; Ger. *Nagel*.]
nainsook *nān'sŏŏk, n* a kind of muslin like jaconet. [Hind. *nainsukh* — *nain*, eye, *sukh*, pleasure.]

NO P

naira *nī'rə*, *n* the standard unit of currency in Nigeria (100 *kobo*).

naive or **naïve** *nī-* or *nä-ēv'*, *adj* with natural or unaffected simplicity, esp. in thought, manners or speech; artless; ingenuous; simplistic. — *adv* **naïve'ly**. — *n* **naïveté** (*nä-ēv'tā*) or **naïvety** (*nī-* or *nä-ēv'ti*) natural simplicity and unreservedness of thought, manner or speech; ingenuosity. — Also **naif**. [Fr. *naïf*, fem. *naïve* — L. *nātīvus*, native — *nāscī*, *nātus*, to be born.]

naked *nā'kid*, *adj* without clothes; uncovered; bare; exposed; unconcealed; evident; defenceless; devoid (of); simple; without the usual covering. — *adv* **na'kedly**. — *n* **na'kedness**. — **naked eye** the eye unassisted by an optical instrument of any kind; **naked lady** the meadow-saffron. [O.E. *nacod*.]

naker *nā'kər*, (*hist*) *n* a kettledrum used in mediaeval music. [O.Fr. *nacre* — Ar. *naqāra*.]

NALGO *nal'gō*, *abbrev* for National and Local Government Officers' Association.

namaste *nä'məs-ti*, *n* (in India) a traditional form of greeting, a slight bow with the palms pressed together before the chest or face. — Also **namaskar** (*nä-məs-kär'*; Sans. *kara*, doing). [Sans. *namas*, obeisance, salutation, bow, and *te*, dative of *tuam*, you.]

namby-pamby *nam'bi-pam'bi*, *adj* feebly wishy-washy; prettily or sentimentally childish. — *n* namby-pamby writing or talk; a namby-pamby person. [Nickname given by Carey or by Swift to *Ambrose* Philips (1674–1749), whose simple odes to children were despised by 18th-cent. Tories.]

name *nām*, *n* that by which a person or a thing is known or called; a designation; reputation; fame; a celebrity; family or clan; seeming or pretension without reality; authority; behalf; assumed character (of). — *vt* to give a name to; to mention the name of; to designate; to speak of or to call by name; to state or specify; to utter (with cognate object); to mention for a post or office; to nominate; to mention formally by name in the House of Commons as guilty of disorderly conduct; to make known the name of (someone implicated in a crime, an accomplice, etc.) to the police, etc. — *adj* **nam'able** or **name'able** capable or worthy of being named. — *adj* **named**. — *adj* **name'less** without a name; anonymous; undistinguished; indescribable; unspeakable. — *adv* **name'lessly**. — *n* **name'lessness**. — *adv* **name'ly** by name; that is to say. — **name brand** a make of an article bearing a manufacturer's distinguishing name; **name'-calling** abuse; **name'-child** a person called after one; **name'-day** the day of the saint of one's name; the day when a ticket bearing the buyer's name, etc. is given to the seller (*stock exchange*); the day on which a name is bestowed; **name'-dropping** trying to impress others by casually mentioning important or well-known persons as if they were one's friends; **name'-dropper**. — *vi* **name'-drop**. — **name'-part** the part that gives the title to a play; the title-rôle; **name'-plate** an attached plate bearing the name of occupant, owner, manufacturer, etc.; **name'sake** a person bearing the same name as another; **name'-tape** a short piece of cloth tape attached to a garment, etc., marked with the owner's name. — **call names** to abuse; **in name** fictitiously, as an empty title; **in name of** on behalf of; by the authority of; **name after** or (*NAm*) **name for** to give (a child) the same name as another person, in honour of that person; **name the day** to fix a day, esp. for a marriage; **proper name** a name given to a particular person, place or thing; **take a name in vain** to use a name lightly or profanely; **the name of the game** (*colloq*) the thing that is important or essential; the central trend or theme; what it's all about; **to one's name** belonging to one; **you name it** this applies to whatever you mention, want, etc. [O.E. *nama*.]

nan *nän*, *n* a type of slightly leavened bread, as baked in India and Pakistan, similar to pitta bread. [Hindi.]

nana[1]. See **nanny**.

nana[2] *nä'nə*, (orig. *Austr slang*) *n* an idiot, fool; the head, as in *off one's nana*. [Prob. ba*nana*.]

nancy *nan'si*, *n* an effeminate young man; a homosexual — also **nan'cy-boy**. — Also *adj*. [From the girl's name, *Nancy*.]

nankeen *nan'kēn* or *-kēn'*, *n* a buff-coloured cotton cloth first made at *Nanking* in China; (in *pl*) clothes, esp. trousers, made of nankeen.

nanny *nan'i*, *n* a she-goat (also **nann'y-goat**); a children's nurse, esp. one trained to take care of children; a pet name for a grandmother. — Also **nana** and **nanna**. — *adj* (*derog*; of institutions, the state, etc.) protective to an intrusive extent. — *vt* to nurse; to overprotect; to supervise to the point of meddlesomeness. — *adj* **nann'yish** overprotective. [From the woman's name.]

nano- *nān-ō-* or *nan-ō-*, *combining form* denoting: one thousand millionth, 10^{-9}, as in **nan'ogram, nan'ometre, nan'osecond**; of microscopic size, as in **nan'oplankton** or **nann'oplankton** very small forms of plankton. [Gr. *nānos*, a dwarf.]

nap[1] *nap*, *vi* to take a short or casual sleep: — *pr p* **napp'ing**; *pa p* **napped**. — *n* a short or casual sleep. — **catch someone napping** to detect someone in error that might have been avoided; to catch someone off their guard or unprepared. [O.E. *nappian*.]

nap[2] *nap*, *n* a woolly surface on cloth, now (distinguished from *pile*) such a surface raised by a finishing process, not made in the weaving; a downy covering or surface on anything. — *vt* to raise a nap on; to remove nap from. — *adj* **nap'less**. — *n* **napp'iness**. [M.E. *noppe*; app. — M.Du. or M.L.G. *noppe*.]

nap[3] *nap*, *n* the card-game *Napoleon*; in that game a call of five; the winning of five tricks; a racing tip that professes to be a certainty — one that one may 'go nap' on. — *vt* to name (a particular horse) as certain to win. — **go nap** to undertake to win all five tricks; to risk all.

napa or **nappa** *nap'ə*, *n* a soft leather made (orig. at *Napa* in California) by a special tawing process, from sheepskin or goatskin.

napalm *nā'päm* or *na'*, *n* a petroleum jelly, highly inflammable, used in bombs and flame-throwers. — *vt* to attack or destroy with napalm bombs. [*naph*thenate *palm*itate.]

nape *nāp*, *n* the back of the neck.

Naperian. See **Napierian**.

napery *nāp'ə-ri*, (*archaic* or *Scot*) *n* linen, esp. for the table. [O.Fr. *naperie* — L. *mappa*, a napkin.]

naphtha *naf'thə* or *nap'tə*, *n* a vague name for the liquid inflammable distillates from coal-tar, wood, etc., esp. the lighter and more volatile ones. — *n* **naph'thalene** a hydrocarbon obtained by distillation of coal-tar, crystallising in plates, used for killing moths, etc. — *adj* **naphthal'ic** (*naf-thal'ik*) pertaining to or derived from naphthalene. [Gr. *naphtha*.]

Napierian or **Naperian** *nā-pē'ri-ən*, *adj* pertaining to John *Napier* of Merchiston (1550–1617), or to his system of logarithms; now applied to natural logarithms. — **Napier's bones** or **rods** an invention of Napier's for multiplying and dividing mechanically by means of rods.

napkin *nap'kin*, *n* a small square of linen, paper, etc., used at table for wiping the mouth and hands, or otherwise; a pad of disposable material or a folded square of towelling, muslin, etc. as placed between a baby's legs and kept in place by a fastening at the waist, for absorbing urine and faeces (usu. shortened to **nappy** (*nap'i*)). — **nap'kin-ring** a ring in which a table-napkin is rolled before and after use. [Dimin. of Fr. *nappe* — L. *mappa*.]

napoleon *nə-pōl'yən* or *-i-ən*, *n* a twenty-franc gold coin issued by *Napoleon*; a French modification of the game of euchre, each player receiving five cards and playing as an individual (commonly **nap**). — *adj* **Napoleonic** (*-i-on'ik*) relating to *Napoleon* (1769–1821), Emperor of the French. — *n* **Napol'eonism**. — *n* **Napol'eonist**.

nappa. See **napa**.

nappe *nap*, *n* a sheet of rock brought far forward by recumbent folding or thrusting (*geol*); one of the two sheets on either side of the vertex forming a cone (*math*). [Fr. *nappe*, tablecloth — L. *mappa*.]

nappy. See **napkin**.

narcissus *när-sis'əs*, *n* a plant of the daffodil genus *Narcissus*, of the Amaryllis family esp. *Narcissus poeticus* (the poet's narcissus): — *pl* **narciss'uses** or **narciss'ī**. — *n* **narciss'ism** sensual gratification found in one's own body; excessive self-admiration. — *n* **narciss'ist**. — *adj* **narcissis'tic**. [L., — Gr. *Narkissos*, a youth who pined away for love of his own image, and was transformed into the flower.]

narco-analysis, etc. See under **narcotic**.

narcolepsy *när'kō-lep-si*, *n* a condition marked by short attacks of irresistible drowsiness. — *adj* **narcolep'tic**. [Gr. *narkē*, numbness, and *lēpsis*, seizure.]

narcotic *när-kot'ik*, *adj* producing torpor, sleep or deadness; affecting the central nervous system so as to produce dizziness, euphoria, loss of memory and of neuromuscular co-ordination, and eventually unconsciousness. — *n* anything having a narcotic effect, e.g. a drug, alcohol, an inert gas. — *n* **narcosis** (*-kō'sis*) drowsiness, unconsciousness or other effects to the central nervous system produced by a narcotic: — *pl* **narco'ses** (*-sēz*). — *adv* **narcot'ically**. — *vt* **nar'cotise** or **-ize** to subject to the influence of a narcotic. — *n* **nar'cotism** the influence of narcotics. — **nar'co-analysis** hypnoanalysis when narcotics are used in producing the hypnotic state; **narcosyn'thesis** the bringing out of repressed emotions by narcotics so that they become freely accepted into the self. [Gr. *narkōtikos* — *narkē*, numbness, torpor.]

nard *närd*, *n* spikenard; a name for matweed; any of several aromatic plants formerly used in medicine. — *vt* to anoint with nard. [L. *nardus* — Gr. *nardos*.]

nardoo *när-dōō'*, *n* an Australian cloverlike fern; its spore-forming, multicellular body, ground into flour and used as a food by aboriginals. [Aboriginal.]

narghile, nargile or **nargileh** *när'gil-i*, *n* a hookah. [Pers. *nārgīleh* — *nārgīl*, a coconut (from which it used to be made).]

narial *nā'ri-əl* or **narine** *nā'rīn*, *adj* of or relating to the nostrils. [L. *nāris*, pl. *-ēs*, nostril.]

nark *närk*, (*slang*) *n* an informer; a police spy, as *copper's nark*; a persistent fault-finder; an annoying or baffling circumstance. — *vi* to grumble. — *vt* to annoy; to tease. — *adj* **nark'y** irritable. — *adj* **narked** annoyed. — **nark at** to annoy with persistent criticism. [Romany *nāk*, nose.]

narrate *nə-* or *na-rāt'*, *vt* to tell of (a series of events); to give a running commentary on (a film, etc.). — *vi* to recount or relate events. — *adj* **narrāt'able**. — *n* **narrā'tion** the act of telling; that which is told; an orderly account of a series of events. — *adj* **narrative** (*nar'ə-tiv*) narrating; giving an account of any occurrence; inclined to narration; story-telling. — *n* that which is narrated; a continued account of any series of occurrences; story. — *adv* **narr'atively**. — *n* **narrā'tor**. — *adj* **narr'atory**. [L. *narrāre*, *-ātum*, prob. — *gnārus*, knowing.]

narrow *nar'ō*, *adj* of little breadth; of small extent from side to side; closely confining; limited; contracted in mind or outlook; bigoted; not liberal; parsimonious (*colloq*); with little to spare; close; strict, precise, thorough; slight; tense (*phon*). — *n* a narrow part or place; (usu. in *pl*) a narrow passage, channel or strait. — *adv* narrowly. — *vt* to make narrow; to contract or confine. — *vi* to become narrow; to reduce the number of stitches in knitting. — *adv* **narr'owly**. — *n* **narr'owness**. — **narr'ow boat** a canal boat. — *vt* **narr'owcast**. — **narr'owcasting** cable television; the production and distribution of material on video tapes, cassettes, etc.; **narrow escape** an escape only just managed. — *adj* **narr'ow-gauge** (of a railway) less than 4 ft. $8\frac{1}{2}$ in. (about 1·4 metres) in gauge. — *adj* **narrow-mind'ed** of a narrow or illiberal mind. — **narrow-mind'edness**; **narrow squeak** a narrow escape. [O.E. *nearu*.]

narthex *när'theks*, *n* a western portico or vestibule in an early Christian or Oriental church or basilica, to which women and catechumens were admitted; a vestibule between the church porch and the nave. [Gr. *narthēx*, giant fennel, a cane or stalk, a casket, a narthex.]

nartjie (orig. **naartje**) *när'chi*, (*Afrik*) *n* a small sweet orange like the mandarin. [Prob. conn. with **orange**.]

narwhal *när'wəl*, *n* a kind of whale (*Monodon*) with one large projecting tusk (occasionally two tusks) in the male. [Dan. *narhval*; O.N. *nāhvalr*, may be from *nār*, corpse, *hvalr*, whale, from its pallid colour.]

nary *nār'i*, (*NAm* and *dialect*) *adv* never; not. — **nary a** never a, not one.

NASA *na'sə*, *abbrev* for National Aeronautics and Space Administration (U.S.).

nasal *nā'zl*, *adj* belonging to the nose; affected by, or sounded through, the nose. — *n* a sound uttered through the nose; a letter representing such a sound. — *n* **nasalisation** or **-z-** (*nā-zə-lī-zā'shən*). — *vi* and *vt* **na'salise** or **-ize** to render nasal, as a sound. — *n* **nasality** (*nā-zal'i-ti*). — *adv* **na'sally**.

nascent *nas'ənt* or *nās'ənt*, (*formal*) *adj* coming into being; beginning to develop. — *n* **nasc'ency**. [L. *nāscēns*, *-entis*, pres. p. of *nāscī*, *nātus*, to be born.]

naso- *nā-zō-*, *combining form* signifying: nose; of the nose (and something else). — *adj* **nasofront'al** pertaining to the nose and the frontal bone. — *adj* **nasolac'rymal** pertaining to the nose and tears, as the duct that carries tears from the eye and the nose. — *n* **nasophar'ynx** that part of the pharynx above the soft palate. [L. *nāsus*, nose.]

nastic *näs'tik* or *nas'*, *adj* (of plant movements) not related to the direction of the stimulus. [Gr. *nastos*, close-pressed.]

nasturtium *nas-tûr'shəm*, *n* (with *cap*) the watercress genus of Cruciferae; (in popular use) the Indian cress, a garden climber with bright orange, yellow or red flowers. [L. *nāsus*, nose, *torquēre*, to twist (from its pungency).]

nasty *näs'ti*, *adj* disgustingly foul; obscene; threatening; ill-natured; difficult to deal with; unpleasant. — *n* (*colloq*) something or someone unpleasant or intractable; an obscene or sadistic film, as in *video nasty*. — *adv* **nas'tily**. — *n* **nas'tiness**. — **a nasty piece (**or **bit) of work** a person very objectionable in character and conduct. [Perh. for earlier *nasky*, or perh. conn. with Du. *nestig*, dirty.]

NAS/UWT *abbrev* for National Association of Schoolmasters/Union of Women Teachers.

natal[1] *nā'tl*, *adj* of or connected with birth; native. — *n* **natality** (*nə-* or *nā-tal'i-ti*) birth; birth-rate. — **natal therapy** (in psychoanalysis) the treatment of rebirthing (q.v.). [L. *nātālis* — *nāscī*, *nātus*, to be born.]

natal[2]. See **nates**.

natality. See **natal**[1].

natant *nāt'ənt*, (*formal*) *adj* floating; swimming. — *n* **natation** (*nat-* or *nāt-ā'shən*) swimming. — *adj* **nātato'rial** or **nā'tatory** pertaining to swimming; having the habit of swimming; adapted or used for swimming. — *n* **nātato'rium** (*NAm*) a swimming-pool. [L. *natāns*, *-antis*, pres. p. of *natāre*, frequentative of *nāre*, to swim.]

natch *nach*, (*slang*) *adv* of course, short for **naturally**.

nates *nā'tēz*, *npl* the buttocks. — *adj* **na'tal**. [L. *natis*, pl. *-ēs*.]

nat. hist. *abbrev* for natural history.

nation *nā'shən*, *n* a body of people marked off by common descent, language, culture or historical tradition, whether or not bound by the defined territorial limits of a state; an American Indian tribe or federation of tribes; a set of people, animals, etc. — *adj* **national** (*nash'nəl* or *-ə-nəl*) pertaining to a nation or nations; belonging or peculiar to, characteristic of, or controlled by a nation; public; general; attached to one's own country. — *n* a member or fellow-member of a nation. — *n* **nationalīsā'tion** or **-z-**. — *vt* **nat'ionalise** or **-ize** to make national; to make the property of the nation; to bring under national management; to naturalise; to make a nation of. — *n* **nat'ionalism**. — *n* **nat'ionalist** a person who favours or strives after the unity, independence, interests or domination of a nation; a member of a political party specially so called. — Also *adj*. — *adj* **nationalist'ic**. — *adv* **nationalist'ically**. — *n* **nationality** (*-al'it-i*) membership of or the fact or state of belonging to a particular nation; nationhood; a group or set having the character of a nation; national character. — *adv* **nat'ionally**. — *n* **nationhood** (*nā'*) the state or fact of being a nation. — *adj* **nationwide'** covering the whole nation. — Also *adv*. — **national anthem** an official song or hymn of a nation, sung or played on ceremonial occasions; **national call** (formerly **trunk call**) a long-distance telephone call within the country, not international; **national debt** money borrowed by the government of a country and not yet paid back; **national grid** the grid (q.v.) of power-lines in, or of lines on maps of, Great Britain; **National Guard** a force which took part in the French Revolution, first formed in 1789; organised militia of individual States (*US*); **national insurance** a system of compulsory insurance paid for by weekly contributions by employee and employer, and yielding benefits to the sick, retired, unemployed, etc.; **national park** an area owned by or for the nation, set apart for preservation and enjoyment of what is beautiful or interesting; **national service** compulsory service in the armed forces; **National Socialism** the policies of the National Socialist Party; **National Trust** and **National Trust for Scotland** charitable bodies concerned with the preservation of historic monuments and buildings and areas of natural beauty in Great Britain and Northern Ireland. — **National Health Service** (in Britain) the system under which medical, dental, etc. treatment is available free, or at a nominal charge, to all, paid for out of public taxation; **National Savings Bank** a department of the Post Office with which money may be deposited to accumulate interest; **National Socialist (German Workers') Party** an extreme nationalistic fascist party, led by Adolf Hitler, which ruled Germany from 1933 to 1945. [L. *nātiō*, *-ōnis* — *nāscī*, *nātus*, to be born.]

native *nā'tiv*, *adj* belonging naturally; innate; natural; in a natural state; occurring naturally as a mineral (not manufactured), or naturally uncombined (as an element); belonging by birth; having a right by birth; born or originating in the place; being the place of birth or origin; belonging to the people originally or at the time of discovery inhabiting the country, esp. when they are not yet fully civilised. — *n* someone born in any place; someone born and for a long time resident in a place; a member of a native race; a member of a non-white race, esp. in a colonised country (*colloq derog*; no longer common); an indigenous species, variety or breed, or an individual of it. — *adv* **na'tively**. — *n* **na'tiveness**. — *n* **na'tivism** the belief that the mind possesses some ideas or forms of thought that are inborn and not derived from sensation. — *n* **na'tivist**. — *adj* **nativis'tic**. — *n* **nativity** (*nə-tiv'i-ti*) the state or fact of being born; the time, place and manner of birth; the birth of Christ, hence the festival commemorating it — Christmas, or a picture representing it; a horoscope. — **native American** an American Indian; **native bear** the koala. — *adj* **na'tive-born** born in the country. — **native cat** a marsupial cat, a carnivorous, cat-sized white-spotted animal of the genus Dasyurus, with a pointed snout; **native land** the land to which one belongs by birth; **native language** the language one acquires first, usu. that of one's native land; **native rock** unquarried rock; **native speaker** a person who speaks the language in question as their native language. — **go native** see under **go**. [L. *nātīvus* — *nāscī*, *nātus*, to be born.]

Nato *nā'tō*, *n* the *N*orth *A*tlantic *T*reaty *O*rganization (see under **north**).

natron *nā'trən*, *n* a hydrated carbonate of sodium found on some lake borders. [Ar. *natrūn* — Gr. *nitron*.]

natter *nat'ər*, (*colloq*) *vi* to rattle on in talk, esp. grumblingly; to chatter, talk much about little. — Also *n*.

natterjack *nat'ər-jak*, *n* a toad with a yellow stripe down the back.

natty *nat'i*, (*colloq*) *adj* dapper; spruce; clever, ingenious. — *adv* **natt'ily**. — *n* **natt'iness**. [Possibly connected with **neat**[1].]

natural *nach'rəl* or *nach'ə-rəl*, *adj* pertaining to, produced by, or according to nature; furnished by or based on nature; not miraculous; not the work of man; not interfered with by man; inborn; having the feelings that may be expected to come by nature, kindly; normal; happening in the usual course; spontaneous; not acquired; without affectation; physical; lifelike, like nature; related by actual birth (not adoption, etc.); illegitimate; in a state of nature, unregenerate; (of classification) according to ancestral relationships (*biol*); according to the usual diatonic scale, not sharp or flat (*mus*). — *n* someone having a natural aptitude (for), or being an obvious choice (for); a thing assured by its very nature of success, a certainty; a tone that is neither sharp nor flat (*mus*); a character (♮) cancelling a preceding sharp or flat (*mus*) a white key in keyboard musical instruments. — *n* **naturalīsā'tion** or **-z-**. — *vt* **nat'uralise** or **-ize** to make natural or easy; to cause an introduced species of plant, animal, etc. to adapt to a different climate or to different conditions of life; to grant the privileges of natural-born citizens to; to adopt into the language; to admit among accepted institutions, usages, etc. — *vi* to acquire citizenship in another country; to study natural history in the field; (of a plant, animal, etc.) to adapt to a new environment. — *n* **nat'uralism** following of nature; a close following of nature without idealisation; the theory that this should be the aim of art and literature, esp. the form of realism advocated or practised by Emile Zola; a world-view that rejects the supernatural. — *n* **nat'uralist** someone who studies nature, more particularly zoology and botany, esp. zoology, and esp. in the field; a believer in naturalism. — *adj* **naturalist'ic** pertaining to, or in accordance with, nature, natural history or naturalism. — *adv* **naturalist'ically**. — *adv* **nat'urally** in a natural manner; by nature; according to nature or one's own nature; in a lifelike manner; normally; in the ordinary course; of course. — *n* **nat'uralness**. — *adj* **nat'ural-born** native. — **natural death** death owing to disease or old age, not violence or accident; **natural gas** gases issuing from the earth, whether from natural fissures or bored wells, applied particularly to the hydrocarbon gases associated with the production of petroleum and used as domestic or industrial fuel in place of town gas (q.v.); **natural**

history originally the description of all that is in nature, now used of the sciences that deal with the earth and its productions — botany, zoology and mineralogy, esp. field zoology; **natural law** a law of nature; the sense of right and wrong which arises from the constitution of the mind of man, as distinguished from the results of revelation or legislation; **natural logarithm** one to the base *e*; **natural magic** see under **magic**; **natural numbers** the whole numbers 1, 2, 3, and upwards, sometimes also including 0; **natural order** (in botany) a category now usually called a family; **natural philosophy** the science of the physical properties of bodies; physics, or physics and dynamics; **natural religion** see **natural theology**; **natural resources** features, properties, etc. of the land such as minerals, an abundance of water, timber, etc. that occur naturally and can be used by man; **natural science** the science of nature, as distinguished from mental and moral science and from mathematics; **natural selection** evolution by the survival of the fittest with inheritance of their fitness by the next generation; **natural theology** religion derived from reasoned facts, not revelation; **natural wastage** (reduction of staff by) non-replacement of those who leave, e.g. through retirement; **natural year** see under **year**. [L. *nātūrālis* — *nātūra*, nature.]

nature *nā'chər*, *n* the power that creates and regulates the world; the power of growth; the established order of things; the external world, esp. as untouched by man; the qualities of anything which make it what it is; essence; being; constitution; kind or order; naturalness; normal feeling; conformity to truth or reality; inborn mind, character, instinct or disposition; course of life; nakedness; a primitive undomesticated condition; the strength or substance of anything. — *adj* **na'tured** having a certain temper or disposition (esp. in compounds, as in *good-natured*). — *n* **na'turism** communal nudity practised in the belief that it encourages self-respect, respect for others and a feeling of being in harmony with nature; nature-worship. — *n* **na'turist**. — *adj* **naturist'ic**. — *n* **nat'uropath** a person who practises naturopathy. — *adj* **naturopath'ic**. — *n* **nāturop'athy** (also *nat-*) the promotion of health and natural healing by a system of diet, exercise, manipulation, care and hydrotherapy; the philosophy of the system. — **na'ture-cure** the practice of or treatment by naturopathy; **na'ture study** a discipline intended to cultivate the powers of seeing and enjoying nature by the observation of natural objects, e.g. plants, animals, etc.; **nature strip** (*Austr*) a strip of grass, etc. bordering a road or footpath or dividing two carriageways; **na'ture-worship** worship of the powers of nature; naturism. — **in the nature of** of the same sort as, that amounts to. [Fr., — L. *nātūra* — *nāscī*, *nātus*, to be born.]

naturopath and **naturopathy**. See under **nature**.

naught *nöt*, *n* nothing (*archaic*); a nought (q.v.) (esp. *NAm*); **bring to naught** (*archaic*) to frustrate, baffle; **come to naught** (*archaic*) to come to nothing, to fail; **set at naught** (*archaic*) to treat as of no account, to despise. [O.E. *nāht*, *nāwiht* — *nā*, never, *wiht*, whit.]

naughty *nöt'i*, *adj* bad; badly-behaved; verging on the indecorous; titillating; now chiefly applied to children in censure. — *n* (*Austr* and *NZ colloq*) an act of sexual intercourse. — *adv* **naught'ily**. — *n* **naught'iness** [**naught**.]

nauplius *nö'pli-əs*, *n* a larval form in many Crustacea, with one eye and three pairs of appendages: — *pl* **nau'plii** (*ī*). [L., a kind of shellfish — Gr. *Nauplios*, a son of Poseidon — *naus*, a ship, *pleein*, to sail.]

nausea *nö'si-ə*, *-shi-ə* or *-zhə*, *n* a feeling of inclination to vomit; sickening disgust or loathing. — *vi* **nau'seate** to feel nausea or disgust. — *vt* to cause to feel sick; to loathe; to strike with disgust. — *adj* **nau'seating** causing nausea or (*fig*) disgust. — *adj* **nau'seous** (*-shəs*, *-shi-əs* or *-si-əs*) producing nausea; disgusting; loathsome. — *adv* **nau'seously**. — *n* **nau'seousness**. [L., — Gr. *nausiā*, seasickness — *naus*, a ship.]

naut. *abbrev* for nautical.

nautch *nöch* or *näch*, *n* (in India) a performance of dancing women known as **nautch'-girls**. [Hind. *nāch*, dance.]

nautical *nö'ti-kəl adj* of or pertaining to ships, to sailors, or to navigation. — *adv* **nau'tically**. — **Nautical Almanac** a periodical book of astronomical tables specially useful to sailors; **nautical mile** see under **mile**. [L. *nauticus* — Gr. *nautikos* — *nautēs*, sailor, *naus*, a ship.]

nautilus *nö'ti-ləs*, *n* a cephalopod (**pearly nautilus**) of southern seas, with a chambered external shell; a Mediterranean cephalopod (**paper nautilus**) wrongly believed by Aristotle to use its arms as sails: — *pl* **nau'tiluses** or **nau'tilī**. [L., — Gr. *nautilos*, a sailor, a paper nautilus — *naus*, ship.]

nav. *abbrev* for: naval; navigable; navigation; navigator.

Navaho or **Navajo** *nav'ə-hō*, *n* a North American Indian people of Utah, Arizona and New Mexico; a member of this people; their language: — *pl* **Nav'ahos** or **Nav'ajos**. [Sp. *Navajó*, name of a particular pueblo.]

naval *nā'vl*, *adj* pertaining to warships or a navy. — **naval officer** an officer in the navy; a custom-house officer of high rank (*US*). [L. *nāvālis* — *nāvis*, a ship.]

navarin *nav'ə-rin* or *nav-a-rē*, *n* a stew of mutton or lamb, with turnip and other root vegetables. [Fr.]

nave[1] *nāv*, (*archit*) *n* the middle or main body of a basilica, rising above the aisles; the main part of a church, generally west of the crossing, including or excluding its aisles. [L. *nāvis*, a ship.]

nave[2] *nāv*, *n* the hub or central part of a wheel, through which the axle passes. [O.E. *nafu*.]

navel *nā'vl*, *n* the umbilicus or depression in the centre of the abdomen; a central point. — **na'vel-orange** a variety of orange with a navel-like depression, and a smaller orange enclosed; **na'vel-string** the umbilical cord; **na'velwort** pennywort. [O.E. *nafela*, dimin. of *nafu*, nave of a wheel.]

navicular *nav-ik'ū-lər*, *adj* boat-shaped; pertaining to the navicular bone. — *n* the navicular bone. — **navicular bone** a boat-shaped bone on the thumb side of the wrist joint, the scaphoid bone; a corresponding bone in the ankle joint; **navicular disease** inflammation of the navicular bone in horses. [L. *nāvicula*, dimin. of *nāvis*, a ship.]

navigate *nav'i-gāt*, *vi* to conduct or manage a ship, aircraft, motor vehicle, etc., in sailing, flying or moving along; to find one's way and keep one's course, esp. by water or air; to sail. — *vt* to direct the course of; to sail, fly, etc., over, on or through. — *n* **navigability** (*-gə-bil'i-ti*). — *adj* **nav'igable** that may be passed by ships, etc.; dirigible. — *n* **nav'igableness**. — *n* **navigā'tion** the act, science or art of conducting ships or aircraft, etc., esp. the finding of position and determination of course by astronomical observations and mathematical computations; travel or traffic by water or air (esp. *NAm*). — *adj* **naviga'tional** pertaining to navigation. — *n* **nav'igator** a person who navigates or sails; a person who directs the course of a ship, etc.; a person who describes the route to, and directs, the driver in car rally or race; an explorer by sea. [L. *nāvigāre*, *-ātum* — *nāvis*, a ship, *agĕre*, to drive.]

navvy *nav'i*, (*colloq*) *n* a labourer. — *vi* to work as a navvy, or like a navvy: — *pr p* **navv'ying**; *pa t* and *pa p* **navv'ied**. [**navigator**.]

navy *nā'vi*, *n* a fleet of ships; the whole of a nation's ships-of-war; the officers and men belonging to a nation's warships. — *adj* of, used by or such as is supplied to the navy. — *n* and *adj* **navy blue** dark blue as in naval dress. — **navy list** a list of officers and ships of a navy; **navy yard** (*US*) a government dockyard. [O.Fr. *navie* — L. *nāvis*, a ship.]

nawab *nə-wäb'* or *-wöb'*, *n* a deputy or viceroy in the Mogul empire; a Muslim prince or noble; an honorary title bestowed by the Indian government. [Hind. *nawwāb* — Ar. *nawwāb*, respectful pl. of *nā'ib*, deputy.]

nay *nā*, (*archaic* or *dialect*) *adv* no; not only so, but; yet more; in point of fact. — *n* a denial; a vote against (*formal*). [O.N. nei.]

Nazarene *naz'ə-rēn*, *n* an inhabitant of *Nazareth*, in Galilee; a follower of Jesus of Nazareth, originally used of Christians in contempt; an early Jewish Christian. — Also *adj*. — Also Naz'arite.

Nazarite *naz'ə-rīt*, *n* a Jewish ascetic under a vow (see Num. vi.) (also **Naz'irite**); a Nazarene. — [Heb. *nāzar*, to consecrate.]

naze *nāz*, *n* a headland or cape. [O.E. *næs*.]

Nazi *nä'tsē*, *n* and *adj* for Ger. *Nazional-sozialist*, National Socialist, Hitlerite. — *n* **Naz'ism** or **Naz'iism**. — *vt* and *vi* **Naz'ify**. [Ger.]

Nazirite. See **Nazarite**.

NB *abbrev* for: Nebraska (U.S. state); New Brunswick (Can. province); North Britain or North British; *nota bene* (L.), note well or take notice (also **nb**).

Nb (*chem*) *symbol* for niobium.

NBA *abbrev* for Net Book Agreement, an agreement within the book trade that net books may not be sold at less than the price fixed by the publisher.

NBC *abbrev* for: National Broadcasting Company (U.S.); nuclear, biological and chemical (warfare, weapons, etc.). — **NBC suit** a suit that protects the wearer against the physical effects of nuclear, biological and chemical weapons.

NC *abbrev* for North Carolina (U.S. state).

NCC *abbrev* for National Consumer Council.

NCCL *abbrev* for National Council for Civil Liberties.

NCO *abbrev* for non-commissioned officer.

ND or **N.Dak.** *abbrev* for North Dakota (U.S. state).

Nd (*chem*) *symbol* for neodymium.

NE *abbrev* for: Nebraska (U.S. state; also **Nebr.**); New England; north-east.

Ne (*chem*) *symbol* for neon.

né *nā*, *adj* (of a man) born, used in giving the original name of a titled man. [Fr.]

Neanderthal *ni-an'dər-täl*, *adj* of a Palaeolithic species of man whose remains were first found in 1857 in a cave in the *Neanderthal*, a valley between Düsseldorf and Elberfeld.

neanic *nē-an'ik*, (*zool*) *adj* pertaining to the adolescent period in the life-history of an individual. [Gr. *neanikos*, youthful.]

neap *nēp*, *adj* (of tides) of smallest range. — *n* a neap tide. — *vi* to tend towards the neap. — *adj* **neaped** left aground between spring tides. — **neap tide** a tide of minimum amplitude, occurring when the sun and moon are working against each other. [O.E. *nēp*, app. meaning helpless; *nēpflōd*, neap tide.]

Neapolitan *nē-ə-pol'i-tən*, *adj* of the city or the former kingdom of Naples. — *n* a native, citizen or inhabitant of Naples. — **Neapolitan ice** ice-cream made in layers of different colours and flavours; **Neapolitan violet** a scented double variety of sweet violet. [L. *Neāpolitānus* — Gr. *Neāpolis*, new town — *neos*, *-ā*, *-on*, new, *polis*, city.]

near *nēr*, *adv* to or at no great distance; close; closely; nearly; almost; narrowly. — *prep* close to. — *adj* (*compar* **near'er**, *superl* **near'est**) not far away in place or time; close in relationship, friendship, imitation, approximation or in any relation; close, narrow, so as barely to escape; short, direct, as of a road; stingy (*colloq*); (of horses, vehicles, roads, etc.) left, left-hand. — *vt* and *vi* to approach; to come nearer. — *adv* **near'ly** at or within a short distance; closely; almost; approximately but rather less. — *n* **near'ness**. — **near beer** (in the U.S) any of several beers containing ½ per cent alcohol or less. — *adj* **near'by** neighbouring. — *adv* (usu. **nearby'**) close at hand. — *prep* (also **near by**) close to. — **Near East** formerly, an area including the Balkans and Turkey, and sometimes also the countries to the west of Iran; now synonymous with **Middle East** (q.v.); **near miss** (*lit* and *fig*) a miss that is almost a hit; **near'side** the side of a vehicle nearer to the kerb e.g. when it is being driven, in Britain the left side; the left side of a horse or other animal, or of a team of horses. — Also *adj*. — *adj* **near-sight'ed** short-sighted. — **near-sight'edness**. — **a near thing** a narrow escape; **near as dammit** (*colloq*) very nearly. [O.E. *nēar*, compar. of *nēah*, nigh (*adv*.), and O.N. *nǣr*, compar. (but also used as positive) of *nā*, nigh.]

Nearctic *nē-ärk'tik*, *adj* of the New World part of the Holarctic region, including the part of N. America to the north of the Tropic of Cancer, and Greenland. [Gr. *neos*, new, *arktikos*, northern.]

neat *nēt*, *adj* unmixed; undiluted; elegant; trim; tidy; fastidious; deft; well and concisely put; ingenious, effective, economical in effort or method. — *adv* neatly. — *vt* **neat'en** to make neat, tidy. — *adv* **neat'ly**. — *n* **neat'ness**. — *adj* **neat-hand'ed** dexterous. [Fr. *net*, clean, tidy — L. *nitidus*, shining, bright — *nitēre*, to shine.]

neath or **'neath** *nēth*, (*dialect* and *poetic*) *prep* beneath. [Aphetic for *aneath*, or for **beneath**.]

NEB *abbrev* for New English Bible.

neb *neb*, (*Scot* and *Northern Eng*) *n* a beak or bill; the nose; the sharp point of anything. [O.E. *nebb*, beak, face.]

nebbich *neb'ihh* or **nebbish** *neb'ish*, *n* a colourless, incompetent person, a perpetual victim. — Also *adj*. [Yiddish.]

Nebr. *abbrev* for Nebraska (U.S. state).

nebula *neb'ū-lə*, *n* a little cloudiness; a slight opacity of the cornea; a liquid for spraying; a faint, misty appearance in the heavens produced either by a group of stars too distant to be seen singly, or by diffused gaseous matter: — *pl* **neb'ulae** (*-lē*). — *adj* **neb'ular** pertaining to nebulae; like or of the nature of a nebula. — *n* **nebulos'ity**. — *adj* **neb'ulous** hazy, vague, formless (*lit* and *fig*); cloudlike; like, of the nature of, or surrounded by a nebula. — *adv* **neb'ulously**. — *n* **neb'ulousness**. — **nebular hypothesis** the theory of Laplace that the solar system was formed by the contraction and breaking up of a rotating nebula. [L. *nebula*, mist.]

NEC *abbrev* for: National Executive Committee; National Exhibition Centre.

necessary *nes'is-ə-ri*, *adj* that must be; that cannot be otherwise; unavoidable; indispensable; (of an agent) not free. — *n* that which cannot be left out or done without (food, etc.) — used chiefly in *pl*; money (*colloq*). — *adv* **nec'essarily** (or *nes-is-e'rə-li*) as a necessary consequence; inevitably; (*loosely*) for certain. — *n* **nec'essariness**. — **necessary truths** such as cannot but be true. [L. *necessārius*.]

necessity *ni-ses'i-ti*, *n* a state or quality of being necessary; that which is necessary or unavoidable; unavoidable compulsion; great need; poverty. — *n* and *adj* **necessitā'rian** or **necessa'rian**. — *n* **necessitā'rianism** or **necessa'rianism** the philosophical theory that human actions are determined by precursory circumstances and cannot be willed. — *vt* **necess'itate** to make necessary; to render unavoidable; to compel. — *n* **necessitā'tion**. — *adj* **necess'itous** in necessity; very poor; destitute. — *adv* **necess'itously**. — *n* **necess'itousness**. — **of necessity** necessarily. [L. *necessitās*, *-ātis*.]

neck *nek*, *n* the part connecting head and trunk; the flesh of that part regarded as food; anything resembling that part; the part connecting the head and body of anything, e.g. a violin; the plain lower part of the capital of a column; any narrow connecting part, e.g. an isthmus; anything narrow and throatlike, such as the upper part of a bottle; the part of a garment on or nearest the neck; a neck's length; impudence, audacity (*slang*). — *vt* to make a neck on. — *vi* (*slang*) to embrace. — *adj* **necked** having a neck. — *n* **neck'ing** the neck of a column (*archit*); a moulding between the capital and shaft of a column (*archit*); embracing, petting (*slang*). — *n* **neck'let** a simple form of necklace. — **neck'band** the part of a shirt, etc., encircling the neck; a band worn on the neck; **neck'cloth** a piece of folded cloth worn round the neck by men as a band or cravat; **neck'erchief** an ornamental cloth, a kerchief, for the neck; **neck'lace** (-*lis* or -*ləs*) a lace, chain, or string of beads or precious stones worn on the neck; (in S. Africa) the punishment of having a petrol-soaked tyre placed round the neck or shoulders and set alight, used by blacks against blacks thought to be government sympathisers (also called **neck'lacing**); **neck'line** the edge of a garment at the neck; **neck'-moulding** a moulding where the capital of a column joins the shaft; **neck'tie** (esp. *NAm*) a band of fabric tied round the neck under the collar and usu. hanging down in front; a tie; a hangman's noose (*US slang*); **necktie party** (*US slang*) a lynching; **neck'wear** apparel for the neck, such as ties or scarves. — **get it in the neck** to be severely dealt with or hard hit; **neck and neck** exactly equal; side by side; **neck of the woods** (*colloq*) a particular area, part of the country; **neck or nothing** risking everything; **save one's neck** to escape narrowly with one's life or reputation; **stick one's neck out** to put oneself at risk, expose oneself to trouble, danger or contradiction; **talk through the back of one's neck** to talk wildly or absurdly wide of the truth; **up to one's neck** deeply involved, esp. in a troublesome situation. [O.E. *hnecca*.]

necro- *nek-rō-* or *-ro-*, *combining form* denoting: dead; dead body. — *n* **necrōbiō'sis** degeneration of living tissue. — *n* **necrol'ater**. — *n* **necrol'atry** worship of, or morbid or sentimental reverence for, the dead. — *adj* **necrōlog'ical**. — *n* **necrol'ogist**. — *n* **necrol'ogy** an obituary list. — *n* **nec'rōmancer** a sorcerer. — *n* **nec'rōmancy** the art of revealing future events by calling up and questioning the spirits of the dead; enchantment; sorcery. — *adj* **necrōman'tic**. — *adv* **necrōman'tically**. — *adj* **necroph'agous** feeding on carrion. — *n* **nec'rophile** (-*fīl*) or **necrophiliac** (-*fil'iak*) someone who is morbidly attracted to, and esp. has sexual intercourse with, corpses. — *n* **necrophilia** (-*fil'*). — *adj* **necrophil'iac** or **necrophil'ic**. — *n* **necroph'ilism** or **necroph'ily** necrophilia. — *adj* **necroph'ilous**. — *n* **necrōphō'bia** a morbid horror of corpses. — *n* **necrop'olis** a cemetery or burial site. — *n* **nec'ropsy** (or -*rop'*) a post-mortem examination. — *adj* **necrōscop'ic**. — *n* **necros'copy** a post-mortem examination, autopsy. [Gr. *nekros*, dead body, dead.]

necrosis *nek-rō'sis*, *n* death of part of the living body, esp. of a concentrated area of cells owing to an interruption of the blood supply, etc. — *vt* and *vi* **necrose** (*nek-rōs'*) to affect with or undergo necrosis. — *adj* **necrot'ic**. — *vt* and *vi* **nec'rōtise** or **-ize** to necrose. [Gr. *nekros*, dead body.]

nectar *nek'tər*, *n* the name given by Homer, etc., to the beverage of the gods, giving life and beauty; the honey of the glands of plants; a delicious beverage; anything very sweet or pleasant. — *adj* **nectā'rean**, **nectā'reous** or **nec'tarous** of or like nectar. — *n* **nec'tarine** (-*ēn* or -*in*) a variety of peach with a smooth skin. — *n* **nec'tary** a glandular organ that secretes nectar [Gr. *nektar*.]

neddy *ned'i*, *n* a donkey; a fool (*colloq*); a racehorse (*Austr slang*). [From *Edward*.]

née *nā*, *adj* (of a woman) born — used in stating a woman's maiden name. [Fr., fem. past. p. of *naître*, to be born.]

need *nēd*, *n* lack of something which one cannot easily do without; necessity; a state that requires relief; lack of the means of living. — *vt* to want; to require; (used before the infinitive with *to*, or in negative, interrogative, conditional, etc. sentences without *to*) to require or be obliged (to do something); (used before a verbal noun) to require (to be dealt with in a particular way). — *adj* **need'ful** necessary; requisite. — *adv* **need'fully**. — *n* **need'fulness**. — *adv* **need'ily**. — *n* **need'iness**. — *adj* **need'less** not needed; unnecessary. — *adv* **need'lessly**. — *n* **need'lessness**. — *adv* **needs** of necessity; indispensably. — *adj* **need'y** very poor. — **must needs** or **needs must** (often *ironic*) must inevitably; **the needful** (*slang*) ready money; whatever is requisite, usu. in *do the needful* (*colloq*). [O.E. *nēd*, *nīed*, *nȳd*.]

needle *nēd'l*, *n* a small, sharp instrument for sewing; any similar slender, pointed instrument, as for knitting, etching, playing gramophone records, dissection, (hooked) for crochet; the suspended magnet of a compass or galvanometer; a pointer on a dial; the pointed end of a hypodermic syringe; anything sharp and pointed; a pinnacle of rock; an obelisk; a long slender crystal; a strong beam passed through a wall as a temporary support; a long, narrow, stiff leaf; a feeling of irritation (*slang*); dislike, enmity (*slang*). — *adj* (of a contest) intensely keen and acutely critical. — *vt* to sew; to pass through; to underpin with needles; to irritate, goad or heckle. — *vi* to pass out and in; to sew. — **need'le-book** a needle-case in book form; **need'le-case** a case for holding needles; **need'lecord** a cotton material with closer ribs and flatter pile than corduroy; **need'le-craft** the art of needlework; lace made with a needle; embroidery on canvas, done with woollen yarns, used on chair-covers, etc.; **needle time** the amount of time allowed to a radio channel for the broadcasting of recorded music; **need'lewoman** a woman who does needlework; **need'lework** work done with a needle; the business of a seamstress. — **get the needle** (*colloq*) to be irritated; **look for a needle in a haystack** to engage in a hopeless search. [O.E. *nǣdl*.]

neep *nēp*, (*Scot*) *n* a turnip. [O.E. *nǣp* — L. *nāpus*.]

ne'er *nār*, *adv* contraction of **never**. — *adj* and *n* **ne'er'-do-well** good-for-nothing.

NEF *abbrev* for National Energy Foundation.

nefarious *ni-fā'ri-əs*, *adj* extremely wicked; villainous. — *adv* **nefā'riously**. — *n* **nefā'riousness**. [L. *nefārius*, *nefāstus* — *nefās*, wrong, crime — *ne-*, not, *fās*, divine law.]

neg. *abbrev* for: negative; negatively; negotiable.

negate *ni-gāt'*, *vt* to deny; to nullify; to imply the non-existence of; to make ineffective. — *n* **negation** (-*gā'shən*) the act of saying no; denial; a negative proposition (*logic*); something that is the opposite (of a positive quality, state, etc.); a thing characterised by the absence of qualities. — *n* **negā'tionist** someone who merely denies, without offering any positive assertion. — *adj* **negative** (*neg'ə-tiv*) denying; expressing denial, refusal or prohibition (opp. to *affirmative*); denying the connection between a subject and a predicate (*logic*); lacking positive quality; opposite, contrary to, neutralising, etc. that which is regarded as positive; defeatist; obstructive, unconstructive; less than nothing (*math*); reckoned or measured in the opposite direction to that chosen as positive (*math*); of, having or producing negative electricity; having dark for light and light for dark (*optics* and *phot*); in complementary colours (*optics* and *phot*); in a direction away from the source of stimulus (*biol*). — *n* a word or statement by which something is denied; a word or grammatical form that expresses denial or opposition; the side of a question or the decision which denies what is affirmed; an image in which the lights and shades are reversed; a photographic plate bearing such an image. — *vt* to prove the contrary of; to veto; to reject by veto; to deny; to neutralise. — *adv* **neg'atively.** — *n* **neg'ativeness.** — *n* **neg'ativism** the doctrine or attitude of a negationist. — *n* **negativ'ity.** — *adj* **neg'atory** expressing denial. — **negative electricity** electricity arising from an excess of electrons; **negative pole** that pole of a magnet which turns to the south when the magnet swings freely; **negative sign** the sign (– read *minus*) of subtraction. [L. *negāre, -ātum,* to deny.]

neglect *ni-glekt',* *vt* to treat carelessly; to pass by without notice; to omit by carelessness; to fail to bestow due care upon. — *n* disregard; slight; omission; uncared-for state. — *n* **neglect'edness.** — *n* **neglect'er.** — *adj* **neglect'ful** careless; accustomed to omit or neglect things; slighting. — *adv* **neglect'fully.** — *n* **neglect'fulness.** [L. *neglegĕre, neglectum* — *neg-* or *nec-*, not, *legĕre,* to gather.]

negligé or **negligee** *nā'gli-zhā* or *ne',* *n* a woman's loose decorative dressing-gown of flimsy material. [Fr., neglected.]

negligence *neg'li-jəns,* *n* the fact or quality of being negligent; lack of proper care; habitual neglect; a slight; carelessness about dress, manner, etc.; omission of duty, esp. such care for the interests of others as the law may require. — *adj* **neg'ligent** neglecting; careless; inattentive, esp. to duties or responsibilities; disregarding ceremony or fashion. — *adv* **neg'ligently.** — *n* **negligibil'ity.** — *adj* **neg'ligible** such as may be ignored because very little or very unimportant. — *adv* **neg'ligibly.** [L. *negligentia* for *neglegentia* — *neglegĕre,* to neglect.]

negotiate *ni-gō'shi-āt,* *vi* to confer for the purpose of mutual arrangement; to bargain. — *vt* to arrange for by agreement; to manage; to transfer or exchange for value; to cope with successfully (*colloq*). — *n* **negotiabil'ity.** — *adj* **nego'tiable** that can be negotiated; not fixed; legally transferable, as bonds, etc. — *n* **negotiā'tion.** — *n* **nego'tiātor.** [L. *negōtiārī, -ātus* — *negōtium,* business — *neg-*, not, *ōtium,* leisure.]

Negrillo *ni-gril'ō,* *n* an African Negrito: — *pl* **Negrill'os.** [Sp., dimin. of *negro,* black.]

Negrito *ni-grē'tō,* *n* a member of any of a number of pygmy negroid peoples of S.E. Asia and Africa: — *pl* **Negri'tos.** [Sp., dimin. of *negro,* black.]

Negro *nē'grō,* *n* (formerly also without *cap*) a member of any of the dark-skinned peoples of Africa or a person racially descended from them: — *pl* **Ne'groes.** — *adj* of or pertaining to Negroes. — *n* **Ne'gress** (formerly also without *cap*) a Negro woman or girl. — *adj* **ne'groid** having physical characteristics associated with Negro races, e.g. full lips, broad nose, tightly curling hair, etc. — *n* a negroid person. — *adj* **negroid'al.** — *n* **ne'grōism** any peculiarity of speech among Negroes, esp. in the southern U.S.; devotion to the causes of the Black civil rights movement (*old fashioned;* sometimes *derog*). [Sp. *negro* — L. *niger, nigra, nigrum,* black.]

Negus *nē'gəs,* (*hist*) *n* the king of Ethiopia. [Amharic.]

negus *nē'gəs,* *n* port or sherry with hot water, sweetened and spiced. [From Colonel *Negus,* its first maker.]

Neh. (*Bible*) *abbrev* for (the Book of) Nehemiah.

neigh *nā,* *vi* to utter the cry of a horse, or a similar cry. — *n* the cry of a horse. [O.E. *hnǣgan.*]

neighbour or in N.Am. **neighbor** *nā'bər,* *n* a person who lives near another; a person or thing that is near another. — *vt* and *vi* to live or be near. — *vi* to associate with one's neighbours. — *n* **neigh'bourhood** or in N.Am. **neigh'borhood** a set of neighbours; a district, locality, esp. with reference to its inhabitants as a community; a district; a region lying near; a near position; all the points that surround a given point in a specified degree of closeness (*math*). — *adj* **neigh'bouring** or in N.Am. **neigh'boring** being near; adjoining. — *n* **neigh'bourliness** or in N.Am. **neigh'borliness.** — *adj* **neigh'bourly** or in N.Am. **neigh'borly** like or becoming a neighbour; friendly; social. — **in the neighbourhood of** approximately, somewhere about; **neighbourhood law centre** see **law centre** under **law**[1]. [O.E. *nēahgebūr* — *nēah,* near, *gebūr* or *būr,* a farmer.]

neither *nī'dhər,* or *nē'dhər,* *adj* and *pron* not either. — *conj* not either; and not; nor yet. — *adv* not at all; in no case. [O.E. *nāther, nāwther,* abbrev. of *nāhwæther* — *nā,* never, *hwæther,* whether.]

nekton *nek'ton,* *n* the assemblage of actively swimming organisms in a sea, lake, etc. [Gr. *nēkton* (neut.), swimming.]

nellie or **nelly** (*nel'i*): **not on your nellie** or **nelly** (*slang*) not on any account — said to be from *not on your Nellie Duff,* rhyming with *puff,* meaning 'life'.

nelly *nel'i,* *n* a large petrel. [Perh. the woman's name.]

nelson *nel'sən,* *n* a wrestling hold in which the arms are passed under both the opponent's arms from behind, and the hands joined so that pressure can be exerted with the palms on the back of his neck. — Also **full nelson.** — **half nelson** this hold applied on one side only, i.e. with one arm under one of the opponent's arms; a disabling restraint (*fig*). [From the proper name.]

nematocyst *nem'ət-ō-sist* or *-at',* *n* a stinging organ in jellyfishes, etc., a sac from which a stinging thread can be everted. [Gr. *nēma, -atos,* a thread, *kystis,* a bladder.]

nematode *nem'ə-tōd,* *n* a roundworm or threadworm. — Also *adj.* — *adj* **nem'atoid.** — *n* **nematol'ogist.** — *n* **nematol'ogy** the study of nematodes. [Gr. *nēma, -atos,* thread, *eidos,* form.]

Nembutal® *nem'bū-təl,* *n* proprietary name for pentobarbitone sodium, used as a sedative, hypnotic and antispasmodic.

nem. con. *abbrev* for **nemine contradicente** (q.v.).

nem. diss. *abbrev* for **nemine dissentiente** (q.v.).

Nemean *nem-ē'ən, nem'i-ən* or *nēm'i-ən,* *adj* of *Nemea* (Gr. *Nĕmĕā*), the valley of Argolis, famous for its games held in the second and fourth years of each Olympiad, and for the lion killed by Herakles.

Nemertinea *nem-ər-tin'i-ə,* *npl* a phylum of wormlike animals, mostly marine, often brightly coloured. — Also **Nemer'tea.** [Gr. *Nēmertēs,* one of the nereids.]

nemesia *nem-ē'zhə* or *nem-ē'zhyə,* *n* a plant of the S. African genus *Nemesia* of the figwort family, including some brightly coloured garden flowers. [Gr. *nemesion,* a kind of catchfly.]

Nemesis *nem'i-sis,* (*Gr mythol*) *n* the Greek goddess of retribution; (without *cap*) retributive justice. [Gr. *nemesis,* retribution — *nemein,* to deal out, dispense.]

nemine contradicente *nem'i-nē kon-trə-di-sen'tē* or *nā'mi-ne kon-trä-dē-ken'te,* (L.; often abbrev. **nem. con.**) without opposition; no-one speaking in opposition; **nemine dissentiente** (*di-sen-shi-en'tē* or *-ti-en'te;* L.; often abbrev. **nem. diss.**) no-one dissenting.

nemophila *nem-of'i-lə,* *n* a plant of the N. American genus *Nemophila,* of popular garden annuals, esp. one with blue, white-centred flowers. [Gr. *nemos,* a glade, wooded pasture, *phileein,* to love.]

neo- *nē-ō-, nē-ə-* or *nē-o-,* *combining form* signifying new, young, or revived in a new form. — *adj* **neoclass'ic** or **neoclass'ical** belonging to a revival of the classical style, esp. in the art and architecture of the late 18th and early 19th cents. — *n* **neoclass'icism.** — *n* **neocolō'nialism** the quasi-colonialism practised by strong powers in dominating weaker, though politically independent, states by means of economic pressure. — *n* and *adj* **neocolō'nialist.** — *n* **Neo-Dar'winism** a later development of Darwinism, laying greater stress upon natural selection and denying the inheritance of acquired characteristics.

— *n* and *adj* **Neo-Dar'winist** or **Neo-Darwin'ian**. — *n* **Neofascism** (*-fash'izm*) a movement attempting to reinstate the policies of fascism. — *n* and *adj* **Neofasc'ist**. — *adj* **Neoplatonic** (*-plə-ton'ik*). — *n* **Neoplā'tonism** a philosophy developed in the 3rd cent. A.D. combining Platonism with oriental elements. — *n* and *adj* **Neoplā'tonist**. — *n* **neorē'alism** a modern form of realism in the arts and literature; esp. an orig. Italian movement in cinematography concentrating on social themes and the realistic depiction of esp. lower-class life. — *n* and *adj* **neorē'alist**. — *adj* **neorealis'tic**. — *adj* **neotrop'ical** (*biol*) belonging to the tropics of the New World, tropical America. [Gr. *neos*, new.]

neoblast *nē'ə-bläst*, (*zool*) *n* (in many of the lower animals, such as the *Annelida* (worms)) any of the large amoeboid cells that play an important part in the phenomena of regeneration. [**neo-** and Gr. *blastos*, shoot, bud.]

neoclassic . . . to . . . **Neo-Darwin'ian**. See under **neo-**.

neodymium *nē-ə-dim'i-əm*, (*chem*) *n* a silvery-grey toxic metallic element (symbol **Nd**; atomic no. 60). [**neo-** and *didymium*, a once-supposed element found to consist of neodymium and praseodymium.]

Neofascism, etc. See under **neo-**.

Neolithic *nē-ə-lith'ik*, (*archaeol*) *adj* relating to the later, more advanced, Stone Age. [**neo-** and Gr. *lithos*, stone.]

neologism *nē-ol'ə-jizm*, *n* a new word or phrase; a new use of an established word; the practice of coining or introducing neologisms. — *vi* **neol'ogise** or **-ize** to introduce new words, coin neologisms. — *n* **neol'ogist**. — *adj* **neologis'tic** or **neologis'tical**. [**neo-** and Gr. *logos*, word.]

neomycin *nē-ə-mī'sin*, (*pharm*) *n* an antibiotic used to treat skin and eye infections. [**neo-**, Gr. *mukēs*, fungus, and sfx. *-in*.]

neon *nē'on*, *n* a gaseous element (symbol **Ne**; atomic no. 10) found in the atmosphere by Sir William Ramsay (1852–1916). — **neon lamp** or **light** an electric discharge lamp containing neon, giving a red glow, used e.g. for advertising signs; (*loosely*) one of a variety of tubular fluorescent lamps giving light of various colours; **neon lighting**. [Neuter of Gr. *neos*, new.]

neonatal *nē-ə-nā'tl*, *adj* relating to the newly born. — *n* **nē'onate** a newly born child. — *n* **neonatol'ogy**. [N.L. *neonātus* — Gr. *neo-* new, L. *nātus*, born.]

neophobia *nē-ə-fō'bi-ə*, *n* dread or hatred of novelty. — *n* **nē'ophobe**. — *adj* **neophō'bic**. [Gr. *neos*, new, *phobos*, fear.]

neophyte *nē'ə-fīt*, *n* a new convert; a person newly baptised; a newly ordained priest; a novice in a religious order; a beginner. — *adj* **neophytic** (*-fit'ik*). [Gr. *neophytos*, newly planted.]

neoplasm *nē'ə-plazm*, (*pathol*) *n* a morbid new growth of tissue. — *adj* **neoplas'tic**. [**neo-** and Gr. *plasma*, something moulded.]

Neoplatonic, etc. See under **neo-**.

neoprene *nē'ə-prēn*, *n* an oil-resisting and heat-resisting synthetic rubber made by polymerising chloroprene. [**neo-** and **chloroprene**.]

neorealism, etc. See under **neo-**.

neoteny *nē-ot'ə-ni*, (*biol*) *n* prolonged retention of larval or immature features in the adult form. — *adj* **neotenic** (*-ten'ik*) or **neot'enous**. [**neo-** and Gr. *teinein*, to stretch.]

neoteric *nē-ō-ter'ik*, *adj* of recent origin, modern. — *adv* **neoter'ically**. [Gr. *neōterikos* — *neōteros*, compar. of *neos*, new.]

neotropical. See under **neo-**.

Neozoic *nē-ə-zō'ik*, (*geol*) *adj* and *n* relating to the period between the Mesozoic and the present age. [**neo-** and Gr. *zōikos*, of animals.]

Nepalese *nep-ə-lēz'*, *adj* of Nepal or its people. — *n* a native or citizen of Nepal.

Nepali *ni-pö'lē*, *n* the official language of Nepal, belonging to the Indic branch of Indo-European languages; a native or citizen of Nepal. — *adj* of Nepal, its people or its language.

nepenthe *ni-pen'thē*, *n* a sorrow-lulling drink or drug (*poetic*); the plant yielding it. — *adj* **nepen'thean**. — *n* **Nepen'thes** (*-thēz*) nepenthe; the pitcher plant genus. [Gr. *nepenthēs, -es* — pfx. *nē-*, not, *penthos*, grief.]

nephelometer *nef-ə-lom'i-tər*, *n* an instrument for measuring cloudiness, esp. in liquids. — *adj* **nephelomet'ric**. — *n* **nephelom'etry**. [Gr. *nephelē*, cloud, *metron*, measure.]

nephew *nev'ū* or *nef'ū*, *n* the son of a brother or sister; extended to a like relation by marriage: — *fem* **niece**. [(O.)Fr. *neveu* — L. *nepōs, nepōtis*, grandson.]

nephology *nef-ol'ə-ji*, *n* the study of clouds in meteorology. — *adj* **nephologic** (*-ə-loj'*) or **nepholog'ical**. — *n* **nephol'ogist**. [Gr. *nephos*, cloud.]

nephro- *nef-ro-* or *-rō-* or **nephr-** *combining form* signifying kidney. — *n* **neph'rīte** the mineral jade, in the narrower sense — an old charm against kidney disease. — *adj* **nephrit'ic** pertaining to the kidneys, or nephritis. — *n* **nephrī'tis** inflammation of the kidneys. — *adj* **nephrological** (*-loj'*). — *n* **nephrol'ogist**. — *n* **nephrol'ogy** the science concerned with structure, functions and diseases, of the kidneys. — *n* **nephrot'omy** incision into the kidney. [Gr. *nephros*, a kidney.]

nepit. See **nit**[4].

ne plus ultra *nē plus ul'trə* or *nā plōōs ōōl'trä*, (L.) nothing further; the uttermost point or extreme perfection of anything.

nepotism *nep'o-tizm*, *n* undue favouritism to one's relations and close friends, orig. by a pope. — *adj* **nepotic** (*ni-pot'ik*) or **nepotis'tic**. — *n* **nep'otist**. [L. *nepōs, nepōtis*, a grandson.]

Neptune *nep'tūn*, *n* the Roman sea-god, identified with the Greek Poseidon; a remote planet of the solar system, discovered in 1846. — *adj* **Neptū'nian**. [L. *Neptūnus*.]

neptunium *nep-tū'ni-əm*, *n* an element (symbol **Np**; atomic no. 93) named as next after uranium, as Neptune is next after Uranus.

NERC *nûrk*, *abbrev* for Natural Environment Research Council.

nerd or **nurd** *nûrd*, (*slang*) *n* a clumsy, foolish, feeble, unathletic, irritating, unprepossessing, etc. person.

nereid *nē'rē-id*, *n* a sea-nymph, daughter of the sea-god *Nereus* (*Gr mythol*); a marine worm. [Gr. *nērēis* or *nērēis* — *Nēreus*.]

nerine *ni-rī'nē*, *n* any plant of the South African genus *Nerine*, with scarlet or rose-coloured flowers, including the Guernsey lily. [L. *nērinē*, a nereid.]

nerk *nûrk*, (*slang*) *n* an irritating fool or idiot. [Poss. **nerd** and **berk**.]

nerka *nûr'kə*, *n* the sockeye salmon.

nero-antico *nā-rō-an-tē'kō*, *n* a deep-black marble found in Roman ruins. [It., ancient black.]

neroli *ner'ə-lē*, *n* an oil distilled from orange flowers — also **neroli oil**. [Said to be named from its discoverer, an Italian princess.]

Neronian *nē-rō'ni-ən*, *adj* pertaining to *Nero*, Roman emperor from A.D. 54 to 68; excessively cruel and tyrannical. [L. *Nĕrō, -ōnis*.]

nerve *nûrv*, *n* a sinew (now chiefly *fig*); a cord that conveys impulses between the brain or other centre and some part of the body (*anat*); a leaf-vein or rib (*bot*); a nervure in an insect's wing (*entom*); cool courage; impudent assurance, audacity (*colloq*); (in *pl*) nervousness. — *vt* to give strength, resolution or courage to. — *adj* **ner'vate** (of a leaf) having veins; nerved. — *adj* **nerved** supplied with nerves. — *adj* **nerve'less** without nerves or nervures; without strength; inert; slack, flabby; without nervousness. — *n* **nerve'lessness**. — *n* **nerv'iness**. — *adj* **nerv'ous** pertaining to the nerves; having the nerves easily excited or weak, agitated and apprehensive (often with *of*); shy; timid; in a jumpy state. — *adv* **nerv'ously**. — *n* **nerv'ousness**. — *n* **nerv'ure** a leaf-vein; a chitinous strut or rib supporting and strengthening an insect's wing (*entom*). — *adj* **nerv'y** nervous; jumpily excited or excitable; impudent or audacious (*NAm colloq*). — **nerve agent** a nerve gas or similar substance; **nerve'-cell** any cell forming part of the nervous system; a neuron; **nerve centre** an aggregation of nerve-cells from which nerves branch out; (in an organisation) the centre from which control is exercised (*fig*); **nerve fibre** an axon; **nerve gas** any of a number of gases, prepared for use in war, having a deadly effect on the nervous system, esp. on nerves controlling respiration. — *adj* **nerve'-racking** or **-wracking** distressfully straining the nerves. — **nerve impulse** or **nervous impulse** the electrical impulse passing along a nerve fibre when it has been stimulated; **nervous breakdown** a loose term indicating nervous debility following prolonged mental or physical fatigue; a euphemism for any mental illness; **nervous system** the brain, spinal cord and nerves collectively. — **bundle of nerves** (*colloq*) a very timid, anxious person; **get on one's nerves** to become oppressively irritating; **live on one's nerves** to be in a tense or nervous state; to be of an excitable temperament; **lose one's nerve** to lose confidence in one's ability; to become suddenly afraid; **war of nerves** see under **war**. [L. *nervus*, sinew.]

NES *abbrev* for National Eczema Society.

nescience *nes'i-əns* or *nes'yəns*, (*formal*) *n* lack of knowledge; ignorance. — *adj* **nesc'ient**. [L. *nescientia* — *nescīre*, to be ignorant — *ne-*, not, *scīre*, to know.]

ness *nes*, *n* a headland. [O.E. *næs*, *næss*.]

nest *nest*, *n* a structure prepared by animals for egg-laying, brooding and nursing, or as a shelter; a den; a comfortable residence; a group of machine-guns in a position fortified or screened by sandbags or anything similar; a place where anything teems, or is fostered; the occupants of a nest, such as a brood, a swarm, a gang, etc.; a set of things (as boxes, tables) fitting one within another. — *vi* to build or occupy a nest; to go bird-nesting. — *vt* and *vi* to lodge or settle. — *n* **nest'er** somone who builds a farm or homestead on land used for grazing cattle (*US hist*); a nest-builder. — **nest'-egg** an egg, real or sham, left or put in a nest to encourage laying; something laid up as the beginning of an accumulation; money saved; **nest'ing-box** a box set up for birds to nest in. — **feather one's nest** see under **feather**. [O.E. *nest*.]

nestle *nes'l*, *vi* to lie or press close or snug as in a nest; to settle comfortably or half hidden. — *vt* to thrust close; to provide a nesting-place for. — *n* **nestling** (*nes'ling*) a young bird in the nest. — Also *adj*. [O.E. *nestlian* — *nest*.]

net[1] *net*, *n* an open fabric, knotted into meshes; a piece, bag, screen or structure of such fabric, used for catching fish, butterflies, etc., carrying parcels, stopping balls, retaining hair, excluding pests; machine-made lace of various kinds; a snare; a plan to trap or catch someone or something. — *adj* of or like net or network. — *vt* to form into network; to mark or cover with network; to set with nets; to form by making network; to take with a net; to capture. — *vi* to form network: — *pr p* **nett'ing**; *pa t* and *pa p* **nett'ed**. — *n* **net'ful** enough to fill a net. — *adj* **nett'ed** made into a net; caught in a net; covered with a net. — *n* **nett'ing** the act or process of forming network; a piece of network. — *adj* **nett'y** like a net. — **net'ball** a game, played mainly by women, in which the ball is thrown into a net hung from a pole; **net'-play** (in tennis, etc.) play near the net; **net'-player**; **nett'ing-needle** a kind of shuttle used in netting; **net'work** any structure in the form of a net; a system of lines, e.g. railway lines, resembling a net; a system of units, as e.g. buildings, agencies, groups of people, constituting a widely spread organisation and having a common purpose; an arrangement of electrical components; a system of stations connected for broadcasting the same programme (*radio* and *TV*); a system of computer terminals and other peripheral devices that can pass information to one another. — *vt* to broadcast on radio or TV stations throughout the country, as opposed to a single station covering only one region. [O.E. *net*, *nett*.]

net[2] or **nett** *net*, *adj* clear of all charges or deductions (opp. to *gross*); (of weight) not including that of packaging; lowest, subject to no further deductions. — *vt* to gain or produce as clear profit: — *pr p* **nett'ing**; *pa t* and *pa p* **nett'ed**. [**neat**.]

Neth. *abbrev* for Netherlands.

nether *nedh'ər*, *adj* lower. — *adj* **neth'ermost** lowest. — **neth'erworld** hell. [O.E. *neothera*, adj. — *nither*, adv., from the root *ni-*, down.]

Netherlander *nedh'ər-land-ər*, *n* an inhabitant of the *Netherlands* formerly also Belgium. — *adj* **Netherland'ic** or **Neth'erlandish** Dutch.

netsuke *net'skē* or *net'sŏŏ-ki*, *n* a small Japanese carved ornament, once used to fasten small objects (e.g. a purse or pouch for tobacco, medicines, etc.) to a sash. [Jap. *ne*, root, bottom, *tsuke* — *tsukeru*, to attach.]

nett. See **net**[2].

nettle *net'l*, *n* any of various common weeds with stinging hairs. — *vt* to sting; to annoy. — *adj* **nett'lesome** irritable. — **nett'le-rash** a rash of red or white weals with irritation like nettle-stings; urticaria. — **grasp the nettle** to set about an unpleasant task, duty, etc. with firmness and resolution. [O.E. *netele*.]

netty, network, etc. See **net**[1].

neume or **neum** *nūm*, *n* (in mediaeval music) a succession of notes sung to one syllable; a sign giving a rough indication of rise or fall of pitch. [O.Fr., — Gr. *pneuma*, breath.]

neur- *nūr-* or **neuro-** *nū-rō-*, *nū-rə-* or *nū-ro'-*, *combining form* signifying: pertaining to a nerve-cell, to a nerve-fibre, to nerve-tissue or to the nervous system (esp. the brain and spinal cord); pertaining to the nerves and some other system, as in *neuromuscular*, *neurovascular*; concerned with, or dealing with, the nervous system, as in *neurophysiology*, *neurosurgery*. — *n* **neuralgia** (*nū-ral'jə*) paroxysmal intermittent pain along the course of a nerve. — *adj* **neural'gic**. — *n* **neurasthenia** (*nū-rəs-thē'ni-ə*; Gr. *astheneia*, weakness) nervous debility. — *n* **neurasthē'niac** someone suffering from neurasthenia. — *adj* **neurasthenic** (*-then'ik* or *-thē'nik*). — Also *n* a neurastheniac. — *n* **neurec'tomy** the surgical excision of part of a nerve. — *n* **neurilemm'a** or **neurolemm'a** (Gr. *eilēma*, covering) the external sheath of a nerve-fibre. — *adj* **neuroen'docrine** pertaining to the nervous and endocrine systems, and to their interaction. — *n* **neuroendocrinol'ogy** the study of the interaction of the nervous and endocrine systems. — *n* **neuroethol'ogy** the description of features of animal behaviour in terms of the mechanisms of the nervous system. — *n* **neurofibrō'ma** a fibroma of the peripheral nerves: — *pl* **neurofibro'mas** or **neurofibro'mata**. — *n* **neurofibromatō'sis** a condition characterised by the formation of neurofibromas and areas of dark pigmentation on the skin. — *adj* **neurog'lia** (Gr. *gliā*, glue) the supporting tissue of the brain and spinal cord, etc. — *n* **neur'olinguist**. — *adj* **neurolinguis'tic**. — *nsing* **neurolinguis'tics** the branch of linguistics which deals with the processing and storage of language in the brain. — *adj* **neurolog'ical**. — *n* **neurol'ogist**. — *n* **neurol'ogy** orig. the study of the nervous system; that branch of medicine concerned with the diagnosis and treatment of diseases of the nervous system. — *adj* **neuromus'cular** relating to both nerves and muscles. — *n* **neur'opath** (*-path*) someone whose nervous system is diseased or in disorder. — *adj* **neuropath'ic** or **neuropath'ical**. — *n* **neuropathist** (*nū-rop'ə-thist*) a specialist in nervous diseases. — *n* **neuropathol'ogy** the pathology of the nervous system. — *n* **neurop'athy** nervous disease generally. — *n* **neuropharmacol'ogist**. — *n* **neuropharmacol'ogy** the scientific study of the effects of drugs on the nervous system. — *n* **neurophysiol'ogy** the physiology of the nervous system. — *n* **neur'oscience** any or all of the scientific disciplines studying the nervous system and/or the mind and mental behaviour. — *n* **neurosci'entist**. — *n* **neur'osurgeon**. — *n* **neurosur'gery** surgery performed on the brain, spinal cord or other parts of the nervous system. — *n* **neurotomy** (*-ot'ə-mi*) the surgical cutting of a nerve. — *n* **neurotransmitt'er** a chemical released from a nerve fibre by means of which an impulse passes to a muscle or another nerve. — *adj* **neurovas'cular** relating to both nerves and blood vessels. [Gr. *neuron*, a nerve.]

neural *nū'rəl*, *adj* of or relating to the nerves; dorsal, as opp. to *haemal*. — **neural plate** the part of the ectoderm of an embryo which develops into the neural tube; **neural tube** the channel formed by the closing of the edges of a fold in the ectoderm of an embryo, later developing into the spinal cord and cerebral hemispheres. [Gr. *neuron*, nerve.]

neuritis *nū-rī'tis*, *n* inflammation of a nerve or nerves, in some cases with defective functioning of the affected part. [Gr. *neuron*, nerve, and **-itis**.]

neuron *nū'ron* or **neurone** *nū'rōn*, *n* a cell with the specialised function of transmitting nerve impulses, a nerve cell. [Gr. *neuron*, nerve.]

Neuroptera *nū-rop'tə-rə*, *npl* a former order of insects, now placed in a superorder, **Neuropteroidea** (*nū-rop-tə-roi'di-ə*), the insects generally having four net-veined wings. — *adj* **neurop'terous**. [Gr. *neuron*, a nerve, *pteron*, a wing, *eidos*, form.]

neurosis *nū-rō'sis*, *n* functional derangement resulting from a disordered nervous system, esp. without lesion of parts; mental disturbance characterised by a state of unconscious conflict, usu. accompanied by anxiety and obsessional fears: — *pl* **neurō'sēs**. — *adj* **neurot'ic** of the nature of, characterised by or affected by neurosis; (*loosely*) obsessive; hypersensitive. — *n* a person suffering from neurosis. — *adv* **neurot'ically**. — *n* **neurot'icism** (*-i-sizm*). [Gr. *neuron* and **-osis**.]

neut. *abbrev* for: neuter; neutral.

neuter *nū'tər*, *adj* neither masculine nor feminine (*gram*); sexless; sexually undeveloped; castrated; without an androecium or a gynaeceum, or a functional one (*biol*). — *n* a neuter word, plant or animal; esp. a worker bee, ant, etc.; a castrated cat. — *vt* to castrate. [L. *neuter*, neither — *ne*, not, *uter*, either.]

neutral *nū'trəl*, *adj* indifferent; taking no part on either side; not siding with either party; pertaining to neither party; not involved in a war or dispute; belonging to neither, esp. of two adjoining countries; of no decided character; having no decided colour; with no noticeable smell; belonging to neither of two opposites, such as acid and alkaline, electrically positive and negative; neuter; (of e.g. a force or gear) without transmission of motion. — *n* a person who or nation that takes no part in a contest; a position of gear in which no power is transmitted; a neuter. — *n* **neutralīsā'tion** or **-z-**. — *vt* **neu'tralise** or **-ize** to declare neutral; to make inert; to render of no effect; to counteract. — *n* **neu'traliser** or **-z-**. — *n* **neu'tralism** the policy of not entering into alliance with other nations or taking sides ideologically. — *n* **neu'tralist**. — *n* **neutrality** (*-tral'i-ti*) the fact or state of being neutral. — *adv* **neu'trally**. [L. *neutrālis* — *neuter*, neither.]

neutron *nū'tron*, (*phys*) *n* an uncharged particle of about the same mass as a proton. — *n* **neutrett'o** a type of neutrino: — *pl* **neutrett'os**. — *n* **neutrino** (*-trē'nō*) an uncharged particle with zero mass when at rest: — *pl* **neutri'nos**. — **neutron bomb** a type of nuclear bomb which destroys life by immediate intense radiation, without blast and heat effects to destroy buildings, etc.; **neutron number** the number of neutrons in the nucleus of an atom; **neutron star** a supposed heavenly body of very small size and very great density, an almost burnt out and collapsed star. [L. *neuter*, neither.]

neutrophil *nū'trō-fil*, *adj* (of a cell, etc.) stainable with a neutral dye. — *n* a neutrophil cell, etc.; a leucocyte with granular cytoplasm and a lobular nucleus. [Ger. — L. *neuter* (see **neuter**) and Gr. *philos* (see **phil-**, **-phil**).]

Nev. *abbrev* for Nevada (U.S. state).

névé *nā'vā*, *n* the granular snow lying on the surface of a glacier. [Fr., — L. *nix*, *nivis*, snow.]

never *nev'ər*, *adv* not ever; at no time; in no degree; not. — *adj* **nev'er-end'ing**. — *adj* **nev'er-fad'ing**. — *adj* **nev'er-fail'ing**. — *adv* **nev'ermore** at no future time. — **never-nev'er** the hire-purchase system (*colloq*). — **never-never land** (also with *caps*) an imaginary place, imaginary conditions, too fortunate ever to exist in reality. — *adv* **nevertheless'** notwithstanding; in spite of that. — **never a** no; — **well I never!** or **I never did!** I never heard anything so surprising, shocking, etc. [O.E. *nǣfre* — *ne*, not, *ǣfre*, ever.]

new *nū*, *adj* very recently made or produced; young; fresh; not much used; having lately become, happened or begun to be; recent, modern; not before seen or known; only lately discovered or experienced; other than the former or preceding, different; additional; strange, unaccustomed; lately begun; beginning afresh; renewed; reformed or regenerated; restored or resumed; (of crops) harvested early. — *n* that which is new; newness. — *adv* (often joined by hyphen to an adj.) newly; anew. — *adj* **new'ish**. — *adv* **new'ly** very lately. — *n* **new'ness**. — *adj* and *n* **New Age** or **new age** (of or relating to) a cultural trend that emerged in the 1980s, concerned with the union of mind, body and spirit, expressed through popular interest in a variety of beliefs and disciplines incl. mysticism, meditation, astrology, holistic medicine, etc.; (of or relating to) a dreamy style of music of the late 1980s usu. using synthesisers. — **new Australian** an immigrant to Australia; **new birth** renewal, esp. spiritual; **new blood** (a person with) fresh talent; a revitalising force. — *adj* **new'-blown** just come into bloom. — *adj* **new'born** newly born. — **new broom** (*fig*) see **new brooms sweep clean** under **broom**. — *adj* **new'come** recently arrived. — **new'comer** someone who has lately come; **New Englander** a native or citizen of any of the New England states. — *adj* **newfangled** see separate article. — *adj* **new-fash'ioned** made in a new way or fashion; lately come into fashion. — *adj* **new'-found** newly discovered or devised. — **New Jerusalem** the heavenly city; heaven. — *adj* **new'-laid** newly laid. — **New Learning** the new studies of the Renaissance; **New Left** an extreme left-wing movement among students, etc., in the 1960s; **New Light** a member of a relatively more advanced or liberal religious school; **new look** a change in women's fashions (1947), notably to longer and fuller skirts; a radical modification in the appearance of something. — *n* and *adj* **new'ly-wed** (a person who is) recently married; **new man** a reformed character; a fitter, healthier man; (sometimes with *caps*) a man who has adopted modern ideas esp. with regard to health, sharing family responsibilities, and environment; **new maths** a method of teaching mathematics which is more concerned with basic structures and concepts than numerical drills; **new moon**

the moment when the moon is directly in line between the earth and sun, and therefore invisible; the time when the waxing moon becomes visible; the narrow waxing crescent itself; **new rich** the recently enriched; parvenus; **New'speak** a type of English described by George Orwell in his book, *Nineteen Eighty-four* (1949), developed by reducing vocabulary to such a point, and forming new words of such ugliness and so little emotive value, that literature and even thought will be impossible; (also without *cap*) any type of language considered similar in style, etc. (esp. *derog*); **New Style** see under **style; new town** a town planned and built by the government to aid housing conditions in nearby large cities, stimulate development, etc.; **New Wave** a movement in French cinema in the late 1950s and 1960s which abandoned the linear narrative and experimented with untypical framing and fluid camera movements — also called **Nouvelle Vague**; a slightly later movement in jazz aiming at freedom from set patterns and styles; (also without *caps*) any similar artistic, musical, cultural, etc. movement or grouping; **New World** North and South America; **New Year** the first few days of the year. — **New Model Army** the Parliamentary army as remodelled by Cromwell (1645); **New Year's Day** the first day of the year. [O.E. *nīwe, nēowe*.]

Newcastle disease *nū'kä-səl diz-ēz'*, *n* an acute, highly contagious viral disease of chickens and other domestic and wild birds, first recorded at *Newcastle*-upon-Tyne in 1926 — also called **fowl-pest**.

newel *nū'əl*, *n* the upright column about which the steps of a circular staircase wind; an upright post at the end or corner of a stair handrail (also **newel post**). — *adj* **new'elled**. [O.Fr. *noual*, fruitstone — L.L. *nucālis*, nutlike — L. *nux, nucis*, a nut.]

newfangled *nū-fang'gld*, *adj* newly but superfluously devised; excessively or ostentatiously modern. — *n* **newfang'ledness**. [M.E. *newefangel* — *newe* (O.E. *nīwe*), new, *fangel*, ready to catch.]

Newfoundland *nū-fownd'lənd* or *nū'fənd-lənd*, *n* a very large, intelligent breed of dog from Newfoundland in Canada, originally black, a strong swimmer.

newmarket *nū'mär-kit*, *n* a card game in which the money bet is won by those who succeed in playing out cards whose duplicates lie on the table; a close-fitting coat, originally a riding-coat, for men or women. [*Newmarket*, the racing town.]

news *nūz*, *n* (orig. *pl*) a report of, or information on, a recent event; something one had not heard before; matter suitable for newspaper readers or for radio and television bulletins. — *n* **news'iness**. — *adj* **news'y** full of news or gossip. — **news agency** an organisation which collects material for newspapers, magazines, etc.; **news'agent** a shop owner who sells newspapers; **news'boy** or **news'girl** a boy or girl who delivers or sells newspapers; **news'cast** a news broadcast or telecast; **news'caster** a person who presents newscasts or telecasts; a machine which gives a changing display of news headlines, etc.; **news'casting; newsflash** see under **flash**; **newsgirl** see **newsboy**; **news'hound** (*jocular*) a reporter in search of news; **news'letter** a sheet of news supplied to members of a particular group or locality; **news'man** or **news'woman** a bringer, collector or writer of news; **news'monger** a person who deals in news; a person who spends much time in hearing and telling news, a gossip; **news'paper** a paper published periodically for circulating news, etc.; **news'paperman** or **news'paperwoman** a journalist; **news'print** paper for printing newspapers on; **news'reader** a person who reads news on radio or television; **news'reel** film showing, or a programme commenting on, news items; **news'-room** a reading-room with newspapers, e.g. in a library; a room, etc., where news is made ready for a newspaper, newscast, etc.; **news'-sheet** a printed sheet of news, esp. an early form of newspaper; **news'-stand** a street stall for the sale of newspapers; **news'-value** interest to the general public as news; **news'-vendor** a street seller of newspapers; **newswoman** see **newsman**. — *adj* **news'-worthy** sufficiently interesting to be told as news. — **news'worthiness; news'-writer** a reporter or writer of news. [Late M.E. *newes*; Fr. *nouvelles*.]

newt *nūt*, *n* a tailed amphibian of the salamander family — formed with initial *n*, borrowed from the article **an**, and *ewt*, a form of archaic or dialect *eft*, newt. [O.E. *efeta, efete*.]

newton *nū'tən*, *n* the SI unit of force — equal to the force which, acting on a mass of one kilogramme, produces an acceleration of one metre per second per second. — *adj* **Newtonian** (*nū-tō'ni-ən*) relating to, according to, formed or discovered by, Sir Isaac *Newton* (1642–1727). — **Newtonian telescope** a form of reflecting telescope.

next *nekst*, *adj* nearest in place, in kinship or other relation; nearest following (or preceding, if explicitly stated) in time or order. — *adv* nearest; immediately after; on the first occasion that follows; in the following place (with *to*). — *adv* **next'ly**. — **next best** next lowest in degree after the best; **next biggest, next dearest**, etc., next lowest (or highest, depending on context) in degree after the previous one mentioned. — *adj* **next'-door** dwelling in, occupying or belonging to the next house, shop, etc.; neighbouring. — *adv* **next-door'**. — **next door** at or in the next house (often with *to*); near, bordering upon, very nearly (with *to*); **next of kin** see under **kin; next to** adjacent to; almost; **next to nothing** almost nothing at all. [O.E. *nēhst* (*nīehst*), superl. of *nēh* (*nēah*), near.]

nexus *nek'səs*, *n* a bond; a linked group. [L. *nexus*, pl. *-ūs* — *nectĕre*, to bind.]

NF *abbrev* for: National Front; Norman French; Northern French.

NF or **Nfld** *abbrev* for Newfoundland (Can. province).

NFER *abbrev* for National Foundation for Educational Research.

NFS *abbrev* for not for sale.

NFSC *abbrev* for National Federation of (Football) Supporters' Clubs.

NFSE *abbrev* for National Federation of Self Employed.

NFU *abbrev* for National Farmers' Union.

NFWI *abbrev* for National Federation of Women's Institutes.

NGA *abbrev* for National Graphical Association.

ngaio *nī'ō*, *n* a New Zealand tree with white wood: — *pl* **ngai'os**. [Maori.]

ngultrum *əng-gul'trəm*, *n* the standard monetary unit of Bhutan (100 *chetrun*).

NH *abbrev* for New Hampshire (U.S. state).

NHBRC *abbrev* for National House-Builders' Registration Council (or Certificate).

NHI *abbrev* for National Health Insurance.

NHS *abbrev* for National Health Service.

NI *abbrev* for: National Insurance; Northern Ireland.

Ni (*chem*) *symbol* for nickel.

niacin *nī'ə-sin*, *n* nicotinic acid.

nib *nib*, *n* a pen-point; a bird's bill; a projecting point or spike; (in *pl*) crushed cocoa-beans; (in *pl*) included particles in varnish, wool, etc. — *vt* to provide with a pen-point; to reduce to nibs. — *adj* **nibbed** having a nib. [Ety. as for **neb**.]

nibble *nib'l*, *vt* to bite gently or by small bites; to eat a little at a time. — *vi* to bite gently; to show signs of accepting, e.g. an offer (with *at*); to find fault. — *n* the act of nibbling; a little bit. — *n* **nibb'ler**. — *n* **nibb'ling**. — *adv* **nibb'lingly**.

niblick *nib'lik*, *n* an old-fashioned golf club with a heavy head with wide face, used for lofting — now a number eight or nine iron.

NIC *abbrev* for: Newly Industrialised Country; Nicaragua (I.V.R.).

nicad *nī'kad*. Short for *ni*ckel-*cad*mium, as applied to rechargeable batteries.

NICAM or **Nicam** *nī'kam*, (*TV*) *abbrev* for near-instantaneously companded audio multiplexing (a system by which digital stereo sound signals are transmitted along with the standard TV signal, to allow the viewer to receive sound of CD quality).

niccolite *nik'əl-īt*, *n* a hexagonal mineral, nickel arsenide, also called *kupfernickel*, copper-nickel. [See **nickel**.]

nice *nīs*, *adj* agreeable, delightful, respectable, good in any way; forming or observing very small differences; calling for very fine discrimination; done with great care and exactness, accurate; delicate; dainty. — *adj* **nice'ish**. — *adv* **nice'ly**. — *n* **nice'ness**. — *n* **nicety** (*nīs'i-ti*) a critical subtlety; a matter of delicate discrimination or refinement; the quality of being nice; precision; fineness of perception or feeling. — **nice and** (used adverbially) pleasantly; **to a nicety** with great exactness. [O.Fr. *nice*, foolish, simple — L. *nescius*, ignorant.]

Nicene *nī'sēn*, *adj* pertaining to the town of *Nicaea*, in Bithynia, Asia Minor, where a council in A.D. 325 dealt with the theological controversy surrounding Arius of Alexandria. — **Nicene Creed** the Christian creed based on the results of the first Nicene Council.

niche *nich* or *nēsh*, *n* a recess in a wall; a suitable or actual place or condition in life; a place in the market not subject to the normal pressures of competition (*commerce*). — *vt* to place in a niche. — *adj* **niched** placed in a niche. — **niche marketing** the marketing of a product aimed at a relatively small, specialised sector, or niche, of consumer society. [Fr., — It. *nicchia*, niche.]

Nick *nik*, *n* the devil, esp. **Old Nick**. [Apparently for *Nicholas*.]

nick *nik*, *n* a notch; a small cut; a prison or a police-station (*slang*); the line formed where two walls meet in a squash, etc. court. — *vt* to notch; to cut (usu. slightly); to snip; to catch (*slang*); to arrest (*slang*); to steal (*slang*); to make a cut in (a horse's tail muscle), so that the tail is carried higher. — *vi* (of breeding animals) to mate well. — *n* **in good nick** (*colloq*) in good health or condition; **in the nick of time** just in time; at the critical moment.

nickel *nik'l*, *n* an element (symbol **Ni**; atomic no. 28), a white, magnetic, very malleable and ductile metal largely used in alloys; a 5-cent piece (of copper and nickel; *NAm*). — *adj* made, composed, etc. of nickel. — *vt* to plate with nickel: — *pr p* **nick'elling**; *pa t* and *pa p* **nick'elled**. — *adj* **nickel-and-dime'** involving only a small amount of money; worth only a small amount of effort, concern, etc. — **nickel-plat'ing** the plating of metals with nickel; **nickel-sil'ver** an alloy of nickel, copper and zinc, white like silver; **nickel-steel'** a steel containing some nickel. [Ger. *Kupfer-nickel*, niccolite — *Kupfer*, copper, *Nickel*, a mischievous sprite, goblin, because the ore looked like copper-ore but yielded no copper.]

nickelodeon *nik-ə-lō'di-ən*, (*US*; *old*) *n* a five-cent cinema; an old form of juke-box. [**nickel** and *odeon*, an ancient Greek theatre.]

nicker *nik'ər*, (*slang*) *n* pound sterling.

nick-nack, etc. Same as **knick-knack**, etc.

nickname *nik'nām*, *n* a name given in contempt, or in jocular or fond familiarity. — *vt* to give a nickname to. [M.E. *neke-name*, for *eke-name*, an additional name, with *n* from the indefinite article; see **eke** and **name**.]

nicotiana *ni-kō-shi-ä'nə* or *-ā'nə*, *n* any plant of the tobacco genus *Nicotiana*. — *n* **nicotinamide** (*-tin'ə-mīd*) a member of the vitamin B complex, deficiency of which can lead to the development of the disease pellagra. — *n* **nicotine** (*nik'ə-tēn*) a poisonous alkaloid obtained from tobacco leaves. — *adj* **nic'otined**. — *adj* **nicotinic** (*-tin'ik*). — *n* **nic'otinism** a morbid state induced by excessive use of tobacco. — **nicotinic acid** a white crystalline substance, a member of the vitamin B complex, deficiency of which is connected with the development of the disease pellagra. [Jean *Nicot*, who sent tobacco to Catherine de Medici.]

nictate *nik'tāt*, *vi* to wink or blink. — Also **nic'titate**. — *n* **nictā'tion** or **nictitā'tion**. — **nictitating membrane** the third eyelid, developed in birds, etc., a thin movable membrane that passes over the eye. [L. *nictāre*, *-ātum* and its L.L. frequentative *nictitāre*, *-ātum*, to wink.]

nidal, nidi. See **nidus**.

nidicolous *nid-ik'ə-ləs*, *adj* (of young birds) staying in the nest for longer than average. [L. *nīdus*, a nest, *colĕre*, to inhabit.]

nidificate. See **nidify**.

nidifugous *nid-if'ū-gəs*, *adj* (of young birds) leaving the nest soon after hatching. [L. *nīdus*, nest, *fugĕre*, to flee.]

nidify *nid'i-fī*, *vi* to build a nest. — Also **nidificate** (*nid'i-fi-kāt*). — *n* **nidificā'tion**. [L. *nīdus*, nest, *facĕre*, to make.]

nidus *nī'dəs*, *n* a nest or breeding-place; a place where anything is originated, harboured, developed or fostered; a point of infection; a nerve-centre: — *pl* **nī'dī**. — *adj* **nī'dal** pertaining to a nest or nidus. [L. *nīdus*, a nest.]

niece *nēs*, *n* a brother's or sister's daughter; extended to a like relation by marriage: — *masc* **neph'ew**. [O.Fr., — L.L. *neptia* — L. *neptis*.]

niello *ni-el'ō*, *n* a method of ornamenting metal by engraving, and filling up the lines with a black compound; a piece of work so produced; the compound used in niello-work, sulphur with silver, lead or copper: — *pl* **niell'i** (*-ē*) or **niell'os**. — *vt* to decorate with niello: — *pr p* **niell'oing**; *pa t* and *pa p* **niell'oed**. [It. *niello* — L.L. *nigellum*, a black enamel — L. *niger*, black.]

Niersteiner *nēr'shtīn-ər* or *-stīn-*, *n* a white Rhine wine, named from *Nierstein*, near Mainz.

Nietzschean *nēch'i-ən*, *adj* of or pertaining to Friedrich *Nietzsche* (1844–1900) or his philosophy. — *n* a follower of Nietzsche. — *n* **Nietzsch'eanism**.

niff *nif*, (*slang*) *n* a stink. — *vi* to smell bad. — *adj* **niff'y**.

nifty *nif'ti*, (*slang*) *adj* fine; smart; quick; agile. — *n* **nif'tiness**.

nigella *nī-jel'ə*, *n* any plant of the genus of plants *Nigella*, with finely dissected leaves, and whitish, blue or yellow flowers, one variety being otherwise known as love-in-a-mist. [Fem. of L. *nigellus*, blackish — *niger*, black, from the black seeds.]

niggard *nig'ərd*, *n* a person who begrudges spending or giving away. — *adj* mean, stingy. — *n* **nigg'ardliness**. — *adj* **nigg'ardly** stingy, mean.

nigger *nig'ər*, (*derog*, now esp. *offensive*) *n* a Negro, or a member of any very dark-skinned race. — *adj* Negro; blackish brown. — **nigger in the wood-pile** a hidden evil influence; **work like a nigger** to work extremely hard. [Fr. *nègre* — Sp. *negro*; see **Negro**.]

niggle *nig'l*, *vi* to busy oneself with petty criticism of detail; to gnaw (at one's thoughts, conscience, etc.). — *n* a minor criticism. — *n* **nigg'ler**. — *n* **nigg'ling** fussiness, esp. over minor detail; petty criticism. — *adj* petty; fussy; persistently annoying. — *adj* **nigg'ly**. [Cf. Norw. *nigle*.]

nigh *nī*, (*poetic*, *dialect*, or *archaic*) *adv* near. — *prep* near to. — **nigh on** almost, nearly. [O.E. *nēah*, *nēh*.]

night *nīt*, *n* the end of the day, evening; (the period of) time from sunset to sunrise; the dark part of the 24-hour day; darkness; obscurity, ignorance, evil, affliction or sorrow (*fig*); death (*euph*). — *adj* belonging to night; occurring or done in the night; working or on duty at night. — *adj* **night'less**. — *adj* and *adv* **night'long** lasting all night. — *adj* **night'ly** done or happening at night or every night. — *adv* at night; every night. — *adv* **nights** (*colloq*) at night. — *n* **night'y** or **night'ie** (*colloq*) a nightgown. — **night'-bell** a doorbell for use at night, esp. at a hotel; **night'-bird** a bird that flies or sings at night; a person who is active, awake or about at night; **night-blind'ness** inability to see in dim light, nyctalopia; **night'cap** a cap worn at night in bed; a drink taken just before going to bed; **night'class** a class at night-school; **night'club** a club for drinking and entertainment, etc., open between evening and morning; **night'clubbing** dining, dancing, etc. at a nightclub; **night'dress** clothes for sleeping in; a nightgown; **night'fall** the onset or beginning of the night; the close of the day; evening; **night'-glass** a small hand-held telescope with concentrating lenses for use at night; **night'gown** a loose robe for sleeping in, for men or women; **night'jar** a bird of the swift family; **night'-latch** a door-lock worked by a key from outside and a knob from inside; **night'life** activity in the form of entertainments at night; **night'-light** a lamp or candle that gives a subdued light all night; **night'mare** (O.E. *mære*, M.E. *mare*, the nightmare incubus; cf. O.H.G. *mara*, incubus, O.N. *mara*, nightmare) an unpleasant dream; a horrifying experience. — *adj* **night'-marish.** — **night'-owl** an exclusively nocturnal owl; a person who sits up very late; **night'-school** classes held at night for people who have left school, esp. for those at work during the day; **night shift** a gang or group of workers that takes its turn at night; the period for which it is on duty; **night'shirt** a shirt for sleeping in; **night'-soil** the contents of privies, cesspools, etc., generally carried away at night and sometimes used for fertiliser; **night'spot** (*colloq*) a nightclub; **night'stand** a bedside table; **night starvation** hunger pangs experienced in the middle of the night; **night'-stick** (*NAm*) a truncheon; **night'-time** (*colloq* or *childish*) the time when it is night; **night'-watch** a watch or guard at night; a person who is on guard at night; time of watch at night; **night-watch'man** a person who is on watch at night, esp. on industrial premises and building sites; a batsman, not a high scorer, put in to defend a wicket until the close of play (*cricket*). — **make a night of it** to spend the night, or a large part of it, in amusement or celebration. [O.E. *niht*.]

nightingale *nīt'ing-gāl*, *n* a small bird of the thrush family celebrated for the rich love-song of the male, heard chiefly at night; a person with a beautiful singing voice. [O.E. *nihtegale* — *niht*, night, *galan*, to sing.]

nightjar, nightlong, nightmare, etc. See under **night.**

nightshade *nīt'shād*, *n* a name given to various plants, chiefly poisonous or narcotic. — **deadly night-shade** the belladonna plant, all parts of which are poisonous; **woody nightshade** bittersweet. [O.E. *nihtscada*.]

nightshirt, nightspot, nightstand, night-stick, etc. See under **night.**

nigrescence *nī-* or *ni-gres'əns*, *n* blackness; dark colouring or pigmentation; blackening. — *adj* **ni-gresc'ent** growing black or dark; blackish. [L. *niger*, black.]

nihilism *nī'il-izm*, belief in nothing; denial of all reality, or of all objective truth (*philos*); extreme scepticism; (sometimes with *cap*) in tsarist Russia, a terrorist movement aiming at the overturn of all the existing institutions of society. — *n* and *adj* **ni'hilist.** — *adj* **nihilist'ic.** — *n* **nihility** (*-hil'*) nothingness; a mere nothing. [L. *nihil*, nothing.]

-nik *-nik*, *combining form* denoting a person who does, practises, advocates, etc. something, as in *beatnik*, *kibbutznik*, *peacenik*. [Russ. suffix, influenced in meaning by Yiddish suffix denoting an agent.]

Nikkei index *nik'ā in'deks*, *n* the indicator of the relative prices of stocks and shares on the Tokyo stock exchange. [From the title of the newspaper publishing it.]

nil *nil*, *n* nothing; zero. [L. *nīl*, *nihil*, nothing.]

Nile green *nīl grēn*, *n* a very pale green colour, thought of as the colour of the River *Nile*.

nilgai *nil'gī*, *n* a large Indian antelope, the male slaty-grey, the female tawny. [Pers. and Hind. *nīl*, blue, Hind. *gāī*, Pers. *gāw*, cow.]

Nilot *nīl'ot* or **Nilote** *nīl'ōt*, *n* an inhabitant of the banks of the Upper Nile; a Negro of the Upper Nile. — *adj* **Nilotic** (*-ot'ik*) of the Nile, or Nilots or their languages. [Gr. *Neilōtēs*.]

nim *nim*, *n* an old and widespread game, perh. orig. Chinese, in which two players take alternately from heaps or rows of objects (now usu. matches). [O.E. *niman*, to take.]

nimbi. See **nimbus.**

nimble *nim'bl*, *adj* light and quick in motion, agile; active; swift. — *n* **nim'bleness.** — *adv* **nim'bly.** — *adj* **nimble-fing'ered.** — *adj* **nimble-foot'ed.** — *adj* **nimble-witt'ed.**

nimbus *nim'bəs*, *n* a cloud or luminous mist encircling a god or goddess; a rain-cloud: — *pl* **nim'bī** or **nim'buses.** — *n* **nimbostratus** (*-strā'* or *-strä'təs*) a low, dark-coloured layer of cloud, bringing rain. [L.]

NIMBY or **Nimby** *nim'bi*, (*slang*) *n* a person who is willing to have something occur so long as it does not affect him or her or take place in his or her locality. — *n* **nim'byism.** [From '*n*ot *i*n *m*y *b*ack *y*ard'.]

niminy-piminy *nim-i-ni-pim'i-ni*, (*derog*) *adj* affectedly fine or delicate. [Imit.]

Nimrod *nim'rod*, *n* any great hunter. [From the son of Cush in the Bible: Gen. x. 8–10.]

nincompoop *ning'kəm-pōōp*, *n* a simpleton; an idiot, stupid person.

nine *nīn*, *n* the cardinal number next above eight; a symbol representing it (9, ix, etc.); a set of that number of things or persons (such as a baseball team); a shoe or other article of size 9; a card with nine pips; a score of nine points, tricks, etc.; the ninth hour after midday or midnight; the age of nine years. — *adj* nine in number; nine years old. — *adj* **ninth** (*nīnth*) last of nine; next after the eighth; equal to one of nine equal parts. — *n* a ninth part; the person or thing in ninth position; an octave and a second (*mus*); a tone at that interval (*mus*). — *adv* **nīnth'ly** in the ninth place, ninth in order. — *adj* **nine'-foot, -metre,** etc., measuring 9 feet, etc. — *adj* **nine'-hole** (of a golf course) having nine holes. — **nine'pin** a bottle-shaped pin set up with eight others for the game of **nine'pins** in which players bowl a ball at them (see **skittle**). — **nine days' wonder** see under **wonder; nine points of the law** worth nine-tenths of all the points that could be raised (proverbially, the value of possession); **to the nines** fully, elaborately. [O.E. *nigon*.]

nineteen *nīn-tēn'* or *nīn'tēn*, *n* and *adj* the total of nine and ten. — *n* and *adj* **nine'teenth** (or *-tēnth'*). — *adv* **nineteenth'ly.** — **nineteenth hole** a golf club-house, esp. the bar or restaurant. — **nineteen to the dozen** (of speaking, done) in great quantity, not necessarily with equal quality. [O.E. *nigontēne* (*-tiene*); see **nine** and **ten.**]

ninety *nīn'ti*, *n* and *adj* nine times ten. — *npl* **nine'ties** the numbers ninety to ninety-nine; the years so numbered in a life or a century; a range of temperature from ninety to just less than one hundred degrees. — *adj* **nine'tieth** last of ninety; next after the eighty-ninth; equal to one of ninety equal parts. — *n* a ninetieth part; the person or thing in ninetieth position. [O.E. *nigontig* (*hundnigontig*).]

ninja *nin'jə*, *n* (also with *cap*) one of a body of trained assassins in feudal Japan: — *pl* **nin'ja** or **nin'jas.** [Jap.]

ninny *nin'i, n* a simpleton, stupid person.
ninon *nē'nɔ̃, n* a silk voile or other thin fabric. [Fr. *Ninon*, a woman's name.]
ninth. See **nine**.
Niobe *nī'ə-bē*, (*Gr mythol*) *n* a daughter of Tantalus, turned into stone as she wept for her children, slain by Artemis and Apollo. — *adj* **Niobē'an.** [Gr. *Niobē*.]
niobium *nī-ō'bi-əm, n* a metallic element (symbol **Nb**; atomic no. 41) discovered in the mineral tantalite and used in certain alloys. — *n* **nī'obate** a salt of niobic acid. — *adj* **nio'bic** (**niobic acid** hydrated niobium pentoxide). — *adj* **nīo'bous.** [**Niobe**, from the connection with tantalite.]
Nip. See **Nippon**.
nip[1] *nip, n* a small quantity of spirits. — *vi* to take a nip.
nip[2] *nip, vt* to pinch; to press between two surfaces; to remove or sever by pinching or biting (often with *off*); to halt the growth or vigour of; to give a smarting or tingling feeling to; to snatch (esp. *US*). — *vi* to pinch; to smart; to go nimbly: — *pr p* **nipp'ing;** *pa t* and *pa p* **nipped** (*nipt*). — *n* an act or experience of nipping; the pinch of cold; a nipping quality. — *n* **nipp'er** a person who or thing which nips; a great claw, as of a crab; a horse's incisor, esp. of the middle four; a little boy or (sometimes) girl (*colloq*); (in *pl*) any of various pincer-tools. — *adj* **nipp'y** pungent, biting; nimble, quick (*colloq*); (esp. of weather) very cold, frosty. — **nip in the bud** see under **bud**[1].
nipple *nip'l, n* the rounded projecting point of the breast, the location of the milk ducts in women and female animals; a teat; a small projection with an orifice, esp. for regulating flow or lubricating machinery. — **nipp'lewort** a tall composite weed with small yellow heads. [A dimin. of **neb** or **nib**.]
Nippon *nipon, n* the Japanese name of Japan. — *n* and *adj* **Nipponese'**. — *n* **Nip** (*offensive slang*) a Japanese. [Jap. *ni*, sun, *pon* — *hon*, origin.]
nippy. See **nip**[2].
NIRC *abbrev* for National Industrial Relations Court.
nirvana *nir-vä'nə, n* the cessation of individual existence — the state to which a Buddhist aspires as the best attainable; a blissful state (*loosely*). — Also **Nirva'na.** [Sans. *nirvāna*, a blowing out.]
nisei *nē-sā', n* a resident in the Americas born of Japanese immigrant parents. [Jap., second generation.]
nisi *nī'sī*, (*law*) *adj* to take effect unless, after a time, some condition referred to is fulfilled. [The L. conj. *nisi*, unless.]
Nissen hut *nis'ən hut, n* a semicylindrical corrugated-iron hut designed by Col. P. N. *Nissen* (1871–1930).
nit[1] *nit, n* the egg of a louse or similar insect; a young louse. — *adj* **nitt'y** full of nits. — **nit'-picking** (*colloq*) petty criticism of minor details. — *vi* **nit'-pick.** [O.E. *hnitu*.]
nit[2] *nit*, (*colloq*) *n* a fool.
nit[3] *nit, n* a unit of luminance, one candela per square metre. [L. *nitor*, brightness.]
nit[4] *nit*, (*comput*) *n* a unit of information (1·44 bits). — Also **nep'it.** [*N*apierian dig*it*.]
niterie or **nitery** *nīt'ə-ri*, (*slang*) *n* a nightclub. [**night**.]
nitid *nit'id*, (*poetic*) *adj* shining, bright. [L. *nitidus* — *nitēre*, to shine.]
Nitinol *nit'in-ol, n* an alloy of nickel and titanium, in particular one which, when shaped and then heated to fix that shape, will, after reshaping or deformation, return to the original shape on reheating. [The chemical symbols *Ni* and *Ti*, and the initial letters of the U.S. *N*aval *O*rdnance *L*aboratory in Maryland where the alloy was discovered.]
nitrazepam *nī-trā'zi-pam, n* a hypnotic drug taken for the relief of insomnia. [*nitro-* and *-azepam* as in **diazepam**.]
nitre *nī'tər, n* potassium nitrate or saltpetre (**cubic nitre** is sodium nitrate, or Chile saltpetre). — *n* **ni'trate** a salt of nitric acid; a fertiliser — natural (potassium or sodium) or synthetic (calcium) nitrate. — *vt* (*-trāt'*) to treat with nitric acid or a nitrate; to convert into a nitrate or nitro-compound. — *n* **nitrā'tion.** — *adj* **ni'tric.** — *n* **ni'tride** a compound of nitrogen with another element. — *vt* to turn into a nitride; to harden the surface of by heating in ammonia gas. — *n* **ni'triding.** — *n* **nitrificā'tion** treatment with nitric acid; conversion into nitrates, esp. by bacteria through the intermediate condition of nitrites. — *vt* and *vi* **ni'trify** to subject to or suffer nitrification: — *pr p* **ni'trifying;** *pa t* and *pa p* **ni'trified.** — *n* **ni'trile** (*-tril* or *-trīl*) any of a group of organic cyanides. — *n* **ni'trite** a salt of nitrous acid. — *adj* **ni'trous.** — **nitric acid** HNO_3; **nitric anhydride** N_2O_5; **nitric oxide** NO; **nitrous acid** HNO_2; **nitrous oxide** laughing gas, N_2O. [Fr., — L. *nitrum* — Gr. *nitron*, sodium carbonate.]
nitric, nitride, nitrile, nitrify, etc. See under **nitre**.
nitro- *nī-trō-, combining form* indicating nitration. — *npl* **nitrobactē'ria** bacteria that convert ammonium compounds into nitrites, and esp. those that convert nitrites into nitrates. — *n* **nitroben'zene** a yellow oily liquid ($C_6H_5NO_2$) obtained from benzene and nitric and concentrated sulphuric acid. — *n* **nitrocell'ulose** cellulose nitrate, used as an explosive, and in lacquers, glues, etc. — *n* **nitro-com'pound** a compound in which one or more hydrogens of a benzene- or methane-derived compound are replaced by nitro-groups. — *n* **nitrocott'on** guncotton, an explosive made from cotton soaked in nitric and sulphuric acids. — *n* **nitroglyc'erine** a powerfully explosive compound produced by the action of nitric and sulphuric acids on glycerine. — *n* **ni'tro-group** the radical NO_2. — *n* **nitromē'thane** a liquid (CH_3NO_2) obtained from methane and used as a solvent and as rocket-fuel.
nitrogen *nī'trə-jən, n* a gaseous element (symbol **N**; atomic no. 7) forming nearly four-fifths of common air, a necessary constituent of every organised body, so called from its being an essential constituent of nitre. — *vt* **nitrogenise** or **-ize** (*-troj'*) to combine or supply with nitrogen. — *adj* **nitrog'enous** of or containing nitrogen. — **nitrogen cycle** the sum total of the transformations undergone by nitrogen and nitrogenous compounds in nature — from free nitrogen back to free nitrogen; **nitrogen fixation** the bringing of free nitrogen into combination with anything else. [Gr. *nitron*, sodium carbonate (but taken as if meaning nitre), and the root of *gennaein*, to generate.]
nitrous. See under **nitre**.
nitty-gritty *nit-i-grit'i*, (*colloq*) *n* the basic or essential details, the fundamentals, esp. in phrase *get down to the nitty-gritty*.
nitwit *nit'wit*, (*slang*) *n* a blockhead, stupid person. — *adj* **nit'witted.**
nix *niks*, (*slang*) *n* nothing. [Colloq. Ger. and Du. for Ger. *nichts*, nothing.]
NJ *abbrev* for New Jersey (U.S. state).
NL *abbrev* for Netherlands (I.V.R.).
NLRB *abbrev* for National Labor Relations Board (U.S.).
NM or **N.Mex.** *abbrev* for New Mexico (U.S. state).
n. mile *abbrev* for (international) nautical mile.
NNE *abbrev* for north-north-east.
NNEB *abbrev* for Nursery Nurses' Examination Board.
NNW *abbrev* for north-north-west.
NO *abbrev* for: natural order; New Orleans.
No (*chem*) *symbol* for nobelium.
no[1] *nō, adv* (with *compar*) in no degree, not at all. — *n* a denial; a refusal; a vote or voter for the negative: — *pl* **noes** or **nos.** — *n* **no'-no** (*colloq*) a failure, non-event; something which must not be done, said, etc.; an impossibility, non-starter: — *pl* **no'-nos, no'-no's** or **no'-noes.** — **no more** destroyed; dead;

never again, not any longer. [O.E. *nā* — *ne*, not, *ā*, ever; cf. **nay**.]

no² *nō*, *adj* not any; not one; by no means properly called, certainly not. — *adj* **no-account'** (*US colloq*) worthless; insignificant. — **no-ball'** (*cricket*) a ball bowled in such a way that it is disallowed by the rules. — *adj* **no'-fault** (of insurance compensation payments, etc.) made without attachment to or admission of blame by any one person or party in particular. — *adj* **no'-frills** basic, not elaborate or fancy. — *adj* **no'-good** bad, worthless. — *n* a bad, worthless person. — **no-hope** and **no-hoper** see under **hope¹**; **no'-man's-land** a waste region to which no one has a recognised claim; neutral or disputed land, esp. between entrenched hostile forces (also *fig*); *n* and *pron* **no one** or **no'-one** nobody. — *adj* **no-non'sense** sensible, tolerating no nonsense. — **no-show'** a person who does not arrive for something he or she has booked, e.g. a restaurant table, or a flight; an instance of such non-arrival; **no-side'** the end of a game at Rugby football; **no-trump'** or **no-trumps'** (*bridge*) a call for the playing of a hand without any trump suit. — *adj* **no-trump'**. — *adv* **no'way, no'ways** or **no'wise** in no way, manner or degree. — *adj* **no-win'** (of a situation) in which one is bound to lose or fail whatever one does. — **no-claims bonus** or **discount** a reduction in the price of an insurance policy because no claims have been made on it; **no end** and **no go** see under **end** and **go¹**; **no one** no single. [O.E. *nān*, none. See **none**.]

no³, nō or **noh** *nō*, *n* (often with *cap*) the traditional Japanese style of drama developed out of a religious dance: — *pl* **no** or **noh**. — Also **nō'gaku** (-*gä-ko͞o*; Jap. *gaku*, music): — *pl* **no'gaku**. [Jap. *nō*.]

no. or **No.** *abbrev* for number.

n.o. (*cricket*) *abbrev* for not out.

nob¹ *nob*, *n* head (*colloq*); the knave of the turned-up suit in cribbage. — **one for his nob** a point scored for holding the knave of the turned-up suit.

nob² *nob*, (*slang*) *n* a socially superior person. — *adv* **nobb'ily**. — *n* **nobb'iness**. — *adj* **nobb'y**.

nobble *nob'l*, (*slang*) *vt* to win over, persuade or dissuade, as by bribery or coercion; to swindle; to injure or drug (a racehorse) to prevent it from winning; to prevent from doing something; to seize, steal.

Nobel prize *nō-bel' prīz*, *n* one of the annual prizes for work in physics, chemistry, medicine, literature, and the promotion of peace, instituted by Alfred B. *Nobel* (1833–96), Swedish discoverer of dynamite. — **Nobel laureate** a (past) winner of the Nobel prize in any category.

nobelium *nō-bēl'i-əm*, *n* the name given to an element of greater atomic number than uranium (symbol **No**; atomic no. 102) in 1957 when its production at the *Nobel* Institute, Stockholm, was claimed.

nobiliary. See under **nobility**.

nobility *nō-bil'i-ti*, *n* the quality of being noble; high rank; dignity; excellence; greatness of mind or character; noble descent; (with *the*) nobles as a body. — *adj* **nobil'iary** of nobility. — **nobiliary particle** a preposition forming part of a title or certain names, e.g. Ger. *von*, Fr. *de*, It. *di*. [See **noble**.]

noble *nō'bl*, *adj* illustrious; high in social rank or character; of high birth; stately; generous; excellent, worthy. — *n* a person of high social title or rank; a peer; an obsolete gold coin. — *n* **no'bleness**. — *adv* **no'bly**. — **noble gas** an inert gas; **no'bleman** a man who is noble or of high social rank; a peer: — *pl* **no'blemen**; *fem* **no'blewoman**: — *pl* **no'blewomen**. — **noble metal** one that does not readily tarnish on exposure to air, such as gold, silver, platinum (opp. to *base metal*). — **noble rot** a mould which forms on over-ripe grapes; **noble savage** a romantic and idealised view of primitive man. [Fr. *noble* — L. (*g*)*nōbilis* — (*g*)*nōscĕre*, to know.]

noblesse *nō-bles'*, *n* nobility; nobles collectively. — **noblesse oblige** (*ō-blēzh*) rank imposes obligations. [Fr.]

nobody *nō'bə-di*, *n* no person, no one; a person of no importance. — **like nobody's business** (*colloq*) very energetically or intensively. [**no²** and **body**.]

NOC *abbrev* for National Olympic Committee.

nociceptive *nō-si-sep'tiv*, *adj* sensitive to pain; causing pain. [L. *nocēre*, to hurt, and re*ceptive*.]

nock *nok*, *n* a notch, or a part carrying a notch, esp. on an arrow or a bow. — *vt* to notch; to fit (an arrow) on the string of a bow.

noct- *nokt-* or **nocti-** *nok-ti-*, *combining form* denoting night. [L. *nox*, *noct-*.]

noctambulation *nok-tam-bū-lā'shən*, *n* sleep-walking. — *n* **noctam'bulism**. — *n* **noctam'bulist**. [L. *nox*, *noctis*, night, *ambulāre*, -*ātum*, to walk.]

noctilucent *nok-ti-lo͞o'sənt*, *adj* phosphorescent, glowing in the dark (*zool*); (of high-altitude dust- or ice-clouds) visible at night in latitudes greater than *c* 50 °, when they reflect light from the sun below the horizon (*meteorol*). — *n* **noctilu'cence**. [L. *nox*, *noctis*, night, *lūcēre*, to shine.]

Noctua *nok'tū-ə*, *n* a generic name sometimes used (without *cap*) as a general name for any member of the **Noctū'idae**, a large family (or group of families) of mostly nocturnal, strong-bodied moths. — *n* and *adj* **noc'tūid**. [L. *noctŭa*, an owl — *nox*, night.]

noctule *nok'tūl*, *n* the great bat, the largest British species. [Fr., — It. *nottola*, L. *nox*, *noctis*, night.]

nocturn *nok'tûrn*, *n* (*RC*) any one of the three sections of the service of Matins. — *adj* **nocturn'al** belonging to night; happening, done, or active by night. — *adv* **nocturn'ally**. — *n* **nocturne** a dreamy or pensive musical piece, generally for the piano; a moonlight or night scene (*painting*). [L. *nocturnus* — *nox*, night.]

nod *nod*, *vi* to give a quick forward motion of the head, esp. in assent, greeting or command; to let the head drop in weariness or dozing; to dance, dip or bob up and down; to make a careless mistake through inattention. — *vt* to move (the head) in assent, greeting or command; to signify or direct by a nod: — *pr p* **nodd'ing**; *pa t* and *pa p* **nodd'ed**. — *n* a quick bending forward of the head; a slight bow; a movement of the head as a gesture of assent, greeting or command. — *n* **nodd'er**. — *n* and *adj* **nodd'ing**. — **nodding acquaintance** slight acquaintance; someone with whom one is only slightly acquainted; **nodding donkey** (*colloq*; esp. US) a type of pump for pumping oil from land-based oil-wells. — **Land of Nod** sleep (in punning allusion to the biblical land, Gen. iv. 16); **nod off** (*colloq*) to fall asleep; **nod through** in parliament, to allow to vote by proxy; to pass without discussion or a vote, etc.; **on the nod** (*slang*) by general assent, i.e. without the formality of voting, etc. [M.E. *nodde*, not known in O.E.]

nodal, etc. See **node**.

noddle *nod'l*, (*slang*) *n* the head.

noddy *nod'i*, *n* a simpleton, stupid person; an oceanic bird akin to the terns, unaccustomed to man and therefore easily caught and so deemed stupid. — **noddy suit** (*mil slang*) an NBC suit.

node *nōd*, *n* a knob or lump; a swelling; a place, often swollen, where a leaf is attached to a stem; a point of intersection of two great circles of the celestial sphere, esp. the orbit of a planet or the moon and the ecliptic (*astron*); a point at which a curve cuts itself, and through which more than one tangent to the curve can be drawn (*geom*); a similar point on a surface, where there is more than one tangent-plane (*geom*); a point of minimum displacement in a system of stationary waves (*electronics*); a point of intersection or junction in any branching system. — *adj* **nō'dal** of or like a node or nodes. — *adj* **nodical** (*nōd'* or *nod'*) pertaining to the nodes of a celestial body. — *adj* **nodose** (*nōd'ōs* or *nōd-ōs'*) having nodes, knots or swellings. — *n* **nodosity** (*nō-dos'i-ti*) knottiness; a knotty swelling. — *adj* **nodular** (*nod'ū-lər*) of or like a nodule; in the form of nodules; having nodules or little knots. — *adj* **nod'ulāted** having nodules. — *n* **nodūlā'tion.** — *n* **nod'ūle** a little rounded lump; a swelling on a root inhabited by symbiotic bacteria. — *adj* **nod'ūled.** — *adj* **nod'ūlose** or **nod'ūlous.** — *n* **nōd'us** (L.) a knotty point, difficulty, complication: — *pl* **nōd'ī.** [L. *nōdus*; dimin. *nōdulus.*]

Noel or **Nōel** *nō-el'*, (*obs* except in Christmas carols, on Christmas cards, etc.) *n* Christmas. [O.Fr. — L. *nātālis*, belonging to a birthday].

noesis *nō-ē'sis*, *n* the activity of the intellect. — *adj* **noetic** (*nō-et'ik*) purely intellectual. [Gr. *noēsis* — *noeein*, to perceive, think.]

nog[1] *nog*, *n* egg-nog or similar drink.

nog[2] *nog*, *n* a wooden peg; a brick-sized piece of wood inserted in a wall to receive nails. — *n* **nogg'ing** brick filling between timbers in a partition or wall.

nogaku. See **no**[3].

noggin *nog'in*, *n* a small mug or wooden cup; its contents, a measure of about a gill; a drink (of beer, spirits, etc.) (*colloq*); the head (*colloq*).

noh. See **no**[3].

nohow *nō'how*, (*colloq*) *adv* not in any way, not at all.

noise *noiz*, *n* sound of any kind; an unmusical sound; (an) over-loud or disturbing sound; frequent or public talk; interference in an electrical current, etc. or communication channel. — *vt* (*literary*; usu. with *about* or *abroad*) to spread by rumour, word of mouth. — *adj* **noise'less.** — *adv* **noise'lessly.** — *n* **noise'lessness.** — *adv* **nois'ily.** — *n* **nois'iness.** — *adj* **nois'y** making a loud noise or sound; accompanied by noise. — **a big noise** a person of great importance. [Fr. *noise*, noise.]

noisette *nwa-zet'*, *n* a small piece of meat (usu. lamb) cut off the bone and rolled; a nutlike or nut-flavoured sweet. [Fr., hazelnut.]

noisome *noi'səm*, *adj* harmful to health; disgusting to sight or smell. — *adv* **noi'somely.** — *n* **noi'someness.**

nolens volens *nō'lenz vō'lenz*, (L.) willy-nilly, giving no choice.

noli-me-tangere *nō-li-mā-tan'jə-ri* (**noli me tangere** *nō-lē mā tang'ge-rā*; from the Vulgate, John xx. 17) *n* warning against touching; a species of balsam that ejects its ripe seeds at a light touch. [L. *nōlī* do not, *mē*, me, *tangĕre*, to touch.]

nolle prosequi *no'le pros'ə-kwī*, (L.; *law*) *n* (an entry on a record to the effect that) the plaintiff or prosecutor will proceed no further with (part of) the suit.

nolo contendere *nō'lō kon-ten'də-ri*, (L.) I do not wish to contend (*lit*) — a legal plea by which the accused does not admit guilt, but accepts conviction.

nom *nɔ̃*, (Fr.) *n* name. — **nom de guerre** (*də ger*) an assumed name; a pseudonym.

nom. or **nomin.** *abbrev* for nominative.

noma *nō'mə*, (*med*) *n* a destructive ulceration of the cheek, esp. that affecting hunger-weakened children. [L. *nomē*, ulcer — Gr. *nemein*, to consume.]

nomad *nōm'ad*, *n* an individual of a wandering pastoral community; a rover, wanderer. — Also *adj.* — *adj* **nomadic** (*nōm-ad'ik*). — *adv* **nomad'ically.** — *n* **nomadisā'tion** or **-z-.** — *vi* **nom'adise** or **-ize** to lead a nomadic or vagabond life. — *vt* to make nomadic, force into a nomadic life. — *n* **nom'adism.** — *n* **nom'ady** living as or like a nomad. [Gr. *nomas*, *nomados* — *nemein*, to drive to pasture.]

nombril *nom'bril*, (*heraldry*) *n* a point a little below the centre of a shield. [Fr., navel.]

nom de plume *nɔ̃ də plüm'* or *ploōm'*, or *nom*, *n* a pen-name, pseudonym. [Would-be Fr. — Fr. *nom*, name, *de*, of, *plume*, pen.]

nomen *nō'men*, (L.) *n* a name, esp. of the *gens* or clan, a Roman's second name, such as Gaius *Julius* Caesar: — *pl* **no'mina** (*nom'*).

nomenclator *nō'mən-klā-tər*, *n* a person who bestows names, or draws up a classified scheme of names; a person who announces or tells the names of persons, esp. (*hist*) in canvassing for a Roman election. — *n* **nomenclature** (*nō-men'klə-chər* or *nō'mən-klā-chər*) a system of names; terminology; a list of names; mode of naming. [L. *nōmenclātor* — *nōmen*, a name, *calāre*, to call.]

-nomic. See **-nomy.**

nominal *nom'in-əl*, *adj* pertaining to, or of the nature of, a name or noun; of names; only in name; so-called, but not in reality; small, minor, hardly more than a minimum; according to plan (*space flight*). — *n* (*gram*) a noun or phrase, etc. standing as a noun. — *n* **nom'inalism** the doctrine that the objects to which general terms refer are related to one another only by the terms. — *adj* **nom'inalist.** — *adj* **nominalist'ic.** — *adv* **nom'inally** in name only; by name; as a noun. [L. *nōminālis* — *nōmen*, *-inis*, a name.]

nominate *nom'in-āt*, *vt* to propose formally for election; to appoint. — *n* **nominā'tion** the act or power of nominating; state or privilege of being nominated; naming; (in horse breeding), the arranged mating of a mare with a stallion. — *adj* **nominatival** (*nom-in-ə-tī'vl* or *nom-nə-*). — *adv* **nominatī'vally.** — *adj* **nominative** (*nom'in-ə-tiv* or *nom'nə-tiv*; *gram*) naming the subject; (in the case) in which the subject is expressed; (also *nom'in-ā-tiv*) nominated, appointed by nomination (not elected). — *n* the nominative case; a word in the nominative case. — *adv* **nom'inatively.** — *n* **nom'ināator** a person who nominates. — **nominative absolute** (*gram*) a nominative combined with a participle, but not connected with a finite verb or governed by any other word. [L. *nōmināre*, *-ātum*, to name — *nōmen.*]

nominee *nom-in-ē'*, *n* a person who is nominated by another; a person on whose life an annuity or lease depends. [L. *nōmināre*, *-ātum*, to nominate, with *-ee* as if from Fr.]

nomography *nom-* or *nōm-og'rə-fi*, *n* the art of making nomograms. — *n* **nom'ogram** a chart or diagram of scaled lines or curves used to help in mathematical calculations, comprising three scales in which a line joining values on two determines a third. — Also called **nom'ograph** or **isopleth.** — *adj* **nomograph'ic** or **nomograph'ical.** [Gr. *nomos*, law, *graphein*, to write.]

nomothete *nom'ō-thēt*, *n* a lawgiver, legislator. — *adj* **nomothetic** (*-thet'ik*) or **nomothet'ical.** [Gr. *nomothetēs* — *nomos*, law, and the root *the-*, as in *tithenai*, to set.]

-nomy *-nə-mi*, *combining form* used to signify a science or field of knowledge, or the discipline of the study of these. — *combining form* **-nom'ic** forming corresponding adjectives. [Gr. *-nomia*, administration, regulation.]

non *non*, *pfx* a Latin word meaning not; sometimes used of someone or something with pretensions who or which, is ludicrously unworthy of the name mentioned, e.g. **non'-hero** and **non'-event**; the words given below include the most common words with *non-* but the prefix is living and many other words using it may be formed. — *n* **non-accept'ance.** — *n* **non-ac'cess** (*law*) lack of opportunity for sexual intercourse. — *n* **non-aggress'ion** abstention from aggression (also *adj*). — *adj* **non-alcohol'ic** not alcoholic; not containing alcohol. — *adj* **non-aligned'** not aligned geometrically; not taking sides in international politics, esp. not supporting either of the main international blocs, i.e. the Warsaw Pact countries or the USA and the western European democracies. — *n* **non-align'ment.** — *n* **non-appear'ance** failure or neglect to appear, esp. in a court of law. — *n* **non-arri'val.** — *n* **non-attend'ance** a failure to attend; absence. — *adj* **non-attrib'utable** (of a press statement, etc.) whose source is not able or permitted to be disclosed. — *adv* **non-attrib'utably.** — *n* **non-Chris'tian**

(also *adj*). — *n* **non-claim'** a failure to make a claim within the time limited by law. — *adj* **non-cog'nisable** (*law*) (of an offence) that cannot be judicially investigated. — *n* **non-com'batant** anyone connected with an army who is there for some purpose other than that of fighting, such as a surgeon or a chaplain; a civilian in time of war. — *adj* **non-commiss'ioned** not having a commission, as an officer in the army below the rank of commissioned officer or warrant officer. — *adj* **non-committ'al** not committing one, or refraining from committing oneself, to any particular opinion or course of conduct; free from any declared preference or pledge; implying nothing, one way or the other, for or against. — *adv* **non-committ'ally.** — *n* **non-commun'icant** a person who does not take communion on any particular occasion or in general (*Christian relig*); a person who has not yet communicated. — *n* **non-complī'ance.** — *adj* **non-conduct'ing** not readily conducting, esp. heat or electricity. — *n* **non-conduct'or** a substance or object that does not readily conduct heat or electricity. — *adj* **nonconform'ing.** — *n* **nonconform'ist** a person who does not conform (esp. one who refused to conform or subscribe to the Act of Uniformity in 1662 making the Book of Common Prayer the only legal form of worship in England); usu. applied in England (with *cap*) to a Protestant separated from the Church of England (also *adj*). — *n* **nonconform'ity.** — *n* **non'-content** a person who is not content; (in the House of Lords) a person casting a negative vote. — *adj* **non-contrib'utory** (of pensions) not funded by the beneficiary. — *n* **non-co-operā'tion** failure or refusal to co-operate. — *adj* **non-custō'dial** (of a legal sentence) not involving imprisonment. — *n* **non-deliv'ery.** — *adj* **non-denominā'tional** not exclusively belonging to or according to the beliefs of any single denomination of the Christian church. — *adj* **non-destruc'tive** having no destructive effect, esp. of tests on products, substances or organisms. — *n* **nondisjunc'tion** (*biol*) the failure of paired chromosomes to separate during meiosis. — *adj* **non-drip'** (of paint) thixotropic, of such a consistency that it does not drip when being applied. — *adj* **non-effect'ive** (*mil*) unfit or unavailable for service. — *n* a member of a force who is unfit or unavailable for active service. — *n* **non-e'go** in metaphysics, the not-I, the object as opposed to the subject, whatever is not the conscious self. — *adj* **non-elec'tive** not chosen by election. — *adj* **non-essen'tial.** — *n* something that is not essential, or is not of extreme importance. — *adj* **non-Euclid'ean** not according to Euclid's axioms and postulates. — *n* **non-event** see above at **non.** — *adj* **non-exec'utive** (of e.g. directors) not employed by a company full-time, but brought in for advisory purposes (also *n*). — *n* **non-exist'ence.** — *adj* **non-exist'ent.** — *n* **non-feasance** see separate article. — *adj* **non-ferr'ous** containing no iron; not iron; relating to metals other than iron. — *adj* **non-fic'tion** (of a literary work) without any deliberately fictitious element, purely factual (also *n*). — *adj* **non-fic'tional.** — *adj* **non-flamm'able** not easily set on fire; not flammable. — *n* **non-fulfil'ment** not fulfilling or not being fulfilled. — *n* **non-interven'tion** a policy of systematic abstention from interference in the affairs of other nations. — *adj* **non-invas'ive** (of medical treatment) not involving surgery or the insertion of instruments, etc., into the patient. — *n* **non-involve'ment.** — *adj* **non-judgmen'tal** or **non-judgemen'tal** relating to or having an open attitude without implicit judgment, esp. moral. — *adv* **non-judgmen'tally** or **non-judgemen'tally.** — *adj* **nonjur'ing** not swearing allegiance. — *n* **nonjur'or** a person who refuses to swear allegiance, esp. (with *cap*) one of the clergy in England and Scotland who would not swear allegiance to William and Mary in 1689. — *adj* **non-lin'ear.** — *adj* **non-marr'ying** not readily disposed to marry. — *n* **non-mem'ber** a person who is not a member. — *n* **non-met'al** an element that is not a metal. — Also *adj.* — *adj* **non-metall'ic.** — *adj* **non-mor'al.** — *adj* **non-nat'ural.** — *adj* **non-objec'tive** (*painting*) non-representational. — *n* **non-observ'ance.** — *adj* **non-operā'tional.** — *adj* **non-partic'ipating** not taking part; (of shares, etc.) not giving the holder the right to a share in profits. — *adj* **non-partisan'** (or *-pärt'*). — *adj* **non-par'ty** independent of party politics. — *n* **non-pay'ment.** — *n* **non-perform'ance.** — *n* **non-per'son** a person previously of political, etc. eminence, now out of favour; a complete nonentity. — *adj* **non-play'ing** (of e.g. the captain of a team). — *adj* **nonpo'lar** without any electrical poles. — *adj* **non-prof'it-making** not organised or engaged in with the purpose of making a profit. — *n* **non-proliferā'tion** lack of proliferation, esp. a limit imposed on the proliferation of (usu. nuclear) weapons. — *adj* **non-representā'tional** (*painting*) not aiming at the realistic depiction of objects. — *n* **non-res'idence** the fact of not (permanently or for the moment) residing at a place, esp. where one's official or social duties require one to reside or where one is entitled to reside. — *adj* and *n* **non-res'ident.** — *n* **non-resist'ance** the principle of not resisting violence by force, or of not resisting authority; passive submission. — *adj* **non-resist'ant** or **non-resist'ing.** — *adj* **non-restric'tive** (*gram*) used of a relative clause that does not restrict the people or things to which its antecedent may refer. — *adj* **non-return'able** (of a bottle, jar or other container) on which a returnable deposit has not been paid. — *n* **non-return valve** a valve incorporating a device to prevent flow in one direction. — *adj* **non-sched'uled** (of an airline) operating between specified points but not to a specific schedule of flights. — *adj* **non-skid'** or **non-slip'** (of a surface) designed to reduce chance of slipping to a minimum. — *n* **non-smo'ker** a person who does not smoke; a railway compartment in which smoking is forbidden. — *adj* **non-smok'ing.** — Also *n.* — *adj* **non-specif'ic** not specific; (of a disease) not caused by any specific agent. — *n* **non-start'er** a horse which, though entered for a race, does not run; a person, idea, etc., with no chance at all of success. — *adj* **non-stick'** (of e.g. a pan) treated so that food or other substance will not stick to it. — *adj* and *adv* **non-stop'** uninterrupted(ly); without any stop or halt. — *adj* **non-U** see under **U.** — *adj* **non-u'nion** not attached to a trade union; not approved of by a union; employing, or produced by, non-union workers. — *n* **non-vi'olence** (the ideal or practice of) refraining from violence on grounds of principle. — *adj* **non-vi'olent.** — *adj* **non-vo'ting** not voting; (of shares, etc.) not giving the holder the right to vote on company decisions. — *n* **non-white'** (a member of) a race other than the white race (also *adj*). [L. *nōn*, not.]

nonage *non'ij* or *nōn'ij*, *n* legal infancy, minority; time of immaturity generally. — *adj* **non'aged.** [O.Fr. *nonage* — pfx. *non-* (L. *nōn*) and *age*, age.]

nonagenarian *nōn-* or *non-ə-ji-nā'ri-ən*, *n* a person who is ninety years old or between ninety and a hundred. — *adj* of that age. [L. *nōnāgēnārius*, relating to ninety — *nōnāgintā*, ninety.]

nonagon *non'ə-gon*, *n* a nine-sided geometrical figure. [L. *nōnus*, ninth, Gr. *gōniā*, angle.]

nonary *nōn'ə-ri*, *adj* (of a mathematical system) based on nine. [L. *nōnārius.*]

nonce¹ *nons*, *n* (almost confined to the phrase *for the nonce*) the occasion; the moment, the time being. — *adj* occurring, adopted or coined for a particular occasion only, as **nonce'-word.** [From *for the nones*, i.e. *for then ones*, for the once.]

nonce² *nons*, (*prison slang*) *n* a sexual offender, esp. one who assaults children.

nonchalance *non'shə-ləns*, *n* unconcern; coolness; indifference. — *adj* **non'chalant**. — *adv* **non'chalantly**. [Fr., — *non*, not, *chaloir*, to matter, interest.]

non-com. *non'kom*, *abbrev* for non-commissioned (officer).

nonconformist and **nonconformity**. See under **non**.

nondescript *non'di-skript*, *adj* not distinctive enough to be described, featureless (*derog*); neither one thing nor another. — *n* a featureless person or thing, or one not easily described. [L. *nōn*, not, *dēscrībĕre*, *-scrīptum*, to describe.]

none *nun*, *pron* (*pl* or *sing*) not one; no person or persons; not any; no portion or amount. — *adv* **nonetheless'** (or **none the less**) nevertheless. — **none other** (often with *than*) no other person; **none the** (followed by *compar adj*) in no way, to no degree; **none too** (*colloq*) not very. [O.E. *nān* — *ne*, not, *ān*, one.]

nonentity *non-en'ti-ti*, *n* the state of not being; a thing which does not exist; a person or thing of no importance (*derog*). [L. *nōn*, not, *entitās* (see **entity**).]

Nones *nōnz*, *npl* in the Roman calendar, the ninth day before the Ides (both days included) — the 7th of March, May, July, and October, and the 5th of the other months; (without *cap*) a church service originally held at the ninth hour, or three o'clock, afterwards earlier. [L. *nōnae* — *nōnus*, ninth.]

nonesuch or **nonsuch** *nun'* or *non'such*, (*literary*) *n* a unique, unparalleled or extraordinary thing. [**none** and **such**.]

nonet *nō-net'*, (*mus*) *n* a composition for nine performers. — Also **nonett'**: — *pl* **nonet'tos** or **nonet'ti** (*-tē*). [It. *nonetto*.]

non-feasance *non-fē'zəns*, (*law*) *n* omission of something which ought to be or have been done. [**non** and O.Fr. *faisance*, doing — *faire* — L. *facĕre*, to do.]

nonillion *nō-nil'yən*, *n* a million raised to the ninth power, one followed by 54 zeros; a thousand raised to the tenth power, one followed by 30 zeros (*NAm*). — *adj* **nonill'ionth**. [L. *nōnus*, ninth, in imitation of **million** and **billion**.]

nonjuring, etc. See under **non**.

no-no. See **no¹**.

nonpareil *non'pə-rel* or *-rəl*, *n* a person or thing without equal; a fine variety of apple; a kind of confectionery. — *adj* unequalled; matchless. [Fr. *non*, not, *pareil*, from a L.L. dimin. of L. *pār*, equal.]

nonplus *non-plus'*, *vt* to perplex completely, make uncertain what to say or do: — *pr p* **nonpluss'ing** (or in U.S. **nonplus'ing**); *pa t* and *pa p* **nonplussed'** (or in U.S. **nonplused'**). — *adj* **nonplussed'** (or **nonplused'**). [L. *nōn*, not, *plūs*, more.]

nonsense *non'səns*, *n* anything which makes no sense; language without meaning; absurdity, foolishness; trivial things; something which is manifestly false; an absurd, illogical or unintelligible statement or action. — Also *interj*. — *adj* **nonsensical** (*-sens'*) without sense; absurd. — *n* **nonsensicality** (*non-sens-i-kal'i-ti*) or **nonsens'icalness**. — *adv* **nonsens'ically**. — **nonsense verse** verse deliberately written to convey an absurd meaning, or without obvious meaning at all. — **no-nonsense** see under **no²**. [**non** and **sense**.]

non sequitur *non sek'wi-tər*, *n* the drawing of a conclusion that does not follow logically from the foregoing premises; (*loosely*) a remark, event or action that has no relation to what has gone before. — *abbrev* **non seq.** [L. *nōn*, not, *sequitur*, follows, 3rd sing. pres. indic. of *sequi*, to follow.]

nonsuch. See **nonesuch**.

noodle¹ *nōōd'l*, (*colloq*) *n* a simpleton; a blockhead, stupid person.

noodle² *nōōd'l*, *n* a flat, usu. string- or ribbon-shaped pasta, usu. made with eggs. [Ger. *Nudel*.]

nook *nŏŏk*, *n* a corner; a narrow place formed by an angle; a recess; a secluded retreat. — **every nook and cranny** (*colloq*) everywhere. [M.E. *nok*, *noke*.]

noon *nōōn*, *n* the ninth hour of the day in Roman and ecclesiastical reckoning, three o'clock p.m.; afterwards (when the church service called *Nones* was shifted to midday) midday. — *adj* belonging to, characteristic or typical of, midday. — **noon'day** midday; the time of greatest prosperity (*fig*). — *adj* of or pertaining to midday. — **noon'tide** (*literary*) the time of noon, midday. — *adj* of or pertaining to noon. [O.E. *nōn* — L. *nōna* (*hōra*), the ninth (hour).]

no-one. See under **no²**.

noose *nōōs*, *n* a loop with running knot which draws tighter the more it is pulled, used for trapping or killing by hanging; a snare or bond generally. — *vt* to tie or catch in a noose. — **put one's head in a noose** to put oneself into a dangerous or vulnerable situation.

NOP *abbrev* for National Opinion Poll or Polls.

nopal *nō'pəl*, *n* a Central American cactus used for rearing cochineal insects. [Sp. *nopal* — Mex. *nopalli*.]

nope *nōp*, (*slang*) *interj* an emphatic, originally American, form of **no¹**, pronounced with a snap of the mouth.

NOR *nör*, (*comput*) *n* a logic circuit that has two or more inputs and one output, the output signal being 1 if all its inputs are 0, and 0 if any of its inputs is 1. — Also *adj*. [*not or*.]

nor *nör*, *conj* and not; neither — used esp. in introducing the second part of a negative proposition — correlative to *neither*.

nor' *nör*, *adj* and *n* a shortened form of **north**.

noradrenalin *nör-ə-dren'ə-lin* or **noradrenaline** *-lin* or *-lēn*, *n* a neurotransmitter hormone related to adrenalin, produced by the adrenal glands. — Also (esp. *US*) **norepinephrine** (*nör-ep-i-nef'rin* or *-rēn*).

Nordic *nör'dik*, *adj* of a tall, blond, long-skulled type of (generally Germanic) peoples in N.W. Europe. — Also *n*. — **Nordic skiing** competitive skiing involving cross-country and jumping events. [Fr. *nord*, north.]

norepinephrine. See **noradrenalin**.

Norfolk *nör'fək*, *adj* belonging to the English county of *Norfolk*. — **Norfolk jacket** a loose pleated man's jacket with a waistband. [O.E. *northfolc*, north folk.]

nori *nö'ri*, *n* a seaweed of the genus *Porphyra* used as a foodstuff in Japan in the form of dried sheets or as paste. [Jap.]

noria *nö'ri-ə*, *n* an endless chain of buckets on a wheel for water-raising. [Sp. *noria* — Ar. *nā'ūrah*.]

nork *nörk*, (*Austr slang*) *n* a woman's breast.

norm *nörm*, *n* a rule; a pattern; an authoritative standard; the ordinary or most frequent value or state; an accepted standard of behaviour. — *adj* **nor'mal** according to rule; not deviating from the standard; ordinary; well-adjusted mentally; functioning regularly; (of a solution) having one gramme-equivalent of dissolved substance to a litre; perpendicular (*geom*). — *n* a perpendicular. — *n* **nor'malcy** (esp. *US*) normality, often of political, economic, etc., conditions. — *n* **normalisā'tion** or **-z-**. — *vt* **nor'malise** or **-ize** to make normal; to bring within or cause to conform to normal standards, limits, etc.; to heat (steel) in order to refine the crystal structure and to relieve internal stress. — *vi* to become normal, regular. — *n* **normalisa'tion** or **-z-** return to normality or the status quo. — *n* **normal'ity**. — *adv* **nor'mally** in a normal manner; usually; typically. — *adj* **nor'mative** of or pertaining to a norm; establishing a standard; prescriptive. — **normal distribution** (*statistics*) a frequency distribution represented by a symmetrical, bell-shaped curve; **normal school** in some countries, esp. France and North America, a training-college for teachers; **normal solution** see **normal** above and also **standard solution**; **norm-ref'erencing** (*education*) comparing a pupil's abilities with those of his or her peers. — *adj* **norm-ref'erenced**. [L. *norma*, a rule.]

normal, etc. See **norm**.

Norman *nör'mən*, *n* a native or inhabitant of Normandy; an individual of that Scandinavian people which settled in northern France about the beginning of the 10th century, founded the Duchy of Normandy, and conquered England in 1066; the Norman-French dialect: — *pl* **Nor'mans**. — *adj* pertaining to the Normans or to Normandy. — **Norman architecture** a massive Romanesque style, prevalent in Normandy (10th–11th cent.) and England (11th–12th), the churches with semicircular apse and a great tower; **Norman Conquest** the conquest of England by Duke William of Normandy (1066). — *n* and *adj* **Norman-French'** French as spoken by the Normans. [O.Fr. *Normanz*, *Normans*, nom. and accus. pl. of *Normant*, Northman, from Scand.]

normative. See under **norm**.

Norse *nörs*, *adj* Norwegian; ancient Scandinavian. — *n* the Norwegian language; the language of the ancient Scandinavians — also **Old Norse**. — *n* **Norse'man** a Scandinavian, a viking. [Perh. Du. *noor(d)sch*.]

north *nörth*, *adv* in the direction of that point of the horizon or that pole of the earth or heavens which at equinox is opposite the sun at noon in Europe or elsewhere on the same side of the equator, or towards the sun in the other hemisphere; in the slightly different direction (*magnetic north*) in which a magnetic needle points. — *n* the point of the horizon in that direction; the region lying in that direction; the part placed relatively in that direction; the north wind. — *adj* lying towards the north; forming the part that is towards the north; blowing from the north; (of a pole of a magnet, usually) north-seeking. — *n* **norther** (*nörth'ər*) a wind or gale from the north. — *n* **north'erliness** (*-dh-*). — *adj* **north'erly** (*-dh-*) being toward the north; blowing from the north. — *adv* toward or from the north. — *n* a north wind. — *adj* **north'ern** (*-dh-*) pertaining to the north; being in the north or in the direction toward it; proceeding from the north. — *n* a native of the north. — *n* **north'erner** (*-dh-*) a native of, or resident in, the north, esp. of the northern United States or the northern counties of England. — *adj* **north'ern-most** (*-dh*) most northerly. — *n* **north'ing** (*-th-*) motion, distance or tendency northward; distance of a heavenly body from the equator northward; difference of latitude made by a ship in sailing; deviation towards the north. — *adj*, *adv* and *n* **northward** (*nörth'wərd*). — *adj* and *adv* **north'-wardly**. — *adv* **north'wards**. — *adj* **north'bound** bound for the north; travelling northwards. — *adj* **north'-country** belonging to the northern part of the country, esp. of England. — **north-coun'try-man**. — *adj* and *adv* **north-east'** (also *nörth'*) midway between north and east. — *n* the direction midway between north and east; the region lying in that direction; the wind blowing from that direction. — **north-east'er** or **nor'-east'er** a strong wind from the north-east. — *adj* and *adv* **north-east'erly** towards or from the north-east. — *adj* **north-east'ern** belonging to the north-east; being in the north-east, or in that direction. — *adj* and *adv* **north-east'ward** toward the north-east. — *n* the region to the north-east. — *adj* and *adv* **north-east'wardly**. — *adv* **north-east'wards**. — **northern lights** the aurora borealis; **north'land** (also *adj*) land, or lands, of the north; **North'man** an ancient Scandinavian. — *n*, *adj* and *adv* **north-north-east'** and **north-north-west'** (in) a direction midway between north and north-east or north-west. — **north pole** the end of the earth's axis in the Arctic regions; its projection on the celestial sphere; (usually) that pole of a magnet which when free points to the earth's north magnetic pole; **North Star** a star very near the north pole of the heavens, the Pole Star. — *adj* and *adv* **north-west'** (also *nörth'*) midway between north and west. — *n* the direction midway between north and west; the region lying in that direction; the wind blowing from that direction. — **north-west'er** or **nor'-west'er** a strong north-west wind. — *adj* and *adv* **north-west'erly** toward or from the north-west. — *adj* **north-west'ern** belonging to the north-west; being in the north-west or in that direction. — *adj*, *adv* and *n* **north-west'ward**. — *adj* and *adv* **north-west'wardly**. — *adv* **north-west'wards**. — **North Atlantic Treaty Organization** a political alliance linking the United States and Canada to a group of European States, established by the **North Atlantic Treaty**, 4 April 1949 (abbrev. **NATO**); **North-east Passage** a passage for ships along the north coasts of Europe and Asia to the Pacific; **North-west Passage** a seaway from the Atlantic into the Pacific north of North America. [O.E. *north*; cf. Ger. *Nord*.]

Northants. *nörth'antz*, *abbrev* for Northamptonshire.

Northumb. *nörth-um'*, *abbrev* for Northumberland.

Northumbrian *nör-thum'bri-ən*, *n* a native of the modern *Northumberland*, or of the old kingdom of *Northumbria* (O.E. *Northhymbre*, *Northhymbraland*) which stretched from the Humber to the Forth, or the modern region of Northumbria comprising Northumberland, Tyne and Wear, Co. Durham and Cleveland; the dialect of Old English spoken in Northumbria, later Northern English (including Scots). — *adj* of Northumberland or Northumbria.

Norway *nör'wā*: **Norway rat** the brown rat; **Norway spruce** *Picea excelsa*; its wood.

Norwegian *nör-wē'jən*, *adj* of Norway, its people, or its language. — *n* a native or citizen of Norway; the language of Norway. [L.L. *Norvegia*, Norway — O.N. *Norvegr* (O.E. *Northweg*) — O.N. *northr*, north, *vegr*, way.]

Nos or **nos** *abbrev* for Numbers or numbers.

nose *nōz*, *n* the projecting part of the face used in breathing, smelling, and to some extent in speaking; the power of smelling; flair, a faculty for tracking out, detecting, or recognising (*fig*); scent, aroma, esp. the bouquet of wine; a projecting forepart of anything; a projection; a beak; a nozzle; an informer (*slang*). — *vi* and *vt* to proceed or cause to proceed gingerly, as if feeling with the nose. — *vt* to smell; to examine by smelling or as if by smelling; to track out, detect or recognise (often with *out*); to touch, press or rub with the nose; to thrust the nose into. — *vi* to pry; to nuzzle; to move nose-first. — *adj* **nosed** having a nose — esp. in combination, as in *bottle-nosed*, *long-nosed*, etc. — *adj* **nose'less**. — *adj* **nos'ey** or **nos'y** long-nosed; large-nosed; prying; bad-smelling; fragrant. — *n* a nickname for a person who pries. — *adv* **nos'ily**. — *n* **nos'iness** a tendency to pry. — *n* **nos'ing**. — **nose'bag** a bag for food, hung on a horse's head; **nose'-band** the part of the bridle coming over the nose; **nose'-bleed** a bleeding from the nose; **nose'-cone** the front, usu. conical, part of a spacecraft, etc.; **nose'-dive** a headlong plunge. — *vi* to plunge nose-first; to drop or decline sharply (*fig*). — **nose'-flute** a flute blown by the nose; **nose'-piece** a nozzle; the end of a microscope tube carrying the objective; a nose-band; **nose'-rag** (*slang*) a handkerchief; **nose'-ring** an ornament worn in the septum of the nose or in either of its wings; a ring in the septum of the nose for controlling a bull, swine, etc.; **nose'-wheel** the single wheel at the front of a vehicle, etc., esp. an aircraft; **Nosey Parker** (*colloq*; also without *caps*) a prying person.

— **by a nose** by a very short distance or small margin; **cut off one's nose to spite one's face** to injure or disadvantage oneself through an act of revenge or anger towards another; **follow one's nose** to go straight forward, or take the obvious or instinctive course; **get up someone's nose** (*colloq*) to annoy, irritate someone; **keep one's nose clean** (*colloq*) to keep out of trouble, i.e. not to behave badly or dishonestly; **lead by the nose** see under **lead[1]**; **look down one's nose at** to look at in a supercilious way; **make a long nose** or **thumb one's nose** see under **long** and **thumb**; **nose out** to move forward slowly into traffic (in a vehicle); **nose to tail** closely following one another; **nose to the grindstone** see under **grind**; **nose up** to direct or turn an aircraft nose upwards; **not see beyond** or **further than (the end of) one's nose** to see only what is immediately in front of one, i.e. not to see the long-term consequences of one's actions, etc.; **on the nose** (in horse-race betting) to win only (not to come second or third); **put someone's nose out of joint** see under **join**; **rub someone's nose in it** (*colloq*) to remind someone continually of something they have done wrong; **through the nose** exorbitantly; **thrust, poke** or **stick one's nose into** to meddle officiously with; **thumb one's nose** see under **thumb**; **turn up one's nose at** to refuse or receive contemptuously; **under one's (very) nose** in full view; close at hand; **with one's nose in the air** in a haughty, superior manner. [O.E. *nosu*.]

nosegay *nōz'gā*, *n* a bunch of fragrant flowers; a posy or bouquet. [**nose** and **gay**.]

nosh *nosh*, (*slang*) *vi* to nibble, eat between meals; to eat. — *n* food. — **nosh'-up** (*slang*) a meal, esp. a large one. [Yiddish.]

no-show. See under **no[2]**.

nosography *nos-og'rə-fi*, *n* the description of diseases. — *n* **nosog'rapher**. — *adj* **nosographic** (*nos-ə-graf'ik*). [Gr. *nosos*, disease, *graphein*, to write.]

nosology *nos-ol'ə-ji*, *n* the branch of medicine which deals with the classification of diseases. — *adj* **nosological** (*-ə-loj'*). — *n* **nosol'ogist**. [Gr. *nosos*, disease, *logos*, discourse.]

nostalgia *nos-tal'ji-ə*, *n* home-sickness; sentimental longing for past times. — *adj* **nostal'gic**. — *adv* **nostal'gically**. [Gr. *nostos*, a return, *algos*, pain.]

nostoc *nos'tok*, *n* an alga of the *Nostoc* genus of blue-green algae, beaded filaments forming gelatinous colonies on damp earth, etc., once thought to be derived from stars. [App. coined by Paracelsus.]

nostril *nos'tril*, *n* either of the openings of the nose. [M.E. *nosethirl* — O.E. *nosthyr(e)l* — *nosu*, nose, *thyrel*, opening.]

nostrum *nos'trəm*, *n* any secret, quack or patent medicine; any favourite remedy or scheme. [L. *nostrum* (neut.), our own — *nōs*, we.]

nosy. See **nose**.

NOT *not*, (*comput*) *n* a logic circuit that has one input and one output, the output signal being 1 if its input is 0, and 0 if its input is 1. [**not**.]

not *not*, *adv* a word expressing denial, negation or refusal: — enclitic form **-n't**. — **not'-being** the state or fact of not existing; **not'-I** that which is not the conscious ego. — *adj* and *adv* **not-out'** (*cricket*) still in; at the end of the innings without having been put out. — **not on** (*colloq*) not possible; not morally, socially, etc. acceptable. [Same as **naught, nought**.]

nota bene *nō'tə ben'i*, or *no'tä ben'e*, (L.) mark well, take notice (often abbrev. **NB**).

notable *nō'tə-bl*, *adj* worthy of being known or noted; remarkable; memorable; distinguished; noticeable; considerable. — *n* a person or thing worthy of note, esp. in *pl* for persons of distinction and political importance in France in pre-Revolution times. — *n* **notabil'ity** the fact of being notable; a notable person or thing. — *n* **no'tableness**. — *adv* **no'tably**. [L. *notābilis* — *notāre*, to mark.]

notaphily *nō-taf'i-li*, *n* the collecting of bank-notes, cheques, etc. as a hobby. — *adj* **notaph'ilic**. — *n* **notaph'ilism**. — *n* **notaph'ilist**. [**note** and **phil-**.]

notary *nō'tə-ri*, *n* an officer authorised to certify deeds, contracts, copies of documents, affidavits, etc. (generally **notary public**). — *adj* **notā'rial**. — *adv* **notā'rially**. — *vt* **no'tarise** or **-ize** to attest to, authenticate (a document, etc.) as a notary. [L. *notārius*.]

notation *nō-tā'shən*, *n* a system of signs or symbols; the act of notating or writing down. — *vt* **notate'** to write (music, etc.) in notation. — *adj* **notā'tional**. [L. *notātiō*, *-ōnis* — *notāre*, *-ātum*, to mark.]

notch *noch*, *n* a nick; an indentation; a narrow pass. — *vt* to make a nick in; to form, fix or remove by nicking; to fit arrow to bowstring (also **nock**); to record by a notch; (often with *up*) to score, achieve. — *adj* **notched** nicked. — *n* **notch'ing** a method of joining timbers, by fitting into a groove or grooves. — *adj* **notch'y**. — **notch'-board** a board that receives the ends of the steps of a staircase. [Supposed to be from Fr. *oche* (now *hoche*) with *n* from the indefinite article; not conn. with **nock**.]

note *nōt*, *n* a significant or distinguishing mark; a characteristic; a significant tone or hint; a mark or sign calling attention; a written or printed symbol other than a letter; a stigma or mark of censure; an observation or remark; a comment attached to a text, explanatory, illustrative, critical, or recording textual variants; a jotting set down provisionally for use afterwards; an impression; a short statement or record; a memorandum; a short informal letter; a diplomatic paper; a small size of paper used for writing; a mark representing a sound (**whole note**, a semibreve) (*mus*); a key of a piano or other instrument; the sound or tone represented by the printed or written note; the song, cry or utterance of a bird or other animal; a bank-note; a promissory note; notice; attention; cognisance; distinction; importance; consequence. — *vt* to make a note of; to notice; to attend to; to indicate; to mark; to mention; to record in writing or in musical notation; to annotate. — *adj* **nōt'ed** marked; well-known; celebrated; eminent; notorious. — *adv* **not'edly**. — *n* **nōt'edness**. — *adj* **note'less**. — *n* **note'let** a short annotation or letter; a folded sheet of note-paper, usu. with printed decoration, for short informal letters. — **note'book** a book for keeping notes or memoranda; **note'case** a wallet for bank-notes; **note'-pad** a pad of paper for writing notes on; **note'paper** writing-paper intended for letters; **note row** a tone row; **note'worthiness**. — *adj* **note'worthy** worthy of note or of notice. — **note of hand** promissory note; **of note** well-known, distinguished; significant, worthy of attention; **strike the right (**or **a false) note** to act or speak appropriately (or inappropriately); **take note** to observe carefully, closely (often with *of*). [Fr., — L. *nota*, a mark.]

nothing *nuth'ing*, *n* no thing; the non-existent; zero number or quantity; the figure representing it, a nought; a thing or person of no significance or value; an empty or trivial utterance; a low condition; a trifle; no difficulty or trouble. — *adv* in no degree; not at all. — *n* **noth'ingness** non-existence; the state of being nothing; worthlessness; insignificance; vacuity; a thing of no value. — **be nothing to** not to be important to or concern (someone); **come to nothing** to have little or no result; to turn out a failure; **for nothing** in vain; free of charge; **make nothing of** see under **make**; **next to nothing** almost nothing; **nothing but** only; **nothing doing** an emphatic refusal; an expression of failure; **nothing for it but** no alternative but; **nothing if not** primarily, above all; at the very least; **nothing**

on (*slang*) no claim to superiority over; no information about (used esp. by police of criminals); no engagement; **nothing to it** having nothing in it worth while; easy; **nothing less than** or **nothing short of** at least; downright; **stop** or **stick at nothing** to be ruthless or unscrupulous; **sweet nothings** (esp. whispered) words of affection and endearment; **to say nothing of** not to mention (see under **mention**); **think nothing of** to regard as easy or unremarkable; to have a low opinion of. [**no**[2] and **thing**.]

notice *nō'tis*, *n* intimation; announcement; information; warning; a writing, placard, board, etc., conveying an intimation or warning; time allowed for preparation; cognisance; observation; heed; a dramatic or artistic review; civility or respectful treatment. — *vt* to mark or observe; to regard or attend to; to make observations upon; to show sign of recognition of; to treat with civility. — *adj* **no'ticeable** that can be noticed; likely to be noticed. — *adv* **no'ticeably**. — **no'tice-board** a board for fixing notices on. — **at short notice** with notification only a little in advance; **give notice** to warn beforehand; to inform; to intimate, esp. the termination of an agreement. [Fr. *notice* — L. *nōtitia* — *nōscĕre*, *nōtum*, to get to know.]

notify *nō'ti-fī*, *vt* to make known; to declare; to give notice or information of: — *pr p* **no'tifying**; *pa t* and *pa p* **no'tified**. — *adj* **no'tifiable** (of diseases) that must be reported to public health authorities. — *n* **notification** (*-fi-kā'shən*). — *n* **not'ifier**. [Fr. *notifier* — L. *nōtificāre*, *-ātum* — *nōtus*, known, *facĕre*, to make.]

notion *nō'shən*, *n* a concept in the mind of the various marks or qualities of an object; an idea; an opinion, esp. one not very well founded; a caprice or whim; a liking or fancy; a small article ingeniously devised (usually in *pl*). — *adj* **no'tional** of the nature of a notion; having a full meaning of its own, not merely contributing to the meaning of a phrase; theoretical; ideal; fanciful; imaginary, unreal. — *n* **no'tionalist** a theorist. — *adv* **no'tionally**. [Fr., — L. *nōtiō*, *-ōnis* — *nōscĕre*, *nōtum*, to get to know.]

notochord *nō'tō-körd*, (*zool*) *n* a simple cellular rod, foreshadowing the spinal column, persisting throughout life in many lower vertebrates. — *adj* **notochord'al**. [Gr. *nōtos*, back, *chordē*, a string.]

notorious *nō-tö'ri-əs*, *adj* publicly known (now only in a bad sense); infamous. — *n* **notorī'ety** the state of being notorious; publicity; public exposure. — *adv* **noto'riously**. — *n* **noto'riousness**. [L.L. *nōtōrius* — *nōtus*, known.]

Notornis *no-tör'nis*, *n* a genus of flightless rails, long thought extinct, but found surviving in New Zealand in 1948; (without *cap*) a bird of this genus. [Gr. *notos*, south, *ornis*, a bird.]

no-trump(s). See under **no**[2].

Notts. *notz*, *abbrev* for Nottinghamshire.

notwithstanding *not-with-stan'ding* or *-widh-*, *prep* in spite of. — *conj* in spite of the fact that, although. — *adv* nevertheless, however, yet. [Orig. a participial phrase in nominative absolute = L. *non obstante*.]

nougat *nōō'gä* or *nug'ət*, *n* a confection made of a sweet paste containing chopped almonds, pistachio nuts, cherries, etc. [Fr., — L. *nux*, *nucis*, a nut.]

nought *nöt*, *n* not anything; nothing; the figure 0. — *adv* in no degree. — *adj* same as **naught**. — **noughts and crosses** a game in which one seeks to make three noughts, the other three crosses, in a row in the spaces of crossed parallel lines; **set at nought** to despise, disregard, flout. [Same as **naught**.]

noumenon *nōō'* or *now'mi-non*, *n* an unknown and unknowable substance or thing as it is in itself: — *pl* **nou'mena**. — *adj* **nou'menal**. [Gr. *nooumenon* , neuter of pres. p. pass. of *noeein*, to think.]

noun *nown*, (*gram*) *n* a word used as a name. — *adj* **noun'al**. — *adj* **noun'y** having many nouns; having the nature or function of a noun. — **noun clause** (or **phrase**) a clause (or phrase) equivalent to a noun. [A.Fr. *noun* (O.Fr. *non*; Fr. *nom*) — L. *nōmen*, *nōminis*, a name.]

nourish *nur'ish*, *vt* to feed; to provide with food; to support; to encourage the growth of in any way; to allow to grow. — *adj* **nour'ishable**. — *n* **nour'isher**. — *adj* **nour'ishing**. — *n* **nour'ishment** the act of nourishing; the state of being nourished; that which nourishes; nutriment. [O.Fr. *norir*, *nourir*, *-iss-* (Fr. *nourrir*) — L. *nūtrīre*, to feed.]

nous *nows*, *n* intellect; common sense (*slang*). [Gr.]

nouveau *nōō-vō*, *fem* **nouvelle** *-vel*, (Fr.) *adj* new. — **nouveau riche** (*rēsh*) a person (or persons collectively) with newly-acquired wealth, but without good taste or manners; an upstart: — *pl* **nouveaux riches**. — Also *adj*. — **nouvelle cuisine** (*kwē-zēn*) a style of simple French cooking excluding rich creamy sauces, etc. in favour of fresh vegetables and light sauces; **Nouvelle Vague** (*väg*) a movement in the French cinema (beginning just before 1960) aiming at imaginative quality in films. — **art nouveau** see under **art**[1].

Nov. *nov*, *abbrev* for November.

nova *nō'və*, *n* a star that suddenly increases in brightness for a number of days or years: — *pl* **no'vae** (*-vē*) or **no'vas**. [L. *nŏva* (*stella*), new (star); fem. of *novus*, new.]

novation *nō-vā'shən*, (*law*) *n* the substitution of a new obligation for the one existing. [L. *novātiō*, *-ōnis* — *novus*, new.]

novel *nov'l*, *adj* new and strange; of a new kind; felt to be new. — *n* a fictitious prose narrative or tale presenting a picture of real life, esp. of the emotional crises in the life-history of the men and women portrayed. — *n* **novelese** (*-ēz'*; *derogatory*) the hackneyed style typical of poor novels. — *n* **novelette'** a short novel, esp. one that is feeble, trite and sentimental; Schumann's name for a short piano piece in free form. — *adj* **novelett'ish**. — *n* **novelett'ist**. — *adj* **nov'elish** savouring of a novel. — *n* **nov'elist** a novel-writer. — *adj* **novelist'ic**. — *n* **novella** (*-el'lə*) a short novel. — *n* **nov'elty** newness; unusual appearance; anything new, strange or different from what was known or usual before; a small, usually cheap, manufactured article of unusual or gimmicky design: — *pl* **nov'elties**. [Partly through O.Fr. *novelle* (Fr. *nouvelle*), partly through It. *novella*, partly direct, from L. *novellus*, fem. *novella* — *novus*, new.]

November *nō-vem'bər*, *n* formerly the ninth, now the eleventh month. [L. *November* — *novem*, nine.]

novena *nō-vē'nə*, (*RC*) *n* a devotion lasting nine days, to obtain a particular request, through the intercession of the Virgin or some saint. [L. *novēnus*, nine each, *novem*, nine.]

novice *nov'is*, *n* someone new in anything; a beginner; a new convert or church member; an inmate of a religious house who has not yet taken the vows; a competitor that has not yet won a recognised prize. — *n* **nov'icehood**. — *n* **nov'iceship**. — *n* **noviciate** or **novitiate** (*-ish'i-āt*) the state of being a novice; the period of being a novice; the novices' quarters in a religious house; a religious novice. [Fr., — L. *novīcius* — *novus*, new.]

Novocaine® *nō'və-kān*, *n* a proprietary name for procaine (q.v.).

now *now*, *adv* at the present time, or the time in question, or a very little before or after; as things are; used meaninglessly, or with the feeling of time lost or nearly lost, in remonstrance, admonition, or taking up a new point. — *adj* present. — *n* the present time or the time in question. — *conj* at this time when and because it is the fact; since at this time. — *interj* expressing admonition, warning or (when repeated) reassurance. — *n* **now'ness** the quality of constantly being in or taking place at the present moment; a lively and up-to-date quality. — **now and then** or **now and again** sometimes; from time to time; **now ... now** at one time ... at another time; **now then!** interjection expressing admonition or rebuke. [O.E. *nū*; Ger. *nun*, L. *nunc*, Gr. *nȳn*.]

nowadays *now'ə-dāz, adv* in these times. — Also *adj*. [**now** and **days**, O.E. *dæges*, genitive of *dæg*, day, to which *a-* (see **a-**[1]) was later added.]

noway, noways, nowise. See under **no**[2].

nowhere *nō'wār* or *nō' hwār, adv* in or to no place; out of the running. — *n* a non-existent place. — **nowhere near** not nearly. [**no**[2] and **where.**]

nowt *nowt*, (*dialect* or *colloq*) *n* nothing. [**naught.**]

noxious *nok'shəs, adj* poisonous; unwholesome; harmful. — *adv* **nox'iously.** — *n* **nox'iousness.** [L. *noxius* — *noxa*, hurt — *nocēre*, to hurt.]

noyau *nwä-yō', n* a liqueur flavoured with bitter almonds or peach-kernels. [Fr., fruit-stone — L. *nucālis*, nutlike — *nux, nucis*, a nut.]

nozzle *noz'l, n* an outlet tube, or spout; an open end of a tube. [Dimin. of **nose.**]

NP *abbrev* for: new paragraph (also **np**); New Providence (Bahamas); Notary Public.

Np (*chem*) *symbol* for neptunium.

np *abbrev* for no place (of publication).

NPFA *abbrev* for National Playing Fields Association.

NPG *abbrev* for National Portrait Gallery.

NPL *abbrev* for National Physical Laboratory.

nr *abbrev* for near.

NRA *abbrev* for: National Rifle Association; National Rivers Authority.

NRDC *abbrev* for National Research Development Corporation.

NRPB *abbrev* for National Radiological Protection Board.

NS *abbrev* for: New Style; Nova Scotia (Can. province).

ns *abbrev* for: nanosecond(s); not specified.

NSAID *abbrev* for non-steroidal anti-inflammatory drug.

NSB *abbrev* for National Savings Bank.

NSPCC *abbrev* for National Society for the Prevention of Cruelty to Children.

NSRA *abbrev* for National Small-bore Rifle Association.

NSU *abbrev* for non-specific urethritis.

NSW *abbrev* for New South Wales (Austr.).

NT *abbrev* for: National Theatre; National Trust; New Testament; Northern Territory (Austr.); no trumps (*cards*).

-n't. Shortened (enclitic) form of **not.**

NTA *abbrev* for National Training Award.

nth. See under **N** (noun).

ntp *abbrev* for normal temperature and pressure.

NTS *abbrev* for National Trust for Scotland.

NU *abbrev* for name unknown.

Nu. *abbrev* for ngultrum (Bhutanese currency).

nu *nū* or *nü, n* the thirteenth letter (Ν, ν) of the Greek alphabet, corresponding to N. [Gr. *nȳ*.]

NUAAW *abbrev* for National Union of Agricultural and Allied Workers.

nuance *nū-äns'* or *nū'əns, n* a delicate degree or shade of difference. — *vt* to give nuances to. — *adj* **nuanced.** [Fr., — L. *nūbēs, nūbis*, a cloud.]

nub *nub, n* the point or gist. [Prob. from *knub*, a knob, small lump — Low Ger. *knubbe*, variant of *knobbe*, knob.]

nubbin *nub'in*, (*US*) *n* a small or underdeveloped ear of corn, fruit, etc. [Dimin. of old *nub*, knob, lump.]

nubile *nū'bīl* or *-bil, adj* (esp. of a woman) marriageable; sexually mature; sexually attractive. — *n* **nubility** (*-bil'i-ti*). [L. *nūbilis* — *nūbere*, to veil oneself, hence to marry.]

nuc. *abbrev* for nuclear.

nucha *nū'kə, n* the nape of the neck. — *adj* **nū'chal.** [L.L. *nucha* — Ar. *nukhā'*, spinal marrow.]

nuciferous *nū-sif'ər-əs*, (*bot*) *adj* nut-bearing. [L. *nux, nucis*, nut, *ferre*, to bear.]

nucivorous *nū-siv'ə-rəs*, (*zool*) *adj* nut-eating. [L. *nux, nucis*, nut, *vorāre*, to devour.]

nuclear *nū'kli-ər, adj* of, or of the nature of, a nucleus; pertaining to the nucleus of an atom or the nuclei of atoms; pertaining to, derived from, or powered by, the fission or fusion of atomic nuclei. — *vt* **nu'clearise** or **-ize** to make nuclear; to supply or fit with nuclear weapons. — *n* **nuclearisa'tion** or **-z-.** — **nuclear energy** energy released or absorbed during reactions taking place in atomic nuclei; **nuclear family** the basic family unit consisting of the mother and father with their children; **nuclear fission** spontaneous or induced splitting of an atomic nucleus; **nuclear fuel** material, such as uranium or plutonium, consumed to produce nuclear energy; **nuclear fusion** the creation of a new nucleus by merging two lighter ones, with the release of energy; **nuclear medicine** diagnosis and treatment of disease using radiation detectors or radioactive materials; **nuclear physics** the science of forces and transformations within the nucleus of the atom; **nuclear power** power obtained from a controlled nuclear reaction. — *adj* **nu'clear-powered.** — **nuclear reaction** a process in which an atomic nucleus interacts with another nucleus or particle, producing changes in energy and nuclear structure; **nuclear reactor** an assembly of fissile material with a moderator, in which a nuclear chain reaction is produced and maintained; the apparatus housing this; **nuclear threshold** the point in an armed conflict when nuclear weapons are resorted to; **nuclear warfare** warfare using nuclear weapons; **nuclear warhead; nuclear weapon** a bomb, missile, etc. deriving its destructive force from the energy released by a nuclear reaction; **nuclear winter** the period of lack of sunlight and resulting severe cold predicted by scientists as the aftermath of a nuclear war. — **nuclear-free zone** an area in which the transport, storage, manufacture and deployment of nuclear weapons, and the transport or disposal of nuclear waste, are officially prohibited; **nuclear magnetic resonance** resonance which can be produced in nuclei or most isotopes of the elements and which helps to identify the particular atoms involved. [**nucleus.**]

nuclease *nū'klē-āz, n* any of a number of enzymes inducing hydrolysis in nucleic acids. [**nucleus.**]

nucleate *nū'kli-āt, vt* and *vi* to form into, or group around, a nucleus. — *vt* to act, in a process of formation, as a nucleus for (e.g. crystals). — *adj* having a nucleus. — *n* **nuc'leation** the action or process of nucleating; seeding clouds to control rainfall and fog formation. [**nucleus.**]

nucleolus *nū-klē-ō'ləs, n* a body (sometimes two bodies) within a cell nucleus, indispensable to growth: — *pl* **nucleoli** (*nū-klē-ō'lī*). — *adj* **nu'cleolar.** — *adj* **nu'cleolate** or **nu'cleolated** having a nucleus or nucleolus; (of a spore) containing one or more conspicuous oil-drops. [**nucleus.**]

nucleon *nū'kli-on, n* a general name for a neutron or a proton. — *nsing* **nucleon'ics** nuclear physics, esp. its practical applications. — *n* **nucleoprot'ein** any of a group of compounds containing a protein molecule combined with a nuclein — important constituents of the nuclei of living cells. — *n* **nu'cleoside** a compound consisting of a purine or pyramidine base bound to a sugar (usu. ribose or deoxyribose). — *n* **nucleosyn'thesis** the process in which atomic nuclei bind together to form chemical elements (e.g. in stars). — *n* **nu'cleotide** a compound of a nucleoside and phosphoric acid, which forms the principal constituent of nucleic acid. [**nucleus.**]

nucleus *nū'kli-əs, n* a central mass or kernel; that around which something may grow; the densest part of a comet's head or a nebula; a rounded body in the protoplasm of a cell, the centre of its life (*biol*); the massive part of an atom, distinguished from the outlying electrons (*phys*); a stable group of atoms to which other atoms may be attached so as to form series of compounds (*phys*): — *pl* **nuclei** (*nū'kli-ī*). — *n* **nuclide** (*-klīd* or *klid*) a species of atom of any element distinguished by the number of neutrons and protons in its nucleus, and its energy state. — **nucleic acid** (*nū-klē'ik* or *-klā'-*) any of the complex acid components of nucleoproteins. [L., — *nux*, *nucis*, a nut.]

NUCPS *abbrev* for National Union of Civil and Public Servants.

nude *nūd*, *adj* naked; bare; without clothes; showing or involving naked or almost naked figures; without consideration (*law*) — *n* a nude figure or figures; the condition of being naked. — *adv* **nude'ly**. — *n* **nude'ness**. — *n* **nu'die** (*colloq*) naked or featuring nudity, esp. of films, shows, magazines, etc. — Also *n*. — *n* **nu'dism** the practice of going naked; (esp. *US*) naturism. — *n* **nu'dist** a person who goes naked, or approves of going naked; (esp. *US*) a naturist. — Also *adj*. — *n* **nu'dity** the state of being nude. [L. *nūdus*, naked.]

nudge *nuj*, *n* a gentle poke or push, as with the elbow. — *vt* to poke or push gently, esp. to draw someone's attention to something. — **nudge, nudge** or **nudge, nudge, wink, wink** (*colloq*) imputing some disreputable practice or indicating a sexual innuendo. — Also **nudge-nudge'**. [Perh. connected with Norw. *nugge*, to rub.]

nudibranch *nū'di-brănch*, *n* a shell-less marine gastropod with gills exposed on the back and sides of the body. [L. *nudus*, naked, *branchia*, gills.]

nugatory *nū'gə-tə-ri*, *adj* trifling; worthless; inoperative; unavailing; futile. — *n* **nu'gatoriness**. [L. *nūgātōrius* — *nūgae*, trifles, trumpery.]

nuggar *nug'ər*, *n* a large boat used to carry cargo on the Nile. [Ar. *nuqqār*.]

nugget *nug'it*, *n* a lump, esp. of gold; anything small but valuable (*fig*). — *adj* **nugg'ety** (*Austr*) stocky, thickset.

NUGMW *abbrev* for National Union of General and Municipal Workers.

NUI *abbrev* for National University of Ireland.

nuisance *nū'səns*, *n* something which annoys or hurts, esp. if there is some legal remedy; something which is offensive to the senses; a person or thing that is troublesome or obtrusive in some way. [Fr., — L. *nocēre*, to hurt.]

NUJ *abbrev* for National Union of Journalists.

nuke *nūk*, (*slang*) *n* a nuclear weapon. — *vt* to attack using nuclear weapons. [Contr. of **nuclear**.]

null *nul*, *adj* of no legal force; void; invalid; having no significance; amounting to nothing. — *n* **null'ity** the state of being null or void; something without legal force or validity; lack of existence, force or efficacy. — *n* **null'ness**. [L. *nūllus*, not any, from *ne*, not, *ūllus*, any.]

nullah *nul'ə*, *n* a ravine; a watercourse; a stream or drain. [Hind. *nālā*.]

nulla-nulla *nul'ə-nul'ə*, *n* an Australian Aborigine's wooden club. [Aboriginal.]

nullifidian *nul-i-fid'i-ən*, *adj* having no faith, esp. religious. — *n* a person who has no faith. [L. *nūllus*, none, *fidēs*, faith.]

nullify *nul'i-fī*, *vt* to make null; to annul; to make void or of no force: — *pr p* **null'ifying**; *pa t* and *pa p* **null'ified**. — *n* **nullification** (*-fi-kā'shən*). — *n* **null'ifier** (*-fī-ər*). [L.L. *nūllificāre* — *nūllus*, none, *facěre*, to make.]

nullipara *nul-ip'ə-rə*, *n* a woman who has never given birth to a child, esp. if she is not a virgin. — *adj* **nullip'arous**. — *n* **nulliparity** (*-i-par'i-ti*). [L. *nūllus*, none, *parěre*, to bring forth.]

nullipore *nul'i-pōr*, *n* a coralline seaweed. [L. *nūllus*, none, *porus*, a passage, pore.]

nullity, nullness. See **null**.

NUM *abbrev* for National Union of Mineworkers.

Num. or **Numb.** (*Bible*) *abbrev* for (the Book of) Numbers.

numb *num*, *adj* having diminished power of sensation or motion; powerless to feel or act; stupefied. — *vt* to make numb; to deaden: — *pr p* **numbing** (*num'ing*); *pa t* and *pa p* **numbed** (*numd*). — *n* **numb'ness**. — **numbskull** see **numskull**. [O.E. *numen*, past participle of *niman*, to take.]

numbat *num'bat*, *n* a small Australian marsupial which feeds on termites. [Aboriginal.]

number *num'bər*, *n* that by which single things are counted or reckoned; quantity reckoned in units; a particular value or sum of single things or units; a representation in arithmetical symbols of such a value or sum; a full complement; a specified or recognised set, class or group; some or many of the persons or things in question (often in *pl*); more than one; numerousness; (in *pl*) numerical superiority; numerability; a numerical indication of a thing's place in a series, or one assigned to it for reference, as in a catalogue; a label or other object bearing such an indication; a person or thing marked or designated in such a way; an item; an issue of a periodical or serial publication; a self-contained portion of an opera or other composition; arithmetical faculty; (in *pl*) rhythm, verses, music; the property in words of expressing singular and plural (*gram*); a single item in a programme, esp. of popular music and/or variety turns; (with *cap*, in *pl*) the fourth book of the Old Testament, in which an account of a census is given. — *vt* to count; to apportion; to have lived through; to reckon as one; (also *vi*) to mark with a number or assign a number to; (also *vi*) to amount to. — *n* **num'berer**. — *adj* **num'berless** without number; more than can be counted. — **number cruncher** (*slang*) a computer designed to carry out large quantities of complex numerical calculations; **number crunching**; **number one** chief, most important; the first in the numbered series; self, oneself (*slang*); lieutenant, first officer (under the rank of commander; *naut slang*); **number plate** the plaque on a motor vehicle showing its registration number; **numbers game, pool** or **racket** (*US*) an illegal form of gambling in which players bet on the appearance of a chosen sequence of numbers in the financial pages of a newspaper, etc.; **number system** (*math*) any set of elements which has two binary operations called addition and multiplication, each of which is commutative and associative, and which is such that multiplication is distributive with respect to addition; **number ten** (*colloq*; also with *caps*) 10 Downing Street, official residence of the British Prime Minister; **number two** second-in-command. — **any number of** many; **beyond** or **without number** too many to be counted; **by numbers** (of a procedure, etc.) performed in simple stages, each stage being identified by a number; **have** or **get someone's number** to size someone up; **his (**or **her) number is up** he (or she) is doomed, has not long to live; **one's (**or **its) days are numbered** one's (or its) end is imminent. [Fr. *nombre* — L. *numerus*.]

numdah *num'dä*, *n* an embroidered felt rug made in India. [Cf. **numnah**.]

numen *nū'men*, *n* a presiding deity: — *pl* **nu'mina** (*-min-ə*). [L. *nūmen*, *-inis*, divinity.]

numerable *nū'mər-ə-bl*, *adj* that may be numbered or counted. — *n* **numerabil'ity**. — *adv* **nu'merably**. — *n* **nu'meracy** the state of being numerate. — *adj* **nu'meral** pertaining to, consisting of, or expressing number. — *n* a figure or mark used to express a number, such as 1, 2, I, V, etc.; a word used to denote a number (*gram*). — *vt* **nu'merate** (*-āt*) to read off as numbers (from figures). — *adj* (*-ət*) having some understanding of mathematics and science; able to solve arithmetical problems; (see also **innumerate**). — Also *n*. — *n* **numerā'tion.** — *n* **nu'merātor** a person who or thing which numbers; the upper number of a vulgar fraction, which expresses the number of fractional parts taken. — *adj* **numeric** (*-mer'ik*) or **numer'ical** belonging to, expressed in, or consisting in, number; in number independently of sign. — *adv* **numer'ically.** — *n* **numerol'ogy** the study of numbers as supposed to show future events. — *adj* **nu'merous** many; consisting of or pertaining to a large number. — *adv* **nu'merously.** — *n* **nu'merousness.** — **numerical analysis** the study of methods of approximation and their accuracy, etc.; **numerical control** automatic control of operation of machine tools by means of numerical data stored on magnetic or punched tape or on punched cards. [L. *numerus*, number.]

numinous *nū'min-əs*, *adj* pertaining to a divinity; suffused with feeling of a divinity. — *n* **nu'minousness.** [L. *nūmen*, *-inis*, divinity.]

numismatic *nū-miz-mat'ik*, *adj* pertaining to money, coins or medals. — *nsing* **numismat'ics** the study or collection of coins and medals. — *n* **numis'matist.** — *n* **numismatol'ogist.** — *n* **numismatol'ogy.** [L. *numisma* — Gr. *nomisma*, current coin — *nomizein*, to use commonly — *nomos*, custom.]

nummary *num'ə-ri*, *adj* relating to coins or money. — *adj* **numm'ūlar** coin-shaped. — *n* **numm'ūlite** a large coin-shaped fossil marine rhizopod, forming limestones. — *adj* **nummūlitic** (*-lit'ik*). [L. *nummus*, a coin.]

numnah *num'nə*, *n* a felt, sheepskin, or quilted cloth or pad placed under a saddle to prevent chafing. [Hind. *namdā*.]

numskull or **numbskull** *num'skul*, *n* a blockhead. [**numb** and **skull**.]

nun *nun*, *n* a female member of a religious order, esp. one who has taken her final vows; a kind of pigeon with feathers on its head like a nun's hood. — *n* **nunn'ery** a house for nuns. — *adj* **nunn'ish.** — *n* **nunn'ishness.** — **nun's-veil'ing** a thin, soft woollen dress-material. [O.E. *nunne* — L.L. *nunna*, *nonna*, a nun, orig. mother.]

nunatak *nōō'na-tak*, *n* a point of rock appearing above the surface of land-ice. [Eskimo.]

nunc dimittis *nungk di-mit'tis*, *n* (also with *caps*) the song of Simeon (from the Bible: Luke ii. 29–32) in the R.C. Breviary and the Anglican evening service. [From the opening words, *nunc dīmittis*, now lettest thou depart.]

nunchaku *nun-cha'kōō*, *n* a weapon consisting of two short thick sticks joined by a length of chain. [Jap.]

nuncio *nun'shi-ō*, *n* an ambassador from the pope: — *pl* **nun'cios.** — *n* **nun'ciature** a nuncio's office or term of office. [It. (now *nunzio*) — L. *nūntius*, a messenger.]

nuncupate *nung'kū-pāt*, *vt* to declare (a will) orally. — *n* **nuncūpā'tion.** — *adj* **nunc'ūpātive.** [L. *nuncupāre*, to call by name — prob. from *nōmen*, name, *capĕre*, to take.]

nunnery. See **nun.**

nuoc mam *nwok mäm*, *n* a spicy sauce made from raw fish. [Viet.]

NUPE *nū'pē*, *abbrev* for National Union of Public Employees.

nuptial *nup'shəl*, *adj* pertaining to marriage; pertaining to mating (*zool*). — *n* (usu. in *pl*) marriage; wedding ceremony. — *n* **nuptiality** (*-shi-al'i-ti*) nuptial character or quality; marriage-rate; (in *pl*) wedding ceremonies and festivities. [L. *nuptiālis* — *nuptiae*, marriage — *nubĕre*, *nuptum*, to marry.]

NUR *abbrev* for National Union of Railwaymen.

nurd. See **nerd.**

nurl. See **knurl.**

nurse[1] *nûrs*, *n* a woman who suckles a child; one who tends a child; a person who has the care of the sick, feeble or injured, or who is trained for the purpose; a worker bee, ant, etc., that tends the young; someone who or that which feeds, rears, tends, saves, fosters or develops anything, or preserves it in any desired condition; the state of being nursed (in the phrases *at nurse*, *out to nurse*). — *vt* to suckle; to tend (e.g. an infant or a sick person); to bring up; to cherish; to manage with care and economy; to play skilfully, manipulate carefully, keep watchfully in touch with, in order to obtain or preserve the desired condition; to hold or carry as a nurse does a child. — *adj* **nurse'like.** — *n* **nurse'ling** or **nurs'ling** that which is nursed or fostered; an infant. — *n* **nurs'er.** — **nurse'maid** a maid servant who takes care of children; **nur'sing-chair** a low chair without arms, used when feeding a baby; **nursing home** a private hospital; **nursing officer** any of several grades of nurses having administrative duties. — **put (or put out) to nurse** to put (a baby) into the care of a nurse, usu. away from home; to put (an estate) under trustees. [O.Fr. *norrice* (Fr. *nourrice*) — L. *nūtrīx*, *-īcis* — *nūtrīre*, to nourish.]

nurse[2] *nûrs*, *n* a shark; a dogfish. — **nurse'-hound** a European dogfish (*Scylliorhinus caniculus*); **nurse shark** any shark of the family *Orectolobidae*. [Earlier *nuss*, perh. for (*an*) *huss*, *husk*, a dogfish.]

nursery *nûr'sə-ri*, *n* a room in a house set aside for children; a place providing residential or day-care for young children; a place where young animals are reared, or where the growth of anything is promoted; a place where plants are reared for sale or transplanting; a race for two-year-old horses (also called **nursery stakes**). — *adj* pertaining to a nursery, or to early training. — **nursery cannon** (*billiards*) a cannon (esp. one of a series) with the three balls close together and being moved as little as possible; **nur'serymaid** a nursemaid; **nur'seryman** a man who owns or works in a nursery for plants; **nursery nurse** a person trained in the care of young children, employed in a nursery; **nursery rhyme** a traditional rhyme or song known to children; **nursery school** a school for very young children (aged two to five). — *npl* **nursery slopes** slopes set apart for novice skiers. [**nurse**[1].]

nurture *nûr'chər*, *n* upbringing; rearing; training; whatever is derived from the individual's experience, training, environment, distinguished from *nature*, or what is inherited; food. — *vt* to nourish; to bring up; to educate. — *adj* **nur'tural.** — *adj* **nur'turant.** — *n* **nur'turer.** [O.Fr. *noriture* (Fr. *nourriture*) — L.L. *nūtritūra* — L. *nūtrīre*, to nourish.]

NUS *abbrev* for: National Union of Seamen; National Union of Students.

NUT *abbrev* for National Union of Teachers.

nut *nut*, *n* popularly, any fruit with an edible seed in a hard shell; a hard dry indehiscent fruit formed from a syncarpous gynaeceum (*bot*); often the hazelnut, sometimes the walnut; the head (*slang*); a hard-headed person, one difficult to deal with, a tough; a crazy person (also **nut'case**; *slang*); a small block, usu. of metal, for screwing on the end of a bolt; an en (*printing*); the ridge at the top of the fingerboard on a fiddle, etc. (*mus*); the mechanism for tightening or slackening a bow (*mus*); a small lump of coal; a small biscuit or round cake; (in *pl*) the testicles (*slang*). — *vi* to look for and gather nuts. — *vt* to butt with the head (*slang*): — *pr p* **nutt'ing**; *pa t* and *pa p* **nutt'ed.** — *adj* **nuts** crazy (*slang*). — Also *interj* expressing defiance, contempt, disappointment, etc. — *n* **nutt'er** a person who gathers nuts; a crazy person (*slang*). — *n* **nutt'ery** an area of nut-trees; a mental hospital (*slang*). — *n* **nutt'iness.** — *n* **nutt'ing** the gathering of nuts. — *adj* **nutt'y** abounding in nuts; having the flavour of nuts; mentally unhinged (*slang*). — *adj* **nut'-brown** brown, like a ripe hazelnut. — **nut butter** a butter-substitute or spread made from nuts; **nut'cracker** a bird (*Nucifraga*) of the crow family which feeds on nuts and pine seeds; (usu. in *pl*) an instrument for cracking nuts. — *adj* like a pair of nutcrackers, e.g. toothless jaws. — **nut-cracker man** a type of early man found in Tanzania in 1959, by some distinguished as a separate species *Zinjanthropus*; **nut'-gall** a nutlike gall, produced by a gall wasp, chiefly on the oak; **nut'hatch** any of various birds of the family *Sittidae* that hack nuts and seek insects on the bark of trees; **nut'house** (*slang*) a mental hospital; a place where people's behaviour is crazy; **nut oil** an oil obtained from walnuts or other nuts; **nut'-pine** the stone-pine or other species with large edible seeds; **nut'shell** the hard covering of a nut; **nut'-tree** any tree bearing nuts, esp. the hazel; **nut'-weevil** a weevil whose larvae live on hazelnuts. — **a (hard) nut to crack** a difficult problem; **be nuts on** or **about** (*slang*) to be very fond of; **do one's nut** (*slang*) to become extremely angry, to rage; **in a nutshell** in very small space; briefly, concisely; **not for nuts** (*colloq*) not very well, incompetently; **nuts and bolts** the basic facts, the essential, practical details; **off one's nut** (*slang*) mentally unhinged, crazy. [O.E. *hnutu*.]

nutant *nū'tənt*, *adj* nodding; drooping. — *vi* **nutate'** to nod; to droop; to perform a nutation. — *n* **nutā'tion** a nodding; a fluctuation in the precessional movement of the earth's pole about the pole of the ecliptic (*astron*); the sweeping out of a curve by the tip of a growing axis (*bot*). — *adj* **nutā'tional.** [L. *nūtāre*, to nod.]

nutmeg *nut'meg*, *n* the aromatic kernel of an East Indian tree, much used as a seasoning in cookery. — *adj* **nut'meggy.** [M.E. *notemuge* — **nut** and inferred O.Fr. *mugue*, musk — L. *muscus*, musk.]

nutria *nū'tri-ə*, *n* the coypu; its fur. [Sp. *nutria*, otter — L. *lutra*.]

nutrient *nū'tri-ənt*, *adj* feeding; nourishing. — *n* any nourishing substance. — *n* **nu'triment** that which nourishes; food. — *adj* **nutrimental** (*-men'tl*). — *n* **nutri'tion** the act or process of nourishing; food. — *adj* **nutri'tional.** — *n* **nutri'tionist** an expert in foods and their nutritional values. — *adj* **nutri'tious** nourishing. — *adv* **nutri'tiously.** — *n* **nutri'tiousness.** — *adj* **nu'tritive** nourishing; concerned in nutrition. — *adv* **nu'tritively.** [L. *nūtrīre*, to nourish.]

nux vomica *nuks vom'ik-ə*, *n* a seed that yields strychnine; the East Indian tree (*Strychnos nux-vomica*) that produces it; the drug made from it. [L. *nux*, a nut, *vomĕre*, to vomit.]

nuzzle *nuz'l*, *vt* and *vi* to poke, press, burrow, root, rub, sniff, caress or investigate with the nose. — *vt* to thrust in (the nose or head). — *vi* to snuggle. [Frequentative verb from **nose**.]

NV *abbrev* for: Nevada (U.S. state); new version.

NVALA or **NVLA** *abbrev* for National Viewers' and Listeners' Association.

nvd *abbrev* for no value declared.

NW *abbrev* for north-west.

NWT *abbrev* for Northwest Territories (Can.).

NY *abbrev* for New York (U.S. city or state).

nyala *n-yä'lə*, *n* a large South African antelope. [Bantu *(i)nyala*.]

NYC *abbrev* for New York City.

nyctalopia *nik-tə-lō'pi-ə*, *n* properly, night-blindness, abnormal difficulty in seeing in a faint light; by confusion sometimes, day-blindness. — *adj* **nyct-alōp'ic.** [Gr. *nyktalōps*, night-blind, day-blind — *nyx*, *nyktos*, night, *alaos*, blind, *ōps*, eye, face.]

nyctitropism *nik-tit'ro-pizm*, *n* the assumption by plants of certain positions at night. — *adj* **nyctitropic** (*-trop'*). [Gr. *nyx*, *nyktos*, night, *tropos*, turning.]

nyctophobia *nik-tō-fō'bi-ə*, *n* morbid fear of the night or of darkness. [Gr. *nyx*, *nyktos*, night, and **phobia**.]

nylon *nī'lən* or *-lon*, *n* any of numerous polymeric amides that can be formed into fibres, bristles or sheets; any material made from nylon filaments or fibres; a stocking made of nylon. [Invented by the original manufacturers.]

nymph *nimf*, *n* one of the divinities who lived in mountains, rivers, trees, etc. (*mythol*); a young and beautiful maiden (often *ironic*); an immature insect, similar to the adult but with wings and sex-organs undeveloped. — *npl* **nymphae** (*-ē*) the labia minora. — *adj* **nymph'al.** — *adj* **nymphē'an.** — *n* **nymph'et** a young nymph; a sexually attractive and precocious young girl. — *adj* **nymph'-like.** — *n* **nymph'o** (*colloq*) a nymphomaniac: — *pl* **nym'-phos.** — *n* **nymph'olepsy** a species of ecstasy or frenzy said to have seized those who had seen a nymph; a yearning for the unattainable. — *n* **nymph'olept** a person so affected. — *adj* **nym-pholept'ic.** — *n* **nymphomā'nia** morbid and uncontrollable sexual desire in women. — *n* and *adj* **nymphomā'niac.** [L. *nympha* — Gr. *nymphē*, a bride, a nymph.]

NYO *abbrev* for National Youth Orchestra.

nystagmus *nis-tag'məs*, *n* a spasmodic, involuntary lateral oscillatory movement of the eyes. — *adj* **nystag'mic** or **nystag'moid.** [Latinised from Gr. *nystagmos* — *nystazein*, to nap.]

NZ *abbrev* for New Zealand (also I.V.R.).

NZBC *abbrev* for New Zealand Broadcasting Corporation.

NZPA *abbrev* for New Zealand Press Association.

O

O[1] or **o** *ō*, *n* the fifteenth letter of the modern English alphabet; (in telephone, etc., jargon) nought or nothing: — *pl* **Oes, O's, oes** or **o's** (*ōz*). — **O'-grade** or **Ordinary Grade** in Scotland, (a pass in) a former examination taken at the end of the 4th year of secondary education; **O'-level** or **Ordinary level** esp. in England and Wales, (a pass in) an examination generally taken at the end of the 5th year of secondary education. — Also *adj.*

O[2] or **oh** *ō*, *interj* used in addressing or apostrophising, marking the occurrence of a thought, reception of information, or expressing wonder, admiration, disapprobation, surprise, protest, pain, or other emotion.

O or **O.** *abbrev* for: Ohio (U.S. state); an ABO blood group.

O *ō* (*chem*) *symbol* for oxygen.

O- (*chem*) *pfx* signifying ortho-.

o' or **o** *ō* or *ə*, a shortened form of **of** and **on**.

-o (*colloq*) *sfx* used to form diminutives and abbreviations, e.g. *wino*, *aggro*.

oaf *ōf*, *n* an idiot or lout: — *pl* **oafs.** — *adj* **oaf'ish** idiotic, doltish; loutish. [O.N. *ālfr*, elf.]

oak *ōk*, *n* a genus (*Quercus*) of trees of the beech family; its timber, valued in shipbuilding, etc.; extended to various other trees, such as **poison-oak, she-oak** (qq.v.). — *adj* made of oak. — *adj* **oak'en** of oak. — *adj* **oak'y** like oak, firm; abounding in oaks. — **oak apple** a gall caused by an insect on an oak; **oak'-gall** a gall produced on the oak; **oak'-mast** acorns collectively; **oak'-nut** a gall on the oak; **oak'-tree**; **oak wilt** a serious fungal disease of oak trees, causing wilting and discoloration of foliage; **oak'-wood.** [O.E. *āc*.]

oakum *ōk'əm*, *n* old (usu. tarred) ropes untwisted and teased out for caulking the seams of ships. [O.E. *ācumba* (*æcumbe*) from *ā-*, away from, and the root of *cemban*, to comb.]

O & M *abbrev* for organisation and method(s).

OAP *abbrev* for old age pensioner.

oar *ör*, *n* a light pole with a blade at one end for propelling a boat; a swimming organ; an oarsman or oarswoman. — *vt* to impel as by rowing. — *vi* to row. — *adj* **oared** provided with oars. — *adj* **oar'less.** — *adj* **oar'y** having the form or use of oars. — **oar fish** a ribbon-fish (*Regalecus*). — *adj* **oar'-footed** having swimming feet. — **oars'man** or **oars'woman** a (male or female) rower; a man or woman skilled in rowing; **oars'manship** skill in rowing. — **lie** or **rest on one's oars** to abstain from rowing without removing the oars from the rowlocks; to rest, take things easily; to cease working; **put one's oar in** to interpose when not asked. [O.E. *ār*.]

OAS *abbrev* for Organization of American States.

oasis *ō-ā'sis*, *n* a fertile spot or tract in a sandy desert; any place of rest or pleasure in the midst of toil and gloom; (with *cap*; ®) a block of soft permeable material used to hold cut flowers, etc. in place in a flower arrangement: — *pl* **oa'ses** (*-sēz*). [Gr. *oasis*, an Egyptian word; cf. Coptic *ouahe*.]

oast *ōst*, *n* a kiln to dry hops or malt. — *n* **oast house.** [O.E. *āst*.]

oat *ōt* (more often in *pl* **oats** *ōts*), *n* a well-known genus (*Avena*) of grasses (esp. *A. sativa*) whose seeds are much used as food; its seeds. — *adj* **oat'en** consisting of an oat stem or straw; made of oatmeal. — **oat'cake** a hard dry biscuit made with oatmeal; **oat grass** a grass of *Avena* or similar genus used more as fodder than for the seed; **oat'meal** meal made of oats. — *adj* of the colour of oatmeal. — **feel one's oats** to be frisky or assertive; **get one's oats** (*slang*) to have sexual intercourse; **off one's oats** without appetite, off one's food (*colloq*); **sow one's wild oats** to indulge in youthful dissipation or excesses. [O.E. *āte*, pl. *ātan*.]

oath *ōth*, *n* a solemn appeal to a god or something holy or reverenced as witness or sanction of the truth of a statement; the form of words used; a more or less similar expression used lightly, exclamatorily, decoratively, or in imprecation; a swear-word; a curse: — *pl* **oaths** (*ōdhz*). — **on, under** or **upon oath** sworn to speak the truth; attested by oath; **take an oath** to pledge formally. [O.E. *āth*.]

OAU *abbrev* for Organization of African Unity.

OB *abbrev* for: Old Boy; outside broadcast.

Obad. (*Bible*) *abbrev* for (the Book of) Obadiah.

obbligato *ob-li-gä'tō* or *ob-bli-*, *n* a musical accompaniment of independent importance, esp. that of a single instrument to a vocal piece: — *pl* **obbliga'tos** or **obbliga'ti** (*-tē*). [It.]

obcompressed *ob'kəm-prest*, (*bot*) *adj* flattened from front to back. [L. pfx. *ob-*, towards; in mod. L., in the opposite direction, reversed.]

obconic *ob-kon'ik* or **obconical** *-kon'ik-əl*, (*bot*) *adj* conical and attached by the point. [L. pfx. *ob-*, as in **obcompressed.**]

obcordate *ob-kör'dāt*, (*bot*) *adj* inversely heart-shaped, as a leaf. [L. pfx. *ob-*, as in **obcompressed.**]

obdurate *ob'dū-rāt*, *adj* hardened in heart or in feelings; difficult to influence, esp. in a moral sense; stubborn; hard. — *n* **ob'dūracy** the state of being obdurate; invincible hardness of heart. — *adv* **ob'dūrately.** — *n* **ob'dūrateness.** [L. *obdūrāre*, *-ātum* — *ob-* (intensive) against, *dūrāre*, to harden — *dūrus*, hard.]

OBE *abbrev* for (Officer of the) Order of the British Empire.

obeah. See **obi**[1].

obedience *ō-bē'dyəns* or *-di-əns*, *n* the act or practice of doing what one is told; the state of being obedient; willingness to obey commands; dutifulness. — *adj* **obē'dient** obeying; ready to obey. — *adv* **obē'diently.** [L. *obēdientia*; see **obey.**]

obeisance *ō-bā'səns*, *n* a bow or act of reverence; an expression of respect. — *adj* **obei'sant.** [Fr. *obéissance* — *obéir* — L. root as **obey.**]

obelisk *ob'ə-lisk*, *n* a tall, four-sided, tapering pillar, usually of one stone, topped with a pyramid; an obelus. [**obelus.**]

obelus *ob'i-ləs*, *n* a sign (— or ÷) used in ancient manuscripts to mark suspected, corrupt or spurious words and passages; a dagger-sign (†) used esp. in referring to footnotes (**double obelus** ‡; *printing*): — *pl* **ob'eli** (*-lī*). [L. — Gr. *obelos* (dimin. *obeliskos*), a spit.]

obese *ō-bēs'*, *adj* abnormally fat. — *n* **obese'ness** or **obesity** (*-bēs'* or *-bes*). [L. *obēsus* — *ob-*, completely, *edĕre*, *ēsum*, to eat.]

obey *ō-bā'*, *vi* to render obedience; to do what one is told; to be governed or controlled. — *vt* to do as told by; to comply with; to be controlled by. [Fr. *obéir* — L. *obēdīre* — *ob-*, towards, *audīre*, to hear.]

obfuscate *ob-fus'kāt*, *vt* to darken; to obscure. — *n* **obfuscā'tion.** — *adj* **obfusca'tory.** [L. *obfuscāre*, *-ātum* — *ob-* (intensive) and *fuscus*, dark.]

obi[1] *ō'bi* or **obeah** *ō'bi-ə*, *n* witchcraft and poisoning practised by Negroes of the West Indies, Guyana, etc.; a fetish or charm. — **o'bi-man; o'bi-woman.** [Of W.Afr. origin.]

obi[2] *ō'bi*, *n* a broad sash worn with a kimono by the Japanese. [Jap. — *obiru*, to wear.]

obit *ob'it* or *ō'bit*, *n* an anniversary or other commemoration of a death; short for **obituary**.

obiter *ōb'it-ər* or *ob'it-er*, (L.) *adv* by the way, cursorily. — **obiter dictum** (*dik'təm* or *-tŏŏm*) something said by the way, a cursory remark: — *pl* **obiter dicta** (*dik'ta*).

obituary *ə-bit'ū-ə-ri*, *adj* relating to or recording the death of a person or persons. — *n* an account of a deceased person; an announcement of someone's death; a collection of death-notices. [L.L. *obitus* — *obīre*, *-itum*, to die — *ob*, in the way of, *īre*, to go.]

obj. *abbrev* for: object; objective.

object *ob'jikt*, *n* a material thing; that which is thought of, regarded as being outside, different from, or independent of, the mind (opposed to *subject*); that upon which attention, interest, or some emotion is fixed; an oddity or deplorable spectacle; that towards which action or desire is directed, an end; part of a sentence denoting that upon which the action of a transitive verb is directed, or standing in an analogous relation to a preposition (*gram*). — *vt* (*əb-jekt'*) to offer in opposition; to bring as an accusation. — *vi* to be opposed, feel or express disapproval (with *to*, *that*, *against*); to refuse assent. — *n* **objectificā'tion** (*-jekt-*). — *vt* **object'ify** to make objective. — *n* **objec'tion** an act of objecting; anything said or done in opposition; argument or reason against (with *to* or *against*); inclination to object, dislike, unwillingness. — *adj* **objec'tionable** capable of being objected to; requiring to be disapproved of; distasteful. — *adv* **objec'tionably.** — *adj* **object'ive** relating to or constituting an object; of the nature of, or belonging to, that which is presented to consciousness (opposed to *subjective*), exterior to the mind, self-existent, regarding or setting forth what is external, actual, practical, uncoloured by one's own sensations or emotions; denoting the object (*gram*); in the relation of object to a verb or preposition (*gram*); objecting; (of lenses) nearest the object. — *n* the case of the grammatical object; a word in that case (*gram*); an object-glass; the point to which the operations (esp. of an army) are directed; a goal, aim. — *adv* **object'ively.** — *n* **object'iveness.** — *vt* **object'ivise** or **-ize** to objectify. — *n* **object'ivism** a tendency to lay stress on what is objective; a theory that gives priority to the objective. — *n* **object'ivist.** — *adj* **object-ivist'ic.** — *n* **objectiv'ity.** — *adj* **ob'jectless** having no object; purposeless. — *n* **object'or.** — **ob'ject-finder** a device in microscopes for locating an object in the field before examination by a higher power; **ob'ject-glass** in an optical instrument, the lens or combination of lenses at the end next to the object; **objective test** a test or examination in which every question is set in such a way as to have only one right answer; **ob'ject-lesson** a lesson in which a material object is before the class; a warning or instructive experience; **money,** etc. **no object** money, etc., not being an obstacle or a problem; **object of virtu** an article valued for its antiquity or as an example of craftsmanship, etc. [L. *objectus*, past p. of *ob(j)icĕre*, or partly the noun *objectus*, *-ūs* (found in the abl.), or the frequentative verb *objectāre* — *ob*, in the way of, *jacĕre*, to throw.]

objet *ob-zhā*, (Fr.) *n* an object. — **objet d'art** (*där*) an article with artistic value; **objet de vertu** (*də ver-tü*) a Gallicised (by the English) version of object of virtu (q.v.); **objet trouvé** (*trŏŏ-vā*) a natural or man-made object displayed as a work of art: — *pl* **objets** (*-zhā*) **d'art, de vertu** and **trouvés** (*-vā*).

objure *ob-jŏŏr'*, *vi* to swear. — *vt* to bind by oath; to charge or entreat solemnly. — *n* **objurā'tion** the act of binding by oath; a solemn charge. [L. *objūrāre*, to bind by oath — *ob-*, down, *jūrāre*, to swear.]

objurgate *ob'jər-gāt* or *-jûr'*, *vt* and *vi* to chide. — *n* **objurgā'tion.** [L. *objurgāre*, *-ātum*, to rebuke — *ob-* (intensive) and *jurgāre*, to chide.]

obl. *abbrev* for: oblique; oblong.

oblanceolate *ob-län'si-ō-lāt*, (*bot*) *adj* like a lance-head reversed, as a leaf — about three times as long as broad, tapering more gently towards base than apex. [Pfx. *ob-*, as in **obcompressed.**]

oblast *ob'läst*, *n* an administrative district of the Soviet Union. [Russ.]

oblate[1] *ob'lāt* or *ob-lāt'*, *adj* dedicated; offered up. — *n* a dedicated person, esp. one dedicated to monastic life but not professed, or to a religious life. — *n* **oblā'tion** an act of offering; a sacrifice; anything offered in worship, esp. a eucharistic offering; an offering generally. [L. *oblātus*, offered up, used as past p. of *offerre*, to offer; see ety. for **offer.**]

oblate[2] *ob'lāt*, *adj* flattened at opposite sides or poles, as a spheroid is, — shaped like an orange (opp. to *prolate*). — *n* **ob'lateness.** [On analogy of **pro-late;** L. pfx. *ob-*, against, or (N.L.) in the opposite direction.]

oblige *ə-* or *ō-blīj'*, *vt* to bind morally or legally; to constrain; to bind by some favour rendered, hence to do a favour to. — *vi* (*colloq*) to do something as a favour. — *vt* **ob'ligate** (*-li-gāt*) to bind by contract or duty; to bind by gratitude. — *n* **obligation** (*ob-li-gā'shən*) act of obliging; a moral or legal bond, tie, or binding power; that to which one is bound; a debt of gratitude; a favour; a bond containing a penalty in case of failure (*law*). — *adv* **obligatorily** (*o-blig'ə-tər-i-li*). — *n* **oblig'atoriness.** — *adj* **oblig'atory** (or *ob'lig-* or *əb-*) binding; imposing duty; imposed as an obligation; obligate. — *n* **oblige'ment** a favour conferred. — *adj* **oblīg'ing** disposed to confer favours; ready to do a good turn; courteous. — *adv* **oblīg'ingly.** — *n* **oblīg'ingness.** [Fr. *obliger* — L. *obligāre*, *-ātum* — *ob-*, down, *ligāre*, to bind.]

oblique *ō-* or *ə-blēk'*, *adj* slanting; neither perpendicular nor parallel; not at right angles; not parallel to an axis; not straightforward; indirect; underhand; not a right angle (*geom*); having the axis not perpendicular to the plane of the base; asymmetrical about the midrib (*bot*); monoclinic (*crystall*). — *n* an oblique line, figure, muscle, etc.; an oblique movement or advance, esp. one about 45° from the original direction. — *vi* to advance obliquely by facing half right or left and then advancing. — *n* **obliqueness** (*-blēk'*) or **obliquity** (*ob-lik'wi-ti*) state of being oblique; a slanting direction; crookedness of outlook, thinking or conduct, or an instance of it. — *adv* **oblique'ly.** — **oblique case** (*gram*) any case other than nominative and vocative. [L. *oblīquus* — *ob-* (intensive) and the root of *līquis*, slanting.]

obliterate *ō-blit'ə-rāt*, *vt* to blot out, so as not to be readily or clearly readable; to efface. — *n* **oblit-erā'tion.** — *adj* **oblit'erative.** [L. *oblitterāre*, *-ātum* — *ob-*, over, *littera* (*lītera*), a letter.]

oblivion *əb-liv'i-ən*, *n* forgetfulness; a state of having forgotten; amnesty; a state of being forgotten. — *adj* **obliv'ious** forgetful; prone to forget; raptly or absent-mindedly unaware (with *of* or *to*). — *adv* **obliv'iously.** — *n* **obliv'iousness.** [L. *oblīviō*, *-ōnis*, from the root of *oblīvīscī*, to forget.]

oblong *ob'long*, *adj* long in one way; longer than broad; nearly elliptical, with sides nearly parallel, ends blunted, two to four times as long as broad (*bot*). — *n* a rectangle longer than broad; any oblong figure, whether angular or rounded. [L. *oblongus* — *ob-* (force obscure), and *longus*, long.]

obloquy *ob'lə-kwi*, *n* reproachful language, censure; calumny; disgrace. [L. *obloquium* — *ob*, against, *loquī*, to speak.]

obnoxious *ob-nok'shəs* or *əb-*, *adj* objectionable, offensive. — *adv* **obnox'iously**. — *n* **obnox'iousness**. [L. *obnoxius* — *ob*, exposed to, *noxa*, hurt.]

obo *ō'bō*, *n* a vessel designed to carry oil and bulk ore, together or separately: — *pl* **o'bos**. [From *o*il/ *b*ulk *o*re.]

oboe *ō'bō*, *n* a double-reed treble woodwind instrument; an organ stop of similar tone; a person who plays the oboe. — *n* **o'bōist** a player on the oboe. [It. *oboe* — Fr. *hautbois*.]

obol *ob'ol*, (*hist*) *n* in ancient Greece, the sixth part of a drachma in weight or in money. [Gr. *obolos*.]

obovate *ob-ō'vāt*, (*bot*) *adj* egg-shaped in outline, with the narrow end next to the base. [N.L. *ob-*, reversed, and **ovate**.]

obs. *abbrev* for: observation, as in **obs.** (*obz*) **ward** (*med*); obsolete.

obscene *ob-sēn'*, *adj* offensive to the senses or the sensibility, disgusting, repellent; indecent, esp. in a sexual sense; offending against an accepted standard of morals or taste; (of publications, etc.) tending to deprave or corrupt (*law*). — *adv* **obscene'ly**. — *n* **obscenity** (*-sen'* or *-sēn'*). [L. *obscēnus*.]

obscure *ob-skūr'*, *adj* dark; not distinct; not easily understood; not clear, legible or perspicuous; unknown; hidden; inconspicuous; not famous; living or enveloped in darkness. — *n* darkness; an obscure place; indistinctness. — *vt* to darken; to make dim; to hide; to make less plain; to render doubtful. — *vi* to become hidden; to darken. — *n* **obscūrant'ism** (or *-skūr'*) opposition to inquiry, reform or new knowledge. — *adj* **obscūrant'ist** (or *-skūr'*) pertaining to obscurantism. — *n* **obscūrā'tion**. — *adv* **obscūre'ly**. — *n* **obscūr'ity** state or quality of being obscure; state of being unknown or not famous; darkness; an obscure place, point or condition. [Fr. *obscur* — L. *obscūrus*.]

obsecrate *ob'si-krāt*, *vt* to beseech; to implore. — *n* **obsecrā'tion** supplication. [L. *obsecrāre*, *-ātum*, to entreat.]

obsequies *ob'si-kwiz*, *npl* funeral rites and solemnities. [L.L. *obsequiae*, a confusion of L. *exsequiae*, funeral rites, and *obsequium*; see next word.]

obsequious *ob-sē'kwi-əs*, *adj* servilely ingratiating; fawning. — *adv* **obsē'quiously**. — *n* **obsē'quiousness**. [L. *obsequiōsus*, compliant.]

observe *ob-zûrv'*, *vt* to keep in view, to watch, esp. systematically; to regard attentively; to watch critically and attentively in order to ascertain a fact; to ascertain by such watching; to notice; to pay attention to; to remark in words; to comply with or act according to; to heed and to carry out in practice; to keep or celebrate, esp. with ceremony; to keep (e.g. silence). — *vi* to take observations; to make remarks. — *adj* **observ'able** discernible, perceptible; worthy of note, notable; to be observed. — *adv* **observ'ably**. — *n* **observ'ance** the keeping of, or acting according to, a law, duty, custom or ceremony; the keeping with ceremony or according to custom; a custom observed or to be observed; a rule of religious life; a deferential act or treatment. — *n* **observ'ancy** observance; observation. — *adj* **observ'ant** observing; having powers of observing and noting; taking notice; keeping an observance; carefully attentive. — *adv* **observ'antly**. — *n* **observā'tion** the or an act of observing; habit, practice or faculty of seeing and noting; attention; the act of recognising and noting phenomena as they occur in nature, as distinguished from *experiment*; a reading of an instrument; the result of such observing; watching; that which is observed; a remark; the fact of being observed. — *adj* **observā'tional** consisting of or containing observations or remarks; derived from observation, as distinguished from *experiment*. — *adv* **observā'tionally**. — *adj* **observ'ative** observant; observational. — *n* **observ'atory** a building or station for making astronomical and physical observations; a viewpoint. — *n* **observ'er** a person who observes in any sense; a person whose function it is to take observations; formerly, an airman who accompanied a pilot to observe, now, a **flying officer** (q.v.); a member of the Royal Observer Corps, a uniformed civilian organisation affiliated to the Royal Air Force; someone deputed to watch proceedings. — *adj* **observ'ing** habitually taking notice; attentive. — **observation car** a railway carriage designed to allow passengers to view scenery; **observation post** a position (esp. military) from which observations are made (and from which artillery fire is directed). [Fr. *observer* — L. *observāre*, *-ātum* — *ob*, towards, *servāre*, to keep.]

obsess *ob-ses'*, *vt* to occupy the thoughts of obstinately and persistently. — *n* **obsession** (*-sesh'ən*) a fixed idea; morbid persistence of an idea in the mind, against one's will (*psychiatry*). — *adj* **obsess'ional**. — *n* **obsess'ionist** someone who is obsessed by a fixed idea. — *adj* **obsess'ive** relating to or resulting from obsession; obsessing. [L. *obsidēre*, *obsessum*, to besiege.]

obsidian *ob-sid'i-ən*, *n* a vitreous acid volcanic rock resembling bottle glass, a coarse green glass used in the making of bottles. [From *obsidiānus*, a wrong reading of L. *obsiānus* (*lapis*), a stone found by one *Obsius* (wrongly *Obsidius*) in Ethiopia, according to Pliny.]

obsolescent *ob-sə-les'ənt*, *adj* going out of use; in course of disappearing or becoming useless; tending to become obsolete. — *vi* **obsolesce** (*-les'*) to be in the process of going out of use. — *n* **obsolesc'ence**. — *adj* **ob'solete** (*-lēt*) gone out of use; antiquated; no longer functional or fully developed. — *adv* **ob'soletely**. — *n* **ob'soleteness**. — **planned obsolescence** the deterioration or the going out of date of a product according to a prearranged plan usu. involving its replacement. [L. *obsolēscĕre*, *obsolētum*, perh. from pfx. *obs-* (*ob-*, completeness) and the root of *alĕre*, to nourish.]

obstacle *ob'stə-kl*, *n* anything that stands in the way (of) or hinders advance. — **obstacle race** a race in which obstacles have to be passed, gone through, etc. [Fr., — L. *obstāculum* — *ob*, in the way of, *stāre*, to stand.]

obstetric *ob-stet'rik* or **obstetrical** *-stet'rik-əl*, *adj* pertaining to the care of women during pregnancy and childbirth. — *n* **obstetrician** (*ob-sti-trish'ən*) a man or woman skilled in practising, or qualified to practise, obstetrics. — *nsing* **obstet'rics** the science of midwifery. [L. *obstetrīcius* (the *-īc-* confused with the sfx. *-ic*) — *obstetrīx*, *-īcis*, a midwife — *ob*, before, *stāre*, to stand.]

obstinate *ob'sti-nit*, *adj* blindly or excessively firm; unyielding; stubborn; not easily subdued or remedied. — *n* **ob'stinacy** (*-nə-si*). — *n* **ob'stinateness**. — *adv* **ob'stinately**. [L. *obstināre*, *-ātum* — *ob*, in the way of, *stanāre* (found in compounds), a form of *stāre*, to stand.]

obstreperous *ob-strep'ə-rəs*, *adj* noisy; unruly; making a loud noise; clamorous. — *adv* **obstrep'erously**. — *n* **obstrep'erousness**. [L. *obstreperus* — *ob*, before, against, *strepěre*, to make a noise.]

obstruct *ob-* or *əb-strukt'*, *vt* to block up; to hinder from passing or progressing; to shut off; to hamper. — *vi* to be an obstruction; to practise obstruction. — *n* **obstruc'tion** the or an act of obstructing; a state of being obstructed; that which hinders progress or action; an obstacle; opposition by delaying tactics, as in a legislative assembly (also **obstruc'tionism**). — *n* **obstruc'tionist** a politician who practises obstructionism. — *adj* **obstruct'ive** tending to obstruct; hindering. — *n* a hindrance; someone who hinders progress. — *adv* **obstruct'ively**. — *n* **obstruct'or**. — *adj* **obstruent** (*ob'stroo-ənt*) obstructing; blocking up. — *n* anything that obstructs, esp. (*med*) in the passages of the body; an astringent drug (*med*); a stop or a fricative (*phon*). — **obstruction lights** (*aeronautics*) lights fixed to all structures near airports that constitute a danger to aircraft in flight. [L. *obstruĕre*, *obstructum* — *ob*, in the way of, *struĕre*, *structum*, to pile up, build.]

obtain *ob-* or *əb-tān'*, *vt* to get; to procure by effort; to gain. — *vi* to be established; to continue in use; to hold good. — *adj* **obtain'able**. — *n* **obtain'er**. — *n* **obtain'ment**. [Fr. *obtenir* — L. *obtinēre*, to occupy — *ob*, against, *tenēre*, to hold.]

obtrude *ob-* or *əb-trood'*, *vt* to thrust forward, or upon one, unduly or in an unwelcome way. — *vi* to thrust oneself forward. — *n* **obtrud'er**. — *n* **obtrud'ing**. — *n* **obtrusion** (*-troo'zhən*) an unwanted thrusting in, forward or upon. — *adj* **obtrusive** (*-troo'siv*) unduly prominent, protruding or projecting; tending to thrust oneself in or forward. — *adv* **obtru'sively**. — *n* **obtru'siveness**. [L. *obtrūdĕre* — *ob*, against, *trūdĕre*, *trūsum*, to thrust.]

obtuse *ob-* or *əb-tūs'*, *adj* blunt; not pointed; blunt or rounded at the tip (*bot*); greater than a right angle and less than 180° (*geom*); dull or dull-witted; insensitive. — *adv* **obtuse'ly**. — *n* **obtuse'ness**. — *n* **obtus'ity**. — *adj* **obtuse-ang'led** or **-ang'ular** having an angle greater than a right angle and less than 180°. [L. *obtūsus* — past p. of *obtundĕre*, to strike upon.]

obverse *ob'vûrs* or *ob-vûrs'*, *adj* turned towards one; complemental, constituting the opposite aspect of the same fact; having the base narrower than the apex (*bot*); obtained by obversion (*logic*). — *n* **obverse** (*ob'vûrs*) the side of a coin containing the head, or principal symbol; the face or side of anything normally presented to view; a counterpart or opposite aspect; a proposition obtained by obversion (*logic*). — *adv* **obverse'ly**. — *n* **obver'sion** the act of turning a thing towards oneself; a species of immediate inference where the contradictory of the original predicate is predicated of the original subject, the quality of the proposition being changed — e.g. to infer from All A is B that No A is not B — also called *permutation* and *equipollence* (*logic*). — *vt* **obvert'** to turn in the direction of, or face to face with, something; to infer the obverse of. [L. *obversus*, turned against or towards — *ob-*, towards, *vertĕre*, to turn.]

obviate *ob'vi-āt*, *vt* to prevent or dispose of in advance; to forestall. — *n* **obviā'tion**. [L. *obviāre*, *-ātum* — *ob*, in the way of, *viāre*, *viātum*, to go — *via*, a way.]

obvious *ob'vi-əs*, *adj* easily discovered or understood; clearly or plainly evident; not subtle. — *adv* **ob'viously**. — *n* **ob'viousness**. [L. *obvius* — *ob*, *via*; see **obviate**.]

OC *abbrev* for: Officer Commanding; Officer in Charge; (Officer of the) Order of Canada; original cover (*philat*).

oc *abbrev* for only child.

ocarina *ok-ə-rē'nə*, *n* a fluty-toned musical toy, egg-shaped, with a long mouthpiece. [It., dimin. of *oca*, a goose, from its shape.]

OCCAM or **occam** *ok'əm*, (*comput*) *n* a software language.

Occamism or **Ockhamism** *ok'əm-izm*, *n* the doctrine of the nominalist schoolman, William of *Occam* or *Ockham* (who died about 1349). — *n* **Occ'amist** or **Ock'hamist**. — **Occam's (or Ockham's) razor** the principle that entities are not to be multiplied beyond necessity.

occasion *ə-kā'zhən*, *n* a case, instance or time of something happening; a suitable time, moment or opportunity; a special time or season; a chance of bringing about something desired; an opportunity; an event which, although not the cause, determines the time at which another happens; a reason, pretext or excuse; requirement; need; (usu. in *pl*) business; a special ceremony, celebration or event. — *vt* to cause or give rise to. — *adj* **occā'sional** happening or occurring infrequently, irregularly, now and then; produced on or for some special event or for special occasions; constituting the occasion. — *n* **occā'sionalism** the Cartesian explanation of the apparent interaction of mind and matter by the direct intervention of God on the occasion of certain changes occurring in one or the other. — *n* **occā'sionalist**. — *adv* **occā'sionally** on or for an occasion; now and then. — **occasional table** a small portable ornamental table. — **occasioned by** caused by; necessitated by; **on occasion** from time to time; in case of need; as opportunity offers; **rise to the occasion** see under **rise**; **take occasion** to take advantage of an opportunity (to). [L. *occāsiō*, *-ōnis*, opportunity — *ob*, in the way of, *cadĕre*, *cāsum*, to fall.]

Occident or **occident** *ok'si-dənt*, *n* the quarter of the sky where the sun, stars and planets set; the west (opp. to *Orient*). — *adj* **Occidental** or **occidental** (*-dent'l*) western; characteristic of the West (esp. Europe, America, the Western United States). — *n* a westerner. — *vt* **occiden'talise** or **-ize** to cause to conform to western ideas or customs. — *n* **Occiden'talism** the culture and ways of Occidental peoples. — *n* **Occiden'talist** a student of Occidental languages; an Oriental who favours western ideas, customs, etc. — *adv* **occiden'tally**. [L. *occidēns*, *-entis*, setting, pres. p. of *occidĕre* — *ob*, towards, down, *cadĕre*, to fall.]

occiput *ok'si-put*, (*anat*) *n* the back of the head or skull. — *adj* **occip'ital** pertaining to the back of the head. — *n* the occipital bone, the bone at the back of the skull. [L. *occiput* — *ob*, over against, *caput*, head.]

occlude *o-* or *ə-klōod*, *vt* to shut in or out; to cut or shut off; to stop or cover (a passage, cavity or opening); to bring together (the teeth or eyelids); to absorb or retain (e.g. a gas by a metal). — *vi* to bite or close (the teeth) together. — *adj* **occlu'dent** causing or resulting in occlusion; occluding. — *n* that which occludes. — *n* **occlu'der** (*med*, *ophthalm* etc.) a device that occludes. — *n* **occlu'sion** (*-zhən*) a closing of an opening, passage or cavity; the act of occluding or absorbing; the bite or mode of meeting of the teeth; the formation or condition of an occluded front (*meteorol*). — *adj* **occlu'sive** (*-siv*) serving to close; characterised by occlusion. — *n* (*phon*) a sound produced by closing the breath passage. — *n* **occlu'sor** (*anat*) that which closes, esp. a muscle for closing an opening. — **occluded front** (*meteorol*) an advancing cold front into which a mass of warm air has been driven obliquely, forming a bulge which narrows as the warm air is lifted up and the cold air flows in beneath. [L. *occlūdĕre*, *-clūsum* — *ob*, in the way of, *claudĕre*, to shut.]

occult *ok-ult'* or *ok'ult*, *adj* hidden, secret; esoteric; unknown; beyond the range of sense or understanding; transcending the bounds of natural knowledge; mysterious; magical; supernatural. — *vt* **occult** (*ok-ult'*) to hide or cause to disappear; to obscure, esp. by occultation (*astron*). — *vi* to become temporarily invisible; (of a heavenly body) to be hidden by occultation (*astron*). — *n* **occultā'tion** a concealing, esp. of one of the heavenly bodies by another; the state of being hidden. — *adj* **occult'ed**. — *n* **occult'ing** (of a lighthouse, beacon, etc. light) becoming temporarily invisible at regular intervals. — *n* **occ'ultism** the doctrine or study of things hidden or mysterious — theosophy, etc. — *n* **occ'ultist** a person who believes in occult things. — *adv* **occ'ultly**. — *n* **occ'ultness**. — **occult**

sciences alchemy, astrology, magic, palmistry, etc. [L. *occultus*, past p. of *occulĕre*, to hide — *ob-*, over, and the root of *celāre*, to hide.]

occupy *ok'ū-pī*, *vt* to take possession of; to capture; to hold; to keep possession of by being present in; to fill (a post, office); to take up, e.g. a space, time, etc.; to tenant; to keep (often oneself) busy: — *pr p* **occ'ūpying**; *pa t* and *pa p* **occ'ūpied**. — *n* **occ'ūpancy** the act or fact of occupying, or of taking or holding possession; possession; the time during which someone occupies. — *n* **occ'ūpant** a person who takes or has possession. — *n* **occūpā'tion** the act of occupying; possession; the state of being employed or occupied; the time during which a country, etc. is occupied by enemy forces; that which occupies or takes up one's attention; a person's habitual employment, profession, craft or trade. — *adj* occupational. — *adj* **occūpā'tional** connected with habitual occupation. — *n* **occ'ūpier** (*-pī-ər*) a person who occupies; an occupant. — **occupational ailment, disease** or **hazard** a disease, injury, etc., common among workers engaged in a particular occupation because encouraged by the conditions of that occupation; **occupational therapy** the treatment of a disease (incl. a mental disease) or an injury by a regulated course of suitable work. — **army of occupation** troops stationed in the territory of a defeated enemy or subject country to keep order, to ensure compliance with the terms of a peace treaty, to prop up a weak or unpopular government, etc. [Fr. *occuper* — L. *occupāre*, *-ātum* — *ob-*, to, on, *capĕre*, to take.]

occur *o-kûr'*, *vi* to come into the mind of (with *to*); to be or be found; to happen; (of festivals) to fall on the same day: — *pr p* **occurr'ing**; *pa t* and *pa p* **occurred'**. — *n* **occurrence** (*-kur'*) the act or fact of occurring; anything that happens; an event, esp. one unlooked for or unplanned. — *adj* **occurr'ent** occurring; happening; turning up; to be found; incidental. [L. *occurrĕre* — *ob*, in the way of, *currĕre*, to run.]

ocean *ō'shən*, *n* the vast expanse of salt water that covers the greater part of the surface of the globe; any one of its great divisions (Atlantic, Pacific, Indian, Arctic and Antarctic; also Southern — i.e. the belt of water round the earth between 40° and 66½° south — and German — i.e. the North Sea); any immense expanse or vast quantity (*fig*). — *adj* of or relating to the ocean generally. — *n* **oceanarium** (*ō-shən-ār'i-əm*) an enclosed part of the sea, or a large salt-water pond, in which dolphins, porpoises, etc. are kept and tamed. — *adj* **Oceanian** (*ō-shi-ā'ni-ən*) pertaining to *Oceania*, which includes Polynesia, Micronesia, Melanesia, with or without Australasia. — *adj* **oceanic** (*ō-shi-an'ik*) pertaining to the ocean; found or formed in the ocean or high seas, pelagic; wide like the ocean. — *n* **oceanographer** (*ō-shi-ən-og'rə-fər*, *ō-shən-* or *ō-si-ən-*). — *adj* **oceanographic** (*ō-shi-an-ō-graf'ik*, *ō-shən-* or *ō-si-an-*) or **oceanograph'ical**. — *n* **oceanog'raphy** the scientific study and description of the ocean. — *adj* **oceanolog'ical**. — *n* **oceanol'ogist**. — *n* **oceanol'ogy** oceanography. — *adj* **o'cean-going** sailing, or suitable for sailing, across the ocean. [O.Fr. *occean* — L. *Ōcĕănus* — Gr. *Ōkĕănos*, the river, or its god.]

ocellus *ō-sel'əs*, *n* a simple eye or eye-spot, distinguished from a compound eye, in insects and other lower animals; an eyelike or ringed spot of colour: — *pl* **ocell'ī**. — *adj* **ocell'ar** of, or of the nature of, an ocellus or ocelli. — *adj* **ocell'ate** (or *os'əl-āt*) or **ocell'ated** (or *-id*) eyelike and ringed; having an eyelike spot or spots. — *n* **ocellation** (*os-ə-lā'shən*). [L. *ŏcellus*, dimin. of *oculus*, an eye.]

ocelot *o'* or *ō'si-lot*, *n* an American cat, like a small leopard; its fur. [Mex. *ocelotl*, jaguar.]

oche *ok'i*, (*darts*) *n* the line, groove or ridge behind which a player must stand to throw. — Also **hockey** or **hockey line**. [Poss. O.E. *oche*, to lop — O.Fr. ocher, to nick, cut a groove in.]

ocher, ocherous, etc. See under **ochre**.

ochone. See **ohone**.

ochre or in U.S. **ocher** *ō'kər*, *n* a native pigment composed of fine clay and an iron oxide (limonite in yellow ochre, haematite in red); a paint manufactured from it; an earthy metallic oxide of various kinds. — *vt* to mark or colour with ochre. — *adj* **ochrā'ceous** or **ochreous** (*ō'kri-əs*), **o'chroid** or **o'chrous** (sometimes **o'cherous**) or **o'chry** (also **o'chrey** or **o'chery**) consisting of, containing or resembling ochre. [Fr. *ocre* — L. *ōchra* — Gr. *ōchrā* — *ōchros*, pale yellow.]

ochrea, etc. See **ocrea**.

ochrous, ochry, etc. See **ochre**.

Ockhamism and **Ockham's razor**. See **Occamism**.

o'clock. See under **clock**.

ocotillo *ō-kō-tē'yō*, *n* a shrub, a native of Mexico and the south-western part of the United States, with spines and clusters of red flowers: — *pl* **ocotillos**. [Am. Sp., dimin. of *ocote*, a type of tree — Nahuatl *ocotl*.]

OCR (*comput*) *abbrev* for optical character recognition or reading.

ocrea (*commonly* **ochrea**) *ok'ri-ə*, (*bot*) *n* sheath formed of two stipules united round a stem: — *pl* **och'reae** or **oc'reae** (*-ē*). — *adj* **och'reāte** or **oc'reāte**. [L., a legging.]

Oct. *abbrev* for October.

oct. *abbrev* for octavo.

oct- *okt-* or **octa-** (*-a-* or *-ə-*), also **octo-** (q.v.) *combining form* denoting eight. — *n* **octachord** (*ok'tə-körd*; Gr. *chordē*, a gut string) a diatonic series of eight tones. — *n* **octagon** (*ok'tə-gon*; Gr. *gōniā*, an angle) a plane figure of eight sides and eight angles. — Also *adj*. — *adj* **octagonal** (*-tag'ən-əl*). — *adv* **octag'onally**. — *n* **octahedron** (*ok-tə-hē'dron*; Gr. *hedrā*, a base) a solid bounded by eight plane faces: — *pl* **octahē'drons** or **octahē'dra**. — *adj* **octahē'dral**. — *adj* **octamerous** (*ok-tam'ə-rəs*; Gr. *meros*, a part) having parts in eights. — *n* **octameter** (*ok-tam'i-tər*) a line of eight feet or measures. — *npl* **Octan'dria** a Linnaean class of plants with eight stamens. — *adj* **octangular** (*ok-tang'gū-lər*) having eight angles. [Gr. *okta-*, combining form of *oktō*, eight.]

octad *ok'tad*, *n* a set of eight things. — *adj* **octad'ic**. [Gr. *oktas*, *-ados*.]

octagon ... to ... **octahedron**. See under **oct-**.

octal *ok'təl*, *adj* pertaining to, or based on, the number eight. [Gr. *oktō*, eight.]

octamerous ... to ... **octandrous**. See under **oct-**.

octane *ok'tān*, *n* any of a group of eighteen isomeric hydrocarbons (C_8H_{18}), eighth in the methane series. — **octane number** or **rating** the percentage by volume of so-called iso-octane (see under **iso-**) in a mixture with normal heptane which has the same knocking characteristics as the motor fuel under test. [Gr. *oktō*, eight, sfx. *-ane*, as in meth*ane*.]

octant *ok'tənt*, *n* an arc of one-eighth of the circumference of a circle; a sector of one-eighth of a circle; an angle-measuring instrument with such an arc; a division of space or of a solid figure or body divided into eight by three planes, usu. at right angles; a position 45° distant from another position, esp. of the moon from conjunction or opposition (*astron*). — *adj* **octantal** (*-tant'əl*). [L. *octāns*, *-antis*, an eighth.]

octaroon. See **octoroon**.

octave *ok'tiv* or *-tāv*, *n* a set of eight; the last day of eight beginning with a church festival; the eight days from a festival to its octave; an eighth, or an interval of twelve semitones (*mus*); a note or sound an eighth above (or below) another (*mus*); the range of notes or keys from any one to its octave (*mus*); an organ stop sounding an octave higher than the keys indicate; an eight-lined stanza; the first eight lines of a sonnet. — *adj* consisting of eight (esp. lines); in octaves; sounding an octave higher. — *adj* **octāv'al** pertaining to an octave; based on the number eight. — **oc'tave-coupler** (*mus*) a device in an organ whereby, when a key is struck, the note played is doubled. [Fr., — L. *octāvus*, eighth.]

octavo *ok-tā'vō*, *adj* having eight leaves to the sheet; of a size so obtained, whether so folded or not. — *n* a book printed on sheets so folded; a book of such a size; contracted **8vo** — usually meaning demy octavo $8\frac{1}{2} \times 5\frac{1}{2}$ in. (216 × 138 mm.): — *pl* **octā'vōs**. [L. *in octāvō*, in the eighth — *octāvus*, eighth.]

octennial *ok-ten'yəl* or *ok-ten'i-əl*, *adj* happening every eighth year; lasting eight years. — *adv* **octenn'ially**. [L. *octennium*, eight years — *annus*, year.]

octet, octett or **octette** *ok-tet'*, *n* a group of eight (lines of verse, electrons, musicians, etc.); a composition for eight musicians. [On analogy of **duet**.]

octillion *ok-til'yən*, *n* a million raised to the eighth power, expressed by a unit with forty-eight ciphers; in U.S., one thousand raised to the ninth power, i.e. a unit with twenty-seven ciphers. — *n* and *adj* **octill'ionth**. [Modelled on **million** — L. *octō*, eight.]

octo- *ok-tō-* or *ok-to-*, also **oct-** or **octa-** (q.v.), *combining form* denoting eight. — *n* **octocentenary** (*ok-tō-sin-tēn'ə-ri*, *-sin-ten'* or *-sen'tin-*) an eight-hundredth anniversary. — *adj* **octogynous** (*ok-toj'i-nəs*; Gr. *gynē*, wife; *bot*) having eight pistils or styles. — *n* **octohe'dron** an octahedron. — *adj* **octopetalous** (*ok-tō-pet'ə-ləs*) having eight petals. — *n* **octopod** (*ok'tō-pod*; Gr. *pous*, *podos*, foot) eight-footed or eight-armed. — *n* an octopus or other member of the **Octopoda** (*-top'*), an order of cephalopods with two gills. — *adj* **octosepalous** (*ok-tō-sep'ə-ləs*) having eight sepals. — *adj* **octosyllabic** (*ok-tō-sil-ab'ik*) consisting of eight syllables. — *n* a line of eight syllables. — *n* **octosyllable** (*-sil'ə-bl*) a word of eight syllables. [Gr. *oktō*, and L. *octō*.]

October *ok-tō'bər*, *n* the tenth month, eighth in the most ancient Roman calendar. — *n* **Octō'brist** (*hist*) a member of a Russian moderate liberal party who made the tsar's manifesto of October 1905 their basis. [L. *octōber* — *octō*.]

octogenarian *ok-tō-ji-nā'ri-ən*, *n* a person who is eighty years old, or between eighty and ninety. — Also *adj*. — *adj* **octogenary** (*ok-tō-jē'nə-ri* or *ok-toj'i-nə-ri*). [L. *octōgēnārius*, pertaining to eighty.]

octogynous, octohedron, octopetalous, octopod, etc. See under **octo-**.

octopus *ok'tə-pəs*, *n* a genus (*Octopus*) of eight-armed cephalopods; any eight-armed cephalopod; (*fig*) a person, organisation, with widespread influence: — *pl* **oc'topuses** (**oc'topī** is wrong). [Gr. *oktō* (L. *octo*), eight, *pous*, a foot.]

octopush *ok'tō-po͝osh*, (*sport*) *n* a kind of underwater hockey, in which a lead puck, called a squid, is used in place of a ball and pushers in place of sticks. — *n* **oc'topusher**. [**octo-** (from **octopus**) and **push**.]

octoroon or **octaroon** *ok-tə-ro͞on'*, *n* the offspring of a quadroon and a person of European descent; a person having one-eighth Negro blood. [Modelled on **quadroon** — L. *octō*, eight.]

octosepalous, octosyllabic, octosyllable. See under **octo-**.

octroi *ok'trwä* or *ok-trwa'*, *n* a toll or tax levied at the gates of a city on articles brought in; the place where, or officials to whom, it is paid; payment for passage of a car on a road. [Fr., — *octroyer*, to grant, from L.L. *auctōrizāre*, to authorise — L. *auctor*, author.]

octuple *ok'tū-pl*, *adj* eightfold. — *vt* or *vi* to multiply by eight. — *n* **oc'tūplet** a group of eight notes to be played in the time of six (*mus*); one of eight (children or animals) born at one birth. [L. *octuplus*; cf. **duple, double**.]

ocular *ok'ū-lər*, *adj* pertaining to the eye or to vision; formed in, addressed to, or known by, the eye; received by actual sight; eyelike. — *n* an eyepiece; an eye (*facetious*). — *n* **oc'ularist** a person who makes artificial eyes. — *adv* **oc'ularly**. — *adj* **oc'ulate** or **oc'ulated** having eyes, or spots like eyes. — *n* **oc'ulist** a specialist in diseases and defects of the eye, an ophthalmologist. — *combining form* **oculo-** (*ok'ū-lō-* or *-lo'-*) of or pertaining to the eye or eyes. — *adj* **oculomō'tor** pertaining to or causing movements of the eye. — *n* **oculus** (*ok'ū-ləs*) a round window: — *pl* **ok'ū-lī**. [L. *oculus*, the eye.]

OD *o-dē'*, (*slang*) *n* an overdose (of drugs). — Also *vi*: — *pr p* **OD'ing**; *pa t* and *pa p* **OD'd**.

OD *abbrev* for: Officer of the Day; Ordnance Datum or Data; (also **O/D**) overdrawn.

ODA *abbrev* for Overseas Development Administration.

oda *ō'də*, *n* a room in a harem. [Turk.; cf. **odalisque**.]

odalisque or **odalisk** *ō'də-lisk* or **odalique** *-lik*, *n* a female slave in a harem. [Fr., — Turk. *ōdaliq* — *ōdah*, a chamber.]

odd *od*, *adj* unpaired; left over; extra; not one of a complete set; not exactly divisible by two (opp. to *even*); strange; casual; out-of-the-way; standing apart. — *n* one stroke above the like (*golf*); a stroke allowed in handicap (*golf*); one trick above book (*whist*): — in *pl* **odds** (*odz*, sometimes treated as *sing*) inequality; difference in favour of one against another; more than an even wager; the amount or proportion by which the bet of one exceeds that of another; the chances or probability; advantage; dispute; scraps or pieces. — *adj* **odd'ish**. — *n* **odd'ity** the state of being odd or singular; strangeness; a strange or odd person or thing. — *adv* **odd'ly**. — *n* **odd'ment** something remaining over; one of a broken set — often in *pl*. — *n* **odd'ness**. — **odd'ball** an eccentric person, nonconformist in some respect. — Also *adj* (of e.g. a thing, plan, circumstance). — **Odd'fellow** a member of a secret benevolent society called Oddfellows. — *adj* **odd'-job**. — **odd jobs** occasional pieces of work such as small house repairs; **odd-jobb'er** or **odd-job'man**. — *adj* **odd'-looking**. — **odd lot** (*stock exchange*) a block of less than one hundred shares; **odd-lott'er** someone who deals in odd lots. — *adj* **odds-on'** (of a chance) better than even. — **at odds** at variance (with); **make no odds** to make no significant difference; **odd man out** or **odd one out** a person who is left out when numbers are made up; a person set apart, willingly or unwillingly, by difference of interests, etc., from a particular group; **odds and ends** miscellaneous pieces, scraps or things; **odds and sods** (*colloq*) miscellaneous people, things, etc.; **over the odds** more than expected, normal, necessary, etc.; **shout the odds** (*slang*) to talk overmuch or too loudly; **what's the odds?** what difference does it make? [O.N. *oddi*, point, a triangle, odd number.]

ode *ōd*, *n* orig., a poem intended to be sung; an elaborate lyric, often of some length, generally addressed to somebody or something. — *n* **o'dist** a writer of odes. [Fr. *ode* — Gr. *ōidē* — *aeidein*, to sing.]

odium *ō'di-əm*, *n* hatred; offensiveness; blame; reproach attaching to (with *of*); the quality of provoking hate. — *adj* **o'dious** hateful; offensive; repulsive; causing hatred. — *adv* **o'diously**. — *n* **o'diousness**. [L. *ŏdium*.]

odograph *od'ō-gräf*, *n* a device for plotting automatically a course travelled; an odometer; a pedometer. [Gr. *hodos*, a way, *graphein*, to write.]

odometer *od-om'i-tər*, *n* an instrument attached to the wheel of a car, etc. for measuring distance travelled. — Also **hodom'eter**. — *n* **odom'etry** or

hodom'etry. [Gr. *hodos*, a way, *metron*, a measure.]

odont- *od-ont-* or **odonto-** *-o-*, *combining form* denoting tooth. — *n* **odontalgia** (*-al'ji-ə*; Gr. *algos*, pain) or **odontal'gy** toothache. — *adj* **odontal'gic** relating to toothache. — *adj* **odon'tic** dental. — *n* **odont'oblast** a dentine-forming cell. — *n* **odontogeny** (*-oj'i-ni*) the origin and development of teeth. — *n* **odontog'raphy** description of teeth. — *adj* **odont'oid** toothlike (**odontoid peg** or **process** a projection from the second vertebra of the neck). — *n* **odont'olite** (Gr. *lithos*, stone) bone turquoise or occidental turquoise, a fossil bone or tooth coloured blue with phosphate of iron. — *adj* **odontolog'ic** or **odontolog'ical**. — *n* **odontol'ogist.** — *n* **odontol'ogy** the science of the teeth. — *n* **odontopho'bia** (*psychol*) fear of teeth. [Gr. *odous*, *odontos*, a tooth.]

odour or in U.S. **odor** *ō'dər*, *n* smell; savour (*fig*); repute (*fig*). — *adj* **o'dorant, o'dorate** or **odorif'erous** emitting a (usually pleasant) smell. — *adv* **odorif'erously.** — *n* **odorif'erousness.** — *adj* **odorous** (*ō'də-rəs*) emitting an odour or scent; sweet-smelling; fragrant; bad-smelling (*colloq*). — *adv* **o'dorously.** — *n* **o'dorousness.** — *adj* **o'doured.** — *adj* **o'dourless.** — **in bad odour** in bad repute or standing (with); (similarly, but less commonly) **in good odour; the odour of sanctity** a fragrance after death alleged to be evidence of saintship; a sanctimonious manner. [A.Fr. *odour* — L. *odor*, *-ōris*.]

Odyssey *od'is-i*, *n* a Greek epic poem, ascribed to Homer, describing the ten years' wanderings of *Odysseus* (Ulysses) on his way home from the Trojan war to Ithaca; (also without *cap*) a long wandering, or a tale of wandering. — *adj* **Odyssē'an.** [Gr. *Odysseia*.]

OECD *abbrev* for Organisation for Economic Co-operation and Development.

oecology, etc., **oecumenic, oecumenical** etc. Alternative spellings **ecology, ecumenic**, etc.

OED *abbrev* for Oxford English Dictionary.

oedema *ē-dē'mə*, *n* dropsy, pathological accumulation of fluid in tissue spaces (*med*); an unhealthy mass of swollen parenchyma (*bot*). — *adj* **oede'matose.** — *adj* **oede'matous.** — Also **edē'ma**, etc. [Gr. *oidēma*, *-atos*, swelling.]

Oedipus *ē'di-pəs*, *n* in Greek legend, a king of Thebes who solved the Sphinx's riddle and unwittingly killed his father and married his mother. — *adj* **Oe'dipal.** — *adj* (*irreg*) **Oedipē'an.** — **Oedipus complex** (*psychol*) the attachment of a son to his mother with unconscious rivalry and hostility towards his father. [Gr. *Oidipous*, lit. Swell-foot.]

oen- *ēn-* or **oeno-** *-ō-*, *combining form* denoting wine. — Also **oin-** or **oino-**. — *adj* **oenolog'ical.** — *n* **oenol'ogist.** — *n* **oenol'ogy** the science of wines. — *n* **oen'ophil** or **oenoph'ilist** a connoisseur of wine — also (now usu.) **oen'ophile** (*-fīl*). — *n* **oenoph'ily** love of and knowledge of wines. [Gr. *oinos*, wine.]

o'er *ör*, (*poetic* or *archaic*) shortened form of **over**. For compounds, see **over-**.

oerlikon *ûr'li-kon*, *n* (also with *cap*) an aircraft or anti-aircraft cannon of Swiss origin. [*Oerlikon*, near Zürich.]

oersted *ûr'sted*, *n* the C.G.S. unit of magnetic field strength. [After H.C. *Oersted* (1777–1851), Danish physicist.]

Oes or **oes** *ōz*, a plural of **O** or **o** (see **O**[1]).

oesophagus or (esp. in U.S.) **esophagus** *ē-sof'ə-gəs*, *n* the gullet: — *pl* **oesophagi** (*gī*). — *adj* **oesophageal** (*-fə-jē'əl*). [Gr. *oisophagos*, gullet; poss. connected with *phagein*, to eat.]

oestrus or (esp. in U.S.) **estrus** *ēs'trəs* or *es'trəs*, *n* heat or sexual impulse, esp. in female mammals; oestrous cycle. — Also **oes'trum.** — *adj* **oes'tral.** — *n* **oestradī'ol** a natural oestrogen, also synthesised for use in cancer treatment and menstrual etc. disorders. — *n* **oestrogen** (*ēs'trō-jən*) any one of the female sex-hormones; a substance found in plants, or synthesised, that has similar effects. — *adj* **oestrogenic** (*-jen'*). — *adj* **oes'trous.** — **oestrous cycle** the series of physiological changes from the beginning of one period of oestrus to the beginning of the next. [L. *oestrus* — Gr. *oistros*, a gadfly, noted for its frenzied activity.]

œuvre *œ-vr'*, (Fr.) *n* work (of an artist, writer, etc.): — *pl* **œuvres** (*œ-vr'*).

of *ov*, *uv* or *əv*, *prep* from; from among; belonging to; among; proceeding or derived from; made from, having for material; having or characterised by; in the manner that characterises; with respect to; owing to; with; over; concerning; during; by; on; in; specified as; constituted by; to (in giving the time, e.g. *quarter of five*) (*US*); measuring; aged; owning. [O.E.]

ofay *ō'fā* or *ō-fā'*, (*US Negro derog slang*) *n* a white person. — Also *adj*.

off *of* or *öf*, *adv* away; in or to a position that is not on something; in motion; out of continuity; out of connection, supply, activity, operation or validity; to a finish, up; no longer available; in deterioration or diminution; into freedom. — *adj* most distant; on the opposite or farther side; on the side of a cricket-field; on the side opposite that on which the batsman stands (normally the bowler's left; *cricket*); (of a horse or vehicle) right; out of condition or form; not devoted to the particular or usual activity (as in *off-day*, *off-season*). — *prep* from; away from; removed from; opening out of; in or to a position or condition that is not on; disengaged from; disinclined to, not wanting; out to sea from; from a dish of; from a ball bowled by (*cricket*); with a handicap of (*golf*); not up to the usual standard of; not eating or drinking; not subject to or following. — *n* the offside. — *vt* to put off; to take off; to kill (*US slang*). — *vi* (or *vt* with *it*) to go off, to take off (with *with*; *colloq*). — *interj* away! depart! — *n* **off'ing** the region some distance offshore; a place or time some way off (**in the offing** in sight, at hand). — *adj* and *adv* **off-and-on'** occasional(ly); intermittent(ly). — *adj* **off-beam** see **off beam** below. — **off'beat** any of the usually unaccented beats in a musical bar. — *adj* away from standard; out of the usual; eccentric. — **off'-break** (*cricket*) (of a ball on pitching) deviation inwards from the offside spin given to a ball to cause such a deviation; a ball bowled so as to have such a deviation. — *adj* **off-cen'tre** not quite central. — **off'-chance** or **off chance** a remote chance (**on the off(-)chance** (with *that* or *of*) just in case, or in the hope that, (something might happen)). — *adj* **off-col'our** or **off-col'oured** unsatisfactory in colour (as a diamond) and so inferior; (**off-colour**) not completely healthy; (of jokes, etc.) smutty, blue. — **off'cut** a small piece cut off or left over from a larger piece of some material (e.g. wood); **off'-day** see **off** (*adj*) above; a day when one is not at one's best or most brilliant; **off'-drive** (*cricket*) a drive to the off side. — Also *vi* and *vt*. — *adj* **off'-duty** not on duty. — *adv* **offhand'** extempore; at once; without hesitating. — *adj* **off'hand** without study; impromptu; free and easy; ungraciously curt or summary. — *adj* **offhand'ed.** — *adv* **offhand'edly.** — **offhand'edness.** — *adj* **off-key'** out of tune (*lit* and *fig*); not in keeping. — **off'-licence** a licence to sell alcoholic liquors for consumption off the premises only; a shop having such a licence (*colloq*). — *adj* **off-lim'its** prohibited, out of bounds. — *adj* **off'-line** (*comput*) not under the direct control of the central processing unit; not connected, switched off. — Also *adv*. — *vt* and *vi* **off'load** (orig. *SAfr*) to unload; to get rid of (something unwanted) by passing to someone else (with *on to*). — *adj* **off'peak** not at the time of highest demand. — *adj* **off'-plan** pertaining to a home, etc. bought before (completion of) building on the basis of plans seen, or to the buyer of such a property. — **off'print** a reprint of a single article from a periodical; **off'-putting** an act of putting off. — *adj* that puts off; disconcerting; causing disinclination or aversion. — **off-sales'** (*SAfr*) a shop where alcoholic drinks can be bought for consumption elsewhere. — *n*, *adj* and *adv* **off'season** (of or at) a time (for e.g. a holiday) other than the most popular and busy. — **off'set** a thing set off against another as equivalent or compensation; a lateral shoot that strikes root and forms a new plant; offset printing (see below). — *vt* (*of-set'* or *of'set*) to set off against something as an equivalent or compensation. — *adj* **offset'able** (or *of'*). — **off-'shoot** a branch or derivative of anything. — *adv* **offshore'** and *adj* **off'shore** from the shore; at a distance from the shore; (operating or placed) abroad. — **off'side** the far side; a horse's or vehicle's right towards the middle of the road; (*cricket*) see **off** *adj*; (*football*, etc.) the field between the ball and the opponents' goal. — *adj* and *adv* (**offside'**) on the offside; between the ball, or the last player who had it, and the opponents' goal. — *adj* and *adv* **off-site'** (working, happening, etc.) away from a site. — **off'spin** (*cricket*) (an) off-break; **off'-spinner** (*cricket*) a person who bowls off-breaks; **off'spring** a child or children; progeny; issue. — *adv* and *adj* **off'-stage** not on the stage as visible to the spectators. — *adj* and *adv* **off'-stream** (of an industrial plant, etc.) not in operation or production. — *adj* **off'-street** (of parking) in a car park. — *adj* **off-the-peg** see under **peg.** — *adj* **off'-white** not quite white. — *n* a colour, paint, etc., which is off-white. — **a bit off** (*colloq*) unfair or unacceptable; **badly off** not well off, poor; **be off** to go away quickly (as a command, also **be off with you**); **from off** from a position on; **ill off** poor or badly provided; **off and on** same as **off-and-on** above; **off beam** or **off'-beam** mistaken, wrong, in what one is thinking; **off duty** see under **duty**; **offset printing** a method of printing lithographs, etc., by firstly taking an impression from a plate on a rubber cylinder and then transferring the impression to paper, or metal, etc.; **off the cuff** see under **cuff**^{2}; **off the face** or **off the shoulder** (of a woman's hat, dress, etc.) so as to reveal the face or shoulder; **off the peg** see under **peg**; **off the wall** (*US slang*) off the cuff, unofficially, without preparation; unorthodox, strange; **off with** take off at once; **tell off** to count; to assign, as for a special duty; to chide; **well off** rich, well provided; fortunate. [Same as **of.**]

off. *abbrev* for: official; officinal.

offal *of'l*, *n* waste or rejected parts, esp. of a carcase; an edible part cut off in dressing a carcase, esp. entrails, heart, liver, kidney, tongue, etc.; anything worthless or unfit for use; refuse. [**off** and **fall**^{1}.]

offbeat . . . to . . . **off-duty**. See under **off**.

offend *o-* or *ə-fend'* *vt* to displease; to make angry; to hurt the feelings of; to affront. — *vi* to sin; to break the law; to cause anger. — *n* **offence'** any cause of anger or displeasure; an injury; a transgression, an infraction of law; a crime; a sin; affront; assault; those players in a team, or (as in *Am football*) the team, assuming the attacking role (*sport*); attacking play, position or style (*sport*). — *n* **offend'er**. — *n* **offense'** (chiefly *US*) same as **offence**. — *adj* **offens'ive** causing offence, displeasure or injury; used in attack (*sport*, *mil*, etc.); making the first attack. — *n* the act or course of action of the attacking party; the posture of one who attacks; a great and sustained effort to achieve an end, as in *peace offensive*. — *adv* **offens'ively**. — *n* **offens'iveness**. — **give offence** to cause displeasure; **take offence** to feel displeasure, be offended. [L. *offenděre*, *offēnsum* — *ob*, against, *fenděre*, *fēnsum*, to strike (found in compounds); cf. **defend** under **defence**.]

offer *of'ər*, *vt* to present, esp. as an act of devotion, homage, charity, etc.; to express willingness; to hold out for acceptance or rejection; to lay before one; to present to the mind; to attempt; to make a show of attempting, make as if; to propose to give, pay, sell or perform. — *vi* to present itself; to be at hand; to incline; to make an offer: — *pr p* **off'ering**; *pa t* and *pa p* **off'ered**. — *n* the act of offering; the state of being offered; the first advance; that which is offered; a proposal made; an attempt, essay; a knob on an antler. — *adj* **off'erable** that may be offered. — *n* **offeree'** the person to whom something is offered. — *n* **off'erer** (*law*) or **off'eror**. — *n* **off'ering** the act of making an offer; that which is offered; a gift; a sacrifice; (in *pl*) in the Church of England, certain dues payable at Easter. — *n* **off'ertory** the act of offering; the thing offered; the verses or the anthem said or sung while the offerings of the congregation are being made; the money collected at a religious service. — **offer up** (in e.g. joinery) to position on a trial basis, in order to test for size and suitability before fixing; **on offer** being offered for sale, consumption, etc.; for sale as a special offer; **special offer** (esp. in a shop) the act of offering something for sale, or that which is offered, usu. for a short time, at a bargain price. [L. *offerre* — *ob*, towards, *ferre*, to bring.]

offhand, etc. See under **off**.

office *of'is*, *n* an act of kindness or attention; (with *ill*, etc.) a disservice; a function or duty; settled duty or employment; a position imposing certain duties or giving a right to exercise an employment; the possession of a post in the government; business; an act of worship; the order or form of a religious service, either public or private; that which a thing is designed or fitted to do; a place where business is carried on; a body or staff occupying such a place. — *n* **off'icer** a person who holds an office; a person who performs some public duty; a person holding a commission in an army, navy or air force; a person who holds a similar post in any force or body organised on a similar plan; a policeman; an office-bearer in a society. — *vt* to command, as officers. — *adj* **official** (*of-ish'əl*) pertaining to an office; depending on the proper office or authority; done by authority; issued or authorised by a public authority or office; (of a drug) recognised in the pharmacopoeia. — *n* a person who holds an office; a subordinate public officer; the deputy of a bishop, etc. — *n* **offic'ialdom** officials as a body; the world of officials; officialism. — *n* **officialese'** stilted, wordy and stereotyped English alleged to be characteristic of official letters and documents. — *n* **offic'ialism** official position; excessive devotion to official routine and detail. — *n* **officiality** (*of-ish-i-al'i-ti*) officialism. — *adv* **officially** (*of-ish'ə-li*). — *n* **officiant** (*of-ish'i-ənt*) someone who officiates at a religious service, someone who administers a sacrament. — *vi* **offic'iate** to perform the duties of an office. — *n* **offic'iator**. — **off'ice-bearer** a person who holds office; someone who has an appointed duty to perform in connection with some company, society, church, etc.; **off'ice-block** a large building in which an office or variety of offices is housed; **off'ice-boy**, *fem* **off'ice-girl**, a young person employed to do minor jobs in an office; **off'iceholder**; **office hours** the time during which an office is open for business (typically 9 a.m. to 5 p.m. Monday to Friday). — **last offices** rites for the dead; the preparation of a corpse for burial; **official list** a list of the current prices of stocks and shares published daily by the London Stock Exchange; **official receiver** see under **receive**. [Fr., — L. *officium*, a favour, duty, service.]

officinal *of-is'in-əl* or *-i-sīn'əl*, *adj* belonging to or used in a shop; used in medicine; sold by pharmacists. [L.L. *officīnālis* — L. *officīna*, a workshop, later a monastic storeroom — *opus*, work, *facĕre*, to do.]

officious *of-ish'əs*, *adj* too forward in offering unwelcome or unwanted services; intermeddling; (in diplomacy) informal, not official. — *adv* **offic'iously**. — *n* **offic'iousness**. [L. *officiōsus* — *officium*.]

offing, offload, offpeak, offprint, offput, offset, offside, offspring, etc. See under **off**.

Ofgas *of'gas*, *abbrev* for Office of Gas Supply.

OFT *abbrev* for Office of Fair Trading.

oft *oft* or *öft*, *adv* (now mainly as *combining form*) often. [O.E.]

Oftel *of'tel*, *abbrev* for Office of Telecommunications.

often *of'n*, *öf'n*, *of'ən* or *of'tən adv* frequently; many times. — *adv* **of'tentimes** many times; frequently. — **as often as not** in about half of the instances; quite frequently. [**oft**.]

Ofwat *of'wat*, *abbrev* for Office of Water Services.

ogam or **ogham** *og'əm* or *ō'əm*, *n* an ancient Celtic alphabet of straight lines meeting or crossing the edge of a stone; any of its twenty characters. — *adj* **ogam'ic** or **ogham'ic** (or *og'* or *ō'*) or **og'mic**. [O.Ir. *ogam*, mod. Ir. *ogham*.]

ogee *ō'jē* or *ō-jē'*, *n* a moulding S-shaped in section (*archit*); an S-shaped curve. — *adj* having S-shaped curves. — *adj* **ogee'd**. [Fr. *ogive*; see **ogive**.]

oggin *og'in* (*naval slang*) *n* the sea. [Said to be from earlier *hogwash*, the sea.]

ogham, oghamic. See **ogam**.

ogive *ō'jīv* or *ō-jīv'*, (*archit*) *n* a diagonal rib of a vault; a pointed arch or window. — *adj* **ogī'val**. [Fr.; poss. — Ar. *auj*, summit.]

ogle *ō'gl*, *vt* to look at fondly, or impertinently, with side glances; to eye greedily. — *vi* to cast amorous glances; to stare impertinently. — *n* **o'gle**. — *n* **o'gler**. — *n* **o'gling**. [Cf. L.G. *oegeln*, frequentative of *oegen*, to look at; Ger. *äugeln*, to leer, *Auge*, eye.]

ogmic. See **ogam**.

ogre *ō'gər*, *fem* **ogress** *ō'gres*, *n* a man-eating monster or giant of fairy tales; an ugly, cruel or bad-tempered person, or one whose sternness inspires fear. — *adj* **o'greish** or **o'grish**. [Fr. *ogre*, prob. invented by Perrault.]

OH *abbrev* for Ohio (U.S. state).

oh *ō*, *interj* denoting surprise, pain, sorrow, etc. [See **O**[2].]

ohm *ōm*, *n* the unit of electrical resistance in the SI and the MKSA systems, the resistance in a conductor in which a potential difference of one volt produces a current of one ampere. — **Ohm's law** the law that strength of electric current is directly proportional to electromotive force and inversely to resistance. [Georg Simon *Ohm*, German electrician (1787–1854).]

OHMS *abbrev* for On Her (or His) Majesty's Service.

oho *ō-hō'*, *n interj* expressing triumphant surprise or gratification: — *pl* **ohos'**.

-oholic or **-oholism**. See **-aholic**.

ohone or **ochone** *ō-hōn'* or *-hhōn'*, (*Ir* and *Highland*) *interj* of lamentation. [Ir. and Gael. *ochoin*.]

-oid *-oid*, *combining form* denoting (something) which resembles or has the shape of, as in *anthropoid*, *asteroid*, *deltoid*. — **-oidal** *combining form* used to form adjectives. [Gr. *-eidēs* — *eidos*, shape, form.]

oil *oil*, *n* the juice from the fruit of the olive-tree; any similar liquid obtained from parts of other plants; any similar (usu. flammable) greasy liquid derived from animals, plants, mineral deposits or by artificial means, and used as a lubricant, fuel, foodstuff, etc.; (in *pl*) oil paints, or painting; (in *pl*) oilskins; news, information, esp. in *the good oil* (*Austr*). — *vt* to smear, lubricate or anoint with oil. — *vi* to take oil aboard as fuel. — *adj* **oiled** smeared, treated, lubricated or impregnated with oil; preserved in oil; tipsy (*slang*). — *n* **oil'er** a person who, or that which, oils; an oilcan; (in *pl*) oilskins; a ship driven by oil; a ship that carries oil. — *adv* **oil'ily**. — *n* **oil'iness**. — *adj* **oil'y** consisting of, containing, or having the qualities of, oil; greasy; unctuous. — **oil'-bath** a receptacle containing lubricating oil through which part of a machine passes; **oil'-cake** a cattle-food made of the residue of oil-seeds when most of the oil has been pressed out; **oil'can** a can for carrying oil or for applying lubricating oil; **oil'cloth** a canvas coated with linseed-oil paint; **oil'-colour** a colouring substance mixed with oil; **oil'-cup** a small cup-like container, usu. attached to machinery, for holding and dispensing lubricating oil; **oil'drum** a cylindrical metal barrel for oil; **oil'field** an area which produces mineral oil. — *adj* **oil'-fired** burning oil as fuel. — **oil'-gland** the uropygial gland in birds, forming a secretion used in preening the feathers; **oil'man** a man who deals in oils; a man who owns an oil well; a man involved in the operation of an oil well, oil rig, etc.; **oil'-mill** a grinding-mill for expressing oil from seeds, etc.; **oil'nut** the North American butternut or other oil-yielding nut; **oil paint** an oil-colour; **oil painting** a picture painted in oil-colours; the art of painting in oil-colours; **oil palm** a palm whose fruit-pulp yields palm-oil; **oil'-pan** the sump in an internal-combustion engine; **oil'-paper** paper which has been oiled, e.g. to make it waterproof; **oil platform** a steel and/or concrete structure, either fixed or mobile, used in offshore drilling to support the rig and to keep stores; **oil rig** the complete plant (machinery, structures, etc.) required for oil well drilling; (*loosely*) a mobile oil platform; **oil sand** sand or sandstone occurring naturally impregnated with petroleum; tar sand; **oil'-seed** any seed that yields oil; **oil'-shale** a shale containing diffused hydrocarbons in a state suitable for distillation into mineral oils; **oil'skin** cloth made waterproof by means of oil; a garment made of oilskin; **oil slick** a patch of oil forming a film on the surface of water or (*rarely*) a road, etc.; **oil'stone** a whetstone used with oil; **oil'-tanker** a vessel constructed for carrying oil in bulk; **oil well** a boring made for extracting petroleum. — **no oil-painting** (*colloq*) not very beautiful; **oil someone's palm** to bribe a person; **oil the wheels** (*fig*) to do something in order to make things go more smoothly, successfully, etc. [O.Fr. *oile* (Fr. *huile*) — L. *oleum* — Gr. *elaion* — *elaiā*, olive-tree, olive.]

OILC *abbrev* for Offshore Industry Liaison Committee.

oink *oi'ngk*, *n* (the representation of) the noise made by a pig. — Also *interj*.

oino- *oi-nō-*, *combining form* occurring as an occasional variant for words beginning **oeno-**.

ointment *oint'mənt*, *n* anything used in anointing; any greasy substance applied to diseased or wounded parts (*med*); an unguent. [Fr. *oint*, past p. of *oindre* — L. *unguĕre*, to anoint.]

Oireachtas *er'əhh-thəs*, *n* the legislature of the Republic of Ireland (President, Seanad, and Dáil). [Ir., assembly.]

OK or **okay** *ō-kā'*, (*colloq*) *adj* all correct; all right; satisfactory. — *adv* yes; all right, certainly. — *n* approval; sanction; endorsement: — *pl* **OK's** or **okays**. — *vt* to mark or pass as right; to sanction: — *pr p* **OK'ing, OKing** or **okaying**; *pa t* and *pa p* **OK'd, OKed** or **okayed**.

OK *abbrev* for Oklahoma (U.S. state).

okapi *ō-kä'pē*, *n* an animal of Central Africa related to the giraffe: — *pl* **oka'pis**. [Native name.]

okay. See **OK**.

okey-dokey *ō'ki-dō'ki*, (*slang*) *adj* and *adv* OK.

Okla. *abbrev* for Oklahoma (U.S. state).

okra *ok'rə* or *ōk'rə*, *n* a tropical plant, of the mallow family, with edible pods; the pods themselves; a dish prepared with the pods. — Also known as **gumbo** and **lady's fingers**. [From a W. African name.]

old *ōld*, *adj* (*compar* **old'er** or **eld'er** (q.v.), *superl* **old'est** or **eld'est**) advanced in years; having been long or relatively long in existence, use or possession; of a specified (or to be specified) age; of long standing; worn or worn out; out of date; superseded or abandoned; former; old-fashioned; antique; ancient; early; belonging to later life; belonging to former times; denoting anyone or anything with whom or with which one was formerly associated, such as *old school*, etc.; (of a language) of the earliest, or earliest known, stage long practised or experienced; having the characteristics of age; familiar, accustomed; in plenty, in excess, or wonderful (esp. in *high old*; *colloq*); a general word of familiar or affectionate approbation or contempt (often *good old* or *little old*; *colloq*); reckoned according to Old Style (see **style**). — *adj* **old'en** former, old, past (now usu. only in phrases *in olden days/times*). — *n* **old'ie** (*colloq*) an old person; a film, song, etc. produced or popularised, etc. a considerable time ago. — *n* **old'ness.** — *n* **old'ster** a man getting old (*colloq*). — **old age** the later part of life; **Old Bailey** the Central Criminal Court in London; **old boy** one's father, husband, etc. (*colloq*); an old or oldish man, esp. one in authority, or one who has some air of youthfulness; a former pupil; an affectionately familiar term of address to a male of any age (*colloq*; also **old bean, old chap, old fellow, old man, old thing**): — *fem* **old girl; Old Catholic** a member of a body that broke away from the Roman Catholic Church on the question of papal infallibility; **old-clothes'-man** a man who buys cast-off garments; **old country** the mother country; **old dear** (*slang*) an old lady. — *adj* **old'-established** long established. — *adj* **olde-worlde** (*ō'ldi-wûrld'i*) self-consciously imitative of the past or supposed past. — *adj* **old-fash'ioned** in a fashion like one of long ago; out of date; clinging to old things and old styles; with manners like those of a grown-up person (said of a child); knowing. — **old-fash'ionedness; old gang** or **old guard** old and conservative element in a political party, etc.; **Old Glory** the Stars and Stripes; **old gold** a dull gold colour like tarnished gold, used in textile fabrics; **old hand** an experienced performer; an old convict; **Old Harry, Old Nick, Old One, Old Poker** or **Old Scratch** the devil. — *adj* **old hat** out-of-date. — **old lady** (*colloq*) a person's mother or wife; **old maid** a spinster, esp. one who is likely to remain a spinster; a woman, or more often a man, of the character supposed to be common among spinsters — fussy, prim, conventional, overcautious, methodical; a simple game played by passing and matching cards; also the player left with the odd card. — *adj* **old-maid'ish** like the conventional old maid, prim. — **old man** a person's husband, father or employer (*colloq*); the captain of a merchant ship; a familiar friendly or encouraging term of address. — *adj* (*Austr*; also with *hyphen*) of exceptional size, intensity, etc. — **old master** (often with *caps*) any great painter or painting of a period previous to the 19th cent. (esp. of the Renaissance); **old Nick** see **Old Harry** above, and **Nick; old salt** an experienced sailor; **old school** those whose ways or thoughts are such as prevailed in the past. — Also *adj.* — **old story** something one has heard before; something that happened long ago, or has happened often. — *adj* **old'-time** of or pertaining to times long gone by; of long standing; old-fashioned. — **old-tim'er** someone who has long been where he is; an experienced person, veteran; an old-fashioned person; (esp. as a form of address; *US*) an old person; **old wife** an old woman; someone who has the character ascribed to old women; a fish of various kinds — alewife, menhaden, etc.; **old woman** a person's wife or mother (*colloq*); an old-womanish person. — *adj* **old-wom'anish** like an old woman, esp. fussy. — *adj* **old'-world** belonging to earlier times; old-fashioned and quaint; (with *cap*) of the Old World. — **Old World** the Eastern hemisphere. — **an old-fashioned look** a knowing or quizzically critical look; **any old** see under **any; of old** long ago; in or of times long past; formerly; **old age pension** see **retirement pension; old age pensioner; Old Boy network** (also without *caps*) the members of a society (usu. upper-class), closely interconnected, who share information, and secure advantages for each other; this form of association; **old man's beard** a name for several plants including traveller's joy; **old school tie** a distinctive tie worn by old boys of a school; the emblem of (esp. upper-class) loyalties shown by such people to each other. [O.E. *ald*.]

olden, etc, **oldster.** See under **old.**

olé *ō-lā'*, (Sp.) *interj* an exclamation of approval, support or encouragement, sometimes used in English as an expression of triumph. [Ar. *wa-llāh*, by God.]

oleaginous *ō-li-aj'in-əs*, *adj* oily. — *n* **oleag'inousness.** [L. *oleāginus* — *oleum*, oil.]

oleander *ō-li-an'dər*, *n* an evergreen shrub with lance-shaped leathery leaves and beautiful red or white flowers, the rose-bay or rose-laurel. [L.L. *oleander*.]

olearia *ō-li-ā'ri-ə*, *n* a plant of the *Olearia* genus of Australasian evergreen shrubs of the family Compositae, bearing white, yellow or mauve daisy-like flowers; a daisy-tree or bush (*colloq*). [After the German theologian and horticulturalist Johann Gottfried *Olearius* (1635–1711).]

oleaster *ō-li-as'tər*, *n* properly the true wild olive; extended to the so-called wild olive, *Elaeagnus*. [L. *oleāster* — *olea*, an olive-tree — Gr. *elaiā*.]

oleate *ō'li-āt*, *n* a salt of oleic acid. — *n* **o'lefin** or **o'lefine** (*-fin* or *-fēn*) any hydrocarbon of the ethylene series. — *adj* **olē'ic** (or *ō'li-ik*) pertaining to or derived from oil (as in **oleic acid**). — *adj* **oleif'erous** producing oil, as e.g. seeds do. — *n* **olein** (*ō'li-in*) a glycerine ester of oleic acid. — *n* **oleo** (*ō'li-ō*) short for oleograph or for oleomargarine: — *pl* **ō'leos.** — *n* **o'leograph** a print in oil-colours to imitate an oil painting. — *n* **oleog'raphy.** — *n* **oleomar'garine** margarine (*US*); a yellow fatty substance got from beef tallow and used in the manufacture of margarine, soap, etc. — *adj* **oleophil'ic** having affinity for oils; wetted by oil in preference to water. — *n* **oleum** (*ōl'i-əm*) a solution of sulphur trioxide in sulphuric acid (also **fuming sulphuric acid**). [L. *oleum*, oil.]

oleraceous *ol-ər-ā'shəs*, *adj* of the nature of a pot-herb, for kitchen use. [L. (*h*)*olerāceus* — (*h*)*olus*, (*h*)*oleris*, a pot-herb, vegetable.]

oleum. See under **oleate.**

olfactory *ol-fak'tə-ri*, *adj* pertaining to, or used in, smelling. — *nsing* **olfactronics** (*-tron'iks*; *electronics*) the precise measurement, analysis and detection of odours using electronic instruments. [L. *olfacĕre*, to smell — *olēre*, to smell, *facĕre*, to make.]

olibanum *ol-ib'ə-nəm*, *n* a gum-resin flowing from incisions in species of *Boswellia*, esp. species in Somaliland and Arabia, frankincense. [L.L., prob. — Gr. *libanos*, frankincense.]

olig- *ol-ig-*, or **oligo-** *-i-gō* or *-i-gə-*, *combining form* denoting little, few. — *n* **ol'igarch** (*-ärk*; Gr. *archē*, rule) a member of an oligarchy. — *adj* **oligarch'al, oligarch'ic** or **oligarch'ical.** — *n* **ol'igarchy** (*-är-ki*) government by a small exclusive class; a state so governed; a small group of people who have the supreme power of a state in their hands. — *adj* **Oligocene** (*ol'i-gō-sēn*; Gr. *kainos*, new; as having few fossil molluscs of living species; *geol*) between Eocene and Miocene. — *n* the Oligocene system, period or strata. — *adj* **oligopolist'ic.** — *n* **oligopoly** (*ol-i-gop'o-li*; Gr. *pōleein*, to sell) a situation in which there are few sellers, and a small number of competitive firms control the market — opp. to **oligopsony** (*ol-i-gop'sə-ni*; Gr. *opsōnia*, purchase of food) a situation in which there are few buyers, each competitive buyer influencing the market. — *adj* **oligopsonist'ic.** — *adj* **oligotrophic** (*-trof'*; Gr. *trophē*, nourishment) (of a lake) having steep, rocky shores and scanty littoral vegetation, lacking in nutrients but rich in oxygen at all levels. [Gr. *oligos*, little, few.]

olio *ō'li-ō*, *n* a savoury dish of different sorts of meat and vegetables; a mixture; a medley; a miscellany; a variety entertainment: — *pl* **o'lios.** [Sp. *olla* — L. *ōlla*, a pot; cf. **olla.**]

olive *ol'iv*, *n* a tree (*Olea europaea*) cultivated round the Mediterranean for its oily fruit; extended to many more or less similar trees; the fruit of the olive-tree; a colour like the unripe olive; a person of olive-coloured complexion; an olive-shaped or oval object of various kinds; a small rolled piece of seasoned meat (usu. in *pl*), esp. as *beef olives*. — *adj* of a brownish-green colour like the olive. — *adj* **olivā'ceous** olive-coloured; olive-green. — *adj* **ol'ivary** olive-shaped. — **olive branch** a symbol of peace; something which shows a desire for peace or reconciliation: **olive drab** the olive green of American military uniforms; **olive green** a dull dark yellowish green; **ol'ive-oil** oil pressed from the fruit of the olive. [Fr., — L. *olīva.*]

Oliver. See **Bath.**

olla (L.) *ol'a* or *ōl'a*, (Sp.) *ōl'yä*, *n* jar or urn; an olio. — **olla-podrida** (*ōl'yä-pō-drē'dä*; Sp., rotten pot) a Spanish mixed stew or hash of meat and vegetables; any incongruous mixture or miscellaneous collection. [L. *ōlla* and Sp. *olla*, pot, Sp. *podrida* — L. *putrida* (fem.) — *puter, putris*, rotten.]

olm *olm* or *ōlm*, *n* a European, blind, cave-dwelling, eel-like salamander (*Proteus anguinus*). [Ger.]

-ology. The combining element is properly **-logy** (q.v.). — *n* **ology** (*ol'ə-ji*) a science whose name ends in *-ology*; any science.

oloroso *ol-ə-rō'sō, -zō* or *ōl-*, *n* a golden-coloured medium-sweet sherry: — *pl* **oloro'sos.** [Sp., fragrant.]

Olympus *ol-im'pəs*, *n* the name of several mountains, esp. of one in Thessaly, traditionally the abode of the greater Greek gods; heaven. — *n* **Olym'piad** in ancient Greece, a period of four years, being the interval from one celebration of the Olympic games to another, used in reckoning time; in ancient Greece, a celebration of the Olympic games; a celebration of the modern Olympic games; (sometimes without *cap*) an international contest in bridge or other mental exercise. — *n* **Olym'pian** a dweller on Olympus, any of the greater gods, esp. Zeus (*Gr mythol*); a godlike person; a competitor in the Olympic games. — *adj* of Olympus; godlike. — *adj* **Olym'pic** of Olympia; of the Olympic games. — *npl* **Olym'pics** the Olympic games, esp. those of modern times; (sometimes without *cap*) an international contest in some mental exercise such as chess. — **Olympic games** in ancient Greece, the games celebrated every four years at Olympia; quadrennial international athletic contests held at various centres since 1896; **Winter Olympics** international contests in skiing, skating, and other winter sports, held in the same years as the Olympics. [Gr. *Olympos.*]

OM *abbrev* for: Old Measurement; Order of Merit.

Om or **om** *ōm* or *om*, *n* a sacred syllable intoned as part of Hindu devotion and contemplation, symbolising the Vedic scriptures, the three worlds (earth, atmosphere and air), and the Absolute. [Sanskrit.]

-oma *-ō-mə*, *n sfx* denoting a tumour, abnormal growth, etc., as in *carcinoma, angioma, glioma*, etc.: — *pl* **-ō'mas** or **-ō'mata.** [Gr., ending of nouns formed from verbs with infinitive *-oun.*]

omasum *ō-mā'səm*, *n* a ruminant's third stomach, the psalterium or manyplies: — *pl* **omā'sa.** — *adj* **omā'sal.** [L. *omāsum*, ox tripe; a Gallic word.]

ombré *om'brā*, *adj* (of a fabric, etc.) with colours or tones shading into each other to give a shaded or striped effect. [Fr., past p. of *ombrer*, to shade.]

ombrometer *om-brom'i-tər*, *n* a rain-gauge. [Gr. *ombros*, a rainstorm, *metron*, measure.]

ombú or **ombu** *om-bōō'*, *n* a South American tree, a species of *Phytolacca*, that grows isolated in the pampas: — *pl* **ombús'** or **ombus'.** [Sp., — Guaraní *umbú.*]

Ombudsman *om'bŏŏdz-man* or *-mən*, *n* (also without *cap*) (orig. in Sweden and Denmark) a 'grievance man', an official who is appointed to investigate complaints against the Administration; in Britain officially 'Parliamentary Commissioner for Administration'; (often without *cap*) any official with a similar function: — *pl* **Om'budsmen.** [Sw.]

-ome *-ōm*, *n sfx* denoting a mass, as in *rhizome, biome*. [Gr. *-ōma.*]

omega *ō'mig-ə* or in U.S. *-mēg'*, *n* the last letter of the Greek alphabet — long o (Ω, ω); the conclusion. [Late Gr. *ō mega*, great O; opposed to omicron; the earlier Gr. name of the letter was *ō.*]

omelet or **omelette** *om'lit* or *-let*, *n* a pancake made of eggs, beaten up, and fried in a pan (with or without cheese, herbs, ham, jam, or other addition). [Fr. *omelette*, earlier *amelette*, apparently by change of sfx. and metathesis from *alemelle* (*l'alemelle* for *la lemelle*), a thin plate — L. *lāmella, lāmina*, a thin plate.]

omen *ō'mən*, *n* a sign of some future event, either good or evil; threatening or prognosticating character. — *vt* to portend. — *adj* **o'mened** affording or attended by omens, esp. in combination, as in *ill-omened*. [L. *ōmen, -inis.*]

omentum *ō-men'təm*, (*zool*) *n* a fold of peritoneum proceeding from one of the abdominal viscera to another: — *pl* **omen'ta.** [L. *ōmentum.*]

omertà or **omerta** *om-er-ta'*, *n* the Mafia code of honour requiring silence about criminal activities and stressing the disgrace of informing; a criminal conspiracy of silence. [It., dialect form of *umiltà*, humility.]

omicron *ō-mī'krən, ōm'i-* or *om'*, *n* the fifteenth letter of the Greek alphabet — short o (*O, o*). [Late Gr. *o mīcron*, little O; opposed to omega; the earlier Greek name of the letter was *ou.*]

ominous *om'in-əs*, *adj* pertaining to, or containing, an omen; portending evil; inauspicious. — *adv* **om'inously.** — *n* **om'inousness.** [See **omen.**]

omit *ō-mit'*, *vt* to leave out; to fail (to); to fail to use, perform: — *pr p* **omitt'ing**; *pa t* and *pa p* **omitt'ed.** — *adj* **omiss'ible** that may be omitted. — *n* **omission** (*-mish'n*) the act of omitting; a thing omitted. [L. *omittĕre, omissum* — *ob-*, in front, *mittĕre, missum*, to send.]

ommateum *om-ə-tē'əm*, (*entom*) *n* a compound eye: — *pl* **ommate'a.** — *n* **ommatid'ium** a simple element of a compound eye: — pl **ommatid'ia.** [Gr. *omma, -atos*, an eye.]

omni- *om-ni-*, *combining form* denoting all. — *n* **omnicom'petence** competence in all matters. — *adj* **omnicom'petent.** — *adj* **omnidirec'tional** acting in all directions. — *n* **omnip'otence** or **omnip'otency** unlimited power. — *adj* **omnip'otent** all-powerful. — *adv* **omnip'otently.** — *n* **omnipres'ence** the quality of being present everywhere at the same time. — *adj* **omnipres'ent.** — *n* **omniscience** (*om-nis'i-əns, -nish'əns* or *-yəns*) knowledge of all things. — *adj* **omnisc'ient** all-knowing. — *adv* **omnisc'iently.** — *n* **om'nivore.** — *adj* **omniv'orous** all-devouring; feeding on both animal and vegetable food (*zool*). — *n* **omniv'ory.** [L. *omnis*, all.]

omnibus *om'ni-bəs*, *n* a large road-vehicle carrying a considerable number of passengers of the general public, etc. (now usually shortened form **bus**); an omnibus book: — *pl* **om'nibuses.** — *adj* widely comprehensive; of miscellaneous contents. — **om-**

nibus book a book containing reprints of several works or items, usually by a single author, or on a single subject, or of the same type; **omnibus clause** (e.g. *insurance*) one that covers many different cases; **omnibus edition** (*TV* and *radio*) a programme comprising or edited from all the preceding week's editions of a particular series. [Lit. for all, dative pl. of L. *omnis*.]

omnicompetence . . . omnipotence . . . omniscience. See under **omni-**.

omnium *om'ni-əm*, *n* a Stock Exchange term for the aggregate value of the different stocks in which a loan is funded. — **om'nium-gath'erum** (*colloq*; *sham Latin*) a miscellaneous collection. [L., of all; genitive pl. of *omnis*, all.]

omnivore, omnivorous, omnivory. See under **omni-**.

on *on*, *prep* in contact with the upper, supporting, outer or presented surface of; to a position in contact with such a surface of; in or to a position or state of being supported by; having for basis, principle or condition; subject to; in a condition or process of; towards or to; against; applied to; with action applied to; with inclination towards; close to, beside; exactly or very nearly at; at the time, date or occasion of; very little short of; just after; concerning, about; with respect to; by (in oaths and adjurations); at the risk of; assigned to; in addition to; at the expense of, to the disadvantage of (*colloq*). — *adv* in or into a position on something; towards something; in advance; forward; in continuance; in, or into, or allowing connection, supply, activity, operation or validity; in progress; on the stage, the table, the fire, the programme, the menu, or anything else; not off. — *interj* forward!, proceed! — *adj* on the side on which the batsman stands (normally the bowler's right) (*cricket*); in a condition expressed by the adverb *on*; agreed upon; willing to participate. — *n* the on side (*cricket*). — *vi* to go on (*colloq*); (with *with*) to put on (*colloq*). — *adj* **on'-board'** or **on'board** on, installed inside or carried aboard a vehicle or craft. — **on'coming** an approach. — *adj* advancing; approaching. — **on'-drive** (*cricket*) a drive to the on side. — Also *vi* and *vt*. — **on'fall** an attack, onslaught; **on'flow** a flowing on; an onward flow; **on'going** a going on; a course of conduct; an event; (in *pl*) proceedings, behaviour, esp. misbehaviour. — *adj* **on'-going** currently in progress; continuing; which will not stop. — *adj* **on'-job** combined with or in the course of normal work duties and conditions. — **on'-licence** a licence to sell alcoholic liquors for consumption on the premises. — *adj* **on'-line** (*comput*) attached to, and under the direct control of, the central processing unit; got from or by means of on-line equipment; taking place as part of, or pertaining to, a continuous (esp. production) process. — **on'looker** a looker on, observer. — *adj* **on'looking.** — *adj* **on'-off** (of a switch, etc.) which can be set to one of only two positions, either *on* or *off*. — **on'rush** a rushing onward; **on'set** a violent attack; an assault; the beginning, outset. — *adj* **onshore** (*on'shör*) towards the land. — *adv* **on'-shore.** — *adj* and *adv* **on'side** not offside. — *n* (*cricket*) see **on** *adj*. — *adj* and *adv* **on'-stage** on a part of the stage visible to the audience. — *adj* and *adv* **on'-stream** (of an industrial plant, etc.) in, or going into, operation or production; passing through or along a pipe, system, etc. (also *fig*). — *prep* **onto** see **on to** below; to the whole of (*math*). — *adj* (*math*) describing a mapping of one set to a second set, involving every element of the latter. — *adj* **onward** (*on'wərd*) going on; advancing; advanced. — *adv* (also **on'wards**) towards a place or time in advance or in front; forward; in continuation of forward movement. — **on and off** same as **off and on; on and on (and on)** used in phrases containing the particle *on* to emphasise duration, distance, etc.; **on stream** same as **on-stream; on to** to a place or position on (also **on'to**); forward to; aware of, cognisant of (*colloq*). [O.E. *on*.]

onager *on'ə-jər*, *n* the wild ass of Central Asia. [L., — Gr. *onagros* — *onos*, an ass, *agrios*, wild — *agros*, a field.]

onanism *ō'nən-izm*, *n* coitus interruptus; masturbation. — *n* **o'nanist.** — *adj* **onanist'ic.** [After biblical *Onan*, son of Judah; see Gen. xxxviii. 9.]

ONC *abbrev* for Ordinary National Certificate (a qualification awarded by BTEC).

once *wuns*, *adv* a single time; on one occasion; at a former time; at any time. — *n* one time. — *adj* former. — *conj* when once; as soon as. — *n* **onc'er** (*slang*) a £1 note. — *adj* **once'-for-all** done, etc., once and for all. — *n* **once-o'ver** a single comprehensive survey; a quick (sometimes casual) examination. — **at once** without delay; alike; at the same time; **for once** on one occasion only; **once and again** more than once; now and then; **once (and) for all** once only and not again; **once in a way** or **while** occasionally; rarely; **once or twice** a few times; **once upon a time** at a certain time in the past — the usual formula for beginning a fairy tale. [O.E. *ānes*, orig. genitive of *ān*, one, used as adv.]

onchocerciasis *ong-kō-sər-kī'ə-sis*, *n* a disease of man, also known as river blindness, common in tropical regions of America and Africa, caused by infestation by a filarial worm (*Onchocerca volvulus*) which is transmitted by various species of black fly, and characterised by subcutaneous nodules and very often blindness. [Gr. *onkos*, a hook, *kerkos*, a tail.]

oncology *ong-kol'ə-ji*, *n* the study of tumours. — *n* **oncogen** (*-ko-jen'*) an agent causing oncogenesis. — *n* **oncogene** (*-ko-jēn'*) a type of gene involved in the onset and development of cancer. — *n* **oncogen'esis** the formation of cancerous tumours. — *n* **oncogenet'icist** someone who studies oncogenes. — *adj* **oncogenic** (*-kō-jen'*) causing tumours. — *n* **oncol'ogist.** [Gr. *onkos*, bulk, mass, tumour.]

OND *abbrev* for Ordinary National Diploma (a qualification awarded by BTEC).

on-dit *ɔ̃-dē*, *n* rumour; hearsay: — *pl* **on-dits** (*-dē* or *-dēz*). [Fr.]

one *wun*, *adj* single; of unit number; undivided; the same; a certain; a single but not specified; first. — *n* the number unity; a symbol representing it; an individual thing or person; a thing bearing or distinguished by the number one. — *pron* somebody; anybody; I (*formal*). — *n* **one'ness** singleness; uniqueness; identity; unity; homogeneity, sameness. — *n* **oner, one'-er** or **wunn'er** (*wun'ər*; all meanings *colloq* or *slang*) a person or thing unique or outstanding in any way; an expert; a single, uninterrupted action; a 1 note; a heavy blow; a big lie. — *pron* **oneself'** or **one's self** the emphatic and reflexive form of **one.** — *adj* **one'-day** (of an event, etc.) lasting for one day. — *adj* **one'-eyed.** — *adj* **one'-handed** with, by, or for, one hand. — *adj* **one'-horse** drawn by a single horse; petty, mean, inferior. — *adj* **one'-legged.** — **one-lin'er** (*colloq*) a short pithy remark; a wisecrack, quip; a joke delivered in one sentence. — *adj* **one'-man** of, for, or done by, one man. — *n* **one-nighter** see **one-night stand** below. — *adj* **one'-off** made, intended, etc. for one occasion only. — Also *n*. — *adj* **one'-one** one-to-one. — *adj* **one'-piece** made in one piece. — *adj* **one'-shot** (intended to be) done, used, etc. on only one occasion or for one particular purpose or project; one-off; not part of a serial. — Also *n*. — *adj* **one-sid'ed** limited to one side; partial; developed on one side only; turned to one side. — *adv* **one-sid'edly.** — **one-sid'edness; one'-step** a dance of U.S. origin danced to quick march time. — *vi* to dance a one-step. — *adj* **one'-stop** or **one stop** providing a variety of goods or services all at one source. — *adj* **one'-time** former, past. — *adj* **one'-to-one** corresponding each one uniquely to one. — *adj* **one'-track** incapable of dealing with more than one idea or activity at a time; obsessed with one idea to the exclusion of others. — **one'-two** (*colloq*) (in boxing, etc.) a blow with one fist followed by a blow with the other (also *fig*); (in football) a movement in which a player passes the ball to another player then runs forward to receive the ball which is immediately passed back to him; **one-up'manship** (*facetious*; *Stephen Potter*) the art of being one up, i.e. scoring or maintaining an advantage over someone. — *adj* **one'-way** proceeding, or permitting, or set apart for traffic, in one direction only; not requiring reciprocal action, etc. — **all one** just the same; of no consequence; **a (or the) one** a person special or remarkable in some way (*colloq*); **a one for** an enthusiast for; **at one** of one mind; reconciled (with); **be one up on** to score an advantage over (another); **in one** or **all in one** combined; as one unit, object, etc.; **just one of those things** an unfortunate happening that must be accepted; **one and all** everyone without exception; **one-armed bandit** a fruit-machine (q.v.); **one by one** singly in order; **one-horse race** (*fig*) a race, competition, etc., in which one particular competitor or participant is certain to win; **one-man band** a musician who carries and plays many instruments simultaneously; (also **one-man show**) an organisation, activity, etc., run very much by one person who refuses the help of others (*fig*); **one-night stand** or **one-night'er** a performance or performances, or anything similar, given on one single evening in one place by one or more people who then travel on to another place; an amorous relationship lasting only one night (*colloq*); **one or two** a few; **one-parent family** a family in which, due to death, divorce, etc., the children are looked after by only one parent; **one-way glass** or **mirror** glass which can be looked through from one side but which appears from the other side to be a mirror. [O.E. *ān*.]

oneiric or **oniric** *ō-nī'rik*, *adj* belonging to dreams. [Gr. *oneiros*, a dream.]

onerous *on'ə-rəs* or *ō'nər-əs*, *adj* burdensome; oppressive. — *adv* **on'erously**. — *n* **on'erousness**. [L. *onerōsus* — *onus*, a burden.]

onfall . . . to . . . **ongoing**. See under **on**.

onion *un'yən*, *n* a pungent edible bulb of the lily family; the plant yielding it; applied also to some related species. — *adj* **on'iony**. — **onion dome** a bulb-shaped dome having a sharp point, characteristic of Eastern Orthodox, esp. Russian, church architecture. — **know one's onions** (*colloq*) to know one's subject or one's job well. [Fr. *oignon* — L. *ūniō*, *-ōnis*, union, a large pearl, an onion.]

oniric. See **oneiric**.

on-licence . . . to . . . **onlooking**. See under **on**.

only *ōn'li*, *adj* single in number; without others of the kind; without others worthy to be counted. — *adv* not more, other, or otherwise than; alone; merely; barely; just. — *conj* but; except that. — **if only** (I, he, etc.) wish (or wished, etc.) ardently that; **only too** very, extremely. [O.E. *ānlic* (adj.) — *ān*, one, *-līc*, like.]

ono or **o.n.o.** *abbrev* for or near(est) offer.

onomastic *on-ə-mas'tik*, *adj* pertaining to a name, esp. pertaining to the signature to a paper written in another hand. — *nsing* **onomas'tics** the study of the history of proper names. [Gr. *onomastikos*, *-on* — *onoma*, a name.]

onomatopoeia *on-ō-mat-ō-pē'ə*, *n* the formation of a word in imitation of the sound of the thing meant; a word so formed; the use of words whose sounds help to suggest the meaning (*rhet*). — *adj* **onomatopoeic** (*-pē'ik*) or **onomatopoetic** (*-pō-et'ik*). [Gr. *onomatopoiiā*, *-poiēsis* — *onoma*, *-atos*, a name, *poieein*, to make.]

onrush . . . to . . . **onside**. See under **on**.

onslaught *on'slöt*, *n* an attack or onset; assault. [Prob. Du. *aanslag* or Ger. *Anschlag*, refashioned as Eng.]

onstream . . . to . . . **onto**. See under **on**.

Ont. *abbrev* for Ontario (Can. province).

ontogenesis *on-tō-jen'i-sis* or **ontogeny** *on-toj'i-ni*, *n* the history of the individual development of an organised being, as distinguished from *phylogenesis*. — *adj* **ontogenet'ic** or **ontogen'ic**. — *adv* **ontogenet'ically** or **ontogen'ically**. [Gr. *ōn*, *ontos*, pres. p. of *einai*, to be, *genesis*, generation.]

ontology *on-tol'ə-ji*, *n* the science that deals with the principles of pure being; that part of metaphysics which deals with the nature and essence of things. — *adj* **ontologic** (*-tə-loj'ik*) or **ontolog'ical**. — *adv* **ontolog'ically**. [Gr. *ōn*, *ontos*, pres. p. of *einai*, to be, *logos*, discourse.]

onus *ō'nəs*, *n* burden; responsibility. [L. *ŏnus*, *-eris*.]

onward, onwards. See under **on**.

onyx *on'iks*, *n* an agate formed of alternate flat layers of chalcedony, white or yellow and black, brown or red, used for making cameos (*mineralogy*); onychite, onyx-marble; a fingernail-like opacity in the cornea of the eye. — **on'yx-marble** a banded travertine or stalagmite, also called oriental alabaster. [Gr. *onyx*, *onychos*, nail, claw, onyx.]

oo- *ō'ə-*, *ō-o-*, *combining form* denoting egg. — *n* **oolite** (*ō'ə-līt*; Gr. *lithos*, a stone; *geol*) a kind of limestone composed of grains like the eggs or roe of a fish; (with *cap*) stratigraphically the upper part of the Jurassic in Britain, consisting largely of oolites. — *adj* **oolitic** (*ō-ə-lit'ik*). — *n* **ool'ogist**. — *n* **oology** (*ō-ol'ə-ji*; Gr. *logos*, discourse) the science or study of birds' eggs. [Gr. *oion*, egg.]

o/o *abbrev* for offers over.

oodles *ōō'dlz*, *nsing* or *npl* abundance. [Perh. **huddle**.]

ooh *ōō*, *interj* expressing pleasure, surprise, etc. — Also *n* and *vi*. [Imit.]

oolite . . . to . . . **oologist**. See **oo-**.

oolong or **oulong** *ōō'long*, *n* a variety of black tea with the flavour of green. [Chin. *wu-lung*, black dragon.]

oompah *ōōm'pä*, *n* a conventional representation of the deep sound made by a large brass musical instrument such as a tuba. — Also *vi* and *vt*.

oomph *ŏŏmf* or *ōōmf*, (*slang*) *n* vitality; enthusiasm; sex-appeal; personal magnetism.

oophoron *ō-of'ər-on*, *n* (*zool*) an ovary. — *n* **oophorec'tomy** (*surg*) removal of one or both ovaries. — *n* **oophorī'tis** (*med*) inflammation of the ovary. [Gr. *ōiophoros*, *-on*, egg-bearing.]

oops *ŏŏps*, *interj* an exclamation drawing attention to or apologising for, etc., a mistake.

oorial. Same as **urial**.

ooze *ōōz*, *n* gentle flow, as of water through sand or earth; slimy mud; a fine-grained, soft, deep-sea deposit, composed of shells and fragments of marine rhizopods, diatoms, and other organisms. — *vi* to flow gently; to percolate, as a liquid through pores or small openings; to leak. — *vt* to exude. — *adv* **ooz'ily**. — *n* **ooz'iness**. — *adj* **ooz'y** resembling ooze; slimy; oozing. [Partly O.E. *wōs*, juice, partly O.E. *wāse*, mud.]

Op. *abbrev* for: Opera; Opus.

op. *op*, *abbrev* for: operation; (in **op art** q.v.) optical; opus.

op or **o/p** *abbrev* for out of print.

opacity. See under **opaque**.

opah *ō'pə*, *n* the kingfish (*Lampris*), a large sea-fish with laterally flattened body, constituting a family of uncertain affinities. [West African origin.]

opal *ō'pl*, *n* amorphous silica with some water, usually milky white with fine play of colour, in some varieties precious; opal-glass; the colouring of opal. — *adj* of opal; like opal. — *adj* **o'paled**. — *n* **opalesc'ence** a milky iridescence. — *adj* **opalesc'ent**. — *adj* **o'pal-**

ine (*-ēn* or *-īn*) relating to, like, or of, opal. — *n* opal-glass; a photographic print fixed on plate-glass. — *adj* **o'palised** or **-z-** converted into opal; opalescent. — **o'pal-glass** white or opalescent glass. [L. *opalus*; Gr. *opallios*, perh. — Sans. *upala*, gem.]

opaque *ō-pāk'*, *adj* shady; dark; dull; that cannot be seen through; impervious to light or to radiation of some particular kind; obscure, hard to understand (*fig*); impervious to sense; doltish. — *vt* to make opaque. — *n* **opacity** (*ō-pas'i-ti*) opaqueness. — *adv* **opaque'ly**. — *n* **opaque'ness**. [L. *opācus*.]

op art *op ärt*, *n* art using geometrical forms precisely executed and so arranged that movement of the observer's eye, or inability to focus, produces an illusion of movement in the painting. [*op*tical.]

op. cit. *abbrev* for *opere citato* (L.), in the work cited.

OPEC *ō'pek*, *abbrev* for Organization of Petroleum Exporting Countries.

open *ō'pn*, *adj* not shut; allowing passage out or in; exposing the interior; unobstructed; free; unenclosed; exposed; uncovered; liable; generally accessible; available; ready to receive or transact business with members of the public; willing to receive or accept (with *to*); public; free to be discussed; obvious; unconcealed; undisguised; unfolded, spread out, expanded; unrestricted; not restricted to any class of persons, as in *open championship*; (of a town) without military defences; not finally decided, concluded, settled or assigned; not dense in distribution or texture; widely spaced; loose; much interrupted by spaces or holes; showing a visible space between (*naut*); clear; unfrozen; not frosty; not hazy; free from trees; frank; unreserved; unstopped (*mus*); without use of valve, crook or key (*mus*); (of an organ pipe) not closed at the top; (of a vowel sound) low, with wide aperture for the breath; (of a consonant) without stopping of the breath stream; (of a syllable) ending with a vowel. — *vt* to make open; to make as an opening; to make an opening in; to clear; to expose to view; to expound; to declare open; to begin. — *vi* to become open; to have an opening, aperture or passage; to serve as passage; to begin to appear; to begin; to give tongue; to speak out. — *n* a clear space; public view; open market; an opening. — *n* **o'pener**. — *n* **o'pening** the act of causing to be, or of becoming, open; an open place; an aperture; a gap; a street or road breaking the line of another; a beginning; a first stage; a preliminary statement of a case in court; the initial moves, or mode of beginning, in a game, etc.; the two pages exposed together when a book is opened; an opportunity for action; a vacancy. — Also *adj*. — *adv* **o'penly**. — *n* **o'penness**. — **open access** public access to the shelves of a library. — *adj* **open-air'** outdoor. — *adj* **o'pen-and-shut** simple, obvious, easily decided. — *adj* **o'pen-armed** cordially welcoming. — **open book** anything that can be read or interpreted without difficulty; **open borstal** a borstal run on the same lines as an open prison (q.v.); **o'pen-cast** (in mining) an excavation open overhead. — Also *adj* and *adv* **o'pencast**. — **open court** a court proceeding in public; **open day** a day on which an institution (esp. a school) is open to the public, usu. with organised exhibitions or events. — *adj* **open-door'**. — *adj* **open-end'** or **open-end'ed** not closely defined, general and adaptable to suit various contingencies; (of question, debate, etc.) allowing free unguided answers or expressions of opinion; (of an investment trust) offering shares in unlimited numbers, redeemable on demand; (**open-end'ed**) without fixed limits. — *adj* **o'pen-eyed** astonished; fully aware of what is involved. — **open fire** an exposed fire on a domestic hearth. — *adj* **open-hand'ed** with an open hand; generous; liberal. — **open-hand'edness**. — *adj* **open-heart'ed** with an open heart; frank; generous. — **open-heart'edness**. — *adj* **o'pen-hearth** making use of, or having, a shallow hearth of reverberating type. — **open house** hospitality to all comers; **opening time** the time when bars, public houses, etc., can begin selling alcoholic drinks; **open letter** a letter addressed to one person but intended for public reading; **open market** a market in which buyers and sellers compete without restriction; **open mind** freedom from prejudice; readiness to receive and consider new ideas. — *adj* **open-mind'ed**. — **open-mind'edness**. — *adj* **open-mouthed'** gaping; expectant; greedy; clamorous; surprised, astonished. — **open note** (*mus*) a note produced by an unstopped string, open pipe, or without a crook, etc. — *adj* **o'pen-plan** having few, or no, internal walls, partitions, etc. — **open prison** a prison without the usual close security, allowing prisoners considerably more freedom of movement than in conventional prisons; **open question** a matter undecided; a question formed so as to elicit a full response or an opinion rather than a yes or no answer; **open sandwich** one which has no bread, etc., on top; **open sea** unenclosed sea, clear of headlands; **open season** a time of the year when one may kill certain game or fish (also *fig*); **open secret** a matter known to many but not explicitly divulged; **open sesame** a spell or other means of making barriers fly open — from the story of Ali Baba and the Forty Thieves in the *Arabian Nights*; **open side** the part of the field between the scrum, etc., and the farther touch-line (*Rugby football*); **open skies** the open air; reciprocal freedom for aerial inspection of military establishments. — *adj* **o'pen-top** (esp. of a vehicle) without a roof or having an open top; **open university** (also with *caps*) a British university having no fixed entry qualifications, whose teaching is carried out by correspondence and by radio and television, etc.; **open verdict** a verdict that death has occurred without specifying the cause; **o'penwork** any work showing openings through it. — *adj* open-cast. — **open fire** to begin to shoot; **open-heart surgery** surgery performed on a heart which has been stopped and opened up while blood circulation is maintained by a heart-lung machine; **open out** to make or become more widely open; to expand; to disclose; to unpack; to develop; to bring into view; to open the throttle, accelerate; **open up** to open thoroughly or more thoroughly; to lay open; to disclose; to make available for traffic, colonisation, or the like; to accelerate; to begin firing; **with open arms** cordially. [O.E. *open*; prob. related to **up**.]

opera[1] *op'ə-rə*, *n* musical drama; a company performing opera. — *adj* used in or for an opera. — *adj* **operatic** (*-at'ik*) pertaining to or resembling opera. — *adv* **operat'ically**. — **opéra comique** (*komēk*) (Fr.) opera with some spoken dialogue. — **opera-glasses** or **-glass** small binoculars used by audiences in theatres; **opera hat** a collapsible top hat; **opera house** a theatre for opera; **opera singer**. — **comic opera** opéra comique; opera of an amusing nature; an absurd emotional situation; **grand opera** opera without dialogue, esp. if the subject is very dramatic or emotional; **light opera** a lively and tuneful opera; an operetta (q.v.); **soap opera** see under **soap**. [It., L. *opera*.]

opera[2] *op'ə-rə*, *pl* of **opus**.

operate *op'ə-rāt*, *vi* to exert strength; to produce any effect; to exert moral power; to be in activity, act, carry on business; to take effect upon the human system (*med*); to perform some surgical act upon the body with the hand or an instrument. — *vt* to effect, bring about, cause to occur; to work; to conduct, run, carry on. — *adj* **op'erable** capable of treatment by a surgical operation; able to be operated; practicable. — *n* **op'erand** something on which an operation is performed, e.g. a quantity in mathematics. — *adj* **op'erant** operative; active; effective. — *n* an operator. — *adj* **op'erāting**. — *n* **operā'tion**

the act or process of operating; that which is done or carried out; agency; influence; a method of working; an action or series of movements; a surgical performance: — shortened to **op**, esp. in military or surgical sense. — *adj* **operā'tional** relating to operations; ready for action. — *adj* **operā'tions** relating to problems affecting operations, esp. military (as in **operations research**). — *adj* **op'erative** having the power of operating or acting; exerting force; producing effects; efficacious. — *n* a worker in a factory; a labourer. — *adv* **op'eratively**. — *n* **op'erativeness**. — *n* **op'erātor** someone who, or that which, operates; a person charged with the operation of a machine, instrument or apparatus; a person employed to connect calls, etc., at a telephone exchange; someone who deals in stocks; a symbol, signifying an operation to be performed (*math*); a crooked or calculating person, a shark (*colloq*, esp. *US*). — **operant conditioning** (*psychol*) a learning procedure in which the subject's spontaneous response to a stimulus is reinforced if it is a desired response; **operating system** (*comput*) a software system which controls a computer's operational processes; **operating table** and **theatre** those for use in surgical operations; **operational research** or **operations research** research to discover how a weapon, tactic or strategy can be altered to give better results; similar research to promote maximum efficiency in industrial spheres; **operative words** the words in a deed legally effecting the transaction (e.g. *devise and bequeath* in a will); (*loosely*; often in *sing*) the most significant word or words. [L. *operārī*, *-ātus* — *opera*, work, closely connected with *opus*, *operis*, work.]

operculum *ō-pûr'kū-ləm*, *n* a cover or lid (*bot*); the plate over the entrance of a shell (*zool*); the gill-cover of fishes: — *pl* **oper'cula**. — *adj* **oper'culate** or **oper'culated** having an operculum. [L. *operculum* — *operīre*, to cover.]

operetta *op-ə-ret'ə*, *n* a short, light, rather trivial, musical drama; often, esp. formerly, light opera (see **opera**[1]). — *n* **operett'ist** a composer of operettas. [It., dimin. of *opera*.]

ophi- *of-i-* or **ophio-** *of-i-ō-* or *-o'-*, *combining form* signifying snake. — *npl* **Ophid'ia** (Gr. *ophidion*, dimin.) the snakes as an order or suborder of reptiles. — *n* and *adj* **ophid'ian**. — *n* **oph'iolite** serpentine; a group of igneous rocks associated with deep-sea sediments. — *adj* **ophiolit'ic**. — *n* **ophiol'ogist**. — *n* **ophiol'ogy** the study of snakes. — *n* **ophioph'ilist** a snake-lover. — *n* **oph'ite** a name given to various rocks mottled with green. — *adj* **ophitic** (*of-it'ik*). [Gr. *ophis*, snake.]

ophthalmo- *of-thal-mō-* or *-o'-*, or before a vowel often **ophthalm-**, *combining form* denoting eye. — *n* **ophthal'mia** inflammation of the eye, esp. of the conjunctiva. — *adj* **ophthal'mic** pertaining to the eye. — *n* **ophthal'mist** an ophthalmologist. — *n* **ophthalmī'tis** ophthalmia. — *adj* **ophthalmolog'ical**. — *n* **ophthalmol'ogist**. — *n* **ophthalmol'ogy** the science of the eye, its structure, functions and diseases. — *n* **ophthal'moscope** an instrument for examining the interior of the eye. — *adj* **ophthalmoscop'ic** or **ophthalmoscop'ical** — *n* **ophthalmos'copy** examination of the interior of the eye with the ophthalmoscope. — **ophthalmic optician** an optician qualified both to prescribe and to dispense spectacles, etc. [Gr. *ophthalmos*, eye.]

opiate *ō'pi-āt* or *-ət*, *n* a drug containing opium or a substance with similar addictive or narcotic properties; that which dulls sensation, physical or mental. — *adj* inducing sleep. — *vt* (*ō'pi-āt*) to treat with opium; to dull. — *adj* **o'piated**. [**opium**.]

opine *ō-pīn'*, *vt* to suppose; to form or express as an opinion. [Fr. *opiner* — L. *opīnārī*, to think.]

opinion *ō-pin'yən*, *n* what seems to one to be probably true; judgment; estimation; favourable estimation. — *adj* **opin'ionāted** unduly attached to and assertive about one's own opinions; stubborn. — **a matter of opinion** a matter about which opinions differ. [L. *opīniō*, *-ōnis*.]

opium *ō'pi-əm*, *n* the dried narcotic juice of the white poppy; anything considered to have a stupefying or tranquillising effect on people's minds, emotions, etc. — **opium den** a place where opium-smokers meet or gather; **o'pium-eater** or **-smoker** a person who habitually takes opium. [L. *ŏpium* — Gr. *opion*, dimin. from *opos*, sap.]

opossum *ō-pos'əm* or (*Austr*, *NZ* and *NAm*) **possum** *pos'əm*, *n* any member of the American genus *Didelphys*, or family *Didelphyidae*, small marsupials, often pouchless, mainly arboreal, with prehensile tail; a phalanger (*Austr* and *NZ*); opossum-fur. [Am. Indian.]

opp. *abbrev* for: oppose; opposed; opposite.

oppidan *op'i-dən*, *n* a townsman; in university towns, someone who is not a member of the university, or a student not resident in a college; at Eton (formerly elsewhere) a schoolboy who is not a foundationer or colleger. — *adj* urban. [L. *oppidānus* — *oppidum*, town.]

opponent *o-pō'nənt*, *adj* opposing; placed opposite or in front. — *n* a person who opposes a course of action, belief, person, etc. — *n* **oppo'nency**. [L. *oppōnēns*, *-entis*, pres. p. of *oppōnĕre* — *ob*, in the way of, *pōnĕre*, to place.]

opportune *op'ər-tūn* or *-tūn'*, *adj* occurring at a fitting time; conveniently presented; timely; convenient; suitable; opportunist. — *adv* **opportune'ly** (or *op'*). — *n* **opportune'ness** (or *op'*). — *n* **opportun'ism** (or *op'*) the practice of regulating actions by favourable opportunities rather than consistent principles. — *n* **opportun'ist** (or *op'*) a person (e.g. a politician) who waits for events before declaring his or her opinions, or shapes his or her conduct or policy to circumstances of the moment; a person without settled principles. — Also *adj*. — *n* **opportun'ity** an occasion offering a possibility; advantageous conditions. — **opportunity cost** (*econ*) the cost of an investment (of money, resources, time, etc.) in terms of its best alternative use. [Fr. *opportun* — L. *opportūnus* — *ob*, before, *portus*, *-ūs*, a harbour.]

oppose *o-pōz'*, *vt* to place in front or in the way (with *to*); to place or apply face to face or front to front; to set in contrast or balance; to set in conflict; to place as an obstacle; to face; to resist; to contend with. — *vi* to make objection. — *n* **opposabil'ity**. — *adj* **oppos'able** that may be opposed; capable of being placed with the front surface opposite (to — as a thumb to other fingers). — *adj* **oppo'sing**. — *n* **oppos'er**. [Fr. *opposer* — L. *ob*, against, Fr. *poser*, to place — L. *pausāre*, to rest, stop; see **pose**[1].]

opposite *op'ə-zit*, *adj* placed, or being, face to face, or at two extremities of a line; facing on the other side; (of leaves) in pairs at each node, with the stem between (*bot*); (of floral parts) on the same radius; directly contrary; diametrically opposed; opposed; corresponding. — *adv* in or to an opposite position or positions. — *prep* in a position facing, opposing, contrary to, etc.; as a lead in the same film or play as (another lead). — *n* that which is opposed or contrary; an opponent. — *adv* **opp'ositely**. — *n* **opp'ositeness**. — *adj* **oppositive** (*-poz'*) characterised by opposing; adversative; inclined to oppose. — **opposite number** (*colloq*) someone who has a corresponding place in another set; a person who is allotted to another as partner, opponent, etc.; living partner. [Fr., — L. *oppositus* — *ob*, against, *pōnĕre*, *positum*, to place.]

opposition *op-ə-zish'ən*, *n* the act of opposing or of setting opposite; the state of being opposed or placed opposite; opposed or opposite position; an opposite; contrast; contradistinction; resistance; a difference of quantity or quality between two propositions having the same subject and predicate (*logic*); a body of opposers; the party that opposes the government or existing administration; the situation of a celestial body, as seen from the earth, when it is directly opposite to another, esp. the sun (*astron*). — *adj* of the parliamentary opposition. — *adj* **opposi'tional.** [L. *oppositiō*, *-ōnis*; cf. **opposite.**]

oppress *o-pres'*, *vt* to distress; to lie heavy upon; to treat with tyrannical cruelty or injustice; to load with heavy burdens (*fig*). — *n* **oppression** (*o-presh'ən*) an act of oppressing; tyranny; a feeling of distress or of being weighed down; dullness of spirits. — *adj* **oppress'ive** tending to oppress; tyrannical; heavy; overpowering. — *adv* **oppress'ively.** — *n* **oppress'iveness.** — *n* **oppress'or.** [Fr. *oppresser* — L.L. *oppressāre*, frequentative of L. *opprimĕre*, *oppressum* — *ob*, against, *premĕre*, to press.]

opprobrium *o-prō'bri-əm*, *n* disgrace, reproach or imputation of shameful conduct; infamy; anything that brings such reproach. — *adj* **oppro'brious** reproachful, insulting, abusive. — *adv* **oppro'briously.** — *n* **oppro'briousness.** [L. *opprobrium* — *ob*, against, *probrum*, reproach.]

oppugn *o-pūn'*, *vt* to dispute; to oppose; to call in question. — *adj* **oppug'nant** opposing; hostile. — *n* an opponent. — *n* **oppugner** (*o-pūn'ər*). [L. *oppugnāre*, to attack — *ob*, against, *pugna*, a fight.]

Ops *abbrev* for: Operations; Operations officer; Operations room.

OP's (*colloq*) *abbrev* for other people's.

opt *opt*, *vi* where there is more than one possibility, to decide (to do), to choose (with *for*). — *n* **opt'ant** a person who opts; someone who has exercised a power of choosing, esp. his or her nationality. — *adj* **optative** (*opt'ə-tiv* or *op-tā'tiv*) expressing a desire or wish. — *n* (*gram*) a mood of the verb expressing a wish. — *adv* **op'tatively.** — **opt'-out** (*TV* and *radio*) a programme broadcast by a regional station which has temporarily opted out of the main network transmission. — **opt out** to choose not to take part (in; also with *of*); (of a school or hospital) to leave local authority control. [L. *optāre*, *-ātum*, to choose, wish.]

opt. *abbrev* for: optative; optic; optical; *optime* (L.), very well indeed; optimum; optional.

Optic® *op'tik*, *n* a device attached to a bottle for measuring liquid poured out (also without *cap*).

optic *op'tik* or **optical** *op'tik-əl*, *adj* relating to sight, or to the eye, or to optics; (**optical**) constructed to help the sight; acting by means of light; amplifying radiation; visual. — *n* **op'tic** an eye (now mainly *facetious*). — *adv* **op'tically.** — *n* **optician** (*op-tish'ən*) a person who makes or sells optical instruments esp. spectacles (see also **ophthalmic optician**). — *nsing* **op'tics** the science of light. — *adj* **optoelectron'ic.** — *nsing* **optoelectron'ics** the study or use of devices involving the interaction of electronic and light signals, or the conversion of one to the other. — *n* **optom'eter** an instrument for testing vision. — *adj* **optomet'rical.** — *n* **optom'etrist** an ophthalmic optician; a person qualified to practise optometry. — *n* **optom'etry** the science of vision and eye-care; the practice of examining the eyes and vision; the prescription and provision of spectacles, contact lenses, etc. for the improvement of vision. — **optical character reader** (*comput*) a light-sensitive device for inputting data directly to a computer by means of optical character recognition; **optical character recognition** the scanning, identification and encoding of printed characters by photoelectric means; **optical computing** the technique of controlling the computer by pulses of light instead of by electronic means; **optical fibre** a thin strand of glass through which light waves may be bounced, used e.g. in some communications systems, fibre optics, etc.; **optical microscope** and **telescope** those which operate by the direct perception of light from the object viewed, as opposed to an electron microscope or radio telescope; **optic axis** the axis of the eye — a line through the middle of the pupil and the centre of the eye; **optic lobe** part of the midbrain concerned with sight. [Gr. *optikos*, optic, *optos*, seen.]

optimism *op'ti-mizm*, *n* a belief that everything is ordered for the best; a disposition to take a bright, hopeful view of things; hopefulness; opp. to *pessimism*. — *adj* **op'timal** optimum. — *vt* **op'timalise** or **-ize** to bring to the most desirable or most efficient state. — *n* **optimalisā'tion** or **-z-**. — *vi* **op'timise** or **-ize** to make the most or best of; to make as efficient as possible, esp. by analysing and planning processes; to prepare or revise (a computer system or program) so as to achieve greatest possible efficiency. — *n* **optimisā'tion** or **-z-**. — *n* **op'timist** a person who believes in optimism; someone with a hopeful, cheerful disposition. — *adj* **optimist'ic.** — *adv* **optimist'ically.** [L. *optimus*, best.]

optimum *op'ti-məm*, *n* that point at which any condition is most favourable: — *pl* **op'tima.** — *adj* (of conditions) best for the achievement of an aim or result; very best. [L., neut. of *optimus*, best.]

option *op'shən*, *n* an act of choosing; the power or right of choosing; a thing that may be chosen; an alternative for choice; a power (as of buying or selling at a fixed price) that may be exercised at will within a time-limit. — *adj* **op'tional** left to choice; not compulsory; leaving to choice. — *adv* **op'tionally.** — **keep** or **leave one's options open** to refrain from committing oneself (to a course of action, etc.). [L. *optiō*, *-ōnis* — *optāre*, to choose.]

optometry, etc. See under **optic.**

opulent *op'ū-lənt*, *adj* wealthy; loaded with wealth; luxuriant; over-enriched. — *n* **op'ulence** conspicuous wealth; luxury. — *adv* **op'ulently.** [L. *opulentus*.]

opuntia *ō-pun'shi-ə*, *n* a plant of the prickly-pear genus (*Opuntia*) of the cactus family. [L. *Opūntia* (*herba*, plant), of *Opūs* (Gr. *Opous*), a town of Locris where Pliny said it grew.]

opus *ō'pəs* or *op'əs*, *n* a work, esp. a musical composition — esp. one numbered in order of publication, e.g. opus 6 (abbrev. op. 6): — *pl* **o'puses** or **opera** (*op'ə-rə*). — **opus Dei** (*dā'ē*) the work of God; liturgical worship; in Benedictine monastic practice, the primary duty of prayer; (with *caps*) an international R.C. organisation of lay people and priests. [L. *ŏpus*, *-eris*, work.]

OR *ör*, (*comput*) *n* a logic circuit that has two or more inputs and one output, the output signal being 1 if any of its inputs is 1, and 0 if all of its inputs are 0. [**or.**]

OR *abbrev* for: operational or operations research; Oregon (U.S. state); other ranks.

or *ör*, *conj* used to mark an alternative. [M.E. *other.*]

-or. Agent *sfx.* from L., corresponding to **-er** from O.E. In most words one or other ending is standard but in some both endings occur (**-or** used esp. in legal terms or in terms for a non-personal agent).

orach or **orache** *or'ich*, *n* an edible plant belonging to a genus of the goosefoot family, sometimes used as spinach is. [O.Fr. *arace* — L. *atriplex* — Gr. *atraphaxys*.]

oracle *or'ə-kl*, *n* a medium or agency of divine revelation; a response by or on behalf of a god; the place where such responses are given; the Jewish sanctuary; the word of God; a person with the reputation or air of infallibility or great wisdom; an infallible indication; a wise, sententious or mysterious utterance; (with *cap*; ®) the teletext (q.v.) service of the Independent Broadcasting Authority. — *adj* **oracular** (*or-ak'ū-lər*) of the nature of an oracle; like an oracle; seeming to claim the authority of an oracle; delivering oracles; equivocal; ambiguous; obscure. [L. *ōrāculum* — *ōrāre*, to speak.]

oral *ö'rəl, adj* relating to the mouth; near the mouth; uttered by the mouth; (e.g. of an examination) spoken, not written; (e.g. of a medicine) taken through the mouth; pertaining to the infant stage of development when satisfaction is obtained by sucking. — *n* an oral examination. — *n* **o'racy** skill in self-expression and ability to communicate freely with others by word of mouth. — *adv* **o'rally.** — **oral contraception** inhibition of the normal process of ovulation and conception by taking orally, and according to a specified course, any of a number of hormone-containing pills; **oral contraceptive** a pill of this type; **oral history** (the study of) information on events, etc. of the past, obtained by interviewing people who participated in them; **oral rehydration therapy** the treatment of dehydration (caused by diarrhoea, etc.) with drinks of a water, glucose and salt solution. [L. *ōs, ōris*, the mouth.]

orang. See **orang-utan.**

Orange *or'inj, adj* relating to the family of the princes of *Orange*, a former principality in southern France from the 11th century, passing by an heiress to the house of Nassau in 1531, the territory ceded to France in 1713; favouring the cause of the Prince of Orange in Holland or in Great Britain and Ireland; of or favouring the Orangemen; extreme Protestant Irish Conservative. — *n* **Or'angism** or **Or'angeism.** — **Or'angeman** a member of a society revived and organised in Ireland in 1795 to uphold Protestant principles and supremacy.

orange *or'inj, n* a gold-coloured fruit within which are juicy segments; the tree (*Citrus* genus of family *Rutaceae*) on which it grows; extended to various unrelated but superficially similar fruits and plants; a colour between red and yellow. — *adj* pertaining to an orange; orange-coloured. — *n* **orangeade** (*or-in-jād'*) a drink made with orange juice. — *n* **or'angery** (*-ri* or *-ər-i*) a building for growing orange-trees in a cool climate. — *adj* **or'angey** (*-ji*). — **or'ange-blossom** the white blossom of the orange-tree, worn by brides; that of the mock-orange, similarly used. — *adj* **or'ange-coloured.** — **or'ange-flower** orange-blossom (**orange-flower water** a solution of oil of neroli); **or'ange-peel** the rind of an orange, often candied; **orange squash** a highly concentrated orange drink; **or'ange-squeezer** an instrument for squeezing out the juice of oranges; **or'ange-tip** a butterfly (*Euchloe* or similar) with an orange patch near the tip of the forewing; **or'ange-tree; bitter, Seville** or **sour orange** *Citrus aurantium* or its fruit, which is used to make marmalade; **sweet orange** *Citrus sinensis*, native of China and S.E. Asia, or any cultivated fruit derived from it. [Fr. ult. from Ar. *nāranj*; the loss of the *n* may be due to confusion with the indef. article (*una, une*), the vowel changes to confusion with L. *aurum*, Fr. *or*, gold.]

orang-utan *ö-rang'-ōō-tan'* or *ö'rang-ōō'tan*, also **orang-outang** *ö-rang'-ōō-tang* or *-tang'*, *n* a reddish-brown anthropoid ape, found only in the forests of Sumatra and Borneo. — Also **orang'.** [Malay *ōranghūtan*, man of the woods (said not to be applied by the Malays to the ape) — *ōrang*, man, *hūtan*, wood, wild.]

oration *ö-rā'shən, n* a formal speech; a harangue. — *vi* **orate'** (*facetious*) to harangue, hold forth. [L. *ōrātiō, -ōnis* — *ōrāre*, to pray.]

orator *or'ə-tər, n* a public speaker; an eloquent person. — *adj* **oratorial** (*or-ə-tō'ri-əl*) of an orator, oratory, or an oratory. — *adj* **orato'rian** of an oratory. — *n* a priest of an oratory. — *adj* **oratorical** (*-tor'*) characteristic of an orator; addicted to oratory; rhetorical; relating to or savouring of oratory. — *adv* **orator'ically.** — *n* **or'atory** the art of the orator; rhetoric; rhetorical utterances or expression; a place for private prayer; a lectern for praying at. [L. *ōrātor, -ōris* — *ōrāre*, to pray.]

oratorio *or-ə-tö'ri-ō, n* a story, usually Biblical, set to music, with soloists, chorus, and full orchestra but without scenery, costumes or acting; the form of such composition: — *pl* **orato'rios.** — *adj* **orato'rial.** [It. *oratorio* — L. *ōrātōrium*, an oratory, because they developed out of the singing at devotional meetings in church oratories.]

orb *örb, n* a circle; a sphere; anything spherical; a celestial body; an eyeball; the mound or globe of a monarch's regalia. — *adj* **orbed** in the form of an orb; circular. — *adj* **orbic'ular** approximately circular or spherical; having the component minerals crystallised in spheroidal aggregates (*petrology*). [L. *orbis*, circle.]

orbit *ör'bit, n* the path in which a celestial body moves round another, or an electron round the nucleus of an atom (also **or'bital**), or the like; a path in space round a celestial body; a regular course or beat, a sphere of action; the hollow in which the eyeball rests; the skin round a bird's eye. — *vt* (of an aircraft) to circle (a given point); to circle (the earth or other planet, etc.) in space; to put into orbit. — *adj* **or'bital.** — *n* **or'biter** a spacecraft or satellite which orbits the earth or another planet without landing on it. — **orbital engine** an axial two-stroke engine with curved pistons in a circular cylinder-block which rotates around a fixed shaft. [L. *orbita*, a wheel-track — *orbis*, a ring, wheel.]

orc *örk, n* a killer-whale; a fierce sea-monster (*mythol*); an ogre. [L. *orca*.]

Orcadian *ör-kā'di-ən, adj* of Orkney. — *n* an inhabitant or a native of Orkney. [L. *Orcadēs* — Gr. *Orkadĕs*, Orkney (Islands).]

orchard *ör'chərd, n* an enclosed garden of fruit-trees. — **or'chardman** a man who grows and sells orchard fruits. [O.E. *ort-geard*, prob. L. *hortus*, garden, and O.E. *geard*, enclosure.]

orchestra *ör'kis-trə, n* a large company of musicians (strings, woodwinds, brasses and percussion) playing together under a conductor; the part of a theatre or concert-room in which the instrumental musicians are placed; loosely applied to a small instrumental group, as in a restaurant; in the Greek theatre, the place in front of the stage where the chorus danced. — *adj* **orchestral** (*-kes'*) of or for an orchestra. — *vt* **or'chestrate** to compose or arrange (music) for performance by an orchestra; to organise so as to achieve the best or greatest overall effect (*fig*). — Also *vi*. — *n* **orchestrā'tion.** — *n* **or'chestrātor.** — **orchestra stalls** theatre seats just behind the orchestra. [Gr. *orchēstrā* — *orcheesthai*, to dance.]

orchid *ör'kid, n* any plant, or flower, of a family of monocotyledons, including many tropical epiphytes, often with showy flowers. — *adj* **orchidā'ceous** or **orchid'eous.** — *n* **or'chidist** a fancier or grower of orchids. — *n* **orchidol'ogist.** — *n* **orchidol'ogy** the knowledge of orchids. — **or'chid-house** a place for growing orchids. [Gr. *orchis, -ios* or *-eōs*, a testicle (from the appearance of the root-tubers; the *d* is a blunder, as if the genitive were *orchidos*.]

orchil. See **archil.**

orchitis *ör-kī'tis, n* inflammation of a testicle. — *adj* **orchitic** (*-kit'ik*). — *n* **orchidec'tomy** or **orchiec'tomy** (*-ki-ek'*) excision of one or both testicles. [Gr. *orchis, -ios* or *-eōs*, testicle.]

ord. *abbrev* for: ordained; order; ordinary; ordnance.

ordain *ör-dān', vt* to establish; to decree; to destine; to order; to assign, set apart; to appoint; to invest with ministerial functions; to admit to holy orders. — *adj* **ordain'able.** — *n* **ordain'er.** — *n* **ordain'ment.** — *n* **ordinee'** a person who is being, or has just been, ordained. [O.Fr. *ordener* — L. *ordināre, -ātum* — *ordō, -inis*, order.]

ordeal *ör-dēl', n* any severe trial or trying experience; an ancient form of referring a disputed question to the judgment of God, by lot, fire, water, etc. [O.E. *ordēl, ordāl* — pfx. *or-*, out, *dǣl*, deal, share.]

order *ör'dər*, *n* arrangement; sequence; proper condition; the condition of normal or proper functioning; a regular or suitable arrangement; a method; a system; tidiness; a restrained or undisturbed condition; a form of procedure or ceremony; the accepted mode of proceeding at a meeting; a practice; grade, degree, rank or position, esp. in a hierarchy; a command; a written instruction to pay money; a customer's instruction to supply goods or perform work; the goods supplied; a pass for admission or other privilege; a class of society; a body of persons of the same rank, profession, etc.; a fraternity, esp. religious or knightly; a body modelled on a knightly order, to which members are admitted as an honour; the insignia of such a body; a group above a family but below a class (*biol*); one of the different ways in which the column and its entablature with their various parts are moulded and related to each other (*archit*); one of the successively recessed arches of an archway; the position of a weapon with butt on ground, muzzle close to the right side; (in *pl*) the several degrees or grades of the Christian ministry. — *vt* to arrange; to set in order; to put in the position of order (*mil*); to regulate; to command; to give an order for. — *vi* to give command; to request the supply of something, esp. food. — *interj* used in calling for order or to order. — *n* **or'derer**. — *n* **or'dering** arrangement; management; the act or ceremony of ordaining, e.g. priests or deacons. — *n* **or'derliness**. — *adj* **or'derly** in good order; regular; well regulated; of good behaviour. — *n* a non-commissioned officer who carries official messages for his superior officer; a hospital attendant; a street cleaner. — **or'der-book** a book for entering the orders of customers, the special orders of a commanding officer, or the motions to be put to the House of Commons; the amount of orders received and awaiting completion; **order form** a printed form on which the details of a customer's order are written; **orderly officer** the officer on duty for the day; **orderly room** a room for regimental, company, etc. business; **order paper** paper showing order of business esp. in parliament. — **full orders** the priesthood; **holy orders** an institution, in the Roman and Greek Churches a sacrament, by which one is specially set apart for the service of religion; the rank of an ordained minister of religion; **in order** with the purpose (with *to*, *that*); in accordance with rules of procedure at meetings; appropriate, suitable, likely; (also in **good, working,** etc. **order**) operating, or able to operate, well or correctly; in the correct, desired, etc. order; **in** or **of the order of** more or less of the size, quantity or proportion stated; **on order** having been ordered but not yet supplied; **order about** or **around** to give orders to in a domineering fashion; **order of battle** arrangement of troops or ships in preparation for a fight; **order of magnitude** the approximate size or number of something, usu. measured in a scale from one value to ten times that value; (*loosely*) a rising scale in terms of size, quantity, etc.; **order of the day** business set down for the day; something necessary, normal, prevalent, especially popular, etc. at a given time (*fig*); **out of order** not in order; (of people, events, behaviour) outside normally acceptable standards, excessive or uncontrolled (*colloq*); **sealed orders** instructions not to be opened until a specified time; **take orders** to be ordained; **tall** or **large order** a very great task or demand; **to order** according to, and in fulfilment of, an order. [Fr. *ordre* — L. *ordō, -inis.*]

ordinaire *ör'din-ār*, (*colloq*) *n* vin ordinaire; table wine. [Fr.]

ordinal *or'din-əl*, *adj* indicating order of sequence; relating to an order. — *n* an ordinal numeral (first, second, third, etc. — distinguished from *cardinal*); a service-book; a book of forms of consecration and ordination. [L.L. *ordinālis* — L. *ordō, -inis*, order.]

ordinance *ör'din-əns*, *n* that which is ordained by authority, fate, etc.; regulation; artistic arrangement; planning; a decree; a religious practice enjoined by authority, esp. a sacrament. — *n* **or'dinand** a candidate for ordination. — *n* **or'dinate** a straight line parallel to an axis cutting off an abscissa; the *y*-co-ordinate in analytical geometry. — *vt* to ordain; to co-ordinate or order. — *adv* **ord'inately** in an ordered manner; restrainedly; with moderation. — *n* **ordinā'tion** the act of ordaining; admission to the Christian ministry by the laying on of hands of a bishop or a presbytery; established order. [L. *ordināre, -ātum* — *ordō*, order.]

ordinary *örd'i-nə-ri* or *örd'nə-ri*, *adj* usual; of the usual kind; customary; plain; undistinguished; commonplace; (of a judge or jurisdiction) by virtue of office, not by deputation; (of a judge in Scotland) of the Outer House of the Court of Session (**Lord Ordinary**). — *n* a judge of ecclesiastical or other causes who acts in his own right, such as a bishop or his deputy; something settled or customary; the common run, mass or course; one of a class of armorial charges, figures of simple or geometrical form, conventional in character (*heraldry*); a reference-book of heraldic charges; a penny-farthing bicycle. — *adv* **or'dinarily**. — **Ordinary grade** and **level** see **O grade** and **level** at **O**[1]; **ordinary seaman** a seaman ranking below an able seaman; **ordinary shares** shares which rank last for receiving dividend, but which may receive as large a dividend as the profits make possible (**preferred ordinary shares** have limited priority). — **in ordinary** in regular and customary attendance; **out of the ordinary** unusual. [L. *ordinārius* — *ordō, -inis*, order.]

ordinate, etc. See **ordinance**.

ordnance *örd'nəns*, *n* munitions; great guns, artillery; a department concerned with supply and maintenance of artillery. — **Ordnance datum** the standard sea level of the Ordnance Survey, now mean sea level at Newlyn, Cornwall; **Ordnance Survey** the preparation of maps of Great Britain and N. Ireland by the *Ordnance Survey* (*Department*). [**ordinance**.]

ordonnance *ör'də-nəns*, *n* co-ordination, esp. the proper disposition of figures in a picture, parts of a building, etc. [Fr.; cf. **ordinance**.]

ordure *örd'yər*, *n* dirt; dung; anything unclean (*fig*). — *adj* **or'durous**. [Fr., — O.Fr. *ord*, foul — L. *horridus*, rough.]

ore *ōr*, *n* a solid, naturally-occurring mineral aggregate, of economic interest, from which one or more valuable constituents may be recovered by treatment. — **ore body** a mass or vein of ore. [O.E. *ār*, brass, influenced by *ōra*, unwrought metal; cf. L. *aes, aeris*, bronze.]

öre *œ'rə*, *n* a coin and monetary unit in Sweden and (**øre**) Norway and Denmark: — *pl* **öres** and **øre**. See **krone**.

Oreg. *abbrev.* for Oregeon (U.S. state).

oregano *ö-ri-gä'nō* or in U.S. *o-reg'ə-nō*, *n* the Mediterranean aromatic herb *Origanum vulgare*, used in cooking: — *pl* **oreganos**. [Am. Sp. *orégano*, wild marjoram — L. *orīganum*; see **origanum**.]

orf *örf*, *n* a viral infection of sheep, etc. and communicable to man, characterised by the formation of vesicles and pustules on the skin and mucous membranes, esp. on lips, nose and feet. [Dialect *hurf*; O.N. *hrūfa*, scab.]

orfe *örf*, *n* a fish — a golden-yellow semi-domesticated variety of id. [Ger. *Orfe* — Gr. *orphōs*, the great sea-perch.]

organ *ör'gən*, *n* an instrument or means by which anything is done; a part of a body fitted for carrying on a natural or vital operation; a means of communicating information or opinions; a keyboard wind instrument consisting of a collection of pipes made to sound by means of compressed air; a system of pipes in such an organ, having an individual keyboard, a partial organ; a musical instrument in some way similar to a pipe-organ, incl. pipeless organ; a barrel organ. — *n* **or'ganist** a person who plays an organ. — **or'gan-bird** the Australian magpie or pied butcher-bird; **or'gan-gallery** a gallery in a church, etc., where an organ is placed; **or'gan-grinder** a person who plays a hand-organ by a crank; **or'gan-pipe** one of the sounding pipes of a pipe-organ; **or'gan-screen** an ornamented stone or wood screen in a church, etc., on which an organ is placed. — **organ of Corti** (*kör'ti*) the organ in the cochlea which contains the auditory receptors. [L. *organum* — Gr. *organon* — *ergon*, work.]

organdie *ör'gən-di*, *n* fine plain-woven cotton dress material with a stiff finish. [Fr. *organdi*.]

organelle *ör-gə-nel'*, (*biol*) *n* a specialised part of a cell serving as an organ. [N.L. *organella*, dimin. of L. *organum*, organ.]

organic *ör-gan'ik*, *adj* pertaining to, derived from, like or of the nature of, an organ (in any sense); of an organism or organisation; organised; inherent in organisation; structural; formed as if by organic process (*art*); instrumental; mechanical; containing or combined with carbon (*chem*); concerned with carbon compounds; (of crops, crop production, etc.) produced without, or not involving, the use of fertilisers and pesticides not wholly of plant or animal origin; governed in its formation or development by inherent or natural factors rather than by a predetermined plan. — *adv* **organ'ically**. — **organic chemistry** the chemistry of carbon compounds; **organic disease** a disease accompanied by changes in the structures involved; **organic sensation** sensation from internal organs, e.g. hunger. [**organ**.]

organise or **-ize** *ör'gə-nīz*, *vt* to form into an organic whole; to co-ordinate and prepare for activity; to arrange; to obtain (*colloq*). — *vi* to be active in organisation; to become organic. — *n* **organīsabil'ity** or **-z-**. — *adj* **organīs'able** or **-z-**. — *n* **organīsā'tion** or **-z-** the act of organising; the state of being organised; the manner in which anything is organised; an organised system, body or society. — *adj* **organīsā'tional** or **-z-**. — *adj* **or'ganīsed** or **-z-** having or consisting of parts acting in co-ordination; having the nature of a unified whole; organic. — *n* **or'ganīser** or **-z-** someone who, or something which, organises; (also **or'ganiser-bag** or **purse**, etc.) a container with separate divisions, pockets, etc. in which the contents can be arranged for ease and speed of access; (also **personal organiser**) a small ring-binder with divisions in which information, diary, personal notes, etc. can be kept to hand; a pocket, desktop or laptop, etc. electronic device for the same purpose. [O.Fr. *organiser* — Med.L. *organizare* — L. *organum*, organ.]

organism *ör'gən-izm*, *n* organic structure, or that which has it; that which acts as a unified whole; a living animal or vegetable. — *adj* **organis'mal** or **organis'mic**. [**organise**.]

organo- *ör-gə-nō-* or *ör-gan'ō-*, *combining form* denoting organ; (of a chemical compound) containing an organic radical, such as **organochlor'ine** any one of a group of compounds of chlorine and carbon used in pest control. — *n* **organogeny** (*ör-gən-oj'i-ni*) or **organogen'esis** the development of living organs. — *n* **organog'raphy** a description of the organs of plants or animals. — *adj* **organolep'tic** affecting a bodily organ or sense; concerned with testing the effects of a substance on the senses, esp. of taste and smell (Gr. root of *lambanein*, to seize). — *adj* **organometall'ic** (or *-gan'*) consisting of a metal and an organic radical; relating to compounds of this type. — *n* **organother'apy** treatment of disease by administration of animal organs or extracts of them, esp. of ductless gland extracts. [L. *organum*; see **organ**.]

organza *ör-gan'zə*, *n* a transparently thin material resembling organdie but made of silk or synthetic fibres.

organzine *ör'gən-zēn*, *n* a silk yarn of two or more threads put together with a slight twist. [Fr. *organsin* — It. *organzino*, poss. — *Urgenj*, Turkestan.]

orgasm *ör'gazm*, *n* culmination of sexual excitement. — *vi* to experience an orgasm. — *adj* **orgas'mic** or **orgas'tic**. [Gr. *orgasmos*, swelling.]

orgy *ör'ji*, *n* a secret rite, as in the worship of Bacchus (usu. in *pl*) esp. a frantic unrestrained celebration; a riotous, licentious or drunken revel; a bout of excessive or frenzied indulgence in some activity. — *n* **or'giast** a person who takes part in orgies. — *adj* **orgias'tic**. [Fr. *orgies* — L. — Gr. *orgia* (pl.).]

oribi *or'i-bi*, *n* a small South African antelope, the palebuck. [Afrik., app. from some native language.]

oriel *ö'ri-əl*, *n* a small room or recess with a polygonal bay window esp. one supported on brackets or corbels; the window of an oriel (in full **oriel-win'dow**). — *adj* **o'rielled**. [O.Fr. *oriol*, porch, recess, gallery.]

orient *ö'ri-ənt*, *adj* eastern. — *n* the part where the sun rises; sunrise; purity of lustre in a pearl; (with *cap*) the East; (with *cap*) the countries of the East. — *vt* **o'rient** (or *-ent'*) to set so as to face the east; to build (lengthwise) east and west; to place in a definite relation to the points of the compass or other fixed or known directions; to determine the position of, relatively to fixed or known directions; to acquaint (someone, oneself) with the present position relative to known points, or (*fig*) with the details of the situation. — *adj* **oriental** or **Oriental** (*-ent'əl*) eastern; pertaining to, in or from the east. — *n* a native of the east; an Asiatic. — *vt* **orient'alise** or **-ize**. — *n* **Orient'alism** an eastern expression, custom, etc.; scholarship in eastern languages and/or cultures. — *n* **Orient'alist** an expert in eastern languages. — *n* **orientality** (*-al'i-ti*). — *adv* **orient'ally**. — *vt* **o'rientāte** to orient. — *vi* to face the east; to be oriented. — *n* **orientā'tion** the act of orienting or orientating; the state of being oriented; determination or consciousness of relative direction; the assumption of definite direction in response to stimulus. — *n* **o'rientātor** an instrument for orientating. — *adj* **o'riented** or **o'rientated** directed (towards); often used in composition as second element of *adj*; normally aware of the elements of one's situation — time, place, persons (*psychiatry*; also *fig*). — *n* **orienteer'** a person who takes part in orienteering. — *vi* to take part in orienteering. — *n* **orienteer'ing** the sport of making one's way quickly across difficult country with the help of map and compass. — **orientation table** an indicator of tabular form for showing the direction of various objects — mountains and the like. [L. *oriēns*, *-entis*, pres. p. of *orīrī*, to rise.]

orifice *or'i-fis*, *n* a mouth-like opening, esp. small; an opening from the body or body cavity. — *adj* **orificial** (*-fish'əl*). [Fr., — L. *ōrificium* — *ōs*, *ōris*, mouth, *facĕre*, to make.]

oriflamme *or'i-flam*, *n* a little banner of red silk split into many points, borne on a gilt staff — the ancient royal standard of France. [Fr., — L.L. *auriflamma* — L. *aurum*, gold, *flamma*, a flame.]

orig. *abbrev* for: origin; original; originally.

origami *or-i-gäm'i*, *n* the orig. Japanese art of folding paper so as to make bird forms, etc. [Jap., paper-folding, — *ori*, folding, *kami*, paper.]

origanum *or-ig'ə-nəm*, *n* any of various aromatic herbs of the marjoram genus (*Origanum*) of labiates or other genus, used in cookery. — *n* **or'igan** (*-gan*) marjoram, esp. wild marjoram. — See also **oregano**. [L. *orīganum* — Gr. *orīganon*.]

origin *or'i-jin, n* the rising or first existence of anything; that from which anything first proceeds; the fixed starting-point or point from which measurement is made (*math*); the point or place from which a muscle, etc. arises (*anat*); source; derivation. — *adj* **orig'inal** pertaining to the origin or beginning; existing from or at the beginning; being such from the beginning; innate; not derived, copied, imitated or translated from anything else; originative; novel; creative. — *n* that which is not itself, or of which something else is, a copy, imitation or translation; a real person, place, etc., serving as model for one in fiction; an inhabitant, member, etc., from the beginning; a person of marked individuality or oddity. — *n* **original'ity**. — *adv* **orig'inally**. — *vt* **orig'inate** to give origin to; to bring into existence. — *vi* to have origin; to begin. — *n* **originā'tion**. — *adj* **orig'inative** having power to originate or bring into existence; originating. — *n* **orig'inātor**. — **original sin** innate depravity and corruption believed to be transmitted to Adam's descendants because of his sin; **originating summons, application,** etc. (*law*) one which originates legal proceedings. [L. *orīgō, -inis — orīrī*, to rise.]

oriole *ör'i-ōl, n* a golden yellow bird (*Oriolus galbula*, the **golden oriole**) with black wings, or other member of the genus or of the Old World family **Oriol'idae**, related to the crows; in America applied to birds of the *Icteridae* (see **Baltimore**). [O.Fr. *oriol* — L. *aureolus*, dimin. of *aureus*, golden — *aurum*, gold.]

orison *or'i-zən*, (*archaic* or *literary*) *n* a prayer. [O.Fr. — L. *ōrātiō, -ōnis — ōrāre*, to pray.]

Oriya *ō-rē'yə, n* the language of Orissa in India; a member of the people speaking it. — Also *adj.*

orle *örl*, (*heraldry*) *n* a border within a shield at a short distance from the edge; a number of small charges set as a border. [O.Fr., border, from a dimin. formed from L. *ōra*, border.]

Orlon® *ör'lon, n* a type of acrylic fibre or crease-resistant fabric made from it.

orlop *ör'lop* or **orlop deck** (*dek*), *n* the lowest deck in a ship, a covering to the hold. [Du. *overloop*, covering.]

ormer *ör'mər, n* an ear-shaped shell, esp. the edible *Haliotis tuberculata*, formerly common in the Channel Islands. [Channel Island Fr. *ormer* (Fr. *ormier*) — L. *auris maris*, sea ear.]

ormolu *ör'mo-lo͞o, n* an alloy of copper, zinc, and sometimes tin; gilt or bronzed metallic ware; gold leaf prepared for gilding bronze, etc. [Fr. *or* — L. *aurum*, gold, and Fr. *moulu*, past p. of *moudre*, to grind — L. *molěre*, to grind.]

ornament *ör'nə-mənt, n* anything meant to add grace or beauty or to bring credit; additional beauty or decoration; a mark of honour; (usu. in *pl*) articles used in the services of the church. — *vt* to adorn. — *adj* **ornament'al** serving to adorn; decorative, pleasantly striking in dress and general appearance. — *n* a plant grown for ornament or beauty. — *adv* **ornament'ally**. — *n* **ornamentā'tion** the act or art of ornamenting; ornamental work. — *n* **ornament'er** or **ornament'ist**. [Fr. *ornement* — L. *ornāmentum — ornāre*, to adorn.]

ornate *ör-nāt'* or *ör'nāt, adj* decorated; much or elaborately ornamented. — *adv* **ornate'ly** (or *ör'*). — *n* **ornate'ness** (or *ör'*). [L. *ornāre, -ātum*, to adorn.]

ornery *ör'nə-ri*, (*NAm dialect* or *colloq*) *adj* commonplace; touchy, cantankerous; stubborn; mean, contemptible. [A variant of **ordinary**.]

ornis *ör'nis, n* the birds collectively of a region, its avifauna. — *adj* **ornithic** (*ör-nith'ik*) relating to birds. — *npl* **Ornithischia** (*-this'ki-ə*; Gr. *ischion*, hip joint) the order of bird-hipped dinosaurs, herbivorous and often heavily armoured. — *n* and *adj* **ornithis'chian**. — *adj* **ornitholog'ical**. — *adv* **ornitholog'ically**. — *n* **ornithol'ogist**. — *n* **ornithol'ogy** the study of birds. — *n* **or'nithopod** a member of the **Ornithop'oda**, a suborder of bipedal ornithischian dinosaurs. — *n* **Ornithorhynchus** (*-ō-ring'kəs*; Gr. *rhynchos*, snout) the duckbill genus; (without *cap*) the duckbill. — *n* **ornithosaur** (*ör-nī'thō-sör*; Gr. *sauros*, lizard) a pterodactyl. — *n* **ornitho'sis** psittacosis. [Gr. *ornis, ornīthos*, a bird.]

orogenesis *or-ō-jen'i-sis*, (*geol*) *n* mountain-building, the processes which take place during an orogeny. — *n* **or'ogen** an orogenic belt. — *adj* **orogenet'ic** or **orogen'ic**. — *n* **orogeny** (*or-oj'ə-ni* or *ōr-*) a period of mountain-building, during which rocks are severely folded, metamorphosed and uplifted; orogenesis. — **orogenic belt** a usu. elongated region of the earth's crust which has been subjected to an orogeny. [Gr. *oros*, mountain, *genesis*, production.]

orography *or-og'rə-fi, n* the description of mountains. — *adj* **orographic** (*-graf'ik*) or **orograph'ical**. — *n* **orol'ogy** the scientific study of mountains. — *adj* **orolog'ical**. — *n* **orol'ogist**. [Gr. *oros, -eos*, mountain, *graphein*, to write, *logos*, discourse.]

oroide *ō'rō-īd, n* an alloy of copper and zinc or tin, etc., imitating gold. [Fr. *or* — L. *aurum*, gold, Gr. *eidos*, form.]

orology, etc. See **orography**.

oropharynx *ö-rō-far'ingks, n* the part of the pharynx between the soft palate and the epiglottis. [L. *ōs, ōris*, a mouth, and **pharynx**.]

orotund *o', ō'* or *ö'rō-tund, adj* (of a voice) full, round, booming; (of an utterance) pompous. — *n* **orotund'ity**. [L. *ōs, ōris*, mouth, *rotundus*, round.]

orphan *ör'fən, n* a child, animal, etc. bereft of father or mother, or (usually) of both; a machine etc. which has been phased out or superseded; same as **club-line**. — Also *adj.* — *vt* to make an orphan. — *n* **or'phanage** the state of being an orphan; a house for orphans. — *n* **or'phanhood** or **or'phanism**. [Gr. *orphanos*.]

Orpheus *ör'fūs* or *-fi-əs*, (*Gr mythol*) *n* a mythical Thracian musician and poet who could move inanimate objects by the music of his lyre, the founder or interpreter of the ancient mysteries. — *adj* **Orphē'an** pertaining to Orpheus; melodious. — *adj* **Or'phic** pertaining to the mysteries associated with Orpheus; esoteric.

orphrey *ör'fri, n* gold or other rich embroidery, esp. bordering an ecclesiastical vestment. [O.Fr. *orfreis* — L. *auriphrygium*, Phrygian gold.]

orpiment *ör'pi-mənt, n* a yellow mineral, arsenic trisulphide, used as a pigment. [O.Fr., — L. *auripīgmentum — aurum*, gold, *pīgmentum*, paint.]

orpine or **orpin** *ör'pin, n* a purple-flowered, broad-leaved stonecrop. [Fr. *orpin*.]

Orpington *ör'ping-tən, n* a breed of poultry (white, black or buff). [*Orpington* in W. Kent.]

orrery *or'ər-i, n* a clockwork model of the solar system. [From Charles Boyle, fourth Earl of *Orrery* (1676–1731) for whom one was made.]

orris *or'is, n* the Florentine or other iris; its dried rootstock (**orr'is-root**) smelling of violets, used in perfumery. [Perh. **iris**.]

ORT *abbrev* for oral rehydration therapy (q.v.).

ortanique *ör'tan-ēk, n* a cross between the orange and the tangerine, or its fruit. [Portmanteau word: *or*ange, *tan*gerine and un*ique*.]

orthicon *örth'i-kon, n* a television camera tube more sensitive than the earlier iconoscope; a further development is the **image orthicon**. [**ortho-** and *icon*oscope.]

ortho- *ör-thō-, combining form* denoting: straight; upright; perpendicular; right; genuine; derived from an acid anhydride by combination with the largest number of water molecules (distinguished from *meta-*; *chem*); having substituted atoms or groups attached to two adjacent carbon atoms of the benzene ring (distinguished from *meta-* and *para-* —

in this sense commonly represented by *o-*; *chem*). — *n* **orthocaine** (*-kā'in* or *-kān*) a white crystalline substance used as a local anaesthetic. — *n* **or'thocentre** the point of intersection of the altitudes of a triangle. — *adj* **orthochromat'ic** correct in rendering the relation of colours, without the usual photographic modifications. — *n* **or'thoclase** (*-klās* or *-klāz*; Gr. *klasis*, fracture) common or potash feldspar, monoclinic, with cleavages at right angles. — *n* **or'tho-compound**. — *n* **orthodontia** (*-don'shi-ə*) or **orthodont'ics** (Gr. *odous, odontos*, tooth) rectification of abnormalities in the teeth. — *adj* **orthodont'ic**. — *n* **orthodont'ist**. — *adj* **or'thodox** (Gr. *doxa*, opinion) sound in doctrine; believing, or according to, the received or established doctrines or opinions, esp. in religion; (with *cap*) of the Greek, Eastern, Church (see **Eastern Church** under **east**). — *n* **or'thodoxy**. — *adj* **orthoepic** (*-ep'ik*) or **orthoep'ical** (Gr. *epos*, a word). — *n* **orthō'epist**. — *n* **orthō'epy** (the study of) correct pronunciation. — *n* **orthogen'esis** the evolution of organisms systematically in definite directions and not accidentally in many directions; determinate variation. — *adj* **orthogenet'ic**. — *adj* **orthog'onal** (Gr. *gōniā*, angle) right-angled (**orthogonal projection** projection by lines perpendicular to the plane of projection). — *adv* **orthog'onally**. — *n* **or'thograph** a drawing in orthographic projection, esp. of the elevation of a building. — *n* **orthog'rapher** a person skilled in orthography; a speller. — *adj* **orthograph'ic** or **orthograph'ical** pertaining or according to spelling; spelt correctly; in perspective projection, having the point of sight at infinity. — *adv* **orthograph'ically**. — *n* **orthog'raphist** an orthographer. — *n* **orthog'raphy** the art or practice of spelling words correctly; spelling; orthographic projection. — *adj* **orthopae'dic** or (*US*) **orthopē'dic**. — *nsing* **orthopaedics** or in U.S. **orthopēdics** (*-pē'diks*; Gr. *pais, paidos*, a child) the art or process of curing deformities arising from disease or injury of bones, esp. in childhood. — *n* **orthopae'dist** or in U.S. **orthopē'dist**. — *npl* **Orthop'tera** (Gr. *pteron*, wing) the cockroach order of insects with firm forewings serving as covers to the fan-wise folded hindwings. — *n* and *adj* **orthop'teran**. — *adj* **orthop'terous** pertaining to the Orthoptera. — *adj* **orthop'tic** relating to normal vision. — *nsing* **orthop'tics** the treatment of defective eyesight by exercises and visual training. — *n* **orthop'tist**. — *adj* **orthorhom'bic** (*crystall*) referable to three unequal axes at right angles to each other. — *adj* **orthoscop'ic** having or giving correct vision, true proportion, or a flat field of view. — *n* **orthō'sis** a device which supports, corrects deformities in, or improves the movement of, the movable parts of the body: — *pl* **orthō'ses**. — *adj* **orthot'ic** of or relating to orthotics. — *nsing* **orthot'ics** the branch of medical science dealing with the rehabilitation of injured or weakened joints or muscles through artificial or mechanical support by orthoses. — *n* **or'thotist** someone skilled in orthotics. — *n* **orthotonē'sis** (Gr. *tonos*, accent) accentuation of a proclitic or enclitic (opp. to *enclisis*). — *adj* **orthoton'ic** taking an accent in certain positions but not in others. — *adj* **orthotop'ic** (*med*; Gr. *topos*, place; of tissue, grafts, organ replacement, etc.) done, put, occurring, etc. at the normal place. — *adj* **orthotrop'ic** manifesting orthotropism; (of a material, such as wood) having elastic properties varying in different planes. — *n* **orthot'ropism** growth in the direct line of stimulus, esp. of gravity. — *n* **orthot'ropy** (of a material, such as wood) the state of being orthotropic. [Gr. *orthos*, straight, upright, right.]

ortolan *ör'tə-lən*, *n* a kind of bunting, common in Europe, eaten as a delicacy. [Fr., — It. *ortolano* — L. *hortulānus*, belonging to gardens — *hortulus*, dimin. of *hortus*, a garden.]

Orwellian *ör-wel'i-ən*, *adj* relating to or in the style of the English writer George *Orwell* (1903–50); characteristic of the dehumanised authoritarian society described in his novel 1984.

oryx *or'iks*, *n* an antelope of the African genus of antelopes (*Oryx*). [Gr. *oryx, -ygos*, a pick-axe, an oryx antelope.]

OS *abbrev* for: Old Style; Ordinary Seaman; Ordnance Survey; outsize.

Os (*chem*) *symbol* for osmium.

Osage *ō-sāj'* or *ō'sāj*, *n* an Indian of a tribe living in Oklahoma, etc. — Also *adj*. — **Osage orange** an ornamental tree (*Maclura*) of the mulberry family often used for hedges, first found in the Osage country; its orange-like inedible fruit. [Osage *Wazhazhe*.]

Oscar *os'kər*, *n* a gold-plated statuette awarded by the American Academy of Motion Picture Arts and Sciences to a film writer, actor, director, etc., for the year's best performance in his or her particular line. [Name fortuitously given, possibly after an Academy employee's uncle.]

oscillate *os'il-āt*, *vi* to swing to and fro like a pendulum; to vibrate; to radiate electromagnetic waves; to vary between certain limits; to fluctuate. — *vt* to cause to swing or vibrate. — *adj* **osc'illating**. — *n* **oscillā'tion**. — *adj* **osc'illātive** having a tendency to vibrate; vibratory. — *n* **osc'illātor** a person who or thing which oscillates; apparatus for producing oscillations. — *adj* **oscillatory** (*os'il-ə-tə-ri*) swinging; moving as a pendulum does; vibratory. — *n* **oscill'ogram** a record made by an oscillograph. — *n* **oscill'ograph** an apparatus for producing a curve representing a number of electrical and mechanical phenomena which vary cyclically. — *n* **oscill'oscope** an instrument which shows on a fluorescent screen the variation with time of the instantaneous values and waveforms of electrical quantities, including voltages translated from sounds or movements. [L. *ōscillāre, -ātum*, to swing.]

Oscines *os'i-nēz*, *npl* the songbirds, forming the main body of the Passeriformes. — *adj* **osc'inine** or **osc'ine**. [L. *oscen, oscinis*, a singing-bird.]

osculant *os'kū-lənt*, *adj* kissing; adhering closely; intermediate between two genera, species, etc., linking (*biol*). — *adj* **os'cular** pertaining to the mouth or to kissing; osculating. — *vt* **os'culāte** to kiss; to have three or more coincident points in common with (*math*). — *vi* to be in close contact; to form a connecting link. — *n* **osculā'tion**. — *adj* **os'culatory** of or pertaining to kissing or osculation. [L. *ōsculārī, -ātus* — *ōsculum*, a little mouth, a kiss, dimin. of *ōs*, mouth.]

osier *ōzh'yər* or *ōz'yər*, *n* any willow whose twigs are used in making baskets, esp. *Salix viminalis*. — *adj* made of or like osiers. — **o'sier-bed** a place where osiers grow. [Fr.; cf. L.L. *ausāria* or *osāria*, willow bed.]

-osis *-ō'sis*, *n sfx* denoting: (1) a condition or process; (2) a diseased condition. [L. *-osis*, Gr. *-ōsis*.]

Osmanli *os-man'li*, *adj* of the dynasty of *Osmān*, who founded the Turkish empire in Asia, and reigned 1288–1326; of the Turkish empire; of the western branch of the Turks or their language. — *n* a member of the dynasty; a Turk of Turkey. [Cf. **Ottoman**.]

osmium *oz'* or *os'mi-əm*, *n* a grey-coloured metal (symbol **Os**; atomic no. 76) the heaviest substance known. — *n* **osmirid'ium** iridosmium. [Gr. *osmē*, smell.]

osmosis *os-* or *oz-mō'sis*, (*chem*) *n* diffusion of liquids through a semi-permeable membrane. — *vt* and *vi* **osmose'** to undergo, or cause to undergo, osmosis. — *n* **osmom'eter** an apparatus for measuring osmotic pressure. — *n* **osmom'etry**. — *n* **osmoregulā'tion** the process by which animals regulate the amount of water in their bodies and the concentration of various solutes and ions in their body fluids. — *adj* **osmotic** (*-mot'ik*). — *adv* **osmot'ically**. — **osmotic pressure** the pressure exerted by a dissolved substance in virtue of the motion of its molecules, or a measure of this in terms of the pressure which must be applied to a solution in order just to prevent osmosis into the solution. [Gr. *ōsmos* = *ōthismos*, impulse — *ōtheein*, to push.]

osp *abbrev* for *obiit sine prole* (L.), died without issue.

osprey *os'pri* or *-prā*, *n* a bird of prey (*Pandion haliaetus*) that feeds on fish; an egret or other plume used in millinery, not from the osprey. [Supposed to be from L. *ossifraga*, misapplied; see **ossifrage**.]

osseous *os'i-əs*, *adj* bony; composed of, or like, bone; of the nature or structure of bone. — *n* **ossein** (*os'i-in*) the organic basis of bone. [L. *os*, *ossis*, bone.]

ossia *ō-sē'a*, (It.) *conj* or (giving an alternative in music).

ossicle *os'i-kl*, (*anat*) *n* a small bone or bonelike plate. [L. *ossiculum*, dimin. of *os*, *ossis*, bone.]

ossifrage *os'i-frāj*, *n* the lammergeier, a rare type of vulture; the osprey. [L. *ossifraga*, prob. the lammergeier — *os*, *ossis*, bone, and the root of *frangĕre*, to break.]

ossify *os'i-fī*, *vt* to turn into bone or into a bonelike substance. — *vi* to become bone; to become rigid, hardened, inflexible or set into a conventional pattern: — *pr p* **oss'ifying**; *pa t* and *pa p* **oss'ified**. — *n* **oss'ificā'tion**. [Fr. *ossifier* — L. *os*, *ossis*, bone.]

ossuary *os'ū-ə-ri*, *n* a place where bones are laid, e.g. a vault or charnel-house; an urn for bones. [L. *ossuārium* — *os*, bone.]

oste-. See **osteo-**.

ostensible *os-ten'si-bl*, *adj* seeming, or outwardly apparent; pretended or professed. — *n* **ostensibil'ity**. — *adv* **osten'sibly**. [Med.L. *ostensībilis* — *ostendere*, *ostensum*, to show.]

ostensive *os-ten'siv*, *adj* of a clearly demonstrative nature (*logic*, etc.); (of a definition) pointing to examples of things to which the defined word or phrase properly applies; ostensible. — *adv* **osten'sively**. [L.L. *ostensīvus*, provable, — L. *ostendere*, *ostensum*, to show.]

ostentation *os-tən-tā'shən*, *n* pretentious display intended to draw attention or admiration. — *adj* **ostentā'tious**. — *adv* **ostentā'tiously**. — *n* **ostentā'tiousness**. [L. *ostentātio*, *-ōnis* — *ostentāre*, frequentative of *ostendere*, to show.]

osteo- *os-ti-ō-*, *-o-* or *-ə-*, or **oste-** *os-ti-*, *combining form* meaning bone. — *adj* **osteal** (*os'ti-əl*) relating to, composed of, or resembling bone; sounding like bone on percussion. — *n* **osteitis** (*os-ti-ī'tis*) inflammation of a bone. — *n* **osteoarthrī'tis** a form of arthritis in which the cartilages of the joint and the bone adjacent are worn away. — *n* **osteoarthrō'sis** chronic non-inflammatory disease of bones. — *n* **os'teoblast** a bone-forming cell. — *n* **osteogen'esis** or **osteogeny** (*-oj'*) formation of bone (**osteogenesis imperfecta** the disease *brittle bones*, in which bones are abnormally liable to fracture). — *adj* **osteogen'ic**. — *adj* **osteolog'ical**. — *n* **osteol'ogist**. — *n* **osteol'ogy** the part of anatomy that deals with the study of bones and the skeleton. — *n* **osteō'ma** a tumour composed of bone or bonelike tissue. — *n* **osteomalacia** (*-mə-lā'shə*) softening of the bones resulting from a deficiency of vitamin D. — *n* **osteomyelitis** (*-mī-ə-lī'tis*) inflammation of bone and bone marrow. — *n* **os'teopath** (*-path*) or **osteop'athist** (*-ə-thist*) a practitioner of osteopathy. — *adj* **osteopathic** (*-path'ik*). — *n* **osteop'athy** a system of healing or treatment consisting largely of manipulation of the bones, and massage. — *adj* **osteoplas'tic**. — *n* **os'teoplasty** plastic surgery of the bones, bone-grafting, etc. — *n* **osteoporō'sis** development of a porous structure in bone due to loss of calcium resulting in brittleness. — *n* **osteosarcō'ma** a malignant tumour derived from osteoblasts, composed of bone and sarcoma cells. [Gr. *osteon*, bone.]

ostinato *os-ti-nä'tō*, (*mus*) *n* a ground bass: — *pl* **ostina'tos**. [It.; root as for **obstinate**.]

ostler *os'lər*, or in U.S. **hostler** *hos'* or *os'lər*, *n* a person who attends to horses at an inn. [**hosteler**.]

Ostmark *ōst'märk*, *n* (prior to unification) the standard monetary unit (100 pfennig) of the Democratic Republic of Germany (E. Germany). [Ger., east mark.]

Ostpolitik *ōst'po-li-tēk*, *n* the West German policy, initiated in the 1960s, of establishing normal trade and diplomatic relations with the East European communist countries; any similar policy. [Ger., Eastern policy.]

ostracise or **-ize** *os'trə-sīz*, *vt* to exclude from society, or from one's social group; (in ancient Greece) to banish by popular vote, the voters writing on potsherds the name of the person they wanted banished. — *n* **os'tracism** (*-sizm*) expulsion from society; banishment by ostracising. [Gr. *ostrakon*, a potsherd, as used in ostracising.]

ostreiculture *os'trē-i-kul-chər*, *n* oyster culture, the artificial breeding of oysters for sale. — *n* **ostrēicul'turist**. [L. *ostrea* — Gr. *ostreon*, oyster.]

ostrich *os'trich* or *os'trij*, *n* the largest living bird (genus *Struthio*), found in Africa, flightless but remarkable for its speed in running, and prized for its feathers; a person who refuses to face, or who ignores, unpleasant facts, from the ostrich's habit of burying its head when chased, in the belief, supposedly, that it cannot be seen. [O.Fr. *ostruche* — L. *avis*, bird, L.L. *struthiō* an ostrich.]

Ostrogoth *os'trə-goth*, *n* a member of the Germanic people who established their power in Italy in the late 5th century A.D. — *adj* **Os'trogothic**. [L.L. *Ostrogothi*, Eastern Goths.]

OT *abbrev* for: occupational therapy; Old Testament.

otalgia *ō-tal'ji-ə*, (*med*) *n* earache. [Gr. *ous*, *ōtos*, ear, *algē*, pain.]

otary *ō'tə-ri*, *n* any of the eared seals, including the sea lions and fur seals, with well-developed external ears. [Gr. *ōtaros*, large-eared — *ous*, *ōtos*, ear.]

OTC *abbrev* for: Officers' Training Corps; over-the-counter.

OTE *abbrev* for on-target earnings, the earnings of a salesman who achieves targeted sales.

other *udh'ər*, *adj* second; alternate; different; different from or not the same as the one in question (often with *than*); not the same; remaining; additional. — *pron* other one; another. — *adv* otherwise (with *than*). — *n* **oth'erness**. — *adv* **oth'erwise** in another way or manner; by other causes; in other respects; under other conditions. — *conj* else; under other conditions. — *adj* **oth'er-directed** (*sociol*) guided by standards set for one by external influences. — *npl* **other ranks** members of the armed services not holding commissions. — **otherworld'liness**. — *adj* **otherworld'ly** concerned with the world to come, or with the world of the imagination, to the exclusion of practical interests. — **every other** each alternate; **in other words** this means; **or otherwise** or the opposite, as in *the efficiency or otherwise of the staff*; **other things being equal** associated circumstances being unchanged; **rather . . . than otherwise** rather than not; **someone, something, somewhere,** etc. **or other** an undefined person thing, place, etc.; **the other day, etc.**, on an unspecified day, etc., not long past. [O.E. *ōther*.]

otic *ō'tik*, (*med*) *adj* of or relating to the ear. — *n* **otī'tis** inflammation of the ear. — *combining form* **otō-** (or *ō-to-* or *ō-tə-*) relating to the ear. — *n* **otol'ogist**. — *n* **otol'ogy** the branch of medicine concerned with the ear. — *n* **otorhinolaryngology** (*-rī-nō-lar-ing-*

gol'ə-ji) the branch of medicine dealing with the ear, nose and larynx, and their diseases, often shortened to **otolaryngol'ogy**. — *n* **o'toscope** an instrument for examining the ear. [Gr. *ous*, *ōtos*, ear.]

otiose *ō'shi-ōs*, *adj* (of a word, expression, etc. in a particular context) superfluous, redundant. — *n* **otiosity** (*-os'i-ti*) or **otiose'ness**. [L. *ōtiōsus* — *ōtium*, leisure.]

otitis, otolaryngology, otology. See under **otic**.

-otomy *combining form* properly **-tomy** (q.v.).

otorhinolaryngology, otoscope. See under **otic**.

OTT *abbrev* for over-the-top.

ottava rima *ō-tä'və rē'mə*, *n* an Italian stanza consisting of eight hendecasyllabic lines, rhyming *a b a b a b c c*. [It., eighth rhyme.]

otter *ot'ər*, *n* an aquatic fish-eating carnivore (genus *Lutra*) of the weasel family with short smooth fur, a long slim body, and webbed feet; a board travelling edge-up, manipulated on the principle of the kite, to carry the end of a fishing-line (or several hooked and baited lines) in a lake, or to keep open the mouth of a trawl (also **otter board**); a device for severing the moorings of mines, a paravane. — **ott'er-hound** a large rough-haired dog formerly bred for otter-hunting. [O.E. *otor*, akin to **water**.]

Ottoman *ot'ə-mən*, *adj* relating to the Turkish Empire, or to the dynasty, founded by *Othmān* or *Osmān*, or to his people, who overran the Near East and pushed into Europe in the 14th century. — *n* a Turk of Turkey; (the following meanings without *cap*) a low, stuffed seat without a back (sometimes in the form of a chest); a variety of corded silk.

OU *abbrev* for: the Open University; Oxford University.

ouakari. See **uakari**.

oubliette *ōō-bli-et'*, *n* a dungeon with no opening except at the top; a secret pit in the floor of a dungeon into which a victim could be precipitated. [Fr., — *oublier*, to forget — L. *oblīvīscī*.]

ouch *owch*, *interj* expressing pain. [Ger. *autsch*.]

ought *öt*, *auxiliary verb* (taking an infinitive with *to*) expressing duty or obligation, rightness or suitability, probability. [O.E. *āhte*, past t. of *āgan*, to owe.]

Ouija® *wē'jə*, *n* a board with signs and the letters of the alphabet on it, used with a planchette in endeavouring to get messages from the dead. — Also without *cap*. [Fr. *oui*, Ger. *ja*, yes.]

oulong. See **oolong**.

ounce[1] *owns*, *n* $\frac{1}{16}$ of a pound avoirdupois; a minute quantity. — **fluid ounce** 0·0284 litre ($\frac{1}{20}$ pint); 0·0295 litre ($\frac{1}{16}$ U.S. pint). [O.Fr. *unce* — L. *uncia*, the twelfth part.]

ounce[2] *owns*, *n* the snow leopard, a big cat of Asia, with markings similar to a leopard's. [Fr. *once*, perh. for *lonce* (as if *l'once*) — Gr. *lynx*.]

our *owr*, *possessive adj* or *pron* belonging to us — when used predicatively or absolutely, **ours** (*owrz*). — *pron* **ourselves'** (used *reflexively*) us; (used emphatically for clarification in apposition to **we** or **us**) personally; our normal or usual selves, as in *we can relax and be ourselves*: — *sing* **ourself'** used regally or (*formerly*) editorially. [O.E. *ūre*, genitive of *wē*, we.]

ourali *ōō-rä'lē* or **ourari** *ōō-rä'rē*. See **wourali**.

ousel. See **ouzel**.

oust *owst*, *vt* to eject or expel. — *n* **oust'er** (*law*) ejection, dispossession. [A.Fr. *ouster*.]

out (see also **out-**) *owt*, *adv* (shading into *adj* predicatively), not within; forth; away from one's home, etc.; to, towards, or at the exterior or a position away from the inside or inner part or from anything thought of as enclosing, hiding or obscuring; from among others; from the mass; beyond bounds; away from the original or normal position or state; at or towards the far end, or a remote position; seawards; away from home or a building; in or into the open air; in or into a state of exclusion or removal; not in office; not in use or fashion; ruled out, not to be considered; no longer in the game; no longer in as a batsman, dismissed; not batting; out of the contest and unable to resume in time; in the condition of having won; away from the mark; at fault; in error; not in form or good condition; at a loss; in or into a disconcerted, perplexed or disturbed state; in or into an unconscious state; not in harmony or amity; in distribution; in or into the hands of others or the public; on loan; to or at an end; in an exhausted or extinguished state; completely; thoroughly; subjected to loss; in or to the field; in quest of or expressly aiming at something; in rebellion; on strike; in an exposed state; no longer in concealment or obscurity; in or into the state of having openly declared one's homosexuality; in or into the open; before the public; in or into society (*old*); in existence; in bloom; at full length; in an expanded state; in extension; loudly and clearly; forcibly; unreservedly. — *adj* external; outlying; remote; outwards; in any condition expressed by the adverb *out*. — *n* a projection or outward bend (as in *outs and ins*); a way out, a way of escape. — *prep* forth from (esp. *US*). — *vt* to put out, throw out; to make public the homosexual inclinations of (esp. *US*). — *vi* to surface, be revealed, emerge publicly, as in *truth* or *murder will out*. — *interj* expressing peremptory dismissal; announcing that a player is out, the ball not in court, etc.; indicating that one has come to the end of one's transmission (*radio*). — **out and about** able to go out, convalescent; active out of doors. — *adj* **out'-and-out** thoroughgoing; utter, absolute. — *n* **out-and-ou'ter** (*colloq*) an extremity. — **out for** abroad in quest of; aiming at obtaining or achieving; dismissed from batting with a score of; **out of** from within; from among; not in; not within; excluded from; from (a source, material, motive, condition, possession, language, etc.); born of; beyond the bounds, range or scope of; deviating from, in disagreement with; away or distant from; without, destitute or denuded of; **out of date** or (as attributive *adj*) **out-of-date'** not abreast of the times, old-fashioned; no longer valid; no longer current; **out of doors** in or into the open air. — *adj* **out-of-doors'** or **out-of-door'** open-air, outdoor. — *n* **out-of-doors'** the open air. — **out of it** excluded from participation; without a chance; **out of pocket** see under **pocket**. — *adj* **out-of-(the-)bod'y** denoting an occurrence in which the individual has the experience of being outside his or her own body. — **out of the way** not in the way, not impeding or preventing progress. — *adj* **out-of-the-way'** uncommon, unusual; secluded, remote. — **out of work** see under **work**. — **out of this world** see under **world**. — **out on one's feet** as good as knocked out; done for, but with a semblance of carrying on; **out to** aiming, working resolutely, to; **out with** let's do away with; **out with it!** (*colloq*) say what you have to say, and be quick about it, spit it out. [O.E. *ūte*, *ūt*.]

Words made with **out-** *adv* are listed above, and those with **out-** *pfx* in the following entry or in the separate panel; other OUT- words follow (p. 741).

out- *owt-*, *pfx* (1) meaning 'outside', 'not within', 'outlying', e.g. *outhouse*, *out-patient*; (2) meaning 'away from the inside or inner part' e.g. *outgoing*, *output*, *outpouring*; (3) with prepositional force, meaning 'outside of', e.g. *outboard*, *outdoor*; (4) meaning 'through, throughout', or 'beyond', or 'completely', e.g. *outwatch*, *outflank*, *outweary*; (5) indicating the fact of going beyond a norm, standard of comparison, or limit, 'more than', 'more successfully than', 'farther than', 'longer than', etc., e.g. *outweigh*, *outmanoeuvre*, *outlast*, etc. — *n* **out'back** the parts of Australia remote from the cities, the bush country. — *vt* **outbal'ance** to outweigh. — *vt* **outbid'** to make a higher bid than. — *adj* **out'board**

(of an engine) designed to be attached to the outside of a ship or boat; towards, or nearer, the side of a ship or aircraft. — *adv* outside, or towards the outside of a ship or aircraft. — *n* **out'break** a breaking out of e.g. violence or illness. — *n* **out'building** a building such as a barn, stable, etc., separate from a house. — *n* **out'burst** an eruption or explosion; a sudden violent expression of feeling. — *n* **out'cast** a person who has been cast out or rejected by society. — *n* **out'caste** a person who is of no caste or has lost caste. — *vt* **outclass'** to surpass by a long way, be markedly better than. — *n* **out'come** the issue or result of something, consequence. — *n* **out'crop** an emergence of rock or of a mineral vein at ground surface; a sudden emergence or occurrence. — *n* **out'cry** a loud cry of protest; a confused noise. — *adj* **outdāt'ed** outmoded, old-fashioned, obsolete. — *vt* **outdis'tance** to leave far behind; to outstrip. — *vt* **outdo'** to surpass; to excel; to overcome. — *adj* **out'door** in or for the open air. — *adv* **outdoors'** in or into the open air. — *n* the world outside houses or buildings, the open air. — *vt* **outface'** to outstare; to confront boldly. — *n* **outfall** (*owt'föl*) the outlet of a river, drain, etc. — *n* **out'field** (*cricket* and *baseball*) the outer part of the field; the players who occupy it. — *n* **out'fit** a set of (esp. selected and matching) clothes; complete equipment; a company travelling, or working, together for any purpose, formerly esp. in charge of cattle (*US*); any set of persons, a gang. — *vt* to fit out, equip. — *vi* to get an outfit. — *n* **out'fitter** a person who makes or provides outfits; a person who deals in clothing, haberdashery, sporting equipment, etc. — *n* **out'fitting**. — *vt* **outflank'** to extend beyond or pass round the flank of; to circumvent. — *n* **out'flow** a flowing out; an outward current; outfall; amount that flows out. — *vt* **outfox'** to get the better of by cunning, to outwit. — *vt* **outgen'eral** to get the better of by generalship. — *n* **out'go** (*pl* **out'goes** expenditure (opp. to *income*). — *n* **out'going** the act of going out. — *adj* departing, leaving or retiring (opp. to *incoming*); friendly, gregarious, extrovert. — *npl* **out'goings** expenditure. — *vt* **outgrow'** to surpass in growth; to grow out of, grow too big for; to eliminate or become free from in course of growth. — *n* **out'growth** that which grows out from anything; an excrescence; a product. — *vt* **outgun'** to defeat by means of superior weapons, forces, strength, etc. — *n* **out'house** a building built near to, or up against, a main building. — *vt* **outjock'ey** to outwit by trickery. — *adj* **outlan'dish** strange, bizarre, foreign. — *adv* **outlan'dishly**. — *n* **outlan'dishness**. — *vt* **outlast'** to last longer than. — *n* **outlaw** see separate entry. — *n* **outlay'** an expenditure of money, resources, etc. — *n* **out'let** a vent or opening allowing the escape of something; a means of full or uninhibited expression; a market for a certain product, etc.; a shop, etc. selling a particular producer's products; an electrical power point (*US*). — *n* **out'lier** a detached portion of anything lying some way off or out; an isolated remnant of rock surrounded by older rocks (*geol*). — *n* **out'line** the line by which any figure or object appears to be bounded; a line representing this in a drawing, etc.; a sketch showing only the main lines; a general statement without details; a statement of the main principles. — *vt* to draw the exterior line of; to delineate or sketch. — *vt* **outlive** (*-liv'*) to live longer than; to survive; to live through; to live down. — *n* **out'look** a place for looking out from; a view, prospect; a prospect for the future; mental point of view. — *adj* **out'lying** remote from the centre or main part. — *vt* **outmanoeu'vre** to surpass in or by manoeuvring. — *n* **out'marriage** marriage to a partner outside one's own group, religion, etc. — *adj* **outmo'ded** outdated, old-fashioned, no longer current. — *adj* **out'most** see **outermost** under **outer**. — *vt* **outnum'ber** to exceed in numbers. — *vt* **outpace'** to go faster than; to outstrip. — *n* **out'patient** a non-resident patient attending a hospital. — *vt* **outperform'** to perform better than. — *n* **out'placement** (*euph*) dismissal from one's job, by sacking or redundancy. — *vt* **outplay'** to play better than, and so defeat. — *vt* **outpoint'** to score more points than. — *n* **out'post** a post or station beyond the main body of the army, etc.; a remote settlement or stronghold. — *n* **out'pouring** a pouring out; a passionate or voluble utterance. — *n* **out'put** quantity produced or turned out; data in either printed or coded form after processing by a computer; punched tape or printed page by which processed data leave a computer; a signal delivered by a telecommunications instrument or system. — *vt* (of a computer, etc.) to send out, supply, produce as output (data, etc.). — *vt* **outrank'** to rank above. — *vt* **outreach'** to reach or extend beyond; to overreach. — *n* the extent or distance something can reach or stretch out; an organisation's involvement in or contact with the surrounding community, esp. that of a church for purposes of evangelism or that of community welfare organisations taking their services out to (esp. disadvantaged) individuals and groups. — *vt* **outride'** to ride beyond; to ride faster than; to ride safely through (a storm). — *n* **out'rider** a man who rides beside a carriage as a guard; a rider sent ahead as a scout, or to ensure a clear passage. — *n* **out'rigger** a projecting contrivance supported on a float, fixed to the side of a canoe, etc. to give stability; a projecting rowlock giving extra leverage to the oar; a boat having such rowlocks; a projecting beam or framework attached to a building, ship or aircraft for any of various purposes. — *adj* **out'right** without qualifications or reservations; total, absolute. — *adv* totally, completely, without qualification; directly, without concealment or circumlocution, unreservedly; at once and completely. — *vt* **outrun'** to go beyond in running; to exceed; to get the better of or to escape by running. — *vt* **outsell'** to be sold in larger quantities than; to fetch a higher price than. — *n* **out'set** a beginning or start, esp. in *at* or *from the*

Some words with **out-** prefix; see **out-** entry for numbered senses

outact' *vt* (5).
outbar'gain *vt* (5).
outbox' *vt* (5).
outburn' *vt* (5), *vi* (4).
outdance' *vt* (5).
outdrink' *vt* (5).
outdrive' *vt* (5).
outeat' *vt* (5).
outfight' *vt* (5).
out'flowing *n*, *adj* (2).
outfly' *vt* (5).
out'goer *n* (2).
out'gush *n* (2).
outhit' *vt* (5).
outjump' *vt* (5).
outmarch' *vt* (4),(5).
outmatch' *vt* (5).
outperform' *vt* (5).
outrace' *vt* (5).
outri'val *vt* (5).
outsail' *vt* (5).
outshine' *vt* (5).
outshoot' *vt* (5).
outsit' *vt* (5).
outsleep' *vt* (4),(5).
outswim' *vt* (5).
out'swing *n* (1).
outtalk' *vt* (5).
outthink' *vt* (5).

outset. — *adj* **out'size** over normal size. — *n* an exceptionally large size; anything, esp. a garment, of exceptionally large size. — *adj* **out'sized**. — *n* **out'skirts** the outlying areas of a town, etc., suburbs; the fringes of a subject, etc. — *vt* **outsmart'** (*colloq*) to show more cleverness or cunning than, to outwit. — *vt* **outspend'** to spend more than or beyond the limits of. — *adj* **outspō'ken** speaking, or spoken, frankly, without circumlocution. — *n* **outspō'kenness**. — *vt* and *vi* **outspread'** to spread out or over. — *adj* **out'spread** (or *owt-spred'*) spread out. — *n* an expanse. — *adj* **outstand'ing** prominent; excellent, superior; unsettled; unpaid; still to be attended to or done. — *adv* **outstand'ingly** noticeably, exceptionally, surpassingly. — *vt* **outstare'** to face the stare of boldly; to outdo in staring. — *n* **out'station** a post or station remote from headquarters. — *vt* **outstay'** to stay longer than; to stay beyond the limit of, as in *outstay one's welcome*. — *adj* **outstretched'** stretched out; extended, proffered. — *vt* **outstrip'** to outrun; to leave behind; to surpass. — *n* **out'swinger** a ball bowled to swerve from leg to off (*cricket*); a ball kicked to swerve away from the goal or from the centre of the pitch. — *n* **out'take** (*cinema*) an unwanted section cut out of a film. — *n* **out'-tray** a shallow container for letters, etc. ready for despatch. — *n* **out'turn** the amount of anything turned out, produced or achieved, output. — *vt* **outvote'** to defeat by a majority of votes to overrule by weight of opinion. — *vt* **outweigh'** to exceed in weight or importance. — *vt* **outwit'** to defeat by superior ingenuity: — *pr p* **outwitt'ing**; *pa t* and *pa p* **outwitt'ed**. — *prep* **outwith'** (*Scot*) beyond the limits of, outside. — *n* **out'work** (often *pl*) a defence work that lies outside the principal line of fortification; work done away from the factory or shop, etc. — *n* **out'worker**. — *adj* **outworn'** (or *owt'*) worn out; obsolete.

outage *ow'tij*, *n* the amount of commodity lost in transport and storage; the amount of fuel used on a flight; stoppage of a mechanism due to failure of power; a period during which electricity fails or is cut off; a period when a reactor is working at a low level (*nuc energy*).

outer *ow'tər*, *adj* further out; external. — *n* the outermost ring on a target, or the shot striking it (*archery*); the unsheltered part of the spectator enclosure at a sportsground (*Austr* and *NZ*). — *adj* **ou'termost** or **out'most** furthest out; most remote from the centre. — **outer bar** (*Eng law*) the junior barristers, who plead outside the bar in court; **outer space** space beyond the earth's atmosphere; **ou'terwear** or **outer garments** clothes such as jackets, suits, worn over other clothes; clothes put on to go out of doors. — **on the outer** (*Austr* and *NZ*) excluded, out in the cold. [O.E. *ūterra*.]

outing *ow'ting*, *n* an outdoor excursion; the act of making public another person's homosexuality (esp. *US*).

outlaw *owt'lö*, *n* a person deprived of the protection of the law; (*loosely*) a bandit; someone banished, exiled or on the run from the law. — *vt* to deprive of the benefit of the law; to ban, make illegal, proscribe. — *n* **out'lawry**. [O.E. *ūtlaga* — O.N. *ūtlāgi* — *ūt*, out, *lög*, law.]

outmost. See **outermost** under **outer**.

outrage *owt'rāj*, *n* gross or violent injury; an act of wanton mischief; an atrocious act; gross offence to moral feelings; great anger or indignation; violation; rape. — *vt* to shock grossly; to injure by violence, esp. to violate, to ravish. — *adj* **outrageous** (*owt-rā'jəs*) iniquitous, disgraceful, shocking; offensive, gross; turbulent, violent; immoderate, wild, extravagant. — *adv* **outrā'geously**. — *n* **outrā'geousness**. [O.Fr. *ultrage* — *outre*, beyond — L. *ultrā*.]

outré *ōō'trā*, *adj* beyond what is customary or proper; extravagant, fantastic. [Fr.]

outside *owt'sīd* or *owt-sīd'*, *n* the outer side; the farthest limit; the outer surface; the exterior; the outer part; an outside player in football, etc. — *adj* **out'side** on or from the outside; carried on the outside; exterior; superficial; external; extreme; (of a possibility) unlikely, remote; beyond the limit; not having membership; (of a criminal activity) carried out by person(s) not having contacts with someone near the victim; at a distance from a major centre of population (*Austr*); of a position near (or nearer) the edge of the field (*Rugby*, etc.). — *adv* **outside'** on or to the outside; not within; out of prison. — *prep* **out'side** or **outside'** to or on the outside of; except for, apart from (*colloq*). — *n* **outsi'der** a person who is not a member of a particular company, profession, etc., a stranger, a layman; a person not considered fit to associate with; a person who is not an inmate; a person who is not participating; a racehorse, competitor, team, etc. not included among the favourites in the betting; a person whose place in a game, at work, etc. is on the outside; (in *pl*) a pair of nippers for turning a key in a keyhole from the outside. — **outside broadcast** a broadcast not made from within a studio; **outside chance** a remote chance; **outside half** (*Rugby football*) a stand-off half; **outside left** and **right** (in some games) forward players respectively on the extreme left and right. — **at the outside** at the most, etc.; **get outside of** (*colloq*) to eat or drink; **outside in** same as **inside out**; **outside of** (*colloq*, esp. *US*) in or to a position external to; apart from, except. [**out** and **side**.]

outward *ow'twərd*, *adj* toward the outside; on the outside; outer; external; apparent or seeming; in a direction away from home or one's base. — *adv* outwards. — *adv* **out'wardly** in outward appearance, apparently, superficially; externally. — *n* **out'wardness**. — *adv* **out'wards** in an outward direction, out.

ouzel or **ousel** *ōō'zl*, *n* (*archaic*) blackbird. — **ring ouzel** a blackish thrush with a broad white band on the throat; **water ouzel** the dipper, an aquatic songbird. [O.E. *ōsle*.]

ouzo *ōō'zō*, *n* an aniseed liqueur: — *pl* **ou'zos**. [Mod. Gr. *ouzon*.]

ova. See **ovum**.

oval *ō'vəl*, *adj* strictly, egg-shaped, like an egg in the round or in projection, rounded, longer than broad, broadest near one end; (*loosely*) elliptical or ellipsoidal, or nearly so; rounded at both ends, about twice as long as broad, broadest in the middle (*bot*). — *n* an oval figure or thing. — *adv* **o'vally**. [L. *ōvum*, egg; *ōvālis* is modern Latin.]

ovary *ō'və-ri*, *n* the female genital gland; the part of the gynaeceum that contains the ovules (*bot*). — *adj* **ovā'rian** of or relating to the ovary. [N.L. *ōvārium* — L. *ōvum*, egg.]

ovate[1] *ov'āt*, *n* an Eisteddfodic graduate who is neither a bard nor a druid. [Welsh *ofydd*, a philosopher, or lord.]

ovate[2] *ō'vāt*, *adj* egg-shaped; having an outline like an egg's, broadest below the middle (*bot*). [L. *ōvātus*, egg-shaped.]

ovation *ō-vā'shən*, *n* an outburst of popular applause, an enthusiastic reception. [L. *ŏvātiō*, *-ōnis* — *ŏvāre*, to exult.]

oven *uv'n*, *n* a closed compartment for baking, heating or drying; a small furnace. — **ov'en-bird** a name for various birds that build domed nests, esp. the S. American genus *Furnarius*; **oven glove** a type of thick reinforced glove worn when handling hot dishes. — *adj* **ov'en-ready** (of food) prepared beforehand so as to be ready for cooking in the oven immediately after purchase. — **ov'enware** dishes, such as casseroles, that will stand the heat of an oven. [O.E. *ofen*.]

over *ō'vər*, *prep* above in place, rank, power, authority, contention, preference, value, quantity, number, etc.; in excess of; above and from one side of to the other; down from or beyond the edge of; from side to side or end to end of; along; throughout the extent of; during; until after; across; on or to the other side of; on, on to, about, or across the surface of, or all or much of; in discussion, contemplation, study of, or occupation with; concerning; on account of; recovered from the effects of; in a sunk, submerged or buried state beyond the level of, as in *over head and ears*. — *adv* on the top; above; across; to or on the other side; from one person, party, condition, etc. to another; into a sleep; outwards so as to overhang, or to fall from; down, away from an upright position; through, from beginning to end, esp. in a cursory or exploratory way; throughout; into a reversed position; again, in repetition; too much; in excess; left remaining; at an end. — *interj* indicating that the speaker now expects a reply (*radio*). — *adj* (usu. as *pfx*) upper or superior. — *n* the series of balls or the play between changes in bowling from one end to the other (*cricket*). — *n* **overage** (*ō'və-rij*) surplus, excess (see also **over-age** under **over-**). — *adv* **o'verly** (*colloq*) excessively. — **over-and-un'der** a double-barrelled gun having the barrels one on top of the other rather than side by side (also **under-and-o'ver**). — *adj* **over-the-count'er** (of securities, etc.) not listed on or traded through a stock exchange, but traded directly between buyers and sellers; (of drugs, etc.) able to be bought or sold without a prescription or licence. — *adj* **over-the-top'** excessive, extreme, too much. — **all over** at an end; everywhere; at his, her, or its, most characteristic; covered with, besmeared or bespattered with; **all over again** again from the beginning, anew; **be all over (someone)** to make a fuss of, fawn on (someone); **not over-** not very, as in *not over-generous*; **over again** all over again; **over against** opposite; **over and above** in addition to; besides; **over and out** an expression used to announce the end of one's transmission (*radio*); **over and over (again)** many times; repeatedly; **over head and ears** completely submerged; **over to you!** used to transfer the initiative in speaking, etc., to another person. [O.E. *ofer*; cf. **up**.]

Words made with **over** *prep* are listed above, and those with **over-** *pfx* in the following entry or in the separate panel; other OVER- words follow (p. 745).

over- *pfx* used with certain meanings of **over** *prep*, *adv*, or *adj*, as (1) above, across, across the surface; (2) beyond an understood limit; (3) down, away from the upright position; (4) upper or outer; (5) beyond what is usual or desirable; (6) completely. — *vi* **overachieve'** to do better than predicted or expected. — *vt* and *vi* **overact'** to act with exaggeration. — *adj* **over-age'** too old, beyond the age limit specified for (see also **overage** under **over**). — *adv* **overall'** altogether; over the whole. — *adj* **o'verall** including everything; everything being reckoned; all-round. — *n* **o'verall** a protective loose coat worn over ordinary clothes for dirty work; (in *pl*) a one-piece protective work garment combining sleeved top and trousers, a boiler suit; dungarees (*US*). — *adj* **o'veralled**. — *vt* **overarch'** to arch over; to form an arch over. — *adj* and *adv* **o'verarm** with the arm raised above the shoulder. — *vt* **overawe'** to daunt by arousing fear or reverence. — *vt* **overbal'ance** to cause to lose balance. — *vi* to lose balance, fall over. — *vt* **overbear'** to bear down, overpower; to overwhelm; to overrule (objections or an objector). — *adj* **overbear'ing** inclined to domineer; arrogant and dogmatic; imperious. — *adv* **overbear'ingly**. — *n* **overbear'ingness**. — *vt* **overbid'** to outbid; to make a bid that is greater than or counts above; to bid more than the value of. — *n* **o'verbid**. — *vi* **overblow'** to produce a harmonic instead of the fundamental tone, by increase of wind-pressure (*mus*). — *adv* **overboard'** over the side (of a ship or boat) into the water; (**go overboard about** or **for** (*slang*) to go to extremes of enthusiasm about or for; **throw overboard** to reject, jettison). — *vt* and *vi* **overbook'** to make more reservations than the number of places (in a plane, ship, hotel, etc.) actually available (also *vi*). — *vt* **overbuild'** to build over the top of; to build too much upon or in. — *vt* **overburd'en** to burden too heavily. — *n* (*ō'vər-*) an excessive burden; rock that must be removed to expose a vein or seam (*mining*). — *vt* **overbuy'** to buy too much of. — *vt* **overcall'** (*bridge*) to outbid. — *n* **o'vercall**. — *vt* **overcast'** to sew stitches over (a raw edge). — *adj* clouded over. — *vt* **overcharge'** to charge too much; to load to excess. — *n* **o'vercharge**. — *vt* **overcloud'** to cover over with clouds; to fill with gloom, sadness or anxiety. — *n* **o'vercoat** an outdoor coat worn over one's indoor clothes, a topcoat. — *vt* **overcome'** to get the better of; to conquer or subdue; to surmount. — *vi* to be victorious. — *vi* **overcom'pensate** to go too far in trying to correct a fault that one (believes one) suffers from (with *for*; *psychol*). — *n* **overcompensā'tion**. — *vt* **overcorrect'** to apply so great a correction to as to deviate in the opposite way. — *n* **overcorrec'tion**. — *vt* **o'vercrop** to take too much out of by cultivation. — *vt* **overcrowd'** to crowd too many people, animals, etc. into. — *adj* **overcrow'ded**. — *vt* **overdevel'op** to develop too far; to leave (a film) too long in the developer (*phot*). — *vt* **overdo'** to do too much (**overdo it** or **things** to tire oneself out); to overact; to exaggerate, carry too far; to cook too much; to use too much of. — *adj* **overdone'**. — *n* **o'verdose** an excessive dose of drugs, medicine, etc. — *vt* and *vi* **overdose'**. — *n* **o'verdraft** the overdrawing of a bank account; the excess of the amount drawn over the sum against which it is drawn. — *vt* **overdraw'** to draw from (one's bank account) beyond one's credit; to exaggerate in depicting. — *vt* and *vi* **overdress'** to dress too ostentatiously or elaborately. — *n* **o'verdrive** a gearing device which transmits to the driving shaft a speed greater than engine crankshaft speed; too long a shot in tennis, golf, etc. — *vt* to work (someone, or oneself) too hard. — *adj* **overdue'** behind time for arrival; still unpaid after the time it is due. — *vi* **overeat'** to eat too much. — *vt* **overexpose'** to give too much publicity to; to expose (a film) to too much light. — *n* **overexpo'sure**. — *vt* **overflow'** to flow over (a bank, rim, etc.); to flow over the edge of; to flow over the surface of; to flood; (of e.g. people) to fill and then spread beyond (e.g. a room). — *vi* to flow over an edge or limit; to abound (with *with*). — *n* **o'verflow** flowing over; that which flows over; an excess number or quantity; a pipe or channel for spare water, etc.; an inundation; a superabundance. — *adj* **overflow'ing** flowing or running over; overfull; abounding (with *with*); exuberant. — *n* **o'verglaze** an additional glaze given to porcelain, etc. — *adj* **overgrown** (*ō'vər-grōn* or *-grōn'*) grown beyond the natural size; covered over with uncontrolled vegetation, weeds, etc. — *n* **o'vergrowth** excessive or abnormally great growth; excess or superfluity resulting from growth; that which grows over and covers anything. — *adv* **overhand'** (or *ō'vər-*) with hand above the object; palm downwards; with hand or arm raised above the shoulders or (in swimming) coming out of the water over the head; from below (*mineralogy*); with stitches passing through in one direction and back round the edges (*needlework*). — *adj* **o'verhand** done or performed overhand. — *vt* **overhang'** to hang or project over; to impend over. — *vi* to hang over, lean out beyond the vertical. — *n* **o'verhang** a projecting part; degree of projection. — *vt* **overhaul'** to examine thoroughly and repair where necessary; to overtake or gain upon (*naut*). — *n* **o'verhaul** a thorough examination with a view to repair. — *adv* **overhead'** above one's head;

aloft; in the zenith. — *adj* **o'verhead** above one's head; well above ground level; (of a projector) designed to sit on a speaker's desk and project transparencies on a screen behind him or her; all-round, general, average. — *n* (often in *pl*; also **overhead costs or charges)** the general expenses of a business, such as heating and lighting of premises, etc. — as distinct from the direct cost of producing an article. — *vt* **overhear'** to hear without being meant to hear, as an eavesdropper does; to hear by accident, as an unintentional or unnoticed listener does. — *vt* **overheat'** to heat to excess; to overstimulate (the economy) with the risk of increasing inflation (*econ*). — *vi* to become too hot. — *adj* **overhea'ted** agitated. — *n* **overhea'ting.** — *adj* **overhung'** overhanging; suspended from above; covered over with hangings, or hanging vegetation. — *n* **overinsur'ance.** — *vt* **overinsure'** to insure for more than the real value. — *vt* **overiss'ue** to issue in excess (e.g. bank-notes or bills of exchange). — *n* **o'verissue.** — *adj* **overjoyed'** filled with great joy; transported with delight or gladness. — *n* **o'verkill** something, e.g. power for destruction, in excess of what is necessary or desirable. — *adj* **o'verland** passing entirely or principally by land. — *vt* or *vi* (*Austr*) to drive (cattle) across country for long distances. — *adv* **overland'** by or over land. — *vt* **overlap'** to extend over the edge of, and partly cover; to coincide in part with. — *n* **o'verlap** an overlapping part or situation; a disposition of strata where the upper beds extend beyond the boundary of the lower beds of the same series (*geol*). — *vt* **overlay'** to cover by laying or spreading something over; to cover to excess, encumber: — *pa t* and *pa p* **overlaid'.** — *n* **o'verlay** a covering; anything laid on or over for the purpose of visual alteration. — *adv* **overleaf'** on the other side of the leaf of a book. — *vt* **overlie'** to lie above or upon; to smother by lying on: — *pr p* **overly'ing**; *pa t* **overlay'**; *pa p* **overlain'.** — *vt* **overload'** to load too heavily or fill too full. — *n* **o'verload** an excessive load. — *vt* and *vi* **o'verlock** to oversew (a fabric edge, hem, seam, etc.) with an interlocking stitch to prevent fraying. — *n* **o'verlocker** a person who or machine which does this. — *n* **o'verlocking** the process of doing this, or the stitching produced. — *vt* **overlook'** to look over; to see from, or afford a view of, from above; to view carefully; to oversee, superintend; to fail to notice or take into account; to allow (a misdemeanour, etc.) to go unpunished. — *n* **o'verlord** a supreme lord. — *n* **o'verlordship.** — *adv* **overly** see under **over**. — *adj* **overly'ing** lying on the top. — *n* **o'verman** an overseer in mining, the man in charge of work below ground. — *vt* **overman'** to supply (a vessel) with too many men, employ uneconomically large numbers of workers in (an industry, etc.). — *n* **o'vermantel** an ornamental structure, often with a mirror, set on a mantelshelf. — *vt* **overmas'ter** to overpower. — *vt* **overmatch'** (esp. *US*) to be more than a match for; to match with a superior opponent. — *adj* and *adv* **o'vermuch** (or *-much'*) too much. — *adj* **overnice'** too fastidious. — *adv* **overnight'** for the duration of the night, till the next morning; during, or in the course of, the night; hence, extraordinarily quickly. — *adj* done or occurring or existing overnight; for the time from evening till next morning; (**overnight bag** or **case** a small case for carrying the clothes, toilet articles, etc., needed for an overnight stay). — *n* **o'vernighter** a person staying overnight; an overnight bag. — *adv* **overpage'** overleaf. — *n* **o'verpass** a road bridging another road or railway, canal, etc., a flyover. — *vt* **overpay'** to pay too much. — *n* **overpay'ment.** — *vi* **overped'al** to make excessive use of the sustaining pedal of a piano. — *vt* **overpitch'** (*cricket*) to bowl (the ball) so that its trajectory would bring it too close to the stumps. — *vt* **overplay'** to overemphasise the importance or value of; to try to gain more than one's assets can be expected to yield (**overplay one's hand**; *fig*). — *vt* and *vi* to exaggerate (an emotion, acting rôle, etc.). — *vt* **overpower'** to overcome, reduce to helplessness, by force; to subdue; to overwhelm; to make (an engine, etc.) too powerful. — *adj* **overpower'ing** excessive in degree or amount; irresistible. — *adv* **overpower'ingly.** — *vt* **overprice'** to ask too high a price for. — *adj* **overpriced'.** — *vt* **overprint'** to print over already printed matter (esp. a postage stamp). — *n* **o'verprint.** — *vt* and *vi* **overproduce'.** — *n* **overproduc'tion** excessive production; production in excess of the demand. — *adj* **overproof'** containing more alcohol than does proof-spirit. — *adj* **overqual'ified** having qualifications and skills in excess of those required for a particular job, etc. — *vt* (*reflexive*) **overreach'** to undo (oneself) by attempting too much, venturing too far, trying to be too clever, etc. — *vi* (of a horse) to strike the hindfoot against the forefoot. — *vi* **overreact'** to react or respond with too much vehemence, or otherwise excessively. — *n* **overreac'tion.** — *vt* **override'** to pass over; to set aside; to be valid against; to be more important than, prevail over; to overlap. — *n* **o'verride** an auxiliary (esp. manual) control capable of temporarily prevailing over the operation of another (esp. automatic) control. — *n* **o'verrider** an attachment on the bumper of a motor vehicle to prevent another bumper becoming interlocked with it. — *adj* **overri'ding** dominant, stronger than anything else. — *vt* **overrule'** to modify or to set aside by greater power; to prevail over the will of, against a previous decision of; to impose an overriding decision upon; to prevail over and set aside; to annul, declare invalid (*law*); to rule against; to disallow. — *vt* **overrun'** to spread over; to infest, swarm over; to infect widely; to spread over and take possession of; to run beyond; to exceed the limit of; to carry over into another line or page; (of a vehicle engine) to slow down in response to a reverse torque transmitted through the gears from the wheels: — *pr p* **overrunn'ing**; *pa t* **overran'**; *pa p* **overrun'.** — *n* **o'verrun** an act or occasion of overrunning; the extent of overrunning; the overrunning of a vehicle engine (**overrun brake** a brake fitted to a trailer that prevents it from travelling faster than the towing vehicle when reducing speed or going downhill). — *adj* **o'versea** or **o'verseas** across, beyond, or from beyond the sea. — *adv* **overseas'** in or to lands beyond the sea; abroad. — *n* foreign lands. — *vt* **oversee'** to superintend. — *n* **o'verseer** (*-sē-ər*) a person who oversees workmen, etc.; a superintendent; the manager of a plantation of slaves (*hist*). — *vt* and *vi* **oversell'** to sell more of than is available; to exaggerate the merits of. — *vt* **o'versew** to sew together overhand. — *vt* **overshad'ow** to throw a shadow over; to cast into the shade by surpassing, to outshine; to darken. — *n* **o'vershoe** a shoe (esp. of waterproof material) worn over another. — *vt* **overshoot'** to shoot over or beyond (one's target); (of a train or aircraft) to fail to come to a halt at (a station) or on (a runway): — *pa t* and *pa p* **overshot'.** — *n* **o'vershoot.** — *adj* **o'vershot** having the upper jaw protruding over the lower; (of a waterwheel) fed from above. — *n* **o'versight** a failure to notice; a mistake; an omission; supervision. — *adj* **o'versize** or **o'versized** very large, or larger than normal. — *vi* **oversleep'** to sleep too long. — *vt* **overspend'** to spend beyond (one's income, budget, etc.). — *vi* to spend too much. — *n* an instance of overspending; the amount by which an allocated budget, etc. is overspent. — *n* **o'verspill** a proportion of the population that leaves a district, displaced by changes in housing, etc.; (in a public bar) beer, etc. that overflows from a glass as it is being filled. — *n* **o'verspin** the spinning of a flying ball in the same direction as if it were rolling on the ground. — *vt*

overstaff' to provide too many people as staff for. — *vt* **overstate'** to state too strongly; to exaggerate. — *n* **overstate'ment**. — *vt* **overstay'** to stay beyond (a time limit). — *n* **overstay'er** an immigrant worker who stays beyond the time allowed by his or her work permit. — *vi* **o'versteer** (of a motor car) to exaggerate the degree of turning applied by the steering-wheel. — *n* the tendency to do this. — *vt* **overstep'** to step beyond; to exceed; to transgress. — *adj* **overstrung'** too highly strung; (of a piano) having two sets of strings crossing obliquely to save space. — *vt* **oversubscribe'** to subscribe for (shares) beyond the number offered. — *n* **oversubscrip'-tion**. — *vt* **overtake'** to draw level with and move past (something or someone travelling in the same direction); to come upon or befall, as in *overtaken by darkness* or *disaster*. — *vt* **overtax'** to tax too heavily; to require too much of. — *vt* **overthrow'** to throw over, overturn, upset; to ruin, subvert; to defeat utterly; to throw too far or too strongly. — *n* **o'verthrow** the act of overthrowing or state of being overthrown; a ball missed at the wicket and returned from the field (*cricket*); a run scored in consequence. — *n* **o'vertime** time spent in working beyond the regular hours; work done in such time; pay for such work. — *adj* and *adv* during, for or concerning such time. — *vt* **overtime'** to exceed the correct allowance of time for (a photographic exposure, etc.). — *n* **o'vertimer** a person who works overtime. — *n* **o'vertone** a harmonic or upper partial (*mus*); (in *pl*) a subtle meaning, additional to the main meaning, or constant association. — *vt* **overtop'** to rise higher than; to surpass; to exceed. — *n* **o'vertrick** (*bridge*) a trick in excess of those contracted for. — *vt* **overtrump'** to trump with a higher card than one already played. — *vt* **overturn'** to throw down or over; to upset; to subvert. — *n* **o'verview** a general survey. — *n* **o'verwash** (*geol*) material carried by glacier-streams over a frontal moraine. — *adj* **over-ween'ing** (of a person) arrogant, conceited; (of pride) inflated, excessive, immoderate. — *n* **o'ver-weight** weight beyond what is required or what is allowed. — *adj* **overweight'** above the weight required; above the ideal or desired weight. — *vt* **overwhelm'** to reduce to helplessness, crush completely; to overpower; to affect overpoweringly; to defeat utterly, usu. with superior numbers; to inundate, submerge, esp. suddenly. — *adj* **over-whel'ming**. — *adv* **overwhel'mingly**. — *vt* **over-wind** (*-wīnd'*) to wind too far: — *pa t* and *pa p* **overwound'**. — *vi* **overwin'ter** to pass the winter. — *vt* and *vi* to keep (animals, etc.), or stay, alive through the winter. — *vt* and *vi* **overwork'** to work too hard. — *n* **overwork'** excessive work. — Also *vi*. — *vt* **overwrite'** to write too much about; to write in a laboured manner. — *vi* to write too much or in too contrived a manner. — *adj* **overwrought'** in an over-emotional state; overdone, too elaborate.

Some words with **over-** prefix; see **over-** entry for numbered senses

overabound' *vi* (5).
overabound'ing *adj* (5).
over-absorp'tion *n* (5).
overabun'dance *n* (5).
over-anxi'ety *n* (5).
over-anx'ious *adj* (5).
over-anx'iously *adv* (5).

o'verblanket *n* (4).
overboil' *vt*, *vi* (2), (5).
overbold' *adj* (5).
overbold'ly *adv* (5).

overcare'ful *adj* (5).
overclad' *adj* (5).
over-con'fidence *n* (5).
over-con'fident *adj* (5).
over-cool' *vt* (5).
overcredu'lity *n* (5).
overcred'ulous *adj* (5).

overdar'ing *adj* (5).
overdram'atise or **-ize** *vt* (5).
o'verdress *n* (4).

overear'nest *adj* (5).
over-emo'tional *adj* (5).
overes'timate *vt*, *n* (5).
overestima'tion *n* (5).
over-exact' *adj* (5).
overexcitabil'ity *n* (5).
overexcit'able *adj* (5).
overexcite' *vt* (5).
overexert' *vt* (5).
overexer'tion *n* (5).

overfamil'iar *adj* (5).
overfamiliar'ity *n* (5).
overfed' *pa t*, *pa p* (5).
overfeed' *vt*, *vi* (5).
overfill' *vt*, *vi* (5).
overfine' *adj* (5).
overfine'ness *n* (5).
overfish' *vt* (5).
overfond' *adj* (5).
overfond'ly *adv* (5).
overfond'ness *n* (5).
overfree' *adj* (5).
overfree'dom *n* (5).
overfree'ly *adv* (5).
overfull' *adj* (5).
overful(l)'ness *n* (5).

o'vergarment *n* (4).
overgraze' *vt*, *vi* (5).
overgrā'zing *n* (5).

overhast'ily *adv* (5).
overhast'iness *n* (5).
overhast'y *adj* (5).
overhit' *vt* (5).

overinclined' *adj* (5).
overindulge' *vt* (5).
overindul'gence *n* (5).
overindul'gent *adj* (5).

overkind' *adj* (5).
overkind'ness *n* (5).

overleav'en *vt* (5).
overlong' *adj*, *adv* (5).
overloud' *adj* (5).

overmul'tiply *vi* (5).

overneat' *adj* (5).

overpaint' *vt* (5).
overpay' *vt* (5).
overpeo'ple *vt* (5).
overpop'ulate *vt* (5).
overpopulā'tion *n* (5).
overpraise' *vt* (5).
overpraise' (or **ō'**) *n* (5).
over-precise' *adj* (5).
overprepare' *vi*, *vt* (5).
overprotec'tive *adj* (5).
overproud' *adj* (5).

overrate' *vt* (2).
o'verrate *n* (2).
over-refine' *vt* (5).
over-refine'ment *n* (5).
over-rev' *vt*, *vi* (5).
overripe' *adj* (5).
overri'pen *vt*, *vi* (5).
overripe'ness *n* (5).
overroast' *vt* (2).

overscru'pulous *adj* (5).
overscrup'ulousness *n* (5).
oversexed' *adj* (5).
o'vershirt *n* (4).
oversimplificā'tion *n* (5).
oversim'plify *vt* (5).
o'verskirt *n* (4).
o'versleeve *n* (4).
overspec'ialise or **-ize** *vi* (5).
overspecialisā'tion or **-z-** *n* (5).
overspread' *vt* (1).
overstain' *vt* (1).
overstock' *vt* (5).
o'verstock *n* (5).
overstrain' *vt* (5).
overstress' *vt* (5).
o'verstress *n* (5).
overstretch' *vt* (5).
overstrong' *adj* (5).
overstud'y *vt*, *vi* (5).
overstuff' *vt* (5).
oversubt'le *adj* (5).
oversubt'lety *n* (5).
oversupply' *vt* (5).
o'versupply *n* (5).

overtire' *vt* (5).
overtrain' *vt*, *vi* (5).

overuse' *vt* (5).
o'veruse *n* (5).

overval'ue *vt* (5).
overvalua'tion *n* (5).
overvi'olent *adj* (5).

overwear'y *adj* (5).
overwise' *adj* (5).

overt *ō'vûrt* or *ō-vûrt'*, *adj* open to view, not concealed; public; evident. — *adv* **overtly**. — **overt act** something obviously done in execution of a criminal intent. [Fr. *ouvert*, past p. of *ouvrir*, to open.]

overtake ... to ... **overtrump**. See under **over-**.

overture *o'vər-tūr*, *n* an instrumental prelude to an opera, etc.; a one-movement musical composition in a similar style; (usu. in *pl*) an introductory proposition or opening move to negotiations, etc. [O.Fr. *overture* (Fr. *ouverture*), opening.]

overturn ... to ... **overwrought**. See under **over-**.

ovi- *ov-i-* or *ō-vi-*, or **ovo-** *-vō-* or *-və-*, *combining form* denoting: egg; ovum. — *n* **oviduct** (*ō'vi-dukt*) the tube by which the egg escapes from the ovary (*zool*). — *adj* **oviform** (*ō'vi-förm*) egg-shaped. — *adj* **oviparous** (*ō-vip'ə-rəs*) egg-laying, as birds, fishes or reptiles are. — *n* **ovipar'ity** (*-par'i-ti*). — *adv* **ovip'arously**. — *vi* **ovipositor** (*ō-vi-poz'i-tər*) an egg-laying organ in female insects and some female fishes. — *adj* **ovoviviparous** (*ō-və-vi-vip'ə-rəs*, or *-vī*) producing eggs which are hatched in the body of the parent, as some reptiles and fishes are. [L. *ōvum*, egg.]

ovine *ō'vīn*, *adj* of, or relating to, sheep; sheeplike. [L. *ŏvis*, sheep, *fōrma*, form.]

ovo- *combining form*. See **ovi-**.

ovoid *ō'void*, *adj* (of a solid or plane figure) egg-shaped; egg-shaped and attached by the broad end (*bot*). — *n* an egg-shaped figure or body. [L. *ōvum*, egg, and **-oid**.]

ovolo *ō'və-lō*, (*archit*) *n* a moulding with the rounded part composed of a quarter of a circle, or of an arc of an ellipse with the curve greatest at the top: — *pl* **ō'voli** (*-lē*). [It., — L. *ōvum*, an egg.]

ovoviviparous. See under **ovi-**.

ovular. See **ovule**.

ovulate *ov'ū-lāt*, *vi* to release ova from the ovary; to form ova. — *n* **ovulā'tion**. [From **ovule**.]

ovule *ov'ūl*, *n* in flowering plants, the body containing the egg cell, which on fertilisation becomes the seed; an unfertilised ovum. — *adj* **ov'ular** of or relating to an ovule. [Med.L. *ōvulum*, dimin. of *ōvum*, egg.]

ovum *ō'vəm*, *n* an egg; the egg-cell, or female gamete (*biol*): — *pl* **o'va**. [L. *ōvum*, egg.]

owe *ō*, *vt* to be under an obligation to repay or render; to feel as a debt or as due; to be indebted for; to have to thank; to bear (a person a grudge). — *vi* to be in debt: — *pa t* and *pa p* **owed**. [O.E. *āgan*, to own, possess.]

owing *ō'ing*, *adj* due; to be paid; imputable. — **owing to** because of; in consequence of.

owl *owl*, *n* any member of the order *Strigiformes*, nocturnal predacious birds with large broad heads, flat faces, large eyes surrounded by discs of feathers, short hooked beaks, silent flight, and a howling or hooting cry; a person who sits up at night; a person who sees badly, or who shuns light; a solemn person. — *n* **owl'et** a young owl. — *adj* **owl'ish** like an owl; solemn, esp. if also bespectacled. — *n* **owl'ishness**. — *adj* **owl'-eyed** having blinking eyes like an owl. — **owl'-light** (*poetic*) dusk, twilight. — *adj* **owl'-like**. [O.E. *ūle*.]

own[1] *ōn*, *vt* to possess, have belonging to one; to acknowledge as one's own; to confess; to allow to be true; to admit, concede; to acknowledge, recognise. — *vi* to confess (with *to*). — *n* **own'er** possessor, proprietor. — *adj* **own'erless**. — *n* **own'ership**. — **owner-occupa'tion**. — *adj* **owner-occ'upied**. — **owner-occ'upier** a person who owns the house he or she lives in. — **own up** to confess (often with *to*). [O.E. *āgnian* — *āgen*, one's own.]

own[2] *ōn*, *adj* and *pron* (preceded by *possessive adj* or *possessive case*) belonging to oneself and no-one else — with intensifying force (as in *her*(*very*) *own room*), an endearment (as in *my own* (*darling*)), with a force similar to the emphatic *oneself*, etc. (as in *he makes his own bed, his own worst enemy*). — *adj* **own-brand'** or **own-la'bel** (of a commodity) carrying the trademark or label of the store that sells it. — **own goal** (in football) a goal scored by mistake for the opposing side; a move that turns out to the disadvantage of the party making it. — **come into one's own** to take possession of one's rights; to have one's talents or merits realised; **get one's own back** to retaliate, get even; **of one's own** belonging to oneself and no-one else; **one's own** what belongs to oneself (as in *I may do what I like with my own*); **on one's own** on one's own account; on one's own initiative; by one's own efforts or resources; independently; set up in independence; alone, by oneself. [O.E. *āgen*, past p. of *āgan*, to possess; cf. **owe**.]

ox *oks*, *n* a general name for male or female of common domestic cattle (bull and cow), esp. a castrated male of the species; extended to other animals of bovine type: — *pl* **ox'en** used for both male and female. — **ox'blood** a dark reddish-brown colour. — Also *adj*. — **ox'bow** (*-bō*) a collar for a yoked ox; a horse-shaped bend in a river (forming an *ox-bow lake* when the neck is pierced and the bend cut off); **ox'eye** a wild chrysanthemum with yellow disc and white ray (*oxeye daisy*); sometimes (*yellow oxeye*) the corn marigold; an elliptical dormer window. — *adj* **ox'-eyed** having large, ox-like eyes. — **ox'tail** the tail of an ox, esp. as used for soup, stew, etc.; **ox'-tongue** the tongue of an ox, used as food; a plant of the daisy family (genus *Picris*) with yellow flowers. [O.E. *oxa*, pl. *oxan*.]

oxalis *ok'sə-lis*, *n* the wood-sorrel. — *adj* **oxalic** (*-sal'ik*) applied to an acid ($C_2H_2O_4$) obtained from wood-sorrel and other plants, used for cleaning metals, and as a bleaching agent. — *n* **ox'alate** a salt of oxalic acid. [Gr. *oxalis* — *oxys*, sharp, acid.]

Oxbridge *oks'brij*, *n* and *adj* (relating to) *Ox*ford and Cam*bridge* (universities), esp. when regarded as typifying an upper-class-oriented kind of education, or as a road to unfair advantages, e.g. in obtaining jobs, or as the home of particular academic attitudes.

Oxfam *oks'fam*, *n* short for Oxford Committee for Famine Relief.

oxford *oks'fərd*, *n* a low-heeled laced shoe (also **Oxford shoe**); a light cotton or synthetic woven fabric (also **Oxford cloth**) used for men's shirts. — **Oxford bags** very wide trousers; **Oxford blue** a dark blue (see also **blue**[1]); **Oxford movement** see **Tractarianism** under **tract**. [*Oxford* (university or city) — O.E. *Oxnaford*, lit. oxen's ford.]

oxide *ok'sīd*, *n* a compound of oxygen and some other element or radical. — *n* **ox'idant** a substance acting as an oxidiser. — *n* **oxidā'tion** oxidising. — *adj* **oxidī'sable** or **-z-**. — *vt* and *vi* **ox'idise** or **-ize** to combine with oxygen; to make, or become, rusty; to put a protective oxide coating on (a metal surface). — *n* **oxidīs'er** or **-z-** an oxidising agent. [Fr. *oxide* (now *oxyde*), formed from *oxygène*, oxygen.]

oxlip *ok'slip*, *n* originally a hybrid between primrose and cowslip; now, a species of the genus *Primula* like a large pale cowslip. [O.E. *oxanslyppe* — *oxan*, genitive of *oxa*, ox, *slyppe*, slime.]

Oxon. *abbrev* for: Oxfordshire; *Oxoniensis* (L.), of Oxford.

Oxonian *ok-sō'ni-ən*, *adj* of or relating to *Oxford* or to its university. — *n* an inhabitant, native, student or graduate of Oxford. [L. *Oxonia*, Oxford.]

oxonium *ok-sō'ni-əm*, (*chem*) *n* a univalent basic radical, H_3O, in which oxygen is tetravalent, forming organic derivatives, **oxonium salts**. [*ox*ygen and amm*onium*.]

oxy-[1] *ok-si-*, *combining form* denoting: sharp; pointed; acid. [Gr. *oxys*.]

oxy-[2] *ok-si-*, *combining form* denoting oxygen. — *adj* **oxy-acet'ylene** involving, using, or by means of, a mixture of oxygen and acetylene, esp. in cutting or welding metals at high temperatures. — *n* **oxy-a'cid**,

oxy-com'pound, oxy-salt', etc., an acid, compound, salt, etc. containing oxygen; one in which an atom of hydrogen is replaced by a hydroxyl-group. [Gr. *oxys*, sharp.]

oxygen *ok'si-jən, n* a gas (atomic no. 8; symbol **O**) without taste, colour or smell, forming part of the air, water, etc., and supporting life and combustion. — *vt* **ox'ygenāte** (or *ok-sij'*) to oxidise; to impregnate or treat with oxygen. — *n* **oxygenā'tion.** — *vt* **ox'ygenise** or **-ize** to oxygenate. — *adj* **oxyg'enous.** — **oxygen debt** a depletion of the body's store of oxygen occurring during bursts of strenuous exercise, replaced after bodily activity returns to normal levels; **oxygen mask** a masklike breathing apparatus through which oxygen is supplied in rarefied atmospheres to aviators and mountaineers; **oxygen tent** a tentlike enclosure in which there is a controllable flow of oxygen, erected round a patient to aid breathing. [Gr. *oxys*, sharp, acid, and the root of *gennaein*, to generate, from the old belief that all acids contained oxygen.]

oxymoron *ok-si-mö'ron, n* a figure of speech by means of which contradictory terms are combined, so as to form an expressive phrase or epithet, such as *cruel kindness*, *falsely true*, etc. [Gr. neut. of *oxymōros*, lit. pointedly foolish — *oxys*, sharp, *mōros*, foolish.]

oxytocin *oks-i-tō'sin, n* a pituitary hormone that stimulates uterine muscle contraction and milk-production, also produced synthetically for use in accelerating labour. — *adj* and *n* **oxytō'cic** (a drug) stimulating uterine muscle contraction. [Gr. *oxys*, sharp, *tokos*, birth.]

oxytone *ok'si-tōn, adj* having the acute accent on the last syllable (*Gr gram*); stressed on the final syllable. — *n* a word so accented. [Gr. *oxys*, sharp, *tonos*, tone.]

oyez *ō-yes'* or *ō-yez' interj* the call of a public crier, or officer of a law-court, for attention before making a proclamation. [O.Fr. *oyez*, imperative of *oir* (Fr. *ouïr*), to hear.]

oyster *ois'tər, n* a bivalve shellfish (genus *Ostrea*) used as food; a secretive person (*colloq*); a source of advantage; the colour of an oyster, a pale greyish beige or pink. — *adj* of this colour. — **oyster bank, bed, farm, field** and **park** places where oysters breed or are bred; **oys'ter-catcher** a black and white wading bird, with red bill and feet, feeding on limpets and mussels (not oysters); **oys'ter-fishery** the business of catching oysters; **oyster knife** a knife for opening oysters; **oyster mushroom** an edible fungus (genus *Pleurotus*) found esp. in clusters on dead wood; **oyster plant** salsify, or a seaside plant (genus *Mertensia*), both supposed to taste like oysters. — **the world is my, your,** etc. **oyster** the world lies before me, you, etc., ready to yield profit or success. [O.Fr. *oistre* — L. *ostrea*, an oyster.]

Oz *oz*, (*Austr slang*) *n* Australia. — Also *adj.*

oz. or **oz** *abbrev* for ounce.

Ozacling® *oz'ə-kling*, (*printing*) *n* transparent adhesive film from which printed material can be cut for application to illustrations, etc.

Ozalid® *oz'ə-lid, n* a method of duplicating printed matter on to chemically treated paper; a reproduction made by this process.

ozokerite *ō-zō'kə-rīt* or **ozocerite** *ō-zō'sə-rīt* or *ō-zos'ə-rīt, n* a waxy natural paraffin. [Gr. *ozein*, to smell, *kēros*, wax.]

ozone *ō'zōn, n* an allotropic form (O_3) of oxygen present in the atmosphere, toxic in concentration, having a pungent smell, formed when ultraviolet light or an electric spark acts on oxygen or air, and used in bleaching, sterilising water, and purifying air; (*loosely*) fresh bracing air. — *n* **ozonisā'tion** or **-z-**. — *vt* **ō'zonise** or **-ize** to turn into, charge with, or treat with, ozone. — *n* **ozoni'ser** or **-z-** apparatus for turning oxygen into ozone. — *n* **ozo'nosphere** or **ozone layer** a layer of the upper atmosphere where ozone is formed in quantity, protecting earth from the sun's ultraviolet rays. — *adj* **ozone-friend'ly** (of aerosols, etc.) not thought to be destructive of the ozone layer, being free of chlorofluorocarbons. [Gr. *ozōn*, pres. p. of *ozein*, to smell.]

P

P or **p** *pē*, *n* the sixteenth letter of the modern English alphabet representing a voiceless labial stop.

P or **P.** *abbrev* for: parking; pedal (*mus*); Portugal (I.V.R.); President; Prince; pula (currency of Botswana).

P (*chem*) *symbol* for phosphorus.

P *symbol* for power.

p or **p.** *abbrev* for: new pence; new penny; page; participle; piano (*mus*); pico-; positive. — *adj* **p'-type** (i.e. 'positive type') (of a semiconductor) having an excess of mobile holes over conduction electrons.

p- (*chem*). See **para-**[1].

PA *abbrev* for; Panama (I.V.R.); Pennsylvania (U.S. state); personal assistant; Press Association; public address (system); Publishers Association.

Pa. *abbrev* for Pennsylvania (U.S. state).

Pa *symbol* for: pascal; protactinium (*chem*).

pa *pä*, *n* a childish or familiar word for father. **[papa.]**

pa. *abbrev* for past.

p.a. or **pa** *abbrev* for per annum.

pa'anga *päng'gə*, *n* the standard unit of currency of Tonga, Tongan dollar (100 *seniti*). [Tongan, from a type of vine yielding disc-shaped seeds.]

pabulum *pab'ū-ləm* or *-yə-*, *n* food of any kind, esp. that of lower animals and of plants; fuel; nourishment for the mind. — *adj* **pab'ūlar.** — *adj* **pab'ūlous.** [L. *pābulum* — *pāscĕre*, to feed.]

paca *pä'kə*, *n* the so-called spotted cavy of South America. [Sp. and Port., — Tupí *paca.*]

pace[1] *pās*, *n* a stride; a step; the space between the feet in walking, about 76 cm.; gait; rate of walking, running, etc. (of a man or animal); rate of speed in movement or work, often applied to fast living; a mode of stepping in horses in which the legs on the same side are lifted together; amble; a step of a stair, or the like. — *vt* to traverse with measured steps; to measure by steps (often with *out*); to train to perform paces; to set the pace for; to perform as a pace or paces. — *vi* to walk; to walk slowly and with measured tread; to amble. — *adj* **paced** having a certain pace or gait. — *n* **pac'er** a person who paces; a horse whose usual gait is a pace; a horse trained to pace in harness racing. — *adj* **pac'ey** or **pac'y** (*colloq*) fast; lively, smart. — **pace'-bowler** in cricket, a bowler who delivers the ball fast; **pace'-bowling; pace'maker** a person who sets the pace as in a race (also *fig*); a small mass of muscle cells in the heart which control the heartbeat electrically; an electronic device (in later models, with radioactive core) used to correct weak or irregular heart rhythms; **pace'-setter** a pacemaker, except in anatomical and electronic senses. — **go the pace** to go at a great speed; to live a fast life; **keep** or **hold pace with** to go as fast as; to keep up with; **make** or **set the pace** to regulate the speed for others by example; **put someone through his** (or **her**) **paces** to set someone to show what he (or she) can do; **show one's paces** to show what one can do; **stand, stay** or **stick the pace** to keep up with the pace or speed that has been set. [Fr. *pas* — L. *passus*, a step — *pandĕre*, *passum*, to stretch.]

pace[2] *pā'sē*, *prep* with or by the leave of (expressing disagreement courteously). [L., abl. of *pāx*, peace.]

pachinko *pə-ching'kō*, *n* a form of pinball popular in Japan. [Jap. *pachin* (onomatopoeic) representing trigger sound.]

pachisi *pä-chē'sē* or *-zē*, *n* an Indian game like backgammon or ludo. [Hindi *pacīsī*, of twenty-five — the highest throw.]

pachy- *pak-i-*, *combining form* signifying thick. — *n* **pach'yderm** (Gr. *derma*, skin) strictly, any animal of the old classification *Pachydermata*, i.e. ungulates that do not ruminate, but usually an elephant, rhinoceros or hippopotamus; an insensitive person. [Gr. *pachys*, thick.]

pacify *pas'i-fī*, *vt* to appease; to calm; to bring peace to. — *adj* **pac'ifīable.** — *adj* **pacif'ic** peacemaking; appeasing; inclining towards peace; peaceful; mild; tranquil; (with *cap*) of, or pertaining to the ocean between Asia and America (so called by Magellan because he happened to cross it in peaceful weather conditions). — *n* (with *cap*) the Pacific Ocean. — *adj* **pacif'ical** pacific. — *adv* **pacif'ically.** — *vt* **pacif'icāte** to give peace to. — *n* **pacificā'tion** peacemaking; conciliation; appeasement; a peace treaty. — *adj* **pacif'icatory** (*-kə-tə-ri*) tending to make peace. — *n* **pacif'icism** (*-sizm*) the beliefs and principles of pacificists. — *n* **pacif'icist** (*-sist*) someone who is opposed to war, or believes all war to be wrong. — *n* **pac'ifīer** a person or thing that pacifies. — *n* **pac'ifism** and *n* **pac'ifist** popularly preferred forms of **pacificism** and **pacificist.** [Partly through Fr. *pacifier* — L. *pācificus*, pacific — *pācificāre* — *pāx*, *pācis*, peace, *facĕre*, to make.]

pack[1] *pak*, *n* a bundle, esp. orig. one made to be carried on the back by a pedlar or pack-animal; a backpack, rucksack; a collection, stock or store; a bundle of some particular kind or quantity; a complete set of playing cards; a number of animals herding together or kept together for hunting; the forwards in a Rugby football team; a group of Cub Scouts or Brownies; a worthless, disreputable or otherwise objectionable set of people; a mass of pack-ice; a sheet for folding round the body to allay inflammation, fever, etc.; the use or application of such a sheet; a cosmetic paste; the act of packing or condition of being packed; mode of packing; a compact package, esp. of something for sale; a group (of e.g. submarines) acting together. — *vt* to make into a bundled pack; to place compactly in a box, bag, or the like; to press together closely; to compress; to fill tightly or compactly; to fill with anything; to cram; to crowd; to envelop; to surround closely; to fill the spaces surrounding; to prepare (food) for preservation, transport and marketing; to send away, dismiss (usu. with *off*); to form into a pack; to load with a pack; to carry in packs; to carry or wear (a gun). — *vi* to form into a pack; to settle or be driven into a firm mass; to form a scrum; to be capable of being put into compact shape; to put one's belongings together in boxes, bags, etc., as for a journey (often with *up*); to travel with a pack; to take oneself off, to depart hastily (usu. with *off*). — *n* **pack'age** the act, manner or privilege of packing; a bundle, packet or parcel; a case or other receptacle for packing goods in; a composite proposition, scheme, offer, etc., in which various separate elements are all dealt with as essential parts of the whole (see also **package deal**); a computer program in general form, to which the user adds such data as are applicable in a particular case. — *vt* to put into a container or wrappings, or into a package. — *adj* **pack'aged** (*lit* and *fig*). — *n* **pack'ager** a specialist in the packaging of books, programs, etc. — *n* **pack'aging** anything used to package goods; the total presentation of a product for sale, i.e. its design, wrapping, etc.; the designing and complete production of e.g. illustrated books, programmes for television, etc. for sale to a publisher, broadcasting company, etc. — *n* **pack'er** a person who packs; someone who packs goods for sending out; an employer or employee in the business of preparing and preserving food; a machine or device for packing. — *n* **pack'et** a small package; a carton; a ship or vessel employed in carrying packets of letters, passengers, etc.; a vessel plying regularly between one port and another (also **pack'et-boat, pack'et-ship,** etc.); a large amount of money (*colloq*); a small group; a block of coded data (*comput*; see **packet-switching** below). — *vt* to parcel up. — *n* **pack'ing** the act of putting into packs or of tying up for carriage or storing; material for packing; anything used to fill an empty space or to make a joint close. — **package deal** a deal which embraces a number of matters and has to be accepted as a whole, the less favourable items along with the favourable; **package holiday** or **tour** one whose details are arranged by the organisers before they advertise it and for which they are paid a fixed price which covers all costs (food, travel, etc.); **pack'-animal** an animal used to carry goods on its back; **pack'-drill** a military punishment of marching about laden with full equipment; **pack'et-switching** (*comput*) a system of communication in which packets of data are transmitted between computers of varying types and compatibility; **pack'-horse,** etc. a horse, etc. used to carry goods on its back; a drudge; **pack'-ice** a mass of large pieces of floating ice driven together by winds and currents; **pack'ing-box** or **-case** a box or framework for packing goods in; **pack'-load** the load an animal can carry; **pack'man** a pedlar or a man who carries a pack; **pack'-rat** a kind of long-tailed rat, native to the western part of North America; **pack'-saddle** a saddle for pack-horses, pack-mules, etc.; **pack'-train** a train of loaded pack-animals; **pack'way** a narrow path fit for pack-horses. — **pack a punch** to be capable of giving a powerful blow; **pack it in** or **up** (*slang*) to stop, give up, doing something; **pack up** (*slang*) to stop; to break down; **send someone packing** to dismiss summarily. [M.E. *packe, pakke*, app. — M. Flem. *pac* or Du. or L.Ger. *pak*.]

pack[2] *pak*, *vt* to fill up (a jury, meeting, etc.) with people of a particular kind for one's own purposes. [Prob. **pact.**]

package, packet. See under **pack**[1].

paco *pä'kō*, *n* an alpaca: — *pl* **pa'cos.** [Sp., — Quechua *paco*.]

pact *pakt*, *n* that which is agreed on; an agreement, esp. informal or not legally enforceable. — **Warsaw Pact** a treaty of friendship, assistance and co-operation signed in Warsaw in May 1955 by the U.S.S.R. and seven other European communist states. [L. *pactum* — *pacīscĕre, pactum*, to contract.]

pad[1] *pad*, *vi* to walk on foot; to trudge along; to walk with quiet or dull-sounding tread: — *pr p* **padd'ing**; *pa t* and *pa p* **padd'ed.** [Du. *pad*, a path.]

pad[2] *pad*, *n* anything stuffed with a soft material, to prevent friction, pressure or injury, for inking, for filling out, etc.; a soft saddle; a cushion; a number of sheets of paper or other soft material fastened together in a block; a leg-guard for cricketers, etc.; the fleshy, thick-skinned undersurface of the foot of many animals, such as the fox; the foot of an animal esp. of chase; its footprint; a waterlily leaf (*US*); a rocket-launching platform; a bed, room or home, esp. one's own (*slang*); a device built into a road surface, operated by vehicles passing over it, controlling changes of traffic lights (**vehicle-actuated signal**) so as to give passage for longer time to the greater stream of traffic. — *vt* to stuff, cover or fill out with anything soft; to furnish with padding; to track by footprints; to impregnate, as with a mordant: — *pr p* **padd'ing**; *pa t* and *pa p* **padd'ed.** — *n* **padd'er** someone who pads, or cushions. — *n* **padd'ing** stuffing; matter of less value introduced into a book or article in order to make it of the length desired; the process of mordanting a fabric. — **pad'-cloth** a cloth covering a horse's loins; **padded cell** a room with padded walls in a mental hospital; **pad'saw** or **keyhole saw** a small saw-blade with detachable handle, used for cutting curves and awkward angles. [Perh. connected with **pod**[1].]

paddle[1] *pad'l*, *vi* to wade about or dabble in liquid or semi-liquid; to walk unsteadily or with short steps. — *n* **padd'ler** someone who paddles; (in *pl*) a protective garment worn by children when paddling. [Cf. **pad**[1] and L. Ger. *paddeln*, to tramp about.]

paddle[2] *pad'l*, *n* a small, long-handled spade; a short, broad, spoon-shaped oar, used for moving canoes; the blade of an oar; one of the boards of a paddle-wheel or water-wheel; a paddle-shaped instrument for stirring, beating, etc.; a small bat, as used in table tennis (*US*). — *vi* to use a paddle, progress by use of paddles; to row gently; to swim about like a duck. — *vt* to propel by paddle; to strike or spank with a paddle or the like (esp. *US*). — *n* **padd'ler.** — *n* **padd'ling.** — **padd'le-board** one of the boards of a paddle-wheel; **padd'le-boat** a paddle-steamer; **padd'le-steamer** a steamer propelled by paddle-wheels; **padd'le-wheel** the wheel of a steam-vessel, which by turning in the water causes the boat to move. — **paddle one's own canoe** to progress independently.

paddock *pad'ək*, *n* an enclosed field under pasture, orig. near a house or stable; a small field in which horses are led around, and mounted before a race. [App. from earlier *parrock* — O.E. *pearroc*, park.]

Paddy *pad'i*, *n* a familiar name for an Irishman; (without *cap*) a rage (*colloq*).

paddy *pad'i*, *n* growing rice; rice in the husk. — **padd'y-field** a rice field. [Malay *pādī*, rice in the straw.]

padlock *pad'lok*, *n* a movable lock with a link turning on a hinge or pivot at one end, catching the bolt at the other. — Also *vt*. [Poss. Eng. dialect *pad*, a basket, and **lock**[1].]

padre *pä'drā*, *n* father, a title given to priests; an army chaplain; a parson. [Port. (also Sp. and It.) *padre* — L. *pater*, a father.]

paean or **pean** *pē'ən*, *n* a song of thanksgiving or triumph; exultation. [L. *Paeān, paeōn* — Gr. *Paiān, -ānos*.]

paed- or **ped-** *pēd-*, **paedo-** or **pedo-** *pē-dō-*, also sometimes **paid-** *pīd-* or **paido-** *pī-dō-*, *combining form* denoting child, boy. — *adj* **paedagog'ic** same as **pedagogic.** — *n* **paed'agogue** same as **pedagogue.** — *n* **paed'erast** same as **pederast.** — *adj* **paederast'ic.** — *n* **paed'erasty** same as **pederasty.** — *n* **paedeut'ic** or **paideut'ic** (also *nsing* **paedeutics** or **paideutics**) educational method or theory. — *adj* **paediat'ric** (Gr. *iātrikos*, medical) relating to the medical treatment of children. — *nsing* **paediat'rics** the treatment of children's diseases. — *n* **paediatrician** (*-ə-trish'ən*). — *n* **paedī'atrist.** — *n* **paedī'atry.** — *n* **paedobap'tism** infant baptism. — *n* **paedobap'tist.** — *adj* **paedolog'ical.** — *n* **paedol'ogist.** — *n* **paedol'ogy** the study of the growth and development of children. — *adj* **paedomor'phic** of paedomorphism or paedomorphosis. — *n* **paedomorph'ism** retention of juvenile characteristics in the mature stage. — *n* **paed'ophile** (*-fīl*) a person affected with paedophilia. — *n* **paedophilia** (*-fil'*) sexual desire towards children. — *adj* and *n*

paedophil'iac or **paedophil'ic.** [Gr. *pais, paidos*, boy, child; *paideutēs*, teacher.]

paella *pī-el'ə* or *pä-el'ya*, *n* a stew containing saffron, chicken, rice, vegetables, seafood, etc. [Sp., — L. *patella*, pan.]

paeony. See **peony**.

pagan *pā'gən*, *n* a heathen; a person who is not a Christian, Jew or Muslim; more recently, someone who has no religion; a person who sets a high value on sensual pleasures. — Also *adj.* — *vt* **pā'ganise** or **-ize** to render pagan or heathen; to convert to paganism. — *adj* **pā'ganish** heathenish. — *n* **pā'ganism** heathenism; the beliefs and practices of the heathen. [L. *pāgānus*, rustic, peasant, also civilian (because the Christians reckoned themselves soldiers of Christ) — *pāgus*, a district.]

page[1] *pāj*, *n* a boy attendant; a boy employed as a messenger in hotels, clubs, etc.; a messenger (boy or girl) in the U.S. Congress, etc.; a youth training for knighthood, receiving education and performing services at court or in a nobleman's household (*hist*). — *vt* to attend as a page; to seek or summon by sending a page around, by repeatedly calling aloud for, or by means of a pager. — *n* **pā'ger** an electronic device which pages a person (cf. **bleeper**). — **page'boy** a page; (also **pageboy hairstyle** or **pageboy haircut**) a hairstyle in which the hair hangs smoothly to about shoulder-level and curls under at the ends. [Fr. *page*.]

page[2] *pāj*, *n* one side of a leaf of a book, etc; the type, illustrations, etc., arranged for printing one side of a leaf; a leaf of a book thought of as a single item; (in *pl*) writings, literature (*rhet*); an incident, episode, or whatever may be imagined as matter to fill a page; one of the blocks into which a computer memory can be divided for ease of reference. — *vt* to number the pages of; to make up into pages (*printing*). — *adj* **paginal** (*paj'*). — *vt* **paginâte** (*paj'*) to mark with consecutive numbers, to page. — *n* **paginā'tion** the act of paging a book; the figures and marks that indicate the numbers of pages. — *n* **pā'ging** the marking or numbering of the pages of a book. — **page'-proof** a proof of a book, etc., made up into pages. — *adj* **page-three'** shown on, or appropriate for, **page three**, the page on which, traditionally, certain popular newspapers print nude or semi-nude photographs of female models with well-developed figures. — **page'-turner** an exciting book, a thriller. [Fr., — L. *pāgĭna*, a page.]

pageant *paj'ənt*, *n* a spectacle, esp. one carried around in procession; a series of tableaux or dramatic scenes connected with local history or other topical matter, performed either on a fixed spot or in procession; a piece of empty show; display. — *n* **page'antry** splendid display; pompous spectacle; a fleeting show. [Anglo-L. *pāgina* may be the classical word transferred from page to scene in a MS; or *pāgina*, in the sense of slab, may have come to mean boarding, framework.]

paginal, paginate, etc. See under **page**[2].

pagoda *pə-gō'də*, *n* an Eastern temple, esp. in the form of a many-storeyed tapering tower, each storey with a projecting roof; an ornamental building in imitation of this. [Port. *pagode* — Pers. *but-kadah*, idol-house, or some other Eastern word.]

pah *pä*, *interj* an exclamation of disgust.

pahoehoe *pə-hō'ē-hō-ē*, *n* a hardened lava with a smooth undulating shiny surface. [Hawaiian.]

paid *pād*, *pa t* and *pa p* of **pay**[1]. — *adj* **paid-up'** paid in full; having fulfilled financial obligations. — **put paid to** to finish; to destroy chances of success in.

paid-. See **paed-**.

pail *pāl*, *n* an open cylindrical or conical vessel with a hooped handle, for holding or carrying liquids (also ice, coal, etc.), a bucket; a pailful. — *n* **pail'ful** as much as fills a pail. [O.E. *pægel*, a gill measure, app. combined with or influenced by O.Fr. *paele*, a pan — L. *patella*, a pan, dimin. of *patera* — *patēre*, to be open.]

paillasse. See **palliasse.**

pain *pān*, *n* suffering; bodily suffering; (now only in *pl*) great care or trouble taken in doing anything; a tiresome or annoying person (*colloq*); penalty. — *vt* to cause suffering to. — *adj* **pained** showing or expressing pain; suffering pain; distressed. — *adj* **pain'ful** full of pain; causing pain; requiring labour, pain or care; distressing, irksome. — *adv* **pain'fully.** — *n* **pain'fulness.** — *adj* **pain'less.** — *adv* **pain'lessly.** — *n* **pain'lessness.** — **pain'killer** anything that does away with pain, esp. an analgesic; **pains'taker** a careful worker. — *adj* **pains'taking** taking pains or care. — *n* careful diligence. — *adv* **pains'takingly.** — **be at pains** or **take pains (to)** to put oneself to trouble, be assiduously careful (to); **for one's pains** as reward or result of trouble taken (usu. ironical); **pain in the neck** (*fig*) an exasperating circumstance; a thoroughly tiresome person; a feeling of acute discomfort; **under** or **on pain of** under liability to the penalty of. [Fr. *peine* — L. *poena*, satisfaction — Gr. *poinē*, penalty.]

paint *pānt*, *vt* to cover over with colouring matter; to represent in a coloured picture; to produce as a coloured picture; to apply with a brush; to apply anything to, with a brush; to describe or present as if in paint (*fig*); to colour; to apply coloured cosmetics to; to adorn, diversify; to represent speciously or deceptively. — *vi* to practise painting. — *n* a colouring substance spread or for spreading on the surface a cake of such matter; coloured cosmetics. — *adj* **paint'able** suitable for painting. — *adj* **painted** covered with paint; ornamented with coloured figures; marked with bright colours; feigned. — *n* **paint'er** someone who paints; an artist in painting; someone whose occupation is painting; a house-decorator; a vivid describer. — *n* **paint'iness.** — *n* **paint'ing** the act or employment of laying on colours; the act of representing objects by colours; a painted picture; vivid description in words. — *adj* **paint'y** overloaded with paint, with the colours too glaringly used; smeared with paint; like paint, in smell, etc. — *n* **paint'ball** (sometimes with *cap*) a type of war game where the ammunition used is paint fired from compressed-air guns; a paint-pellet as used in this; **paint'-box** a box in which different paints are kept in compartments; **paint'-brush** a brush for putting on paint; **painted lady** the *thistle-butterfly*, orange-red spotted with white and black; **paint roller** roller used in house-painting, etc. instead of a brush. — *nsing* **paint'works** a paint-making factory. — **fresh as paint** very fresh and bright; **paint the town red** to break out in a boisterous spree. [O.Fr. *peint*, past p. of *peindre*, to paint — L. *pingĕre*, to paint.]

painter *pānt'ər*, (*naut*) *n* a rope for fastening a boat. — **cut the painter** to sever ties; **lazy painter** a small painter for use in fine weather only.

pair *pār*, *n* two things equal, or suited to each other, or growing, grouped or used together; a set of two equal or like things forming one instrument, garment, etc., such as a pair of scissors, tongs, trousers; the other of two matching things; a set of like things generally; a couple; husband and wife; two people engaged to or in love with each other; a male and a female animal mated together; two persons or things associated together; a partner; two horses harnessed together; two cards of the same designation; (in *pl* with *sing v*) another name for **Pelmanism;** two voters on opposite sides who have an agreement to abstain from voting; either of such a pair; a duck in both innings (*cricket*); a boat rowed by two; (in *pl*) a contest, etc. in which competitors take part in partnerships of two: — *pl* **pairs** or **pair** (*colloq*). — *vt* to couple; to sort out in pairs. — *vi* to be joined in couples; to be a counterpart or counterparts; to mate; (of two opposing voters) to arrange to abstain, on a motion or for a period (also *vt*; usu. *passive*). — *adj* **paired** arranged in pairs; set by twos of a similar kind; mated (**paired reading** a teaching method in which a child and an adult read together until the child is confident enough to read on alone). — *n* **pair'ing.** — *adv* **pair'wise** in pairs. — **pair'-bond** a continuing and exclusive relationship between a male and female; **pair'-bonding; pair-roy'al** three cards of the same denomination, esp. in cribbage; a throw of three dice all falling alike; a set of three (also **pairī'al** and **prī'al**). — **pair of colours** two flags carried by a regiment, one the national ensign, the other the flag of the regiment; an ensigncy; **pair off** to arrange, set against each other, or set aside in pairs; to become associated in pairs. [Fr. *paire*, a couple — L. *paria*, neut. pl. of *pār*, afterwards regarded as a fem. sing., equal.]

paisa *pī'sä*, *n* in India and Pakistan (a coin worth) one one-hundredth of a rupee; in Bangladesh, (a coin worth) one one-hundredth of a taka: — *pl* **pai'se** (*-sā*).

paisano *pī-zä'nō*, *n* among people of Spanish or American descent in America, a person from the same area or town; hence, a friend: — *pl* **paisa'nos.** [Sp., — Fr. *paysan*, peasant.]

paisley *pāz'li*, *n* a woollen or other fabric with a pattern resembling Paisley pattern. — **paisley pattern** or **design** a type of pattern whose most characteristic feature is an ornamental device known as a 'cone' (rather like a tree cone), used in the **Paisley shawl**, a shawl made in *Paisley*, Scotland in the 19th cent.

pajamas. See **pyjamas.**

PAK *abbrev* for Pakistan (I.V.R.).

pakapoo *pak-ə-pōō'*, (*Austr* and *NZ*) *n* a Chinese version of lotto, in which betting tickets are filled up with Chinese characters. [Chin.]

pak-choi cabbage *päk'-choi kab'ij*, *n*. Same as **Chinese cabbage.**

Pakistani *pä-kis-tän'i*, *n* a citizen of Pakistan; an immigrant from, or a person whose parents, etc. are immigrants from, Pakistan. — Also *adj*. — *n* **Paki** (*pak'i*; *offensive British slang*) a Pakistani. — Also *adj*.

pakora *pə-kö'rə*, *n* an Indian dish consisting of chopped vegetables, etc. formed into balls, coated with batter and deep-fried. [Hindi.]

pal *pal*, (*colloq*) *n* a partner, mate; chum. — *vi* to associate as a pal: — *prp* **pall'ing;** *pa t* and *pa p* **palled** (*pald*). — *adj* **pally** (*pal'i*). — *adj* **pal'sy** (*-zi*) or **palsy-wal'sy** (*colloq*) over-friendly; ingratiatingly intimate. [Gypsy.]

palace *pal'is*, *n* the house of a king or a queen; a very large and splendid house; a bishop's official residence; a large and usually showy place of entertainment or refreshment. — **palace guard** (one of) those responsible for the personal protection of a monarch; the group of intimates and advisers around a head of government, etc.; **palace revolution** a revolution within the seat of authority. — **palace of culture** in the U.S.S.R., a cultural and recreational centre; **palais de danse** (*pa-le də dãs*; Fr.) a dance-hall. [Fr. *palais* — L. *Palātium*, the Roman emperor's residence on the *Palatine* Hill at Rome.]

palae- or **palaeo-**, in U.S. also **pale-** or **paleo-** *pal-i-* or *-ō-*, also *pāl-*, *combining form* meaning: old; of, or concerned with, the very distant past. — *adj* **palae(o)anthrop'ic** (Gr. *anthrōpos*, man) of the earliest types of man. — *adj* **palae(o)anthropolog'ical.** — *n* **palae(o)anthropolog'ist.** — *n* **palae(o)anthropol'ogy.** — *adj* **palaeobiolog'ic** or **palaeobiolog'ical.** — *n* **palae(o)biol'ogist.** — *n* **palae(o)biol'ogy** the biological study of fossil plants and animals. — *adj* **palaeobotan'ic** or **palaeobotan'ical.** — *n* **palaeobot'anist.** — *n* **palaeobot'any** the study of fossil plants. — *adj* **Pal'aeocene** (*geol*) of or from the oldest epoch of the Tertiary period (also *n*). — *n* **palaeoclī'mate** the climate at any stage in the geological development of the earth. — *adj* **palaeoclimat'ic.** — *adj* **palaeoclimatolog'ic** or **palaeoclimatolog'ical.** — *n* **palaeoclimatol'ogist.** — *n* **palaeoclimatol'ogy.** — *n* **palaeoecol'ogist.** — *n* **palaeoecol'ogy** the ecology of fossil animals and plants. — *n* **palaeoenvī'ronment** the environment in earlier ages. — *adj* **palaeoenvironment'al.** — *adj* **palaeoethnolog'ic** or **palaeoethnolog'ical.** — *n* **palaeoethnol'ogist.** — *n* **palaeoethnol'ogy** the science of early man. — *n* **palaeog'rapher** an expert in or student of palaeography. — *adj* **palaeograph'ic** or **palaeograph'ical.** — *n* **palaeog'raphist.** — *n* **palaeog'raphy** ancient modes of writing; the study of ancient modes of handwriting. — *adj* **Palaeolith'ic** of the earlier Stone Age. — *n* **palaeontol'ogist.** — *n* **palaeontol'ogy** (Gr. *onta*, neut. pl. of pres. p. of *einai*, to be, *logos*, discourse) the study of fossils. — *adj* **Palaeozo'ic** of the division of fossil-bearing rocks, from Cambrian to Permian. — *adj* **palaeozoolog'ical.** — *n* **palaeozool'ogist.** — *n* **palaeozool'ogy** the study of fossil animals. [Gr. *palaios*, old.]

palais de danse. See under **palace.**

palamino *pal-ə-mē'nō*, *n*. Same as **palomino.**

palanquin *pal-ən-kēn'*, *n* a light litter for one passenger, carried on poles on men's shoulders. [Port. *palanquim*.]

palate *pal'it* or *-ət*, *n* the roof of the mouth, consisting of the *hard palate* in front and the *soft palate* behind; sense of taste; relish; mental liking, taste; ability to appreciate the finer qualities of wine, etc. (also *fig*). — *adj* **pal'atable** pleasant to the taste; acceptable to mind or feelings. — *n* **palatabil'ity.** — *n* **pal'atableness.** — *adv* **pal'atably.** — *adj* **pal'atal** pertaining to the palate; uttered by bringing the tongue to or near the hard palate (*phon*). — *n* (*phon*) a sound so produced. — *n* **palatalisā'tion** or **-z-.** — *vt* **pal'atalise** or **-ize** to make palatal. — *adj* **palatō-alvē'olar** (*phon*) produced by bringing the tongue to a position at or close to the hard palate and the roots of the upper teeth. — **cleft palate** a congenital defect of the palate, leaving a longitudinal fissure in the roof of the mouth. [L. *palātum*.]

palatial *pə-lā'shl*, *adj* of or like a palace. [See **palace.**]

palatine *pal'ə-tīn*, *adj* of the Palatine Hill or the palace of emperors there; of a palace; having royal privileges or jurisdiction. [L. *palātīnus*.]

palaver *pə-lä'vər*, *n* a long, boring, complicated and seemingly pointless exercise; a fuss; idle copious talk; talk intended to deceive; a conference, esp. orig. with African or other native tribespeople. — *vi* to hold a palaver; to chatter idly. — *vt* to flatter. — *n* **pala'verer.** [Port. *palavra*, word — L. *parabola*, a parable, later a word, speech — Gr. *parabolē*.]

palazzo *pə-lat'sō*, *n* an Italian palace, often one converted into a museum; a house built in this style: — *pl* **palazzi** (*-at'sē*). [It., — L. *palātium*.]

pale[1] *pāl*, *n* a stake of wood driven into the ground for fencing; any thing that encloses or fences in; a limit; the limit of what can be accepted as decent or tolerable (*fig*); an enclosure; a marked-off district; a broad stripe from top to bottom of a shield (*heraldry*). — *vt* to enclose with stakes; to fence. — *adv* **pale'wise** (*heraldry*) vertically, like a pale. — *n* **pāl'ing** the act of fencing; wood or stakes for fencing; a fence of stakes connected by horizontal pieces; an upright stake or board in a fence. — *adj* **pāl'y** (*heraldry*) divided by vertical lines. — **beyond the pale** intolerable; unacceptable. [Fr. *pal* — L. *pālus*, a stake.]

pale[2] *pāl*, *adj* whitish; not ruddy or fresh; wan; of a faint lustre, dim; lacking colour. — *vt* to make pale. — *vi* to turn pale. — *n* paleness. — *adv* **pale'ly.** — *n* **pale'ness.** — *adj* **pāl'ish** somewhat pale. — **pale**

ale a light-coloured bitter ale; **pale'buck** the oribi; **pale'face** (attributed to American Indians) a white person. [O.Fr. *palle*, pale (Fr. *pâle*) — L. *pallidus*, pale.]

pale-, paleo-, etc. See **palae-**.

Palestinian *pal-is-tin'i-ən, adj* pertaining to *Palestine*. — *n* a native or inhabitant of Palestine; a member of a guerrilla movement or political body one of whose aims is to reclaim former Arab lands from Israelis. [Cf. **Philistine.**]

palette *pal'it, n* a little board, usu. with a thumb-hole, on which a painter mixes colours; the assortment or range of colours used by a particular artist or for any particular picture; a range or selection (*fig*); a plate against which one leans in working a drill. — **pal'ette-knife** a thin round-ended knife for mixing colours, cooking ingredients, etc. [Fr., — It. *paletta* — *pala*, spade — L. *pāla*, a spade.]

Pali *pä'lē, n* the sacred language of the Buddhists of India, etc., closely related to Sanskrit. [Sans. *pāli*, canon.]

palimony *pal'i-mən-i,* (*colloq*) *n* alimony or its equivalent demanded by one partner when the couple have been cohabiting without being married. [**pal** and **alimony.**]

palimpsest *pal'imp-sest, n* a manuscript in which old writing has been rubbed out to make room for new; a monumental brass turned over for a new inscription. [Gr. *palimpsēston* — *palin*, again, *psāein*, to rub.]

palindrome *pal'in-drōm, n* a word, verse or sentence that reads the same backward and forward. — *adj* **palindromic** (*-drom'* or *-drōm'*) or **palindrom'ical.** — *n* **pal'indromist** (or *pə-lin'drom-ist*) an inventor of palindromes. [Gr. *palindromos*, running back.]

paling. See under **pale**[1].

palingenesis *pal-in-jen'i-sis, n* a new birth; reincarnation; a second creation; regeneration; unmodified inheritance of ancestral characters; the re-formation of a rock by refusion: — *pl* **palingen'eses** (*-sēz*). [Gr. *palin*, again, *genesis*, birth.]

palisade *pal-i-sād', n* a fence of stakes; a stake so used (*mil*). — *vt* to surround or defend with a palisade. [Fr. *palissade* and Sp. *palizada* — L. *pālus*, a stake.]

palish. See under **pale**[2].

pall[1] *pöl, n* a cloth spread over a coffin or tomb; a cloak, mantle, outer garment (esp. ecclesiastical); a curtain, covering or cloak, e.g. of smoke or darkness (*fig*). — *vt* to cover with, or as though with, a pall. — **pall'-bearer** one of the people carrying, or walking beside, a coffin at a funeral. [O.E. *pæll*, a rich robe — L. *pallium*; see **pallium.**]

pall[2] *pöl, vi* to become vapid, insipid or tiresome; to lose relish. — *vt* to make vapid; to cloy. [Prob. from **appal.**]

palladium *pə-lā'di-əm, n* a metallic element (symbol **Pd**; atomic no. 46) resembling platinum, remarkable for power of occluding hydrogen. — *adj* **palladic** (*-lad'ik*) containing palladium in smaller or greater proportion respectively. [Named by its discoverer Wollaston (in 1803 or 1804) after the newly discovered minor planet *Pallas.*]

pallescent *pə-les'ənt, adj* turning pale. — *n* **pallesc'ence.** [L. *pallēscēns, -entis*, pres. p. of *pallēscĕre*, to turn pale.]

pallet[1] *pal'it, n* a platform or tray for lifting and stacking goods, used with the fork-lift truck, and having a double base into which the fork can be thrust; a piece of wood built into a wall for the nailing on of joiner-work; a board for carrying newly moulded bricks; a flat wooden tool with a handle, such as that used for shaping pottery; (in a timepiece) the surface or part on which the teeth of the escape wheel act to give impulse to the pendulum or balance; a valve of an organ wind-chest, regulated from the keyboard; a palette. — *adj* **pall'eted** carried on pallet(s). — *n* **palletisa'tion** or **-z-** the adoption of pallets for moving goods; the packing of goods on pallets. — *vi* and *vt* **pall'etise** or **-ize.** — *n* **pall'etiser** or **-z-.** [**palette.**]

pallet[2] *pal'it, n* a mattress, or couch, properly a mattress of straw; a small or poorly furnished bed. [Dialect Fr. *paillet*, dimin. of Fr. *paille*, straw — L. *palea*, chaff.]

palliasse or **paillasse** *pal-i-as', pal-yas'* or *pal', n* a straw mattress; an under-mattress. [Fr. *paillasse* — *paille*, straw — L. *palea.*]

palliate *pal'i-āt, vt* to excuse, extenuate; to soften by pleading something in favour; to mitigate; to alleviate. — *n* **palliā'tion.** — *adj* **pall'iative** (*-ə-tiv*) serving to extenuate; mitigating; alleviating. — *n* that which lessens pain, etc., or gives temporary relief. — *adj* **pall'iatory.** [L. *palliāre, -ātum*, to cloak — *pallium*, a cloak.]

pallid *pal'id, adj* pale, wan. — *n* **pallid'ity.** — *adv* **pall'idly.** — *n* **pall'idness.** [L. *pallidus*, pale.]

pallium *pal'i-əm, n* a white woollen vestment like a double Y, embroidered with crosses, worn by the Pope, and conferred by him upon archbishops: — *pl* **pall'ia.** [L.]

pallor *pal'ər, n* paleness. [L. *pallēre*, to be pale.]

pally. See **pal.**

palm[1] *päm, n* the inner surface of the hand between wrist and fingers; the corresponding part of a forefoot, or of a glove; a sailmaker's instrument used instead of a thimble; a flat expansion, as of an antler, or the inner surface of an anchor fluke; an act of palming. — *vt* to touch, or stroke with the palm; to hold or conceal in the palm; to impose, pass off (esp. with *off*, and *on* or *upon*); to bribe. — *adj* **palmar** (*pal'mər*) relating to the palm. — *adj* **palmate** (*pal'*) or **pal'mated** hand-shaped; having lobes radiating from one centre (*bot*); web-footed (*zool*). — *adv* **pal'mately.** — *n* **palmā'tion** palmate formation; a palmate structure or one of its parts or divisions. — *adj* **palmed** (*pämd*) having a palm; held or concealed in the palm. — *n* **palmiped** (*pal'mi-ped*) or **pal'mipede** (*-pēd*) a web-footed bird. — *adj* web-footed. — *n* **palmist** (*päm'ist*) someone who tells a person's fortune from the lines on their palm. — *n* **palm'istry.** — **grease someone's palm** to bribe someone; **in the palm of one's hand** in one's power; at one's command. [L. *palma.*]

palm[2] *päm, n* any tree or shrub of the **Palmae** (*pal'mē*), a large tropical and subtropical family of usually branchless trees with a crown of pinnate or fan-shaped leaves; a leaf of this tree carried or waved as a sign of rejoicing or of victory; (emblematically) pre-eminence, the prize; a branch of willow or other substitute in symbolic or ceremonial use. — *adj* **palmaceous** (*pal-mā'shəs*) of the palm family. — *n* **palmificā'tion** (*pal-*) artificial fertilisation of dates by hanging a wild male flower-cluster on a cultivated female tree. — *n* **palmitate** (*pal'*) a salt of **palmitic acid** (*-mit'*), a fatty acid ($C_{15}H_{31}{\cdot}COOH$) obtained from palm-oil, etc. — *adj* **palm'y** bearing palms; flourishing; palmlike. — **palma Christi** (*pal'mə*) the castor-oil plant; **palm'-branch** a palm-leaf; **palm'-butter** palm-oil in a solid state; **palm'-cat** or **-civet** the paradoxure. — *adj* **palm'-court** suitable to a **palm court**, a large, palm-tree-decorated room or conservatory in a hotel, etc., in which, traditionally, light music is played by a small orchestra, a **palm-court orchestra.** — **palm'-honey** evaporated sap of the Chilean *coquito-palm*; **palm'house** a glass house for palms and other tropical plants; **palmitic acid** see **palmitate** above; **palm'-leaf; palm'-oil** an oil or fat obtained from the pulp of the fruit of palms, esp. of the oil-palm; **palm'-sugar** jaggery; **Palm Sunday** the Sunday before Easter, in commemoration of the strewing of palm-branches when Christ entered Jerusalem; **palm'-tree; palm'-wine** fermented palm sap. [O.E. *palm, palma, palme*, also directly — L. *palma*, palm-tree, from the shape of its leaves; see **palm**[1].]

palmar, palmate, etc., **palmiped, palmipede, palmist,** etc. See under **palm**[1].

palmy. See under **palm**[2].

palmyra *pal-mī'rə*, *n* an African and Asiatic palm yielding toddy, jaggery and **palmy'ra-nuts**. — **palmy'ra-wood** properly the wood of the palmyra palm; any palm timber. [Port. *palmeira*, palm-tree, confused with *Palmyra* in Syria.]

palolo *pa-lō'lō*, *n* an edible sea-worm that burrows in coral-reefs: — *pl* **palo'los.** — Also called **palolo worm.** [Samoan.]

palomino *pal-ə-mē'nō*, *n* a horse of largely Arab blood, pale tan, yellow or gold, with white or silver mane and tail: — *pl* **palomi'nos.** [Am. Sp., — Sp., of a dove.]

palooka *pə-lōō'kə*, (*US slang*) *n* a stupid or clumsy person, esp. in sports.

palp[1] *palp* or **palpus** *pal'pəs*, (*zool*) *n* a jointed sense-organ attached in pairs to the mouth-parts of insects and crustaceans: — *pl* **pal'pī.** — *adj* **pal'pal.** [L.L. *palpus*, a feeler (L. a stroking) — L. *palpāre*, to stroke.]

palp[2] *palp*, *vt* to feel, examine or explore by touch. — *n* **palpabil'ity.** — *adj* **palp'able** that can be touched or felt; perceptible; easily found out, as of lies, etc.; obvious, gross. — *n* **palp'ableness.** — *adv* **palp'ably.** — *vt* **palp'āte** to examine by touch. — *n* **palpā'tion.** [L. *palpāre*, *-ātum*, to touch softly, stroke, caress, flatter.]

palpi. See **palp**[1].

palpitate *pal'pi-tāt*, *vi* to throb; to beat rapidly; to pulsate; to quiver. — *vt* to cause to throb. — *adj* **pal'pitant** palpitating. — *n* **palpitā'tion** the act of palpitating; abnormal awareness of heartbeat. [L. *palpitāre*, *-ātum*, frequentative of *palpāre*; cf. **palp**[1,2].]

palpus. See **palp**[1].

palsy[1] *pöl'zi*, *n* loss of control or of feeling, more or less complete, in the muscles of the body; paralysis. — *vt* to affect with palsy; to deprive of action or energy; to paralyse. — *adj* **pal'sied.** [From **paralysis.**]

palsy[2], **palsy-walsy.** See under **pal.**

paltry *pöl'tri*, *adj* of poor quality; trashy; worthless; not worth considering. — *adv* **pal'trily.** — *n* **pal'triness.** [Cf. Dan. *pialter*, rags, L.G. *paltrig*, ragged.]

paludal *pal-ū'dl* or *-ōō'*, *adj* pertaining to marshes; marshy; malarial. — *adj* **palu'dic** of marshes. — *adj* **palustral** (*-us'trəl*), **palus'trian** or **palus'trine** (*-trīn*) of marshes; inhabiting marshes. [L. *palus*, *palūdis*, a marsh; *palūster*, *-tris*, marshy.]

paly. See under **pale**[1,2].

pam. *abbrev* for pamphlet.

pampa *pam'pə* (usu. in *pl* **pampas** (*pam'pəs*), also used as *nsing*) *n* a vast treeless plain in southern S. America. — **pampas grass** a tall, ornamental, reed-like grass (*Gynerium*, or *Cortaderia*) with large thick silvery panicles. [Sp., — Quechua *pampa*, *bamba*, plain.]

pamper *pam'pər*, *vt* to gratify to the full; to over-indulge. — *n* **pam'peredness.** — *n* **pam'perer.** [A frequentative from (obs.) *pamp*, *pomp*.]

pamphlet *pam'flit*, *n* a small book stitched but not bound; a separately published treatise on some subject of the day; a small booklet of information. — *n* **pamphleteer'** a writer of pamphlets. — *vi* to write pamphlets. — *n* and *adj* **pamphleteer'ing.** [Anglo-L. *panfletus*, possibly from a Latin erotic poem *Pamphilus* (— Gr. *Pamphilos*, beloved of all) very popular in the Middle Ages.]

Pamyat *pam'yət*, *n* a Russian anti-Semitic nationalist organisation.

Pan *pan*, *n* the Greek god of pastures, flocks and woods, with goat's legs and feet, and sometimes horns and ears; later (from association with *pān*, the whole) connected with pantheistic thought. — **Pan's-pipes** or **Pan's pipes** the syrinx, a musical instrument attributed to Pan, made of reeds of different lengths, fastened in a row. [Gr. *Pān*.]

pan[1] *pan*, *n* a broad, shallow vessel for use in the home or in arts or manufactures; a saucepan; anything of a similar shape, such as the upper part of the skull (*brainpan*), the patella (*knee-pan*); a lavatory bowl; a hollow in the ground, a basin, in which water collects in the rainy season, leaving a salt deposit on evaporation; a salt pan; a salt-work; the part of a firelock that holds the priming; a hard layer (*hard-pan*) in or under the soil; a small ice-floe; a hollow metal drum as played in a steel band; a panful. — *vt* to wash in a goldminer's pan; to obtain by evaporating in a pan; to yield; to obtain; to review, criticise, harshly (*colloq*). — *vi* to wash earth for gold; to yield gold (usu. with *out*); to result, turn out (with *out*); to come to an end, be exhausted (with *out*); to cake: — *pr p* **pann'ing;** *pa t* and *pa p* **panned.** — *n* **pan'ful:** — *pl* **pan'fuls.** — *n* **pann'ikin** a small metal cup; a little pan or saucer. — *n* **pann'ing** washing for gold; the gold so obtained; harsh criticism (*colloq*). — **pan'cake** a thin cake of eggs, flour, sugar and milk, fried in a pan; pancake make-up; an aeroplane descent or landing with wings nearly horizontal (also *adj*). — *vi* to descend or alight in such a way. — *vt* to cause to make a pancake (descent or landing). — **pan'handle** a strip of territory stretching out from the main body like the handle of a pan. — **flash in the pan** a mere flash in the pan of a flintlock without discharge; a fitful show of beginning without accomplishing anything; a brief success; **pancake ice** polar sea ice in thin flat slabs, found as winter draws near; **pancake make-up** cosmetic make-up in cake form, moist, or moistened before application; **Pancake Tuesday** Shrove Tuesday. [O.E. *panne*.]

pan[2] *pän* or **pawn** *pön*, *n* betel leaf; betel. [Hind. *pān*.]

pan[3] *pan*, *vt* to move (a cinema, television, still or video camera) about, or as if pivoting about, an axis while taking a picture so as to follow a particular object or to produce a panoramic effect; in broadcasting or recording, to cause (sound) apparently to move by electronic means. — Also *vi*: — *pr p* **pann'ing;** *pa t* and *pa p* **panned.** [**pan(orama)**.]

pan- *pan-*, **pant-** *pant-* or **panto-** *pan-tō-*, *combining form* meaning all. [Gr. *pās*, *pāsa*, *pān*, genitive *pantos*, *pāsēs*, *pantos*.]

panacea *pan-ə-sē'ə*, *n* a cure for all things. [Gr. *panakeia* — *akos*, cure.]

panache *pa-näsh'* or *-nash'*, *n* a plume (*hist*); swagger; grand manner, theatricality, sense of style. [Fr., — It. *pennacchio* — *penna*, feather.]

panada *pə-nä'də*, *n* a dish made by boiling bread to a pulp in water, and flavouring; a thick binding sauce of breadcrumbs or flour and seasoning. [Sp. *pan*, bread.]

Pan-African *pan-af'ri-kən*, *adj* including or relating to all Africa, esp. concerning policies of political unity among African states. — *n* **Pan-Af'ricanism.** [**pan-**.]

Pan Am *pan-am'*, *abbrev* for Pan-American (World Airways Incorporated).

panama *pan-ə-mä'* or *pan'ə-mä*, also **panama hat,** *n* a hand-plaited hat made, not in Panama but in Ecuador, of plaited strips of the leaves of a South American plant; an imitation version of this. [Sp. *Panamá*, Panama in Central America.]

Pan-American *pan-ə-mer'i-kən*, *adj* including all America or Americans, North and South. — *n* **Pan-Amer'icanism.** [**pan-**.]

Pan-Arab *pan-ar'əb* or **Pan-Arabic** *-ar'əb-ik*, *adj* of or relating to the policy of political unity between all Arab states. — *n* **Pan-Ar'abism.** [**pan-**.]

panatella *pan-ə-tel'ə*, *n* a long, thin cigar. [Am. Sp. *panetela*, a long, thin biscuit, — It., small loaf — L. *pānis*.]

pancake. See under **pan**[1].

panchax *pan'chaks*, *n* any of several kinds of brightly coloured fish (genus *Aplocheilus*) native to Africa and S.E. Asia — often stocked in aquariums. [L., former generic name.]

panchromatic *pan-krō-mat'ik*, *adj* equally or suitably sensitive to all colours; rendering all colours in due intensity. — *n* **panchro'matism**. [Gr. *chrōma*, *-atos*, colour.]

pancreas *pang'kri-əs* or *pan'kri-əs*, *n* the sweetbread, a large gland discharging into the duodenum and containing islands of endocrine gland tissue. — *adj* **pancreat'ic**. — *n* **pan'creatin** the pancreatic juice; a medicinal substance to aid the digestion, prepared from extracts of the pancreas of certain animals. — *n* **pancreatec'tomy** surgical removal of all or part of the pancreas. — *n* **pancreatī'tis** inflammation of the pancreas. — **pancreatic juice** the alkaline secretion from the pancreas into the duodenum to aid the digestive process. [Gr. *kreas*, *-atos*, flesh.]

panda *pan'də*, *n* a raccoon-like animal (*Ailurus fulgens*) of the Himalayas (also called the **common** or **lesser panda**); (also, more correctly, **giant panda**) a larger animal, with distinctive black and white markings (*Ailuropoda melanoleuca*) of Tibet and China, apparently linking the lesser panda with the bears. — **panda car** a police patrol car (formerly white with black markings). [Said to be its name in Nepal.]

Pandean *pan-dē'ən*, *adj* of the god Pan; of Pan-pipes (q.v. at **Pan**). [Irregularly formed from *Pān*.]

pandect *pan'dekt*, *n* a treatise covering the whole of any subject. — *n* **pandect'ist**. [L. *pandecta* — Gr. *pandektēs* — *pās*, *pān*, all, *dechesthai*, to receive.]

pandemic *pan-dem'ik*, *adj* affecting a whole people, epidemic over a wide area. — *n* a pandemic disease. — *n* **pandemia** (*-dē'mi-ə*) a widespread epidemic. [Gr. *pandēmios* — *dēmos*, people.]

pandemonium *pan-di-mō'ni-əm*, *n* any very disorderly or noisy place or assembly; tumultuous uproar. — *adj* **pandemonic** (*-mon'ik*). [Title given by Milton to the capital of Hell in *Paradise Lost* — Gr. *pās*, *pān*, all, *daimōn*, a spirit.]

pander *pan'dər*, *n* someone who procures for another the means of gratifying his or her base passions; a pimp. — *vt* to play the pander for. — *vi* to act as a pander; to minister to the passions; to indulge, gratify (with *to*). [*Pandarus*, in the story of Troilus and Cressida as told by Boccaccio (*Filostrato*), Chaucer and Shakespeare.]

pandit. See **pundit**.

P and O or **P & O** *abbrev* for Peninsular and Oriental (Steamship Navigation Company).

Pandora *pan-dō'rə*, (*Gr mythol*) *n* the first woman, made for Zeus so that he might through her punish man for the theft by Prometheus of heavenly fire, given a box from which escaped and spread all the ills of human life. — **Pandora's box** any source of great and unexpected troubles. [Gr. *pās*, *pān*, all, *dōron*, a gift.]

p and p or **p & p** *abbrev* for postage and packing.

pane *pān*, *n* a rectangular compartment; a panel; a slab of window glass; a flat side or face. — *vt* to insert panes or panels in. — *adj* **paned** (*pānd*) made of panes or small squares; variegated. [Fr. *pan* — L. *pannus*, a cloth, a rag.]

panegyric *pan-i-jir'ik* (or in U.S. sometimes *-jīr'ik*), *n* a eulogy, esp. public and elaborate (on or upon); laudation. — *adj* **panegyr'ic** or **panegyr'ical**. — *adv* **panegyr'ically**. — *vt* **pan'egyrise** or **-ize** (or *-ej'ər-*) to write or pronounce a panegyric on; to praise highly. — *n* **pan'egyrist** (or *-jir'*, or *-ej'ər-*). [Gr. *panēgyrikos*, fit for a national festival — *pās*, *pān*, all, *agyris*, an assembly.]

panel *pan'l*, *n* a rectangular piece of any material; rectangular divisions on a page, esp. for the illustrations in children's comics, etc.; a bordered rectangular area; a thin flat piece sunk below the general surface of a door, shutter, wainscot, etc., often with a raised border; a board with dials, switches, etc. for monitoring or controlling the operation of an electrical or other apparatus; a compartment or hurdle of a fence; a strip of material inserted in a dress; a thin board on which a picture is painted; a large long photograph; a group of persons chosen for some purpose, e.g. to judge a competition, serve on a brains trust, or be the guessers in radio and television guessing games (**panel games**); a jury; prior to the introduction of the national health service, a list of doctors available to treat those who paid into a national health insurance scheme; such a doctor's list of patients. — *vt* to furnish with a panel or panels: — *pr p* **pan'elling**; *pa t* and *pa p* **pan'elled**. — *n* **pan'elling** panel-work. — *n* **pan'ellist** a member of a panel, esp. in panel games. — **panel beater**; **panel beating** the shaping of metal plates for vehicle bodywork, etc.; **panel doctor** a doctor who was on the panel or had a panel; **panel heating** indoor heating diffused from floors, walls or ceilings; **panel pin** a light, narrow-headed nail of small diameter used chiefly for fixing plywood or hardboard to supports; **panel saw** a fine saw for cutting very thin wood. [O.Fr., — L.L. *pannellus* — L. *pannus*, a cloth.]

panettone *pan-e-tōn'ā*, *n* a kind of spiced cake, usu. containing sultanas, traditionally eaten at Christmas in Italy: — *pl* **panettōn'i** (*-ē*). [It. *panetto*, a small loaf.]

pang *pang*, *n* a violent but not long-continued pain; a painful emotion.

panga *pang'gə*, *n* a broad, heavy African knife used as a tool and as a weapon.

Pangaea or **Pangea** *pan-jē'ə*, *n* the postulated super-continent that began to break up, forming the present continents of the Earth. [**pan-** and Gr. *gē*, the Earth.]

pan-galactic *pan-gə-lak'tik*, *adj* of or pertaining to all the galaxies in the universe. [**pan-** and **galactic**.]

Pan-German *pan-jûr'mən*, *adj* pertaining to or including all Germans. — *n* **Pan-Ger'manism** a movement for a Greater Germany or union of all German peoples. [**pan-** and **German**.]

pangolin *pang-gō'lin*, *n* the scaly ant-eater, a member of the class of mammals having no (front) teeth (edentates), of Asia and Africa. [Malay *peng-gōling*, roller, from its habit of rolling up.]

pangrammatist *pan-gram'ə-tist*, *n* a writer who contrives verses or sentences containing all the letters of the alphabet. — *n* **pan'gram** a sentence containing all the letters of the alphabet, e.g. *the quick fox jumps over the lazy brown dog*. [Gr. *gramma*, *-atos*, letter.]

panhandle. See under **pan**[1].

panhellenic *pan-hel-en'ik*, *adj* pertaining to all Greece; including all Greeks; (with *cap*) of or relating to Panhellenism. — *n* **Panhell'enism** (*-ən-izm*) a movement or aspiration for the union of all Greece or all Greeks. — *n* **Panhell'enist**. — *adj* **Panhellenis'tic**. [Gr. *Hellēnikos*, Greek — *Hellas*, Greece.]

panic[1] *pan'ik*, *n* frantic or sudden fright; contagious fear; great terror, often without any visible reason or foundation. — *adj* of the nature of a panic; inspired, caused by panic. — *vt* to throw into a panic. — *vi* to be struck by panic: — *pr p* **pan'icking**; *pa t* and *pa p* **pan'icked**. — *adj* **pan'icky** inclined to, affected by, resulting from, or of the nature of, panic. — **pan'ic-bolt** an easily moved bolt for emergency exits; **panic button** a button operating a distress or other emergency device or signal. — *vi* and *vt* **panic-buy'** to buy up stocks of a commodity which threatens to be in short supply (often precipitating a greater shortage than might otherwise have occurred). — **panic-buy'ing.** — *adj* **pan'ic-stricken** or **pan'ic-struck** struck with panic or sudden fear. [Gr. *pānikos*, belonging to the god Pan; *pānikon (deima)*, panic (fear), fear associated with Pan.]

panic[2] *pan'ik*, *n* any grass of the genus Panicum (see below), or of various closely related genera (also **pan'ic-grass**); the edible grain of some species. — Also **pan'ick** or **pann'ick.** — *n* **pan'icle** (*bot*) a raceme, or florescence in which the flowers occur on the main stalk, whose branches are themselves racemes; (*loosely*) a lax irregular inflorescence. — *adj* **pan'icled, panic'ūlate** or **panic'ulated** having, arranged in, or like, panicles. — *adv* **panic'ūlately.** — *n* **Pan'icum** a large genus of grasses having the one- or two-flowered spikelets in spikes, racemes or panicles — including several of the millets. [L. *pānicum*, Italian millet.]

panislam *pan-iz'läm*, *n* the whole Muslim world; panislamism. — *adj* **panislam'ic.** — *n* **panis'lamism** an aspiration or movement for the union of all Muslims. — *n* **panis'lamist.** [**pan-** and **Islam.**]

Panjabi. See **Punjabi.**

panjandrum *pan-jan'drəm*, *n* an imaginary figure of great power and self-importance, a burlesque potentate, from the Grand Panjandrum in a string of nonsense made up by Samuel Foote, 18th cent. English wit, actor and dramatist. — Also **panjan'darum.**

panleucopenia *pan-lū-kō-pē'ni-ə*, *n* a viral disease of cats marked by a deficiency of white blood cells and causing fever, diarrhoea and dehydration. [**pan-** and *leucopenia*.]

panne *pan*, *n* a fabric resembling velvet, with a long nap. [Fr.]

pannick. See **panic**[2].

pannier *pan'i-ər*, *n* a provision-basket; a basket carried on one's back; one of a pair of baskets slung over a pack-animal's back or over the rear wheel of a bicycle, motorcycle, etc.; a sculptured basket (*archit*); a system of hoops formerly used for spreading out a woman's dress at the hips. — *adj* **pann'iered.** [Fr. *panier* — L. *pānārium*, a bread-basket — *pānis*, bread.]

pannikin. See under **pan**[1].

pannose *pan'ōs*, (*bot*) *adj* like felt. [L. *pannōsus* — *pannus*, cloth.]

pannus *pan'əs*, (*pathol*) *n* a layer of new connective tissue that forms over the joints in rheumatoid arthritis, or over the cornea in trachoma. [L. *pannus*, cloth.]

panocha *pa-nō'chə*, *n* a Mexican coarse sugar. [Sp.]

panophobia *pan-ō-fō'bi-ə*, *n* a form of melancholia marked by groundless fears; erroneously used for **pantophobia.** [Gr. *Pān*, the god who inspired fears, *phobos*, fear.]

panoply *pan'ə-pli*, *n* complete armour, a full suit of armour; full or brilliant covering or array. — Also *fig.* — *adj* **pan'oplied** in panoply. [Gr. *panopliā*, full armour of a heavy-armed Greek foot-soldier — *pās*, *pān*, all, *hopla* (pl.), arms.]

panoptic *pan-op'tik*, *adj* all-embracing; viewing all aspects. — Also **panop'tical.** [Gr. *panoptēs*, all-seeing.]

panorama *pan-ə-rä'mə*, *n* a wide or complete view; a picture projected around the interior of a room, viewed from within in all directions; a picture unrolled and made to pass before the spectator. — *adj* **panoramic** (*-ram'ik*). — **panoramic camera** one which takes very wide-angle views, generally by rotation about an axis and by exposing a roll of film through a vertical slit; **panoramic sight** a gun-sight that can be rotated, so enabling the user to fire in any direction. [Gr. *horāma*, a view, from *horaein*, to see.]

Pan-Slav *pan-släv'*, *adj* of, including, or representing, all Slavs. — *adj* **Pan-Slav'ic.** — *n* **Pan-Slav'ism** a movement for the union of all Slav peoples. — *n* and *adj* **Pan-Slav'ist.** — *adj* **Pan-Slavon'ic.** [**pan-** and **Slav.**]

pansophy *pan'sə-fi*, *n* universal knowledge. — *adj* **pansophic** (*-sof'ik*) or **pansoph'ical.** — *n* **pan'sophism.** — *n* **pan'sophist.** [Gr. *sophiā*, wisdom.]

panspermatism *pan-spûr'mə-tizm*, **pansper'mism** *-mizm*, **pansper'my** *-mi* or **pansper'mia** *-mi-ə*, *n* the theory that life could be diffused through the universe by means of germs carried by meteorites or that life was brought to earth by this means. — *adj* **panspermat'ic** or **pansper'mic.** — *n* **pansper'matist** or **pansper'mist.** [Gr. *sperma*, *-atos*, seed.]

pansy *pan'zi*, *n* a name for various multicoloured species of violet, esp. the heart's-ease and garden kinds derived from it, as well as other species with upturned side petals and large leafy stipules; an effeminate or namby-pamby man (*derog slang*); a male homosexual (*derog slang*, often *offensive*). — *adj* (*derog slang*) effeminate. [A fanciful use of Fr. *pensée*, thought — *penser*, to think — L. *pēnsāre*, to weigh.]

pant *pant*, *vi* to gasp for breath; to run gasping; to wish ardently, to long, to yearn (with *for*). — *vt* to gasp out (an utterance). — *n* a gasping breath. — *n* and *adj* **pant'ing.** — *adv* **pant'ingly.**

pant-. See **pan-.**

Pantagruelism *pan-tə-groo͞'əl-izm*, *n* the theories and practice of *Pantagruel* as described by Rabelais (d. 1553), i.e. burlesque ironical buffoonery as a cover for serious satire. — *adj* and *n* **Pantagruelian** (*-el'i-ən*).

pantaloons *pan-tə-lo͞onz'*, *npl* various kinds of trousers such as the wide breeches of the Restoration, later combined breeches and stockings, later 18th-century trousers fastened below the calf or under the shoe, children's trousers resembling these (usu. **pants**), trousers generally or long woollen underpants. — *adj* **pantalooned'.** [Fr. *pantalon* — It. *pantalone*, from St *Pantaleone*, a favourite saint of the Venetians.]

pantechnicon *pan-tek'ni-kon*, *n* orig., a building in London intended for the sale of all kinds of artistic work, turned into a furniture-store; a furniture-van (in full **pantech'nicon-van**). [Gr. *technē*, art.]

pantheism *pan'thē-izm*, *n* the doctrine that identifies God with the universe; belief in many or all gods. — *n* **pan'thēist.** — *adj* **panthēist'ic** or **panthēist'ical.** — *n* **Pantheon** (*pan'thi-on* or *pan-thē'on*) a temple of all the gods, esp. the rotunda erected by Hadrian at Rome (on the site of Agrippa's of 27 B.C.), now the church of Santa Maria Rotonda, a burial-place of great Italians; a building serving as a general burial-place or memorial of the great dead, as Sainte Geneviève at Paris; all the gods collectively; a complete mythology. [Gr. *theos*, a god, *pantheion*, a Pantheon.]

panthenol *pan'thin-ol*, *n* a vitamin of the B-complex, affecting the growth of hair.

panther *pan'thər*, *n* a leopard, esp. a large one or one in its black phase, formerly believed to be a different species; a puma (*NAm*): — *fem* **pan'theress.** — *adj* **pan'therine** (*-īn*) or **pan'therish.** — **Black Panther** a member of a militant U.S. Black political movement dedicated to ending domination by whites. [Gr. *panthēr*.]

panties. See **pants.**

pantihose *pan'ti-hōz*, (esp. *US*) *npl* tights worn by women or children with ordinary dress, i.e. not theatrical, etc. [**panties** and **hose**[1].]

pantile *pan'tīl*, *n* a roofing tile whose cross-section forms an S-shaped curve; a tile concave or convex in cross-section. — *adj* **pan'tiled.** — *n* **pan'tiling.** [**pan**[1] and **tile.**]

panto. See **pantomime.**

panto-. See **pan-.**

Pantocrator *pan-tok'rə-tər*, *n* the ruler of the universe, esp. Christ enthroned, as in icons, etc. [Gr. *kratos*, power.]

pantograph *pan'tə-gräf*, *n* a jointed framework of rods, based on the geometry of a parallelogram, for copying drawings, plans, etc., on the same, or a different, scale; a similar-shaped framework for other purposes, as for collecting a current from an overhead wire on electric locomotives, trams, etc. — *n* **pantographer** (*-tog'rə-fər*). — *adj* **pantographic** (*-tō-graf'ik*) or **pantograph'ical**. — *n* **pantog'raphy.** — **laser pantography** a technique of tracing a circuit pattern on to a microchip by means of a laser beam. [Gr. *graphein*, to write.]

pantomime *pan'tə-mīm*, *n* a play or an entertainment in mime; a theatrical entertainment, usu. about Christmas-time, developed out of this, no longer in mime, with showy scenery, topical allusions, songs and star attractions of the day, buffoonery and dancing strung loosely upon a nursery story (also **pan'to**: — *pl* **pan'tos**); mime; a situation of fuss, farce or confusion (*derog*). — *adj* of pantomime. — *adj* **pantomimic** (*-mim'ik*) or **pantomim'ical**. — *adv* **pantomim'ically.** — *n* **pan'tomīmist** an actor in or writer of pantomime. [L. *pantomīmus* — Gr. *pantomīmos*, imitator of all — *pās*, *pantos*, all, *mīmos*, an imitator.]

pantophagy *pan-tof'ə-ji*, *n* omnivorousness. — *n* **pantoph'agist.** — *adj* **pantoph'agous** (*-gəs*). [Gr. *phagein*, to eat.]

pantophobia *pan-tə-fō'bi-ə*, *n* morbid fear of everything; (by confusion with **panophobia**) causeless fear. [Gr. *pās*, *pantos*, all, *phobos*, fear.]

pantothenic *pan-tə-then'ik*, *adj* lit. from all quarters. — **pantothenic acid** a member of the vitamin B complex, so ubiquitous that the effects of its deficiency in man are not known. [Gr. *pantothen*, from everywhere.]

pantry *pan'tri*, *n* a room or cupboard for provisions and table furnishings, or where plate, knives, etc., are cleaned. — **pan'trymaid**: — *masc* **pan'tryman.** [Fr. *paneterie* — L.L. *pānitāria* — L. *pānis*, bread.]

pants *pants*, *npl* knickers or underpants; trousers (esp. *NAm*). — *npl* **pant'ies** short knickers for children and women. — **pants suit** or (esp. *NAm*) **pant suit** a woman's suit of trousers and jacket. — **(be caught) with one's pants down** (*colloq*) (to be caught) at an embarrassing and unsuitable moment, in a state of extreme unpreparedness; **(fly) by the seat of one's pants** (*colloq*) (to get through a difficult or dangerous situation) by a combination of resourcefulness and sheer luck; **scare, bore,** etc. **the pants off someone** (*slang*) to scare, bore, etc. someone to a great degree. [Ety. as for **Pantaloon.**]

panty girdle *pan'ti gûr'dl*, *n* a woman's foundation garment consisting of panties made of elasticated material. [**panties.**]

pap[1] *pap*, *n* soft food for infants, such as bread boiled with milk; trivial, rubbishy ideas, entertainment, etc. (*fig*); mash, pulp. — *adj* **papp'y**. [Imit.]

pap[2] *pap*, (*dialect*) *n* a nipple; (in place names) a round conical hill.

papa *pə-pä'* or (esp. in U.S.) *pä'pə*, *n* father (*old-fashioned pet-name*, *jocular* or *genteel*). [Partly through Fr. *papa*, partly directly from L.L. *pāpa*, Gr. *papās*, *pappās*, father.]

papacy *pā'pə-si*, *n* the office of pope; a pope's tenure of office; papal government. [L.L. *pāpātia* — *pāpa*, pope.]

papain *pə-pā'in*, *n* a digestive enzyme in the juice of pawpaw (*Carica*) fruits and leaves, used for tenderising meat. [Sp. *papaya*, papaw.]

papal *pā'pl*, *adj* of or pertaining to the pope or the papacy. — *n* **pa'palism** the papal system. — *n* **pa'palist** a supporter of the pope and of the papal system. — *adv* **pa'pally.** — **papal cross** a cross with three cross-bars; **Papal knighthood** a title of nobility conferred by the Pope. [L.L. *pāpālis* — *pāpa*, pope.]

Papanicolaou smear *pap-ə-nik'o-low* (or *-nēk'*) *smēr* or **Papanicolaou test** (*test*), *n* a smear test for detecting cancer, esp. of the womb, devised by George *Papanicolaou*, 20th cent. U.S. anatomist.

paparazzo *pa-pa-rat'sō*, *n* a photographer who specialises in spying on or harassing famous people in order to obtain photographs of them in unguarded moments, etc.: — *pl* **paparazz'i** (*-sē*). [It.]

Papaver *pə-pā'vər*, *n* the poppy genus, giving name to the family **Papaverā'ceae**. — *adj* **papaveraceous** (*pə-pav-* or *-pāv-ə-rā'shəs*) of the poppy family. — *n* **papaverine** (*pə-pav'ə-rēn*, *-rīn* or *-pāv'*) an alkaloid derived from poppy juice and used medicinally. [L. *papāver*, the poppy.]

papaw. See **pawpaw**.

papaya *pə-pä'yə*, *n* a tree, or its fruit, native to South America but common in the tropics, the trunk, leaves and fruit yielding papain, the leaves providing a powerful anti-worm preparation. — Also called **paw'paw** or **papaw'**. [Sp. *papayo* (tree), *papaya* (fruit).]

paper *pā'pər*, *n* a material made in thin sheets as an aqueous deposit from linen rags, esparto, wood-pulp, or other form of cellulose, used for writing, printing, wrapping, and other purposes; extended to other materials of similar purpose or appearance, e.g. to papyrus, rice paper, to the substance of which some wasps build their nests, to cardboard, and even to tinfoil ('silver paper'); a piece of paper; a written or printed document or instrument, note, receipt, bill, bond, deed, etc.; (in *pl*) documents, esp. for the purpose of personal identification, customs or passport controls, etc.; a newspaper; an essay or literary contribution, esp. one read before a society or submitted for a degree examination; a set of examination questions; paper money; stocks and shares (*stock exchange slang*); wallpaper; a quantity of anything wrapped in or attached to a paper. — *adj* consisting or made of paper; papery; on paper. — *vt* to cover with paper; to treat in any way by means of any type of paper, e.g. to sandpaper, etc. — *n* **pa'perer.** — *n* **pa'pering** the operation of covering with paper; the paper so used. — *adj* **pa'perless** using esp. electronic means instead of paper for communication, recording, etc. — *adj* **pa'pery** like paper. — **pa'perback** a book with a flexible paper cover. — Also *adj*. — *vt* to publish in paperback form. — **pa'perboard** a type of strong, thick cardboard, pasteboard; **pa'per-boy** or **-girl** a boy or girl who delivers newspapers; **pa'per-chase** the game of hare and hounds, in which some runners (*hares*) set off across country strewing paper by which others (*hounds*) track them; **pa'per-clip** a clip of bent wire or the like, for holding pieces of paper together; **pa'per-cutter** a paper-knife or guillotine; **pa'per-fastener** a button with two blades that can be forced through papers and bent back to hold the papers together; **pa'per-hanger** a professional hanger of wallpaper; **pa'per-knife** a thin, flat blade for cutting open the leaves of books or using as a letter-opener; **pa'per-mâché** papier-mâché; **pa'per-maker** a manufacturer of paper; **pa'per-making**; **pa'per-mill** a mill where paper is made; **paper money** pieces of paper stamped or marked by government or by a bank, as representing a certain value of money, which pass from hand to hand; **paper nautilus** a type of mollusc with a papery spiral shell, the argonaut; **paper profits** the appreciation in value of a bond, share, etc.; **pa'per-pulp** pulpy material for making paper; **pa'per-reed** the papyrus; **pa'per-ruler** a person who, or an instrument which, makes straight lines on paper; **paper tape** (*comput*) paper data-recording tape, which records information by means of punched holes (**paper tape punch** a machine that perforates paper tape; **paper tape reader** a device that senses and translates the holes punched in paper tape into machine-processable form); **paper tiger** a person or organisation that appears to be powerful but is in fact not; **pa'perweight** a small, often decorative, weight for keeping loose papers from blowing away or being moved; **pa'perwork** clerical work; keeping of records as part of a job. — **on paper** planned, decreed, existing in theory only; apparently, judging by statistics, but perhaps not in fact; **paper over (the cracks in)** to create the impression that there is or has been no dissent, error or fault in (something doubtful). [A.Fr. *papir*, O.Fr. (Fr.) *papier* — L. *papyrus* — Gr. *papȳros*, papyrus.]

Papiamento *pap-i-ə-men'tō*, *n* a creole language derived from Spanish, spoken in the Dutch Antilles. [Sp. *papia*, talk.]

papier-mâché *pap-yā-ma'shā*, *n* a material consisting of paper-pulp or of sheets of paper pasted together, often treated so as to resemble varnished or lacquered wood or plaster. — *adj* made of papier-mâché. [Would-be French, — Fr. *papier* (see **paper**) *mâché*, chewed — L. *masticātus*.]

papilio *pə-pil'i-ō*, *n* a butterfly of the swallow-tailed *Papilio* genus: — *pl* **papil'ios**. — *adj* **papilionā'ceous** of butterflies; butterfly-like; of a form of corolla which is somewhat butterfly-like (*bot*); of a family of plants characterised by such a corolla, including pea, bean, clover, gorse, laburnum, etc. [L. *pāpiliō*, *-ōnis*, butterfly.]

papilla *pə-pil'ə*, *n* a small nipple-like protuberance; a minute elevation on the skin, esp. of the fingertips, the inner surface of the eyelids, and upper surface of the tongue, in which a nerve ends; a protuberance at the base of a hair, feather, tooth, etc.; a minute conical protuberance as on the surface of a petal: — *pl* **papill'ae** (*-ī*). — *adj* **papill'ary** like, of the nature of, or having, papillae. — *adj* **papill'ate**, **papill'ated** or **papillif'erous** (*pap-*) having papillae. — *adj* **papill'iform** in the form of a papilla. — *n* **papillō'ma** a tumour formed by abnormal enlargement of a papilla or papillae, such as a wart, etc. [L., dimin. of *papula*.]

papillon *pap-ē-yɔ̃*, *n* (a dog of) a breed of toy spaniel with erect ears. [Fr., butterfly.]

papillote *pap'il-ōt*, *n* a curl-paper for the hair; a frilled paper used to decorate the bones of chops, etc. (*cookery*); oiled or greased paper in which meat is cooked and served (*cookery*; also *pap-ē-yot'*). [Fr.]

papist *pā'pist*, *n* a follower or advocate of the pope; a name slightingly given to a Roman Catholic (*derog*). — *n* **pā'pism** (often *derog*) popery. — *n* **pā'pistry** (often *derog*) popery. [L.L. *pāpa*, pope.]

papoose *pə-pōōs'*, *n* a North American Indian baby or young child. [Narraganset *papoos*.]

pappadom. Same as **poppadum**.

pappus *pap'əs*, (*bot*) *n* a ring or parachute of fine hair or down, which grows above the seed and helps in wind-dissemination in composites and some other plants, e.g. dandelions. [L. *pappus* — Gr. *pappos*, a grandfather, down, a pappus.]

pappy[1]. See **pap**[1].

pappy[2] *pap'i*, (*US colloq*) *n* father. [**papa**.]

paprika *pa-prēk'ə* or *pap'ri-kə*, *n* (a hot spice obtained from) Hungarian red pepper, a species of capsicum. [Hung.]

papula *pap'ū-lə* or **papule** *pap'ūl*, *n* a pimple; a papilla: — *pl* **pap'ūlae** (*-lē*) or **pap'ules**. — *adj* **pap'ūlar**. [L. *papula*, a pimple.]

papyrus *pə-pī'rəs*, *n* the paper-reed, a tall plant of the sedge family, once common in Egypt; its stems cut in thin strips and pressed together as a writing material of ancient times; a manuscript on papyrus: — *pl* **papy'ri** (*-rī*). — *n* **papyrologist** (*pap-i-rol'ə-jist*). — *n* **papyrol'ogy** the study of ancient papyri. [L. *papȳrus* — Gr. *papȳros*.]

par[1] *pär*, *n* state of equality; equal value; norm or standard; state or value of bills, shares, etc., when they sell at exactly the price marked on them — i.e. without *premium* or *discount*; the number of strokes that should be taken for a hole or a round by good play (*golf*). — **par value** value at par. — **above par** at a premium, or at more than the nominal value; **at par** at exactly the nominal value; **below par** at a discount, or at less than the nominal value; out of sorts, not particularly good in health, spirits, etc. (*fig*); **on a par with** equal to; **par for the course** a normal, average result or (*colloq fig*) normal or predictable occurrence, state of affairs, etc. [L. *pār*, equal.]

par[2] *pär*, *n*. Same as **parr**.

par. *abbrev* for: paragraph; parallel; parish.

para[1] *pär'ə*, *n* a small Turkish coin; the 40th part of a piastre; in Yugoslavia the 100th part of a dinar. [Turk. *pārah*.]

para[2] *par'ə*, (*colloq*) *n* a short form of **paratrooper** or **paragraph**.

para-[1] *par-ə-*, *combining form* denoting: beside; faulty; abnormal; a polymer of; a compound related to; closely resembling, or parallel to (as in **paramedic**, **paramilitary**); (in organic chemistry) having substituted atoms or groups attached to two opposite carbon atoms of the benzene ring — commonly represented by *p-* (as in a **pa'ra-compound**, e.g. *p*-xylene). [Gr. *para*, beside.]

para-[2] *par'ə-*, *pfx* denoting parachute. — *n* **par'abrake** a parachute used to help brake an aircraft when it has landed. — *n* **par'adoctor** a doctor who parachutes to patients. — *n* **par'afoil** a form of steerable parachute, consisting of air-filled nylon cells. — *n* **par'amedic** or **par'amedico** a paradoctor (see also **paramedic**[1]).

parable *par'ə-bl*, *n* a fable or story of something which might have happened, told to illustrate some doctrine, or to make some duty clear. — *vt* to represent by a parable. [Gr. *parabolē*, a placing alongside, comparison, parabola, etc. — *para*, beside, beyond, *ballein*, to throw.]

parabola *pə-rab'ə-lə*, *n* a curve, one of the conic sections, the intersection of a cone and a plane parallel to its side, or the locus of a point equidistant from a fixed point (the *focus*) and a fixed straight line (the *directrix*): — *pl* **parab'olas**. — *adj* **parabolic** (*par-ə-bol'ik*) or **parbol'ical** of or like a parable or a parabola; expressed by a parable; belonging to, or in the form of, a parabola. — *adv* **parabol'ically**. [Ety. as for **parable**.]

paracentesis *par-ə-sen-tē'sis*, (*surg*) *n* tapping of a body cavity to remove gas, fluid, etc. [Gr. *parakentēsis* — *para*, beside, beyond, *kenteein*, to pierce.]

paracetamol *par-ə-sēt'ə-mol* or *-set'*, *n* a mild analgesic and anti-fever drug, often used instead of aspirin. [Gr. *para*, beside, beyond, *acetam*ide.]

parachronism *par-ak'rən-izm*, *n* an error in dating, esp. when anything is represented as later than it really was. [Gr. *para*, beside, beyond, *chronos*, time.]

parachute *par'ə-shōōt*, *n* an apparatus like an umbrella for descending safely from a great height, esp. when jumping from an aeroplane (*colloq* short form **chute**); any structure serving a similar purpose. — *vi* to descend by parachute. — *vt* to take and drop by parachute (also *fig*). — *n* **par'achutist**. [Fr. *parachute* — It. *para*, imper. of *parare*, to ward (— L. *parāre*, to prepare) and Fr. *chute*, fall.]

paraclete *par'ə-klēt*, *n* an advocate or legal helper, or intercessor, pleader on behalf of another — applied in the Bible (with *cap*) to the Holy Ghost (John xiv. 26). [Gr. *paraklētos* — *parakaleein*, to call in, also to comfort.]

paracrostic *par-ə-kros'tik*, *n* a poem whose initial letters reproduce its first verse. [**para-**[1] and **acrostic**.]

parade *pə-rād'*, *n* show; display; ostentation; an assembling in order for exercise, inspection, etc.; a procession; a public promenade; a row (of shops or houses); a parry (*fencing*). — *vt* to show off; to thrust to the attention of others; to traverse a square, etc. in parade; to marshal in military order for inspection, etc. — *vi* to march up and down (as if) for show; to march, drive, etc. in procession or military order; to show off. — **parade'-ground** a square, etc., for the parading of troops. [Fr., — Sp. *parada* — *parar*, to halt — L. *parāre*, *-ātum*, to prepare.]

paradigm *par'ə-dīm*, *n* an example, exemplar; (an example of) the inflection of a word (*gram*); a basic theory, a conceptual framework within which scientific theories are constructed. — *adj* **paradigmatic** (*-dig-mat'ik*) or **paradigmat'ical**. — *adv* **paradigmat'ically**. [Fr. *paradigme* — Gr. *paradeigma* — *paradeiknynai*, to exhibit side by side — *para*, beside, beyond, *deiknynai*, to show.]

paradise *par'ə-dīs*, *n* the garden of Eden; heaven; the place (intermediate or final) where the blessed dead go; any place or state of bliss. — *adj* **paradisaic** (*par-ə-dis-ā'ik*), **paradisa'ical, paradisal** (*-dī'səl*), **paradisean** (*-dis'i-ən*), **paradisiac** (*-dis'i-ak* or *-diz'i-ak*), **paradisiacal** (*-dis-ī'ə-kl*), **paradisial** (*-dis'* or *-diz'*), **paradisian** (*-dis'* or *-diz'*) or **paradisic** (*-dis'* or *-diz'*). — **par'adise-fish** a Chinese freshwater fish, often kept in aquaria for its beauty of form and colouring. — **bird of paradise** any bird of the family **Paradisē'idae**, inhabitants chiefly of New Guinea, closely related to the crows but extremely gorgeous in plumage. [Gr. *paradeisos*, a park — O.Pers. *pairidaēza*, park.]

parador *par'ə-dör*, *n* any of several types of (usu. country) dwellings, e.g., castles, convents, etc. converted for use as tourist accommodation in Spain: — *pl* **paradores** (*-dör'ās*). [Sp.]

paradox *par'ə-doks*, *n* something which is contrary to received, conventional opinion; something which is apparently absurd but is or may be really true; a self-contradictory statement; paradoxical character. — *adj* **paradox'al**. — *n* **par'adoxer**. — *adj* **paradox'ical**. — *adv* **paradox'ically**. — *n* **par'adoxist**. — *n* **paradoxol'ogy** the utterance or maintaining of paradoxes. — *n* **par'adoxy** the quality of being paradoxical. [Gr. *paradoxos*, *-on*, contrary to opinion — *para*, beside, beyond, *doxa*, opinion.]

paradoxure *par-ə-dok'sūr*, *n* a civet-like carnivore of Southern Asia and Malaysia. [Gr. *paradoxos*, paradoxical — *para*, beside, beyond, *ourā*, tail.]

paraesthesia or in U.S. **paresthesia** *par-is-thē'zi-ə* or *-es-*, (*med*) *n* abnormal sensation in any part of the body. [Gr. *para*, beyond, *aisthēsis*, sensation.]

paraffin *par'ə-fin*, *n* originally, paraffin-wax — so named by its discoverer, Reichenbach, from its having little chemical affinity for other bodies; generalised to mean any saturated hydrocarbon of the methane series, gaseous, liquid, or solid, the general formula being C_nH_{2n+2}; paraffin-oil. — Also **par'affine**. — *vt* to treat with paraffin. — *adj* **paraffin'ic, par'affinoid** or **par'affiny**. — **par'affin-oil** any of the mineral burning oils associated with the manufacture of paraffin, mixtures of liquid paraffin and other hydrocarbons; **paraffin test** a test using paraffin to detect trace elements left on the skin of someone who has been in contact with explosives, etc.; **par'affin-wax** a white transparent crystalline substance got by distillation of shale, coal, tar, wood, etc., a mixture of solid paraffins. — **liquid paraffin** a liquid form of petroleum jelly, used as a mild laxative. [L. *parum*, little, *affīnis*, having affinity.]

parafoil. See under **para-**[2].

paragenesis *par-ə-jen'i-sis* or **paragenesia** *par-ə-jin-ē'zi-ə*, (*geol*) *n* the order in which minerals have developed in a given mass of rock; the development of minerals in such close contact that their formation is affected and they become a joined mass. — *adj* **paragenet'ic**. [**para-**[1].]

paraglider *par'ə-glīd-ər*, *n* a glider with inflatable wings. — *n* **par'agliding** the sport of being towed through the air by plane while wearing a modified type of parachute, then being allowed to drift to the ground. [**para-**[2].]

paragon *par'ə-gon* or *-gən*, *n* a model of perfection or supreme excellence. [O.Fr. *paragon* — It. *paragone*, touchstone.]

paragraph *par'ə-gräf*, *n* a sign (in ancient MSS. a short horizontal line, in the Middle Ages ℂ, now ¶, ⁋) marking off a section of a book, etc.; a distinct part of a discourse or writing marked by such a sign or now usually by indenting or extra space between lines; a musical passage forming a unit; a short separate item of news or comment in a newspaper. — *vt* to form into paragraphs; to write or publish paragraphs about. — *n* **par'agrapher** or **par'agraphist** a person who writes paragraphs, news items, esp. for newspapers. — *adj* **paragraphic** (*-graf'*) or **paragraph'ical**. — *adv* **paragraph'ically**. [Gr. *paragraphos*, written alongside — *para*, beside, beyond, *graphein*, to write.]

paragraphia *par-ə-graf'i-ə*, *n* writing of wrong words and letters, owing to disease or injury of the brain. — *adj* **paragraphic** (*-graf'ik*). [Gr. *para*, beside, beyond, *graphein*, to write.]

parainfluenza virus *par-ə-in-flōō-en'zə vī'rəs*, *n* any of a number of viruses causing influenza-like symptoms, esp. in children.

parakeet or **parrakeet** *par'ə-kēt*, *n* a small long-tailed parrot of various kinds. [Sp. *periquito*, It. *parrocchetto*, or O.Fr. *paroquet* (Fr. *perroquet*).]

parakiting *par'ə-kīt-ing*, *n* the sport of soaring suspended from a parachute which is being towed. [**para-**[2].]

paralalia *par-ə-lā'li-ə*, *n* a form of speech disturbance, particularly that in which a different sound or syllable is produced from the one intended. [Gr. *para*, beside, beyond, *lalia*, speech.]

paralanguage *par'ə-lang-gwij*, *n* elements of communication other than words, i.e. tone of voice, gesture, facial expression, etc. — *adj* **paralinguist'ic**. — *nsing* **paralinguist'ics** the study of paralanguage. [**para-**[1].]

paraldehyde *par-al'di-hīd*, *n* a polymer, $(C_2H_4O)_3$, of *acetaldehyde* (acetic aldehyde), a liquid with a characteristic smell, used to induce sleep. [**para-**[1] and **aldehyde**.]

paralegal *par-ə-lē'gl*, *adj* of, concerning or being a person who assists a professional lawyer. — Also *n* (*par'ə-lē-gl*). [**para-**[1].]

paraleipsis *par-ə-līp'sis* or **paralipsis** *-lip'sis*, *n* a rhetorical figure by which one fixes attention on a subject by pretending to neglect it, as 'I will not speak of his generosity', etc. — *pl* **paraleip'ses** or **paralip'ses** (*-sēz*). — *n* **paraleipom'enon** or **paralipom'enon** a thing left out, added in supplement: — *pl* **paraleipom'ena** or **paralipom'ena**, esp. (in the Septuagint, etc.) the Books of Chronicles. [Gr. *paraleipsis*, *paraleipomenon* (neut. pres. p. pass.) — *paraleipein*, to leave aside.]

paralinguistic, paralinguistics. See **paralanguage**.

paralipsis, etc. See **paraleipsis**.

parallax *par'ə-laks*, *n* an apparent change in the position of an object caused by change of position in the observer; (in astronomy) the apparent change in the position of a heavenly body when viewed from different points — when viewed from opposite points on the earth's surface this change is called the *daily*, *diurnal* or *geocentric parallax*; when viewed from opposite points of the earth's orbit, the *annual* or *heliocentric parallax*. — *adj* **parallac'tic** or **parallac'tical**. — **parallactic motion** see **proper motion** under **proper**. [Gr. *parallaxis* — *para*, beside, beyond, *allassein*, to change — *allos*, another.]

parallel *par'ə-lel, adj* (of lines, etc.) extended in the same direction and equidistant in all parts; analogous, corresponding; alongside in time; exactly contemporary; having a constant interval (major and minor being reckoned alike; *mus*). — *adv* in parallel motion, pattern, etc. — *n* a parallel line; a line of latitude; an analogue, or like, or equal; an analogy; a tracing or statement of resemblances; parallel arrangement. — *vt* to place so as to be parallel; to represent as parallel; to liken in detail; to find a parallel to; to match; to be or run parallel to. — *vi* to be or run parallel: — *pr p* **par'alleling**; *pa t* and *pa p* **par'alleled**. — *vt* **par'allelise** or **-ize** to provide a parallel to. — *n* **par'allelism** the state or fact of being parallel; resemblance in corresponding details; a balanced construction of a verse or sentence, where one part repeats the form or meaning of the other; comparison; development along parallel lines. — *n* **par'allelist** a person who draws a parallel or comparison. — *adj* **parallelis'tic**. — *adv* **par'allelwise**. — **parallel bars** a pair of fixed bars used in gymnastics; **parallel imports** imports brought into a country through other than official channels, thus circumventing regulations, etc.; **parallel importer**; **parallel motion** a name given to any linkage by which circular motion may be changed into straight-line motion; **parallel processing** (*comput*) the processing of several elements of an item of information at the same time; **parallel ruler** or **rulers** rulers joined by two pivoted strips, for drawing straight parallel lines; **parallel slalom** a slalom race in which two competitors ski down parallel courses. — **in parallel** (of electrical apparatus) so arranged that terminals of like polarity are connected together; simultaneously (*fig*). [Gr. *parallēlos*, as if *par' allēloin*, beside each other.]

parallelepiped *par-ə-lel-ep'i-ped* (or *-lel'ə-* or *-ə-pī'*), *n* a solid figure bounded by six parallelograms, opposite pairs being identical and parallel. [Gr. *parallēlepipedon* — *parallēlos*, *epipedon*, a plane surface — *epi*, on, *pedon*, ground.]

parallelogram *par-ə-lel'ō-gram, n* a two-dimensional four-sided figure whose opposite sides are parallel. — *adj* **parallelogrammat'ic, parallelogrammat'ical, parallelogramm'ic** or **parallelogramm'ical**. [Gr. *parallēlogrammon* — *grammē*, a line.]

paralysis *pə-ral'i-sis, n* a loss of power of motion, or sensation, in any part of the body; deprivation of the power of action. — *vt* **paralyse** or in U.S. **paralyze** (*par'ə-līz*) to afflict with paralysis; to deprive of the power of action. — *n* **par'alyser** or in U.S. **-z-**. — *adj* **paralytic** (*par-ə-lit'ik*) of or pertaining to paralysis; afflicted with or inclined to paralysis; helplessly drunk (*slang*). — *n* a person who is affected with paralysis. [Gr. *paralysis*, secret undoing, paralysis — *lyein*, to loosen.]

paramatta or **parramatta** *par-ə-mat'ə, n* a fabric like merino wool made of worsted and cotton. [From *Parramatta* in New South Wales.]

paramedic[1] *par-ə-med'ik, n* a person helping doctors or supplementing medical work, esp. in emergency teams. — *adj* **paramed'ic** or **paramed'ical**. [**para-**[1] and **medic**[1].]

paramedic[2], **paramedico**. See under **para-**[2].

paramenstruum *par-ə-men'strōō-əm, n* the four days before and the four days after the onset of menstruation. [**para-**[1].]

parameter *pə-ram'i-tər, n* a line or quantity which serves to determine a point, line, figure or quantity, in a class of such things (*math*); a boundary or limit (*lit* and *fig*); a quantity to which an arbitrary value may be given as a convenience in expressing performance or for use in calculations (*electr*); a variable; a variable which is given a series of arbitrary values in order that a family of curves of two other related variables may be drawn; any constant in learning or growth curves that differs with differing conditions (*psychol*). — *adj* **param'etral, parametric** (*par-ə-met'rik*) or **paramet'rical**. [Gr. *para*, beside, beyond, *metron*, measure.]

paramilitary *par-ə-mil'i-tər-i, adj* on military lines and intended to supplement the strictly military; organised as a military force. — Also *n*. [**para-**[1].]

paramnesia *par-am-nē'zhə, n* a memory disorder in which words are remembered but not their proper meaning; the condition of believing that one remembers events and circumstances which have not previously occurred. [Gr. *para*, beside, beyond, and the root of *mimnēskein*, to remind.]

paramo *pa'rə-mō, n* a bare, windswept, elevated plain in South America: — *pl* **par'amos**. [Sp. *páramo*.]

paramount *par'ə-mownt, adj* superior to all others; supreme. — *n* a paramount chief; a superior. — *n* **par'amountcy**. — *adv* **par'amountly**. — **paramount chief** a supreme chief. [O.Fr. *paramont*, *par* (L. *per*) *à mont* (L. *ad montem*); see **amount**.]

paramour *par'ə-mōōr, n* a lover (of either sex), formerly in an innocent, now usually in the illicit, sense. [Fr. *par amour*, by or with love.]

parang *pär'ang, n* a heavy Malay knife. [Malay.]

paranoia *par-ə-noi'ə, n* a form of mental disorder characterised by constant delusions, esp. of grandeur, pride, persecution; intense (esp. irrational) fear or suspicion. — *adj* **paranoi'ac** (*-ak*) of paranoia. — *n* a victim of paranoia. — *adj* **par'anoid** or **paranoid'al** resembling or suffering from paranoia. [Gr. *paranoiă* — *para*, beside, beyond, *noos*, mind.]

paranormal *par-ə-nör'məl, adj* abnormal, esp. psychologically; not susceptible to normal explanations. — *n* that which is paranormal; (with **the**) paranormal occurrences or phenomena. [**para-**[1] and **normal**.]

paranym *par'ə-nim, n* a word whose meaning is altered to conceal an evasion or untruth, e.g. *liberation* used for *conquest*. [**para-**[1] and Gr. *onyma*, *onoma*, name.]

parapenting *par'ə-pent-ing* or *-pãt-ing, n* a cross between hang-gliding and parachuting, a sport in which the participant jumps from a high place wearing a modified type of parachute, which is then used as a hang-glider. [**para-**[2] and Fr. *pente*, slope.]

parapet *par'ə-pit, n* a bank or wall to protect soldiers from the fire of an enemy in front; a low wall along the side of a bridge, edge of a roof, etc. — *adj* **par'apeted** having a parapet. [It. *parapetto*, from pfx. *para-* (see **parachute**) and It. *petto* — L. *pectus*, the breast.]

paraph *par'af, n* a mark or flourish under one's signature. — *vt* to append a paraph to, to sign with initials. [Fr. *paraphe*; cf. **paragraph**.]

paraphasia *par-ə-fā'zhə* or *-zi-ə, n* a form of aphasia in which one word is substituted for another. — *adj* **paraphasic** (*-fā'zik*). [**para-**[1] and **aphasia**.]

paraphernalia *par-ə-fər-nāl'i-ə, npl* or *nsing* trappings; equipment; miscellaneous accessories. [Late L. *paraphernālia* — *parapherna* — Gr., from *para*, beside, beyond, *phernē*, a dowry — *pherein*, to bring.]

paraphonia *par-ə-fō'ni-ə, n* a morbid change of voice; an alteration of the voice, as at puberty. — *adj* **paraphonic** (*-fon'ik*). [Gr. *para*, beside, beyond, *phōnē*, voice.]

paraphrase *par'ə-frāz, n* (an) expression of the same thing in other words. — *vt* to express in other words. — *vi* to make a paraphrase. — *n* **par'aphraser** or **par'aphrast** (*-frast*) a person who paraphrases. — *adj* **paraphrast'ic** or **paraphras'tical**. — *adv* **paraphrast'ically**. [Gr. *paraphrasis* — *para*, beside, beyond, *phrasis*, a speaking — *phrazein*, to speak.]

paraphrenia *par-ə-frē'ni-ə, n* any mental disorder of the paranoid type. [**para-**[1] and Gr. *phrēn*, mind.]

paraplegia *par-ə-plē'jə, n* paralysis of the lower part of the body. — *adj* **paraple'gic**. — *n* a person suffering from paraplegia. [Ionic Gr. *paraplēgiē*, a stroke on the side — *para*, beside, beyond, *plēgē*, a blow.]

parapsychology *par-ə-sī-kol'ə-ji*, *n* psychical research; the study of phenomena such as telepathy and clairvoyance which seem to suggest that the mind can gain knowledge by means other than the normal perceptual processes. — *adj* **parapsycholog'ical**. — *adv* **parapsycholog'ically**. — *n* **parapsychol'ogist**. [**para-**[1].]

paraquat® *par'ə-kwot*, *n* a weedkiller very poisonous to human beings. [**para-**[1] and *quat*ernary, part of its formula.]

parasailing *par'ə-sā-ling*, *n* a sport similar to paragliding, the participant wearing water-skis and a modified type of parachute, and being towed into the air by motorboat. [**para-**[2].]

parascending *par'ə-sen-ding*, *n* a sport similar to paragliding, the participant being towed into the wind behind a motor vehicle. [**para-**[2] and **ascending**.]

parascience *par'ə-sī-əns*, *n* the study of phenomena which cannot be investigated by rigorous traditional scientific method. [**para-**[1].]

paraselene *par-ə-sə-lē'nē*, *n* a mock moon, a bright patch on a lunar halo: — *pl* **paraselē'nae** (*-nē*). [Gr. *para*, beside, beyond, *selēnē*, moon.]

parasite *par'ə-sīt*, *n* a hanger-on or sycophant; a person who lives at the expense of society or of others and contributes nothing; an organism that lives in or on another organism and derives subsistence from it without rendering it any service in return; in literary but not scientific use extended to an epiphyte. — *n* **parasitaemia** (*-ē'mi-ə*) the presence of parasites in the blood. — *adj* **parasitic** (*-sit'ik*) or **parasit'ical** of, of the nature of, caused by, or like, a parasite. — *adv* **parasit'ically**. — *n* **parasit'icalness**. — *n* **parasiticide** (*-sit'i-sīd*) anything which destroys parasites. — *vt* **par'asitise** or **-ize** to be a parasite on (another organism); to infect or infest with parasites. — *n* **par'asitism** (*-sīt-izm*) the act or practice of being a parasite. — *n* **parasitol'ogist** (*-si-* or *-sī-*). — *n* **parasitol'ogy** (*-si-* or *-sī-*). [Gr. *parasītos* — *para*, beside, *sītos*, corn, bread, food.]

parasol *par'ə-sol*, *n* a sunshade similar to an umbrella. — **parasol mushroom** a tall white edible mushroom resembling a parasol. [Fr., — It. *parasole* — *para*, imper. of *parare*, to ward — L. *parāre*, to prepare, *sole* — L. *sōl*, *sōlis*, the sun.]

parastatal *par-ə-stā'tl*, *adj* indirectly controlled by the state. [**para-**[1].]

parasuicide *par-ə-sōō'i-sīd*, *n* a deliberate harmful act (such as taking an overdose of drugs) which appears to be an attempt at suicide but which was probably not intended to be successful; a person who performs such an act. [**para-**[1] and **suicide**.]

parasympathetic *par-ə-sim-pə-thet'ik*. See under **sympathy**.

parasynthesis *par-ə-sin'thi-sis*, *n* derivation of words from compounds, e.g. *come-at-able*, where *come* and *at* are first compounded and then the derivative suffix *-able* added. — *adj* **parasynthetic** (*-thet'ik*). — *n* **parasyn'theton** a word so formed: — *pl* **parasyn'theta**. [Gr.]

parataxis *par-ə-tak'sis*, (*gram*) *n* the arrangement of clauses or propositions without connectives. — *adj* **paratac'tic** or **paratac'tical**. — *adv* **paratac'tically**. [Gr., — *para*, beside, beyond, *taxis*, arrangement.]

paratha *pə-rä'tə*, *n* a thin cake made of flour, water and clarified butter, originating in India. [Hindi.]

parathyroid *par-ə-thī'roid*, (*anat*) *adj* beside the thyroid. — *n* any of a number of small ductless glands apparently concerned with calcium metabolism. [**para-**[1].]

paratroops *par'ə-trōōps*, *npl* troops carried by air, to be dropped by parachute. — *n* **par'atrooper**. [**para-**[2].]

paratyphoid *par-ə-tī'foid*, *n* a disease (of various types) resembling typhoid. — Also *adj*. [**para-**[1].]

paravane *par'ə-vān*, *n* a fish-shaped device, with fins or vanes, towed from the bow of a vessel, for deflecting mines along a wire and severing their moorings — sometimes called an 'otter'; an explosive device of similar design for attacking submerged submarines. [**para-**[1].]

parawalker *par'ə-wök-ər*, *n* a metal structure like an external skeleton worn by a paraplegic to enable him or her to walk. [**para-**[1] and **walker** (see **walk**).]

Parazoa *par-ə-zō'ə*, *npl* a division of the animal kingdom, the sponges, of the same rank as *Protozoa* and *Metazoa* (also without *cap*). — *n* and *adj* **parazō'an**. — *n* **parazō'on** any member of the group Parazoa: — *pl* **parazō'a**. [Gr. *para*, beside, beyond, *zōion*, animal.]

parboil *pär'boil*, *vt* to part-cook by boiling. [O.Fr. *parboillir* — L.L. *perbullīre*, to boil thoroughly; influenced by confusion with **part**.]

parcel *pär'sl*, *n* a package, esp. one wrapped in paper and tied with string; a little part; a portion; a quantity; a group; a continuous stretch (of land). — *vt* to divide into portions (esp. with *out*); to make up into parcels or a parcel (esp. with *up*): — *prp* **par'celling**; *pa t* and *pa p* **par'celled**. — **parcel bomb** a bomb wrapped in a parcel and designed to detonate when unwrapped. — **parcel post** a Post Office service forwarding and delivering parcels. [Fr. *parcelle* (It. *particella*) — L. *particula*, dimin. of *pars*, *partis*, a part.]

parch *pärch*, *vt* to make hot and very dry; to roast slightly; to scorch. — *vi* to be scorched; to become very dry. — *adj* **parched** very dry; very thirsty (*colloq*). — *n* **parch'edness**.

parchment *pärch'mənt*, *n* the skin of a sheep, goat or other animal, prepared for writing on, etc.; a piece of this material; a manuscript written on it; a parchment-like membrane or skin. — *adj* of parchment. — *vt* **parch'mentise** or **-ize** to make like parchment, esp. by treating with sulphuric acid. — *adj* **parch'menty** like parchment. — **parchment paper** or **vegetable parchment** unsized paper made tough and transparent by dipping in sulphuric acid. [Fr. *parchemin* — L. *pergamēna* (*charta*), Pergamene (paper) — from Gr. *Pergamos*, Bergama, in Asia Minor.]

pard *pärd* or **pardner** *pärd'nər*, (*US*) *n* slang forms of **partner**.

pardon *pär'dn*, *vt* to forgive; to allow to go unpunished; to excuse; to tolerate; to grant remission of sentence to (even if the condemned person has been found innocent). — *vi* to forgive; to grant pardon. — *n* forgiveness, either of an offender or of his or her offence; remission of a penalty or punishment; a warrant declaring that a pardon has been given; a papal indulgence. — *adj* **par'donable** that may be pardoned; excusable. — *n* **par'donableness**. — *adv* **par'donably**. — *n* **par'doner** a person who pardons; a licensed seller of papal indulgences (*hist*). — *n* and *adj* **par'doning**. — **I beg your pardon** what did you say? (also **Pardon?**); **pardon me** excuse me — used in apology and to soften a contradiction. [Fr. *pardonner* — L.L. *perdōnāre* — L. *per*, through, away, *dōnāre*, to give.]

pare *pār*, *vt* to cut or shave off the outer surface or edge of; to trim; to remove by slicing or shaving; to diminish by small amounts. — *n* **pār'er**. — *n* **par'ing** the act of trimming or cutting off; a piece which is pared off; the cutting off of the surface of grassland for cultivation. — **paring chisel** a long, thin chisel with bevelled edges. [Fr. *parer* — L. *parāre*, to prepare.]

paregoric *par-i-gor'ik*, *adj* soothing, lessening pain. — *n* a medicine that soothes pain, esp. an alcoholic solution of opium, benzoic acid, camphor, and oil of anise. [Gr. *parēgorikos* — *parēgoreein*, to exhort, comfort.]

pareira *pə-rā'rə*, *n* (the root of a climbing plant of South America, used to prepare) a tonic diuretic drug. [Port. *parreira*, a climber of walls.]

parencephalon *par-en-sef'ə-lon*, (*anat*) *n* a cerebral hemisphere. [Gr. *para*, beside, beyond, *enkephalon*, brain.]

parent *pā'rənt*, *n* someone who begets or brings forth offspring; a father or a mother; a person who or that which produces; that from which anything springs or branches; an author; a cause. — *adj* (of an organisation, etc.) which has established a branch or branches, over which it usu. retains some control. — *vt* and *vi* to be or act as a parent (to). — *n* **pā'rentage** descent from parents; extraction; rank or character derived from one's parents or ancestors; the relation of parents to their children; the state or fact of being a parent. — *adj* **parental** (*pə-rent'əl*). — *adv* **parent'ally**. — *n* **pā'renthood** the state of being a parent; the duty or feelings of a parent. — *n* **pā'renting**. — *adj* **pā'rentless** without a parent. — **parental leave** a period of time off work allowed by an employer to a parent of a (usu. newborn) baby; **parent company** a company that holds most of the shares of another company. [Fr. *parent*, kinsman — L. *parēns*, *-entis*, old pres. p. of *parĕre*, to bring forth.]

parenteral *par-en'tər-əl*, (*med*) *adj* not intestinal; (said of the administration of a drug) not by way of the alimentary tract. — *adv* **paren'terally**. [Gr. *para*, beside, and **enteral**.]

parenthesis *pə-ren'thi-sis*, *n* a word or passage of comment or explanation inserted in a sentence which is grammatically complete without it; a figure of speech consisting of the use of such insertion; a digression; an interval, space or interlude; (usu. in *pl*) a round bracket ( ) used to mark off a parenthesis: — *pl* **paren'theses** (*-sēz*). — *vi* **parenth'esise** or **-ize**. — *adj* **parenthetic** (*par-ən-thet'ik*) or **parenthetical** (*-thet'ik-əl*) of the nature of a parenthesis; using or being a parenthesis. — *adv* **parenthet'ically**. [Gr., — *para*, beside, beyond, *en*, in, *thesis*, a placing.]

pareo. See **pareu**.

paresis *par'i-sis*, (*med*) *n* a partial form of paralysis affecting muscle movements but not diminishing sensation. — *adj* **paretic** (*-et'ik*). — **general paresis** the manifestation of a syphilitic infection of long standing, consisting of progressive dementia and generalised paralysis. [Gr., — *parienai*, to relax.]

paresthesia. See **paraesthesia**.

pareu *pa-rā'ōō* or **pareo** *pa-rā'ō*, *n* a wraparound skirt worn by men and women in Polynesia. [Tahitian.]

par excellence *pär ek'se-lās* or *ek'sə-ləns*, (Fr.) as an example of excellence; superior to all others of the same sort.

parfait *pär-fe'*, *n* a kind of frozen dessert containing whipped cream, fruit and eggs. [Fr., lit. perfect.]

parget *pär'jit*, *vt* to plaster over; to cover with ornamental plasterwork: — *pr p* **par'geting**; *pa t* and *pa p* **par'geted**. — *n* plaster spread over a surface; ornamental work in plaster; surface decoration; cow-dung plaster for chimney flues. — *n* **par'geter**. — *n* **par'geting**. [App. O.Fr. *parjeter*, to throw all over.]

parhelion *pär-hēl'i-ən*, *n* a bright spot on the parhelic circle, the result of diffraction caused by the crystals in the atmosphere: — *pl* **parhē'lia**. — *adj* **parhelic** (*-hē'lik* or *-he'lik*) or **parheliacal** (*-hē-lī'ə-kl*). — **parhelic circle** a band of luminosity parallel to the horizon, the result of diffraction caused by ice crystals in the atmosphere. [Irregularly — Gr. *parēlion* — *para*, beside, beyond, *hēlios*, sun.]

pariah *pə-rī'ə* or *par'i-ə*, *n* a member of a caste in Southern India lower than the four Brahminical castes; a person of low or no caste; a social outcast (*fig*); an ownerless half-wild dog of Eastern towns (in full **pariah dog**), a pye-dog. [Tamil *paraiyar*.]

parietal *pə-rī'i-tl*, (*anat*) *adj* of a wall or walls of any bodily cavity; pertaining to or near the parietal bone. — *n* either of the two bones (**parietal bones**) which form part of the sides and top of the skull, between the frontal and the occipital. — **parietal cells** cells in the stomach lining that produce hydrochloric acid. [L. *parietālis* — *pariēs*, *parietis*, a wall.]

pari-mutuel *par-ē-mü-tü-el*, (Fr.) *n* a betting-machine which automatically pools stakes and distributes winnings — a totalisator; the system of betting in which the winners receive a proportion of the total money staked, less the management charge.

pari passu *pa'rē pas'ōō* or *pā'rī pas'ū*, (L.) with equal pace; together.

paripinnate *par-i-pin'it* or *-āt*, (*bot*) *adj* pinnate without a terminal leaflet. [L. *pār*, equal.]

Paris *par'is*, *adj* of or originating in Paris. — *adj* **Parisian** (*pə-ri'zyən* or esp. in N.Am. *-zhyən* or *-zhən*) of or pertaining to Paris. — *n* a native or resident of Paris: — Fr. *fem* **Parisienne** (*pa-rē-zē-en'*). — **Paris green** copper arsenite and acetate, a pigment and insecticide. [L. *Parīsiī*, the Gallic tribe of the Paris district.]

parish *par'ish*, *n* a district having its own church and minister or priest of the Established Church; a district assigned by a church to a minister or priest; a division of a county for administrative and local government purposes (not now in Scotland). — *adj* belonging or relating to a parish; employed or supported by the parish; for the use of the parish. — *n* **parishioner** (*pə-rish'ə-nər*) someone who belongs to or is connected with a parish; a member of a parish church. — **parish church** the church of the establishment for a parish; **parish clerk** the clerk or recording officer of a parish; the one who leads the responses in the service of the Church of England; **parish council** a body elected to manage the affairs of a parish; **parish councillor**; **parish minister** or **priest** a minister or priest who has charge of a parish; **parish pump** the symbol of petty local interests; **parish register** a book in which the baptisms, marriages and burials in a parish are recorded. — **on the parish** (*hist*) in receipt of food, shelter, etc. provided by the parish. [A.Fr. *paroche* (Fr. *paroisse*) — L. *parochia* — Gr. *paroikiā*, an ecclesiastical district — *para*, beside, *oikos*, a dwelling; altered by confusion with Gr. *parochos*, a purveyor.]

parison *par'i-sən*, *n* a lump of glass before it is moulded into its final shape. [Fr. *paraison* — *parer*, to prepare — L. *parāre*.]

parisyllabic *par-i-si-lab'ik*, *adj* (of a noun or verb) having the same number of syllables in (almost) all inflected forms. [L. *pār*, equal.]

parity *par'i-ti*, *n* equality in status; parallelism; equivalence; a standard equivalence in currency; (of two or more numbers) the property of being both odd or even (*math*). [Fr. *parité* — L. *paritās* — *pār*, equal.]

park *pärk*, *n* a piece of country kept in its natural condition as a nature-reserve or for public recreation; a piece of land in a town reserved for public recreation; a tract of land surrounding a mansion, constituting a private estate; hence often (with *cap*) part of the name of a house, street or district; a football, etc. pitch (*colloq*); a piece of ground where motor cars or other vehicles may be left untended; (an area containing) a group of buildings housing related enterprises, e.g. a *science park*. — *vt* to place and leave (a vehicle) in a parking-place or elsewhere; to enclose in a park; to deposit and leave (*colloq*). — *vi* to leave a vehicle in a car park, parking-place or elsewhere. — *n* **park'ing** the action of the verb park. — *adj* **park-and-ride'** (of a transport system) designed to encourage the maximum use of public transport within a city, etc. by providing bus and train links from large car parks on the outskirts. — Also *n*. — **parking lot** (*NAm*) a car park; **parking meter** a coin-operated meter that charges for motor car parking-time; **park'ing-place** a place where one may temporarily stop and leave a vehicle; **park'ing-ticket** a notice of a fine, or summons to appear in court, for a parking offence; **park'-keeper** a person employed to patrol a public park, keep order, etc. (also *colloq* called **park'ie**); **park'land** parklike grassland dotted with trees; **park'way** (*NAm*) a broad road adorned with turf and trees, often connecting the parks of a town. [O.Fr. *parc*, of Gmc. origin.]

parka *pärk'ə*, *n* orig. a fur shirt or coat with a hood, now a similar garment made of a windproof material, worn by hikers, etc. [Aleutian Eskimo word.]

parkie *pär'ki*, *n* (*colloq*) a park-keeper.

parkin *pär'kin* or **perkin** *pûr'kin*, (*Scot* and *Northern Eng dialect*) *n* a biscuit or gingerbread made of oatmeal and treacle.

Parkinson's disease *pär'kin-sənz diz-ēz'*, *n* shaking palsy, a disease characterised by rigidity of muscles, tremor of hands, etc., studied by James *Parkinson* (1755–1824). — Also **Par'kinsonism.**

Parkinson's law *pär'kin-sənz lö*, (*facetious*) *n* any one of the laws propounded by C. Northcote *Parkinson*, esp. the law that in officialdom work expands so as to fill the time available for its completion.

parkleaves *pärk'lēvz*, *n* a woodland shrub with yellow flowers, once considered a panacea; tutsan. [App. **park** and **leaf**.]

parky *pär'ki*, (*colloq*) *adj* chilly.

parlance *pär'ləns*, *n* a manner of speaking; an idiom. [Ety. as for **parley**.]

parlando *pär-län'dō*, (*mus*) *adj* and *adv* in declamatory style; recitative. [It., speaking.]

parley *pär'li*, *vi* to speak with another; to confer; to hold discussions with an enemy. — *n* talk; a conference with an enemy; a conference. [Fr. *parler*, to speak — L.L. *parlāre* — *parabolāre* — Gr. *parabolē*, a parable, word.]

parliament *pär'lə-mənt*, *n* an assemblage of the political representatives of a nation, often forming the supreme legislative body. — *n* **parliamentā'rian** an adherent of parliament in opposition to Charles I (*hist*); a member of a parliament; a person skilled in the ways of parliament. — *adj* (*hist*) on the side of parliament during the Civil War. — *adv* **parliamentarily** (*-ment'ər-i-li*). — *n* **parliamenta'rianism** or **parliament'arism** the principles of parliamentary government; the parliamentary system. — *adj* **parliament'ary** pertaining to parliament; enacted, enjoined or done by parliament; according to the rules and practices of legislative bodies; (of language) civil, decorous; (in the Civil War) for Parliament against the Royalists. — **par'liament-house** a building where parliament sits or has sat. — **act of parliament** a statute that has passed through both the House of Commons and the House of Lords, and received the formal royal assent; **Parliamentary Commissioner for Administration** see **Ombudsman.** [Fr. *parlement* — *parler*, to speak.]

parlour or (esp. in N.Am.) **parlor** *pär'lər*, *n* a family sitting-room or living-room (*old-fashioned*); a more or less private room in a public house; a room where conversation is allowed in a monastery or nunnery; a room or shop providing a particular service or selling certain specified goods, such as a beauty parlour or an ice-cream parlour. — *adj* used in or suitable for a parlour. — **parlour game** an (esp. informal) indoor game; **par'lour-maid** a maid-servant who waits at table; **parlour tricks** minor social accomplishments; performances intended to impress. — **milking parlour** a special room or building in which cows are milked. [A.Fr. *parlur* (Fr. *parloir*) — *parler*, to speak.]

Parmesan *pär-mi-zan'* or *pär'mi-zan*, *adj* pertaining to *Parma* in N. Italy. — *n* Parmesan cheese, a hard dry cheese made from skimmed milk mixed with rennet and saffron, used grated as a garnish on pasta dishes and in soups. — **Parma violet** Neapolitan violet.

Parnassus *pär-nas'əs*, *n* a mountain in Greece, sacred to Apollo and the Muses; a collection of poems. — *adj* **Parnass'ian** of Parnassus; of the Muses; of a school of French poetry supposed to believe in art for art's sake (from the collections published as *le Parnasse contemporain*, 1866–76). — *n* a member of the Parnassian school.

paroccipital *par-ok-sip'i-tl*, (*anat*) *adj* near the occiput. [**para-**[1] and **occiput**.]

parochial *pə-rō'ki-əl*, *adj* of or relating to a parish; (of sentiments, tastes, etc.) restricted or confined within narrow limits. — *vt* **parō'chialise** or **-ize** to make parochial; to form into parishes. — *vi* to do parish work. — *n* **parō'chialism** a system of local government which makes the parish the unit; provincialism, narrowness of view (also **parōchiality** (*-al'*)). — *adv* **parō'chially**. [L. *parochiālis* — *parochia*; see **parish**.]

parody *par'ə-di*, *n* a burlesque or satirical imitation; a poor imitation, which seems to be a mockery. — *vt* to make a parody of: — *pr p* **par'odying**; *pa t* and *pa p* **par'odied**. — *adj* **parod'ic** or **parod'ical**. — *n* **par'odist**. [Gr. *parōidiā* — *para*, beside, *ōidē*, an ode.]

parol. See **parole.**

parole *pə-rōl'*, *n* conditional release of a prisoner; the condition of having given one's word of honour, or privilege of having it accepted; word of honour (esp. by a prisoner of war, to fulfil certain conditions; *mil*); officers' daily password in a camp or garrison (*mil*); word of mouth; language as manifested in the speech of individuals (*linguis*). — *adj* pertaining to parole; (usu. **parol**, usu. *par'*) given by word of mouth, as in *parol* evidence (opp. of *documentary*). — *vt* to put on parole; to release on parole. — *vi* to give parole. — *n* **parolee'** a prisoner who has been conditionally released. [Fr. *parole*, word — L. *parabola*, a parable, saying — Gr.; see **parable**.]

paronomasia *par-on-o-mā'syə*, *-zyə* or *-zh(y)ə*, *n* a play on words. — *adj* **paronomastic** (*-mas'tik*) or **paranomastical** (*-mas'tik-əl*). — *n* **paronym** (*par'o-nim*) a word from the same root, or having the same sound, as another. — *adj* **paron'ymous.** — *n* **paron'ymy**. [Gr. *para*, beside, *onoma*, *onyma*, name.]

paronychia *par-o-nik'i-ə*, (*med*) *n* a whitlow. — *adj* **paronych'ial**. [Gr. *para*, beside *onyx*, *onychos*, nail.]

parotid *pə-rot'id* or *-rōt'*, *adj* near the ear. — *n* the parotid gland, a salivary gland in front of the ear. [Gr. *parōtis*, *-idos* — *para*, beside, *ous*, *ōtos*, ear.]

parousia *pə-roo'zi-ə* or *-row'zi-ə*, (*theol*) *n* the second coming of Christ. [Gr. *parousiā*, presence, arrival.]

paroxysm *par'oks-izm*, *n* a fit of acute pain; a sudden recurrence of symptoms; a fit of passion, laughter, coughing, etc.; any sudden violent action. — *adj* **paroxys'mal**. [Gr. *paroxysmos* — *para*, beyond, *oxys*, sharp.]

paroxytone *par-ok'si-tōn*, *adj* (in ancient Greek) having the acute accent on the last syllable but one; having a heavy stress on the penultimate syllable. — *n* a word so accented. [Gr. *paroxytonos* — *para*, beside, *oxys*, acute, *tonos*, tone.]

parpen *pär'pən*, *n* a stone passing through a wall from face to face; a wall of such stones; a partition; a bridge parapet. [O.Fr. *parpain*.]

parquet *pär'kā* or *pär'kē*, *n* a floor-covering of wooden blocks fitted in a pattern. — *adj* of parquetry. — *vt* to cover or floor with parquetry: — *pa p*

parqueted (*pär'kə-tid* or *pär'kād*) or **parquetted** (*pär-ket'id*). — *n* **par'quetry** (*-ki-tri*) flooring in parquet. [Fr. *parquet*, dimin. of *parc*, an enclosure.]

parr *pär*, *n* a young salmon up to two years of age before it becomes a smolt; the young of several other kinds of fish.

parrakeet. See **parakeet.**

parramatta. See **paramatta.**

parricide *par'i-sīd*, *n* the murder of a parent or near relative, or the murder of anyone to whom reverence is considered to be due; a person who commits such a crime. — *adj* **parricīd'al.** [Fr., — L. *parricīdium*, *pāricīdium* (the offence), *parricīda*, *pāricīda* (the offender) — *caedĕre*, to slay.]

parrot *par'ət*, *n* one of a family of tropical and subtropical birds with brilliant plumage, hooked bill and zygodactyl feet, good imitators of human speech; an uncritical repeater of the words of others. — *vt* to repeat by rote. — *vi* to talk like a parrot (also *vt* with *it*): — *pa p* **parr'oted.** — *n* **parr'oter.** — *n* **parr'otry** unintelligent imitation. — *adj* **parr'oty** like a parrot. — **parr'ot-cry** a catch-phrase senselessly repeated from mouth to mouth. — *adv* **parr'ot-fashion** by rote. — **parr'ot-fish** a name applied to various fishes, esp. of the family *Scaridae*, from their colours or their powerful jaws; **parrot mouth** a congenital malformation of the jaw that occurs in horses and other grazing animals preventing normal feeding. [Poss. Fr. *Perrot*, dimin. of *Pierre*, Peter.]

parry *par'i*, *vt* to ward or keep off; to turn aside, block or evade; to avert: — *pr p* **parr'ying**; *pa t* and *pa p* **parr'ied.** — *n* a turning aside of a blow or a thrust or of an attack of any kind, e.g. an argument or a jibe. [Perh. from Fr. *parez*, imper. of *parer* — L. *parāre*, to prepare, in L.L. to keep off.]

parse *pärz* or *pärs*, (*gram*) *vt* to describe (a word) fully from point of view of classification, inflexion and syntax; to analyse (a sentence). — *n* **pars'er.** — *n* **pars'ing.** [L. *pars* (*ōrātiōnis*), a part (of speech).]

parsec *pär'sek* or *pär-sek'*, *n* the distance (about 19 billion miles) at which half the major axis of the earth's orbit subtends an angle of one second, a unit for measurement of distances of stars. [*par*allax and *sec*ond.]

Parsee or **Parsi** *pär'sē* or *-sē'*, *n* a descendant of the Zoroastrians who emigrated from Persia to India in the 8th century; a Persian dialect dominant during the time of the Sassanidae, *Pahlari*. — Also *adj*. — *n* **Par'seeism** or **Par'siism** (or *-sē'*) the religion of the Parsees. [Pers. *Pārsī* — *Pārs*, Persia.]

parsimony *pär'si-mən-i*, *n* sparingness or reluctance in the spending of money; avoidance of excess; frugality; niggardliness. — *adj* **parsimonious** (*-mō'ni-əs*). — *adv* **parsimō'niously.** — *n* **parsimō'niousness.** [L. *parsimōnia* — *parcĕre*, *parsus*, to spare.]

parsley *pärs'li*, *n* a bright green umbelliferous herb with finely divided, strongly scented leaves, used in cookery. — **parsley fern** a fern with bright green crisped leaves similar in appearance to parsley. [O.E. *petersilie*, modified by Fr. *persil*, both — L. *petroselīnum* — Gr. *petroselīnon* — *petros*, a rock, *selīnon*, parsley.]

parsnip *pärs'nip*, *n* an umbelliferous plant or its edible carrot-like root. [L. *pastināca* — *pastinum*, a dibble; prob. affected by **neep.**]

parson *pär'sn*, *n* the priest or incumbent of a parish; a rector; any minister of religion; a person who is licensed to preach. — *n* **par'sonage** the residence appropriated to a parson. — *adj* **parsonic** (*-son'ik*) or **parsonical** (*-son'ik-əl*). — **par'son-bird** the tui; **parson's nose** the piece of flesh at the tail-end of a (cooked) fowl (also **pope's nose**). [O.Fr. *persone* — L. *persōna*, a person, prob. in legal sense, or a mouthpiece.]

part *pärt*, *n* a portion; that which along with others makes up, has made up, or may at some time make up, a whole; a constituent; a component; a member or organ; an equal quantity; an equal or nearly equal division, constituent, etc., as in e.g. *three parts oil to one part vinegar*; share; region; direction, hand or side; participation; concern; interest; a role or duty; a side or party; a character taken by an actor in a play; the words and actions of a character in a play or in real life; a voice or instrument in concerted music; that which is performed by such a voice or instrument; a copy of the music for it; a constituent melody or succession of notes or harmony; a section of a work in literature (see also **partwork** below), or in music; a separately published portion or number (see also **partwork** below); (in *pl*) intellectual qualities, talents or conduct; the place where the hair is parted, a parting (*NAm*). — *adj* in part; partial. — *adv* in part; partly. — *vt* to divide; to separate; to break; to set in different directions; to distribute; to share. — *vi* to become divided or separated; to separate; to go different ways; to depart; to come or burst apart; to relinquish (with *with*). — *adj* **part'ed** divided; separated; departed; (of a leaf) deeply cleft (*bot*). — *n* **partibil'ity.** — *adj* **part'ible** that may or must be parted or divided up (esp. of inherited property). — *n* **part'ing** the action of the verb to part; a place of separation or division; a dividing line; a line of skin showing between sections of hair brushed in opposite directions on the head; leave-taking. — *adj* separating; dividing; departing; leave-taking; of or at leave-taking. — *adv* **part'ly** in part; in some degree. — **part-exchange'** a transaction in which an article is handed over as part of the payment for another article. — Also *adj* and *adv*. — **part'-off** (*WIndies*) a screen used to divide a room into two separate areas; **part-own'er** a joint owner; **part-pay'ment** payment in part; **part'-singing**; **part'-song** a melody with parts in harmony, usu. unaccompanied. — *adj* and *adv* **part'-time** (done) for part of the usual working time only. — *vi* to work part-time. — **part-tim'er**; **part'work** one of a series of publications (esp. magazines) issued at regular intervals, eventually forming a complete course or book. — **for my part** as far as concerns me; **for the most part** commonly; **in good part** favourably; without taking offence; **in great part** to a great extent; **in part** partly; not wholly but to some extent; **on the part of** so far as concerns; as done or performed by; in the actions of; on the side of; **part and parcel** essentially a part; **part company** to separate; **parting of the ways** a point at which a fateful decision must be made; **part of speech** one of the various classes of words; **part way** some way, not all the way, approaching but not reaching, as e.g. *go part way towards an objective*; **take part in** to share or to assist in; **take part with** to take the side of; **take someone's part** to support or side with someone (in an argument, etc.). [O.E. and Fr. *part* — L. *pars*, *partis*.]

partake *pär-* or *pər-tāk'*, *vi* to take or have a part or share (usu. with *of* or *in*); to take some, esp. of food or drink; to have something of the nature or properties (of). — *vt* to have a part in; to share; to have a share in the knowledge of: — *pr p* **partā'king**; *pa t* **partook'**; *pa p* **partā'ken.** — *n* **partā'ker.** — *n* **partā'king.** [Back-formation from **partaker** — **part** and **taker.**]

parterre *pär-ter'*, *n* an arrangement of flower-beds; the pit of a theatre, esp. the part under the galleries. [Fr., — L. *per*, along, *terra*, the ground.]

parthenogenesis *pär-thi-nō-jen'i-sis*, *n* reproduction by means of an unfertilised ovum. — *adj* **parthenogenetic** (*-ji-net'ik*). [Gr. *parthenos*, a virgin, *genesis*, production.]

Parthian *pär'thi-ən*, *adj* of *Parthia*, in ancient Persia. — *n* native of Parthia. — **a Parthian shot** a parting hostile remark, gesture, etc., from the Parthian habit of turning round in the saddle to discharge an arrow at a pursuer.

parti *par-tē*, (Fr.) *n* a marriageable person considered as a match or catch. — **parti pris** (*prē*) bias, preconceived opinion.

partial *pär'shl, adj* relating to a part only; not total or entire; inclined to favour one person or party; having a preference or fondness (with *to*); component; subordinate (*bot*). — *n* (*acoustics*) a partial tone, one of the single-frequency tones which go together to form a sound actually heard. — *n* **par'tialism**. — *n* **par'tialist** someone who is biased; someone who sees or knows only part. — *n* **partiality** (*-shi-al'i-ti*). — *adv* **par'tially**. — **partial derivative** (*math*) a derivative obtained by letting only one of several independent variables vary; **partial fraction** one of a number of simple fractions whose sum is a complex fraction. — **partial out** (*statistics*) to eliminate (a factor) so as to assess other factors when they are independent of its influence. [Fr., — L.L. *partiālis* — L. *pars*, a part.]

partible, partibility. See under **part**.

participate *pär-tis'i-pāt, vi* to have a share, or take part (in); to have some of the qualities (of). — *adj* **partic'ipant** participating; sharing. — *n* a person, group, etc. taking part. — *adj* **partic'ipating** (of insurance) entitling policy-holders to a share of the company's additional profits. — *n* **participā'tion** the act of participating; (as in the phrase **worker participation**, the involvement of employees at all levels in the policy-making decisions of a company, etc.). — *n* **partic'ipator** someone who participates; a person who has a share in the capital or income of a company. — *adj* **participā'tory**. [L. *participāre, -ātum* — *pars, partis*, part, *capěre*, to take.]

participle *pär'ti-sip-l*, (*gram*) *n* a word combining the functions of adjective and verb. — **present participle** and **past** or **perfect participle** referring respectively to an action roughly contemporaneous or past, the present participle is active, the past usually passive. — *adj* **particip'ial**. — *adv* **particip'ially**. [O.Fr. (Fr. *participe*), — L. *participium* — *pars, partis*, a part, *capěre*, to take.]

particle *pär'ti-kl, n* a little part; a very small portion; a minute piece of matter; a little hard piece; a material point (*mech*); a smallest amount; a short, usu. indeclinable word, such as a preposition, a conjunction or an interjection; a prefix or suffix; a crumb of consecrated bread or a portion used in the communion of the laity (*RC*). — *adj* **partic'ulate** having the form of or relating to particles. — *n* a particulate substance. — **particle accelerator** a device by means of which the speed of atomic particles may be greatly accelerated. [L. *particula*, dimin. of *pars partis*, a part.]

parti-coated, particoloured. See under **party**.

particular *pər-tik'ū-lər, adj* pertaining to a single person or thing; worthy of special attention; individual; special; relating to a part; detailed; noteworthy; definite; concerned with or marking things single or distinct; minutely attentive and careful; fastidious in taste; particularist; predicating of part of the class denoted by the subject (*logic*). — *n* a distinct or minute part; a single point; a single instance; a detail; an item. — *n* **particularīsā'tion** or **-z-**. — *vt* **partic'ularise** or **-ize** to render particular; to mention the particulars of; to enumerate in detail; to mention as a particular or particulars. — *vi* to mention or attend to minute details. — *n* **partic'ularism** attention to one's own interest or party; attention to the interest of a federal state before that of the confederation; the policy of allowing much freedom in this way; the doctrine that salvation is offered only to particular individuals, the elect, and not to the race (*theol*). — *n* and *adj* **partic'ularist**. — *adj* **particularist'ic**. — *n* **particularity** (*-lar'i-ti*) the quality of being particular; minuteness of detail; a single instance or case; a detail; peculiarity. — *adv* **partic'ularly** in a particular manner; individually; severally; in detail; in the manner of a particular proposition; intimately; notably; in a very high degree. — *n* **partic'ularness**. — **in particular** especially; in detail. [Ety. as for **particle**.]

partisan or **partizan** *pär-ti-zan'* or *pär'ti-zan, n* an adherent, esp. a blind or unreasoning adherent, of a party or a faction; a light irregular soldier who scours the country and forays; (in World War II) a member of a resistance group within the enemy occupation lines. — Also *adj*. — *n* **par'tisanship** (or *-zan'*). [Fr. *partisan*, from a dialect form of It. *partigiano* — *parte* (L. *pars, partis*), part.]

partita *pär-tē'tə*, (*mus*) *n* (esp. 18th cent.) a suite; a set of variations. [It.]

partite *pär'tīt, adj* divided; (esp. of plant leaves) cut nearly to the base. — *n* **partition** (*-tish'ən*) the act of dividing; the division of a country into politically autonomous states; the state of being divided; a separate part; that which divides; a wall between rooms; a barrier, septum or dissepiment (*bot*). — *vt* to divide into shares; to divide into parts by walls, septa or anything similar. — *n* **parti'tioner** a person who partitions property. — *n* **parti'tionist** a person who favours the partition of a country. — *n* **parti'tionment**. — *adj* **par'titive** parting; dividing; distributive; indicating that a part is meant (*gram*). — *n* a partitive word. — *adv* **par'titively**. — **partition-wall'** an internal wall. [L. *partītus*, past p. of *partīrī* or *partīre*, to divide — *pars*, part.]

partly. See under **part**.

partner *pärt'nər, n* an associate; a person who plays on the same side with another in a game; a person engaged with another in business; a person who dances or goes in to a formal dinner with another; a husband or wife; either member of a couple living together in a sexual relationship; an associate in commensalism or symbiosis (*bot*); (in *pl*; *naut*) a wooden framework round a hole in the deck, supporting a mast, etc. — *vt* to join as a partner; to be the partner of. — *n* **part'nership** the state of being a partner; a contract between persons engaged in any business.

partook *pär-tŏŏk', pa t* of **partake**.

partridge *pär'trij, n* any member of a genus of game birds of the pheasant family; extended to many other birds: — *pl* **par'tridge** or **par'tridges**. [Fr. *perdrix* — L. *perdīx* — Gr. *perdix*.]

parturient *pär-tū'ri-ənt, adj* of or related to childbirth; giving or about to give birth; bringing or about to bring about anything new. — *n* **partūri'tion** the act of giving birth. [L. *parturīre* — *parěre*, to bring forth.]

party *par'ti, n* a side in a battle, game, lawsuit or other contest; a body of persons united in favour of a political or other cause; a small body of persons associated together in any occupation or amusement; a detachment (*mil*); a company; a meeting or entertainment of guests; a person concerned in any affair, as in *third party*; a person who enters into a contract, e.g. of marriage. — *adj* pertaining to a party; parted or divided (*heraldry*). — *vi* (*colloq*) to attend, hold or take part in parties or similar entertainments; to have a good time. — *adj* **par'ti-coated** or **par'ty-coated** having on a coat of various colours. — *adj* **par'ticoloured** or **par'ty-coloured** variegated. — **party line** a telephone exchange line shared by two or more subscribers; boundary between properties; the policy rigidly laid down by the party leaders; **party man** a faithful member of a political party; **party politics** politics viewed from a party standpoint, or arranged to suit the views or interests of a party; **par'ty-pooper** someone who spoils the enjoyment of others at a party or social occasion by their lack of enthusiasm, or by their inability or unwillingness to participate. — *adj* **par'ty-size** (of an item of food, etc.) smaller than the usual size, intended to be used as a snack at parties. — **party spirit** the unreasonable spirit of a party man; a festive atmosphere. — *adj* **party=spir'ited.** — **party wall** a wall between two adjoining properties or houses. — **the party's over** a favourable, enjoyable, carefree, etc. situation has ended. [Fr. *partie*, fem. (and also *parti*, masc.), past p. of *partir* — L. *partīre, partīrī*, to divide — *pars*, a part.]

parulis *pə-rōō'lis*, (*med*) *n* a gumboil. [Gr. *para*, beside, *oulon*, the gum.]

parure *pa-rür'*, *n* a set of jewels, ornaments, etc. [Fr.]

parvenu *pär'və-nü* or *-nū*, *n* an upstart; someone newly risen into wealth, notice or power, esp. if vulgar or exhibiting an inferiority complex. — Also *adj*. [Fr. past p. of *parvenir* — L. *pervenīre*, to arrive.]

parvis *pär'vis* or **parvise** *pär'vēs*, *n* an enclosed space, or sometimes a portico, at the front of a church; a room over a church porch (*erron*). [O.Fr. *parevis*.]

pas *pä*, (Fr.) *n* a step or dance, esp. in ballet; action: — *pl* **pas** (*pä*). — **pas de bourrée** (*də bōō-rā*) a ballet movement in which one foot is swiftly placed behind or in front of the other; **pas de chat** (*də sha*) a ballet leap in which each foot is raised in turn to the opposite knee; **pas de deux, trois, quatre,** etc. (*də dø, trwä, kätr'*) a ballet dance for two, three, four, or more people; **pas redoublé** (*rə-dōōb-lā*) a quickstep; **pas seul** (*sœl*) a dance for one person, a solo ballet dance. [Fr., — L. *passus*.]

PASCAL *pas-kal'*, *n* a high-level computer programming language.

pascal *pas'kal*, *n* a unit of pressure, the newton per square metre, a supplementary SI unit. — **Pascal's triangle** a group of numbers arranged to form a triangle in which each number is the sum of the two numbers to its right and left in the line above. [Blaise *Pascal*, French philosopher and scientist.]

Pasch *pask*, *n* the Passover; Easter (*archaic*). — *adj* **pasch'al**. [L. *pascha* — Gr. *pascha* — Heb. *pesach*, the Passover — *pāsach*, to pass over.]

pash *pash*, *n* a slang contraction of **passion**.

pasha *pa'shə* or *pä-shä'*, (*hist*) *n* a Turkish title (abolished 1934) given to governors and high military and naval officers. [Turk. *paşa*.]

pashm *push'əm*, *n* the fine underfleece of the goats of Northern India, used for making rugs, shawls, etc. [Pers., wool.]

Pashto or **Pushto** *push'tō* or **Pushtu** *push'tōō*, *n* an official language of Afghanistan, also spoken in parts of Pakistan; a native speaker of this, a Pathan. — *adj* of or pertaining to this language or people.

paso doble *pä'sō dō'blā*, (Sp.) *n* a march usu. played at bullfights; a two-step; the music for this dance.

pasque-flower *päsk'-flowr*, *n* a species of anemone with bell-shaped purple flowers; extended to some other species. [Fr. *passefleur*, app. — *passer*, to surpass, modified after **Pasch**, as flowering about Easter.]

pass *päs*, *vi* to proceed; to go or be transferred from one place to another; to transfer the ball to another player (*football*, etc.); to make one's way; to reach, extend or have a course; to undergo change from one state to another; to be transmitted, communicated or transacted; to change ownership; to change; to circulate; to be accepted or reputed or known; to go by; to go unheeded or neglected; to elapse, to go away; to disappear, come to an end, fade out; to die; to move over, through or onwards; to go or get through an obstacle, difficulty, test, ordeal, examination, etc.; to get through an examination without honours; to be approved; to meet with acceptance; to be sanctioned; to be made law; to come through; to happen; to be pronounced; to exceed bounds; to perform a pass (see noun below); to abstain from making a call or declaration (*cards*). — *vt* to go or get by, over, beyond, through, etc.; to undergo, experience; to undergo successfully; to spend (time); to omit; to disregard; to exceed; to surpass; to cause or allow to pass; to transfer, transmit; to transfer (the ball) to another player (*football*, etc.); to hand; to pronounce; to circulate; to emit, discharge; to perform a pass with or upon; to perform as a pass: — *pa t* and *pa p* **passed** (*päst*). — *n* a way by which one may pass or cross; a narrow passage, esp. through or over a range of mountains or some other difficult region; an act of passing; the passing of an examination, without honours at degree level; a state or condition (as in *pretty* or *sad pass*); a predicament, critical position; a passport; a written permission to go somewhere or do something; a free ticket; a thrust (*fencing*); transference of the ball to another team-member (*football*, etc.); transference in a juggling trick; an amorous advance (*colloq*); a movement of the hand over anything, e.g. by a magician or mesmerist. — *adj* **pass'able** that may be passed, travelled over or navigated; that may bear inspection; that may be accepted or allowed to pass; tolerable. — *n* **pass'ableness**. — *adv* **pass'ably**. — *adj* **passing** (*päs'ing*) going by, through or away; transient, fleeting. — *n* the action of the verb to pass; a place of passing; a coming to an end; death. — **pass-back'** an act of passing (a ball, etc.) to a member of one's own team nearer one's own goal-line; **pass band** (*radio*) a frequency band in which there is negligible attenuation; **pass'book** a book that passes between a trader and their customer, in which credit purchases are entered; a bank-book; **passed pawn** (*chess*) a pawn having no opposing pawn before it on its own or an adjacent file; **pass'-er-by** someone who passes by or near: — *pl* **pass'ers-by**; **passing note** (*mus*) a note forming an unprepared discord in an unaccented place in the measure (also in N.Am. **passing tone**); **passing shot** (*tennis*) a shot hit past, and beyond the reach of, an opponent; **pass'key** a key enabling one to enter a house; a key for opening several locks. — *adj* **pass'out** entitling someone who goes out to return. — **pass'word** (*mil*) a secret word by which a friend may pass or enter a camp, etc. — **bring to pass** to bring about, cause to happen; **come to pass** to happen (apparently originally a noun in these expressions); **in passing** while doing, talking about, etc. something else; **make a pass at** (*colloq*) to aim a short blow at, esp. ineffectually; to make an amorous advance to; **pass as** or **for** to be mistaken for or accepted as; **pass away** to come to an end, go off; to die; to elapse; **pass by** to move, go beyond or past; to ignore or overlook; **pass off** to impose fraudulently, to palm off; to take its course satisfactorily; to disappear gradually; **pass on** to go forward; to proceed; to die; to transmit, hand on; **pass out** to distribute; to die; to faint, become unconscious (*colloq*); to go off; to complete military, etc. training; **pass over** to overlook, to ignore; to die; **pass the time of day** to exchange any ordinary greeting of civility; **pass through** to undergo, experience; **pass up** to renounce, to have nothing to do with; to neglect (an opportunity). [Fr. *pas*, step, and *passer*, to pass — L. *passus*, a step.]

pass. *abbrev* for passive.

passacaglia *pas-a-käl'ya*, (*mus*) *n* a slow solemn old Spanish dance-form, slower than the chaconne, in triple time, usually on a ground bass. [Italianised from Sp. *pasacalle* — *pasar*, to pass, *calle*, street, app. because often played in the streets.]

passade *pä-säd'*, *n* the motion of a horse to and fro over the same ground in dressage exercises. [Fr. *passade*, Sp. *pasada* — L. *passus*, step.]

passage[1] *pas'ij*, *n* a means or way of passing; an alley; a corridor or lobby; a navigable channel or route; a crossing-place, ford, ferry, bridge, or mountain pass; an act of passing; transit; a crossing; migration;

transition; lapse, course; a journey (now only by water or air; also *fig*); that which passes; an occurrence, incident, episode; a continuous but indefinite portion of a book, piece of music, etc., of moderate length; a run, figure or phrase in music; a stage in the maintenance or controlled development of micro-organisms under analysis, in which they are introduced into the host or culture, allowed to multiply, and extracted (*biol*). — *vt* (*biol*) to submit (a micro-organism) to a passage. — **pass'ageway** a way of access; a corridor; an alley. — **bird of passage** a migratory bird; a transient visitor (*fig*); **passage of arms** any armed struggle; an encounter, esp. in words. [Fr. *passage* — L. *passus*, step.]

passage[2] *pas-äzh'* or *pas'ij*, (*dressage*) *n* a slow sideways walk; a rhythmical trot with diagonal pairs of legs lifted high. — *vi* to move at a passage. — *vt* to cause (a horse) to move at a passage. [Fr. *passager* — *passéger* — It. *passeggiare*, to walk — L. *passus*, step.]

passant *pas'ənt*, (*heraldry*) *adj* walking towards the dexter side, with dexter forepaw raised. [Fr.]

passé, *fem* **passée** *pa-sā*, (Fr.) *adj* past one's best, faded; out of date; no longer fashionable.

passement *pas'mənt* or **passementerie** *pas'mā-tə-rē*, *n* decorative trimming of beads, braid, etc. [Fr.]

passenger *pas'in-jər*, *n* someone who travels in a private or public conveyance (as opposed to one who drives or operates the vehicle, etc.); someone carried along by others' efforts (*fig*). — *adj* of or for passengers. [O.Fr. *passagier* (Fr. *passager*), with inserted *n*, as in *messenger*, *nightingale*.]

passe-partout *päs-pär-too'*, *n* a means of passing anywhere; a master-key; a card or something similar cut as a mount for a picture; a kind of simple picture-frame, usually of pasteboard, the picture being fixed by strips pasted over the edges; adhesive tape or paper used in this way. [Fr., a master-key, from *passer*, to pass, *par*, over, *tout*, all.]

Passeriformes *pas-ər-i-för'mēz*, *npl* the huge order of perching birds (sparrow-like in form) including amongst others all British songbirds. — *adj* and *n* **pass'erine** (*-īn*). [L. *passer*, a sparrow.]

passible *pas'i-bl*, *adj* susceptible to or capable of suffering or feeling. — *n* **passibil'ity** or **pass'ibleness**. [L. *passibilis* — *patī*, *passus*, to suffer.]

passim *pas'im*, (L.) *adv* everywhere; throughout (esp. a cited piece of writing).

passion *pash'n*, *n* strong feeling or agitation of mind, esp. rage, often sorrow; a fit of such feeling, esp. rage; ardent love; sexual desire; an enthusiastic interest or direction of the mind; the object of such a feeling; (usu. with *cap*) the sufferings (esp. on the Cross) and death of Christ; martyrdom; suffering; a painful bodily ailment (as in *iliac passion*); the fact, condition or manner of being acted upon; passivity (*philos*). — *adj* **pass'ional** of or relating to the sufferings of a Christian martyr. — *n* **pass'ional** or **pass'ionary** a book of the sufferings of saints and martyrs. — *adj* **pass'ionate** moved by passion; showing strong and warm feeling; easily moved to passion; intense, fervid. — *adv* **pass'ionately**. — *n* **pass'ionateness**. — *adj* **pass'ioned** moved by passion; expressing passion; expressed with passion. — *adj* **pass'ionless** free from or lacking passion, esp. sexual desire; not easily excited to anger. — **pass'ion-flower** any flower or plant of genus *Passiflora*, consisting mostly of climbers of tropical and warm temperate America, from a fancied resemblance of parts of the flower to the crown of thorns, nails, and other emblems of Christ's Passion; the plant itself; **passion fruit** any edible passion-flower fruit, esp. the granadilla; **Passion play** a religious drama representing the sufferings and death of Christ; **Passion Sunday** the fifth Sunday in Lent; **Pass'iontide** the two weeks preceding Easter; **Passion week** Holy week; the week before Holy week. [O.Fr. *passiun* and L. *passiō*, *-ōnis* — *patī*, *passus*, to suffer.]

passive *pas'iv*, *adj* acted upon, not acting; inert; lethargic; not reacting; not actively resisting; bearing no interest (*finance*); (of that voice) which expresses the suffering of an action by the person or thing represented by the subject of the verb (*gram*). — *n* (*gram*) the passive voice; a passive verb. — *adv* **pass'ively**. — *n* **pass'iveness**. — *n* **pass'ivism** passive resistance. — *n* **pass'ivist** a passive resister. — *n* **passiv'ity**. — **passive immunity** the short-term immunity acquired either artificially, through the administration of antibodies, or naturally, as in the very young who receive antibodies through the placenta or in colostrum; **passive resistance** deliberate refusal (on principle) to do what law or regulation orders, and submission to the consequent penalties; **passive resister**; **passive smoking** the involuntary inhalation of tobacco smoke that has been produced by others. [L. *passīvus* — *patī*, *passus*, to suffer.]

Passover *päs'ō-vər*, *n* an annual feast of the Jews, to commemorate the exodus of the Israelites from captivity in Egypt, so named from the destroying angel passing over the houses of the Israelites when he slew the first-born of the Egyptians. — *adj* pertaining to the Passover.

passport *päs'pört*, *n* a permit for entering a country; that which gives privilege of entry to anything (*fig*). [Fr. *passeport*.]

past *päst*, *adj* bygone; elapsed; ended; in time already passed; expressing action or being in time that has passed, preterite (*gram*); just before the present; past one's best; having served a term of office. — *n* time that has passed; things that have already happened; (one's) early life or bygone career, esp. if marked by tragedy or scandal; the past tense; a verb or verbal form in the past tense. — *prep* after; after the time of; beyond, in place, position, etc.; beyond the possibility of. — *adv* by. — **past master** someone who has held the office of master (as among freemasons); someone thoroughly proficient. — **I, etc. would not put it past him**, etc. (*colloq*) I, etc. regard him, etc. as (esp. morally) capable of (some action disapproved of); **past it** (*colloq*) or **past one's best** having decreased strength, ability, etc. due to advancing age; **past praying for** beyond hope of redemption or recovery. [An old past p. of **pass**.]

pasta *päs'tə* or *pas'tə*, *n* flour dough in fresh, processed (e.g. spaghetti, macaroni, lasagne), and/or cooked form. [It., paste.]

paste *pāst*, *n* a soft plastic mass; a smooth preparation of food suitable for spreading on bread; a cement made of flour, water, etc.; dough for piecrust, etc.; a doughy sweetmeat; a fine kind of glass for making artificial gems; material for making pottery. — *adj* of paste. — *vt* to fasten or cover with paste; to thrash (*slang*). — *n* **pāst'iness**. — *n* **pāst'ing** (*slang*) a beating. — *adj* **pāst'y** like paste in texture; (of a complexion) pale and unhealthy-looking. — **paste'board** a stiff board made of sheets of paper pasted together; a visiting-card, playing-card or ticket (*slang*). — *adj* of pasteboard; sham. — **paste'down** the outer leaf of an endpaper that is pasted down on the inside cover of a book; **paste'-up** a draft of a printed page consisting of text, artwork, photographs, etc. pasted onto a sheet, for photographing or as a plan for a printing plate. — *adj* **past'y-faced** pale and dull of complexion. [O.Fr. *paste* (Fr. *pâte*) — L.L. *pasta* — Gr. *pasta*, barley porridge.]

pastel *pas'təl* or *-tel*, *n* chalk mixed with other materials and coloured for crayons; a drawing made with pastels; the process or art of drawing with pastels. — *adj* in pastel; (of colour) soft, quiet. — *n* **pastellist** (*pas'* or *-tel'*). [Fr. *pastel* — It. *pastello* — L. *pasta*, paste.]

pastern *pas'tərn, n* the part of a horse's foot from the fetlock to the hoof, where the shackle is fastened. [O.Fr. *pasturon* (Fr. *paturon*) — O.Fr. *pasture*, pasture, a tether for a horse.]

Pasteurian *pas-tûr'i-ən, adj* relating to Louis *Pasteur* (1822–95), French chemist and bacteriologist, or his methods. — *n* **Pasteurell'a** a genus of bacteria which cause various serious infectious diseases, including plague; (without *cap*) a bacterium of this genus: — *pl* **Pasteurell'as** or **Pasteurell'ae** (*-ē*). — *n* **Pasteurellō'sis** a disease caused by organisms of the genus *Pasteurella*: — *pl* **Pasteurellō'sēs**. — *n* **pasteurīsā'tion** or **-z-** sterilisation of milk, etc., by heating. — *vt* **pas'teurise** or **-ize**. — *n* **pas'teuriser** or **-z-** an apparatus for sterilising milk, etc.

pastiche *pas-tēsh', n* a jumble; a pot-pourri; a composition (in literature, music or painting) made up of bits of other works or imitations of another's style. [Fr. (from It.) and It. — It. *pasta*, paste; see **paste**.]

pastille *pas'til* or *pas-tēl', n* a small (often medicated) sweet; a small cone of charcoal and aromatic substances, burned as incense, or for fumigation or fragrance. [Fr., — L. *pāstillus*, a little loaf.]

pastime *päs'tīm, n* that which serves to pass away the time; a hobby or recreation. [**pass** and **time**.]

pastis *pas-tēs', n* an alcoholic drink flavoured with anise. [Fr.]

pastor *päs'tər, n* a clergyman; the rose-coloured starling. — *adj* **pas'toral** relating to, depicting or evoking rural life, the countryside, etc.; of the nature of pastureland; of or pertaining to the pastor of a church and his obligations to his congregation; addressed to the clergy of a diocese by their bishop. — *n* a poem, play, romance, opera, piece of music or picture depicting the life of (usually idealised or conventionalised) shepherds, or rural life in general; such writing as a genre; a pastoral letter; a book on the care of souls; a pastoral staff. — *n* **pastorale** (*päs-to-rä'lā*; It.) a pastoral composition in music; a pastoral, rustic or idyllic opera or cantata. — *n* **pas'toralism** pastoral character, fashion, cult or mode of writing. — *n* **pas'toralist**. — *adv* **pas'torally**. — *n* **pas'torate** the office of a pastor; a pastor's tenure of office; a body of pastors. — *adj* **pas'torly** becoming a pastor. — *n* **pas'torship**. — **pastoral address** or **letter** an address or a letter by a pastor to his people, or by a bishop to his clergy; **pastoral staff** a crosier, a tall staff forming part of a bishop's insignia, headed like a shepherd's crook. [L. *pāstor* — *pāscĕre*, *pāstum*, to feed.]

pastrami *pəs-trä'mi, n* a smoked, highly seasoned (esp. shoulder) cut of beef. [Yiddish — Rumanian *pastramă* — *a păstra*, to serve.]

pastry *pās'tri, n* articles made of paste or dough collectively; crust of pies, tarts, etc.; a small cake. — **pas'trycook** a maker or seller of pastry. [**paste**.]

pasture *päs'chər, n* growing grass for grazing; grazing land; a grazing ground, piece of grazing land. — *vi* to graze. — *vt* to put to graze; to graze on. — *adj* **pas'turable** fit for pasture. — *n* **pas'turage** the business of feeding or grazing cattle; pasture-land; grass for feeding; right of pasture. — *adj* **pas'tural** of pasture. — *adj* **pas'tureless**. — **pas'ture-land** land suitable for pasture. [O.Fr. *pasture* (Fr. *pâture*) — L. *pāstūra* — *pāscĕre*, *pāstum*, to feed.]

pasty[1] *pās'ti, adj*. See under **paste**.

pasty[2] *pas'ti* or *päs'ti, n* a meat-pie baked without a dish. [O.Fr. *pastée* — L. *pasta*; see ety. for **paste**.]

pat *pat, n* a gentle stroke with a flat surface, such as the palm of the hand; such a stroke as a caress or mark of approbation; a sound as of such a stroke; a small lump, esp. of butter, such as might be moulded by patting. — *vt* to strike (now only to strike gently) with the palm of the hand or other flat surface; to shape by patting. — *vi* to tap; to make the sound of pats, as with the feet: — *pr p* **patt'ing**; *pa t* and *pa p* **patt'ed**. — *adv* and *adj* hitting the mark precisely; at the right time or place; exactly to the purpose; with or ready for fluent or glib repetition. — *n* **pat'ness**. — **pat'ball** rounders; gentle hitting in other games. — **off pat** exactly memorised; pat; **pat on the back** a mark of encouragement or approbation; **stand pat** (in poker) to decide to play one's hand as it is; to refuse to change. [Prob. imit.]

pat. *abbrev* for: patent; patented.

pataca *pə-tä'kə, n* the basic unit of currency in the Portuguese colonies of Macao and Timor (100 *avos*); a coin of one pataca in value. [Port.]

patch *pach, n* a piece put on or to be put on to mend a defect; a piece of plaster for a cut or sore; a pad for a hurt eye; a piece of ground or plot of land; an area, district, etc. regularly visited, patrolled, traded in, etc.; a scrap or fragment; a scrap pieced together with others; a group of instructions added to a computer program to correct a mistake (*comput*); a small piece of black silk, etc., stuck by ladies on the face, to bring out the complexion by contrast, an imitation beauty spot; a smallish area differing in colour or otherwise from its surroundings. — *vt* to mend with a patch; to put a patch on; to apply as a patch; to join in patchwork; to mend or construct hastily, clumsily or temporarily (commonly with *up*); to construct as a patchwork; to mark with patches; to connect (a telephone call) using a patchboard (with *through*), to put through. — *adj* **patch'able**. — *adj* **patched**. — *n* **patch'er**. — *adv* **patch'ily**. — *n* and *adj* **patch'ing**. — *adj* **patch'y** covered with patches; diversified in patches; inharmonious, incongruous, irregular. — **patch'board** (*telecomm*, etc.) a panel with multiple electric terminals into which wires may be plugged to form a variety of electric circuits; **patch'-pocket** a flat, usu. square piece of material attached to the outside of a garment as a pocket; **patch test** a test for allergy in which allergenic substances are applied to areas of skin which are later examined for signs of irritation; **patch-up'** a provisional repairing; **patch'work** work formed of patches or pieces sewn together; an incongruous combination; work patched up or clumsily executed; a surface diversified in patches. — **hit** or **strike a bad patch** to experience a difficult time, encounter unfavourable conditions, etc.; **not a patch on** not fit to be compared with. [M.E. *pacche*.]

patchouli or **patchouly** *pach'o͞o-lē* or *pə-cho͞o'lē, n* a labiate shrub of S.E. Asia; a perfume derived from its dried branches. [Tamil *pacculi*.]

pate *pāt, n* the crown of the head, esp. when bald; the head; intelligence (*fig*).

pâté *pät'ā* or *pat'ā, n* a paste made of blended meat, herbs, etc. — **pâté de foie gras** (*də fwä grä*) a paste made of fat goose liver. [Fr.]

patella *pə-tel'ə, n* the knee-cap (*anat*); a little pan (*archaeol*): — *pl* **patell'as** or **patell'ae** (*-ē*). — *adj* **patell'ar** of the knee-cap. — *adj* **patell'ate** (or *pat'*) saucer-shaped; limpet-shaped. — *n* **patellec'tomy** the surgical removal of the patella. — *adj* **patell'iform** patellate. [L., dimin. of *patina*, a pan.]

paten *pat'ən, n* a communion plate; a metal disc. [O.Fr. *patene* — L. *patena*, *patina*, a plate — Gr. *patanē*.]

patent *pā'tənt*, or (esp. in *letters-patent* and *Patent Office*, and in U.S.) *pat'ənt, adj* lying open; conspicuous, obvious, evident; generally accessible; protected by a patent; spreading (*bot*); expanding; ingenious (*colloq*). — *n* an official document, open, and having the official seal of the government attached to it, conferring an exclusive right or privilege, such as a title of nobility, or the sole right for a term of years to the proceeds of an invention; something invented and protected by a patent; a privilege; a certificate. — *vt* to secure a patent for. — *n* **pā'tency** openness; obviousness. — *adj* **pā'tentable**. — *n* **pātentee'** a person who holds a patent, or to whom a patent is granted. — *adv* **pā'tently** openly, obviously. — *n* **pā'tentor** a person, body, authority, etc. that or who grants a patent. — **patent agent** someone who obtains patents on behalf of inventors; **patent leather** finely varnished leather; **patent medicine** (*strictly*) a medicine protected by a patent; (*loosely*) any proprietary medicine, esp. one liable to stamp duty, as made by secret process or for some other reason; **Patent Office** an office for the granting of patents for inventions; **pā'tent-right** the exclusive right reserved by letters patent (q.v). — *npl* **pā'tent-rolls** the register of letters patent (q.v.) issued in England. [L. *patēns*, *-entis*, pres. p. of *patēre*, to lie open.]

pater *pā'tər*, (*slang*, usu. *facetious*) *n* father. [L. *păter*.]

paterfamilias *pā-tər-fə-mil'i-as* or *pat'ər-*, *n* the father or head of a family or household: — *pl* strictly **patresfamil'ias** (*-trās-*), sometimes **paterfamil'-iases**. [L. *păter*, a father, *familiās*, old genitive of *familia*, a household.]

paternal *pə-tûr'nəl*, *adj* of a father; on the father's side; derived or inherited from the father; fatherly; showing the disposition or manner of a father. — *n* **pater'nalism** a system or tendency in which well-meaning supervision, regulation, etc. is apt to become unwelcome interference. — *adj* **paternalis'tic**. — *adv* **pater'nally**. — *n* **pater'nity** the state or fact of being a father; fatherhood; the relation of a father to his children; origin on the father's side; origination or authorship. — **paternity leave** leave of absence from work granted to a husband so that he can be with his wife and assist her during and after childbirth. [L. *pater* (Gr. *patēr*), a father.]

paternoster *pat-ər-nos'tər* or *pāt'*, *n* (with *cap*) the Lord's Prayer; a muttered formula or spell; a large bead in a rosary, at which, in telling, the Lord's Prayer is repeated; a rosary; anything strung like a rosary; a lift for goods or passengers, consisting of a series of cars moving on a continuous belt, the floors remaining horizontal at the top and bottom of travel. [L. *Pater noster*, 'Our Father', the first words of the Lord's Prayer.]

Paterson's curse *pat'ər-sənz kûrs*, *n* (*Austr*) any of various naturalised orig. European herbs regarded as harmful to livestock.

path *päth*, *n* a way trodden out by the feet; a footpath; a course, route, line, etc. along which anything moves; a course of action, conduct: — *pl* **paths** (*pädhz*). — **path'finder** a person who explores the route, a pioneer; a radar device used as an aircraft navigational aid; a radar device for guiding missiles into a target area. — *n* **path'way** a path; (in neurology) the route of a sensory impression to the brain, or of a motor impulse from the brain to the musculature. [O.E. *pæth*; Ger. *Pfad*.]

path. or **pathol.** *abbrev* for: pathological; pathology.

-path *path*, *n combining form* used to denote: a sufferer from a particular disorder, as in *psychopath*; a therapist for a particular disorder, as in *osteopath*. — *combining form* **patho-** denoting disease or disorder, as in *pathology*. — *n combining form* **-pathy** denoting: mental or emotional sensitivity or receptiveness; disease, disorder; therapy for a particular disorder. — *adj combining form* **-pathet'ic** or **-path'ic**. — *n combining form* **-pathist** denoting a therapist for a particular disorder. — *n* **pathogen** (*path'ə-jen*) an organism or substance that causes disease. — *n* **pathogen'esis** or **pathogeny** (*pə-thoj'ə-ni*) (mode of) production or development of disease. — *adj* **pathogenetic** (*path-ō-ji-net'ik*) or **pathogenic** (*-jen'ik*) producing disease. — *n* **pathogenicity** (*-is'i-ti*) the quality of producing, or the ability to produce, disease. — *adj* **patholog'ical** relating to pathology; relating to or caused by disease; (*loosely*) habitual or compulsive. — *adv* **patholog'ically**. — *n* **pathol'ogist** a person skilled in pathology, usu. having as a duty the performing of post-mortems. — *n* **pathol'ogy** the study of diseases or abnormalities or, more particularly, of the changes in tissues or organs that are associated with disease; a deviation from the normal, healthy state. [Ety. as for **pathos**.]

Pathan *pə-tan'* or *put-än'*, *n* an Afghan; a person of Afghan race settled in India. — Also *adj*. [Afghan *Pakhtun*.]

patho-. See under **path-**.

pathos *pā'thos*, *n* the quality that arouses pity. — *adj* **pathetic** (*pə-thet'ik*) affecting the emotions of pity, grief or sorrow; touching; sadly inadequate; contemptible, derisory (*colloq*). — *n* the style or manner fitted to excite emotion; (in *pl*) attempts at pathetic expression. — *adv* **pathet'ically**. — **pathetic fallacy** (in literature, etc.) the transference of human emotions to inanimate objects. [Gr. *pathos*, experience, feeling, pathos.]

patible *pat'i-bl*, *adj* capable of suffering or being acted on; passible. [L. *patibilis* — *patī*, to suffer.]

patience *pā'shəns*, *n* the quality of being able calmly to endure suffering, toil, delay, vexation, or any similar condition; a card-game of various kinds, generally for one person, the object being to fit the cards, as they turn up, into some scheme. — *adj* **pā'tient** sustaining pain, delay, etc., without fretting; not easily provoked; persevering in long-continued or minute work; expecting with calmness; long-suffering; enduring. — *n* a person under medical or surgical treatment. — *adv* **pā'tiently**. [Fr., — L. *patientia* — *patī*, to bear.]

patina *pat'i-nə*, *n* a film of basic copper carbonate that forms on exposed surfaces of copper or bronze; a similar film of oxide, etc., on other metals; a film or surface appearance that develops on other substances (wood, flint, etc.) on long exposure or burial; a sheen acquired from constant handling or contact (also *fig*). — *adj* **pat'ināted**. — *n* **patinā'tion**. — *adj* **pat'ined**. [L. *patina*, a dish.]

patio *pa'ti-ō*, *n* a courtyard; a paved area usu. adjoining a house, where outdoor meals can be served, etc.: — *pl* **pa'tios**. [Sp., a courtyard.]

pâtisserie *pa-tēs'ə-rē*, (Fr.) *n* a shop which sells fancy cakes, etc.; such cakes.

Patna rice *pat'nə rīs*, *n* a long-grained rice, originally grown at *Patna* in India, served with savoury dishes.

patois *pat'wä*, *n* spoken regional dialect; (*loosely*) jargon: — *pl* **pat'ois** (*-wäz*). [Fr.]

patresfamilias. See **paterfamilias**.

patrial *pā'* or *pa'tri-əl*, *adj* pertaining to one's native land; (of a word) denoting a native or inhabitant of the place from whose name the word was formed; pertaining to the legal right to enter and stay in the U.K., or to one who has this right. — *n* a patrial word; a citizen of the U.K., a British colony or the British Commonwealth, who for certain reasons, e.g. because a parent was born in the U.K., has a legal right to enter and stay in the U.K. — *n* **patrialisā'tion** or **-z-**. — *vt* **pa'trialise** or **-ize**. — *n* **patrial'ity** the condition of being a patrial. [Obs. Fr. — L. *patria*, fatherland.]

patriarch *pā'tri-ärk*, *n* a male head of a family; one of the early heads of families from Adam downwards to Abraham, Jacob, and his sons (*OT*); a bishop ranking above primates and metropolitans; the head of certain Eastern Churches; a father or founder; a venerable old man; an oldest inhabitant. — *adj* **patriarch'al** belonging or subject to a patriarch; like a patriarch; of the nature of a patriarch. — *n* **patriarch'alism** the condition of tribal government by a patriarch. — *n* **pa'triarchate** the province, dignity, office, term or residence of a church patriarch; patriarchy. — *n* **pa'triarchism** government by a patriarch. — *n* **pa'triarchy** a community of related families under the authority of a patriarch; the patriarchal system. — **patriarchal cross** a cross with two horizontal bars. [Gr. *patriarchēs* — *patriā*, family — *patēr*, father, *archē*, rule.]

patriation *pā-tri-ā'shən*, *n* the transferring of responsibility for the Canadian constitution (as enshrined in the British North America Act of 1867) from the British parliament to the Canadian parliament. — *vt* **pāt'riate**. [L. *patria*, fatherland.]

patrician *pə-trish'ən*, *n* a member or descendant by blood or adoption of one of the original families of citizens forming the Roman people (opp. to *plebeian*); a nobleman of a new order nominated by the emperor in the later Roman Empire; an imperial Roman provincial administrator in Italy or Africa; a hereditary noble; an aristocrat. — Also *adj*. — *adj* **patri'cianly**. — *n* **patriciate** (*pə-trish'i-āt*) the position of a patrician; the patrician order. [L. *patrĭcius* — *pater*, *patris*, a father.]

patricide *pat'ri-sīd*, *n* the murder of one's own father; a person who murders their own father. — *adj* **patricī'dal**. [Doubtful L. *patricīda*, as if from *pater*, *patris*, father, *caedĕre*, to kill; prob. an error for *parricīda*; see ety. for **parricide**.]

patrifocal *pat'ri-fō-kəl*, (*anthrop*, etc.) *adj* centred on the father; (of societies, families, etc.) in which authority and responsibility rest with the father. — *n* **patrifocal'ity**. [L. *pater*, *patris*, father, *fŏcus*, a hearth.]

patrilineal *pat-ri-lin'i-əl* or **patrilin'ear** *-ər*, *adj* traced through the father or through males alone. — *adv* **patrilin'eally**. — *n* **pat'riliny** patrilineal descent. [L. *pater*, *patris*, father, *līnea*, line.]

patrilocal *pat-ri-lō'kl*, *adj* (of a form of marriage) in which the wife goes to live with the husband's group. [L. *pater*, *patris*, father, *locālis* — *locus*, place.]

patrimony *pat'ri-mən-i*, *n* an inheritance from a father or from ancestors; a church estate or revenue. — *adj* **patrimonial** (*-mō'ni-əl*). — *adv* **patrimō'nially**. [L. *patrimōnium*, a paternal estate — *pater*, *patris*, a father.]

patriot *pā'tri-ət* or *pat'ri-ət*, *n* a person who truly, though sometimes injudiciously, loves and serves their fatherland. — *adj* **patriotic** (*pat-ri-ot'ik* or *pāt-*) devoted to one's country; like a patriot; actuated by a love of one's country. — *adv* **patriot'ically**. — *n* **pā'triotism** (or *pat'*). [Gr. *patriōtēs*, fellow-countrymen — *patrios* — *patēr*, a father.]

patristic *pə-tris'tik* or **patristical** *-tris'tik-əl*, *adj* pertaining to the Fathers of the Christian Church. [Gr. *patēr*, *pat(e)ros*, a father.]

patrol *pə-trōl'*, *vi* to move systematically round an area, for purpose of watching, repressing, protecting, inspecting, etc.; (of a police officer) to be on duty on a beat. — *vt* to keep (an area) under surveillance by patrolling; to perambulate: — *pr p* **patrōll'ing**; *pa t* and *pa p* **patrōlled'**. — *n* the act or service of patrolling; perambulation; a person or group of people patrolling an area; a body of aircraft, ships, etc. having patrolling duties; a small detachment of soldiers, etc. sent on reconnaissance or to make an attack, etc.; one of the units of eight or so Scouts or Guides forming a troop. — *n* **patroll'er**. — **patrol car** that used by police to patrol an area; **patrol'-man**, *fem* **patrol'woman** a police officer on duty on a beat (*NAm*); a member of the police force without rank (*NAm*); (or **patrol'**) a man on patrol to help motorists in difficulties. [O.Fr. *patrouiller*, to patrol, orig. to paddle in the mud.]

patron *pā'trən*, *n* a protector; a person, group, organisation, etc. which gives support, encouragement and often financial aid; a (regular) customer; a habitual attender; an upholder; a proprietor of a restaurant, etc.; a person who has the right to appoint to any office, esp. to a living in the church (*C of E*); a guardian saint. — *n* **patronage** (*pat'*) support given by a patron; guardianship of saints; the right of bestowing offices, privileges or church benefices (*C of E*); habitual commercial dealings. — *adj* **patronal** (*pə-trō'nl*). — *vt* **patronise** or **-ize** (*pat'* or in N.Am. *pāt'*) to act as a patron toward; to give encouragement to; to frequent as a customer; to assume the condescending air of a patron toward.

patronymic *pat-rə-nim'ik*, *adj* derived from the name of a father or an ancestor. — *n* a name so derived. [Gr. *patrōnymikos* — *patēr*, a father, *onyma* (*onoma*), a name.]

patsy *pat'si*, (*slang*, esp. *NAm*) *n* an easy victim, a sucker; a scapegoat, fall guy.

patten *pat'n*, (*hist*) *n* a wooden shoe, a clog; a wooden sole mounted on an iron ring to raise the shoe above the mud. — *adj* **patt'ened** with pattens. [O.Fr. *patin*, clog (now skate), perh. — *patte*, paw.]

patter[1] *pat'ər*, *vi* to pat or strike often, as hailstones do; to make the sound of a succession of light pats; to run with short quick steps. — *n* the sound of pattering. [Frequentative of **pat**.]

patter[2] *pat'ər*, *vi* to talk or sing rapidly and glibly. — *vt* to repeat hurriedly, to gabble. — *n* glib talk, chatter, esp. the insincere speech of salesmen, etc.; the jargon of a particular class, group, etc. — **patt'er-song** a comic song in which a great many words are sung or spoken very rapidly. [**paternoster**.]

pattern *pat'ərn*, *n* a decorative design; a particular disposition of forms and colours; a design or figure repeated indefinitely; a design or guide with help of which something is to be made (e.g. a dressmaker's paper pattern); a person or thing to be copied; a model; a sample; the distribution of shot on a target; a model of an object to be cast, from which a mould is prepared; a typical example. — *vt* to fashion after a pattern; to make a pattern upon. — **patt'ern-maker** a person who makes the patterns for moulders in foundry-work; **pattern race** a horse-race open to all-comers in a particular category, e.g. of a certain age or weight, usu. contested by top-class horses, the object being to find the best; **patt'ern-shop** the place in which patterns for a factory are prepared. [Fr. *patron*, patron, pattern; cf. **patron**.]

patty *pat'i*, *n* a little pie; a small flat cake of minced beef or other food. — **patt'y-pan** a pan for baking patties. [Fr. *pâté*; cf. **pasty**.]

patzer *pats'ər*, *n* a poor chess player. [Ger. *patzen*, to bungle, make a mess of.]

pauciloquent *pö-sil'ə-kwənt*, *adj* of few words, speaking little. [L. *paucus*, little, *loquī*, to speak.]

paucity *pö'sit-i*, *n* fewness; smallness of quantity, insufficiency, dearth. [L. *paucitās*, *-ātis* — *paucus*, few.]

Pauline *pö'līn*, *adj* of the apostle Paul. — *n* a member of any religious order named after him. — *adj* **Paulinian** (*-in'i-ən*) Pauline. — *n* **Paul'inism** the teaching or theology of Paul. — *n* **Paul'inist**. — *adj* **Paulinist'ic**.

Paul Jones *pöl jōnz*, *n* a dance in the course of which each man takes a number of partners in succession — perh. from the Scottish-American seaman Paul Jones (1747–92), who excelled in the capture of prizes.

paunch *pönch* or *pönsh*, *n* the belly; a protuberant belly; the first and largest stomach of a ruminant; a rope mat to prevent chafing (*naut*). — *adj* **paunch'y** big-bellied. [O.Fr. *panche*.]

pauper *pö'pər*, *n* a destitute person; a person not required to pay costs in a law suit (*hist*); a person supported by charity or by some public provision (*hist*). — *n* **pauperisā'tion** or **-z**. — *vt* **pau'perise** or **-ize** to reduce to pauperism; to accustom to expect or depend on support from without. — *n* **pau'perism**. [L., poor.]

pause *pöz*, *n* a temporary stop; a short break; cessation caused by doubt; hesitation; a mark for suspending the voice (*prosody*); a continuance of a note or rest beyond its time, or a mark indicating this (*mus*). — *vi* to make a pause. — *adj* **paus'al**. — *adj* **pause'ful**. — *adv* **pause'fully**. — *adj* **pause'less**.

— *adv* **pause'lessly**. — *n* **paus'er**. — *n* and *adj* **paus'ing**. — *adv* **paus'ingly**. — **give pause to** to cause to hesitate. [Fr., — L. *pausa* — Gr. *pausis*, from *pauein*, to cause to cease.]

pavane *pav-än'* or **pavan** *pav'ən*, *n* a slow dance, once much practised in Spain; music for it, in 4-4 time. [Fr. *pavane*, or Sp. or It. *pavana*, prob. — L. *pāvō*, *-ōnis*, peacock.]

pave *pāv*, *vt* to cover with slabs or other close-set pieces, so as to form a level surface for walking on; to cover with anything close-set; to be such a covering for. — *adj* **paved**. — *n* **pave'ment** a paved surface, or that with which it is paved; a footway by the side of a street (sometimes even when unpaved); a paved road or its surface (*NAm*). — *n* and *adj* **pā'ving**. — *n* **pā'viour** or in N.Am. **pa'vior** a person who or a machine which lays pavements. — **pavement artist** a person who seeks a living by drawing coloured pictures on the pavement; **pavement light** a window of glass blocks in the pavement to light a cellar; **pa'ving-stone** a slab of stone or concrete used in a pavement, etc. — **pave the way for** to prepare the way for; to make easier; to help to bring on. [Fr. *paver*, prob. a back-formation from *pavement* — L. *pavīmentum* — *pavīre*, to beat hard.]

pavilion *pə-vil'yən*, *n* a tent, esp. a large or luxurious one; a tentlike covering; a light building at a sports ground for players and spectators of the game; an ornamental or showy building often turreted or domed for pleasure purposes; a projecting section of a building, usually with a tentlike roof and much decorated; a hospital block; an exhibition building; (in gem-cutting) the under-surface of a brilliant, opposite to the crown. — *vt* to provide with pavilions; to cover, as with a tent. [Fr. *pavillon* — L. *pāpiliō*, *-ōnis*, a butterfly, a tent.]

pavior, paviour. See under **pave**.

pavlova *pav-lō'və*, *n* a type of sweet dish consisting of a meringue base topped with whipped cream and fruit (also with *cap*). [Named in honour of the Russian ballerina Anna *Pavlova*.]

Pavlovian *pav-lō'vi-ən*, (*psychol* and *physiol*) *adj* relating to the work of the Russian physiologist, Ivan *Pavlov*, on conditioned reflexes; (of reactions, responses, etc.) automatic, unthinking.

paw *pö*, *n* a clawed foot; a hand (*facetious* or *derog*). — *vi* to draw the forefoot along the ground; to strike the ground with the forefoot; to strike out with the paw. — *vt* to scrape, feel, handle or strike with the forefoot; to handle indecently, coarsely or clumsily. [O.Fr. *poe*, *powe*, prob. Gmc.]

pawl *pöl*, *n* a catch engaging with the teeth of a ratchet wheel to prevent backward movement. [Poss. connected with Du. or Fr. *pal*, L. *pālus*, stake.]

pawn[1] *pön*, *n* something deposited as security for repayment or performance; the state of being pledged (as *in* or *at pawn*). — *vt* to give as security for repayment of borrowed money, esp. to a pawnbroker; to pledge or stake. — *n* **pawnee'** a person who takes anything in pawn. — *n* **pawn'er** a person who gives a pawn or pledge as security for money borrowed. — **pawn'broker** a broker who lends money on pawns; **pawn'broking**; **pawn'shop** a shop of a pawnbroker. [O.Fr. *pan*.]

pawn[2] *pön*, *n* a small piece in chess of lowest rank and range; an easily manipulated person. [O.Fr. *paon*, a foot-soldier — L.L. *pedō*, *-ōnis* — L. *pēs*, *pedis*, the foot.]

pawn[3]. See **pan**[2].

pawnee. See **pawn**[1].

pawpaw *pö'pö* or **papaw** *pə-pö'*, *n* a tree of the custard-apple family or its fruit, native to the U.S.; the papaya.

pax[1] *paks*, *n* the kiss of peace. — *interj* (*colloq*) (let's call a) truce. [L. *pāx*, peace.]

pax[2] *paks*, (L.) *n* peace. — **pax vobiscum** (*vō-bis'kəm*) peace be with you.

pay[1] *pā*, *vt* to give what is due (in satisfaction of a debt, in exchange, in compensation, in remuneration, etc.) to (the person, etc. to whom it is owed); to give (money, etc.) in satisfaction of a debt, in exchange, compensation, remuneration, etc.; to settle, discharge (a claim, bill, debt, etc.); to hand over money, etc., for; (of a sum of money, etc.) to be or yield satisfactory remuneration or compensation for, or enough to discharge; to yield (a certain sum, profit, etc.); to be profitable to, to benefit; to render, confer (attention, heed, court, a visit, etc.); (of a rope) to allow or cause to run out (*naut*). — *vi* to hand over money or other equivalent, compensation, etc. (with *for*); to afford, constitute, etc. a means of making payment (with *for*); to be worth one's trouble; to be profitable; to suffer or be punished (with *for*); to be the subject of payment: — *pr p* **pay'ing**; *pa t* and *pa p* **paid** or (in the nautical sense) **payed** (*pād*). — *n* money given for service; salary, wages; receipt of wages, etc., service for wages, etc., hire or paid employment (esp. for an evil purpose). — *adj* **paid** see separate article. — *adj* **pay'able** that may or should be paid; due; profitable. — *n* **payee'** someone to whom money is paid. — *n* **pay'er**. — *n* and *adj* **pay'ing**. — *n* **pay'ment** the act of paying; the discharge of a debt by money or its equivalent in value; that which is paid; recompense; reward; punishment. — **pay-as-you-earn'** a method of income tax collection in which the tax is paid by deduction from earnings before they are received (abbrev. **PAYE**); **pay bed** a bed, *specif* in a National Health Service hospital, available to a patient who pays for its use (also called *private paybed* or **amenity bed**); **pay'day** a regular day for payment, as of wages; **pay'-dirt** or **pay-grav'el** gravel or sand containing enough gold to be worth working (**pay-dirt** also *fig*); **paying guest** (*euph*) a lodger; **pay'list** or **pay'roll** a list of people entitled to receive pay, with the amounts due to each; (**payroll**) the money for paying wages; **pay'load** that part of the cargo of an aeroplane or other conveyance for which revenue is obtained; the part of a rocket's equipment that is to fulfil the purpose of the rocket, such as a warhead, or apparatus for obtaining information; **pay'master** the official in an organisation, government, etc. who pays out money; **pay'-off** (time of) payment — reward or punishment; outcome; an esp. useful or desirable result; dénouement; **pay-out** see **pay out** below; **pay'phone** a coin-operated public telephone; **pay'roll** see **paylist**; **pay'slip** a note to a worker (giving an analysis) of the sum they have been paid. — **in the pay of** receiving payment in return for services, used esp. in a sinister sense; **pay back** to pay in return (a debt); to give tit for tat; **pay down** to pay (e.g. a first instalment) in cash on the spot; **pay for** to make amends for; to suffer for; to bear the expense of; **pay in** to contribute to a fund; to deposit money in a bank account; **pay off** to pay in full and discharge; to take revenge upon; to requite; to fall away to leeward (*naut*); to yield good results, justify itself (see also **pay-off** above); **pay one's** (or **its**) **way** to have, or bring, enough to pay expenses; to compensate adequately for initial outlay; **pay out** to cause to run out (e.g. rope); to disburse (*n* **pay'-out**); to punish deservedly; **payroll giving** contributions to charity which are deducted from one's wages and paid by one's employer directly to the charity concerned; **pay the piper** see under **pipe**[1]; **pay through the nose** to pay dearly; **pay up** to pay in full; to pay arrears; to pay on demand. [Fr. *payer* — L. *pācāre*, to appease; cf. *pāx*, peace.]

pay[2] *pā*, (*naut*) *vt* to smear (a wooden boat) with tar, etc., as waterproofing: — *pa t* and *pa p* **payed**. [O.Fr. *peier* — L. *picāre*, to pitch.]

PAYE *abbrev* for pay-as-you-earn.

payola *pā-ō'lə*, *n* secret payment, a bribe, etc. to secure a favour, esp. the promotion of a commercial product by a disc-jockey; the practice of making or receiving payments of this kind. [Facetiously coined from **pay**[1] and Victr*ola*, a make of gramophone, or pian*ola*.]

paysage *pā-ē-zäzh'*, (*art*) *n* a landscape or landscape painting. — *n* **paysagist** (*pā'zə-jist*) a landscape-painter. [Fr.]

pazzazz or **pazazz**. See **pizzazz**.

Pb (*chem*) *symbol* for lead.

PBX (*telecomm*) *abbrev* for private branch exchange, a private telephone switching apparatus which routes calls between extensions and the public telephone network, and internally between extensions.

PC *abbrev* for: personal computer; Police Constable; Privy Councillor.

pc *abbrev* for: per cent; personal computer.

PCAS *pē'kas*, *abbrev* for Polytechnics Central Admissions System.

PCB *abbrev* for polychlorinated biphenyl, any of several compounds with various industrial applications, regarded as environmental pollutants.

PCN *abbrev* for personal communications network, a network for mobile telephone users.

PCP® *abbrev* for phencyclidine, a depressant drug taken illegally as a hallucinogen. — Also called (*colloq*) **angel dust**.

pct *abbrev* (esp. in N.Am.) for per cent.

Pd (*chem*) *symbol* for palladium.

pd *abbrev* for paid.

pdq *abbrev* (*colloq*) for pretty damn quick.

PE *abbrev* for: Peru (I.V.R.); physical education; Protestant Episcopal.

pea *pē*, *n* the nutritious seed of the papilionaceous climbing plants *Pisum sativum* (garden pea) and *P. arvense* (field pea); the plant itself (also **pea'-plant**); extended to various similar seeds and plants and to various rounded objects, e.g. roe of salmon. — *n* and *adj* **pea'-green** (or *-grēn'*) yellowish-green, the colour of soup made from split peas; bright green like fresh peas. — **peanut** see separate entry; **pea'pod** the seed case of a pea; **pea'shooter** a small tube for blowing peas through, used as a toy weapon; **pea-soup, pea-souper** see under **pease**; **pea'-trainer** an erection for pea-plants to climb on; **pea-vin'er** a machine that picks, washes and grades peas. — **split peas** peas stripped of their membranous covering, dried and halved. [Singular formed from **pease**, which was mistaken for a plural.]

peace *pēs*, *n* a state of quiet; freedom from disturbance, war or contention; cessation of war; a treaty that ends a war; ease of mind or conscience; tranquillity; quiet; stillness; silence. — *adj* **peace'-able** disposed to peace; peaceful. — *n* **peace'-ableness**. — *adv* **peace'ably**. — *adj* **peace'ful** enjoying peace; tending towards or favouring peace; inclined to peace; belonging to time of peace; consistent with peace; tranquil; calm; serene. — *adv* **peace'fully**. — *n* **peace'fulness**. — **Peace Corps** (in the U.S.) a government agency that sends volunteers to developing countries to help with agricultural, technological and educational schemes; **peace dividend** money left over from a government's defence budget as a result of negotiated arms reduction policies, available for peaceable (esp. social) use; the fact of having such surplus money; **peace'keeper**. — *adj* **peace'keeping** (**peace-keeping force** a military force sent into an area with the task of preventing fighting between opposing factions). — **peace'maker** a person who makes or produces peace; a person who reconciles enemies; **peace'making; peace'-offering** a gift offered towards reconciliation; **peace'-pipe** the calumet; **peace'time** time when there is no war. — *adj* of peacetime. — **at peace** in a state of peace; not at war; **hold one's peace** to remain silent; **in peace** in enjoyment of peace; **keep the peace** to refrain from disturbing the public peace; to refrain from, or to prevent, contention; **make one's peace with** to reconcile or to be reconciled with; **make peace** to end a war. [O.Fr. *pais* (Fr. *paix*) — L. *pāx*, *pācis*, peace.]

peach[1] *pēch*, *vi* (with *on*) to betray one's accomplice; to become informer. [Obs. *appeach*, to accuse.]

peach[2] *pēch*, *n* a sweet, juicy, velvety-skinned stone-fruit; the tree bearing it, closely related to the almond; extended to other fruits and fruit-trees; anything regarded as a very choice example of its kind, esp. a girl (*slang*); a yellow slightly tinged with red. — *adj* of the peach; of the colour of a peach. — *adj* **peach'y** coloured or tasting somewhat of peach; very good, excellent (*slang*). — **peach'-blow** a pinkish glaze on porcelain. — Also *adj*. — **peach-brand'y** a spirit distilled from the fermented juice of the peach. — *adj* **peach'-coloured** of the colour of a ripe peach (yellowish, tinged with red) or of peach-blossom (pink). — **peach Melba** a dish named in honour of the Australian soprano Dame Nellie *Melba*, consisting of peach halves served with ice-cream and usu. a raspberry sauce; **peach'-stone; peach'-tree**. [O.Fr. *pesche* (Fr. *pêche*, It. *persica*, *pesca*) — L. *Persicum* (*mālum*), the Persian (apple).]

pea-chick *pē'-chik*, *n* a young peacock or peahen.

pea-coat *pē'-kōt*, *n*. Same as **pea-jacket**.

peacock *pē'kok*, *n* a genus (*Pavo*) of large birds of the pheasant kind, consisting of the common peacock (*P. cristatus*) and the Javan (*P. muticus*), noted for their showy plumage, esp., in the former, the deep iridescent greenish blue in the neck and tail coverts; the male of either species; a vain person; peacock-blue (also *adj*); a peacock butterfly. — *vt* (*Austr*) to pick the best parts out of. — *vi* to strut about or behave like a peacock; to acquire the choicest pieces of land (i.e. near water) (*Austr*). — *adj* **pea'cockish**. — *adj* **pea'cock-like**. — *adj* **pea'cocky**. — **peacock-blue'** the deep greenish blue of the peacock's neck. — Also *adj*. — **peacock-butt'erfly** a butterfly (*Inachis io*) with wingspots like those of the peacock's train. [Obs. *pea*, a peafowl, and **cock**[1].]

peafowl *pē'fowl*, *n* a male or female peacock. — **pea'hen** the female of the peacock. [Obs. *pea*, a peafowl, and **fowl, hen**.]

pea-jacket *pē'-jak-it*, *n* a sailor's coarse thick overcoat. [Du. *pîe* (now *pij*), coat of coarse stuff, and **jacket**.]

peak[1] *pēk*, *n* a point; the pointed end or highest point of anything; the top of a mountain, esp. when sharp; a summit; a maximum point in a curve or the corresponding value in anything capable of being represented by a curve, e.g. a point or time of maximum use by the public of a service, etc.; the projecting front of a cap; a projecting point of hair on the forehead; a pointed beard; the upper outer corner of a sail extended by a gaff or yard (*naut*); the upper end of a gaff (*naut*). — *adj* maximum; of a maximum. — *vi* to rise in a peak; to reach the height of one's powers, popularity, etc.; (of prices, etc.) to reach a highest point or level (sometimes with *out*). — *adj* **peaked** having a peak or peaks. — *adj* **peak'y** having a peak or peaks; like a peak. — **peak'-load** the maximum demand of electricity, or load on a power-station. — **peak (viewing** or **listening) hours** or **time** the period in the day when the maximum number of people are watching television or listening to the radio. [Found from the 16th cent. (*peked* in the 15th); app. connected with **pike**[1].]

peak[2] *pēk*, *vi* to droop, to look thin or sickly. — *adj* **peak'y** having a pinched or sickly look.

peal *pēl*, *n* a loud sound; a number of loud sounds one after another; a set of bells tuned to each other; a chime or carillon; the changes rung upon a set of bells. — *vi* to resound in peals. — *vt* to give forth in peals. [App. aphetic for **appeal**.]

pean[1]. U.S. spelling of **paean**.

pean[2]. Same as **peen**.

peanut *pē'nut*, *n* the monkey-nut or groundnut (*Arachis*); (in *pl*) something very trifling or insignificant, esp. a paltry sum of money (*colloq*). — **peanut butter** a paste made from ground roasted peanuts. [**pea** and **nut**.]

pear *pār*, *n* a fruit, a pome tapering towards the stalk and bulged at the end; the tree (*Pyrus communis*) of the apple genus, which bears it; extended to various fruits (such as **alligator-pear, anchovy-pear** and **prickly-pear**); (in gem-cutting) a pear-shaped brilliant. — **pear'-drop** a sweet shaped and flavoured like a pear; a pear-shaped pendant. — *adj* **pear'-shaped** tapering towards one end and bulged at the other; in the shape of a pear; (of a vocal quality) mellow, resonant, non-nasal. — **pear'-tree**. — **go pear-shaped** (*colloq*) to put on weight around the hips, waist or bottom; to go awry or out of kilter. [O.E. *pere, peru* — L.L. *pira* — L. *pirum* (wrongly *pyrum*), pear.]

pearl[1] *pûrl*, *n* a rounded, solidified mass of nacre formed in a pearl-oyster, pearl mussel, or other shellfish, around a foreign body, etc. prized as a gem; nacre; a paragon or prized example; a lustrous globule; a granule. — *adj* made of or like pearl; granulated; (of an electric light bulb) made from a frosted, rather than clear, glass as a precaution against glare. — *vt* to set or adorn with pearls or pearly drops; to make pearly; to make into small round grains. — *vi* to fish for pearls; to become like pearls. — *adj* **pearled**. — *n* **pearl'er** a pearl-fisher or a pearl-fisher's boat. — *n* **pearl'iness**. — *n* and *adj* **pearl'ing**. — *adj* **pearl'ised** or **-ized** treated so as to give a pearly or lustrous surface. — *adj* **pearl'y** like pearl, nacreous; rich in pearls. — *n* (in *pl*) pearl-buttons; (in *pl*) costermongers' clothes covered with pearl-buttons; a costermonger, or a member of his family, wearing such clothes: — *pl* **pearl'ies**. — **pearl barley** see under **barley; pearl-butt'on** a mother-of-pearl button; **pearl'-diver** someone who dives for pearls; **pearl'-fisher** someone who fishes for pearls; **pearl'-fishery; pearl'-fishing; pearl'-gray** or **-grey** a pale grey. — Also *adj*. — **pearl-mill'et** the bulrush millet or spiked millet, a grain much grown in India; **pearl'-mussel** a freshwater mussel that yields pearls; **pearl'-oyster** any oyster that produces pearls; **pearl'-shell** mother-of-pearl; pearly or pearl-bearing shell; **pearl-tapiō'ca** tapioca granulated and graded according to its size; a potato-starch imitation; **pearl'wort** a member of a genus (*Sagina*) of small plants related to chickweed; **pearly gates** (from the Bible: Rev. xxi) the entrance to heaven; **pearly king** a costermonger whose costume is considered the most splendidly decorated with pearl-buttons: — *fem* **pearly queen**. — **cultured pearl** a true pearl formed by artificial means, as by planting a piece of mother-of-pearl wrapped in oyster epidermis in the body of an oyster; **false, imitation** or **simulated pearl** an imitation, e.g. a glass bulb coated with pearl essence. [Fr. *perle*, prob. from dimin. of L. *perna*, leg, leg-of-mutton-shaped.]

pearl[2] *pûrl*, *n* a small loop on the edge of lace, ribbon, etc. [Cf. **purl**[3].]

pearlite *pûr'līt*, *n* a constituent of steel composed of alternate plates of ferrite and cementite. — *adj* **pearlit'ic**. [**pearl**[1].]

pearmain *pār'mān*, *n* a variety of apple. [App. O.Fr. *parmain, permain*.]

peasant *pez'ənt*, *n* a small farmer (*hist*); a countryman, a rustic (*colloq*); an ignorant or low fellow (*derog*). — *adj* of or relating to peasants, rustic, rural. — *n* **peas'antry** peasants as a class; the condition or quality of a peasant. — *adj* **peas'anty** in the style of a peasant. [O.Fr. *paisant* (Fr. *paysan*) — *pays* — assumed L. *pāgēnsis* — *pāgus*, a district.]

pease *pēz*, *n* (*archaic*) a pea or pea-plant (*pl* **pease**; old *pl* **peason** *pēz'ən*). — **pease'-meal, pease'-porridge** or **pease'-pudding** meal, porridge or pudding made from pease; **pease'-soup** or **pea'-soup** soup made from pease; a thick yellow heavy-smelling fog (also **pea-soup'er**). [M.E. *pēse*, pl. *pēsen* — O.E. *pise*, pl. *pisan* — L.L. *pisa*, L. *pĭsum* — Gr. *pĭson* or *pĭsos*.]

peat *pēt*, *n* a shaped block dug from a bog and dried or to be dried for fuel; the generally brown or nearly black altered vegetable matter (chiefly bog-moss) found in bogs, from which such blocks are cut. — **peat'-bank, -bed, -bog, -land, -moor, -moss** an area, bog, moor, etc., covered with peat; a place from which peat is dug. — *adj* **peat'y** like, of the nature of, abounding in, or composed of, peat. [From the 13th cent. in S.E. Scotland in Anglo-Latin as *peta*, a peat.]

peau de soie *pō-də-swä'*, *n* a type of smooth silk or rayon fabric. [Fr., lit. skin of silk.]

peavey or **peavy** *pē'vi*, (*NAm*) *n* a lumberman's spiked and hooked lever. [Joseph *Peavey*, its inventor.]

pebble *peb'l*, *n* a small roundish stone, esp. worn down by water; transparent and colourless rock-crystal; a lens made of it; a semi-precious agate; a grained appearance on leather, as if pressed by pebbles. — *adj* of pebble. — *vt* to cover with pebbles; to impart pebble to (leather). — *adj* **pebb'led**. — *n* **pebb'ling**. — *adj* **pebb'ly** full of pebbles. — **pebb'ledash** a method of coating exterior walls with small pebbles set into the mortar; this coating. — *vt* to treat or coat with pebbledash. [O.E. *papol(-stān)*, a pebble(-stone).]

PEC *abbrev* for photoelectric cell. — Also *n* **pec** (*pek*).

pec *pek*, *n* colloq. short form for a pectoral muscle (usu. in *pl*).

pecan *pi-kan'*, *n* a North American hickory (also **pecan'-tree**); its edible, smooth-shelled nut (also **pecan'-nut**). [Indian name; cf. Cree *pakan*.]

peccable *pek'ə-bl*, *adj* liable to sin. — *n* **peccabil'ity**. — *n* **pecc'ancy** sinfulness; transgression. — *adj* **pecc'ant** sinning; offending; morbid, unhealthy. — *adv* **pecc'antly**. [L. *peccāre, -ātum*, to sin.]

peccadillo *pek-ə-dil'ō*, *n* a trifling fault, a small misdemeanour: — *pl* **peccadill'os** or **peccadill'oes**. [Sp. *pecadillo*, dimin. of *pecado* — L. *peccātum*, a sin.]

peccant, etc. See **peccable**.

peccary *pek'ə-ri*, *n* either of two species of hog-like South American animals. [Carib *pakira*.]

peccavi *pek-ä'vē*, *n* an admission of guilt or sin: — *pl* **pecca'vis**. [L. *peccavi*, I have sinned.]

peck[1] *pek*, *n* formerly a measure of capacity for dry goods, 2 gallons, or one-fourth of a bushel; a measuring vessel holding this quantity; a great amount (as in *a peck of troubles*). [M.E. *pekke, pek* — O.Fr. *pek*, generally a horse's feed of oats.]

peck[2] *pek*, *vt* to strike or pick up with the point of the beak or other sharp instrument; to make (a hole, etc.), or cause to be (damaged, pierced, etc.) by a quick movement of the beak, etc.; to eat sparingly or daintily; to kiss in a quick or cursory manner or movement. — *vi* to strike or feed with the beak or in similar manner; to eat daintily or sparingly (with *at*); to nit-pick, quibble (with *at*); to nag, criticise (with *at*). — *n* an act of pecking; a hole made by pecking; a quick or cursory kiss. — *n* **peck'er** that which pecks; a woodpecker; spirit, resolve, humour (as in *keep your pecker up*; *slang*); a penis (*slang*, orig. *US*). — *adj* **peck'ish** somewhat hungry (*colloq*); irritable (*US slang*). — *n* **peck'ishness**. — **pecking** (or **peck) order** a social order among poultry (or other birds) according to which any bird may peck a less important bird but must submit to being pecked by a more important one; order of prestige, power or importance in a human social group. [App. a form of **pick**.]

pecten *pek'tən*, *n* a comb-like structure of various kinds, e.g. in a bird's or reptile's eye: — *pl* **pec'tines** (*-tin-ēz*). — *adj* **pec'tinate** or **pec'tinated** toothed like a comb; having narrow parallel segments or lobes; like the teeth of a comb. — *n* **pectinā'tion**. [L. *pecten*, *-inis*, a comb.]

pectic *pek'tik*, *adj* of, relating to, or derived from, pectin. — *n* **pec'tin** a mixture of carbohydrates found in the cell-walls of fruits, used for the setting of jellies. — *n* **pec'tōse** a substance yielding pectin contained in the fleshy pulp of unripe fruit. [Gr. *pēktikos*, congealing — *pēgnynai*, to fix.]

pectinate, pectination, pectines, etc. See **pecten.**

pectoral *pek'tə-rəl*, *adj* of, for, on, or near, the breast or chest. — *n* either of the two muscles (*pectoralis major* and *pectoralis minor*) situated on either side of the top half of the chest and responsible for certain arm and shoulder movements (colloq. short form **pec**); armour for the breast of man or horse; an ornament worn on the breast, esp. the breastplate worn by the ancient Jewish high-priest, and the square of gold, embroidery, etc., formerly worn on the breast over the chasuble by bishops during mass; a pectoral fin. — *adv* **pec'torally**. — **pectoral cross** a gold cross worn on the breast by bishops, etc.; **pectoral fins** the anterior paired fins of fishes. [L. *pectorālis* — *pectus*, *pectoris*, the breast.]

pectose. See under **pectic.**

peculate *pek'ū-lāt*, *vt* and *vi* to appropriate dishonestly to one's own use, pilfer, embezzle. — *n* **peculā'tion**. — *n* **pec'ulātor**. [L. *pecūlārī*, *-ātus* — *pecūlium*, private property.]

peculiar *pi-kū'lyər*, *adj* belonging exclusively (to); characteristic, special (to); very particular; odd, strange; (of one's) own; having eccentric or individual variations in relation to the general or predicted pattern, as in *peculiar motion*, *velocity* (*astron*). — *n* a parish or church exempt from the jurisdiction of the ordinary or bishop in whose diocese it is placed; anything exempt from ordinary jurisdiction. — *vt* **pecu'liarise** or **-ize** to set apart, distinguish. — *n* **peculiarity** (*-li-ar'i-ti*) the quality of being peculiar or singular; that which is found in one and in no other; something which distinguishes anything from others; individuality; oddity. — *adv* **pecu'liarly**. — **peculiar motion** see **proper motion** under **proper**. [L. *pecūlium*, private property.]

pecuniary *pi-kū'nyə-ri* or *-ni-ə-ri*, *adj* relating to money; consisting of money. [L. *pecūnia*, money.]

ped-[1]. See **paed-**.

ped-[2]. See **pedi-**.

-ped *-ped* or **-pede** *-pēd*, *combining form* denoting foot. — *adj combining form* **-pedal** (*-ped'l*). [L. *pēs*, *pedis*, foot.]

pedagogue *ped'ə-gog*, *n* a teacher; a pedant. — *adj* **pedagogic** (*-gog'* or *-goj'*) or **pedagog'ical**. — *adv* **pedagog'ically**. — *nsing* **pedagog'ics** (*-gog'* or *-goj'*) the science and principles of teaching. — *adj* **ped'agoguish**. — *n* **ped'agogy** (*-gog-i* or *-goj-i*) the science of teaching; instruction; training. [Partly through Fr. and L. from Gr. *paidagōgos*, a slave who led a boy to school.]

pedal *ped'l* (in *zool* also *pē'dəl*), *adj* of the foot; of, with, or pertaining to, a pedal or pedals; of the feet of perpendiculars (*geom*). — *n* (*ped'l*) a lever pressed by the foot. — *vi* to use a pedal or pedals; to advance by use of the pedals. — *vt* to drive or operate by using the pedals: — *pr p* **ped'alling** (or in U.S. **ped'aling**); *pa t* and *pa p* **ped'alled** (or in U.S. **ped'aled**). — *n* **ped'aller** a person who uses pedals. — *n* **ped'alling**. — **ped'al-organ** the division of an organ played by means of pedals; **ped'al-point** a tone or tones sustained normally in the bass, while other parts move independently (also called **organ point**); **ped'al-pushers** women's knee-length breeches. — **pedal steel guitar** an electric steel guitar with foot pedals for adjusting pitch, creating glissando effects, etc. [L. *pedālis* — *pēs*, *pedis*, foot.]

pedalo *ped'ə-lō*, *n* a small pedal-propelled boat used (esp. on lakes) for pleasure.

pedant *ped'nt*, *n* someone who attaches too much importance to merely formal matters in scholarship; an over-educated person who parades his or her knowledge. — *adj* **pedantic** (*pid-ant'ik*) of the character or in the manner of a pedant. — *adv* **pedant'ically**. — *n* **ped'antry** the character or manner of a pedant; a pedantic expression; unduly rigorous formality. [It. *pedante* (perh. through Fr. *pédant*).]

pedate *ped'āt*, *adj* footed; foot-like; palmately lobed with the outer lobes deeply cut, or ternately branching with the outer branches forked (*bot*). — *adv* **ped'ately**. [L. *pedātus*, footed — *pēs*, *pedis*, foot.]

peddle *ped'l*, *vi* to go from place to place or house to house selling (small goods); to trifle. — *vt* to sell or offer as a pedlar; to deal in, sell (illegal drugs), usu. in small quantities. — *n* (esp. *US*) **pedd'ler**. [App. partly a back-formation from **pedlar**, partly from **piddle**.]

-pede. See **-ped**.

pederast *ped'ə-rast*, *n* a man who practises pederasty. — *adj* **pederas'tic**. — *n* **ped'erasty** sexual relations of a man with a boy. [Gr. *pais*, *paidos*, boy, *erastēs*, lover.]

pedestal *ped'is-tl*, *n* the support of a column, statue, vase, etc.; the fixed casting which holds the brasses in which a shaft turns. — *vt* to place on a pedestal. — *adj* **ped'estalled**. — **pedestal desk** a desk for which sets of drawers act as the side supports for the writing surface. [Fr. *piédestal* — It. *piedistallo*, for *piè di stallo*, foot of a stall.]

pedestrian *pi-des'tri-ən*, *adj* on foot; of walking; prosaic, uninspired; flat or commonplace. — *n* a walker, someone travelling on foot. — *n* **pedestrianisā'tion** or **-z-**. — *vt* **pedes'trianise** or **-ize** to convert (a street) to use by pedestrians only. — *n* **pedes'trianism**. — **pedestrian crossing** a part of a roadway (often controlled by traffic lights) marked for the use of pedestrians who wish to cross, and on which they have right of way; **pedestrian precinct** see under **precinct**. [L. *pedester*, *-tris* — *pēs*, *pedis*.]

pedi- *ped-i-* or **ped-** *ped-*, *combining form* used to denote foot. [L. *pēs*, *pedis*, foot.]

pediatrics. N.Am. spelling of **paediatrics** (see under **paed-**).

pedicab *ped'i-kab*, *n* a light vehicle consisting of a tricycle with the addition of a seat, usu. behind, covered by a half hood, for passenger(s). [L. *pēs*, *pedis*, the foot, and **cab**.]

pedicel *ped'i-sel*, (*biol*) *n* the stalk of a single flower in an inflorescence; the stalk of a sedentary animal; the stalk of an animal organ, e.g. a crab's eye. [Dimin. of L. *pēs*, *pedis*, the foot.]

pedicle *ped'i-kl*, *n* a short stalk or pedicel (*bot*); a narrow stalklike structure or short bony process (*zool*); in deer, a bony protrusion of the skull from which an antler grows. — *adj* **ped'icled**. — *adj* **pedic'ūlate**. — *adj* **pedic'ulated**. [L. *pediculus*, a little foot — *pēs*, *pedis*, foot.]

pedicure *ped'i-kūr*, *n* the treatment of corns, bunions, or the like; a person who treats the feet. — *n* **ped'icurist**. [L. *pēs*, *pedis*, foot, *cūra*, care.]

pedigree *ped'i-grē*, *n* a line of ancestors; a scheme or record of ancestry; genealogy; distinguished and ancient lineage; derivation, descent. — *adj* of known descent, pure-bred, and of good stock. — *adj* **ped'igreed** having a pedigree. [App. Fr. *pied de grue*, crane's-foot, from the arrow-head figure in a family-tree.]

pediment *ped'i-mənt*, (*archit*) *n* a triangular structure crowning the front of a Greek building, less steeply sloped than a gable; in later architecture a similar structure, triangular, rounded, etc., over a portico, door, window or niche. — *adj* **pedimental** (*-ment'l*). — *adj* **ped'imented** furnished with a pediment; like a pediment. [Earlier *periment*, prob. for **pyramid**.]

pedlar *ped'lər*, *n* a person who goes about with a small stock or selection of goods for sale; a person who peddles. — *n* **ped'lary** the wares or occupation of a pedlar. [Prob. from M.E. *pedder*.]

pedo-. See **paed-**.

pedology[1] *ped-ol'ə-ji*, *n* the study of soils. — *adj* **pedological** (*-ə-loj'*). — *n* **pedol'ogist.** [Gr. *pedon*, ground, *logos*, discourse.]

pedology[2]. N.Am.spelling of **paedology** (see **paed-**).

pedometer *pid-om'i-tər*, *n* an instrument for counting paces and so approximately measuring distance walked. [L. *pēs*, *pedis*, foot — Gr. *metron*, measure.]

peduncle *pi-dung'kl*, (*biol*) *n* the stalk of an inflorescence or of a solitary flower; the stalk by which a sedentary animal is attached; a stalklike part in a body (*zool*); a narrow stalklike connecting part (e.g. between the thorax and abdomen of insects); a tract of white fibres in the brain; a narrow process of tissue linking a tumour to normal tissue. — *adj* **pedun'cular, pedun'culate** or **pedun'culated.** [Botanists' L. *pedunculus* — L. *pēs*, *pedis*, the foot.]

pee *pē*, (*colloq*) *vi* to urinate. — Also *n*. [For **piss**.]

peek *pēk*, *n* a sly look, a peep. — *vi* to peep. — *n* **peek'aboo** a child's peeping game.

peel[1] *pēl*, *vt* to strip off the skin, bark, or other covering from; to strip (e.g. skin or other covering layer) off. — *vi* to come off like skin; to lose, shed the skin; to undress (*colloq*). — *n* rind, esp. that of oranges, lemons, etc., in the natural state or candied. — *adj* **peeled.** — *n* **peel'er** a person who peels; an instrument or machine for peeling or husking. — *n* **peel'ing** the act of stripping; a piece, strip or shred stripped off. — **peel off** to leave a flying formation by a particular manoeuvre (*aeronautics*); (of a ship) to veer away from a convoy; (of a person or group of persons) to veer off, separate from the mass. [O.E. *pilian* — L. *pīlāre*, to deprive of hair — *pīlus*, a hair; perh. influenced by Fr. *peler*, to skin.]

peel[2] *pēl*, *n* a shovel, esp. a baker's wooden shovel; an instrument for hanging up paper to dry. [O.Fr. *pele* — L. *pāla*, a spade.]

peel[3] or **pele** *pēl*, also **peel'-house** or **-tower** (or **pele'-house** or **-tower**), *n* a fortified dwelling-house, usu. entered by a ladder to the first floor, with vaulted ground floor for cattle, common on the Borders (*hist*); now a loosely used term. [Obs. *peel*, *pele*, a stake — A.Fr. *pel* — L. pālus.]

peen or **pein** *pēn*, *n* the end of a hammer head opposite the hammering face. — *vt* to strike or work (metal) with a peen; to fix (e.g. a rivet) by hammering into place (usu. with *in* or *over*).

peep[1] *pēp*, *vi* to cheep like a chicken. — *n* a high feeble sound. — *n* **peep'er.** — **not a peep** (*colloq*) no noise, not a sound. [Imit.]

peep[2] *pēp*, *vi* to look through a narrow opening; to look out from a hiding-place; to look slyly, surreptitiously, or cautiously; to be just showing; to begin to appear. — *vt* to cause to project slightly from a concealed place. — *n* a sly or cautious look; a beginning to appear; a speck of light or flame; a glimpse. — *n* **peep'er** someone who peeps; a prying person; the eye (*slang*); a glass, for various purposes (*slang*). — **peep'-hole** a hole through which one may look without being seen; **peeping Tom** a man who furtively spies on other people, esp. one who peeps in at windows; a voyeur; **peep'-show** a small entertainment, film or series of pictures, esp. of erotic or pornographic nature, viewed through a small hole, usually fitted with a magnifying glass.

peepul. See **pipal**.

peer[1] *pēr*, *n* an equal, fellow; a nobleman of the rank of baron upward, or (generally) a nobleman; a member of the House of Lords: — *fem* **peer'ess.** — *adj* **peer** pertaining to a peer group. — *n* **peer'age** the rank or dignity of a peer; the body of peers; a book of the genealogy, etc., of the different peers. — *adj* **peer'less** unequalled; matchless. — *adv* **peer'lessly.** — *n* **peer'lessness.** — **peer group** a group of people equal in age, rank, merit, etc.; **peer pressure** compulsion towards doing or obtaining the same things as others in one's peer group. — **life peer** or **peeress** a person invested with a non-hereditary peerage, entitling them to the title of baron or baroness and a seat in the House of Lords; **spiritual peer** a bishop or archbishop qualified to sit in the House of Lords; **temporal peer** any other member. [O.Fr. (Fr. *pair*) — L. *pār*, *paris*, equal.]

peer[2] *pēr*, *vi* to look narrowly or closely; to look with strain, or with half-closed eyes. — *adj* **peer'y.**

peevish *pēv'ish*, *adj* fretful, complaining; irritable; perverse. — *vt* **peeve** (back-formation) to irritate. — *vi* to be fretful; to show fretfulness. — *n* a fretful mood; a grievance, grouse. — *adj* **peeved** (*colloq*) annoyed. — *adv* **peev'ishly.** — *n* **peev'ishness.**

peewit *pē'wit*, *n* the lapwing. [Imit.]

peg *peg*, *n* a pin (esp. of wood); a fixture for hanging a hat or coat on; a pin for tuning a string (*music*); a small stake for securing tent-ropes, marking a position, boundary, claim, etc.; a pin for scoring as in cribbage; a drink measure, esp. of brandy and soda; a degree or step; a set level applied to e.g. an exchange rate or a price (*econ*); a wooden or other pin used in shoemaking; a clothes-peg; a cricket stump; a piton; a peg-top; a wooden leg (*colloq*); a leg (*colloq*); a theme (*fig*). — *vt* to fasten, mark, score, furnish, pierce or strike with a peg or pegs; to pin down; to insert or fix like a peg; to score (as at cribbage); to keep from falling or rising by buying or selling at a fixed price (*stock exchange*); to hold (prices, pensions, etc.) at a fixed level, or directly related to the cost of living; to stabilise; to throw or target. — *vi* (usu. with *away*) to keep on working assiduously; to make one's way vigorously: — *pr p* **pegg'ing**; *pa t* and *pa p* **pegged.** — *adj* **pegged.** — *n* **pegg'ing.** — **peg'board** a board having holes into which pegs are placed, used for playing and scoring in games or for display or storage purposes; **peg'-box** part of the head of a musical instrument in which the pegs are inserted; **peg'-leg** (*colloq*) a simple wooden leg; a man with a wooden leg. — **off the peg** of a garment, (bought) ready to wear from an already-existing stock; of an item, (bought) ready to use, not purpose-built; not adjusted to suit the circumstances, etc. (*fig*; *adj* **off-the-peg**'); **peg away** to work on assiduously; **peg back** (in sport, esp. racing) to gain an advantage over an opponent; **peg down** to restrict (someone) to an admission, following a certain course of action; **peg out** (in croquet) to finish by driving the ball against the peg; (in cribbage) to win by pegging the last hole before show of hands; to mark off with pegs; to become exhausted, be ruined, or die (*slang*); **round peg in a square hole** or **square peg in a round hole** someone who is unsuited to the particular position he or she occupies; **take down a peg (or two)** to bring down, deflate, humiliate or humble. [Cf. L.G. *pigge*, Du. dialect *peg*, Dan. *pig*.]

pegmatite *peg'mə-tīt*, *n* graphic granite, a granite with markings like Hebrew characters; a very coarsely crystallised granite, as in dykes and veins (*geol*); any very coarse-grained igneous rock occurring this way. — *adj* **pegmatitic** (*-tit'ik*). [Gr. *pēgma*, a bond, framework, from the root of *pēgnynai*, to fasten.]

PEI *abbrev* for Prince Edward Island.

peignoir *pen'wär*, *n* a woman's dressing-gown, esp. a fine, lightweight one. [Fr., — *peigner* — L. *pectināre*, to comb.]

pein. See **peen.**

peirastic *pī-ras'tik, adj* experimental; tentative. — *adv* **peiras'tically.** [Gr. *peirastikos* — *peira*, a trial.]

pejorate *pē'jər-āt* or *pi'jə-rāt, vt* to make worse. — *n* **pejorā'tion** a making or becoming worse; deterioration. — *adj* **pejor'ative** depreciating, disparaging. — *n* a depreciating word or suffix. — *adv* **pejor'atively.** [L. *pējor*, worse.]

pekan *pek'ən, n* a large North American marten with dark brown fur. [Can. Fr. *pékan* — Algonquin *pékané*.]

Pekingese or **Pekinese** *pē-kin-ēz', n* a native or inhabitant of Peking (now Beijing); esp. formerly, the chief dialect of Mandarin; a dwarf pug-dog of a breed brought from Peking (also *colloq* short form **peke**). — *adj* of *Peking*, China. — **Pekin** or **Pekin duck** a large white breed of duck, bred esp. for food; **Peking man** a type of fossil man first found (1929) S.W. of Peking, related to Java man.

pekoe *pēk'ō* or *pek'ō, n* a scented black tea. [Chin. *pek-ho*, white down.]

pelage *pel'ij, n* an animal's coat of hair or wool. [Fr.]

pelagic *pi-laj'ik, adj* of, inhabiting, or carried out in, the deep or open sea; living in the surface waters or middle depths of the sea; (of sediments) deposited under deep-water conditions. — *adj* **pelagian** (*pi-lā'ji-ən*) pelagic. — *n* a pelagic animal. [Gr. *pelagos*, sea.]

pelargonium *pel-ər-gō'ni-əm, n* any plant of a vast genus (*Pelargonium*) of the geranium family, having clusters of red, pink or white flowers, often cultivated under the name of geranium. [Gr. *pelargos*, stork, the beaked capsules resembling a stork's head.]

pelf *pelf*, (*derog*) *n* riches; money. [O.Fr. *pelfre*, booty; cf. **pilfer.**]

pelham *pel'əm, n* (often with *cap*) a type of bit on a horse's bridle, a combination of the curb and snaffle designs. [Perh. the name *Pelham*.]

pelican *pel'i-kən, n* a large water fowl, with enormous pouched bill. — **pel'ican-fish** a deep-sea fish (*Eurypharynx*) with an enormous mouth and a very little body; **pelican's-foot'** a type of marine gastropod mollusc, or its shell which has a lip like a webbed foot. [L.L. *pelicānus* — Gr. *pelekan*, *-ānos*, pelican.]

pelican crossing *pel'i-kən kros'ing, n* a pedestrian-operated street crossing, having a set of lights including an amber flashing light which indicates that motorists may proceed only if the crossing is clear. [Adapted from *pe*destrian *li*ght *con*trolled *crossing*.]

pelisse *pe-lēs', n* a lady's long mantle; orig. a fur-lined or fur garment, esp. a military cloak. [Fr., — L.L. *pellicea* (*vestis*) — L. *pellis*, a skin.]

pelite *pē'līt, n* any rock derived from clay or mud. — *adj* **pēlitic** (*-lit'ik*). — *n* **pēlother'apy** therapeutic treatment using mud. [Gr. *pēlos*, clay, mud.]

pellagra *pel-ag'rə* or *-āg'rə, n* a chronic disease marked by shrivelled skin, wasted body, mental illness and paralysis, caused by a dietary deficiency of certain vitamin-B, elements. — *n* **pellag'rin** someone afflicted with pellagra. — *adj* **pellag'rous** connected with, like, or afflicted with, pellagra. [Gr. *pella*, skin, *agrā*, seizure; or It. *pelle agra*, rough skin.]

pellet *pel'it, n* a little ball; a small rounded mass of compressed iron ore, waste material, etc.; a small pill; a ball of shot; a mass of undigested waste thrown up by a hawk or owl. — *vt* to form (e.g. seeds for planting) into a pellet by surrounding with a substance; to bombard with pellets. — *vt* **pell'etify, pell'etise** or **-ize** to form (esp. solid waste material, iron ore, etc.) into pellets. — *n* **pelletīsā'tion** or **-z-.** [O.Fr. *pelote* — L. *pīla*, a ball.]

pellicle *pel'i-kl, n* a thin skin or film. — *adj* **pellic'ūlar.** [L. *pellicula*, dimin. of *pellis*, skin.]

pellitory[1] *pel'i-tə-ri, n* a plant of the nettle family, growing esp. on walls (called *pellitory of the wall*), or another member of the genus *Parietaria*. [L. (*herba*) *parietāria* — *parietārius* — *pariēs*, *parietis*, a wall.]

pellitory[2] *pel'i-tə-ri, n* a North African and South European plant, known as *pellitory of Spain*, related to camomile; extended to various similar plants, such as yarrow. [M.E. *peletre* — L. *pyrethrum* — Gr. *pyrethron*, pellitory of Spain; see **pyrethrum.**]

pell-mell *pel-mel', adv* confusedly, promiscuously; headlong; helter-skelter; vehemently. — *adj* confusedly mingled; promiscuous, indiscriminate; headlong. — *n* disorder; confused mingling. [O.Fr. *pesle-mesle* (Fr. *pêle-mêle*), *-mesle* being from O.Fr. *mesler*, to mix, meddle; and *pesle*, a rhyming addition, perh. influenced by Fr. *pelle*, shovel.]

pellucid *pe-lū'sid* or *-lōō'sid, adj* perfectly clear; transparent. — *n* **pellucid'ity** or **pellu'cidness.** — *adv* **pellu'cidly.** [L. *pellūcidus* — *per*, through, *lūcidus*, clear.]

Pelmanism *pel'mən-izm, n* a system of mind training to improve the memory; (usu. without *cap*) a card game in which the cards are spread out face down and must be turned up in matching pairs. [The *Pelman* Institute, founded 1898, which devised the system.]

pelmet *pel'mit, n* a fringe, valance, or other device hiding a curtain rod. [Perh. Fr. *palmette*.]

Peloponnesian *pel-ō-pə-nē'zhən, -zhyən* or *-zyən, adj* of the Peloponnese, the southern peninsula of Greece. — *n* a native of the Peloponnese. — **Peloponnesian War** a war between Athens and Sparta, 431–404 B.C. [Gr. *Peloponnēsos*, Peloponnese — *Pelops* son of Tantalus, *nēsos*, an island.]

pelorus *pel-ör'əs, n* a kind of compass from which bearings can be taken. [Perh. *Pelorus*, Hannibal's pilot.]

pelota *pel-ō'tə, n* a ball-game, of Basque origin, resembling fives, using a basket catching and throwing device (also **jai alai**); the ball used for this game. [Sp. *pelota*, ball.]

pelotherapy. See under **pelite.**

pelt[1] *pelt, n* a raw animal hide; a hawk's prey when killed, especially when torn. — *n* **pelt'ry** the skins of animals with the fur on them; furs. [App. a back-formation from *peltry* — O.Fr. *pelleterie* — L. *pellis*, a skin.]

pelt[2] *pelt, vt* to hurl, or fire, in a persistent or rapid stream; to assail with a torrent of missiles or blows, or of words, reproaches, pamphlets, etc.; to shower. — *vi* to shower blows or missiles; (of rain, hail, etc.) to beat vigorously (sometimes with *down*); to speak angrily; to speed. — *n* a blow; a pelting; a downpour, as of rain; a storm of rage; a rapid pace. — *n* **pelt'er.** — *vi* to go full pelt. — *n* and *adj* **pelt'ing.** — **full pelt** or **at full pelt** at full speed.

peltry. See **pelt**[1].

pelvis *pel'vis*, (*anat*) *n* the bony cavity at the lower end of the trunk; the bony frame enclosing it; the cavity of the kidney: — *pl* **pel'vises** or **pel'ves** (*-vēz*). — *adj* **pel'vic.** — **pelvic fin** a fish's paired fin homologous with a mammal's hindleg; **pelvic girdle** or **arch** the posterior limb-girdle of vertebrates, with which the hind-limbs articulate, consisting of the haunch-bones (ilium, pubis and ischium united), which articulate with the sacrum. — **pelvic inflammatory disease** a damaging inflammatory condition affecting a woman's pelvic organs, esp. the Fallopian tubes, caused by a bacterial infection. [L. *pelvis*, a basin.]

pemmican or **pemican** *pem'i-kən, n* a North American Indian preparation of lean flesh-meat, dried, pounded, and mixed with fat and other ingredients; a highly condensed, nutritious preparation of dried ingredients, used esp. as emergency rations. [Cree *pimekan*.]

pemoline *pem'ə-lēn, n* a stimulant of the central nervous system, used esp. in the treatment of fatigue, depression and memory loss.

pemphigus *pem'fi-gəs, n* a diseased condition of the skin with watery vesicles. — *adj* **pem'phigoid.** — *adj* **pem'phigous.** [False Latin — Gr. *pemphix, -īgos,* blister.]

PEN *pen, abbrev* for (the International Association of) Poets, Playwrights, Editors, Essayists and Novelists.

Pen. *abbrev* for Peninsula.

pen[1] *pen, n* a small enclosure, esp. for animals; a covered dock, as for servicing submarines; animals kept in, and enough to fill, a pen; a cattle farm (*Caribb*); an estate or plantation (*Caribb*). — *vt* to put or keep in a pen; to confine; to dam: — *pr p* **penn'ing;** *pa t* and *pa p* **penned** or **pent.** — **pen'fold** a fold for penning cattle or sheep; a pound. — **submarine pen** a dock for a submarine, esp. if protected from attack from above by a deep covering of concrete. [O.E. *penn,* pen.]

pen[2] *pen, n* an instrument used for writing (with ink or otherwise), formerly made of a quill, but now of other materials; a quill; a large feather; a nib; writing, literary style; a cuttle-bone. — *vt* to write, to commit to paper: — *pr p* **penn'ing;** *pa t* and *pa p* **penned.** — *n* **pen'ful** as much ink as a pen can hold. — *adj* **penned** written; quilled. — **pen-and-ink'** writing materials; a pen drawing. — *adj* writing; written; (of a drawing) executed with pen and ink. — **pen'-case** a receptacle for a pen or pens; **pen friend** or **pen pal** an otherwise unknown person (usu. abroad) with whom one corresponds; **pen'knife** a small pocket-knife; orig. a knife for making or mending pens; **pen'light** a small pen-shaped electric torch (**pen-light battery** a long, thin battery, as used in a penlight); **pen'man,** *fem* **pen'woman** a person skilled in handwriting; a writer or author; **pen'-manship; pen name** a writer's assumed name; **pen'-nib** a nib for a pen. [O.Fr. *penne* — L. *penna,* a feather.]

pen[3]. Slang short form of **penitentiary.**

pen[4] *pen, n* a female swan.

penal *pē'nl, adj* pertaining to, liable to, imposing, constituting, or used for, punishment; constituting a penalty; very severe. — *n* **pēnalīsā'tion** or **-z-.** — *vt* **pē'nalise** or **-ize** to impose a penalty or disadvantage on (e.g. someone guilty of an offence or lapse); to make (something) punishable. — *adv* **pē'nally.** — **penal code** a codified system of law relating to crime and punishment; **penal laws** laws imposing penalties, esp. (*hist*) in matters of religion; **penal servitude** hard labour in a prison under different conditions from ordinary imprisonment, substituted in 1853 for transportation, abolished 1948; **penal settlement** a settlement peopled by convicts. [L. *poenālis* — *poena* — Gr. *poinē,* punishment.]

penalty *pen'l-ti, n* suffering or loss imposed for breach of a law; a fine or loss agreed upon in case of non-fulfilment of some undertaking; punishment; a fine; a disadvantage imposed upon a competitor for breach of a rule of the game, for failing to attain what is aimed at, as a handicap, or for any other reason arising out of the rules; a penalty kick, shot or stroke; a loss or suffering brought upon one by one's own actions or condition; a score for an opponent's failure to complete a contract or for the bidder's success when the call is doubled (*bridge*). — **penalty area** or **box** (in association football) the area or box in front of the goal in which a foul by the defending team may result in a penalty kick being awarded against them; **penalty bench** or **box** (in ice-hockey) an area or box beside the rink in which a player must stay for his or her allotted penalty period; **penalty corner** (in hockey) a free stroke taken on the goal line; **penalty goal** one scored by a penalty kick or shot; **penalty kick** a free kick, or the privilege granted to a player to kick the ball as he or she pleases, because of some breach of the rules by the opposing side; **penalty shot; penalty spot** (in association football and men's hockey) a spot in front of the goal from which a penalty kick or shot is taken. — **death penalty** punishment by putting to death; **under** or **on penalty of** with liability in case of infraction to the penalty of. [L.L. *poenālitās;* see ety. for **penal.**]

penance *pen'əns, n* an act of humiliation or punishment, either self-imposed or imposed by a priest, to express or show evidence of sorrow for sin; the sacrament by which absolution is conveyed (*RC* and *Orthodox Church*); expiation; hardship. [O.Fr.; cf. **penitence.**]

penannular *pen-an'ū-lər, adj* in the form of an almost complete ring. [L. *paene,* almost, *annulāris,* annular.]

pence *pens, n* a plural of **penny;** a new penny (*colloq*).

penchant *pã'shã, n* inclination; decided taste; bias. [Fr., pres. p. of *pencher,* to incline — assumed L.L. *pendicāre* — L. *pendēre,* to hang.]

pencil *pen'sl, n* a writing or drawing instrument that leaves a streak of blacklead, chalk, slate, or other solid matter, esp. one of blacklead enclosed in wood and sharpened as required; a small stick of various materials shaped like a lead-pencil, for medical, cosmetic, or other purpose; a system of straight lines meeting in a point (*geom*); a set of rays of light diverging from or converging to a point (*optics*); a narrow beam of light (*phys*); something long, fine and narrow in shape. — *vt* to paint, draw, write or mark with a pencil; (with *in*) to enter provisionally, as in a diary; to note (something) allowing for or expecting later alteration (*fig*); to apply a pencil to: — *pr p* **pen'cilling;** *pa t* and *pa p* **pen'cilled.** — *adj* **pen'cilled.** — *n* **pen'ciller.** — *n* **pen'cilling** the art or act of painting, writing, sketching or marking with a pencil; marks made with a pencil; fine lines; the marking of joints in brickwork with white paint. — **pen'cil-case** a case for pencils; metal case used to hold a piece of blacklead, etc., for writing; **pen'cil-lead** graphite for pencils; a stick of it for a metal pencil-case; **pen'cil-sharpener** an instrument for sharpening lead-pencils by rotation against a blade or blades; **pencil skirt** a straight, close-fitting skirt. [O.Fr. *pincel* (Fr. *pinceau*) — L. *pēnicillum,* a painter's brush, dimin. of *pēnis,* a tail.]

pend *pend, vi* to hang, as in a balance, to impend. — *adj* **pend'ing** hanging; impending; remaining undecided; not fully dealt with or completed. — *prep* during; until, awaiting. [Fr. *pendre* or L. *pendēre,* to hang; sometimes aphetic for **append** or for **depend.**]

pendant or sometimes **pendent** *pen'dənt, n* anything hanging, especially for ornament; a hanging ornament, esp. one worn around the neck; a lamp hanging from the roof; an ornament of wood or of stone hanging downwards from a roof; a pennant (*naut*); anything attached to another thing of the same kind. — *n* **pen'dency** a state or quality of being pendent. — *adj* **pen'dent** (sometimes **pen'dant**) hanging; dangling; drooping; overhanging; not yet decided; grammatically incomplete, left in suspense. — *n* **pendentive** (*pen-dent'iv; archit*) a spherical triangle formed by a dome springing from a square base. — *adv* **pen'dently.** [Fr. *pendant,* pres. p. of *pendre,* to hang — L. *pendēns, -entis* — pres. p. of *pendēre,* to hang.]

pendente lite *pen-den'tē lī'tē* or *pen-den'te li'te,* (L.) during the process of litigation.

pendulum *pen'dū-ləm, n* any weight hung from a fixed point so as to swing freely; the swinging weight which regulates the movement of a clock; anything that undergoes obvious and regular shifts or reversals in direction, attitude, opinion, etc.: — *pl* **pen'dulums.** — *adj* **pen'dular** relating to a pendulum. — *n* **pendulos'ity.** — *adj* **pen'dulous** hanging loosely; swinging freely; drooping; dangling; suspended from the top; floating in air or space. — *adv*

pen'dulously. — *n* **pen'dulousness.** [Neut. of L. *pendulus*, hanging — *pendēre*, to hang.]

peneplain *pē'ni-plān*, *n* a land surface so worn down by denudation as to be almost a plain. [L. *paene*, almost, and **plain**.]

penes. See **penis.**

penetrate *pen'i-trāt*, *vt* to thrust or force a way into the inside of; to pierce into or through; to insert the penis into the vagina of; to force entry within a country's borders or through an enemy's front line (*mil*); to gain access into and influence within (a country, organisation, market, etc.) for political, financial, etc., purposes; to permeate; to reach the mind or feelings of; to pierce with the eye or understanding, see into or through, whether with the eye or with the intellect (*fig*); to understand. — *vi* to make way or pass inwards. — *n* **penetrability** (*-trə-bil'i-ti*) or **pen'etrableness.** — *adj* **pen'etrable.** — *adv* **pen'etrably** so as to be penetrated. — *n* **pen'etrance** (*genetics*) the frequency, expressed as a percentage, with which a gene exhibits an effect. — *n* **pen'etrancy.** — *adj* **pen'etrant** penetrating. — *n* (*chem*) a substance which increases the penetration of a liquid into porous material or between contiguous surfaces, by lowering its surface tension. — *adj* **pen'etrāting** piercing; having keen and deep insight; sharp; keen; discerning. — *adv* **pen'etrātingly.** — *n* **penetrā'tion** the act or power of penetrating or entering; acuteness; discernment; the sexual act of inserting the penis into the vagina; the process and practices of espionage or infiltration within an organisation, country, etc.; the space-penetrating power of a telescope. — *adj* **pen'etrātive** tending or able to penetrate; piercing; having keen and deep insight; reaching and affecting the mind. — *adv* **pen'etrātively.** — *n* **pen'etrātiveness.** — *n* **pen'etrātor.** — **penetration agent** a person employed to penentrate and obtain information within an organisation, country, etc. [L. *penetrāre, -ātum* — *penes*, in the house, possession, or power of.]

penfold. See **pen**[1].

penguin *peng'gwin* or *pen'gwin*, *n* any bird of a family of flightless sea birds (*Spheniscidae*) of the Southern Hemisphere, with modified flipper-like wings used for swimming, and black or bluish plumage except for the white breast. — *n* **pen'guinery** or **pen'guinry** a penguin breeding-place. [According to some, Welsh *pen*, head, *gwyn*, white, or the corresponding Breton words; others suggest *pin-wing*, or L. *pinguis*, fat.]

penial. See **penis.**

penicillate *pen-i-sil'it, -āt* or *pen'*, *adj* tufted; forming a tuft; brush-shaped. — *adj* **penicill'iform** paint-brush-shaped. — *n* **penicill'in** a group of substances that stop the growth of bacteria, extracted from moulds, esp. of the genus of fungi, **Penicill'ium** (**Ascomycetes**; see under **ascus**), which includes also the mould of jam, cheese, etc. — *n* **penicill'inase** an enzyme, produced by certain bacteria, that inactivates the effect of some penicillins. [L. *pēnicillus*, paint-brush, dimin. of *pēnis*, tail.]

penile. See **penis.**

penillion. See **pennill.**

peninsula *pen-in'sū-lə*, *n* a piece of land that is almost an island. — *adj* **penin'sular.** — *n* **peninsular'ity.** — **Peninsular War** the war in Spain and Portugal carried on by Great Britain against Napoleon's marshals (1808–14). [L. *paenīnsula* — *paene*, almost, *īnsula*, an island.]

penis *pē'nis*, *n* the external male organ used for copulation, and also (in mammals) for the excretion of urine: — *pl* **pē'nises** or **pē'nes** (*-nēz*). — *adj* **pē'nial** or **pē'nile.** — **penis envy** (*psychol*) the Freudian concept of a woman's subconscious wish for male characteristics. [L. *pēnis*, orig. a tail.]

penitent *pen'i-tənt*, *adj* suffering pain or sorrow for past sin, and feeling a desire to reform; contrite; repentant; undergoing penance. — *n* a person who repents of his or her sin; someone who has confessed sin, and is undergoing penance; a member of one of various orders devoted to penitential exercises, etc. (*RC*). — *n* **pen'itence.** — *adj* **penitential** (*pen-i-ten'shl*). — *n* a book of rules relating to penance; a penitent. — *adv* **peniten'tially.** — *adj* **penitentiary** (*-ten'shə-ri*) relating to penance; penal and reformatory; penitential. — *n* a reformatory prison or house of correction; a prison (*US*); a book for guidance in imposing penances; a R.C. office (under the *Grand Penitentiary*) at Rome dealing with cases of penance, dispensations, etc. — *adv* **pen'itently.** [L. *paenitēns, -entis*, pres. p. of *paenitēre*, to cause to repent, to repent.]

penknife, penlight, penman. See under **pen**[2].

Penn. *abbrev* for Pennsylvania (U.S. state).

penna *pen'ə*, (*ornithol*) *n* a feather, esp. one of the large feathers of the wings or tail: — *pl* **penn'ae** (*-ē*). — *adj* **penn'ate** pinnate; winged, feathered, or like a wing in shape. [L. *penna*, feather.]

pennant *pen'ənt* or (*naut*) *pen'ən*, *n* a dangling line from the masthead, etc., with a block for tackle, etc. (*naut*); a long narrow flag; a signalling or identifying flag; a pennon. — **broad pennant** a long swallow-tailed flag flown by a commodore. [A combination of **pendant** and **pennon.**]

pennate. See **penna.**

penniless. See **penny.**

pennill *pen'il* or in Welsh *pen'ihl*, *n* a form of Welsh improvised verse: — *pl* **penill'ion.** [Welsh, lit. a verse or stanza.]

pennon *pen'ən*, *n* a long narrow flag or streamer. [O.Fr. *penon*, streamer, arrow-feather, prob. — L. *penna*, feather.]

penn'orth. See **pennyworth** under **penny.**

penny *pen'i*, *n* a bronze coin, equal to a hundredth part of £1 (also **new penny**), until 1971 worth 1/12 of a shilling, or 1/240 of a pound; its value; applied to various more or less similar coins; a cent (*US colloq*); a small sum; money in general: — *pl* **pennies** *pen'iz* (as material objects) or **pence** *pens* (as units of value). — *adj* sold for a penny; costing a penny. — *adj* **penn'iless** without a penny; without money; poor. — *n* **penn'ilessness.** — **penny arcade** an amusement arcade with slot machines orig. operated by a penny; **penny black** the first adhesive postage stamp, issued by Britain, 1840; **penn'ycress** a cruciferous plant of the genus *Thlaspi*, with round flat pods; **penny dreadful** see under **dread; penny-far'thing** an old-fashioned bicycle with a big wheel and a little one. — *adj* **penny-in-the-slot'** worked by putting a penny (or other coin) in a slot. — **penn'y-piece** a penny. — *adj* **penn'y-pinching** miserly, too concerned with saving money; **penny share** or **stock** (*stock exchange*) a share or stock trading for less than £1 or $1, usu. bought very speculatively; **penn'yweight** a unit equal to twenty-four grains of troy weight; **penny-whist'le** a tin whistle or flageolet. — *adj* **penn'y-wise** saving small sums at the risk of larger; niggardly on unsuitable occasions. — **penn'ywort** a name given to various plants with round leaves; **penn'yworth** a penny's worth of anything; the amount that can be got for a penny; a good bargain. — Also **penn'orth** (*pen'ərth*; *colloq*). — **a penny for your thoughts** (*colloq*) what are you thinking so deeply about?; **a pretty penny** a considerable sum of money; **in penny numbers** a very few, or a very little, at a time; **pennies from heaven** money obtained without effort and unexpectedly; **Peter's pence** a tax or tribute of a silver penny paid to the Pope — in England perhaps from the time of Offa of Mercia, in Ireland from Henry II, abolished under Henry VIII; a voluntary contribution to the Pope in modern times; **spend a penny** (*euph*) to urinate; **the penny drops** now I (etc.)

understand; **turn an honest penny** to earn some money honestly; **two a penny** in abundant supply and of little value. [O.E. *penig*.]

pennyroyal *pen-i-roi'əl*, *n* a species of mint once valued medicinally. [M.E. *puliol real* — A.Fr. — L. *pūleium*, *pūlegium*, pennyroyal.]

penology or **poenology** *pē-nol'ə-ji*, *n* the study of punishment in its relation to crime; the management of prisons. — *adj* **penological** (*-nə-loj'*). — *n* **penologist** (*-nol'ə-jist*). [Gr. *poinē*, punishment, *logos*, discourse.]

pensile *pen'sīl* or *-sil*, *adj* hanging; suspended; overhanging; (of birds) building a hanging nest. — *n* **pen'sileness** or **pensility** (*-sil'i-ti*). [L. *pēnsilis* — *pendēre*, to hang.]

pension *pen'shən*, *n* a Government allowance of money to a person who has retired or has been disabled, has reached old age, been widowed or orphaned, etc.; an allowance paid by an employer to a retired employee; an allowance paid as a bribe for future services, as a mark of favour, or in reward for one's own or another's merit; (now pronounced as Fr., *pã-syɔ̃*) a continental boarding-house; board. — *vt* to grant a pension to. — *adj* **pen'sionable** entitled, or entitling, to a pension. — *adj* **pen'sionary** receiving a pension; of the nature of a pension. — *n* a person who receives a pension; someone whose interest is bought by a pension. — *n* **pen'sioner** a person who receives a pension; a dependent. — **pension off** to dismiss, or allow to retire, with a pension. [Fr., — L. *pēnsiō*, *-ōnis* — *pendĕre*, *pēnsum*, to weigh, pay.]

pensive *pen'siv*, *adj* meditative; expressing thoughtfulness with sadness. — *adv* **pen'sively**. — *n* **pen'siveness**. [Fr. *pensif*, *-ive* — *penser*, to think — L. *pēnsāre*, to weigh — *pendĕre*, to weigh.]

penstemon *pen-stē'mən* or **pentstemon** *pen(t)-stē'mən*, *n* any plant of a mainly N. American showy-flowered genus of Scrophulariaceae, with a sterile fifth stamen. [Gr. *pente*, five, *stēmōn*, warp, as if stamen.]

penstock *pen'stok*, *n* a sluice; (in a hydroelectric or other plant) a valve-controlled water conduit. [**pen**[1] and **stock**[1].]

pent *pa t* and *pa p* of **pen**[1], to shut up. — *adj* **pent'-up** held in; repressed.

pent- *pent-* or **penta-** *pen-tə-*, *combining form* denoting five. [Gr. *pente*, five.]

pentachord *pen'tə-kōrd*, *n* a musical instrument with five strings; a diatonic series of five notes. [**penta-** and Gr. *chordē*, string.]

pentacle *pent'ə-kl*, *n* a pentagram or similar figure (sometimes a hexagram) or amulet used as a defence against demons. [L.L. *pentaculum*, or O.Fr. *pentacol* — *pendre*, to hang, *ā*, on, *col*, the neck.]

pentad *pent'ad*, *n* a set of five things; a period of five years or five days. — Also *adj*. — *adj* **pentad'ic**. [Gr. *pentas*, *-ados*.]

pentadactyl *pen-tə-dak'til*, *n* having five digits. — *n* a person with five fingers and five toes. — *adj* **pentadactyl'ic** or **pentadac'tylous**. — *n* **pentadac'tylism**. — *n* **pentadac'tyly**. [**penta-** and Gr. *daktylos*, finger, toe.]

pentagon *pen'tə-gon*, *n* a rectilineal plane figure having five angles and five sides (*geom*); (with *cap*) the headquarters of the U.S. armed forces at Washington — from the shape of the building. — *adj* **pentagonal** (*pen-tag'ən-əl*). — *adv* **pentag'onally**. [Gr. *pentagōnon* — *pente*, five, *gōnia*, angle.]

pentagram *pent'ə-gram*, *n* a stellate pentagon or five-pointed star; a magic figure of that form. [Gr. *pentagrammon* — *pente*, five, *gramma*, a letter.]

pentahedron *pen-tə-hē'drən*, *n* a five-faced solid figure: — *pl* **pentahē'drons** or **pentahē'dra**. — *adj* **pentahē'dral**. [**penta-** and Gr. *hedrā*, a seat.]

pentamerism *pen-tam'ər-izm*, *n* the condition of being pentamerous. — *adj* **pentam'erous** having five parts or members; having parts in fives. — *n* **pentam'ery**. [**penta-** and Gr. *meros*, a part.]

pentameter *pen-tam'ə-tər*, *n* a verse of five measures or feet. [Gr. *pentametros* — *pente*, five, *metron*, a measure.]

pentamidine *pen-tam'i-dēn*, (*pharm*) *n* a drug first used to combat tropical diseases such as sleeping-sickness, later found effective against a form of pneumonia common in AIDS patients. [*pent*ane, *amid*e and chem. sfx. *-ine*.]

pentane *pent'ān*, (*chem*) *n* a hydrocarbon (C_5H_{12}), fifth member of the methane series. [**penta-**.]

pentangle *pent'ang-gl*, *n* a pentacle; a pentagon. — *adj* **pentang'ular**. [**pent-** and **angle**[1].]

pentaprism *pent'ə-prizm*, (*phot*) *n* a five-sided prism that corrects lateral inversion by turning light through an angle of 90°, used on reflex cameras to allow eye-level viewing. [**penta-**.]

pentasyllabic *pen-tə-si-lab'ik*, *adj* five-syllabled. [**penta-**.]

Pentateuch *pen'tə-tūk*, *n* the first five books of the Old Testament. — *adj* **pentateuch'al**. [Gr. *pentateuchos*, five-volumed — *teuchos*, a tool (later, a book).]

pentathlon *pen-tath'lon*, *n* a sporting contest made up of five exercises — wrestling, disc-throwing, spear-throwing, leaping, running; a five-event contest at the modern Olympic games from 1906–24; a five-event Olympic games contest for women; **(modern pentathlon)** an Olympic games contest consisting of swimming, cross-country riding and running, fencing and revolver-shooting. [Gr. *penthalon* — *pente*, five, *athlon*, contest.]

pentatomic *pent-ə-tom'ik*, (*chem*) *adj* having five atoms, esp. five atoms of replaceable hydrogen; pentavalent. [**pent-**.]

pentatonic *pent-ə-ton'ik*, (*mus*) *adj* consisting of five tones or notes — applied esp. to a scale, a major scale with the fourth and seventh omitted. [**penta-** and Gr. *tonos*, tone.]

pentavalent *pen-tə-vā'lənt* or *pen-tav'ə-lənt*, (*chem*) *n* having a valency of five. [**penta-**.]

Pentecost *pent'i-kost*, *n* a Jewish festival held on the fiftieth day after the second day of the Passover (also called the **Feast of Weeks** and **Shabuoth**); the Christian festival of Whitsuntide, seven weeks after Easter. — *adj* **Pentecost'al** of or relating to Pentecost; of or relating to any of several fundamentalist Christian groups placing great emphasis on the spiritual powers of the Holy Spirit. — *n* **Pentecost'alist** a member of a Pentecostal church. [Gr. *pentēkostē* (*hēmerā*), fiftieth (day).]

penthouse *pent'hows*, *n* a separate room or dwelling on a roof; a (small) select top flat; a protection from the weather over a door or a window; (in real tennis) a roofed corridor surrounding the court: — *pl* **pent'houses** (*-how-ziz*). — *vt* to provide or cover with, or as with, a penthouse. [For *pentice* — Fr. *appentis* — L.L. *appendicium*, an appendage.]

pentimento *pen-ti-men'tō*, (*art*) *n* something painted out of a picture which later becomes visible again: — *pl* **pentimen'ti** (*-tē*). [It. — *pentirsi*, to repent.]

pentobarbitone *pen-tə-bär'bit-ōn*, or in U.S. **pentobarbital** *-bär'bi-tal*, (*pharm*) *n* a barbiturate drug with hypnotic, sedative and anticonvulsant effects.

pentode *pent'ōd*, (*electr*) *n* a thermionic tube with five electrodes. [Gr. *pente*, five, *hodos*, way.]

pentose *pent'ōs*, (*chem*) *n* a sugar (of various kinds) with five oxygen atoms. [**pent-** and chem. sfx. *-ose*, to denote a sugar.]

Pentothal® *pen'tō-thal*, *n* thiopentone sodium (in N.Am. thiopental sodium), an intravenous anaesthetic, a sodium thiobarbiturate compound.

pentoxide *pent-ok'sīd*, (*chem*) *n* a compound having five atoms of oxygen combined with another element or radical. [**pent-**.]

pentroof *pent'ro͞of*, *n* a roof that slopes one way only. [From **penthouse**, app. influenced by Fr. *pente*, slope.]

pentstemon. See **penstemon**.

penuchle. See **pinochle**.

penult *pi-nult'* or **penultima** *-ult'i-mə*, *n* the last but one syllable. — *adj* **penult'imate** last but one. — *n* the penult; the last but one. [L. *paene*, almost, *ultimus*, last.]

penumbra *pen-um'brə*, *n* a partial or lighter shadow round the perfect or darker shadow of an eclipse; the less dark border of a sunspot or any similar spot; the part of a picture where the light and shade blend into each other. — *adj* **penum'bral** or **penum'brous.** [L. *paene*, almost, *umbra*, shade.]

penury *pen'ū-ri*, *n* great poverty; want, lack. — *adj* **penū'rious** niggardly; miserly. — *adv* **penū'riously.** — *n* **penū'riousness.** [L. *pēnūria*.]

peon *pē'on*, *n* a day-labourer, esp. formerly in Spanish-speaking America, one working off a debt by bondage; in India (*pūn*), a foot-soldier (*hist*), policeman (*hist*), or messenger; in S.E. Asia, a minor office worker. — *n* **pē'onage** or **pē'onism** agricultural servitude of the above kind. [Sp. *peón* and Port. *peão* — L.L. *pedō*, *-ōnis*, a foot-soldier.]

peony or **paeony** *pē'ə-ni*, *n* any plant of the genus *Paeonia*, of the buttercup family, with large showy crimson or white globular flowers; its flower. [O.E. *peonie* and O.Fr. *pione* — L. *paeōnia* — Gr. *paiōniā* — *Paiōn*, *Paiān*, physician of the gods, from its use in medicine.]

people *pē'pl*, *n* a set of persons; a nation; a community; a body of persons held together by belief in common origin, speech, culture, political union, or by a common leadership, headship, etc.; the mass of the nation; general population; populace; the citizens; voters; subjects; followers; employees; congregation; attendants; members of one's household or family; parents; ancestors and descendants; inhabitants of a place; the persons associated with any business; laity; (approaching a *pronoun*) they, one, folks — in these senses used as *pl*. — Often used in combination to denote belonging or relating to the people, general populace (as in *people-power*, *people-oriented*, etc.). — *vt* to stock with people or inhabitants; to inhabit; to occupy as if inhabiting. — **people's democracy** a form of government in which the proletariat, represented by the Communist Party, holds power — seen ideologically as a transitional state on the way to full socialism; **people's front** same as **popular front**; **People's Republic** a name adopted by some socialist or communist states. [O.Fr. *poeple* — L. *pŏpulus*.]

PEP *pep*, *abbrev* for: personal equity plan; political and economic planning.

pep *pep*, (*colloq*) *n* vigour, go, spirit, life. — *vt* to put pep into (usu. with *up*). — *adj* **pep'ful** or **pepp'y.** — **pep pill** a pill containing a stimulant drug; **pep talk** a strongly-worded talk designed to arouse enthusiasm for a cause or course of action. [**pepper.**]

peperomia *pep-ər-ō'mi-ə*, *n* any plant of the large genus of subtropical herbaceous plants *Peperomia*, many grown as house plants for their ornamental foliage. [Gr. *peperi*, pepper, *homoios*, like, similar.]

pepino *pə-pē'nō*, *n* a purple-striped pale yellow fruit with sweet flesh, oval (often elongated) in shape; the spiny-leaved S. American plant (*Solanum muricatum*) that bears this fruit. — Also called **mel'on-pear.** [Sp., cucumber.]

peplos *pep'los* or **peplus** *pep'ləs*, *n* a draped outer robe worn usu. by women in ancient Greece. — *n* **pep'lum** a short skirt-like section attached to the waistline of a dress, blouse or jacket; an overskirt supposed to be like the peplos. [Gr. *peplos*.]

pepo *pē'pō*, *n* a large many-seeded berry, usually with hard epicarp — the type of fruit found in the melon and cucumber family: — *pl* **pē'pos.** [L. *pĕpō*, *-ōnis*.]

pepper *pep'ər*, *n* a pungent aromatic condiment consisting of the dried berries of the pepper plant, whole or ground (*black pepper*), or ground with the outer parts removed (*white pepper*); any plant of the genus *Piper*, esp. *P. nigrum*, or of the family *Piperaceae*; a plant of the genus *Capsicum* or one of its pods (*red*, *yellow* or *green pepper*; also called **sweet pepper**); cayenne (also **cayenne pepper**); extended to various similar condiments and the plants producing them. — *vt* to sprinkle or flavour with pepper; to sprinkle, spray; to pelt with bullets, etc.; to pelt thoroughly. — *vi* to pelt; to shower liberally; to fire bullets, etc., in showers. — *n* **pepp'eriness.** — *n* **pepp'ering.** — *adj* **pepp'ery** having the taste or qualities of pepper; pungent; hot, choleric, irritable. — *adj* **pepper-and-salt'** mingled black and white; (of hair) flecked with grey. — **pepp'ercorn** the dried berry of the pepper plant; something of little value. — *adj* like a peppercorn; trivial, nominal, as in *peppercorn rent*; **pepp'ermill** a small handmill in which peppercorns are ground; **pepp'ermint** an aromatic and pungent species of mint (*Mentha piperita*); the essence distilled from it; a sweet flavoured with it (**peppermint cream** a sweet creamy peppermint-flavoured substance; a sweet made of this; **pepp'ermint-drop** a peppermint-flavoured, usu. hard, sweet); **pepp'er-pot** a pot or container with a perforated top for sprinkling pepper; a West Indian dish of the juice of a bitter cassava, meat or dried fish, and vegetables, esp. green okra and chillies. [O.E. *pipor* — L. *piper* — Gr. *peperi* — Sans. *pippali*.]

pepperoni or **peperoni** *pep-ə-rō'ni*, *n* a hard, spicy beef and pork sausage. [It. *peperoni*, pl. of *peperone*, chilli, pepper — L. *piper*, pepper.]

peppy. See **pep**.

pepsin *pep'sin*, (*biol*) *n* any of a group of digestive enzymes in the gastric juice of vertebrates, which breaks down proteins under acidic conditions. — *vt* **pep'sinate** to treat, mix or combine with pepsin. — *n* **pep'sinogen** a zymogen found in granular form in the mucous membrane of the stomach mucosa which converts into pepsin in a slightly acid medium. — *adj* **pep'tic** relating to or promoting digestion; of or relating to pepsin or the digestive juices. — *n* **pep'tidase** an enzyme which breaks down peptides into their constituent amino acids. — *n* **pep'tide** any of a number of substances formed from amino-acids in which the amino-group of one is joined to the carboxyl group of another. — *n* **pep'tōne** a product of the action of enzymes on proteins, used e.g. as a bacteriological culture medium. — **peptic ulcer** an ulcer of the stomach or duodenum, etc. [Gr. *pepsis*, digestion — *peptein*, to digest.]

per[1] *pûr* or *pər*, *prep* for each, a; (chiefly commercial) by. — **as per usual** (*colloq* or *illit*) as usual. [L. and O.Fr. *per*.]

per[2] *pûr* or *per*, (L.) *prep* through, by means of, according to (also **as per**). — **per annum, diem** or **mensem** (*an'əm* or *-o͞om*, *dī'əm* or *dē'em*, *men'səm* or *-sem*) yearly, daily or monthly; **per capita** (*kap'i-tə*) (counting) by heads; for each person; all sharing alike; **per contra** (*kon'trə* or *kon'trä*) on the contrary; as a contrast; **per impossibile** (*im-po-si'bi-le*) by an impossibility; if it were so, which it is not; **per procurationem** (*prok-ū-rā-shi-ō'nem* or *prō-ko͞o-rä-ti-ō'nem*) by the agency of another, by proxy; **per se** (*sē* or *sā*) by himself, etc.; essentially; in itself.

per- *pûr-* or *pər-*, *combining form* denoting: (1) the highest degree of combination with oxygen or other element or radical (*chem*); (2) in words from Latin, through, beyond or thoroughly, or indicating destruction.

peradventure *pûr-əd-ven'chər*, *adv* by chance; perhaps. [O.Fr. *per* (or *par*) *aventure*, by chance.]

perambulate *pər-am'bū-lāt, vt* to walk through, about, around, up and down, or over; to pass through for the purpose of surveying; to wheel in a perambulator. — *vi* to walk about. — *n* **perambulā'tion**. — *n* **peram'bulātor** a person who perambulates; a wheel for measuring distances on roads; a light carriage for a baby (now usu. **pram**). — *adj* **peram'bulatory**. [L. *perambulāre, -ātum* — *per*, through, *ambulāre*, to walk.]

per an. *abbrev* for per annum (see **per**[2]).

Perca. See **perch**[1].

percale *per-käl'* or *pər-kāl', n* a closely woven French cambric. — *n* **percaline** (*pûr-kə-lēn'* or *pûr'-*) a glossy cotton cloth. [Fr.; cf. Pers. *purgālah*, rag.]

perceive *pər-sēv', vt* to become or be aware of through the senses; to get knowledge of by the mind; to see; to understand; to discern. — **perceived noise decibel** a unit used to measure the amount of annoyance caused to people by noise. [O.Fr. *percever* — L. *percipěre, perceptum* — pfx. *per-*, thoroughly, *capěre*, to take.]

per cent (sometimes written or printed with a point after it as if an abbreviation for *per centum*, but pronounced as a complete word, *pər-sent'*) in the hundred; for each hundred or hundred pounds. — *n* a percentage; (in *pl*) securities yielding a specified percentage (e.g. *three-percents*). — *n* **percent'age** rate per hundred; an allowance of so much for every hundred; a proportional part; commission (*colloq*); profit, advantage (*colloq*). — *adj* **percen'tile**. — *n* the value below which falls a specified percentage (as 25, 50, 75) of a large number of statistical units (e.g. scores in an examination); percentile rank. — **percentile rank** grading according to percentile group. — **play the percentages** (in sport, gambling, etc.) to play, operate or proceed by means of unspectacular safe shots, moves, etc. as opposed to spectacular but risky ones which may not succeed, on the assumption that this is more likely to lead to success in the long run. [L. *per centum*.]

percept *pûr'sept, n* an object perceived by the senses; the mental result of perceiving. — *n* **perceptibil'ity**. — *adj* **percep'tible** that can be perceived; that may be known by the senses; discernible. — *adv* **percep'tibly**. — *n* **percep'tion** the act or power of perceiving; discernment; apprehension of any modification of consciousness; the combining of sensations into a recognition of an object; direct recognition; a percept; reception of a stimulus (*bot*). — *adj* **percep'tional**. — *n* **percep'tive** able or quick to perceive; discerning; active or instrumental in perceiving. — *n* **percep'tiveness** or **perceptiv'ity**. — *adj* **percep'tūal** of the nature of, or relating to, perception. [L. *percipěre, perceptum*; see **perceive**.]

perch[1] *pûrch, n* a spiny-finned freshwater fish of the genus **Perca** (*pûr'kə*); extended to various similar or related fishes. — *adj* **per'coid** (*-koid*). [L. *perca* (partly through Fr. *perche*) — Gr. *perkē*, a perch.]

perch[2] *pûrch, n* a rod for a bird to alight, sit or roost on; anything serving that purpose for a bird, a person, or anything else; a rod or pole, a measure of $5\frac{1}{2}$ yards (5·03 metres). — *vi* to alight, sit or roost on a perch; to be set on high; to be balanced on a high or narrow footing; to settle. — *vt* to place, as on a perch. — *adj* **perch'ing** with feet adapted for perching. — **perching birds** the Passeriformes. [Fr. *perche* — L. *pertica*, a rod.]

perchance *pər-chäns', adv* by chance; as it may happen; perhaps. [A.Fr. *par chance*.]

percheron *per'shə-rɔ̃* or *pûr'shə-ron, n* a draught-horse of a breed originating in La *Perche* in Southern Normandy. — Also *adj*. [Fr.]

perchloric *pər-klō'rik*, (*chem*) *adj* containing more oxygen than chloric acid — applied to an oily explosive acid, $HClO_4$. — *n* **perchlō'rate** a salt of perchloric acid. [**per-** (1).]

percipient *pər-sip'i-ənt, adj* perceiving; having the faculty of perception. — *n* a person who perceives or can perceive; someone who receives impressions telepathically or by other means outside the range of the senses. — *n* **percip'ience**. [L. *percipiēns, -entis*, pres. p. of *percipěre*.]

percoid *pûr'koid*. See **perch**[1].

percolate *pûr'kə-lāt, vt* and *vi* to pass through pores, small openings, etc.; to filter. — *n* a filtered liquid. — *n* **percolation** (*pûr-kō-lā'shən*). — *n* **per'colātor** an apparatus for percolating, esp. for making coffee. [L. *percōlāre, -ātum* — *per*, through, *cōlāre*, to strain.]

percuss *pər-kus', vt* to strike or tap sharply; to tap for purposes of diagnosis. — *n* **percussion** (*-kush'ən*) striking; impact; tapping directly or indirectly upon the body to find the condition of an organ by the sound (*med*); massage by tapping; the striking or sounding of a discord, etc., as distinguished from preparation and resolution (*mus*); collectively, instruments played by striking — drum, cymbals, triangle, etc. (*mus*); a device for making an organ-pipe speak promptly by striking the reed (*mus*). — *adj* **percuss'ional**. — *n* **percuss'ionist** a musician who plays percussion instruments. — *adj* **percussive** (*-kus'*). — *adv* **percuss'ively**. — *n* **percuss'or** a percussion hammer. — **percussion bullet** a bullet that explodes on striking; **percussion cap** a metal case containing a substance which explodes when struck, formerly used for firing rifles, etc. (see also **cap**); **percuss'ion-hammer** a small hammer for percussion in diagnosis. [L. *percussiō, -ōnis* — *percutěre, percussum* — pfx. *per-*, thoroughly, *quatěre*, to shake.]

percutaneous *pər-kū-tā'ni-əs, adj* done or applied through the skin. — *adv* **percutā'neously**. [**per-** (2), L. *cutis*, the skin.]

perdition *pər-dish'ən, n* the utter loss of happiness in a future state; hell. [L. *perditiō, -ōnis* — *perděre, perditum* — pfx. *per-*, entirely, *dăre*, to give, give up.]

père *per*, (Fr.) *n* father. — **Père David's** (*dä'vidz, dä'vēdz* or *-vēdz'*) **deer** a breed of large grey deer discovered in China by Father A. *David*, 19th-cent. French missionary, and now surviving only in captivity.

peregrinate *per'i-grin-āt, vi* to travel about; to go on pilgrimage. — *vt* to traverse. — *n* **peregrinā'tion** travelling about; wandering; pilgrimage; a complete and systematic course or round. — *n* **per'egrinātor** someone who travels about. — *adj* **per'egrinatory** of or pertaining to a peregrinator; wandering. [L. *peregrīnus*, foreign — *peregre*, abroad — *per*, through, *ager*, field.]

peregrine *per'i-grin* or **peregrin falcon** (*fŏl'kən*) *n* a small falcon with a dark back and streaked under-parts, noted for its acrobatic flight. [Ety. as for **peregrinate** (young birds being captured in flight rather than taken from the nest).]

pereira *pə-re'rə* or **pereira bark** (*bärk*) *n* a Brazilian tree, the bark of which is used medicinally; the bark itself. [From Jonathan *Pereira*, 19th-cent. English pharmacologist.]

peremptory *pər-emp'tə-ri* or *per'əmp-, adj* imperious; arrogantly commanding. — *adv* **peremp'torily** (or *per'*). — *n* **peremp'toriness** (or *per'*). [L. *peremptōrius* — *periměre, peremptum*, to destroy, prevent — pfx. *per-*, entirely, and *eměre*, to take, to buy.]

perennial *pər-en'yəl, adj* lasting through the year; perpetual; never failing; growing constantly; lasting more than two years (*bot*); (of insects) living more than one year. — *n* a plant that lives more than two years. — *adv* **perenn'ially**. — *n* **perennial'ity**. [L. *perennis* — *per*, through, *annus*, a year.]

perestroika *per-i-stroy'kə, n* reconstruction, restructuring (of society, the state, etc.). [Russ.]

perf. *abbrev* for perfect.

perfect *pûr'fekt* or *pûr'fikt*, *adj* without flaw, blemish or fault; complete; having all organs in a functional condition; having androecium and gynaeceum in the same flower (*bot*); completely skilled or versed; thoroughly known or acquired; exact; exactly conforming to definition or theory; sheer, utter; absolute; of the simpler kind of consonance (*mus*). — *n* the perfect tense; a verb in the perfect tense. — *vt* **perfect** (*pər-fekt'*) to make perfect; to finish; to teach fully, to make fully skilled in anything. — *n* **perfect'er**. — *n* **perfectibil'ity**. — *adj* **perfect'ible** capable of becoming perfect. — *n* **perfec'tion** the state of being perfect; a quality in perfect degree; the highest state or degree; an embodiment of the perfect; (*loosely*) a degree of excellence approaching the perfect. — *n* **perfec'tionism**. — *n* **perfec'tionist** a person who aims at or calls for nothing short of perfection; someone who thinks that moral perfection can be attained in this life. — *adj* **perfectionist'ic**. — *adj* **perfect'ive** tending to make perfect; of a verb aspect, denoting completed action (*gram*). — *adv* **perfect'ively**. — *adv* **per'fectly**. — *n* **per'fectness**. — **perfect binding** an unsewn bookbinding in which the backs of the gathered sections are sheared off and the leaves held in place by glue; **perfect cadence** (*mus*) one passing from the chord of the dominant to that of the tonic; **perfect fifth** (*mus*) the interval between two sounds whose vibration frequencies are as 2 to 3; **perfect fourth** (*mus*) the interval between sounds whose vibration frequencies are as 3 to 4; **perfect insect** the imago or completely developed form of an insect; **perfect interval** (*mus*) the fourth, fifth, or octave; **perfect number** (*math*) a number equal to the sum of its aliquot parts, as $6 = 1 + 2 + 3$, $28 = 1 + 2 + 4 + 7 + 14$; **perfect pitch** (*mus*) the pitch of a note as determined by the number of vibrations per second; the ability to identify or remember a note accurately; a term often used for *absolute pitch*; **perfect tense** a tense signifying action completed in the past (e.g. *I have said*) or at the time spoken of (**past perfect** or **pluperfect** e.g. *I had said*; **future perfect** e.g. *I shall have left by then*). — **to perfection** perfectly. [M.E. *parfit* — O.Fr. *parfit*.]

perfecta *pər-fek'tə*, (orig. *US*) *n* a form of bet in which the punter has to select, and place in the correct order, the two horses, dogs, etc. which will come first and second in a race. [Am. Sp. (*quiniela*) *perfecta*, perfect (quiniela); cf. **quinella** and **trifecta**.]

perfervid *pər-fûr'vid*, (*poetic*) *adj* very fervid; ardent; eager. — *n* **perfervidity** (*pûr-fər-vid'i-ti*) or **perfer'vidness**. [L. *perfervidus* — *prae*, before, *fervidus*, fervid.]

perfidious *pər-fid'i-əs*, *adj* faithless; deceitful; treacherous. — *adv* **perfid'iously**. — *n* **perfid'iousness** or **perfidy** (*pûr'fid-i*). [L. *perfidiōsus* — *perfidia*, faithlessness — pfx. *per-*, implying destruction, *fidēs*, faith.]

perfluorocarbon *pər-flōō-rō-kär'bən*, *n* an organic compound in which much of the hydrogen has been replaced by fluorine; any binary compound of carbon and fluorine, similar to a hydrocarbon. [**per-** (1), **fluorine** and **carbon**.]

perfoliate *pər-fō'li-āt*, *adj* (of a leaf) having the base joined around the stem, so as to appear pierced by the stem — orig. said of the stem passing through the leaf, or of the plant. — *n* **perfoliā'tion**. [**per-** (2) and L. *folium*, a leaf.]

perforans *pûr'fər-ans*, (*anat*) *n* the long flexor muscle of the toes, or the deep flexor muscle of the fingers, whose tendons pass through those of the perforatus. — *n* **perforatus** (*pûr-fər-ā'təs*) the short flexor of the toes or the superficial flexor of the fingers. [Ety. as for **perforate**.]

perforate *pûr'fə-rāt*, *vt* to pierce or to make a hole through; to make a series of small holes in (paper, etc.) to facilitate tearing; to penetrate; to pass through by a hole. — *adj* **per'forable**. — *adj* **perforation** (*pûr-fə-rā'shən*) the act of making a hole; the formation of a hole or aperture; the condition of being perforated; a hole through or into anything; a series, or one of a series, of small holes, as for ease in tearing paper. — *adj* **per'forātive** having the power to pierce. — *n* **per'forātor**. [L. *perforāre*, *-ātum* — *per*, through, *forāre*, to bore.]

perforce *pər-fōrs'*, *adv* by force; of necessity. [O.Fr. *par force*.]

perform *pər-förm'*, *vt* to do; to carry out duly; to act in fulfilment of; to bring about; to execute; to go through duly; to act. — *vi* to do what is to be done; to execute a function; to act, behave; to act a part; to play, sing, dance; to do tricks, etc. for an audience. — *adj* **perform'able** capable of being performed; practicable. — *n* **perform'ance** the act of performing; a carrying out of something; something done; a piece of work; manner or success in working; execution, esp. as an exhibition or entertainment; an act or action; the power or capability of a machine (esp. a motor vehicle) to perform; an instance of awkward, aggressive, embarrassing, etc., behaviour (*colloq*). — *n* **perform'er** a person who performs; someone who does or fulfils what is required; an executant; someone who takes part in a performance or performances; an entertainer. — *adj* **perform'ing** that performs; trained to perform tricks. — *n* performance. — **performance art** a theatrical presentation in which several art forms, such as acting, music, photography, etc., are combined; **performing arts** those in which an audience is present, such as drama, ballet, etc.; **performing right** the right to give a public performance of a piece of music or play. [A.Fr. *parfourmer*, app. an altered form of *parfourner* — O.Fr. *parfournir*, *par* — L. *per*, through, *fournir*, to furnish.]

perfume *pûr'fūm*, formerly and still sometimes *pər-fūm'*, *n* a fragrant substance, usu. a liquid, applied to the body, etc. to give a pleasant smell; any substance made or used for the sake of its fragrance; fragrance. — *vt* **perfume** (*pər-fūm'* or *pûr'fūm*) to scent. — *adj* **per'fumed** (or *pər-fūmd'*). — *adj* **per'fumeless** (or *-fūm'*). — *n* **perfū'mer** a maker or seller of perfumes. — *n* **perfū'mery** perfumes in general; the art of preparing perfumes; the shop or place in a shop where perfumes are sold. — *adj* **per'fūmy**. [Fr. *parfum* — L. *per*, through, *fūmus*, smoke.]

perfunctory *pər-fungk'tə-ri*, *adj* done merely as a duty to be got through; done for form's sake, or in mere routine; acting without zeal or interest; merely formal; hasty and superficial. — *adv* **perfunc'torily**. — *n* **perfunc'toriness**. [L. *perfunctōrius* — *perfunctus*, past p. of *perfungī*, to execute — *per-*, thoroughly, *fungī*, to do.]

perfuse *pər-fūz'*, *vt* to pour or diffuse through or over; to pass (a liquid) through an organ or tissue. — *n* **perfusate** (*-fūz'āt*) that which is perfused. — *n* **perfusion** (*-fū'zhən*) the pouring on or diffusion through; treatment by continuous blood transfusion (*med*). — *n* **perfu'sionist** the member of a surgical team administering this. — *adj* **perfu'sive**. [L. *perfūsus*, poured over — *per*, through, *fundĕre*, *fūsus*, to pour.]

pergola *pûr'gə-lə*, *n* a structure with climbing plants, usu. along a walk. [It., — L. *pergula*, a shed.]

perh. *abbrev* for perhaps.

perhaps *pər-haps'*, *adv* it may be; possibly; as it may happen. [From the pl. of **hap**, chance — O.N. *happ*, good luck, after the model of **peradventure** and **perchance**.]

peri- *per-i-* or *pə-ri'-*, *combining form* denoting: (1) around; (2) (esp. in *astron*) near. [Gr. *peri*, around.]

perianth *per'i-anth*, (*bot*) *n* calyx and corolla together, esp. when not clearly distinguishable. [**peri-** (1) and Gr. *anthos*, flower.]

periastron *per-i-as'tron*, (*astron*) *n* that stage in the orbit of a comet, one component of a binary star, etc. when it is closest to the star around which it revolves. [**peri-** (2) and Gr. *astron*, star.]

periblast *per'i-blast*, (*biol*) *n* the outer layer of protoplasm surrounding the nucleus of a cell or ovum; cytoplasm. [**peri-** (1) and Gr. *blastos*, a sprout.]

periblem *per'i-blem*, (*bot*) *n* the layer of primary meristem from which the cortex is formed, covering the plerome. [Gr. *periblēma*, garment, mantle — *peri*, around, *ballein*, to throw.]

pericardium *per-i-kär'di-əm*, (*anat*) *n* the sac round the heart. — *adj* **pericar'diac** or **pericar'dial**. — *n* **pericardī'tis** inflammation of the pericardium. [Latinised from Gr. *perikardion* — *peri*, around, *kardiā*, heart.]

pericarp *per'i-kärp*, (*bot*) *n* the wall of a fruit, derived from that of the ovary. — *adj* **pericar'pial**. [Gr. *perikarpion* — *peri*, around, *karpos*, fruit.]

perichondrium *per-i-kon'dri-əm*, *n* the fibrous membrane covering a cartilage. — *adj* **perichon'drial**. [**peri-** (1) and Gr. *chondros*, cartilage.]

periclase *per'i-klāz* or *-klās*, (*chem*) *n* magnesium oxide occurring naturally in isometric crystals. [Gr. *peri-*, very, *klasis*, fracture (from its perfect cleavage).]

periclinal *per-i-klī'nəl*, *adj* sloping downwards in all directions from a point (*geol*); parallel to the outer surface (*bot*). [Gr. *periklīnēs*, sloping on all sides — *peri*, around, *klīnein*, to slope.]

pericranium *per-i-krā'ni-əm*, *n* the membrane that surrounds the cranium; (*loosely*) skull or brain. — *adj* **pericrā'nial**. [Latinised from Gr. *perikrānion* — *peri*, around, *krānion*, skull.]

pericycle *per'i-sī-kl*, (*bot*) *n* the outermost layer or layers of the central cylinder. — *adj* **pericy'clic**. [Gr. *perikyklos*, all round — *peri*, around, *kyklos*, a circle.]

pericynthion *per-i-sin'thi-ən*, *n*. Same as **perilune**. [**peri-** (2) and *Cynthia*, a name of the goddess of the moon.]

peridesmium *per-i-des'mi-əm*, (*anat*) *n* the areolar tissue round a ligament. [**peri-** (1) and Gr. *desmos*, a band.]

peridot *per'i-dot*, *n* olivine; a green olivine used in jewellery. — *adj* **peridot'ic**. — *n* **peridotite** (*-dō'tīt*) a coarse-grained igneous rock mainly composed of olivine, usu. with other ferromagnesian minerals but little or no feldspar. [Fr. *péridot*.]

perigastric *per-i-gas'trik*, (*med*) *adj* surrounding the alimentary canal. — *n* **perigastrī'tis** inflammation of the outer surface of the stomach. [**peri-** (1) and Gr. *gastēr*, belly.]

perigee *per'i-jē*, (*astron*) *n* the point of the moon's, or any artificial satellite's, orbit at which it is nearest the earth (opp. to *apogee*). — *adj* **perigē'al** or **perigē'an**. [Gr. *perigeion*, neut. of *perigeios*, round or near the earth — *peri*, around, *gē*, earth.]

periglacial *per-i-glā'si-əl*, *-glās'yəl* or *-glā'shəl*, *adj* bordering a glacier; of, like or pertaining to a region bordering a glacier. [**peri-** (1) and L. *glaciālis*, icy — *glaciēs*, ice.]

Perigordian *per-i-gör'di-ən*, *adj* pertaining to the Palaeolithic epoch to which the Lascaux Cave paintings and other examples of primitive art belong. [*Périgord*, region in S.W. France.]

perihelion *per-i-hē'li-ən*, *n* the point of the orbit of a planet or a comet at which it is nearest to the sun (opp. to *aphelion*); culmination (*fig*). [**peri-** (2) and Gr. *hēlios*, the sun.]

perihepatic *per-i-hi-pat'ik*, (*med*) *adj* surrounding the liver. — *n* **perihepatitis** (*-hep-ə-tī'tis*) inflammation of the peritoneum covering the liver. [**peri-** (1) and Gr. *hēpar*, *hēpatos*, liver.]

perikaryon *per-i-kar'i-on*, *n* that part of a nerve cell which contains the nucleus: — *pl* **perikar'ya**. [**peri-** (1) and Gr. *karyon*, kernel.]

peril *per'il*, *n* danger. — *adj* **per'ilous** dangerous. — *adv* **per'ilously**. — *n* **per'ilousness**. [Fr. *péril* — L. *perīculum*.]

perilune *per'i-lūn* or *-lōōn*, *n* the point in a spacecraft's orbit round the moon where it is closest to it. — Also **pericynthion**. [**peri-** (2) and Fr. *lune* — L. *luna*, moon.]

perimeter *pər-im'i-tər*, *n* the circuit or boundary of any plane figure, or the sum of all its sides (*geom*); an instrument for measuring the field of vision (*med*); the boundary of a camp, field or enclosure; the outer edge of any area. — *adj* **perimetric** (*per-i-met'rik*) or **perimet'rical**. — *n* **perim'etry**. [Gr. *perimetros* — *peri*, around, *metron*, measure.]

perimorph *per'i-mörf*, *n* a mineral enclosing another. [**peri-** (1) and Gr. *morphē*, form.]

perimysium *per-i-miz'i-əm*, (*anat*) *n* the connective tissue which surrounds and binds together muscle fibres. [**peri-** (1) and *-mysium* — Gr. *mus*, muscle.]

perinatal *per-i-nā'tl*, *adj* pertaining to the period between the seventh month of pregnancy and the first week of life. [**peri-** (1) and **natal**[1].]

perinephrium *per-i-nef'ri-əm*, (*med*) *n* the fatty tissue surrounding the kidney. — *adj* **perineph'ric**. — *n* **perinephrī'tis** inflammation of the perinephrium. [**peri-** (1) and Gr. *nephros*, kidney.]

perineum *per-i-nē'əm*, (*zool*) *n* the lower part of the body between the genital organs and the anus. — *adj* **perinē'al**. [Latinised from Gr. *perinaion*.]

perineurium *per-i-nū'ri-əm*, (*zool*) *n* the sheath of connective tissue surrounding a bundle of nerve fibres. — *adj* **perineu'ral**. — *n* **perineurī'tis** inflammation of the perineurium. [**peri-** (1) and Gr. *neuron*, nerve.]

period *pē'ri-əd*, *n* the time in which anything runs its course; an interval of time at the end of which events recur in the same order; the time required for a complete oscillation — reciprocal of the frequency; the time of a complete revolution of a heavenly body about its primary; the difference between two successive values of a variable for which a function has the same value; the recurring part of a circulating decimal; a set of figures (usu. three) in a large number marked off e.g. by commas; a series of chemical elements represented in a horizontal row of the periodic table; a stretch of time; a long stretch, an age; one of the main divisions of geological time; a stage or phase in history, in a person's life and development, in a disease, or in any course of events; a time; a division of the school day, the time of one lesson; the end of a course; a recurring time; the menstrual discharge or the time it occurs; a complete sentence, esp. one of elaborate construction; a division analogous to a sentence (*mus*); a mark (.) at the end of a sentence — a full stop; a rhythmical division in Greek verse. — *adj* (of e.g. architecture, furniture, a play) characteristic, representative, imitative of, belonging to, or dealing with, a past period. — *adj* **periodic** (*pē-ri-od'ik*) relating to a period or periods; of revolution in an orbit; having a period; recurring regularly in the same order; (*loosely*) occurring from time to time; characterised by or constructed in periods. — *adj* **period'ical** periodic; published in numbers at more or less regular intervals; of, for, or in such publications. — *n* a magazine or other publication that appears at stated intervals (not usu. including newspapers). — *adv* **period'ically** at regular intervals; in a periodic manner; in a periodical publication; (*loosely*) from time to time. — *n* **periodicity** (*-dis'*) the fact or character of being periodic; frequency. — *n* **periodīsā'tion** or **-z-** division into periods. — **periodic function** (*math*) one whose values recur in a cycle as the variable increases; **periodic law** that the properties of atoms are periodic functions of their atomic numbers; **periodic sentence** a sentence so constructed that it is not until the final clause that the requirements of sense and grammar are met; **periodic system** the classification of chemical elements according to the periodic law; **periodic table** a table of chemical elements in order of atomic number arranged in horizontal series and vertical groups, showing how similar properties recur at regular intervals; **period piece** an object belonging to a past age esp. with charm or value; a person ludicrously behind the times; a play, novel, etc., set in a past time. — **period of grace** a specific time allowed to both parties to a contract to fulfil any obligations arising from it. [Fr. *période* — L. *periodus* — Gr. *periodos* — *peri*, around, *hodos*, a way.]

periodontal *per-i-ō-dont'əl, adj* (pertaining to tissues or regions) round about a tooth. — *nsing* **periodont'ics** or *n* **periodontol'ogy** the branch of dentistry concerned with periodontal diseases. — *n* **periodont'ist**. — *n* **periodontī'tis** the inflammation of the tissues surrounding the teeth. [**peri-** (1) and *odous, odontos*, tooth.]

perionychium *per-i-o-nik'i-əm,* (*med*) *n* the skin surrounding a fingernail or toenail. [**peri-** (1) and Gr. *onux*, a nail.]

periosteum *per-i-os'ti-əm,* (*zool*) *n* a tough fibrous membrane covering the surface of bones. — *adj* **perios'teal** or **periostit'ic**. — *n* **periostī'tis** inflammation of the periosteum. [Gr. *periosteon* (neut. adj.) — *peri*, around, *osteon*, a bone.]

peripatetic *per-i-pə-tet'ik, adj* walking about; (of e.g. a teacher) itinerant. — *n* a pedestrian; an itinerant. — *adj* **peripatet'ical**. [Gr. *peripatētikos* — *peripatos*, a walk — *peri*, around, *pateein*, to walk.]

peripeteia or **peripetia** *per-i-pe-tī'ə, n* a sudden change of fortune, esp. in drama. [Gr. *peripeteia* — *peri*, and *pet-* the root of *piptein*, to fall.]

periphery *pər-if'ə-ri, n* line or surface acting as a boundary; the outside of anything; a surrounding region. — *adj* **periph'eral** of or relating to a periphery; not of the most important; incidental; minor. — *n* a peripheral unit. — **peripheral unit** or **device** in a computer system, the input (e.g. card reader), output (e.g. magnetic tape), and storage devices, which are connected to or controlled by the central processing unit. [Gr. *periphereia* — *peri*, around, *pherein*, to carry.]

periphonic *per-i-fon'ik, adj* of or pertaining to a sound system with many speakers. [**peri-** (1) and Gr. *phōnē*, voice.]

periphrasis *pər-if'rə-sis, n* circumlocution; a roundabout expression: — *pl* **periph'rases** (*-sēz*). — *vt* **periphrase** (*per'i-frāz*) to say with circumlocution. — *vi* to use circumlocution. — *adj* **periphrastic** (*per-i-fras'tik*) using periphrasis; using at least two words instead of a single inflected form, esp. of a verb tense involving an auxiliary. — *adv* **periphras'tically**. [Gr. *periphrasis* — *peri*, around, *phrasis*, speech.]

periplast *per'i-pläst,* (*zool*) *n* intercellular substance; the ectoplasm of flagellates; cuticle covering the ectoplasm. [**peri-** (1) and Gr. *plastos*, moulded.]

perique *pə-rēk', n* a strongly-flavoured tobacco from Louisiana. [Perh. *Périque*, nickname of a grower.]

periscope *per'i-skōp, n* a tube with mirrors by which an observer in a trench, a submarine, etc., can see what is going on above. — *adj* **periscopic** (*-skop'ik*). [Gr. *periskopeein*, to look around.]

perish *per'ish, vi* to decay; to lose life; to be destroyed; to be ruined or lost. — *vt* to destroy; to ruin; to cause to decay; to distress with cold, hunger, etc. — *n* **perishabil'ity**. — *adj* **per'ishable** subject to speedy decay. — *n* that which is perishable; (in *pl*) food or other stuff liable to rapid deterioration. — *n* **per'ishableness**. — *adv* **per'ishably**. — *adj* **per'ished** distressed by cold, hunger, etc. (*colloq* or *dialect*); (of materials such as rubber) weakened or injured by age or exposure. — *n* **per'isher** (*slang*) a reprehensible and annoying person. — *adj* **per'ishing** (*colloq* or *dialect*) freezing cold; vaguely used as a pejorative. — Also *adv*. — *adv* **per'ishingly**. [O.Fr. *perir*, pres. p. *perissant* — L. *perīre*, *perītum*, to perish — *per-* and *īre*, to go.]

perisperm *per'i-spûrm,* (*bot*) *n* nutritive tissue in a seed derived from the nucellus. — *adj* **perisper'mal** or **perisper'mic**. [**peri-** (1) and Gr. *sperma*, seed.]

perissodactyl *pər-is-ō-dak'til,* (*zool*) *adj* having an odd number of toes. — *n* an animal of the **Perissodac'tyla**, a division of ungulates with an odd number of toes — horse, tapir, rhinoceros, and extinct kinds (distinguished from the *Artiodactyla*). — *adj* **perissodac'tylate, perissodactyl'ic** or **perissodac'tylous**. [Gr. *perissos*, odd, *daktylos*, a finger, toe.]

peristalith *pər-is'tə-lith, n* a stone circle. [Irreg. formed from Gr. *peri*, around, *histanai*, to set up, *lithos*, a stone.]

peristaltic *per-i-stalt'ik, adj* forcing onward by waves of contraction, as the alimentary canal and other organs do their contents. — *n* **peristal'sis**. — *adv* **peristalt'ically**. [Gr. *peristaltikos* — *peristellein*, to wrap round — *peri*, around, *stellein*, to place.]

peristyle *per'i-stīl, n* a range of columns round a building or round a square; a court, square, etc., with columns all round. — *adj* **peristy'lar**. [L. *peristȳl(i)um* — Gr. *peristȳlon* — *peri*, around, *stȳlos*, a column.]

peritoneum *per-i-tən-ē'əm,* (*zool*) *n* a serous membrane enclosing the viscera in the abdominal and pelvic cavities. — *adj* **peritonē'al**. — *n* **peritonēos'copy** (*med*) the visual examination of the peritoneal cavities by means of an endoscope inserted through an incision in the abdomen. — *adj* **peritonitic** (*-it'ik*) of peritonitis; suffering from peritonitis. — *n* **peritonī'tis** (*med*) inflammation of the peritoneum. [Gr. *peritonaion* — *peri*, around, *teinein*, to stretch.]

peritrich *per-it'rik, n* a bacterium bearing a ring of cilia around the body: — *pl* **perit'richa** (*-kə*). — *adj* **perit'richous** of or pertaining to peritricha; bearing a ring of cilia around the body. [**peri-** (2) and Gr. *thrix, trichos*, hair.]

periwinkle[1] *per'i-wingk-l, n* a creeping evergreen plant, growing in woods; the light blue colour of some of its flowers. — *adj* of this colour. [M.E. *peruenke* — O.E. *peruince*, from L. *pervinca*.]

periwinkle[2] *per'i-wingk-l, n* an edible gasteropod with a spiral shell, abundant between tide-marks, esp. *Littorina littorea*. [O.E. (pl.) *pinewinclan* (or perh. *winewinclan*) — *wincle*, a whelk.]

perjure *pûr'jər, vi* (*reflexive*) to swear falsely. — *adj* **per'jured** having sworn falsely; being sworn falsely (e.g. of an oath). — *n* **per'jurer**. — *adj* **perjurious** (*-jōō'ri-əs*) guilty of or involving perjury. — *n* **per'jury** false swearing; the breaking of an oath; the crime of wilfully giving false evidence on oath or affirmation as a witness in judicial proceedings. [O.Fr. *parjurer* — L. *perjūrāre* — *per-* and *jūrāre*, to swear.]

perk[1] *pûrk*, (with *up*) *vi* and *vt* to recover or cause to recover spirits and energy, esp. in sickness; to jerk up, cock up. — *vt* to decorate so as to look newer, smarter, or more interesting.

perk[2] *pûrk,* (*colloq*) *n*. Short for **perquisite**.

perk[3] *pûrk, vt* and *n*. Short for **percolate** or **percolator** (of coffee).

perkin. See **parkin**.

perky *pûr'ki, adj* in good spirits; self-assertive; pert. — *adv* **perk'ily**. — *n* **perk'iness**. [**perk**[1].]

perlite *pûrl'īt, n* any acid volcanic glass with perlitic structure; pearlite. — *adj* **perlitic** (*-it'ik*) showing little concentric spheroidal or spiral cracks between rectilineal ones. [Fr. *perle*, Ger. *Perle*, pearl.]

perlocution *pûr-lə-kū'shən,* (*philos*) *n* an act that is the effect of an utterance, such as frightening, persuading, comforting, etc. (cf. **illocution**). — *adj* **perlocū'tionary**. [**per-** (2) and **locution**.]

perm[1] *pûrm*, (*colloq*) *n* short for **permutation**. — *vt* to permute; to arrange a forecast according to some defined system of combination or permutation.

perm[2] *pûrm*, (*colloq*) *n* short for **permanent wave**. — *adj* (esp. of a job) short for **permanent**. — *vt* (*colloq*) to give a permanent wave to.

permafrost *pûr'mə-frost*, *n* permanently frozen subsoil. [*perma*nent *frost*.]

permalloy *pûrm'a-loi*, *n* any of various alloys of iron and nickel, often containing other elements, e.g. copper, molybdenum, chromium, which has high magnetic permeability. [*perm*eable *alloy*.]

permanent *pûr'mə-nənt*, *adj* remaining, or intended to remain, indefinitely. — *n* **per'manence** the fact or state of being permanent. — *n* **per'manency** permanence; a thing that is permanent. — *adv* **per'manently**. — **permanent teeth** the adult teeth, which come after the milk teeth lost in childhood; **permanent wave** a long-lasting artificial wave in hair. [L. *permanēns*, *-entis*, pres. p. of *permanēre* — *per*, through, *manēre*, to continue.]

permanganate *pər-mang'gə-nāt*, *n* a salt of permanganic acid, esp. **potassium permanganate** which is used as an oxidising and bleaching agent and as a disinfectant. — **permanganic acid** (*-gan'*) an acid containing more oxygen than manganic acid. [**per-** (1) and **manganese**.]

permeate *pûr'mi-āt*, *vt* to pass through the pores of; to penetrate and fill the pores of; to pervade; to saturate. — *vi* to diffuse. — *n* **permeabil'ity**. — *adj* **per'meable**. — *adv* **per'meably**. — *n* **per'meance** the act of permeating; the reciprocal of the reluctance of a magnetic circuit. — *n* **per'mease** any enzyme which acts to assist the entry of certain sugars into cells. — *n* **permeā'tion**. — *adj* **per'meative** having power to permeate. — **magnetic permeability** the ratio of flux density to magnetising force. [L. *permeāre* — *per*, through, *meāre*, to pass.]

Permian *pûr'mi-ən*, (*geol*) *n* the uppermost Palaeozoic system. — *adj* of that system. [*Perm*, in Russia, where it is widely developed.]

per mil. or **per mill.** *abbrev* for *per mille* (L.), by the thousand, or in each thousand.

permissible, etc. See **permit**.

permit *pər-mit'*, *vt* and *vi* to allow: — *pr p* **permitt'ing**; *pa t* and *pa p* **permitt'ed**. — *n* (*pûr'mit*) permission, esp. in writing. — *n* **permissibil'ity**. — *adj* **permiss'ible** that may be permitted; allowable. — *adv* **permiss'ibly**. — *n* **permission** (*-mish'ən*) an act of permitting; leave. — *adj* **permiss'ive** granting permission or liberty; permitted, optional; lenient, indulgent; allowing much freedom in social conduct (as in **the permissive society** — from *c* 1960). — *adv* **permiss'ively**. — *n* **permiss'iveness**. [L. *permittĕre*, *-missum*, to let pass through — *per*, through, *mittĕre*, to send.]

permutate *pər'mūt-āt* or **permute** *pər-mūt'*, *vt* to change the order of; to subject to permutation. — *n* **permūtabil'ity**. — *adj* **permūt'able** interchangeable. — *n* **permutā'tion** the arrangement of a set of things in every possible order (*math*); any one possible order of arrangement of a given number of things taken from a given number; immediate inference by obversion (*logic*); esp. in football pools, a forecast of a specified number of results from a larger number of matches based on some defined system of combination or permutation (often shortened to **perm**); any such system. [L. *permūtāre*, to change thoroughly — *per-* and *mūtāre*, to change.]

pernancy *pûr'nən-si*, (*law*) *n* receiving. [A.Fr. *pernance* (O.Fr. *prenance*).]

pernicious *pər-nish'əs*, *adj* destructive; highly injurious; malevolent. — *adv* **perni'ciously**. — *n* **perni'ciousness**. — **pernicious anaemia** see under **anaemia**. [L. *perniciōsus* — *per-* and *nex*, *necis*, death by violence.]

pernickety *pər-nik'i-ti*, *adj* finical; exacting minute care. — *n* **pernick'etiness**. [Scot.]

pernoctate *pûr'nok-tāt*, (usu. *facetious*) *vi* to pass or spend the night. — *n* **pernocta'tion** passing the night; a watch, vigil. [**per-** (2) and L. *nox*, *noctis*, night.]

Pernod® *per'nō*, *n* an alcoholic drink made in France, flavoured with aniseed.

peroneal *per-ō-nē'əl*, (*anat*) *adj* of or relating to the fibula. — *n* **peronē'us** one of several fibular muscles. [Gr. *peronē*, fibula.]

peroration *per-ə-rā'shən* or *-ö-*, *n* the conclusion of a speech; a rhetorical performance. — *vi* **per'orate** to make a peroration; to harangue (*colloq*). [L. *perōrātiō*, *-ōnis* — *per*, through, *ōrāre*, to speak.]

peroxide *pər-oks'īd*, *n* an oxide with the highest proportion of oxygen; one that yields hydrogen peroxide on treatment with an acid; the bleach hydrogen peroxide (*colloq*). — *vt* to treat or bleach with hydrogen peroxide. [**per-** (1) and **oxide**.]

perpendicular *pûr-pən-dik'ū-lər*, *adj* erect; vertical; upright; in the direction of gravity or at right angles to the plane of the horizon; at right angles to a given line or surface (*geom*). — *n* an instrument for determining the vertical line; a straight line or plane perpendicular to another line or surface; verticality or erectness; (in a ship) a vertical line from each end of the waterline. — *n* **perpendicularity** (*-lar'i-ti*) the state of being perpendicular. — *adv* **perpendic'ularly**. [L. *perpendiculāris* — *perpendiculum*, a plumb-line — *per-* and *pendēre*, to hang.]

perpetrate *pûr'pi-trāt*, *vt* to execute or commit (esp. an offence or a pun). — *n* **perpetrā'tion**. — *n* **per'petrātor**. [L. *perpetrāre*, *-ātum* — *per-* and *patrāre*, to achieve.]

perpetual *pər-pet'ū-əl*, *adj* never ceasing; everlasting; not temporary; incessant; (of a sports trophy, etc.) awarded every year; continuously blooming; perennial. — *adv* perpetually. — *n* a perennial; a continuously blooming hybrid rose. — *n* **perpet'ualism**. — *n* **perpet'ualist** a person who advocates the perpetual continuation of anything. — *n* **perpetuality** (*-al'i-ti*). — *adv* **perpet'ually**. — **perpetual calendar** a calendar by means of which it may be ascertained on which day of the week any given day has fallen or will fall; one which may be used for any year, or for more than a year; **perpetual check** (*chess*) a situation in which one player's king is continually placed in check by the other player who may thereby claim a draw; **perpetual motion** a hypothetical machine, or motion of such a machine, that should do work indefinitely without an external source of energy; **perpetual screw** an endless screw. [L. *perpetuālis* — *perpetuus*, continuous.]

perpetuate *pər-pet'ū-āt*, *vt* to cause to last for ever or for a very long time; to preserve from extinction or oblivion; to pass on, cause to continue to be believed, known, etc. — *n* **perpetūā'tion**. — *n* **perpet'ūātor**. [L. *perpetuāre*, *-ātum* — *perpetuus*, perpetual.]

perpetuity *pûr-pi-tū'i-ti*, *n* the state of being perpetual; endless time; duration for an indefinite period; something lasting for ever; the sum paid for a perpetual annuity; the annuity itself; an arrangement whereby property is tied up, or rendered inalienable, for all time or for a very long time. [L. *perpetuitās*, *-ātis* — *perpetuus*, perpetual.]

perplex *pər-pleks'*, *vt* to embarrass or puzzle with difficulties or intricacies; to bewilder; to tease with suspense or doubt; to complicate. — *adv* **perplex'edly**. — *n* **perplex'edness**. — *adj* **perplex'ing**. — *adv* **perplex'ingly**. — *n* **perplex'ity** the state of being perplexed; confusion of mind arising from doubt, etc. [L. *perplexus*, entangled — *per-* and *plexus*, involved, past p. of *plectĕre*.]

per pro. *abbrev* for *per procurationem* (L.) (see **per[2]**).

perquisite *pûr'kwi-zit*, *n* (often *colloq* shortened to **perk**) an incidental benefit from one's employment;

a tip expected upon some occasions; something regarded as falling to one by right. [L. *perquīsītum*, from *perquīrĕre*, to seek diligently — *per-* and *quaerĕre*, to ask.]

Perrier® *per'i-ā*, *n* a sparkling mineral water from a spring of that name in Southern France.

perron *per'ən* or *per-ɔ̃'*, *n* a raised platform or terrace at an entrance door; an external flight of steps leading up to it. [Fr., — L. *petra*, stone.]

perry *per'i*, *n* a drink made from fermented pear juice. [O.Fr. *peré* — L.L. *pēra* (L. *pirum*), pear.]

Pers. *abbrev* for Persian.

pers. *abbrev* for: person; personal.

perse *pûrs*, *adj* dark blue, bluish-grey. — *n* a dark-blue colour; a cloth of such colour. [O.Fr. *pers*.]

persecute *pûr'si-kūt*, *vt* to harass, afflict, hunt down, or put to death, esp. for religious or political opinions. — *n* **persecū'tion**. — *adj* **per'secūtive**. — *n* **per'secūtor**. — *adj* **per'secūtory**. — **persecution complex** (*psychiatry*) a morbid fear that one is being plotted against by other people. [L. *persequī*, *persecūtus* — *per-* and *sequī*, to follow.]

persevere *pûr-si-vēr'*, *vi* to continue steadfastly; to keep on striving. — *n* **persevē'rance** the act or state of persevering; continued application to anything which one has begun; persistence despite setbacks. — *adj* **persev'erant** steadfast. — *vi* **persev'erate** to recur or tend to recur (*psychiatry*); to repeat the same actions or thoughts. — *n* **perseveration** (*pûr-sev-ər-ā'shən*) meaningless repetition of an action, utterance, thought, etc.; the tendency to experience difficulty in leaving one activity for another. — *n* **persev'erātor**. — *adj* **persevē'ring**. — *adv* **persevē'ringly**. [Fr. *persévérer* — L. *persevērāre* — *persevērus*, very strict — *per-* and *sevērus*, strict.]

Persian *pûr'shən*, *-shyən* or *-zh-*, *adj* of, from, or relating to *Persia* (now Iran), its inhabitants, or language. — *n* a native or citizen of Persia; the language of Persia; a Persian cat. — *vt* and *vi* **Per'sianise** or **-ize**. — **Persian blinds** persiennes; **Persian carpet** a rich, soft carpet of the kind woven in Persia; **Persian cat** a kind of cat with long, silky hair and bushy tail; **Persian Gulf** the Arabian Gulf, the arm of the Arabian Sea which separates Iran (to the N.) from (to the S.) Saudi Arabia and the Arab States; **Persian lamb** a lamb of the Karakul or Bukhara breed; its black, curly fur used to make coats, hats, etc.

persienne *per-si-en'*, *n* an Eastern cambric or muslin with coloured printed pattern; (in *pl*) Persian blinds, outside shutters of thin movable slats in a frame. [Fr., Persian (fem.).]

persiflage *pûr'si-fläzh*, *n* banter; flippancy. [Fr., — *persifler*, to banter — L. *per*, through, Fr. *siffler* — L. *sībilāre*, to whistle, to hiss.]

persimmon *pər-sim'ən*, *n* a tree of the American or African genus *Diospyros*; its plumlike fruit. [From an Am. Ind. word.]

persist *pər-sist'*, *vi* to continue steadfastly or obstinately, esp. against opposition (often with *in*); to persevere; to insist; to continue to exist; to remain in the mind after the external cause is removed. — *vt* to assert or repeat insistently. — *n* **persis'tence** or **persis'tency**. — *adj* **persis'tent** persisting; pushing on, esp. against opposition; tenacious; fixed; constant or constantly repeated; remaining after the usual time of falling off, withering, or disappearing (*zool*, *bot*); continuing to grow beyond the usual time. — *adv* **persis'tently**. — *adv* **persis'tingly**. — **persistent cruelty** (*law*) (in matrimonial proceedings) behaviour likely to cause danger to the life or health of a spouse. [L. *persistĕre* — *per* and *sistĕre*, to cause to stand, to stand — *stāre*, to stand.]

person *pûr'sn*, *n* a living soul or self-conscious being; a character represented, as on the stage; a capacity in which one is acting; a personality; a human being, sometimes used contemptuously or patronisingly; the outward appearance of a human being; bodily form; the human figure (often including clothes); a hypostasis of the Godhead (*theol*); a form of inflexion or use of a word according as it, or its subject, represents the person, persons, thing or things speaking (*first person*), spoken to (*second person*), or spoken about (*third person*) (*gram*): — *pl* in the sense of an individual human being, usu. **people** (q.v.); in formal, technical, etc. use **per'sons**. — **-person** (*pûr-sn*) used in combination instead of *-man* to avoid illegal or unnecessary discrimination on grounds of sex, e.g. *chairperson*. — *adj* **per'sonable** of good appearance. — *n* **per'sonableness**. — *n* **per'sonage** a person, esp. an important or august one. — *n* **per'sonpower** manpower, applying to either sex. — *adj* **person-to-per'son** (of a telephone call) personal; involving meeting or contact. — Also *adv*. — **in person** in actual bodily presence; by one's own act, not by an agent or representative; **on** or **about one's person** with one, worn or carried about one's body. [L. *persōna*, a player's mask.]

persona¹ *pər-sōn'ə*, *n* Jung's term for a person's manner assumed when dealing with the world, masking one's inner thoughts, feelings, etc.; a character in fiction, esp. in drama: — *pl* **person'ae** (*-ē* or *-ī*) or **person'as**. [Ety. as for **person**.]

persona² *pər-sōn'ə* or *-a*, (L.) *n* person. — **persona grata** (*grä'tə*) a person who is acceptable, liked or favoured, esp. one who is diplomatically acceptable to a foreign government. — **persona non grata** opp. of **persona grata**.

personal *pûr'sən-l*, *adj* of or relating to a person or personality; relating, referring or pointing to a particular person or persons; aiming offensively at a particular person or persons; belonging or perculiar to a person; one's own; relating to private concerns; bodily; in bodily presence; (of a telephone call) made to a particular person; by one's own action; indicating person (*gram*); tailored to the needs of a particular person; done in person. — *n* **personalisā'tion** or **-z-**. — *vt* **per'sonalise** or **-ize** to apply to, or take as referring to, a definite person; to tailor to, or cater for, the desires of a particular person; to mark with a person's name, initials, monogram, etc.; to give a mark or character to anything so that it is identifiable as belonging to a certain person (*colloq*); to personify. — *n* **per'sonalism** the character of being personal; a philosophical system emphasising the importance of individuals. — *n* **per'sonalist**. — *adj* **personalist'ic**. — *adv* **per'sonally** in a personal or direct manner; in person; individually; for my part (*colloq*). — *n* **per'sonalty** (*law*) personal estate. — **personal chair** a university chair created for the period of tenure of a particular person; **personal column** a newspaper column containing personal messages, advertisements, etc.; **personal computer** a single-user microcomputer; **personal effects** those belongings worn or carried about one's person; private or intimate possessions; **personal estate** or **property** property other than land or buildings (opp. to *real*) passing at death to one's executor, not to one's heir-at-law; **personal identity** the continued sameness of the individual person, through all changes, as testified by consciousness; **personal organiser** see **organiser**; **personal pronoun** (*gram*) a pronoun which stands for a definite person or thing; **personal remark** a remark, esp. derogatory, made to, referring to, or aimed at a particular person or persons; **personal rights** rights which belong to a person as a living, rational being; **personal service** attention or service of the proprietor of a concern, rather than an employee or assistant; **personal stereo** a small lightweight cassette-player designed to be carried around and listened to through earphones. — **personal identification number** see **PIN**. [**person**.]

personality *pər-sən-al'i-ti, n* the fact or state of being a person or of being personal; existence as a person; individuality; distinctive or well-marked character; a person, esp. a remarkable one; a celebrity; a personal remark; the integrated organisation of all the physical, mental and emotional characteristics of an individual, esp. as they are presented to others (*psychol*); the sum of such characteristics which make one attractive socially. — **personality cult** excessive adulation of the individual, esp. one in public life; **personality disorder** (*psychiatry*) any of various types of mental illness in which one tends to behave in ways which are harmful to oneself or others. [**person.**]

personate *pûr'sən-āt, vt* to play the part of; to impersonate, esp. with criminal intent; to represent in the form of a person. — *n* **personā'tion.** — *n* **per'sonātor.** [**person.**]

personify *pər-son'i-fī, vt* to represent as a person; to ascribe personality to; to be the embodiment of: — *pr p* **person'ifying**; *pa t* and *pa p* **person'ified.** — *n* **personificā'tion.** — *n* **person'ifīer.** [L. *persōna*, a person, *facĕre*, to make.]

personnel *pər-sən-el', n* the persons employed in any service; (*loosely*) people in general; an office or department that deals with employees' appointments, records, welfare, etc. — **personnel carrier** a military vehicle, often armoured, for carrying troops. [Fr., personal.]

perspective *pər-spek'tiv, n* the art or science of drawing objects on a surface, so as to give the picture the same appearance to the eye as the objects themselves; appearance, or representation of appearance, of objects in space, with effect of distance, solidity, etc.; just proportion in all the parts; a picture in perspective; a vista; a prospect of the future; a way of regarding facts and their relative importance; point of view. — *adj* pertaining or according to perspective. — *n* **perspec'tivism** the theory that things can only be known from an individual point of view at a particular time (*philos*); the use of subjective points of view in literature and art. — *n* **perspec'tivist** an artist whose work emphasises the effects of perspective; someone who studies the rules of perspective. — **perspective plane** the surface on which the picture of the objects to be represented in perspective is drawn. — **in (or out of) perspective** according to (or against) the laws of perspective; in correct (or incorrect) proportion. [L. (*ars*) *perspectīva*, perspective (art) — *perspicĕre, perspectum* — *per, specĕre*, to look.]

Perspex® *pûr'speks, n* a thermoplastic resin of exceptional transparency and freedom from colour, used for windscreens, etc.

perspicacious *pûr-spi-kā'shəs, adj* clear-minded. — *adv* **perspicā'ciously.** — *n* **perspicacity** (*-kas'i-ti*). [L. *perspicāx, -ācis*; see **perspective.**]

perspicuous *pər-spik'ū-əs, adj* expressed or expressing clearly; lucid. — *n* **perspicū'ity.** — *adv* **perspic'ūously.** — *n* **perspic'ūousness.** [L. *perspicuus*; see **perspective.**]

perspire *pər-spīr', vi* to sweat. — *n* **perspiration** (*-spir-ā'shən*) the act of perspiring; sweat. [L. *perspīrāre, -ātum* — *per*, through, *spīrāre*, to breathe.]

persuade *pər-swād', vt* to induce by argument, advice, etc.; to bring to any particular opinion; to convince. — *vi* to use persuasive methods. — *adj* **persuād'able.** — *n* **persuād'er** a person who or thing which persuades; a gun (*slang*); a device used to fit metal type into a chase (*printing*). — *n* **persuasibility** (*-swās-i-bil'i-ti*). — *adj* **persuās'ible** capable of being persuaded. — *n* **persuasion** (*-swā'zhən*) the act, process, method, art or power of persuading; an inducement; the state of being persuaded; settled opinion; a creed; a party adhering to a creed; a kind (*facetious*). — *adj* **persuasive** (*-swās'*) having the power to persuade; influencing the mind or passions. — *adv* **persuā'sively.** — *n* **persuā'siveness.** [L. *persuādēre, -suāsum* — *per-* and *suādēre*, to advise.]

PERT (*business*) *abbrev* for programme evaluation and review technique.

pert *pûrt, adj* saucy; impertinent; jaunty. — *adv* **pert'ly.** — *n* **pert'ness.** [Aphetic for archaic *apert*, open, public.]

pertain *pûr-tān', vi* to belong; to relate (with *to*). — *n* **per'tinence** (*pûr'*) the state of being pertinent. — *adj* **per'tinent** pertaining or related; to the point; fitted for the matter on hand; fitting or appropriate. — *n* (chiefly *Scot*) anything that goes along with an estate. — *adv* **per'tinently.** [O.Fr. *partenir* — L. *pertinēre* — *per-* and *tenēre*, to hold.]

pertinacious *pûr-ti-nā'shəs, adj* thoroughly tenacious; holding obstinately to an opinion or a purpose; obstinate; unyielding. — *adv* **pertinā'ciously.** — *n* **pertinā'ciousness** or **pertinacity** (*-nas'i-ti*) the quality of being pertinacious or unyielding; obstinacy; resoluteness. [L. *pertināx, -ācis*, holding fast — *per-* and *tenāx*, tenacious — *tenēre*, to hold.]

pertinence, pertinent, etc. See **pertain.**

perturb *pər-tûrb', vt* to disturb greatly; to agitate. — *adj* **pertur'bable.** — *n* **pertur'bance** perturbation. — *n* **pertur'bant** anything that perturbs. — *adj* perturbing. — *n* **perturbā'tion** the act of perturbing or state of being perturbed; disquiet of mind; irregularity; the disturbance produced in the simple elliptic motion of one heavenly body about another by the action of a third body, or by the non-sphericity of the principal body (*astron*); a perturbing agent. — *adj* **perturbā'tional.** — *adj* **pertur'bative.** — *n* **per'turbātor.** — *adj* and *n* **pertur'batory.** — *adj* **perturbed'.** — *adv* **pertur'bedly.** — *n* **pertur'ber.** [L. *perturbāre, -ātum* — *per-* and *turbāre*, to disturb — *turba*, a crowd.]

pertussis *pər-tus'is*, (*med*) *n* whooping-cough. — *adj* **pertuss'al.** [**per-** (2) and L. *tussis*, cough.]

peruse *pər-ōōz', vt* to examine in detail; to read attentively or critically; to read. — *n* **perus'al.** — *n* **perus'er.** [L. *per-*, thoroughly, *ūtī, ūsus*, to use.]

Peruvian *pə-rōō'vi-ən, adj* of Peru or its inhabitants. — *n* a native or inhabitant of *Peru*, in S. America.

perv or **perve** *pûrv*, (*colloq*) *n* a (sexual) pervert; an act of perving (*Austr*); someone who pervs (*Austr*). — *vi* to behave as a perv; (with *at* or *on*) to look at lustfully or for sexual pleasure (*Austr*). — Also *adj.* [**pervert.**]

pervade *pər-vād', vt* to spread or extend through the whole of, to permeate. — *n* **pervasion** (*-vā'zhən*). — *adj* **pervasive** (*-vā'siv*) tending or having the power to pervade. — *adv* **perva'sively.** — *n* **perva'siveness.** [L. *pervādĕre* — *per*, through, *vādĕre*, to go.]

perverse *pər-vûrs', adj* obstinately determined when in the wrong; capricious and unreasonable in opposition; stubborn; deliberately wicked; against the evidence or judge's direction on point of law (*legal*). — *adv* **perverse'ly.** — *n* **perverse'ness.** — *n* **perversion** (*-vûr'shən*) the act or process of perverting; the condition of being perverted; the product of having been perverted; a diverting from the true object; a turning from right or true; a distortion; a misapplication; a pathological deviation of sexual instinct; the formation of a mirror-image (*math*); the mirror-image itself. — *n* **pervers'ity** the state or quality of being perverse. — *adj* **pervers'ive** tending to pervert. — *vt* **pervert'** to turn wrong or from the right course; to misconstrue, interpret wrongly; to corrupt; to turn from truth or virtue; to form a mirror-image of (*math*). — *vi* to go wrong or off the right course. — *n* (*pûr'vûrt*) someone whose sexual instinct is perverted. — *n* **pervert'er.** — *adj* **pervert'ible.** [L. *pervertĕre, perversum* — *per-*, wrongly, *vertĕre*, to turn.]

Pes. *abbrev* for peseta (Spanish currency).
Pesach or **Pesah** *pā'sahh, n* the festival of Passover. [Heb.]
pesade *pə-zäd, -sād'* or *-zād'*, *n* a dressage manoeuvre in which a horse rears up on its hindlegs without forward movement. [Fr.; from It.]
peseta *pe-sā'ta* or *-ə, n* the Spanish standard monetary unit (100 *céntimos*). [Sp., dimin. of *pesa*, weight.]
pesky *pes'ki*, (*colloq*) *adj* annoying. — *adv* **pes'kily**. [Perh. **pest**.]
peso *pā'sō, n* in S. and Central America and the Philippines, a coin worth 100 centavos: — *pl* **pe'sos**. [Sp., — L. *pēnsum*, weight.]
pessary *pes'ə-ri, n* a surgical plug, or medicated device, esp. one worn in the vagina. [Fr. *pessaire* — L.L. *pessārium* — Gr. *pessos*, a pebble, pessary.]
pessimism *pes'i-mizm, n* the doctrine that the world is bad rather than good (*philos*); a tendency to look on the dark side of things; a depressing view of life; despondency, hopelessness. — *n* **pess'imist** a person who believes that everything is tending to the worst; a person who looks too much on the dark side of things (opp. to *optimist*). — *adj* **pessimis'tic**. — *adv* **pessimis'tically**. [L. *pessimus*, worst.]
pessimum *pes'i-məm, n* that point at which any condition is least favourable: — *pl* **pess'ima**. — *adj* (of conditions) worst, least favourable. — Also **pess'imal**. [L., neut. of *pessimus*, worst.]
pest *pest, n* any insect, fungus, etc., destructive of cultivated plants; a troublesome person or thing; any deadly epidemic disease; plague (*rare*). — *n* **pesti'cide** (*pes'ti-sīd*) a substance for killing pests. — *adj* **pestolog'ical**. — *n* **pestol'ogist**. — *n* **pestol'ogy** the study of agricultural pests and methods of combating them. [Fr. *peste* — L. *pestis*.]
pester *pes'tər, vt* to annoy persistently. — *n* an annoyance. — *n* **pes'terer**. — *adv* **pes'teringly**. [App. from O.Fr. *empestrer*, to entangle; infl. by **pest**.]
pesticide. See under **pest**.
pestilence *pes'ti-ləns, n* any deadly epidemic disease; bubonic plague; anything that is hurtful to the morals. — *adj* **pest'ilent** deadly; producing pestilence; harmful to health and life; pernicious; mischievous; vexatious. — *adj* **pestilential** (*-len'shl*) of the nature of pestilence; producing or infested with pestilence; destructive; baneful; detestable; pestering. — *adv* **pestilen'tially** or **pes'tilently**. [Fr. — L. *pestilentia*.]
pestle *pes'l*, also *pest'l, n* an instrument for pounding. — *vt* to pound. — *vi* to use a pestle. [O.Fr. *pestel* — L. *pistillum*, a pounder — *pīnsĕre, pistum*, to pound.]
pesto *pes'tō, n* an Italian sauce made chiefly of basil and cheese, with nuts, olive oil, etc., originating in Liguria. [It.]
pestology. See under **pest**.
PET (*med*) *abbrev* for positron emission tomography (brain scanner).
Pet. (*Bible*) *abbrev* for (the Letters of) Peter.
pet[1] *pet, n* a tame animal kept as a companion or for amusement; an indulged favourite; used as an endearment. — *adj* kept as a pet; for or of pet animals; indulged, cherished; favourite. — *vt* to treat as a pet; to fondle; to pamper, indulge. — *vi* (*colloq*) to caress amorously: — *pr p* **pett'ing**; *pa t* and *pa p* **pett'ed**. — *n* **pett'er**. — *n* **pett'ing**. — **pet aversion** or **hate** a chief object of dislike; **pet name** a name used in familiar affection.
pet[2] *pet, n* an offended feeling; a slight fit of aggrieved or resentful sulkiness; the sulks, huff. — *vi* to be peevish, to sulk. — *adj* **pett'ed** in a pet; apt to be in a pet. — *adv* **pett'edly**. — *n* **pett'edness**. — *adj* **pett'ish** peevish; sulky; inclined to sulk; of or expressing sulkiness. — *adv* **pett'ishly**. — *n* **pett'ishness**.
peta- *pe-tə-, combining form* denoting one thousand million million, 10^{15}, as in *petajoule, petametre*. [Prob. Gr. **penta-**.]
petal *pet'l, n* one of the usu. brightly-coloured leaflike parts of a flower, a corolla leaf. [Gr. *petalon*, a leaf.]
pétanque *pā-tãk', n* a French (Provençal) game in which steel bowls are rolled or hurled towards a wooden marker ball.
petard *pe-tär'* or *pe-tärd', n* a case containing an explosive, used for blowing in doors, etc.; a moving firework. — **hoist with one's own petard** see under **hoist**. [O.Fr. — *péter*, to crack or explode — L. *pēdĕre*, to break wind.]
petechia *pe-tē'ki-ə*, (*med*) *n* a small red or purple spot on the skin: — *pl* **pete'chiae** (*-ē*). — *adj* **petech'ial**. [Latinised from It. *petecchia*.]
peter[1] *pē'tər, vi* to dwindle away to nothing, be dissipated or exhausted (with *out*). [Orig. U.S. mining slang.]
peter[2] *pē'tər, n* the Blue Peter (flag); a call for trumps (*whist*); a high card followed by a low card, so played as a signal to one's partner (*bridge*). — *vi* to signal that one has a short suit (*whist*); to play a high card followed by a low card (*bridge*). — **Peter principle** (*facetious*) the theory that in a hierarchy people rise to the level at which they are incompetent; **Peter's pence** see under **penny**; **Peters' projection** (*cartog*) an equal area map, one that shows accurately the relative sizes of continents, oceans, etc.
peter[3] *pē'tər*, (*slang*) *n* a safe; a prison cell. — **pe'terman** a safe-blower.
Peterloo *pē-tər-lōō', n* a popular term for the incident at St Peter's Fields, Manchester, in 1819, in which a peaceable demonstration for reform was charged by cavalry. [St *Peter*'s Fields and Water*loo*.]
peterman. See **peter**[3].
Peter Pan *pē'ter pan, n* a character in J.M. Barrie's play of that name (1904), a typical example of the person who never grows up. — **Peter Pan collar** a flat collar with rounded ends.
petersham *pē'tər-shəm, n* a heavy corded ribbon used for belts, hat-bands, etc.; a heavy greatcoat; rough-napped cloth, generally dark blue, of which it was made. [Lord *Petersham*, a 19th-cent. English army officer.]
pethidine *peth'ə-dēn, n* a synthetic analgesic and hypnotic, acting like morphine. — Also called **meperidine**. [Perh. mixture of *piperidine* and *ethyl*.]
pétillant *pā-tē-yã*, (Fr.) *adj* (of wine) slightly sparkling.
petiole *pet'i-ōl, n* a leaf-stalk (*bot*); a stalklike structure, esp. that of the abdomen in wasps, etc. (*zool*). — *adj* **pet'iolar** of or of the nature of a petiole. — *adj* **pet'iolāte, pet'iolated** or **pet'ioled** stalked. [L. *petiolus*, a little foot, a petiole.]
petit *pet'i, pə-tē'*, or as Fr. *pə-tē, adj* form of **petty**, insignificant (*obs* except in legal and other French phrases). — *adj* **petite** (*pə-tēt'*) applied to a woman, small-made and neat. — **petit battement** (*bat-mã*; *ballet*) a light tapping or beating with the foot; **petit bourgeois** (*bōōr-zhwä*) a member of the lower middle class; **petite bourgeoisie** (*bōōr-zhwä-zē*) the lower middle class; **petit four** (*för* or *fōōr*) a small very fancy biscuit; **petit jury** (*legal*) a jury of twelve persons, in Britain now the only form of jury (also **petty jury**; see **grand jury** under **grand**[1]); **petit mal** (*mal*) a mild form of epilepsy without convulsions; **petit point** (*point* or *pwɛ̃*) tapestry work using small stitches diagonal to the canvas threads; **petits pois** (*pə-tē pwä*) small green peas. [Fr. *petit*, -e.]
petition *pə-tish'ən, n* a supplication; a prayer; a formal request to an authority; a written supplication signed by a number of persons; a written application to a court of law; the thing asked for. — *vt* to address a petition to; to ask for. — *adj*

peti'tionary. — *n* **peti'tioner.** — *n* **peti'tioning.** — *n* **peti'tionist.** [L. *petītiō, -ōnis* — *petĕre*, to ask.]

petitio principii *pe-tish'i-ō prin-sip'i-ī*, (*logic*) *n* a begging of the question. [L.]

Petrarchan *pe-trär'kən* or **Petrarchian** *-trär'ki-ən*, *adj* pertaining to or in the style of the Italian poet Francesco *Petrarca* or *Petrarch* (1304–74).

petrel *pet'rəl*, *n* any bird of the genus *Procellaria* related to the albatrosses and fulmars, esp. the **storm (popularly stormy) petrel** or Mother Carey's chicken, a dusky sea-bird, rarely landing except to lay its eggs, the smallest web-footed bird known. [L. *Petrus*, Peter, from the fact that it appears to walk on the water; see Matt. xiv. 29.]

Petri (or petri) dish *pē'tri, pā'tri* or *pet'ri dish*, *n* a shallow glass dish with an overlapping cover used for cultures of bacteria. — Also **Petri plate.** [R.J. *Petri*, German bacteriologist.]

petrify *pet'ri-fī*, *vt* to turn into stone; to fossilise (*geol*); to encrust with stony matter; to make hard like a stone; to fix in amazement, horror, etc. — *vi* to become stone, or hard like stone: — *pr p* **pet'rifying**; *pa t* and *pa p* **pet'rified.** — *n* **petrifac'tion** turning or being turned into stone; a petrified object; a fossil. — *adj* **petrifac'tive** or **petrif'ic** petrifying. — *n* **petrificā'tion** petrifaction. [L. *petra* — Gr. *petrā*, rock, L. *facĕre, factum*, to make.]

Petrine *pē'trīn*, *adj* of the apostle Peter. [L. *Petrinus* — *Petrus*, Gr. *Petros*, Peter.]

petro-[1] *pet-rō-*, *combining form* signifying petroleum. — *n* and *adj* **petrōchem'ical** (of or relating to) any chemical obtained from petroleum. — *n* **petro-chem'istry.** — *n* **pet'rocurrency, pet'romoney, pet'rodollars** and **pet'ropounds** currency, etc., acquired by the oil-producing countries as profit from the sale of their oil to the consumer countries. [*petro*leum.]

petro-[2] *pet-rō-* or *pi-tro'-*, *combining form* signifying rock. — *n* **petrogen'esis** (the study of) the origin, formation, etc., of rocks. — *adj* **petrogenet'ic.** — *n* **pet'rōglyph** a rock-carving, esp. prehistoric. — *adj* **petrōglyph'ic.** — *n* **pet'rōglyphy.** — *n* **pet'rō-gram** a picture on stone. — *n* **petrog'rapher.** — *adj* **petrograph'ic** or **petrograph'ical.** — *n* **petrog'-raphy** the systematic description and classification of rocks. — *adj* **petrolog'ical.** — *n* **petrol'ogist.** — *n* **petrol'ogy** the science of the origin, chemical and mineral composition and structure, and alteration of rocks. — *adj* **petrōphys'ical.** — *n* **petrōphys'icist.** — *n* **petrōphys'ics** that branch of physics concerning the physical properties of rocks. [Gr. *petrā*, rock.]

petrol *pet'rol* or *-rəl*, *n* formerly, petroleum; now a mixture of light volatile hydrocarbons obtained by fractional distillation or cracking of petroleum, used for driving motor cars, aeroplanes, etc. (U.S. **gasoline**); petrol blue. — *vt* to supply with petrol: — *pr p* **pet'rolling**; *pa t* and *pa p* **pet'rolled.** — *n* **petrolatum** (*-ā'təm*) petroleum jelly. — *adj* **petroleous** (*pi-trō'li-əs*) containing or rich in petroleum. — *n* **petroleum** (*pi-trō'li-əm*) a (usu. liquid) mineral oil containing a mixture of hydrocarbons obtained from oil wells, and used to make petrol, paraffin, lubricating oil, fuel oil, etc. — *adj* **petrolic** (*pi-trol'ik*) of petrol or petroleum. — *adj* **petrolif'erous** (*pet-*) yielding petroleum. — **petrol blue** a vibrant blue colour; **petrol bomb** a petrol-filled Molotov cocktail or similar small explosive device; **petroleum jelly** soft paraffin, a mixture of petroleum hydrocarbons used in emollients, as a lubricant, etc. (see also **liquid paraffin** under **paraffin**); **petrol pump** a machine for transferring measured amounts of petrol to motor vehicles; **petrol station** a garage which sells petrol, a filling station. [L. *petra*, rock, *oleum*, oil.]

petrology. See under **petro-**[2].

petrous *pet'rəs*, *adj* stony. [L. *petrōsus* — *petra* — Gr. *petrā*, rock.]

pe-tsai cabbage *pā-tsī' kab'ij*. Same as **Chinese cabbage.**

petted. See **pet**[2].

petticoat *pet'i-kōt*, *n* a skirt, esp. an underskirt, or a garment of which it forms part; a bell-shaped structure, as in telegraph insulators, etc. (*electr eng*). — *adj* (usu. *facetious*) feminine, female or of women. — *adj* **pett'icoated.** — **petticoat government** domination by women. [**petty** and **coat.**]

pettifogger *pet'i-fog-ər*, *n* a lawyer who deals, often deceptively and quibblingly, with trivial cases. — *vi* **pett'ifog** to play the pettifogger. — *n* **pett'ifoggery.** — *n* and *adj* **pett'ifogging** paltry, trivial, cavilling (behaviour). [**petty**, and M.L.G. *voger*, a person who does things.]

pettish. See **pet**[2].

petty *pet'i*, *adj* small; of less importance; minor; trifling; lower in rank, power, etc.; inconsiderable, insignificant; contemptible; small-minded. — *adv* **pett'ily.** — *n* **pett'iness.** — **petty bourgeois** and **bourgeoisie** variants of **petit bourgeois** and **petite bourgeoisie**; **petty cash** a sum of money kept for minor expenses which usu. do not need to be referred to a higher authority; miscellaneous small sums of money received or paid; **petty jury** see **petit jury**; **petty officer** a naval officer ranking with a non-commissioned officer in the army. [Fr. *petit.*]

petulant *pet'ū-lənt*, *adj* showing peevish impatience, irritation or caprice; forward, impudent in manner. — *n* **pet'ulance** or **pet'ulancy.** — *adv* **pet'ulantly.** [L. *petulāns, -antis* — assumed *petulāre*, dimin. of *petĕre*, to seek.]

petunia *pē-tū'nyə* or *-ni-ə*, *n* a plant of the South American genus *Petunia* of ornamental plants closely related to tobacco. [Tupí *petun*, tobacco.]

pew *pū*, *n* an enclosed compartment or fixed bench in a church; a box or stall in another building; a seat (*slang*). [O.Fr. *puie*, raised place, balcony — L. *podia*, pl. of *podium* — Gr. *podion*, dimin. of *pous*, *podos*, foot.]

pewit *pē'wit* or *pū'it*, *n*. Same as **peewit.**

pewter *pū'tər*, *n* tin with a little copper, antimony and/or bismuth; a vessel made of pewter, esp. a beer-tankard; the bluish-grey colour of pewter. — *adj* made of pewter. — *n* **pew'terer** a worker with pewter. — **pew'ter-mill** a lapidary's pewter polishing-wheel for amethyst, agate, etc. [O.Fr. *peutre.*]

peyote *pā-yō'tā*, *n* a Mexican intoxicant made from cactus tops — also called **mescal.** — *n* **peyō'tism** the taking of peyote, esp. as part of a religious ceremony; the N. American Indian religion in which peyote is taken sacramentally, a form of Christianity. — *n* **peyō'tist.** [Nahuatl *peyotl.*]

PF *abbrev* for: Patriotic Front; Procurator Fiscal.

Pf *abbrev* for pfennig (German currency).

pfennig *pfen'ig* or *-ihh*, *n* a German coin, the hundredth part of a mark.

PG *abbrev* for: Parental Guidance (a certificate denoting a film in which some scenes may be unsuitable for young children); paying guest.

PGA *abbrev* for Professional Golfers' Association.

pH *pē-āch'* or **pH value** (*val'ū*), *n* a number used to express degrees of acidity or alkalinity in solutions, related by formula to a standard solution of potassium hydrogen phthalate, which has value 4 at 15°C.

PHAB *fab*, *abbrev* for Physically Handicapped and Able Bodied.

phacoid *fak'* or *fāk'oid*, or **phacoidal** *fə-koi'dl*, *adj* lentil-shaped; lens-shaped. [Gr. *phakos*, a lentil, *eidos*, form.]

Phaedra complex *fēd'rə kom'pleks*, (*psychol*) *n* the difficult relationship which can arise between a new step-parent and the (usu. teenage) son or daughter of the original marriage. [Greek story of *Phaedra* who fell in love with her stepson and committed suicide after being repulsed by him.]

phaen- *fēn-* or **phaeno-** *fē-no-*. Now usu. **phen-** or **pheno-** (q.v.).

phaeton *fā'i-tən* or *fā'tən*, *n* an open four-wheeled carriage for one or two horses. [Gr. *Phaethon*, son of the Greek god Helios, who drove his father's chariot so close to the earth that he was destroyed by Jupiter (Gr. mythol.); Gr. *phaethōn*, *-ontos*, shining.]

phag- *fag-* or **phago-** *fag-ō-*, *combining form* denoting 'feeding' or 'eating', as in *phagocyte*. — **-phaga** in zoological names, denoting 'eaters'; **-phage** (*-fāj* or *-fäzh*) eater or destroyer; **-phagous** (*-fəg-əs*) feeding on; **-phagus** (*-fəg-əs*) one feeding in a particular way or on a particular thing; **-phagy** (*-fə-ji*) eating of a specified nature. [Gr. *phagein*, to eat.]

phage. Short for **bacteriophage.**

phagedaena or **phagedena** *faj-* or *fag-i-dē'nə*, (*med*) *n* rapidly spreading destructive ulceration, once common in hospitals — hospital gangrene. — *adj* **phagedae'nic** or **phagedē'nic.** [Gr. *phagedaina* — *phagein*, to eat.]

phagocyte *fag'ō-sīt*, *n* a white blood corpuscle that engulfs bacteria and other harmful particles. — *adj* **phagocytic** (*-sit'*) or **phagocyt'ical.** — *n* **phag'o-cytism** (*-sīt-*) the nature or function of a phagocyte. — *n* **phagocytō'sis** destruction by phagocytes. [Gr. *phagein*, to eat, *kytos*, a vessel.]

phagophobia *fag-ō-fō'bi-ə*, *n* fear of or aversion to eating. [**phag(o)-** and **phobia.**]

-phagous, -phagus or **-phagy.** See under **phag-.**

phalange, etc. See under **phalanx.**

phalanger *fal-an'jər*, *n* any one of a group of small tree-dwelling Australasian mammals whose young are usu. carried in a pouch by the female, an opossum. [Gr. *phalangion*, spider's web, from their webbed toes.]

phalanx *fal'angks* or *fāl'angks*, *n* a solid formation of soldiers, etc.; a solid body of supporters or partisans; a solid body of people generally; a bone of a digit; the part of a finger or toe corresponding to it; a joint of an insect's leg; a bundle of stamens: — *pl* **phal'anxes** or (*biol*) **phalanges** (*fal-an'jēz*). — *adj* **phalangal** (*fal-ang'gl*) phalangeal. — *n* **phalange** (*fal'anj*) a phalanx (in any of its biological senses); the Christian right-wing group in Lebanon, modelled on the Spanish Falange: — *pl* **phal'anges.** — *adj* **phal-an'geal.** — *n* **phalangid** (*fal-an'jid*) a harvester spider. — *n* **phalan'gist** a member of the Lebanese phalange. [Gr. *phalanx*, *-angos*, a roller, phalanx, phalange, spider.]

phalarope *fal'ə-rōp*, *n* a wading bird (*Phalaropus*) with feet like a coot. [Gr. *phalaris*, a coot, *pous*, a foot.]

phallus *fal'əs*, *n* the penis; the symbol of generation in primitive religion: — *pl* **phall'ī** or **phall'uses.** — *adj* **phall'ic.** — *adj* **phallocen'tric** centred on the phallus; dominated by or expressive of male attitudes. — *n* **phallocentric'ity.** [L., — Gr. *phallos*.]

Phanariot *fa-nar'i-ot*, (*hist*) *n* one of the Greeks inhabiting the *Fanar* quarter of Constantinople, or of a Greek official class — in Turkish history mostly diplomatists, administrators and bankers. — *adj* **Phanar'iot.** — Also **Fanariot.** [Gr. *phānarion*, lighthouse, from that on the Golden Horn.]

phanerogam *fan'ər-ō-gam*, (*biol*; *old*) *n* a spermatophyte. — *adj* **phanerogam'ic** or **phanerog'a-mous.** [Gr. *phaneros*, visible, *gamos*, marriage.]

Phanerozoic *fan-ər-ə-zō'ik*, (*geol*) *adj* denoting the geological period of time from the Cambrian period to the present. — Also *n*. [Gr. *phaneros*, visible, *zōion*, an animal.]

phantasm *fan'tazm*, *n* a vision, an illusion; an apparition; a spectre: — *pl* **phan'tasms.** — Also **phantas'ma**: — *pl* **phantas'mata.** — *adj* **phan-tas'mal.** — *n* **phantasmal'ity.** — *adv* **phantas'-mally.** — *adj* **phantas'mic** or **phantas'mical.** [Gr. *phantasma* — *phantazein*, to make visible.]

phantasmagoria *fan-taz-mə-gö'ri-ə*, *n* a fantastic series of illusory images or of real forms. — *adj* **phantasmago'rial** pertaining to or resembling a phantasmagoria. — *adj* **phantasmagor'ic** or **phantasmagor'ical.** [Fr. *phantasmagorie* — Gr. *phantasma*, an appearance, and perh. *agorā*, an assembly.]

phantasy, phantastic, phantastry. Same as **fantasy,** etc.

phantom *fan'təm*, *n* an immaterial form, a spectre; a deceitful appearance; a visionary experience, such as a dream. — *adj* illusory, imaginary; unreal, non-existent; spectral, like a ghost. — **phantom limb** the sensation of feeling in a limb that has been amputated; **phantom pregnancy** false pregnancy (q.v.). [O.Fr. *fantosme* — Gr. *phantasma*.]

phar. or **pharm.** *abbrev* for: pharmaceutical; pharmacopoeia; pharmacy.

Pharaoh *fā'rō*, *n* a title of the kings of ancient Egypt. — *adj* **pharaonic** (*fā-rā-on'ik*). — **Pharaoh's serpent** the coiled ash of burning mercuric thiocyanate, a type of indoor firework; **Pharaonic circumcision** the ancient practice of female circumcision by the removal of the clitoris and labia majora and minora. [L. and Gr. *pharaō* — Heb. *par'ōh* — Egyp. *pr-'o*, great house.]

Pharisee *far'i-sē*, *n* a member of an ancient Jewish sect, whose strict interpretation of the Mosaic law led to an obsessive concern with the rules covering the details of everyday life; anyone more careful of the outward forms than of the spirit of religion; a very self-righteous or hypocritical person. — *adj* **pharisā'ic** or **pharisā'ical** pertaining to, or like, the Pharisees; hypocritical. — *adv* **pharisā'ically.** — *n* **pharisā'icalness.** — *n* **phar'isāism** (also **phar'i-seeism**). [O.E. *phariseus* — L.L. *pharisaeus* — Gr. *pharisaios* — Heb. *pārūsh*, separated.]

pharm. (*abbrev*.). See **phar.**

pharmaceutic *fär-mə-sū'tik* (or *-kū'tik*) or **pharmaceu'tical** *-əl*, *adj* pertaining to the knowledge or art of preparing medicines. — *n* **pharmaceu'tical** a chemical used in medicine. — *adv* **pharmaceu'tically.** — *nsing* **pharmaceu'tics** the science of preparing medicines. — *n* **pharmaceu'tist.** [Gr. *pharmakeutikos*.]

pharmacology, etc. See **pharmacy.**

pharmacopoeia *fär-mə-kə-pē'ə* or *-pē'yə*, *n* a book or list of drugs with directions for their preparation; a collection of drugs. [Gr. *pharmakopoiiā* — *pharmakon*, a drug, *poieein*, to make.]

pharmacy *fär'mə-si*, *n* the art, practice or science of collecting, preparing, preserving and dispensing medicines; the art of preparing and mixing medicines; a druggist's shop; a dispensary. — *n* **phar'macist** (*-sist*) a druggist, someone skilled in pharmacy; someone legally qualified to sell drugs and poisons. — *n* **pharmacol'ogist.** — *n* **pharmacol'ogy** the science of drugs. [Gr. *pharmakeiā*, use of drugs, *pharmakon*, a drug.]

pharynx *far'ingks*, (*anat*) *n* the cleft or cavity forming the upper part of the gullet, lying behind the nose, mouth and larynx: — *pl* **phar'ynges** (*-in-jēz*) or **phar'ynxes.** — *adj* **pharyngal** (*fa-ring'gl*) or **pharyngeal** (*fa-rin'ji-əl* or *-jē'əl*). — *n* **pharyngitis** (*far-in-jī'tis*) inflammation of the mucous membrane of the pharynx. — *n* **pharyngol'ogy** the study of the pharynx and its diseases. — *n* **pharyngoscope** (*fa-ring'gə-skōp*) an instrument for inspecting the pharynx. — *n* **pharyngoscopy** (*far-ing-gos'kə-pi*). — *n* **pharyngot'omy** the operation of making an incision into the pharynx. [Gr. *pharynx*, *-ygos*, later *-yngos*.]

phase *fāz*, *n* a stage in growth or development (*lit* and *fig*); the aspect or appearance of anything at any stage; the stage of advancement in a periodic change, measured from some standard point; the appearance at a given time of the illuminated surface exhibited by the moon or a planet — also **phasis** (*fā'sis*); *pl* **phases** (*fā'ziz* or *fā'sēz*); a morph (*zool*); one of the circuits in an electrical system in which there are two or more alternating currents out of phase with each other by equal amounts (*electr*). — *vt* to do by phases or stages. — *adj* **phased** adjusted to be in the same phase at the same time; by stages. — *n* **phā'sic** (or *-sik'*). — **phase-contrast (or phase-difference) microscope** one in which the clear detail is obtained by means of a device that alters the speed of some of the rays of light, so that staining is unnecessary. — **in** or **out of phase** in the same phase together, or in different phases; **phase in** or **out** to begin or cease gradually to use, make, etc. [Gr. *phasis* — *phaein*, to shine.]

phaseolin *fə-sē'ə-lin*, *n* a protein found in kidney-beans used to increase the protein content and nutritional value of other crops. [L. *phaseolus*, a kidney-bean.]

phasic. See **phase**.

phasis[1]. See **phase**.

phasis[2]. See **phatic**.

phatic *fat'ik*, *adj* using speech for social reasons, to communicate feelings rather than ideas. — *n* **phasis** (*fā'sis*). [Gr. *phasis*, utterance.]

PhD *abbrev* for *Philosophiae Doctor* (L.), Doctor of Philosophy.

pheasant *fez'nt*, *n* a richly-coloured, long-tailed (of the male), gallinaceous bird, a half-wild game bird in Britain; extended to others of the same or related genus (such as *golden*, *silver*, *Argus*, *Amherst's* pheasant) and to other birds; the flesh of the bird as food: — *pl* **pheas'ant** or **pheas'ants**. — *n* **pheas'antry** an enclosure for rearing pheasants. — **pheas'ant's-eye** a plant with deep-red dark-centred flowers. [A.Fr. *fesant* — L. *phāsiānus* — Gr. *phāsiānos* (*ornis*), (bird) from the river Phasis, in Colchis, ancient Asia.]

phellem *fel'əm*, (*bot*) *n* cork. [Gr. *phellos*, cork.]

phen- *fēn-* or **pheno-** *fēn-ō-*, *combining form* denoting: showing, visible; related to benzene (see **phene**). [Gr. *phainein*, to show.]

phenacetin *fin-as'i-tin*, *n* a drug that counteracts fevers, an antipyretic, $C_{10}H_{13}NO_2$. [**acetic** and **phene**.]

phencyclidine *fen-sī'kli-dēn*, *n* an analgesic and anaesthetic drug, $C_{17}H_{25}N{\cdot}HCl$, also used as a hallucinogen. [*phen-*, *cyclo-* and piper*idine*.]

phene *fēn*, *n* an old name for benzene. — *adj* **phēn'ic** (or *fen'*) of benzene or of phenyl. [Gr. *phainein*, to show, because obtained in the manufacture of illuminating gas.]

phenetics *fi-net'iks*, (*biol*) *nsing* a system of classification of organisms based on observable similarities and differences irrespective of whether or not the organisms are related. — *adj* **phenet'ic**. [*phen*otype and gen*etics*.]

phengophobia *fen-gō-fō'bi-ə*, *n* fear of or aversion to daylight, photophobia. [Gr. *phainein*, to show, and **phobia**.]

phenobarbitone *fē-nō-bär'bi-tōn*, *n* a sedative and hypnotic drug.

phenocryst *fē'nō-krist*, *n* a larger crystal in a porphyritic rock. [Gr. *phainein*, to show, and **crystal**.]

phenol *fē'nol*, *n* carbolic acid, obtained from coal-tar, a strong disinfectant; extended to the class of aromatic compounds with one or more hydroxyl groups directly attached to the benzene nucleus, weak acids with reactions of alcohols. — *n* **phenolphthalein** (*fē-nol-fthal'i-in* or *-thal'*) a substance obtained from phenol and phthalic anhydride, brilliant red in alkalis, colourless in acids, used as an indicator. [See **phene**; *-ol* from **alcohol**.]

phenology *fē-nol'ə-ji*, *n* the study of organisms as affected by climate, esp. dates of seasonal phenomena, such as opening of flowers, arrival of migrants. — *adj* **phenological** (*-ə-loj'*). — *n* **phenol'ogist**. [Gr. *phainein*, to show, *logos*, discourse.]

phenom *fē-nom'*, (*slang*) *n* someone or something phenomenally good.

phenomenon *fi-nom'i-nən* or *-non*, *n* a remarkable or unusual person, thing or appearance, a prodigy; anything directly apprehended by the senses or one of them; an event that may be observed; the appearance which anything makes to our consciousness, as distinguished from what it is in itself (*philos*): — *pl* **phenom'ena**. — *adj* **phenom'enal** pertaining to a phenomenon; of the nature of a phenomenon; very or unexpectedly large, good, etc. (*colloq*). — *vt* **phenom'enalise** or **-ize** to represent as a phenomenon. — *n* **phenom'enalism** the doctrine that phenomena are the only realities, or that knowledge can only comprehend phenomena — also called *externalism* (*philos*). — *n* **phenom'enalist**. — *adj* **phenomenalist'ic**. — *n* **phenomenality** (*-al'i-ti*) the character of being phenomenal. — *adv* **phenom'enally**. — *adj* **phenomenolog'ical**. — *n* **phenomenol'ogist**. — *n* **phenomenol'ogy** the science of observing, or a description of, phenomena; the philosophy of Edmund Husserl (1859–1938), concerned with the experiences of the self. [Gr. *phainomenon*, neut. pres. p. pass. of *phainein*, to show.]

phenothiazine *fē-nō-* or *fen-ō-thī'ə-zēn*, *n* a toxic, heterocyclic compound, $C_{12}H_9NS$, used as a veterinary anthelminthic; any of a number of derivatives of this, used as tranquillisers. [**pheno-**, **thio-**, **azo-** and *-ine*.]

phenotype *fēn'ō-tīp*, *n* the observable characteristics of an organism produced by the interaction of genes and environment; a group of individuals having the same characteristics of this kind. — *vt* to categorise by phenotype. — *adj* **phenotypic** or **phenotypical** (*-tip'*). [Gr. *phainein*, to show, and **type**.]

phenyl *fē'nil*, *n* an organic radical, C_6H_5, found in benzene, phenol, etc. — *adj* **phenyl'ic**. — *n* **phenylal'anin** or **phenylal'anine** an amino-acid present in most food proteins. — **phenylbutazone** (*-būt'ə-zōn*) an analgesic and antipyretic used in the treatment of rheumatic disorders and also (illegally) in horse-doping. — *n* **phenylketonuria** (*-kē-tō-nū'ri-ə*) an inherited metabolic disorder in infants in which there is an inability to break down phenylalanine, commonly later resulting in mental defect, unless a phenylalanine-free diet is given. — *n* **phenylketonū'ric** a person who suffers from phenylketonuria. — Also *adj*. [**phene** and Gr. *hȳlē*, material.]

pheromone *fer'ə-mōn*, *n* a chemical substance secreted by an animal which influences the behaviour of others of its species, e.g. queen bee substance. [Gr. *pherein*, to bear, and **hormone**.]

phew *fū*, *interj* an exclamation of relief, astonishment, vexation, unexpected difficulty, impatience, contempt, etc. [A half-formed whistle.]

phi *fī* or *fē*, *n* the twenty-first letter (Φ, φ) of the Greek alphabet. [Gr. *phei*.]

phial *fī'əl*, *n* a vessel for liquids, esp. now a small medicine bottle. [L. *phiala* — Gr. *phialē*, a broad shallow bowl.]

Phi Beta Kappa *fī'* (or *fē'*) *bē'* (or *bā'*)*'tə kap'ə*, *n* the oldest of the American college societies. [Gr. *Φ.B.K.*, the initial letters of its motto — *Philosophiā biou kybernētēs*, Philosophy is the guide of life.]

Phil. *abbrev* for: Philadelphia (U.S. state); (the Letter to the) Philippians (*Bible*); philology; philosophy.

phil- *fil-* or **philo-** *fil-ō-*, *combining form* denoting: loving; lover. — **-phil** (*-fil*) or **-phile** (*-fīl*) lover of; loving; **-philia** or **-phily** love of; **-philic** (also, as *n sfx*, lover of) or **-philous** loving; **-philus** in zoological names, lover of (usu. a specified food). [Gr. *philos*, friend — *phileein*, to love.]

philabeg. Same as **filibeg.**

philadelphus *fil-ə-del'fəs, n* any shrub (esp. mock-orange) of the genus *Philadelphus*, tall deciduous shrubs with showy flowers. [N.L. — Gr. *philadelphon*, loving one's brother.]

philander *fil-an'dər, vi* to womanise; to flirt or have casual affairs with women. — *n* **philan'derer** a man who enjoys, and often has a reputation for, philandering. [Gr. *philandros*, fond of men or of a husband; misapplied as if meaning a loving man.]

philanthropy *fil-an'thrə-pi, n* love of mankind esp. as shown by contributing (money, time, etc.) to general welfare. — *n* **philan'thropist** someone who tries to benefit mankind. — Also **philanthrope** (*fil'ən-thrōp*). — *adj* **philanthropic** (*-throp'ik*) doing good to others, benevolent. — *adv* **philanthrop'ically.** [**phil-**, and Gr. *anthrōpos*, a man.]

philately *fil-at'i-li, n* the study and collection of postage and revenue stamps, related labels, etc.; stamp-collecting. — *adj* **philatelic** (*fil-ə-tel'ik*). — *n* **philat'elist.** [Fr. *philatélie*, invented in 1864 — Gr. *atelēs*, tax-free — *a-* (privative) and *telos*, tax.]

-phile. See **phil-.**

Philem. (*Bible*) *abbrev* for (the Letter to) Philemon.

philharmonic *fil-är-mon'ik*, also *-här-* or *-ər-*, *adj* fond of music. [**phil-** and Gr. *harmoniā*, harmony.]

philhellenic *fil-hel-ēn'ik* or *-en'ik, adj* loving or having an enthusiasm for Greece, esp. Greek culture; favouring the Greeks. — *n* **philhellene** (*-hel'ēn*) or **philhellenist** (*-hel'in-ist*) a supporter of Greece, esp. in 1821–32. — *n* **philhell'enism.** [**phil-** and Gr. *Hellēn*, a Greek.]

-philia. See **phil-.**

philibeg. Same as **filibeg.**

Philippian *fil-ip'i-ən, n* a native of *Philippi* in Macedonia. — Also *adj.*

Philippic *fil-ip'ik, n* one of the three orations of Demosthenes against Philip of Macedon; (without *cap*) any discourse full of invective. [Gr. *philippikos* — *Philippos*, Philip.]

Philistine *fil'is-tīn* or in U.S. *fil-is'tīn, n* one of the ancient inhabitants of south-west Palestine, enemies of the Israelites; (usu. without *cap*) a person of material outlook, usu. indifferent or hostile to culture. — Also *adj* (sometimes without *cap*). — *n* **Phil'istinism** (sometimes without *cap*). [Gr. *Philistīnos, Palaistīnos* — Heb. *P'lishtīm.*]

phillabeg, phillibeg. Same as **filibeg.**

phillumeny *fil-ōō'mən-i, n* the collecting of matchbox labels. — *n* **phillu'menist.** [L. *lūmen, -inis*, light.]

philo-. See **phil-.**

philogyny *fil-oj'i-ni, n* love of women. — *adj* **philog'ynous.** — *n* **philog'ynist.** [Gr. *philogyniā* — *gynē*, a woman.]

philology *fil-ol'ə-ji, n* the science of language; the study of etymology, grammar, rhetoric and literary criticism; the study of literary and non-literary texts; the study of culture through texts. — *n* **philol'oger, philologian** (*fil-ə-lō'*), **philol'ogist** or **phil'ologue** (*-log*) a person who studies philology. — *adj* **philologic** (*-ə-loj'ik*) or **philolog'ical.** — *adv* **philolog'ically.** — **comparative philology** the study of languages by comparing their history, forms, and relationships with each other. [Gr. *philologiā* — **phil-**, *logos*, word.]

philosopher *fi-los'ə-fər, n* someone who studies or is versed in or devoted to philosophy; a metaphysician; someone who acts calmly and rationally in changing or trying situations. — *adj* **philosophic** (*-sof'* or *-zof'*) or **philosoph'ical** pertaining or according to philosophy; skilled in or devoted to philosophy; befitting or suitable for a philosopher; tending to philosophise; rational; calm. — *adv* **philosoph'ically.** — *vi* **philos'ophise** or **-ize** to reason like a philosopher; to form philosophical theories. — *vt* to explain philosophically. — *n* **philos'ophiser** or **-z-** a would-be philosopher. — *n* **philos'ophy** investigation of the nature of being; knowledge of the causes and laws of all things; the principles underlying any department of knowledge; reasoning; a particular philosophical system; calmness of temper. — **philosopher's stone** an imaginary stone or mineral compound, long sought after by alchemists as a means of transforming other metals into gold. — **moral** and **natural philosophy** see under **moral** and **natural.** [Gr. *philosophos* — *sophiā*, wisdom.]

-philous. See **phil-.**

philoxenia *fil-ok-sē'ni-ə, n* hospitality. [Gr. *xenos*, guest, stranger.]

philtre or **philter** *fil'tər, n* a drink, or (*rarely*) a spell, to excite love. [Fr. *philtre* — Gr. *philtron* — *phileein*, to love, *-tron*, agent-sfx.]

-phily. See **phil-.**

phimosis *fī-mō'sis*, (*med*) *n* narrowness or constriction of the foreskin, which prevents it being drawn back over the glans penis. [Gr. *phīmōsis*, muzzling — *phīmos*, a muzzle.]

phiz *fiz* or **phizog** *fiz-og'*, (*slang*) *n* the face. [**physiognomy.**]

phlebitis *fli-bī'tis*, (*med*) *n* inflammation of a vein. — *vt* **phlebot'omise** or **-ize** to bleed. — *n* **phlebot'omist** a blood-letter. — *n* **phlebot'omy** blood-letting. [Gr. *phleps, phlebos*, a vein.]

phlegm *flem, n* the thick, slimy matter secreted in the throat, and discharged by coughing; one (cold and moist) of the four humours or bodily fluids (*old physiol*); the temperament supposed to be due to the predominance of this humour, sluggish indifference; calmness. — Following words are pronounced *fleg-* unless indicated otherwise. — *adj* **phlegmat'ic** or **phlegmat'ical** having a great deal of or generating phlegm; cold and sluggish; not easily excited. — *adv* **phlegmat'ically.** — *adj* **phlegmy** (*flem'i*). [L. *phlegma* — Gr. *phlegma, -atos*, flame, inflammation, phlegm (regarded as produced by heat), inflammation — *phlegein*, to burn.]

phloem *flō'əm*, (*bot*) *n* the bast or sieve-tube portion of a vascular bundle, by which synthesised food materials are transported in a plant. [Gr. *phloos*, bark.]

phlomis *flō'mis, n* a plant of the *Phlomis* genus of labiate herbs and shrubs with whorls of white, yellow or purple flowers and wrinkled, often woolly, leaves. [Gr. *phlomis*, mullein.]

phlox *floks, n* a plant of the Siberian and American *Phlox* genus of Polemoniaceae, well-known garden plants: — *pl* **phlox** or **phlox'es.** [Gr. *phlox*, flame, wallflower — *phlegein*, to burn.]

phlyctaena or **phlyctena** *flik-tē'nə*, (*med*) *n* a small blister or vesicle: — *pl* **phlyctae'nae** or **phlycte'nae** (*-nē*). [Gr. *phlyktaina*, a blister — *phlyein*, to swell.]

phobia *fō'bi-ə, n* a fear, aversion or hatred, esp. a morbid and irrational one. — Also **phobism** (*fō'bizm*). — **-phobe** *combining form* denoting someone who has a (specified) phobia. — **-phobia** *combining form* denoting a fear or hatred of (a specified object, condition, etc.). — *adj* **phō'bic.** [Gr. *phobos*, fear.]

phocine *fō'sīn, adj* relating to seals. [Gr. *phōkē*, a seal.]

phoebe *fē'bi, n* a N. American flycatcher of the genus *Sayornis.* [Imit.]

Phoenician *fi-nish'ən* or *-yen, adj* of ancient *Phoenicia*, on the coast of Syria, its people, colonies (including Carthage), language and arts. — *n* one of the people of Phoenicia; their Semitic language. [Gr. *Phoinix, -īkos.*]

phoenix *fē'niks, n* a legendary Arabian bird, worshipped in ancient Egypt, the only individual of its kind, that burned itself every 500 years or so and rose rejuvenated from its ashes; anything that rises from its own or its predecessor's ashes. — *n* **phoen'ixism** (*stock exchange*) the practice of forming, usu. with the same directors, workforce, premises, etc. of a bankrupted company, a new company that is therefore able to continue the same trading debt-free. [O.E. *fenix*, later assimilated to L. *phoenīx* — Gr. *phoinix*.]

phon *fon*, (*acoustics*) *n* a unit of loudness, the number of phons of a particular sound being equal to the number of decibels of a pure tone (with a frequency of 1000 hertz) judged, or proved by measurement, to be of the same loudness. — *n* **phonom'eter** (*fə-nom'i-tər*) or **phon'meter** (*fon'mē-tər*) an apparatus for estimating loudness level in phons. [From Gr. *phōnē*, sound.]

phon. *abbrev* for phonetics.

phonate *fō-nāt'*, *vi* to utter vocal sounds. — *n* **phonā'tion.** — *n* **phō'natory.** [From Gr. *phōnē*, sound.]

phone[1] *fōn*, (*phon*) *n* a single or elementary speech sound. [Gr, *phōnē*, sound.]

phone[2] or **'phone** *fōn*, *n* short for **telephone.** — *vt* and *vi* to telephone. — *n* **phō'ner** a person who telephones. — **phone call; phone'card** a card, purchasable from newsagents, post offices, etc., that can be used instead of cash to pay for phone calls from appropriate telephone kiosks; **phone freak** (*slang*) a person who misuses the telephone, by telephoning obscene messages to strangers, trying to make free calls, etc.; **phone freaking; phone'-in** a radio or television programme in which phone calls are invited from listeners or viewers and are broadcast live, with discussion by an expert, panel, etc. in the studio; **phoner-in'.**

-phone *-fōn*, *adj* and *n combining form* used to signify speaking, as in *Francophone* (speaking, or a person who speaks, French). [Gr. *phōnē*, voice, sound.]

phoneme *fō'nēm*, (*linguis*) *n* the smallest significant unit of sound in a language; any of the speech sounds in a language that serve to make one word different from another. — *adj* **phonē'mic.** — *adv* **phonē'mically.** — *n* **phonē'micist.** — *nsing* **phonē'mics** the science or study of the phonemes of a language; the phonemes of a language and the patterns and structures in which they occur. [Gr. *phōnēma*, an utterance, sound made.]

phonetic *fə-net'ik*, *adj* of, concerning, according to, or representing, the sounds of spoken language. — *adv* **phonet'ically** according to pronunciation. — *n* **phoneti'cian** or **phō'netist** a person who is expert in phonetics. — *n* **phoneticisā'tion** or **phonetisa'tion.** — *vt* **phonet'icise** or **phō'netise** to represent phonetically; to make phonetic. — *nsing* **phonet'ics** that branch of linguistic science that deals with pronunciation, speech production, etc. — *npl* phonetic representations. — **phonetic alphabet** a list of symbols used in phonetic transcriptions; a system (used in voice communications) in which letters of the alphabet are identified by means of code words; **phonetic spelling** the writing of a language by means of a separate symbol for every sound; an unconventional spelling system adopted as a guide to pronunciation. [Gr. *phōnētikos*, relating to speech.]

phoney or in U.S. **phony** *fō'ni*, (*colloq*) *adj* fake, counterfeit; unreal. — *n* someone insincere, a fraud; something not genuine, a fake. — *n* **phon'eyness** or in U.S. **phon'iness.** [Perh. — Ir. *fáinne*, a ring, from the old practice of tricking people into buying gilt rings which they believed to be genuine gold.]

phonic *fon'ik* or *fō'nik*, *adj* relating to sounds, esp. vocal sound. — *adv* **phon'ically** (or *fō'nik-*). — *nsing* **phon'ics** (or *fō'niks*) the science of sound or of spoken sounds; the phonic method. — **phonic ear®** a type of radio microphone system, for the benefit of the deaf, in which the teacher wears a transmitter and the student wears a receiver, either with a built-in or an individual hearing-aid; **phonic method** a method of teaching reading through the phonetic value of letters or groups of letters. [Gr. *phōnikos*, relating to speech.]

phono- *fō-nō-*, *fō-no-* or *fō-nə-*, *combining form* denoting voice or sound. — *n* **phō'nofiddle** a one-stringed musical instrument which sounds through a metal amplifying horn. — *n* **phonogram** (*fō'nə-gram*) a character representing a sound. — *n* **phonograph** (*fō'nə-gräf*) a character used to represent a sound; Edison's instrument for recording sounds on a cylinder and reproducing them; a gramophone (*US old*). — *adj* **phonographic** (*fō-nə-graf'ik*) phonetic; of phonography; of or by means of the phonograph. — *adv* **phonograph'ically.** — *n* **phonography** (*fə-nog'rə-fi*) the art of representing each spoken sound by a distinct character; Pitman's phonetic shorthand; the use of the phonograph. — *n* **phonology** (*fə-nol'ə-ji*) the study of the system of sounds in a language, and sometimes the history of their changes. — *adj* **phonolog'ical.** — *n* **phonol'ogist.** — *nsing* **phonotac'tics** (the study of) the ways in which the sounds of a language can appear in the words of that language. [Gr. *phōnē*, sound, voice.]

phonolite *fō'nə-līt*, *n* clinkstone, a fine-grained intermediate igneous rock that rings when struck by a hammer. — *adj* **phonolit'ic** (*-lit'ik*). [Gr. *phōnē*, sound, *lithos*, stone.]

phony. See **phoney.**

phooey *fōō'i*, *interj* an exclamation of contempt, scorn, disbelief, etc. [Perh. conn. with **phew,** or a similar exclamation, or perh. from Yiddish *fooy*, Ger. *pfui*.]

-phore or **-phor** *-fōr*, *combining form* used to denote 'carrier', as in *semaphore, chromatophore.* — *adj combining form* **-phorous.** — *n combining form* **-phoresis** (*-fə-rē'sis*) denoting a transmission, migration, as in *electrophoresis.* [Gr. *phoros*, bearing — *pherein*.]

phosgene *fos'jēn*, *n* a poisonous gas, carbonyl chloride ($COCl_2$). [Gr. *phōs*, light, and the root of *gignesthai*, to be produced.]

phosphate, etc., **phosphatide, phosphide.** See under **phosphorus.**

phosphorus *fos'fə-rəs*, *n* a non-metallic element (symbol **P**; atomic no. 15) a waxy, poisonous and inflammable substance giving out light in the dark. — *n* **phosphate** (*fos'fāt*) a salt of phosphoric acid. — *vt* to treat or coat with a phosphate as a means of preventing corrosion. — *adj* **phosphatic** (*fos-fat'ik*) of the nature of, or containing, a phosphate. — *n* **phos'phatide** a phospholipid. — *vt* **phos'phatise** or **-ize** to phosphate. — *n* **phos'phide** (*-fīd*) a compound of phosphorus and another element. — *n* **phos'phine** (*-fēn* or *-fīn*) phosphuretted hydrogen gas (PH_3); extended to substances analogous to amines with phosphorus instead of nitrogen. — *n* **phos'phite** a salt of phosphorous acid. — *n* **phospholip'id** a lipid which contains a phosphate group and usu. also a nitrogenous group, a component of cell membranes. — *n* **phosphopro'tein** any of a number of compounds formed by a protein with a substance containing phosphorus, other than a nucleic acid or lecithin. — *vt* **phos'phorate** to combine or impregnate with phosphorus; to make phosphorescent. — *vi* **phosphoresce'** to shine in the dark like phosphorus. — *n* **phosphoresc'ence.** — *adj* **phosphoresc'ent.** — *adj* **phos'phoretted** (or *-et'*) see **phosphuretted.** — *adj* **phosphoric** (*fos-for'ik*) of or like phosphorus; phosphorescent; containing phosphorus in higher valency (*chem*). — *vt* **phos'phorise** or **-ize** to combine or impregnate with phosphorus; to make phosphorescent. — *adj* **phos'phorous** phosphorescent; containing phosphorus in lower valency (*chem*). — *adj* **phos'phuretted** (or *-et'*) combined with phosphorus (**phosphuretted** or **phosphoretted hydrogen** phosphine). [L. *phōsphorus* — Gr. *phōsphoros*, light-bearer — *phōs*, light, *phoros*, bearing, from *pherein*, to bear.]

phot *fot* or *fōt*, *n* the CGS unit of illumination, 1 lumen per square centimetre. [Gr. *phōs*, *phōtos*, light.]

phot. *abbrev* for: photographic; photography.

photic *fō'tik*, *adj* of light; light-giving; sensitive to light; accessible to light (as e.g. the uppermost layer of sea). [Gr. *phōs*, *phōtos*, light.]

photism *fō'tizm*, *n* a hallucinatory vision of light; a visual sensation that results from the experience of hearing, feeling, tasting, smelling or thinking something. [Gr. *phōs*, *phōtos*, light.]

photo *fō'to*, *n* short for **photograph**: — *pl* **phō'tos.** — As *combining form* see **photo-**[2].

photo-[1] *fō-tō-*, *fō-to-* or *fō-tə-* or **phot-** *fōt-*, *combining form* signifying light. — *adj* **photoac'tive** affected physically or chemically by light or other radiation. — *n* **phō'to-ageing** ageing of the skin caused by exposure to ultraviolet light. — *n* **photocatal'ysis** the promotion, acceleration or retardation of a chemical reaction by light. — *adj* **photocatalyt'ic.** — *n* **pho'tocell** a photoelectric cell. — *adj* **photochem'ical.** — *n* **photochem'ist.** — *n* **photochem'istry** the part of chemistry dealing with changes brought about by light, or other radiation, and with the production of radiation by chemical change. — *adj* **photoconduct'ing** or **photoconduct'ive** relating to, or showing, photoconductivity. — *n* **photoconductiv'ity** the property of varying conductivity under influence of light. — *n* **photodi'ode** a two-electrode semiconductor device, used as an optical sensor. — *n* **photoelectric'ity** electricity or a change of electric condition, produced by light or other electromagnetic radiation. — *adj* **photoelec'tric** relating to photoelectricity, to photoelectrons, or to electric light (**photoelectric cell** any device in which incidence of light of suitable frequency causes an alteration in electrical state, esp. by photo-emission). — *n* **photoelec'trode** an electrode which is activated by light. — *n* **photoelec'tron** an electron ejected from a body by the incidence of ultraviolet rays or X-rays upon it. — *nsing* **photoelectron'ics** the science dealing with the interactions of electricity and electromagnetic radiations, esp. those that involve free electrons. — *n* **photo-emiss'ion** emission of electrons from the surface of a body on which light falls. — *adj* **photogenic** (*-jen'* or *-jēn'*) producing light; produced by light. — See also **photogenic** under **photo-**[2]. — *n* **photokinesis** (*-ki-nē'sis* or *-kī-*) movement occurring in response to variations in light intensity. — *vi* **photoluminesce'** to produce photoluminescence. — *n* **photoluminesc'ence** luminescence produced by exposure to visible light or infrared or ultraviolet radiation. — *adj* **photoluminesc'ent.** — *vt* **pho'tolyse** to cause photolysis in. — *vi* to undergo photolysis. — *n* **photolysis** (*fə-tol'i-sis*) decomposition or dissociation under the influence of radiation (*chem*). — *adj* **photolytic** (*fō-tə-lit'ik*). — *n* **photom'eter** an instrument for measuring luminous intensity, usu. by comparing two sources of light. — *adj* **photomet'ric.** — *n* **photom'etry** (the branch of physics dealing with) the measurement of luminous intensity. — *n* **photope'riod** the period during every 24 hours when an organism is exposed to daylight. — *adj* **photoperiod'ic.** — *n* **photope'riodism** the physiological and behavioural reactions of organisms to changes in the length of the daylight period. — *n* **photopho'bia** phengophobia. — *n* **photopolarim'eter** a telescopic instrument for photographing planets and other distant objects and measuring the polarisation of light from them. — *n* **photop'sia** or **photop'sy** the appearance of flashes of light, owing to irritation of the retina. — *n* **photorecep'tor** a nerve-ending receiving light stimuli. — *adj* **photoresist'** (of an organic material) that polymerises on exposure to ultraviolet light and in that form resists attack by acids and solvents. — Also *n*. — *vt* **photosens'itise** or **-ize** to make photosensitive by chemical or other means. — *n* **photosens'itiser** or **-z-**. — *adj* **photosens'itive** affected by light, visible or invisible. — *n* **photosensitiv'ity.** — *n* **pho'tosphere** the luminous envelope of the sun's globe, the source of light. — *n* **photosynthesis** (*fō-tō-sin'thi-sis*; *bot*) the building up of complex compounds by the chlorophyll apparatus of plants by means of the energy of light. — *adj* **photosynthet'ic.** — *n* **phototax'is** (*biol*) locomotory response or reaction of an organism or cell to the stimulus of light. — *adj* **phototac'tic.** — *n* **photot'ropism** orientation in response to the stimulus of light (*bot*); reversible colour change on exposure to light (*chem*). — *n* **phō'totrope** a substance that changes thus. — *adj* **phototrop'ic.** — *n* **photot'ropy** change of colour due to the wavelength of incident light. — *adj* **photovoltaic** (*fō-tō-vol-tā'ik*) producing an electromotive force across the junction between dissimilar materials when it is exposed to light or ultraviolet radiation, e.g. in a **photovoltaic cell.** — *nsing* **photovolta'ics** the science and technology of photovoltaic devices and substances. [Gr. *phōs*, *phōtos*, light.]

photo-[2] *fō-tō-*, *fō-to-* or *fō-tə-*, *combining form* denoting: photographic; made by, or by the aid of, photographic means; representing **photo**, shortening of **photograph.** — *n* **photo call** an arranged opportunity for press photographers to take publicity photographs of e.g. a celebrity. — *n* **pho'tocomposition** (*printing*) setting of copy by projecting images of letters successively on a sensitive material from which printing plates are made. — *adj* **pho'tocopiable.** — *n* **pho'tocopier** a machine which makes photocopies. — *n* **phō'tocopy** a photographic reproduction of written matter, etc. — *vt* to make a photocopy of. — *n* **pho'tocopying.** — *n* **pho'to-engraving** or **-etching** any process of engraving by aid of photography, esp. from relief plates. — *n* **photo finish** a race finish in which a special type of photography is used to show the winner, etc.; a neck and neck finish of any contest. — *n* **Pho'tofit®** (also without *cap*) a method of making identification pictures, an alternative to identikit (q.v.). — *adj* **photogen'ic** (or *-jē'nik*) having the quality of photographing well; (*loosely*) attractive, striking. — *n* **pho'togram** a type of picture produced by placing an object on or near photographic paper which is then exposed to light. — *n* **photogramm'etry** (*image tech*) the use of photographic records for precise measurement of distances or dimensions — e.g. aerial photography for surveying. — *n* **photogravure** (*fō-tō-grə-vūr'*) a method of photo-engraving in which the design etched on the metal surface is intaglio, not relief; a picture produced by this method. — *n* **photojour'nalism** journalism in which written material is subordinate to photographs. — *n* **photojour'nalist.** — *n* and *vt* **photolith'ograph.** — *n* **photolithog'rapher.** — *adj* **photolithograph'ic.** — *n* **photolithog'raphy** a process of lithographic printing from a photographically produced plate. — *n* **photomac'rograph** a photograph of an object that is unmagnified or only slightly magnified. — *adj* **photomacrograph'ic.** — *n* **photomacrog'raphy.** — *n* **photomī'crograph** an enlarged photograph of a microscopic object taken through a microscope. — *n* **photomicrog'rapher.** — *adj* **photomicrograph'ic.** — *n* **photomicrog'raphy.** — *n* **photomon'tage** (*-täzh*) (the art of making) a picture made by cutting up photographs, etc., and arranging the parts so as to convey, without explicitly showing, a definite meaning. — *n* **photo opportunity** an opportunity for press photographers to get good or interesting pictures of a celebrity, either arranged by the celebrity (esp. for publicity purposes) or arising more or less by chance during some event the celebrity is participating in. — *n* **pho'torealism** (*art*) an esp. detailed, precise painting style (suggestive of and often worked from a photograph), giving an effect of (often exaggerated) realism. — *n* **pho'tosetting** photocomposition. — *n* **Photostat®** (*fō'tō-stat*) a photographic apparatus for making facsimiles of MSS., drawings, etc., directly; a facsimile so made. — *vt* and *vi* to photograph by Photostat. — *n* **phototel'egraph** an instrument for transmitting drawings, photographs, etc., by telegraphy. — *n* **phototeleg'raphy**. — *n* **phō'totype** a printing block on which the material is produced photographically; a print made from such a block; the process of making such a block. — *vt* to reproduce by phototype. — *adj* **phototypic** (*-tip'ik*). — *n* **phototypy** (*fō'tō-tī-pi* or *fō-tot'i-pi*). [**photograph.**]

photography *fə-tog'rə-fi, n* the art or process of producing permanent and visible images by the action of light, or other radiant energy, on chemically prepared surfaces. — *n* **photograph** (*fō'tə-gräf*) an image so produced. — *vt* to make a picture of by means of photography. — *vi* to take photographs; to be capable of being photographed. — *n* **photog'rapher**. — *adj* **photographic** (*-graf'ik*). — *adv* **photograph'ically**. [Gr. *phōs, phōtos*, light, *graphein*, to draw.]

photon *fō'ton, n* a quantum of light or other radiation. — *nsing* **photon'ics** the study of the applications of photons, e.g. in communication technology. [Gr. *phōs, phōtos*, light, with *-on* after **electron**.]

phrase *frāz, n* manner of expression in language; an expression; a group of words generally not forming a clause but felt as expressing a single idea or constituting a single element in the sentence; a pithy expression; a catchword; an empty or high-sounding expression; a short group of notes felt to form a unit (*mus*). — *vt* to express in words; to style; to flatter, wheedle (*Scot*); to mark, bring out, or give effect to the phrases of (*mus*). — *adj* **phrās'al** consisting of, or of the nature of, a phrase. — *adj* **phrase'less** incapable of being described. — *n* **phraseogram** (*frā'zi-ō-gram*) a single sign, written without lifting the pen, for a whole phrase (esp. in shorthand). — *n* **phra'seograph** a phrase that is so written. — *n* **phraseol'ogy** style or manner of expression or arrangement of phrases; peculiarities of diction; a collection of phrases in a language. — *n* **phra'sing** the wording of a speech or passage; the grouping and accentuation of the sounds in performing a melody (*mus*). — *adj* **phra'sy** inclining to emptiness and verbosity of phrase. — **phrasal verb** a phrase, consisting of a verb and one or more additional words, having the function of a verb; **phrase book** a book containing or explaining phrases of a language. — **turn of phrase** an expression; one's manner of expression. [Gr. *phrăsis* — *phrazein*, to speak.]

phreatic *frē-at'ik, adj* pertaining to underground water supplying, or probably able to supply, wells or springs, or to the soil or rocks containing it, or to wells; (of underground gases, etc.) present in, or causing, volcanic eruptions. — *n* **phreat'ophyte** a deep-rooted plant drawing its water from the water table or just above it. [Gr. *phrear*, well, *phreătia*, cistern.]

phrenic *fren'ik, adj* of, near or relating to the midriff or diaphragm. [Fr. *phrénique* — Gr. *phrēn, phrenos*, midriff.]

phrenology *fri-nol'ə-ji, n* a would-be science of mental faculties supposed to be located in various parts of the skull and investigable by feeling the bumps on the outside of the head. — *adj* **phrenologic** (*fren-ə-loj'ik*) or **phrenolog'ical**. — *adv* **phrenolog'ically**. — *vt* **phrenol'ogise** or **-ize** to examine phrenologically. [Gr. *phrēn, phrenos*, midriff (supposed seat of passions, mind, will) and **-logy**.]

Phrygian *frij'i-ən, adj* pertaining to *Phrygia* in ancient Asia Minor, or to its people. — *n* a native of Phrygia; the language of the ancient Phrygians. — **Phrygian cap** an ancient type of conical cap with the top turned forward, which in the French Revolution came to symbolise liberty.

phthalic *thal'ik* or *fthal'ik*, (*chem*) *adj* applied to three acids, $C_6H_4(COOH)_2$, and an anhydride, derived from naphthalene. — *n* **phthal'ate** a salt or ester of phthalic acid. — *n* **phthal'ein** (*-i-in*) any one of a very important class of dye-yielding materials formed by the union of phenols with phthalic anhydride. [**naphthalene.**]

phthisis *thī'sis*, also *fthī'* or *tī'sis*, (*med*; *old*) *n* wasting disease; tuberculosis, esp. of the lungs. — *n* **phthisic** (*tiz'ik*, sometimes *thī'sik, fthī'sik* or *tī'sik*) phthisis; vaguely, a lung or throat disease. — *adj* **phthisical** (*tiz'*) or **phthis'icky**. [Gr. *phthĭsis* — *phthi(n)ein*, to waste away.]

phut *fut, n* a dull sound esp. of collapse, deflation, etc. — Also *adv*, as in **go phut** to break, become unserviceable; to come to nothing. — *vi* to make, go, or land with, a phut or phuts. [Hind. *phatnā*, to split.]

pH value. See **pH**.

phyco- *fī-kō-, combining form* denoting seaweed. — *n* **phycocyan** (*-sī'an*) or **phycocy'anin** (*-ə-nin*; Gr. *kyanos*, dark blue) a blue pigment found in algae. — *n* **phycoerythrin** (*-e-rith'rin*; Gr. *erythros*, red) a red pigment found in algae. — *adj* **phycolog'ical**. — *n* **phycologist** (*-kol'ə-jist*). — *n* **phycol'ogy** the study of algae. — *n* **phycomy'cete** a fungus of the class (*Phycomycetes*) that shows affinities with the green seaweeds. — *n* **phycophaein** (*-fē'in*; Gr. *phaios*, grey) a brown pigment found in seaweeds. — *n* **phycoxan'thin** (Gr. *xanthos*, yellow) a yellow pigment found in diatoms, brown seaweeds, etc. [Gr. *phȳkos*, seaweed.]

phyla. See **phylum**.

phylactery *fi-lak'tə-ri, n* a charm or amulet; (among the Jews) a slip of parchment inscribed with certain passages of Scripture, worn in a box on the left arm or forehead; a reminder; ostentatious display of religious forms; a case for relics; (in mediaeval art), a scroll at the mouth of a figure in a picture bearing the words he is supposed to speak. [Gr. *phylaktērion* — *phylax*, a guard.]

phyletic *fī-let'ik*, (*biol*) *adj* pertaining to a phylum; according to presumed evolutionary descent. [Gr. *phȳletikos* — *phȳlē*, a tribe.]

phyllary *fil'ə-ri*, (*bot*) *n* an involucral bract. [Gr. *phyllarion*, dimin. of *phyllon*, leaf.]

phyllo. See **filo**.

phylloclade *fil'ō-klād*, (*bot*) *n* a flattened branch, with the shape and functions of a leaf. [Gr. *phyllon*, leaf, *klados*, shoot.]

phyllode *fil'ōd*, (*bot*) *n* a petiole with the appearance and function of a leaf-blade. [Gr. *phyllon*, leaf.]

phyllomania *fil-ō-mā'ni-ə*, (*bot*) *n* excessive production of leaves, at the expense of flower or fruit production. [Gr. *phyllon*, leaf, *maniā*, madness.]

phylloquinone *fil-ō-kwin'ōn, n* vitamin K_1, one of the fat-soluble vitamin K group essential for normal blood coagulation. [Gr. *phyllon*, leaf, and **quinone**.]

phyllotaxis *fil-ō-tak'sis*, (*bot*) *n* the disposition of leaves on the stem. — Also **phyll'otaxy**. — *adj* **phyllotact'ic** or **phyllotact'ical**. [Gr. *phyllon*, a leaf, *taxis*, arrangement.]

phylloxera *fil-ok-sē'rə, n* an insect of the genus *Phylloxera*, similar to greenfly, very destructive to vines. [Gr. *phyllon*, a leaf, *xēros*, dry.]

phylogeny *fī-loj'i-ni* or **phylogenesis** *fī-lō-jen'i-sis, n* evolutionary pedigree or genealogical history. —

adj **phylogenet'ic**. — *adv* **phylogenet'ically**. [Gr. *phȳlon*, race, *genesis*, origin.]

phylum *fī'ləm*, *n* a main division of the animal or the vegetable kingdom: — *pl* **phy'la**. [N.L. — Gr. *phȳlon*, race.]

phys. *abbrev* for: physician; physics; physiology.

physalia *fī-sā'li-ə*, *n* a member of the genus (*Physalia*) of large oceanic colonial hydrozoans with a floating bladder — including the Portuguese man-of-war. [Gr. *phȳsallis*, a bladder, *phȳsētēr*, a blower, a whale, bellows — *phȳsaein*, to blow.]

physic *fiz'ik*, *n* anything healing or wholesome (*fig*); a medicine; the science, art or practice of medicine (*obs*). — *adj* **phys'ical** pertaining to the world of matter and energy, or its study, natural philosophy; material; bodily; requiring bodily effort; involving bodily contact. — *n* a physical examination of the body, e.g. to ascertain fitness. — *n* **phys'icalism** the theory that all phenomena are explicable in spatio-temporal terms and that all statements are either analytic or reducible to empirically verifiable assertions. — *n* **phys'icalist**. — *n* **physical'ity** preoccupation with the bodily. — *adv* **phys'ically**. — *n* **physician** (*fi-zish'n*) a doctor; someone legally qualified to practise medicine; a person skilled in the use of physic or the art of healing; someone who makes use of medicines and treatment, distinguished from a surgeon who practises manual operations. — *n* **physi'cianship**. — *n* **phys'icism** (*-sizm*) belief in the material or physical as opp. to the spiritual. — *n* **phys'icist** (*-sist*) an expert or student in physics; someone who believes the phenomena of life are purely physical. — *adj* **physicochem'ical** relating to or involving both physics and chemistry; pertaining to physical chemistry (see below). — *nsing* **phys'ics** the science of the properties (other than chemical) of matter and energy, and the forces and interrelationships between them; orig. natural science in general. — **physical astronomy** the study of the physical condition and chemical composition of the heavenly bodies; **physical chemistry** the study of the dependence of physical properties on chemical composition, and of the physical changes accompanying chemical reactions; **physical force** force applied outwardly to the body, as distinguished from persuasion, etc.; **physical geography** the study of the earth's natural features — its mountain chains, ocean currents, etc.; **physical jerks** (*colloq*) bodily exercises. [Gr. *physikos*, natural — *physis*, nature.]

physi- *fiz-i-* or **physio-** *fiz-i-ō-*, *combining form* signifying nature. — *n* **phys'io** short for **physiotherapist**: — *pl* **phys'ios**. [Gr. *physis*, nature.]

physiocracy *fiz-i-ok'rə-si*, *n* government, according to François Quesnay (1694–1774) and his followers, by a natural order inherent in society, land and its products being the only true source of wealth, direct taxation of land being the only proper source of revenue. — *n* **phys'iocrat** (*-ō-krat*) a person who maintains these opinions. — *adj* **physiocrat'ic**. [**physio-** and Gr. *krateein*, to rule.]

physiognomy *fiz-i-on'ə-mi* or *-og'nə-mi*, *n* the art of judging character from appearance, esp. from the face; the face as an index of the mind; the face (*colloq*); the general appearance of anything; character, aspect. — *adj* **physiognomic** (*-nom'ik*) or **physiognom'ical**. — *adv* **physiognom'ically**. — *n* **physiogn'omist**. [Gr. *physiognōmiā*, a shortened form of *physiognōmoniā* — *physis*, nature, *gnōmōn*, *-onos*, an interpreter.]

physiography *fiz-i-og'rə-fi*, *n* description of nature, descriptive science; physical geography. — *n* **physiog'rapher**. — *adj* **physiographic** (*-ō-graf'ik*) or **physiograph'ical**. [**physio-** and Gr. *graphein*, to write.]

physiology *fiz-i-ol'ə-ji*, *n* the science of the processes of life in animals and plants. — *adj* **physiologic** (*-ə-loj'ik*) or **physiolog'ical**. — *adv* **physiolog'ically**. — *n* **physiol'ogist**. [**physio-** and Gr. *logos*, discourse.]

physiotherapy *fiz-i-ō-ther'ə-pi*, *n* treatment of disease by remedies such as massage, fresh air, electricity, rather than by drugs. — Also *nsing* **physiotherapeutics** (*-pūt'iks*). — *adj* **physiotherapeut'ic**. — *n* **physiother'apist**. [**physio-** and Gr. *therapeiā*, treatment.]

physique *fiz-ēk'*, *n* bodily type, build or constitution. [Fr.]

phyto- *fī-tō-* or *-to-*, *combining form* denoting plant. — *combining form* **-phyte** used to indicate a plant belonging to a particular habitat, or of a particular type. — *adj combining form* **-phytic** (*-fit-ik*). — *n* **phytoalex'in** (Gr. *alexein*, to ward off) any substance produced by a plant as a defence against disease. — *n* **phytochem'ical** a chemical derived from a plant. — *adj* of chemicals in plants. — *n* **phytogen'esis** or **phytogeny** (*-toj'i-ni*) evolution of plants. — *adj* **phytogenet'ic** or **phytogen'ical** relating to phytogenesis. — *adj* **phytogenic** (*-jen'ik*) of vegetable origin. — *n* **phytog'rapher**. — *adj* **phytograph'ic**. — *n* **phytog'raphy** descriptive botany. — *n* **phytohor'mone** a plant hormone regulating growth, etc. — *adj* **phytolog'ical**. — *n* **phytol'ogist** a botanist. — *n* **phytol'ogy** botany. — *n* **phytonadione** (*fī-tō-nə-dī'ōn*) phylloquinone, vitamin K_1. — *n* **phytopathol'ogist**. — *n* **phytopathol'ogy** the study of plant diseases. — *n* **phyto'sis** the presence of vegetable parasites or disease caused by them. — *n* **phytot'omist**. — *n* **phytotomy** (*-tot'ə-mi*) plant anatomy. — *adj* **phytotox'ic** poisonous to plants; pertaining to a phytotoxin. — *n* **phytotoxic'ity** harmfulness to plants. — *n* **phytotox'in** a toxin produced by a plant. [Gr. *phyton*, plant.]

PI *abbrev* for: Philippines (I.V.R.); Private Investigator.

pi[1] *pī* or *pē*, *n* the sixteenth letter (Π, π) of the Greek alphabet, answering to the Roman P; a symbol for the ratio of the circumference of a circle to the diameter, approx. 3·14159 (*math*). — **pi-** (or π-) **meson** (*phys*) the source of the nuclear force holding protons and neutrons together. — Also called **pion**. [Gr. *pei*, *pī*.]

pi[2] (*printing*). Same as **pie**[2].

pi[3] *pī*, (*slang*) *adj* a short form for **pious**; religious; sanctimonious. — *n* a pious, religious or sanctimonious person or talk.

PIA *abbrev* for Pakistan International Airlines.

piacevole *pyə-chā'vo-lā*, (*mus*) *adj* pleasant, playful. [It.]

piaffe *pi-af'* or *pyaf*, (*dressage*) *vi* to advance at a piaffer. — *n* **piaff'er** a gait in which the horse's feet are lifted in the same succession as a trot, but more slowly. — Also called *Spanish-walk*. [Fr. *piaffer*.]

pia mater *pī'ə mā'tər*, (*anat*) *n* the vascular membrane surrounding the brain and spinal cord. [L. *pīa māter*, tender mother, a mediaeval trans. of Ar. *umm raqīqah*, thin mother.]

pianoforte *pya'nō-fōr-ti*, *pē-a'*, *pyä'* or *pē-ä'*, *n* generally shortened to **piano** (*pya'nō*, *pē-a'nō* or *pi-ä'nō*) a musical instrument with wires struck by hammers moved by keys: — *pl* **pia'nofortes** and **pia'nos**. — *n* **pianette** (*pē-ə-net'*) or **pianino** (*pya-nē'nō* or *pē-ə-nē'nō*) a small upright piano: — *pl* **piani'nos**. — *adj* and *adv* **pianissimo** (*pya-nēs'si-mō* or *pē-ə-nis'i-mō*) very soft. — *n* **pianist** (*pē'ə-nist* or *pyan'ist*; also *pē-an'ist*) a person who plays the pianoforte, esp. expertly. — *adj* **pianist'ic**. — *adv* **pianist'ically**. — *adj* and *adv* **piano** (*pyä'nō* or *pē-ä'nō*) soft, softly. — *n* a soft passage. — *n* **Pianola®** (*pyan-ō'lə* or *pē-ə-nō'lə*) a type of piano with a pneumatic mechanism for playing it by means of a perforated roll (a **piano roll**). — *n* **pianō'list**. — **piano-accord'ion** a sophisticated type of accordion with a keyboard like that of a piano; **pia'no-organ**

a piano like a barrel-organ, played by mechanical means; **pia'no-player** a mechanical contrivance for playing the piano; a pianist; **piano roll** see at **Pianola®** above; **pia'no-stool** a stool usu. adjustable in height for a pianist; **pia'no-wire** wire used for piano strings, and for deep-sea soundings, etc. — **player piano** a piano with a piano-player. [It. — *piano*, soft — L. *plānus*, level, *forte*, loud — L. *fortis*, strong.]

piano nobile *pyä'nō nō'bi-lā*, (*archit*) *n* the main floor of a large house or villa, usu. on the first floor. [It., noble storey.]

piassava *pē-əs-ä'və* or **piassaba** *-ä'bə*, *n* a coarse stiff fibre used for making brooms, etc., obtained from Brazilian palms; the tree yielding it. [Port. from Tupí.]

piastre *pi-as'tər*, *n* a unit of currency in current or former use in several N. African and Middle Eastern countries, equal to 1/100 of a (Sudanese, Egyptian, Syrian, etc.) pound; a coin of this value. [Fr., — It. *piastra*, a leaf of metal; see **plaster**.]

piazza *pē-ät'sə*, also *pē-ad'zə* or *pē-az'ə*, *n* a place or square surrounded by buildings; (*erron*) a walk under a roof supported by pillars; a veranda (*US*). — *adj* **piazz'ian**. [It., — L. *platea* — Gr. *plateia*, a street (fem. of *platys*, broad).]

pibroch *pē'brohh*, *n* the classical music of the bagpipe, free in rhythm and consisting of theme and variations. [Gael. *piobaireachd*, pipe-music — *piobair*, a piper — *piob*, from Eng. **pipe**[1].]

pic *pik*, (*colloq*) *n* a short form of **picture**: — *pl* **pics** or **pix**.

pica[1] *pī'kə*, (*printing*) *n* an old type size, approximately, and still used synonymously for, 12-point, giving about 6 lines to the inch, much used in typewriters. [Poss. used for printing *pies*; see **pie**[2].]

pica[2] *pī'kə*, (*med*) *n* unnatural craving for unsuitable food. [L. *pīca*, magpie.]

picador *pik'ə-dör*, *n* a mounted bullfighter with a lance. [Sp., — *pica*, a pike.]

picaroon *pik-ə-rōōn'*, *n* someone who lives by his wits; a cheat; a pirate. — *adj* **picaresque** (*-resk'*). — **picaresque novels** the tales of Spanish rogue and vagabond life, much in vogue in the 17th cent.; novels of similar type. [Sp. *picarón*, augm. of *pícaro*, rogue.]

picayune *pik-ə-ūn'*, *n* anything of little or no value (*US colloq*); a five-cent piece, or other small coin; a small coin worth 6¼ cents, current in the U.S. before 1857. — *adj* (*US colloq*) petty. — *adj* **picayun'ish**. [Prov. *picaioun*, an old Piedmontese copper coin.]

piccalilli *pik-ə-lil'i*, *n* a pickle of various vegetable substances with mustard and spices.

piccaninny or **pickaninny** *pik-ə-nin'i*, *n* a little child; a Negro child; an Aborigine child (*Austr*). — *adj* very little. — *n* **picc'anin** (*SAfr*) a piccaninny. [Port. *pequenino*, dimin. of *pequeno*, little, or poss. Sp. *pequeño niño*, little child.]

piccolo *pik'ə-lō*, *n* a small flute, an octave higher than the ordinary flute; an organ stop of similar tone: — *pl* **picc'olos**. [It., little.]

piccy *pik'i*, (*colloq*) *n* short for **picture**, esp. a photograph: — *pl* **picc'ies**.

pice *pīs*, *nsing* and *pl* a (former) small Indian coin, ¼ anna. — **new pice** 1/100 rupee, paisa (q.v.). [Hind. *paisā*.]

piceous *pis'i-əs*, *adj* like pitch; inflammable; black; reddish black. [L. *piceus* — *pix*, pitch.]

pichurim *pich'ōō-rim*, *n* a S. American tree of the laurel family; its aromatic kernel (also **pichurim bean**). [Port. *pichurim* — Tupí *puchury*.]

pick *pik*, *n* a tool for breaking ground, rock, etc., with a head pointed at one end or both, and a handle fitted to the middle; a pointed hammer; an instrument of various kinds for picking; an act, opportunity or right of choice; a portion picked; the best or choicest. — *vt* to break up, dress or remove with a pick; to make with a pick or by plucking; to poke or pluck at, as with a sharp instrument or the nails; to clear, remove or gather by single small acts; to detach, extract, or take separately and lift or remove; to pluck; to pull apart; to cull; to choose; to select, esp. one by one or bit by bit; to peck, bite or nibble; to eat in small quantities or delicately; to open (e.g. a lock) by a sharp instrument or other unapproved means; to seek and find a pretext for (e.g. a quarrel). — *vi* to use a pick; to eat small or delicate mouthfuls; to pilfer. — *adj* **picked** (*pikt*) selected; choice or best; plucked, as flowers or fruit. — *n* **pick'edness**. — *n* **pick'er** a person who picks or gathers up; a tool or machine for picking; someone who removes defects from and finishes electrotype plates; a pilferer. — *n* **pick'ing** the action of the verb to pick; the quantity picked; that which is left to be picked; dabbing in stoneworking; the final finishing of woven fabrics by removing burs, etc.; removing defects from electrotype plates; (in *pl*) odd gains or perquisites. — *adj* **pick'y** (*colloq*) fussy or choosy, esp. excessively so; able to pick out or pick over dexterously. — **pick'er-up**; **pick'lock** an instrument for picking or opening locks; a person who picks locks; **pick'-me-up** a stimulating drink; a medicinal tonic. — *n* and *adj* **pick-'n'-mix'** (an assortment of loose sweets) chosen by the individual customer from a range of types available at a self-service counter; (a discriminatory selection) chosen to suit one's individual taste or needs (*fig*). — **pick'-pocket** someone who picks or steals from other people's pockets; **pick'-up** an act of picking up; reception; a stop to collect something or someone; a recovery; something picked up; a light motor vehicle with front part like a private car and rear in form of a truck; a man's casual, informal acquaintance with a woman, usu. implying a sexual relationship; the woman in such a relationship; accelerating power; a device for picking up an electric current; (also **pick-up head**) a transducer, activated by a sapphire or diamond stylus following the groove on a gramophone record, which transforms the mechanical into electrical impulses. — *adj* for picking up; picked up. — **pick-your-own'** a method of selling fruit or vegetables by which private customers pick the produce they wish to buy at the place where it is grown; produce sold in this way. — *adj* sold or operating by the pick-your-own system. — **pick at** to find fault with; to nibble (food) without enthusiasm; **pick holes in someone** or **something** to find fault with someone or something; **pick off** to select from a number and shoot; to detach and remove; **pick on** to single out, esp. for anything unpleasant; to nag at; to carp at; **pick one's way** to choose carefully where to put one's feet, as (or as if) on dirty or dangerous ground; **pick out** to make out, distinguish; to pluck out; to select from a number; to mark with spots of colour, etc.; **pick over** to go over and select; **pick someone's brains** to make use of another's brains or ideas for one's own ends; **pick to pieces** to pull apart; to criticise adversely in detail; **pick up** to lift from the ground, floor etc.; to improve gradually; to gain strength bit by bit; to take into a vehicle, or into one's company; to scrape acquaintance informally with, esp. of a man with a woman; to acquire as occasion offers; to gain; to come upon, make out, distinguish (e.g. a signal, a track, a comet, etc.); **pick up the pieces** to restore balance and order after an (esp. emotional) upset, collapse, or period of disruption.

pickaback. See **piggyback**.

pickaninny. See **piccaninny**.

pickaxe *pik'aks*, *n* a picking tool, with a point at one end of the head and a cutting blade at the other, used in digging. [M.E. *pikois* — O.Fr. *picois*, a mattock, *piquer*, to pierce, *pic*, a pick.]

pickerel *pik'ər-əl*, *n* a young pike. [**pike**[1].]

picket *pik'it*, *n* a pointed stake or peg driven into the ground; a surveyor's mark; a small outpost, patrol, or body of men set apart for some special duty; picket-duty; a person or group set to watch and dissuade those who go to work during a strike. — *vt* to tether to a stake; to strengthen or surround with pickets; to peg down; to post as a picket; to deal with as a picket or by means of pickets; to place pickets at or near. — *vi* to act as picket: — *pr p* **pick'eting**; *pa t* and *pa p* **pick'eted**. — *n* **pick'eter** a person who pickets in a labour dispute. — **pick'et-duty**; **pick'et-fence** (*US*) a fence made of pales; **pick'et-guard** a guard kept in readiness in case of alarm; **pick'et-line** a line of people acting as pickets in a labour dispute. — **picket out** (in a labour dispute) to close or bring to a standstill by picketing. [Fr. *piquet*, dimin. of *pic*, a pickaxe.]

pickle *pik'l*, *n* a liquid, esp. brine or vinegar, in which food is preserved; an article of food preserved in such liquid; (in *pl*) preserved onions, cucumber, etc., as a condiment; acid or other liquid used for cleansing or treatment in manufacture; a tricky situation, predicament or muddle (*colloq*); a troublesome child (*colloq*). — *vt* to preserve with salt, vinegar, etc.; to clean or treat with acid or other chemical. — *adj* **pick'led** treated with a pickle; drunk (*slang*). — *n* **pick'ler** someone who pickles; a container for pickling; an article suitable, or grown, for pickling. — **pick'le-herring** a pickled herring. [M.E. *pekille*, *pykyl*, *pekkyll*, *pykulle*.]

picnic *pik'nik*, *n* an open-air meal taken by a number of persons on a country excursion, etc.; an undertaking that is mere child's play (often *ironically*). — *adj* of or for a picnic; picnicking. — *vi* to have a picnic: — *pr p* **pic'nicking**; *pa t* and *pa p* **pic'nicked**. — *n* **pic'nicker**. — *adj* **pic'nicky**. [Fr. *pique-nique*.]

pico- *pē-kō-* or *pī-kō-*, *combining form* denoting a millionth of a millionth part, a million millionth, as in **picocurie**, **picosecond**, etc. [Sp. *pico*, a small quantity.]

picornavirus *pi-kör'nə-vī-rəs*, *n* any of a group of viruses including the enteroviruses and rhinoviruses. [**pico-**, **RNA** and **virus**.]

picot *pē'kō*, *n* a loop in an ornamental edging; a raised knot in embroidery. — *vt* to ornament with picots. — *adj* **picoté** (*pē-kō-tā*). [Fr. *picot*, point, prick.]

picotee *pik-ə-tē'*, *n* a variety of carnation, orig. speckled, now edged with a different colour. [Fr. *picoté*, prickled.]

picric acid *pik'rik as'id*, (*chem*) *n* *trinitrophenol*, $C_6H_2(NO_2)_3.OH$, used as a yellow dyestuff and as the basis of high explosives. — *n* **pic'rate** a (highly explosive) salt of picric acid. [Gr. *pikros*, bitter.]

Pict *pikt*, *n* one of an ancient people of Britain, esp. north-eastern Scotland. — *adj* **Pict'ish**. — *n* the language of the Picts. — **Picts' house** an earth-house. [L. *Pictī*, Picts; poss. the same as *pictī*, past p. of *pingĕre*, to paint.]

pictograph *pik'tə-gräf*, *n* a picture used as a symbol in picture-writing. — *n* **pic'togram** a pictograph; a graphic representation. — *adj* **pictographic** (*-graf'ik*). — *adv* **pictograph'ically**. — *n* **pictography** (*pik-tog'rə-fi*) picture-writing. [L. *pictus*, painted; Gr. *graphein*, to write, *gramma*, a letter, figure.]

pictorial *pik-tö'ri-əl*, *adj* of or relating to painting or drawing; of, by means of, like, or of the nature of, a picture or pictures. — *n* a periodical in which pictures are prominent. — *adv* **picto'rially**. [L. *pictor*, *-ōris*, painter — *pingĕre*, *pictum*, to paint.]

picture *pik'chər*, *n* the art or act of painting; an imitative representation of an object on a surface; (*loosely*) a photograph; a portrait; a visible or visual image; a mental image; (an image on) a television screen; a person who appears to be exactly like another; an impressive or attractive sight, like a painting or worthy of being painted; a visible embodiment; a vivid verbal description; a cinema film; (in *pl*) a cinema show, or the building in which it is given. — *vt* to depict, represent in a picture; to form a likeness of in the mind; to describe vividly in words. — *adj* **pic'tural** relating to, illustrated by, or consisting of pictures. — **pic'ture-book** a book of pictures; **pic'ture-card** (*cards*) a card bearing the representation of a king, queen or knave; **pic'ture-frame** a frame for surrounding a picture; **pic'ture-gallery** a gallery, hall or building where pictures are exhibited; **pic'ture-house** or **-palace** a building for cinema shows; **Picturephone®** a device which allows speakers on the telephone to see each other; **picture postcard** a postcard bearing a picture, commonly a local view. — *adj* **pict'ure-postcard** like a postcard in traditional or idealised prettiness. — **pic'ture-restorer** a person who cleans and restores old pictures; **pic'ture-rod**, **-rail** or **-moulding** a rod, rail or moulding from which pictures may be hung; **picture-win'dow** a usu. large window designed to act as a frame to an attractive view; **pic'ture-writing** the use of pictures to express ideas or relate events. — **get the picture** (*colloq*) to understand the situation; **in the picture** having a share of attention; adequately briefed; **put me** (etc.) **in the picture** give me (etc.) all the relevant information. [L. *pictūra* — *pingĕre*, *pictum*, to paint.]

picturesque *pik-chə-resk'*, *adj* like a picture; such as would make a striking picture, implying some measure of beauty with much quaintness or immediate effectiveness; (of language) vivid and colourful, or (*facetiously*) vulgar; having taste or feeling for the picturesque. — *adv* **picturesque'ly**. — *n* **picturesque'ness**. [It. *pittoresco* — *pittura*, a picture — L. *pictūra*.]

PID *abbrev* for pelvic inflammatory disease.

piddle *pid'l*, *vi* (esp. with *about*) to trifle, toy; to urinate (*colloq*). — *n* (*colloq*) urine; an act of urination. — *n* **pidd'ler** a trifler. — *adj* **pidd'ling** trifling, paltry.

pidgin *pij'in*, *n* a Chinese corruption of **business** (also **pidg'eon** or **pig'eon**); affair, concern (*colloq*; also **pidg'eon** or **pig'eon**); any combination and distortion of two languages as a means of communication. — *n* **pidginīsā'tion** or **-z-**. — **pidgin English** a jargon, mainly English in vocabulary with Chinese arrangement, used in communication between Chinese and foreigners; any jargon consisting of English and another language.

pi-dog, pie-dog. See **pye-dog**.

pie[1] *pī*, *n* a magpie; extended to other pied animals, esp. birds. [Fr., — L. *pīca*.]

pie[2] or **pi** *pī*, *n* confusedly mixed type (*printing*); a mixed state; confusion.

pie[3] *pī*, *n* a quantity of meat, fruit or other food baked within or under a crust of prepared pastry; an easy thing (*slang*); a welcome luxury, prize or spoil (*colloq*). — **pie chart, diagram** or **graph** a circle divided into sections by radii so as to show relative numbers or quantities; **pie'crust** the paste covering or enclosing a pie; **piecrust table** a Chippendale table with carved raised edge; **pie'dish** a deep dish in which pies are made. — *adj* **pie'-eyed** (*colloq*) drunk. — **pie'man** a man who sells pies, esp. in the street; **pie'-shop**. — **pie in the sky** some improbable future good promised without guarantee.

piebald *pī'böld*, *adj* black and white in patches; (*loosely*) of other colours in patches; motley; heterogeneous. — *n* a piebald horse or other animal. [**pie**[1] and **bald**.]

piece *pēs*, *n* a part or portion of anything, esp. detached; a separate lump, mass or body of any material, considered as an object; a span of time; a single article; a definite quantity or length as of cloth or paper; a literary, dramatic, musical or artistic composition; a production, specimen of work; an exemplification or embodiment; a gun; a coin; a man in chess, draughts, or other game (in chess sometimes excluding pawns); (*disrespectfully*) a woman; a work executed in graffiti (*slang*). — *vt* to enlarge by adding a piece; to patch; to combine. — *vi* to have a between-meal snack (*US slang*); to create a piece in graffiti (*slang*). — (in combination) **-piece'** consisting of a given number of separate parts, pieces, members, etc., as in *three-piece suite*. — *adv* **piece'meal** in pieces; to pieces; bit by bit. — *adj* done bit by bit; fragmentary. — **piece'-goods** textile fabrics made in standard lengths; **piece'-rate** a fixed rate paid according to the amount of work done; **piece'work** work paid for by the piece or quantity, not by time. — **all to pieces** or **to pieces** into a state of disintegration or collapse; **a piece** each; **a piece of** an instance of; a bit of, something of; **a piece of one's mind** a frank outspoken reprimand; **go to pieces** to break up entirely (*lit* and *fig*); completely to lose ability to cope with the situation; **in pieces** in, or to, a broken-up state; **of a piece** as if of the same piece, the same in nature; homogeneous, uniform; in keeping, consistent (with *with*); **piece of eight** see under **eight**; **piece of work** a task; a person (usu. with *nasty*, etc.); **piece together** to put together bit by bit; **to pieces** see **all to pieces** above. [O.Fr. *piece* — L.L. *pecia*, *petium*, a fragment, a piece of land.]

pièce *pyes*, (Fr.) *n* a piece, item; (a barrel of) about 220 litres (of wine). — **pièce de résistance** (*də rā-zē-stās*) the best item; the substantial course at dinner, the joint; **pièce d'occasion** (*do-ka-zyɔ̃*) something, usu. a literary or musical work, composed, prepared or used for a special occasion.

pied *pīd*, *adj* variegated like a magpie; of various colours. — *n* **pied'ness**. [**pie**[1].]

pied-à-terre *pyā-da-ter*, (Fr.) *n* a dwelling kept for temporary, secondary or occasional lodging: — *pl* **pieds-à-terre**.

pied noir *pyā nwär*, (Fr.) *n* a North African (esp. Algerian) person of French descent: — *pl* **pieds noirs**.

pier *pēr*, *n* a mass of stone, ironwork or woodwork projecting into the sea or other water, such as a breakwater, landing-stage or promenade; a jetty or a wharf; the mass of stonework between the openings in the wall of a building; the support of an arch, bridge, etc.; a masonry support; a buttress. — *n* **pier'age** a toll paid for using a pier. — **pier'-glass** a tall mirror, orig. hung between windows; **pier'head** the seaward end of a pier. [M.E. *pēr*, L.L. *pēra*.]

pierce *pērs*, *vt* to thrust or make a hole through; to enter, or force a way into; to touch or move deeply; to penetrate; to perforate; to make by perforating or penetrating. — *vi* to penetrate. — *n* a perforation; a stab; a prick. — *adj* **pierce'able**. — *adj* **pierced'**. — *n* **pierc'er**. — *adj* **pierc'ing** penetrating; very acute; keen, sharp. — *adv* **pierc'ingly**. — *n* **pierc'ingness**. [O.Fr. *percer*.]

Pierrot *pē'ə-rō* or *pyer-ō*, *n* a white-faced buffoon with a loose long-sleeved costume; (without *cap*; *formerly*) a member of a group of entertainers in similar dress at seaside resorts, etc.: — *fem* **Pierrette'**. [Fr., dimin. of *Pierre*, Peter.]

pietà *pyā-tä'*, (*art*) *n* a representation of the Virgin with the dead Christ across her knees. [It., — L. *pietās*, *-ātis*, pity.]

pietra-dura *pyā-trə-dōō'rə*, *n* inlaid mosaic work with hard stones — jasper, agate, etc.: — *pl* **pietre dure** (*pyā'tre dōō're*) used as *nsing* for this type of (usu. relief) mosaic work. [It., hard stone.]

piety *pī'i-ti*, *n* the quality of being pious; dutifulness; devoutness; sense of duty towards parents, benefactors, etc.; dutiful conduct. — *n* **pī'etism**. — *n* **pī'etist** a person marked by strong devotional feeling; a name first applied to a sect of German religious reformers of deep devotional feeling (end of 17th cent.). — *adj* **pietist'ic** or **pietist'ical**. [O.Fr. *piete* — L. *pietās*, *-ātis*.]

piezo- *pī-i-zō-* or *pī-ē-zō-*, *combining form* denoting pressure. — *adj* **piezo** short for **piezoelectric**. — *n* **piezochem'istry** the chemistry of substances under high pressure. — *adj* **piezoelec'tric**. — *n* **piezoelectri'city** electricity developed in certain crystals by mechanical strain, and the effect of an electric field in producing expansion and contraction along different axes. [Gr. *piĕzein*, to press.]

piffle *pif'l*, (*colloq*) *n* nonsense; worthless talk. — *vi* to trifle; to act ineffectually. — *n* **piff'ler**. — *adj* **piff'ling** trivial, petty.

pig *pig*, *n* any omnivorous ungulate mammal of the family *Suidae*, with thick, bristly skin, esp. the domesticated *Sus scrofa*, a farm animal bred as food for humans; its flesh used as food, esp. that of the young animal; someone who is like a pig, dirty, greedy, gluttonous, cantankerous, unpleasant, etc.; an oblong mass of unforged metal, as first extracted from the ore; the mould into which it is run, esp. one of the branches, the main channel being the *sow*; a device that is propelled through a pipeline or duct by pneumatic, hydraulic or gas pressure, for clearing, cleaning, tracking or scanning purposes, etc. (*tech*); a policeman (*slang*; *derog*); something very difficult or unpleasant (*slang*). — *vi* to give birth to pigs; to live, herd, huddle, sleep or feed like pigs; to eat greedily (*slang*): — *pr p* **pigg'ing**; *pa t* and *pa p* **pigged**. — *n* **pigg'ery** a place where pigs are kept; piggishness. — *n* **pigg'ing** (*tech*) operating a pig (q.v.) or running a pig along a pipeline. — *adj* (*slang*) expressing aversion of something troublesome, unpleasant or difficult. — *adj* **pigg'ish** like a pig; greedy; dirty; cantankerous or mean. — *adv* **pigg'ishly**. — *n* **pigg'ishness**. — *n* **pigg'ie**, **pigg'y**, **pig'let** or **pig'ling** a little pig. — *adj* **pigg'y** like a pig. — **pig'deer** the babiroussa. — *adj* **pig'-eyed** having small, pinkish, dull eyes with heavy lids. — *adj* **pig'-faced**. — **pig'feed** food for pigs; **piggyback** see separate entry; **pigg'y-bank** a child's moneybox, shaped like a pig; sometimes a child's moneybox of any design. — *adj* **pighead'ed** stupidly obstinate. — *adv* **pighead'edly**. — **pighead'edness**. — *adj* **pig-ig'norant** (*colloq*; *derog*) very ignorant. — **pig-** or **piggy-in-the-midd'le** a children's game in which a person standing between two others tries to intercept a ball, etc. that is passing back and forth between them; a person caught between opposing viewpoints, strategies, etc.; **pig'-iron** iron in pigs or rough bars; **pig'meat** bacon, ham or pork; **pig'nut** the earth-nut (*Conopodium*); **pig'pen** a pigsty; **pig'-rat** the bandicoot rat; **pig'skin** the skin of a pig prepared as a strong leather; a saddle (*slang*); a football (*NAm slang*); **pig'-sticker**; **pig'-sticking** boar-hunting with spears; **pig'sty** a pen for keeping pigs; **pig swill** or **pig'swill** kitchen, etc. waste fed to pigs; **pig'tail** the tail of a pig; the hair of the head plaited behind or at the side; a short length of rope or cable. — **a pig in a poke** see under **poke**[1]; **make a pig of oneself** (*colloq*) to overindulge in food or drink; **make a pig's ear of something** (*colloq*) to make a mess of something, to do something badly or clumsily; **pig it** (*colloq*) to live squalidly or in dirty surroundings; **pig out** to overeat, go on a binge; **when pigs fly** (*colloq*) never. [M.E. *pigge*.]

pigeon[1] *pij'ən* or *pij'in*, *n* a dove; any bird of the dove family; extended to various other birds (e.g. the *Cape pigeon*); a person who is fleeced (*slang*); short for **stool-pigeon** (see **stool**). — *vt* to gull. — *n* **pig'eonry** a place for keeping pigeons. — *adj* **pig'eon-breasted** or **-chested** having a narrow chest with the breastbone projecting. — **pig'eon-fancier** a person who keeps and breeds pigeons for racing or exhibiting. — *adj* **pig'eon-hearted** timid. — **pig'eon-hole** or **pig'eonhole** a niche for a pigeon's nest; a compartment for storing and classifying papers, etc.; a compartment of the mind or memory. — *vt* to provide with or make into pigeon-holes; to put into a pigeon-hole; to classify methodically, or too rigidly; to lay aside and delay action on, or treat with neglect. — **pig'eon-holer; pig'eon-house** a dovecot; **pig'eon-pea** dal; **pig'eon-post** transmission of letters by pigeons; **pigeon's milk** partly digested food regurgitated by pigeons to feed their young. — *adj* **pig'eon-toed** having the toes more or less turned inward. [O.Fr. *pijon* — L. *pīpiō, -ōnis* — *pīpīre*, to cheep.]

pigeon[2]. Same as **pidgin**.

piggy. See under **pig**.

piggyback *pig'i-bak* or **pickaback** *pik'ə-bak*, *adv* and *adj* (carried) on the back like a pack; (of a vehicle or plane, etc.) conveyed on top of one another. — *n* a ride on one's back (as given to children). — *adj* **pigg'yback** of a method of heart transplant surgery in which the patient's own heart is not removed and continues to function in tandem with that of the donor. [Conn. with dialect *pick*, pitch, **pack** and **back** obscure.]

piggy-bank . . . to . . . **pigmeat**. See under **pig**.

pigmean. See under **pygmy**.

pigment *pig'mənt*, *n* any substance used for colouring; that which gives colour to animal and vegetable tissues; paint or dye. — *adj* **pigmental** (*-men'tl*), **pig'mentary** or **pig'mented.** — *n* **pigmentā'tion** coloration or discoloration by pigments in the tissues. [L. *pīgmentum* — *pingĕre*, to paint.]

pigmy. See **pygmy**.

pignut . . . to . . . **pigtail**. See under **pig**.

pika *pī'kə*, *n* the tailless hare (*Ochotona*), a small mammal found in mountain regions. [Tungus *piika*.]

pike[1] *pīk*, *n* a sharp point; a weapon with a long shaft and a sharp head like a spear, formerly used by foot-soldiers; a spiked staff; a sharp-pointed hill or summit; a voracious freshwater fish (*Esox lucius*) with pointed snout; extended to various other fishes. — *vt* to kill or pierce with a pike. — *adj* **piked** (*pīkt* or *pīk'id*) spiked; ending in a point. — *n* **pīk'er** (*slang*) someone who bets, gambles, speculates or does anything else in a very small way; a shirker or a mean character. — **pike'man** a man armed with a pike; someone who wields a pick; **pike'staff** the staff or shaft of a pike; a staff with a pike at the end. — **plain as a pikestaff** perfectly plain or clear. [O.E. *pīc*, pick, spike; but also partly from Fr. *pic* with the same meaning, and *pique* the weapon.]

pike[2] *pīk*, *n* a turnpike; a toll; a main road (*US*). — **pike'man** a turnpike keeper. [Short for **turnpike**.]

pike[3] *pīk* or **piked position** *pīkd pə-zi'shən*, (*diving* and *gymnastics*) *n* a posture in which the body is bent sharply at the hips with legs kept straight at the knees and toes pointed. — *vi* to adopt this position. — *adj* **piked**.

pilaff. See **pilau**.

pilaster *pi-las'tər*, (*archit*) *n* a square column, partly built into, partly projecting from, a wall. — *adj* **pilas'tered**. [Fr. *pilastre* — It. *pilastro* — L. *pīla*, a pillar.]

pilau, pilaw *pi-low'* or **pilaff** *pi-laf'*, *n* a highly spiced Eastern dish of rice with chicken, meat, vegetables, shellfish or the like, boiled together or separately. [Pers. *pilāw*, Turk. *pilāw*, *pilāf*.]

pilchard *pil'chərd*, *n* a European sea-fish like the herring, but smaller, thicker and rounder.

pile[1] *pīl*, *n* a set of things fitted, laid or resting one over another; a set of weights fitting one within another; a series of alternate plates of two metals for generating an electric current; a nuclear reactor, orig. the graphite blocks forming the moderator for the reactor; a great amount of money, a fortune (*slang*); a large supply (*colloq*); a tall building. — *vt* to lay in a pile or heap; to collect in a mass; to heap up, or load in a heap or heaps; to accumulate. — *vi* to come into piles; to accumulate; to go in crowds; to get in or out (with *in* or *out*). — *n* **pī'ler**. — **pile'-cap** the top of a nuclear reactor; see also under **pile**[2]; **pile'-up** a collision involving several motor vehicles, players in Rugby football, etc. — **pile it on** (*colloq*) to overdo, exaggerate (something); **pile on (or up) the agony** (*colloq*) to overdo painful effects by accumulation, etc.; **pile up** to run ashore; to form a disorderly mass or heap; to become involved in a pile-up (q.v.); to accumulate. [Fr., — L. *pīla*, a pillar.]

pile[2] *pīl*, *n* a large stake or cylinder driven into the earth to support foundations. — *vt* to drive piles into; to support with or build on piles. — **pile'-cap** (*civ eng*) a reinforced concrete block cast around a set of piles to create a unified support; see also under **pile**[1]; **pile'-driver** an engine for driving in piles; (in games) a very heavy stroke, kick, etc.; **pile shoe** the iron or steel point fitted to the foot of a pile to give it strength to pierce the earth and so assist driving. [O.E. *pīl* — L. *pīlum*, a javelin.]

pile[3] *pīl*, *n* a covering of hair, esp. soft, fine or short hair; down; human body-hair; a single hair; the raised or fluffy surface of a fabric, carpet, etc.; (as distinguished from *nap*) the raised surface of a fabric made not in finishing but in weaving, either by leaving loops (which may be cut) or by weaving two cloths face to face and cutting them apart. — *adj* **pīlif'erous** bearing hairs; ending in a hairlike point. — *adj* **pīl'iform** hairlike. [L. *pīlus*, a hair.]

pile[4] *pīl*, *n* (usu. in *pl*) a haemorrhoid. [L. *pīla*, a ball.]

pileum *pī'li-əm*, *n* the top of a bird's head: — *pl* **pil'ea**. — *n* **pi'leus** the expanded cap of a mushroom or toadstool, or other fungus: — *pl* **pilei** (*pī'li-ī*). — *adj* **pi'leate** or **pi'leated** cap-shaped; capped; crested. [L. *pīleum*, *pīleus*, for *pilleum*, *pilleus*, a felt cap.]

pilfer *pil'fər*, *vi* and *vt* to steal in small quantities. — *n* **pil'ferage** or **pil'fering** petty theft. — *n* **pil'ferer**. — *adv* **pil'feringly**. [O.Fr. *pelfrer*, pillage.]

pilgrim *pil'grim*, *n* a person who travels esp. a distance to visit a holy place; allegorically or spiritually, someone journeying through life as a stranger in this world; a Pilgrim Father. — *adj* of or pertaining to a pilgrim; like a pilgrim; consisting of pilgrims. — *n* **pil'grimage** the journeying of a pilgrim; a journey to a shrine or other holy place or place venerated for its associations; the journey of life; a lifetime. — *adj* visited by pilgrims. — *vi* to go on pilgrimage; to wander. — **Pilgrim Fathers** the Puritans who sailed for America in the *Mayflower*, and founded Plymouth, Massachusetts, in 1620. [Assumed O.Fr. *pelegrin* (Fr. *pèlerin*) — L. *peregrīnus*, foreigner, stranger; see ety. for **peregrinate.**]

piliferous, piliform. See under **pile**[3].

Pilipino *pil-i-pē'nō*, *n* the official language of the Philippines, based on Tagálog. [Pilipino — Sp. *Filipino*, Philippine.]

pill *pil*, *n* a little ball of medicine; a ball, e.g. a cannon-ball, tennis ball; anything disagreeable that must be accepted; a tiresome person; a doctor (*slang*; also in *pl*). — *vt* to form into pills; to dose with pills. — **pill'box** a box for holding pills; a small blockhouse (*mil slang*); a small round brimless hat; **pill'head** or **pill'popper** (*slang*) a regular, usu. addicted, taker of sedative and/or stimulant pills. — **the pill** any of various contraceptive pills (see **oral contraception**); **on the pill** taking contraceptive pills regularly. [L. *pila*, perh. through O.Fr. *pile*, or from a syncopated form of the dimin. *pilŭla*.]

pillage *pil'əj*, *n* the act of plundering; plunder. — *vt* and *vi* to plunder. — *n* **pill'ager**. [Archaic verb *pill* — O.E. *pylian* and O.Fr. *peler*, both — L. *pilāre*, to deprive of hair.]

pillar *pil'ər*, *n* a detached support, not necessarily cylindrical or of classical proportions (*archit*); a structure of similar form erected as a monument, ornament, object of worship, etc.; a tall upright rock; a mass of coal or rock left in a mine to support the roof; anything in the form of a column; a supporting post; the post supporting a bicycle saddle; (in a car) a vertical column of bodywork, e.g. the *door pillar* separating the front and rear doors; a cylinder holding the plates of a watch or clock in position; a person who, or anything that, sustains. — **pill'ar-box** a short hollow pillar for posting letters in (**pillar-box red** the bright red colour of most British pillar-boxes). — **from pillar to post** hither and thither; **Pillars of Islam** the five major Islamic duties — the statement of faith, prayer, fasting, almsgiving, and pilgrimage to Mecca. [O.Fr. *piler* (Fr. *pilier*) — L.L. *pīlāre* — L. *pīla*, a pillar.]

pillion *pil'yən*, *n* a cushion behind a horseman for a second rider (usu. a woman) or for a bag; the passenger-seat of a motorcycle, or a baggage-carrier, usable as an extra seat. — *adv* on a pillion. — *vt* to seat on or supply with a pillion. — **pill'ion-rider; pill'ion-seat**. [Prob. Ir. *pillín*, Gael. *pillin*, *pillean*, a pad, a pack-saddle — *peall*, a skin or mat, L. *pellis*, skin.]

pillock *pil'ək*, (*slang*) *n* a stupid or foolish person. [Obs. *pillicock*, penis and dialect forms *pillick*, *pilluck*.]

pillory *pil'ə-ri*, *n* (*hist*) a wooden frame, supported by an upright pillar or post, with holes through which the head and hands were put as a punishment, abolished in England in 1837. — *vt* to set in the pillory (*hist*); to hold up to ridicule: — *pr p* **pill'orying**; *pa t* and *pa p* **pill'oried**. — Also **pill'orise** or **-ize**. [O.Fr. *pilori*.]

pillow *pil'ō*, *n* a cushion for a sleeper's head; any object used for that purpose; a support for part of a structure; something resembling a pillow in shape or feel. — *vt* to lay or rest for support; to serve as pillow for; to provide or prop with pillows. — *adj* **pill'owed** supported by, or provided with, a pillow. — *adj* **pill'owy** like a pillow; round and swelling; soft. — **pill'ow-case** or **-slip** a cover for a pillow; **pill'ow-fight; pill'ow-fighting** the sport of thumping one another with pillows; **pill'ow-lace** lace worked with bobbins on a padded cushion; **pillow talk** talk between lovers in bed. [O.E. *pyle*, also *pylu* — L. *pulvīnus*.]

pilose *pī'lōs*, *adj* hairy; having scattered soft or moderately stiff hairs. — *n* **pilosity** (*-los'i-ti*). — *adj* **pī'lous** hairy. [L. *pīlōsus* — *pīlus*, hair.]

pilot *pī'lət*, *n* a person who conducts ships in and out of a harbour, along a dangerous coast, etc.; a person who operates the controls of an aircraft, hovercraft, spacecraft, etc.; someone who is qualified to act as pilot; a guide; a pilot film, project, broadcast, etc. — *adj* pertaining to pilot(s); acting as guide or control; trial (of e.g. a model on a smaller scale) serving to test the qualities or future possibilities of a machine, plant, etc., or (of a film or broadcast) to test the popularity of a projected radio or television series. — *vt* to act as pilot to. — *n* **pī'lotage** piloting; a pilot's fee. — *adj* **pī'lotless** without a pilot; (of an automatic aeroplane) not requiring a pilot. — **pi'lot-balloon** a small balloon sent up to find how the wind blows; **pi'lot-boat** a boat used by pilots on duty; **pilot burner, jet** or **light** (see also below) a small gas-burner kept alight to light another; **pi'lot-fish** a fish that accompanies ships and sharks; **pi'lot-flag** or **-jack** the flag hoisted at the fore by a vessel needing a pilot; **pi'lot-house** a shelter for steering-gear and pilot — also *wheel-house*; **pi'lot-jacket** a pea-jacket; **pilot lamp** or **light** a small electric light to show when the current is on, or for other purpose; **pil'otman** a railway employee assigned to guide trains across a section of single-track line; **pilot officer** (in the Air Force) an officer ranking with an army second-lieutenant; **pi'lot-plant** prototype machinery set up to begin a new process; **pilot project** or **scheme** a project or scheme serving as a guide on a small scale to a full-scale project or scheme. [Fr. *pilote* — It. *pilota*, app. for earlier *pedota*, which may be — Gr. *pēdon*, oar, in pl. rudder.]

pilotis *pi-lot'ē* or *pi-lo-tēz'*, (*archit*) *npl* a series of slender columns or stilts used on the ground floor of a building to raise the main floor to first-floor level, and leaving open space below (e.g. for car-parking). [Fr. *pillars*, stilts.]

pilous. See **pilose**.

Pils *pils* or *pilz*, *n* a lager beer similar to Pilsener.

Pilsener or **Pilsner** *pilz'nər* or *pils'nər*, (also without *cap*) *n* a light, strongly-flavoured lager beer. [Ger., from *Pilsen*, a city in Czechoslovakia.]

Piltdown man *pilt'down man*, *n* a once-supposed very early form of man represented by parts of a skull found at *Piltdown*, Sussex (1912), but exposed as a hoax in 1953.

pilule *pil'ūl*, *n* a little pill. — Also **pil'ula**. — *adj* **pil'ular**. [L. dimin. of *pīla*, ball.]

pimento *pi-men'tō*, *n* allspice or Jamaica pepper, the dried unripe fruits of a W. Indian tree (*Pimenta officinalis*) of the myrtle family; the tree itself; its wood: — *pl* **pimen'tos**. — *n* **pimiento** (*pi-mē-en'tō*) the sweet, red, yellow or green pepper, capsicum: — *pl* **pimien'tos**. [O.Fr. *piment*, Sp. *pimiento* — L. *pīgmentum*, paint.]

pimp *pimp*, *n* a man who lives with, and sometimes solicits for, a prostitute and lives off her earnings, or one who solicits for a prostitute or brothel and is paid for his services; a person who procures gratifications for the lust of others, a pander. — *vi* to act or live as a pimp; to pander. [Perh. rel. to Fr. *pimpant*, well-dressed, smart — O.Fr. *pimper*, to dress smartly.]

pimpernel *pim'pər-nel*, *n* a plant of the primrose family, with scarlet (or blue, etc.) flowers. — **water pimpernel** a water plant of the primrose family, also called *brookweed*; **yellow pimpernel** the wood loosestrife. [O.Fr. *pimpernelle*, mod. Fr. *pimprenelle*, and It. *pimpinella*, burnet.]

pimple *pim'pl*, *n* a pustule; a small swelling, protuberance, etc. — *adj* **pim'pled** or **pim'ply** having pimples.

PIN *abbrev* for personal identification number, a multi-digit number for use with a debit card and computerised cash dispenser to authorise access to information, withdrawal of cash, etc.

pin *pin*, *n* a piece of wood or of metal used for fastening things together; a peg or nail; a sharp-pointed piece of wire with a rounded head for fastening clothes, etc.; a cylindrical part inserted into something, such as the stem of a key, or part of a lock that a hollow-stemmed key fits; the projecting part of a dovetail joint; a peg aimed at in quoits; a peg in the centre of an archery target; the rod of a golf flag; a skittle or ninepin; a tuning peg in a stringed instrument; a leg (*colloq*); short for clothes-pin, rolling-pin, etc.; an act of pinning or state of being pinned; anything of little value. — *vt* to fasten with a pin; to fix, to fasten, to enclose, to hold down (*fig*); to make a small hole in; to cause an opponent's piece to be unable to move without checking its own king (*chess*): — *pr p* **pinn'ing**; *pa t* and *pa p* **pinned**. — **pin'ball** a scoring game, played on a slot-machine, in which a ball runs down a sloping board set with pins or other targets; a form of bagatelle; **pin curl** a lock of hair made to curl by winding it around one's finger, etc., and securing it with a hairpin; **pin'-cushion** a small cushion for holding pins; **pin'-feather** a young, unexpanded feather; **pin'head** the head of a pin; a stupid person (*slang*); **pin'hole** a hole for or made by a pin, or such as a pin might make; **pinhole camera**; **pinhole photography** the taking of photographs by the use of a pinhole instead of a lens; **pin'hooker** (*slang*) a speculator who buys up foals hoping to make a profit on them when selling them as yearlings for racing; **pin'-money** extra money earned by a man or woman to spend on incidental or luxury items; a trifling amount of money; **pin'point** the point of a pin; anything very sharp or minute. — *vt* to place or define, very exactly. — **pin'-prick** the prick of a pin; (an act of) petty irritation; **pin'stripe** a very narrow stripe in cloth; cloth with such stripes. — *adj* **pin'striped** (of fabric or garments) having pinstripes; (of a person) wearing a pinstriped suit (*colloq*). — **pin'table** a pinball machine; **pin'tail** a type of duck with a pointed tail; a sand-grouse. — *adj* **pin'tailed** having a long, narrow tail. — **pin tuck** a very narrow ornamental tuck. — *adj* **pin'-up** (of a person) such as might have their photograph pinned up on a wall for admiration. — *n* a person of such a kind; a photograph or picture so pinned up for admiration. — **pin'-wheel** a wheel with pins at right angles to its plane, to lift the hammer of a striking clock; a paper toy windmill; a revolving firework. — **on pins and needles** in agitated expectancy; **pin it on** or **pin it on to (someone)** to prove, or seem to prove, that (that person) did it; **pin one's faith on** to put entire trust in; **pin one's hopes on** to place one's entire hopes on; **pins and needles** a tingling feeling in arm, hand, leg, foot, due to impeded circulation (see also **on pins and needles** above); **pin someone down** to get someone to commit themselves (to), to make someone express a definite opinion. [O.E. *pinn*, prob. — L. *pinna*, a feather, a pinnacle.]

piña colada or **pina colada** *pē'nə kəl-ä'də* (Sp. *pē'nyə*), *n* a drink made from pineapple juice, rum and coconut. [Sp., strained pineapple.]

pinafore *pin'ə-för*, *n* a loose, protective or decorative garment worn over a dress. — *adj* **pin'afored**. — **pinafore dress** or **skirt** a skirt hung loose from the shoulders, or combined with a sleeveless bodice. [**pin** and **afore**.]

pinaster *pī-* or *pi-nas'tər*, *n* the cluster-pine. [L. *pīnāster* — *pīnus*, pine.]

pinball. See under **pin**.

pince-nez *pɛ̃s'-nā*, *n* a pair of glasses to assist sight with a spring for catching the nose: — *pl* **pince'-nez** (*-nāz* or *-nā*). — *adj* **pince'-nezed** (*-nād*). [Fr., pinch nose.]

pincer *pin'sər*, *n* a grasping claw or forceps-like organ; (in *pl*) a gripping tool with jaws and handles on a pivot, used for drawing out nails, squeezing, etc.; (in *pl*) a twofold advance that threatens to isolate part of an enemy's force (*fig*). — *vt* to pinch with pincers. — **pin'cer-movement**. [O.Fr. *pincier*, to pinch.]

pinch *pinch* or *pinsh*, *vt* to compress a small part of between fingers and thumb or between any two surfaces, to nip; to squeeze; to nip off; to bring or render by squeezing or nipping; (e.g. of cold or hunger) to affect painfully or injuriously; to cause to show the effects of such pain or injury; to harass; to hamper; to restrict; to be miserly or frugal with; to steal; (*slang*); to arrest (*slang*); to over-urge (*horse-racing*); to pluck, play pizzicato. — *vi* to nip or squeeze; to be painfully tight; to encroach; to narrow, taper off (*mining*, etc.). — *n* an act or experience of pinching; a critical time of difficulty or hardship; an emergency; a place of narrowing, folding, difficulty or steepness; a quantity taken up between the finger and thumb. — *adj* **pinched** having the appearance of being tightly squeezed; hard pressed by want or cold; (of the face, or general appearance) haggard with cold, tiredness, hunger, etc.; narrowed; straightened. — *n* and *adj* **pinch'-ing**. — *adv* **pinch'ingly**. — **pinch'cock** a clamp that stops the flow of liquid by pinching a tube. — *vi* **pinch'-hit** (*baseball*) to bat in place of another in an emergency (also *fig*). — **pinch'-hitter**; **pinch'-point** a constricted, awkward or congested point, as in the traffic system. — **at a pinch** in a case of necessity or emergency; **feel the pinch** (*colloq*) to be in financial difficulties, to find life, work, etc. difficult because of lack of money; **know where the shoe pinches** to know by direct experience what the trouble or difficulty is. [O.Fr. *pincier*.]

pinchbeck *pinch'* or *pinsh'bek*, *n* a yellow alloy of copper with much less zinc than ordinary brass, simulating gold, invented by Christopher *Pinchbeck* (*c* 1670–1732), watchmaker. — *adj* sham; in bad taste.

pin-cushion. See under **pin**.

pine[1] *pīn*, *n* any tree of the north temperate coniferous genus *Pinus*, with pairs or bundles of needle-leaves on short shoots and scale-leaves only on long shoots; extended to various more or less similar trees and to some plants only superficially similar; the timber of the pine; a pineapple plant or its fruit. — *adj* of pines or pinewood. — *adj* **pī'ny** (wrongly **pī'ney**) of, like, or covered in pine trees. — **pine'apple** see separate entry; **pine'-beauty** and **pine'-carpet** kinds of moths whose larvae feed on pine trees; **pine'-beetle** any beetle that attacks pine trees, esp. the **pine'-chāfer**; **pine cone** the cone or strobilus of a pine tree; **pine'-finch** an American finch like the goldfinch; a large grosbeak of pine forests; **pine kernel** the edible seed of a pine tree of various species; **pine marten** a British species of marten (*Mustela martes*) now rare, dark brown, with yellowish throat, and partly arboreal in habit; **pine needle** the slender, sharp-pointed leaf of the pine tree; **pine tar** a dark, oily substance obtained from pinewood, used in paints, etc., and medicines; **pine tree**; **pinewood** a wood of pine trees; pine timber. [O.E. *pīn* — L. *pīnus*.]

pine[2] *pīn*, *vi* to waste away, esp. under pain or mental distress; to long; to languish listlessly or fretfully. [O.E. *pīnian*, to torment — L. *poena*, punishment.]

pineal *pin'i-əl* or *pīn'i-əl*, *adj* shaped like a pine cone; connected with the pineal body. — *n* **pinealec'tomy** surgical removal of the pineal body. — **pineal body** or **gland** a small body at the end of a stalk growing up from the optic thalami of the brain; **pineal eye** a vestigial third eye in front of the pineal body, best developed in the New Zealand reptile, the tuatara. [L. *pīnea*, a pine cone — *pīnus*, pine.]

pineapple *pīn'ap-l*, *n* a large tropical fruit shaped like a large pine cone, with sweet, yellow juicy flesh; the plant (*Ananas*) that bears it; a finial shaped like a pine cone or a pineapple; a hand grenade (*slang*). [M.E. *pinappel*, pine cone.]

ping *ping*, *n* a sharp ringing or whistling sound as of a bullet. — *vi* to make such a sound. — *vt* to cause to make such a sound. — *n* **ping'er** a domestic clockwork device set to give a warning signal at a chosen time; any of various devices sending out an acoustic signal for directional or timing, etc. purposes. — **Ping'-Pong**® a trademark for table tennis. — *adj* (without *cap*) moving backwards and forwards, to and fro (*fig*). [Imit.]

pingo *ping'gō*, *n* a large cone-shaped mound having a core of ice formed by the upward expansion of freezing water surrounded by permafrost: — *pl* **ping'os** or **ping'oes**. [Eskimo.]

pinguid *ping'gwid*, *adj* fat. [L. *pinguis*, fat.]

pinguin *ping'gwin*, *n* a W. Indian plant, *Bromelia pinguin*; its fruit.

pinhead, pinhole. See under **pin**.

pinion[1] *pin'yən*, *n* a wing; the last joint of a wing; a flight feather, esp. the outermost. — *vt* to cut a pinion of; to confine the wings of; to confine by holding or binding the arms. [O.Fr. *pignon* — L. *pinna* (*penna*), wing.]

pinion[2] *pin'yən*, (*horology*) *n* a small wheel with teeth (or 'leaves'). [Fr. *pignon*, pinion, in O.Fr. battlement — L. *pinna*, pinnacle.]

pink[1] *pingk*, *vt* to make a serrated edge on; to decorate by cutting small holes or scallops. — *adj* **pinked** with the edge serrated; pierced or worked with small holes. — **pink'ing-shears** scissors with serrated cutting edges. [Cf. L.G. *pinken*, to peck.]

pink² *pingk*, *n* any plant or flower of the genus *Dianthus*, including carnation and sweet-william; extended to some other plants; the colour of a wild pink, a light red; a scarlet hunting-coat or its colour; the person wearing it; someone who is something of a socialist but hardly a red (also **pink'ō**: — *pl* **pink'os** or **pink'oes**); the fine flower of excellence; perfect condition; the highest point, the extreme. — *adj* of the colour pink; slightly socialistic; slightly pornographic, somewhat blue (*cinema* etc.). — *vt* and *vi* to make or become pink. — *n* **pink'iness**. — *adj* **pink'ish** somewhat pink. — *n* **pink'ishness**. — *n* **pink'ness**. — *adj* **pink'y** inclining to pink. — **pink elephants** see under **elephant**; **pink'-eye** acute contagious conjunctivitis; an acute contagious infection in horses due to a virus, the eye sometimes becoming somewhat red; a red discoloration in salt fish, etc.; **pink gin** gin with angostura bitters. — **in the pink** in perfect health or condition.

pink³ *pingk*, *n* a tinkling sound; a chaffinch's note. — *vi* (of an engine) to detonate or knock. — *n* (in an engine) a characteristic metallic knocking noise caused by detonation. [Imit.]

pinko, pinky. See **pink²**.

pinna *pin'ə*, (*biol*) *n* a leaflet of a pinnate leaf, or similar expansion; a wing, fin, feather, or similar expansion; the outer ear, esp. the upper part: — *pl* **pinn'ae** (-*ē*). — *adj* **pinn'ate** shaped like a feather; having a row of leaflets on each side of the rachis, or other expansions arranged in a similar way; having wings, fins or winglike tufts. — *adv* **pinn'ately**. — *adj* **pinnatifid** (*pin-at'i-fid*) pinnately cut nearly or about halfway down. — *adj* **pinnat'iped** (of birds) with lobate feet. — *adj* **pinn'ūlate** or **pinn'ūlated**. — *n* **pinn'ūle** a lobe of a leaflet of a pinnate leaf; a branchlet of a crinoid arm. [L. *pinna*, a feather, dimin. *pinnula*.]

pinnace *pin'is* or *pin'əs*, *n* a small vessel with oars and sails; a boat with eight oars; a man-of-war's tender; (*loosely*) a small boat. [Fr. *pinasse*.]

pinnacle *pin'ə-kl*, *n* a slender turret or spiry structure in architecture; a high pointed rock or mountain like a spire; the highest point. — *vt* to be the pinnacle of; to set on a pinnacle; to raise as a pinnacle; to provide with pinnacles. — *adj* **pinn'acled**. [Fr. *pinacle* — L.L. *pinnāculum*, dimin. from L. *pinna*, a feather.]

pinnate, etc. See under **pinna**.

pinnie *pin'i*, *n*. Short for **pinafore**.

pinnule, etc. See under **pinna**.

pinny *pin'i*, *n*. Short for **pinafore**.

pinochle, pinocle or **penuchle** *pin'* or *pēn'ək-l*, *n* a game like bezique; in this game, a declaration of queen of spades and knave of diamonds.

pinole *pē-nō'lā*, *n* parched Indian corn or other seeds ground and eaten with milk. [Sp., — Aztec *pinolli*.]

piñon *pin'yon* or *pēn'yōn*, (*US*) *n* an edible pine seed; the tree bearing it. [Sp.]

pinpoint. See under **pin**.

pinscher. See **Doberman pinscher**.

pint *pīnt*, *n* a measure of capacity in imperial measure (liquid or dry), about 568 cm³, 0·568 litre, 20 fluid ounces — in U.S. measure (liquid) 473 cm³, 16 U.S. fluid ounces, (dry) 551 cm³; a pint of beer (*colloq*). — *n* **pint'a** (*colloq*; **pint of**) a drink, esp. a pint, of milk. — **pint'-pot** a pot for holding a pint, esp. a pewter pot for beer. — *adj* **pint'-size** or **-sized** (*colloq*) very small (usu. used of a person). [Fr. *pinte*.]

pinta¹. See under **pint**.

pinta² *pin'tə*, *n* a contagious skin disease occurring in the tropics, characterised by loss of skin pigmentation. [Sp., — L.L. *pinctus* — L. *pictus*, painted.]

pintable, pintail. See under **pin**.

pintle *pin'tl*, *n* a bolt or pin, esp. one on which something turns; the plunger or needle of the injection valve of an oil engine, opened by oil pressure on an annular face, and closed by a spring. [O.E. *pintel*.]

pinto *pin'tō*, (*US*) *adj* mottled; piebald. — *n* a piebald horse: — *pl* **pin'tos**. — **pinto bean** a kind of bean resembling a kidney bean, mottled in colour. [Sp., painted.]

pinxit *pingk'sit*, (L.) (he or she) painted (this) (abbrev. **pinx.**).

piny. See **pine¹**.

Pinyin *pin-yin'*, *n* an alphabetic system (using Roman letters) for the transcription of Chinese, esp. Mandarin. [Chin., phonetic, alphabetic (transcription).]

piolet *pyo-lā'* or *pyō-lā'*, *n* an ice-axe, spiked staff for climbing. [Fr., — Piedmontese dialect *piola*.]

pion *pī'on*, *n* a *pi*-meson (see **pi¹** and **meson**). — *adj* **pīon'ic**.

pioneer *pī-ə-nēr'*, *n* someone who is among the first in new fields of enterprise, exploration, colonisation, research, etc.; a military engineer, employed in peacetime in painting and repairing barracks, in war in preparing the way for an army, and minor engineering works, such as trenching; (of a species) characteristically among the first to establish itself on bared ground (*bot*). — *vt* to act as pioneer to; to prepare as a pioneer. [O.Fr. *peonier* (Fr. *pionnier*) — *pion*, a foot-soldier — L.L. *pedō*, *pedōnis*.]

pious *pī'əs*, *adj* showing, having or resulting from piety; professing to be religious. — *adv* **pi'ously**. [L. *pius*.]

pip¹ *pip*, *n* roup in poultry, etc.; spleen, hump, disgust, offence (*colloq*). — *vt* to affect with the pip. — **give someone the pip** (*colloq*) to annoy or offend someone. [App. — M.Du. *pippe* — L.L. *pipīta* — L. *pītuīta*, rheum.]

pip² *pip*, *n* a small hard seed or fruitlet in a fleshy fruit. — *adj* **pip'less**. — *adj* **pipp'y**. [App. from **pippin**.]

pip³ *pip* or *pēp*, *n* a spot on dice, cards or dominoes; a star as a mark of rank (*colloq*); a speck; (on a radar screen) an indication, e.g. spot of light, of presence of object; a single blossom or corolla in a cluster (*bot*).

pip⁴ *pip*, *n* a short, high-pitched signal analogous in sound to the word 'pip', esp. as used in radio time signals, the speaking clock, payphones, etc. — **the pips** (*colloq*) the six pips broadcast by the BBC, made up of five short (counting down from 55 to 59 seconds) and one long (marking the start of the new minute and hour).

pip⁵ *pip*, (*slang*) *vt* to blackball; to foil, thwart, get the better of; to wound, hit with a bullet or the like; to defeat: — *pr p* **pipp'ing**; *pa t* and *pa p* **pipped**. — **pipped at the post** defeated at the point when success seemed certain, or at the last moment. [Perh. from **pip²**.]

pip⁶ *pip*, *vi* to chirp, as a young bird does. [Cf. **peep¹**.]

pipa *pē'pə*, *n* a S. American toad of the genus *Pipa*, the female of which is noted for carrying her developing young on her back; also called the *Surinam toad*. [Surinam dialect.]

pipage. See under **pipe¹**.

pipal, pipul or **peepul** *pē'pul* or *-pəl*, *n* the bo tree. [Hind. *pīpul*.]

pipe¹ *pīp*, *n* a metal or plastic tube for the conveyance of water, gas, etc.; a musical wind instrument consisting of a tube; any of an organ's upright metal tubes; (in *pl*) a bagpipe; a pipelike volcanic vent; a cylindrical mass of ore, etc.; a tube with a bowl at one end for smoking; a fill of tobacco; the smoking of a fill of tobacco; any of various hollow organs in an animal body; (in *pl*) the windpipe (*colloq*); a boatswain's whistle. — *vi* to play upon a pipe; to whistle (as the wind or as a boatswain does); to speak or sing, esp. in a high voice; to sing, as a bird does. — *vt* to play on a pipe; to lead, call, by means of a pipe; to accompany or summon ceremonially with pipe music (with *in*, *aboard*, etc.); to propagate by piping (*hort*); to ornament with piping; to supply with pipes; to convey by pipe; to transmit (television or radio signals) by electricity along a wire. — *n* **pī'page** conveyance or distribution by pipe. — *adj* **piped**

(*pīpt*) transported by means of a pipe; transmitted simultaneously to many outlets from a central control location by means of an audio system, telephone or electricity line, etc. — *n* **pipe'ful** enough to fill a pipe. — *adj* **pipe'less.** — *adj* **pipe'like.** — *n* **pī'per** a player on a pipe, esp. a bagpipe. — *adj* **pī'ping** playing a pipe; producing a shrill sound; whistling; thin and high-pitched; (of food) very hot. — *n* pipe-playing; a system of pipes; tubing; small cord used as trimming for clothes; strings and twists of icing ornamenting a cake; a slip or cutting from a joint of a stem (*hort*). — **pipe'clay** a fine, white, nearly pure kaolin, free from iron, used for making tobacco pipes and fine earthenware, and for whitening belts, etc. — *vt* to whiten with pipeclay. — **pipe'-cleaner** a length of wire with tufts of fabric twisted into it, used to clean tobacco-pipe stems; **piped music** continuous background music played in a restaurant, etc. or piped from a central studio to other buildings; **pipe dream** a futile and unreal hope or fancy such as one has when relaxing while smoking a pipe; **pipe'-dreamer; pipe'fish** a fish (of several species) of the sea-horse family, a long thin fish covered with hard plates, the jaws forming a long tube; **pipe'line** a long continuous line of piping to carry water from a reservoir, oil from an oilfield, etc.; a line of piping to carry solid materials; any continuous line of communication or supply; see **in the pipeline** below. — *adj* (*comput*; of a processor, program, etc.) carrying out two or more instructions simultaneously by performing processes in one sequence. — **pipe'lining; pipe major** the chief of a band of bagpipers; **pipe organ** a musical organ with pipes; **pipe rack** a rack for tobacco pipes; **pipe stem** the tube of a tobacco pipe; **pipe'stone** a red clayey stone used by North American Indians for making tobacco pipes; **pipe'work** a vein of ore in the form of a pipe; piping or pipes collectively, as in an organ. — **boatswain's pipe** see under **whistle; in the pipeline** waiting to be considered or dealt with; in preparation; **pay the piper** to bear the expense (and so **call the tune,** have control); to have to pay heavily; **pipe down** to subside into silence; to stop talking or be quiet (*colloq*); **pipe of peace** see **calumet; pipe up** (*colloq*) to begin to speak, to say something; **piping hot** (of food, usu. when served) very hot, (*lit*) so hot as to make a hissing noise. [O.E. *pīpe* — L. *pīpāre*, to cheep.]

pipe[2] *pīp*, *n* a cask or butt of varying capacity, usu. about 105 gallons in Britain, 126 U.S. gallons, used for wine or oil; the measure of a pipe. [O.Fr. *pipe*, cask, tube.]

piperazine *pi-per'ə-zēn*, *n* a crystalline nitrogen compound used in medicine, insecticides and anti-corrosion substances. [*piperidine* and **az-**, nitrogen.]

piperidine *pi-per'i-dēn*, *n* a liquid base ($C_5H_{11}N$) with a peppery odour, obtained from piperine. [L. *piper*, pepper.]

piperine *pip'ə-rīn*, *n* an alkaloid ($C_{17}H_{19}O_3N$) found in pepper. [L. *piper*, pepper.]

piperonal *pip'ə-rō-nal*, *n* a phenolic aldehyde of very pleasant odour, used as a perfume and in flavourings, etc. — also called *heliotropin*. [L. *piper*, pepper.]

pipette *pi-pet'*, *n* a tube for transferring and measuring fluids. [Fr., dimin. of *pipe*, pipe.]

piping. See under **pipe**[1].

pipistrelle *pip-i-strel'*, *n* a small reddish-brown bat, the commonest British bat. [Fr., — It. *pipistrello* — L. *vespertiliō*, bat — *vesper*, evening.]

pipit *pip'it*, *n* any member of a lark-like genus (*Anthus*) of birds related to wagtails. [Prob. imit.]

pipkin *pip'kin*, *n* a small pot, now only of earthenware. [Poss. a dimin. of **pipe**[2].]

pippin *pip'in*, *n* an apple of various varieties. [O.Fr. *pepin*.]

pippy. See **pip**[2].

pipsqueak *pip'skwēk*, (*slang*) *n* something or someone insignificant, contemptible.

pipul. See **pipal.**

piquant *pē'kənt*, *adj* pleasantly pungent; appetising; stimulating, provocative. — *n* **pi'quancy.** — *adv* **pi'quantly.** [Fr., pres. p. of *piquer*, to prick.]

pique[1] *pēk*, *n* a feeling of anger or vexation caused by a slight, wounded pride, etc. — *vt* to wound the pride of; to nettle; to arouse, stir, provoke; (*reflexive*) to pride (oneself; with *on* or *upon*). [Fr. *pique*, a pike, pique, *piquer*, to prick.]

pique[2] *pēk*, *n* in piquet, the scoring of 30 points in one hand before the other side scores at all. — *vt* to score a pique against. — *vi* to score a pique. [Fr. *pic*; see **piquet.**]

piqué *pē'kā*, *n* a stiff corded cotton fabric. [Fr., past p. of *piquer*, to prick.]

piquet *pi-ket'*, *n* a game for two with 32 cards, with scoring for declarations and tricks. [Fr.]

Pir *pēr*, (also without *cap*) *n* a Muslim title of honour given to a holy man or religious leader. [Pers. *pīr*, old man, chief.]

piracy. See **pirate.**

piranha or **piraña** *pē-rän'yə*, *n* a ferocious S. American river-fish (genus *Serrasalmo*). [Port. from Tupí *piranya*, *piraya*.]

pirate *pī'rət*, *n* a robber or marauder operating at sea; a pirates' ship; a person who publishes a work without authority of the copyright owner or otherwise makes use of or takes over another person's work without legal sanction; a person who runs an unlicensed radio station. — *vt* to publish or reproduce without permission of the copyright owner, or otherwise usurp (someone else's work or ideas). — *n* **piracy** (*pī'rə-si*) the crime of a pirate; robbery on the high seas; unauthorised publication; infringement of copyright. — *adj* **piratic** (*pī-rat'ik*) or **pirat'ical.** — *adv* **pirat'ically.** [L. *pīrāta* — Gr. *peirātēs* — *peiraein*, to attempt.]

piri-piri[1] *pir-ē-pir'ē*, *n* a sauce made with red peppers. [Perh. from Swahili *pilipili*, pepper.]

piri-piri[2] *pēr-ē-pēr'ē*, *n* a New Zealand weed with prickly burrs (genus *Acaena*) used medicinally and as a tea. [Maori.]

pirouette *pir-o͞o-et'*, *n* in dancing, a spin performed on tiptoe or the ball of the foot. — *vi* to spin round in the manner of a dancer. [Fr.]

piscatorial *pis-kə-tö'ri-əl* or **piscatory** *pis'kə-tə-ri*, *adj* of or relating to fishing or fishermen. [L. *piscātor*, fisherman, and *piscātōrius*, relating to fishermen.]

Pisces *pī'sēz*, *n* the Fishes, the twelfth sign of the zodiac, or the constellation that formerly coincided with it (*astron*); a person born between 20 February and 21 March, under the sign of Pisces. [L., the Fishes, pl. of *piscis*, a fish.]

pisci- *pis-i-*, *combining form* denoting fish. — *n* **pisc'iculture** the rearing of fish by artificial methods. — *n* **pisc'iculturist.** — *n* **piscifau'na** the assemblage of fishes in a region, formation, etc. — *adj* **pisc'iform** having the form of a fish. [L. *piscis*, a fish.]

piscina *pi-sē'nə*, *n* a fish-pond; a swimming-pool (as in Roman baths); a basin and drain in old churches, usu. in a niche south of an altar, into which water used in washing the sacred vessels was emptied: — *pl* **pisci'nas** or **pisci'nae** (*-nē*). [L. *piscīna* — *piscis*, a fish.]

piscine *pis'īn*, *adj* of fishes; of the nature of a fish. — *adj* **pisciv'orous** fish-eating, living on fish. [L. *piscis*, a fish.]

pisé *pē'zā*, *n* rammed earth or clay for walls or floors. [Fr.]

pish *pish*, (*old-fashioned*) *interj* expression of impatience or contempt. [Imit.]

pisiform *pī'si-förm* or *piz'i-förm*, *adj* pea-shaped. — *n* a pea-shaped bone of the carpus. [L. *pisum*, pea, *fōrma*, shape.]

piss *pis*, (*vulg*) *vi* to urinate. — *vt* to discharge as urine; to urinate on. — *n* urine. — *adj* **pissed** (*slang*) extremely drunk. — **piss artist** (*slang*) someone who drinks heavily; a person who is all talk, a foolish show-off; **piss'head** (*slang*) a heavy drinker, a habitual drunkard. — **piss about** or **around** (*slang*) to behave in a foolish or time-wasting way; **pissed off** (*slang*) annoyed; fed up; **piss off** (*interj*; *vulg*) go away; **piss (someone) off** (*slang*) to annoy or upset (someone); **take the piss out of** (*slang*) to mock, tease, scoff at (*n* **piss'-taker**; *n* **piss'-taking**). [Fr. *pisser*.]

pissoir *pē-swär*, (Fr.) *n* a public urinal.

pistachio *pi-stash'iō* or *pi-stä'shi-ō*, *n* the nut of a small western Asiatic tree (genus *Pistacia*) having a green, almond-flavoured kernel: — *pl* **pista'chios**. [Sp. *pistacho* and It. *pistacchio* — L.L. *pistāquium* — Gr. *pistăkion* — Pers. *pistah*.]

piste *pēst*, *n* a beaten track, esp. a ski trail in the snow; a strip of ground used for some sporting activity, etc. [Fr.]

pistil *pis'til*, (*bot*) *n* the ovary of a flower, with its style and stigma. — *adj* **pis'tillary**. — *adj* **pis'tillate** having a pistil but no (functional) stamens, female. [L. *pistillum*, a pestle.]

pistol *pis'tl*, *n* a small handgun, held in one hand when fired. — **pistol grip** a handle (usu. with a trigger mechanism) for a camera, etc., shaped like the butt of a pistol; **pistol shot**. — *vt* **pis'tol-whip** to hit (someone) with a pistol. — **hold a pistol to someone's head** to use threats to force someone to do what one wants. [Through Fr. and Ger. from Czech.]

pistole *pis-tōl'*, *n* an old (esp. Spanish) gold coin. [O.Fr., earlier *pistolet*.]

piston *pis'tən*, *n* a cylindrical part moving to and fro in a hollow cylinder, as in engines and pumps; a valve mechanism for altering the effective length of tube in brass and musical instruments; a push-key for combining a number of organ stops. — **piston ring** a split ring fitted in a circumferential groove around a piston rim forming a spring-loaded seal against the cylinder wall; **piston rod** the rod to which the piston is fixed, and which moves up and down with it. [Fr., — It. *pistone* — *pestare*, to pound — L. *pinsĕre*, *pistum*.]

pit[1] *pit*, *n* a hole in the earth; a mine shaft; a mine, esp. a coalmine; a place whence minerals are dug; a cavity in the ground or in a floor for any purpose, such as reception of ashes, inspection of motor cars; a place beside the course where cars in a race can be refuelled and repaired; a grave, esp. one for many bodies; a hole used as a trap for wild animals; an enclosure in which animals are kept (esp. bears); an enclosure for cockfights or the like; orig., the ground floor of a theatre, or its occupants, or the part of the ground floor behind the stalls, now usu. the area in front of the stage reserved for the orchestra in a theatre (also **orchestra pit**); part of an exchange allotted to trading in a particular commodity (*US*); any hollow or depression, e.g. the *pit of the stomach* below the breastbone; an indentation left by smallpox; a minute depression in a surface. — *vt* to mark with little hollows; to set to fight, as cocks in a cockpit; to match (with *against*). — *vi* to become marked with pits; to retain an impression for a time after pressing (*med*): — *pr p* **pitt'ing**; *pa t* and *pa p* **pitt'ed**. — *adj* **pitt'ed** marked with small pits. — **pit brow** the top of a shaft; **pit bull terrier** a large breed of bull terrier developed orig. for dogfighting; **pit'fall** a hidden danger or unsuspected difficulty; a lightly covered hole as a trap; **pit'head** the ground at the mouth of a pit, and the machinery, etc., on it; **pit'man** a coalminer, collier; **pit pony** a pony used for haulage in a coalmine; **pit'prop** a support, esp. of timber, in the workings of a coalmine; **pit stop** a stop a racing-car makes during a motor race when it goes into the pits for repairs; **pit viper** any member of an American group of snakes, including the rattlesnake, able to detect prey in the dark by means of a pit, sensitive to body heat, between eye and nose. — **the pits** (*slang*) the absolute worst place, conditions, thing, person, etc. possible. [O.E. *pytt* — L. *puteus*, a well.]

pit[2] *pit*, (esp. *NAm*) *n* a fruit stone. — *vt* to remove the stone from: — *pr p* **pitt'ing**; *pa t* and *pa p* **pitt'ed**. [App. Du. *pit*.]

pitapat *pit'ə-pat*, *adv* with a pattering or tapping noise; with a palpitating sensation. — *n* a pattering noise; a palpitating sensation; a succession of light taps. — *vi* to patter or tap lightly; to palpitate: — *pr p* **pit-a-patt'ing**; *pa t* and *pa p* **pit-a-patt'ed**. [Imit.]

pitch[1] *pich*, *n* the black shining residue of distillation of tar, etc.; extended to various bituminous and resinous substances; resin from certain pine trees. — *vt* to smear, cover or caulk with pitch. — *n* **pitch'iness**. — *adj* **pitch'y** like pitch; smeared with, or full of, pitch; black. — *adj* **pitch'-black** black as pitch. — *adj* **pitch-dark'** utterly dark. — **pitch'pine** a name for several American pines that yield pitch and timber. [O.E. *pic* — L. *pix*, *picis*.]

pitch[2] *pich*, *vt* to set up (a tent, camp, etc.) and fix firmly; to set in position; to pave (a road) with stones set on end or on edge; to establish the slope of; to set in a key, to give this or that musical pitch, emotional tone, or degree of moral exaltation, etc. to; to fling, throw or toss, esp. in such a manner as to fall flat or in a definite position; to loft so as not to roll much on falling (*golf*); in bowling, to make (the ball) land close to the batsman (*cricket*); to deliver to the batsman by an overhand or underhand throw (*baseball*). — *vi* to fix the choice (on); to encamp; to plunge forward; (of a ship) to plunge and lift alternately at bow and stern; to oscillate about a transverse axis (*aeronautics*); to slope down; to descend or fall away abruptly. — *n* the act or manner of pitching; a throw or cast; degree, esp. of elevation or depression; height; a descent; slope or degree of slope; ground between the wickets (*cricket*); a place set apart for playing or practising a game; the point where a ball alights; a station taken by a street trader, etc.; a salesman's particular line of persuasive talk; the degree of acuteness of a sound that makes it a high, low, etc. note, or the standard degree of acuteness assigned to a particular note (*mus*); degree of intensity; distance between successive points or things, such as the centres of teeth in a wheel or a saw, or the threads of a screw; the angle between the chord of the blade of a propeller and the plane of rotation; the distance a propeller would advance in one revolution. — *n* **pit'cher** a person who pitches, esp. a baseball player who delivers the ball to the batsman; a paving-stone or sett. — **pitch-and-toss'** a game in which coins are thrown at a mark, the player who throws nearest having the right of tossing all, and keeping those that come down heads up; **pitch circle** in a toothed wheel, an imaginary circle along which the tooth pitch is measured and which would put the wheel in contact with another that meshed with it; **pitched battle** a deliberate battle on chosen ground between duly arranged sides; a violent confrontation generally; **pitched roof** a roof having two downward-sloping surfaces meeting in a central ridge; **pitch'fork** a fork with two prongs, for tossing hay, etc.; a tuning-fork. — *vt* to lift with a pitchfork; to throw suddenly into a position or situation. — **pitch'man** (also **pitch'-person**; *fem* **pitch'woman**) a street or market trader (*NAm*); an advertising man, esp. in the media; someone who delivers a strong sales pitch; **pitch'-pipe** a small pipe to pitch the voice or tune with; **pitch'-wheel** a toothed wheel which operates with another of the same design. — **pitch in** to set to work briskly; to join in, cooperate; **pitch into** to assail vigorously; to throw oneself into (work, a task, etc.); **pitch on** or **upon** to let one's choice fall on or upon.

pitchblende *pich'blend*, *n* a black mineral composed of uranium oxides, a source of uranium and radium. [Ger. *Pechblende*, **pitch**[1], **blende**.]

pitcher[1] *pich'ər*, *n* a tall jug, usu. of earthenware, for holding or pouring liquids; a modified leaf or part of a leaf in the form of a pitcher, serving to catch insects. — *n* **pitch'erful**. — **pitcher plant** any of several insectivorous plants with pitchers, esp. one of genus *Nepenthes*. [O.Fr. *picher* — L.L. *picārium*, a goblet — Gr. *bīkos*, a wine-vessel.]

pitcher[2]. See **pitch**[2].

pitch-pole or **pitch-poll** *pich'-pōl*, *vi* to go head over heels; to somersault; to flip over lengthways; (of a boat) to turn stern over bow. [**pitch**[2] and **poll**.]

pitchy. See **pitch**[1].

piteous *pit'i-əs*, *adj* arousing or deserving pity. — *adv* **pit'eously**. — *n* **pit'eousness**. [O.Fr. *pitos*, *piteus*.]

pitfall. See under **pit**[1].

pith *pith*, *n* the soft tissue within the ring of vascular bundles in the stems of dicotyledonous plants; similar material elsewhere, such as the white inner skin of an orange; the soft, spongy interior of a feather; the innermost, central, or most important part, the essence; substance, weight, significance; vigour. — *vt* to remove the pith of; to sever, pierce or destroy the marrow or central nervous system of; to kill (animals) in this way. — *adv* **pith'ily**. — *n* **pith'iness**. — *adj* **pith'less**. — *adj* **pith'like**. — *adj* **pith'y** full of pith; expressed briefly but forcefully. — **pith helmet** a sun helmet of sola pith. [O.E. *pitha*.]

pithead. See under **pit**[1].

Pithecanthropus *pith-i-kan-thrō'pəs*, *n* a fossil hominid discovered in Java in 1891–92, a former genus of primitive man, now included in the genus *Homo*. [Gr. *pithēkos*, ape, *anthrōpos*, man.]

pithecoid *pi-thē'koid*, *adj* apelike. [Gr. *pithēkos*, ape, *eidos*, form.]

pitiable, pitiless, etc. See **pity**.

pitman. See under **pit**[1].

piton *pē'ton* or Fr. *pē-tɔ̃*, *n* an iron peg or stanchion to which a rope may be attached, used in mountaineering. [Fr.]

pitta *pit'ə*, *n* (also **pitta bread**) a type of slightly leavened bread, originating in the Middle East, usu. made in the form of flat hollow ovals; one of these ovals. [Mod. Gr., a cake.]

pittance *pit'əns*, *n* a very small quantity, esp. of money as wages. [O.Fr. *pitance* — L. *pietās*, pity.]

pitter-patter *pit'ər-pat-ər*, *adv* with light pattering sound. — *vi* to make, or move with, such a sound. — *n* such a sound. [Imit.]

pittosporum *pi-tos'pə-rəm*, *n* an evergreen shrub native to Australasia and parts of Africa and Asia, with leathery leaves and purple, white or greenish-yellow flowers (also called *parchment bark*). [N.L. — Gr. *pitta*, pitch, *sporos*, seed.]

pituitary *pi-tū'i-tə-ri*, *adj* of or relating to the pituitary gland. — **pituitary gland** or **body** an endocrine gland at the base of the brain, affecting growth. [L. *pītuīta*, phlegm, once thought to be produced by this gland.]

pity *pit'i*, *n* a feeling for the sufferings and misfortunes of others; a cause or source of pity or grief; an unfortunate chance; a matter for regret. — *vt* to feel pity for: — *pr p* **pit'ying**; *pa t* and *pa p* **pit'ied**. — *adj* **pit'iable** arousing pity; miserable, contemptible. — *n* **pit'iableness**. — *adv* **pit'iably**. — *adj* **pit'iful** exciting pity; wretched; despicable. — *adv* **pit'i-fully**. — *n* **pit'ifulness**. — *adj* **pit'iless** without pity; merciless, cruel. — *adv* **pit'ilessly**. — *n* **pit'ilessness**. — *adj* **pit'ying**. — *adv* **pit'yingly**. [O.Fr. *pite* — L. *pietās*, *pietātis* — *pius*, pious.]

pityriasis *pit-i-rī'i-sis*, (*med*) *n* any of several skin diseases marked by the formation and flaking away of branny scales. [Gr. *pityron*, bran.]

più *pyōō*, (It.; *mus*) *adv* more, as *più mosso*, quicker.

piupiu *pē'ōō-pē-ōō*, *n* a skirt, traditionally made from strips of flax, worn by Maori men and women for dances, celebrations and ceremonial occasions. [Maori.]

pivot *piv'ət*, *n* a pin or shaft on which anything turns; a soldier upon whom, or position on which, a body wheels; a centre-half in football or similarly placed player in other games; a person or thing on which anything depends or turns; the action of turning the body using one foot as a pivot. — *vt* to mount on a pivot. — *vi* to turn on or as if on a pivot. — *adj* **piv'otal** of, containing, or acting like, a pivot; crucially important. — *adv* **piv'otally**. — **pivot bridge** a swing-bridge moving on a vertical pivot in the middle. [Fr., perh. rel. to It. *piva*, pipe, peg, pin.]

pix[1] *piks*, *n*. Same as **pyx**.

pix[2] *piks*, (*colloq*) *npl* short for **pictures**, usu. in sense of photographs: — *nsing* **pic**.

pixel *pik'səl*, (*comput*, *image tech*) *n* the smallest element with controllable colour and brightness in a video display or in computer graphics. [**pix**[2] and *el*ement.]

pixie or **pixy** *pik'si*, *n* a small fairy. — **pixie hood** a child's hood with a point, usu. tied under the chin. [Cf. Sw. *pysk*, *pyske*, a small fairy.]

pixilated or **pixillated** *pik'si-lā-tid*, (esp. *US*) *adj* bemused, bewildered; slightly crazy; intoxicated. — *n* **pixilā'tion** or **pixillā'tion**. [*Pix*ie and poss. tit*illated*.]

pixilation or **pixillation** *pik-si-lā'shən*, *n* a technique for making human figures or animals appear to be animated artificially e.g. by the use of stop-frame camera methods, usu. to create a whimsical effect (*cinema*, *theatre*, *TV*; from *pixill*ated and anim*ation*); a video effect in which the whole picture is broken down into a comparatively small number of square elements (*image tech*; associated with **pixel**); see also under **pixilated**.

pixy. See **pixie**.

pizazz. See **pizzazz**.

pizza *pēt'sə*, *n* an open pie of bread dough topped with tomatoes, cheese, etc. — *n* **pizzeria** (*pēt-sə-rē'ə*) a bakery or restaurant where pizzas are sold and/or made. [It.]

pizzazz, pizazz, pazzazz or **pazazz** *pə-zaz'*, (*colloq*) *n* a combination of flamboyance, panache and vigour, in behaviour, display or performance. [Onomatopoeic coinage by Diana Vreeland, U.S. fashion editor (*c* 1903–89).]

pizzicato *pit-si-kä'tō*, (*mus*) *adj* played by plucking the string, not with the bow. — *adv* by plucking. — *n* a passage so played; the manner of playing by plucking: — *pl* **pizzica'tos**. [It., twitched — *pizzicare*, to twitch.]

Pk *abbrev* for Park (in place and street names).

PL *abbrev* for Poland (I.V.R.).

Pl. *abbrev* for Place (in street names, etc.).

pl. *abbrev* for plural.

placable *plak'ə-bl*, *adj* easily appeased; relenting, forgiving. — *n* **placabil'ity** or **plac'ableness**. — *adv* **plac'ably**. [L. *plācabilis* — *plācāre*, to appease.]

placard *plak'ärd*, *n* a written or printed notice stuck up on a wall or otherwise publicly displayed; a notice written or printed on wood, cardboard or other stiff material, and carried, hung, etc., in a public place. — *vt* to publish or notify by placard; to post or set up as a placard; to put placards on or in. [O.Fr. *plackart*, *placard*, etc. — *plaquier*, to lay flat, plaster — M.Flem. *placken*, to plaster.]

placate *plə-kāt'*, *vt* to conciliate. — *n* **placā'tion** propitiation. — *adj* **placā'tory** conciliatory. [L. *plācāre*, to appease, rel. to *placēre*.]

place *plās, n* a portion of space; a portion of the earth's surface, or any surface; a position in space, or on the earth's surface, or in any system, order or arrangement; a point, e.g. in a book, narrative, conversation, etc.; a building, room, piece of ground, etc., assigned to some purpose (such as *place of business, entertainment* or *worship*); a particular locality; a town, village, etc.; a dwelling or home; a mansion with its grounds; (with *cap*) used in street names, esp. for a short street, a circus or a row of houses; an open space or square, as in *market place*; a seat or accommodation in a theatre, train, at table, etc.; space occupied; room; the position held by anybody, employment, office, a situation, esp. under government or in domestic service; due or proper position or dignity; that which is incumbent on one; precedence; position in a series; high rank; position attained in a competition or assigned by criticism; position among the first three in a race; stead. — *vt* to put in any place; to assign to a place; to find a place, home, job, publisher, etc., for; to find a buyer for (usu. a large quantity of stocks or shares; *commerce*); to propose, lay, put (with *before*); to appoint; to identify; to invest; to arrange (a loan, bet, etc.); to put (trust, etc., in); to assign the finishing positions in a race. — *vi* (esp. *US*) to finish a race or competition (in a specified position); to finish a race in second (if otherwise unspecified) position (*horse-racing*). — *adj* **placed** among the first three in a race. — *n* **place'ment** placing or setting; assigning to places; assigning to a job; a job so assigned. — *n* **pla'cing** position, esp. a finishing position in a race or competition; the process of finding an intermediary buyer for large numbers of (usu. newly issued) shares, etc. (*commerce*). — **place card** a card placed before each setting on the table at a banquet, formal dinner, etc., with the name of the person who is to sit there; **place kick** (in football) a kick made when the ball has been placed on the ground for that purpose; **place'-kicker; place mat** a table mat set at a person's place setting; **place name** a geographical proper name; **place setting** each person's set of crockery, cutlery and glassware at a dining table. — **all over the place** scattered; in a muddle or mess, confused, disorganised (*colloq*); **fall into place** to be resolved; **give place (to)** to make room (for); to be superseded (by); **go places** see under **go**; **in place** in position; opportune; **in place of** instead of; **in the first place** firstly, originally; **know one's place** to show proper subservience; **lose one's place** to falter in following a text, etc., not know what point has been reached; to become angry; **lose the place** (*colloq*) to flounder, be at a loss, be all at sea; **out of place** out of due position; inappropriate, unseasonable; **put** or **keep someone in his** or **her place** to humble someone who is arrogant, presumptuous, etc. or keep him or her in subservience; **take one's place** to assume one's usual or rightful position; **take place** to come to pass, to occur; **take someone's place** to act as substitute for, or successor to, someone; **take the place of** to be a substitute for. [Partly O.E. *plæce*, market-place, but mainly Fr. *place*, both from L. *platea* — Gr. *plateia* (*hodos*), broad (street).]

placebo *plə-sē'bō, n* a medicine given to humour or gratify a patient rather than to exercise any physically curative effect; a pharmacologically inactive substance administered as a drug either in the treatment of psychological illness or in the course of drug trials; the vespers for the dead (*RC*): — *pl* **placē'bos.** [From the first words of the first antiphon of the vespers service, *Placēbō Dominō*, I shall please the Lord.]

placenta *plə-sen'tə, n* the structure that unites the unborn mammal to the womb of its mother and establishes a nutritive connection between them; the part of the carpel that bears the ovules (*bot*); any mass of tissue bearing sporangia or spores: — *pl* **placen'tae** (*-tē*) or **placen'tas.** — *adj* **placen'tal.** [L. *placenta*, a flat cake.]

placer *plas'ər* or *plā'sər, n* a superficial deposit from which gold or other mineral can be washed. — **plac'er-gold.** [Sp. *placer*, sandbank — *plaza*, place.]

placet *plā'set, n* a vote of assent in a governing body; permission given, esp. by a sovereign, to publish and carry out an ecclesiastical order, such as a papal bull or edict. [L. *plăcet*, it pleases, 3rd sing. pres. indic. of *placēre*, to please.]

placid *plas'id, adj* calm. — *n* **placid'ity** or **plac'idness.** — *adv* **plac'idly.** [L. *placidus* — *placēre*, to please.]

placket *plak'it, n* an opening in a skirt, for a pocket, or at the fastening; a piece of material sewn behind this. [Orig. a breastplate; as such a variant of *placard*, formerly breastplate.]

placoderm *plak'ə-dûrm, adj* covered with bony plates (like some fossil fishes). — *n* a fish so covered. [Gr. *plax, plakos*, anything flat, *derma*, skin.]

placoid *plak'oid, adj* (of scales) plate-like; (of fish, e.g. sharks) having placoid scales, irregular plates of hard bone, not overlapping. [Gr. *plax, plakos*, anything flat and broad, *eidos*, form.]

plafond *pla-fɔ̃, n* a ceiling, esp. decorated; an earlier version of contract bridge. [Fr., ceiling, score above the line in bridge — *plat*, flat, *fond*, bottom.]

plage *pläzh, n* a fashionable beach; a bright, highly disturbed area in the chromosphere, the outer gaseous layers of the sun, usu. presaging, or associated with, a sunspot. [Fr.]

plagiarise or **-ize** *plā'jə-rīz, vt* and *vi* to steal from the writings or ideas of another. — *n* **pla'giarism** the act or practice of plagiarising. — *n* **pla'giarist.** [L. *plagiārius*, a kidnapper, plagiarist — *plăga*, a net.]

plagio- *plā-ji-ō-, -o-* or *-ə-, combining form* meaning oblique. — *n* **plagiocephaly** (*-sef'ə-li; med*) a twisted condition of the head, the front of the skull being larger on one side, the back larger on the other. — *n* **plā'gioclase** (*-klās*) a feldspar whose cleavages are not at right angles. — *n* **plā'giostome** (*-stōm*) a fish, such as the shark, whose mouth is a transverse slit on the underside of the head. [Gr. *plagios*, oblique.]

plague *plāg, n* a deadly epidemic or pestilence, esp. a fever caused by a bacillus transmitted by rat-fleas from rats to man, characterised by buboes, or swellings of the lymphatic glands; murrain; a sudden abnormal infestation, such as *a plague of greenfly*; any troublesome thing or person; a nuisance or vexation (*colloq*); an affliction regarded as a sign of divine displeasure. — *vt* to pester or annoy. — *adj* **plague'some** (*colloq*) troublesome, annoying. — **a plague on** may a curse fall on; **avoid like the plague** (*colloq*) to keep well away from, shun absolutely. [O.Fr. *plague* — L. *plāga*, a blow.]

plaice *plās, n* a brown flatfish with orange spots, used as food; any of several related fishes (*N Am*). [O.Fr. *plaïs* — L.L. *platessa*, a flatfish.]

plaid *plād* or *plad, n* a long piece of woollen cloth, worn over the shoulder, usu. in tartan as part of Scottish Highland dress, or checked as formerly worn by Lowland shepherds; cloth for it. — *adj* like a plaid in pattern or colours. [Perh. Gael. *plaide*, a blanket; but that may be from the Scots word.]

plain *plān, adj* flat; level; even; unobstructed; clear; obvious; simple; downright, utter; not ornate; unembellished; unvariegated; uncoloured; unruled; without pattern, striation, markings, etc.; without gloss; not twilled; in knitting, denoting a straightforward stitch with the wool passed round the front of the needle (opp. to *purl*); not elaborate; without addition; not highly seasoned; deficient in beauty; without subtlety; candid; outspoken; straightforward; undistinguished; ordinary; other than a picture-card; other than trumps. — *n* an extent of level land. — *adv* clearly; distinctly. — *adv* **plain'ly.** — *n* **plain'ness.** — **plain'chant** plainsong; **plain chocolate** dark chocolate, made with some sugar added but without milk. — *adj* **plain'clothes** wearing ordinary clothes, not uniform, as a policeman on detective work. — **plain dealer** a person who is candid and outspoken. — *n* and *adj* **plain dealing.** — **plain Jane** (*colloq derog*) a plain, dowdy girl. — *adj* **plain'-Jane** ordinary, unremarkable; plain, esp. of a garment. — **plain language** straightforward, understandable language; **plain sailing** sailing in open, unrestricted waters (*naut*); an easy, straightforward task, procedure, etc. (see also **plane²**); **plains'man** a dweller in a plain, esp. in N. America: — *pl* **plain'smen; plain'song** unmeasured music sung in unison in ecclesiastical modes from early times, and still in use in R.C. and some Anglican churches; **plain speaking** straightforwardness or bluntness in speech. — *adj* **plain'-spoken** frank, candid, esp. if rather blunt. — **plain as a pikestaff** see under **pike¹**. [Fr., — L. *plānus*, plain.]

plaint *plānt*, *n* lamentation (*literary*); a statement of grievance, esp. the exhibiting of an action in writing by a complainant in a court of law. [O.Fr. *pleinte* — L. *plangere, planctum*, to lament.]

plaintiff *plān'tif*, (*Eng law*) *n* a person who commences a suit against another — opp. to *defendant*. [O.Fr. *plaintif*, complaining.]

plaintive *plān'tiv*, *adj* mournful; querulous. — *adv* **plaint'ively.** — *n* **plaint'iveness.** [Ety. as for **plaintiff.**]

plait *plat* or in U.S. *plāt*, *n* a braid in which strands are passed over one another in turn; material so braided; a braided tress of hair. — *vt* to braid or intertwine. — *adj* **plait'ed.** — *n* **plait'er.** — *n* **plait'ing.** [O.Fr. *pleit, ploit* — L. *plicāre, -itum*, to fold.]

plan *plan*, *n* a figure or representation of anything projected on a plane or flat surface, esp. that of a building, floor, etc., as disposed on the ground; a large-scale detailed map of a small area; a scheme for accomplishing a purpose; an intended method; a scheme drawn up beforehand; a scheme of arrangement. — *vt* to make a plan of; to design; to lay plans for; to devise; to purpose. — *vi* to make plans: — *pr p* **plann'ing;** *pa t* and *pa p* **planned.** — *adj* **planned** intended; in accordance with, or achieved by, a careful plan made beforehand. — *n* **plann'er** a person who plans, esp. the development of a town, etc.; a calendar showing the whole year, etc., at a glance, used for forward planning. — **planning permission** permission from a local authority to erect or convert a building or to change the use to which a building or piece of land is put. [Fr., — L. *plānus*, flat.]

planar. See under **plane².**

planarian *plə-nār'i-ən*, *n* any of several kinds of aquatic flatworm. [N.L. *Planāria*, genus name, — L. *planārius*, flat.]

planchet *plan'shit*, *n* a blank metal disc to be stamped as a coin. [Dimin. of *planch*, slab of metal.]

planchette *plã-shet* or *plan-shet'*, *n* a board mounted on two castors and a pencil-point, used as a medium for automatic writing and supposed spirit messages. [Fr., dimin. of *planche*, plank.]

plane¹ *plān*, *n* any tree of the genus *Platanus*; the name given in Scotland to the sycamore or the great maple. — **plane tree.** [Fr. *plane* — L. *platanus*; see ety. for **platane.**]

plane² *plān*, *n* a surface of which it is true that, if any two points on the surface be taken, the straight line joining them will lie entirely on the surface (*geom*); any flat or level material surface; one of the thin horizontal structures used as wings and tail to sustain or control aeroplanes in flight; short for aeroplane or airplane (also **'plane**); any grade of life or of development or level of thought or existence. — *adj* having the character of a plane; pertaining to, lying in, or confined to a plane; level; smooth. — *vi* to soar; (of a boat) to skim across the surface of the water. — *adj* **planar** (*plā'nər*) relating to a plane; lying in a single plane, flat. — *n* **plane chart** a chart used in plane sailing, the lines of longitude and latitude being projected on to a plane surface, so being represented parallel; **plane sailing** the calculation of a ship's place in its course as if the earth were flat instead of spherical (see also **plain sailing** under **plain**). [L. *plānum*, a flat surface, neut. of *plānus*, flat.]

plane³ *plān*, *n* a carpenter's tool for producing a smooth surface by paring off shavings; a tool or machine for smoothing other things. — *vt* to smooth or remove with a plane. — *n* **plā'ner** a person who uses a plane; a tool or machine for planing. — **plā'ning-machine** a machine for planing wood or metals. [Fr. *plane* — L.L. *plāna* — *plānāre*, to smooth.]

planet *plan'it*, *n* any of the celestial bodies (including the earth) that revolve about the sun, reflecting the sun's light and generating no heat or light of their own, these being Mercury, Venus, Earth, Mars, Jupiter, Saturn, Uranus, Neptune and Pluto; a satellite of a planet (*secondary planet*); an astrological influence vaguely conceived. — *n* **planetā'rium** a machine showing the motions and orbits of the planets, often by projection of their images on to a (domed) ceiling; a hall or building containing such a machine: — *pl* **planetā'ria.** — *adj* **plan'etary** relating to the planets or a planet, or this planet; consisting of, or produced by, planets; under the influence of a planet (*astrol*); erratic; revolving in an orbit. — *n* **plan'etoid** a minor planet. — *n* **planetol'ogist.** — *n* **planetol'ogy** the science of the planets. — **minor planets** the numerous group of asteroids between the orbits of Mars and Jupiter. [Fr. *planète* — Gr. *planētēs*, wanderer.]

plangent *plan'jənt*, *adj* resounding mournfully; loud, resonant, ringing. — *n* **plan'gency.** — *adv* **plan'gently.** [L. *plangēns, -entis*, pres. p. of *plangĕre*, to beat.]

plani- *plan-i-*, *combining form* signifying plane (see **plane²**). — *n* **planimeter** (*plə-nim'i-tər*) an instrument for measuring the area of a plane figure. — *n* **planim'etry.** — *n* **planisphere** (*plan'i-sfēr*) a sphere projected on a plane; a map of the celestial sphere, which can be adjusted so as to show the area visible at any time. — *adj* **planispher'ic.** [L. *plānus*, flat.]

planish *plan'ish*, *vt* to polish (metal, etc.); to flatten. — *n* **plan'isher** a person who, or tool that, planishes. [Obs. Fr. *planir, -issant* — *plan*, flat.]

planisphere. See under **plani-.**

plank *plangk*, *n* a long piece of timber, thicker than a board; one of the principles or aims that form the platform or programme of a political party. — *vt* to cover with planks; to put down with a thump (often with *down*). — *n* **plank'ing** the act of laying planks; a series of planks; work made up of planks. — **walk the plank** to walk (compulsorily) along a plank projecting over the ship's side into the sea. [L. *planca*, a board.]

plankton *plangk'tən*, *n* the drifting organisms in oceans, lakes or rivers. — *adj* **planktonic** (*-ton'ik*). [Neut. of Gr. *planktos, -ē, -on*, wandering.]

plano- *plān-ō-* or *plan-o-*, *combining form* signifying plane (see **plane²**). — *adj* **plānō-con'cave** (of a lens) plane on one side and concave on the other. — *adj* **plānō-con'vex** (of a lens) plane on one side and convex on the other. — *n* **planometer** (*plə-nom'ə-tər*) a flat device used as a gauge for flat surfaces. [L. *plānus*, flat.]

plant *plänt*, *n* a vegetable organism, or part of one, ready for planting or lately planted; a slip, cutting or scion; any member of the vegetable kingdom, esp. (*popularly*) one of the smaller kinds; something deposited beforehand for a purpose; equipment, machinery, apparatus, for an industrial activity; a factory; the buildings, equipment, etc. of e.g. a school, university or other institution; a deceptive trick, put-up job (*slang*); a shot in which one pockets, or tries to pocket, a red ball by causing it to be propelled by another red ball which has been struck by the cue ball or by some other red ball (*snooker*). — *vt* to put into the ground for growth; to introduce; to insert; to place firmly; to set in position; to station, post; to found; to settle; to locate; to place or deliver (as a blow, a dart); to bury (*slang*); to hide (*slang*); to deploy (stolen goods, etc.) in such a way as to incriminate someone; to place as a spy, etc. (*slang*); to interpose (a question or comment) as a snare or stumbling-block; to instil or implant; to supply with plants; to colonise; to stock; to furnish or provide (with things disposed around). — *vi* to plant trees, etc. — *adj* **plant'able**. — *n* **plantā'tion** a place planted, esp. with trees; (*formerly*) a colony; an estate used for growing cotton, rubber, tea, sugar, or other product of warm countries; the act or process of introduction. — *n* **plant'er** a person who plants or introduces; the owner or manager of a plantation; a pioneer colonist; a settler; an instrument for planting; an ornamental pot or other container for plants. — *n* **plant'ing** the act of setting in the ground for growth; the art of forming plantations of trees. — **plant louse** an aphis or greenfly: — *pl* **plant lice**; **plant pot** a pot for growing a plant in; **plants'man** or **plants'woman** a man or woman who has great knowledge of and experience in gardening. — **plant out** to transplant to open ground, from pot or frame; to dispose at intervals in planting. [O.E. *plante* (noun) — L. *planta*, shoot, slip, cutting, and O.E. *plantian* (verb), and partly from or affected by Fr. *plante* and L. *planta*, plant.]

plantain[1] *plan'tin, n* a plant (genus *Plantago*) that presses its leaves flat on the ground and has greenish flowers on a slim stem. — **plantain lily** a plant of the *Hosta* genus. [L. *plantāgō, -inis* — *planta*, the sole of the foot.]

plantain[2] *plan'tin, n* a plant related to the banana; its fruit, a coarse, green-skinned banana, used as a staple food in tropical countries. — **plan'tain-eater** an African bird, the touraco. [Sp. *plátano*, the plantain or plane tree.]

plantar *plan'tər*, (*anat*) *adj* of, or relating to, the sole of the foot. [L. *plantāris* — *planta*, sole of the foot.]

plantation. See under **plant**.

plantigrade *plan'ti-grād*, (*zool*) *adj* walking fully on the soles of the feet. — *n* an animal that walks on the soles of the feet. [N.L. *plantigrādus* — L. *planta*, sole of the foot, and *-gradus*, walking.]

plaque *pläk* or *plak, n* a plate, tablet, or slab hung on, applied to, or inserted in, a surface as an ornament, memorial, etc.; a tablet worn as a badge of honour; a patch, such as a diseased area (*med*); a film composed of saliva and bacteria that forms on teeth (*dentistry*); an area in a bacterial or tissue culture where the cells have been destroyed by infection with a virus. [Fr.]

plash *plash, n* a dash of water; a splashing sound. — *vi* to dabble in water; to splash. — *vt* to splash. — *adj* **plash'y**. [Cf. M.L.G. *plaschen*, early Mod. Du. *plasschen*.]

plasm *plazm, n* (also as *combining form*) a formative substance, protoplasm, as in *cytoplasm, germ plasm*; another word for **plasma**. — *n* **plas'ma** the liquid part of blood, lymph or milk; a very hot ionised gas, having approx. equal numbers of positive ions and of electrons, highly conducting (*phys*); a bright green chalcedony (*geol*). — *n* **plasmapherē'sis** the process of taking plasma only from a blood donor — the blood is drawn, the blood cells separated from the plasma by a centrifuge and returned to the donor. — *adj* **plasmat'ic** or **plas'mic** of, or occurring in, plasma; protoplasmic. — *n* **plas'mid** a circular piece of DNA which can exist and reproduce autonomously in the cytoplasm of cells. — *n* **plas'min** fibrinolysin, an enzyme that breaks down the fibrous protein (*fibrin*) in blood clots. — *n* **plasmin'ogen** (*-ə-jən*) the substance in blood plasma from which plasmin is formed. — *n* **plasmodesm** (*plaz'mə-dezm*) a thread of protoplasm connecting cells: — *pl* **plasmodes'mata**. — *n* **plasmo'dium** naked mass of protoplasm with many nuclei, as in myxomycetes: — *pl* **plasmo'dia**. — *n* **plasmog'amy** fusion of cytoplasm only, i.e. without, or as distinct from, fusion of cell nuclei. — *vt* **plas'molyse** or **-yze** (*-līz*). — *n* **plasmolysis** (*-mol'i-sis*) removal of water from a cell by osmosis, with resultant shrinking. — *adj* **plasmolytic** (*-mə-lit'ik*). — *n* **plasmosō'ma** or **plas'mosome** a nucleolus. [Gr. *plasma, -atos*, a thing moulded — *plassein*, to mould.]

plaster *pläs'tər, n* a strip of fabric coated with an adhesive substance for protection of a cut, etc.; a pasty composition that sets hard, esp. a mixture of slaked lime, sand, and sometimes hair, used for coating walls, etc.; (esp. *formerly*) a curative substance spread on linen and applied locally; plaster of Paris; calcium sulphate, gypsum. — *adj* made of plaster. — *vt* to apply plaster, a plaster or a plaster cast to; to bedaub, smear, or cover excessively; to stick (with *on* or *over*); to damage by a heavy attack; to smooth (hair) down; to attach with plaster. — *adj* **plas'tered** (*slang*) intoxicated. — *n* **plas'terer** a person who plasters, or works in plaster. — *n* **plas'tering**. — *adj* **plas'tery** like plaster. — *n* **plas'teriness**. — **plas'terboard** a building slab of plaster faced with paper or fibre; **plaster cast** a copy obtained by pouring a mixture of plaster of Paris and water into a mould formed from the object; an immobilising and protective covering of plaster of Paris for a broken limb, etc.; **plaster saint** a virtuous person; someone who pretends hypocritically to be virtuous; **plas'terwork**. — **plaster of Paris** gypsum (orig. found near *Paris*) partially dehydrated by heat, which dries into a hard substance when mixed with water. [O.E. *plaster* (in medical sense) and O.Fr. *plastre* (builder's plaster) both — L.L. *plastrum* — Gr. *emplastron* — *en*, on, *plassein*, to mould, apply as a plaster.]

plastic *plas'tik* or *plä'stik, adj* shaping, formative; mouldable; of or relating to moulding or modelling; modifiable; capable of permanent deformation without giving way; capable of, or relating to, metabolism and growth; made of plastic; unattractively synthetic or artificial. — *n* a mouldable substance, esp. now any of a large number of polymeric substances, most of them synthetic, mouldable at some stage under heat or pressure, used to make domestic articles and many engineering products. — *nsing* **plas'tics** the scientific study, or industrial production, of plastic materials. — *vt* and *vi* **plas'ticise** or **-ize** (*-ti-sīz*) to make or become plastic. — *n* **plas'ticiser** or **-z-** a substance that induces plasticity. — *n* **plasticity** (*-tis'i-ti*) the state or quality of being plastic; the quality in a picture of appearing to be three-dimensional. — **plastic art** the art, or any of the arts, of shaping in three dimensions, such as sculpture, ceramics, modelling; **plastic bomb** a bomb made with a certain explosive chemical that can be moulded; **plastic bullet** a four-inch cylinder of PVC fired for the purpose of riot control; **plastic explosive** an adhesive explosive material of jelly-like consistency; **plastic money** (*colloq*) credit cards; **plastic surgeon**; **plastic surgery** the branch of surgery concerned with restoring a lost part, or repairing a deformed or disfigured part, of the body. [Gr. *plastikos* — *plassein*, to mould.]

Plasticene® *plas'ti-sēn, n* a kind of modelling material that remains soft and can be reworked, used esp. by children.

plastique *plas-tēk'*, *n* graceful poses and movements in dancing. [Fr. — Gr. *plastikos* (see **plastic**).]

plastron *plas'trən*, *n* the ventral section of the shell of a turtle or tortoise; a fencer's wadded breast-shield; the front of a dress shirt; a separate ornamental front part of a woman's bodice; a steel breastplate (*hist*). [Fr. — It. *piastrone* — *piastra*, breastplate.]

platane or **platan** *plat'ən*, *n* a plane tree. [L. *platanus* — Gr. *platanos* — *platys*, broad.]

platanna *plə-tan'ə* or **platanna frog** (*frog*), *n* an African frog (*Xenopus laevis*) used in research, and formerly used in tests for pregnancy. [Afrik. — *plat-hander*, flat-handed.]

plat du jour *pla dü zhōōr*, *n* a dish on a restaurant menu specially recommended that day. [Fr.]

plate *plāt*, *n* a sheet, slab, or lamina of metal or other hard material, usu. flat or flattish; metal in the form of sheets; a broad piece of armour; a separate portion of an animal's shell; a broad thin piece of a structure or mechanism; a platelike section of the earth's crust; a piece of metal, wood, etc., bearing or to bear an inscription to be affixed to anything; an engraved piece of metal for printing from; an impression printed from it, an engraving; a whole-page illustration in a book, separately printed and inserted; a mould from type, etc., for printing from, as an electrotype or stereotype; part of a denture fitting the mouth and carrying the teeth; the whole denture; a device worn in the mouth by some children in order to straighten the teeth; a film-coated sheet of glass or other material to photograph on; a horizontal supporting timber in building; a five-sided white slab at the home base (*baseball*); wrought gold or silver; household utensils in gold or silver; plated ware such as *Sheffield plate*, a silver-plated copper ware; a cup or other prize for a race or other contest; a race or contest for such a prize; a shallow dish of any of various sizes according to purpose, e.g. *side plate*, *dessert plate*, *dinner plate*; a plateful; a portion served on a plate; a church collection; (in *pl*) the feet (*slang*; orig. rhyming slang for *plates of meat*). — *vt* to overlay with metal; to armour with metal; to cover with a thin film of another metal; to make a printing plate of. — *adj* **plā'ted** covered with plates of metal; covered with a coating of another metal, esp. gold or silver; armoured with hard scales or bone (*zool*). — *n* **plate'ful** as much as a plate will hold. — *n* **plate'let** a minute body in blood, concerned in clotting. — *n* **plā'ter** a person who, or that which, plates; a moderate horse entered for a minor, esp. selling, race. — *n* **plā'ting**. — **plate armour** protective armour of metal plates; **plate glass** a fine kind of glass used for mirrors and shop-windows, orig. poured in a molten state on an iron plate. — *adj* **plate'-glass** made with, or consisting of, plate glass; of a building, having large plate-glass windows, appearing to be built entirely of plate glass; hence used of any very modern building or institution, esp. recently-founded British universities. — **plate'-layer** a person who lays, fixes, and attends to the rails of a railway; **plate rack** one for draining plates after washing; **plate rail** a flat rail with a flange; **plate tectonics** (*geol*) the inter-relating movements of the rigid plates or sections that make up the earth's crust, riding on the semi-molten rock of the interior; the science or study of these movements. — **hand** or **give (someone something) on a plate** to cause or allow (someone) to achieve or obtain (something) without the least effort; **on one's plate** in front of one, waiting to be dealt with. [O.Fr. *plate*, fem. (and for the dish *plat*, masc.), flat — Gr. *platys*, broad.]

plateau *plat'ō* or *pla-tō'*, *n* a large level tract of elevated land, a tableland; a temporary stable state reached in the course of upward progress; the part of a curve representing this: — *pl* **plateaux** (*-tōz*) or **plateaus**. — *vt* to reach a level, even out (sometimes with *out*). [Fr., — O.Fr. *platel*, dimin. of *plat*, plate.]

platen *plat'n*, *n* a flat part that in some printing-presses pushes the paper against the forme; the roller of a typewriter. [Fr. *platine* — *plat*, flat.]

platform *plat'förm*, *n* a raised floor for speakers, musicians, etc.; a raised pavement alongside the track at a railway station, giving access to trains; a position prepared for mounting a gun; a floating installation, usu. moored to the sea bed, for drilling for oil, marine research, etc.; an open part at the back of some buses, trams, etc. by which passengers enter or leave the vehicle; a very thick, rigid sole on a boot or shoe (esp. *attrib*, as in *platform sole*); the publicly declared principles and intentions of a political party, taken as forming the basis of its policies; any situation giving one access to an audience, that one can exploit as an opportunity for promoting one's views; the people occupying the platform at a meeting, etc. [Fr. *plateforme*, lit. flat form.]

platinum *plat'i-nəm*, *n* a noble metal (symbol **Pt**; atomic no. 78), a steel-grey element, very valuable, malleable and ductile, very heavy and hard to fuse. — *adj* made of platinum. — *adj* **platinic** (*plə-tin'ik*) of platinum, esp. tetravalent. — *vt* **plat'inise** or **-ize** to coat with platinum. — *adj* **plat'inous** of bivalent platinum. — **platinum black** platinum in the form of a velvety black powder. — *adj* **platinum-blond'** (of hair) silvery blond. — **platinum blonde** a woman with hair of this colour. — **go platinum** (*slang*) (usu. of a long-playing record) to sell at least a million copies, earning for the artist a framed platinum disc from the recording company. [Sp. *platina* — *plata*, silver.]

platitude *plat'i-tūd*, *n* a dull commonplace or truism; an empty remark made as if it were important. — *n* **platitu'dinise** or **-ize**. — *adj* **platitu'dinous**. [Fr., — *plat*, flat.]

Platonic *plə-ton'ik*, *adj* relating to Plato, the Greek philosopher or to his philosophy; (of love; often without *cap*) without sensual desire; relating to Platonic love. — *n* **Plā'tonism** the philosophy of Plato. — *n* **Plā'tonist** a follower of Plato. — **Platonic solid** any of the five regular polyhedrons (tetrahedron, hexahedron or cube, octahedron, dodecahedron, and icosahedron). [Gr. *platōnikos* — *Platōn*, Plato.]

platoon *plə-tōōn'*, *n* a subdivision of a company (*mil*); a squad; a group of people acting together. [Fr. *peloton*, ball, knot of men — L. *pĭla*, ball.]

platteland *plä'tə-länt*, (*SAfr*) *n* rural districts. [Afrik.]

platter *plat'ər*, *n* a large flat plate or dish; a gramophone record (*slang*, esp. *US*). [A.Fr. *plater* — *plat*, a plate.]

platy- *plat-i-*, *combining form* signifying flat, broad. [Gr. *platys*, broad.]

platypus *plat'i-pəs*, *n* an aquatic burrowing and egg-laying Australian mammal (genus *Ornithorhynchus*), with broadly webbed feet and ducklike bill: — *pl* **plat'ypuses**. [**platy-** and Gr. *pous*, *podos*, a foot.]

platyrrhine *plat'i-rīn* or **platyrrhinian** *plat-i-rin'i-ən*, *adj* broad-nosed; belonging to the division of the monkeys found in South America, with widely spaced nostrils. — *n* a New World monkey. [Gr. *platyrrīs*, *-īnos* — *rhīs*, *rhīnos*, nose.]

plaudit *plö'dit*, *n* (now usu. in *pl*) an act of applause; praise bestowed, enthusiastic approval. [Shortened from L. *plaudite*, applaud, an actor's call for applause at the end of a play, pl. imper. of *plaudĕre*, *plausum*, to clap the hands.]

plausible *plöz'i-bl*, *adj* likely, reasonable, seemingly true; seemingly worthy of approval or praise; specious; smooth-tongued, ingratiating. — *n* **plausibil'ity** or **plaus'ibleness**. — *adv* **plaus'ibly**. [L. *plaudĕre*, to clap the hands.]

play *plā*, *vi* to move about irregularly, lightly or freely; to flicker, flutter, shimmer, pass through rapid alternations; to appear faintly and fleetingly (usu.

with *round*); to move in, discharge, or direct a succession, stream or shower (as of water, light, waves, missiles); to perform acts not part of the immediate business of life but in mimicry or rehearsal or in display; to amuse oneself; to trifle; to behave without seriousness; to behave amorously or sexually; to take part in a game; (with *for*) to compete on the side of; to proceed with the game, perform one's part in turn; to deliver a ball, etc. in the course of a game; to perform on a musical instrument; to produce or emit music; (of music) to issue forth; to act a part; to co-operate (*colloq*). — *vt* to perform; to ply, wield; to cause or allow to play; to set in opposition, pit; to send, let off, or discharge in succession or in a stream or shower; to allow (a fish) to tire itself by its struggles to get away; to engage in (a game); to proceed through (a game, part of a game — as a stroke, trick — or an aggregate of games — as a rubber, set); to stake or risk in play; to gamble on (*colloq*); to bring into operation in a game, as by striking (a ball), throwing on the table (a card), moving (a man); to compete against in a game, sport, etc.; to act (e.g. comedy, a named play); to act the part of, in a play or in real life; to act or perform in (e.g. a circuit of theatres, halls); to pretend for fun; to perform music on; to perform on a musical instrument; to cause (a radio, record-player, etc.) to emit sound; to lead, bring, send, render or cause to be by playing. — *n* activity; operation; action of wielding; light fluctuating movement or change; limited freedom of movement; scope; recreative activity; display of animals in courtship; amusement; fun; the playing of a game; manner of playing; procedure or policy in a game; gambling; a drama or dramatic performance; manner of dealing, as in *fair play*. — *adj* **play'able** capable (by nature or by the rules of the game) of being played, or of being played on. — *n* **play'er** a person who plays; a person participating in, or skilled at, esp. a game or sport; an actor; an instrumental performer; an apparatus for playing records, etc., as in *record-player, cassette-player*; in Northern Ireland, a terrorist, esp. one who is young and unknown. — *adj* **play'ful** full of fun, frolicsome, frisky; high-spirited, humorous. — *adv* **play'fully**. — *n* **play'fulness**. — **play'-acting** performance of plays; pretence; **play'-actor** or **-actress** a professional actor or actress (usu. *derog*); **play'back** the act of reproducing a recording of sound or visual material, esp. immediately after it is made; a device for doing this (see also **play back** below); **play'bill** a bill announcing a play; **play'boy** a light-hearted irresponsible person, esp. rich and leisured. — *adj* **played out** or (*attrib*) **played-out'** exhausted; no longer good for anything. — **player piano** a mechanical piano, a Pianola® (q.v. under **pianoforte**); **play'fellow** a playmate; **play'-ground** a place for playing in, esp. one connected with a school; a holiday region; **play'group** an informal, usu. voluntarily-run group having morning or afternoon sessions attended by mothers and preschool children, for creative and co-operative play; **play'house** a theatre; a child's toy house, usu. big enough for a child to enter; **play'ing-card** one of a pack (usu. of fifty-two cards, divided into four suits) used in playing games; **play'ing-field** a grass-covered space set apart, marked out, and kept in order for games (**a level** or **flat playing-field** (*colloq*) fair competition); **play'leader** a person trained to supervise and organise children's play in a playground, etc.; **play'mate** a companion in play, esp. child's play; **play'-off** a game to decide a tie; a game between the winners of other competitions; see also **play off** below; **play'pen** an enclosure within which a young child may safely play; **play'room** a room for children to play in; **play'school** a nursery school or playgroup; **play'thing** a toy; a person or thing treated as a toy; **play'time** a time for play; in schools, a set period for playing, usu. out of doors; **play'wright** a dramatist. — **bring, call** or **come into play** to bring, call or come into exercise, operation or use; **in** or **out of play** (of a ball, etc.) in, or not in, a position in which it may be played; **make a play for** (*colloq*) to try to get; **make great play with** to make a lot of; to treat, or talk of, as very important; **play about** to behave irresponsibly, not seriously; **play along (with)** to cooperate, agree (with), usu. temporarily; **play a part (in)** to be instrumental (in), take part (in); **play around** to play about; to have amorous affairs with men or women other than one's spouse; **play at** to engage in the game of; to make a pretence of; to practise without seriousness; **play back** to play a sound, video, etc. recording that has just been made; **play ball** (*colloq*) to co-operate; **play it (or one's cards) close to the chest** to be secretive about one's actions or intentions in a particular matter; **play down** to treat (something) as not very important or probable, esp. as less so than it is; **play fair** (sometimes with *with*) to act honestly; **play fast and loose** to act in a shifty, inconsistent and reckless fashion; **play for safety** to play safe; **play for time** to delay action or decision in the hope or belief that conditions will become more favourable later; **play hard to get** to make a show of unwillingness to co-operate with a view to strengthening one's position; **play havoc** or **hell with** to upset, disorganise; to damage; **play into the hands of** to act so as to give, usu. unintentionally, an advantage to; **play it** (*colloq*; followed by an *adj*) to behave in, or manage, a particular situation in a stated way, as in *play it cool*; **play it by ear** to improvise a plan of action to meet the situation as it develops; **play off** to manipulate so as to counteract; to play from the tee (*golf*); **play on words** a pun or other manipulation of words depending on their sound; **play out** to play to the end; to wear out, to exhaust; **play safe** to take no risks; **play the field** (*colloq*) to spread one's interests, affections or efforts over a wide range of subjects, people, activities, etc., rather than concentrate on any single one; **play the game** to act strictly honourably; **play up** to function faultily (*colloq*); to behave unco-operatively (*colloq*); (of an impaired part of the body) to give one pain (*colloq*); to redouble one's efforts, play more vigorously; to give (esp. undue) prominence to, or to boost; **play upon** or **on** to rouse, manipulate, work upon; **play up to** to act so as to afford opportunities to (another actor); to flatter; **play with** to play in company of, or as partner or opponent to; to flirt or philander with; to stimulate (the genitals of), to masturbate (oneself or someone else). [O.E. *pleg(i)an*, verb, *plega*, noun.]

playa *plä'yə, n* a basin which becomes a shallow lake after heavy rainfall and dries out again in hot weather. [Sp.]

plaza *plä'zə, n* a public square or open, usu. paved, area in a city or town. [Sp.]

PLC or **plc** *abbrev* for public limited company.

plea *plē, n* a prisoner's or defendant's answer to a charge or claim; an excuse; a pretext; an urgent entreaty. — **plea bargaining** the (esp. *US*) legal practice of arranging more lenient treatment by the court in exchange for the accused's admitting to the crime, turning State's evidence, etc. [O.Fr. *plai, plaid, plait* — L.L. *placitum*, a decision — L. *placēre, -ĭtum*, to please.]

plead *plēd, vi* to carry on a plea or lawsuit; to argue in support of a cause against another; to put forward an allegation or answer in court; to make an entreaty (with *with*). — *vt* to maintain by argument; to allege in pleading; to put forward as a plea; to offer in excuse: — *pa t* and *pa p* **plead'ed**, also (*Scot* and *US*) **pled**. — *adj* **plead'able**. — *n* **plead'er** a person who pleads; an advocate. — *adj* **plead'ing** imploring. — *n* the act of putting forward or conducting a plea; (in *pl*) the statements of the two parties in a lawsuit; entreaty. — *adv* **plead'ingly**. — **plead guilty** or **not guilty** to state that one is guilty, or innocent, of a crime with which one is charged; **special pleading** unfair or one-sided argument aiming rather at victory than at truth. [O.Fr. *plaidier*; cf. **plea**.]

pleasant *plez'ənt*, *adj* pleasing; agreeable; affable; good-humoured; cheerful. — *adv* **pleas'antly**. — *n* **pleas'antness**. — *n* **pleas'antry** jocularity; a facetious utterance. [O.F. *plaisant* — pres. p. of *plaisir*, to please.]

please *plēz*, *vt* to give pleasure to; to delight; to satisfy; to be the will or choice of (to do something). — *vi* to give pleasure; to like, think fit, choose. — *interj* used in making polite requests, or in politely accepting an offer, etc., as in *yes, please*. — *adj* **pleased** (*plēzd*) grateful; delighted; willing or inclined (to do something). — *adj* **pleas'ing**. — *adv* **pleas'ingly**. — **if you please** a polite formula of request or acceptance (*old*); certainly (*ironic*); **pleased as Punch** delighted; **please yourself** do as you like. [O.Fr. *plaisir*, to please.]

pleasure *plezh'ər*, *n* agreeable emotions; gratification of the senses or of the mind; sensuality; dissipation; a source of gratification; what the will prefers; purpose; command. — *vt* (*archaic*) to give pleasure to. — **pleasure boat** a boat used for pleasure or amusement; **pleasure ground** ground laid out in an ornamental manner for pleasure; **pleasure-pain principle** the principle that dominates the instincts, directing one's behaviour towards seeking pleasure and avoiding pain; **pleas'ure-seeker** someone who seeks pleasure; a holiday-maker; **pleas'ure-seeking**; **pleasure trip** an excursion for pleasure. — **at pleasure** when, if, or as, one pleases. [O.Fr. *plesir*.]

pleat *plēt*, *n* any of several types of fold sewn or pressed into cloth. — *vt* to make pleats in. — *adj* **pleat'ed**. — *n* **pleat'er**. [From **plait**.]

pleb. See **plebeian**.

plebeian *pli-bē'ən*, *adj* of the Roman plebs (see separate entry); of the common people; low-born; undistinguished; lacking taste or refinement, vulgar. — *n* a member of the plebs (q.v.) of ancient Rome; one of the common people; a boor, a vulgarian. — *n* **pleb** (*colloq*) a person of unpolished manners. — *adj* **plebb'y** (*colloq*). [L. *plēbēius* — *plēbs, plēbis*.]

plebiscite *pleb'i-sit* or *-sīt*, *n* a direct vote of the whole nation or of the people of a district on a special point; an ascertainment of general opinion on any matter. — *adj* **plebisc'itary**. [Partly through Fr. *plébiscite* — L. *plēbiscītum* — *plēbs*, plebs, *scītum*, decree.]

plebs *plebz*, *n* one of the two divisions of the Roman people, orig. the less privileged politically. — See also **plebeian**. [L. *plēbs, plēbis*.]

plectrum *plek'trəm*, *n* a pointed device held in the fingers or on the thumb, with which to strike or pluck the strings of e.g. a guitar. [L. *plēctrum* — Gr. *plēktron* — *plēssein*, to strike.]

pled *pled*. See **plead**.

pledge *plej*, *n* something given as a security; a gage; a token or sign of assurance; a solemn promise; a friendly sentiment expressed by drinking; a state of being given, or held, as a security. — *vt* to give as security; to bind by solemn promise; to vow; to give assurance of; to drink to the health of, drink a toast to. — *adj* **pledge'able**. — *n* **pledgee'** the person to whom a thing is pledged. — *n* **pledger, pledgeor** or **pledgor** (*plej'ər*). — **take** or **sign the pledge** to give a written promise to abstain from intoxicating liquor. [O.Fr. *plege* — L.L. *plevium, plivium*.]

pledget *plej'it*, *n* a wad of lint, cotton, etc., as for a wound or sore; an oakum string used in caulking.

pledgor. See **pledge**.

-plegia *-plē-ji-ə*, *combining form* denoting paralysis, as in *paraplegia, quadriplegia*. — *adj* and *n combining form* **-plēgic**. [Gr. *plēgē*, stroke — *plēssein*, to strike.]

pleiad *plī'ad*, *n* a brilliant group of seven, esp. a group of 16th-cent. French poets, including Ronsard, Du Bellay, Baïf, Daurat, and others variously selected. [Fr. *Pléiade*, from Gr. *Pleiades*, the cluster of stars in Taurus, in mythology the seven daughters of Atlas changed into stars after their deaths.]

pleio-, plio- *plī-ō-*, *-o-* or *-ə-* or **pleo-** *plē-ō-*, *-o-* or *-ə-*, *combining form* signifying more. [Gr. *pleiōn* or *pleōn*, compar. of *polys*, many, much.]

Pleiocene *plī'ō-sēn*, *adj*, *n*. Same as **Pliocene**.

Pleistocene *plīs'tə-sēn*, *adj* of the geological period following the Pliocene, having the greatest proportion of fossil molluscs of living species. — *n* the Pleistocene system, period or strata. [Gr. *pleistos*, most (numerous), *kainos*, recent — from the proportion of living species of molluscs.]

plenary *plē'nə-ri*, *adj* full, entire, absolute, unqualified; (of an assembly, session, etc.) to be attended by all members or delegates. — *adv* **plē'narily**. — **plenary indulgence** in the R.C. Church, full or complete remission of temporal penalties to a repentant sinner; **plenary powers** full powers to carry out some business or negotiations. [L.L. *plēnārius* — L. *plēnus*, full.]

plenipotentiary *plen-i-pə-ten'shə-ri*, *adj* having or conferring full powers; (of authority or power) absolute. — *n* a person invested with full powers, esp. a special ambassador or envoy to some foreign court. [L. *plēnus*, full, *potentia*, power.]

plenitude *plen'i-tūd*, *n* fullness; completeness; plentifulness. — *adj* **plenitu'dinous**. [L. *plēnitūdō, -inis* — *plēnus*, full.]

plenty *plen'ti*, *n* a full supply; all that can be needed; an abundance, a substantial number or amount. — *adj* (*Scot*) in abundance. — *adv* (*colloq*) abundantly. — *adj* **plenteous** (*plen'tyəs*) (*literary*) abundant; fruitful; rich; producing plentifully. — *adv* **plen'teously**. — *n* **plen'teousness**. — *adj* **plen'tiful** copious; abundant; yielding abundantly. — *adv* **plen'tifully**. — *n* **plen'tifulness**. — **horn of plenty** see **cornucopia**; **in plenty** abundant, as in *food in plenty*. [O.Fr. *plente* — L. *plēnitās, -ātis* — *plēnus*, full.]

plenum *plē'nəm*, *n* a space completely filled with matter (opp. to *vacuum*); (also **plenum chamber**) a sealed chamber containing pressurised air (*aeronautics*, etc.); a full assembly. — *n* **plenum system** or **ventilation** (*archit*) an air-conditioning system in which the air propelled into a building is maintained at a higher pressure than the atmosphere. [L. *plēnum* (*spatium*), full (space).]

pleo-. See **pleio-**.

pleomorphic *plē-ō-mör'fik* or **pleomorphous** *-mör'fəs*, *adj* occurring in several different forms, polymorphic; changing form several times during its life history (*biol*). — *n* **pleomorph'ism** or **plē'omorphy**. [Gr. *pleōn*, more, *morphē*, shape.]

pleonasm *plē'ə-nazm*, *n* redundancy, esp. of words; a redundant expression. — *adj* **pleonas'tic**. — *adv* **pleonas'tically**. [Gr. *pleonasmos* — *pleōn*, more.]

pleroma *pli-rō'mə*, *n* fullness; abundance; in Gnosticism, divine being. — *adj* **pleromatic** (*-mat'ik*). [Gr. *plērōma* — *plērēs*, full.]

plerome *plē'rōm*, (*bot*) *n* the central part of the apical meristem, the part of the primary tissue from which growth takes place. [Gr. *plērōma*, filling.]

plesiosaur *plē'si-ō-sör*, *n* a great Mesozoic fossil reptile with long neck, short tail, and four flippers. [Gr. *plēsios*, near, *sauros*, lizard.]

plessor, plessimeter, etc. See **plexor**.

plethora *pleth'ər-ə*, *n* excessive fullness of blood (*med*); over-fullness or excess in any way; (*loosely*) a large amount. — *adj* **plethoric** (*pli-thor'ik*). — *adv* **plethor'ically**. [Gr. *plēthōrā*, fullness — *pleos*, full.]

pleura *ploo͞'rə, n* a delicate membrane that covers the lung and lines the cavity of the chest: — *pl* **pleu'rae** (*-rē*). — *adj* **pleu'ral**. — *n* **pleurisy** (*ploo͞'ri-si*) inflammation of the pleura. — *adj* **pleurit'ic** of, affected with, or causing pleurisy. — *n* a sufferer from pleurisy. — *n* **pleurodynia** (*ploo͞-rə-din'i-ə*) neuralgia of the muscles between the ribs. — *n* **pleuro-pneumo'nia** pleurisy complicated with pneumonia. — *n* **pleurot'omy** (*med*) incision into the pleura. [Gr. *pleurā* and *pleuron*, rib, side.]

plexor *pleks'ər* or **plessor** *ples'ər*, (*med*) *n* a percussion hammer. — *n* **plexim'eter** or **plessim'eter** a small plate to receive the tap in examination by percussion. [Gr. *plēxis*, a stroke, *plēssein*, to strike.]

plexus *plek'səs*, (*anat*) *n* a complex network of nerves, ganglia, blood vessels and lymphatic vessels anywhere in the body, such as the *solar plexus* behind the stomach, serving the abdominal viscera; an involved network: — *pl* **plex'uses** or **plex'us**. [L. *plexus*, *-ūs*, a weaving.]

pliable *plī'ə-bl, adj* easily bent or folded; flexible; adaptable; easily persuaded; yielding to influence. — *n* **plīabil'ity** or **plī'ableness**. — *adv* **plī'ably**. [From Fr. *plier*, to fold.]

pliant *plī'ənt, adj* bending easily; flexible; tractable; easily influenced. — *n* **plī'ancy**. — *adv* **plī'antly**. [Ety. as for **pliable**.]

plié *plē'ā, n* a movement in ballet, in which the knees are bent while the body remains upright. [Fr., bent.]

plied, plier, plies. See **ply**[1,2].

pliers *plī'ərz, npl* a tool like a pair of pincers, with serrated jaws for gripping small objects, and for bending or cutting wire. [From **ply**[1].]

plight[1] *plīt, vt* to pledge. — **plight one's troth** to pledge oneself in marriage. [O.E. *pliht*, risk.]

plight[2] *plīt, n* a difficult or dangerous situation, an alarming predicament. [Assimilated to **plight**[1], but deriv. from O.Fr. *pleit* — L. *plicāre*, to fold, as **plait**.]

plimsoll or **plimsole** *plim'səl, n* a rubber-soled canvas shoe (the line of the sole having been supposed to resemble the Plimsoll line). — **Plimsoll line** or **mark** a ship's load line, or set of load lines for different waters and conditions, required by the Merchant Shipping Act (1876) passed at the instigation of Samuel *Plimsoll* (1824–98).

plinth *plinth, n* the square block under the base of a column; a block serving as a pedestal; a flat-faced projecting band at the bottom of a wall; a similar projecting base in furniture. [L. *plinthus*, Gr. *plinthos*, a brick, squared stone, plinth.]

plio-. See **pleio-**.

Pliocene *plī'ō-sēn*, (*geol*) *adj* of the Tertiary period following the Miocene, and having a greater proportion of molluscan species now living. — *n* the Pliocene system, period or strata. [Gr. *pleiōn*, greater, more numerous, *kainos*, recent.]

pliosaur *plī'ə-sör, n* a fossil marine reptile similar to the plesiosaur, with a shorter neck, larger head, and more powerful jaws. [Gr. *pleōn*, more, *sauros*, lizard.]

plissé *plē-sā*, (Fr.) *adj* (of a fabric) chemically treated to produce a shirred effect.

PLO *abbrev* for Palestine Liberation Organisation.

plod *plod, vi* to walk heavily and laboriously; to study or work on steadily and laboriously. — *vt* to traverse or make (one's way) by slow and heavy walking: — *pr p* **plodd'ing**; *pa t* and *pa p* **plodd'ed**. — *n* a heavy walk. — *n* **plodd'er** a person who keeps on plodding; a person who gets on more by sheer toil than by inspiration. — *adj* and *n* **plodd'ing**. — *adv* **plodd'ingly**. [Prob. imit.]

plonk[1] *plongk, vt* to put down, etc. heavily or emphatically. — *vi* to plump down, plonk oneself. — *n* the action or sound of plonking. — *adv* with a plonk, as in *it landed plonk on the desk*. — *n* **plonk'er** anything large, esp. a smacking kiss (*colloq*); a stupid person, a clot, idiot (*slang*). — *adj* **plonk'ing** (*colloq*) enormous (sometimes *adverbially* or *intensively* with *great*); relating to the practice of plonking. — *n* the practice of uttering jejune or pedestrian remarks in a deliberate and portentous tone. — *adj* **plonk'y** relating to or in the style of such a practice. [Imit.]

plonk[2] *plongk*, (orig. *Austr slang*) *n* wine, esp. cheap. [Poss. — Fr. *blanc*, white, from *vin blanc*, white wine.]

plop *plop, n* the sound of a small object falling vertically into water; the sound of the movement of small bodies of water; the sound of a cork coming out of a bottle, or of a bursting bubble. — *adv* with a plop. — *vi* to make the sound of a plop; to drop into water. — *vt* to let drop with a plop: — *pr p* **plopp'ing**; *pa t* and *pa p* **plopped**. [Imit.]

plosive *plō'siv* or *-ziv*, (*phon*) *adj* and *n* (a consonantal sound) accompanied by plosion. — *n* **plo'sion** (*phon*) the release of breath after stoppage in articulating certain consonantal sounds.

plot *plot, n* a small piece of ground; a ground plan of a building, plan of a field, etc.; the story or scheme of connected events running through a play, novel, etc.; a secret scheme, usu. in combination, to bring about something, often illegal or evil, a conspiracy; a stratagem or secret contrivance. — *vt* to lay out in plots, dispose; to make a plan of; to create the plot of (a play, etc.); to represent on or by a graph; to conspire or lay plans for. — *vi* to conspire: — *pr p* **plott'ing**; *pa t* and *pa p* **plott'ed**. — *adj* **plot'ful**. — *adj* **plot'less**. — *n* **plott'er**. — *n* and *adj* **plott'ing**. [O.E. *plot*, a patch of ground; infl. by (or partly from) Fr. *complot*, a conspiracy.]

plough or in U.S. **plow** *plow, n* an instrument for turning up the soil in ridges and furrows; a joiner's plane for making grooves; agriculture (*fig*); a plough-team; ploughed land; (with *cap*) seven stars of the Great Bear. — *vt* to turn up with the plough; to make furrows or ridges in; to make with a plough; to put into or render with a plough (also *fig*); to tear, force or cut a way through; to furrow; to wrinkle; to reject in an examination (*university slang*); to fail in (a subject) (*university slang*). — *vi* to work with a plough; (with *through* or *into*) to crash, force one's way, move, drive, etc., violently or uncontrollably (through or into) (see also **plough (one's way) through** below); to fail (*slang*). — **plough'boy** a boy who drives or guides horses in ploughing; **plough'land** land suitable for tillage; **plough'man** a man who ploughs: — *pl* **plough'men**; **plough-man's lunch** a cold meal of bread, cheese, cold meat, pickle, etc.; **ploughman's spikenard** see **spike-nard**; **plough'share** (O.E. *scear*, ploughshare — *scieran*, to shear, cut) the detachable part of a plough that cuts the under surface of the sod from the ground; **plough'-team** the team of horses, oxen, etc. (usu. two), that pulls a simple plough; **plough'-wright** someone who makes and mends ploughs. — **plough a lonely furrow** to be separated from one's former friends and associates and go one's own way; **plough back** (*fig*) to reinvest (profits of a business) in that business; **plough in** to cover with earth by ploughing; **plough (one's way) through** to work, read, eat, etc., steadily but slowly and laboriously through; **put one's hand to the plough** to begin an undertaking. [Late O.E. *plōh*, *plōg*, a ploughland.]

plover *pluv'ər, n* a general name for birds of the family (*Charadriidae*) to which the lapwing and dotterel belong; extended to some related birds. [Fr. *pluvier* — L. *pluvia*, rain; poss. from their restlessness before rain.]

plow. See **plough**.

ploy *ploi, n* an employment, doings, affair, frolic, escapade, or engagement for amusement; a method or procedure used to achieve a particular result; a manoeuvre in a game, conversation, etc. [Prob. **employ**.]

PLP *abbrev* for Parliamentary Labour Party.
PLR *abbrev* for public lending right (see under **public**).
plu. *abbrev* for plural.
pluck *pluk*, *vt* to pull off, out or away; to snatch away; to rescue; to pull, tug; to twitch; to strip, esp. of feathers; to rob, fleece; to swindle (*slang*). — *vi* to make a pulling or snatching movement (at). — *n* a single act of plucking; the heart, liver and lungs of an animal — hence heart, courage, spirit. — *adj* **plucked**. — *adj* **pluck'ily**. — *n* **pluck'iness**. — *adj* **pluck'y** having courageous spirit and pertinacity. — **pluck up** to pull out by the roots; to summon up, esp. courage; to gather strength or spirit. [O.E. *pluccian*.]
plug *plug*, *n* a peg or piece of rubber, plastic, etc. stopping, or for stopping, a hole; a bung; a stopper; a mechanism releasing the flow of water in a lavatory; filling for a tooth; volcanic rock stopping a vent; a fitting for a socket for giving electrical connection; a piece of wood inserted in a wall to take nails; a fire-plug; a spark plug; a piece of favourable publicity, esp. one incorporated in other material (*colloq*); anything worn-out or useless; an instance of dogged plodding; a blow or punch; a compressed cake of tobacco; a piece of it cut for chewing. — *vt* to stop with a plug or as a plug; to insert a plug in; to insert as a plug; to shoot (*slang*); to punch with the fist (*slang*); to force into familiarity by persistent repetition, esp. for advertising purposes (*slang*); to din into the ears of the public. — *vi* (*slang*) to go on doggedly: — *pr p* **plugg'ing**; *pa t* and *pa p* **plugged**. — *n* **plugg'er** someone who plugs in any sense; that which plugs, esp. a dentist's instrument. — *n* **plugg'ing** the act of stopping with a plug, or punching (*slang*), or promoting (*slang*); material of which a plug is made. — **plug-ug'ly** (*US*) a street ruffian; a thug, tough. — **plug in** to complete an electric circuit by inserting a plug into a socket (*adj* **plug'-in**); **pull the plug on** (*colloq*) to end, put a stop to. [App. Du. *plug*, a bung, a peg.]
plum *plum*, *n* a drupe or stone-fruit, or the tree producing it (*Prunus domestica* or similar species) of the rose family; extended to various fruits and trees more or less similar (e.g. *sapodilla plum*, *coco-plum*, *date-plum*); a raisin as a substitute for the true plum; plum-colour; a sugar-plum; something choice that may be extracted or attained to. — *adj* plum-colour; choice, cushy. — *adj* **plumm'y** full of plums; plum-like; desirable, profitable; (of voice) too rich and resonant. — **plum'-cake** a cake containing raisins, currants, etc. — *n* and *adj* **plum'-colour** dark purple. — **plum-pudd'ing** an English national dish made of flour and suet, with raisins, currants, and various spices; **plum'-stone**; **plum'-tree**. [O.E. *plūme* — L. *prūnum*.]
plumage *plōōm'ij*, *n* a natural covering of feathers; feathers collectively. — *adj* **plum'aged**. [Fr., — *plume* — L. *plūma*, a feather, down.]
plumassier, plumate. See under **plume**.
plumb *plum*, *n* a heavy mass, as of lead, hung on a string to show the vertical line, or for other purpose; verticality; a sounding lead, plummet. — *adj* vertical; level, true (*cricket*); sheer, thoroughgoing, out-and-out. — *adv* vertically; precisely; utterly (esp. *US*, now *archaic* or *dialect*). — *vt* to test by a plumb-line; to make vertical; to sound as by a plumb-line; to pierce the depth of, fathom, by eye or understanding; to weight with lead; to seal with lead; to do or furnish the plumber-work of. — *vi* to hang vertically; to work as a plumber. — *n* **plumbate** (*plum'bāt*) a salt of plumbic acid. — *adj* **plumbeous** (*plum'bi-əs*) leaden; lead-coloured; lead-glazed. — *n* **plumber** (*plum'ər*) someone who installs and mends pipes, cisterns, and other fittings for supply of water and gas and for household drainage. — *n* **plumb'ery** plumber-work; a plumber's workshop. — *adj* **plumbic** (*plum'bik*) due to lead; of quadrivalent lead. — *adj* **plumbiferous** (*-bif'*) yielding or containing lead. — *n* **plumbing** (*plum'ing*) the operation of making plumb; the craft of working in lead; the system of pipes in a building for gas, water and drainage; (the design, style, working etc. of) lavatories (*euph*); the work of a plumber. — *n* **plum'bism** (*-bizm*) lead poisoning. — *n* **plum'bite** (*-bīt*) a salt of the weak acid lead hydroxide. — *adj* **plumb'less** incapable of being sounded. — *adj* **plumbous** (*plum'bəs*) of bivalent lead. — **plumb bob** a weight at the end of a plumb-line; **plumb'er-work** the work of a plumber; **plumbic acid** an acid of which lead dioxide is the anhydride; **plumb'-line** a line to which a bob is attached to show the vertical line; a vertical line; a plummet; **plumb'-rule** a board with plumb-line and bob, for testing the verticality of walls, etc. [Fr. *plomb* and its source L. *plumbum*, lead.]
plumbago *plum-bā'gō*, *n* graphite: — *pl* **plumbā'gos**. — *adj* **plumbaginous** (*-baj'i-nəs*). [L. *plumbāgō*, *-inis* — *plumbum*, lead.]
plumbate, etc., **plumber**, etc. See under **plumb**.
plume *plōōm*, *n* a feather, esp. a large showy feather; a feather, or anything similar, used as an ornament, symbol, crest, etc.; the vane of a feather; a bunch or tuft of feathers; anything resembling a feather, like smoke, etc. — *vt* to preen; (*reflexive*) to pride, take credit to (with *on* or *upon*; *fig*); to adorn with plumes. — *n* **plumassier** (*plōō-mä-sēr'*) a worker in feathers; a feather-seller. — *adj* **plum'ate**, **plu'mose** or **plu'mous** feathered; feathery; plumelike. — *adj* **plumed** feathered; adorned with a plume. — *adj* **plume'less**. — *n* **plume'let** a plumule; a little tuft. — *n* **plum'ery** plumes collectively. — *adj* **plu'my** covered or adorned with down or plume; like a plume. — **plume'-bird** a long-tailed bird of paradise; **plume'-grass** a tall grass (*Erianthus*) related to sugar-cane, with great silky panicles, grown for ornament. [O.Fr., — L. *plūma*, a small soft feather.]
plummet *plum'it*, *n* leaden or other weight, esp. on a plumb-line, sounding-line, or fishing-line; plumb-rule. — *vt* to fathom, sound. — *vi* to plunge headlong. [O.Fr. *plomet*, dimin. of *plomb*, lead; see **plumb**.]
plump[1] *plump*, *vi* to fall or drop into liquid, esp. vertically, passively, resoundingly, without much disturbance; to flop down; to come suddenly or with a burst; to give all one's votes without distribution; to choose, opt, decisively or abruptly (with *for*). — *vt* to plunge or souse; to fling down or let fall flat or heavily; to blurt. — *n* the sound or act of plumping; a sudden heavy fall of rain (esp. *Scot*); a blow (*slang*). — *adj* and *adv* with a plump; in a direct line; downright; in plain language; without hesitation, reserve or qualification. [L.G. *plumpen* or Du. *plompen*, to plump into water; prob. infl. by **plumb** and **plump**[2].]
plump[2] *plump*, *adj* pleasantly fat and rounded; well filled out. — *vt* and *vi* to make or grow plump; to swell or round. — *n* **plump'ness**. [App. the same word as Du. *plomp*, blunt, L.G. *plump*.]
plumula *plōōm'ū-lə*, *n* a plumule: — *pl* **plum'ulae** (*-lē*). — *adj* **plumulā'ceous**. — *adj* **plum'ular**. — *adj* **plum'ulate** downy. — *n* **plum'ule** a little feather or plume; a down feather; the embryo shoot in a seed. — *adj* **plum'ulose**. [L. *plūmula*, dimin. of *plūma*, a feather.]
plumy. See under **plume**.
plunder *plun'dər*, *vt* to carry off the goods of by force; to pillage; to carry off as booty; to carry off booty from. — *vi* to pillage, carry off plunder. — *n* pillage; booty. — *n* **plun'derage** the stealing of goods on board ship. — *n* **plun'derer**. — *adj* **plun'derous**. [Ger. *plündern*, to pillage — *Plunder*, household stuff, now trash.]
plunge *plunj*, *vt* to put or thrust suddenly under the surface of a liquid, or into the midst of, the thick of, or the substance of, anything; to immerse. — *vi* to fling oneself or rush impetuously, esp. into water, downhill, or into danger or discourse; to turn

suddenly and steeply downward; to fire down upon an enemy from a height; to gamble or squander recklessly; (of a ship) to pitch; (of an animal) to pitch suddenly forward and throw up the hindlegs. — *n* an act of plunging. — *n* **plung'er** a person who plunges; part of a mechanism with a plunging movement, as the solid piston of a force-pump; a suction instrument for cleaning blockages in pipes. — *adj* and *n* **plung'ing.** — **plunge bath** a bath large enough to immerse the whole body; **plunging neckline** (in a woman's dress) a neckline which is cut low. — **take the plunge** to commit oneself definitely after hesitation. [O.Fr. *plonger* — L. *plumbum*, lead.]

plunk *plungk*, *vt* to twang; to pluck the strings of (a banjo, etc.); to plonk. — *vi* to plump. — Also *n*, *adv* and *interj.* [Imit.]

plup. *abbrev* for pluperfect.

pluperfect *plōō-pûr'fekt*, *-fikt* or *plōō'*, (*gram*) *adj* denoting that an action happened before some other past action referred to. — *n* the pluperfect tense; a pluperfect verb or form. [L. *plūs quam perfectum* (*tempus*) more than perfect (tense).]

plur. *abbrev* for plural (also **pl.**).

plural *plōōr'l*, *adj* numbering more than one; more than onefold; expressing more than one, or, where dual is recognised, more than two (*gram*). — *n* (*gram*) the plural number; a plural word form. — *n* **pluralīsā'tion** or **-z-**. — *vt* **plur'alise** or **-ize** to make plural. — *n* **plur'alism** plurality; the holding by one person of more than one office at once, esp. ecclesiastical livings; a system allowing this; a philosophy that recognises more than one principle of being (opp. to *monism*) or more than two (opp. to *monism* and *dualism*); a (condition of) society in which different ethnic, etc. groups preserve their own customs, or hold equal power. — *n* **plur'alist** someone who holds more than one office at one time; a believer in pluralism. — Also *adj.* — *adj* **pluralist'ic.** — *n* **plurality** (*-al'i-ti*) the state or fact of being plural; numerousness; a plural number; the greater number, more than half; the holding of more than one benefice at one time; a living held by a pluralist. — *adv* **plu'rally.** — **plural society** one in which pluralism is found. [L. *plūrālis* — *plūs*, *plūris*, more.]

pluri- *plōōr-i-*, *combining form* denoting: several; usu. more than two. [L. *plūs*, *plūris*, more.]

plus *plus*, (*math* and *colloq*) *prep* with the addition of. — *adj* positive; additional; having an adverse handicap. — *n* an addition; a surplus; a positive quality or term; the sign (also **plus sign**) of addition or positivity (+); opp. to *minus* (−): — *pl* **plus'es** or **pluss'es.** — *vt* and *vi* to increase (in value): — *pr p* **plus'ing** or **pluss'ing**; *pa t* and *pa p* **plused** or **plussed.** — *adv* (*colloq*) moreover; and more, or more. [L. *plūs*, more.]

plus-fours *plus-fōrz'*, *npl* baggy or a suit with knickerbockers. [**plus** and **four**; from the four additional inches of cloth required.]

plush *plush*, *n* a fabric with a longer and more open pile than velvet; (in *pl*) footman's breeches. — *adj* made of plush; pretentiously luxurious (also **plush'y**). [Fr. *pluche* for *peluche* — L. *pīla*, hair; cf. **pile**[3].]

Pluto *plōōt'ō*, *n* the Greek god of the underworld (*Gr mythol*); a planet beyond Neptune, discovered 1930. — *n* **plutō'nium** the element (symbol **Pu**; atomic no. 94) named as next after neptunium (93), as the planet Pluto is beyond Neptune. [L. *Plūtō*, *-ōnis* — Gr. *Ploutōn*, *-ōnos*, Pluto.]

plutocracy *plōō-tok'rə-si*, *n* government by the wealthy; a ruling body or class of rich men. — *n* **plutocrat** (*plōō'tō-krat*) a person who is powerful because of their wealth. — *adj* **plutocrat'ic.** [L. *Plūtus*, Gr. *Ploutos*, the Greek god of wealth (Gr. *ploutos*, wealth).]

pluvial *plōō'vi-əl*, *adj* of or by rain; rainy. — *n* a period of prolonged rainfall (*geol*). — *adj* **plu'vious** or **plu'viose** rainy. — **pluvius insurance** insurance cover taken out, e.g. by the organiser of a fête, against loss of takings due to rain. [L. *pluvia*, rain.]

ply[1] *plī*, *n* a fold, a layer or thickness; a layer of hard rock or of hard or soft rocks in alternation (*mineralogy*); a bend; a bend or set; a strand: — *pl* **plies.** — *vt* and *vi* to bend or fold: — *pr p* **ply'ing**; *pa t* and *pa p* **plied**; *3rd pers sing* **plies.** — *n* **pli'er** someone who plies. — **ply'wood** boarding made of thin layers of wood glued together, the grain of each at right angles to that of the next. [(O.)Fr. *pli*, a fold, *plier*, to fold — L. *plicāre*.]

ply[2] *plī*, *vt* to work at steadily; to use or wield diligently or vigorously; to keep supplying or assailing (with); to importune; to row or sail over habitually. — *vi* to work steadily; to make regular journeys over a route; to be in attendance for hire; to beat against the wind; to make one's way, direct one's course: — *pr p* **ply'ing**; *pa t* and *pa p* **plied**; *3rd pers sing* **plies.** — *n* **pli'er** someone who plies. [Aphetic, from **apply**.]

Plymouth *plim'əth*, *n* a port in Devon; a port named after it in Massachusetts, with the supposed landing-place of the Pilgrims (Plymouth Rock). — **Plymouth Brethren** a religious sect, founded in Dublin *c* 1825, out of a reaction against High Church principles and against a dead formalism associated with unevangelical doctrine — its first congregation was established at Plymouth in 1831.

plywood. See **ply**[1].

PM *abbrev* for: Past Master; Postmaster; (or **pm**) *post meridiem* (L.), after noon; (or **pm**) *post mortem* (L.), after death; Prime Minister; Provost-Marshal.

Pm (*chem*) *symbol* for promethium.

pm *abbrev* for: premium; see also under **PM**.

PMG *abbrev* for: Paymaster-General; Postmaster-General.

PMO *abbrev* for Principal Medical Officer.

Pmr *abbrev* for Paymaster.

PMRAFNS *abbrev* for Princess Mary's Royal Air Force Nursing Service.

PMS *abbrev* for premenstrual syndrome.

PMT *abbrev* for premenstrual tension.

pn *abbrev* for promissory note.

PNdB *abbrev* for perceived noise decibel.

pneum- *nūm-*, **pneumo-** *nūm-ō-*, **pneumon-** *nūm-on-* or **pneumono-** *nūm-ə-nō-*, *combining form* signifying lung. — *n* **pneumococc'us** a bacterium in the respiratory tract which is a causative agent of pneumonia. — *n* **pneumoconiosis** (*nū-mō-kō-ni-ō'sis*; Gr. *konia*, dust) any of various diseases caused by habitually inhaling mineral or metallic dust, as in coalmining. — *n* **pneumō'nia** inflammation of the lung. — *adj* **pneumonic** (*-mon'*) pertaining to the lungs. — *n* a medicine for lung diseases. — *n* **pneumonī'tis** pneumonia. — *n* **pneumotho'rax** (*med*) the existence, or introduction of, air between the lung and chest-wall; lung collapse resulting from the escape of air from the lung into the chest cavity — a potential hazard of working in compressed air, e.g. when deep-sea diving. [Gr. *pneumōn*, *-ōnos*, lung — *pneein*, to breathe.]

pneumatic *nū-mat'ik*, *adj* relating to air or gases; containing or inflated with air; worked or driven by compressed air; containing compressed air; with air-cavities (*zool*); spiritual. — *adv* **pneumat'ically.** — *n* **pneumaticity** (*nū-mə-tis'i-ti*) the condition of having air-spaces. — *nsing* **pneumat'ics** the science of the properties of gases. — *n* **pneumatom'eter** an instrument for measuring the quantity of air breathed or the force of breathing. [Gr. *pneuma*, *-atos*, breath — *pneein*.]

PNG *abbrev* for Papua New Guinea (also I.V.R.).

PO *abbrev* for: Petty Officer; Pilot Officer; Post Office.

Po (*chem*) *symbol* for polonium.

po[1] *pō*, (*colloq*) *n* a shortening of **chamberpot**: — *pl* **pos.** [**pot** — prob. from a euph. Fr. pronunciation.]

po[2] *pō*, (*colloq*) *adj* a shortening of **po-faced**.
po or **p.o.** *abbrev* for postal order.
po. *abbrev* for pole.
POA *abbrev* for Prison Officers' Association.
poa *pō'ə*, *n* any plant of a large genus of grasses, meadow-grass (*Poa*). — *adj* **pōā'ceous**. [Gr. *pŏā*, grass.]
poach[1] *pōch*, *vt* to cook slowly in simmering liquid. — *n* **poach'er** someone who poaches eggs; a vessel with hollows for poaching eggs in. — **poached egg flower** Romneya; an annual, *Limnanthes douglasii*, with yellow and white flowers. [App. Fr. *pocher*, to pocket — *poche*, pouch, the white forming a pocket about the yolk.]
poach[2] *pōch*, *vi* to intrude on another's preserves in order to pursue or kill game, or upon another's fishing to catch fish (also *fig*); to encroach upon another's rights, profits, area of influence, etc., or on a partner's place or part in a game; to seek an unfair advantage. — *vt* to take illegally on another's ground or in another's fishing; to seek or take game or fish illegally on; to take in unfair encroachment. — *n* **poach'er**. — *n* **poach'iness**. — *n* **poach'ing**. — *adj* **poach'y** spongy and sodden. [A form of **poke**[2] or from O.Fr. *pocher*, to poke.]
po'chaise. See **pochay**.
pochard *pōch'ərd* or *poch'ərd*, *n* a red-headed diving-duck esp. the male, the female being the dun-bird.
pochay *pō'shā*, **po'chaise** *pō'shāz*. See **post-chaise** (under **post**[2]).
pochette *posh-et'*, *n* a small bag, esp. one carried by women; a pocket notecase or wallet. [Fr., dimin. of *poche*, pocket.]
pochoir *posh'wär*, *n* a form of colour stencilling, by hand, on to a printed illustration. [Fr., stencil.]
pock *pok*, *n* a small elevation of the skin containing pus, as in smallpox. — *adj* **pocked**. — *adj* **pock'y** marked with pustules; infected with pox. — **pock'-mark** or **pock'pit** the mark, pit or scar left by a pock. — *adj* **pock'marked**. — *adj* **pock'pitted**. [O.E. *poc*, a pustule; see **pox**.]
pocket *pok'it*, *n* a little pouch or bag, esp. one fitted in or attached to a garment, or a billiard-table or book-cover; a cavity; a rock cavity filled with ore, etc.; a portion of the atmosphere differing in pressure or other condition from its surroundings; a small isolated area or patch, as of military resistance, unemployment, etc.; the innermost compartment of a pound-net. — *adj* for the pocket; of a small size. — *vt* to put in one's pocket or a pocket; to appropriate; to take stealthily; to conceal; to enclose; to hem in; to play into a pocket (*billiards*). — *vi* to form a pocket: — *pr p* **pock'eting**; *pa t* and *pa p* **pock'eted**. — *n* **pock'etful** as much as a pocket will hold: — *pl* **pock'etfuls**. — **pocket battleship** a small battleship, built to specifications limited by treaty, etc.; **pock'et-book** a notebook; a wallet for papers or money carried in the pocket; a small book for the pocket; a handbag (*US*); **pocket gopher** any American burrowing rodent with outward-opening cheek-pouches; **pocket-hand'kerchief**; **pock'et-knife** a knife with one or more blades folding into the handle, thus safe to carry in the pocket; **pock'et-money** money carried for occasional expenses; an allowance, esp. to a boy or girl; **pocket mouse** a small rodent of genus *Perognathus*, native to the N. American desert. — *adj* **pock'et-sized** small enough for the pocket. — **in one's pocket** (*fig*) under one's control or influence; **in (or out of) pocket** with (or without) money; the richer (or the poorer) by a transaction (*adj* **out'-of-pocket** (of expenses, etc.) paid in cash); **line one's pockets** to make or take money dishonestly from business entrusted to one; **pick a person's pocket** to steal from their pocket; **pocket an insult** or **affront**, etc., to submit to or put up with it without protest; **pocket one's pride** to humble oneself to accept a situation. [A.Fr. *pokete* (Fr. *pochette*, dimin. of *poche*, pocket).]
pocky, etc. See **pock**.
poco *pō'kō*, (It.) *adj* little. — *adj* **pococuran'te** (*-kōō-ran'tā* or *-kū-ran'ti*; It. *curante*, pres. p of *curare*, to care) uninterested; indifferent; nonchalant. — *n* a habitually uninterested person. — *n* **pococurant-ism** (*-kū-rant'izm*) or **pococuranteism** (*-kū-rant'i-ism*). — *n* **pococurant'ist**. — **poco a poco** little by little.
poculiform *pok'ū-li-förm*, *adj* cup-shaped. [L. *pōculum*, cup.]
pod[1] *pod*, *n* the fruit, or its shell, in peas, beans and other leguminous plants — the legume; sometimes extended to the siliqua; a silk cocoon; a paunch; a groove along an auger or bit; the socket into which a bit, etc., fits; a protective housing for (external) engineering equipment, e.g. aircraft engines, nuclear reactor, space or submarine instruments, or for weapons carried externally e.g. on an aircraft; a decompression compartment. — *vt* to shell or hull. — *vi* to form pods; to fill as pods: — *pr p* **podd'ing**; *pa t* and *pa p* **podd'ed**.
pod[2] *pod*, *n* a school, esp. of whales or seals; sometimes applied to groups of other animals and birds.
pod or **p.o.d.** *abbrev* for pay on delivery.
pod- *combining form*. See **podo-**.
-pod *-pod* or **-pode** *-pōd*, *combining form* denoting foot. [Gr. *pous*, *podos*, foot.]
podagra *pod-ag'rə*, also *po'*, (*med*) *n* gout, properly in the feet. — *adj* **podag'ral**, **podag'ric**, **podag'rical** or **podag'rous** gouty. [Gr. *podagrā* — *pous*, *podos*, foot, *agrā*, a catching.]
podge *poj* or **pudge** *puj*, *n* a squat, fat and flabby person or thing. — *n* **podg'iness** or **pudg'iness**. — *adj* **podg'y** or **pudg'y**.
podiatrist, **podiatry**. See under **podo-**.
podium *pō'di-əm*, *n* a continuous pedestal, a stylobate (*archit*); a platform, dais; a foot or hand (*anat*). [Latinised from Gr. *pŏdion*, dimin. of *pous*, *podos*, foot.]
podo- *pod-ō-* or *pōd-ō-*, also **pod-** *pod-* or *pōd-*, *combining form* denoting foot. — *adj* **pō'dal** or **podal'ic** of the feet. — *n* **podiatry** (*pod-ī'ə-tri*; Gr. *īātros*, *īātros*, physician) treatment of disorders of the foot. — *n* **podi'atrist**. — *n* **podol'ogist**. — *n* **podol'ogy** the scientific study of the feet. [Gr. *pous*, *podos*, foot.]
podsol or **podzol** *pod-zol'* or *pod'-*, *n* any of a group of soils characterised by a greyish-white leached and infertile topsoil and a brown subsoil, typical of regions with a subpolar climate. — *adj* **podsol'ic**. [Russ., — *pod*, under, *zola*, ash.]
poem *pō'im* or *-əm*, *n* a composition in verse; a composition of high beauty of thought or language and artistic form, typically, but not necessarily, in verse; anything supremely harmonious and satisfying (*fig*). [Fr. *poème* — L. *poēma* — Gr. *poiēma* — *poieein*, to make.]
poenology. See **penology**.
poesy *pō'i-zi*, *n* poetry collectively or in the abstract. [Fr. *poésie* — L. *poēsis* — Gr. *poiēsis* — *poieein*, to make.]
poet *pō'it* or *-ət*, *fem* **poetess** *pō-it-es'*, *n*, the author of a poem; a verse-writer; someone skilled in making poetry; someone with a poetical imagination. — *adj* **poetic** (*pō-et'ik*) or **poet'ical** of the nature or having the character of poetry; pertaining or suitable to a poet or to poetry; expressed in poetry; in the language of poetry; imaginative. — *nsing* **poet'ics** the branch of criticism that relates to poetry. — *adv* **pōet'ically**. — *vt* and *vi* **poet'icise** or **-ize** to make poetic; to write poetry about; to write, speak or treat poetically. — *n* **pō'etry** the art of the poet; the essential quality of a poem; poetical composition or writings collectively (rarely in *pl*); poetical quality. — *n* **pō'etship**. — **poetic justice** ideal administration

of reward and punishment; **poetic licence** a departing from strict fact or rule by a poet for the sake of effect. — Also *fig*. — **Poet Laureate** the poet appointed as Court Poet, commissioned to write poems to mark state occasions, etc. — **poetry in motion** exceedingly beautiful, harmonious, rhythmical, etc. movement. [Fr. *poète* — L. *poēta* — Gr. *poiētēs* — *poieein*, to make.]

POEU *abbrev* for Post Office Engineering Union.

po-faced *pō'-fāst*, (*colloq*) *adj* stupidly solemn and narrow-minded; stolid, humourless. [Perh. *pot-faced* or *poor-faced*.]

pogo stick *pō'gō stik*, *n* a child's toy consisting of a stick with a crossbar on a strong spring on which one stands in order to bounce along the ground. [*Pogo*, a trademark.]

pogrom *pog'rom* or *pog-rom'*, *n* an organised massacre, orig. (late 19th cent.) esp. of Russian Jews. [Russ., destruction, devastation.]

poignant *poin'yənt*, *adj* stinging, pricking; sharp; acutely painful; penetrating; pungent; piquant; touching, pathetic. — *n* **poign'ancy**. — *adv* **poign'antly**. [O.Fr. *poignant*, pres. p. of *poindre* — L. *pungĕre*, to sting.]

poikilotherm *poi'kil-o-thərm*, *n* a cold-blooded animal. — *adj* **poikilotherm'al** or **poikilotherm'ic** having variable blood-temperature, or cold-blooded. — *n* **poikilotherm'y** (or *poi'*) cold-bloodedness. [Gr. *poikilos*, variegated.]

poinciana *poin-si-ä'nə*, *n* a tree of the tropical genus *Poinciana* of the *Caesalpinia* family — flamboyant tree, etc. [After De *Poinci*, a French W. Indian governor.]

poinsettia *poin-set'i-ə*, *n* a spurge, *Euphorbia pulcherrima*, with petal-like bracts (usu. scarlet) and small yellow flowers, orig. from Mexico and Central America. [From Joel Roberts *Poinsett* (1779–1851), American Minister to Mexico.]

point *point*, *n* a dot; a small mark used in Semitic alphabets to indicate a vowel, to differentiate a consonant, or for other purpose; a dot separating the integral and fractional parts of a decimal; a mark of punctuation; that which has position but no magnitude (*geom*); a place or station, considered in relation to position only; a place or division in a scale, course or cycle (as *boiling point*, *dead-point*); a moment of time, without duration; a precise moment; a state; a juncture; a critical moment; the verge; a culmination; a conclusion; a unit in scoring, judging or measurement; a unit used in quoting changes in prices of stocks and securities; a character taken into account in judging; a distinctive mark or characteristic; a unit of measurement of type, approximately $\frac{1}{72}$ inch; one of thirty-two divisions of the compass (**points of the compass**) or the angle between two successive divisions ($\frac{1}{8}$ of a right angle); a particular; a head, clause or item; a position forming a main element in the structure of an argument or discourse; a matter in debate, under attention, or to be taken into account; that which is relevant; that upon which one insists or takes a stand; the precise matter; the essential matter; that without which a story, joke, etc. is meaningless or ineffective; a clearly defined aim, object or reason; a particular imparted as a hint; lace made with a needle (also **point'-lace**); a sharp end; a tip, or free end; a thing, part or mark with a sharp end; a piercing weapon or tool; an etching-needle; the sharp end of a sword; a tine; a spike; a cape or headland; the tip of the chin (*boxing*); a horse's or other animal's extremity; a nib; a movable rail for passing vehicles from one track to another; a tapering division of a backgammon board; a fielder or his position, on the offside straight out from and near the batsman (as if at the point of the bat) (*cricket*); a socket for making connection with electric wiring; pointedness; pungency; sting; the act or position of pointing; the vertical rising of a hawk, indicating the position of the prey; pointe; $\frac{1}{100}$ part of a carat. — *adj* (*phon*) articulated with the tip of the tongue. — *vt* to insert points in; to mark with points; to mark off in groups of syllables for singing; to sharpen; to give point to; to prick in or turn over with the point of a spade; to show the position or direction of or draw attention to (now usu. with *out*); to place in a certain direction, direct (with *at*); to indicate; to insert white hairs in (a fur); to rake out old mortar from, and insert new mortar in, the joints of. — *vi* to have or take a position in a direction (with *at*, *to*, *toward*, etc.); to indicate a direction or position by extending a finger, a stick, etc.; (of dogs) to indicate the position of game by an attitude; to hint; to aim. — *adj* **point'ed** having a sharp point; sharp; keen; telling; epigrammatic; precise; explicit; aimed at particular persons; having marked personal application. — *adv* **point'edly**. — *n* **point'edness**. — *n* **point'er** someone who points, in any sense; a rod for pointing to a blackboard, map, screen, etc.; an index-hand; a hint, tip, suggestion, indication; a tool for clearing out old mortar from joints; a breed of dogs that point on discovering game; (in *pl*) two stars of the Great Bear nearly in a straight line with the Pole Star. — *n* **point'ing**. — *adj* **point'less**. — *adv* **point'lessly**. — *n* **point'lessness**. — *adj* **point'y**. — **point after** (*Am football*) a goal kick taken after a touch-down is scored; **point'-duty** the duty of a policeman stationed at a particular point to regulate traffic; **point'-lace** (see under **point** above). — *adj* **point'-of-sale** of, relating to, or occurring at the place where (and time when) a sale is made. — **points'man** someone on point-duty; someone in charge of rail points. — *adj* **point'-to-point** from one fixed point to another; across country. — *n* a cross-country race, a steeplechase. — **at the point of** on the verge of; **carry one's point** to gain what one contends for; **in point** apposite; **in point of** in the matter of; **in point of fact** as a matter of fact; **make a point of** to treat as essential, make a special object of; **not to put too fine a point on it** to speak bluntly; **on the point of** close upon; very near; **point for point** exactly in all particulars; **point of no return** that point on a flight from which one can only go on, for want of fuel to return (also *fig*); **point of order** a question raised in a deliberative society, whether proceedings are according to the rules; **point of view** the position from which one looks at anything, literally or figuratively; **point out** to point to, show, bring someone's attention to; **point up** to emphasise; **score points off someone** to advance at the expense of another; to outwit, get the better of someone in an argument or repartee; **stand upon points** to be punctilious; **to the point** apposite; **up to a point** partly, not wholly. [Partly Fr. *point*, point, dot, stitch, lace, partly Fr. *pointe*, sharp point, pungency — L. *punctum* and L.L. *puncta*, respectively — L. *pungĕre*, *punctum*, to prick.]

point-blank *point'-blangk*, *adj* aimed directly at the mark without allowing for the downward curve of the trajectory; permitting such an aim, i.e. at very close range; direct; straightforward; blunt. — *adv* with point-blank aim; directly; bluntly; flat. — *n* a point-blank shot or range. [App. from **point** (verb) and **blank** (of the target).]

pointe *pwɛ̃t*, (Fr.) (*ballet*) *n* the extreme tip of the toe, or the position of standing on it.

pointillism *pwan'til-izm* or (Fr.) **pointillisme** *pwɛ̃-tē-yēzm*, (*art*) *n* the use of separate dots of pure colour instead of mixed pigments. — *adj* **pointillé** (*pwɛ̃-tē-yā*) ornamented with a pattern of dots made by a pointed tool. — *n* and *adj* **poin'tillist**, (Fr.) **pointilliste** (*-tē-yēst*). [Fr. *pointillisme* — *pointille*, dimin. of *point*, point.]

poise *poiz*, *vt* to hold so as to get some notion of the weight; to balance; to carry or hold in equilibrium. — *vi* to hang in suspense; to hover. — *n* balance;

equilibrium; bias; carriage or balance of body; dignity and assurance of manner; suspense. — *adj* **poised** having or showing poise or composure; balanced. — *n* **pois'er.** [O.Fr. *poiser* (Fr. *peser*) — L. *pēnsāre*, frequentative of *pendĕre*, to weigh, and O.Fr. *pois* — L. *pēnsum*, weight.]

poison *poi'zn*, *n* any substance which, taken into or formed in the body, destroys life or impairs health; any malignant influence; a substance that inhibits the activity of a catalyst (*chem*); a material that absorbs neutrons and so interferes with the working of a nuclear reactor. — *vt* to administer poison to; to injure or kill with poison; to put poison on or in; to taint; to mar; to embitter; to corrupt. — *adj* poisonous. — *adj* **poi'sonable.** — *n* **poi'soner.** — *adj* **poi'sonous** having the quality or effect of poison; noxious; offensive (*colloq*). — *adv* **poi'sonously.** — *n* **poi'sonousness.** — **poi'son-fang** one of two large tubular teeth in the upper jaw of venomous snakes, through which poison passes from glands at their roots when the animal bites; **poi'son-gas** any injurious gas used in warfare; **poi'son-gland** a gland that secretes poison; **poi'son-ivy, poi'son-oak** or **poi'son-sumac(h)** names for various North American sumacs with ulcerating juice; **poi'son-nut** nux vomica; **poison pen** a writer of malicious anonymous letters; **poison pill** (*colloq*) any of various actions, such as merger, takeover, recapitalisation, taken by a company to prevent or deter a threatened takeover bid; a clause or clauses in a company's articles of association put into effect by an unwanted takeover bid, and making such a takeover less attractive. — **what's your poison?** (*colloq*) what would you like to drink? [O.Fr. *puison*, poison — L. *pōtiō*, *-ōnis*, a draught — *pōtāre*, to drink; cf. **potion.**]

Poisson distribution *pwä-sɔ̃ dis-tri-bū'shən* or **Poisson's** (*pwä-sɔ̃z*) **distribution** (*statistics*) *n* a distribution that, as a limiting form of binomial distribution, is characterised by a small probability of a specific event occurring during observations over a continuous interval (e.g. of time or distance); **Poisson's ratio** (*phys*) one of the elastic constants of a material, defined as the ratio of the lateral contraction per unit breadth to the longitudinal extension per unit length when a piece of material is stretched. [After S. Denis *Poisson* (1781–1840), French mathematician.]

poke[1] *pōk*, (now chiefly *dialect*) *n* a bag; a pouch; a pokeful; a pocket. — **a pig in a poke** a blind bargain, as of a pig bought without being seen. [M.E. *poke*.]

poke[2] *pōk*, *vt* to thrust or push the end of anything against or into; to prod or jab; to cause to protrude; to thrust forward or endwise; to make, put, render or achieve by thrusting or groping; to stir up, incite; (of a man) to have sexual intercourse with (*slang*); to change a number in the memory of a computer. — *vi* to thrust, make thrusts; to protrude; to feel about, grope; to bat gently and cautiously (*cricket*); to potter; to stoop; to pry about; to live a dull or secluded life. — *n* an act of poking. — *n* **pō'ker** someone who pokes; a rod for poking or stirring a fire; an instrument for doing poker-work; a stiff person. — *adj* like a poker; stiff. — *adv* **pō'kerishly.** — *adj* **pō'ky** (of a room, etc.) cramped, small, confined. — **pō'ker-work** work done by burning a design into wood with a heated point. — **poke fun at** to banter; **poke one's nose** to pry; **red-hot poker** kniphofia or *Tritoma*. [M.E. *pōken*; app. of L.G. origin.]

poke[3] *pōk*, *n* a name for various American species of *Phytolacca* (also **poke'weed** or **poke'berry**); American or white hellebore (**Indian poke**). [Of Am. Ind. origin.]

poker *pō'kər*, *n* a round game at cards. — **po'ker-face** an inscrutable face, useful to a poker-player; its possessor. — *adj* **po'ker-faced.**

pokey *pō'ki*, (*US slang*) *n* jail.

Polack *pōl'ak*, (*slang*; usu. *derog*) *n* a Pole. — *adj* Polish. [Pol. *Polak*; Ger. *Polack*.]

polar *pō'lər*, *adj* of, or pertaining to, a pole (see **pole**[1]) or poles; belonging to the neighbourhood of a pole; referred to a pole; of the nature of, or analogous to, a pole; axial; having polarity; directly opposed. — *n* **polarim'eter** an instrument for measuring the rotation of the plane of polarisation of light, or the amount of polarisation of light. — *adj* **polarimetric** (*pō-lar-i-met'rik*). — *n* **polarimetry** (*pō-lər-im'i-tri*). — *n* **Polaris** (*pō-lä'ris*) the Pole Star. — *n* **polarisation** or **-z-** (*pō-lər-ī-zā'shən*) an act of polarising; the state of being polarised; development of poles; (*loosely*) polarity; the effect of deposition of products of electrolysis upon electrodes, resulting in an opposing electromotive force; the restriction (according to the wave theory) of the vibrations of light to one plane. — *n* **polariscope** (*pō-lar'i-skōp*) an instrument for showing phenomena of polarised light. — *vt* **polarise** or **-ize** (*pō'lər-īz*) to subject to polarisation; to give polarity to; to develop new qualities or meanings in (*fig*); to split into opposing camps (also *vi*). — *vi* to acquire polarity. — *adj* **po'larised** or **-z-**. — *n* **po'larīser** or **-z-** a device for polarising light. — *n* **polarity** (*pō-lar'i-ti*) the state of having two opposite poles; the condition of having properties different or opposite in opposite directions or at opposite ends; particular relation to this or that pole or opposed property rather than the other; directedness (*fig*); opposedness or doubleness of aspect or tendency. — *n* **Po'laroid**® a trademark applied to photographic equipment, light-polarising materials, etc. — *n* **po'laron** (*electronics*) a free electron trapped by polarisation charges on surrounding molecules. — **polar axis** (*astron*) that diameter of a sphere which passes through the poles; (in an equatorial telescope) the axis, parallel to the earth's axis, about which the whole instrument revolves in order to keep a celestial object in the field; **polar bear** a large white bear found in the Arctic regions; **polar body** (*biol*) one of two small cells detached from the ovum during the maturation divisions; **polar circle** the Arctic or the Antarctic Circle; **polar co-ordinates** (*math*) co-ordinates defining a point by means of a radius vector and the angle which it makes with a fixed line through the origin; **polar equation** (*math*) an equation in terms of polar co-ordinates. [L. *polāris* — *polus*; see **pole**[1].]

polder *pōl'dər*, *n* a piece of low-lying reclaimed land; the first stage in its reclamation. — Also *vt*. [Du.]

Pole *pōl*, *n* a native or citizen of Poland; a Polish-speaking inhabitant of Poland.

pole[1] *pōl*, *n* the end of an axis, esp. of the earth, the celestial sphere or any rotating sphere; either of the two points of a body in which the attractive or repulsive energy is concentrated, as in a magnet; an electric terminal or electrode; a fixed point (*geom*); a point from which a pencil of rays radiates; an opposite extreme (*fig*). — **Pole Star** Polaris, a star near the N. pole of the heavens; a guide or director. — **poles apart** widely separated, very different. [L. *polus* — Gr. *polos*, pivot, axis, firmament.]

pole[2] *pōl*, *n* a long rounded shaft, rod or post, usu. of wood; a single shaft to which a pair of horses may be yoked; a measure of length ($5\frac{1}{2}$ yards) or of area ($30\frac{1}{4}$ square yards); the position next to the inner boundary-fence in a race-course, on a race-track, etc. (now usu. **pole position**). — *vt* to propel, push, strike, or stir with a pole; to furnish or support with poles. — *vi* to use a pole. — *n* **pō'ler** (*Austr*) one of a pair of bullocks harnessed to the pole; a shirker. — *n* **pō'ling** supplying, propelling or stirring with a pole or poles; poles collectively. — **pole position** the most advantageous position in any competition, race, etc. (see also above); **pole'-vault** an athletic event in which the competitor uses a pole to achieve great height in jumping over a cross-bar. — Also *vi*. — **pole'-vaulter**. — **pole on** (*Austr slang*) to impose on; **up the pole** (*slang*) in a predicament; drunk; crazed. [O.E. *pāl*, *pālus*, a stake.]

pole-axe or **pole-ax** *pōl'-aks*, *n* a battle-axe, orig. short-handled; a long-handled axe or halbert; a sailor's short-handled axe for cutting away rigging; a butcher's axe with a hammer-faced back. — *vt* to strike, knock down or concuss with (or now usu. as if with) a pole-axe. [Orig. *pollax*, from **poll**, head, and **axe**, confused with **pole**[2].]

polecat *pōl'kat*, *n* a large relative of the weasel, which emits a stink. — **pole'cat-ferret** the hybrid offspring of the ferret and polecat. [M.E. *polcat*; poss. Fr. *poule*, hen, and **cat**.]

Pol. Econ. *abbrev* for Political Economy.

polemic *po-lem'ik*, *adj* given to disputing; controversial. — *n* a controversialist; a controversy; a controversial writing or argument. — *adj* **polem'ical**. — *adv* **polem'ically**. — *n* **polem'icist** or **pol'emist** a person who writes polemics or engages in controversy. — *nsing* **polem'ics** the practice or art of controversy. [Gr. *polemikos* — *polemos*, war.]

polenta *po-len'tə*, *n* an Italian porridge of maize, barley, chestnut, or other meal. [It., — L. *polenta*, peeled barley.]

police *pəl-ēs'*, *n* a body of men and women employed to maintain order, etc.; its members collectively. — *adj* of the police. — *vt* to control as police; to provide with police; to guard, or to put or keep in order. — **police-con'stable** a policeman of ordinary rank; **police dog** a dog trained to help the police; **police force** a separately organised body of police; **police inspector** a superior officer of police who has charge of a department, next in rank to a superintendent; **police'man** a member of a police force; **police office** or **police station** the headquarters of the police of a district, used also as a temporary place of confinement; **police officer** a member of a police force esp. one of ordinary rank; **police state** a country in which secret police are employed to detect and stamp out any opposition to the government in power; **police'woman** a woman member of a police force. [Fr., — L. *polītīa* — Gr. *polīteiā* — *polītēs*, a citizen — *polis*, a city.]

policy[1] *pol'i-si*, *n* a course of action; a system of administration guided more by interest than by principle; dexterity of management; prudence; cunning; in Scotland (sometimes in *pl*), the pleasure-grounds around a mansion. [O.Fr. *policie* (Fr. *police*) — L. *polītīa* — Gr. *polīteiā* (see **police**); in Scots perh. infl. by L. *polītus*, embellished.]

policy[2] *pol'i-si*, *n* a document containing a contract of insurance. — **pol'icy-holder** someone who holds a contract of insurance. [Fr. *police*, policy, app. — L.L. *apodissa*, a receipt — Gr. *apodeixis*, proof.]

poliomyelitis *pōl-i-ō-mī-ə-lī'tis* or *pol-*, (*med*) *n* inflammation of the grey matter of the spinal cord; infantile paralysis. — *n* **polio** (*pōl'i-ō* or *pol'*) short for poliomyelitis; a sufferer from this: — *pl* **pol'ios**. — Also *adj*. [Gr. *polios*, grey, *myelos*, marrow.]

Polish *pō'lish*, *adj* of Poland, or its people or its language. — *n* the Slavonic language of the Poles.

polish *pol'ish*, *vt* to make smooth and glossy by rubbing; to bring to a finished state; to impart culture and refinement to. — *vi* to take a polish. — *n* an act of polishing; gloss; refinement of manners; a substance applied to produce a polish. — *adj* **pol'ishable**. — *adj* **pol'ished** cultured, refined; accomplished. — *n* **pol'isher**. — **pol'ishing-paste**; **pol'ishing-powder**; **pol'ishing-slate** a diatomaceous slaty stone used for polishing glass, marble and metals. — **polish off** (*colloq*) to finish off; to dispose of finally; **polish up (on)** to work at, study in order to improve. [O.Fr. *polir*, *polissant* — L. *polīre*, to polish.]

Politburo or **Politbureau** *po-lit'bū-rō* or *pol'it-bū-rō*, *n* in Communist countries, the policy-making committee, effectively the most powerful organ of the Communist Party's executive. [Russ. *politicheskoe*, political, *byuro*, bureau.]

polite *po-līt'*, *adj* refined, cultivated; having courteous manners. — *adv* **polite'ly**. — *n* **polite'ness**. — *n* **politesse** (*pol-ē-tes'*; Fr.) superficial politeness. [L. *polītus*, past p. of *polīre*, to polish.]

politic *pol'i-tik*, *adj* in accordance with good policy; acting or proceeding from motives of policy; prudent; discreet; astutely contriving or intriguing. — *adj* **polit'ical** pertaining to policy or government; pertaining to parties differing in their views of government; interested or involved in politics. — *adv* **polit'ically**. — *n* **politician** (*-tish'ən*) someone versed in the science of government; someone engaged in political life or statesmanship; someone interested in party politics; a politic person; someone who makes a profession or a game of politics. — *n* **politicīsā'tion** or **-z-**. — *vt* **polit'icise** or **-ize** (*-i-sīz*) to make political. — *vi* to play the politician; to discuss politics. — *vi* **pol'itick**. — *n* **pol'iticking** engaging in political activity, such as seeking votes. — *adv* **pol'iticly**. — *combining form* **polit'ico-** used to form nouns or adjectives, denoting politics or political, as in *politico-economic*, *politico-industrial*. — *adj* **politico-econom'ic** of political economy; of politics and economics. — *n* **pol'itics** (as *sing*) the art or science of government; (as *sing*) the management of a political party; (as *sing* or *pl*) political affairs or opinions; (as *pl*) manoeuvring and intriguing; (as *pl*) policy-making, as opp. to administration; (as *pl*) the civil rather than the military aspects of government. — **political animal** in the orig. Aristotelian sense, a social animal, one which lives in communities; someone who is enthusiastic about or involved in politics; someone who enjoys politicking; **political economy** the science of the production, distribution and consumption of wealth; **political geography** that part of geography which deals with the division of the earth for purposes of government, e.g. states, colonies, counties, and the work of man, e.g. towns, canals, etc.; **political prisoner** someone imprisoned for his or her political beliefs, activities etc.; **political science** the science or study of government, as to its principles, aims, methods, etc.; **political status** the status of a political prisoner. [Gr. *polītikos* — *polītēs*, a citizen.]

politico *pō-lit'i-kō*, (*colloq*) *n* a politician, or a person who is interested in politics (usu. *derog*): — *pl* **polit'icos** or **polit'icoes**. — **politico-** see under **politic**. [It. or Sp.]

polity *pol'i-ti*, *n* political organisation; form of political organisation, constitution; a body of people organised under a system of government. [Gr. *polīteiā*.]

polka *pōl'kə* or *pol'kə*, *n* a Bohemian dance or a tune for it, in 2-4 time with accent on the third quaver, invented about 1830. — *vi* **polk** to dance a polka. — **pol'ka-dot** a pattern of dots. [Perh. Czech. *půlka*, half-step; or from Pol. *polka*, a Polish woman.]

poll *pōl*, *n* a head as a unit in numbering, an individual; a register, esp. of voters; a voting; an aggregate of votes; the taking of a vote; a taking of public opinion by means of questioning (also **opinion poll**); the blunt end of the head of a hammer, miner's pick, etc.; a polled animal. — *adj* polled; cut evenly (as in **deed poll**, opp. to *indenture*). — *vt* to cut the hair, horns, top (of a tree), edge (of a deed) from; to receive or take the votes of; to receive, take or cast (a vote); to receive (a stated number of votes); to question (someone) in a poll. — *vi* to vote. — *adj* **polled** shorn; pollarded; deprived of horns; hornless. — *n* **poll'er**. — *n* **poll'ing** (*comput*) a technique by which each of several terminals connected to the same central computer is periodically interrogated in turn by the computer to determine whether it has a message to transmit. — *n* **poll'ster** someone who carries out, or puts their faith in, a public opinion poll. — **poll'ing-booth** the place, esp. the partially-enclosed cubicle, where a voter records his or her vote; **poll tax** a tax of so much a head — i.e. on each person alike (also **poll money**); (also with *caps*) the community charge (*colloq*). — **at the head of the poll** having the greatest number of votes at an election. [Earlier sense of head, or hair of the head, cf. obs. Du. and L.G. *polle*, top of the head.]

pollack or **pollock** *pol'ək*, *n* a common fish of the cod family.

pollan *pol'ən*, *n* a whitefish, esp. that found in Lough Neagh, Northern Ireland. [Perh. Ir. *poll*, lake; cf. **powan.**]

pollard *pol'ərd*, *n* a tree having the whole crown cut off, leaving it to send out new branches from the top of the stem; a hornless animal of horned kind. — *adj* pollarded; not having an awn; bald. — *vt* to make a pollard of. [**poll.**]

pollen *pol'ən*, *n* the fertilising powder formed in the anthers of flowers. — *vt* **poll'inate** to convey pollen to. — *n* **pollinā'tion.** — *n* **poll'inātor.** — *adj* **pollin'ic** of or pertaining to pollen. — *adj* **pollinif'erous** bearing or producing pollen. — **poll'en-basket** a hollow in a bee's hindleg in which pollen is carried; **pollen count** the amount of pollen in the atmosphere, estimated from deposits on slides exposed to the air; **poll'en-sac** a cavity in an anther in which pollen is formed; **poll'en-tube** an outgrowth from a pollen-grain by which the gametes are conveyed to the ovule. [L. *pollen*, *-inis*, fine flour.]

pollex *pol'eks*, *n* the thumb or its analogue: — *pl* **pollices** (*pol'i-sēz*). — *adj* **poll'ical.** [L. *pollex*, *-icis*.]

pollination, pollinic, etc. See under **pollen.**

pollock. See **pollack.**

pollster. See under **poll.**

pollute *po-lōōt'* or *-lūt'*, *vt* to make dirty physically; to contaminate, make (any feature of the environment) offensive or harmful to human, animal or plant life; to make unclean morally; to defile ceremonially, profane. — *adj* defiled. — *n* **pollu'tant** something that pollutes. — *adj* **pollut'ed.** — *adv* **pollut'edly.** — *n* **pollut'edness.** — *n* **pollut'er.** — *n* **pollution** (*po-lōō'shən* or *-lū'*). — *adj* **pollu'tive** causing pollution. [L. *polluĕre*, *pollūtus* — *pol-*, a form of *prō* or *per*, *luĕre*, to wash.]

Polly *pol'i*, *n* a form of the name *Molly*; a parrot.

pollyanna *pol-i-an'ə*, *n* someone whose naive optimism may verge on the insufferable (also with *cap*). — *adj* **pollyann'aish** or **pollyann'ish.** — *n* **pollyann'aism** a pollyannaish observation. [From *Pollyanna*, fictional creation of Eleanor Hodgman Porter (1868–1920).]

polo *pō'lō*, *n* a game like hockey on horseback — of Oriental origin; a similar aquatic (*water-polo*), bicycle (*bicycle polo*), or skating (*rink polo*) game; a jersey with a polo neck: — *pl* **pō'los.** — *n* **po'loist.** — **polo neck** a pullover collar fitting the neck closely and doubling over, as orig. in a polo jersey; a jersey with such a collar. [Balti (Tibetan dialect in Kashmir) *polo*, polo ball; Tibetan *pulu*.]

polonaise *pol-ə-nāz'*, *n* a woman's bodice and skirt in one piece, showing an underskirt; a Polish national dance or promenade of slow movement in 3-4 time; a musical form in the same rhythm. [Fr., Polish (fem.).]

polonium *pol-ō'ni-əm*, *n* a radioactive element (symbol **Po**; atomic no. 84) discovered by Mme Curie (a Pole). [Med.L. *Polōnia*, Poland.]

polony *po-lō'ni*, *n* a dry sausage of partly cooked meat. [Prob. *Bologna*, in Italy.]

poltergeist *pōl'* or *pol'tər-gīst*, *n* a mysterious invisible force thought to throw or move objects about; a noisy ghost. [Ger. *poltern*, to make a racket, *Geist*, ghost.]

poltroon *pol-trōōn'*, *n* a despicable coward. [Fr. *poltron* — It. *poltrone* — *poltro*, lazy.]

poly *pol'i*, (*colloq*) *n* (and *adj*) short for **polytechnic** (and **polytechnical**): — *pl* **pol'ys.**

poly- *pol-i-*, *combining form* denoting: many; several; much; a polymer, such as *polyethylene* (see below); affecting more than one part (*med*). — *adj* **pol'yact** (Gr. *aktīs*, *-īnos*, ray), **polyactī'nal** (also *-akt'in-əl*) or **polyact'ine** (of a marine animal) having many rays or tentacles. — *n* **polyam'ide** a polymeric amide, such as nylon. — *adj* **polyan'drous** having or allowing several husbands or male mates (at a time); having a large and indefinite number of stamens or of antheridia (*bot*). — *n* **pol'yandry** (or *-an'*) the condition or practice of being polyandrous; the social usage of some peoples in which a woman normally has several husbands. — *n* **polyan'thus** (Gr. *anthos*, flower) a many-flowered supposed hybrid between cowslip and primrose; also applied to certain hybrid roses: — *pl* **polyan'thuses.** — *adj* **polyatom'ic** (*chem*) having many atoms, or replaceable atoms or groups; multivalent. — *adj* **polyax'ial** having many axes or several axis cylinders. — *adj* **polybās'ic** capable of reacting with several equivalents of an acid; (of acids) having several replaceable hydrogen atoms. — *adj* **polycarp'ic** (Gr. *karpos*, fruit) fruiting many times, or year after year). — *adj* **polycarp'ous** polycarpic. — *n* **polychlorinated biphenyl** see **PCB.** — *adj* **pol'ychrome** (*-krōm*; Gr. *chrōma*, colour) many-coloured. — *n* a work of art (esp. a statue) in several colours; varied colouring. — *adj* **polychromat'ic** or **polychrom'ic.** — *n* **pol'ychromy** the art of decorating in many colours. — *n* **pol'yclinic** a general clinic or hospital. — *adj* **polycon'ic** pertaining to or composed of many cones. — *adj* and *n* **pol'ycotton** (of) a material made from polyester and cotton. — *adj* **polycotylē'donous** (*bot*) with more than two cotyledons. — *adj* **polycyclic** (*-sī'klik*; Gr. *kyklos*, wheel) having many circles, rings, whorls, turns or circuits; containing more than one ring of atoms in the molecule. — *adj* **polydac'tyl** having more than the normal number of fingers or toes. — Also *n*. — *n* **polydac'tylism** or **polydac'tyly.** — *adj* **polydac'tylous.** — *n* **polyde'monism** or **polydae'monism** the belief in and worship of numerous supernatural powers. — *n* **polyes'ter** any of a range of polymerised esters, some thermoplastic, some thermosetting. — *n* **polyeth'ylene** or **pol'ythene** a generic name for certain thermoplastics, polymers of ethylene. — *n* **polygamist** (*pol-ig'*). — *adj* **polyg'amous.** — *adv* **polyg'amously.** — *n* **polygamy** (*pol-ig'ə-mi*) the rule, custom or condition of marriage to more than one person at a time; mating with more than one in the same breeding season (*zool*); occurrence of male, female and hermaphrodite flowers on the same or on different plants (*bot*). — *n* **pol'ygene** (*-jēn*) any of a group of genes that control a single continuous character (e.g. height). — *n* **polygen'esis** multiple origin, esp. of mankind. — *adj* **pol'yglot** (Gr. *polyglōttos* — *glōtta*, tongue) in, of, speaking or writing many languages. — *n* a person who speaks or writes many languages; a collection of versions in different languages of the same work, esp. a Bible. — *adj* **polyglott'al.** — *n* **pol'ygon** (*-gon* or *-gən*; Gr. *gōniā*, angle) a plane figure bounded by straight lines, esp. more than four. — *adj* **polyg'onal.** — *n* **pol'ygraph** a copying, multiplying or tracing apparatus; an instrument which measures very small changes in body temperature, pulse rate, respiration, etc., and which is often used as a lie detector. — *adj* **polygraph'ic.** — *adj* **polygynous** (*-lij'* or *-lig'i-nəs*) having several wives; mating with several females; (of flowers) having several styles. — *n* **polygyny** (*-lij'* or *-lig'*) the custom, practice or condition of having a plurality of wives or styles; the habit of mating with more than one female. — *adj* **polyhed'ral** or **polyhed'ric** (*-hēd'* or *-hed'*). — *n* **polyhē'dron** (or *-hed'*; Gr. *hedrā*, seat) a solid figure or body bounded by plane faces (esp. more than six): — *pl* **poly=hed'rons** or **polyhed'ra.** — *n* **polyhy'brid** a cross between parents differing in several heritable characters. — *adj* **polyhy'dric** having several hydroxyl groups. — *n* **pol'ymath** (Gr. *polymathēs* — the root of *manthanein*, to learn) a person whose knowledge covers a wide variety of subjects. — *adj* **polymath'ic.** — *n* **polym'athy** much and varied learning. — *n* **pol'ymer** (Gr. *meros*, part; *chem*) one of a series of substances alike in percentage composition, but differing in molecular weight, esp. one of those of higher molecular weight as produced by polymerisation. — *adj* **polymeric** (*-mer'ik*) of, in a relation of, or manifesting polymerism. — *n* **polym'eride** a polymer. — *n* **polymerīsā'tion** or **-z-.** — *vt* **polym'erise** or **-ize** to combine to form a more complex molecule having the same empirical formula as the simpler ones combined; to cause to form a polymer; to make polymerous. — *vi* to change into a polymer. — *n* **polym'erism.** — *adj* **polym'erous** having many parts; having many parts in a whorl (*bot*). — *n* **polym'ery** the condition of being polymerous. — *n* **pol'ymorph** (Gr. *polymorphos*, many-formed — *morphē*, form) any one of several forms in which the same thing may occur; an organism occurring in several forms; a substance crystallising in several systems. — *adj* **polymorph'ic.** — *n* **polymorph'ism.** — *adj* **polymorph'ous.** — *n* **polymyositis** (*-mī-ō-sī'tis*; Gr. *mȳs*, *mȳos*, muscle) inflammation of several muscles at the same time. — *adj* **Polynē'sian** (Gr. *nēsos*, an island) of *Polynesia*, its prevailing race of light brown-skinned people or their languages. — *n* a native of Polynesia; a member of the pale brown-skinned race of Polynesia. — *n* **polyneuritis** (*-nūr-ī'tis*) simultaneous inflammation of several nerves. — *adj* and *n* **polynō'mial** (*math*) (an expression) consisting of a sum of terms each containing a constant and one or more variables raised to a power. — *n* **polynō'mialism.** — *n* **polynucleotide** (*pol-i-nū'kli-ə-tīd*) a compound (e.g. nucleic acid) that is made up of a number of nucleotides. — *n* **polyomino** (*pol-i-om'in-ō*; on the false analogy of *domino*) a flat, many-sided shape made up of a number of identical squares placed edge to edge: — *pl* **polyom'inos.** — *n* **polypep'tide** a peptide in which many amino-acids are linked to form a chain. — *n* **polyphagia** (*-fā'ji-ə*; Gr. *phagein* (aorist), to eat) bulimia; the habit in animals, esp. certain insects, of eating many different kinds of food. — *adj* **polyphagous** (*po-lif'ə-gəs*) (of an animal) eating many different kinds of food; given to eating excessive amounts of food, esp. as the result of a pathological condition. — *n* **polyph'agy** (*-ji*) the character of being polyphagous. — *adj* **pol'yphase** having several alternating electric currents of equal frequency with uniformly spaced phase differences. — *adj* **polyphasic** (*-fāz'ik*) going through several phases of activity followed by rest in any twenty-four hours. — *n* **pol'yphone** (*phon*) a letter having more than one phonetic value, able to be pronounced or sounded in more than one way. — *adj* **polyphonic** (*-fon'ik*) many-voiced; of polyphones; of polyphony. — *n* **pol'yphonist** a contrapuntist. — *n* **polyph'ony** the composition of music in parts each with an independent melody of its own. — *adj* **polyploid** (*pol'i-ploid*; on the analogy of *haploid*, *diploid*) having more than twice the normal haploid number of chromosomes. — *n* **pol'yploidy** the polyploid condition. — *n* **polypod** (*pol'i-pod*) an animal with many feet. — *n* **polypody** (*pol'i-pod-i*) any fern of the genus *Polypodium*, esp. *P. vulgare*. — *adj* **pol'ypoid** (*med*) pedunculated. — *n* **polyprop'ylene** a polymer of propylene, similar in properties to polyethylene. — *n* **polyprō'todont** (Gr. *prōtos*, first, *odous*, *odontos*, tooth) any member of the suborder of marsupials, including opossums, dasyures, etc., with many small incisors. — *n* **polyptych** (*pol'ip-tik*; Gr. *ptychos*, a fold) a picture, altarpiece, etc. consisting of four or more panels hinged or folding together. — *n* **pol'yrhythm** the simultaneous combination of different rhythms in a piece of music. — *adj* **polyrhyth'mic.** — *n* **polysaccharide** (*-sak'ə-rīd*) a carbohydrate of a class including starch, insulin, etc., that hydrolyses into more than one simple sugar. — *n* (*linguis*) **polysemant** (*-sē'*) or **pol'yseme** (*-sēm*) a word with more than one meaning. — *n* **pol'ysemy.** — *adj* **polysep'alous** having the sepals separate from each other. — *n* **pol'ysome** a group of cell particles linked by a molecule of ribonucleic acid and functioning as a unit in the synthesis of proteins. — *n* **pol'ysomy** a condition in which one or more extra chromosomes, esp. sex chromosomes, are present in the cells of the body. — *n* **polysty'rene** a polymer of styrene resistant to moisture and to chemicals, with many commercial and industrial applications. — *adj* **polysyllabic** (*-ab'ik*) or **polysyllab'ical.** — *n* **polysyll'able** a word of many or of more than three syllables. — *n* **polysyndeton** (*pol-i-sin'di-tən*; Gr. *syndeton*, a conjunction; *rhet*) figurative repetition of connectives or conjunctions. — *n* **polysynthesis** (*-sin'thi-sis*). — *adj* **polysynthet'ic** made up of many separate elements; combining many simple words of a sentence in one, as in the native languages of America — also called *incorporating* (*philol*). — *adv* **polysynthet'ically.** — *n* **polysynthet'icism** (*-i-sizm*) or **polysyn'thetism** the character of being polysynthetic. — *adj* **polytechnic** (*-tek'nik*; Gr. *technikos* — *technē*, art) of many arts or technical subjects. — *n* a college where such subjects are taught to an advanced level. — *adj* **polytech'nical.** — *adj* **polytene** (*pol'i-tēn*; L. *taenia*, band) (of abnormally large chromosomes) composed of many reduplicated strands. — *n* **polytetrafluoroeth'ylene** a plastic with non-adhesive surface properties. — *n* **polytheism** (*pol'i-thē-izm*; Gr. *theos*, a god) the doctrine of a plurality of gods. — *n* **pol'ytheist.** — *adj* **polytheist'ic** or **polytheist'ical.** — *adv* **polytheist'ically.** — *n* **pol'ythene** see **polyethylene.** — *adj* **polytocous** (*pol-it'ə-kəs*; Gr. *tokos*, birth) producing many or several at a birth or in a clutch. — *adj* **polyton'al.** — *n* **polytonal'ity** use at the same time of two or more musical keys. — *adj* **polyunsat'urated** (*chem*) containing more than one carbon-carbon double bond in the molecule (**polyunsaturated fats** or **oils** glycerides of polyunsaturated fatty acids, containing no cholesterol). — *n* **polyur'ethane** any of a range of resins, both thermoplastic and thermosetting, used in production of foamed materials, coatings, etc. — *adj* **polyvalent** (*pol-i-vā'lənt* or *pol-iv'ə-lənt*) multivalent. — *n* **polyvi'nyl** a vinyl polymer. — Also *adj* (**polyvinyl acetate** a colourless resin used in paints, adhesives, and as a coating for porous surfaces; **polyvinyl chloride** a vinyl plastic used as a rubber substitute for coating electric wires, cables, etc., and as a dress and furnishing fabric; abbrev. **PVC**). — *n* **pol'ywater** a supposed form of water, said to be a polymer, with properties different from those of ordinary water. [Gr. *polys*, *poleia*, *poly*, much.]

polyact ... to ... **polynucleotide.** See under **poly-.**

polynya *polin'yə*, *n* open water among sea ice, esp. Arctic. [Russ. *polyn'ya.*]

polyomino. See under **poly-.**

polyp *pol'ip*, *n* an individual of a colonial animal; a pedunculated tumour growing from mucous membrane (*med*): — *pl* **polyps** (*pol'ips*) or **polypi** (*pol'i-pī*). — *n* **pol'ypary** the common supporting structure of a colony of polyps. — *n* **polypō'sis** the presence or development of polyps. — *adj* **pol'ypous** of the nature of a polyp. [L. *polypus*, *-ī*, adopted, and transformed to 2nd declension, from Gr. *polypous*, *-podos* — *pous*, foot.]

polypeptide ... to ... **polywater**. See under **poly-**.

pom[1] *pom*, (*colloq*) *n* short for Pomeranian dog.

pom[2] *pom*, (*Austr* and *NZ colloq*) *n* and *adj* short for pommy (q.v.).

pomace *pum'is*, *n* crushed apples for cider-making, or the residue after pressing; anything crushed to pulp, esp. after oil has been expressed. [App. L.L. *pōmācium*, cider — L. *pōmum*, apple, etc.]

pomaceous. See **pome**.

pomade *pom-äd'*, *n* ointment for the hair — Latinised as **pomā'tum**. — *vt* to put pomade on. [Fr. *pommade* — It. *pomada*, *pomata*, lip-salve — L. *pōmum*, an apple.]

pomander *pom-* or *pōm-an'dər*, *n* a ball of perfumes, or a perforated globe or box in which this or a similarly perfumed preparation is kept or carried. [O.Fr. *pomme d'ambre*, apple of amber.]

pomatum. See **pomade**.

pombe *pom'be*, *n* any of various Central and East African alcoholic drinks. [Swahili.]

pome *pōm*, (*bot*) *n* any of the fruits of the apple family, e.g. apple, pear, quince, the enlarged fleshy receptacle enclosing a core formed from the carpels. — *adj* **pomaceous** (*-ā'shəs*) relating to, consisting of, or resembling apples; of the apple family or the apple section of the rose family. — *adj* **pomif'erous** bearing apples, pomes or fruit generally. — *adj* **pomolog'ical**. — *n* **pomol'ogist**. — *n* **pomol'ogy** the study of fruit-growing. [L. *pōmum*, a fruit, an apple.]

pomegranate *pom'i-gran-it* or *pom'ə-gran-it*, *n* an Oriental fruit much cultivated in warm countries, with a thick leathery rind and numerous seeds with pulpy edible seed-coats; the tree bearing it. [O.Fr. *pome grenate* — L. *pōmum*, an apple, *grānātum*, having many grains.]

pomelo *pum'* or *pom'il-ō*, *n* the grapefruit-like fruit of a tropical tree grown in Eastern countries; the tree that bears it; a grapefuit (*NAm*); a similar pear-shaped fruit or the tree that bears it, also called **shaddock**: — *pl* **pom'elos**.

Pomeranian *pom-i-rā'ni-ən*, *adj* of *Pomerania*. — *n* a native of Pomerania; a spitz or Pomeranian dog, a cross from the Eskimo dog, with a sharp-pointed face and an abundant white, creamy or black coat.

pomfret *pom'* or *pum'frit*, or **pomfret-cake** (*-kāk*) *n* a flat round liquorice sweet made in *Pontefract* (orig. pronounced *pum'frit*) in W. Yorkshire. [A.Fr. *Pontfret*, L. *pōns*, *pontis*, bridge, *fractus*, broken.]

pomiferous. See **pome**.

pommel *pum'l*, *n* a ball-shaped finial; a knob on a sword-hilt; the high part of a saddle-bow; a heavy-headed ramming tool; either of two handles on top of a gymnastics horse. — *vt* (usu. spelt **pummel**, q.v.). [O.Fr. *pomel* — L. *pōmum*, an apple.]

pommy *pom'i*, (*Austr* and *NZ colloq*; often *derog*) *n* a British (esp. English) person, often shortened to **pom**. — Also *adj*. [Perh. from **pomegranate**, alluding to the colour of the immigrants' cheeks or rhyming slang for *jimmygrant*, immigrant.]

pomologist, etc. See under **pome**.

pomp *pomp*, *n* great show or display; ceremony; ostentation; vanity or self-importance. — *n* **pomposity** (*-os'i-ti*) solemn affectation of dignity; a ridiculously pompous action, expression or person. — *adj* **pomp'ous** self-important. — *adv* **pomp'ously**. — *n* **pomp'ousness**. [Fr. *pompe* — L. *pompa* — Gr. *pompē*, a sending, escort, procession.]

pompadour *pom'pə-dōōr*, (*hist*) *n* a fashion of dressing women's hair by rolling it back from the forehead over a cushion. — *adj* in or pertaining to the style of hairdressing or dress described above, associated with Mme de Pompadour's time. [Marquise de *Pompadour* (1721–64).]

pompano *pomp'ə-nō*, *n* a general name for fishes of the *Carangidae* family, esp. edible American fishes of the genus *Trachynotus*: — *pl* **pomp'ano** or **pomp'anos**. [Sp. *pámpano*, a fish of another family.]

pompom[1] *pom'pom*, (*colloq*) *n* a machine-gun; a usu. multi-barrelled anti-aircraft gun. [Imit.]

pompom[2] *pom'pom* or **pompon** *pom'pon*, *n* a fluffy or woolly ball, tuft or tassel worn on a shoe, hat, etc. [Fr. *pompon*.]

pomposity, pompous. See **pomp**.

ponce *pons*, *n* a man who lives on the earnings of a prostitute; a pimp; an effeminate, posturing man. — *vi* to act as or like a pimp. — *adj* **pon'cy** or **pon'cey**. — **ponce about** or **around** to act the ponce or in a showy manner.

ponceau *pɔ̃-sō'*, *n* and *adj* poppy colour. — *n* a red dye: — *pl* **ponceaux** (*-sōz'*). [Fr.]

poncho *pon'chō*, *n* a South American cloak, a blanket with a hole for the head; a cyclist's waterproof cape of similar design; any similar garment: — *pl* **pon'chos**. [Sp. from Araucanian.]

pond *pond*, *n* a small, usu. artificial lake; the stretch of water between locks in a canal; (also with *cap*) the Atlantic (*facetious*). — **pond'-life** animal life in ponds; **pond'-lily** a waterlily; **pond'-snail** a pond-dwelling snail, esp. *Limnaea*; **pond'weed** any plant of the genus *Potamogeton*. [M.E. *ponde*.]

ponder *pon'dər*, *vt* to weigh in the mind; to think over; to consider. — *vi* to think (often with *on* and *over*). — *n* **ponderabil'ity**. — *adj* **pon'derable** appreciable; able to be weighed or measured. — *vt* and *vi* **pon'derate** (*lit*) to weigh; to ponder. — *n* **ponderā'tion** (*lit*) weighing or weighing up. — *n* **pon'derer**. — *adv* **pon'deringly**. — *n* **ponderosity** (*-os'i-ti*). — *adj* **pon'derous** heavy; weighty; massive; unwieldy; lumbering; (of a speech, etc.) solemnly laboured. — *adv* **pon'derously**. — *n* **pon'derousness**. [L. *ponderāre*, to weigh, and *pondus*, *ponděris*, a weight.]

pondok *pon'dok* or **pondokkie** *pon-dok'i*, (*SAfr*) *n* a crude dwelling, a hut, shack, etc. [Hottentot *pondok*, a hut, or perh. Malay *pondók*, a leaf shelter.]

pone[1] *pōn*, (*US*) *n* maize bread; a maize loaf or cake. [Algonquian.]

pone[2] *pō'ni* or *pōn*, (*cards*) *n* the player to the right of the dealer who cuts the cards; sometimes the player to the left. [L. *pōně*, imper. of *pōněre*, to place.]

pong *pong*, (*colloq*) *vi* to smell bad. — *n* a bad smell. — *adj* **pong'y**. [Prob. Romany *pan*, to stink.]

pongee *pun-* or *pon-jē'*, *n* a soft unbleached silk, made from cocoons of a wild silkworm; a fine cotton similar to this. [Perh. Chin. *pun-chī*, own loom.]

pongo *pong'gō*, *n* an anthropoid ape, orig. prob. the gorilla, but transferred to the orang-utan; a monkey: — *pl* **pong'os** or (*Austr*) **pong'oes**. [Congo *mpongi*.]

pongy. See **pong**.

poniard *pon'yərd*, *n* a small dagger. — *vt* to stab with a poniard. [Fr. *poignard* — *poing* — L. *pugnus*, fist.]

pons *ponz*, (*anat*) *n* a connecting part, esp. the *pons Varolii*, a mass of fibres joining the hemispheres of the brain: — *pl* **pon'tēs**. — *adj* **pon'tal**, **pon'tic** or **pon'tile** relating to the pons of the brain. [L. *pōns*, *pontis*, a bridge.]

pont *pont*, *n* in S. Africa, a small ferry boat guided across narrow stretches of water by a rope or cable. [O.E. *punt*, shallow boat.]

pontal, pontes, pontic. See **pons**.

ponticello *pon-ti-chel'ō*, *n* the bridge of a stringed instrument: — *pl* **ponticell'os**. [It., dimin. of *ponte*, bridge — L. *pōns*, *pontis*.]

pontifex *pon'ti-feks*, *n* in ancient Rome, a member of a college of priests that had control of matters of religion, their chief being *Pontifex Maximus*; a pontiff: — *pl* **pontifices** (*-tif'i-sēz* or *-kās*). [Ety. as for **pontiff**.]

pontiff *pon'tif, n* a high-priest; a bishop, esp. the pope or *sovereign pontiff* (*RC*). — *adj* **pontif'ical** of or belonging to a pontiff; splendid; pompously dogmatic. — *n* an office-book for bishops. — *n* **pontifical'ity**. — *adv* **pontif'ically**. — *npl* **pontif'icals** the dress of a priest, bishop or pope. — *n* **pontificate** (*-if'ik-it*) the dignity of a pontiff or high-priest; the office and dignity or reign of a pope. — *vi* (*-if'ik-āt*) to perform the duties of a pontiff; to behave in a pompous, self-important way. — *vi* **pon'tify** to play the pontiff. — **pontifical mass** mass celebrated by a bishop while wearing his full vestments. [L. *pontifex, pontificis* (partly through Fr. *pontife*), which was supposed to be from *pōns, pontis*, a bridge, *facěre*, to make, but is poss. from an Oscan and Umbrian word *puntis*, propitiatory offering.]

pontile. See **pons**.

Pont-l'Évêque *pɔ̃-lā-vek*, (Fr.) *n* a soft Cheddar cheese originating in *Pont-l'Évêque* in north-west France.

pontoon¹ *pon-tōōn', n* a flat-bottomed boat, ferry-boat, barge or other lighter vessel; such a boat, or a float, used to support a bridge; a bridge of boats; a low vessel carrying plant, materials and men for work at sea or on rivers; the floating gate of a dock; a boat-like float of a seaplane. — **pontoon'-bridge** a platform or roadway supported on pontoons. [Fr. *ponton* — L. *pontō, -ōnis*, a punt, pontoon — *pōns*, a bridge.]

pontoon² *pon-tōōn', n* a card game of chance or the winning score of 21 points which is its object. — Also called **twenty-one**. [**vingt-et-un** (q.v.).]

pony *pō'ni, n* any of several breeds of small horse — usu. one less than 14·2 hands high; £25 (*slang*); a small glass, esp. of beer; crib notes for a translation in an exam (*US slang*). — *vt* and *vi* to pay or settle (with *up*; *slang*). — **pony express** (in the U.S.) a former method of long-distance postal delivery employing relays of horses and riders; **po'nytail** a hair style in which the hair is gathered together at the back and hangs down like a pony's tail; **po'ny-trekking** cross-country pony-riding in groups as a pastime. [Scots *powny, pownie*, prob. — O.Fr. *poulenet*, dimin. of *poulain* — L.L. *pullānus*, a foal — L. *pullus*, a young animal.]

poo *pōō*, (*slang*) *n* and *vi* same as **poop⁴**. — **in the poo** (*Austr*) in an awkward situation.

pooch *pōōch*, (*slang*) *n* a dog, esp. a mongrel.

poodle *pōōd'l, n* a breed of domestic dog of various sizes which has curly hair (often clipped to a standard pattern); a lackey. [Ger. *Pudel*; L.G. *pudeln*, to paddle, splash.]

poof *pōōf*, (*slang*) *n* a male homosexual. — Also **poof'tah** or **poof'ter** (*-tə* or *-tər*). — *adj* **poof'y** effeminate. [Fr. *pouffe*, puff.]

poogye or **poogyee** *pōō'gē, n* an Indian nose-flute. [Hindi *pūgī*.]

pooh *pōō* or *pōō*, *interj* an exclamation of disdain, dismissal or disgust (as at an offensive smell). — *vt* **pooh-pooh'** or **poo-poo'** to make light of; to ridicule, dismiss contemptuously. [Imit.]

pooka *pōō'kə, n* (in Irish folklore) a malevolent goblin or spirit, sometimes assuming an animal form, said to haunt bogs and marshes. [Ir. *púca*.]

pool¹ *pōōl, n* a small body of still water; a temporary or casual collection of water or other liquid; a puddle; a deep part of a stream; an underground accumulation (in the pores of sedimentary rock) of petroleum or gas. — *n* and *adj* **pool'side**. [O.E. *pōl*.]

pool² *pōōl, n* the stakes in certain games; the collective stakes of a number of persons who combine in a betting arrangement; an organised arrangement for betting in this way; a group of persons so combining; a game or contest of various kinds in which the winner receives the pool; any of various games played on a billiard-table, each player trying to pocket a number of (esp. coloured and numbered) balls; a common stock or fund; a combination of interests; an arrangement for eliminating competition; a group of people who may be called upon as required, e.g. a pool of typists; (in *pl*) football pools, betting by post on the results of a number of football games. — *vt* to put into a common fund or stock. — *vi* to form a pool. [Fr. *poule*, a hen, also stakes (poss. through an intermediate sense of plunder), but associated in Eng. with **pool¹**.]

poontang *pōōn'tang*, (*US slang*) *n* sexual intercourse. [Fr. *putain*, a prostitute.]

poop¹ *pōōp, n* the stern of a ship; a high deck at the stern (also called **poop deck**). — *vt* (of a wave) to break over the stern of; to ship (waves) over the stern. — *adj* **pooped** having a poop. [Fr. *poupe* — L. *puppis*, the poop.]

poop² *pōōp, n* short for **nincompoop**.

poop³ *pōōp*, (*slang*) *vt* to make out of breath; to exhaust. — *vi* to become winded or exhausted; (often with *out*) to cease or give up.

poop⁴ *pōōp*, (*slang*) *n* faeces; defecation. — *vi* to defecate. — **poop scoop** or **poop'er-scooper** an implement for lifting and removing faeces (esp. one used by dogs' owners to remove faeces deposited on pavements, in parks, etc.).

poo-poo. See **pooh**.

poor *pōōr, adj* possessing little or nothing; without the means, esp. financial, of subsistence; needy; deficient; lacking; unproductive; scanty; mere; inferior; sorry; spiritless; in sorry condition; (in modest or ironical self-depreciation) humble; unfortunate, to be pitied. — *adj* **poor'ish**. — *adv* **poor'ly** in a poor manner; badly; inadequately; in a small way; meanly. — *adj* unwell. — *n* **poor'ness**. — **poor'-box** a moneybox for gifts for the poor; **poor'house** a house established at the public expense for sheltering the poor — a workhouse; **poor law** (*hist*; often in *pl*) the law or laws relating to the support of the poor. — *adj* **poor'-law**. — *vi* **poor'mouth** to claim poverty. — *vt* to malign. — **poor rate** (*hist*) a rate or tax for the support of the poor; **poor relation** any person or thing similar but inferior or subordinate to another; **poor'-relief** money, food, etc. for the poor. — *adj* **poor-spir'ited** lacking in spirit. — **poor white** (often *derog*) a member of a class of poor, improvident and incompetent white people in the Southern States of America, South Africa and elsewhere, often called by the blacks *poor white trash*. [O.Fr. *poure, povre* (Fr. *pauvre*) — L. *pauper*, poor.]

poori. See **puri**.

poorwill *pōōr'wil, n* a Western North American nightjar smaller than the whip-poor-will. [From its note.]

pooter *pōō'tər, n* an entomological collecting bottle into which small arthropods are introduced by suction.

poove *pōōv*, (*slang*) *n* same as **poof** (q.v.). — *n* **poo'very**. — *adj* **poo'vy**.

POP *abbrev* for Post Office preferred (of a kind of envelope).

pop¹ *pop, n* a mild explosive sound, as of drawing a cork; a shot; ginger-beer or any other non-alcoholic effervescing drink (*colloq*); pawn, or an act of pawning (*slang*). — *vi* to make a pop; to burst with a pop; (of eyes) to protrude; to come, go, slip or pass, suddenly, unexpectedly or unobtrusively; to pitch or alight. — *vt* to cause to make a pop or to burst with a pop; to thrust or put suddenly or quickly; to pawn (*slang*); to inject a drug or swallow it in pill form (*drug-taking slang*): — *pr p* **popp'ing**; *pa t* and *pa p* **popped**. — *adv* with a pop; suddenly. — *n* **popp'er** anything that makes a pop; a press-stud; a utensil for popping corn; (in *pl*) amyl nitrate or butyl nitrate inhaled from a crushed capsule. — *n* **popp'it** or

popp'et one of usu. a number of beads each having a small protrusion on one side and a hole on the other, by means of which they can be linked together. — **pop'corn** maize burst open and swelled by heating; a kind of maize suitable for this. — *adj* **pop'-eyed** having prominent or protruding eyes; open-eyed, agog (as from interest, excitement, etc.). — **pop-fastener** (*-fäs'nər*) a press-stud; **pop'-gun** a toy gun consisting of a tube which shoots pellets by compressed air; **pop-lacrosse** see under **lacrosse**; **pop'over** (esp. *US*) a thin hollow cake or pudding made from batter. — *adj* **pop'-up** (of appliances, books, etc.) having mechanisms, pages, etc., that rise or move quickly upwards. — **pop off** (*colloq*) to make off; to die; to fall asleep; **pop the question** (*colloq*) to make an offer of marriage. [Imit.]

pop[2] *pop*, (*colloq*) *adj* popular. — *n* currently popular music (also **pop music**), esp. the type characterised by a strong rhythmic element and the use of electrical amplification. — **pop art** art drawing deliberately on commonplace material of modern urbanised life; **pop'-artist**; **pop concert** a concert at which pop music is played; **pop festival**; **pop group** a (usu. small) group of musicians who play pop music; **pop record**; **pop singer**; **pop song**. — **top of the pops** (*old-fashioned*) (of a record) currently (among) the most popular in terms of sales; currently very much in favour (*fig*).

pop[3] *pop*, (*colloq*, esp. *NAm*) *n* (a) father; (a term of address used for) any older man.

pop. *abbrev* for: popular; popularly; population.

pope[1] *pōp*, *n* the bishop of Rome, head of the R.C. Church (often with *cap*); a person wielding, assuming or thought to assume authority like that of the pope; a parish priest in the Greek Orthodox Church; the head of the Coptic Church. — *n* **pope'dom** the office, dignity or jurisdiction of the pope; a pope's tenure of office. — *n* **pope'hood** or **pope'ship** the condition of being pope. — *n* **pop'ery** a hostile term for Roman Catholicism or whatever seems to savour of it. — *adj* **pop'ish** (*hostile*) relating to the pope or to popery. — **pope's eye** the gland surrounded with fat in the middle of the thigh of an ox or a sheep; a cut of steak (also called **popeseye steak**); **pope's nose** a parson's nose (q.v.). [O.E. *pāpa* — L.L. *pāpa* — Gr. *pappas* (late Gr. *papās*), hypocoristic for father.]

pope[2] *pōp*, *n* the ruff, a European freshwater fish.

popinjay *pop'in-jā*, *n* a figure of a parrot set up to be shot at (*hist*); a conceited person; a fop or coxcomb. [O.Fr. *papegai*.]

popish. See under **pope**[1].

poplar *pop'lər*, *n* any of a genus of rapidly growing trees of the willow family, widespread in northern temperate regions. — **trembling poplar** the aspen. [O.Fr. *poplier* — L. *pōpulus*, poplar-tree.]

poplin *pop'lin*, *n* a corded fabric with silk warp and worsted weft; an imitation in cotton or other material. [Perh. Fr. *popeline* — It. *papalina*, papal, from the papal town of Avignon, where it was made.]

popliteal *pop-lit'i-əl* or *pop-lit-ē'əl*, *adj* of the back of the knee. [L. *poples*, *-itis*.]

poppa *pop'ə*, (*colloq*, esp. *NAm*) *n* father; papa. — Short form **pop** or **pops**.

poppadum or **poppadom** *pop'e-dəm*, *n* a thin circular piece of dough, fried or grilled crisp and served with Indian food. [Tamil, Malayalam, *poppatam*.]

popper. See under **pop**[1].

poppet[1] *pop'it*, *n* a darling; a timber support used in launching a ship; a lathe head; a valve that is lifted bodily (also **popp'et-valve**). [An earlier form of **puppet**.]

poppet[2], **poppit.** See under **pop**[1].

popple *pop'l*, *vi* to flow tumblingly; to make the sound of rippling or bubbling, or of repeated shots. — *n* a poppling movement or sound. [Imit.; or a frequentative of **pop**[1].]

poppy *pop'i*, *n* a cornfield plant (of several species) or its large scarlet flowers; any other species of the genus Papaver, such as the opium poppy, or of the related genera *Glaucium*, extended to various unrelated plants. — **Poppy Day** orig. Armistice Day (q.v.), later the Saturday nearest Armistice Day, or (later) Remembrance Sunday (q.v.), when artificial poppies are sold for war charity; **popp'y-head** a capsule of the poppy; a finial in wood, esp. at a pew end. — **Flanders poppy** an emblem, from the 1st World War, of the fallen British soldiers. [O.E. *popig* — L. *papāver*, poppy.]

poppycock *pop'i-kok*, (*slang*) *n* balderdash. [Du. *pappekak*, lit. soft dung.]

popsy *pop'si*, (*old-fashioned*) *n* term of endearment for a girl or young woman. — Also **popsy-wop'sy**. [Prob. dimin. abbrev. of **poppet**.]

populace *pop'ū-ləs*, *n* the common people; those not distinguished by rank, education, office, etc. [Fr., — It. *popolazzo* — L. *pŏpulus*, people.]

popular *pop'ū-lər*, *adj* pleasing to, enjoying the favour of, or prevailing among, the people; liked by one's associates; suited to the understanding or the means of ordinary people. — *n* a popular newspaper, etc. — *n* **popularīsā'tion** or **-z-**. — *vt* **pop'ularise** or **-ize** to make popular; to present in a manner suited to ordinary people; to spread among the people. — *n* **pop'ularīser** or **-z-**. — *n* **popularity** (*-lar'i-ti*) the fact or state of being popular. — *adv* **pop'ularly**. — *vt* **pop'ulate** to people; to supply with inhabitants. — *n* **populā'tion** the act of populating; the number of the inhabitants; the number of inhabitants of a particular class; the plants or animals in a given area; a group of people, objects, items, etc. considered statistically. — *n* **pop'ulism**. — *n* **pop'ulist** a person who believes in the right and ability of the common people to play a major part in governing themselves; a supporter, wooer or student of the common people. — *adj* (of a political or social programme, cause, etc.) appealing to the mass of the people. — *adj* **pop'ulous** full of people; numerously inhabited. — *adv* **pop'ulously**. — *n* **pop'ulousness**. — **popular front** an alliance of the more progressive or left-wing political parties in the state; **population explosion** see under **explode**; **population inversion** (*phys*) the reversal of the normal ratio of populations of two different energy states, i.e., that normally fewer and fewer atoms occupy states of successively higher energies. [L. *pŏpulus*, the people.]

poral. See **pore**[1].

porbeagle *pör'bē-gl*, *n* a North Atlantic and Mediterranean shark. [From Cornish dialect.]

porcelain *pörs'lin*, *-lən*, *-lān* or *pörs'ə-*, *n* a fine earthenware, white, thin, transparent or semitransparent, first made in China; objects made of this. — *adj* of porcelain. — *adj* **porcell'anous** or **porcelain'ous** (or *pör'*) like porcelain — also **porcellā'neous** or **porcelaineous** (*pör-sə-lā'ni-əs*). — **porcelain cement** cement for mending china; **porcelain clay** kaolin. [O.Fr. *porcelaine* — It. *porcellana*, cowrie.]

porch *pörch*, *n* a building forming an enclosure or protection for a doorway; a portico or colonnade. [O.Fr. *porche* — L. *porticus* — *porta*, a gate.]

porcine *pör'sīn*, *adj* (characteristic) of pigs. [L. *porcīnus* — *porcus*, a swine.]

porcupine *pör'kū-pīn*, *n* a large spiny rodent of various kinds. [O.Fr. *porc espin* — L. *porcus*, a pig, *spīna*, a spine.]

pore[1] *pör*, *n* a minute passage or interstice, esp. the opening of a sweat-gland. — *adj* **por'al** of or pertaining to pores. — *adj* **poromer'ic** permeable to water vapour, as some synthetic leather is. — *n* **porosity** (*-os'i-ti*) the quality or state of being porous; the ratio of the volume of pores to the total volume (of e.g. a rock). — *adj* **por'ous** having many pores; permeable by fluids, etc. — *n* **por'ousness**. [Fr., — L. *porus* — Gr. *poros*, a passage.]

pore[2] *pör*, *vi* (usu. with *over*, *on* or *upon*) to gaze with close and steady attention; to ponder. — *n* **por'er**.

porge *pörj*, *vt* (in Jewish ritual) to cleanse (a slaughtered animal) ceremonially by removing the forbidden fat, sinews, etc. [Ladino (Jewish Spanish) *porgar* (Sp. *purgar*) — L. *pūrgāre*, to purge.]

porgy or **porgie** *pör'gi*, *n* a name given to many fishes, chiefly American species of sea-bream. [Partly Sp. and Port. *pargo*, app. — L. *pargus*, a kind of fish; partly from Am. Indian names.]

Porifera *por-if'ə-rə*, *npl* a phylum of animals, the sponges. — *n* **por'ifer** a member of the Porifera. [L. *porus*, a pore, *ferre*, to bear.]

pork *pörk*, *n* pig's flesh as food. — *n* **pork'er** a young pig; a pig fed to be slaughtered and used for pork. — *adj* **pork'y** pig-like; fat. — **pork barrel** (*US slang*) a project or bill which requires national government spending in a particular town or area where the citizens will benefit from increased employment, etc. and the political representative from increased local support; **pork'-butcher** someone who sells pork; **pork chop** a slice from a pig's rib; **pork pie** a pie made of minced pork. — **pork pie hat** a hat with a low flat circular crown, shaped somewhat like a pie. [Fr. *porc* — L. *porcus*, a hog.]

pornography *pör-nog'rə-fi*, *n* books, magazines, films, etc. dealing with or depicting sexual acts, in a more or less explicit way, intended to arouse sexual excitement (often shortened to **porn** or **por'no**). — *n* **pornog'rapher**. — *adj* **pornographic** (*pör-nə-graf'ik*) — often shortened to **porn** or **por'no**). — *adv* **pornograph'ically**. — **porn shop** a shop selling pornographic literature, etc.; **porn squad** the branch of the police force that enforces the law as regards obscene publications. [Gr. *pornē*, a whore, *graphein*, to write.]

poromeric. See under **pore**[1].

porosis *pö-rō'sis*, (*med*) *n* the formation of a callus, the knitting together of broken bones: — *pl* **poro'ses**. [Gr. *pōrōsis* — *pōros*, callus.]

porosity, **porous**, etc. See under **pore**[1].

porphyra *pör'fir-ə*, *n* a seaweed (genus *Porphyra*) with flat translucent red or purple fronds, purple laver. [Gr. *porphȳrā*, purple (dye).]

porphyria *pör-fi'ri-ə*, (*pathol*) *n* an inborn error of metabolism resulting in the excretion of an abnormal pigment in the urine and characterised by great pain, abnormal skin pigmentation and photosensitivity. [Gr. *porphȳrā*, purple (dye).]

Porphyrogenite *pör-fir-oj'ən-īt*, *n* a Byzantine emperor's son born in the purple or porphyry room assigned to empresses (*hist*); a prince born after his father's accession; a person born into the nobility, or a position of high rank. — *n* **Porphyrogenitism** (*-ō-jen'it-izm*) the Byzantine principle of the first son born after his father's accession succeeding to the throne. [L. *porphyrogenitus* for Gr. *porphyrogennētos* — *porphyros*, purple, *gennētos*, born.]

porphyry *pör'fir-i*, *n* a very hard, variegated rock, of a purple and white colour, used in sculpture; (*loosely*) an igneous rock with large crystals in a fine-grained ground mass (*geol*). — *adj* **porphyritic** (*-it'ik*) like or of the nature of porphyry; having large crystals scattered among small, or in a fine-grained or glassy groundmass. [Gr. *porphyrītēs* — *porphyros*, purple.]

porpoise *pör'pəs*, *n* a short-snouted genus (*Phocaena*) of the dolphin family, 1.2 to 2.5 metres (4 to 8 feet) long; extended to similar forms, esp. (*loosely*) the dolphin. [O.Fr. *porpeis* — L. *porcus*, a hog, a pig, and *piscis*, a fish.]

porridge *por'ij*, *n* a kind of dish usually made by slowly stirring oatmeal in boiling water or milk; jail, or a jail sentence, esp. in the phrase **do porridge**, to serve a jail sentence (*slang*). [**pottage** altered by influence of obs. or dialect *porray*, vegetable soup. — O.Fr. *poree* — L.L. *porrāta* — L. *porrum*, leek.]

porringer *por'in-jər*, *n* a small dish for soup, porridge, etc. [**porridge**, **pottage**.]

port[1] *pört*, *n* a harbour; a town with a harbour. — **port of call** a port where vessels can call for stores or repairs; **port of entry** a port where merchandise is allowed by law entry to and exit from a country. [O.E. *port* — L. *portus*, *-ūs*, akin to *porta*, a gate.]

port[2] *pört*, *n* a fortified wine (dark-red or tawny, sometimes white) of the Douro valley, shipped from *Oporto*, Portugal. — Also called **port-wine**.

port[3] *pört*, (*naut*) *n* the left side of a ship. — *adj* left. — *vt* and *vi* to turn left.

port[4] *pört*, *n* a town gate, or its former position (now chiefly *Scot*); an opening in the side of a ship; a porthole or its cover; a passage-way for a ball or curling-stone; an outlet or inlet for a fluid; any socket on a data processor by means of which electronic information can pass to and from peripheral units (*comput*); part of a bit curved for the tongue. [Fr. *porte* (perh. also O.E. *port*) — L. *porta*, gate.]

port[5] *pört*, *n* bearing; demeanour; carriage of the body; the position of a ported weapon. — *vt* (*mil*) to hold in a slanting direction upward across the body. — *n* **portabil'ity**. — *adj* **port'able** easily or conveniently carried or moved about; (of a computer program) easily adapted for use on a wide range of computers. — *n* a portable article. — *n* **port'age** an act of carrying; carriage; the price of carriage; a space, track or journey over which goods and boats have to be carried or dragged overland. — *adj* **port'ative** easily carried. [Fr. *port*, *porter* — L. *portāre*, to carry.]

portage. See **port**[5].

Portakabin® *pör'tə-kab-in*, *n* a *portable* structure used as a temporary office, etc.

portal *pört'əl*, *n* a gate or doorway, esp. a great or magnificent one; any entrance. [O.Fr. *portal* — L.L. *portāle* — L. *porta*, a gate.]

Portaloo® *pör'tə-lōō*, *n* a *portable* lavatory. [**loo**[1].]

portamento *pör-ta-men'tō*, (*mus*) *n* a continuous glide from one tone to another; sometimes applied to an execution between staccato and legato: — *pl* **portamen'ti** (*-tē*). — Also *adj* and *adv*. [It.]

portcullis *pört-kul'is*, *n* a grating that can be let down to close a gateway of a castle, fortress, etc. [O.Fr. *porte coleïce*, sliding gate.]

port de bras *por də bra*, (Fr.) *n* the practice or technique of arm movements in ballet; a balletic figure illustrating this technique.

Porte *pört*, (*hist*) *n* the Turkish imperial government, so called from the Sublime Porte or High Gate, the chief office of the Ottoman government at Constantinople. [Fr. *porte* — L. *porta*, gate.]

portend *pör-tend'*, *vt* to warn of as something to come; to presage. — *n* **portent** (*pör'tent*) that which portends or foreshows; a foreshadowing import; an evil omen; a prodigy, marvel. — *adj* **portentous** (*-tent'*) ominous; prodigious, extraordinary; self-conciously impressive or solemn; pompous. — *adv* **portent'ously**. — *n* **portent'ousness**. [L. *portendĕre*, *portentum* — *por-*, equivalent to *prō* or *per*, *tendĕre*, to stretch.]

porter[1] *pört'ər*, *n* a caretaker in a college, university, etc., or in a block of flats; a person at the door or entrance to an office block, factory, etc. who greets visitors, takes messages, allows or monitors entrance, etc. — **porter's lodge** a house or an apartment near a gate for the use of the porter. [O.Fr. *portier* — L.L. *portārius* — L. *porta*, a gate.]

porter[2] *pört'ər*, *n* a person employed at a railway station, hotel, etc. to carry passengers' luggage, incoming parcels, etc.; a dark-brown malt liquor, prob. so-called because a favourite drink with London porters. — *n* **port'erage** carriage; the charge made by a porter for carrying goods. — **port'erhouse** a public house where porter was sold; a chop-house; a choice cut of beefsteak next to the sirloin (also called **porterhouse steak**). [O.Fr. *porteour* (Fr. *porteur*) — L. *portātor, -ōris* — *portāre*, to carry.]

portfolio *pört-fō'li-ō, n* a case or pair of boards for loose papers, drawings, etc.; a collection of such papers; a list of securities held; the office of a cabinet minister with responsibility for a government department: — *pl* **portfo'lios**. [It. *portafogli(o)* — L. *portāre*, to carry, *folium*, a leaf.]

porthole *pört'hōl, n* a hole or opening in a ship's side for light and air, or (formerly) for pointing a gun through. [**port**[4] and **hole**.]

portico *pör'ti-kō, n* a range of columns along the front or side of a building (*archit*); a colonnade forming a porch at the entrance to a building: — *pl* **por'ticos** or **por'ticoes**. — *adj* **por'ticoed** having a portico. [It., — L. *porticus*, a porch.]

portière *por-tyer', n* a curtain hung over the door or doorway of a room. [Fr.]

portion *pör'shən, n* a part; an allotted part; an amount of food served to one person; destiny; the part of an estate descending to an heir; a dowry. — *vt* to divide into portions; to allot as a share; to provide with a portion. — *adj* **por'tioned**. [O.Fr., — L. *portiō, -ōnis*.]

Portland *pört'lənd, adj* belonging to or associated with the Isle of *Portland*, a peninsula of Dorset. — **Portland cement** a cement made by burning a mixture of clay and chalk of the colour of Portland stone; **Portland sheep** a breed of small, black-faced sheep found in the Isle of Portland; **Portland stone** building-stone which is quarried in the Isle of Portland.

portly *pört'li, adj* corpulent; stout. — *n* **port'liness**. [**port**[5].]

portmanteau *pört-man'tō, n* a large travelling-bag that folds back flat from the middle; Lewis Carroll's term for a word into which are packed the sense (and sound) of two words (also called **portman'teau word** and **blend** — e.g. *slithy* for *lithe* and *slimy*): — *pl* **portman'teaus** or **portman'teaux** (*-tōz*). — *adj* combining or covering two or more things of the same kind. [Fr., — *porter*, to carry, *manteau*, a cloak.]

portrait *pör'trit* or *-trāt, n* a painting, photograph or other likeness of a real person; a vivid description in words. — *n* **por'traitist** or **por'trait-painter**. — *n* **por'traiture** the art or act of making portraits; a collection of portraits; verbal description. — *vt* **portray** (*pör-trā'*) to paint or draw the likeness of; to describe in words. — *n* **portray'al** the act of portraying; a representation. — *n* **portray'er**. — **por'trait-gallery**; **por'trait-painting**. [O.Fr. *po(u)rtrait, po(u)rtraire* — L. *prōtrahĕre, -tractum*; see **protract**.]

Portuguese *pör-tū-gēz', adj* of Portugal, its people or its language. — *n* a native or citizen of Portugal; the language of Portugal: — *pl* **Portuguese'**. — **Portuguese man-of-war** any of several hydrozoans (genus *Physalia*) having tentacles able to give a painful, sometimes deadly, sting.

port-wine. See **port**[2].

POS *pos* (in acronyms), *abbrev* for point of sale.

pos *poz*, (*slang*) *adj* short for **positive**.

pos. *abbrev* for: position; positive.

pose[1] *pōz, n* an attitude; an assumed attitude; an affectation of a mental attitude. — *vi* to assume or maintain a pose; to attitudinise. — *vt* to put in a suitable attitude; to assert or claim; to put forward, propound. — *adj* **pose'able**. — *n* **pos'er** a person who poses, esp. (*colloq*) a person who dresses, behaves, etc. so as to be noticed. — *n* **poseur** (*pō-zœr'*; Fr.), *fem* **poseuse** (*-oez'*) an attitudiniser; a person who adopts poses, affects opinions, etc. in order to impress others. — *adj* **pos'ey** (*derog*) affected, adopting poses for effect. [Fr. *poser*, to place — L.L. *pausāre*, to cease — L. *pausa*, pause — Gr. *pausis*; between Fr. *poser* and L. *pōnĕre, positum*, there has been confusion, which has influenced the derivatives of both words.]

pose[2] *pōz, vt* to puzzle or perplex by questions. — *n* **pos'er** someone who or something which poses; a difficult question. — *n* and *adj* **pos'ing**. — *adv* **pos'ingly**. [Aphetic for **oppose**, or **appose**, confused with it.]

poser. See **pose**[1,2].

poseur, poseuse. See **pose**[1].

posh *posh*, (*colloq*) *adj* smart, stylish, top-class; expensive and therefore of the wealthy classes. — *adv* in a way associated with the upper classes, as in *talk posh*. — *vt* and *vi* (usu. with *up*) to smarten up, to polish. — *adv* **posh'ly**. — *n* **posh'ness**. [Popularly supposed to be from '*p*ort *o*utward *s*tarboard *h*ome', the most desirable position of cabins when sailing to and from the East before the days of air-conditioning, but no evidence has been found to support this; poss. linked with obs. *posh*, a dandy.]

posigrade *poz'i-grād*, (*aeronautics* and *astronautics*) *adj* having or producing positive thrust; of or pertaining to a posigrade rocket. — **posigrade rocket** a small propellant rocket that is fired to give forward acceleration when required, esp. on a multi-stage rocket when jettisoning a redundant stage. [*Posi*tive in contrast to retro*grade*.]

posit *poz'it, vt* to set in place, dispose; to postulate, assume as true, definitely or for argument's sake: — *pr p* **pos'iting**; *pa t* and *pa p* **pos'ited**. [L. *pōnĕre, positum*, to lay down.]

position *poz-ish'ən, n* situation; place occupied; attitude, disposition, arrangement; state of affairs; a proposition or thesis; the ground taken in argument or in a dispute; principle laid down; place in society; high standing; a post or appointment. — *adj* of or defining position. — *vt* to set in place; to determine the position of. — *adj* **posi'tional**. — *adj* **posi'tioned** placed. [Fr., — L. *positiō, -ōnis* — *pōnĕre, positum*, to place.]

positive *poz'i-tiv, adj* definitely, formally or explicitly laid down; beyond possibility of doubt; absolute; affirmative; expressing a quality simply without comparison (*gram*); downright; fully convinced; concrete; material; actual; characterised by the presence of some quality, not merely absence of its opposite; feeling or expressing agreement to or approval of something; having a good or constructive attitude; having qualities worthy of approval; (of a bacteriological test) confirming the presence of the suspected organism, etc.; greater than zero, or conventionally regarded as greater than zero, indicating such a quantity (*math*); in a direction towards the source of stimulus (*biol*); having the lights and shades not reversed (*phot* and *optics*); having a relatively high potential (*electr*). — *n* that which is positive; reality; a positive quantity; a positive quality; the positive degree, or an adjective or adverb in it; an image in which lights and shades or colours, or both, are unchanged; a photographic plate with the lights and shades of the original. — *adv* **pos'itively**. — *n* **pos'itiveness**. — *n* **pos'itivism** actual or absolute knowledge; certainty; assurance; positive philosophy (see below). — *n* **pos'itivist** a believer in positivism. — *adj* **positivist'ic**. — *n* **positiv'ity**. — **positive action** same as **affirmative action**; **positive angle** one generated by a straight line moving anticlockwise; **positive discrimination** see under **discriminate**; **positive philosophy** the philosophical system originated by Comte (1798–1857) — its foundation being the doctrine that man can have no knowledge of anything but phenomena, and that the knowledge of phenomena is relative, not absolute; also 20th-century developments of this (**logical positivism**) much concerned with determining whether or not statements are meaningful; **positive pole** (of a magnet) that end (or pole) which turns to the north when the magnet swings freely; **positive rays** a stream of positively electrified particles towards the cathode of a vacuum-tube; **positive sign** the sign (+ read *plus*) of addition; **positive vetting** a method of screening individuals to ensure their suitability for highly responsible positions. [L. *positīvus*, fixed by agreement — *pōnĕre*, *positum*, to place.]

positron *poz'i-tron*, (*phys*) *n* a particle differing from the electron in having a positive charge; a *positive* elec*tron*. — *n* **positronium** (*-trōn'i-əm*) a positron and an electron bound together as a short-lived unit, similar to a hydrogen atom.

posology *pos-ol'ə-ji*, *n* the science of quantity; the science of dosage. — *adj* **posological** (*-ə-loj'i-kl*). [Gr. *posos*, how much, *logos*, a word, discourse.]

poss[1] *pos*, *adj* a slang shortening of **possible.**

poss[2] *pos*, (*hist*) *vt* to agitate (clothes) in washing them, with a stick, etc. — *n* **poss'er** or **poss'-stick** a wooden stick, usu. with a perforated metal plate on the bottom, for possing clothes in a wash-tub. [Perh. imit. modification of Fr. *pousser*, to push — L. *pulsāre*, to beat.]

posse *pos'i*, *n* a force or body (of constables); any group temporarily established for some purpose. — **in posse** (*law*) in potentiality; possibly. [L. *posse*, to be able, *comitātūs*, of the county.]

possess *poz-es'*, *vt* to have or hold as owner, or as if owner; to have as a quality, etc.; to be master of; to occupy and dominate the mind of; to put in possession (with *of*). — *adj* **possessed'** in possession; self-possessed; dominated by a spirit that has entered one, or by some other irresistible influence. — *n* **possession** (*poz-esh'ən*) the act, state or fact of possessing or being possessed; a thing possessed; a subject foreign territory. — *adj* **possess'ional** pertaining to possession. — *adj* **possess'ionary.** — *adj* **possess'ionate** (*formal*) holding or allowed to hold possessions (opp. to *mendicant*). — *n* a possessionate monk. — *adj* **possess'ive** pertaining to or denoting possession; unwilling to share what one has with others; reluctant to allow another person to be independent of oneself, too inclined to dominate; genitive (*gram*). — *n* (*gram*) a possessive adjective or pronoun; the possessive case or a word in it. — *adv* **possess'ively.** — *n* **possess'iveness** extreme attachment to one's possessions; desire to dominate another emotionally. — *n* **possess'or.** — *adj* **possess'ory.** — **what possesses him** or **her?** what causes him or her to act so foolishly?, what has come over him or her? [O.Fr. *possesser* — L. *possidēre*, *possessum*.]

posset *pos'it*, *n* a drink, milk curdled with e.g. wine, ale or vinegar, formerly used as a remedy for colds, etc. [M.E. *poschot*, *possot*.]

possible *pos'i-bl*, *adj* that may be or happen; that may be done; not contrary to the nature of things; contingent; potential; practicable; such as one may tolerate, accept, or get on with. — *n* a possibility; someone who or something which is possible; the highest possible score in shooting. — *n* **poss'ibilism** the policy of confining efforts to what is immediately possible or practicable. — *n* **poss'ibilist.** — *n* **possibil'ity** the state of being possible; that which is possible; a contingency; a candidate, etc. capable of winning or being successful; (in *pl*) potential, promise for the future. — *adv* **poss'ibly** perhaps; by any possible means. [L. *possibilis* — *posse*, to be able.]

possum *pos'əm*, *n* an (orig. colloquial) aphetic form of **opossum.** — **play possum** to feign death, sleep, illness or ignorance; to dissemble. — **stir the possum** (*Austr*) to liven things up.

post[1] *pōst*, *n* a stout, stiff stake or pillar of timber or other material, usually fixed in an upright position; an upright member of a frame; a winning-post, starting-post, etc.; the pin of a lock; a solid thickish stratum; a pillar of coal left in a mine as a support. — *vt* to stick up on a post, hence on a board, door, wall, hoarding, etc.; to announce or advertise by placard, etc.; to affix a bill or bills to. — *n* **post'er** a bill-sticker; a large printed bill or placard for posting on a board or wall, etc. — *vt* to stick bills on; to advertise or publish by posters. — **poster colours** matt water colours for designing posters and other reproduction work; **post'-mill** a windmill pivoted on a post. — **between you and me and the (bed-, lamp-, gate-, etc.) post** in confidence, between ourselves only; **first past the post** having reached the winning-post first, having won the race (see also **first-past-the-post** under **first**). [O.E. *post* — L. *postis*, a doorpost — *pōnĕre*, to place.]

post[2] *pōst*, *n* an established system of conveying letters; a despatch, delivery, or batch of letters; a post-office, or post-office letter-box; an office, employment or appointment; a fixed place or station, esp. a place where a soldier or body of soldiers is stationed; a body of men stationed at a post; a trading station; a fixed place or stage on a road, for forwarding letters and change of horses (*hist*); a messenger carrying letters by stages or otherwise (*hist*); a mail-coach (*hist*); a bugle-call (*first* or *last*) summoning soldiers to their quarters or (*last post*) performed at a military funeral; full rank as naval captain (see **post-captain** below). — *vt* to entrust to the post-office for transmission; to station; to appoint to a post; to move (personnel, a military unit, etc.) to a new location; to supply with necessary information; to send or appoint (to a ship) as full captain; to transfer to another book, or enter in a book, or carry to an account (*bookkeeping*). — *vi* to move up and down in the saddle, in time with the horse's movements. — *adv* with posthorses; with speed. — *n* **post'age** money paid for conveyance by post. — *adj* **post'al** of or pertaining to the mail-service. — *adv* **post'ally.** — *n* and *adj* **post'ing.** — **post'age-stamp** an embossed or printed stamp or an adhesive label to show that the postal charge has been paid; something very tiny in area (*facetious*); **postal ballot** the submission of votes by post; **postal note** (*Austr* and *NZ*) a postal order; **postal order** an order issued by the postmaster authorising the holder to receive at a post-office payment of the sum printed on it; **postal union** an association of the chief countries of the world for international postal purposes; **postal vote** a vote submitted by post rather than placed directly into a ballot-box; **post'-bag** a mail-bag; a term used collectively for letters received; **post'-box** a letter-box; **post'-bus** a small bus used for delivering mail and for conveying passengers, esp. in rural areas; **post'-captain** formerly, a naval officer posted to the rank of captain, a full captain distinguished from a commander (called captain by courtesy); **post'card** a card on which a message may be sent by post; **post'-chaise** (popularly **po''chay, po'chay** or **po''chaise**; *hist*) a carriage, usually four-wheeled, for two or four passengers with a postilion, used in travelling with posthorses; **post'code** or **postal code** a short series of letters and numbers denoting a very small area used for sorting mail by machine. — *vt* to affix or provide with a postcode. — *adj* and *adv* **post-free'** without charge for postage; with postage prepaid. — **posthaste'** (from the old direction on letters, *haste, post, haste*) haste in travelling like that of a mail-carriage. — *adj* speedy; immediate. — *adv* with the utmost haste or speed. — **post'-horn** (*hist*) a postman's horn; a long straight brass horn blown by a coach guard; **post'horse** a horse formerly kept for conveying the post; **post'house** an inn, orig. where horses were kept for posting; **post'man** a man who delivers and handles the mail; **post'mark** the mark stamped upon a letter at a post-office defacing the postage-stamp or showing the date and place of despatch or of arrival; **post'master**, *fem* **post'-mistress** the manager or superintendent of a post-office; **Postmaster-Gen'eral** the head of the postal service in various countries; **post'-office** an office for receiving and transmitting letters by post, and other business; **Post Office** a government department or national authority in charge of the conveyance of letters, etc. in various countries. — *adj* **post-paid'** having the postage prepaid. — **post'-person** a postman or postwoman; **post'-road** (*hist*) a road with stations for posthorses; **post'-woman** a female postman. — **postman's knock** an old party game in which you must kiss the 'postman' if he or she knocks the number allotted to you; **post-office box** a box in a post-office to which are letters addressed to a particular person or firm may be sent. [Fr. *poste* — It. *posta* and *posto* — L. *pōnĕre*, *positum*, to place.]

post- *pōst-*, *pfx* signifying: after (as in *post-classical*, *post-Reformation*, *post-war*, etc.); behind (as in *post-nasal*). — *vt* **postdate'** to date after the real time; to mark with a date (as for payment) later than the time of signing. — *adj* **post-doc'toral** pertaining to academic work carried out after obtaining a doctorate. — *adj* **post-exil'ian** or **post-exil'ic** after the time of the Babylonian captivity of the Jews. — *n* **post'face** something added by way of a concluding note at the end of a written work (opp. to *preface*). — *vt* **postfix'** to add at the end; to suffix. — *adj* **post-glā'cial** after the glacial epoch. — *adj* **post-grad'uate** belonging to study pursued after graduation. — Also *n.* — *adj* **post-hypnot'ic** (**post-hypnotic suggestion** a suggestion made to a hypnotised subject but not acted upon till some time after they emerge from their trance). — *n* **Post-Impress'ionism** a movement in painting that came after Impressionism, aiming at the expression of the spiritual significance of things rather than mere representation. — *n* and *adj* **Post-Impress'ionist.** — *n* **post'lude** (*mus*) a concluding movement or voluntary. — *adj* **post-merid'ian** coming after the sun has crossed the meridian; in the afternoon. — *n* **post-millenā'rian** a believer in post-millennialism. — *adj* **post-millenn'ial.** — *n* **post-millenn'ialism** the doctrine that the Second Advent will follow the millennium. — *n* **post-mod'ernism** a style (in any of the arts) following upon, and showing movement away from, or reaction against, a style, theory, etc. termed 'modernist'. — *adj* **post-mod'ern.** — *n* and *adj* **post-mod'ernist.** — *adj* and *adv* **post-mor'tem** (L. *mortem*, accus. of *mors*, *mortis*, death) (coming, happening, etc.) after death. — *n* a post-mortem examination, autopsy; an after-the-event discussion. — *adj* **post-na'sal** behind the nose. — *adj* **post-na'tal** after birth. — *adj* **post-op'erative** relating to the period just after a surgical operation. — *n* **postposi'tion** (*gram*) the position of a word after another word that it modifies to which it is syntactically related; such a word. — *adj* **post-posi'tional.** — *adv* **postposi'tionally.** — *adj* **postpos'itive** (*gram*) used in postposition. — *n* a word used in postposition. — *adv* **postpos'itively.** — *adj* **post-pran'dial** (L. *prandium*, a repast) after-dinner. — *n* **postscē'nium** the part of the stage behind the scenery. — *n* **post'script** (L. *scrīptum*, written, *pa p* of *scrībĕre*, to write) a part added to a letter after the signature; an addition to a book after it is finished; a talk following e.g. a news broadcast; additional comment or information provided. — *n* **post-synchronisā'tion** or **-z-** (*cinematography*) the process of recording and adding a soundtrack to a film after it has been shot (*colloq* short forms **post-synch'** and **post-synch'ing**). — *vt* **post-synch'ronise** or **-ize.** — *vt* **post-ten'sion** to stretch the reinforcing wires or rods (in pre-stressed concrete) after the concrete is set. — *adj* **post-ten'sioned.** — *adj* **post-war'** (**post-war credit** portion of income tax credited to an individual for repayment after World War II). — **post-viral syndrome** a condition, following a viral infection, characterised by periodic fatigue, diminished concentration, depression, dizziness, etc. [L. *post*, after, behind.]

postage, postal. See under **post²**.

poster. See under **post¹,²**.

poste restante *pōst res-tãt'*, *n* a department of a post-office where letters are kept until called for. [Fr., remaining post.]

posterior *pos-tē'ri-ər*, *adj* coming after in time; later; at the back or behind; on the side next to the main stem (*bot*). — *n* rear parts, buttocks. — *n* **posteriority** (*pos-tē-ri-or'i-ti*). — *adv* **postē'riorly.** — *n* **posterity** (*-ter'i-ti*) those coming after; succeeding generations; a race of descendants. [L. *postĕrior*, compar. of *posterus*, coming after — *post*, after.]

postern *post'ərn*, *n* a back door or gate; a small private door. — *adj* back; private. [O.Fr. *posterne*, *posterle* — L. *posterula*, a dimin. from *posterus*, coming after.]

posthorse, posthouse. See under **post²**.

posthumous *post'ū-məs*, *adj* after death; born after the father's death; published after the author's or composer's death. — *adv* **post'humously.** [L. *posthumus*, *postumus*, superl. of *posterus*, coming after — *post*, after; the *h* inserted from false association with *humāre*, to bury.]

postiche *pos-tēsh'*, *adj* (esp. of a piece of architectural decoration) superfluously and inappropriately superadded to a finished work; counterfeit or false. — *n* a superfluous and inappropriate addition; a false hairpiece, wig. [Fr., — It. *posticio* — L. *postīcus*, hinder.]

postilion or **postillion** *pos-til'yən*, *n* a person who guides posthorses, or horses pulling any carriage, riding on one of them. [Fr. *postillon* — It. *postiglione* — *posta*, post.]

postliminy *pōst-lim'i-ni*, *n* the right of a returned exile, prisoner, etc. to resume their former status; the right by which persons or things taken in war are restored to their former status. — *adj* **post-limin'iary.** [L. *postlīminium*, lit. return behind the threshold — *līmen*, *-inis*, threshold.]

postlude. See under **post-**.

postmaster. See under **post²**.

post meridiem *pōst mer-id'i-em*, (L.) after noon, p.m.

postpone *pōst-pōn'*, *pōs-pōn'* or *pəs-*, *vt* to put off to a future time; to defer; to delay; to subordinate. — *n* **postpone'ment.** — *n* **postpōn'er.** [L. *postpōnĕre*, *-positum* — *post*, after, *pōnĕre*, to put.]

postscenium, postscript, post-synchronisation, etc., **post-tension,** etc. See under **post-**.

postulate *pos'tū-lāt*, *vt* to claim; to take for granted, assume; to assume as a possible or legitimate operation without preliminary construction (*geom*). — *n* a stipulation; an assumption; a fundamental principle; a position assumed as self-evident; an operation whose possibility is assumed (*geom*); an axiom; a necessary condition. — *n* **pos'tulancy** the state or period of being a postulant. — *n* **pos'tulant** a petitioner; a candidate, esp. for holy orders, or admission to a religious community. — *n* **postulā'tion.** — *adj* **postulā'tional.** — *adv* **postulā'tionally.** — *adj* **pos'tulatory** assuming or assumed as a postulate. [L. *postulāre*, *-ātum*, to demand — *poscĕre*, to ask urgently.]

posture *pos'chər*, *n* relative disposition of parts, esp. of the body; attitude of body or mind; carriage or bearing; pose. — *vt* to place in a particular manner. — *vi* to assume a posture; to pose; to attitudinise. — *adj* **pos'tural.** — *n* **pos'turer** a person who attitudinises. [Fr., — L. *positūra* — *pōnere*, *positum*, to place.]

posy *pō'zi*, *n* a small bunch of flowers. [**poesy**.]

pot[1] *pot*, *n* a deep or deepish vessel for manufacturing, cooking or preserving purposes, or for growing plants, or holding jam, etc., or holding or pouring liquids; the contents or capacity of such a vessel; a chamber-pot; a stroke in which the object ball enters a pocket in billiards, snooker, etc.; a prize (*colloq*); a large sum of money; the total amount bet; a pot-shot; a simple helmet; a wicker trap for lobsters, etc. — *vt* to put in pots, for preserving, etc.; to cook in a pot; to plant in a pot; to shoot for the pot, by a pot-shot, or generally, to bag, win, secure; to pocket (e.g. a billiard-ball). — *vi* to have a pot-shot: — *pr p* **pott'ing**; *pa t* and *pa p* **pott'ed**. — *n* **pot'ful**: — *pl* **pot'fuls**. — *adj* **pott'ed** cooked or preserved in a pot; condensed, concentrated; abridged; (of music, etc.) recorded for reproduction. — *n* **pott'y** a chamber-pot (esp. as a child's expression or *facetious*); a similar article especially intended for children too young to use a full-size toilet (**pott'y-chair** a child's chair fitted with a potty; **pott'y-training** teaching (a child) to use a potty). — **pot-bar'ley** barley whose outer husk has been removed by millstones. — *adj* **pot'-bellied**. — **pot-bell'y** a protuberant belly; **pot'-boiler** a work in art or literature produced merely to make money; a producer of such works; **pot'-boiling**. — *adj* **pot'-bound** (of a houseplant) having roots compressed in a mass without room for growth. — **pot'-herb** a vegetable (esp) for flavouring — e.g. parsley; **pot'-hole** a hole worn in rock in a stream bed by eddying detritus; a deep hole eroded in limestone; a hole worn in a road surface; **pot'holer**; **pot'holing** the exploration of limestone potholes; **pot'hook** a hook for hanging a pot over a fire; a hooked stroke in writing; **pot'-liquor** (esp. *NAm*) a thin broth in which meat has been boiled; **pot-luck'** what may happen to be in the pot, or available, for a meal, without special preparation for guests (also *fig*); **pot'-metal** an alloy of copper and lead; scraps of old iron pots, etc.; **pot'-plant** a plant grown in a pot; **pot'-roast** braised meat. — *vt* to braise. — **pot'-shot** a shot within easy range; a casual or random shot. — **pot'-still** a still in which heat is applied directly to the pot containing the wash; **pott'ing-shed** a garden shed in which plants are grown in pots before being planted out in beds; **potty-chair, potty-training** see **potty** above. — **go to pot** to go to ruin; to go to pieces (orig. in allusion to the cooking-pot, not the melting-pot); **keep the pot boiling** to procure the necessaries of life; to keep going briskly without stop; **pot on** to transfer (a plant) into a larger pot; **the pot calling the kettle black** criticism of the faults of one person by another who has the same shortcomings. [Late O.E. *pott*.]

pot[2] *pot*, (*colloq*) *n* the drug cannabis in any form. [Perh. shortened Mex. Ind. *potiguaya*.]

pot[3] *pot*, *n* short for **potentiometer**.

potable *pō'tə-bl*, *adj* fit to drink. [L. *pōtābilis* — *pōtāre*, to drink.]

potage *po'täzh*, *n* thick soup. — *n* **potager** (*pot'ə-jər* or *pot'ə-zhā*) a vegetable garden laid out in a decorative way, often incorporating flowers. [Fr.]

potamic *pot-am'ik*, *adj* of rivers. — *n* **potamologist** (*-mol'ə-jist*). — *n* **potamol'ogy** the scientific study of rivers. [Gr. *potamos*, a river.]

potash *pot'ash*, *n* a powerful alkali, potassium carbonate, originally obtained in a crude state by leaching wood *ash* and evaporating in *pots* — hence **pot'-ashes** or **pot'-ash**; potassium hydroxide (*caustic potash*); sometimes the monoxide or (vaguely) some other compound of potassium. — *adj* containing, or rich in, potassium. — *adj* **potass'ic** of potassium. — *n* **potass'ium** an element (symbol **K**, for *kalium*; atomic no. 19), an alkali metal discovered by Davy in 1807 in potash. — **potassium-argon dating** estimating the date of prehistoric mineral formation from the proportion of potassium-40 to argon-40, the latter having developed from the former by radioactive decay and being trapped in the rock. [Eng. **pot** and **ash**, or the corresponding Du. *pot-asschen* (mod. *potasch*).]

potation *pō-tā'shən*, (*formal*) *n* drinking; a draught; liquor. — *adj* **potā'tory**. [L. *pōtātiō*, *-ōnis* — *pōtāre*, *-ātum*, to drink.]

potato *pə-tā'tō*, *n* originally the sweet potato, plant or tuber (see under **sweet**); now usu. a S. American plant, widely grown in temperate regions, or its tuber, cooked and eaten as a vegetable: — *pl* **potā'toes**. — **pota'to-blight** a destructive disease of the potato caused by the parasitic fungus *Phytophthora infestans*; **pota'to-chips** long pieces of potato fried in fat; chips; potato crisps (*NAm* and elsewhere); **potato crisps** very thin, crisp, fried slices of potato, widely produced commercially; crisps; **hot potato** (*slang*) a controversial issue; a tricky problem or assignment that one passes on as quickly as possible, or would prefer not to touch; **small potatoes** (*US*) anything of no great worth. [Sp. *patata* — Haitian *batata*, sweet potato.]

potatory. See **potation**.

poteen or **potheen** *po-tyēn'*, *-chēn'* or *-tēn'*, *n* Irish whiskey illicitly distilled, esp. from potatoes. [Ir. *poitín*, dimin. of *pota*, pot, from Eng. **pot** or Fr. *pot*.]

potent *pō'tənt*, *adj* powerful; mighty; strongly influential; (of a male) capable of sexual intercourse; cogent; formed of or terminating in crutch heads (*heraldry*). — *n* **pō'tence** a structure shaped like a gibbet; (in watchmaking) a bracket for supporting the lower pivot; a revolving ladder in a dovecot; a right-angled military formation. — *adj* **pō'tencé** (*-sā*; *heraldry*) potent. — *n* (*heraldry*) a marking of the shape of T. — *n* **pō'tency** power; potentiality; (in a male) the ability to have sexual intercourse. — *n* **pō'tentate** a person who possesses power; a ruler. — *adj* **pōtential** (*-ten'shl*) powerful, efficacious; latent; existing in possibility, not in reality; expressing possibility (*gram*). — *n* anything that may be possible; a possibility; of a point in a field of force, the work done in bringing a unit (of mass, electricity, etc.) from infinity to that point; powers or resources not yet developed; a verb or verb form expressing possibility (*gram*). — *n* **pōtentiality** (*pō-ten-shi-al'i-ti*). — *adv* **pōten'tially**. — *n* **pōtentiom'eter** (shortened form **pot**) an instrument for measuring difference of electric potential; a rheostat. — *adj* **potentiōmet'ric**. — *vt* **po'tentise** or **-ize** to make potent. — *adv* **pō'tently**. — **potential difference** a difference in the electrical states existing at two points, which causes a current to tend to flow between them; **potential energy** the power of doing work possessed by a body in virtue of its position. [L. *potēns*, *-entis*, pres. p. of *posse*, to be able — *potis*, able, *esse*, to be.]

potentilla *pō-tən-til'ə*, *n* any plant of the *Potentilla* genus of the rose family, including barren strawberry. [L.L., dimin. of L. *potēns*, powerful, from its once esteemed medicinal virtues.]

potentiometer. See under **potent**.

potheen. See **poteen**.

pother *podh'ər*, *n* choking smoke or dust; fuss; commotion; turmoil. — *vt* to fluster, to perplex. — *vi* to make a pother.

pot-herb, pothole, pothook. See under **pot**[1].

potion *pō'shən*, *n* (a dose of) liquid medicine or poison. [Fr., — L. *pōtiō*, *-ōnis* — *pōtāre*, to drink.]

potlatch *pot'lach*, *n* (in north-west U.S.) an Indian winter festival, the occasion for competition in extravagant gift-giving and, in one tribe, even property-destruction; any feast or gift (*colloq*). [Chinook.]

potoroo *pot-ə-roo'*, *n* a rat-kangaroo, a marsupial of rabbit size related to the kangaroo. [Aboriginal.]

pot-pourri *pō-pōō'ri, pō'* or *-rē'*, *n* a mixture of sweet-scented materials, chiefly dried petals; a selection of tunes strung together; a literary production composed of unconnected parts; a hotch-potch; orig. mixed stew. [Fr. *pot*, pot, *pourri*, rotten — past p. of *pourrir* — L. *putrēre*, to rot.]

potsherd *pot'shûrd*, (*archaeol*) *n* a piece of broken pottery. [**pot**[1] and **shard**.]

pottage *pot'ij*, *n* thick vegetable or meat soup. [Fr. *potage*, food cooked in a pot, later, soup — *pot*, jug, pot.]

potter[1] *pot'ər*, *n* a person who makes articles of baked clay, esp. earthenware vessels. — *n* **pott'ery** articles of baked clay collectively, esp. earthenware vessels; a place where such goods are manufactured; the art of the potter. [**pot**[1].]

potter[2] *pot'ər*, *vi* to busy oneself in a desultory way (with *about* or *around*); to dawdle. — *n* pottering. — *n* **pott'erer**. — *n* and *adj* **pott'ering**. — *adv* **pott'eringly**. [O.E. *potian*, to thrust.]

pottle *pot'l*, *n* a chip-basket for strawberries. [O.Fr. *potel*, dimin. of *pot*, pot.]

potto *pot'ō*, *n* a member of a West African genus of lemurs; also applied to the kinkajou: — *pl* **pott'os**. [Said to be a W. Afr. name.]

Pott's disease *pots diz-ēz'*, (*pathol*) *n* a weakening disease of the spine caused by tuberculous infection, often causing curvature of the back. — **Pott's fracture** a fracture and dislocation of the ankle-joint in which the lower tibia and fibula are damaged. [Named after Sir Percival(l) *Pott*, English surgeon (1714–88), who first described them.]

potty[1] *pot'i*, (*colloq*) *adj* crazy; dotty; trifling; petty. — *n* **pott'iness**.

potty[2]. See under **pot**[1].

pouch *powch*, *n* a poke, pocket or bag; any pocket-like structure, such as a kangaroo's marsupium, a monkey's cheek-pouch, etc. — *vt* to pocket; to form into a pouch. — *vi* to form a pouch; to be like a pouch. — *adj* **pouched** having a pouch. — *n* **pouch'ful**: — *pl* **pouch'fuls**. — *adj* **pouch'y** baggy. [O.N.Fr. *pouche* (O.Fr. *poche*).]

pouf or **pouffe**, *pōōf*, *n* a soft ottoman or large hassock, usu. cylindrical; (in dressmaking) material gathered up into a bunch. [Fr. *pouf*.]

poulard *pōō-lärd'*, *n* a spayed and fattened hen. [Fr. *poularde* — *poule*, hen.]

poult *pōlt*, *n* a chicken; the young of the common domestic fowl or of other farmyard or game bird. — *n* **poult'erer** a person who deals in dead fowls and game. — *n* **poult'ry** domestic or farmyard fowls collectively. [Fr. *poulet*, dimin. of *poule* — L.L. *pulla*, hen, fem. of L. *pullus*, young animal.]

poultice *pōl'tis*, (*med*) *n* a usu. hot, soft composition applied on a cloth to the skin, to reduce inflammation. — *vt* to put a poultice on. [L. *pultēs*, pl. of *puls*, *pultis* (Gr. *poltos*), porridge.]

pounce[1] *powns*, *n* a sudden spring or swoop with attempt to seize; a hawk's claw. — *vt* to emboss (metal) by blows on the other side. — *vi* to make a pounce (with *on* or *upon*). [Derived in some way from L. *punctiō*, *-ōnis* — *pungĕre*, *punctum*, to prick.]

pounce[2] *powns*, *n* fine powder for preparing a writing surface or absorbing ink; coloured powder shaken through perforations to mark a pattern on a surface beneath. — *vt* to prepare with pounce; to trace, transfer or mark with pounce. — **pounce'-bag** or **-box** a perforated bag or box for sprinkling pounce. [Fr. *ponce*, pumice — L. *pūmex*, *pūmicis*.]

pound[1] *pownd*, *n* a unit of weight of varying value, long used in western and central Europe, more or less answering to the Roman *libra*, whose symbol **lb** is used for pound; in avoirdupois weight, 16 ounces avoirdupois, 7000 grains, or 0·45359237 kilogram; a unit of money, originally the value of a pound-weight of silver, now worth 100 (new) pence (the pound sterling, written £1, for *libra*); the Australian (formerly), New Zealand (formerly), and Jamaican pound (written £A, £NZ, £J); the unit of currency in certain other countries, including Israel, Egypt, Syria, Lebanon and Turkey; formerly a unit of troy weight, 12 ounces troy, 5760 grains, or about 373·242 grams: — *pl* formerly **pound**, now **pounds** (except *colloq* and in compounds and certain phrases). — *n* **pound'age** a charge or tax made on each pound; a commission, or a share in profits, of so much a pound. — *n* **pound'al** the foot-pound-second unit of force, equal to the force required to accelerate a mass of one pound by one foot per second in a second. — **-pound'er** used in combination to denote anything weighing, worth or carrying, or a person who has, receives or pays, so many pounds. — **pound'-cake** a sweet cake originally containing about a pound of each chief ingredient. — *adj* **pound-fool'ish** neglecting the care of large sums in attending to little ones. — **pound force** the gravitational force of 1 lb. weight and mass; a unit of such force (abbrev. **lbf**); **pound scots** a former unit of currency (1 s. 8 d. at Union); **pound-weight'** as much as weighs a pound; a weight of one pound used in weighing. — **pound of flesh** strict exaction of one's due in fulfilment of a bargain, etc., to the point of making the other party suffer beyond what is reasonable. [O.E. *pund* — L. (*libra*) *pondō*, (pound) by weight, *pondō*, by weight — *pendĕre*, to weigh.]

pound[2] *pownd*, *n* an enclosure in which strayed animals are confined, or distrained goods kept; any confined place. — *vt* to put in a pound; to enclose, confine. — **pound'-net** an arrangement of nets for trapping fish. [O.E. *pund* (in compounds), enclosure.]

pound[3] *pownd*, *vt* to beat into pulp; to beat heavily and often (also *fig*); to thump; to walk repeatedly. — *vi* to beat; to thump; to beat the ground; to make one's way heavily; to struggle on. — *n* the act or sound of pounding. — *n* **pound'er**. [O.E. *pūnian*, to beat; *-d* excrescent, as in **sound**[3] and **bound**[4].]

poundal. See under **pound**[1].

pour *pör*, *vt* to cause or allow to flow in a stream; to send forth or emit in a stream or like a stream; to serve (wine, etc.) by pouring. — *vi* to stream; to rain heavily; to pour out tea, coffee, etc.; (of a container) to allow liquid contents to run out duly; to come, go, etc. in large numbers. — *n* a pouring; an amount poured at a time. — *adj* **pour'able**. — *n* **pour'er**. — *n* and *adj* **pour'ing**. — **it never rains but it pours** bad things never happen singly; **pouring wet** raining hard; **pour oil on troubled waters** to soothe or calm a person or situation. [M.E. *pouren*.]

pourboire *pōōr-bwär'*, (Fr.) *n* a tip or gratuity.

pourpoint *pōōr'point*, (*hist*) *n* a mediaeval quilted doublet. [Fr.]

pousse-café *pōōs-ka-fā*, (Fr.) *n* a liqueur, served with coffee. [Lit. push-coffee.]

poussette *pōōs-et'*, *n* a figure in country-dancing in which couples hold both hands and move up or down the set, changing places with the next couple. — *vi* to perform a poussette. [Fr., dimin of *pousse*, push.]

poussin *pōō-sẽ'*, *n* a chicken reared for eating at four to six weeks old; a small whole poussin, served as an individual serving, roasted, or split and fried or grilled. [Fr.]

pout[1] *powt*, *vi* to push out the lips, in sullen displeasure or otherwise; to protrude. — *vt* to protrude. — *n* a protrusion, esp. of the lips. — *n* **pout'er** someone who pouts; a variety of pigeon having its breast inflated. — *adv* **pout'ingly**. — *adj* **pout'y** given to pouting; sulky. [M.E. *powte*.]

pout[2] *powt*, *n* a fish of the cod family, the bib. — Also **whit'ing-pout**. — *n* **pout'ing** the whiting-pout. [O.E. (*æle-*)*pūte*, (eel-)pout — perh. connected with **pout**[1] with reference to the bib's inflatable membrane on the head.]

poverty *pov'ər-ti, n* the state of being poor; necessity; want; lack; deficiency. — *adj* **pov'erty-stricken** suffering from poverty. — **poverty trap** a poor financial state from which there is no escape as any realistic increase in income will result in a diminution or withdrawal of low-income government benefits. [O.Fr. *poverte* (Fr. *pauvreté*) — L. *paupertās, -ātis* — *pauper*, poor.]

POW *abbrev* for prisoner of war.

powan *pow'ən* or *pō'ən, n* a species of whitefish found in Loch Lomond and Loch Eck, Scotland. [Scots form of **pollan**.]

powder *pow'dər, n* dust; any solid in fine particles; gunpowder; hair-powder; face-powder; a medicine in the form of powder. — *vt* to reduce to powder; to sprinkle, daub or cover with (or as if with) powder. — *adj* **pow'dered** reduced to powder e.g., of food, through dehydration and crushing; sprinkled, daubed or dusted with powder. — *adj* **pow'dery** of the nature of powder; covered with powder; dusty; easily crumbled. — **pow'der-box** box for face-, hair-powder, etc.; **pow'der-flask** or **-horn** a flask (originally a horn) for carrying gunpowder; **pow'der-monkey** a boy carrying powder to the gunners on a ship-of-war; **pow'der-puff** a soft, downy ball, etc. for dusting powder onto the skin; an effeminate homosexual male (*old-fashioned slang*); **pow'der-room** (*euph*) a lavatory for women. — **keep one's powder dry** to keep one's energies ready for action, play a waiting game; to observe all practical precautions. [O.Fr. *poudre* — L. *pulvis, pulveris*, dust.]

power *pow'ər* or *powr, n* ability to do anything — physical, mental, spiritual, legal, etc.; capacity for producing an effect; strength; energy; faculty of the mind; moving force of anything; authority; rule; influence; control; governing office; permission to act; potentiality; a wielder of authority, strong influence, or rule; that in which such authority or influence resides; a spiritual agent; a being of the sixth order of the celestial hierarchy; a state influential in international affairs; a great deal or great many (now *dialect* or *colloq*); the rate at which a system absorbs energy from, or passes energy into, another system, esp. the rate of doing mechanical work, measured in watts or other unit of work done per unit of time (*mech, physics*, etc.); an instrument serving as means of applying energy; the product of a number of equal factors, generalised to include negative and fractional numbers (*math*); the potency of a point with respect to a circle (*geom*); magnifying strength, or a lens possessing it (*optics*). — *adj* concerned with power; worked, or assisted in working, by mechanical power; involving a high degree of physical strength and skill (esp. *sport*, e.g. *power tennis*). — *vt* to equip with mechanical energy. — *vi* and *vt* (*slang*) to move, or propel, with great force, energy or speed. — *adj* **pow'ered**. — *adj* **pow'erful** having great power; mighty; forcible; efficacious; intense; impressive, esp. in a disagreeable way; very great (*colloq*). — *adv* (*colloq*) exceedingly. — *adv* **pow'erfully**. — *n* **pow'erfulness**. — *adj* **pow'erless** without power; weak; impotent; helpless. — *adv* **pow'erlessly**. — *n* **pow'erlessness**. — *adj* **power-assis'ted** helped by, or using, mechanical power. — **power block** a politically important and powerful group or body; **pow'erboat** a boat propelled by a motor, a motorboat; **power breakfast, lunch** or **tea** (*colloq*) a high-level business discussion held over breakfast, lunch or tea; **power cut** an interruption of, or diminution in, the electrical supply in a particular area; **power dive** a usu. steep dive of an aeroplane, made faster by use of engine(s). — *vi* and *vt* **pow'er-dive**. — **pow'er-diving**. — **pow'er-drill, -lathe, -loom** or **-press** a drill, lathe, loom or press worked by mechanical power, such as water, steam or electricity. — *adj* **pow'er-driven** worked by (esp. mechanical or electrical) power. — **power'-house** (also *fig*) or **power'-station** a place where mechanical power (esp. electric) is generated; **power pack** a device for adjusting an electric current to the voltages required by a particular piece of electronic equipment; **power plant** an industrial plant for generating power; the assemblage of parts generating motive power in a motor car, aeroplane, etc.; **pow'erplay** strong, attacking play designed to pressure the defence by concentrating players and action in one small area (*team sport*); similarly concentrated pressure applied in e.g. military, political or business tactics; **power point** a point at which an appliance may be connected to the electrical system; **pow'er-politics** international politics in which the course taken by states depends upon their knowledge that they can back their decisions with force or other compulsive action; **power-station** see **power-house**; **power steering** a type of steering system in a vehicle, in which the rotating force exerted on the steering wheel is supplemented by engine power. — **in one's power** at one's mercy; within the limits of what one can do; **in power** in office; **the powers that be** the existing ruling authorities (from the Bible: Rom. xiii. 1). [O.Fr. *poer* (Fr. *pouvoir*) — L.L. *potēre* (for L. *posse*), to be able.]

powwow *pow'wow, n* a conference. — *vi* **powwow'** to hold a powwow; to confer. [Algonquian *powwaw, powah*.]

pox *poks, n* (*pl* of **pock**) pustules; an eruptive disease, esp. smallpox or syphilis (as *nsing*); sheep-pox. — *vt* to infect with pox. — *interj* (*old*) plague. — *adj* **pox'y** suffering from pox; spotty; dirty, diseased, rotten (*slang*); (*loosely*) applied to anything unpleasant or troublesome (*slang*). — **pox'virus** any one of a group of DNA-containing animal viruses, including those which cause smallpox, cowpox, myxomatosis and certain fibromata.

pozzolana *pot-sō-lä'nə* or **pozzuolana** *-swō-lä'nə, n* a volcanic dust first found at *Pozzuoli*, near Naples, which forms with mortar a cement that will set in air or water.

PP *abbrev* for: parish priest; past President; present pupil.

pp *abbrev* for: pages; *per procurationem* (L.), by proxy (also *per pro* (L.), for and on behalf of); pianissimo (*mus*).

PPA *abbrev* for Pre-school Playgroups Association.

ppc *abbrev* for picture postcard.

PPE *abbrev* for Philosophy, Politics and Economics.

PPI *abbrev* for Plan Position Indicator.

ppm *abbrev* for parts per million.

PPP *abbrev* for Private Patients' Plan.

PPS *abbrev* for: Parliamentary Private Secretary; *post postscriptum* (L.), a later additional postscript.

PQ *abbrev* for Province of Quebec (Canada).

PR *abbrev* for: prize ring; proportional representation; public relations; Puerto Rico.

Pr. *abbrev* for: priest; Prince; Provençal.

Pr (*chem*) *symbol* for praseodymium.

pr *abbrev* for: pair; per.

pr. *abbrev* for: present; price.

praam. See **pram**[2].

practicable *prak'tik-əbl, adj* that may be practised, carried out, accomplished, used or followed; passable, as a road; (of a stage window, light-switch, etc.) functioning, practical (q.v.). — *n* **practicabil'ity**. — *n* **prac'ticableness**. — *adv* **prac'ticably**. [Fr. *praticable* — *pratiquer*, to put into practice.]

practical *prak'tik-əl, adj* in, relating to, concerned with, well adapted to, or inclining to look to, actual practice, actual conditions, results or utility; practised; practising, actually engaged in doing something; efficient in action; workable; virtual; (of a piece of stage equipment, esp. electric lights, etc.) that can be operated on stage (*theat*). — *n* a practical class or examination. — *n* **prac'ticalism** devotion to what is practical. — *n* **prac'ticalist.** — *n* **practical'ity** practicalness; a practical matter, feature or aspect of an affair. — *adv* **prac'tically** in a practical way; by a practical method; to all intents and purposes; very nearly, as good as. — *n* **prac'ticalness.** — **practical joke** a joke that consists in action, not words, usually an annoying trick. [Archaic *practic* — obs. Fr. *practique*, L. *practicus* — Gr. *prāktikos*, fit for action.]

practice *prak'tis, n* action, performance; actual doing; proceeding; habitual action; custom; legal procedure; repeated performance as a means of acquiring skill, esp. in playing a musical instrument; form so acquired; the exercise of a profession; a professional man's business, as a field of activity or a property; scheming; plotting; trickery; working upon the feelings. — *n* **practician** (*-tish'ən*) a practiser or practitioner; a practical man. — *n* **prac'ticum** (*-ti-kəm*; *US*) a course of practical work undertaken to supplement academic studies. — *n* **prac'tisant** an agent or fellow in conspiracy. — *vt* **practise** or in U.S. **practice** (*prak'tis*) to put into practice; to perform; to carry out; to do habitually; to exercise, as a profession; to exercise oneself in, or on, or in the performance of, in order to acquire or maintain skill; to train by practice; to put to use. — *vi* to act habitually; to be in practice (esp. medical or legal); to exercise oneself in any art, esp. instrumental music; to proceed, esp. to seek to injure, by underhand means; to tamper, work (with *upon* or *on*); to scheme; to have dealings; to use artifices; to work by artifice (on the feelings). — *adj* **prac'tised** skilled through practice. — *n* **prac'tiser.** — *adj* **prac'tising** actually engaged, e.g. in professional employment; holding the beliefs, following the practices, demanded by a particular religion, etc. — *n* **practitioner** (*-tish'ən-ər*; irreg. from *practician*) someone who is in practice, esp. in medicine; someone who practises. — **general practitioner** see under **general.** [Ety. as for **practical.**]

praecoces, praecocial. See under **precocious.**

Praesepe *prī-sē'pi, n* a cluster of stars in the constellation Cancer.

praesidium. See under **presidial.**

pragmatic *prag-mat'ik, adj* relating to, or of the nature of, pragmatism; having concern more for matters of fact than for theories; pragmatical; relating to affairs of state (*hist*). — *adj* **pragmat'ical** practical; matter of fact; interfering with the affairs of others; officious; self-important; opinionative; pragmatic. — *n* **pragmatical'ity.** — *adv* **pragmat'ically.** — *n* **pragmat'icalness.** — *nsing* **pragmat'ics** the study of inherent practical usage, and social and behavioural aspects of language; a study of linguistic sign-systems and their use. — *vt* **prag'matise** or **-ize** to interpret or represent as real; to rationalise. — *n* **prag'matiser** or **-z-**. — *n* **prag'matism** pragmatical quality; matter-of-factness; concern for the practicable rather than for theories and ideals; a treatment of history with an eye to cause and effect and practical lessons; humanism or practicalism, a philosophy, or philosophic method, that makes practical consequences the test of truth (*philos*). — *n* **prag'matist** a pragmatic person; someone who advocates the practicable rather than the ideal course; a believer in pragmatism. [Gr. *prāgma, -atos*, deed — *prāssein*, to do.]

prahu. See **prau.**

prairie *prā'ri, n* a treeless plain, flat or rolling, naturally grass-covered. — **prairie-chick'en** or **-hen'** an American genus of grouse; the sharp-tailed grouse of the western United States; **prai'rie-dog** a gregarious burrowing and barking North American marmot (*Cynomys*); **prai'rie-wolf** the coyote. [Fr., — L.L. *prātaria* — L. *prātum*, a meadow.]

praise *prāz, vt* to speak highly of; to commend; to extol; to glorify, as in worship. — *n* commendation; glorifying; the musical part of worship; that for which praise is due. — *n* and *adj* **prais'ing.** — *adv* **prais'ingly.** — *adv* **praise'worthily.** — *n* **praise'worthiness.** — *adj* **praise'worthy** worthy of praise; commendable. [O.Fr. *preiser* — L.L. *preciāre* for L. *pretiāre*, to prize — *pretium*, price.]

Prakrit *prä'krit, n* a name for (any of) the Indo-Aryan dialects contemporary with Sanskrit, or for (any of) the later languages derived from them. — *adj* **Prakrit'ic.** [Sans. *prākṛta*, the natural — *prakṛti*, nature.]

praline *prä'lēn, n* an almond or nut kernel with a brown coating of sugar, or a similar confection made with crushed nuts. [Fr. *praline*, from Marshal Duplessis-*Praslin*, whose cook invented it.]

pram[1] *pram, n* short for **perambulator**, a light carriage for a baby, pushed by hand.

pram[2] or **praam** *präm, n* a flat-bottomed Dutch or Baltic boat; a flat-bottomed dinghy with squared-off bow; a barge fitted as a floating battery. [Du. *praam.*]

prana *prä'nə, n* the breath of life; in Hindu religion, esp. yoga, breath as the essential life force. — *n* **pranaya'ma** (*yoga*) controlled breathing. [Sans.]

prance *präns, vi* to bound from the hind legs; to go with a capering or dancing movement; to move with exaggerated action and ostentation; to swagger; to ride a prancing horse. — *vt* to cause to prance. — *n* an act of prancing; swagger. — *n* **pranc'er.** — *adj* and *n* **pranc'ing.** — *adv* **pranc'ingly.** [M.E. *praunce.*]

prandial *pran'di-əl*, (esp. *facetious*) *adj* relating to dinner. [L. *prandium*, a morning or midday meal.]

prang *prang*, (*slang*, orig. *airmen's slang*) *n* a crash; a bombing-attack. — *vt* to crash or smash; to bomb heavily; to crash into (e.g. another car). [App. imit.]

prank *prangk, n* a malicious or mischievous trick; a trick; a practical joke; a frolic. — *n* **prank'ster.**

praseodymium *prāz-ī-ō-dim'i-əm, n* an element (symbol **Pr**; atomic no. 59), a metal with green salts, separated from the once-supposed element didymium. [Gr. *prasios*, leek-green — *prason*, leek, and **didymium.**]

prat[1] *prat*, (*slang*) *n* the buttocks. — *n* **prat'fall** (*US slang*) a fall landing on the buttocks; a humiliating blunder or experience.

prat[2] *prat*, (*slang*) *n* (used *abusively*) a fool, an ineffectual person. [Poss. conn. with **prat**[1].]

prate *prāt, vi* to talk foolishly; to talk boastfully or insolently; to tattle; to be loquacious. — *vt* to utter pratingly; to blab. — *n* **pra'ter.** — *n* and *adj* **pra'ting.** — *adv* **pra'tingly.** [Cf. L.G. *praten*, Dan. *prate*, Du. *praaten.*]

pratincole *prat'ing-kōl, n* a bird similar to the plovers, with swallow-like wings and tail. [L. *prātum*, meadow, *incola*, an inhabitant.]

prattle *prat'l, vi* to talk much and idly; to speak in child's talk. — *vt* to utter in a prattling way. — *n* empty talk. — *n* **pratt'ler.** [Dimin. and frequentative of **prate.**]

prau *prä'o͞o* or *prow*, **prahu** *prä'o͞o* or *-ho͞o*, or **proa** *prō'ə, n* Malay sailing- or rowing-boat, esp. a fast sailing-vessel with both ends alike, and a flat side with an outrigger kept to leeward. [Malay *prāū.*]

prawn *prön, n* a small edible shrimp-like crustacean. — *vi* to fish for prawns. [M.E. *prayne, prane.*]

praxis *praks'is, n* practice; an example or a collection of examples for exercise; a model or example. [Gr. *prāxis* — *prāssein*, to do.]

pray *prā, vi* to ask earnestly (often with *for*); to entreat; to express one's desires to, or commune with, a god or some spiritual power. — *vt* to ask earnestly and reverently, as in worship; to supplicate; to present as a prayer; to render, get, put, or cause to be, by praying: — *pa t* and *pa p* **prayed.** — *interj* (now usu. *ironic*) I ask you, may I ask. — *n* **pray'er** someone who prays; (*prār* or *prā'ər*) the act of praying; entreaty; a petition to, or communing with, a god or spiritual power; the wish put forward or the words used; a form used or intended for use in praying; public worship; (in *pl*) (a time set aside for) worship in a family, school, etc.; (in Parliament) a motion addressed to the Crown asking for the annulment of an order or regulation; the thing prayed for. — *adj* **prayerful** (*prār'fo͞ol*) given to prayer; in a spirit or mental attitude of prayer. — *adv* **prayer'fully.** — *n* **prayer'fulness.** — *adj* **prayer'less.** — *n* and *adj* **pray'ing.** — (Position of accent on following compounds depends on whether one says *prār'* or *prā'ər*) **prayer'-bead** one of the beads on a rosary; a jequirity bean; **prayer'-book** a book containing prayers or forms of devotion, esp. the Book of Common Prayer of the Church of England; **prayer'-flag** in Tibetan Buddhism, a flag on which a prayer is inscribed; **prayer'-mat** same as **prayer-rug; prayer'-meeting** a short and simple form of public religious service, in which laymen often take part; **prayer'-rug** a small carpet on which a Muslim kneels at prayer; **prayer'-wheel** a drum wrapped with strips of paper inscribed with prayers deemed by Buddhists of Tibet to be proffered when the drum is turned; **praying insect** or **praying mantis** the mantis. [O.Fr. *preier* (Fr. *prier*), to pray, and O.Fr. *preiere*, prayer (— L.L. *precāria*) — L. *precārī* — *prex, precis*, a prayer.]

pre- *prē-*, *pfx* denoting: (1) in front, in front of, the anterior part of, as in *predentate, premandibular, presternum*; (2) before in time, beforehand, in advance, as in *prehistoric, pre-war, prewarn*; (3) surpassingly, to the highest degree, as in *pre-eminent, pre-potent.* — used without hyphen as *prep* (*colloq*) before, prior to. [L. *prae*, in front of.]

preach *prēch*, *vi* to deliver a sermon; to discourse earnestly; to give advice in an offensive, tedious or obtrusive manner. — *vt* to set forth in religious discourses; to deliver, as a sermon; to proclaim or teach publicly or by preaching. — *n* (*colloq*) a sermon. — *n* **preach'er** a person who discourses publicly on religious matters; a minister or clergyman; an assiduous inculcator or advocate. — *vi* **preach'ify** to preach tediously; to sermonise; to weary with lengthy advice. — *adj* **preach'y** given to tedious moralising; savouring of preaching. [Fr. *prêcher* — L. *praedicāre, -ātum*, to proclaim.]

preadmonish *prē-ad-mon'ish*, *vt* to forewarn. — *n* **preadmoni'tion.** [**pre-** (2).]

preamble *prē-am'bl*, *n* a preface; an introduction, esp. that of an Act of Parliament, giving its reasons and purpose; a prelude. — Also *vt* and *vi.* [Fr. *préambule* — L. *prae*, in front of, *ambulāre*, to go.]

preamplifier *prē-amp'li-fī-ər* or (*colloq*) **preamp** *prē'amp*, *n* an electronic device that boosts and clarifies the signal from a radio, microphone, etc. before it reaches the main amplifier. [**pre-** (2).]

preannounce *prē-ə-nowns'*, *vt* to announce beforehand. [**pre-** (2).]

preappoint *prē-ə-point'*, *vt* to appoint in advance. [**pre-** (2).]

prearrange *prē-ə-rānj'*, *vt* to arrange beforehand. — *n* **prearrange'ment.** [**pre-** (2).]

preaudience *prē-ö'di-əns*, *n* right to be heard before another; precedence at the bar among lawyers. [**pre-** (2).]

Preb. *abbrev* for: Prebend; Prebendary.

prebend *preb'ənd*, *n* the share of the revenues of a cathedral or collegiate church allowed to a clergyman who officiates in it at stated times. — *adj* **prebendal** (*pri-bend'l*). — *n* **preb'endary** a resident clergyman who enjoys a prebend, a canon; the honorary holder of a disendowed prebendal stall. [L.L. *praebenda*, an allowance — L. *praebēre*, to allow, grant.]

Pre-Cambrian *prē-kam'bri-ən*, (*geol*) *adj* and *n* (of or relating to) the earliest geological era; Archaean. [**pre-** (2).]

pre-cancel *prē-kan'səl*, *vt* to cancel a postage stamp (e.g. by applying a postmark) before use. — Also *n.* [**pre-** (2).]

pre-cancerous *prē-kan'sər-əs*, *adj* that may become cancerous. [**pre-** (2).]

precarious *pri-kā'ri-əs*, *adj* depending on chance; insecure; uncertain; dangerous, risky. — *adv* **precā'riously.** — *n* **precā'riousness.** [L. *precārius* — *precārī*, to pray.]

precast *prē'käst*, *adj* (of concrete blocks, etc.) cast before putting in position. [**pre-** (2).]

precatory *prek'ə-tə-ri*, *adj* of the nature of, or expressing, a wish, request or recommendation. — *adj* **prec'ative** supplicatory; expressing entreaty (*gram*). [L. *precārī*, to pray.]

precaution *pri-kö'shən*, *n* a caution or care beforehand; a measure taken beforehand. — *adj* **precau'tional.** — *adj* **precau'tionary.** — *adj* **precau'tious.** [**pre-** (2).]

precede *prē-sēd'*, *vt* to go before in position, time, rank or importance; to cause to be preceded. — *vi* to be before in time or place. — *n* **precedence** (*pres'i-dəns* or *prēs'*) the act of going before in time; the right of going before; priority; the state of being before in rank; the place of honour; the foremost place in ceremony — also **precedency** (*pres'i-, prēs'i-* or *pri-sē'dən-si*). — *n* **precedent** (*pres'i-dənt*; also *prēs'*) that which precedes; a past instance that may serve as an example; a previous judicial decision or proceeding. — *adj* (*pri-sē'dənt*) preceding. — *adj* **precedented** (*pres'*; also *prēs'*) having a precedent; warranted by an example. — *adj* **precedential** (*pres-i-den'shl*) of the nature of a precedent. — *adj* **precē'ding** going before in time, rank, etc.; antecedent; previous; foregoing; immediately before. — **take precedence of** or **over** to precede in ceremonial order. [Fr. *précéder* — L. *praecēdĕre, -cēssum*, — *prae, cēdĕre*, to go.]

precentor *pri-* or *prē-sen'tər*, (*eccles*) *n* the leader of the singing of a church choir or congregation; in some English cathedrals, a member of the chapter who deputes this duty to a succentor: — *fem* **precen'tress** or **precen'trix.** — *n* **precen'torship.** [L.L. *praecentor, -ōris* — L. *prae, canĕre*, to sing.]

precept *prē'sept*, *n* a rule of action; a commandment; a principle, or maxim; the written warrant of a magistrate (*law*); a mandate; an order to levy money under a rate. — *adj* **precep'tive** containing or giving precepts; directing in moral conduct; didactic. — *n* **precep'tor,** *fem* **precep'tress** someone who delivers precepts; a teacher; an instructor; a tutor (*US*); the head of a school. — *adj* **precepto'rial** (*prē-*). — *adj* **precep'tory** (*pri-*) giving precepts. [L. *praeceptum*, past p. neut. of *praecipĕre*, to take beforehand — *prae, capĕre*, to take.]

precession *pri-sesh'ən*, *n* the act of going before; a moving forward; the precession of the equinoxes (see below); the analogous phenomenon in spinning-tops and the like, whereby the wobble of the spinning object causes its axis of rotation to become cone-shaped. — *adj* **precess'ional.** — **precession of the equinoxes** a slow westward motion of the equinoctial points along the ecliptic, caused by the greater attraction of the sun and moon on the excess of matter at the equator, such that the times at which the sun crosses the equator come at shorter intervals than they would otherwise do. [L.L. *praecessiō, -ōnis* — *praecēdĕre*; see **precede.**]

pre-Christian *prē-kris'chən*, *adj* before Christ or Christianity. [**pre-** (2).]

precinct *prē'singkt*, *n* a space, esp. an enclosed space, around a building or other object (also in *pl*); a district or division within certain boundaries; a district of jurisdiction or authority; a division for police or electoral purposes (*US*); (in *pl*) environs. — **pedestrian precinct** a traffic-free area of a town, esp. a shopping centre; **shopping precinct** a shopping centre, esp. if traffic-free. [L.L. *praecinc-*

tum, past p. neut. of *praecingĕre* — *prae*, *cingĕre*, to gird.]

precious *presh'əs*, *adj* of great price or worth; cherished; very highly esteemed; often used in irony for arrant, worthless, 'fine'; affecting an over-refined choiceness. — *adv* (*colloq*) extremely, confoundedly. — *n* **preciosity** (*presh-i-os'i-ti* or *pres-*) fastidious over-refinement. — *adv* **prec'iously**. — *n* **prec'iousness**. — **precious metals** gold, silver (sometimes mercury, platinum, and others of high price); **precious stone** a stone of value and beauty for ornamentation; a gem or jewel. [O.Fr. *precios* (Fr. *précieux*) — L. *pretiōsus* — *pretium*, price.]

precipice *pres'i-pis*, *n* a high vertical or nearly vertical cliff. — *adj* **precip'itable** (*chem*) that may be precipitated. — *n* **precip'itance** or **precip'itancy** the quality of being precipitate; a headlong fall; headlong haste or rashness; an impulsively hasty action. — *adj* **precip'itant** falling headlong; rushing down with too great velocity; impulsively hasty. — *n* anything that brings down a precipitate. — *adv* **precip'itantly**. — *vt* **precip'itate** to hurl headlong; to force into hasty action; to bring on suddenly or prematurely; to bring down from a state of solution or suspension. — *vi* to rush in haste; to come out of solution or suspension; to condense and fall, as rain, hail, etc. — *adj* (*-āt* or *-it*) falling, hurled, or rushing headlong; sudden and hasty; without deliberation; rash. — *n* (*-āt* or *-it*) a substance separated from solution or suspension, usually falling to the bottom; moisture deposited as rain, snow, etc. — *adv* **precip'itately**. — *n* **precipitā'tion** the act of precipitating; a headlong fall or rush; an impulsive action; great hurry; impulsiveness; rain, hail and snow (sometimes also dew); the amount of rainfall, etc.; the formation or coming down of a precipitate; separation of suspended matter; a precipitate. — *adj* **precip'itātive**. — *n* **precip'itātor** someone who precipitates; a precipitating agent; an apparatus or tank for precipitation. — *adj* **precip'itous** like a precipice; sheer. — *adv* **precip'itously**. — *n* **precip'itousness**. [L. *praeceps*, *praecipitis*, headlong, *praecipitium*, precipice, *praecipitāre*, *-ātum*, to precipitate — *prae*, *caput*, *-itis*, head.]

précis or **precis** *prā'sē*, *n* an abstract, summary: — *pl* **précis** or **precis** (*-sēz*). — *vt* to make a précis of: — *pr p* **précising** (*prā'sē-ing*); *pa t* and *pa p* **précised** (*prā'sēd*). [Fr.]

precise *pri-sīs'*, *adj* definite; exact; accurate; free from vagueness; very, identical; scrupulously exact; scrupulous in religion; puritanical; over-exact; prim; formal. — *adv* **precise'ly**. — *n* **precise'ness**. — *n* **precisian** (*pri-sizh'ən*) an over-precise person; a formalist. — *n* **precis'ianism**. — *n* **precis'ianist** a precisian. — *n* **preci'sion** the quality of being precise; exactness; minute accuracy. — *adj* for work of, or carried out with, accuracy. — *n* **precis'ionist** a person who insists on precision; a purist. [Fr. *précis*, *-e* — L. *praecīsus*, past p. of *praecīdĕre* — *prae*, *caedĕre*, to cut.]

preclassical *prē-klas'i-kəl*, *adj* (in music and the arts) before the classical period. [**pre-** (2).]

preclinical *prē-klin'i-kəl*, (*med*) *adj* taking place before, or without yet having gained, practical clinical experience with patients; of, relating to or occurring during the stage before the symptoms of a disease are recognisable; (of a drug) prior to clinical testing. [**pre-** (2).]

preclude *pri-klōōd'*, *vt* to close beforehand; to shut out beforehand; to hinder by anticipation; to prevent. — *n* **preclusion** (*pri-klōō'zhən*). — *adj* **preclusive** (*-klōō'siv*) tending to preclude; hindering beforehand. [L. *praeclūdĕre*, *-clūsum* — *claudĕre*, to shut.]

precocious *pri-kō'shəs*, *adj* early in reaching some stage of development, such as flowering, fruiting, ripening, mental maturity (esp. *derog* when used of a child with early talents or confidence); precocial; flowering before leaves appear; showing unusually early development. — *npl* **praecoces** (*prē'kō-sēz* or *prī'ko-kās*) praecocial birds (opp. to *altrices*). — *adj* **precocial** or **praecocial** (*-kō'shl* or *-shyəl*) hatched with complete covering of down, able to leave the nest at once and seek food; premature; forward. — *adv* **precō'ciously**. — *n* **precō'ciousness** or **precocity** (*pri-kos'i-ti*) the state or quality of being precocious; early development or too early maturity of the mind. [L. *praecox*, *-ŏcis* — *prae*, *coquĕre*, to cook, ripen.]

precognition *prē-kog-nish'ən*, *n* foreknowledge; a preliminary examination of witnesses as to whether there is ground for prosecution (*Scots law*); evidence so obtained; a formally-prepared statement of evidence, etc., submitted in advance to an inquiry or court, usu. read out by the submitter at the inquiry (*Scots law*). — *adj* **precog'nitive** (*pri-*). [**pre-** (2).]

preconceive *prē-kən-sēv'*, *vt* to conceive or form a notion of, before having actual knowledge. — *n* **preconceit'** a preconceived notion. — *n* **precon-cep'tion** the act of preconceiving; a previous opinion formed without actual knowledge. [**pre-** (2).]

precondemn *prē-kən-dem'*, *vt* to condemn beforehand, in advance. [**pre-** (2).]

precondition *prē-kən-dish'ən*, *n* a condition that must be satisfied beforehand. — *vt* to prepare beforehand. [**pre-** (2).]

preconise or **-ize** *prē'kən-īz*, *vt* to proclaim; to summon publicly; (of the pope) to proclaim and ratify the election of as bishop. — *n* **preconisation** or **-z-** (*prē-kən-ī-zā'shən*, or *-kon-i-*). [L. *praecō*, *-ōnis*, a crier, a herald.]

preconscious *prē-kon'shəs*, *adj* (of material) currently absent from, but which can be readily recalled to, the conscious mind (*psychol*); (of something that occurred, existed, etc.) before consciousness, or the conscious self, developed. — *n* **precon'sciousness**. [**pre-** (2).]

preconstruct *prē-kən-strukt'*, *vt* to construct beforehand. — *n* **preconstruc'tion**. [**pre-** (2).]

precook *prē-kŏŏk'*, *vt* to cook partially or completely beforehand. [**pre-** (2).]

precursor *prē-kûr'sər*, *n* something that exists or goes in advance of another; a predecessor; an indication of the approach of an event; a compound from which another substance is derived or manufactured (*chem*). — *adj* **precur'sory**. [L. *praecurrĕre*, *-cursum* — *currĕre*, to run.]

predacious or (*irreg*) **predaceous** *pri-dā'shəs*, *adj* living by prey; predatory. — *n* **predā'ciousness**. — *n* **predac'ity**. [L. *praeda*, booty.]

predate[1] *prē-dāt'*, *vt* to date before the true date; to antedate; to be earlier than. [**pre-** (2).]

predate[2] *pri-dāt'*, *vt* to eat, prey upon. — *vi* to hunt prey. — *n* **predator** (*pred'*). — *adv* **pred'atorily**. — *n* **pred'atoriness**. — *adj* **pred'atory** of, relating to, or characterised by, plundering; living by plunder or on prey. [**predacious**.]

predecease *prē-di-sēs'*, *n* death before another's death, or before some other time. — *vt* to die before. — *adj* **predeceased'** deceased at an earlier time. [**pre-** (2).]

predecessor *prē-di-ses'ər* or *prē'*, *n* someone who has been before another; a thing that has been supplanted or succeeded; an ancestor. [L. *praedēcessor* — *dēcessor*, a retiring officer — *dē*, away, *cēdĕre*, to go, depart.]

predella *pri-del'ə*, *n* the platform or uppermost step on which an altar stands; a retable; a painting or sculpture on the face of either of these; a painting in a compartment along the bottom of an altarpiece or other picture. [It., prob. — O.H.G. *pret*, board.]

predentate *prē-den'tāt*, *adj* having teeth in the forepart of the jaw only. [**pre-** (1).]

predestine *prē-* or *pri-des'tin, vt* to destine or decree beforehand; to foreordain. — *adj* **predestinā'rian** believing in, or pertaining to, the doctrine of predestination. — *n* a person who holds the doctrine of predestination. — *n* **predestinā'tion** the act of predestinating; God's decree fixing unalterably from all eternity whatever is to happen, esp. the eternal happiness or misery of men (*theol*); fixed fate. — *n* **predes'tiny** irrevocably fixed fate. [**pre-** (2).]

predetermine *prē-di-tûr'min, vt* to determine or settle beforehand. — *adj* **predeter'minable.** — *adj* **predeter'minate** determined beforehand. — *n* **predeterminā'tion.** [**pre-** (2).]

predevelop *prē-də-vel'əp, vt* to develop beforehand. — *n* **predevel'opment.** [**pre-** (2).]

predicable *pred'i-kə-bl, adj* that may be predicated or affirmed of something; attributable. — *n* anything that can be predicated of another, or esp. of many others; one of the five attributes — genus, species, difference, property and accident (*logic*). — *n* **predicabil'ity.** [L. *praedicabilis* — *praedicāre*, to proclaim, *-abilis*, able.]

predicament *pri-dik'ə-mənt, n* a condition; an unfortunate or trying position. [L.L. *praedicāmentum*, something predicated or asserted.]

predicant *pred'i-kənt, adj* predicating; preaching. — *n* someone who affirms anything; a preacher; a preaching-friar or Dominican; a predikant. [L. *praedīcāns*, *-antis*, pres. p. of *praedicāre*; see **predicate.**]

predicate *pred'i-kāt, vt* to affirm; to assert; to state as a property or attribute of the subject (*logic*). — *n* (*-it*) that which is predicated of the subject (*logic*); the word or words by which something is said about something (*gram*). — *n* **predicā'tion.** — *adj* **predicative** (*pri-dik'ə-tiv* or *pred'i-kā-tiv*) expressing predication or affirmation; affirming; asserting. — *adv* **predic'atively.** — *adj* **pred'icatory** affirmative. — **predicate calculus** see under **calculus.** [L. *praedīcāre*, *-ātum*, to proclaim — *prae*, forth, *dīcāre*, (orig.) to proclaim.]

predict *pri-dikt', vt* to foretell. — *n* **predictabil'ity.** — *adj* **predic'table** that can be predicted; happening, or prone to act, in a way that can be predicted. — *n* **predic'tableness.** — *adv* **predic'tably.** — *n* **predic'tion** (*-shən*). — *adj* **predic'tive** foretelling; prophetic. — *n* **predic'tor** that which predicts; an anti-aircraft rangefinding and radar device. [L. *praedictus*, past p. of *praedīcĕre* — *dīcĕre*, to say.]

predigest *prē-di-jest'* or *-dī-*, *vt* to digest artificially before introducing into the body. — *n* **predigestion** (*-jest'yən*) digestion beforehand. [**pre-** (2).]

predikant *prā-di-känt'*, *n* a Dutch Reformed preacher, esp. in South Africa. [Du., — L. *praedīcāns*, *-antis*; see **predicant** and **preach.**]

predilection *prē-di-lek'shən* or *pred-i-*, *n* favourable prepossession of mind; preference. [L. *prae*, *dīligĕre*, *dīlectum*, to love — *dī-*, *dis-*, apart, *legĕre*, to choose.]

predispose *prē-dis-pōz'*, *vt* to dispose or incline beforehand; to make favourable or liable. — *n* **predisposition** (*-pəz-ish'ən*). [**pre-** (2).]

predominate *pri-dom'in-āt, vi* to surpass in strength or authority; to be most numerous or abounding; to have a commanding position. — *n* **predom'inance.** — *n* **predom'inancy.** — *adj* **predom'inant** ruling; having superior power; ascendant; preponderating; prevailing; commanding in position or effect. — *adv* **predom'inantly.** — *n* **predominā'tion.** [**pre-** (3).]

pre-eclampsia *prē-i-klamp'si-ə*, (*med*) *n* a toxic condition occurring in late pregnancy, characterised by high blood pressure, excessive weight gain, proteins in the urine, oedema, and sometimes severe headaches and visual disturbances. [**pre-** (2) and **eclampsia.**]

pre-elect *prē-i-lekt'*, *vt* to choose beforehand. — *n* **pre-elec'tion.** — *adj* before election. [**pre-** (2).]

pre-embryo *prē-em'bri-ō*, (*med*) *n* a human embryo in the first fourteen days after fertilisation: — *pl* **pre-em'bryos.** — *adj* **pre-embryon'ic.** [**pre-** (2).]

preemie, premie or **premy** *prē'mē*, (*US slang*) *n* short for *pre*mature baby.

pre-eminent *prē-em'in-ənt, adj* eminent above others; more important or influential than others; surpassing others in good or bad qualities; outstanding; extreme. — *n* **prē-em'inence.** — *adv* **prē-em'inently.** [**pre-** (3).]

pre-emption *prē-emp'shən* or *-em'shən, n* the act or right of purchasing in preference to others; a belligerent's right to seize neutral contraband at a fixed price; seizure; the act of attacking first to forestall hostile action. — *vt* **pre-empt** (*prē-empt'* or *-emt'*) to secure as first-comer; to secure by preemption; to take possession of. — *vi* (*bridge*) to make a pre-emptive bid. — *adj* **prē-empt'ible.** — *adj* **prē-empt'ive.** — *n* **prē-empt'or.** — **prē-emptive bid** (*bridge*) an unusually high bid intended to deter others from bidding. [L. *prae*, *emptiō*, *-ōnis*, a buying — *emĕre*, to buy.]

preen *prēn, vt* (of a bird) to clean and arrange (the feathers), or to clean and arrange the feathers of (a part of the body); to adorn, dress or slick (oneself) (*fig*); to plume, pride or congratulate (oneself) (with *on*). — **preen gland** the uropygial gland that secretes oil used in preening the feathers. [App. archaic *prune*, to preen, assimilated to Scot. *preen*, to pin.]

pre-engage *prē-en-gāj'*, *vt* to engage beforehand. — *n* **pre-engage'ment.** [**pre-** (2).]

pre-establish *prē-is-tab'lish, vt* to establish beforehand. [**pre-** (2).]

pre-exist *prē-ig-zist'*, *vi* to exist beforehand, esp. in a former life. — *n* **prē-exist'ence.** — *adj* **prē-exist'ent.** [**pre-** (2).]

pref. *abbrev* for preface.

prefab *prē'fab*, (*colloq*) *n* a *prefab*ricated house.

prefabricate *prē-fab'ri-kāt, vt* to make standardised parts of beforehand, for assembling later. — *adj* **prefab'ricated** composed of such parts. — *n* **prefabricā'tion.** — *n* **prefab'ricātor.** [**pre-** (2).]

preface *pref'is, n* something said by way of introduction or preliminary explanation; a statement, usually explanatory, placed at the beginning of a book, not regarded as forming (like the introduction) part of the composition; the ascription of glory, etc., in the liturgy of consecration of the eucharist (*eccles*); anything preliminary or immediately antecedent. — *vt* to say by way of preface; to precede; to front. — *vi* to make preliminary remarks. — *adj* **prefatorial** (*pref-ə-tö'ri-əl*) serving as a preface or introduction. — *adv* **prefato'rially** or **prefatorily** (*pref'ə-tər-i-li*). — *adj* **pref'atory** pertaining to a preface; serving as an introduction; introductory. [Fr. *préface* — L.L. *prēfātia* for L. *praefātiō* — *prae*, *fārī*, *fātus*, to speak.]

prefect *prē'fekt, n* someone placed in authority over others; a school pupil with some measure of authority over others; the administrative head of a department in France, of a province in Italy, or of any similar administrative district elsewhere. — *adj* **prefectorial** (*prē-fek-tö'ri-əl*). — *n* **prē'fectship.** — *adj* **prefect'ural** (*pri-*). — *n* **prē'fecture** the office, term of office, or district of a prefect; in Japan, any of 46 administrative districts headed by a governor; the house or office occupied by a prefect. — **prefect of police** the head of the Paris police. [O.Fr. *prefect* (Fr. *préfet*) and L. *praefectus*, past p. of *praeficĕre* — *prae*, *facĕre*, to make.]

prefer *pri-fûr'*, *vt* to put forward, offer, submit or present for acceptance or consideration; to promote; to advance; to hold in higher estimation; to choose or select before others; to like better (with *to*, or *rather than*; not with *than* alone): — *pr p* **preferring** (*pri-fûr'ing*); *pa t* and *pa p* **preferred** (*pri-fûrd'*). — *n*

preferabil'ity (*pref-*). — *adj* **pref'erable** to be preferred; having priority. — *adv* **pref'erably** by choice; in preference. — *n* **pref'erence** the act of choosing, favouring or liking one above another; estimation above another; the state of being preferred; that which is preferred; priority; an advantage given to one over another. — *adj* **preferential** (*pref-ər-en'shl*) having, giving or allowing a preference. — *n* **preferen'tially**. — *n* **prefer'ment** advancement; promotion; superior place, esp. in the Church. — *n* **preferr'er**. — **preference shares** or **stock** shares or stock on which the dividends must be paid before those on other kinds. [Fr. *préférer* — L. *praeferre* — *ferre*, to bear.]

prefigure *prē-fig'ər*, *vt* to imagine beforehand; to foreshadow by a type. — *n* **prefigūrā'tion**. [**pre-** (2).]

prefix *prē-fiks'* or *prē'fiks*, *vt* to put before, or at the beginning; to add as a prefix; to fix beforehand. — *n* **pre'fix** an affix added at the beginning of a word; a title placed before a name, such as *Mr*, *Sir*. [L. *praefigere*, *-fīxum* — *fīgĕre*, to fix.]

preflight *prē'flīt*, *adj* before flight, prior to take-off. [**pre-** (2).]

preform *prē-förm'*, *vt* to determine the shape of beforehand. — *n* **prēformā'tion**. [**pre-** (2).]

prefrontal *prē-front'l* or *-frunt'l*, *adj* in front of, or in the forepart of, the frontal bone, lobe, scale, etc.; pertaining to such a part. — *n* a bone or scale so situated. [**pre-** (1).]

preggers *preg'ərz*, (*colloq*, esp. upper-class) *adj* pregnant.

pre-glacial *prē-glā'shl*, *adj* earlier than the glacial period. [**pre-** (2).]

pregnable *preg'nə-bl*, *adj* that may be taken by assault or force; vulnerable. [Fr. *prenable* — *prendre*, to take; see **impregnable**.]

pregnant *preg'nənt*, *adj* carrying an unborn child or young in the womb; fruitful; fruitful in results; momentous; significant; threatening; freighted; swelling; full of thoughts, ready-witted, inventive; full of promise; pithy and to the purpose; conveying a compressed meaning beyond what the grammatical construction can strictly carry; weighty; cogent; obvious; clear. — *n* **preg'nancy**. — *adv* **preg'nantly**. [L. *praegnāns*, *-antis*, from earlier *praegnās*, *-ātis*, app. — *prae* and the root of *gnāscī*, to be born; but in some meanings from or confused with O.Fr. *preignant* — L. *premĕre*, to press.]

preheat *prē-hēt'*, *vt* to heat before using, before heating further, or before subjecting to some other process or treatment. [**pre-** (2).]

prehensile *prē-hen'-sīl*, *adj* capable of grasping — also **prehen'sive**, **prehensō'rial** (*prē-*) and **prehen'sory** (*pri-*). — *n* **prehensility** (*prē-hen-sil'i-ti*). — *n* **prehension** (*pri-hen'shən*). [L. *praehendĕre*, *-hēnsum*, to seize.]

prehistoric *prē-his-tor'ik* or **prehistor'ical** *-əl*, *adj* of a time before extant historical records. — *n* **prēhistō'rian**. — *adv* **prēhistor'ically**. — *n* **prēhis'tory**. [**pre-** (2).]

pre-ignition *prē-ig-nish'ən*, *n* too-early ignition of the charge in an internal-combustion engine. [**pre-** (2).]

prejudge *prē-juj'*, *vt* to judge or decide upon before hearing the whole case; to condemn unheard. — *n* **prejudg'ment** or **prejudge'ment**. — *adj* **prejudicant** (*prē-jōōd'i-kənt*). — *vt* **prejud'icāte** to judge beforehand. — *vi* to form an opinion beforehand. — *n* **prejudicā'tion**. [L. *praejūdicāre*.]

prejudice *prej'ŏŏ-dis*, *n* a judgment or opinion formed beforehand or without due examination; prepossession in favour of or (usu.) against anything; bias; injury or hurt; disadvantage. — *vt* to fill with prejudice; to prepossess; to bias the mind of; to injure or hurt. — *adj* **prej'udiced** having prejudice; biased. — *adj* **prejudicial** (*-dish'l*) injurious; detrimental; (*prē-jōō-*) relating to matters to be decided before a case comes into court. — *adv* **prejudic'ially**. — **without prejudice** a phrase used to require an understanding that nothing said at this stage is to detract from one's rights, to damage claims arising from future developments, or to constitute an admission of liability. [Fr. *préjudice*, wrong, and L. *praejūdicium* — *jūdicium*, judgment.]

prelacy. See **prelate**.

prelapsarian *prē-lap-sā'ri-ən*, *adj* of or pertaining to the time before the Fall of Man (sometimes *fig*). [**pre-** (2) and L. *lāpsus*, a fall.]

prelate *prel'it*, *n* an ecclesiastic of high rank; a chief priest; a clergyman. — *n* **prelacy** (*prel'ə-si*) the office of a prelate; the order of bishops or the bishops collectively; church government by prelates; episcopacy. — *n* **prel'ateship**. — *adj* **prelatial** (*pri-lā'shəl*) of a prelate. — *adj* **prelatic** (*pri-lat'ik*) or **prelat'ical** pertaining to prelates or prelacy; (in hostility) episcopal or episcopalian. — *adv* **prelat'ically**. — *n* **prelā'tion** preferment; promotion; eminence. — *vt* and *vi* **prel'atise** or **-ize** to make or to become prelatical. — *n* **prel'atism** (usu. *hostile*) episcopacy or episcopalianism; domination by prelates. — *n* **prel'atist** an upholder of prelacy. — *n* **prel'aty** prelacy. [Fr. *prélat* — L. *praelātus* — *prae*, before, *lātus*, borne.]

preliminary *pri-lim'in-ə-ri*, *adj* introductory; preparatory; preceding or preparing for the main matter. — *n* that which precedes; an introduction (often in *pl*, **prelim'inaries**); a preliminary or entrance examination (in *student slang* shortened to **prelim'** or **prē'lim**; often in *pl*); (in *pl*) preliminary pages — titles, preface, contents, introduction, etc. (*in printers' slang* **prelims'** or **prē'lims**). [L. *prae*, *līmen*, *-inis*, threshold.]

prelude *prel'ūd*, *n* a preliminary performance or action; an event preceding and leading up to another of greater importance; a preliminary strain, passage or flourish, often improvised (*mus*); an introduction or first movement of a suite (*mus*); a movement preceding a fugue (*mus*); an overture (*mus*); an introductory voluntary (*mus*); a short independent composition such as might be the introduction to another, or developed out of the prelude in the literal sense. — *vt* (*prel'ūd*, formerly and still by some *pri-lūd'* or *-lōōd'*) to precede as a prelude, serve as prelude to; to introduce with a prelude; to perform as a prelude. — *vi* to provide a prelude; to perform a prelude; to serve as a prelude. — *adj* **prelusive** (*-lōō'* or *-lū'siv*) of the nature of a prelude; introductory. — *adj* **prelu'sory** (*-sə-ri*) introductory. [Fr. *prélude* — L.L. *praelūdium* — L. *lūdĕre*, to play.]

premarital *prē-mar'i-təl*, *adj* before marriage. [**pre-** (2).]

premature *prem'ə-tūr* or *prēm'* or *-tūr'*, *adj* ripe before the time; unduly early; (of a human baby) born less than 37 weeks after conception, or (sometimes) having a birth weight of less than 2.495 kg. ($5\frac{1}{2}$lb.) irrespective of length of gestation. — *adv* **prematurely**. — *n* **prematureness**. — *n* **prematur'ity**. [L. *praemātūrus* — *prae*, *mātūrus*, ripe.]

premedical *prē-med'i-kl*, *adj* of or pertaining to a course of study undertaken before medical studies. — *adj* and *n* **prē'med** (*colloq*) short for **premedical** or **premedication**. — *n* (also **premed'ic**) a premedical student; premedical studies; premedication. — *vt* **premed'icate**. — *n* **premedicā'tion** drugs given to sedate and prepare a patient, esp. for the administration of a general anaesthetic. [**pre-** (2).]

premeditate *prē-med'i-tāt*, *vt* to think about beforehand; to design previously. — *vi* to deliberate beforehand. — *adj* **premed'itated**. — *adv* **premed'itātedly**. — *n* **premeditā'tion**. — *adj* **premed'itātive**. [L. *praemeditārī*, *-ātus* — *prae*, *meditārī*, to meditate.]

premenstrual *prē-men'strŏŏ-əl*, *adj* preceding menstruation. — **premenstrual syndrome** (abbrev.

PMS) or **premenstrual tension** (abbrev. **PMT**) a state of emotional anxiety, etc. caused by hormonal changes preceding menstruation. [**pre-** (2).]

premia. See **premium.**

premie. See **preemie.**

premier *prem'i-ər, -yər*, or by some *prēm'i-ər, adj* prime or first; chief. — *n* the first or chief; the prime minister. — *n* **première** or **premiere** (*prəm-yer'* or *prem'yər*; from the Fr. *fem*) a leading actress, dancer, etc.; the first performance of a play or film. — Also *adj.* — *vt* to give a first performance of. — Also *vi.* — *n* **prem'iership**. [Fr., — L. *prīmārius*, of the first rank — *prīmus*, first.]

premillenarian *prē-mil-ən-ā'ri-ən, n* a believer in the premillennial coming of Christ. — Also *adj.* — *n* **premillena'rianism**. [**pre-** (2).]

premillennial *prē-mil-en'yəl, adj* before the millennium. — *n* **premillenn'ialism** premillenarianism. — *n* **premillenn'ialist**. [**pre-** (2).]

premise *prem'is, n* a proposition stated or assumed for subsequent reasoning, esp. one of the two propositions in a syllogism from which the conclusion is drawn (*logic*; also **prem'iss**); (usu. in *pl*) the matter set forth at the beginning of a deed; (in *pl*) the beginning of a deed setting forth its subject-matter; (in *pl*) a building and its adjuncts, e.g. a public house, a clubhouse and grounds; a presupposition (also **prem'iss**). — *vt* **premise** (*pri-mīz'*, also *prem'is*) to mention or state first, or by way of introduction; to prefix; to state or assume as a premise; to perform or administer beforehand (*med*). [Fr. *prémisse* and L. (*sententia*, etc.) *praemissa*, (a sentence, etc.) put before — *mittĕre, missum*, to send.]

premium *prē'mi-əm, n* a reward; a prize; a bounty; payment made for insurance; a fee for admission as a pupil for a profession; excess over original price or par (opp. to *discount*); anything offered as an incentive: — *pl* **pre'miums** or (*rare*) **pre'mia**. — **Premium Bond** or **Premium Savings Bond** a Government bond, the holder of which gains no interest, but is eligible for a money prize allotted by draw held at stated intervals. — **at a premium** above par; in great demand. [L. *praemium* — *prae*, above, *emĕre*, to buy.]

premix *prē-miks', vt* to mix in advance. [**pre-** (2).]

premolar *prē-mō'lər, adj* in front of the true molar teeth. — *n* a tooth between the canine and molars (called molar or milk-molar in the milk dentition). [**pre-** (1).]

premonition *prem-* or *prē-mən-ish'ən, n* a forewarning; a feeling that something is going to happen. — *adj* **premonitive** (*pri-mon'*) or **premon'itory** giving warning or notice beforehand. [On the model of **admonish** — L. *praemonēre* — *monēre*, to warn.]

Premonstratensian *pri-mon-strə-ten'shyən* or *-si-ən, adj* of an order of canons regular, founded by St Norbert, in 1119, at *Prémontré*, near Laon, or of a corresponding order of nuns. — *n* a member of the order. — Also (*n* and *adj*) **Premon'strant**. [L. *prātum mōnstrātum*, the meadow pointed out, or (*locus*) *praemōnstrātus*, (the place) foreshown (in a vision), i.e. *Prémontré*.]

premorse *pri-mörs', adj* ending abruptly, as if bitten off. [L. *praemorsus*, bitten in front — *prae, mordēre, morsum*, to bite.]

premy. See **preemie.**

prenatal *prē-nā'tl, adj* before birth. [**pre-** (2).]

prenubile *prē-nū'bīl, adj* before sexual maturity; not yet nubile. [**pre-** (2).]

preoccupy *prē-ok'ū-pī, vt* to occupy or fill beforehand or before others; to take or have possession of to the exclusion of others or other things; to fill the mind of. — *n* **prēoccupā'tion.** — *adj* **prēocc'upied** already occupied; lost in thought, abstracted; having one's attention wholly taken up by (with *with*); (of a genus or species name) not available for adoption because it has already been applied to another group. [**pre-** (2).]

preordain *prē-ör-dān', vt* to ordain, appoint or determine beforehand. — *n* **preordain'ment.** — *vt* **preor'der** to arrange or ordain beforehand. — *n* **preor'dinance** a rule previously established; that which is ordained beforehand. — *n* **preordinā'tion** preordaining. [**pre-** (2).]

prep *prep, adj* colloq. short form of *prep*aratory. — *n* school slang for *prep*aration of lessons; a preparatory school (also **prep school**); a pupil in a preparatory school. — Also *vt.* — *adj* **prepp'y** (esp. *NAm*) vaguely denoting the values, mores, dress, etc. of a class of people who (might wish to seem to) have attended a (*NAm*) preparatory school (q.v.), specifically upper-class and conservative. — Also *n.*

prep. *abbrev* for preposition.

prepack *prē-pak', vt* to pack (e.g. food) before offering for sale. — *participial adj* **prē-packed'**. [**pre-** (2).]

prepaid. See **prepay.**

prepare *pri-pār', vt* to make ready or fit; to bring into a suitable state; to dispose; to adapt; to train, as for an examination; to learn; to make a preliminary study of (work prescribed for a class); to subject to a process for bringing into a required state; to make or produce; to cook and dress; to anticipate (a dissonant note) by including it in a preceding chord as a consonance (*mus*). — *vi* to make oneself ready; to carry out preparation. — *n* **preparation** (*prep-ə-rā'shən*) the act of preparing; a preliminary arrangement; the process or course of being prepared; the preliminary study of prescribed classwork; readiness; that which is prepared or made up, as a medicine; an anatomical or other specimen prepared for study or preservation. — *adj* **preparative** (*pri-par'ə-tiv*) serving to prepare; preliminary. — *n* that which prepares the way; preparation. — *n* **prepar'ator.** — *adv* **prepar'atorily.** — *adj* **prepar'atory** preparing; previous; introductory. — *adv* preparatorily (with *to*). — *adj* **prepared** (*pri-pārd'*) made ready, fit or suitable; ready. — *adv* **prepā'redly.** — *n* **prepā'redness.** — *n* **prepā'rer.** — **preparatory school** one which prepares pupils for a public or other higher school; a private school that prepares young people for college (*NAm*). — **be prepared to** to be ready, or be willing, to (do something). [Fr. *préparer* — L. *praeparāre* — *prae, parāre*, to make ready.]

prepay *prē-pā', vt* to pay before or in advance: — *pa t* and *pa p* **prē-paid'**. — *adj* **pre-paid'**. — *adj* **pre-pay'able.** — *n* **pre-pay'ment.** [**pre-** (2).]

prepense *pri-pens'*, (esp. *law*) *adj* premeditated; intentional, chiefly in the phrase *malice prepense*, malice aforethought or intentional. [O.Fr. *purpense.*]

preponderate *pri-pon'də-rāt, vi* to weigh more; to turn the balance; to prevail or exceed in number, quantity, importance, influence or force (with *over*). — *n* **prepon'derance** or **prepon'derancy.** — *adj* **prepon'derant.** — *adv* **prepon'derantly.** [L. *praeponderāre, -ātum* — *prae, ponderāre, -ātum*, to weigh — *pondus*, a weight.]

preposition *prep-ə-zish'ən, n* a word placed usually before a noun or its equivalent to mark some grammatical or semantic relation; (*prē-*) position in front. — *vt* **prepose** (*prē'pōz*) to place (a word) before (another) — see also **postpose** under **post-position.** — *adj* **preposi'tional** (*prep-*). — *adv* **preposi'tionally.** — *adj* **prepositive** (*pri-poz'i-tiv*) put before; prefixed. [L. *praepositiō, -ōnis* — *praepōnĕre, -positum* — *prae, pōnĕre*, to place.]

prepossess *prē-poz-es', vt* to fill beforehand, esp. the mind with some opinion or feeling; to preoccupy; to bias or prejudice, esp. favourably. — *adj* **prepossessed'** biased, prejudiced. — *adj* **prepossess'ing** tending to prepossess; making a favourable impression. — *adv* **prepossess'ingly.** — *n* **pre-**

possession (*-esh'ən*) previous possession; preoccupation; bias, usually favourable. [**pre-** (2).]

preposterous *pri-pos'tə-rəs, adj* contrary to the order of nature or reason; utterly absurd. — *adv* **prepos'terously.** — *n* **prepos'terousness.** [L. *praeposterus* — *prae*, before, *posterus*, after — *post*, after.]

prepotent *prē-pō'tənt, adj* powerful to a very high degree, esp. more powerful than others. — *n* **prepo'tency** the quality of being prepotent; the ability or tendency, of one parent, of having a stronger fertilising influence and of transmitting more hereditary characteristics to offspring (*biol*). [**pre-** (3).]

preprogrammed *prē-prō'gramd, adj* programmed beforehand. [**pre-** (2).]

preppy. See under **prep.**

prepuce *prē'pūs, n* the loose skin of the penis, the foreskin; a similar fold of skin over the clitoris. — *adj* **preputial** (*pri-pū'shyəl* or *-shəl*). [L. *praepūtium*.]

prequel *prē'kwəl*, (*colloq*) *n* a film or book produced after some other film or book has proved a success, based on the same leading characters but depicting events happening before those of the first one. [**pre-** (2) and **sequel.**]

Pre-Raphaelite *prē-raf'əl-īt, n* an artist who seeks to return to the spirit and manner of painters before the time of *Raphael* (1483–1520); a member of a group (the Pre-Raphaelite Brotherhood, or 'P.R.B.', 1848) of painters and others (Rossetti, Holman Hunt, Millais, etc.) who practised or advocated a truthful, almost rigid, adherence to natural forms and effects. — Also *adj.* [**pre-** (2), *Raphael* and **-ite.**]

prerecord *prē'rə-körd, vt* to record beforehand. — *adj* **prerecor'ded.** [**pre-** (2).]

pre-Reformation *prē-ref-ər-mā'shən, adj* before the Reformation; dating from before the Reformation. [**pre-** (2).]

prerelease *prē-ri-lēs', n* the release of a cinema film before the normal date; a film so released. — Also *adj.* [**pre-** (2).]

prerequisite *prē-rek'wi-zit, n* a condition or requirement that must previously be satisfied. — *adj* required as a condition of something else. [**pre-** (2).]

prerogative *pri-rog'ə-tiv, n* a peculiar privilege shared by no other; a right arising out of one's rank, position or nature. — *adj* holding, arising out of, or held by, a prerogative. — **royal prerogative** the rights which a sovereign has by right of office, which are different in different countries. [L. *praerogātīvus*, asked first for his vote — *prae*, *rogāre*, *-ātum*, to ask.]

Pres. *abbrev* for President.

pres. *abbrev* for present.

presa *prā'sä, -sə* or *pre'*, (*mus*) *n* a symbol (·X·, ·S· or :S:) used to indicate the points at which successive voice or instrumental parts enter a round, canon, etc.: — *pl* **pre'se** (*-sā*). [It., an act of taking up.]

presage *pres'ij, n* a prognostic; an omen; an indication of the future; a foreboding; a presentiment. — *vt* **presage** (*pres'-ij* or *pri-sāj'*) to portend; to forebode; to warn of as something to come; to forecast; to have a presentiment of. [L. *praesāgium*, a foreboding — *prae*, *sāgus*, prophetic.]

presbyopia *prez-bi-ō'pi-ə, n* difficulty in accommodating the eye to near vision, a defect increasing with age. — *n* **pres'byope** a person suffering from presbyopia. — *adj* **presbyopic** (*-op'ik*). [Gr. *presbys*, old, *ōps*, *ōpos*, the eye.]

presbyter *prez'bi-tər, n* (in the Presbyterian Church) an elder; (in Episcopal churches) a minister or priest in rank between a bishop and a deacon; a member of a presbytery. — *adj* **presbyterial** (*-tē'ri-əl*) of a presbytery; of church government by elders. — *adv* **presbytē'rially.** — *adj* **Presbytē'rian** pertaining to, or maintaining the system of, church government by elders of equal rank in this way; of a church so governed. — *n* a member of such a church; an upholder of the Presbyterian system. — *n* **Presbytē'rianism** the form of church government by presbyters. — *n* **pres'bytership.** — *n* **pres'bytery** a church court ranking next above the kirk session, consisting of the ministers and one ruling elder from each church within a certain district; the district so represented; the Presbyterian system; part of a church reserved for the officiating priests, the eastern extremity; a priest's house (*RC*). [Gr. *presbyteros*, compar. of *presbys*, old.]

preschool *prē'skōōl, adj* before school; not yet at school. — *n* **prē'schooler** a preschool child. [**pre-** (2).]

prescience *pre'shəns* or *-si-əns, n* foreknowledge; foresight. — *adj* **pre'scient.** — *adv* **pre'sciently.** [L. *praesciēns*, *-entis*, pres. p. of *praescīre* — *prae*, *scīre*, to know.]

prescind *pri-sind', vt* to cut off, cut short or separate; to abstract. — *vi* to withdraw the attention (usu. with *from*). — *n* **prescission** (*pri-sish'ən*). [L. *praescindĕre*, to cut off in front.]

prescribe *pri-skrīb', vt* to lay down as a rule or direction; to give as an order; to appoint; to give directions for, esp. as a remedy (*med*); to limit or set bounds to. — *vi* to lay down rules; to give or make out a prescription (*med*); to assert a rightful claim (with *to* or *for*). — *n* **prescrip'tion** the act of prescribing or directing; a written direction for the preparation or dispensing of a medicine (*med*); the medicine itself; any claim based on long use, or an established custom taken as authoritative. — *adj* **prescrip'tive** prescribing, laying down rules; consisting in, or acquired by, custom or long-continued use; customary. — *adv* **prescrip'tively.** — *n* **prescrip'tiveness.** [L. *praescrībĕre*, *-scrīptum*, to write before, lay down in advance, demur to — *prae*, *scrībĕre*, to write.]

prese. See **presa.**

preselect *prē-si-lekt', vt* to select beforehand. — *n* **preselec'tion.** — *n* **preselec'tor** a component of a radio receiver, improving reception. [**pre-** (2).]

pre-sell *prē-sel', vt* to sell (something), or advertise (something) for sale, before it has been produced. [**pre-** (2).]

presence *prez'əns, n* the fact or state of being present (opp. to *absence*); immediate proximity; the impression made by one's bearing, esp. imposing bearing; military or political representation or influence; something felt or imagined to be present. — **presence of mind** the power of keeping one's wits about one; coolness and readiness in emergency, danger or surprise; **real presence** the true and substantial presence, according to the belief of Roman Catholics, Eastern Orthodox, etc., of the body and blood of Christ in the eucharist. [O.Fr., — L. *praesentia*; see **present**[1,2,3].]

presension. See **presentient.**

present[1] *prez'ənt, adj* in the place in question or implied (opp. to *absent*); at hand; ready; found or existing in the thing in question; now under view or consideration; now existing; not past or future; denoting time just now, or making a general statement in which no time is explicitly stated (*gram*); in or of the present tense (*gram*). — *n* that which is present; the present time; the present tense; a verb in the present tense; the present business or occasion; the present document or (in *pl*) writings (*law*). — *adv* **pres'ently** before long, soon; at present, now (*Scot* and *NAm*). — *n* **pres'entness.** — *adj* **pres'ent-day** belonging to or found in the present time, contemporary. — **at present** at the present time, now; **for the present** for the moment; now, for the time being. [O.Fr., — L. *praesēns*, *-sentis*, present.]

present[2] *prez'ənt, n* a gift. [O.Fr. *present*, orig. presence, hence gift (from the phrase *mettre en present à*, to put into the presence of, hence to offer as a gift to).]

present[3] *pri-zent', vt* to set before (someone), introduce into presence or to notice, cognisance or acquaintance; to exhibit to view; to put forward; to proffer; to make a gift of; to bestow something upon, endow (with *with*); to put forward or bring up for examination, trial, dedication, a degree, consideration, etc.; to introduce to the public, e.g. on the stage; to put on the stage; to have as a characteristic; to appoint to a benefice; to nominate to a foundation; to represent, depict or symbolise; to hold vertically in front of the body in salute to a superior (*mil*); (*reflexive*) to come into presence, attend, appear; (*reflexive*) to offer (oneself); (*reflexive*) to offer (itself), occur. — *vi* to be in position for coming first (*obstetrics*). — *n* the position of a weapon in presenting arms or in aiming. — *n* **presentabil'ity**. — *adj* **present'able** fit to be presented; fit to be seen; passable. — *n* **present'ableness.** — *adv* **present'ably.** — *n* **presentation** (*prez-ən-tā'shən*) the act of presenting; the mode of presenting; the right of presenting; that which is presented; a setting forth, as of a truth; representation. — *adj* that has been presented; of or for presentation. — *n* **presenter** (*pri-zent'ər*). — *n* **present'ment** the act of presenting; a statement; a jury's statement to a court of matters within its knowledge; a theatrical representation; an image, delineation or picture; a presentation to the consciousness. — **at present** in the position of presenting arms; **present arms** to bring the weapon to a vertical position in front of the body. [O.Fr. *presenter* — L. *praesentāre* — *praesēns*, present (in place or time).]

presentient *prē-sen'shənt* or *-shi-ənt*, *adj* having a presentiment. — *n* **prēsen'sion.** [**pre-** (2).]

presentiment *pri-zent'i-mənt* or *-sent'*, *n* a foreboding, esp. of evil. [**pre-** (2).]

presentment. See under **present**[3].

preserve *pri-zûrv'*, *vt* to keep safe from harm or loss; to keep alive; to keep in existence; to retain; to maintain, keep up; to guard (game) against shooting or fishing by unauthorised persons; to keep sound; to keep from or guard against decay; to pickle, season, or otherwise treat (food) for keeping. — *n* preserved fruit or jam (often in *pl*); a place or water where shooting or fishing is preserved; anything regarded as closed or forbidden to outsiders. — *n* **preservabil'ity.** — *adj* **preserv'able.** — *n* **preservā'tion** (*prez-*). — *n* **preservā'tionist** a person who is interested in preserving traditional and historic things. — *adj* **preserv'ative** serving to preserve. — *n* a preserving agent, esp. a chemical added to food; a safeguard. — *adj* and *n* **preserv'atory.** — *n* **preserv'er.** — **preservation order** a legally binding directive ordering the preservation of a building deemed to be historically important; **preserv'ing-pan** a large pan usu. with a hooped handle and a lip, in which jams, etc. are made. — **well preserved** (*colloq*; of a person) not showing the signs of ageing one would expect in a person of such an age. [Fr. *préserver* — L. *prae*, *servāre*, to keep.]

preset *prē-set'*, *vt* to set beforehand. [**pre-** (2).]

pre-shrink *prē-shringk'*, *vt* to shrink (cloth) before it is made up into garments, etc. [**pre-** (2).]

preside *pri-zīd'*, *vi* to be in the position of authority or control (with *over* or *at*); to be at the head; to superintend; to be at the organ or piano (orig. as a kind of conductor). — *n* **presidency** (*prez'i-dən-si*) the office of a president, or their dignity, term of office, jurisdiction or residence. — *n* **pres'ident** a person who is chosen to preside over the meetings of a society, conference, etc.; the elected head of a republic; the head of a board, council or department of government; the title of the head of certain colleges, universities and other institutions; the head of an organisation generally (esp. *NAm*). — *adj* **presidential** (*-den'shl*) presiding; of a president or presidency. — **presiding officer** a person in charge of a polling-place. — **Lord President** the presiding judge of the Court of Session; **Lord President of the Council** a member of the House of Lords who presides over the privy council. [Fr. *présider* — L. *praesidēre* — *prae*, *sedēre*, to sit.]

presidial *pri-sid'i-əl*, *adj* pertaining to a garrison, a presidio or a president. — *n* **presid'io** (in Spanish-speaking countries) a military post or penal settlement: — *pl* **presid'ios.** — *n* **presid'ium** a standing committee in the Soviet system (also **praesidium**): — *pl* **presid'iums** or **presid'ia.** [L. *praesidium*, a garrison — *praesidēre*, to preside.]

press[1] *pres*, *vt* to exert a pushing force upon; to squeeze; to compress; to clasp; to thrust onwards or downwards; to squeeze out; to imprint, stamp or print; to flatten, condense, dry, shape or smooth by weight or other squeezing force; to put to death by application of heavy weights (*hist*); to bear heavily on; to harass; to beset; to urge strongly; to invite with persistent warmth; to offer urgently or abundantly (with *on* or *upon*); to throng, crowd; to present to the mind with earnestness; to lay stress upon; to hurry on with great speed; to raise to the shoulders and then lift above the head (*weightlifting*). — *vi* to exert pressure; to push with force; to crowd; to go forward with violence; to be urgent in application, entreaty or effort; to strive; to strain; to strive to do too much, to the loss of ease and effectiveness (*golf*). — *n* an apparatus for pressing, esp. one that produces solid articles from soft metal, clay, etc.; a printing-machine; newspapers and periodicals collectively; the journalistic profession; a printing organisation; often extended to a publishing house; printing activities; (with *cap*) a common name for a newspaper; (favourable or unfavourable) reception by newspapers and periodicals generally (also *fig*); an act of pressing; crowding; a crowd; a cupboard or shelved closet or recess. — *n* **press'er.** — *n* **press'ful.** — *n* **press'ing** the action of the verb *press*; an article, articles, esp. gramophone records, made from the same mould or press. — *adj* urgent; crowding. — *adv* **press'ingly.** — **press'-agent** someone who arranges for newspaper advertising and publicity, esp. for an actor or theatre; **press association** an association of newspapers formed to act as a news agency for the members of the association, each supplying local news, etc. to the association; (with *caps*) a British news agency formed as a press association in 1868; **press'-box** an erection provided for the use of reporters at sports, shows, etc.; **press conference** a meeting of a person in the public eye with the press for making an announcement or to answer questions; **press'-cutting** a paragraph or article cut out of a newspaper or magazine; **pressed glass** glass given shape and pattern by pressure in a mould; **press'-gallery** a reporters' gallery at a sports stadium, theatre, etc.; **press'man** a person who works a printing-press; a journalist or reporter; **press'-mark** a mark on a book to show its place in a library; **press'-proof** the last proof before printing; **press release** an official statement or report supplied to the press; **press'-room** a room where printing-presses are worked; a room for the use of journalists; **press'-stud** a form of button fastening in two parts, one of which is pressed into the other; **press'-up** a gymnastic exercise in which the prone body is kept rigid while being raised and lowered by straightening and bending the arms; **press'-work** the operation of a printing-press; printed matter; journalistic work. — **at press** or **in the press** in course of printing; about to be published; **freedom of the press** right of publishing material without submitting it to a government authority for permission; **go to press** to begin to print or to be printed; **press ahead, forward** or **on** to continue, esp. energetically, often in spite of difficulties or opposition; **press flesh** or **press the flesh** (*colloq*; orig. *US*) esp. of politicians, to shake hands, esp. with many people; **press of**

canvas or **sail** as much sail as can be carried; **the press** printed matter generally, esp. newspapers; journalists as a class. [Fr. *presser* — L. *pressāre* — *premĕre, pressum*, to press.]

press² *pres, vt* to carry off and force into service, esp. in the navy; to requisition; to turn to use in an unsuitable or provisional way. — *n* recruitment by force into service, esp. in the navy. — **press'-gang** a gang or body of sailors under an officer, empowered to forcibly recruit men into the navy. — Also *vt* (also *fig*).

pressie or **prezzie** *prez'i*, (*colloq*) *n* a present or gift.

pressor *pres'ər*, (*physiol*) *adj* causing an increase in blood pressure. [L.L., one who presses — *premĕre, pressum*, to press.]

pressure *presh'ər, n* the act of pressing or squeezing; the state of being pressed; constraining force or influence; that which presses or afflicts; urgency; a strong demand; a force directed towards the thing it acts upon, measured as so much weight upon a unit of area (*mech* and *phys*). — *vt* to compel by pressure (with *into*). — *n* **pressurisā'tion** or **-z-**. — *vt* **press'urise** or **-ize** (of an aeroplane, etc.) to fit with a device that maintains nearly normal atmospheric pressure; to subject to pressure; to force by pressure (into doing something). — **press'ure-cabin** a pressurised cabin in an aircraft. — *vt* **press'ure-cook** to cook in a pressure cooker. — **pressure cooker** a sealed pot in which food can be cooked more quickly than usual, using increased air pressure and above-boiling water temperatures; **pressure group** an organisation established in order to put pressure on a government for a particular purpose; **press'ure-helmet** a pilot's helmet for use with a pressure-suit; **pressure point** any of various points on the body on which pressure may be exerted to relieve pain, control bleeding, etc.; **pressure ridge** a ridge formed by lateral pressure in floating ice in polar waters; **press'ure-suit** an automatically inflating suit worn by pilots against pressure-cabin failure at very high altitudes. [L. *pressura* — *premĕre*, to press.]

Prestel® *pres'tel, n* the viewdata (q.v.) system of British Telecom.

prestidigitation *pres-ti-dij-i-tā'shən, n* sleight of hand. — *n* **prestidig'itātor**. [Fr. *prestidigitateur* — *preste*, nimble, L. *digitus*, finger.]

prestige *pres-tēzh', n* standing or reputation in people's minds owing to associations, influence, success, etc. — *adj* consisting in, or for the sake of, prestige; considered to have or give prestige; superior in quality, style, etc. — *adj* **prestigious** (*-tij'əs*) having prestige, esteemed. [Fr., — L. *praestigium*, delusion.]

presto *pres'tō*, (*mus*) *adj* (to be played) very fast. — *n* a presto movement or passage: — *pl* **pres'tos**. — *adv* quickly, quicker than *allegro*. — *adv* or *interj* (usu. **hey presto** as in conjuring tricks) at once. [It., — L. *praestō*, at hand.]

pre-stressed *prē-strest', adj* (of concrete) strengthened with stretched wires or rods instead of large steel bars as in reinforced concrete. [**pre-** (2).]

presume *pri-zūm', -zōōm'* or *-zh-, vt* to take as true without examination or proof; to take for granted; to assume provisionally; to take upon oneself, esp. with over-boldness. — *vi* to venture beyond what one has ground for; to act forwardly or without proper right; to rely or count (with *on* or *upon*), esp. unduly. — *adj* **presūm'able** that may be presumed or supposed to be true. — *adv* **presūm'ably**. — *adj* **presūm'ing** venturing without permission; unreasonably bold. — *conj* (often with *that*) making the presumption (that). — *n* **presumption** (*-zum'shən* or *-zump'shən*) the act of presuming; supposition; strong probability; that which is taken for granted; an assumption or belief based on facts or probable evidence; confidence grounded on something not proved; a ground or reason for presuming; arrogant or insolent conduct. — *adj* **presumptive** (*-zump'* or *-zum'tiv*) grounded on probable evidence; giving grounds for presuming. — *adj* **presumptuous** (*-zump'tū-əs* or *-zum'*) tending to presume, esp. boldly or arrogantly. — *adv* **presump'tuously**. — *n* **presump'tuousness**. [L. *praesūmĕre, -sūmptum* — *prae, sūmĕre*, to take — *sub*, under, *emĕre*, to buy.]

presuppose *prē-sə-pōz', vt* to assume or take for granted; to involve as a necessary antecedent. — *n* **presupposition** (*prē-sup-ə-zish'ən*). [**pre-** (2).]

pret. *abbrev* for preterite.

pre-tax *prē-taks', adj* (of profits, etc.) calculated before tax has been deducted. [**pre-** (2).]

pre-teen *prē-tēn', n* (usu. in *pl*) a child slightly younger than a teenager. — Also *adj*. [**pre-** (2).]

pretend *pri-tend', vt* to profess, now only falsely; to feign; to allege falsely; to make believe. — *vi* to make believe; to feign; to make a claim (with *to*); to aspire (with *to*). — *n* **pretence'** or in N.Am. **pretense'** an act of pretending; something pretended; an allegation; appearance or show to hide reality; false show; a false allegation; a pretext; claim. — *adj* **preten'ded**. — *n* **preten'der** a claimant, esp. to a throne; a candidate; a person who pretends. — *n* **preten'dership**. — *n* **preten'sion** pretence; show; pretext; a claim, esp. one that cannot be supported; aspiration, esp. to marriage; pretentiousness. — *adj* **preten'tious** (*-shəs*) giving a false appearance of importance or great worth; ostentatious. — *adv* **preten'tiously**. — *n* **preten'tiousness**. — **Old Pretender** and **Young Pretender** the son and grandson of James II and VII as claimants to the British throne. [L. *praetendĕre* — *prae, tendĕre, tentum, tēnsum*, to stretch.]

pre-tension *prē-ten'shən, vt* to stretch (the reinforcing wires or rods in pre-stressed concrete) before the concrete is cast. — *adj* **pre-ten'sioned**. [**pre-** (2).]

pretension, etc. See under **pretend**.

preter- *prē-tər-, combining form* meaning beyond. — *adj* **preternat'ural** out of the ordinary course of nature; abnormal; supernatural. [L. *praeter*.]

preterite or (esp. in N.Am.) **preterit** *pret'ə-rit, adj* denoting a tense of verbs used to signify past action. — *n* this tense of verbs (also called **preterite tense**); a word in the past tense. — **preterite-pres'ent** a verb which has an original preterite still preterite in form but present in meaning (now usually referrred to as a **modal verb** or **modal auxiliary**). — Also *adj*. [L. *praeteritus* — *īre, ĭtum*, to go.]

preterm *prē'tûrm, adj* (of a baby) born prematurely. [**pre-** (2).]

pretermit *prē-tər-mit', vt* to omit; to leave undone; to desist from for a time: — *pr p* **prētermitt'ing**; *pa t* and *pa p* **prētermitt'ed**. — *n* **pretermission** (*-mish'ən*). [L. *praetermittĕre, -missum* — *mittĕre*, to send.]

pretext *prē'tekst, n* an ostensible motive or reason, put forward as an excuse or to conceal the true one. [L. *praetextus, -ūs*, pretext, outward show, *praetextum*, pretext.]

pretty *prit'i, adj* (of a woman or child) having some superficial attractiveness but not striking beauty; attractive because of being small, neat, dainty or graceful; pleasing in a moderate way but not deeply; (esp. ironically) fine; insipidly graceful. — *n* a pretty thing or person; a knick-knack. — *adv* fairly. — *vt* to make pretty (with *up*). — *n* **prettificā'tion**. — *vt* **prett'ify** to make pretty in an excessively ornamental or over-delicate way. — *adv* **prett'ily** in a pretty manner; pleasingly; elegantly; neatly. — *n* **prett'iness**. — *adj* **pretty-prett'y** insipidly pretty, overpretty. — **a pretty penny** a large sum; **pretty much** very nearly; **pretty well** almost entirely; **sitting pretty** in an advantageous position. [O.E. *prættig*, tricky — *prætt*, trickery.]

pretzel *pret'səl, n* a crisp salted biscuit made in rope shape and twisted into a kind of loose knot. [Ger.]

prevail *pri-vāl', vi* to gain the victory (with *over* or *against*); to succeed; to have the upper hand; to urge successfully (with *on* or *upon*); to be usual or most usual; to hold good, be in use or be customary. — *adj* **prevail'ing** very general or common; most common; predominant. — *adv* **prevail'ingly.** — *n* **prevalence** (*prev'ə-ləns*) the state of being prevalent or widespread; superior strength or influence; preponderance. — *adj* **prev'alent** widespread; most common; prevailing; having great power; victorious. — *adv* **prev'alently.** [L. *praevalēre — prae, valēre*, to be powerful.]

prevaricate *pri-var'i-kāt, vi* to evade the truth; to act so as to mislead or deceive; to quibble. — *n* **prevaricā'tion.** — *n* **prevar'icātor.** [L. *praevāricārī, -ātus*, to walk straddlingly or crookedly, to act collusively — *prae, vāricus*, straddling — *vārus*, bent.]

prevent *pri-vent', vt* to stop, keep or hinder effectually; to keep from coming to pass; to balk; to preclude. — *n* **prevē'nience.** — *adj* **prevē'nient** antecedent; predisposing; preventive. — *n* **preventabil'ity.** — *adj* **preven'table** or **prevent'ible.** — *n* **preven'ter.** — *n* **preven'tion** the act of preventing; anticipation or forethought; obstruction. — *adj* **preven'tive** (also, irregularly, **preven'tative**) tending to prevent or hinder; prophylactic. — *n* that which prevents; a prophylactic. — **preventive detention** specially prolonged imprisonment for persistent offenders of 30 or over for periods of from 5 to 14 years. [L. *praevenīre, -ventum — venīre*, to come.]

preverb *prē'vûrb*, (*linguis*) *n* a particle or prefix which precedes a verb or verb-root. — *adj* **prever'bal** occurring or standing before a verb; pertaining to a time before the development of speech. [**pre-** (2).]

preview *prē'vū, n* a view of a performance, exhibition, etc., before it is open to the public; an advance showing to the public of excerpts from a film, play, etc. (also in N.Am. **pre'vue**). — *vt* (*prē-vū'*) to view in advance of public performance or exhibition; (*prē'vū*) to give a preview of. [**pre-** (2).]

previous *prē'vi-əs, adj* going before in time; former; premature (*facetious*). — *adv* previously (usu. with *to*). — *adv* **prē'viously.** — *n* **prē'viousness.** — **previous question** (in the House of Commons) a motion to end the present debate before a vote takes place; (in the House of Lords and U.S. assemblies) a motion to vote without delay on the matter presently under debate. [L. *praevius — prae, via*, a way.]

previse *prē-vīz'*, (*literary*) *vt* to foresee; to forewarn. — *n* **prevision** (*-vizh'ən*) foresight; foreknowledge. [L. *praevidēre, -vīsum — prae, vidēre*, to see.]

pre-war *prē-wör', adj* and *adv* (which happened, etc.) before a (particular) war, esp. the First or Second World War. [**pre-** (2).]

pre-warn *prē-wörn', vt* to warn in advance. [**pre-** (2).]

pre-wash *prē'-wosh, n* a preliminary wash before the main wash, esp. in a washing-machine; an instruction setting for this on an automatic washing-machine. [**pre-** (2).]

prey *prā, n* an animal that is, or may be, killed and eaten by another; a victim (with *to*). — *vi* (commonly with *on* or *upon*) to seek, kill and feed; to live (on) as a victim; to have a distressing or otherwise harmful effect. — **beast** and **bird of prey** one that devours other creatures. [O.Fr. *preie* (Fr. *proie*) — L. *praeda*, booty.]

prezzie. See **pressie.**

prial. See **pair-royal.**

Priapus *prī-ā'pəs, n* an ancient deity personifying male generative power, the guardian of gardens, later regarded as the chief god of lasciviousness and sensuality. — *adj* **Priapean** (*prī-ə-pē'ən*) or **Priapic** (*-ap'ik*) of or relating to Priapus; (without *cap*) of, relating to, exhibiting, etc. a phallus; (without *cap*) overly concerned or preoccupied with virility and male sexuality. — *n* **prī'apism** persistent painful erection of the penis (*pathol*); licentiousness, lewdness. [Latinised from Gr. *Priāpos.*]

price *prīs, n* the amount, usually in money, for which a thing is sold or offered; that which one forgoes or suffers for the sake of or in gaining something; money offered for the capture or killing of anybody; (the size of) the sum, etc. by which one can be bribed; betting odds. — *vt* to fix, state or mark the price of; to ask the price of (*colloq*). — *adj* **priced** having a price assigned; valued at a (particular) price. — *adj* **price'less** beyond price; invaluable; supremely and delectably absurd. — *adv* **price'lessly.** — *n* **price'lessness.** — *n* **pric'er.** — *adj* **pric'ey** or **pric'y** (*colloq*; *compar* **prī'cier**, *superl* **prī'ciest**) expensive. — *n* **prī'ciness.** — **price control** the fixing by a government of maximum, or sometimes minimum, prices chargeable for goods or services; **price'-fixing** the establishing of the price of a commodity, etc. by agreement between suppliers or by government price control, rather than by the operation of a free market; **price index** an index number which relates current prices to those of a base period or base date, the latter usu. being assigned the value of 100; **price'-list** a list of prices of goods offered for sale; **price ring** a group of manufacturers who co-operate for the purpose of raising or maintaining the price of a commodity above the level that would be established by a free market; **price'-tag** a tag or the like attached to an article showing its price (also *fig*). — **above** or **beyond price** so valuable that no price can or would be enough; **at a price** at a somewhat high price; **of price** of great value; **price-earnings ratio** the ratio of the market price of a common stock share to its earnings; **price of money** the rate of discount in lending or borrowing capital; **price oneself out of the market** to charge more than customers or clients are willing to pay; **price on one's head** reward for one's capture or slaughter; **what price — ?** what is the chance of (this or that) happening now?; **without price** priceless; without anything to pay. [O.Fr. *pris* (Fr. *prix*) — L. *pretium*, price.]

prick *prik, n* anything sharp and piercing, such as a thorn, spine, etc.; the act, experience or stimulus of piercing or puncturing; a puncture; a mark or wound made by puncturing; a hare's footprint; a penis (*vulg*); a term of abuse used of a person one dislikes or thinks a fool (*vulg*). — *vt* to pierce slightly with a fine point; to give a feeling as of pricking, esp. a sharp emotional distress; to make by puncturing; to urge with, or as with, a spur or goad; to trace with pricks; to insert (e.g. seedlings) in small holes (usu. with *in*, *out*, etc.); to stick, stick over; to erect, cock, stick up (sometimes with *up*). — *vi* to pierce, make punctures; to have a sensation of puncture or prickling; to begin to turn sour; to stand erect. — *n* **prick'er.** — *n* **prick'ing.** — *n* **prickle** (*prik'l*) a little prick; a sharp point growing from the epidermis of a plant or from the skin of an animal. — *vt* and *vi* to prick slightly. — *vi* to have a prickly feeling. — *n* **prick'liness.** — *n* and *adj* **prick'ling.** — *adj* **prick'ly** full of prickles; tingling as if prickled; easily annoyed. — *adj* **prick'-eared** having erect or noticeable ears. — **prick'ly-heat** a skin disease, inflammation of the sweat-glands with intense irritation; **prick'ly-pear** a cactaceous genus of plants with clusters of prickles; the pear-shaped fruits they produce. — **kick against the pricks** to hurt oneself by resisting someone or something, to no avail (from the Bible: Acts ix. 5); **prick up one's ears** to begin to listen intently. [O.E. *prica*, point.]

pride *prīd, n* the state or feeling of being proud; too great self-esteem; haughtiness; a proper sense of what is becoming to oneself and scorn of what is unworthy; a feeling of pleasure on account of something worthily done or anything connected with oneself; that of which one is proud; a peacock's attitude of display; a group of lions. — *vt* (*reflexive*) to take pride in (with *on*). — **pride of place** the culmination of an eagle's or hawk's flight; the distinction of holding the highest position; **take pride** or **take a pride in** to make (a thing) an object of which one can be proud. [O.E. *prȳde, prȳte* — *prūd, prūt*, proud.]

pried. See **pry**.

prie-dieu *prē'-dyø, n* a praying-desk or chair for praying on. [Fr., pray-God.]

pries, prier. See **pry**.

priest *prēst, n* an official conductor of rites in any religion; a mediator between a god and worshippers (*Christian relig*); (in Episcopal churches) a minister above a deacon and below a bishop. — *n* **priest'-craft** priestly policy directed to worldly ends. — *n fem* **priest'ess** (becoming *old-fashioned*) a woman priest. — *n* **priest'hood** the office or character of a priest; the priestly order. — *adj* **priest'ly** pertaining to or like a priest. — **priest's hole** or **priest hole** a secret room for a priest in time of persecution or repression. [O.E. *prēost* — L. *presbyter* — Gr. *presbyteros*, an elder.]

prig *prig, n* a conceited person who is over-precise in regard to morals, speech, manners, etc. — *n* **prigg'-ery**. — *adj* **prigg'ish**. — *adv* **prigg'ishly**. — *n* **prigg'ishness**.

prill *pril, vt* to turn into pellet form, e.g. by melting and letting the drops solidify in falling. — *n* a pellet, or pelleted material, formed by prilling. [Orig. a Cornish mining term.]

prim[1] *prim, adj* exact and precise; stiffly formal; over-modest. — *vt* to decorate with great nicety; to form, set or purse (esp. the mouth) into primness. — *vi* to look prim; to prim the mouth: — *pr p* **primm'ing**; *pa t* and *pa p* **primmed**. — *adv* **prim'ly**. — *n* **prim'ness**. [Late 17th-cent. cant.]

prim[2] *prim*, (*med colloq*) *n* contraction of **primi-gravida** (q.v.), as in **elderly prim** (one of 30 and over).

prima. See **primo**.

primacy *prī'mə-si, n* (the state of being in) the position which is first in importance, rank, etc.; the office or dignity of a primate.

primaeval. Same as **primeval**.

prima facie *prī'mə fāsh'ē* or *prē'mä fak'i-ā*, (L.) on the first view; at first sight; (of evidence) sufficient to support the bringing of a charge (*law*); (of a case) supported by prima facie evidence (*law*).

primal. See **prime**[1].

primary *prī'mə-ri, adj* first; original; of the first order (e.g. in a system of successive branchings) first-formed; primitive; chief; fundamental; belonging to the first stages of education, elementary; (of a feather) growing on the manus; relating to primaries (*US politics*); (with *cap*) Palaeozoic (*geol*). — *n* that which is highest in rank or importance; a primary school; a primary feather; a substance obtained directly, by extraction and purification e.g. from natural, or crude technical, raw material — cf. *intermediate*; a meeting of the voters of a political party in an electoral division e.g. to nominate candidates, or to elect delegates to a nominating convention representing a larger area (*US politics*). — *adv* **prī'marily**. — *n* **prī'mariness**. — **primary battery** or **cell** one producing an electric current by irreversible chemical action; **primary colours** those from which all others can be derived — physiologically red, green, violet or blue — for pigments, red, yellow, blue, which can be mixed to produce any other colour; also red, orange, yellow, green, blue, indigo and violet; **primary planet** a planet distinguished from a satellite. [L. *prīmārius* — *prīmus*, first.]

primate *prī'māt* or *-mit, n* a bishop or archbishop to whose see was formerly annexed the dignity of vicar of the holy see (*RC*); an archbishop over a province (*C of E*); a member of the order Primates (*zool*). — *npl* **Primates** (*prī-mā'tēz*) the highest order of mammals, including lemurs, monkeys, anthropoid apes, and man. — *n* **pri'mateship**. — *n* **prima-tol'ogist**. — *n* **primatol'ogy** the study of the Primates. [L.L. *prīmās, -ātis* — L. *prīmus*, first.]

prime[1] *prīm, adj* first in order of time, rank or importance; primary; chief; main; of the highest quality; (of the time of broadcasting of a radio or television programme) occurring during peak viewing or listening time and (therefore) having the highest advertising rates; (of a number other than one) divisible by no whole number except unity and itself (*arith*); (of two or more numbers) relatively prime (with *to*; *arith*). — *n* the height of perfection; full health and strength; the best part; a prime number; a first subdivision or symbol marking it (*math*, etc.); the beginning; the first hour of the day, esp. when considered an hour of prayer, usually 6 a.m., but sometimes sunrise at any hour; the first guard against sword-thrusts, also the first and simplest thrust (*fencing*). — *adj* **prī'mal** first; primitive; original; chief, fundamental. — **prime lending rate** or **prime rate** the lowest rate of interest charged by a bank at any given time, usu. available only to large concerns with high credit ratings, and forming the base figure on which other rates are calculated; **prime meridian** that chosen as zero for reference; **prime minister** the chief minister of state; **prime mover** the main cause or instigator of an action, project, etc. (*fig*); **prime number** a number, other than one, divisible only by itself or unity. — *adj* **prime'-time** pertaining to prime time (see **prime** *adj* above). — **relatively prime** (*arith*) having no common integral factor but unity. [L. *prīmus*, first; partly through O.E. *prīm* — L. *prīma* (*hōra*), first (hour).]

prime[2] *prīm, vt* to charge or fill; to supply with powder or other means of igniting the charge (of a firearm, bomb, etc.); to bring into activity or working order by a preliminary charge (as a man by giving him liquor, a pump by pouring in water, an internal-combustion engine by injecting gas or oil); to coach or cram beforehand with information or instructions; to put on a primer in painting. — *vi* to prime a gun; (of a boiler) to send water with the steam into the cylinder (of the tides) to recur at progressively shorter intervals. — *n* **prī'mer** a person who primes; a priming-wire; a detonator; a preparatory first coat of paint, etc.; the particular type of paint used for this. — *n* **prī'ming** the action of the verb in any sense; the progressive shortening of the interval between tides as spring tide approaches; a detonating charge that fires a propellant charge; a tube for priming an internal-combustion engine; a priming-wire; a first coat of paint. — **prī'ming-iron** or **-wire** (*hist*) a wire passed through the touch-hole of a cannon to clear it and pierce the cartridge; **prī'ming-powder** detonating powder; a train of powder.

primer *prī'mər* or *prim'ər, n* a first reading-book; an elementary introduction to any subject. [L. *prīmārius*, primary.]

primeval or **primaeval** *prī-mē'vl, adj* belonging to the first ages of the world. [L. *prīmaevus* — *prīmus*, first, *aevum*, an age.]

primigravida *prī-mi-grav'i-də*, (*obstetrics*) *n* a woman pregnant for the first time: — *pl* **primigrav'idae** (*-dē*) or **primigrav'idas**. — See also **prim**[2]. [L. fem. adjectives *prīma*, first, *gravida*, pregnant.]

primipara *prī-mip'ə-rə*, (*obstetrics*) *n* a woman who has given birth for the first time only, or is about to do so: — *pl* **primip'arae** (*-rē*) or **primip'aras**. [L. *prīma* (fem.), first, *parĕre*, to bring forth.]

primitiae *prī-mish'i-ē*, (*formal* or *relig*) *npl* first-fruits; the first year's revenue from a benefice. — *adj* **primitial** (*-mish'l*) of first-fruits; (*loosely*) primeval, original. [L. *prīmitiae* — *prīmus*, first.]

primitive *prim'i-tiv*, *adj* belonging to the beginning, or to the first times; crude; first-formed, of early origin (*biol*); (of a culture or society) not advanced, lacking a written language and having only fairly simple technical skills; not derivative (*linguis*). — *n* that from which other things are derived; a root-word; a painter or picture of pre-Renaissance date or manner; a 19th- and 20th-century school of painting, characterised by a complete simplicity of approach to subject and technique. — *adv* **prim'itively**. — *n* **prim'itiveness**. — *n* **prim'itivism** approbation of primitive ways, primitive Christianity, primitive art, etc. — *n* **prim'itivist**. [L. *prīmitīvus*, an extension of *prīmus*.]

primo *prē'mō*, *adj*, *fem* **pri'ma** first. — *n* **pri'mo** (*mus*) the first or principal part in a duet or trio: — *pl* **pri'mos**. — **prima ballerina** (*bal-ə-rēn'ə* or It. *ba-le-rē'na*) the leading ballerina: — *pl* **prima ballerinas** or **prime** (*-ā*) **ballerine; prima donna** (*don'ə* or It. *don'na*) the leading female singer in an opera company; a person, esp. a woman, who is temperamental, over-sensitive and hard to please: — *pl* **prima donnas** or **prime** (*-ā*) **donne**. [It., — L. *prīmus*.]

primogeniture *prī-mō-jen'i-tūr*, *n* the state or fact of being first-born; inheritance by or of the first-born child or (*male primogeniture*) son. [L. *prīmōgenitus* — *prīmō*, first (adv.), *genitus*, born.]

primordial *prī-mör'di-əl*, *adj* existing from the beginning; original; rudimentary; first-formed. — *n* the first principle or element. — *n* **primordiality** (*-al'i-ti*). — *adv* **primor'dially**. [L. *prīmordium* — *prīmus*, first, *ordīrī*, to begin.]

primp *primp*, *vi* to dress in a fussy or affected manner. — *vt* (*reflexive*) to preen or titivate (oneself). [Connected with **prim**.]

primrose *prim'rōz*, *n* a temperate plant, or its pale yellow flower, common in spring in woods and meadows; extended to others of the genus *Primula*. — *adj* pale yellow, like a primrose. [O.Fr. *primerose*, as if — L. *prīma rosa*; perh. really through M.E. and O.Fr. *primerole* — L.L. *prīmula* — *prīmus*, first.]

primula *prim'ū-lə*, *n* a plant of the *Primula* genus of flowers including the primrose, cowslip, oxlip, etc. [L.L., little first one or firstling, — L. *prīmus*, first.]

Primus® *prī'məs*, *n* a portable cooking stove burning vaporised oil. — Also **Primus stove**.

primus[1] *prī'məs* or *prē'mŏŏs*, *n* a presiding bishop in the Scottish Episcopal Church. [L., first.]

primus[2] *prī'məs* or *prē'mŏŏs*, (L.) *n* first. — **primus inter pares** (*in'tər pār'ēz* or *pär'ās*) first among equals.

prin. *abbrev* for principal.

prince *prins*, *n* a non-reigning male member of a royal or imperial family; a sovereign (of some small countries); a title of nobility, as formerly in Germany (*Fürst*); a person of the highest rank; a chief; anybody or anything that is first in merit or demerit, or most outstanding. — *n* **prince'dom** a principality; the estate, jurisdiction, sovereignty or rank of a prince. — *adj* **prince'like** like a prince; becoming a prince. — *n* **prince'liness**. — *n* **prince'ling** a young or petty prince; the ruler of some minor principality. — *adj* **prince'ly** of a prince or princess; of the rank of prince; princelike; becoming a prince; magnificent; sumptuous; lavish. — Also *adv*. — *n* **prin'cess** (or *-ses'*) a non-reigning female member of a royal or imperial family; a prince's wife (of recognised rank); a woman outstanding in some way, esp. an extremely beautiful woman; a woman's garment with skirt and bodice in one piece — in this sense also (Fr.) **princesse** (*prin'* or *-ses'*) or **princess-dress** or **-skirt**, the style being known as **princess line**. — **prince-con'sort** a prince who is husband of a reigning queen; **princess-roy'al** a title which may be conferred on the eldest daughter of a sovereign. — **prince of darkness** or **prince of this world** Satan; **Prince of Peace** Christ; the Messiah; **Prince of Wales** since 1301, a title usu. conferred on the eldest son of the English, and later British, sovereign. [Fr., — L. *prīnceps* — *prīmus*, first, *capĕre*, to take.]

principal *prin'si-pl*, *adj* taking the first place; highest in rank, character or importance; chief; of the nature of principal or a principal. — *n* a principal person; the head of a college or university, or sometimes of a school; a person who takes a leading part; money on which interest is paid; a main beam, rafter, girder or timber; the person who commits a crime, or one who aids and abets another in doing it (*law*); a person for whom another becomes surety (*law*); a person who employs another to act as their agent (*law*); an actor who takes the leading role in a play; an organ-stop like the open diapason but an octave higher (*mus*). — *n* **principality** (*-pal'i-ti*) the territory of a prince or the country that gives him title; the status, dignity or power of a prince; the condition of being a prince. — *adv* **prin'cipally**. — *n* **prin'cipalship**. — **principal boy** (*theat*) an actress (now sometimes an actor) who plays the role of the hero in pantomime; **principal clause** (*gram*) a clause which could function as an independent sentence; **principal parts** (*gram*) those forms (of a verb) from which all other forms may be deduced. [L. *prīncipālis* — *prīnceps*, *-ipis*, chief.]

principate *prin'si-pāt*, *n* princehood; principality; the Roman empire in its earlier form in which something of republican theory survived. [L. *prīncipātus* — the emperor's title *prīnceps* (*cīvitātis*), chief (of the city or state).]

principle *prin'si-pl*, *n* consistent regulation of behaviour according to moral law; a law or doctrine from which others are derived; a theoretical basis; a fundamental truth on which others are founded or from which they spring; that which is fundamental; a source, root, origin; essential nature; a constituent part from which some quality is derived (*chem*). — *adj* **prin'cipled** holding certain principles; having, or behaving in accordance with, good principles; invoking or founded on a principle. — **first principles** fundamental principles, not deduced from others; **in principle** so far as general character or theory is concerned without respect to details or particular application; in theory; **on principle** on grounds of principle; for the sake of obeying or asserting a principle. [L. *prīncipium*, beginning — *prīnceps*.]

prink *pringk*, *vt* (*reflexive*) and *vi* to dress (oneself) up, to smarten (oneself). [App. connected with archaic *prank*, to dress showily.]

print *print*, *n* an impression; a mould or stamp; printed state; printed characters or lettering; an edition; a printed copy; a printed picture; an engraving; printed matter, esp. newspapers or books; a positive photograph made from a negative (or negative from positive); a printed cloth, esp. calico stamped with figures; a plaster cast in low relief (*archit*); a fingerprint. — *adj* of printed cotton. — *vt* to impress on paper, etc., by means of types, plates or blocks; to produce or reproduce by such means; to cause to be so printed; to stamp a pattern on or transfer it to; to mark by pressure; to produce as a positive picture from a negative, or as a negative from a positive (*phot*); to write in imitation of type. — *vi* to practise the art or business of printing; to publish a book; to yield an impression, or give a positive, etc. — *adj* **print'able** capable of being printed; fit to print. — *n* **print'er** someone who or that which prints; a person who is employed in printing books, etc.; a device for printing e.g. telegraph messages, photographs, the output from a computer, etc. — *n* **print'ing** the act, art or business of the printer; the whole number of copies printed at one time, an impression. — **printed circuit** a wiring circuit, free of loose wiring, formed by printing the design of the wiring on copper foil bonded to a flat base and etching away the unprinted foil (**printed circuit board** the combined circuit and supporting base); **printer's mark** an engraved device used by printers as a trademark; **print'ing-house** a building where printing is carried on; a printing-office; **print'ing-ink** ink used in printing — a usually thickish mixture of pigment (as carbon black) with oil and sometimes varnish; **print'ing-machine** a printing-press worked by power; **print'-ing-office** an establishment where books, etc. are printed; **print'ing-press** a machine by which impressions are taken in ink upon paper from types, plates, etc.; **print'-out** the printed information given out by a computer, etc.; **print'-run** a single printing of a book, etc. — **in print** existing in printed form; printed and still to be had; **out of print** no longer in print; no longer available from a publisher; **print out** to produce a print-out of. [M.E. *print*, *prente*, etc. — O.Fr. *preinte*, *priente* — *preindre*, *priembre* — L. *premĕre*, to press.]

prion *prī'on*, *n* any petrel of the genus *Pachyptila*, blue-grey above and white below, feeding on the plankton of the southern oceans. [Gr. *priōn*, a saw.]

prior *prī'ər*, *adj* previous. — *adv* previously, before (with *to*). — *n* the officer next under the abbot in an abbey (*claustral prior*); the head of a priory of monks (*conventual prior*) or of a house of canons regular or of friars. — *n* (*fem*) **prī'oress** the officer next under the abbess in an abbey; the head of a priory of nuns. — *n* **prioritisa'tion** or **-z-**. — *vt* and *vi* **prior'itise** or **-ize** to arrange, deal with, etc. according to priority (importance, urgency, etc.). — *n* **priority** (*prī-or'i-ti*) the state of being first in time, place or rank; preference; the privilege of preferential treatment; something that ought to be considered, dealt with, etc. in the earliest stage of proceedings. — *adj* having, entitling to, or allowed to those who have priority. — *n* **prī'orship** the office or tenure of office of a prior. — *n* **prī'ory** a convent of either sex subject to an abbey. [L. *prĭor*, *-ōris*, former.]

prise. See **prize**[1].

prism *prizm*, *n* a solid whose ends are similar, equal and parallel polygons, and whose sides are parallelograms (*geom*); an object of that shape, esp. a triangular prism of glass or the like for resolving light into separate colours; (*loosely*) prismatic colours or spectrum. — *adj* **prismat'ic** resembling or pertaining to a prism; built up of prisms; separated or formed by a prism. — *n* **pris'moid** a figure like a prism, but with similar unequal ends. — **prismatic colours** the seven colours into which a ray of white light is refracted by a prism — red, orange, yellow, green, blue, indigo and violet; **prismatic compass** a surveying instrument which by means of a prism enables the compass-reading to be taken as the object is sighted. [Gr. *prīsma*, *-atos*, a piece sawn off.]

prison *priz'n*, *n* a building for the confinement of criminals or others; a jail; any place of confinement; confinement. — *vt* (*poetic*) to imprison. — *n* **pris'-oner** a person under arrest or confined in prison; a captive, esp. in war; anyone involuntarily kept under restraint. — **prison officer** the official title of a warder (still so-called unofficially) in prison. — **prisoner of conscience** see under **conscience**; **prisoner of war** a person captured during a war, esp. a member of the armed forces, but also including militia, irregular troops and, under certain conditions, civilians; **take prisoner** to capture. [O.Fr. *prisun* — L. *prēnsiō*, *-ōnis*, for *praehēnsiō*, seizure — *praehendĕre*, *-hēnsum*, to seize.]

prissy *pris'i*, *adj* prim, prudish, fussy; effeminate. [Prob. **prim** and **cissy**.]

pristine *pris'tīn* or *-tēn*, *adj* original; former; belonging to the earliest time; pure, unspoilt, unchanged. [L. *prīstinus*.]

privacy *priv'ə-si* or *prīv'*, *n* avoidance of notice or display; seclusion; secrecy. [**private**.]

private *prī'vit*, *adj* relating to personal affairs; not public; not made known generally; confidential; peculiar to oneself; not open to the public; retired from observation; belonging to, or concerning, an individual person or company; not part of, not receiving treatment under, etc. the National Health Service or any similar state scheme; independent; own; (of a member of parliament) not holding government office; (of a soldier) not an officer or non-commissioned officer. — *n* privacy; (in *pl*) private parts; a private soldier. — *adv* **prī'vately**. — *n* **privatisā'tion** or **-z-**. — *vt* **prī'vatise** or **-ize** to transfer from ownership by the state into private ownership; to denationalise. — *n* **prī'vatiser** or **-z-**. — **private company** a company, with restrictions on the number of shareholders, whose shares may not be offered to the general public; **private detective** see **detective** under **detect**; **private enterprise** an economic system in which individual private firms operate and compete freely; **private eye** (*colloq*) a private detective; **private income** private means, not wages; **private investigator** (esp. *NAm*) a private detective; **private means** income from investments, etc. as opposed to salary or fees for work done; **private parts** (*euph*) the external sexual organs; **private school** a school run independently of the state by an individual or a group, especially for profit; **private sector** the part of a country's economy owned, operated, etc. by private individuals and firms (opp. to *public sector*). — **in private** not in public; away from public view; secretly; **private member's bill** one introduced and sponsored by a private member in parliament. [L. *prīvātus*, past p. of *prīvāre*, to deprive, to separate.]

privateer *prī-və-tēr'*, *n* a private vessel commissioned by a government to seize and plunder an enemy's ships in time of war; the commander or one of the crew of a privateer. — *vi* to serve as a privateer. — *n* **privateer'ing**. — *n* **privateers'man** a crew member on a privateer. [**private**.]

privation *prī-vā'shən*, *n* the state of being deprived of something, esp. of what is necessary for comfort; the absence of any quality. — *adj* **privative** (*priv'ə-tiv*) causing privation; consisting in the absence or removal of something; expressing absence or negation (*gram*). — *n* that which is privative or depends on the absence of something else; a term denoting the absence of a quality (*logic*); a privative affix or word (*gram*). — *adv* **priv'atively**. [L. *prīvātiō*, *-ōnis*, *prīvātivus* — *prīvāre*, to deprive.]

privet *priv'it*, *n* European shrub of the olive family, used for hedges; also applied to other members of the genus *Lingustrum*.

privilege *priv'i-lij*, *n* an advantage, right or favour granted to or enjoyed by an individual, or a few; a happy advantage; a prerogative; a sacred and vital civil right. — *vt* to grant a privilege to; to exempt (with *from*); to authorise, license. — *adj* **priv'ileged**. — **breach of privilege** any interference with or slight done to the rights or privileges of a legislative body; **privilege of parliament** or **parliamentary privilege** special rights or privileges enjoyed by members of parliament, as freedom of speech (not subject to slander laws), and freedom from arrest except on a criminal charge. [Fr. *privilège* — L. *prīvilēgium* — *prīvus*, private, *lēx*, *lēgis*, a law.]

privy *priv'i*, *adj* sharing the knowledge of something secret (with *to*). — *n* a person having an interest in an action, contract, conveyance, etc. (*law*); a lavatory, esp. one in an outhouse (*old-fashioned*). — *adv* **priv'ily** (*literary*) privately; secretly. — **privy council** (also with *caps*) originally the private council of a sovereign to advise in the administration of government — its membership now consisting of all present and past members of the Cabinet and other eminent people, but with its functions mainly formal or performed by committees, etc.; **privy councillor** or **counsellor** (also with *caps*); **privy purse** (also with *caps*) an allowance for the private or personal use of the sovereign; **privy seal** see under **seal**[1]. — **Lord Privy Seal** see under **seal**[1]. [Fr. *privé* — L. *prīvātus*, private.]

prize[1] or **prise** *prīz*, *vt* to force (with *up* or *open*) with a lever (also *fig*; with *out*). [Fr. *prise*, hold, grip.]

prize[2] *prīz*, *n* something that is taken by force, or in war, esp. a ship. — *vt* to make a prize of. [Fr. *prise*, capture, thing captured — L. *praehēnsa* — *praehendĕre*, to seize.]

prize[3] *prīz*, *n* a reward or symbol of success offered or won in a competition by contest or chance, or granted in recognition of excellence; anything well worth striving for; a highly valued acquisition. — *adj* awarded, or worthy of, a prize. — *vt* to value highly. — *adj* **prized** considered or valued highly. — **prize'list** a list of winners; **prize'-winner**. [A differentiated form of **price** and **praise** — O.Fr. *pris*, *prisier* — L. *pretium*, price.]

prize[4] *prīz*, *n* (*old-fashioned*) a match. — **prize'-fight** a public boxing-match for money; **prize'-fighter** a professional boxer; orig. someone who fights in a prize; **prize'-fighting**. [Possibly from **prize**[3].]

PRO *abbrev* for: Public Records Office; public relations officer.

pro[1] *prō*, (L.) *prep* for. — **pro bono publico** (*bo'nō pub'li-kō* or *bō'nō pōō'bli-kō*) for the public good; **pro forma** (*fōr'mə*) as a matter of form; (also with *hyphen*) of an account, etc., made out to show the market price of specified goods; with goods being paid for before dispatch. — *n* a pro forma invoice; (*loosely*) an official form or record for completion. — Also **profor'ma**. — **pro patria** (*pā'tri-ə* or *pä'tri-ä*) for one's country; **pro rata** (*rā'tə* or *rä'tä*) in proportion; **pro tempore** (*tem'pə-rē* or *tem'po-re*) for the time being.

pro[2] *prō*, *n* a colloq. contraction of **professional** (golfer, cricketer, actor, etc.), of **probationary** (nurse), and of **prostitute**: — *pl* **pros** (*prōz*). — *adj* of or pertaining to a pro or pros. — *adj* **pro-am'** involving both professionals and amateurs. — Also *n*.

pro[3] *prō*, *n* a person who favours or votes for some proposal; a reason or argument in favour: — *pl* **pros** (*prōz*). — **pros and cons** reasons or arguments for and against. [L. *prō*, for.]

pro-[1] *prō*, *pfx* signifying: before (in time or place); earlier than; in front of; the front part of; primitive; rudimentary. [Gr. prep. *prŏ*, before; cf. L. *prō*, Eng. **for** and **fore**.]

pro-[2] *prō*, *pfx* used: (1) as an etymological element with the senses before (in place or time), forward, forth, publicly; (2) as a living pfx. with the sense instead of, in place of, acting on behalf of; (3) as a living pfx. (in new formations) with the sense in favour of — as in *pro-Boer*, *pro-German*, *pro-slavery*. [L. prep. *prō*, earlier *prōd*, in compar. sometimes *prŏ*-; cf. **pro-**[1].]

proa. See **prau**.

pro-active *prō-ak'tiv*, *adj* taking or ready to take the initiative, acting without being prompted by others (*loosely* opp. to *reactive*). [**pro-**[1] and **active**.]

pro-am. See **pro**[2].

prob. *abbrev* for probably.

probable *prob'ə-bl*, *adj* having more evidence for than against; giving ground for belief; likely; plausible. — *n* probable opinion; a candidate, etc. who has a good chance of success, selection, etc. — *n* **probabil'ity** the quality of being probable; the appearance of truth; that which is probable; the chance or likelihood of something happening: — *pl* **probabil'ities**. — *adv* **prob'ably**. — **in all probability** quite probably. [Fr., — L. *probābilis* — *probāre*, *-ātum*, to prove.]

probang *prō'bang*, (*med*) *n* an instrument for pushing obstructions down the oesophagus. [Called *provang* by its inventor; prob. influenced by **probe**.]

probate *prō'bāt* or *-bit*, (*law*) *n* the proof before a competent court that a written paper purporting to be the will of a person who has died is indeed their lawful act; the official copy of a will, with the certificate of its having been proved lawful. — *adj* relating to the establishment of wills and testaments. — *vt* (*NAm*) to establish the validity of (a will) by probate; to place a probate on; to place a probation sentence on. — *n* **probation** (*prə-* or *prō-bā'shən*) testing; proof; suspension of prison sentence, allowing liberty under supervision on condition of good behaviour (esp. to young, or first offenders); a preliminary time or condition appointed to allow fitness or unfitness for a job, position, etc. to appear; noviciate. — *adj* **probā'tional** relating to or serving the purpose of probation or trial. — *adj* **probā'tionary** probational; on probation. — *n* a probationer. — *n* **probā'tioner** a person who is on probation or trial; an offender under probation; a novice; a person licensed to preach, but not ordained to a pastorate (esp. *Scot*). — *n* **probā'tionership**. — *adj* **probative** (*prō'bə-tiv*) testing; affording proof. — **probation officer** one appointed to advise and supervise offenders under probation. [L. *probāre*, *-ātum*, to test, prove.]

probe *prōb*, *n* an instrument for exploring a wound, locating a bullet, and the like; an act of probing; an exploratory bore; a prod; a thorough investigation; any of various instruments of investigation in space research (as a multi-stage rocket), electronics, etc.; a pipelike device attached to an aircraft for making connection with a tanker aeroplane so as to refuel in flight; a device used in docking two space modules. — *vt* to examine with or as with a probe; to examine searchingly. — *vt* and *vi* to pierce. [L. *proba*, proof, later examination — *probāre*, to prove.]

probit *prō'bit*, (*statistics*) *n* a unit for measuring probability in relation to an average frequency distribution. [*Prob*ability un*it*.]

probity *prob'i-ti* or *prōb'*, *n* uprightness; moral integrity; honesty. [L. *probitās*, *-ātis* — *probus*, good, honest.]

problem *prob'ləm*, *n* a matter difficult to settle or solve; a question or puzzle propounded for solution; a source of perplexity. — *adj* **problemat'ic** or **problemat'ical** of the nature of a problem; questionable. — *adv* **problemat'ically**. — **problem child** one whose character presents an exceptionally difficult problem to parents, teachers, etc. [Gr. *problēma*, *-atos* — *pro*, before, *ballein*, to throw.]

proboscis *prə-* or *prō-bos'is*, *n* a trunk or long snout; a trunk-like process, such as the suctorial mouth-parts of some insects; a nose (*facetious*): — *pl* **probosc'ises** or **probosc'ides** (*-i-dēz*). — *npl* **Proboscid'ea** the elephant order of mammals. — *adj* and *n* **proboscid'ean** or **proboscid'ian**. — **proboscis monkey** a very long-nosed monkey. [L., — Gr. *proboskis*, a trunk — *pro*, expressing motive, *boskein*, to feed.]

procaine *prō'kān*, *n* a crystalline substance used as a local anaesthetic. [**pro-**[2] (2) and **cocaine**.]

procathedral *prō-kə-thē'drəl*, *n* a church used temporarily as a cathedral. [**pro-**[2] (2).]

proceed *prə-* or *prō-sēd'*, *vi* to go on; to continue; to advance; to begin and go on (often with *with*); to act according to a method; to go from point to point; to come forth; to result (often with *from*); to be descended; to take measures or action; to take legal action. — *n* **prō'ceed** (usu. in *pl*) outcome; money got from anything. — *adj* **procedural** (*-sēd'yə-rəl*). — *n* **procē'dure** a mode of proceeding; a method of conducting business, esp. in a law case or a meeting;

a course of action; a step taken or an act performed. — *n* **proceed'ing** a going forward; progress; advancement; a course of conduct; a step; an operation; a transaction; (in *pl*) a record of the transactions of a society. [Fr. *procéder* — L. *prōcēdĕre* — *prō*, before, *cēdĕre*, *cēssum*, to go.]

process *prō'ses* or (esp. in N.Am.) *pros'es*, *n* a state of being in progress or being carried on; course; a series of actions or events; a sequence of operations or changes undergone; a writ by which a person or matter is brought into court (*law*); an action, suit, or the proceedings in it as a whole; progression; proceeding; a projecting part, esp. on a bone (*biol*). — *vt* to subject to a special process; to prepare (e.g. agricultural produce) for marketing, by some special process, e.g. canning or bottling; to arrange (documents, etc.) systematically; to examine and analyse; (of a computer) to perform operations on (data supplied); to subject (data) to such operations; to serve a summons on; to sue or prosecute. — *adj* **prō'cessed** produced by a special process, e.g. synthetically. — *n* **prō'cessor** a person or thing that processes something; a device which processes data (*comput*); a central processing unit (*comput*). — **data processing** the handling and processing of information by computers; **in (the) process of** carrying out or on (an activity), or being carried out or on. [Fr. *procès* — L. *prōcēssus*, *-ūs*, advance; cf. **proceed**.]

procession *prə-* or *prō-sesh'ən*, *n* a train of persons, boats, etc. moving forward together as in ceremony, display, demonstration, etc.; the movement of such a train; the act of proceeding. — *vi* **process** (*prō-ses'*) to go in procession. — *adj* **process'ional.** — *n* a book of litanies, hymns, etc., for processions; a hymn sung in procession. — *n* **process'ionalist.** — *adj* **process'ionary.** — **processionary moth** a European moth whose caterpillars go out seeking food in great processions. [L. *prōcēssiō*, *-ōnis*; cf. **proceed**.]

processor. See under **process**.

prochronism *prō'kron-izm*, *n* a dating of an event before the time it actually occurred. [Gr. *pro*, before, *chronos*, time.]

proclaim *prə-* or *prō-klām'*, *vt* to cry aloud; to publish abroad; to announce officially; to denounce; to announce the accession of. — *n* **proclaim'er.** — *n* **proclamation** (*prok-lə-mā'shən*) the act of proclaiming; that which is proclaimed; an official notice given to the public. — *adj* **proclamatory** (*-klam'ə-tər-i*). [Fr. *proclamer* — L. *prōclāmāre*, *prŏclāmāre* — *prō*, out, *clāmāre*, to cry.]

proclitic *prō-klit'ik*, *adj* so closely attached to the following word as to have no stress. — *n* a proclitic word. — *n* **pro'clisis** (or *prok'*). [A modern coinage on the analogy of **enclitic** — Gr. *pro*, forward, *klīnein*, to lean.]

proclivity *prə-* or *prō-kliv'i-ti*, *n* inclination; propensity. [L. *prōclīvis* — *prō*, forward, *clīvus*, a slope.]

proconsul *prō-kon'sl*, *n* a Roman magistrate with almost consular authority outside the city, orig. one whose consulate had expired, often governor of a province; sometimes applied to a colonial or dominion governor. — *adj* **procon'sular** (*-sū-lər*). — *n* **procon'sulate** (*-sū-lit* or *-lāt*). — *n* **procon'sulship** (*-sl-ship*) the office, or term of office, of a proconsul. [L. *prōcōnsul*.]

procrastinate *prō-kras'ti-nāt*, *vi* to defer action; to put off what should be done immediately. — *n* **procrastinā'tion.** — *adj* **procras'tinātive, procras'tināting** or **procras'tinatory.** — *n* **procras'tinātor.** [L. *procrāstināre*, *-ātum* — *prō*, onward, *crāstīnus*, of tomorrow — *crās*, tomorrow.]

procreate *prō'kri-āt*, *vt* to engender; to beget; to generate. — *vi* to produce offspring. — *n* **prō'creant** (*-kri-ənt*) a generator. — *adj* generating; connected with or useful in reproduction. — *n* **prōcreā'tion.** — *adj* **prō'creātive** having the power to procreate; generative; productive. — *n* **prō'creātiveness.** — *n* **prō'creātor** a parent (*lit* and *fig*). [L. *prōcreāre*, *-ātum* — *prō*, forth, *creāre*, to produce.]

Procrustean *prō-krus'ti-ən*, *adj* violently enforcing conformity to a standard — from *Procrustes* (Gr. *Prŏkroustēs*) a legendary Greek robber, who stretched or cut his captives' legs to make them fit a bed. — Hence **Procrustean bed** (*fig*). [Gr. *prokrouein*, to lengthen out.]

proct- *prokt-* or **procto-** *prok-to-*, (*med*) *combining form* denoting rectum. — *n* **proctalgia** (*-al'ji-ə*; Gr. *algos*, pain) neuralgic pain in the rectum. — *n* **proctī'tis** inflammation of the rectum. — *n* **proctol'ogist.** — *n* **proctol'ogy** the medical study and treatment of the rectum. — *n* **proc'toscope** an instrument for examining the rectum. [Gr. *prōktos*, anus, rectum.]

proctor *prok'tər*, *n* an attorney in ecclesiastical courts; a representative of the clergy in the Church of England Convocation; an official in some English universities whose functions include enforcement of university regulations. — *adj* **proctorial** (*-tö'ri-əl*). — *adv* **procto'rially.** — *n* **proc'torship.** — **king's** or **queen's proctor** an official who intervenes in divorce cases in England if collusion or fraud is suspected. [**procurator**.]

procumbent *prō-kum'bənt*, *adj* lying or leaning forward; prone; prostrate; growing along the ground (*bot*). [L. *prōcumbēns*, *-entis*, pres. p. of *prōcumbĕre* — *prō*, forward, *cumbĕre*, to lie down.]

procurator *prok'ū-rā-tər*, *n* a financial agent in a Roman imperial province, sometimes administrator of part of it; an agent in a law court. — *adj* **procuratorial** (*-rə-tö'ri-əl*). — *n* **proc'uratorship.** — *n* **proc'uratory** (*-rə-tər-i*) authorisation to act for another (*law*). — **procurator fiscal** see under **fiscal**. [L. *prōcūrātor*, *-ōris*; see **procure**.]

procure *prə-* or *prō-kūr'*, *vt* to contrive to obtain or bring about; to bring upon someone; to induce; to obtain (women) to act as prostitutes. — *vi* to pimp. — *adj* **procur'able** to be had. — *n* **procuracy** (*prok'ū-rə-si*) the office of a procurator. — *n* **procurā'tion** (an act of) procuring; a sum paid by incumbents to the bishop or archdeacon on visitations. — *n* **procure'ment** the act of procuring in any sense. — *n* **procur'er** a person who procures; a pimp (*fem* **procur'ess**). [Fr. *procurer* — L. *prōcūrāre*, to manage — *prō*, for, *cūrāre*, *-ātum*, to care for.]

Prod *prod*, (*offensive slang*) *n* (esp. in Ireland) a Protestant.

prod *prod*, *vt* to poke, as with the end of a stick; to urge to act: — *pr p* **prodd'ing**; *pa t* and *pa p* **prodd'ed.** — *n* an act of prodding; a sharp instrument, such as a goad, an awl, a skewer.

prodigal *prod'i-gl*, *adj* wasteful of one's means; squandering; lavish (with *of*). — *n* a waster; a spendthrift; a wanderer returned (also **prodigal son**). — *n* **prodigality** (*-gal'i-ti*) the state or quality of being prodigal; extravagance; profusion; great liberality. — *adv* **prod'igally.** [Obs. Fr., — L. *prōdigus* — *prōdigĕre*, to squander.]

prodigy *prod'i-ji*, *n* any person or thing that causes great wonder; a wonder; a child of precocious genius or virtuosity. — *n* **prodigios'ity.** — *adj* **prodig'ious** astonishing; more than usually large in size or degree. — *adv* **prodig'iously.** — *n* **prodig'iousness.** [L. *prōdigium*, a prophetic sign.]

prodnose *prod'nōz*, (*slang*) *n* a prying, meddlesome person; a detective. [**prod** and **nose.**]

produce *prə-dūs'*, *vt* to bring into being; to bring about; to bring forth; to make; to yield; to put on the stage; to prepare for exhibition to the public; to extend (*geometry*). — *vi* to give birth; to yield; to create value. — *n* **produce** (*prod'ūs*) that which is produced; product; proceeds; crops; yield, esp. of fields and gardens. — *n* **produc'er** someone who produces, esp. commodities, or a play or similar exhibition; a person who exercises general administrative and financial control over, but does not actually make, a motion picture (cf. **director**). — *adj* **produc'ible**. — *n* **product** (*prod'əkt* or *-ukt*) a thing produced; a result; a work; offspring; a quantity got by multiplying (*math*); a substance obtained from another by chemical change (*chem*). — *n* **productibil'ity** (*prə-dukt-*) the capability of being produced. — *n* **produc'tion** the act of producing; that which is produced; product; a work, esp. of art; a putting upon the stage; a bringing out. — *adj* **produc'tional**. — *adj* **produc'tive** having the power to produce; bringing good results; generative (often with *of*); that produces; producing richly; fertile; efficient. — *adv* **produc'tively**. — *n* **produc'tiveness**. — *n* **productiv'ity** (*prod-* or *prōd-*) the rate or efficiency of work, esp. in industrial production. — **producer gas** chiefly a mixture of hydrogen and carbon monoxide diluted with nitrogen, used esp. as a fuel. — *npl* **producer** (or **producer's) goods** goods, such as raw materials and tools, used in the production of consumer goods. — **production line** an assembly line (q.v.); **production platform** an oil platform (q.v.); **productivity deal** an agreement whereby employees receive increased wages or salaries if they agree to improve their efficiency and increase their output. — **make a production of** or **out of** (*colloq*) to make an unnecessary fuss or commotion about (something). [L. *prōdūcĕre*, *-ductum* — *prō*, forward, *dūcĕre*, to lead.]

proem *prō'em*, *n* an introduction; a prelude; a preface. [Fr. *proème* — L. *prooemium* — Gr. *prooimion* — *pro*, before, *oimē*, a song, *oimos*, a way.]

Prof. *abbrev* for Professor.

prof *prof*, *n* a familiar contraction of **professor**.

profane *prə-* or *prō-fān'*, *adj* not sacred; secular; showing contempt of sacred things; uninitiated; unhallowed; (esp. of language) vulgar or irreverent. — *vt* to treat with contempt or insult in spite of the holiness attributed; to desecrate; to violate; to put to an unworthy use. — *n* **profanation** (*prof-ə-nā'shən*). — *adj* **profanatory** (*prō-fan'ə-tər-i*). — *adv* **profane'ly**. — *n* **profane'ness**. — *n* **profān'er**. — *n* **profanity** (*-fan'*) irreverence; that which is profane; profane language or conduct. [L. *profānus*, outside the temple, not sacred, unholy — *prō*, before, *fānum*, a temple.]

profess *prə-fes'*, *vt* to make open declaration of; to declare in strong terms; to claim (often insincerely) to have a feeling of; to pretend to; to claim to be expert in; to receive into a religious order by profession. — *vi* to enter publicly into a religious state. — *adj* **professed'** openly declared; avowed; acknowledged; alleged; having made a religious profession. — *adv* **profess'edly**. — *adj* **profess'ing** avowed; pretending. — *n* **profession** (*-fesh'ən*) the act of professing; an open declaration; an avowal; a declaration of religious belief made upon entering a religious order; a pretence. — *n* **professor** (*prə-fes'ər*) a university or sometimes a college teacher of the highest grade, esp. the head of a department (prefixed to the name); (in the U.S.) a university or college teacher of any grade (prefixed to the name), rising from *assistant professor*, *associate professor* to full *professor* — see also **associate professor**. — *n* **profess'orate** professoriate. — *adj* **professorial** (*prof-es-ö'ri-əl*). — *adv* **professo'rially**. — *n* **professo'riate** the office or chair of a professor; a professor's period of office; body of professors. — *n* **profess'orship**. [L. *professus*, perf. p. of *profitērī* — *prō*, publicly, *fatērī*, to confess.]

profession *prə-fesh'-ən*, *n* a non-manual occupation requiring some degree of learning; a calling or habitual employment; the collective body of people engaged in any profession. — *adj* **profess'ional** pertaining to a profession; engaged in a profession or in the profession in question; competing for money prizes or against those who sometimes do so; undertaken as a means of subsistence (opp. of *amateur*); showing the skill, artistry, demeanour or standard of conduct apporopriate in a member of a (particular) profession; (of a foul in football, etc.) deliberate, intended to prevent the opposition from scoring (*euph*; *sport*). — *n* a person who makes his or her living by engaging in some activity also carried on at an amateur level. — *n* **professionalisa'tion** or **-z-**. — *vt* **profess'ionalise** or **-ize** to give a professional character to; to give over to professionals. — *n* **profess'ionalism** the status of a professional; the competence or the correct demeanour of those who are highly trained and disciplined; the outlook, aim or restriction of the mere professional; the predominance of professionals in sport. — *adv* **profess'ionally**. [Ety. as for **profess**.]

proffer *prof'ər*, *vt* to offer for acceptance, to tender, present: — *pr p* **proff'ering**; *pa t* and *pa p* **proff'ered**. — *n* an offer, tender; the act of proffering. — *n* **proff'erer**. [A.Fr. *proffrir* — L. *prō*, forward, *offerre*; see **offer**.]

proficient *prə-fish'ənt*, *adj* competent; well-skilled; thoroughly qualified. — *n* an adept; an expert. — *n* **profi'ciency**. — *adv* **profi'ciently**. [L. *prōficiēns*, *-entis*, pres. p. of *prōficĕre*, to make progress.]

profile *prō'fīl*, *n* a head or portrait in a side-view; the side-face; an outline; a short biographical sketch, e.g. in a newspaper or magazine; an outline of the characteristic features (of e.g. a particular type of person); one's manner, attitude or behaviour considered with regard to the extent to which it attracts attention to oneself and one's activities or reveals one's feelings, intentions, etc., or the extent of one's involvement, etc. (as in *low*, *high*, etc. *profile*); a public image, esp. one created and controlled by design; the outline of any object without foreshortening; a drawing of a vertical section of land, an engineering work, etc. — *vt* to draw, make or give in profile; to show in profile. [It. *profilo* — L. *prō*, before, *fīlum*, a thread.]

profit *prof'it*, *n* gain; the gain resulting from the employment of capital; the excess of selling price over first cost; advantage; benefit; improvement. — *vt* to benefit or to be of advantage to. — *vi* to gain advantage; to receive profit; to be of advantage. — *n* **profitabil'ity**. — *adj* **prof'itable** yielding or bringing profit or gain; lucrative; productive. — *n* **prof'itableness**. — *adv* **prof'itably**. — *n* **profiteer'** (*derog*) a person who takes advantage of an emergency to make exorbitant profits. — *vi* to act as a profiteer. — *n* **profiteer'ing**. — *n* **prof'iter**. — *adj* **prof'itless**. — **prof'it-sharing** a voluntary agreement under which the employee receives a share, fixed beforehand, in the profits of a business; **prof'it-taker**; **prof'it-taking** selling off shares, commodities, etc. in order to profit from a rise in the purchase price. [Fr., — L. *prōfectus*, progress — *prōficĕre*, *prōfectum*, to make progress.]

profiterole *prə-fit'ə-rōl*, *n* a small puff of choux pastry, usu. filled with cream and covered with a chocolate sauce. [Fr.; perh. — *profiter*, to profit.]

profligate *prof'li-git* or *-gāt*, *adj* debauched; dissolute; prodigal, rashly extravagant. — *n* a person leading a profligate life; someone who is recklessly extravagant or wasteful. — *n* **prof'ligacy** (*-gə-si*). — *adv* **prof'ligately**. [L. *prōflīgātus*, past p. of *prōflīgāre* — *prō*, forward, *flīgĕre*, to dash.]

Pr. of Man. (*Bible*) *abbrev* for (the Apocryphal Book of the) Prayer of Manasses.

proforma. See **pro forma** under **pro**[1].

profound *prə-* or *prō-fownd'*, *adj* deep; deep-seated; far below the surface; intense; abstruse; intellectually deep; penetrating deeply into knowledge. — *adv* **profound'ly**. — *n* **profound'ness** or **profundity** (*-fund'*) the state or quality of being profound; depth of place, of knowledge, etc.; that which is profound. [Fr. *profond* — L. *profundus* — *pro*, forward, *fundus*, bottom.]

profuse *prə-* or *prō-fūs'*, *adj* liberal to excess; lavish; extravagant; over-abounding. — *adv* **profuse'ly**. — *n* **profuse'ness**. — *n* **profusion** (*-fū'zhən*) the state of being profuse; extravagance; prodigality. [L. *prōfūsus*, past p. of *prōfundĕre* — *prō*, forth, *fundĕre*, to pour.]

progenitor *prō-jen'i-tər*, *n* an ancestor. — *n* **progeny** (*proj'ə-ni*) offspring; descendants; race. [L. *prōgenitor*, *prōgeniēs* — *prōgignĕre* — *prō*, before, *gignĕre*, *genitum*, beget.]

progesterone *prō-jes'tər-ōn*, *n* a female sex hormone that prepares the uterus for the fertilised ovum and maintains pregnancy. — *n* **proges'tin** (**pro-**[1], *gestation* and *-in*) any hormone concerned with changes before pregnancy, esp. **proges'togen**, any of a range of hormones of the progesterone type; several synthetic progestogens are used in oral contraceptives. [*progestin*, *sterol* and *-one*.]

prognathous *prog'nə-thəs* or *prog-nā'thəs*, (*zool*) *adj* with projecting jaw. [Gr. *pro*, forward, *gnathos*, a jaw.]

prognosis *prog-nō'sis*, *n* a forecasting, or forecast, esp. of the course of a disease: — *pl* **prognō'ses** (*-ēz*). — *n* **prognostic** (*prog-* or *prəg-nost'ik*) a foretelling; an indication of something to come; a presage; a symptom on which prognosis can be based. — *adj* indicating what is to happen by signs or symptoms; of prognosis. — *vt* **prognos'ticāte** to foretell; to foreshadow. — *n* **prognosticā'tion**. — *adj* **prognos'ticātive**. — *n* **prognost'icātor** a predictor, esp. a weather prophet. [Gr. *prognōsis* — *pro*, before, *gignōskein*, to know.]

prograde *prō'grād*, *adj* (of metamorphism) from a lower to a higher metamorphic level, or caused by a rise in temperature or pressure (*geol*); (of movement or rotation) in a forward direction, i.e. in the same direction as that of adjacent bodies (*astron*). — *vi* (*geog*) (of a coastline, etc.) to advance seawards because of a build-up of sediment. — *n* **progradā'tion**. [**pro-**[2] (1) and contrast with retro *grade*.]

programme or (*NAm* and *comput*) **program** *prō'gram*, *n* a paper, booklet, or the like, giving a scheme of proceedings arranged for an entertainment, conference, course of study, etc., with relevant details; the items of such a scheme collectively; a plan of things to be done; a TV or radio presentation produced for broadcast singly or as one of a series; the sequence of actions to be performed by a computer in dealing with data of a certain kind; a sequence of encoded instructions to a computer to fulfil a task or series of actions; a course of instruction in which subject-matter is broken down into a logical sequence of short items of information, and a student can check immediately the suitability of his or her responses. — *vt* to provide with, enter in, etc. a programme; to prepare a program for (a computer, etc.); to create a certain pattern of thought, reaction, etc. in the mind of (*fig*). — *n* **programmabil'ity**. — *adj* **programm'able** capable of being programmed to perform a task, calculation, etc. automatically. — *n* a programmable calculator. — *adj* **programmatic** (*-grə-mat'ik*) of a programme; of, or of the nature of, programme music. — *adj* **pro'grammed**. — *n* **pro'grammer** (*comput*). — *n* **pro'gramming**. — **programmed learning** learning by programme (see definition of **programme** above); **programme music** music that seeks to depict a scene or tell a story; **program trader**; **program trading** the automatic buying or selling of securities, etc. by computer when the price reaches pre-set limits; **programming language** a system of codes, symbols, rules, etc. designed for communicating information to, on or by a computer. — **programme evaluation and review technique** a method of planning, monitoring and reviewing the progress, costs, etc. of a complex project. [Gr. *programma*, proclamation — *pro*, forth, *gramma*, a letter.]

progress *prō'gres*, sometimes (esp. in U.S.) *pro'gres*, *n* a forward movement; an advance to something better or higher in development; a gain in proficiency; a course; a passage from place to place. — *vi* **progress'** to go forward; to make progress; to go on, continue; travel in state; to go. — *vt* to cause (esp. building or manufacturing work) to proceed steadily. — *n* **progression** (*prə-* or *prō-gresh'ən*) motion onward; the act or state of moving onward; progress; movement by successive stages; a regular succession of chords (*mus*); movements of the parts in harmony; a change from term to term according to some law (*math*); a series of terms so related (see under **arithmetic**, **geometry**, **harmonic**). — *adj* **progress'ional**. — *adj* **progress'ive** moving forward; making progress; of the nature of progress; advancing by successive stages; (of a disease, condition, etc.) increasing steadily in severity or extent; (in dancing, card games, etc.) involving a change of partners according to rule after each set, hand, etc. advancing towards better and better or higher and higher; in favour of social and political progress or reform; (usu. with *cap*) applied to a political party with progressive policies; (of taxation) in which the rate increases as the amount to be taxed increases. — *n* a person who favours progress or reform; (usu. with *cap*) a member of a party called progressive. — *adv* **progress'ively**. — *n* **progress'iveness**. — **in progress** going on; in course of publication. [Fr. *progresse* (now *progrès*) — L. *prōgressus*, *-ūs* — *prō*, forward, *gradī*, *gressus*, to step.]

prohibit *prə-* or *prō-hib'it*, *vt* to forbid; to prevent. — *n* **prohib'iter** or **prohib'itor**. — *n* **prohibition** (*prō-hi-bi'shən* or *prō-i-*) the act of prohibiting, forbidding or interdicting; an interdict; the forbidding by law of the manufacture and sale of alcoholic drinks. — *adj* **prohibi'tionary**. — *n* **prohibi'tionism**. — *n* **prohibi'tionist** a person who favours prohibition, esp. of the manufacture and sale of alcoholic drinks. — *adj* **prohibitive** (*-hib'*) tending to make impossible or preclude. — *adv* **prohib'itively**. — *n* **prohib'itiveness**. — *adj* **prohib'itory** that prohibits or forbids; forbidding. [L. *prohibēre*, *prohibitum* — *prō*, before, *habēre*, to have.]

project *proj'ekt*, *n* a scheme of something to be done; a proposal for an undertaking; an undertaking. — *vt* **project** (*prə-jekt'* or *prō-jekt'*) to throw out or forward; to speak or sing in such a way as to aim (the voice) at the rear of the auditorium (*theat*); to throw, propel; to cause to jut out, stretch out; to scheme, plan, devise; to cast (e.g. a light, a shadow, an image) upon a surface or into space; to show outlined against a background; to predict or expect on the basis of past results or present trends; to derive a new figure from, so that each point corresponds to a point of the original figure according to some rule (*geom*); to externalise; to make objective. — *vi* to jut out. — *adj* **projec'tile** caused by projection; impelling; capable of being thrown or thrust forth. — *n* a body projected by force; a missile, esp. one discharged by a gun. — *n* and *adj* **projec'ting**. — *n* **projec'tion** (*-shən*) an act or method of projecting; the fact or state of being projected; planning; that which is projected; a jutting out; that which juts out; the standing out of a figure; a figure obtained by projecting another (*geom*); a method of representing geographical detail upon a plane, or the representation so obtained (also **map projection**); a projected image; the reading of one's own emotions and experiences into a particular situation (*psychol*); a person's unconscious attributing to other people of certain attitudes towards himself or herself, usu. as a defence against their own guilt, inferiority, etc. (*psychol*). — *adj* **projec'tional**.

— *n* **projec'tionist** a person who projects, or makes projections, esp. in map-making; an operator of a film-projector; an operator of certain television equipment. — *n* **projectisa'tion** or **-z-** the direction of aid to developing countries towards a specific project, without regard to wider issues or needs. — *adj* **projec'tive** projecting; of projection; derivable by projection; unchanged by projection. — *n* **projectivity** (*proj-ək-tiv'i-ti*). — *n* **projec'tor** a person who projects enterprises; a promoter of speculative schemes for money-making; an apparatus for projecting, esp. an image or a beam of light; a straight line joining a point with its projection (*geom*). — *n* **projec'ture** a jutting out. [L. *prōjicĕre*, *prōjectum* — *prō*, forth, *jacĕre*, to throw.]

prokaryon *prō-kar'i-ən*, (*biol*) *n* the nucleus of a blue-green alga, bacterium, etc., with no membrane separating the DNA-containing area from the rest of the cell (cf. *eukaryon*). — *n* **prokar'yote** (*-ōt*) a cell or organism with such a nucleus or nuclei. — Also *adj*. — *adj* **prokaryot'ic**. [**pro-**[1] and Gr. *karyon*, a kernel.]

prolapse *prō-laps'* or *prō'laps*, (*med*) *n* a falling down, or out of place. — *vi* **prolapse'** to slip out of place. [L. *prōlābī*, *prōlāpsus*, to slip forward — *prō*, forward, *lābī*, to slip.]

prolate *prō'lāt*, *adj* drawn out along the polar diameter, as a spheroid (opp. to *oblate*); widespread. [L. *prōlātus*, produced — *prō*, forward, *lātus*, used as perf. p. of *ferre*, to carry.]

prole *prōl*, (*colloq*) *n* and *adj* proletarian.

proleg *prō'leg*, (*zool*) *n* an insect larva's abdominal leg, distinguished from a thoracic or 'true' leg. [**pro-**[2] (2) and **leg**.]

prolegomena *prō-leg-om'in-ə*, *npl* an introduction, esp. to a treatise: — *nsing* **prolegom'enon**. — *adj* **prolegom'enary** or **prolegom'enous**. [Gr. *prolegomenon*, pl. *-a*, pass. p. neut. of *prolegein* — *pro*, before, *legein*, to say.]

prolepsis *prō-lep'sis* or *-lēp'sis*, *n* the rhetorical figure of anticipation, use of a word not literally applicable till a later time; a figure by which objections are anticipated and answered: — *pl* **prolep'sēs**. — *adj* **prolep'tic** or **prolep'tical**. — *adv* **prolep'tically**. [Gr. *prolēpsis* — *pro*, before, *lambanein*, to take.]

proletarian *prō-li-tā'ri-ən*, *adj* of the proletariat. — *n* a member of the proletariat. — *n* **proletarianisā'tion** or **-z-**. — *vt* **proletā'rianise** or **-ize**. — *n* **proletā'riat** (*-ət*) the poorest labouring class; the wage-earning classes, esp. those without capital. [L. *prōlētārius*, (in ancient Rome) a citizen of the sixth and lowest class, who served the state not with his property but with his *prōlēs*, offspring.]

pro-lifer *prō-lī'fər*, *n* a person in favour of protecting and promoting the life of unborn children; a campaigner against abortion, experiments on embryos, etc. — *adj* **pro-life'**. [**pro-**[2] (3) and **life**.]

proliferate *prō-lif'ə-rāt*, *vi* to grow or to reproduce by multiplication of parts (cells, buds, shoots, etc.); to reproduce abundantly; to increase in numbers greatly and rapidly. — *vt* to produce by multiplication of parts; to cause to grow or increase rapidly. — *n* **proliferā'tion**. — *adj* **prolif'erative** or **prolif'erous**. — *adv* **prolif'erously**. [L. *prōlēs*, progeny, *ferre*, to bear.]

prolific *prə-* or *prō-lif'ik*, *adj* producing much or many offspring; (of an author, artist, etc.) producing many works; fruitful; abounding. — *n* **prolif'icacy** (*-ə-si*). — *adv* **prolif'ically**. — *n* **prolificā'tion** the generation of young; development of a shoot by continued growth of a flower (*bot*). — *n* **prolificity** (*-is'i-ti*) or **prolif'icness**. [L. *prōlēs*, offspring, *facĕre*, to make.]

proline *prō'lēn* or *-lin*, (*chem*) *n* an amino-acid commonly occurring in proteins. [Ger. *Prolin*, contracted from *Pyrrolidin*, pyrrolidine.]

prolix *prō'liks* or *-liks'*, *adj* long and wordy; long-winded; dwelling too long on particulars. — *n* **prolix'ity**. — *adv* **prolix'ly** (or *prō'*). — *n* **prolix'ness** (or *prō'*). [L. *prōlixus* — *pro*, forward, *līquī*, to flow.]

prolocutor *prō-lok'ū-tər*, *n* a spokesman; a chairman, esp. of the lower house of Convocation in the Anglican church: — *fem* **prōloc'utrix**. — *n* **prolocu'tion** (*prō-* or *pro-*) an introductory speech or saying. — *n* **prōloc'utorship**. [L. *prōlocūtor* — *prōloquī*, *-locūtus*, to speak out — *loquī*, to speak.]

prologue *prō'log*, *n* in a Greek play, the part before the entry of the chorus; an introduction to a poem, etc.; a speech before a play; the speaker of a prologue; an introductory event or action. — *vt* to introduce; to preface. [Fr., — L. *prologus* — Gr. *prologos* — *logos*, speech.]

prolong *prə-* or *prō-long'*, *vt* to lengthen out. — *adj* **prolongable** (*prō-long'ə-bl*). — *vt* **prolongate** (*prō'long-gāt*) to lengthen. — *n* **prolongation** (*-long-gā'shən*) lengthening out; a piece added in continuation; continuation. [L. *prōlongāre* — *prō*, forward, *longus*, long.]

prolusion *prō-lōō'zhən* or *-lū'*, *n* a preliminary performance, activity or display; an essay preparatory to a more solid treatise. — *adj* **prolu'sory** (*-sə-ri*). [L. *prōlūsiō*, *-ōnis* — *prō*, before, *lūdĕre*, *lūsum*, to play.]

prom *prom*, *n* short for **promenade** (q.v.); a promenade concert; a school or college dance (*NAm*). — **The Proms** a series of promenade concerts held annually in London.

pro-marketeer *prō-mär-ki-tēr'*, *n* a person in favour of Britain's entry into, or continued membership of, the European Common Market. [**pro-**[2] (3).]

promenade *prom-i-näd'* or *-nād'*, *n* a walk, ride, or drive for pleasure, show, or gentle exercise; a processional dance; a school dance, a prom (*NAm*); a place where people walk to and fro; a paved terrace on a sea front; an esplanade. — *vi* to walk, ride or drive about; to perform a promenade. — *vt* to lead about and exhibit; to walk, ride or drive about or through. — *n* **promenader** (*-äd'ər*) someone who promenades; a member of the standing portion of the audience at a promenade concert. — **promenade concert** one in which part of the audience stands throughout and can move about; **promenade deck** a deck on which passengers may walk about. [Fr., — *promener*, to lead about (*se promener*, to take a walk) — L. *prōmināre*, to drive forwards.]

prometal *prō'met-l*, *n* a kind of cast-iron highly resistant to heat.

Promethean *prō-mē'thi-ən* or *-thyən*, *adj* pertaining to *Prometheus* (*-thi-əs*) who stole fire from heaven, for which Zeus chained him to a rock, to be tortured by a vulture; daringly innovative. — *n* **promē'thium** a radioactive lanthanide element (symbol **Pm**; atomic no. 61). [Gr. *Promētheus*.]

prominent *prom'i-nənt*, *adj* standing out; projecting; most easily seen; catching the eye or attention; in the public eye. — *n* **prom'inence** state or quality of being prominent; a prominent point or thing; a projection. — *n* **prom'inency** a prominence. — *adv* **prom'inently**. [L. *prōminēns*, *-entis*, pres. p. of *prōminēre*, to jut forth — *prō*, forth, *minae*, projections, threats.]

promiscuous *pro-mis'kū-əs*, *adj* confusedly or indiscriminately mixed; indiscriminate (now usu. referring to someone indulging in indiscriminate sexual intercourse); haphazard; belonging to a mixed set; casual (*colloq*). — *n* **promiscū'ity** mixture without order or distinction; promiscuous sexual intercourse. — *adv* **promis'cuously**. [L. *prōmiscuus* — *prō* (intensive) and *miscēre*, to mix.]

promise *prom'is*, *n* an engagement to do or keep from doing something; expectation, or that which raises expectation; a ground for hope of future excellence. — *vt* to engage by promise to do, give, etc.; to betroth; to encourage to expect; to give reason to expect; to assure; to engage to bestow. — *vi* to make a promise or promises; to give rise to hopes or expectations. — *n* **promisee'** the person to whom a promise is made. — *n* **prom'iser**. — *adj* **prom'ising** giving ground for hope or expectation; likely to turn out well. — *adv* **prom'isingly**. — *n* **prom'isor** (*law*) the person making a promise. — *adj* **prom'issory** containing a promise of some engagement to be fulfilled. — **promised land** the land promised by God to Abraham and his descendants; Canaan; heaven; **promissory note** a written promise to pay a sum of money on some future day or on demand. [L. *prōmissum*, neut. past p. of *promittĕre*, to send forward — *prō*, forward, *mittĕre*, to send.]

prommer *prom'ər*, (*colloq*) *n* a (regular) attender of promenade concerts, esp. a promenader.

promo *prō'mō*, (*slang*) *n* a shortening of **promotion**; a promotional video recording: — *pl* **pro'mos**.

promontory *prom'ən-tər-i* or *-tri*, *n* a headland or high cape; a projection, ridge or eminence (*anat*). [L.L. *prōmontōrium*.]

promote *prə-* or *prō-mōt'*, *vt* to further; to further the progress of; to raise to a higher grade; to take steps for the passage or formation of; to set in motion (as the office of a judge in a criminal suit); to encourage the sales of by advertising. — *n* **promō'ter** a person who promotes; someone who takes part in the setting up of companies; the organiser of a sporting event, esp. a boxing match; a substance that increases the efficiency of a catalyst (*chem*); a substance that encourages the formation or growth of tumour cells (*med*). — *n* **promotion** (*-mō'shən*) the act of promoting; advancement in rank or in honour; encouragement; preferment; a venture, esp. in show business; advertising in general, or an effort to publicise and increase the sales of a particular product. — *adj* **promo'tional**. [L. *prōmovēre*, *-mōtum* — *prō*, forward, *movēre*, to move.]

prompt *prompt* or *promt*, *adj* ready in action; performed at once. — *adv* promptly, punctually, to the minute. — *vt* to incite; to instigate; to move to action; to supply forgotten words to, esp. in a theatrical performance; to help with words or facts when one is at a loss; to suggest to the mind. — *n* a time limit for payment; an act of prompting; words provided by the prompter; a question or statement which appears on a computer screen, inviting the operator to proceed or to choose from set options. — *n* **prompt'er** a person who prompts, esp. actors. — *n* **prompt'ing**. — *n* **prompt'itude** promptness; readiness; quickness of decision and action. — *adv* **prompt'ly**. — *n* **prompt'ness**. [L. *prōmptus* — *prōmĕre*, to bring forward.]

promulgate *prom'əl-gāt* or in U.S. *prə-mul'*, *vt* to proclaim, publish abroad; to make widely known; to put (e.g. a law) in execution by proclamation. — *n* **promulgā'tion**. — *n* **prom'ulgātor**. [L. *prōmulgāre*, *-ātum*.]

prone *prōn*, *adj* with the face, ventral surface, or palm of the hand downward prostrate; directed downward; (*loosely*) lying or laid flat; sloping downwards; disposed, inclined, naturally tending; willing. — **-prone** (in combination) meaning liable to suffer a specified thing, as in *accident-prone*. [L. *prōnus*, bent forward.]

prong *prong*, *n* a tine, tooth or spike of a fork or forked object; a tine, spur or projection, as on an antler. — *adj* **pronged** having prongs. — **prong'buck** the pronghorn (properly the male); **prong'horn** an American antelope-like ruminant with deciduous horns pronged in front. [M.E. *prange*.]

pronoun *prō'nown*, *n* a word used instead of a noun, i.e. to indicate without naming. — *adj* **pronominal** (*prə-* or *prō-nom'in-əl*) belonging to, or of the nature of, a pronoun. — *adv* **pronom'inally**.

pronounce *prə-* or *prō-nowns'*, *vt* to proclaim; to utter formally or rhetorically; to declare; to utter; to articulate. — *vi* to pass judgment; to articulate one's words. — *adj* **pronounce'able** capable of being pronounced. — *adj* **pronounced'** marked with emphasis; marked. — *adv* **pronoun'cedly** (*-səd-li*). — *n* **pronounce'ment** a confident or authoritative assertion or declaration; the act of pronouncing. — *n* **pronoun'cer**. — *n* and *adj* **pronoun'cing**. — *n* **pronunciation** (*prō-nun-si-ā'shən*) mode of pronouncing; articulation. [Fr. *prononcer* — L. *prōnūntiāre* — *prō*, forth, *nūntiāre*, to announce — *nūntius*, a messenger.]

pronto *pron'tō*, (*slang*) *adv* promptly, quickly. [Sp. *pronto* — L. *prōmptus*, at hand.]

pronunciamento *prō-nun-si-ə-men'tō*, *n* a manifesto; a proclamation: — *pl* **pronunciamen'tos** or **pronunciamen'toes**. [Sp. *pronunciamiento*.]

pronunciation. See under **pronounce**.

proof *prōōf*, *n* that which proves or establishes the truth of anything; the fact, act or process of proving or showing to be true; demonstration; evidence that convinces the mind and goes toward determining the decision of a court; an instrument of evidence in documentary form; a checking operation (*arith*); a test; testing, esp. of guns; ability to stand a test; invulnerability; impenetrability; a standard strength of spirit (alcohol and water of relative density 12/13 at 51°F. — i.e. 49·28 per cent of alcohol); an impression taken for correction (*printing*); an early impression of an engraving; a coin, intended for display, etc., rather than circulation, struck from polished dies on polished blanks (also **proof coin**); the first print from a negative (*phot*): — *pl* **proofs**. — *adj* impervious; invulnerable; of standard strength (of alcohol). — *vt* to make impervious, esp. to water; to take a proof of; to test. — (In combination) **-proof** able to withstand or resist; to make so, as in *waterproof*, *childproof*, *weatherproof*, etc. — *n* **proof'ing** the process of making waterproof, gas-proof, etc.; material used for the purpose. — **proof'-mark** a mark stamped on a gun to show that it has stood the test. — *vt* and *vi* **proof'read** to read and correct in proof. — **proof'reader** a person who reads printed proofs to discover and correct errors; **proof'reading**; **proof'-sheet** an impression taken on a slip of paper for correction before printing finally; **proof'-spirit** a standard mixture of alcohol and water; **proof'-text** a passage of the Bible adduced in proof of a doctrine. — **artist's proof** a first impression from an engraved plate or block; **over (or under) proof** containing in 100 volumes enough alcohol for so many volumes more (or less) than 100. [O.Fr. *prove* (Fr. *preuve*).]

PROP *prop*, *abbrev* for Preservation of the Rights of Prisoners.

prop[1] *prop*, *n* a rigid support; a supplementary support; a stay; a strut; a timber supporting a mine roof; a supporter, upholder; (in Rugby football) either of the two forwards at the ends of the front row of the scrum (also **prop-for'ward**). — *vt* to hold up by means of something placed under or against; to support or to sustain; to keep (a failing enterprise, etc.) going; to hit straight or knock down (*slang*). — **prop'-root** a root growing down from a trunk or branch, serving to prop up a tree. [M.E. *proppe*.]

prop[2] *prop*, *n* a colloq. or slang short form for: propeller; (theatrical) property. — *n* **props** a property-man. — **prop shaft** see **propeller shaft**.

prop. *abbrev* for: proper; properly; property; proposition.

propaedeutic *prō-pē-dū'tik*, *n* (often in *pl*) a preliminary study. — *adj* **propaedeu'tic** or **propaedeu'tical**. [Gr. *propaideuein*, to teach beforehand.]

propaganda *prop-ə-gan'də*, *n* the organised spreading of doctrine, true or false information, opinions, etc., esp. to bring about change or reform; an association or scheme for this; the information, etc. spread; (with *cap*) a Roman Catholic congregation, founded 1622, responsible for foreign missions and the training of missionaries. — *vt* and *vi* **propagan'dise** or **-ize.** — *n* **propagan'dism** the practice of propagating tenets or principles; zeal in the spreading of one's opinions; proselytism. — *n* and *adj* **propagan'dist.** — **propaganda machine** all the means employed in the process of spreading opinions; the process itself. [L. *congregatio dē propāgandā fidē*, congregation for propagating the faith, the full title of the Propaganda.]

propagate *prop'ə-gāt*, *vt* to increase by natural process; to multiply; to pass on; to transmit; to spread from one to another. — *vi* to multiply; to breed. — *adj* **prop'agable.** — *n* **propagā'tion.** — *adj* **prop'agātive.** — *n* **prop'agātor** a person who, or thing which, propagates; a heated, covered box in which plants may be grown from seed or cuttings. [L. *prōpāgāre, -ātum*.]

propane *prō'pān*, *n* a hydrocarbon gas (C_3H_8), third member of the methane series, used as fuel. [**propionic.**]

proparoxytone *prō-par-ok'si-tōn*, *adj* (in ancient Greek) having the acute accent on the third last syllable; having heavy stress on the third last syllable. — *n* a word accented or stressed in this way. [Gr. *proparoxytonos*; see **paroxytone.**]

propel *prə-* or *prō-pel'*, *vt* to drive forward: — *pr p* **propell'ing;** *pa t* and *pa p* **propelled'.** — *n* **propell'ant** that which propels; an explosive for propelling projectiles; the fuel used to propel a rocket, etc.; the gas in an aerosol spray. — *adj* **propell'ent** driving. — *n* a driving agent; a motive. — *n* **propell'er** a person who, or something which, propels; driving mechanism; a shaft with blades radiating from it (*screw-propeller*) for driving a ship, aeroplane, etc.; a helical blower (*air-propeller, propeller fan*). — *n* **propel'ment** propulsion; propelling mechanism. — **propeller shaft** the shaft of a propeller; the driving shaft between gearbox and rear axle in a motor vehicle (also **prop shaft**); **propelling pencil** one having a replaceable lead held within a casing that can be turned to push the lead forward as it is worn down. [L. *prōpellĕre* — *prō*, forward, *pellĕre*, to drive.]

propensity *prə-* or *prō-pen'si-ti*, *n* inclination of mind; tendency to good or evil. [L. *prōpendēre, -pēnsum*, to hang forward.]

proper *prop'ər*, *adj* appropriate; peculiar; confined to one; strict; strictly applicable; strictly so-called (usu. after *n*); thorough, out-and-out (*colloq*); actual, real; befitting; decorous, seemly; conforming strictly to convention. — *adv* (*colloq*) very, exceedingly. — *adv* **prop'erly** in a proper manner; strictly; entirely, extremely (*colloq*). — *n* **prop'erness.** — **proper fraction** a fraction that has a numerator of a lower value than the denominator; **proper motion** a star's apparent motion relative to the celestial sphere, due partly to its own movement (peculiar motion), partly to that of the solar system (parallactic motion); **proper noun** or **name** the name of a particular person, animal, thing, place, etc. (opp. to *common* noun). [Fr. *propre* — L. *prŏprĭus*, own.]

property *prop'ər-ti*, *n* a quality that is always present; a characteristic; that which is one's own; the condition of being one's own; a piece of land or building owned by somebody; right of possessing, employing, etc.; ownership; an article required on the stage (abbrev. **prop**). — *adj* of the nature of a stage property. — *adj* **prop'ertied** possessed of property. — **property man** one who has charge of stage properties (abbrev. **props**); **property** (or **props) room** the room in which stage properties are kept; **property tax** a tax levied on property, at the rate of so much per cent on its value. [O.Fr. *properte*; see **propriety.**]

prophecy *prof'i-si*, *n* inspired or prophetic utterance; prediction. [O.Fr. *prophecie* — L. *prophētīa* — Gr. *prophēteia* — *prophētēs*, prophet.]

prophesy *prof'i-sī*, *vi* to utter prophecies; to speak prophetically; to foretell the future. — *vt* to foretell: — *pa t* and *pa p* **proph'esīed.** — *n* **proph'esīer.** — *n* **proph'esying.** [A variant of **prophecy.**]

prophet *prof'it*, *n* a spokesman of deity; someone who proclaims a divine message; an inspired teacher, preacher or poet; the spokesman of a group, movement or doctrine; a minister of the second order of the Catholic Apostolic Church; a foreteller, whether claiming to be inspired or not: — *fem* **proph'etess.** — *n* **proph'ethood.** — *adj* **prophetic** (*prə-fet'ik*) or **prophet'ical.** — *adv* **prophet'ically.** — **prophet of doom** a person who continually predicts unfortunate events, disasters, etc.; **the Prophet** Mohammed. [Fr. *prophète* — L. *prophēta* — Gr. *prophētēs* — *pro*, for, *phanai*, to speak.]

prophylactic *pro-fi-lak'tik*, *adj* guarding against disease. — *n* a preventive of disease; a condom (usu. *US*). — *n* **prophylax'is** preventive treatment against diseases, etc. [Gr. *prophylaktikos* — *pro*, before, *phylax*, a guard.]

propinquity *prə-ping'kwi-ti*, *n* nearness. [L. *propinquitās, -ātis* — *propinquus*, near — *prope*, near.]

propionic acid *prō-pi-on'ik as'id*, *n* one of the fatty acids, a colourless liquid used to control the growth of certain moulds. [**pro-**[1] and *piōn, -on*, fat.]

propitiate *prə-pish'i-āt*, *vt* to render favourable; to appease. — *adj* **propi'tiable.** — *n* **propitiā'tion** an act of propitiating; atonement; atoning sacrifice. — *adj* **propi'tiātive.** — *n* **propi'tiātor.** — *adv* **propi'tiatorily** (*-shi-ə-tər-i-li*). — *adj* **propi'tiatory** propitiating; expiatory. — *adj* **propitious** (*-pish'əs*) favourable; disposed to be gracious; of good omen. — *adv* **propi'tiously.** — *n* **propi'tiousness.** [L. *propitiāre, -ātum*, to make favourable — *propitius*, well-disposed.]

propjet *prop'jet*, (*aeronautics*) *n* a jet aeroplane with a turbine-driven propeller. — *adj* having such a propeller. [Cf. **turboprop.**]

propolis *prop'ə-lis*, *n* a brown sticky resinous substance gathered by bees from trees and used by them as cement and varnish. [Gr. *propolis*.]

propone *prə-pōn'*, *vt* (now *Scot*) to put forward, propose. — *n* **propōn'ent** a propounder or proposer; a favourer, advocate. [L. *prōpōnĕre* — *prō*, forward, *pōnĕre*, to place.]

proportion *prə-pör'shən*, *n* the relation of one thing to another in magnitude; fitness of parts to each other; due relation; relation of rhythm or of harmony; ratio; the identity or equality of ratios (*math*); equal or just share; relative share, portion, inheritance, contribution, fortune; a part or portion (*colloq*); (in *pl*) dimensions. — *vt* to adjust or fashion in due proportion; to regulate the proportions of; to divide proportionally. — *adj* **propor'tionable** that may be proportioned; having a due or definite relation. — *adj* **propor'tional** relating to proportion; in proportion; having the same or a constant ratio (*math*); proportionate, in suitable proportion. — *n* (*math*) a number or quantity in a proportion. — *n* **proportional'ity.** — *adv* **propor'tionally.** — *adj* **propor'tionate** in fit proportion; proportional. — *vt* to adjust in proportion. — *adv* **propor'tionately.** — *n* **propor'tioning** adjustment of proportions. — *adj* **propor'tionless** ill-proportioned. — **proportional representation** a system intended to give parties in an elected body a representation as nearly as possible proportional to their voting strength; often loosely applied to the system of transferred vote. — **in proportion** (often with *to*) in a (given) ratio; having a correct or harmonious relation (with something); to a degree or extent which seems appropriate to the importance, etc. of the matter in hand; **out of (all)**

proportion not in proportion. [L. *prōportiō, -ōnis* — *prō*, in comparison with, *portiō*, part, share.]

propose *prə-pōz'*, *vt* to offer for consideration or acceptance; to suggest as something to be done; to intend; to move formally; to nominate; to invite the company to drink (a health); to enunciate. — *vi* to form or put forward an intention or design; to offer, especially marriage. — *n* **propōs'al** an act of proposing; an offer, esp. of marriage; anything proposed; a plan. — *n* **propōs'er.** [Fr. *proposer* — pfx. *pro-*, *poser*, to place; see **pose**[1].]

proposition *prop-ə-zish'ən*, *n* an act of propounding or (more rarely) proposing; the thing propounded or proposed; a statement of a judgment; a form of statement in which a predicate is affirmed or denied of a subject (*logic*); a premise, esp. a major premise; a statement of a problem or theorem for (or with) solution or demonstration (*math*); a possibility, suggestion, course of action, etc. to be considered; any situation, thing or person considered as something to cope with, such as an enterprise, job, opponent, etc. (*slang*; orig. *US*); an invitation to sexual intercourse (*colloq*). — *vt* to make a proposition to someone, esp. to solicit a woman for sexual relations. — *adj* **proposi'tional.** — **propositional calculus** see under **calculus.** [L. *prōpositiō, -ōnis* — *prō*, before; see **position.**]

propound *prə-pownd'*, *vt* to offer for consideration; to set forth as aim or reward; to produce for probate (*law*). — *n* **propound'er.** [**propone.**]

propranolol *prop-ran'ə-lol*, *n* a beta-blocker (q.v.) used esp. in the treatment of cardiac arrhythmia, angina and hypertension.

proprietor *prō-prī'ə-tər*, *fem* **proprietress** *-prī'ə-*, *n* an owner, esp. of a small business. — *adj* **pro-prī'etary** of the nature of property; legally made only by a person or body of persons having special rights, esp. a patent or trademark; pertaining to or belonging to the legal owner; (of a company, etc.) privately owned and run; owning property. — *adj* **proprīetorial** (*-tö'*). — *n* **proprī'etorship.** [L.L. *proprietārius* — *proprius*, own; **proprietor** has been formed irregularly; it is not a Latin word.]

propriety *prō-prī'ə-ti*, *n* rightness, as in the use of words; appropriateness; seemliness; decency; conformity with good manners; conformity with convention in language and conduct. [Fr. *propriété* — L. *proprietās, -ātis* — *proprius*, own.]

proprioceptive *prō-pri-ō-sep'tiv*, (*biol*) *adj* of, pertaining to, or made active by, stimuli arising from movement in the tissues. — *n* **propriocep'tor** a sensory nerve-ending receptive of such stimuli. — **proprioceptive sense** the sense of muscular position. [L. *proprius*, own, after **receptive.**]

propulsion *prə-pul'shən*, *n* driving forward. — *adj* **propul'sive** or **propul'sory.** [L. *prōpellĕre, prō-pulsum*, to push forward; see **propel.**]

propyl *prō'pil*, *n* the alcohol radical C_3H_7. — *n* **pro'pylamine** an amine of propyl. — *n* **pro'pylene** or **pro'pene** a gaseous hydrocarbon (C_3H_6). — *adj* **propyl'ic.** [**propionic** and Gr. *hȳlē*, matter.]

pro rata. See under **pro**[1].

prorate *prō-rāt'* or *prō'rāt*, (mainly *US*) *vt* to distribute proportionately. — *n* **prorā'tion.** [**pro rata.**]

prorogue *prə-* or *prō-rōg'*, *vt* to discontinue the meetings of (a legislative assembly) for a time without dissolving. — *n* **prōrogā'tion.** [L. *prōrogāre, -ātum* — *prō*, forward, *rogāre*, to ask.]

prosaic *prō-zā'ik*, *adj* like prose; unpoetical; matter-of-fact; commonplace; dull. — *adv* **prosā'ically.** — *n* **prosā'icness.** [L. *prosa*, prose.]

prosauropod *prō-sör'ə-pod*, *n* a reptile-like dinosaur of the division *Prosauropoda* which lived in the Triassic period. — Also *adj.*

proscenium *prō-sē'ni-əm*, *n* the part of the stage in front of the curtain; the curtain and its framework, esp. the arch that frames the more traditional type of stage (**proscenium arch**). [Latinised from Gr. *proskēnion* — *pro*, before, *skēnē*, stage.]

prosciutto *pro-shōō'tō*, *n* finely cured uncooked ham, often smoked: — *pl* **prosciu'tti** or **prosciu'ttos.** [It., lit. pre-dried.]

proscribe *prō-skrīb'*, *vt* to outlaw; to prohibit. — *n* **prōscrib'er.** — *n* **prōscrip'tion.** — *adj* **prōscrip'-tive.** [L. *prōscrībĕre* — *prō-*, before, publicly, *scrībĕre, scrīptum*, to write.]

prose *prōz*, *n* ordinary spoken and written language with words in direct straightforward arrangement without metrical structure; all writings not in verse; a passage of prose for translation from or, usu., into a foreign language, as an exercise. — *adj* of or in prose; not poetical; plain; dull. — *vi* to write prose; to speak or write tediously. — *vt* to compose in prose; to turn into prose. — *n* **prō'ser.** — *adv* **prō'sily.** — *n* **prō'siness.** — *adj* **prō'sy.** — **prose poem** a prose work or passage having some of the characteristics of poetry; **prose'-writer.** [Fr., — L. *prōsa* — *prorsus*, straightforward — *prō*, forward, *vertĕre, versum*, to turn.]

prosecute *pros'i-kūt*, *vt* to follow onwards or pursue, in order to reach or accomplish to pursue by law; to bring before a court. — *vi* to carry on a legal prosecution. — *adj* **pros'ecūtable.** — *n* **prosecū'-tion** the act of prosecuting in any sense; the prosecuting party in legal proceedings. — *n* **pros'-ecūtor**, *fem* **pros'ecūtrix**, a person who prosecutes or pursues any plan or business; someone who instigates a civil or criminal suit. — **director of public prosecutions** or **public prosecutor** an official appointed to conduct criminal prosecutions in the public interest (in U.S. **prosecuting attorney, district attorney**). [L. *prōsequī, -secūtus* — *prō*, onwards, *sequī*, to follow.]

proselyte *pros'i-līt*, *n* a person who has come over from one religion or opinion to another; a convert, esp. from paganism to Judaism. — *vt* **pros'elytise** or **-ize** to convert. — *vi* to make proselytes. — *n* **pros'elytiser** or **-z-.** — *n* **pros'elytism** being, becoming or making a convert; conversion. [Gr. *prosēlytos*, a newcomer, resident foreigner — *pros*, to, and the stem *elyth-*, used to form aorists for *erchesthai*, to go.]

prosencephalon *pros-en-sef'ə-lon*, (*zool*) *n* the forebrain, comprising the cerebral hemispheres and olfactory processes. [Gr. *pros*, to, used as if for *pro*, before, *enkephalon*, brain — *en*, in, *kephalē*, head.]

prosimian *prō-sim'i-ən*, *n* a primate of the suborder **Prosimii**, e.g. the lemur, loris, tarsier. — Also *adj.* [**pro-**[1] and L. *simia*, ape.]

prosit *prō'sit*, *interj* good luck to you, a salutation in drinking healths customary among German students. [L. *prōsit*, used as 3rd pers. sing. pres. subj. of L. *prōdesse*, to be of use — *prō(d)-*, for, *esse*, to be.]

prosody *pros'ə-di*, *n* the study of versification. — *adj* **prosodial** (*pros-* or *prəs-ō'di-əl*), **prosodic** (*-od'ik*) or **prosod'ical.** — *n* **prosō'dian** or **pros'odist** someone skilled in prosody. [L. *prosōdia*, Gr. *prosōidiā* — *pros*, to, *ōidē*, a song.]

prosopagnosia *pros-ō-pag-nō'si-ə*, *n* inability to recognise faces of persons well-known to the sufferer. [L.L. *prosopagnosia* — Gr. *prosōpon*, face, *a*, without, *gnōsis*, knowledge.]

prosopography *pros-ō-pog'rə-fi*, *n* a biographical sketch, description of a person's appearance, character, life, etc.; the compiling or study of such material. — *adj* **prosopograph'ical.** [Gr. *prosōpon*, face, person, *graphein*, to write.]

prosopon *pros-ō-pon'*, (*theol*) *n* the outer appearance, personification or embodiment of one of the persons of the Trinity. — *n* **prosopopoeia** or **prosopopeia** (*pros-ō-pō-pē'ə*) personification. — *adj* **prosopo-poe'ial** or **prosopope'ial.** [Gr. *prosōpopoiiā* — *prosōpon*, face, person, *poieein*, to make.]

prospect *pros'pekt, n* outlook; direction of facing; a wide view; view, sight, field of view; a scene; a pictorial representation, view; a survey or mental view; outlook upon the probable future; expectation; chance of success; a wide street (Russ. *prəs-pyekt'*); a place thought likely to yield a valuable mineral (*mining*); a sample, or a test, or the yield of a test of a sample from such a place; a probable source of profit. — *vi* **prospect'** to look around; (*prəs-pekt'* or in U.S. *pros'*) to make a search, esp. for chances of mining; to promise or yield results to the prospector. — *vt* (*-pekt'* or *pros'pekt*) to explore, search, survey or test for profitable minerals. — *n* **prospect'ing** (or in U.S. *pros'*) searching a district for minerals with a view to further operations. — *n* **prospec'tion** looking to the future; foresight. — *adj* **prospec'tive** probable or expected future; looking forward; yielding distant views; looking to the future. — *n* prospect. — *adv* **prospec'tively.** — *n* **prospec'tiveness.** — *n* **prospec'tor** (or in U.S. *pros'*) a person who prospects for minerals. — *n* **prospec'tus** the outline of any plan submitted for public approval, particularly of a literary work, a joint-stock concern, or an issue of shares; an account of the organisation of a school: — *pl* **prospec'tuses.** [L. *prōspectus, -ūs* — *prōspicĕre, prōspectum* — *prō-*, forward, *specĕre*, to look.]

prosper *pros'pər, vi* to thrive; to experience favourable circumstances; to flourish; to turn out well. — *vt* to cause to prosper. — *n* **prosperity** (*-per'i-ti*) the state of being prosperous; success; good fortune. — *adj* **pros'perous** thriving; affluent; successful. — *adv* **pros'perously.** — *n* **pros'perousness.** [L. *prosper, prosperus.*]

prostaglandin *pros-tə-gland'in, n* any one of a group of chemical substances secreted by various parts of the body into the bloodstream and having a wide range of effects on the body processes, e.g. on muscle contraction. [*prostate gland*, a major source of these.]

prostate *pros'tāt, n* a gland in males at the neck of the bladder. — Also **prostate gland.** — *n* **prostatec'tomy** surgical removal of all or part of the prostate gland. — *adj* **prostatic** (*pros-tat'ik*). [Gr. *prostatēs*, one who stands in front, the prostate — *pro*, before, *sta*, root of *histanai*, to set up.]

prosthesis *pros'thə-sis* or *pros-thē'sis, n* addition of a prefix to a word, e.g. for ease of pronunciation (*linguis*; also **prothesis**, q.v.); the fitting of artificial parts to the body; such an artificial part: — *pl* **prostheses** (*-sēz*). — *adj* **prosthetic** (*-thet'ik*) relating to prosthesis. — *n* an artificial part of the body. — *nsing* **prosthet'ics** the surgery or dentistry involved in supplying artificial parts to the body. — *n* **prosthet'ist.** [Gr. *prosthesis*, adj. *prosthetikos* — *pros*, to, *thesis*, putting.]

prosthodontia *pros-thō-don'shi-ə, n* provision of false teeth. — Also *nsing* **prosthodon'tics.** — *n* **prosthodon'tist.** [Gr. *prosthesis*, addition — *pros*, to, *thesis*, putting, *odous, odontos*, tooth.]

prostitute *pros'ti-tūt, vt* to devote to, or offer or sell for, evil or base use; to hire out for sexual intercourse; to devote to such intercourse as a religious act; to degrade by publicity or commonness. — *adj* openly devoted to lewdness; given over (to evil); basely venal. — *n* a person (usu. a woman or a homosexual man) who accepts money in return for sexual intercourse; someone who offers skills, efforts or reputation for unworthy ends. — *n* **prostitū'tion** the act or practice of prostituting; devotion to base purposes. — *n* **pros'titūtor.** [L. *prōstituĕre, -ūtum*, to set up for sale — *prō*, before, *statuĕre*, to place.]

prostrate *pros'trāt, adj* prone; lying or bent with face on the ground; (*loosely*) lying at length; procumbent, trailing (*bot*); reduced to helplessness; completely exhausted. — *vt* **prostrate'** (or *pros'*) to throw forwards on the ground; to lay flat; to overthrow; to reduce to impotence or exhaustion; to bend in humble reverence (*reflexive*). — *n* **prostrā'tion.** [L. *prōstrātus*, past p. of *prōsternĕre* — *prō*, forwards, *sternĕre*, to spread.]

prosy. See under **prose.**

Prot. *abbrev* for Protestant.

prot-. See **proto-.**

protactinium *prōt-ak-tin'i-əm, n* radioactive element (symbol **Pa**; atomic no. 91) that yields actinium on disintegration. [Gr. *prōtos*, first, and **actinium.**]

protagonist *prō-tag'ən-ist, n* orig., the chief actor, character or combatant; now, often applied to any (or in *pl*, all) of the main personages or participants in a story or event; (*loosely*) a champion, advocate. [Gr. *prōtos*, first, *agōnistēs*, a combatant, actor.]

protamine *prō'tə-mēn, n* any of the simplest proteins, found esp. in the sperm of certain fish. [**proto-** and **amine.**]

protanopia *prō-tən-op'i-ə, n* a form of colour-blindness in which red and green are confused because the retina does not respond to red. — *n* **prō'tanope** a sufferer from protanopia. — *adj* **prōtanop'ic** colour-blind to red. [N.L. *protanopia.*]

protasis *prot'ə-sis, n* the conditional clause of a conditional sentence (opp. to *apodosis*); the first part of a dramatic composition: — *pl* **prot'asēs.** [Gr. *protasis*, proposition, premise, protasis — *pro*, before, *tasis*, a stretching, *teinein*, to stretch.]

protea *prō'ti-ə, n* a plant of the large South African *Protea* genus of shrubs or small trees with big cone-shaped heads of flowers. [*Proteus*, Greek sea-god who assumed many shapes (from the varied character of the family).]

protean. See under **proteus.**

protease. See under **protein.**

protect *prə-* or *prō-tekt', vt* to shield from danger, injury, change, capture, loss; to defend; to strengthen; to seek to foster by import duties; to screen off for safety (e.g. machinery). — *adj* **protect'ed.** — *n* **protec'tion** the act of protecting; the state of being protected; defence; that which protects; a fostering of home produce and manufactures by import duties; patronage; concubinage. — *n* **protec'tionism.** — *n* **protec'tionist** a person who favours the protection of trade by duties on imports — also *adj.* — *adj* **protec'tive** giving protection; intended to protect; defensive; sheltering. — *n* that which protects; a condom. — *adv* **protec'tively.** — *n* **protec'tiveness.** — *n* **protec'tor,** *fem* **protec'tress,** a person who protects from injury or oppression; a protective device; a means of protection; a guard; a guardian; a regent; the head of the state during the Commonwealth (*Lord Protector*). — *adj* **protec'toral.** — *n* **protec'torāte** the position, office, term of office, or government of a protector; (with *cap*) the Commonwealth period (*hist*); guardianship; authority over a vassal state; relation assumed by a state over a territory which it administers without annexation and without admitting the inhabitants to citizenship. — *adj* **protectorial** (*prō-tek-tör'i-əl*). — *adj* **protec'torless.** — *n* **protec'torship.** — *n* **protec'tory** an institution for destitute or delinquent children. — **protection money** money extorted from shopkeepers, businessmen, etc. as a bribe for leaving their property, business, etc. unharmed; **protective coloration** likeness in the colour of animals to their natural surroundings tending to prevent them from being seen by their enemies; **protective custody** detention of a person for his or her personal safety or from doubt as to his possible actions. [L. *prōtegĕre, -tēctum* — *prō-*, in front, *tegĕre*, to cover.]

protégé *prō'* or *pro'tə-zhā, fem* **pro'tégée,** *n* a person under the protection or patronage of another; a pupil; a ward. [Fr., — past p. of *protéger*, to protect — L. *prōtegĕre.*]

protein *prō'tēn*, *n* any member of a group of complex nitrogenous substances that play an important part in the bodies of plants and animals, easily hydrolysed into mixtures of amino-acids. — *n* **pro'tease** (*-tē-ās* or *-āz*) any enzyme that splits up proteins. — *adj* **proteinaceous** (*prō-tēn-ā'shəs*), **proteinic** (*prō-tēn'ik*) or **protein'ous**. [Gr. *prōteios*, primary — *prōtos*, first.]

pro tem *prō tem*, short for **pro tempore** (q.v. under **pro**[1]).

Proterozoic *prot-ər-ō-zō'ik* or *prōt-*, *n* and *adj* orig., Lower Palaeozoic (Cambrian to Silurian); Pre-Cambrian; Upper Pre-Cambrian. [Gr. *proteros*, earlier, *zōē*, life.]

protest *prə-* or *prō-test'*, *vi* to express or record dissent or objection; to make solemn affirmation, professions or avowal. — *vt* to make a solemn declaration of; to declare; to note, as a bill of exchange, on account of non-acceptance or non-payment; to make a protest against. — *n* **prō'test** an affirmation or avowal; a declaration of objection or dissent; the noting by a notary-public of an unpaid or unaccepted bill. — *adj* expressing, in order to express, dissent or objection. — *n* **Protestant** (*prot'is-tənt*) a member, adherent or sharer of the beliefs of one of those churches which separated from the Roman Catholic church at the Reformation, or their offshoots; orig., one of those who, in 1529, protested against an edict of Charles V and the Diet of Spires denouncing the Reformation. — *adj* of, or pertaining to, Protestants, or more usually, Protestantism. — *vt* **Prot'estantise** or **-ize**. — *n* **Prot'estantism** the Protestant religion; the state of being a Protestant. — *n* **protestation** (*prō-tes-tā'shən*) an avowal; an asseveration; a declaration in pleading. — *n* **protest'er** or **protest'or** a person who protests. — *adv* **protest'ingly**. — **Protestant work ethic** an attitude to life stressing the virtue of hard work over enjoyment, popularly associated with the Protestant denominations; **under protest** unwillingly, having made a protest. [Fr. *protester* — L. *prōtestārī*, *-ātus*, to bear witness in public — *prō*, before, *testārī* — *testis*, a witness.]

proteus *prō'tūs* or *-ti-əs*, *n* a member of the *Proteus* genus of rodlike bacteria found in the intestines and in decaying organic matter: — *pl* **pro'teuses**. — *adj* **protean** (*prō-tē'ən* or *prō'ti-ən*) readily assuming different shapes; variable; inconstant. [Gr. *Prōteus*, a sea-god able to assume different shapes.]

prothesis *proth'i-sis*, *n* in the Greek Church the preliminary oblation of the eucharistic elements before the liturgy; the table used; the chapel or northern apse where it stands; development of an inorganic initial sound (*linguis*). — *adj* **prothetic** (*prə-* or *prō-thet'ik*). [Gr. *prothesis* — *pro*, before, and the root of *tithenai*, to place.]

Protista *prō-tis'tə*, *npl* a large group of unicellular organisms, protozoa, bacteria, etc. not classified as plants or animals. — *n* **prō'tist** any member of the Protista. [Gr. *prōtistos*, very first — *prōtos*, first.]

protium *prō'ti-əm* or *-shi-əm*, *n* ordinary hydrogen of atomic weight 1, distinguished from deuterium and tritium. [Gr. *prōtos*, first.]

proto- *prō-tō-* or before a vowel **prot-** *prōt-*, *combining form* signifying: first; first of a series; first-formed; primitive; ancestral; denoting a protolanguage. [Gr. *prōtos*, first.]

protocol *prō'tō-kol*, *n* an original note, minute or draft of an instrument or transaction; a draft treaty; an official or formal account or record; an official formula; a body of diplomatic etiquette; a set of rules governing the transmission of data between two computers which cannot communicate directly. — *vi* to issue or form protocols. — *vt* to make a protocol of: — *pr p* **pro'tocolling**; *pa t* and *pa p* **pro'tocolled**. — *adj* **protoco'lic**. [Fr. *protocole* — L.L. *prōtocollum* — Late Gr. *prōtokollon*, a glued-on descriptive first leaf of a manuscript — Gr. *prōtos*, first, *kolla*, glue.]

protogalaxy *prō-tō-gal'ək-si*, *n* a large cloud of gas supposed to be slowly condensing into stars, an early stage in the formation of a galaxy. [**proto-**.]

protohistoric *prō-tō-his-tor'ik*, *adj* belonging to the earliest age of history, just after the prehistoric and before the development of written records, etc. — *n* **protohis'tory**. [**proto-**.]

protohuman *prō-tō-hū'mən*, *n* a prehistoric primate, a supposed ancestor of modern man. — Also *adj*. [**proto-**.]

protolanguage *prō'tō-lang-gwij*, *n* a hypothetical language (such as *Proto-Indo-European*) regarded as the ancestor of other recorded or existing languages, and reconstructed by comparing these. [**proto-**.]

protolithic *prō-tō-lith'ik*, *adj* of or pertaining to the earliest Stone Age. [**proto-** and Gr. *lithos*, stone.]

protomartyr *prō'tō-mär-tər*, *n* the first martyr in any cause, esp. St Stephen. [Late Gr. *prōtomartyr*.]

proton *prō'ton*, (*phys*) *n* an elementary particle of positive charge and unit atomic mass — the atom of the lightest isotope of hydrogen without its electron. — *adj* **protonic** (*-ton'ik*). [Gr., neut. of *prōtos*, first.]

protopathic *prō-tə-path'ik*, *adj* of or relating to a certain type of nerve which is only affected by the coarser stimuli, e.g. pain; of or relating to this kind of reaction. — *n* **protop'athy**. [**proto-** and **pathic** (see **-path**).]

Protophyta *prōt-of'i-tə*, *npl* a group of unicellular plants. — *n* **protophyte** (*prō'tə-fīt*) one of the Protophyta. — *adj* **protophytic** (*-fit'ik*). [**proto-** and Gr. *phyton*, a plant.]

protoplasm *prō'tə-plazm*, *n* living matter, the physical basis of life. — *adj* **protoplas'mic**, **protoplas'mal** or **protoplasmat'ic**. [**proto-** and Gr. *plasma*, form.]

protostar *prō'tō-stär*, *n* a condensing mass of gas, a supposed early stage in the formation of a star. [**proto-**.]

Prototheria *prō-tə-thē'ri-ə*, *npl* the monotremes. — *adj* **protothē'rian**. [**proto-** and Gr. *thēr*, wild beast.]

prototrophic *prō-tō-trof'ik*, *adj* feeding only on inorganic matter. [**proto-** and Gr. *trophē*, food.]

prototype *prō'tə-tīp*, *n* the first or original type or model from which anything is copied; an exemplar; a pattern; an ancestral form. — *vt* to make or use a prototype of. — *adj* **pro'totypal** or **prototypical** (*-tip'*). [Fr., — Gr. *prōtos*, first, *typos*, a type.]

Protozoa *prō-tō-zō'ə*, *npl* the lowest and simplest of animals, unicellular forms or colonies multiplying by fission. — *n* **protozō'an** or **protozō'on** one of the Protozoa: — *pl* **protozō'ans** or **protozō'a**. — *adj* **protozō'an** or **protozō'ic**. [**proto-** and Gr. *zōion*, an animal.]

protract *prō-trakt'*, *vt* to draw out or lengthen in time; to prolong; to lengthen out; to protrude; to draw to scale. — *adj* **protrac'ted** drawn out in time; prolonged; lengthened out; drawn to scale. — *adv* **protrac'tedly**. — *adj* **protrac'tile** (*-tīl* or in U.S. *-til*) or **protrac'tible** capable of being thrust out. — *n* **protrac'tion** (*-shən*) act of protracting or prolonging; the delaying of the termination of a thing; the plotting or laying down of the dimensions of anything on paper; a plan drawn to scale. — *adj* **protrac'tive** drawing out in time; prolonging; delaying. — *n* **protrac'tor** an instrument for laying down angles on paper; a muscle whose contraction draws a part forward or away from the body. [L. *prōtrahĕre*, *-tractum* — *prō*, forth, *trahĕre*, to draw.]

protrude *prō-trood'*, *vt* to thrust or push out or forward; to obtrude. — *vi* to stick out, project. — *n* **protru'sion** (*-zhən*) the act of protruding; the state of being protruded; that which protrudes. — *adj* **protru'sive**. — *adv* **protru'sively**. — *n* **pro-**

tru'siveness. [L. *prōtrūděre, -trūsum* — *prō*, forward, *trūděre*, to thrust.]

protuberance *prō-tūb'ər-əns, n* a bulging out; a swelling. — *adj* **protū'berant.** — *adv* **protū'berantly.** — *vi* **protū'berate** to bulge out. — *n* **protūberā'tion.** [L. *prōtūberāre, -ātum* — *prō*, forward, *tūber*, a swelling.]

proud *prowd, adj* having excessive self-esteem; arrogant, haughty; having a proper sense of self-respect; having an exulting sense of credit due to or reflected upon oneself; having a glowing feeling of gratification (because of; with *of*); giving reason for pride or boasting; manifesting pride; having an appearance of pride, vigour, boldness, and freedom; stately; mettlesome; swollen; projecting, standing out, as from a plane surface, e.g. a nail-head. — *adj* **proud'ish.** — *adv* **proud'ly.** — *n* **proud flesh** a growth or excrescence of flesh in a wound. — **do someone proud** (*colloq*) to treat someone sumptuously; to give honour to someone. [O.E. *prūd, prūt*, proud; perh. from a L.L. word connected with L. *prōdesse*, to be of advantage.]

Prov. *abbrev* for: (the Book of) Proverbs (*Bible*); Provincial; Provost.

prove *prōōv, vt* to test, experience or suffer; to test the genuineness of; to ascertain; to establish or ascertain as truth by argument or otherwise; to demonstrate; to check by the opposite operation (*arith*); to obtain probate of (a will); to cause or allow (dough) to rise. — *vi* to make trial; to turn out; to be shown afterwards: — *pa p* **proved** or **prov'en** (*prōōv'n* or as used, *specif* for *Scots law prōv'n*). — *adj* **prove'able** or **prov'able.** — *adv* **prove'ably** or **prov'ably.** — *n* **prov'er.** — *adj* **prov'ing** testing, as in **proving ground** a place for testing scientifically (also *fig*), and **proving flight** test flight. — **the exception proves the rule** the existence of an exception proves that the rule holds good otherwise. [O.Fr. *prover* — L. *probāre* — *probus*, excellent; partly perh. — O.E. *prōfian*, to assume to be — L. *probāre*.]

proven *prōv'n* or *prōōv'n*. See **prove.** — **not proven** a Scottish legal verdict declaring that guilt has been neither proved nor disproved.

provenance *prov'i-nəns, n* source, esp. of a work of art. [Fr., — L. *prō-*, forth, *venīre*, to come.]

Provençal *prov-ã-säl, adj* of or pertaining to *Provence*, in France, or to its inhabitants or language. — *n* a native or the language of Provence, *langue d'oc*. — *adj* **Provençale** (*prov-ã-säl*) in cooking, prepared with oil and garlic and usu. tomatoes. [L. *prōvinciālis* — *prōvincia*, province.]

provender *prov'in-dər* or *-ən-dər, n* dry food for animals, such as hay or corn; esp. a mixture of meal and cut straw or hay; food (*facetious*). — *vt* and *vi* to feed. [O.Fr. *provendre* for *provende* — L.L. *provenda*.]

provenience *prō-vē'ni-əns*, (chiefly *US*) *n* provenance. [L. *prōvenīre*.]

proverb *prov'ərb, n* a short familiar sentence expressing a supposed truth or moral lesson; a byword; (in *pl* with *cap*) a book of maxims in the Old Testament. — *adj* **prover'bial** (*prə-vûr'bi-əl*) like or of the nature of a proverb; expressed or mentioned in a proverb; notorious. — *adv* **prover'bially.** [Fr. *proverbe* — L. *prōverbium* — *prō-*, publicly, *verbum*, a word.]

provide *prə-* or *prō-vīd', vt* to supply; to afford, yield; to appoint or give a right to a benefice, esp. before it is actually vacant; to stipulate. — *vi* to procure supplies, means, or whatever may be desirable, make provision; to take measures (for or against). — *adj* **provī'dable.** — *pa p* or *conj* **provi'ded.** — *pr p* or *conj* **provī'ding** (often with *that*) on condition; upon these terms; with the understanding. — *n* **provī'der.** [L. *prōvidēre* — *prō*, before, *vidēre*, to see.]

providence *prov'i-dəns, n* foresight; prudent management and thrift; timely preparation; the foresight and benevolent care of God (*theol*); (usu. with *cap*) God, considered in this relation (*theol*). — *adj* **prov'ident** seeing beforehand, and providing for the future; prudent; thrifty; frugal. — *adj* **providential** (*-den'shl*) affected by or proceeding from divine providence. — *adv* **providen'tially.** — *adv* **prov'idently.** — **provident society** same as **friendly society.** [L. *prōvidēns, -entis*, pres. p. of *prōvidēre* — *prō*, before, *vidēre*, to see.]

province *prov'ins, n* a portion of an empire or a state marked off for purposes of government or in some way historically distinct; the district over which an archbishop has jurisdiction; a territorial division of the Jesuits, Templars, and other orders; a faunal or floral area; a region; vaguely, a field of duty, activity or knowledge; a department; (in *pl*) all parts of the country but the capital. — *adj* **provincial** (*prə-vin'shl*) relating to a province; belonging to a province or the provinces; local; showing the habits and manners of a province; unpolished; narrow. — *n* an inhabitant of a province or country district; an unsophisticated person; the superintendent of the heads of the religious houses in a province (*RC*). — *vt* **provin'cialise** or **-ize** to render provincial. — *n* **provin'cialism** a manner, a mode of speech, or a turn of thought peculiar to a province or a country district; a local expression; the state or quality of being provincial; ignorance and narrowness of interests shown by a person who gives their attention entirely to local affairs. — *n* **provin'cialist.** — *n* **provinciality** (*-shi-al'i-ti*). — *adv* **provin'cially.** [Fr., — L. *prōvincia*, an official charge, hence a province.]

provirus *prō-vī'rəs, n* the form of a virus when it is integrated into the DNA of a host cell. — *adj* **provī'ral.** [pro-[2] (2).]

provision *prə-vizh'ən, n* the act of providing; that which is provided or prepared; measures taken beforehand; a clause in a law or a deed; a stipulation; a rule for guidance; an appointment by the pope to a benefice not yet vacant; preparation; previous agreement; a store or stock; (commonly in *pl*) store of food; (in *pl*) food. — *vt* to supply with provisions or food. — *adj* **provi'sional** provided for the occasion; to meet necessity; (of e.g. an arrangement) adopted on the understanding that it will probably be changed later; containing a provision. — *adj* and *n* **Provi'sional** (a member) of the Provisional Irish Republican Army, the militant breakaway wing of the Official IRA (colloq. shortening **Prō'vō**: — *pl* **Pro'vos**). — *adv* **provi'sionally.** — *n* **provisional'ity.** — **provisional order** an order granted by a secretary of state, which, when confirmed by the legislature, has the force of an act of parliament. [Fr., — L. *prōvīsiō, -ōnis* — *prōvidēre*; see **provide.**]

proviso *prə-vī'zō, n* a provision or condition in a deed or other writing; the clause containing it; any condition: — *pl* **provī'sos** or **provī'soes** (*-zōz*). — *adv* **provī'sorily** (*-zə-ri-li*). — *adj* **provī'sory** containing a proviso or condition; conditional; making provision for the time; temporary. [From the L. law phrase *prōvīsō quod*, it being provided that.]

Provo. See **Provisional** under **provision.**

provocable, etc. See under **provoke.**

provoke *prə-vōk, vt* to call forth, evoke (feelings, desires, etc.); to excite, stimulate; to incite, bring about; to excite with anger or sexual desire; to annoy, exasperate. — *adj* **provocable** (*prov'ək-ə-bl*). — *n* **provocateur** (*pro-vo-ka-tœr'*) a person who provokes unrest and dissatisfaction for political ends. — *n* **provocā'tion** the act of provoking; that which provokes; any cause of danger. — *adj* **provocative** (*-vok'*) tending, or designed, to provoke or excite. — *n* anything that provokes. — *adv* **provoc'atively.** — *n* **provoc'ativeness.** — *n* **prov'ocātor.** — *adj* **provoc'atory.** — *adj* **provōk'ing** irritating; stimulating. — *adv* **provōk'ingly.** [L. *prōvocāre, -ātum* — *prō-*, forth, *vocāre*, to call.]

provost *prov'əst, n* the dignitary set over a cathedral or collegiate church; in certain colleges, the head; in Scotland, the chief magistrate of a burgh, answering to mayor in England. — *n* **prov'ostship.** — *n* **provost-mar'shal** (*prə-vō'*; or in U.S. *prō'*) (in the army) head of military police, an officer with special powers for enforcing discipline and securing prisoners until trial; (in the navy) officer (master-at-arms) having charge of prisoners; **provost-ser'geant** (*prə-vō'*) sergeant of military police. — **Lord Provost** the chief magistrate of Edinburgh, Glasgow, Perth, Aberdeen or Dundee. [O.E. *profast* (*prafost*), O.Fr. *provost* (Fr. *prévôt*) — L.L. *prō-positus* — *prō-* for *prae*, at the head, *positus*, set.]

prow *prow, n* the forepart of a ship; the nose of an aeroplane; a projecting front part. [Fr. *proue*, or Port., Sp., or Genoese *proa* — L. *prōra* — Gr. *prōiră*.]

prowess *prow'es, n* bravery; valour; daring; accomplishment. [O.Fr. *prou* (Fr. *preux*).]

prowl *prowl, vi* to keep moving about as if in search of something; to rove in search of prey or plunder. — *n* the act of prowling. — *n* **prowl'er.** — *n* and *adj* **prowl'ing.** — *adv* **prowl'ingly.** — **on the prowl** occupied in prowling. [M.E. *prollen*.]

proximate *proks'i-mit* or *-māt, adj* nearest or next; without anything between, as a cause and its effect; near and immediate. — *adj* **prox'imal** (*biol*) at the near, inner, or attached end (opp. to *distal*). — *adv* **prox'imally.** — *adv* **prox'imately.** — *n* **proxim'ity** immediate nearness in time, place, relationship, etc. — *adv* **prox'imo** next month (often abbrev. **prox**) (for L. *proximō mēns*). [L. *proximus*, next, superl. from *propior* (compar.) — *prope*, near.]

proxy *prok'si, n* the agency of one who acts for another; a person who acts or votes for another; the writing by which they are authorised to do so; a substitute. [**procuracy**.]

PRS *abbrev* for Performing Rights Society.

prude *prōōd, n* a person of priggish or affected modesty; a person who pretends to be very correct and proper. — *n* **pru'dery** manners of a prude. — *adj* **pru'dish.** — *adv* **pru'dishly.** — *n* **pru'dishness.** [O.Fr. *prode*, fem. of *prou*, *prod*, excellent.]

prudent *prōō'dənt, adj* cautious and wise in conduct; discreet; characterised by, behaving with, showing, having or dictated by forethought. — *n* **pru'dence** the quality of being prudent; wisdom in practical matters; attention to self-interest; caution. — *adj* **prudential** (*-den'shl*) having regard to considerations of prudence; relating to prudence; prudent. — *n* **prudentiality** (*-den-shi-al'i-ti*). — *adv* **pruden'tially.** — *adv* **pru'dently.** [L. *prūdēns*, *prūdentis*, contr. of *prōvidēns*, pres. p. of *prōvidēre*, to foresee.]

prudery, prudish, etc. See **prude.**

pruina *prōō-ī'nə*, (*bot*) *n* a powdery bloom or waxy secretion. — *adj* **pruinose** (*prōō'i-nōs*). [L. *pruīna*, hoar-frost.]

prune[1] *prōōn, vt* to trim by lopping off superfluous parts; to divest of anything superfluous (*fig*); to remove by pruning. — *n* **pru'ner.** — *n* **pru'ning** the act of pruning or trimming. — **pru'ning-bill** or **-hook** a hooked bill for pruning with; **pru'ning-knife** a large knife with a slightly hooked point for pruning. — *npl* **pru'ning-shears** shears for pruning shrubs, etc. [O.Fr. *proignier*.]

prune[2] *prōōn, n* a dried plum; the dark purple colour of prune juice; a despised or silly person (*colloq*). [Fr., — L. *prūna*, pl. of *prūnum* (taken for a *nsing*); cf. Gr. *prou(m)non*, plum.]

prunella *prōō-nel'ə, n* a strong silk or woollen material, formerly used for academic and clerical gowns and women's shoes. — *adj* made of prunella. [App. Fr. *prunelle*, sloe, dimin. of *prune*, plum.]

prurient *prōō'ri-ənt, adj* having an unhealthy interest in sexual matters; arousing such interest. — *n* **pru'rience** or **pru'riency.** — *adv* **pru'riently.** [L. *prūriēns*, *-entis*, pres. p. of *prūrīre*, to itch.]

prurigo *prōō-rī'gō, n* an eruption on the skin, causing great itching: — *pl* **prurī'gos.** — *adj* **pruriginous** (*-rij'i-nəs*). — *adj* **prurit'ic** pertaining to pruritus. — *n* **prurī'tus** itching. [L. *prūrīgō*, *-inis*, *prūrītus*, *-ūs* — *prūrīre*, to itch.]

Prussian *prush'ən, adj* of or pertaining to *Prussia*, a former state of N. Central Europe. — *n* an inhabitant, native, or citizen of Prussia. — *vt* and *vi* **Pruss'ianise** or **-ize** to make or become Prussian. — *n* **Pruss'ianiser** or **-z-**. — *n* **Pruss'ianism** spirit of Prussian nationality; often used for arrogant militarism. — *n* **prussiate** (*prus'* or *prush'i-āt*) a cyanide; one of several compounds of iron. — *adj* **pruss'ic** (also sometimes *prōōs'ik*), pertaining to Prussian blue. — **Prussian** (also without *cap*) **blue** a colour pigment, discovered in Berlin; the very dark blue colour of this; **prussic acid** a deadly poison, first obtained from Prussian blue.

pry *prī, vi* to peer or peep into that which is private (also *fig*); to examine things with impertinent curiosity: — *pr p* **prying**; *pa t* and *pa p* **pried**; *3rd pers sing pr t* **pries.** — *n* **prī'er** or **pry'er.** — *n* and *adj* **pry'ing.** — *adv* **pry'ingly.** — **pry out** to investigate or find out by prying. [M.E. *prien*.]

Przewalski's horse *pr-zhe-val'skiz hörs, n* a wild horse discovered in Central Asia by Nikolai *Przewalski* (1839–88). — Various other spellings exist.

PS *abbrev* for: Police Sergeant; postscript; private secretary; prompt side.

Ps. (*Bible*) *abbrev* for (the Book of) Psalms.

PSA *abbrev* for Property Services Agency.

psalm *säm, n* a devotional song or hymn, esp. one of those included in the Old Testament **Book of Psalms.** — *n* **psalmist** (*säm'ist*) a composer of psalms, esp. (with *cap*) David. — *adj* **psalmodic** (*sal-mod'ik*) or **psalmod'ical** pertaining to psalmody. — *n* **psalmodist** (*sal'* or *sä'mə-dist*) a singer of psalms. — *n* **psalmody** (*sal'* or *säm'*) the singing of psalms, esp. in public worship; psalms collectively. — **psalm'-book.** [O.E. (*p*)*salm*, (*p*)*sealm* — L.L. *psalmus* — Gr. *psalmos*, music of or to a stringed instrument.]

Psalter *söl'tər, n* the Book of Psalms, esp. when separately printed; (without *cap*) a book of psalms. — *n* **psal'tery** an ancient and mediaeval stringed instrument like the zither, played by plucking. [O.E. *saltere* — L. *psaltērium* — Gr. *psaltērion*, a psaltery.]

psalterium *söl-tē'ri-əm*, (*zool*) *n* the third division of a ruminant's stomach, the omasum or manyplies: — *pl* **psaltē'ria.** [From the appearance of its lamellae, like a stringed instrument; see **Psalter.**]

p's and q's *pēz ən(d) kyōōz', npl* social manners or behaviour, esp. in the phrase **to mind one's p's and q's.** [Alteration of *p(lea)se* and (*than*)*kyou's*.]

PSBR (*econ*) *abbrev* for Public Sector Borrowing Requirement.

PSDR (*econ*) *abbrev* for Public Sector Debt Repayment.

psephism *sē'fizm, n* (*antiq*) a decree of the Athenian assembly (from the practice of voting with pebbles). — *n* **pse'phite** a rock composed of pebbles, a conglomerate. — *adj* **psephit'ic.** — *n* **psēphol'ogy** sociological and statistical study of election results and trends. — *adj* **psepholog'ical.** — *n* **psephol'ogist.** [Gr. *psēphos*, a pebble.]

pseud[1] *s(y)ōōd*, (*colloq*) *n* a pretentious person, esp. intellectually.

pseud[2] (adj.). See under **pseud-**.

pseud. *abbrev* for pseudonym.

pseud- *sūd-* or **pseudo-** *sū-dō-* or in N.Am. *sōō-dō-*, *combining form* signifying: sham, false, spurious; deceptively resembling; isomerous with; temporary, provisional. — As a separate word, *adj* **pseu'do** or **pseud** (*colloq*) false, sham, pretentious. — *n* **pseu'dery** (*colloq*) falseness. — *adj* **pseud'ish** pretentious; spurious. — *n* **pseudaesthē'sia** imaginary feeling, as in an amputated limb. — *n* **pseudepig'rapha** (*pl*) books ascribed to Old Testament characters, but not judged genuine by scholars. — *adj* **pseudepigraph'ic, pseudepigraph'ical** or **pseudepig'raphous.** — *n* **pseu'docarp** a fruit formed from other parts in addition to the gynaeceum. — *n* **pseudocyesis** (*-sī-ē'sis*) a psychosomatic condition marked by many of the symptoms of pregnancy. — Also called **false pregnancy, hysterical pregnancy.** — *n* **pseu'dograph** a writing falsely ascribed. — *n* **pseu'domorph** a portion of a mineral showing the outward form of another which it has replaced by molecular substitution or otherwise. — *adj* **pseudomor'phic** or **pseudomor'phous.** — *n* **pseudomor'phism.** — *n* **pseu'donym** a fictitious name assumed, as by an author. — *n* **pseudonym'ity.** — *adj* **pseudon'ymous.** — *adv* **pseudon'ymously.** — *n* **pseudopod'ium** a process protruding from the cell of a protozoan, etc. used for locomotion of feeding: — *pl* **pseudopō'dia.** [Gr. *pseudēs*, false.]

pshaw *pshö, shö* or *pshə, interj* expressing contempt or impatience. — *vi* to say 'pshaw'. — *vt* to say 'pshaw' at. [Spontaneous expression.]

psi *psī, psē, sī* or *sē, n* the twenty-third letter (Θ, θ) of the Greek alphabet, equivalent to *ps.* — *n* **psī'on** a psi particle. — *adj* **psion'ic.** — *nsing* **psion'ics** the use of the paranormal in the treatment of illness, disease, etc. — **psi particle** an elementary particle with a very long life, formed by an electron-positron collision; **psi phenomena** the phenomena of parapsychology. [Gr. *psei.*]

psi *abbrev* for pounds per square inch.

psilocybin *sī-lō-sī'bin, n* a hallucinogenic drug, obtained from the Mexican mushroom *Psilocybe mexicana.* [Gr. *psīlos*, bare, *kybē*, head.]

psilosis *psī-lō'sis* or *sī-lō'sis, n* loss of hair; sprue (from loss of epithelium). — *adj* **psilot'ic.** [Gr. *psīlōsis* — *psīlos*, bare.]

psionic, psionics. See **psi** (noun).

Psittacus *psit'a-kəs* or *sit'a-kəs, n* the grey parrot genus. — *adj* **psitt'acine** (*-sīn*) of or like parrots. — *n* **psittacosis** (*-kō'sis*) a contagious disease of birds, strictly of parrots, also used of other birds, communicable to man. [Gr. *psittakos*, parrot.]

psoas *psō'əs* or *sō'əs*, (*anat*) *n* a muscle of the loins and pelvis; the tenderloin. [Gr. (pl.) *psoai*, the accus. *psoās* being mistaken for a nom. sing.]

psoriasis *sör-* or *sər-ī'ə-sis*, (*med*) *n* a skin disease in which red scaly papules and patches appear. — *adj* **psoriat'ic.** [Gr. *psōrā, psōriāsis*, itch.]

psst or **pst** *pst, interj* used to draw someone's attention quietly or surreptitiously. [Imit.]

PSV *abbrev* for Public Service Vehicle.

psyche *sī'kē, n* the soul, spirit, mind; the principle of mental and emotional life, conscious and unconscious. — *vt* **psych** or **psyche** (*sīk*; *slang*) to subject to psychoanalysis; to work out a problem, the intentions of another person, etc. psychologically (often with *out*); to defeat or intimidate by psychological means (sometimes with *out*); to get (oneself) psychologically prepared for (usu. with *up*); to stimulate (usu. with *up*). — *n* **psychedelia** (*-dēl'i-ə*) the production of, or the culture associated with, psychedelic experiences. — *npl* (objects, etc. associated with) psychedelic experiences. — Also **psychodel'ia.** — *adj* **psychedelic** (*-del'*) pertaining to a state of relaxation and pleasure, with heightened perception and increased mental powers generally; pertaining to drugs which cause, or are believed to cause, the taker to enter such a state; pertaining to visual effects and/or sound effects whose action on the mind is a little like that of psychedelic drugs; dazzling in pattern. — *adj* **psychiat'ric** or **psychiat'rical.** — *n* **psychī'atrist** a person who is medically qualified to treat diseases of the mind. — *n* **psychī'atry.** — *adj* **psych'ic** or **psych'ical** pertaining to the psyche, soul or mind; spiritual; spiritualistic; beyond, or apparently beyond, the physical; sensitive to or in touch with that which has not yet been explained physically. — *n* **psych'ic** that which is of the mind or psyche; a spiritualistic medium. — *adv* **psych'ically.** — *n* **psy'chicism** (*-kəs-*) psychical research. — *n* **psy'chicist.** — *nsing* **psy'chics** the science of psychology; psychical research. — **psychical research** investigation of phenomena apparently implying a connection with another world; **psychic force** a power not physical or mechanical, supposed to cause certain so-called spiritualistic phenomena. [Gr. *psȳchē*, soul, butterfly.]

psycho *sī'kō*, (*colloq*) *n* short for **psychopath**: — *pl* **psy'chos.**

psycho- *sī-kō-, combining form* denoting: soul, spirit; mind, mental; psychological. — *adj* **psychoac'tive** or **psychotrop'ic** (of a drug) affecting the brain and influencing behaviour. — *vt* **psychoan'alyse** or **-yze** to subject to psychoanalysis. — *n* **psychoanal'ysis** a method of investigation and psychotherapy whereby nervous diseases or mental ailments are traced to forgotten hidden concepts in the patient's mind and treated by bringing these to light. — *n* **psychoan'alyst** someone who practises psychoanalysis. — *adj* **psychoanalyt'ic** or **psychoanalyt'ical.** — *n* **psy'chobabble** excessive or needless use of psychologists' jargon; needless or meaningless use of jargon generally. — *n* **psych'ochemical** a psychoactive chemical. — Also *adj.* — *adj* **psychodel'ic** see **psychedelic** under **psyche.** — *n* **psychodra'ma** a method of mental treatment in which the patient is led to objectify and understand their difficulty by spontaneously acting it out. — *adj* **psychodramat'ic.** — *adj* **psychodynam'ic** pertaining to mental and emotional forces, their source in past experience, and their effects. — *n* **psychodynam'ics.** — *n* **psychogen'esis** (the study of) the origin or development of the mind (also **psychogenet'ic**); origination in the mind. — *adj* **psychogenet'ic** or **psychogenet'ical.** — *adj* **psychogen'ic** having origin in the mind or in a mental condition. — *adj* **psychogeriat'ric.** — *n* **psychogeriatri'cian.** — *nsing* **psychogeriat'rics** the study of the psychological problems of old age. — *adj* **psychograph'ic.** — *nsing* **psychograph'ics** the quantitative study of personalities and attitudes, used as a tool in marketing. — *adj* **psychohistor'ical.** — *n* **psychohis'tory** history studied from a psychological point of view. — *n* **psychokinē'sis** movement by psychic agency. — *adj* **psychokinet'ic.** — *n* **psycholing'uist.** — *adj* **psycholinguis'tic.** — *nsing* **psycholinguis'tics** the study of language development, language in relation to the mind, thought, etc. — *adj* **psycholog'ic** or **psycholog'ical.** — *adv* **psycholog'ically.** — *n* **psychol'ogist** someone who has studied and qualified in psychology. — *n* **psychol'ogy** science of mind; study of mind and behaviour; attitudes, etc., characteristic of individual, type, etc., or animating specific conduct. — *n* **psychom'eter** a person who has occult power of psychometry; an instrument for measuring reaction-times, etc. — *adj* **psychomet'ric** or **psychomet'rical.** — *n* **psychometrician** (*-trish'ən*) or **psychom'etrist.** — *nsing* **psychomet'rics** a branch of psychology dealing with measurable factors. — *n* **psychom'etry** psychometrics; occult power of divining properties of things by mere contact. — *adj* **psy'chomōtor** pertaining to such mental action as induces muscular contraction. — *n* **psychoneurō'sis** mental disease without any apparent anatomical lesion; a functional disorder of the mind in a person who is legally sane and shows insight into his or her condition: — *pl* **psychoneurō'sēs.** — *n* and *adj* **psychoneurot'ic.** — *n* **psy'chopath** (*-path*) a person who shows a pathological degree of specific emotional instability without specific mental disorder; someone suffering from a behavioural disorder resulting in inability to form personal relationships and in indifference to or ignorance of their obligations to society, often manifested by antisocial behaviour, such as acts of violence, sexual perversion, etc. — *adj* **psychopath'ic** pertaining to psychopathy (also *n*). — *n* **psychopathol'ogist.** — *n* **psychopathol'ogy** the branch of psychology that deals with the abnormal workings of the mind; an abnormal psychological condition. — *n* **psychop'athy** derangement of mental functions. — *n* **psychopharmacol'ogist.** — *n* **psychopharmacol'ogy** the study of the effects of drugs on the mind. — *adj* **psychophys'ical.** — *nsing* **psychophys'ics** the study of the relation between physical processes and mental processes. — *n* **psychoprophylax'is** a method of training for childbirth aimed at making labour painless. — *adj* **psychosex'ual** of or relating to the psychological aspects of sex, e.g. sexual fantasies. — *n* **psychō'sis** mental condition; a serious mental disorder characterised by e.g. illusions, delusions, hallucinations, mental confusion and a lack of insight into his or her condition on the part of the patient: — *pl* **psychō'sēs.** — *adj* **psychosō'cial** of or relating to matters both psychological and social. — *adj* **psychosomat'ic** (Gr. *sōma*, body) of mind and body as a unit; concerned with physical diseases having a psychological origin. — *n* **psychosur'gery** brain-surgery in the treatment of mental cases. — *n* **psychotherapeut'ics** or **psychother'apy** treatment of mental illness by hypnosis, psychoanalysis and similar psychological means. — *n* **psychother'apist.** — *adj* **psychot'ic** relating to psychosis. — *n* a person suffering from a psychosis. — *adj* **psychotrop'ic** same as **psychoactive** (also *n*). — **psychological block** an inability to think about, remember, etc., a particular subject, event, etc., for psychological reasons; **psychological moment** the most suitable moment for achieving a purpose; **psychological warfare** the use of propaganda to influence enemy opinion or morale. [Gr. *psȳchē*, soul, butterfly.]

psychrometer *sī-krom'it-ər, n* a wet-and-dry-bulb hygrometer; orig. a thermometer. — *adj* **psychrometric** (*sī-krō-met'rik*) or **psychromet'rical.** — *n* **psychrom'etry.** [Gr. *psȳchros*, cold, *metron*, a measure.]

PT *abbrev* for: physical therapy; physical training; postal telegraph.

Pt (*chem*) *symbol* for platinum.

pt *abbrev* for: part; past tense; pint(s).

PTA *abbrev* for Parent-Teacher Association.

ptarmigan *tär'mi-gən, n* a mountain-dwelling grouse, white in winter; extended to other species of *Lagopus*, such as willow-grouse. [Gael. *tàrmachan*.]

Pte (*mil*) *abbrev* for Private.

pter- *ter-* or **ptero-** *ter-ō-, combining form* denoting feather or wing. — *n combining form* **-ptera** in zoological names, denoting organism(s) having a specified type or number of wings or winglike parts. — *adj combining form* **-pteran** or **-pterous.** [Gr. *pteron*, wing.]

pteranodon *ter-an'ə-don, n* a toothless flying reptile of the Cretaceous period with a horn-like crest. [Gr. *pteron*, wing, *an-*, without, *odous*, *odontos*, tooth.]

pteridology. See under **Pteris.**

pteridophyte *ter'id-ō-fīt, n* a vascular cryptogam or a member of the **Pteridophyta** (*-of'i-tə*), one of the main divisions of the vegetable kingdom. [Gr. *pteris*, *-idos*, a fern, *phyton*, a plant.]

pterin *ter'in, n* any of a group of substances occurring as pigments in butterfly wings, important in biochemistry. — *n* **pteroic** (*ter-ō'ik*) **acid** the original folic acid found in spinach. — *n* **pteroylglutamic** (*ter'ō-il-gloo-tam'ik*) **acid** the folic acid that is therapeutically active in pernicious anaemia. [Gr. *pteron*, a wing.]

pterion *ter'* or *tēr'i-on, n* (in craniometry) the suture where the frontal, temporal, and parietal bones meet the wing of the sphenoid: — *pl* **pter'ia.** [Gr. dimin. of *pteron*, wing.]

Pteris *ter'is* or *tē'ris, n* a genus of ferns with spore-clusters continuous along the pinnule margin, usually taken to include bracken, which some separate as **Pterid'ium.** — *n* **pteridol'ogist.** — *n* **pteridol'ogy** the science of ferns. — *n* **pteridoph'ilist** a fern-lover. [Gr. *pteris*, *-idos*, or *-eōs*, male-fern — *pteron*, a feather.]

pterodactyl *ter-ə-dak'til, n* a fossil (Jurassic and Cretaceous) flying reptile with large and birdlike skull, long jaws, and a flying-membrane attached to the long fourth digit of the forelimb. [Gr. *pteron*, wing, *daktylos*, finger.]

pteroic acid. See under **pterin.**

pterosaur *ter'ə-sör, n* a member of the **Pterosaur'ia,** an extinct order of flying reptiles, including the pterodactyls. [Gr. *pteron*, wing, *sauros*, lizard.]

-pterous. See under **pter-.**

pteroylglutamic acid. See under **pterin.**

pterygium *tər-ij'i-əm, n* a vertebrate limb; a winglike growth; a wing-shaped area of thickened conjunctiva which spreads over part of the cornea and sometimes over the eyeball (*med*): — *pl* **pteryg'ia.** — *adj* **pteryg'ial.** — *n* a bone in a fin. [Latinised from Gr. *pterygion*, dimin. of *pteryx*, *-ygos*, wing.]

pterygoid *ter'i-goid, adj* winglike; of or near the pterygoid. — *n* **pterygoid bone, plate** or **process** in various vertebrates, a paired bone of the upper jaw. [Gr. *pteryx*, *-ygos*, wing.]

ptisan or **tisane** *tiz'n* or *tiz-an', n* a medicinal drink made from barley; a decoction. [Gr. *ptisanē*, peeled barley, barley-gruel — *ptissein*, to winnow.]

PTO *abbrev* for please turn over.

Ptolemaic *tol-i-mā'ik, adj* pertaining to the *Ptolemies*, Greek kings of Egypt (from Alexander's general to Caesar's son), or to *Ptolemy* the astronomer (*fl* A.D. 150).

ptomaine *tō'mān* or *tō-mān', n* a loosely used name for amino-compounds, some poisonous, formed from putrefying animal tissues. [It. *ptomaina* — Gr. *ptōma*, a corpse.]

ptosis *tō'sis, n* downward displacement; drooping of the upper eyelid: — *pl* **ptō'ses** (*-sēz*). [Gr. *ptōsis* — *piptein*, to fall.]

pty *abbrev* for proprietary.

Pu (*chem*) *symbol* for plutonium.

pub *pub, n* a place where alcoholic liquors are sold to be consumed on the premises. — **pub'-crawl** a progression from pub to pub. — Also *vi.* [Short for **public house.**]

puberty *pū'bər-ti, n* the beginning of sexual maturity. — *adj* **pū'bertal.** — *n* **pū'bes** (*-bēz*) the lower part of the hypogastric region; the hair that grows on it at puberty. — *n* **pūbescence** (*-es'əns*) puberty; a soft downy covering, esp. in plants, of closely pressed together hairs. — *adj* **pūbes'cent** or **pū'bic** of the pubes or the pubis. — *n* **pū'bis** (for L. *os pūbis*, bone of the pubes) a bone of the pelvis which in man forms the anterior portion of the *os innominatum*: — *pl* **pū'bises.** — As a prefix **pū'biō-** (wrongly **pū'bo-**). [L. *pūber* and *pūbēs*, *-eris*, grown-up, downy, and *pūbēs*, *-is*, grown-up youth, the pubes.]

public *pub'lik, adj* of or belonging to the people; pertaining to a community or a nation; general; common to, shared in by, or open to, all; generally known; in open view, unconcealed, not private; engaged in, or concerning, the affairs of the community; devoted or directed to the general good (as in *public spirit*); international; open to members of a university as a whole, not confined to a college; of a public house. — *n* the people; the general body of mankind; the people, indefinitely; a part of the community regarded from a particular viewpoint, e.g. as an audience or a target for advertising; public view of a public place, society, or the open. — *n* **pub'lican** the keeper of an inn or public house; a tax-collector (*Roman hist*). — *n* **publicā'tion** the act of publishing or making public; a proclamation; the act of sending out (a book, etc.) for sale; something that is published as a book, etc. — *vt* **pub'licise** or **-ize** (*-sīz*) to give publicity to; to make known to the general public, to advertise. — *n* **pub'licist** (*-sist*) a person who publicises; an advertising agent. — *n* **publicity** (*-lis'i-ti*) state of being open to the knowledge of all; the process of making something known to the general public; advertising; notoriety or acclaim. — *adv* **pub'licly.** — **public bar** one serving drinks more cheaply than a lounge bar and usu. less well furnished; **public company** a company whose shares can be purchased on the stock exchange by members of the public; **public convenience** see **convenience** under **convenient; public corporation** one owned by the government and run on business principles, being for the most part self-ruling; **public domain** the status of a published word which is not, or is no longer, subject to copyright; **public enemy** someone whose behaviour is considered to be a menace to a community in general; **public expenditure** spending by government, local authorities, etc.; **public funds** government funded debt; **public health** the maintenance of the health of a community, e.g. by sanitation, hygienic food preparation, etc. and the measures to achieve this; **public holiday** a general holiday; **public house** a pub; an inn or tavern; **public image** see under **image**; **public inquiry** an investigation held in public into various aspects (e.g. safety, environmental effect) of a proposed engineering or building project; **public law** the law governing relations between public authorities, such as the state, and the individual; **public nuisance** an illegal act harming the general community rather than an individual; an annoying, irritating person (*colloq*); **public opinion** the opinion of the general public on matters which affect the whole community; **public ownership** ownership by the state as of nationalised industry; **public prosecutor** an official whose function is to prosecute persons charged with offences; **public relations** the relations between a person, organisation, etc., and the public; the business of setting up and maintaining favourable relations; a department of government, an industrial firm, etc., dealing with this. — Also *adj.* — **public school** a school under the control of a publicly elected body; an endowed classical school for providing a liberal education for those who can afford it — Eton, Harrow, Rugby, etc. — *adj* **pub'lic-school.** — **public sector** government-financed industry, social service, etc.; **public servant** a person employed by the government; **public speaking** the making of formal speeches to a large audience; the art of making such speeches; **public spending** spending by the government. — *adj* **public-spir'ited** having a spirit actuated by regard to the public interest; with a regard to the public interest. — **public utility** a service or supply provided in a town, etc. for the public, such as gas, electricity, water or transport; (in *pl*) public utility shares. — **go public** to become a public company; **in public** openly, publicly; **public address system** a system that enables (large) groups of people to be addressed clearly, consisting of some or all of the following — microphones, amplifiers, loudspeakers; **public health inspector** former designation (previously **sanitary inspector**) of environmental health officer (q.v.); **public lending right** an author's right to payment when his or her books are borrowed from public libraries; **public opinion poll** a taking of public opinion based on the answers of scientifically selected elements in the community to questioning. [L. *pūblicus* — *pop(u)lus*, the people.]

publican, publication, publicity, etc. See under **public.**

publish *pub'lish*, *vt* to proclaim; to send forth to the public; to produce and offer for sale books, newspapers, etc.; to put into circulation; (of an author) to get published. — *vi* to publish a work, newspaper, etc. — *adj* **pub'lishable.** — *n* **pub'lisher** a person who or company that publishes books; someone who attends to the issuing and distributing of a newspaper. [Fr. *publier* — L. *pūblicāre*, with *-ish* on the model of other verbs.]

puce *pūs*, *n* and *adj* brownish-purple. [Fr. *puce* — L. *pūlex*, *-icis*, a flea.]

puck[1] *puk*, *n* a goblin or mischievous sprite. — *adj* **puck'ish** impish; full of mischief. [O.E. *pūca*.]

puck[2] *puk*, *n* a rubber disc used instead of a ball in ice-hockey.

pucka or **pukka** *puk'ə*, (*Anglo-Indian*) *adj* out-and-out good; thorough, complete; straightforward, genuine. — **pucka sahib** a gentleman. [Hind. *pakkā*, cooked, ripe.]

pucker *puk'ər*, *vt* to wrinkle; to make gathers in. — Also *vi.* — *n* a corrugation or wrinkle; a group of wrinkles, esp. irregular ones. — *adj* **puck'ery.** [Cf. **poke**[1].]

puckish. See **puck**[1].

pud *pŏŏd*, (*colloq*) *n* a shortened form of **pudding.**

pudding *pŏŏd'ing*, *n* the dessert course of a meal; meat, fruit, etc., cooked in a casing of flour; a soft kind of cooked dish, usually farinaceous, commonly with sugar, milk, eggs, etc.; a skin or gut filled with seasoned minced meat and other materials (such as blood, oatmeal), a kind of sausage; a pad of rope, etc., used as a fender on the bow of a boat or elsewhere; a fat, dull or heavy-witted person (*colloq*). — *adj* **pudd'ingy** (*-ing-i*). — *adj* **pudd'ing-faced** having a fat, round, smooth face. — *n* **pudd'ing-plate** a shallow bowl-like plate, usu. smaller than a soup-plate. — **in the pudding club** (*slang*) pregnant. [M.E. *poding*.]

puddle *pud'l*, *n* a small muddy pool; a non-porous mixture of clay and sand. — *vt* to make muddy; to work into puddle, to stir and knead; to cover with puddle; to make watertight by means of clay; to convert from pig-iron into wrought-iron by stirring in a molten state. — *vi* to make a dirty stir. — *n* **pudd'ler.** — *n* **pudd'ling.** — *adj* **pudd'ly.** [App. dimin. of O.E. *pudd*, ditch.]

pudendum *pū-den'dəm*, *n* (*pl* **puden'da**) the external genital organs, esp. female. [L. *pudēre*, to make (or be) ashamed, *pudendum*, something to be ashamed of.]

pudge, pudgy. See **podge.**

pueblo *pweb'lō*, *n* a town or settlement (in Spanish-speaking countries); a communal habitation of the Indians of New Mexico, etc.: — *pl* **pueb'los.** [Sp., town — L. *populus*, a people.]

puerile *pū'ər-īl* or in U.S. *-il*, *adj* childish; trifling; silly. — *n* **pūerility** (*-il'i-ti*). [L. *puerīlis* — *puer*, a boy.]

puerperal *pū-ûr'pər-əl*, *adj* relating to childbirth. — **puerperal fever** fever occurring following childbirth — formerly a common and serious form of septicaemia, but now confined to fever due to introduction of organisms into the genital tract. [L. *puerpera*, a woman in labour — *puer*, a child, *parĕre*, to bear.]

puff *puf*, *vi* to blow in whiffs; to breathe out vehemently or pantingly; to emit puffs; to make the sound of a puff; to go with puffs; to swell up (usu. with *up*). — *vt* to drive with a puff; to blow; to emit in puffs; to play (e.g. a wind instrument) or smoke (e.g. a pipe) with puffs; to inflate or swell (usu. with *up*); to extol, esp. in insincere advertisement (usu. with *up*); to put out of breath. — *n* a sudden, forcible breath, blast or emission; a gust or whiff; a cloud or portion of vapour, dust, air, etc., emitted at once; a sound of puffing; a downy pad for powdering; anything light and porous, or swollen and light; a biscuit or cake of puff-pastry or the like; praise intended as, or serving as, advertisement; a male homosexual (*slang*). — *adj* **puffed** distended, inflated; gathered up into rounded ridges, as a style of sleeve; out of breath (*colloq*). — *n* **puff'er** a person or thing that puffs; a steam engine; a steamboat; a globe fish. — *adv* **puff'ily**. — *n* **puff'iness**. — *n* **puff'ing**. — *adj* **puff'y** puffed out with air or any soft matter; tumid; coming in puffs; puffing; short-winded. — **puff'-adder** a thick, venomous African snake that puffs out its upper body when irritated; **puff'ball** a fungus with a ball-shaped spore-case filled when ripe with a snuff-like mass of spores; a tight-waisted full skirt gathered in at the hem to an underskirt, so as to be shaped like a ball; **puff'erfish** or **puff'er** a globe fish; **puff'-pastry** or in U.S. **puff'-paste** pastry composed of thin flakey layers. — **puffed out** quite out of breath; inflated, distended, expanded; **puffed up** swollen with pride, presumption, or the like. [O.E. *pyffan*, or related form.]

puffin *puf'in*, *n* a sea-bird (esp. *Fratercula*) of the auk family, with brightly coloured parrot-like beak.

pug[1] *pug*, *n* a small short-haired dog with wrinkled face, upturned nose, and short curled tail. — *adj* **pugg'ish** or **pugg'y**. — **pug'-nose** a short, thick nose with the tip turned up. — *adj* **pug'-nosed**.

pug[2] *pug*, *n* clay ground and worked with water. — *vt* to beat; to grind with water and make plastic; to pack with pugging. — *n* **pugg'ing** clay, sawdust, plaster, etc., put between floors to deaden sound.

puggy. See **pug**[1].

pugilism *pū'jil-izm*, *n* the art or practice of boxing; prize-fighting. — *n* **pu'gilist**. — *adj* **pugilist'ic**. — *adv* **pugilist'ically**. [L. *pugil*, a boxer.]

pugnacious *pug-nā'shəs*, *adj* given to fighting; combative; quarrelsome. — *adv* **pugnā'ciously**. — *n* **pugnā'ciousness** or **pugnacity** (*-nas'i-ti*) inclination to fight; fondness for fighting; quarrelsomeness. [L. *pugnāx*, *-ācis* — *pugnāre*, to fight.]

puisne *pū'ni*, *adj* (as applied to certain judges) junior. — *n* a puisne judge. [Obs. form of **puny** — O.Fr.— *puis* — L. *posteā*, after, *né* — L. *nātus*, born.]

puissant *pū'is-ənt*, *pwis'* or (*poetic*) *pū-is'ənt*, *adj* powerful. — *n* **puissance** (*pwē'sãs*, *-səns* or *-säns*) (a showjumping competition with very high jumps showing) the power of a horse. — *adv* **puiss'antly** (*-ənt-li*). [Fr. *puissant*, app. formed as a pres. p. from a vulgar L. substitute for L. *potēns*, *-entis*; see **potent**.]

puke *pūk*, (*slang*) *vt* and *vi* to vomit. — *n* vomit. [Poss. conn. with Flem. *spukken*, Ger. *spucken*.]

pukeko *puk'ə-kō*, *n* a New Zealand wading bird with bright plumage: — *pl* **puk'ekos**. [Maori.]

pukka. See **pucka**.

pula *pōō'lä*, *n* the standard unit of currency in Botswana (100 *thebes*). [Tswana, rain.]

pulchritude *pul'kri-tūd*, (*formal* or *literary*) *n* beauty. — *adj* **pulchritud'inous**. [L. *pulchritūdō*, *-inis* — *pulcher*, beautiful.]

pule *pūl*, *vt* and *vi* to whimper or whine. — *n* **pū'ler**. — *n* and *adj* **pū'ling**. — *adv* **pū'lingly**. — *adj* **pū'ly**. [Imit.; cf. Fr. *piauler*.]

Pulitzer prize *pōōl'it-sər* (or *pū'lit-sər*) *prīz*, *n* any of various annual prizes for American literature, journalism and music. [J. *Pulitzer* (1847–1911), U.S. newspaper publisher who instituted them.]

pulka *pul'kə*, *n* a Laplander's boat-shaped sledge. [Finnish *pulkka*, Lappish *pulkke*, *bulkke*.]

pull *pōōl*, *vt* to pluck; to remove by plucking; to extract, withdraw; to strip, deprive of feathers, hair, etc.; to move, or try or tend to move, towards oneself or in the direction so thought of; to draw, make or bring to be, by pulling; to row or transport by rowing; to move in a particular direction when driving (usu. with *out*, *over*, etc.); to stretch; to hold back (e.g. a boxing blow, a racehorse to prevent its winning); to take as an impression or proof, orig. by pulling the bar of a hand-press; (in cricket and golf) to strike to the left (right for left-handed person); to bring down; to carry out, execute; to take a draught of; to draw or fire (a weapon); to snatch, steal (*slang*); to succeed in forming a (sexual) relationship with (a girl) (*slang*); to arrest or stop (*slang*); to raid (*slang*); to attract (e.g. a crowd) (*slang*). — *vi* to give a pull; to perform the action of pulling anything; to tear, pluck; to drag, draw; to strain at the bit; to exert oneself; to go with a pulling movement; to move in a particular direction, esp. when in a motor vehicle (usu. with *away*, *out*, *over*, etc.); to row; to suck; to strike the ball to the left, etc. — *n* an act, bout or spell of pulling; a pulling force; a row; a stiff ascent; a draught of liquor; a proof, single impression (*printing*); advantage; influence; an apparatus for pulling; the quantity pulled at one time; resistance. — *n* **pull'er**. — **pull'back** a retreat, withdrawal; **pull'-in** a stopping-place (also *adj*); a transport café (see also **pull in** below). — *adj* **pull'-on** requiring only to be pulled on, without fastening. — *n* a pull-on garment of any kind. — *adj* **pull'-out** (of a section of a magazine, etc.) that can be removed and kept separately (see also **pull out** below). — **pull'over** a jersey, a jumper or garment put on over the head. — **pull about** to distort; to treat roughly; **pull a face** to grimace; **pull a fast one on** (*slang*) to take advantage of by an unexpected trick; **pull ahead** to move into the lead; **pull apart** or **to pieces** to tear into separate parts by pulling; to criticise harshly; **pull away** to pull ahead; to withdraw; **pull back** to retreat, withdraw (see also *n* **pull'back** above); **pull down** to take down or apart; to demolish; to bring down; **pull for** to row for; to support; **pull in** to draw in; to make tighter; to draw a motor vehicle into the side of the road, or drive into the carpark of a café, etc., and halt (see also *n* and *adj* **pull'-in** above); to arrest; to earn; to attract (a crowd); (of a train) to arrive at a station; **pull off** to carry through successfully; **pull oneself together** to regain one's self-control; to collect oneself, preparing to think or to act; **pull one's punches** see under **punch**[3]; **pull one's weight** to give full effect to one's weight in rowing; to do one's full share of work, co-operate wholeheartedly; **pull out** to draw out; to drive a motor vehicle away from the side of the road or out of a line of traffic; (of a train) to leave a station; to abandon a place or situation which has become too difficult to cope with (*colloq*; *n* **pull'-out**; see also *adj* above); **pull over** to draw over to the side of the road, either to stop or to allow other vehicles to pass; **pull round** to bring, or come, back to good health or condition or to consciousness; **pull someone's leg** see under **leg**; **pull through** to bring or get to the end of something difficult or dangerous with some success; **pull together** (*fig*) to co-operate; **pull up** to pull out of the ground; to tighten the reins; to bring to a stop; to halt; to take to task; to gain ground; to arrest. [O.E. *pullian*, to pluck, draw.]

pullet *pōōl'it*, *n* a young hen, esp. from first laying to first moult. [Fr. *poulette*, dimin. of *poule*, a hen — L.L. *pulla*, a hen, fem. of L. *pullus*, a young animal.]

pulley *pōōl'i*, *n* a wheel turning about an axis, and receiving a rope, chain or band on its rim, used for raising weights, changing direction of pull, transmission of power, etc.; a block; a combination of pulleys or blocks: — *pl* **pull'eys**. [M.E. *poley*, *puly* — O.Fr. *polie* (Fr. *poulie*) — L.L. *polegia*.]

Pullman *pōōl'mən*, *n* a luxuriously-furnished railway saloon or sleeping-car, first made by George M. *Pullman* (1831–97) in America. — In full, **Pullman car**.

pullulate *pul'ū-lāt*, (*biol*) *vi* to sprout; to sprout or breed abundantly; to teem; to increase vegetatively. — *n* **pullulā'tion**. [L. *pullulāre*, *-ātum* — *pullulus*, a young animal, sprout — *pullus*.]

pulmonary *pul'mən-ər-i*, *adj* of the lungs or respiratory cavity; leading to or from the lungs; of the nature of lungs; having lungs; diseased or weak in the lungs. — *adj* **pulmonic** (*-mon'ik*) of the lungs. [L. *pulmō*, *-ōnis*, lung.]

pulp *pulp*, *n* any soft fleshy part of an animal, e.g. the tissue in the cavity of a tooth; the soft part of plants, esp. of fruits; any soft structureless mass; the soft mass obtained from the breaking and grinding of rags, wood, etc. before it is hardened into paper; crushed ore; nonsense; sentimentality; a cheap magazine printed on wood-pulp paper, or of a paltry and sentimental or sensational character (also **pulp magazine**); fiction of the type published in such a magazine; a film, etc. of such a type. — *vt* to reduce to pulp; to make pulpy; to deprive of pulp. — *vi* to become pulp or like pulp. — *n* **pulp'er** a machine for reducing various materials to pulp. — *adj* **pulp'y**. — **pulp'-cavity** the hollow of a tooth containing pulp; **pulp'mill** a machine or factory for pulping wood, roots, or other material; **pulp novel**; **pulp novelist**; **pulp'wood** wood suitable for paper-making; a board of compressed wood-pulp and adhesive. [L. *pulpa*, flesh, pulp.]

pulpit *pōōl'pit*, *n* a raised structure for preaching from (also *fig*); an auctioneer's desk or similar. [L. *pulpitum*, a stage.]

pulque *pōōl'kā* or *-kē*, *n* a fermented drink made in Mexico from agave sap. [Am. Sp.]

pulsate *pul'sāt*, *vi* to beat, throb; to vibrate; to change repeatedly in force or intensity; to thrill with life or emotion. — *n* **pul'sar** (for 'pulsating star') any of a number of interstellar sources of regularly pulsed radiation, which may be rotating neutron stars. — *adj* **pul'satile** (*-sə-tīl* or in U.S. *-til*) capable of pulsating; pulsatory; rhythmical; played by percussion (*mus*). — *n* **pulsā'tion** a beating or throbbing; a motion of the heart or pulse; any measured beat; vibration. — *adj* **pulsative** (*pul'sə-tiv*). — *n* **pulsā'tor** a machine, or part of a machine, that pulsates or imparts pulsation, as for separating diamonds from earth, for regulating the rhythmical suction of a milking machine, for pumping. — *adj* **pulsatory** (*pul'sə-tər-i* or *-sā'*) beating or throbbing. [L. *pulsāre*, *-ātum*, to beat.]

pulse[1] *puls*, *n* a beating or throbbing; a measured beat or throb; a vibration; a single variation, beat or impulse; a signal of very short duration (*radio*); the beating of the heart and the arteries; bustle, activity; a thrill (*fig*). — *vi* to beat, as the heart; to throb, to pulsate. — *vt* to drive by pulsation; to produce, or cause to be emitted, in the form of pulses. — *adj* **pulsed**. — *adj* **pulsif'ic** producing a single pulse. — *n* **pulsim'eter** an instrument for measuring the strength or quickness of the pulse. — **pulse rate** the number of beats of a pulse per minute; **pulse'-wave** the expansion of the artery, moving from point to point, like a wave, as each beat of the heart sends the blood to the extremities. — **feel someone's pulse** to test or measure someone's heartbeat, usu. by holding their wrist; to explore a person's feelings or inclinations in a tentative way; **keep one's finger on the pulse** (*fig*) to keep in touch with current events, ideas, etc. [L. *pulsus* — *pellĕre*, *pulsum*; partly O.Fr. *pouls*, *pous*, remodelled on Latin.]

pulse[2] *puls*, *n* seeds of leguminous plants as food collectively — beans, peas, lentils, etc.; the plants yielding them. [L. *puls*, *pultis*, porridge; cf. Gr. *poltos*, and **poultice**.]

pulverise or **-ize** *pul'və-rīz*, *vt* to reduce to dust or fine powder; to defeat thoroughly, destroy (*fig*). — *vi* to fall into dust or powder. — *n* **pul'verīser** or **-z-** a person who pulverises; a machine for pulverising or for spraying. — *adj* **pul'verous** dusty or powdery. — *adj* **pul'verīsable** or **-z-**. — *n* **pulverīsā'tion** or **-z-**. — *n* **pulverulence** (*-vûr'ū-ləns*). — *adj* **pulver'ūlent** consisting of fine powder; powdery; dusty-looking; readily crumbling. [L. *pulvis*, *pulveris*, powder.]

puly. See **pule**.

puma *pū'mə*, *n* the cougar, a large reddish-brown American cat — also called **mountain lion**: — *pl* **pu'mas**. [Am. Sp., — Quechua.]

pumelo. Same as **pomelo**.

pumice *pum'is* or **pumice stone** (*stōn*), *n* an acid glassy lava so full of gas-cavities as to float in water; a frothy portion of any lava; a piece of such lava used for smoothing or cleaning. — *vt* to smooth or clean with pumice-stone. — *adj* **pumiceous** (*-mish'əs*). [O.E. *pumic*(*-stān*), pumice(-stone); reintroduced — O.Fr. *pomis*; both — L. *pūmex*, *-icis*.]

pummel *pum'l*, *n* a less usual spelling of **pommel**. — *vt* (the usual spelling) to beat, pound, thump, esp. with the fists: — *pr p* **pumm'elling**; *pa t* and *pa p* **pumm'elled**. [**pommel**.]

pump[1] *pump*, *n* a machine for raising and moving fluids, orig. esp. bilge-water in ships, or for compressing, rarefying or transferring gases; a stroke of a pump; an act of pumping. — *vt* to raise, force, compress, exhaust, empty, remove or inflate with a pump; to discharge by persistent effort; to move in the manner of a pump; to subject to, or elicit by, persistent questioning. — *vi* to work a pump; to work like a pump; to move up and down like a pump-handle; to spurt; to propel, increase the speed of, a sailing boat by rapidly pulling the sails in and out (*naut*). — *n* **pump'er**. — *adj* **pump'-action** of a repeating rifle or shotgun whose chamber is fed by a pump-like movement. — **pumped storage** in a hydroelectric system, the use of electricity at times of low demand to pump water up to a high storage reservoir, to be used to generate electricity at times of high demand; **pump gun** a pump-action gun; **pump priming** starting a pump working efficiently by introducing fluid to drive out the air; investing money in order to stimulate commerce, local support, etc.; **pump room** the apartment at a mineral spring in which the waters are drunk; **pump'-water** water from a pump; **pump'-well** a well from which water is got by pumping; the compartment in which a pump works. — **pump iron** (*colloq*) to do exercise with weights, to develop one's muscles.

pump[2] *pump*, *n* a light shoe without fastening, worn esp. for dancing.

pumpernickel *pump'ər-nik-l* or *pōōmp'*, *n* a coarse, dark rye bread, esp. from Westphalia. [Ger.; the Ger. word means a rackety goblin, a coarse lout, rye bread (poss. from its giving forth a sound like *pump* when struck).]

pumpkin *pum'kin* or *pump'kin*, *n* a plant of the gourd family, or its fruit. [O.Fr. *pompon* — L. *pepō* — Gr. *pepōn*, ripe.]

pun *pun*, *vi* to play upon words alike or nearly alike in sound but different in meaning, or upon words with more than one meaning: — *pr p* **punn'ing**; *pa t* and *pa p* **punned**. — *n* a play upon words. — *n* **punn'ing**. — *n* **pun'ster** a maker of puns. [A late-17th-century word; poss. — It. *puntiglio*, fine point.]

punch[1] *punch* or *punsh*, *n* a short-legged draught-horse, chestnut in colour, long bred in Suffolk. [Poss. shortened from **puncheon**[1], or from **Punchinello**, or a variant of **bunch**.]

punch[2] *punch* or *punsh*, *n* a drink ordinarily of spirits, water, sugar, lemon-juice and spice (with variations). — **punch'bowl** a large bowl for making punch in; a large bowl-shaped hollow in the ground; **punch'-ladle** a ladle for filling glasses from a punchbowl. [Traditionally from the five original ingredients, from Hindi *pā̃c*, five — Sans. *pañca*.]

punch[3] *punch* or *punsh, vt* to strike with a forward thrust, as of the fist; to thump; to stamp, pierce, perforate or indent by a forward thrust of a tool or part of a machine; to make, obtain or remove by such a thrust (often with *out*); to press in vigorously the keys or button of; to record by pressing a key. — *vi* to perform an act of punching; to clock (*in* or *out*). — *n* a vigorous thrust or forward blow; striking power; effective forcefulness; a tool or machine for punching; a prop for a mine-roof. — *n* **punch'er** a person who punches; an instrument for punching. — *adj* **punch'y** vigorous, powerful; punch-drunk (*colloq*). — **punch'-bag** or in U.S. **punch'ing-bag** a large stuffed bag used for boxing practice; **punch'ball** a suspended ball used for boxing practice; **punch'-card** or **punched card** a card with perforations representing data, used in the operation of automatic computers. — *adj* **punch'-drunk** having a form of cerebral concussion from past blows in boxing, with results resembling drunkenness; dazed. — **punched tape** (*comput*) same as **paper tape**; **punch line** the last line or conclusion of a joke, in which the point lies; the last part of a story, giving it meaning or an unexpected twist; **punch'-up** a fight with fists. — **pull one's punches** to hold back one's blows (also *fig*). [**pounce**[1]; or from **puncheon**[1]; possibly in some senses for **punish**.]

puncheon[1] *pun'chn* or *-shn, n* a tool for piercing, or for stamping; a short supporting post; a split trunk with one face smoothed for flooring, etc. [O.Fr. *poinson* — L. *pungĕre, punctum*, to prick.]

puncheon[2] *pun'chn* or *-shn, n* a cask; a liquid measure of from 70 to 120 gallons. [O.Fr. *poinson*, a cask.]

Punchinello *punch-* or *punsh-i-nel'ō, n* a hook-nosed character in an Italian puppet-show; a buffoon, etc.: — *pl* **Punchinell'os** or **Punchinell'oes**. [It. *Pulcinella*, a Neapolitan buffoon.]

punchy. See **punch**[3].

punctate *pungk'tāt* or **punc'tated** *-id*, (*biol*) *adj* dotted; pitted. — *n* **punctā'tion**. [L. *punctum*, a point, puncture — *pungĕre, punctum*, to prick.]

punctilio *pungk-til'i-ō* or *-yō, n* a nice point in behaviour or ceremony; nicety in, or exact observance of, etiquette: — *pl* **punctil'ios**. — *adj* **punctil'ious** scrupulous and exact; attentive to punctilio. — *adv* **punctil'iously**. — *n* **punctil'iousness**. [It. *puntiglio* and Sp. *puntillo*, dimins. of *punto* — L. *punctum*, a point.]

punctual *pungk'tū-əl, adj* of the nature of a point; pertaining to a point, or points (*math*); exact in keeping time and appointments; done at the exact time; on time. — *n* **punctuality** (*-al'i-ti*). — *adv* **punc'tually**. [L.L. *punctuālis* — *punctum*, a point.]

punctuate *pungk'tū-āt, vt* to mark off with the usual stops, points of interrogation, and the like; to intersperse; to emphasise. — *n* **punctuā'tion** the act or art of dividing sentences by points or marks. — *n* **punctuā'tionist** a believer in punctuated equilibrium. — *adj* **punc'tuative**. — *n* **punc'tuator**. — **punctuated equilibrium** or **equilibria** (*biol*) a theory which states that evolution happens in short bursts of major change punctuating long periods of stability. [L.L. *punctuāre, -ātum*, to prick — L. *punctum* (see **punctum**).]

punctum *pungk'təm*, (*anat*) *n* a point, dot; a minute aperture: — *pl* **punc'ta**. [L. *punctum* — *pungĕre, punctum*, to prick.]

puncture *pungk'chər, n* a small hole made with a sharp point; perforation of a pneumatic tyre; a flat tyre. — *vt* to make a puncture; to deflate someone's pride, self-confidence, etc. (*fig*). — *vi* to get a puncture. — *adj* **punc'tured** perforated; pierced; marked with little holes; consisting of little holes. — *n* **puncturā'tion**. [L. *punctūra* — *pungĕre*, to prick.]

pundit *pun'dit, n* a learned man; an authority, now, commonly, someone who considers himself or herself an authority; (also **pandit** *pan'dit*) a Hindu learned in Sanskrit and in Hindu culture, philosophy and law. — *n* **pun'ditry**. [Hindi *paṇḍit* — Sans. *paṇḍita*.]

pungent *pun'jənt, adj* sharp; bitter or acrid to taste or smell; keenly touching the mind; painful; sarcastic; ending in a hard sharp point (*bot*). — *n* **pun'gency**. — *adv* **pun'gently**. [L. *pungēns, -entis*, pres. p. of *pungĕre*, to prick.]

Punic *pū'nik, adj* of ancient Carthage; Carthaginian; faithless, treacherous, deceitful. — **Punic faith** treachery. [L. *Pūnicus* — *Poenī*, the Carthaginians.]

punily. See **puny**.

punish *pun'ish, vt* to cause (someone) to suffer for an offence; to cause someone to suffer for (an offence); to handle roughly or beat (*colloq*); to consume a large quantity of (*colloq*). — *vi* to inflict punishment. — *n* **punishabil'ity**. — *adj* **pun'ishable**. — *adj* **pun'ishing** causing suffering or retribution; severe, testing (*colloq*). — *adv* **pun'ishingly**. — *n* **pun'ishment** act or method of punishing; penalty imposed for an offence; rough handling, beating (*colloq*). [Fr. *punir, punissant* — L. *pūnīre*, to punish — *poena*, penalty.]

punitive *pū'ni-tiv, adj* concerned with, inflicting, or intended to inflict, punishment. [L. *pūnīre*, to punish.]

Punjabi or **Panjabi** *pun-jä'bē, n* a native or inhabitant of the *Punjab* in India and Pakistan; the language of the Punjab. — *adj* of the Punjab. [Hindi *Pañjābī*.]

punk[1] *pungk, n* a worthless person or thing; balderdash; a foolish person; a follower of punk rock, often recognisable by the use of cheap, utility articles (e.g. razor blades, plastic rubbish bags, safety-pins) as clothes or decoration. — *adj* rotten; worthless; miserable. — **punk rock** a style of popular music of the late 1970s, rhythmical and aggressive, with violent, often obscene lyrics, inspired by a feeling of despair at the cheapness and ugliness of life — also called **new wave**.

punk[2] *pungk, n* touchwood; tinder.

punka or **punkah** *pung'kə, n* a fan, esp. palm-leaf fan; a large mechanical fan for cooling a room. [Hindi *pākhā*.]

punnet *pun'it, n* a small basket or open container for soft fruit.

punning, punster. See **pun**.

punt[1] *punt, n* a flat-bottomed boat with square ends. — *vt* to propel by pushing a pole against the river-bed; to transport by punt. — *vi* to go in a punt; to go shooting in a punt; to pole a punt or boat. — *n* **punt'er**. — **punt'-pole** a pole for propelling a punt. [O.E. — L. *pontō, -ōnis*, punt, pontoon; cf. **pontoon**[1].]

punt[2] *punt, vi* to bet against the bank; to back a horse. — *n* **punt'er** a person who punts; a professional gambler; customer (*colloq*); an ordinary person (*colloq*). [Fr. *ponter*.]

punt[3] *punt, n* the act of kicking a dropped rugby- or football before it touches the ground. — *vt* to kick in this manner. — *n* **punt'er**.

punt[4] *po͞ont, n* the Irish pound.

puny *pū'ni, adj* (*compar* **pū'nier**, *superl* **pū'niest**) stunted; feeble. — *adv* **pū'nily**. — *n* **pū'niness**. [**puisne**.]

pup *pup, n* a shortened form of **puppy**. — *vt* and *vi* to whelp: — *pr p* **pupp'ing**; *pa t* and *pa p* **pupped**. — **buy** or **be sold a pup** to be swindled; **in pup** (of a bitch) pregnant; **sell a pup** to inveigle someone into a specious bad bargain; to swindle.

pupa *pū'pə, n* an insect in the usually passive stage between larva and imago; an intermediate stage of development in some other invertebrates: — *pl* **pupae** (*pū'pē*) or **pū'pas**. — *adj* **pū'pal**. — *vi* **pū'pate** to become a pupa. — *n* **pūpā'tion**. [L. *pūpa*, a girl, a doll.]

pupil[1] *pū'pl* or *-pil*, *n* a ward (*law*); someone who is being taught; a person who is being or has been taught by a particular teacher. — *n* **pu'pillage** the state of being a pupil or student; the time during which one is a pupil or student. — *n* **pupillar'ity** (*law*) the state or time of being legally a pupil. — *adj* **pu'pillary** pertaining to a pupil or ward, or one under academic discipline. (The above words are sometimes spelt with one *l*). — **pupil teacher** a pupil who does some teaching as part of his or her training for later entry into the profession. [Fr. *pupille* — L. *pūpillus*, *pūpilla*, dimins. of *pūpus*, boy, *pūpa*, girl.]

pupil[2] *pū'pl* or *-pil*, *n* the round opening in the eye through which the light passes; a central spot, esp. within a spot. — *adj* **pu'pillary**. — *adj* **pu'pillate** (*zool*) having a central spot of another colour. (The above words sometimes with one *l*). [L. *pūpilla*, pupil of the eye, orig. the same as in **pupil**[1], from the small image to be seen in the eye.]

puppet *pup'it*, *n* a doll or image moved by wires or hands in a show; a marionette; a person, state, etc. under the control of another. — *adj* behaving like a puppet; manipulated by others. — *n* **puppeteer'** a person who manipulates puppets. — *n* **pupp'etry** play of, or with, puppets; puppets collectively; puppet-like action; puppet-shows; anything like or associated with puppets; **pupp'et-valve** same as **poppet-valve** (see **poppet**[1]). [Earlier **poppet**; cf. O.Fr. *poupette*, dimin. from L. *pūpa*.]

puppodum *pup'ə-dəm*, *n*. Same as **poppadum**.

puppy *pup'i*, *n* a young dog; a whelp; a young seal; a young rat; a conceited young man. — *vt* and *vi* to pup. — **pupp'y-dog; pupp'y-fat** temporary fatness in childhood or adolescence; **puppy love** same as **calf-love; pupp'y-walker** a person who brings up a puppy until it is ready for training as a working dog; an experienced policeman who introduces a new recruit to his or her beat (*slang*). [App. Fr. *poupée*, a doll or puppet — L. *pūpa*.]

Purana *pōō-rä'nə*, *n* any one of a class of sacred books of Hindu mythology, cosmology, etc. written in Sanskrit. — *adj* **Puranic** (*-rä'nik*). [Sans. *purāṇa* — *purā*, of old.]

purblind *pûr'blīnd*, *adj* nearly blind; dim-sighted, esp. spiritually. — *adv* **pur'blindly**. — *n* **pur'blindness**. [App. orig. wholly blind — **pure** (or perh. O.Fr. pfx. *pur-*), and **blind**.]

purchase *pûr'chəs*, *vt* to acquire; to get in any way other than by inheritance (*law*); to buy; to obtain by labour, danger, etc.; to raise or move by a mechanical power. — *vi* to make purchases. — *n* an act of purchasing; that which is purchased; acquisition; annual rent; any mechanical advantage in raising or moving bodies or apparatus; advantageous hold, or means of exerting force advantageously. — *adj* **pur'chasable**. — *n* **pur'chaser**. — **so many years' purchase** value or price of a house, an estate, etc., equal to the amount of so many years' rent or income. [O.Fr. *porchacier*, to seek eagerly, pursue.]

purdah *pûr'də*, *n* a curtain, esp. for screening women's apartments; seclusion of women; seclusion generally (*fig*). — **purdah bus, carriage**, etc. one for women only, in which the occupants are screened by shutters or blinds. [Urdu and Pers. *pardah*.]

pure *pūr*, *adj* clean, unsoiled; unmixed; free from guilt or defilement; chaste; free from bad taste, bad grammar, bad manners, insincerity, barbarism, etc.; modest; that and that only; utter, sheer; (of a study) confined to that which belongs directly to it; non-empirical, involving an exercise of mind alone; homozygous, breeding true (*biol*); unconditional (*law*). — *adv* purely; utterly, completely; without mixture. — *adv* **pure'ly** chastely; unmixedly; unconditionally; wholly, entirely. — *n* **pure'ness**. — *adj* **pure'-blood, pure'-blooded** or **pure'-bred** of unmixed race. — **pure mathematics** mathematics treated without application to observed facts of nature or to practical life; **pure science** science considered apart from practical applications. [Fr. *pur* — L. *pūrus*, pure.]

purée or **puree** *pū'rā*, *n* food matter reduced to pulp, e.g. by being processed in a liquidiser; a soup without solid pieces. — *vt* to make a purée of. [Fr.]

purfle *pûr'fl*, *vt* to ornament the edge of. — *n* a decorated border. — *n* **pur'fling** a purfle, esp. around the edges of a fiddle. [O.Fr. *pourfiler* — L. *prō*, before, *fīlum*, a thread.]

purge *pûrj*, *vt* to purify; to remove impurities from; to clear of undesirable elements or persons; to remove as an impurity; to clarify; to clear from accusation; to expiate; to evacuate (the bowels); to make (someone) evacuate the bowels; to atone for, wipe out (esp. a contempt of court) (*law*). — *vi* to become pure by clarifying; to evacuate the bowels; to have frequent evacuations; to take a purgative. — *n* act of purging; an expulsion or massacre of those who are not trusted; a purgative. — *n* **purga'tion** a purging; a clearing away of impurities; the act of clearing from suspicion or imputation of guilt (*law*); a cleansing. — *adj* **purgative** (*pûr'gə-tiv*) cleansing; having the power of evacuating the intestines. — *n* a medicine that evacuates. — *adv* **pur'gatively**. — *adj* **purgato'rial** or **purgato'rian**. — *adj* **pur'gatory** purging or cleansing; expiatory. — *n* a place or state in which souls are after death purified from venial sins (*RC*); any kind or state of suffering for a time; intense discomfort (*colloq*). [Fr. *purger* — L. *pūrgāre*, *-ātum* — earlier *pūrigāre* — *pūrus*, pure.]

puri or **poori** *pōō'ri*, *n* a small cake of unleavened Indian bread, deep-fried and served hot; a small round cake filled with a spicy vegetable mixture and deep-fried in oil. [Hind.]

purify *pū'ri-fī*, *vt* to make pure; to cleanse from foreign or harmful matter; to free from guilt, from ritual uncleanness or from improprieties or barbarisms in language. — *vi* to become pure: — *pr p* **pu'rifying**; *pa t* and *pa p* **pu'rified**. — *n* **purificā'tion**. — *adj* **pu'rificātive**. — *adj* **pu'rificātory** tending to purify or cleanse. — *n* **pu'rifier**. [Fr. *purifier* — L. *pūrificāre* — *pūrus*, pure, *facĕre*, to make.]

purim *pū'rim* or *pōōr'ēm*, *n* the Feast of Lots held about 1 March, in which the Jews commemorate their deliverance from the plot of Haman, as related in the Book of Esther (see esp. iii. 7). [Heb. *pūrīm* (sing. *pūr*), lots.]

purin *pūr'in* or **purine** *pūr'ēn*, *n* a white crystalline substance which with oxygen forms uric acid and is the nucleus of many other derivatives. [Contracted from L. *pūrum ūricum* (*acidum*), pure uric (acid).]

purism *pūr'izm*, *n* fastidious, esp. over-fastidious, insistence upon purity (esp. of language in vocabulary or idiom). — *n* and *adj* **pur'ist**. — *adj* **puris'tic**. — *adv* **puris'tically**. [L. *pūrus*, pure.]

Puritan *pūr'i-tən*, *n* a person who in the time of Elizabeth and the Stuarts wished to carry the reformation of the Church of England further by purifying it of ceremony; an opponent of the Church of England because of its retention of much of the ritual and belief of the Roman Catholics; an opponent of the Royalists in the 17th century; (the following meanings also without *cap*) a person of like views with, or in sympathy with, the historical Puritans; a person strictly moral in conduct; (*slightingly*) someone professing a too-strict morality or disapproving of luxury or amusement; an advocate of purity in any sense. — *adj* (also without *cap*) pertaining to the Puritans. — *adj* **puritanic** (*-tan'ik*) or **puritan'ical** (usu. *derog*). — *adv* **puritan'ically**. — *n* **pur'itanism**. [L. *pūrus*, pure.]

purity *pūr'i-ti*, *n* condition of being pure; freedom from mixture of any kind, or from sin, defilement, or ritual uncleanness; chastity; sincerity; freedom from foreign or improper idioms or words. [L. *pūritās*, *-ātis* — *pūrus*.]

purl[1] *pûrl, vi* to flow with a murmuring sound; to flow in eddies; to curl or swirl. — *n* a trickling rill; a movement or murmuring as of a stream among stones; an eddy or ripple. [Cf. Norw. *purla*, to babble, Sw. dialect *porla*, to purl, ripple.]

purl[2] *pûrl, vi* to spin round; to capsize; to go head over heels; to fall headlong or heavily. — *vt* to throw headlong. — *n* a heavy or headlong fall; an upset. — *n* **purl'er** a headlong or heavy fall or throw, esp. in *go* or *come a purler*. [Perh. conn. with **purl**[1].]

purl[3] *pûrl, vt* to embroider or edge with gold or silver thread; to provide with a decorative edging, such as lace. — *vt* and *vi* to knit with a purl stitch. — *n* twisted gold or silver wire; a loop or twist, esp. on an edge (also **pearl**); a succession of such loops, or a lace or braid having them; a fold, pleat or frilling; knitting with a purl stitch. — *adj* (in knitting) denoting an inverted stitch made with the wool passed behind the needle (opp. to *plain*).

purlieu *pûr'lū, n* (frequently in *pl*) one's usual haunts; (in *pl*) borders or outskirts. [A.Fr. *puralee*, land severed by perambulation — O.Fr. *pur* (= L. *prō*), *allee*, going; infl. by Fr. *lieu*, place.]

purlin or **purline** *pûr'lin, n* a piece of timber stretching across the principal rafters to support the common or subsidiary rafters.

purloin *pər-loin'* or *pûr', vt* to filch, steal. — *vi* to practise theft. [A.Fr. *purloigner*, to remove to a distance.]

purple *pûr'pl, n* any mixture of blue and red; crimson (*hist*); the dignity of king or emperor; the red robe of a cardinal; the office of cardinal; (with **the**) bishops collectively; a purple pigment; (in *pl*) purpura. — *adj* of the colour purple, mixed red and blue; (of writing) fine or over-ornate. — *vt* to make purple. — *vi* to become purple. — *adj* **pur'plish** or **pur'ply** somewhat purple. — **purple heart** the purple-coloured wood of species of *Copaifera* (family *Caesalpiniaceae*) (also **purple wood**); a mauve heart-shaped tablet of a stimulant drug of amphetamine type; (with *caps*) a U.S. decoration awarded for wounds received on active service; **purple patch** a passage of fine, or (often) over-ornate, writing. — **born in the purple** born in the purple chamber (see **Porphyrogenite**); of royal or noble birth. [O.E. (Northumbrian) *purpl(e)*, purple (adj.) — *purpur* (n.) — L. *purpura* — Gr. *porphyrā*, purple-fish.]

purport *pûr'pərt* or *-pört, n* meaning conveyed; substance, gist, tenor. — *vt* **purport'** to give out as its meaning; to convey to the mind; to seem, claim, profess (to mean, be, etc.). — *adv* **purport'edly**. [O.Fr., from *pur* (Fr. *pour*) — L. *prō*, for, *porter* — L. *portāre*, to carry.]

purpose *pûr'pəs, n* the idea or aim kept before the mind as the end of effort; power of seeking the end desired; the act or fact of purposing; an end desired; a useful function; a definite intention. — *vt* to intend. — *adj* **pur'posed** intentional; intended; purposeful. — *adj* **pur'poseful** directed towards a purpose; actuated by purpose. — *adv* **pur'posefully**. — *n* **pur'posefulness**. — *adj* **pur'poseless**. — *adv* **pur'poselessly**. — *n* **pur'poselessness**. — *adv* **pur'posely** intentionally. — *adj* **pur'posive** directed towards an end; showing intention or resolution, purposeful. — *adj* **purpose-built'** specially made or designed to meet particular requirements. — **on purpose** with design, intentionally; **to good (**or **some) purpose** with good effect; **to the purpose** to the point, or material to the question. [O.Fr. *pourpos, propos* — L. *prōpositum*, a thing intended — *prō*, forward, *pōnĕre, positum*, to place; cf. **propose**.]

purpura *pûr'pū-rə*, (*med*) *n* purples, an eruption of small purple spots, caused by subcutaneous bleeding. [L. *purpura* — Gr. *porphyrā*.]

purr *pûr, vi* to utter a low, vibrant sound, as a cat does when pleased. — *vt* to express with or by purring. — *n* **purr**. — *n* and *adj* **purr'ing**. — *adv* **purr'ingly**. [Imit.]

purse *pûrs, n* a small bag for carrying money; a sum of money in a purse; a sum given as a present or offered as a prize; funds; a woman's handbag (*US*); a purse-like receptacle or cavity. — *vt* to contract (one's lips) into a rounded, puckered shape, esp. in order to express displeasure, etc.; to contract or draw into folds or wrinkles. — *vi* to pucker. — *n* **purs'er** an officer on a ship, etc. who keeps accounts and is responsible for services to passengers. — *n* **purs'ership**. — **purse'-bearer** a person who carries in a bag the Great Seal for the Lord Chancellor, or the royal commission for the Lord High Commissioner; **purse'-net** a bag-shaped net that closes by a drawstring at the neck; **purse'-seine** a seine net that can be drawn into the shape of a bag; **purse'-seiner** a fishing-vessel equipped with such nets; **purse sharing** the sharing-out of an individual fee or prize between all members of the recipient's firm or team; **purse'-strings** the strings fastening a purse (usu. *fig*). — **privy purse** an allowance for a sovereign's private expenses; **public purse** the nation's finances. [O.E. *purs*, app. — L.L. *bursa* — Gr. *byrsa*, a hide.]

purslane *pûrs'lin, n* a pot and salad herb of the *Portulacaceae*; any member of that genus or family. [O.Fr. *porcelaine* — L. *porcilāca, portulāca*.]

pursue *pər-sū'* or *-sōō', vt* to harass, persecute, persist in opposing or seeking to injure; to follow in order to overtake and capture or kill; to chase, hunt, follow up; to follow the course of; to be engaged in; to carry on; to seek to obtain or attain; to proceed with. — *vi* to follow; to go on or continue; to act as a prosecutor at law. — *adj* **pursu'able**. — *n* **pursu'ance** pursuit; act of carrying out or (e.g. *in pursuance of this policy*) furthering. — *adj* **pursu'ant** pursuing; in pursuance (with *to*; approaching an *adv*). — *n* **pursu'er**. — *n* and *adj* **pursu'ing**. [A.Fr. *pursuer, pursiwer* — popular L. forms *pro-, per-sequĕre, -ēre*, for L. *prōsequī, persequī* — *prō-, per-* (the prefixes being confused), and *sequī*, to follow.]

pursuit *pər-sūt'* or *-sōōt', n* the act of pursuing; endeavour to attain; occupation; employment; that which is pursued; a cycle race in which two riders start at opposite sides of a track and try to overtake each other. — **pursuit plane** a type of military aeroplane used in pursuing enemy aeroplanes. [A.Fr. *purseute*, fem. past p.; see **pursue**.]

pursuivant *pûr'si-vənt* or *-swi-vənt, n* a state messenger with power to execute warrants; an officer ranking below a herald. [Fr. *poursuivant*, pres. p. of *poursuivre*, to pursue.]

pursy *pûrs'i, adj* puffy; short-winded. — *n* **purs'iness**. [O.Fr. *poulsif*, broken-winded — *poulser* — L. *pulsāre*, to drive.]

purulent *pū'rū-lənt* or *-rōō-, adj* consisting of, of the nature of, forming, full of, characterised by, or like pus. — *n* **pū'rulence** or **pū'rulency**. — *adv* **pū'rulently**. [L. *pūrulentus* — *pūs, pūris*, pus.]

purvey *pûr-vā', vt* to provide or furnish; to supply. — *vi* to provide meals or provisions as one's business. — *n* **purvey'ance** the act of purveying; a procuring of victuals; that which is supplied. — *n* **purvey'or** a person whose business is to provide food or meals. [A.Fr. *purveier* — L. *prōvidēre*; see **provide**.]

purview *pûr'vū, n* the body or enacting part of a statute distinguished from the preamble; enactment; scope, range; field of activity or view. [A.Fr. *purveu*, provided, past p. of *purveier*, to purvey, provide.]

pus *pus, n* a thick yellowish fluid formed by an inflamed wound or sore, consisting of serum, white blood cells, bacteria, and debris of tissue. [L. *pūs, pūris*.]

push *pōōsh, vt* to thrust or press against; to drive by pressure; to press or drive forward; to urge; to press hard; to advance or carry to a further point; to promote, or seek to promote, vigorously and persistently; to make efforts to promote the sale of; to effect by thrusting forward; to peddle or to use illegal drugs; to come near (an age or number). — *vi* to make a thrust; to exert pressure; to make an effort; to press forward; to make one's way by exertion; to be urgent and persistent. — *n* a thrust; an impulse or effort; pressure; a help to advancement; enterprising or aggressive pertinacity; an onset or offensive; dismissal or rejection (*colloq*). — *adj* **pushed** (*colloq*) in a hurry; short of money. — *n* **push'er** a person who pushes; a machine or part that pushes; a child's table implement, or a finger of bread, used for pushing food on to a fork; a self-assertive person or one who pushes for social advancement; a drug pedlar. — *adj* **push'ful** energetically or aggressively enterprising. — *adv* **push'fully.** — *n* **push'fulness.** — *adj* **push'ing** pressing forward, e.g. in business; self-assertive. — *n* **push'iness.** — *adj* **push'y** aggressive; self-assertive. — **push'-bike** (*colloq*) a bicycle driven by pedals; **push'-button** a knob which when pressed puts on or cuts off an electric current, as for bells, etc. — *adj* operated by, or using, a push-button or push-buttons. — **push'chair** a folding chair with wheels, for a child; **push'over** an easy thing; a person or side easily overcome; **pushover try** (*Rugby*) one in which the attacking side of a scrum pushes the defenders back until the ball crosses the goal line. — *adj* **push'-pull** of any piece of apparatus in which two electrical or electronic devices act in opposition to each other, as, e.g., of an amplifier using two valves or transistors working in phase opposition, serving to reduce distortion. — **push'-rod** a metal rod in an internal combustion engine that opens and closes the valves. — *vt* **push'-start** to start (a motor car) by pushing it while it is in gear. — *n* the act of starting the car this way. — **push'-up** a press-up (see under **press**[1]). — **at a push** when circumstances urgently require; if really necessary; **give (or get) the push** to dismiss (or be dismissed), to reject (or be rejected); **push along** (*colloq*) to depart, to go on one's way; **push around** to bully; **push for** to make strenuous efforts to achieve; **push off** (of a rower or a boat) to leave the bank, shore, etc.; to depart (*colloq*); **push one's luck** see under **luck; push out** (of person or boat) to row or be rowed out towards open water; **push-pull train** one which can be pulled or pushed by the same locomotive; **push the boat out** see under **boat; push through** to force the acceptance of; **push up the daisies** (*colloq*) to be dead and buried. [Fr. *pousser* — L. *pulsāre*, frequentative of *pellĕre*, *pulsum*, to beat.]

Pushto, Pushtu. See **Pashto.**

pusillanimous *pū-si-lan'i-məs*, *adj* lacking firmness or determination; mean-spirited; cowardly. — *n* **pusillanim'ity.** — *adv* **pusillan'imously.** [L. *pusillanimis* — *pusillus*, very little, *animus*, mind.]

puss[1] *pōōs*, *n* a familiar name for a cat; (in hunting or coursing) a hare; a playfully pejorative name for a child or a girl. — *n* **puss'y** a dimin. of **puss** (also **puss'y-cat**); anything soft and furry; a willow-catkin; the female genitalia (*slang*). — **puss'moth** a thick-bodied hairy moth whose caterpillar feeds on willow or poplar leaves. — *vi* **puss'yfoot** to move stealthily; to act timidly, cautiously or non-committally. — **puss'yfooter; puss'y-willow** a common American willow (*Salix discolor*) or other species with silky spring catkins.

puss[2] *pōōs*, (*slang*) *n* the face. [Ir. *pus*, a mouth.]

pustule *pus'tūl*, *n* a pimple containing pus; a pimple-like or warty spot or elevation. — *adj* **pus'tular** or **pus'tulous.** [L. *pustula.*]

put[1] *pōōt*, *vt* to push or thrust; to place, or cause to be, in such and such a position, state, predicament, relation, etc.; to apply; to append, affix; to connect or add; to commit; to assign; to assign or suggest a course of action to (with *on*, as a diet, a study, a track; or *to*, as a task); to cast, throw, hurl (esp. by a thrusting movement of the hand from the shoulder); to subject; to reduce; to convert; to render; to express; to assert, have; to propound; to submit to a vote; to impose; to impute; to call upon, oblige, stake, venture, invest; to repose (e.g. trust or confidence). — *vi* to proceed, make one's way (*naut*); to set out, esp. hurriedly: — *pr p* **putting** (*pōōt'*); *pa t* and *pa p* **put.** — *n* a push or thrust; a cast, throw, esp. of a heavy object from the shoulder; (on the stock exchange) an option of selling within a certain time certain securities or commodities, at a stipulated price (also **put option**). — *n* **putter** (*pōōt'ər*). — *n* **putting** (*pōōt'*) or **putting the shot** the act or sport of hurling a heavy stone or weight from the hand by a sudden thrust from the shoulder (see also under **putt**). — **put'-down** a snub; an action intended to assert one's superiority; **put'-in** (*Rugby football*) the act of throwing the ball into a set scrum; **put'-off** an excuse or evasion; a postponement; **put'-on** a hoax. — *adj* **put-up'** arranged beforehand in a false but deceptively plausible way. — **put about** to publish, circulate; (of a ship, etc.) to change the course; **put across** to carry out successfully, bring off; to perform so as to carry the audience with one; **put an end (or a stop) to** to cause to discontinue; **put away** to renounce; to divorce; to stow away, pack up, set aside; to put into the proper or desirable place; to imprison; to admit to a mental hospital (*colloq*); to eat (*colloq*); **put back** to push backward; to delay; to turn and sail back for port (*naut*); to reduce one's finances (*colloq*); **put by** to store up; **put down** to crush, quell; to kill, esp. an old or sick animal; to snub, humiliate; to enter, write down on paper; to reckon; to attribute; to surpass, outshine; (of an aeroplane) to land (often with *at*); to pay (a deposit); to put (a baby) to bed (*colloq*); **put forth** to propose; to set out from port; (of a plant) to produce (leaves, etc.); **put forward** to propose; to advance; **put in** to introduce; to insert; to lodge, deposit, hand in; to make a claim or application (*for*); to enter; to enter a harbour; to interpose; to perform towards completing a total; to spend, pass, fill up with some occupation; to appoint; **put in an appearance** see under **appear; put in mind** to remind; **put it across someone** to defeat or trick someone by ingenuity; **put it on** to pretend (to be ill, etc.); **put it past someone** to judge it inconsistent with someone's character; **put off** to lay aside; to lay aside the character of; to palm off; to turn aside with evasions, excuses or unsatisfactory substitutes; to divert, turn aside from a purpose; to postpone; to disconcert; to cause aversion or disinclination; to push from shore; **put on** to don, clothe with; to assume, esp. deceptively; to mislead, deceive; to impose; to affix, attach, apply; to add (e.g. weight, charges, etc.); to stake; to move forward; to set to work; to set in operation; to incite; to turn on the supply of; to score; to stage; **put (someone) on to** to make (someone) aware of; to connect (someone) with by telephone; **put out** to expel; to dismiss from a game and innings; to send or stretch forth; to extinguish; to place at interest; to expand; to publish; to disconcert; to inconvenience; to offend; to dislocate; to exert; to produce; to place with others or at a distance; to go out to sea, leave port; to remove bodily or blind (an eye); to render unconscious (*slang*); **put over** to carry through successfully; to impress an audience, spectators, the public, favourably with; to impose, pass off; **put through** to bring to an end; to accomplish; to put in telephonic communication; to process (*comput*); **putting the shot, stone** or **weight** putting (q.v. under **putt**); **put to** to apply; to add to; to connect with; to harness; to shut; to set to; **put to death** see under **death; put to it** to press hard; to distress; **put to rights** see under **right; put to sea** to begin a voyage; **put to the sword** see under **sword; put two and two together** to draw a conclusion from various facts; **put up** to accommodate with lodging; to take lodgings; to nominate or stand for election; to expose for sale; to present (e.g. a good game, fight or defence, or a prayer); to supply and pack (an order, a picnic, etc.); to preconcert; to sheathe; to compound; **put-up job** a dishonest scheme prearranged usu. by several people; **put upon** to take undue advantage of; to impose upon; **put up to** to incite to; to supply with useful information or tips about; **put up with** to endure; **stay put** to remain passively where one is put or in the required position. [Late O.E. *putian*.]

put² *put*. See **putt**.

putative *pū'tə-tiv*, *adj* supposed; reputed; commonly supposed to be. [L. *putātīvus* — *putāre*, *-ātum*, to suppose.]

putlog *put'log* or **putlock** *put'lok*, *n* a crosspiece in a scaffolding, the inner end resting in a hole left in the wall.

putrefy *pū'tri-fī*, *vt* to cause to rot; to corrupt. — *vi* to rot: — *pr p* **pu'trefying**; *pa t* and *pa p* **pu'trefied**. — *adj* **putrefacient** (*-fā'shənt*) causing putrefaction. — *n* **putrefaction** (*-fak'shən*) rotting. — *adj* **putrefac'tive**. — *adj* **putrefī'able**. — *n* **putrescence** (*-tres'əns*) incipient rottenness. — *adj* **putresc'ent**. — *adj* **pu'trid** rotten; wretchedly bad (*slang*). — *adv* **pu'tridly**. — *n* **putrid'ity** or **pu'tridness**. [L. *putrefacĕre*, *putrēscĕre*, *putridus* — *puter*, *putris*, rotten.]

putsch *pōōch*, *n* a sudden revolutionary outbreak; a coup d'état. [Swiss Ger. dialect.]

putt (also **put**) *put*, *vt* to hurl (a weight, stone) in putting (*Scot*; see **put¹**); to strike in making a putt (*golf*). — *vi* to make a putt or putts: — *pr p* **putting** (*put'*); *pa p* and *pa t* **putted** (*put'*). — *n* a throw or cast (*Scot*; see **put¹**); a delicate stroke such as is made with a putter on, or sometimes near, a putting-green, with the object of rolling the ball, if possible, into the hole (*golf*). — *n* **putter** (*put'ər*) a person who putts or can putt; a usu. short stiff golf club with upright striking-face, used in putting. — *n* **putt'ing** the exercise of hurling a heavy weight (*Scot*; see **put¹**; also called **putting the shot**); the act or art of making a putt; a game played with putters and golf balls on a small course with several holes. — **putt'ing-green** the turf, made firm and smooth for putting, round each of the holes of a golf course — by the rules all within 20 yards of the hole, hazards excluded; a small golf course with several holes for practice or for putting as an informal game. [A Scot. form of **put¹**.]

puttee or **puttie** *put'ē*, *n* a cloth strip wound round the leg from ankle to knee, as a legging. [Hindi. *paṭṭī*.]

putter. See **put¹**, **putt**.

puttie. See **puttee**.

puttier. See **putty**.

putto *pōōt'ō*, *n* very young boy, often winged, in Renaissance or Baroque art: — *pl* **putti** (*pōōt'ē*). [It.]

putty *put'i*, *n* a fine cement of slaked lime and water only (*plasterers' putty*); a cement of whiting and linseed oil (*glaziers'* or *painters' putty*); orig. putty-powder (*polishers'* or *jewellers' putty*); a yellowish grey colour; a weak-willed, easily manipulated person (*fig*). — *vt* to fix, coat or fill with putty: — *pr p* **putt'ying**; *pa t* and *pa p* **putt'ied**. — *n* **putt'ier** a glazier. — *adj* **putt'y-coloured**. — **putt'yknife** a blunt, flexible tool for laying on putty; **putt'y-powder** stannic oxide (often with lead oxide) used for polishing glass. [Fr. *potée*, potful, puttypowder — *pot*.]

puzzle *puz'l*, *vt* to perplex, bewilder; to cause difficulty in solving or comprehending to; to set a problem that causes difficulty to; to entangle, complicate; to solve by systematic and assiduous thinking (with *out*). — *vi* to be bewildered; to work hard at solving; to search about. — *n* perplexity, bewilderment; anything that puzzles; a problem; a riddle or toy designed to test skill or ingenuity. — *n* **puzz'lement** the state of being puzzled. — *n* **puzz'ler**. — *adj* **puzz'ling** perplexing. — *adv* **puzz'lingly**.

puzzolana *pōōt-sō-lä'nə*, *n*. Same as **pozzolana**.

PVA *abbrev* for polyvinyl acetate (see under **poly-**).

PVC *abbrev* for polyvinyl chloride (see under **poly-**).

PVFS *abbrev* for post-viral fatigue syndrome (see under **post-**).

Pvt. (*mil*) *abbrev* for Private.

pw *abbrev* for per week.

PWR *abbrev* for pressurised water reactor.

PX *pē eks*, *n* a shop selling goods for U.S. servicemen and their families overseas. [Abbrev. of **post²** and **exchange**.]

pxt *abbrev* for pinxit (q.v.).

PY *abbrev* for Paraguay (I.V.R.).

pyaemia or in U.S. **pyemia** *pī-ē'mi-ə*, (*med*) *n* infection of the blood with bacteria from a septic focus, with abscesses in different parts of the body. — *adj* **pyae'mic** or **pye'mic**. [Gr. *pyon*, pus, *haima*, blood.]

pycnic *pik'nik*, *adj*. Same as **pyknic**.

pye-dog, **pi-dog** or **pie-dog** *pī'-dog*, *n* (in Asia) an ownerless or pariah dog. [Hind. *pāhī*, outsider.]

pyelitis *pī-ə-lī'tis*, (*med*) *n* inflammation of the pelvis of the kidney. — *adj* **pyelitic** (*-lit'ik*). — *n* **pyelonephritis** (*-nef-rī'tis*) inflammation of the kidney and the renal pelvis. — *adj* **pyelonephritic** (*-rit'ik*). [Gr. *pyelos*, a trough.]

pyemia. See **pyaemia**.

pygmy or **pigmy** *pig'mi*, *n* a member of any of the actual dwarf human races, Negritos, Negrillos and others; a dwarf; any person, animal or thing relatively diminutive or in some way insignificant. — *adj* dwarfish; (esp. of a breed or species) diminutive; of the pygmies. — *adj* **pygmaean** or **pygmean**, **pigmaean** or **pigmean** (*-mē'ən*). — *adj* **pyg'moid** or **pig'moid**. [Gr. *pygmaios*, measuring a *pygmē* (13½ inches, distance from elbow to knuckles).]

pygostyle *pī'gō-stīl*, *n* the bone of a bird's tail. [Gr. *pȳgē*, rump, *stȳlos*, a column.]

pyjamas or in U.S. **pajamas** *pə-* or *pi-jä'məz*, *npl* light, loose-fitting trousers and a jacket or top, worn esp. for sleeping in; loose trousers tied round the waist, worn in the East. — *adj* **pyja'ma'd** or **pyja'maed** wearing pyjamas. — **pyjama cricket** (*Austr*) cricket played under floodlights and in coloured clothing; **pyja'ma-jacket**; **pyja'ma-trousers**. [Pers. and Hind. *pāējāmah* — *pāē*, leg, *jāmah*, clothing.]

pyknic *pik'nik*, *adj* characterised by short squat stature, small hands and feet, relatively short limbs, domed abdomen, short neck, round face. [Gr. *pyknos*, thick.]

pylon *pī'lon*, *n* a structure for support of power-cables; a guiding mark at an aerodrome; an external structure on an aeroplane for attaching an engine, etc.; a gateway, gate-tower, gatehouse, or mass of building through which an entrance passes, esp. the gateway of an Egyptian temple (*archit*). [Gr. *pylōn*, *-ōnos* — *pylē*, a gate.]

pylorus *pī-* or *pi-lö'rəs*, (*anat*) *n* the opening from the stomach to the intestines. — *adj* **pyloric** (*-lor'*). [L., — Gr. *pylōros*, gatekeeper, pylorus — *pylē*, an entrance, *ōrā*, care.]

pyogenic *pī-ə-jen'ik*, (*med*) *adj* pus-forming. — *n* **pyogen'esis**. — *adj* **py'oid** resembling pus. — *n* **pyorrhoea** (*-rē'ə*) discharge of pus; suppuration in the sockets of teeth. — *adj* **pyorrhoe'al** or **pyorrhoe'ic**. [Gr. *pyon*, pus.]

pyracantha *pī-rə-kan'thə*, *n* a thorny evergreen shrub of the genus *Pyracantha*, having bright red, yellow or orange berries. [Gr. *pȳrakantha* — *pȳr*, fire, *akanthos*, thorn.]

pyramid *pir'ə-mid*, *n* a solid figure on a triangular, square or polygonal base, with triangular sides meeting in a point; any object or structure of that or similar form, esp. a great Egyptian monument; a crystal form of three or more faces each cutting three axes (*crystall*); (in *pl*) a game played on a billiard-table in which the balls are arranged in a pyramid shape. — *vi* (chiefly *US*) to increase one's holdings, profits, etc. during a boom period by using paper profits for further purchases. — *adj* **pyram'idal, pyramid'ic** or **pyramid'ical** having the form of a pyramid. — *adv* **pyram'idally** or **pyramid'ically**. — *n* **pyram'idist** or **pyramidol'ogist** a person who studies the Egyptian Pyramids. — *n* **pyramidol'ogy**. — **pyramid selling** a method of distributing goods by selling batches to agents who then sell batches at increased prices to sub-agents, and so on. [Gr. *pyramis, -idos.*]

pyre *pīr*, *n* a pile of combustible material for burning a dead body. [L. *pyra* — Gr. *pyrā* — *pyr*, fire.]

Pyrenean *pir-ə-nē'ən*, *adj* of the *Pyrenees*, the mountains between France and Spain. — *n* a native of the Pyrenees. — **Pyrenean mountain dog** a large dog with a dense white coat, bred in the Pyrenees to guard flocks. [L. *Pȳrēnaeus* — Gr. *Pȳrēnaios.*]

pyrethrum *pī-rēth'rəm* or *pī-reth'rəm*, *n* any of various garden flowers, esp. varieties of *Chrysanthemum coccineum*; an insecticide made from the flower-heads of various species of pyrethrum; (in pharmacy) the root of pellitory of Spain. — *n* **pyrēth'rin** (or *-reth'*) either of two insecticidal oily esters prepared from pyrethrum flowers. — *n* **pyrēth'roid** (or *-reth'*) any of various synthetic compounds related to the pyrethrins, and sharing their insecticidal properties. [L., — Gr. *pyrĕthron*, pellitory of Spain.]

pyretic *pī-ret'ik* or *pir-et'ik*, *adj* of, of the nature of, or for the cure of, fever. — *n* **pyretol'ogy** study of fevers. — *n* **pyretother'apy** treatment by inducing high body temperature. [Gr. *pyretikos*; ety. as for **pyrexia**.]

Pyrex® *pī'reks*, *n* a type of glassware containing oxide of boron and so resistant to heat. [Gr. *pȳr*, fire, and L. *rēx*, king.]

pyrexia *pī-rek'si-ə*, (*med*) *n* fever. — *adj* **pyrex'ial** or **pyrex'ic**. [Gr. *pyretos*, fever — *pȳr*, fire.]

pyridine *pir'*, *pīr'i-dēn* or *-dīn*, *n* a strong-smelling, colourless, strongly basic liquid, C_5H_5N, distilled from bone-oil, coal-tar, etc. — *n* **pyridox'in** or **pyridox'ine** a pyridine derivative, a member of the vitamin B complex. — *n* **pyrim'idine** one of a group of heterocyclic compounds forming an essential part of nucleic acids. [Gr. *pȳr*, fire.]

pyrimethamine *pi-ri-meth'ə-mēn* or *pī-*, *n* a powerful antimalarial drug. [Gr. *pȳr*, fire, *methyl*, and **amine**.]

pyrimidine. See under **pyridine**.

pyrites *pīr-* or *pir-ī'tēz*, *n* a brassy yellow mineral, iron disulphide (also called **pyrite** (*pī'rīt*) or **iron pyri'tes**); extended to a large class of mineral sulphides and arsenides. — *adj* **pyritic** (*pir-* or *pīr-it'ik*) or **pyrit'ical**. — *adj* **pyritif'erous**. [Gr. *pȳrītēs*, striking fire — *pȳr*, fire.]

pyro *pī'rō*, (*phot*) *n* a familiar short form of **pyrogallol**.

pyro- *pī-rō-*, *combining form* signifying: fire, heat or fever; obtained by heating or as if by heating, or by removing (theoretically) a molecule of water (*chem*). — *adj* **pyrochem'ical** relating to, producing, or produced by chemical changes at high temperatures. [Gr. *pȳr*, in compounds *pȳr-*, fire.]

pyroelectric *pī-rō-i-lek'trik*, *adj* becoming positively and negatively electrified at opposite poles on heating or cooling; of pyroelectricity. — *n* **pyroelectricity** (*-el-ik-tris'i-ti*) the property of being pyroelectric; the study of the phenomema shown by pyroelectric crystals. [Gr. *pȳr*, fire, and **electric**.]

pyrogallol *pī-rō-gal'ol*, *n* a phenol obtained by heating *gallic* acid, used in photographic developing; also called **pyrogallic acid**.

pyrogenic *pī-rō-jen'ik*, **pyrogenetic** *-jin-et'ik* or **pyrogenous** *-roj'ə-nəs*, *adj* produced by, or producing, heat or fever. — *n* **py'rogen** a substance causing heat or fever. [Gr. *pȳr*, fire, and the root of *gignesthai*, to become.]

pyrography *pī-rog'rə-fi*, *n* poker-work (q.v. under **poke**[2]). — *n* **pyrogravure'**. [Gr. *pȳr*, fire, *graphein*, to write.]

pyrokinesis *pī-rō-kī-nē'sis* or *-ki-*, *n* the ability to start fires by thought alone. [Gr. *pȳr*, fire, *kīnēsis*, movement.]

pyrolysis *pi-rol'is-is*, *n* decomposition of a substance by heat. — *vt* **py'rolyse** or in U.S. **py'rolyze** to decompose by pyrolysis. — *adj* **pyrolytic** (*-lit'ik*). [Gr. *pȳr-*, fire, *lysis*, loosing.]

pyromania *pī-rō-mā'ni-ə*, *n* an obsessive urge to set light to things. — *n* and *adj* **pyromaniacal** (*-mə-nī'ə-kl*). [Gr. *pȳr*, fire, and **mania**.]

pyrometer *pī-rom'i-tər*, *n* an instrument for measuring high temperatures. — *adj* **pyrometric** (*pī-rō-met'rik*) or **pyromet'rical**. — *n* **pyrom'etry**. [Gr. *pȳr*, fire, *metron*, measure.]

pyrope *pī'rōp*, *n* a fiery red gemstone; a red magnesia-alumina garnet, used in jewellery. [Gr. *pyrōpos*, fiery-eyed — *ōps*, *ōpos*, eye, face.]

pyroscope *pī'rō-skōp*, *n* an instrument for measuring the intensity of radiant heat. [Gr. *pȳr*, fire, *skopeein*, to view.]

pyrosis *pī-rō'sis*, *n* water brash. [Gr. *pȳrōsis* — *pȳr*, fire.]

pyrostat *pī'rō-stat*, *n* a type of themostat for use at high temperatures. — *adj* **pyrostat'ic**. [Gr. *pȳr*, fire, and thermo*stat*.]

pyrotechnics *pī-rō-tek'niks*, *nsing* the art of making fireworks; (*nsing* or *npl*) display of fireworks; (*nsing* or *npl*) showy display in talk, music, etc. — *adj* **pyrotech'nic** or **pyrotech'nical**. — *adv* **pyrotech'nically**. — *n* **pyrotech'nist** a maker of fireworks; someone skilled in, or given to, pyrotechnics. — *n* **py'rotechny** pyrotechnics. [Gr. *pȳr*, fire, *technikos*, skilled — *technē*, art.]

pyroxene *pī'rok-sēn*, *n* a general name for a group of minerals, silicates of calcium, magnesium, aluminium and other metals, usu. green or black, very common in igneous rocks. — *adj* **pyroxenic** (*-sen'ik*). — *n* **pyrox'enite** (*-ən-īt* or *-ēn'īt*) a rock compound essentially of pyroxene. [Gr. *pȳr*, fire, *xenos*, stranger (because Haüy thought that pyroxene crystals in lava had only been accidentally caught up).]

pyrrhic *pir'ik*, *adj* of or pertaining to *Pyrrhus*, king of Epirus (318–272 B.C.). — **Pyrrhic victory** a victory gained at too great a cost (in allusion to Pyrrhus's exclamation after his defeat of the Romans at Heraclea on the Siris (280), 'Another such victory and we are lost'.

Pyrrhonism *pir'ən-izm*, *n* the complete scepticism of the Greek philosopher *Pyrrhō* of Elis (3rd cent. B.C.). — *adj* and *n* **Pyrrhonian** (*pir-ō'ni-ən*). — *adj* **Pyrrhonic** (*-on'ik*). — *n* **Pyrrh'onist**.

pyrrole *pi'rōl*, (*chem*) *n* a colourless toxic liquid found in many naturally-occurring compounds, e.g. porphyrins and chlorophyll. — *n* **pyrrolidine** (*pi-rol'i-dēn*) a colourless strongly alkaline base, C_4H_9N, both occurring naturally and produced from pyrrole. [Gr. *pyrros*, flame-coloured, L. *oleum*, oil.]

pyruvate *pī-roo'vāt*, (*chem*) *n* a salt or ester of pyruvic acid. — **pyruvic acid** (*-roo'vik*) an organic acid, an intermediate in the metabolism of proteins and carbohydrates. [Gr. *pȳr*, fire, and L. *ūva*, grape.]

Pythagorean *pī-thag-ər-ē'ən*, *adj* pertaining to *Pythagoras* of Samos (6th cent. B.C.), the Greek philosopher, or to his philosophy, incl. transmigration of the soul; of a diatonic scale perfected by Pythagoras, with its intervals based on mathematical ratios (*mus*). — *n* a follower of Pythagoras. — *n*

Pythagorē'anism or **Pythag'orism** his doctrines. — **Pythagorean theorem** that the square on the hypotenuse of a right-angled triangle is equal to the sum of the squares on the other two sides.

python *pī'thən*, *n* a large snake that crushes its victims, esp. and properly one of the Old World genus *Python*. — *adj* **python'ic**. [L., — Gr. *Puthōn*, a huge serpent or dragon killed by Apollo.]

Pythonesque *pī-thən-esk'*, *adj* (of humour) bizarre and surreal, as in the BBC television comedy programme *Monty Python's Flying Circus*.

pyx *piks*, *n* a vessel in which the host is kept after consecration, now usu. that in which it is carried to the sick (*RC*); a box at the Royal Mint in which sample coins are kept for testing. — *vt* to test the weight and fineness of, as the coin deposited in the pyx. — *n* **pyxid'ium** (*bot*) a capsule that opens by a transverse circular split: — *pl* **pyxid'ia.** — *n* **pyx'is** a little box or casket as for jewels, drugs, toilet materials, etc.: — *pl* **pyx'ides** (*-id-ēz*). — **trial of the pyx** periodic official testing of sterling coinage. [L. *pyxis*, a box — Gr. *pyxis*, *-idos*, dimin. of *pyxidion* — *pyxos*, box-tree.]

pzazz. Same as **pizzazz**.

Q

Q or **q** *kū*, *n* the seventeenth letter of the modern English alphabet; in English followed by *u* (*qu* being sounded as *kw*). [L. *cū*.]
Q or **Q.** *abbrev* for: quality; Quebec (also **Que.**); queen (*cards* and *chess*); Queensland (also **Qld**); query; question; quetzal (Guatemalan currency).
Q symbol for: electric charge (*phys*); quality or quality-value.
q or **q.** *abbrev* for: quart; quarter; query; quintal.
qa-, qe-, qi-, qo-, qu-. Arabic and Hebrew words spelt this way are in most cases given at **k-** or **c-**.
Qaddish and **qadi**. Same as **Kaddish** and **cadi**.
Qajar *ka-jär'*, *n* the dynasty that united and ruled Iran from 1779 to 1925. — *adj* of the dynasty, its time, esp. its art, porcelain, etc.
qanat *kä-nät'*, *n* an underground tunnel for carrying irrigation water. [Ar. *qanāt*, pipe.]
Q & A *abbrev* for question and answer.
QANTAS *kwon'təs*, *abbrev* for Queensland and Northern Territory Aerial Service (the Australian international airline).
QARANC *abbrev* for Queen Alexandra's Royal Army Nursing Corps.
QARNNS *abbrev* for Queen Alexandra's Royal Naval Nursing Service.
qat. See **khat**.
QB *abbrev* for Queen's Bench.
QC *abbrev* for: Queen's College; Queen's Counsel.
QE2 *abbrev* for Queen Elizabeth the Second (the liner).
QED *abbrev* for *quod erat demonstrandum* (L.), which was to be demonstrated (or proved). — Also **q.e.d.**
QEF *abbrev* for *quod erat faciendum* (L.), which was to be done.
QEH *abbrev* for Queen Elizabeth Hall (on London's South Bank).
QEI *abbrev* for *quod erat inveniendum* (L.), which was to be found.
Q-fever *kū'-fē-vər*, *n* an acute disease characterised by fever and muscular pains, transmitted by the rickettsia *Coxiella burnetii*. [*Q* as abbrev. for query.]
qibla *kib'lä*, *n*. Same as **kiblah**.
qid *abbrev* for (in prescriptions) *quater in die* (L.), four times a day.
qigong *chē-gōōng*, *n* a system of exercises for promoting physical and mental health by deep breathing. [Chin. *qì*, breath, *gong*, skill, exercise.]
ql *abbrev* for (in prescriptions) *quantum libet* (L.), as much as you please.
Qld *abbrev* for Queensland (Australian state).
QM *abbrev* for Quartermaster.
QMG *abbrev* for Quartermaster-General.
QMS *abbrev* for Quartermaster-Sergeant.
Qoran. Same as **Koran**.
QPM *abbrev* for Queen's Police Medal.
QPR *abbrev* for Queen's Park Rangers (Football Club).
qq *abbrev* for quartos.
qqv *abbrev* for *quae vide* (L.), which (*pl*) see. — In *sing* **qv**.
qr *abbrev* for quarter.
qs *abbrev* for (in prescriptions) *quantum sufficit* (L.), a sufficient quantity.
QSM *abbrev* for Queen's Service Medal (N.Z.).
QSO *abbrev* for: quasi-stellar object (quasar); Queen's Service Order (N.Z.).
qt *abbrev* for: quantity; quart.
q.t. (*colloq*) *abbrev* for quiet.
qto *abbrev* for quarto.
QTS *abbrev* for Qualified Teacher Status.
qty *abbrev* for quantity.
Qu. *abbrev* for: Queen; question.
qu. or **quar.** *abbrev* for: quart; quarter; quarterly.
qua *kwā* or *kwä*, *adv* in the capacity of. [L. *quā*, adverbial abl. fem. of *quī*, who.]
quack[1] *kwak*, *n* the cry of a duck. — *vi* to make the sound of a quack. — *n* **quack'er**. [Imit.]
quack[2] *kwak*, *n* someone who claims, and sets themselves up as having, knowledge and skill (esp. in medicine) that they do not possess; a doctor (*slang*); a charlatan. — Also *adj*. — *n* **quack'ery** the pretensions or practice of a quack, esp. in medicine. [Orig. *quacksalver*, perh. someone who quacks about their salves (remedies) — Du. (now *kwakzalver*).]
quad[1] *kwod*, *n* a shortening of **quadrangle, quadraphonics, quadrat** and **quadruplet**. — *adj* short for **quadruple**.
quad[2] or **Quad** *kwod*, *n* a small, powerful four-wheel drive vehicle, used e.g. in military, agricultural and sporting activities. [**quadruple**.]
quadr- *kwod-r-* or **quadri-** *kwod-ri-*, *combining form* denoting: four; square. — *adj* **quad'ric** of the second degree. [L. *quadri-* — *quattuor*, four.]
quadragenarian *kwod-rə-ji-nā'ri-ən*, *n* a person who is forty years old, or between forty and fifty. — Also *adj*. [L. *quadrāgēnārius* — *quadrāgēnī*, forty each.]
Quadragesima *kwod-rə-jes'i-mə*, *n* the first Sunday in Lent. — *adj* **quadrages'imal**. [L. *quadrāgēsimus,-a, -um*, fortieth — *quadrāgintā*, forty — *quattuor*, four.]
quadrangle *kwod-rang'gl*, also *kwod'rang-gl*, *n* a plane figure with four angles (and therefore four sides); an object or space of that form; a court or open space, usu. rectangular, enclosed by a building (such as a college). — *adj* **quadrang'ular** (*-gū-lər*). — *adv* **quadrang'ularly**. [Fr., — L. *quadrangulum* — *quattuor*, four, *angulus*, an angle.]
quadrant *kwod'rənt*, *n* the fourth part of a circle or its circumference, a sector or an arc of 90° (also *adj*); an area, object or street of that form; an instrument with an arc of 90° for taking altitudes. — *adj* **quadrantal** (*-rant'l*). [L. *quadrāns, -antis*, a fourth part — *quattuor*, four.]
quadraphonics or **quadrophonics** *kwod-rə-fon'iks* or *kwod-ro-fon'iks*, *nsing* a system of sound transmission using a minimum of four speakers fed by four, or sometimes three, separate channels. — Also **quadrophony** (*-rof'*) or **quadraph'ony**. — *adj* **quadraphon'ic** or **quadrophon'ic**.
quadrat *kwod'rat*, (*printing*) *n* a piece of type-metal lower than the letters, used in spacing between words and filling out blank lines (commonly called a **quad**) — distinguished as *en* and *em*. — *adj* **quad'rate** (*-rāt* or *-rit*) square; rectangular; squarish; square, as a power or root (*math*). — *n* a square or quadrate figure or object; the quadrate bone, suspending the lower jaw in vertebrates other than mammals. — *vt* and *vi* to square; to conform. — *adj* **quadratic** (*-rat'ik*) of

Q R

or like a quadrate; involving the square but no higher power, as a *quadratic equation* (*alg*). — *n* a quadratic equation. — *n* **quad'rature** (*-rə-chər*) the finding of a square equal to a given figure; an angular distance of 90°; the position of a heavenly body at such an angular distance, or the time of its being there. [L. *quadrātus*, past p. of *quadrāre*, to square — *quattuor*, four.]

quadratura *kwod-rə-tōōr'ə*, (*art*) *n* a work having a trompe l'œil effect, e.g. a wall or ceiling painted with arches, colonnades, etc. in strong perspective: — *pl* **quadratur'e** (*-re*). [It.]

quadrella *kwod-rel'ə*, (*Austr*) *n* a group of four (esp. the last four) horse-races at a meeting, for which the punter selects the four winners. [L. *quadr-*, four, *-ella*, dimin. sfx.]

quadrennium *kwod-ren'i-əm*, *n* four years: — *pl* **quadrenn'ia**. — *adj* **quadrenn'ial** lasting four years; once in four years. — *n* a quadrennial event. — *adv* **quadrenn'ially**. — The forms **quadrienn'ium**, **quadriennial** etc., are etymologically correct but now less usual. [**quadri-** and L. *annus*, a year.]

quadri-, **quadric**. See **quadr-**.

quadriceps *kwod'ri-seps*, (*anat*) *n* the large thigh muscle that extends the leg. — *adj* **quadricipital** (*-sip'i-tl*). [L. *quadri-*, four-, *caput*, *-itis*, head (from its four insertions).]

quadriennium, etc. See **quadrennium**.

quadrifid *kwod'ri-fid*, (*bot*) *adj* split in four. [L. *quadrifidus* — *quadri-*, four, *-fid* from the root of *findĕre*, to cleave.]

quadrilateral *kwod-ri-lat'ər-l*, *adj* four-sided. — *n* a plane figure bounded by four straight lines (*geom*); a group of four fortresses, esp. Mantua, Verona, Peschiera and Legnaga. [**quadri-** and L. *latus*, *lateris*, a side.]

quadrilingual *kwod-ri-ling'gwəl*, *adj* using four languages. — *n* a word or a root of four letters. [**quadri-** and L. *lingua*, tongue.]

quadrille[1] *kwə-dril'* or *kə-*, *n* a square dance for four couples or more, in five movements; music for such a dance. [Fr., — Sp. *cuadrilla*, a troop, app. — L. *quadra*, a square.]

quadrille[2] *kwə-dril'* or *kə-*, *n* a four-handed game with 40 cards. — *vi* to play quadrille. [Fr., perh. — Sp. *cuatrillo*, the game of quadrille, or *cuartillo*, fourth part.]

quadrillion *kwod-* or *kwəd-ril'yən*, *n* (modelled on **million**) a million raised to the fourth power, represented by a unit and 24 ciphers; (in U.S.) a thousand to the fifth power, a unit with 15 ciphers. — *n* and *adj* **quadrill'ionth**. [**quadr-**.]

quadrinomial *kwod-ri-nō'mi-əl*, (*alg*) *adj* made up of four terms. — *n* an expression of four terms. [**quadri-** and L. *nōmen*, *-inis*, a name.]

quadripartite *kwod-ri-pär'tīt*, *adj* in four parts; having four parties; (of e.g. a leaf) deeply cleft into four parts (*bot*); divided, as a vault, into four compartments (*archit*). — *n* **quadriparti'tion**. [**quadri-** and L. *partīrī*, *-ītum*, to divide.]

quadriplegia *kwod-ri-plē'jə* or *-plē'jyə*, (*med*) *n* paralysis of both arms and both legs. — *n* and *adj* **quadripleg'ic**. [**quadri-** and Gr. *plēgē*, a blow.]

quadrivalent *kwod-riv'ə-lənt* or *-vā'lənt*, (*biol*) *n* having a valency of four. — *n* **quadriv'alence** (or *-vā'*). [**quadri-**.]

quadrivium *kwod-riv'i-əm*, *n* in mediaeval education, the four branches of mathematics (arithmetic, geometry, astronomy and music). — *adj* **quadriv'ial**. [L., the place where four roads meet — **quadri-**, four-, *via*, a way.]

quadroon *kwod-rōōn'*, *n* a person of one-quarter Negro descent; extended to refer to any person or animal of similarly mixed ancestry. [Sp. *cuarterón* — *cuarto*, a fourth.]

quadrophonic(s), **quadrophony**. See **quadraphonics**.

quadru- *kwod-rōō-*. A variant of **quadr(i)-**.

quadrumanous *kwod-rōō'mən-əs*, (*zool*) *adj* four-handed; of the Primates other than man. [**quadru-** and L. *manus*, a hand.]

quadruped *kwod'rōō-ped*, *n* a four-footed animal, usu. a mammal, esp. a horse. — *adj* four-footed. — *adj* **quadrupedal** (*-rōō'pi-dəl*). [**quadru-** and L. *pes*, *pedis*, a foot.]

quadruple *kwod'rōō-pl*, also (esp. in Scotland) *kwod-rōō'pl*, *adj* fourfold; having four parts, members or divisions. — *n* four times as much. — *vt* to increase fourfold; to equal four times. — *vi* to become four times as much. — *n* **quad'ruplet** (or *-rōō'*) any combination of four things; a group of four notes performed in the time of three (*mus*); a cycle for four riders; one of four (children or animals) born at one birth. — *n* **quad'ruplex** a videotape recording and reproduction system using four rotating heads to produce transverse tracks on magnetic tape. — *adv* **quad'ruply** (*-pli* or *-rōō'pli*) in a fourfold manner. — **quadruple time** (*mus*) a time with four beats to the bar. [Fr., — L. *quadruplus*, from the root of *plēre*, to fill.]

quadruplicate *kwod-rōō'pli-kit*, *adj* fourfold. — *n* one of four corresponding things; fourfoldness. — *vt* to make fourfold. — *n* **quadruplicā'tion**. — *n* **quadruplicity** (*-plis'i-ti*). [L. *quadruplex*, *-icis*, fourfold — *plicāre*, *-ātum*, to fold.]

quaestor *kwēs'tör* or *kwīs'tor*, *n* an ancient Roman magistrate, in early times an investigator, prosecutor or judge in murder cases, later a treasurer with various other functions. — *adj* **quaestor'ial**. — *n* **quaes'torship**. [L. *quaestor*, *-ōris* — *quaerĕre*, *quaesītum*, to seek.]

quae vide. See **qqv**.

quaff *kwäf* or *kwof*, *vt* to drink or drain in large draughts. — *vi* to drink deeply or eagerly. — *n* a draught. — *n* **quaff'er**.

quag *kwag* or *kwog*, *n* a boggy place, esp. one that moves or quivers underfoot. — *n* **quagg'iness**. — *adj* **quagg'y**. [Cf. **quake**.]

quagga *kwag'ə*, *n* an extinct S. African wild ass, less fully striped than the zebras, to which it was related. [Perh. Hottentot *quacha*.]

quagmire *kwag'mīr* or *kwog'mīr*, *n* wet, boggy ground that yields, moves or quivers under the feet. [App. **quag** and **mire**.]

quahog or **quahaug** *kwö'hog* or *-hög*, *n* an edible lamellibranch mollusc (*Venus mercenaria*) of the N. American Atlantic coast — also known as *round clam*. [Narraganset Ind. *poquauhock*.]

quaich or **quaigh** *kwāhh*, (*Scot*) *n* a drinking-cup, orig. made of staves and hoops, now usu. of silver or pewter. [Gael. *cuach*, a cup.]

quail[1] *kwāl*, *vi* to flinch; to fail in spirit. [M.E. *quayle*.]

quail[2] *kwāl*, *n* a genus (*Coturnix*) of small birds of the partridge family; in N. America extended to various small game birds. [O.Fr. *quaille*; prob. Gmc.]

quaint *kwānt*, *adj* pleasantly odd; whimsical; charmingly old-fashioned. — *adv* **quaint'ly**. — *n* **quaint'ness**. [O.Fr. *cointe* — L. *cognitus*, known.]

quake *kwāk*, *vi* to quiver or vibrate; to tremble, esp. with cold or fear. — *n* a tremor; an earthquake; a shudder. — *n* **quā'kiness**. — *n* **quā'king**. — *adv* **quā'kingly**. — *adj* **quā'ky** shaky. — **quaking ash** the aspen; **quā'king-grass** a moorland grass of the genus *Briza*, with pendulous, panicled, quivering spikelets. [O.E. *cwacian*.]

Quaker *kwā'kər*, *n* one of the Religious Society of Friends, founded by George Fox (1624–91); a dummy cannon (also called a **Quaker gun**). — *adj* of Quakers. — *n* **Quā'keress**. — *n* **Quā'kerism**. — *adj* **Quā'kerish** or **Quā'kerly** like a Quaker. [Nickname given to them because Fox would tell them to *quake* at the word of the Lord.]

qualify *kwol'i-fī*, *vt* to ascribe a quality to; to characterise; to render capable or suitable; to provide with legal power; to limit by modifications; to moderate. — *vi* to take the necessary steps to fit oneself for a certain position, activity or practice; to fulfil a requirement; to have the necessary qualities or qualifications: — *pr p* **qual'ifying**; *pa p* and *pa t* **qual'ified.** — *adj* **qual'ifiable** (*-fī-ə-bl*). — *n* **qualification** (*-fi-kā'shən*) qualifying; modification; restriction; that which qualifies; a quality that fits a person for a place, etc.; a necessary condition. — *adj* **qual'ificātory.** — *adj* **qual'ified** (*-fīd*) fitted; competent; having the necessary qualification; modified; limited. — *adv* **qual'ifiedly** (*-fīd-li*). — *n* **qual'ifier** (*-fī-ər*). — *n* and *adj* **qual'ifying.** — **qualifying round** a preliminary round in a competition, to limit the number of competitors. — **Qualified Teacher Status** accredited status (awarded by the Department of Education and Science) required by any school teacher wishing to teach in England and Wales. [Fr. *qualifier* or L.L. *quālificāre* — L. *quālis*, of what sort, *facĕre*, to make.]

quality *kwol'i-ti*, *n* nature; character; kind; property; attribute; high social status; persons of the upper class collectively; grade of goodness; excellence; skill, accomplishment; timbre, that character of a sound that depends on the overtones present, distinguished from loudness and pitch (*acoustics*); the character of a proposition as affirmative or negative (*logic*). — *adj* of high grade of excellence; of recognisably high quality. — *adj* **qual'itātive** relating to, or concerned with, quality (esp. opp. to *quantitative*). — *adv* **qual'itātively.** — *adj* **quality control** inspection, testing, etc. of samples of a product to ensure maintenance of high standards. [O.Fr. *qualité* — L. *quālitās, -tātis* — *quālis*, of what kind.]

qualm *kwäm* or *kwöm*, *n* an uneasiness, e.g. of conscience; a misgiving; a sickly feeling. — *adj* **qualm'ish.** — *adv* **qualm'ishly.** — *n* **qualm'ishness.** — *adj* **qualm'less.** — *adj* **qualm'y.** [Perh. O.E. *cwealm*, death, murder, torment, pain.]

quandang. See **quandong.**

quandary *kwon'də-ri*, *n* a state of perplexity; dilemma.

quandong *kwan'* or *kwon'dong*, *n* a small Australian tree of the sandalwood family; its edible drupe (*native peach*) or edible kernel (**quan'dong-nut**); an Australian tree (*Elaeocarpus grandis*) (**silver, blue** or **brush quandong**). — Also **quan'dang.** [Aboriginal.]

quango *kwang'gō*, *n* a board funded by, and with members appointed by, central government, to supervise or develop activity in areas of public interest: — *pl* **quan'gos.** [*qu*asi-*a*utonomous *n*on-*g*overnmental *o*rganisation.]

quant *kwant*, *n* a punting or jumping pole, with a flat end. — *vt* to punt. [Perh. conn. with L. *contus*, Gr. *kontos*, (boat-)pole.]

quanta, quantal. See **quantum.**

quantic *kwon'tik*, (*math*) *n* a rational integral homogeneous function of two or more variables. — *adj* **quan'tical.** [L. *quantus*, how great.]

quantify *kwon'ti-fī*, *vt* to fix or express the quantity of; to express as a quantity; to qualify (a term in a proposition) by stating the quantity (*logic*). — *adj* **quan'tifiable.** — *n* **quantification** (*-fi-kā'shən*). — *n* **quan'tifier.** [L. *quantus*, how great, *facĕre*, to make.]

quantise, -ize. See under **quantum.**

quantity *kwon'ti-ti*, *n* the amount of anything; size; a sum; a determinate amount; an amount, portion; a considerable amount; length or shortness of duration of a sound or syllable (*acoustics*); extension (*logic*); the character of a proposition as universal or particular; anything which can be increased, divided or measured. — *adj* **quan'titātive** (or **quan'titive**) relating to, or concerned with, quantity (esp. opp. to *qualitative*). — *adv* **quan'titātively.** — **quantity surveyor** a person who estimates quantities required, obtains materials, evaluates work done, etc. for construction work. — **unknown quantity** a quantity whose mathematical value is not known; a factor, person or thing whose importance or influence cannot be foreseen. [O.Fr. *quantité* — L. *quantitās, -tātis* — *quantus*, how much.]

quantum *kwon'təm*, *n* quantity; amount; a naturally fixed minimum amount of some entity, which is such that all other amounts of that entity occurring in physical processes in nature are integral multiples of it (*phys*): — *pl* **quan'ta.** — *adj* **quan'tal** of, or pertaining to, a quantum (*phys*); having one of only two possible states or values. — *n* **quantisā'tion** or **-z-.** — *vt* **quan'tise** or **-ize** to express in terms of quanta or in accordance with the quantum theory. — **quantum jump** or **leap** the sudden transition of an electron, atom, etc. from one energy state to another; a sudden spectacular advance, as one which dramatically skips over intermediate stages of understanding or development (*fig*); **quantum mechanics** a branch of mechanics based on the quantum theory, used in predicting the behaviour of elementary particles; **quantum number** any of a set of integers or half-integers which together describe the state of a particle or system of particles; **quantum theory** Planck's theory of the emission and absorption of energy not continuously but in finite steps. [L. *quantum*, neut. of *quantus*, how much.]

quaquaversal *kwā-kwə-vûr'sl* or *kwä-kwä-*, *adj* dipping outward in all directions from a centre (*geol*); facing or bending all ways. — *adv* **quaquaver'sally.** [L. *quāquā*, whithersoever, *vertĕre, versum*, to turn.]

quarantine *kwor'ən-tēn*, *n* a time (orig. for a ship forty days) of compulsory isolation or detention to prevent spread of contagion or infection; isolation or detention for such a purpose; the place where the time is spent; any period of enforced isolation. — *vt* to subject to quarantine. — **quarantine flag** a yellow flag displayed by a ship in quarantine, with a black spot if there is a contagious disease on board. [It. *quarantina* — *quaranta*, forty — L. *quadrāgintā*.]

quark[1] *kwörk* or *kwärk*, (*phys*) *n* a fundamental subatomic particle (currently seen as any of six types: *bottom, top, up, down, charmed* and *strange*), not yet observed directly, but suggested as the units out of which all other subatomic particles are formed. [From word coined by James Joyce in *Finnegans Wake*.]

quark[2] *kwärk* or *kwörk*, *n* a low-fat, soft cheese made from skim-milk. [Late M.H.G. *twarc, quarc*, or *zwarc*.]

quarrel[1] *kwor'əl*, *n* ground of complaint or action; a cause that is fought for; an unfriendly contention or dispute; a breach of friendship. — *vi* to cavil, find fault (with); to dispute violently; to fall out; to disagree violently: — *pr p* **quarr'elling**; *pa t* and *pa p* **quarr'elled.** — *n* **quarr'eller.** — *n* and *adj* **quarr'elling.** — *adj* **quarr'elsome** disposed to quarrel. — *adv* **quarr'elsomely.** — *n* **quarr'elsomeness.** [O.Fr. *querele* — L. *querēla* — *querī, questus*, to complain.]

quarrel[2] *kwor'əl*, *n* a square-headed arrow as for a crossbow; a diamond pane of glass; a square tile. — **quarr'el-pane.** [O.Fr. (Fr. *carreau*) — L.L. *quadrellus* — *quadrus*, a square.]

quarry[1] *kwor'i*, *n* an open excavation for building-stone, slate, etc.; any source of building-stone, etc.; a source from which information can be extracted. — *vt* to dig from, or as if from, a quarry; to cut into or cut away: — *pr p* **quarr'ying**; *pa t* and *pa p* **quarr'ied.** — *adj* **quarr'iable.** — *n* **quarr'ier** a quarryman. — **quarr'yman** a man who works in a quarry; **quarr'ymaster** the owner of a quarry. [L.L. *quareia*, for *quadrāria* — L. *quadrāre*, to square.]

quarry² *kwor'i, n* a hunted animal; prey; a victim; a hunter's heap of dead game. [Formerly a deer's entrails given (on a hide) to the dogs, — O.Fr. *cuiree, curee*, said to be from *cuir* — L. *corium*, hide.]

quarry³ *kwor'i, n* a quarrel of glass; a square paving-tile or slab. — **quarry tile** a square unglazed floor tile. [A form of **quarrel²**; or perh. from O.Fr. *quarré* — L. *quadrātus*, squared.]

quart¹ *kwört, n* the fourth part of a gallon, or two pints (1·14 litres); in U.S., 0.946 litre in liquid measure, 1.1 litre in dry measure; a vessel containing two pints; as much as will fill it. [Fr. *quart, -e* — L. *quārtus, -a, -um*, fourth — *quattuor*, four.]

quart² or **quarte** *kärt, n* a sequence of four cards in piquet, etc.; the fourth of eight parrying or attacking positions in fencing (also called **carte**). [Fr. *quarte* — It. and L. *quarta*, fourth.]

quartan *kwör'tən, adj* (of a fever) occurring every third (by inclusive reckoning fourth) day. — *n* quartan malaria. [L. *quārtānus*, of the fourth.]

quarte. See **quart²**.

quarter *kwör'tər, n* a fourth part; a 25-cent piece, 25 cents, quarter of a dollar (*US*); the fourth part of an hour, of the year, of the moon's cycle (or the moon's position at the end of it), of the world, etc.; the fourth part of a cwt. = 28 (in U.S. 25) lb. avoirdupois; 8 bushels (perh. orig. a fourth of a ton of corn); a quarter of a pound, 4 oz. (*colloq*); a cardinal point, or any point, of the compass; the region about any point of the compass; a region generally, and also figuratively; a town district inhabited by a particular class; (usu. in *pl*) lodging, esp. for soldiers; an assigned station or position; mercy granted to a beaten opponent (perh. from sending to quarters); the part of a ship's side abaft the beam; a limb with adjacent parts of the trunk, esp. (*hist*) of the dismembered body of an executed person, or of an animal carcass; a haunch; one of the four parts of a quartered shield (*heraldry*); an ordinary occupying one-fourth of the field (*heraldry*). — *vt* to divide into four equal parts; to divide into parts or compartments; to station, lodge or impose in quarters; to bear, place or divide quarterly (*heraldry*); (of a dog) to beat or range as for game, search thoroughly. — *vi* to be stationed; to lodge; (of a dog) to range for game; (of the wind) to blow on to a ship's quarter. — **quar'ter-** used in combination: (*adjectivally*) to denote one-fourth part (of); (*adverbially*) to denote to the extent of one-fourth. — *n* **quar'terage** a quarterly payment; quarters, lodging. — *adj* **quar'tered.** — *adj* **quar'tering** sailing nearly before the wind; (of a wind) striking on the quarter of a ship. — *n* assignment of quarters; series of small upright posts for forming partitions, lathed and plastered only, or boarded also (*archit*); the division of a coat by horizontal and vertical lines (*heraldry*); one of the divisions so formed; the marshalling of coats in these divisions, indicating family alliances; any one of the coats so marshalled. — *adj* **quar'terly** relating to a quarter, esp. of a year; recurring, or published, once a quarter; divided into or marshalled in quarters (*heraldry*). — *adv* once a quarter; in quarters or quarterings (*heraldry*). — *n* a quarterly periodical. — **quart'erback** (*Am football*) a player between the forwards and the half-backs, who directs the attacking play of his team. — *adj* **quar'ter-bound** having leather or cloth on the back only, not the corners. — **quar'ter-day** the first or last day of a quarter, on which rent or interest is paid; **quar'terdeck** the part of the deck of a ship abaft the mainmast — used by cabin passengers and by superior officers (and saluted on warships); **quarter-fi'nal** the round before the semi-final in a knockout competition; **quarter hour** or **quarter of an hour** a period of fifteen minutes. — *adv* **quarter-hour'ly.** — **quarter light** a small window in a car, beside the front seat, for ventilation; **quar'termaster** an officer who finds quarters for soldiers, and attends to supplies; a petty officer who attends to the helm, signals, etc. (*naut*): — *fem* **quar'termistress** (or **quartermaster**); **quartermaster-gen'eral** a staff-officer who deals with questions of transport, marches, quarters, fuel, clothing, etc.; **quarter-master-ser'geant** a non-commissioned officer who assists the quartermaster; **quarter-mil'er** an athlete whose speciality is the quarter-mile race; **quar'ter-note** a crotchet (*US*); a quarter-tone; **quarter section** (*US*) an area of land half a mile square, 160 acres; **quar'ter-sessions** a court formerly held quarterly by justices of the peace (superseded in 1972 by crown courts); **quar'terstaff** a long wooden pole, an old weapon of defence; **quar'ter-tone** half a semitone. — **(a) quarter after** or **past** (a specified hour) fifteen minutes after that hour; **(a) quarter to** fifteen minutes before the hour; **at close quarters** in very near proximity; hand-to-hand. [O.Fr. — L. *quārtārius*, a fourth part — *quārtus*, fourth.]

quartern *kwör'tən* or *-tərn, n* an old measure — a quarter, esp. of a peck, a stone, a pound (weight), a pint, or a hundred. — **quar'tern-loaf** a four-pound loaf. [A.Fr. *quartrun*, O.Fr. *quarteron* — *quart(e)*, fourth part.]

quartet *kwör-tet', n* a set of four; a composition for four voices or instruments; a set of performers or instruments for such compositions. [It. *quartetto*, dimin. of *quarto* — L. *quārtus*, fourth.]

quartic *kwör'tik, (math) adj* of the fourth degree. — *n* a function, curve or surface of the fourth degree. [L. *quārtus*, fourth.]

quartile *kwör'tīl, n* an aspect of planets when their longitudes differ by 90° (*astrol*); in frequency-distribution, a value such that a fourth, a half, or three-quarters of the numbers under consideration fall below it. — Also *adj*. [L. *quārtus*, fourth.]

quarto *kwör'tō, (printing) adj* having the sheet folded into four leaves or eight pages (often written **4to**). — *n* a book of sheets so folded, or of such a size: — *pl* **quar'tos.** [L. (*in*) *quārtō*, (in) one-fourth.]

quartz *kwörts, n* the commonest rock-forming mineral, composed of silica, occurring in hexagonal crystals (clear and colourless when pure) or of microscopically crystalline structure. — *adj* of quartz. — *adj* **quartzif'erous** quartz-bearing. — *n* **quartz'ite** a metamorphosed sandstone with the grains welded together. — *adj* **quartzitic** (*-it'ik*). — *adj* **quartz'y.** — **quartz crystal** a disc or rod cut in certain directions from a piece of piezoelectric quartz and ground so that it vibrates naturally at a particular frequency; **quartz glass** fused quartz resistant to high temperatures and transparent to ultraviolet radiation; **quartz-crystal clock** or **watch** one in which a quartz crystal, energised by a microcircuit, does the work of the pendulum or hairspring of the traditional clock or watch; **quartz-iodine lamp** (using iodine) a compact source of light used for high-intensity flooding of large areas, car (fog-)lamps, cine-projectors, etc. — Also **quartz-hal'ogen lamp** (using halogen). [Ger. *Quarz* — M.H.G. *quarz* — W.Slav. *kwardy*, hard.]

quasar *kwā'sär, -zär* or *-sər, n* a point (star-like) source of radiation (radio waves, etc.) outside our galaxy, usu. with a very large red shift; quasars are the most distant and most luminous bodies so far known. [*quasi*-stell*ar* object.]

quash *kwosh, vt* to crush; to subdue or extinguish suddenly and completely; to annul. [O.Fr. *quasser* — L. *quassāre*, intensive of *quatĕre*, to shake.]

quasi *kwā'sī* or *kwä'zē, adv* as if, as it were. — *combining form* **quasi-** denoting: in a certain manner, sense or degree; in appearance only, as in **quasi-historical** and **quasi-stellar.** [L.]

quassia *kwosh'yə* or *kwosh'ə, n* a South American tree (*Quassia amara*), whose bitter wood and bark are used as a tonic; now generally a West Indian tree of the same family (*Picraena excelsa*). [Named by Linnaeus from a Negro *Quassi*, who discovered its value against fever.]

quatercentenary *kwat-ər-sen-tēn'ər-i, n* a 400th anniversary, or its celebration. [L. *quater*, four times.]

quaternary *kwo-tûr'nər-i, adj* consisting of four; by fours; in fours; of the fourth order; based on four; with four variables; (with *cap*; *geol*) Post-Tertiary. — *n* the number four; a set of four; (with *cap*; *geol*) the Post-Tertiary era or group of strata (Pleistocene and Recent). — *n* **quater'nion** a set or group of four; the operation of changing one vector into another, or the quotient of two vectors, depending on four geometrical elements and expressible by an algebraical quadrinomial (*math*). — *n* **quatern'ity** fourfoldness; a set of four. [L. *quaternī*, four by four.]

quatorze *kə-törz', n* (in piquet) the four aces, kings, queens, knaves or tens, counting 14. [Fr. *quatorze*, *quatorzaine*.]

quatrain *kwot'rān*, (*poetry*) *n* a stanza of four lines usu. rhyming alternately. [Fr.]

quatrefoil *kat'ər-foil* or *kat'rə-foil, n* a four-petalled flower or leaf of four leaflets; an openwork design or ornament divided by cusps into four lobes (*archit*). [O.Fr. *quatre*, four, *foil*, leaf.]

quattrocento *kwät-rō-chen'tō, n* the 15th century in reference to Italian art and literature. — *n* **quattrocent'ism**. — *n* **quattrocen'tist**. [It., four (for fourteen) hundred.]

quaver *kwā'vər, vi* to tremble, quiver; to speak or sing with tremulous uncertainty; to trill. — *vt* to speak or sing tremulously. — *n* a trembling, esp. of the voice; half a crotchet (*mus*). — *n* **quā'verer**. — *n* and *adj* **quā'vering**. — *adv* **quā'veringly**. — *adj* **quā'very**. [Frequentative from obs. or dialect *quave*, M.E. *cwavien*, to shake.]

quay *kē, n* a landing-place; a wharf for the loading or unloading of vessels. — *n* **quay'age** provision of quays; space for, or system of, quays; payment for use of a quay. — *n* and *adj* **quay'side**. [O.Fr. *kay*, *cay*, perh. Celt.; partly assimilated to mod. Fr. spelling *quai*.]

Que. *abbrev* for Quebec (also **Q**).

queasy or **queazy** *kwē'zi, adj* uneasy; causing nausea; squeamish; inclined to vomit. — *adv* **quea'sily**. — *n* **quea'siness**. [Poss. O.Fr. *coisier*, to hurt, or O.N. *kveisa*, a boil.]

Quebecker or **Quebecer** *kwi-bek'ər, n* an inhabitant of *Quebec*, in Canada. — *n* **Québecois** (*kā-bek-wa*; Fr.) an inhabitant of Quebec, esp. a French-speaking one. — Also *adj*.

quebracho *kā-brä'chō, n* the name of several S. American trees yielding very hard wood; their wood or bark: — *pl* **quebra'chos**. [Sp., — *quebrar*, to break, *hacha*, axe.]

Quechua *kech'wə, n* a Peruvian Indian of the race that was dominant in the Inca empire; the language of the Quechua. — Also *adj*. — *adj* and *n* **Quech'uan**. [Sp. *Quechua*, *Quichua*.]

queen *kwēn, n* a female monarch; the consort or wife of a king; a presiding goddess; a woman or (*fig*) anything that is pre-eminent in excellence, beauty, etc.; a sexually functional female social insect; a female cat; a male homosexual, esp. if adopting female role (*slang*); a playing-card bearing the figure of a queen, in value next below a king; (in chess) a piece that can be moved any distance in any straight line. — *vt* to make a queen of; to substitute a queen for; to play the queen (with *it* or *it up*). — *adj* **queen'like**. — *n* **queen'liness**. — *adj* **queen'ly** becoming or suitable to a queen; like a queen. — *n* **queen'ship**. — **Queen Anne** (*archit*) the simplified Renaissance style of the early 18th cent., or an imitation of it, plain and simple, with classical cornices and details; **queen bee** a fertile female bee; a woman who dominates, or is centre of attention amidst, her associates; a woman in an important business position; **queen cake** a small, soft, sweet cake with currants; **queen-con'sort** the wife of a reigning king; **queen-dow'ager** a king's widow; **queen'fish** a Californian blue and silver fish, *Seriphus politus* (also known as *drum-fish*); a tropical food and game fish of the *Carangidae*; **queen mother** a queen-dowager who is mother of the reigning king or queen; **queen'-post** one of two upright posts in a trussed roof, resting upon the tie-beam, and supporting the principal rafter; **queen-rē'gent** a queen who reigns as regent; **queen-reg'nant** a queen reigning as monarch; **Queen's Bench** (or **King's Bench** in a king's reign) a division of the High Court of Justice; **Queen's Counsel** (or **King's Counsel**) an honorary rank of barristers and advocates; a barrister or advocate of this rank; **Queen's English** see **King's English**; **queen's evidence** (or **king's evidence**) evidence given for the Crown by a criminal against his or her accomplices (**turn queen's evidence** to give such evidence); **Queen's Guide** the rank awarded to a (Girl) Guide upon reaching the highest level of proficiency and in recognition of service to the community; a Guide of this rank. — *adj* **queen'-size** larger than standard size, but smaller than the largest sizes, used of furnishings, etc. — **Queen's Regulations** (or **King's Regulations**) the regulations governing the British Armed Forces; **Queen's Scout** (or **King's Scout**) a Scout who has reached the highest level of proficiency, etc.; **queen's speech** (or **king's speech**) the sovereign's address to parliament at its opening and closing; **queen's ware** cream-coloured Wedgwood ware. — **queen bee substance** a substance secreted by a queen bee which attracts drones and affects workers; **queen of puddings** a pudding made with egg, breadcrumbs, fruit or jam, etc., topped with meringue. [O.E. *cwēn*; Goth. *qēns*; O.N. *kvæn*, *kvān*; Gr. *gynē*.]

Queensberry Rules *kwēnz'bər-i rōōlz, npl* rules applied to boxing, originally drawn up in 1867 and named after the Marquess of *Queensberry*, who took a keen interest in sport; (*loosely*) standards of proper behaviour in any fight, physical or verbal.

Queenslander *kwēns'lən-dər, n* a person born in and/or permanently resident in the N.E. Australian state of *Queensland*.

Queensland nut *kwēnzlənd nut, n* the macadamia nut. [Orig. found in *Queensland* and New South Wales.]

queer *kwēr, adj* odd, singular, quaint; open to suspicion; slightly mad; vaguely unwell, faint or giddy; homosexual (*slang*). — *vt* (*slang*) to spoil. — *n* (*slang*) a male homosexual. — *adj* **queer'ish**. — *adv* **queer'ly**. — *n* **queer'ness**. — **Queer Street** debt or other difficulties; (*specif*) the imaginary place where debtors, etc. live. — **queer someone's pitch** to spoil someone's chances. [Perh. Ger. *quer*, across, cf. **thwart**.]

quell *kwel, vt* to extinguish; to crush; to subdue. — *n* **quell'er**. [O.E. *cwellan*, to kill.]

quena *kā'nə, n* a type of bamboo flute from the Andes, held vertically for playing. [Am. Sp. — Quechua.]

quench *kwentsh* or *kwensh, vt* to put out; to put out the flame, light, or sight of, or the desire for; to stop (a discharge of electrically charged particles); to cool with liquid; to slake; to damp down; to put an end to. — *n* quenching. — *adj* **quench'able**. — *n* **quench'er** a person who, or a thing which, quenches. — *n* and *adj* **quench'ing**. — *adj* **quench'less** not to be extinguished. — *adv* **quench'lessly**. [O.E. *cwencan*, found only in the compound *ācwencan*, to quench.]

quenelle *kə-nel', n* a poached forcemeat dumpling of chicken, veal or fish. [Fr.]

querist. See **query**.

quern *kwûrn*, *n* a stone mill turned by hand. — **quern'stone**. [O.E. *cweorn*.]

querulous *kwer'ū-ləs*, *adj* complaining; peevish. — *adv* **quer'ulously**. — *n* **quer'ulousness**. [L.L. *querulōsus* — *querī*, to complain.]

query *kwē'ri*, *n* an inquiry; a doubt; an interrogation mark (?). — *vt* to inquire into; to question; to doubt; to mark with a query. — *vi* to question: — *pa t* and *pa p* **que'ried**. — *n* **que'rist** an inquirer. — *n* and *adj* **que'rying**. — *adv* **que'ryingly**. [L. *quaere*, imper. of *quaerěre*, *quaesītum*, to inquire.]

quest *kwest*, *n* the act of seeking; search; an undertaking in to order to achieve or find some definite object; the object sought for. — *vi* to go in search; (of dogs) to search for game. — *vt* to go in quest of or after. — *n* **quest'er**. — *n* and *adj* **quest'ing**. — *adv* **quest'ingly**. [O.Fr. *queste* — L. (*rēs*) *quaesīta*, (a thing) sought.]

question *kwes'chən*, *n* an inquiry; an interrogation; a demand for an answer; an interrogative sentence or other form of words in which it is put; a unit task in an examination; the putting of a problem; a problem; a subject of doubt or controversy; a subject of discussion, esp. the particular point actually before the house, meeting or company; objection; doubt; the measure to be voted upon; (vaguely) a relevant matter; subjection to examination; examination by torture (*hist*). — *vt* to put questions to; to call to account; to examine by questions; to inquire; to inquire concerning; to throw doubt upon; to challenge, take exception to. — *vi* to ask questions; to inquire. — *adj* **quest'ionable** that may be questioned; doubtful; open to suspicion. — *n* **questionabil'ity**. — *n* **quest'ionableness**. — *adv* **quest'ionably**. — *n* **quest'ioner**. — *n* and *adj* **quest'ioning**. — *adv* **quest'ioningly**. — *adj* **quest'ionless** unquestioning; beyond question or doubt. — *adv* certainly. — **ques'tion-begging** begging the question (see **beg**[2]). — Also *adj*. — **ques'tion-mark** a point of interrogation (?); a query or unresolved doubt (*fig*); **ques'tion-master** someone who presides over a quiz, discussion programme or meeting, and puts the questions to the participants; **question time** (in parliament) a period during each day when members can put questions to ministers. — **in question** under consideration; in dispute, open to question; **out of the question** not to be thought of; **question of fact** (*Eng law*) that part of the issue which is decided by the jury; **question of law** that part decided by the judge. [O.Fr., — L. *quaestiō*, *-ōnis* — *quaerěre*, *quaesītum*, to ask.]

questionnaire *kwes-chə-nār'* or *kest-yə-nār'*, *n* a prepared set of written questions, for purposes of compilation or comparison of the information gathered; a series of questions. [Fr. — *questionner*, to question, *-aire*, -ary.]

quetzal *ket-säl'* or *kwet'səl*, *n* a golden green Central American bird with long tail-feathers; the Guatemalan currency unit, or dollar (100 centavos). [Aztec *quetzalli*.]

queue *kū*, *n* a line of people, etc. awaiting their turn for service or attention; a set of data processing tasks waiting to be processed in order (*comput*); a braid of hair hanging down at the back of the head, a pigtail. — *vi* to form, or take one's place in, a queue. — *n* **queu'ing** or **queue'ing**. — *vi* and *vt* **queue'-jump**. — **queue'-jumping** going straight to the head of a queue, waiting list, etc. instead of taking one's proper place in it (*lit* and *fig*). [Fr., — L. *cauda*, a tail.]

quia timet *kwē'ə tim'et*, (*law*) of or denoting an (action to obtain an) injunction to prevent a possible future harmful act. [L., because he/she fears.]

quibble *kwib'l*, *n* an evasive turning away from the point in question to something irrelevant, merely verbal, trivial or insignificant; a petty complaint or observation; a pun, play on words. — *vi* to raise petty or irrelevant objections; to argue over an unimportant detail; to pun or evade the issue by punning. — *n* **quibb'ler**. — *n* and *adj* **quibb'ling**. — *adv* **quibb'lingly**. [Perh. dimin. of obs. *quib*, quibble, which may be from L. *quibus* (dat. or abl. pl. of *quī*, who) a word frequent in legal use; or a variant of **quip**.]

quiche *kēsh*, *n* a flan of plain pastry filled with a cooked egg mixture usu. containing cheese, onion or other vegetable, and/or ham, etc. [Fr., — Ger. dialect *küche*, dimin. of *Kuche*, cake.]

quick *kwik*, *adj* swift; nimble; ready; sensitive; readily responsive; ready-witted; prompt in perception; hasty; living (*archaic*, *Bible*, *liturgical*, etc.). — *adv* without delay; rapidly; soon. — *n* the sensitive parts, esp. under the nails; the tenderest or deepest feelings; the living (*archaic*, *Bible*, *liturgical*, etc.). — *vt* **quick'en** to impart energy or liveliness to; to stimulate; to accelerate; to revive; to give life to. — *vi* to become alive or lively; to revive; to be stimulated; to reach the stage in pregnancy when the mother becomes conscious of the movement of the child; to move faster. — *n* **quick'ener**. — *n* and *adj* **quick'ening**. — *n* **quick'ie** (*colloq*) something that takes, or is to be done in, a short time; an alcoholic drink to be rapidly consumed; brief or hurried sexual intercourse. — Also *adj*. — *adv* **quick'ly**. — *n* **quick'ness**. — **quick assets** readily realisable assets. — *adj* **quick'-change** quick in making a change, esp. (of a performer) in appearance (**quick-change artist** such a performer; a person who changes rapidly or frequently in mood or opinion). — **quick'-fire** rapid and continuous gunfire. — *adj* following in rapid succession (as of questions, etc.); (also **quick'-firing**) designed to allow a quick succession of shots. — **quick'-firer**; **quick'-freeze** very rapid freezing of food so that its natural qualities are unimpaired. — Also *vt* and *vi*. — *adj* **quick'-frozen**. — **quick'lime** unslaked lime, calcium oxide; **quick march** (*mil*) a march at a fast pace. — *interj* the command to start such a march. — **quick'sand** a loose watery sand which swallows up anyone who walks on it, or boats, etc. placed on it; anything similarly treacherous. — *adj* **quick'-sandy**. — *adj* **quick'-selling**. — *adj* **quick'set** formed of living plants set into place. — *n* a living plant, slip or cutting, esp. of hawthorn, or a series of them, set to grow for a hedge; a quickset hedge. — *adj* **quick'-sighted** having quick sight or discernment. — **quick-sight'edness**; **quick'silver** mercury. — *vt* to overlay or to treat with quicksilver or amalgam. — *adj* **quick'silvered**. — **quick'silvering** the mercury on the back of a mirror. — *adj* **quick'-silverish** or **quick'silvery**. — **quick'step** a march step or tune in fast time; a fast foxtrot. — *vi* to dance a quickstep. — *adj* **quick-tem'pered** irascible, fiery. — **quick'thorn** hawthorn; **quick time** (*mil*) a rate of about 120 steps per minute in marching; **quick trick** (*bridge*) a card that should win a trick in the first or second round of the suit. — *adj* **quick-witt'ed** with the ability to think quickly and effectively. — **quick-witt'edness**. — **a quick one** a quick drink; a quickie; **quick on the draw** swift to draw a gun from its holster; prompt in response or action. [O.E. *cwic*; O.N. *kvikr*, living.]

quid[1] *kwid*, (*slang*) *n* a pound (1): — *pl* **quid**. — **quids in** (*slang*) in a very favourable or profitable situation.

quid[2] *kwid*, *n* something chewed or kept in the mouth, esp. a piece of tobacco. [**cud**.]

quiddity *kwid'i-ti*, *n* the essence of anything; any trifling nicety; a quibble. [Med. L. *quidditās*, *-tātis*.]

quid pro quo *kwid prō kwō*, (L.) something for something; something given or taken as equivalent to another, often as retaliation; the action or fact of giving or receiving in this way.

quiescent *kwē-es'ənt*, *adj* resting; (of a consonant) not sounded; inactive; still. — *n* **quiesc'ence** or **quiesc'ency** rest; inactivity; silence of a consonant. — *adv* **quiesc'ently.** [L. *quiēscĕre*, to rest.]

quiet *kwī'ət*, *adj* (*compar* **qui'eter**, *superl* **qui'etest**) at rest; calm; undisturbed; free from disturbing noise; without loudness, gaudiness, ostentation, formality or obtrusiveness of any kind; still; without bustle or restlessness; without much activity; peaceful; gentle; inoffensive. — *n* freedom from noise or disturbance; calm; stillness; rest; peace. — *vt* and *vi* to quieten. — *vt* and *vi* **quī'eten** to make or become quiet. — *n* and *adj* **quī'etening.** — *n* **quī'eter.** — *n* and *adj* **quī'eting.** — *n* **quī'etism** mental tranquillity; the doctrine that religious perfection on earth consists in passive and uninterrupted contemplation of the Deity. — *n* **quī'etist.** — *adj* **quīetist'ic.** — *adv* **quī'etly.** — *n* **quī'etness.** — *n* **quī'etude** quietness. — **on the quiet** (*colloq*) secretly, furtively; unobtrusively. [L. *quiētus*, quiet, calm.]

quietus *kwī-ē'təs* or *kwi-ā'tōōs*, *n* a release or discharge, e.g. from debts or duties; a finishing stroke; extinction, death; silencing. [L. *quiētus est*, he is quiet.]

quiff *kwif*, *n* a lock of hair oiled and brushed down on the forehead or turned up and back from it. [Poss. **coif.**]

quill *kwil*, *n* the hollow basal part of a feather; a large feather; a porcupine's spine; a goose or other feather used as a writing pen; a pen generally; something made from a quill feather, such as a toothpick, an angler's float or a plectrum; a weaver's bobbin (orig. made of reed or other material); a musical pipe made from a hollow stem; a roll of curled bark, as of cinnamon; a hollow non-rotating shaft (also **quill drive**; *eng*). — *vt* to goffer, crimp; to wind on a bobbin. — *adj* **quilled** provided with, or formed into quills; tubular. — *n* **quill'ing** a ribbon or strip gathered into flutings. — **quill drive** see **quill** above; **quill'-feather** a large stiff wing or tail feather; **quill-pen'** a quill used as a pen. — *adj* using or suggestive of old-fashioned, slow and protracted methods or style (in office or literary work). [Cf. L.G. *quiele*, Ger. *Kiel.*]

quilt *kwilt*, *n* a bed-cover of two thicknesses with padding sewn in compartments; any material or piece of material treated in such a way; a thick coverlet; a duvet, continental quilt. — *vt* to pad, cover or line with a quilt; to form into a quilt; to stitch in; to seam like a quilt. — *adj* **quilt'ed.** — *n* **quilt'er.** — *n* **quilt'ing** the act of making a quilt or quilted material; something which is quilted; a cloth for making quilts; a cloth with a pattern like a quilt. [O.Fr. *cuilte* — L. *culcita*, a cushion.]

quin *kwin*, *n* short for **quintuplet.**

quinacrine *kwin'ə-krēn*, (*pharm*) *n* another name for **mepacrine.** [*quinine* and *acridine.*]

quinary *kwī'nər-i*, *adj* fivefold; by or in fives; of the fifth order; based on five; with five variables. — *adj* **qui'nate** (*bot*) with five leaflets arising at one point. [L. *quīnī*, five by five.]

quince *kwins*, *n* a golden, round or pear-shaped, fragrant, acid fruit, used esp. for jellies, marmalade, etc.; the tree or shrub (genus *Cydonia*) that bears it; extended to the *Japanese quince* (see **japonica**). [Orig. pl. of *quine* — O.Fr. *coin* — L. *cotōneum* — Gr. *kydōnion* — *Kydōniā* (in Crete).]

quincentenary *kwin-sin-tēn'ər-i* or *-sin-ten'ər-i*, *n* and *adj* a five-hundredth anniversary or its celebration. [Irreg. formed — L. *quīnque*, five, and **centenary.**]

quincunx *kwin'kungks*, *n* an arrangement of five things at the corners and centre of a square (e.g. as seen on cards and dice) or of a great number of things (esp. trees) spaced in the same way. — *adv* **quincun'cially.** [L. *quīncunx* — *quīnque*, five, *uncia*, a twelfth part.]

quinella *kwi-nel'ə*, (orig. *US*, now esp. *Austr*) *n* a form of bet in which the punter has to select the two horses, (dogs, etc.) which will come in first and second but not give their order of placing. [Am. Sp. *quiniela.*]

quinine *kwin-ēn'* or *kwin'ēn*, or in U.S. *kwī'nīn*, *n* a colourless, inodorous, very bitter alkaloid obtained from cinchona bark, or one of its salts, used as an antipyretic and analgesic, formerly widely used to treat malaria. — *n* **quin'idine** (*-i-dēn*) a crystalline alkaloid drug, used to treat irregularities in the heart rhythm. [Sp. *quina*, cinchona bark — Quechua *kina*, bark.]

quinol *kwin'ol*, *n* a reducing agent and photographic developer, produced by reduction of quinone, hydroquinone. — *n* **quin'oline** (*-ō-lēn*) a pungent, colourless, oily liquid, used e.g. as a food preservative. — *n* **quin'olone** any of a group of antibiotics esp. effective against infections of the urinary and respiratory tracts resistant to conventional antibiotics. — *n* **quinone** (*kwin'ōn* or *kwin-ōn'*) a golden-yellow crystalline compound usu. prepared by oxidising aniline; a reddish or colourless isomer of this; a general name for a benzene derivative in which two oxygen atoms replace two hydrogen.

quinqu- *kwin-kw-* or **quinque-** *kwin-kwi-*, *combining form* signifying five. — *n* **quinquagenarian** (*kwin-kwə-ji-nā'ri-ən*) a person who is fifty years old, or between fifty and fifty-nine. — Also *adj.* — *n* **quinquennium** (*kwin-kwen'i-əm*) a period of five years: — *pl* **quinquenn'ia.** — *adj* **quinquenn'ial** occurring once in five years; lasting five years. — *n* a fifth anniversary or its celebration. — *adv* **quinquenn'ially.** — *n* **quinquereme** (*kwin'kwi-rēm*; L. *rēmus*, an oar) an ancient ship with five sets of oars. — *adj* **quinquevalent** (*kwin-kwev'ə-lənt* or *-kwi-vā'lənt*) having a valency of five. — *n* **quinquev'alence** (or *-vā'ləns*). [L. *quīnque*, five.]

Quinquagesima *kwin-kwə-jes'i-mə*, *n* (also **Quinquagesima Sunday**) the Sunday preceding Lent — app. as fifty days before Easter Sunday (both counted). — *adj* **quinquages'imal** of the number fifty; of fifty days. [L. *quīnquāgēsimus, -a, -um*, fiftieth.]

quinque-, quinquennium, etc. See **quinqu-.**

quinsy *kwin'zi*, *n* suppurative tonsillitis. — *adj* **quin'sied** suffering from quinsy. [L.L. *quinancia* — Gr. *kynanchē.*]

quint *kwint*, *n* an organ stop a fifth above the foundation stops; (*kint*) a sequence of five cards in piquet. [Fr. *quinte* — L. *quīntus, -a, -um*, fifth.]

quint- *kwint-*, *combining form* denoting fifth. [L. *quīntus*, fifth.]

quinta *kin'tə*, *n* in Spain or Portugal, a country house. [Sp. and Port.]

quintain *kwin'tin*, *n* a post for tilting at; the sport of tilting at such a post. [O.Fr. *quintaine*, perh. — L. *quintana*, the market place of a military camp.]

quintal *kwin'tl*, *n* 100 kilograms; (*formerly*) a hundredweight. [Fr. and Sp. *quintal* — Ar. *qintār* — L. *centum*, a hundred.]

quintan *kwin'tən*, *adj* (of a chill or fever) occurring every fourth day. [L. *quintānus*, of the fifth.]

quinte *kɛ̃t*, (*fencing*) *n* the fifth of eight parrying or attacking positions. [Fr.]

quintessence *kwin-tes'əns*, *n* the pure concentrated essence of anything; the most essential part, form or embodiment of anything; orig. a fifth entity (i.e. in addition to the four elements). — *adj* **quintessential** (*-ti-sen'shl*). [Fr., — L. *quīnta essentia*, fifth essence.]

quintet *kwin-tet'*, *n* a composition for five voices or instruments; a set of performers or instruments for such compositions; a group of five people or things. [It. *quintetto*, dimin. of *quinto* — L. *quīntus*, fifth.]

quintillion *kwin-til'yən*, *n* the fifth power of a million, represented by a unit and thirty ciphers; in the U.S., the sixth power of one thousand — a unit with eighteen ciphers. — *n* and *adj* **quintill'ionth.** [Modelled on **million.**]

quintuple *kwin'tū-pl* or *-tū'pl, adj* fivefold; having five parts, members or divisions. — *n* five times as much. — *vt* and *vi* to increase fivefold. — *n* **quin'tūplet** (also *-tū'plət*) a set of five things; a group of five notes played in the time of four; one of five (children or animals) born at one birth. [L. *quīntus*, fifth, on the model of **quadruple.**]

quintuplicate *kwin-tū'pli-kāt, adj* fivefold. — *n* one of five corresponding things; fivefoldness. — *vt* to make fivefold. — *n* **quintuplicā'tion.** [L. *quīntuplex, -icis* — *quīntus*, fifth, *plicāre*, to fold.]

quip *kwip, n* a short, clever remark; a gibe. — *vi* to make quips. — *adj* **quipp'ish.** — *n* **quip'ster** a person given to making clever remarks. [Perh. from obs. *quippy*, which may be — L. *quippe*, forsooth.]

quire *kwīr, (printing) n* the twentieth part of a ream, 24 sheets of paper (now often 25) of the same size and quality; *(formerly)* four sheets of paper or parchment folded together in eight leaves. — *vt* to fold in quires. [O.Fr. *quaier* (Fr. *cahier*), prob. from L.L. *quaternum*, a set of four sheets — L. *quattuor*, four.]

quirk *kwûrk, n* a trick or peculiarity of action, style or behaviour; a sudden turn, twist, jerk or flourish; an acute sharp-edged groove alongside a moulding (*archit*). — *n* **quirk'iness.** — *adj* **quirk'ish.** — *adj* **quirk'y.**

quirt *kwûrt, n* a braided hide riding-whip. — *vt* to strike with a quirt. [Mex.-Sp. *cuarta.*]

quisling *kwiz'ling, n* a person who aids the enemy; a native puppet prime minister set up by an occupying foreign power. [Vidkun *Quisling*, who played that part in Norway during German occupation (1940–45).]

quit *kwit, vt* to depart from; to cease to occupy; to clear off; (with *of*) to rid (oneself) of; to leave off, cease (esp. *US*); (with *of*) to behave, acquit (oneself) of; to discharge (e.g. a debt or charge). — *vi* to leave off, cease (esp. *US*); to depart: — *pr p* **quitt'ing**; *pa t* and *pa p* **quitt'ed** or **quit.** — *adj* **quit** set free; clear, rid; quits; released from obligation. — *adj* **quits** even; neither owing nor owed. — *n* **quitt'er** a shirker; a person who gives up easily. — **quit'-claim** (*law*) a deed of release. — *vt* to relinquish claim or title to. — **call it quits** or **cry quits** to declare oneself even with another, and so satisfied; **double or quits** see under **double.** [O.Fr. *quiter* — L.L. *quiētāre*, to pay.]

quitch *kwich, n* couch grass. — Also **quitch grass.** [O.E. *cwice*; cf. **couch grass.**]

quite *kwīt, adv* completely, wholly, entirely; enough fully to justify the use of the word or phrase qualified; somewhat, fairly; exactly, indeed, yes (*colloq*; often **quite so**). — **quite something** (*colloq*) something remarkable or excellent. [**quit.**]

quiver[1] *kwiv'ər, vi* to shake with slight and tremulous motion; to tremble; to shiver. — *vt* (of a bird) to cause (the wings) to move rapidly. — *n* **quiv'er** or **quiv'ering.** — *adv* **quiv'eringly.** — *adj* **quiv'erish.** — *adj* **quiv'ery.** [Perh. conn. with **quiver**[2].]

quiver[2] *kwiv'ər, n* a case for arrows. — *n* **quiv'erful.** [O.Fr. *cuivre*; prob. Gmc. in origin.]

qui vive *kē vēv*: **on the qui vive** on the alert; lively and ready for action. [From the French sentry's challenge, lit. (long) live who? (corresponding to 'who goes there?').]

quixotic *kwiks-ot'ik, adj* like Don *Quixote*, the knight in the romance by Cervantes (1547–1616), i.e. extravagantly romantic in ideals or chivalrous in action; (of ideals, actions) absurdly generous. — *adv* **quixot'ically.** — *n* **quix'otism.** — *n* **quix'otry.**

quiz *kwiz, n* a set of questions (designed for amusement or entertainment), such as a test on general knowledge or on a special subject; a TV or radio programme, or organised event, in which contestants are asked a prepared set of questions; an interrogation: — *pl* **quizz'es.** — *vt* to question, interrogate. — *vi* and *vt* to eye, examine (esp. with an air of mockery): — *pr p* **quizz'ing**; *pa t* and *pa p* **quizzed.** — *n* **quizz'er.** — *n* **quizz'ery.** — *adj* **quizz'ical** amusing, comical; mocking, questioning. — *n* **quizzical'ity.** — *adv* **quizz'ically.** — **quiz'-master** question-master; **quiz show** a TV or radio quiz.

quod[1] *kwod*, neut. of L. *quī*, which. — **quod erat demonstrandum** (*er'at dem-ən-stran'dəm* or *er-at'*; abbrev. **QED**) which was to be proved or demonstrated; **quod erat faciendum** (*fā-shē-en'dəm* or *fa-ki-en'do͝om*; abbrev. **QEF**) which was to be done; **quod** (in *pl* **quae** *kwē* or *kwī*) **vide** (*vī'dē* or *vē'de*; abbrev. **qv** and (*pl*) **qqv**) which see.

quod[2] *kwod, (slang) n* prison. — *vt* to imprison.

quodlibet *kwod'li-bet, n* a scholastic argument; a humorous medley of tunes. [L., what you please — *quod*, what, *libet*, it pleases.]

quoin *koin, n* a wedge, esp. for locking type in a forme (*printing*), or for raising a gun; a salient angle, esp. of a building; a cornerstone, esp. a dressed cornerstone; a keystone; a voussoir. — *vt* to wedge; to secure, or raise by wedging. [See **coin.**]

quoit *koit* or *kwoit, n* a heavy flat ring for throwing as near as possible to a hob or pin; (in *pl*, treated as *sing*) the game played with quoits. — *vi* to play at quoits. — *vt* to throw as a quoit. — *n* **quoit'er.**

quokka *kwok'ə, n* a small short-tailed wallaby found in W. Australia. [Aboriginal.]

quondam *kwon'dam, adj* former. [L., formerly.]

Quonset hut® *kwon'set hut, n* the U.S. equivalent of the Nissen hut.

Quorn® *kwörn, n* a vegetable protein composed of minute filaments, derived from a type of microscopic plant, used as a low-calorie, cholesterol-free meat substitute that absorbs flavours in cooking. [Coined by the marketing company.]

quorum *kwö'rəm, n* a minimum number of persons necessary for transaction of business in any body. — *adj* **quo'rate** having or being (at least) a quorum. [L. *quōrum*, of whom, from the wording of the commission, of whom we wish that you, so-and-so, be one (two, etc.).]

quot. *abbrev* for quotation.

quota *kwō'tə, n* a proportional share, a part assigned; a regulated quantity of goods allowed by a government to be manufactured, exported, imported, etc.; a prescribed number of immigrants allowed into a country per year, students allowed to enrol for a course, fish allowed to be caught, etc.: — *pl* **quo'tas.** — **quota sample** a proportional sample of people in a specific category of the population defined in terms of age, sex, social class, etc.; **quota sampling** the use of quota samples to obtain data, as for opinion polls and marketing purposes. [L. *quota* (*pars*), the howmanieth (part) — *quotus*, of what number — *quot*, how many.]

quote *kwōt, vt* to refer to; to cite as evidence, authority, illustration or example; to give the actual words of; to note, set down or mention, in writing or mentally; to give the current price of; to state the market price of (shares, etc.) on the Stock Exchange list; to enclose within quotation-marks. — *vi* to make quotations. — *interj* used to indicate that what follows immediately is a quotation. — *n* a quotation; a quotation-mark. — *adj* **quō'table** lending itself, herself or himself, to quotation; fit to quote. — *n* **quō'tableness** or **quōtabil'ity.** — *adv* **quō'tably.** — *n* **quōtā'tion** the act of quoting; something that is quoted; a short passage of music, written or played, extracted from a longer piece; an estimated price submitted to a prospective purchaser; the current price of shares, etc., on the Stock Exchange list; a quadrat for filling blanks in type (*printing*). — *n* **quō'ter.** — *adj* **quōte'worthy.** — **quōtā'tion-mark** one of the marks (in *printing*, **quotes**) used to note the beginning and end of a quotation (see also **inverted**

commas under **comma**); **quoted company** one whose shares are quoted on the Stock Exchange. [L.L. *quotāre*, to divide into chapters and verses — L. *quotus*, of what number — *quot*, how many.]

quotidian *kwot-id'i-ən, adj* daily; everyday, commonplace; of any activity of a living creature or a living part, that follows a regular recurrent pattern. — *n* a fever or chill that recurs daily. [L. *quotīdiānus* — *quotīdiē*, daily — *quot*, how many, *diēs*, day.]

quotient *kwō'shənt, (math) n* the number of times one quantity is contained in another; a ratio, usu. multiplied by 100, used in giving a numerical value to ability, etc. (see **intelligence quotient**). [L. *quotiēns, quotiēs*, how often — *quot*, how many (with *t* from false appearance of being a participle).]

quo vadis? *kwō vä'dis*, (L.) where are you going?, the words used by Peter to Christ (John xvi, 5: Vulgate version) and, in tradition, by Christ later appearing to Peter as he fled from Rome.

quo warranto *kwō wo-ran'tō, (law)* a writ calling upon a person to show by what warrant he or she holds (or claims) a franchise or office. [L. *quō warrantō*, by what warrant.]

Qurân, Quran or **Qur'an** *koo-rän', n.* Same as **Koran**. — *adj* **Quran'ic** or **Qur'anic**.

qv or **q.v.** *abbrev* for: *quantum vis* (L.), as much as you wish; *quod vide* (L.), which see (*pl* **qqv** or **qq.v.**).

qwerty *kwûr'ti, n* a standard arrangement of keys on a typewriter keyboard; a keyboard having its keys laid out as on a standard typewriter (also **qwerty keyboard**). — *adj* of or having such a keyboard. [From the letters at the top left-hand side of the keyboard.]

qy *abbrev* for query.

R

R or **r** *är*, *n* the eighteenth letter in the modern English alphabet. — **R months** the time when oysters are in season (from the spelling of the names of the months from September to April); **the three R's** reading, writing and arithmetic. [L. *er*.]

R or **R.** *abbrev* for: rand (S.Afr. currency); Réaumur's thermometric scale (also **Reáu**); *rex* (King) or *regina* (Queen); River; Röntgen unit. — **R18** *symbol* for (a certificate) designating a film for restricted distribution only, in venues (or from premises) to which no one under eighteen may be admitted.

R symbol for electric resistance.

® *symbol* for registered trademark.

r or **r.** *abbrev* for: radius; right.

RA *abbrev* for: Rear Admiral; Republic of Argentina (I.V.R.); Royal Academician; Royal Academy; Royal Artillery.

Ra (*chem*) *symbol* for radium.

RAAF *abbrev* for Royal Australian Air Force.

rabbet *rab'it*, *n* a groove cut to receive an edge, a rebate. — *vt* to groove; to join by a rabbet: — *pr p* **rabb'eting**; *pa t* and *pa p* **rabb'eted**. — **rabb'eting-machine**; **rabb'eting-plane**; **rabb'eting-saw**; **rabb'et-joint**. [Fr. *rabat* — *rabattre*, to beat back.]

rabbi (with *cap* when prefixed, as in *Chief Rabbi*) *rab'ī*, *n* a Jewish expounder or doctor of the law; the leader of a Jewish congregation: — *pl* **rabb'is**. — *n* **rabb'inate** the post or tenure of office of a rabbi; a body or gathering of rabbis. — *adj* **rabbin'ic** or **rabbin'ical** pertaining to the rabbis or to their opinions, learning and language. — *n* **Rabbin'ic** the late Hebrew language. — *adv* **rabbin'ically**. [Heb. *rabbi*, my great one — *rabh*, great, master.]

rabbit *rab'it*, *n* a small burrowing animal of any of several genera of the family *Leporidae*, related to the hare; its flesh (as food); its fur, esp. as used in clothing; a persistent but incurably inferior player at lawn tennis or other game; a timid person. — *vi* to hunt rabbits; to talk at length and in a rambling fashion (*derog slang*; often with *on*; orig. rhyming slang *rabbit and pork*, talk). — *n* **rabb'iter**. — *n* **rabb'itry** a place where rabbits are kept. — *adj* **rabb'ity**. — **rabb'it-punch** a blow on the back of the neck; **rabb'it-warren** see under **warren**. — **Welsh rabbit** see **rarebit** at **rare**[1]. [M.E. *rabet*.]

rabble[1] *rab'l*, *n* a disorderly gathering or crowd; a mob; (with **the**) the lowest class of people. — *vi* **rabb'le-rouse**. — **rabb'le-rouser** a person who stirs up the common people to discontent and violence, esp. by inflammatory speeches; **rabb'le-rousing**. [Cf. Du. *rabbelen*, to gabble, L.G. *rabbeln*.]

rabble[2] *rab'l*, *n* a device for stirring molten iron, etc. in a furnace. [Fr. *râble* — L. *rutābulum*, a poker.]

Rabelaisian *rab-ə-lā'zi-ən*, *n* a follower, admirer or student of François *Rabelais* (d. 1553 or 1554). — *adj* of or like Rabelais; robustly satirical; (*loosely*) coarsely indecent. — *n* **Rabelais'ianism**.

rabi *rub'ē*, *n* the spring grain harvest in India, Pakistan, etc. [Ar. *rabī'*, spring.]

rabid *rab'id*, *adj* raging; fanatical (*fig*); affected with rabies. — *adv* **rab'idly**. — *n* **rabid'ity** or **rab'idness**. — *n* **rabies** (*rā'biz* or *-bi-ēz*) the disease called hydrophobia, (fear of water being a symptom) caused by a virus transmitted by the bite of an infected animal. [L. *rabidus* (adj.), *rabiēs* (noun) — *rabĕre*, to rave.]

RAC *abbrev* for: Royal Armoured Corps; Royal Automobile Club.

raccoon or **racoon** *rə-kōōn'*, *n* a smallish American animal with black-striped tail and face, related to the bears; its fur. [From an Am. Ind. name.]

race[1] *rās*, *n* the descendants of a common ancestor, esp. those who inherit a common set of characteristics; such a set of descendants, narrower than a species; a breed; ancestry, lineage, stock; a class or group, defined otherwise than by descent. — *adj* **racial** (*rā'shl*) of or relating to race. — *n* **ra'cialism** hatred, rivalry or bad feeling between races; belief in the inherent superiority of some races over others, usu. with the implication of a right to be dominant; discriminatory treatment based on such belief. — *n* and *adj* **ra'cialist**. — *adv* **ra'cially**. — *n* **rac'ism** racialism. — *n* **rac'ist**. — **race-ha'tred** animosity accompanying difference of race; **race relations** social relations between members of different races living in the same country or community; **race riot** a riot caused by perceived discrimination on the grounds of race; **race-su'icide** voluntary cessation of reproduction, leading to the extinction of the race. [Fr., — It. *razza*.]

race[2] *rās*, *n* a fixed course, track or path over which anything runs; a channel bringing water to or from a millwheel; a groove in which anything runs (such as ball-bearings or a rope); a regular traverse of a fixed course, as of the sun; a rapid flow or current of the tides; a competitive trial of speed, as by running, driving, sailing, etc.; (in *pl*) a meeting for horse-racing; a competition in getting ahead of others figuratively. — *vi* to run, go, drive, sail, etc. swiftly; to contend in speed with others; to run wildly fast (as an engine or a propeller) when resistance is removed. — *vt* to cause (a car, horse, etc.) to race; to rush (an action); to contend in speed with. — *n* **ra'cer** a person, animal or thing that races or is raced; any of several non-venomous N. American snakes of the genus *Coluber*. — *n* **ra'cing**. — **race'-card** a programme for a race-meeting; **race'-course** or **race'-track** a course for running races over; **race'goer** an attender at race-meetings; **race'-going**; **race'horse** a horse bred for racing; **race meeting** an organised occasion for horse-racing; **race'way** a millrace; a track for running (usu. motorised) races over. [O.N. *rās*; O.E. *rǣs*.]

raceme *ra-*, *rə-* or *rā-sēm'*, (*bot*) *n* an indefinite formation in which stalked flowers are borne on an unbranched main stalk; a similar group of spore-cases. — *n* **racemate** (*ras'i-māt*) a racemic mixture. — *n* **racemation** (*ras-i-mā'shən*) a residue; a cluster or bunch of grapes or of anything else. — *adj* **racemed'** (or *ras'* or *rās'*) consisting of, or having, racemes. — *adj* **racemic** (*rə-sē'mik* or *-sem'ik*) applied to an acid obtained from a certain kind of grape, an optically inactive form of tartaric acid. — *n* **racemisā'tion** or **-z-** a change into a racemic form. — *vt* and *vi* **rac'emise** or **-ize**. — *n* **rac'emism** the quality of being racemic. — *adj* **racemose** (*ras'i-mōs*) of the nature of, or like, a raceme or racemes;

having racemes; like a bunch of grapes. [L. *racēmus*, a bunch of grapes.]

rachis *rā'kis*, *n* the spine; an axis, as of a feather, an inflorescence, a feather-shaped leaf: — *npl* **ra'chises** or **rachides** (*rak'* or *rāk'i-dēz*). — *n* **rachischisis** (*ra-kis'ki-sis*; Gr. *schisis*, cleavage) a severe form of spina bifida. [Gr. *rhachis*, spine.]

rachitis *ra-* or *rə-kī'tis*, (*med*) *n* rickets. — *adj* **rachitic** (*-kit'ik*). [Gr. *rhachītis*, inflammation of the spine.]

Rachmanism *rak'man-izm*, *n* conduct of a landlord who charges extortionate rents for property in slum condition. — *adj* **Rach'manite.** [From the name of one such landlord exposed in 1963.]

racial, etc., **racism**, etc. See **race[1]**.

rack[1] *rak*, *n* a framework, grating, shelf, etc. on or in which articles are laid or set aside; a grating from which farm animals may pull down fodder; a bar with teeth to work into those of a wheel, pinion, cog, etc.; an instrument for stretching, esp. an instrument of torture; an extreme pain, anxiety or doubt. — *vt* to stretch, move forcibly or excessively; to torture; to put in a rack; to move or adjust by rack and pinion. — *adj* **racked** (also, *erroneously*, **wracked**) tortured, tormented; (in combination) denoting tortured, distressed by, as in *disease-racked*, etc. — *n* **rack'er.** — *n* and *adj* **rack'ing.** — **rack'-rail** a cogged rail, as on a rack-and-pinion railway; **rack-rail'way** a mountain railway with a rack in which a cog-wheel on the locomotive works; **rack'-rent** a rent stretched to the utmost annual value of the house, etc. rented, an exorbitant rent; a rack-renter. — *vt* to subject to such rents. — **rack'-renter.** — **rack and pinion** a means of turning rotatory into linear or linear into rotatory motion by a toothed wheel engaging in a rack; **rack one's brains** to use one's memory or reasoning powers to the utmost.

rack[2] *rak*, *n* same as **wrack**, destruction. — **rack and ruin** a state of neglect, collapse or poverty. [**wrack[1]**, or O.N. *rek*, wreckage.]

rack[3] *rak*, *vt* to draw off (wine) from its sediment. [Prov. *arracar* — *raca*, husks, dregs.]

rack[4] *rak*, *n* the neck and spine of a forequarter of a carcass, esp. as a cut of meat.

rack[5] *rak*, (esp. *US*) *n* a horse's gait in which the legs at the same side move nearly together. — *vi* to walk with such a gait. — *n* **rack'er.**

racket[1] *rak'it*, *n* a bat with usu. roughly elliptical head, of wood or metal strung with catgut or nylon, for playing tennis, badminton, etc.; a snow-shoe of similar design. — *nsing* **rack'ets** a simplified derivative of the old game of tennis, similar to squash, played by two or four people in a four-walled court. — **rack'et-press** a press for keeping a racket in shape; **rack'et-tail** a humming-bird with two long racket-shaped feathers. — *adj* **rack'et-tailed.** [Fr. *raquette.*]

racket[2] *rak'it*, *n* din, hubbub, noise (*colloq*); noisy gaiety; fraudulent, violent, or otherwise unscrupulous money-making activities. — *vi* to go about making a great, unnecessary noise. — *n* **racketeer'** a person who extorts money or other advantage by threats or illegal interference. — *vi* to perform the actions of a racketeer. — *n* **racketeer'ing.** — *n* **rack'eter.** — *adj* **rack'ety** noisy. — **stand the racket** to endure the strain, noise; to pay expenses or (*fig*) penalties of a deed.

raclette *rak-let'*, *n* a dish of melted cheese and jacket potatoes, orig. from the Valais region of Switzerland. [Fr., a small scraper.]

racon *rā'kon*, *n* a radar beacon. [*ra*dar and bea*con*.]

raconteur *ra-kon-tûr'* or *ra-kɔ̃-tœr*, *n* a teller of anecdotes: — *fem* **raconteuse** (*-tœz*). — *n* **raconteur'ing.** [Fr.]

racoon. See **raccoon.**

racquet *rak'it*, *n*. Same as **racket[1]**. — **racq'uetball** (*US*) a game played by or two or four players in a walled court with rubber balls and short-handled strung rackets.

racy *rās'i*, *adj* (of wine) having a distinctive flavour imparted by the soil; spirited, esp. of writing, lifestyle, etc.; slightly risqué. — *n* **ra'ciness.** [**race[1]**.]

rad[1] *rad*, *n* (sometimes with *cap*) short for **radical** (in politics). — *adj* (*slang*, esp. and orig. *US*) excellent, radically and admirably up to date (short for **radical**).

rad[2] *rad*, *n* a unit of dosage of any radiation, equal to 100 ergs of energy for one gram of mass of the material irradiated. [**rad(iation)**.]

rad[3] *rad*, *n* short for radian.

rad. *abbrev* for *radix* (L.), root.

RADA *rä'də*, *abbrev* for Royal Academy of Dramatic Art.

radar *rā'där*, *n* the use of high-powered radio pulses for locating objects or determining one's own position; equipment for sending out and receiving such pulses. — **radar beacon** a fixed radio transmitter whose signals enable an aircraft, by means of its radar equipment, to determine its position and direction; **radar gun** a gun-like device used by police which, when pointed at a moving vehicle and 'fired', records (by means of radar) the speed of the vehicle; **ra'darscope** a cathode-ray oscilloscope on which radar signals can be seen; **radar trap** a device using radar which enables the police to identify motorists exceeding the speed limit over a particular section of road (see also **speed trap**). [Acronym from *ra*dio *d*etection *a*nd *r*anging.]

RADC *abbrev* for Royal Army Dental Corps.

raddle *rad'l*, *n* ruddle or reddle (red ochre). — *vt* to colour or mark with red ochre; to rouge coarsely. — *adj* **radd'led** (of a person) aged and deteriorated by debauchery. [**ruddle.**]

radial *rā'di-əl*, *adj* pertaining to a ray or radius; along, or in the direction of, a radius or radii; having rays, spokes, or parts diverging from a centre; arranged like spokes or radii; near the radius of the arm (*med*). — *n* a radiating part; a radial artery, nerve, engine, plate, tyre, etc. — *n* **radialisation** or **-z-** (*rād-yəl-ī-zā'shən*). — *vt* **ra'dialise** or **-ize** to arrange radially. — *n* **rādiality** (*-al'*) radial symmetry. — *adv* **rā'dially** in the manner of radii or of rays. — **radial engine** one with its cylinders radially arranged (as opp. to in line); **radial symmetry** symmetry about several planes intersecting in a common axis; **radial velocity** the speed of motion along the observer's line of sight, esp. to or from a star. — **radial-ply tyre** a tyre in which layers of fabric in the carcass are wrapped in a direction radial to the centre of the wheel. [L.L. *radiālis* — L. *radius.*]

radian *rā'di-ən*, (*geom*) *n* a constant unit of circular measure, nearly 57.3°, the angle between two lines which, when drawn from the centre of a circle, divide off on its circumference an arc equal to its radius. [L. *radius.*]

radiant *rā'di-ənt* or *rā'dyənt*, *adj* emitting rays; issuing in rays; transmitted by radiation; glowing or shining; beaming, lit up with happy emotion. — *n* that which emits radiations; a point from which rays emanate; the centre from which meteoric showers seem to emanate. — *n* **rā'diance** or **rā'diancy** the state of being radiant; a measure of the amount of electromagnetic radiation being transmitted from or to a point (on a surface). — *adv* **rā'diantly.** — **radiant energy** energy given out as electromagnetic radiation; **radiant heat** heat transmitted by electromagnetic radiation. [L. *radiāns, -antis*, pres. p. of *radiāre*, to radiate — *radius.*]

radiate *rā'di-āt*, *vi* to emit rays; to shine; to issue in rays; to diverge (from a point or points); to transmit without the use of cables, by radio. — *vt* to send out in or by means of rays; to communicate by radio, without wires. — *n* **rādiā'tion** the act of radiating;

the emission and diffusion of rays; that which is radiated; energy, esp. nuclear rays, transmitted in electromagnetic waves; radial arrangement. — *adj* **rā'diātive** or **rā'diatory**. — *n* **rā'diātor** that which radiates; an apparatus for radiating or diffusing heat, as for warming a room, or cooling an engine; a radio transmitting aerial. — **radiation oncologist** see **radiologist** under **radiology; radiation sickness** an illness due to excessive absorption of radiation in the body, marked by diarrhoea, vomiting, internal bleeding, decrease in blood cells, loss of teeth and hair, reduction of sperm in the male, etc. [L. *radiāre*, to shine, *radiātus*, rayed — *radius*.]

radical *rad'i-kl*, *adj* pertaining to, constituting, proceeding from or going to the root of anything; fundamental; favouring, involving or necessitating thoroughgoing but constitutional social and political reform; (with *cap*) of or pertaining to a political party holding such beliefs; thorough; proceeding from near the root (*bot*); of or concerning the root of a word (*linguis*); of or concerning the roots of numbers (*math*); see also under **rad**[1] (*slang*). — *n* a root, in any sense; an advocate of radical reform; a member of the Radical party; a group of atoms behaving like a single atom and passing unchanged from one compound to another (*chem*; sometimes **rad'icle**). — *n* **radicalīsā'tion** or **-z-**. — *vt* and *vi* **rad'icalise** or **-ize**. — *n* **Rad'icalism** the principles or beliefs of a Radical. — *adv* **rad'ically**. — *n* **rad'icalness**. — *n* **rad'icle** a little root; the part of a seed that becomes the root; a rhizoid, a short hairlike type of root in some plants; a radical (*chem*). — **free radical** see under **free**; **radical sign** the symbol $\surd$, indicating a square root. [L. *rādīx*, *-īcis*, a root.]

radicchio *rə-dē'ki-ō*, *n* a purple-leaved variety of chicory from Italy, used raw in salads. [It.]

radices. See **radix**.

radicle. See **radical**.

radii. See **radius**.

radio- *rā-di-ō-*, *combining form* (some of the following words may also be hyphenated) denoting: rays; radiation; radium; radius; radio, wireless; (of product or isotope) radioactive. — *n* **rā'dio** a generic term applied to methods of signalling through space, without connecting wires, by means of electromagnetic waves generated by high-frequency alternating currents; a wireless receiving, or receiving and transmitting, set; wireless broadcasting; the business of sound broadcasting: — *pl* **rā'dios**. — *adj* of, for, transmitted or transmitting by, electromagnetic waves. — *vt* and *vi* to communicate by transmitting a radio message. — *adj* **rādioact'ive**. — *n* **rādioactiv'ity** spontaneous disintegration, first observed in certain naturally occurring heavy elements (radium, actinium, uranium, thorium) with emission of α-rays, β-rays, and γ-rays; disintegration effected by high-energy bombardment. — **radio altimeter** see **altimeter**. — *n* **radio astronomy** astronomical study by means of radar; the study of radio waves generated in space. — *n* **radio beacon** an apparatus that transmits signals for direction-finding. — *n* **radiobiol'ogy** the study of the effects of radiation on living tissue. — *n* **radiocar'bon** a radioactive isotope of carbon, *specif* carbon-14, used in **radiocarbon dating**, a method of establishing the age of any organic material, e.g. wood, paper, by measuring content of carbon-14. — *n* **rādiochem'istry** the chemistry of radioactive elements and compounds. — *n* **radio-com'pass** a radio direction-finding instrument. — *n* **rādioel'ement** a radio-isotope. — *n* **radio frequency** a frequency in the range suitable for radio transmission, about 3 kHz to 300 GHz (**radio-frequency heating** heating, such as non-conducted heating, by means of a radio-frequency electric current). — *n* **radio galaxy** a galaxy emitting a particularly high level of radio-frequency energy. — *n* **rā'diogram** an X-ray photograph, radiograph; a telegram sent by radio; (for **rādio-gram'ophone**) a combined radio and record-player. — *n* **radio immunoass'ay** an assessment of the comparative effectiveness of a drug, etc. which has had one of its atoms replaced by a radioactive substance for identification purposes. — *n* **radio-ī'sotope** a radioactive isotope of a stable element. — *adj* **radiola'belled** having had an atom replaced by a radioactive substance, for ease of subsequent identification in tests. — *n* **radiolocā'tion** position-finding by radio signals; radar. — *n* **radioluminesc'ence** light arising from radiation from a radioactive material. — *n* **radio microphone** a microphone with a miniature radio transmitter, and therefore not requiring any cable. — *n* **rādionū'clide** any radioactive atom of an element identified by the number of neutrons and protons in its nucleus, and its energy state. — *n* **rā'diopager** a radio receiver which functions as a paging device. — *n* **rā'diopaging**. — *adj* **rādiophonic** (*-fon'ik*) of music, produced electronically; producing electronic music. — *npl* **rādiophon'ics**. — *n* **rādiophonist** (*-of'ə-nist*). — *adj* **rādiosen'sitive** readily injured or changed by radiation. — *n* **ra'diosonde** (Fr. *sonde*, plummet, probe) apparatus for ascertaining atmospheric conditions at great heights, consisting of a hydrogen-filled balloon, radio transmitter(s), etc. — *n* **rādiotel'egram**. — *n* **rādiotel'egraph**. — *n* **radioteleg'raphy**. — *n* **rādiotelem'eter** see **telemeter**. — *n* **rādiotel'ephone** a device which receives and transmits by means of radio waves (rather than wires) and which functions as a telephone (e.g. in cars and other vehicles). — *n* **radio telescope** an apparatus for the reception, analysis and transmission of radio waves from and to outer space. — *n* **rādiotel'etype** a teleprinter that receives and transmits by radio. — *n* **rādiotherapeut'ics** or **radiother'apy** treatment of disease, esp. cancer, by radiation. — *n* **radio wave** an electromagnetic wave of radio frequency. [L. *rădius*, a rod, spoke, radius, ray.]

radiography *rā-di-og'rə-fi*, *n* photography of the interior of a body or specimen by radiations other than light, such as X-rays, etc. — *n* **rā'diograph** (*-grāf*) a photograph produced by means of such radiations. — *n* **rādiog'rapher** a technician involved in radiology, in the taking of photographs or in radiotherapy. — *adj* **radiographic** (*-graf'ik*). [**radio-** and Gr. *graphein*, to write.]

Radiolaria *rā-di-ō-lā'ri-ə*, *npl* an order of marine Protozoa, or unicellular animals, with fine radial tentacles for feeding and movement. — *adj* and *n* **radiola'rian**. — **radiolarian ooze** a deep-sea deposit in which the silica skeletons of Radiolaria predominate. [L.L. *radiolus*, dimin. of L. *rădius*, radius.]

radiology *rā-di-ol'ə-ji*, *n* the study of radioactivity and radiation or their application to medicine, e.g. as X-rays, or as treatment for certain diseases. — *adj* **radiolog'ic** or **radiolog'ical**. — *n* **radiol'ogist** a doctor specialising in the diagnostic or therapeutic use of X-rays and in other methods of imaging the internal structure of the body, now often called a **radiation oncologist** or **radiation therapist**. [**radio-** and **-logy**.]

radish *rad'ish*, *n* a plant of the *Cruciferae*, the pungent root of which is eaten as a salad vegetable. [Fr. *radis* — Prov. *raditz* or It. *radice* — L. *rādīx*, *-īcis*, a root.]

radium *rā'di-əm*, *n* a radioactive metallic element (symbol **Ra**; atomic no. 88) discovered by the Curies in 1898, found in pitchblende and other minerals, remarkable for its active spontaneous disintegration. — **radium emanation** radon. [L. *rădius*, a ray.]

radius *rā'di-əs*, *n* a straight line from the centre to the circumference of a circle or surface of a sphere (*geom*); a radiating line; anything placed like a radius, such as the spoke of a wheel; the outer bone (in supine position) of the forearm in man, or its equivalent in other animals; a distance from a centre, conceived as limiting an area or range: — *pl* **radii** (*rā'di-ī*; L. *ra'di-ē*) or **ra'diuses**. — *adj* **ra'dial** (q.v.). — **radius vector** (*pl* **radii vectō'res** *-rēz*) a straight line joining a fixed point and a variable point. [L. *rădius*, a rod, spoke, ray.]

radix *rā'diks*, *n* a source, root, basis; the quantity on which a system of numeration, or of logarithms, etc. is based: — *pl* **radices** (*rā'di-sez*). [L. *rādīx*, *-īcis*, root.]

radome *rā'dōm*, *n* a protective covering for microwave radar antennae. [*ra*dar *dome*.]

radon *rā'don*, *n* a gaseous radioactive element (symbol **Rn**; atomic no. 86), the first disintegration product of radium — radium emanation. [**radium** and chem. sfx. *-on*, of an elementary particle.]

radula *rad'ū-lə*, *n* a mollusc's tongue or rasping ribbon: — *pl* **rad'ulae** (*-lē*). — *adj* **rad'ūlar**. [L. *rādula*, a scraper — *rādĕre*.]

RAEC *abbrev* for Royal Army Educational Corps.

RAeS *abbrev* for Royal Aeronautical Society.

RAF *är-ā-ef* or (*colloq*) *raf*, *abbrev* for Royal Air Force.

raffia *raf'i-ə*, *n* the ribbon-like fibre of the Raphia palm, used for weaving. [**Raphia**.]

raffish *raf'ish*, *adj* rakish, dashing; flashy. — *adv* **raff'ishly**. — *n* **raff'ishness**. [Cf. **riff-raff**.]

raffle *raf'l*, *n* a lottery for an article. — *vt* to dispose of by raffle. — *n* **raff'ler**. — **raffle-ticket** a ticket with a number printed on it, bought by raffle participants and drawn to determine the winner(s). [Fr. *rafle*, a pair-royal.]

raft *räft*, *n* a flat floating mass of logs or other material (ice, vegetation, etc.); a flat structure of logs, etc. for support or conveyance on water; a wide layer of concrete to support a building on soft ground. — *vt* to transport on a raft; to form into a raft; to cross, travel down, etc. by raft. — *vi* to travel by raft; to form into a raft. — *n* **raft'er**. — **rafts'man** a person who works on a raft. [O.N. *raptr*, rafter.]

rafter[1] *räf'tər*, *n* an inclined beam supporting a roof. — *vt* to provide with rafters. — *adj* **raf'tered** having (esp. visible) rafters. — *n* **raf'tering**. [O.E. *ræfter*, a beam.]

rafter[2], **raftsman**. See **raft**.

rag[1] *rag*, *n* a worn, torn or waste scrap of cloth; a shred, scrap or tiny portion; a flag, handkerchief, garment or newspaper (*jocular* or *derog*); (in *pl*) tattered clothing; a piece of ragtime music. — *adj* of, for or dealing in rags. — *vt* to perform in ragtime: — *pr p* **ragg'ing**; *pa p* and *pa t* **ragged** (*ragd*). — *adj* **ragg'ed** rough-edged; jagged; uneven in performance, ability, etc.; torn or worn into rags; wearing rags. — *adv* **ragg'edly**. — *n* **ragg'edness**. — *adj* **ragg'edy**. — **rag-and-bone'-man** a person who collects or deals in rags, bones, or other goods of little worth; **rag'-bag** a bag for rags and thrown-away garments; a random or confused collection (*fig*; *derog*); **rag'bolt** a bolt with barb-like projections to prevent withdrawal once locked in position; **rag'=book** a child's scrapbook mounted on cloth; **rag doll** a doll made of rags; **ragged-Rob'in** a campion with ragged-edged petals; **ragged school** (*hist*) a voluntary school for destitute children; **rag'=paper** paper made from rags; **rag'-rolling** a technique, used in house decoration, of rolling a folded cloth over a specially painted surface to produce a randomly shaded effect; **rag'tag** the rabble, the common herd. — Also *adj*. — **rag'time** a form of jazz music of American Negro origin, highly syncopated in the melody; **rag trade** the trade concerned with designing, making and selling clothes; **rag'weed** ragwort: **rag'worm** a pearly white burrowing marine worm used as bait by fishermen; **rag'wort** a common coarse yellow-headed composite weed of pastures. — **ragtag and bobtail** riff-raff. [O.E. *ragg*, inferred from the adj. *raggig*, shaggy; O.N. *rögg*, shagginess, tuft.]

rag[2] or **ragg** *rag*, *n* a rough hard stone of various kinds, esp. one naturally breaking into slabs; a large rough slate (3 ft. by 2). — **rag'stone; rag'work** undressed masonry in slabs.

rag[3] *rag*, *vt* to banter; to assail or beset with silly questions, ridicule or horseplay. — *vi* to wrangle, argue; to indulge in a rag: — *pr p* **ragg'ing**; *pa t* and *pa p* **ragged** (*ragd*). — *n* an outburst of organised horseplay, usu. in defiance of authority; riotous festivity, esp. and orig. of undergraduates — now, in British universities, associated with the raising of money for charity. — *n* **ragg'ing**. — *adj* **ragg'y** (*slang*) irritated. — **rag day** or **rag week** in British universities the particular day or week during which money-making activities, processions, etc. for charity are organised. — **lose one's rag** (*colloq*) to lose one's temper.

raga *rä'gə*, *n* a traditional Hindu musical form or mode, a rhythmic or melodic pattern used as the basis for improvisation; a piece composed in such a mode. [Sans. *rāga*, colour, tone (in music).]

ragamuffin *rag'ə-muf-in* or *-muf'*, *n* a ragged, disreputable child.

rage *rāj*, *n* madness; overpowering passion of any kind, such as desire or (esp.) anger; a fit of any of these; a mania or craze (for something), a vogue (*colloq*); something in vogue; violence, stormy or furious activity. — *vi* to behave or speak with passion, esp. with furious anger; to be violent; to storm; to scold (with *at*). — *n* **rā'ger**. — *adj* **rā'ging**. — *adv* **rā'gingly**. — **all the rage** very much in fashion. [Fr., — L. *rabiēs* — *rabĕre*, to rave.]

ragee. See **ragi**.

ragg. See **rag**[2].

ragged, raggedy. See **rag**[1].

ragi, ragee, raggee or **raggy** *rä'gē* or *rag'i*, *n* a millet much grown in India, Africa, etc. [Hind. (and Sans.) *rāgī*.]

raglan *rag'lən*, *n* an overcoat with the sleeve in one piece with the shoulder. — *adj* (of a sleeve) in one piece with the shoulder. [From Lord *Raglan* (1788–1855), commander in the Crimea.]

ragout *ra-goo'*, *n* a highly seasoned stew of meat and vegetables. — *vt* to make a ragout of. [Fr. *ragoût* — *ragoûter*, to restore the appetite.]

ragstone, ragwork. See under **rag**[2].

ragtag, ragtime, ragweed, ragworm, ragwort. See under **rag**[1].

raguly *rag'ū-li*, (*heraldry*) *adj* with projections like oblique stubs of branches. — Also **rag'ūled**.

rah or **'rah** *rä*, *interj*, *n* and *vi*. Short form of **hurrah**.

raid *rād*, *n* a sudden swift incursion, orig. by horsemen, for assault or seizure; an air attack; an invasion unauthorised by government; an incursion of police for the purpose of making arrests; an onset or onslaught for the purpose of obtaining or suppressing something; concerted selling by a group of speculators in order to lower the price of a particular stock. — *vt* to make a raid on. — *vi* to go on a raid. — *n* **raid'er**. — **raid the market** to upset prices of stocks artificially for future gain. [Scots form of **road** — O.E. *rād*, riding.]

rail[1] *rāl*, *n* a bar extending horizontally or at a slope between supports or on the ground, often to form a support, a fence, a guard, or a track for wheels; railways as a means of travel or transport; a horizontal member in framing or panelling (as in a door). — *vt* to enclose or separate with rails (often with *off*); to provide with rails. — *n* **rail'ing** fencing; fencing materials; (often in *pl*) a barrier or ornamental fence, usu. of upright iron rods secured by horizontal connections. — **rail'car** a railway carriage (*US*); a single motorised railway carriage; **rail'card** any of various cards entitling its holder (e.g. a student, old age pensioner, etc.) to reduced train fares; **rail'-head** the furthest point currently reached by a railway under construction; the end of a railway line, its terminus; **rail'man** a man employed on the railway; **rail'road** (chiefly *NAm*) a railway. — *vt* (*colloq*) to force, e.g. a person into a particular course of action, a bill through parliament, etc. (orig. *US*); to get rid of, esp. by sending to prison on a false charge. — **rail'way** a track laid with rails for wheels to run on, esp. for trains of passenger coaches and goods wagons; a system of such tracks together with their equipment and organisation; the company owning such a system. — Also *adj*. — **rail'way-carriage** a railway vehicle for passengers; **rail'way-crossing** an intersection of railway lines or of road and railway, esp. without a bridge; **rail'wayman** a railman. — **off the rails** disorganised; not functioning; mad. [O.Fr. *reille* — L. *rēgula*, a ruler.]

rail[2] *rāl*, *vi* to revile, express great anger or frustration (usu. with *at* or *against*). — *n* **rail'er**. — *adj* and *n* **rail'ing**. — *adv* **rail'ingly**. — *n* **raillery** (*rāl'ər-i*) the act of railing, or the language used; banter or mild satire. [Fr. *railler*.]

rail[3] *rāl*, *n* any bird of the wader genus *Rallus*, esp. the water-rail, or other member of the family *Rallidae*, esp. the corncrake or landrail. [O.Fr. *rasle* (Fr. *râle*).]

raiment *rā'mənt*, (*poetic* or *archaic*) *n* clothing. [**arrayment**.]

rain *rān*, *n* water that falls from the clouds in drops; a fall of anything in the manner of rain; (in *pl*) the rainy season in tropical countries. — *vi* to fall as or like rain; to send down rain. — *vt* to shower, drop (something) in such large quantities as to resemble rain. — *n* **rain'iness**. — *adj* **rain'less**. — *adj* **rain'y**. — **rain'bird** a bird, such as the green woodpecker and various kinds of cuckoo, supposed to foretell rain when it calls; **rain'bow** a coloured arch in the sky caused by refraction and internal reflection of light in raindrops; any similar array of colours covering the whole spectrum. — *adj* of, or coloured like, the rainbow. — *adj* **rain'bow-coloured**. — **rainbow trout** a finely marked and coloured Californian trout. — *adj* **rain'bowy**. — **rain'check** (*US*) a ticket for future use given to spectators when a game or a sports meeting is cancelled or stopped because of bad weather (**take a raincheck (on)** (*colloq*, orig. *US*) to promise to accept an invitation at a later date); **rain'-cloud** nimbus, a dense dark sheet of cloud that may shed rain or snow; **rain'coat** a light overcoat protective against moderate rain; **rain'-doctor** a rain-maker; **rain'drop** a drop of rain; **rain'fall** a shower of rain; the amount (by depth of water) of rain that falls in a given area in a stated period; **rain'forest** broad-leaved, evergreen tropical forest with very heavy rainfall; **rain'-gauge** an instrument for measuring rainfall; **rain'-maker** a person in tribal societies who professes to bring rain; a high-powered employee who generates a great deal of income for his or her employers (*slang*); **rain'-making** attempting to cause rainfall by techniques such as seeding clouds. — *adj* **rain'proof** more or less impervious to rain. — *vt* to make rainproof. — **rain'-shadow** an area sheltered by hills from the prevailing winds and having a lighter rainfall than the windward side of the hills; **rain'-tree** a S. American tree of the mimosa family, under which there is a constant rain of juice ejected by cicadas; **rain'water** water that falls or has recently fallen as rain. — **a rainy day** (*fig*) a possible future time of need; **come rain or shine** whatever the weather or circumstances; **rained off** (of a sport, outdoor activity, etc.) cancelled because of rain; **rain in** (of rain) to penetrate a roof, tent, covering, etc.; **right as rain** (*colloq*) perfectly well or in order; **take a raincheck (on)** see **raincheck** above. [O.E. *regn*.]

raise *rāz*, *vt* to cause to rise; to make higher or greater; to lift; to advance, further; to elevate; to cause to stand up or upright, to erect; to rouse, awaken; to stir up; to rear, grow or breed (children, animals, etc.); to give rise to; to bring to life (from the dead); to utter (esp. a question); to establish; to bring into consideration; to intensify (hopes, expectations, etc.); to cause (land) to rise into view by approaching (*naut*); to contact by radio or telephone; to levy, get together, collect (e.g. taxes, an army); to cause (a lump) to swell; to produce a nap on. — *n* an increase in wages or salary (*colloq*; esp. *US*). — *adj* **rais'able** or **raise'able**. — *n* **rais'er**. — *n* **rais'ing**. — **raised beach** (*geol*) an old sea-margin above the present water level. — **raise a hand to** to hit, or generally treat badly; **raise an eyebrow** or **raise one's eyebrows** to look surprised (at); **raise a siege** to abandon, or put an end to, a siege; **raise Cain** or **raise the roof** (*colloq*) to make a lot of noise; to be extremely angry; **raise hell** or **raise the devil** (*colloq*) to make a lot of trouble, esp. by youthful irresponsibility; **raise money on** to get money for, by pawning or selling, esp. privately; **raise one's glass** to drink a health (to); **raise one's hat** to take one's hat off in greeting; **raise the market (upon)** (*stock exchange*) to bring about a rise in prices (to the disadvantage of); **raise the wind** (*slang*) to get together the necessary money by any means. [M.E. *reisen* — O.N. *reisa*, causative of *rīsa*, to rise; cf. **rise**, **rear**[2].]

raisin *rā'zn*, *n* a dried grape. [Fr., grape — L. *racēmus*, a bunch of grapes.]

raison d'être *rā-zɔ̃ detr'*, (Fr.) *n* reason for existence (purpose or cause).

raisonné *rā-zon-ā*, (Fr.) *adj* logically set out, systematically arranged, and (usu.) provided with notes.

raisonneur *rā-zon-œr'*, *n* (in a play or novel) a character who embodies the author's point of view and expresses his or her opinions. [Fr., an arguer.]

raj *räj*, *n* rule, sovereignty; government, esp. (with *cap*) the British government of India, 1858–1947. — *n* **ra'ja** or **ra'jah** an Indian prince or king; a Malay chief. — *n* **ra'jaship** or **ra'jahship**. — *n* **Rajput** or **Rajpoot** (*räj'po͞ot*) a member of a race or class claiming descent from the original Hindu military and ruling caste. [Hind. *rāj*, *rājā*, *Rājpūt* — Sans. *rājan*, a king (cognate with L. *rēx*), *putra*, son.]

rake[1] *rāk*, *n* a toothed bar on a handle, for scraping, gathering together, smoothing, etc., in gardens, on golf courses, etc.; a tool for various purposes, toothed, notched or bladed and with a long handle (e.g. a croupier's implement for drawing in money); a wheeled field implement with long teeth for gathering hay, scraping up weeds, etc.; a connected set (of railway carriages or wagons). — *vt* to use a rake on or perform the action of a rake on; to cover (a fire) with ashes so as to keep smouldering; to graze, scrape; to pass over violently and swiftly; to fire (bullets, etc.) across the entire line of one's enemy; to provide or take a view all over or completely through. — *vi* to work with or as if with a rake; to search minutely. — *n* **rā'ker** a person or thing that rakes. — *n* and *adj* **rā'king**. — **rake'-off** monetary share, esp. unearned or dishonest. — **rake in** (*colloq*) to acquire rapidly and in great quantity; **rake up** to revive from oblivion (usu. something scandalous); to collect together. [O.E. *raca*.]

rake[2] *rāk*, *n* a debauched or dissolute person, esp. a fashionable man. — *n* **rā'kery** dissoluteness. — *adj* **rā'kish**. — *adv* **rā'kishly**. — *n* **rā'kishness**.

rake[3] *rāk*, *n* inclination from the vertical or horizontal, slope of a ship's funnel(s) or a theatre stage; an angle, between the face of a cutting-tool and the surface on which it is working, or between the wings and body of an aircraft. — *vi* to incline, slope. — *vt* to slope; to cut on a slope or at an angle. — *adj* **rā'kish** with raking masts; swift-looking; dashing, jaunty. — *adv* **rā'kishly**.

rakee. See **raki**.

rakery. See **rake**[2].

raki *räk'ē*, *n* an alcoholic liquor drunk in the Levant and Greece. — Also **rak'ee**. [Turk. *rāqī*.]

rakish. See **rake**[2,3].

râle or **rale** *räl*, (*pathol*) *n* a sound from a diseased lung. [Fr.]

rall. *ral*, (*mus*) *abbrev* for rallentando.

rallentando *ral-ən-tan'dō*, (*mus*) *adj* and *adv* becoming slower. — *n* a slowing: — *pl* **rallentan'dos**. [It., pres. p. of *rallentare*, to slacken.]

rallier. See **rally**[1,2].

rally[1] *ral'i*, *vt* to assemble or reassemble; to gather to one's support or cause; to bring together for united effort; to muster (e.g. the faculties) by an effort; to pull together, revive. — *vi* to come together, esp. from being dispersed, or for renewed effort, or in support of a leader, friend or cause; to recover in some degree lost health, power, vigour, value, etc.: — *pr p* **rall'ying**; *pa p* and *pa t* **rall'ied**. — *n* an assembly or reassembly for renewed effort; a gathering for a common purpose; a mass meeting; a competition to test skill in driving, and ability to follow an unknown route, or to test quality of motor vehicles; a temporary or partial recovery (from an illness, etc.); a quick exchange of blows in boxing; a series of to and fro strokes in deciding a point, as in tennis. — *n* **rall'ier**. — *n* **rall'ying** long-distance motor racing over public roads. — *n* **rall'yist**. — **rall'ycross** motor racing round a circuit consisting partly of paved road and partly of rough ground; **rall'ying-cry** a slogan to attract support for a cause, etc.; **rall'ying-point** a place of assembly, esp. for a mass meeting. — **rally round** to support, help (someone in need). [O.Fr. *rallier* — pfx. *re-* and *allier*; see **ally**.]

rally[2] *ral'i*, *vt* and *vi* to banter: — *pr p* **rall'ying**; *pa t* and *pa p* **rall'ied**. — *n* **rall'ier**. — *adv* **rall'yingly**. [Fr. *railler*; cf. **rail**[2].]

RAM *abbrev* for: random access memory (*comput*; *ram*); Royal Academy of Music.

ram *ram*, *n* a male sheep, a tup; Aries (*astrol*); a battering-ram; a ship's beak, a pointed device for striking holes in an enemy ship's hull; the falling weight of a pile-driver; the striking head of a steam hammer; a piston applying pressure, operated by hydraulic or other power; an act of ramming. — *vt* to thrust roughly, cram (also *fig*); to drive hard down; to strike, batter, pierce; to strike, dash into, violently: — *pr p* **ramm'ing**; *pa t* and *pa p* **rammed**. — *n* **ramm'er**. — **ram'jet** or **ram'jet engine** a simple form of aero-engine, consisting of forward air intake, combustion chamber, and rear expansion nozzle, in which thrust is generated by compression due solely to forward motion; **ram'rod** a rod for ramming down a charge into, or for cleaning, a gun-barrel; a stern, inflexible person; a strict disciplinarian. — *adj* rigid, inflexible; stern. [O.E. *ram*, *rom*.]

r.a.m. *abbrev* for relative atomic mass.

Ramadan or **Ramadhan** *ram-ə-dän'*, *n* the ninth month of the Muslim calendar, the month of fasting by day; the fast. [Ar. *Ramadān*.]

ramal, ramate, etc. See **ramus**.

Raman effect *räm'ən i-fekt'*, *n* a change in frequency of light passing through a transparent medium — used in the study of molecules. [From Sir Chandrasekhara *Raman* (1888–1970), Indian physicist.]

Ramapithecus *rä-mə-pith'i-kəs*, *n* an early Pliocene genus of primates, possibly an ancestor of modern man, known from fossil remains found in N. India. — *n* and *adj* **ramapith'ecine**. [*Rāma*, an incarnation of Vishnu, with reference to his birth as a prince of Oudh, and Gr. *pithēkos*, ape.]

ramble *ram'bl*, *vi* to go wherever one's fancy leads one; to wander; to walk for recreation or pleasure; to wander in mind or discourse; to be incoherent or delirious; to straggle or trail randomly, e.g. of a plant. — *n* a roving about; an irregular, unorganised excursion; a walk for pleasure. — *n* **ram'bler** a person who rambles, esp. for recreation; a trailing climbing plant, esp. a rose with small clustered flowers. — *n* and *adj* **ram'bling**. — *adv* **ram'blingly**. [M.E. *romblen*.]

rambunctious *ram-bungk'shəs*, *adj* difficult to control, boisterous, exuberant. — *adv* **rambunc'tiously**. — *n* **rambunc'tiousness**.

rambutan *ram-bōō'tən*, *n* a lofty Malayan tree similar to the longan; its hairy edible fruit. [Malay *rambūtan* — *rambut*, hair.]

RAMC *abbrev* for Royal Army Medical Corps.

ramekin *ram'ə-kin*, *n* a mixture of cheese, eggs, etc., baked in small moulds; a baking dish for one person. [Fr. *ramequin* — obs. Flem. *rammeken*.]

ramification *ram-i-fi-kā'shən*, *n* branching; arrangement of branches; a single branch or part of a complex arrangement, or of a situation or problem, esp. a consequence that must be taken into account. — *adj* **ram'iform** having a branched shape. — *vt* and *vi* **ram'ify** to divide into branches (also *fig*): — *pr p* **ram'ifying**; *pa t* and *pa p* **rami'fīed**. [Ety. as for **ramus**.]

ramin *ram'in*, *n* a hardwood commonly used in making mouldings, frames, etc.

ramjet, rammer. See under **ram**.

ramose, ramous. See under **ramus**.

ramp *ramp*, *vi* to slope from one level to another; to dash about wildly. — *vt* to provide with a ramp. — *n* an inclined plane, a slope; a low hump made across a road, e.g. to slow down traffic; the slope of a wall-top, or anything similar, between two levels; a swindle; an exploitation of a special situation to increase prices or the like. — *n* **ramp'er**. — **ramp up** to increase (the price of something) dishonestly, and to a large extent. [Fr. *ramper*, to creep, to clamber.]

rampage *ram-pāj'*, *n* turbulently or aggressively excited behaviour or rushing about. — *vi* to storm; to rush about wildly. — *adj* **rampā'geous**. — *n* **rampā'geousness** or **rampag'ing**. — **on the rampage** storming about, behaving wildly and violently in anger, exuberance, etc. [Ety. as for **ramp**.]

rampant *ram'pənt*, *adj* rearing; standing in profile, on the left hindleg (*heraldry*); unrestrained, unchecked in growth or prevalence. — *n* **ram'pancy**. — *adv* **ramp'antly**. [Ety. as for **ramp**.]

rampart *ram'pärt*, *n* a flat-topped defensive mound; anything performing such a defensive role (*lit* or *fig*). — *vt* to fortify or surround with ramparts. [Fr. *rempart* — O.Fr. *rempar* — *remparer*, to defend — L. pfx. *re-*, *ante*, *parāre*, to prepare.]

rampion *ramp'i-ən*, *n* a bell-flower whose root is eaten as a salad vegetable. [Cf. It. *raponzolo*, Ger. *Rapunzel*, Fr. *raiponce*.]

ramrod. See under **ram**.

ramshackle *ram'shak-l*, *adj* tumbledown; badly constructed, organised, etc.

ramus *rā'məs*, *n* a branch of anything, esp. a nerve: — *pl* **rā'mī**. — *adj* **rā'mal** or **rā'mous** of a branch. — *adj* **rā'mate** or **ramose** (*rə-mōs'* or *rā'mōs*) branched. [L., a branch.]

ran *ran*, *pa t* of **run**.

ranch *räntsh* or *ränsh*, *n* a stock-farm, as in western N. America, often taken to include its buildings and the persons employed on it; an establishment for rearing any other commercially-important animal, such as a mink ranch, etc. — *vi* to own, manage or work on a ranch. — *n* **ranch'er**. — **ranch'-hand**; **ranch'man**. [From Am. Sp. — Sp. *rancho*, mess, mess-room.]

rancid *ran'sid*, *adj* rank in smell or taste, as of butter or oil that is going bad. — *n* **rancid'ity** or **ran'cidness**. [L. *rancidus*.]

rancour or in U.S. **rancor** *rang'kər*, *n* bitterness of mind, speech, etc.; deep-seated enmity. — *adj*

ran'corous. — *adv* **ran'corously.** [O.Fr., — L. *rancor, -ōris*, an old grudge — *rancēre*, to be rancid.]

rand *rand, n* a border, margin; a ridge overlooking a valley (in S. Afr. *ront* or *rand*); the basic unit of the South African decimal coinage (100 *cents*), introduced in 1961 as equivalent to ten shillings: — *pl* **rand** or **rands.** — **the Rand** the Witwatersrand goldfield. [O.E. and Du. *rand*, border.]

R & A *abbrev* for Royal and Ancient (Golf Club of St Andrews).

R & B *abbrev* for rhythm and blues.

R & D *abbrev* for research and development.

randem *ran'dəm, n, adj* and *adv* tandem with three horses in line, one in front of the other.

random *ran'dəm adj* haphazard, chance; uncontrolled; irregular. — *vt* **ran'domise** or **-ize** to arrange or set up so as to occur in a random manner. — *n* **randomīsā'tion** or **-z-.** — *n* **ran'domiser** or **-z-.** — *adv* **ran'domly** or **ran'domwise.** — **random access** (*comput*) access to any data in a large store of information without affecting other data; **random access memory** measure of the amount of data available by random access from the memory of a given computer; **random variable** (*statistics*) one which can take any one of a range of values which occur randomly. [O.Fr. *randon* — *randir*, to gallop.]

R and R *abbrev* (*colloq*; orig. *US*) for rest and recreation.

randy *ran'di, adj* sexually excited; lustful.

ranee. See **rani.**

rang *rang, pa t* of **ring**[2,3].

range *rānj, vt* to set in a row or rows; to assign a place among others to; to arrange; to straighten, level, align; to traverse freely or in all directions. — *vi* to lie in a stated direction; to extend; to take or have a position in a line, or alongside; to take sides; to lie evenly, align; to move, have freedom of movement, occur or vary within limits; to rove freely, in all directions; to be inconstant, fluctuate; to have a range. — *n* anything extending in line, such as a chain of mountains, or a row of connected buildings; a stretch of open country, esp. one used for grazing; scope, compass, extent, limits; movement, freedom of movement, or variation between limits; space or distance between limits; area or distance within which anything moves, can move, occurs, is possible, acts efficiently, or varies; a place for practice in shooting; effective shooting distance of a gun, etc.; an enclosed kitchen fireplace fitted with appliances of various kinds; a row or rank; a system of points in a straight line. — *n* **ran'ger** a forest or park officer; a member of a body of troops, usu. mounted and employed in policing an area; a soldier specially trained for raiding combat; (with *cap*) a member of a senior branch of the Girl Guide organisation (also **Ranger Guide**); (with *cap* in *pl*) a name sometimes taken by football clubs. — *n* **rang'ership.** — *n* **rang'iness.** — *adj* **ran'gy** long-legged and thin; well adapted to roaming; roomy. — **range'finder** an instrument for finding the distance away of an object; **range'finding; range'land** (often *pl*) land suitable for grazing, but too dry for growing crops; **range pole, range rod, ranging pole** or **ranging rod** a pole or rod used to mark positions in surveying. — **range oneself** to side (with), to take sides. [Fr. *ranger*, to range — *rang*, a rank.]

rani or **ranee** *rän'ē, fem* of **raja.** [Hind. *rānī* — Sans. *rājñī*, queen, fem. of *rājan*.]

rank[1] *rangk, n* a row; a row of soldiers standing side by side (as opp. to *file*); any row thought of as so placed (e.g. of squares along the player's side of a chess-board); (in *pl*) soldiers, esp. private soldiers — often (with *the*) private soldiers collectively; (in *pl*) persons of ordinary grade; a row of cabs awaiting hire; a place where taxis are allowed to stand for hire; order, grade or degree; an official post ordered in superiority (esp. *mil*); position in society, etc.; high standing. — *vt* to place in a line; to assign to a particular class or grade; to be superior to in position, grade, etc., outrank (*US*). — *vi* to have a place in a rank, grade, scale or class. — *n* **rank'er** a person who serves or has served as a private soldier; an officer who has risen from the ranks. — *adj* **rank'ing** having a high military, political, etc. position; highest in rank of those present. — *n* a position or grade. — **pull rank** to use one's superior position to exert authority, get one's own way; **rank and file** common soldiers; ordinary people; those in an organisation, etc. not involved in its management. [O.Fr. *renc*.]

rank[2] *rangk, adj* coarsely overgrown; out-and-out, arrant, utter; offensively strong-scented or strong-tasted; foul, highly offensive. — *adv* **rank'ly.** — *n* **rank'ness.** [O.E. *ranc*, proud, strong.]

rankle *rangk'l, vi* to continue to vex, irritate or embitter. [O.Fr. *rancler, raoncler* — L.L. *dra(cu)nculus*, an ulcer, dimin. of L. *dracō*, dragon.]

ransack *ran'sak* or *-sak', vt* to search thoroughly and violently; to plunder, pillage. — *n* **ran'sacker** (or *-sak'*). [O.N. *rannsaka* — *rann*, house, *sǣkja*, to seek.]

ransom *ran'səm, n* a sum of money demanded in return for release from captivity; atonement, redemption (*relig*); an extortionate price. — *vt* to pay, demand or accept a ransom for; to redeem, atone (*relig*). — *adj* **ran'somable.** — *n* **ran'somer.** — *adj* **ran'somless.** — **a king's ransom** an enormous sum of money; **hold to ransom** to retain until a ransom be paid; to blackmail into concessions (*fig*). [Fr. *rançon* — L. *redemptiō, -ōnis*, redemption.]

rant *rant, vi* to declaim bombastically; to storm or scold with great anger. — *vt* to utter in a high-flown, self-important way. — *n* empty speechifying; a tirade. — *n* **ran'ter** a person who rants, esp. an extravagant preacher. — *n* and *adj* **rant'ing.** — *adv* **rant'ingly.** [Obs. Du. *ranten*, to rave.]

RAOC *abbrev* for Royal Army Ordnance Corps.

rap[1] *rap, n* a sharp blow; the sound of a knock; a crime or criminal charge (*slang*). — *vt* and *vi* to strike or knock sharply; to communicate or sound out by raps. — *vt* to censure, reprove (*colloq*); to utter sharply: — *pr p* **rapp'ing;** *pa t* and *pa p* **rapped.** — *n* **rapp'er** a person who raps; a door-knocker. — **rap sheet** (*slang*) a criminal record; a charge sheet. — **beat the rap** (*US slang*) to be acquitted of a crime (whether guilty of not); to avoid punishment; **take the rap** (*slang*) to take the blame or punishment, esp. in place of another. [Imit.]

rap[2] *rap, n* a type of worthlessness, a whit, esp. in *not worth a rap.* [18th-cent. Irish counterfeit halfpenny.]

rap[3] *rap*, (*colloq*) *n* an informal talk, discussion, chat, etc.; a rhythmic monologue delivered over a musical background; a type of music consisting of such monologues. — *vi* to have a talk, discussion, etc.; to get along well, sympathise; to deliver a rhythmic monologue to music. — *n* **rapp'er.** — *n* **rapp'ing.** — **rap session** an informal discussion.

rapacious *rə-pā'shəs, adj* grasping; greedy for gain; living by taking prey. — *adv* **rapā'ciously.** — *n* **rapā'ciousness** or **rapacity** (*-pas'*). [L. *rapāx, -ācis* — *rapěre*, to seize and carry off.]

rape[1] *rāp, n* unlawful sexual intercourse (by force or, technically, with a minor) with another person without that person's consent; violation, despoliation. — *vt* to commit rape upon; to violate, despoil. — *n* **rā'pist.**

rape[2] *rāp, n* a plant related to the turnip, brilliantly yellow-flowered, and cultivated for its herbage and oil-producing seeds; applied to various closely allied species or varieties. — **rape'-cake** refuse of rape-seed after the oil (**rape-oil**) has been expressed; **rape'-seed.** [L. *rāpa, rāpum*, a turnip.]

rape[3] *rāp*, *n* the refuse left after wine-making. [Fr. *râpe*.]

Raphia *rā'fi-ə* or *raf'i-ə*, *n* a genus of handsome palms with featherlike leaves; (without *cap*) raffia. [Malagasy.]

rapid *rap'id*, *adj* swift; quickly accomplished; requiring short exposure (*phot*). — *n* (usu. in *pl*) a very swift-flowing part of a river with steep descent and often broken water but no vertical drop. — *n* **rapidity** (*rə-pid'i-ti*). — *adv* **rap'idly**. — *n* **rap'idness**. — **rapid fire** the quickly repeated firing of guns, asking of questions, etc. — *adj* **rap'id-fire**. — **rapid eye movement** (abbrev. **REM**) an observable manifestation of a phase of sleep during which dreams are particularly vivid. [L. *rapidus* — *rapěre*, to seize.]

rapier *rā'pi-ər*, *n* a long slender sword, suitable for thrusting. [Fr. *rapière*.]

rapine *rap'īn* or *-in*, *n* plundering; ravishment. [L. *rapīna* — *rapěre*, to seize.]

rapist. See **rape**[1].

rappel *rə-pel'*, *n* call to arms by beating of a drum (*mil*); abseiling. — *vi* same as **abseil**: — *pr p* **rappell'ing**; *pa t* and *pa p* **rappell'ed**. [Fr.]

rapper, rapping. See **rap**[1,3].

rapport *ra-pör'*, *n* sympathy; emotional bond. [Fr.]

rapporteur *ra-pör-tœr'*, *n* a person whose task it is to carry out an investigation and/or draw up a report (for a committee, etc.). — *n* **rapportage** (*ra-pör-täzh'*) the description of real events in writing; flat description, lacking in imagination. [Fr. — *rapporter*, to bring back.]

rapprochement *ra-prosh'mã*, *n* a drawing together or closer; establishment or renewal of cordial relations. [Fr.]

rapscallion *rap-skal'yən*, *n* a rascal; (*jocular*) a low, mean wretch. [**rascal**.]

rapt *rapt*, *adj* enraptured, entranced; wholly engrossed. [L. *raptus*, past p. of *rapěre*, to seize and carry off.]

raptor *rap'tər*, (*ornithol*) *n* a bird of prey. — *adj* **raptō'rial**. [L. *raptor*, *-ōris*, a plunderer — *rapěre*, to seize.]

rapture *rap'chər*, *n* extreme delight; ecstasy. — *adj* **rap'turous**. — *adv* **rap'turously**. [**rapt**.]

ra-ra skirt *rä'-rä skûrt*, *n* a very short gathered or pleated skirt, orig. as worn by cheerleaders. [Prob. — **hurrah**.]

rare[1] *rār*, *adj* (of the atmosphere) thin; seldom encountered; uncommon; excellent; especially good; extraordinary. — *n* **rarefac'tion** (*rār-i-*) the action of rarefying. — *adj* **rarefac'tive**. — *adj* **rar'efīable**. — *vt* and *vi* **rar'efy** to make or become less dense, to refine: — *pr p* **rar'efying**; *pa t* and *pa p* **rar'efied**. — *adv* **rāre'ly** seldom; remarkably well. — *n* **rāre'ness**. — *n* **rār'ity** state of being rare; something valued for its scarcity; uncommonness. — **rare bird** (*colloq*) an exceptional person or thing; **rare'bit** (often called **Welsh rarebit**) melted cheese with or without ale, on hot toast (also **rabbit** or **Welsh rabbit**); **rare earth** an oxide of a **rare-earth element**, any of a group of metallic elements (some of them rare) closely similar in chemical properties and very difficult to separate; now more usu. a rare-earth element itself; **rare gas** an inert gas. [Fr., — L. *rārus*.]

rare[2] *rār*, *adj* (of meat) undercooked, still bloody. [Obs. *rear*, lightly cooked, infl. by **rare**[1].]

rarebit. See under **rare**[1].

raring *rā'ring*, *adj* eager (to do something), full of enthusiasm and sense of urgency, esp. in the phrase **raring to go**. [**rear**[2].]

rarity. See under **rare**[1].

RAS *abbrev* for Royal Astronomical Society.

rascal *räs'kl*, *n* a knave, rogue, scamp; (*playfully*) a fellow. — *n* **ras'caldom**. — *n* **rascality** (*-kal'*) the rabble, common people; the character or conduct of rascals. — *adj* **ras'cal-like** or **ras'cally**. [O.Fr. *rascaille*, scum of the people.]

raschel *räsh'əl*, *n* a type of light, loosely-knitted fabric. [Ger. *Raschelmaschine*, a kind of knitting-machine.]

rase. See **raze**.

rash[1] *rash*, *adj* over-hasty; lacking in caution. — *adv* **rash'ly**. — *n* **rash'ness**. [Cf. Dan. and Sw. *rask*.]

rash[2] *rash*, *n* an eruption on the skin; a large number of instances (of something happening) at the same time or in the same place.

rasher *rash'ər*, *n* a thin slice of bacon.

rasp[1] *räsp*, *n* a coarse file; any similar surface; a mollusc's tongue; an insect's apparatus for making chirping sounds; a grating sound or feeling. — *vt* to grate as with a rasp; to utter gratingly. — *vi* to have a grating effect; to scrape, as on a fiddle. — *n* **rasp'er**. — *n* **rasp'ing**. — *adj* grating, harsh. — *adv* **rasp'ingly**. — *adj* **rasp'y**. [O.Fr. *raspe* (Fr. *râpe*).]

rasp[2] *räsp*, (*colloq*) *n* a raspberry. — *n* **raspberry** (*räz'bər-i*) the berry fruit of shrubs of the *Rubus* genus; the plant producing it; extended to some similar species; a rude sign of disapproval, esp. a noise produced by blowing hard with the tongue between the lips (*slang*). — *adj* of, made with, or like raspberries. [Earlier *raspis*.]

rasse *ras* or *ras'i*, *n* a small civet. [Jav. *rase*.]

Rastafarian *ras-tə-fār'i-ən*, *n* a member of a West Indian, esp. Jamaican, cult, which rejects western culture and ideas and regards Haile Selassie, the former Emperor of Ethiopia, as divine. — Also **Ras'ta** and **Ras'taman**. — *adj* **Rastafā'rian, Rastafari** (*-ä'ri*) and **Ras'ta** (all also without *cap*). [From Haile Selassie's title and name, *Ras Tafari*.]

raster *ras'tər*, (*TV*) *n* a complete set of scanning lines appearing at the receiver as a rectangular patch of light on which the image is reproduced. [Perh. — L. *rāstrum*, a rake.]

rasure or **razure** *rā'zhər*, *n* the act of scraping or shaving; erasure; obliteration. [L. *rāsūra*.]

rat *rat*, *n* a genus of animals closely allied to mice, but larger; extended to various related or superficially similar animals; a renegade or turncoat (from the rat's alleged desertion of a doomed ship; *colloq*); a strike-breaker (*colloq*); someone who works for less than recognised wages (*colloq*); a miserable or ill-looking specimen (*colloq*); a despicable person (*colloq*). — *vi* to hunt or catch rats; to desert or change sides for unworthy motives; (of a workman) to work as a rat: — *pr p* **ratt'ing**; *pa t* and *pa p* **ratt'ed**. — *adj* **rat'proof**. — *interj* **rats** (*colloq*) expressing contemptuous incredulity, annoyance, etc. — *n* **ratt'er** a killer of rats, esp. a dog; a person who rats. — *n* **ratt'ery** a place where rats are kept or abound. — *n* **ratt'ing** rat-hunting. — *adj* **ratt'ish**. — *adj* **ratt'y** ratlike; rat-infested; angry, irritable (*colloq*). — **rat'bag** (*slang*) a term of, esp. gentle, abuse; a despicable person; **rat'-catcher** a professional killer of rats; unconventional hunting garb (*slang*); **rat'-catching**; **rat'-kangaroo** a marsupial about the size of a rabbit, similar in appearance to the kangaroo (also **potoroo'**); **rat'pack** (*slang*) a rowdy gang of young people; **rat race** a continual round of hectic and futile activity; the scramble to get on in the world by fair means or foul; **rats'bane** poison for rats, esp. white arsenic; a name for many poisonous plants; **rat's'-tail** or **rat'-tail** a thin dangling lock of hair; an excrescence on a horse's leg; **rat'-tail** a deep-sea fish of the *Macrouridae* family. — *adj* **rat's'-tail, rat'-tail** or **rat'-tailed** having a tail like a rat; like a rat's tail; (of a spoon) ridged along the back of the bowl. — **rat on** to inform against; to betray the interests of; to desert; **smell a rat** to have a suspicion that foul play is afoot. [O.E. *ræt*.]

rata *rä'tə*, *n* a New Zealand tree of the myrtle genus, with hard wood. [Maori.]

ratable or **rateable**. See under **rate**[1].

ratafia *rat-ə-fē'ə*, *n* a flavouring essence made with the essential oil of almonds; a cordial or liqueur flavoured with fruit-kernels; an almond biscuit or cake. [Fr.]

ratan. See **rattan**.

rat-a-tat *rat'-ə-tat'*, *n*. Same as **rat-tat**.

ratatouille *rat-ə-too'i* or *ra-ta-twē'*, *n* a stew of tomatoes, aubergines, peppers, onions and other vegetables, with olive oil. [Fr. — *touiller*, to stir.]

ratbag. See under **rat**.

ratch *rach*, *n* a ratchet; a ratchet-wheel. — *n* **ratch'et** a pawl and/or ratchet-wheel. — *vt* and *vi* to move by, or as if by, a rachet mechanism, by steady, progressive degrees (*up* or *down*). — **ratch'et-wheel** a wheel with inclined teeth with which a pawl engages. [Cf. Ger. *Ratsche*, Fr. *rochet*.]

rate[1] *rāt*, *n* price or cost; amount corresponding; ratio, esp. time-ratio, speed; amount determined according to a rule or basis; a standard; a class or rank, esp. of ships or of seamen; manner, mode; extent, degree; (often in *pl*) an amount levied by a local authority according to the assessed value of a (commercial) property; a clock's gain or loss in unit time. — *vt* to estimate; to value; to settle the relative rank, scale or position of; to esteem, regard as; to deserve, be worthy of; to value for purpose of rate-paying. — *vi* to be placed in a certain class. — *n* **rāteabil'ity** or **ratabil'ity.** — *adj* **rāte'able** or **rat'able.** — *n* **rāt'er** a person who makes an estimate; (in combination) a ship, etc. of a given rate (as in *second-rater*). — *n* **rāt'ing** a fixing of rates; classification according to grade; the class of any member of a crew; a sailor of such a class; the tonnage-class of a racing yacht; the proportion of viewers or listeners who are deemed to watch or listen to a particular programme or network. — **rateable (or rat'able) value** a value placed on a commercial property, and used to assess the amount of rates payable to the local authority each year. — *vt* **rate'-cap.** — **rate'-capping** the setting by central government of an upper limit on the rate that can be levied by a local authority; **rate'payer; rate support grant** money contributed by central government to make up the difference between the rate levied and the amount required for local authority spending. — **at any rate** in any case, anyhow. [O.Fr., — L.L. (*pro*) *ratā* (*parte*), according to a calculated part — *rērī*, *rătus*, to think, judge.]

rate[2] *rāt*, *vt* to scold, rebuke. [M.E. *raten*.]

ratel *rā'təl* or *rä'təl*, *n* an animal of the badger-like genus (*Ratel*) of Africa and India. [Afrikaans.]

ratfink *rat'fingk*, (*derog slang*, esp. *NAm*) *n* a mean, deceitful, despicable person. — Also *adj*. [**rat** and **fink**.]

rath *räth*, *n* a prehistoric hill-fort. [Ir.]

rather *rä'dhər*, *adv* more readily; more willingly; in preference; more than otherwise; more properly; somewhat, in some degree. — *interj* **ra'ther** (sometimes affectedly *rä-dhûr'*) yes, indeed. [Compar. of archaic *rath*, quick, ready, eager; O.E. *hrathor*.]

ratify *rat'i-fī*, *vt* to approve and sanction, esp. by signature; to give validity or legality to: — *pr p* **rat'ifying**; *pa t* and *pa p* **rat'ified.** — *n* **ratificā'tion.** — *n* **rat'ifier.** [Fr. *ratifier* — L. *rătus*, past p. of *rērī* (see **rate**[1]), *facĕre*, to make.]

rating. See under **rate**[1].

ratio *rā'shi-ō* or *rāsh'yō*, *n* the relation of one thing to another of which the quotient is the measure; quotient; proportion; (also **ratio decidendi**; *law*) the reason or principle on which a decision is based: — *pl* **rā'tios.** — **inverse ratio** see under **inverse.** [L. *rătiō*, *-ōnis*, reason — *rērī*, *rătus*, to think.]

ratiocinate *rat-* or *rash-i-os'i-nāt*, *vi* to reason formally and logically. — *n* **ratiocinā'tion.** — *adj* **ratioc'inative** or **ratioc'inatory.** [L. *ratiōcinārī*, *-ātus*.]

ration *ra'shən*, *n* a fixed allowance or portion esp. of food and other provisions in time of shortage; (in *pl*) food (*colloq*). — *vt* to put on an allowance; to supply with rations; to restrict the supply of to so much for each. — **ra'tion-book** or **-card** a book or card of coupons or vouchers for rationed commodities. [Fr., — L. *ratiō*, *-ōnis*.]

rational *rash'ən-əl*, *adj* endowed with reason; agreeable to, in accordance with, etc. reason; sane; intelligent; judicious; commensurable with natural numbers. — *n* a rational being or quantity; (in *pl*) rational dress, i.e. knickerbockers instead of skirts for women (*hist*). — *n* **rationale** (*rash-ə-näl'*) underlying principle; a rational account; a theoretical explanation or solution. — *n* **rationalisation** or **-z-** (*rash-nəl-ī-zā'shən*). — *vt* **rat'ionalise** or **-ize** to make rational; to free from irrational quantities; to conform to reason; to reorganise scientifically; to interpret rationalistically; to substitute conscious reasoning for unconscious motivation in explaining; to organise (an industry) so as to achieve greater efficiency and economy. — *vi* to think or argue rationally or rationalistically; to employ reason, rationalism or rationalisation. — *n* **rat'ionalism** a system of belief regulated by reason, not intuition or experience; a disposition to apply to religious doctrines the same critical methods as to science and history, and to attribute all phenomena to natural rather than miraculous causes. — *n* **rat'ionalist.** — *adj* **rationalist'ic.** — *adv* **rationalist'ically.** — *n* **rationality** (*rash-ən-al'i-ti*) the quality of being rational; the possession or due exercise of reason; reasonableness. — *adv* **rat'ionally.** — **rational dress** (*hist*) knickerbockers for women instead of skirts; **rational horizon** see **horizon; rational number** a number expressed as the ratio of two integers. [L. *ratiōnālis*, *-e* — *ratiō*.]

ratite *rat'īt*, *adj* (of flightless birds) having a keel-less breastbone; of the **Ratitae** (*rä-tī'tē*) family of flightless birds — ostrich, rhea, emu, kiwi, etc. [L. *ratis*, raft.]

ratlin, ratline or **ratling** *rat'lin*, *n* one of the small lines forming steps of the rigging of ships.

ratoon *rat-* or *rət-oon'*, *n* a new shoot from the ground after cropping, esp. of sugar-cane or cotton. — *vi* to send up ratoons. — *vt* to cut down so as to obtain ratoons. [Sp. *retoño*, shoot.]

rattan or **ratan** *ra-tan'*, *n* any of various climbing palms with a very long thin stem; a cane made from the stem; the stems collectively as wickerwork. [Malay *rōtan*.]

rat-tat *rat'-tat'*, *n* a knocking sound. [Imit.]

ratter, rattery, ratting, etc. See **rat**.

rattle *rat'l*, *vi* to make a quick succession or alternation of short hard sounds; to move along rapidly with a rattle; to chatter briskly and emptily. — *vt* to cause to rattle; to utter glibly, as by rote (often with *off*); to perform or push through to completion in a rapid, perfunctory or noisy manner; to fluster, disconcert or irritate (*colloq*). — *n* an instrument or toy for rattling; an instrument for making a whirring noise, formerly used by watchmen; a similar device used at football matches or other gatherings of people; a plant whose seeds rattle in the capsule — applied to two plants, **yell'ow-rattle** (*Rhinanthus*) and **red'-rattle** or marsh lousewort; the rings of a rattlesnake's tail; a vivacious prattler; the sound of rattling; a sound in the throat of a dying person. — *n* **ratt'ler** (*colloq*) a rattlesnake; an excellent specimen of the kind. — *n* **ratt'ling.** — *adj* smart, lively; strikingly good (*colloq*). — Also *adv*. — *adj* **ratt'ly** making a rattling noise; inclined to rattle. — **ratt'lebag** a rattle or rattling apparatus; **ratt'le=brain, -head** or **-pate** a shallow, voluble, volatile person. — *adj* **ratt'le-brained, -headed** or **-pated.** — **ratt'lesnake** a venomous American viper with rattling horny rings on the tail; **ratt'le-trap** (*colloq*) a rickety vehicle. — **rattle someone's cage** (*colloq*) to stir someone up to anger or excitement. [M.E. *ratelen*.]

ratty. See **rat**.

ratu or **ratoo** *rä'too*, *n* a chief or petty prince in Indonesia and Fiji.

raucous *rö'kəs*, *adj* hoarse, harsh. — *adv* **rau'cously**. — *n* **rau'cousness**. [L. *raucus*, hoarse.]

raunchy *rön'chi*, (*colloq*) *adj* coarse, earthy, smutty or lewd. — *n* **raunch'iness**.

rauwolfia *rö-wol'fi-ə*, *n* any of a tropical genus of trees and shrubs, of which *R. serpentina* and other species yield valuable drugs. [After the German botanist Leonhard *Rauwolf* (d. 1596).]

ravage *rav'ij*, *vt* and *vi* to lay waste; to destroy; to pillage. — *n* devastation; ruin. — *n* **rav'ager**. [Fr. *ravager* — *ravir*, to carry off by force — L. *rapěre*.]

rave[1] *rāv*, *vi* to rage; to talk as if mad or delirious; to write or speak with extreme enthusiasm (with *about*; *colloq*). — *vt* to utter wildly. — *n* (*colloq*) infatuation; extravagant praise; a rave-up. — *adj* (*colloq*) extravagantly enthusiastic; crazy. — *n* **rā'ver** a person who raves; a lively, uninhibited person (*colloq*). — *n* and *adj* **rā'ving**. — *adv* **rā'vingly**. — **rave'-up** (*slang*) a lively celebration; a wild, uninhibited, thoroughly enjoyable party. — **raving mad** frenzied; very angry (*colloq*). [Perh. O.Fr. *raver*, which may be — L. *raběre*, to rave.]

rave[2] *rāv*, *n* a side piece of a wagon.

ravel *rav'l*, *vt* to entangle; to disentangle, untwist, unweave, unravel (usu. with *out*). — *vi* to become entangled: — *pr p* **rav'elling**; *pa t* and *pa p* **rav'elled**. — *n* a tangle or complication; a broken thread. — *n* **rav'elling**. [App. Du. *ravelen*.]

ravelin *rav'lin*, (*fort*) *n* a detached work with two embankments raised before the counterscarp. [Fr.]

raven[1] *rā'vn*, *n* a large glossy black species of crow. — *adj* shiny black like a raven. [O.E. *hræfn*.]

raven[2] *rav'in*, *vt* to devour hungrily or greedily. — *vi* to prey rapaciously; to be intensely hungry; to hunger intensely (*for*). — *n* **rav'ener**. — *adj* **rav'enous** voracious; intensely hungry. — *adv* **rav'enously**. — *n* **rav'enousness**. [O.Fr. *ravine*, plunder — L. *rapīna*, plunder.]

ravine *rə-vēn'*, *n* a deep, narrow gorge. — *adj* **ravined'** scored with ravines; trenched. [Fr., — L. *rapīna*, rapine, violence.]

ravioli *rav-i-ōl'ē*, *n* little edible pasta cases with a savoury filling of meat, etc. [It., pl. of *raviòlo*.]

ravish *rav'ish*, *vt* to rape; to enrapture. — *n* **rav'isher**. — *adj* **rav'ishing** delightful; lovely; transporting. — *adv* **rav'ishingly**. — *n* **rav'ishment**. [Fr. *ravir*, *ravissant* — L. *rapěre*, to seize and carry off.]

raw *rö*, *adj* not altered from its natural state; not cooked or dressed; unwrought; not prepared or manufactured; not refined; not mixed; having the skin abraded or removed (also *fig*); crude; hard, harsh, cruel; untrained; red and inflamed; immature; inexperienced; chilly and damp; naked; (of statistics, data for a computer, etc.) not yet checked, sorted, corrected, etc. — *n* (with *the*) a skinned, sore or sensitive place (usu. with *on*); the raw state. — *adj* **raw'ish**. — *adv* **raw'ly**. — *n* **raw'ness**. — *adj* **raw'boned** with little flesh on the bones; gaunt. — *adj* **raw'hide** of untanned leather. — *n* a rope or whip of untanned leather. — **raw material** material (often in its natural state) that serves as the starting-point of a manufacturing or technical process; that out of which something is made, or makable, or may develop (*fig*); **raw silk** natural untreated silk threads; fabric made from these. — **a raw deal** harsh, inequitable treatment; **in the raw** in its natural state; naked. [O.E. *hrēaw*.]

ray[1] *rā*, *n* a line along which light or other energy, or a stream of particles, is propagated; a narrow beam; a gleam of intellectual light; a radiating line or part; the radially extended fringing outer part of an inflorescence; a supporting spine in a fin. — *vt* to radiate; to provide with rays. — *vi* to radiate. — *adj* **rayed**. — *adj* **ray'less**. — *n* **ray'let** a small ray. — **ray flower** or **floret** any of the small flowers radiating out from the margin of the flower head of certain composite plants; **ray'-fungus** a bacterium that forms radiating threads, some species pathogenic. — **ray of sunshine** a happy person, someone who cheers up others. [O.Fr. *rais* (accus. *rai*) — L. *radius*, a rod.]

ray[2] *rā*, *n* a skate, thornback, torpedo or any similar flat-bodied elasmobranch fish. [Fr. *raie* — L. *raia*.]

ray[3]. Same as **re**[1].

raylet, etc. See under **ray**[1].

rayon *rā'ən*, *n* fabric made from cellulose; artificial silk (see **silk**). [Fr. *rayon*, ray.]

raze or **rase** *rāz*, *vt* to lay (a building) level with the ground; to demolish. — *adj* **razed** or **rased**. [Fr. *raser* — L. *rāděre*, *rāsum*, to scrape.]

razee *rā-zē'*, (*hist*) *n* a ship cut down by reducing the number of decks. — *vt* to remove the upper deck or decks of. [Fr. *rasé*, cut down.]

razoo *rə-zoo'*, (*Austr* and *NZ colloq*) *n* a (non-existent) coin of insignificant value, esp. in phrases *not have a (brass) razoo*, *give someone every last razoo*, etc.

razor *rā'zər*, *n* a sharp-edged implement for shaving. — *adj* (*fig*) sharp, keen, precise. — **rā'zor-back** a rorqual; a ridge-backed pig. — *adj* sharply ridged. — **rā'zor-bill** a species of auk, with a compressed bill; **rā'zor-cut** a haircut done with a razor. — *vt* **rā'zor-cut**. — **rā'zor-edge** a very fine sharp edge, such as that on which a balance swings; a critically balanced situation; **rā'zor-fish** a mollusc with shell like a razor handle; **rā'zor-shell** its shell, or the animal itself; **razor wire** thick wire with sharp pieces of metal attached, used like barbed-wire, for fences, etc. — **Occam's razor** see **Occamism**. [O.Fr. *rasour*; see **raze**.]

razz *raz*, (*slang*) *n* a raspberry. — *vt* and *vi* (*NAm*) to jeer (at).

razzamatazz. See **razzmatazz**.

razzia *raz'ya*, *n* a pillaging incursion, esp. one carried out by N. African Moors. [Fr., — Algerian Ar. *ghāzīah*.]

razzle-dazzle *raz'l-daz'l*, (*slang*) *n* a rowdy frolic or spree; dazzling show, confusion, etc. — Also **razz'le**. — **on the razzle** having a spree or bout of heavy drinking. [App. from **dazzle**.]

razzmatazz *raz-mə-taz'* or **razzamatazz** *raz-ə-mə-taz'*, *n* to-do, hullabaloo; razzle-dazzle.

RB *abbrev* for Republic of Botswana (I.V.R.).

Rb (*chem*) *symbol* for rubidium.

RC *abbrev* for: Red Cross; Roman Catholic (Church); Taiwan (official name *Republic of China*; I.V.R.).

RCA *abbrev* for: Central African Republic (*Republique Centafricaine*; I.V.R.); Radio Corporation of America; Royal Canadian Academy; Royal College of Art.

RCAF *abbrev* for Royal Canadian Air Force.

RCB *abbrev* for Republic of the Congo (Brazzaville) (I.V.R.).

RCD *abbrev* for residual current device.

RCH *abbrev* for Republic of Chile (I.V.R.).

RCM *abbrev* for Royal College of Music.

RCMP *abbrev* for Royal Canadian Mounted Police.

RCN *abbrev* for: Royal Canadian Navy; Royal College of Nursing.

RCOG *abbrev* for Royal College of Obstetricians and Gynaecologists.

RCP *abbrev* for Royal College of Physicians.

RCR *abbrev* for Royal College of Radiologists.

RCS *abbrev* for: Royal College of Science; Royal College of Surgeons; Royal Corps of Signals.

RCT *abbrev* for Royal Corps of Transport.

RCVS *abbrev* for Royal College of Veterinary Surgeons.

RD *abbrev* for: refer to drawer (written on a returned bank cheque); Rural Dean.

Rd *abbrev* for Road (in addresses).
rd *abbrev* for rutherford.
RDA *abbrev* for recommended daily (or dietary) allowance.
RDC *abbrev* for Rural Development Council.
RDF *abbrev* for refuse-derived fuel.
RDX *abbrev* for Research Department Explosive (also called **cyclonite**).
RE *abbrev* for: Reformed Episcopal; religious education (in schools); Royal Engineers; Royal Exchange.
Re (*chem*) *symbol* for rhenium.
re[1] *rā*, (*mus*) *n* the second note of the scale in sol-fa notation — also anglicised in spelling as **ray**.
re[2] *rē*, (*commercial jargon*) *prep* concerning, with reference to. [L. *in rē* (abl. of *rēs*, thing), in the matter.]
re- *rē-*, *pfx* denoting: again; again and in a different way. [L.]

Words with the prefix **re-** are listed in the following text or in the separate panels.

're *r*, a shortened form of **are**[2].
reach *rēch*, *vt* to stretch forth, hold out; to hand, pass; to succeed in touching or getting; to communicate with; to arrive at; to extend to; to get at. — *vi* to stretch out the hand; to extend; to amount; to attain to (usu. with *for* or *after*); to succeed in going or coming: — *pa t* and *pa p* **reached**. — *n* act or power of reaching; extent of stretch; range, scope; a stretch or portion between defined limits, as of a stream between bends; the distance traversed between tacks (*naut*). — *adj* **reach'able**. — *n* **reach'er**. — *adj* **reach'-me-down** ready-made. — *n* (often in *pl*) ready-made or second-hand clothes. [O.E. *rǣcan* (past t. *rǣhte*, *rāhte*; past p. *gerǣht*).]
react *ri-akt'*, *vi* to respond to a stimulus; to undergo chemical change produced by a reagent; to return an impulse in the opposite direction; to act in return; to act with mutual effect; to act in resistance; to swing back in the opposite direction; (*loosely*) to act, behave; (of share prices) to fall sharply after a rise. — *n* **reac'tance** (*electr*) the component of impedance due to inductance or capacitance. — *n* **reac'tant** (*chem*) a substance taking part in a reaction. — *n* **reac'tion** response to stimulus; the chemical action of a reagent; action resisting other action; mutual action; an action or change in an opposite direction; backward tendency from revolution, reform or progress; a physical or mental effect caused by medicines, drugs, etc.; a transformation within the nucleus of an atom; acidity or alkalinity; (*loosely*) feeling or thought aroused by, or in response to, a statement, situation, person, etc. — *adj* **reac'tional**. — *adj* **reac'tionary** of or favouring reaction, esp. against revolution, reform, etc. — *n* a person who tends to oppose political change or who attempts to revert to past political conditions. — *n* and *adj* **reac'tionist** reactionary. — *adj* **reac'tive** of or pertaining to reaction; readily acted upon or responsive to stimulus; produced by emotional stress; pertaining to or having a reactance. — *adv* **reac'tively**. — *n* **reac'tiveness** or **reactiv'ity**. — *n* **reac'tor** someone who or that which undergoes a reaction; a device which introduces reactance into an electric circuit; a container in which a chemical reaction takes place; a nuclear reactor (see under **nuclear**). [L.L. *reagĕre*, *-actum* — *agĕre*, to do.]
re-act *rē'-akt*, *vt* to act a second, etc. time.
reactivate *rē-ak'ti-vāt*, *vt* to restore to an active state. — *n* **reactivā'tion**. [**re-**.]
reactive. See under **react**.
read *rēd*, *vt* to look at and comprehend the meaning of written or printed words in; to go over progressively with silent understanding of symbols or with utterance aloud of words or performance of notes; to make out; to interpret; to understand as by interpretation of signs; to accept or offer as that which the writer intended; to learn from written or printed matter; to find recorded; to observe the indication of; to register, indicate; to teach, lecture on; to study; to impute by inference (as to read a meaning into); to retrieve (data) from a storage device (*comput*). — *vi* to perform the act of reading; to practise much reading; to study; to find mention; to give the reader an

Some words with **re-** prefix

rēaccus'tom *vt.*
rēacquaint' *vt.*
rēacquaint'ance *n.*
rēacquire' *vt.*
rēadapt' *vt.*
rēadaptā'tion *n.*
rēaddress' *vt.*
rēadjust' *vt.*
rēadjust'ment *n.*
rēadmiss'ion *n.*
rēadmit' *vt.*
rēadmitt'ance *n.*
rēadopt' *vt.*
rēadop'tion *n.*
rēadvance' *n*, *vt* and *vi.*
rēad'vertise or **-ize** *vt* and *vi.*
rēadver'tisement or **-z-** *n.*
rēadvise' *vt* and *vi.*
rēaffirm' *vt.*
rēaffirmā'tion *n.*
rēaffor'est *vt.*
rēafforestā'tion *n.*
rēall'ocate *vt.*
rēallocā'tion *n.*
rēallot' *vt.*
rēallot'ment *n.*
rēappear' *vi.*
rēappear'ance *n.*
rēapplicā'tion *n.*
rēapply' *vi.*
rēappoint' *vt.*
rēappoint'ment *n.*
rēappor'tion *vt.*
rēappor'tionment *n.*
rēapprais'al *n.*
rēappraise' *vt.*
rēarm' *vt* and *vi.*
rēarm'ament *n.*
rēarrange' *vt.*
rēarrange'ment *n.*
rēarrest' *n* and *vt.*
rēassem'ble *vt* and *vi.*
rēassem'bly *n.*
rēassert' *vt.*
rēasser'tion *n.*
rēassess' *vt.*
rēassess'ment *n.*
rēassign' *vt.*
rēassign'ment *n.*
rēassume' *vt.*
rēassump'tion *n.*
rēattach' *vt* and *vi.*
rēattach'ment *n.*
rēattain' *vt.*
rēattempt' *vt*, *vi* and *n.*
rēawake' *vt* and *vi.*
rēawak'en *vt* and *vi.*
rēawak'ening *n.*
rēboil' *vt* and *vi.*
rēbroad'cast *vt* and *n.*
rēbuild' *vt.*
rēbur'ial *n.*
rēbur'y *vt.*
rēbutt'on *vt.*
rēcal'culate *vt.*
rēcen'tre *vt.*
rēcharge' *vt.*
rēcharge'able *adj.*
rēcheck *vt* and *vi.*
rēchrist'en *vt.*
rēcir'culate *vt* and *vi.*
rēclassificā'tion *n.*
rēclass'ify *vt.*
rēclimb' *vt.*
rēclothe' *vt.*
rēcolonisā'tion or **-z-** *n.*
rēcol'onise or **-ize** *vt.*
rēcommence' *vt* and *vi.*
rēcommence'ment *n.*
rēcommit' *vt.*
rēcommit'ment *n.*
rēcommitt'al *n.*
rēconfirm' *vt.*
rēconnect' *vt.*
rēcon'quer *vt.*

impression; to endure the test of reading; to deliver lectures; to have a certain wording: — *pa t* and *pa p* **read** (*red*). — *n* **read** (*rēd*) a spell of reading; reading matter. — *adj* **read** (*red*) versed in books; learned. — *n* **readabil'ity** (*rēd-*) or **read'ableness.** — *adj* **read'able** legible; easy to read; interesting without being of highest quality. — *adv* **read'ably.** — *n* **read'er** a person who reads or reads much; a person who reads prayers in church (see also **lay reader** under **lay**[4]); a lecturer, esp. a higher grade of university lecturer; a proof-corrector; a person who reads and reports on manuscripts for a publisher; a reading-book; a device which projects a large image of a piece of microfilm on to a screen, for reading; a document reader (*comput*). — *n* **read'ership** the post of reader in a university; the total number of readers (of a newspaper, etc.). — *adj* **read'ing** addicted to reading. — *n* perusal; study of books; public or formal recital, esp. of a bill before Parliament (see **first, second** and **third reading** below); the actual word or words that may be read in a passage of a text; the indication that can be read off from an instrument; matter for reading; an interpretation; a performer's conception of the meaning, rendering. — **read'-in** input of data to a computer or storage device; **reading age** reading ability calculated as equivalent to the average ability at a certain age; **read'ing-book** a book of exercises in reading; **read'ing-desk** a desk for holding a book or paper while it is read; a lectern; **read'ing-lamp** a lamp for reading by; **read'ing-machine** a reader for microfilm; a document reader (*comput*); **reading matter** printed material, e.g. books, magazines; **read'ing-room** a room for consultation, study or investigation of books; a room with papers, periodicals, etc.; a proof-readers' room. — *adj* **read'-only** (*comput*) referring to a type of storage device whose contents have been built in and cannot be altered by programming. — **read'-out** output unit of a computer; the retrieval of data from a computer; data from a computer, printed or registered on magnetic tape or punched paper tape, or displayed on a screen; data from a radio transmitter. — **first, second** and **third reading** the three successive formal readings of a bill before parliament, when (in Britain) it is introduced, discussed in general, and reported on by a committee; **read between the lines** to detect a meaning not expressed but implied; **read into** to find in a person's writing, words, behaviour, etc. (meanings which are not overtly stated and may not have been intended); **read off** to take as a reading from an instrument; **read out** to read aloud; to retrieve data from a computer, etc.; **read someone's mind** to guess accurately what someone is thinking; **read up (on)** to amass knowledge (of) by reading; **read-write head** (*comput*) a head in a disc drive which can retrieve data and also record it; **read-write memory** (*comput*) one which allows retrieval and input of data; **take as read** (*red*) to presume; to understand to be, and accept as, true. [O.E. *rǣdan*, to discern, read — *rǣd*, counsel.]

ready *red'i, adj* prepared; willing; inclined; dexterous; prompt; handy; at hand; immediately available; about or liable (to). — *n* (usu. with *the*) the position of a firearm ready to be fired; ready money (*slang*). — *vt* to make (usu. oneself) ready. — *adv* **read'ily** willingly; quickly and without difficulty. — *n* **read'iness.** — **ready-** or **ready-to-** used in combination to signify ready to (as in **read'y-mix, read'y-to-eat, read'y-to-sew read'y-to-wear,** etc.). — *adj* **read'y-made** made before sale, not made to order. — *n* a ready-made article, esp. a garment. — **ready money** money ready at hand; cash. — *adj* **read'y-money** paying, or for payment, in money on the spot. — **ready reckoner** a book of tables used as a calculation aid, esp. one giving the value of so many things at so much each, and interest on any sum of money from a day upwards. — *adj* **read'y-witted.** — **at the ready** (of a firearm) ready to be fired; prepared for instant action; **ready, steady, go!** words used by the starter of a race to the competitors. [O.E. (*ge*)-*rǣde*.]

Some words with **re-** prefix

rēcon'secrate *vt.*
rēconsecrā'tion *n.*
rēcontin'ue *vt* and *vi.*
rēconvene' *vt* and *vi.*
rēcross' *vt* and *vi.*

rēdeal' *vt*, *vi* and *n.*
rēdec'orate *vt.*
rēdefine' *vt.*
rēdesign' *vt.*
rēdevel'op *vt.*
rēdevel'opment *n.*
rēdi'al *vt* and *vi.*
rēdid'. See **redo**.
rēdirect' *vt.*
rēdiscount' *vt.*
rēdis'count *n.*
rēdiscov'er *vt.*
rēdiscov'ery *n.*
rēdistrib'ute *vt.*
rēdistribu'tion *n.*
rēdo' *vt*: — *pa t* **rēdid'**; *pa p* **rēdone'**.
rēdraw' *vt* and *vi.*
rēdrive' *vt.*

rē-elect' *vt.*
rē-elec'tion *n.*
rē-embark' *vt* and *vi.*
rē-embarkā'tion *n.*
rē-emerge' *vi.*
rē-emer'gence *n.*
rē-endorse' *vt.*
rē-endorse'ment *n.*
rē-engage' *vt* and *vi.*
rē-engage'ment *n.*
rē-enlist' *vt* and *vi.*
rē-enlist'ment *n.*
rē-equip' *vt* and *vi.*
rē-erect' *vt.*
rē-erec'tion *n.*
rē-estab'lish *vt.*
rē-estab'lishment *n.*
rē-examinā'tion *n.*
rē-exam'ine *vt.*
rē-export' *vt.*
rē-ex'port *n.*
rē-exportā'tion *n.*

rēfash'ion *vt.*
rēfloat' *vt.*
rēflow'er *vi.*
rēflow'ering *n.*
rēfo'cus *vt.*
rēfor'mat *vt.*
rēform'ulate *vt.*
rēframe' *vt.*
rēfreeze' *vt.*
rēfū'el *vt.*
rēfur'nish *vt* and *vi.*

rēgrade' *vt.*
rēgrind' *vt.*
rēgroup' *vt.*
rēgrowth' *n.*

rēimport' *vt.*
rēinhab'it *vt.*
rēinsert' *vt.*
rēinser'tion *n.*
rēinter'pret *vt.*
rēinterpretā'tion *n.*
rēinter'pretative *adj.*
rēintroduce' *vt.*
rēintroduc'tion *n.*
rēiss'uable *adj.*
rēiss'ue *vt* and *n.*

rēkin'dle *vt* and *vi.*

rēlet' *vt*: — *pa t* and *pa p* **rēlet'**.
rēlight' *vt* and *vi.*
rēload' *vt* and *vi.*

rē'match *n.*
rēmarr'iage *n.*
rēmarr'y *vt* and *vi.*
rēmod'el *vt.*
remort'gage *vt* and *n.*

rēname' *vt.*
rēnegō'tiable *adj.*
rēnegō'tiate *vt.*
rēnegōtiā'tion *n.*

reagent *rē-ā'jənt*, *n* a substance with characteristic reactions, used as a chemical test. — *n* **reā'gency**. [See ety. for **react**.]

real[1] *rē'əl* or *ri'əl*, *adj* actually existing; not counterfeit or assumed; true; genuine; sincere; authentic; pertaining to things fixed, such as lands or houses (*law*). — *adv* (*colloq*, *NAm* and *Scot*) really, quite. — *n* **rē'alism** the mediaeval philosophical doctrine that general terms stand for real existences (opp. to *nominalism*); the philosophical doctrine that in external perception the objects immediately known are real existences; the tendency to look to or accept things as they really are (often in their most ignoble aspect); a style in art, literature, etc. that seeks to present an unglamorised, unromanticised view of the world; literalness and precision of detail, with the effect of reality; the taking of a practical view in human problems; (of prices, wages, etc.) considered in relation to their purchasing power (*econ*). — *n* **rē'alist**. — *adj* **rēalist'ic** pertaining to the realists or to realism; lifelike. — *adv* **rēalist'ically**. — *n* **reality** (*ri-al'i-ti* or *rē-*) the state or fact of being real; that which is real and not imaginary; truth; verity; the fixed permanent nature of real property (*law*). — *adv* **rē'ally** in reality; actually; in truth. — *n* **Realtor**® or **rē'altor** (*NAm*; irreg. formed) an estate agent, esp. one who is a member of the National Association of Realtors. — *n* **rē'alty** (*law*) land, with houses, trees, minerals, etc. on it; the ownership of, or property in, lands — also (esp. in U.S.) **real estate**. — **real ale** or **beer** beer which continues to ferment and mature in the cask after brewing. — *adj* **re'al-estate** (esp. *NAm*) concerned with or dealing in property in land. — **real life** everyday life as lived by ordinary people, as opp. to glamorous fictional life; **real number** any rational or irrational number; **real presence** see under **presence**. — *adj* **real'time** (*comput*) of or relating to a system in which the processing of data occurs as it is generated. — **for real** (*slang*) in reality; serious or seriously; intended to be carried out or put into effect; **get real** (*NAm slang*; usu. in imper.) to awaken to the realities of the situation; **the real McCoy** or **Mackay** the genuine article, esp. good whisky (the expression has been variously explained); **the real thing** the genuine thing, not an imitation or a cheap substitute. [L.L. *reālis* — L. *rēs*, a thing.]

real[2] *rā-äl'* or *rē'əl*, (*hist*) *n* a former Spanish coin, one-eighth of a dollar. [Sp., — L. *rēgālis*, royal.]

realgar *ri-al'gär* or *-gər*, *n* a bright red monoclinic mineral, arsenic monosulphide. [Med. L. — Ar. *rahj-al-ghār*, powder of the mine or cave.]

realign *rē-ə-līn'*, *vt* to align afresh; to group or divide on a new basis. — *n* **realign'ment**. [**re-**.]

realise or **-ize** *rē'ə-līz*, *vt* to make real, or as if real; to bring into being or act; to accomplish; to convert into real property or money; to obtain, as a possession; to comprehend completely; to provide the drawings for an animated cartoon. — *adj* **realī'sable** or **-z-** (or *rē'*). — *n* **realīsā'tion** or **-z-** (or *-li-*). — *n* **rē'aliser** or **-z-**. — *adj* **rē'alising** or **-z-**. [Fr. *réaliser*; see ety. for **real**[1].]

realist, etc., **reality**, **really**. See under **real**[1].

realm *relm*, *n* a kingdom; a domain, province or region; a field of study or sphere of action. — *adj* **realm'less**. [O.Fr. *realme* — L. *rēgālis*, royal.]

realpolitik *rā-äl-po-lē-tēk'*, *n* practical politics based on the realities and necessities of life, rather than moral or ethical ideas. [Ger.]

real tennis. See **tennis**.

realtor, **realty**. See under **real**[1].

ream[1] *rēm*, *n* 500 sheets of paper or 20 quires; (in *pl*) a large quantity (*colloq*). — **printer's ream** 516 sheets of paper (to allow for waste). [Ar. *rizmah*, a bundle.]

ream[2] *rēm*, *vt* to enlarge the bore of. — *n* **ream'er** a rotating instrument for enlarging, shaping or finishing a bore. — **ream'ing-bit**. [App. O.E. *rȳman*, to open up, to make room — *rūm*, room.]

reanimate *rē-an'i-māt*, *vt* to restore to life; to infuse new life or spirit into. — *vi* to revive. — *n* **reanimā'tion**. [**re-**.]

reap *rēp*, *vt* to cut down (e.g. grain); to clear by cutting a crop; to derive as an advantage or reward. — *n* **reap'er** a person who reaps; a reaping-machine. —

Some words with **re-** prefix

rēnum'ber *vt*.

rēoccupā'tion *n*.
rēocc'upy *vt*.
rēoccur *vi*.
rēoffend' *vi*.
rēop'en *vt* and *vi*.
rēor'der *vt*.
rēorganisā'tion or **-z-** *n*.
rēor'ganise or **-ize** *vt*.

repack' *vt* and *vi*.
rēpā'per *vt*.
rēpeo'ple *vt*.
rēplan' *vt* and *vi*.
rēplant' *vt*.
rēpopulate *vt*.
rēpot' *vt*.
rēpott'ing *n*.
rēpro'gramme *vt*.
rēpublicā'tion *n*.
rēpub'lish *vt*.
rēpur'chase *vt* and *n*.

rēquote' *vt* and *vi*.

rēreg'ulate *vt*.
rē-roof' *vt*.
rēregulā'tion *n*.
rēroute' *vt*.

rēsay' *vt*: — *pa t* and *pa p* **rēsaid'**.

rēseal' *vt*.
rēseal'able *adj*.
rēselect' *vt*.
rēselect'ion *n*.
rēsell' *vt*: — *pa t* and *pa p* **rēsold'**.
rēsent'ence *vt*.
rēset *vt*.
rēsett'le *vt* and *vi*.
rēsett'lement *n*.
rēshape' *vt*.
rē-site' *vt*.
rēsole' *vt*.
rēspell' *vt*.
rēspray' *vt* and *n*.
rēstage' *vt*.
rēstate' *vt*.
rēstate'ment *n*.
rēstock' *vt*.
rēstring' *vt*.
rēstruc'ture *vt*.
rēstyle' *vt*.
rēsubmit' *vt*.
rēsurvey' *vt*.
rēsur'vey *n*.
rēsynchronisā'tion or **-z-** *vt*.
rēsyn'chronise or **-ize** *vt*.
rētell' *vt*: — *pa p* **rētold'**.
rētell'er *n*.

rētie' *vt*.
rētile' *vt*.
rētī'tle *vt*.
rētrain' *vt* and *vi*.
rētune' *vt*.
rēturf' *vt*.
rē-type' *vt*.

rēūnificā'tion *n*.
rēū'nify *vt*.
rēuphol'ster *vt*.
rēūs'able *adj*.
rēuse' (*-ūz'*) *vt*.
rēuse' (*-ūs'*) *n*.

rēvictual (*rē-vit'l*) *vt* and *vi*: — *pr p* **revict'ualling**; *pa t* and *pa p* **revict'ualled**.
rēvis'it *vt* and *n*.
rēvīt'alise or **-ize** *vt*.

rēwind' *vt*: — *pa t* and *pa p* **rēwound'**.
rēwire' *vt*.
rēwork' *vt*.
rēwrap' *vt*.
rēwrite' *vt*: — *pa t* **rēwrote'**; *pa p* **rēwritt'en**.
rē'write *n*.

reap'ing-hook a sickle. — **the grim reaper** (*fig*) death. [O.E. *rīpan* or *ripan*.]

rear[1] *rēr*, *n* the back or hindmost part or position, esp. of an army or fleet; a position behind; the buttocks (*euph*); a latrine (*slang*). — *adj* placed behind; hinder. — *adj* **rear'most** last of all. — *adj* **rear'ward** in or toward the rear. — *adv* backward; at the back. — **rear-ad'miral** an officer next in rank below a vice-admiral — orig. one in command of the rear; **rear'guard** the rear of an army; a body of troops protecting it. — *adj* from a defensive or losing position; from the rear, as characteristic of a rearguard. — **rear'-lamp** or **-light** a light carried at the back of a vehicle; **rear-view mirror** a mirror that shows what is behind a vehicle. — **bring up the rear** to come last (in a procession, etc.). [Aphetic for *arrear*, an old word for that which is in the rear or behind; also partly from O.Fr. *rere* (Fr. *arrière*).]

rear[2] *rēr*, *vt* to bring up; to breed and foster; to raise, cause or help to rise; to erect. — *vi* (esp. of a horse) to rise on the hindlegs. — *n* **rear'er**. [O.E. *rǣran*, to raise (causative of *rīsan*, to rise).]

reason *rē'zn*, *n* ground, support or justification for an act or belief; a motive or inducement; an underlying explanatory principle; a cause; the mind's power of drawing conclusions and determining right and truth; the exercise of this power; a premise, esp. when placed after its conclusion; sanity; conformity to what is fairly to be expected or called for; moderation. — *vi* to exercise the faculty of reason; to deduce inferences from premises; to argue; to debate. — *vt* to examine or discuss; to debate; to think out; to set forth logically; to bring by reasoning. — *adj* **rea'sonable** endowed with reason; rational; acting according to reason; agreeable to reason; just; not excessive; not expensive; moderate. — *n* **rea'sonableness**. — *adv* **rea'sonably**. — *adj* **rea'soned** argued out. — *n* **rea'soner**. — *n* **rea'soning**. — *adj* **rea'sonless**. — **by reason of** on account of; in consequence of; **it stands to reason** it is obvious, logical; **listen to reason** to listen to, and take heed of, the reasonable explanation, course of action, etc.; **pure reason** reason absolutely independent of experience; **within (or in) reason** within the bounds of what is possible, sensible, etc. [Fr. *raison* — L. *ratiō*, *-ōnis* — *rērī*, *rătus*, to think.]

reassure *rē-ə-shoo͞r'*, *vt* to give confidence to; to relieve apprehension or worry; to confirm. — *n* **reassur'ance**. — *n* **reassur'er**. — *adj* **reassur'ing**. — *adv* **reassur'ingly**. [**re-**.]

Réau. *abbrev* for Réaumur's thermometric scale.

Réaumur *rā-ō-mür*, *adj* (of a thermometer or thermometer scale) having the freezing-point of water marked 0° and boiling-point 80°. [From the French physicist, R.A.F. de *Réaumur* (1683–1757), who introduced the scale.]

re-bar *rē'-bär*, *n* a steel bar in reinforced concrete. [*re*inforcing *bar*.]

rebarbative *ri-bärb'ə-tiv*, (*literary*) *adj* repellent. [Fr. *rébarbatif* — *barbe*, beard.]

rebate[1] *ri-bāt'*, *vt* to repay a part of; to diminish by removal of a projection (*heraldry*). — *n* (or *rē'bāt*) discount; refund. — *n* **re'bater**. [Fr. *rabattre*, to beat back — pfx. *re-*, *abattre*, to abate.]

rebate[2] *rē'bāt* or *rab'it*. Same as **rabbet**.

rebbetzin *reb'ət-sən*, *n* a rabbi's wife. [Yiddish.]

rebeck or **rebec** *rē'bek*, *n* a mediaeval instrument of the viol class shaped like a mandoline, usu. with three strings. [O.Fr. *rebec* — Ar. *rebāb*, *rabāb* (change of ending unexplained).]

rebel *reb'əl*, *n* a person who rebels; a person who resents and resists authority or oppressive conditions; a person who refuses to conform to the generally accepted modes of behaviour, dress, etc. — *adj* rebellious. — *vi* (*ri-bel'*; often with *against*) to renounce the authority of the laws and government, or to take up arms and openly oppose them; to oppose any authority; to revolt; to offer opposition; to feel repugnance: — *pr p* **rebell'ing**; *pa t* and *pa p* **rebelled'**. — *n* **rebell'ion** (*-yən*) an act of rebelling; revolt. — *adj* **rebell'ious** engaged in rebellion; characteristic of a rebel or rebellion; inclined to rebel; refractory. — *adv* **rebell'iously**. — *n* **rebell'iousness**. [Fr. *rebelle* — L. *rebellis*, insurgent — pfx. *re-*, *bellum*, war.]

rebid *rē-bid'*, *vt* and *vi* to bid again, esp. (*bridge*) on the same suit as a previous bid. — *n* a renewed bid, esp. on one's former suit. [**re-**.]

rebind *rē-bīnd'*, *vt* to give a new binding to; to bind again. — *adj* **rēbound'**. [**re-**.]

rebirth *rē-bûrth'*, *n* reincarnation; revival of, e.g. an interest; spiritual renewal. — *n* **rebirth'ing** a type of psychotherapy involving the reliving of the experience of being born, in order to release anxieties, etc. [**re-**.]

rebore *rēbör'*, *vt* to bore again (the cylinder of a car engine) so as to clear it. — Also *n*. [**re-**.]

reborn *rē-börn'*, *adj* born again (q.v.).

rebound[1]. See **rebind**.

rebound[2] *ri-bownd'*, *vi* to bound back from collision; to spring back (*lit* and *fig*); to re-echo; to recover quickly after a setback. — *n* (*rē'bownd*) an act of rebounding. — **on the rebound** while reacting against a setback, disappointment, etc., esp. in love affairs; after bouncing. [Fr. *rebondir*.]

rebuff *ri-buf'*, *n* a sudden check, curb or setback; unexpected refusal or rejection; a snub or slight. — *vt* to check; to repulse or reject; to snub. [O.Fr. *rebuffe* — It. *ribuffo*, a reproof — It. *ri-* (= L. *re-*), back, *buffo*, puff.]

rebuke *ri-būk'*, *vt* to reprimand sternly. — *n* a reproach; stern reproof or reprimand. — *adj* **rebūk'able**. — *n* **rebūk'er**. — *adv* **rebūk'ingly**. [A.Fr. *rebuker* (O.Fr. *rebucher*) — pfx. *re-*, *bucher*, to strike.]

rebus *rē'bəs*, *n* an enigmatical representation of a word or name by pictures which punningly represent parts of the word, as in a puzzle or a coat of arms; such a puzzle: — *pl* **re'buses**. [L. *rēbus*, by things, abl. pl. of *rēs*, thing.]

rebut *ri-but'*, *vt* to drive back; to repel; to meet in argument or proof; to disprove; to refute: — *pr p* **rebutt'ing**; *pa t* and *pa p* **rebutt'ed**. — *n* **rebut'ment**. — *adj* **rebutt'able**. — *n* **rebutt'al**. — *n* **rebutt'er** a person, or an argument, that rebuts; a defendant's reply to a plaintiff's surrejoinder (*law*). [O.Fr. *rebo(u)ter*, *rebuter*, to repulse; see **butt**[1].]

REC *abbrev* for regional electricity company.

rec *rek*, (*colloq*) *n* a recreation ground.

rec. *abbrev* for: receipt; recipe; record.

recalcitrance *ri-kal'si-trəns*, *n* disobedience or opposition; refractoriness. — *adj* **recal'citrant** refractory; obstinate in opposition. [L. *recalcitrāre*, to kick back — *calx*, *calcis*, the heel.]

recalesce *rē-kal-es'*, *vt* to display again a state of glowing heat. — *n* **recales'cence** (*phys*) the renewed glowing of iron at a certain stage of cooling from white-heat. — *adj* **recales'cent**. [L. *re-*, again, *calēscĕre*, to grow hot.]

recall *ri-köl'*, *vt* to call back; to command to return; to bring back as by a summons; to remove from office by vote (*US*); to revoke; to call back to mind. — *n* act, power or possibility of recalling or revoking; a signal or order to return; a right of electors to dismiss an official by a vote (*US*); remembrance of things learned or experienced (esp. in the phrase **total recall**, (power of) remembering accurately in full detail). — *adj* **recall'able** capable of being recalled. [**re-**.]

recant *ri-kant'*, *vt* to retract (a statement, belief, etc.). — *vi* to revoke a former declaration; to unsay what has been said, esp. to declare one's renunciation of one's former religious belief. — *n* **recantā'tion** (*rē-*).

— *n* **recant'er** (*ri-*). [L. *recantāre*, to revoke — *cantāre*, to sing, to charm.]

recap *rē-kap'*. Short for **recapitulate** and **recapitulation.**

recapitulate *rē-kə-pit'ū-lāt, vt* to go over again the chief points of; (of an embryo) to repeat (stages in the development of the species) during embryonic development; to repeat (an earlier passage) in a musical work. — *n* **recapitūlā'tion** the act of recapitulating; summing up; the reproduction, in the developmental stages of an individual embryo, of the evolutionary stages in the life history of the race or type (*biol*); the final repetition of the subjects in sonata form after development (*mus*). — *adj* **recapit'ūlātive** or **recapit'ūlatory.** [L. *recapitulāre, -ātum* — *re-*, again, *capitulum*, heading, chapter — *caput*, head.]

recapture *rē-kap'chər, vt* to capture back (e.g. a prize from a captor); to recover by effort. — *n* the act of retaking; recovery. — *n* **recap'turer.** [**re-**.]

recast *rē-käst', vt* to cast or mould again; to reconstruct; to reassign parts in a theatrical production; to give (an actor) a different part: — *pa t* and *pa p* **recast'**. — *n* (*rē'käst* or *rē-käst'*) shaping again or afresh; that which has been shaped again or afresh. [**re-**.]

recce *rek'i*, (*mil slang*) *n* reconnaissance: — *pl* **recc'es.** — Also (esp. *air force*) **recc'ō**: — *pl* **recc'ōs.** — *vt* and *vi* **recce** to reconnoitre: — *pr p* **recc'eing;** *pa t* and *pa p* **recc'ed** or **recc'eed.**

reccy *rek'i*, (*mil slang*) *n* another spelling of **recce.** — Also *vt* and *vi*: — *pr p* **recc'ying;** *pa t* and *pa p* **recc'ied.**

recd *abbrev* for received.

recede[1] *ri-sēd', vi* to go back, go farther off, become more distant; to go or draw back (from); to grow less, decline; to bend or slope backward; to give up a claim, renounce a promise, etc. (usu. with *from*). — *adj* **reced'ing.** [L. *recēdĕre, recēssum* — *re-*, back, *cēdĕre*, to go, yield.]

re-cede or **recede**[2] *rē'sēd, vt* to cede again or back. [**re-**.]

receipt *ri-sēt', n* receiving; place of receiving; a written acknowledgment of anything received; that which is received (often in *pl*). — *vt* to mark as paid; to give a receipt for (usu. *NAm*). [O.Fr. *receite, recete* — L. *recepta*, fem. past p. of *recipĕre*, to receive, with *p* restored after L.]

receive *ri-sēv', vt* to take, get or catch, usu. more or less passively; to have given or delivered to one; to experience; to take in or on; to admit; to accept; to meet or welcome on entrance; to harbour (ideas, etc.); to bear the weight of; to experience, or learn of, and react towards; to take into the body; to buy, or deal in, (stolen goods); to be acted upon by, and transform, electrical signals. — *vi* to be a recipient; to participate in communion (*Christian relig*); to receive signals; to hold a reception of visitors. — *n* **receivabil'ity** or **receiv'ableness.** — *adj* **receiv'able.** — *adj* **received'** generally accepted. — *n* **receiv'er** a person who receives; an officer who receives taxes; a person appointed by a court to manage property under litigation, receive money, etc.; an official receiver (see below); a person who receives stolen goods (*colloq*); a vessel for receiving the products of distillation, or for containing gases (*chem*); an instrument by which electrical signals are transformed into audible or visual form, such as a telephone receiver; a receiving-set. — *n* **receiv'ership** the state of being in the control of a receiver; the office or function of a receiver. — *n* and *adj* **receiv'ing.** — **Received Standard English** or **Received English** the English generally spoken by educated British people and considered the standard of the language; **Received Pronunciation** the particular pronunciation of British English which is generally regarded as being least regionally limited, most socially acceptable, and is considered the standard; **receiv'er-general** an officer who receives revenues; **receiv'ing-house** a depot; a house where letters, etc. are left for transmission; **receiv'ing-line** a number of people standing in line formally to receive a V.I.P., guests, etc. on arrival; **receiv'ing-set** apparatus for receiving wireless communications. — **official receiver** an official appointed by the Department of Trade and Industry to manage the estate of a person, company, etc. declared bankrupt, until a trustee has been appointed. [A.Fr. *receivre* — L. *recipĕre, receptum* — *re-*, back, *capĕre*, to take.]

recency. See **recent.**

recension *ri-sen'-shən, n* a critical revision of a text; a text so revised. [L. *recēnsiō, -ōnis* — *re-*, again, *cēnsēre*, to value, assess.]

recent *rē'sənt, adj* done, made, etc. not long ago or not long past; fresh; modern; (with *cap*) of the present geological period — Post-Glacial. — *n* **rē'cency.** — *adv* **rē'cently.** — *n* **rē'centness.** [L. *recēns, recentis.*]

receptacle *ri-sep'tə-kl, n* that in which anything is or may be received or stored; the enlarged end of an axis bearing the parts of a flower or the crowded flowers of an infloresence; (in flowerless plants) a structure bearing reproductive organs, spores or gemmae. — *n* **receptibil'ity** (*ri-*). — *adj* **recept'ible.** [Ety. as for **receive.**]

reception *ri-sep'shən, n* the act, fact or manner of receiving or of being received; taking in; act or manner of taking up signals; the quality of received radio or television signals; a social function (e.g. *wedding reception*) at which guests are usu. received formally; a formal receiving, as of guests; the part of a hotel, suite of offices, etc. where visitors, guests, etc. are received; a reception room; treatment on arrival. — *n* **recep'tionist** a person employed to receive callers, hotel guests, patients, customers or the like, and make arrangements. — *adj* **recep'tive** capable of receiving; quick to receive or take in esp. ideas; pertaining to reception or receptors. — *n* **recep'tiveness** or **receptivity** (*res-ep-tiv'i-ti*). — *n* **recep'tor** an element of the nervous system adapted for reception of stimuli, a sense-organ or sensory nerve-ending; a chemical grouping on the surface of the cell to which a specific antigen may attach itself; a site in or on a cell to which a drug or hormone can become attached, stimulating a reaction inside the cell. — **reception centre** a building, etc. where people are received for immediate assistance, as in the case of drug-addicts, or victims of fire, etc.; **reception class** a class for the new intake of children at a school; **reception order** an order for the reception and detention of a person in a mental hospital; **reception room** a room for formal receptions; any public room in a house. [L. *recipĕre, receptum*, to receive.]

recess *rē-ses', n* a going back or withdrawing; remission of business; a break, interval during a school day; a holiday period during the academic year; part of a room formed by a receding of the wall; a niche or alcove; an indentation; a nook. — *vt* to make a recess in; to put into a recess. — *vi* to adjourn. — *adj* **recessed'.** — *n* **recession** (*ri-sesh'ən*) the or an act of receding; withdrawal; the state of being set back; a temporary decline in trade. — *n* **recessional** (*ri-sesh'ən-əl*) hymn sung during recession or retirement of clergy and choir after a service. — *adj* **recess'ional.** — *adj* **recessive** (*-ses'*) tending to recede; (of an ancestral character) apparently suppressed in crossbred offspring in favour of the alternative character in the other parent, though it may be transmitted to later generations (*genetics*; also *n*); (of stress) tending to move toward the beginning of the word (*linguis*). — *adv* **recess'ively.** — *n* **recess'iveness.** — **recessed arch** one arch within another. [**recede.**]

recession[1] *rē-sesh'ən*, *n* a ceding again or back. [**re-**.]

recession[2]. See under **recess**.

réchauffé *rā-shō'fā*, *n* a warmed-up dish; a fresh concoction of old material. [Fr.]

recherché *rə-sher'shā*, *adj* particularly choice; (too) far-fetched or tenuous. [Fr.]

recidivism *ri-sid'i-vizm*, *n* the habit of relapsing into crime. — *n* and *adj* **recid'ivist**. [Fr. *récidivisme* — L. *recidīvus*, falling back.]

recipe *res'i-pi*, *n* directions for making something, esp. a food or drink; a method laid down for achieving a desired end: — *pl* **rec'ipes**. [L. *recipe*, take, imper. of *recipĕre*.]

recipient *ri-sip'i-ənt*, *adj* receiving; receptive. — *n* a person who or thing which receives. — *n* **recip'ience** or **recip'iency**. [L. *recipiēns*, *-entis*, pres. p. of *recipĕre*, to receive.]

reciprocal *ri-sip'rə-kl*, *adj* acting in return; mutual; complementary; interchangeable; giving and receiving or given and received; expressing mutuality (*gram*). — *n* that which is reciprocal; the multiplier that gives unity (*math*). — *n* **reciprocality** (*-kal'i-ti*). — *adv* **recip'rocally**. — *vt* **recip'rocāte** to give and receive mutually; to requite; to interchange; to alternate. — *vi* to move backward and forward; to make a return or interchange (*colloq*). — *n* **reciprocā'tion**. — *adj* **recip'rocātive**. — *n* **recip'rocātor**. — *n* **reciprocity** (*res-i-pros'i-ti*) reciprocal action; mutual relation; concession of mutual privileges or advantages, esp. mutual tariff concessions. — **reciprocating engine** an engine in which the piston moves to and fro in a straight line. [L. *reciprocus*.]

récit *rā-sē*, *n* a narrative, esp. the narrative in a book as opposed to the dialogue; a book consisting largely of narrative; a solo part, for voice or instrument (*mus*); a principal part in a concerted piece (*mus*); a swell organ (*mus*). [Fr.]

recite *ri-sīt'*, *vt* to repeat from memory, esp. to an audience, a teacher, etc.; to enumerate; to narrate; to give (the details of). — *vi* to give a recitation; to repeat a lesson (*NAm*). — *n* **recī'tal** an act of reciting; setting forth; enumeration; narration; a public performance of music, usu. by one performer or one composer; that part of a deed which recites the circumstances (*law*). — *n* **recitation** (*res-i-tā'shən*) the or an act of reciting; a piece for declaiming; the repeating or hearing of a prepared lesson (*NAm*). — *n* **recitative** (*-tə-tēv'*) a style of song resembling speech in its succession of tones and freedom from melodic form; a passage to be sung in this manner. — *adj* in the style of recitative. — *n* **reciter** (*ri-sīt'ər*). [L. *recitāre* — *citāre*, *-ātum*, to call.]

reckless *rek'ləs*, *adj* careless; heedless of consequences; rash. — *adv* **reck'lessly**. — *n* **reck'lessness**. [Obs. *reck*, care, heed (— O.E. *reccan*, *rēcan*) and **-less**.]

reckon *rek'n* or *-ən*, *vt* to count; to calculate (often with *up*); to include (in an account); to place or class; to estimate, judge to be; to think, believe, suppose or expect. — *vi* to calculate; to judge; to go over or settle accounts (with); to concern oneself (with); to count or rely (on or upon). — *n* **reck'oner**. — *n* **reck'oning** counting; calculation; a bill; settlement of accounts; judgment. [O.E. *gerecenian*, to explain; Ger. *rechnen*.]

reclaim *ri-klām'*, *vt* to win back; to convert from evil, wildness, waste or submersion; (*rē-klām'*) to claim back. — *n* recall; possibility of reform. — *adj* **reclaim'able**. — *adv* **reclaim'ably**. — *n* **reclaim'ant** or **reclaim'er**. [O.Fr. *reclamer* — L. *reclāmāre*.]

reclamation *rek-lə-mā'shən*, *n* act of reclaiming; state of being reclaimed. [L. *reclāmātiō*, *-ōnis* — *reclāmāre* — *clāmāre*, to cry out.]

réclame *rā-kläm*, *n* the art or practice by which publicity or notoriety is secured; publicity. [Fr.]

recline *ri-klīn'*, *vt* to lay on the back; to incline or bend (properly backwards). — *vi* to lean in a recumbent position, on the back or side. — *adj* **reclī'nable**. — *adj* **reclinate** (*rek'li-nāt*) (esp. of a plant leaf or stem) bent down or back. — *n* **reclinā'tion** (*rek-li-*). — *adj* **reclīned'**. — *n* **reclī'ner** someone or something that reclines, esp. a type of easy chair with a back that can be lowered towards a horizontal position. — *adj* **reclī'ning**. [L. *reclīnāre*, *-ātum* — *clīnāre*, to bend.]

recluse *ri-kloos'*, *adj* enclosed; secluded; retired; solitary. — *n* a religious devotee who lives shut up in a cell; a person who lives retired from the world. — *n* **reclusion** (*-kloo'zhən*). — *adj* **reclu'sive** (*-siv*). [L. *reclūsus*, past p. of *reclūdĕre*, to open, in later L., shut away — *re-*, back, away, *claudĕre*.]

recognise or **-ize** *rek'əg-nīz*, *vt* to identify as known or experienced before; to show sign of knowing (a person); to see, or acknowledge, the fact of; to acknowledge (that); to acknowledge the validity of (a claim); to acknowledge the status or legality of (e.g. a government); to reward (meritorious conduct). — *adj* **recognīs'able** or **-z-** (or *rek'*). — *adv* **recognīs'ably** or **-z-** (or *rek'*). — *n* **recognisance** or **-z-** (*ri-kog'ni-zəns* or *ri-kon'i-zəns*) a legal obligation entered into before a magistrate to do, or not to do, some particular act; money pledged for the performance of such an obligation. — *n* **recogniser** or **-z-** (*rek'əg-nīz-ər* or *-nīz'ər*). — *n* **recognition** (*rek-əg-nish'ən*) act of recognising; state of being recognised; acknowledgment; acknowledgment of status; a sign, token or indication of recognising. — *adj* **recognitive** (*ri-kog'*) or **recog'nitory**. [L. *recognōscĕre* and O.Fr. *reconoistre*, *reconoiss-*; see **cognition**.]

recoil *ri-koil'*, *vi* to start back; to stagger back; to shrink in horror, etc.; to rebound; (of a gun) to kick. — *n* a starting or springing back; rebound; the kick of a gun; change in motion of a particle caused by ejection of another particle, or (sometimes) by a collision (*nuc*). — *n* **recoil'er**. — *adj* **recoil'less**. [Fr. *reculer* — *cul* — L. *cūlus*, the hind parts.]

recollect[1] *rek-əl-ekt'*, *vt* to recall to memory; to remember, esp. by an effort; to recall to the matter in hand, or to composure or resolution (usu. *reflexive*). — *adj* **recollect'ed**. — *n* **recollec'tion** (*rek-*) act or power of recollecting; a memory, reminiscence; a thing remembered. — *adj* **recollec'tive**. — *adv* **recollec'tively**. [L. *recolligĕre*, to gather again or gather up — *colligĕre*; see **collect**.]

recollect[2] or **re-collect** *rē'kol-ekt*, *vt* to gather together again. [**re-** and **collect**.]

recombine *rē-kəm-bīn'*, *vt* and *vi* to join together again. — *adj* and *n* **recombinant** (*ri-kom'bi-nənt*). — *n* **recombinā'tion**. — **recombinant DNA** genetic material produced by the combining of DNA molecules from different organisms. [**re-**.]

recommend *rek-ə-mend'*, *vt* to commend or introduce as suitable for acceptance, favour, appointment or choice; to make acceptable or attractive; to advise. — *adj* **recommend'able**. — *adv* **recommend'ably**. — *n* **recommendā'tion**. — *adj* **recommend'atory**. — *n* **recommend'er**. [**re-**.]

recompense *rek'əm-pens*, *vt* to return an equivalent to or for; to repay. — *n* return of an equivalent; that which is so returned; reward; retribution; requital. [O.Fr. *recompenser* — L. *compēnsāre*, to compensate.]

reconcile *rek'ən-sīl*, *vt* to restore or bring back to friendship or union; to bring to agreement or contentment; to pacify; to make or prove consistent. — *n* **rec'oncilability** (or *-sīl'*). — *adj* **rec'oncilable** (or *-sīl'*). — *n* **rec'oncilableness**. — *adv* **rec'oncilably** (or *-sīl'*). — *n* **rec'oncilement** (or *-sīl'*). — *n* **rec'onciler**. — *n* **reconciliā'tion** (*-sil-*). — *adj* **reconciliatory** (*-sil'i-ə-tər-i*). [L. *reconciliāre*, *-ātum* — *conciliāre*, to call together.]

recondite *ri-kon'dīt* or *rek'ən-dīt, adj* hidden; obscure; abstruse; profound. [L. *recondĕre, -itum,* to put away — *re-,* again, *condĕre,* to establish, store.]
recondition *rē-kən-dish'ən, vt* to repair and refit; to restore to original or sound condition. **[re-.]**
reconnaissance *ri-kon'i-səns, n* reconnoitring; a preliminary survey. [Fr.]
reconnoitre or (esp in N.Am.) **reconnoiter** *rek-ə-noi'tər, vt* to examine with a view to military operations or other purpose. — *vi* to make a preliminary examination. — *n* a reconnaissance. — *n* **reconnoi'trer** or (esp. in N.Am.) **reconnoi'terer.** — *n* **reconnoi'tring.** [Fr. *reconnoître* (now *reconnaître*) — L. *recognōscĕre,* to recognise.]
reconsider *rē-kon-sid'ər, vt* to consider (a decision, etc.) again, with a view to altering or reversing it. — *n* **reconsiderā'tion. [re-.]**
reconstitute *rē-kon'sti-tūt, vt* to construct anew; to reorganise; to restore the constitution of (esp. dried foods by adding water). — *adj* **reconstit'ūent** (*-kən-*). — *n* **reconstitū'tion. [re-.]**
reconstruct *rē-kən-strukt', vt* to construct again; to rebuild; to remodel; to restore (past events, esp. in crime) in imagination or theory. — *n* **reconstruc'tion** the act of reconstructing; a thing reconstructed; reorganisation; a model representing a series of sections; a theoretical representation or view of something unknown. — *adj* **reconstruc'tive.** — *n* **reconstruc'tor. [re-.]**
reconvert *rē-kən-vûrt', vt* to convert again to a former state, religion, etc. — *n* **reconver'sion. [re-.]**
record *ri-körd', vt* to set down in writing or other permanent form; to register (on an instrument, scale, etc.); to trace a curve or other representation of; to perform before a recording instrument; to make a recording of (music, etc., person speaking, etc.); to mark or indicate; to bear witness to; to put on record (an offence, etc.) without taking further measures against the offender; to register (as a vote or verdict); to celebrate. — *vi* to make a record. — *n* **record** (*rek'örd*) a register; a formal writing of any fact or proceeding; a book of such writings; past history; a witness, a memorial; memory, remembrance; anything entered in the rolls of a court, esp. the formal statement or pleadings of parties in a litigation; a curve or other representation of phenomena made by an instrument upon a surface; a disc (or formerly a cylinder) on which sound is registered for reproduction by an instrument such as a gramophone; a performance or occurrence not recorded to have been surpassed; a list of a person's criminal convictions. — *adj* not surpassed. — *adj* **record'able** (*ri-*). — *n* **record'er** (*ri-*) a person who records or registers, esp. the rolls, etc. of a city; a judge of a city or borough court of quarter-sessions; a musician, etc. who performs before a recording instrument; a recording apparatus; a fipple-flute, once called the 'English flute'. — *n* **record'ership** the office of recorder, or the time of holding it. — *n* **record'ing** a record of sound or images made for later reproduction, e.g. on magnetic tape, film or gramophone disc. — Also *adj.* — *n* **record'ist** a person who records (esp. the sound for a cinema film). — **recorded delivery** a service of the Post Office in which a record is kept of the collection and delivery of a letter, parcel, etc.; **recording angel** an angel supposed to keep a book in which every misdeed is recorded against the doer; **record office** a place where public records are kept; **rec'ord-player** an instrument for playing gramophone records, run on batteries or mains; **rec'ord-sleeve** a cardboard cover for a gramophone record. — **beat (or break) a (or the) record** to outdo the highest achievement yet recorded; **court of record** a court whose acts and proceedings are permanently recorded, and which has the authority to fine or imprison people for contempt; **for the record** (*colloq*) in order to get the facts straight; **go on record** to make a public statement; **off the record** not for publication in the press, etc. (*adj* **off'-the-record**); **on record** recorded in a document, etc.; publicly known; **public records** contemporary officially authenticated statements of acts and proceedings in public affairs, preserved in the public interest; **set the record straight** to put right a mistake or false impression. [O.Fr. *recorder* — L. *recordārī,* to call to mind, get by heart — *cor, cordis,* the heart.]
recount[1] *ri-kownt', vt* to narrate the particulars of; to detail. [O.Fr. *reconter* — *conter,* to tell.]
recount[2] or **re-count** *rē-kownt', vt* and *vi* to count over again. — *n* (*rē'kownt*) a second or new counting (e.g. of votes). **[re-.]**
recoup *ri-ko͞op', vt* to deduct or keep back (from what is claimed by a counterclaim; *law*); to make good (a loss); to indemnify, compensate. — *n* **recoup'ment.** [Fr. *recouper,* to cut back — *couper,* to cut.]
recourse *ri-körs', n* resort; a source of aid or protection; right to payment, esp. by the drawer or endorser of a bill of exchange not met by the acceptor. — **have recourse to** to go to for help, protection, etc.; **without recourse** a qualified endorsement of a bill or promissory note indicating that the endorser takes no responsibility for non-payment (*law* or *commerce*). [Fr. *recours* — L. *recursus* — *re-,* back, *currĕre, cursum,* to run.]
recover[1] *ri-kuv'ər, vt* to get or find again; to regain; to reclaim; to extract (a valuable substance) from an ore, etc., or (usable material) from waste; to retrieve; to restore; to rescue; to obtain as compensation; to obtain for injury or debt. — *vi* to regain health or any former state; to get back into position. — *n* return to a former position, as in rowing or exercise with a weapon; the position so resumed. — *n* **recoverabil'ity.** — *adj* **recov'erable.** — *n* **recov'erableness** or **recoverabil'ity.** — *n* **recov'erer.** — *n* **recov'ery** the act, fact, process, possibility or power of recovering, or state of having recovered, in any sense. [O.Fr. *recover* — L. *recuperāre*; see **recuperate.**]
re-cover or **recover**[2] *rē-kuv'ər, vt* to cover again. **[re-.]**
recpt *abbrev* for receipt.
recreate *rē-krē-āt', vt* to create again; (in the following senses *rek'ri-āt*; *rare*) to reinvigorate; to amuse by sport or pastime. — *n* **recreation** (*rē-krē-ā'shən*) the act of creating anew; a new creation; (in the following senses *rek-ri-ā'shən*), refreshment after work, etc.; pleasurable occupation of leisure time; an amusement or sport. — *adj* **recreā'tional** (*rek-*) or **rēcreā'tive** (also *rek'ri-ā-tiv*). — **recreation ground** (*rek-*) an open area for games, sports, etc. **[re-.]**
recriminate *ri-krim'in-āt, vi* to return an accusation against an accuser. — *n* **recriminā'tion** the or an act of accusing in return; countercharge. — *adj* **recrim'inative.** — *n* **recrim'inator.** — *adj* **recrim'inatory.** [L. *crīminārī,* to accuse.]
recrudesce *rē-kro͞o-des', vi* (of a disease, troubles, etc.) to break out afresh. — *n* **recrudesc'ence.** — *adj* **recrudesc'ent.** [L. *recrūdēscĕre* — *crūdus,* raw.]
recruit *ri-kro͞ot', n* a newly enlisted member, e.g. a soldier, police officer, etc. — *vi* to obtain fresh supplies; to enlist new soldiers. — *vt* to enlist or raise; to replenish. — *n* **recruit'al.** — *n* **recruit'er.** — *adj* **recruit'ing.** — *n* **recruit'ment** the act or practice of recruiting, esp. for employment; (in deafness of neural cause) the distressing exaggeration of loud sounds, while soft sounds may be audible. — **recruit'ing-ground** a place where recruits may be obtained. [Obs. Fr. *recrute,* reinforcement, prob. past p. fem. of *recroître* — L. *recrēscĕre,* to grow again.]

Rect. *abbrev* for: Rector; Rectory.
recta, rectal, etc. See **rectum.**
rectangle *rek'tang-gl* or *rek-tang'l, n* a four-sided plane figure with all its angles right angles. — *adj* **rec'tangled.** — *adj* **rectang'ūlar** of the form of a rectangle; at right angles; right-angled. — *n* **rectangūlar'ity.** — *adv* **rectang'ūlarly.** — **rectangular hyperbola** one whose asymptotes are at right angles. [L.L. *rēct(i)angulum* — L. *angulus*, an angle.]
recti. See **rectus.**
recti- *rekt'i-* or **rect-** *rekt-, combining form* denoting: right; straight. — *adj* **rectilineal** (*rek-ti-lin'i-əl*) or **rectilinear** (*-lin'i-ər*) in a straight line or lines; straight; bounded by straight lines. — *n* **rectilinearity** (*-ar'i-ti*). — *adv* **rectilin'early.** [L. *rēctus*, straight, right.]
rectify *rek'ti-fī, vt* to set right; to correct; to redress; to adjust; to purify by distillation (*chem*); to determine the length of (an arc); to change (an alternating current) to a direct current: — *pr p* **rec'tifying;** *pa t* and *pa p* **rec'tified.** — *adj* **rec'tifiable.** — *n* **rectificā'tion.** — *n* **rec'tifier** someone who rectifies; a component for rectifying an alternating current (*electr*). [Fr. *rectifier* — L.L. *rēctificāre* — *facĕre*, to make.]
rectilineal, etc. See under **recti-.**
rectitude *rek'ti-tūd, n* rightness; uprightness, literal and moral; integrity. — *adj* **rectitū'dinous** manifesting moral correctness; over-obviously righteous. [Fr., — L.L. *rēctitūdō* — L. *rēctus*, straight.]
recto *rek'tō,* (*printing*) *n* the right-hand page of an open book, the front page of a leaf (opp. to *verso*): — *pl* **rec'tōs.** [L. *rēctō* (*foliō*), on the right (leaf).]
recto- *rek'tō-, combining form* signifying of or relating to the rectum.
rector *rek'tər, n* (in the Church of England) a clergyman of a parish where the tithes would formerly have all come to him; an Episcopal clergyman with charge of a congregation in the US or Scotland; the headmaster of certain schools in Scotland; the chief elective officer of many Scottish (*Lord Rector*) and foreign universities; a college head; an ecclesiastic in charge of a congregation, a mission or a religious house, esp. the head of a Jesuit seminary (*RC*). — *n* **rec'torate** a rector's office or term of office. — *adj* **rectorial** (*-tō'ri-əl*) of a rector. — *n* an election of a Lord Rector. — *n* **rec'torship.** — *n* **rec'tory** the province or residence of a rector. [L. *rēctor, -ōris* — *regĕre, rēctum*, to rule.]
rectrix *rek'triks, n* a bird's long tail-feather, used in steering: — *pl* **rectrices** (*rek'tri-sēz* or *rek-trī'sēz*). — *adj* **rectricial** (*-trish'l*). [L. *rēctrīx, -īcis*, fem. of *rēctor*.]
rectum *rek'təm, n* the terminal part of the large intestine: — *pl* **rec'ta** or **rec'tums.** — *adj* **rec'tal.** — *adv* **rec'tally.** [L. neut. of *rēctus*, straight.]
rectus *rek'təs,* (*anat*) *n* a straight muscle: — *pl* **rec'tī.** [L., straight, direct.]
recumbent *ri-kum'bənt, adj* reclining; (of an organ, etc.) resting against the anatomical structure from which it extends. — *n* **recum'bence** or **recum'bency.** — *adv* **recum'bently.** [L. *recumbĕre* — *cubāre*, to lie down.]
recuperate *ri-kū'pər-āt, vi* to recover from an illness, etc. — *vt* to recover (a loss). — *adj* **recu'perable** recoverable. — *n* **recuperā'tion.** — *adj* **recu'perative** (*-ə-tiv*). [L. *recuperāre*, to recover.]
recur *ri-kûr', vi* to come up or come round again, or at intervals; to come back into one's mind: — *pr p* **recurr'ing** (or *-kur'*); *pa t* and *pa p* **recurred'** (*-kûrd*). — *n* **recurr'ence** (*-kur'*). — *adj* **recurr'ent** (*-kur'*) returning at intervals; running back in the opposite direction or toward the place of origin (*anat*). — *adv* **recurr'ently.** — *n* **recur'sion** (*-kûr'*) a going back, return. — *adj* (*math*) (of a formula) enabling a term in a sequence to be computed from one or more of the preceding terms. — *adj* **recur'sive** (*math*) (of a definition) consisting of rules which allow values or meaning to be determined with certainty. — **recurring decimal** a decimal fraction in which after a certain point one figure (*repeating decimal*) or a group of figures (*circulating*) is repeated to infinity. [L. *recurrĕre* — *currĕre*, to run.]
recurve *ri-kûrv', vt* and *vi* to bend back. [L. *recurvāre*.]
recusant *rek'ū-zənt* or *ri-kū'zənt, n* a person (esp. a Roman Catholic) who refused to attend the Church of England when it was legally compulsory (*hist*); a dissenter; a person who refuses, esp. to submit to authority. — Also *adj.* [L. *recūsāre* — *causa*, a cause.]
recycle *rē-sī'kl, vt* to pass again through a series of changes or treatment; (*loosely*) to remake into something different; to cause (material) to be broken down by bacteria and then reconstitute it. — *adj* **recy'clable.** [**re-.**]
red *red, adj* (*compar* **redd'er,** *superl* **redd'est**) of a colour like blood; extended to other colours more or less near red; having a red face (from shame, heat, embarrassment, etc.; communist, or supposedly communist (*derog*). — *n* the colour of blood; an object of this colour in a set of similar objects; a red pigment; red clothes; the red traffic-light, meaning 'stop'; a revolutionary or someone who favours sweeping changes, applied to socialist, communist, etc. — *vt* **redd'en** to make red. — *vi* to grow red; to blush. — *adj* **redd'ish.** — *n* **redd'ishness.** — *adj* **redd'y.** — *adv* **red'ly.** — *n* **red'ness.** — **red admiral** a common butterfly of Europe, America and Asia with reddish-banded wings; **red alert** a state of readiness for imminent crisis, e.g. war, natural disaster; **red algae** one of the great divisions of seaweeds, containing a red pigment; **red'back** (*Austr*) a poisonous spider with a red strip on its back; **red biddy** (*colloq*) a drink made of red wine and methylated spirit. — *adj* **red-blood'ed** having red blood; abounding in vitality and/or virility. — *adj* **red'brick** (**redbrick university** a general name given to a more modern type of British university, usu. one founded in the 19th or first half of the 20th century, contrasted with Oxford and Cambridge). — **red cabbage** a purplish cabbage, often used for pickling; **red'-cap** a goldfinch; military policeman (*slang*); railway porter (*NAm*); **red card** (*football*) a red-coloured card that a referee holds up to show that he is sending a player off; **red carpet** a strip of carpet put out for the highly favoured to walk on; treatment as a very important person. — *adj* **red-car'pet.** — **red cedar** a name for various species of *Cedrela* and of juniper; **red cent** a cent (formerly made of copper) considered as a very small amount (*colloq*, esp. *NAm*); a whit; **red'coat** (*hist*) a British soldier; **red corpuscle** an erythrocyte, a blood cell which carries oxygen in combination with the pigment haemoglobin, and removes carbon dioxide; **Red Crescent** the Red Cross Society in Muslim countries; **Red Cross** a red cross on a white ground, the national flag of England; the Swiss flag with colours reversed, the copyrighted symbol of an organisation (known as **the Red Cross**) for tending sick, wounded in war, etc.; **redcurr'ant** the small red berry of a shrub of the gooseberry genus. — *adj* **red'currant.** — **red deer** the common stag or hind, reddish-brown in summer; **Red Ensign** (*slang* **Red Duster**) a red flag with the Union Jack in the top left corner; **red'-eye** the rudd; poor quality whisky (*US*); an overnight aeroplane journey (*NAm slang*; also *adj*); **red face** a blushing from embarrassment or disconcertion (*adj* **red'-faced**); **red'fish** a male salmon when, or just after, spawning; any of various red-fleshed fish, of the genus *Sebastes*; **red flag** a flag used as a signal of danger, defiance, no mercy; the banner of socialism or of revolution; a socialist's song; **red giant** and

red dwarf a red star of high and low luminosity respectively; **Red Guard** a member of a strict Maoist youth movement in China, esp. active in the cultural revolution of the late 1960s. — *adj* **red'-haired**. — *adj* and *adv* **redhand'ed** in the very act, or immediately after, as if with bloody hands. — **red'-hat** a cardinal; a cardinal's hat; **red'head** a person with red hair. — *adj* **red'-headed**. — **red'-heat** the temperature at which a thing is red-hot; **red herring** a herring cured and dried, of reddish appearance; a subject introduced to divert discussion or attention (as a herring drawn across a track would throw hounds out). — *adj* **red'-hot** heated to redness; extreme; marked by extreme emotion of any kind; (of information) very recently received (*colloq*); (of a telephone line) very busy with calls (*colloq*); **red-hot poker** the plant kniphofia or *Tritoma*; **Red Indian** (often considered *offensive*) an American Indian, esp. of North America; **red lead** an oxide of lead of a fine red colour, used in paint-making — also called *minium*. — *adj* **red'-letter** marked with red letters (as holidays or saints' days were in old calendars); deserving to be so marked, special. — **red light** a rear-light; a danger-signal; the red traffic-light, meaning 'stop'; a red light in a window indicating a brothel. — *adj* **red-light'** (*colloq*) of or relating to brothels, as in *red-light district*; **red meat** dark-coloured meat, such as beef and lamb; **red mud** a type of industrial waste resulting from alumina processing, consisting of silicone oxide, iron oxide, etc.; **red mullet** see **mullet**; **red'neck** (*US*) a derogatory term for a poor white farm labourer in the south-western states. — *adj* ignorant, intolerant, narrow-minded; pertaining to or characteristic of this class of labourers. — **red pepper** see **pepper**; **red'poll** a name for two birds (*lesser* and *mealy redpoll*) similar to the linnet; an animal of a red breed of polled cattle. — *adj* **red'-polled**. — **red rag** the tongue (*slang*); a cause of infuriation (as red is said to be to a bull); **red'-rattle** a marsh-growing herb once supposed to cause grazing animals to have lice; **red salmon** any of various types of salmon with red flesh, esp. the sockeye salmon; **red sanders** a papilionaceous tree of tropical Asia, with heavy dark-red heartwood, used as a dye, etc. (see also **sandalwood**); **red'shank** a sandpiper with red legs; a Highlander or an Irishman (*colloq derog*); **red shift** a shift of lines in the spectrum toward the red, usu. considered to occur because the source of light is receding (see under **dopplerite**); **red'shirt** a follower of Garibaldi (from his dress; *hist*); a revolutionary or anarchist; **red'skin** (*derog*) a Red Indian; **red snapper** fish of the *Lutianidae* with reddish colouring, common off the east coast of America; **red snow** snow coloured by a microscopic red alga; **red spider** or **red spider mite** a spinning mite that infests leaves; **red squirrel** a squirrel of reddish-brown colour native to Europe and Asia, in Britain now rarely found outside the Scottish highlands; **red'start** (O.E. *steort*, tail) a European bird with a conspicuous chestnut-coloured tail; an American warbler, superficially similar; **red tape** rigid formality of intricate official routine (from the red tape used to bind official documents, etc.); bureaucracy. — *adj* **red'-tape**. — **red'water** a cattle disease due to a protozoan parasite in the blood, that is transmitted by ticks and destroys the red blood cells, causing red-coloured urine to be passed; **red wine** wine coloured by (red) grape skins during fermentation; **red'wing** a thrush with reddish sides below the wings; **red'wood** a species of sequoia with reddish wood much used commercially; any wood or tree yielding a red dye. — **in the red** overdrawn at the bank, in debt; **see red** to grow furious; to thirst for blood; **the Red Planet** Mars. [O.E. *rēad*.]

redact *ri-dakt'*, *vt* to edit, work into shape. — *n* **redac'tion**. — *n* **redac'tor**. — *adj* **redactō'rial** (*re-* or *rē-*). [L. *redigĕre*, *redactum*, to bring back.]

redan *ri-dan'*, (*fort*) *n* a fieldwork of two faces forming a salient. [O.Fr. *redan*—L. *re-*, *dēns*, *dentis*, a tooth.]

redd *red*, (chiefly *Scot*) *vt* to put in order, make tidy; to clear up. — *vi* to set things in order, tidy up (usu. with *up*): — *pr p* **redd'ing**; *pa t* and *pa p* **redd**. — *n* an act of redding; refuse, rubbish. — *n* **redd'er**. — *n* **redd'ing**. — **redding-up'** setting in order, tidying up. [Partly O.E. *hreddan*, to free, rescue, prob. partly from or infl. by O.E. *rǣdan*.]

redden, etc. See **red**.

reddle. See **ruddle**.

redeem *ri-dēm'*, *vt* to buy back; to act so as to settle or discharge (a burden, obligation, etc.); to recover or free by payment; to free oneself from (a promise) by fulfilment; to ransom; to rescue, deliver, free; to reclaim; to exchange (tokens, vouchers, etc.) for goods, or (bonds, shares, etc.) for cash; to pay the penalty of; to atone for; to compensate for; to put (time) to the best advantage; (of God or Christ) to deliver from sin. — *n* **redeemabil'ity**. — *adj* **redeem'able**. — *n* **redeem'ableness**. — *adv* **redeem'ably**. — *n* **redeem'er**. — *adj* **redeem'ing**. — **the Redeemer** the Saviour, Jesus Christ. [L. *redimĕre* (perh. through Fr. *rédimer*) — *red-*, back, *emĕre*, to buy.]

redemption *ri-demp'shən* or *-dem'shən*, *n* act of redeeming; atonement. — *adj* **redemp'tible**. — *adj* **redemp'tive** or **redemp'tory**. [L. *redimĕre*, *redemptum*; cf. **redeem**.]

redeploy *rē-di-ploi'*, *vt* to transfer (e.g. military forces, supplies, industrial workers) from one area to another. — Also *vi*. — *n* **redeploy'ment**. [**re-**.]

Rediffusion® *rē-di-fū'zhən*, *n* a system by which television or radio programmes are transmitted by electricity along a wire rather than by direct broadcast.

redingote *red'ing-gōt*, *n* a long double-breasted (orig. man's, later woman's) overcoat. [Fr.,—Eng. *riding-coat*.]

redivivus *red-i-vī'vəs* or *re-di-wē'wŏŏs*, (*formal* or *literary*) *adj* resuscitated; come to life again. [L.,—*red-*, again, *vivus*, alive — *vivĕre*, to be alive.]

redolent *red'ə-lənt*, *adj* fragrant; smelling (of or with); suggestive (of), imbued (with). — *n* **red'olence** or **red'olency**. — *adv* **red'olently**. [L. *redolēns*, *-entis* — *red-*, again, *olēre*, to emit smell.]

redouble *ri-dub'l*, *vt* and *vi* to double; to repeat; to increase; to double after previous doubling (*bridge*). — *n* (*rē'dub-l*) an act or fact or redoubling (as in *bridge*). — *n* **redoub'lement** (*ri-*). [**re-**.]

redoubt *ri-dowt'*, (*fort*) *n* a fieldwork enclosed on all sides, its ditch not flanked from the parapet; an inner last retreat. [Fr. *redoute* — It. *ridotto* — L.L. *reductus*, refuge — L., retired — *redūcĕre*; the *b* from confusion with next word.]

redoubtable *ri-dowt'ə-bl*, *adj* formidable; valiant. [O.Fr. *redouter*, to fear greatly — L. *re-*, back, *dubitāre*, to doubt.]

redound *ri-downd'*, *vi* to have a beneficial or detrimental effect (with *to*); to come back (to) as a result or consequence. [Fr. *rédander* — L. *redundāre* — *red-*, back, *undāre*, to surge — *unda*, a wave.]

redox *rē'doks*, *adj* of a type of chemical reaction in which one of the reagents is reduced, while another is oxidised. [*red*uction and *ox*idation.]

redress *ri-dres'*, *vt* to set right; to readjust; to remedy; to compensate. — *n* relief; reparation. — *n* **redress'er** (*ri-*). [Fr. *redresser* (see **dress**); partly from **re-** and **dress**.]

re-dress *rē'-dres*, *vt* and *vi* to dress again; to dress in different clothes. [**re-**.]

reduce *ri-dūs'*, *vt* to lessen in size, weight, number, extent, level, etc.; to weaken; to bring into a lower state; to drive into (a condition; with *to*); to change to another form; to express in other terms; to impoverish; to subdue; to bring to the metallic state; to remove oxygen from, or combine with hydrogen, or lessen the positive valency of (an atom or ion) by adding electrons; to put back into a normal condition or place, e.g. a dislocation or fracture (*surg*); to put into (writing, practice; with *to*); to bring to a lower rank (*mil*). — *vi* to resolve itself; to slim, or lessen weight or girth. — *n* **reduc'er** a means of reducing; a joint-piece for connecting pipes of varying diameter. — *n* **reducibil'ity**. — *adj* **reduc'ible** that may be reduced. — *n* **reduc'ibleness**. — *adj* **reduc'ing**. — *n* **reduc'tase** an enzyme which brings about the reduction of organic compounds. — *n* **reduction** (*-duk'shən*) the act of reducing or state of being reduced; diminution; lowering of price; subjugation; changing of numbers or quantities from one denomination to another (*arith*); a settlement of S. American Indians converted by the Jesuits to Christianity, and governed by them (*hist*). — *n* **reduc'tionism** the belief that complex data and phenomena can be explained in terms of something simpler. — *n* and *adj* **reduc'tionist**. — *adj* **reduc'tive** reducing. — *adv* **reduc'tively**. — *n* **reduc'tiveness**. — **reducing agent** (*chem*) a substance with a strong affinity for oxygen, or the like, serving to remove it from others. — **in reduced circumstances** (*euph*) impoverished; **reduce to the ranks** to demote, for misconduct, to the condition of a private soldier. [L. *redūcĕre, reductum* — *re-*, back, *dūcĕre*, to lead.]

reductio ad absurdum *ri-duk'shi-ō ad ab-sûr'dəm* or *re-do͝ok'ti-ō ad ab-so͞or'do͝om*, reduction to absurdity; the proof of a proposition by proving the falsity of its contradictory; the application of a principle so strictly that it is carried to absurd lengths. [L.]

redundant *ri-dun'dənt*, *adj* superfluous; (of workers) no longer needed and therefore dismissed; (of a word or phrase) excessive, able to be removed from the sentence, etc. without affecting meaning. — *n* **redun'dancy**. — *adv* **redun'dantly**. [L. *redundāns, -antis*, pres. p. of *redundāre*, to overflow.]

reduplicate *ri-dū'pli-kāt*, *vt* to double; to repeat. — *vi* to double; to exhibit reduplication (*gram*). — *adj* doubled; showing reduplication (*gram*); with edges turned outwards (*bot*). — *n* **reduplicā'tion** a doubling; the doubling or repetition of the initial part in a word (*gram*); the reduplicated element in a word; the combination of two rhyming, alliterative, etc. words (one of which may be a coinage for the purpose) to form one (as in *hurry-skurry, popsy-wopsy, mish-mash*). — *adj* **redū'plicātive**. [L. *reduplicāre, -ātum* — *duplicāre*, to double.]

reebok *rē'bok*, *n* a South African antelope. [Du.]

re-echo *rē-ek'ō*, *vt* to echo back; to repeat as if an echo. — *vi* to give back echoes; to resound. — *n* a re-echoing. [**re-**.]

reed *rēd*, *n* a tall stiff marsh or water grass of various kinds; a thing made (or formerly made) of a reed or reeds — an arrow, a music pipe, the vibrating tongue of an organ pipe or woodwind instrument (with or without the parts to which it is attached), a weaver's appliance for separating the warp threads and beating up the weft; thatching; a small reedlike moulding; a reed instrument; the metal reed of an organ pipe used as the plate of a capacitor for electronic amplification. — *vt* to thatch. — *adj* having a vibrating reed (*mus*); milled, ribbed. — *n* **reed'iness**. — *n* **reed'ing** the milling on the edge of a coin; a reed moulding. — *adj* **reed'y**. — **reed'-band** a band of reed instruments; **reed'bed; reed'-bird** the bobolink; **reed bunting** a European bunting which breeds in marshy places and reedbeds; **reed'-grass** a reedlike grass of various kinds (such as *Phalaris* or *Arundo*); **reed instrument** a woodwind with reed, e.g. clarinet, oboe, bassoon; **reed'mace** a tall marsh-plant of the family *Typhaceae*, resembling the bulrush; **reed'-organ** a keyboard instrument with free reeds, e.g. harmonium, or American organ; **reed'pipe** an organ pipe whose tone is produced by the vibration of a reed, the pipe acting as resonator; **reed'stop** a set of reedpipes controlled by a single organ-stop; **reed warbler** a warbler that frequents marshy places and builds its nest on reeds. — **broken reed** (*fig*) a person who is too weak or unreliable to be depended upon. [O.E. *hrēod*.]

re-educate *rē-ed'ū-kāt*, *vt* to educate again; to change a person's (esp. political) beliefs. — *n* **re-educa'tion**. — **re-education camp** a detention camp in some totalitarian states where dissidents and others are sent to be re-educated. [**re-**.]

reedy. See **reed**.

reef[1] *rēf*, *n* a chain of rocks at or near the surface of water; a shoal or bank; a gold-bearing lode or vein (orig. *Austr.*). [Du. *rif* — O.N. *rif*.]

reef[2] *rēf*, *n* a portion of a sail that may be rolled or folded up. — *vt* to reduce the exposed surface of (a sail); to gather up in a similar way. — *n* **reef'er** someone who reefs; a midshipman (*slang*); a reefing-jacket (also **reef'er-jacket**); a cigarette containing cannabis (*slang*). — *n* **reef'ing**. — **reef band** a reinforcing strip across a sail; **reef'ing-jacket** a short thick double-breasted jacket; **reef'-knot** a flat knot used in tying reef points consisting of two loops passing symmetrically through each other; **reef point** a short rope on a reef band to secure a reefed sail. [O.N. *rif*.]

reefer[1] *rē'fər*, (*slang*) *n* a refrigerated railway car, ship or van. [**refrigerator**.]

reefer[2]. See **reef**[2].

reek *rēk*, *n* a (esp. bad) smell; smoke; vapour; fume. — *vi* to emit smoke, fumes, or (esp. bad) smell; to exhale. — *adj* **reek'ing**. — *adj* **reek'y**. [O.E. *rēc*.]

reel *rēl*, *n* a cylinder, drum, spool, bobbin or frame on which thread, fishing-line, wire, cables, photographic film, or the like may be wound; a length of material so wound; a lively dance, esp. Highland or Irish; a tune for it, usu. in 4–4, sometimes in 6–8 time. — *vt* to wind on a reel; to take off by or from a reel; to draw (in) by means of a reel. — *vi* to whirl; to seem to swirl or sway; to totter; to stagger; (of line of battle) to waver; to dance a reel. — *n* **reel'er**. — *n* and *adj* **reel'ing**. — *adv* **reel'ingly**. — **reel'man** (*Austr*) the member of a surf life-saving team who operates the reel on which the line is wound. — **off the reel** (*colloq*) one after another, without interruption; **reel off** to utter rapidly and fluently; **Virginia reel** an American country-dance. [O.E. *hrēol*, but poss. partly of other origin.]

re-enact *rē-in-akt'*, *vt* to enact over again; to re-construct in action. — *n* **re-enact'ment**. [**re-**.]

re-enter *rē-en'tər*, *vt* and *vi* to enter again or in a different way. — *adj* **re-en'trant** re-entering (opp. to *salient*); reflex (*math*); returning upon itself at the ends (*electr*). — *n* a re-entering angle; a valley, depression, etc. running into a main feature; the concavity between two salients. — *n* **re-en'try** entering again, esp. of a spacecraft, entering the earth's atmosphere again; resumption of possession; the re-opening of an oil well for further drilling; a card allowing a hand to take the lead again. [**re-**.]

reeve[1] *rēv*, *vt* to pass the end of a rope through; to pass through any hole; to thread one's way through; to fasten by reeving: — *pa t* and *pa p* **reeved** or **rove**.

reeve[2] *rēv*. See **ruff**[2].

ref *ref*, (*colloq*) *n*, *vt* and *vi* short for **referee**: — *pr p* **reff'ing**; *pa t* and *pa p* **reffed**.

ref. *abbrev* for: referee; reference.

Ref. Ch. *abbrev* for Reformed Church.

refection *ri-fek'shən*, *n* refreshment or relief; a meal. — *n* **refectory** (*ri-fek'tər-i*) a dining-hall, esp. in a monastery or college. — **refectory table** a long narrow dining-table supported on two shaped pillars each set in a base. [L. *reficĕre, refectum*—*facĕre*, to make.]

refer *ri-fûr'*, *vt* to assign (to); to impute (to); to attribute (to); to bring into relation (to); to deliver, commit or submit (to); to hand over for consideration (to); to direct for information, confirmation, testimonials, or whatever is required (to); to direct the attention of (to); to direct to sit an examination again, fail. — *vi* (with *to* in all cases) to have relation or application, to relate; to direct the attention; to turn for information, confirmation, etc.; to turn, apply, or have recourse; to make mention or allusion: — *pr p* **referr'ing**; *pa t* and *pa p* **referred'**. — *adj* **referable** or **referrable** (*ref'ər-ə-bl* or *ri-fûr'-i-bl*) that may be referred or assigned. — *n* **referee** (*ref-ə-rē'*; colloq. shortening **ref**) a person to whom anything is referred; an arbitrator, umpire or judge; a person willing to provide a testimonial. — *vt* to act as referee for (a game, etc.). — *vi* to act as umpire or judge. — *n* **ref'erence** the act of referring; a submitting for information or decision; the act of submitting a dispute for investigation or decision (*law*); relation; allusion; a person or thing that is referred to; a testimonial; a person willing to provide this; a direction to a book or passage; a book or passage used for reference. — *vt* to make a reference to; to provide (a book, etc.) with references to other sources. — *adj* (of a price, point on a scale, etc.) providing a standard to which others may be referred for comparison. — *n* **referen'dum** the principle or practice of submitting a question directly to the vote of the entire electorate: — *pl* **referen'da** or **referen'dums**. — *n* **ref'erent** the object of reference or discussion; the first term in a proposition. — *adj* **referential** (*-en'shl*) containing a reference; having reference (to); used for reference. — *adv* **referen'tially**. — *n* **referr'al** an act or instance of referring or being referred, esp. to another person or organisation for e.g. consideration, treatment, etc. — **reference book** a book to be consulted on occasion, not for consecutive reading; a pass book (*SAfr*); **ref'erence-mark** a character, such as *, †, or a figure written above the line, used to refer to notes; **referred pain** pain felt in a part of the body other than its source. — **terms of reference** a guiding statement defining the scope of an investigation or similar piece of work; the scope itself. [L. *referre*, to carry back — *ferre*, to carry.]

reffo *ref'ō*, (*Austr slang*) *n* a refugee: — *pl* **reff'os**.

refill *rē-fil'*, *vt* to fill again. — *n* (*rē'fil*) a fresh fill; a duplicate, or duplicate quantity, for refilling purposes. [**re-**.]

refine *ri-fīn'*, *vt* to purify; to clarify; (usu. with *out*) to get rid of (impurities, etc.) by a purifying process; to free from coarseness, vulgarity, crudity; to make more cultured. — *vi* to become more fine, pure, subtle or cultured; to improve by adding refinement or subtlety (with *on* or *upon*). — *adj* **refined'**. — *adv* **refin'edly**. — *n* **refin'edness**. — *n* **refine'ment** act or practice of refining; state of being refined; culture in feelings, taste, and manners; an improvement; a subtlety; an excessive nicety. — *n* **refin'er**. — *n* **refin'ery** a place for refining. — *n* **refin'ing**. [L. *re-*, denoting change of state, and **fine**[1].]

refit *rē-fit'*, *vt* to fit out afresh and repair. — *vi* to undergo refitting. — *n* **re'fit, refit'ment** or **refitt'ing**. [**re-** and **fit**[1].]

reflag *rē-flag'*, *vt* to replace the national flag of (a ship) with that of a more powerful nation, so it sails under its protection; to change the country of registration of (a ship), usu. for commercial advantage: — *pr p* **reflagg'ing**; *pa t* and *pa p* **reflagged'**. [**re-**.]

reflation *rē-flā'shən*, *n* increase in the amount of currency, economic activity, etc. after deflation; a general increase, above what would normally be expected, in the spending of money. — *vt* (back-formation from *n*) **rēflate'**. — *adj* **reflā'tionary**. [**re-** and in*flation*.]

reflect *ri-flekt'*, *vt* to bend or send back or aside; to throw back after striking; to give an image of in the manner of a mirror; to express, reproduce (*fig*); to cast, shed (e.g. credit, discredit) (*fig*); to consider meditatively (that, how, etc.). — *vi* to bend or turn back or aside; to be mirrored; to meditate (on); to cast reproach or censure (on or upon); to bring harmful results. — *n* **reflect'ance** or **reflecting factor** ratio of reflected radiation to incident radiation. — *adj* **reflect'ed**. — *adj* **reflect'ing**. — *adv* **reflect'ingly**. — *n* **reflection**, also (now chiefly in scientific use) **reflexion** (*ri-flek'shən*) a turning, bending or folding aside, back, or downwards; folding upon itself; rebound; change of direction when an electromagnetic wave or sound wave strikes on a surface and is thrown back; reflected light, colour, heat, etc.; an image in a mirror; the action of the mind by which it is conscious of its own operations; attentive consideration; contemplation; a thought or utterance resulting from contemplation; censure or reproach. — *adj* **reflec'tionless**. — *adj* **reflect'ive** reflecting; reflected; meditative. — *adv* **reflect'ively**. — *n* **reflect'iveness**. — *n* **reflectiv'ity** ability to reflect rays; reflectance. — *n* **reflect'or** a reflecting surface, instrument or body; a reflecting telescope; **reflecting factor** see **reflectance** above; **reflecting microscope** one using a system of mirrors instead of lenses; **reflecting telescope** one which has a concave mirror instead of a lens or lenses. [L. *reflectĕre, reflexum* — *flectăre*, to bend.]

reflet *rə-fle'* or *rə-flā*, (Fr.) *n* an iridescent or metallic lustre. [It. *riflesso*, reflection.]

reflex *rē'fleks*, *adj* bent or turned back; reflected; reciprocal; (of an angle) more than 180°; turned back upon itself; involuntary, produced by or concerned with response from a nerve centre to a stimulus from outside; illuminated by light from another part of the same picture (*painting*); using the same valve or valves for high- and low-frequency amplification (*radio*). — *n* reflection; reflected light; a reflected image; an expression, manifestation or outward representation; an involuntary action in response to an external stimulus. — *vt* (*-fleks'*) to bend back. — *adj* **reflexed'** (*bot*) bent abruptly backward or downward. — *n* **reflexibil'ity**. — *adj* **reflex'ible**. — *adj* **reflex'ive** (*gram*) indicating that the action turns back upon the subject. — *adv* **reflex'ively**. — *n* **reflex'iveness** or **reflexiv'ity**. — *adv* **reflex'ly** (or *rē'*). — *adj* **reflexolog'ical**. — *n* **reflexol'ogy** a form of therapy for particular ailments and general stress, carried out through massage on the soles of the feet, specific areas of which are believed to relate to specific parts or organs of the body. — **reflex arc** the simplest functional unit of the nervous system, by which an impulse produces a reflex action; **reflex camera** one in which the image is reflected on to a glass screen for composing and focusing. — **reflex anal dilatation** involuntary widening of the anus on examination. [L. *reflexus*, ety. as for **reflect**.]

reflux *rē'fluks*, *n* a flowing back, an ebb; the process of boiling a liquid in a flask with a condenser attached so that the vapour condenses and flows back into the flask, avoiding loss by evaporation. — Also *vi* and *vt*. [L. *refluĕre* — *fluĕre, fluxum*, to flow; *fluxus, -ūs*, a flow.]

re-form *rē'-förm*, *vt* and *vi* to form again or in a new way. — *n* **rē-formā'tion**. — *adj* **rē-formed'**. [**re-**.]

reform *ri-förm'*, *vt* to transform; to make better; to remove defects from; to bring to a better way of life. — *vi* to abandon evil ways. — *n* amendment or transformation, esp. of a system or institution; an extension or better distribution of parliamentary representation. — *n* **reformabil'ity**. — *adj* **re-**

form'able. — *n* **reformation** (*ref-ər-mā'shən*) the act of reforming; amendment; improvement; (with *cap*) the great religious revolution of the 16th cent., which gave rise to the various evangelical or Protestant organisations of Christendom. — *n* **reform-ā'tionist**. — *adj* **reformative** (*ri-fōrm'ə-tiv*). — *adj* **reform'atory** reforming; tending to produce reform. — *n* (*US* and *Br hist*) an institution for reclaiming young delinquents. — *adj* **reformed'**. — *n* **reform'er** a person who reforms; someone who advocates political reform; (with *cap*) one of those who took part in the Reformation of the 16th cent. — *n* **reform'ism**. — *n* **reform'ist** a reformer; an advocate of (esp. moderate) reform. — **Reform flask** a salt-glazed stoneware flask made in the likeness of one of the figures connected with the 1832 parliamentary Reform Bill; **Reform Judaism** a form of Judaism, originating in the 19th cent., in which the Jewish Law is adapted so as to be relevant to contemporary life; **reform school** reformatory. [L. *refōrmāre*, *-ātum* — *fōrmāre*, to shape — *fōrma*, form.]

refract *ri-frakt'*, *vt* (of a medium) to deflect (rays of light, sound, etc., passing into it from another medium). — *adj* **refract'able**. — *adj* **refrac'ted**. — *n* **refrac'tion**. — *adj* **refrac'tive**. — *n* **refractivity** (*rē-frak-tiv'i-ti*). — *n* **rēfractom'eter** an instrument for measuring refractive indices. — *n* **refrac'tor** anything that refracts; a refracting telescope. — **refracting telescope** one in which the principal means of focusing the light is an object glass; **refraction correction** (*astron*) the correction made in the calculation of the altitude of a star, planet, etc. to allow for the refraction of its light by the earth's atmosphere; **refractive index** the ratio of the sine of the angle of incidence to that of the angle of refraction when a ray passes from one medium to another. — **angle of refraction** the angle between a refracted ray and the normal to the bounding surface; **double refraction** the separation of an incident ray of light into two refracted rays, polarised in perpendicular planes. [L. *refringĕre*, *refrāctum* — *frangĕre*, to break.]

refractory *ri-frak'tər-i*, *adj* unruly; unmanageable; perverse; resistant to ordinary treatment, stimulus, etc., esp. difficult of fusion; fire-resisting. — *n* a substance that is able to resist high temperatures, etc., used in lining furnaces, etc. — *adv* **refrac'torily**. — *n* **refrac'toriness**. [L. *refrāctārius*, stubborn.]

refrain[1] *ri-frān'*, *n* a line or phrase recurring, esp. at the end of a stanza; the music of such a line or phrase. [O.Fr. *refrain* — *refraindre* — L. *refringĕre* — *frangĕre*, to break.]

refrain[2] *ri-frān*, *vi* to keep oneself from action, forbear; to abstain (from). [O.Fr. *refrener* — *L.L. refrēnāre* — *re-*, back, *frēnum*, a bridle.]

refrangible *ri-fran'ji-bl*, *adj* that may be refracted. — *n* **refrangibil'ity** or **refran'gibleness**. [Ety. as for **refract**.]

refresh *ri-fresh'*, *vt* to make fresh again; to freshen up; to give new vigour, life, liveliness, spirit, brightness, fresh appearance, coolness, moistness, etc. to. — *vi* to take refreshment, esp. drink (*colloq*). — *n* **refresh'er** a person or thing that refreshes; a cool drink (*colloq*); a fee paid to counsel for continuing their attention to a case, esp. when adjourned; a douceur to encourage further exertions (*colloq*); a subsequent course of training or instruction to maintain or reattain one's former standard, study new developments, etc. — Also *adj*. — *adj* **refresh'ing** pleasantly cooling, energising, reviving, invigorating. — *adv* **refresh'ingly**. — *n* **refresh'ment** the act of refreshing; state of being refreshed; renewed strength or spirit; that which refreshes, esp. food or rest; (in *pl*) drink or a light meal. [O.Fr. *refrescher* — *re-*, *freis* (fem. *fresche*), fresh.]

refrigerant *ri-frij'ə-rənt*, *adj* cooling. — *n* a freezing or cooling agent. — *vt* **refrig'erāte** to freeze; to make cold; to expose to great cold (as food for preservation). — *vi* to become cold. — *n* **refrigerā'tion**. — *adj* **refrig'erative** (*-rə-tiv*). — *n* **refrig'erator** (*-rā-tər*) an apparatus or chamber for producing and maintaining a low temperature (contracted to **fridge**, esp. when in domestic use). — *adj* **refrig'eratory** (*-rə-tər-i*) cooling. [L. *refrigerāre*, *-ātum* — *re-*, denoting change of state, *frīgerāre* — *frīgus*, cold.]

refuge *ref'ūj*, *n* shelter or protection from danger or trouble; an asylum or retreat; a street island for pedestrians; recourse in difficulty. — *n* **refugee** (*ref-ū-jē'*) a person who flees for refuge to another country, esp. from religious or political persecution; a fugitive. — *n* **refugium** (*ri-fū'ji-əm*) a region that has retained earlier geographical, climatic, etc. conditions, and thus becomes a haven for older varieties of flora and fauna: — *pl* **refū'gia** (*-ji-ə*). — **house of refuge** a shelter for the destitute. [Fr., — L. *refugium* — *fugĕre*, to flee.]

refulgent *ri-ful'jənt*, *adj* casting a flood of light; radiant; beaming. — *n* **reful'gence** or **reful'gency**. [L. *refulgēns*, *-entis*, pres. p. of *refulgēre* — *re-* (intensive) and *fulgēre*, to shine.]

refund[1] *ri-* or *rē-fund'*, *vt* to repay. — *vi* to restore what was taken. — *n* **refund** (*rē'fund*). — *n* **refund'er**. — *n* **refund'ment** (*ri-*). [L. *refundĕre* — *fundĕre*, to pour.]

refund[2] *rē-fund'*, *vt* to replace (an old issue) by a new; to borrow so as to pay off (an old loan). [**re-**.]

refurbish *rē-fûr'bish*, *vt* to renovate; to brighten up, redecorate. [**re-**.]

refuse[1] *ri-fūz'*, *vt* to decline to take or accept; to renounce; to decline to give or grant; (of a horse) to decline to jump over; to fail to follow suit to (*cards*). — *vi* to make refusal. — *adj* **refus'able**. — *n* **refus'al** the act of refusing; the option of taking or refusing. — *n* **refus'er**. [Fr. *refuser* — L. *refūsum*, past p. of *refundĕre* — *fundĕre*, to pour; cf. **refund[1]**.]

refuse[2] *ref'ūs*, *n* that which is rejected or left as worthless; rubbish, waste. [Fr. *refuse*; see ety. for **refuse[1]**.]

refute *ri-fūt'*, *vt* to disprove; to deny. — *adj* **refut'able**. — *adv* **refut'ably**. — *n* **refu'tal** or **refutā'tion** (*ref-*) act of refuting; that which disproves. — *n* **refu'ter**. [L. *refūtāre*, to drive back.]

regain *ri-* or *rē-gān'*, *vt* to gain or win back; to get back to. — *n* recovery. — *adj* **regain'able**. — *n* **regain'er**. — *n* **regain'ment**. [Fr. *regaigner* (now *regagner*).]

regal *rē'gl*, *adj* royal; kingly. — *n* **regality** (*ri-gal'i-ti*) state of being regal; royalty. — *adv* **re'gally**. [L. *rēgālis* — *rēx*, a king — *regĕre*, to rule.]

regale *ri-gāl'*, *vt* to feast; to entertain with (stories, etc.; with *with*). — *n* **regale'ment**. [Fr. *régaler* — It. *regalare*, perh. — *gala*, a piece of finery.]

regalia *ri-gā'li-ə*, *npl* the insignia of royalty — crown, sceptre, etc.; insignia or special garb generally, as of the Freemasons. [L. *rēgālis*, royal, neut. sing. *-e*, pl. *-ia*.]

regard *ri-gärd'*, *vt* to look at; to observe; to heed; to consider; to esteem; to have respect or relation to. — *n* attention with interest; observation; estimation; esteem; kindly, affectionate or respectful feeling; care; consideration; repute; respect; relation; reference; (in *pl*) in messages of greeting, respectful good will. — *n* **regard'er**. — *adj* **regard'ful** heedful; respectful. — *adv* **regard'fully**. — *n* **regard'fulness**. — *prep* **regard'ing** concerning. — *adj* **regard'less** without regard to consequences; careless (of). — *adv* nevertheless, anyway; despite or without concern for the consequences. — *adv* **regard'lessly**. — *n* **regard'lessness**. — **as regards** with regard to, concerning; **in this regard** in this respect; **with regard to** concerning; so far as relates to. [Fr. *regarder* — *garder*, to keep, watch.]

regatta *ri-gat'ə*, *n* a yacht or boat race-meeting. [It. (Venetian) *regata*.]

regelation *rē-ji-lā'shən*, *n* freezing together again (as of ice melted by pressure when the pressure is released). — *vt* and *vi* **rē'gelāte.** [**re-** and L. *gelāre*, to freeze.]

regency *rē'jən-si*, *n* the office, term of office, jurisdiction or dominion of a regent; a body entrusted with vicarious government; (*specif*, with *cap*) (1) in French history, 1715–23, when Philip of Orleans was regent; (2) in English history, 1811–20, when the Prince of Wales was Prince Regent. — *adj* (also with *cap*) of, or in the style prevailing during, the French or English Regency. — *adj* **regent** ruling; invested with interim or vicarious sovereign authority. — *n* a ruler; a person invested with interim authority on behalf of another; a master or doctor who takes part in the regular duties of instruction and government in some universities. — *n* **rē'gentship.** [L. *regēns*, *-entis*, pres. p. of *regĕre*, to rule.]

regenerate *ri-jen'ər-āt*, *vt* to produce again or newly; to renew spiritually (*theol*); to put new life or energy into; to reform completely; to reproduce (a part of the body); to magnify the amplitude of an electrical output by relaying part of the power back into the input circuit (*electr*). — *vi* to undergo regeneration, to be regenerated. — *adj* (*-it* or *-āt*) regenerated, renewed; changed from a natural to a spiritual state. — *adj* **regen'erable.** — *n* **regen'eracy** (*-ə-si*). — *n* **regenerā'tion.** — *adj* **regen'erative.** — *adv* **regen'eratively.** — *n* **regen'erātor.** — *adj* **regen'eratory** (*-ə-tər-i*). [L. *regenerāre*, *-ātum*, to bring forth again — *re-*, again, *generāre*, to generate.]

regent. See under **regency.**

reggae *reg'ā* or *rā'gā*, *n* a simple, lively, strongly rhythmic rock music of the West Indies, imported into Britain by immigrants in the mid-1960s.

regicide *rej'i-sīd*, *n* the killing or killer of a king. — *adj* **regicī'dal.** [L. *rēx*, *rēgis*, a king, on the analogy of **homicide, parricide,** etc.]

regime or **régime** *rā-zhēm'*, *n* regimen; system of government; a particular government; administration. [Fr., — L. *regimen*.]

regimen *rej'i-men*, *n* course of treatment, such as (*med*) a prescribed combination of diet, exercise, drugs, etc. [L. *regimen*, *-inis* — *regĕre*, to rule.]

regiment *rej'i-mənt*, *n* a body of soldiers constituting the largest permanent unit, commanded by a colonel; a large number (*fig*). — *vt* (*rej'i-ment* or *-ment'*) to form into a regiment or regiments; to systematise, classify; to subject to excessive control. — *adj* **regimental** (*-i-ment'l*) of or belonging to a regiment. — *n* (in *pl*) the uniform of a regiment. — *n* **regimentation** (*-i-men-tā'shən*). [L.L. *regimentum* — L. *regĕre*, to rule.]

regina *ri-jī'nə*, *n* queen; (with *cap*) title of a reigning queen, abbreviated **R** in signature. [L. *rēgīna*.]

region *rē'jən*, *n* a tract of country; any area or district, esp. one characterised in some way; the larger of the two local government administrative units in Scotland (see also **district**); a realm; a portion or division, as of the body; a portion of space. — *adj* **rē'gional.** — *n* **regionalīsā'tion** or **-z-** the dividing of England (in 1972) and Scotland (in 1973) into regions for local government administration. — *vt* **re'gionalise** or **-ize.** — *n* **rē'gionalism** regional patriotism. — *n* **rē'gionalist.** — *adv* **rē'gionally.** — *adj* **rē'gionary.** — **in the region of** near; about, approximately. [A.Fr. *regiun* — L. *rĕgiō*, *-ōnis* — *regĕre*, to rule.]

régisseur *rā-zhē-sœr*, (Fr.) *n* (in a ballet company) a director.

register *rej'is-tər*, *n* a written record or official list regularly kept; the book containing such a record; a recording or indicating apparatus, such as a cash register; apparatus for regulating a draught; an organ stop or stop-knob; the set of pipes controlled by an organ stop; part of the compass of any instrument having a distinct quality of tone; the compass of an instrument or voice; the range of tones of a voice produced in a particular manner; the form of language used in certain situations, e.g. legal, technical, journalistic; exact adjustment of position, as of colours in a picture, or letterpress on opposite sides of a leaf (*printing*); a device for storing small amounts of data (*comput*). — *vt* to enter or cause to be entered in a register; to record; to indicate; to put on record; to express; to represent by bodily expression; to adjust in register; to send by registered post. — *vi* to enter one's name (esp. as a hotel guest); to correspond in register; to make an impression, reach the consciousness (*colloq*). — *adj* **reg'istered.** — *adj* **reg'istrable.** — *n* **reg'istrar** (*-trär* or *-trär'*) a person who keeps a register or official record; someone who makes an official record of births, deaths and marriages registered locally; a hospital doctor in one of the intermediate grades. — *n* **reg'istrarship** office of a registrar. — *n* **reg'istry** registration; an office or place where a register is kept. — **register office** a record-office; a registry office (see below); **Registrar-Gen'eral** an officer who superintends the registration of all births, deaths and marriages; **registration number** the combination of letters and numbers shown on a motor vehicle's number plates, by which its ownership is registered; **registry office** a registrar's office (strictly, **register office**) where births, etc. are recorded and civil marriages are celebrated. — **Registered General Nurse** (abbrev. **RGN**) a nurse who has passed the examination of the General Nursing Council for Scotland; **ship's register** a document showing the ownership of a vessel. [O.Fr. *registre* or L.L. *registrum*, for L. pl. *regesta*, things recorded — *re-*, back, *gerĕre*, to carry.]

regius *rē'ji-əs*, *adj* royal, as in **regius professor** one whose chair was founded by Henry VIII, or, in Scotland, by the Crown. [L. *rēgius* — *rēx*, king.]

reglet *reg'lit*, *n* a flat, narrow moulding (*archit*); a fillet; a strip for spacing between lines (*printing*). [Fr. *réglet*, dimin. of *règle* — L. *rēgula*, a rule.]

regnal *reg'nl*, *adj* of a reign. — *adj* **reg'nant** reigning (often after the noun, as in *queen-regnant* a reigning queen, not a *queen consort*); prevalent. [L. *rēgnālis* — *rēgnum*, a kingdom.]

regorge *ri-* or *rē-görj'*, *vt* to disgorge, regurgitate. — *vi* to gush back. [**re-** and **gorge**; or Fr. *regorger*, to overflow.]

Reg. Prof. *abbrev* for Regius Professor.

regress *rē'gres*, *n* return; reversion; backward movement. — *vi* (*ri-gres'*) to go back; to return to a former place or state; to revert. — *n* **regression** (*ri-gresh'ən*) an act of regressing; reversion; return to an earlier stage of development, as in an adult's or adolescent's behaving like a child. — *adj* **regressive** (*ri-gres'iv*) going back; reverting; returning; (of taxation) in which the rate decreases as the amount to be taxed increases. — *adv* **regress'ively.** — *n* **regress'iveness** (*ri-*). — *n* **regressiv'ity** (*rē-*). [L. *regressus* — *regredī* — *re-*, **re-** and *gradi*, to go.]

regret *ri-gret'*, *vt* to remember with sense of loss or feeling of having done wrong; to wish otherwise: — *pr p* **regrett'ing**; *pa t* and *pa p* **regrett'ed.** — *n* sorrowful wish that something had been otherwise; sorrowful feeling of loss; compunction; an intimation of regret or refusal. — *adj* **regret'ful.** — *adv* **regret'fully.** — *adj* **regrett'able** to be regretted. — *adv* **regrett'ably** in a regrettable way; I'm sorry to say, unfortunately. [O.Fr. *regreter*, *regrater*; poss. conn. with **greet**[2].]

regt *abbrev* for regiment.

regular *reg'ū-lər*, *adj* subject to a monastic rule (opp. to *secular*); governed by or according to rule, law, order, habit, custom, established practice, mode prescribed, or the ordinary course of things; placed, arranged, etc. at uniform intervals in space or time; normal; ordinary; habitual; constant; steady; uniform; periodical; duly qualified; inflected in the usual way, esp. of weak verbs (*gram*); symmetrical; having all the sides and angles equal or all faces equal, equilateral and equiangular, the same number meeting at every corner (*geom*); (of a pyramid) having a regular polygon for base and the other faces similar and equal isosceles triangles; permanent, professional or standing (*mil*; opp. to *militia*, *volunteer* and *territorial*); (of a satellite) that keeps or scarcely deviates from a circular orbit around its planet (*astron*); thorough, out-and-out. — *n* a member of a religious order who has taken the three ordinary vows; a soldier of the regular army; a regular customer; a loyal supporter of the party leader (*US politics*). — *n* **regularīsā'tion** or **-z-**. — *vt* **reg'ularise** or **-ize** to make regular. — *n* **regularity** (*-lar'i-ti*). — *adv* **reg'ularly**. — *vt* **reg'ulate** to control; to adapt or adjust continuously; to adjust by rule. — *n* **regulā'tion** act of regulating; state of being regulated; a rule or order prescribed. — *adj* prescribed by regulation. — *adj* **reg'ulātive** tending to regulate. — *n* **reg'ulātor** a person or thing that regulates; a controlling device, esp. for the speed of a clock or watch; a change in the taxation rate introduced by the Chancellor of the Exchequer between budgets to regulate the economy. — *adj* **reg'ulatory** (*-lə-tər-i*). [L. *rēgula*, a rule — *regĕre*, to rule.]

reguline. See **regulus**.

Regulo® *reg'ū-lō*, *n* a thermostatic control system for gas ovens; (with a given numeral and usu. without *cap*) one of the graded scale of temperatures on a gas oven.

regulus *reg'ū-ləs*, *n* an impure metal, an intermediate product in smelting of ores; antimony. — *adj* **reg'uline**. [L. *rēgulus*, dimin. of *rēx*, a king.]

regurgitate *ri-* or *rē-gûr'ji-tāt*, *vt* to cast out again; to pour back; to bring back into the mouth after swallowing. — *vi* to gush back. — *adj* **regur'gitant**. — *n* **regurgitā'tion**. [L.L. *regurgitāre*, *-ātum* — *re*, back, *gurges*, *gurgitis*, a gulf.]

rehab *rē'hab*, (chiefly *US*) *abbrev* for: rehabilitate; rehabilitation; rehabilitation centre.

rehabilitate *rē-hə-bil'i-tāt*, *vt* to reinstate, restore to former privileges, rights, rank, etc.; to clear the character of; to bring back into good condition, working order, prosperity; to make fit, after disablement, illness or imprisonment for earning a living or playing a part in the world; (of buildings or housing areas) to rebuild, restore to good condition. — *n* **rehabilitā'tion**. — *adj* **rehabil'itative**. — *n* **rehabil'itator**. [L.L. *rehabilitāre*, *-ātum*; see **habilitate**.]

rehash *rē-hash'*, *n* something made up of materials formerly used, esp. a restatement in different words of ideas already expressed by oneself or someone else. — Also *vt*. [**re-** and **hash[1]** (noun).]

rehear *rē-hēr'*, *vt* to hear again; to retry (a lawsuit). — *n* **rehear'ing**. [**re-**.]

rehearse *ri-hûrs'*, *vt* to repeat, say over; to enumerate; to recount, narrate in order; to perform privately for practice or trial; to practise beforehand; to train by rehearsal. — *vi* to take part in rehearsal. — *n* **rehears'al** the act of rehearsing; a performance for trial or practice. — *n* **rehears'er**. — *n* **rehears'ing**. [O.Fr. *rehercer*, *reherser* — *re-*, again, *hercer*, to harrow — *herce* — L. *hirpex*, *-icis*, a rake, a harrow.]

reheat *rē-hēt'*, *vt* to heat again. — *n* (*rē'hēt*) a device to inject fuel into the hot exhaust gases of a turbojet in order to obtain increased thrust; the use of this. — *n* **reheat'er**. [**re-**.]

rehoboam *rē-hō-bō'əm*, *n* a large liquor measure or vessel (esp. for champagne), the size of six normal bottles (approx. 156 fl.oz.). [*Rehoboam*, king of Israel.]

rehouse *rē-howz'*, *vt* to provide with new housing or premises. — *n* **rehous'ing**. [**re-**.]

rehydrate *rē-hī'drāt*, *vi* to absorb water after dehydration. — *vt* to add water to (a dehydrated substance); to enable a dehydrated person to absorb water. — *n* **rehydra'tion**. [**re-**.]

Reich *rīhh*, *n* the German state; Germany as an empire — the **First Reich** Holy Roman Empire, 962–1806, **Second Reich** under Hohenzollern emperors, 1871–1918, and **Third Reich** as a dictatorship under the Nazi regime, 1933–45. — *n* **Reichstag** (*-täg*) the lower house of the parliament of Germany during the Second Reich and the Weimar Republic; the building in which it met. [Ger., O.E. *rīce*, kingdom.]

Reichian *rīhh'i-ən*, *adj* of or pertaining to the theory or practice of Wilhelm *Reich*, Austrian-born psychiatrist (1897–1957), esp. the concept of a universal, sexually-generated life energy termed 'orgone'. — **Reichian therapy** (also without *cap*) therapy designed to release inhibited or disturbed energies by the use of massage, controlled breathing, etc. — also called **bioenerget'ics**.

reify *rē'i-fī*, *vt* to think of as a material thing; to materialise. — *n* **reification** (*-fi-kā'shən*) materialisation, turning into an object; depersonalisation (esp. in Marxist terminology). [L. *rēs*, a thing.]

reign *rān*, *n* rule, actual or nominal, of a monarch; predominating influence; time of reigning. — *vi* to be a monarch; to prevail. [O.Fr. *regne* — L. *rēgnum* — *regĕre*, to rule.]

reimburse *rē-im-bûrs'*, *vt* to repay; to pay an equivalent to for loss or expense. — *adj* **reimburs'able**. — *n* **reimburse'ment**. [L.L. *imbursāre* — *in*, in, *bursa*, purse.]

reimplant *rē-im-plänt'*, (*med*) *vt* to replace severed body tissue, esp. an organ or member, in its original site surgically. — *n* (*-im'-*) a section of the body which has been reimplanted. — *n* **reimplantā'tion**. [**re-**.]

rein *rān*, *n* the strap or either half of the strap from the bit, by which a horse is controlled; (in *pl*) a device with a similar strap for guiding a small child (also called **walking reins**); any means of curbing or governing. — *vt* to provide with reins; to govern with the rein; to restrain or control; to stop or check (with *in*). — *vi* to stop or slow up. — **draw rein** (of a horseman) to pull up; **give rein (or a free rein) to** to allow free play to; **keep a tight rein (on)** to control closely; **rein back** to make a horse step backwards by pressure on the reins; (of a horse) step backwards (also *fig*); **take the reins** to take control. [O.Fr. *rein*, *resne*, *rene* (Fr. *rêne*).]

reincarnate *rē-in-kär'nāt*, *vt* to cause to be born again in another body or form; to embody again in flesh. — *adj* reborn. — *n* **rēincarnā'tion**. — *n* **rēincarnā'tionism** belief in reincarnation of the soul. — *n* **rēincarnā'tionist**. [**re-**.]

reindeer *rān'dēr*, *n* a large heavy deer (*Rangifer*), wild and domesticated, of northern regions, antlered in both sexes, the American variety (or species) called the caribou: — *pl* **rein'deer** or **rein'deers**. — **reindeer moss** a lichen which is the winter food of the reindeer. [O.N. *hreinndȳri*, or O.N. *hreinn* and **deer**.]

reinforce *rē-in-fōrs'*, *vt* to strengthen with new force or support; to strengthen; to increase by addition. — *n* **reinforce'ment** the act of reinforcing; additional force or assistance, esp. of troops (commonly in *pl*). — **reinforced concrete** concrete strengthened by embedded steel bars or mesh. [Alteration (by 17th cent.) of obs. *renforce*, to reinforce.]

reinstate *rē-instāt'*, *vt* to instate again; to restore to or re-establish in a former station or condition. — *n* **reinstāte'ment**. [**re-**.]

reinsure *rē-in-shōōr'*, *vt* to insure against the risk undertaken by underwriting an insurance; to insure again. — *n* **reinsur'ance**. — *n* **reinsur'er**. [**re-**.]

reintegrate *rē-in'ti-grāt*, *vt* to integrate again. — *n* **reintegrā'tion**.

re-invent *rē-in-vent'*, *vt* to invent again; to recreate in a different or spurious form. — *n* **re-inven'tion**. — **re-invent the wheel** to return, usu. by a circuitous and complex process, to a simple device or method. [**re-**.]

reinvest *rē-in-vest'*, *vt* to invest again. — *n* **re-invest'ment**. [**re-**.]

reinvigorate *rē-in-vig'ər-āt*, *vt* to put new vigour into. — *n* **reinvigorā'tion**. [**re-**.]

reistafel. See **rijstafel**.

reiterate *rē-it'ər-āt*, *vt* to repeat; to repeat again and again. — *n* **reiterā'tion**. — *adj* **reit'erative**. [**re-**.]

reject *ri-jekt'*, *vt* to throw away; to discard; to refuse to accept, admit or accede to; to refuse; to renounce; (of the body) not to accept tissue, a transplanted organ, etc. from another source (*med*). — *n* (usu. *rē'jekt*) a person or thing that is rejected; an imperfect article, not accepted for export, normal sale, etc., and often offered for sale at a discount. — *adj* **rejec'table** or **reject'ible**. — *n* **rejec'tion**. — *adj* **rejec'tionist** (of a policy, attitude, etc.) rejecting or clearly inclined toward rejection of an offer, proposal or (esp. peace) plan; (*specif*) refusing to accept peace with Israel. — Also *n*. — *adj* **rejec'tive** tending to reject. — *n* **reject'or** or **reject'er**. [L. *rejicĕre*, *rejectum* — *re-*, back, *jacĕre*, to throw.]

rejig *rē-jig'* or **rejigger** *-jig'ər*, *vt* to re-equip; to change or rearrange in a new or unexpected way that is sometimes regarded as unethical (*commerce*). — *n* **re'jig**.

rejoice *ri-jois'*, *vt* to gladden. — *vi* to feel joy; to exult; to make merry. — *n* **rejoic'er**. — *n* **rejoic'ing** an instance of being joyful; expression, subject or experience of joy; (in *pl*) festivities, celebrations, merrymakings. — *adv* **rejoic'ingly**. — **rejoice in** to be happy because of; to have (*facetious*). [O.Fr. *resjoir*, *resjoiss-* (Fr. *réjouir*) — L. *re-*, *ex*, *gaudēre*, to rejoice.]

rejoin[1] *ri-join'*, *vi* (*law*) to reply to a charge or pleading, esp. to a plaintiff's replication. — *vt* to say in reply, retort. — *n* **rejoin'der** the defendant's answer to a plaintiff's replication (*law*); an answer to a reply; an answer, esp. a sharp or clever one. [O.Fr. *rejoindre*.]

rejoin[2] *ri-* or *rē-join'*, *vt* and *vi* to join again.

rejon *re-hhōn'*, (Sp.) *n* a lance with a wooden handle, used in bullfighting: — *pl* **rejo'nes**. — *n* **rejoneador** (*re-hhōn-ā-ad-ör'*) a mounted bullfighter who uses rejones: — *pl* **rejoneador'es**: — *fem* **rejoneador'a**. — *n* **rejoneo** (*re-hhōn-ā'ō*) the art of bullfighting on horseback using rejones.

rejuvenate *ri-jōō'vi-nāt*, *vt* to make young again; to restore to youthful condition or appearance, or to activity. — *vi* to rejuvenesce. — *n* **rejuvenā'tion**. — *n* **reju'venator**. — *vi* **rejuvenesce** (*-es'*) to grow young again; to recover youthful character; to undergo change in cell-contents to a different, usu. more active, character (*biol*). — *vt* to rejuvenate. — *n* **rejuvenesc'ence**. — *adj* **rejuvenesc'ent**. [**re-** and L. *juvenis*, young, *juvenēscĕre*, to become young.]

rel. *abbrev* for: related; relating; relation; relative.

relapse *ri-laps'*, *vi* to slide, sink or fall back, esp. into evil or illness; to return to a former state or practice; to backslide; to fall away. — *n* a falling back into a former bad state; the return of a disease after partial recovery. — *adj* **relapsed'**. — *n* **relap'ser**. — *adj* **relap'sing**. — **relapsing fever** an infectious disease characterised by recurrent attacks of fever with enlargement of the spleen, caused by a spirochaete transmitted by ticks and lice. [L. *relābī*, *relāpsus* — *lābī*, to slide.]

relate *ri-lāt'*, *vt* to recount, narrate, tell; to refer, bring into connection or relation. — *vi* to date back in application (*law*); to have reference or relation; to connect; to get on well (with) (often with *to*; *colloq*). — *adj* **relā'ted** narrated; connected; allied by relationship or marriage. — *n* **relā'tedness**. — *n* **relā'ter**. — *n* **relā'tion** state or mode of being related; way in which one thing is connected with another; respect, reference; a relative by birth or marriage; (in *pl*) mutual dealings; (in *pl*) sexual intercourse (*euph*); the act of relating; narrative or recital; statement; an information (*law*); a quality that can be predicated, not of a single thing, but only of two or more together (*philos*). — *adj* **relā'tional**. — *adv* **relā'tionally**. — *adj* **relā'tionless**. — *n* **relā'tionship** a state or mode of being related; an emotional or sexual affair. — *adj* **relatival** (*rel-ə-tī'vl*) pertaining to relation, esp. grammatical relation. — *adj* **rel'ative** (*rel'ə-tiv*) in or having relation; correlative; corresponding; having the same key signature (*mus*); relevant; comparative; not absolute or independent; relating, having reference (to); referring to an antecedent (*gram*). — *n* that which is relative; a relative word, esp. a relative pronoun; a person who is related by blood or marriage. — *adv* **rel'atively**. — *n* **rel'ativeness**. — *vt* and *vi* **rel'ativise** or **-ize** to make or become relative. — *n* **rel'ativism** a doctrine of relativity; the view that accepted standards of right and good vary with environment and from person to person. — *n* **rel'ativist**. — *adj* **relativis'tic** pertaining to relativity, or to relativism. — *n* **relativ'itist** someone who studies or accepts relativity. — *n* **relativ'ity** the state or fact of being relative; (in *pl*) related aspects of pay, working conditions, etc., between different jobs or the same job in different areas; a principle which asserts that only relative, not absolute, motion can be detected in the universe (Einstein's **Special Theory of Relativity**, 1905, starts from two fundamental postulates: (a) that all motion is relative, (b) that the velocity of light is always constant relative to an observer; his **General Theory of Relativity**, 1916, which embraces the Special Theory, deals with varying velocities or accelerations — whereas the Special Theory dealt with constant relative velocity, or zero acceleration — and it is much concerned with gravitation). — *n* **relator** (*ri-lā'tər*) a person who relates; a narrator; a person who lays an information before the Attorney-General, enabling him to take action (*law*). — **relational database** a computer database which can be interrogated using different or multiple criteria; **relative aperture** (in a camera) the ratio of the diameter of the lens to the focal length; **relative density** the weight of any given substance as compared with the weight of an equal bulk or volume of water or other standard substance at the same, or at standard, temperature and pressure; **relative humidity** the ratio of the amount of water vapour in the air to the amount that would saturate it at the same temperature. — **relative atomic mass** the inferred weight of an atom of an element relative to that of oxygen as 16 or, more recently, carbon-12 taken as 12; **relative molecular mass** weight of a molecule relative to that of an atom of carbon-12 taken as 12. [L. *relātus*, *-a*, *-um*, used as past p. of *referre*, to bring back — *re*, *ferre*.]

relax *ri-laks'*, *vt* and *vi* to loosen; to slacken; to make or become less close, tense, rigid, strict or severe. — *adj* **relax'ant** having the effect of relaxing. — *n* a substance having this effect. — *n* **relaxā'tion** (*ri-* or *rē-*) act of relaxing; state of being relaxed; partial remission (*law*); recreation. — *adj* **relax'ative**. — *n* **relax'in** a hormone which has a relaxing effect on the pelvic muscles, and is used to facilitate childbirth. — *adj* **relax'ing**. [L. *relaxāre*, *-ātum* — *laxus*, loose.]

relay[1] *ri-lā'*, also *rē'lā* or *rē-lā'*, *n* a supply of horses, etc., to relieve others on a journey; a relieving shift of men; a relay race; an electrically-operated switch employed to effect changes in an independent circuit; any device by which a weak electric current or other small power is used to control a strong one; a relayed programme, or act or fact of relaying it. — *vt* to place in, relieve, control, supply or transmit by relay; to rebroadcast (a programme received from another station or source). — *vi* to obtain a relay; to operate a relay: — *pa t* and *pa p* **relayed**. — **relay race** a race between teams, each person running part of the total distance. [O.Fr. *relais*, a relay of horses or dogs.]

relay² *rē-lā'*, *vt* to lay again: — *pa t* and *pa p* **rēlaid'**. [**re-**.]

rel.d. *abbrev* for relative density.

release¹ *rē-lēs'*, *vt* to grant a new lease of. [**re-**.]

release² *ri-lēs'*, *vt* to let loose; to set free; to let go; to relieve; to slacken; to undo; to remit; to surrender, convey, give up a right to (*law*); to make available, authorise sale, publication, exhibition, etc. of; to make available for public knowledge. — *n* a setting free; discharge or acquittance; remission; the giving up of a claim, conveyance; a catch for holding and releasing; authorisation to make available on a certain date; a thing made available in this way; a film, record or other recording made available for sale by its production company — esp. *new release*. — *adj* **releas'able**. — *n* **releasee'** a person to whom an estate is released. — *n* **release'ment** release. — *n* **releas'er** or (*law*) **releas'or**. [O.Fr. *relaissier* — L. *relaxāre*, to relax.]

relegate *rel'i-gāt*, *vt* to banish; to consign (to a, usu. unimportant, place or position); to remove to a lower league (*football*); to refer (to another, others) for decision or action. — *adj* **rel'egable**. — *n* **relegā'tion**. [L. *relēgāre*, *-ātum* — *re-*, away, *lēgāre*, to send.]

relent *ri-lent'*, *vi* to soften, become less severe; to give way. — *n* and *adj* **relent'ing**. — *adj* **relent'less** unrelenting; inexorable; merciless. — *adv* **relent'lessly**. — *n* **relent'lessness**. [L. *re-*, back, *lentus*, sticky, sluggish, pliant.]

relevant *rel'i-vənt*, *adj* bearing upon, or applying to, the matter in hand, pertinent; related, proportional (to); sufficient legally. — *n* **rel'evance** or **rel'evancy**. — *adv* **rel'evantly**. [L. *relevāns*, *-antis*, pres. p. of *relevāre*, to raise up, relieve; from the notion of helping; cf. **relieve**.]

reliable, reliant, etc. See under **rely**.

relic *rel'ik*, *n* that which is left after loss or decay of the rest; any personal article of a saint, or a part of the saint's body, kept in reverence as an incentive to faith and piety (*RC*); a memorial of antiquity or object of historic interest; (of e.g. a custom) a survival from the past. [Fr. *relique* — L. *reliquiae*; see **reliquiae**.]

relict *rel'ikt*, *n* an object or species surviving in a primitive form. — *adj* (*ri-likt'*) left behind; surviving; formed by removal of surrounding materials (*geol*). [L. *relictus*, *-a*, *-um*, left, past p. of *relinquěre*, to leave.]

relied. See **rely**.

relief *ri-lēf'*, *n* the lightening or removal of any burden, discomfort, evil, pressure or stress; release from a post or duty; a person who releases another by taking his or her place; that which relieves or mitigates; aid in danger, esp. deliverance from siege; assistance to the poor; fresh supply of provisions; anything that gives diversity; projection or standing out from the general surface, ground or level; a sculpture or other work of art executed in relief; appearance of standing out solidly; distinctness by contrast, esp. in outline. — *adj* providing relief in cases of overloading, distress, danger, difficulty. — *adj* **relief'less**. — **relief map** a map in which the form of the country is shown by elevations and depressions of the material used, or by the illusion of such elevations and depressions. [O.Fr. *relef* — *relever*; see **relieve**, also **relievo**.]

relieve *ri-lēv'*, *vt* to bring, give or afford relief to; to release; to release from duty by taking the place of; to ease (e.g. a burden); (*reflexive*) to urinate or to defecate; to mitigate; to raise the siege of; to set off by contrast; to break the sameness of; to bring into relief. — *adj* **reliev'able**. — *n* **reliev'er**. — *adj* **reliev'ing**. — **relieve someone of** to take from someone's possession, with or without the person's approval; to steal from someone; to free someone from (a necessity, restriction, etc.). [O.Fr. *relever* — L. *relevāre*, to lift, relieve — *levāre*, to raise.]

relievo *ri-lē'vō*, also (from It.) **rilievo** *rē-lyā'vō*, (*art*) *n* relief; a work in relief; appearance of relief: — *pl* **relie'vos** and **rilie'vi** (*-vē*).

religio- *re-lij'i-ō-*, *combining form* relating to religion or religious matters.

religion *ri-lij'ən*, *n* belief in, recognition of, or an awakened sense of, a higher unseen controlling power or powers, with the emotion and morality connected with such; rites or worship; any system of such belief or worship; devoted fidelity; monastic life. — *vt* **relig'ionise** or **-ize** to imbue with religion. — *n* **relig'ionism** religiosity; bigotry. — *n* **relig'ionist** a person attached to a religion; a bigot; someone professionally engaged in religion. — *adj* **relig'ionless**. — *adj* **religiose** (*-lij'i-ōs* or *-ōs'*) morbidly or sentimentally religious. — *n* **religiosity** (*-i-os'it-i*) spurious or sentimental religion; religious feeling. — *adj* **relig'ious** (*-əs*) of, concerned with, devoted to, or imbued with, religion; scrupulous; bound to a monastic life (*RC*); strict, very exact. — *n* a person bound by monastic vows. — *adv* **relig'iously**. — *n* **relig'iousness**. [L. *religiō*, *-ōnis* (noun), *religiōsus* (adj.), perh. conn. with *religāre*, to bind.]

reline *rē-līn'*, *vt* to mark with new lines; to renew the lining of. [**re-**.]

relinquish *ri-ling'kwish*, *vt* to give up; to let go. — *n* **relin'quishment**. [O.Fr. *relinquir*, *relinquiss-* — L. *relinquěre*, *relictum* — *re-*, *linquěre*, to leave.]

reliquary *re-lik'wə-ri*, *n* a container for holy relics. [Fr. *reliquaire*; ety. as for **relic**.]

reliquiae *ri-lik'wi-ē* or *re-lik'wi-ī*, *npl* remains, esp. fossil remains. [L. — *relinquěre*, to leave.]

relish *rel'ish*, *n* a flavour; characteristic flavour; appetising flavour; zest-giving quality; an appetiser, condiment; zestful enjoyment; gusto. — *vt* to like the taste of; to enjoy; to appreciate discriminatingly. — *adj* **rel'ishable**. [O.Fr. *reles*, *relais*, remainder — *relaisser*, to leave behind.]

relive *rē-liv'*, *vt* and *vi* to live again; to experience again.

relocate *rē-lō-kāt'*, *vt* to locate again; to move (a firm, workers, etc.) to a different area or site. — *vi* to move one's place of business or residence. — *n* **relocā'tion**. [**re-**.]

reluctance *ri-lukt'əns*, *n* unwillingness; magnetomotive force applied to whole or part of a magnetic circuit divided by the flux in it. — *adj* **reluc'tant** unwilling; resisting. — *adv* **reluct'antly**. [L. *reluctārī* — *re-*, against, *luctārī*, to struggle.]

rely *ri-lī'*, *vi* to depend confidently (on, or upon): — *pr p* **rely'ing**; *pa t* and *pa p* **relied'**. — *n* **reliabil'ity**. — *adj* **relī'able** to be relied on, trustworthy. — *n* **relī'ableness**. — *adv* **relī'ably**. — *n* **relī'ance** trust; something or someone in which one trusts. — *adj* **relī'ant**. [O.Fr. *relier* — L. *religāre*, to bind back.]

REM *rem*, *abbrev* for rapid eye movement.

rem *rem*, *n* a unit of radiation dosage, the amount which has the same effect as one rad of X-radiation. [*r*öntgen *e*quivalent *m*an or *m*ammal.]

remain *ri-mān'*, *vi* to stay or be left behind; to continue in the same place; to be left after or out of a greater number; to continue in one's possession or mind; to continue unchanged; to continue to be; to be still to be dealt with (often without subject *it*); to await. — *n* **remain'der** that which remains or is left behind after the removal of a part or after division; the residue, rest; an interest in an estate to come into effect after a certain other event happens (*legal*); right of next succession to a post or title; residue of an edition when the sale of a book has fallen off. — *vt* to sell (a book) as a remainder. — *npl* **remains'** what is left; relics; a corpse; the literary productions of one dead. [O.Fr. *remaindre* — L. *remanēre* — *re-*, back, *manēre*, to stay.]

remake *rē-māk'*, *vt* to make again or in a new way. — *n* **rē'make** a thing (e.g. a gutta golf ball) made over again from the original materials; something made again, esp. (a new version of) a film. **[re-.]**

remand *ri-mänd'*, *vt* to send back (esp. a prisoner into custody or on bail to await further evidence). — *n* the act of remanding; recommittal. — **remand centre** in England, a place of detention for persons on remand or awaiting trial; **remand home** (*formerly*) a place where young people were to be detained as punishment. — **on remand** having been remanded. [O.Fr. *remander*, or L.L. *remandāre* — *mandāre*, to order.]

remanent *rem'ən-ənt*, *adj* remaining; (of magnetism) remaining after removal of magnetising field (*phys*). — *n* **rem'anence** or **rem'anency**. [L. *remanēns*, *-entis*, pres. p. of *remanēre*.]

remark[1] *ri-märk'*, *vt* to notice; to comment (that), or say incidentally (that). — *vi* to comment, make an observation (often with *on* or *upon*). — *n* noteworthiness; observation; comment; a distinguishing mark on an engraving or etching indicating an early state of the plate. — *adj* **remark'able** noteworthy; unusual, singular, strange, distinguished. — *n* **remark'ableness**. — *adv* **remark'ably**. — *adj* **remarked'** conspicuous; (of e.g. an etching) bearing a remark. — *n* **remark'er**. [O.Fr. *remarquer* — *re-* (intensive) and *marquer*, to mark.]

remark[2] or **re-mark** *rē-märk'*, *vt* to mark again. **[re-.]**

REME *rē'mi*, *abbrev* for Royal Electrical and Mechanical Engineers.

remeasure *rē-mezh'ər*, *vt* to measure again. — *n* **remeas'urement**. **[re-.]**

remedy *rem'i-di*, *n* any means of curing a disease, redressing, counteracting or repairing any evil or loss; reparation; redress; range of tolerated variation in the weight of a coin. — *vt* to put right, repair, counteract: — *pr p* **rem'edying**; *pa t* and *pa p* **rem'edied**. — *adj* **remē'diable**. — *adv* **remē'diably**. — *adj* **remē'dial** tending or intended to remedy; of or concerning the teaching of slow-learning children. — *adv* **remē'dially**. — *adj* **rem'ediless**. [A.Fr. *remedie*, O.Fr. *remede* — L. *remedium*.]

remember *ri-mem'bər*, *vt* to keep in or recall to memory or mind; to bear in mind as something to be mentioned; to bear in mind as someone or something deserving of honour or gratitude, or as someone to be rewarded, tipped, or prayed for; to regain one's good manners after a temporary lapse (*reflexive*); to recall to the memory of another (often as a greeting). — *vi* to have the power or perform the act of memory. — *adj* **remem'berable**. — *adv* **remem'berably**. — *n* **remem'berer**. — *n* **remem'brance** memory; that which serves to bring to or keep in mind; a souvenir; the reach of memory; (in *pl*) a message of friendly greeting. — *n* **remem'brancer** an officer of exchequer responsible for collecting debts due to the Crown (**King's** or **Queen's Remembrancer**); an official representative of the City of London to Parliamentary committees, etc. — **Remembrance Sunday** the Sunday nearest to 11 November, kept in commemoration of the fallen of the two World Wars (see **Armistice Day**). [O.Fr. *remembrer* — L. *re-*, again, *memor*, mindful.]

remex *rē'meks*, (*ornithol*) *n* one of the large feathers of a bird's wing — primary or secondary: — *pl* **remiges** (*rem'i-jēz*). — *adj* **remigial** (*ri-mij'i-əl*). [L. *rēmex*, *-igis*, a rower.]

remind *ri-mīnd'*, *vt* to put in mind (of), to cause to remember. — *n* **remind'er** something which reminds. — *adj* **remind'ful**. [**re-** and **mind** (trans. verb).]

remineralise or **-ize** *rē-min'ər-əl-īz*, (*med*) *vi* (of bone) to regain depleted minerals, e.g. calcium. — *n* **remineralisā'tion** or **-z-**. **[re-.]**

reminiscence *rem-i-nis'əns*, *n* recollection; (often *pl*) an account of something remembered; the recurrence to the mind of the past. — *vi* **reminisce** (*-nis'*; back-formation) to recount reminiscences. — *adj* **reminisc'ent** suggestive, remindful; addicted to reminiscences; pertaining to reminiscence. — Also *n*. — *adj* **reminiscen'tial** (*-sen'shl*). — *adv* **reminisc'ently**. [L. *reminīscēns*, *-entis*, pres. p. of *reminīscī*, to remember.]

remise *ri-mīz'*, *n* surrender of a claim (*law*); (*rə-mēz'*) an effective second thrust after the first has missed (*fencing*). — *vt* (*ri-mīz'*) to surrender. [Fr. *remis*, *remise* — *remettre* — L. *remittĕre*, to send back, remit, relax.]

remiss *ri-mis'*, *adj* negligent, slack; lax; lacking vigour. — *adv* **remiss'ly**. — *n* **remiss'ness**. [L. *remittĕre*, *remissum*; see **remit**.]

remission *ri-mish'ən*, *n* the act of remitting; abatement; relinquishment of a claim; the lessening of a term of imprisonment; pardon; forgiveness. — *n* **remissibil'ity**. — *adj* **remiss'ible** capable of being remitted. — *adj* **remiss'ive** remitting; forgiving. **[remit.]**

remit *ri-mit'*, *vt* to relax; to refrain from exacting or inflicting; to give up; to transfer; to transmit, as money, etc.; to refer to another court, authority, etc.; to refer; to send or put back. — *vi* (esp. of pain, an illness, etc.) to abate; to relax; to desist: — *pr p* **remitt'ing**; *pa t* and *pa p* **remitt'ed**. — *n* (*rē'mit* or *ri-mit'*) reference of a case or matter to another (*law*); scope, terms of reference; a matter submitted (to a conference or other body) for consideration (*politics*, esp. *NZ*). — *n* **remit'ment** or **remitt'al** remission; reference to another court, etc. — *n* **remitt'ance** the sending of money, etc., to a distance; the sum or thing sent. — *n* **remittee** (*-ē'*) the person to whom a remittance is sent. — *adj* **remitt'ent** (of an illness) becoming less severe at intervals. — *adv* **remitt'ently**. — *n* **remitt'er** or **remitt'or** someone who makes a remittance. — **remitt'ance-man** a man dependent upon remittances from home. [L. *remittĕre*, *remissum* — *re-*, back, *mittĕre*, to send.]

remnant *rem'nənt*, *n* a fragment or a small number surviving or remaining after destruction, defection, removal, sale, etc. of the greater part; esp. a remaining piece of cloth; a surviving trace. **[remanent.]**

remonetise or **-ize** *rē-mun'ə-tīz* or *-mon'*, *vt* to re-establish as legal tender. — *n* **remonetīsā'tion** or **-z-**. **[re-.]**

remonstrance *ri-mon'strəns*, *n* a strong or formal protest, expostulation. — *adj* **remon'strant** remonstrating. — *n* someone who remonstrates. — *vi* **remonstrate** (*rem'ən-strāt*) to make a remonstrance. — *vt* to say in remonstrance. — *adv* **rem'onstratingly**. — *n* **remonstrā'tion** (*rem-ən-*). — *adj* **remon'strative** or **remon'stratory** (*-strə-tər-i*) expostulatory. — *n* **rem'onstrator**. [L. *re-*, again, *mōnstrāre*, to point out.]

remontant *ri-mon'tənt*, (*bot*) *adj* blooming more than once in the same season. — *n* a remontant plant, esp. a rose. [Fr.]

remora *rem'ə-rə*, *n* the sucking-fish, formerly believed to stop ships by attaching its sucker. [L. *rĕmŏra*, delay, hindrance — *mora*, delay.]

remoralise or **-ize** *rē-mor'əl-īz*, *vt* to restore morality to. — *n* **remoralisā'tion** or **-z-**. **[re-.]**

remorse *ri-mörs'*, *n* feeling of regret and guilt for past wrongdoing; compunction. — *adj* **remorse'ful**. — *adv* **remorse'fully**. — *n* **remorse'fulness**. — *adj* **remorse'less** without remorse; cruel; without respite. — *adv* **remorse'lessly**. — *n* **remorse'less-**

ness. [O.Fr. *remors* — L.L. *remorsus* — L. *remordēre, remorsum,* to bite again.]

remote *ri-mōt',* *adj* far removed in place, time, chain of causation or relation, resemblance or relevance; widely separated; very indirect; aloof, distant; located separately from the main processor but having a communication link with it (*comput*). — *n* an outside broadcast (*TV* and *radio*, esp. *US*); a remote control device (e.g. for a TV). — *adv* **remote'ly.** — **remote control** control of a device from a distance by the making or breaking of an electric circuit or by means of radio waves. — *adj* **remote controlled.** — **remote sensing** a method in which remote sensors are used to collect data for transmission to a central computer; observation and collection of scientific data without direct contact, esp. observation of the earth's surface from the air or from space using electromagnetic radiation. — **remote job entry** (*comput*) input of data or programs to a computer from a distant input device (e.g. a card reader). [L. *remōtus*, past p. of *removēre*; see **remove.**]

remoulade or **rémoulade** *rā-mōō-läd',* *n* a sauce made with eggs, herbs, capers, etc., or sometimes with mayonnaise, and served with fish, salad, etc. [Fr. dialect *ramolas*, horse-radish, — L. *armoracea.*]

remould *rē'mōld,* *n* a used tyre which has had a new tread vulcanised to the casing and the walls coated with rubber. — Also *vt.* — Cf. **retread.** **[re-.]**

remount *rē-mownt',* *vt* and *vi* to mount again. — *n* a fresh horse, or supply of horses. **[re-.]**

remove *ri-mōōv',* *vt* to put or take away; to transfer; to withdraw; to displace; to make away with. — *vi* to go away; to change one's home or location. — *n* removal; step or degree of remoteness or indirectness; (in some schools) an intermediate class. — *n* **removabil'ity.** — *adj* **remov'able.** — *adv* **remov'ably.** — *n* **remov'al** the act of taking away; displacing; change of place; transference; going away; change of home or location; murder (*euph*). — *adj* **removed'** remote; distant by degrees, as in descent or relationship. — *n* **remov'edness.** — *n* **remov'er** a person who or thing which removes; a person who conveys furniture from house to house. [O.Fr. *remouvoir* — L. *removēre, remōtum* — *re-*, away, *movēre*, to move.]

remuage *rə-mü-äzh'* or *-mōō-*, *n* the process of turning or shaking wine bottles so that the sediment collects at the cork end for removal. — *n* **remueur** (*rə-mü-œr'* or *-mōō-ûr'*) in wine-making, the person who turns the bottles. [Fr. — *remuer*, to move or turn.]

remunerate *ri-mū'nə-rāt,* *vt* to recompense; to pay for service rendered. — *adj* **remū'nerable.** — *n* **remūnerā'tion** recompense; reward; pay. — *adj* **remū'nerative** profitable. — *n* **remū'nerativeness.** — *n* **remū'nerātor.** — *adj* **remū'neratory** (*-ə-tər-i*) giving a recompense. [L. *remunerārī* (late *-āre*), *-ātus* — *mūnus, -ĕris*, a gift.]

renaissance *ri-nā'səns, ren'i-säns* or *-säns',* *n* a new birth, esp. of culture and learning; (with *cap*) the revival of arts and letters, the transition from the Middle Ages to the modern world. — *adj* of the Renaissance. — **Renaissance man** a man who typifies the Renaissance ideal of wide-ranging culture and learning. [Fr.; cf. **renascence.**]

renal *rē'nl,* *adj* of the kidneys. [L. *rēnālis* — *rēnēs* (sing. *rēn*, is rare), the kidneys.]

renascent *ri-nas'ənt,* also *-nās',* *adj* coming into renewed life or vitality. — *n* **renasc'ence** being born again or into new life. [L. *renāscēns*, pres. p. of *renāscī* — *nāscī*, to be born.]

rend *rend,* *vt* to tear apart with force; to split; to tear away; to disturb with a loud, piercing sound. — *vi* to become torn: — *pa t* and *pa p* **rent.** [O.E. *rendan*, to tear.]

render *ren'dər,* *vt* to give up; to give back, return, give in return; to make up; to deliver; to hand over; to give, surrender or yield; to tender or submit; to show forth; to represent or reproduce, esp. artistically; to perform; to translate; to perform or pay as a duty or service; to cause to be or become; to melt; to extract, treat or clarify by melting; to plaster with a first coat. — *adj* **ren'derable.** — *n* **ren'derer.** — *n* **ren'dering** a first coat of plaster, etc. — *n* **rendi'tion** surrender; rendering; a performance. [O.Fr. *rendre* — L.L. *rendĕre*, app. formed by influence of *prendĕre*, to take — L. *reddĕre* — *re-*, back, *dăre*, to give.]

rendezvous *rā'dā-vōō* or *ron'di-,* *n* appointed meeting-place; a meeting by appointment; a general resort; an arranged meeting, and usu. docking, of two spacecraft (*space tech*): — *pl* **rendezvous** (*-vōōz*). — *vi* to assemble at any appointed place: — *pa t* and *pa p* **rendezvoused** (*rā'dā-vōōd* or *ron'di-*). [Fr. *rendez-vous*, present yourselves — *rendre*, to render.]

rendition. See under **render.**

renegade *ren'i-gād,* *n* someone faithless to principle or party; a turncoat; esp. a Christian turned Muslim. — *vt* **renege** or **renegue** (*ri-nēg'* or *-nāg'*) to renounce; to apostatise from. — *vi* to deny (often with *on*); to refuse (often with *on*); to revoke at cards. — *n* **reneg'er** or **reneg'uer.** [L.L. *renegātus* — L. *re-*, *negāre*, to deny; partly through Sp. *renegado.*]

renew *ri-nū',* *vt* to renovate; to begin again; to repeat; to invigorate; to substitute new for; to restore; to extend (e.g. the period of a loan, validity of a lease, etc.). — *vi* to be made new; to begin again. — *adj* **renew'able.** — *n* (often in *pl*) an alternative source of energy, such as waves, wind or sun, that can be considered inexhaustible. — Also called *alternative energy* or **renewable energy.** — *n* **renew'al.** — *n* **renew'er.** — *n* **renew'ing.** **[re-** and **new** (adj.).]

reni- *ren'i-* *combining form* relating to the kidneys. **[renal.]**

reniform *ren'i-fōrm,* *adj* kidney-shaped. [L. *rēnēs* (sing. *rēn*), the kidneys, and *fōrma*, form: see **renal.**]

renin *rē'nin,* *n* a protein enzyme secreted by the kidneys into the bloodstream, where it helps to maintain the blood pressure. [L. *rēnēs* (sing. *rēn*), the kidneys.]

renminbi *ren-min-bē,* (also with *cap*) *n* the currency of the Peoples' Republic of China since 1948; a Chinese monetary unit, also called **yuan** or **renminbi yuan** (100 *fen*, 10 *jiao*). [Chin. *renmin*, the people, *bi*, money.]

rennet *ren'it,* *n* any means of curdling milk, esp. a preparation of calf's stomach. [O.E. *rinnan*, to run.]

rennin *ren'in,* *n* an enzyme found in gastric juice, which causes coagulation of milk. [*renn*et.]

renormalisation or **-z-** *rē-nör-məl-īz-ā'shən,* (*phys*) *n* a method of obtaining finite answers to calculations (rather than infinities) by redefining the parameters, esp. of mass and charge. — *vt* **renorm'alise** or **-ize** to subject to or calculate using renormalisation. **[re-.]**

renounce *ri-nowns',* *vt* to disclaim; to disown; to reject publicly and finally; to recant; to abjure. — *vi* to fail to follow suit at cards. — *n* a failure to follow suit. — *n* **renounce'ment.** — *n* **renoun'cer.** [O.Fr. *renuncer* — L. *renuntiāre* — *re-*, away, *nuntiāre, -ātum*, to announce.]

renovate *ren'ō-vāt,* *vt* to renew or make new again; to make as if new; to regenerate. — *n* **renovā'tion.** — *n* **ren'ovātor.** [L. *re-*, again, *novāre, -ātum*, to make new — *novus*, new.]

renown *ri-nown',* *n* fame. — *adj* **renowned'** famous. [O.Fr. *renoun* — L. *re-*, again, *nōmen*, a name.]

rent[1] *rent,* *n* an opening made by rending; a fissure. — Also *pa t* and *pa p* of **rend.** **[rend.]**

rent[2] *rent,* *n* periodical payment for use of another's property, esp. houses and lands; revenue. — *vt* to hold or occupy by paying rent; to let or hire out for a rent; to charge with rent. — *vi* to be let at a rent. — *n* **rentabil'ity.** — *adj* **rent'able.** — *n* **rent'al** a rent-roll; rent; annual value; something rented or hired (*US*). — *n* **rent'er** a tenant who pays rent; a person who lets out property; a distributor of commercial films to cinemas. — **rent-a-** or **rent-an-** (*facetious*) used in combination to denote (as if) rented, hired or organised for a specific occasion or purpose, instantly or artificially created, etc., as in **rent'-a-crowd, rent'-a-mob, rent'-an-army**. — **rental library** (*US*) lending-library which takes fees for books borrowed; **rent boy** a young male homosexual prostitute; **rent'-collector; rent'-day**. — *adj* and *adv* **rent'-free** without payment of rent. — **rent'-restriction** restriction of landlord's right to raise rent; **rent'-roll** list of property and rents; total income from property. — **for rent** (orig. *US*) to let. [Fr. *rente* — L. *reddita* (*pecūnia*), money paid — *redděre*, to pay.]

renunciation *ri-nun-si-ā'shən*, *n* act of renouncing; self-resignation. — *adj* **renun'ciative** or **renun'ciatory**. [L. *renūntiāre*, proclaim; see **nuncio**.]

reopen *rē-ō'pn*, *vt* and *vi* to open again; to begin again. — **reopening clause** in collective bargaining, a clause enabling any issue in a contract to be reconsidered before the contract expires (also **re-ō'pener** or **reopener clause**). [**re-**.]

reorient *rē-ö'ri-ent*, *vt* to orient again. — *vt* **re-ö'rientate** to reorient. — *n* **reörientā'tion**. [**re-**.]

rep[1] or **repp** *rep*, *n* a corded cloth used in furnishings. [Fr. *reps*.]

rep[2] *rep*, (*colloq*) *n* short for: repertory; representative; reputation.

rep[3] *rep*, (*colloq*) *n* commercial representative. — *vi* to work or act as a rep: — *pr p* **repp'ing**; *pa t* and *pa p* **repped**. — *n* **repp'ing**.

rep. *abbrev* for: report; reporter; republic.

repaid *rē-pād'*, *pa t* and *pa p* of **repay**.

repaint *rē-pānt'*, *vt* to paint again. — *n* **repaint'ing**. [**re-**.]

repair[1] *ri-pār'*, *vi* to betake oneself; to go; to resort. [O.Fr. *repairer*, to return to a haunt — L.L. *repatriāre*, to return to one's country.]

repair[2] *ri-pār'*, *vt* to mend, fix, put right (something broken, out of order or condition, etc.); to make amends for; to make good. — *n* restoration after injury, loss or deterioration; sound condition; condition in terms of soundness; a part that has been mended or made sound. — *adj* **repair'able**. — *n* **repair'er**. — *n* **reparability** (*rep-ər-ə-bil'i-ti*). — *adj* **reparable** (*rep'ər-ə-bl*) capable of being made good. — *adv* **rep'arably**. — *n* **reparā'tion** an act of making amends; compensation; fresh supply of what has been wasted; repair. — *adj* **reparative** (*ri-par'ə-tiv*). — *adj* **repar'atory**. — **repair'man** a man who does repairs, esp. on something mechanical. [O.Fr. *reparer* — L. *reparāre* — *parāre*, to prepare.]

repand *ri-pand'*, (*bot* and *zool*) *adj* slightly wavy. [L. *repandus* — *re-*, back, *pandus*, bent.]

reparable, etc. See under **repair**[2].

repartee *rep-är-tē'*, *n* a ready and witty retort; skill in making such retorts. [O.Fr. *repartie* — *repartir* — *partir*, to set out — L. *partīrī*, to divide.]

repass *rē-päs'*, *vt* and *vi* to pass again; to pass in the opposite direction. — *n* **repassage** (*rē-pas'ij*). [**re-**.]

repast *ri-päst'*, (*formal*) *n* a meal. [O.Fr. — L.L. *repastus* — L. *pascěre*, *pastum*, to feed.]

repatriate *rē-* or *ri-pāt'ri-āt*, or *-pat'*, *vt* to restore or send (someone) back to his or her own country. — *n* a repatriated person. — *n* **repatriā'tion**. [L.L. *repatriāre*, *-ātum*, to return to one's country — L. *patria*.]

repay *rē-pā'* or *ri-pā'*, *vt* to pay back; to make return for; to recompense; to pay or give in return. — *vi* to make repayment: — *pr p* **repay'ing**; *pa t* and *pa p* **repaid'**. — *adj* **repay'able** that is to be repaid; due. — *n* **repay'ment**. [**re-**.]

repeal *ri-pēl'*, *vt* to revoke; to annul. — *n* a revocation or annulment. — *adj* **repeal'able**. — *n* **repeal'er**. [O.Fr. *rapeler* — pfx. *re-*, *apeler*, to appeal.]

repeat *ri-pēt'*, *vt* to say, do, perform or go over again; to quote from memory; to say off; to recount; to say or do after another; to tell to others, divulge; to cause to recur; to reproduce. — *vi* to recur; to make repetition; to strike the last hour, quarter, etc. when required; to fire several shots without reloading; to rise so as to be tasted after swallowing; to vote (illegally) more than once (*US*). — *n* a repetition; a retracing of one's course; a passage repeated or marked for repetition (*mus*); dots or other mark directing repetition; an order for more goods of the same kind; a radio or television programme broadcast for the second, third, etc. time. — *adj* done or occurring as a repetition. — *adj* **repeat'able** able to be done again; fit to be told to others. — *adj* **repeat'ed** done, said, etc. again and again; continual. — *adv* **repeat'edly** many times repeated; again and again. — *n* **repeat'er** someone who, or that which, repeats; a decimal fraction in which the same figure (or sometimes figures) is repeated to infinity (also **repeating decimal**); a watch or clock, or a firearm, that repeats; an instrument for automatically retransmitting a message (*teleg*). — *n* and *adj* **repeat'ing**. — **repeat oneself** to say again what one has said already. [Fr. *répéter* — L. *repetěre*, *repetītum* — *re-*, again, *petěre*, to seek.]

repechage *rep'ə-shäzh*, or Fr. *rə-pesh-äzh*, (*rowing*, *fencing*, etc.) *adj* and *n* (pertaining to) a supplementary competition in which second-bests in earlier eliminating competitions get a second chance to go on to the final. [Fr. *repêchage*, a fishing out again.]

repel *ri-pel'*, *vt* to drive off or back; to repulse; to reject; to hold off; to fail to absorb or mix with; to provoke aversion in: — *pr p* **repell'ing**; *pa t* and *pa p* **repelled'**. — *n* **repell'ence** or **repell'ency**. — *adj* **repell'ent** able or tending to repel; distasteful. — *n* that which repels. — *adv* **repell'ently**. — *n* **repell'er**. — *adj* **repell'ing**. — *adv* **repell'ingly**. [L. *repellěre* — *pellěre*, to drive.]

repent[1] *ri-pent'*, *vi* to regret, or wish to have been otherwise, what one has done or left undone (with *of*); to change from past evil or misconduct; to feel contrition. — *vt* to regret, or feel contrition for (an action). — *n* **repent'ance**. — *adj* **repent'ant** experiencing or expressing repentance. — *adv* **repent'antly**. — *n* **repent'er**. [O.Fr. *repentir* — L. *paenitēre*, to cause to repent.]

repent[2] *rē'pənt*, (*bot*) *adj* lying on the ground and rooting. [L. *repēns*, *-entis*, pres. p. of *repěre*, to creep.]

repercussion *rē-pər-kush'ən*, *n* driving back; reverberation; echo; reflection; a return stroke, reaction or consequence. — *adj* **repercussive** (*-kus'iv*). [L. *repercutěre*, *-cussum* — *re-*, *per*, *quatěre*, to strike.]

repertory *rep'ər-tər-i*, *n* a stock of pieces that a person or company is prepared to perform; repertory theatre or company. — Also *adj*. — *n* **repertoire** (*rep'ər-twär*) performer's or company's repertory; the whole range of things used or available for a certain activity or practice; a full set of the codes and instructions which a computer can accept and execute (*comput*). — **repertory theatre** a theatre with a repertoire of plays and a company of actors, called a **repertory company**. [L.L. *repertōrium* — L. *reperīre*, to find again — *parěre*, to bring forth.]

repetend *rep'i-tend* or *rep-i-tend'*, *n* the figure(s) that recur(s) in a recurring decimal number (*math*); a recurring note, word, refrain, etc.; anything that recurs or is repeated. — *adj* to be repeated. [L. *repetendum*, that which is to be repeated — L. *repetere*, to repeat.]

répétiteur *rā-pā-tē-tœr'*, *n* a coach, tutor who rehearses opera singers, etc. [Fr.; cf. **repeat**.]

repetition *rep-i-tish'ən*, *n* the act of repeating; recital from memory; a thing repeated; power of repeating a note promptly. — *adj* **repetitious** (*-tish'əs*) or **repetitive** (*ri-pet'i-tiv*) iterative; overinclined to repetition. — *adv* **repeti'tiously** or **repet'itively**. — *n* **repeti'tiousness** or **repet'itiveness**. — **repetitive strain injury** inflammation of the tendons and joints of the hands and lower arms, caused by repeated performance of identical manual operations. [L. *repetěre*; see **repeat**.]

rephrase *rē-frāz'*, *vt* to put in different words, usu. so as to make more understandable, acceptable, etc. [**re-**.]

repine *ri-pīn'*, *vi* to fret (with *at* or *against*); to feel discontent. — *n* and *adj* **repīn'ing**. [App. from **pine**[2].]

replace *ri-* or *rē-plās'*, *vt* to put back; to provide a substitute for; to take the place of, supplant. — *adj* **replace'able**. — *n* **replace'ment** an act of replacing; a person or thing that takes the place of another. — *n* **replac'er** a substitute. — **replaceable hydrogen** hydrogen atoms that can be replaced in an acid by metals to form salts. [**re-**.]

replay *rē-plā'*, *vt* to play again (a game, match, record, recording, etc.) — *n* (*rē'plā*) a game, match, played again; a recording played again, esp. (also **action replay**) of a part of a broadcast game or match, often in slow motion. [**re-**.]

replenish *ri-plen'ish*, *vt* to fill again; to fill completely; to stock abundantly; to people. — *n* **replen'isher**. — *n* **replen'ishment**. [O.Fr. *replenir*, *-iss-*, from *replein*, full — L. *re-*, again, *plēnus*, full.]

replete *ri-plēt'*, *adj* full; filled to satiety; abounding (with *with*). — *n* **replete'ness** or **replē'tion**. [L. *replētus*, past p. of *replēre* — *plēre*, to fill.]

replevy *ri-plev'i*, (*law*) *vt* to recover, or restore to the owner (goods distrained) upon pledge to try the right in legal proceedings. — *adj* **replev'iable** or **replev'isable** (*-i-səb-l*). — *n* **replev'in** replevying; a writ or action in such a case. [O.Fr. *replevir* — *plevir*, to pledge.]

replica *rep'li-kə*, *n* a duplicate, properly one by the original artist; a facsimile. [It., — L. *replicāre*, to repeat.]

replicate *rep'li-kāt*, *vt* to make a replica of; to repeat; to fold back. — *vi* (of molecules of living material) to reproduce molecules identical with themselves. — *n* (*mus*) a tone one or more octaves from a given tone. — *adj* folded back. — *n* **replicā'tion** the plaintiff's answer to the defendant's plea (*law*); a repetition of an experiment, procedure, etc.; doubling back; copy, reproduction. [L. *replicāre*, *-ātum*, to fold back — *plicāre*, to fold.]

reply *ri-plī'*, *vt* to say in answer. — *vi* to answer; to respond in action, e.g. by returning gunfire; to echo; to answer a defendant's plea: — *pr p* **reply'ing**; *pa t* and *pa p* **replied'**. — *n* an answer, response. — *n* **replī'er**. [O.Fr. *replier* — L. *replicāre*; see **replicate**.]

repo *rē'pō*, (*colloq*) *n* short for **repossession**: — *pl* **rē'pōs**.

repoint *rē-point'*, *vt* to repair (stone or brickwork) by renewing the mortar, etc. [**re-**.]

répondez s'il vous plaît *rā-pɔ̃-dā sēl vo͞o ple*, or *abbrev* **RSVP** (Fr.) please answer (this invitation).

report *ri-pört'*, *vt* to bring back, as an answer, news, or account of anything; to give an account of, esp. a formal, official or requested account; to state in such an account; to relate; to circulate publicly; to transmit as having been said, done or observed; to write down or take notes of, esp. for a newspaper or radio or television programme; to lay a charge against; (*reflexive*) to make personal announcement of the presence and readiness of. — *vi* to make a statement; to write an account of occurrences; to make a formal report; to report oneself; to act as a reporter. — *n* a statement of facts; a formal or official statement, e.g. of results of an investigation or matter referred; a statement on a school pupil's work and behaviour, etc.; an account of a matter of news, esp. the words of a speech; general talk; hearsay; an explosive noise. — *adj* **report'able**. — *n* **report'age** journalistic reporting, style or manner. — *adv* **report'edly** according to report. — *n* **report'er** a person who reports, esp. for a newspaper or legal proceedings. — *n* and *adj* **report'ing**. — **reported speech** indirect speech; **report stage** the stage at which a parliamentary bill as amended in committee is reported to the House, before the third reading. [O.Fr. *reporter* — L. *reportāre* — *re-*, back, *portāre*, to carry.]

repose *ri-pōz'*, *vt* to lay at rest; to give rest to, refresh by rest; to place (e.g confidence) in a person or thing; to place in trust. — *vi* to rest; to be still; to rely, to be based (with *on* or *upon*). — *n* rest; calm; restful feeling or effect. — *adj* **repōsed'** calm; settled. — *adv* **repō'sedly**. — *n* **repōs'edness**. — *adj* **repōse'ful**. — *adv* **repōse'fully**. [Fr. *reposer* — L.L. *repausāre*.]

reposition *rē-pəz-ish'ən*, *vt* to put in a different position. [**re-**.]

repository *ri-poz'it-ər-i*, *n* a place or receptacle in which anything is laid up; a collection or museum; a tomb; a storehouse, magazine, as of information; a confidant. [L. *repōněre*, *repositum*, to put back, lay aside — *pōněre*, to put.]

repossess *rē-pəz-es'*, *vt* to regain possession of; to take back (goods acquired on credit or by hire-purchase) because payment has not been made; to put again in possession. — *n* **repossession** (*-esh'ən*). [**re-**.]

repoussé *rə-po͞o'sā*, *adj* raised in relief by hammering from behind or within. — *n* repoussé work. — *n* **repoussage** (*-säzh'*). [Fr.]

repp. See **rep**[1].

reprehend *rep-ri-hend'*, *vt* to find fault with; to reprove. — *n* **reprehend'er**. — *adj* **reprehen'sible** blameworthy. — *adv* **reprehen'sibly**. — *n* **reprehen'sion**. — *adj* **reprehen'sory**. [L. *repraehenděre*, *-hēnsum* — *re-* (intensive) and *praehenděre*, to lay hold of.]

represent *rep-ri-zent'*, *vt* to use, or serve, as a symbol for; to stand for; to exhibit, depict, personate, or show an image of, by imitative art; to act; to be a substitute, agent, deputy, member of parliament, or the like, for; to correspond or be in some way equivalent or analogous to; to serve as a sample of, typify; to present earnestly to mind; to give out, allege (that). — *adj* **represent'able**. — *n* **representation** (*-zən-tā'shən*) the act, state or fact of representing or being represented; anything which represents; an image; picture; dramatic performance; a presentation of a view of facts or arguments; a petition, expostulation; a body of representatives. — *adj* **representā'tional** (*rep-ri-zən-*) esp. of art which depicts objects in a realistic rather than an abstract form. — *n* **representā'tionalism** or **representā'tionism** representational art; the doctrine that in the perception of the external world the immediate object represents another object beyond the sphere of consciousness. — *n* **representā'tionist**. — *adj* **representative** (*rep-ri-zent'ə-tiv*) representing; exhibiting a likeness; typical. — *n* a sample; a typical example or embodiment; a person who represents another or others, such as a deputy, delegate, ambassador, member of parliament, agent, successor, heir; a travelling salesperson. — *adv* **represent'atively**. — *n* **represent'ativeness**. — *n* **represent'er**. — **House of Representatives** the lower branch of the United States Congress, consisting of members chosen biennially by the people. [L. *repraesentāre*, *-ātum* — *praesentāre*, to place before.]

re-present *rē-pri-zent'*, *vt* to present again. — *n* **rē-presentā'tion**. [**re-**.]

repress *ri-pres'*, *vt* to restrain; to keep under control; to put down; to banish to the unconscious. — *adj* **repress'ed** having a tendency to repress unacceptable thoughts, feelings, etc. — *adj* **repress'ible**. — *adv* **repress'ibly**. — *n* **repression** (*-presh'ən*). — *adj* **repress'ive**. — *adv* **repress'ively**. — *n* **repress'or**. [L. *reprimĕre*, *repressum* — *premĕre*, to press.]

re-press *rē-pres'*, *vt* to press again. [**re-**.]

reprieve *ri-prēv'*, *vt* to delay the execution of; to give a respite to. — *n* a suspension of a criminal sentence, esp. a death sentence; interval of ease or relief. [Supposed to be from A.Fr. *repris*, past p. of *reprendre*, to take back (see **reprisal**).]

reprimand *rep'ri-mänd*, *n* a severe reproof. — *vt* to reprove severely, esp. publicly or officially. [Fr. *réprimande* — L. *reprimĕre*, *repressum*, to press back — *premĕre*, to press.]

reprint *rē-print'*, *vt* to print again; to print a new impression of, esp. with little or no change. — *vi* to be reprinted. — *n* **rē'print** a later impression (of e.g. a book); printed matter used as copy.

reprisal *rə-prīs'əl*, *n* seizure in retaliation; (an act of) retaliation. [Fr. *reprise* — *reprendre* — L. *reprae-hendĕre*.]

reprise *ri-prīz'*, *vt* to repeat (esp. a musical theme). — *n* (*mus*) resumption of an earlier subject.

reprivatize *rē-prī'vət-īz*, *vt* to return (a company, etc.) to private ownership.

repro *rē'prō* or *rep'rō*, *n* and *adj* short for **reproduction**, esp. of modern copies of period styles of furniture. — *n* (*rē'prō*) short for **reproduction proof**: — *pl* **re'pros**.

reproach *ri-prōch'*, *vt* to rebuke; to blame (oneself, etc., *for* or *with*). — *n* upbraiding; reproof; censure; disgrace; a source or matter of disgrace or shame. — *adj* **reproach'able**. — *n* **reproach'er**. — *adj* **reproach'ful** reproving. — *adv* **reproach'fully**. — *n* **reproach'fulness**. — **above** or **beyond reproach** excellent, too good to be criticised. [Fr. *reprocher*, perh. from L. *prope*, near; cf. **approach**; or from *reprobāre*; see **reprobate**.]

reprobate *rep'rō-bāt*, *adj* given over to sin; depraved; unprincipled. — *n* an abandoned or profligate person; a villain or rogue. — *vt* to reject; to disapprove of; to censure. — *n* **rep'robacy** (*-bə-si*). — *n* **rep'robāter**. — *n* **reprobā'tion**. [L. *reprobāre*, *-ātum*, to reprove, contrary of *approbāre* — *probāre*, to prove.]

reprocess *rē-prō'ses*, *vt* to process again, esp. to remake used material, e.g. spent nuclear fuel, into a new material or article. [**re-**.]

reproduce *rē-prə-dūs'*, *vt* to produce a copy or imitation of; to form anew; to propagate; to reconstruct in imagination. — *vi* to produce offspring; to prove suitable for copying in some way; to turn out (well, badly, etc.) when copied. — *n* **reprodū'cer**. — *adj* **reprodū'cible**. — *n* **reproduction** (*-duk'shən*) the act of reproducing; the act of producing new organisms — the whole process whereby life is continued from generation to generation; regeneration; a copy, facsimile; a representation. — Also *adj* (of furniture, etc.). — *adj* **reproduc'tive**. — *adv* **reproduc'tively**. — *n* **reproduc'tiveness** or **reproductiv'ity**. — **reproduction proof** (*printing*) a high-quality proof made from strips of typeset copy and photographed to produce a plate for printing from (commonly abbrev. as **repro proof** or **repro**). [**re-**.]

reprography *ri-prog'rə-fi*, *n* the reproduction of graphic or typeset material, e.g. by photocopying. — *n* **reprog'rapher**. — *adj* **reprograph'ic**. [Fr. *reprographie*.]

reproof[1] *ri-prōōf'*, *n* a reproving; rebuke, censure. — *n* **reproval** (*ri-prōō'vl*) reproof. — *vt* **reprove'** to rebuke; to censure, condemn. — *n* **repro'ver**. — *adj* **repro'ving**. — *adv* **repro'vingly**. [O.Fr. *reprover* — L. *reprobāre*; see **reprobate**.]

reproof[2] *rē-prōōf'*, *vt* to make waterproof again. — *n* a second or new proof.

rept *abbrev* for: receipt; report.

reptant *rep-tənt*, (*biol*) *adj* creeping. [L. *reptāre*, to creep.]

reptile *rep'tīl*, *n* any animal of the class **Reptilia** (*-til'i-ə'*), vertebrates with scaly integument, cold blood, pulmonary respiration, and pentadactyl limbs (sometimes lacking); a creeping thing; a base, malignant or treacherous person. — *adj* creeping; like a reptile in nature. — *adj* **reptilian** (*-til'i-ən*). — *adj* **reptilif'erous** bearing fossil reptiles. — *adj* **reptil'ious** like a reptile. [L.L. *reptilis*, *-e* — *repĕre*, to creep.]

republic *ri-pub'lik*, *n* a form of government without a monarch, esp. one in which the supreme power is vested in the people and their elected representatives; a state or country so governed. — *adj* **repub'lican** of or favouring a republic; (with *cap*) of the Republican party. — *n* a person who advocates a republican form of government; (in the U.S.) a member of the political party opposed to the *Democrats*, and favouring an extension of the powers of the national government. — *vt* **repub'licanise** or **-ize**. — *n* **repub'licanism**. [L. *rēspublica*, commonwealth — *rēs*, affair, *publica* (fem.), public.]

repudiate *ri-pū'di-āt*, *vt* to cast off, disown; to refuse, or cease, to acknowledge (debt, authority, claim) to deny as unfounded (a charge, etc.). — *adj* **repū'diable**. — *n* **repūdiā'tion**. — *adj* **repū'diative**. — *n* **repū'diātor**. [L. *repudiāre*, *-ātum* — *repudium*, divorce — *re-*, away, and the root of *pudēre*, to be ashamed.]

repugnant *ri-pug'nənt*, *adj* distasteful, disgusting; (of things) incompatible; inconsistent with (with *to*). [L. *repugnāre* — *re-*, against, *pugnāre*, to fight.]

repulse *ri-puls'*, *vt* to drive back; to rebuff, reject. — *n* a driving back; a check; a refusal; a rebuff. — *n* **repulsion** (*-pul'shən*) driving off; a repelling force, action or influence. — *adj* **repul'sive** tending to repulse or drive off; cold, reserved, forbidding; causing aversion and disgust. — *adv* **repul'sively**. — *n* **repul'siveness**. [L. *repulsus*, past p. of *repellĕre* — *re-*, back, *pellĕre*, to drive.]

repute *ri-pūt'*, *vt* to account, deem. — *n* general opinion or impression; attributed character; widespread or high estimation; fame. — *adj* **reputable** (*rep'ūt-ə-bl*) in good repute; respectable; honourable. — *adv* **rep'ūtably**. — *n* **repūtā'tion** (*rep-*) repute; estimation; character generally ascribed; good report; fame; good name. — *adj* **reputed** (*ri-pūt'id*) supposed, reckoned to be such; of repute. — *adv* **repūt'edly** in common repute or estimation. [L. *reputāre*, *-ātum* — *putāre*, to reckon.]

request *ri-kwest'*, *n* the asking of a favour; a petition; a favour asked for; the state of being sought after. — *vt* to ask as a favour; to ask politely; to ask for. — *n* **request'er**. — **request stop** a stop at which a bus will stop only if signalled to do so. — **on request** if, or when, requested. [O.Fr. *requeste* — L. *requīsītum*, past p. of *requīrĕre* — *re-*, away, *quaerĕre*, to seek.]

requiem *rek'wi-əm* or *rē'kwi-əm*, (*Christian relig* and *mus*) *n* a mass for the rest of the soul of the dead; music for it. [L., accus. of *requiēs* (*re-* (intensive) and *quiēs*, rest); first word of the introit.]

requiescat *re-kwi-es'kat*, (*Christian relig*) *n* a prayer for the rest of the soul of the dead. — **requiescat in pace** (*in pä'chā*; abbrev. **RIP**) may he (or she) rest in peace. [L., third pers. sing. subj. of *requiescĕre*.]

require *ri-kwīr'*, *vt* to demand, exact; to direct (a person to do something); to call for, necessitate. — *vi* to ask. — *adj* **requir'able**. — *adj* **required'** compulsory, e.g. as part of a curriculum. — *n* **require'ment** a need; a thing needed; a necessary condition; a demand. — *n* **requir'er**. — *n* **requir'ing**. [L. *requīrĕre*; partly through O.Fr. *requerre*, later assimilated to L.]

requisite *rek'wi-zit, adj* required, needed; indispensable. — *n* that which is required, necessary or indispensable. — *n* **req'uisiteness.** — *n* **requisi'tion** the act of requiring; a formal demand or request; a formal call for the doing of something that is due; a demand for the supply of anything for military purposes; a written order for the supply of materials; the state of being in use or service. — *vt* to demand or take by requisition; to press into service. — *adj* **requisi'tionary.** — *n* **requisi'tionist.** [L. *requīsītus*, past p. of *requīrere*; see **require.**]

requite *ri-kwīt', vt* to repay (an action); to avenge; to repay (a person, for): — *pa t* and *pa p* **requit'ed.** — *adj* **requī'table.** — *n* **requī'tal** the act of requiting; payment in return; recompense. — *n* **requite'ment.** — *n* **requī'ter.** [**re-** and **quit.**]

reread *rē-rēd', vt* to read again: — *pa t* and *pa p* **reread'** (*-red*). [**re-.**]

reredos *rēr'dos, n* a screen or panelling behind an altar or seat; a choir-screen. [O.Fr. *areredos* — *arere*, behind, *dos*, back.]

rerun *rē-run', vt* to run (a race, etc.) again; to broadcast (a series) again. — Also *n* (*rē'run*). [**re-.**]

res. *abbrev* for: research; reserve; residence; resolution.

resale *rē'sāl* or *rē-sāl', n* the selling again of an article. — **resale price maintenance** (abbrev. **RPM**) the setting of a fixed minimum price on an article by the manufacturer. [**re-.**]

reschedule *rē-shed'ūl* or *-sked'ūl, vt* to schedule again; to arrange a new time or timetable for; to rearrange (a country's debt repayment programme) usu. to alleviate liquidity problems (*econ*). — *n* **resched'uling.** [**re-.**]

rescind *ri-sind', vt* to annul, abrogate. — *n* **rescind'ment** or **rescission** (*-sizh'ən*). [L. *rescindĕre, rescissum* — *rē*, back, *scindĕre*, to cut.]

rescore *rē-skör', vt* to rewrite a musical score for different instruments, voices, etc. [**re-.**]

rescript *rē'skript, n* the official answer of a pope or an emperor to any legal question; an edict or decree; a rewriting. — Also *vt.* [L. *rescrīptum* — *re-*, *scrībĕre, scrīptum*, to write.]

rescue *res'kū, vt* to free from danger, captivity, or evil plight; to deliver forcibly from legal custody; to recover by force: — *pr p* **res'cuing**; *pa t* and *pa p* **res'cued.** — *n* the act of rescuing; deliverance from danger or evil; forcible recovery; forcible release from arrest or imprisonment; relief of a besieged place. — *adj* **res'cuable.** — *n* **res'cuer.** [O.Fr. *rescourre* — L. *re-*, *excutĕre* — *ex*, out, *quatĕre*, to shake.]

research *ri-sûrch', n* a careful search; investigation; systematic investigation towards increasing the sum of knowledge. — *vi* and *vt* to make researches (into or concerning); **re-search** (*rē'*) to search again. — *n* **research'er.** [Obs. Fr. *recerche* (mod. Fr. *recherche*); see **search.**]

resect *ri-sekt', vt* to cut away part of, esp. the end of a bone. — *n* **resection** (*-sek'shən*) cutting away, esp. bone (*surg*); a positional fix of a point by sighting it from three or more known stations (*surveying*). [L. *resecāre, -sectum*, to cut off — *secāre*, to cut.]

reseda *re'si-də, n* a plant of the mignonette genus; a pale green colour. — Also *adj.* [L. *resēda*, said to be from *resēdā morbīs*, assuage diseases, first words of a charm used in applying it as a poultice.]

resemble *ri-zem'bl, vt* to be like. — *n* **resem'blance** likeness; appearance; an image. — *adj* **resem'blant.** — *n* **resem'bler.** — *adj* **resem'bling.** [O.Fr. *resembler* — *re-*, again, *sembler*, to seem — L. *simulāre*, to make like.]

resent *ri-zent', vt* to take, consider as an injury or affront; to feel bitterness or indignation about. — *n* **resent'er.** — *adj* **resent'ful.** — *adv* **resent'fully.** — *n* **resent'ment.** [O.Fr. *ressentir* — L. *re-*, in return, *sentīre*, to feel.]

reserpine *ri-zûr'pin, n* a drug (obtained from the plant *Rauwolfia serpentina*) used against high blood pressure, and as a tranquilliser.

reserve *ri-zûrv', vt* to hold back; to save up, esp. for a future occasion or special purpose; to keep or retain; to preserve; to set apart; to book or engage. — *n* the keeping of something reserved; state of being reserved; something that is reserved; a reserved store or stock; a reserve price; a tract of land reserved for a special purpose; a substitute kept in readiness (*sport*); (esp. in *pl*) a military force kept out of action until occasion serves; (esp. in *pl*) a force not usually serving but liable to be called up when required; (often *pl*) resources of physical or spiritual nature available in abnormal circumstances; part of assets kept readily available for ordinary demands; (usu. in *pl*) an unexploited quantity of a mineral (esp. oil, gas or coal) calculated to exist in a given area; (in *pl*) amounts of gold and foreign currencies held by a country; artistic restraint; restrained manner; aloofness. — *adj* kept in reserve; of the reserves. — *adj* **reserv'able.** — *n* **reservā'tion** (*rez-*) the act of reserving or keeping back; an expressed, or tacit, proviso, limiting condition, or exception; something withheld; the booking of a seat, room, passage, etc.; a booked seat, room, etc.; the strip of grass, etc. between the two roads of a dual carriageway; a tract of public land reserved for some special purpose, e.g. for Indians, schools, game, etc.; the pope's retention to himself of the right to nominate to a benefice; a clause of a deed by which a person reserves for himself a right, interest, etc. in a property he is granting (*legal*). — *adj* **reserv'ed** reticent; booked. — *adv* **reserv'edly.** — *n* **reservedness** (*ri-zûrvd'nis*). — *n* **reserv'ist** a member of a reserve force. — **reserve bank** one of the U.S. Federal Reserve banks; a central bank holding reserves for other banks (esp. *Austr* and *NZ*); **reserve currency** one ranking with gold in world banking transactions; **reserved list** a list of retired officers in the armed services who may be recalled for active service in the event of war; **reserved occupation** employment of national importance that exempts from service in the armed forces; **reserve price** the minimum price acceptable to the vendor of an article for sale or auction. — **judgment reserved** see under **judge**; **without reserve** frankly; fully, without reservation; without restrictions or stipulations regarding sale; without a reserve price. [O.Fr. *reserver* — L. *reservāre* — *re-*, back, *servāre*, to save.]

reservoir *rez'ər-vwär, n* an artificial lake or tank for storing water; a receptacle for fluids, esp. a large basin; a large supply of anything. [Fr.]

res gestae *rēz jes'tē* or *rās ges'tī*, (L.) exploits; facts relevant to the case and admissible in evidence (*law*).

reshuffle *rē-shuf'l, vt* to shuffle again; to rearrange, esp. cabinet or government offices. — Also *n.* [**re-.**]

reside *ri-zīd', vi* to dwell permanently; to be in residence; to abide; to inhere. — *n* **residence** (*rez'i-dəns*) act or duration of dwelling in a place; the act of living in the place required by regulations or performance of functions; a stay in a place; a dwelling-place; a dwelling-house, esp. one of some pretensions; that in which anything permanently inheres or has its seat. — *n* **res'idency** a residence; the official abode of a resident or governor of a protected state; an administrative district under a resident; a resident's post at a hospital, or the period during which it is held. — *adj* **res'ident** dwelling in a place for some time; residing on one's own estate, or the place of one's duties, or the place required by certain conditions; not migratory; inherent. — *n* a person who resides; an animal that does not migrate; a doctor who works in, and usu. resides at, a hospital to gain experience in a particular field; a registered guest at a hotel; a representative of a governor in a protected state; the governor of a residency or administrative district. — *adj* **residential** (*-den'shl*) of, for, or connected with, residence; suitable for or occupied by houses, esp. of a better kind. — *adj* **residentiary** (*-den'shə-ri*) resident; officially bound to reside; pertaining to or involving official residence. — *n* a person bound to reside, such as a canon. — *n* **res'identship**. — *n* **resī'der**. [L. *residēre* — *re-*, back, *sedēre*, to sit.]

residue *rez'i-dū*, *n* that which is left, remainder; what is left of an estate after payment of debts, charges and legacies. — *adj* **resid'ual** remaining as residue or difference. — *n* that which remains as a residue or as a difference; a payment to an artist, etc. for later use of a film, etc. in which he or she appears. — *adj* **resid'uary** of, or of the nature of, a residue, esp. of an estate. — *n* **residuum** (*rez-id'ū-əm*) a residue: — *pl* **resid'ua**. — **residual current device** a circuit-breaker used to protect electrical equipment or its operator. [L. *residuum* — *residēre*, to remain behind.]

resign *ri-zīn'*, *vt* to give up (one's employment, etc.); to yield up; to submit calmly; to relinquish; to entrust. — *vt* to give up office, employment, etc. — *n* **resignation** (*rez-ig-nā'shən*) an act of giving up; the state of being resigned or quietly submissive. — *adj* **resigned** (*ri-zīnd'*) calmly submissive. — *adv* **resignedly** (*ri-zīn'id-li*). — *n* **resign'edness**. — *n* **resign'er**. [O.Fr. *resigner* — L. *resignāre*, *-ātum*, to unseal, annul.]

re-sign *rē-sīn'*, *vt* to sign again. **[re-.]**

resile *ri-zīl'*, *vi* to recoil; to rebound; to recover form and position elastically; to draw back from a statement, agreement or course. [L. *resilīre*, to leap back — *salīre*, to leap.]

resilient *ri-zil'i-ənt*, *adj* able to recover form and position elastically; able to withstand shock, suffering, disappointment, etc. — *n* **resil'ience** or **resil'iency** the quality of being resilient. **[resile.]**

resin *rez'in*, *n* any of a number of substances, products obtained from the sap of certain plants and trees (*natural resins*), used in plastics, etc.; any of a large number of substances made by polymerisation or condensation (*synthetic resins*) which, though not related chemically to natural resins, have some of their physical properties, very important in the plastics industry, etc. — *vt* to treat with resin; to rosin. — *n* **res'ināte** a salt of any of the acids occurring in natural resins. — *adj* **resinif'erous** yielding resin. — *n* **resinificā'tion**. — *vt* and *vi* **res'inify** to make or become a resin or resinous. — *adj* **res'inous**. [Fr. *résine* — L. *rēsīna*.]

resipiscence *res-i-pis'əns*, *n* recognition of error, change to a better frame of mind. — *adj* **resipisc'ent**. [L. *resipīscentia* — *resipīscěre* — *re-*, again, *sapěre*, to be wise.]

res ipsa loquitur *rēz ip'sə lok'wi-tər* or (L.) *rās ip'sə lok'wi-tōōr*, (*law*) the thing speaks for itself — applied in cases in which the mere fact that an accident has happened is deemed to be evidence of negligence unless the defendant proves otherwise. [L.]

resist *ri-zist'*, *vt* to strive against, oppose; to withstand; to refuse; to hinder the action of; to be little affected by. — *vi* to make opposition. — *n* a protective coating, esp. one on parts of a textile to protect the blank areas of the design that is being printed, or a light-sensitive coating on a silicon wafer. — Also *adj*. — *n* **resis'tance** an act or power of resisting; opposition; the body's ability to resist disease; (with *cap*) an organisation of (armed) opposition to an occupying enemy force; the opposition of a body to the motion of another; that property of a substance in virtue of which the passage of an electric current through it is accompanied with a dissipation of energy; an electrical resistor. — *n* **resis'tant** a person who or thing which resists. — *adj* making resistance; (often used in combination) withstanding adverse conditions, as parasites, germs, antibiotics, corrosion. — *n* **resistibil'ity**. — *adj* **resis'tible**. — *adv* **resis'tibly**. — *adj* **resis'tive**. — *adv* **resis'tively**. — *n* **resistiv'ity** (*rez-*) capacity for resisting; (also **specific resistance**) a property of a conducting material expressed as resistance multiplied by cross-sectional area over length. — *n* **resist'or** anything that resists; a piece of apparatus used to offer electric resistance. — **resistance thermometer** a device for measuring high temperatures by means of the variation in the electrical resistance of a wire as the temperature changes. — **line of least resistance** the easiest course of action. [L. *resistěre* — *re-*, against, *sistěre*, to make to stand.]

resit *rē-sit'*, *vi* and *vt* to sit (an examination) again after failing. — *n* (*rē'sit*) an opportunity or act of resitting. **[re-.]**

resoluble *ri-zol'ū-bl*, *adj* that may be resolved, dissolved or analysed. — *adj* **resolute** (*rez'əl-ōōt* or *-ūt*) having a fixed purpose; constant in pursuing a purpose; determined. — *adv* **res'olutely**. — *n* **res'oluteness**. — *n* **resolution** (*rez-əl-ōō'shən* or *-ū-shən*) the act of resolving; analysis; separation of components; melting; solution; the definition of a picture in TV or facsimile (measured by the number of lines used to scan the image of the picture); the smallest measurable difference, or separation, or time interval (*phys, electronics, nucleonics*); resolving power (q.v.); the state of being resolved; fixed determination; that which is resolved; removal of or freedom from doubt; progression from discord to concord (*mus*); a formal proposal put before a meeting; a formal determination on a proposal; substitution of two short syllables for a long (*prosody*); the making visible of detail; the disappearance or dispersion of a tumour or inflammation (*med*). — *adj* **res'olutive**. — *n* **resolvabil'ity**. — *adj* **resolvable** (*ri-zolv*). — *vt* **resolve'** to separate into components; to make visible the details of; to analyse; to break up; to melt; to transform; to relax; to solve; to dissipate; to free from doubt or difficulty; to pass as a resolution; to determine; to disperse (e.g. a tumour) (*med*); to make (a discord) pass into a concord (*mus*). — *vi* to undergo resolution; to come to a determination (often with *on* to indicate the course chosen). — *n* resolution; fixed purpose; firmness of purpose. — *adj* **resolved'** fixed in purpose. — *adv* **resolvedly** (*ri-zol'vid-li*) resolutely. — *n* **resol'vedness**. — *adj* **resol'vent** having power to resolve. — *n* and *adj* (a drug) causing or helping resolution (*med*). — *n* **resol'ver**. — **resolving power** the ability of telescope, microscope, etc. to distinguish very close, or very small, objects; the ability of a photographic emulsion to produce finely-detailed images. [L. *resolvěre*, *resolūtum* — *re-* (intensive) and *solvěre*, to loose.]

resolve, etc. See under **resoluble**.

resonance *rez'ən-əns*, *n* resounding; sonority; the sound heard in auscultation (*med*); sympathetic vibration; the ringing quality of the human voice when produced in such a way that sympathetic vibration is caused in the air-spaces in the head, chest and throat; the state of a system in which a large vibration is produced by a small stimulus of approx. the same frequency as that of the system (*phys, electr*); such a large vibration (*phys, electr*); increased probability of a nuclear reaction when the energy of an incident particle or photon is around a certain value appropriate to the energy level of the compound nucleus; a property of certain compounds, in which the most stable state of the molecule is a combination of theoretically possible bond arrangements or distributions of electrons (*chem*). — *adj* **res'onant** resounding, ringing; giving its characteristic vibration in sympathy with another body's vibration. — *adv* **res'onantly**. — *vi* **res'onate** to resound; to vibrate sympathetically. — *n* **res'onā-**

tor a resonating body or device, as for increasing sonority or for analysing sound. [L. *resonāre, -ātum* — *re-*, back, *sonāre*, to sound.]

resorb *ri-sörb'*, *vt* to absorb back. — *n* **resorb'ence.** — *adj* **resorb'ent.** [L. *resorbēre*, to suck back.]

resorcin *ri-zör'sin*, *n* a colourless phenol, $C_6H_4(OH)_2$, used in dyeing, photography and medicine. — Also **resor'cinol.** [**resin** and *orcin*, a phenol found in archil.]

resorption *ri-sörp'shən*, *n* resorbing, esp. of a mineral by rock magma; the breaking-down and assimilation of a substance (*med*). — *adj* **resorp'tive.** [See **resorb.**]

resort[1] *ri-zört'*, *vi* to have recourse; to go or be, esp. habitually (*formal*). — *n* an act of resorting; a place often visited, esp. for holidays, a specified reason, etc.; that which one has or may have recourse to, an expedient. — *n* **resort'er.** — **in the last resort** as a last expedient. [O.Fr. *resortir*, to rebound, retire — *sortir*, to go out.]

resort[2] or **re-sort** *rē-sört'*, *vt* to sort again. [**re-**.]

resound *ri-zownd'*, *vt* to echo; to sound with reverberation; to sound or spread (the praises of a person or thing). — *vi* to echo; to re-echo, reverberate; to sound sonorously. — *adj* **resound'ing** echoing; thorough, decisive (as in *resounding victory*). — *adv* **resound'ingly.** [**re-**.]

resource *ri-sörs'* or *-zörs*, *n* source or possibility of help; an expedient; (in *pl*) money or means of raising money; means of support; means of occupying or amusing oneself; resourcefulness. — *vt* to provide the (esp. financial) resources for. — *adj* **resource'ful** fertile in expedients; clever, ingenious; rich in resources. — *n* **resource'fulness.** — *adj* **resource'less.** [O.Fr. *ressource* — *resourdre* — L. *resurgĕre*, to rise again.]

respect *ri-spekt'*, *vt* to heed; to treat with consideration, refrain from violating; to feel or show esteem, deference or honour to; to value. — *n* a particular; reference; consideration; partiality or favour towards (with *of*); deferential esteem; (often in *pl*) a greeting or message of esteem. — *n* **respectabil'ity.** — *adj* **respec'table** worthy of respect; considerable; passable; fairly well-to-do; decent and well-behaved; reputable; seemly; presentable. — *n* **respec'tableness.** — *adv* **respec'tably.** — *n* **respec'ter** someone who respects, esp. in *respecter of persons*, someone who or something that singles out individual(s) for unduly favourable treatment (usu. in *neg*). — *adj* **respect'ful** showing or feeling respect. — *adv* **respect'fully.** — *n* **respect'fulness.** — *prep* **respect'ing** concerning; considering. — *adj* **respec'tive** relative; particular or several, relating to each distributively. — *adv* **respec'tively.** — **in respect of** in the matter of; **with (or with all) due respect** a polite expression of disagreement; **with respect to** with regard to. [L. *respicĕre, respectum* — *re-*, back, *specĕre*, to look.]

respire *ri-spīr'*, *vi* to breathe; to take breath. — *vt* to breathe; to exhale. — *adj* **respirable** (*res'pər-ə-bl* or *ri-spīr'ə-bl*) fit for breathing. — *n* **respiration** (*res-pər-ā'shən*) breathing; the taking in of oxygen and giving out of carbon dioxide, with associated physiological processes; a breath. — *n* **res'pirātor** an appliance worn on the mouth or nose to filter or warm the air breathed; a gas mask. — *adj* **respiratory** (*ri-spir'ə-tər-i, res'pər-ə-tər-i* or *ri-spī'rə-tər-i*). — *n* **respirom'eter** an apparatus for measuring breathing. [L. *respīrāre, -ātum* — *spīrāre*, to breathe.]

respite *res'pīt* or *-pit*, *n* temporary cessation of something that is tiring or painful; postponement requested or granted; temporary suspension of the execution of a criminal (*law*). — *vt* to grant a respite to; to delay or put off; to grant postponement to. [M.E. *respit* — O.Fr. — L. *respectus, respicĕre*; see ety. for **respect.**]

respond *ri-spond'*, *vi* to answer; to utter liturgical responses; to act in answer; to react. — *n* a response to a versicle in liturgy; a half-pillar or half-pier attached to a wall to support an arch (corresponding to one at the other end of an arcade, etc.). — *n* **respond'ence** or **respond'ency** correspondence. — *adj* **respond'ent** answering; responsive. — *n* a person who answers; a person who refutes objections; a defendant, esp. in a divorce suit. — *n* **respond'er, respons'er** or **respons'or** (*ris-*) someone who or something which responds. — *n* **response'** an answer; an answer made by the congregation to the priest during divine service; a responsory; a reaction, esp. sympathetic; the ratio of the output to the input level of a transmission system at any particular frequency (*electronics*). — *adj* **response'less.** — *adj* **respon'sive** ready to respond; answering. — *adv* **respon'sively.** — *n* **respon'siveness.** — *adj* **respon'sory** making answer. — *n* an anthem sung after a lesson; a liturgical response. [L. *respondēre, respōnsum* — *re-*, back, *spondēre*, to promise.]

responsible *ri-spon'si-bl*, *adj* liable to be called to account as being in charge or control; answerable (*to* a person, etc., or *for* something); deserving the blame or credit of (with *for*); governed by a sense of responsibility; being a free moral agent; morally accountable for one's actions; trustworthy; able to pay; involving responsibility. — *n* **responsibil'ity** state of being responsible; a trust or charge for which one is responsible. — *adv* **respon'sibly.** [Ety. as for **respond.**]

rest[1] *rest*, *n* repose, refreshing inactivity; intermission of or freedom from motion or disturbance; tranquillity; repose of death; a place for resting; a prop or support (e.g. for a book, a billiard cue, a violinist's chin); motionlessness; a pause in speaking or reading; an interval of silence in music, or a mark indicating it. — *vi* to repose; to be at ease; to be still; to be supported (on); to lean (on); to have foundation in (with *on*); to remain; to be unemployed (*slang*, esp. *theatrical*). — *vt* to give rest to; to place or hold in support (on); to base (on). — *n* **rest'er.** — *adj* **rest'ful** at rest; rest-giving; tranquil. — *adv* **rest'fully.** — *n* **rest'fulness.** — *n* and *adj* **rest'ing.** — *adj* **rest'less** unresting, not resting, sleeping or relaxing; never still; uneasily active; never-ceasing; allowing no rest. — *adv* **rest'lessly.** — *n* **rest'lessness.** — **rest'-cure** treatment consisting of inactivity and quiet; **rest'-home** an establishment for those who need special care and attention, e.g. invalids, old people, etc.; **rest'-house** house of rest for travellers; **rest mass** (*phys*) the mass of an object when it is at rest; **rest'-room** a room in a building (not a private house) with lavatories, etc. — **at rest** stationary; in repose; free from disquiet; **lay to rest** to bury, inter. [O.E. *rest, ræst*; converging and merging in meaning with the following words.]

rest[2] *rest*, *n* remainder; all others; reserve fund. — *vi* to remain. — **for the rest** as regards other matters. [Fr. *reste* — L. *restāre*, to remain — *re-*, back, *stāre*, to stand.]

restaurant *rest'(ə-)rã, -rong, -ront* or *-rənt*, *n* a place where food or meals are prepared and served, or are available, to customers. — *n* **restaurateur** (*res-tər-ə-tûr'* or *-tœr'*) the keeper of a restaurant. — *n* **restaura'tion** a business, skill or art of a restaurateur. — **res'taurant-car** a dining-car. [Fr., — *restaurer*, to restore.]

rest-harrow *rest'-har-ō*, *n* a papilionaceous plant (*Ononis*) with long, tough, woody roots. [**rest** (aphetic for **arrest**), and **harrow.**]

restitution *res-ti-tū'shən*, *n* a restoring, return; compensation; (also **restitū'tionism**) restorationism. — *n* **restitū'tionist.** — *adj* **restitūtive** (*ri-stit'* or *res'tit-*). — *n* **res'titūtor.** — *adj* **restit'ūtory.** [L. *restituĕre, -ūtum* — *re-*, *statuĕre*, to make to stand.]

restive *res'tiv*, *adj* obstinate, refractory; uneasy, as if ready to break from control. — *adv* **res'tively**. — *n* **res'tiveness**. [O.Fr. *restif* — L. *restāre*, to rest.]

restore *ri-stör'*, *vt* to repair; to bring, put or give back; to make good; to reinstate; to bring back to a (supposed) former state, or to a normal state; to reconstruct mentally, by inference or conjecture. — *adj* **restor'able**. — *n* **restor'ableness**. — *n* **restoration** (*res-tö-rā'shən*, or *-tə-* or *-to-*) act or process of restoring; a reinstatement of or to kingship (as the Restoration of the Stuarts, the Bourbons; usu. with *cap*); renovations and reconstruction of a building, painting, etc.; a reconstructed thing or representation. — *adj* (with *cap*) of the time of the Restoration of Charles II. — *n* **restorā'tionism** (*theol*) receiving of a sinner to divine favour; the final recovery of all men. — *n* **restorā'tionist**. — *adj* **restorative** (*ris-tor'ə-tiv* or *-tör'*) tending to restore, esp. to strength and vigour. — *n* a medicine that restores. — *adv* **restor'atively**. — *n* **restor'er**. [O.Fr. *restorer* — L. *restaurāre*, *-ātum*.]

restrain *ri-strān'*, *vt* to hold back; to control; to subject to forcible repression. — *adj* **restrain'able**. — *adj* **restrained'** controlled; self-controlled; showing restraint. — *adv* **restrain'edly**. — *n* **restrain'edness**. — *n* **restrain'er**. — *n* and *adj* **restrain'ing**. — *n* **restraint'** the act of restraining; the state of being restrained; restriction; forcible control; want of liberty; reserve. — **restraint of trade** interference with free play of economic forces. [O.Fr. *restraindre*, *restrai(g)n-* — L. *restringĕre*, *restrictum* — *re-*, back, *stringĕre*, to draw tightly.]

restrict *ri-strikt'*, *vt* to limit; to confine within limits; to limit circulation or disclosure of for security reasons. — *adj* **restrict'ed**. — *adv* **restrict'edly**. — *n* **restric'tion**. — *n* **restric'tionist**. — Also *adj*. — *adj* **restric'tive** tending to restrict; expressing restriction, as in relative clauses, etc., in which the application of the verb is limited to the subject (*gram*). — *adv* **restric'tively**. — **restricted area** one from which the general public is excluded; one within which there is a speed limit; **restrictive practice** a trade practice that is against the public interest, as e.g. an agreement to sell only to certain buyers, or to keep up resale prices; used also of certain trade union practices, such as the closed shop, demarcation, or working to rule. [L. *restringĕre*, *restrictum*.]

result *ri-zult'*, *vi* to issue (with *in*); to follow as a consequence; to be the outcome. — *n* consequence; outcome; outcome aimed at; quantity obtained by calculation; in games, the (usu. final) score; in games, etc., a successful final score, a win (*colloq*; as in *get a result*). — *adj* **result'ant** resulting. — *n* a force compounded of two or more forces; a sum of vector quantities. — *adj* **result'ing**. — *adj* **result'less**. [L. *resultāre*, to leap back — *saltāre*, to leap.]

resume *ri-zūm'* or *-zōōm'*, *vt* to assume again; to take up again; to begin again. — *vi* to take possession again; to begin again in continuation. — *adj* **resum'able**. — *n* **résumé** (*rā-zü-mā*; Fr. past p.) a summary; a curriculum vitae (*US*). — *n* **resumption** (*ri-zump'shən* or *-zum'*) the act of resuming. — *adj* **resumptive** (*-zump'* or *-zum'*). — *adv* **resump'tively**. [L. *resūmĕre*, *-sūmptum* — *re-*, *sūmĕre*, to take.]

resupinate *ri-sōō'* or *-sū'pin-āt*, (*bot*) *adj* upside down by twisting. — *n* **resupinā'tion**. [L. *resupīnāre*, *-ātum*, and *resupīnus* — *re-*, back, *supīnus*, bent backward.]

resurgent *ri-sûrj'ənt*, *adj* rising again. — *n* **resur'gence**. [L. *resurgĕre*, *resurrēctum* — *re-*, *surgĕre*, to rise.]

resurrect *rez-ər-ekt'*, *vt* to restore to life; to revive; to disinter. — *vi* to come to life again. — *n* **resurrection** (*-ek'shən*) a rising from the dead, esp. (with *cap*) that of Christ; resuscitation; revival; a thing resurrected. — *adj* **resurrec'tional**. — *adj* **resurrec'tionary**. — *vt* **resurrec'tionise** or **-ize**. — *n* **resurrec'tionism**. — *n* **resurrec'tionist** (*old*) someone who stole bodies from the grave for dissection. — *adj* **resurrect'ive**. — *n* **resurrect'or**. — **resurrection plant** a plant that curls into a ball during a drought and spreads out again when moist. [Ety. as for **resurgent**.]

resuscitate *ri-sus'i-tāt*, *vt* and *vi* to bring back to life or consciousness; to revive. — *adj* **resusc'itable**. — *n* **resusc'itant**. — *n* someone who or something that resuscitates. — *n* **resuscitā'tion**. — *adj* **resusc'itātive**. [L. *resuscitāre*, *-ātum* — *re-*, *sus-*, *sub-*, from beneath, *citāre*, to put into quick motion.]

ret *ret*, *vt* to expose (e.g. flax, hemp) to moisture. — *vt* and *vi* to soak; to soften, spoil or rot by soaking or exposure to moisture; to rot: — *pr p* **rett'ing**; *pa t* and *pa p* **rett'ed**. [App. related to **rot**.]

retable *ri-tā'bl*, *n* a shelf or ornamental setting for panels, etc. behind an altar. [Fr. *rétable* — L.L. *retrōtabulum*.]

retail *rē'tāl*, *n* the sale directly to the consumer or in small quantities. — *adj* in, of, engaged in or concerned with such sale. — *adv* by retail. — *vt* (*ri-* or *rē-tāl'*) to sell by retail; to repeat in detail; hand on by report. — *vi* to sell. — *n* **retail'er**. — *n* **retail'ment**. — **retail park** a landscaped shopping complex. [O.Fr. *retail*, piece cut off — *tailler*, to cut.]

retain *ri-tān'*, *vt* to keep; to hold back; to continue to hold; to keep up; to employ or keep engaged, as by a fee paid; to keep in mind. — *adj* **retain'able**. — *n* **retain'er** someone who or something that retains; a dependent of a person of rank; a family servant of long standing; an authorisation; a retaining fee (in legal usage, **general** to secure a priority of claim on a counsel's services, **special** for a particular case). — *n* **retain'ership**. — *n* **retain'ment**. — **retaining fee** the advance fee paid to a lawyer to defend a cause; **retaining wall** a wall to hold back earth or water. [Fr. *retenir* — L. *retinēre* — *re-*, back, *tenēre*, to hold.]

retake *rē-tāk'*, *vt* to take again; to take back, recapture: — *pa t* **retook'**; *pa p* **retā'ken**. — *n* (*rē'*) a second or repeated photographing or photograph, esp. for a motion picture. — *n* **retāk'er**. — *n* **retāk'ing**. [**re-**.]

retaliate *ri-tal'i-āt*, *vt* to repay in kind (usu. an injury). — *vi* to return like for like (esp. in hostility). — *n* **retaliā'tion** return of like for like; imposition of a tariff against countries that impose a tariff. — *n* **retaliā'tionist**. — *adj* **retal'iātive**. — *n* **retal'iātor**. — *adj* **retal'iatory** (*-āt-ər-i* or *-ət-ər-i*). [L. *retāliāre*, *-ātum* — *re-*, *tāliō*, *-ōnis*, like for like — *tālis*, such.]

retard *ri-tärd'*, *vt* to slow; to keep back development or progress of; to delay; to delay the timing of (an ignition spark). — *vi* to slow down; to delay. — *adj* **retar'dant** serving to delay, slow down or impede something, e.g. rusting, fire, etc. — Also *n*. — *n* **retardā'tion** (*rē-*) or **retard'ment** slowing; impedance or delay; lag. — *adj* **retardative** (*ri-tard'ə-tiv*). — *adj* **retar'datory**. — *adj* **retar'ded** delayed or slowed down; slow in development, esp. mental, or having made less than normal progress in learning. — *n* **retar'der** a substance that delays or prevents setting of cement; a retardant. [L. *retardāre*, *-ātum* — *re-*, *tardāre*, to slow.]

retch *rech*, also *rēch*, *vi* to strain as if to vomit. — *n* an act of retching. [O.E. *hræcan* — *hrāca*, a hawking.]

retd *abbrev* for: retired; returned.

rete *rē'tē*, (*anat*) *n* a network (as of blood-vessels or nerves). — *adj* **retial** (*rē'shi-əl*). [L. *rēte*, net.]

retention *ri-ten'shən*, *n* the act or power of retaining; memory; custody; inability to void or get rid of (e.g. fluid) (*med*). — *n* **reten'tionist** a person who advocates the retaining of a policy, etc., esp. that of capital punishment. — *adj* **reten'tive** retaining;

tenacious; retaining moisture. — *adv* **reten'tively**. — *n* **reten'tiveness** or **retentiv'ity** (*rē-*). [L. *retentiō, -ōnis*; O.Fr. *retentif*; see **retain**.]

rethink *rē-thingk'*, *vt* to consider again and come to a different decision about. — Also *n*. **[re-.]**

retial. See **rete**.

retiarius *rē-shi-ā'ri-əs* or *rā-ti-ä'ri-ōōs*, (*hist*) *n* a gladiator armed with a net. [L. *rētiārius* — *rēte*, net.]

reticent *ret'i-sənt*, *adj* reserved or communicating sparingly or unwillingly. — *n* **ret'icence**. [L. *reticēns, -ēntis*, pres. p. of *reticēre* — *re-*, *tacēre*, to be silent.]

reticle *ret'i-kl*, *n* an attachment to an optical instrument consisting of a network of lines of reference. — *adj* **reticular** (*ri-tik'ū-lər*) netted; netlike; reticulated; of the reticulum (*zool*). — *adv* **retic'ularly**. — *vt* **retic'ulate** to form into or mark with a network. — *vi* to form a network. — *adj* netted; marked with network; net-veined. — *adj* **retic'ulated** reticulate; of lozenge-shaped stones, or of squares placed diamond-wise (*masonry*). — *adv* **retic'ulately**. — *n* **reticulā'tion**. — *n* **reticule** (*ret'i-kūl*) a reticle; a small bag carried by ladies. — *n* **retic'ulum** a network; the second stomach of a ruminant (*zool*). [L. *rēticulum*, dimin. of *rēte*, net.]

retiform *rē'ti-förm*, *adj* having the form of a net. [L. *rēte*, net, *fōrma*, form.]

retina *ret'i-nə*, *n* the sensitive layer of the eye: — *pl* **ret'inas** or **ret'inae** (*-nē*). — *adj* **ret'inal**. — *n* **retinī'tis** inflammation of the retina. — *n* **retinoblastōma** a cancerous tumour of the eye. — *n* **ret'inoscope** an optical instrument used in **retinos'copy**, examination of the eye by observing a shadow on the retina. — *n* **retinula** (*ri-tin'ū-lə*) a cell acting as a retina in an ommatidium: — *pl* **retin'ulae** (*-lē*). — *adj* **retin'ular**. [L.L. *rētina*, app. — L. *rēte*, net.]

retinue *ret'i-nū*, *n* a body accompanying and often attending an important person. [Fr. *retenue*, fem. past p. of *retenir*; see **retain**.]

retire *ri-tīr'*, *vi* to withdraw; to retreat; to recede; to withdraw from society, office, public or active life, business, profession, etc.; to go into seclusion or to bed. — *vt* to withdraw; withdraw from currency; to cause to retire. — *n* **retī'ral** (esp. *Scot*) giving up of work, office, business, etc.; withdrawal. — *adj* **retired'** secluded; withdrawn from business or profession. — *n* **retired'ness** (or *ri-tī'rid-nis*). — *n* **retire'ment** the act of retiring; the state of being or having retired; solitude; a time or place of seclusion. — *adj* **retī'ring** reserved; unobtrusive; modest. — *adv* **retī'ringly**. — *n* **retī'ringness**. — **retired list** a list of officers who are relieved from active service but receive a certain amount of pay (**retired pay**); **retirement pension** (*Brit*) a state pension paid to men of 65, and women of 60, and over (*formerly* **old age pension**). [Fr. *retirer* — *re-*, back, *tirer*, to draw.]

retook. See **retake**.

retool *rē-tōōl'*, *vt* to re-equip with new tools (in a factory, etc.; also *vi*); to remake, refashion (chiefly *US*). **[re-.]**

retort *ri-tört'*, *vt* to throw back; to return upon an assailant or opponent; to answer in retaliation or wittily; to purify or treat in a retort (*chem*); to sterilise (food in sealed container) by heating it by steam, etc. (*US*). — *vi* to make a sharp reply. — *n* a ready and sharp or witty answer; the art or act of retorting; a vessel in which substances are placed for distillation, typically a flask with long bent-back neck (*chem*). — *adj* **retor'ted** turned back. — *n* **retor'ter**. — *n* **retortion** (*-tör'shən*). — *adj* **retor'tive**. [L. *retorquēre*, *retortum* — *re-*, back, *torquēre*, to twist.]

retouch *rē-tuch'*, *vt* to touch again; to touch up with a view to improving. — *n* an act of touching up, esp. of a photograph by pencil-work on the negative. — *n* **retouch'er**. **[re-.]**

retrace *ri-* or *rē-trās'*, *vt* to trace back; to go back upon; to run over with the eye or in the memory; (*rē-*) to trace again; (*rē-*) to renew the outline of. — *adj* **retrace'able** (*ri-*). [Fr. *retracer*.]

retract *ri-trakt'*, *vt* to withdraw; to revoke; to undo (the previous move) (*chess*). — *vi* to take back, or draw back from, what has been said or granted. — *adj* **retrac'table** able to be retracted; that can be drawn up into the body or wings (*aeronautics*); that can be drawn up towards the body of a vehicle. — *n* **retractā'tion** (*rē-*) revoking; recantation. — *adj* **retrac'ted** drawn in; turned back. — *adj* **retrac'tile** (*-tīl*) that may be drawn back (as a cat's claws). — *n* **retractility** (*rē-trak-til'i-ti*). — *n* **retraction** (*ri-trak'shən*) drawing back; retractation. — *adj* **retrac'tive**. — *adv* **retrac'tively**. — *n* **retrac'tor** a device or instrument for holding parts back, esp. a surgical instrument for this purpose; a muscle that pulls in a part. [L. *retrahĕre*, *retractum* — *re-*, back, *trahĕre*, to draw.]

retral *rē'trəl* or *ret'rəl*, (*biol*) *adj* at or towards the rear. — *adv* **re'trally**. [L. *retro*, backwards.]

retread *rē-tred'*, *vt* to tread again: — *pa t* **retrod'**; *pa p* **retrodd'en**; to remould (a tyre): — *pa t* and *pa p* **retread'ed**. — *n* (*rē'tred*) a used tyre which has been given a new tread (cf. **remould**); someone or something returned, or someone hoping to return, to use, service or office. **[re-.]**

retreat[1] *ri-trēt'*, *n* a withdrawal; an orderly withdrawal before an enemy, or from a position of danger or difficulty; a signal (by bugle or drum) for withdrawal or for retirement to quarters; seclusion; retirement for a time for religious meditation; a time of such retirement; a place of privacy, seclusion, refuge or quiet; an institution for the care and treatment of the elderly, the mentally ill, alcoholics. — *vi* to draw back; to relinquish a position; to retire; to recede. — *n* **retreat'ant** a person taking part in a religious, etc. retreat. [O.Fr. *retret*, *-e*, past p. of *retraire* — L. *retrahĕre*, to draw back.]

re-treat or **retreat**[2] *rē-trēt'*, *vt* to treat again. **[re-.]**

retrench *ri-trench'* or *-trensh'*, *vt* to cut off, out or down. — *vi* to cut down expenses. — *n* **retrench'ment**. [O.Fr. *retrencher* — *re-*, off, *trencher*; see **trench**.]

retrial. See **retry**.

retribution *ret-ri-bū'shən*, *n* requital (now esp. of evil). — *adj* **retrib'ūtive** (*ri-*) repaying; rewarding or punishing suitably. — *adv* **retrib'ūtively**. — *n* **retrib'ūtor**. — *adj* **retrib'ūtory**. [L. *retribuĕre*, *-ūtum*, to give back — *re-*, back, *tribuĕre*, to give.]

retrieve *ri-trēv'*, *vt* to search for and fetch (something), as a dog does game; to recover, repossess; to rescue (from, out of); to save (time); to restore (honour, fortune); to make good (a loss, error); to return successfully (in tennis) a shot which is difficult to reach. — *vi* to find and fetch (as a dog does). — *adj* **retriev'able**. — *n* **retriev'ableness**. — *adv* **retriev'ably**. — *n* **retriev'al** retrieving; the extraction of data from a file (*comput*). — *n* **retriev'er** a dog (of a breed that can be) trained to find and fetch game that has been shot; someone who retrieves. — *n* and *adj* **retriev'ing**. [O.Fr. *retroev-*, *retreuv-*, stressed stem of *retrover* — *re-*, again, *trouver*, to find.]

retro or **Retro** *ret'rō*, *adj* reminiscent of, reverting to, or recreating the past, esp. for effect. — *n* short for retro-rocket. [Ety. as for **retro-**.]

retro- *ret-rō-* or *rē-trō-*, *pfx* denoting: backwards; behind. [L. *retrō*.]

retroact *rē-trō-akt'* or *ret'rō-akt*, *vi* to act retrospectively, or apply to the past (*law*); to react. — *n* **retroac'tion**. — *adj* **retroac'tive** applying to, or affecting, things past; operating retrospectively. — *adv* **retroac'tively**. — *n* **retroactiv'ity**. [L. *retroagĕre*, *-actum* — *agĕre*, to do.]

retrocede *ret-rō-* or *rē-trō-sēd'*, *vi* to move back. — *vt* to grant back. — *adj* **retrocē'dent.** — *n* **retrocession** (*-sesh'ən*). — *adj* **retrocess'ive.** [L. *retrōcēdĕre, -cēssum* — *cēdĕre*, to go, yield; partly from **retro-** and **cede**, or Fr. *céder*.]

retrochoir *rē'trō-kwīr* or *ret'rō-*, (*archit*) *n* an extension of a church behind the position of the high altar. [**retro-**.]

retrod, retrodden. See **retread.**

retrofit *ret'rō-fit*, *vt* to modify (a house, car, aircraft, etc.) some time after construction or maunufacture by incorporating or substituting more up-to-date parts, etc.: — *pr p* **ret'rofitting;** *pa t* and *pa p* **ret'rofitted.** — *n* and *adj* **ret'rofit.** — *n* **ret'rofitting.** [**retro-**.]

retroflex *ret'rō-fleks* or *rē'trō-*, *adj* bent back (also **retroflect'ed** or **ret'roflexed**); cacuminal (*phon*; also **ret'roflexed**). — *n* **retroflexion** or **retroflection** (*-flek'shən*). [L.L. *retroflexus* — L. *retro-*, back — L. *flectĕre, flexum*, to bend.]

retrograde *ret'rō-grād* or *rē'trō-*, *adj* moving or directed backward or (*astron*) from east to west, relatively to the fixed stars; inverse; habitually walking or swimming backwards; degenerating; reverting. — *n* someone who goes back or degenerates. — *vi* to go back or backwards; to have a retrograde movement (*astron*). — *n* **retrogradation** (*-grə-dā'shən*) retrogression (esp. *astron*). — *vi* **retrogress'** to retrograde. — *n* **retrogression** (*-gresh'ən*). — *adj* **retrogress'ive.** — *adv* **retrogress'ively.** [L. *retrōgradus*, going backward, *retrōgressus*, retrogression — *retrō-*, backward, *gradī, gressus*, to go.]

retroject *ret'rō-jekt*, *vt* to throw backwards (opp. to *project*). — *n* **retrojec'tion.** [**retro-** and **(pro)ject.**]

retroreflector *ret-rō-rə-flect'ər*, *n* a device, placed on a satellite or a heavenly body, that reflects light or radiation back to its source. — *adj* **retroreflect'ive.**

retro-rocket *ret'* or *rēt'rō-rok'it*, *n* a rocket whose function is to slow down a spacecraft or an artificial satellite, fired in a direction opposite to that in which that vehicle is travelling. [**retro-**.]

retrorse *ri-trörs'*, *adj* turned back or downward. — *adv* **retrorse'ly.** [L. *retrōrsus* — *retrōversus*.]

retrospect *ret'rō-* or *rēt'ō-spekt*, *n* reference, regard; a backward view; a view or a looking back; a contemplation of the past. — *n* **retrospec'tion.** — *adj* **retrospec'tive** looking back; retroactive. — *n* an exhibition, etc. presenting the life's work of an artist, etc. — *adv* **retrospec'tively.** [L. *retrōspicĕre* — L. *specĕre, spectum*, to look.]

retroussé *rə-trōō's'ā*, *adj* turned up (esp. of the nose). [Fr. (past p. *retroussé*), to turn up.]

retrovert *ret-rō-*, *rē-trō-vûrt'* or *rē'trō-vûrt*, *vt* to turn back. — *n* **retrover'sion.** [L. *retrōvertĕre, -versum* — *vertĕre*, to turn.]

retrovirus *ret'rō-vī-rəs*, *n* any of a group of eukaryotic viruses whose genetic material is encoded in the form of RNA rather than DNA and which are known to cause a number of diseases. [*re*verse *tr*anscriptase (the active enzyme in these viruses) and **virus.**]

retry *rē-trī'*, *vt* to try again (judicially): — *pr p* **retry'ing;** *pa t* and *pa p* **retried'.** — *n* **rētrī'al.** [**re-**.]

retsina *ret-sēn'ə*, *n* a Greek resin-flavoured wine. [Gr.]

retted, retting. See **ret.**

return *ri-tûrn'*, *vi* to come or go back; to revert; to recur; to continue with change of direction (*archit*). — *vt* to make a turn at an angle (*archit*); to give, put, cast, bring or send back; to answer; to retort; to report officially; to report as appointed or elected; to elect to parliament; to give in return; to lead back or hit back (*sport*); to requite; to repay; to render; to yield. — *n* the act of returning; a recurrence; reversion; continuation, or a continuing stretch, at an angle, esp. a right angle (*archit*, etc.); that which comes in exchange; proceeds, profit, yield; recompense; an answer; an answering performance; a thing returned, esp. an unsold newspaper; the rendering back, with the sheriff's report, of a writ (*law*); an official report or statement, e.g. of one's taxable income (*tax return*) or (esp. in *pl*) of the votes cast in an election; election to parliament; a return ticket. — *adj* returning; for return; in return; at right angles. — *adj* **return'able.** — *n* **returnee'** someone who returns or is returned, esp. home from abroad or war service. — *n* **return'er.** — *adj* **return'less.** — **returning officer** the officer who presides at an election; **return match** a second match played at a different venue by the same teams of players; **return ticket** a ticket entitling a passenger to travel to a place and back to the starting-point. — **by return (of post)** by the next post leaving in the opposite direction; **many happy returns (of the day)** a conventional expression of good wishes said to a person on his or her birthday. [Fr. *retourner* — *re-*, back, *tourner*, to turn.]

re-turn *rē-tûrn'*, *vt* and *vi* to turn again or back. [**re-**.]

retuse *ri-tūs'*, (*bot*) *adj* with the tip blunt and broadly notched. [L. *retūsus* — *retundĕre*, to blunt.]

reunion *rē-ūn'yən*, *n* a union, or a meeting, after separation; a social gathering of friends or people with something in common. [Fr. *réunion* — *re-*, again, *union*, union.]

reunite *rē-ū-nīt'*, *vt* and *vi* to join after separation. [**re-**.]

Rev. *abbrev* for: (the Book of) the Revelation of St. John, Revelations (*Bible*); Reverend (also **Revd**); revise, revised or revision (also **rev.**).

rev *rev*, *n* a revolution in an internal-combustion engine. — *vt* to increase the speed of revolution in (often with *up*). — *vi* to revolve; to increase in speed of revolution: — *pr p* **revv'ing;** *pa t* and *pa p* **revved.** [**revolution.**]

revalorise or **-ize** *rē-val'ər-īz*, *vt* to give a new value to, esp. to restore the value of (currency). — *n* **rēvalorīsā'tion** or **-z-**. [**re-**.]

revalue *rē-val'ū*, *vt* to make a new valuation of; to give a new value to. — *n* **rēvalūā'tion.** [**re-**.]

revamp *rē-vamp'*, *vt* to renovate, revise or give a new appearance to. — Also *n*. [**re-**.]

revanche *ri-vänch'*, *n* a policy directed towards recovery of territory lost to an enemy. — *n* **revanch'ism.** — *n* and *adj* **revanch'ist.** [Fr.; conn. with **revenge** (q.v.).]

Revd. See **Rev.**

reveal[1] *ri-vēl'*, *vt* to make known, as by divine agency or inspiration; to disclose; to allow to be seen. — *adj* **reveal'able.** — *n* **reveal'er.** — *n* and *adj* **reveal'ing.** [O.Fr. *reveler* — L. *revēlāre* — *re-*, back, *vēlāre*, to veil — *vēlum*, a veil.]

reveal[2] *ri-vēl'*, *n* the side surface of a recess or of the opening for a doorway or window between the frame and the outer surface of the wall. [O.Fr. *revaler*, to lower.]

reveille *ri-val'i* or in U.S. *rev'ə-lē*, *n* the sound of the drum or bugle at daybreak to awaken soldiers; the time when this sound is made. [Fr. *réveillez*, awake, imper. of *réveiller*.]

revel *rev'l*, *vi* to feast or make merry in a riotous or noisy manner; to take intense delight, to luxuriate (with *in*): — *pr p* **rev'elling;** *pa t* and *pa p* **rev'elled.** — *n* a riotous feast; merrymaking; a festival or (often in *pl*) occasion of merrymaking, dancing, masking, etc. — *n* **rev'eller.** — *n* **rev'elling.** — *n* **rev'elry** revelling. [O.Fr. *reveler* — L. *rebellāre*, to rebel.]

revelation *rev-i-lā'shən*, *n* the act or experience of revealing; that which is revealed; a disclosure; an enlightening experience; divine or supernatural communication; **Revelation (of St John)** or, popularly, **Revelations** (*nsing*) the Apocalypse or last book of the New Testament. — *adj* **revelā'tional.** — *n* **revelā'tionist** a believer in divine revelation; the author of the Apocalypse. — *adj* **rev'elatory.** [L. *revēlāre*, *-ātum*; see **reveal**[1].]

revenant *rəv-nã'* or *rev'ə-nənt*, *n* someone who returns after a long absence, esp. supposedly from the dead; a ghost. [Fr., pres. p. of *revenir*, to come back.]

revenge *ri-venj'*, *vt* to inflict injury in retribution for; (esp. *reflexive*) to avenge. — *vi* to take vengeance: — *n* (the act of inflicting) malicious injury in return for injury received; the desire for opportunity of retaliation. — *adj* **revenge'ful.** — *adv* **revenge'fully.** — *n* **revenge'fulness.** — *adj* **revenge'less.** — *n* **reveng'er.** — *n* and *adj* **reveng'ing.** — *adv* **reveng'ingly.** [O.Fr. *revenger*, *revencher*.]

revenue *rev'in-ū*, *n* receipts or return from any source; income; the income of a state; a government department concerned with it. — *adj* **rev'enued.** — **revenue cutter** (*hist*) an armed vessel employed in preventing smuggling. [Fr. *revenue*, past p. (fem.) of *revenir*, to return.]

reverb *ri-vûrb'* or **reverb unit** (*ū'nit*), (*mus*) *n* a device which creates an effect of reverberation, used in recording or with electrically amplified instruments. [Colloq. abbrev. of **reverberate** and **reverberation.**]

reverberate *ri-vûr'bər-āt*, *vt* to echo; to reflect; to heat in a reverberatory furnace. — *vi* to be reflected; to re-echo, to resound. — *adj* **rever'berant** reverberating. — *n* **reverberā'tion.** — *adj* **rever'berātive** (or *-ət-*). — *n* **rever'berātor.** — *adj* **rever'beratory** (*-ət-ər-i* or *-āt-*). — **reverberatory furnace** a furnace in which the flame is turned back over the substance to be heated. [L. *reverberāre*, *-ātum* — *re-*, back, *verberāre*, to beat.]

revere *ri-vēr'*, *vt* to regard with high respect; to venerate. — *adj* **revēr'able.** — *n* **reverence** (*rev'ər-əns*) high respect; veneration; a gesture or observance of respect. — *vt* to venerate. — *n* **rev'erencer.** — *adj* **rev'erend** worthy of reverence; (with *cap*; usu. written **Rev.**) a title prefixed to a clergyman's name. — *n* a clergyman. — *adj* **rev'erent** feeling or showing reverence. — *adj* **reverential** (*-en'shl*) respectful; submissive. — *adv* **reveren'tially.** — *adv* **rev'erently.** — *n* **reverer** (*ri-vēr'ər*). — **His** or **Your Reverence** (now *Ir* or *playful*) a mode of referring to or addressing a clergyman; **Most Reverend** is used of an archbishop, **Right Reverend** of a bishop or a Moderator of the Church of Scotland, **Very Reverend** of a dean or a former Moderator; **Reverend Mother,** a Mother Superior of a convent. [O.Fr. *reverer* — L. *reverērī* — *re-* (intensive) and *verērī*, feel awe.]

reverie *rev'ə-ri*, *n* mental abstraction; an undirected train of thoughts or fancies in meditation; a piece of music expressing such a state of mind. [Fr. *rêverie* — *rêver*, to dream.]

revers *ri-vēr'*, *n* any part of a garment that is turned back, such as a lapel: — *pl* **revers** (*ri-vērz'*). [Fr., — L. *reversus*.]

reverse *ri-vûrs'*, *vt* to turn the other way about, e.g. upside down, outside in, in the opposite direction, etc.; to invert; to set moving backwards; to move (something) backwards; to annul. — *vi* to move backwards or in the opposite direction; to set an engine, etc. moving backwards. — *n* the contrary, opposite; the back, esp. of a coin or medal (opp. to *obverse*); a setback, misfortune, defeat; an act of reversing; a backwards direction; reverse gear. — *adj* contrary, opposite; turned about; acting in the contrary direction; of the rear (*mil*). — *n* **rever'sal** an act or instance of reversing; a change (e.g. in fortune; esp. for the worse). — *adj* **reversed'.** — *adv* **rever'sedly.** — *adv* **reverse'ly.** — *n* **rever'ser.** — *n* **reversibil'ity.** — *adj* **rever'sible** able to be reversed (in any sense); allowing of restoration (of tissues, etc.) to a normal state (*med*). — *n* a fabric having both sides equally well finished. — *n* and *adj* **rever'sing.** — *n* **rever'sion** (*-shən*) the act or fact of reverting or of returning; something which reverts or returns; the right to return or succeed to possession or office; a sum payable on death; that which is left over, remains; return to ancestral type (*biol*). — *adj* **rever'sional.** — *adv* **rever'sionally.** — *adj* **rever'sionary.** — **reverse engineering** the taking apart of a competitor's product to see how it works, with a view to copying it or improving on it; **reverse gear** a gear combination which causes an engine, etc. to go in reverse; **reverse transcriptase** the enzyme in a retrovirus which makes a DNA copy of an RNA genome; **reversing light** a light on the back of a motor vehicle which comes on when the vehicle is put into reverse gear. — **go into reverse** to engage reverse gear; to move backwards; **reverse the charges** to charge a telephone call to the one who receives it instead of to the caller. [L. *reversāre*, to turn round.]

revert *ri-vûrt'*, *vt* to turn back. — *vi* to return; to fall back to a former state; to return to the original owner or to his or her heirs. — *adj* **rever'ted.** — *adj* **rever'tible.** [L. *re-*, *vertĕre*, to turn.]

revetment *ri-vet'mənt*, (esp. *fort*) *n* a retaining wall, a facing. [Fr. *revêtir*, to reclothe.]

review *ri-vū'*, *n* a viewing again (also **re-view** *rē'-vū*); a looking back; a reconsideration; a survey; a revision; a critical examination; a critique; a periodical with critiques of books, etc.; a display and inspection of troops or ships; the judicial revision of a higher court (*law*). — *vt* to see, view or examine again (also **rē-view'**); to look back on or over; to survey; to examine critically; to write a critique on; to inspect, (e.g. troops); to revise. — *vi* to write reviews. — *adj* **review'able.** — *n* **review'al.** — *n* **review'er** a writer of critiques. — **review body** a committee set up to review (salaries, etc.); **review copy** a copy of a book sent by the publisher to a periodical for review. [Partly pfx. **re-** and **view;** partly Fr. *revue*, past p. (fem.) of *revoir*.]

revile *ri-vīl'*, *vt* to assail with bitter abuse. — *vi* to rail, use abusive language. — *n* **revile'ment** the act of reviling; a reviling speech. — *n* **revil'er.** — *n* and *adj* **revil'ing.** — *adv* **revil'ingly.** [O.Fr. *reviler* — L. *re-*, *vīlis*, worthless.]

revise *ri-vīz'*, *vt* to examine and correct; to make a new, improved version of; to study again (esp. for an examination, something already learned). — Also *vi.* — *n* a proof in which previous corrections have been given effect to (*printing*); a revision. — *adj* **revīs'able** liable to revision. — *n* **revī'sal.** — *n* **revī'ser** (also **revīs'or**). — *n* **revision** (*-vizh'ən*) the act or product of revising. — *adj* **revi'sional.** — *adj* **revi'sionary.** — *n* **revi'sionism.** — *n* **revi'sionist** an advocate of revision (e.g. of established doctrines, etc.); a Communist favouring modification of stricter orthodox Communism and evolution, rather than revolution; (*abusively*) a Communist who does not hold to orthodox Communism. — *adj* **revī'sory.** — **Revised Version** an English translation of the Bible issued 1881–85 (Apocrypha 1895). [Fr. *reviser* and L. *revīsĕre* — *re-*, back, *vīsĕre*, intensive of *vidēre*, to see.]

revive *ri-vīv'*, *vt* and *vi* to bring back or come back to life, vigour, being, activity, consciousness, memory, good spirits, freshness, vogue, notice, currency, use, or the stage. — *n* **revīvabil'ity.** — *adj* **revī'vable.** — *adv* **revī'vably.** — *n* **revī'val** the act or fact of reviving; recovery from languor, neglect, depression, etc.; a renewed performance, e.g. of a play; a time of religious awakening; a series of meetings to encourage this; renewal; awakening. — *n* **revī'valism.** — *n* **revī'valist** a person who promotes religious revival; an itinerant preacher. — *adj* **revivalist'ic.** — *n* **revī'ver** someone who or something that revives; a preparation that renovates or restores; a stimulant, esp. an alcoholic drink (*colloq*). — *n* and *adj* **revī'ving.** — *adv* **revī'vingly.** — *n* **revī'vor** (*law*) the revival of a suit which was abated by the death of a party or other cause. — **Gothic Revival** the resuscitation of Gothic architecture in (and before) the 19th century; **Revival of Learning** the Renaissance. [L. *revīvĕre*, to live again — *vīvĕre*, to live.]

revivify *ri-viv'i-fī*, *vt* to restore to life; to put new life into; to reactivate: — *pr p* **reviv'ifying**; *pa t* and *pa p* **reviv'ified.** — *n* **revivificā'tion.** [L.L. *re-vīvificāre* — *re-*, *vīvus*, alive, *facĕre*, to make.]

revocable, etc. See **revoke.**

revoke *ri-vōk'*, *vt* to annul; to retract. — *vi* to neglect to follow suit at cards. — *n* the act of revoking at cards. — *adj* **revocable** (*rev'ō-kə-bl*). — *n* **rev'ocableness.** — *n* **revocabil'ity.** — *adv* **rev'ocably.** — *n* **revocā'tion** the act of revoking. — *adj* **rev'ocatory.** [L. *revocāre* — *vocāre*, to call.]

revolt *ri-vōlt'*, *vi* to renounce allegiance; to rise in opposition; to turn or rise up with feelings of hate, loathing or repugnance. — *vt* to inspire revulsion or repugnance in. — *n* a rebellion; secession. — *adj* **revolt'ed** insurgent; shocked, outraged. — *n* **revol'ter.** — *adj* **revol'ting** horrible, repulsive, disgusting; rising in revolt, rebellious. — *adv* **revol'tingly.** [Fr. *révolter* — L. *re-*, *volūtāre*, frequentative of *volvĕre*, *volūtum*, to turn.]

revolute. See under **revolve.**

revolution *rev-əl-ōō'shən* or *-ū'shən*, *n* the act or condition of revolving; movement in an orbit, as distinguished from rotation; rotation; a complete turn by an object or figure, through four right angles, about an axis; a cycle of phenomena or of time; recurrence in cycles; a great upheaval; a complete change, e.g. in outlook, social habits or circumstances; a radical change in government; a time of intensified change in the earth's features (*geol*). — *adj* **revolu'tionary** of, favouring, or of the nature of, revolution, esp. in government or conditions. — *n* someone who takes part in or supports a revolution. — *vt* **revolu'tionise** or **-ize** to cause radical change or a revolution in; to make revolutionary. — *n* **revolu'tionism.** — *n* **revolu'tionist.** — **Revolutionary Calendar** the calendar used in France from 1793 to 1805. — **the American Revolution** the change from the condition of British colonies to national independence effected by the thirteen states of the American Union in 1776; **the French Revolution** the overthrow of the old French monarchy and absolutism (1789). [L.L. *revolūtiō*, *-ōnis*.]

revolve *ri-volv'*, *vt* and *vi* to ponder; to move about a centre; to rotate. — *adj* **revolute** (*rev'əl-ūt* or *-ōōt*; *bot*) rolled backward and usu. downward. — *n* and *adj* **revol'ving.** — **revolving credit** credit which is automatically renewed as the sum previously borrowed is paid back, so allowing the borrower to make repeated use of the credit so long as the agreed maximum sum is not exceeded; **revolving door** a door consisting of usu. four leaves fixed around a central axis. [L. *revolvĕre*, *revolūtum* — *volvĕre*, to roll.]

revolver *ri-volv'ər*, *n* a pistol with a rotating magazine. [Ety. as for **revolve.**]

revue *ri-vū'*, *n* a loosely constructed theatrical show, topical, musical and usu. amusing. [Fr., review.]

revulsion *ri-vul'shən*, *n* disgust; a sudden change or reversal; withdrawal; diversion to another part, esp. by counter-irritation (*med*). — *adj* **revul'sive** (*-siv*). [L. *revellĕre*, *revulsum*, to pluck back — *vellĕre*, to pluck.]

revved, etc. See **rev.**

reward *ri-wörd'*, *n* something given in return for good (sometimes evil), or in recognition of merit, or for performance of a service. — *vt* to give or be a reward to or for. — *adj* **reward'able.** — *n* **reward'ableness.** — *n* **reward'er.** — *adj* **reward'ing** profitable; yielding a result well worth while. — *adj* **reward'less.** [O.Fr. *rewarder*, *regarder* — *re-*, again, *warder*, *garder*, to guard.]

rewarewa *rē'wə-rē'wə* or *rā'wə-rā'wə*, *n* a New Zealand tree (*Knightia excelsa*) whose wood is used in furniture-making — also known as **honeysuckle.** [Maori.]

reword *rē-wûrd'*, *vt* to put into different words. [**re-**.]

Rex *reks*, *n* king, the title used by a reigning king, abbrev. to **R** in signature. [L. *rex*, king.]

Reye's syndrome *rīz sin'drōm*, (*med*) *n* a rare, acute and often fatal disease of children, affecting the brain and the liver. [R.D.K. *Reye* (1912–78), Australian paediatrician.]

Reynard or **reynard** *rān'* or *ren'ärd* or *-ərd*, *n* a fox, from the name given to the fox in the mediaeval epic *Reynard the Fox*. [M.Du. *Reynaerd* — O.H.G. *Reginhart*, lit. strong in counsel.]

Reynolds number *ren'əldz num'bər*, (*mech*) *n* a number designating the type of flow of a fluid in a system. [Osborne *Reynolds* (1842–1912), British physicist.]

RF *abbrev* for radio frequency.

Rf (*chem*) *symbol* for rutherfordium.

RFU *abbrev* for Rugby Football Union.

RGN *abbrev* for Registered General Nurse.

RGV *abbrev* for Remote Guidance Vehicle.

RH *abbrev* for: Republic of Haiti (I.V.R.); Royal Highness.

Rh *symbol* for: rhesus; rhodium (*chem*).

rh *abbrev* for right hand or right-hand.

RHA *abbrev* for: Royal Hibernian Academy; Royal Horse Artillery.

rhabdomancy *rab'də-man-si*, *n* divination by rod, esp. divining for water or ore. — *n* **rhab'domantist.** [Gr. *rhabdos*.]

Rhaeto-Romanic *rē'tō-rō-man'ik*, *n* a general name for a group of Romance dialects spoken from south-eastern Switzerland to Friuli. — Also **Rhae'tic** or **Rhae'to-Romance.** — Also *adj*.

rhagades *rag'a-dēz*, (*med*) *npl* cracks or fissures in the skin. — *adj* **rhagad'iform.** [Gr. *rhagas*, pl. *rhagades*, a tear, rent.]

rhapsody *raps'ə-di*, *n* an irregular emotional piece of music; an ecstatic utterance of feeling. — *adj* **rhapsodic** (*-od'ik*). — *adj* **rhapsod'ical** rhapsodic; unrestrainedly enthusiastic, rapt. — *adv* **rhapsod'ically.** — *vt* **rhaps'odise** or **-ize** (*-ə-dīz*) to recite in rhapsodies. — *vi* to write or utter rhapsodies. — *n* **rhaps'odist.** [Gr. *rhapsōidiā*, an epic, a rigmarole — *rhaptein*, to sew, *ōidē*, a song.]

rhatany *rat'ə-ni*, *n* either of two South American plants (species of *Krameria*); the astringent, thick, fleshy root of either plant. [Sp. *ratania* — Quechua *rataña*.]

rhea *rē'ə*, *n* a small flightless South American bird of the genus *Rhea*, resembling the ostrich. [Gr. *Rhĕā*.]

Rhenish *ren'ish* or *rēn'ish*, *adj* of the river *Rhine*, a river of Europe. — *n* Rhine wine.

rhenium *rē'ni-əm*, *n* a chemical element (symbol **Re**; atomic no. 75) discovered by X-ray spectroscopy in Germany in 1925. [L. *Rhēnus*, the Rhine.]

rheo- *rē'ō-* or *rē-ō'-*, *combining form* signifying current, flow. — *n* a wire rheostat. — *adj* **rheolog'ic** or **rheolog'ical.** — *n* **rheol'ogist.** — *n* **rheol'ogy** the science of the deformation and flow of matter. — *n* **rhē'ostat** an instrument for varying an electric resistance. — *adj* **rheotrop'ic.** — *n* **rheot'ropism** (*biol*) response to the stimulus of flowing water. [Gr. *rheos*, flow.]

rhesus *rē'səs*, *n* a macaque (*Macacus rhesus*, or *Macaca mulatta*), an Indian monkey. — Also **rhesus monkey.** — **Rhesus factor, Rh-factor** or **Rh** an antigen usu. found in human red blood cells and in those of rhesus monkeys, **Rh-pos'itive** persons being those who have the factor and **Rh-neg'ative** those (a very much smaller number) who do not. [Gr. *Rhēsos*, a king of Thrace, arbitrarily applied.]

rhet. *abbrev* for rhetoric.

rhetoric *ret'ər-ik*, *n* the theory and practice of eloquence, whether spoken or written, the whole art of using language so as to persuade others; the art of literary expression; false, showy, artificial or declamatory expression. — *adj* **rhetoric** (*ri-tor'ik*). — *adj* **rhetor'ical** pertaining to rhetoric; oratorical; inflated or insincere in style. — *adv* **rhetor'ically.** — *n* **rhetorician** (*ret-ər-ish'ən*) a person who teaches the art of rhetoric; an orator; a user of rhetorical language. — **rhetorical question** a question in form, for rhetorical effect, not calling for an answer. [Gr. *rhētōr*, a teacher of rhetoric, or professional orator.]

rheum *rōōm*, *n* a mucous discharge, esp. from the nose. — *adj* **rheumatic** (*rōō-mat'ik*) of the nature of, pertaining to, apt to cause, or affected with, rheumatism. — *n* someone who suffers from rheumatism; (in *pl*) rheumatic pains (*colloq*). — *adv* **rheumat'ically.** — *adj* **rheumat'icky.** — *n* **rheumatism** (*rōō'mə-tizm*) a condition characterised by pain and stiffness in muscles and joints. — *adj* **rheum'atoid.** — *adj* **rheumatolog'ical.** — *n* **rheumatol'ogist.** — *n* **rheumatol'ogy** the study of rheumatism. — *adj* **rheumed.** — *adj* **rheum'y** of or like rheum; esp. of air, cold and damp. — **rheumatic fever** an acute disease characterised by fever, multiple arthritis, and liability of the heart to be inflamed, caused by a streptococcal infection; **rheumatoid arthritis** a disease characterised by inflammation and swelling of joints. [Gr. *rheuma*, *-atos*, flow — *rheein*, to flow.]

Rh-factor. See under **rhesus.**

RHG *abbrev* for Royal Horse Guards.

rhin- *rīn-* or **rhino-** *rīn-ō-* *combining form* denoting nose. — *adj* **rhī'nal** of the nose. — *n* **rhinī'tis** inflammation of the mucous membrane of the nose. — *adj* **rhīnolog'ical.** — *n* **rhīnol'ogist** a nose specialist. — *n* **rhīnol'ogy** the study of the nose; nasal pathology. — *adj* **rhīnoplas'tic.** — *n* **rhī'noplasty** plastic surgery of the nose. — *n* **rhī'noscope** an instrument for examining the nose. — *adj* **rhīnoscop'ic.** — *n* **rhīnos'copy.** — *n* **rhī'novirus** a virus belonging to a subgroup picornaviruses thought responsible for the common cold and other respiratory diseases. [Gr. *rhīs*, *rhīnos*, nose.]

Rhinestone *rīn'stōn*, *n* (also without *cap*) a rock-crystal; a paste diamond. — **Rhine wine** wine made from grapes grown in the *Rhine* valley. [*Rhine*, a river of Europe; Ger. *Rhein*; Du. *Rijn*.]

rhinitis. See under **rhin-.**

rhino[1] *rī'nō*, *n* short for **rhinoceros**: — *pl* **rhī'nos.**

rhino[2] *rī'nō*, (*slang*) *n* money.

rhinoceros *rī-nos'ər-əs*, *n* a large, thick-skinned mammal of several ungulate species in Africa and southern Asia which form a family characterised by one or two horns on the nose: — *pl* **rhinoc'eroses.** — *adj* **rhinocerot'ic.** [Gr. *rhīnokerōs* — *rhīs*, *rhīnos*, nose, *keras*, horn.]

rhinological . . . to . . . **rhinovirus.** See under **rhin-.**

rhiz- *rīz-* or **rhizo-** *rī-zō-*, *combining form* denoting root. — *n* **rhī'zocarp** (Gr. *karpos*, fruit) a perennial herb; a plant fruiting underground. — *adj* **rhīzocar'pic** or **rhīzocar'pous.** — *n* **rhī'zoid** a short hairlike organ in the lower plants, serving as a root. — *adj* **rhīzoi'dal.** — *adj* **rhīzō'matous.** — *n* **rhī'zome** a rootstock, an underground stem producing roots and leafy shoots. — *n* **rhī'zopod** protozoa with rootlike pseudopodia. [Gr. *rhiza*, root.]

Rh-negative. See under **rhesus.**

rho *rō*, *n* the seventeenth letter (Ρ, ρ) of the Greek alphabet, answering to R: — *pl* **rhos.** [Gr. *rhō*.]

rhod- *rōd-* or **rhodo-** *rō-dō-* *combining form* signifying: rose; rose-coloured. [Gr. *rhodon*, rose.]

rhodamine *rō'də-mēn*, *n* a synthethic dyestuff, usually red. — *n*. [**rhod-** and **amine.**]

Rhode Island Red *rōd ī'lənd red*, *n* an American breed of domestic fowl, with browny-red plumage.

Rhodesian man *rō-dē'zhyən man*, *n* an extinct type of man represented by a skull found at Broken Hill, in Northern Rhodesia, in 1921.

rhodium *rō'di-əm*, *n* a metallic element (symbol **Rh**; atomic no. 45) of the platinum group, forming rose-coloured salts. [Gr. *rhodon*, rose.]

rhodochrosite *rō-dō-krō'sīt*, *n* manganese spar, a pink rhombohedral mineral, manganese carbonate. [Gr. *rhodochrōs*, rose-coloured, and **-ite** (3).]

rhododendron *rō-* or *rod-ə-den'drən*, *n* any member of the **Rhododen'dron** genus of trees and shrubs of the heath family, with leathery leaves and large showy slightly zygomorphic flowers, some species being called *Alpine rose*. [Gr. *rhodon*, rose, *dendron*, tree.]

rhodolite *rō'də-līt*, *n* a pink or purple garnet (gemstone). [**rhodo-** and *-lite*, sfx. denoting stone.]

rhodonite *rō'də-nīt*, *n* a rose-red anorthic pyroxene, manganese silicate. [Gr. *rhodon*, rose, and **-ite** (3).]

rhodopsin *rō-dop'sin*, *n* a purple-red pigment in the retinal rods of vertebrates. [Gr. *rhodon*, rose, *opsis*, sight.]

rhodora *rō-dö'rə*, *n* a handsome N. American species of rhododendron. [L. *rhodōra*, meadowsweet.]

rhomb *rom* or *romb*, *n* an equilateral parallelogram (usu. excluding the square); a lozenge-shaped object; a rhombohedron (*crystall*). — *adj* **rhombic** (*rom'bik*) shaped like a rhombus; orthorhombic (*crystall*). — *adj* **rhombohē'dral.** — *n* **rhombohē'dron** a crystal form of six rhombi: — *pl* **rhombohē'dra** or **rhombohē'drons.** [**rhombus** or Fr. *rhombe*.]

rhomboid *rom'boid*, *adj* like a rhombus; nearly square, with the petiole at one of the acute angles (*bot*). — *n* a figure approaching a rhombus, a parallelogram, usu. one that is not a rhombus nor a rectangle. — *adj* **rhomboid'al.**

rhombus *rom'bəs*, *n* a rhomb (*geom*); an object shaped like a rhomb: — *pl* **rhom'bī** or **rhom'buses.** [Gr. *rhombos*, bull-roarer, magic wheel, rhombus.]

Rh-positive. See under **rhesus.**

RHS *abbrev* for: Royal Highland Show; Royal Historical Society; Royal Horticultural Society; Royal Humane Society.

rhubarb *rōō'bärb* or *-bərb*, *n* any species of the genus *Rheum*, of the dock family; the leaf-stalks (chiefly of *R. rhaponticum*) cooked and used as if fruit; the rootstock (chiefly of *R. officinale*) used for its purgative properties; nonsense; hubbub (*slang*); a word muttered repeatedly to give the impression of indistinct background conversation (*theat*). — *n* **rhu'barbing** (*theat*) the use or practice of muttering rhubarb or a similar sound. [O.Fr. *reubarbe* — Gr. *rhā*, rhubarb — *Rhā*, the Volga, and L. *barbarum* (neut.), foreign.]

rhumb *rum*, (*naut*) *n* (also **rhumb'-line**) a loxodromic curve; a course following such a fixed line; any point of the compass. [Fr. *rumb*, or Sp. or Port. *rumbo* — L. *rhombus*; see **rhombus.**]

rhumba. See **rumba.**

rhyme *rīm*, *n* in two (or more) words, identity of sound from the last stressed vowel to the end, the consonant or consonant group preceding not being the same in both (or all) cases; extended to other correspondences in sound, such as *head-rhyme* or *eye-rhyme*; a word or group of words agreeing in this way with another; versification, verses, a poem or a short piece of verse, in which this correspondence occurs; a jingle. — *vi* to be in rhyme; to correspond in sound; to make or find a rhyme or rhymes; to make rhymes or verses. — *vt* to put into rhyme; to use or treat as a rhyme. — *adj* **rhymed** (*rīmd*). — *adj* **rhyme'less.** — *n* **rhy'mer** a user of rhyme; a poet; an inferior poet; a minstrel. — *n* **rhyme'ster** a would-be poet. — *n*

rhym'ist a versifier. — **rhyme-roy'al** a seven-line stanza borrowed by Chaucer from the French, its lines rhyming in the pattern *a b a b b c c*; **rhyme'-scheme** the pattern of rhymes in a stanza, etc.; **rhyming slang** a form of slang in which a word is replaced by another word, or part or all of a phrase, which rhymes with it. — **without rhyme or reason** without reasonable or sensible purpose or explanation. [In archaic usage *rime* — O.Fr. — L. *rhythmus* — Gr. *rhythmos*.]

rhyolite *rī'ō-līt*, *n* a fine-grained igneous rock, with a chemical composition similar to granite, generally containing large quartz and alkali-feldspar crystals in a glassy groundmass. — *adj* **rhyolitic** (*-lit'ik*). [Irregularly — Gr. *rhyax*, *-ākos*, a (lava) stream, *lithos*, a stone.]

rhythm *ridhm* or *rithm*, *n* regular recurrence, esp. of stress or of long and short sounds; a pattern of recurrence; an ability to sing, move, etc. rhythmically. — *adj* **rhythmed** (*ridhmd* or *rithmd*), **rhyth'mic** or **rhyth'mical**. — *n* **rhyth'mic** (also **rhyth'mics** *nsing*) the science or theory of rhythm. — *adv* **rhyth'mically**. — *n* **rhythmic'ity**. — *vt* **rhyth'mise** or **-ize** to subject to rhythm. — *vi* to act in or observe rhythm. — *n* **rhyth'mist** a person skilled in rhythm. — *adj* **rhythm'less**. — **rhythm method** a method of birth control requiring the avoidance of sexual intercourse during the period in which conception is most likely to occur; **rhythm section** in a band, those instruments whose main function is to supply the rhythm (usu. percussion, guitar, double-bass and piano); the players of such instruments. — **rhythm and blues** a type of music combining the styles of rock and roll and the blues. [L. *rhythmus* — Gr. *rhythmos* — *rheein*, to flow.]

rhytidectomy *rī-ti-dek'tə-mi*, *n* an operation for smoothing the skin of the face by removing wrinkles, a face-lift. [Gr. *rhytis*, a wrinkle, *ektomē*, cutting out.]

RI *abbrev* for: religious instruction; Republic of Indonesia (I.V.R.); Rhode Island (U.S. state); (Member of the) Royal Institute of Painters in Water Colours; Royal Institution.

RIA *abbrev* for Royal Irish Academy. — **RIAM** *abbrev* for Royal Irish Academy of Music.

ria *rē'ə*, (*geol*) *n* a normal drowned valley. [Sp. *ría*, river-mouth.]

rial *rē'əl*, *rī'əl* or *rē-äl'*, *n* the unit of currency in Iran (100 *dinars*), Oman (1000 *baizas*) and (also as **riyal**, q.v.) Saudi Arabia (100 *halalah*) and the Yemen Arab Republic (100 *fils*). [Pers. *rial*, Ar. *riyal*; see **riyal**.]

rib[1] *rib*, *n* one of the bones that curve round and forward from the backbone; a piece of meat containing one or more ribs; a curved member of the side of a ship running from keel to deck; a strengthening bar; a rodlike structure supporting or strengthening a membrane, etc., such as the vein of a leaf, or a spoke supporting the fabric of an umbrella; the shaft of a feather; one of the parallel supports of a bridge; a framing timber; a raised band; a ridge; a ridge raised in knitting, by alternating plain and purl stitches (e.g. as used for a waistband or wristband on a jumper), or a similar ridge raised in weaving; the pattern of ribs so formed (also called **ribb'ing**); a moulding or projecting band on a ceiling; a wife (from the Bible: Gen. ii. 21–23; *facetious*). — *vt* to provide, form, cover or enclose with ribs): — *pr p* **ribb'ing**; *pa t* and *pa p* **ribbed**. — *adj* **ribbed**. — *n* **ribb'ing** an arrangement of ribs. — *adj* **ribb'y**. — *adj* **rib'less**. — *n* **rib'let** a small, narrow or shallow rib. — *adj* **rib'like**. — **rib'-bone**; **rib'cage** the enclosing wall of the chest formed by the ribs, etc.; **rib'-tickler** a very funny joke or story. — *adj* **rib'-tickling** very funny, making one laugh uproariously. — **rib'-vaulting**; **rib'wort** or **ribwort plantain** a common weed with narrow strongly ribbed leaves and short brown heads. — **false rib** one joined indirectly to the breastbone or (**floating rib**) not at all; **true rib** one joined directly by its cartilage. [O.E. *ribb*, rib, *ribbe*, ribwort.]

rib[2] *rib*, (*slang*) *vt* to tease, ridicule, make fun of. [Perh. **rib**[1] — the tickling of one's ribs causing laughter.]

RIBA *abbrev* for Royal Institute of British Architects.

ribald *rib'əld*, *adj* foul-mouthed or derisive; indecently abusive. — *n* an obscene speaker or writer. — *n* **rib'aldry** obscenity; coarse talk or behaviour. [O.Fr. *ribald*, *ribaut*.]

riband *rib'ənd*, *n* a spelling of **ribbon** used (esp. in *heraldry* or *sport*) in derivatives and compounds, e.g. **blue riband**.

ribbon *rib'ən*, *n* material woven in a narrow band or strip; a strip of such or other material, e.g. metal or timber; anything resembling such a strip, such as a road, a stripe of colour; a torn strip, tatter or shred; a strip of inking cloth, as for a typewriter. — *adj* made of ribbon; like a ribbon; having bands of different colours. — *vt* to decorate with, mark into, or make into ribbon. — *adj* **ribb'ony**. — **ribb'on-building** or **-development** unplanned building, growth of towns, in long strips along the main roads; **ribb'on-fish** a long, slender, laterally compressed fish, esp. the oar fish; **ribbon microphone** a microphone in which the sound is picked up by a thin metallic strip; **ribb'on-seal** a banded North Pacific seal; **ribb'on-worm** one of the Nemertinea. [O.Fr. *riban*.]

riboflavin *rī-bō-flā'vin*, *n* a member of vitamin B complex, in yellowish-brown crystals, promoting growth in children. [*ribose* and *flavin*, a yellow dye.]

ribonuclease *ri-bō-nū'kli-ās* or *-āz*, *n* an enzyme in the pancreas, etc., the first enzyme to be synthesised (1969). [*ribonucleotide* and chem. sfx. *-ase* denoting an enzyme.]

ribonucleic acid *rī'bō-nū-klē'ik as'id*, *n* a nucleic acid containing ribose, present in the living cells, where it plays an important part in the development of proteins (abbrev. **RNA**).

ribose *rī'bōs*, (*chem*) *n* a pentose, $C_5H_{10}O_5$. [From *arabinose*, a sugar in gum arabic, by transposition of letters.]

RIC *abbrev* for Royal Irish Constabulary.

rice *rīs*, *n* a grass (*Oryza sativa*) grown in warm climates, usu. in flooded paddy-fields; its grain, an important cereal food. — *vt* (esp. *US*) to form soft food, esp. cooked potatoes, into strands by passing through a ricer, sieve, etc. — *n* **rīc'er** a utensil for ricing food. — *adj* **rice'y** or **ri'cy**. — **rice'-beer** a fermented drink made from rice; **rice flour**; **rice paper** sliced and flattened pith of an Asiatic tree used as an edible paper in baking, etc., and as a delicate art paper; a similar material made from other plants, or from linen trimmings; **rice pudding**. [O.Fr. *ris* — L. *oryza* — Gr. *oryza*.]

rich *rich*, *adj* having abundant possessions; wealthy; well provided or supplied; having any ingredient or quality in great abundance; productive, fertile; deep in colour, full-toned; full-flavoured; abounding in fat, sugar, fruit or seasonings; full; splendid and costly; elaborately decorated. — (In combination) **-rich** abundantly supplied with a specified thing, as in *oil-rich*. — *adv* **rich'ly**. — *n* **rich'ness**. [O.E. *rīce*, great, powerful.]

riches *rich'iz*, *n* (now usu. treated as *pl*) wealth. [O.Fr. *richesse* — *riche*, rich.]

Richter scale *rihht'ər skāl*, *n* a scale of measurement from 1 to 10, used to indicate the magnitude of an earthquake (8 is a major quake). [From its inventor, Dr Charles F. *Richter* (born 1900).]

rick[1] *rik*, *n* a stack; a heap. — *vt* to stack. — *n* **rick'er** an implement for shocking hay (see **shock**[2]). — **rick'yard**. [O.E. *hrēac*; O.N. *hraukr*.]

rick[2] *rik*, *vt* to sprain or strain. — *n* a sprain or strain. [App. a variant of **wrick**.]

ricker *rik'ər, n* a spar or young tree-trunk. [Perh. Ger. *Rick*, pole.]

rickets *rik'its, nsing* a disease of children, characterised by softness of the bones caused by deficiency of vitamin D. — *adv* **rick'etily** shakily. — *n* **rick'etiness** unsteadiness. — *adj* **rick'ety** affected with rickets; feeble, unstable; tottery, threatening to collapse. [Perh. M.E. *wrikken*, to twist; or Gr. *rhachitis* (see **rachitis**).]

Rickettsia *rik-et'si-ə, n* a genus of micro-organisms found in lice and ticks and, when transferred to man by a bite, causing typhus and other serious diseases; (without *cap*) a member of the genus Rickettsia. — *adj* **rickett'sial**. [After Howard Taylor *Ricketts* (1871–1910), American pathologist.]

rick-rack or **ric-rac** *rik'-rak, n* a decorative braid in even zigzag form, or openwork made with it. [**rack**[1].]

ricksha or **rickshaw** *rik'shä* or *-shö, n* a small two-wheeled, hooded carriage drawn by a man or men, or powered by a man on a bicycle or motor-bicycle. — Also **jinrick'sha** or **jinrick'shaw**. [Jap. *jin*, man, *riki*, power, *sha*, carriage.]

ricochet *rik'ō-shā* or *-shet*, also *-shā'* or *-shet', n* a glancing rebound or skip, as of a projectile flying low. — *vi* to glance; to skip along the ground: — *pr p* **ricocheting** (*rik'ə-shā-ing*) or **ricochetting** (*rik'ə-shet-ing*); *pa t* and *pa p* **ricocheted** (*rik'ə-shād*); **ricochetted** (*rik'ə-shet-id*). [Fr.]

ric-rac. See **rick-rack**.

RICS *abbrev* for Royal Institution of Chartered Surveyors.

rictus *rik'təs*, (*zool*) *n* the gape, esp. of a bird; unnatural gaping of the mouth. — *adj* **ric'tal**. [L. *rictus, -ūs*.]

rid[1] *rid, vt* to free; to clear; to disencumber: — *pr p* **ridd'ing**; *pa t* and *pa p* **rid** or **ridd'ed**. — *n* **ridd'ance** clearance; removal; disencumberment; deliverance. — *n* **ridd'er**. — **a good riddance** a welcome relief; **get rid of** to disencumber oneself of. [O.N. *rythja*, to clear.]

rid[2], **ridden**. See **ride**.

riddle[1] *rid'l, n* an obscure description of something which the hearer is asked to name; a puzzling question; anything puzzling. — *vt* to solve; to puzzle. — *vi* to make riddles; to speak obscurely. — *n* **ridd'ler**. — *n* **ridd'ling**. — *adj* enigmatic, obscure, puzzling. — *adv* **ridd'lingly**. [O.E. *rǣdelse* — *rǣdan*, to guess, to read — *rǣd*, counsel.]

riddle[2] *rid'l, n* a large coarse sieve. — *vt* to separate with a riddle; to make full of holes like a riddle, e.g. with shot. — *vi* to use a riddle; to sift. — *n* **ridd'ler**. — *n* **ridd'ling**. [O.E. *hriddel*, earlier *hridder*.]

ride *rīd, vt* to sit on and control; to travel on; to traverse, trace, ford or perform on horseback, on a bicycle, etc.; to sit on; to bestride; to control at will, or oppressively; to rest or turn on; to sustain, come through, esp. while riding at anchor (*naut*); to give a ride to, or cause to ride; to convey by vehicle (*US*); to copulate with (*vulg*). — *vi* to travel or be carried along on the back of an animal, on a bicycle, or in a vehicle, boat, on a broomstick, the waves, etc.; to float buoyantly; to lie at anchor (*naut*); to remain undisturbed, unchanged; to work up out of position; to allow (itself) to be ridden; to copulate (*vulg*): — *pa t* **rōde**; *pa p* **ridd'en**. — *n* a journey on horseback, on a bicycle, or in a vehicle; a spell of riding; an experience or course of events of a specified nature, e.g. a *rough ride*; a fairground entertainment on or in which people ride; a road for horse-riding, esp. one through a wood; an act of copulation (*vulg*); a partner (esp. female) in copulation (*vulg*). — *n* **rīdabil'ity**. — *adj* **rī'dable** or **ride'able**. — (In combination) **-ridden** oppressed by the dominance or prevalence of a specified thing (e.g. **hag-ridden, cliché-ridden**). — *n* **rī'der** a person who rides or can ride; an object that rests on or astride of another; an added clause or corollary; a proposition that a pupil or candidate is asked to deduce from another. — *adj* **rī'derless**. — *n* **rī'ding** the action of the verb to ride; the art or practice of horse-riding; a track for riding on; anchorage. — Also *adj*. — **ri'ding-boot** a high boot. — *npl* **ri'ding-breeches** breeches for riding, with loose-fitting thighs and tight-fitting legs. — **ri'ding-crop; ri'ding-habit** a woman's outfit for riding, esp. one with a long skirt for riding side-saddle; **ri'ding-hood** a hood formerly worn by women when riding; **ri'ding-light** a light hung out in the rigging at night when a vessel is riding at anchor; **ri'ding-school**. — **let (something) ride** to let (something) alone, not try to stop it; **ride down** to overtake by riding; to charge and overthrow or trample; **ride for a fall** to court disaster; **ride (someone) off** (*polo*) to bump against (another player's horse) moving in the same direction; **ride out** to keep afloat throughout (a storm); to survive, get safely through or past (a period of difficulty, etc.); **ride to hounds** to take part in fox-hunting; **ride up** to work up out of position; **take for a ride** to play a trick on, dupe. [O.E. *rīdan*.]

ridge *rij, n* the earth thrown up by the plough between the furrows; a long narrow top or crest; the horizontal line of a rooftop; a narrow elevation; a hill-range. — *vt* and *vi* to form into ridges; to wrinkle. — *adj* **ridged**. — *n* **ridg'ing**. — *adj* **ridg'y**. — **ridge'-piece** or **ridge'-pole** the timber forming the ridge of a roof; **ridge'-tile** a tile shaped to cover the ridge of a roof; **ridge'way** a track along the crest of a hill. [O.E. *hrycg*; O.N. *hryggr*, Ger. *Rücken*, back.]

ridicule *rid'i-kūl, n* derision; mockery. — *vt* to laugh at; to deride; to mock. — *n* **rid'icūler**. — *adj* **ridic'ūlous** deserving or provoking ridicule; absurd. — *adv* **ridic'ūlously**. — *n* **ridic'ūlousness**. [L. *rīdiculus* — *rīdēre*, to laugh.]

Riding *rī'ding, n* one of the three former divisions of Yorkshire (**West, East** and **North Riding**); a political constituency (*Can*). [For *thriding* — O.N. *thrithi*, third.]

riding. See **ride**.

RIE *abbrev* for Recognised Investment Exchanges.

riel *rē'əl, n* the basic monetary unit (100 *sen*) of Cambodia (formerly Kampuchea).

rien ne va plus *ri-ɛ̃ ne va plōō*, (Fr.) a term used by croupiers to indicate that no more bets may be placed. [Lit., nothing goes any more.]

Riesling *rēz'ling, n* a dry white table wine, named from a type of grape. [Ger.]

rife *rīf, adj* prevalent; abounding; current. — Also *adv*. — *adv* **rife'ly**. — *n* **rife'ness**. [O.E. *rȳfe, rīfe*.]

riff *rif*, (*jazz, rock* and *pop music*) *n* a phrase or figure played repeatedly. [Perh. *refrain*.]

riffle *rif'l, n* (*US*) a shallow section in a river where the water flows swiftly. — *vt* to riffle; to turn or stir lightly and rapidly (e.g. the pages of a book), often in cursory search for something; to treat the pages of (a book) in this way; to shuffle by allowing the corner of a card from one part of the pack to fall alternately with that of a card in the other. — Also *vi*. — *n* (e.g. in gold-washing) a groove or slat in a sluice to catch free particles of ore. [Cf. **ripple**[1].]

riff-raff *rif'-raf, n* undesirable, common people, scum. [M.E. *rif and raf* — O.Fr. *rif et raf*.]

rifle[1] *rī'fl, vt* to plunder; to ransack. — *n* **rī'fler**. [O.Fr. *rifler*.]

rifle[2] *rī'fl, vt* to groove spirally. — *n* a firearm with a spirally grooved barrel. — *n* **rī'fling** the spiral grooving of a gun-bore. — **ri'fle-bird** an Australian bird of paradise; **ri'fle-green** a dark green, the colour of a rifleman's uniform (also *adj*); **ri'fleman**; **ri'fle range** the range of a rifle; a place for rifle practice; **ri'fle-shot**. [O.Fr. *rifler*, to scratch.]

rift *rift, n* a cleft; a fissure. — *vt* and *vi* to cleave or split. — *adj* **rift'less**. — *adj* **rift'y**. — **rift valley** a valley formed by subsidence of a portion of the earth's crust between two faults. [Cf. Dan. and Norw. *rift*, a cleft.]

rig[1] *rig*, *vt* to fit with sails and tackling (*naut*); to fit up or fit out; to equip; to set up, set in working order; to dress, clothe (now *colloq*): — *pr p* **rigg'ing**; *pa t* and *pa p* **rigged**. — *n* the form and arrangement of masts, sails and tackling; an outfit; garb; general appearance; equipment; an articulated lorry (*colloq*); a well-boring plant, an oil rig. — (In combination) **-rigged** with masts and sails arranged in the manner indicated. — *n* **rigg'er** a person who rigs ships; a person who attends to the rigging of aircraft; someone who puts up and looks after scaffolding, etc., used for building operations; outrigger. — (In combination) **-rigger** denoting a ship rigged in manner indicated. — *n* **rigg'ing** tackle; the system of cordage which supports a ship's masts and extends the sails; the system of wires and cords in an aircraft. — **rig'-out** an outfit, costume, get-up. — **rig out** to furnish with complete dress, full equipment, etc.; **rig up** to dress or equip; to put up quickly from available materials. [Perh. conn. with Norw. *rigga*, to bind.]

rig[2] *rig*, *vt* to manipulate unscrupulously or dishonestly; to set up fraudulently. — *n* a frolic, prank, trick. — *n* **rigg'ing** manipulating unscrupulously or dishonestly, as in *price-rigging*, *vote-rigging*.

rigadoon *rig-ə-dōōn'*, *n* a lively jig-like dance for one couple, or its music. [Fr. *rigaudon*.]

right *rīt*, *adj* straight; direct; perpendicular; forming one-fourth of a revolution; with axis perpendicular to base; true; genuine; characteristic; truly judged or judging; appropriate; in accordance, or identical, with what is true and fitting; not mistaken; accurate; fit; sound; intended to be exposed (as a side, e.g. of cloth); morally justifiable; just; equitable; justly to be preferred or commended; at or towards that side at which in a majority of people is the better-developed hand (of a river, this side in relation to a person going downstream, or on the stage, from the point of view of an actor looking at the audience); for a part of the body, etc. on the right side; sitting at the president's right hand (in Continental assemblies); hence, conservative or inclined towards conservatism, right-wing. — *adv* straight; straightway; quite; just, exactly; in a right manner; justly; correctly; very (*archaic* or *dialect* or in special phrases); to or on the right side. — *n* that which is right or correct; rightness; fair treatment; equity; truth; justice; just or legal claim; what one has a just claim to; due; the right hand; the right side; the region on the right side; the right wing; the conservatives. — *vt* to set in order; to rectify; to redress; to vindicate; to set right side up or erect. — *vi* to recover an erect position. — *interj* expressing agreement, acquiescence, or readiness. — *adj* **right'able**. — *n* **right'er** someone who sets right or redresses wrong. — *adj* **right'ful** having a just claim; according to justice; belonging by right. — *adv* **right'fully**. — *n* **right'fulness**. — *n* **right'ing**. — *n* **right'ish**. — *n* **right'ist** an adherent of the political right (conservatives). — Also *adj*. — *adj* **right'less**. — *adv* **right'ly**. — *n* **right'ness**. — *interj* **righto'** (*pl* **rightos'**) or **right-oh'** (*colloq*) expressing (esp. cheerful) compliance or acceptance. — *adj* and *adv* **right'ward** towards the right; more right-wing. — *adv* **right'wards**. — **right about** the directly opposite quarter (in drill or dismissal; also **right-about face**). — *adv* in the opposite direction. — *vi* to turn to face the opposite direction. — *adj* **right'-and-left'** having a right and a left side, part, etc.; on both sides; from both barrels. — *n* a shot or a blow from each barrel or hand. — *adv* on both sides; on all hands; towards one side, then the other; in all directions. — *adj* **right'-angled** having a **right angle**, an angle of 90°, formed by the intersection of a vertical and a horizontal straight line. — *adj* **right'-hand** at the right side; towards the right; performed with the right hand; with thread or strands turning to the right; chiefly relied on (as **right-hand man**, an assistant who is most heavily relied upon and trusted, etc.). — *adj* **right-hand'ed** using the right hand more easily than the left; with or for the right hand; with rotation towards the right, or clockwise. — *adv* towards the right. — **right-hand'edness**; **right-hand'er** a blow with the right hand; a right-handed person; **right-hand man** see **right-hand** above. — *n* and *adj* **Right Honourable** a title of distinction given to peers below the rank of marquis, to privy councillors, to present and past cabinet ministers, and to certain Lord Mayors and Lord Provosts, etc. — *adj* **right'-minded** having a mind disposed towards what is right, just, or according to good sense; sane. — **right-mind'edness**; **right'-of-way** a track over which there is a **right of way** (see in phrases below); the strip of land occupied by a railway track, a road, etc. (*US*): — *pl* **right'-of-ways'** or **rights'-of-way'**. — *n* and *adj* **Right Reverend** see **reverend**. — **rights issue** (*commerce*) an issue of new shares which shareholders of a company may buy, usu. below the market price, in proportion to their current holdings. — *adj* **right'-thinking** of approved opinions; right-minded. — **right whale** a whale of the typical genus *Balaena*, esp. the Greenland whale; **right wing** the political right; the wing on the right side of an army, football pitch, etc. — *adj* **right'-wing** of or on the right wing; pertaining to the political right; (having opinions which are) conservative, opposed to socialism, etc. — **right-wing'er**. — **all right** see under **all**; **at right angles** forming or in such a way as to form a right angle; **bill of rights** (often with *caps*) an accepted statement of the rights and privileges of the people or of individuals, which the government or state must not infringe (e.g. that embodied in the Bill of Rights, 1689, or in the U.S. Constitution); **by rights** rightfully; if all were right; **civil rights** see under **civil**; **have a right** (or **no right**) to be entitled (or not entitled); **in one's own right** by absolute and personal right, not through another; **in one's right mind** quite sane; **in the right** right; maintaining a justifiable position; **put** or **set to rights** to set in order; **right as rain** see under **rain**; **right away** straight away; without delay; **right, left and centre** same as **left, right and centre**; **right of common** (*law*) a right to take something from, or pasture animals on, another person's land; **right of entry** a legal right to enter a place; **right off** without delay; **right of way** the right of the public to pass over a piece of ground (see also **right-of-way** above); **right on** (*US colloq*) an exclamation expressing enthusiastic agreement or approval. [O.E. *riht* (noun and adj.), *rihte* (adv.), *rihten* (verb).]

righteous *rī'chəs*, *adj* just, upright; provoked or supported by a moral standpoint or premise; excellent, honest (*US slang*). — *adv* **right'eously**. — *n* **right'eousness**. [O.E. *rihtwīs* — *riht*, right, *wīs*, wise, prudent, or *wīse*, wise, manner.]

rigid *rij'id*, *adj* stiff; unbending; unyielding; rigorous; strict; (of an airship) having a rigid structure; (of a truck or lorry) not articulated. — *vt* and *vi* **rigid'ify** to make or become rigid: — *pr p* **rigid'ifying**; *pa t* and *pa p* **rigid'ified**. — *n* **rigid'ity**. — *adv* **rig'idly**. — *n* **rig'idness**. [L. *rigidus* — *rigēre*, to be stiff.]

rigmarole *rig'mə-rōl*, *n* a long, complicated series of actions, instructions, etc., often rather pointless, boring or irritating; a long rambling discourse. [From the *Ragman Rolls* in which the Scottish nobles subscribed allegiance to Edward I.]

rigor *rig'ər* or *rī'gör*, *n* a sense of chilliness with contraction of the skin, a preliminary symptom of many diseases (*med*); a rigid irresponsive state caused by a sudden shock. — *n* **rigorism** (*rig'ər-izm*) extreme strictness; the doctrine that in doubtful cases the strict course should be followed. — *n* **rig'orist**. — *adj* **rig'orous** rigidly strict or scrupulous; exact;

unsparing; severe. — *adv* **rig'orously.** — *n* **rig'orousness.** — *n* **rigour** (*rig'ər*) stiffness; hardness; rigor; severity; unswerving enforcement of law, rule or principle; strict exactitude; austerity; extreme strictness; severity of weather or climate. — **rigor mortis** (*mör'tis*; L.) stiffening of the body after death. [L. *rigor* — *rigēre*, to be stiff.]

Rig-veda *rig-vā'də* or *-vē'də*, *n* the first and oldest of the four Hindu Vedas, comprised of ancient hymns to various Aryan deities. [Sans. *ṛic*, a hymn, *veda*, knowledge.]

rijstafel or **reistafel** *rīs'tä-fəl*, *n* an Indonesian rice dish served with a variety of foods. [Du. *rijst*, rice, *tafel*, table.]

rile *rīl*, *vt* to annoy or irritate. [Obs. or dialect *roil*, to make turbid, irritate.]

rilievo. See **relievo.**

rill *ril*, *n* a very small brook; a small trench; a narrow furrow on the moon or Mars (also **rille** from Ger. *Rille*). [Cf. Du. *ril*, Ger. (orig. L.G.) *Rille*, channel, furrow.]

rillettes *ri-yet'*, *npl* a French type of potted meat made by simmering shreds of lean and fat pork, etc. till crisp, and pounding them to form a paste. [Fr.]

RIM *abbrev* for Mauritania (*République Islamique de Mauretanie*; I.V.R.).

rim *rim*, *n* an edge, border, brim or margin, esp. when raised or more or less circular; an encircling band, mark or line; the outermost circular part of a wheel, not including the tire. — *vt* to form or provide a rim to; to edge: — *pr p* **rimm'ing**; *pa t* and *pa p* **rimmed.** — *adj* **rim'less.** — *adj* **rimmed.** — **rim'-brake** a brake acting on the rim of a wheel; **rim'-lock** a lock mechanism in a metal case that is screwed to the inner face of a door (as opp. to a *mortise lock*). [O.E. *rima* (found in compounds).]

rime *rīm*, *n* hoar-frost or frozen dew; ice deposited by freezing of fog (*meteorol*). — *vt* to cover with rime. — *adj* **rī'my.** [O.E. *hrīm*.]

rimu *rē'mōō*, *n* a coniferous tree of New Zealand, *Dacrydium cupressinum*. [Maori.]

rind *rīnd*, *n* the peel (as of a fruit); the crust (as of a cheese); the outer bark (as of a tree); the tough outer layer of skin (as of bacon, etc.). — *vt* to bark. — *adj* **rīnd'ed.** — *adj* **rīnd'less.** — *adj* **rīnd'y.** [O.E. *rinde*.]

rinderpest *rin'dər-pest*, *n* a malignant and contagious disease of cattle causing fever, severe diarrhoea, and discharges from the mucous membranes, etc. [Ger., cattle-plague.]

ring[1] *ring*, *n* a small circular band or hoop, esp. one of metal, worn on the finger, in the ear, nose, or elsewhere; any object, mark, arrangement, group or course of a similar form; an encircling band; a rim; an encircling cut in bark; a zone of wood added in a season's growth, as seen in sections a mark of fungus growth in turf (**fair'y-ring**); a segment of a worm, caterpillar, etc.; a closed chain of atoms; a system of elements in which addition is associative and commutative and multiplication is associative and distributive with respect to addition (*math*); a circular ripple; a circular earthwork or rampart; an arena; a space set apart for boxing, wrestling, circus performance, riding display of animals, etc.; an enclosure for bookmakers at a race-course; pugilism; a combination or clique, esp. organised to control the market or for other self-seeking purpose; a system operated by some antique dealers who arrange not to bid against each other at an auction, so that one of their number may buy cheaply, and then share the profit made by subsequent resale; a computer system suitable for local-network use, with several microcomputers or peripheral devices connected by cable in a ring. — *vt* to encircle; to put a ring on or in; to cut a ring in the bark of; to cut into rings; to go in rings round: — *pa t* and *pa p* **ringed.** — *adj* **ringed.** — *n* **ringer** (*ring'ər*) someone who rings; a throw of a quoit that encircles the pin; a quoit so thrown. — *n* and *adj* **ring'ing.** — *adj* **ring'less.** — *n* **ring'let** a long curl of hair; a type of satyrid butterfly with small ring-marks on its wings. — *adj* **ring'leted.** — *n* **ring'ster** a member of a ring, esp. in a political or price-fixing sense. — *adv* **ring'wise.** — *vt* **ring'-bark** to strip a ring of bark from. — **ring'-bolt** a bolt with a ring through a hole at one end; **ring'bone** a bony callus on a horse's pastern-bone; the condition caused by this; **ring circuit** (*electr*) an electrical supply system in which a number of power-points are connected to the main supply by a series of wires, forming a closed circuit; **ring'-dove** the wood-pigeon, which has a broken white ring or line on its neck; **ringed'-plover** a ring-necked plover of various kinds; **ring'-fence** a fence continuously encircling an estate; a complete barrier; the compulsory reservation of funds for use within a specific, limited sector or department (of government, of a company, etc.). — *vt* to enclose within a ring-fence; to apply a ring-fence to. — **ring'-fencing; ring'-finger** the third finger, esp. of the left hand, on which the wedding-ring is worn; **ring fort** (*archaeol*) a dwelling-site of the Iron Age with a strong circular wall; **ring'leader** a person who takes the lead in mischief or trouble; **ring main** (*electr*) an electrical supply system in which the power-points and the mains are connected in a ring circuit; **ring'-mark** a ring-shaped mark; **ring'master** a person in charge of performances in a circus-ring. — *adj* **ring'-necked** (*-nekt*) having the neck marked with a ring. — **ring network** (*comput*) one forming a closed loop of connected terminals; **ring ouzel** or **ousel** see **ouzel; ring pull** the tongue of metal and the ring attached to it, which one pulls from or on the top of a can of beer, lemonade, etc. to open it; **ring road** a road or bypass encircling a town or its inner part; **ring'side** the side of the prize-ring; **ring'-snake** a common English snake, the grass snake; **ring'tail** the female or young male of the hen-harrier, from the rust-coloured ring on its tail-feathers; a ringtailed cat (see **cacomistle**). — *adj* **ring'tail** or **ring'tailed** (*-tāld*) having the tail marked with bars or rings of colour, as a lemur does; having a prehensile tail curled at the end, as certain species of opossum do. — **ring'way** a ring road; **ring'worm** a skin disease characterised by ring-shaped patches, caused by fungi. — **a ringside seat** or **view** (*fig*) (a position which allows one to have) a very clear view; **make** or **run rings round** to be markedly superior to, get the better of; **throw one's hat into the ring** (*colloq*) to offer oneself as a candidate or challenger; to issue a challenge, institute an attack. [O.E. *hring*.]

ring[2] *ring*, *vi* to give a metallic or bell-like sound; to sound loudly and clearly; to give a characteristic or particular sound; to resound, re-echo; to be filled with sound, or a sensation like sound; to cause a bell or bells to sound, esp. as a summons or signal. — *vt* to cause to give a metallic or bell-like sound; to sound in the manner of a bell; to summon, usher or announce by a bell or bells; to call on the telephone; to re-echo, resound, proclaim: — *pa t* **rang**; *pa p* **rung.** — *n* a sounding of a bell; the characteristic sound or tone, as of a bell or a metal, or of a voice; a ringing sound; a set of bells. — *n* **ring'er** a person who or a thing which rings; a horse raced under the name of another horse, or an athlete or other contestant competing under a false name or otherwise disguised (esp. *US*); an outsider, an impostor (*US slang*); (also **dead ringer**) a person or thing (almost) identical to some other person or thing (with *for*; *colloq*). — *n* and *adj* **ring'ing.** — *adv* **ring'ingly.** — **ring a bell** to cause a vague memory of having been seen, heard, etc. before; **ring back** to telephone (a previous caller) in response to his or her call; to follow up a telephone call with a second one; **ring down the curtain** to give the signal for lowering the curtain (*theat*); (with *on*) to bring (something) to a close (*fig*); **ring in** or **out** to usher in or out (esp. the year) with bell-ringing; **ring off** to put an end to a telephone conversation by replacing the receiver; **ring out** to sound loudly, clearly and suddenly; **ring true** to sound genuine (like a tested coin); **ring up** to call (someone) on the telephone; **ring up the curtain** to give the signal for raising the curtain (*theat*); (with *on*) to open, set (something) in motion (*fig*). [O.E. *hringan*.]

ringhals *ring'hals*, *n* a snake of Southern Africa, which spits or sprays its venom at its victims. [Afrik. *ring*, a ring, *hals*, a neck.]

rink *ringk*, *n* a piece of ice prepared for skating; a building or floor for roller-skating or ice-skating; a portion of a bowling-green, curling-pond, etc., allotted to one set of players; a division of a bowls or curling team playing on such a portion. [Orig. Scots.]

rinky-dink *ring'ki-dingk*, (*US slang*) *n* something old and run down or worn out; something corny, trite or trivial. — Also *adj*.

rinse *rins*, *vt* to wash lightly by pouring, shaking or dipping; to wash in clean water to remove soap traces. — *n* an act of rinsing; liquid used for rinsing; a solution used in hairdressing, esp. one to tint the hair slightly and impermanently. — *adj* **rins'able** or **rinse'able**. — *n* **rins'er**. — *n* **rins'ing**. [O.Fr. *rinser* (Fr. *rincer*).]

riot *rī'ət*, *n* a disturbance of the peace by a crowd (legally three or more); tumult; wild revelry; unrestrained squandering or indulgence; a great, usu. boisterous, success; (of colour) a striking display; a wildly enjoyable or amusing event or occasion (*slang*); a hilarious person (*slang*). — *vi* to take part or indulge in a riot; to revel. — *n* **rī'oter**. — *n* **rī'oting**. — *adj* **rī'otous**. — *adv* **rī'otously**. — *n* **rī'otousness**. — **Riot Act** (*law*; *hist*) a statute designed to prevent riotous assemblies; a form of words read as a warning to rioters to disperse; **riot police** police specially equipped with **riot gear** (shields, tear-gas grenades, etc.) for dealing with rioting crowds. — **read the riot act** (*fig*) to give an angry warning that the bad behaviour must stop; **run riot** to act or grow wild, without restraint. [O.Fr. *riot*, *riotte*.]

RIP *abbrev* for *requiescat in pace* (L.), may he (or she) rest in peace.

rip[1] *rip*, *vt* to slash or tear open, apart, off or out; to make by such an action; (with *up*) to shred, tear into pieces; to split or saw (timber) with the grain; (with *out*) to utter explosively. — *vi* to come apart in shreds; to break out violently; to rush, go forward unrestrainedly: — *pr p* **ripp'ing**; *pa t* and *pa p* **ripped**. — *n* a tear, rent; an unchecked rush. — *n* **ripp'er** a person who rips; a tool for ripping; a person or thing especially admirable (*slang*, esp. *Austr*). — *adj* **ripp'ing** (*old-fashioned slang*) excellent. — Also *adv*. — *adv* **ripp'ingly**. — **rip'-cord** a cord for enabling a parachute to open, or for opening a balloon's gas-bag; **rip'-off** (*slang*) (financial) exploitation; a theft, stealing, cheating, etc.; a swindle, confidence trick; a film, commercial, etc. that exploits the success of another by imitating it; **rip'-saw** a saw for cutting along the grain of timber. — *adj* **rip'-roaring** wild and noisy. — **rip'snorter** (*slang*) a fast and furious affair, or person. — *adj* **rip'snorting**. — **let it rip** to allow an action or process to go on in an unrepressed or reckless way; **let rip** to express oneself, or to act, violently or without restraint; to make a sudden increase in speed, volume, etc.; **rip off** (*slang*) to steal; to steal from; to exploit, cheat, overcharge, etc. [Cf. Fris. *rippe*, Flem. *rippen*, Norw. *rippa*.]

rip[2] *rip*, *n* stretch of broken water; a disturbed state of the sea. — *n* **rip'tide** tidal rip. [Perh. **rip**[1].]

RIPA *abbrev* for Royal Institute of Public Administration.

riparian *rī-pā'ri-ən*, *adj* of or inhabiting a riverbank. — *n* an owner of land bordering a river. — *adj* **ripā'rial**. [L. *rīpārius* — *rīpa*, a riverbank.]

ripe *rīp*, *adj* ready for harvest; fit for use; fully developed; ready for a particular purpose or action; resembling ripe fruit; arrived at perfection; mature; (of cheese) mature, strong-smelling; (of language, etc.) somewhat indecent or over-colourfully expressive; rich and strong in quality. — *adv* **ripe'ly**. — *vt* and *vi* **rī'pen** to make or grow ripe or riper. — *n* **ripe'ness**. [O.E. *rīpe*, ripe, *rīpian*, to ripen.]

RIPHH *abbrev* for Royal Institute of Public Health and Hygiene.

ripieno *ri-pyā'nō*, (*mus*) *adj* supplementary. — *n* a supplementary instrument or performer: — *pl* **ripie'nos**. [It.]

riposte *ri-post'* or *-pōst'*, *n* a quick return thrust after a parry (*fencing*); a retort. — *vt* and *vi* to answer with a riposte. [Fr., — It. *risposta*, reply.]

ripper, ripping. See **rip**[1].

ripple[1] *rip'l*, *n* light agitation of the surface of a liquid; a little wave; a similar appearance in anything; small periodic variations in a steady current or voltage (*electronics*); a sound as of rippling water; (in *pl*) repercussions, reverberations. — *vt* to ruffle the surface of; to mark with ripples. — *vi* to move or run in ripples; to sound like ripples. — *n* and *adj* **ripp'ling**. — *adv* **ripp'lingly**. — *adj* **ripp'ly**. — **ripple effect** a process in which a trend or situation spreads outward from its initial location to affect areas distant from it; **ripp'le-mark** an undulatory ridging produced in sediments by waves, currents and wind, often preserved in sedimentary rocks. — *adj* **ripp'le-marked**.

ripple[2] *rip'l*, *n* a toothed implement for removing seeds, etc., from flax or hemp. — *vt* to clear of seeds by drawing through a ripple; to remove by a ripple. — *n* **ripp'ler**. [Cf. L.G. and Du. *repel*, a ripple, hoe, Ger. *Riffel*.]

Rip Van Winkle *rip van wing'kl*, *n* someone very much behind the times, as was a character of that name in a story by Washington Irving: according to the story he returned home after having slept in the mountains for twenty years.

RISC *abbrev* for reduced instruction set computer (i.e. one having a central processor with a very small instruction set, allowing faster processing, etc.).

rise *rīz*, *vi* to get up; to become erect, stand up; to come back to life; to revolt (often with *up*); to close a session; to move upward; to come up to the surface; to fly up from the ground; to come above the horizon; to grow upward; to advance in rank, fortune, etc.; to swell; to increase; to increase in price; to become more acute in pitch; to be excited; to be cheered; to come into view, notice or consciousness; to spring up; to take origin; to have source; to come into being; to extend upward; to tower; to slope up; to come to hand, chance to come; to respond (e.g. to provocation, or to a demanding situation); to feel nausea: — *pa t* **rose** (*rōz*); *pa p* **risen** (*riz'n*). — *n* rising; ascent; increase in height; vertical difference or amount of elevation or rising; increase of salary, price, status, etc.; an upward slope; a sharpening of pitch; source, origin; a response, esp. an angry or excited one; the riser of a step. — *n* **rīs'er** someone who rises, esp. from bed; that which rises; the upright portion of a step; a vertical pipe, e.g. in a building or an oil rig. — *n* **rīs'ing** the action or process of the verb in any sense; a revolt, uprising. — *adj* and *pr p* ascending; increasing; coming above the horizon; advancing; growing up; approaching the age of. — **give rise to** to cause, bring about; **on the rise** in the process of rising or increasing, esp. in price; **rise and shine** a facetiously cheerful invitation to get out of bed briskly, esp. in the morning; **rise from the ranks** to work one's way up from private soldier to commissioned officer; to become a self-made man; **rise to the bait** (*fig*, from fishing) to take the lure, do what someone has intended to make one do; **rise to the occasion** to prove able to cope in an emergency or special circumstance; **take a rise out of** to lure into reacting to provocation, or (*loosely*) to tease or mock; **take rise** to originate. [O.E. *rīsan*.]

risible *riz'i-bl*, *adj* inclined to laughter; of or relating to laughter; ludicrous. — *n* **risibil'ity**. [L. *rīsibilis* — *rīdēre*, *rīsum*, to laugh.]

risk *risk*, *n* hazard, danger, chance of loss, failure or injury; the degree of probability of loss; a person, thing or factor likely to cause loss or danger. — *vt* to expose to risk; to incur the chance of unfortunate consequences, loss or danger by (doing something). — *n* **risk'er**. — *adj* **risk'ful**. — *adv* **risk'ily**. — *n* **risk'iness**. — *adj* **risk'y** dangerous, liable to accident or mishap. — **risk analysis** a methodical investigation process undertaken to assess the financial and physical risks affecting a business venture; **risk capital** see **venture capital** under **venture**; **risk'-money** allowance to a cashier to compensate for ordinary errors. — **at risk** in a situation or circumstances where loss, injury, physical abuse, etc. are possible; susceptible; **run a risk** to be in, get into, a risky situation; **run a (or the) risk of** to risk (failing, etc.). [Fr. *risque* — It. *risco*.]

risorgimento *ri-sör-ji-men'tō*, (*hist*) *n* the liberation and unification of Italy in the 19th century. [It., — L. *resurgĕre*, to rise again.]

risotto *ri-zot'ō*, *n* a dish of rice cooked in stock with meat or seafood, onions and other vegetables, and cheese, etc.: — *pl* **risott'os**. [It., — *riso*, rice.]

risqué *rēs'kā* or *ris-kā'*, *adj* audaciously bordering on the unseemly. [Fr., past p. of *risquer*, to risk.]

rissole *ris'ōl*, *n* a fried ball or cake of minced seasoned meat coated in breadcrumbs. [Fr.]

ritardando *rē-tär-dan'dō*, (*mus*) *adj* and *adv* with diminishing speed. — *n* a ritardando passage; a slowing down: — *pl* **ritardan'dos**. [It.]

rite *rīt*, *n* a ceremonial form or observance, esp. religious; a liturgy. — *adj* **rite'less**. — **rite of passage** a term for any of the ceremonies — such as those associated with birth, puberty, marriage or death — which mark or ensure a person's transition from one status to another within his or her society. [L. *rītus*.]

ritenuto *rit-ə-nū'tō*, (*mus*) *adj* restrained — indicating a sudden slowing-down of tempo. — *n* a ritenuto passage: — *pl* **ritenū'tos**. [It., past p. of *ritenere*, to restrain, hold back.]

ritornello *rit-ör-nel'ō*, (*mus*) *n* a short instrumental passage in a vocal work, e.g. a prelude or refrain: — *pl* **ritornel'li** (*-lē*) or **ritornell'os**. [It.]

ritual *rit'ū-əl*, *adj* relating to, or of the nature of, rites. — *n* the manner of performing divine service, or a book containing it; a body or code of ceremonies; an often repeated series of actions; the performance of rites; ceremonial. — *n* **ritualisā'tion** or **-z-**. — *vi* **rit'ualise** or **-ize** to practise or turn to ritualism. — *vt* to make ritualistic. — *n* **rit'ualism** attachment of importance to ritual, esp. an excessive amount. — *n* **rit'ualist**. — *adj* **ritualist'ic**. — *adv* **ritualist'ically**. — *adv* **rit'ually**. — **ritual murder** the killing of a human being as part of a tribal religious ceremony. [L. *rituālis* — *rītus*; see **rite**.]

ritzy *rit'zi*, (*slang*) *adj* stylish, elegant, ostentatiously rich. [The *Ritz* hotels.]

rival *rī'vl*, *n* a person who pursues an object in competition with another; someone who strives to equal or excel another; someone for whom, or something for which, a claim to equality might be made. — *adj* standing in competition; having similar pretensions or comparable claims. — *vt* to stand in competition with; to try to gain the same object against; to try to equal or excel; to be worthy of comparison with: — *pr p* **rī'valling**; *pa t* and *pa p* **rī'valled**. — *adj* **rī'valless**. — *n* **rī'valry** the state of being a rival; competition; emulation; the feeling of a rival. [L. *rīvālis*, said to be from *rīvus*, river, as one who draws water from the same river.]

rive *rīv*, (*poetic* or *archaic*) *vt* to tear apart; to tear; to rend; to split. — *vi* to split: — *pa t* **rīved**; *pa p* **riven** (*riv'n*) or **rived** (*rīvd*). [O.N. *rīfa*.]

river *riv'ər*, *n* a large stream of water flowing over the land; sometimes extended to a strait or inlet; a stream, plentiful flow. — *adj* of a river or rivers; dwelling or found in or near a river or rivers. — *adj* **riv'ered** watered by rivers. — *adj* **riv'erine** (*-īn* or *-ēn*) of, on, or dwelling in or near a river. — *adj* **riv'erless**. — *adj* **riv'erlike**. — *adj* **riv'ery**. — **riv'erbank**; **riv'er-basin** the whole region drained by a river with its affluents; **riv'er-bed** the channel in which a river flows; **river blindness** see **onchocerciasis**; **riv'er-boat** a boat with a flat bottom or shallow draft; **riv'er-bottom** (*US*) alluvial land along the margin of a river; **riv'er-head** the source of a river; **riv'er-mouth**; **riv'erside** the bank or neighbourhood of a river. — *adj* beside a river. — **riv'er-terrace** a terrace formed when a river eats away its old alluvium deposited when its flood-level was higher. [O.Fr. *rivere* — L. *ripārius*, adj. — *rīpa*, bank.]

rivet *riv'it*, *n* a bolt with a head at one end, used to join two or more pieces of metal, etc. by hammering down the projecting, headless end. — *vt* to fasten with rivets; to fix immovably; to attract or fix (one's attention, etc.) on something; to enthral or fascinate; to clinch or hammer out the end of: — *pr p* **riv'eting**; *pa t* and *pa p* **riv'eted**. — *n* **riv'eter**. — *n* **riv'eting**. — *adj* gripping, enthralling, arresting. [O.Fr. *rivet* — *river*, to clinch.]

riviera *riv-i-ā'rə*, *n* a warm coastal district reminiscent of the Riviera in France and Italy on the Mediterranean Sea.

rivière *rē-vyer* or *riv-i-er'*, *n* a necklace of diamonds or other precious stones, usu. in several strings. [Fr., river.]

rivulet *riv'ū-lit*, *n* a small river. [L. *rīvulus*, dimin. of *rīvus*, a stream.]

riyal *ri-yäl'*, *n* the unit of currency in Qatar (100 *dirhams*), and (also spelt **rial**, q.v.) in Saudi Arabia and the Yemen Arab Republic. [Ar., — Sp. *real*; see **real**^{2}.]

RJE (*comput*) *abbrev* for remote job entry. — **RJET** *abbrev* for remote job entry terminal.

RL *abbrev* for: reference library; Republic of Lebanon (I.V.R.); Rugby League.

rly *abbrev* for railway.

RM *abbrev* for: Republic of Madagascar (I.V.R.); Resident Magistrate; Royal Mail; Royal Marines.

rm *abbrev* for: ream (*printing*); room.

RMA *abbrev* for Royal Military Academy, Sandhurst.

RMetS *abbrev* for Royal Meteorological Society.

RMM *abbrev* for Republic of Mali (I.V.R.).

RMN *abbrev* for Registered Mental Nurse.

RMO *abbrev* for Resident Medical Officer.

rms (*math*) *abbrev* for root-mean-square.

RN *abbrev* for: Registered Nurse (*NAm*); Republic of Niger; Royal Navy.

Rn (*chem*) *symbol* for radon.

RNA (*biochem*) *abbrev* for ribonucleic acid.

RNAS *abbrev* for Royal Naval Air Service(s).

RNCM *abbrev* for Royal Northern College of Music.

RNIB *abbrev* for Royal National Institute for the Blind.

RNID *abbrev* for Royal National Institute for the Deaf.

RNLI *abbrev* for Royal National Lifeboat Institution.

RNR *abbrev* for Royal Naval Reserve.

RNVR *abbrev* for Royal Naval Volunteer Reserve.

RNZAF *abbrev* for Royal New Zealand Air Force.

RNZN *abbrev* for Royal New Zealand Navy.
RO *abbrev* for Romania (I.V.R.).
ro *abbrev* for: recto (*printing*); run out (*cricket*).
roach[1] *rōch*, *n* a silvery freshwater fish of the carp family, with pale red ventral and tail fins; applied to various American fishes. [O.Fr. *roche*.]
roach[2] *rōch*, (*naut*) *n* a concave curve in the foot of a square sail.
roach[3] *rōch*, *n* a cockroach (*US*); the butt of a marijuana cigarette (*slang*; esp. *US*).
road *rōd*, *n* a track with a surface (esp. tarmac, etc.) suitable for wheeled traffic, esp. for through communication (often in street-names); a highway; a way of approach; course; a passage in a mine; (often in *pl*) a roadstead; a railway (*US*); journeying; tour, wayfaring. — *n* **road'ie** (*slang*) a member of the crew who transport, set up and dismantle equipment for musicians, esp. a pop group, on tour. — *adj* **road'less.** — *n* **road'ster** a horse, cycle or car, suitable for ordinary use on the road; an open car (orig. *US*) with a rumble seat or large boot instead of a rear seat, and a single seat for two or three in front. — **road'-bed** the foundation of a railway track; the material laid down to form a road; **road'block** an obstruction set up across a road, e.g. to enable an inspection of vehicles or an inquiry to be conducted. — *adj* **road'-borne.** — **road'-bridge** a bridge carrying a road; **road'-hog** a selfish, inconsiderate or reckless motorist. — Also *vi.* — *adj* **road'-hoggish.** — **road'holding** the extent to which a motor vehicle holds the road when in motion; **road'house** a roadside public house catering for motorists, cyclists, etc.; **road hump** one of a series of low ridges built into a road surface to slow traffic down, a sleeping policeman; **road'-maker; road'-making; road'man** a man who keeps a road in repair; **road manager** the tour manager for a rock band or other group, entertainer, etc., responsible for organising venues, equipment, crew, etc.; **road'-map; road'-mender; road'-mending; road'-metal** broken stones for making roads; **road'-metalling; road pricing** the system of charging the driver of a vehicle for the use of a road (e.g. to reduce traffic in a city centre); **road'-roller** a heavy roller used on roads; **road'-runner** an American bird, the chaparral cock, that runs fast; **road'-sense** aptitude for doing the right thing in driving or road-using in general; **road'show** a touring group of theatrical or musical performers; (a live broadcast from one of a series of venues, presented by) a touring disc jockey and his or her retinue, or a programme presenter or team; a promotional tour undertaken by any body or organisation seeking publicity for its policies or products; their performances; **road'side** the border of a road; wayside. — *adj* by the side of a road. — **road sign** a sign along a road, motorway, etc. giving information on routes, speed limits, etc. to travellers; **road'stead** a place near a shore where ships may ride at anchor. — *vt* **road'-test** to test (a vehicle) on the road for performance and roadworthiness (also *fig*). — Also *n.* — **road'-train** (*Austr*) a number of linked trailers towed by a truck, for transporting cattle, etc.; **road'way** the way or part of a road or street used by traffic; the road surface. — *npl* **roadworks** the building or repairing of a road, or work involving the digging up, etc. of part of a road. — **road'-worthiness.** — *adj* **road'worthy** fit for the road. — **in** (or **out of**) **the** (or **one's**) **road** (*colloq*) in (or out of) the way; **one for the road** a last alcoholic drink before setting off; **on the road** travelling, esp. as a commercial traveller, tramp, musician on tour, etc.; on the way to some place; **road fund licence** a round certificate, usu. stuck on a vehicle's windscreen, showing that the vehicle excise duty (or **road fund licence fee**) payable on that vehicle has been paid; **road up** road surface being repaired; **take the road** to set off, depart; **take to the road** to become a tramp; to set off for, travel to, somewhere. [O.E. *rād*, a riding, raid; cf. **raid, ride.**]
roam *rōm*, *vi* to rove about; to ramble. — *vt* to wander over; to range. — *n* a wandering; a ramble. — *n* **roam'er.** [M.E. *romen.*]
roan[1] *rōn*, *adj* bay or dark, with spots of grey and white; of a mixed colour, with a decided shade of red. — *n* a roan colour; a roan animal, esp. a horse. [O.Fr. *roan.*]
roan[2] *rōn*, *n* grained sheepskin leather. — *adj* made of roan. [Poss. *Roan*, early form of *Rouen.*]
roan[3]. See **rone.**
roar *rör*, *vi* to make a full, loud, hoarse, low-pitched sound (like a lion, fire, wind, the sea, or cannon); to bellow; to bawl; to guffaw; (of a diseased horse) to take in breath with a loud noise; to rush forward with loud noise from the engine. — *vt* to utter loudly; to shout (encouragement, abuse, etc.); to encourage by shouting (esp. with *on*). — *n* a sound of roaring. — *n* **roar'er.** — *n* **roar'ing** the action of the verb in any sense; a disease of horses marked by roaring. — *adj* uttering or emitting roars; riotous; proceeding with very great activity or success (as a *roaring trade*). — *adv* **roar'ingly.** — **roaring drunk** very drunk (and typically rowdy); **roaring forties** see under **forty.** [O.E. *rārian*; partly from M.Du. *roer*, disturbance.]
roast *rōst*, *vt* to cook before a fire or in an oven (esp. of meat cooked dry but usu. basted); to bake, parch by heat; to heat strongly; to dissipate the volatile parts of (esp. sulphur) by heat; to criticise excessively. — *vi* to undergo roasting; (of a person) to be very hot (*colloq*). — *adj* roasted. — *n* a joint, esp. of beef, roasted or to be roasted; an operation of roasting. — *n* **roas'ter** apparatus for roasting; a pig, etc., suitable for roasting; a very hot day (*colloq*). — *n* and *adj* **roast'ing.** — **roast'-beef; roast'-meat.** [O.Fr. *rostir*; of Gmc. origin.]
rob *rob*, *vt* to deprive wrongfully and forcibly; to steal from; to plunder; to deprive. — *vi* to commit robbery: — *pr p* **robb'ing**; *pa t* and *pa p* **robbed.** — *n* **robb'er.** — *n* **robb'ery** theft from the person, aggravated by violence or intimidation; an incidence of robbing. — **robb'er-crab** a large coconut-eating land-crab of the Indian Ocean. — **daylight robbery** glaring extortion; **rob Peter to pay Paul** to deprive one person in order to satisfy another. [O.Fr. *rober*; of Gmc. origin.]
robe *rōb*, *n* a gown or loose outer garment; a gown or dress of office, dignity or state; a rich dress; a woman's dress (esp. *US*); a dressing-gown. — *vt* to dress; to invest in robes. — *vi* to assume official vestments. — *n* **rob'ing.** — **robe-de-chambre** (*rob-də-shā-br'*; Fr.) a dressing-gown: — *pl* **robes-de-chambre** (same pronunciation); **robe'-maker** a maker of official robes; **rob'ing-room** a room in which official robes may be put on. — **Mistress of the Robes** the head of a department in a queen's household. [Fr. *robe*, orig. booty.]
robin *rob'in*, *n* the redbreast or **robin redbreast** (*Erithacus rubecula*), a widely-spread singing bird with reddish-orange breast; extended to other birds such as a red-breasted thrush of N. America. — **Robin Hood** a legendary mediaeval English outlaw who robbed the rich to give to the poor. [A form of *Robert.*]
robinia *ro-bin'i-ə*, *n* any plant of the locust or false acacia genus *Robinia*. [From the Paris gardener Jean *Robin* (1550–1629).]
roborant *rob'ər-ənt*, *n* a strengthening drug or tonic. — *adj* **rob'orant** or **rob'orating.** [L. *rōborāns*, *-antis*, pres. p. of *rōborāre*, to strengthen, invigorate.]
robot *rō'bot*, *n* a mechanical man; a more than humanly efficient automaton; esp. in S. Africa, an automatic traffic signal. — *adj* **robot'ic.** — *nsing* **robot'ics** the branch of technology dealing with the design, construction and use of robots; a form of street dance in which a mechanical effect is achieved

by making short sharp movements keeping the body stiff (also called **robotic dancing**). — *vt* **rō'botise** or **-ize** to cause (a job, etc.) to be done by, or (a house, etc.) to be looked after by, a robot or robots. [Czech *robota*, statute labour; from Karel Čapek's play *R.U.R.* (1920).]

robust *rō-bust'*, *adj* stout, strong and sturdy; constitutionally healthy; vigorous; thickset; over-hearty. — *adv* **robust'ly**. — *n* **robust'ness**. [L. *rōbustus* — *rōbur*, strength, oak.]

robusta *rō-bus'tə*, *n* coffee produced from the shrub *Coffea robusta*, grown esp. in E. Africa.

ROC *abbrev* for Royal Observer Corps.

roc *rok*, *n* an enormous bird told of in Arabian legend, strong enough to carry off an elephant. [Pers. *rukh*.]

rocaille *rō-kä'ē*, *n* artificial rockwork or similar ornamental work; scroll ornament; rococo. [Fr.]

rocambole *rok'əm-bōl*, *n* a plant with a bulb similar to and used like garlic. [Fr.]

Roche limit *rōsh* or *rosh lim'it*, (*astron*) *n* the lowest orbit which a satellite can maintain around its parent planet without being pulled apart by the tidal forces it creates. [Discovered by French astronomer Edouard *Roche* (1820–83).]

roche moutonnée *rosh mōō-to-nā'*, *n* a smooth, rounded hummocky rock-surface due to glaciation: — *pl* **roches moutonnées** (same pronunciation, or *-nāz*). [Fr. *roche*, a rock, *moutonnée*, a kind of wig.]

rochet *roch'it*, *n* a close-fitting surplice-like vestment worn by bishops and abbots. [O.Fr., of Gmc. origin.]

rock[1] *rok*, *n* a large outstanding natural mass of stone; a natural mass of one or more minerals consolidated or loose (*geol*); any variety or species of such an aggregate; a diamond or other precious stone (*slang*); crack, the drug (*slang*); a stone, pebble or lump of rock; (in *pl*) testicles (*vulg slang*); a type of hard confectionery made in sticks; a sure foundation or support, anything immovable; a danger or obstacle. — *adj* made of rock; found on, in, or among rocks. — *n* **rock'ery** a heap of soil and rock fragments in a garden, for growing rock plants. — *n* **rock'iness**. — *adj* **rock'y** full of rocks; like rocks; rough, difficult (*colloq*). — **rock'-badger** a dassie; **rock'-bird** a puffin or other bird that nests or lives on rocks; **rock bottom** bedrock; the very bottom, esp. of poverty or despair. — *adj* the lowest possible; to or at the lowest possible level. — *adj* **rock'-bound** hemmed in by rock; rocky. — **rock cake** a small hard bun, irregular on top; **rock'-climber**; **rock'-climbing** mountaineering on rocky faces; **rock crystal** colourless quartz, esp. when well crystallised; **rock dove** a pigeon that nests on rocks, source of the domestic varieties; **rock drill** a tool for boring rock; **rock'fish** a fish of various types that live among rocks; rock salmon; **rock garden** a rockery. — *adj* **rock'-hewn** hewn out of rock. — **rock'-hopper** a crested penguin; **rock house** (*slang*) a crack- or cocaine-dealer's den; **rock melon** the cantaloupe; **rock pigeon** the rock dove; **rock plant** a plant adapted to growing on or among rocks; **rock'-rabbit** a hyrax; **rock rose** a roselike plant of either of the genera *Cistus* and *Helianthemum*; **rock salmon** dogfish or wolf-fish when being sold as food fish; **rock salt** salt as a mineral, halite; salt in crystalline form; **rock snake** a python. — *adj* **rock'-sol'id** steady; dependable; firm; unwavering; unbeatable. — **rock tripe** an edible arctic lichen of various kinds; **rock wool** mineral wool, used as an insulating material; **rock'work** masonry in imitation of rock (*archit*); rocks in rockery; rock-climbing. — **on the rocks** penniless; (of whisky, etc.) on ice; **Rocky Mountain goat** a white N. American animal, between a goat and an antelope; **the Rock** Gibraltar; **the Rockies** the Rocky Mountains. [O.Fr. *roke* — L.L. *rocca*.]

rock[2] *rok*, *vt* and *vi* to sway to and fro, tilt from side to side; to startle, stagger (*colloq*). — *vi* to dance to, or play in, rock-and-roll style. — *n* a rocking movement; (also **rock music**) a form of music with a strong beat, which developed from rock-and-roll. — *adj* pertaining to rock music. — *n* **rock'er** someone who rocks; an apparatus that rocks; a curved support on which anything rocks; a rocking-chair; (with *cap*) a member of a teenage faction of the 1960s who wore leather jackets, rode motorcycles, etc.; a mining cradle; a skate with curved blade; a 180°-turn in skating, so that the skater continues backwards in the same direction. — *adv* **rock'ily**. — *n* **rock'iness**. — *n* and *adj* **rock'ing**. — *adj* **rock'y** tending to rock; shaky; unpleasant, unsatisfactory (*slang*). — **rock-and-roll** see **rock-'n'-roll** below; **rocker switch** an electric light, etc. switch on a central pivot; **rock'ing-chair** a chair mounted on rockers; **rock'ing-horse** the figure of a horse mounted on rockers or on some other supports which allow the horse to rock when a child rides on it; **rock'ing-stone** finely poised boulder that can be made to rock; **rock'-'n'-roll'** or **rock'-and-roll'** a simple form of music deriving from jazz, country-and-western and blues music, with a strongly accented, two-beat rhythm; dancing to this music; **rock'shaft** (in engines) a shaft that oscillates instead of revolving; **rock'steady** a style of dance music orig. from Jamaica, slow in tempo with a heavily stressed off-beat. — **off one's rocker** out of one's right mind; **rock the boat** to make things difficult for one's colleagues, create trouble. [O.E. *roccian*.]

rockery. See under **rock**[1].

rocket[1] *rok'it*, *n* a cylinder full of inflammable material, projected through the air for signalling, carrying a line to a ship in distress, or for firework display; a missile projected by a rocket system; a system or vehicle obtaining its thrust from a backward jet of hot gases, all the material for producing which is carried within the rocket; a severe reprimand (*slang*). — *vi* to move like a rocket; to fly straight up rapidly; (of e.g. prices) to rise very rapidly; to come to an important position with remarkable speed. — *vt* to attack with rockets. — *n* **rocketeer'** a rocket technician or pilot of rockets; a specialist in rocketry, especially a designer. — *n* **rock'etry** the scientific study and use of rockets. — **rocket engine** or **motor** a jet engine or motor which uses an internally stored oxidiser instead of atmospheric oxygen, for combustion; **rocket'-launcher**; **rock'et-range** a place for experimentation with rocket projectiles; **rocket scientist** (*stock exchange slang*) a person who devises schemes to take advantage of price differentials on money markets. [It. *rocchetta*; of Gmc. origin.]

rocket[2] *rok'it*, *n* a salad plant (*Eruca sativa*) of Mediterranean countries; extended to other plants, the cruciferous wall-rocket (*Diplotaxis*) or yellow-rocket (*Barbarea*). [O.Fr. *roquette* — L. *ērūca*.]

rockling *rok'ling*, *n* a small fish of the cod family with barbels on both jaws. [**rock**[1] and **-ling**.]

rococo *rə-kō'kō* or *rō-kō-kō'*, *n* a style of architecture, decoration and furniture-making prevailing in Louis XV's time, marked by ornamental details unrelated to structure and unsymmetrical and broken curves, a freer development of the baroque; the musical equivalent to this style: — *pl* **rococos**. — *adj* in the style of rococo; florid, extravagant in style. [Fr., prob. — *rocaille*, rockwork.]

rod *rod*, *n* a slender stick; a slender bar of metal or other material; a stick as instrument of punishment; a slender pole or structure, or a fisherman, carrying a fishing-line; a long straight shoot; a stick or wand for magic or divination; a metal bar forming part of the framework under a railway carriage (see also **ride the rods** below); a sceptre or similar emblem of authority; a rod-shaped body of the retina of the eye, sensitive to light; a rod-shaped bacterium; a revolver, a pistol (*US slang*); a penis (*slang*); a pole or perch ($5\frac{1}{2}$ yards, or $16\frac{1}{2}$ feet); a square pole ($272\frac{1}{4}$ sq. ft.). — *vt* to push a rod through (a drain, etc.) so as to clear it: — *pr p* **rodd'ing**; *pa t* and *pa p* **rodd'ed**. — *n* **rodd'ing**. — *adj* **rod'less**. — *adj* **rod'like**. — **rod'fisher**; **rod'fishing**; **rod puppet** a glove puppet held on one hand, its arms being manipulated by rods held in the other hand. — **make a rod for one's own back** to create trouble for oneself; **ride the rods** (*US*) to travel illegitimately on the railway, on the rods (q.v.) under railway carriages. [O.E. *rodd*.]

rode *rōd*, *pa t* of **ride**.

rodent *rō'dənt*, *n* a mammal of the order **Rodentia** (*rō-den'shə* or *-shyə*), which have prominent incisor teeth and no canines, e.g. the squirrel, beaver or rat. — *adj* gnawing; belonging to the Rodentia. — *n* **roden'ticide** a substance that kills rodents. — *adj* **ro'dent-like**. — **rodent officer** an official rat-catcher. [L. *rōdēns*, *-entis*, pres. p. of *rōdĕre*, to gnaw.]

rodeo *rō'di-ō* or *rō-dā'ō*, *n* an exhibition of cowboy skill; a round-up of cattle; a place where cattle are assembled; a contest suggestive of a cowboy rodeo involving, e.g. motorcycles: — *pl* **ro'deos**. [Sp., — *rodear*, to go round — L. *rotāre*, to wheel.]

rodomontade *rod-ō-mon-tād'*, *n* extravagant boasting. — *vi* to bluster or brag. — *n* **rodomontā'der**. [After the boasting of *Rodomonte* in Ariosto's *Orlando Furioso*.]

roe[1] *rō*, *n* a mass of fish-eggs (also called **hard roe**); the testis of a male fish containing mature sperm (also called **soft roe**). — *adj* **roed** containing roe. [M.E. *rowe*.]

roe[2] *rō*, *n* a small species of deer. — **roe'buck** the male roe; **roe deer** a roe. [O.E. *rā*, *rāha*.]

roentgen. See **röntgen**.

rogation *rō-gā'shən*, (*eccles*) *n* supplication, esp. in ceremonial form. — **Rogation Days** the three days before Ascension Day, when supplications were recited in procession; **Rogation Sunday** that before Ascension Day; **Rogation Week** the week in which the Rogation Days occur. [L. *rogātiō*, *-ōnis* — *rogāre*, to ask.]

roger *roj'ər*, *n* a word used in signalling and radio-communication for R, in the sense of *r*eceived (and understood). — *vt* and *vi* (*vulg slang*) (of a man) to copulate (with). — *n* **rog'ering**. [Obs. slang meaning a penis — *Roger* (a man's name) — Fr., of Gmc. origin.]

rogue *rōg*, *n* a rascal; a mischievous person (often *playfully* or *affectionately*); a plant that falls short of a standard, or is of a different type from the rest of the crop; a variation from type; a horse, person or object that is troublesome, unruly or unco-operative; a savage elephant or other animal cast out or withdrawn from its herd. — *adj* mischievous; disruptive; diverging from type. — *vt* to eliminate rogues from (e.g. a crop). — *n* **roguery** (*rōg'ər-i*). — *adj* **roguish** (*rōg'ish*). — *adv* **rog'uishly**. — *n* **rog'uishness**. — **rogue-el'ephant**; **rogues' gallery** a police collection of photographs of criminals. [Cant.]

roister *rois'tər*, *vi* to bluster, swagger; to revel noisily. — *n* **rois'terer**. — *n* **rois'tering**. — *adj* **rois'terous**. [O.Fr. *rustre*, a rough, rude fellow — O.Fr. *ruste* — L. *rusticus*, rustic.]

ROK *abbrev* for Republic of Korea (I.V.R.).

rolag *rō'lag*, *n* a roll of combed sheep's wool ready for spinning. [Gael. *ròlag*, dimin. of *rola*, a roll.]

Roland *rō'lənd*, *n* a worthy match (with allusion to a drawn contest between Roland, hero of the Charlemagne legend, and his comrade-in-arms, Oliver). — **a Roland for an Oliver** tit for tat; as good as one got.

role or **rôle** *rōl*, *n* a part played by an actor; a function, part played in life or in any event. — **role model** a person whose character behaviour, etc. is imitated by others who would like to be in the same or a similar position, situation, etc.; **role'-play** or **role'-playing** the performing of imaginary roles, as a method of instruction, training or therapy. [Fr.]

Rolfing *rolf'ing*, *n* a therapeutic technique for correcting postural faults and improving physical wellbeing through manipulation of the muscles and connective tissue, so that the body is realigned symmetrically and the best use of gravity made in maintaining balance. [Dr Ida *Rolf* (1897–1979), originator of the technique.]

roll *rōl*, *n* an act of rolling; a sheet of paper, parchment, cloth or other material bent spirally upon itself into a nearly cylindrical form; a document in such form; a scroll; a register; a list, esp. of names; a small, individually-baked portion of bread formed into any of various shapes, that can be cut open and filled with other foods; a spirally wound cake, or one of dough turned over to enclose other material; a roller; a more or less cylindrical package, mass or pad; a part turned over in a curve; a swaying about an axis in the direction of motion; a full rotation about an axis in the direction of motion, as an aeronautical manoeuvre; a continuous reverberatory or trilling sound; an undulation; a wavelike flow. — *vi* to move like a ball, a wheel, a wheeled vehicle or a passenger in one; to perform revolutions; to sway on an axis in the direction of motion; to turn over or from side to side; to swagger; to wallow; to move in, on, or like waves; to flow; to undulate; to sound with a roll; to use a roller; to curl; to start; to get under way, start operating; to make (esp. fast and sustained) progress. — *vt* to cause to roll; to turn on an axis; to move with a circular sweep (esp. of the eyes); to wrap round on itself; to enwrap; to curl; to wind; to move upon wheels; to press, flatten, spread out, thin or smooth with a roller or between rollers; to pour in waves; to rob (someone drunk or asleep) (*NAm* and *NZ slang*); to have sexual intercourse with (*slang*, esp. *NAm*). — *adj* **roll'able**. — *adj* **rolled**. — *n* **roll'er** someone who or something that rolls; a revolving or rolling cylinder; a contrivance including a heavy cylinder or cylinders for flattening roads or turf; a long, coiled-up bandage (**roll'er-bandage**); a long heavy wave; a small solid wheel; a cylinder on which hair is wound to curl it; a kind of pigeon that rolls or tumbles backward as it flies. — *n* **roll'ing**. — *adj* (of landscape) characterised by a gentle undulation; extremely rich (*slang*); staggering with drunkenness (*slang*); (of a contract, etc.) subject to periodic review; occurring in different places in succession; (of planned events, etc.) organised to take place successively, on a relay or rota system, with a steadily maintained or escalating effect. — **roll'-bar** a metal bar that strengthens the frame of a vehicle, lessening the danger to the vehicle's occupants if the vehicle overturns; **roll'-call** the calling of a list of names, to ascertain attendance; **roll'collar** a collar of a garment turned back in a curve; **rolled gold** metal coated with gold rolled very thin; **roll'er-bearing** a bearing consisting of two grooves between which a number of parallel or tapered rollers are located, usu. in a cage, suitable for heavier loads than ball-bearings; **roll'er-coaster** a type of switchback railway at carnivals, etc., along which people ride in open cars at great speed; **roll'er-hockey** a form of hockey played by teams on roller-skates; **roll'er-skate** a skate with wheels instead of a blade. — Also *vi*. — **roll'er-skater**; **roll'er-skating**; **roll'er-towel** a continuous towel on a roller; **roll'ing-mill** factory or machine for rolling metal into various shapes between rolls; **roll'ing-pin** a cylinder for rolling dough; **roll'ing-stock** the stock or store of engines and vehicles that run upon a railway; **rolling stone** see phrase below. — *adj* **roll'-neck** (of a jersey, etc.) having a high neck which is made to be folded over loosely on itself. — *adj* **roll'-on** (of a deodorant, etc.) contained in a bottle which has a rotating ball in its neck, by means of which the deodorant is applied. — *n* a roll-on deodorant, etc.; a corset that fits on by stretching. — *adj* and *n* **roll-on-roll-off'** (a ferry-boat, cargo boat or service) designed to allow goods vehicles to embark and disembark without unloading, and passenger traffic to drive straight on and off. — **roll'-out** the first public display of a prototype of an aircraft; that part of an aeroplane's landing during which it slows down after touch-down. — *adj* **roll'-top** having a flexible cover of slats that rolls up. — **roll'-up** a hand-rolled cigarette (*colloq*); attendance, turn-out (*Austr*). — **a rolling stone gathers no moss** a wandering person does not accumulate wealth or possessions but is free from responsibilities and ties; **a roll in the hay** (*colloq*) an act of sexual intercourse; **be rolling in** to have large amounts of (e.g. money); **heads will roll** severe punishments will be meted out, esp. loss of status or office; **Master of the Rolls** the head of the Record Office, one of the judges in the Court of Appeal; **roll along** to arrive by chance, or with a casual air; **rolled into one** combined in one person or thing; **roll in** to arrive in quantity; **roll on!** may (a specified event) come quickly!; **roll over** to defer demand for repayment of (a loan or debt) for a further term (*n* and *adj* **roll'-over**); **roll up** (*colloq*) to assemble, arrive; **roll with the punches** (of a boxer) to move the body away to cushion the impact of the opponents blows (also *fig*); **strike off the roll** to remove the right to practise from (a doctor, solicitor, etc.) after professional misconduct. [O.Fr. *rolle* (n.), *roller* (vb.) — L. *rotula*, dimin. of *rota*, a wheel.]

rollick[1] *rol'ik*, *vi* to behave in a careless, swaggering, playful manner. — *adj* **roll'icking.**

rollick[2] *rol'ik*, (*slang*) *vt* to rebuke severely. — *n* a severe scolding. — *n* **roll'icking** (also **roll'ocking**). [Perh. alteration of **bollock**.]

rollmop *rōl'mop*, *n* a fillet of herring rolled up, usu. enclosing a slice of onion, and pickled in spiced vinegar. [Ger. *Rollmops* — *rollen*, to roll, *Mops*, a pug-dog.]

rollocking. See **rollick**[2].

roly-poly *rōl'i-pōl'i*, *n* a pudding made of a sheet of dough, covered with jam or fruit, rolled up, and baked or steamed (also **roly-poly pudding**); a round, podgy person; any of several bushy plants (esp. *Salsola kali*) that break off and roll in the wind (*Austr*). — *adj* round, podgy. [Prob. **roll**.]

ROM *rom*, (*comput*) *n* acronymic abbreviation of read-only memory, a storage device whose contents cannot be altered by a programmer.

Rom. (*Bible*) *abbrev* for (the Letter to the) Romans.

rom *rom*, *n* (also with *cap*) a male gypsy: — *pl* **rom'a** or **rom'as.** [Romany, man, husband.]

rom. *abbrev* for roman (type).

Romaic *rō-mā'ik*, *n* and *adj* modern Greek. [Mod. Gr. *Rhōmaikos*, Roman (i.e. of the Eastern Roman Empire) — *Rhōmē*, Rome.]

Roman *rō'mən*, *adj* pertaining to Rome, esp. ancient Rome, its people, or the empire founded by them; pertaining to the Roman Catholic religion, papal; (without *cap*) (of type) of the ordinary upright kind (as opp. to *italic*); (of numerals) written in letters (as IV, iv), opp. to *Arabic*; (of a nose) high-bridged. — *n* a native or citizen of Rome; a Roman Catholic; (without *cap*) roman letter or type. — *adj* **Romanic** (*rō-man'ik*) of Roman or Latin origin; Romance. — *n* the Romance language or languages collectively. — *n* **Romanisation** or **-z-** (*rō-mə-nī-zā'shən*). — *vt* **Ro'manise** or **-ize** to make Roman or Roman Catholic; to bring under Roman or Roman Catholic influence; to represent by the Roman alphabet. — *vi* to accept Roman or Roman Catholic ways, laws, doctrines, etc. — *n* **Ro'maniser** or **-z-**. — *n* **Ro'manism** Roman Catholicism or a slavish adherence to its doctrine. — *n* **Ro'manist** a Roman Catholic; a person versed in Romance philology or Roman law or antiquities. — *adj* Roman Catholic. — *adj* **Romanist'ic.** — *combining form* **Romano-** (*rō-mä'nō-*) signifying Roman and (as in **Roma'no-British**). — **Roman candle** a firework discharging a succession of white or coloured stars. — *adj* **Roman Catholic** recognising the spiritual supremacy of the Pope or Bishop of Rome. — *n* a member of the Roman Catholic Church. — **Roman Catholicism** the doctrines and polity of the Roman Catholic Church collectively; **Roman Empire** the ancient empire of Rome, divided in the 4th century into the Eastern and Western Empires (see also under **Holy**); **Roman law** the system of law developed by the ancient Romans — civil law. [L. *Rōmānus* — *Rōma*, Rome.]

roman à clef *ro'mā ä klā'*, *n* a novel about real people under disguised names. [Fr., novel with a key.]

Romance *rō-mans'*, *n* a general name for the vernaculars that developed out of popular Latin — French, Provençal, Italian, Spanish, Portuguese, Romanian, Romansch, with their various dialects. — Also *adj.* — *n* **romance'** a tale of chivalry, orig. one in verse, written in one of these vernaculars; any fictitious and wonderful tale; a fictitious narrative in prose or verse which passes beyond the limits of ordinary life; a piece of romantic fiction; romantic fiction as a literary genre; a romantic occurrence or series of occurrences; a love affair; romantic atmosphere or feeling; an imaginative lie; romanticism; a composition of romantic character (*mus*). — *vi* to talk extravagantly or with an infusion of fiction; to lie. — *n* **roman'cer.** — *n* and *adj* **roman'cing.** [L.L. *rōmānicē* (adv.), in (popular) Roman language.]

Romanes. See **Romany.**

Romanesque *rō-mən-esk'*, *adj* of the transition from Roman to Gothic architecture, characterised by round arches and vaults. — *n* the Romanesque style, art or architecture. [Fr.]

roman-fleuve *ro'mā-flœv*, *n* a novel in a series of self-contained narratives telling the story of a family, etc. over successive generations (also **saga novel**). [Fr., river novel.]

Romani. See **Romany.**

Romanian *rō-mā'ni-ən*, **Rumanian** or **Roumanian** *ro͞o-*, *adj* pertaining to *Romania* or its language. — *n* a native or citizen of Romania, or member of the same people; the (Romance) language of Romania. [Romanian *România* — L. *Rōmānus*, Roman.]

Romanise, Romanism, etc. See under **Roman.**

Romansch or **Romansh** *rō-*, *ro͞o-mansh'* or *-mänsh'*, *n* and *adj* Rhaeto-Romanic; sometimes confined to the Upper Rhine dialects. [Romansch.]

romantic *rō-man'tik*, *adj* pertaining to, of the nature of or inclining towards romance, esp. feelings of love or the idea of sentimentalised love; extravagant, wild; fantastic. — *n* a romanticist. — *adv* **roman'tically.** — *n* **romanticīsā'tion** or **-z-**. — *vt* **roman'ticise** or **-ize** (*-ti-sīz*) to make seem romantic. — *vi* to have or express romantic ideas. — *n* **roman'ticism** (*-sizm*) romantic quality, feeling, tendency, principles or spirit. — *n* **roman'ticist.** — **Romantic Revival** the late 18th-century and early 19th-century revolt against classicism to a more picturesque, original, free and imaginative style in literature and art. [Fr. *romantique* — O.Fr. *romant*, romance.]

Romany or **Romani** *rom'ə-ni* or *rōm'*, *n* a gypsy; (also **Romanes** *rom'ə-nes*) the Indic language of the gypsies (in pure form not now common in Britain). — *adj* of Romanies or their language; gypsy. [Gypsy, — *rom*, man.]

Rome *rōm*, *n* the capital of the Roman Empire, now of Italy; often used for the Roman Catholic Church or Roman Catholicism. — *adj* **Rōm'ish** (*hostile*) Roman Catholic. [L. *Rōma*.]

Romeo *rō'mi-ō, n* a young man very much in love; a Don Juan in the making: — *pl* **Rō'meos.** [Shakespearean character.]

romneya *rom'ni-ə, n* any plant of the *Romneya* genus of shrubs, with large white poppy-like flowers with yellow centres. [Thomas *Romney* Robinson (1792–1882), British astronomer.]

romp *romp, vi* to frolic actively; to move along easily and quickly, esp. in winning a race. — *n* a young person, esp. a girl, who romps; a tomboy; a vigorous frolic; a swift easy run. — *n* **romp'er** someone who romps; (usu. in *pl*) a child's garb for play (also **romp'er-suit**). — *adv* **romp'ingly.** — **romp home** to win easily; **romp through** to do (something) quickly and easily. [**ramp.**]

rondavel *ron-dav'əl* or *ron', n* (in S. Africa) a round hut, usu. with grass roof. [Afrik. *rondawel.*]

rondeau *ron'dō* or *rɔ̃-dō, n* a form of poem characterised by closely-knit rhymes, consisting of thirteen lines (sometimes ten), the burden (repeating the first few words) after the eighth and thirteenth lines: — *pl* **ron'deaux** (*-dōz*). — *n* **ron'del** a verse-form of thirteen or fourteen lines on two rhymes, the seventh and thirteenth being identical with the first, and the eighth and (if present) the fourteenth with the second. — *n* **ron'do** (orig. It., from Fr.) a musical composition whose principal subject recurs in the same key in alternation with other subjects, often the last movement of a sonata: — *pl* **ron'dos.** — *n* **rondolet'to** a short rondo: — *pl* **rondolet'tos.** [Fr. *rondeau*, earlier *rondel* — *rond*, round.]

rone or **roan** *rōn*, (*Scot*) *n* a roof-gutter.

Roneo® *rō'ni-ō, n* a duplicating machine: — *pl* **Rō'neos.** — *vt* **rō'neo** to produce copies of by duplicating machine.

ronggeng *rong'geng, n* a Malaysian dancing-girl; a kind of dancing, often with singing, in Malaysia. [Malay *rônggeng.*]

röntgen or **roentgen** *rœnt'yən, rent', ront'* or *runt'*, also *-gən*, (sometimes with *cap*) *adj* of the German physicist Wilhelm Conrad *Röntgen* (1845–1923), discoverer of the **röntgen rays** or X-rays. — *n* the international unit of dose of X-rays or gamma rays, defined in terms of the ionisation it produces in air under stated conditions. — *n* **röntgenog'raphy** photography by these rays. — *n* **röntgenol'ogy** the study of the rays.

roo *rōō*, (*Austr colloq*) *n* short form of kangaroo. — **roo'-bar** a strong metal bar or grid fitted to the front of a road vehicle as protection in case of collision with a kangaroo or other animal on an outback road, etc.

rood *rōōd, n* Christ's cross; a cross or crucifix, esp. at the entrance to a church chancel; a quarter of an acre or 0.10117 hectares. — **rood'-beam** a beam for supporting the rood; **rood'-loft** a gallery over the rood-screen; **rood'-screen** an ornamental partition separating choir from nave. [O.E. *rōd*, gallows, cross.]

roof *rōōf, n* the top covering of a building or vehicle; a ceiling; the overhead surface, structure or stratum of a vault, arch, cave, etc.; the upper covering of the mouth (the palate); a dwelling; a high or highest plateau (as in *the roof of the world*); an upper limit: — *pl* **roofs.** — *vt* to cover with a roof; to shelter. — *adj* **roofed.** — *n* **roof'er** a person who makes or mends roofs. — *n* **roof'ing** materials for a roof; the roof itself. — *adj* **roof'less.** — *adj* **roof'like.** — **roof'-garden** a garden on a flat roof; **roof'-rack** a rack which may be fitted to the roof of a car, etc. to carry luggage, etc.; **roof'top** the outside of a roof; **roof'-tree** the ridge-pole of a roof. — **have a roof over one's head** to have somewhere to live; **hit** (or **go through**) **the roof** to become very angry; **raise the roof** to make a great noise or commotion; to hit the roof. [O.E. *hrōf.*]

rooinek *rō'i-nek, n* an Afrikaans nickname for an Englishman. [Afrik., red neck — Du. *rood, nek.*]

rook[1] *rŏŏk, n* a gregarious species of crow; a card sharp (*slang*). — *vt* to cheat, swindle or fleece. — *n* **rook'ery** a breeding-place of rooks in a group of trees; a breeding-place of penguins, seals, etc. — *adj* **rook'ish.** — *adj* **rook'y.** [O.E. *hrōc.*]

rook[2] *rŏŏk, n* a chess-piece which is moved in a vertical or horizontal line, its shape usu. being that of a tower with battlements. [O.Fr. *roc* — Pers. *rukh.*]

rookie *rŏŏk'i*, (*slang*) *n* a raw beginner; a callow recruit. — Also *adj.* [App. from **recruit.**]

room *rōōm* or *rŏŏm, n* space; necessary or available space; space unoccupied; opportunity, scope or occasion; appointment, office; a compartment; a chamber. — *vt* and *vi* (chiefly *NAm*) to lodge; to share a room or rooms (with *with*). — *adj* **roomed** having rooms. — *n* **room'er** (*NAm*) a lodger, usu. taking meals elsewhere. — *n* **roomette'** (*NAm*) a sleeping compartment in a train. — *n* **room'ful**: — *pl* **room'fuls.** — *adv* **room'ily.** — *n* **room'iness.** — *npl* **rooms** a set of rooms in a house, etc. rented as a separate unit. — *adj* **room'y** having ample room; wide; spacious. — **room'-divider** a low wall or piece of furniture serving to divide a room into two separate sections; **room'ing-house** (*NAm*) a house with furnished rooms to let; **room'-mate** a fellow-lodger, with whom one shares a room; **room service** the serving of food, etc. to people in their room(s) in a hotel, etc.; **room temperature** the average temperature of a living-room, taken to be be about 20°C. — **leave the room** (*euph*) (esp. of children in school) to go to the toilet. [O.E. *rūm.*]

roost[1] *rōōst, n* a perch or place for a sleeping bird; a henhouse; a sleeping-place; a set of fowls resting together. — *vi* to settle or sleep on a roost or perch; to perch; to go to rest for the night. — *n* **roost'er** a domestic cock. — **come home to roost** to recoil upon oneself (**the chickens have come home to roost** one's actions have had unpleasant consequences); **rule the roost** to lord it, to predominate. [O.E. *hrōst*; Du. *roest.*]

roost[2] *rōōst*, (*Orkney and Shetland*) *n* a strong tidal current. [O.N. *röst.*]

root[1] *rōōt, n* ordinarily and popularly, the underground part of a plant, esp. when edible; that part of a higher plant which never bears leaves or reproductive organs, ordinarily underground and descending, and serving to absorb salts in solution, but often above-ground, often arising from other parts, often serving other functions, though morphologically comparable (*bot*); the source, cause, basis, foundation or occasion of anything, as of an ancestor, or an element from which words are derived; an embedded or basal part, e.g. of a tooth or a hair; a growing plant with its root; the factor of a quantity which, taken so many times, produces that quantity (*math*); any value of the unknown quantity for which an equation is true (*math*); the fundamental note on which a chord is built (*mus*); (in *pl*) one's ancestry, family origins; (in *pl*) a feeling of belonging in a community, etc. — *vi* to fix the root; to be firmly established; to develop a root; to have sexual intercourse (*Austr* and *NZ slang*). — *vt* to plant in the earth; to implant deeply; to fix by the root; to uproot (usu. with *up*); to remove entirely by uprooting, eradicate, extirpate (usu. with *out*). — *n* **root'age** the act of striking root; the state of being rooted; a root-system. — *adj* **root'ed** having roots; fixed by roots or as by roots; firmly established. — *adv* **root'edly.** — *n* **root'edness.** — *n* **root'er.** — *adj* **root'less** having no roots; belonging nowhere, constantly shifting about. — *n* **root'let.** — *adj* **root'like.** — *adj* **root'y.** — *adj* and *adv* **root-and-branch'** without leaving any part; thorough(ly), complete(ly). — **root'-ball** the spherical mass formed by the roots of a plant, with the surrounding soil; **root'-beer** a drink made from roots of dandelion, sassafras, etc.; **root'-cause** fundamental cause; **root'-climber** a plant that climbs by means of roots, such as ivy; **root'-crop** a crop cultivated for its edible roots; **root'-hair** a fine tubular outgrowth from a cell by which a young root absorbs water; **roots music** popular music with a folk influence and a more or less discernible ethnic identity; **root'stock** rhizome, esp. if short, thick, and more or less erect (*bot*); **root'-system; root vegetable** a vegetable which has an edible root; the root itself. — **root mean square** (*math*) the square root of the sum of the squares of a set of quantities divided by the total number of quantities; **strike (**or **take) root** to root, to become established. [Late O.E. *rōt* — O.N. *rōt*.]

root[2] *ro͞ot, vi* (of pigs) to burrow into the ground with the snout; to grub; to rummage; to poke about. — *n* **root'er.** — *n* and *adj* **root'ing.** — *vt* and *vi* **root'le** to root. [O.E. *wrōtan* — *wrōt*, a snout; see also **rout**[2].]

root[3] *ro͞ot*, (orig. *US*) *vi* to shout, applaud, support or encourage (a contestant, etc.) (with *for*). — *n* **root'er.** [Prob. from archaic *rout*, to roar.]

rope *rōp, n* a stout twist of fibre, wire, etc., technically over 1 in. round; a string of pearls, onions, etc.; a glutinous stringy formation. — *vt* to fasten, bind, enclose, mark off, or (*US* and *Austr*) catch with a rope. — *vi* to form into a rope. — *adj* **rop'able** or **rope'able** (*Austr*) (of cattle or horses) wild, unmanageable; very angry. — *adj* **roped** (*rōpt*). — *adv* **rōp'ily.** — *n* **rōp'iness.** — *n* and *adj* **rōp'ing.** — *adj* **rō'py** or **rō'pey** stringy; glutinous; inferior of its kind (*slang*). — **rope'-dance** a tightrope performance; **rope'-dancer; rope'-ladder** a ladder of ropes; **rope's end** (*hist*) the end of a rope used for flogging. — *vt* (*hist*) **rope's-end'** to beat with a rope's end. — *adj* **rope'-soled** having a sole of rope. — **rope'-trick** a conjuring or other magic trick with a rope; **rope'-walk** a long narrow shed or alley used for making rope; **rope'-walker** a tightrope performer; **rope'way** a means of transmission by ropes; **rope'-yarn** yarn for making ropes, or obtained by untwisting ropes; **roping-down'** abseiling. — **give someone (enough) rope (to hang themselves)** to allow a person full scope to defeat their own ends; **know the ropes** see under **know; on the ropes** driven back against the ropes of a boxing ring; nearing defeat, desperate; **rope in** to bring in, enlist (esp. one who has some reluctance); **the rope** capital punishment by hanging. [O.E. *rāp*.]

Roquefort *rok'fȯr, n* a blue cheese orig. made (of ewe's milk) at *Roquefort* in France.

roquet *rō'kā, n* (in croquet) a stroke by which the player's ball strikes an opponent's. — *vt* to strike by a roquet. — *vi* to play a roquet. [Prob. formed from **croquet.**]

ro-ro *rō'-rō, adj* and *n* short for roll-on-roll-off (q.v. under **roll**): — *pl* **ro'-ros.**

rorqual *rör'kwəl, n* any whale of the genus *Balaenoptera* (finback). [Fr., — Norw. *røyrkval* — O.N., lit. red whale.]

Rorschach test *rör'shak test, n* a test, designed to show intelligence, personality and mental state, in which the subject interprets ink-blots of standard type. [Hermann *Rorschach* (1884–1922), Swiss psychiatrist.]

rorty *rör'ti*, (*Austr colloq*) *adj* lively and enjoyable; rowdy. — *n* **rort** a racket (**racket**[2]).

Rosa *rōz'ə* or *roz'ə, n* the rose genus, giving name to the family **Rosā'ceae.** — *n* **rosace** (*rō-zās'* or *-zäs'*; from Fr.; *archit*) a rosette; a rose-window. — *n* **rosā'cea** see **acne rosacea** under **acne.** — *adj* **rosaceous** (*rō-zā'shəs*) of the rose family; roselike. — *n* **rosā'rian** a rose-fancier. — *n* **rosā'rium** a rose-garden. — *n* **rosary** (*rō'zər-i*) a rose-garden or rose-bed (also **rō'sery**). [L. *rŏsa*, rose; *rosārium*, rose-garden.]

rosaniline *rō-zan'i-lin, -lēn* or *-līn, n* a base derived from aniline, with red salts used in dyeing. [**rose**[2] and **aniline.**]

rosarian, rosarium. See under **Rosa.**

rosary[1]. See under **Rosa.**

rosary[2] *rō'zə-ri*, (*RC*) *n* a series of prayers; a string of beads used as a guide to devotions. [L. *rosārium*, rose-garden — *rosa*, rose.]

rose[1], *pa t* of **rise.**

rose[2] *rōz, n* the flower of any species of the genus Rosa — national emblem of England; a shrub bearing it, mostly prickly, with white, yellow, pink, orange or red flowers, numerous stamens and carpels, achenes enclosed in the receptacle; extended to various flowers or plants (see **black hellebore** under **hellebore, guelder-rose, rock**[1]); a paragon; a rosette, esp. on a shoe; a rose-cut stone; a rose-window; a perforated nozzle; a circular moulding from which a door-handle projects; a circular fitting in a ceiling from which an electric light flex hangs; the typical colour of the rose — pink or light crimson; (in *pl*; in white-skinned peoples) the pink glow of the cheeks in health. — *adj* of, for, or like the rose or roses; rose-coloured. — *vt* to make like a rose, in colour or scent. — *adj* **rō'seate** (*-zi-it* or *-zi-āt*) rosy; of roses; unduly favourable or sanguine. — *adj* **rose'less.** — *adj* **rose'like.** — *n* **rō'sery** a rose-garden (cf. **rosary**[1]). — *adv* **rō'sily.** — *n* **rōsiness.** — *adj* **rō'sy** of roses; roselike; rose-red; blooming; blushing; bright, hopeful; promising. — **rose'-apple** an E. Indian tree of the clove genus; its edible fruit; **rose'-bay** the oleander (**rose-bay laurel, rose-laurel**); any rhododendron; a willow-herb (**rose-bay willow-herb**); **rose'-beetle** the rose-chafer; **rose'bud; rose'bush; rose'-campion** a garden species of campion; **rose'-chafer** a beetle that eats roses. — *adj* **rose'-colour** pink. — *adj* **rose'-coloured** pink; seeing or representing things in too favourable a light. — **rose'-comb** a fowl's low red crest. — *adj* **rose'-cut** (of a gem) cut in nearly hemispherical form, with flat base and many small facets rising to a low point above. — **rose'-diamond** a rose-cut diamond; **rose'-engine** a lathe attachment for carving swirling patterns; **rose'fish** a red northern sea-fish; **rose'-garden; rose geranium** a pelargonium with small pink flowers and fragrant leaves; **rose'hip** the fruit of the rose. — *adj* **rose'-hued.** — **rose'-laurel** oleander; **rose'-leaf** the leaf of a rose; usu. a rose-petal; **rose'-mallow** hollyhock; hibiscus. — *adj* **rose'-pink.** — *n* a pink colour; a pink pigment; **rose'-quartz** a rose-coloured quartz. — *adj* **rose'-red.** — **rose'-root** a rock-plant with rose-scented root. — *adj* **rose'-tinted** rose-coloured (*lit* and *fig*). — **rose'-tree; rose'water** water distilled from rose-leaves. — *adj* sentimental; superfine. — **rose-win'dow** a round window with tracery of radiating compartments; **rose'wood** a valuable heavy dark-coloured wood of many trees, said to smell of roses when fresh-cut. — *adj* **ro'sy-cheeked.** — **rosy cross** the emblem of the Rosicrucians. — **all roses** see **roses all the way; bed of roses** see under **bed**[1]; **look (**or **see) through rose-coloured (**or **rose-tinted) spectacles** to view matters over-optimistically; **rose of Jericho** a plant of N. Africa and Syria, that curls in a ball in drought; **rose of Sharon** probably a narcissus (*OT*); now applied to a species of hibiscus; **roses all the way** or **all roses** pleasant, happy; without difficulties, problems, etc.; **under the rose** in confidence; privately; **Wars of the Roses** a disastrous dynastic struggle in England (1455–85) between the Houses of Lancaster and York, from their emblems, the red and the white rose. [O.E. *rōse* — L. *rŏsa*, prob. — Gr. *rhŏdeā*, a rose-bush, *rhodon*, rose.]

rosé *rō'zā, n* a pinkish table wine produced either by removing red grape skins or by mixing red and white wines early in fermentation. [Fr. lit., pink.]

roseate, etc. See under **rose²**.

rosella *rō-zel'ə*, *n* a handsome Australian parakeet, first observed at Rose Hill near Sydney. [For *rosehiller*.]

rosemary *rōz'mə-ri*, *n* a small fragrant pungent Mediterranean labiate shrub whose leaves are widely used as a flavouring in food, and in perfumes. [L. *rōs marīnus*, sea dew.]

roseola *rō-zē'ə-lə*, *n* rose-coloured rash; German measles (also **rubella**). [Dimin. from L. *roseus*, rosy.]

rosery. See under **Rosa** and **rose²**.

rosette *rō-zet'*, *n* a knot of radiating loops of ribbon or the like in concentric arrangement, esp. worn as a badge showing affiliation, or awarded as a prize; a close radiating group of leaves, usu. pressed to the ground; a rose-shaped ornament (*archit*); any structure, arrangement or figure of similar shape. — *adj* **rosett'ed**. [Fr., dimin. of *rose*.]

Rosh Hashanah *rosh hə-shä'nə*, *n* the Jewish festival of New Year. [Heb., lit. head of the year.]

Rosicrucian *roz'* or *rōz'i-kroo'shyən* or *-shən*, *n* a member of an alleged secret society whose members made pretensions to knowledge of the secrets of Nature, transmutation of metals, etc. — affirmed to have been founded (1459) by Christian *Rosenkreuz*; a member of one or other of various modern esoteric quasi-religious fraternities. — Also *adj*. — *n* **Rosicru'cianism**. [Prob. a Latinisation of *Rosenkreuz*, rose cross, L. *rŏsa*, rose, *crux*, cross.]

rosily, rosiness. See under **rose²**.

rosin *roz'in*, *n* a resin obtained when turpentine is prepared from dead pine wood, used to make waxes, varnishes, etc. and for preparing the bows used to play stringed musical instruments. — *vt* to rub with rosin. — *adj* **ros'ined**. — *adj* **ros'iny**. **[resin.]**

rosolio *rō-zō'lyō*, *n* a sweet cordial made with raisins. [It. *rosolio* — L. *rōs sōlis*, dew of the sun.]

RoSPA *ros'pə*, *abbrev* for Royal Society for the Prevention of Accidents.

roster *ros'tər*, *n* a list; any roll of names. — *vt* to put in a roster. — *n* **ros'tering**. [Du. *rooster*, orig. gridiron (from the ruled lines) — *roosten*, to roast.]

rostrum *ros'trəm*, *n* a platform for public speaking, etc. (from the *Rostra* in the Roman forum, adorned with the beaks of captured ships); a part resembling a beak (*biol*); a raised platform on a stage (*theat*); a platform carrying a camera (*cinema, TV*). — *adj* **ros'tral**. — *adj* **ros'trāte** or **restra'ted**. [L. *rōstrum*, beak — *rōdĕre*, *rōsum*, to gnaw.]

rosy. See under **rose²**.

rot *rot*, *vi* to putrefy; to decay; to become weak; to become corrupt; to suffer from wasting disease. — *vt* to cause to rot, to ret: — *pr p* **rott'ing**; *pa t* and *pa p* **rott'ed**. — *n* decay; putrefaction; corruption; collapse, disintegration (often *fig*); applied to various diseases of sheep, timber, etc.; worthless or rotten stuff (*colloq*); nonsense (*colloq*). — *interj* expressing contemptuous disagreement. — *n* **rott'er** a thoroughly depraved or worthless person. — **rot'gut** bad liquor. [O.E. *rotian*, past p. *rotod*; cf. **rotten**.]

rota *rō'tə*, *n* a roster; a course, round, routine, cycle of duty, etc.; (with *cap*) the Roman Catholic supreme ecclesiastical tribunal. — *n* **Rō'tameter®** a device for measuring the rate of flow of a fluid in which a tapered float moves vertically in a transparent tube in accordance with the speed of flow. — *n* **Rōtarian** (*-tā'ri-ən*) a member of a Rotary club. — Also *adj*. — *n* **Rōtā'rianism**. — *adj* **rotary** (*rō'tər-i*) turning like a wheel; of the nature of rotation; working by rotation of a part; (with *cap*) of an international system of clubs, formed to encourage service to and within the community, with a wheel as a badge. — *n* a rotary apparatus; (with *cap*) a Rotary club; (with *cap*) Rotarianism; a traffic roundabout (*NAm*). — *adj* **rōtāt'able**. — *vt* and *vi* **rōtāte'** to turn like a wheel; to put, take, go or succeed in rotation. — *adj* **rō'tate** (*bot*) wheel-shaped — with united petals in a plane with almost no tube. — *n* **rotā'tion** a turning round like a wheel; succession in definite order, as of crops; recurrent order; the conformal transformation (q.v.) in which a particular arrangement is rotated about a fixed point (*math*, etc.). — *adj* **rotā'tional**. — *adj* **rotative** (*rō'tə-tiv*). — *n* **rotā'tor** someone who or something that rotates; a muscle which rotates a part of the body on its axis (*anat*). — *adj* **rotatory** (*rō'tə-tər-i* or *rō-tāt'ər-i*) rotary. — *vt* **rō'tavate** or **rō'tovate** (*back-formation*) to till by means of a rotavator. — *n* **Rō'tavator®** or **Rō'tovator®** (*rotary cultivator*; also without *cap*) a motor-powered, hand-operated soil-tilling machine. [L. *rŏta*, a wheel, *rotāre*, *-ātum*, to run.]

rotch or **rotche** *roch*, *n* the little auk. — Also **rotch'ie**. [Cf. Du. *rotje*, petrel.]

rote *rōt*, *n* mechanical memory, repetition or performance without regard to the meaning. — **by rote** by repetition. [L. *rŏta*, a wheel, and O.Fr. *rote*, road, have been conjectured.]

rotenone *rō'ti-nōn*, *n* an insecticide and fish poison prepared from derris and other plants.

roti *rō'tē*, *n* (in Indian and Caribbean cooking) a cake of unleavened bread. [Hind.]

rotifer *rōt'if-ər*, *n* any minute aquatic animal whose rings of waving cilia suggest a rotating wheel. — *adj* **rotif'eral** or **rotif'erous**. [L. *rŏta*, a wheel, *ferre*, to carry.]

rotisserie *rō-tis'ə-ri*, *n* a cooking apparatus incorporating a spit; a shop or restaurant in which meats are cooked by direct heat. [Fr., cookshop — *rôtir*, to roast.]

rotogravure *rō-tō-grə-vūr'*, *n* a photogravure process using a rotary press; a print so produced. [L. *rŏta*, a wheel, Fr. *gravure*, engraving.]

rotor *rō'tər*, *n* a rotating part, esp. of a dynamo, motor or turbine; a revolving cylinder for propulsion of a ship; a revolving aerofoil. [For **rotator**.]

rotovator. See under **rota**.

rotten *rot'n*, *adj* putrefied; decaying; affected by rot; corrupt; unsound; disintegrating; deplorably bad (*colloq*); miserably out of sorts (*colloq*). — *adv* **rott'enly**. — *n* **rott'enness**. — **rotten apple** a corrupt person; **rotten borough** a borough that still (till 1832) sent members to parliament though it had few or no inhabitants; **rott'enstone** a decomposed silicious limestone, used for polishing metals. [O.N. *rotinn*; cf. **rot**.]

rotter, rotting, etc. See **rot**.

Rottweiler *rot'vīl-ər*, *n* a large powerfully built black German dog with smooth coat and tan markings on the chest and legs (also without *cap*). [*Rottweil*, in S.W. Germany.]

rotund *rō-tund'*, *adj* round; rounded; convexly protuberant; (of speech, etc.) impressive or grandiloquent; plump. — *n* **rotund'a** a round (esp. domed) building or hall. — *n* **rotund'ity** roundness. — *adv* **rotund'ly**. [L. *rotundus* — *rŏta*, a wheel.]

ROU *abbrev* for Republic of Uruguay.

rouble or **ruble** *roo'bl*, *n* the Russian standard monetary unit (100 kopecks). [Russ. *rubl'*.]

roucou *roo-koo'*, *n* annatto. [Fr., — Tupí *urucú*.]

roué *roo'ā*, *n* a profligate, rake or debauchee. [Fr. *roué*, broken on the wheel — past p. of *rouer* — *roue* — L. *rŏta*, a wheel.]

rouge *roozh*, *n* cosmetic powder used to redden the face, orig. a mixture of safflower and talc; a polishing powder of hydrated ferric oxide (also *jeweller's rouge*); French red wine (for *vin rouge*). — *vt* to colour with rouge. — *vi* to use rouge. — **Rouge Croix** (*krwä*) and **Rouge Dragon** two of the pursuivants of the Heralds' College; **rouge-et-noir** (*roozh-ā-nwär*) a gambling card-game played on a table with two red and two black diamond marks on which stakes are laid. [Fr. *rouge* — L. *rubeus*, red.]

rough *ruf*, *adj* uneven; rugged; unshaven; unpolished; crude; unelaborated; without attention to minute correctness; coarse; unrefined; ungentle; turbulent; aspirate; feeling unwell, tired or hung over (*colloq*). — *adv* roughly; with roughness or risk of discomfort. — *n* rough state; that which is rough; rough ground, esp. uncut grass, etc., beside a golf fairway; a hooligan, a rowdy; a crude preliminary sketch, etc. — *vt* to make rough; to ruffle; to shape roughly; to treat roughly (usu. with *up*). — *n* **rough'age** refuse of grain or crops; bran, fibre, etc. in food; coarse food that promotes intestinal movement. — *vt* **rough'en** to make rough. — *vi* to become rough. — *adj* **rough'ish.** — *adv* **rough'ly.** — *n* **rough'ness.** — *adj* **rough'-and-ready** ready to hand or easily improvised, and serving the purpose well enough; (of a person) lacking refinement or social graces but pleasant enough. — *adj* **rough'-and-tumble** haphazard and scrambling. — Also *adv*. — *n* a scuffle; haphazard struggling. — **rough breathing** (in ancient Greek) the sound *h*. — *vt* **rough'cast** to shape roughly; to cover with roughcast. — *n* plaster mixed with small stones, used to coat walls. — *adj* coated with roughcast. — *adj* **rough-coat'ed.** — **rough diamond** see under **diamond.** — *vt* **rough'=draft** or **-draw** to draft roughly. — *vt* **rough'-dry** to dry without smoothing. — *adj* **rough-foot'ed** with feathered feet. — **rough grazing** uncultivated ground, used for pasture. — *vt* **rough-grind'** to grind roughly. — *vt* **rough-hew'** to hew to the first appearance of form. — **rough-hew'er.** — *adj* **rough-hewn'.** — **rough'house** (*colloq*; orig. **rough house**) a disturbance; a brawl. — *vi* to brawl; to make a disturbance. — *vt* to maltreat. — **rough justice** approximate justice, hastily assessed and carried out. — *adj* **rough'-legged** with feathered or hairy legs. — **rough'neck** an unmannerly lout; a hooligan or tough a member of an oil rig crew employed to deal with equipment on the rig floor; **rough passage** a stormy sea voyage; a difficult, trying time; **rough'-rider** a rider of untrained horses; a horse-breaker. — *adj* **rough'shod** provided with horse-shoes with projecting nails to afford extra grip. — **rough shooting** shooting over moorland (mainly grouse). — *adj* **rough'-spoken** rough in speech. — **rough'-stuff** coarse paint laid on after]the priming, and before the finish; violent behaviour; **rough trade** (*slang*) casual sexual partner(s), esp. homosexual; violent or sadistic male prostitute(s). — *adj* **rough'-wrought** shaped out or done roughly, or in a preliminary way. — **cut up rough** see under **cut; ride roughshod over** to domineer over without consideration; **rough in** to sketch in roughly; **rough it** to live in rough or basic conditions (to which one is unaccustomed); to take whatever hardships come; **rough on** hard luck for; **rough out** to shape out roughly; **sleep rough** to sleep out-of-doors. [O.E. *rūh*.]

roulade *rōō-läd'*, *n* melodic embellishment (*mus*); a run, turn, etc. sung to one syllable (*mus*); a rolled slice, usu. of meat, usu. with a filling (*cookery*). [Fr.]

rouleau *rōō-lō'*, *n* a roll or coil, often of ribbon; a cylindrical pile or column of coins, or other discs: — *pl* **rouleaus** or **rouleaux** (*-lōz'*). [Fr.]

roulette *rōōl-et'*, *n* a game of chance in which a ball rolls from a rotating disc into one or other of a set of compartments answering to those on which the players place their stakes; a tool with a toothed disc for engraving rows of dots, for perforating paper, etc.; a cylinder for curling hair or wigs; the locus of a point carried by a curve rolling upon a fixed curve (*geom*). [Fr.]

round *rownd*, *adj* having a curved outline or surface; approaching a circular, globular or cylindrical form; in a course returning upon itself; with horizontal swing; plump; pronounced with lips contracted to a circle; smooth and full-sounding; sonorous; finished off; approximate, without regarding minor denominations; (of a number) without fractions; full; not inconsiderable in amount; plain-spoken; candid; (of a pace) vigorous. — *adv* about; on all sides; every way; in a ring; in a curve; along the circumference; in rotation; from one to another successively; indirectly; circuitously; towards the opposite quarter; in the neighbourhood. — *prep* about; around; on every side of; all over; to every side of in succession; past, beyond. — *n* a round thing or part; a ring, circumference, circle or globe; a whole slice of bread or toast; a sandwich made with two complete slices of bread; a cut of beef across the thigh-bone; a coil; a course returning upon itself; a dance in a ring, or its tune; a canon sung in unison; a cycle or recurring series of events or doings; a complete revolution or rotation; an accustomed walk; a prescribed circuit; a patrol; (often in *pl*) a series of calls (esp. one regularly repeated, as of a doctor, postman); a complete series of holes in golf; routine; a volley, esp. of firearms or applause; ammunition of one shot; a successive or simultaneous action of each member of a company or player in a game; a portion dealt around to each; a set of drinks bought at one time for all the members of a group; a subdivision of a bout, as in boxing; a defined stage in a competition; roundness; the condition of being visible from all sides, not merely in relief (*sculp*). — *vt* to make round; to go round; to finish off. — *vi* to become round; to go round. — *adj* **round'ed** made round or curved; (of a sound) round; finished, complete, developed to perfection. — *n* **round'edness.** — *n* **round'er** a person who or thing which rounds; a complete circuit in rounders; (in *pl*) a bat-and-ball game in which players run from station to station. — *adj* **round'ing.** — *n* the process of raising (*up*) or lowering (*down*) a number to an approximation which has fewer decimal places (*comput*). — *adj* **round'ish.** — *adv* **round'ly.** — *n* **round'ness.** — *adj* **round'about** circuitous; indirect. — *n* a circular revolving platform with handles, seats, etc., at playgrounds, etc.; a merry-go-round; a place where traffic circulates in one direction. — *adj* **round'-arm** with nearly horizontal swing of the arm. — **round dance** a dance in a ring; a dance in which couples revolve about each other; **round'-down** an instance of rounding down (q.v. above under **rounding** *n*). — *adj* **round game** a game, esp. a card-game, in which each plays for their own hand. — **round'hand** a style of penmanship in which the letters are well rounded and free; **Round'-head** a supporter of Parliament during the English Civil War, a Puritan (from the close-cut hair); **round'house** a cabin on the after part of the quarterdeck; an engine-house with a turntable; (a boxing style using) a wild swinging punch (orig. *US*); **rounding error** (*comput*) an error in a computation caused by repeated rounding; **round robin** (or **Robin)** a paper with signatures in a circle, that no one may seem to be a ringleader; any letter, petition, etc. signed by many people; (in sports) a tournament in which each player plays every other player (also called *American tournament*). — *adj* **round=shoul'dered** with shoulders bending forward from the back. — **rounds'man** a man who goes round esp. one sent by a shopkeeper to take orders and deliver goods; a policeman who acts as a supervisor (*US*). — *adj* **round'-table** meeting on equal terms (like the inner circle of King Arthur's knights, who sat at a round table). — *adj* **round-the-clock'** lasting through the day and night (also *adv*, without hyphens). — **round'-top** a mast-head platform; **round-trip'** a trip to a place and back again. — *adj* (*NAm*) return. — **round'-up** a driving together or assembling, as of all the cattle on a ranch, a set of persons wanted by the police, a collection of facts or information, etc.; an instance of rounding up (q.v. above under **rounding** *n*). — **round'-worm** a threadworm or nematode, a member of the *Nematoda*, unsegmented animals with long rounded body, mostly parasitic. — **bring round** and **come round** see under **bring** and **come; get round to** to have the time or inclination to do (something) after delay; **go** or **make the rounds** to go or be passed from place to place or person to person; to circulate; to patrol; **in round numbers** or **figures** to the nearest convenient large number; approximately; **in the round** capable of being viewed from all sides, not merely in relief; taking everything into consideration; **round about** an emphatic form of round; the other way about; approximately; **round down** to lower (a number) to the nearest convenient figure; **round off** to finish off neatly; **round on** to turn on, assail in speech; **round out** to fill out to roundness; **round the bend** or **twist** see under **bend** and **twist; round the clock** see **round-the-clock** above; **round to** to turn the head of a ship to the wind; **round up** to ride round and collect; to gather in (wanted persons, facts, etc.); to raise (a number) to the nearest convenient figure. [O.Fr. *rund* — L. *rotundus* — *rŏta*, a wheel.]

roundel *rown'dl*, *n* a disc; a rondel; a circular device. — *n* **roun'delay** a song with a refrain; a dance in a ring. [O.Fr. *rondel*, *-le*, *rondelet*, dimins. of *rond*, round.]

roup[1] *rowp*, (*Scot and Northern Eng*) *n* a sale by auction. — *vt* to sell by auction. [Scand.]

roup[2] *ro͞op*, *n* an infectious disease of the respiratory passages of poultry. — *adj* **roup'y**. [Perh. imit.]

rouse *rowz*, *vt* to bring out, e.g. from cover or a lair; to stir up; to awaken; to excite; to haul in (as a cable). — *vi* to awake; to be excited to action. — *n* **rouse'about** (*Austr*) an odd-job man on a sheep station. — *n* **rous'er**. — *adj* **rous'ing** awakening; stirring. — *adv* **rous'ingly**. — *vt* **roust** to stir up; to rout out. — *n* **roust'about** a wharf labourer (*NAm*); someone who does odd jobs (*NAm*); a rouseabout (*NAm* and *Austr*); a general labourer employed on an oil rig or in a circus.

rout[1] *rowt*, *n* a rabble; an utter defeat; disorderly flight; a gathering of three or more people for the purpose of committing an unlawful act (*legal*). — *vt* to defeat utterly; to put to disorderly flight. [O.Fr. *route*, from the past p. of L. *rumpĕre*, *ruptum*, to break.]

rout[2] *rowt*, *vt* to grub up; to scoop out; to turn out, fetch out; to rummage out; to bring to light. — *vi* to grub; to poke about. — *n* **rout'er**. [An irreg. variant of **root**[2].]

route *ro͞ot*, *n* a way or course that is or may be traversed; any regular journey; a regular series of calls, a round (*NAm*). — *vt* to fix the route of; to send by a particular route: — *pr p* **route'ing** or (esp. in N.Am.) **rout'ing**; *pa t* and *pa p* **rout'ed**. — **route'-man** (*NAm*) a shopkeeper's roundsman; **route'= march** a long march of troops in training; **route'= step** an order of march in which soldiers are not required to keep step. [Fr., — L. *rupta* (*via*), broken (way); see **rout**[1].]

routine *ro͞o-tēn'*, *n* regular, unvarying or mechanical course of action or round; the set series of movements gone through in a dancing, skating or other performance; a comedian's, singer's, etc. act (*colloq*); a part of a program performing a specific and separate function (*comput*). — *adj* unvarying; keeping an unvarying round; forming part of a routine. — *adv* **routine'ly**. — *vt* **routinise'** or **-ize'** to render mechanical or uniform; to remove interest from. — *n* **routi'nism**. — *n* **routi'nist** a person who advocates or is fond or routine. [Fr.]

roux *ro͞o*, (*cookery*) *n* a thickening for sauces made of equal quantities of butter and flour cooked together: — *pl* **roux** (*ro͞o* or *ro͞oz*). [Fr. (*beurre*) *roux*, brown (butter).]

rove[1] *rōv*, *vt* to wander over or through. — *vi* to wander about; to ramble; to change about inconstantly. — *n* wandering. — *n* **rō'ver** a pirate; a robber; (in archery) a random or distant mark; a wanderer; an inconstant person; a croquet ball or player ready to peg out; (*formerly*) a member of a senior branch of the (Boy) Scout organisation (also **rover scout**). — *adj* **rō'ving** wandering; not confined to a particular place, e.g. *roving ambassador* or *commission*. — Also *n*. — *adv* **rō'vingly**. — **have a roving eye** to tend to show a fleeting sexual interest in successive members of the opposite sex. [Partly from Du. *rooven*, to rob, *roofer*, robber — *roof*, plunder; perh. partly from a Midland form of obs. Northern Eng. *rave*, to wander.]

rove[2] *rōv*, *vt* to twist (fibres) slightly in preparation for spinning. — *n* a roved strand of fibre.

rove[3] *rōv*, *pa t* and *pa p* of **reeve**[1].

rove[4] *rōv*, *n* a metal plate or ring through which a rivet is put and clenched over. [O.N. *ró*.]

rove-beetle *rōv'-bē-tl*, *n* the devil's coach-horse, or other beetle of the family *Staphylinidae*.

row[1] *rō*, *n* a line or rank of people or things, such as seats, houses or vegetables in a plot; a series in line, or in ordered succession; (often in street-names) of a single or double line of houses. — **row house** (*NAm*) a terraced house. — **a hard row to hoe** a destiny fraught with hardship; **in a row** in unbroken sequence. [O.E. *rāw*.]

row[2] *rō*, *vt* to propel with an oar; to transport by rowing; to achieve, render, perform, effect or compete in by use of oars. — *vi* to work with the oar; to be moved by oars. — *n* an act or spell of rowing; a journey in a rowing-boat. — *adj* **row'able**. — *n* **row'er**. — **row'boat** (*NAm*); **row'ing-boat**. [O.E. *rōwan*.]

row[3] *row*, *n* a noisy squabble; a brawl; a din, hubbub; a chiding. — *vi* to quarrel. [A late 18th-cent. word, poss. a back-formation from archaic *rouse*, a carousal.]

rowan *row'ən* or *rō'ən*, *n* the mountain-ash, a tree of the rose family with pinnate leaves; its small red berrylike fruit. — **row'an-berry; row'an-tree**. [Cf. Norw. *raun*, Sw. *rönn*.]

rowdy *row'di*, *n* orig. a lawless American backwoodsman; a noisy, turbulent person. — *adj* noisy and disorderly, or having a tendency to behave so. — *adv* **row'dily**. — *n* **row'diness**. — *adj* **row'dyish**. — *n* **row'dyism**.

rowel *row'əl*, *n* a little spiked wheel on a spur; a disc used as a seton for animals. — *vt* to prick or treat with the rowel: — *pr p* **row'elling**; *pa t* and *pa p* **row'elled**. — **row'el-spur** a spur with a rowel. [Fr. *rouelle* — L.L. *rotella*, dimin. of L. *rŏta*, a wheel.]

rowen *row'ən*, *n* a second mowing of grass in the same season, an aftermath. [From a Northern form of O.Fr. *regain*.]

rowlock *rol'*, *rul'* or *rōl'ək*, *n* a contrivance serving as fulcrum for an oar. [Prob. for *oar-lock* — O.E. *ārloc*.]

royal *roi'əl*, *adj* of a king or queen; kingly; being a king or queen; of a reigning family; founded, chartered or patronised by a king or queen; magnificent; of more than common size or excellence; (of writing-paper) 19 by 24 in.; (of printing-paper) 20 by 25 in. — *n* a royal person (*colloq*); a gold coin of various kinds; a sail immediately above the top-gallant sail; a stag with antlers of twelve or more points. — *n* **roy'alism** attachment to monarchy. — *n* **roy'alist** an adherent of royalism; a cavalier during the English civil war; (in American history) an adherent of the British government; (in French history) a supporter of the Bourbons. — Also *adj*. — *adv* **roy'ally**. — *n* **roy'-alty** the character, state or office of a king or queen;

members of royal families collectively; royal authority; a right or prerogative granted by a king or queen, esp. a right over minerals; a payment made by oil companies, etc. to the owners of the mineral rights in the area in which they operate; payment to an author, composer, etc. for every copy sold or every public performance. — **Royal Academy** an academy of fine arts in London, to which members and associates are elected; **royal assent** see under **assent; royal blue** a bright, deep-coloured blue; **royal commission** (also with *caps*) a body of persons nominated by the Crown to inquire into and report on some matter; **royal fern** the most striking of British ferns, with large fronds; **royal flush** see under **flush**[4]**; royal icing** a kind of hard icing made with white of egg, used esp. on rich fruit cakes; **royal jelly** a secretion produced by worker bees, the food of young larvae and of a developing queen bee; **royal mast** the fourth and highest part of the mast, commonly made in one piece with the top-gallant mast; **royal palm** a palm of the cabbage-palm genus; **royal standard** a banner bearing the British royal arms, flown wherever the monarch is present; **royal tennis** the earlier form of the game of tennis, distinguished from lawn tennis, and played in a wall court (also **real** or **court tennis**); **royal warrant** an official authorisation to supply goods to a royal household; **Royal We** (also without *caps*) a monarch's use of the first person plural when speaking of himself or herself. [Fr., — L. *rēgālis*, regal.]

rozzer *roz'ər*, (*slang*) *n* a policeman.

RP *abbrev* for: Received Pronunciation; Reformed Presbyterian; Regius Professor; Republic of the Philippines (I.V.R.); Royal Society of Portrait Painters.

RPB *abbrev* for recognised professional body.

RPI *abbrev* for retail price index.

RPM *abbrev* for retail price maintenance.

rpm *abbrev* for revolutions per minute.

RPO *abbrev* for Royal Philharmonic Orchestra.

RPS *abbrev* for Royal Photographic Society.

rps *abbrev* for revolutions per second.

rpt *abbrev* for: repeat; report.

RR *abbrev* for Right Reverend.

RRP *abbrev* for recommended retail price.

RS *abbrev* for Royal Society.

RSA *abbrev* for: Republic of South Africa; Royal Scottish Academy or Academician; Royal Society of Arts.

RSC *abbrev* for: Royal Shakespeare Company; Royal Society of Chemistry.

RSFSR *abbrev* for Russian Socialist Federated Socialist Republic.

RSI *abbrev* for: repetitive strain injury; repetitive stress injury.

RSL *abbrev* for: Returned Services League (*Austr*); Royal Society of Literature.

RSM *abbrev* for: Regimental Sergeant-Major; Republic of San Marino (I.V.R.); Royal School of Music; Royal Society of Medicine.

RSNC *abbrev* for Royal Society for Nature Conservation.

RSNO *abbrev* for Royal Scottish National Orchestra (formerly **SNO**).

RSPB *abbrev* for Royal Society for the Protection of Birds.

RSPCA *abbrev* for Royal Society for the Prevention of Cruelty to Animals.

RSSA *abbrev* for Royal Scottish Society of Arts.

RSSPCC *abbrev* for Royal Scottish Society for the Prevention of Cruelty to Children.

RSV *abbrev* for Revised Standard Version (of the Bible).

RSVP *abbrev* for *répondez s'il vous plaît* (Fr.), please reply.

RTE *abbrev* for *Radio Telefís Éireann* (Ir. Gael.), Irish Radio and Television.

Rt Hon. *abbrev* for Right Honourable.

Rt Rev. *abbrev* for Right Reverend.

RU *abbrev* for: Republic of Burundi (formerly *Urundi*; I.V.R.); Rugby Union.

Ru (*chem*) *symbol* for ruthenium.

rub *rub*, *vt* to apply friction to; to move something with pressure along the surface of; to move with pressure along the surface of something; to clean, polish or smooth by friction; to remove, erase or obliterate by friction (usu. with *away*, *off* or *out*); to grind, sharpen, chafe or treat by friction; to cause to pass by friction (with *in*, *through*, etc.). — *vi* to apply, or move with, friction; to meet an impediment (esp. of a bowl); to chafe; to be capable of being rubbed: — *pr p* **rubb'ing**; *pa t* and *pa p* **rubbed**. — *n* process or act of rubbing; an impediment, or a meeting with an impediment (*bowls*); an uneven place; a difficulty; a hitch. — *n* **rubb'er**. — *n* **rubb'ing** application of friction; an impression of an inscribed surface produced by rubbing heel-ball or plumbago upon paper laid over it. — **rub'down** an act of rubbing down. — **rub along** to get along, to manage somehow; to be on more or less friendly terms (with) (*colloq*); **rub down** to rub from head to foot; to remove (a surface) by rubbing in order to repaint, etc.; **rub in** to force into the pores by friction; to be unpleasantly insistent in emphasising; **rub off on** (*fig*) to pass to (someone or something else) by close contact, association, etc.; **rub one's hands** to rub one's palms together, esp. as a sign of satisfaction; **rub out** to erase; to murder (*slang*); **rub shoulders** to come into social contact (with); **rub someone's nose in it** (*colloq*) to remind someone insistently of a mistake, etc.; **rub (**or **rub up) the wrong way** to irritate by tactless handling; **rub up** to polish; to freshen one's memory of. [Cf. L.G. *rubben*.]

rubaiyat *rōō'bä-yat*, *n* a Persian verse form consisting of four-line stanzas. [Arabic *rubā'īyāt*, pl. of *rubā'īyah*, quatrain.]

rubato *rōō-bä'tō*, (*mus*) *adj*, *adv* and *n* (in) modified or distorted rhythm: — *pl* **ruba'ti** (*-tē*) or **ruba'tos**. [It., past p. of *rubare*, to steal.]

rubber[1] *rub'ər*, *n* an eraser; caoutchouc, india-rubber or a synthetic substitute; a condom (*NAm*); (in *pl*) plimsolls or india-rubber overshoes (*NAm*); a cabinetmaker's pad for polishing. — *adj* of, yielding or concerned with india-rubber. — *vt* **rubb'erise** or **-ize** to treat or coat with rubber. — *adj* **rubb'ery**. — **rubber band** a thin loop of rubber used to hold things together; **rubber cement** an adhesive made of rubber dissolved in a solvent; **rubber goods** (*euph*) condoms; **rubb'erneck** (*slang*) an over-inquisitive or gaping person. — *vi* to behave in this way. — *vt* to stare or gape at. — **rubber plant** any of various plants from whose sap rubber is made, often grown as an ornamental pot-plant; **rubber stamp** a stamp of rubber for making inked impressions; an automatic or unthinking agreement or authorisation; a person or people making such an agreement, etc. — *vt* **rubber-stamp'** to imprint with a rubber stamp; to approve without exercise of judgment. — Also *adj*. — **rubber tree** an tropical American tree grown for its latex, a source of rubber. [**rub**.]

rubber[2] *rub'ər*, *n* formerly in bowls (also **rubbers**, *nsing* or *pl*), now chiefly in bridge and whist, the winning of, or play for, the best of three games (sometimes five); (vaguely) a session of card-playing; used generally of a series of games in various sports, such as cricket, tennis, etc.

rubbish *rub'ish*, *n* waste matter; litter; trash; nonsense; a worthless or despicable person or people. — Also *adj*. — *vt* to criticise, think of or talk about as rubbish. — *adj* (*colloq*) **rubb'ishing**. — *adj* **rubb'ishy** worthless; trashy. — **rubb'ish-heap**.

rubble *rub'l*, *n* loose fragments of rock or ruined buildings; undressed irregular stones used in rough masonry and in filling in; masonry of such a kind. — *adj* composed of rubble. — *adj* **rubb'ly**. — **rubb'le-work** coarse masonry.

rube *rōōb*, (*NAm slang*) *n* a country bumpkin; an uncouth, unsophisticated person. [*Reuben*, the personal name.]

rubefy *rōō'bi-fī*, *vt* to redden (esp. the skin). — *adj* **rubefacient** (*-fā'shənt*) reddening. — *n* an external application that reddens the skin. — *n* **rubefaction** (*-fak'shən*). [L. *rubefacĕre* — *rubeus*, red, *facĕre*, to make.]

rubella *rōō-bel'ə*, *n* German measles, an infectious disease with pink rash, like measles but milder, except for its possible effect on the foetus of an expectant mother infected early in pregnancy. — *n* **rubell'ite** a red kind of a mineral with varying composition, red tourmaline. [Dimin. from L. *rubeus*, red.]

rubeola *rōō-bē'ə-lə*, *n* measles. [Dimin. from L. *rubeus*, red.]

rubicon *rōōb'i-kon* or *-kən*, *n* (in piquet) the winning of a game before one's opponent scores 100. — *vt* to defeat in this way. — **cross the Rubicon** to take a decisive, irrevocable step. [L. *Rubicō*, *-ōnis*, a stream of Central Italy separating Caesar's province of Gallia Cisalpina from Italia proper — its crossing by Caesar (49 B.C.) being thus a virtual declaration of war against the republic.]

rubicund *rōō'bi-kund* or *-kənd*, *adj* (esp. of the complexion) ruddy. — *n* **rubicund'ity**. [L. *rubicundus* — *rubēre*, to be red.]

rubidium *rōō-bid'i-əm*, *n* a soft silvery-white metallic element (symbol **Rb**; atomic no. 37). [L. *rubidus*, red (so called from two red lines in its spectrum).]

rubiginous *rōō-bij'i-nəs*, *adj* rusty-coloured. [L. *rūbīgō* or *rōbīgō*, *-inis*, rust.]

ruble. See **rouble**.

rubric *rōō'brik*, *n* a heading, guiding rule, entry or liturgical direction, orig. one in red; something definitely settled. — *adj* **ru'brical**. — *adv* **ru'brically**. — *vt* **ru'bricate** to mark with red; to write or print in red; to furnish with rubrics. — *n* **rubricā'tion**. — *n* **ru'bricātor**. — *n* **rubrician** (*-brish'ən*) a person versed in liturgical rubrics. [L. *rubrīca*, red ochre — *ruber*, red.]

ruby *rōō'bi*, *n* a highly-prized stone, a pure transparent red corundum; redness. — *adj* red as a ruby. — *adj* **ru'by-coloured**. — *adj* **ruby-red'**. [O.Fr. *rubi* and *rubin* — L. *rubeus* — *ruber*, red.]

RUC *abbrev* for Royal Ulster Constabulary.

ruche *rōōsh*, *n* a pleated or gathered frilling of lace, etc. — *vt* to trim with ruche. — *n* **ruch'ing**. [Fr.; prob. Celt.]

ruck[1] *ruk*, *n* a wrinkle, fold or crease. — *vt* and *vi* to wrinkle (often with *up*). — *n* **ruck'le** a pucker or crease. [O.N. *hrukka*, a wrinkle.]

ruck[2] *ruk*, *n* a heap, stack, mass, etc. of anything; a multitude; the common run; (in Rugby) a gathering of players around the ball when it is on the ground; (in Australian rules football) the three players who do not have fixed positions but follow the ball about the field. — *vt* to heap. — *vi* (in Rugby) to form a ruck. [Prob. Scand.]

ruckle. See **ruck**[1].

rucksack *ruk'sak*, *n* a bag carried on the back by hikers, campers, etc. [Ger. dialect *ruck*, back, and Ger. *Sack*, bag.]

ruckus *ruk'əs*, (*colloq*) *n* a disturbance. [Perh. a combination of **ruction** and **rumpus**.]

ruction *ruk'shən*, (*slang*) *n* a disturbance; a rumpus. [Poss. for **insurrection**.]

rudbeckia *rud-* or *rŏŏd-bek'i-ə*, *n* any of the N. American composite plants of the genus *Rudbeckia*, of the sunflower subfamily. [Swedish botanist(s) *Rudbeck*.]

rudd *rud*, *n* the red-eye, a fish very similar to the roach. [Prob. O.E. *rudu*, redness.]

rudder *rud'ər*, *n* a flat structure hinged to the stern of a ship or boat for steering; a vertical control surface for steering an aeroplane to right or left; anything that steers; a principle that guides a person in life. — *adj* **rudd'erless**. — **rudd'er-fish** the pilot-fish, or any other fish that accompanies ships. [O.E. *rōthor*, oar.]

ruddle *rud'l*, **raddle** *rad'l* or **reddle** *red'l*, *n* red ochre. — *vt* to mark (sheep) with ruddle; to rouge coarsely.

ruddy *rud'i*, *adj* (*compar* **rudd'ier**, *superl* **rudd'iest**) red; reddish; of the colour of healthy skin in white-skinned peoples; rosy, glowing, bright; bloody (*euph*). — *vt* to make red: — *pr p* **rudd'ying**; *pa t* and *pa p* **rudd'ied**. — *adv* **rudd'ily**. — *n* **rudd'iness**. [O.E. *rudig*.]

rude *rōōd*, *adj* uncultured; unskilled; discourteously unmannerly; vulgar; harsh; crude; undeveloped; unwrought; coarse; rugged; roughly or unskilfully fashioned; (of health) robust. — *adv* **rude'ly**. — *n* **rude'ness**. — *n* **rud'ery** (*colloq*). — *adj* **rud'ish**. [L. *rudis*, rough.]

ruderal *rōō'dər-əl*, (*bot*) *n* and *adj* (a plant) growing in waste places or among rubbish. [L. *rūdus*, *-eris*, rubbish.]

rudiment *rōōd'i-mənt*, *n* (usu. in *pl*) a first principle or element; anything in a rude or first state; an organ in the first discernible stage (*biol*); often applied to an organ that never develops beyond an early stage (*biol*). — *adj* **rudimental** (*-ment'l*) rudimentary. — *adv* **rudimen'tarily**. — *n* **rudimen'tariness**. — *adj* **rudimen'tary** elementary; crude, primitive or makeshift; in an early or arrested stage of development (*biol*); of rudiments (*biol*). [L. *rudīmentum* — *rudis*, rough, raw.]

rue[1] *rōō*, *n* a strong-smelling shrubby Mediterranean plant with pinnately divided leaves and greenish-yellow flowers, punningly (see next word) symbolic of repentance. [Fr. *rue* — L. *rūta* — Peloponnesian Gr. *rhȳtē*.]

rue[2] *rōō*, *vt* to repent of; to wish not to have been or happened: — *pr p* **rue'ing** or **ru'ing**; *pa t* and *pa p* **rued**. — *adj* **rue'ful** sorrowful; mournful. — *adv* **rue'fully**. — *n* **rue'fulness**. [O.E. *hrēowan* (verb).]

rufescent *rōō-fes'ənt*, (*bot* and *zool*) *adj* inclining to redness. [L. *rūfescens*, *-entis*, pres. p. of *rūfescere*, to turn reddish — *rūfus*, reddish.]

ruff[1] *ruf*, *n* a frill, usu. starched and pleated, worn round the neck, esp. in the reigns of Elizabeth I and James; a beast's or bird's collar of long hair or feathers; a ruffed breed of domestic pigeons. — *adj* **ruffed** (*ruft*) having a ruff.

ruff[2] *ruf*, *fem* **reeve** *rē'v* or **ree** *rē*, *n* a kind of sandpiper, the male having an erectile ruff during the breeding season. [Poss. **ruff**[1].]

ruff[3] *ruf*, *n* an old card-game similar to whist or trumps; an act of trumping. — *vt* and *vi* to trump. [Perh. connected with O.Fr. *roffle*, It. *ronfa*, a card-game.]

ruff[4] or **ruffe** *ruf*, *n* the pope, a small freshwater fish of the perch family, with one dorsal fin. [Perh. **rough**.]

ruffian *ruf'i-ən* or *-yən*, *n* a coarse, brutal or violent person; a bully. — *adj* brutal; violent. — *adj* **ruff'ianish**. — *n* **ruff'ianism**. — *adj* **ruff'ianly**. — *adj* **ruff'ian-like**. [O.Fr. (Fr. *rufien*).]

ruffle *ruf'l*, *vt* to make uneven, disturb the smoothness of; to set up (as feathers); to disorder; to agitate; to turn the leaves of hastily; to disturb the equanimity of, to irritate, discompose. — *vi* to grow rough; to flutter. — *n* a frill, esp. at the wrist or neck; a ruff; a rippled condition; annoyance; agitation. — *adj* **ruff'led**. — *n* and *adj* **ruff'ling**. [Cf. L.G. *ruffelen*.]

rufiyaa *rōō'fi-yä*, *n* the standard monetary unit of the Maldives (100 *laaris*) — also **rupee** (q.v.).

rufous *rōō'fəs*, *adj* (mainly of an animal) reddish or brownish-red. [L. *rūfus*, akin to *ruber*, red.]

rug *rug*, *n* a thick, heavy mat for laying on a floor; a thick covering or wrap, e.g. for travelling. — **pull the rug (out) from under** (*fig*) by a sudden action, argument, discovery, etc., to leave (a person) without support, defence, a standpoint, etc. [Cf. Norw. *rugga, rogga*, coarse coverlet, Sw. *rugg*, coarse hair.]

Rugby or **rugby** *rug'bi*, *n* a form of football using an oval ball which (unlike *Association*) permits carrying the ball (also *colloq* **rugg'er**). — **Rugby football** or **Rugby Union football** the original form of the game, with 15 players; **Rugby League football** a modified form of the game subject to professional rules, with 13 players. [From *Rugby* school, Warwickshire.]

rugged *rug'id*, *adj* rough; uneven; uncouth; toilsome; (of facial features) giving an appearance of strength or suggesting experience of (esp. physical) hardships; sturdy and rough; massively irregular; robust, vigorous. — *vt* **rugg'edise** or **-ize** to render rugged; to make so as to withstand rough handling. — *adv* **rugg'edly**. — *n* **rugg'edness**. [Prob. related to **rug**.]

rugger. See **Rugby**.

rugose *rōō'gōs* or *-gōs'*, *adj* wrinkled; covered with sunken lines. — *adv* **ru'gosely** (or *-gōs'*). — *n* **rugosity** (*-gos'i-ti*). [L. *rūgōsus* — *rūga*, a wrinkle.]

ruin *rōō'in*, *n* downfall; collapse; overthrow; complete destruction; wreck; loss of fortune or means; bankruptcy; undoing; downfallen, collapsed, wrecked or irretrievably damaged state (often in *pl*); cause of ruin; broken-down remains, esp. of a building (often in *pl*); devastation. — *vt* to reduce or bring to ruin; to spoil. — *adj* **ru'inable**. — *n* **ruinā'tion** act of ruining; state of being ruined. — *adj* **ru'ined**. — *n* **ru'iner**. — *n* and *adj* **ru'ining**. — *adj* **ru'inous** fallen to ruins; decayed; bringing ruin. — *adv* **ru'inously**. — *n* **ru'inousness**. [L. *ruīna* — *ruĕre*, to tumble down.]

ruing. See **rue²**.

rule *rōōl*, *n* a straight-edged strip used as a guide in drawing straight lines, or as a measuring-rod or means of mechanical calculation; a straight line printed or drawn on paper, etc.; a straight-edge used for securing a flat surface in plaster or cement; government; control; prevalence; that which is normal or usual; conformity to good or established usage; well-regulated condition; a principle; a standard; a code of regulations, e.g. of a religious order; a regulation, whether imposed by authority or voluntarily adopted; an order of a court; a guiding principle; a method or process of achieving a result; a maxim or formula that it is generally best, but not compulsory, to follow; (in *pl*) an area around a prison in which privileged prisoners were allowed to live (*hist*); the privilege of living there (*hist*); (in *pl*) Australian football (see **Australian rules**). — *vt* to draw with a ruler; to mark with (esp. parallel) straight lines; to govern; to control; to manage; to prevail upon; to determine or declare authoritatively to be; to determine or decree. — *vi* to exercise power (with *over*); to decide; to be prevalent; to stand or range in price. — *adj* **ru'lable** governable; allowable (*US*). — *adj* **rule'less**. — *n* **ru'ler** a strip or roller for ruling lines; a person who rules. — *n* **ru'lership**. — *adj* **ru'ling** predominant; prevailing; reigning; exercising authority. — *n* a determination by a judge, esp. an oral decision; the act of making ruled lines. — *adj* **rule-of-thumb'** according to rule of thumb (see below). — **as a rule** usually; **be ruled** take advice; **rule of the road** the regulations to be observed in traffic by land, water or air; **rule of three** the mathematical method of finding the fourth term of a proportion when three are given; **rule of thumb** any rough-and-ready practical method; **rule out** to exclude as a choice or possibility. [O.Fr. *reule* — L. *rēgula* — *regĕre*, to rule.]

rum¹ *rum*, *n* a spirit distilled from fermented sugar-cane juice or from molasses; alcoholic liquor generally (*NAm*). — *adj* **rumm'y**. — **rum-butt'er** a mixture of butter and sugar with rum, etc.; **rum-punch'** punch made with rum; **rum'-runner** (*hist*) a person who smuggled rum; **rum'-running**; **rum baba** baba au rhum (see **baba**). [Perh. from its now obs. name *rumbullion* or some similar form.]

rum² *rum*, (*slang*) *adj* queer, droll, odd. — *adv* **rum'ly**. — *n* **rum'ness**. [Cant.]

Rumanian. See **Romanian**.

rumba or **rhumba** *rōōm'bə* or *rum'bə*, *n* a lively Cuban dance or a ballroom dance based on a modification of it; a piece of music for the dance. — *vi* to dance the rumba. [Sp.]

rumble¹ *rum'bl*, *vi* to make a low heavy grumbling or rolling noise; to move with such a noise; to be involved in a gang fight (*slang*, esp. *NAm*). — *vt* to give forth, or to agitate or move, with such a sound. — *n* a sound of rumbling; a seat for servants behind a carriage, or for extra passengers in a two-seater car (also **rumble seat**); a quarrel, disturbance or gang fight (*slang*, esp. *NAm*). — *n* **rum'bler**. — *n* and *adj* **rum'bling**. — *adv* **rum'blingly**. — *adj* **rum'bly**. — **rumble strip** one of a set of rough-textured strips set into a road surface to warn drivers (by tyre noise) of a hazard ahead; **rumble-tum'ble** a tumbling motion. [Cf. Du. *rommelen*, Ger. *rummeln*.]

rumble² *rum'bl*, (*slang*) *vt* to grasp; to see through, discover the truth about.

rumbustious *rum-bust'yəs*, (*colloq*) *adj* loud and boisterous. [Prob. **robust**.]

rumen *rōō'men*, (*zool*) *n* the paunch or first stomach of a ruminant: — *pl* **ru'mina** or **ru'mens**. [L. *rūmen*, *-inis*, gullet.]

ruminant *rōō'min-ənt*, *n* an animal that chews the cud. — *adj* cud-chewing; meditative. — *adv* **ru'minantly**. — *vi* **ru'mināte** to chew the cud; to regurgitate for chewing; to meditate on or upon. — *adv* **ru'minātingly**. — *n* **ruminā'tion**. — *adj* **ru'minative**. — *adv* **ru'minatively**. — *n* **ru'minātor**. [L. *rūmināre*, *-ātum* — *rūmen*, *-inis*, the gullet.]

rummage *rum'ij*, *n* a thorough search; an overhauling search. — *vt* to ransack; to search. — *vi* to make a search (often with *through*). — *n* **rumm'ager**. — **rummage sale** a sale at which buyers are allowed to rummage among the goods; also a sale of odds and ends or undesired goods. [Fr. *arrumage* (now *arrimage*), stowage.]

rummer *rum'ər*, *n* a large drinking-glass. [Du. *roemer*; Ger. *Römer*.]

rummy¹. See **rum¹**.

rummy² *rum'i*, *n* a card-game in which cards are drawn from the pack and sequences, triplets, etc. are laid on the table.

rumour or in N.Am **rumor** *rōō'mər*, *n* general talk, repute; hearsay; gossip; a current story. — *vt* to put about by report. — *n* **ru'mourer**. [O.Fr. — L. *rūmor*, *-ōris*, a noise.]

rump *rump*, *n* the hinder part of an animal's body; a cut of beef between the loin and the round; the buttocks; a remnant (usu. *contemptuous*). — **rump steak** steak cut from the thigh near the rump. — **the Rump** the remnant of the long Parliament, after Pride's expulsion (1648), of about a hundred Presbyterian royalist members. [Scand.]

rumple *rum'pl*, *n* a fold or wrinkle. — *vt* to crush out of shape; to make uneven. [Du. *rompel*; cf. O.E. *hrimpan*, to wrinkle.]

rumpus *rum'pəs*, *n* an uproar; a disturbance. — **rumpus room** (orig. *NAm*) a room in which children can play freely.

run *run*, *vi* to proceed by lifting one foot before the other is down; to go swiftly, at more than a walking pace; to hasten; to proceed quickly; to flee; to progress, esp. smoothly and quickly; to go about freely; to ride at a running pace; to revolve; to go with a gliding motion; to slip; to go on wheels; to travel, cover a distance; to make a short journey; to swim in shoals; to ascend a river for spawning; to ply; to have a definite sequence, e.g. of notes or words; to proceed through a sequence of operations, to work, or go, as a machine; to follow a course; to flow; to spread, diffuse; to emit or transmit a flow; to melt; to fuse; to have a course, stretch or extent; to range; to average; to elapse; to tend; to be current; to be valid; to recur repeatedly or remain persistently (in the mind, in the family, etc.); to come undone, e.g. by the dropping or breaking of a stitch; to compete in a race; to be a candidate (*NAm*). — *vt* to cause to run; to chase, hunt; to drive forward; to thrust; to pierce; to drive; to pass quickly; to enter, promote, put forward (e.g. a horse, candidate or protégé); to render, by running or otherwise; to conduct, manage; to traverse; to cause to extend, form in a line; to sew slightly; to shoot along or down; to perform, achieve or score by running, or as if by running; to incur; to risk and pass the hazard of; to smuggle; to have or keep current or running; to publish (a regular paper, magazine, etc.); to publish (an article or advertisement) in a newspaper or magazine, esp. in successive issues; to show (a film or TV programme); to fuse; to emit, discharge, flow with; to execute (a program) (*comput*): — *pr p* **runn'ing**; *pa t* **ran**; *pa p* **run.** — *n* an act, spell or manner of running; a journey, trip; distance, time or quantity run; a circuit of duty, such as a delivery round, etc.; a continuous stretch, spell, series or period; a shoal, migration or migrating body; a spell of being in general demand; a rush for payment, as upon a bank; a unit of scoring in cricket; a batsman's passage from one popping-crease to the other; a circuit in baseball; flow or discharge; course; prevalence; the ordinary or average kind, the generality; a track; a path made by animals; a range of feeding-ground; a tract of land used for raising stock (*Austr* and *NZ*); an enclosure for chickens, etc.; freedom of access to all parts; general direction; a ladder in knitting or knitted fabrics, esp. stockings; the complete execution of a program (*comput*); (in *pl* with **the**) diarrhoea (*colloq*). — *n* **run'let** a runnel. — *adj* **runn'able** (of a stag) fit for hunting. — *n* **runn'er** a person who or that which runs or can run; a racer; a messenger; a rooting stem that runs along the ground; a rope to increase the power of a tackle; a smuggler; a Bow Street officer (*hist*); a ring or the like, through which anything slides or runs; the part on which a sledge, a skate or a drawer slides; a strip of cloth as a table ornament; a revolving millstone; a climbing plant of the kidney-bean genus also called **runn'er-bean** or **scarlet runner**; a long narrow strip of carpet used for passages and staircases. — *adj* **runn'ing** racing; habitually going at a run; current; successive; continuous; flowing; discharging; cursive; done at or with a run. — *n* the action of the verb; the pace; the lead; the competitive state. — *adv* **runn'ingly**. — *adj* **runn'y**. — **run'about** a small light car, boat or aeroplane; **run'around** a runabout (car); see also **get** and **give the runaround** (below); **run'away** a fugitive; a horse that bolts; a flight. — *adj* fleeing; done by or in flight; uncontrolled; overwhelming. — *adj* **run-down'** in weakened health; (of a building, etc.) dilapidated. — *n* (usu. **run'down**) a reduction in numbers; a statement bringing together all the main items, a summary (see also **run down** below). — *adj* **run'flat** (of a tyre) able, after being punctured, to be safely driven on for a distance. — **run'-in** an approach; a quarrel or argument (*colloq*; see also **run in** below). — **runner-up'** the competitor next after the winner; one of a number of contestants coming close behind the winner: — *pl* **runners-up'**. — **running back** (*Am football*) a back who is expected to advance the ball from the scrimmage by running with it; **running battle** a battle between pursuers and pursued; a continuing skirmish; **runn'ing-board** a footboard along the side of a car; **running commentary** a broadcast description of a game or other event in progress; **running dog** (*derog*) (in political jargon) a slavish follower; **runn'ing-knot** a knot that will form a noose on pulling; **running lights** the lights shown by vessels between sunset and sunrise; small lights at the front and rear of a car which remain on while the engine is running; **running mate** a horse teamed with another, or making the pace for another; the candidate for the less important of two associated offices, esp. the candidate for the vice-presidency considered in relation to the presidential candidate (*US politics*); **running stitch** a simple stitch usu. made in a line, in order to gather fabric, etc.; **running title** the title of a book, etc., continued from page to page on the upper margin; **run'-off** a race held to resolve a dead heat or other uncertain result (also *fig*); rainwater which drains into rivers, rather than being absorbed into the soil; urination (*slang*). — *adj* **run-of-the-mill'** constituting an ordinary fair sample, not selected; mediocre. — *adj* **run'-resist** (of stockings or tights) knitted with a stitch which does not ladder readily. — **run'-through** an instance of running through (see **run through** below); **run time** the time needed for the execution of a computer program; **run'-up** an approach (*lit* and *fig*; see also **run up** below); **run'way** a trail, track or passageway; a firm strip of ground for aircraft to take off from and land on. — **do a runner** (*colloq*) to run away, esp. to leave a shop, restaurant, etc. quickly, without paying; **give (someone) the runaround** (*colloq*) to repeatedly behave in a deceptive or evasive way towards; to question or meet a request with evasion; **get the runaround** (*colloq*) to be treated thus; **in the long run** in the end or final result; **in (or out of) the running** competing with (or without) a fair chance of success; **make (or take up) the running** to take the lead; to set the pace; **on the run** (*colloq*) pursued, esp. by the police; **run across** to come upon by accident; **run after** to pursue; **run along!** (*colloq*) off you go!; **run a temperature** to be feverish; **run away with** to take away; to win (a prize, etc.) easily; **run down** to pursue to exhaustion or capture; to collide with and knock over or sink; to treat or speak to disparagingly; to become unwound or exhausted; **run dry** to cease to flow; to come to an end; **run for it** (*colloq*) to attempt to escape, run away; **run hard** or **close** to press hard behind; **run in** to arrest and take to a lock-up; to bring (new machinery, car) into full working condition by a period of careful operation; **run in (the blood** or**) the family** to be a hereditary characteristic; **run into** to meet, come across; to extend into; **run into debt** to get into debt; **run it fine** to allow very little margin (of time); **run itself** (of a business enterprise, etc.) to need little supervision or active direction; **run low** to run short; **run off** to cause to flow out; to take impressions of, to print; **run off one's feet** exhausted by overwork; **run off with** (*colloq*) to take away, steal; to elope with; **run on** to talk on and on; to continue in the same line, and not in a new paragraph (*printing*); **run one's eyes over** to look at cursorily; **run out** to run short; to terminate, expire; to leak, let out liquid; to put out (a batsman running between the wickets and not yet in his ground); dismissed thus; **run out of** to have no more of; **run out on** (*colloq*) to abandon, desert; **run over** to overflow; to go over cursorily; (of a road vehicle) to knock down (a person or animal); **run scared** (*slang*) to be frightened; **run short** to come to be short, lacking or exhausted; **run through** to spend wastefully; to pierce through with a sword, etc.; to read or perform quickly or cursorily but completely; **run to** to be sufficient for; **run to**

earth or **ground** see under **earth** or **ground**[2]; **run together** to mingle or blend; **run to seed** see under **seed**; **run up** to make or mend hastily; to build hurriedly; to string up, hang; to incur increasingly; **take a running jump** (*slang*) an expression of impatience, contempt, etc. [O.E. *rinnan*, *irnan*, *iernan*, to run; causative *rennan*, to curdle.]

runcible *run'si-bl*, *adj* apparently a nonsense-word of Edward Lear's, whose phrase *runcible spoon* has been applied to a pickle-fork with broad prongs and one sharp curved prong.

rune *ro͞on*, *n* a letter of the futhork or ancient Germanic alphabet; a mystical symbol; a song, stanza or canto of a Finnish poem, esp. of the *Kalevala* (Finn. *runo*, akin to O.N. *rūn*). — *adj* **runed**. — *adj* **ru'nic** of, pertaining to, written in or inscribed with runes. [O.E. and O.N. *rūn*, mystery, rune.]

rung[1] *rung*, *n* a spoke; a cross-bar or rail; a ladder step. [O.E. *hrung*.]

rung[2]. See **ring**[2].

runlet, runnable. See under **run**.

runnel *run'l*, *n* a little brook. [O.E. *rynel*, dimin. of *ryne*, a stream — *rinnan*, to run.]

runner, running and **runny**. See under **run**.

runt *runt*, *n* a small pig, esp. the smallest of a litter; anything undersized; a large breed of domestic pigeon; a small stunted or old ox or cow.

rupee *ro͞o-pē'*, *n* the standard monetary unit of India and Pakistan (100 *paisa*), Bhutan (100 *chetrum*), Nepal (100 *paise* or *pice*), Sri Lanka, Mauritius and the Seychelles (100 *cents*) and the Maldive Islands (100 *laaris*). [Urdu *rūpiyah* — Sans. *rūpya*, wrought silver.]

rupiah *ro͞o'pi-ə*, *n* the standard unit of currency of Indonesia (100 *sen*): — *pl* **ru'piah** or **ru'piahs**. [Hindi, rupee.]

rupture *rup'chər*, *n* a breach, breaking or bursting; the state of being broken; a breach of harmony, relations or negotiations; a hernia, esp. abdominal. — *vt* and *vi* to break or burst. [L.L. *ruptūra* — L. *rumpěre*, *ruptum*, to break.]

rural *ro͞o'rl*, *adj* of, relating to or suggesting the country or countryside. — *n* **ruralisā'tion** or **-z-**. — *vt* **ru'ralise** or **-ize** to render rural. — *vi* to adopt rural habits, way of life, etc. — *n* **rurality** (*-al'i-ti*). — *adv* **ru'rally**. — *n* **ru'ralness**. — *adj* **ruridecanal** (*ro͞o-ri-di-kā'nl*, or sometimes *-dek'ən-l*) of a rural dean or deanery. — **rural dean** see under **dean**[2]. [L. *rūrālis* — *rūs*, *rūris*, the country.]

Ruritania *ro͞or-i-tān'yə*, *n* a fictitious land of historical romance (in S.E. Europe) created by Anthony Hope; any idealistically exciting or romantic place situation, etc. — *n* and *adj* **Ruritān'ian**.

rurp *rûrp*, (orig. *US*) *n* a very small hook-like piton used in mountaineering. [Acronym of *r*ealised *u*ltimate *r*eality *p*iton.]

rusa *ro͞o'sə*, *n* any large E. Indian deer of the genus *Rusa*, esp. the sambar. [Malay *rūsa*.]

ruse *ro͞oz*, *n* a trick, stratagem or artifice. [O.Fr. *ruse* — *ruser*, *reüser*, to get out of the way, double on one's tracks.]

rush[1] *rush*, *vi* to move forward with haste, impetuosity or rashness. — *vt* to force out of place; to hasten or hustle forward, or into any action; to move, transport, drive or push in great haste; to capture or secure by a rush; to overcharge (*colloq*). — *n* a swift impetuous forward movement; a sudden simultaneous or general movement (such as a *gold rush*); an onset; a stampede; a migratory movement or body; a run upon anything; an unedited print of a motion picture scene or series of scenes for immediate viewing by the film makers; rapidly increased activity; bustling activity; a feeling of euphoria experienced after the taking of a drug (*slang*); a sound of rushing; a collective name for a group of pochards. — *adj* (*colloq*) done or needing to be done quickly. — *n* **rush'er**. — **rush hour** one of the times during the day of maximum activity or traffic. — **rush one's fences** to act precipitately. [A.Fr. *russcher*, O.Fr. *reusser*, *reüser*, *ruser*; see ety. for **ruse**.]

rush[2] *rush*, *n* any plant of the grasslike marsh-growing genus *Juncus*; a stalk or round stalklike leaf of such a plant; extended to various more or less similar plants (see **bulrush**); a thing of no value or importance. — *adj* made of rush or rushes. — *n* **rush'iness**. — *adj* **rush'like**. — *adj* **rush'y**. — *adj* **rush'-bottomed** having a seat made with rushes. — **rush'-candle** or **rush'light** a candle or night-light having a wick of rush-pith; a small, feeble light. [O.E. *risce*.]

rusk *rusk*, *n* a small cake like a piece of very hard toast. [Sp. *rosca*, a roll.]

russel *rus'l*, *n* a ribbed cotton and woollen material. — **russ'el-cord** a kind of corded cloth made of cotton and wool. [Poss. Flem. *Rijssel*, Lille.]

russet *rus'it*, *n* a coarse homespun cloth; a reddish-brown colour; a reddish-brown variety of apple. — *adj* made of russet; reddish-brown. — *adj* **russ'ety**. [O.Fr. *rousset* — L. *russus*, red.]

Russian *rush'ən*, *adj* of *Russia* or the Soviet Union, its people or their language. — *n* a native or citizen of Russia or the Soviet Union; the Slavonic language of most Russians, the official language of the Soviet Union. — *n* **russ'ia** russia leather. — *n* **Russianīsā'tion** or **-z-**. — *vt* **Russ'ianise** or **-ize** to give Russian characteristics to. — *n* **Russification** (*rus-i-fi-kā'shən*). — *vt* **Russ'ify** to Russianise. — *n* **Russ'ky** or **Russ'ki** (*derog slang*, esp. *NAm*) Russian. — *n* **Russ'ophile** or **Russ'ophil** a person who shows admiration for or is enthusiastic about the culture, language, political system, etc. of Russia or the Soviet Union (also *adj*). — *n* **Russ'ophobe** someone who dreads or hates the Soviet Union, its citizens, political system, etc. (also *adj*). — *n* **Russophō'bia**. — **russia (or Russia) leather** a fine brownish-red leather with a characteristic odour; **Russian boots** wide, calf-length leather boots; **Russian dressing** mayonnaise sharpened with chilli sauce, chopped pickles, etc.; **Russian roulette** an act of bravado, *specif* that of loading a revolver with one bullet, spinning the cylinder, and firing at one's own head; **Russian salad** a salad of mixed vegetables, diced and served with a Russian dressing; **Russian tea** tea with lemon and no milk, usu. served in a glass.

rust *rust*, *n* the reddish-brown coating on iron exposed to moisture; any similar coating or appearance; a plant disease characterised by a rusty appearance, caused by various fungi; a fungus causing such disease; injurious influence or consequence, esp. of mental inactivity or idleness; the colour of rust. — *vi* to become rusty; to affect with rust; to become dull or inefficient by inaction. — *vt* to make rusty; to impair by time and inactivity. — *adj* **rust'ed**. — *adv* **rust'ily**. — *n* **rust'iness**. — *n* and *adj* **rust'ing**. — *adj* **rust'less**. — *adj* **rust'y** covered with rust; impaired by inactivity, out of practice; rust-coloured; time-worn; rough; raucous; discoloured. — **rust'-bucket** (*colloq*) a badly rusted car. — *adj* **rust'-coloured**. — *adj* **rust'proof**. — *adj* **rust'-resistant**. — **rusty nail** (*colloq*) an alcoholic cocktail containing whisky and Drambuie®. [O.E. *rūst*.]

rustic *rus'tik*, *adj* of, or characteristic of, the country or country-dwellers; country-dwelling; like country-folk or their works; simple and plain; awkward; uncouth; unrefined; roughly made; made of rough branches; (of masonry) with sunken or chamfered joints, sometimes with roughened face. — *n* a peasant. — *adv* **rus'tically**. — *vt* **rust'icate** to send into the country; to give (masonry) a rough surface, and usu. sunken joints; to build in rustic masonry. — *vi* to live in the country; to become rustic. — *adj* **rust'icated**. — *n* **rusticā'tion**. — *n* **rust'icātor**. —

n **rust'icism** (*-sizm*) a rustic saying or custom. — *n* **rusticity** (*-tis'i-ti*) rustic manner; simplicity. — **rustic capitals** a type of Roman script using simplified, squared capital letters; **rus'tic-work** rusticated masonry. [L. *rūsticus* — *rūs*, the country.]

rustle *rus'l*, *vi* to make a soft, whispering sound, as of dry leaves; to go about with such a sound; to steal cattle (*US*). — *vt* to cause to rustle; to get by rustling (*US*). — *n* a quick succession of small sounds, such as that of dry leaves; a rustling. — *n* **rus'tler.** — *n* and *adj* **rus'tling.** — *adv* **rus'tlingly.** — **rustle up** to arrange, gather together or prepare, esp. at short notice. [Imit.]

rusty. See under **rust.**

rut[1] *rut*, *n* a furrow made by wheels; a fixed course that is difficult to get out of or depart from. — *vt* to furrow with ruts: — *pr p* **rutt'ing**; *pa t* and *pa p* **rutt'ed.** — *adj* **rutt'y.** — **in a rut** following a tedious routine from which it is difficult to escape.

rut[2] *rut*, *n* sexual excitement in male deer and other ruminants. — *vi* to be in such a period of sexual excitement. — *n* and *adj* **rutt'ing.** — *adj* **rutt'ish.** [O.Fr. *ruit*, *rut* — L. *rugītus* — *rugīre*, to roar.]

rutabaga *rōō-tə-bā'gə*, (*NAm*) *n* a swede. [Sw. dialect *rotabagge.*]

ruthenium *rōō-thē'ni-əm*, *n* a metallic element (symbol **Ru**; atomic no. 44) of the platinum group, found in the Ural Mountains. [L.L. *Ruthenia*, Russia.]

rutherford *rudh'ər-fərd*, *n* a unit of radioactive disintegration, equal to a million disintegrations a second (abbrev. **rd**). — *n* **rutherford'ium** the name coined in the U.S. for a transuranic element (symbol **Rf**; atomic no. 104), called by the Russians kurchatovium. [After the physicist Baron *Rutherford* (1871–1937).]

ruthless *rōōth'ləs*, *adj* pitiless; unsparing. — *adv* **ruth'lessly.** — *n* **ruth'lessness.** [Now rare *ruth*, pity (— M.E. *ruthe*, *reuth*) and **-less.**]

rutile *rōō'tīl*, *n* a reddish-brown mineral of the tetragonal system, titanium oxide. [L. *rutilus*, reddish.]

rutty. See under **rut**[1].

RV *abbrev* for Revised Version (of the Bible).

RW *abbrev* for: Right Worshipful; Right Worthy.

RWA *abbrev* for Rwanda (I.V.R.).

Rwy or **Ry** *abbrev* for Railway.

rya *rē'ə*, *n* a type of Scandinavian knotted-pile rug with a distinctive colourful pattern (also **rya rug**); the weave, pattern or style typical of a rya. — Also *adj.* [Sw., connected with Finn. *ryijy.*]

rye *rī*, *n* a grass allied to wheat and barley; its grain, used for making bread; rye whisky. — *adj* made of or with rye. — **rye'bread**; **rye'flour**; **rye grass** a pasture and fodder grass; **rye whisky** whisky distilled chiefly from rye. [O.E. *ryge.*]

ryokan *rē-ō'kən*, *n* a traditional Japanese inn. [Jap.]

ryot *rī'ət*, *n* an Indian peasant. [Hind. *raiyat*, Ar. *ra'īyah*, a subject.]

RZS *abbrev* for Royal Zoological Society.

S

S or **s** *es, n* the nineteenth letter in the modern English alphabet, a consonant, its usual sound a voiceless sibilant (pronounced *s*), but often voiced (pronounced *z*); any mark or object of the form of the letter.

S or **S.** *abbrev* for: Sabbath; Saint; schilling (Austrian currency); siemens; Society; South; square; stokes; sun; Sweden (I.V.R.). — **S4C** *abbrev* for *Sianel Pedwar Cymru*, the Welsh language television channel.

S *symbol* for: sulphur (*chem*); (in the form **$**) dollar.

s or **s.** *abbrev* for second(s).

's *z* or *s*, a sentence element used to form the possessive (e.g. *John's*, *the dog's*, *the children's*); often also to form the plural of numbers or symbols (e.g. 3'*s*); a shortened form of **has** or **is** (e.g. *she's taken it*, *he's not here*); a shortened form of **us** (pronounced *s*; e.g. *let's go*).

SA *abbrev* for: Salvation Army; sex-appeal; *Societé anonyme* (Fr.), limited liability company; Society of Antiquaries; Society of Arts; South Africa; South America; South Australia.

sa *abbrev* for: *secundum artem* (L.), according to art; *sine anno* (L.), without date (lit., year).

sabadilla *sab-ə-dil'ə, n* the seeds of a plant of the lily genus, yielding veratrine. — Also **cebadill'a** or **cevadill'a.** [Sp. *cebadilla*, dimin. of *cebada*, barley.]

Sabahan *səb-ä'hən, n* a citizen or inhabitant of *Sabah*, a Malaysian state. — *adj* of, from or pertaining to Sabah.

Sabaoth *sa-bā'oth* or *sab'a-ōt*, (*Bible*) *npl* armies, used only in the phrase, 'Lord of Sabaoth'. [Heb. *tsebāōth* (transliterated *sabaōth* in Gr.), pl. of *tsabā*, an army.]

Sabbath *sab'əth, n* (among the Jews) Saturday, set apart for rest from work; (among most Christians) Sunday; a time of rest; (also **sabb'at**) a witches' midnight meeting. — *adj* of or appropriate to the Sabbath. — *n* **Sabbatā'rian** a person who observes Saturday as the Sabbath; a person who believes in or practises observance, or strict observance, of the Sabbath (Saturday or Sunday). — Also *adj.* — *n* **Sabbatā'rianism.** — *adj* **sabbatical** (*səb-at'ik-l*) pertaining to or resembling the Sabbath; on or pertaining to leave from one's work (as in *sabbatical leave*, etc.). — *n* a period of leave from one's work, esp. for teachers and lecturers, also esp. to undertake a separate or related project. — *vt* **sabb'atise** or **-ize** to observe as a Sabbath. — *vi* to keep a Sabbath. — *n* **sabb'atism** sabbatical rest; observance of the Sabbath. — **sabbatical year** every seventh year, in which the Israelites allowed their fields and vineyards to lie fallow; a year off, for study, travel, etc. [Heb. *Shabbāth*.]

saber. See **sabre.**

sabin *sab'in* or *sā'bin*, (*phys*) *n* a unit of acoustic absorption. [From Wallace C. *Sabine* (1868–1919), U.S. physicist.]

Sabine *sab'īn*, (*hist*) *n* one of an ancient people of central Italy, afterwards united with the Romans. — Also *adj.* [L. *Sabīnus*.]

sable[1] *sā'bl, n* an arctic and subarctic marten; its lustrous dark brown fur; a paint-brush made with its hair. — *adj* made of sable fur. [O.Fr.]

sable[2] *sā'bl, n* and *adj* black (orig. *heraldry*, now chiefly *poetic*); dark. — **sable antelope** a large South African antelope, black above, white below. — *adj* **sa'ble-coloured.** [Fr.; poss. **sable**[1].]

sabot *sab'ō, n* a wooden shoe, as formerly worn by the French peasantry. [Fr.]

sabotage *sab'ə-täzh, n* malicious destruction for political, etc. reasons; action taken to prevent the achievement of any aim. — Also *vt* and *vi.* — *n* **saboteur** (*-tœr'*) a person who sabotages. [Fr. *sabot.*]

sabra *sä'brə, n* a native-born Israeli, not an immigrant. [Mod. Hebrew *sābrāh*, type of cactus.]

sabre or in U.S. **saber** *sā'bər, n* a curved, single-edged, cavalry sword; a light sword used in fencing. — *vt* to wound or kill with a sabre. — *vi* **sa'bre-rattle.** — **sa'bre-rattling** military bluster as an attempt to convince of one's intentions; **sa'bre-tooth** (in full **sabre-toothed tiger**) a fossil carnivore with extremely long upper canine teeth. [Fr. *sabre.*]

sabretache *sab'ər-tash, n* a flat bag slung from a cavalry officer's sword-belt. [Fr., — Ger. *Säbeltasche* — *Säbel*, sabre, *Tasche*, pocket.]

sac *sak*, (*biol*) *n* a pouch or bag. — *adj* **sacc'ate** pouchlike; enclosed in a sac. — *adj* **sacciform** (*sak'si-förm*) or **sacc'ūlar** saclike. — *adj* **sacc'ūlated** formed in a series of saclike enclosures; enclosed in a sac. — *n* **sacculā'tion.** — *n* **sacc'ūle** or **sacc'ūlus** a small sac: — *pl* **sacc'ules** or **sacc'ulī.** [L. *saccus*, a bag; see **sack**[1].]

saccade *sak-äd', n* a short jerky movement, esp. of the eye; a short rapid tug on a horse's reins. — *adj* **saccad'ic** jerky; consisting of or pertaining to saccades. — *adv* **saccad'ically.** [Fr. *saccade*, a jerk — O.Fr. *saquer*, to pull.]

saccate. See **sac.**

Saccharum *sak'ə-rəm, n* the sugar-cane genus of grasses. — *n* **sacch'aride** a carbohydrate; a compound with sugar. — *n* **saccharim'eter** an instrument for testing the concentration of sugar solutions. — *n* **saccharim'etry.** — *n* **sacch'arin** or **sacch'arine** (*-in* or *-ēn*) an intensely sweet, white crystalline substance used as an artificial sweetener; sickly sweetness. — *adj* **sacch'arine** (*-īn* or *-ēn*) of sickly sweetness. — *n* **saccharinity** (*-in'i-ti*). — *n* **saccharom'eter** a hydrometer or other instrument for measuring the concentration of sugar solutions. — *n* **sacch'arose** (*-ōs*) any carbohydrate, esp. cane sugar. [L. *saccharum* — Gr. *sakcharon*, sugar, a word of Eastern origin.]

sacciform, saccular, etc. See **sac.**

sacerdotal *sas-ər-dō'tl, adj* priestly. — *vt* **sacerdō'talise** or **-ize** to render sacerdotal. — *n* **sacerdō'talism** the spirit, principles, etc. of the priesthood; devotion to priestly interests; priestcraft; attribution to the priesthood of special or supernatural powers; excessive influence of priests (*derog*). — *n* **sacerdō'talist.** — *adv* **sacerdō'tally.** [L. *sacerdōs, -ōtis*, a priest — *sacer*, sacred, *dăre*, to give.]

sachem *sā'chəm*, (*US*) *n* a N. American Indian chief; a political leader. [Algonquian.]

sachet *sa'shā, n* a small usu. plastic envelope, containing a liquid, cream, etc., such as shampoo; a small bag containing pot-pourri or other scented material; a bag for holding handkerchiefs, etc. [Fr.]

S

sack[1] *sak*, *n* a large bag made of coarse material; a sackful; a varying, usu. large, measure of capacity; (with **the**) dismissal (*colloq*); an instance of sacking (*Am football*). — *vt* to put into a sack; to dismiss (*colloq*); to tackle the quarterback while he still holds the ball and is behind the line of scrimmage (*Am football*). — *n* **sack'ful**: — *pl* **sack'fuls**. — *n* **sack'ing** sackcloth. — **sack'cloth** coarse cloth for sacks; coarse material, formerly worn in mourning or penance; **sack'-race** one in which each racer's legs are encased in a sack. — **hit the sack** (*slang*) go to bed; **in, wearing,** etc. **sackcloth and ashes** showing extreme regret, mourning, etc. [O.E. *sacc* — L. *saccus* — Gr. *sakkos*.]

sack[2] *sak*, *n* plundering or devastation (of a town); pillage. — *vt* to plunder; to pillage. [Fr. *sac*; according to some the same as **sack**[1] (putting in a bag).]

sack[3] *sak*, *n* the old name of a Spanish wine. [Fr. *sec* — L. *siccus*, dry.]

sackbut *sak'but*, *n* an early wind instrument with a slide like the trombone. [Fr. *saquebute*.]

sacra. See **sacrum.**

sacral[1] *sā'krəl*, *adj* of or relating to sacred rites. — *n* **sacralisā'tion** or **-z-** endowing (something) with sacred status or properties; treating (something) as if it were sacred. — *vt* **sac'ralise** or **-ize.** [L. *sacrum*, a sacred object.]

sacral[2]. See **sacrum.**

sacrament *sak'rə-mənt*, *n* a Christian religious rite variously regarded as a channel to and from God or as a sign of grace — amongst Protestants generally *Baptism* and the *Lord's Supper* — amongst Roman Catholics also *Confirmation*, *Penance*, *Holy Orders*, *Matrimony* and *Extreme Unction*; the Lord's Supper especially; the bread or wine taken in celebration of the Lord's Supper; a symbol of something spiritual or secret; a sign, token or pledge. — *adj* **sacramental** (*-men'tl*). — *n* (*RC*) an act or object which may transmit or receive grace. — *n* **sacramen'talism**. — *n* **sacramen'talist** a person who attaches importance to the spiritual nature of the sacraments. — *adv* **sacramen'tally**. [L. *sacrāmentum*, an oath, pledge — *sacrāre*, to consecrate — *sacer*, sacred.]

sacrarium *sə-krā'ri-əm* or (L.) *sa-krä'ri-o͝om*, *n* the sanctuary of a church: — *pl* **sacra'ria**. [L. *sacrārium* — *sacer*, holy.]

sacred *sā'krid*, *adj* consecrated; set apart or dedicated, esp. to God; holy; emanating from God; religious; entitled to veneration, worship; not to be violated, breached, etc. — *adv* **sa'credly**. — *n* **sa'credness**. — **Sacred College** the body of cardinals; **sacred cow** an institution, custom, etc. so revered that it is regarded as above criticism (*colloq*); **Sacred Heart** (*RC*) the physical heart of Christ, adored with special devotion. [Past p. of obs. *sacre* — O.Fr. *sacrer* — L. *sacrāre* — *sacer*, sacred.]

sacrifice *sak'ri-fīs*, *n* the offering of a slaughtered animal on an altar to a god; any offering, tangible or symbolic, to a god; Christ's offering of himself as mankind's saviour (*theol*); destruction, surrender or giving up of anything valued for the sake of anything or anyone else, esp. a higher consideration; a victim offered in sacrifice. — *vt* to offer up in sacrifice; to make a sacrifice of; to give up, surrender, for a higher good or for mere advantage; to make a victim of; to allow to come to destruction or evil. — *vi* to offer sacrifice(s). — *n* **sac'rificer**. — *adj* **sacrificial** (*-fish'l*) of or pertaining to sacrifice; (of an object or substance) which protects another from corrosion by its own exposure to and damage by the corrosive (as esp. **sacrificial anode, sacrificial metal** (*tech*)). — *adv* **sacrifi'cially**. [L. *sacrificium* — *sacer*, sacred, *facĕre*, to make.]

sacrilege *sak'ri-lij*, *n* profanation of anything holy; the breaking into a place of worship and stealing from it; extreme disrespect of anything regarded as worthy of extreme respect. — *adj* **sacrilegious** (*-lij'əs*). — *adv* **sacrile'giously**. — *n* **sacrile'giousness**. — *n* **sacrilē'gist**. [Fr. *sacrilège* — L. *sacrilegium* — *sacer*, sacred, *legĕre*, to gather.]

sacrist *sak'rist* or *sā'krist*, or **sacristan** *sak'ris-tən*, *n* an officer in a church who has care of the sacred vessels and other movables; a sexton. — *n* **sacristy** (*sak'*) an apartment in a church where the sacred utensils, vestments, etc. are kept; a vestry. [L.L. *sacrista*, *sacristānus*, a sacristan, *sacristia*, a vestry — L. *sacer*.]

sacro-. See under **sacrum.**

sacrosanct *sak'rō-sangkt*, *adj* inviolable, protected by sacred or quasi-sacred rules. — *n* **sacrosanc'tity** or **sac'rosanctness**. [L. *sacrōsanctus* — *sacer*, sacred, *sanctus*, past p. of *sancīre*, to hallow.]

sacrum *sā'krəm* or *sak'rəm*, (*anat*) *n* a triangular bone composed of fused vertebrae forming the keystone of the pelvic arch in humans: — *pl* **sa'cra**. — *adj* **sa'cral**. — *adj combining form* **sacrō-** denoting sacrum, as in **sacrōil'iac** pertaining to the sacrum and ilium. — *n* this joint. [L. (*os*) *sacrum*, holy (bone).]

sad *sad*, *adj* (*compar* **sadd'er**, *superl* **sadd'est**) sorrowful; deplorable (often *jocularly*); (of baking) heavy, stiff, doughy; sober, dark-coloured. — *vt* **sadd'en** to make sad. — *vi* to grow sad. — *adj* **sadd'ish**. — *adv* **sad'ly** in a sad manner; unfortunately, sad to relate. — *n* **sad'ness**. [O.E. *sæd*, sated.]

saddhu. See **sadhu.**

saddle *sad'l*, *n* a seat for a rider on a horse, bicycle, etc.; a pad for the back of a draught animal; anything of similar shape, e.g. a mountain col between two peaks; that part of the back of an animal on which the saddle is placed; a butcher's cut including a part of the backbone with the ribs; the rear part of a cock's back; (in a structure, e.g. a bridge) a support having a groove shaped to hold another part. — *vt* to put a saddle on; to impose upon (someone) as a burden or encumbrance; (of a trainer) to be responsible for preparing and entering (a racehorse) for a race; to ride or mount (a horse, bicycle, etc.). — *adj* **sadd'leless**. — *n* **sadd'ler** a maker or seller of horse saddles and related goods; a soldier who has charge of cavalry saddles. — *n* **sadd'lery** the occupation of a saddler; a saddler's shop or stock-in-trade; a saddle-room at a stables, etc. — **sadd'leback** a saddle-shaped hill or animal; a saddle roof. — *adj* (also **sadd'lebacked**) saddle-shaped; having a depression in the middle (of the back); having a saddle-shaped mark on the back. — **sadd'lebag** a bag carried at, or attached to, the saddle of a horse or bicycle; **sadd'le-bow** (*-bō*) the arched front of a saddle; **sadd'le-cloth** a cloth placed under a horse saddle to avoid rubbing; **sadd'le-girth** a strap that holds the saddle in place; **saddle roof** a roof with two gables and a ridge; **sadd'le-room** a room where saddles and harness are kept; **saddle soap** a kind of soap used for cleaning and treating leather. — *adj* **sadd'le-sore** (of a rider) chafed with riding. — **saddle stitch** needlework consisting of long stitches on the top surface and short stitches on the underside of the material; one such stitch; a method of stitching or stapling (a booklet, magazine, etc.) together through the back centre fold. — *vt* and *vi* to sew using saddle stitch. — **sadd'le-tree** the frame of a saddle. — **in the saddle** in control. [O.E. *sadol*, *sadel*.]

Sadducee *sad'ū-sē*, (*hist*) *n* one of a Jewish priestly and aristocratic party of traditionalists, whose reactionary conservatism resisted the progressive views of the Pharisees, and who rejected, among various other beliefs, that of life after death. — *adj* **Sadducaean** or **Sadducean** (*-sē'ən*). — *n* **Sadd'uceeism** or **Sadd'ucism** scepticism. [Gr. *Saddoukaios* — Heb. *Tsadūqīm*, from *Zadok* the High Priest, the founder.]

sadhu or **saddhu** *sä'doo*, *n* a Hindu holy man, living a life of austerity and existing on charity. [Sans. *sādhu*, — adj., straight, pious.]

sadism *säd'izm*, *n* love of cruelty, esp. to the point of sexual gratification. — *n* **sad'ist.** — *adj* **sadistic** (*sə-dis'tik*). — *n* **sado-mas'ochism** obtaining pleasure by inflicting pain on oneself or others. — *n* **sado-mas'ochist.** — *adj* **sado-masochist'ic.** [Comte (called Marquis) de *Sade* (1740–1814), who died insane, notoriously depicted this form of pleasure in his novels.]

SAE or **sae** *abbrev* for stamped addressed envelope.

saeter *set'ər* or *sāt'ər*, *n* (in Norway) an upland meadow which provides summer pasture for cattle. [Norw.]

safari *sə-fä'ri*, *n* an expedition for hunting or animal-watching in Africa; a long expedition involving difficulty and requiring planning, usu. in tropical climes. — **safari park** an enclosed park where wild animals (mostly non-native) are kept uncaged on view to the public; **safari suit** a suit for men, boys or women, typically of khaki cotton and consisting of long square-cut **safari jacket** and long or short trousers. [Swahili.]

safe *sāf*, *adj* unharmed; free from danger; secure; sound, free from risk; certain, sure; reliable; cautious. — *n* a metal box, often set in a wall, secure against thieves, fire, etc.; a ventilated box or cupboard for meat, etc. — *adv* **safe'ly.** — *n* **safe'ness.** — *n* **safe'ty** the state or fact of being safe; the most deeply-placed member of a defensive side (*Am football*; also **safe'tyman**); a play where a player from one side is tackled on or behind his own goal-line, scoring two points for the other side (*Am football*); **safe'-blower; safe'-blowing** forcing of safes, using explosives; **safe'-breaker** or **-cracker; safe'-breaking** or **-cracking** illegal opening of safes; **safe-con'duct** a permit to pass or travel with guarantee of freedom from interference or arrest; **safe'-deposit** or **safe'ty-deposit** a vault, etc. offering safe storage for valuables; **safe'guard** a device, condition or arrangement ensuring safety; a safe-conduct. — *vt* to protect, ensure the safety of. — **safe house** a place (esp. one kept by the intelligence services or care agencies) unknown to one's pursuers, where one can safely hide; **safe-keep'ing** safe custody; **safe period** that part of the menstrual cycle during which conception is most unlikely; **safe seat** a parliamentary seat that the incumbent political party will almost certainly win again in an election; **safe sex** sexual intercourse which is protected against disease, e.g. by the use of condoms; **safe'ty-belt** a belt for fastening a workman, etc. to a fixed object while he carries out a dangerous operation; one fastening a passenger to his or her seat as a precaution against injury in a crash; **safe'ty-catch** any catch to provide protection against something, such as the accidental firing of a gun; **safety curtain** a fireproof curtain between stage and audience in a theatre; **safety factor** the ratio between the breaking stress in a member, structure or material, and the safe permissible stress in it; **safety film** photographic or cine film with a non-flammable or slow-burning base of cellulose acetate or polyester; **safety fuse** a slow-burning fuse that can be lit at a safe distance; a fuse inserted for safety in an electric circuit; **safety glass** a laminate of plastic between sheets of glass, used e.g. in vehicle windscreens; glass reinforced with wire, or toughened to avoid shattering; **safety lamp** a miners' lamp that will not ignite inflammable gases; **safety match** a match that can be ignited only on a prepared surface; **safe'ty-net** a net stretched beneath an acrobat, etc. during a rehearsal or performance, in case he or she should fall; any precautionary measure (*fig*); **safe'ty-pin** a pin in the form of a clasp with a guard covering its point; a pin for locking a piece of machinery, etc. e.g. that used to prevent the explosion of a grenade, a mine, etc.; **safety razor** a razor with protected blade, largely proof against cutting the user; **safety valve** a valve that opens when the pressure becomes too great; any outlet that gives relief (*fig*); **safe'ty-wear** protective clothing. — **be** or **err on the safe side** to choose the safer alternative; **place of safety order** a legal order, effective for not more than 28 days, allowing a child to be taken into care to avoid further or possible physical harm by parents, etc.; **safe and sound** secure and unharmed; **safe as houses** (*colloq*) very safe. [O.Fr. *sauf* — L. *salvus*.]

saffian *saf'i-ən*, *n* leather tanned with sumac and dyed in bright colours. [Russ. *saf'yan*.]

safflower *saf'lowr*, *n* a thistle-like composite plant cultivated in India; its dried petals, used for making a red dye and rouge. — **safflower oil** an oil produced from this plant and used in cooking, etc. [Cf. Du. *saffloer*, O.Fr. *saffleur*.]

saffron *saf'rən*, *n* a species of crocus; its dried stigmas, used as a dye and flavouring; its colour, orange-yellow. — *adj* **saff'roned.** — *adj* **saff'rony.** — *n* **saf'ranin** or **saf'ranine** (*-nēn*) a coal-tar dye, giving various colours. — **saffron cake** a cake flavoured with saffron. — **saffron milk cap** an edible orange toadstool. [O.Fr. *safran* — Ar. *za'farān*.]

sag *sag*, *vi* to bend, sink or hang down, esp. in the middle; to yield or give way, from or as though from weight or pressure; to droop: — *pr p* **sagg'ing;** *pa p* and *pa t* **sagged.** — *n* a droop. — *n* and *adj* **sagg'ing.** — *adj* **sagg'y** inclined to sag. [Cf. Sw. *sacka*, to sink down.]

saga *sä'gə*, *n* a prose tale of the deeds of Icelandic or Norwegian heroes in the old literature of Iceland; a body of legend about some subject; a long, detailed story (*colloq*). — **saga novel** see **roman fleuve.** [O.N. *saga*; cf. **saw**^{3}.]

sagacious *sə-gā'shəs*, *adj* keen in perception or thought; discerning and judicious; wise. — *adv* **sagā'ciously.** — *n* **sagā'ciousness** or **sagacity** (*-gas'i-ti*). [L. *sagāx*, *-ācis*.]

sagamore *sag'ə-mör*, *n* an American Indian chief. [Penobscot *sagamo*; cf. **sachem.**]

sage^1 *sāj*, *n* a garden plant whose grey-green leaves are used as flavouring and as stuffing for goose, etc. — **sage'brush** a shrubby aromatic plant found on dry American plains; **sage Derby** a kind of cheese flavoured (and coloured) with sage. — *adj* **sage-green'** greyish green, like sage leaves. — **sage'-grouse** a large North American grouse that feeds on sagebrush. [O.Fr. *sauge* (It. *salvia*) — L. *salvia* — *salvus*, safe.]

sage^2 *sāj*, *adj* wise. — *n* a (usu. old) man of great wisdom. — *adv* **sage'ly.** — *n* **sage'ness.** [Fr. *sage*, ult. — L. *sapĕre*, to be wise.]

saggar or **sagger** *sag'ər*, *n* a clay box in which pottery is packed for baking.

sagged, sagging. See **sag.**

sagger. See **saggar.**

sagittal *saj'it-l*, *adj* arrow-shaped; pertaining or parallel to the sagittal suture. — *adv* **sag'ittally.** — *n* and *adj* **Sagittār'ian** (of) a person born under Sagittarius. — *n* **Sagittār'ius** the Archer, a constellation and sign of the zodiac; a person born between 23 November and 22 December, under the sign of Sagittarius. — **sagittal suture** the join between the two parietal bones forming the top and sides of the skull. [L. *sagitta*, an arrow.]

sago *sā'gō*, *n* a nutritive cereal substance produced from the pith of certain palms. — **sa'go-palm.** [Malay *sāgū*.]

saguaro *sə-gwä'rō*, *n* the giant cactus: — *pl* **sagua'ros.** [From an Am. Indian language.]

Saharan *sə-hä'rən*, *adj* of, resembling, or characteristic of, the *Sahara* desert.

sahib *sä'ib*, *n* a term of respect given in India; Sir or Mr. [Ar. *sāhib*, orig. friend.]

said *sed*, *pa t* and *pa p* of **say**. — *adj* previously- or already-mentioned.

saiga *sī'gə*, *n* a W. Asian antelope. [Russ.]

sail *sāl*, *n* a sheet of canvas, framework of slats, or other structure, spread to catch the wind, so as to propel a ship, drive a windmill, etc.; sails collectively; a ship or ships; a trip in a vessel (which may or may not have sails); an act or distance of sailing. — *vi* to progress, travel or make trips by sailing craft or other ship; to set out on a voyage; to glide or float smoothly along (*fig*). — *vt* to navigate; to cause (a toy boat, etc.) to sail; to pass over or along in a ship; to go or get through effortlessly (*fig*). — *adj* **sail'able** navigable. — *adj* **sailed** having sails. — *n* **sail'er** a boat or ship that can sail in a stated manner. — *n* **sail'ing** travelling or journey by sails or on water; (the time of) a ship's departure from port; the act or mode of directing a ship's course. — Also *adj.* — *adj* **sail'less.** — *n* **sail'or** a person who is employed in the management of a ship, esp. one who is not an officer; a mariner, seaman. — *n* **sail'oring** occupation as a sailor. — *adj* **sail'orlike** or **sail'orly.** — **sail'board** a small, light, flat-hulled sailing-craft usu. consisting of a surfboard fitted with a single flexible mast, the sail being controlled by a hand-held boom; **sail'-boarder; sail'boarding** the sport of sailing a sailboard (also called **wind'surfing**); **sail'-boat** (esp. *NAm*) a (usu. small) sailing-boat; **sail'-cloth** a strong cloth for sails; **sail'-fish** a fish that shows a large dorsal fin, esp. the basking shark; **sail'ing-boat** a boat moved by sails, though often having auxiliary motor power; **sail'ing-master** an officer in charge of navigation, esp. of a yacht; **sailing orders** instructions to the captain of a ship when setting out on a voyage; **sail'ing-ship** a ship driven by sails; **sail'-maker; sail'or-hat** a round hat with a wide, upturned brim; **sail'or-man** a seaman; **sail'or-suit** a child's or woman's outfit resembling that of a sailor; **sail'plane** a glider that can rise with an upward current. — **full sail** with all sails raised and filled with the wind; **good (or bad) sailor** a person who is unaffected (or made ill) by the motion of a ship; **make sail** to spread more canvas, raise more sails; **put on sail** to set more sails in order to travel more quickly; **sail close to (or near) the wind** see under **wind**[1]; **set sail** to spread the sails; to set forth on a voyage (for); **shorten sail** to reduce its open extent; **strike sail** to lower a sail or sails; **under sail** having the sails spread; moved by sails. [O.E. *segel.*]

sainfoin *sān'foin*, *n* a variety of pulse vegetable used as fodder. — Also **saint'foin.** [Fr. *sainfoin* — L. *sānum fēnum*, healthy hay.]

saint *sānt* or when prefixed to a name *sint* or *snt*, *adj* (or *n* in apposition) holy. — *n* a holy person; a person famed for their virtue; an Israelite, a Christian, or one of the blessed dead (*Bible*); a person who has been canonised; a member of various religious bodies, esp. Puritans, as used of themselves or as a nickname. — *vt* to make a saint of; to hail as a saint. — *n* **saint'dom.** — *adj* **saint'ed** made a saint, holy; gone to heaven. — *n* **saint'hood.** — *adj* **saint'like.** — *n* **saint'liness.** — *adj* **saint'ly** of, like, characteristic of, or befitting a saint. — *n* **saint'ship.** — **saint's day** a day set apart for the commemoration of a particular saint; **St Agnes's Eve** 20 January; **St Andrew's cross** a cross in the form of the letter X; a white cross of this type on a blue background, as borne on the banner of Scotland; **St Bernard's dog** or **St Bernard** a breed of very large dogs, named after the hospice of the Great St Bernard, used, esp. formerly, to rescue travellers lost in the snow; **St Christopher** a medallion showing a likeness of St Christopher, the patron saint of travellers; **St Elmo's fire** an electrical discharge forming a glow around a church spire, ship's mast, etc.; **St George's cross** a red upright cross on a white background; **St James's** the British royal court; **St John's wort** any of the plants of the *Hypericum* genus; **St Leger** a horse-race run annually at Doncaster, named after a Col. *St Leger*; **St Swithin's Day** 15 July; **St Vitus's dance** chorea, a nervous disease causing facial and bodily twitching. [Fr., — L. *sanctus*, holy.]

saintfoin. See **sainfoin.**

saintpaulia *sānt-pö'li-ə*, *n* a plant of the *Saintpaulia* genus to which the African violet belongs. [Baron Walter von *Saint Paul*, who discovered it.]

sake[1] *sä'ki*, *n* a Japanese alcoholic drink made from fermented rice. — Also **saké** or **saki.** [Jap.]

sake[2] *sāk*, *n* a cause; account, behalf; advantage, benefit; purpose, aim, object. — **for old time's sake** because of what happened in the past; **for the sake of** in order to, for the purpose of. [O.E. *sacu*, strife, a lawsuit.]

saker *sā'kər*, *n* a species of falcon used in hawking, esp. the female. — *n* **sa'keret** the male saker. [Fr. *sacre.*]

saki[1] *sä'ki*, *n* a S. American monkey of the genus *Pithecia*, with long bushy non-prehensile tail. [Fr., for Tupí *sai*, or *saguin.*]

saki[2]. See **sake**[1].

sal[1] *säl*, *n* a tree of N. India with teak-like wood. [Hind. *sāl.*]

sal[2] *sal*, (*chem* and *pharm*) *n* a salt. — **sal ammoniac** ammonium chloride; **sal volatile** (*vol-at'i-li*) ammonium carbonate, or a solution of it in alcohol and/or ammonia in water; smelling salts. [L. *sāl.*]

salaam *sa-läm'*, *n* a word and gesture of salutation in the East, chiefly among Muslims; obeisance; greeting. — *vi* to perform the salaam, a low bow with the palm of the hand on the forehead. — **salaam eleikum** or **aleichem** (*a-lā'kōōm*) peace be upon you. [Ar. *salām*, peace; cf. Heb. *shālōm.*]

salable, salableness, salably. See **sale.**

salacious *sə-lā'shəs*, *adj* lustful, lecherous; arousing lustful or lecherous feelings. — *adv* **salā'ciously.** — *n* **salā'ciousness** or **salacity** (*-las'i-ti*). [L. *salāx*, *-ācis* — *salīre*, to leap.]

salad *sal'əd*, *n* a cold dish of vegetables or herbs (either raw or pre-cooked), generally mixed; a plant grown for or used in salad dishes; a confused mixture. — **salad cream** a type of bottled mayonnaise for dressing salad; **salad days** one's youth, esp. if carefree and showing inexperience; **salad dressing** or **oil** sauce, olive-oil, etc., used in dressing salads. — **fruit salad** see under **fruit.** [Fr. *salade* — L. *sāl*, salt.]

salamander *sal'ə-man-dər*, *n* a member of a genus of tailed amphibians, closely related to the newts, harmless, but long dreaded as poisonous, once supposed able to live in fire or to put out fire; an elemental spirit believed to live in fire; a hot metal plate for browning meat, etc. — *adj* **salaman'drian** or **salaman'drine.** — *adj* **salaman'droid** (also *n*). [Fr. *salamandre* — L. *salamandra* — Gr. *salamandrā.*]

salami *sə-lä'mi*, *n* a highly seasoned Italian sausage, usu. sliced very thinly. — **salami technique** a fraud involving the deduction of almost indiscernable sums of money from numerous and scattered transactions (esp. *comput*). [It.]

salary *sal'ə-ri*, *n* a periodic payment (usually at longer intervals than a week) for one's (usu. non-manual) labour. — *vt* to pay a salary to. — *adj* **sal'aried.** [O.Fr. *salarie* — L. *salārium*, money given to soldiers to buy salt — *sāl*, salt.]

salbutamol *sal-bū'tə-mol*, *n* a broncho-dilator, used in the treatment of bronchial asthma.

salchow *sal'kō* or *sal'kov*, (*ice-skating*) *n* a jump in which the skater takes off from the inside back edge of one skate, spins in the air and lands on the outside back edge of the other skate. [From Ulrich *Salchow*, 20th-cent. Swedish skater.]

sale *sāl*, *n* an act or occasion of selling; the exchange of anything for money; power or opportunity of selling; demand, volume of selling; (an occasion of) public offer of goods to be sold, esp. at reduced prices or by auction; the state of being offered to buyers. — *adj* intended for selling, esp. at reduced prices or by auction. — *n* **salabil'ity** (also **saleabil'ity**). — *adj* **sale'able** or **sal'able** that can be sold; in good demand. — *n* **sale'ableness** or **sal'ableness.** — *adv* **sale'ably** or **sal'ably.** — **sale price** price asked at a sale; **sale'ring** an open market where livestock for sale are paraded; **sale'room** an auction-room; **sales'-clerk** (*NAm*) a sales assistant in a store or shop; **sales'man** or **sales'person** a man (or person) who sells goods, esp. in a shop; a commercial traveller: — *fem* **sales'girl** or **sales'lady; sales'-manship** the art of selling; skill in presenting wares in the most attractive light or in persuading purchasers to buy; **sales resistance** unwillingness to buy; **sales'-talk** persuasive talk to effect a sale; **sales tax** (esp. *NAm*) a tax on the sale of goods and services, esp. one general in character and standard in rate. — **sale of work** a sale of things made by members of a church congregation or association so as to raise money; **sale or return** or **sale and return** an arrangement by which a retailer may return to the wholesaler any goods he or she does not sell. [Late O.E. *sala*.]

salep *sal'ep*, *n* dried orchid tubers; a food or drug prepared from them. [Turk. *sālep*, from Ar.]

Salesian *sə-lē'zhən*, (*RC*) *adj* of St Francis of *Sales* or his order, the Visitants. — *n* a follower of St Francis; a member of his order.

Salian *sā'li-ən*, (*hist*) *adj* pertaining to a tribe of Franks on the lower Rhine. — *n* one of this tribe. — *adj* **Salic** (*sal'ik* or *sā'lik*). — **Salic law** a law among the Salian Franks limiting the succession of certain lands to males — held later to apply to the succession to the crown of France. [L. *Saliī*, Salians.]

Salicaceae *sal-i-kā'si-ē*, *npl* a family of willows and poplars. — *adj* **salicā'ceous** (*-shəs*). — *n* **sal'icet** (*-set*) and **salicional** (*səl-ish'ə-nəl*) organ stops with tones like those of willow pipes. — *n* **sal'icin** or **sal'icine** (*-sin*) a bitter crystalline glucoside obtained from willow-bark, etc. — *n* **salicylate** (*sə-lis'i-lāt*) a salt of salicylic acid. — *adj* **salicylic** (*sal-i-sil'ik*; Gr. *hylē*, matter, material). — **salicylic acid** an acid originally prepared from salicin. [L. *salix*, *salicis*, a willow.]

salices. See **salix**.

salient *sā'li-ənt*, *adj* outstanding, prominent, striking; projecting outwards, as an angle (*archit*); leaping or springing (*biol* or *heraldry*). — *n* an outward-pointing angle, esp. of a fortification or line of defences. — *n* **sā'lience** or **sā'liency.** — *npl* **Salientia** (*-en'shyə*) the frog and toad order of Amphibia. — *adv* **sā'liently.** [L. *saliēns*, *-entis*, pres. p. of *salīre*, to leap.]

saliferous *sə-lif'ər-əs*, *adj* salt-bearing. [L. *sāl*, *salis*, salt, *ferre*, to bear.]

salina *sə-lē'nə* or *-lī'nə*, *n* a salt lagoon, lake, marsh or spring. [Sp., — L. *salīna* — *sāl*, salt.]

saline *sā'līn*, *adj* salt; salty, containing salt; of the nature of a salt; abounding in salt; of the salts of alkali metals and magnesium. — *n* a salina; a salt solution. — *n* **salinity** (*sə-lin'i-ti*). — *n* **salinometer** (*sal-i-nom'i-tər*) a hydrometer for measuring the saltness of water. [L. *salīnus*, cf. **salina.**]

saliva *sə-lī'və*, *n* spittle, a liquid secreted in the mouth to soften food and begin the process of digestion. — *adj* **salivary** (*sal'i-vər-i* or *sə-lī'*) pertaining to, secreting or conveying saliva. — *vi* **sal'ivate** to produce or discharge saliva, esp. in excess. — *vt* to cause to secrete excess of saliva. — *n* **salivā'tion** flow of saliva, esp. in excess, and esp. in anticipation (of food, etc.). [L. *salīva*.]

salix *sal'iks* or *sā'liks*, *n* any tree of plant of the willow genus *Salix*: — *pl* **salices** (*sa'li-sēz* or *sā'*). [L. *sălix*, *-icis*.]

Salk vaccine *sölk vak'sēn*, *n* a vaccine developed by the American Dr Jonas E. *Salk* and others, used against poliomyelitis.

sallenders *sal'ən-dərz*, (*vet*) *n* a skin disease affecting the hocks of horses. [Cf. Fr. *solandre*.]

sallow[1] *sal'ō*, *adj* (esp. of a person's skin) of a pale yellowish colour. — *vt* to make sallow. — *adj* **sall'owish.** — *n* **sall'owness.** [O.E. *salo*, *salu*.]

sallow[2] *sal'ō*, *n* a willow, esp. the broader-leaved kinds. — *adj* **sall'owy** abounding in sallows. [O.E. (Anglian) *salh* — L. *salix*.]

sally[1] *sal'i*, *n* a sudden rushing forth of troops to attack besiegers; a going forth, an excursion, outing. — *vi* (*archaic* or *facetious*; usu. with *forth*) to rush out suddenly; to go or come forth, set off on an excursion, outing: — *pr p* **sall'ying**; *pa t* and *pa p* **sall'ied.** — **sall'yport** (*hist*) a gateway for making a sally from a fortified place; a large port for the escape of the crew from a fireship. [Fr. *saillie* — *saillir* (It. *salire*) — L. *salīre*, to leap.]

sally[2] *sal'i*, *n* the raising of a bell by pull of the rope; the woolly grip of a bell rope.

Sally Lunn *sal'i lun*, *n* a sweet tea cake, usu. served hot with butter. [From a girl who sold them in the streets of Bath, *c* 1797.]

sallyport. See under **sally**[1].

salmagundi *sal-mə-gun'di*, *n* a dish of minced meat with eggs, anchovies, vinegar, pepper, etc.; a medley, miscellany. — Also **salmagun'dy.** [Fr. *salmigondis*.]

salmanazar *sal-man-ā'zr*, *n* (also with *cap*) a large wine bottle, usu. holding the equivalent of 12 standard bottles. — Also **salmana'ser.** [Allusion to Shalmaneser, King of Assyria, II Kings xvii. 3.]

salmi or **salmis** *sal'mē*, (*cookery*) *n* a ragout, esp. of game: — *pl* **salmis** (*sal'mē*). [Fr.]

salmon *sam'ən*, *n* a large, highly prized fish with silvery sides, that ascends rivers to spawn; extended to many closely allied fishes, and to some that resemble it superficially in some respects; the flesh of any of these as food; the colour of salmon flesh, a pinkish orange: — *pl* **salmon** or (of kinds of salmon) **salmons.** — *adj* salmon-coloured. — **salm'on-colour** an orange-pink. — *adj* **salm'on-coloured.** — **salmon ladder** a series of steps to permit a salmon to pass upstream past obstructions; **salmon leap** a waterfall ascended by salmon at a leap; **salmon trout** a fish like the salmon, but smaller and thicker in proportion; applied to various kinds of trout (*US*). [O.Fr. *saumon* — L. *salmō*, *-ōnis*, from *salīre*, to leap.]

Salmonella *sal-mə-nel'ə*, *n* a large genus of bacteria many of which are associated with poisoning by contaminated food; (without *cap*) a member of the genus: — *pl* **salmonell'as** or **salmonell'ae** (*-ē*). — *n* **salmonellō'sis** food poisoning caused by Salmonella bacteria. [Daniel E. *Salmon* (1850–1914), veterinarian.]

salon *sal-ɔ̃'* or *sal'on*, *n* a drawing-room; a reception-room; a periodic gathering of notable persons in the house of a society queen, literary hostess, etc.; a somewhat elegant shop, or a business establishment whose purpose is to render the customer more beautiful, etc. (e.g. *hairdressing salon*); a room or hall for the exhibiting of paintings, sculptures, etc.; (with *cap*) a great annual exhibition of works by living artists in Paris. [Fr.]

saloon *sə-lōōn'*, *n* a spacious hall for receptions, etc.; a large public room (for billiards, for dancing, for hairdressing, etc.); a large public cabin or dining-room for passengers on a ship, luxury train, etc.; a saloon car; a drinking-bar (*NAm*). — **saloon bar** a quieter and more comfortably furnished part of a public house than the public bar, usu. (esp. formerly) separated from it; **saloon car** a motor car with enclosed body, not an estate, coupé or sports model; **saloon deck** an upper deck reserved for saloon users. [Fr. *salon.*]

salopette *sal-ə-pet'*, *n* a type of ski suit consisting of usu. quilted trousers extending to the shoulders and held up with shoulder-straps. [Fr.]

Salopian *sal-ō'pi-ən*, *adj* of or from Shropshire (formerly called *Salop*); of or from Shrewsbury School. — *n* a native or inhabitant of Shropshire; a person educated at Shrewsbury School. [*Salop* — A.Fr. *Sloppesberie* — O.E. *Scrobbesbyrig.*]

salpiglossis *sal-pi-glos'is*, *n* any plant of the genus *Salpiglossis*, some of which bear bright, trumpet-shaped flowers. [Gr. *salpinx*, a trumpet, *glōssa*, tongue.]

salpinx *sal'pingks*, (*anat*) *n* the Eustachian tube, leading from the middle ear to the pharynx; either of the Fallopian tubes, leading from the ovary to the uterus. — *n* **salpingectomy** (*-pin-jek'tə-mi*) surgical removal of a Fallopian tube. — *n* **salpingitis** (*-jī'tis*) inflammation of a Fallopian tube. [Gr. *salpinx*, *-ingos*, a trumpet.]

salsa *sal'sə*, *n* the name given to a type of rhythmic Latin-American music; a dance performed to this music. — *vi* to dance the salsa. [Sp. *salsa*, sauce.]

salsify *sal'si-fi*, *n* a purple-flowered species of goat's-beard, cultivated for its root, tasting like oysters or asparagus. — **black salsify** scorzonera, a plant like a dandelion, with an edible root. [Fr. *salsifis.*]

SALT *sölt*, *abbrev* for Strategic Arms Limitation Talks or Treaty.

salt *sölt*, *n* chloride of sodium, occurring naturally as a mineral (rock-salt) and in solution in sea-water, salt-water springs, etc., used as a condiment and preservative; a salt-cellar; a compound in which metal atoms or radicals replace one or more of the replaceable hydrogen atoms of an acid — generalised to include the acid itself; piquancy; wit and good sense; a salt-marsh or salting; a sailor, esp. an old sailor; (in *pl*) smelling-salts; Epsom salts or other salt or mixture of salts used in medicine, esp. as a purgative. — *adj* containing salt; tasting of salt; seasoned or cured with salt; covered over with, or immersed in, salt water; growing in salt soil; inhabiting salt water. — *vt* to sprinkle, season, preserve or impregnate with salt; to season; to add gold, ore, etc. to, in order to give a false appearance of riches (*mining slang*). — *adj* **salt'ed**. — *n* **salt'er** a person who makes or deals in salt or salted foods; a dealer in gums, dyes, etc. — *adv* **salt'ily**. — *n* **salt'iness**. — *n* **salt'ing** the act of preserving, seasoning, etc. with salt; a meadow flooded by the tides (sfx. *-ing*, indicating a meadow in place names). — *adj* **salt'ish**. — *n* **salt'ishness**. — *adj* **salt'less**. — *adv* **salt'ly**. — *n* **salt'ness**. — *adj* **salt'y** tasting of, containing, etc. salt; piquant, racy, witty. — **salt'-bush** any Australian shrubby plant related to the beet family; **salt'-cellar** (O.Fr. *saliere* — L. *salārium* — *sāl*, salt) a container for holding salt when it is used as a condiment; a depression behind the collar-bone; **salt flat** a stretch of flat, salt-covered land formed by the evaporation of an area of salt water; **salt'-glaze** a glaze produced on pottery by the use of common salt; pottery produced with this glaze; **salt'-glazing; salt lake** an inland lake of saline water; **salt lick** a place to which animals go to obtain salt; an object coated in salt, given to pets deficient in salt; **salt'-marsh** land liable to be flooded with salt water; **salt'-mine** a mine of rock-salt; **salt pan** a large basin for obtaining salt by evaporation; a natural land depression in which salt accumulates or has accumulated by evaporation; **salt'-spoon** a small spoon for taking salt at table; **salt water**. — *adj* **salt'-water** of or containing salt water. — **salt'-works** a place where salt is made; **salt'wort** a fleshy, prickly plant of sandy seashores, related to the beet family, or other plant of the genus. — **above (or below) the salt** among those of high (or low) social class, the salt-cellar marking the boundary at table when all dined together; **lay, put** or **cast salt on someone's tail** to find or catch someone, from the jocularly recommended method of catching a bird; **like a dose of salts** (*colloq*) very quickly; **rub salt in a wound** to aggravate someone's sorrow, shame, regret, etc.; **salt away** to store away; to hoard, esp. in a miserly way; **salt down** to preserve with salt; to lay by, store away; **salt of the earth** the choice few people of the highest excellence (from the Bible: Matt. v. 13); **take with a grain (**or **pinch) of salt** to believe (something or someone) only with great reservations; **worth one's salt** valuable, useful. [O.E. (Anglian) *salt.*]

saltant *sal'tənt* or *söl'tənt*, *adj* (*heraldry*) leaping. — *n* **saltā'tion** a leaping or jumping; an abrupt variation or mutation in appearance from one generation to another (*genetics*). — *n* **saltā'tionism** the process or concept of saltation, *specif* the evolutionary theory that new species come about by saltation. — *n* **saltā'tionist** a person who believes in saltationism. — *adj* **saltato'rial, saltato'rious** or **sal'tatory** leaping or jumping (*biol*); displaying genetic saltation. [L. *saltāre*, *-ātum*, intensive of *salīre*, to leap.]

saltarello *sal-tə-rel'ō*, *n* a lively dance with skips, for two dancers; its music, in triple time: — *pl* **saltarell'os**. [It. *saltarello*, Sp. *saltarelo* — L. *saltāre*, to dance.]

saltern *sölt'ərn*, *n* a salt-works. [O.E. *s(e)altern* — *s(e)alt*, salt, *ærn*, house.]

saltigrade *sal'ti-grād*, (*biol*) *adj* progressing by leaps. — *n* a jumping spider. [L. *saltus*, *-ūs*, a leap, *gradī*, to go.]

saltimbocca *sal-tim-bok'ə*, *n* and *adj* (of) an Italian dish containing veal and ham, with cheese or other ingredients. [It.]

saltire *söl'* or *sal'tīr*, *n* a heraldic design in the form of a St Andrew's (diagonal) cross. [O.Fr. *saultoir*, *sautoir* — L.L. *saltātōrium*, a stirrup.]

saltpetre or in U.S. **saltpeter** *sölt-pē'tər*, *n* potassium nitrate. — **Chile saltpetre** or **cubic saltpetre** sodium nitrate; **Norway saltpetre** calcium nitrate. [O.Fr. *salpetre* — L.L. *salpetra.*]

saltus *sal'təs*, (*logic*) *n* a breach of continuity; a jump to a conclusion. [L., a leap, pl. *saltūs.*]

salubrious *sə-lōō'bri-əs*, *adj* healthful, health-giving. — *adv* **salu'briously**. — *n* **salu'briousness** or **salu'brity**. [L. *salūbris* — *salūs*, *salūtis*, health.]

saluki *sə-lōō'ki*, *n* a silky-haired Persian or Arabian greyhound. [Ar. *seluqi.*]

salutary *sal'ū-tər-i*, *adj* promoting health or safety; wholesome; containing, bringing, etc. a timely warning. — *adv* **sal'ūtarily**. — *n* **sal'ūtariness**. [L. *salūtāris* — *salūs*, health.]

salute *səl-ōōt'* or *-ūt'*, *vt* to greet with words or (now esp.) with a gesture or with a kiss; to honour formally, e.g. by a discharge of cannon, etc. — *vi* to perform the act of saluting, esp. in the military manner. — *n* the act or position of saluting; a greeting, esp. by gesture or a kiss; a discharge of cannon, presenting arms, etc., e.g. to honour a person or occasion. — *n* **salutation** (*sal-ū-tā'shən*) the act or words of greeting. — *adj* **salūtā'tional**. — *n* **salutatorian** (*sə-lōō-tə-tö'ri-ən*) in American colleges, the graduand who pronounces the address of welcome. — *adj* **salu'tatory**. — *n* an address of welcome, esp. in American colleges. — *n* **salu'ter**. [L. *salūtāre*, *-ātum* (verb), and *salūs*, *salūtis* (noun), partly through Fr. *salut.*]

salvable, etc. See **salve**[1].

salvage *sal'vij*, *n* compensation paid by the owner for the rescue of a ship or cargo from danger of loss; the raising of sunken or wrecked ships; rescue of property from fire or other peril; saving of waste material for utilisation; the goods saved in any of these ways. — *vt* to save from danger of loss or destruction; to manage to retain (e.g. one's pride); to recover or save as salvage. — *adj* **sal'vageable**. — **sal'vage-corps** a body of men employed in salvage work. [L.L. *salvāgium* — *salvāre*, to save.]

salve[1] *salv*, *vt* to salvage (also *n*). — *n* **salvabil'ity**. — *adj* **salv'able**. — *n* **salvā'tion** the act of saving; the means of preservation from any serious evil; the saving of man from the power and penalty of sin, the conferring of eternal happiness (*theol*). — *n* **Salvā'tionism**. — *n* **Salvā'tionist** a member of the Salvation Army. — **Salvation Army** an organisation for the spread of religion among the poor masses, founded by William Booth in 1865. [L.L. *salvāre*, to save; partly back-formation from **salvage**.]

salve[2] *salv*, also *sav*, *n* an ointment; a remedy; anything to soothe the feelings or conscience. — *vt* to anoint, to smear; to heal; to soothe. — *n* and *adj* **salv'ing**. [O.E. *s(e)alf*, ointment.]

salve[3] *sal'vi*, L. *sal'wā* or *-vā*, *n* a piece of church music beginning *Salve Regina* (*RC*). — *interj* hail! (addressed to one person). — *interj* and *n* **salvē'tē** (L. *sal-wā'tā* or *-vā'*) (addressed to more than one person). [L. *salvē*, imper. of *salvēre*, to be well.]

salver[1] *sal'vər*, *n* a tray or (silver) plate on which anything is presented. [Sp. *salva*, the precautionary tasting of food, as by a prince's taster, hence the tray on which it was presented to the prince — *salvar*, to save.]

salver[2]. See **salvor**.

salvia *sal'vi-ə*, *n* a plant of the sage genus (*Salvia*). [L. *salvia*, sage.]

salvo *sal'vō*, *n* a simultaneous discharge of artillery, in salute or otherwise; a simultaneous discharge of bombs, etc.; a sudden round of applause; a burst (of repeated critisms, insults, attacks, etc.): — *pl* **sal'vos** or **sal'voes**. [It. *salva*, salute — L. *salvē*, hail.]

sal volatile. See **sal**[2].

salvor or **salver** *sal'vər*, *n* a person who salvages.

SAM *sam*, *abbrev* for surface-to-air missile.

Sam. (*Bible*) *abbrev* for (the Books of) Samuel.

saman *sam-än'*, *n* the rain-tree, a member of the mimosa family. — Also **samaan'**. [Am. Sp. *samán* — Carib *zamang*.]

samara *sə-mä'rə*, *n* a dry usu. one-seeded fruit, with a winglike appendage for distribution on air currents. [L. *samara*, *samera*, elm seed.]

Samaritan *sə-mar'i-tən*, *adj* of *Samaria*, in Palestine. — *n* a native of Samaria, an adherent of the religion of Samaria, differing from Judaism in that only the Pentateuch is accepted as holy scripture; the Aramaic dialect of Samaria; a member of a voluntary organisation formed to help people who are distressed or despairing, esp. by talking to them on the telephone. — *n* **Samar'itanism**. — **good Samaritan** a person who charitably gives help in need (from the Bible: Luke x. 30–37). [L. *Samāritānus*.]

samarium *sə-mā'ri-əm*, *n* a metallic element (symbol **Sm**; atomic no. 62) observed spectroscopically in samarskite. — *n* **samarskite** (*sə-mär'skīt*) a black mineral containing uranium. [Named in honour of Col. *Samarski*, Russian engineer.]

samba *sam'bə*, *n* a Brazilian dance in duple time with syncopation; a ballroom development of the dance; a tune for either.

sambal *säm'bäl*, *n* any of various foods served with curries in Malaya and Indonesia — peppers, pickles, salt fish, coconut, etc. [Malay.]

sambar or **sambur** *sam'bər*, *n* a large Indian deer. [Hindi *sā̃bar*.]

Sam Browne *sam brown*, *n* a military officer's belt with shoulder strap. [Invented by General Sir Samuel James *Browne* (1824–1901).]

sambuca *sam-bū'kə*, *n* an ancient musical instrument like a harp. [L. *sambūca* — Gr. *sambȳkē*, cf. Aramaic *sabbekā*.]

sambur. See **sambar**.

same *sām*, *adj* identical (commonly with *as*, also with *with* or a relative clause or pronoun); not different; unchanged, unvaried; (esp. with *the*) mentioned before. — *pron* (*colloq*) the aforesaid, it, them, they, etc. — *n* **same'ness** being the same; tedious monotony. — *adj* **sā'mey** (*colloq*) (boringly) alike; monotonous. — **all the same** for all that, nevertheless; **at the same time** still, however; **same here!** (*colloq*) me too!; **the same** the same thing or person; the aforesaid or aforementioned; in the same way. [O.E. *same* (only in phrase *swā same*, likewise); Goth. *sama*.]

samfoo or **samfu** *sam'fo͞o*, *n* an outfit worn by Chinese women, consisting of a jacket and trousers. [Cantonese.]

Samian *sā'mi-ən*, *adj* of or from the Greek island of *Samos*. — *n* a native of Samos. — **Samian ware** brick-red or black pottery, with lustrous glaze; a later imitation made in Roman Gaul, etc.

samisen *sam'i-sen*, *n* a Japanese guitar. [Jap.]

samite *sam'īt*, *n* a kind of heavy silk fabric. [O.Fr. *samit* — L.L. *examitum* — Gr. *hexamiton* — *hex*, six, *mitos*, thread.]

samizdat *sam'iz-dat*, *n* in the Soviet Union, the secret printing and distribution of government-banned literature; such literature. — Also *adj*. [Russ.]

samlet *sam'lit*, *n* a young salmon. [**salmon**, sfx. **-let**.]

samlor *sam'lör*, *n* a three-wheeled vehicle common in Thailand, usu. motorised and used as a taxi. [Thai.]

Samnite *sam'nīt*, *n* a member of an ancient people of central Italy. — Also *adj*. [L. *Samnīs*, *-ītis*.]

samosa *sa-mō'sə* or *-zə*, *n* a small, fried, pastry turnover stuffed with spiced vegetable or meat, an Indian savoury: — *pl* **samo'sas** or **samo'sa**. [Hindi.]

samovar *sam'ə-vär*, *n* a Russian water boiler, used for making tea, etc., traditionally heated by charcoal in a tube that passes through it. [Russ. *samovar*, lit. self-boiler.]

Samoyed *sam-ō-yed'* or *sam'*, *n* one of a Ugrian people of north-west Siberia; their language; (*samoi'ed*) a thickly white-coated dog of a breed used by them. — Also *adj*. — *adj* **Samoyed'ic**. [Russ. *Samoyed*.]

sampan *sam'pan*, *n* a small Chinese motorless boat. — Also **san'pan**. [Chin. *san*, three, *pan*, board.]

samphire *sam'fīr* or **sampire** *sam'pīr*, *n* a plant of sea-cliffs, whose fleshy leaves are used in pickles; extended to other plants used in the same way. [Fr. (*herbe de*) *Saint Pierre*, Saint Peter('s herb).]

sample *säm'pl*, *n* a specimen, a small portion to show the quality or nature of the whole. — *adj* serving as a sample. — *vt* to take, try, or offer, a sample or samples of; (in popular music) to mix a (short) extract from one recording into a different backing track; to record (a sound) and program it into a synthesiser which can then reproduce it at the desired pitch. — *n* **sam'pler** a collection of samples; the equipment that samples sounds as described above. — *n* **sam'pling**. [M.E. *essample*; see **example**.]

sampler[1] *säm'plər*, *n* a test-piece of embroidery, commonly including an alphabet, with figures, often names, etc. [O.Fr. *essemplaire* — L. *exemplar*; see **exemplar**.]

sampler[2]. See **sample**.

Samson *sam'sn*, *n* an abnormally strong man (from the biblical Hebrew champion of Judges xiii-xvi).

samurai *sam'o͝o-rī* or *-ū-rī*, (*Jap hist*) *n* a military retainer of a feudal Japanese nobleman; a member of the military caste: — *pl* **sam'urai**. [Jap., — *samurau*, to attend (one's lord).]

sanative *san'ə-tiv*, *adj* healing. — *n* **sanatō'rium** or (esp. in U.S.) **sanitā'rium** (imitation Latin) a hospital, esp. for consumptives or convalescents; a health farm: — *pl* **sanato'riums** or **sanato'ria.** — *adj* **san'atory** healing; of healing. [L. *sānāre, -ātum*, to heal.]

sanctify *sangk'ti-fī, vt* to make, declare, regard as, or show to be, sacred or holy; to set apart for sacred use; to free from sin or evil; to consecrate, bless; to invest with sacredness: — *pr p* **sanc'tifying**; *pa t* and *pa p* **sanc'tified.** — *n* **sanctificā'tion.** — *adj* **sanc'tified** made holy. — *adv* **sanc'tifiedly** (*-fī-id-li*). — *n* **sanc'tifier** (*-fī-ər*) a person who sanctifies; (usu. with *cap*) the Holy Spirit. — *n* and *adj* **sanc'tifying.** — *adv* **sanc'tifyingly.** [Fr. *sanctifier* — L. *sanctificāre* — *sanctus*, holy, *facĕre*, to make.]

sanctimonious *sangk-ti-mō'ni-əs, adj* simulating holiness, esp. hypocritically. — *adv* **sanctimō'niously.** — *n* **sanctimō'niousness.** [L. *sanctimōnia* — *sanctus*.]

sanction *sangk'shən, n* motive, rationale for obedience to any moral or religious law (*ethics*); a penalty or reward expressly attached to non-observance or observance of a law or treaty (*law*); a military or economic measure taken by one country in order to persuade another to follow a certain course of action; the act of ratifying, or giving permission or authority; support; permission, authority. — *vt* to authorise; to countenance, permit. — **sanc'tions-busting** the breaching (usu. by commercial concerns) of economic sanctions imposed on a country. [L. *sanctiō, -ōnis* — *sancīre, sanctum*, to ratify.]

sanctitude *sangk'ti-tūd, n* saintliness. [L. *sanctitūdō, -inis*.]

sanctity *sangk'ti-ti, n* the quality of being sacred or holy; purity; godliness; inviolability; saintship; (in *pl*) holy feelings, obligations or objects. [L. *sanctitās, -ātis*, sanctity.]

sanctuary *sangk'tū-ər-i, n* a holy place, e.g. a place of worship; the most holy part of a temple, church, etc.; a place affording immunity from arrest, persecution, etc.; the privilege of refuge in such a place; a nature, animal or plant reserve. [L. *sanctuārium*.]

Sanctus *sangk'təs* or *-to͝os, n* the hymn *Holy, holy, holy* (from the Bible: Isaiah vi); music for it. — *n* **sanc'tum** (esp. in the phrase *inner sanctum*) a sacred place; a (very) private room. — **sanctum sanctorum** (*sangk-tö'rəm*) the holy of holies, the inner chamber of the Jewish tabernacle; any specially reserved retreat or room; **sanctus bell** a bell rung at the singing of the Sanctus; in R.C. churches, a small bell rung to call attention to the more solemn parts of the Mass. [L. *sanctus, -a, -um*, holy.]

sand *sand, n* a mass of tiny rounded grains of rock, esp. quartz; (in *pl*) a tract covered with this, as on a sea-beach or desert. — *adj* made of sand. — *vt* to sprinkle, cover or mix with sand; to smooth or polish with abrasive material, esp. sandpaper. — *adj* **sand'ed** sprinkled, covered or mixed with sand; smoothed or polished with sandpaper, etc. — *n* **sand'er** a tool (esp. power-driven) with an abrasive surface, used to sand wood, etc. — *n* **sand'iness.** — *n* **sand'ing.** — *adj* **sand'y** consisting of, covered with, containing or like sand; coloured like sand, reddish beige. — **sand'bag** a bag of sand or earth, used esp. to protect against bomb blasts, floods, etc.; a small bag of sand, etc. used as a cosh. — *vt* to provide with sandbags; to attack with a cosh: — *pa p* **sand'bagged.** — **sand'bagger; sand'bank** a bank of sand in a river or river mouth, etc., often above water at low tide; **sand'-bar** a long sandbank in a river or sea; **sand'-bath** a bath in sand; a vessel for heating something without direct exposure to the source of heat; **sand'-bed** a layer of sand, esp. one used in founding or moulding; **sand'blast** sand driven by a blast of air or steam for glass-engraving, finishing metal surfaces, cleaning stone and metal surfaces, etc. — Also *vt*. — **sand'blasting.** — *adj* **sand'-blind** see separate entry. — **sand'-box** a box of sand, e.g. for sprinkling on railway lines or roads; a sandpit; **sand'-boy** a boy selling sand, proverbially happy; **sand'castle** a model of a castle made in sand by children at play on the beach or in a sandpit; **sand'-dollar** a flat sea-urchin; **sand'-dune** a hill of sand on the beach or in the desert; **sand'-eel** an eel-like fish living in wet sand at low tide; **sand'-flea** the chigoe or jigger, a West Indian or S. American flea; a sand-hopper; **sand'-fly** a small biting midge; a small mothlike midge that transmits **sand-fly fever,** a fever due to a viral infection; **sand'-glass** a glass instrument for measuring time by the running out of sand, an hourglass; **sand'-grouse** any bird of the genera *Pterocles* and *Syrrhaptes*, with long pointed wings, once mistaken for grouse because of their feathered legs but now considered similar to pigeons; **sand'-hopper** a crustacean of the seashore that jumps by suddenly straightening its bent body; **sand'man** (with **the**) a fairy who supposedly throws sand into children's eyes towards bedtime; **sand'-martin** a bird of the martin family that nests in sandy banks; **sand painting** the making of designs with coloured sand, as in various American Indian ceremonies; **sand'paper** paper or cloth coated with sand, used as an abrasive polisher. — *vt* to smooth or polish with sandpaper. — **sand'piper** the name for a large number of ground-dwelling, wading birds intermediate between plovers and snipe, haunting sandy shores and river banks and uttering a clear piping note; **sand'pit** a place from which sand is dug; a pit filled with sand for children to play in; **sand'-pump** a pump for raising wet sand or mud; **sand'shoe** a shoe for walking or playing on the sands, a plimsoll; **sand'-skipper** a sand-hopper; **sand'stone** a type of rock formed of compacted and hardened sand; **sand'storm** a storm of wind carrying along clouds of sand; **sand'-table** a tray for moulding sand on or for demonstration of military tactics; an inclined trough for separating heavier particles from smaller in a flow of liquid, as in ore-dressing, paper-making (also **sand'-trap**); **sand'-trap** a bunker (*golf*); a sand-table; **sand'wort** any species of *Arenaria*, plants related to chickweed; **sand'-yacht, sand'-yachting** see under **yacht.** [O.E. *sand*.]

sandal[1] *san'dl, n* a type of footware consisting of a sole bound to the foot by straps; an ornate shoe or slipper. — *adj* **san'dalled** wearing sandals. [L. *sandalium* — Gr. *sandalion*, dimin. of *sandalon*.]

sandal[2] *san'dl* or **sandalwood** *san'dl-wo͝od, n* a compact and fine-grained very fragrant East Indian wood; the parasitic tree yielding it (**white sandalwood**), or other species; extended to certain other woods. [L.L. *santalum* — Gr. *sandanon*, — Sans. *candana*, of Dravidian origin.]

sandarach or **sandarac** *san'dər-ak, n* arsenic monosulphide; the resin (in full **gum sandarach** or **sandarac resin**) of the Moroccan **sandarach tree,** powdered to form pounce and used in making varnish. [L. *sandaraca* — Gr. *sandărākē, -chē*.]

sand-blind *sand'blīnd, adj* half-blind.

sanderling *san'dər-ling, n* a species of sandpiper without a hind toe.

Sandinista *san-di-nis'tə, n* a member of the left-wing revolutionary movement in Nicaragua which overthrew President Samoza in 1979. — *n* **Sandinismo** (*-niz'mō*) beliefs and practices of the Sandinistas. [Named after the Nicaraguan rebel general Augusto César *Sandino*, murdered in 1933.]

S and T *abbrev* for Signalling and Telecommunications.

sandwich *sand'wich* or *-wij*, or *san'*, *n* any sort of food between two slices of bread, said to be named from the fourth Earl of *Sandwich* (1718–92), who ate a snack of this kind in order not to have to leave the gaming-table; anything in a similar arrangement. — *vt* to lay or place between two layers; to fit tightly or squeeze between two others or two of another kind. — *adj* of a sandwich or sandwich course. — **sandwich course** an educational course consisting of alternating periods of academic and industrial work; **sand'wich-man** a man who perambulates the streets carrying two advertising boards (**sand'-wich-boards**) hung over his shoulders, so that one is in front, the other behind.

sane *sān, adj* sound in mind; rational. — *adv* **sane'ly**. — *n* **sane'ness**. [L. *sānus*.]

sang *sang, pa t* of **sing**.

sangar or **sungar** *sung'gər, n* a stone breastwork; a look-out post. [Pushtu *sangar*.]

sangaree *sang-gə-rē', n* a West Indian drink of wine, diluted, sweetened, spiced, etc. [**sangria**.]

Sangraal, Sangrail or **Sangreal** *san-grāl'* or *san'grāl, sang-* or *sang', n* the holy grail (see **grail**). [**saint** and **grail**.]

sangria *sang-grē'ə, n* a Spanish drink similar to sangaree. [Sp. *sangría*.]

sangui- *sang-gwi-, combining form* denoting blood. — *n* **sanguificā'tion** blood-making. — *vi* **san'guify** (*-fī*) to make blood. — *vt* to turn into blood. — *adv* **san'guinarily** (*-gwin-ə-ri-li*). — *n* **san'guinariness**. — *adj* **san'guinary** bloody. — *adj* **sanguine** (*sang'gwin*) of the complexion or temperament in which blood was supposed to predominate over the other humours; ardent, confident and inclined to hopefulness; blood-red; bloody; ruddy. — *n* a blood-red colour; a red chalk; a drawing in red chalks. — *adv* **san'guinely**. — *n* **san'guineness**. — *adj* **sanguin'eous** of or having blood; blood-red; bloody; full-blooded. — *n* **sanguin'ity** sanguineness. [L. *sanguis, -inis*, blood; adjs. *sanguineus, sanguinārius*; partly through Fr. *sanguin*.]

Sanhedrim *san'i-drim* or **Sanhedrin** *san'i-drin* or *san-hed'rin*, (*hist*) *n* a Jewish council or court, esp. the supreme council and court at Jerusalem. [Heb. *sanhedrīn* — Gr. *synedrion* — *syn*, together, *hedrā*, a seat.]

sanicle *san'ik-l, n* a woodland plant (in full **wood'-sanicle**) with glossy leaves, headlike umbels, and hooked fruits; any plant of the genus; extended to various other plants. [O.Fr., perh. L. *sānāre*, to heal, from once-supposed power.]

sanies *sā'ni-ēz*, (*med*) *n* a thin discharge from wounds or sores. — *adj* **sa'nious**. [L. *saniēs*.]

sanitary *san'i-tər-i, adj* pertaining to, or concerned with the promotion of health, esp. connected with drainage and sewage disposal; conducive to health. — *n* **sanitā'rian** a person who favours or studies sanitary measures. — Also *adj*. — *adv* **san'itarily**. — *n* **sanitā'rium** (esp. *US*) a sanatorium: — *pl* **sanita'ria** or **sanita'riums**. — *n* **sanitā'tion** measures for the promotion of health and prevention of disease, esp. drainage and sewage disposal. — *n* **sanitā'tionist**. — *n* **sanitīsā'tion** or **-z-**. — *vt* **san'itise** or **-ize** to make sanitary; to clean up, make more acceptable by removing offensive elements, words, connotations, etc. — **sanitary engineer**; **sanitary engineering** the branch of civil engineering dealing with provision of pure water supply, disposal of waste, etc.; **sanitary inspector** see **public health inspector** under **public**; **sanitary towel** a pad of absorbent material for wearing during menstruation, etc.; **sanitary ware** plumbing fixtures such as sinks, baths, lavatories, etc. [Fr. *sanitaire* — L. *sānitās*, health.]

sanity *san'i-ti, n* soundness of mind; rationality. [L. *sānitās*, health — *sānus*, healthy.]

sank *sangk, pa t* of **sink**.

sannyasi *sun-yä'si, n* a Hindu religious hermit who lives by begging. [Hindi, — Sans. *saṁnyāsin*, casting aside.]

sanpan. See **sampan**.

sans *sã* or *sanz, prep* without. [Fr.]

sansculotte *sã-kü-lot, n* in the French Revolution, the nickname for a democrat (apparently as wearing long trousers instead of knee-breeches); hence generally (usu. in hostility) a strong republican, democrat or revolutionary. — *n* **sansculott'ism**. — *n* **sansculott'ist**. [**sans**, Fr. *culotte*, knee-breeches.]

sansei *san'sā, n* a resident of the Americas born of the offspring of Japanese immigrant parents — cf. **issei, nisei**. [Jap., third generation.]

sanserif *san-ser'if*, (*printing*) *n* a type without serifs. — Also *adj*. [**sans** and **serif**.]

Sanskrit *sans'krit, n* the ancient Indo-European literary language of India. — Also *adj*. — *adj* **Sanskrit'ic**. — *n* **Sans'kritist** a person skilled in Sanskrit. [Sans. *saṁskrta*, put together, perfected — *sam*, together, *karoti*, he makes.]

Santa Claus *san'tə klöz, n* a fat rosy old fellow who by tradition brings children Christmas presents, also known as **Father Christmas**; an improbable source of improbable benefits. [Orig. U.S. modification of Du. dialect *Sante Klaas*, St Nicholas.]

santolina *san-tō-lē'nə, n* a plant of the *Santolina* genus of fragrant Mediterranean shrubs related to the camomile. [It. *santolina*, — L. *sanctus*, holy, *līnum*, flax.]

santonica *san-ton'i-kə, n* the dried unexpanded flower-heads of a species of wormwood. — *n* **san'tonin** (*-tən-*) an anthelmintic extracted from it. [Gr. *santonikon*, as found in the country of the *Santones* in Gaul.]

sap[1] *sap, n* vital juice that circulates in plants; juice generally; sapwood; a weak or foolish person (*colloq*). — *vt* to drain or withdraw the sap from; to drain the energy from, exhaust. — *adj* **sap'ful**. — *adj* **sap'less**. — *n* **sap'lessness**. — *n* **sap'ling** a young tree (also *adj*); a young greyhound. — *n* **sapp'iness**. — *adj* **sapp'y**. — **sap'-green** a green paint made from the juice of buckthorn berries; its colour (also *adj*); **sap'wood** alburnum. [O.E. *sæp*.]

sap[2] *sap, n* sapping; a trench (usually covered or zigzag) by which approach is made towards a hostile position. — *vt* to undermine or weaken. — *vi* to make a sap; to proceed insidiously: — *pr p* **sapp'ing**; *pa p* and *pa t* **sapped**. — *n* **sapp'er** someone who saps; a private in the Royal Engineers. [It. *zappa* and Fr. *sappe* (now *sape*).]

sapajou *sap'ə-jōō, n* a capuchin monkey. [Fr., from a Tupí name.]

sapan. See **sappan**.

sapele *sa-pē'lē, n* a wood resembling mahogany, used for furniture; a tree of the genus *Entandrophragma* that yields such wood. [W. African name.]

saphena *sə-fē'nə*, (*anat*) *n* either of two large prominent veins in the leg. [N.L., from Ar. *sāfin*.]

sapid *sap'id, adj* having a decided taste; savoury; relishing, exhilarating. — *n* **sapid'ity**. [L. *sapidus* — *sapĕre*, to taste.]

sapience *sā'pi-əns, n* discernment; wisdom (often ironical); judgment. — *adj* **sā'pient**. — *adj* **sāpien-tial** (*-en'shl*). — *adv* **sā'piently**. [L. *sapientia* — *sapĕre*, to be wise.]

sapling. See **sap**[1].

sapodilla *sap-ō-dil'ə, n* a large evergreen tree of the West Indies, etc.; its edible fruit (**sapodilla plum**); its durable timber. [Sp. *zapotilla*.]

saponaceous *sap-ō-* or *sap-ə-nā'shəs, adj* soapy; soaplike. — *n* **sapogenin** (*-jen'in*) a compound derived from saponin, often used in synthesising steroid hormones. — *adj* **saponifiable** (*sap-on'i-fī-ə-bl*). — *n* **saponificā'tion** the turning into or forming of soap; hydrolysis of esters. — *vt* **sapon'ify**: — *pr p* **sapon'ifying**; *pa t* and *pa p* **sapon'ified**. — *n* **saponin** (*sap'ə-nin*) a glucoside from soapwort, etc. that gives a soapy froth. [L. *sāpō, -ōnis*, soap.]

sapor *sā'pör*, (*formal*) *n* taste. — *adj* **sā'porous** (*-pər-əs*). [L. *sapor, -ōris*.]

sappan or **sapan** *sap'an* or *sap'ən*, *n* brazil-wood (*Caesalpinia sappan*) — usu. **sapp'an-** or **sap'an-wood**. [Malay *sapang*.]

sapped, sapper, sapping. See **sap**[2].

Sapphic *saf'ik*, *adj* of or pertaining to *Sappho*, a great Greek lyric poetess (*c* 600 B.C.) of Lesbos. — *n* (usu. in *pl*; also without *cap*) verses in a form said to have been invented by Sappho in stanzas of four lines each. — *n* **Sapph'ism** (also without *cap*) lesbianism, with which she was charged by ancient writers. — *n* **sapph'ist** a lesbian. [Gr. *Sapphō*.]

sapphire *saf'īr*, *n* a brilliant precious variety of corundum, generally of a beautiful blue; the blue colour of a sapphire. — *adj* made of sapphire; deep pure blue. — **sapph'ire-wing** a blue-winged humming-bird. [O.Fr. *safir* — L. *sapphīrus* — Gr. *sappheiros*, lapis lazuli.]

sappy. See **sap**[1].

sapr- *sapr-* or **sapro-** *sap-rō-*, *combining form* denoting rotten, decayed. — *adj* **saprogenic** (*sap-rō-jen'ik*) or **saprogenous** (*sə-proj'i-nəs*) growing on decaying matter; causing or caused by putrefaction. — *adj* **saprophagous** (*sə-prof'ə-gəs*) feeding on decaying organic matter. — *n* **saprophyte** (*sap'rō-fīt* or *-rə-*) a plant that feeds upon decaying organic matter. — *adj* **saprophytic** (*-fit'ik*). — *adv* **saprophyt'ically**. — *n* **sap'rophȳtism**. — *adj* **saprozō'ic** feeding on dead or decaying organic material. [Gr. *sapros*, rotten.]

sapsucker *sap'suk-ər*, *n* a N. American woodpecker which feeds on the sap from trees. [**sap**[1] and **suck**.]

saraband *sar'ə-band*, *n* a slow Spanish dance, or dance-tune; a suite-movement in its rhythm, in 3–4 time strongly accented on the second beat (a dotted crotchet or minim). [Sp. *zarabanda*.]

Saracen *sar'ə-sən*, *n* a Syrian or Arab nomad; a Muslim, esp. an opponent of the Crusaders; a Moor or Berber. — Also *adj*. — *adj* **Saracenic** (*-sen'ik*). — **Saracenic architecture** a general name for Muslim architecture; **Saracen's-stone** same as **sarsen**. [O.E. *Saracene* (pl.) — L. *Saracēnus* — late Gr. *Sarakēnos*.]

sarangi *sä'rung-gē*, *n* an Indian fiddle. [Hind.]

sarcasm *sär'kazm*, *n* language expressing scorn or contempt, often but not necessarily ironical; a jibe; the quality of such language. — *adj* **sarcas'tic** containing or inclined to sarcasm. — *adv* **sarcas'tically**. [L. *sarcasmus* — Gr. *sarkasmos* — *sarkazein*, to tear flesh like dogs, to speak bitterly — *sarx*, *sarkos*, flesh.]

sarcenet. See **sarsenet**.

sarco- *sär-kō-* or *-ko'-*, *combining form* signifying flesh. — *n* **sarcocarp** (*sär'kō-kärp*; *bot*) the fleshy pericarp of a stone fruit. — *n* **sar'coplasm** the protoplasmic substance separating the fibrils in muscle fibres. — *adj* **sarcoplas'mic**. — *adj* **sarcous** (*sär'kəs*) of flesh or muscle. [Gr. *sarx*, *sarkos*, flesh.]

sarcoid *sär'koid*, *adj* fleshlike; resembling a sarcoma. — *n* (*med*) short for sarcoidosis. — *n* **sarcoidō'sis** a chronic disease of unknown cause characterised by the formation of nodules in the lymph nodes, lungs, skin, etc. [Gr. *sarkōdēs*, *sarkoeides* — *eidos*, form.]

sarcoma *sär-kō'mə*, *n* a tumour derived from connective tissue: — *pl* **sarco'mas** or **sarcō'mata**. — *n* **sarcomatō'sis** a condition characterised by the formation of sarcomas in many areas of the body. — *adj* **sarcō'matous**. [Gr. *sarkōma* — *sarx*, flesh.]

sarcophagus *sär-kof'ə-gəs*, *n* a limestone used by the Greeks for coffins, thought to consume the flesh of corpses; a stone coffin, esp. one with carvings; a tomb or cenotaph of similar form: — *pl* **sarcoph'agi** (*-jī* or *-gī*) or **sarcoph'aguses**. [Latinised from Gr. *sarkophagos* — *phagein* (aorist), to eat.]

sarcoplasm, sarcoplasmic, sarcous. See under **sarco-**.

sard *särd* or **sardius** *särd'i-əs*, *n* a deep-red chalcedony. [L. *sarda*, *sardius*, and Gr. *sardion*, also *sardios* (*lithos*), the Sardian (stone) — *Sardeis*, Sardis, in Lydia.]

sardel *sär-del'* or **sardelle** *-del'* or *-del'ə*, *n* a small fish related to the sardine.

sardine *sär'dēn* or *sär-dēn'*, *n* a young pilchard, commonly tinned in oil; applied at various times and places to other fishes. — **packed like sardines** crowded closely together. [Fr. *sardine* — It. *sardina* — L. *sardīna*; Gr. *sardīnos*, or *-ē*.]

Sardinian *sär-din'i-ən* or *-yən*, *adj* of the island or former kingdom of *Sardinia* or of the inhabitants. — *n* a native, citizen or member of the people of Sardinia; their language or dialect of Italian.

sardonic *sär-don'ik*, *adj* mockingly scornful, heartless or bitter; sneering. — *adv* **sardon'ically**. [Fr. *sardonique* — L. *sardonius* — late Gr. *sardonios*, doubtfully referred to *sardonion*, a plant of Sardinia (Gr. *Sardō*) which was said to screw up the face of the eater.]

sardonyx *sär'də-niks*, *n* an onyx with layers of cornelian or sard. [Gr. *sardonyx* — *Sardios*, Sardian, *onyx*, a nail.]

saree. See **sari**.

sargasso *sär-gas'ō*, *n* gulfweed (genus *Sargassum*); a floating mass or expanse of it, like the **Sargasso Sea** in the North Atlantic: — *pl* **sargass'os**. [Port. *sargaço*.]

sarge *särj*, (*colloq*) *n* short for **sergeant**.

sari or **saree** *sär'ē*, *n* a Hindu woman's chief garment, a long cloth wrapped round the waist and passed over the shoulder and head. [Hind. *sārī*.]

sarking *särk'ing*, *n* a lining for a roof. [O.E. *serc*.]

sarky *sär'ki*, (*colloq*) *adj* short for **sarcastic**.

Sarmatia *sär-mā'shyə* or *-shi-ə*, *n* anciently a region reaching from the Vistula and Danube to the Volga and Caucasus; Poland (*poetic*). — *n* and *adj* **Sarma'tian**. — *adj* **Sarmat'ic**.

sarmentose *sär'mən-tōz* or **sarmentous** *sär-ment'əs*, *adj* having sarmenta or runners; creeping. — *n* **sarmentum** (*-ment'əm*) a runner: — *pl* **sarment'a**. [L. *sarmentum*, a twig — *sarpĕre*, to prune.]

sarod *sa'rod*, *n* an Indian instrument like a cello, with strings that are plucked. [Hind.]

sarong *sä'rong* or *sə-rong'*, *n* a Malay skirtlike garment for a man or woman; a cloth for making it. [Malay *sārung*.]

saros *sā'ros* or *sä'ros*, *n* an astronomical cycle of 6585 days and 8 hours, after which relative positions of the sun and moon recur; a Babylonian cycle of 3600 years. [Gr. *saros* — Babylonian *shāru*, 3600.]

sarrusophone *sə-rus'ō-fōn*, *n* a reed instrument of brass, devised by a French bandmaster, *Sarrus*. [Gr. *phōnē*, voice.]

sarsaparilla *sär-sə-pə-ril'ə*, *n* any tropical American smilax plant; its dried root; a soft drink flavoured with this (*US*); a medicinal preparation from it; extended to various plants or roots of similar use. [Sp. *zarzaparilla* — *zarza*, bramble (from Basque), and a dimin. of *parra*, vine.]

sarsen *sär'sn*, *n* a sandstone boulder. [App. a form of **Saracen**.]

sarsenet or **sarcenet** *särs'nit* or *-net*, *n* a thin tissue of fine silk. — *adj* made of sarsenet. [A.Fr. *sarzinett*, probably *Sarzin*, Saracen.]

sartorial *sär-tö'ri-əl*, *adj* of or relating to a tailor, tailoring, dress, or to the sartorius. — *adv* **sarto'rially**. — *n* **sarto'rius** (*anat*) a thigh muscle that crosses the leg, helping to flex the knee. [L. *sartor*, a patcher.]

Sarum use *sā'rum ūs*, *n* the medieval rites of Salisbury cathedral. [Ancient name of Salisbury.]

Sarvodaya *sär-vō'da-ya*, *n* in India, the promotion of the welfare of the community. [Sans. *sārva*, all, *udayā*, prosperity.]

SAS *abbrev* for Special Air Service.

sash[1] *sash, n* a band or scarf, worn round the waist or over the shoulder. — *vt* to dress or adorn with a sash. [Ar. *shāsh.*]

sash[2] *sash, n* a frame, esp. a sliding frame, for window-panes. — *vt* to provide with sashes. — **sash cord** a cord attaching a weight to the sash in order to balance it at any height; **sash window** a window with a sash or sashes (opp. to *casement window*). [Fr. *châssis.*]

sashay *sa-shā', vi* to walk or move in a gliding or ostentatious way. — *n* an excursion (esp. *fig*). [Alteration of **chassé**.]

sashimi *sash'ə-mi, n* a Japanese dish of thinly-sliced raw fish. [Jap.]

sasin *sas'in, n* the common Indian antelope. [Nepalese.]

sasine *sā'sin,* (*Scots law*) *n* the act of giving legal possession of feudal property. [A variant of **seisin**, Law L. *sasina.*]

Sask. *abbrev* for Saskatchewan (Canadian province).

sasquatch *sas'kwach* or *sas'kwoch, n* a large hairy manlike creature thought by some to inhabit parts of North America. [Indian name.]

sass *sas,* (*US colloq*) *n* impertinent talk or behaviour. — *vt* to be impertinent to. — *adj* **sass'y** impertinent. [**sauce**.]

sassaby *sə-sā'bi, n* the bastard hartebeest, a large S. African antelope. [Tswana *tsessébe.*]

sassafras *sas'ə-fras, n* a tree of the laurel family common in N. America; the bark, esp. of its root, a powerful stimulant; an infusion of it; extended to various plants with similar properties. — **sassafras oil** a volatile aromatic oil distilled from sassafras. [Sp. *sasafrás.*]

Sassenach *sas'ə-nahh,* (esp. *Scot*; usu. *derog*) *n* an English person. [Gael. *Sasunnach.*]

sassy. See **sass**.

sastruga. See **zastruga**.

SAT *abbrev* for: scholastic aptitude test (*US*); standard assessment task (*educ*).

Sat. *abbrev* for Saturday.

sat *sat, pa t* and *pa p* of **sit**.

Satan *sā'tən, n* the chief evil spirit, adversary of God and tempter of men, the Devil; the chief fallen angel, Lucifer. — *adj* **satanic** (*sə-tan'ik*) or **satan'ical**. — *adv* **satan'ically**. — *n* **sā'tanism** Satan-worship; devilish disposition. — *n* and *adj* **Sā'tanist**. [Gr. and L. *Satān, Satanās* — Heb. *sātān,* enemy — *sātan,* to be adverse.]

satay *sat'ā, n* a Malaysian dish of spicy meat barbecued on skewers. [Malay.]

SATB *abbrev* for soprano, alto, tenor, bass (when combined in choral music.)

satchel *sach'l, n* a small bag, esp. with shoulder strap, as for school-books. — *adj* **satch'elled**. [O.Fr. *sachel* — L. *saccellus,* dimin. of *saccus*; see **sack**[1], **sac**.]

sate *sāt, vt* to satisfy fully; to glut. — *adj* **sāt'ed**. — *n* **sāt'edness**. [Blend of M.E. *sade* (cf. **sad**) and L. *sat,* enough, or **satiate** shortened.]

sateen *sa-tēn', n* a glossy cotton or woollen fabric resembling *satin.*

satellite *sat'ə-līt, n* a body revolving about a planet, esp. now a man-made device used for communication, etc. (see **artificial satellite** below); a smaller companion to anything; a subordinate or dependent state, community, etc.; an obsequious follower; an attendant. — Also *adj.* — *adj* **satellitic** (*-lit'ik*). — **satellite broadcasting** or **television** the broadcasting of television programmes via artificial satellite; **satellite dish** saucer-shaped receiver for satellite television; **satellite state** or **country** one which relies on and obeys the dictates of a larger, more powerful state; **satellite town** a town, often a garden city, limited in size, built near a great town to check overgrowth. — **artificial** or **earth satellite** any man-made body, including spacecraft, launched by rocket into space and put into orbit round the earth. [L. *satelles, satellitis,* an attendant.]

sati. Same as **suttee**.

satiate *sā'shi-āt, vt* to gratify fully; to satisfy to excess. — *n* **sātiabil'ity**. — *adj* **sā'tiable**. — *n* **sātiā'tion** or **satiety** (*sə-tī'ə-ti*) the state of being satiated; surfeit. [L. *satiāre, -ātum* — *satis,* enough.]

satin *sat'in, n* a closely woven silk with a lustrous and unbroken surface showing much of the warp. — *adj* of or like satin. — *vt* to make satiny. — *n* **satinet'** or **satinette'** a thin satin; a modification of satin with a slightly different weave; a cloth with a cotton warp and a woollen weft. — *adj* **sat'iny**. — **satin bird** a satiny blue and black bower-bird; **satin finish** a satiny polish; **satin paper** a fine, glossy writing-paper; **satin stitch** an embroidery stitch, repeated in parallel lines, giving a satiny appearance; **sat'in-wood** a beautiful, smooth, satiny ornamental wood from India; the tree (*Chloroxylon swietenia*) yielding it; extended to several more or less similar woods and trees. [Fr. *satin,* app. — L.L. *sēta,* silk (L. *saeta,* bristle), or from Ar. *zaytūnī,* — *Zaitūn,* a town in China where it was produced.]

satire *sat'īr, n* a literary composition, orig. in verse, essentially a criticism of folly or vice, which it holds up to ridicule or scorn — its chief instruments, irony, sarcasm, invective, wit and humour; satirical writing as a genre; its spirit; the use of, or inclination to use, its methods; satirical denunciation or ridicule. — *adj* **satiric** (*sə-tir'ik*) or **satir'ical** pertaining to, or conveying, satire; sarcastic; abusive. — *adv* **satir'ically**. — *n* **satir'icalness**. — *vt* **satirise** or **-ize** (*sat'ər-īz*) to make the object of satire. — *vi* to write satire. — *n* **sat'irist** a writer of satire. [L. *satira, satura* (*lanx*), full (dish), a medley.]

satisfy *sat'is-fī, vt* to pay in full; to compensate or atone for; to give enough to; to be enough for; to supply fully; to fulfil the conditions of; to meet the requirements of; to content; to free from doubt; to convince. — *vi* to give content; to make payment or atonement: — *pr p* **sat'isfying**; *pa t* and *pa p* **sat'isfied**. — *n* **satisfaction** (*-fak'shən*) the act of satisfying; the state of being satisfied, content; payment; quittance; gratification; comfort; something which satisfies; atonement; satisfying of honour, as by a duel; conviction. — *adv* **satisfac'torily**. — *n* **satisfac'toriness**. — *adj* **satisfac'tory** satisfying; giving contentment; such as might be wished; making amends or payment; atoning; convincing. — *adj* **sat'isfīable**. — *adj* **sat'isfied**. — *n* **sat'isfier**. — *adj* **sat'isfying**. — *adv* **sat'isfyingly**. [O.Fr. *satisfier* — L. *satisfacĕre* — *satis,* enough, *facĕre,* to make.]

satori *sa-tö'rē, n* sudden enlightenment — sought in Zen Buddhism. [Jap., — *toshi,* be quick.]

satrap *sat'rap, n* a viceroy or governor of an ancient Persian province; a provincial governor, esp. if powerful or ostentatiously rich. — *adj* **sat'rapal**. — *n* **sat'rapy** a satrap's province, office or time of office. [Gr. *satrapēs,* from O.Pers. *khshathrapāvan-,* country-protector.]

Satsuma *sat-soo'mə, n* a province of S.W. Japan; Satsuma ware. — **satsuma** or **satsuma orange** a thin-skinned seedless type of mandarin orange, or its tree; **Satsuma ware** a yellowish pottery with gilding and enamel made in Satsuma from the end of the 16th century.

saturate *sat'ū-rāt* or *sa'chə-rāt, vt* to soak; to imbue; to charge to the fullest extent possible; to satisfy all the valencies of (*chem*); to cover (a target area) completely with bombs dropped simultaneously. — *adj* saturated; deep in colour, free from white. — *n* a saturated compound (*chem*). — *adj* **sat'urable**. — *adj* **sat'urant** tending to saturate. — *n* a saturating substance. — *adj* **sat'urated** (of a solution) containing as much of a solute as can be dissolved at a particular temperature and pressure; (esp. of a fat) containing no carbon-carbon double bonds in the molecule and consequently not susceptible to addition reactions (*chem*); thoroughly wet; soaked. — *n* **saturā'tion** the state of being saturated; the state of the atmosphere when fully saturated with water vapour at any given temperature. — Also used as *adj*, meaning of very great, or greatest possible, intensity (e.g. *saturation bombing*). — *n* **sat'urātor**. — **saturated fat** an animal fat (usu. solid, e.g. lard, butter) containing a high proportion of saturated fatty acids; **saturation point** the point at which saturation is reached; dewpoint; the limit in numbers that can be taken in, provided with a living, used, sold, etc.; the limit of emotional response, endurance, etc. [L. *saturāre*, *-ātum* — *satur*, full.]

Saturday *sat'ər-di*, *n* the seventh day of the week (dedicated by the Romans to Saturn), the Jewish Sabbath. [O.E. *Sæter-*, *Sætern(es)dæg*, Saturn's day.]

Saturn *sat'ərn*, *n* the ancient Roman god of agriculture; commonly used for the Greek Kronos, with whom he came to be identified; the second in size and sixth in distance from the sun of the major planets, believed by the astrologers to induce a cold, melancholy, gloomy temperament; the metal lead (*alchemy*). — *npl* **Saturnā'lia** (*Roman hist*) the festival of Saturn in mid-December, a time of great revelry and gift-giving when slaves had temporary freedom; hence (often as *nsing* without capital) an orgy. — *adj* **saturnā'lian**. — *n* **Satur'nia** (*sat-* or *sət-*) a genus of very large moths. — *adj* **Satur'nian** pertaining to Saturn, whose fabulous reign was called the golden age; thus happy, pure or simple; of the planet Saturn. — *n* a person born under Saturn, or of saturnine temperament. — *adj* **satur'nic** (*med*) affected with lead-poisoning. — *adj* **sat'urnine** grave; gloomy; phlegmatic; caused or poisoned by lead. — *n* **sat'urnism** lead-poisoning. [L. *Sāturnus* — *serěre*, *sătum*, to sow.]

satyagraha *sut'yə-gru-hə* or *-grä'hə*, *n* orig. Mahatma Gandhi's policy of passive resistance to British rule in India, now any non-violent campaign for reform. — *n* **sat'yagrahi** (*-hi*) an exponent of this. [Sans., reliance on truth.]

satyr *sat'ər*, *n* a Greek god of the woodlands, with tail and long ears, represented by the Romans as part goat; a very lecherous person; any butterfly of the *Satyridae* family. — *n* **satyrī'asis** (*med*) a morbid, overpowering sexual desire in men, corresponding to nymphomania in women. — *adj* **satyric** (*sə-tir'ik*) or **satyr'ical**. [L. *satyrus* — Gr. *satyros*.]

sauce *sös*, *n* a dressing poured over food; anything that gives relish; stewed fruit (*US*); pert or impertinent language or behaviour (*colloq*). — *vt* to add or give sauce to; to make piquant or pleasant; to be impertinent to. — *adv* **sauc'ily**. — *n* **sauc'iness**. — *adj* **sauc'y** (*compar* **sauc'ier**, *superl* **sauc'iest**) like or tasting of sauce; pert, forward; piquantly audacious, esp. arousing sexual desire; smart and trim; disdainful. — **sauce boat** a vessel for sauce; **sauce'box** (*colloq*) an impudent person; **sauce'pan** a handled and usu. lidded metal pan for boiling, stewing, etc. [Fr. *sauce* — L. *salsa* — *sallěre*, *salsum*, to salt — *sāl*, salt.]

saucer *sö'sər*, *n* a shallow dish, esp. one placed under a tea or coffee cup; anything of similar shape. — *n* **sau'cerful**: — *pl* **sau'cerfuls**. [O.Fr. *saussiere* — L.L. *salsārium* — L. *salsa*, sauce.]

sauerkraut *sow'ər-* or *zow'ər-krowt*, *n* a German dish of cabbage allowed to ferment with salt, etc. [Ger., sour cabbage.]

sauger *sö'gər*, *n* a small American pike-perch.

sauna *sö'nə*, *n* (a building or room equipped for) a Finnish form of steam bath. [Finn.]

saunter *sön'tər*, *vi* to wander about idly; to lounge or stroll. — *n* a sauntering gait; a leisurely stroll. — *n* **saun'terer**. — *n* **saun'tering**. — *adv* **saun'teringly**.

saurian *sö'ri-ən*, *n* a lizard. — *adj* **saurischian** (*-is'ki-ən*) of or belonging to the **Sauris'chia** (lit. 'lizard-hipped'), an order of dinosaurs. — *n* any dinosaur of the Saurischia. — *npl* **Saurop'oda** a suborder of gigantic quadrupedal herbivorous dinosaurs, one of the two main groups of lizard-hipped dinosaurs. [Gr. *saurā*, *sauros*, a lizard.]

saury *sö'ri*, *n* a long, sharp-beaked, marine fish. [Perh. Gr. *sauros*, lizard.]

sausage *sos'ij*, *n* chopped or minced meat with fat, cereal, etc. seasoned and stuffed into a tube of gut or the like or formed into the shape of a tube; anything of similar shape. — **sausage dog** (*colloq*) a dachshund; **sausage meat** meat prepared for making sausages; **sausage roll** minced meat cooked in a roll of pastry. — **not a sausage** (*colloq*) nothing at all. [Fr. *saucisse* — L.L. *salsīcia* — L. *salsus*, salted.]

sauté *sō'tā*, *adj* fried lightly and quickly. — Also *vt*: — *pa p* and *pa t* **sau'téed**; *pr p* **sau'téing** or **sau'téeing**. — *n* a dish of food that has been sautéed. [Fr. *sauter*, to jump.]

Sauterne or **Sauternes** *sō-tûrn'* or *-tern'*, *n* sweet white wine produced at *Sauternes* in the Gironde, France.

Sauvignon *sō'vē-nyɔ̃*, *n* a variety of grape originally grown in Bordeaux and the Loire valley; wine made from this.

savable, etc. See under **save**.

savage *sav'ij*, *adj* in a state of nature; untamed, wild; uncivilised; ferocious; furious. — *n* a human being in a wild or primitive state; a brutal, fierce or cruel person; an enraged horse or other animal. — *vt* to attack savagely, esp. with the teeth. — *adv* **sav'agely**. — *n* **sav'ageness** the state of being savage. — *n* **sav'agery** (*-ri* or *-ər-i*) fierceness; ferocity; uncivilised condition; wildness; savage behaviour. [O.Fr. *salvage* — L. *silvāticus*, pertaining to the woods — *silva*, a wood.]

savanna or **savannah** *sə-van'ə*, *n* a tract of level land, covered with low vegetation, treeless, or dotted with trees or patches of wood. [Sp. *zavana* (now *sabana*), said to be from Carib.]

savant *sa'vã* or *sä-vã'*, *n* a learned person. — **savant syndrome** the syndrome observed in an **idiot savant**. [Fr. obs. pres. p. of *savoir*, to know.]

savate *sä-vät'*, *n* boxing with the use of the feet. [Fr.]

save *sāv*, *vt* to bring safe out of evil; to rescue; to bring or keep out of danger; to protect, to preserve; to prevent or avoid the loss, expenditure, or performance of, or the gain of by an opponent; to reserve; to spare; to deliver from the power of sin and from its consequences; to be economical in the use of; to hoard; to store (data) on a tape or disk; to prevent (a goal) from being scored; to obviate, to prevent. — *vi* to act as a saviour; to be economical; to reserve (esp. money) for future use. — *prep* except. — *conj* were it not that; unless. — *n* an act of saving, esp. in games; a computer instruction to save material onto a tape or disk. — *adj* **sav'able**. — *n* **sav'ableness**. — *adj* **saved**. — *n* **sa'ver**. — *adj* **sa'ving** protecting; preserving; redeeming; securing salvation (*theol*); frugal; making a reservation (esp. *law*). — *prep* excepting. — *n* the action of the verb; something which is saved; (in *pl*) money laid aside for future use. — *adv* **sa'vingly**. — **saving clause** a legal clause, or a statement, in which a reservation or condition is made; **saving grace** see under **grace; savings and loan association** (*US*) a building society; **savings bank** a bank established to encourage thrift by taking small deposits, investing under regulations for safety, and giving compound interest; **savings certificate** a certificate of having invested a small sum in government funds. — **save appearances** to keep up an appearance of wealth, comfort, consistency, harmony, propriety, etc.; **save as you earn** (abbrev.

SAYE) a government-operated savings scheme in which regular deductions are made from one's earnings; **save one's bacon, save one's face** see under **bacon, face**; **save up** to accumulate or hold for some purpose by refraining from spending or using. [Fr. *sauver* — L. *salvāre* — *salvus*, safe.]

saveloy *sav'ə-loi*, *n* a highly seasoned sausage, orig. made of brains. [Fr. *cervelat*, *cervelas*, a saveloy — L. *cerebellum*, dimin. of *cerebrum*, the brain.]

savin or **savine** *sav'in*, *n* a species of juniper with very small leaves; its tops, yielding an irritant volatile oil, anthelmintic and abortifacient; extended to Virginian juniper ('red cedar') and other plants. [O.Fr. *sabine* — L. *sabīna* (*herba*), Sabine (herb).]

saviour *sā'vyər*, *n* someone who saves from evil; (with *cap*) a title applied by Christians to Jesus Christ. [M.E. *sauveur* — O.Fr. *sauveour* — L. *salvātor* — *salūs*, *salūtis*, health, wellbeing, safety.]

savoir-faire *sav-wär-fer'*, *n* the faculty of knowing just what to do and how to do it; tact. [Fr.]

savoir-vivre *sav-wär-vē'vr'*, *n* good breeding; knowledge of polite usages. [Fr.]

savory *sā'vər-i*, *n* a labiate flavouring herb (genus *Satureia*, esp. *S. hortensis*, summer savory, or *S. montana*, winter savory). [App. — L. *saturēia*.]

savour or in U.S. **savor** *sā'vər*, *n* taste; odour; the distinctive quality of something; relish. — *vi* to taste or smell (*of* something); to have a flavour; to have a suggestion (*of*). — *vt* to flavour, season; to taste, smell; to be conscious of; to relish; to taste with conscious direction of the attention. — *adj* **sā'voured.** — *adv* **sā'vourily.** — *n* **sā'vouriness.** — *adj* **sā'vourless.** — *adj* **sā'voury** of good savour or relish; fragrant; having savour or relish; appetising; wholesome; attractive; salty, piquant or spiced (opp. to *sweet*). — *n* a savoury course or dish or small item of food. [O.Fr. *sav(o)ur* — L. *sapor* — *sapěre*, to taste.]

Savoy *sə-voi'*, *n* a district of S.E. France, giving its name to a former palace and sanctuary and to a theatre in London; (without *cap*) a winter cabbage with a large close head and wrinkled leaves — originally from *Savoy*. — *n* **Savoyard** (*sav'oi-ärd*) a native or inhabitant of Savoy; a performer in, or devotee of, the Gilbert and Sullivan operas produced at the Savoy theatre. — Also *adj*. [Fr. *Savoie*, *Savoyard*.]

savvy *sav'i*, (*slang*) *vt* and *vi* to know; to understand. — *n* general ability; common sense; know-how, skill. — *adj* knowledgeable, shrewd. [Sp. *sabe* — *saber*, to know — L. *sapěre*, to be wise.]

saw[1] *sö*, *pa t* of **see**[1].

saw[2] *sö*, *n* a toothed cutting instrument. — *vt* to cut with, or as if with, or as, a saw; to shape by sawing; to play harshly or crudely (as a fiddler). — *vi* to use a saw; to make to and fro movements, as if with a saw: — *pa t* **sawed**; *pa p* **sawed** or (usu.) **sawn.** — *adj* **sawed.** — *n* and *adj* **saw'ing.** — *adj* **sawn.** — *n* **saw'yer** a person who saws timber, esp. at a sawpit; a stranded tree that bobs in a river (*US*). — **saw'-bones** (*slang*) a surgeon; **saw'dust** dust or small particles of wood, etc. detached in sawing. — *vt* to sprinkle with sawdust. — *adj* **saw'dusty.** — **saw'-edge.** — *adj* **saw'-edged** serrated. — **saw'fish** a ray (*Pristis*) or (sometimes) a shark (*Pristiophorus*; **saw'shark**) with a flattened bony beak toothed on the edges; **saw'fly** a hymenopterous insect of various kinds with sawlike ovipositor; **saw'-frame** the frame in which a saw is set; **saw'horse** a trestle for supporting wood that is being sawn; a straight-line diagram showing the three-dimensional structure of a molecule; **saw'mill** a mill for sawing timber. — *adj* **sawn'-off** (or **sawed off**) shortened by cutting with a saw; short in stature (*colloq*). — **saw'pit** a pit in which one sawyer stands while another stands above; **saw set** an instrument for turning sawteeth to right and left; **saw'tooth.** — Also *adj*. — *adj* **saw'toothed** serrated, like the edge of a saw. — **saw'-wort** a name for various composites with serrated leaves. [O.E. *saga*.]

saw[3] *sö*, *n* a saying; a proverb. [O.E. *sagu*, from the root of *secgan*, to say, tell.]

sawah *sa'wa*, *n* an irrigated paddy-field. [Malay.]

sawn *sön*, *pa p* of **saw**[2].

sawyer. See **saw**[2].

sax[1] *saks*, *n* a chopper for trimming slates. [O.E. *sæx*, a knife.]

sax[2] *saks*, (*colloq*) *n* short for **saxophone.**

saxatile *sak'sə-tīl* or *-til*, *adj* rock-dwelling. [L. *saxātilis* — *saxum*, a rock.]

Saxe *saks*, *adj* made in, or characteristic of, Saxony (of china, etc); of a deep shade of light blue (**Saxe blue,** also **Saxon** or **Saxony blue**). — *n* Saxon blue, a dye colour. [Fr. *Saxe*, Saxony.]

saxhorn *saks'hörn*, *n* a brass wind-instrument with a long winding tube with bell opening, invented by Antoine or Adolphe *Sax* (1814–94).

saxicolous *sak-sik'ə-ləs* or **saxicoline** *-sik'ə-lēn*, *adj* living or growing among rocks. [L. *saxum*, a rock, *colěre*, to inhabit.]

saxifrage *sak'si-frij* or *-frāj*, *n* any species of the genus *Saxifraga*, Alpine or rock plants with tufted foliage and small white, yellow or red flowers; extended to other plants. — *adj* **saxifragā'ceous.** [L. *saxifraga* — *saxum*, a stone, *frangěre*, to break (from growing in clefts of rock).]

Saxon *saks'ən*, *n* one of a N. German people that conquered most of Britain in the 5th and 6th centuries; the language of that people on the Continent (Old Saxon) or in Britain (Anglo-Saxon, Old English); a native, inhabitant or citizen of Saxony in the later German sense (now in S. Germany). — *adj* pertaining to the Saxons in any sense, their language, country or architecture. — *vt* and *vi* **Sax'onise** or **-ize** to make or become Saxon. — *n* **Sax'onism** a Saxon or English idiom; a preference for native English words, institutions, etc. — *n* **Sax'onist** a scholar in Old English. — *n* **sax'ony** a soft woollen yarn or cloth. — **Saxon architecture** a style of building in England before the Norman Conquest, with characteristics of the woodwork of the period; **Saxon** (or **Saxony**) **blue** see **Saxe**; **Saxon Shore** (L. *Litus Saxonicum*) in Roman times, the coast districts from Brighton to the Wash. [L. *Saxŏnēs* (pl.); of Ger. origin.]

saxophone *sak'sə-fōn*, *n* a jazz, military and dance band instrument with reed, (properly) metal tube, and about twenty finger-keys. — *n* **saxophonist** (*-sof'ən-ist*). [*Sax*, the inventor (see **saxhorn**), Gr. *phōnē*, the voice.]

say *sā*, *vt* to utter or set forth, as words or in words; to speak; to assert, affirm, state, declare; to express; to tell; to suppose as a hypothesis; to go through in recitation or repetition. — *vi* to make a statement; to speak; to declare, set forth in answer to a question: — *3rd pers sing* **says** (*sez* or *səz*); *pr p* **say'ing**; *pa p* and *pa t* **said** (*sed*). — *n* something said; a remark; a speech; what one wants to say; opportunity of speech; a voice, part or influence in a decision. — *adv* approximately; for example. — *interj* (*US*) expressing surprise, protest, sudden joy, etc. — *adj* **say'able.** — *n* **say'er.** — *n* **say'ing** something said; an expression; a maxim. — **say'-so** an authoritative saying; authority; a rumour; hearsay. — **I'll say!** (*colloq*) a response expressing wholehearted agreement; **I say!** an exclamation calling attention or expressing surprise, protest, sudden joy, etc.; **it is said** or **they say** it is commonly reputed; **it says (that)** the text runs thus (*colloq*); **nothing to say for oneself** no defence of oneself to offer; no small-talk; **not to say** indeed one might go further and say; **says I, says you, he,** etc. (in *illit* or *jocular* use) ungrammatical substitutes for said I, you, he, etc.; **says you** *interj* expressing incredulity; **that is to say**

in other words; **to say nothing of** not to mention; **to say the least** at least; without exaggeration; **what do you say to?** how about?; are you inclined towards?; **you can say that again** (*colloq*) you are absolutely right, I agree entirely. [O.E. *secgan* (*sægde, gesægd*).]

SAYE *abbrev* for save as you earn.

sayyid, sayid or **said** *sī'* or *sä'(y)id*, or *säd*, *n* a descendant of Mohammed's daughter Fatima; an honorary title given to some Muslims. [Ar.]

saz *saz*, *n* a stringed instrument of Turkey, N. Africa and the Middle East. [Pers. *sāz*, a musical instrument.]

sazerac® *saz'ə-rak*, (*US*) *n* a cocktail based on Pernod and whisky.

Sb (*chem*) *symbol* for antimony (from L. *stibium*).

SBN *abbrev* for Standard Book Number.

SBS *abbrev* for Special Boat Squadron.

SC *abbrev* for: School Certificate (*Austr* and *NZ*); Signal Corps; South Carolina (U.S. state).

Sc (*chem*) *symbol* for scandium.

sc (*printing*) *abbrev* for small capitals.

sc. *abbrev* for: *scilicet* (L.), namely; *sculpsit* (L.), (he/she) sculptured (this).

s/c *abbrev* for self-contained.

scab *skab*, *n* a skin disease, esp. with scales or pustules, and esp. one caused by mites (as in *sheep scab*); a fungous disease of various kinds in potatoes, apples, etc.; a crust formed over a sore, or in any of these diseases; a scoundrel (*derog*); a blackleg (*colloq*). — *vi* to develop a scab; to play the scab, act as a blackleg. — *n* **scabb'iness.** — *adj* **scabb'y.** [App. from an O.N. equivalent of O.E. *scæb, sceabb* (see **shabby**) infl. by assoc. with L. *scabiēs*.]

scabbard *skab'ərd*, *n* a sheath, esp. for a sword. — *vt* to sheathe. — *adj* **scabb'ardless.** — **scabbard fish** a long narrow fish (genus *Lepidopus*) of the family having a whiplike tail. [M.E. *scauberc*, app. — A.Fr. *escaubers* (pl.), prob. Gmc.]

scabies *skā'bi-ēz* or *-bēz*, *n* a skin disease causing intense itching. [L. *scăbiēs* — *scabĕre*, to scratch.]

scabious *skā'bi-əs*, *n* a plant of the teasel family, long thought to be effective in treating scaly eruptions; a plant of the bell-flower family, of similar appearance. [L. *scăbiōsus* — *scăbiēs*, the itch.]

scabrous *skā'brəs*, *adj* rough; scurfy; beset with difficulties; bordering on the indecent. — *adv* **scab'rously.** — *n* **scā'brousness.** [L. *scăbrōsus*, *scăbridus* — *scăber*, rough.]

scad[1] *skad*, *n* a fish with armoured and keeled lateral line, superficially like a coarse mackerel (also called *horse mackerel*). [App. Cornish dialect.]

scad[2] *skad*, (esp. *US*) *n* a large amount, a lot (usu. in *pl*).

scaffold *skaf'əld*, *n* a temporary erection for people at work on a building, and their tools and materials; a raised platform (as for performers, spectators or executions); a framework; capital punishment. — *vt* to supply with a scaffold. — *n* **scaff'older.** — *n* **scaff'olding** a framework for painters, builders, etc. at work; materials for scaffolds; a frame or framework. [O.Fr. *escadafault*.]

scag *skag*, (*US slang*) *n* heroin.

scagliola *skal-i-ō'-lə*, *n* a polished imitation marble consisting of ground gypsum bound with glue. [It., dimin. of *scaglia*, a chip of marble.]

scalar *skā'lər*, (*phys* or *math*) *adj* having magnitude only, not direction. — *n* a scalar quantity. [L. *scāla*, a ladder.]

scalawag or **scallawag.** See **scallywag.**

scald *sköld*, *vt* to injure with hot liquid; to cook or heat short of boiling; to treat with very hot water. — *vi* to be scalded; to be hot enough to scald. — *n* a burn caused by hot liquid. — *n* **scald'er.** — *n* and *adj* **scald'ing.** [O.Fr. *escalder* — L.L. *excaldāre*, to bathe in warm water — *ex*, from, *calidus*, warm, hot.]

scaldfish *sköld'fish*, *n* a small European flatfish with large scales.

scale[1] *skāl*, *n* a graduated series or order; a graduated measure; a system of definite tones used in music; a succession of these performed in ascending or descending order of pitch through one octave or more; the compass or range of a voice or instrument; a numeral system; a system or scheme of relative values or correspondences; the ratio of representation to object; relative extent. — Also used as *adj* (as in *scale model*). — *vt* to mount (as by a ladder); to climb; to change according to scale (often with *up* or *down*). — *adj* **scal'able.** — *n* **scal'er** an instrument that counts very rapid pulses, by recording at the end of each group of specified numbers instead of after individual pulses. — *n* **scal'ing.** — **scal'ing-ladder** a ladder for climbing the walls of a fortress, etc.; a fireman's ladder. — **full-scale** see under **full; on a large, small,** etc. **scale** in a great, small, etc. way; **on the scale of** in the ratio of; **to scale** in proportion to actual dimensions. [L. *scāla*, a ladder — *scandĕre*, to mount.]

scale[2] *skāl*, *n* a thin plate on a fish, reptile, etc.; a readily detached flake; a lamina; an overlapping plate in armour; a small, flat, detachable piece of cuticle; a reduced leaf or leaf-base; a small flat structure clothing a butterfly's or moth's wing; an encrustation, esp. that left inside a kettle, etc. by hard water; a film, as on iron being heated for forging. — *vt* to clear of scales; to peel off in thin layers. — *vi* to come off in thin layers or flakes; to become encrusted with scale. — *adj* **scaled.** — *adj* **scale'less.** — *adj* **scale'like.** — *n* **scal'er** a person who scales fish, boilers, etc.; an instrument for scaling, as for removing tartar from the teeth. — *n* **scal'iness.** — *n* **scal'ing.** — Also *adj.* — *adj* **scal'y.** — **scale armour** armour of overlapping scales; **scale board** a very thin slip of wood; **scale fern** a fern whose back is densely covered with rusty-coloured scales; **scale insect** any insect of the homopterous family Coccidae, in which the sedentary female fixes on a plant and secretes a waxy shield; **scale moss** a liverwort with small leaflike structures, such as *Jungermannia*. [M.E. *scāle* — O.Fr. *escale*, husk, chip of stone, of Gmc. origin.]

scale[3] *skāl*, *n* a balance pan; (usu. in *pl*) a balance; (in *pl*) Libra, a constellation and a sign of the zodiac. — *vt* to weigh; to weigh up. — *vi* to weigh or be weighed, as a jockey (often *scale in*). — **turn** or **tip the scale(s)** see under **turn** and **tip**[4]. [A Northern form from O.N. *skāl*, bowl, pan of balance.]

scalene *skāl'ēn*, *adj* (of a triangle) with three unequal sides; (of a cone or cylinder) with axis oblique to the base (*math*); denoting the muscles that connect the upper ribs to the cervical vertebrae, being obliquely situated and unequal-sided (*anat*). [Gr. *skalēnos*, uneven, *hedrā*, seat.]

scallion *skal'yən*, *n* the leek; an onion with a slim bulb; a spring onion. [O.N.Fr. *escalogne* — L. *Ascalōnia* (*cēpa*), Ascalon (onion).]

scallop *skol'əp* or *skal'əp*, *n* a bivalve (esp. genus *Pecten*) having a sub-circular shell with radiating ridges and eared hinge-line; a valve of its shell; a dish or other object of similar form; a shallow dish in which oysters, etc. are cooked, baked and browned; the cooked oysters, etc. themselves; a potato slice cooked in batter; one of a series of curves in the edge of anything; an escalope. — *vt* to cut into scallops or curves; to cook in a scallop with sauce and usu. breadcrumbs. — *vi* to gather or search for scallops. — *adj* **scall'oped** having the edge or border cut into scallops or curves. — **scallop shell** the shell of a scallop, esp. that of a Mediterranean species used (*hist*) as the badge of a pilgrim to the shrine of St James of Compostela. [O.Fr. *escalope*; of Gmc. origin.]

scallywag, scallawag or **scalawag** *skal'i-wag* or *-ə-wag*, *n* an undersized animal of little value; a good-for-nothing; a rascal, scamp.

scalp *skalp*, *n* the outer covering of the skull; the top or hairy part of the head; the skin on which the hair of the head grows; a piece of that skin torn off as a token of victory by the N. American Indians; a bare rock or mountain-top. — *vt* to cut the scalp from; to buy cheap in order to resell quickly at a profit; (of theatre, travel, or other tickets) to buy up and sell at other than official prices (*US*); to destroy the political influence of (*US*). — *n* **scalp'er**. — *adj* **scalp'less**. — **scalp'-lock** a long tuft of hair left unshaven as a challenge by N. American Indians. [M.E. *scalp*.]

scalpel *skal'pəl*, *n* a small knife for dissecting or operating. — *adj* **scalpell'iform** shaped like a scalpel. — *adj* **scalp'riform** chisel-shaped. — *n* **scalp'rum** a surgeon's rasping instrument. [L. *scalpĕre*, to scrape, cut, *scalper*, *scalprum*, dimin. *scalpellum*, a knife.]

scaly. See **scale^2**.

scam *skam*, (esp. *US slang*) *n* a swindle.

scammony *skam'ən-i*, *n Convolvulus scammonia*, a twining Asian plant with arrow-shaped leaves; its dried root; a cathartic gum-resin obtained from its root or that of a substitute. [Gr. *skammōniā*.]

scamp^1 *skamp*, a rascal; a lively, mischievous person, esp. a child. — *adj* **scamp'ish**. — *adv* **scamp'ishly**. — *n* **scamp'ishness**. [O.Fr. *escamper* or It. *scampare*, to decamp.]

scamp^2 *skamp*, *vt* to do or execute perfunctorily or without thoroughness. — *n* **scamp'er**. — *n* **scamp'ing**. [Poss. O.N. *skemma*, to shorten.]

scamper *skam'pər*, *vi* to run or skip about briskly. — *n* an act of scampering. [**scamp^1**.]

scampi *skam'pi*, *npl* crustaceans of the species *Nephrops norvegicus*, esp. (treated as *sing*) when cooked and served as a dish. [Pl. of It. *scampo*, a shrimp.]

scan *skan*, *vt* to analyse metrically; to recite so as to bring out the metrical structure; to examine critically or closely; to glance over quickly; to examine all parts of in systematic order; (in television) to pass a beam over every part of in turn; to make pictorial records of (part of) the body by various techniques, e.g. ultrasonics (*med*); to examine data on (a magnetic disk, etc.); to cast an eye negligently over; to search out by swinging the beam (*radar*). — *vi* to agree with the rules of metre: — *prp* **scann'ing**; *pa t* and *pa p* **scanned**. — *n* a scanning; the image, etc. produced by scanning. — *n* **scann'er** a person who scans or can scan; a perforated disc (also **scann'ing-disc**) used in television; the rotating aerial by which the beam is made to scan (*radar*); an instrument which scans, esp. one that makes an image of an internal organ. — *n* and *adj* **scann'ing**. — *n* **scan'sion** the act, art, or a mode, of scanning verse; scanning in television. — **scanning electron microscope** an electron microscope that produces a three-dimensional image. [L. *scandĕre*, *scānsum*, to climb.]

scandal *skan'dl*, *n* anything that causes moral discredit or injury to reputation; something said which is injurious to reputation; a false imputation; malicious gossip; slander; a disgraceful fact, thing or person. — *n* **scandalīsā'tion** or **-z-**. — *vt* **scan'dalise** or **-ize** to give scandal or offence to; to shock. — *adj* **scan'dalous** giving scandal or offence; openly vile; defamatory. — *adv* **scan'dalously**. — *n* **scan'dalousness**. — **scan'dalmonger** a person who deals in defamatory reports; **scan'dalmongering**; **scandal sheet** a newspaper with a reputation for publishing scandal or gossip. [L. *scandalum* — Gr. *skandalon*, a stumbling-block.]

Scandinavian *skan-di-nā'vi-ən*, *adj* of, or characteristic of, *Scandinavia*, the peninsula divided into Norway and Sweden, but, in a historical sense, applying also to Denmark and Iceland; North Germanic (*philol*). — *n* a native of Scandinavia; a member of the dominant Nordic race of Scandinavia. [L. *Scandināvia* (from Gmc. word) and its shortened form *Scandia*.]

scandium *skan'di-əm*, *n* a rare metallic element (symbol **Sc**; atomic no. 21) found in various rare minerals including the Scandinavian mineral *euxenite* in which it was discovered in 1879. [**Scandinavian**.]

scanner, scansion. See under **scan**.

scant *skant*, *adj* not full or plentiful; scarcely sufficient; deficient; short, poorly supplied. — *adv* barely; scantily. — *vt* to stint; to restrict; to reduce; to dispense sparingly; to treat inadequately. — *npl* **scant'ies** (*colloq*) underwear, esp. women's brief panties. — *adv* **scant'ily**. — *n* **scant'iness**. — *adv* **scant'ly**. — *n* **scant'ness**. — *adj* **scant'y** meagre; deficient; skimped; lacking fullness. [O.N. *skamt*, neut. of *skammr*, short.]

scantling *skant'ling*, *n* dimensions of a cross-section; a sample or pattern; a narrow piece of timber; a small quantity or amount. [O.Fr. *escantillon*, *eschantillon*.]

scanty. See under **scant**.

scape *skāp*, *n* a flower stalk rising from the ground, without foliage leaves (*bot*); the basal part of an antenna (*entom*); the shaft or stem of a feather; the shaft of a column (*archit*). [L. *scāpus*, a shaft.]

-scape *-skāp*, *sfx* indicating a type of scene or view, as in *seascape*, *streetscape*. [**landscape**.]

scapegoat *skāp'gōt*, *n* a goat on which, once a year, the Jewish high-priest laid symbolically the sins of the people, and which was then allowed to escape into the wilderness (Lev. xvi); someone who is made to bear or take the blame for the failings or misdeeds of another. — *vt* to make into or treat as a scapegoat. — *n* **scape'goating** the practice of making (someone) into or using (someone) as a scapegoat, esp. involving harsh or violent treatment; a psychological syndrome of this nature. [**escape** and **goat**.]

scapegrace *skāp'grās*, *n* an incorrigible rascal. [**escape**.]

scaphoid *skaf'oid*, *adj* boat-shaped. — *n* **scaphoid bone** or **scaphoid** the navicular bone. [Gr. *skaphē*, a boat, *eidos*, form.]

scapula *skap'ū-lə*, *n* the shoulder blade. — *adj* **scap'ūlar** of the shoulder blade or shoulder. — *n* originally an ordinary working garb, now the mark of the monastic orders, a long strip of cloth with an opening for the head, worn hanging before and behind over the habit; two pieces of cloth tied together over the shoulders, worn by members of certain lay confraternities (*RC Church*); a supporting bandage worn over the shoulder; a shoulder feather. — *adj* and *n* **scap'ūlary** scapular. [L. *scapulae*, the shoulder blades.]

scar^1 *skär*, *n* the mark left by a wound or sore; any mark or blemish; any mark, trace or result of injury, material, moral or psychological, etc. (*fig*); a mark at a place of former attachment, as of a leaf. — *vt* to mark with a scar. — *vi* to become scarred: — *prp* **scarr'ing**; *pa t* and *pa p* **scarred**. — *adj* **scar'less**. — *adj* **scarred**. — *n* and *adj* **scarr'ing**. — *adj* **scarr'y**. [O.Fr. *escare* — L. *eschara* — Gr. *escharā*, a hearth, brazier, burn, scar.]

scar^2 *skär* or **scaur** *skör*, *n* a precipitous bare place on a hill-face; a cliff; a reef in the sea. — *adj* **scarr'y**. [App. O.N. *sker*, *skera*, to cut.]

scarab *skar'əb*, *n* a dung-beetle, esp. the sacred beetle of the ancient Egyptians; a gem cut in the form of a beetle. — *n* **scarabaeid** (*skar-ə-bē'id*) any beetle of the *Scarabaeidae*, a large family of beetles, some of them of great size (chafers, dung-beetles). [L. *scarabaeus*.]

scarce *skārs*, *adj* not often found; hard to get; in short supply. — *adv* scarcely; hardly ever. — *adv* **scarce'ly** only just; not quite; not at all. — *n* **scarce'ness**. — *n* **scarc'ity** the state or fact of being scarce; shortness of supply, esp. of necessaries; dearth; deficiency.

— **make oneself scarce** (*colloq*) to leave quickly, unobtrusively, for reasons of prudence, tact, etc. [O.N.Fr. *escars*, niggardly, from a L.L. substitute for L. *excerptus*, past p. of *excerpĕre* — *ex*, out, *carpĕre*, to pick.]

scare *skār*, *vt* to startle, to frighten; to drive or keep off by frightening. — *vi* to become frightened. — *n* a fright; a panic; a baseless public alarm. — *adj* **scared.** — *n* **scar'er.** — *adj* **scar'y** or **scar'ey** frightening; timorous. — **scare'crow** anything set up to scare birds; a shabbily-dressed person; a very thin person; **scare'-head, scare'-heading** or **scare'-line** a newspaper heading designed to raise a scare; **scare'monger** an alarmist, a person who causes panic by initiating or encouraging rumours of trouble; **scare'mongering.** — **run scared** to panic; **scare the (living) daylights out of** or **scare the pants off** (*colloq*) to frighten considerably. [M.E. *skerre* — O.N. *skirra*, to avoid — *skiarr*, shy.]

scarf[1] *skärf*, *n* a light, usually decorative piece of material thrown loosely on the shoulders about the neck, or tied around the head, etc.; a military or official sash; a necktie; a muffler; a cravat: — *pl* **scarfs** or **scarves.** — **scarf'-pin** an ornamental pin worn in a scarf; **scarf'-ring** an ornamental ring through which the ends of a scarf are drawn. [Perh. O.N.Fr. *escarpe*, sash, sling.]

scarf[2] *skärf*, *n* a joint between pieces placed end to end, cut so as to fit with overlapping like a continuous piece; an end so prepared; a longitudinal cut in a whale's carcase. — *vt* to join with a scarf-joint; to make a scarf in. — *n* **scarf'ing.** — **scarf'-joint.** [Perh. Scand.]

scarfskin *skärf'skin*, *n* the surface skin. [Perh. **scarf**[1]; perh. related to **scurf.**]

scarify *skar'i-fī*, *vt* to make a number of scratches or slight cuts in; to break up the surface of; to lacerate; to criticise severely: — *pr p* **scar'ifying;** *pa t* and *pa p* **scar'ified.** — *n* **scarification** (*-fi-kā'shən*). — *n* **scar'ificātor** a surgical instrument for scarifying. — *n* **scar'ifier** an implement for breaking the surface of the soil or of a road. [L.L. *scarīficāre, -ātum* — Gr. *skarīphos*, an etching tool.]

scarious *skā'ri-əs*, (*bot*) *adj* thin, dry, stiff and membranous.

scarlatina *skär-lə-tē'nə*, *n* scarlet fever. [It. *scarlattina.*]

scarlet *skär'lit*, *n* a brilliant red; a brilliant red cloth, garment, or clothing, or its wearer. — *adj* scarlet in colour; dressed in scarlet. — **scarlet fever** an infectious fever, usually marked by a sore throat and a scarlet rash; **scarlet hat** a red hat formerly worn by cardinals; the rank or office of cardinal; **scarlet runner** a scarlet-flowered climbing plant of the kidney-bean genus, with edible beans; **scarlet woman** the woman referred to in the Bible (Rev. xvii) — variously taken as pagan Rome, Papal Rome, or the world in its anti-Christian sense; a whore. [O.Fr. *escarlate* thought to be from Pers. *saqalāt*, scarlet cloth.]

scarp *skärp*, *n* an escarp; an escarpment. — *vt* to cut into a scarp. — *adj* **scarped.** — *n* **scarp'ing.** [It. *scarpa.*]

scarper *skär'pər*, (*slang*) *vi* to run away, escape, leave without notice. [It. *scappare.*]

scarred, scarring, scarry. See **scar**[1,2].

scat[1] *skat*, *interj* be off! — *vt* to scare away.

scat[2] *skat*, *n* singing a melody to nonsense syllables. — Also *vt* and *vi.* [Perh. imit.]

scathe *skādh*, (usu. in *neg*) *vt* to injure; to blast; to scorch with invective. — *adj* **scathe'less** without injury. — *adj* **scath'ing.** — *adv* **scath'ingly.** [O.N. *skathe*, injury.]

scatology *ska-tol'ə-ji*, *n* the study of excrement, esp. in order to assess diet; a morbid interest in excrement or with obscene literature referring to it; such literature. — *adj* **scatolog'ical.** [Gr. *skōr, skatos*, dung.]

scatophagy *ska-to'fə-ji*, *n* the practice of feeding on dung. — *adj* **scato'phagous.** [Gr. *skōr, skatos*, dung, and *phagein*, to eat.]

scatter *skat'ər*, *vt* to disperse; to throw loosely about; to strew; to sprinkle; to dispel; to reflect or disperse irregularly (waves or particles). — *vi* to disperse; to throw shot loosely. — *n* a scattering; a sprinkling; dispersion; the extent of scattering. — *adj* **scatt'ered** dispersed irregularly, widely, in all directions, or here and there; thrown about; (of one's thoughts, etc.) distracted. — *adv* **scatt'eredly** (*-ərd-li*). — *n* **scatt'erer.** — *n* **scatt'ering** dispersion; that which is scattered; a small proportion occurring sporadically; the deflection of photons or particles as a result of collisions with other particles (*phys*). — *adv* **scatt'eringly.** — *adj* **scatt'ery.** — **scatt'erbrain** someone incapable of sustained attention or thought. — *adj* **scatt'erbrained.** — **scatt'er-gun** (*US*) a shotgun; **scatter rugs** and **cushions** small rugs and cushions which can be placed anywhere in the room. — *adj* **scatt'ershot** random, indiscriminate, wide-ranging, like shot from a gun. — **elastic** and **inelastic scattering** see **elastic** and **inelastic collision** under **collide.**

scatty *skat'i*, (*colloq*) *adj* slightly crazy and unpredictable in conduct. — *n* **scatt'iness.** [Poss. *scatter*brain.]

scauper or **scorper** *skö'pər*, *n* a tool with semicircular face, used by engravers. [**scalper**[2].]

scaur. See **scar**[2].

scavenge *skav'inj* or *-inzh*, *vi* to act as scavenger; to search (for useful items) among refuse. — *vt* to cleanse, to remove impurities from (a substance) (*chem*). — *n* the sweeping out of waste gases from an internal-combustion engine. — *n* **scav'enger** (*-jər*) a person who searches for and gathers discarded items, from garbage bins, etc.; a person or apparatus that removes waste; an animal that feeds on garbage or carrion; a person who deals or delights in filth. — *n* **scav'engery.** — *n* **scav'enging.** [A.Fr. *scawage*, inspection.]

scawtite *skö'tīt*, *n* a carbonate or silicate of calcium, occurring naturally as small colourless crystals. [*Scawt* Hill, C. Antrim, where it is found.]

ScB *abbrev* for *Scientiae Baccalaureus* (L.), Bachelor of Science.

SCCL *abbrev* for Scottish Council for Civil Liberties.

ScD *abbrev* for *Scientiae Doctor* (L.), Doctor of Science.

SCE *abbrev* for Scottish Certificate of Education.

scena *shā'na*, *n* an operatic scene; an elaborate dramatic recitative followed by an aria: — *pl* **scene** (*shā'nā*). [It., — L. *scēna.*]

scenario *si-, se-* or *shā-nä'ri-ō*, *n* a skeleton of a dramatic work, film, etc., scene by scene; an outline of future development, or of a plan to be followed; (loosely) any imagined or projected sequence of events, etc.: — *pl* **scena'rios.** [**scena.**]

scend. See **send.**

scene *sēn*, *n* the place of action in a play (hence in a story, an actual occurrence, etc.); its representation on the stage; a painted slide, hanging, or other object, used for this purpose; a division of a play marked off by the fall of the curtain, by a change of place, or by the entry or exit of an important character; an episode; a dramatic or stagy incident, esp. an uncomfortable, untimely, or unseemly display of hot feelings; a landscape, picture of a place or action; a view or spectacle; the activity, publicity, etc. surrounding a particular business or profession, e.g. *the pop music scene* (*colloq*); area of interest or activity (*colloq*); a situation, state of affairs (*colloq*). — *vt* to set in a scene. — *n* **scēn'ery** theatrical slides, hangings, etc. collectively; views of beautiful, picturesque or impressive country. — *adj* **scenic** (*sē'nik* or *sen'ik*) pertaining to scenery; having beautiful or remarkable scenery. — *adv* **scen'ically.** — *adj* **scēnograph'ic** or **scēnograph'ical.** — *adv* **scēnograph'ically.** — *n* **scēnog'raphy** perspective drawing; scene-painting. — **scene dock** or **bay** the space where scenery is stored; **scene'-man** a scene-shifter; **scene-of-crime officer** a police officer responsible for gathering evidence at the scene of a crime; **scene'-painter** a person who paints scenery for theatres; **scene'-shifter** a person who sets and removes the scenery in a theatre; **scenic railway** a railway on a small scale, running through artificial representations of picturesque scenery; a roller-coaster. — **behind the scenes** at the back of the visible stage; away from the public view (*lit* and *fig*); in a position to know what goes on; **come on the scene** to arrive; **set the scene** to describe the background to an event, etc. [L. *scēna* — Gr. *skēnē*, a tent, stage building.]

scent *sent*, *vt* to track, find or discern by smell, or as if by smell; to perfume. — *vi* to give forth a smell; to sniff; to smell. — *n* odour; sense of smell; a substance used for the sake of its smell; the smell left by an animal, etc., by which it may be hunted; paper strewn by the pursued in hare and hounds. — *adj* **scent'ed** having a smell, fragrant; impregnated or sprinkled with perfumery. — *n* and *adj* **scent'ing.** — *adj* **scent'less.** — **scent'-bag** a scent-gland; a sachet; a bag of strong-smelling stuff dragged over the ground for a drag-hunt; **scent'-bottle** a small bottle for holding perfume; **scent'-gland** a gland that secretes a substance of distinctive smell, for recognition, attraction, or defence; **scent'-organ** a scent-gland; a smelling organ. — **put (or throw) someone off the scent** to mislead someone. [Fr. *sentir* — L. *sentīre*, to perceive.]

scepsis or (esp. in U.S.) **skepsis** *skep'sis*, *n* philosophic doubt. [Gr.; see **sceptic**.]

sceptic or (esp. in U.S.) **skeptic** *skep'tik*, *n* a person who doubts prevailing doctrines, esp. in religion; a person who tends to disbelieve; a sceptic philosopher. — *adj* pertaining to the ancient Greek philosophical school of Pyrrho and his successors, who asserted nothing positively and doubted the possibility of knowledge. — *adj* **scep'tical** of or inclined to scepticism; doubtful, or inclined towards incredulity. — *adv* **scep'tically** or (esp. *US*) **skep'tically.** — *n* **scep'ticism** or (esp. *US*) **skep'ticism** doubt; the doctrine that no facts can be certainly known; agnosticism; sceptical attitude towards Christianity; general disposition to doubt. [L. *scepticus* — Gr. *skeptikos*, thoughtful, *skeptesthai*, to consider.]

sceptre *sep'tər*, *n* a staff or baton carried as an emblem of kingship. — *adj* **scep'tral** regal. — *adj* **scep'tred** bearing a sceptre; regal. — *adj* **scep'treless.** [L. *scēptrum* — Gr. *skēptron*, a staff — *skēptein*, to prop, stay.]

SCF *abbrev* for Save the Children Fund.

Sch. *abbrev* for: schilling (q.v.); school.

schadenfreude *shä'dən-froi-də*, *n* pleasure in others' misfortunes. [Ger., — *Schade*, hurt, *Freude*, joy.]

schappe *shap'ə*, *n* a fabric of waste silk with gum, etc., partly removed by fermentation. — *vt* to subject to this process. [Swiss Ger.]

schechita, shechita, shehita, or **-tah**, *she-hēt'a*, (*Judaism*) *n* the slaughtering of animals in accordance with rabbinical law. [Heb. *shěhītāh*, slaughter.]

schedule *shed'ūl* or (esp. in U.S.) *sked'ūl*, *n* a slip or scroll with writing; a list, inventory, or table; a supplementary, explanatory, or appended document; an appendix to a bill or act of parliament; a form for filling in particulars, or such a form filled in; a timetable, plan, programme or scheme. — *vt* to set as in a schedule; to plan, appoint, arrange. — *adj* **sched'uled** entered in a schedule; planned, appointed, arranged (to happen at a specified time). — **scheduled castes** (in India) the former untouchables; **scheduled territories** sterling area; **scheduled tribes** (in India) aboriginal tribes officially given some protection and privileges. — **behind schedule** not keeping up to an arranged programme; late; **on schedule** on time. [O.Fr. *cedule* — L.L. *sc(h)edula*, dimin. of *scheda*, a strip of papyrus.]

scheelite *shē'līt*, *n* native calcium tungstate. [From the Swedish chemist K.W. *Scheele* (1742–86).]

schefflera *shef'lə-rə*, *n* any of various evergreen tropical or sub-tropical shrubs of the family *Auraliceae*, having large compound leaves and clusters of small flowers followed by berries.

schema *skē'mə*, *n* a scheme, plan; a diagrammatic outline or synopsis; the image of the thing with which the imagination aids the understanding in its procedure; a kind of standard which the mind forms from past experiences, and by which new experiences can be evaluated to a certain extent: — *pl* **schē'mata.** — *adj* **schematic** (*ski-mat'ik*) or **schemat'ical** following, or involving, a particular plan or arrangement; representing something by a diagram, plan, etc. — *adv* **schemat'ically.** — *n* **schematisā'tion** or **-z-.** — *vt* **schē'matise** or **-ize** to reduce to or represent by a scheme. — *n* **schē'matism** form or outline of a thing; arrangement, disposition in a scheme. — *n* **schē'matist.** [Gr. *schēma*, *-atos*, form, from the reduced grade of the root of *echein*, to have.]

scheme *skēm*, *n* a plan of purposed action for achieving an end; a plan for building operations of various kinds, or the buildings etc. constructed, or the area covered (e.g. *housing scheme*, *irrigation scheme*); a plan pursued secretly, insidiously, by intrigue, or for private ends; a project; a programme of action; a system; a diagram or table; a diagram of positions, esp. (*astrol*) of planets. — *vt* to plan; to lay schemes for. — *vi* to form a plan; to lay schemes. — *n* **schē'mer.** — *n* and *adj* **schē'ming.** [**schema**.]

Schengen agreement *sheng'gən a-grē'mənt*, *n* an agreement between France, Germany, Belgium, Luxembourg and the Netherlands to remove all border controls between these countries and to exchange information on criminal activities, etc. [From the Luxembourg village of *Schengen*, where the agreement was first discussed.]

scherzo *sker'tsō* or *skûr'tsō*, (*mus*) *n* a lively busy movement in triple time, usually with a trio, in a sonata or a symphony: — *pl* **scher'zos** or **scher'zi** (*-ē*). — *adj* and *adv* **scherzan'do** with playfulness. — *n* a scherzando passage or movement: — *pl* **scherzan'dos** or **scherzan'di** (*-ē*). [It., — Gmc.]

Schick test *shik test* or **Schick's test** (*shiks*), *n* a test for susceptibility to diphtheria, made by injecting the skin with a measured amount of diphtheria toxin. [From Bela *Schick* (1877–1967), U.S. doctor.]

schilling *shil'ing*, *n* the Austrian standard monetary unit (100 *groschen*). [Ger.; cf. **shilling**.]

schipperke *skip'ər-kə* or *-ki*, also *ship'*, *n* a small tailless breed of dogs (orig. watchdogs on barges). [Du., little boatman.]

schism *sizm* or *skizm*, *n* a breach, esp. in the unity of a church; promotion of such a breach; a body so formed. — *n* **schismatic** (*siz-mat'ik* or *skiz-*) a person who favours a schism or belongs to a schismatic body. — *adj* **schismat'ic** or **schismat'ical.** — *adv* **schismat'ically.** — *n* **schismat'icalness.** — **great Eastern** (or **Greek**) **schism** the separation of the Greek church from the Latin, finally completed in 1054; **(great) Western schism** the division in the Western church from 1378 to 1417, when there were antipopes under French influence at Avignon. [Gr. *schisma*, a split, rent, cleft, partly through O.Fr. (*s*)*cisme*.]

schist *shist*, *n* any crystalline foliated metamorphic rock such as mica-schist, hornblende-schist; sometimes extended to shaly rocks. — *adj* **schist'ose.** [Fr. *schiste* — Gr. *schistos*, split; pronunciation due to German influence.]

Schistosoma *shis-tə-sō'mə* or *skis-*, *n* the Bilharzia genus. — *n* **schis'tosome** a member of the genus. — *n* **schistosomī'asis** the disease bilharzia. [Gr. *schistos*, split.]

schizo- *skits-ō-* or *skīz-ō-*, or before a vowel **schiz-** *skiz-*, *combining form* signifying division, split. — *n* **schizanthus** (*-an'thəs*) a showy Chilean plant (genus *Schizanthus*). — *adj* **schizo-affect'ive** marked by symptoms of schizophrenia and manic-depressiveness. — *n* **schiz'ocarp** (*-kärp*) a dry fruit that splits into several one-seeded portions. — *adj* **schizocar'pous** or **schizocar'pic.** — *adj* **schizognathous** (*-og'nə-thəs*) of some birds, having the bones of the palate separate. — *n* **schizoid** (*skits'oid*) showing qualities of a schizophrenic personality, such as asocial behaviour, introversion, tendency to fantasy, but without definite mental disorder. — *n* a schizoid person. — *adj* **schizoid'al.** — *npl* **Schizomycetes** (*-mī-sē'tēz*) a class of micro-organisms which includes the bacteria: — *sing* **schizomy'cete** (*-sēt*). — *adj* **schizomycet'ic** or **schizomycē'tous.** — *n* **schizophrenia** (*-frē'ni-ə*) a psychosis marked by introversion, dissociation, inability to distinguish reality from unreality, delusions, etc. — *adj* **schizophrenic** (*-fren'ik*). — *n* **schizothymia** (*-thī'mi-ə*) manifestation of schizoid traits within normal limits. — *adj* **schizothy'mic.** [Gr. *schizein*, to split, cleave.]

schlemiel, schlemihl or **shlemiel** *shlə-mēl'*, (*slang*) *n* a clumsy or unlucky person. [Yiddish.]

schlep or **shlep** *shlep*, (*slang*) *vt* to pull, drag: — *pr p* **schlepp'ing** or **shlepp'ing**; *pa t* and *pa p* **schlepped** or **shlepped.** — *n* a clumsy, stupid, incompetent person. — *adj* **schlepp'y.** [Yiddish.]

schlieren *shlē'rən*, *npl* streaks of different colour, structure or composition in igneous rocks; streaks in a transparent fluid, caused by the differing refractive indices of fluid of varying density. — **schlieren photography** the technique of photographing a flow of air or other gas, the variations in refractive index according to density being made apparent under a special type of illumination. [Ger.]

schlimazel or **shlimazel** *shli-mä'zl*, (*US slang*) *n* a persistently unlucky person. [Yiddish; see **shemozzle.**]

schlock or **shlok** *shlok'*, (*US slang*) *adj* of inferior quality. — *n* (also **schlock'er**) a thing or things of inferior quality. [Yiddish.]

schloss *shlos*, *n* a castle, palace, manor house. [Ger.]

schmaltz *shmölts* or *shmälts*, *n* a production in music or other art that is very sentimental, or showy; sentimentality; mush; fat (esp. chicken) used in cooking. — *adj* **schmaltz'y** old-fashioned, old-style, outmoded; sentimental. [Yiddish — Ger. *Schmalz*, cooking fat, grease.]

schmuck *shmuk* or **schmock** *shmok*, (*US slang*) *n* a stupid person. [Yiddish.]

schmutter *shmut'ər*, (*slang*) *n* clothing; rag. [Yiddish *schmatte*, rag.]

schnapper *shnap'ər*. Same as **snapper** (Australian fish). [Germanised.]

schnapps or **schnaps** *shnaps*, *n* any of various spirits, esp. Hollands. [Ger. *Schnapps*, a dram.]

schnauzer *shnowt'sər*, *n* a German breed of wire-haired terrier. [Ger. *Schnauze*, snout.]

schnitzel *shnit'sl*, *n* a veal cutlet. [Ger.]

schnorkel *shnör'kl* or **snorkel** *snör'kl*, *n* a retractable tube or tubes containing pipes for discharging gases from, or for taking air into, a submerged submarine; a tube for bringing air to a submerged swimmer. [Ger., *Schnörkel*, a spiral ornament.]

schnorrer *shnō'* or *shno'rər*, (*US slang*) *n* a beggar. — *vi* **schnorr** (*shnōr*) to beg, esp. in such a way as to make the giver feel in some way beholden. [Yiddish.]

schnozzle *shnoz'əl*, (*slang*) *n* nose. [Yiddish.]

scholar *skol'ər*, *n* a pupil; a disciple; a student; (in times of less widespread education) someone who could read and write, or an educated person; a person whose learning (formerly esp. in Latin and Greek) is extensive and exact, or whose approach to learning is scrupulous and critical; a holder of a scholarship. — *n* **schol'arliness.** — *adj* **schol'arly** of or natural to a scholar; having the learning of a scholar. — *n* **schol'arship** scholarly learning; a foundation or grant for the maintenance of a pupil or student; the status and emoluments of such a pupil or student. — **scholar's mate** (*chess*) a simple mate accomplished in four moves. [O.E. *scōlere*, and (in part) O.Fr. *escoler*, both from L.L. *scholāris* — *schola*; see **school**[1].]

scholastic *skol-* or *skəl-as'tik*, *adj* pertaining to schools or universities, to their staffs or teaching, or to schoolmen; subtle; pedantic. — *n* a schoolman, a person who adheres to the method or subtleties of the Mediaeval schools; a Jesuit who has taken first vows only; a university teacher (esp. with implication of pedantry). — *adv* **scholas'tically.** — *n* **scholas'ticism** (*-sizm*) the aims, methods and products of thought which constituted the main endeavour of the intellectual life of the Middle Ages; the method or subtleties of the schools of philosophy; the collected body of doctrines of the schoolmen. [Gr. *scholastikos* — *scholē*; see **school**[1].]

scholion *skō'li-on* or **scholium** *skō'li-əm*, *n* an explanatory note, such as certain ancient grammarians wrote on passages in manuscripts; often in *pl* **scho'lia.** — *n* **scho'liast** a writer of scholia. — *adj* **scholias'tic.** [Gr. *schŏlion* (N.L. *scholium*), *schŏliastēs* — *schŏlē*; see **school**[1].]

school[1] *skōōl*, *n* a place for instruction; an institution for education, esp. primary or secondary, or for teaching of special subjects; a division of such an institution; a building or room used for that purpose; the work of a school; the time given to it; the body of pupils of a school; the disciples of a particular teacher; those who hold a common doctrine or follow a common tradition; a group of people meeting in order to play card games, usu. for money (*slang*); a method of instruction; the body of instructors and students in a university, or department; a group of studies in which honours may be taken; (in Oxford, in *pl*) the BA examinations. — *adj* of school, schools, or the schools. — *vt* to educate in a school; to train, to drill; to instruct; to coach in a part to be played; to teach overbearingly; to discipline. — *adj* **schooled** trained; experienced. — *n* **school'ing** instruction or maintenance at school; tuition; training; discipline. — *adj* and *adv* **school'ward.** — *adv* **school'wards.** — **school age** the age at which children attend school. — *adj* **school'-age.** — **school'bag** a bag for carrying school-books; **school'-book** a book used in school; **school'boy** a boy attending school. — Also *adj.* — *adj* **school'-boyish.** — **school'child**; **school'-day** a day on which schools are open; (in *pl*) time of being a school pupil; **school'-divine**; **school-divin'ity** scholastic or seminary theology; **school'fellow** someone taught at the same school at the same time; **school'-friend** someone who is or has been a friend at school; **school'girl** a girl attending school. — Also *adj.* — *adj* **school'girlish.** — **school'house** a building used as a school; a house provided for a school-teacher (**school house** a headmaster's or headmistress's boarding-house; its boarders); **school'-inspector** an official appointed to examine schools; **school'-leaver** someone who is leaving school because he or she has reached the statutory age, or the stage, for doing so. — *n* and *adj* **school'-leaving.** — **school'-ma'am** a school-marm; **school'man** a philosopher or theologian of mediaeval scholasticism; **school'-marm** (*colloq*; a form of **school-**

ma'am) a schoolmistress (*US*); a prim pedantic woman (*colloq*). — *adj* **school'-marmish**. — **school'master** the master or one of the masters of a school. — Also *vt* and *vi*. — *n* and *adj* **school'-mastering**. — *adj* **school'masterish** or **school'-masterly**. — **school'mastership; school'-mate** a school-friend; a schoolfellow; **school'mistress; school nurse** a person employed to visit schools and promote children's health through screening procedures, immunisation, etc.; **school phobia** an irrational fear of attending school; **school'room** a school classroom; (in a house) a room for receiving or preparing lessons in; **school ship** a training-ship; **school'teacher** a person who teaches in a school; **school'teaching; school term** a division of the school year; **school'-time** the time at which a school opens, or during which it remains open; school-days; **school'-work; school year** the period of (more or less) continual teaching during the year comprising an academic unit during which a child or student remains in the same basic class, i.e., in Britain, from autumn to early summer. — **old school** see **old**. [O.E. *scōl* — L. *schŏla* — Gr. *schŏlē*, leisure, a lecture, a school.]

school[2] *skōōl*, *n* a shoal of fish, whales or other swimming animals; a flock, troop or assemblage (esp. of birds). — *vi* to gather or go in schools. — *adj* going in schools. — *n* and *adj* **school'ing**. [Du. *school*; cf. **shoal**[1].]

schooner *skōōn'ər*, *n* a swift-sailing vessel, generally two-masted, fore-and-aft rigged, or with top and top-gallant sails on the foremast; a large beer glass (esp. *US* and *Austr*); also a large sherry glass. — *adj* **schoon'er-rigged**. [Early 18th-century *skooner*, *scooner*, said to be from a dialect Eng. word *scoon*, to skim.]

schorl *shörl*, *n* black tourmaline. [Ger. *Schörl*.]

schottische *sho-tēsh'*, *n* a dance, or dance-tune, similar to the polka. [Ger. *der schottische Tanz*, the Scottish dance; pronunciation sham French.]

schtook, schtuck. See **shtook**.

schtoom. See **shtoom**.

schuss *shŏŏs*, (*skiing*) *n* a straight slope on which it is possible to make a fast run; such a run. — *vi* to make such a run. [Ger.]

schwa or **shwa** *shwä*, (*phon*) *n* an indistinct vowel sound; a neutral vowel (ə). — Cf. **sheva**. [Ger., — Heb. *schĕwa*.]

Schwann cell *shvan sel*, (*zool*) *n* a large nucleated cell that produces myelin in peripheral nerve fibres. [Theodor *Schwann* (1810–82), German physiologist.]

scia- *sī'-ə-* or *sī-a'-* or **skia-** *skī'-ə-* or *skī-a'-*, *combining form* denoting shadow. For various words see under **skia-**.

sciatic *sī-at'ik*, *adj* of, or in the region of, the hip. — *n* **sciat'ica** neuritis of the great sciatic nerve which passes down the back of the thigh. [L.L. *sciaticus*, fem. *-a* — Gr. *ischion*, hip-joint.]

science *sī'əns*, *n* knowledge ascertained by observation and experiment, critically tested, systematised and brought under general principles; a department or branch of such knowledge or study. — *adj* **sciential** (*-en'shl*) of, having or producing science; scientific. — *adj* **scientif'ic** of, relating to, based on, devoted to, according to, used in, or versed in, science. — *adv* **scientif'ically**. — *vt* **sci'entise** or **-ize** to treat in a scientific way. — *n* **sci'entism** the methods or mental attitudes of men of science; a belief that the methods used in studying natural sciences should be employed also in investigating all aspects of human behaviour and condition, e.g. in philosophy and social sciences. — *n* **sci'entist** a person who studies or practises any science, esp. natural science. — *adj* **scientis'tic**. — *n* **Scientol'ogist**. — *n* **Scientol'ogy**® a religious system founded in 1952 by L. Ron Hubbard which, it is claimed, improves the mental and physical well-being of its adherents by scientific means. — **science fiction** fiction dealing with life on the earth in future, with space or time travel, and with life on other planets, or the like; **science park** a centre for industrial research, etc., attached to a university, set up for the purpose of co-operation between the academic and the commercial world; **scientific whaling** whaling carried out actually or ostensibly for the purposes of research. [L. *scientia* — *sciēns*, *-entis*, pres. p. of *scīre*, to know.]

scienter *sī-en'tər*, (*legal*) *adv* having knowledge, being aware; wilfully. [L.]

sci-fi *sī'-fī*, (*colloq*) *n* short for **science fiction**.

scilicet *sī'li-set* or *skē'li-ket*, *adv* to wit, namely (abbrev. **scil**. or **sciz**.). [L. *scīlicet* — *scīre licet*, it is permitted to know.]

scilla *sil'ə*, *n* the squill genus (*Scilla*) of the lily family, including some bright blue spring flowers. [L., — Gr. *skilla*, the officinal squill.]

Scillonian *si-lō'ni-ən*, *adj* of, belonging to or concerning, the *Scilly* Isles, off the south-west coast of Britain. — *n* an inhabitant of these islands.

scimitar *sim'i-tər*, *n* a short, single-edged, curved sword, broadest at the point end, used by the Turks and Persians.

scintigraphy *sin-tig'rə-fi*, *n* a diagnostic technique in which a pictorial record of the pattern of gamma ray emission after injection of isotope into the body gives a picture of an internal organ. — *n* **scin'tigram** a picture so produced. [*scint*illation.]

scintillate *sin'til-āt*, *vi* to sparkle; to talk wittily. — *vt* to emit in sparks; to sparkle with. — *adj* **scin'tillating** brilliant, sparkling; full of interest or wit. — *n* **scintillā'tion** a flash of light produced in a phosphor by an ionising particle, e.g. an alpha particle, or a photon. — *n* **scin'tillātor** an instrument for detecting radioactivity. — *n* **scintillom'eter** an instrument for detecting and measuring radioactivity. — *n* **scintill'oscope** an instrument which shows scintillations on a screen. — **scintillation counter** a scintillometer. [L. *scintilla*, a spark.]

scio-. For various words see **skia-**.

sciolism *sī'ə-lizm*, *n* superficial pretensions to knowledge. — *n* **sci'olist** a pretender to science. — *adj* **sciolis'tic** or **sci'olous**. [L. *sciolus*, dimin. of *scius*, knowing — *scīre*, to know.]

scion *sī'ən*, *n* a detached piece of a plant capable of propagating, esp. by grafting; a young member of a family; a descendant, offshoot. [O.Fr. *sion*, *cion*.]

scire facias *sī'ri fā'shi-as* or *skē're fa'ki-äs*, (*law*) *n* a writ requiring a person to appear and show cause why a record should not be enforced or annulled. [L. *scīre faciās*, make him to know.]

scirocco. See **sirocco**.

scirrhus *skir'əs* or *sir'əs*, (*med*) *n* a hard swelling; a hard cancer. — *adj* **scirr'hoid** or **scirr'hous**. [Latinised from Gr. *skirros*, *skīros*, a tumour.]

scissel *sis'l*, *n* metal clippings; scrap left when blanks have been cut out. [O.Fr. *cisaille* — *ciseler* — *cisel*, a chisel; for the spelling cf. ety. for **scissors**.]

scissile *sis'īl*, *adj* capable of being cut; readily splitting. — *n* **scission** (*sish'ən* or *sizh'ən*) cutting; division; splitting; schism. [L. *scissilis*, *scissiō*, *-ōnis* — *scindĕre*, *scissum*, to cut, to split, cleave.]

scissors *siz'ərz*, *npl* a cutting instrument with two blades pivoted to close together and overlap — smaller than shears; a position or movement like that of scissors; movement of the legs suggesting opening and closing of scissors (*gymnastics*); locking the legs round body or head of an opponent (*wrestling*); a style of high jump in which the leg nearest the bar leads throughout; a pass in Rugby football from one running player to another who is crossing his or her path. — *vt* **sciss'or** to cut with scissors. — *adv* **sciss'orwise**. — **sciss'or-bill** a skimmer;

scissors-and-paste' literary or journalistic matter collected from various sources with little or no original writing. — Also *adj*. — **sciss'ortail** an American flycatcher; **sciss'or-tooth** a usu. long, large tooth in a carnivore, used for tearing flesh. [O.Fr. *cisoires* — L.L. *cīsōrium*, a cutting instrument — *caedĕre*, *caesum*, to cut; the spelling *sc-* is due to erroneous association with *scindĕre*, *scissum*.]

Sciurus *sī-ū'rəs*, *n* the squirrel genus, giving name to the family **Sciu'ridae**. — *adj* **sciurine** (*sī-ūr'īn*, or *sī'*). — *n* **sciuroid** (*-ū'*). [L. *sciūrus* — Gr. *skiouros* — *skiā*, shadow, *ourā*, tail.]

sciz. See under **scilicet**.

SCL *abbrev* for Student of Civil Law.

sclera *sklē'rə*, *n* the outermost membrane of the eyeball. — *adj* **sclē'ral**. — *n* **sclerenchyma** (*sklər-eng'ki-mə*; Gr. *enchyma*, in-filling) plant tissue with thick, lignified cell-walls; hard skeletal tissue, as in corals. — *adj* **sclerenchymatous** (*skler-eng-kim'ə-təs*). — *n* **scleroder'mal** or **scleroder'mia** hardness and rigidity of skin by substitution of fibrous tissue for subcutaneous fat. — *adj* **scleroder'mic** or **scleroder'mous** hard-skinned. — *adj* **sclē'roid** (*bot* and *zool*) hard; hardened. — *n* **sclerō'ma** hardening; morbid hardening; formation of nodules in the nose, etc. — *n* **sclerom'eter** an instrument for measuring the hardness of minerals. — *n* **sclerophyll** (*sklēr'ō-fil*) a hard, stiff leaf. — *adj* **sclerophyll'ous**. — *n* **scleroprō'tein** insoluble protein forming the skeletal parts of tissues. — *vt* **sclerose** (*sklər-ōs'* or *sklēr'ōs*) to harden; to affect with sclerosis. — *vi* to become sclerotic. — *n* **sclerosis** (*sklər-ō'sis*) hardening; morbid hardening, as of arteries (*med*); hardening of tissue by thickening or lignification (*bot*). — *adj* **sclerot'ic** hard, firm, applied esp. to the outer membrane of the eyeball; of sclerosis; sclerosed. — *n* the sclera. — *n* **sclerotī'tis** (*skler-* or *sklēr-*) inflammation of the sclera. — *n* **sclerot'omy** (*med*) incision into the sclera. — *adj* **sclē'rous** hard or indurated; ossified or bony. — **disseminated (or multiple) sclerosis** see under **disseminate**. [Gr. *sklēros*, hard.]

scliff or **skliff** *sklif*, (*Scot*) *n* a small segment or piece. [Imit.]

SCM *abbrev* for: State Certified Midwife; Student Christian Movement.

SCODA *skō'də*, *abbrev* for Standing Conference on Drug Abuse.

scoff[1] *skof*, *n* mockery; a jibe, jeer; an object of derision. — *vi* to jeer (with *at*). — *n* **scoff'er**. — *n* and *adj* **scoff'ing**. — *adv* **scoff'ingly**. [Cf. obs. Dan. *skof*, jest, mockery, O.Fris. *schof*.]

scoff[2] *skof*, (*dialect* and *slang*) *vt* to devour. — *vi* to feed quickly or greedily. — *n* food; a meal. [App. Scots *scaff*, food, reinforced from S. Africa by Du. *schoft*, a meal.]

scofflaw *skof'lö*, (*US colloq*) *n* a person who is contemptuous of the law. [**scoff**[1] and **law**[1].]

scold *skōld*, *n* a rude clamorous woman or other person; a scolding. — *vi* to brawl; to vituperate; to find fault vehemently or at some length. — *vt* to chide; to rebuke. — *n* **scold'er**. — *n* and *adj* **scold'ing**. [App. O.N. *skāld*, poet (through an intermediate sense, lampooner).]

scolex *skō'leks*, *n* a tapeworm head: — *pl* **scoleces** (*skō-lē'sēz*; erroneously **scō'lices**). — *adj* **scōlecoid** (*-lē'koid*) like a scolex. [Gr. *skolēx*, *-ēkos*, a worm.]

scoliosis *skol-i-ō'sis*, (*pathol*) *n* lateral spinal curvature. — Also **scoliom'a**. — *adj* **scoliotic** (*-ot'ik*). [Gr. *skoliōsis*, obliquity.]

scollop. Same as **scallop**.

scomber *skom'bər*, *n* any member of the *Scombroidea*, a family of spiny-finned marine fish, which includes the mackerel, tunny and swordfish. — *adj* **scom'brid** or **scom'broid**. [L. *scomber* — Gr. *skombros*, a mackerel.]

sconce[1] *skons*, *n* a small fort or earthwork; a shelter. [Du. *schans*.]

sconce[2] *skons*, *n* a candlestick or lantern with a handle; a bracket candlestick; a street wall-lamp. [O.Fr. *esconse* — L.L. *absconsa*, a dark lantern — *abscondĕre*, to hide.]

scone *skon*, in the South of England often pronounced *skōn*, (orig. *Scot*) *n* a flattish, usually round or quadrant-shaped plain cake of dough without much fat, with or without currants, baked on a griddle or in an oven. [Perh. from Du. *schoon* (*brot*), fine (bread).]

SCONUL *skō'nəl* or *-nŏŏl*, *abbrev* for Standing Conference of National and University Libraries.

scoop *skōōp*, *n* a bailing-vessel; a concave shovel or lipped vessel for skimming or shovelling up loose material; an instrument for gouging out apple-cores, samples of cheese, etc.; anything of similar shape; an act of scooping; a sweeping stroke; a scooped-out place; anything got by or as if by scooping, a haul; the forestalling of other newspapers in obtaining a piece of news; an item of news so secured (also *adj*). — *vt* to bail out; to lift, obtain, remove, hollow, or make with, or as if with, a scoop; to secure in advance of or to the exclusion of others. — *adj* **scooped**. — *n* **scoop'er**. — *n* **scoop'ful**: — *pl* **scoop'fuls**. — *n* **scoop'ing**. — *adj* **scooped'-out**. — **scoop neck** a low rounded neckline; **scoop'-net** a long-handled dipping net; a net for scooping along the bottom. [Prob. partly M.L.G. or M.Du. *schôpe*, bailing-vessel, partly M.Du. *schoppe*, shovel.]

scoot *skōōt*, *vi* and *vt* to make off speedily (*colloq*); to travel on a scooter (*colloq*). — *vt* to propel by kicking the ground. — *n* an act of scooting. — *n* **scoot'er** a child's toy, a wheeled footboard with steering handle, propelled by kicking the ground; a small-wheeled motorcycle with a protective front fairing (also **mo'tor-scooter**); a boat for sailing on ice and water (*US*). [Prob. from O.N., related to **shoot**.]

scopa *skō'pə*, *n* a bee's pollen-brush: — *pl* **sco'pae** (*-pē*). — *adj* **scō'pate** tufted. — *n* **scopula** (*skop'ū-lə*; *entom*) a little tuft of hairs. — *adj* **scop'ulate**. [L. *scōpae*, twigs, a broom.]

scope[1] *skōp*, *n* point aimed at; aim; range; field or opportunity of activity; room for action; potential or natural ability; spaciousness; length of cable at which a vessel rides at liberty. [It. *scopo* — Gr. *skopos*, watcher, point watched, (*fig*) aim — *skopeein*, to view.]

scope[2] *skōp*, *n* short for **microscope**, **telescope**, **horoscope**, etc.; a visual display unit, esp. a radar screen. — *vt* to examine the internal organs with a viewing instrument.

-scope *-skōp*, *combining form* denoting an instrument for viewing, examining or detecting, as in *telescope*, *oscilloscope*, *stethoscope*. [Gr. *skopeein*, to view.]

scopolamine *sko-pol'ə-mēn*, *n* an alkaloid derived from the genus **Scopolia** and other plants (see **hyoscine** under **Hyoscyamus**) with sedative properties, used e.g. to prevent travel sickness and as a truth drug. [Named after *Scopoli* (1723–88), Italian naturalist; and **amine**.]

scopula, scopulate. See under **scopa**.

-scopy *-skə-pi*, *combining form* indicating viewing, examining or observing, as in *autoscopy*, *poroscopy*, *ornithoscopy*. [Gr. *skopeein*, to view.]

scorbutic *skör-bū'tik*, *adj* of, like, of the nature of, or affected with, scurvy. [L.L. *scorbūticus*, poss. from M.L.G. *schorbuk*, scurvy.]

scorch *skörch*, *vt* to burn slightly or superficially; to parch; to dry up, wither, or affect painfully or injuriously by heat or as if by heat; to wither with scorn, censure, etc. — *vi* to be burned on the surface; to be dried up; to cycle or drive furiously (*colloq*). — *n* an act of scorching; damage or an injury by scorching. — *adj* **scorched**. — *n* **scorch'er** a person who or thing which scorches; a day of scorching heat (*colloq*). — *n*, *adj* and *adv* **scorch'ing**. — *adv*

scorch'ingly. — *n* **scorch'ingness**. — **scorched earth** country devastated before evacuation so as to be useless to an advancing enemy; **scorched-earth policy**. [Perh. M.E. *skorken*; cf. O.N. *skorpna*, to shrivel.]

scordato *skör-dä'tō*, (*mus*) *adj* put out of tune. — *n* **scordatura** (*-tōō'rə*) a temporary departure from normal tuning. [It.]

score *skör*, *n* a notch, gash or scratch; an incised line; a boldly drawn line, esp. one marking a deletion; a line marking a boundary, starting-place, or defined position; an arrangement of music on a number of staves (perh. orig. with the bar divisions running continuously through all); a composition so distributed; a notch in a tally; an account of charges incurred; a debt incurred; a reckoning, account; the total or record of points made in a game; an addition made thereto; a set of twenty (sometimes verging upon numeral *adj*); applied also to an indefinitely large number. — *vt* to mark with or by scores; to record in or with a score; to make a score through as a mark of deletion (with *out*); to write in score; to distribute among the instruments of the orchestra; to make as a score; to add to a score; to achieve; to enumerate; to record. — *vi* to make a point; to achieve a success; to be worth a certain number of points; (of a man) to achieve sexual intercourse (*slang*); to obtain drugs (*slang*). — *n* **scor'er** a person who or thing that scores; someone who keeps the marks in a game. — *n* **scor'ing**. — **score'-board** or **scor'ing-board** a board on which the score is exhibited, as at cricket; **score'-card**, **scor'ing-card** or **score'-sheet** a card or sheet, for recording the score in a game; **score'-draw** (esp. *football*) a drawn result other than nil all; **score'line** a score in a match, etc. — **know the score** to know the hard facts of the situation; **on that score** as regards that matter; **pay off (or settle) old scores** to repay old grudges; **score an own goal** (*colloq*) to do something unintentionally to one's own disadvantage; **score off** or **score points off** (*colloq*) to achieve a success against, get the better of. [Late O.E. *scoru* — O.N. *skor*, *skora*.]

scoria *skō'ri-ə*, *n* dross or slag from metal-smelting; a piece of lava with steam-holes: — *pl* **sco'riae** (*-ri-ē*). — *adj* **scoriaceous** (*-ri-ā'shəs*). — *n* **scorificā'tion** reduction to scoria; assaying by fusing with lead and borax. — *n* **sco'rifier** a dish used in assaying. — *vt* **sco'rify** to reduce to scoria; to rid metals of (impurities) by forming scoria. — *adj* **sco'rious**. [L., — Gr. *skōriā* — *skōr*, dung.]

scorn *skörn*, *n* hot or extreme contempt. — *vt* to feel or express scorn for; to refuse with scorn. — *n* **scorn'er**. — *adj* **scorn'ful**. — *adv* **scorn'fully**. — *n* **scorn'fulness**. — *n* **scorn'ing**. [O.Fr. *escarn*, mockery; of Gmc. origin.]

scorper. See **scauper**.

Scorpio *skör'pi-ō*, *n* a constellation (the scorpion); a sign of the zodiac; a person born between 24 Oct. and 22 Nov., under the sign of Scorpio. [Ety. as for **scorpion**.]

scorpioid *skör'pi-oid*, *adj* (*zool*) like a scorpion, or a scorpion's curled tail. — *n* (*bot*) inflorescence in which the plane of each daughter axis is at right angles, to right and left alternately, with its parent axis, that of the whole coiled in bud. [Gr. *skorpios*, scorpion, *eidos*, form.]

scorpion *skör'pi-ən*, *n* an arachnid with head and thorax united, pincers, four pairs of legs, and a segmented abdomen including a tail with a sting; a form of scourge (*Bible*); (with *cap*) the constellation or the sign Scorpio (*astron*). — *adj* **scorpion'ic**. — **scorpion fish** any fish of the family *Scorpaenidae*, having venomous spines on the fins; **scorpion fly** an insect of the *Mecoptera* (from the male's upturned abdomen); **scorpion grass** forget-me-not; **scor'pion-spider** a whip-scorpion. [L. *scorpiō*, *-ōnis* — Gr. *skorpios*.]

scorzonera *skör-zō-nē'rə*, *n* a plant like a dandelion, with edible root — black salsify. [It.]

Scot *skot*, *n* a native or inhabitant of Scotland; one of a Gaelic-speaking people of Ireland, afterwards also in Argyllshire (now part of Strathclyde) (*hist*). — *n* **Scotland** (*skot'lənd*) the country forming the northern member of the United Kingdom; Ireland (*hist*). — *n* **Scott'y** or **Scott'ie** a nickname for a Scotsman; a Scotch terrier. — **Scotland Yard** the earliest or (New Scotland Yard) two more recent headquarters (1890 and 1967) of the Metropolitan Police; hence the London Criminal Investigation Department. [O.E. *Scottas* (pl.) — L.L. *Scottus*; see also **Scotch, Scots, Scottish**.]

Scot. *abbrev* for: Scotland; Scottish.

scot *skot*, (*hist*) *n* a payment, esp. a customary tax; a share of a reckoning. — *adj* **scot-free'** free from scot (*hist*); entirely free from expense, injury, etc. [O.E. *scot*, *sceot*.]

Scotch *skoch*, *adj* a form of **Scottish** or **Scots**, disliked by many Scots; applied esp. to products of Scotland; having the character popularly attributed to a Scot — an excessive leaning towards defence of oneself and one's property. — *n* Scotch whisky, or a glass of it; the Scottish (Northern English) dialect; (as *pl*) the Scots collectively. — *n* **Scotch'ness**. — **Scotch bluebell** the harebell; **Scotch broth** broth made with pot-barley and plenty of various vegetables chopped small; **Scotch catch** or **snap** (*mus*) a short accented note followed by a longer; **Scotch collops** minced beef; **Scotch egg** a hard-boiled egg enclosed in sausage-meat; **Scotch fir** Scots pine; **Scotch'man** a Scotsman; **Scotch mist** a fine rain; **Scotch pebble** an agate or similar stone; **Scotch snap** a Scotch catch (see above); **Scotch tape**® a transparent tape, adhering to paper, etc. when pressure is applied; **Scotch terrier** a rough-haired, prick-eared, strongly-built little dog (also **Scottish terrier, Scottie** or **Scotty**); **Scotch verdict** not proven; **Scotch'woman**. [From **Scottish**.]

scotch[1] *skoch*, *vt* to maim, cripple for the time without killing; to frustrate; to quash. — *n* a line marked on the ground (as for hopscotch).

scotch[2] *skoch*, *n* a strut, wedge, block, etc. to prevent turning or slipping, e.g. of a wheel, gate or ladder. — *vt* to stop or block. [Perh. a form of **scratch**.]

scoter *skō'tər*, *n* any of several black or almost-black sea-ducks of the genus *Melanitta*.

scotia *sko'ti-ə* or *-shi-ə*, *n* a hollow moulding, esp. at the base of a column. [Gr. *skŏtiā* — *skotos*, darkness.]

Scoticise, Scoticism, Scotify. See **Scottish**.

Scotism *skō'tizm*, *n* the metaphysical system of Johannes Duns *Scotus* (*c* 1265–1308), who saught the foundation of Christian theology in practice, not in speculation. — *n* **Scō'tist** a follower of Duns Scotus. — *adj* **Scotist'ic**.

scoto- *skot-ō-*, *combining form* signifying dark. — *n* **scotodinia** (*-din'i-ə*; Gr. *dīnos*, whirling) dizziness with headache and impairment of vision. — *n* **scotoma** (*-ō'mə*) a blind spot due to disease of the retina or optic nerve: — *pl* **scotō'mata** or **scotō'mas**. — *adj* **scotō'matous**. [Gr. *skotos*, darkness.]

Scots *skots*, *adj* Scottish (almost always used of money, measures, law and language). — *n* the form of English spoken in Lowland Scotland. — **Scots fir** Scots pine (see below); **Scots Greys** a famous regiment of dragoons, established in 1683; **Scots Guards** a Scottish force which served the kings of France from 1418 to 1759; a regiment of Guards in the British army; **Scots'man**; **Scots pine** the only native British pine, *Pinus sylvestris*; **Scots'woman**. [Shortened form of Scots *Scottis*, Scottish.]

Scottie. See **Scot**.

Scottish *skot'ish*, *adj* of Scotland or Scots. — *n* Scots (q.v.); (as *pl*) the Scots collectively. — *vt* **Scott'icise** or **-ize** to render Scottish or into Scots. — (the following words are sometimes spelt with one *t*) *n* **Scott'icism** a Scottish idiom; Scottish feeling. — *vt* **Scott'ify** to make Scottish: — *pr p* **Scott'ifying**; *pa t* and *pa p* **Scott'ified**. — **Scottish Certificate of Education** (in secondary education in Scotland) a certificate obtainable at Ordinary or Higher grades (see **O level** and **Higher**) for proficiency in one or more subjects; **Scottish Office** the government department that deals with Scottish affairs and oversees the work of several Scottish government ministries and agencies. [O.E. *Scottisc* — *Scottas*; see **Scot**.]

scoundrel *skown'drəl*, *n* an unprincipled or villainous person. — *adj* **scoun'drelly**.

scour[1] *skowr*, *vt* to clean, polish, remove or form by hard rubbing; to scrub; to cleanse; to free from grease, dirt or gum; to flush or cleanse by a current; to purge, esp. drastically (also *vi*); to clear out. — *n* the action, place or means of scouring; diarrhoea in cattle, etc. — *n* **scour'er**. — *n* **scour'ing** scrubbing; vigorous cleansing; clearing; erosion; purging; (often in *pl*) matter removed or accumulated by scouring. — Also *adj*. [Prob. M.Du. or M.L.G. *schûren* — O.Fr. *escurer* — L. *ex cūrāre*, take care of.]

scour[2] *skowr*, *vi* to range about, esp. in quest or pursuit. — *vt* to range over or traverse swiftly, vigorously, or in pursuit; to search thoroughly. [Poss. O.N. *skūr*, storm, shower; cf. **shower**.]

scourge *skûrj*, *n* a whip; an instrument of divine punishment; a cause of widespread affliction. — *vt* to whip severely; to afflict. — *n* **scourg'er**. [A.Fr. *escorge* — L. *excoriāre*, to flay — *corium*, leather (perh. as made of a strip of leather, perh. as a flaying instrument).]

Scouse *skows*, (*colloq*) *n* a native or inhabitant of Liverpool (also **scous'er**); the northern English dialect spoken in and around Liverpool; (without *cap*) a stew or hash, often made with meat scraps. [Short for *lobscouse*, a vegetable stew, a sea dish.]

scout[1] *skowt*, *n* someone sent out to bring in information; a (military) spy; a member of the Scout Association (formerly **Boy Scout**); (in U.S.) a member of the Girl Scouts, an organisation similar to the Girl Guides); a person who seeks out new recruits, sales opportunities, etc.; a ship for reconnoitring; a small light aeroplane orig. intended for reconnaissance; a light armoured car for reconnaissance (now usu. **scout car**); a person who watches or attends at a little distance; a person (usu. term of approbation; *slang*); a college servant, esp. at Oxford. — *vi* to act as scout; to reconnoitre (often with *about* or *around*). — *n* **scout'er** an adult working with instructors, etc. in the Scout Association. — *n* **scout'ing**. — **Scout Association** (formerly, the **Boy Scouts**) a worldwide movement for young people, intended to develop character and a sense of responsibility, founded (for boys) by Lord Baden-Powell in 1908; **scout'master** the leader of a band of scouts; **scout's pace** alternately walking and running for a set number of paces. [O.Fr. *escoute* — *escouter* — L. *auscultāre*, to listen.]

scout[2] *skowt*, *vt* to mock, flout; to dismiss or reject with disdain. [Cf. O.N. *skūta*, a taunt.]

scow *skow*, *n* a flat-bottomed boat. [Du. *schouw*.]

scowl *skowl*, *vi* to contract the brows in a malevolent and menacing look; to look gloomy and threatening. — *n* a scowling look. — *adj* **scow'ling**. — *adv* **scow'lingly**. [Cf. Dan. *skule*, to cast down the eyes, look sidelong.]

SCPS *abbrev* for Society of Civil and Public Servants.

SCR *abbrev* for Senior Common Room.

Scrabble® *skrab'l*, *n* a word-building game. [**scrabble**.]

scrabble *skrab'l*, *vt* to scratch; to scrape; to scrawl. — *vi* to scramble. — *n* a scrawl. — *n* **scrabb'ler**. [Du. *schrabben*, to scratch, frequentative *schrabbelen*.]

scrag *skrag*, *n* a sheep's or (*slang*) human neck; the bony part of the neck; a lean person or animal. — *vt* to hang; to throttle; to wring the neck of; to tackle by the neck: — *pr p* **scragg'ing**; *pa t* and *pa p* **scragged**. — *adv* **scragg'ily**. — *n* **scragg'iness**. — *adj* **scragg'y** lean, skinny, and gaunt. — **scrag'-end** the scrag of a neck. [Prob. **crag**[2].]

scram *skram*, (*slang*) *vi* (esp. in the *imper*) to be off: — *pr p* **scramm'ing**; *pa t* and *pa p* **scrammed**. [Perh. **scramble**.]

scramble *skram'bl*, *vi* to make one's way with disorderly struggling haste; to get along somehow; to clamber; to dash or struggle for what one can get before others; (of a military aircraft or its crew) to take off immediately, as in an emergency. — *vt* to put, make or get together, scramblingly; to change the frequency of (a transmission) so that it can be made intelligible only by means of an electronic decoding device; to beat (eggs) up and heat to thickness with milk, butter, etc.; to make (a radiotelephone conversation) unintelligible to third parties by a device that alters frequencies; to order (a military aircraft or its crew) to take off immediately. — *n* act of scrambling; a dash or struggle for what can be had; a disorderly performance; an emergency take-off by a military aircraft; a form of motor car or motorcycle trial. — *n* **scram'bler** a person who, or thing which, scrambles, esp. a telephone device. — *adj* **scram'bling**. — *n* the action of the verb scramble; participation in motor-cycle, etc. scrambles. — *adv* **scram'blingly**. — **scrambled eggs** eggs cooked as described above; the gold braid on a military officer's cap (*slang*). [Cf. the dialect verb *scramb*, to rake together with the hands.]

scramjet *skram'jet*, *n* a jet engine in which the fuel burns at a supersonic speed. [*s*upersonic *c*ombustion *ramjet*.]

scrap[1] *skrap*, *n* a small fragment; a piece of left-over food; a remnant; a cut-out picture, newspaper cutting, or the like, intended or suited for preservation in a scrapbook; metal clippings or other waste; anything discarded as worn-out, out of date, or useless; residue after extraction of oil from blubber, fish, etc. — *adj* consisting or of the value of scrap. — *vt* to consign to the scrap-heap; to discard, cease to use, do away with, abandon: — *pr p* **scrapp'ing**; *pa p* and *pa t* **scrapped**. — *adv* **scrapp'ily**. — *n* **scrapp'iness**. — *adj* **scrapp'y** fragmentary; disconnected, disorganised; made up of scraps. — **scrap'book** a book of blank pages for pasting in scraps, cuttings, etc.; **scrap'-heap** a place where old iron or useless material is collected; rubbish-heap; **scrap iron** or **scrap metal** scraps of iron or other metal, of use only for remelting; **scrap'-man** or **scrap'-merchant** a person who deals in scrap-metal; **scrap'yard** a scrap-merchant's premises. — **not a scrap** not even a tiny amount; **throw on the scrap-heap** to reject as useless (*lit* and *fig*). [O.N. *skrap*, scraps; cf. **scrape**.]

scrap[2] *skrap*, (*slang*) *n* a fight, usu. physical; a battle (*euph*). — Also *vi* (*pr p* **scrapp'ing**; *pa t* and *pa p* **scrapped**). — *adj* **scrapp'y** belligerent.

scrape *skrāp*, *vt* to press a sharp edge over; to move over with a grating sound; to smooth, clean, clear, reduce in thickness, abrade, remove, form, collect, etc. by such an action; to get together, collect by laborious effort (often with *together* or *up*). — *vi* to graze (the skin); to scratch the ground; to make a grating sound; to play the fiddle; to save as much as possible, through hardship; to get with difficulty (with *through*, *along*, *home*, etc.). — *n* an act, process or spell of scraping; a grating sound; a scraped place in the ground; a graze of the skin; a backward movement of one foot accompanying a bow; a scraping or thin layer; a predicament that threatens disgrace, friction with authority, minor illegality, etc. (*colloq*). — *n* **scrāp'er** a person who scrapes; a scraping instrument or machine. — *n* **scrāp'ie** a virus disease of sheep causing degeneration of the central nervous system and acute itching, the animals rubbing against trees, etc. to relieve it. — *n* **scrāp'ing** the action of the verb; its sound; a thin piece scraped off. — **scrap'erboard** a clay-surface board on which drawings can be made by scraping layers off as well as applying them; such a drawing; this method of making drawings. — **bow and scrape** to be over-obsequious; **scrape acquaintance with** to contrive somehow to get to know; **scrape the bottom of the barrel** to utilise the very last and worst of one's resources, opinions, etc. [O.E. *scrapian* or O.N. *skrapa*.]

scrapie. See under **scrape.**

scrapple *skrap'l*, (*US*) *n* a type of meat loaf made with scraps of meat or minced meat, usu. pork, cornmeal, seasonings, etc., served sliced and fried. [**scrap**[1].]

scratch *skrach*, *vt* to draw a sharp point over the surface of; to hurt, mark, seek to relieve an itch in, by so doing; to dig or scrape with the claws; to erase or delete (usu. with *out*); to withdraw from a competition or (esp. musical) engagement. — *vi* to use the nails or claws, esp. in order to hurt someone, relieve an itch, etc.; to scrape; to make a grating or screechy noise; to retire from a contest or engagement; to get (along or through) somehow (*colloq*). — *n* an act, mark or sound of scratching; a slight wound or graze; the line up to which boxers are led — hence test, trial, as in *come up to scratch* (q.v. below); the starting-point for a competitor without handicap; a competitor who starts from scratch; (in *pl*) a disease in horses with the appearance of scratches on the pastern or ankle. — *adj* improvised; casual; hastily or casually got together; (of a competitor) having no handicap. — *n* **scratch'er.** — *adv* **scratch'ily.** — *n* **scratch'iness.** — *n* and *adj* **scratch'ing.** — *adv* **scratch'ingly.** — *adj* **scratch'less.** — *adj* **scratch'y** like scratches; ready or likely to scratch; grating or screechy. — *vt* **scratch'build** to build (usu. models) from the raw materials, as opposed to from kits or buying ready-made. — *n* **scratch'-builder.** — *n* **scratch'building.** — *adj* **scratch-built'.** — **scratch pad** a note-pad, jotter; **scratch test** (*med*) a test for allergy to a certain substance, made by introducing it to an area of skin that has been scratched. — **come up to scratch** (*fig*) to reach an expected standard; to fulfil an obligation; **start from scratch** (*fig*) to start at the beginning; to embark on (a task, career, etc.) without any advantages, experience, etc.; **you scratch my back and I'll scratch yours** (*colloq*) do me a favour and I'll do you one in return.

scrawl *skröl*, *vt* and *vi* to draw or write illegibly, untidily or hastily; to scribble. — *n* untidy, illegible, or bad writing; a letter, etc. written thus. — *n* **scrawl'er.** — *n* and *adj* **scrawl'ing.** — *adv* **scrawl'ingly.** — *adj* **scrawl'y.**

scrawny *skrö'ni*, (orig. *US*) *adj* lean, meagre.

scream *skrēm*, *vt* and *vi* to cry out in a loud shrill voice, as in fear or pain; to laugh shrilly and uncontrolledly; to shriek. — *vi* (of colours) to clash acutely (*colloq*); to be all too loudly evident (*colloq*); to move with a screaming noise. — *n* a shrill, sudden cry, as in fear or pain; a shriek; a loud whistling sound; anything or anyone supposed to make one scream with laughter (*colloq*). — *n* **scream'er** a person who screams; a large spur-winged S. American bird (*crested* and *black-necked screamer*) with loud harsh cry; a different S. American bird, the seriema (sometimes known as *crested screamer*); a sensational headline (*slang*); an exclamation mark (*printing slang*). — *adj* **scream'ing.** — *adv* **scream'ingly.** [Late O.E. *scræmen*.]

scree *skrē*, *n* a sloping mass of debris at the base of a cliff. [O.N. *skritha*, a landslip — *skrītha*, to slide.]

screech *skrēch*, *vi* to utter a harsh, shrill, and sudden cry or noise, or to speak in that way. — *vt* to utter in such tones. — *n* a harsh, shrill and sudden cry, noise, or tone of voice. — *n* **screech'er.** — *adj* **screech'y** shrill and harsh, like a screech. — **screech'-owl** the barn-owl. [M.E. *scrichen*.]

screed *skrēd*, *n* a long passage, spoken or written; a band of plaster laid on the surface of a wall as a guide to the thickness of a full coat of plaster to be applied subsequently (*building*); a layer of mortar finishing off the surface of a floor (also **screed'ing**); a strip of wood or metal for levelling off mortar, sand, etc. — *n* **screed'er.** [O.E. *scrēade*, shred.]

screen *skrēn*, *n* a shield against danger, observation, wind, heat, light, or other outside influence; a piece of room furniture in the form of a folding framework or of a panel on a stand; a windscreen; a sheltering row of trees, shrubs, etc.; a body of troops or formation of ships intended as a cover for some activity; a wall (also **screen wall**) masking a building; a partial partition separating off part of a room, a church choir, or side chapel; a coarse sifting apparatus; in some cameras, a glass plate with a pattern of various kinds on it to aid in focusing the object of a photograph; the surface on which a cinema film, television image or slide projection is seen; a glass plate with rules or dots of a given coarseness or frequency for printing half-tone photographs; a mosaic of primary colours for colour photography; a screen grid. — *vt* to shelter or conceal; to sift coarsely; to sort out by, or subject to, tests of ability, trustworthiness, desirability, etc.; to test for illness, etc.; to protect from stray electrical interference; to prevent from causing outside electrical interference; to project or exhibit on a cinema, television or slide screen or on cinema or TV screens generally; to make a motion picture of. — *n* **screen'er.** — *n* **screen'ing.** — *npl* **screen'ings** material eliminated by sifting. — **screen door** (in the U.S.) a frame of wood or metal with netting panels, to exclude insects when the door proper is open; **screen grid** an electrode placed between the control grid and anode in a valve, having an invariable potential to eliminate positive feedback and instability; **screen'play** the written text for a film, with dialogue, stage directions, and descriptions of characters and setting; **screen printing** and **screen process** see **silk-screen printing**; **screen test** a trial filming to determine whether an actor or actress is suitable for cinema work; **screen'writer** a writer of screenplays. — **screen off** to hide behind, or separate by, a screen; to separate by sifting.

screw *skrōō*, *n* a cylinder with a helical groove or ridge (the *thread*), used as a fastening driven into wood, etc. by rotation (a *male screw*; for *female screw*, see **female**), mechanically or otherwise; anything of similar form; a screw propeller or ship driven by one; a thumbscrew, an instrument of torture; a twisted cone of paper, or the portion of a commodity contained in it; a turn of a screw; a twist; (esp. in billiards or snooker) a spin imparted to a ball; a prison officer (*slang*); an act of sexual intercourse (*vulg*); salary, wages (*colloq*). — *vt* to fasten, tighten, compress, force, adjust or extort by a screw or screws, a screwing motion, or as if by screws; to twist; to turn in the manner of a screw; to pucker (often with *up*); to summon (courage, etc.; with *up*); to have sexual intercourse with (*vulg*); to practise extortion upon; to cheat (*slang*); to disrupt, spoil, make a mess or disaster of (often with *up*; *colloq*); to burgle (*slang*). — *vi* to be capable of being screwed; to wind (*in*, *up*, etc.); to have sexual intercourse (*vulg*). — *adj* **screwed** (*slang*) messed up, spoiled; tipsy. — *n* **screw'er.** — *n* and *adj* **screw'ing.** — *adj* **screw'y** (*colloq*) eccentric, slightly mad. — **screw'ball** (*US*) (in baseball) a ball that breaks contrary to its swerve; a crazy person, an eccentric. — Also *adj*. — **screw cap** a lid that screws on to a container. — *adj* **screw'-down** closed by screwing. — **screw'driver** an instrument for turning and driving screws; **screw eye** a screw formed into a loop for attaching string, rope, wire, etc.; **screw jack** a jack for lifting heavy weights, operated by a screw; **screw'-pile** a pile for sinking into the ground, ending in a screw; **screw'=pine** a plant of the genus *Pandanus* or its family — from the screwlike arrangement of the leaves; **screw propeller** a propeller with helical blades; **screw=steam'er** a steam ship driven by screw; **screw thread** the helical ridge of a screw; **screw top** a bottle with a stopper that screws in or on, esp. a beer-bottle of this kind with its contents. — Also *adj*. — **screw'-up** (*slang*) something disastrous, a failure, etc.; a person who has made such a mess (of their life, etc.); **screw'-wrench** a tool for gripping screw-heads. — **have a screw loose** to be defective (esp. mentally); **put on** or **turn the screw** to apply pressure (physical, moral, etc.) progressively; to exact payment; **put the screws on** to coerce; **screwed up** (*slang*) messed up; psychologically disturbed, in mental turmoil, etc.; **screw it, them, you,** etc. (*vulg slang*) an interjection expressing disgust, scorn, frustration, etc.; **screw up** (*slang*) to make a mess of something, fail, etc. [Earlier *scrue*.]

scribble[1] *skrib'l*, *vt* to scrawl; to write illegibly, carelessly, or worthlessly (in handwriting or substance). — *n* careless writing; a scrawl. — *n* **scribb'ler** (*derog*) a worthless author. — *n* **scribb'ling.** — *adv* **scribb'lingly.** — *adj* **scribb'ly.** [A frequentative of **scribe**, or L.L. *scrībillāre* — L. *scrībĕre*, to write.]

scribble[2] *skrib'l*, *vt* to comb wool roughly. — *n* **scribb'ler** a wool-combing machine; a person who tends it. — *n* **scribb'ling.**

scribe *skrīb*, *n* an expounder and teacher of the traditional law and that of Moses (*Bible*); a writer; a public or official writer; a medieval clerk, amanuensis, secretary; a copyist; a penman, calligrapher; a pointed instrument to mark lines on wood, metal, etc. — *vt* to mark or score with a scribe, etc. — *adj* **scrī'bal.** — *n* **scrī'ber** a scribing tool. — *n* **scrī'bing.** [L. *scrība*, a scribe, and *scrībĕre*, to write.]

scrim *skrim*, *n* open fabric used in upholstery, bookbinding, for curtains, etc.

scrimmage *skrim'ij* or **scrummage** *skrum'ij*, *n* an untidy mêlée, a struggle; (in Rugby football) a scrum (*old*); (in American football) play between the two teams beginning with the snap (q.v.) and ending when the ball is dead; a practice session of this; a line of scrimmage. — *vi* to take part in a scrimmage. — *n* **scrimm'ager** or **scrumm'ager.** — **line of scrimmage** or **scrimmage line** (*Am football*) an imaginary line, parallel to the goal lines, behind which the linemen of a team position themselves for start of play, and on which the end of the ball nearest that team's goal line rests. [**skirmish.**]

scrimp *skrimp*, *vt* to stint; to keep limited, often perforce. — *vi* to be sparing or niggardly, often perforce (usu. in the phrase *scrimp and save*). — *adj* **scrimped.** — *adv* **scrimp'ily.** — *n* **scrimp'iness.** — *adj* **scrimp'y** scanty. [Cf. Sw. and Dan. *skrumpen*, shrivelled, O.E. *scrimman*, to shrink.]

scrimshank *skrim'shangk*, (*mil slang*) *vi* to evade work or duty. — *n* evasion of work or duty. — *n* **scrim'shanker.**

scrimshaw *skrim'shö*, *n* a sailors' spare-time handicraft, as engraving or carving fanciful designs on shells, whales' teeth, etc.; anything crafted in this way. — *vt* and *vi* to work or decorate in this way.

scrip *skrip*, *n* a scrap of paper or of writing; (for *subscription*) a preliminary certificate, as for shares allotted but not yet paid for; share certificates, or shares or stock collectively; a paper token issued instead of currency in special e.g. emergency circumstances (*US*). — *n* **scripoph'ily** the collecting of bond and share certificates as a hobby; the items thus collected. — **scrip issue** a bonus issue (q.v. at **bonus**). [**script** and **subscription.**]

Script. *abbrev* for Scripture.

script *skript*, *n* a piece of writing; the actors', director's, etc. written copy of the text of a play or film; a text for broadcasting; handwriting, system or style of handwriting; a set of characters used in writing a language (as *Cyrillic script*); type in imitation of handwriting; handwriting in imitation of type; an original document (*law*). — *vt* to write a script for, or make a script from (e.g. a novel), esp. for broadcasting or the theatre or cinema. — *adj* **script'ed.** — **script'writer.** [L. *scrīptum* — *scrībĕre*, to write.]

scriptorium *skrip-tö'ri-əm*, *n* a writing-room, esp. in a monastery: — *pl* **scripto'ria.** — *adj* **scripto'rial.** [L. *scrīptōrium* — *scrībĕre*.]

scripture *skrip'chər*, *n* (*sing* or *pl*) sacred writings of a religion, esp. (with *cap*) the Bible. — Also *adj*. — *adj* **scrip'tural** of, in, or according to Scripture; of writing. — *n* **scrip'turalism** literal adherence to the Scriptures. — *adv* **scrip'turally.** [L. *scrīptūra* — *scrībĕre*, to write.]

scrivener *skriv'nər*, (*hist*) *n* a scribe; a copyist; a person who draws up contracts, etc. — *n* **scriv'enership.** — *n* **scriv'ening** writing. — **scrivener's palsy** writer's cramp. [O.Fr. *escrivain* — L.L. *scrībānus* — L. *scrība*, a scribe.]

scrofula *skrof'ū-lə*, *n* tuberculosis, esp. of the lymphatic glands, called also king's-evil. — *adj* **scrof'ulous.** [L. *scrōfulae* — *scrōfa*, a sow (supposed to be prone to it).]

scroll *skrōl*, *n* a roll of paper, parchment, etc.; a ribbonlike decorative strip in painting, architecture, etc., partly coiled or curved, sometimes bearing a motto; a writing in the form of a roll; a spiral ornament or part, such as a flourish to a signature. — *vt* to roll into a scroll or scrolls; to cut into scrolls from a length of material; to move (a text) up or down or from side to side in order to view data that cannot all be seen on a VDU at the same time (*comput*). — *vi* (*comput*) (of a text) to move in such a way. — *adj* **scrolled** formed into a scroll; ornamented with scrolls; moved across a VDU screen as described above. — *n* **scroll'ery** or **scroll'work** ornament in scrolls. — *adv* **scroll'wise.** — **scroll'=saw** a saw for cutting scrolls. [Earlier *scowl(e)*.]

Scrooge *skrōōj*, *n* a miser. [From Ebenezer Scrooge in Dickens's *A Christmas Carol*.]

scrophularia *skrof-ū-lā'ri-ə*, *n* any plant of the figwort genus (*Scrophularia*), giving name to the **Scrophulariaceae** (*-lar-i-ā'si-ē*), a family including foxglove, mullein, speedwell, eyebright. — *adj* **scrophulariā'ceous.** [L. *scrōfulae*, as reputedly cure for scrofula.]

scrotum *skrō'təm*, *n* the bag of skin that contains the testicles in mammals. — *adj* **scrō'tal.** [L. *scrōtum*.]

scrounge *skrownj*, *vt* to cadge, beg. — *vi* to hunt around (with *for*); to sponge off others. — *n* **scroung'er.** — *n* **scroung'ing.**

scrub[1] *skrub*, *vt* to rub hard; to wash or clean by hard rubbing with e.g. a stiff brush; to purify (*gas-making*); to cancel, abandon (*slang*). — *vi* to use a scrubbing-brush; to make a rapid to-and-fro movement as if scrubbing: — *pr p* **scrubb'ing**; *pa t* and *pa p* **scrubbed.** — *n* an act of scrubbing. — *n* **scrubb'er** a person who scrubs; apparatus for freeing gas from tar, ammonia, and hydrogen-sulphur combinations; any device that filters out impurities; an unattractive woman or one with loose morals (*derog slang*). — *n* **scrubb'ing.** — **scrubb'-ing-board** a washboard; **scrubb'ing-brush** a brush with short stiff bristles for scrubbing floors, etc.

— **scrub round** (*slang*) to cancel; to ignore intentionally; **scrub up** (of a surgeon, etc.) to wash the hands and arms thoroughly before performing or assisting at an operation.

scrub[2] *skrub*, *n* stunted trees and shrubs collectively; country covered with bushes or low trees, esp. the Australian evergreen dwarf forest or bush of Eucalyptus, Acacia, etc.; hence, a remote place, far from civilisation (*Austr colloq*); an undersized or inferior animal, esp. one of indefinite breed; a player in a second or inferior team (*NAm*); a team of inferior players, or one with too few players (*NAm*); an insignificant or undersized person; anything small or insignificant. — *adj* insignificant; undersized; (of a player) in a second or inferior team (*NAm*). — *adj* **scrubb'y**. — **scrub'land** an area covered with scrub; **scrub-tur'key** or **scrub'-fowl** a mound-bird; **scrub typhus** a typhus-like disease transmitted by a mite. — **the Scrubs** colloq. abbrev. for **Wormwood Scrubs**, an English prison. [A variant of **shrub**[1].]

scruff[1] *skruf*, *n* the nape (of the neck).

scruff[2] *skruf*, (*colloq*) *n* an untidy, dirty person. — *n* **scruff'iness**. — *adj* **scruff'y** untidy, dirty. [Ety. as for **scurf**.]

scrum *skrum*, *n* an untidy struggle, a mêlée; a closing-in of rival forwards round the ball on the ground, or in readiness for its being inserted (by the scrum-half) between the two packs (*Rugby football*); a large number of people crushed into a relatively small space (*colloq*). — **scrum'down** an act of forming a rugby scrum; **scrum-half'** (*Rugby football*) a half-back whose duty it is to put the ball into the scrum and get possession of it as soon as it emerges again. — **scrum down** to form a rugby scrum: — *pr p* **scrumm'ing**; *pa t* and *pa p* **scrummed**. [Abbrev. of **scrummage**; see **scrimmage**, **skirmish**.]

scrummage. See **scrimmage**.

scrummy. See **scrumptious**.

scrumptious *skrump'shəs*, *adj* (*colloq*) delightful; delicious. — Also **scrumm'y**. — *adv* **scrump'tiously**.

scrumpy *skrum'pi*, *n* very strong cider made from small, sweet apples. [*scrump*, a withered apple.]

scrunch *skrunch* or *skrunsh*, variant of **crunch**. — *adj* **scrunch'y**. — *vt* **scrunch'-dry** to crumple (hair) while blow-drying it, in order to give it more body and shape.

scruple *skrōō'pl*, *n* a small weight — in apothecaries' weight, 20 grains; a difficulty, objection or consideration, usu. moral, obstructing or preventing action; scrupulousness. — *vi* to hesitate because of scruples. — *vt* to have scruples about (followed by infinitive). — *n* **scrupulosity** (*-pū-los'i-ti*). — *adj* **scru'pulous** directed by scruples; having scruples, doubts or objections; extremely conscientious or exact. — *adv* **scru'pulously**. — *n* **scru'pulousness**. — **make no scruple** (or **no scruples**) **about** or **make scruples about** to offer (no) moral objections to. [L. *scrūpulus*, dimin. of *scrūpus*, a sharp stone, anxiety.]

scrutiny *skrōō'ti-ni*, *n* close, careful or minute investigation or examination, esp. of election procedures, etc.; a searching look. — *n* **scrutā'tor** a close examiner; a scrutineer. — *n* **scrutineer'** someone who makes a scrutiny, esp. of votes. — *vt* and *vi* **scru'tinise** or **-ize** to examine closely. — *n* **scru'tiniser** or **-z-**. — *adj* **scru'tinising** or **-z-**. — *adv* **scru'tinisingly** or **-z-**. [L. *scrūtinium*, and *scrūtārī*, to search even to the rags — *scrūta*, rags, trash.]

scuba *skōō'bə* or *skū'bə*, *n* a device used by skin-divers, consisting of compressed-air cylinders and a mouthpiece for underwater breathing. — Also *adj*. — *vi* to swim using scuba gear. — Also **scu'ba-dive**. — **scu'ba-diver**; **scu'ba-diving**. [*s*elf-*c*ontained *u*nderwater *b*reathing *a*pparatus.]

scud *skud*, *vi* (esp. of clouds) to sweep along easily and swiftly; (esp. of sailing vessels) to drive before the wind: — *pr p* **scudd'ing**; *pa t* and *pa p* **scudd'ed**. — *n* act of scudding; driving cloud, shower or spray. — *n* **scudd'er**.

scuff *skuf*, *vt* and *vi* to shuffle, dragging or scraping the feet on the ground; to brush, graze, scrape (esp. shoes or heels whilst walking); to make or become shabby by wear. [Ety. as for **scuffle**.]

scuffle *skuf'l*, *vi* to struggle confusedly, esp. while fighting. — *n* a confused struggle. — *n* **scuff'ler**. [Cf. Sw. *skuffa*, to shove; Du. *schoffelen*; **shove**, **shovel**, **shuffle**.]

sculduggery. Same as **skulduggery**.

scull[1] *skul*, *n* a short, light spoon-bladed oar for one hand, used in pairs; an oar used over the stern of a boat; a small, light rowing-boat propelled by sculls; an act or spell of sculling; (in *pl*) a race between small, light rowing-boats rowed by one person. — *vt* to propel with sculls, or with one oar worked like a screw over the stern. — *vi* to row using sculls. — *n* **scull'er** a person who sculls; a small boat pulled by one person with a pair of sculls. — *n* **scull'ing**.

scull[2] or **skull** *skul*, *n* a shallow basket for fish, etc.

scullery *skul'ər-i*, *n* a room for rough kitchen work, such as cleaning of utensils. — **scull'ery-maid**. [O.Fr. *escuelerie* — L. *scutella*, a tray.]

sculp. or **sculpt.** *abbrev* for: sculpsit (q.v.); sculptor; sculpture.

sculpin *skul'pin*, (*NAm*) *n* the dragonet, a large-headed, spiny fish.

sculpsit *skulp'sit* or *skŏŏlp'sit*, (L.) (he or she) sculptured (this), sometimes appended to the signature of the sculptor on the sculpture.

sculpt *skulpt*, *vt* and *vi* to sculpture; to carve. [Fr. *sculpter* — L. *sculpĕre*, to carve.]

sculptor *skulp'tər*, *fem* **sculp'tress**, *n* an artist in carving, esp. in stone. — *adj* **sculp'tural** (*-chər-əl*). — *adv* **sculp'turally**. — *n* **sculp'ture** the act of carving, esp. in stone; extended to clay-modelling or moulding for casting metals; work, or a piece of work, in this art; shaping in relief; spines, ridges, etc. standing out from the surface (*biol*). — *vt* to carve, shape in relief; to represent in sculpture; to mould, or form, so as to have the appearance or (*fig*) other quality of sculpture; to modify the form of (the earth's surface). — *adj* **sculp'tured** carved; engraved; (of features) fine and regular, like a classical sculpture; having ridges, etc. on the surface (*bot* and *zool*). — *adj* **sculpturesque'**. — *n* **sculp'turing**. [L. *sculptor*, *-ōris*, *sculptūra* — *sculpĕre*, *sculptum*, to carve.]

scum *skum*, *n* waste matter coming to or floating on the surface of liquid, esp. in the form of foam or froth; worthless, despicable people. — *vt* to remove the scum from. — *vi* to form or throw up a scum: — *pr p* **scumm'ing**; *pa t* and *pap* **scummed**. — *n* **scumm'er** an instrument for removing scum. — *npl* **scumm'ings** scum removed from a liquid. — *adj* **scumm'y**. — **scum'bag** (*vulg slang*) a condom (*US*); a general term of abuse (esp. *US*). [Cf. Dan. *skum*, Ger. *Schaum*, foam.]

scumble *skum'bl*, *vt* to soften the effect of (a painting) by a very thin coat of opaque or semi-opaque colour, or by light rubbing or by applying paint with a dry brush. — *n* colour laid down in this way; the effect produced. — *n* **scum'bling**. [Frequentative of **scum**.]

scuncheon *skun'* or *skon'shən*, *n* the inner part of a door or window jamb. [O.Fr. *escoinson*.]

scupper[1] *skup'ər*, *n* (usu. in *pl*) a hole to drain a ship's deck.

scupper[2] *skup'ər*, (*colloq*) *vt* to do for; to ruin; to sink (a ship).

scurf *skûrf*, *n* small flakes or scales of dead skin, esp. on the scalp. — *n* **scurf'iness**. — *adj* **scurf'y**. [O.E. *scurf*, *sceorf*.]

scurrilous *skur'ə-ləs*, *adj* indecently abusive and unjustifiably defamatory. — *adv* **scurr'ilously**. — *n* **scurril'ity** or **scurr'ilousness**. [L. *scurrīlis* — *scurra*, a buffoon.]

scurry *skur'i*, *vi* to hurry briskly or in a panicky way; to scuttle. — *n* flurried haste; a flurry, e.g. of wind, snow. [From **hurry-scurry**, reduplication of **hurry**.]

scurvy *skûr'vi*, *adj* scurfy; vile, contemptible. — *n* a disease marked by bleeding under the skin and sponginess of the gums, due to lack of fresh vegetables and consequently of vitamin C. — *adv* **scur'vily**. — *n* **scur'viness**. — **scur'vy-grass** a cruciferous plant used by sailors as an anti-scurvy preparation. [**scurf**; the application to the disease helped by similarity of sound; see **scorbutic**.]

'scuse *skūz*, (*colloq*) *vt* short form of **excuse**.

scut *skut*, *n* a short erect tail like a hare's.

scuta. See **scute**.

scutal, scutate. See **scute**.

scutch[1] *skuch*, *vt* to prepare (e.g. flax) by beating, so as to extract the fibres. — *n* a tool for dressing flax. — *n* **scutch'er** a person, tool, or part of a machine that scutches; the striking part of a threshing-mill. — *n* **scutch'ing**.

scutch[2] *skuch* or **scutch grass**. Forms of **quitch** or **quitch grass** (see **couch grass**).

scutcheon *skuch'ən*, *n* a form of **escutcheon**.

scute *skūt*, *n* a scutum; a hard skin plate. — *adj* **scū'tal**. — *adj* **scū'tate** protected by scutes; shield-shaped. — *adj* **scū'tiform**. — *n* **scu'tum** a scute; the second dorsal plate of a segment of an insect's torso or thorax: — *pl* **scū'ta**. [L. *scūtum*, a shield.]

scutellum *skū-tel'əm*, *n* a scale of a bird's foot; the third dorsal plate of a segment of an insect's torso or thorax; a structure, supposed to be the cotyledon, by which a grass embryo absorbs nutritive matter: — *pl* **scūtell'a**. — *adj* **scūtell'ar**. — *adj* **scū'tellate**. — *n* **scūtellā'tion** (*zool*) arrangement of scales. [L. *scutella*, a tray, dimin. of *scutra*, a platter, confused in scientific use with *scūtulum*, dimin. of *scūtum*, a shield.]

scutiform. See **scute**.

scutter *skut'ər*, *vi* to run hastily, scurry. — *n* a hasty run. [A variant of **scuttle**[3].]

scuttle[1] *skut'l*, *n* a shallow basket, esp. a vessel for holding coal. — *n* **scutt'leful**. [O.E. *scutel* — L. *scutella*, a tray.]

scuttle[2] *skut'l*, *n* an opening in a ship's deck or side; its lid; a shuttered hole in a wall, roof, etc.; its shutter or trap-door. — *vt* to make a hole in, or open the lids of the scuttles of, esp. in order to sink; to destroy, ruin (e.g. plans). — **scutt'lebutt** a cask with a hole cut in it for drinking-water on board ship (also **scutt'le-cask**); rumour, gossip (*US*). [O.Fr. *escoutille*, hatchway.]

scuttle[3] *skut'l*, *vi* to dash with haste, scurry. — *n* an act of scuttling. — *n* **scutt'ler**. [**scud**.]

scutum. See **scute**.

Scylla *sil'ə*, (*mythol*) *n* a six-headed monster who sat over a dangerous rock opposite Charybdis — used in the phrase **between Scylla and Charybdis**, forced to steer a hopeless course between evil and disaster. [Gr. *Skylla*.]

scyphus *sīf'əs*, *n* a large ancient Greek drinking-cup; a cup-shaped structure (*bot*): — *pl* **scyph'ī**. — *adj* **scyph'iform**. [Gr. *skyphos*, cup.]

scythe *sīdh*, *n* an instrument with a large curved blade attached to a wooden handle, for mowing by hand; a blade attached to a war-chariot wheel. — *vt* and *vi* to mow (down) with a scythe. — *adj* **scythed** armed or cut down with scythes. — *n* **scyth'er**. [O.E. *sīthe*.]

SD *abbrev* for: South Dakota (U.S. state; also **S. Dak.**); Swaziland (I.V.R.).

sd *abbrev* for *sine die* (L.), without a day, without (fixed) date.

SDA *abbrev* for Scottish Development Agency.

SDLP *abbrev* for Social Democratic and Labour Party (of Northern Ireland).

SDP *abbrev* for: (former) Social Democratic Party; (of motor insurance) social, domestic and pleasure.

SDR *abbrev* for special drawing rights.

SE *abbrev* for: Society of Engineers; south-east.

Se (*chem*) *symbol* for selenium.

sea *sē*, *n* the great mass of salt water covering the greater part of the earth's surface; the ocean; any great expanse of water; a great (esp. salt) lake — mainly in proper names; (a given height of) swell or roughness; a great wave; the tide; a wide expanse (*fig*). — *adj* marine. — *adj* **sea'-like** like the sea. — *adv* in the manner of the sea. — *adj* and *adv* **sea'ward** towards the (open) sea. — *n* the seaward side, direction or position. — *adj* and *adv* **sea'wardly**. — *adv* **sea'wards**. — **sea air** the air at sea or at the seaside; **sea anchor** a floating anchor used at sea to slow a boat down, or maintain its direction; **sea anemone** a solitary soft-bodied polyp of the *Zoantharia* genus, having many tentacles; **sea'bank** the seashore; an embankment to keep out the sea; **sea'-bather**; **sea'-bathing**; **sea'-beach** a strip of sand, gravel, etc. bordering the sea; **sea bed** the bottom, floor of the sea; **sea'bird**; **sea'board** the country bordering the sea. — Also *adj*. — **sea'boots** long, waterproof boots worn by sailors. — *adj* **sea'borne** carried on, transported by, the sea. — **sea bottom** the sea bed; **sea breeze**; **sea cabbage** seakale; **sea'-captain** the captain of a merchant ship; **sea change** a complete transformation; **sea'chest** a seaman's trunk; **sea cliff**; **sea'-coal** small pieces of coal from marine deposits, washed up on the shore; **sea'coast**; **sea'-cock** a gurnard, a type of fish; a valve communicating with the sea through a vessel's hull; **sea'-cook** a ship's cook; **sea'craft** skill in navigation; seamanship; a sea-going craft; **sea cucumber** any burrowing sea animal of the genus *Holothuria* (such as trepang, bêche-de-mer); **sea'-dog** an old sailor; **sea eagle** any of several fish-eating eagles living by the sea; **sea elephant** the elephant-seal; **sea'farer** a traveller by sea, usu. a sailor; **sea'faring**. — Also *adj*. — **sea'-fight** a battle between ships at sea; **sea'-fisher**; **sea'fishing**; **sea floor** the bottom of the sea; **sea fog** a fog coming inland off the sea; **sea'food** food got from the sea, esp. shellfish; **sea fret** a fog coming inland off the sea; **sea front** the side of the land, of a town, or of a building that looks towards the sea; a promenade with its buildings fronting the sea. — *adj* **sea'-girt** (*poetic*) surrounded by sea. — **sea god** or **sea goddess**. — *adj* **sea'-going** sailing on the seas; suitable for deep-sea voyages. — **sea-green'** green like the sea. — Also *adj* (see also **sea-green incorruptible** below). — **sea'gull** any bird of the gull family; **sea'-holly** a seashore plant bearing a certain resemblance to the thistle, eryngo; **sea'horse** the fabulous hippocampus, a sea-monster with the body of a horse and the tail of a fish; any of several types of fish with horselike heads. — *adj* **sea'island** (of cotton) of the kind grown on the islands off the coast of South Carolina. — **sea'kale** a fleshy, sea-green, cruciferous seaside plant cultivated for its blanched sprouts, eaten as food; **sea'-keeping** the maintenance of navigational control and stability on (rough) seas. — Also *adj*. — **sea'-king** a Viking chief; **sea'-lane** a navigable passage, delineated on charts, etc., between islands, ships, ice-floes, etc.; **sea law** maritime law; **sea-law'yer** a captious, fault-finding sailor; **sea legs** ability to walk on a ship's deck when it is pitching; resistance to seasickness; **sea leopard** a spotted seal of the southern seas; **sea lettuce** a seaweed with flat translucent green fronds — green laver (see under **laver**[2]); **sea'-level** the mean level of the surface of the sea; **sea'-lily** see **crinoid**; **sea'-lion** a seal with external ears and with hind flippers turned forward; **sea'-loch** a lakelike arm of the sea; **sea lord** (often with *caps*) a naval member of the Board of Admiralty, a division of the Ministry of Defence; **sea'man** a sailor; a man other than an officer or apprentice, employed aboard ship. — *adj* **sea'manlike** showing good seamanship. — *adj* **sea'manly** characteristic of a seaman. — **sea'manship** the art of handling ships at sea; **sea'-margin** the land along the edge of the sea; **sea'-mew** any bird of the gull family; **sea-mile'** a geographical or nautical mile; **sea'-monster; sea'-mount** or **sea'mount** a mountain under the sea of at least 3 000 ft; **sea'-nymph; sea'-otter** a N. Pacific animal akin to the true otters; its silvery brown fur, now very rare; **sea passage** (the cost of) a journey by sea; **sea pink** any of several perennial plants generally known as thrift; **sea'plane** an aeroplane with floats instead of wheels, for landing on water; **sea'port** a port or harbour by the sea; a place with such a harbour; **sea'power** naval strength; **sea power** a nation with great naval strength; **sea'-quake** a seismic disturbance at sea; **sea'-road** a designated route followed by ships, a sea-lane; **sea'-room** space to manoeuvre a ship safely; **sea'-rover** a pirate or pirate ship; **sea'-salt** salt got from seawater; **sea'scape** a painting or photograph of the sea; **sea scorpion** a scorpion-fish, having spiny head and fins; **Sea Scout** a member of a marine branch of the Scout movement; **sea'-serpent** (*mythol*) an enormous marine animal of serpentlike form; **sea'-shell** the shell of a crustacean or mollusc; **sea'-shore** the land immediately adjacent to the sea; the foreshore (*law*). — *adj* **sea'sick** nauseous owing to the rolling of a vessel at sea. — **seasick'ness; sea'side** the neighbourhood of the sea. — Also *adj*. — **sea slug** a type of shell-less marine mollusc; a sea cucumber; **sea snail** any snail-like marine mollusc; **sea'-squirt** a marine animal shaped like a double-mouthed flask, an ascidian; **sea'-surgeon** a tropical genus (*Acanthurus*) of spiny-finned fishes with a lancetlike spine ensheathed on each side of the tail; **sea swallow** a tern; **sea trout** the salmon trout; **sea'-urchin** one of a class of marine animals with globular, ovoid or heart-shaped, sometimes flattened body and shell of calcareous plates, without arms; **sea wall** a wall to keep out the sea; **sea'water; sea'way** progress through the waves; a heavy or high sea; a regular route taken by ocean traffic; an inland waterway on which ocean-going vessels can sail; **sea'weed** marine algae collectively; any marine alga. — *adj* **sea'-worn** worn by the sea or by seafaring. — **sea'worthiness.** — *adj* **sea'worthy** (of a vessel) fit for travel on sea; able to endure stormy weather. — **all at sea** totally disorganised; completely at a loss; **at sea** away from land; on the ocean; disorganised, bewildered; **go to sea** to become a sailor; **heavy sea** a sea in which the waves run high; **sea-green incorruptible** a person honestly and unshakably devoted to an ideal or purpose, esp. in public life (orig. used by Carlyle of Robespierre); **short sea** a sea in which the waves are choppy, irregular and interrupted; **the Seven Seas** see **seven.** [O.E. *sǣ*.]

Seabee *sē'bē* (the letters *cb* phonetically represented), *n* a member of a U.S. Navy construction *b*attalion.

SEAC *sē'ak*, *abbrev* for South-East Asia Command.

seal[1] *sēl*, *n* a piece of wax, lead or other material, stamped with a design and attached as a means of authentication or attestation; a piece of wax, etc., stamped or not, used as a means of keeping something closed; the design stamped; an engraved stone or other stamp for impressing a design, or a trinket of similar form; an adhesive label, esp. decorative, for a Christmas parcel, etc., sold for charity; a token or symbol to confirm a bargain, etc.; that which keeps something closed; an obligation to secrecy; an impression; a device to prevent passage of a gas, air, water, etc. — *vt* to put a seal on; to fasten with a seal; to give confirmation of; to ratify; to close, esp. permanently or for a long time; to enclose; to decide, settle irrevocably; to tarmac (*Austr* and *NZ*). — *vi* to set one's seal to something. — *n* **seal'ant** a substance that seals a place where there is a leak. — *adj* **sealed.** — *n* **seal'er** a person or thing that seals; a substance used to coat a surface for protection, impermeability, etc. — *n* **seal'ing.** — *adj* **sealed-beam'** (of car headlights) consisting of a complete unit sealed within a vacuum. — **sealed book** something beyond one's knowledge or understanding; **seal'-engraving** the art of engraving seals; **seal'ing-wax** formerly beeswax, now usually a composition of shellac, turpentine, vermilion or other colouring matter, etc., for making decorative seals; **seal'-ring** a signet-ring. — **Great Seal** (also without *caps*) the state seal of the United Kingdom; **Lord Privy Seal** the senior cabinet minister without official duties (formerly the keeper of the Privy Seal); **Privy Seal** (also without *caps*) the seal formerly appended to state documents that were to receive, or did not require, authorisation by the Great Seal, in Scotland used esp. to authenticate royal grants of personal rights; **seal off** to make it impossible for any thing or person to leave or enter (e.g. an area); **set one's seal to** or **on** to give one's authority or assent to; **under sealed orders** under orders only to be opened at a stated time. [O.Fr. *seel* — L. *sigillum*, dimin. of *signum*, a mark.]

seal[2] *sēl*, *n* any of the paddle-footed varieties of the genus *Carnivora* usually excluding the walrus and often excluding the sea-lions; sealskin. — *adj* made of seal or sealskin. — *vi* to hunt seals. — *n* **seal'er** a seal-fisher. — *n* **seal'ing.** — **seal'-fisher** a hunter of seals; a sealing ship; **seal'-fishing; seal'point** a variety of Siamese cat, with dark brown face, paws and tail; **seal rookery** a seals' breeding-place; **seal'skin** the prepared fur of the fur-seal, or an imitation (as of rabbit-skin, or of mohair); a garment made of this. — Also *adj*. [O.E. *seolh* (genitive *sēoles*); O.N. *selr*.]

Sealyham *sēl'i-əm*, *n* (also without *cap*; in full **Sealyham terrier**) a long-bodied, short-legged, hard-coated terrier, first bred at *Sealyham* in Pembrokeshire.

seam *sēm*, *n* a join between edges sewn, welded, etc. together, or between other edges generally; the turned-up edges of such a join on the wrong side of a piece of material; (the mark of) a surgical incision whose edges are rejoined; a wrinkle; a stratum (of a mineral), esp. if thin or valuable; (in cricket) seam bowling (*colloq*). — *vt* to join, provide, or mark with seams. — *n* **seam'er** a person or thing that seams; a ball delivered by seam bowling (*cricket*). — *adj* **seam'less.** — *n* **seam'stress** a woman who sews. — **seam allowance** (in dressmaking) the margin allowed for the seams along the edge of the pieces of a garment; **seam bowler; seam bowling** (*cricket*) bowling in which the seam of the ball is used in delivery to make the ball swerve in flight, or first to swerve and then to break in the opposite direction on pitching; **seam welding** welding of overlapping sheets of metal using wheels or rollers as electrodes. [O.E. *sēam* — *sīwian*, to sew.]

seamy *sēm'i*, *adj* sordid; disreputable. — *adj* **seam'iness.** — **seamy side** the disreputable, sordid or unpleasant side or aspect (of something). [Ety. as for **seam.**]

Seanad *shan'edh* or **Seanad Eireann** (*e'rən*), *n* the upper house of the legislature of the Republic of Ireland. [Ir., senate.]

séance *sā'ãs*, *n* lit. a sitting, esp. of psychical researchers or others who attempt contact with the spirits of the dead, or Spiritualists. [Fr., — L. *sedēre*, to sit.]

SEAQ or **Seaq** *sē'ak*, *abbrev* for Stock Exchange Automated Quotations.

sear[1] *sēr*, *n* the catch that holds a gun at cock or half-cock. [Cf. O.Fr. *serre* — L. *sera*, a bar.]

sear[2] *sēr*, *vt* to scorch; to brand; to cauterise; to render callous or unfeeling. — *n* a mark of searing. — *adj* **seared**. — *n* **seared'ness**. — *n* and *adj* **sear'ing**. — *n* **sear'ness**. — **sear'ing-iron**. [O.E. *sēar*, dry, *sēarian*, to dry up.]

search *sûrch*, *vt* to explore all over in trying to find something; to examine closely; to examine for hidden articles; to ransack; to scrutinise (e.g. one's conscience); to probe (e.g. by thorough questioning); to put to the test; to seek out (usu. with *out*). — *vi* to make examination, etc. — *n* the act or power of searching; thorough examination; a quest. — *adj* **search'able**. — *n* **search'er**. — *adj* **search'ing** penetrating; thorough. — *adv* **search'ingly**. — *n* **search'ingness**. — **search'light** a lamp and reflector throwing a strong beam of light for illuminating a target or quarry by night; the beam of light so projected; **search'-party** a group of people sent out in search of somebody or something missing; **search'-warrant** a legal warrant authorising the searching of a house, etc. — **right of search** the right of a warring country to search neutral ships for contraband of war; **search me** (*slang*) I don't know. [O.Fr. *cerchier* — L. *circāre*, to go about — *circus*, a circle.]

season *sē'zn*, *n* one of the four natural divisions of the year, spring, summer, autumn and winter; the usual, natural, legal or appropriate time, or time of year (for anything); any particular period of time. — *vt* to mature; to temper, reduce somewhat; to bring into suitable condition, e.g. wood by drying it out; to add herbs, spices, etc. to, to flavour; to add as an ingredient. — *vi* to become mature or experienced. — *adj* **sea'sonable** appropriate to the particular season; timely. — *n* **sea'sonableness**. — *adv* **sea'sonably**. — *adj* **sea'sonal** according to the seasons. — *n* **seasonal'ity** the quality of being seasonal. — *adv* **sea'sonally**. — *adj* **sea'soned**. — *n* **sea'soner**. — *n* **sea'soning** the process or act by which anything is seasoned; herbs and spices, salt and pepper, added to food to improve its flavour. — *adj* **sea'sonless** without difference in the seasons. — **season ticket** a ticket valid any number of times within a specified period. — **close season** see under **close**[1]; **in season** (of vegetables, fruit, etc.) ripe, fit and ready for use; (of game, etc.) legally allowed to be killed; (of a bitch) ready to mate, on heat; fit to be eaten; **open season** see under **open**; **out of season** unripe, not normally grown; (of game, etc.) not legally killable. [O.Fr. *seson* — L. *satiō*, *-ōnis*, a sowing.]

seat *sēt*, *n* anything used or intended for sitting on; a chair, bench, saddle, etc.; the part of a chair on which a person sits; a mode of sitting, esp. on horseback; a place where one may sit, as in a theatre, cinema, etc., or a ticket for this; a parliamentary or local government constituency; membership, e.g. of a committee; that part of the body or of a garment on which one sits; that on or in which something rests; site, situation; a place where anything is located, settled or established; a throne; (usu. country) abode, mansion. — *vt* to place on a seat; to cause to sit down; to place in any situation, site, location, etc.; to establish, fix; to assign a seat to; to provide with a seat or seats; to fit accurately. — *adj* **seat'ed**. — (In combination) **-seat'er** denoting a vehicle, sofa, etc. with seats for a given number. — *n* **seat'ing** the taking, provision, allocation or arrangement of seats; a supporting surface; fabric material for covering seats. — *adj* **seat'less**. — **seat'-belt** a belt which can be fastened to hold a person firmly in his or her seat in a car or aircraft, for safety. — **by the seat of one's pants** instinctively, by intuition (*adj* **seat-of-the-pants'** instinctive); **lose one's seat** to fail to be re-elected to Parliament or local council; **take a seat** to sit down; **take one's seat** to take up one's allocated place, esp. in Parliament. [O.N. *sǣti*, seat; cf. O.E. *sǣt*, ambush.]

SEATO *sē'tō*, *abbrev* for South-East Asia Treaty Organisation.

seaward, seawardly, seawards. See under **sea**.

sebum *sē'bəm*, *n* the fatty secretion that lubricates the hair and skin. — *adj* **sebaceous** (*si-bā'shəs*) like tallow; of, like, of the nature of, or secreting sebum. — *n* **seborrhoea** (*seb-ə-rē'ə*) a disorder causing excessive discharge from the sebaceous glands. — *adj* **seborrhoe'ic**. [L. *sēbum*, suet.]

Sec. or **Secy** *abbrev* for Secretary.

sec[1] *sek*, *adj* (of wines) dry. [Fr.]

sec[2] *sek*, *n* short for: secant; second (of time) (*colloq*).

SECAM *sē'kam*, *abbrev* for *séquentiel couleur à mémoire* (Fr.), a broadcasting system for colour television.

secant *sē'kənt*, *n* a straight line which cuts a curve in two or more places (*geom*); the ratio of the hypotenuse to the base of a right-angled triangle formed by dropping a perpendicular from a point on one side of the angle to the other (negative if the base is the side produced) — in trigonometrical notation written **sec**. [L. *secāns*, *-antis*, pres. p. of *secāre*, to cut.]

secateur *sek'ə-tûr* or *-tûr'*, *n* (usu. in *pl*) pruning-shears. [Fr.]

secede *si-sēd'*, *vi* to withdraw, esp. from a party, religious body, federation, or the like. — *n* **secē'der** a country, etc., which secedes; any of a body of Presbyterians who seceded from the Church of Scotland about 1733. — *n* **secession** (*-sesh'ən*) the act of seceding; a body of seceders. — Also *adj*. — *adj* **secess'ional**. — *n* **secess'ionism**. — *n* **secess'ionist** a person who favours or joins in secession. — Also *adj*. — **War of Secession** the American Civil War. [L. *sēcēdĕre*, *sēcēssum* — *sē-*, apart, *cēdĕre*, to go.]

sech *sesh*, *n* a conventional abbreviation of *h*yperbolic *sec*ant.

seclude *si-klōōd'*, *vi* to shut off, esp. from contact, association or influence. — *adj* **seclud'ed** withdrawn, protected from observation or contact from society. — *adv* **seclud'edly**. — *n* **seclusion** (*si-klōō'zhən*) the act of secluding; the state of being secluded; privacy; solitude. [L. *sēclūdĕre*, *-clūsum* — *sē-*, apart, *claudĕre*, to shut.]

second *sek'ənd*, *adj* next after or below the first; (with *every*) other, alternate; additional; supplementary; inferior; subordinate; referring to the person or persons addressed (*gram*); singing or playing a part in harmony slightly below others of the same voice or instrument, as *second soprano*, *second violin*. — *adv* next after the first; in the second place, as the second matter, etc. — *n* a person or thing that is second or of the second class; a place in the second class or rank; second gear; a person who acts as assistant to a protagonist in a duel or a prize fight; a supporter; the 60th part of a minute of time, or of a minute of angular measurement (abbreviated as **sec**); a very small amount of time (*colloq*; esp. in short form **sec**); a second class university degree; the second person (*gram*); the interval between successive tones of the diatonic scale (*mus*); (in *pl*) goods of inferior quality; (in *pl*) a second helping of food (*colloq*). — *vt* to follow; to act as second to (a duellist or prize-fighter); to back, give support to; to support (the mover of) a nomination or resolution; to transfer temporarily to some special employment (*si-kond'*; esp. *mil*). — *adv* **sec'ondarily**. — *n* **sec'ondariness**. — *adj* **sec'ondary** subordinate; subsidiary; of lesser importance; of a second stage, esp. of an electric circuit; not original; (of a voltage, magnetic field, etc.) induced; (of education) between primary and higher or tertiary; (of a feather) growing in the second joint of the wing; (with *cap*; *geol*) Mesozoic, of the period between 225 million and 70 million years ago. — *n* a subordinate; a delegate or deputy; a feather growing in the second wing-joint; (the coil or windings of) the second stage of a transformer, etc. — *n* **secondee** (*sek-on-dē'*) a person who is on secondment. — *n* **sec'onder** a person who seconds a motion, resolution, etc. — *adv* **sec'ondly** as regards the second matter. — *n* **second'ment** temporary transfer to another position, organisation, etc. — **Second Advent** or **Second Coming** a second coming of Christ to earth; **secondary battery** or **secondary cell** one on which the chemical action is reversible, and which can therefore be recharged; **secondary coil** one carrying an induced current; **secondary colours** those produced by mixing two primary colours; **secondary electron** an electron in a beam of secondary emission; **secondary emission** emission of electrons from a surface or particle caused by bombardment with electrons, etc. from another source; **secondary growth** a cancer somewhere other than at the original site; **secondary modern** (formerly) a type of secondary school offering a less academic, more technical education than a grammar school; **secondary picket; secondary picketing** the picketing by workers of a firm with which they are not directly in dispute but which has a trading connection with their own firm, in order to maximise the effects of a strike; **secondary school** any of several types of school for secondary education; **secondary smoking** inhalation of tobacco smoke by non-smokers, passive smoking; **second ballot** a system of election whereby a second vote is taken, the candidate or candidates who received fewest votes in the first ballot being eliminated. — *n* and *adj* **second-best'** next to the best (**come off second-best** to get the worst of a contest). — **second chamber** in a legislature of two houses, the house with fewer powers, usu. acting as a check on the other; **second childhood** mental weakness in extreme old age; **second class** the class next in inferiority to the first. — *adj* **second-class'** (see also below). — **Second Coming** see **Second Advent**; **second cousin** a cousin who has the same pair of great-grandparents, but different grandparents; loosely, a first cousin's child, or a parent's first cousin (properly, first cousin once removed); **second degree** see **degree**; **second floor** (see **floor** for British and U.S. senses). — *adj* **sec'ond-floor.** — **second growth** a new growth of a forest after cutting, fire, etc.; a second crop of grapes in a season. — *vt* and *vi* **second-guess'** (*colloq*) to criticise, find fault with using hindsight; to predict. — *adj* **second-hand'** derived from an original, not original; already used by a previous owner; dealing in second-hand goods. — *n* (*sek'*) a hand on a watch or clock that indicates seconds (see also **seconds-hand** below). — *adv* (*-hand'*) indirectly, at one remove; after use by a previous owner. — **second home** a holiday home; a house owned in addition to one's main residence; a place where one feels as much at home as in one's own house; **second-in-command'** the next under the commanding officer or other person in charge; **second-lieuten'ant** an army officer of lowest commissioned rank; **second man** a man assisting the driver of a locomotive, esp. a steam loco; **sec'ond-mark** the character ″, used for seconds of arc or time or for inches; **second nature** a deeply ingrained habit or tendency. — *adj* **second-rate'** inferior; mediocre. — **second-rat'er; second self** a person with whom one has the closest possible ties, almost intuitively sharing beliefs, attitudes, feelings, ways of behaving; **sec'onds-hand** a hand on a watch or clock that indicates seconds; **second sight** a gift of prophetic vision attributed to certain persons, esp. Scots Highlanders; **second storey** the first floor; **second strike** a counterattack (in nuclear warfare) following an initial attack by an enemy. — *adj* (also with *hyphen*; of a nuclear weapon) specially designed so as to be ready to be used to strike back after a first attack by an enemy and to withstand such an attack. — **second string** an alternative choice, course of action, etc.; **second thoughts** reconsideration. — *adj* **second-to-none'** supreme, best; unsurpassed. — **second wind** recovery of breath after a time, during prolonged exertion. — **at second hand** through an intermediate source, indirectly; by hearsay; **second-class citizen** a member of a community who is not given the full rights and privileges enjoyed by the community as a whole; **second-class mail** or **post** mail sent at a cheaper rate either because of its nature or because the sender is prepared to accept slower delivery. [Fr., — L. *secundus* — *sequī, secūtus*, to follow.]

seconde *si-kond'* or *sə-gɔ̃d*, (*fencing*) *n* a position in parrying. [Fr.]

secret *sē'krit*, *adj* kept away from knowledge of others; guarded against discovery or observation; unrevealed, unidentified; hidden; secluded; preserving secrecy or privacy. — *adv* (*poetic*) secretly. — *n* a fact, purpose, method, etc. that is kept undivulged; anything unrevealed or unknown; secrecy; a key or principle that explains or enables something; an inaudible prayer, esp. in the Mass. — *n* **secrecy** (*sē'kri-si*) the state or fact of being secret; concealment; seclusion; confidentiality; power or habit of keeping secrets; the keeping of secrets. — *vt* **secrete** (*si-krēt'*) to hide; to take away (usu. an object) secretly; to form and emit by means of bodily functions (*biol* or *zool*). — *n* **secrē'tion** the act of secreting; anything which is secreted by an organ, etc. in the body. — *adj* **secrē'tional.** — *adj* **sē'cretive** (also *si-krē'tiv*) inclined to, fond of, secrecy; very reticent; indicative of secrecy. — *adv* **sē'cretively.** — *n* **sē'cretiveness.** — *adv* **sē'cretly** in secret; (of players) inaudibly, to oneself. — *n* **sē'cretness.** — *adj* **secrē'tory** (of a gland, etc.) secreting. — **secret agent** one employed in (the) secret service; **secret police** a police force which operates in secret, usu. dealing with matters of politics, national security, etc.; **Secret Service** a department of the U.S. government service whose operations are covert, not disclosed; (without *caps*) espionage. — **in secret** with precautions against being known, found out, etc.; in confidence, as a secret; secretly; **in on (or in) the secret** admitted to, participating in, having knowledge of, the secret; **keep a secret** not to divulge a secret; **open secret** see under **open.** [L. *sēcernĕre, sēcrētum* — *sē-*, apart, *cernĕre*, to separate.]

secretaire *sek'ri-tār* or *sek-rə-ter'*, *n* a cabinet folding out to form a writing desk, escritoire. [Fr.; cf. **secretary.**]

secretary *sek'ri-tə-ri*, *n* a person, usu. female, who types and deals with correspondence, and does general clerical and administrative work for a company or individual; a person employed to write or transact business for a society, company, etc.; the minister at the head of certain departments of state; an ambassador's or government minister's assistant. — *adj* **secretarial** (*-tā'ri-əl*). — *n* **secretā'riat** (*-ət*) the administrative department of a council, organisation, legislative or executive body; a secretary's office. — *n* **sec'retaryship** the position, duties or art of being a secretary. — **sec'retary-bird** a long-legged snake-eating African bird of prey said to be named from the tufts of feathers at the back of its head like pens stuck behind the ear; **secretary-gen'eral** the chief administrator of an organisation, e.g. the United Nations. — **secretaire à abattant** (*a ab-at-ã*) a writing cabinet with a desk-flap that closes vertically; **Secretary of State** a cabinet minister holding one of the more important portfolios; in the U.S., the foreign secretary. [M.E. *secretarie* — L.L. *sēcrētārius* — L. *sēcrētum*; see **secret.**]

secrete, etc. See **secret**.

sect *sekt*, *n* a body of followers, esp. of an extreme political movement; a school of opinion or belief, esp. in religion or philosophy; a subdivision of one of the main religious divisions of mankind; an organised denomination, used esp. by members of the established churches to express their disapproval of the less established or smaller. — *adj* **sectā'rian** of or pertaining to a sect, or between sects; narrow, exclusive, rigidly adhering to the beliefs of a given sect. — *n* a member of a sect; a person strongly imbued with the characteristics of a sect, esp. if bigoted. — *vt* **sectā'rianise** or **-ize**. — *n* **sectā'rianism**. — *n* **sectary** (*sekt'ər-i*) a member of a sect; a dissenter from the established faith. [L. *secta*, a school or following — *sequī*, *secūtus*, to follow, influenced by *secāre*, to cut.]

sect. *abbrev* for section.

section *sek'shən*, *n* the act of cutting; a division; a portion; one of the parts into which anything may be considered as divided or of which it may be composed; the line of intersection of two surfaces; the surface formed when a solid is cut by a plane; an exposure of rock in which the strata are cut across (*geol*); a plan of anything represented as if cut by a plane or other surface; a thin slice for microscopic examination; any process involving cutting (*surg*); a one-mile square of U.S. public lands; a subdivision of a company, platoon, battery, etc.; a number of men detailed for a special service; a subdivision of an orchestra or chorus, containing (players of) similar instruments or singers of similar voice; a section-mark (*printing*); a building plot (*NZ*). — *vt* to divide into sections; to draw a sectional plan of; to cut a section through (*surg*). — *adj* **sec'tional**. — *n* **sectionalisā'tion** or **-z-**. — *vt* **sec'tionalise** or **-ize** to divide into sections. — *n* **sec'tionalism** a narrow-minded concern for the interests of a particular group, area, etc. — *adj* **sec'tionalist** (also *n*). — *adv* **sec'tionally**. — **sec'tion-cutter** an instrument for making sections for microscopic work; **sec'tion-mark** the sign §, used to mark the beginning of a section of a book or as a reference mark. [L. *secāre*, *sectum*, to cut.]

sector *sek-tər*, *n* a plane figure bounded by two radii and an arc; an object of similar shape, esp. one for measuring angular distance (*astron*); a length or section of a fortified line, army front, guarded area, etc.; a mathematical instrument consisting of two graduated rules hinged together, originally with a graduated arc; a division, section, of (usu.) a nation's economic operations. — *vt* to divide into sectors. — *adj* **sec'toral**. — *adj* **sectorial** (*-tö'ri-əl*) sectoral; adapted for cutting (*zool*). — *n* a tooth designed for flesh-eating. [Ety. as for **section**.]

secular *sek'ū-lər*, *adj* pertaining to the present world, or to things not spiritual; civil, not ecclesiastical; lay, not concerned with religion; (of clergy) not bound by monastic rules (opp. to *regular*); of the secular clergy; lasting for a long time; pertaining to or coming or observed once in a lifetime, generation, century, age. — *n* a layman; a clergyman (such as a parish priest) not bound by monastic rules. — *n* **secūlarīsā'tion** or **-z-**. — *vt* **sec'ularise** or **-ize** to make secular. — *n* **sec'ularism** the belief that the state, morals, education, etc. should be independent of religion. — *n* and *adj* **sec'ularist**. — *adj* **secularist'ic**. — *n* **secularity** (*-lar'*). — *adv* **sec'ularly**. — **secular arm** the civil power, authority, courts. [L. *saeculāris* — *saeculum*, a lifetime, generation.]

secund *sē'kund*, also *sek'und* or *si-kund'*, (*bot*) *adj* (of e.g. leaves) all turned to, positioned on, the same side. [L. *secundus*, following, second.]

secure *si-kūr'*, *adj* having no care or anxiety; free from danger; safe; confident; assured; providing safety; stable; firmly fixed or held; in (police, etc.) custody. — *vt* to make safe, or certain; to assure the possession of; to seize and guard; to get hold of; to contrive to get; to guarantee; to fasten. — *adj* **secūr'able**. — *adv* **secure'ly**. — *n* **secure'ment**. — *n* **secure'ness**. — *n* **secūr'er**. — *n* **securitisā'tion** or **-z-** the procedure, practice or policy of making (loans, mortages, etc.) into negotiable securities. — *vt* **secur'itise** or **-ize** to make (debts) into securities. — *n* **secūr'ity** the state, feeling or means of being secure; protection from espionage, theft, attack, etc.; staff providing such protection; certainty; a pledge, a guarantee; a right conferred on a creditor to make him or her sure of recovering a debt; (usu. in *pl*) a bond or certificate forming evidence of debt or property. — *adj* providing security. — **secure unit** a government-run institution for the confinement of difficult or mentally disordered persons, juvenile offenders, etc.; **security blanket** a blanket, piece of material, etc. that a child comes to depend upon for a sense of comfort and security; something that (irrationally) makes one feel secure or happy (*fig*); an official set of measures, a policy, etc. applied to conceal a matter of (often national) security; **Security Council** a body of the United Nations charged with the maintenance of international peace and security; **security risk** a person considered from his or her political affiliations or other leanings to be likely to divulge (esp. state) secrets. [L. *sēcūrus* — *sē-*, without, *cūra*, care.]

Securitate *si-kūr-i-tä'tā*, *npl* the secret police of Romania.

SED *abbrev* for Scottish Education Department.

sedan *si-dan'*, *n* a covered chair for one person, carried on two poles by servants (also **sedan chair**; *hist*); a large closed motor car, a saloon-car (*NAm* and *NZ*).

sedate *si-dāt'*, *adj* composed; dignified or staid. — *vt* to calm or quieten by means of sedatives. — *adv* **sedāte'ly**. — *n* **sedāte'ness**. — *n* **sedā'tion** the act of calming, or state of being calmed, by means of sedatives. — *adj* **sedative** (*sed'ə-tiv*) calming; composing; allaying excitement or pain. — *n* a sedative medicine or agent. [L. *sēdātus*, past p. of *sēdāre*, to still.]

sedentary *sed'ən-tə-ri* or *sed'ən-tri*, *adj* sitting much and taking little exercise; requiring much sitting; inactive; stationary; not migratory; lying in wait, as a spider; attached to a substratum (*zool*). [L. *sedēns*, *-entis* (pres. p.), and *sedentārius* — *sedēre*, to sit.]

Seder *sā'dər*, (*Judaism*) *n* the ceremonial meal and its rituals on the first night or first two nights of the Passover. [Heb., order.]

sederunt *si-dē'runt*, *si-dā'rənt* or *sā-dā'ro͝ont*, *n* (in Scotland) a sitting, as of a court; a list of persons present. [L. *sēdērunt*, there sat — *sedēre*, to sit.]

sedge *sej*, *n* any species of a family of plants distinguished from grasses by their solid triangular stems and leaf-sheaths without a slit; extended to iris and other plants. — *adj* **sedg'y** of, like or abounding with sedge. — **sedge warbler** a common British warbler found in watery places. [O.E. *secg*.]

sedilia *si-dil'i-ə*, *npl* seats (usu. three, often in niches) for the officiating clergy, on the south side of the chancel: — *nsing* **sedile** (*si-dī'li*, L. *se-dē'le*). [L. *sedīle*, pl. *sedīlia*, seat.]

sediment *sed'i-mənt*, *n* what settles at the bottom of a liquid; dregs; a deposit; material deposited by water, wind or ice and formed into rock (*geol*). — *vt* to deposit as sediment; to cause or allow to deposit sediment. — *adj* **sedimentary** (*-men'tər-i*). — *n* **sedimentā'tion** deposition of sediment; the formation of sedimentary rocks. — **sedimentary rocks** those formed by accumulation and deposition of fragmentary materials or organic remains. [L. *sedimentum* — *sedēre*, to sit.]

sedition *si-di'shən*, *n* public speech or actions intended to promote disorder; (vaguely) any offence against the state short of treason. — *adj* **sedi'tious**. — *adv*

sedi'tiously. — *n* **sedi'tiousness**. [O.Fr., — L. *sēditiō, -ōnis* — *sēd-*, away, *īre, ītum*, to go.]

seduce *si-dūs'*, *vt* to draw aside from party, belief, allegiance, service, duty, etc.; to lead astray; to entice; to corrupt; to induce to have sexual intercourse. — *n* **sedūce'ment** the act of seducing or drawing aside; allurement. — *n* **sedū'cer**, *fem* **seduc'tress**. — *n* and *adj* **sedū'cing**. — *adv* **sedū'cingly**. — *n* **seduction** (*si-duk'shən*) the act or practice of seducing; allurement. — *adj* **seduc'tive** tending or intended to seduce; alluring. — *adv* **seduc'tively**. — *n* **seduc'tiveness**. [L. *sēdūcere, sēductum* — *sē-*, aside, *dūcere*, to lead.]

sedulous *sed'ū-ləs*, *adj* assiduous or diligent; painstaking. — *n* **sedulity** (*si-dū'li-ti*) or **sed'ulousness**. — *adv* **sed'ulously**. [L. *sēdulus* — *sē dolō*, without deception, hence in earnest.]

sedum *sē'dəm*, *n* any rock plant of the genus *Sedum*, with white, yellow or pink flowers. [L. *sēdum*, houseleek.]

see[1] *sē*, *vt* to perceive by the sense seated in the eye; to perceive mentally; to apprehend; to recognise; to understand; to learn; to be aware by reading; to look at; to judge, to deem; to refer to; to ascertain; to make sure; to make sure of having; to wait upon, escort; to spend time with, or meet with regularly, esp. romantically; to call on; to receive as a visitor; to meet; to consult; to experience; to meet and accept (another's bet) by staking a similar sum. — *vi* to have power of vision; to see things well enough; to look or inquire; to be attentive; to consider: — *pa t* **saw**; *pa p* **seen**. — *imper* passing into *interj* look; behold. — *adj* **see'able**. — *n* **see'ing** sight; vision; clear-sightedness; atmospheric conditions for good observation (*astron*). — *adj* having sight, or insight; observant; discerning. — *conj* (also **seeing that**) since; in view of the fact. — *n* **seer** (*sē'ər*) a person who sees; (*sēr*) a person who sees into the future. — *adj* **see'-through** transparent. — **have seen better days** or **one's best days** to be now on the decline; **let me see** a phrase employed to express reflection; **see about** to consider; to do whatever is to be done about; to attend to; **see fit** to think it appropriate (to); **see off** to accompany (someone) at their departure; to get rid of (*colloq*); **see one's way clear to** (*colloq*) to feel that one will be able to; **see out** to conduct to the door; to see to the end; to outlast; **see over** or **round** to look or be conducted all through e.g. premises, property; **see red** see under **red**; **see someone right** (*colloq*) to take care of someone, usu. in the sense of giving them a tip or reward; **see the light** to experience a religious conversion; to come round to another's way of thinking, to come to understand and agree with someone (usu. *facetious*); **see things** see under **thing**; **see through** to participate in to the end; to back up till difficulties end; to understand the true nature of, esp. when faults or bad intentions are concealed by a good appearance; **see to** to look after; to make sure about; **see what I can do** do what I can; **see you (later)** or **be seeing you** (*colloq*) goodbye for now. [O.E. *sēon*.]

see[2] *sē*, *n* the office of bishop of a particular diocese; (wrongly according to some) a cathedral city, also a diocese. — **Holy See** the papal court. [O.Fr. *se, sied* — L. *sēdēs, -is* — *sedēre*, to sit.]

seed *sēd*, *n* a multicellular structure by which flowering plants reproduce, consisting of embryo, stored food and seed-coat, derived from the fertilised ovule (*bot*); a small hard fruit or part in a fruit, a pip; a seedlike object or aggregate; semen (*literary* or *poetic*); the condition of having or proceeding to form seed; sown land; a first principle; origin, beginning or germ; a crystal introduced to start crystallisation; offspring, descendants, race; a tournament player who has been seeded (*colloq*). — *vi* to produce seed; to run to seed. — *vt* to sow; to remove seeds from; (in lawn-tennis tournaments, etc.) to arrange (the draw) so that the best players do not meet in the early rounds; to deal with (good players) in this way; to introduce particles of material (into something, e.g. a chemical solution) to induce crystallisation or precipitation; (*specif*) to induce rainfall, disperse a storm or freezing fog, etc. by scattering cloud with particles of an appropriate substance (also **cloud seed**). — *adj* **seed'ed** with the seeds removed; having seeds; bearing seed; sown; showing seeds or carpels (*heraldry*); (of a tournament player) who has been seeded. — *n* **seed'er** a seed-drill; an apparatus for removing seeds from fruit; a seed-fish. — *adv* **seed'ily**. — *n* **seed'iness**. — *n* and *adj* **seed'ing**. — *adj* **seed'less**. — *adj* **seed'like**. — *n* **seed'ling** a plant reared from the seed; a young plant ready for planting out from a seedbed; a seed-oyster. — Also *adj*. — *adj* **seed'y** abounding with seed; run to seed; out of sorts; shabby. — **seed'bed** a piece of ground for receiving seed; an environment, etc. that fosters a particular thing (esp. something considered undesirable); **seed'box** or **seed'case** the part of a plant in which the seeds are encased; **seed'cake** a cake flavoured with caraway seeds; **seed'-coat** the hard protective covering of the seeds of flowering plants; the testa; **seed'-coral** coral in small irregular pieces; **seed'-corn** grain for sowing; assets likely to bring future profit; **seed'-drill** a machine for sowing seeds in rows; **seed'-fish** a fish about to spawn; **seed'-leaf** a cotyledon, leaf contained in a seed; **seed'lip** a sower's basket (O.E. *lēap*, basket); **seed'-lobe** a cotyledon; **seed money** money with which a project or enterprise is set up; **seed'-oyster** a very young oyster; **seed'-pearl** a very small pearl; **seed'-plot** a piece of nursery ground, a hotbed; **seed'-potato** a potato tuber for planting; **seed'-vessel** a dry fruit; the ovary of a flower. — **go** or **run to seed** to grow rapidly and untidily in preparation for seeding, instead of producing the vegetative growth desired by the grower; to disappoint expectation of development; to become exhausted; to go to waste; (usu. **go**) to become unkempt or shabby; **sow the seed(s) of** to initiate. [O.E. *sǣd*.]

seek *sēk*, *vt* to look for; to try to find, get or achieve; to ask for; to aim for; to resort to, betake oneself to; to try. — *vi* to make search: — *pa t* and *pa p* **sought** (*sōt*). — *n* **seek'er**. — **seek after** to go in quest of; **seek out** to look for and find; to bring out from a hidden place; **sought after** in demand; **to seek** not to be found; lacking. [O.E. *sēcan* (past t. *sōhte*, past p. *gesōht*).]

seem *sēm*, *vi* to appear; to appear to; to appear to be. — *n* **seem'er**. — *n* **seem'ing** appearance; semblance; a false appearance. — *adj* apparent; ostensible. — *adv* apparently; in appearance only (esp. in composition, e.g. **seem'ing-simple**). — *adv* **seem'ingly** apparently; as it would appear. — *n* **seem'ingness**. — *n* **seem'liness**. — *adj* **seem'ly** (*compar* **seem'lier**, *superl* **seem'liest**) becoming; suitable. — **it seems** it appears; it would seem; **it would seem** it turns out; I have been told. [O.N. *sǣma*, to seem.]

seen. See **see**[1].

seep *sēp*, *vi* to ooze, percolate. — *n* **seep'age**. — *adj* **seep'y**.

seer[1] *sēr*, *n* an Indian weight of widely ranging amount, officially about 2 lb. [Pers. *sīr*.]

seer[2]. See **see**[1].

seersucker *sēr'suk-ər*, *n* a thin crinkly Indian linen or cotton fabric. [Pers. *shīr o shakkar*, lit. milk and sugar.]

seesaw *sē'sö*, *n* alternate up-and-down or back-and-forth motion; repeated alternation; a plank balanced so that its ends may move up and down alternately, used in play; the activity of rising and sinking on it. — *adj* going like a seesaw. — *adv* in the manner of a seesaw. — *vi* to play at seesaw; to move or go like a seesaw. [Prob. a reduplication of **saw**[2].]

seethe *sēdh*, *vi* to boil; to surge; to be agitated (by anger, excitement, etc.): — *pa t* and *pa p* **seethed**. — *n* and *adj* **seeth'ing**. [O.E. *sēothan*, past p. *soden*.]

segment *seg'mənt*, *n* a part cut off; a portion; part of a circle, ellipse, etc. cut off by a straight line, or of a sphere, ellipsoid, etc. by a plane; a section; one of a linear series of similar portions, as of a somite or metamere of a jointed animal, or a joint of an appendage; a lobe of a leaf-blade not separate enough to be a leaflet; the smallest sound unit of speech (*phon*). — *vt* and *vi* (*-ment'*) to divide into segments. — *adj* **segmental** (*-men'tl*). — *adv* **segmen'tally**. — *adj* **seg'mentary**. — *n* **segmentā'tion**. — *adj* **segmen'ted** (or *seg'*). — **segmental arch** an arch forming an arc of a circle whose centre is below the springing. [L. *segmentum* — *secāre*, to cut.]

sego *sē'gō*, *n* a showy liliaceous plant of the western U.S.: — *pl* **sē'gos**. [Ute Indian name.]

segregate *seg'ri-gāt*, *vt* to set apart; to seclude; to isolate; to group apart. — *vi* to separate out in a group or groups or mass; to separate into dominants and recessives (*genetics*). — *adj* set apart. — *n* that which is segregated. — *adj* **seg'regable**. — *n* **segregā'tion** the act of segregating; the state of being segregated; separation of dominants and recessives in the second generation of a cross (*genetics*); the separation of hereditary factors from one another during spore formation; separation of one particular class of persons from another, as on grounds of race. — *n* **segregā'tionist** a believer in racial or other segregation. — *adj* **seg'regative**. [L. *sēgregāre*, *-ātum* — *sē-*, apart, *grex*, *gregis*, a flock.]

segue *sā'gwä*, (*mus*) *vi* to proceed without pause, to follow on, usu. (in imperative) as a musical direction to proceed immediately with the next song, movement, etc. without a pause (also *fig*: — *pr p* **se'gueing**; *pa t* and *pa p* **se'gued**. — *n* the term or direction to segue; the act or result of segueing; segued music (live or recorded); a compilation, esp. in popular recorded music, in which tracks follow on continuously. [It.]

seguidilla *seg-i-dēl'yä*, *n* a Spanish dance; a tune for it, in triple time. [Sp.]

sei *sā*, *n* a kind of rorqual (also called **sei whale**). [Norw. *sejhval*, sei whale.]

seicento *sā-chen'tō*, *n* (in Italian art, literature, etc.) the seventeenth century. [It., abbrev. of *mille seicento*, one thousand six hundred.]

seiche *sāsh* or *sesh*, *n* a periodic fluctuation from side to side of the surface of lakes, usu. caused by changes in barometric pressure. [Swiss Fr.]

Seidlitz *sed'lits*, *adj* applied to a laxative powder (or rather pair of powders), Rochelle salt and sodium bicarbonate mixed together, and tartaric acid — totally different from the mineral water of *Sedlitz* in Bohemia.

seif *sāf* or *sīf*, *n* a long sand-dune lying parallel to the direction of the wind that forms it. [Ar. *saif*, sword.]

seignior *sā'* or *sē'nyər*, or **seigneur** *sen-yœr*, *n* a feudal lord, lord of a manor, esp. in France or French Canada. — *n* **seign'iorage** or **seign'orage** lordship; a right, privilege, etc. claimed by an overlord; an overlord's royalty on minerals; a percentage on minted bullion. — *adj* **seignio'rial, seigneu'rial, seignoral** (*sān'* or *sen'*) or **signo'rial** (*sin-*). — *n* **seign'iorship**. — *n* **seign'ory** or **seign'iory** feudal lordship; the council of an Italian city-state (*hist*); (also **seigneurie** *sen'yə-rē*) a domain. — **grand** (*grã*) **seigneur** a great lord; a man of aristocratic dignity and authority. [Fr. *seigneur* — L. *senior*, *-ōris*, compar. of *senex*, old. In L.L. *senior* is sometimes equivalent to *dominus*, lord.]

seine *sān* or *sēn*, *n* a large vertical fishing-net whose ends are brought together and hauled. — *vt* and *vi* to catch or fish with a seine. — *n* **sein'er**. — *n* **sein'ing**. [O.E. *segne* — L. *sagēna* — Gr. *sagēnē*, a fishing-net.]

seise *sēz*, *vt* an old spelling of **seize**, still used legally in the sense of to put in possession. — *n* **seis'in** possession (now, as freehold); an object handed over as a token of possession; sasine (*Scots law*).

seismo- *sīz-mō-* or **seism-** *combining form* denoting earthquake. — *adj* **seis'mal, seis'mic** or **seis'mic**. — *n* **seismicity** (*-mis'i-ti*) liability to or frequency of earthquakes. — *n* **seis'mism** earthquake phenomena. — *n* **seis'mogram** a seismograph record. — *n* **seis'mograph** an instrument for registering earthquakes. — *n* **seismog'rapher**. — *adj* **seismograph'ic** or **seismograph'ical**. — *n* **seismog'raphy** the study of earthquakes. — *adj* **seismolog'ic** or **seismolog'ical**. — *n* **seismol'ogist**. — *n* **seismol'ogy** the science of earthquakes. — *n* **seismom'eter** an instrument for measuring earth-movements. — *adj* **seismomet'ric** or **seismomet'rical**. — *n* **seismom'etry**. — *n* **seis'moscope** an instrument for detecting earthquakes. — *adj* **seismoscop'ic**. [Gr. *seismos*, a shaking — *seiein*, to shake.]

seize or (*formerly* and *legal*) **seise** *sēz*, *vt* to grasp suddenly, eagerly or forcibly; to take by force; to take prisoner; to apprehend; to take possession of; to take legal possession of; to lash or make fast (*naut*). — *vi* to lay hold (with *on* or *upon*; to jam or weld partially, because of lack of lubrication. — *adj* **seiz'able**. — *n* **seiz'er**. — *n* **seiz'ing** the action of the verb; a cord to seize ropes with (*naut*). — *n* **seizure** (*sē'zhər*) the act of seizing; capture; a sudden fit or attack of illness. — **be seized with** or **by** to have a sudden strong attack of (e.g. remorse, pneumonia); **seize** or **seise of** to put in possession of; **seized** or **seised of** in (legal) possession of; aware of; in the process of considering; **seize up** to jam, seize, become immoveable or stuck. [O.Fr. *seisir*, *saisir* — L.L. *sacīre*, prob. Gmc.]

Sejm *sām*, *n* the unicameral parliament of the Polish People's Republic. [Pol., assembly.]

Sekt or **sekt** *sekt*, *n* German sparkling wine or champagne. [Ger.]

selachian *si-lā'ki-ən*, *n* any fish of the shark class, including rays, skates and dogfish. — Also *adj*. [Gr. *selachos*.]

seldom *sel'dəm*, *adv* rarely. — *adj* infrequent. [O.E. *seldum*, altered.]

select *si-lekt'*, *vt* to pick out from a number by preference. — *adj* picked out; choice; exclusive. — *adj* **selec'ted**. — *n* **selec'tion** the act of selecting; a thing or collection of things selected; a number or group of things from which to select; a horse selected as likely to win a race. — *adj* pertaining to or consisting of collection. — *adj* **selec'tive** having or exercising power of selection; able to discriminate, e.g. between different frequencies; choosing, involving, etc. only certain things or people. — *adv* **selec'tively**. — *n* **selectiv'ity** (*sel-*) ability to discriminate. — *n* **select'ness** the quality of being select. — *n* **select'or**. — *adj* **selecto'rial**. — **select committee** a number of members of parliament chosen to report and advise on some matter; **selective weedkiller** a weedkiller that does not destroy garden plants. [L. *sēligěre*, *sēlectum* — *sē-*, aside, *legěre*, to choose.]

Selenic *si-lē'nik* or *-len'ik* (*chem*), *adj* of selenium in higher valency (**selenic acid**). — *adj* **selē'nious** or **selē'nous** of selenium in lower valency (**selenious acid**). — *n* **selenite** (*sel'i-nīt*) gypsum, esp. in transparent crystals (anciently supposed to wax and wane with the moon); a salt of selenious acid. — *adj* **selenitic** (*sel-i-nit'ik*). — *n* **selenium** (*si-lē'ni-əm*) a non-metallic element (symbol **Se**; atomic no. 34) discovered in 1817. — *adj* **selē'nodont** having crescent-shaped ridges on the crowns of the molar teeth. — *n* **selē'nograph** a map of the moon. — *n* **selenographer** (*sel-in-og'rə-fər*) a student of selenography. — *adj* **selenographic** (*si-lē-nə-graf'ik*) or **selenograph'ical**. — *n* **selenography** (*sel-i-nog'rə-fi*) the mapping of the moon; the study of the moon's physical features. — *adj* **selēnolog'ical**. — *n* **selenol'ogist** a selenographer. — *n* **selenol'ogy** the scientific study of the moon. — **selenium cell** a photoelectric cell depending on the fact that light increases the electric conductivity of selenium. [Gr. *selēnē*, moon, *Selēnē*, the moon-goddess.]

self *self*, *pron* (*loosely*) oneself, myself, himself, etc. — *n* personality, ego; a side of one's personality; identity; personality; what one is; self-interest; a self-coloured plant or animal: — *pl* **selves** (*selvz*) or, of things in one colour, **selfs**. — *adj* uniform in colour; made in one piece; made of the same material. — *n* **self'hood** personal identity; existence as a person; personality. — *adj* **self'ish** chiefly or wholly regarding one's own self; having no regard to others. — *adv* **self'ishly**. — *n* **self'ishness**. — *adj* **self'less** having no regard to self, altruistic. — *n* **self'lessness**. — *n* **self'ness** egotism; personality. — **one's self** see **oneself**; **second self** see **second**. [O.E.]

self- *self-* *combining form* indicating: action upon the agent; action by, of, in, in relation to, etc. oneself or itself; automatic action. — *n* **self-aban'donment** disregard of self. — *n* **self-abase'ment** self-humiliation. — *n* **self-abnegā'tion** renunciation of one's own interest; self-denial. — *adj* **self-absorbed'** wrapped up in one's own thoughts or affairs. — *n* **self-absorp'tion** the state of being self-absorbed; self-shielding (*phys*). — *n* **self-abuse'** revilement of oneself; masturbation. — *ns* **self-abus'er**; **self-accusā'tion**. — *adj* **self-act'ing** automatic. — *adj* **self-addressed'** addressed to oneself. — *adj* **self-adhē'sive** able to stick to a surface without the use of (additional) glue, etc. — *adj* **self-adjust'ing** requiring no external adjustment. — *adj* **self-admin'istered**. — *ns* **self-admirā'tion**; **self-advance'ment**; **self-advert'isement**; **self-ad'vertiser**; **self-aggrand'isement**. — *adj* **self-aggrand'ising**. — *n* **self-anal'ysis**. — *adj* **self-appoint'ed**. — *ns* **self-appreciā'tion**; **self-approbā'tion**; **self-appro'val**. — *adj* **self-approv'ing**. — *adj* **self-assert'ing** or **self-asser'tive** given to asserting one's opinion or to putting oneself forward. — *ns* **self-asser'tion**; **self-assū'rance** assured self-confidence. — *adj* **self-assured'**. — *adj* **self-aware'**. — *ns* **self-aware'ness**; **self-betray'al**; **self-bind'er** a reaping-machine with automatic binding apparatus. — *adj* **self-cat'ering** (of a holiday, accommodation, etc.) in which one cooks, etc. for oneself. — *adj* **self-cen'tred** preoccupied with oneself; selfish. — *adj* **self-clean'ing**. — *adj* **self-clōs'ing** shutting automatically. — *n* **self-cock'er** a firearm in which the hammer is raised by pulling the trigger. — *adj* **self-cock'ing**. — *n* **self'-colour** uniform colour; natural colour. — *adj* **self-col'oured**. — *n* **self-command'** self-control. — *n* **self-complā'cence** satisfaction with oneself, or with one's own performances. — *adj* **self-complā'cent**. — *n* **self-conceit'** an inflated opinion of oneself, one's own abilities, etc.; vanity. — *adj* **self-conceit'ed**. — *ns* **self-concern'**; **self-condemna'tion**. — *adj* **self-condemned'** condemned by one's own actions or out of one's own mouth. — *adj* **self-condemn'ing**. — *adj* **self-confessed'** admitted, openly acknowledged (by oneself). — *n* **self-con'fidence** confidence in, or reliance on, one's own powers; self-reliance. — *adj* **self-con'fident**. — *adv* **self-con'fidently**. — *n* **self-congratulā'tion**. — *adj* **self-congrat'ulatory** congratulating oneself. — *adj* **self-con'scious** conscious of one's own mind and its acts and states; conscious of being observed by others. — *n* **self-con'sciousness**. — *n* **self-consis'tency** consistency of each part with the rest; consistency with one's principles. — *adj* **self-consis'tent**. — *adj* **self-contained'** wrapped up in oneself, reserved; (of a house, flat, room, etc.) not approached by an entrance common to others; complete in itself. — *n* **self-contempt'**. — *n* **self-contradic'tion** the act or fact of contradicting oneself; a statement whose terms are mutually contradictory. — *adj* **self-contradic'tory**. — *n* **self-control'** power of controlling oneself. — *adj* **self-convict'ed** convicted by one's own acts or words. — *n* **self-convic'tion**. — *adj* **self-correct'ing**. — *adj* **self-crit'ical**. — *n* **self-crit'icism** critical examination and judgment of one's own works and thoughts. — *n* **self-deceit'** self-deception. — *n* **self-deceiv'er**. — *n* **self-decep'tion** the act or practice of deceiving oneself. — *adj* **self-defeat'ing** that defeats its own purpose. — *n* **self-defence'** defending one's own person, rights, etc. (**art of self-defence** orig. boxing, now used more loosely to refer to any of a number of martial arts). — *n* **self-degradā'tion**. — *n* **self-delu'sion** the delusion of oneself by oneself. — *n* **self-denī'al** forbearing to gratify one's own appetites or desires. — *adj* **self-deny'ing**. — *adv* **self-deny'ingly**. — *adj* **self-destroy'ing**. — *vi* **self-destruct'**. — *n* **self-destruc'tion** the destruction of anything by itself; suicide. — *adj* **self-destruc'tive**. — *n* **self-determinā'tion** direction of the attention or will to an object; the power of a population to decide its own government and political relations or of an individual to live his or her own life. — *n* **self-dispar'agement**. — *adj* **self-displeased'**. — *ns* **self-dispraise'**; **self-distrust'**; **self-doubt'**; **self-dramatisā'tion** or **-z-** presentation of oneself as if a character in a play; seeing in oneself an exaggerated dignity and intensity. — *adj* **self-drive'** (of a motor vehicle) to be driven by the hirer. — *adj* **self-driv'en** driven by its own power. — *adj* **self-ed'ucated** educated by one's own efforts. — *n* **self-efface'ment** keeping oneself in the background out of sight; withdrawing from notice or rights. — *adj* **self-effac'ing**. — *adj* **self-elect'ive** having the right to elect oneself or itself, as by co-option of new members. — *n* **self-elec'tion**. — *adj* **self-employed'** working independently in one's own business. — *n* **self-employ'ment**. — *n* **self-esteem'** good opinion of oneself; self-respect. — *n* **self-ev'idence**. — *adj* **self-ev'ident** evident without proof. — *n* **self-examinā'tion** a scrutiny into one's own state, conduct, etc. — *adj* **self-explan'atory** or **self-explain'ing** obvious, bearing its meaning in its own face. — *n* **self-express'ion** the giving of expression to one's personality, as in art. — *n* **self-feed'er** a device for supplying anything automatically, esp. a measured amount of foodstuff for cattle, etc. — *adj* **self-feed'ing**. — *n* **self-fertilīsā'tion** or **-z-**. — *adj* **self-finan'cing**. — *adj* **self-flatt'ering**. — *n* **self-flatt'ery**. — *adj* **self-fo'cusing**. — *adj* **self-forget'ful** unselfishly forgetful of self. — *adv* **self-forget'fully**. — *adj* **self-fulfill'ing**. — *n* **self-fulfil'ment**. — *adj* **self-gen'erating**. — *adj* **self-giv'ing**. — *adj* **self-glazed'** glazed in one tint. — *n* **self-glorificā'tion**. — *adj* **self-gov'erning**. — *n* **self-gov'ernment** autonomy; government without outside interference. — *n* **self-hate'** or **self-hāt'red**. — *adj* and *n* **self-heal'ing**. — *n* **self-help'** doing things for oneself without help of others. — Also *adj*. — *n* **self-hypnō'sis** or **self-hyp'notism**. — *n* **self-im'age** one's own idea of oneself. — *n* **self-immolā'tion** offering oneself up in sacrifice; suttee. — *n* **self-import'ance** an absurdly high sense of one's own importance; pomposity. — *adj* **self-import'ant**. — *adv* **self-import'antly**. — *n* **self-improve'ment** improvement, by oneself, of one's status, education, job, etc. — *adj* **self-imposed'** taken voluntarily on oneself. — *adj* **self-induced'** induced by oneself; produced by self-induction (*electr*). — *n* **self-induc'tance** the property of an electric circuit whereby self-induction occurs. — *n* **self-induc'tion** the property of an electric circuit by which it resists any change in the current flowing in it. — *n* **self-indul'gence** undue gratification of one's appetites or desires. — *adj* **self-indul'gent.** — *adj* **self-inflict'ed** inflicted by oneself on oneself. — *vi* **self-inject'.** — *n* **self-in'terest** private interest; regard to oneself. — *n* **self-justificā'tion.** — *adj* **self-jus'tifying** justifying oneself; automatically arranging the length of the lines of type (*printing*). — *n* **self-knowl'edge** knowledge of one's own nature. — *adj* **self-light'ing** igniting automatically. — *adj* **self-lim'ited** (*pathol*) running a definite course. — *adj* **self-load'ing** (of a gun) automatically reloading itself. — *adj* **self-lock'ing** locking automatically. — *n* **self-love'** the love of oneself; tendency to seek one's own welfare or advantage. — *adj* **self'-made** risen to a high position from poverty or obscurity by one's own exertions. — *n* **self-mas'tery** self-command; self-control. — *adj* **self-op'erating.** — *adj* **self-opin'ionated** obstinately adhering to one's own opinion. — *adj* **self-perpet'uating.** — *n* **self-pit'y** pity for oneself. — *n* **self-pollinā'tion** transfer of pollen to the stigma of the same flower (or sometimes the same plant or clone). — *n* **self-por'trait** a portrait of oneself painted by oneself. — *n* **self-por'traiture.** — *adj* **self-possessed'** having self-possession. — *n* **self-possess'ion** collectedness of mind; calmness. — *n* **self-praise'.** — *n* **self-preservā'tion** care, action or instinct for the preservation of one's own life. — *adj* **self-preser'vative** or **self-preser'ving.** — *adj* **self-proclaimed'.** — *adj* **self-professed'.** — *adj* **self-prop'agating** propagating itself when left to itself. — *adj* **self-propelled'.** — *adj* **self-propell'ing** carrying its own means of propulsion. — *ns* **self-propul'sion; self-protec'tion** self-defence. — *adj* **self-protect'ing.** — *adj* **self-protec'tive.** — *adj* **self-rais'ing** (of flour) already mixed with something that causes it to rise. — *n* **self-realīsā'tion** or **-z-** attainment of such development as one's mental and moral nature is capable of. — *n* **self-regard'** self-interest; self-respect. — *adj* **self-reg'ulating** or **self-reg'ulatory** regulating itself. — *ns* **self-regulā'tion; self-relī'ance** healthy confidence in one's own abilities. — *adj* **self-relī'ant.** — *n* **self-renunciā'tion** self-abnegation. — *n* **self-repress'ion** restraint of expression of the self. — *n* **self-reproach'** prickings of conscience. — *n* **self-respect'** respect for oneself or one's own character. — *n* **self-restraint'** a refraining from excess; self-control. — *adj* **self-reveal'ing.** — *n* **self-revelā'tion.** — *adj* **self-right'eous** righteous in one's own estimation. — *n* **self-right'eousness.** — *adj* **self-right'ing** (of a boat, etc.) righting itself when capsized. — *n* **self-rule'.** — *adj* **self-rul'ing.** — *n* **self-sac'rifice** forgoing one's own good for the sake of others. — *adj* **self-sac'rificing.** — *adj* **self'-same** the very same. — *ns* **self-same'ness; self-satisfac'tion** satisfaction with oneself; complacency. — *adj* **self-sat'isfied.** — *adj* **self-seal'ing** (of envelopes, etc.) that can be sealed by pressing two adhesive surfaces together; (of tyres) that seal automatically when punctured. — *n* **self-seed'er** a plant that propagates itself by growing from its own seeds shed around it. — *n* **self-seek'er** a person who looks mainly to their own interests; a device which automatically tunes a radio to required wavelengths by means of a push-button control. — *n* and *adj* **self-seek'ing.** — *n* **self-ser'vice** helping oneself, as in a restaurant, petrol station, etc. — Also *adj.* — *adj* **self-ser'ving** taking care of one's own interests above all others. — *adj* **self-sown'** sown naturally without man's agency. — *adj* **self-stan'ding** independent, standing or functioning alone, without support. — *n* **self-star'ter** an automatic contrivance for starting a motor; a car fitted with one; a person with initiative and drive. — *adj* **self'-styled** called by oneself; pretended. — *n* **self-suffi'ciency.** — *adj* **self-suffi'cient** requiring nothing from without; excessively confident in oneself. — *adj* **self-suffīc'ing.** — *n* **self-support'** support or maintenance without outside help; paying one's way. — *adj* **self-support'ing.** — *adj* **self-taught'.** — *ns* **self-tor'ment; self-treat'ment; self-will'** obstinacy. — *adj* **self-willed'.** — *adj* **self-wind'ing** (of a watch) wound by the wearer's spontaneous movements. — *n* **self-wor'ship.** [O.E. *self.*]

-self *-self,* used in combination to form reflexive and emphatic pronouns: — *pl* **-selves** (*selvz*). — **be oneself, himself,** etc. to be in full possession of one's powers; to be (once more) at one's best; **by oneself,** etc. alone.

Seljuk *sel-jo͞ok',* *n* a member of any of the Turkish dynasties (11th–13th cent.) descended from *Seljūq.* — *adj* **Seljuk'** or **Seljuk'ian.**

sell *sel,* *vt* to give or give up for money or other equivalent; to betray; to trick; to promote the sale of; to make acceptable; to cause someone to accept (e.g. an idea, plan); to convince someone of the value of. — *vi* to make sales; to be sold, to be in demand for sale: — *pa t* and *pa p* **sold.** — *n* (*colloq*) a deception; let-down; an act of selling; stocks to be sold; an order to sell stocks. — *adj* **sell'able.** — *n* **sell'er** a person who sells; that which has a sale. — **sell-by date** a date, indicated on a manufacturer's or distributor's label, after which goods, esp. foods, are considered no longer fit to be sold (also *fig*); **sellers'** or **seller's market** one in which sellers control the price, demand exceeding supply; **sell'ing-price** the price at which a thing is sold; **selling race** or **plate** a race of which the winning horse must be put up for auction at a price previously fixed; **sell'-out** a betrayal; a show for which all seats are sold. — **sell down the river** to play false, betray; **sell off** to sell cheaply in order to dispose of (*n* **sell'-off**); **sell on** to sell (what one has bought) to someone else; **sell one's life dearly** to do great injury to the enemy before one is killed; **sell out** to dispose entirely of; to betray; **sell short** to belittle, disparage; to sell (stocks, etc.) before one actually owns them, when intending to buy at a lower price; **sell up** to sell the goods of, for debt; to sell all; **to sell** for sale. [O.E. *sellan,* to give, hand over.]

Sellotape® *sel'ə-tāp,* (also without *cap*) *n* a brand of usu. transparent adhesive tape. — *vt* to stick with Sellotape.

seltzer *selt'sər,* *n* a mineral water from Nieder-*Selters* near Wiesbaden in Germany, or a commercial imitation of it.

selva *sel'və,* *n* (usu. in *pl* **selvas**) a wet forest in the Amazon basin. [Sp., Port. — L. *silva,* wood.]

selvage or **selvedge** *sel'vij,* *n* a differently finished edging of cloth; a border, esp. one sewn or woven so as not to fray. — *n* **sel'vagee** (or *-jē'*) a marked hank of rope, used as a strap or sling. [**self** and **edge.**]

selves *selvz,* *pl* of **self.**

Sem. *abbrev* for: Seminary; Semitic.

sem. *abbrev* for: semester; semi-colon.

semantic *si-man'tik,* *adj* relating to meaning, esp. of words. — *nsing* **seman'tics** the area of linguistics dealing with the meaning of words. — *npl* (*loosely*) differences in, and shades of, meaning of words. — *adv* **seman'tically.** — *n* **seman'ticist.** — *n* **sememe** (*se'mēm* or *sē'mēm*) a unit of meaning, usu. specif. the smallest linguistically analysable unit. [Gr. *sēmantikos,* significant.]

semaphore *sem'ə-fōr,* *n* a signalling apparatus, an upright with arms that can be turned up or down — often the signaller's own body and arms with flags. —

vt and *vi* to signal in this way. [Fr. *sémaphore* — Gr. *sēma*, sign, signal, *-phoros*, bearing, bearer.]

semasiology *si-mā-zi-ol'ə-ji* or *-si-ol'*, *n* the science of semantics. — *adj* **semasiolog'ical**. [Gr. *sēmăsia*, meaning.]

sematic *si-mat'ik*, (*biol*) *adj* (of an animal's colouring) serving for recognition, attraction or warning. [Gr. *sēma*, sign.]

semeiology. Same as **semiology**.

sememe. See under **semantic**.

semen *sē'mən*, *n* the liquid that carries spermatozoa. — See also **seminal**. [L. *sēmen*, *-inis*, seed.]

semester *si-mes'tər*, *n* an academic half-year course or term. [L. *sēmēstris* — *sex*, six, *mēnsis*, a month.]

semi- *sem-i-*, *pfx* denoting: half; (*loosely*) nearly, partly, incompletely. — *n* **sem'i** (colloq. shortening) a semi-detached house; a half-angle. — *adj* **semi-ann'ual** (chiefly *NAm*) half-yearly. — *adv* **semi-ann'ually**. — *adj* **semi-automat'ic** partly automatic but requiring some tending by hand. — *adj* **semi-auton'omous**. — *adv* **semi-auton'omously**. — *n* and *adj* **semi-barbā'rian**. — *n* **semi-bar'barism**. — *n* **sem'ibrēve** half a breve (2 minims or 4 crotchets). — *n* **sem'ibull** a pope's edict issued between election and coronation. — *n* **sem'ichōrus** half, or part of, a chorus; a passage sung by it. — *n* **sem'icircle** half a circle, bounded by the diameter and half the circumference. — *adj* **semicir'cular** (**semicircular canals** the curved tubes of the inner ear concerned with equilibrium). — *adv* **semicir'cularly**. — *n* **sem'icolon** (or *-kō'lon*) the point (;) marking a division greater than the comma. — *adj* **semiconduct'ing**. — *n* **semiconductiv'ity**. — *n* **sem'iconductor** any solid, non-conducting at low temperatures or in pure state, which is a conductor at high temperatures or when very slightly impure; (formerly) any substance with electrical conductivity between that of metals and of non-conductors. — *adj* **semicon'scious**. — *n* **sem'icylinder** a longitudinal half-cylinder. — *adj* **semidepō'nent** (*gram*) passive in form in the perfect tenses only. — Also *n*. — *adj* **semi-detached'** partly separated; joined by a party wall to one other house only. — *n* such a house. — *n* **semi-diam'eter** half the diameter, esp. the angular diameter. — *adj* **semi-diur'nal** accomplished in twelve hours; pertaining to half the time or half the arc traversed between rising and setting. — *adj* **semi-divine'** half-divine; of, or of the nature of, a demigod. — *n* **semidocument'ary** a cinema film with an actual background but an invented plot. — *n* **semi-dome'** half a dome, esp. as formed by a vertical section. — *adj* **semidomes'ticated** partially domesticated; half-tame. — *adj* **semi-doub'le** having only the outermost stamens converted into petals. — *adj* **semi-dry'ing** (of oils) thickening without completely drying on exposure. — *n* **semi-ellipse'** half of an ellipse, bounded by a diameter, esp. the major axis. — *adj* **semi-ellip'tical**. — *n* **semi-ev'ergreen** a plant which is evergreen in its original habitat but not completely so in other places it is now grown, dropping leaves in severe weather conditions. — Also *adj*. — *adj* **semifī'nal** (in competitions, sports contests, etc.) of the contest immediately before the final. — *n* a last round but one. — *n* **semifī'nalist** a competitor in a semifinal. — *adj* **semi-fin'ished** partially finished, *specif* of metal shaped into rods, sheets, etc., in preparation for further processing into finished goods. — *adj* **semiflu'id** nearly solid but able to flow to some extent. — Also *n* (*sem'*). — *adj* **semiglob'ular**. — *n* and *adj* **semi-im'becile**. — *adj* **semi-independ'ent** not fully independent. — *adj* **semi-liq'uid** half-liquid. — Also *n* (*sem'*). — *adj* **semi-lu'nar** or **-lu'nate** half-moon shaped. — *n* **sem'ilune** (*-lo͞on*) a half-moon-shaped object, body or structure. — *adj* **semimen'strual** half-monthly. — *adj* **semi-month'ly** (chiefly *NAm*) half-monthly. — *n* a half-monthly periodical. — *adj* **semi-nūde'** half-naked. — *adj* **semi-offic'ial**. — *adv* **semi-offic'ially**. — *adj* **semi-opaque'**. — *adj* **semiovip'arous** producing imperfectly developed young. — *adj* **semi-per'meable** permeable by a solvent but not by the dissolved substance. — *n* **sem'iplume** a feather with ordinary shaft but downy web. — *adj* **semi-prec'ious** valuable, but not valuable enough to be reckoned a gemstone. — *n* **sem'iquāver** half a quaver. — *adj* **semi-rig'id** (of an airship) having a flexible gas-bag and stiffened keel. — *n* **sem'itone** half a tone — one of the lesser intervals of the musical scale, as from B to C. — *adj* **semiton'ic**. — *n* **semi-transpā'rency**. — *adj* **semitranspā'rent** imperfectly transparent. — *adj* **semi-trop'ical** subtropical. — *adj* **semi-tū'bular** like half of a tube divided longitudinally. — *n* **sem'ivowel** a sound having the nature of both a vowel and a consonant; a letter representing it, in English, chiefly *w* and *y*, and sometimes used of the liquid consonants *l* and *r*. — *adj* **semi-week'ly** issued or happening twice a week. — Also *n* and *adv*. [L. *sēmi-*, half-.]

seminal *sem'in-l*, *adj* pertaining to, or of the nature of, seed or semen; of or relating to the beginnings, first development, etc. of an idea, study, etc.; generative; notably creative or influential in future development. — *adj* **seminif'erous** seed-bearing; producing or conveying semen. [L. *sēmen*, *-inis*, seed.]

seminar *sem'i-när*, *n* a group of advanced students working in a specific subject of study under a teacher; a class at which a group of students and a tutor discuss a particular topic; a discussion group on any particular subject. — *adj* **seminarial** (*-ā'ri-əl*) of a seminary. — *n* **seminā'rian** or **sem'inarist** (*-ər-ist*) a student in a seminary. — *n* **sem'inary** (*-ə-ri*) formerly, a pretentious name for a school (esp. for young ladies); now, usu. a theological college providing training and instruction to ministers, priests, rabbis, etc. [L. *sēminārium*, a seed-plot — *sēmen*, seed.]

semiology *sem-i-ol'ə-ji* or **semiotics** *sem-i-ot'iks*, *n* the science of signs or symbols, esp. of spoken or written words as signs and their relationships with the objects, concepts, etc. they refer to (*linguis*); the scientific study of symptoms (*pathol*). — *adj* **semiolog'ical** or **semiot'ic**. [Gr. *semeion*, sign.]

Semite *sem'* or *sē'mīt*, *n* a member of any of the peoples said (in the Bible: Gen. x) to be descended from Shem, or speaking a Semitic language. — *adj* **Semitic** (*sem-*, *sim-* or *səm-it'ik*). — *n* any Semitic language. — *n* **Sem'itism** a Semitic idiom or characteristic; Semitic ways of thought; the cause of the Semites, esp. the Jews. — *n* **Sem'itist** a Semitic scholar. — **Semitic languages** Assyrian, Aramaic, Hebrew, Phoenician, Arabic, Ethiopic, and other ancient languages of this Afro-Asiatic sub-family. [Gr. *Sēm*, Shem.]

semolina *sem-ə-lē'nə* or *-lī'nə*, *n* the particles of fine, hard wheat that do not pass into flour in milling, used to make puddings, thicken soups, etc. [It. *semolino*, dimin. of *semola*, bran — L. *simila*, fine flour.]

sempervivum *sem-pər-vī'vəm*, *n* any plant of the *Crassulaceae*, including the houseleek and various ornamental plants.

sempiternal *sem-pi-tûr'nl*, *adj* everlasting. [L. *sempiternus* — *semper*, ever.]

semplice *sem'plē-che*, (*mus*) *adj* and *adv* simple or simply, without embellishments. [It.]

sempre *sem'pre*, (*mus*) *adv* always, throughout. [It., — L. *semper*, always.]

Semtex *sem'teks*, *n* a very powerful kind of plastic explosive (q.v.).

SEN *abbrev* for: Special Educational Needs; State Enrolled Nurse.

Sen. *abbrev* for: senate; senator; senior.

sen *sen, n* a hundredth part of the Japanese yen and of the currencies of several S.E. Asian countries; a coin of this value. [Chin. *ch'ien*, coin.]

senary *sēn'* or *sen'ər-i, adj* of, involving or based on six. — *n* a set of six. [L. *sēnārius* — *sēnī*, six each — *sex*, six.]

senate *sen'it, n* the governing body of ancient Rome; a legislative or deliberative body, esp. the upper house of a national or state legislature; a body of venerable or distinguished people; the governing body of certain British universities (in Scotland, **Senā'tus Academ'icus**). — *n* **senator** (*sen'ə-tər*) a member of a senate (**Senator of the College of Justice** a Lord of Session). — *adj* **senatorial** (*sen-ə-tö'ri-əl*). — *adv* **senato'rially** with senatorial dignity. — *n* **sen'atorship.** — **sen'ate-house** the meeting-place of a senate. — **senātus consultum** a decree of the senate, esp. in ancient Rome. [L. *senātus* — *senex, senis*, an old man.]

send *send, vt* to cause, direct, or tell to go; to propel; to cause to be conveyed; to dispatch; to forward; to grant; (orig. of jazz) to rouse (someone) to ecstasy. — *vi* to dispatch a message or messenger (often with *for*); to pitch into the trough of the sea (*naut*; sometimes **scend**): — *pa t* and *pa p* **sent**; *naut* **send'ed.** — *n* the sound or a movement of breaking waves; a swash. — *n* **send'er.** — *n* **send'ing** dispatching; pitching; transmission. — **send'-off** a gathering to express good wishes at departing or starting a journey; **send'-up** a process of making fun of someone or something; a play, film, novel, etc. doing this. — **send down** to send to prison (*colloq*); to expel from university; **send for** to require by message to come or be brought; **send in** to submit (an entry) for a competition, etc.; **send off** (in football, etc.) to order a player to leave the field and take no further part in the game, usu. after an infringement of the rules; **send on** to send in advance; to re-address and re-post (a letter or package); **send up** to make fun of; to sentence to imprisonment (*colloq*); **send word** to send an intimation. [O.E. *sendan*.]

sendal *sen'dəl, n* a thin silk or linen; a garment made of this. [O.Fr. *cendal*.]

senescent *si-nes'ənt, adj* verging on old age; ageing. — *n* **senesc'ence.** [L. *senēscēns, -entis*, pres. p. *of senēscēre*, to grow old — *senex*, old.]

seneschal *sen'i-shl, n* a steward or major-domo in a great house (*hist*); an administrative and judicial title still retained for certain cathedral officials and a judicial position on Sark (Channel Islands). — *n* **sen'eschalship.** [O.Fr., lit. old servant.]

Senhor *se-nyör', fem* **Senhora** *senyör'a* and **Senhorita** *-ē'ta, n* the Portuguese forms corresponding to the Spanish **Señor**, *fem* **Señora** and **Señorita**.

senile *sē'nīl, adj* characteristic of or accompanying old age; showing the decay or imbecility of old age. — *adv* **sēn'ilely.** — *n* **senility** (*si-nil'i-ti*) old age; the imbecility of old age. — **senile dementia** mental decay in old age, senility. [L. *senīlis* — *senex, senis*, old.]

senior *sēn'yər, adj* elder; older or higher in standing; more advanced. — *n* a person who is senior; a fourth-year student (*US*). — *n* **seniority** (*sē-ni-or'i-ti*) the state or fact of being senior; priority by age, time of service, or standing. — **senior citizen** an old age pensioner; **senior common room** see under **junior**; **senior service** the navy. [L. *senior, -ōris*, compar. of *senex*, old.]

senna *sen'ə, n* any tropical shrub of the genus *Cassia*; its purgative dried leaflets. — **senna pods** the dried fruits of the shrub, widely used as a laxative; **senna tea** an infusion of senna. [Ar. *sanā*.]

sennit *sen'it* or **sinnet** *sin'it, n* a braid of rope strands.

Señor *se-nyör', n* a gentleman; (in address) sir; (prefixed to a name) Mr: — *fem* **Señora** (*ra*) a lady; madam; (as a title) Mrs. — *n* **Señorita** (*-rē'ta*) a young lady; Miss. [Sp., — L. *senior*, older.]

sense *sens, n* faculty of receiving sensation, general or particular; immediate consciousness; inward feeling; impression; opinion; mental attitude; discernment; understanding; appreciation; feeling for what is appropriate; discerning feeling for things of some particular kind; (usu. in *pl*) one's right wits; soundness of judgment; reasonableness; sensible or reasonable discourse; that which is reasonable; plain matter of fact; the realm of sensation and sensual appetite; meaning; interpretation; gist; direction. — *adj* pertaining to a sense or senses. — *vt* to have a sensation, feeling or appreciation of; to appreciate, grasp or comprehend; to become aware (that); (of computers) to detect (e.g. a hole, constituting a symbol, in punched card or tape). — *adj* **sen'sate** perceived by the senses. — *n* **sensation** (*sen-sā'shən*) awareness of a physical experience, without any element derived from previous experiences; awareness by the senses generally; an effect on the senses; power of sensing; an emotion or general feeling; a thrill; a state, or matter, of general excited interest in the public, audience, etc.; melodramatic quality or method. — *adj* **sensā'tional** causing or designed to cause strong feelings, esp. of excitement or horror; excellent (*colloq*); related to sensation. — *n* **sensā'tionalism** the doctrine that our ideas originate solely in sensation; a striving after wild excitement and melodramatic effects. — *n* **sensā'tionalist.** — *adj* **sensātionalist'ic.** — *adv* **sensā'tionally.** — *adj* **sense'less** unconscious; without good sense; meaningless. — *adv* **sense'lessly.** — *n* **sense'lessness.** — *n* and *adj* **sen'sing.** — **sense'-datum** what is received immediately through the stimulation of a sense-organ (also called **sen'sum**: — *pl* **sen'sa**); **sense'-organ** a structure specially adapted for the reception of stimuli, such as eye, ear and nose; **sense-percep'tion** perception by the senses. — **bring someone to their senses** to make someone recognise the facts; to let someone understand they must mend their behaviour; **come to one's senses** to regain consciousness; to start behaving sensibly (again); **common sense** see under **common**; **five senses** the senses of sight, hearing, smell, taste and touch; **in a sense** in a sense other than the obvious one; in a way; after a fashion; **make sense** to be understandable, sensible or rational; **make sense of** to understand; to see the purpose in, or explanation of; **sixth sense** an ability to perceive what lies beyond the powers of the five senses; **take leave of one's senses** to go mad, start behaving unreasonably. [L. *sēnsus* — *sentīre*, to feel.]

sensible *sen'si-bl, adj* having or marked by good sense, judicious; perceptible by sense; perceptible, appreciable; having power of sensation. — *n* **sensibil'ity** sensitiveness, sensitivity; capacity of feeling or emotion; readiness and delicacy of emotional response; sentimentality; (usu. in *pl*) feelings that can be hurt. — *n* **sen'sibleness.** — *adv* **sen'sibly** in a sensible manner; to a sensible or perceptible degree; so far as the senses show. [M.E. — O.Fr. — L.L. *sēnsibilis*.]

sensitise or **-ize** *sen'si-tīz, vt* to render sensitive, or more sensitive, or sensitive in a high degree. — *n* **sensitisā'tion** or **-z-**. — *adj* **sen'sitised** or **-z-**. — *n* **sen'sitiser** or **-z-**.

sensitive *sen'si-tiv, adj* having power of sensation; feeling readily, acutely or painfully; capable of receiving stimuli; reacting to outside influence; ready and delicate in reaction; sensitised; susceptible to the action of light (*phot*); pertaining to, or depending on, sensation; (of documents, etc.) with secret or controversial contents. — *adv* **sen'sitively.** — *n* **sen'sitiveness** or **sensitiv'ity** response to stimulation of the senses; heightened awareness of oneself and others within the context of personal and social relationships; abnormal responsiveness as to an allergen; degree of responsiveness to electric current, radio waves or light; (of an instrument) readiness and delicacy in recording changes. — **sensitive plant** a plant, esp. *Mimosa pudica*, that shows more than usual irritability when touched or shaken, by movement of its leaves, etc. [M.E. — O.Fr. — Med. L. *sēnsitīvus*.]

sensitometer *sen-si-tom'i-tər, n* an instrument for measuring sensitivity, as of photographic films. [*sensit*ive and **-meter**.]

sensor *sen'sər, n* a device that detects a change in a physical stimulus and turns it into a signal which can be measured or recorded, or which operates a control. [**sense** and noun-forming sfx. *-or* used for agentlike nouns.]

sensori- *sen-sə-ri-* or **senso-** *sen-sō-* or *-sə-*, *combining form* indicating the senses, as in *sensorineural*, *sensorimotor* and *sensoparalysis*.

sensorium *sen-sör'i-əm*, (*biol*) *n* the seat of sensation in the brain; the brain; the mind; the nervous system. — *adj* **sensor'ial** sensory. — *adj* **sensory** (*sen'sə-ri*) of the sensorium; of sensation. — **sensory deprivation** the reduction to a minimum of all external stimulation reaching the body, a situation used in psychological experiments, etc. [L.L.]

sensual *sen'sū-əl* or *-shōō-əl*, *adj* of the senses, as distinct from the mind; not intellectual or spiritual; carnal; connected with gratification, esp. undue gratification of bodily sense; voluptuous. — *n* **sensualīsā'tion** or **-z-**. — *vt* **sen'sualise** or **-ize** to make sensual; to debase by carnal gratification. — *n* **sen'sualism** sensual indulgence; the doctrine that all our knowledge is derived originally from sensation; the regarding of the gratification of the senses as the highest end. — *n* **sen'sualist** a person given to sensualism or sensual indulgence; a debauchee; a believer in the doctrine of sensualism. — *adj* **sensualist'ic**. — *n* **sensual'ity** the quality of being sensual; indulgence in sensual pleasures. — *adv* **sen'sually**. — *n* **sen'sualness**. [L.L. *sensuālis* — L. *sēnsus*, sense.]

sensum. See **sense-datum** under **sense**.

sensuous *sen'sū-əs, adj* pertaining to sense without implication of lasciviousness or grossness (apparently coined by Milton to distinguish this sense from those of **sensual**); connected with sensible objects; easily affected by or pleasing to the medium of the senses. — *adv* **sen'suously**. — *n* **sen'suousness**. [L. *sēnsu(s)* and *-ous* adj. sfx.]

sent *sent, pa t* and *pa p* of **send**.

sentence *sen'təns, n* determination of punishment pronounced by a court or a judge; a judgment, decision; a number of words making a complete grammatical structure, in writing generally begun with a capital letter and ended with a full stop or its equivalent. — *vt* to pronounce judgment on; to condemn. — *n* **sen'tencer**. — *adj* **sentential** (*-ten'shl*). — *adv* **senten'tially**. — *adj* **senten'tious** full of meaning; aphoristic, abounding in maxims; tending to moralise. — *adv* **senten'tiously**. — *n* **senten'tiousness**. [Fr., — L. *sententia* — *sentīre*, to feel.]

sentient *sen'shyənt* or *-shənt, adj* conscious; capable of sensation; aware; responsive to stimulus. — *n* **sen'tience** or **sen'tiency**. [L. *sentiēns, -entis*, pres. p. of *sentīre*, to feel.]

sentiment *sen'ti-mənt, n* a thought or body of thought tinged with emotion; a thought expressed in words; emotion; feeling bound up with some object or ideal; regard to ideal considerations; sensibility, refined feelings; consciously worked-up or partly insincere feeling; sentimentality. — *adj* **sentimental** (*-men'tl*) pertaining to, given to, characterised by or expressive of sentiment; given to, indulging in or expressive of sentimentality. — *vi* **sentimen'talise** or **-ize** to behave sentimentally; to indulge in sentimentality. — *vt* to make sentimental; to treat sentimentally. — *n* **sentimentality** (*-mən-tal'i-ti*) or **sentimen'talism** disposition to wallow in sentiment; self-conscious working up of feeling; affectation of fine feeling; sloppiness. — *n* **sentimen'talist**. — *adv* **sentimen'tally**. [L.L. *sentīmentum* — L. *sentīre*, to feel.]

sentinel *sen'ti-nl, n* a person posted on guard, a sentry. — *adj* acting as a sentinel. — *vt* to watch over; to post as a sentinel; to supply with sentinels. — **sentinel crab** a crab of the Indian Ocean with long eye-stalks. [Fr. *sentinelle* — It. *sentinella*, watch, sentinel.]

sentry *sen'tri, n* a sentinel; a soldier on guard; watch, guard. — **sen'try-box** a box to shelter a sentry; **sen'try-go** or **-duty** a sentry's beat or duty.

senza *sen'tsä*, (*mus*) *prep* without. [It.]

Sep. or **Sept.** *abbrev* for: September; Septuagint.

sep. *abbrev* for separate.

sepal *sep'l* or *sē'pl*, (*bot*) *n* a member of a flower calyx. — *adj* **sep'alous** having sepals. — *adj* **sep'aline** (*-īn*) or **sep'aloid** of the form of sepals. [Fr. *sépale*, invented by N.J. de Necker (1790) from Gr. *skepē*, cover.]

separate *sep'ə-rāt, vt* to divide; to part; to sever; to disconnect; to disunite; to remove; to isolate; to keep apart; to seclude; to set apart for a purpose; to shut off from cohabitation, esp. by judicial decree; to remove cream from, using a separator. — *vi* to part; to withdraw; to secede; to come out of combination or contact; to become disunited. — *adj* (*sep'ə-rit* or *sep'rit*) separated; divided; apart from another; distinct. — *n* an offprint; (in *pl*) items of dress, e.g. blouse, skirt, etc., forming separate parts of an outfit. — *n* **separability** (*-ə-bil'i-ti*). — *adj* **sep'arable**. — *n* **sep'arableness**. — *adv* **sep'arably**. — *adv* **sep'arately**. — *n* **sep'arateness**. — *n* **separā'tion** act of separating or disjoining; state of being separate; disunion; chemical analysis; cessation of cohabitation by agreement or judicial decree, without a formal dissolution of the marriage tie. — *n* **sep'aratism** (*-ə-tizm*). — *n* **sep'aratist** a person who withdraws or advocates separation from an established church, federation, organisation, etc. — Also *adj*. — *adj* **sep'arative** (*-ə-tiv*) tending to separate. — *n* **sep'arātor** a person who or thing which separates; a machine for separating cream from milk by whirling. — **separate development** segregation of different racial groups, each supposed to progress in its own way; **separate maintenance** a provision made by a husband for his separated wife; **separation allowance** government allowance to a serviceman's wife and dependents. [L. *sēparāre, -ātum* — *sē-*, aside, *parāre*, to put.]

Sephardim *si-fär'dēm* or *-dim, npl* Jews of Spanish and Portuguese descent. — *adj* **Sephar'dic**. [Heb.]

sepia *sē'pi-ə, n* cuttlefish ink; a pigment made from it, or an artificial imitation; its colour, a fine brown; a sepia drawing. — *adj* of the colour of sepia; done in sepia. [L., — Gr. *sēpiā*, cuttlefish.]

sepoy *sē'poi*, (*hist*) *n* an Indian soldier in European service. [Urdu and Pers. *sipāhī*, horseman.]

seppuku *sep-ōō'kōō, n* hara-kiri. [Jap.]

seps *seps, n* a very venomous skink with a serpentlike body, the serpent-lizard. [Gr. *sēps*.]

sepsis *sep'sis*, (*med*) *n* putrefaction; invasion by pathogenic bacteria: — *pl* **sep'sēs**. [Gr. *sēpsis*, putrefaction.]

sept *sept, n* (orig. in Ireland) a division of a tribe; a clan. — *adj* **sept'al**. [Prob. for **sect**, infl. by L. *saeptum*.]

sept- *sept-*, **septi-** *sep-ti-*, **septem-** *sep-tem'-* or *sep'təm-*, *combining form* denoting the quantity or amount seven. — *adj* **septilateral** (*sep-ti-lat'ər-əl*) seven-sided. — *n* **septillion** (*sep-til'yən*; modelled on **million**) the seventh power of a million; the eighth power of a thousand (*NAm*). [L. *septem*.]

septate *sep'tāt, adj* partitioned; having septa (*biol*). — *n* **septā'tion** division by partitions. [Ety. as for **septum**.]

September *səp-* or *sep-tem'bər, n* the ninth (earlier seventh) month of the year. — *n* **Septem'brist** a participator in the September massacres of royalist prisoners in Paris, 2–7 Sept. 1792. [L. *September, -bris*.]

septenarius *sep-ti-nā'ri-əs, n* a seven-metrical-foot verse. — *adj* **septenary** (*sep-tē'nə-ri* or *sep'tə-nə-ri*) numbering or based on seven. — *n* a seven, set of seven (esp. years); a septenarius. [L. *septēnārius*, of seven.]

septennium *sep-ten'i-əm, n* a period of seven years: — *pl* **septenn'ia**. — *adj* **septenn'ial**. — *adv* **septenn'ially**. [L. *septennis — annus*, a year.]

septet or **septette** *sep-tet', n* a composition for seven performers; a set of seven (esp. musicians). [Ger. *Septett* — L. *septem*.]

sept-foil *set'-foil, n* tormentil; a figure divided by seven cusps (*archit*). [Fr. *sept*, seven, O.Fr. *foil* — L. *folium*, a leaf.]

septic *sep'tik, adj* putrefactive. — *n* **septicaemia** (*sep-ti-sē'mi-ə*) presence of pathogenic bacteria in the blood. — *adv* **sep'tically**. — *n* **septicity** (*-tis'i-ti*). — **septic tank** a tank, usually below ground, in which sewage is decomposed by anaerobic bacteria. [Gr. *sēptikos — sēpein*, to putrefy.]

septilateral and **septillion**. See under **sept-**.

septimal *sep'ti-ml, adj* relating to or based on the number seven. — *n* **septime** (*sep'tēm*) the seventh parrying position in fencing. [L. *septimus*, seventh — *septem*, seven.]

septuagenarian *sep-tū-ə-ji-nā'ri-ən, n* a person seventy years old, or between seventy and eighty. — *adj* of that age. [L. *septuāgēnārius — septuāgēnī*, seventy each.]

Septuagesima *sep-tū-ə-jes'i-mə, n* the third Sunday before Lent (also **Septuagesima Sunday**). [L. *septuāgēsimus, -a, -um*, seventieth.]

Septuagint *sep'tū-ə-jint, n* the Greek Old Testament, traditionally attributed to 72 translators at Alexandria in the 3rd century B.C. — usually expressed by LXX. — *adj* **Septuagin'tal**. [L. *septuāgintā — septem*, seven.]

septum *sep'təm*, (*biol*) *n* a partition: — *pl* **sep'ta**. [L. *saeptum* (used in pl.), a fence, enclosure — *saepīre*, to fence.]

septuple *sep'tū-pl, -tū', -tōō-* or *-tōō', adj* sevenfold. — *vt* to multiply sevenfold. — *n* **sep'tūplet** one of seven children or animals born at one birth; a group of seven notes played in six or eight time (*mus*). [L.L. *septuplus* — L. *septem*, seven.]

sepulchre or in N.Am. **sepulcher** *sep'əl-kər, n* a tomb; a recess, usually in the north chancel wall, or a structure placed in it, to receive the reserved sacrament and the crucifix from Maundy Thursday or Good Friday till Easter (**Easter sepulchre**); burial. — *vt* to entomb; to enclose as a tomb. — *adj* **sepulchral** (*si-pul'krəl*) of, or of the nature of, a sepulchre; as if of or from a sepulchre; funereal, gloomy, dismal; hollow-toned. — *adj* **sepul'tural**. — *n* **sep'ulture** burial. — **whited sepulchre** see under **white**. [L. *sepulcrum, sepultūra — sepelīre, sepultum*, to bury.]

seq. *abbrev* for (L.) *sequens*, following: — *pl* **seqq.** for (L.) *sequentes* or *sequentia*.

sequacious *si-kwā'shəs, adj* ready to follow a leader or authority; compliant; pliant; observing logical sequence or consistency. — *n* **sequā'ciousness** or **sequacity** (*si-kwas'i-ti*). [L. *sequāx, sequācis — sequī*, to follow.]

sequel *sē'kwəl, n* that which follows; consequences; upshot; a resumption of a story already complete in itself, in book, play, film, etc. form. — *n* **sequela** (*si-kwē'lə*) any abnormal condition following or related to a previous disease; the psychological, etc. after-effect of any trauma: — often in *pl* **sequē'lae** (*-lē*). [L. *sequēla — sequī*, to follow.]

sequence *sē'kwəns, n* a state or fact of being sequent or consequent; succession; order of succession; a series of things following in order; a succession of quantities each derivable from its predecessor according to a law (*math*); a set of three or more cards consecutive in value; successive repetition in higher or lower parts of the scale or in higher or lower keys (*mus*); (in cinematography) a division of a film; (in liturgics) a hymn in rhythmical prose, sung after the gradual and before the gospel. — *adj* **sē'quent** following; consequent; successive; consecutive. — *n* that which follows. — *adj* **sequential** (*si-kwen'shl*) in, or having, a regular sequence; sequent; (of data) stored one after another in a system (*comput*). — *n* **sequentiality** (*-shi-al'i-ti*). — *adv* **sequen'tially**. — **sequence of tenses** the relation of tense in subordinate clauses to that in the principal. [L. *sequēns, -entis*, pres. p. of *sequī*, to follow.]

sequester *si-kwes'tər, vt* to set aside; to seclude; to set apart; to confiscate; to remove from someone's possession until a dispute can be settled, creditors satisfied, etc.; to hold the income of for the benefit of the next incumbent; to sequester the estate or benefice of the next incumbent (*eccles*); to remove or render ineffective (a metal ion) by adding a reagent that forms a complex with it (e.g. as a means of preventing or getting rid of precipitation in water). — *adj* **seques'tered** retired, secluded. — *n* **seques'trant** (*chem*) a substance which removes an ion or renders it ineffective, by forming a complex with the ion. — *vt* **sequestrate** (*sek', sēk'* or *si-kwes'*) to sequester; to make bankrupt. — *n* **sequestrā'tion** (*sek-* or *sēk-*) act of sequestering; the action of a sequestrant (*chem*). — *n* **seq'uestrātor**. [L.L. *sequestrāre, -ātum* — L. *sequester*, a depositary — *secus*, apart.]

sequin *sē'kwin, n* a spangle used to decorate a garment; an old Italian gold coin. — *adj* **se'quined** or **se'quinned**. [Fr., — It. *zecchino — zecca*, the mint; of Ar. origin.]

sequoia *si-kwoi'ə, n* either of the gigantic conifers of the genus *sequoia*, the Californian big tree and the redwood — sometimes called *Wellingtonia*. [After the Cherokee Indian scholar *Sequoiah*.]

ser. *abbrev* for: serial; series; sermon.

sera. See **serum**.

sérac or **serac** *sā-rak'* or *sā'rak, n* one of the cuboidal or pillarlike masses into which a glacier breaks on a steep incline. [Swiss Fr., orig. a kind of cheese.]

seraglio *sə-, se-rä'li-ō* or *-lyō, n* women's quarters in a Muslim house or palace; a harem; a collection of wives or concubines; a Turkish palace, esp. that of the sultans at Constantinople: — *pl* **sera'glios**. [It. *serraglio* — L. *sera*, a door-bar, confused with Turk. *saray, serāī*, a palace.]

seral. See **sere**.

serape *se-rä'pā, n* a Spanish-American woollen blanket or poncho worn as a man's outer garment when riding, etc.; a similar (usu. woman's) woollen blanket-style wrap, esp. for outdoor wear. [Sp. *sarape*.]

seraph *ser'əf, n* a six-winged celestial being (from the Bible: Isaiah vi); an angel of the highest of the nine orders; a person of angelic character or mien: — *pl* **ser'aphs** or **ser'aphim**. — *adj* **seraphic** (*-af'*) or **seraph'ical**. — *adv* **seraph'ically**. [Heb. *Serāphīm* (pl.).]

seraskier *ser-as-kēr'*, (*hist*) *n* a Turkish commander-in-chief or war minister. — *n* **seraskier'ate** the office of seraskier. [Turk. pron. of Pers. *ser'asker — ser*, head, Ar. *'asker*, army.]

Serb *sûrb* or **Serbian** *sûr'bi-ən, n* a native or citizen of Serbia (formerly a kingdom, now a republic of Yugoslavia); a member of the people principally inhabiting Serbia; the South Slav language of Serbia.

— *adj* of Serbia, its people or their language. — *n* and *adj* **Serbo-Cro'at** or **Serbo-Croatian** (*-krō-ā'shən*) (of) the official language of Yugoslavia. [Serb. *Srb.*]

SERC *abbrev* for Science and Engineering Research Council.

sere *sēr*, *n* a series of plant communities following each other. — *adj* **sēr'al**. [L. *seriēs*, series.]

serein *sə-rē'*, *n* fine rain from a cloudless sky. [Fr., — L. *sērum*, evening, *sērus*, late.]

serenade *ser-i-nād'*, *n* a composition like a symphony, usually lighter in tone and in more movements; a performance in the open air by night, esp. at a woman's window; a piece suitable for such performance. — *vt* to entertain with a serenade. — *vi* to perform a serenade. — *n* **serenā'der**. — *n* **serenata** (*-i-nä'tä*) a (symphonic) serenade; a pastoral cantata. [Fr. *sérénade*, and It. *serenata* — L. *serēnus*, bright clear sky; meaning influenced by L. *sērus*, late.]

serendipity *ser-ən-dip'i-ti*, *n* the faculty of making happy chance finds. — *n* **serendip'itist** a person who believes in serendipity; a person who has this faculty. — *adj* **serendip'itous** discovered by luck or chance; pertaining to or having serendipity. — *adv* **serendip'itously**. [*Serendip*, a former name for Sri Lanka. Horace Walpole coined the word (1754) from the tale 'The Three Princes of Serendip'.]

serene *sə-rēn'*, *adj* calm; unclouded; unruffled; (with *cap*) an adjunct to the titles of members of some European royal families. — *n* (*poetic*) calm brightness; serene sky or sea. — *adv* **serēne'ly**. — *n* **serēne'ness**. — *n* **serenity** (*-ren'i-ti*). — **all serene** (*colloq*) everything as it should be. [L. *serēnus*, clear.]

serf *sûrf*, *n* a person in modified slavery, esp. one bound to work on the land; a villein: — *pl* **serfs**. — *n* **serf'dom** or **serf'hood**. [Fr., — L. *servus*, a slave.]

Serg. *abbrev* for Sergeant.

serge *sûrj*, *n* a strong twilled fabric, now usually of worsted. — *adj* of serge. [Fr., — L. *sērica*, silk.]

sergeant or **serjeant** *sär'jənt*, *n* (usu. with *g*) a non-commissioned officer next above a corporal; (with *g*) an officer of police; (usu. with *g*) alone or as a prefix, designating certain officials; (with *j*) (*formerly*) a barrister of highest rank (in full **serjeant-at-law'**). — *n* **ser'geancy** or **ser'jeancy** office or rank of sergeant or serjeant. — *n* **ser'geantship** or **ser'jeantship**. — **sergeant-** or **serjeant-at-arms'** an officer of a legislative body or the Court of Chancery, for making arrests, etc.; **ser'geant-fish** a fish with stripes, similar to the mackerels; **sergeant-mā'jor** the highest non-commissioned officer; (formerly) an officer of rank varying from major to major-general (**company sergeant-major** the senior warrant-officer in a company; **regimental sergeant-major** a warrant-officer on the staff of a battalion, regiment, etc.). — **Common Serjeant** (in London) an assistant to the Recorder, a judge of the quarter-session court. [Orig., a servant — Fr. *sergent* — L. *serviēns*, *-entis*, pres. p. of *servīre*, to serve.]

Sergt *abbrev* for Sergeant.

serial, seriate and **seriatim**. See **series**.

sericeous *sə-rish'əs*, *adj* silky; covered with soft silky hairs (*bot*); with silky sheen. — *n* **ser'iculture** silkworm breeding. — *n* **sericul'turist**. — *n* **ser'igraph** a print made by silk-screen process. — *n* **serig'rapher**. — *adj* **serigraph'ic**. — *n* **serig'raphy**. [L.L. *sericeus* — L. *sēricus*, Chinese, silken — Gr. *Sēr*, a Chinese, a silkworm (pl. *Sērĕs*).]

seriema *ser-i-ē'mə* or *-ā'mə*, *n* either of two S. American birds of the family *Cariamidae*, related to the cranes and the rails, somewhat like a small crested crane in form. [Tupí *çariama*.]

series *sē'rēz* or *-riz*, *n* a set of things in line or in succession, or thought of in this way; a set of things having something in common, e.g. of books in similar form issued by the same publishing house; a set of things differing progressively; the sum where each term of a sequence is added to the previous one (*math*); a taxonomic group (of various rank); a geological formation; succession; sequence; linear or end-to-end arrangement; a set of notes in a particular order, taken, instead of a traditional scale, as the basis of a composition (*mus*): — *pl* **se'ries**. — *adj* **se'rial** forming a series; in series; in a row; in instalments; of publication in instalments; using series as the basis of composition (*mus*); (of supernumerary buds) one above another. — *n* a publication, esp. a story, in instalments; a motion picture, television or radio play appearing in instalments. — *n* **serialisā'tion** or **-z-** publication in instalments; the use of notes and/or other elements of music in regular patterns. — *vt* **se'rialise** or **-ize** to arrange in series; to publish serially. — *n* **se'rialism** (*mus*) serial technique, or use of it. — *n* **se'rialist** a writer of serials, or of serial music. — *n* **seriality** (*-al'i-ti*). — *adv* **se'rially**. — *adj* **se'riate** in rows. — *vt* to arrange in a series, or in order. — *adv* **se'riately**. — *adv* **seriā'tim** one after another. — *n* **seriā'tion**. — **serial number** the individual identification number marked on each one of a series of identical products. — **arithmetical series** a series progressing by constant difference; **geometrical series** a series progressing by constant ratio. [L. *seriēs* — *serĕre*, *sertum*, to join.]

serif *ser'if*, *n* the short cross-line at the end of a stroke in a letter. [Poss. Du. *schreef*, stroke.]

serigraph, serigrapher, etc. See under **sericeous**.

serin *ser'in*, *n* a smaller species of canary. — *n* **serinette'** a small barrel-organ for training songbirds. [Fr., canary.]

seringa *sə-ring'gə*, *n* a Brazilian rubber-tree; a tall shrub with strongly scented flowers, mock-orange or syringa. [Port.]

serious *sē'ri-əs*, *adj* grave; staid; earnest; disinclined to lightness of mood; in earnest; not to be taken lightly; showing firmness of intention or commitments; approaching the critical or dangerous; concerned with weighty matters. — *adj* **seriocom'ic** or **seriocom'ical** partly serious and partly comic. — *adv* **se'riously**. — *n* **se'riousness**. [L.L. *sēriōsus* — L. *sērius*.]

serj. or **serjt** *abbrev* for serjeant.

serjeant. See **sergeant**.

sermon *sûr'mən*, *n* a discourse, esp. one delivered, or intended to be delivered, from the pulpit, on a Biblical text; a harangue, reproof or moralising lecture. — *vi* **ser'monise** or **-ize** to compose sermons; to preach. — *vt* to preach to. — *n* **ser'moniser** or **-z-**. [L. *sermō*, *sermōnis*, speech, prob. ult. from *serĕre*, to join.]

sero- *sē-ro-*, *combining form* denoting serum. — *adj* **serolog'ical**. — *adv* **serolog'ically**. — *n* **serol'ogist**. — *n* **serol'ogy** the study of serums and their properties. — *n* **seros'ity**. — *n* **serotaxon'omy** serological analysis as a source of information for taxonomic classification. — *n* **serother'apy** treatment or prevention of disease by injecting blood-serum containing the appropriate antibodies.

serosa *si-rō'zə*, (*zool*) *n* the chorion; the serous membrane (see **serum**): — *pl* **serō'sas** or **-sae** (*-zē*). [N.L.; fem. of *serōsus* — *serum* (see **serum**).]

serosity, serotherapy, etc. See under **sero-**.

serotine *ser'ō-tīn* or *-tin*, *n* a small reddish bat. — *adj* late, in occurrence, development, flowering, etc. (*biol*). — *adj* **serotinous** (*si-rot'i-nəs*). — *n* **serotō'nin** a potent vasoconstrictor and neurotransmitter found particularly in brain and intestinal tissue and blood-platelets. [L. *sērōtinus* — *sērus*, late.]

serous, etc. See **serum**.

serow *ser'ō*, *n* a Himalayan antelope-like goat. [Lepcha (Tibeto-Burman language) *sa-ro*.]

serpent *sûr'pənt*, *n* (formerly) any reptile or creeping thing, esp. if venomous; (now) a snake; a treacherous or malicious person; an obsolete wooden leather-covered bass wind instrument shaped like a writhing snake. — *adj* **ser'pentine** (*-tīn*) snakelike; winding; tortuous. — *n* a soft, usually green mineral, occurring in winding veins and in masses, etc.; a rock (in full **ser'pentine-rock**), composed mainly of the mineral serpentine. — *vi* to wind. — *adv* **ser'pentinely.** — *adj* and *adv* **ser'pentlike.** — **ser'pent-eater** the secretary-bird; **ser'pent-lizard** the seps. — **the old serpent** Satan. [L. *serpēns, -entis*, pres. p. of *serpĕre*, to creep.]

serpigo *sər-pī'gō*, (*pathol*) *n* any spreading skin disease: — *pl* **serpigines** (*-pij'in-ēz*) or *serpī'goes*. — *adj* **serpiginous** (*-pij'*). [L.L. *serpīgō* — L. *serpĕre*, to creep.]

SERPS or **Serps** *sûrps*, *abbrev* for state earnings-related pension scheme.

serpula *sûr'pū-lə*, *n* a marine worm which constructs twisted calcareous tubes for living in: — *pl* **ser'pulae** (*-lē*). [L., a snake — *serpĕre*, to creep.]

serra *ser'ə*, *n* (*zool*) a sawlike organ: — *pl* **serr'ae** (*-ē*) or **serr'as.** — *n* **serradill'a** (Port.) a species of clover grown as fodder. — *n* **serr'an** a fish of the *Serranidae* family similar to the perches. — *n* and *adj* **serranid** (*ser'ən-id*) or **serr'anoid.** — *vt* **serrate'** to notch. — *adj* **serr'āted** or **serrā'te** notched like a saw; with sharp forward-pointing teeth (*bot* and *zool*). — *n* **serrā'tion** saw-edged condition; (usu. in *pl*) a sawlike tooth. — *adj* **serr'ulate** or **serr'ulated** finely serrated. — *n* **serrulā'tion.** [L. and Port. (from L.) *serra*, a saw.]

serrate, serrated, etc. See **serra.**

serried *ser'id*, *adj* close-set; packed or grouped together without gaps. [Fr. *serrer* or its past p. *serré* — L. *sera*, bar, lock.]

serrulate, etc. See **serra.**

serum *sē'rəm*, *n* a watery liquid, esp. that which separates from coagulating blood; blood-serum containing antibodies, taken from an animal that has been inoculated with bacteria or their toxins, used to immunise people or animals; the watery part of a plant fluid: — *pl* **sē'rums** or **sē'ra.** — *adj* **se'rous** pertaining to, like or of the nature of serum. — **serous membrane** a thin membrane, moist with serum, lining a cavity and enveloping the viscera within; **serum hepatitis** a virus infection of the liver, usu. transmitted by transfusion of infected blood or use of contaminated instruments, esp. needles, consequently often occurring in drug addicts. [L. *sĕrum*, whey.]

serval *sûr'vl*, *n* a large, long-legged, short-tailed African cat or tiger-cat. [Port. (*lobo*) *cerval*, lit. deer-wolf, transferred from another animal.]

servant *sûr'vənt*, *n* a person who is hired to perform service, especially personal or domestic service of a menial kind, or farm labour, for another or others; a person who is in the service of the state, the public, a company or other body; someone who serves in any capacity; in formal letter-writing, formerly in greeting and leave-taking, now jokingly, applied in apparent humility to oneself. — *adj* **ser'vantless.** — **servants' hall** a servants' dining- and sitting-room. — **civil servant** a member of the civil service (see under **civil**). [Fr., pres. p. of *servir* — L. *servīre*, to serve.]

serve *sûrv*, *vt* to be a servant to; to be in the service of; to work for; to render service to; to perform the duties or do the work connected with; (of a male animal) to copulate with; to attend as assistant; to be of use to or for; to avail; to suffice for; to satisfy; to further; to minister to; to attend to the requirements of; to supply; to provide with materials; to help to food, etc.; to send or bring to table; to put into play by striking (*tennis*, etc.); to be opportune to; to conform one's conduct to; to bind (rope, etc.) with cord, etc.; to deliver or present formally, or give effect to (*law*). — *vi* to be a servant; to be in service or servitude; to render service; to be a member, or take part in the activities, of an armed force; to perform functions; to wait at table; to attend to customers; to act as server; to answer a purpose, be of use, do; to be opportune or favourable; to suffice. — *n* service of a ball. — *n* **serv'er** a person who serves, esp. at meals, mass, or tennis; a salver; a fork, spoon or other instrument for distributing or helping at table. — *n* **serv'ery** a room or rooms adjoining a dining-room, from which meals and liquors are served and in which utensils are kept. — *n* and *adj* **serv'ing.** — **serve as** to act as; to take the place of; **serve one's time** to pass through an apprenticeship or a term of office; **serve out** to deal or distribute; to punish; to retaliate on; **serve someone right** (of something unpleasant) to be no more than deserved; **serve the** (or **one's**) **turn** to suffice for one's immediate purpose or need; **serve time** to undergo a term of imprisonment, etc.; **serve up** to bring to table. [Fr. *servir* — L. *servīre*, to serve.]

service[1] *sûr'vis*, *n* the condition or occupation of a servant or of any person who serves; work; the act or mode of serving; employ; employment as a soldier, sailor, or airman, or in any public organisation or department; the personnel so employed; the force, organisation or body employing it (in *pl* usu. the fighting forces); that which is required of its members; that which is required of a feudal tenant; performance of a duty or function; actual participation in warfare; a performance of religious worship; a liturgical form or office or a musical setting of it; a good turn, good offices, benefit to another; duty or homage ceremonially offered, as in health-drinking, correspondence or greeting; use; hard usage; availability; disposal; supply, e.g. of water, railway trains, etc.; waiting at table; a set, e.g. of dishes for a particular meal; the checking, and (if necessary) repairing and/or replacing of parts of machinery, etc. to ensure efficient operation; cord or other material for serving a rope. — *adj* of the army, navy or air force; (sometimes in *pl*) of the army, navy and air force collectively; for the use of servants; providing services rather than manufactured products (see e.g. **service industry** below). — *vt* to provide or perform service for (e.g. motor cars). — *n* **serviceabil'ity** or **ser'viceableness.** — *adj* **ser'viceable** able or willing to serve; advantageous; useful; capable of rendering long service, durable. — *adv* **ser'viceably.** — *adj* **ser'viceless.** — **ser'vice-book** a book of forms of religious service; a prayer-book; **service charge** a charge made for service in a restaurant or hotel, usu. a percentage of the bill; **ser'vice-court** (in lawn tennis) the area outside of which a served ball must not fall; **service flat** a flat in which domestic service is provided, its cost being included in rent; **service hatch** one connecting dining-room to kitchen, etc., through which dishes, etc. may be passed; **service industry** an industry which provides a service rather than a product, e.g. catering, entertainment, transport; **ser'vice-line** the boundary of the service-court, in lawn tennis 21 feet from the net; **ser'viceman** or (*fem*) **ser'vicewoman** a member of a fighting service; **ser'vice-pipe, -wire,** etc. a branch from a gas, electric, etc. main to a building; **ser'vice-reservoir** a reservoir for supplying water to a particular area; **service road** a minor road parallel to a main road and serving local traffic without obstructing the main road; **service station** an establishment providing general services, esp. the supply of fuel for motorists. — **active service** service of a soldier, etc. in the field (widely interpreted by the authorities); **at your service** at your disposal; also a mere phrase of civility; **civil service** see under **civil; have seen service** to have fought in war; to have been put to long or hard use. [Fr., — L. *servitium*.]

service² *sûr'vis, n* a European tree very like the rowan (also called **sorb**). — **ser'vice-berry** its pear-shaped fruit; shadbush or its fruit (*NAm*); **ser'vice-tree.** — **wild service** a similar tree to the domestic service tree with sharp-lobed leaves. [O.E. *syrfe* — L. *sorbus*.]

serviette *sûr-vi-et', n* table-napkin. [Fr.]

servile *sûr'vīl, adj* pertaining to slaves or servants; slavish; fawning or submissive; slavishly or unintelligently imitative. — *adv* **ser'vilely.** — *n* **servility** (*-vil'i-ti*) slavishness of manner or spirit; slavish deference. [L. *servīlis* — *servus*, a slave.]

servitor *sûr'vi-tər, n* a servant (*poetic*); (formerly, in Oxford) an undergraduate partly supported by the college, his duty to wait on the fellows and gentlemen commoners at table. — *adj* **servitorial** (*-ö'ri-əl*). — *n* **ser'vitorship.** [L.L. *servītor, -ōris* — L. *servīre*, to serve.]

servitude *sûr'vi-tūd, n* a state of being a slave; subjection; compulsory labour; subjection to irksome conditions; a burden on property obliging the owner to allow another person or thing an easement (*legal*). [L. *servitūdō*.]

servo *sûr'vō, adj* of a system in which the main mechanism is set in operation by a subsidiary mechanism and is able to develop a force greater than the force communicated to it. — **ser'vocontrol** a reinforcing mechanism for the pilot's effort, usu. a small auxiliary aerofoil; **ser'vomechanism** a closed-cycle control system in which a small input power controls a larger output power in a strictly proportionate manner; **ser'vomotor** a motor using a servomechanism. [L. *servus*, a servant, slave.]

sesame *ses'ə-mi, n* a plant (*Sesamum indicum*), probably native to S.E. Asia, cultivated for its seeds which yield an edible oil. — *adj* **ses'amoid** shaped like a sesame seed. — *n* a small rounded bone in the substance of a tendon. — **sesame seed.** — **open sesame** see under **open.** [Gr. *sēsamē*, a dish of sesame (Gr. *sēsamon*).]

sesqui- *ses-kwi-, combining form* denoting in the ratio of one and a half to one. — *n* **sesquicenten'ary** or **sesquicentenn'ial** a hundred and fiftieth anniversary. — Also *adj*. — *n* **sesquiox'ide** (*chem*) an oxide with three atoms of oxygen to two of the other constituent. — *adj* **sesquip'edal** or **sesquipedā'lian** (of objects or words) a foot and a half long — of words, very long and pedantic. — *n* **sesquipedā'lianism** or **sesquipedality** (*-pi-dal'i-ti*). — *adj* **sesquip'licate** (*math*) of, or as, the square roots of the cubes. — *n* **sesquisul'phide** a compound with three atoms of sulphur to two of the other element or radical. [L. *sēsqui* — *sēmisque* — *sēmis* (for *sēmi-as*), half a unit, *que*, and.]

Sess. *abbrev* for Session.

sessile *ses'īl*, or (esp. in U.S.) *ses'il, adj* stalkless; sedentary; fixed and stationary. — *adj* **sess'ile-eyed.** [L. *sessilis*, low, squat — *sedēre, sessum*, to sit.]

session *sesh'ən, n* a sitting, series of sittings, or time of sitting, as of a court or public body; a period of time spent engaged in any one activity (*colloq*); the time between the meeting and prorogation of Parliament; a school year (sometimes a school day); in Scotland, etc., a division of the academic year; (in *pl*) quarter-sessions. — *adj* **sess'ional.** — *adv* **sess'ionally.** — **sess'ion-house** a building where sessions are held; the room where a kirk session meets; **session singer** or **musician** a person who provides vocal or instrumental backing at recording sessions. — **Court of Session** the supreme civil court of Scotland. [Fr., — L. *sessiō, sessiōnis*, a sitting — *sedēre, sessum*, to sit.]

sesterce *ses'tərs*, (*hist*) *n* a Roman coin, the *sestertius*, worth $2\frac{1}{2}$ asses, later 4 asses. [L. *sestertius*, two and a half — *sēmis*, half, *tertius*, third.]

sestet *ses-tet', n* a group of six; the last six lines of a sonnet; a composition for six performers (*mus*). [It. *sestetto* — *sesto* — L. *sextus*, sixth.]

sestina *ses-tē'nə*, (*poetry*) *n* an old verse-form of six six-lined stanzas having the same end-words in different orders, and a triplet introducing all of them. [It., — L. *sextus*, sixth.]

set *set, vt* to put, place, or fix, in position or required condition; to dispose, array, arrange; to apply; to cause to be; to plant; to stake; to embed; to frame; to mount; to stud, dot, sprinkle, variegate; to put in type (*printing*); to compose (type); to form or represent, as in jewels; to adjust to show the correct (or a specified) time, etc.; to spread, lay, cover (a table) with the food, dishes, etc. for a meal, or (*Scot* and *dialect*) to cover the table with the food, dishes, etc. for (a meal); to regulate; to appoint; to ordain; to assign; to prescribe; to propound; to put upon a course, start off; to incite, direct; to put in opposition; to cause to become solid, coagulated, rigid, fixed, or motionless; to begin to form (as fruit or seed); to rate, value; to pitch (e.g. a tune); to compose or fit music to; to position (a sail) to catch the wind; to arrange (hair) in a particular style when wet, so that it will remain in it when dry; to seat; to put (a hen) on eggs; to put (eggs) under a hen; (of a gun dog) to indicate by crouching; to sharpen, e.g. a razor; to defeat (one's opponents' contract), usu. by a stated number of tricks (*bridge*). — *vi* to go down towards or below the horizon, to decline; to offer a stake; to become rigid, fixed, hard, solid or permanent; to coagulate; (of a bone) to knit; (of e.g. fruit) to begin to develop; to have, take or start along a course or direction; to dance in a facing position; (of dogs) to point out game: — *pr p* **sett'ing**; *pa t* and *pa p* **set.** — *adj* in any of the senses of the participle; prescribed; deliberate, intentional; prearranged; formal; settled; fixed; rigid; determined; regular; established; ready. — *n* a group of persons or things, esp. of a type that associate, occur, or are used together or have something in common; a clique, exclusive group; a complete series, collection or complement; a company performing a dance; a series of dance movements or figures; a complete apparatus, esp. for receiving radio or television signals; an act, process, mode, or time of setting; a setting; a direction; the scenery, properties, etc. set up for a scene (*cinematography*); the place where filming takes place (*cinematography*); any collection of objects, called 'elements', defined by specifying the elements (*math*); habitual or temporary form, posture, carriage, position or tendency; the items performed by a singer or band at a concert; a group of games in which the winning side wins six, with such additional games as may be required in the case of deuce (*tennis*); a set hairstyle; the hang of a garment; a young plant-slip, bulb or tuber, for planting; a gun dog's indication of game; (for the following senses, **set** or **sett**) the number of a weaver's reed, determining the number of threads to the inch; the texture resulting; a square or a pattern of tartan; a paving-block of stone or wood; a tool for setting in various senses; a badger's burrow. — *n* **set'ness.** — *n* **sett'er** someone who or something that sets; a dog that sets; a dog of a breed derived from the spaniel and (probably) pointer. — *n* **sett'ing** surroundings; environment; a level of power, volume, etc. to which a machine or other device can be set; mounting of jewellery; the period of time in which a play, novel, etc. is set; adaptation to music; music composed for a song, etc.; a system of dividing pupils in mixed-ability classes into ability groups for certain subjects only; the period of play after a game has been set (to two, three or five) (*badminton*). — **set'-aside** or **land set-aside** the practice or policy of taking agricultural land out of production (**set-aside scheme** *specif* that introduced to reduce EEC grain surpluses, with compensatory payments to farmers); **set'back**

a check, reverse or relapse; a disappointment or misfortune; **set'line** any of various kinds of fishing-line suspended between buoys, etc., and having shorter baited lines attached to it; **set'-off** a claim set against another; a cross-claim which partly offsets the original claim; a counterbalance; an ornament; a contrast, foil; an offset (*archit* and *printing*); **set piece** a painstakingly prepared performance; an elaborately arranged display in fireworks; **set'-screw** a screw used to prevent relative motion by exerting pressure with its point; **set speech** a studied oration; **set'-square** a right-angled triangular drawing instrument; **setter-forth'**; **setter-off'**; **setter-out'**; **setter-up'**; **set-to'** a bout; a hot contest: — *pl* **set-tos'** or **set-to's'**; **set'-up** configuration, arrangement, structure, situation (see **set up** below). — **dead set** determined (on); **set about** to begin, take in hand; to attack; **set (a game) to two, three, five** (*badminton*) to set, in the final stages of a game, a new deciding score of two, three, or five points; **set alight, set light to, set fire to** or **set on fire** to cause to break into flame and burn; **set apart** to put aside, or out of consideration; to separate, distinguish; **set aside** to put away or to one side; to reject, annul; to reserve, lay by; to take (agricultural land) out of production, to leave fallow; **set at naught** see **naught**; **set back** to check, delay, reverse; to cost (in money; *slang*); to place at some distance behind; to surprise, take aback; **set by** to lay up; to put aside; **set down** to lay on the ground; to put in writing; to judge, esteem; to snub; to attribute, charge; to lay down authoritatively; **set eyes on** to see, catch sight of; **set fair** (of weather) steadily fair; **set fire to** see **set alight** above; **set forth** to exhibit, display; to expound, declare; to praise, recommend; to start on a journey; **set free** to release, liberate; **set going** to put in motion; **set hand to** to set to work on; **set in** to begin; to become prevalent; **set in hand** to undertake; **set little, much,** etc. **by** to regard or value little, much, etc.; **set off** to start off; to send off; to show in relief or to advantage; to counterbalance; to make an offset, mark an opposite page; to mark off, lay off; **set on** to attack or incite to attack; to instigate; bent, determined upon; **set oneself** to bend one's energies; **set oneself against** to oppose; **set one's face against** see under **face**; **set one's hand to** to start work on, set about; to sign; **set one's heart on** see under **heart**; **set on fire** see **set alight** above; **set out** to start, go forth; to display; to begin with an intention; to expound; to mark off; to adorn; **set sail** see under **sail**; **set to** to affix; to apply oneself; **set up** to erect; to put up; to exalt, raise up; to arrange; to begin; to enable to begin; to place in view; to put in type; to begin a career; to make pretensions; to arrange matters so that another person is blamed, embarrassed, made to look foolish, etc. (*slang*; *n* **set'-up**); **set upon** to set on; set on. [O.E. *settan*.]

seta *sē'tə*, (*biol*) *n* a bristle; a bristle-like structure: — *pl* **se'tae** (*-tē*). — *adj* **setaceous** (*si-tā'shəs*) or **setose** (*sē'tōs* or *-tōs'*). [L. *saeta* (*sēta*), bristle.]

SETI *abbrev* for search for extraterrestrial intelligence.

seton *sē'tn*, (*surg*) *n* a thread or similar filament passed through the skin as a counter-irritant and means of promoting drainage; a flow obtained in this way. [L.L. *sētō*, *-ōnis*, appar. — L. *sēta*, *saeta*, bristle.]

sett. See **set**.

settee *se-tē'*, *n* a long seat with a back. [Prob. **settle**.]

setter, setting. See **set**.

settle *set'l*, *n* a long high-backed bench. — *vt* to place in a stable, secure, restful or comfortable situation; to adjust; to lower; to compact, cause to subside; to regulate; to fix; to establish, set up or install (e.g. in residence, business, marriage, a parish); to colonise; to determine; to decide; to put beyond doubt or dispute; to restore to good order; to quiet; to compose; to secure by gift or legal act; to make final payment of; to dispose of, put out of action. — *vi* to alight; to come to rest; to subside; to sink to the bottom (or form a scum); to dispose oneself; to take up permanent abode; to become stable; to fix one's habits (often with *down*); to grow calm or clear; to come to a decision or agreement; to adjust differences; to settle accounts (often with *up*). — *adj* **sett'led.** — *n* **sett'ledness.** — *n* **sett'lement** act of settling; state of being settled; payment; arrangement; placing of a minister; a subsidence or sinking; a settled colony; a local community; an establishment of social workers aiming at benefit to the surrounding population; a settling of property, an instrument by which it is settled, or the property settled, esp. a marriage-settlement; residence in a parish or other claim for poor-relief in case of becoming destitute. — *n* **sett'ler** someone who settles; a colonist; a decisive blow, argument, etc. — *n* **sett'ling.** — *n* **sett'lor** (*law*) a person who settles property on another. — **settling day** a date fixed by the stock exchange for completion of transactions. — **settle for** to agree to accept (usu. as a compromise); **settle in** to adapt to a new environment; to prepare to remain indoors for the night; **settle with** to come to an agreement with; to deal with. [O.E. *setl*, seat, *setlan*, to place.]

seven *sev'n*, *n* the cardinal number next above six; a symbol representing it (7, vii, etc.); a set of that number of persons or things; a shoe or other article of a size denoted by that number; a card with seven pips; a score of seven points, tricks, etc.; the seventh hour after midday or midnight; the age of seven years. — *adj* of the number seven; seven years old. — *adj* **sev'enth** last of seven; next after the sixth; equal to one of seven equal parts. — *n* a seventh part; a person or thing in seventh position; a tone or semitone less than an octave; a note at that interval. — *adv* **sev'enthly** in the seventh place. — **seven-a-side'** a form of Rugby football played by seven men on each side instead of fifteen. — Also *adj.* — *adj* **sev'en-day** for seven days. — *adj* and *adv* **sev'enfold** in seven divisions; seven times as much. — **seven deadly sins** pride, covetousness, lust, anger, gluttony, envy and sloth; **Seven Seas** the Arctic, Antarctic, North and South Atlantic, North and South Pacific, and Indian Oceans; all the seas of the world generally; **Seventh-Day Adventists** a sect that expect the second coming of Christ and observe Saturday as the Sabbath; **seventh heaven** see under **heaven**; **Seven Wonders of the World** the seven monuments regarded as the most remarkable in the ancient world: the Pyramids, the Hanging Gardens of Babylon, the Temple of Artemis at Ephesus, Phidias's statue of Zeus at Olympia, the Mausoleum at Halicarnassus, the Colossus of Rhodes, and the Pharos of Alexandria; **Seven Years' War** the struggle for Silesia between Frederick the Great and the Empress Maria Theresa (1756–63). [O.E. *seofon*.]

seventeen *sev-n-tēn'* or *sev'n-tēn*, *n* and *adj* seven and ten. — *adj* and *n* **sev'enteenth** (or *-tēnth'*). — *adv* **seventeenth'ly**. [O.E. *seofontīene* — *seofon*, *tīen*, ten.]

seventy *sev'n-ti*, *n* and *adj* seven times ten: — *pl* **sev'enties** the numbers seventy to seventy-nine; the years so numbered in a life or any century; a range of temperature from seventy to just less than eighty degrees. — *adj* **sev'entieth** last of seventy; next after the sixty-ninth; equal to one of seventy equal parts. — *n* a seventieth part; a person or thing in seventieth position. — **seventy-eight'** an old type of gramophone record designed to be played at 78 revolutions per minute, standard before the introduction of long-playing microgroove records (usu. written 78). [O.E. (*hund*)*seofontig*.]

sever *sev'ər, vt* and *vi* to separate; to divide, part; to split; to cut off. — *adj* **sev'erable.** — *n* **sev'erance.** — **severance pay** an allowance granted to an employee on the termination of his or her employment. [Fr. *sevrer*, to wean — L. *sēparāre*, to separate.]

several *sev'ər-l, adj* various; more than one (usu. more than three), but not very many; separate; belonging or pertaining distributively, not jointly (*law*); particular. — *pron* a few. — *adv* **sev'erally** separately. — *n* **sev'eralty** separateness; individual ownership. [O.Fr., separate — L. *sēparāre*, to separate.]

severance. See **sever.**

severe *si-vēr', adj* rigorous; very strict; unsparing; pressing hard; hard to endure; austerely restrained or simple. — *adv* **sevēre'ly.** — *n* **severity** (*si-ver'i-ti*). [L. *sevērus.*]

severy *sev'ə-ri*, (*archit*) *n* a compartment of vaulting. [O.Fr. *civoire* — L. *cibōrium*; see ety. for **ciborium.**]

Sèvres *sev'r', adj* (of porcelain) made at *Sèvres*, near Paris. — *n* Sèvres porcelain.

sew *sō, vt* to join, attach, enclose or work on with a needle and thread, with wire, or with a sewing-machine. — *vi* to work with needle and thread, sewing-machine or similar: — *pa t* **sewed** (*sōd*); *pa p* **sewn** (*sōn*) or **sewed.** — *n* **sew'er.** — *n* **sew'ing** the act of sewing; something that is being sewn. — **sew'ing-machine** a machine for sewing, esp. an electric machine for sewing clothes, etc. — **sew up** to enclose or close up by sewing; to complete satisfactorily, or secure a satisfactory result (*slang*). [O.E. *sīwian, sēowian.*]

sewage *sōō'ij* or *sū'ij, n* waste or refuse carried off by sewers. — *n* **sewer** (*sōō'ər* or *sū'ər*) a channel (esp. underground) for receiving the discharge from house-drains and streets. — *vt* to provide with sewers. — *n* **sew'erage** a system, or the provision, of sewers; sewage. — *n* **sew'ering.** — **sew'age-farm** a place where sewage is treated so as to be used as manure; also a farm on which sewage is used as fertiliser; **sew'age-works** a place where sewage is treated and purified before being discharged; **sew'er-gas** the contaminated air of sewers; **sew'er-rat** the brown rat. [O.Fr. *essever*, to drain off — L. *ex*, out, *aqua*, water.]

sewellel *si-wel'əl, n* an American rodent linking beavers and squirrels, also called the *mountain beaver*. [Chinook *shewallal*, a robe made of its skin.]

sewen. See **sewin.**

sewer[1]. See **sew.**

sewer[2], **sewerage.** See under **sewage.**

sewin or **sewen** *sū'in, n* a Welsh sea-trout grilse.

sewn. See **sew.**

sex *seks, n* the sum of the characteristics which distinguish an animal or plant as male or female; the quality of being male or female; either of the divisions according to this, or its members collectively; the whole area connected with this distinction; sexual intercourse. — Also *adj.* — *vt* to ascertain the sex of. — *adj* **sexed** (*sekst*) having sex; being male or female; having sexual characteristics, feelings or desires to a specified degree (as in **over-, under-, highly-,** etc., **sexed**). — *n* **sex'er** a person who ascertains the sex of birds, etc. — *n* **sex'iness.** — *n* **sex'ism** discrimination against, stereotyping of, patronising or otherwise offensive behaviour towards (orig. women, now women or men) on the grounds of sex. — *n* and *adj* **sex'ist.** — *adj* **sex'less** of neither sex; without sex; without sexual feelings. — *n* **sex'lessness.** — *adj* **sexolog'ical.** — *n* **sexol'ogist.** — *n* **sexol'ogy** the study of (human) sexual behaviour and relationships. — *adj* **sex'ūal** of, by, having or characteristic of sex, one sex or other, or organs of sex. — *n* **sex'ūalism** emphasis on sex. — *n* **sex'ūalist.** — *n* **sexūal'ity.** — *adv* **sex'ūally.** — *adj* **sex'y** (of a person) very attractive to the opposite sex; stimulating sexual instincts; involved in, or concerned with, sexual activity, esp. sexual intercourse; (of an object, idea, etc.) exciting, attractive, fascinating, tempting. — **sex aid** any of various artificial items used to aid or heighten sexual arousal, as sold in sex shops; **sex'-appeal** power of attracting, esp. of exciting desire in, the other sex; **sex'-bomb** (*colloq*) a person, esp. female, with a lot of sex-appeal; **sex'-cell** an egg-cell or sperm; **sex'-change** (esp. of humans) a changing of sex. — Also *adj.* — **sex'-chromosome** a chromosome that determines sex; **sex drive** the natural impulse and appetite for sexual relations. — *adj* **sexed-up'** made sexy or extra sexy; sexually excited. — **sex'-kitten** a young woman (mischievously) playing up her sex-appeal. — *adj* **sex'-limited** developed only in one sex. — *adj* **sex'-linked** inherited along with sex, that is, by a factor located in the sex-chromosome. — **sexploitā'tion** the ex*ploitation* of *sex* for commercial gain in literature and the performing arts, esp. films; **sex'pert** (esp. *US*) an expert in human sexual behaviour; **sex'pot** (*slang*) a person of very great or obvious physical attraction; **sex'-reversal** change from male to female or female to male in the life of the individual; **sex shop** a shop selling items connected with sexual arousal, behaviour, etc. — *adj* **sex'-starved** suffering from a lack and need of the pleasures and satisfactions of sexual activity. — **sex (or sexual) therapist** a person who deals with problems relating to sexual intercourse; **sex (or sexual) therapy; sexual athlete** someone who performs sexual intercourse skilfully and/or frequently; **sexual harassment** that consisting of misplaced and unwelcome sexual advances, remarks, etc., esp. from a senior colleague in the workplace; **sexual intercourse** the uniting of sexual organs, esp. involving the insertion of the male penis into the female vagina and the release of sperm; **sexual reproduction** the union of gametes or gametic nuclei preceding the formation of a new individual; **sexual system** the Linnaean system of plant classification according to sexual organisation. — **sexually transmitted disease** venereal disease. [L. *sexus, -ūs.*]

sex- *seks-* or **sexi-** *sek-si-*, *combining form* denoting six. — *adj* **sexivā'lent** or **sexvā'lent** (*chem*) with a valency of six. — *adj* **sexpart'ite** parted in six; involving six participants, groups, etc. [L. *sex*, six.]

sexagenarian *sek-sə-ji-nā'ri-ən, n* a person sixty years old, or between sixty and seventy. — *adj* of that age. [L. *sexāgēnārius*, pertaining to sixty — *sexāgintā*, sixty.]

Sexagesima *sek-sə-jes'i-mə, n* the second Sunday before Lent (also **Sexagesima Sunday**). — *adj* **sexages'imal** pertaining to, or based on, sixty. — *n* a sexagesimal fraction. — *adv* **sexages'imally.** [L. *sexāgēsimus, -a, -um*, sixtieth.]

sexcentenary *sek-sin-tēn'ər-i* or *-ten'ər-i, n* a 600th anniversary, or a celebration of this. — Also *adj.*

sexennial *sek-sen'yəl, adj* lasting six years; recurring every six years. — *adv* **sexenn'ially.** [L. *sex*, six, *annus*, year.]

sext *sekst, n* (*eccles*) the office of the sixth hour, said at midday, afterwards earlier. — *adj* **sex'tan** (*med*) (of a fever) recurring every fifth (formerly every sixth) day. [L. *sextus*, sixth — *sex*, six.]

sextant *seks'tənt, n* the sixth part of a circle or its circumference, a sector or an arc of 60°; an instrument with an arc of a sixth of a circle, for measuring angular distances. [L. *sextāns, -antis*, a sixth.]

sextet *seks-tet', n* altered form (partly through Ger.) of **sestet.**

sextillion *seks-til'yən, n* the sixth power of a million; the seventh power of a thousand (*US*). [For *sexillion*, after **billion,** etc.]

sextodecimo *seks-tō-des'i-mō*, (*printing*) *n* a book or a size of book made by folding each sheet into sixteen leaves: — *pl* **sextodec'imos**. — Also *adj*. [L. (*in*) *sextō decimō* (in) one-sixteenth.]

sexton *seks'tən*, *n* an officer who rings a church bell, attends the clergyman, digs graves, etc.; a burying-beetle (also called the **sex'ton-beetle**). [**sacristan**.]

sextuple *seks'tū-pl*, *adj* sixfold. — *n* six times as much. — *vt* and *vi* to increase or multiply sixfold. — *n* **sex'tūplet** one of six children or animals born at one birth. [L.L. *sextuplus*.]

sexual, sexy, etc. See **sex**.

Seyfert galaxy *sī'fərt* or *sē'fərt gal'ək-si*, (*astron*) *n* one of a small class of galaxies with intensely bright nuclei and inconspicuous spiral arms. [After Carl *Seyfert*, U.S. astrophysicist (1911–60).]

SF *abbrev* for: (Suomi) Finland (I.V.R.); science fiction; signal frequency; Sinn Fein.

SFA *abbrev* for: Scottish Football Association; Sweet Fanny Adams (= nothing at all; *slang*).

SFO *abbrev* for Serious Fraud Office.

sforzando *sför-tsän'dō* or **sforzato** *sför-tsä'tō*, (*mus*) *adj* and *adv* forced, with sudden emphasis. — Also *n*: — *pl* **sforzan'dos** or **sforzan'di** (*-dē*), **sforza'tos** or **sforza'ti** (*-tē*). [It., pres. p. and past p. of *sforzare*, to force — L. *ex*, out, L.L. *fortia*, force.]

sfumato *sfōō-mä'tō*, (*painting* or *drawing*) *n* a misty, indistinct effect obtained by gradually blending together areas of different colour or tone: — *pl* **sfuma'tos**. [It., past p. of *sfumare*, to shade off, — L. *ex*, out, *fūmāre*, to smoke.]

sfz. *abbrev* for sforzando.

sfx *abbrev* for suffix.

SG *abbrev* for Solicitor-General.

sg *abbrev* for specific gravity.

SGHWR *abbrev* for steam-generating heavy water reactor.

SGP *abbrev* for Singapore (I.V.R.).

sgraffito *zgräf-fē'tō*, *n* decorative work in which different colours are revealed by removal of the parts of outer layers of material (plaster, slip, etc.) laid on; pottery with such decoration: — *pl* **sgraffi'ti** (*-tē*). [It., — L. *ex-*, and It. *graffito*, q.v.]

Sgt *abbrev* for Sergeant.

sh *sh*, *interj* hush: — *pl* **sh's**.

s/h *abbrev* for shorthand and typing.

shabby *shab'i*, *adj* dingy, threadbare or worn (e.g. of clothes); having a look of poverty; mean in look or conduct; low; paltry. — *adv* **shabb'ily**. — *n* **shabb'iness**. [Obs. or dialect *shab*, scab — O.E. *sceabb*.]

shabrack *shab'rak*, (*hist*) *n* a trooper's housing or saddle-cloth. [Ger. *Schabracke*, prob. — Turk. *çāprāq*.]

Shabuoth, Shavuoth or **Shavuot** *shav-ū'oth* or *-ot*, *n* the Jewish Feast of Weeks, celebrated 7 weeks after the first day of Passover, orig. marking the end of harvest, now generally taken as a commemoration of the giving of the Law to Moses. — Also called **Pentecost**. [Heb. *shabuot(h)*, weeks.]

shack *shak*, *n* a roughly-built hut. — **shack up with** (*slang*) (esp. of an unmarried person) to live with someone (as a lover). [Am.]

shackle *shak'l*, *n* a prisoner's or slave's ankle-ring or wrist-ring, or the chain connecting a pair; (in *pl*) fetters, manacles; a hindrance, constraint; a hobble; a staple-like link, closed with a pin; the curved movable part of a padlock; a coupling of various kinds. — *vt* to fetter; to couple; to hamper. — **shack'le-bolt** the pin of a shackle. [O.E. *sceacul*.]

shad *shad*, *n* an anadromous fish similar to the herring; extended to various other fishes. — **shad'berry** the fruit of the **shad'bush**, a N. Am. shrub of the rose family that flowers at shad spawning-time. [O.E. *sceadd*.]

shaddock *shad'ək*, *n* an Oriental citrus fruit like a very large orange, the pomelo; the tree that bears it. [Introduced to the W. Indies *c* 1700 by Captain *Shaddock*.]

shade *shād*, *n* partial or relative darkness; interception of light; obscurity; a shady place or area; shelter from light or heat; that which casts a shadow; a screen; a window-blind (*US*); a cover to modify or direct light of a lamp or the sun; a projecting cover to protect the eyes from glare; (in *pl*; *slang*) sunglasses; a variety or degree of colour; a hue mixed with black; a dark or shaded part of a picture; a slight difference or amount; a ghost (*lit*). — *vt* to screen; to overshadow; to mark with gradations of colour or shadow; to soften down; to darken; to lower very slightly, as a price (orig. *US*). — *vi* to pass imperceptibly (*away*, *into*, etc.). — *adj* **shā'ded**. — *adj* **shade'less**. — *adv* **shā'dily**. — *n* **shā'diness**. — *n* **shā'ding** the marking of shadows or shadowlike appearance; the effect of light and shade; fine gradations; nuances; toning down; slight lowering of prices. — *adj* **shā'dy** having, or in, shade; sheltered from light or heat; underhand, disreputable (*colloq*); shadowy, mysterious, sinister. — **in the shade** sheltered from strong light; overlooked, forgotten, in relative obscurity; **on the shady side of** over (a specified age); **put in the shade** to outdo or overshadow completely; **shades of** (a specified person or thing) an exclamation greeting something which reminds one in some way of (a specified person or thing). [O.E. *sceadu*; see **shadow**.]

shadoof or **shaduf** *shä-dōōf'*, *n* a machine for raising water by a bucket on a counterpoised pivoted rod. [Egyp. Ar. *shādūf*.]

shadow *shad'ō*, *n* shade cast by the interception of light by an object; the dark shape so projected on a surface in this way, mimicking the object; the dark part of a picture; a reflected image; a mere appearance; an unreal thing; a representation; a person or thing wasted away almost to nothing; an inseparable or constant companion; a spy, detective, etc. who follows one; shade; protective shade, shelter; darkness; gloom; trouble; a ghost, spirit. — *adj* unreal; feigned; existing only in skeleton; inactive, or only partly active, but ready for the time when opportunity or need arises; denoting, in the main opposition party, a political counterpart to a member or section of the party in power. — *vt* to shade; to cloud or darken; to represent as by a shadow; to typify; to hide; to attend like a shadow, follow and watch; to maintain a position close to, follow every movement of. — *n* **shad'ower**. — *n* **shad'owiness**. — *n* **shad'owing**. — *adj* **shad'owless**. — *adj* **shad'owy** shady; like a shadow; secluded, dim; unsubstantial. — **shadow box** a frame or boxlike structure (often with shelves and a clear protective front) used to display articles; **shad'ow-boxing** sparring practice with an imaginary opponent; making a show of opposition or other action, as a cover for taking no effective steps; **shadow cabinet** a body of opposition leaders holding shadow ministerial positions and ready to take office should their party assume power; **shad'ow-fight** a fight between or with shadows or imaginary enemies; **shad'owgraph** an image produced by throwing a shadow on a screen; a radiograph; **shad'ow-play** one in which the spectators see only shadows on a screen. — **afraid of one's own shadow** extremely timid; **shadow of death** the threatening approach of darkness or death. [O.E. *sceadwe*, genitive, dat., and accus. of *sceadu* (**shade** representing the nom.).]

SHAEF *shāf*, *abbrev* for Supreme Headquarters Allied Expeditionary Force.

shaft *shäft*, *n* anything long and straight; a stem; an arrow; a missile; the main, upright, straight or cylindrical part of anything; a pole; a ray or beam of light; a rotating rod that transmits motion; a well-like excavation or passage; the part of a cross below the arms; the part of a column between the base and the capital; the rachis of a feather; the thill of a carriage on either side of the horse; a straight handle; the penis (*vulg slang*); a woman's body (purely as a sexual object) (*US vulg slang*). — *vt* to have sexual intercourse with (a woman) (*vulg slang*); to dupe, swindle, treat unfairly (*US slang*). — *adj* **shaft'ed**. — *n* **shaft'er** or **shaft'-horse** a horse harnessed between shafts. — *n* **shaft'ing** the action of the verb in either sense; a system of shafts. — *adj* **shaft'less**. [O.E. *sceaft*.]

shag *shag*, *n* a ragged mass of hair, or the like; a long coarse nap; a kind of tobacco cut into shreds; the green cormorant (app. from its crest), or other species; an act of sexual intercourse (*vulg slang*); a partner, usually female, in sexual intercourse (*vulg slang*); a whore (*vulg slang*); a U.S. dance related to the jitterbug but with shuffling footwork, first popular in the 1950s and 60s; an earlier lively dance of the 1930s. — *vt* and *vi* to have sexual intercourse (with) (*vulg slang*). — *vi* to dance the shag: — *pr p* **shagg'ing**; *pa t* and *pa p* **shagged** (*shagd*). — *adj* **shagged** (*shagd*) tired out, exhausted (*colloq*). — *adv* **shagg'ily**. — *n* **shagg'iness**. — *adj* **shagg'y** long, rough and coarse; having long, rough, coarse hair, wool, vegetation, etc.; unkempt, rough. — **shag'bark** a kind of hickory tree; **shaggy cap**, **shaggy ink cap** or **shaggy mane** an edible fungus with a white, cylindrical, shaggy-scaled cap. — *adj* **shag'haired**. — **shaggy dog story** a whimsically long-drawn-out story humorous because of its length and the inconsequence of its ending. [O.E. *sceacga*.]

shagreen *shə-grēn'*, *n* a granular leather made from horse's or ass's skin; the skin of shark, ray, etc., covered with small nodules. [Fr. *chagrin* — Turk. *sagri*, horse's rump, shagreen.]

shah *shä*, *n* the king of Persia (now Iran); also formerly of certain other Eastern countries. [Pers. *shāh*.]

shake *shāk*, *vt* to move with quick, short, to-and-fro movements; to brandish; to tremble or to totter; to disturb the stability of; to cause to waver; to disturb; to put, send, render or cause to be, by shaking; to scatter or send down by shaking; to split. — *vi* to be agitated; to tremble; to shiver; to shake hands; to trill (*mus*): — *pa t* **shook**, *pa p* **shāk'en**. — *n* a shaking; tremulous motion; a damaging or weakening blow; a shaken-up drink (esp. a milk-shake); a trillo, rapid alternation of two notes a tone or semitone apart (*mus*); a fissure (esp. in rock or in growing timber); a moment (*colloq*). — *adj* **shake'able** or **shak'able**. — *adj* **shāk'en**. — *n* **shāk'er** a person who shakes; someone lively or influential (*slang*); a device for shaking (e.g. drinks); a perforated container from which something is shaken; (*cap*) a name popularly applied to a member of an American religious sect, the United Society for Believers in Christ's Second Appearing, as a result of their ecstatic dancing. — *n* **Shāk'erism**. — *adv* **shāk'ily**. — *n* **shāk'iness**. — *n* and *adj* **shāk'ing**. — *adj* **shāk'y** shaking or inclined to shake; loose; tremulous; precarious; uncertain; wavering; unsteady; full of cracks or clefts. — **shake'down** a temporary bed (orig. made by shaking down straw); a trial run, operation, etc. to familiarise personnel with procedures and machinery (chiefly *US*); **shake'-up** a disturbance or major reorganisation (*colloq*). — **great shakes** or **no great shakes** of great account or of no great account; **shake a leg** (*colloq*) to hurry up, get moving; **shake down** (*slang*) to extort money from; to search thoroughly; to frisk (a person for weapons, etc.); to go to bed (esp. in a temporary bed); to settle by shaking; **shake hands with** to greet (someone) by grasping his or her hand and (often) moving it up and down; **shake** or **shiver in one's shoes** to be extremely afraid, shiver with fear; **shake off** to get rid of; **shake one's head** to turn one's head from side to side in token of reluctance, rejection, denial, disapproval, etc.; **shake out** to empty or cause to spread or unfold by shaking; **shake up** to rouse, mix, disturb or loosen by shaking; to reorganise thoroughly (*colloq*); **two shakes** (**of a lamb's tail**, etc.) (*colloq*) a very short time. [O.E. *sc(e)acan*.]

Shakespearian or **Shakespearean** *shāk-spē'ri-ən*, *adj* of or relating to William *Shakespeare* (1564–1616), or his literary works, etc. — *n* a student of Shakespeare.

shako *shak'ō*, *n* a tall, nearly cylindrical military cap with a plume: — *pl* **shak'os** or **shak'oes**. [Hung. *csákó*.]

shakudo *shak'o͞o-dō* or *-dō'*, *n* an alloy of copper and a small percentage of gold, used in Japanese decorative art, esp. in sword fittings, to give a blue-black patina. — *adj* made of or with shakudo. [Jap.]

shakuhachi *shäk-o͞o-häch'ē*, *n* a Japanese, end-blown, bamboo flute. [Jap.]

shale *shāl*, *n* clay rock that splits readily into thin layers along the bedding-planes. — *adj* **shā'ly**. — **shale'oil** oil distilled from oil-shale. [Ger. *Schale*, lamina; or obs. *shale*, a shell — O.E. *scealu*.]

shall *shal* or *shəl*, *vt* used with the infinitive of a verb (without *to*) to form (in sense) a future tense, expressing in the first person mere futurity (as **will** in the second and third), in the second and third person implying also promise, command, decree or control on the part of the speaker (rules for use of *shall*, *will* are often ignored); must, will have to, is to, etc. (in 2nd and 3rd persons, and interrogatively 1st); may be expected to, may chance to, may well (in all persons); may in future contingency, may come to (in all persons). — No *participles*; *3rd pers sing* **shall**; *pa t* **should** (*sho͝od* or *shəd*). [O.E. *sculan*, pres. t. *sceal*, *scealt*, *sceal*; past t. *sceolde*.]

shallop *shal'əp*, *n* a dinghy; a small or light boat. [Fr. *chaloupe*.]

shallot *shə-lot'*, *n* a garlic-flavoured species of onion, with clusters of small, oval bulbs. [O.Fr. *eschalote*, variant of *escalogne*.]

shallow *shal'ō*, *adj* of no great depth, concavity, profundity or penetration; superficial. — *adv* at or to no great depth. — *n* a shallow place; (used in plural with **the**) the shallow part. — *vt* to make shallow. — *vi* to grow shallow. — *n* and *adj* **shall'owing**. — *adv* **shall'owly** simply, foolishly; in a shallow or superficial manner. — *n* **shall'owness**. [M.E. *schalowe*, perh. related to **shoal²**.]

shalom *shal-ōm'* or *shal-om'*, (Heb.) *interj* peace (be with you) — a greeting or valediction used esp. by Jewish people: — in full **shalom aleichem** (*əl-āhh'əm*).

shalwar *shul'vär* or *shal'war*, *n* loose-fitting trousers worn (by both sexes) in many parts of S. Asia. — **shalwar-kameez'** a S. Asian outfit (for women) of loose-fitting trousers and a long tunic. [Urdu *shalwār*, Hindi *salvar* — Pers. *shalwar*; Urdu *kamis* — Ar. *qamīs*, shirt.]

shaly. See **shale**.

sham *sham*, *n* a counterfeit, pretence. — *adj* pretended; false. — *vt* to pretend; to feign. — *vi* to make false pretences; to pretend to be (as in *to sham dead* or *sick*): — *pr p* **shamm'ing**; *pa t* and *pa p* **shammed**. — *n* **shamm'er**. [First found as slang, late 17th cent.]

shaman *shäm'an* or *shäm'ən*, *n* a doctor-priest working by magic, primarily of N. Asia: — *pl* **sham'ans**. — Also *adj*. — *n* **Sham'anism** (also without *cap*) the religion of N. Asia, based essentially on magic spiritualism and sorcery. — *n* **sham'anist**. — *adj* **shamanist'ic**. [Russ., — Tungus.]

shamateur *sham'ə-tœr* or *-tūr*, *n* a person rated as an amateur in sport who yet makes money from playing or competing. — *n* **sham'ateurism**. [**sham** and **amateur**.]

shamble *sham'bl*, *vi* to walk with an awkward, unsteady gait. — *n* a shambling gait. — *n* and *adj*

sham'bling. [Poss. from **shambles**, in allusion to trestle-like legs.]

shambles *sham'blz, npl* (usu. treated as *nsing*) a flesh-market, hence, a slaughterhouse; a place of carnage (*fig*); a mess or muddle (*colloq*). — *adj* **shambol'ic** (*slang*) chaotic. [O.E. *scamel*, stool — L.L. *scamellum*, dimin. of *scamnum*, a bench.]

shame *shām, n* the humiliating feeling of having appeared unfavourably in one's own eyes, or those of others, as a result of shortcoming, offence, or unseemly exposure, or a similar feeling on behalf of anything one associates with oneself; susceptibility to such feeling; fear or scorn of incurring disgrace or dishonour; modesty; bashfulness; disgrace, ignominy; cause or source of disgrace; a thing to be ashamed of; an instance or a case of hard or bad luck (*colloq*). — *interj* how shameful, what a disgrace!; an expression of affection, warmth or sympathy (*SAfr*). — *vt* to make ashamed; to disgrace; to put to shame by greater excellence; to drive or compel by shame. — *adj* **shamed** ashamed. — *adj* **shame'ful** disgraceful. — *adv* **shame'fully.** — *n* **shame'fulness.** — *adj* **shame'less** immodest, brazen; done without shame. — *adj* **shame'lessly.** — *n* **shame'lessness.** — *adj* **shame'faced** very modest or bashful; showing shame; abashed. — *adv* **shame'facedly** (*-fāst-li* or *-fā'sid-li*). — **shame'facedness** modesty. — **for shame** you should be ashamed; **put to shame** to disgrace, esp. by excelling; **shame on (you, them,** etc.) (you, they, etc.) should be ashamed. [O.E. *sc(e)amu*.]

shammy *sham'i, n* (in full **shammy-leath'er**) a soft leather, originally made from chamois-skin, now usually from sheepskin, by working in oil; a piece of it, used for polishing, etc. — Also *adj*. [**chamois.**]

shampoo *sham-pōō', vt* to wash and rub (the scalp and hair) with a special lathering preparation; to clean (a carpet, etc.) by rubbing likewise with a detergent: — *pa t* and *pa p* **shampooed'** or **shampoo'd'**. — *n* an act or process of shampooing; a preparation for the purpose: — *pl* **shampoos'**. — *n* **shampoo'er.** [Hindi *cāpnā*, to squeeze.]

shamrock *sham'rok, n* the national emblem of Ireland, a trifoliate leaf or plant. [Ir. *seamróg*, Gael. *seamrag*, dimin. of *seamar*, trefoil.]

shandy *shan'di, n* a mixture of beer and ginger beer or lemonade.

Shang *shang, n* a Chinese dynasty (17th–11th cent. B.C. — *adj* of the dynasty, its time or esp. its pottery, bronzes, etc.

shanghai[1] *shang-hī', vt* to drug or make drunk and send to sea as a sailor; to trick into performing an unpleasant task: — *pr p* **shanghai'ing**; *pa t* and *pa p* **shanghaied'** or **shanghai'd'**. — *n* **shanghai'er.** [*Shanghai* in China.]

shanghai[2] *shang-hī', (Austr* and *NZ) n* a catapult. — *vt* to shoot with a shanghai.

Shangri-la *shang-gri-lä', n* an imaginary pass in the Himalayas, an earthly paradise, described in James Hilton's *Lost Horizon* (1933); any remote or imaginary paradise.

shank *shangk, n* the leg from knee to foot; the corresponding part in other vertebrates; the lower part of the foreleg, esp. as a cut of meat; a shaft, stem, straight or long part; the part of a shoe connecting sole with heel; the leg of a stocking; an act of shanking a golf ball. — *vi* to be affected with disease of the footstalk (*bot*). — *vt* to strike with the junction of the shaft (*golf*). — *adj* **shanked** having a shank; affected with disease of the shank or footstalk (*bot*). — **shank'-bone.** — **on Shanks's mare, nag, pony,** etc. on foot. [O.E. *sceanca*, leg.]

shanny *shan'i, n* a fish, the smooth blenny.

shan't *shänt, (colloq)* a contraction of **shall not.**

shantung *shan-tung'* or *-tōōng', n* a plain rough cloth of wild silk; a similar cotton or rayon fabric. [*Shantung* province in China.]

shanty[1] *shan'ti, n* a roughly built hut; a ramshackle dwelling; a rough public-house or (*hist*) a place selling alcohol illicitly (*Austr*). — **shanty town** a town, or an area of one, where housing is makeshift and ramshackle. [Perh. Fr. *chantier*, a timber-yard (in Canada a woodcutters' headquarters); perh. Ir. *sean tig*, old house.]

shanty[2] *shan'ti, n* a rhythmical song with chorus and solo verses (often extempore), sung by sailors while heaving at the capstan, etc. — *n* **shant'yman** the solo-singer in shanties. [Said to be from Fr. *chantez* (imper.), sing.]

SHAPE *shāp, abbrev* for Supreme Headquarters Allied Powers Europe.

shape *shāp, vt* to form; to fashion; to give form to; to embody; to devise; to direct; to determine. — *vi* to take shape; to develop; to become fit: — *pa t* and *pa p* **shaped.** — *n* form; figure; disposition in space; guise; form or condition; that which has form or figure; a pattern; a mould (*cookery*); a jelly, pudding, etc. turned out of a mould. — *adj* **shāp'able** or **shape'able.** — *adj* **shaped.** — Also in composition, as *L-shaped*. — *adj* **shape'less** of ill-defined or unsatisfactory shape; without shape. — *n* **shape'lessness.** — *n* **shape'liness.** — *adj* **shape'ly** well-proportioned. — *n* **shap'er.** — *n* and *adj* **shap'ing.** — **in any shape or form** at all; **in good shape** or **in shape** in good condition; **in the shape of** in the guise of; of the nature of; **out of shape** deformed, disfigured; in poor physical condition, unfit; **shape one's course** to direct one's way; **shape up** to assume a shape; to develop, to be promising; **take shape** to assume a definite form or plan; to be embodied or worked out in practice. [O.E. *scieppan*.]

sharawaggi or **sharawadgi** *shar-ə-waj'i, n* (in design, architecture, etc.) the use of irregularity, discordance or incongruity for deliberate, artful, contrastive effect. [Used orig. in the late 17th cent. in the context of Chinese landscape gardening.]

shard *shärd* or **sherd** *shûrd, n* a scrap, broken piece, esp. of pottery. [O.E. *sceard*, cleft, potsherd.]

share[1] *shār, n* a part allotted, contributed, owned or taken; a division, section, portion; a fixed and indivisible section of the capital of a company, which also constitutes a part-ownership of the company and the right to receive a portion of the profits. — *vt* to divide into shares; to apportion; to give or take a share of; to participate in; to have in common. — *vi* to have, receive or give a share. — *n* **shar'er.** — *n* **shar'ing.** — **share'-capital** money derived from the sale of shares in a business, and used for carrying it on. — *vi* **share'crop.** — **share'cropper** (esp. *US*) a tenant farmer who supplies, in lieu of rent, a share of the crop; **share'farmer** (esp. *Austr*) a tenant farmer who pays a share of the proceeds as rent; **share'holder** someone who owns a share, esp. in a company; **share'holding; share'milker** (*NZ*) a sharefarmer on a dairy farm; **share'-out** a distribution in shares; **share'-pusher** a person who seeks to sell shares otherwise than through recognised channels, or by dubious advertisement, etc.; **share shop** a shop at which shares and bonds are traded quickly and informally without investment advice. — **go shares** (*colloq*) to divide; **lion's share** see under **lion; share and share alike** in equal shares. [O.E. *scearu*; cf. **shear.**]

share[2] *shār, n* a ploughshare or corresponding part of another implement. [O.E. *scear*; cf. **share**[1] and **shear.**]

Sharia *shə-rē'ə* or **Shariat** *shə-rē'ət, n* same as **Sheria, Sheriat.** — Also without *cap*.

shark *shärk, n* a general name for elasmobranchs other than skates, rays, and chimaeras — voracious fishes, with lateral gill-slits, and mouth on the under side; sometimes confined to the larger kinds, excluding the dogfishes; an extortioner; a financial swindler, underhand or predatory dealer; a sharper. — **shark'skin** a heavy rayon material with dull finish; shagreen. [Ger. *Schurke*, scoundrel, Austrian Ger. *Schirk*, sturgeon, have been suggested.]

Sharon fruit *shar'ən frōōt*, *n* a persimmon. [From the *Sharon* valley in Israel where it is esp. grown.]

sharp *shärp*, *adj* cutting; piercing; penetrating; acute; having a thin edge or fine point; affecting the senses as if pointed or cutting; severe; harsh; keen; eager; alive to one's own interests; barely honest; of keen or quick perception; alert; fit, able; pungent, sarcastic; brisk; abrupt; having abrupt or acute corners, etc.; sudden in onset; clear-cut; unblurred; well-defined; stylish (*slang*); high in pitch, or too high. — *adv* high or too high in pitch; punctually, precisely; sharply. — *n* a note raised a semitone; the symbol for it; the key producing it; a long slender needle; a sharper; (in *pl*) hard parts of wheat. — *vt* and *vi* **sharp'en** to make or become sharp in any sense. — *n* **sharp'ener**. — *n* **sharp'er** a cheat or hoaxer. — *n* **sharp'ie** one of a set of stylishly dressed teenagers (*Austr* and *NZ*). — *n* and *adj* **sharp'ing** cheating. — *adj* **sharp'ish**. — *adv* **sharp'ly**. — *n* **sharp'ness**. — *adj* **sharp'-cut** well-defined; clear-cut. — *adj* **sharp-edged'**. — *adj* **sharp-eyed'**. — *adj* **sharp'-nosed** having a pointed nose; keen of scent. — **sharp practice** unscrupulous dealing, verging on dishonesty. — *adj* **sharp'-set** keen in appetite for anything, esp. food or sexual indulgence; set with a sharp edge. — *adj* **sharp'-shod** (of a horse) having spikes in the shoes to prevent slipping. — **sharp'shooter** a good marksman; a soldier set apart for work as a marksman; (*loosely*) someone with a talent for scoring in any sport; **sharp'shooting**. — *adj* **sharp-sight'ed** having acute sight; shrewd. — *adj* **sharp-tongued'** critical, sarcastic or harsh in speech. — *adj* **sharp-toothed'**. — *adj* **sharp-witted'** having an alert intelligence, wit or perception. — **at the sharp end** in the position of direct action, confrontation, challenge or pressure; **look sharp** be quick; hurry up. [O.E. *scearp*.]

Shar-Pei *shär-pā'*, *n* a large muscular dog of a Chinese breed, with distinctive wrinkled skin. [Chin. dialect, sand fur.]

shashlik *shash-lik'* or *shash'lik*, *n* a type of lamb kebab. [Russ. *shashlyk*.]

shaster *shas'tər* or **shastra** *shäs'trä*, (*Hinduism*) *n* a holy writing. [Sans. *śāstra* — *śās*, to teach.]

shat. See **shit**.

shatter *shat'ər*, *vt* to dash to pieces; to wreck. — *vi* to break into fragments. — *adj* **shatt'ered** exhausted; extremely upset. — *adj* **shatt'erproof** made specially resistant to shattering. [Perh. L.G.]

shave *shāv*, *vt* to scrape or pare off a superficial slice, hair (esp. of the face), or other surface material from; to remove by scraping or paring; to pare closely; to graze the surface of. — *vi* to remove hair with a razor: — *pa p* **shāved**. — *n* the act or process of shaving; a paring; a narrow miss or escape (esp. *close shave*); a tool for paring or slicing. — *adj* **shā'ven** shaved; close-cut; smoothed; tonsured. — *n* **shā'ver** a person who shaves; an electric razor; a chap, a youngster (*colloq*). — *n* **shā'ving** the act of scraping or using a razor; a thin slice, esp. a curled piece of wood planed off. — **shā'ving-brush** a brush for lathering the face; **shā'ving-soap** soap for lathering in preparation for shaving; **shā'ving-stick** a cylindrical piece of shaving-soap. [O.E. *sc(e)afan*.]

Shavian *shā'vi-ən*, *adj* pertaining to the dramatist George Bernard *Shaw* (1856–1950). — *n* a follower or admirer of Shaw.

Shavuot, Shavuoth. See **Shabuoth**.

shaw *shö*, *n* the above-ground parts of a potato plant, turnip, etc.

shawl *shöl*, *n* a loose covering for the shoulders, etc. — *vt* to wrap in a shawl. — *n* **shawl'ing**. — **shawl collar** a large rolled collar tapering from the neck towards the waistline; **shawl'-pattern** a pattern like that of an Eastern shawl such as those woven in Kashmir. — **Paisley shawl** see **paisley**. [Pers. *shāl*.]

shawm *shöm*, (*mus*) *n* a predecessor of the oboe, an instrument with a double reed and a flat circular piece against which the lips are rested. [O.Fr. *chalemie*, *-mel* — L. *calamus*, reed.]

Shawnee *shö-nē'*, *n* a N. American Indian of an Algonquin tribe now mostly in Oklahoma; the language of this tribe. — **shawnee'-wood** a species of catalpa. [Shawnee *Shawunogi*.]

she *shē* (or when unemphatic *shi*), *nominative* (irregularly, in dialect, or ungrammatically *accusative* or *dative*) *fem pronoun* of the *3rd pers* the female (or thing spoken of as female) named before, indicated or understood (*pl* **they**). — *n* (*nominative*, *accusative* and *dative*) a female (*pl* **shes**). — *adj* female (esp. in composition, as in **she'-ass, she'-bear, she'-devil**). [Prob. O.E. *sēo*, fem. of the definite article, which in the 12th cent. came to be used instead of the pronoun *hēo*.]

s/he. A form representing *she or he*.

shea *shē*, *n* an African tree (**shea'-tree**, *Butyrospermum*) whose seeds (**shea'-nuts**) yield **shea-butt'er**. [Mandingo (W.Afr. language) *si*.]

sheading *shē'ding*, *n* one of the six divisions or districts of the Isle of Man. [**shedding**.]

sheaf *shēf*, *n* a bundle of things bound side by side, esp. stalks of corn; a bundle of papers; a bundle of arrows: — *pl* **sheaves** (*shēvz*). — *vt* **sheaf** or **sheave** to bind in sheaves. — *vi* to make sheaves. — *adj* **sheaved**. [O.E. *scēaf*.]

shear *shēr*, *vt* to cut, or clip esp. with shears; to cut superfluous nap from; to achieve or make by cutting; to subject to a shear (*eng* and *phys*); to strip, fleece (also *fig*). — *vi* to separate; to cut; to penetrate: — *pa t* **sheared**; *pa p* **shorn**, also, less commonly in ordinary senses, but always of deformation and usually of metal-cutting, **sheared**. — *n* a shearing or clipping; a strain, stress or deformation in which parallel planes remain parallel, but move parallel to themselves (*eng* and *phys*). — *n* **shear'er** a person who shears sheep. — *n* **shear'ing**. — *n* **shear'ling** a sheep that has been shorn for the first time; the fleece of such a sheep. — *npl* **shears** a large pair of clippers, or scissorlike cutting instrument with a pivot or spring; a hoisting apparatus (see **sheers** under **sheer**[2]). — **shear'-leg** see **sheer**[2]; **shear pin** (in a machine) a pin which, as a safety mechanism, will shear and halt the machine when the correct load or stress is exceeded; **shear'water** one of a genus of oceanic birds that skim the water. [O.E. *sceran*.]

sheatfish *shēt'fish*, *n* a gigantic fish (*Silurus glanis*), the European catfish of European rivers. [Ger. *Scheidfisch*.]

sheath *shēth*, *n* a case for a sword or blade; a close-fitting (esp. tubular or long) covering; (also **sheath dress**) a close-fitting, usu. simple, straight dress; a clasping leaf-base, or similar protective structure; an insect's wing-case; a condom: — *pl* **sheaths** (*shēdhz*). — *vt* **sheathe** (*shēdh*) to put into or cover with a sheath or casing. — *adj* **sheathed** (*shēdhd*) having or enclosed in a sheath. — *n* **sheath'ing** (*-dh-*) that which sheathes; casing; the covering of a ship's bottom. — *adj* **sheath'less**. — **sheath'-bill** either of two Antarctic sea-birds (*Chionis*) with white plumage and a horny sheath at the base of the bill; **sheath'-knife** a knife encased in a sheath. [O.E. *scēath*, *scǣth*.]

sheave[1] *shēv*, *n* a grooved wheel, pulley-wheel.

sheave[2], **sheaves**, etc. See **sheaf**.

shebang *shi-bang'*, (*slang*, orig. *US*) *n* a vehicle; affair, matter, etc., esp. as in *the whole shebang*. [Perh. conn. with **shebeen**.]

shebeen *shi-bēn'*, *n* an illicit liquor-shop. [Anglo-Ir.]

shechita, shechitah. See **schechita.**
shed[1] *shed, vt* to part, separate; to cast off; to drop; to emit; to pour forth; to cast, throw (e.g. light); to impart; to cause effusion of: — *pr p* **shedd'ing;** *pa t* and *pa p* **shed.** — *adj* cast; spilt, emitted. — *n* **shedd'er** a person who or thing that sheds; a female salmon or the like after spawning. — *n* **shedd'ing.** [O.E. *scādan, scēadan* (strong verb), to separate.]
shed[2] *shed, n* a structure, often open-fronted, for storing or shelter; an outhouse. [App. a variant of **shade.**]
she'd *shēd,* (*colloq*) a contraction of **she had** or **she would.**
sheen *shēn, n* shine; lustre; radiance; a very thin slick of oil (on water). — *adj* **sheen'y** lustrous; glistening. [O.E. *scēne,* beautiful; infl. by **shine.**]
sheep *shēp, n* a beardless, woolly, ruminant animal (*Ovis*) of the goat family; a sheepish person; someone who is like a sheep, as e.g. a member of a flock (or congregation), a creature that follows meekly, is at the mercy of the wolf or the shearer, etc.: — *pl* **sheep.** — *adj* **sheep'ish** like a sheep; embarrassed through having done something foolish or wrong. — *adv* **sheep'ishly.** — *n* **sheep'ishness.** — **sheep'cote** an enclosure for sheep; **sheep'-dip** a disinfectant insecticidal preparation used in washing sheep; a place for dipping sheep, specif. the trough of sheep-dip through which they are driven; **sheep'dog** a dog trained to watch sheep, or of a breed used for that purpose; **sheep'-farmer; sheep'fold; sheep'hook** a shepherd's crook; **sheep'-pox** a contagious eruptive disease of sheep, resembling smallpox; **sheep'-run** a tract of grazing country for sheep; **sheep's'-bit** (or **sheep's scabious**) a plant (*Jasione*) with blue heads resembling scabious; **sheep'-scab** a mange in sheep transmitted by mites. — *npl* **sheep's-eyes'** wishful amorous gazes. — **sheep's fescue** a temperate tufted pasture grass; **sheep'shank** a nautical knot for shortening a rope; **sheep's'-head** the head of a sheep, esp. as food (also *adj*); an American fish similar to the porgie; **sheep'shearer; sheep'-shearing; sheep'skin** the skin of a sheep, with or without the fleece attached; leather or parchment prepared from it; an item made of it (e.g. a coat or a horse's noseband). — Also *adj.* — **sheep station** (*Austr*) a large sheep farm; **sheep'stealer; sheep'-stealing; sheep'-track; sheep'-walk** a range of pasture for sheep. — **black sheep** the disreputable member of a family or group; **separate the sheep from the goats** to identify (esp. by some test) the superior members of any group. [O.E. *scēap.*]
sheer[1] *shēr, adj* thin; pure; unmingled; mere, downright; unbroken; vertical or very nearly. — *adv* clear; quite; plumb; vertically. — *adv* **sheer'ly** completely, thoroughly, wholly, etc. [M.E. *schēre,* perh. from O.N. *skœrr* infl. by O.E. *scīr.*]
sheer[2] *shēr, vi* (with *off* or *away*) to deviate; to take oneself off, esp. to evade something disagreeable; to swerve. — *vt* to cause to deviate. — *n* a deviation; an oblique position; the fore-and-aft upward curve of a ship's deck or sides. — *npl* **sheers** or **shears** an apparatus for hoisting heavy weights, having legs or spars spread apart at their lower ends, and hoisting tackle at their joined tops. — **sheer'-leg** or **shear'leg** one of the spars of sheers; (in *pl*) sheers. [Partly at least another spelling of **shear.**]
sheet[1] *shēt, n* a large wide expanse or thin piece of something; a large broad rectangular piece of cloth, esp. for a bed; a piece of paper, esp. large and broad; a section of a book printed upon one piece of paper, a signature; a pamphlet, broadsheet, or newspaper, etc. — *adj* in the form of a sheet; printed on a sheet. — *vt* to wrap or cover with, or as with, a sheet; to provide with sheets; to form into sheets. — *vi* to form or run in a sheet. — *adj* **sheet'ed** wrapped or covered with a sheet. — *n* **sheet'ing** cloth for sheets; protective boarding or metal covering; formation into sheets. — **sheet-copp'er, -i'ron, -lead', -met'al, -rubb'er, -tin',** etc., copper, iron, etc. in thin sheets. — *vt* and *n* **sheet feed.** — **sheet feeder** (*comput* and *word processing*) a storage cassette that feeds single sheets of paper automatically into a printer as required; **sheet-glass'** a kind of glass made in a cylinder and flattened out; **sheet-light'ning** the diffused appearance of distant lightning; **sheet music** music written or printed on (unbound) sheets. [O.E. *scēte* , *scēat*; cf. **sheet.**]
sheet[2] *shēt,* (*naut*) *n* a rope attached to the lower corner of a sail; (in *pl*) the part of a boat between the thwarts and the stern or bow. — **sheet bend** a type of knot used esp. for joining ropes of different sizes. — **a sheet** (or **three sheets**) **in** or **to the wind** half-drunk (or drunk). [O.E. *scēata,* corner; related to **sheet**[1].]
sheet-anchor *shēt'-angk-ər, n* an extra anchor for an emergency (*naut*); a chief support; a last refuge. [Formerly *shut-, shot-,* or *shoot-anchor.*]
Sheffield plate *shef'ēld plāt, n* a type of metalware developed in Sheffield and produced between the mid-18th and mid-19th century, of copper coated with silver. [*Sheffield* (city in S. Yorkshire) and **plate.**]
shehita, shehitah. See **schechita.**
sheikh or **sheik** *shāk* or *shēk, n* an Arab chief. — *n* **sheikh'a** the chief wife or consort of a sheikh; a high-class Arab lady. — *n* **sheik'dom** or **sheikh'dom** a sheik's territory. [Ar. *shaikh* — *shākha,* to be old.]
sheila *shē'lə,* (*Austr colloq*) *n* a young girl or a woman. [From the proper name.]
shekel *shek'l, n* a Jewish weight (about 14 grams) and coin of this weight; the standard unit of currency of Israel (100 *agorot*); (in *pl*) money (*slang*). [Heb. *sheqel* — *shāqal,* to weigh.]
shelduck *shel'duk, n* (*fem* or *generic*) a large duck (genus *Tadorna*) with a free hind-toe. — Also (esp. *masc*) **shel'drake.** [Prob. dialect *sheld,* variegation, and **duck, drake.**]
shelf *shelf, n* a board fixed on a wall, in a bookcase, etc., for laying things on; a shelf-ful; a ledge; a shoal; a sandbank: — *pl* **shelves** (*shelvz*). — *n* **shelf'-ful** enough to fill a shelf: — *pl* **shelf'-fuls.** — *adj* **shelf'like.** — **shelf'-catalogue** a library catalogue arranged by shelves; **shelf'-life** the length of time a product can be stored without deterioration occurring; **shelf'-mark** an indication on a book of its place in a library; **shelf'room** space or accommodation on shelves; **shelf'talker** a marketing device, e.g. a notice or mini-poster, attached to a shelf in a shop, to promote a specific product. — **on the shelf** no longer likely to have the opportunity to marry; removed from further prospect of employment. [O.E. *scylf,* shelf, ledge, pinnacle, or L.G. *schelf.*]
shell *shel, n* a hard outer covering, esp. of a shellfish, a tortoise, an egg, or a nut; a husk, pod or rind; an outer framework; a crust; a hollow sphere or the like; a mere outside, empty case, or lifeless relic; any frail structure; a type of light racing boat; an explosive projectile shot from a cannon; a cartridge containing explosive for small-arms, fireworks, etc.; in some schools, an intermediate class (from one that met in an apse at Westminster). — *adj* of, with, or like shell or shells. — *vt* to separate from the shell; to case; to throw, fire, etc. shells at. — *vi* to peel or scale; to separate from the shell. — *adj* **shelled** having a shell; separated from the shell, pod, etc. — *n* **shell'er.** — *n* **shell'ful.** — *n* **shell'iness.** — *n* **shell'ing.** — *adj* **shell'-less.** — *adj* **shell'-like.** — *n* (*slang*) a person's ear. — *adj* **shell'y** of or like shell or shells; abounding in shells; having a shell. — **shell'back** an old sailor; **shell company** (*commerce*) a company that exists on paper only, e.g. one set up as a potential takeover subject, to hold assets, or for corrupt financial

purposes; **shell'-crater** a hole in the ground made by a bursting shell; **shell'-egg** one in the shell, in its natural state; **shell'fire** bombardment with shells; **shell'fish** a shelled aquatic invertebrate, esp. a mollusc or crustacean, or such animals collectively; **shell'-hole** a shell-crater; **shell'-jacket** a tight, short undress military jacket; **shell'-lime** lime made from seashells; **shell'-money** wampum; **shell-pink'** a pale yellow-tinged shade of pink. — Also *adj*. — *adj* **shell'proof** able to resist shells or bombs. — **shell'shock** mental disturbance, or a stunned state, due to war experiences, once thought to be caused by the bursting of shells; mental disturbance due to similar violent, etc. experiences. — *adj* **shell'-shocked**. — **shell suit** a fashionable type of tracksuit, often used as everyday casual wear, with an outer layer of one material and a lining of another. — **come out of one's shell** to cease to be shy and reticent; **shell out** (*slang*) to pay up; to disburse. [O.E. *scell*.]

she'll *shēl*, (*colloq*) a contraction of **she shall** or **she will**.

shellac or **shell-lac** *shel-ak'* or *shel'ak*, *n* lac (q.v.) in thin plates, obtained by melting seed-lac, straining and dropping; (*loosely*) lac, the resin, used e.g. as a spirit varnish. — *vt* to coat with shellac; (*shel-ak'*) to trounce (*US*): — *pr p* **shellacking**; *pa t* and *pa p* **shellacked**. — *n* **shellacking**.

Shelta *shel'tə*, *n* a secret jargon used by vagrants in Britain and Ireland. [*Shelrū*, poss. O.Ir. — *béulra*, language.]

shelter *shel'tər*, *n* a shielding or screening structure, esp. against weather; (a place of) refuge, retreat or temporary lodging in distress; asylum; screening; protection. — *vt* to screen; to shield; to give asylum, protection or lodging to; to harbour. — *vi* to take shelter. — *adj* **shel'tered** affording shelter. — *n* **shel'terer**. — *n* and *adj* **shel'tering**. — *adj* **shel'terless**. — **sheltered housing** housing for the elderly or disabled consisting of separate units with a resident housekeeper or similar person to look after the tenants' wellbeing.

sheltie or **shelty** *shel'ti*, *n* a Shetland pony or sheepdog. [Perh. O.N. *Hjalti*, Shetlander.]

shelve *shelv*, *vt* to furnish with shelves; to place on a shelf; to put aside, postpone. — *vi* to slope, incline. — *npl* **shelves** (*pl* of **shelf**). — *n* **shel'ving** provision of, or material for, shelves; shelves collectively; the act of putting upon a shelf or setting aside; a slope. — *adj* shallowing; sloping. — *adj* **shel'vy** having sand-banks; overhanging. [See ety. for **shelf**.]

shemozzle *shi-moz'l*, (*slang*) *n* a mess; a scrape; a rumpus. [Yiddish, — Ger. *schlimm*, bad, Heb. *mazzāl*, luck; cf. **schlimazel**.]

shenanigan *shi-nan'i-gən*, (*slang*; usu. in *pl*) *n* trickery; humbug.

she-oak *shē'-ōk*, (*Austr*) *n* a casuarina tree. [**she** (denoting inferior) and **oak**, from its grain.]

Sheol or **She'ol** *shē'ōl*, *n* the place of departed spirits. [Heb. *she'ōl*.]

shepherd *shep'ərd*, *n* a person who tends sheep (*fem* **shep'herdess**); a pastor. — *vt* to tend or guide as or like a shepherd; to watch over, protect the interests of, or one's own interests in. — *adj* **shep'herdless**. — **shepherd's check, plaid** or **tartan** small black-and-white check; cloth with this pattern; **shepherd's pie** a dish of minced lamb or beef cooked with potatoes on the top; **shepherd's purse** a weed with flat pods and white flowers. — **the Good Shepherd** Jesus Christ (from the Bible: John x. 11). [O.E. *scēaphirde*; see **sheep** and **herd**.]

sherardise or **-ize** *sher'ərd-īz*, *vt* to coat with zinc by heating with zinc-dust in absence of air. [From *Sherard* Cowper-Coles, the inventor of the process.]

Sheraton *sher'ə-tən*, *n* a kind or style of furniture designed by Thomas *Sheraton* (1751–1806). — Also *adj*.

sherbet *shûr'bət*, *n* an effervescent drink, or powder for making it; a kind of water-ice; a fruit-juice drink; beer (*Austr colloq*). [Turk. and Pers. *sherbet*, from Ar.]

sherd *shûrd*, *n*. See **shard**.

Sheria *shə-rē'ə* or **Sheriat** *shə-rē'ət*, *n* the body of Islamic religious law. — Also without *cap*. [Turk. *sherīʿat*, law.]

sherif or **shereef** *shə-rēf'*, *n* a descendant of Mohammed through his daughter Fatima; a prince, esp. the Sultan of Morocco; the chief magistrate of Mecca. [Ar. *sharīf*, noble, lofty.]

sheriff *sher'if*, *n* in England, the chief officer of the crown in the shire or county, with duties chiefly honorary rather than judicial; in Scotland, the chief judge of the sheriff court of a town or region; in the United States, the chief executive officer of the county, mainly responsible for maintaining peace and order, attending courts, serving processes and executing judgments; the king's representative in a shire, with wide judicial and executive powers (*hist*). — *n* **sher'iffalty** shrievalty. — *n* **sher'iffdom** the office, term of office, or territory under the jurisdiction of a sheriff; in Scotland, one of six divisions of the judicature, made up of sheriff court districts. — *n* **sher'iffship**. — **sheriff clerk** in Scotland, the registrar of the sheriff court, who has charge of the records of the court, organises its work, etc.: — *pl* **sheriff clerks**; **sheriff court** the sheriff's court; **sheriff depute** in Scotland, sometimes applied to the sheriff or sheriff principal: — *pl* **sheriff deputes**; **sheriff officer** in Scotland, an officer of the sheriff court, who is responsible for raising actions, enforcing decrees, ensuring attendance of witnesses, etc.; **sheriff principal** in Scotland, the chief judge of a sheriffdom. — **high sheriff** an English sheriff proper; the chief executive officer of a district (*US*); **un'der-sheriff** an English sheriff's deputy who performs the execution of writs. [O.E. *scīrgerēfa* — *scīr*, shire, *gerēfa*, reeve.]

Sherlock Holmes *shûr'lok hōmz*, *n* someone who shows highly developed powers of observation and deduction, as did the detective, Sherlock Holmes, in the stories of Conan Doyle (1859–1930) — often used ironically.

Sherpa *shûr'pə*, *n* one of an eastern Tibetan people living high on the south side of the Himalayas: — *pl* **Sher'pa** or **Sher'pas**. [Tibetan *shar*, east, *pa*, inhabitant.]

sherry *sher'i*, *n* a fortified wine from the neighbourhood of Jerez de la Frontera in Spain; a wine of this type or similar. — **sherry-cobb'ler** a drink made of sherry, lemon, sugar, ice, etc.; **sherry party** a gathering at which sherry is drunk. — **cream sherry** sweet sherry. [*Xeres*, earlier form of Jerez.]

she's *shēz*, (*colloq*) a contraction of **she is** or **she has**.

Shetland *shet'lənd*, *adj* pertaining to the Shetland Islands off the N. coast of Scotland. — *n* **Shet'lander**. — *adj* **Shetlan'dic**. — *n* Shetland dialect. — **Shetland pony** a small, hardy pony with a thick coat, originating in the Shetland Islands; **Shetland sheep** a breed of sheep of Shetland and formerly Aberdeenshire; **Shetland sheepdog** a breed of dog resembling the collie, though smaller in size and with a thicker coat; **Shetland wool** a fine loosely twisted wool from Shetland sheep.

sheva *shə-vä'*, *n* Hebrew point or sign indicating absence of vowel; a schwa (*phon*). [Heb. *shewā*.]

shewbread *shō'bred*, *n* the twelve loaves offered weekly in the sanctuary by the Jews.

Shia or **Shiah** *shē'ə*, *n* the branch of Islam, or a member of it, that recognises Ali, Mohammed's son-in-law, as his successor. — **Shiism** (*shē'izm*). — **Shiite** (*shē'īt*) a member of this (now chiefly Iranian) sect. — Also *adj*. — *adj* **Shiitic** (*-it'ik*). [Ar. *shīʿa*, sect.]

shiatsu *shi-at'sōō*, *n* a Japanese healing, relaxing and health-promoting therapy using massage with fingers, palms, etc. [Jap., lit. finger pressure.]

shibboleth *shib'ə-leth*, *n* the criterion, catchword or catchphrase of a group; a peculiarity of speech; orig., the Gileadite test-word for an Ephraimite, who could not pronounce *sh* (from the Bible: Judg. xii. 5–6); any such test. [Heb. *shibbōleth*, an ear of corn, or a stream.]

shibuichi *shi-bōō-i'chē*, *n* an alloy of three parts copper to one part silver, widely used in Japanese decorative art to give a silver-grey patina. — *adj* made of or with shibuichi. [Jap. *shi*, four, *bu*, part, *ichi*, one.]

shied. See **shy**[1,2].

shiel *shēl* or **shieling** *shē'ling*, (*Scot*) *n* a shepherd's summer hut; (now only **shie'ling**) a summer pasture. [Prob. from a lost O.E. equivalent of O.N. *skāli*, hut.]

shield *shēld*, *n* a broad plate carried to ward off weapons, esp. one with a straight top and tapering curved sides; a protective plate, screen, pad or other guard; a protection; any shield-shaped design or object, e.g. an escutcheon used for displaying arms, a piece of plate as a prize; a large stable area of Pre-Cambrian rock in the earth's crust. — *vt* to protect by sheltering; to ward off. — *n* **shield'er.** — *adj* **shield'less.** — **shield'-bearer; shield'-bug** an insect with a well-developed scutellum. — *adj* **shield'-shaped.** [O.E. *sceld* (W. Saxon *scield*).]

shieling. See **shiel.**

shier, shies, shiest. See **shy**[1,2].

shift *shift*, *vt* to change; to change the position of; to remove; to dislodge; to transfer; to rid; to quit; to swallow, consume (*slang*); to put off. — *vi* to manage, get on, do as one can; to change position; to fluctuate; to take appropriate or urgent action; to move; to go away; to move quickly (*colloq*); to undergo phonetic change. — *n* an expedient; a set of persons taking turns (esp. in working) with another set; the time of working of such a set; a change; a change of position; provision of things for use in rotation or substitution; displacement of an ordered set of data to the left or right (*comput*); a smock, or a loose dress roughly triangular or oblong (*old-fashioned*); a general or bodily displacement of a series (as of lines in the spectrum, consonant or vowel sounds, faulted strata); a removal; (in violin-playing) any position of the left hand except that nearest the nut. — *adj* **shift'ed.** — *n* **shift'er.** — *adv* **shift'ily.** — *n* **shift'iness.** — *n* **shift'ing.** — *adj* moving about; unstable. — *adj* **shift'less** without resource or expedient; inefficient; feckless. — *adv* **shift'lessly.** — *n* **shift'lessness.** — *adj* **shift'y** evasive, tricky, suggesting trickery; dubious, shady, furtive; ready with shifts or expedients. — **shift'-key** a typewriter key used to bring a different set of letters (such as capitals) into play; **shift register** (*comput*) a register (q.v.) which carries out shifts on data (bits or digits); **shift work** (a system of) working in shifts; **shift worker; shift working.** — **shift about** to move from side to side; to turn quite round to the opposite point; **shift for oneself** to depend on one's own resources; **shift one's ground** (usu. *fig*) to change the position one has taken, e.g. in a discussion. [O.E. *sciftan*, to divide, allot.]

shigella *shig-el'ə*, *n* a rod-shaped bacterium (genus *Shigella*), esp. one of the species which cause dysentery. [After K. *Shiga* (1870–1957), the Jap. bacteriologist who discovered it.]

shih tzu *shē dzōō*, *n* a small long-haired dog of Tibetan and Chinese breed.

Shiism, Shiite, Shiitic. See **Shia.**

shiitake *shi-it-äk'ā*, *n* the variety of mushroom most widely used in Oriental cookery: — *pl* **shiitak'e.** [Jap. *shii*, a type of tree, *take*, mushroom.]

shikar *shi-kär'*, (*Anglo-Indian*) *n* hunting, sport. — *n* **shikar'ee** or **shikar'i** a hunter. [Urdu, from Pers. *shikār*.]

shillelagh *shi-lā'li* or *-lā'lə*, *n* in Ireland, an oak or blackthorn cudgel, or any similar stout club, etc. [*Shillelagh*, an oak wood in County Wicklow, Ireland, or *sail*, willow, *éille* (genitive), thong.]

shilling *shil'ing*, *n* a coin or its value, 12 old pence (equiv. to 5 (new) pence) (*hist*); (in Kenya, Tanzania, Uganda, etc.) a coin worth 100 cents. — *adj* costing or offered for a shilling; also in compounds, such as **two'-shilling, three'-shilling,** etc. — *n* **shill'ings-worth** as much as can be purchased for a shilling. — **take the (king's** or **queen's) shilling** (*hist*) to enlist as a soldier by accepting a recruiting officer's shilling — discontinued in 1879. [O.E. *scilling*.]

shilly-shally *shil'i-shal-i*, *vi* to be indecisive, vacillate. — *adv* indecisively. — *n* vacillation. — *n* **shill'y-shallier.** — *n* **shill'y-shallying.** [A reduplication of **shall I?**]

shim *shim*, *n* a slip of metal, wood, etc. used to fill in space or to adjust parts. — *vt* to fill in or adjust with a shim or shims.

shimmer *shim'ər*, *vi* to gleam tremulously, to glisten. — *n* **shimm'er** or **shimm'ering** a tremulous gleam. — *adj* **shimm'ery.** [O.E. *scimerian* — *scimian*, to shine.]

shimmy *shim'i*, *n* a shivering dance (also **shimm'y-shake**); a shaking of the hips; vibration in a motor car or an aeroplane. — *vi* to dance the shimmy, or make similar movements; to vibrate. [App. from **chemise.**]

shin *shin*, *n* the forepart of the leg below the knee; the lower part of a leg of beef. — *vi* to swarm, climb by gripping with the hands and legs (usu. with *up*). — *vt* to climb by gripping with the hands and legs; to kick on the shins. — **shin'bone** the tibia; **shin'plaster** (*US*) a brown-paper patch for a sore on the shin; paper money of small value. [O.E. *scinu*, the shin.]

shindig *shin'dig*, (*colloq*) *n* a lively celebration or party; a row. [Cf. **shindy.**]

shindy *shin'di*, (*colloq*) *n* a row, rumpus. — **kick up a shindy** to make a disturbance. [Perh. **shinty.**]

shine *shīn*, *vi* to give or reflect light; to beam with steady radiance; to glow; to be bright; to be clear or conspicuous; to excel. — *vt* to cause to shine; to direct the light of a torch, etc.: — *pa t* and *pa p* **shone** (*shon*) or (in the sense of polished) **shined.** — *n* brightness; lustre; a dash, brilliant appearance; an act or process of polishing; fine weather. — *adj* **shine'less.** — *n* **shīn'er** a person or thing that shines; a small glittering fish of various kinds; a black eye (*slang*). — *n* **shīn'iness.** — *adj* **shīn'ing** bright or gleaming; excellent or distinguished. — *adj* **shīn'y** clear, unclouded; glossy. — **shine at** to be very good at; **take a shine to** (*colloq*) to fancy, take a liking to; **take the shine out of** (*slang*) to outshine, eclipse; to take the brilliance or pleasure-giving quality out of. [O.E. *scīnan*.]

shingle[1] *shing'gl*, *n* a wooden slab (or substitute) used as a roofing-slate; these slabs collectively; a board; a small signboard or plate (*US*); a mode of hair-cutting showing the form of the head at the back (from the overlap of the hairs). — *vt* to cover with shingles; to cut in the manner of a shingle. — *adj* **shing'led.** — *n* **shing'ler.** — *n* **shing'ling.** — *adj* **shing'le-roofed.** [L.L. *scindula*, a wooden tile — L. *scindĕre*, to split.]

shingle[2] *shing'gl*, *n* coarse gravel; small water-worn pebbles found esp. on beaches; a bank or bed of gravel or stones. — *adj* **shing'ly.**

shingles *shing'glz*, *npl* the disease *Herpes zoster*, an eruption usu. running along an intercostal nerve with acute inflammation of the nerve ganglia. [L. *cingulum*, a belt — *cingĕre*, to gird.]

Shinto *shin'tō*, *n* the Japanese nature and hero cult, the indigenous religion of the country. — *n* **Shin'tōism.** — *n* **Shin'tōist.** [Jap., — Chin. *shin tao* — *shin*, god, *tao*, way, doctrine.]

shinty *shin'ti*, *n* a game like hockey, of Scot. origin, played by teams of 12; the slim curved club (also **shin'ty-stick**) or leather-covered cork ball (or substitute) used for this. [Perh. from Gael. *sinteag*, a bound, pace.]

shiny. See **shine**.

ship *ship*, *n* a large vessel, esp. a three-masted square-rigged sailing vessel; a racing-boat; any floating craft; an aircraft; a ship's crew; a spaceship. — *vt* to put, receive, or take on board; to send or convey by ship; to send by land or air; to dispatch, send (off); to engage for service on board; to fix in position. — *vi* to embark; to engage for service on shipboard: — *pr p* **shipp'ing**; *pa t* and *pa p* **shipped**. — *n* **ship'ful**. — *adj* **ship'less**. — *adj* **shipped** embarked. — *n* **shipp'er** a person or company that sends goods by ship. — *n* **shipp'ing** ships collectively; accommodation on board ship; (the act of) putting aboard ship; transport by ship. — **ship'board** a ship's side, hence a ship; **ship'broker** a broker for sale, insurance, etc. of ships; **ship'builder**; **ship'building**; **ship canal** a canal large enough for ships; **ship (or ship's) carpenter** a carpenter employed on board ship or in a shipyard; **ship (or ship's) chandler** a dealer in supplies for ships; **ship chandlery**; **ship fever** typhus; **ship'lap** an arrangement of boards or plates in which the lower edge of one overlaps the upper edge of the next below it. — Also *vt* and *vi*. — **ship'load** the actual or possible load of a ship; **ship'master** the captain of a ship; **ship'mate** a fellow sailor; **ship'-money** a tyrannical tax imposed by the king on seaports, revived without authorisation of parliament by Charles I in 1634–37; **ship'owner** the owner of, or owner of a share in, a ship or ships; **shipping agent** a person (or company) that manages the administrative business of a ship on behalf of the owner; **shipping articles** articles of agreement between the captain and his crew; **shipping clerk** a person employed to deal with the receiving and dispatching of goods by ship. — *adj* **ship'-rigged** having three masts with square sails and spreading yards. — **ship's biscuit** hard biscuit for use on shipboard. — *adj* **ship'shape** in a seamanlike condition; trim, neat, proper. — **ship's husband** an owner's agent who manages the affairs of a ship in port; **ship's papers** documents that a ship is required to carry; **ship'way** a sliding way for launching ships; a support for ships under examination or repair; a ship canal; **ship'worm** a wormlike mollusc that makes shell-lined tunnels in wood; **ship'wreck** a wrecked ship; the wreck or destruction (esp. by accident) of a ship; destruction, ruin, disaster. — *vt* to wreck; to cause ruin or destruction to. — **ship'wright** a wright or carpenter employed in shipbuilding; **ship'yard** a yard where ships are built or repaired. — **on shipboard** upon or within a ship; **ship a sea** or **ship water** to have a wave come aboard; **ship of the desert** the camel; **ship of the line** before steam navigation, a man-of-war large enough to take a place in a line of battle; **ship the oars** to put the oars in the rowlocks; to bring the oars into the boat; **ship water** see **ship a sea**; **take ship** or **shipping** to embark; **when one's ship comes home** or **in** when one becomes rich. [O.E. *scip*.]

-ship *-ship*, *sfx* denoting: a condition or state, e.g. *friendship*, *fellowship*; position, rank, status, e.g. *lordship*; a specified type of skill, e.g. *craftsmanship*, *scholarship*; a group of people having something in common, e.g. *membership*. [O.E. *-scipe*, conn. with **shape**.]

shipment *ship'mənt*, *n* the act of putting on board; a consignment, orig. by ship, now extended to other forms of transport. [**ship**.]

shiralee *shir'ə-lē*, (*Austr*) *n* a swagman's bundle.

shire *shīr* (in combination *-shir* or *-shər*), *n* a county; a rural district having its own elected council (*Austr*). — **shire horse** a large, strong draught-horse, once bred chiefly in the Midland shires. — **the Shires** those English counties whose names end in *-shire*, esp. (for hunting) Leicestershire, Northamptonshire, and part of Lincolnshire. [O.E. *scīr*, office, authority.]

shirk *shûrk*, *vt* to evade; to slink out of facing or shouldering (responsibility, etc.). — *vi* to go or act evasively; to avoid work or duty. — *n* a person who shirks. — *n* **shirk'er**.

shirr *shûr*, *n* a puckering or gathering. — *vt* to pucker, make gathers in; to bake (eggs broken into a dish). — *adj* **shirred**. — *n* **shirr'ing**.

shirt *shûrt*, *n* a man's loose sleeved garment for the upper part of the body, typically with fitted collar and cuffs; a woman's blouse of similar form; an undershirt; a nightshirt. — *n* **shirt'ing** cloth for shirts. — *adj* **shirt'less**. — **shirt'band** the neckband of a shirt; **shirt dress** a straight dress with a shirt-type collar, resembling an elongated shirt; a shirtwaister (*US*); **shirt front** the breast of a shirt, esp. a starched false one; **shirt pin** an ornamental pin fastening a shirt at the neck; **shirt'sleeve**; **shirt stud**; **shirt'tail** the longer flap at the back of a shirt; **shirt'waist** (*US*) a woman's blouse; **shirt'waister** a tailored dress with shirtwaist top. — **Black Shirt** or **Black'-shirt** a fascist; **Brown Shirt** or **Brown'shirt** a Nazi; **in one's shirtsleeves** with one's jacket or jersey off; **keep one's shirt on** to keep calm; **lose one's shirt** to lose all one has; **put one's shirt on** to bet all one has on. [O.E. *scyrte*; cf. **short**.]

shirty *shûrt'i*, (*colloq*) *adj* ill-tempered, annoyed. [**shirt**.]

shish kebab. See **kebab**.

shit *shit*, (*vulg*) *n* excrement; the act of defecating; a contemptuous term for a person; rubbish, nonsense. — *vi* to evacuate the bowels. — *vt* to produce by defecating: — *pr p* **shitt'ing**; *pa t* and *pa p* **shit**, **shitt'ed** or **shat**. — *interj* expressing annoyance, disappointment, etc. — *n* **shitt'iness**. — *adj* **shitt'y** soiled with or like shit; very bad or unpleasant. — **shit'head** contemptible or unpleasant person. — **no shit** (*US slang*) no fooling; goodness me (often *ironic*); **shit oneself** (*slang*) to be very scared. [O.E. *scitan*, to defecate.]

shiv. See **chiv**.

Shiva. See **Siva**.

shiver[1] *shiv'ər*, *n* a splinter or small fragment. — *vt* and *vi* to shatter. — *adj* **shiv'ery** brittle. — **shiver my timbers** a stage sailor's oath. [Early M.E. *scifre*.]

shiver[2] *shiv'ər*, *vi* to quiver; to make an involuntary muscular movement as with cold. — *vt* to cause to quiver. — *n* a shivering movement or feeling. — *n* and *adj* **shiv'ering**. — *adv* **shiv'eringly**. — *adj* **shiv'ery** inclined to shiver or to cause shivers. — **shiver in one's shoes** see **shake**; **the shivers** (*colloq*) a shivering fit; the ague; a thrill of horror or fear. [M.E. *chivere*.]

shivoo *shə-vōō'*, (*Austr colloq*) *n* a (noisy) party. [From N. Eng. dialect *sheevo*, a shindy.]

shlemiel. See **schlemiel**.

shlep. See **schlep**.

shlimazel. See **schlimazel**.

shlock. See **schlock**.

shmaltz. See **schmaltz**.

shoal[1] *shōl*, *n* a multitude of fishes, etc. swimming together; a flock, swarm, great assemblage. — *vi* to gather or go in shoals, swarm. [O.E. *scolu*, troop; cf. **school**[2].]

shoal[2] *shōl*, *adj* shallow. — *n* a shallow; a sandbank, esp. one exposed at low tide. — *vi* to grow shallow; to come to shallow water. — *vt* to make shallow. — *n* **shoal'ing**. — *adj* **shoal'y** full of shallows. [O.E. *sceald*, shallow.]

shoat *shōt*, *n* a young hog. [From M.E.]

shochet *shohh'ət*, *n* a slaughterer qualified to kill cattle or poultry according to prescribed Jewish ritual: — *pl* **shoch'etim** (*-tim*). [Heb. *shōḥet*, pres. p. of *shāḥat*, to slaughter.]

shock[1] *shok*, *n* a violent impact, orig. of charging warriors; a dashing together; a shaking or unsettling blow; a sudden shaking or jarring as if by a blow; a blow to the emotions or its cause; outrage at something regarded as improper; a convulsive excitation of nerves, as by electricity; the prostration of voluntary and involuntary functions caused by trauma, a surgical operation, or excessive sudden emotional disturbance. — *vt* to meet or assail with a shock; to shake or impair by a shock; to give a shock to; to cause to feel outrage, indignation, disgust, etc. — *vi* to outrage feelings. — *adj* **shocked**. — *n* **shock'er** (*colloq*) a very sensational tale; any unpleasant, offensive, etc. person or thing. — *adj* **shock'ing** giving a shock; revolting to the feelings, esp. to oversensitive modesty; execrable; deplorably bad. — *adv* (*colloq*) deplorably. — *adv* **shock'ingly**. — *n* **shock'ingness**. — **shock absorber** a contrivance for damping shock, as in an aeroplane alighting or a car on a bad road. — *adj* **shock'proof** protected in some way from giving, or suffering the effects of, shock; unlikely to be upset, or to feel moral outrage. — **shock tactics** orig. tactics of cavalry attacking in masses and depending for their effect on the force of impact; any action that seeks to achieve its object by means of suddenness and force; **shock therapy** or **treatment** the use of electric shocks in treatment of mental disorders; the use of violent measures to change one's way of thinking; **shock troops** troops trained or selected for attacks demanding exceptional physique and bravery; **shock wave** a wave of the same nature as a sound wave but of very great intensity, caused e.g. by an atomic explosion, or by a body moving with supersonic velocity; the reaction to a sensation or a scandal, thought of as spreading in ever-widening circles. — **shock horror** (*colloq*) an ironic expression denoting boredom, lack of interest, etc. (e.g. toward news that lacks impact or novelty), alluding esp. to banner headlines in tabloid newspapers. — *adj* **shock horror** or **shock'-horror**. [App. Fr. *choc* (n.), *choquer* (vb.), or perh. directly from a Gmc. source.]

shock[2] *shok*, *n* a stook, or propped-up group of sheaves, commonly twelve. — *vt* to set up in shocks. — *n* **shock'er**. [M.E. *schokke*.]

shock[3] *shok*, *n* a mass of shaggy hair. — **shock'-head**. — *adj* **shock'head** or **shock'headed**.

shod. See **shoe**.

shoddy *shod'i*, *adj* inferior and pretentious; cheap and nasty; sham; made of shoddy. — *n* wool from shredded rags; cloth made of it, alone or mixed; anything inferior seeking to pass for better than it is. — *adv* **shodd'ily**. — *n* **shodd'iness**.

shoe *shōō*, *n* a stiff outer covering for the foot, not coming above the ankle; a rim of iron nailed to a hoof; anything in form, position, or use like a shoe, as in a metal tip or ferrule, a piece attached where there is friction, a drag for a wheel, the touching part of a brake, the block by which an electric tractor collects current: — *pl* **shoes** (*shōōz*). — *vt* to put shoes or a shoe on: — *pr p* **shoe'ing**; *pa t* and *pa p* **shod** (*shod*) or **shoed** (*shōōd*). — *adj* **shod**. — *n* **shoe'ing**. — *adj* **shoe'less**. — *n* **shoer** (*shōō'ər*) a horse-shoer. — **shoe'black** a bootblack; **shoe'-horn** an instrument for helping the heel into the shoe. — *vt* (*fig*) to fit, squeeze or compress into a tight or insufficient space. — **shoe'lace** a string passed through eyelet holes to fasten a shoe; **shoe leather** leather for shoes; shoes or shoeing generally; **shoe'-maker** a person who makes (now more often only sells or mends) shoes and boots; **shoe'making**; **shoe nail** a nail for fastening a horseshoe; **shoe'-shine** (the act of) polishing shoes; **shoe'string** a shoelace (*US*); a minimum of capital. — *adj* operated, produced, etc. on a minimum of capital; petty, paltry (*US*); **shoe'-tree** a support, usu. of wood or metal, inserted in a shoe when it is not being worn in order to preserve its shape. — **be in** or **step into someone's** (or **a dead man's**) **shoes** to be in, or succeed to, someone's place. [O.E. *scōh* (pl. *scōs*).]

shofar *shō'fär*, *n* a kind of trumpet made from a ram's horn, blown in Jewish religious ceremonies and in ancient times as a call to battle, etc.: — *pl* **shō'fars** or **shōfroth** (*-frōt'*). [Heb. *shōphār*, ram's horn.]

shogi *shō'gē*, *n* the Japanese form of chess. [Jap. *shōgi*.]

shogun *shō'gōōn* or *shō'gōōn*, *n* the commander-in-chief and real ruler of feudal Japan. — *adj* **shō'gunal**. — *n* **shō'gunate** the office, jurisdiction or state of a shogun. [Jap., — *sho*, to lead, *gun*, army.]

shone *shon*, *pa t* and *pa p* of **shine**.

shoo *shōō*, *interj* an exclamation used to scare away fowls, etc. — *vi* to cry 'Shoo!'. — *vt* to drive away by calling 'Shoo!'. — *n* **shoo'-in** (*US slang*) a horse that is allowed to win; any certain winner of a race, competition, etc.; a sure thing. [Instinctive.]

shook[1] *shŏŏk*, *pa t* of **shake**.

shook[2] *shŏŏk*, *n* a bundle of sheaves, a shock, stook; a set of cask staves and heads, or of parts for making a box, etc.

shoot *shōōt*, *vt* to let fly with force; to discharge (a bullet, missile, etc.); to hit, wound or kill in this way; to precipitate, launch forth; to tip out, dump; to cast; to kick or hit at goal (*games*); to score, for a hole or the round (*golf*); to thrust forward; to pull (one's shirt cuffs) forward so that they project from the sleeves of one's jacket; to slide along; to slide the bolt of; to put forth in growth; to pass rapidly through, under, or over; to pass through (traffic lights) without stopping; to photograph, esp. for motion pictures; to variegate; to produce a play of colour in (usu. in *pa p*); to inject (esp. oneself) with (a drug) (*slang*); to play (a round of golf, game of pool, etc.); to detonate. — *vi* to dart forth or forward; (of a cricket ball) to start forward rapidly near the ground; to send darting pains; to sprout; (of vegetables) to bolt; to elongate rapidly; to jut out far or suddenly; to begin, esp. to speak one's mind or to tell what one knows (*colloq*; usu. in *imper*); to tower; to send forth a missile, etc.; to discharge a shot or weapon; to use a bow or gun in practice, competition, hunting, etc.: — *pa t* and *pa p* **shot**; see also **shott'en**. — *n* a shooting; a shooting match, party, expedition; the shooting of a film; new growth; a sprout; the stem and leaf parts of a plant; a dump; a chute (see **chute**[1]). — *adj* **shoot'able** capable of being shot, or shot over. — *n* **shoot'er** a cricket ball that shoots (see above); a gun, etc. (*colloq*). — *n* **shoot'ing** the action of the verb in any sense; the killing of game with firearms over a certain area; the right to do so; the district so limited. — Also *adj*. — *n* **shoot'ist** (*slang*; now esp. *US*) someone who shoots; a skilled marksman. — **shoot'ing-box** or **-lodge** a small house in the country for use in the shooting season; **shoot'ing-brake** (*old*) an estate car; **shooting gallery** a long room used for practice or amusement with firearms; a place where addicts gather to inject drugs (*slang*); **shooting iron** (*slang*) a firearm, esp. a revolver; **shooting jacket** a short coat for shooting in; **shooting range** a place for shooting at targets; **shooting star** a meteor; **shooting stick** a printer's tool for driving quoins; a walking-stick with a head that opens out into a seat; **shooting war** actual war as distinct from cold war; **shoot'-out** a gunfight, esp. to the death or other decisive conclusion (also *fig*). — **get shot of** (*slang*) to get rid of; **have shot one's bolt** see **bolt**[1]; **shoot a line** (*slang*) to brag, exaggerate (*n* **line'-shooter**); **shoot down** to kill, or to bring down (an aeroplane) by shooting; to rout in argument; **shoot down in flames** (*slang*) to reprimand severely; **shoot from the hip** (*colloq*) to speak bluntly or hastily, without preparation or without caring about the consequences; **shoot home** to hit the target; **shoot it out** to settle by military action; **shoot off** to discharge a gun; to begin; to rush away; **shoot oneself in the foot** (*colloq*) to harm one's own interests through ineptitude; **shoot one's mouth off** see under **mouth**; **shoot through** (*slang*) leave quickly; **shoot up** to kill or injure by shooting; to grow very quickly; to inject (heroin, etc.) (*slang*); **the whole (bang) shoot** or **shooting-match** (*colloq*) the whole lot. [O.E. *scēotan*; in some senses merging with Fr. *chute*, fall.]

shop *shop*, *n* a building or room in which goods are sold; a place where mechanics work, or where any kind of industry is pursued; a place of employment or activity, esp. a theatre; prison (*slang*); talk about one's own business. — *vi* to visit shops, esp. for the purpose of buying. — *vt* to imprison, or cause to be imprisoned (*slang*); to betray (someone), e.g. to inform against (him) to the police (*slang*): — *pr p* **shopp'ing**; *pa p* **shopped**. — *n* **shopahol'ic** a compulsive shopper (see **-aholic**). — *n* **shop'ful**. — *n* **shopp'er** a person who shops; a shopping bag, basket. — *n* **shopp'ing** visiting shops to buy or see goods; goods thus bought. — *adj* for shopping. — *adj* **shopp'y**. — **shop assistant** a person who sells goods in a shop; **shop bell** a bell that rings at the opening of a shop-door; **shop'breaker** a person who breaks into a shop; **shop'breaking**; **shop floor** that part of a factory, etc. housing the production machinery and the main part of the workforce; the people who work on the shop floor. — *adj* **shop'-floor**. — **shop'-front**; **shop'keeper** a person who keeps a shop of his or her own; **shop'keeping**; **shop'lifter**; **shop'lifting** stealing from a shop; **shop'man** a man who serves in a shop; **shopping bag** or **basket** a receptacle for goods bought; **shopping centre** a place where there is a concentration of shops of different kinds; **shopping list** a list of items to be bought; a list of items to be obtained, done, acted upon, considered, etc. (*fig*); **shopping precinct** see under **precinct**; **shop sign** indication of trade and occupier's name over a shop. — *adj* **shop'soiled** somewhat faded or worn by display in a shop. — **shop steward** a representative of factory or workshop hands elected from their own number; **shop'walker** a shop employee who walks about in a shop to see customers attended to; **shop window** a window of a shop in which wares are displayed; any means of displaying something to advantage. — *adj* **shop'worn** shopsoiled. — **all over the shop** dispersed all around; **on the shop floor** among the workers in a factory or workshop; **set up shop** to open a trading establishment; to begin operations generally; **shop around** to compare prices and quality of goods at various shops before making a purchase; **talk shop** to talk about one's own work or business. [O.E. *sceoppa*, a treasury.]

shoran *shör'an*, *n* a system of aircraft navigation using the measurement of the time taken for two dispatched radar signals to return from known locations. [*Sho*rt *ra*nge *n*avigation.]

shore[1] *shör*, *n* the land bordering on the sea or a great sheet of water; the foreshore. — *vt* to set on shore. — *adj* **shore'less** having no shore, unlimited. — *adj* and *adv* **shore'ward**. — *adv* **shore'wards**. — **shore crab** a crab (*Carcinus maenas*) very common between tidemarks. — *adj* **shore'-going** going, or for going, ashore; land-dwelling. — **shore leave** leave of absence to go ashore; **shore'line** the line of meeting of land and water; a rope connecting a net with the land; **shore'man** a dweller on the shore; a landsman; **shore weed** a plant of lake margins of the plantain family. — **on shore** on the land; ashore. [M.E. *schore*.]

shore[2] *shör*, *n* a prop. — *vt* to prop (often with *up*). — *n* **shor'er**. — *n* **shor'ing** propping; a set of props. [Cf. Du. *schoor*, O.N. *skortha*.]

shorn *shörn*, *pa p* of **shear**.

short *shört*, *adj* of little length, tallness, extent, or duration; in the early future (as *short day*, *date*); concise; curt or abrupt; snappish; (of pastry) crisp yet readily crumbling; brittle; on the hither side; (of memory) not retentive; failing to go far enough or reach the standard; deficient; lacking; scanty, in inadequate supply; in want, ill supplied; in default; unable to meet engagements; pertaining to the sale of what one cannot supply; in accentual verse, loosely, unaccented (*prosody*); (of an alcoholic drink) undiluted with water, neat (*colloq*); of certain fielding positions, relatively near the batsman (*cricket*). — *adv* briefly; abruptly; on this or the near side; at a disadvantage (e.g. *taken short*); see **sell short** under **sell**. — *n* that which is short; shortness, abbreviation, summary; a short circuit; (in *pl*) short trousers (i.e. thigh-length, as opp. to ankle-length); (in *pl*) undershorts (*US*); (in *pl*) the bran and coarse part of meal, in mixture; (in *pl*) short-dated securities; short circuit (*colloq*); a short film subordinate to a main film in a programme; a short alcoholic drink (*colloq*). — *vt* to short-change. — *vt* and *vi* to short-circuit. — *n* **short'age** a lack, deficiency. — *vt* **short'en** to make shorter; to make to seem short or to fall short; to draw in or back; to check; to make friable (by adding butter, lard, etc.). — *vi* to become shorter. — *n* **short'ener**. — *n* **short'ening** making or becoming shorter; fat for making pastry short. — *n* **short'ie** or **short'y** (*colloq*) a very short person, garment, etc. — Also *adj*. — *adj* **short'ish**. — *adv* **short'ly** soon; briefly; curtly; a little. — *n* **short'ness**. — *adj* **short'-arm** (*boxing*, etc.; of a blow) using a bent (rather than extended) arm. — **short'bread** a brittle crumbling cake of flour and butter; **short'cake** shortbread or other friable cake; a light cake, prepared in layers with fruit between, served with cream (*US*). — *vt* **short-change'** to give less than the correct change to; to deal dishonestly with (a person). — *adj* **short'-change** pertaining to cheating. — **short-chan'ger**; **short circuit** a new path of comparatively low resistance between two points of a circuit (*electr*); a deviation of current by a path of low resistance. — *vt* **short-cir'cuit** to establish a short circuit in; to interconnect where there was obstruction between (*surg*); to provide with a short cut. — *vi* to cut off current by a short circuit; to save a roundabout passage. — **short'coming** an act of coming or falling short; a neglect of, or failure in, duty; a defect; **short commons** minimum rations; **short covering** (*stock exchange*) the buying of securities, etc. to cover a short sale; the securities, etc. bought for this purpose. — *adj* **short'-cut**. — **short cut** a shorter way than the usual. — *adj* **short-dāt'ed** having little time to run from its date, as a bill; (of securities) redeemable in under five years. — **short division** division without writing down the working out; **short'fall** the fact or amount of falling short; **short fuse** (*colloq*) quick temper; **short game** (in golf) play on and around the green(s); **short'hand** a method of swift, coded writing to keep pace with speaking; writing of such a kind. — Also *adj*. — *adj* **short-hand'ed** short of workers; with a small or reduced number on the team, in the crew, etc. — *adj* **short'-haul** involving transportation, etc. over (relatively) short distances. — *vt* **short'-head** (*colloq*) to beat by a short head (see below). — Also *adj*. — **short'horn** one of a breed of cattle having very short horns — *Durham* or *Teeswater*; **short leg** (*cricket*) the fielder or the field near (and in line with) the batsman on the leg side. — *adj* **short'-life** having a short duration, existence, etc. — **short list** (see also

leet) a selected list of candidates for an office. — *vt* **short'-list** to include (someone) in a short list. — *adj* **short'-līved** (or *-livd*) living or lasting only for a short time. — **short measure** less than the amount promised or paid for; **short odds** in betting, a nearly even chance, favourable odds in terms of risk, unfavourable in terms of potential gain; **short order** (*US*) (an order for) food that can be prepared quickly. — *adj* **short'-order**. — *adj* **short'-range** of or relating to a short distance or period of time. — **short score** a musical score with some of the parts omitted; **short selling** see **sell short** under **sell**; **short shrift** see under **shrift**. — *adj* **short-sight'ed** having clear sight only of near objects; lacking foresight. — *adv* **short-sight'edly**. — **short-sight'edness; short slip** (*cricket*) the fielder, or the field, near the batsman on the off side behind the wicket. — *adj* **short-spō'ken** curt in speech. — *adj* **short-staffed'** having a reduced or inadequate staff. — **short'sword** a sword with a short blade. — *adj* **short-tem'pered** easily put into a rage. — **short tennis** a form of tennis for young children, using a smaller court and modified equipment and rules. — *adj* **short'-term** extending over a short time; concerned with the immediate present and future as distinct from time further ahead. — **short-term'ism** (a tendency toward) the adopting of only short-term views, solutions to problems, etc.; **short time** (the condition of) working fewer than the normal number of hours per week. — *adj* **short'-time**. — **short wave** an electronic wave with a length of 50 metres or less. — *adj* **short'-wave**. — *adj* **short-wind'ed** soon becoming breathless. — **by a short head** by a distance less than the length of a horse's head; narrowly, barely; **caught** or **taken short** (*colloq*) having a sudden need to relieve oneself; **cut short** see under **cut; fall short** see **fall**; **for short** as an abbreviation; **in short** in a few words; **in short order** very quickly; **in short supply** not available in desired quantity, scarce; **in the short run** over a brief period of time; **make short work of** to settle or dispose of promptly; **run short** see under **run; short for** a shortened form of; **short of** less than; without going so far as; (also **short on**; *colloq*) having insufficient supplies of; **stop short** to come to a sudden standstill; **take (or take up) short** to take by surprise or at a disadvantage; to interrupt curtly. [O.E. *sc(e)ort*.]

shot[1] *shot, pa t* and *pa p* of **shoot**. — *adj* hit or killed by shooting; exhausted (*colloq*); elongated by rapid growth; with warp and weft of different colours, as *shot silk*; showing play of colours; rid (with *of*; *colloq*).

shot[2] *shot, n* act of shooting; a blast; an explosive charge; a photographic exposure, esp. for motion pictures; a unit in film production; a stroke or the like in a game; an attempt; a spell; a turn; a guess; an aggressive remark; an injection (*colloq*); a dram (*colloq*); a marksman; a projectile, esp. one that is solid and spherical, without bursting charge; a cannonball; a weight for putting (*athletics*); a small pellet of which several are shot together; such pellets collectively; flight of a missile, or its distance; range, reach; a contribution. — *vt* to load with shot: — *pr p* **shott'ing**; *pa t* and *pa p* **shott'ed**. — *adj* **shott'ed**. — **shot'-blasting** the cleaning of metal, etc. by means of a stream of shot; **shot'gun** a smooth-bore gun for small shot, a fowling-piece. — *adj* pertaining to a shotgun; involving coercion (e.g. *a shotgun merger, marriage*). — **shot put** in athletics, the event of putting the shot; **shot'-putter; shot tower** a tower where small shot is made by dropping molten lead into water. — **a shot across the bows** a shot thus directed so as to warn a ship off rather than damage it; **a shot in the arm** an injection in the arm (*med*); a revivifying injection, as of money, new effort, fresh talent (*fig*); **a shot in the dark** a random guess; **big shot** (*colloq*) a person of importance; **call the shots** see **call**; **like a shot** instantly, quickly; eagerly, willingly. [O.E. *sc(e)ot, gesc(e)ot*; cf. **shoot**.]

shotten *shot'n, adj* (of a herring, etc.) having ejected the spawn; effete, exhausted; bursting or shooting out, as something violently dispersed.

should *shŏŏd, pa t* of **shall**. [O.E. *sceolde*.]

shoulder *shōl'dər, n* the part about the junction of the body with the forelimb; the upper joint of a foreleg cut as meat; part of a garment covering the shoulder; a bulge, protuberance, offshoot like the human shoulder; a curve like that between the shoulder and the neck or side; either edge of a road. — *vt* to thrust with the shoulder; to take upon the shoulder or in a position of rest against the shoulder; to undertake; to take responsibility for. — *vi* to jostle. — *adj* **shoul'dered** having a shoulder or shoulders (**shouldered arch** a lintel on corbels). — *n* and *adj* **shoul'dering**. — **shoulder bag** a bag suspended from a strap worn over the shoulder; **shoulder belt** a belt that passes across the shoulder; **shoulder blade** the broad, flat, bladelike bone forming the back of the shoulder, the scapula; **shoulder bone** shoulder blade; **shoulder girdle** the pectoral girdle; **shoulder height**. — *adj* and *adv* **shoulder-high'** as high as the shoulder. — **shoulder joint; shoulder knot** a knot worn as an ornament on the shoulder; **shoulder mark** (*US*) a badge of naval rank worn on the shoulder; **shoulder note** a note at the upper outside corner of a page; **shoulder pad** a pad inserted into the shoulder of a garment to raise and square it; **shoulder strap** a strap worn on or over the shoulder esp. on suspending a garment, etc.; a narrow strap of cloth edged with gold lace worn on the shoulder with uniform to indicate rank (*US*). — **put one's shoulder to the wheel** to set to work in earnest; **shoulder-of-mutton sail** a triangular sail; **shoulder to shoulder** side by side; in unity; **(straight) from the shoulder** frank(ly) and forceful(ly). [O.E. *sculdor*.]

shouldn't *shŏŏd'ənt*, (*colloq*) a contraction of **should not**.

shout *showt, n* a loud cry; a call; a call for a round of drinks (*slang*); a turn to buy a round of drinks (*slang*). — *vi* to utter a shout; to speak in a raised, esp. angry, voice (with *at*); to stand drinks all round (*slang*). — *vt* to utter with or as a shout. — *n* **shout'er**. — *n* and *adj* **shout'ing**. — *adv* **shout'ingly**. — **shouting match** (*colloq*) a quarrel or argument in which both sides loudly insult each other. — **all over bar the shouting** of a happening, contest, etc., as good as over, virtually finished or decided; **shout down** to make (another speaker) inaudible by shouting or talking loudly.

shove *shuv, vt* and *vi* to thrust; to push; to jostle; to place roughly. — *n* a push or thrust. — *n* **shov'er**. — **shove-half'penny** a game similar to shovel board. — **shove off** to push (a boat) from the shore; to go away (*colloq*). [O.E. *scūfan*.]

shovel *shuv'l, n* a broad spadelike tool for scooping, the blade usu. curved forward at the sides; a (part of) a machine having a similar shape or function; a scoop; a shovelful. — *vt* to move with, or as if with, a shovel; to gather in large quantities. — *vi* to use a shovel: — *pr p* **shov'elling**; *pa t* and *pa p* **shov'elled**. — *n* **shov'elful**: — *pl* **shov'elfuls**. — *n* **shov'eler** or **shov'eller** someone who shovels; a duck with expanded bill. — **shovel hat** a hat with a broad brim, turned up at the sides, and projecting in front — worn by Anglican clergy; **shov'elhead** a shark with a flattish head, related to the hammerhead. [O.E. *scofl*, from *scūfan*, to shove.]

shovel board *shuv'l bōrd* or **shuffle-board** *shuf'l-bōrd, n* an old game in which a coin or other disc was driven along a table by the hand; a modern development played in America; a deck game played with wooden discs and cues; a table for the game. [App. **shove** and **board**, confused with **shovel** and **shuffle**.]

show *shō*, *vt* to present to view; to exhibit, display or set forth; to cause or allow to be seen or known; to instruct by demonstrating; to prove; to manifest; to indicate; to usher or conduct (with *in*, *out*, *over*, *round*, *up*, etc.). — *vi* to appear; to come into sight; to be visible; to take part in an exhibition, etc.; to arrive, turn up (*slang*): — *pa t* **showed** (*shōd*); *pa p* **shown** (*shōn*) or **showed**. — *n* act of showing; display; exhibition; a sight or spectacle; an entertainment; parade; a demonstration; appearance; plausibility; pretence; a sign, indication; an indication of the presence of oil or gas in an exploratory well; performance; any thing, affair or enterprise; in childbirth, a small discharge of blood and mucus at the start of labour; a chance (*US*). — *adj* of the nature of, or connected with, a show; for show. — *n* **shower** (*shō'ər*). — *adv* **show'ily**. — *n* **show'iness**. — *n* **show'ing** act of displaying, pointing out, etc.; performance; a setting forth, representation. — *adj* **show'y** cutting a dash; making a show; ostentatious; gaudy; flashy. — **show'boat** a steamer serving as a travelling theatre. — *vi* to behave in an ostentatious manner; to show off. — **show'boater**; **show'bread** same as **shewbread**; **show business** the entertainment business, esp. the branch of the theatrical profession concerned with variety entertainments — also (*colloq*) **show'biz** or **show biz** (*adj* **show'bizzy**). — **show'card** a shopkeeper's advertising card; **show'case** a glass case for a museum, shop, etc.; any setting in which something or someone can be displayed to advantage; **show'-down** in poker, putting one's cards face-up on the table; the name of a card game similar to poker; an open disclosure of plans, means, etc.; an open clash; **show'girl** a girl who takes part in variety entertainments usu. as a dancer or singer; **show'ground** ground where a show is held; **show house** a house, usu. on a new housing estate, opened for public viewing as an example of the builders' work; **show'jumper** a horse or rider in a showjumping competition; **show'jumping** a competition in which riders on horseback have to jump a succession of obstacles (also *adj*); **show'man** a man who exhibits, or owns, a show; a man who is skilled in publicly showing off things (e.g. his own merits). — *adj* **show'manly**. — **show'manship** skilful display, or a talent for it; **show'-off** a person who behaves in an ostentatious manner in an effort to win admiration; **show'piece** something considered an especially fine specimen of its type, etc.; an exhibit, something on display, etc.; **show'place** a place visited or shown as a sight; a place where shows are exhibited; **show'room** a room where goods or samples are displayed; **show'-stopper** see **stop the show** below; **show trial** one held purely for propaganda, the charges usu. being false, and the confession forcibly extracted. — **for show** for the sake of outward appearances; to attract notice; **give the show away** to let out a secret; **good** (or **bad**) **show** well (or not well) done; fortunate (or unfortunate) occurrence or circumstances; **run the show** (*colloq*) to take or be in charge; to take over, dominate; **show a leg** (*colloq*) to get out of bed; **show-and-tell'** (*US*) educational exercise in which a pupil shows an item and talks about it; **show fight** to show a readiness to resist; **show forth** to manifest, proclaim; **show off** to display or behave ostentatiously; **show of hands** a vote indicated by raising hands; **show up** to expose; to appear to advantage or disadvantage; to show clearly by contrast; to be present; to arrive (*colloq*); **steal the show** to win the most applause; to attract the most publicity or admiration; **stop the show** to be applauded with so much enthusiasm as to interrupt the show, play, etc. (hence *n* **show'-stopper** the act, line, etc. applauded in such a way). [O.E. *scēawian*, to look.]

shower *show'ər* or *showr*, *n* a short fall, as of rain; a fall of drops of liquid; a fall, flight, or accession of many things together, such as meteors, arrows, blows, volcanic dust or (esp. *US*) wedding gifts; a party at which gifts are presented (*US*); a device for spraying water from above to wash the body; a wash thus taken; fast particles in number arising from a high-energy particle; a disparaging term for a particular group of people (*slang*). — *vt* and *vi* to drop in a shower or showers; to sprinkle. — *vi* to wash under a shower. — *adj* **shower'ful**. — *n* **shower'iness**. — *adj* **shower'y** marked by showers; raining by fits and starts. — **shower bath** (a bath taken under) a shower. — *adj* **shower'proof** impervious to showers. — *vt* to render showerproof. [O.E. *scūr*.]

shrank *shrangk*, *pa t* of **shrink**.

shrapnel *shrap'nl*, *n* a shell filled with musketballs with a bursting-charge, invented by General *Shrapnel* (1761–1842); pieces scattered by the bursting of a shrapnel or other shell; any later improved version of the orig. shell.

shred *shred*, *n* a scrap, fragment; a paring, esp. a curled paring; a ragged strip. — *vt* to cut or cut off; to cut, tear or scrape into shreds. — *vi* to be reduced to shreds: — *pr p* **shredd'ing**; *pa t* and *pa p* **shredd'ed** or **shred**. — *adj* **shredd'ed**. — *n* **shredd'er** a device or machine for shredding, e.g. vegetables, waste paper. — *n* **shredd'ing**. — *adj* **shredd'y**. — *adj* **shred'less**. [O.E. *scrēade*.]

shrew *shroo*, *n* a small mouselike animal, formerly thought venomous; a brawling, troublesome person, now only a woman, a scold. — *adj* **shrew'ish** of the nature of a shrew or scold; ill-natured. — *adv* **shrew'ishly**. — *n* **shrew'ishness**. — **shrew'-mouse** a shrew: — *pl* **shrew'mice**. [O.E. *scrēawa*, a shrewmouse.]

shrewd *shrood*, *adj* showing keen practical judgment, astute; wily, crafty. — *n* **shrewd'ie** (*colloq*) a shrewd person. — *adv* **shrewd'ly**. — *n* **shrewd'ness**. [**shrew**.]

Shri. See **Sri**.

shriek *shrēk*, *vi* to utter a shriek. — *vt* to utter shriekingly. — *n* a shrill outcry; a wild piercing scream. — *n* **shriek'er**. — *n* and *adj* **shriek'ing**. — *adv* **shriek'ingly**. [Cf. **screech**.]

shrieval *shrē'vl*, *adj* pertaining to a sheriff. — *n* **shriev'alty** the office, term of office, or area of jurisdiction, of a sheriff. [*shrieve*, obs. form of **sheriff**.]

shrift *shrift*, *n* absolution; confession. — **short shrift** short time for confession before execution; summary treatment of a person or a matter. [O.E. *scrift* — *scrīfan*, to shrive.]

shrike *shrīk*, *n* a butcher-bird, a passerine bird, of which some kinds impale small animals on thorns. [App. O.E. *scrīc*, perh. thrush.]

shrill *shril*, *adj* high-pitched and piercing; keen; excessively strident. — *vt* and *vi* to sound or cry shrilly. — *n* and *adj* **shrill'ing**. — *n* **shrill'ness**. — *adv* **shrill'y**. — *adj* **shrill-tongued'**. — *adj* **shrill-voiced'**. [Cf. L.G. *schrell*.]

shrimp *shrimp*, *n* a small edible crustacean, esp. a decapod of *Crangon* or a related genus; the colour of a shrimp, a bright pink; a very small person (*colloq*). — *vi* to fish for shrimps. — *n* **shrimp'er**. — *n* and *adj* **shrimp'ing**.

shrine *shrīn*, *n* orig. a chest or cabinet; a casket for relics or an erection over it; a place hallowed by its associations. — *vt* to enshrine. — *adj* **shrī'nal**. [O.E. *scrīn* — L. *scrīnium*, a case for papers — *scrībere*, to write.]

shrink *shringk*, *vi* to contract; to shrivel; to give way; to draw back; to withdraw; to feel repugnance; to recoil; to shrinkwrap (*colloq*). — *vt* to cause to contract; to withdraw; to fix by allowing to contract: — *pa t* **shrank** or **shrunk**; *pa p* **shrunk**. — *n* an act of shrinking; contraction; withdrawal or recoil; a psychiatrist, contracted from **head'shrinker** (*slang*, orig. *US*). — *adj* **shrink'able**. — *n* **shrink'age** a contraction into a smaller compass; extent of such diminution; in meat marketing, the loss of carcase weight during shipping, preparation for sale, etc.; in manufacturing, etc., the loss of goods resulting from pilfering, breakages, etc. — *n* **shrink'er**. — *adv* **shrink'ingly**. — *adj* **shrunk** or **shrunk'en** contracted, reduced, shrivelled. — **shrink'pack** a shrinkwrapped package. — *adj* **shrink'-proof** or **-resis'tant** that will not shrink on washing. — **shrink'-resistance**. — *vt* **shrink'wrap** to package (goods) in a clear plastic film that is subsequently shrunk (e.g. by heating) so that it fits tightly. — Also *n*. [O.E. *scrincan, scranc, gescruncen*.]

shrive *shrīv*, (*RC*) *vt* to hear a confession from and give absolution to; to disburden by confession or otherwise. — *vi* to receive or make confession: — *pa t* **shrōve** or **shrīved**; *pa p* **shriven** (*shriv'ən*) or **shrīved**. — *n* **shrī'ver**. [O.E. *scrīfan*, to write, to prescribe penance — L. *scrībĕre*.]

shrivel *shriv'l*, *vi* and *vt* to contract into wrinkles: — *pr p* **shriv'elling**; *pa t* and *pap* **shriv'elled**. [Cf. Sw. dialect *skryvla*, to wrinkle.]

shroud *shrowd*, *n* a winding-sheet; a covering, screen, shelter or shade; (in *pl*) a set of ropes from the masthead to a ship's sides to support the mast. — *vt* to enclose in a shroud; to cover; to hide; to shelter. — *adj* **shroud'ed**. — *n* and *adj* **shroud'ing**. — *adj* **shroud'less**. — **shroud line** any one of the cords of a parachute by which the load is suspended from the canopy. [O.E. *scrūd*.]

shrove *shrōv*, *pa t* of **shrive**.

Shrovetide *shrōv'tid*, *n* the days preceding Ash Wednesday. — **Shrove Tuesday** the day before Ash Wednesday. [Rel. to O.E. *scrīfan*, to shrive.]

shrub[1] *shrub*, *n* a low woody plant, a bush, esp. one with little or no trunk. — *n* **shrubb'ery** a plantation of shrubs. — *n* **shrubb'iness**. — *adj* **shrubb'y** of, like or having the character of, a shrub; covered with shrubs. — *adj* **shrub'less**. [O.E. *scrybb*, scrub.]

shrub[2] *shrub*, *n* a drink of lemon or other juice with spirits, esp. rum, or (*US*) of fruit juice (such as raspberry) and vinegar. [Ar. *sharāb*, for *shurb*, drink.]

shrug *shrug*, *vi* to draw up the shoulders, a gesture expressive of doubt, indifference, etc. — *vt* to raise (one's shoulders) in a shrug: — *pr p* **shrugg'ing**; *pa t* and *pa p* **shrugged**. — *n* an expressive drawing up of the shoulders. — **shrug off** to shake off; to show indifference to or unwillingness to tackle (e.g. responsibility, a difficulty).

shrunk, shrunken. See **shrink**.

shtick *shtik*, *n* a familiar routine, line of chat, etc. adopted by, and associated with, a particular comedian, etc. [Yiddish *shtik*, piece, slice — M.H.G. *stücke*.]

shtook, schtook, shtuck or **schtuck** *shtŏŏk*, (*slang*) *n* trouble, bother. — **in shtook**, etc. (*slang*) in trouble.

shtoom, schtoom, shtum, shtumm or **stumm** *shtŏŏm*, (*slang*) *adj* silent, quiet. — **keep shtoom**, etc. remain silent. [Yiddish, — Ger. *stumm*, silent.]

shubunkin *shōō-bung'kin* or *-bŏŏng'kin*, *n* a type of variegated large-finned goldfish. [Jap.]

shuck *shuk*, (*US*) *n* a husk, shell or pod. — *vt* to remove the shuck from. — *n* **shuck'er**. — *n* **shuck'ing**. — *interj* **shucks** (*slang*) expressive of disappointment, irritation or embarrassment. — **shuck off** to remove, shed (clothing, etc.).

shudder *shud'ər*, *vi* to shiver as from cold or horror; to vibrate. — *n* a tremor as from cold or horror; an instance of vibrating or trembling. — *n* and *adj* **shudd'ering**. — *adv* **shudd'eringly**. — *adj* **shudd'ery**. [Cf. Ger. (orig. L.G.) *schaudern*.]

shuffle *shuf'l*, *vt* to mix at random (esp. playing-cards); to jumble; to put (*out, in, off*, etc.) surreptitiously, evasively, scramblingly, or in confusion; to manipulate unfairly; to patch up; to shove (the feet) along without lifting clear; to perform with such motions. — *vi* to mix cards in a pack; to shift ground; to evade fair questions; to move by shoving the feet along; to shamble. — *n* act of shuffling; a shuffling gait or dance; an evasion or artifice. — *n* **shuff'ler**. — *n* and *adj* **shuff'ling**. — *adv* **shuff'lingly**. — **shuffle off** to thrust aside, put off, wriggle out of. [Early modern; cf. **scuffle, shove, shovel**.]

shuffle-board. See **shovel board**.

shufti or **shufty** *shŏŏf'ti*, (*colloq*) *n* a look. [Colloq. Ar. *shufti*, have you seen? — *shaffa*, to see.]

shun *shun*, *vt* to avoid: — *pr p* **shunn'ing**; *pa t* and *pa p* **shunned**.

shunt *shunt*, *vt* and *vi* to turn or move aside; to move to another track, esp. a side track. — *vt* to bypass; to sidetrack; to shelve; to get rid of; to crash (a car) (*slang*). — *n* an act of shunting; a conductor diverting part of an electric current; a switch; a road accident, crash, mishap (orig. *racing motorists' slang*). — *n* **shunt'er**. — *n* and *adj* **shunt'ing**. [Perh. conn. with **shun**.]

shush *shush*, *vt* and *vi* to (cause to) be quiet. — *interj* be quiet!

shut *shut*, *vt* to place so as to stop an opening, close; to stop or cover the opening of; to lock; to fasten; to bar; to forbid entrance into; to bring together the parts or outer parts of; to confine; to catch or pinch in a fastening; to end the operations of (a business, etc.). — *vi* to become closed; to admit of closing; to close in; (of a business, etc.) to cease to operate: — *pr p* **shutt'ing**; *pa t* and *pa p* **shut**. — *adj* made fast; closed; rid (with *of*; *colloq*). — **shut'down** a temporary closing, as of a factory; the reduction of power in a nuclear reactor to the minimum; **shut'-eye** (*colloq*) sleep; **shut'-in** (*US*) an invalid or cripple confined to his or her house; **shut'-off** a device that stops the flow or operation of something; a stoppage. — *adj* **shut'-out** intended to exclude, as (*bridge*) a bid to deter opponents from bidding. — Also *n*. — **shut away** to keep hidden or repressed; to isolate; to confine; **shut down** to close down, or stop the operation of, often temporarily; **shut in** to enclose, to confine; **shut off** to exclude; to switch off; to stop the flow of; **shut out** to prevent from entering; **shut up** to close finally or completely; to confine; to cease speaking (*colloq*); to reduce to silence. [O.E. *scyttan*, to bar.]

shutter *shut'ər*, *n* a person or thing which shuts; a close cover for a window; a device for regulating the opening of an aperture, as in photography, cinematography; a removable cover, gate, or piece of shuttering. — *vt* to close or fit with a shutter or shutters. — *adj* **shutt'ered**. — *n* **shutt'ering** closing and fitting with a shutter; material used as shutters; temporary support for concrete work. [**shut**.]

shuttle *shut'l*, *n* an instrument used for shooting the thread of the woof between the threads of the warp in weaving or through the loop of thread in a sewing-machine; anything that makes similar movements; rapid movement to and fro between two points; a shuttle service or the vehicle, craft, etc. used for this; a shuttlecock. — *vt* and *vi* to move to and fro like a shuttle; to move regularly between two points. — **shutt'lecock** a cork stuck with feathers to be driven to and fro with battledores or badminton rackets; the game played with battledores; something tossed to and fro repeatedly. — *vt* and *vi* to shuttle. — **shuttle diplomacy** shuttle-like travelling between two heads of states by an intermediary, in order to bring about agreement between them; **shuttle service** a train or other transport service moving constantly between two points. [O.E. *scytel*, dart.]

shwa. See **schwa.**

shy[1] *shī, adj* (*compar* **shy'er** or **shi'er**, *superl* **shy'est** or **shi'est**) shrinking from notice or approach; bashful; chary; disposed to avoidance (with *of*; also used in combination, as in *workshy*); warily reluctant; (esp. in poker) short in payment; short, lacking (with *of*) (*US colloq*). *vi* to recoil, to shrink (with *away, off*); to start aside, like a horse from fear: — *3rd pers sing* **shies**; *pr p* **shy'ing**; *pa t* and *pa p* **shied** (*shīd*). — *n* a sudden swerving aside: — *pl* **shies.** — *n* **shi'er** or **shy'er.** — *adj* **shy'ish.** — *adv* **shy'ly.** — *n* **shy'ness.** — **fight shy of** to shrink from. [O.E. *scēoh*, timid.]

shy[2] *shī, vt* and *vi* to fling, toss: — *3rd pers sing* **shies**; *pr p* **shy'ing**; *pa t* and *pa p* **shied.** — *n* a throw; a gibe; an attempt, shot; a thing to shy at: — *pl* **shies.** — *n* **shi'er** or **shy'er.**

Shylock *shī'lok, n* a ruthless creditor, or a very grasping person. [From Shylock in *The Merchant of Venice*.]

shyster *shī'stər*, (*slang*) *n* an unscrupulous or disreputable lawyer; an unscrupulous practitioner in any profession or business. [Prob. from *Scheuster*, 19th cent. New York lawyer famous for pettifoggery.]

SI units *es ī ū'nits* or **SI**, *n* the modern scientific system of units, used in the measurement of all physical quantities. [*S*ystème *I*nternational (d'Unités).]

Si (*chem*) *symbol* for silicon.

si *sē*, (*mus*) *n* the seventh note of the scale (superseded by *ti*).

sial *sī'əl, n* the lighter partial outer shell of the earth, rich in *si*lica and *al*umina. — *adj* **sial'ic.**

siala- *sī-əl-ə-* or *sī-al'ə-*, **sialo-** *sī-al'ō-* or *-o'-*, *combining form* denoting saliva. — *adj* **sial'ic** of or relating to saliva. — *n* **sialagogue** (*sī-al'ə-gog*) anything that stimulates flow of saliva. — Also *adj.* — *adj* **sialagog'ic.** [Gr. *sialon*, saliva.]

sialic. See **sial** and **siala-.**

sialon *sī'ə-lon, n* any of various ceramic materials consisting of silicon, aluminium, oxygen and nitrogen. [From the chemical symbols of the constituent elements — *Si, Al, O, N*.]

siamang *sē'ə-mang, n* the largest of the gibbons, found in Sumatra and Malacca. [Malay.]

Siamese *sī-əm-ēz', adj* of *Siam*, the former name of Thailand. — *n* a native, a citizen, or the language of Siam; a Siamese cat. — **Siamese cat** a domestic fawn-coloured cat, with blue eyes and a small head, prob. descended from the jungle cat of India, Africa, etc.; **Siamese twins** orig. a set of Chinese twins (1811–74), born in Siam, joined from birth by a fleshy ligature; any set of twins joined in this way.

SIB *abbrev* for Securities and Investments Board.

sib *sib, n* a blood relation; a brother or sister. — *adj* akin; related by blood; (of canaries) inbred. — *n* **sib'ling.** — Also *adj.* — *n* **sib'ship** group of sibs. [O.E. *sibb*, relationship, *gesibb*, related.]

sibilate *sib'i-lāt, vt* and *vi* to pronounce (words) with, or produce, a hissing sound. — *n* **sib'ilance** or **sib'ilancy.** — *adj* **sib'ilant** hissing; pronounced with a hissing sound. — *n* a hissing consonant sound, as of *s* and *z*. — *n* **sibilā'tion.** [L. *sībilāre, -ātum*, to hiss.]

sibling. See **sib.**

Sibyl *sib'il, n* one of several ancient prophetesses (*mythol*); (without *cap*) a prophetess, sorceress or witch. — *adj* **Sib'ylline** (*-īn*). — **Sibylline Books** prophetic books supposedly produced by the Sibyl of the Greek colony of Cumae in Italy. [Gr. *Sibylla*.]

sic[1] *sik* or *sēk*, (L.) *adv* so, thus — printed within brackets in quoted matter to show that the original is being faithfully reproduced even though it is incorrect or apparently so. — **sic passim** (*pas'im*) so throughout.

sic[2]. Same as **sick**[2].

siccative *sik'ə-tiv, adj* drying. — *n* a drying agent. [L. *siccus*, dry.]

sice *sīs, n* the number six in a game of dice. [O.Fr. *sis*.]

sick[1] *sik, adj* unwell, ill; diseased; vomiting or inclined to vomit; pining; mortified; thoroughly wearied; sickly; of or for the sick; (of humour, comedy, a joke, etc.) gruesome, macabre, tending to exploit topics not normally joked about, such as illness, death, etc.; disappointed (*colloq*). — *vt* (*colloq*) to vomit (with *up*). — *vt* **sick'en** to make sick; to disgust; to make weary of anything. — *vi* to become sick; to display symptoms (with *for*); to be disgusted (with *at*). — *n* **sick'ener.** — *n* and *adj* **sick'ening.** — *adv* **sick'eningly.** — *n* **sick'ie** (*colloq*) a day's sick leave (*Austr* and *NZ*); a sick person, whether mentally or physically (*NAm*). — *adj* **sick'ish.** — *n* **sick'liness.** — *adj* **sick'ly** inclined to be ailing; feeble; pallid; suggestive of sickness; mawkish; of sickness or the sick. — *n* **sick'ness.** — *n* **sick'o** (*NAm*) a sick person, esp. someone mentally ill or disturbed, or a pervert. — **sick'-bay** a compartment for sick and wounded on a ship (also **sick'-berth**); an infirmary at a boarding-school, etc.; **sick'-bed** a bed on which someone lies sick; **sick'-benefit** a benefit paid to someone who is out of work through illness; **sick headache** headache with nausea; **sick'-leave** leave of absence owing to sickness; **sick'-list** a list of sick employees, pupils, soldiers, etc. — *adj* **sick'-listed** entered on the sick-list. — *adj* **sick'-making** (*colloq*) sickening. — **sick'nurse** a nurse who attends the sick; **sick'nursing**; **sick'room** a room to which one is confined by sickness. — **be sick** to vomit; **sick (and tired) of** tired of; **sick as a dog** (*colloq*) vomiting profusely and unrestrainedly; **sick as a parrot** (*colloq*) extremely disappointed; **sick to one's stomach** about to vomit. [O.E. *sēoc*.]

sick[2] *sik, vt* to set upon, chase; to incite (e.g. dog) to make an attack (on). [A variant of **seek.**]

sickle *sik'l, n* a reaping-hook, an implement with a curved blade and a short handle. — **sick'lebill** a bird of paradise, humming-bird, etc., with sickle-shaped bill; **sick'le-feather** a cock's tail feather. — *adj* **sick'le-shaped.** — **sickle-cell** (or **-celled**) **anaemia** a severe anaemia in which sickle-shaped red blood-cells appear in the blood. [O.E. *sicol, sicel*, perh. — L. *secula* — *secāre*, to cut.]

sidalcea *si-dal'si-ə* or *-dal'ki-ə, n* a plant of the *Sidalcea* genus of the mallow family, a perennial with white, pink or purple flowers. [*Sida* and *Alcea*, related genera.]

siddhi *sid'i, n* (in Hinduism, Buddhism and Jainism) the supernatural powers that come with the spiritual perfection attained by meditation, etc. — Also with *cap* and in *pl.* — *n* **sidd'ha** a person who has attained spiritual perfection (also **sid'ha**). [Sans., fulfilment.]

siddur *si'dŏŏr, n* a Jewish prayer-book: — *pl* **siddur'im** or **-im'.** [Heb., order.]

side *sīd, n* a line or surface forming part of a boundary; the part near such a boundary; a surface or part turned in some direction, esp. one more or less upright, or one regarded as right or left, not front or back, top or bottom; the part of the body between armpit and hip; half of a carcase divided along the medial plane; either of the extended surfaces of anything in the form of a sheet; a page; a portion of space lying in this or that direction from a boundary or a point; the father's or mother's part of a genealogy; an aspect; a direction; a particular district; a border or bank; the slope of a hill; the wall of a vessel or cavity; any party, team, interest or opinion opposed to another; part (as in *on my side*, for my part); spin given to a billiard ball causing it to swerve and regulating its angle of rebound; a pretentious air (*slang*). — *adj* at or toward the side; sidewise; subsidiary. — *vi* to take sides (with *with*). —

adj **sid'ed** having sides; flattened on one or more sides. — *adj* **side'long** oblique; sloping; sideways. — *adv* in the direction of the side; obliquely; on the side. — *n* **sid'er** someone who takes a side in a dispute, etc. — *adj* and *adv* **side'ward.** — *adv* **side'wards.** — *adj* and *adv* **side'ways** or **side'-wise** toward or on one side. — *n* **sid'ing** a short railway track for shunting or lying by. — *n* and *adj* taking sides. — **side'arm** (usu. in *pl*) a weapon worn at the side; **side'-band** (*radio*) a band of frequencies not much above or below the carrier frequency; **side'-bar** (in South Africa) solicitors, as opp. to barristers (who belong to the bar); **side'board** a piece of dining-room furniture for holding plates, etc., often with drawers and cupboards; a board at the side, as of a cart; (in *pl*) side-whiskers; **side'-burns** short side-whiskers, a modification of the rather more extensive growth pioneered by General *Burnside* of America; **side'car** a small car attached to the side of a motorcycle usu. for the carriage of a passenger; a kind of cocktail containing brandy, orange liqueur and lemon juice; **side'-chain** a chain of atoms forming a branch attached to a ring; **side'=dish** a supplementary dish; **side door** a door at the side of a building or of a main door; **side'-drum** a small double-headed drum with snares, slung from the drummer's side or from a stand; **side effect** a subsidiary effect; an effect, often undesirable, additional to the effect sought; **side'-face** profile; **side'-glance** a sidelong glance; a passing allusion; **side issue** something subordinate, incidental, not important in comparison with the main issue; **side'kick** (*colloq*) partner, deputy; a special friend; **side'light** a light carried on the side of a vessel or vehicle; a window above or at the side of a door; light coming from the side; any incidental illustration; **side'line** a line attached to the side of anything; a branch route or track; a subsidiary trade or activity; (in *pl*) (the area just outside) the lines marking the edge of a football pitch, etc., hence, a peripheral area to which spectators or non-participants are confined. — *vt* to remove (a player) from a team; to suspend from normal operation or activity. — *adj* and *adv* **side-on'** with the side presented. — **side plate** a small plate used for food which accompanies the main meal; **side'-road** a by-road; **side'-saddle** a saddle for riding with both feet on one side (also *adv*); **side'shoot** (*bot*); **side'-show** an exhibition subordinate to a larger one; any subordinate or incidental activity; **side'-slip** a skid; a lateral movement of an aircraft; a side-on downward slide (*skiing*). — *vi* to slip sideways. — **sides'man** a deputy church-warden. — *adj* **side'-splitting** extremely funny, making one laugh till one's sides ache. — **side'-step** a step taken to one side; a step attached to the side. — *vi* to step aside. — *vt* to avoid, as by a step aside. — **side'street** a minor street, esp. if opening off a main street; **side'-stroke** a stroke given sideways; a stroke performed by a swimmer lying on their side; **side'swipe** a blow dealt from the side, not struck head-on; a criticism made in passing, incidentally to the main topic; **side'-table** a table used as a sideboard, or placed against the wall, or to the side of the main table; **side'-track** a siding. — *vt* **side'track** to divert or turn aside; to shelve. — **side'-view** a view on or from one side; **side'walk** (*NAm*) pavement or foot-walk; **side'wall** the side portion of a tyre, between tread and wheel rim; **side'-whiskers** hair grown by a man down either side of the face, in front of the ears; **side'winder** a rattlesnake of the southern U.S. that progresses by lateral looping motions; the name of an air-to-air missile directed at its target by means of a homing device. — **choose sides** to pick teams; **let the side down** to fail one's colleagues, associates, etc. by falling below their standard; **on the side** in addition to ordinary occupation, income, etc.; **on the short, long, tight,** etc. **side** rather too short, long, etc. than the contrary; **put on one side** to shelve; **put on side** to assume pretentious airs; **side by side** close together; abreast; **take sides** to range oneself with one party or other; **the other side** the spiritual world, to which one passes after death; **this side (of)** between here and ...; short of. [O.E. *sīde*.]

sidereal *sī-dē'ri-əl*, *adj* of, like, or relative to the stars. — *n* **sid'erostat** a mirror, or telescope with a mirror, for reflecting the rays of a star in a constant direction. — **sidereal day** the time the earth takes to make a revolution on its axis, relative to the time between two successive transits of a particular star; **sidereal year** see **year**. [L. *sīdus*, *sīderis*, a star, constellation.]

siderite *sid'ər-īt*, *n* a meteorite consisting mainly of iron; ferrous carbonate, one of the ores of iron. — *adj* **sideritic** (*-it'ik*). — *n* **sid'erolite** a meteorite, partly stony, partly of iron. — *n* **siderō'sis** lung disease caused by breathing in iron or other metal fragments. [Gr. *sidēros*, iron.]

siderostat. See under **sidereal.**

sidesman, siding, etc. See under **side.**

sidha. See under **siddhi.**

sidle *sīd'l*, *vi* to go or edge along sideways, esp. in a furtive or ingratiating manner. [Prob. back-formation from *sideling*, sideways.]

siege *sēj*, *n* persistent attack against a town or fortress with the intention of taking it; any persistent attack, offensive, attempt to gain control, etc. — **lay seige to** to besiege; **state of siege** a condition of suspension of civil law or its subordination to military law. [O.Fr. *sege*, seat — L. *sēdēs*, seat.]

siemens *sē'mənz*, *n* unit of electrical conductance (an SI additional unit; abbrev. **S**), the equivalent of mho and reciprocal of ohm.

Sienese *sē-ə-nēz'*, *adj* of *Siena* or its school of painting. — *n* **sienna** (*sē-en'ə*) a fine pigment made from ferruginous ochreous earth — browny-yellow when *raw*, warm reddish-brown when *burnt* (i.e. roasted); its colour.

sierra *si-er'ə*, *n* a mountain range, esp. in Spanish-speaking countries and the U.S. — *adj* **sierr'an.** [Sp., — L. *serra*, saw.]

siesta *si-es'tə*, *n* a midday or afternoon nap. [Sp., — L. *sexta* (*hōra*), sixth (hour).]

sieve *siv*, *n* a utensil with a meshed or perforated bottom for sifting or straining — generally finer than a riddle. — *vt* and *vi* to sift. — **have a head** (or **memory) like a sieve** to be very forgetful. [O.E. *sife*.]

sievert *sē'vərt*, *n* the SI unit (abbrev. **Sv**) of radiation dose equivalent (see under **dose**), equal to one joule per kilogram (or 100 rems). [R.M. *Sievert* (1896–1966), Sw. physicist.]

sifaka *sif-ä'kə*, *n* a lemur, typically long-tailed and black and white (genus *Propithecus*), native to Madagascar. [Malagasy.]

sift *sift*, *vt* to separate as by passing through a sieve; to sprinkle as from a sieve; to examine closely and discriminatingly. — *vi* to use a sieve; to find passage as through a sieve. — *n* a sifting. — *n* **sift'er.** — *n* **sift'ing** putting through a sieve; separating or sprinkling by a sieve; (in *pl*) material separated by a sieve. — *adj* **sift'ing.** — *adv* **sift'ingly.** — **sift through** to examine by sifting. [O.E. *siftan* — *sife*, a sieve.]

Sig. *abbrev* for: Signor; Signore.

sig. *abbrev* for signature.

sigh *sī*, *vi* to produce a long, deep, audible respiration expressive of yearning, dejection, relief, etc. — *vt* to utter, regret, while away, bring or render with sighs. — *n* an act of, or the sound made by, sighing. — *n* **sigh'er.** — *adj* **sigh'ing.** — *adv* **sigh'ingly.** — **sigh for** to yearn for. [Prob. a back-formation from the weak past tense of M.E. *siche* — O.E. (strong) *sīcan*.]

sight *sīt*, *n* act, opportunity or faculty of seeing; view; estimation; a beginning or coming to see; an instrumental observation; visual range; that which is seen; a spectacle; an object of especial interest; an unsightly, odd or ridiculous object; a guide to the eye on a gun or optical or other instrument; a sight-hole; a great many or a great deal (*colloq*). — *vt* to catch sight of; to view; to adjust the sights of (a gun, etc.). — *adj* **sight'ed** having sight, not blind; (of a gun, etc.) equipped with a sight; used in combination denoting sight of a particular kind, as in *long-sighted*. — *n* **sight'er** a practice shot in archery, etc. — *n* **sight'ing** an instance or the act of taking or catching sight. — *adj* **sight'less** blind. — *adv* **sight'lessly**. — *n* **sight'lessness**. — *n* **sight'liness**. — *adj* **sight'ly** pleasing to look at; comely. — *adj* **sight'worthy** worth looking at. — **sight'-hole** an aperture for looking through; **sight'-line** the line from the eye to the perceived object; (in *pl*) the view afforded e.g. of the stage in a theatre; **sight'-player, -reader** and **-singer** a musician who can read or perform music at first sight of the notes; **sight'-reading** and **-singing**. — *vi* and *vt* **sight'-read**. — *vi* **sight'-sing**. — **sight'-screen** a screen placed behind the bowler in cricket to help the batsman see the ball. — *vi* **sight'see** to go about visiting sights, buildings, etc. of interest. — **sight'seeing; sight'seer** (*-sē-ər*). — **at sight** without previous view or study; as soon as seen; on presentation; **catch sight of** to get a glimpse of, begin to see; **keep sight of** or **keep in sight** to keep within seeing distance of; to remain in touch with; **lose sight of** to cease to see; to get out of touch with; **on sight** as soon as seen, at sight; **out of sight** not in a position to be seen or to see; out of range of vision; **put out of sight** to remove from view; **sight for sore eyes** a most welcome sight; **sight unseen** without having seen the object in question. [O.E. *sihth, gesiht*.]

sigla *sig'lə*, *npl* abbreviations and signs, as in manuscripts, seals, etc. [L.]

sigma *sig'mə*, *n* the eighteenth letter (Σ, early form C; σ, or when final, ς) of the Greek alphabet, answering to S. — *adj* **sig'mate** (*-māt*) shaped like Σ, C, or S. — *adj* **sig'moid** or **sigmoid'al** C-shaped; S-shaped. — **sigmoid flexure** (*zool*, etc.) a C-shaped or S-shaped bend; (also **sigmoid colon**) the convoluted part of the large intestine, between the descending colon and the rectum. [Gr. *sīgma*.]

sign *sīn*, *n* a gesture expressing a meaning; a signal; a mark with a meaning; a symbol; an emblem; a token; a portent; a miraculous token; an indication of positive or negative value, or that indicated; a device marking an inn, etc., instead of a street number; a board or panel giving a shopkeeper's name, trade, etc.; an indication; an outward evidence of disease, perceptible to an examining doctor, etc.; a trail or track of a wild animal, perceptible to a tracker; a trace; a twelfth part (30°) of the zodiac, bearing the name of, but not now coincident with, a constellation. — *vt* to indicate, convey, communicate, direct, mark, by a sign or signs; to attach a signature to; to write as a signature; to designate by signature; to engage by signature; to mark; to cross, make the sign of the cross over. — *vi* to make a sign; to sign one's name; to use sign language. — *n* **signary** (*sig'nə-ri*) a system of symbols, as an alphabet or syllabary. — *adj* **signed**. — *n* **sign'er**. — *n* **signet** (*sig'nit*) a small seal; the impression of such a seal; a signet-ring; one of the royal seals for authenticating grants (for **Writer to the Signet** see under **write**); **sign'board** a board bearing a notice or serving as a shop or inn sign; **sig'net-ring** a ring with a signet; **sign'-painter** a person who paints signs for shops, etc.; **sign'post** a post for an inn sign; a finger-post or post supporting road-signs; an indication, clue. — *vt* to provide with a signpost; to point out as a signpost does. — **sign'-writer** an expert in lettering for shop-signs, etc.; **sign'-writing**. — **sign away** to transfer by signing; **sign in** or **out** to sign one's name on coming in or going out; **sign off** to record departure from work; to stop work, etc.; to discharge from employment; to leave off broadcasting; to signal that one does not intend to bid further (*bridge*); **sign of the cross** a gesture of tracing the form of a cross as an invocation of God's grace; **sign on** to engage (*vt* or *vi*) for a job, etc., by signature (also **sign up**); to register for unemployment benefit (*colloq*); **sign on the dotted line** to give one's consent, thereby binding oneself, to a proposed scheme, contract, etc. [Fr. *signe* — L. *signum*.]

signal *sig'nl*, *n* an intimation, e.g. of warning, conveyed over a distance; a transmitted effect conveying a message; the apparatus used for the purpose; an intimation of, or event taken as marking, the moment for action; an initial impulse; a piece of play intended to give information to one's partner (*cards*). — *vt* to intimate, convey or direct by signals; to signalise. — *vi* to make signals: — *pr p* **sig'nalling** or in N.Am. **sig'naling**; *pa t* and *pa p* **sig'nalled** or in N.Am. **sig'naled**. — *vt* **sig'nalise** or **-ize** to mark or distinguish signally. — *n* **sig'naller** or in N.Am. **sig'naler**. — *n* **sig'nalling** or in N.Am. **sig'naling**. — *adv* **sig'nally** notably. — **sig'nal-box** a railway signalman's cabin; **sig'nalman** a person who transmits signals; a person who works railway signals. [Fr. *signal* — L. *signum*.]

signary. See **sign**.

signatory. See **signature**.

signature *sig'nə-chər*, *n* a signing; a signed name; an indication of key, also of time, at the beginning of a line of music, or where a change occurs; a letter or numeral at the foot of a page to indicate sequence of sheets; a sheet so marked; the pages formed by such a sheet when folded and cut. — *n* **sig'natory** a person who has signed a document, agreement, treaty, etc. — Also *adj*. — **sig'nature-tune** a tune used to introduce, and hence associated with, a particular radio or television programme, group of performers, etc. [L.L. *signātūra* — L. *signāre, -ātum*, to sign.]

signet. See under **sign**.

signify *sig'ni-fī*, *vt* to be a sign for; to mean; to denote, betoken; to indicate or declare. — *vi* to be of consequence: — *pr p* **sig'nifying**; *pa t* and *pa p* **sig'nified**. — *adj* **sig'nifiable**. — *n* **signif'icance** (*-i-kəns*) meaning; import; the quality of being significant (also **signif'icancy**). — *adj* **signif'icant** having a meaning; full of meaning; important, worthy of consideration; indicative. — *adv* **signif'icantly**. — *n* **significā'tion** meaning; that which is signified; importance. — *adj* **signif'icative** (*-kə-tiv*) indicative; significant. — *adv* **signif'icatively**. — *n* **sig'nifier**. — **significant figures** (*arith*) the figures 1 to 9, or ciphers occurring medially (the following numbers are expressed to three significant figures — 3·15, 0·0127, 1·01). [L. *significāre, -ātum* — *signum*, a sign, *facĕre*, to make.]

Signor *sē'nyör* or **Signore** *sē-nyö'rā*, *n* an Italian word of address equivalent to Mr or sir; (without *cap*) a gentleman. — *n* **Signora** (*sē-nyö'rä*) feminine of *Signor*, Mrs, madam; (without *cap*) a lady. — *n* **Signorina** (*sē-nyö-rē'nä*) Miss, miss; (without *cap*) an unmarried lady. — *n* **signoria** (*-rē'ä*; *hist*) a seignory, the governing body of an Italian city-state. — *n* **si'gnory** seignory; a signoria. [It. *signor, signore*.]

signorial. See **seignior**.

sika *sē'kə*, *n* a small Japanese deer, spotted white in summer. [Jap. *shika*.]

sike or **syke** *sīk*, (*Scot*) *n* a rill or small ditch. [Northern, — O.E. *sīc*.]

Sikh *sēk*, *n* one of a North Indian monotheistic sect, founded by Nának (1469–1539), later a military confederacy; a Sikh soldier in the Indian army. — Also *adj*. — *n* **Sikh'ism**. [Hind., disciple.]

silage *sī'lij, n* fodder preserved in a silo. — *vt* to put in a silo. [**ensilage**, after **silo**.]

Silastic® *sil-as'tik, n* a flexible silicone rubber, used in the manufacture of artificial limbs, etc. — Also without *cap*.

sild *sild, n* a young herring. [Norw.]

silence *sī'ləns, n* absence of sound; abstention from sounding, speech, mention or communication; a time of such absence or abstention; a state of not, or no longer, being spoken about; taciturnity. — *vt* to cause to be silent. — *interj* be silent. — *adj* **si'lenced**. — *n* **si'lencer** a person who or a thing that silences; a device for reducing the sound of escaping gases by gradual expansion, used e.g. for small-arms and internal combustion engines. — *adj* **si'lent** noiseless; without sound; unaccompanied by sound; refraining from speech, mention or divulging; taciturn; not pronounced; inoperative. — *n* a silent film. — *adv* **si'lently**. — *n* **si'lentness**. — **silent film** a cinema film which has no accompanying synchronised soundtrack; **silent majority** those, in any country the bulk of the population, who are assumed to have sensible, moderate opinions though they do not trouble to express them publicly; **silent partner** a sleeping partner (q.v.). [L. *silēre*, to be silent.]

silenus *sī-lē'nəs, (mythol) n* a woodland god or old satyr (**Silenus** their chief, foster-father of Bacchus, pot-bellied, bald and snub-nosed). [L. *Sīlēnus* — Gr. *Seilēnos*.]

silesia *sī-lē'zhə, n* a thin, twilled cotton or linen used for lining clothes, etc., orig. made in *Silesia* (now part of Poland).

silex *sī'leks, n* silica of quartz; a heat-resistant and shock-resistant glass formed of fused quartz. [L. *silex, silicis*, flint.]

silhouette *sil-ōō-et', n* a pictorial representation of an object or esp. a person, in profile, consisting of an outline filled in with black; the shadow of anything. — *vt* to represent or show in silhouette. [Étienne de *Silhouette* (1709–67), French minister of finance in 1759 — reason disputed.]

silica *sil'i-kə, n* silicon dioxide or silicic anhydride, occurring in nature as quartz, chalcedony, etc. and (amorphous and hydrated) as opal. — *adj* composed of silica. — *n* **sil'icate** a salt of silicic acid. — *adj* **siliceous** or **silicious** (*-ish'əs*) of or containing silica. — *adj* **silicic** (*-is'ik*) pertaining to, or obtained from, silica (**silicic acid** a general name for a group of acids containing silicon). — *n* **sil'icide** (*-sīd*) a compound of silicon and another element. — *n* **silicification** (*si-lis-i-fi-kā'shən*). — *adj* **silicified** (*-lis'*). — *vt* **silic'ify** to render siliceous; to impregnate or cement with or replace by silica. — *vi* to become siliceous. — *n* **sil'icon** (*-kon* or *-kən*) a non-metallic element (symbol **Si**; atomic no. 14), most abundant of all except oxygen, forming grey crystals or brown amorphous powder and having semi-conducting properties. — *n* **sil'icone** any of a number of extremely stable organic derivatives of silicon, used in rubbers, lubricants, polishes, etc. — *n* **silicosis** (*-kō'sis*) a disease caused by inhaling silica dust. — *n* and *adj* **silicot'ic**. — **silicon chip** see **chip**. [L. *silex, silicis*, flint.]

silicle, silicula, etc. See **siliqua**.

siliqua *sil'i-kwə* or **silique** *sil-ēk', (bot) n* a long pod of two carpels divided by a partition, characteristic of cruciferous plants. — *n* **silicula** (*-ik'ū-lə*) a short pod of the same kind. — Also **sil'icle** or **sil'icule**. — *adj* **silic'ulose**. — *adj* **sil'iquose**. [L. *siliqua*, pod, dimin. *silicula*.]

silk *silk, n* a fibre produced by the larva of a silkworm moth, formed by the hardening of a liquid emitted from spinning-glands; a similar fibre from another insect or a spider; an imitation (**artificial silk**) made by forcing a viscous solution of modified cellulose through small holes; a thread, cloth, garment or clothing made from such fibres; the silk gown, or the rank, of a king's or queen's counsel. — *adj* of or pertaining to silk. — *vt* to cover or clothe with silk. — *adj* **silk'en** of, like or clad in silk; glossy; soft and smooth; luxurious. — *vt* to make silken. — *adv* **silk'ily**. — *n* **silk'iness**. — *adj* **silk'y**. — **silk-hat'** a top-hat; **silk'worm** the moth whose larva produces silk. — **silk-screen printing** or **process** a stencil process in which the colour applied is forced through silk or other fine-mesh cloth; **take silk** to become a QC or KC. [O.E. *seolc* — L. *sēricum*.]

sill *sil, n* the timber, stone, etc. at the foot of an opening, as for a door, window, embrasure, port, dock-entrance, or the like; the bottom (of a title-page, a plough, a ledge); a bed of rock (*mining*); a sheet of intrusive rock more or less parallel to the bedding (*geol*). [O.E. *syll*.]

sillabub. Same as **syllabub**.

sillimanite *sil'i-mən-īt, n* aluminium silicate in the form of orthorhombic crystals, occurring in argillaceous metamorphic rocks. [After Benjamin *Silliman* (1779–1864), Am. scientist.]

silly *sil'i, adj* feeble-minded; frivolous; not well thought-out; senseless; close-in (*cricket*; e.g. *silly mid-off*). — *n* a silly person. — *adv* **sill'ily**. — *n* **sill'iness**. — **sill'y-billy** (*colloq*) a foolish person; **silly season** a season, usu. late summer, when newspapers print trivial matter for want of more newsworthy material. [O.E. *sælig*.]

silo *sī'lō, n* a pit or airtight chamber for storing grain, or for ensilage, or for storing other loose materials; a storage tower above ground, typically tall and cylindrical; an underground chamber housing a guided missile ready to be fired: — *pl* **si'los**. — *vt* to put or keep in a silo: — *pa p* **si'lo'd** or **si'loed**. [Sp., — L. *sīrus* — Gr. *siros, sīros, seiros*, a pit.]

silt *silt, n* fine sediment deposited by a body of water. — *vt* to choke, block, cover, etc. with silt (with *up*). — *vi* to become silted up. — *n* **siltā'tion**. — *adj* **silt'y**. [M.E. *sylt*.]

Silurian *sil-ōō'ri-ən* or *-ū', adj* of the *Silūrēs*, a British tribe of S. Wales, etc.; applied by Murchison in 1835 to the geological system preceding the Devonian. — Also *n*.

silva or **sylva** *sil'və, n* the assemblage of trees in a region: — *pl* **sil'vas, syl'vas, sil'vae** or **syl'vae** (*-vē*). — *adj* **sil'van** or **syl'van** of woods; woodland; wooded. — *n* a wood-god; a forest-dweller. — *adj* **silvat'ic, sylvat'ic, silves'trian** or **sylves'trian** of the woods; woodland; rustic. — *adj* **silvicul'tural** or **sylvicul'tural**. — *n* **sil'viculture** or **syl'viculture** forestry. [L. *silva* (sometimes *sylva*), a wood.]

silver *sil'vər, n* a white precious metal (symbol **Ag**, for L. *argentum*; atomic no. 47); silver money; silverware; cutlery, sometimes even when not of silver; a silver medal. — *adj* of or like silver; silver-coloured; clear and ringing in tone. — *vt* to cover with silver; to make silvery. — *vi* to become silvery. — *n* **sil'veriness**. — *n* **sil'vering** coating with, or of, silver or quicksilver. — *vt* **sil'verise** or **-ize** to coat or treat with silver. — *adj* **sil'vern** (*poetic*) made of silver; silvery. — *adj* **sil'very** like silver; silver-coloured; light in tone; having a clear ringing sound. — **sil'ver-bath** (*phot*) a solution of a silver salt, or a vessel for it, for sensitising plates; **sil'ver-bell** the snowdrop-tree; **sil'verbill** the name of two species of the genus *Lonchura* of weaver-finches, with a silvery sheen to their bills; **silver birch** a species of birch with silvery-white peeling bark; **sil'verfish** an insect of the *Thysanura*, an order of small wingless insects; **silver-foil'** silver-leaf; **silver fox** an American fox with white-tipped black fur; **silver-gilt'** gilded silver. — Also *adj*. — **sil'ver-glance** native sulphide of silver; **silver iodide** a yellow powder that darkens when exposed to light, is used in photography, is scattered on clouds to cause rainfall, and has various medical uses; **silver jubilee** a twenty-fifth anniversary; **silver-leaf'** silver beaten into thin leaves; (*sil'*) a disease of plum-trees; **silver lining** a redeeming aspect of an otherwise unpleasant or unfortunate situation; **silver medal** (in athletics competitions, etc.) the medal awarded as second prize; **silver nitrate** a poisonous colourless crystalline salt that turns grey or black in the presence of light or organic matter, and has uses in photography, as an antiseptic, etc.; **silver paper** silver-foil; (usu.) tinfoil (sometimes with a backing of greaseproof paper); **silver=plate'** utensils of silver; electroplate. — *adj* **silver=plā'ted.** — **sil'ver-point** the process or product of drawing with a silver-tipped pencil; **silver screen** the cinema screen; **sil'verside** the top of a round of beef; **sil'versmith** a worker in silver. — *adj* **silver=tongued'** plausible, eloquent. — *adj* **silver=voiced'.** — **silver wedding** the twenty-fifth wedding anniversary; **sil'ver-white.** — **born with a silver spoon in one's mouth** born to affluence. [O.E. *silfer, seolfor.*]

silvestrian and **silviculture.** See under **silva.**

sima *sī'mə,* (*geol*) *n* the part of the earth's crust underlying the sial. [From *si*licon and *ma*gnesium.]

simian *sim'i-ən, adj* of the apes; apelike. — Also *n.* [L. *sīmia,* ape.]

similar *sim'i-lər, adj* (with *to*) like; resembling; exactly corresponding in shape, without regard to size (*geom*). — *n* **similarity** (*-lar'i-ti*). — *adv* **sim'ilarly.** [Fr. *similaire* — L. *similis,* like.]

simile *sim'i-li,* (*rhet*) *n* (an) explicit likening of one thing to another: — *pl* **sim'iles.** — *adj* **sim'ilātive** expressing similarity. — *n* **simil'itude** likeness; semblance; comparison; parable. [L. neuter of *similis,* like.]

simillimum *si-mil'i-mum, n* (in homoeopathy) a remedy chosen because it would produce in a healthy person the same symptoms as those exhibited by the patient. [L., neuter superl. of *similis,* like.]

similor *sim'i-lör, n* a yellow alloy used for cheap jewellery. [Fr., — L. *similis,* like, *aurum,* gold.]

simmer *sim'ər, vi* and *vt* to boil gently. — *vi* to be near boiling or breaking out. — *n* a simmering state. — **simmer down** to calm down. [Earlier *simper.*]

simnel *sim'nl, n* a sweet cake usu. covered with marzipan for Easter, or sometimes Christmas or Mothering Sunday. — Also **sim'nel-bread** or **-cake.** [O.Fr. *simenel* — L. *simila,* fine flour.]

simony *sī'mən-i* or *sim'ən-i, n* the buying or selling of an ecclesiastical benefice. — *n* **simō'niac** a person guilty of simony. — *adj* **simonī'acal.** — *adv* **simonī'acally.** — *n* **si'monist** a person who practises or defends simony. [*Simon* Magus (from the Bible: Acts viii).]

simoom *si-mōōm'* or **simoon** *-mōōn', n* a hot suffocating desert wind in Arabia and N. Africa. [Ar. *samûm* — *samm,* to poison.]

simp. See **simpleton** under **simple.**

simpatico *sim-pat'i-kō,* (*colloq*) *adj* sympathetic in the sense of congenial. [It. and Sp.]

simper *sim'pər, vi* to smile in a silly, affected manner. — *n* a silly or affected smile. — *adj* **sim'pering.** — *adv* **sim'peringly.** [Cf. Norw. *semper,* smart.]

simple *sim'pl, adj* consisting of one thing or element; not complex or compound; not divided into leaflets (*bot*); easy; plain; unornate; unpretentious; mean, sorry; mere, sheer; ordinary; unlearned or unskilled; of humble rank or origin; unaffected; artless; guileless; unsuspecting; credulous; weak in intellect; silly. — *n* a medicine of one constituent; hence a medicinal herb. — *n* **sim'pleness.** — *n* **sim'pleton** a weak or foolish person, one easily imposed on (*colloq* short form **simp**). — *n* **simplicity** (*-plis'*). — *n* **simplificā'tion** the process, or an instance, of making simple or simpler. — *adj* **sim'plificātive.** — *n* **sim'plifīer.** — *vt* **sim'plify** to make simple, simpler, or less difficult: — *pr p* **sim'plifying**; *pa t* and *pa p* **sim'plified.** — *n* **sim'plism** affected simplicity; oversimplification of a problem or situation. — *adj* **simplis'tic** tending to oversimplify, making no allowances for problems and complexities; naive. — *adv* **simplis'tically.** — *adv* **sim'ply** in a simple manner; considered by itself; alone; merely; without qualification; veritably; absolutely; really (*colloq*). — **simple fraction** a fraction that has whole numbers as numerator and denominator; **simple fracture** see **fracture**; **simple interest** interest calculated on the principal only. — *adj* **simple=mind'ed** lacking intelligence; foolish. — **simple=mind'edness; simple sentence** a sentence with one predicate. [Fr. *simple,* and L. *simplus, simplex.*]

simpliste *sẽ-plēst, sim-plēst'* or *sim'plist, adj* simplistic, naive. [Fr.]

simulacrum *sim-ū-lā'krəm, n* an image; a semblance: — *pl* **simula'cra** or **simula'crums.** [L. *simulācrum.*]

simulate *sim'ū-lāt, vt* to feign; to have or assume a false appearance of; to mimic; to re-create the conditions of, for the purposes of training or experimentation. — *adj* **sim'ulated** (of a material, e.g. fur, leather, wood) not of such a material but made (usu. in an inferior material) to look like it; not genuine, feigned. — *n* **simulā'tion** feigning; mimicry; the making of working replicas or representations of machines or the re-creation of a situation, environment, etc. for demonstration or for analysis of problems. — *adj* **sim'ulātive.** — *n* **sim'ulātor** someone who or something that simulates; a device used for simulating required conditions, etc., e.g. for training purposes. — *adj* **sim'ulatory.** — **simulated pearl** a bead resembling a pearl. [L. *simulāre, -ātum*; cf. **similar, simultaneous.**]

simulcast *sim'əl-käst, n* a programme broadcast simultaneously on radio and television; the transmission of such a programme. — Also *vt.* [*simultaneous* and broad*cast.*]

simulium *si-mū'li-əm, n* a small blood-sucking fly of the genus *Simulium.* — *npl* **Simulī'idae** (*-dē*) the family of flies of which the Simulium is the type-genus, some species of which are the carriers of diseases such as onchocerciasis. [L. *simulāre,* to imitate.]

simultaneous *sim-əl-tā'ni-əs* or in N.Am. *sīm', adj* being or happening at the same time; (of equations) satisfied by the same roots (*math*). — *n* **simultaneity** (*-tə-nē'i-ti* or *-nā'-*) or **simultā'neousness.** — *adv* **simultā'neously.** [L. *simul,* at the same time.]

sin[1] *sin, n* a moral offence or shortcoming, esp. from the point of view of religion; the condition of offending in this way; an offence generally; a shame or pity. — *vi* to commit sin (often with *against*): — *pr p* **sinn'ing;** *pa t* and *pa p* **sinned.** — *adj* **sin'ful** wicked; involving sin; morally wrong. — *n* **sin'fulness.** — *adj* **sin'less.** — *adv* **sin'lessly.** — *n* **sin'lessness.** — *n* **sinn'er.** — **sin bin** (in ice-hockey, etc.) an enclosure to which a player is sent for a statutory length of time when suspended from a game for unruly behaviour; a room or other place to which disruptive school pupils are sent; **sin'-offering** a sacrifice in expiation of sin. — **live in sin** to cohabit in an unmarried state; **original sin** see under **origin.** [O.E. *synn.*]

sin[2]. See **sine**[1].

Sinanthropus *sin-, sīn-an'thrō-pəs* or *-thrō', n* Peking (fossil) man. [Gr. *Sīnai,* (the) Chinese, *anthrōpos,* man.]

sinapism *sin'ə-pizm,* (*med*) *n* a mustard plaster. [Gr. *sinăpi.*]

sinarchism *sin'är-kizm* or **sinarquism** *sin'är-kizm* or *-kwizm, n* (also with *cap*) the fascist movement in Mexico prominent around the time of the Second World War. — *n* and *adj* **sin'archist** or **sin'arquist.** [Sp. *sinarquismo* — *sin,* without, *anarquismo,* anarchism.]

since *sins*, *adv* from that time on; after that time; past; ago. — *prep* after; from the time of. — *conj* from the time that; seeing that; because. [M.E. *sins*, *sithens*.]

sincere *sin-sēr'*, *adj* unfeigned; genuine; free from pretence; the same in reality as in appearance. — *adv* **sincēre'ly**. — *n* **sincēre'ness** or **sincerity** (*-ser'*). [Fr. *sincère* — L. *sincērus*, clean.]

sinciput *sing'si-put*, (*anat*) *n* the forepart of the head or skull. — *adj* **sincip'ital**. [L., — *sēmi-*, half, *caput*, head.]

Sindhi or **Sindi** *sin'dē*, *n* a native or inhabitant of *Sind*, in S.E. Pakistan; the Indic language spoken mainly in Sind. — Also *adj*.

sine[1] *sīn*, (*math*) *n* (as a function of an angle) the ratio of the side opposite it (or its supplement) in a right-angled triangle to the hypotenuse (short form **sin**); orig. the perpendicular from one end of an arc to the diameter through the other. — *adj* **sinical** (*sin'i-kl*). — **sine curve** a curve showing the relationship between the size of an angle and its sine; **sine wave** any oscillation whose graphical representation is a sine curve. [L. *sinus*, a bay.]

sine[2] *sī'nē* or *si'ne*, (L.) *prep* without. — **sine die** (*dī'ē* or *dē'ā*) without a day (appointed); (of a meeting or other business) indefinitely adjourned; **sine dubio** (*dū'bi-ō* or *dōō'bi-ō*) without doubt; **sine prole** (*prō'lē* or *prō'le*) without issue, without children; **sine qua non** (*kwā non* or *kwä nōn*) an indispensable condition.

sinecure *sī'ni-kūr* or *sin'*, *n* a benefice without cure of souls; an office without work, a cushy job. — Also *adj*. — *n* **sin'ecurism**. — *n* **sin'ecurist**. [L. *sine*, without, *cūra*, care.]

sinew *sin'ū*, *n* that which joins a muscle to a bone, a tendon; strength or that which it depends on (*fig*). — *vt* (*poetic*) to bind as by sinews; to strengthen. — *adj* **sin'ewed**. — *adj* **sin'ewy**. [O.E. *sinu*, genitive *sinwe*.]

sinfonia *sin-fō-nē'ə*, *n* a symphony; a symphony orchestra. — *n* **sinfonietta** (*-nē-et'tə*) a simple, or light, little symphony; a small symphony orchestra. — **sinfonia concertante** (*kon-chər-tan'ti*) an orchestral work with parts for more than one solo instrument. [It.]

sing *sing*, *vi* to utter melodious sounds in musical succession in articulating words; to perform songs; to emit more or less songlike sounds; to give a cantabile or lyrical effect; (of the ears) to ring; to be capable of being sung; to write (of) in poetry; to confess, to turn informer, to squeal (*slang*, esp. *US*). — *vt* to utter or perform by voice, musically; to chant; to celebrate; to proclaim, relate, in song or verse or in comparable manner; to bring, drive, render, pass, etc. by singing: — *pa t* **sang**; *pa p* **sung**. — *adj* **sing'able**. — *n* **sing'er** a person, bird, etc. that sings; a person who sings as a profession; an informer (*slang*, esp. *US*). — *n* **sing'ing**. — *adv* **sing'ingly**. — **singer-song'writer** a person who performs songs that they have also written; **sing'-ing-bird** a songbird; **sing'-sing** (in New Guinea) a tribal get-together for singing, dancing and feasting; **sing'song** a ballad; jingly verse; monotonous up-and-down intonation; an informal concert where the company sing; a meeting for community singing. — *adj* of the nature of a singsong. — *vt* and *vi* to sing, speak or utter in a singsong way. — **sing along** (orig. *US*) of an audience, to join in the familiar songs with the performer (with *with*; *n* **sing'along**); **sing another song** or **tune** to change to a humbler tone; **sing out** to call out distinctly; to inform, peach; **sing small** to assume a humble tone. [O.E. *singan*.]

sing. *abbrev* for singular.

singe *sinj*, *vt* to burn on the surface; to scorch; to remove by scorching. — *vi* to become scorched: — *pr p* **singe'ing**; *pa t* and *pa p* **singed**. — *n* a burning on the surface; a slight burn. [O.E. *sen(c)gan*.]

Singhalese. See **Sinhalese**.

single *sing'gl*, *adj* consisting of one only or one part; unique; one-fold; uncombined; unmarried; for one; (of combat) man-to-man; (of ale) weak, small (*old-fashioned*); undivided; unbroken; (of a flower) without development of stamens into petals or of ligulate instead of tubular florets; (of a travel ticket) valid for the outward journey only, not return. — *adv* singly. — *n* anything single; (usu. in *pl*) an unmarried, unattached person; (in *pl*; in tennis, etc.) a game played by one against one; a hit for one run; a gramophone record with usu. only one tune, or other short recording, on each side; a one-pound or one-dollar note. — *vt* to separate; to pick (out); to take aside. — *n* **sing'lehood** the state of being unmarried. — *n* **sing'leness** (*-gl-nis*). — *n* **sing'let** (*-glit*) a thing that is single; an undershirt. — *n* **sing'leton** (*-gl-tən*) a single card of its suit in a hand; anything single. — *adv* **sing'ly** (*-gli*) one by one; alone; by oneself. — *adj* **sing'le-breasted** with one thickness over the breast and one row of buttons. — **single cream** cream with a low fat-content that will not thicken when beaten; **single-deck'er** a vessel or vehicle, esp. a bus, with only one deck. — *adj* **sing'le-figure**. — **single figures** a score, total, etc. of any number from 1 to 9; **single file** see under **file**[1]. — *adj* and *adv* **single-hand'ed** by oneself; unassisted; with or for one hand. — *adj* **sing'le-hearted** sincere; without duplicity; dedicated, devoted in one's attitude. — *adj* **single-mind'ed** ingenuous; bent upon one sole purpose. — **single-mind'edness; single parent** a mother or father bringing up children alone (in a **single-parent family**). — *adj* **sing'le-phase** (of an alternating electric current) requiring one outward and one return conductor for transmission. — **singles bar** or **club** one especially for unmarried or unattached people, where friendships (and implicitly sexual relationships) can be formed; **single-seat'er** a car, aeroplane, etc. having seats for one only. [O.Fr., — L. *singulī*, one by one.]

singletree. Same as **swingletree**.

sing-sing, singsong. See under **sing**.

singular *sing'gū-lər*, *adj* single; unique; denoting or referring to one; pre-eminently good or efficacious; extraordinary; peculiar; strange, odd. — *adv* singularly. — *n* an individual person or thing; the singular number or a word in the singular number. — *n* **singularīsā'tion** or **-z-**. — *vt* **sing'ularise** or **-ize** to make singular; to signalise. — *n* **singularity** (*-lar'i-ti*) fact or state of being singular; peculiarity; individuality; oddity; oneness; anything curious or remarkable; a point in space-time at which matter is compressed to an infinitely great density (*astron*). — *adv* **sing'ularly** in a singular manner; peculiarly; strangely; singly. [L. *singulāris*.]

sinh *shīn* or *sīn-āch'*, (*math*) *n* a conventional abbreviation of *h*yperbolic *sine*.

Sinhalese *sin'ə-lēz* or *-lēz'*, or **Singhalese** *sing'gə-lēz* or *-lēz'*, *adj* of the majority population of Sri Lanka (formerly Ceylon); of or in their language, similar to Pali. — *n* a member of the Sinhalese people; their language. [Sans. *Siṁhala*, Ceylon.]

sinical. See under **sine**[1].

sinister *sin'is-tər*, *adj* suggestive of threatened evil; malign; underhand; inauspicious; on the left side from the point of view of the bearer of the shield, not the beholder, and similarly sometimes in description of an illustration, etc. (*heraldry*). — *adv* **sin'isterly**. — *adj* **sin'istral** turning to the left; (of a shell) coiled contrary to the normal way. — *n* **sinistral'ity**. [L.]

sinistrorse *sin-is-trörs'* or *sin'*, (*biol*) *adj* rising spirally and turning to the right, i.e. crossing an outside observer's field of view from right to left upwards (like an ordinary spiral stair). — Also **sinistrors'al**. — *adv* **sinistrorse'ly**. [L. *sinistrōrsus*, *sinistrōversus*, towards the left side — *sinister*, left, *vertĕre*, *versum*, to turn.]

sink *singk*, *vi* to become submerged, wholly or partly; to subside; to fall slowly; to go down passively; to pass to a lower level or state; to penetrate or be absorbed; to slope away, dip; to diminish; to collapse; to be or become withdrawn inwards. — *vt* to cause or allow to sink; (in games) to cause (a ball) to run into the hole (*colloq*); to excavate; to let in, insert; to abandon; to abolish; to merge; to pay (a debt); to invest, esp. unprofitably or beyond easy recovery; to damn or ruin (esp. in imprecation); to drink quickly (*colloq*): — *pa t* **sank**; *pa p* **sunk** or **sunk'en**. — *n* a kitchen or scullery trough or basin with a drain, for washing dishes, etc.; a receptacle or drain for filth or dirty water; a place where things are engulfed or where foul things gather; a cesspool; a depression in a surface; an area without surface drainage; a swallow-hole (*geol*); a shaft; a natural or artificial means of absorbing or discharging heat, fluid, etc. (*phys*, etc.). — *n* **sink'age** act or process of sinking; amount of sinking; a sunken area or depression; shrinkage. — *n* **sink'er** a person who sinks; a weight for sinking anything, e.g. a fishing-line. — *n* and *adj* **sink'ing**. — *adj* **sink'y** yielding underfoot. — **sink'-hole** a hole for filth; **sink'ing-fund** a fund formed by setting aside income to accumulate at interest to pay off debt; **sink unit** a fitting consisting of a sink, draining-board, and cupboards, etc. underneath. — **sink in** to be absorbed; to be understood. [O.E. *sincan*, intransitive verb.]

sinner, etc. See **sin[1]**.

Sino- *sin-ō-* or *sī-nō-*, *pfx* denoting Chinese. — *n* **Sinol'ogist**. — *n* **Sinol'ogy** the study of Chinese culture, language, etc. [Gr. *Sīnai*, Chinese (pl.).]

sinter *sin'tər*, *n* a deposit from hot springs. — *vt* to heat a mixture of powdered metals, sometimes under pressure, to the melting-point of the metal in the mixture which has the lowest melting-point, the melted metal binding together the harder particles. — *vi* to coalesce under heat without liquefaction. [Ger. *Sinter*.]

sinuate *sin'ū-āt* or **sinuated** *sin'ū-āt-id*, *adj* wavy-edged; winding. — *adv* **sin'uately**. — *n* **sinuā'tion** winding. [Ety. as for **sinus**.]

sinuous *sin'ū-əs*, *adj* wavy; winding; bending in a supple manner. — *adj* **sinuose** (*sin'ū-ōs*) sinuous. — *n* **sinuosity** (*-os'*). — *adv* **sin'uously**. — *n* **sin'uousness**. [Ety. as for **sinus**.]

sinus *sī'nəs*, *n* an air-filled cavity in the bones of the skull, connecting with the nose; a narrow cavity through which pus is discharged; a cavity; a notch between two lobes in a leaf (*bot*): — *pl* **si'nuses**. — *n* **sinusī'tis** (*sin-* or *sī-nəs-*) inflammation of a sinus of the skull communicating with the nose. [L. *sĭnus*, *-ūs*, a bend, fold, bay.]

Sioux *sōō*, *n* an American Indian of a tribe now living in the Dakotas, Minnesota and Montana; any of the group of languages spoken by them: — *pl* **Sioux** (*sōō* or *sōōz*). — Also *adj*. — *adj* **Siou'an** pertaining to the Sioux, or to a larger group to which the Sioux belong; pertaining to the languages of this group. — *n* the group of languages spoken by the Siouan peoples. [Fr., from a native word.]

sip *sip*, *vt* and *vi* to drink, or drink from, in small quantities by action of the lips: — *pr p* **sipp'ing**; *pa t* and *pa p* **sipped**. — *n* the act of sipping; the quantity sipped at once. — *n* **sipp'er**. [Cf. **sup**; O.E. *sypian*.]

sipe *sīp*, *n* a tiny groove or slit in the tread of a tyre, aiding water dispersal and improving the tyre's grip. [Dialect *sipe*, to ooze.]

siphon or **syphon** *sī'fən*, *n* a bent tube or channel by which a liquid may be drawn off by atmospheric pressure; a tubular organ for intake and output of water, as in lamellibranchs; an aerated-water bottle that discharges by a siphon. — *vt* (often with *off*) to convey, remove by means of (or as if by means of) a siphon; to divert (funds, money, etc.). [Gr. *sīphōn*, *sĭphōn*, siphon.]

sippet *sip'it*, *n* a morsel, esp. of bread with soup. [Cf. **sip** and **sup**.]

si quis *sī* or *sē kwis*, *n* a public notice, esp. one announcing the impending ordination of a parish priest, allowing for objections to be raised. [L. *sī quis*, if anybody (wants, knows, has found, etc.).]

Sir. (*Bible*) *abbrev* for (the Apocryphal Book) Wisdom of Jesus the Son of Sirach (also called *Ecclesiasticus*).

sir *sûr*, *n* a word of respect (or disapprobation) used in addressing a man; a gentleman; (with *cap*) prefixed to the Christian name of a knight or baronet; (with *cap*) a word of address to a man in a formal letter. — *vt* to address as 'sir': — *pr p* **sirr'ing**; *pa t* and *pa p* **sirred**. [O.Fr. *sire*, from L. *senior*, an elder.]

sire *sīr*, *n* a father, esp. of a horse or other beast; an ancestor; a term of address to a king (*hist*). — *vt* (of animals) to father. [See **sir**.]

siren *sī'rən*, *n* a signalling or warning instrument that produces sound by the escape of air or steam through a rotating perforated plate; a fascinating woman, insidious and deceptive; a bewitching singer; a mermaid; (with *cap*) one of certain sea-nymphs, part woman, part bird, whose songs lured sailors to death (*Gr mythol*). — Also *adj*. — *npl* **Sirē'nia** an order of aquatic mammals now represented by the dugong and the manatee. — *n* and *adj* **sirē'nian**. — *adj* **sirenic** (*-ren'*). [Gr. *Seirēn*, a Siren.]

sirloin *sûr'loin*, *n* the loin or upper part of a loin of beef. [From a by-form of Fr. *surlonge* — *sur*, over, and *longe* (cf. **loin**).]

sirocco *si-rok'ō* or **scirocco** *shi-rok'ō*, *n* (in Southern Italy) a hot, dry, dusty and gusty wind from N. Africa, becoming moist further north; any oppressive south or south-east wind; a wind from the desert; a drying machine: — *pl* **sirocc'os** or **scirocc'os**. [It. *s(c)irocco* — Ar. *sharq*, east wind.]

sirup. See **syrup**.

sirvente *sēr-vãt'*, *n* a troubadour's short narrative, often politically satirical poem. [Fr.]

sis or **siss** *sis*, (esp. *NAm*) *n* a contracted form of **sister** (used in addressing a girl). — *n* and *adj* **siss'y** (orig. chiefly *NAm*) cissy.

-sis *-sis*, *n sfx* signifying: action, process; condition caused by: — *pl* **-ses** (*-sēz*). [Gr.]

sisal *sī'səl* or *sī'zəl*, *n* (in full **sis'al-hemp** or **-grass**) agave fibre, used for making rope, etc. [First exported from *Sisal*, in Yucatán.]

siskin *sis'kin*, *n* a yellowish-green Eurasian finch. [Ger. dialect *sisschen*; app. Slav.]

siss and **sissy**. See **sis**.

sister *sis'tər*, *n* a daughter of the same parents; a half-sister; (formerly) a sister-in-law; a female fellow; a member of a sisterhood; a nun; a senior nurse, esp. one in charge of a ward. — *adj* of the same origin; fellow; built on the same model. — *vt* to be a sister to. — *adj* **sis'terless**. — *n* **sis'terhood** the act or state of being a sister; the relationship of sister; a society, esp. a religious community, of women; a set or class of women. — *n* **sis'terliness**. — *adj* **sis'terly** like or becoming a sister; kind, affectionate. — *n* **sis'ter-in-law** a husband's or wife's sister, or a brother's wife; a husband or wife's brother's wife: — *pl* **sis'ters-in-law**. — *adj* **sis'terlike**. [App. O.N. *systir*.]

Sistine *sis'tīn*, *-tēn* or *-tin*, *adj* of Pope *Sixtus*, esp. Sixtus IV (1471–84) or V (1585–90). — **Sistine Chapel** the Pope's chapel in the Vatican, built by Sixtus IV.

Sisyphean *sis-i-fē'ən*, *adj* endless, laborious and futile (*fig*); relating to *Sisyphus*, king of Corinth, condemned in Tartarus to roll ceaselessly up a hill a huge stone which would roll back to the foot of the hill again each time he neared the top.

sit *sit*, *vi* to rest on the buttocks and thighs with the upper body more or less vertical; to perch, as birds; to brood; to have a seat, as in parliament; to be in session; to reside; to be a tenant; to be located, have station or (as the wind) direction; to pose, be a model; to undergo an examination, be a candidate; to weigh, bear, press; to be disposed in adjustment, hang, fit; to befit. — *vt* to seat; to have a seat on, ride; to undergo or be examined in; (often in combination) to stay in or with in order to look after: — *pr p* **sitt'ing**; *pa t* and *pa p* **sat**. — *n* a mode or spell of sitting. — *n* **sitt'er** someone who sits; a person who sits as a model for an artist or with a medium; a babysitter; a sitting bird; an easy shot; an easy dupe (*slang*); anything difficult to fail in; a sitting-room (*slang*). — *n* **sitt'ing** the state of being seated or act of taking a seat; brooding on eggs; a clutch; one or two or more groups into which a large number of diners are divided, or the period set aside for each group to occupy the dining-room, etc.; a continuous meeting of an official body; a spell of posing for an artist, etc. — *adj* seated; brooding; in the course of a parliamentary session. — **sit'-down** a spell of sitting. — *adj* (of a meal) that one sits down to; (of a strike) in which workers down tools but remain in occupation of the plant, workshop, etc. — **sit'-in** the occupation of a building, etc. as an organised protest against some (supposed) injustice, etc. (also *adj*); **sitt'ing-room** a room in which members of a family commonly sit; a space for sitting; **sitting target** an easy target or victim; **sitting tenant** the tenant currently occupying a property; **sit'-upon** (*colloq*) the buttocks. — **sit back** to take no active part, or no further active part; **sit by** to look on without taking any action; **sit down** to take a seat; to pause, rest; to take up positions prior to beginning a siege; to accept meekly (with *under*); **sit in** to act as a babysitter; to be present as a visitor, and (usu.) take part, as at a conference or discussion; to have or take part in a sit-in; **sit on** or **upon** to hold an official inquiry regarding; to repress, check or delay dealing with (*slang*); **sit out** to sit apart without participating; to sit to the end of; to outstay; **sit tight** to maintain one's seat; to keep one's position quietly and unobtrusively; **sit up** to rise from a recumbent to a sitting position, or from a relaxed to an erect seat; to become alert or startled; to remain up instead of going to bed; to keep watch during the night. [O.E. *sittan*.]

sitar *si-tär'*, *n* a Hindu plucked-string instrument with a long neck and a rounded body. [Hind. *sitār*.]

sitatunga *si-tə-tōōng'gə* or *-tung'gə*, *n* a species of African antelope notable for its elongated hooves which allow it to walk on marshy ground. [Swahili.]

sitcom *sit'kom*, (*colloq*) *n* a *sit*uation *com*edy.

site *sīt*, *n* situation, esp. of a building; an area set aside for some specific purpose, activity, etc. — *vt* to locate, position. [L. *situs*, set — *sinĕre*.]

sitology *sī-tol'ə-ji* or **sitiology** *sit-i-ol'ə-ji*, *n* dietetics. — *n* **sitophō'bia** or **sitiophō'bia** morbid aversion to food. [Gr. *sītos*, dimin. *sītion*, grain, food.]

sitrep *sit'rep*, (*colloq*) *n* a report on the current military position (also *fig*). [*sit*uation *rep*ort.]

sitter, sitting, etc. See **sit**.

situate *sit'ū-āt*, *vt* to set, place, locate; to circumstance. — *adj* (*-ū-it*; *law*) situated. — *adj* **sit'uated** set, located; circumstanced. — *n* **situā'tion** location; place; position; momentary state; condition; a set of circumstances, a juncture; a critical point in the action of a play or the development of the plot of a novel; office, employment. — *adj* **situā'tional**. — **situation comedy** a comedy, now esp. in a television or radio series in which the same characters appear in each episode, which depends for its humour on the behaviour of the characters in particular, sometimes contrived, situations. [L.L. *situātus* — L. *situĕre*, to place.]

sit. vac. *sit vak*, *abbrev* for situation vacant: — *pl* **sits vac**.

sitz-bath *sits'-bäth*, *n* a therapeutic hip-bath in hot water. [Ger. *Sitzbad*.]

Siva *shē'və* or *sē'və*, *n* the third god of the Hindu triad, destroyer and reproducer. — *n* **Si'vaism**. — *n* **Shi'vaite**.

six *siks*, *n* the cardinal numeral next above five; a symbol representing it (6, vi, etc.); a set of that number; an article of size denoted by it; a card with six pips; a score of six points, tricks, etc.; the sixth hour after midnight or after midday; a division of a Brownie Guide or Cub Scout pack; the age of six years. — *adj* of the number six; six years old. — *n* **six'er** anything counting for six or indicated by six; the leader of a Brownie Guide or Cub Scout six. — *adj* and *adv* **six'fold** in six divisions; six times as much. — *adj* **sixth** last of six; next after the fifth; equal to one of six equal parts. — *n* a sixth part; a person or thing in sixth position; an interval of five (conventionally called six) diatonic degrees (*mus*); a combination of two tones that distance apart (*mus*). — *adv* **sixth'ly** in the sixth place. — *adj* **six'-day** of or for six days (i.e. usu. excluding Sunday). — *adj* **six'-foot** measuring six feet. — **six-foot'er** a person six feet tall; **sixth form** (the classes studying in) the (usu.) two years of preparation for A-level examinations or, in Scotland, higher level examinations and sixth-year studies; **six'-gun** a six-shooter; **six'-pack** a pack which comprises six items sold as one unit, esp. a pack of six cans of beer; **six'pence** a coin worth six old pence; its value. — *adj* **six'penny** costing or worth sixpence; cheap; worthless. — *n* and *adj* **six'score**. — **six'-shooter** a six-chambered revolver. — **at sixes and sevens** in disorder; **hit** or **knock for six** to overcome completely; to take by surprise; **six (of one) and half a dozen (of the other)** equal, attributable to both parties equally; having alternatives which are considered equivalent, equally acceptable, etc.; **sixth form college** a school which provides the sixth form education for the pupils of an area; **the Six Counties** Northern Ireland. [O.E. *siex*.]

sixain or **sixaine** *siks-ān'*, (*poetry*) *n* a stanza of six lines. [Fr.]

sixte *sikst*, (*fencing*) *n* a parry with hand on guard opposite the right breast, sword point a little raised to the right. [Fr.]

sixteen *siks-tēn'* or *siks'tēn*, *n* and *adj* six and ten. — *n* and *adj* **sixteen'mo** sextodecimo: — *pl* **sixteen'mos**. — *adj* **sixteenth'** (or *siks'*) last of sixteen; next after the fifteenth; equal to one of sixteen equal parts. — *n* a sixteenth part; a person or thing in sixteenth position. — *adv* **sixteenth'ly**. [O.E. *siextēne* (*-tīene*); see **six** and **ten**.]

sixty *siks'ti*, *adj* and *n* six times ten: — *pl* **six'ties** the numbers sixty to sixty-nine; the years so numbered in a life or century; a range of temperature from sixty to just less than seventy degrees. — *adj* **six'tieth** last of sixty; next after the fifty-ninth; equal to one of sixty equal parts. — *n* a sixtieth part; a person or thing in sixtieth position. — **sixty-four (thousand) dollar question** (from a U.S. quiz game) the final and most difficult question one has to answer, from the sixty-four (thousand) dollar top prize money awarded. [O.E. *siextig*.]

size[1] *sīz*, *n* bigness; magnitude; any of a series of graded measurements into which esp. clothes are divided. — *vt* to arrange according to size; to measure. — *adj* **sī'zable** or **size'able** of a fair size; quite large. — *n* **sī'zar** (also **sī'zer**) at Cambridge and Dublin, a student receiving an allowance from their college towards their expenses. — *n* **sī'zarship**. — *adj* (usu. in combination) **sized** having a particular size. — *n* **sī'zer** a measurer; a gauge; a thing of considerable or great size (*slang*). — *n* **sī'zing** sorting by size. — **of a size** of the same size; **size up** to take mental measure of (also *fig*); **the size of it**

(*colloq*) an accurate description of the present situation or state of affairs. [**assize.**]

size[2] *sīz*, *n* a weak glue or gluey material, used for stiffening paper and fabric and for preparing walls before plastering or wallpapering. — *vt* to cover or treat with size. — *adj* **sized.** — *n* **sī'zer.** — *n* **sī'ziness.** — *n* **sī'zing** application of size, or material for the purpose. — *adj* **sī'zy.**

sizzle *siz'l*, *vi* to make a hissing sound of frying; to be in a state of intense emotion, esp. anger or excitement (*colloq*). — *vt* and *vi* to fry, scorch, sear. — *n* a hissing sound; extreme heat. — *n* **sizz'ler** a sizzling heat or day; a thing strikingly fierce or effective. — *n* **sizz'ling** a hissing. — *adj* very hot; very striking. [Imit.]

SJ *abbrev* for Society of Jesus.

sjambok *sham'bok*, (*SAfr*) *n* a whip of dried hide. — *vt* to flog. [Afrik. — Malay *samboq* — Urdu *chābuk*.]

ska *skä*, *n* a form of Jamaican music similar to reggae.

skank *skangk*, *vi* to dance to reggae music, lifting the knees up with fast movements. — *n* such a dance, or a period of dancing in this way. — *n* **skank'ing.**

skat *skät*, *n* a three-handed card-game. [O.Fr. *escart*, laying aside.]

skate[1] *skāt*, *n* a sole or sandal mounted on a blade (for moving on ice); the blade itself; a boot with such a blade fixed to it; a roller-skate; a spell of skating. — *vi* to move on skates. — *n* **skā'ter.** — *n* **skā'ting.** — **skate'board** a narrow wooden, fibreglass, etc. board mounted on roller-skate wheels, on which one balances to ride; **skate'boarder; skate'boarding; skā'ting-rink.** — **get one's skates on** (*colloq*) to hurry; **skate on thin ice** see under **ice; skate over** (*fig*) to hurry over lightly; **skate round** (*fig*) to avoid discussing or answering. [Du. *schaats* — O.N.Fr. *escache*, stilt — L.G. *schake*, shank.]

skate[2] *skāt*, *n* a large edible kind of ray of tropical and temperate waters. [O.N. *skata*.]

skean. See **skene.**

skedaddle *ski-dad'l*, (*colloq*) *vi* to scamper off. — *n* a scurrying off.

skeet *skēt*, *n* a form of clay-pigeon shooting. [O.N. *skōta*, to shoot.]

skeeter *skēt'ər*, (*US*) *n* a colloq. short form of **mosquito.**

skeg *skeg*, (*naut*) *n* a brace between keel and rudder; a projection from, or in place of, a keel; a stabilising fin projecting from the underside of a surfboard. [Du. *scheg*.]

skein *skān*, *n* a loosely tied coil or standard length of thread or yarn; a tangle; a web; a loose or confused bundle of things; a tangle (also *fig*); a flock of wild geese in flight. [O.Fr. *escaigne*.]

skeleton *skel'i-tn*, *n* the internal or external framework of bones of a person or an animal; the veins of a leaf; a framework or outline of anything; a scheme reduced to its essential or indispensable elements; a workforce, etc. reduced to its lowest strength; an emaciated person or animal (*colloq*). — Also *adj*. — *adj* **skel'etal.** — *vt* **skel'etonise** or **-ize** to reduce to a skeleton. — **skeleton key** a key with its serrated edge or the shaped part of its bit filed down, so that it can open many locks. — **skeleton in the cupboard, closet, house,** etc. a hidden domestic sorrow or shame. [Gr. *skeleton* (*sōma*), dried (body) — *skellein*, to dry.]

skelp *skelp*, (*Scot*) *vt* to slap. — *vi* to move briskly along; to bound along. — *n* a slap. — *adj* **skelp'ing** very big or full; smacking; lusty. — *n* a smacking. [Gael. *sgealp*, a slap with the palm of the hand.]

skelter *skel'tər*, *vi* to scurry. — *n* a scurry.

skene *skēn* or **skean** *skē'ən*, *n* an Irish or Highland dagger, knife or short sword. — **skene-dhu** or **skean-dhu** (*-do͞o'*) a dirk, a dagger stuck in the stocking (q.v.) in full Highland dress. [Ir. and Gael. *sgian*, knife, *dhu*, black.]

skep *skep*, *n* a basket; a beehive. — *vt* to collect into a hive: — *pr p* **skepp'ing;** *pa t* and *pa p* **skepped.** — *n* **skep'ful.** [O.N. *skeppa*.]

skerrick *sker'ik*, (*dialect*; esp. *US*, *Austr* and *NZ*) *n* (chiefly with *negative*) a minute quantity, a scrap.

skerry *sker'i*, *n* a reef of rock. [O.N. *sker*.]

sketch *skech*, *n* a drawing, slight, rough or without detail, esp. as a study towards a more finished work; an outline or short account; a short and slightly constructed play, dramatic scene, musical entertainment, etc.; a short descriptive essay. — *vt* to make or give a sketch of; to outline, or give the principal points of. — *vi* to practise sketching. — *n* **sketchabil'ity.** — *adj* **sketch'able** worth sketching. — *n* **sketch'er.** — *adv* **sketch'ily.** — *n* **sketch'iness.** — *adj* **sketch'y** like a sketch; incomplete, slight; imperfect, inadequate. — **sketch'book** a book of or for sketches (in drawing, literature or music). [Du. *schets*, prob. — It. *schizzo* — L. *schedium*, an extempore — Gr. *schedios*, offhand.]

skeuomorph *skū'ə-mörf*, *n* a decoration or decorative feature in architecture, etc., derived from the nature of the material (originally) used, or the way of working it; a retained but no longer either functional or incidental characteristic of an artefact, e.g. the 'casting seams' cut on to a flint knife, imitated from those on a cast bronze knife (*archaeol*); (or modernly) the imitation stitching on plastic upholstery. — *adj* **skeuomorph'ic.** — *n* **skeuomorph'ism.** [Gr. *skeuos*, vessel, tool, *morphe*, shape.]

skew *skū*, *adj* oblique; (of statistics or a curve representing them) not symmetrical about the mean. — *adv* awry. — *n* obliquity. — *vt* and *vi* to set, go, or look obliquely. — *adj* **skewed** distorted; skew. — *n* **skew'ness.** — *adj* and *adv* **skew-whiff'** (*colloq*) crooked, awry. [App. O.N.Fr. *eskiu(w)er* — O.Fr. *eschuer*; see **eschew;** or M.Du. *schuwe*, to shun.]

skewbald *skū'böld*, *adj* (of an animal, esp. a horse) marked in white and another colour (not black). — *n* a skewbald horse.

skewer *skū'ər*, *n* a long pin of wood or metal, esp. for holding pieces of meat together for cooking. — *vt* to fasten or pierce with a skewer; to transfix. [Dialect *skiver*.]

ski *skē*, *n* a long narrow runner orig. of wood, now also of metal, etc., fastened to the foot to enable the wearer to slide across snow, etc.: — *pl* **skis** or **ski.** — *vi* to travel on skis: — *pr p* **ski'ing;** *pa t* and *pa p* **skied** or **ski'd.** — *adj* **ski'able** (of a surface) in condition for skiing on. — *n* **ski'er.** — *n* **ski'ing.** — **ski'-bob** a vehicle used for gliding down snow-slopes, consisting of a short front-pivoting ski, turned by handlebars, and a longer fixed rear ski with a seat attached. — Also *vi*. — **ski'-bobbing; ski'-flying** ski-jumping from a high take-off point, so that a longer time is spent in the air; **ski-joring** (*-jör'*) the sport of being towed on skis by a horse or motor vehicle; **ski'-jumping; ski'-lift** and **ski'-tow** devices for taking skiers uphill; **ski pants** trousers made of stretch material, worn for skiing or leisure, kept taut by a band under the foot; **ski'-run** a slope for skiing on; **ski'-slope; ski'-stick** one of a pair of sticks, usu. pointed with a disc near the tip, used by skiers for balance or propulsion. [Norw., — O.N. *skīth*, snow-shoe, piece of split wood.]

skia- *skī-ə-* or *skī-a'-*, or **scia-** *sī-ə-* or *sī-a'-*, *combining form* denoting shadow. — *n* **ski'agram** or **ski'agraph** an X-ray photograph. — *n* **skiamachy** (*-am'ə-ki*; Gr. *machē*, a fight) a sham fight; a fight with shadows. — *n* **skias'copy** retinoscopy. — *n* **ski'atron** a cathode-ray tube in which an electron beam varies the transparency of a phosphor, which is illuminated from behind so that its image is projected on to a screen. [Gr. *skiā*, a shadow.]

skid *skid*, *vi* to slide along without revolving; to slip, esp. sideways. — *vt* to check with a skid; to make to skid: — *pr p* **skidd'ing;** *pa t* and *pa p* **skidd'ed.** — *n* a side-slip; a skidding; a support on which something rests, is brought to the desired level, or slides; an aeroplane runner; a ship's wooden fender; a shoe or other device to check a wheel on a down-slope. — **skid'-lid** (*slang*) a crash helmet; **skid pan** or **pad** a piece of slippery ground on which motorists can learn to control a skidding car; **skid row** or **road** (esp. *US*) a squalid quarter where vagrants, chronic drunks, etc. live. — **put the skids on** or **under** (*slang*) to cause to hurry; to put a stop to, thwart; **the skids** (*fig*; *colloq*) a downward path. [Prob. rel. to **ski**.]

Ski-doo® or **skidoo** *ski-dōō'*, *n* a motorised sledge, fitted with endless tracks at the rear and steerable skis at the front.

skier[1]. See **ski**.

skier[2] and **skiey**. See under **sky**.

skiff *skif*, *n* a small light boat. [Rel. to **ship**.]

skiffle *skif'l*, *n* a strongly accented jazz type of folk-music played with guitars, drums, and often unconventional instruments, etc., popular about 1957.

ski-joring. See under **ski**.

skill *skil*, *n* expertness; a craft or accomplishment; (in *pl*) aptitudes and competencies appropriate for a particular job. — *adj* **skil'ful**. — *adv* **skil'fully**. — *n* **skil'fulness**. — *adj* **skilled** expert; skilful; (of a job) requiring special training. — *adj* **skill'-less** or **skil'less**. [O.N. *skil*, distinction, *skilja*, to separate.]

skillet *skil'it*, *n* a small, long-handled pan; a frying-pan (esp. *NAm*).

skilly *skil'i*, *n* thin gruel.

skim *skim*, *vt* to remove floating matter from the surface of; to take off by skimming (often with *off*; also *fig*); to glide lightly over; to read superficially and skippingly. — *vi* to pass over lightly; to glide along near the surface; to become coated over: — *pr p* **skimm'ing**; *pa t* and *pa p* **skimmed**. — *n* the act of skimming; skim-milk. — *n* **skimm'er** someone who or that which skims; a utensil for skimming milk; an apparatus for clearing a water-surface of debris, e.g. in a swimming-pool; a seabird that skims the water. — *n* **skimm'ing**. — *adv* **skimm'ingly**. — **skim'-milk** or **skimmed milk** milk from which the cream has been skimmed. [App. rel. to **scum**.]

skimmia *skim'i-ə*, *n* any Asiatic shrub of the genus *Skimmia*, cultivated for its holly-like leaves and drupes. [Jap. *shikimi*.]

skimp *skimp*, *vt* and *vi* to scrimp; to stint. — *adj* scanty, spare. — *adv* **skimp'ily**. — *adj* **skimp'ing**. — *adv* **skimp'ingly**. — *adj* **skimp'y** (of clothes) made with too little material, not covering much of the body; tending to skimp. [Poss. **scamp[2]** combined with **scrimp**.]

skin *skin*, *n* the natural outer covering of tissue of a person or an animal; a hide; a thin outer layer or covering; an integument; a membrane; a wine vessel made of an animal's skin; a drum (*slang*); short for **skinhead** (q.v. below) (*slang*). — *adj* of skin. — *vt* to cover with a skin; to strip the skin from; to swindle or fleece. — *vi* to become covered with skin; to slip through or away: — *pr p* **skinn'ing**; *pa t* and *pa p* **skinned**. — *n* **skin'ful** as much liquor as one can hold. — *adj* **skin'less**. — *adj* **skinned** (usu. in combination). — *n* **skinn'er** a person who prepares hides. — *n* **skinn'iness**. — *adj* **skinn'y** of or like skin; too thin; (of a pullover, etc.) tight-fitting (*colloq*). — *adj* **skin-deep'** superficial; shallow, not deeply fixed. — **skin'-diver** a person involved in skin-diving; orig., a naked pearl-diver; **skin'-diving** diving and swimming under water, with simple equipment, not wearing the traditional diver's helmet and suit, and not connected with a boat; **skin'flick** (*slang*) a film in which some of the characters appear in the nude and which usu. includes scenes of sexual intercourse; **skin'flint** a very niggardly person; **skin'food** a cosmetic intended to nourish the skin; **skin'-game** a swindling trick; **skin'head** a member of certain gangs of young people wearing simple, severe clothes, and having closely cropped hair. — *vi* **skinn'y-dip** (esp. *NAm*) to bathe naked. — **skinn'y-dipper**; **skinn'y-dipping**. — *vi* **skin'-pop** (*slang*) to inject drugs. — **skin'-popping**; **skin test** a test made by applying a substance to, or introducing a substance beneath, a person's skin, to test for an allergy, immunity from a disease, etc. — *adj* **skin'-tight** fitting close to the skin. — *n* (in *pl*) tights. — **by** or **with the skin of one's teeth** very narrowly; **get under someone's skin** to annoy someone; to interest someone seriously; **no skin off one's nose** (*colloq*) a matter about which one feels unconcerned or indifferent because it does not harm or inconvenience one, or because it may be to one's benefit; **save one's skin** to save one's life. [O.N. *skinn*.]

skink *skingk*, *n* a lizard of Asia and Africa with an elongated body. [L. *scincus* — Gr. *skinkos*.]

skinny. See **skin**.

skint *skint*, (*slang*) *adj* without money, hard up. [**skinned**.]

skip[1] *skip*, *vi* to progress by hopping on each foot alternately; to spring or hop lightly; to make jumps over a twirling rope; to pass discontinuously. — *vt* to overleap; to omit; to cut, not go to (e.g. a class): — *pr p* **skipp'ing**; *pa t* and *pa p* **skipped**. — *n* an act of skipping; a belt of inaudibility in wireless transmission; a college servant in some older universities. — *n* **skipp'er** a person who skips; a hairy-bodied butterfly of the family *Hesperiidae*, with short jerky flight; the saury. — *adj* **skipp'ing**. — *n* the art or activity of jumping over a twirling rope. — *adv* **skipp'ingly**. — **skip'jack** any of a number of species of fish that jump out of, or swim at the surface of, the water, such as the bonitos, the bluefish, the saurel, and either of two species of tuna (the **skipjack tuna** and the **black skipjack**); **skipp'ing-rope** a rope for skipping with; **skip zone** an area round a broadcasting station where transmissions cannot be received. — **skip it!** (*colloq*) never mind, forget it! [Cf. O.N. *skopa*, to run.]

skip[2] *skip*, *n* a box or truck for raising minerals from a mine; a large container for transporting building materials, etc., theatrical costumes or refuse. [**skep**.]

skip[3] *skip*, *n* the captain of a rink in bowls or curling. — *vt* and *vi* to act as a skip. [**skipper**.]

skipper[1] *skip'ər*, *n* a ship's captain; the captain of an aeroplane; the captain of a team. — *vt* to act as skipper of. — **skipper's daughters** white-topped waves. [Du. *schipper*.]

skipper[2]. See **skip[1]**.

skippet *skip'it*, *n* a flat box for protecting a seal (as of a document).

skirl *skirl* or *skûrl*, (*Scot*) *vt* and *vi* to shriek or sing shrilly. — *vi* to make the sound of the bagpipes. [Scand.]

skirmish *skûr'mish*, *n* any minor irregular fight between small or marginal parties. — *vi* to fight slightly or irregularly. — *n* **skir'misher**. — *n* **skir'mishing**. [O.Fr. *escarmouche*.]

skirret *skir'it*, *n* a water-parsnip with edible roots. [M.E. *skirwhit*, as if *skire white*, pure white, but perh. altered from O.Fr. *eschervis*.]

skirt *skûrt*, *n* a garment, or part of a garment, generally a woman's, that hangs from the waist; the lower part of a gown, coat or other garment, or anything suggesting this; a saddle-flap; a midriff (of meat); a rim, border or margin; a part of, or attachment to, an object that suggests a skirt, e.g. the flap of material hanging down around the base of a hovercraft to contain the air-cushion, or a similar flap around a racing-car; a woman (*slang*; also **bit of skirt**). — *vt* to border; to pass along the edge of; to scour the outskirts of. — *vi* to be on or pass along the border (usu. with *along*, *around*, etc.). — *adj* **skirt'ed** wearing or having a skirt. — *n* **skir'ting** material for skirts; skirting-board; (in *pl*) dirty wool from the skirts of a fleece. — Also *adj*. — *adj* **skirt'less**. —

skir'ting-board the narrow board next to the floor round the walls of a room. — **divided skirt** trousers made to look like a skirt. [O.N. *skyrta*, a shirt, kirtle; cf. **shirt**.]

skit *skit*, *n* a piece of satire or burlesque, esp. in dramatic or literary form. [Perh. rel. to O.N. *skjōta*, to shoot.]

skitter *skit'ər*, *vi* to skim over the surface of water; to fish by drawing the bait over the surface; to scamper lightly. [**skit**.]

skittish *skit'ish*, *adj* unsteady; light-headed; frivolous; frisky; lively; changeable; wanton. — *adv* **skitt'ishly**. — *n* **skitt'ishness**. [Perh. conn. with **skit**.]

skittle *skit'l*, *n* a pin for the game of **skittles**, a form of ninepins in which a ball or cheese (see **cheese**[1]) is used. — *vt* to knock down. — **skitt'le-alley**, **-ball** and **-ground**. — **beer and skittles** see under **beer**. [Prob. alteration of *kail* (see ety. for **squail**), through intermediate *kittle*.]

skive[1] *skīv*, *vt* to pare or split (leather). — *n* **skī'ver** split sheepskin leather; a person or machine that skives. — *n* **skī'ving**. [O.N. *skīfa*.]

skive[2] *skīv*, (*colloq*) *vt* and *vi* (often with *off*) to evade (a duty, work, etc.). — Also *n*. — *n* **skī'ver**. — *adj* **skī'vy**.

skivvy[1] *skiv'i*, *n* (*colloq*) a disrespectful word for a maidservant.

skivvy[2] *skiv'i*, *n* a man's undervest (esp. *US slang*); a knitted cotton polo-necked sweater (*Austr* and *NZ*).

skoal *skōl* or **skol** *skol*, *interj* hail!; a friendly exclamation in salutation before drinking, etc. [O.N. *skāl*; Norw. *skaal*, a bowl, Sw. *skå*.]

skokiaan *skö'ki-än*, (*SAfr*) *n* a strong home-brewed drink made from yeast. [Afrik.]

skol. See **skoal**.

skolly or **skollie** *skol'i*, (*SAfr derog*) *n* a Coloured hooligan, esp. a member of a gang. [*Afrik.*, prob. from Du. *schoelje*, rascal.]

skoosh *skōōsh*, (*Scot*) *vt* and *vi* to squirt, spurt. — *n* a squirt or spurt. [Imit.]

skrimshank or **scrimshank** *skrim'shangk*, (*mil slang*) *vi* to evade work or duty. — *n* evasion of work. — *n* **skrim'shanker**.

skua *skū'ə*, *n* any of several large predatory gull-like birds. [O.N. *skūfr*.]

skulduggery or in N.Am. **skullduggery** *skul-dug'ə-ri*, *n* underhand malpractices; trickery. [Perh. Scot. *sculduddery*, unchastity.]

skulk *skulk*, *vi* to sneak out of the way; to lurk; to malinger. — *n* **skulk** or **skulk'er** a person who skulks. — *n* and *adj* **skulk'ing**. — *adv* **skulk'ingly**. [Scand., as Dan. *skulke*.]

skull[1] *skul*, *n* the bony case that encloses the brain; a skullcap, esp. of metal; a crust of solidified metal on a ladle, etc. — **skull'cap** a close-fitting cap; a protective cap of metal for the top of the head; the top of the skull; any plant of the genus *Scutellaria*, with helmet-shaped flowers. — **skull and cross-bones** see **crossbones** under **cross**. [M.E. *scolle*.]

skull[2]. See **scull**[2].

skulpin. Same as **sculpin**.

skunk *skungk*, *n* a small American animal of the *Mustelidae* that emits an offensive fluid; its fur; a despised person. [Algonkian *segonku*.]

sky *skī*, *n* the apparent canopy over our heads; the heavens; the weather; the upper rows of pictures in a gallery; sky-blue: — *pl* **skies**. — *vt* to raise aloft; to hit high into the air. — *n* **sky'er** or **skī'er** (*cricket*) a hit high into the air. — *adj* **sky'ey** or **skī'ey** of the weather; of or like the sky. — *adj* and *adv* **sky'ward**. — *adv* **sky'wards**. — *n* and *adj* **sky-blue'** light blue like the sky. — *adj* **sky'-coloured**. — **sky'-diver**; **sky'-diving** or **-jumping** jumping by parachute as a sport, using a special steerable parachute, and delaying opening it for a specified time. — *adj* **sky-high'** very high. — Also *adv*. — *vt* **sky'jack** (*colloq*) to hijack (an aeroplane). — **sky'jacker**; **sky'-jacking**; **sky'lab** an orbiting experimental space-station, *specif* (with *cap*) that launched and manned by the U.S., 1973–74; **sky'lark** the common lark. — *vi* to frolic boisterously. — *vt* to trick. — **sky'larking** running about the rigging of a ship in sport; frolicking; **sky'light** a window in a roof or ceiling; **sky'line** the horizon; a silhouette or outline against the sky; **sky marshal** an armed plain-clothes officer on an air-flight, having the job of protecting passengers and dealing with hijacking attempts; **sky'rocket** a firework that bursts high in the sky. — *vi* to shoot up high; to rise high and fast. — **skysail** (*skī'sl*) a sail above the royal; **sky'scape** a view or a picture of the sky; **sky'scrāper** a very lofty building; a triangular skysail; anything very high; **sky'way** a route for aircraft; **sky'-writing** tracing of words by smoke from an aircraft. — **the sky's the limit** (*colloq*) there are no restrictions on amount or extent (of something); **to the skies** (*colloq*) in a lavish or enthusiastic manner. [O.N. *ský*, cloud.]

Skye *skī*, *n* (in full, **Skye terrier**) a small long-haired Scotch terrier. [From the island of *Skye*.]

SL *abbrev* for: Sergeant-at-Law; Solicitor at Law.

slab *slab*, *n* a plane-sided plate; a large thick slice of cake, etc.; an outer plank sawn from a log; a thin flat piece of stone, etc. — *vt* to cut slabs from; to form into slabs; to cover with slabs. — *adj* **slabbed**. — *adj* **slab'stone** flagstone.

slack[1] *slak*, *adj* lax or loose; not firmly extended or drawn out; not holding fast; remiss; not strict; not eager or diligent, inattentive; not busy; not violent or rapid, slow. — *adv* in a slack manner; partially; insufficiently. — *n* the slack part of a rope, belt, etc.; a time, occasion, or place of relaxed movement or activity; a slack-water haul of a net; (in *pl*) long, loose trousers for casual wear. — *vi* **slack** or **slack'en** to become loose or less tight; to be remiss; to abate; to become slower; to fail or flag; to be inactive or lax. — *vt* to make slack or less tight; to loosen; to slow, retard; to be remiss or dilatory in; to relax; to slake. — *n* and *adj* **slack'ening**. — *n* **slack'er** an idler; a person who is reprehensibly inactive; a shirker. — *adv* **slack'ly**. — *n* **slack'ness**. — *adj* **slack-hand'ed** remiss. — **slack water** turn of the tide; a stretch of still or slow-moving water. — *adj* pertaining to slack water. — **slack off** or **slacken off** to ease off; **slack up** or **slacken up** to ease off; to slow. [O.E. *slæc*.]

slack[2] *slak*, *n* coal-dross. [Cf. Ger. *Schlacke*.]

slag[1] *slag*, *n* solid scum on melted metal; vitrified cinders; scoriaceous lava; coal-mining waste. — *vt* and *vi* to form into slag: — *pr p* **slagg'ing**; *pa p* and *pa p* **slagged**. — *adj* **slagg'y**. — **slag'-heap** a small hill of coal-mining waste; **slag'-wool** fibre made from molten slag; mineral wool. [M.L.G. *slagge*.]

slag[2] *slag*, (*slang*) *n* a slovenly or dissolute woman (or, more recently, man). [**slag**[1].]

slag[3] *slag*, (*slang*) *vt* to criticise, mock, deride (esp. with *off*). [**slag**[1].]

slag[4] *slag*, (*Austr slang*) *n* spit. — *vi* to spit. [Prob. **slag**[1].]

slain *slān*, *pa p* of **slay**.

slàinte *slän'chə*, (Gael.) *interj* good health!

slake *slāk*, *vt* to quench; to extinguish; to refresh with moisture; to abate, mitigate, allay, reduce, moderate (*poetic*); to hydrate (as lime). — *adj* **slake'less** that cannot be slaked. [O.E. *slacian*, *sleacian*, to grow slack — *slæc*, *sleac*, slack.]

slalom *slä'ləm*, *n* a race in which tactical skill is required, esp. a downhill or zigzag ski-run among posts or trees or an obstacle race in canoes. — *vi* and *vt* (*fig*) to move in a zigzag course. [Norw.]

slam[1] *slam*, *vt* or *vi* to shut or strike with violence and noise; to bang; to censure, criticise (*colloq*): — *pr p* **slamm'ing**; *pa t* and *pa p* **slammed**. — *n* the act or sound of slamming; a harsh criticism (*colloq*). — *adv* with a slam (also *fig*). — *n* **slamm'er** (*slang*) prison. [Cf. Norw. *slemma*.]

slam[2] *slam*, *n* (in whist) the winning of every trick; (in bridge) the winning of every trick (*grand slam*) or of all but one (*small* or *little slam*). — *vt* to inflict a slam upon.

slander *slän'* or *slan'dər*, *n* a false or malicious report; injurious defamation by spoken words or by looks, signs, or gestures (distinct from *libel*); calumny. — *vt* to defame; to calumniate. — *n* **slan'derer**. — *adj* **slan'derous**. — *adv* **slan'derously**. — *n* **slan'derousness**. [O.Fr. *esclandre* — L. *scandalum* — Gr. *skandalon*, snare, scandal.]

slang *slang*, *n* orig. a jargon of thieves and disreputable people; the jargon of any class, profession or set; words and usages not accepted for dignified use. — Also *adj*. — *vt* to scold, vituperate. — *n* **slang'iness**. — *n* **slang'ing** a scolding. — Also *adj*. — *adj* **slang'y**. — **slanging match** a bitter verbal quarrel, usu. involving an exchange of insults. [Of cant origin.]

slangy. See **slang**.

slant *slänt* or *slant*, *vt* and *vi* to slope; to turn, strike, fall, obliquely; to be biased. — *vt* to bias in a certain direction in presentation. — *n* a slope; obliquity; a sloping surface, line, ray, or movement; a divergence from a direct line; a jibe; a point of view, way of looking at a thing; bias. — *adj* sloping; oblique; inclined from a direct line. — *adj* **slant'ed** biased, prejudiced. — *adj* **slant'ing**. — *adv* **slan'tingly**, **slant'ways** or **slant'wise**. — *adj* **slant-eyed'** having slanting eyes, esp. (*offensive*) S.E. Asian. [M.E. *slent*.]

slap *slap*, *n* a blow with the hand or anything flat; the sound made by this; a snub, rebuke; stage make-up (*theat*). — *vt* to give a slap to; to bring or send with a slap; to rebuke (also with *down*); to apply without much care or attention (usu. with *on*): — *pr p* **slapp'ing**; *pa t* and *pa p* **slapped**. — *adv* with a slap; suddenly, violently; directly, straight. — *adv* **slap=bang'** violently, all at once; directly, straight. — *adj* dashing, violent. — *adv* **slap'dash** in a hasty, careless way. — *adj* hastily and carelessly done. — *n* roughcast; careless work. — *vt* to do in a hasty, imperfect manner; to roughcast. — *adj* **slap-happy'** (*colloq*) recklessly or boisterously happy; slap-dash, happy-go-lucky; punch-drunk. — *n* a card game in which players try to win the pack by being the first to slap a hand over the jack, as it is turned over on top of the pile; **slap'stick** (also **slapstick comedy**) knockabout low comedy or farce. — *adj* **slap'-up** (*colloq*) first class. — **slap and tickle** (*colloq*) amorous play between humans, with kissing, petting, etc.; **slap in the face** (*colloq*; *fig*) a sharp insult or rebuff; **slap on the back** (*colloq*) a mark of congratulations; **slap on the wrist** (*colloq*) a mild reprimand. [Allied to L.G. *slapp*, Ger. *Schlappe*; imit.]

slash[1] *slash*, *vt* to cut by striking with violence and often at random; to make long cuts in; to slit so as to show lining or material underneath; to cut down, reduce drastically or suddenly (*colloq*). — *vi* to strike violently and at random with a cutting or sharp instrument. — *n* a long cut; a slant or solidus (/); a cut in cloth designed to show colours or material underneath. — *adj* **slashed** cut with slashes; drastically or suddenly reduced (*colloq*). — *n* **slash'er** a person or thing that slashes. — *n* **slash'ing** a slash or slashes. — *adj* cutting mercilessly, unsparing. — **slash-and-burn'** a method of agriculture involving the cutting down and burning of trees, undergrowth, etc. before planting.

slash[2] *slash*, (*US*) *n* a low-lying, swampy area.

slash[3] *slash*, (*vulg slang*) *vi* to urinate. — *n* an act of urinating. [Cf. Scot. *slash*, a large splash.]

slat *slat*, *n* a thin strip of wood, etc. — *adj* **slatt'ed** having, or composed of, slats. [O.Fr. *esclat*.]

slate[1] *slāt*, *n* a fine-grained rock usu. a dull blue, grey, purple, or green, easily split into thin layers; a slab of this material (or a substitute) for roofing, or for writing on with chalk; a preliminary list (e.g. of political candidates); slate-colour. — *adj* made of slate; slate-coloured, esp. dull dark blue. — *vt* to cover with slate; to enter on a list. — *adj* **slat'ed** covered with slates. — *n* **slat'er** a person who covers roofs with slates. — *n* **slat'iness**. — *n* **slat'ing** covering with slates; a covering of slates; materials for slating. — *adj* **slat'y**. — *adj* **slate'-coloured** dark greenish or bluish grey. — *adj* **slate-gray'** or **-grey'**. — **a clean slate** see under **clean**; **have a slate loose** (*slang*) to be mentally deranged; **on the slate** (*colloq*) on credit; **wipe the slate clean** to allow a person to make a fresh start (in a job, relationship, etc.) by ignoring past mistakes, crimes, etc. [O.Fr. *esclate*; cf. **slat**.]

slate[2] *slāt*, *vt* to abuse; to review or comment on very unfavourably; to reprimand. — *n* **slā'ting**. [From the O.N. word answering to O.E. *slǣtan*, to bait.]

slattern *slat'ərn*, *n* a slut, a dirty untidy woman. — *n* **slatt'ernliness**. — *adj* **slatt'ernly** sluttish. — Also *adv*.

slaughter *slö'tər*, *n* killing of animals, esp. for food; killing of great numbers (of animals, people, etc.); wanton or inexcusable killing, esp. of the helpless; carnage. — *vt* to kill in any of these ways. — *adj* **slaugh'terable** fit or due for slaughter. — *n* **slaugh'terer**. — *adj* **slaugh'terous** inclined to slaughter, murderous; destructive. — *adv* **slaugh'terously**. — **slaugh'terhouse** a place where animals are killed for the market; **slaugh'terman** a man employed in killing or butchering animals. [O.N. *slātr*, butchers' meat, whence *slātra*, to slaughter (cattle).]

Slav *släv*, *n* a person whose language is Slavonic, i.e. belongs to that division of the Indo-European languages that includes Russian, Polish, Wendish, Czech, Slovak, Serbian, Slovenian and Bulgarian. — *adj* **Slav** or **Slav'ic**. — *n* **Sla'vism** a Slavonic idiom; enthusiasm for Slavic ways or culture; anything characteristic of the Slavs. — *adj* **Slavonic** (*-von'ik*) of the group of languages indicated above, or the peoples speaking them. — *n* the forerunner of the group of languages indicated above, or the umbrella term for the group. [Med. L. *Sclavus* — Late Gr. *Sklabos*, from the stem of Slav *slovo*, word, *sloviti*, to speak; cf. **Slovene**.]

slave *slāv*, *n* a person kept as property; a person who is submissive under domination; a person who is submissively devoted to another; a person whose will has lost power of resistance, esp. to an influence, drug, etc.; a person who works like a slave, a drudge; a mechanism controlled by another mechanism, e.g. in computing, by the central processor, or by remote control, etc. — Also *adj*. — *vi* to work like or as a slave. — *n* **slāv'er** a slave-trader; a ship employed in the slave-trade. — *n* **slāv'ery** the state of being a slave or enslaved; the institution of ownership of slaves; drudgery. — *adj* **slāv'ish** of or belonging to slaves; befitting a slave; servile; servilely following or conforming (e.g. to fashion). — *adv* **slāv'ishly**. — *n* **slāv'ishness**. — **slave'-driver** a person who superintends slaves at their work; a hard taskmaster (*fig*); **slave'-holder** an owner of slaves; **slave labour** (the work of) people employed as slaves (*lit* or *fig*); **slave'-ship** a ship used for transporting slaves; **slave states** those states of the American Union which maintained domestic slavery before the Civil War; **slave'-trade** or **slave'-traffic** the buying and selling of slaves; **slave'-trader** or **slave'-trafficker**. [O.Fr. (Fr.) *esclave*, orig. a Slav.]

slaver[1] *slav'ər*, *n* spittle running from the mouth. — *vi* to let spittle run out of the mouth, esp. in anticipation of food; to drivel; to fawn over (a person), esp. with lust. — *n* **slav'erer.** — *adj* **slav'ering.** — *adv* **slav'eringly.** — *adj* **slav'ery.**

slaver[2]. See **slave.**

Slavic, Slavonic. See **Slav.**

slaw *slö*, *n* cabbage salad, coleslaw. [Du. *sla* — *salade*.]

slay *slā*, (*literary* or *archaic*) *vt* and *vi* to kill: — *pa t* **slew** (*sloo*); *pa p* **slain** (*slān*). — *vt* (*slang*) to amuse very much; to impress very much: — *pa t* **slayed,** sometimes **slew**; *pa p* **slayed.** — *n* **slay'er.** [O.E. *slēan*, to strike, to kill.]

sld *abbrev* for sailed.

sleazy *slē'zi*, *adj* squalid, esp. in a sexual way. — *n* **sleaze** (*colloq back-formation*) sleaziness. — *adv* **sleaz'ily.** — *n* **slea'ziness.**

sled *sled*, *n* a sledge, esp. a small one; a wheelless structure for conveying goods, esp. on snow. — *vt* to convey by sled. — *vi* to go on a sled: — *pr p* **sledd'ing**; *pa t* and *pa p* **sledd'ed.** — *n* **sledd'ing.** [M.Du. or M.L.G. *sledde*; cf. **sledge**[1], **sleigh, slide.**]

sledge[1] *slej*, *n* a conveyance with runners for sliding on snow; a framework without wheels for dragging goods along; an iron- or flint-studded board for threshing corn (*hist*). — *vt* and *vi* to convey, or travel, by sledge. — *n* **sledg'er.** — *n* **sledg'ing.** [M.Du. *sleedse*; cf. **sled.**]

sledge[2] *slej*, *n* a sledgehammer. — *n* **sledg'ing** (*cricket slang*, esp. *Austr*) the practice of baiting a batsman in order to spoil his concentration. — **sledge'hammer** a large heavy hammer wielded in both hands. [O.E. *slecg* — *slēan*, to strike, kill.]

sleek *slēk*, *adj* pleasingly smooth; glossy; having an oily, plastered-down look; insinuating, slick in manner; prosperous in appearance. — *vt* to make smooth or glossy. — *adv* smoothly, oilily. — *vt* **sleek'en** to make sleek. — *n* **sleek'er.** — *n* **sleek'ing.** — *adv* **sleek'ly.** — *n* **sleek'ness.** [A later form of **slick.**]

sleep *slēp*, *vi* to take rest by surrendering consciousness; to slumber; to be motionless, inactive, or dormant; to appear still or restful; to be dead (*euph*); to rest in the grave (*euph*); (of muscles) to go or be numb through inactivity. — *vt* to spend (time) in sleep; to outsleep; to provide, contain sleeping accommodation for: — *pa t* and *pa p* **slept** (*slept*). — *n* the state of being asleep; a period of sleeping; dormancy; death (*euph*); mucous matter which collects at the corners of the eyes (*colloq*). — *n* **sleep'er** a person who sleeps; a horizontal beam supporting and spreading a weight, esp. a support for railway rails; a sleeping-car; a compartment or berth in a sleeping-car; a Communist (or other) agent who spends a long time (often years) establishing himself as an inoffensive citizen preparing for the moment when he will be required to pass on information, spy for a foreign power, etc.; a record, film, etc. which becomes popular after an initial period of not being so (*colloq*). — *adv* **sleep'ily.** — *n* **sleep'iness.** — *n* **sleep'ing.** — *adj* in a state of, occupied with, or for, sleeping; dormant. — *adj* **sleep'less** without sleep; unable to sleep. — *adv* **sleep'lessly.** — *n* **sleep'lessness.** — *adj* **sleep'y** inclined to sleep, drowsy; inducing or suggesting sleep. — **sleep'ing-bag** a quilted bag for sleeping in, used by travellers, campers, etc.; **sleep'ing-car, -carriage** or **-coach** a railway carriage with berths for sleeping in; **sleep'ing-draught** a medicated drink to induce sleep; **sleeping partner** a person who has money invested in a business but takes no part in its management; **sleep'ing-pill** one containing a sleep-inducing drug; **sleeping policeman** a low hump across a road intended to slow down traffic (*colloq*); **sleeping sickness** a deadly disease of tropical Africa, characterised by headache, great drowsiness, and exhaustion, caused by a parasite introduced by the bite of a tsetse-fly; sometimes erroneously applied to sleepy-sickness; **sleep'-out** (*Austr* and *NZ*) a partitioned-off section of a veranda for use as a sleeping area; **sleep'walker** a person who walks in their sleep; **sleep'walking; sleep'y-head** a lazy or sleepy-looking person; **sleep'y-sickness** a form of encephalitis, a feature of which is great drowsiness; formerly applied to sleeping sickness. — **get to sleep** to manage to fall asleep; **go to sleep** to fall asleep; (of the muscles of a limb) to become numb; **in one's sleep** while asleep; **put to sleep** to anaesthetise; to kill (an animal) painlessly (*euph*); **sleep around** to be sexually promiscuous; **sleep in** to oversleep, wake or get up later than intended; to sleep later than usual; **sleep off** to recover from by sleeping; **sleep on** to consider overnight, postpone a decision on; **sleep together** to have sexual relations with each other; **sleep with** to have sexual relations with. [O.E. *slǣpan* (verb), *slǣp* (noun).]

sleet *slēt*, *n* rain mingled with snow or hail; a coating of ice formed when rain or sleet freezes on a cold surface (*US*). — *vi* to hail or snow simultaneously with rain. — *n* **sleet'iness.** — *adj* **sleet'y.**

sleeve *slēv*, *n* the part of a garment covering the arm; a tube into which a rod or other tube is inserted; a tube, esp. of a different metal, fitted inside a metal cylinder or tube, as protection or to decrease the diameter (*eng*); a thin, paper and cardboard container for a gramophone record; a wind-sock. — *vt* to provide with sleeves. — *adj* **sleeved** having sleeves. — (In combination) **-sleeved** having sleeves of a stated type. — *adj* **sleeve'less** without sleeves. — *n* **sleev'ing** tubular flexible insulation for threading over bare conductor wires. — **sleeve'-board** a board for ironing sleeves on; **sleeve'-nut** a double nut for attaching the joint-ends of rods or tubes. — **laugh up one's sleeve** to laugh privately or secretly, unperceived; **roll up one's sleeves** to get down wholeheartedly to a job, esp. an unattractive manual one; **up one's sleeve** in secret reserve, available in case needed. [O.E. (Anglian) *slēfe*.]

sleigh *slā*, *n* (esp. in *NAm*) a sledge. — *vi* to travel by sleigh. — *n* **sleigh'ing.** — **sleigh'-bell** a small bell attached to a sleigh or its harness. [Du. *slee*.]

sleight *slīt*, *n* dexterity; trickery. — **sleight of hand** deceptive movement of the hands, esp. during conjuring. — Also *adj*. [O.N. *slǣgth*, cunning, *slǣgr*, sly.]

slender *slen'dər*, *adj* thin or narrow; slim; slight. — *vt* and *vi* **slen'derise** or **-ize** to make or become slender. — *adv* **slen'derly.** — *n* **slen'derness.**

slept *slept*, *pa t* and *pa p* of **sleep.**

sleuth *slooth*, (esp. *jocular*) *n* a relentless tracker, a detective. — *vt* and *vi* to track, work as a detective. [O.N. *slōth*, track.]

slew[1] *sloo*, *pa t* of **slay.**

slew[2] or **slue** *sloo*, *vt* and *vi* to turn about the axis; to swing round, esp. suddenly and uncontrollably. — *n* a turn, twist or swing round. — *adj* **slewed** or **slued** (*slang*) very drunk. [First recorded as a sailor's word.]

slice *slīs*, *n* a thin broad piece or segment; a flat or broad-bladed instrument of various kinds, esp. for serving fish; a slash, swipe; a sliced stroke (*golf*); a share (of something) (*colloq*); a representative section. — *vt* to cut into slices; to cut as a slice; in golf, to strike or play so as to send the ball curving to the right (left for left-handed players). — *vi* to slash; to cut in the manner of slicing; (of a boat) to move through the water in a smooth, cutting manner; to slice a stroke (*golf*). — *n* **slī'cer.** — *n* and *adj* **slī'cing.** [O.Fr. *esclice* — O.H.G. *slīzan*, to split.]

slick *slik*, *adj* sleek; smooth; smooth-tongued, glib; adroit; trim, smart. — *n* a film or area of spilt oil; a smooth racing-car tyre. — *vt* to polish, make glossy; to smooth (hair; with *back* or *down*). — *n* **slick'er** a swindler, shifty person; a sophisticated city-dweller.

— *adv* **slick'ly**. — *n* **slick'ness**. [M.E. *sliken* — O.E. *slician*, (in composition) to smooth.]

slid. See **slide**.

slide *slīd*, *vi* to slip or glide; to pass along, over, down, etc. smoothly; to glide or slip (without skates or snow-shoes) over ice or other slippery surface; to lapse, fall out of use; to pass quietly, smoothly, or gradually. — *vt* to cause to slip or glide along: — *pa t* and *pa p* **slid** (*slid*). — *n* a slip; a polished slippery track (on ice); a chute; a slippery sloping surface e.g. in a park, for children to slide down; a bed, groove, rail, etc. on or in which a thing slides; a sliding part, e.g. of a trombone; a sliding clasp, esp. for women's hair; a flat piece of glass for mounting objects on for the microscope; a translucent photograph for projection on a screen, a transparency; a sliding seat, esp. in a rowing-boat; a landslip; a gliding from one note to another (*mus*); a falling (in value, popularity, etc.); (with **the**) a rhythmic hyperactive dance. — *adj* **slīd'able**. — *n* **slīd'er** a person or thing that slides. — *n* and *adj* **slīd'ing**. — *adv* **slīd'ingly**. — **slide'= rule** a mechanical calculating device consisting of two logarithmic graduated scales sliding against one another; **slide trombone** a conventional trombone; **sliding keel** the centreboard of a yacht; **sliding scale** a scale, e.g. of duties or fees charged, varying according to something else, e.g. difficulty, complication, etc.; a slide-rule. — **let something slide** to take no action over something, allow it to get worse. [O.E. *slīdan*, to slide.]

slight *slīt*, *adj* flimsy; lacking solidity, massiveness, weight, significance; slim; slender; small. — *vt* to ignore or overlook disrespectfully; to insult. — *n* discourteous disregard; an insult by showing neglect or lack of respect. — *adv* **slight'ingly**. — *adj* **slight'ish**. — *adv* **slight'ly** a little. — *n* **slight'ness**. — **(not) in the slightest** (not) at all, (not) to the smallest extent. [Cf. O.E. *eorthslihtes*, close to the ground.]

slily *slī'li*, *adv*. See under **sly**.

slim *slim*, *adj* (*compar* **slimm'er**, *superl* **slimm'est**) (of people) pleasingly thin; slender; only slight. — *vt* to make thin; to decrease (*fig*). — *vi* to use means to become more slender or (of e.g. a company) less inefficient, staffed with fewer people, etc.: — *pr p* **slimm'ing**; *pa t* and *pa p* **slimmed**. — *n* (*EAfr*) Aids. — *adv* **slim'ly**. — *n* **slimm'er**. — *n* **slimm'ing**. — *adj* **slimm'ish**. — *n* **slim'ness**. — *adj* **slim'line** slim, or helping to achieve slimness (also *fig*). — **slimmers' disease** anorexia nervosa. — **slim down** to become or make slimmer (usu. *fig*; *adj* **slimmed= down'**). [Du. *slim*, crafty.]

slime *slīm*, *n* ooze; very fine, thin, slippery, or gluey mud; any thick organic semi-liquid secretion, as mucus; moral filth; oily servility. — *vt* to smear or cover with slime. — *adv* **slim'ily**. — *n* **slim'iness**. — *adj* **slim'y** thick and slow-flowing, only semi-liquid; covered with slime; disgusting; obsequiously servile (*colloq*). [O.E. *slīm*.]

sling[1] *sling*, *n* a strap or pocket of material with a string attached to each end, for hurling a stone; a catapult; a ballista, a large Roman war machine like a crossbow; a loop for hoisting, lowering, or carrying a weight; a hanging support for an injured arm or foot; a strap attached to something, for carrying it; an act of throwing; a sweep or swing. — *vt* to throw with a sling; to hang loosely; to move or swing by means of a rope; to hurl, toss, fling (*colloq*); to pass, give, etc. (*slang*). — *vi* to discharge, e.g. stones from a sling: — *pa t* and *pa p* **slung**. — *n* **sling'er**. — **sling'back** or **slingback shoe** one from which the back is absent except for a strap fastening round the heel. — **sling off at** (*Austr* and *NZ colloq*) to jeer at; **sling one's hook** (*slang*) to go away, remove oneself.

sling[2] *sling*, *n* an American drink, spirits and water sweetened and flavoured.

slink *slingk*, *vi* to go sneakingly or ashamedly: — *pa t* and *pa p* **slunk** (*slungk*). — *n* a slinking gait. — *adj* **slink'y** slinking; pleasingly lean or sinuous; attractively close-fitting. [O.E. *slincan*.]

slip[1] *slip*, *vi* to escape; to move quietly, easily, unobtrusively, or stealthily; to glide; to get out of position accidentally; to slide, fall, etc., esp. accidentally; to lose one's former skill, grip, or control of a situation (*colloq*); to lose one's footing; to make a slight mistake inadvertently rather than from ignorance; to lapse morally; (of a motor clutch) to fail to engage correctly. — *vt* to cause or allow to slide or fall; to put with a sliding motion; to convey quietly or secretly; to disengage, let loose; to escape from, elude; to dislocate (a spinal disc): — *pr p* **slipp'ing**; *pa t* and *pa p* **slipped**. — *n* an act of slipping; an inadvertent mistake; a slight error or transgression; an escape; an incline, sloping down to the water, e.g. for launching boats; a slight dislocation; a landslide; a garment worn under a dress, a full-length version of a petticoat; a leash; (in cricket) any of three fielders (*first slip*, *second slip*, *third slip*) positioned on the off side somewhat behind the wicket-keeper or (often in *pl*) their position; (in *pl*) the place at the side of a stage for sliding scenery from. — *n* **slipp'age** (the extent of) failure to reach a set target; act, instance or amount of slipping. — *n* **slipp'eriness**. — *adj* **slipp'ery** or **slipp'y** so smooth, slimy, wet, etc. as to allow or cause slipping; elusive; evasive; apt to slip; uncertain, unpredictable. — *n* **slipp'iness**. — **slip'= case** a boxlike case for a book or set of books, open at one end to leave the spine(s) visible; **slip'-dock** a dock with a slipway; **slip'-knot** a knot that adjusts tightness by slipping along a rope; a knot easily untied by pulling an end. — *adj* **slip'-on** or **slip'= over** slipped on or over; (of a garment) slipped easily over the head without unbuttoning. — *n* a garment easily slipped on; one slipped over the head. — **slipp'erwort** a South American genus of flowers, calceolaria; **slip road** a local bypass; a road by which vehicles move off or on to a motorway. — *adj* **slip'shod** careless, carelessly executed. — **slip stitch** a concealed sewing stitch used on hems, facings, etc. in which only a few threads of the material forming the main body of the garment are caught up by the needle for each stitch; **slip'stream** the stream of air driven back by an aircraft propeller, or the stream of air behind any (usu. quickly) moving vehicle or other object. — *vi* to follow in the slipstream of, in order to take advantage of the decreased wind resistance. — **slip'-up** (*colloq*) an error or failure; **slip'way** a ramp in a dock or shipyard that slopes down into the water. — **give someone the slip** to escape from someone, usu. by cunning; **let slip** to reveal accidentally; to miss (an opportunity); **look slippy** (*colloq*, esp. in *imper*) to be quick, hurry; **slip a cable** or **mooring** to let it go overboard instead of waiting to weigh the anchor; **slip off** to fall off; to take off quickly or easily; to go away quietly; **slip of the tongue** (or **pen**) a word, etc. said (or written) in error when something else was intended; **slip on** to put on loosely or in haste; **slip up** (*colloq*) to make a mistake, to err.

slip[2] *slip*, *n* a young or slender person; anything slender or narrow; a small piece of paper, etc. for a memorandum, or for indexing, etc.; a memorandum giving details of the kind of cover required, to be signed by the underwriters (*insurance*).

slip[3] *slip*, *n* a creamy paste for coating and decorating pottery. — **slip'ware** pottery decorated with slip. [O.E. *slipa*, *slypa*, slime, paste.]

slippage, slippery, etc. See **slip**[1].

slipper *slip'ər*, *n* a loose (usu. indoor) shoe easily slipped on; a person who slips. — *vt* to provide with slippers; to beat with a slipper. — *adj* **slipp'ered**. [**slip**[1].]

slipshod, slipstream, etc. See under **slip**[1].

slipware. See under **slip**[3].

slit *slit, vt* to make a long cut in, esp. lengthwise; to split; to cut into strips: — *pr p* **slitt'ing**; *pa t* and *pa p* **slit.** — *n* a long cut; a narrow opening. — *adj* cut with a long opening, esp. lengthwise; cut open; having a slit. — *n* **slitt'er.** — **slit pocket** an overcoat pocket with a slit to give access to a pocket within; **slit'-trench** (*mil*) a narrow trench for one person or a few people. [M.E. *slitten.*]

slither *slidh'ər, vi* to slide, esp. on the belly. — *adj* **slith'ery** slippery.

sliver *sliv'ər, vt* to split, to tear off lengthwise, to slice thinly. — *n* a thin or small piece cut or torn off, a slice, splinter; a continuous strand of loose untwisted wool or other fibre. [O.E. (*tō-*)*slīfan*, to cleave.]

slivovitz *sliv'ə-vits, n* a dry plum brandy. — Also **sliv'ovic** (*-vits*), **sliv'ovica** (*-sə*) or **sliv'owitz.** [Serbo-Croatian *šljivovica* — *šljiva*, plum.]

Sloane Ranger *slōn rān'jər, n* a young person, typically upper- or upper-middle-class and female, favouring expensively casual clothing suggestive of rural pursuits, speaking in distinctively clipped tones, evincing certain predictable enthusiasms and prejudices and resident (during the week) in the *Sloane* Square area of London or a comparable part. — Also **Sloane.** [Coined in mid-1970s by P. Yorke, punning on *The Lone Ranger*, a television cowboy hero.]

slob *slob, n* a boor, lazy (esp. male) person (*slang*). — *adj* **slobb'y.** [Ir. *slab.*]

slobber *slob'ər, vt* and *vi* to slaver. — *adj* **slobb'ery.** [Cf. Du. *slobberen*, to eat or work in a slovenly way.]

sloe *slō, n* the blackthorn fruit or bush. — *adj* of blackthorn wood; made with sloes; black. — **sloe'-bush.** — *adj* **sloe-eyed'** dark-eyed, slant-eyed, or both. [O.E. *slā, slāg, slāh.*]

slog *slog, vt* and *vi* to hit hard. — *vi* to work or walk doggedly, with great effort: — *pr p* **slogg'ing**; *pa t* and *pa p* **slogged.** — *n* a hard blow (generally with little regard to direction); a strenuous spell of work; something which requires strenuous, esp. protracted, effort. — *n* **slogg'er.**

slogan *slō'gən, n* a party political catchword; an advertising catch-phrase; orig., a clan war-cry. — *n* **sloganeer'** an enthusiastic inventor and user of slogans. — *vi* to invent or make heavy use of slogans. — *n* **sloganeer'ing.** — *vi* **slo'ganise** or **-ize** to utter or repeat slogans, esp. as a substitute for reasoned discussion. — *n* **slo'ganising** or **-z-.** [Earlier *slog(h)orne, sloggorne*; from Gael. *sluagh*, army, *gairm*, cry.]

sloop *sloop, n* a light boat; a one-masted cutter-rigged vessel, differing from a cutter in having proportionally smaller sails and sometimes no bowsprit; (also **sloop-of-war'**) formerly a vessel (of whatever rig) between a corvette and a gun vessel, under a commander, carrying from ten to eighteen guns. [Du. *sloep.*]

slop[1] *slop, n* slush; spilled liquid; a puddle; (in *pl*) liquid refuse; (in *pl*) weak or insipid liquor; (in *pl*) semi-liquid food, esp. as fed to pigs; gushy, wishy-washy sentiment. — *vt* and *vi* to spill; to splash with slops. — *vt* to wash away. — *vi* to walk carelessly in slush or water: — *pr p* **slopp'ing**; *pa t* and *pa p* **slopped.** — *adv* **slopp'ily.** — *n* **slopp'iness.** — *adj* **slopp'y** wet or muddy; wishy-washy, watery; slipshod (of work or language); very over-sentimental. — **slop'-basin** or **slop'-bowl** a basin for waste liquids at table; **slop'-bucket** or **slop'-pail** a pail for removing bedroom slops. — **slop out** (of a prisoner) to take away and empty out one's slops (urine, etc.); to take slops from (a cell). [O.E. (*cū-*)*sloppe*, (cow-)droppings (cowslip) — *slūpan*, to slip.]

slop[2] *slop, n* a loose garment, esp. (in *pl*) wide baggy trousers or breeches; the wide part of these; (in *pl*) poor-quality ready-made clothing; (in *pl*) clothes and bedding issued to seamen. — **Sloppy Joe** (*slang*) a large, loose sweater; a runny mixture of minced beef and sauce served on a half roll (*US*); **slop'-shop** a shop for poor-quality ready-made clothes; **slop'-work** the making of slop clothing; cheap inferior work. [Cf. O.E. *oferslop*, loose outer garment.]

slope *slōp, n* an incline; an inclined surface; an inclination, upward or downward slant. — *vt* to form with a slope, or obliquely; to put in a sloping position or positions; to turn downwards, bow. — *vi* to have or take a sloping position or direction; to move down a slope. — *adj* **slop'ing.** — *adv* **slop'ingly.** — *adj* **slop'y** sloping. — **at the slope** (of a rifle) on the shoulder with the barrel sloping back and up; **slope arms** to place or hold a rifle in this position; **slope off** (*slang*) to go away, esp. suddenly or furtively, decamp. [Aphetic from *aslope* — O.E. *āslopen*, past p. of *āslūpan*, to slip away.]

sloppy. See **slop**[1,2].

slosh *slosh, n* slush; a watery mess; a heavy blow (*slang*). — *vi* to flounder or splash in slush; to hit (*slang*). — *vt* to splash; to hit hard, beat (*slang*). — *adj* **sloshed** (*colloq*) drunk, intoxicated. — *adj* **slosh'y.** [**slush.**]

slot *slot, n* a long narrow depression or opening, as one to receive a coin, an armature winding, or part of a mechanism, or opening into the conduit of an electric or cable tramway or railway; a slit; a (usu. regular) time, place or position in e.g. a radio or television programme; a niche in an organisation; a point in an airport's timetable at which a given aircraft may take off. — *vt* to make a slot in, provide with a slot; to pass through a slot; to put into a slot; to fit into a small space (*lit* or *fig*; with *in* or *into*). — *vi* to fit into a slot in something (with *in* or *into*); to fit into a story, puzzle, etc. (*fig*): — *pr p* **slott'ing**; *pa t* and *pa p* **slott'ed.** — *n* **slott'er** a person or machine that cuts slots. — **slot'-machine** one operated by inserting a coin in a slot, as a vending machine or a fruit machine. [O.Fr. *esclot.*]

sloth *slōth* or *sloth, n* laziness, sluggishness; a sluggish tree-dwelling tropical American toothless mammal. — *vt* and *vi* to pass, spend (time) in idleness. — *adj* **sloth'ful** inclined to sloth, inactive, lazy. — *adv* **sloth'fully.** — *n* **sloth'fulness.** — **sloth'-bear** a black Indian bear, with extended snout and lips. [M.E. *slawthe*, altered from O.E. *slǣwth* — *slāw*, slow.]

slouch *slowch, n* a loose, ungainly, stooping gait. — *adj* drooping. — *vi* to go or carry oneself slouchingly; to droop. — *vt* to turn down the brim of (a hat). — *n* **slouch'er.** — *adj* **slouch'ing.** — *adj* **slouch'y.** — **be no slouch** (*colloq*) (of a person) to be very good, efficient, etc. (usu. with *at*). [Cf. O.N. *slōkr*, a slouching fellow.]

slough[1] *slow, n* a hollow filled with mud; a marsh. — **the Slough of Despond** (the state of) extreme despondency, great depression. [O.E. *sloh.*]

slough[2] *sluf, n* a cast skin; dead tissue in a sore. — *vi* to come away as a slough (with *off*); to cast the skin. — *vt* to cast off, as a snake's skin. — *adj* **slough'y.** [M.E. *sloh.*]

Slovak *slō'vak, n* a member of a Slavonic people living E. of the Czechs; their language. — Also *adj.* — *adj* **Slovakian** (*-vak'*). [Slovak *Slovák.*]

sloven *sluv'n, n* a person carelessly or dirtily dressed, or slipshod in work. — *n* **slov'enliness.** — *adj* and *adv* **slov'enly.** [Cf. O.Du. *slof, sloef*, L.G. *sluf*, slow, indolent.]

Slovene *slō-vēn'* or *slō'vēn, n* a member of a branch of the Southern Slavs found chiefly in Slovenia, the northernmost constituent republic of Yugoslavia, and adjoining areas. — Also *adj.* — *n* and *adj* **Slovē'nian.** [O.Slav.]

slow *slō, adj* not swift, not quick; late; behind in time; not hasty; not ready; not progressive; (of wit or intellect) dull; (of a road lane) for slow-moving traffic; (of business) slack; (of a cooker, etc.) heating gently, cooking slowly; (of photographic film) comparatively less sensitive to light. — *n* anything that is slow. — *adv* (or in compounds) slowly. — *vt* to delay, retard, reduce the speed of. — *vi* to reduce speed. — *n* **slow'ing** a lessening of speed. — *adj* **slow'ish**. — *adv* **slow'ly**. — *n* **slow'ness**. — **slow burn** (*colloq*) a delayed but finally strong response, reaction, etc.; **slow'coach** a slow or sluggish person; **slow'down** see **slow down** below; **slow match** a slowly burning rope for firing explosives. — *adj* **slow-mo'tion** much slower than normal or (*cinematography*) actual motion. — **slow'poke** (esp. *US*) an irritatingly slow person, a slowcoach. — *adj* **slow-release'** (of a medicinal capsule, etc.) releasing its active ingredient little by little over a period of time. — **slow virus** a viral disease which may take years to induce symptoms. — **go slow, go-slow** see **go**[1]; **slow down** or **up** to go more slowly (*n* **slow'-down**). [O.E. *slāw*.]

slow-worm *slō'-wûrm*, *n* the blindworm, a harmless snakelike legless lizard. [O.E. *slāwyrm*, assimilated to **slow** and *wyrm*, worm.]

SLR *abbrev* for single-lens reflex (camera).

slub[1] or **slubb** *slub*, *vt* to twist after carding, so as to prepare for spinning. — *n* a piece of fibre twisted in this way. — *n* **slubb'er**. — *n* **slubb'ing**.

slub[2] *slub*, *n* a lump in yarn. — *adj* lumpy, knobbly in texture. — *adj* **slubbed** or **slubb'y**.

sludge *sluj*, *n* soft mud or mire; half-melted snow; a slimy precipitate, as from sewage; a dark yellowish or brownish green. — *adj* **sludg'y**. [Cf. **slush**.]

slue. Same as **slew**[2].

slug[1] *slug*, *n* a heavy, lazy person; a land mollusc with shell rudimentary or absent; a sea slug; anything slow-moving. — *n* **slugg'ard** a person who is habitually inactive. — Also *adj*. — *adj* **slugg'ish** habitually lazy, slothful; slow-moving, -acting, etc.; inactive. — *adv* **slugg'ishly**. — *n* **slugg'ishness**. [Cf. Norw. dialect *slugg*, a heavy body, *sluggje*, a slow heavy person, Sw. dialect *slogga*, to be sluggish.]

slug[2] *slug*, *n* a lump of crude ore (*mining*); a lump of metal, esp. one for firing from a gun; a bullet (*colloq*); a metal token used in a slot machine; a solid line or section of type cast by a composing machine (*printing*); a strip of metal thicker than a lead, for separating type (*printing*); the gravitational unit of mass, approx. 32·174 pounds (= 14·5939 kg) in the **slug-foot-second** system (47·88 kg in slug-metre-second reckoning).

slug[3] *slug*, *vt* and *vi* to slog; to hit heavily. — *n* a heavy blow. — *n* **slugg'er**. — **slug it out** to fight (esp. in boxing) in a hard-hitting, not particularly skilful, way. [Cf. **slog**.]

slug[4] *slug*, (now esp. *US*) *n* a gulp, a swallow; an alcoholic drink.

sluggard, sluggish, etc. See **slug**[1].

sluice *sloos*, *n* a structure with a gate for stopping or regulating flow of water; a floodgate or water-gate; a regulated outlet or inlet; a drain or channel for water; a trough for washing gold out of sand, etc.; an act of sluicing. — *vt* to let out or drain by a sluice; to wet or drench copiously; to wash in or by a sluice; to flush or swill by flinging water on. — **sluice'-gate**. [O.Fr. *escluse* — L.L. *exclūsa* (*aqua*), a sluice, i.e. (water) shut out, past p. of L. *exclūdĕre*, to shut out.]

slum *slum*, *n* an overcrowded, squalid neighbourhood. — *vi* (also *vt* with *it*) to adopt a lower standard of social behaviour, a less sophisticated level of cultural or intellectual activity, etc. than is or would be normal for oneself. — *n* **slumm'er**. — *n* **slumm'ing**. — *adj* **slumm'y**. — **slum'-dweller**. [Cant.]

slumber *slum'bər*, *vi* to sleep, esp. lightly; to be inattentive or inactive (*fig*). — *vt* to spend in slumber. — *n* light sleep; repose. — *n* **slum'berer**. — *n* and *adj* **slum'bering**. — *adv* **slum'beringly**. [M.E. *slūmeren* — O.E. *slūma*, slumber.]

slummy. See **slum**.

slump *slump*, *vi* to fall or sink suddenly into water or mud; (of prices, trade, etc.) to fall suddenly or heavily; to flop, relax carelessly. — *n* a sinking into mud, etc.; the sound so made; a (time of) sudden or serious fall in prices, business, etc. — opp. to *boom*; a slumped position. — *adj* **slumped**. [Cf. Norw. *slumpe*, to slump, plump, L.G. *schlump*, marshy place.]

slung *slung*, *pa t* and *pa p* of **sling**[1].

slunk *slungk*, *pa t* and *pa p* of **slink**.

slur *slûr*, *n* an aspersion, slight, stain, imputation of blame or wrongdoing; disparagement; discredit to one's reputation; a blur; a running together resulting in indistinctness in writing or speech; a smooth or legato effect (*mus*); a curved line indicating that musical notes are to be sung to one syllable, played with one bow, or with a smooth gliding effect. — *vt* to disparage, cast aspersions on; to glide over slyly so as to mask or to avert attention; to blur; to sound (esp. speech) indistinctly; to sing or play legato: — *pr p* **slurr'ing**; *pa t* and *pa p* **slurred**. — *adj* **slurred**.

slurp *slûrp*, *vt* to drink (liquid) or eat (semi-liquid food) noisily. — *vi* to flow with, or produce the sound of, a slurp or slurps. — *n* the noise produced by, or similar to that produced by, slurping food or drink. — *n* **slurp'er**. [Du. *slurpen*, *slorpen*, to sip audibly, gulp.]

slurry *slur'i*, *n* a thin paste or semi-liquid mixture; liquid manure for spreading on fields. [Ety. as for **slur**.]

slush *slush*, *n* liquid mud; melting snow; worthless sentimental drivel or gush. — *adj* **slush'y**. — **slush fund** or **money** (*slang*; orig. *US*) a fund of money used, usu. corruptly, in political campaigning and propaganda, bribery, undeclared commissions, etc. [Cf. **slosh**.]

slut *slut*, *n* a dirty, untidy, often immoral woman. — *adj* **slutt'ish**. — *adv* **slutt'ishly**. — *n* **slutt'ishness** or **slutt'ery**. [Cf. Ger. dialect *schlutt*(*e*).]

sly *slī*, *adj* (*compar* **sly'er** or **sli'er**, *superl* **sly'est** or **sli'est**) skilful in doing anything (esp. anything wrong) without being observed; cunning, wily; secretive; surreptitious. — *adj* **sly'ish**. — *adv* **sly'ly** (also **slī'ly**). — *n* **sly'ness**. — **on the sly** surreptitiously. [O.N. *slægr*; cf. **sleight**.]

SM *abbrev* for: sado-masochism (also **s-m**); Sergeant-Major; Short Metre.

Sm (*chem*) *symbol* for samarium.

smack[1] *smak*, *n* taste; a distinctive or distinguishable flavour; a trace, tinge. — *vi* to taste or have the flavour (of); to have a suggestion or trace (of) (*fig*). [O.E. *smæc*.]

smack[2] *smak*, *n* a small decked or half-decked coaster or fishing vessel, usu. rigged as a cutter, sloop or yawl; a fishing vessel containing a well in which fish can be kept alive (esp. *US*). [Du. *smak*.]

smack[3] *smak*, *vt* to strike smartly, slap loudly; to kiss roughly and noisily; to make a sharp noise with, as the lips by parting them; to taste with relish or with a smacking sound. — *vi* to make such a sound. — *n* a sharp sound; a crack; a slap; a hearty kiss. — *adv* sharply, straight. — *n* **smack'er** (*slang*) a £1 sterling; a dollar (bill); an enthusiastic kiss. — *n* and *adj* **smack'ing**. [Du. or L.G. *smakken*, to smite, Ger. *schmatzen*, to smack.]

smack[4] *smak*, (*slang*) *n* heroin.

smacker, smacking. See **smack**[3].

small *smöl*, *adj* little in size, extent, quantity, value, power, importance or degree; slender; narrow; fine in grain, texture, gauge, etc.; unimposing, humble; (of thought or action) petty, ignoble; short of full standard; operating on no great scale; soft or gentle in sound; minor. — *n* the narrow part (e.g. of the back); (in *pl*; *euph* or *jocular*) underclothes. — *adv* in a low tone; gently; in small pieces; on a small scale. — *adj* **small'ish**. — *n* **small'ness**. — **small ads** classified advertisements; **small'-arm** (commonly in *pl*) a weapon that can be carried by a person, esp. a handgun or short weapon; **small beer** see **beer.** — *adj* **small'-bore** (of a firearm) having a barrel with a small bore, of a calibre not more than ·22 inch. — **small capitals** (*colloq* **small caps**) capital letters of the height of lower case *x* (*printing*); **small chop** (*WAfr*) snacks served with drinks; **smallest room** (*euph*) a domestic lavatory; **small'holder; small'-holding** a holding of land smaller than an ordinary farm, esp. one provided by a local authority; the working of such land; **small hours** the hours immediately after midnight, small in numbers o'clock; **small letter** (usu. in *pl*) a lower-case letter. — *adj* **small-mind'ed** petty. — **small'pox** (orig. *pl*) a contagious disease, characterised by fever and pock-marks on the skin. — *adj* **small-scale'** (of maps, models, etc.) made in accordance with a series of smaller measurements; (of enterprises, etc.) small in size, scope, etc. — **small screen** television (*adj* **small-screen'**); **small'-sword** a light thrusting sword for fencing or duelling. — *adj* **small'-time** unimportant, small-scale. — *adj* **small'-town** provincial, petty; naive, unsophisticated. — **feel small** to feel insignificant, cheap, ashamed, etc.; **in a small way** with little capital or stock; unostentatiously, on a small scale; **look small** to look silly or insignificant; **the small print** (the location of) the fine but important details of a contract, etc., usu. printed very small. [O.E. *smæl.*]

smarm *smärm*, *vi* to fawn ingratiatingly and fulsomely; to be unctuous, oilily complimentary, etc. — *adv* **smarm'ily.** — *n* **smarm'iness.** — *adj* **smarm'y.**

smart *smärt*, *vi* to feel a smart (also *fig*). — *n* a prolonged stinging pain. — *adj* sharp and stinging; brisk; acute, witty; clever, brainy; pert, vivacious; trim, spruce, fine; fashionable; keen, quick, and efficient in business; technologically advanced (*comput*); computer-guided or electronically controlled (as a *smart house*, *smart bomb*) (*colloq*). — *adv* smartly. — *vt* and *vi* **smart'en** to make or become smart, to brighten (with *up*). — *adv* **smart'ly.** — *n* **smart'ness.** — *n* **smart'y** or **smart'ie** a would-be smart fellow. — **smart Alick, Alec, Aleck** or **alec** a would-be clever person, or one too clever for their own good. — Also *adj* (with hyphen). — **smart'ass** or **smart'arse** (*derog slang*) a smarty. — Also *adj.* — **smart card** a plastic card like a banker's card fitted with a microprocessor (including a memory) rather than a magnetic strip, used in commercial transactions, telecommunications, etc., its design intended to combat fraud; **smart money** money staked or invested by experienced or clever gamblers or investors; the people staking or investing this money; **smart'ypants** or **smart'y-boots** (*colloq*; *pl* the same) a smarty. — **look smart** (*colloq*) to be quick. [O.E. *smeortan.*]

smash *smash*, *vt* to shatter violently; to ruin; (in lawn tennis, etc.) to strike overhand with great force. — *vi* to fly into pieces; to be ruined, to fail; to be dashed or shattered violently; to smash a tennis ball, etc. — *n* an act or occasion of smashing, destruction, ruin, bankruptcy; an accident, esp. in road traffic; a smash hit. — *adj* **smashed** (*slang*) drunk, or intoxicated on drugs. — *n* **smash'er** a person or thing that smashes; anything great or extraordinary (*slang*); a person of dazzling charm (*slang*). — *n* **smash'ing.** — *adj* crushing, shattering, etc.; strikingly good, wonderful (*slang*). — *adj* and *n* **smash-and-grab'** (a robbery) effected by smashing a shop-window and grabbing goods. — **smash hit** an overwhelming success, esp. in entertainment of any kind; **smash'-up** a serious accident. [Imit.]

smatter *smat'ər*, *n* a smattering. — *adj* **smatt'ered** sprinkled, scattered sparingly. — *n* **smatt'ering** a scrappy, superficial knowledge or distribution (of something). [M.E. *smateren*, to rattle, to chatter.]

SME *abbrev* for Suriname (I.V.R.).

smear *smēr*, *n* a rub with, or a mark or patch of, anything sticky or oily; the matter so applied, esp. to a slide for microscopic study; a slur, defamatory accusation. — *vt* to anoint; to overspread with anything sticky or oily; to apply in a smear or smears; to defame. — *adv* **smear'ily.** — *n* **smear'iness.** — *adj* **smear'y** sticky; greasy; showing smears. — **smear campaign** a series of verbal or written attacks intended to defame or discredit someone; **smear'-dab** see **lemon²**; **smear tactics** tactics employed in a smear campaign; **smear test** a test involving the microscopic study of a smear, as for example a cervical smear (q.v.) [O.E. *smeru*, fat, grease.]

smectic *smek'tik*, (*chem*) *adj* used of a substance whose state is intermediate between solid and liquid, and whose atoms or molecules are oriented in parallel planes. [L. *smecticus*, cleansing — Gr. *smektikos*, detergent (from the soapy consistency of a smectic substance).]

smegma *smeg'mə*, *n* a fatty secretion, esp. that under the foreskin. [Gr. *smēgma*, *-atos*, soap.]

smell *smel*, *n* the sense by which the odours of gases, vapours, substances very finely divided, are perceived, located in the higher animals in the mucous membrane of the nose; the specific sensation excited by such a substance; a pleasant scent or (often) an unpleasant one; the property of exciting it; an act or instance of exercising the sense; a smack, savour, sense, property of suggesting, intimation (*fig*). — *vi* to affect the sense of smell; to have odour (esp. unpleasant), or an odour (of); to have or use the sense of smell; to have a savour, give a suggestion (of something; *fig*). — *vt* to perceive, detect, find, by smell (often with *out*); to take a smell at: — *pa t* and *pa p* **smelled** or **smelt.** — *n* **smell'er.** — *n* **smell'iness.** — *n* and *adj* **smell'ing.** — *adj* **smell'-less.** — *adj* **smell'y** having an unpleasant smell. — **smell'ing-salts** a preparation of ammonium carbonate with lavender, etc., used as a stimulant in cases of fainting, etc. — **smell at** to sniff at, take a smell at; **smell of** to have the smell of; to savour of; **smell out** to find out (e.g. a scandal) by prying. [Very early M.E. *smel.*]

smelt¹ *smelt*, *n* a fish of or related to the salmon family, with cucumber-like smell. [O.E.]

smelt² *smelt*, *vt* to melt in order to separate metal from ore. — *n* **smel'ter.** — *n* **smel'ting.**

smew *smū*, *n* a sea duck, a small species of merganser.

smidgen, smidgeon or **smidgin** *smij'ən* or *smij'in*, (*colloq*) *n* a very small amount.

smilax *smī'laks*, *n* a usu. climbing plant of the *Smilax* genus of the lily family, with net-veined leaves, some yielding sarsaparilla; a southern African twining plant of the asparagus family, with bright green foliage, much used by florists as decoration. [Gr. *smīlax.*]

smile *smīl*, *vi* to express amusement, pleasure, slight contempt, favour, etc., by a slight drawing up of the corners of the lips; to look joyous; to be favourable (*fig*). — *vt* to express, drive (away), etc. by smiling; to give (a smile). — *n* an act of smiling; the expression of the features in smiling; favour (*fig*). — *n* **smil'er.** — *n* and *adj* **smil'ing.** — *adv* **smil'ingly.** — **smile at** to show amusement at, disregard of; **smile on** (*fig*) to show favour to, be a good omen for. [M.E. *smīlen.*]

smilodon *smīl'ə-don*, *n* a member of an extinct genus (*Smilodon*) of large, short-limbed, sabre-toothed tigers which inhabited the Americas during the Pleistocene period. [L.L. — Gr. *smilē*, a knife, *odous*, *odontos*, a tooth.]

smirch *smûrch*, *vt* to besmear, dirty; to sully. — *n* a stain. [Earlier *smorch*, supposed to be from O.Fr. *esmorcher*, to hurt, infl. by **smear.**]

smirk *smûrk*, *vi* to smile affectedly, smugly or foolishly. — *n* an affected, smug or foolish smile. — *adv* **smirk'ingly.** — *adj* **smirk'y** simpering. [O.E. *smercian.*]

smite *smīt*, (*literary*, esp. *Bible*) *vt* to strike; to beat; to kill; to overthrow in battle; to affect with feeling; to afflict. — *vi* to strike: — *pa t* **smōte**; *pa p* **smitt'en**. — *n* **smī'ter**. [O.E. *smītan*, to smear.]

smith *smith*, *n* a person who forges metals with the hammer; a worker in metals. — *n* (often in combination) a person who makes anything. — *vt* to forge; to fashion. — *vi* to do a smith's work. — *n* **smith'ery** a smithy; a smith's work, smithing. — *n* **smithy** (*smidh'i* or *smith'i*) a smith's workshop. — *vt* and *vi* to smith. — **smith'craft**. [O.E.]

smithereens *smidh-ə-rēnz'*, *npl* tiny fragments. [Ir. *smidirín*, dimin. of *smiodar*, a fragment.]

smithy. See **smith**.

smitten *smit'n*, *pa p* of **smite**.

SMM *abbrev* for *Sancta Mater Maria* (L.), Holy Mother Mary.

SMMT *abbrev* for Society of Motor Manufacturers and Traders.

SMO *abbrev* for Senior Medical Officer.

smock *smok*, *n* an outer garment of coarse white linen formerly worn by farm-workers in the south of England; a loose, protective garment, usu. of coarse cloth, worn by artists, etc. — *vt* to clothe in a smock; to decorate with smocking. — *n* **smock'ing** honeycomb stitching, as on the yoke and cuffs of a smock. — **smock'-frock** a farm-worker's smock; **smock'=mill** a windmill with a fixed tower and revolvable cap above it bearing the sails (also called **tower-mill**). [O.E. *smoc*.]

smog *smog*, *n* smoky fog. — *adj* **smogg'y**.

smoke *smōk*, *n* the gases, vapours and fine particles that are emitted by burning material; solid particles suspended in a gas; fumes; vapour; a cloud or column of fumes; that which may be smoked — tobacco, a cigarette or cigar (*colloq*); an instance or spell of smoking; tear gas (*colloq*). — *vi* to exhale or emit smoke, vapour, dust, etc.; to reek; to send smoke (esp. in a wrong direction); to take into the mouth and puff out the smoke of tobacco or similar; to lend itself to, permit of, smoking. — *vt* to dry, scent, preserve, fumigate, suffocate, blacken, taint, drive or render by smoke; to inhale and emit the smoke from. — *adj* **smok'able** fit to be smoked. — *adj* **smoked**. — *adj* **smoke'less** emitting little or no smoke; containing little or no smoke. — *adv* **smoke'lessly**. — *n* **smoke'lessness**. — *n* **smok'er** a person who smokes tobacco; a smoking carriage or compartment; a person who smoke-dries meat. — *adv* **smok'ily**. — *n* **smok'iness**. — *n* and *adj* **smok'ing**. — *adj* **smok'y** giving out smoke; like smoke; coloured like or by smoke; filled with smoke, esp. unpleasantly so. — **smoke'-ball** a shell emitting smoke as a screen or to drive out an enemy; **smoke'=bomb** a bomb that emits smoke on bursting; **smoke'-bush** or **-tree** a type of shrub with light, feathery or cloudlike, tiny massed flowers; **smoke'=detector** a device that activates an alarm when it detects smoke in the air of a room, etc. — *adj* **smoke'-dried**. — *vt* **smoke'-dry** to cure or dry by means of smoke. — **smoke'-helmet** a head-covering for firemen or others who work in dense smoke; **smoke'-hole** a volcanic hole emitting smoke and gases; (e.g. in the roof of a primitive dwelling) a hole for the escape of smoke; **smoke hood** an airbag or mask for the head, to prevent or delay the effects of smoke on airline passengers during cabin fires; **smoke'-house** a building where meat or fish is cured by smoking, or where smoked meats are stored; **smokeless zone** a smoke control area. — *adj* **smoke'proof** impervious to smoke. — **smoke'=screen** a cloud of smoke raised to conceal movements (also *fig*); **smoke signal** (often in *pl*) a signal or message conveyed by means of patterns of smoke (also *fig*); **smoke'-stack** the funnel of a ship or railway engine; a tall industrial chimney; **smoke=tree** see **smoke-bush**; **smoke tunnel** a wind tunnel into which smoke is put at certain points in order to make wind effects visible; **smoking cap** or **jacket** a light dress cap or jacket formerly worn by smokers; **smoking carriage, compartment** or **room** a railway carriage, compartment or room set apart for smokers. — **go up in smoke** (of e.g. hopes) to vanish; (of e.g. plans) to fail to bear fruit, come to nothing; **smoke control area** one in which the emission of smoke from chimneys is prohibited; **smoke out** to discover; to drive out of a place of concealment by smoke or fire (*lit* or *fig*); **the Smoke** or **the Big Smoke** (*colloq*; also without *caps*) a metropolitan area (formerly) characterised by atmospheric pollution, esp. London; in Australia, the (nearest) city or major town (orig. a phrase used by the Australian aborigines), now esp. Melbourne or Sydney. [O.E. *smoca* (noun), *smocian* (verb).]

smolt *smōlt*, *n* a young river salmon when it is bluish along the upper half of the body and silvery along the sides. [Orig. Scot.]

smooch *smōōch*, (*colloq*) *vi* to kiss, pet.

smooth *smōōdh*, *adj* having an even surface; without roughness; evenly spread; glossy; hairless; of even consistency; easy; classy or elegant (*slang*). — *adv* smoothly. — *vt* to make smooth, not rough, lumpy, etc.; to free from obstruction, difficulty, harshness; to remove by smoothing (often with *away*; often *fig*); to calm, soothe; to make (difficulties or problems) seem less serious or less important (often with *over*). — *vi* to become smooth. — *n* a smooth place, part or side. — *vt* **smooth'en** to make smooth. — *n* **smooth'er** a person or thing that smooths. — *n* **smooth'ie** (*slang*) a person elegant or suave in manner or appearance, esp. insincerely or excessively so. — *n* and *adj* **smooth'ing**. — *adv* **smooth'ly**. — *n* **smooth'ness**. — *adj* **smooth'-bore** (of a firearm) not rifled (also **smooth'-bored**). — *n* a gun with a smooth-bored barrel. — *adj* **smooth-coat'ed** not shaggy-haired. — **smooth dab** see **lemon²**. — *adj* **smooth'-faced** having a smooth face or surface; pleasant-looking; beardless; unwrinkled. — **smoothing plane** a small fine plane used for finishing wood; **smooth muscle** muscular tissue (e.g. in the walls of the intestines) whose action is slow rhythmic contraction and relaxation, independent of the will. — *adj* **smooth-spo'ken** or **smooth=tongued'** conciliatory, flattering, or soft in speech, esp. excessively so. [O.E. *smōth* (usu. *smēthe*).]

smørbrød *smör'brōō* or *smœr'brō*, (Norw.), or **smørrebrød** *smœr'ə-brœdh* or *smör'ə-bröd*, (Dan.) *n* (*lit*) bread and butter; hors d'œuvres served on slices of buttered bread.

smörgåsbord *smör'gas-börd* or (Sw.) *smœr'gōs-bōōrd*, *n* Swedish-style buffet assortment of hors d'œuvres and many other dishes. [Sw.]

smorzando *smört-san'dō* or (It.) *zmort-sän'dō* or **smorzato** *-sä'tō*, *adj* and *adv* with a gradual fading away; growing slower and softer. [It.; gerund and past p. of *smorzare*, to tone down, extinguish.]

smote *smōt*, *pa t* of **smite**.

smother *smudh'ər*, *vt* to suffocate by excluding the air, esp. by a thick covering; to stifle (*lit* and *fig*); to envelop closely; to cover up thickly; to suppress, to conceal. — *vi* to be suffocated or suppressed. — *adj* **smoth'ered**. — *n* **smoth'erer**. — *n* and *adj* **smoth'ering**. — *adv* **smoth'eringly**. — *adj* **smoth'ery** tending to smother; stifling. [M.E. *smorther* — O.E. *smorian*, to smother.]

smoulder *smōl'dər*, *vi* to burn slowly or without flame; to linger on in a suppressed or hidden state (*fig*). — *n* smouldering fire. — *n* and *adj* **smoul'dering**. [M.E. *smolder*.]

smudge *smuj*, *n* a smear; a blur; a rubbed blot. — *vt* to smear; to blur. — *n* **smudg'er**. — *adv* **smudg'ily**. — *n* **smudg'iness**. — *adj* **smudg'y**.

smug *smug*, *adj* offensively self-complacent. — *adv* **smug'ly**. — *n* **smug'ness**. — *adj* **smug-faced'**.

smuggle *smug'l*, *vt* to import or export illegally or without paying duty; to convey secretly. — *adj* **smugg'led**. — *n* **smugg'ler** a person who smuggles; a ship or boat used in smuggling. — *n* and *adj* **smugg'ling**. [L.G. *smuggeln*.]

smut *smut*, *n* soot; a flake or spot of dirt, soot, etc.; a black spot; a disease of plants, esp. cereals, giving an appearance of soot; the fungus causing it; mildly obscene conversation, remarks, materials, etc. — *vt* to dirty, spot, or affect with smut; to become smutty. — *adj* **smutt'ed**. — *adv* **smutt'ily**. — *n* **smutt'iness**. — *adj* **smutt'y** stained with smut; affected with smut disease; midly obscene, improper. [Cf. L.G. *schmutt*; Ger. *Schmutz*, dirt.]

SN *abbrev* for Senegal (I.V.R.).

Sn (*chem*) *symbol* for *stannum* (L.), tin.

sn *abbrev* for *secundum naturam* (L.), according to nature.

snack *snak*, *n* a light meal. — *vi* to eat a snack. — **snack'-bar** or **-counter** a place where light meals can be bought. — **snack on** to make a light meal from. [Cf. M.Du. *snacken*, to snap; **snatch**.]

snaffle *snaf'l*, *n* a bit for horses (rather mild without a curb). — *vt* to put a snaffle on; to control by a snaffle; (the following meanings *slang*) to arrest; to capture; to purloin, steal; to get possession of.

snafu *sna-fōō'*, (*US slang*) *n* chaos. — *adj* chaotic. [*s*ituation *n*ormal — *a*ll *f*ouled (or *f*ucked) *u*p.]

snag *snag*, *n* a stump, as of a branch or tooth; a jag; a short tine; an embedded tree, dangerous for boats; hence a catch, a hidden obstacle or drawback; a caught thread in a stocking; (usu. *pl*) sausage (*Austr slang*). — *vt* to catch on a snag; to tear on a snag; to hack so as to form snags; to clear of snags: — *pr p* **snagg'ing**; *pa t* and *pa p* **snagged**. — *adj* **snagged**. — *adj* **snagg'y**. [Cf. O.N. *snagi*, peg.]

snaggletooth *snag'l-tōōth*, *n* a broken, irregular or projecting tooth: — *pl* **snagg'leteeth**. — *adj* **snagg'letoothed**. [App. from **snag** and **tooth**.]

snail *snāl*, *n* any terrestrial or air-breathing gasteropod mollusc with well-developed coiled shell; extended to other shelled gasteropods; a sluggish person or animal; a snail-wheel. — *adj* and *adv* **snail'-like**. — *adj* **snail'y**. — **snail darter** a small American freshwater fish. — *adj* **snail'-paced**. — **snail'-shell**; **snail'-wheel** a cam that controls the striking of a clock. — **a snail's pace** a very slow speed. [O.E. *snegl*, *snægl*, *snǣl*.]

snake *snāk*, *n* a serpent, or member of the *Ophidia*, a class of elongated limbless scaly carnivorous reptiles, often venomous, with forked tongue, no eyelids or external ears, and teeth fused to the bones that bear them; an ungrateful or treacherous person (in allusion to Aesop); anything snakelike in form or movement; the band (narrower than the *tunnel* allowed by the IMF on the world market) within which the relative values of certain EEC currencies are allowed to float. — *vi* to wind; to creep. — *adj* **snake'like**. — *adv* **snake'wise** in the manner of a snake. — *adv* **snāk'ily**. — *n* **snāk'iness**. — *adj* **snāk'y**. — **snake'bird** the darter; the wryneck; **snake'bite** the bite of a venomous snake; the condition or symptoms of a victim of a snakebite; a drink made of beer and cider in equal measures; **snake'-charmer** a person who handles snakes and sets them to perform rhythmical movements; **snake'-pit** (*fig*) a mental hospital; a place, or circumstances, characterised by disordered emotions and relationships; **snakeweed** see **bistort**. — **snake in the grass** (*fig*) a person who injures furtively; a lurking danger; **snakes and ladders** a board game played with counters and dice in which 'ladders' afford short cuts to the finish, but 'snakes' oblige one to descend to nearer the starting-point. [O.E. *snaca*.]

snap *snap*, *vi* to make a bite (often with *at*); to speak tartly in sudden irritation; to grasp (with *at*); to shut suddenly, as by a spring; to make a sharp noise; to go with a sharp noise; to break suddenly. — *vt* to bite suddenly; to seize, secure promptly (usu. with *up*); to answer or interrupt sharply (often with *up*); to shut with a sharp sound; to cause to make a sharp sound; to send or put with a sharp sound; to utter snappishly (sometimes with *out*); to break suddenly; to take an instantaneous photograph of, esp. with a hand-camera: — *pr p* **snapp'ing**; *pa t* and *pa p* **snapped**. — *n* an act, instance or noise of snapping; a small catch or lock; a crack; a crisp ginger biscuit (also **gingersnap**); a crisp, incisive quality in style; lively energy; a snapshot; a sudden cold spell (also **cold snap**); a type of card game in which the first player to shout 'snap' on spotting a matching pair of cards wins the cards; the play which involves the passing of the ball from the line of scrimmage back to the quarterback (*Am football*). — *adj* sudden, unexpected; offhand; (of decision, judgment) taken or made, on the spur of the moment without deep consideration of all possibilities; snapping shut. — *adv* with a snap. — *interj* used in the game of snap; also, on meeting or discovering two matching items, circumstances, etc. — *n* **snapp'er** an animal that snaps; a person who snaps or snaps up; a snapping-turtle; any fish of the family *Lutjanidae*, similar to the basses; (also **schnapp'er**) any of several highly esteemed food-fish of the family *Sparidae*, found in Australian and New Zealand waters; a Christmas or party cracker (*US*). — *adv* **snapp'ily**. — *n* and *adj* **snapp'ing**. — *adv* **snapp'ingly**. — *adj* **snapp'ish** inclined to snap; quick and tart. — *adj* **snapp'y** snappish; snapping; instantaneous; smart, fashionable, polished (as in *snappy dresser*). — **snap'-dragon** a plant (genus *Antirrhinum*) of the figwort family whose flower when pinched and released snaps like a dragon; **snap'-fastener** a press-fastener, a press-stud; **snap'-link** a link with a side opening closed by a spring; **snapp'ing-turtle** a large aggressive North American freshwater tortoise; **snap'shot** a hasty shot; a photograph taken quickly and informally, with simple equipment; an instant record of an event, situation, etc. at a particular time, esp. a stage in a process or sequence (*fig*); a visual record of the placement of stored data at a specific stage in a program run (*comput*). — **look snappy** or **make it snappy** to hurry; **snap into it** to get going quickly; **snap out of it** (*colloq*) to give it (e.g. a mood, habit) up at once; **snap someone's head (or nose) off** to answer irritably and rudely; **snap up** to take or purchase eagerly and quickly. [Prob. Du. *snappen*, to snap; Ger. *schnappen*.]

snare *snār*, *n* a running noose for trapping; a trap; an allurement, temptation, entanglement or moral danger; a loop for removing tumours, etc.; a string stretched across the lower head of a side-drum. — *vt* to catch, entangle or trap in a snare; to remove with a snare. — *n* **snar'er**. — *n* **snar'ing**. — *adj* **snar'y**. — **snare drum** a side-drum. [O.E. *sneare* or O.N. *snara*; prob. partly from Du. *snaar* or L.G. *snare*.]

snarl[1] *snärl*, *vi* to make a surly resentful noise with show of teeth; to speak in a surly manner. — *vt* to utter snarlingly. — *n* an ill-natured growling sound or facial expression; an act of snarling. — *n* **snarl'er**. — *n* and *adj* **snarl'ing**. — *adv* **snarl'ingly**. — *adj* **snarl'y**.

snarl[2] *snärl*, *n* a knot; a tangle; a knot in wood. — *vt* to tangle; to raise with a snarling-iron. — *vi* to tangle. — *adj* **snarled**. — *n* **snarl'er**. — *n* **snarl'ing**. — **snarl'ing-iron** or **-tool** a curved tool for raised work in hollow metalware. — **snarl up** (used esp. in *pa p* and *participial adj* forms) to make muddled or tangled and thus stop operating, moving, etc. smoothly (*n* **snarl'-up** a tangle; a traffic jam). [**snare**.]

snatch *snach*, *vt* to seize suddenly; to pluck away quickly; to grab; to take as opportunity occurs. — *vi* to make a snap or seizure. — *n* an act of snatching; a grab; a fragment, as of song, verse, etc.; (in weight-lifting) a type of lift in which the weight is raised from the floor to an overhead position in one movement. — *n* **snatch'er**. — *adv* **snatch'ily** or **snatch'ingly**. — *adj* **snatch'y** irregular. — **snatch at** to try to snatch or seize; **snatch squad** a group of police, etc. who move in swiftly to take specific persons (e.g. ringleaders) from a crowd. [M.E. *snacchen*.]

snazzy *snaz'i*, (*slang*) *adj* very attractive or fashionable; flashy.

SNCF *abbrev* for *Société Nationale des Chemins de Fer français* (Fr.), French national railways.

sneak *snēk*, *vi* to go furtively, to slink or skulk; to cringe; to behave meanly; to tell tales. — *vt* to pass furtively; to steal (*slang*). — *n* a person who sneaks or sneaks away; a tell-tale; a ball bowled along the ground (*cricket*). — *n* **sneak'er** a person who or thing that sneaks; a soft-soled, usu. canvas, shoe. — *adv* **sneak'ily**. — *n* **sneak'iness**. — *adj* **sneak'ing** mean, crouching; secret, underhand, not openly avowed; lurking under other feelings. — *adv* **sneak'ingly**. — *adj* **sneak'ish**. — **sneak'-raid** a bombing or other raid made under conditions of concealment; **sneak'-thief** a thief who steals through open doors or windows without breaking in.

sneck *snek*, (*Scot* and *Northern*) *n* a latch; a door-catch. — *vt* to fasten with a sneck. [Cf. **snack** and **snatch**.]

sneer *snēr*, *vi* to show cynical contempt by the expression of the face, as by drawing up the lip (sometimes with *at*); to express such contempt in other ways. — *vt* to utter sneeringly. — *n* a sneering expression; an act of sneering. — *n* **sneer'er**. — *n* and *adj* **sneer'ing**. — *adv* **sneer'ingly**. — *adj* **sneer'y**.

sneeze *snēz*, *vi* to make a sudden, involuntary and audible expiration through the nose and mouth, due to irritation of the inner nasal membrane. — *n* an act of sneezing. — *n* **sneez'er**. — *n* **sneez'ing**. — *adj* **sneez'y**. — **sneeze'wort** a species of yarrow (*Achillaea ptarmica*) once used as a substitute for snuff; a plant of this species; white hellebore. — **not to be sneezed at** not to be despised. [M.E. *snesen*, *fnesen* — O.E. *fnēsan*, to sneeze.]

Snell's law. See **law[1]**.

SNG *abbrev* for synthetic natural gas.

snib *snib*, (chiefly *Scot*) *n* a small bolt; a catch for a window-sash. — *vt* to fasten with a snib. [Cf. L.G. *snibbe*, beak.]

snick *snik*, *vt* to cut out, snip or nick; to deflect slightly by a touch of the bat (*cricket*). — *n* a small cut; a glancing stroke in cricket.

snicker *snik'ər*, *vi* to snigger; to nicker or neigh. — *vt* to say gigglingly. — *n* a giggle. [Imit.; *nicker*, a Scots word meaning to neigh, and **snigger**.]

snide *snīd*, *adj* sham; counterfeit; dishonest; derogatory in an insinuating way; showing malice. — *adv* **snide'ly**. — *n* **snide'ness**.

sniff *snif*, *vt* to draw in with the breath through the nose; to smell; to suspect or detect by smell or as if by smell. — *vi* to draw in air sharply and audibly through the nose; to draw up mucus or tears escaping into the nose; to smell tentatively; to express disapprobation with reticence by a slight sound in the nose; to snuffle; to inhale a dangerous or addictive substance (e.g. glue, cocaine). — *n* an act or a sound of sniffing; a smell; a small quantity inhaled by the nose; a slight intimation or suspicion (*fig*). — *n* **sniff'er**. — *adj* trained, designed, etc. to seek out or locate (esp. illicit or dangerous substances). — *adv* **sniff'ily**. — *n* **sniff'iness**. — *n* and *adj* **sniff'ing**. — *vi* **sniff'le** to snuffle slightly, to sniff. — *n* an act of sniffling; the sound made by sniffling; (often in *pl* with **the**) a slight cold; (often in *pl* with **the**) liquid mucus running out of or blocking the nose. — *n* **sniff'ler**. — *adj* **sniff'y** inclined to be disdainful. — **sniffer dog** a dog trained to smell out drugs or explosives. — **not to be sniffed at** not to be despised. [Imit.; cf. **snuff[1]**.]

snifter *snif'tər*, *n* a dram (*slang*); a brandy glass (*US*). — **snif'ter-** or **snif'ting-valve** an air-valve in a steam cylinder, etc. [Dialect *snift*, to sniff.]

snigger *snig'ər*, *vi* to laugh in a half-suppressed way, often offensively. — *vt* to say with a snigger. — *n* a half-suppressed laugh. — *n* **snigg'erer**. — *n* and *adj* **snigg'ering**. — *adv* **snigg'eringly**. [Imit.]

snip *snip*, *vt* to cut as with scissors: — *pr p* **snipp'ing**; *pa t* and *pa p* **snipped**. — *n* a small cut, as with scissors; a small shred; a small, slender or despicable person; a small piece; a notch, slit, or slash; the sound of a stroke of scissors; a small white or light patch or stripe on a horse, esp. on the head; a certainty; a bargain. — *n* **snipp'er**. — *n* **snipp'ing** a clipping. — *adj* **snipp'y** fragmentary; stingy; snappish. — *npl* **snips** hand-shears for sheet-metal. [L.G. or Du. *snippen*.]

snipe *snīp*, *n* any of several wading-birds of the genus *Gallinago*, breeding in marshes and having a long straight bill; any of several similar or related species; a sniping shot; a verbal attack, criticism. — *vi* to shoot snipe for sport; to shoot at single men from cover; to attack or criticise, esp. from a position of security (*fig*; often with *at*). — *vt* to pick off by rifle-fire from (usu. distant) cover. — *n* **snip'er**. — *n* **snip'ing**. [Prob. Scand.; the O.E. word is *snīte*.]

snipper. See **snip**.

snippet *snip'it*, *n* a little piece snipped off; a scrap, as of literature, news, etc. — *n* **snipp'etiness**. — *adj* **snipp'ety** trivial, fragmentary. [**snip**.]

snitch *snich*, (*slang*) *n* the nose; an informer. — *vi* to inform, sneak. — *vt* to pilfer. — *n* **snitch'er** an informer.

snivel *sniv'l*, *n* mucus of the nose; a sniff; a hypocritical snuffle; cant. — *vi* to run at the nose; to sniff; to snuffle; to whimper, cry like a child. — *vt* to utter with snivelling: — *pr p* **sniv'elling**; *pa t* and *pa p* **sniv'elled**. — *n* **sniv'eller**. — *adj* **sniv'elling**. — *adj* **sniv'elly**. [O.E. *snofl*, mucus.]

SNO *abbrev* for Scottish National Orchestra (now **RSNO**, Royal Scottish National Orchestra).

snob *snob*, *n* a person who sets too much value on social standing, wishing to be associated with the upper class and treating them obsequiously, while treating those perceived as inferior with condescension or contempt; one having similar pretensions as regards (usu. specified) tastes, as *wine snob*. — *n* **snobb'ery** snobbishness; snobbish behaviour. — *adj* **snobb'ish**. — *adv* **snobb'ishly**. — *n* **snobb'ishness**. — *n* **snobb'ism**. — *adj* **snobb'y**.

snoek. See **snook[1]**.

snog *snog*, (*slang*) *vi* to embrace, caress and kiss amorously. — Also *n*.

snood *snōōd*, *n* an ornamental hair-net supporting the back-hair; a tube of knitted or other material worn as a hood; the hair-line, gut, etc. by which a fish-hook is fixed to the line. — *vt* to bind, dress or fasten with a snood. [O.E. *snōd*.]

snook[1] *snōōk*, *n* any of several fishes — a garfish, or (in S. Africa and now elsewhere also **snoek** *snōōk*) the barracouta. [Du. *snoek*, pike.]

snook[2] *snōōk* or *snōōk*, *n* the gesture of putting the thumb to the nose, to express derision, defiance, etc. — **cock a snook** to make that gesture (also *fig*).

snooker *snōōk'ər*, *n* a variety of the game of pool, played with 15 red balls, 1 white cue ball and 6 balls of other colours, the object being to pocket the non-white balls in a certain order and gain more points in so doing than one's opponent; a situation in snooker where the path between the cue ball and the ball to be played is blocked, forcing an indirect shot to be played. — *vt* to render a direct stroke impossible for; to thwart (a person or plan) by placing an obstacle in the way (*fig*).

snoop *snōōp*, *vi* to go about sneakingly, to pry. — *n* a person who snoops; an act of snooping. — *n* **snoop'er.** — **snoop'erscope** (*US*) a device which converts infrared radiation reflected from an object into a visible image, used for seeing in darkness. [Du. *snoepen*, to eat, steal.]

snoot *snōōt*, *n* (*slang*) the nose. — *n* **snoot'ful** (*colloq*) enough alcohol to make one drunk. — *adj* **snoot'y** (*colloq*) haughtily supercilious. [Cf. Du. *snuit*, snout, face.]

snooze *snōōz*, *vi* to doze. — *n* a nap. — *n* **snoo'zer.** — *adj* **snoo'zy.** — **snooze button** a device on an alarm clock which stops the alarm and allows a few minutes' respite before it sounds again.

snore *snōr*, *vi* to breathe roughly and hoarsely in sleep with vibration of uvula and soft palate or of the vocal chords; to snort. — *n* a noisy breathing of this kind. — *n* **snōr'er.** — *n* **snōr'ing.** [Imit.; cf. **snort.**]

snorkel *snör'kl*, *n* an anglicised form of **schnorkel.** — *n* **snor'kelling** swimming with a snorkel.

snort *snört*, *vi* to force the air with violence and noise through the nostrils, as horses do; to inhale a drug through the nose (*slang*). — *vt* to express by or utter with a snort; to force out, as by a snort; to inhale (a powdered drug, esp. cocaine) through the nose (*slang*). — *n* an act or sound of snorting; a quick drink (*slang*); the snorkel of a submarine. — *n* **snort'er** someone who or something that snorts; anything characterised by extreme force, esp. a gale (*colloq*). — *n* and *adj* **snort'ing.** — *adv* **snort'ingly.** — *adj* **snort'y** snorting; inclined to snort (*colloq*); contemptuous and ready to take offence. [Imit.]

snot *snot*, *n* mucus of the nose; a contemptible person. — *vi* **snott'er** to breathe through an obstruction in the nostrils; to sob, snuffle, blubber. — *adv* **snott'ily.** — *n* **snott'iness.** — *adj* **snott'y** like, or foul with, snot; superciliously stand-offish; mean, of no importance. — *adj* **snott'y-nosed.** [O.E. *gesnot*; *snȳtan*, to blow the nose.]

snout *snowt*, *n* the projecting muzzle of an animal, esp. a pig; any similar projection; a cigarette, tobacco (*slang*); a police informer (*slang*). — *vt* to provide with a snout. — *adj* **snout'ed.** — *adj* **snout'y** like a snout; snouted. [M.E. *snūte*, prob. rel. to **snot.**]

snow *snō*, *n* atmospheric vapour frozen in crystalline form, whether in single crystals or aggregated in flakes; a snowfall; any similar substance, as carbonic acid snow (frozen carbon dioxide); snowlike specks on the screen caused by electrical interference (*TV*); cocaine, morphine or heroin (*slang*). — *adj* of snow. — *vi* to shower snow; to fall as snow or like snow. — *vt* to shower like snow; to strew as with snow; to whiten, whiten the hair of (*fig*); (with *up* or *under*) to bury, block, shut in or overwhelm, with or as if with snow. — *adv* **snow'ily.** — *n* **snow'iness.** — *adj* **snow'less.** — *adj* **snow'like.** — *adj* **snow'y** abounding or covered with snow; white, like snow; pure. — **snow'ball** a ball made of snow pressed hard together; (also **snow'ball-tree**) a sterile *Viburnum opulus*; a round white pudding, cake, or sweetmeat; a drink of advocaat and lemonade; something that grows like a snowball rolled in snow, esp. a distribution of begging letters, each recipient being asked to send out so many copies. — *vt* to throw snowballs at. — *vi* to throw snowballs; to grow greater ever more quickly. — **snow'-bird** any finch of the N. American genus *Junco*, white underneath, familiar in winter; applied to various other birds that appear in winter; one of these birds. — *adj* **snow'-blind.** — **snow'-blindness** amblyopia caused by the reflection of light from snow; **snow'-blink** a reflection from fields of snow, like ice-blink; **snow'-blower** a snow-clearing machine which takes in the snow in front of it and blows it to the side of the road; **snow'boarding** skiing on a **snow'board**, a board similar to a skateboard for use on snow; **snow'-boot** a boot or overshoe for walking in snow. — *adj* **snow'bound** shut in or prevented from travelling, by snow. — **snow bunting** a black-and-white (in summer partly tawny) bunting of the Arctic regions, a winter visitor in Britain; **snow'cap** a cap of snow as on the polar regions or a mountain-top. — *adj* **snow'-capped.** — **snow'drift** a bank of snow drifted together by the wind; **snow'drop** a drooping white flower of early spring, or the plant that bears it; **snow'fall** a quiet fall of snow; the amount falling in a given time; **snow'field** a wide expanse of snow, esp. where permanent; **snow finch** a finchlike Alpine sparrow; **snow'flake** a feathery clump of snow crystals; **snow'-goggles** goggles to guard against snow-blindness; **snow goose** a white Arctic American goose; **snow gun** a device for spreading artificial snow on to ski-slopes; **snow-in-summ'er** a white-flowered garden mouse-ear chickweed; **snow job** (*US slang*) an attempt to mislead, persuade or convince by means of insincere or flattering words, exaggeration, inaccurate or complex information, etc.; **snow leopard** the ounce (*Panthera uncia*), an animal related to the leopard, found in the mountainous regions of Central Asia; **snow'line** the limit of perpetual snow; **snow'man** a great snowball made in human form; the abominable snowman (see under **abominate**); **snow'mobile** a motorised sleigh or a tractorlike vehicle capable of travelling over snow; **snow'-plough** an implement for clearing snow from roads and railways; a skiing position in which the skis form a V, with the tips touching. — *vi* (in skiing) to assume the snow-plough position in order to reduce speed, stop, etc. — **snow'shoe** a long broad framework strapped to the foot for walking on snow; **snowshoe rabbit** or **snowshoe hare** a North American hare, white in winter, brownish with white feet in summer; **snow'-slip** a small avalanche of snow; **snow'-spectacles** spectacles worn as a protection against the glare of snow; **snow'storm; snow'-water** water from melted snow. — *adj* **snow-white'** as white as snow. — **snowy owl** a great white owl of northern regions. — **not a snowball's chance (in hell** or **in an oven)** (*colloq*) no chance at all; **snowed in** or **up** blocked or isolated by snow; **snowed under with** overwhelmed with rapid accumulation of. [O.E. *snāw*.]

SNP *abbrev* for Scottish National Party.

snub *snub*, *vt* to take up, cut short, rebuff, in a humiliating or mortifying manner; to check; to bring to a sudden stop; to cut or break short; to make snub: — *pr p* **snubb'ing;** *pa t* and *pa p* **snubbed.** — *n* an act of snubbing; a check; a snub nose; a stub, snag or knob. — *adj* flat, broad, blunt; (of a polyhedron) having undergone secondary truncation (*geom*). — *n* and *adj* **snubb'ing.** — *adv* **snubb'ingly.** — *adj* **snubb'ish** or **snubb'y** inclined to snub or check; somewhat snub. — **snub cube** a polyhedron obtained by repeated truncation of a cube, having 38 faces, six of which are squares, the rest being equilateral triangles; **snub nose** a short turned-up nose. — *adj* **snub-nosed'.** [O.N. *snubba*, to chide.]

snuff[1] *snuf*, *vi* to draw in air violently and noisily through the nose; to sniff; to smell at anything doubtfully; to take snuff. — *vt* to draw into the nose; to smell, to examine, suspect or detect by smelling. — *n* a powdered preparation of tobacco or other substance for snuffing; a pinch of snuff or act of snuffing; a sniff; resentment, huff. — *n* **snuff'er.** — *n* **snuff'iness.** — *n* and *adj* **snuff'ing.** — *adj* **snuff'y** like, smelling of, soiled with or showing traces of snuff; touchy, huffy. — **snuff'box** a box for snuff; **snuff'-colour** or **-brown'** a yellowish or greyish brown, slightly paler than bistre. — *adj* **snuff'-coloured.** — **snuff'-mill** a factory or a hand-mill for grinding tobacco into snuff. — **up to snuff** alert, knowing, not likely to be taken in; up to scratch, in good order; of a high, or suitable standard. [M.Du. *snuffen*.]

snuff[2] *snuf*, *n* the burnt part of a wick. — *vt* to remove the snuff from; to make brighter; to put out as with snuffers (with *out*; also *fig*). — *n* **snuff'er** (in *pl*) an instrument like a pair of scissors for removing snuffs from the wicks of candles, or of oil-lamps; one with a cap-shaped part for extinguishing candles. — **snuff film, movie, novel** or **video** a pornographic film, video recording or book which has as its climax the real-life murder of one of the participants. — **snuff it** (*slang*) to die. [M.E. *snoffe*.]

snuffle *snuf'l*, *vi* to breathe hard or in an obstructed manner through the nose; to sniff; to speak through the nose. — *vt* to sniff; to say or utter nasally. — *n* an act or sound of snuffling; a snuffling tone; (in *pl*) an obstructed condition of the nose. — *n* **snuff'ler** (*snuf'lər* or *snuf'l-ər*). — *n* and *adj* **snuffling** (*snuf'ling* or *snuf'l-ing*). [Frequentative of **snuff**[1].]

snug *snug*, *adj* lying close and warm; comfortable; sheltered; not exposed to view or notice; in good order; compact; fitting close. — *n* a snuggery. — *vi* to lie close. — *vt* to make snug; to stow away snugly: — *pr p* **snugg'ing**; *pa t* and *pa p* **snugged**. — *n* **snugg'ery** a snug room or place, esp. a bar-parlour. — *vi* **snugg'le** to nestle. — *vt* to hug close; to wrap close. — *adv* **snug'ly**. — *n* **snug'ness**.

SO *abbrev* for Signal Officer; special order; Staff Officer; standing order.

so[1] *sō*, *adv* merging into *conj* or *interj* in this, that, or such manner, degree or condition; to such an extent; likewise; accordingly; well; therefore; in due course, thereupon, thereafter; as; soever; thus; for like reason; in a high degree; as has been stated; provided; in case; in order that. — **so'-and-so** such-and-such a person or thing; used to replace a descriptive oath (*colloq*; also *adj*). — *adj* **so'-called** styled or known as such — usu. implying doubt or denial of the meaning or implications of the following term, or a wish to disassociate oneself from the implications of the term. — **so many** such-and-such a number of; **so much** such-and-such an amount; in such a degree; to such an extent; such an amount (of); that amount of; an equal amount. — **and so on** (or **forth**, or as one phrase **and so on and so forth**) and more of the same or the like; and the rest of it; **just so** exactly right, impeccable; quite so; **or so** approximately; **quite so** just as you have said, exactly; **so as** in such a manner as or that; in order (with *to*); if only, on condition that; **so be it** used to express acceptance or resignation; **so far** to that, or to such an, extent, degree or point; **so far so good** everything is all right up to this point; **so long!** and **so long as** see under **long**; **so much as** as much as; even; **so much for** that disposes of; that is the end of; no more of; **so much so** to such an extent (that); **so so** see **so-so** (separate article); **so that** with the purpose that; with the result that; **so to say** (or **speak**) if one may use that expression; **so what** see under **what**. [O.E. *swā*.]

so[2] *sō*. See **sol**[1].

s.o. (*stock exchange*, *finance*) *abbrev* for seller's option.

soak *sōk*, *vt* to steep in a liquid; to drench; to saturate; to absorb liquid (with *up*); to draw through the pores; to charge or tax heavily (*colloq*). — *vi* to be steeped in a liquid; to pass through pores; to drink (usu. alcohol) to excess; to soften by heating. — *n* the process or act of soaking; a drenching; a marshy place; a heavy or habitual drinker. — *n* **soak'age** soaking; liquid that has percolated. — *n* **soak'er**. — *n* and *adj* **soak'ing**. — *adv* **soak'ingly**. — **soak'-away** a depression into which water percolates. [M.E. *soke* — O.E. *socian*, rel. to *sūcan*, to suck.]

soap *sōp*, *n* an alkaline salt of a higher fatty acid; esp. such a compound of sodium (*hard soap*) or potassium (*soft soap*), used in washing; smooth words, flattery (*slang*); soap opera. — *vt* to rub with soap; to flatter. — *n* **soap'ie** (*Austr*) a soap opera. — *adv* **soap'ily**. — *n* **soap'iness**. — *adj* **soap'less**. — *adj* **soap'y**. — **soap'box** a box for packing soap; a wayside orator's improvised platform; **soap'-bubble** a globe of air enclosed in a film of soap-suds; **soap'-dish**; **soap flakes**; **soap opera** a sentimental, melodramatic radio or television serial concerning the domestic and emotional lives of a family or other small group (also *fig*; orig. American and often sponsored by soap manufacturers); broadcast drama of this sort; **soap powder**; **soap'stone** steatite, or French chalk, a compact kind of talc with soapy feel; **soap'-suds** soapy water, esp. when frothy; **soap'wort** a tall herb of the pink family, whose roots and leaves contain saponin, esp. *saponaria officinalis*. [O.E. *sāpe*.]

soar *sōr*, *vi* to rise or fly high in the air; to rise to a great height (*lit* or *fig*); to glide high in the air, esp. on a rising current; to increase rapidly in number or amount. — *n* and *adj* **soar'ing**. — *adv* **soar'ingly**. — *adj* **soar'away** making spectacular progress. [Fr. *essorer*, to expose to air, raise into air — L. *ex*, out, *aura*, air.]

Soay *sō'ā* or in full **Soay sheep** (*shēp*), *n* a breed of small, wild, dark-coloured sheep found esp. on the island of *Soay* in the Outer Hebrides; one of this breed.

sob *sob*, *vi* to catch the breath convulsively in distress or other emotion; to make a similar sound; to weep noisily. — *vt* to utter with sobs; to bring (oneself) to a certain state by sobbing: — *pr p* **sobb'ing**; *pa t* and *pa p* **sobbed**. — *n* a convulsive catch of the breath; any similar sound. — *n* and *adj* **sobb'ing**. — *adv* **sobb'ingly**. — **sob'-story** a pitiful tale told to arouse sympathy; **sob'-stuff** cheap and extravagant pathos, to stir tears; maudlin films or scenes. [Imit.]

s.o.b. *abbrev* for son of a bitch.

sober *sō'bər*, *adj* not drunk; temperate, esp. in use of intoxicants; moderate; restrained; without excess or extravagance; serious; sedate; quiet in colour; sombre. — *vt* to make sober (often with *up*). — *vi* to become sober (often with *up*). — *adj* **so'bering** making sober; causing to become serious, grave or thoughtful. — *adv* **so'berly**. — *n* **so'berness** or **sobriety** (*sō-* or *sə-brī'i-ti*) the state or habit of being sober; calmness; gravity. [Fr. *sobre* — L. *sōbrius* — *sē-*, apart, not, *ēbrius*, drunk.]

sobole *sō'bōl* or **soboles** *sob'ō-lēz*, (*bot*) *n* a creeping underground stem producing roots and buds: — *pl* **sob'ōlēs**. [L. *sobolēs*, *subolēs*, a shoot — *sub*, under, and the root of *alĕre*, to nourish, sustain.]

sobriety. See **sober**.

sobriquet *sō'bri-kā* or **soubriquet** *sōō'-*, *n* a nickname. [Fr. *sobriquet*, earlier *soubriquet*, a chuck under the chin.]

Soc. *abbrev* for: Socialist; Society.

soca *sō'kə*, *n* a form of popular music from the Caribbean, a mixture of *so*ul and *ca*lypso.

so-called. See under **so**[1].

soccer *sok'ər*, *n* association football. — *npl* **Socceroos'** (*soccer* and kangaroos) the Australian national association football team.

sociable *sō'shə-bl*, *adj* inclined to society; companionable; favourable to social intercourse; friendly, fond of others' company. — *n* **sociabil'ity** or **so'ciableness**. — *adv* **so'ciably**. [Fr. — L. *sociābilis* — *sociāre*, to unite, — *socius*, companion.]

social *sō'shl*, *adj* pertaining to life in an organised community; pertaining to welfare in such; growing or living in communities; pertaining to, or characterised by, friendly association; convivial; gregarious, sociable; pertaining to fashionable circles. — *n* an informal party or gathering of a club, church, etc.; (with **the**) social security (*colloq*). — *n* **socialīsā'tion** or **-z-** the act or process of socialising; the process by which infants and young children become aware of society and their relationships with others.

— *vt* **so'cialise** or **-ize** to make social; to put on a socialistic footing. — *vi* (*colloq*) to behave in a sociable manner, e.g. at parties, etc. — *n* **so'cialism** the theory, principle, or scheme of social organisation which places means of production and distribution in the hands of the community. — *n* **so'cialist** an adherent of socialism. — Also *adj*. — *adj* **socialist'ic.** — *adv* **socialist'ically.** — *n* **so'cialite** a person having a place in fashionable society. — *n* **sociality** (*sō-shi-al'i-ti*) the quality or fact of being social; social relations, association or intercourse; sociability. — *adv* **so'cially.** — *n* **so'cialness.** — *adj* **so'ciātive** expressing association. — **social anthropology** the branch of anthropology which deals with the culture, customs and social structure of (esp. primitive) societies; **social climber** (often *derog*) a person who tries to become accepted into a higher social stratum by a deliberate policy of getting to know and associating with people belonging to it; **social contract** the voluntary agreement between individuals upon which an organised society, its rights, functions and the relationships within it are founded; **social democracy** the practices and policies of socialists who believe that socialism can and should be achieved by a gradual and democratic process; **social democrat** a supporter of social democracy; (with *caps*) a member or supporter of a Social Democratic party. — *adj* **social democratic.** — **social engineer**; **social engineering** the furtherance of social change and the development of social institutions in accordance with an overall plan; **social insurance** state insurance by compulsory contributions against sickness, unemployment and old age; **social science** the scientific study of human society and behaviour, including such disciplines (the *social sciences*) as anthropology, sociology, economics, political science and history; **social secretary** a person who is responsible for organising the social activities of a person, club, association, etc.; **social security** security against sickness, unemployment, old age, provided by a social insurance scheme; supplementary benefit; **social service** welfare work (also in *pl*); (in *pl*) the public bodies carrying out such work; **social work** any of various forms of welfare work intended to promote the well-being of the poor, the aged, the handicapped, etc.; **social worker.** [L. *socius*, a companion.]

society *so-sī'it-i*, *n* fellowship, companionship; company; association; a community; the conventions and opinions of a community; the fashionable world; a corporate body; any organised association. — *adj* of fashionable society. — *adj* **soci'etal** pertaining to society, social. — *adv* **soci'etally.** — **the Society of Jesus** see **Jesuit**. [O.Fr. *societé* — L. *societās* — *socius*, a companion.]

socio- *sō-si-ō-* or *sō-shi-ō-*, *combining form* denoting social, of or pertaining to society, as *sociocultural*, *socioeconomic*, *sociopolitical*. — *n* **sociobiol'ogist.** — *n* **sociobiol'ogy** a scientific discipline combining biology and the social sciences which attempts to establish that social behaviour and organisation in humans and animals has a genetic basis and is to be explained in terms of evolution and genetics. — *n* **socioling'uist.** — *adj* **sociolinguis'tic** of or pertaining to sociolinguistics; pertaining to language as it functions as a social tool. — *nsing* **sociolinguis'tics** the study of language as it functions in society and is affected by social and cultural factors. — *adj* **sociolog'ic** or **sociolog'ical** pertaining to sociology; dealing solely with environmental factors in considering a human problem; social. — *n* **sociol'ogist.** — *n* **sociol'ogy** the study of the structure and functioning of human society. — *adj* **sociomet'ric.** — *n* **sociom'etry** the measurement of social phenomena; the study of personal inter-relationships within a social group. — *n* **so'ciopath.** — *adj* **sociopath'ic.** — *n* **sociop'athy** any of several personality disorders resulting in asocial or antisocial behaviour. [L. *socius*, a companion.]

sock[1] *sok*, *n* a covering for the foot and part or all of the lower leg; an insole placed in a shoe for warmth, to improve the fit, etc. — *n* **sockette** (*sok'et*) a covering for the foot only. — **pull up one's socks** to brace oneself for doing better; **put a sock in it** (*slang*; usu. *imper*) to become silent, stop talking, etc. [O.E. *socc* — L. *soccus*.]

sock[2] *sok*, (*slang*) *vt* to strike hard. — *n* a violent blow, esp. with the fist. — *adj* **sock'ō** (*US* and *theat slang*) excellent, successful, knockout; having a strong impact, full of energy. — **sock it to** (*slang*) to speak, behave, etc. in a vigorous manner towards.

socket *sok'it*, *n* a hollow into which something is inserted or in which something fits, such as the receptacle of the eye, a bone, a tooth, or the shaft of an iron golf club, the hollow of a candlestick, etc.; a device in which an electric plug or light bulb may be inserted to make a connection. — *vt* to provide with or place in a socket; to strike with the socket (*golf*): — *pr p* **sock'eting**; *pa t* and *pa p* **sock'eted.** — *adj* **sock'eted.** — **socket chisel** a robust chisel with a socketed metal shaft into which the wooden handle is fitted; **socket spanner** a spanner with a socketed head made to fit over a nut or a bolt; **socket wrench** a wrench with a handle to which a variety of socketed heads can be fitted. [O.Fr. *soket*, dimin. of *soc*.]

sockette. See **sock**[1].

sockeye *sok'ī*, *n* the blueback salmon. [Am. Ind. *sukai*, the fish of fishes, the native name on the Fraser River.]

socking *sok'ing*, (*colloq*) *adj* huge, whacking (usu. followed by *great*). [Prob. **sock**[2].]

socle *sō'kl* or *sok'l*, (*archit*) *n* a plain face or plinth at the foot of a wall, column, etc. [Fr., — It. *zoccolo* — L. *socculus*, dimin. of *soccus*, a shoe.]

Socratic *sō-krat'ik* or *so-*, *adj* pertaining to *Socrates*, the Greek philosopher (d. 399 B.C.), to his philosophy, or to his method of teaching, by a series of simple questions revealing to his interlocutors their own ignorance.

sod[1] *sod*, *n* a turf, usu. one cut in rectangular shape; sward. — *vt* to cover with sods. [M.L.G. *sode*; Ger. *Sode*.]

sod[2] *sod*, (*vulg*) *n* a term of abuse, affection, etc. — *interj* a term expressing annoyance, etc. (sometimes behaving as a verb with *it*, *him*, etc. as object). — *adj* **sodd'ing.** — **sod off** to go away; **Sod's law** (*facetious*) the law that states that the most inconvenient thing is the most likely to happen, or if there is a possibility that something may go wrong, it will. [Abbrev. of **sodomite.**]

soda *sō'də*, *n* any of a number of common sodium compounds, including sodium oxide (Na_2O), sodium hydroxide (*caustic soda*), sodium carbonate (*washing soda*), and sodium bicarbonate (*baking soda*); soda water (*colloq*); a drink made of soda water with flavouring, ice-cream, etc. (*US*). — *adj* of or containing soda or sodium. — *adj* **sodaic** (*sō-dā'ik*) containing or pertaining to soda. — **soda-ash** anhydrous sodium carbonate; **so'da-fountain** an apparatus for supplying soda water; a shop or counter where sodas, ice-cream, etc. are served; **so'da-lime** a mixture of caustic soda and quicklime; **soda pop** (*US*) a carbonated soft drink of any flavour; **so'da-scone** a scone made with baking soda; **soda siphon** a siphon which dispenses soda water; **soda water** water made effervescent by charging with carbon dioxide (formerly made with sodium bicarbonate). [It. and L.L. *soda*.]

sodality *sō-dal'i-ti*, *n* a fellowship or fraternity. [L. *sodālitās* — *sodālis*, a comrade.]

sodden *sod'n*, *pa p* of **seethe.** — *adj* soaked thoroughly; boggy; doughy, not well baked; bloated or saturated with drink.

sodium *sō'di-əm, n* a bluish-white alkaline metal (symbol **Na**; atomic no. 11). — **sodium amytal** (*am'i-tal*; ® with *caps*) a sodium salt used as a sedative and hypnotic; **sodium ascorbate** a compound used as a meat preservative and also in the treatment of vitamin C deficiency; **sodium bicarbonate** see under **bicarbonate**; **sodium carbonate** a soluble compound widely used in the making of glass, ceramics, etc. and as a cleaning agent; **sodium chlorate** a colourless crystalline compound used in explosives, as an antiseptic, and as weedkiller; **sodium chloride** common salt; **sodium lamp** a street lamp using sodium vapour and giving yellow light. [**soda**.]

Sodom *sod'əm, n* one of the 'cities of the plain' (in the Bible: Genesis xviii, xix); any place of utter depravity (*fig*). — *vt* **sod'omise** or **-ize** to practise sodomy upon. — *n* **Sod'omite** (*-īt*) an inhabitant of Sodom; (without *cap*) someone who practises sodomy. — *adj* **sodomitic** (*-it'ik*). — *n* **sod'omy** anal intercourse (with a man or woman) or copulation with an animal, imputed to the inhabitants of Sodom.

SOE *abbrev* for Special Operations Executive.

soever *sō-ev'ər, adv* generally used to extend or make indefinite the sense of (and esp. as *combining form* **-soever** added to) *who*, *what*, *where*, *how*, etc.

sofa *sō'fə, n* a long upholstered seat with back and arms. — **sofa bed** a piece of furniture serving as a sofa by day and a bed at night. [Ar. *suffah*.]

soffit *sof'it, n* a ceiling, now generally restricted to the ornamented underside of a stair, entablature, archway, etc. [It. *soffitto* — L. *suffixus*, past p. of *suffigĕre*, to fasten beneath — *sub*, under, *figĕre*, to fix.]

S. of S. (*Bible*) *abbrev* for Song of Songs, or Song of Solomon.

soft *soft, adj* easily yielding to pressure; easily cut; easily scratched (*mineralogy*); malleable; yielding; not rigorous enough; not loud; not glaring; diffused; weak in muscle or mind; out of training; smooth; pleasing or soothing to the senses; tender; mild; sympathetic; gentle; effeminate; unable to endure rough treatment or hardship; (relatively) unprotected; gently moving; easy; (of water) free from calcium and magnesium salts; (of coal) bituminous; pronounced with a somewhat sibilant sound, not guttural or explosive; voiced or sonant; apt to fall in price; (of drugs) not habit-forming in an obvious degree; (of radiation) having short wavelengths and therefore not highly penetrating; (in computer typesetting and word processing) of a space or hyphen that can be automatically removed when its environment changes to make it redundant. — *adv* softly; gently; quietly. — *vt* **soften** (*sof'n*) to tone down, make less glaring or smoother. — *vi* to grow soft or softer. — *n* **softener** (*sof'nər*). — *n* and *adj* **softening** (*sof'ning*). — *n* **soft'ie** a softy. — *adv* **soft'ly**. — *n* **soft'ness**. — *n* **soft'y** a silly person, a weak fool; someone who is soft-hearted or sentimental. — **soft'back** a paperback. — Also *adj*. — **soft'ball** an American game similar to baseball, played on a smaller diamond with a soft ball. — *adj* **soft-billed'**. — *adj* **soft-bod'ied**. — *vt* **soft'-boil**. — *adj* **soft-boiled'** boiled not long enough to be quite solid; soft-hearted (*colloq*). — *adj* **soft=cen'tred**. — **soft commodities** foodstuffs, coffee, cotton, etc., as opp. to metals. — *adj* **soft'-core** not explicit, blatant or graphic. — **soft currency** one unstable in value in the international money-market through fluctuation in its gold backing; **soft drink** a non-alcoholic drink. — *adj* **soft-finned'** without fin-spines. — **soft focus** deliberate slight blurring of a picture or scene (*phot*, *cinematography*). — *adj* **soft-foot'ed** softly treading. — **soft fruit** small, stoneless, edible fruit, such as berries and currants; **soft furnishings** curtains, coverings, rugs, etc.; **soft'-goods** cloth, and cloth articles (as opp. to *hardware*, etc.). — *adj* **soft-heart'ed** kind, generous; tender-hearted. — **soft hyphen** (in word-processing) one inserted in a word only if necessary for word division at the end of a line; **soft landing** a landing by a spacecraft, etc. without damage (also *fig*); **soft lens** a flexible contact lens of a hydrophylic material which allows some oxygen to reach the cornea; **soft line** a flexible or lenient attitude, policy, etc.; **soft loan** one without conditions attached; a cheap or interest-free loan, usu. to a developing country. — *adj* **softly-soft'ly** cautious, careful, delicate. — *adj* **soft-nosed'** (of a bullet) with a tip that expands on striking. — **soft option** an alternative that is easy to carry out, undergo, etc.; **soft palate** the back part of the palate; **soft pedal** a pedal for reducing tone in the piano, esp. by causing the hammer to strike only one string (*una corda*). — *vt* and *vi* **soft-ped'al** to play with the soft pedal down; to subdue, tone down, avoid emphasising or alluding to (*slang*). — **soft porn** or **pornography** mild, soft-core pornography; **soft sell** selling or sale by preliminary softening up or other indirect method; mild persuasion, or mildly persuasive tactics. — *adj* **soft-sell'**. — *adj* **soft'-shell** or **-shelled'** having a soft shell; moderate in policy or principles. — *adj* **soft'-shoe** characteristic of or pertaining to a form of tap-dancing done in soft-soled shoes. — **soft soap** a kind of soap containing potash; flattery; blarney. — *vt* **soft'-soap** to rub or cover with soft soap; to flatter for some end. — *adj* **soft-spo'ken** having a mild or gentle voice; affable; suave; plausible in speech. — **soft spot** see under **spot**; **soft touch** see under **touch**; **soft underbelly** the vulnerable part; **soft'ware** computer programs, esp. general ones for routine operations (compare *hardware*); computer program (or analogous) accessories (other than the actual parts of a computer, etc.); material recorded in microform; **soft'wood** timber of a conifer (also *adj*). — **be** or **go soft on** to be lenient with; **softening of the brain** a softening of brain tissues; marked deterioration of mental faculties (*colloq*); **soften up** to lessen resistance in (*colloq*); to wear down by continuous shelling and bombing. [O.E. *sōfte*, *sēfte*.]

SOGAT *sō'gat*, now properly **SOGAT 82** *abbrev* for Society of Graphical and Allied Trades.

soggy *sog'i, adj* soaked; soft or heavy with moisture; boggy; soppy; sultry; spiritless. — *adv* **sogg'ily**. — *n* **sogg'iness**.

soh. See **sol**[1].

soi-disant *swä-dē-zã, adj* self-styled, pretended, would-be. [Fr.]

soigné, *fem* **soignée**, *swa-nyā, adj* well groomed. [Fr.]

soil[1] *soil, n* the ground; the mould in which plants grow; the mixture of disintegrated rock and organic material which nourishes plants; land, country. — *adj* **soil'-bound** attached to the soil. — **soil creep** (*geol*) the very slow but continuous movement of soil and rock fragments down a slope; **soil science** the study of the composition and uses of soil. [O.Fr. *soel*, *suel*, *sueil* — L. *solum*, ground.]

soil[2] *soil, n* dung; filth; sewage; a spot or stain. — *vt* to make dirty; to stain; to manure. — *vi* to become dirty or stained; to tarnish. — *adj* **soiled**. — **soil'-pipe** an upright discharge-pipe which receives the general refuse from water-closets, etc. in a building. [O.Fr. *soil*, *souil*, wallowing-place.]

soil[3] *soil, vt* to feed (cattle) on fresh-cut green food; to purge by so doing; to fatten. [O.Fr. *saouler* — *saol*, *saoul* — L. *satullus* — *satur*, full; or from **soil**[2].]

soirée *swär'ā, n* an evening party; an evening social meeting with tea, etc. [Fr., — *soir*, evening — L. *sērus*, late.]

soixante-neuf *swa-sãt-nœf*, (Fr.) *n* a sexual position in which both partners simultaneously orally stimulate each other's genitalia. [Lit. sixty-nine, from the position adopted.]

sojourn *so'* or *su'jərn*, or *-jûrn'*, *vt* to stay for a day; to dwell for a time. — *n* a temporary residence. — *n* **so'journer**. [O.Fr. *sojourner* — L. *sub*, under, *diurnus*, of a day — *diēs*, a day.]

Sol. or **Solr** *abbrev* for Solicitor.

sol[1] *sol*, *n* the fifth note of the scale in sol-fa notation. — Also **so** or **soh** (*sō*).

sol[2] *sol*, *n* a colloidal suspension in a liquid. — *n* **solā'tion** liquefaction of a gel. [Short for **solution**.]

sol. *abbrev* for solution.

sola *sō'lə*, *n* spongewood, an Indian plant, also known as the *hat-plant*; its pithlike stems. — *adj* of sola. — **sola hat, helmet** or **topi** a sun-helmet made of sola pith (also, incorrectly, **solar**). [Hindi *solā*.]

solace *sol'is* or *sol'əs*, *n* consolation, comfort in distress; pleasure, amusement; a source of comfort or pleasure. — *vt* to comfort in distress; to console; to allay. — *vi* to take comfort. — *n* **sol'acement**. [O.Fr. *solas* — L. *sōlātium* — *sōlārī*, *-ātus*, to comfort in distress.]

solan *sō'lən* or **solan goose** (*gōōs*), *n* the gannet. [O.N. *sūla*.]

solar[1] *sō'lər*, *adj* of, from, like, or pertaining to the sun; measured by the sun; influenced by the sun; powered by energy from the sun's rays; with branches radiating like the sun's rays. — *n* **solarimeter** (*-im'it-ər*) a device for measuring solar radiation. — *n* **sōlarīsā'tion** or **-z-** the act, process or effect of solarising; the reversal of an image by over-exposure (*phot*). — *vt* **sō'larise** or **-ize** to expose to sunlight or affect by such exposure, esp. excessive or injurious exposure. — *vi* to be so affected. — *n* **solā'rium** a place for sunbathing or equipped with sun-beds; a sun-bed. — **solar battery** a battery of solar cells; **solar cell** a photoelectric cell converting the energy of sunlight into electric power; **solar day** see under **day**; **solar energy** energy obtained from the sun's rays, esp. when used for home-heating, etc.; **solar panel** a panel of solar cells; **solar plexus** (*anat*) a network of nerves behind the stomach (so called from its radiating nerves); **solar power** solar energy (*adj* **sō'lar-powered**); **solar prominences** large prominent or protruding parts of the great volumes of heated gas surrounding the sun; **solar system** the sun with its attendant bodies — major and minor planets, meteors, comets, satellites; **solar time** see under **time**; **solar wind** charged particles from the sun travelling at about one and a half million kilometres an hour. [L. *sōlāris*, solar, *sōlārium*, a sundial — *sōl*, the sun.]

solar[2] *sō'lər*. See **sola**.

solation. See under **sol**[2].

solatium *sō-lā'shi-əm* or *sō-lä'ti-ŏŏm*, *n* compensation for disappointment, inconvenience or wounded feelings. [L. *sōlātium*.]

sold *sōld*, *pa t* and *pa p* of **sell**. — **sold on** extremely enthusiastic or convinced about.

solder *sōl'dər* or *sol-*, in U.S. also *sod'ər* or *sōd'ər*, *n* a fusible alloy for uniting metals. — *vt* to attach with solder; to join; to mend, patch up. — *vi* to adhere. — *n* **sol'derer**. — *n* **sol'dering**. — **sol'dering-iron** a tool with pointed or wedge-shaped copper bit for use in soldering. [O.Fr. *soudre*, *souldure* — *souder*, *soulder*, to consolidate — L. *solidāre*, to make solid.]

soldier *sōl'jər* or *sōld'yər*, *n* a person engaged in military service; a private; a person of military skill; an ant, or white ant, of a specialised fighting caste; a scarlet, pugnacious, or armoured animal of various kinds (beetle, fish, etc.); a diligent worker for a cause; a brick set upright in a wall; a narrow strip of bread-and-butter or toast, esp. for a child to eat (*colloq*). — *vi* to serve as a soldier. — *n* **sol'diering**. — *n* **sol'dierliness**. — *adj* **sol'dierly** befitting a soldier; having the qualities of or befitting a soldier. — *n* **sol'diery** soldiers collectively; a military body or class; military qualities. — **sol'dier-crab** a hermit crab. — **soldier of fortune** a mercenary; someone ready to serve anywhere for pay or their own advancement; **soldier on** to continue doggedly in face of difficulty or discouragement. [O.Fr. *soldier* — L. *solidus*, a piece of money, the pay of a soldier.]

sole[1] *sōl*, *n* the underside of the foot; the bottom of a boot or shoe; the undersurface of a golf club head; the bottom, understructure, floor or undersurface of various things. — *vt* to put a sole on. — **sole'-plate** a bed-plate or similar object. [O.E. and O.Fr. *sole* — L. *solea*, sole, sandal — *solum*, bottom.]

sole[2] *sōl*, *n* an elliptical flat fish (genus *Solea*) used as food. [Fr. *sole* — L. *solea*.]

sole[3] *sōl*, *adj* alone; only; without husband or wife (*law*); without another; consisting of one person; exclusive; uniform. — *adv* **sole'ly** alone; only; singly. — *n* **sole'ness**. [Fr., — L. *sōlus*, alone.]

solecism *sol'i-sizm*, *n* a breach of syntax; any absurdity, impropriety or incongruity. — *n* **sol'ecist**. — *adj* **solecist'ic** or **solecist'ical**. — *adv* **solecist'ically**. [Gr. *soloikismos*, said to come from the corruption of the Attic dialect among the Athenian colonists (*oikizein*, to colonise) of *Soloi* in Cilicia.]

solemn *sol'əm*, *adj* accompanied by or marked by special (esp. religious) ceremonies, pomp, or gravity; accompanied by an appeal to God, as an oath; grave; in serious earnestness; with formal dignity; awed; awe-inspiring; stately; pompous; glum; sombre. — *vt* **solemnify** (*sə-lem'ni-fī*) to make solemn. — *n* **solemnisation** or **-z-** (*sol-əm-nī-zā'shən*). — *vt* **sol'emnise** or **-ize** (*-nīz*) to perform religiously or solemnly; to celebrate with rites; to make solemn. — *n* **sol'emniser** or **-z-**. — *n* **solemnity** (*-lem'ni-ti*) a solemn ceremony; high seriousness; affected gravity. — *adv* **sol'emnly**. — *n* **sol'emnness**. — **solemn mass** high mass. [O.Fr. *solempne*, *solemne* — L. *sollemnis*, customary, appointed.]

solenoid *sō'lə-noid*, *n* a cylindrical coil of wire, acting as a magnet when an electric current passes through it, converting electrical energy to mechanical energy. — *adj* **solenoid'al**. [Gr. *sōlēn*, a pipe.]

solera *sō-lā'rä*, *n* a system of sherry production involving blending wines of various ages from a series of graded casks to achieve uniformity; (*collectively*) the casks used in this process. [Sp., — L. *solus*, ground, base.]

soleus *sō'li-əs*, (*anat*) *n* the flat muscle of the leg beneath the muscle that bulges the calf: — *pl* **so'lei** (*-ē-ī*) or **so'leuses**. [N.L., — L. *soles*, sole.]

sol-fa *sol-fä'*, (*mus*) *n* a system of syllables (*do* or *ut*; *re*, *mi*, *fa*; *sol*, *soh* or *so*; *la*; *si* or *ti*) representing and sung to the notes of the scale. — *adj* belonging to the system. — *vt* and *vi* to sing to sol-fa syllables: — *pr p* **sol-faing** (*-fä'ing*); *pa t* and *pa p* **sol-faed** or **-fa'd** (*-fäd'*). — *n* **solfeggio** (*-fed'jō*; It.) an exercise in sol-fa syllables: — *pl* **solfeggi** (*-fed'jē*). — **tonic sol-fa** see under **tone**. [**sol**[1] and **fa**.]

solfatara *sol-fä-tä'rə*, *n* a volcanic vent emitting only gases, esp. one emitting acid gases (hydrochloric acid and sulphur dioxide): — *pl* **solfata'ras**. — *adj* **solfata'ric**. [From the *Solfatara* (lit. sulphur-mine, sulphur-hole) near Naples — It. *solfo*, sulphur.]

solfeggio. See **sol-fa**.

Sol.-Gen. *abbrev* for Solicitor-General.

solicit *sə-lis'it*, *vt* to petition; to importune; to seek after; to call for, require; to invite to immorality; to conduct, manage. — *vi* to petition; to act as solicitor; (of prostitutes) to make advances; (of beggars) to importune for alms. — *n* **solic'itant** a person who solicits (also *adj*). — *n* **solicitā'tion** a soliciting; an earnest request; an invitation. — *n* **solic'iting** any action of the verb, esp. (of prostitutes) the making of advances. — *n* **solic'itor** a lawyer who advises, prepares deeds, manages cases, instructs counsel in the higher courts, and acts as an advocate in the lower courts; a person who asks earnestly. — *n* **solic'itorship**. — *adj* **solic'itous** soliciting or earnestly asking or desiring; anxious; concerned; considerate; careful. — *adv* **solic'itously**. — *n* **solic'itousness** or **solic'itude** the state of being solicitous; anxiety or uneasiness of mind; trouble. — **Solicitor-Gen'eral** in England, the law-officer of the crown next in rank to the Attorney-General — in Scotland, to the Lord-Advocate. [L. *sōlicitāre, sollicitāre* — *sō-, sollicitus* — *sollus*, whole, *citus*, aroused.]

solid *sol'id, adj* resisting change of shape, having the particles firmly cohering (opp. to *fluid*; distinguished from *liquid* and *gaseous*); hard; compact; full of matter; not hollow; strong; having or pertaining to three dimensions; substantial; worthy of credit; weighty; of uniform undivided substance; financially sound, wealthy; reliable; sensible; unanimous; unbroken; unvaried. — *n* a substance, body or figure that is solid; a solid mass or part. — *n* **solidarity** (*-dar'i-ti*) unity of interests, aims, etc. — *adj* **sol'idary** (*-dər-i*) marked by solidarity; jointly responsible; joint and several. — *adj* **solidifiable** (*sə-lid'i-fī-ə-bl*). — *n* **solidificā'tion**. — *vt* **solid'ify** to make solid or compact. — *vi* to grow solid: — *pr p* **solid'ifying**; *pa t* and *pa p* **solid'ified**. — *n* **solid'ity** the state of being solid; fullness, substance, actuality; strength or firmness, moral or physical; soundness, sturdiness; volume. — *adv* **sol'idly**. — *n* **sol'idness**. — *adj* **solid-hoofed'** with uncloven hoofs. — *adj* **solid-state'** of, consisting of, or relating to solid substances; of, consisting of or relating to semiconductor materials (and their electrical properties). — **solid-state physics** a branch of physics which covers all properties of solid materials, now esp. electrical conduction in crystals of semiconductors, and superconductivity and photoconductivity; **solid with** packed tight with; on a firm footing of understanding with; supporting fully. [L. *solidus, -a, -um*, solid.]

solidungulate *sol-id-ung'gū-lāt*, (*zool*) *adj* with uncloven hoofs. [L. *solidus*, solid, *ungula*, a hoof.]

solidus *sol'i-dəs, n* the stroke, oblique or slash (/), a sign used for various purposes, as in writing fractions and to separate alternatives, ratios, etc. (e.g. 3/4, and/or); a Roman gold coin, or a mediaeval silver coin (*hist*): — *pl* **sol'idi** (*-dī*). [M.E. — L.L. *solidus* (*nummus*), a solid (coin); used to denote the former English shilling, representing the old lengthened *s* (£. s. d. = *librae, solidi, denarii*, pounds, shillings, pence).]

soliloquy *sə-lil'ə-kwi, n* an act of talking to oneself; a speech of this nature made by a character in a play, etc. — *vi* **solil'oquise** or **-ize** to speak to oneself; to utter a soliloquy in a play, etc. — *n* **solil'oquiser** or **-z-**, or **solil'oquist**. [L. *sōliloquium* — *sōlus*, alone, *loquī*, to speak.]

solipsism *sol'ip-sizm, n* the theory that self-existence is the only certainty, absolute egoism — the extreme form of subjective idealism. — *n* and *adj* **sol'ipsist**. — *adj* **solipsis'tic**. [L. *sōlus*, alone, *ipse*, self.]

solitaire *sol-i-tār', n* a recluse; a game played by one person with a board and balls, pegs, etc.; patience (the card game); a diamond, etc. set by itself. — **solitaire'-board** a board with cups, holes, etc. for playing solitaire. [Fr., see **solitary**.]

solitary *sol'i-tər-i, adj* alone; single, separate; living alone, not social or gregarious; without company; retired, secluded; lonely; growing single (*bot*). — *n* someone who lives alone; a hermit; solitary confinement (*colloq*). — *adv* **sol'itarily**. — *n* **sol'itariness**. — **solitary confinement** imprisonment in a cell by oneself. [L. *sōlitārius* — *sōlus*, alone.]

soliton *sol'it-ən*, (*phys*) *n* a solitary wave; a quantum which corresponds to a solitary wave in its transmission. [**solitary**.]

solitude *sol'i-tūd, n* solitariness; absence of company. — *adj* **solitūd'inous**. [L. *sōlitūdō* — *sōlus*.]

solmisation or **-z-** *sol-mi-zā'shən*, (*mus*) *n* sol-faing; a recital of the notes of the scale. [**sol**[1] and **mi**.]

solo *sō'lō, n* a piece or passage for one voice or instrument, accompanied or unaccompanied; any performance in which no other person or instrument participates; a single-seater motorcycle or bicycle as opp. to motorcycle with sidecar, tandem, etc.; a card game (**solo whist**) based on whist, in which various declarations are made and the declarer may or may not have a partner: — *pl* **sō'lōs** or (*mus*) **soli** (*sō'lē*). — *adj* performed, or for performances, as a solo; performing a solo; for one; single. — *adv* alone. — *vi* to fly solo; to play (a) solo. — *n* **sō'lōist**. [It., — L. *sōlus*, alone.]

Solomon *sol'ə-mən, n* a person of unusual wisdom, from *Solomon*, king of Israel (from the Bible: 1 Kings iii. 5–15). — *adj* **Solomonian** (*-mō'ni-ən*) or **Solomonic** (*-mon'ik*). — **Solomon's-seal'** any species of *Polygonatum*, a genus of the lily family, with small dangling greenish flowers; a symbol formed of two triangles interlaced or superposed, forming a six-pointed star.

so-long or **so long** *sō-long'*, (*colloq* or *slang*) *interj* good-bye. [Prob. **so**[1] and **long**; poss. **salaam**.]

Solr *abbrev* for Solicitor.

solstice *sol'stis, n* the time when the sun reaches its maximum distance from the equator (*summer solstice* when it touches the tropic of Cancer, about 21 June; the *winter solstice* when it touches that of Capricorn, about 21 December); the turning-point reached then. — *adj* **solstitial** (*-stish'l*) pertaining to, or happening at, a solstice, esp. at the summer solstice. [Fr., — L. *sōlstitium* — *sōl*, the sun, *sistĕre, stătum*, to make to stand.]

soluble *sol'ū-bl, adj* capable of being solved, dissolved or resolved. — *n* **solubilisā'tion** or **-z-**. — *vt* **sol'ubilise** or **-ize** to make soluble; to make more soluble. — *n* **solūbil'ity** (a measure of) the ability of a substance to dissolve. — *adv* **sol'ubly**. — *n* **sol'ūte** a dissolved substance. — *adj* (*sol'* or *-ūt'*) loose; free; not adhering; dissolved. — *n* **solution** (*səl-ōō'shən* or *-ū'shən*) the act of solving or dissolving; the condition of being dissolved; the preparation resulting from this; the separating of parts; abnormal separation; an explanation; the removal of a doubt; the solving of, answer to, a problem; the payment of a debt, or similar discharge of an obligation. [L. *solvĕre, solūtum*, to loosen.]

solve *solv, vt* to dissolve; to settle; to clear up or explain; to find an answer to or a way out of. — *n* **solvabil'ity**. — *adj* **sol'vable**. — *n* **sol'vate** a definite combination of solute and solvent. — *n* **sol'vency**. — *adj* **sol'vent** able to solve or dissolve; able to pay all debts. — *n* a substance that dissolves another; that component of a solution which is present in excess, or whose physical state is the same as that of the solution; something which provides a solution. — *n* **sol'ver**. — **solvent abuse** self-intoxication by inhaling the fumes given off by various solvents — adhesives, petrol, etc. [L. *solvĕre*, to loosen, prob. from *sē-, sĕ-*, aside, *luĕre*, to loosen.]

Som. *abbrev* for Somerset.

soma[1] or **Soma** *sō'mə, n* a plant or its intoxicating juice, used in ancient Indian religious ceremonies, and personified as a god. [Sans. *soma* (Avestan *haoma*, juice).]

soma[2] *sō'mə, n* the body; the body of an animal or plant excluding the germ-cells (*biol*): — *pl* **so'mas** or **somata** (*-mä'tə*). — *n* **somascope** (*sō'mə-skōp*) an instrument using ultrasonic waves converted into a television image to show the character of diseased internal tissues of the body. — *adj* **somatic** (*-mat'ik*). — *adv* **somat'ically**. — *adj* **somatotroph'ic** or **-trop'ic** promoting bodily growth. — *n* **somato-**

troph'in or **-trop'in** growth hormone. — *n* **somat'otype** a type consisting of a physical build paired with a particular temperament. — *vt* to assign a somatotype to. — *n* **so'mite** (*zool*) a body-segment of a vertebrate embryo or of a segmented invertebrate. [Gr. *sōma*, body.]

sombre *som'bər*, *adj* dark and gloomy; melancholy, dismal. — *vt* and *vi* to make or become sombre. — *adv* **som'brely**. — *n* **som'breness**. [Fr. (cf. Sp. *sombra*, shade) — perh. L. *sub*, under, *umbra*, a shade.]

sombrero *som-brā'rō*, *n* a broad-brimmed hat: — *pl* **sombre'ros**. [Sp., hat — *sombra*, shade.]

some *sum*, *indefinite pron* an indefinite part of the whole number or quantity; (a) certain (undetermined) one(s). — *adj* one or other; in an indefinite number or quantity; a little; not a little; considerable; a certain; certain unspecified; several; a few; in approximate number, length, etc., more or less; remarkable, outstanding, of note (*colloq*, esp. *US*; also *ironical*). — *adv* very much (*US*). — *n* (or *pron*) **some'body** some person; a person of importance: — *pl* **some'bodies**. — *adv* **some'day** at an unspecified time in the future. — *adv* **some'how** in some way or other. — *n* (or *pron*) **some'one** somebody. — *adv* **some'place** (*US*) somewhere. — *n* (or *pron*) **some'thing** an undefined thing; a thing of some account; a portion. — *adv* in some degree. — Also used as a substitute for any word (*n*, *adj* or *v*) or component of any word forgotten, indefinite or avoided. — *adv* **some'time** at a time not fixed; at one time or other; formerly. — *adj* former; late. — *adv* **some'times** at times; now and then. — *adv* **some'what** in some degree. — *n* an unfixed quantity or degree. — *adv* **some'where** in or to some place. — **someone else** some other person; **someone else's** some other person's. [O.E. *sum*.]

-some[1] *-sum* or *-səm*, *sfx* (1) forming adjectives with the meaning full of, e.g. *troublesome*, *wholesome*; (2) forming nouns denoting a group with a certain number of members, e.g. *twosome*, *threesome*. [O.E. *-sum*; cf. **same**.]

-some[2] *-sōm*, *sfx* forming nouns denoting a body, e.g. *chromosome*. [Gr. *soma*, body.]

somersault *sum'ər-sölt*, *n* a leap or other movement in which a person turns heels over head. — *vi* to turn a somersault. [O.Fr. *sombre saut* — L. *suprā*, over, *saltus*, *-ūs*, a leap.]

somite. See under **soma**[2].

somnambulance *som-nam'bū-ləns*, *n* sleep-walking. — *adj* and *n* **somnam'būlant**. — *adj* **somnam'būlar** or **somnam'bulary**. — *vi* **somnam'būlate** to walk in one's sleep. — *n* **somnambūlā'tion**. — *n* **somnam'būlātor** or **somnam'būle** a sleepwalker. [L. *somnus*, sleep, *ambulare*, to walk.]

somnifacient *som-ni-fā'shənt* or *-shi-ənt*, *adj* sleep-inducing or promoting. — Also **somnif'erous** or **somnif'ic**. — *n* a somnifacient drug. [L. *somnus*, sleep, *faciens*, *facientis*, pres. p. of *facĕre*, to do.]

somniloquence *som-nil'ə-kwəns*, **somniloquism** *-nil'ə-kwizm* or **somniloquy** *-nil'ə-kwi*, *n* talking in one's sleep. — *vi* **somnil'oquise** or **-ize**. — *n* **somnil'oquist**. [L. *somnus*, sleep, *loquī*, to talk.]

somnolence *som'nə-ləns*, *n* sleepiness. — Also **som'nolency**. — *adj* **som'nolent**. [M.E. *sompnolence* — O.Fr. — L. *somnolentia* — *somnus*, sleep.]

son *sun*, *n* a male child or offspring; a descendant, or one so regarded or treated; a disciple; a native or inhabitant; the product of anything; a familiar (sometimes patronising) mode of address to a boy or to a male younger than oneself. — *n* **sonn'y** a little son; a familiar form of addressing a boy. — *n* **son'ship** the state or character of a son. — **son'-in-law** a daughter's husband: — *pl* **sons'-in-law**. — **son of a bitch** see **sonofabitch**; **son of a gun** see under **gun**; **son of man** a man; applied to Jesus Christ or the Messiah; **the Son** the second person in the Trinity, Jesus Christ. [O.E. *sunu*.]

sonant *sō'nənt*, (*phon*) *adj* voiced; syllabic. — *n* a voiced sound; a syllabic consonant. — *n* **so'nance** a sounding. — *n* **so'nancy**. [L. *sonāns*, *-antis*, pres. p. of *sonāre*, to sound.]

Sonar *sō'nər*, *n* the American equivalent of Asdic; (without *cap*) the natural equipment that provides echo location in bats and some marine animals; (without *cap*) echo-sounding equipment in general. — **sonar buoy** same as **sonobuoy**. [*so*und *nav*igation *a*nd *r*anging.]

sonata *sə-* or *so-nä'tə*, (*mus*) *n* a composition usu. of three or more movements designed chiefly for a solo instrument. — *n* **sonatina** (*son-ə-tē'nə*) a short sonata. — **sonata form** the form usual in the first movement of a sonata or symphony, divided into three sections: exposition, development and recapitulation. [It., fem. past p. of *sonare* — L. *sonāre*, to sound.]

sondage *sɔ̃-däzh*, (*archaeol*) *n* a trial bore or excavation. [Fr.]

sonde *sond*, *n* any device for obtaining information about atmospheric and weather conditions at high altitudes. [Fr.]

son et lumière *son ā lüm-yār'*, *n* a dramatic spectacle presented after dark, involving lighting effects on natural features of the country or on a chosen building and an appropriate theme illustrated by spoken words and by music. [Fr.]

song *song*, *n* that which is sung; a short poem or ballad suitable for singing or set to music; the melody to which it is sung; an instrumental composition of a similar form and character; singing; the melodious outburst of a bird; a theme of song; a habitual utterance, manner or attitude towards anything; a mere trifle (as in **going for a song** being sold for a trifling sum). — *adj* **song'ful** melodious; songlike; like singing; ready to break into song. — *adj* **song'less**. — *adj* **song'like**. — *n* **song'ster**, *fem* **song'stress**, a singer. — **song'bird** a bird that sings; any bird of the suborder Oscines; **song'book** a book of songs; **song cycle** a sequence of songs connected in subject; **song'smith** a composer of songs; **song thrush** the mavis or throstle (see also **thrush**[1]); **song'writer** a person who composes music and/or words for (esp. popular) songs. — **make a song and dance about** to make an unnecessary fuss about; **Song of Songs** or **of Solomon** Canticles, a book of the Old Testament long attributed to Solomon. [O.E. *sang* — *singan*, to sing.]

sonic *son'ik*, *adj* pertaining to or using sound waves; travelling at about the speed of sound. — *nsing* **son'ics** the study of the technological application of sounds, esp. supersonic waves. — **sonic bang** or **boom** (*aeronautics*) a loud double report caused by shock waves projected outward and backward from the leading and trailing edges of an aircraft travelling at supersonic speed; **sonic barrier** the sound barrier; **sonic mine** an acoustic mine. [L. *sonus*, sound.]

sonnet *son'it*, *n* a short poem of fourteen lines of ten or eleven syllables, rhymed according to one or other of certain definite schemes, forming an octave and a sestet, properly expressing two successive phases of one thought. [It. *sonetto*, dimin. of *suono* — L. *sonus*, a sound.]

sonny. See **son**.

sono- *son-ō-*, *combining form* meaning sonic. — *n* **sonobuoy** (*son'ō-boi* or in U.S. also *-bōō-ē*) sonar equipment dropped to float on the sea, pick up underwater noise, and transmit bearings of the source to aircraft. — *n* **son'ogram** a visual representation of a sound, produced by a sonograph (*acoustics*); a sonogram produced by ultrasonography (*med*). — *n* **son'ograph** an instrument for scanning and recording sound and its component frequencies. — *n* **sonog'rapher**. — *n* **sonog'raphy**. [L. *sonus*, sound.]

sonofabitch *sun-əv-ə-bich'*, (*slang*; esp. *US*) *n* son of a bitch, an abusive term of address or of description, or vulgar exclamation: — *pl* **sons of bitches**.

sonorous *sə-nö'rəs* or *son'ə-rəs*, *adj* sounding, esp. loudly; deeply, impressively, etc.; full-sounding; sounding or ringing when struck. — *n* **son'orant** (*phon*) a frictionless continuant or nasal (*l*, *r*, *m*, *n*, *ng*) capable of fulfilling a vocalic or consonantal function; the consonants represented by *w*, *y*, having consonantal or vocalic articulations. — *n* **sonority** (*sō-* or *sə-nor'i-ti*) sonorousness; type, quality, etc. of sound. — *adv* **sono'rously** (or *son'*). — *n* **sono'rousness** (or *son'*) sonorous quality or character. [L. *sonōrus* — *sonor*, *-ōris*, a sound — *sonāre*, to sound.]

sook *so͝ok*, *n* a soft, timid or cowardly person (*slang*, esp. *Austr*); someone who sucks up fawningly, a toady (*Brit dialect*). [Perh. from earlier *suck(-calf)*, a hand-reared calf, infl. by Scot. pronunciation of **suck**.]

soon *so͞on*, *adv* (*compar* **soon'er**, *superl* **soon'est**) in a short time; without much delay; early; readily; willingly. — *adv* **soon'est** (*telegraphese* and *mil jargon*) as soon as possible. — **no sooner ... than** immediately; **sooner or later** eventually. [O.E. *sōna*.]

soot *so͝ot*, *n* a black deposit from imperfect combustion of carbonaceous matter (wood, coal, etc.); a smut. — *vt* to cover, smear, dirty, clog or treat with soot. — *adv* **soot'ily**. — *n* **soot'iness**. — *adj* **soot'less**. — *adj* **soot'y**. [O.E. *sōt*.]

soothe *so͞odh*, *vt* to calm, comfort, compose, tranquillise; to appease; to allay, soften. — *vi* to have a tranquillising effect. — *n* **sooth'er** someone who, or something that, soothes; a dummy teat for a baby, a comforter. — *n* and *adj* **sooth'ing**. — *adv* **sooth'ingly**. [O.E. *(ge)sōthian*, to confirm as true — *sōth*, true.]

soothsayer *so͞oth'sā-er*, *n* someone who foretells, a diviner or prognosticator. — *vi* **sooth'say** to foretell, to divine. — *n* **sooth'saying**. [Archaic *sooth*, truth — O.E. *sōth*, truth, true, and **say**.]

sootily, sootiness, sooty. See **soot**.

SOP *abbrev* for: significant other person (e.g. a cohabiting partner); standard operating procedure.

sop *sop*, *n* bread or other food dipped or soaked in liquid; a propitiatory gift or concession (from the drugged sop the Sibyl gave to Cerberus to gain passage for Aeneas to Hades, *Aeneid* vi. 420). — *vt* to take up by absorption (with *up*); to soak. — *vi* to soak in, percolate; to be soaked: — *pr p* **sopp'ing**; *pa t* and *pa p* **sopped**. — *adv* **sopp'ily**. — *n* **sopp'iness**. — *n*, *adj*, and *adv* **sopp'ing**. — *adj* **sopp'y** sloppily sentimental; thoroughly wet. [O.E. *sopp* (noun), *soppian* (verb).]

sop. *abbrev* for soprano.

sophism *sof'izm*, *n* a plausibly deceptive fallacy. — *n* **soph'ist** a captious or intentionally fallacious reasoner; orig. one of a class of public teachers of rhetoric, philosophy, etc. in ancient Greece. — *adj* **sophis'tic** or **sophis'tical** pertaining to, or of the nature of, a sophist or sophistry; fallaciously subtle. — *adv* **sophis'tically**. — *n* **soph'istry** plausibly deceptive or fallacious reasoning; an instance, or the art, of this. [Gr. *sophiā*, wisdom, *sophisma*, skill.]

sophisticate *so-fis'ti-kāt*, *vt* to give a fashionable air of worldly wisdom to; to make (e.g. a machine) highly complex and efficient; to make sophistic; to adulterate, falsify. — *vi* to practise sophistry. — *adj* **sophis'ticāte** or **sophis'ticāted** very refined and subtle; devoid or deprived of natural simplicity, complex; with qualities produced by special knowledge and skill; (of a person) accustomed to an elegant, cultured way of life; with the most up-to-date devices; worldly-wise; adulterated, falsified. — *n* **sophis'ticāte** a sophisticated person. — *n* **sophisticā'tion**. — *n* **sophis'ticātor**. [Med. L. *sophisticāre*, to adulterate — *sophisticus*, sophistic; see **sophism**.]

sophistry. See **sophism**.

sophomore *sof'ə-mör*, (esp. *US*) *n* a second-year student. — Also *adj*. — *adj* **sophomoric** (*-mor'*) or **sophomor'ical** of a sophomore; bombastic. [Prob. from *sophom* (obs. form of *sophism*) and *-or*, as if from *sophos*, wise, *mōros*, foolish.]

sopor *sō'pör*, (*pathol*) *n* unnaturally deep sleep. — *adj* **soporif'ic** inducing sleep. — *n* a sleep-bringing agent. [L. *sopor*, *-ōris*, deep sleep, *facĕre*, to make.]

sopped, sopping, soppy. See **sop**.

soprano *sə-prä'nō*, *n* the highest variety of voice, treble; a singer with such a voice; a part for such a voice: — *pl* **sopra'nos** or **sopra'ni** (*-nē*). — *adj* of, or possessing, a treble voice or a part for it; in a group of instruments of the same type but of different sizes, that with the range close to the range of a soprano voice. — *adj* **sopranino** (*sō-prə-nē'nō*) (of an instrument) higher than the corresponding soprano. — Also *n*: — *pl* **soprani'nos** or **soprani'ni** (*-nē*). [It., from *sopra* — L. *suprā* or *super*, above.]

SOR *abbrev* for sale or return.

sorb[1] *sörb*, *n* the service-tree, the wild service-tree, or (sometimes) the rowan-tree; its fruit (also **sorb'-apple**). — *n* **sor'bate** a salt of sorbic acid. — **sorbic acid** an acid obtained from the rowan-berry, used in food preservation. [L. *sorbus* (the tree), *sorbum* (the fruit).]

sorb[2] *sörb*, *vt* to absorb or adsorb. — *adj* **sorbefacient** (*-i-fā'shənt*) promoting absorption. — Also *n*. — *n* and *adj* **sor'bent**. [L. *sorbēre*, to suck in, *faciēns*, *-entis*, pres. p. of *facĕre*, to make.]

sorbaria *sörb-ā'ri-ə*, *n* any shrub of the small Asiatic genus (*Sorbaria*) of deciduous shrubs of the family Rosaceae, with long pinnate leaves and large clusters of white flowers. [L. *sorbus*; see **sorb**[1].]

sorbate. See **sorb**[1].

sorbefacient, sorbent. See **sorb**[2].

sorbet *sör'bət* or *sör'bā*, *n* sherbet; water-ice. [Fr., — It. *sorbetto*; cf. **sherbet**.]

sorbic acid. See under **sorb**[1].

sorbitol *sör'bi-tol*, *n* a white crystalline substance ($C_6H_8(OH)_6$) derived from, and used as a substitute for, sugar. [**sorb**[1].]

sorbus *sörb'əs*, *n* any plant of the large genus (*Sorbus*) of deciduous shrubs and trees of the family **Rosaceae** including the service-tree and the rowan: — *pl* **sorb'uses**. [L.; see **sorb**[1].]

sorcery *sör'sə-ri*, *n* divination by the assistance of evil spirits; magic; witchcraft. — *n* **sor'cerer**, *fem* **sor'ceress**. — *adj* **sor'cerous**. [O.Fr. *sorcerie* — L. *sors*, *sortis*, lot.]

sordamente. See under **sordo**.

sordid *sör'did*, *adj* dirty, squalid; meanly avaricious; mercenary; of low or unworthy ideals. — *adv* **sor'didly**. — *n* **sor'didness**. [L. *sordidus*, dirty.]

sordo *sör'dō*, (*mus*) *adj* muted, damped: — *fem* **sor'da**. — *adv* **sordamente** (*-dä-men'tā*) gently, softly. — *n* **sordino** (*-dē'nō*) a mute or damper to soften or deaden the sound of an instrument: — *pl* **sordi'ni** (*-nē*). — **con sordino** with mute; **senza sordino** without mute. [It., — L. *surdus*, deaf, noiseless.]

sore *sör*, *n* a painful or tender injured or diseased spot; an ulcer or boil; an affliction. — *adj* tender; readily sensitive to pain; irritable; painful; vexed; irritated; painful to contemplate; grievous (*archaic* or *Bible*); bringing pain, sorrow or regret; aggrieved (*colloq*). — *adv* painfully; severely; distressingly; in distress; very much. — *adv* **sore'ly**. — *n* **sore'ness**. — **sore point** a subject about which someone feels touchy, angry or aggrieved. — **a sore thumb** something obtrusive, too painful or too awkward to be ignored;

stick out like a sore thumb (*colloq*) to be painfully obvious, noticeable, etc. [O.E. *sār*.]

sorghum *sör'gəm*, *n* any grass of the tropical Old World genus (*Sorghum*) of grasses closely related to sugar-cane, including durra and kaffir corn; molasses made from its juice (*US*). [It. *sorgo*, prob. from an E. Ind. word, or poss. from (unattested) vulg. L. *Syricum* (*grānum*), Syrian (grain).]

sorites *sō-rī'tēz*, *n* a string of propositions in which the predicate of one is the subject of the next (or the same in reverse order) (*logic*); a sophistical puzzle on the model of 'How many grains make a heap?'. — *adj* **sorit'ic** or **sorit'ical**. [Gr. *sōreitēs* — *sōros*, a heap.]

Soroptimist *sor-opt'i-mist*, *adj* of an international organisation of clubs for professional women. — *n* a member of one of these clubs. [L. *soror*, sister, and **optimist**.]

sororal *sor-ō'rəl* or **sororial** *-ō'ri-əl*, *adj* sisterly; of, or of the nature of, a sister. — *n* **sororicide** (*-or'i-sīd*) the killing or killer of a sister. — *n* **sorority** (*sor-or'i-ti*) a sisterhood; a women's academic society (*US*). [L. *soror*, sister.]

sorosis *so-*, *sō-* or *sə-rō'sis*, (*bot*) *n* a fleshy fruit formed from a crowd of flowers, e.g. the pineapple. [Gr. *sōros*, a heap.]

sorption *sörp'shən*, *n* ab*sorption* and/or ad*sorption*.

sorrel[1] *sor'l*, *n* any of the acid-tasting herbs of the dock genus applied also to other plants. [O.Fr. *sorele*, *surele* — *sur*, sour — O.H.G. *sûr*, sour.]

sorrel[2] *sor'l*, *adj* reddish-brown or light chestnut. — *n* a reddish-brown colour; a sorrel horse. [O.Fr. *sorel* — *sor*, sorrel.]

sorrow *sor'ō*, *n* grief, sadness; affliction; pain of mind; a person or thing causing sorrow. — *vt* and *vi* to grieve. — *n* **sorr'ower**. — *adj* **sorr'owful** full of sorrow; causing, showing or expressing sorrow; sad; dejected. — *adv* **sorr'owfully**. — *n* **sorr'owfulness**. — *n* and *adj* **sorr'owing**. [O.E. *sorg*, *sorh*.]

sorry *sor'i*, *adj* (*compar* **sorr'ier**, *superl* **sorr'iest**) regretful; expressing pity, sympathy, etc.; (often merely formally) apologetic; poor, miserable, wretchedly bad, contemptible, worthless. — *interj* expressing (often slight) apology; (as a question) I beg your pardon?, what did you say? (*colloq*). — *n* **sorr'iness**. — *adj* **sorr'yish**. [O.E. *sārig*, wounded — *sār*, pain; infl. in meaning by **sorrow**, but not conn. in origin.]

sort *sört*, *n* a class, kind or species; quality or rank; one, a specimen or instance, of a kind (often ungrammatically in the singular with *these* or *those*, to denote examples of this or that kind); something of the nature but not quite worthy of the name; a letter, stop or other character in a fount of type (*printing*); manner; a woman, esp. an attractive one (*slang*, orig. *Austr*). — *vt* to separate into lots or classes; to group, classify, arrange; to select; to put in good order; to beat, punish (*colloq*); to take effective action upon or about (esp. in a vague threat) (*colloq*). — *adj* **sort'able**. — *n* **sort'er** someone who (or something that) separates and arranges (e.g. letters). — *n* and *adj* **sort'ing**. — **after a sort** to some extent; **a good sort** a decent fellow; **in some sort** in a way; as it were; **of a sort** or **of sorts** vague, rough, inexact; inferior; **out of sorts** out of normal temper or order, slightly unwell; **sort of** (*colloq*) as it were; to an extent; rather; **sort out** to classify, separate, arrange, etc.; to deal with, punish, etc. [L. *sors*, *sortis*, a lot, *sortīrī*, to draw lots; partly through O.Fr.]

sortie *sör'ti*, *n* a sally from a besieged party to attack their besiegers; a raiding excursion. — *vi* to sally. [Fr., — *sortir*, to go out, to issue.]

sortilege *sor'ti-lij*, *n* divination by drawing lots. — *n* **sortil'eger**. — *n* **sortil'egy**. [L. *sortilegus*, a diviner.]

SOS *es-ō-es'*, *n* an appeal for help or rescue, esp. at sea by Morse code (. . . - - - . . .). — *vi* to make such an appeal. [Chosen for ease of transmission in Morse.]

so-so (or **so so**) *sō-sō'*, (*colloq*) *adj* neither very good nor very bad; tolerable; indifferent. — Also *adv*. [**so[1]**.]

sostenuto *sos-te-nōō'tō* or *-nū'to*, (*mus*) *adj* sustained. — *adv* with full time allowed for each note. [It.]

SOT *abbrev* for stay-on tab (see under **stay**).

sot *sot*, *n* someone stupefied by alcohol; a habitual drunkard. — *adj* **sott'ish** like a sot; foolish; stupid with drink. [O.Fr. *sot*.]

soterial *sō-tē'ri-əl*, (*theol*) *adj* pertaining to salvation. — *adj* **sōtēriolog'ical**. — *n* **sōtēriol'ogy** the doctrine of salvation. [Gr. *sōtēriā*, salvation — *sōtēr*, a saviour.]

Sotho *sōō'tōō* or *sō'tō*, *n*. See **Basuto**.

sottish. See **sot**.

sotto voce *sot'tō vō'che*, *adv* in an undertone, aside. [It., below the voice.]

sou *sōō*, *n* a French five-centime piece (*hist*); a tiny amount of money (*colloq*). [Fr., — L. *solidus*.]

souari-nut. Same as **butternut** under **butter[1]**.

soubrette *sōō-bret'*, *n* a pert, coquettish, intriguing maid-servant in comedy (*theat*); a singer of light songs, or any woman, of this type. [Fr., — Prov. *soubreto* (fem.), coy.]

soubriquet. See **sobriquet**.

souchong *sōō'chong* or *sōō-shong'*, *n* a fine sort of black China tea. [Chin. *hsiao*, small, *chung*, sort.]

Soudanese. Same as **Sudanese**.

souffle *sōō'fl*, (*med*) *n* a murmuring in auscultation. [Fr.]

soufflé *sōō'flā*, *n* a light dish, properly one made with white of egg whisked into a froth. — *adj* prepared in this style. [Fr., past p. of *souffler* — L. *sufflāre*, to blow.]

sough[1] *sow* or *suf*, *vi* to sigh, as the wind does. — *vt* to whine out; to sigh out. — *n* a sighing of the wind; a deep sigh; a whining tone of voice. [O.E. *swōgan*, to rustle.]

sough[2] *suf*, *n* a drain, sewer. [Cf. Flem. dialect *zoeg*, a small ditch.]

sought *söt*, *pa t* and *pa p* of **seek**.

souk *sōōk*, *n* among Eastern Muslim people, a market-place. — Also **suk**, **sukh** or **suq**. [Ar. *sūq*.]

soul *sōl*, *n* that which thinks, feels, desires, etc.; a spirit, embodied or disembodied; innermost being or nature; moral and emotional nature, power or sensibility; nobleness of spirit; a complete embodiment or exemplification; the essential part; an indwelling or animating principle; the moving spirit, inspirer; a person (colloq); (also **soul music**) the popular music orig. and esp. of black Americans, typically emotional and earthy, a blend of blues, jazz, gospel and pop elements. — *adj* of or relating to soul music; of or characteristic of black Americans or their food, music, culture, etc. — *adj* **soul'ful** having or expressive of deep or elevated feeling or emotion. — *adv* **soul'fully**. — *n* **soul'fulness**. — *adj* **soul'less** without a soul; (of a person, etc.) lacking animation, spirit, or nobleness of mind; (of a place, etc.) empty, lifeless, bleak; (of a job, etc.) mechanical, dehumanised. — *adv* **soul'lessly**. — *n* **soul'lessness**. — **soul brother** or **sister** a fellow Negro or Negress. — *adj* **soul'-destroying** (of a task, situation, etc.) extremely monotonous, unrewarding, etc. — **soul food** (*US colloq*) food traditionally eaten by black Americans of the Southern states; **soul'-force** (a term for) satyagraha; **soul mate** a person to whom one is deeply emotionally or spiritually attached; **soul music** see **soul** above; **soul'-searching** a critical examination of one's actions, motives, etc. — Also *adj*. — **upon my soul!** an exclamation of surprise, etc. [O.E. *sāwol*.]

sound[1] *sownd*, *adj* uninjured, unimpaired; in good condition; healthy, wholesome; safe; (of sleep) deep;

whole or solid; (of e.g. a beating) thorough; well-founded; well-grounded; of the right way of thinking, orthodox. — *adv* soundly, completely fast (as in sleep). — *adv* **sound'ly**. — *n* **sound'ness**. — **sound as a bell** see under **bell**. [O.E. *gesund*.]

sound² *sownd*, *n* a strait; a fish's air-bladder. [O.E. *sund*, swimming.]

sound³ *sownd*, *n* the sensation of hearing; a transmitted disturbance perceived or perceptible by the ear; mere noise, without meaning or sense; a mental impression; quality or level of noise; (in *pl*) music, esp. popular (*slang*); spoken commentary, music, etc. accompanying visual material such as filmed news footage (*broadcasting* and *cinematography*); radio as opp. to television (*broadcasting*); earshot. — *vi* to give out a sound; to resound; to be audible; to be sounded; to give an impression on hearing; to call, as by trumpet. — *vt* to cause to make a sound; to produce, utter or make the sound of; to pronounce; to announce, publish, proclaim, celebrate, signal or direct by sound; to examine by percussion and listening (see also **sound⁴**); to tease, goad, provoke (*US slang*). — *n* **sound'er** that which sounds; a telegraph-receiving instrument in which Morse signals are translated into sound signals. — *n* **sound'ing** emission of sound; a signal by trumpet, bell, alarm, etc.; examination by percussion. — *adj* making a sound; sonorous; resounding. — *adv* **sound'ingly**. — *adj* **sound'less**. — *adv* **sound'lessly**. — **sound barrier** (*aeronautics*) the resistance met at about the speed of sound, when the power required to increase speed rises steeply; **sound'bite** or **sound'-bite** a brief segment on television news in which a reporter, or political figure, etc. delivers a short succinct report or statement; **sound board** a thin resonating plate of wood or metal in a musical instrument; (in an organ) the apparatus that conveys the air from the windchest to the appropriate pipes; **sound effects** sounds other than dialogue or music used in films, radio and television; **sound engineer** (*broadcasting*, etc.) one responsible for sound; **sound film** a cinematograph film with sychronised soundtrack; **sound hole** an *f*-shaped hole or similar in the belly of a stringed musical instrument; **sound'ing-board** a structure for carrying a speaker's voice towards the audience; a sound board; any person, object or institution used to test the acceptability or effectiveness of an idea, plan, etc. — *adj* **sound'proof** impenetrable by sound. — *vt* to render soundproof. — **sound'proofing**; **sound'-ranging** (*acoustics*) the calculation of position by timing the arrival of sound waves from (three or more) known positions; **sound spectrogram** a record produced by a **sound spectrograph**, an electronic instrument which makes a graphic representation of the qualities of a sound, e.g. frequency, intensity, etc.; **sound spectrography**; **sound stage** the floor of a motion-picture studio on which the actors perform and sets are built; **sound system** an electronic system, including amplifier, speakers and one or more devices for playing recorded sound; a highly sophisticated or accessorised music system, e.g. a mobile discothèque; **sound'track** a recording of the sound (esp. musical) accompaniment to a film; (on a cinematograph film) the magnetic tape on which sounds are recorded; **sound wave** a longitudinal disturbance propagated through air or other medium. — **sound off** (**about** or **on**) to speak loudly and freely (about or on), esp. in complaint; to boast. [M.E. *soun* — A.Fr. — L. *sonus*; for *d* cf. **pound³**.]

sound⁴ *sownd*, *vt* to measure the depth of; to probe; to examine with a sound (*med*); to try to discover the inclinations, thoughts, etc. of (esp. with *out*). — *vi* to take soundings; to dive deep (of e.g. a whale). — *n* (*med*) a probe for examining the bladder, etc. — *n* **sound'er** a person who sounds; apparatus for taking soundings. — *n* **sound'ing** the action of something which or someone who sounds; an ascertained depth; (in *pl*) waters in which an ordinary sounding-line will reach the bottom; a test or measurement of depth, esp. of water by means of an echo-sounder or sounding line; penetrating a particular environment to obtain sample readings, e.g. of temperature; (usu. in *pl*; also with *out*) sample testing of opinion, inclination, etc., usu. of an unofficial kind. — **sound'ing-lead** the weight at the end of a sounding-line; **sound'ing-line** a line with a plummet at the end for soundings; **sounding rocket** a rocket devised to gather high-altitude meteorological data and to radio it back to earth. [O.E. *sund-* (in compounds), cf. **sound²**; or perh. O.Fr. *sonder*, to sound.]

soup *sōōp*, *n* the nutritious liquid obtained by boiling meat or vegetables, etc. in stock; (*loosely*) anything resembling soup in consistency, etc.; a photographic developer (*slang*); nitroglycerine (*US slang*). — *adj* **soup'y**. — *adj* **soup'ed-up** (*slang*) (of e.g. an engine) having had the power increased; enlivened. — **soup'-kitchen** a place for supplying soup, etc. to the poor. — **in the soup** in difficulties or trouble; **soup up** (*slang*) to increase the power of; to enliven. [O.Fr. *soupe*.]

soupçon *sōōp-sɔ̃*, *n* a hardly perceptible quantity. [Fr., suspicion.]

sour *sowr*, *adj* having an acid taste or smell; turned, rancid or fermented; embittered, crabbed or peevish; disagreeable; inharmonious (*lit* and *fig*); bad, unsuccessful; containing sulphur compounds. — *vt* to make sour; to treat with dilute acid. — *vi* to become sour. — *n* an acid drink, as a gin or whisky cocktail that contains lemon or lime-juice; an acid solution used in bleaching, curing skins, etc. — *n* **sour'ing** the process of turning or becoming sour; treatment with dilute acid in bleaching. — *adj* **sour'ish**. — *adv* **sour'ishly**. — *adv* **sour'ly**. — *n* **sour'ness**. — **sour'dough** a piece of dough reserved to leaven a new batch; in Canada and Alaska, an old-timer; **sour mash** (*US*) new mash mixed with old to increase acidity and promote fermentation; **sour'puss** (*slang*) a sour-tempered person. [O.E. *sūr*.]

source *sörs*, *n* a spring, the head of a stream; an origin, a rise; something from which anything rises or originates; a book or document serving as authority for history, or providing material or inspiration for an author; any person, publication, etc. providing information. — *vt* (in *passive*) to come from, originate; to obtain (from a particular source). — *n* **sourc'ing**. — **source'book** a book of original documents for (esp. historic) study. [O.Fr. *sorse* from *sourdre* — L. *surgĕre*, to rise.]

soursop *sow'ər-sop*, *n* a W. Indian tree of the *Anona* species; its large, sour, pulpy fruit. [**sour** and **sop**.]

sousaphone *sōō'zə-fōn*, *n* a large tuba-like brass wind instrument invented by the American bandmaster and composer J.P. *Sousa* (1854–1932).

souse *sows*, *vt* to pickle; to marinade and cook in spiced wine or vinegar; to plunge, immerse or duck; to drench or soak; to make drunk. — *vi* to be drenched or soaked; to get drunk. — *n* pickled meat, esp. pig's feet or ears; pickling liquid; a ducking or drenching; a getting drunk (*slang*). — *adj* **soused** pickled; very wet; drunk (*slang*). — *n* and *adj* **sous'ing**. [Partly O.Fr. *sous*, *souce* — O.H.G. *sulza*, from the root of **salt**; partly imit.]

souslik. Same as **suslik**.

soutache *sōō-täsh*, *n* a narrow braid, used as a decorative trim. [Fr.]

soutane *sōō-tän'*, *n* a cassock. [Fr., — It. *sottana* — L. *subtus*, beneath.]

souterrain *sōō-te-rɛ̃* or *sōō'tə-rān*, *n* an underground chamber; an earth-house. [Fr.]

south *sowth*, *adv* in the direction directly opposite to (i.e. 180° from) north. — *n* the point of the horizon, the region, or the part, in that direction; (with *cap* and **the**) the Southern States of the U.S. — *adj* lying towards the south; forming the part, or that one of two, that is towards the south; blowing from the south; (of a pole of a magnet, usu.) south-seeking. — *adj* and *adv* **southerly** (*sudh'ər-li*) towards or (of wind) from the south. — *adj* **southern** (*sudh'*) of the south; in the south or in the direction toward it; (of wind) from the south; (with *cap*) of, from or pertaining to the South. — *n* a southerner. — *n* **southerner** (*sudh'*) a native or inhabitant of the south; (with *cap*) an inhabitant of the U.S. South. — *adj* (*superl*) **southernmost** (*sudh'*). — *adj, adv* and *n* **southward** (*sowth'wərd*; *naut sudh'ərd*). — *adj* and *adv* **south'wardly**. — *adv* **south'wards**. — *adj* **southbound** (*sowth'*) travelling in a southward direction. — *adj* and *adv* **south-east'** (or *sowth'*) midway between south and east. — *n* the direction midway between south and east; the region lying in, the wind blowing from, that direction. — **south-east'er** a strong wind from the south-east. — *adj* and *adv* **south-east'erly** towards or (of wind) from the south-east. — *adj* **south-east'ern** belonging to, or being in, the south-east, or in that direction. — *adj* and *adv* **south-east'ward** towards the south-east. — *n* the region to the south-east. — *adj* and *adv* **south-east'wardly**. — *adj* **south-east'wards**. — **Southern Cross** a conspicuous southern constellation with four bright stars placed crosswise; **southernwood** (*sudh'*) an aromatic plant of the wormwood genus (*Artemisia*). — *adj* (*colloq*) **south'paw** left-handed; (in boxing) leading with the right hand. — *n* (*colloq*) a left-handed person, esp. in sport; a boxer who leads with his right hand; **south pole** the end of the earth's axis in Antarctica; its projection on the celestial sphere (*astron*); (usu.) the south-seeking pole of a magnet (logically the north-seeking); **South Sea** the Pacific ocean. — *adj* **south-seeking** (*sowth'*) turning towards the earth's magnetic south pole. — *n, adj* and *adv* **south-south-east'** in a direction midway between south and south-east. — *n, adj* and *adv* **south-south-west'** (in) a direction midway between south and south-west. — *adj* and *adv* **south-west** (*sowth'* or *sow'*, also *-west'*) midway between south and west. — *n* the direction between south and west; the region lying that way; the wind blowing from that direction. — *adj* and *adv* **south-west'erly** toward or (of wind) from the south-west. — *adj* **south-west'ern** belonging to, or lying in, the south-west or in that direction. — *adj, adv* and *n* **south-west'ward**. — *adj* and *adv* **south-west'wardly**. — *adv* **south-west'wards**. — **south by east** (or **west**) one compass point east (or west) of south. [O.E. *sūth*.]

Southdown *sowth'down*, *adj* pertaining to the *South Downs* in Hampshire and Sussex, the famous breed of sheep so named. — *n* a sheep of this breed.

southerly, southern, etc. See **south**.

souvenir *sōō'və-nēr* or *-nēr'*, *n* a memento; an item kept as a reminder of a place, occasion, etc. — *vt* (*Austr* and *NZ*; *colloq*) to collect as a 'souvenir', to steal. [Fr. *souvenir* — L. *subvenīre*, to come up, to come to mind — *sub*, under, *venīre*, to come.]

sou'-wester *sow-wes'ter*, *n* a gale from the south-west; a waterproof hat with a large flap at the back of the neck, as worn by seamen. [Orig. *southwester* — **south-west**.]

sov *sov*, (*colloq*) *n* a short form for **sovereign**, pound sterling.

sovereign *sov'rin* or *sov'rən*, *n* a supreme ruler or head; a monarch; a gold coin (from the time of Henry VII to Charles I worth 22s.6d. to 10s., from 1817–1914 a pound sterling). — *adj* excelling all others; having supreme power residing in itself, himself or herself; of sovereignty; highly efficacious. — *adv* **sov'ereignly**. — *n* **sov'ereignty** pre-eminence; supreme and independent power; the territory of a sovereign or of a sovereign state. [O.Fr. *sovrain* and It. *sovrano* — L. *super*, above.]

soviet *sō'vi-ət* or *sov'yet*, *n* a council, esp. one of those forming since 1917 the machinery of local and national government in Russia (the Union of Soviet Socialist Republics) — the local councils elected by workers, peasants and soldiers, the higher councils consisting of deputies from the lower. — *adj* (with *cap*) of the U.S.S.R. — *vt* **so'vietise** or **-ize** to transform to the soviet model. — *n* **so'vietism** the principles and practices of a soviet government; a characteristic mannerism indicative of soviet ideology. — *n* **Sovietol'ogist** (also without *cap*) a person who has made a special study of the theory and practice of government in the U.S.S.R. and of current affairs there. — **Supreme Soviet** see under **supreme**. [Russ. *sovet*, council.]

sow¹ *sow*, *n* a female pig; a female badger, etc.; an abusive term for a fat, lazy, greedy or sluttish person, esp. a woman; a main channel along which molten iron flows, leading to metal pigs (q.v.); the metal solidified there. — **sow thistle** a thistle-like genus of plants (*Sonchus*) with milky juice and yellow flowers. [O.E. *sū*, *sugu*.]

sow² *sō*, *vt* to scatter or put in the ground, as seed; to plant by strewing; to scatter seed over; to spread, strew, disseminate. — *vi* to scatter seed for growth: — *pa t* **sowed** (*sōd*); *pa p* **sown** (*sōn*) or **sowed**. — *n* **sow'er**. — *n* **sow'ing**. — **sow the seeds of** to initiate or implant. [O.E. *sāwan*.]

sox *soks*, *npl* a slang spelling of **socks**.

soy *soi* or **soya** *soi'ə*, *n* a dark, salty sauce made from fermented soy beans and wheat flour (also **soy (**or **soya) sauce**); the soy bean, rich in oil and protein; the eastern Asiatic plant producing it. — *adj* made from soy beans or soy flour. — **soy (**or **soya) bean**; **soy (**or **soya) flour**. [Jap. *shō-yu*, colloq. *soy*, Du. *soya*, *soja* — Chin. *shi-yu*, salt bean oil.]

sozzled *soz'ld*, (*colloq*) *adj* drunk.

SP *abbrev* for starting price.

sp *abbrev* for *sine prole* (L.), without issue.

sp. *abbrev* for: species (pl. **spp.**); spelling.

spa *spä*, *n* a mineral spring; a resort where such a spring is located; a heated bath or pool of aerated water (also **spa bath** or **pool**; *US*). — *vi* to stay at a spa. — *n* **spa'ing**. — **spa town**. [*Spa* in Belgium.]

SPAB *abbrev* for the Society for the Protection of Ancient Buildings.

space *spās*, *n* that in which material bodies have extension; a portion of such; room; intervening distance; an interval; an open or empty place; the near-vacuum surrounding all bodies in the universe; regions remote from the earth; an interval between lines or words; a type used for making such an interval (*printing*); a portion, extent or interval of time; a short time. — *vt* to make, arrange or increase intervals between. — *adj* **spaced**. — *adj* **space'less**. — *n* **spac'er** someone who, or something which, spaces; an instrument for reversing a telegraphic current; a space-bar. — *adj* **spacial** (*spā'shl*) spatial. — *n* **spacing** (*spās'ing*) a space or spatial arrangement; the existence or arrangement of spaces, or of objects in spaces. — *adj* **spacious** (*spā'shəs*) extensive; ample; roomy; wide. — *adv* **spa'ciously**. — *n* **spa'ciousness**. — **space age** the present time when exploration of, and ability to travel in, space up to the limit of and beyond the earth's atmosphere are increasing. — *adj* **space'-age** very modern, up-to-date; characteristic of the space age; using sophisticated modern technology. — **space'-bar** a bar for making spaces in typewriting; **space cadet** a trainee spaceman or -woman; a space travel enthusiast; a person habitually high on drugs (*slang*); **space'craft** a vehicle, manned or unmanned, designed for putting into space, orbiting the earth, or reaching other planets; **space'-heater** a device which warms the air in a room or similar enclosed area; **Space Invaders®** an electronic game played on a machine with a screen, involving 'shooting' at graphic representations of supposed invaders from outer space; **space'man** or **-woman** a traveller in space; **space'plane** a craft (e.g. HOTOL and the space shuttle) designed to take off like a plane, enter into space orbit (e.g. to deliver payloads) and return to earth landing horizontally like a glider; **space platform** or **space station** a platform in space planned as an observatory and/or a landing-stage in space travel; **space probe** a spacecraft designed to obtain, and usu. transmit, information about the environment into which it is sent; **space'ship** a spacecraft; **space shuttle** a spaceplane used to transport men and materials to and from space stations, in-orbit experiments, satellite repair, etc.; **space station** see **space platform**; **space'suit** a suit devised for use in space travel; **space-time'** normal three-dimensional space plus dimension of time, modified by gravity in relativity theory; **space-time continuum** physical space or reality, regarded as having four dimensions (length, breadth, height and time) in which an event can be represented as a point fixed by four co-ordinates; **space travel**; **space traveller**; **space vehicle** see under **vehicle**; **space'walk** an excursion by an astronaut outside the spacecraft while in space connected to it by a life-line. — Also *vi*. — **space out** to set wide apart or wider apart; to lapse into a drugged, dazed, delirious or light-headed state; **spaced out** (*slang*) in a dazed or stupefied state (as if) caused by the taking of drugs. [Fr. *espace* — L. *spatium*.]

spade[1] *spād*, *n* a broad-bladed digging tool; a whaler's knife; a spade's depth or spit. — *vt* to dig or remove with a spade. — *n* **spade'ful**: — *pl* **spade'fuls**. — *adj* **spade'like**. — *n* **spa'der**. — **spade'work** preparatory drudgery. — **call a spade a spade** to speak out plainly without euphemism. [O.E. *spadu*, *spædu*.]

spade[2] *spād*, *n* a playing-card with black leaf-shaped (on Spanish cards, sword-shaped) pips; (*offensive*) a Negro or other coloured person. [Sp. *espada*, sword — L. *spatha* — Gr. *spathē*, a broad blade.]

spadix *spā'diks*, (*bot*) *n* a fleshy spike of flowers: — *pl* **spādices** (*-dī'sēz*). — *adj* **spadiceous** (*spā-dish'əs*) having, like, or of the nature of, a spadix; coloured like a date; shaped like a palm-branch. [Gr. *spādix*, *-īkos*, a torn-off (palm) branch, in L. date-coloured, bay.]

spaghetti *spə-get'i*, *n* an edible, cordlike form of pasta between macaroni and vermicelli in breadth. — *adj* denoting similarity to spaghetti, esp. in terms of numerous intertwining strands, etc. — **spaghetti bolognese** (*bol-on-yāz'* or *bol-ən-āz'*) or **spaghetti alla bolognese** (*a'la*) spaghetti served with a meat and tomato sauce; **spaghetti junction** a complex motorway junction at which many roads intersect at different levels, specif. that near Birmingham, orig. given this nickname; any similar mass of dauntingly intertwining strands (*fig*); **spaghetti western** an internationally-financed western, typically filmed in Europe by an Italian producer, characterised by a violent and melodramatic content and a baroque style. [It., pl. of *spaghetto*, dimin. of *spago*, a cord.]

spahi *spä'hē*, *n* formerly a Turkish, now a French Algerian cavalryman. [Turk. (from Pers.) *sipāhi*.]

spall *spöl*, *vt* and *vi* to split, splinter, chip. — *n* a chip or splinter, esp. of stone. — *n* **spallā'tion** a nuclear reaction in which bombardment by high-energy particles produces a large number of disintegration particles not entirely identifiable. [Cf. M.E. *spalden*, to split.]

Spam® *spam*, *n* a type of luncheon meat made from pork, spices, etc. — *adj* **spamm'y** tasting of, containing or like Spam or luncheon meat; (*loosely*) bland, unexciting, corny (*colloq*). [*Sp*iced h*am*.]

span[1] *span*, *n* the total spread or stretch; the distance between abutments, piers, supports, etc., or the portion of a structure (e.g. a bridge) between; the distance between the wing tips of an aeroplane; a stretch of time, esp. of life; the space from the end of the thumb to the end of the little finger when the fingers are extended; nine inches. — *vt* to measure by spans; to arch over; to stretch over; to bridge; to encompass: — *pr p* **spann'ing**; *pa t* and *pa p* **spanned**. [O.E. *spann*.]

span[2] *span*, *n* a pair of horses; a team of oxen. [Du. and L.G. *span*.]

span[3] *span*, *adj* fresh, short for **span'-new** quite new, new as a fresh-cut chip. — **spick and span** see **spick**[1]. [O.N. *spān-nýr* — *spān*, chip (cf. **spoon**[2]), *nýr*, new.]

spandex *span'deks*, *n* a synthetic elastic fibre made chiefly from polyurethane; (with *cap*; ®) a fabric made from this fibre. [Metathesis of **expand**.]

spandrel or **spandril** *span'drəl*, *n* the space between the curve of an arch and the enclosing mouldings, string-course, etc. (*archit*); a self-contained area of surface space (esp. triangular) available for decorative use, e.g. in graphic design or forming part of a structure. [Poss. conn. with **expand**.]

spangle *spang'gl*, *n* a small, thin, glittering plate of metal; a sparkling speck, flake or spot. — *vt* to decorate with spangles. — *vi* to glitter. — *adj* **spang'led**. — *n* and *adj* **spang'ling**. — *adj* **spang'ly**. [O.E. *spang*, clasp.]

Spaniard *span'yərd*, *n* a native or citizen of *Spain* in S.W. Europe. [M.E. *Spaignarde* — O.Fr. *Espaignart*.]

spaniel *span'yəl*, *n* a kind of dog, usu. liver-and-white, or black-and-white, with large hanging ears; a fawning person. — *adj* like a spaniel; fawning, mean. [O.Fr. *espaigneul* — Sp. *Español*, Spanish.]

Spanish *span'ish*, *adj* of or pertaining to *Spain*. — *n* the language of Spain and Spanish America. — **Spanish fly** see **cantharides**; **Spanish Main** (i.e. mainland) the mainland coast of the Caribbean Sea; often popularly the Caribbean Sea itself; **Spanish moss** any of various tropical and sub-tropical plants growing in long, trailing strands from tree-branches; **Spanish onion** a large mild type of onion. [*Spain*, with vowel-shortening.]

spank[1] *spangk*, *vt* and *vi* to move or drive with speed or spirit. — *n* **spank'er** any person or thing that spanks; any person or thing particularly striking or dashing; a fore-and-aft sail on the aftermost mast (*naut*). — *adj* **spank'ing** spirited, going freely; striking, beyond expectation; very; very large. — *adv* **spank'ingly**. [Poss. back-formation from **spanking**.]

spank[2] *spangk*, *vt* to strike with the flat of the hand, to smack. — *n* a loud slap, esp. on the buttocks. — *n* **spank'ing**. [Prob. imit.]

spanner *span'ər*, *n* a wrench for nuts, screws, etc. — **throw a spanner in the works** to cause confusion or difficulty, upset plans. [Ger. *Spanner* — *spannen*, to stretch; cf. **span**[1].]

spar[1] *spär*, *n* a rafter; a pole; a general term for masts, yards, booms, gaffs, etc.; a bar or rail (chiefly *Scot*). — *vt* to fasten with a spar; to fasten, shut; to fit with spars. — **spar deck** a light upper deck of a ship. [O.E. *gesparrian*, to bar.]

spar[2] *spär*, *n* any transparent to translucent, lustrous, non-metallic mineral, with clean cleavage planes (esp. in compounds, e.g. *calc-spar*, *fluorspar*, *feldspar*); a crystal or fragment of this. — *adj* **sparry** (*spär'i*). [M.L.G. *spar*, rel. to O.E. *spærstān*, gypsum.]

spar[3] *spär*, *vi* to box, or make the actions of boxing; to dispute; (of game cocks) to fight with spurs: — *pr p* **sparr'ing**; *pa t* and *pa p* **sparred**. — *n* a boxing-match or demonstration; a cock-fight; a dispute. — *n* **sparr'er**. — *n* **sparr'ing**. — **sparring partner** a person with whom a boxer practises; a friend with whom one enjoys lively arguments. [Perh. O.Fr. *esparer*, to kick out.]

sparable *spar'ə-bl*, *n* a small headless nail used by shoemakers. — Also **sparr'ow-bill**.

sparaxis *spar-ak'sis*, *n* any plant of the S. African *Sparaxis* genus of cormous plants, having colourful star-shaped flowers with lacerated spathes. [L.L. — Gr. *sparassein*, to tear, lacerate.]

spare *spār*, *vt* to do without, part with voluntarily; to afford; to abstain from using; to refrain from hurting, injuring, punishing, killing or ending; to relieve or save from; to avoid; to avoid incurring. — *adj* not in actual use; not required; kept or available for others or for such purposes as may occur; lean; frugal, scanty; sparing. — *adv* sparely. — *n* a spare part, thing or person; a duplicate kept or carried for emergencies; (in skittles or ten-pin bowling) overturning all the pins with the first two balls — i.e. with a ball to spare (a *double spare*, with first ball only); the score for so doing. — *adv* **spare'ly**. — *n* **spare'ness**. — *n* **spār'er**. — *adj* **spār'ing**. — *adv* **spār'ingly**. — **spare part** a part for a machine ready to replace an identical part if it becomes faulty (**spare-part surgery** surgery involving the replacement of organs, by transplants or artificial devices); **spare rib** a piece of pork consisting of ribs with a little meat adhering to them; **spare room** a bedroom for visitors; **spare time** leisure time (*adj* **spare'-time**); **spare tyre** an extra tyre for a motor vehicle, carried in case of a puncture; a roll of fat around the midriff (*colloq*). — **go spare** (*slang*) to become furious or frenzied; **to spare** over and above what is required. [O.E. *sparian*, to spare, *spær*, sparing.]

sparganium *spär-gā'ni-əm*, *n* a plant, growing in wet or marshy ground, of the genus *Sparganium*, constituting a family **Sparganiā'ceae**. [Gr. *sparganion*.]

sparge *spärj*, *vt* to sprinkle (with moisture). [L. *spargĕre*, to sprinkle.]

spark *spärk*, *n* a glowing or glittering particle; anything of this appearance or character, e.g. something easily extinguished, ready to cause explosion, or burning hot; a flash; an electric discharge across a gap; anything active or vivid; a bright, sprightly person. — *vi* to emit sparks, or like sparks; to sparkle; to send sparks through. — *nsing* **sparks** a ship's wireless operator (*naut slang*); an electrician (*slang*). — *adj* **spark'y**. — **spark coil** an induction coil; a connection of high-resistance used to prevent sparking in electrical apparatus; **spark plug** or **spark'ing-plug** in an internal-combustion engine, a plug carrying wires between which an electric spark passes to fire the explosive mixture of gases. — **make sparks fly** to cause or arouse sudden anger; **spark off** to cause to begin, kindle, animate; **spark out** (*slang*) to fall asleep; to pass out; to die (*adj* **sparked out**). [O.E. *spærca*, *spearca*.]

sparkle *spärk'l*, *n* a little spark; glitter; scintillation; emission of sparks; the appearance of effervescence (as of carbon dioxide in wine); vivacity; scintillating wit. — *vi* to emit sparks; to glitter; to effervesce with glittering bubbles; to be bright, animated, vivacious or witty. — *vt* to cause to sparkle; to throw out as, in, or like sparks. — *n* **spark'ler** something which sparkles; a small firework which can be held in the hand; a diamond or other gem (*slang*). — *n* and *adj* **spark'ling**. — *adv* **spark'lingly**. — *adj* **spark'ly** having sparkles; sparkling. — *n* (*colloq*) something that sparkles: — *pl* **spark'lies**. [Dimin. and frequentative of **spark**.]

sparrer, sparring, etc. See **spar**[3].

sparrow *spar'ō*, *n* any member of a family of small finchlike birds; extended to many other (usu. brown) birds, such as the hedge-sparrow; a spry, chirpy person (*fig*). — **sparr'ow-bill** see **sparable**; **sparr'ow-hawk** a genus (*Accipiter*) of long-legged, short-winged falcons, like the goshawks, but smaller. [O.E. *spearwa*.]

sparrow-grass *spar'ō-gräs*, (*colloq*) *n* a corruption of **asparagus**.

sparry. See **spar**[2].

sparse *spärs*, *adj* thinly scattered; scanty. — Also *adv*. — *adv* **sparse'ly**. — *n* **sparse'ness**. — *n* **spars'ity**. [L. *sparsus*, past p. of *spargĕre*, to scatter.]

spartan *spär'tən*, *adj* simple, hardy, rigorous, frugal, laconic, militaristic, despising culture — i.e. characteristic of the ancient Greek city *Sparta*, capital of Laconia; bleak, rigorous, austere. — *n* someone or something displaying spartan qualities; (with *cap*) a citizen or native of Sparta or Laconia. [Gr. *Spartē* (Doric *Spartā*).]

spasm *spaz'm*, *n* a violent involuntary muscular contraction; a sudden convulsive action, movement or emotion. — *vi* to go into spasm; to experience a spasm or spasms. — *adj* **spas'mic**. — *adj* **spasmod'ic** or **spasmod'ical** relating to, or consisting in, spasms; convulsive; intermittent. — *adv* **spasmod'ically**. [Gr. *spasma*, *-atos*, and *spasmos*, *-ou*, convulsion; adj. *spasmōdēs*, *spaein*, to draw, convulse.]

spastic *spas'tik*, *adj* of the nature of spasm; characterised or affected by spasms; spasmodic; awkward, clumsy, useless (*derog slang*). — *n* a person affected with spastic paralysis; a useless or stupid person (*derog slang*). — *adv* **spas'tically**. — *n* **spasticity** (*-tis'i-ti*). — **spastic paralysis** permanent muscle constriction or involuntary jerky muscle movement caused by injury to the muscle-controlling part of the brain. [Gr. *spastikos* — *spaien*, to draw, convulse; see ety. at **spasm**.]

spat[1] *spat*, *pa t* and *pa p* of **spit**[2].

spat[2] *spat*, *n* a large drop, as of rain; a splash, spattering; a petty quarrel. — *vi* to engage in a petty quarrel. [Prob. imit.]

spat[3] *spat*, *n* a short gaiter; a fairing covering an aircraft wheel. [Abbrev. of **spatterdash**.]

spatchcock *spach'kok*, *n* a chicken or other fowl killed and cooked at once, now specif. one slit lengthways, opened out, and cooked (usu. grilled) flat. — *vt* to treat in this way; to interpolate, slot in, add, etc., esp. incongruously or inappropriately. — Also *adj*. [Prob. **dispatch** and **cock**[1]; cf. **spitchcock**.]

spate *spāt*, (orig. *Scot*) *n* a flood; a sudden rush or increased quantity. — **in spate** (of a river) in a swollen, fast-flowing condition.

spathe *spādh*, (*bot*) *n* a sheathing bract, usu. a conspicuous one enclosing a spadix. — *adj* **spathaceous** (*spə-thā'shəs*) or **spathed** (*spādhd*). [Gr. *spathē*, a broad blade.]

spathic *spath'ik*, (*mineralogy*) *adj* of the nature of, or like, spar; lamellar. [Ger. *Spat(h)*, spar.]

spatial or **spacial** *spā'shl*, *adj* relating to space. — *n* **spatiality** (*spā-shi-al'i-ti*). — *adv* **spā'tially**. — *adj* **spatiotemp'oral** of space-time or space and time together. [L. *spatium*, space.]

Spätlese *shpāt'lā-zə*, (Ger.) *n* lit., a late harvest; a sweet white wine made from grapes harvested after the main vintage.

spatter *spat'ər*, *vt* to throw out or scatter upon or about; to sprinkle, esp. with mud or liquid. — *vi* to fly or fall in drops; to let drops fall or fly about. — *n* a spattering; what is spattered. — **spatt'erdash** roughcast (*US*); an old type of long gaiter to protect the trouser-leg from being spattered. [Cf. Du. and L.G. *spatten*.]

spatula *spat'ū-lə*, *n* a broad blunt blade or flattened spoon. — *adj* **spat'ular**. — *adj* **spat'ulate** shaped like a spatula; broad and rounded at the tip and tapering at the base. [L. *spatula*, *spathula*, dimin. of *spatha* — Gr. *spathē*, a broad blade.]

spavin *spav'in*, *n*. See **bone-spavin**. [O.Fr. *espavain*, *esparvain*.]

spawn *spön, n* a mass of eggs laid in water; fry; brood; (*contemptuously*) offspring; mushroom mycelium. — *vt* to produce as spawn; (*contemptuously*) to generate, esp. in mass. — *vi* to produce or deposit spawn; to teem; to come forth as or like spawn. — *n* **spawn'er**. — *n* and *adj* **spawn'ing**. — **spawn'ing-bed** or **-ground** a bed or place in the bottom of a stream on which fish deposit their spawn. [O.Fr. *espandre*, to shed — L. *expandĕre*, to spread out.]

spay *spā, vt* to remove or destroy the ovaries of. [A.Fr. *espeier* — *espee* (Fr. *épée*), sword.]

SPCK *abbrev* for Society for Promoting Christian Knowledge (now **USPG**).

SPD *abbrev* for *Sozialdemokratische Partei Deutschlands*, the (W.) German Social Democratic Party.

speak *spēk, vi* to utter words; to talk or converse; to make a speech; to give expression, information or intimation by any means. — *vt* to pronounce; to utter; to express; to use or talk in (a language); to bring or render by speaking: — *pa t* **spoke**; *pa p* **spō'ken**. — (In combination) **-speak** (*colloq*) used to denote a particular jargon or style of language, such as *techno-speak*, *doublespeak*, *airspeak*, etc. — *adj* **speak'able** able or fit to be spoken or expressed in speech. — *n* **speak'er** a person who speaks; the president (orig. the mouthpiece) of a legislative body such as the House of Commons; a loudspeaker. — *n* **speak'ership**. — *n* **speak'ing** the act of expressing ideas in words; conversation, discussion. — *adj* uttering or transmitting speech; seeming to speak, lifelike. — *adv* **speak'ingly**. — **speak'easy** (*US*) during Prohibition, an illicit bar selling alcohol, a shebeen; **speaking clock** a British telephone service which states the exact time when dialled; **speaking terms** see under **term**; **speak'ing-tube** a tube for speaking through to another room; **speak'ing-voice** the kind of voice normally used in speaking. — **so to speak** as one might put it, as it were; **speak for** to speak on behalf of or in favour of; to be a proof of or witness to; to bespeak or engage; **speak out** to speak boldly, freely, unreservedly, or so as to be easily heard (*n* **speak'out**); **speak the same language** see under **language**; **speak to** to converse with, address; to rebuke, scold; to attest, testify to; **speak up** to speak so as to be easily heard; to state one's opinions boldly; **to speak of** worth mentioning. [Late O.E. *specan* (for *sprecan*).]

speakerine *spēk-rēn*, (Fr.) (*TV* and *radio*) *n* a female announcer or programme hostess. [Fem. form of *speaker*, announcer — Eng. **speaker**.]

spear *spēr, n* a long weapon made of a pole with a pointed head; a barbed fork for catching fish; anything sharp or piercing; a spiky shoot or blade. — *vt* to pierce with a spear. — *adj* **speared** armed with a spear. — *adj* **spear'y**. — **spear'fish** marlin or similar large game fish; **spear gun** an underwater sporting gun which fires spears; **spear'head** the head of a spear; the front of an attack. — Also *vt*. — **spear'man** a man armed with a spear; **spear'mint** a common garden mint used in cooking and flavouring; **spear'-point**; **spear'-thistle** a common thistle. [O.E. *spere*; with some senses from **spire**[1].]

spec[1] *spek*, (*colloq*) *n* a short form for **speculation**. — *adj* **spec'-built** built speculatively, in the hope of finding a purchaser, rather than on a contract basis. — **on spec** as a gamble, on the chance of achieving something speculatively.

spec[2] *spek*, (*colloq*) *n* a short form for **specification**.

speccy *spek'i*, (*colloq*) *n* and *adj* (someone who is) wearing spectacles. [Cf. **specs, spectacle**.]

special *spesh'l, adj* particular; peculiar; distinctive; exceptional; additional to ordinary; detailed; intimate; designed for a particular purpose; confined or mainly applied to a particular subject. — *n* any special or particular person or thing; any person or thing set apart for a particular duty — a constable, a railway-train, etc.; a particular dish offered in a restaurant, often at a lower price, etc.; a newspaper extra, a dispatch from a special correspondent. — *n* **specialīsā'tion** or **-z-**. — *vt* **spec'ialise** or **-ize** to make special or specific; to differentiate; to adapt to conditions; to specify; to narrow and intensify. — *vi* to become or be a specialist; to become differentiated; to be adapted to special conditions. — *n* **spec'ialiser** or **-z-**. — *n* **spec'ialism** (devotion to) some particular study or pursuit. — *n* **spec'ialist** a person whose work, interest or expertise is concentrated on a particular subject. — *adj* **specialist'ic**. — *n* **speciality** (*spesh-i-al'i-ti*) the particular characteristic skill, use, etc. of a person or thing; a special occupation or object of attention. — *adv* **specially** (*spesh'ə-li*). — *n* **spec'ialogue** a mail order catalogue aimed at a specific target group of customers. — *n* **specialty** (*spesh'əl-ti*) a special contract under seal (*law*); a speciality (chiefly *US* or *med*). — **Special Branch** a British police department which deals with political security; **special constable** see under **constable**; **special correspondent** a person employed to send reports to a particular newspaper, agency, etc.; **special delivery** the delivery of mail by special messenger outside normal delivery times; **special licence, offer, pleading, verdict** see under **licence**, etc.; **special school** a school designed for the teaching of children with particular needs, esp. the mentally or physically handicapped. — **Special Drawing Rights** (also without *caps*; abbrev. **SDR** or **SDRs**) a reserve of International Monetary Fund assets which members of the fund may draw on in proportion to their IMF contributions; **Special Theory of Relativity** see under **relate**. [L. *speciālis* — *speciēs*, species.]

specie *spē'shē* or *-shi-ē, n* coined money. — **in specie** in coin; in kind. [L., abl. of *speciīs*, kind; formerly used of payment or requital in the same kind (*in speciē*).]

species *spē'shēz* or *-shi-ēz, n* a group of individuals having common characteristics, specialised from others of the same genus (*logic*); a group of closely allied mutually fertile individuals showing constant differences from allied groups, placed under a genus (*biol*); a kind, sort, type: — *pl* **spē'cies**. — *n* **speciā'tion** formation of new biological species. — *vt* **spē'ciate**. — *n* **speciesism** (*spē'shēz-izm*) the assumption that man is superior to all other species of animals and is therefore justified in exploiting them. — *adj* **spe'ciesist**. — *n* **speciocide** (*spē'shē-ə-sīd*) the destruction of a whole animal species. [L. *speciēs*, pl. *-ēs*, appearance, kind, species — *specĕre*, to look at.]

specify *spes'i-fī, vt* to mention particularly; to make specific; to set down as required: — *pr p* **spec'ifying**; *pa t* and *pa p* **spec'ified**. — *adj* **spec'ifiable** (or *-fī'*). — *adj* **specific** (*spi-sif'ik*) of special application or origin; specifying; precise; constituting or determining a species; pertaining to or peculiar to a species; (of a parasite) restricted to one particular host; (of a stain) colouring certain structures or tissues only; (of a physical constant) being the ratio per unit volume, area, (or esp.) mass, etc. — *n* anything that is specific, esp. a specific detail or factor. — *adj* **specif'ical**. — *adv* **specif'ically**. — *vt* **specif'icate** to specify. — *n* **specificā'tion** (*spes-*) making, becoming or being specific; the act of specifying; any point or particular specified; a detailed description of requirements, etc.; the description of an invention presented by the inventor applying for a patent. — *n* **specificity** (*spes-i-fis'i-ti*). — *adj* **spec'ified**. — **specific gravity** relative density; **specific heat** or **specific heat capacity** (*phys*) the number of heat-units necessary to raise the unit of mass of a given substance one degree in temperature. [O.Fr. *specifier* — L.L. *specificāre* — L. *speciēs*, kind, *facĕre*, to make.]

specimen *spes'i-min, n* an object or portion serving as a sample, esp. for purposes of study, collection or consideration; a urine, blood or tissue sample (*med*); derogatorily, a person (*colloq*). — *adj* for use as, or of the nature of, a specimen; representative. [L. *specimen* — *specĕre*, to see.]

specious *spē'shəs, adj* looking good at first sight; plausibly deceptive. — *n* **speciosity** (*-shi-os'i-ti*) or **spe'ciousness.** — *adv* **spe'ciously.** [L. *speciōsus*, showy — *speciēs*, form — *specĕre*, to look at.]

speck *spek, n* a small spot; a particle. — *adj* **speck'less.** — *adj* **speck'y.** [O.E. *specca.*]

speckle *spek'l, n* a little spot, esp. of colour; a grainy pattern on or forming a photographic image, caused by atmospheric interference (*astron* and *phys*). — *vt* to mark with speckles. — *adj* **speck'led.** — **speckle interferogram** a visual record produced by speckle interferometry; **speckle interferometry** (*astron* and *phys*) a method of obtaining information (esp. a visual image) of a distant stellar object by processing and analysis of a number of short-exposure speckle photographs. [Dimin. **speck.**]

specs *speks*, (*colloq*) *npl* a pair of spectacles.

spectacle *spek'tə-kl, n* a sight; a show, pageant or exhibition; (in *pl*) a pair of lenses (for correcting the eyesight) mounted in frames with side-pieces extending over the ears to grip the temples; (in *pl*) a marking (on an animal) resembling spectacles. — *adj* **spec'tacled** wearing spectacles; having rings around the eyes (*fig*). — *adj* **spectacular** (*-tak'ū-lər*) of the nature of, or marked by, display; sensational, very impressive. — *n* a theatrical show, esp. on television, or any display, that is large-scale and elaborate. — *n* **spectacularity** (*-lar'i-ti*). — *adv* **spectac'ularly.** [L. *spectāculum* — *spectāre, -ātum*, intensive of *specĕre*, to look at.]

spectator *spek-tā'tər, n* a person who looks on. — *vi* **spectate'** (*back-formation*) to look on. — *adj* **spectatorial** (*-tə-tö'ri-əl*). — *n* **spectā'torship.** — **spectator sport** a sport that has great appeal for spectators. [L. *spectātor* — *spectāre*, to look.]

spectra, spectral[2], **spectrality**[2], etc. See under **spectrum.**

spectre or in U.S. **specter** *spek'tər, n* an apparition: a ghost; a haunting fear or premonition. — *adj* **spec'tral** relating to, or like, a spectre. — *n* **spectral'ity.** — *adv* **spec'trally.** — *n* **spectrol'ogy** the study of ghosts. [Fr. *spectre* — L. *spectrum* — *specĕre*, to look at.]

spectro- *spek'-trō-* or *-tro'-*, *combining form* signifying: spectre; spectrum.

spectrum *spek'trəm, n* an after-image; the range of colour produced by a prism or diffraction-grating; any analogous range of radiations in order of wavelength; range of frequencies of sound or a sound; range of opinions, activities, etc. (*fig*): — *pl* **spec'tra.** — *adj* **spec'tral** relating to, or like, a spectrum. — *n* **spectral'ity.** — *n* **spec'trochemistry** chemical spectroscopy. — *n* **spec'trogram** a photograph of a spectrum; a sound spectrogram (see at **sound**[3]). — *n* **spec'trograph** a spectroscope designed for use over a wide range of frequencies (well beyond visible spectrum) and recording the spectrum photographically (see also **mass spectrograph** at **mass**[1]). — *adj* **spectrograph'ic** or **spectrograph'ical.** — *n* **spectrog'raphy.** — *n* **spectrol'ogy** the science of the spectrum or spectrum analysis. — *n* **spectrom'eter** an instrument for measuring refractive indices; one used for measurement of wavelength or energy distribution in a heterogeneous beam of radiation (see also **mass spectrometer** at **mass**[1]). — *n* **spectrom'etry.** — *n* **spec'troscope** a general term for an instrument (*spectrograph, spectrometer*, etc.) used in spectroscopy, the basic features of which are a slit and collimator for producing a parallel beam of radiation, a prism or grating for 'dispersing' different wavelengths through differing angles of deviation, and a telescope, camera or counter tube for observing the dispersed radiation. — *adj* **spectroscop'ic** or **spectroscop'ical.** — *adv* **spectroscop'ically.** — *n* **spectroscopist** (*spek-tros'kə-pist* or *spek'trə-skop-ist*). — *n* **spectros'copy** (or *spek'*) the study of spectra. — **spectrum analysis** determination of chemical composition by observing the spectrum of light or X-rays coming from or through the substance. [L. *spectrum*, an appearance — *specĕre*, to look at.]

specular *spek'ū-lər, adj* mirrorlike; having a speculum; by reflection; visual; giving a wide view. [L. *speculāris* — *speculum*, a mirror, and *specula*, a watch-tower.]

speculate *spek'ū-lāt, vi* to reflect; to theorise; to make conjectures or guesses; to take risk in hope of gain, esp. in buying and selling. — *n* **speculā'tion** act of speculating or its result; theorising; conjecture; mere guesswork; a more or less risky investment of money for the sake of unusually large profits. — *adj* **spec'ulātive** (or *-lət-*) of the nature of, based on, or given to, speculation or theory. — *adv* **spec'ulātively.** — *n* **spec'ulātiveness.** — *n* **spec'ulātor** someone who speculates in any sense. — *adj* **spec'ulatory** exercising speculation. [L. *speculātus*, past p. of *speculārī* — *specula*, a lookout — *specĕre*, to look at.]

speculum *spek'ū-ləm, n* a mirror; a reflector, usu. of polished metal; an instrument with which to view cavities of the body (*med*); a bright patch on a wing, esp. a duck's: — *pl* **spec'ula.** — **speculum metal** an alloy of copper and tin, with or without other ingredients, which can be highly polished and used for mirrors, lamp reflectors, etc. [L. *speculum*, a mirror — *specĕre*, to look at.]

sped *sped, pa t* and *pa p* of **speed.**

speech *spēch, n* that which is spoken; language; the power of speaking; manner of speaking; a continuous spoken utterance; a discourse, oration; talk; colloquy; mention; the sounding of a musical instrument. — *vi* **speech'ify** to make speeches, harangue (implying contempt). — *adj* **speech'less** lacking or deprived of the power of speech. — *adv* **speech'lessly.** — *n* **speech'lessness.** — **speech community** a community based on a common language or dialect; **speech day** the public day at the close of a school year, or on which prizes won during the previous year are presented; **speech'maker** someone accustomed to speak in public; **speech'-song** (*mus*) sprechgesang; **speech therapy** treatment of speech and language defects; **speech'-training** training in clear speech. [Late O.E. *spēc*, *spǣc*, O.E. *sprēc*, *sprǣc.*]

speed *spēd, n* quickness, swiftness, dispatch; the rate at which a distance is covered; the time taken for a photographic film to accept an image; amphetamine (*slang*). — *vi* to move quickly; to hurry; to drive at high, or at dangerously, unduly or illegally high, speed. — *vt* to send swiftly; to push forward; to haste; to betake with speed; to urge to high speed; to set or regulate the speed of: — *pa t* and *pa p* **sped** (also **speed'ed**). — *n* **speed'er** someone who, or something that, speeds or promotes speed. — *adv* **speed'ily.** — *n* **speed'iness** quickness. — *n* **speed'ing** success; promotion, furtherance; progressive increase of speed (often with *up*); motoring at excessive speed. — Also *adj.* — *adj* **speed'less.** — *n* **speedom'eter** a device indicating the speed at which a vehicle is travelling (colloq. shortening **speed'ō**, *pl* **speed'ōs**). — *n* **speed'ster** a speedboat; a fast (sports) car; someone who speeds. — *adj* **speed'y** swift; prompt; soon achieved. — **speed'balling** injecting or sniffing **speed'ball**, a mixture of cocaine and usually heroin or morphine (*slang*); **speed'boat** a very swift motorboat; **speed'boating; speed bump** a low hump across a road intended to slow down traffic; **speed'-cop** (*slang*) a policeman who watches out for motorists who are exceeding a speed limit; **speed limit** the maximum speed at which motor vehicles may be driven legally on certain roads; **speed merchant** someone who drives a motor vehicle exceedingly fast (*slang*); **speed skating** a sport in which two ice- or roller-skaters race on a track for a number of separate distances, the winner being the skater who accumulates the fewest overall time points; **speed trap** a section of road over which the police (often using radar) check the speed of passing vehicles and identify drivers exceeding the limit (see also **radar trap**); **speed'-up** an acceleration, esp. in work; **speed'way** a road for fast traffic; a motorcycle racing track; the sport of motorcycle racing; **speed'well** any species of the genus *Veronica*, typically blue-flowered, posterior petals united, lacking posterior sepal. — **speed up** to quicken the rate of working. [O.E. *spēd*.]

speiss *spīs*, *n* a mass of arsenides and commonly antimony compounds, a first product in smelting certain ores. [Ger. *Speise*.]

spelaean or **spelean** *spi-lē'ən*, *adj* cave-dwelling. — *adj* **spelaeological** or **speleological** (*spē-li-ə-loj'i-kl* or *spel-*). — *n* **spelaeol'ogist** or **speleol'ogist**. — *n* **spelaeol'ogy** or **speleol'ogy** the scientific study of caves; exploration of caves. [Gr. *spēlaion*, cave.]

spell[1] *spel*, *n* a magic formula; a magic influence; enchantment; entrancement. — *vt* to say a spell over; to bind with a spell; to enchant. — *vt* **spell'bind** (*back-formation*). — **spell'binder** an orator, usu. political or evangelical, who holds his or her audience spellbound; any person or thing that entrances. — *adj* **spell'bound** bound by a spell; entranced. [O.E. *spell*, narrative, *spellian*, to speak, announce.]

spell[2] *spel*, *vt* to read laboriously, letter by letter; to name or set down in order the letters of; to constitute or represent orthographically; to import, amount to (*fig*). — *vi* to spell words, esp. correctly: — *pa t* and *pa p* **spelled** or **spelt**. — *adj* **spell'able**. — *n* **spell'er**. — *n* **spell'ing**. — **spell'ing-bee** a spelling competition; **spell'ing-book** a book for teaching to spell; **spelling pronunciation** (*linguis*) a pronunciation of a word that, as a side effect of literacy, closely represents its spelling, superseding the traditional pronunciation, e.g. *forehead* as *fōr'hed* (orig. *for'id*). — **spell it out** or **spell out** to be extremely specific in explaining something. [O.Fr. *espeller* of Gmc. origin; cf. **spell[1]**.]

spell[3] *spel*, *vt* to take the place of at work; to relieve, give a rest to; to take a turn at. — *vi* to take turns; to rest: — *pr p* **spell'ing**; *pa t* and *pa p* **spelled**. — *n* a shift; a turn at work; a bout, turn; a short time; a stretch of time; a rest; a fit (of irritation, illness, etc.). [O.E. *spelian*, to act for another.]

spellican. See under **spill[2]**.

spelt[1] *spelt*, *n* an inferior species of wheat, grown in the mountainous parts of Europe. [O.E. *spelt*.]

spelt[2]. See under **spell[2]**.

spelter *spel'tər*, *n* zinc, esp. impure zinc. [Cf. L.G. *spialter*.]

spencer[1] *spens'ər*, *n* a short double-breasted overcoat; a woman's short undergarment. [After various persons of the name.]

spencer[2] *spens'ər*, *n* (in ships and barques) a fore-and-aft sail abaft the fore and main masts. [Perh. the name Spencer, as **spenser[1]**.]

spend *spend*, *vt* to expend; to pay out; to give, bestow, employ, for any purpose; to shed; to consume; to use up; to exhaust; to waste; to pass (time, etc.). — *vi* to make expense: — *pa t* and *pa p* **spent**. — *n* an act of, or the sum of money available (usu. on a regular basis) for, spending. — *adj* **spen'dable**. — *n* **spen'der**. — *n* **spen'ding**. — *adj* **spent** used up; exhausted; (of fish) exhausted by spawning. — **spending money** pocket money; **spend'thrift** someone who spends the savings of thrift; a prodigal. — *adj* excessively lavish. — **spent force** a person or thing whose former strength, usefulness, etc. is exhausted. — **spend a penny** (*euph*) to urinate. [O.E. *spendan* — L. *expendĕre* or *dispendĕre*, to weigh out.]

spent *spent*. See under **spend**.

sperm *spûrm*, *n* seed or semen; generative substance; a male gamete or germ-cell; a sperm-whale; sperm-oil; spermaceti. — *combining form* **-sperm** denoting seed. — *adj combining forms* **-spermal** and **-spermous.** — For some compounds beginning **sperma-** or **spermo-** see **spermato-** (*spûr'mə-tō-*) below. — *n* **sper'maduct** or **sper'miduct** a duct conveying spermatozoa. — *n* **spermā'rium** (*pl* **spermā'ria**) or **sper'mary** the male germ-gland. — *adj* **spermat'ic** or **spermat'ical** of, pertaining to or conveying sperm; generative. — *n* **spermat'ic** a spermatic vessel. — *n* **sper'matid** a cell that develops directly into a spermatozoon. — *n* **sper'matoblast** a spermatid. — *adj* **spermatoblas'tic.** — *n* **sper'matocyte** a sperm mother-cell or its predecessor. — *n* **spermatogenesis** (*-jen'*) or **spermatogeny** (*-mə-toj'i-ni*) sperm-formation. — *adj* **spermatogenet'ic, spermatogen'ic** or **spermatog'enous.** — *n* **spermatogonium** (*-gō'ni-əm*) one of the cells that by repeated division form the spermatocytes. — *n* **sper'matophore** a case enclosing the spermatozoa. — *npl* **Spermatoph'yta** (also **Spermaph'yta** or **Spermoph'yta**) the flowering plants as one of the four phyla of the vegetable kingdom. — *n* **spermat'ophyte** (or **sper'maphyte**, etc.). — *adj* **spermatophytic** (*-fit'ik*; also **spermaphyt'ic** or **spermophyt'ic**). — *adj* **spermatozō'al, spermatozō'an** or **spermatozō'ic.** — *n* **spermatozō'id** or **spermatozō'on** (*pl* **spermatozō'a**) a male germ-cell. — *adj* **sper'mic** spermatic. — *n* **sper'micide** any substance which kills spermatozoa. — *adj* **spermicī'dal.** — For some compounds beginning **spermo-** see **spermato-** above. — *adj* **sper'mous** spermatic. — **sperm bank** a store of semen for use in artificial insemination; **sperm'-cell** a male gamete; **sperm oil** oil from the sperm whale; **sperm whale** the cachalot, a whale from which spermaceti is obtained. [Gr. *sperma*, *-atos*, seed, semen — *speirein*, to sow.]

spermaceti *spûr-mə-set'i*, *n* a waxy matter obtained mixed with oil from the head of the sperm-whale and others. — Also *adj*. [L. *sperma cētī* (genitive of *cētus*, a whale — Gr. *kētos*), whale's sperm, from a wrong notion of its origin.]

spermarium, spermatic, etc. See under **sperm**.

Spetsnaz or **Spetznaz** *spets'naz*, *n* a select force, controlled by Soviet military intelligence, highly-trained for undercover activities, raids, etc. — Also without *cap*. — *adj* (usu. without *cap*) of or pertaining to the Spetsnaz. [Russ.]

spew, *spū*, *vt* to vomit. — *vi* to vomit; to ooze, run. — *n* vomited matter. — *n* **spew'er**. [O.E. *spīwan*, *spīowan*, to spit.]

SPF *abbrev* for sun protection factor (of a sunscreen, lotion, etc.).

SPG *abbrev* for Special Patrol Group.

sp.gr. *abbrev* for specific gravity (now relative density).

sphagnum *sfag'nəm*, *n* mosses of the genus *Sphagnum*: — *pl* **sphag'na**. [Gr. *sphagnos*, a name for various plants.]

sphalerite *sfal'ər-īt*, *n* zinc blende. [Gr. *sphaleros*, deceptive, from its resemblance to galena.]

sphene *sfēn*, *n* titanite. — *adj* **sphē'nic** wedgelike. — *npl* **Sphenisciformes** (*sfē-nis-i-fōr'mēz*) the penguin order of birds. — *n* **Sphē'nodon** the genus, also known as *Hatteria*, to which the tuatara (q.v.) belongs; (without *cap*) an animal of this genus. — *adj* **sphē'noid** wedge-shaped, applied to a set of bones at the base of the skull. — *n* a sphenoid bone; a wedge-shaped crystal form of four triangular faces. — *adj* **sphenoid'al.** [Gr. *sphēn, sphēnos*, a wedge.]

sphere *sfēr*, *n* a solid figure bounded by a surface of which all points are equidistant from a centre; its bounding surface; the apparent sphere of the heavens, upon which the stars are seen in projection; any one of the concentric spherical shells which were once supposed to carry the planets in their revolutions; a circle of society, orig. of the higher ranks (as if a planetary sphere); domain, scope, range; a field of activity; condition of life; a world, mode of being; a ball; a spherical object, esp. a planet. — *adj* **sphēr'al.** — *adj* **sphered.** — *adj* **sphere'less.** — *adj* **spheric** (*sfer'ik*) or **spher'ical** of a sphere or spheres; having the form of a sphere. — *n* **spherical'ity.** — *adv* **spher'ically.** — *n* **spher'icalness** or **sphericity** (*-is'i-ti*) a state or quality of being spherical. — *n* **sphē'roid** a body or figure nearly spherical, but not quite so. — *adj* **sphēroi'dal.** — *n* **sphēroidi'city.** — *n* **sphērom'eter** an instrument for measuring curvature of surfaces. — *adj* **spherūlar** (*sfer'*). — *n* **spher'ūle** a little sphere. — **spherical aberration** loss of image definition which occurs when light strikes a lens or mirror with a spherical surface. — **music (**or **harmony) of the spheres** the music, inaudible to mortal ears, produced according to Pythagoras by the motions of the celestial spheres in accordance with the laws of harmony. [Gr. *sphairă*.]

sphincter *sfingk'tər*, (*anat*) *n* a ringlike muscle whose contraction narrows or shuts an orifice. — *adj* **sphinc'teral** or **sphincterial** (*-tē'ri-əl*) or **sphincteric** (*-ter'ik*). [Gr. *sphinktēr* — *sphingein*, to bind tight.]

Sphinx or **sphinx** *sfingks*, *n* a monster with the head of a woman and the body of a lioness, that proposed riddles to travellers, and strangled those who could not solve them (*Gr mythol*); any similar monster or representation of one; an enigmatic or inscrutable person: — *pl* **sphinx'es** or **sphinges** (*sfin'jēz*). [Gr., — *sphingein*, to draw tight.]

sphragistic *sfrə-jist'ik*, *adj* pertaining to seals and signets. — *nsing* **sphragist'ics** the study of seals. [Gr. *sphrāgistikos* — *sphrāgis*, a seal.]

sphygmus *sfig'məs*, *n* the pulse. — *n* **sphyg'mogram** a sphygmograph record. — *n* **sphyg'mograph** an instrument for recording pulse-beat. — *n* **sphygmog'raphy.** — *n* **sphygmōmanom'eter** or **sphygmom'eter** an instrument for measuring arterial blood-pressure. [Latinised from Gr. *sphygmos*, pulse.]

spic, spick or **spik** *spik*, (esp. *US derog*) *n* a person from a Spanish-speaking American country, or of Mexican or S. American, etc. origin; a member of one of the Mediterranean races.

spica *spī'kə*, *n* a spiral bandage with reversed turns suggesting an ear of barley. — *adj* **spī'cate** or **spī'cated** in, having or forming a spike; spikelike. — *adj* **spic'ūlar** of the nature of or like a spicule. — *adj* **spic'ūlate** having spicules. — *n* **spic'ūle** a minute needle-like body, crystal, splinter or process; one of the spikelike forms seen forming and re-forming on the edge of the sun, caused by ejections of hot gas several thousand miles above its surface. [L. *spīca*, an ear of corn.]

spiccato *spik-kä'tō*, (*mus*) *adj* and *adv* half staccato. — *n* spiccato playing or passage: — *pl* **spicca'tos.** [It.]

spice *spīs*, *n* an aromatic and pungent vegetable substance used as a condiment and for seasoning food — pepper, nutmeg, ginger, cinnamon, etc.; such substances collectively or generally; a characteristic smack, flavour; anything that adds piquancy or interest; an aromatic odour; a touch, tincture (*fig*). — *vt* to season with spice; to tincture, vary or diversify. — *adj* **spiced** impregnated with a spicy odour; seasoned with spice. — *adv* **spīc'ily.** — *n* **spīc'iness.** — *adj* **spīc'y** producing or abounding with spices; fragrant; pungent; piquant, pointed; racy; risqué; showy. — **spice'-box** a box, often ornamental, for keeping spices; **spice'bush** an aromatic American shrub (genus *Lindera*) of the laurel family; **spice'-cake** a spiced cake. [O.Fr. *espice* — L.L. *speciēs*, kinds of goods, spices — L. *speciēs*, a kind.]

spick[1]: **spick and span** trim and speckless (like a newly cut spike and a newly split chip); **spick and span new** brand-new. [**spike**[2].]

spick[2]. See under **spic.**

spicule, etc. See under **spica.**

spicy. See under **spice.**

spider *spī'dər*, *n* an arachnid of the order *Araneida*, the body divided into two distinct parts; a frying-pan, properly one with feet; any of various spiderlike radiating structures, instruments, tools, etc.; a rest for a cue in billiards; an arrangement of elastic straps with hooks attached, used to fasten luggage, etc. on to the roof-rack of a car or on to a motorcycle, etc. — *adj* **spi'derlike.** — *adj* **spī'dery** spiderlike; abounding in spiders. — **spi'der-line** a thread of silk spun by a spider; any fine thread in an optical instrument, for measurement, position-marking, etc.; **spi'derman** an erector of steel building structures; **spider monkey** an American monkey with long slender legs and tail; **spider plant** any of various plants (genus *Chlorophytum*) with spiky, variegated leaves, especially one which grows new plantlets on trailing stems; **spi'der-stitch** a stitch in lace or netting in which threads are carried diagonally and parallel to each other; **spi'der-web** the snare spun by a spider; **spi'der-wheel** in embroidery, a circular pattern with radiating lines; **spi'der-work** lace worked by spider-stitch. [O.E. *spīthra* — *spinnan*, to spin.]

spiegeleisen *spē'gl-ī-zn*, *n* a white cast-iron containing manganese, largely used in the manufacture of steel by the Bessemer process. [Ger., — *Spiegel* — L. *speculum*, a mirror, Ger. *Eisen*, iron.]

spiel *spēl* or *shpēl*, *n* a (esp. plausible) story or line of talk. — *vi* to talk glibly, tell the tale. — Also *vt*. — *n* **spiel'er** person with a glib, persuasive line of talk; a swindler or a card sharper. [Ger. *spielen*, to play.]

spies. See under **spy.**

spiffing *spif'ing*, (*old-fashioned colloq*) *adj* excellent.

spiflicate or **spifflicate** *spif'li-kāt*, (*slang*) *vt* to do for; to quell; to confound; to handle roughly. — *n* **spiflicā'tion** or **spifflicā'tion.**

spigot *spig'ət*, *n* a peg for stopping the end of a barrel or for controlling a faucet; a faucet (*US*). [Prov. *espigot* — L. *spīculum*.]

spik. See under **spic.**

spike[1] *spīk*, *n* an ear of corn; an inflorescence in which sessile flowers or spikelets are arranged on a long axis (*bot*); a kind of lavender (**spike'-lavender**). — *n* **spike'let** (in grasses, etc.) a small crowded spike, itself forming part of a greater inflorescence. — **spike'-oil** the oil of spike-lavender. [L. *spīca*, an ear of corn.]

spike[2] *spīk*, *n* a hard thin pointed object; a large nail; a sharp metal projection, e.g. one of those forming a row along the top of a railing, etc.; a sharp-pointed metal rod set upright on a base, on which to impale documents requiring attention, etc.; (in *pl*) spiked shoes, worn to prevent slipping; an electric impulse, esp. a very brief, potentially damaging surge of power on an electronic circuit. — *vt* to fasten, set, pierce or damage with a spike or spikes; to make (e.g. a gun) useless, orig. by driving a spike into the vent; to frustrate, put a stop to; to make (a drink) stronger by adding spirits or other alcohol (*colloq*); to contaminate (e.g. food) by the addition of a harmful substance; to inject with a drug. — *vi* to form a spike or peak; to inject oneself with a drug. — *adj* **spiked.** — *adv* **spīk'ily.** — *n* **spīk'iness.** — *adj* **spīk'y** having or provided with spikes; having a sharp point; irritable, acerbic; characterised by irritable, difficult or jarring disagreements or incidents. — **spike heel** a very narrow metal heel on a woman's shoe; **spike'-nail** a large small-headed nail. [O.E. *spīcing*, a spike-nail; poss. from L. *spīca*, an ear of corn.]

spikenard *spīk'närd*, *n* an aromatic oil or balsam yielded by an Indian herb (*Nardostachys*) also called **nard**, or a substitute; the plant itself. — **ploughman's spikenard** a European and N. African spikenard with yellow flowers and aromatic roots. [L. *spīca nardi*.]

spile *spīl*, *n* a plug; a spigot; a pile for a foundation; a stake, or post for fencing. — *vt* to pierce and provide with a spile. [Cf. L.G. *spile*, Du. *spijl*, Ger. *Speil*.]

spilikin. See under **spill²**.

spill¹ *spil*, *vt* to allow to run out of a vessel; to shed; to waste; to throw from a vehicle or the saddle (*colloq*); to empty from the belly of a sail or empty of wind for reefing. — *vi* to overflow; to be shed; to be allowed to fall, be lost, or wasted: — *pa t* and *pa p* **spilled** or **spilt**. — *n* a fall, a throw; a spilling. — *n* **spill'age** the act of spilling; that which is spilt. — *n* **spill'er**. — *n* **spill'ing**. — *n* **spilth** spilling; anything spilt or poured out lavishly; excess. — **spill'over** an overflow (also *fig*). — **spill over** to overflow (also *fig*); **spill the beans** to let out a secret. [O.E. *spillan*.]

spill² *spil*, *n* a spile; a thin strip of wood or paper for lighting a candle, a pipe, etc. — *n* **spill'ikin, spil'ikin** or **spell'ican** a small slip of wood, ivory, etc. to be picked out from a heap without disturbing the others in the game of **spillikins**, etc.

spillage, etc. See under **spill¹**.

spilt *spilt*, *pa t* and *pa p* of **spill¹**. — Also *adj*.

spilth. See under **spill¹**.

spin *spin*, *vt* to draw out and twist into threads; to draw out a thread as spiders do; to form by spinning; to draw out; to make to last (usu. with *out*); to send hurtling; to twirl, set revolving rapidly; to fish with a swivel or spoon-bait. — *vi* to practise the art or trade or perform the act of spinning; to rotate rapidly; to whirl; to hurtle; to go swiftly, esp. on wheels; to spirt; to stream vigorously; to lengthen out, last (usu. with *out*); to fish with rotating bait: — *pr p* **spinn'ing;** *pa t* and *pa p* **spun**. — *n* act or result of spinning; a rotatory motion; a cycle ride; a short trip in a motor car; a spurt at high speed; a spiral descent (*lit* and *fig*); confused excitement. — *n* **spinn'er** someone who or something that spins; a spinneret; a spinning-machine; a ball with imparted spin, causing it to swerve or break (*cricket*); a spin-bowler; an artificial fly that revolves in the water (*fishing*); a rotating display stand (e.g. for books) in a shop, etc. — *n* **spinn'eret** a spinning organ in spiders, etc.; a plate with holes from which filaments of plastic material are expressed (also **spinn'erette**). — *n* and *adj* **spinn'ing**. — **spin'-bowling** (in cricket) a style of bowling in which the ball is give a twisting motion by the bowler's wrist or fingers, in order to make its speed and direction as it rises after striking the ground, unpredictable; **spin'-bowler; spin doctor** or **spin'-doctor** (orig. *US*) someone (often a public relations expert) employed by a politician, etc. to try to influence public opinion; **spin-dri'er** or **-dry'er** a device that dries washed clothes without wringing, by forcing the water out of them under pressure of centrifugal force in a rapidly revolving drum. — *vt* **spin-dry'**. — **spinn'ing-mill** a factory where thread is spun; **spinn'ing-wheel** a machine for spinning yarn, consisting of a wheel driven by the hand or by a treadle, which drives one or two spindles; **spin'-off** a by-product that proves profitable on its own account. — Also *adj*. — **spin stabilisation** the stabilising of the flight of a projected bullet, space rocket, etc. by giving it a spinning motion. — **flat spin** a state of panic; **spin a yarn** to tell a story; **spin out** to prolong, protract. [O.E. *spinnan*.]

spina bifida *spī'nə bif'id-ə*, *n* a congenital condition in which imperfect development of a vertebra or vertebrae at the embryo stage results in exposure of the spinal cord. [See **spine** and **bifid.**]

spinach *spin'ij* or *spin'ich*, *n* a plant of the goosefoot family; its young leaves used as a vegetable; extended to various other plants. [O.Fr. *espinage*, *espinache*.]

spinal, spinate. See under **spine**.

spindle *spin'dl*, *n* the pin by which thread is twisted; a pin on which anything turns; the fusee of a watch; anything very slender; a spindle-shaped structure formed in mitosis (*biol*). — *adj* **spin'dly** disproportionally long and slender. — *adj* **spin'dle-legged** or **-shanked** having long slender legs, like spindles. — *npl* **spin'dle-legs** or **-shanks** long slim legs; hence (as *nsing*) an overlong and slender person. — **spin'dle-oil** very light and fluid lubricating oil. — *adj* **spin'dle-shaped** shaped like a spindle, thickest in the middle and tapering to both ends. — **spin'dle-tree** a shrub (*Euonymus europaeus*) whose hard-grained wood was used for making spindles. [O.E. *spinel* — *spinnan*, to spin; Ger. *Spindel*.]

spindrift *spin'drift*, *n* the spray blown from the crests of waves. [See **spoon¹**.]

spine *spīn*, *n* a thorn, esp. one formed by a modified branch or leaf; a long sharp process of a leaf; a thin, pointed spike, esp. in fishes; the spinal column; any ridge extending lengthways; heartwood; the back of a book. — *adj* **spī'nal** of the backbone. — *adj* **spī'nate** or **spined** having a spine or spines. — *adj* **spine'less** having no spine; weak; vacillating; lacking courage, esp. moral courage. — *adv* **spine'-lessly**. — *n* **spine'lessness**. — *n* **spīnesc'ence**. — *adj* **spīnesc'ent** tapering or developing into a spine; tending to become spinous; somewhat spiny. — *n* **spī'niness**. — *adj* **spī'nose** (or *-nōs'*) full of spines; thorny. — *adj* **spī'nous** spinose; like a thorn or spine in appearance (*anat*, etc.). — *adj* **spin'ūlāte**. — *n* **spinūle** (*spin'* or *spīn'*) a minute spine. — *adj* **spin'ūlōse**. — *adj* **spin'ūlous**. — *adj* **spī'ny** full of spines; thorny; troublesome; perplexed. — **spinal anaesthesia** injection of an anaesthetic into the spinal canal, producing loss of sensation but not unconsciousness; **spinal canal** a passage running through the spinal column, containing the spinal cord; **spinal column** in vertebrates, the articulated series of vertebrae extending from the skull to the tip of the tail, forming the axis of the skeleton and enclosing the spinal cord; **spinal cord** or **chord** the main neural axis in vertebrates; **spine'-chiller** a frightening story, thought or happening. — *adj* **spine'-chilling**. [L. *spīna*, a thorn.]

spinel *spi-nel'* or *spin'əl*, *n* a mineral, magnesium aluminate or other member of a group of aluminates, ferrates and chromates, crystallising in octahedra. — **spinel ruby** ruby-spinel, a precious variety of typical spinel formerly confounded with ruby. [It. *spinella*.]

spinescence, etc. See under **spine**.

spinet or **spinette** *spin'it* or *spi-net'*, *n* an instrument like a small harpsichord. [It. *spinetta*, poss. from maker G. *Spinetti* (fl. 1500).]

spinnaker *spin'ə-kər*, *n* a triangular sail carried on the side opposite to the mainsail by vessels sailing before the wind; large sail carried by racing yachts. [Prob. **spin**, not *Sphinx* (yacht that carried a spinnaker).]

spinner, spinneret, etc. See under **spin**.

spinney *spin'i*, *n* a small clump of trees or copse: — *pl* **spinn'eys**. [O.Fr. *espinei* — L. *spīnētum*, a thorn-hedge, thicket — *spīna*, thorn.]

spino- *spī-nō-*, *combining form* signifying spine.

spinode *spī'nōd*, (*geom*) *n* a cusp or stationary point of a curve. [L. *spīna*, thorn, *nōdus*, knot.]

spinose, spinous, etc. See under **spine**.

spinster *spin'stər*, *n* an unmarried woman; an old maid. — *n* **spin'sterhood**. — *adj* **spinsterial**

(-*stē'ri-əl*). — *adj* **spinstē'rian**. — *adj* **spin'sterish**. — *adj* **spin'sterly**. [**spin**, and sfx. *-ster*.]

spinule, spiny, etc. See under **spine**.

spiracle *spīr'ə-kl*, *n* a breathing-hole; a vent, orifice, passage. — *n* **spīrac'ulum**: — *pl* **spīrac'ula**. [L. *spīrāculum* — *spīrāre*, to breathe.]

spiraea or (esp. in U.S.) **spirea** *spī-rē'ə*, *n* a plant or shrub of the meadow-sweet genus (*Spiraea*) of the rose family. [Gr. *speiraiā*, meadow-sweet, or privet — *speira*, a coil (from its coiled fruits).]

spiral, etc. See under **spire**[2].

spirant *spī'rənt*, (*phon*) *adj* fricative, open, produced by narrowing without stopping the air-passage. — *n* a spirant consonant (including or excluding nasals, liquids, and semi-vowels). — *n* **spīrā'tion** breathing. [L. *spīrāre*, to breathe.]

spirated. See under **spire**[2].

spire[1] *spīr*, *n* a tapering or conical body, esp. a tree-top; a flower-spike; a tall slender architectural structure tapering to a point. [O.E. *spīr*, shoot, sprout.]

spire[2] *spīr*, *n* a coil; a spiral; the spiral part of a shell, excluding the body-whorl. — *vi* to wind, mount or proceed in spirals. — *adj* **spīr'al** winding like the thread of a screw; with parts arranged in spirals (*bot*). — *n* a spiral line, course or object; a curve (usu. plane), the locus of a point whose distance from a fixed point varies according to some rule as the radius vector revolves (*math*); a helix; a gradual but continuous rise or fall, as of prices. — *vi* to go in a spiral. — *vt* to make spiral. — *adj* **spīr'aliform** in or based on the shape of a spiral. — *n* **spīrality** (*-al'i-ti*). — *adv* **spīr'ally**. — *adj* **spīr'āted** spirally twisted. — *adj* **spī'roid** with the form of, or like, a spiral. — *adj* **spīr'y** spirally coiled. — **spiral arm** (*astron*) an arm of a spiral galaxy; **spiral galaxy** (*astron*) one of a large class of galaxies, with two spiral arms emerging from a bright central ellipsoidal nucleus about which they rotate. [Gr. *speira*, a coil, a tore.]

spirit *spir'it*, *n* vital principle; the principle of thought; the soul; a disembodied soul; a ghost; an incorporeal being; enthusiasm; actuating emotion, disposition, frame of mind; a leading, independent or lively person; animation, verve; courage, mettle; real meaning; essence, chief quality; (in *pl*) cheerful or exuberant vivacity; (in *pl*) state of mind, mood; (in *pl*) spirituous liquor; (the following also in *pl*, sometimes with verb in *sing*) a distilled liquid; an aqueous solution of ethyl alcohol; a solution in alcohol. — *vt* to give spirit to; to inspirit, encourage, cheer; to convey away secretly, to kidnap (often with *away* or *off*). — *adj* **spir'ited** full of spirit, life or fire; animated; possessed by a spirit. — *adv* **spir'itedly**. — *n* **spir'iting** the action of someone who spirits in any sense; the offices of a spirit or sprite. — *n* **spir'itism** spiritualism; animism. — *n* **spir'itist**. — *adj* **spiritist'ic**. — *adj* **spir'itless** without spirit, cheerfulness or courage; dejected; dead. — *adv* **spir'itlessly**. — *adj* **spir'itous** of the nature of spirit, pure; ardent, spirituous. — *adj* **spir'itūal** of, of the nature of, or relating to, spirit, a spirit, spirits, the mind, the higher faculties, the soul; highly refined in thought and feeling, habitually or naturally looking to things of the spirit; incorporeal; ecclesiastical, religious. — *n* that which is spiritual; an American Negro religious song. — *n* **spiritualīsā'tion** or **-z-**. — *vt* **spir'itualise** or **-ize** to make spiritual; to imbue with spirituality; to refine; to free from sensuality; to give a spiritual meaning to. — *n* **spir'itualiser** or **-z-**. — *n* **spir'itualism** a being spiritual; the interpretation of a varied series of abnormal phenomena as for the most part caused by spiritual beings acting upon specially sensitive persons or mediums (also **spir'itism**). — *n* **spir'itualist** someone who has a regard only to spiritual things; (with *cap*) someone who holds the doctrine of spiritualism or spiritism. — *adj* **spiritualist'ic**. — *n* **spirituality** (*-al'i-ti*) state of being spiritual; that which is spiritual. — *adv* **spir'itually**. — *n* **spir'itualness** the state or quality of being spiritual. — *n* **spirituos'ity** spirituous character; immateriality. — *adj* **spir'ituous** alcoholic. — *n* **spir'ituousness**. — **spir'it-gum** a preparation used by actors for attaching false beards, etc.; **spir'it-lamp** lamp burning methylated or other spirit to give heat; **spir'it-level** a glass tube nearly filled with, (usu.) alcohol, showing perfect levelness when the bubble is central; **spir'it-varnish** shellac or other resin in a volatile solvent, usu. alcohol; **spir'it-world** the world of disembodied spirits. — **Holy Spirit** or **the Spirit** see **Holy Ghost** under **holy**; **in spirits** cheerfully vivacious; **out of spirits** depressed; **spirit(s) of ammonia** sal volatile; **spirit(s) of salt** hydrochloric acid in water; **spirit(s) of wine** alcohol. [L. *spīritus*, a breath — *spīrāre*, to breathe.]

spirochaete *spī'rō-kēt*, *n* a spirally coiled bacterium, the cause of syphilis and other diseases. [Gr. *speira*, a coil, *chaitē*, hair, mane.]

spirograph *spī'rō-gräf*, *n* an instrument for recording breathing movements. [L. *spīrāre*, to breathe.]

spiroid. See under **spire**[2].

spirt *spûrt*, *vi* to shoot out forcibly, or in a fine strong jet. — *vt* to squirt in a fine strong jet. — *n* a sudden fine jet.

spiry. See under **spire**[2].

spit[1] *spit*, *n* a long thin rod on which a joint of meat, etc. is skewered for roasting; a sword (*jocularly*); a long narrow tongue of land or sand running into the sea; a wire or spindle holding a spool in a shuttle. — *vt* to transfix; to string on a rod or wire: — *pr p* **spitt'ing**; *pa t* and *pa p* **spitt'ed**. — *adj* **spitt'ed**. [O.E. *spitu*.]

spit[2] *spit*, *vt* to throw out from the mouth; to eject with violence; to utter with hate, scorn or violence; to spawn. — *vi* to throw out saliva from the mouth; to rain in scattered drops; to make a spitting sound; to sputter; to feel or be furious (*colloq*): — *pr p* **spitt'ing**; *pa t* and *pa p* **spat**. — *n* saliva, spume; a light fall of rain or snow; an exact replica (*slang*; usu. *dead* or *very spit*). — *n* **spitt'er**. — *n* **spitt'ing**. — Also *adj*. — *n* **spitt'le** spit, saliva. — *n* **spittoon'** a vessel for spitting in. — **spit'fire** that which emits fire, e.g. a volcano, cannon; (with *cap*) a type of fighting aeroplane used in World War II; a hot-tempered person; **spitting image** the exact likeness of; **spitt'lebug** or **spittle insect** a frog-hopper or froth-fly. — **spit and polish** cleaning up of uniform and equipment, esp. to excess; **spit and sawdust** of or referring to a floor left rough and covered with sawdust, wood chippings, etc., or esp. a bar having this type of floor; the character, quality, etc. of such a bar; **spit blood** to rage, be furious; **spit (it) out** to speak out, tell (it). [Northern O.E. *spittan*.]

spit[3] *spit*, *vt* and *vi* to dig; to plant with a spade. — *n* a spade's depth; this amount of earth, a spadeful. [O.E. *spittan*, or (M.)Du. and (M.)L.G. *spit*.]

spitchcock *spich'kok*, *n* an eel split and broiled. — *vt* to split and broil (an eel). [Cf. **spatchcock**.]

spite *spīt*, *n* grudge; lasting ill-will; hatred. — *vt* to vex; to thwart; to hate. — *adj* **spite'ful** full of spite; desirous to vex or injure; malignant. — *adv* **spite'fully**. — *n* **spite'fulness**. — **in spite of** in opposition to all efforts of, in defiance of, in contempt of; notwithstanding. [**despite**.]

spitter, spittle, spittoon. See under **spit**[2].

spitz *spits*, *n* a Pomeranian dog; a group of breeds of dog generally having long hair, pointed ears and a tightly curled tail, incl. husky, samoyed, Pomeranian, etc. [Ger.]

spiv *spiv*, (*slang*) *n* a flashy black-market hawker; someone who makes money by dubious means; an idler. — *adj* **spivv'y**.

splanchnic *splangk'nik*, (*zool*) *adj* visceral, intestinal. [Gr. *splanchnon*, pl. *splanchna*, entrails.]

splash *splash*, *vt* to spatter, as with water or mud; to throw about brokenly, as liquid; to dash liquid on or over; to effect by or with splashing; to variegate as if by splashing; to display, print very prominently. — *vi* to dabble; to dash liquid about; to move, or go, with throwing about of broken liquid; to fly about dispersedly. — *n* the dispersion of liquid suddenly disturbed, as by throwing something into it or by throwing it about; liquid thrown on anything; a spot formed by or as if by throwing liquid; a little soda-water, tonic, etc. (with a spirit); ostentation, publicity, display; a sensation, excitement, dash; a prominently printed slogan or (a story or article introduced by such a) headline. — *n* and *adj* **splash'ing.** — *adj* **splash'y** splashing; with splashing; wet and muddy; full of puddles; ostentatious, showy. — **splash'-back** a piece of glass, plastic, etc., or area of tiles covering the part of a wall behind a wash-basin to protect against splashing; **splash'board** a mudguard; a dashboard; **splash'down** (the moment of) the landing of a spacecraft on the sea. — *adj* **splash'proof.** — **splash down** (of spacecraft) to land on the sea on completion of a mission; **splash out (on)** (*colloq*) to spend a lot of money (on). [**plash.**]

splat[1] *splat*, *n* a thin strip forming the upright middle part of a chair-back. [*plat*, an old word meaning something flat.]

splat[2] *splat*, *n* the sound made by a soft, wet object striking a surface. — *vi* to strike a surface with a splat; to cause (droplets of molten metal) to strike and spread over a metal surface, driven by shock waves (*metallurgy*). — *adv* with this sound. — *n* **splatt'ing.** — **splat cooling** or **splat quenching** the technical process of cooling metal rapidly by splatting. [Onomatopoeic.]

splatter *splat'ər*, *vt* and *vi* to spatter; to splash; to sputter. — *n* a splash; a spattering. [Cf. **spatter.**]

splay *splā*, *vt* and *vi* to slope, slant or bevel (*archit*); to spread out. — *n* a slant or bevel, as of the side of a doorway, window, or the like. — *adj* having a splay; turned outwards. — **splay foot** a flat foot turned outward. — *adj* **splay'-foot** or **-footed.** [**display.**]

spleen *splēn*, *n* a soft, pulpy, blood-modifying organ close to the stomach, once thought the seat of anger and melancholy; hence spite, melancholy. — *n* **splenec'tomy** (*splin-*) excision of the spleen. — *adj* **splenetic** (*splin-et'ik*) of the spleen; affected with spleen; peevish; melancholy. — *n* a splenetic person. — *adj* **splenet'ical.** — *adv* **splenet'ically.** — *adj* **splenic** (*splē'nik* or *splen'*) of the spleen. — *n* **splenī'tis** (*splin-*) inflammation of the spleen. [L. *splēn* — Gr. *splēn.*]

splendid *splen'did*, *adj* brilliant, resplendent; magnificent; excellent (*colloq*). — *adv* **splen'didly.** — *n* **splen'didness.** — *adj* **splendif'erous** (now only *colloq*). — *adj* **splen'dorous** or **splen'drous.** — *n* **splen'dour** or in U.S. **splendor** (*-dər*) brilliance; magnificence. [L. *splendēre*, to shine, *splendidus*, *splendor.*]

splenectomy, splenetic, etc. See under **spleen.**

splenial *splē'ni-əl*, (*anat*) *adj* of the splenius. — *n* **splē'nius** a large thick muscle on the back of the neck. [Gr. *splēnion*, pad, compress.]

splenic, etc. See under **spleen.**

splice *splīs*, *vt* to unite by interweaving the strands; to join together by overlapping; to unite, esp. (*slang*; also *vi*) in matrimony. — *n* the act of splicing; a joint made by splicing; the part of the handle of a cricket-bat or the like that fits into the blade. — **splice the mainbrace** (*nautical slang*) to serve out an allowance of spirits; to fall to drinking. [Du. (now dialect) *splissen.*]

spliff *splif*, (*slang*, esp. *Rastafarian*, orig. *West Indian*) *n* a marijuana cigarette; the act of smoking such a cigarette.

spline *splīn*, *n* a key to make wheel and shaft revolve together; a thin strip or slat. — *vt* to put splines on. [Orig. E. Anglian.]

splint *splint*, *n* a strip, slip of wood, lath; a splinter; a contrivance for holding a broken bone, or the like, in position; a bony enlargement on a horse's leg between knee and fetlock; splint-coal. — *vt* to put in splints. — *n* **splint'er** a piece of wood, metal, etc. split off, esp. a needle-like piece; a slender strip of wood, esp. one used as a torch. — *vt* and *vi* to split into splinters. — *adj* **splint'ery** made of, or like, splinters; apt to splinter. — **splint'-coal** a hard coal of uneven fracture that does not cake; **splint'er-bar** the cross-bar of a coach, supporting the springs; **splint'er-bone** the fibula; **splinter group** a party or group formed by a breakaway from a larger body. — *adj* **splint'erproof** proof against the splinters of bursting shells or bombs, or against splintering. [M.Du. *splinte* or (M.)L.G. *splinte*, *splente.*]

split *split*, *vt* to break in pieces, wreck; to rend; to cleave lengthwise; to divide, share; to disunite; to divulge (*colloq*). — *vi* to be dashed to pieces (often with *up*); to suffer shipwreck; to divide or part asunder (often with *up*); to divulge secrets (*colloq*); to divide one's votes instead of plumping; to burst with laughter; to go at full speed; to break off relations (with) (*slang*; often with *up*): — *pr p* **splitt'ing**; *pa t* and *pa p* **split.** — *n* a crack or rent lengthwise; a schism; a half-bottle of aerated water, etc., a half-glass of spirits; (in *pl*) the acrobatic feat of going down to the floor with the legs spread out laterally or one forward and one back; a division, share-out (usu. of money, stolen goods, etc.) (*colloq*); a sweet dish, usu. of sliced-open fruit and cream, ice-cream, etc.; a piece of wood for kindling (*Can*); a split-level house or apartment (*US*). — *adj* having been split; having a split or break. — *n* **splitt'er** someone who, or that which, splits; someone who splits hairs in argument, classification, etc.; a splitting headache (*colloq*). — *adj* **splitt'ing** rending; cleaving; ear-splitting; (of a headache) very severe; very rapid. — **split image** a bisected image, produced in a focusing system in which the two halves are displaced if the camera is out of focus (*phot*); a spitting image (also **splitting image**); **split infinitive** an infinitive with an adverb between 'to' and the verb. — *adj* **split-lev'el** on more than one level (see also below). — **split mind** a mental disorder in which the thoughts may become separated from the emotions; (*loosely*) a divided or dual opinion or feeling (about something); **split peas** see under **pea**; **split personality** dual personality; **split pin** a pin made of a doubled piece of metal formed into a ring at the head to give tension and usu. inserted in a hole in a bolt to hold a nut, etc. firmly; **split ring** a ring formed as if split spirally, as for keeping keys together; **split screen** a cinematic technique of showing different scenes simultaneously on separate parts of the screen, also used in television; a facility whereby separate areas of the screen may be used to display and carry out separate functions simultaneously. — *adj* **split'-screen.** — **split second** a fraction of a second. — *adj* **split'-second** timed to a fraction of a second. — **full split** at full speed; **split on** (*colloq*) to betray, give (a person) away; **split one's sides** to laugh immoderately; **split the difference** to divide equally the sum of matter in dispute, to take the mean. [Du. *splitten.*]

splodge, splodgily, etc. See under **splotch.**

splosh *splosh*, *n*, *vi* and *vt* a usu. humorous variant of **splash.**

splotch *sploch* or **splodge** *sploj*, *n* a big or heavy splash, spot or stain. — *vt* to mark with splotches or splodges. — *vi* to trudge flounderingly or splashily. — *adv* **splotch'ily** or **splodg'ily.** — *n* **splotch'iness** or **splodg'iness.** — *adj* **splotch'y** or **splodg'y.** [Perh. conn. with O.E. *splott*, spot.]

splurge *splûrj, n* any boisterous or extravagant display. — *vi* to make such a display; to spend a lot of money (on). — *adj* **splur'gy.** [Imit.]

splutter *splut'ər, vi* to eject drops; to scatter ink upon a paper, as a bad pen does; to scatter liquid with spitting noises; to articulate confusedly as in rage. — *vt* to utter splutteringly. — *n* an act or noise of spluttering. — *n* **splutt'erer.** — *n* and *adj* **splutt'ering.** — *adv* **splutt'eringly.** — *adj* **splutt'ery.** [Prob. imit.; cf. **sputter.**]

Spode *spōd, n* (also without *cap*) a porcelain made with addition of bone-ash by Josiah *Spode* (1754–1827) at Stoke-on-Trent. — Also *adj.*

spoil *spoil, n* (usu. in *pl*) plunder, booty; acquisitions, prizes; spoliation; pillage; material cast out in excavation. — *vt* to mar; to impair; to make useless; to treat over-indulgently; to harm the character by so doing; to plunder; to strip; to deprive; to corrupt. — *vi* to go bad; to deteriorate; to practise spoliation: — *pa t* and *pa p* **spoiled** or (only in sense of damage) **spoilt.** — *n* **spoil'age** waste by spoiling; material so wasted. — *adj* **spoiled.** — *n* **spoil'er** any thing or person that spoils; an aerodynamic device fitted to the wings of an aircraft to reduce lift and assist descent; a similar device fitted to motor vehicles, esp. racing cars, to lessen drag and reduce the tendency to become unstable through a lifting effect at high speeds. — **spoil'sport** someone who stops or interferes with sport or other people's pleasure; a meddler; **spoilt paper** (in a ballot) a voting paper marked, esp. deliberately, in such a way as to be invalid. — **spoiling for** (a fight, etc.) more than ripe or ready for; intent on. [O.Fr. *espoille* — L. *spolium*, spoil.]

spoke[1] *spōk, pa t* of **speak.**

spoke[2] *spōk, n* one of the radiating bars of a wheel. — *adv* **spoke'wise.** — **spoke'shave** a two-handled planing tool for curved work. — **put a spoke in someone's wheel** to thwart someone. [O.E. *spāca.*]

spoken *spōk'n, pa p* of **speak.** — Used in combination to denote speech or speaking, as in *plain-spoken.* — **spoken for** chosen, reserved.

spokesman *spōks'mən* or **spokes'person,** *fem* **spokes'woman,** *n* a person who speaks for another, or for others: — *pl* **spokes'men, spokes'persons** or **spokes'people,** *fem* **spokes'women.**

spoliate *spō'li-āt, vt* and *vi* to despoil, to plunder. — *n* **spōliā'tion.** — *adj* **spō'liātive** serving to take away or diminish. — *n* **spō'liātor.** — *adj* **spō'liatory** (*-ə-tər-i*). [L. *spoliāre, -ātum* — *spolium*, spoil.]

spondee *spon'dē,* (*prosody*) *n* a foot of two long syllables. — *adj* **spondaic** (*-dā'ik*). — *adj* **spondā'ical.** [L. *spondēus* (*pēs*) — Gr. *spondeios* (*pous*), (a foot) used in the slow solemn hymns sung at a *spondē* or drink-offering.]

spondyl *spon'dil,* (*zool*) *n* a vertebra. — *adj* **spondylit'ic** affected by spondylitis. — *n* a person suffering from spondylitis. — *n* **spondylī'tis** (*med*) inflammation of a vertebra. [Gr. *sp(h)ondylos*, a vertebra.]

sponge *spunj, n* any member of the phylum *Porifera*, sessile aquatic animals with a single cavity in the body, with numerous pores; the fibrous skeleton of such an animal, remarkable for its power of sucking up water; a piece of such a skeleton, or a substitute, used for washing, obliterating, absorbing, etc.; any spongelike substance, such as leavened dough, a cake or pudding, or swampy ground; a hanger-on or parasite (*colloq*); a drunkard (*colloq*); an application of a sponge; the life or behaviour of a sponger upon others (*colloq*). — *vt* to wipe, wipe out, soak up or remove with a sponge; to drain, as if by squeezing a sponge; to gain by the art of the parasite. — *vi* to suck in, as a sponge does; to fish for sponges; to live on others parasitically (often with *on* or *off*). — *adj* **spon'geable.** — *adj* **spongeous** (*spun'jəs*) spongy. — *n* **spong'er** a person who uses a sponge; a sponge-fisher; a sponge-fishing boat; an apparatus for sponging cloth; a sponge or parasite. — *adv* **spon'gily** in a spongy way or manner. — *n* **spon'giness.** — *adj* **spongy** (*spun'ji*) absorptive; porous; wet and soft; drunken; (of vehicle suspension, brakes, etc.) lacking firmness. — **sponge'bag** a waterproof bag for carrying a toilet articles; **sponge'bath** a washing of the body with a sponge, as for a bedridden person; **sponge cake** a very light sweet cake of flour, eggs and sugar; **sponge cloth** a cotton cloth of open texture; **sponge finger** a finger-shaped sponge cake; **sponge fisher; sponge fishing; sponge rubber** rubber processed into sponge-like form; **sponge'wood** sola, an Indian plant also known as the hat-plant. — **sponge down** to clean or wipe with a sponge (*n* **sponge'-down**); **throw up the sponge** to acknowledge defeat by throwing into the air the sponge with which a boxer is rubbed down between rounds; to give up any struggle. [O.E. *sponge, spunge*, and O.Fr. *esponge* — L. *spongia* — Gr. *spongiā.*]

sponsion *spon'shən, n* the act of becoming surety for another. [L. *spondēre, spōnsum*, promise.]

sponson *spon'sn, n* an outward expansion from a ship's deck; a short projecting length of plane; a wing-section giving extra lift; an air-filled tank on the side of a canoe to give buoyancy; a structure to give a seaplane steadiness on the water.

sponsor *spon'sər, n* a person who promises solemnly for another; a surety; a godfather or godmother; a promoter; a person or organisation who pays for a radio or television broadcast introducing advertisements; a person or organisation who promises to pay a specified sum to a person for taking part in a fund-raising event or activity on behalf of a charity, etc. — *vt* to act as a sponsor. — *adj* **sponso'rial.** — *n* **spon'sorship.** [Ety. as for **sponsion.**]

spontaneous *spon-tā'nyəs* or *-ni-əs, adj* of one's free will; acting by its own impulse or natural law; produced of itself; impulsive; unpremeditated. — *n* **spontaneity** (*-tə-nē'i-ti* or *-nā'i-ti*). — *adv* **spontā'neously.** — *n* **spontā'neousness.** — **spontaneous combustion** catching fire by causes at work within, esp. slow oxidation of a mass of matter. [L. *spontāneus* — *sponte*, of one's own accord.]

spoof *spo͞of,* (*slang*) *n* a parody, take-off. — *adj* bogus. — *vt* and *vi* to hoax; to parody. — *n* **spoof'er.** — *n* **spoof'ery.** [Name of a hoaxing game invented and named by Arthur Roberts (1852–1933), comedian.]

spook *spo͞ok, n* a ghost; a spy, an undercover agent (*slang*, orig. *US*). — *vi* to play the spook; to take fright; (of a horse) to shy away. — *vt* to frighten, startle. — *adv* **spook'ily.** — *n* **spook'iness.** — *adj* **spook'ish.** — *adj* **spook'y.** [App. L.G.]

spool *spo͞ol, n* a cylinder, bobbin or reel for winding yarn, etc. upon. — *vt* and *vi* to wind on spools. — *n* **spool'er.** [L.G. *spôle.*]

spoon[1] *spo͞on, vi* to scud before the wind. — **spoon'-drift** see **spin'drift.**

spoon[2] *spo͞on, n* an (eating, or serving, etc.) instrument with a shallow bowl and a handle; anything of similar shape, such as an oar; (a stroke with) a wooden-headed golf club with face slightly hollowed; a spoon-bait (*colloq*). — *vt* to transfer with, or as if with, a spoon; to shove, scoop or hit softly up into the air, instead of striking cleanly and definitely; to dally sentimentally with; to catch with a spoon-bait. — *vi* to be sentimentally amorous; to fish with a spoon-bait. — *n* **spoon'ful** as much as fills a spoon; a small quantity: — *pl* **spoon'fuls.** — *adj* **spoon'y** or **spoon'ey** silly; foolishly and demonstratively fond. — **spoon'-bait** or **-hook** a lure on a swivel, used in trolling for fish; **spoon'bill** any bird of a family akin to the ibises, with long, flat, broad bill, spoon-shaped at the tip; a shoveller (genus *Spatula*). — *adj* **spoon'-fed** fed with a spoon; artificially fostered (*fig*); taught by doled-out doses of cut-and-dried information. — *vt* **spoon'feed**. — **born with a silver spoon in one's mouth** see under **silver**. [O.E. *spōn*, sliver, chip, shaving.]

spoonerism *spoo'nər-izm*, *n* a transposition of initial sounds of spoken words — e.g. 'shoving leopard' for 'loving shepherd'. [Rev. W.A. *Spooner* (1844–1930), a noted perpetrator of transpositions of this kind.]

spoor *spoor*, *n* track, esp. of a hunted animal. [Du. *spoor*, a track.]

sporadic *spor-ad'ik*, *adj* scattered; occurring here and there or now and then; occurring casually. — *adv* **sporad'ically**. [Gr. *sporadikos* — *sporas*, *sporados*, scattered — *speirein*, to sow.]

spore *spör*, (*bot*) *n* a unicellular asexual reproductive body; sometimes extended to other reproductive bodies. — *n* **sporan'gium** (*-ji-*) a spore-case, sac in which spores are produced: *pl* **sporan'gia**. — Also **spore'-case**. — *n* **spor'ophyte** the spore-bearing or asexual generation in the life-cycle of a plant. — *adj* **sporophytic** (*-fit'ik*). — *npl* **Sporozō'a** a parasitic group of Protozoa reproducing by spores, including the organisms that cause malaria. — *n* **sporozō'ite** (Gr. *zōion*, an animal) in Sporozoa, a minute, mobile, pre-adult, usu. infective stage developed within a spore. — *n* **sporūlā'tion** formation of spores; breaking up into spores. [Gr. *sporā*, a seed — *speirein*, to sow.]

sporran *spor'ən*, *n* in Scottish Highland dress, an ornamental pouch of leather, fur, etc. worn in front of the kilt by men. [Gael. *sporan*.]

sport *spört*, *vi* to enjoy oneself, have a good time; to take part in a specific amusement, activity or recreation, esp. outdoor; to trifle; to deviate from the normal (*biol*). — *vt* to wear, use, exhibit, set up, publicly or ostentatiously. — *n* recreation; pastime; amorous behaviour; play; a game, esp. one involving bodily exercise; amusement, fun, good-humoured mirth; contemptuous mirth; a laughing-stock; a specific, esp. outdoor, amusement, activity or recreation; success in or pleasure from shooting, fishing, or the like; a sportsman; a person of sportsmanlike character; an animal or plant that varies from the normal type (*biol*). — *adv* **sport'ily**. — *n* **sport'iness**. — *adj* **sport'ing** relating to, engaging in, or fond of, sports; willing to take a chance; sportsmanlike; in the U.K., pertaining to one of the two major classes of dogs recognised by the Kennel Club (the other being *non-sporting*), comprising hounds, gun dogs and terriers; in the U.S., pertaining to one of the six recognised groups of breeds, essentially comprising the gun dogs (as opposed to hounds, terriers, etc.). — *adv* **sport'ingly**. — *adj* **sport'ive** inclined to sport; playful; merry; amorous, wanton. — *npl* **sports** a meeting for races and other competitive events. — *adj* suitable for sport. — *adj* **sport'y** sportsmanlike (*colloq*); (of a person) who enjoys, takes part in or is proficient at sport; (of a car) that looks or handles like a sports car; stylish, lively. — **sporting chance** as good a chance of winning or being successful as of losing or failing; **sports car** a low car, usu. for two, capable of attaining high speed; **sports'caster** or **sport'caster** (*TV* and *radio*; orig. *US*) a commentator on a sports programme; **sports day** a day on which a school, college, etc., usu. annually, holds its own competitive athletic events; **sports ground** an area with equipment and facilities, designed for esp. competitive outdoor sports; **sports jacket** a man's jacket, usu. tweed, for casual wear; **sports'man**, **sports'person** or (*fem*) **sports'woman** someone who practises, or is skilled in, sport; someone who shows fairness and good humour in sport. — *adj* **sports'manlike**. — **sports'manship**; **sports shirt** a man's casual shirt; **sports'wear** clothing designed to be worn for sport; designer clothes, esp. matching separates, for casual wear. [Aphetic for **disport**.]

sporula, etc. See under **spore**.

spot *spot*, *n* a mark made by a drop of something wet; a blot; a small discoloured or differently coloured place; a locality, place or limited area; precise place; an eruption on the skin; a moral flaw; one of the marked points on a billiard-table, from which balls are played; a relatively dark place on the sun; a small quantity of anything (*colloq*); a spotlight; a place on e.g. a television or radio programme; a turn, performance, esp. a short one; a spot deal or commodity (*finance*). — *vt* to mark with spots; to tarnish, e.g. a reputation; to pick out, detect, locate, identify (*colloq*); to place on a spot, as in billiards. — *vi* to become spotted; to rain slightly, with few and intermittent drops (*colloq*): — *pr p* **spott'ing**; *pa t* and *pa p* **spott'ed**. — *adj* on the spot, random (see **spot check** below); of monetary or commodity transactions, etc., to be paid (usu. in cash) or delivered immediately (as in *spot deal*, *spot market*, *spot price*, etc.); involving payment in cash only. — *adj* **spot'less** without a spot; untainted; pure. — *adv* **spot'lessly**. — *n* **spot'lessness**. — *adj* **spott'ed**. — *n* **spott'edness**. — *n* **spott'er** someone who or something (such as a plane) that spots, observes or detects. — *n* **spott'ing**. — *adj* **spott'y**. — (In combination) **-spotting** used to signify noting or identifying, as in *train-spotting*. — *verb combining form* **-spot**. — *noun combining form* **-spotter**. — **spot cash** money down; **spot check** a check on the spot without warning; a check of random samples to serve in place of a general check; **spot dealer** (*finance*); **spot'light** (apparatus for projecting) a circle of light on an actor or a small part of a stage (also *fig*); an adjustable, focused-beam car lamp additional to fixed lights. — *vt* to turn the spotlight on; to draw attention to (*fig*). — *adj* **spot-on'** (*colloq*) on the target; exactly right, accurate. — **spotted dick** a suet pudding with currants; **spotted dog** a Dalmatian dog; spotted dick; **spotted flycatcher** a European songbird (*Muscicapa striata*). — *vt* **spot'-weld** to join metal with single circular welds. — *n* a weld of this kind. — **spot'-welder**. — **high spot** an outstanding feature, happening, occasion, etc.; **in a spot** in a difficult situation; **knock (the) spots off** to surpass easily; **on the spot** at the very place; there and then; immediately; alert, equal to the occasion; in difficulty or danger (e.g. *put on the spot*, orig. to doom to be murdered) (*adj* **on-the-spot'**); **soft spot** (*colloq*) affectionate feeling; **tight spot** (*colloq*) a dangerous or difficult situation; **weak spot** (*colloq*) weakness; an area in which one is not knowledgeable. [O.N. *spotti*, a small bit.]

spouse *spows* or *spowz*, *n* a husband or wife. [O.Fr. *spus*, *-e*, — L. *spōnsus*, past p. of *spondēre*, to promise.]

spout *spowt*, *vt* to throw out in a jet; to declaim. — *vi* to issue in a jet; to blow as a whale; to declaim (*derog*). — *n* a projecting lip or tube for discharging liquid from a vessel, a roof, etc.; a gush, discharge or jet; an undivided waterfall; a waterspout; the blowing or the blow-hole of a whale; a chute. — *n* **spout'er** someone who or something that spouts; a declaimer; a spouting oil-well; a spouting whale; a whaling ship. — *adj* **spout'less**. — **spout'-hole** a blow-hole. — **up the spout** (*slang*) pawned; failed, gone wrong; pregnant. [M.E. *spouten*.]

SPQR *abbrev* for *Senatus Populusque Romanus* (L.), the Senate and People of Rome.

SPR *abbrev* for Society for Psychical Research.

sprag *sprag*, *n* a mine prop; a bar inserted to stop a wheel; a device to prevent a vehicle from running backwards. — *vt* to prop or stop by a sprag: — *pr p* **spragg'ing**; *pa t* and *pa p* **spragged**.

sprain *sprān*, *vt* to overstrain the muscles of. — *n* a wrenching of a joint with tearing or stretching of ligaments.

sprang *sprang*, *pa t* of **spring**.

sprat *sprat*, *n* a fish like the herring, but much smaller. — **a sprat to catch a mackerel, herring** or **whale** a small risk taken in order to make a great gain. [O.E. *sprot*.]

sprauncy *sprön'si*, *adj* smart, dapper. [Poss conn. with dialect *sprouncey*, cheerful, jolly.]

sprawl *spröl*, *vi* to lie or crawl with limbs flung about; to straggle. — *vt* to spread stragglingly. — *n* a sprawling posture, movement, or mass. — *n* **sprawl'er**. — *adj* **sprawl'ing**. — *adj* **sprawl'y**. [O.E. *sprēawlian*, to move convulsively.]

spray[1] *sprā*, *n* a cloud of small flying drops; an application or dispersion of such a cloud; an apparatus or a preparation for so dispersing. — *vt* to sprinkle in or with fine mistlike jets. — *n* **spray'er**. — *adj* **spray'ey**. — *adj* **spray'-dried**. — **spray drift** spray, esp. a chemical pesticide or herbicide, which remains suspended in the air and is blown away from the original site of spraying by the wind; **spray drying** the rapid drying of a liquid by spraying it into a flow of hot gas; **spray'-gun** a device for applying paint, etc. by spraying. — *adj* **spray'-on** applied in a spray, usu. by an aerosol. — **spray'-paint** paint that is applied in the form of a spray, usu. an aerosol. — *vt* to use spray-paint (on something); to apply with spray-paint. — **spray'-painting**. [M.Du. *sprayen*.]

spray[2] *sprā*, *n* a shoot or twig, esp. one spreading out in branches or flowers; an ornament, casting, etc. of similar form. — *vi* to spread or branch in a spray. — *adj* **spray'ey** branching. [Poss. conn. with **sprig** or with O.E. *spræc*, twig.]

sprayey. See under **spray**[1,2].

spread *spred*, *vt* to cause to extend more widely or more thinly; to scatter abroad or in all directions; to stretch; to extend, esp. over a surface; to apply (a soft substance) by smoothing it over a surface; to open out so as to cover a wider surface; to overlay; to set with provisions, as a table. — *vi* to extend or expand; to be extended or stretched; to become bigger or fatter; to open out; to go further apart; to unfold; to be capable of being spread; to be propagated or circulated: — *pa t* and *pa p* **spread**. — *n* extent; compass; reach; expanse; an expanded surface; the act or degree of spreading; an expansion; the process of becoming bigger or fatter; that which is spread out, a feast; anything for spreading on bread; a cover, esp. a bedcover; a ranch (*US*); a double page, i.e. two facing pages (*printing*); a large property with grounds (*colloq*); the gap between the bid and offer price of shares (*stock exchange*). — *adj* extended; flat and shallow (as a gem). — *n* **spread'er**. — *n* and *adj* **spread'ing**. — *adv* **spread'ingly**. — **spread-ea'gle** a heraldic eagle with the wings and legs stretched out. — *vt* to tie up with outstretched limbs; to spread out; to outrun. — *vi* to cut, do or make spreadeagled; to lie, fall, etc. with outstretched limbs; **spread'sheet** or **spreadsheet program** (*comput*) a program with which data, formatted in rows and columns of cells, can be viewed on a screen and manipulated to make projections, calculations, etc. — **spread one's wings** to try one's powers or capabilities; to increase the area of one's activities. [O.E. *sprǣdan*.]

sprechgesang *shprehh'gə-zang*, (*mus*) *n* a style of vocalisation between singing and speaking, originated by Arnold Schoenberg. — *n* **sprech'-stimme** (*-shtim-ə*) music using this form of vocalisation. [Ger., speaking-song, speaking-voice.]

spree *sprē*, *n* a merry frolic; a drunken bout. — *vi* to carouse. [Orig. slang.]

sprig *sprig*, *n* a small shoot or twig; a scion, a young person (usu. *disparagingly*); an ornament like a spray; a spriglike object, ornament or design, esp. embroidered or applied. — *vt* to embroider with representations of twigs: — *pr p* **sprigg'ing**; *pa t* and *pa p* **sprigged**.

sprightly *sprīt'li*, *adj* vivacious; animated; lively; brisk. — *n* **spright'liness**. [*spright*, unhistoric spelling of **sprite**.]

spring *spring*, *vi* to move suddenly, as by elastic force; to bound; to start up suddenly; to break forth; to appear; to issue; to come into being; to take origin; to sprout; to branch off; to give way, split, burst, explode, warp or start. — *vt* to cause to spring up; to start; to release the elastic force of; to let off, allow to spring; to cause to explode; to make known suddenly (with *on* or *upon*); (of a leak) to open; (of a mast) to crack; to bend by force, strain; to leap over; to set together with bevel-joints; to attach or fit with springs; to procure the escape of (a prisoner) from jail (*slang*): — *pa t* **sprang**; *pa p* **sprung**. — *n* a leap; a sudden movement; a recoil or rebound; elasticity; an elastic contrivance usu. for setting in motion or for reducing shocks; a source of action or life; rise; beginning; cause or origin; a source; an outflow of water from the earth; (often with *cap*) the season when plants spring up and grow — in North temperate regions roughly February or March to April or May, astronomically from the spring equinox to the summer solstice; high water; spring tide; a split, bend, warp, etc., esp. a crack in a mast. — *adj* of the season of spring; sown, appearing or used in spring; having or worked by a spring. — *n* **spring'er** someone who or that which springs; a kind of spaniel. — *adv* **spring'ily**. — *n* **spring'iness**. — *n* **spring'ing** the act of leaping, sprouting, starting, rising or issuing; a place of branching; providing with springs. — *adj* leaping; arising; dawning; sprouting; with the freshness of youth; resilient; starting. — *adj* **spring'less**. — *adj* **spring'like**. — *adj* **spring'y** elastic; resilient; abounding with springs. — See also **sprung**. — **spring balance** an instrument for weighing by the elasticity of a spiral spring; **spring'-bed** a spring-mattress; **spring'-beetle** a click beetle. — *adj* **spring'-bladed** (of a knife) having a blade that springs out on pressure of a button. — **spring'board** a springy board for jumping or diving from; anything which serves as a starting-point, or from which one can launch ideas, projects, etc.; **spring'bok** (from Du.) a S. African antelope (also **spring'buck**); (with *cap*) a South African international sportsman (from emblems of sporting teams, orig. 1906 rugby team; shortened to **Bok**); hence also any South African, esp. when overseas; **spring'-box** the frame of a sofa, etc. in which the springs are set; **spring'-carriage**; **spring'-cart** one mounted upon springs; **spring chicken** a young chicken, usu. between two and ten months old, particularly tender when cooked (chiefly *US*; also **spring'er**); a young, lively, sometimes naive, person. — *vt* and *n* **spring-clean'**. — **spring-clean'ing** a thorough cleaning, (esp. of a house) usu. in spring; **spring'-clip** a spring-loaded clip; **spring fever** spring lassitude (*facetious*); restlessness; **spring'halt** a jerking lameness in which a horse suddenly twitches up its leg or legs; **spring'-hare** the jumping hare; **spring'-ligament** a ligament of the sole of the foot. — *adj* **spring-load'ed** having or operated by a spring. — **spring'-lock** a lock that fastens by a spring; one that opens when a spring is touched; **spring mattress** a mattress of spiral springs in a frame; **spring onion** a type of onion, its small bulb and long leaves being eaten raw in salads; **spring roll** a deep-fried savoury pancake enclosing a mixture of vegetables, pork, prawns, etc., orig. Chinese; **spring'tail** any member of the *Collembola* order of wingless, primitive insects; **spring'tide** springtime; **spring tide** a tide of maximum amplitude after new and full moon, when sun and moon pull together; **spring'time** the season of spring. —

spring a leak to begin to leak; **spring a mine** to cause it to explode. [O.E. *springan*.]

springe *sprinj*, *n* a snare with noose and spring; a gin. — *vt* to catch in a springe: — *pr p* **spring'ing**; *pa t* and *pa p* **springed** (*sprinjd*). [Earlier *sprenge*, from a probable O.E. *sprencg*.]

sprinkle *spring'kl*, *vt* to scatter in small drops or particles; to scatter on; to baptise with a few drops of water; to strew, dot, diversify. — *vi* to scatter in drops. — *n* a utensil for sprinkling. — *n* **sprin'kle** or **sprin'kling** the act of someone who sprinkles; a small quantity sprinkled (also *fig*); (in bookbinding) mottling of edges by scattering a few drops of colour. — *n* **sprin'kler** any thing or person that sprinkles; any of various devices for scattering water in drops, e.g. over growing plants, as fire-extinguishers, etc. (**sprinkler system** a system of such fire-extinguishers which operate automatically on a sudden rise in temperature). [Frequentative from O.E. *sprengan*, the causative of *springan*, to spring.]

sprint *sprint*, *n* a short run, row, cycle or race at full speed. — *vi* to run at full speed. — *vt* to perform a sprint over (a given distance). — *n* **sprin'ter** a person who sprints; name given to a vehicle (esp. a small bus or train with limited passenger capacity) designed to travel quickly over short distances. — *n* **sprin'ting**. [Cf. O.N. *spretta*, Sw. *spritta*.]

sprit *sprit*, (*naut*) *n* a spar set diagonally to extend a fore-and-aft sail. — **spritsail** (*sprit'sl*) a sail extended by a sprit. [O.E. *sprēot*, pole.]

sprite *sprīt*, *n* a goblin, elf, imp, impish or implike person; (in computer graphics) an icon formed of pixels, which can be moved around a screen by means of a software program. [O.Fr. *esprit*; cf. **spirit**.]

spritsail. See under **sprit**.

spritzer *sprit'sər*, *n* a drink of white wine and soda water. [Ger. *spritzen*, to spray, squirt.]

spritzig *shprit'sig*, (Ger.) *adj* sparkling (esp. of wine). — *n* a slightly sparkling (usu. German) white wine; the tangy quality of such a wine.

sprocket *sprok'it*, *n* a tooth on the rim of a wheel or capstan for engaging the chain; a toothed cylinder for driving a film, tape, etc.; a sprocket-wheel; a piece of wood used to build a roof out over eaves. — **sprock'et-wheel** a wheel with sprockets.

sprog *sprog*, *n* a recruit (*RAF slang*); a child, infant (*colloq*). [Poss. a reversed portmanteau form of *frog spawn* or a recruit's confusion of **sprocket** and **cog**.]

sprout *sprowt*, *n* a new growth; a young shoot; a side bud, as in **Brussels sprouts** (see **Brussels**); a scion, descendant; sprouting condition. — *vi* to shoot; to push out new shoots. — *vt* to put forth as a sprout or bud; to cause to sprout. [O.E. *sprūtan* (found in compounds).]

spruce[1] *sproōs*, *adj* smart; neat, dapper; over-fastidious, finical. — *adv* sprucely. — *vt* to smarten. — *vi* to become spruce or smart (often with *up*). — *adv* **spruce'ly**. — *n* **spruce'ness**. [Prob. from **spruce**[2], from the vogue of 'spruce leather' (obtained from *Pruce* or Prussia) in the 16th century.]

spruce[2] *sproōs*, *n* any conifer of the genus *Picea*, with long shoots only, four-angled needles, and pendulous cones (also **spruce fir**); its wood. — *adj* of spruce or its wood. [Orig. *Spruce*, for obs. *Pruce*, Prussia.]

sprue[1] *sproō*, *n* a passage by which molten metal runs into a mould; the metal that solidifies in it — *deadhead*.

sprue[2] *sproō*, *n* a tropical disease affecting mouth, throat and digestion. [Du. *spruw*.]

spruik *sproŏk*, (*Austr* and *NZ*) *vi* (of a showman, etc.) to harangue people in public. — *n* **spruik'er**.

sprung *sprung*, *pa t* and *pa p* of **spring**. — *adj* strained; split; loosed; furnished with springs; tipsy (*colloq*). — **sprung rhythm** a poetic rhythm close to the natural rhythm of speech, with mixed feet, and frequent single stressed syllables.

spry *sprī*, *adj* (*compar* **spry'er**, *superl* **spry'est**) nimble; agile. — *adv* **spry'ly**. — *n* **spry'ness**.

SPUC *abbrev* for Society for the Protection of the Unborn Child.

spud *spud*, *n* a small narrow digging tool; a stumpy person or thing; a potato (*slang*). — *vt* and *vi* to dig with a spud; (esp. with *in*) to start drilling (an oil well). — *n* **spudd'ing** or **spudding-in'** the process of starting to drill an oil well by boring a hole in the seabed. — **spud'-bashing** (*slang*) peeling potatoes.

spume *spūm*, *n* foam; scum. — *vi* to foam. — *vt* to throw up or off as foam or scum. — *adj* **spū'my**. [L. *spūma* — *spuĕre*, to spew.]

spun *spun*, *pa t* and *pa p* of **spin**, and *adj*. — *adj* **spun-out'** unduly lengthened. — **spun silk** a fabric made from waste silk fibres, sometimes mixed with cotton; **spun sugar** sugar spun into fine fluffy threads, as in candy floss; **spun'-yarn** rope-yarn twisted into a cord.

spunk *spungk*, (*colloq*) *n* spirit, mettle, courage; semen (*vulg slang*). — *adj* **spunk'y**. [Cf. Ir. *sponc*, tinder, sponge — L. *spongia*, a sponge — Gr. *spongiā*.]

spur *spûr*, *n* a goading instrument on a rider's heel; incitement, stimulus; a hard sharp projection; a clawlike projection at the back of a cock's or other bird's leg; an artificial substitute for this on a game cock; a short, usu. flowering or fruit-bearing, branch; a great lateral root; anything that projects in the shape of a spur; an extension from an electrical circuit; a lateral branch, as of a hill range; a siding or branch line of a railway; a strut; a structure to deflect the current from a bank. — *vt* to apply the spur to; to urge on; to provide with a spur or spurs; to prune into spurs. — *vi* to press forward with the spur; to hasten; to kick out: — *pr p* **spurr'ing**; *pa t* and *pa p* **spurred**. — *adj* **spur'less**. — *adj* **spurred** having or wearing spurs or a spur; in the form of a spur; urged; (of e.g. rye) affected with ergot. — *n* and *adj* **spurr'ing**. — *adj* **spurr'y**. — **spur'-gear** or **-gear'ing** a system of spur-wheels; **spur'-wheel** a cog-wheel. — *adj* **spur'-winged** with a horny spur on the pinion of the wing. — **on the spur of the moment** without premeditation; **set spurs to** to apply the spur and ride off quickly; **win one's spurs** to gain distinction by achievement; orig. to earn knighthood. [O.E. *spura*, *spora*.]

spurge *spûrj*, *n* any species of *Euphorbia*, a genus of very varied habit, with milky, generally poisonous, juice, and an inflorescence (*cyathium*) of flowers so reduced as to simulate a single flower. — **spurge'-laurel** a European evergreen shrub (*Daphne laureola*) with yellowish-green flowers, thick leaves, and poisonous berries. [O.Fr. *espurge* — L. *expurgāre*, to purge — *ex*, off, *purgāre*, to clear.]

spurious *spūr'i-əs*, *adj* not genuine; false; sham; forged; simulating but essentially different; bastard, illegitimate. — *n* **spurios'ity**. — *adv* **spūr'iously**. — *n* **spūr'iousness**. [L. *spurius*, false.]

spurn *spûrn*, *vt* to reject with contempt. — *n* and *adj* **spurn'ing**. [O.E. *spornan*, *spurnan*, related to **spur**.]

spurrey or sometimes **spurry** *spur'i*, *n* any plant of the genus *Spergula*; applied to similar plants. [Du. *spurrie*.]

spurry[1]. See under **spur**.

spurry[2]. See under **spurrey**.

spurt *spûrt*, *vt* to spout, or send out in a sudden stream or jet. — *vi* to gush out suddenly in a small stream; to flow out forcibly or at intervals; to make a sudden short intense effort. — *n* a sudden or violent gush; a jet; a short spell, esp. of intensified effort, speed, etc. [Variant of **spirt**.]

sputa. See under **sputum**.

sputnik *spoŏt'nik*, *n* a Russian man-made earth satellite. [After the Russian *Sputnik* ('travelling companion') 1, the first such satellite, put in orbit in 1957.]

sputter *sput'ər, vi* to spit or throw out moisture in scattered drops; to speak rapidly and indistinctly, to jabber; to make a noise of sputtering. — *vt* to spit out or throw out in or with small drops; to utter hastily and indistinctly; to remove atoms from a cathode by positive ion bombardment — the unchanged atoms being deposited on a surface, and the process being used for coating glass, plastic, another metal, etc. with a thin film of metal. — *n* sputtering; matter sputtered out. — *n* **sputt'erer**. — *n* and *adj* **sputt'ering**. — *adj* **sputt'ery**. [Imit.; cf. Du. *sputteren*, and **spit**[2].]

sputum *spū'təm, n* matter spat out: — *pl* **spū'ta**. [L. *spūtum* — *spuĕre*, to spit.

sp. vol. *abbrev* for specific volume.

spy *spī, n* a secret agent employed to watch others or to collect information, esp. of a military nature; a spying; a look: — *pl* **spies**. — *vt* to watch, observe, investigate or ascertain secretly (often with *out*); to catch sight of, make out; to discover. — *vi* to play the spy: — *pr p* **spy'ing**; *pa t* and *pa p* **spied**; *3rd pers pres indicative* **spies**. — *n* and *adj* **spy'ing**. — **spy'glass** a small hand-telescope; **spy'hole** a peephole; **spy'master** a person who controls and coordinates the activities of undercover agents. [O.Fr. *espie* (n.), *espier* (vb.); cf. **espy**.]

sq. *abbrev* for: *sequens* (L.), following (in pl. **sqq.** *sequentes* or *sequentia*); square; (or **Sq.**) Square (in addresses).

squab *skwob, adj* fat, clumsy; unfledged, newly hatched. — *n* a young pigeon or rook; a fledgling; a short stumpy person. [Poss. Scand.]

squabble *skwob'l, vi* to dispute in a noisy manner; to wrangle. — *n* a noisy, petty quarrel; a brawl. — *n* **squabb'ler**. [Cf. Sw. dialect *sqvabbel*.]

squacco *skwak'ō, n* a small crested heron: — *pl* **squacc'os**. [It. dialect *sguacco*.]

squad *skwod, n* a small group of soldiers drilled or working together; any working party; a set or group; a team or a set of players trained in readiness for the selection of a team (*sport*). — *n* **squadd'y** (*mil colloq*) a private, an ordinary soldier. — **squad car** a police car. [Fr. *escouade*.]

squadron *skwod'rən, n* a detachment, body, group; a division of a cavalry regiment under a major or captain; a section of a fleet under a flag-officer; a group of aeroplanes forming a unit under one command. — *vt* to form into squadrons. — *adj* **squad'ronal**. — *adj* **squad'roned**. — **squadron-lead'er** an air force officer corresponding in rank to a lieutenant-commander or major. [It. *squadrone* — *squadra*, square.]

squail *skwāl, n* a counter for playing squails; (in *pl*) a parlour-game in which small discs are snapped from the edge of the table to a centre mark. [Cf. *kail* (obs. *skail, skayle*), a ninepin.]

squalid *skwol'id, adj* filthy, foul; neglected, uncared-for, unkempt; sordid and dingy; poverty-stricken. — *n* **squalid'ity**. — *adv* **squal'idly**. — *n* **squal'idness**. — *n* **squal'or** the state of being squalid; dirtiness; filthiness. [L. *squālidus*, stiff, rough, dirty, *squālor*, *-ōris*.]

squall *skwöl, vi* to cry out violently; to yell; to sing loudly and unmusically; (of wind) to blow in a squall. — *vt* to sing or utter loudly and unmusically. — *n* a loud cry or yell; a short violent wind. — *n* **squall'er**. — *n* and *adj* **squall'ing**. — *adj* **squall'y** abounding or disturbed with squalls or gusts of wind; gusty, blustering; threatening a squall. [Prob. imit.]

squalor. See under **squalid**.

squama *skwā'mə* or *skwä'mə, n* a scale; a scale-like structure: — *pl* **squa'mae** (*-mē* or *-mī*). — *adj* **squā'mose** or **squā'mous** scaly. [L. *squāma*, a scale.]

squander *skwon'dər, vt* to spend lavishly or wastefully. — *n* a squandering. — *adj* **squan'dered**. — *n* **squan'derer**. — *n* and *adj* **squan'dering**.

square *skwār, n* an equilateral rectangle; an object, piece, space, figure, of approximately that shape, e.g. a window-pane, paving-stone, space on a chess-board; an open space, commonly but not necessarily of that shape, in a town, along with its surrounding buildings; the product of a quantity multiplied by itself; an instrument for drawing or testing right angles; a carpenter's measure; squareness; due proportion; order; honesty, equity, fairness; a person of narrow, traditional outlook and opinions, esp. in musical taste or dress (*slang*). — *adj* having or approaching the form of a square; relatively broad, thick-set; right-angled; (in football, etc.) in a line, position, etc. across the pitch; equal to a quantity multiplied by itself; measuring an area in two dimensions; exact, suitable, fitting; true, equitable, fair, honest; even, leaving no balance, equal in score; directly opposed; complete, unequivocal; solid, full, satisfying; (of taste in music, dress, etc.) traditional and orthodox (*slang*); bourgeois in attitude (*slang*). — *vt* to make square or rectangular, esp. in cross-section; to make nearly cubical; to form into squares; to construct or determine a square equal to; to multiply by itself; to reduce to any given measure or standard, to adjust, regulate; to bring into accord, reconcile; to place at right angles with the mast or keel (*naut*); to make equal; to pay; to bribe; (with *with*) to get (someone's) agreement, approval or permission for something. — *vi* to suit, fit; to accord or agree; to take an attitude of offence and defence, as a boxer (often with *up to* — see below); to make the score or account even. — *adv* at right angles; solidly; directly; evenly; fairly, honestly. — *adj* **squared**. — *adv* **square'ly**. — *n* **square'ness**. — *adv* **square'-wise**. — *n* and *adj* **squar'ing**. — *adj* **squar'ish**. — **square'-bashing** parade-ground drill (*mil slang*). — *adj* **square'-built** of a form suggesting squareness; broad in proportion to height. — **square centimetre** or **metre**, etc. an area equal to that of a square whose side measures a centimetre, metre, etc.; **square dance** a folk-dance done by a group of couples in a square formation; **square'-dancing**; **square deal** (*colloq*) a fair and honest arrangement, transaction, etc.; **square knot** a reef-knot; **square leg** (*cricket*) a fielder to the left of, and in line with, the batsman; **square meal** a full, satisfying meal; **square number** a number of which the square root is an integer. — *adj* **square-rigged'** having the chief sails square, and extended by yards suspended by the middle at right angles to the masts (opp. to *fore-and-aft*). — **square-rigg'er** a square-rigged ship; **square root** that quantity which being multiplied by itself produces the quantity in question; **square sail** a four-sided sail extended by yards suspended by the middle generally at right angles to the mast. — *adj* **square-shoul'dered** with broad, straight shoulders. — *adj* **square-toed'** ending square at the toes. — **back to square one** back to the original position with the problem, etc. unchanged; **on the square** honestly; **square up** (*colloq*) to settle (a bill, account, etc.); **square up to** to face up to and tackle; **squaring the circle** finding a square of the same area as a circle — for hundreds of years this was attempted by Euclidian means (i.e. with straight-edge and compass) until in 1882 it was proved impossible; any impossible task. [O.Fr. *esquarre* — L. *ex* and *quadra*, a square.]

squarial *skwār'iəl, n* a square satellite dish. [**square** and **aerial**.]

squarrose *skwar'ōs, skwor'ōs* or *-ōs'*, (*biol*) *adj* rough with projecting or deflexed scales, bracts, etc.; standing out straight or deflexed. [L. *squarrōsus*, scurfy.]

squash[1] *skwosh, vt* to press into pulp; to crush flat; to squeeze; to put down, suppress; to snub. — *vi* to form a soft mass as from a fall; to crowd; to squelch; to become crushed or pulpy. — *n* anything soft and unripe or easily crushed; a crushed mass; a drink made from fruit juice; a crushed condition; a close crowd; a squeezing; a ball for playing squash; a game for two or four players played with a small rather soft rubber ball, which is struck with a racket against the walls of an enclosed court (also called **squash rackets** or **racquets**). — *adv* with a squash. — *adj* **squash'able**. — *n* **squash'er**. — *n* **squash'iness**. — *adj* **squash'y** pulpy; squelching; sopping. — **squash tennis** a game for two players similar to squash (see above) but played with an inflated ball and larger rackets. [O.Fr. *esquacer*, to crush — L. *ex quassāre*.]

squash[2] *skwosh*, *n* the gourd of several species of the Cucurbitaceae; the plant bearing it. [Narragansett *askutasquash*.]

squat *skwot*, *vi* to sit down upon the hams or heels; to crouch in a compact position like an animal; to settle on land or in unoccupied buildings without legal right. — *vt* to cause to squat: — *pr p* **squatt'ing**; *pa t* and *pa p* **squatt'ed**. — *adj* crouching; short and thick, dumpy. — *n* the act of squatting; a building in which people are squatting (*colloq*). — *n* **squat'ness**. — *n* **squatt'er** someone who squats; a large landowner (*Austr*). — *n* **squatt'iness**. — *adj* **squatt'y** short and thick. [O.Fr. *esquatir*, to crush.]

squaw *skwö*, *n* an American Indian woman, esp. a wife. — **squaw'man** a white man with an American Indian wife. [Massachusett *squa*.]

squawk *skwök*, *n* a croaky call or cry; a complaint, protest (*slang*). — *vi* to utter a squawk; to complain (*slang*). — *vt* to utter with a squawk. — *n* **squawk'er**. — *n* and *adj* **squawk'ing**. — *adj* **squawk'y**. [Imit.]

squeak *skwēk*, *vi* to give forth a high-pitched nasal-sounding note or cry; to inform or confess (*slang*). — *vt* to utter, sing or render squeakily. — *n* a squeaky sound; a narrow escape; a bare chance; the slimmest of margins; a tiny amount. — *n* **squeak'er** someone who or that which squeaks; a squeaking toy. — *adv* **squeak'ily**. — *n* **squeak'iness**. — *n* and *adj* **squeak'ing**. — *adj* **squeak'y**. — *adj* **squeaky-clean'** orig., of wet hair, so clean that it squeaks when pulled; spotlessly clean; (often slightly *derog*) (of a person, storyline, etc.) impeccable, wholesome, virtuous. — **squeak through** to succeed, pass, win, etc. only by a narrow margin. [Imit.]

squeal *skwēl*, *vi* to utter a high-pitched cry; to cry out in pain; to complain; to turn informer (*slang*). — *vt* to utter, sing, render or express with squealing. — *n* a high sustained cry. — *n* **squeal'er** someone who squeals; an informer (*slang*). — *n* and *adj* **squeal'ing**. [Imit.]

squeamish *skwēm'ish*, *adj* sick; easily nauseated; easily shocked, disgusted or offended; fastidious; coy. — *adv* **squeam'ishly**. — *n* **squeam'ishness**. [M.E. *scoymous* — A.Fr. *escoymous*.]

squeegee *skwē'jē* or *-jē'*, *n* an implement with edge of rubber, leather, etc. for clearing water or mud from decks, floors, windows, etc.; a photographer's roller or brush for squeezing out moisture. — *vt* to clear, press or smooth with a squeegee. [App. **squeeze**.]

squeeze *skwēz*, *vt* to crush, press hard, compress; to grasp tightly; to embrace; to force by pressing; to effect, render or put by pressing; to crush the juice or liquid from; to force to discard winning cards; to fleece, extort from. — *vi* to press; to crowd; to crush; to force a way; to yield to pressure. — *n* the act of squeezing; pressure; a restriction or time of restriction (usually financial or commercial); a crowded assembly; an embrace; a close grasp; a few drops got by squeezing; play that forces an opponent to discard a potentially winning card (also **squeeze play**) (*bridge*). — *n* **squeezabil'ity**. — *adj* **squeez'able**. — *n* **squeez'er** someone who squeezes; an instrument, machine or part for squeezing. — *n* and *adj* **squeez'ing**. — *adj* **squeez'y** squeezable; confined, cramped, contracted. — **squeeze'-box** (*slang*) a concertina. — **squeeze home** to win, succeed, etc. with difficulty or narrowly.

squelch *skwelch* or *skwelsh*, *n* the gurgling and sucking sound of walking in wet mud; a heavy blow on, or fall of, a soft body; its sound; a pulpy mass; a disconcerting or quashing retort or rebuff. — *vi* to make, or walk with, the sound of a squelch. — *vt* to crush under heel; to put down, suppress, snub, crush. — *n* **squelch'er** someone who squelches; an overwhelming blow, retort, etc. — *n* and *adj* **squelch'ing**. — *adj* **squelch'y**. [Imit.]

squib *skwib*, *n* a firework, consisting of a paper tube fitted with explosive powder, which burns noisily and explodes; a petty lampoon. — **damp squib** see **damp**. [Perh. imit.]

squid *skwid*, *n* any ten-armed cephalopod, esp. *Loligo*; a bait or lure of, or in imitation of, a squid: — *pl* **squid** or **squids**.

squidge *skwij*, *vt* to squeeze or squash (something soft, moist, pulpy, etc.). — *adj* **squidg'y** squashy; soft, wet and springy; gooey. [Imit.]

squiffy *skwif'i*, (*colloq*) *adj* tipsy. — Also **squiff**.

squiggle *skwig'l*, *vi* to squirm or wriggle; to make wriggly lines. — *n* a twist, wriggle or wriggly line. — *adj* **squigg'ly**. [Imit., or poss. from *squ*irm and *wriggle*.]

squill *skwil*, *n* any plant of the liliaceous genus *Scilla*. [L. *squilla*, *scilla*, shrimp — Gr. *skilla*.]

squint *skwint*, *adv* obliquely, to one side. — *adj* looking obliquely; looking askance; squinting; strabismic, having a squint; oblique; indirect. — *vi* to look obliquely; to peer (*colloq*); to have the eyes focusing in different directions, either by purposely crossing them, or by strabismus; to have a side reference or allusion; to glance aside or casually; to glance (*colloq*); to give an impression of disapproval in one's glance. — *n* the act or habit of squinting; strabismus; an oblique look; a glance; a peep; an oblique reference, hint, tendency or aim. — *n* **squint'er**. — *n* and *adj* **squint'ing**. — *adv* **squint'ingly**. — *adj* **squint'-eyed**. [Perh. Du. *schuinte*, slant.]

squire *skwīr*, *n* an esquire, a knight's attendant (*hist*); a man who escorts or attends a lady; an English or Irish landed gentleman, esp. of old family; in some parts of Britain, a form of sometimes ironically respectful address. — *vt* to escort or attend. [**esquire**.]

squirm *skwûrm*, *vi* to writhe or go writhing. — *n* a wriggle. — *adj* **squirm'y**. [Prob. imit.]

squirrel *skwir'əl*, *n* a nimble, bushy-tailed arboreal rodent (*Sciurus* or related genus); the pelt of such an animal; a person who hoards things (*fig*). — *adj* made of squirrel pelts. — *vt* to hoard (usu. with *away*). — *adj* **squirr'elly** or **squirr'ely** like a squirrel; nervous, jumpy. — **squirr'el-cage** a cage with a treadwheel for a squirrel; in an induction motor, a rotor whose winding suggests this; **squirr'el-monkey** a small golden-haired S. American monkey. [O.Fr. *escurel* — L.L. *scurellus*, dimin. of L. *sciūrus* — Gr. *skiouros* — *skiā*, shade, *ourā*, tail.]

squirt *skwûrt*, *vt* to throw out in a jet; to splash or spray with (water, etc. from) a jet. — *vi* to spirt. — *n* an instrument for squirting; a jet; an unimportant and irritatingly pretentious person (*slang*). — *n* **squirt'er**. — *n* and *adj* **squirt'ing**. [Cf. L.G. *swirtjen*, *swürtjen*.]

squish *skwish*, *vi* to make a squelching or squirting sound. — *n* the sound of squishing. — *adj* **squish'y**. — **squish lip system** a type of diesel engine combustion chamber designed to lessen fumes and noise pollution.

squit *skwit*, (*slang*) *n* a contemptible person; nonsense. [Cf. **squirt**.]

squitch *skwich*, *n* quitch grass.

SR *abbrev* for Southern Region.
Sr *abbrev* for: senior; Señor; Sir; Sister.
Sr (*chem*) *symbol* for strontium.
sr (*math*) *abbrev* for steradian.
SRC *abbrev* for Student Representative Council.
SRCh *abbrev* for State Registered Chiropodist.
Sri or **Shri** *shrē*, *n* in India a title of great respect given to a man, now generally used as the equivalent of *Mr.* [Sans. *śrī*, majesty, holiness.]
SRN *abbrev* for State Registered Nurse.
SRO *abbrev* for self-regulatory organisation.
SRU *abbrev* for Scottish Rugby Union.
SS *abbrev* for: Saints; *Schutzstaffel* (Ger.), Hitler's bodyguard.
ss *abbrev* for: screw steamer; steamship.
SSA *abbrev* for standard spending assessment (a government assessment of the funds that a local authority will require for its services in a given year).
SSAFA *abbrev* for Soldiers' Sailors' and Airmen's Families Association.
SSC *abbrev* for *Societas Sanctae Crucis* (L.), Society of the Holy Cross; Solicitor in the Supreme Court (of Scotland).
SSD *abbrev* for *Sanctissimus Dominus* (L.), Most Holy Lord (the Pope).
SSE *abbrev* for south-south-east.
SSM *abbrev* for surface to surface missile.
SSN *abbrev* for Standard Serial Number.
SSP *abbrev* for statutory sick pay.
SSR *abbrev* for Soviet Socialist Republic.
SSSI *abbrev* for site of special scientific interest.
SST *abbrev* for supersonic transport.
SSW *abbrev* for south-south-west.
St or **St.** *abbrev* for: Saint; Strait; Street.
st. *abbrev* for stone (the weight).
stab *stab*, *vt* to wound or pierce by driving in a pointed weapon; to give a sharp pain (also *fig*). — *vi* to thrust or pierce with a pointed weapon: — *pr p* **stabb'ing**; *pa t* and *pa p* **stabbed**. — *n* an act of stabbing; a wound with a pointed weapon. — *n* **stabb'er**. — *n* and *adj* **stabb'ing**. — *adv* **stabb'ingly**. — **have a stab at** (*colloq*) to have a go at, attempt; **stab in the back** (*lit* and *fig*) to injure in a treacherous manner.
stabile, stabilise, etc., **stability**. See under **stable**[1].
stable[1] *stā'bl*, *adj* standing firm; firmly established; durable; firm in purpose or character; constant; not ready to change; not radioactive. — *adj* **stā'bile** (*-bīl* or *-bil*) not moving; not fluctuating; not decomposing readily, e.g. under moderate heat. — *n* an abstract art construction differing from a mobile in having no movement. — *n* **stabilisation** or **-z-** (*stab-* or *stāb-i-lī-zā'shən*, or *-li-*). — *vt* **stabilise** or **-ize** (*stab'* or *stāb'*) to render stable or steady; to fix; to fix the value of; to establish, maintain or regulate the equilibrium of. — *n* **stab'iliser** or **-z-** anything that stabilises; an additional plane or other device for giving stability to an aircraft; a gyroscope or other means of steadying a ship; a substance that retards chemical action; (in *pl*) an extra pair of small wheels attached to a child's bicycle. — *n* **stability** (*stə-bil'i-ti*) the state of being stable; steadiness; fixity; the power of recovering equilibrium; the fixing by vow of a monk or nun to one convent for life. — *n* **stā'bleness**. — *adv* **stā'bly**. — **stable equilibrium** the condition in which a body will return to its old position after a slight displacement. [Fr., — L. *stabilis* — *stāre*, to stand.]
stable[2] *stā'bl*, *n* a building for horses, or sometimes other animals; a set of horses kept together; a horse-keeping establishment, organisation or staff (as a horse-keeping establishment often *pl* in form but treated as *sing*); a number of skilled trained (esp. young) persons who work together under one head or one manager; a group of commercial (esp. publishing) enterprises under the same ownership or management; an establishment responsible for the training, management, etc. of a group of sumo wrestlers. — *vt* to put or keep in a stable. — *n* **sta'bling** the act of putting into a stable; accommodation for horses, cattle, cycles, etc. — **sta'ble-boy, -girl** or **sta'bleman** someone who works at a stable; **stable lad** or **lass** someone whose job is to look after the horses at a racing-stable; **sta'blemate** a horse from the same stable as another; anything manufactured, originated, produced, etc. in the same place as another (e.g. different models of the same car), or a person from the same club, etc. as another (*fig*). [O.Fr. *estable* — L. *stabulum* — *stāre*, to stand.]
staccato *stə-kä'tō* or *stäk-kä'tō*, (*mus*) *adj* and *adv* with each note detached. — *n* a staccato performance, manner or passage: — *pl* **stacca'tos**. [It., past p. of *staccare*, for *distaccare*, to separate.]
stack *stak*, *n* a large built-up pile (e.g. of hay, corn, wood, etc. or of goods or equipment); a group or cluster of chimneys or flues, or a single tall chimney; the chimney or funnel of a steamer, steam-engine, etc.; an isolated pillar of rock, often rising from the sea; a set of compactly arranged bookcases for storing books not on the open shelves of a library; a temporary storage area for data in a computer memory; an ordered, built-up pile; a standard quantity of gambler's chips bought at one time; aircraft waiting to land and circling at definite heights according to instructions; a large amount (*slang*). — *vt* to pile into a stack; to shuffle (cards) for cheating; to arrange (aircraft waiting to land) in a stack (see above). — *adj* **stacked** piled in a stack; (of shoe-heels) made of horizontal layers of leather; (also **well-stacked'**; of a woman) having a large bust (*slang*). — *n* **stack'er** a person who stacks; a machine for stacking (e.g. products in a manufactory). — *n* **stack'ing**. — **stack'-room** (in a library) a room where books are stored in stacks; **stack system** a modular hi-fi system which stacks one component on top of the other. — **stack against** (or **in favour of**) to arrange (circumstances) to the disadvantage (or advantage) of (**have the cards stacked against** (or **in favour of**) to be faced with circumstances arranged in this way); **stack up** to pile or load high. [O.N. *stakkr*, a stack of hay.]
stadium *stā'di-əm*, *n* a race-course, sports ground: — *pl* **stā'dia** or **sta'diums**. [Latinised from Gr. *stadion*.]
staff *stäf*, *n* a stick carried in the hand; a prop or support; a long piece of wood; a pole; a flagstaff; a long handle; a stick or ensign of authority; a token authorising an engine-driver to proceed; a set of lines and spaces on which music is written or printed; a stanza; (in a watch or clock) the spindle of a balance-wheel (these meanings have *pl* **staffs** or **staves** *stāvz*; see also **stave**); a body of officers who help a commanding officer, or perform special duties: a body of persons employed in an establishment, usu. on management, administration, clerical, etc. work as distinct from manual; the body of teachers or lecturers in a school, college, university, etc. (these three meanings have *pl* **staffs** *stäfs*). — *adj* (or in combination) belonging or attached to the staff; applied also to officers of a higher grade. — *vt* to provide with a staff. — *n* **staff'er** a member of the permanent staff of a business, etc., usu. as opposed to temporary or casual employees. — **staff coll'ege** a college that trains officers for staff appointments (*mil*); **staff'-corps** a body of officers and men assisting a commanding officer and his staff (*mil*); **staff'-duty** the occupation of an officer who serves on a staff, having been detached from his regiment (*mil*); **staff notation** musical notation in which a staff is used, as opposed to the tonic sol-fa system; **staff nurse** a nurse immediately below a sister in rank; **staff officer** an officer serving on a staff (*mil*); **staff'room** a room for the use of the staff, as of a school; **staff sergeant** a non-commissioned officer

serving on a regimental staff (*mil*). — **staff of life** (*fig*) staple food, esp. bread. [O.E. *stæf*.]

Staffs. *stafs*, *abbrev* for Staffordshire.

stag *stag*, *n* a male deer, esp. a red deer over four years old; a male of various kinds (cock, turkey-cock, etc.); a man who goes to a social event unaccompanied by a woman; a person who applies for shares in order to sell them at once for a profit (*stock exchange slang*). — *adj* male; of or for males. — **stag'-beetle** any beetle of the family *Lucanidae*, from the large antlerlike mandibles of the males; **stag'hound** the buck-hound; the Scottish deer-hound; **stag'-hunt**; **stag night** or **stag'-party** a party of men only, esp. one held for a man about to be married. [O.E. *stagga*, stag.]

stage *stāj*, *n* a tier, shelf, floor, storey; an elevated platform, esp. for acting on; the theatre; theatrical representation; the theatrical calling; any field of action, scene; the portion of a journey between two such places; one of a series of divisions of a bus route for which there is a fixed scale of fares; a place of rest on a journey or road; a point reached in, or a section of, life, development, or any process; one of the elements in a complex piece of electronic equipment; one of the sections in a rocket jettisoned during flight; a subdivision of a geological series or formation; (in a microscope, etc.) the support for an object to be examined; a tiered structure for plants. — *adj* pertaining to the stage; as conventionally represented on the stage (e.g. *a stage rustic*). — *vt* to represent or put on the stage; to contrive dramatically, organise and bring off. — *adj* **staged** in storeys or tiers; put on the stage. — *n* **sta'ger** someone who has had much experience in anything, an old hand (*old stager*); a stage-horse. — *n* **sta'ging** scaffolding; putting on the stage; the jettisoning of any of the stages of a rocket. — *adj* **sta'gy** or **sta'gey** savouring of the stage; artificially histrionic. — **stage'coach** formerly, a coach that ran regularly with passengers from stage to stage; **stage'-coaching**; **stage'coachman**; **stage'craft** skill in the technicalities of the theatre; **stage direction** in a copy of a play, an instruction to the actor to do this or that; **stage door** the entrance to a theatre for actors and support staff; **stage effect** theatrical effect; **stage fright** nervousness before an audience, esp. for the first time (also *fig*); **stage hand** a workman employed about the stage. — *vt* **stage-man'age** (back-formation) used *lit*; also *fig*, to arrange (an event) effectively as if it were a stage scene. — **stage'-manager** a person who superintends the production of plays, with general charge behind the curtain; **stage'-name** a name assumed professionally by a performer; **stage whisper** an audible utterance conventionally understood by the audience to represent a whisper; a loud whisper meant to be heard by people other than the person addressed; **staging area** or **base** a point for the assembly of troops en route for an operation; **staging post** a regular point of call on an air-route. — **stage left** (or **right**) at the left (or right) of the stage, facing the audience. [O.Fr. *estage*, a storey of a house — inferred L.L. *staticus* — L. *stāre*, to stand.]

stagger *stag'ər*, *vi* to reel; to go reeling or tottering; to waver. — *vt* to cause to reel; to give a shock to; to cause to waver; to nonplus, confound; to dispose alternately or variously or to arrange so that one thing or part is ahead of another. — *n* a staggering; a wavering; a staggered arrangement; (in *pl*, often treated as *sing*) giddiness, also any of various kinds of disease causing horses, sheep, etc. to stagger. — *adj* **stagg'ered**. — *n* **stagg'erer**. — *n* and *adj* **stagg'ering**. — *adv* **stagg'eringly**. [Earlier *stacker* — O.N. *stakra*, frequentative of *staka*, to push.]

stagnant *stag'nənt*, *adj* still, standing, without current; foul, unwholesome or dull from stillness; inert. — *n* **stag'nancy**. — *adv* **stag'nantly**. — *vi* **stagnate'** (or *stag'*) to be stagnant. — *n* **stagnā'tion**. [L. *stagnāre*, *-ātum* — *stagnum*, pond.]

stagy. See under **stage**.

staid *stād*, *adj* steady; sober; grave; sedate. — *adv* **staid'ly**. — *n* **staid'ness**. [**stayed** — past t. and past p. of **stay**[1].]

stain *stān*, *vt* to impart a new colour to; to tinge; to tarnish; to impregnate with a substance that colours some parts so as to show composition and structure; to bring reproach on. — *vi* to take or impart a stain. — *n* a dye or colouring-matter; discoloration; a spot; taint of guilt; pollution; a cause of reproach; shame. — *adj* **stained**. — *n* **stain'er**. — *n* and *adj* **stain'ing**. — *adj* **stain'less** free from stain; not liable to stain, rust or tarnish. — *adv* **stain'lessly**. — *n* **stain'lessness**. — **stained glass** glass painted with certain pigments fused into its surface; **stainless steel** a steel that will not rust, containing 8 to 25 per cent of chromium. [M.E. *steynen*, to paint.]

stair *stār*, *n* a series of steps, usu. in *pl*, a flight from landing to landing, but in Scotland, in *sing*, the whole series from floor to floor; one such step. — **stair'case** the structure enclosing a stair; stairs with banisters, etc.; **stair'head** the level place at the top of stairs; **stair'-rod** a rod for holding a stair-carpet in place; **stair'way** a staircase; a passage by stairs; **stair well** the well of a staircase; the floor area at the foot of a winding stairway. — **below stairs** in the basement; among the servants. [O.E. *stǣger* — *stīgan*, to ascend.]

stake[1] *stāk*, *n* a stick or pole pointed at one end; a post; a post to which one condemned to be burned was tied (*hist*); hence, death or martyrdom by burning. — *vt* to fasten to or with, to protect, shut, support, furnish, pierce, with a stake or stakes; to mark the bounds of with stakes (often with *off* or *out*). — **stake'-boat** a boat anchored as a marker for a boat-race, or to which other boats may be moored. — **stake a claim** (*for* or *to*) to intimate one's right to or desire to possess; **stake out** (*colloq*) to place (a person, etc.) under surveillance (*n* **stake'-out**). [O.E. *staca*, stake.]

stake[2] *stāk*, *vt* to deposit as a wager; to risk, hazard; to furnish, supply, fit out, whether free or in expectation of return (with *with* or *to*; *US*). — *n* anything pledged as a wager; a prize; anything to gain or lose; an interest, concern; the condition of being at hazard; a grubstake; (in *pl*) a race for money staked or contributed. — **at stake** hazarded; in danger; at issue. [Perh. M.Du. *staken*, to place.]

stalactite *stal'ək-tīt* or *sta-lak'tīt*, *n* an icicle-like pendant of calcium carbonate, formed by evaporation of water percolating through limestone, as on a cave roof; the material it is composed of; anything of similar form. — *adj* **stalactitic** (*-tit'ik*). — *adv* **stalactit'ically**. — *n* **stal'agmite** (or *-lag'*) an upward-growing conical formation on the floor, formed by the drip from the roof or from a stalactite. — *adj* **stalagmitic** (*-mit'ik*) or **stalagmit'ical**. [Gr. *stalaktos*, *stalagma*, *stalagmos*, a dropping — *stalassein*, to drip.]

stalag *stal'ag* or *shtä'lak*, *n* a German camp for prisoners of war (non-commissioned officers and men). [Ger. *Stamm*, base, *Lager*, camp.]

stalagmite. See under **stalactite**.

stale[1] *stāl*, *adj* no longer fresh; past the best; out of condition by over-training or overstudy; impaired by lapse of time; tainted; vapid or tasteless from age. — *adv* **stale'ly**. — *n* **stale'ness**. [Perh. from the root *sta-*, as in **stand**.]

stale[2] *stāl*, *n* urine, now esp. of horses. — *vi* (of horses) to urinate. [Cf. Du. *stalle*, Ger. *Stall*, O.Fr. verb *estaler*.]

stalemate *stāl'māt*, *n* an unsatisfactory draw resulting when a player not actually in check has no possible legal move (*chess*); deadlock. — *vt* to subject to a stalemate.

Stalinism *stä'lin-izm*, *n* the rigorous rule of the Russian Communist dictator Josef *Stalin* (1879–1953), esp. in its concentration of all power and authority in the Communist world in Russia. — *n* and *adj* **Sta'linist.**

stalk[1] *stök*, *n* the stem of a plant; a slender connecting part; a shaft; a tall chimney. — *vt* to remove the stalk from. — *adj* **stalked** having a stalk. — *adj* **stalk'-less.** — *adj* **stalk'y** running to stalk; like a stalk. [Dimin. from the root of O.E. *stela, stalu*, stalk.]

stalk[2] *stök*, *vi* to stride stiffly or haughtily; to go after game, keeping under cover; to follow a person, esp. an enemy, in a similar manner. — *vt* to approach under cover; to stalk over or through (a tract of country, etc.). — *n* an act of stalking; a stalking gait. — *n* **stalk'er.** — *n* and *adj* **stalk'ing.** — **stalk'ing-horse** a horse or substitute behind which a sportsman hides while stalking game; anything put forward to mask plans or efforts. [O.E. (*bi*)*stealcian*, frequentative of **steal.**]

stall[1] *stöl*, *n* a standing-place; a stable, cowshed, or the like; a compartment for one animal; a bench, table, booth or stand for display or sale of goods, or used as a working-place; a church-seat with arms, usu. one of those lining the choir or chancel on both sides, reserved for cathedral clergy, for choir, for monks, or for knights of an order; an office entitling one to such a seat; a doorless pew; an individual armed seat in a theatre, etc., esp. an orchestra stall; a starting stall (q.v. at **start**); a working place in a mine; a covering for a finger (as in *fingerstall*); an instance of stalling an aircraft or engine; a standstill. — *vt* to put or keep in a stall; to induct, install; to bring to a standstill; to cause (an aeroplane) to fly in such a way that the angle between the aerofoils and the direction of motion is greater than that at which there is maximum lift and so lose control; to stop (an engine) by sudden braking, overloading, etc.; to cause (a vehicle) to become stuck in mud or snow. — *vt* to come to a standstill; to stick in mud or snow; (of an aircraft or engine) to be stalled. — *n* **stallage** (*stöl'ij*) rent paid for erecting a stall in a fair or market place. — *vt* **stall'-feed** to confine (an animal) to its stall and fatten it. — **stall'holder** a person having charge of a stall in a market place, etc. [O.E. *stall, steall.*]

stall[2] *stöl*, *n* a ruse, trick; an evasive manoeuvre. — *vt* to delay or obstruct; to stave off (with *off*). — *vi* to hang back, play for time; to be obstructive, evasive or deceptive. [Old word *stale*, a decoy.]

stallage. See under **stall[1].**

stallion *stal'yən*, *n* an uncastrated male horse, esp. one kept for breeding. [O.Fr. *estalon* — O.H.G. *stal*, stall.]

stalwart *stöl'wərt*, *adj* stout, strong, sturdy; determined in partisanship. — *n* a resolute person. — *adv* **stal'wartly.** — *n* **stal'wartness.** [Orig. Scots form of *stalworth* — O.E. *stælwierthe*, serviceable — *stǣl*, place, *wierthe*, worth.]

stamen *stā'mən*, *n* the pollen-producing part of a flower, consisting of anther and filament: — *pl* **stā'mens** or **stamina** (*stam'i-nə*). — *adj* **stam'inate** (*-nət* or *-nāt*) having stamens but no carpels, male. — *adj* **staminif'erous** having stamens. [L. *stāmen, stāminis*, a warp thread (upright in an old loom) — *stāre*, to stand.]

stamina[1] *stam'i-nə*, *n* sustained energy, staying power, whether physical, mental or emotional. [Pl. of *stamen*, warp, understood as the threads of life spun out by the Fates.]

stamina[2]. See under **stamen.**

stammer *stam'ər*, *vi* to falter in speaking; to speak with involuntary hesitations, to stutter. — *vt* to utter falteringly or with a stutter. — *n* involuntary hesitation in speech, a stutter; a faltering mode of utterance. — *n* **stamm'erer.** — *n* and *adj* **stamm'ering.** — *adv* **stamm'eringly.** [O.E. *stamerian.*]

stamp *stamp*, *vt* to bring the foot forcibly down upon; to trample; to bring the sole of (the foot) down flat, heavily or with force; to impress, imprint, or cut with a downward blow, as with a die or cutter; to mint, make, shape by such a blow; to crush, grind or pound (ore, etc.); to fix or mark deeply; to impress with a mark attesting official approval, ratification, payment, etc.; to affix an adhesive stamp to; to attest, declare, prove to be; to characterise. — *vi* to bring the foot down forcibly and noisily; to walk with a heavy tread. — *n* the act of stamping; an impression; a stamped device, mark, imprint; an adhesive piece of paper used as a substitute for stamping; attestation; authorisation; cast, form, character; distinguishing mark, imprint, sign, evidence; an instrument or machine for stamping; national insurance contribution, formerly recorded by sticking a stamp on to an official card (*colloq*). — *n* **stamp'er.** — *n* and *adj* **stamp'ing.** — **Stamp Act** an act of parliament imposing or regulating stamp duties, esp. that of 1765 imposing them on the American colonies; **stamp album** a book for keeping a collection of postage stamps in; **stamp'-collector** a person who makes a hobby of collecting postage stamps; **stamp duty** a tax imposed on legal documents, its payment being confirmed by the affixation of a stamp; **stamp hinge** see **hinge; stamp'ing-ground** an animal's usual resort; a person's habitual place of resort; **stamp mill** a crushing-mill for ores. — **stamp out** to put out, extinguish by tramping; to extirpate; to make by stamping from a sheet with a cutter. [M.E. *stampen*, from an inferred O.E. *stampian.*]

stampede *stam-pēd'*, *n* a sudden rush of a panic-stricken herd; a headlong scramble by a crowd of people; any mass rush to do something. — *vi* to rush in a stampede. — *vt* to send rushing in a stampede. [Sp. *estampida*, crash — *estampar*, to stamp.]

stance *stans*, *n* a posture adopted in standing; the standing position of someone about to play the ball in golf, etc.; a point of view taken, an attitude; a place occupied by market stalls, a taxi rank, etc. (*Scot*). [Fr. *stance* (now meaning 'stanza') — It. *stanza*, a stopping-place, station — L. *stāre*, to stand.]

stanch *stänch* or *stänsh*, or **staunch** *stönch* or *stönsh*, *vt* to stop the flowing of (esp. blood); to quench, allay. — *adj* **stanch'able** or **staunch'able.** — *n* **stanch'er** or **staunch'er.** [O.Fr. *estancher* — L.L. *stancāre*, to stanch.]

stanchion *stän'shən* or *stan'shən*, *n* an upright beam, bar, rod, shaft, etc. acting as a support, a strut. — *vt* to support by means of, or fasten to, a stanchion. [O.Fr. *estançon* — *estance*, prop — L. *stāre*, to stand.]

stand *stand*, *vi* to be, become or remain upright, erect, rigid or still; to be on, or rise to, one's feet; to be a particular height, as in *He stood six feet five*; to be steadfast; to have or take a position; to assume the attitude and duties of (guard, sentinel); to be or remain; to be set or situated; to be likely, be in a position (to lose or gain something); to come to a stop, be stationary or remain still; used with *and* to introduce a second verb, e.g. *stand and stare*; to be set down; to hold a course or direction (with *for*; *naut*); to hold good; to endure, continue to exist; to be, at the moment in question, as in *the score stands at* 3 *to* 1, *as things stand*; to be a representative, representation or symbol (with *for*); to be a candidate (with *for*); (of a vehicle) to park, wait (*US*). — *vt* to withstand; to tolerate; to endure; to sustain; to suffer, undergo; to abide by; to be at the expense of, offer and pay for; to station, cause to stand; to set erect, in place, or in any position: — *pa t* and *pa p* **stood.** — *n* an act, manner or place of standing; a taking up of a position for resistance; resistance; an attitude or position adopted; the partnership of any two batsmen at the wicket, the period of time of the partnership, or the runs made during it (*cricket*); a standing position; a standstill; a stoppage; a post, station; a stall or position occupied by a trader or an organisation at an exhibition, for the display of goods, etc.; a place for vehicles awaiting hire; an erection with sitting or standing accommodation for spectators; a stop on tour to give one or more performances, or the place where it is made (*theat*); a platform; a witness-box (*US*); a base or structure for setting things on; a piece of furniture for hanging things from; a shearer's position in a shed (*Austr* and *NZ*); a standing growth or crop. — *n* **stand'er**. — *adj* **stand'ing** established; settled; permanent; fixed; stagnant; erect; having a base; done as one stands; from a standing position, without preliminary movement (e.g. *standing jump, start*). — *n* duration or continuance; a place to stand in or on; position, status or reputation in one's profession or in society; a current ranking within a graded scale, esp. in sport; a right or capacity to sue or maintain an action. — *adj* **stand'-alone** (*comput*) (of a system, device, etc.) that can operate unconnected to and unaided by any other. — *n* **stand'-by** that which, or someone whom, one relies on or readily resorts to; something, or someone, available for use in an emergency (see also **on stand-by** below). — *adj* (of an airline passenger, ticket, fare, etc.) occupying, for, an aircraft seat not booked in advance but taken as available, usu. with some price reduction, at the time of departure. — **stand'-in** a substitute; **standing committee** one permanently established to deal with a particular matter; **standing joke** a subject that raises a laugh whenever it is mentioned; **standing order** an instruction from a customer to his or her bank to make regular payments from his or her account; an order placed with a shopkeeper, etc. for the regular supply of a newspaper or other goods; a military order with long-term application; (in *pl*) regulations for procedure adopted by a legislative assembly (also **standing rules**); **standing ovation** a burst of applause from an audience that rises to its feet in its enthusiasm; **stand'ing-room** room for standing, without a seat; **standing stone** (*archaeol*) a great stone set erect in the ground; **stand'-off** a Rugby half-back who stands away from the scrum as a link between scrum-half and the three-quarters (also **stand-off half**); a tie, draw or deadlock (*NAm*); any object that stands, projects or holds another a short distance away, e.g. on a ladder, an attachment that holds it away from the surface supporting it. — *adj* standoffish (*NAm*); (of a missile) capable of being released at a long distance from its target. — *adj* **standoff'ish** inclined to hold aloof, keep others at arm's length. — *adv* **standoff'ishly**. — *n* **standoff'ishness**. — **stand'pipe** an open vertical pipe connected to a pipeline, to ensure that the pressure head at that point cannot exceed the length of the pipe; a pipe fitted with a tap, used to obtain water e.g. for an attached hose; **stand'point** a viewpoint; **stand'still** a complete stop. — *adj* **stand'-up** erect; done or taken in a standing position; (of a fight) in earnest; delivering, or consisting of, a comic monologue without feed or other support. — **it stands to reason** it is only logical to assume; **make a stand** to halt and offer resistance; **one-night stand** see under **one**; **on stand-by** in readiness to help in an emergency; **stand by** to support; to adhere to, abide by; to be at hand; to hold oneself in readiness; **stand down** to leave the witness box; to go off duty; to withdraw from a contest or from a controlling position; **stand fast** to be unmoved; **stand for** to be a candidate for; to represent, symbolise; to champion; to put up with, endure (*colloq*); **stand in** to deputise, act as a substitute (with *for*); **stand off** to keep at a distance; to direct the course from (*naut*); to suspend temporarily from employment; **stand on** to continue on the same tack or course (*naut*); to insist on; to set store by (see **ceremony**); **stand one's ground** to maintain one's position; **stand on one's own feet** to manage one's own affairs without help; **stand out** to project, to be prominent; not to comply, to refuse to yield, take an independent stand (with *against* or *for*); **stand over** to keep (someone who is working, etc.) under close supervision; to postpone or be postponed; **stand to** to fall to, set to work; to back up; to uphold; to take up position in readiness for orders; **stand up** to get to one's feet; to take one's position for a dance; to be clad (with *in*); to fail to keep an appointment with (*colloq*); **stand up for** to support or attempt to defend; **stand upon** to stand on; **stand up to** to meet (an opponent, etc.) face to face, to show resistance to; to fulfil (an obligation, etc.) fairly; to withstand (hard wear, etc.); **stand well** to be in favour. [O.E. *standan*.]

standard *stand'ərd*, *n* an established or accepted model; (often in *pl*) a principle of behaviour or morality; a criterion; a definite level of excellence or adequacy required, aimed at, or possible; an overall level achieved; an authorised model for a unit of measurement; the legally required weight and fineness of the metal used in coins; the commodity, e.g. gold or silver, that is taken as the basis of value in a currency; a measure of wood in board form, equivalent to 165 cubic feet, 4.7 cubic metres or 1980 board feet (board foot = a piece of wood one foot square and one inch thick); a flag or symbolic figure on a pole, marking a rallying point; a rallying point; a flag generally; a standing shrub or tree not trained on an espalier or wall; a fruit tree or other tree grafted and trained so as to have an upright stem without branches; an upright post or support; a class or grade in an elementary school; a song or piece of music that has remained popular over the years. — *adj* serving as or conforming to a standard; of the normal, regular quality, size, etc., without additions or variations; of accepted and enduring value; (of a tree) growing as a standard; standing upright. — *n* **standardīsā'tion** or **-z-**. — *vt* **stand'ardise** or **-ize** to make, or keep, of uniform size, shape, etc. — *n* **stand'ardiser** or **-z-**. — **standard atmosphere** 101 325 newtons per sq. m., or 1 013 250 dynes per sq. cm.; a standard of measurement of atmospheric conditions used in comparing the performance of aircraft (*aeronautics*, etc.); **stand'ard-bearer** a person who carries a standard or banner; an outstanding leader; **Stand'ardbred** a breed of horse orig. developed in the U.S. as harness racehorses for trotting or pacing to a standard minimum speed; (also without *cap*) a horse of this breed; **standard deviation** in a frequency distribution, the root of the average of the squares of the differences from their mean of a number of observations, used as a measure of dispersion; **standard English** the form of English taught in schools, etc. and used, esp. in formal situations, by the majority of educated English-speakers; **standard error** standard deviation divided by the root of the number of observations; **Standard grade** a form of examination introduced into Scotland in 1989, intended to replace O grade, and to assess candidates' application rather than merely assimilation of knowledge; a subject offered, or satisfactory assessment in it obtained, at Standard grade; **standard lamp** a lamp on a tall support; **standard solution** a solution of known concentration, used for purposes of comparison. — **by any standards** in the probable estimation of anyone at all, as anyone would agree; **(international) standard book number** a number allotted to a book by agreement of (international) publishers which shows area, publisher and individual title. [O.Fr. *estandart*; prob. conn. either with **extend** or **stand**; infl. by **stander**.]

standee *stan-dē'*, (esp. *US*) *n* a person standing as opposed to sitting, e.g. on a bus when all seats are occupied. [**stand** and sfx. **-ee**.]

stanhope *stan'əp, n* a light open one-seated carriage first made for Fitzroy *Stanhope* (1787–1864).

Stanislavski *stan-i-släf'ski* **method** or **system** *n* method acting (q.v.). [K. *Stanislavski* (1863–1938), Russian actor and director.]

stank *stangk, pa t* of **stink.**

stannary *stan'ə-ri, n* a tin-mining district (esp. the **Stannaries** in Cornwall and Devon). — **Stannary Parliament** the ancient parliament of tinners, comprising twenty-four representatives (**stannā'tors**) for all Cornwall. [L. *stannum*, tin.]

stannic *stan'ik, (chem) adj* relating to tin in its quadrivalent state. [L. *stannum*, tin.]

stannite *stan'it*, a mineral composed of tin, copper, iron and sulphur, occurring in tin-bearing veins. [L. *stannum*, tin.]

stannous *stan'əs, (chem) adj* relating to tin in its bivalent state. [L. stannum, tin.]

stanza *stan'zə, n* a group of lines of verse forming a definite pattern, usu. constituting one of a series of units in a poem. [It. *stanza* — L. *stāre*, to stand.]

stapedectomy, stapedes. See under **stapes.**

stapes *stā'pēz, n* a stirrup-shaped bone, the innermost of the three small bones of the middle ear. — *pl* **stā'pēs** or **stapē'dēs.** — *n* **stapedectomy** (*stap-i-dek'tə-mi*) the surgical excision of this bone. [L.L. *stapēs, -edis*, a stirrup.]

staphylococcus *staf-i-lə-kok'əs, n* a pus-causing bacterium of the genus *staphylococcus*, found in clustered masses: — *pl* **staphylococci** (*-kok'sī*). — *adj* **staphylococc'al.** [Gr. *staphylē*, a bunch of grapes, a swollen uvula, *kokkos*, grain, berry.]

staple[1] *stā'pl, n* a leading commodity or raw material; a main element (as of diet, reading, conversation); unmanufactured wool or other raw material; textile fibre, or its length and quality. — *adj* constituting a staple; leading, main. — *vt* to grade (wool, cotton, etc.) according to staple. [O.Fr. *estaple* — L.G. *stapel*, heap, mart.]

staple[2] *stā'pl, n* a U-shaped rod or wire for driving into a wall, post, etc. as a fastening; a similarly-shaped piece of wire that is driven through sheets of paper and compressed, to fasten them together; the curved bar, etc. that passes through the slot of a hasp, receives a bolt, etc.; the metallic tube to which the reed is fastened in the oboe, etc. — *vt* to fasten with a staple. — *n* **stā'pler** an instrument for (dispensing and) inserting staples into papers, etc. — **staple gun** a hand-held tool that propels staples into a surface; **sta'pling-machine** a machine that stitches paper with wire. [O.E. *stapol*, post, support.]

star *stär, n* any of those celestial bodies visible by night that are really gaseous masses generating heat and light, whose places are relatively fixed (**fixed stars**); (more loosely) these and the planets, comets, meteors and even, less commonly, the sun, moon and earth; a planet as a supposed influence, hence (usu. in *pl*) one's luck; an object or figure with pointed rays, most commonly five; an asterisk; a star-shaped badge or emblem, denoting rank, honour or merit, used e.g. in grading or classification, as in *four-star petrol, five-star* (i.e. luxurious) *hotel*; a white mark on an animal's forehead, esp. a horse's; a pre-eminent or exceptionally brilliant person; a leading performer; a networking conformation in which the central control point is linked individually to all workstations (*comput*). — *adj* of stars; marked by a star; leading, pre-eminent, brilliant. — *vt* to have (a specified person) as a star performer; to mark with a star; to set with stars; to bespangle. — *vi* to appear as a star performer: — *pr p* **starr'ing**; *pa t* and *pa p* **starred.** — *n* **star'dom** the state of being or status of a star performer esp. of stage or screen. — *adj* **star'less.** — *n* **star'let** a little star; a young film actress, esp. one hailed as a future star. — *adj* and *adv* **star'like.** — *adj* **starred** decorated or marked with a star. — *n* **starr'iness.** — *adj* **starr'y** abounding or adorned with stars; like, or shining like, the stars. — **star billing** prominent display of the name of a performer, etc. on posters, etc. — *adj* **star-bright'** bright as a star or with stars. — **star'burst** an explosion, e.g. of a firework, having the appearance of a radiating shower of stars; the explosion of a star; **star chart** a chart of the heavens showing the positions of the stars; **star connection** (*electr*) a Y-shaped connection for use in a three-phase system, with one terminal of each phase connected to a common point. — *adj* **star'-crossed** thwarted by the stars; ill-fated. — **star'dust** distant stars seen like dust grains; an imaginary dust that blinds the eyes to reality and fills them with romantic illusions; **star'fish** any member of the *Asteroidea*, a class of echinoderms with five arms merging in a disc, and tube-feet on the under surface; **star fruit** the fruit of the carambola, star-shaped in cross-section. — *vi* **star'-gaze.** — **star'-gazer** an astrologer; an astronomer; a dreamer or wool-gatherer; **star'light** light from the stars. — *adj* of or with starlight; lighted by the stars; bright as a star. — *adj* **star'lit** lighted by the stars. — **star-nosed mole** a N. American mole with star-shaped nose tip. — *adj* **starry-eyed'** out of touch with reality; innocently idealistic; radiantly happy. — **star ruby** or **star sapphire** a ruby or sapphire manifesting asterism. — *adj* **star'-shaped** shaped like a conventional star, with pointed rays. — **star shell** a shell that explodes high in the air, lighting up the scene so as to reveal the enemy position. — *adj* **star'-spangled** spangled or studded with stars (**Star-spangled Banner** the Stars and Stripes; the American national anthem). — **star'-spot** an area of relative darkness on the surface of a star. — *adj* **star'-studded** covered with stars; of the cast of a film, play, etc., having a high proportion of famous performers. — **star turn** the chief item in an entertainment; a pre-eminent performer; **Star Wars** a colloquial term for the Strategic Defence Initiative (q.v.); **star wheel** a spur wheel with V-shaped teeth; **star'wort** any plant of the genus *Aster*; stitchwort; a water plant (**water starwort** *Callitriche*). — **see stars** (*colloq*) to see spots of light, as result e.g. of blow on the head; to be in a dazed condition; **star of Bethlehem** a plant (*Ornithogalum*) of the lily family with starlike flowers; **Star of David** the Jewish religious symbol — Solomon's seal — a six-pointed star formed by superimposing one equilateral triangle on another); **Stars and Stripes** the flag of the United States of America, with thirteen stripes alternately red and white, and a blue field containing as many stars as there are states. [O.E. *steorra*.]

starboard *stär'bərd* or *stär'börd, n* the right-hand side of a ship. — *adj* and *adv* of, to, towards or on the right. — *vt* to turn to the right — opp. to *port*. [O.E. *stēorbord* — *stēor*, steering, *bord*, board, side of a ship (ancient Gmc. ships being steered by a paddle at the right side).]

starch *stärch, n* the principal reserve food material stored in plants, chemically a carbohydrate, $(C_6H_{10}O_5)_x$, used in the laundry as a stiffener; stiffness, formality. — *adj* made of starch; stiff, rigid, formal. — *vt* to stiffen or stick with starch. — *adj* **starched.** — *n* **starch'er.** — *adv* **starch'ily.** — *n* **starch'iness.** — *adj* **starch'y** of or like starch; stiff, formal, strait-laced, prim. — *adj* **starch-reduced'** (of bread, etc. for the use of slimmers) containing less than the usual amount of starch. [O.E. *stercan*, to stiffen, inferred from *stercedferhth*, stiff-spirited; cf. **stark.**]

Star Chamber *stär chām'bər, n* a court (abolished 1641) with a civil and criminal jurisdiction, which met in the old council chamber at Westminster and was empowered to act without a jury and to use torture; (also without *caps*) generally, an overzealous or secret inquiry or investigation; a closed meeting in which important decisions, resolutions, etc. are made, esp. on matters of public concern. [Prob. named from the gilt *stars* on the ceiling, not from the Jewish bonds (*starrs*) kept in it.]

stare *stār, vi* to look with a fixed gaze; to be all too obvious, to glare. — *vt* to put into a particular state by staring. — *n* a fixed look. — *n, adj* and *adv* **star'ing.** — **stare down** or **out** to force (someone) to drop his or her gaze through the steadiness and power of one's own; **stare (someone) in the face** to be perfectly evident; to be imminent or apparently inevitable. [O.E. *starian.*]

stark *stärk, adj* stern; harsh; plain, bare, unadorned; sheer, out-and-out; harshly apparent, all too clear; stark-naked (q.v.). — *adv* utterly. — *adj* **starkers** see **stark-na'ked.** — *adv* **stark'ly.** — *n* **stark'ness.** [O.E. *stearc*, hard, strong.]

stark-naked *stärk-nā'kid, adj* utterly naked; quite bare — shortened to **stark** or (*colloq*) **stark'ers.** [M.E. *stert-naked* — O.E. *steort*, tail, *nacod*, naked; infl. by **stark.**]

starlet. See under **star.**

starling[1] *stär'ling, n* a bird with black, brown-spotted, iridescent plumage, a good mimic; any other member of its genus, *Sturnus.* [O.E. *stærling*, dimin. of *stær*, starling.]

starling[2] *stär'ling, n* piling protecting a bridge pier. [Prob. for *staddling* from *staddle*, a support for a stack of hay.]

starrily, starry, etc. See under **star.**

START *stärt, abbrev* for Strategic Arms Reduction Talks (or Treaty).

start *stärt, vi* to begin, commence; to shoot, dart, move suddenly forth, or out; to spring up or forward; to make a sudden involuntary movement as of surprise or becoming aware; to spring open, out of place, or loose; to begin to move; (of a car, engine, etc.), to begin to work, to fire; to set forth on a journey, race, career; to take to grumbling (*colloq*). — *vt* to begin; to set going; to set on foot; to set up; to cause to begin (doing something); to conceive (a baby) (*colloq*); to drive from lair or hiding-place; to cause displacement or loosening of; to pour out. — *n* a beginning; a beginning of movement, esp. of a journey, race or career; a setting in motion; the time or place at which something starts, e.g. a race; a help in or opportunity of beginning; an advantage in being early or ahead; the extent of such an advantage in time or distance; a sudden involuntary motion of the body; a startled feeling; a queer occurrence (*colloq*); a spurt, spasm, burst; a beginning of building work on a new house site (esp. as *house* or *housing starts*). — *n* **start'er** one of the competitors or horses assembled for the start of a race; a person who gives the signal for starting; an apparatus or device for starting a machine, such as that (also **self-start'er**) for starting an internal-combustion engine; anything used to begin a process; the first course of a meal; a potentially successful or profitable idea, project, etc. (*commercial jargon*). — **starter home** a small house or flat built, or considered by the seller, to suit and be affordable by a first-time buyer, esp. a young couple; **starting block** (usu. in *pl*) a device for helping a sprinter make a quick start in a race, consisting of a framework with blocks of wood or metal attached, on which the sprinter braces his or her feet; **starting gate** a movable barrier behind which the runners in a horse race are contained till the start; starting stalls (*US*); **starting point** the point from which anything starts, or from which motion begins; **starting post** the post or barrier from which the competitors start in a race; **starting price** odds on a horse when the race begins; **starting stalls** the line of compartments in which runners wait before the start of a horse race, fitted with gates that are sprung open at the start. — **for a start** in the first place, as a preliminary consideration; **for starters** (*colloq*) as the first course of a meal; in the first place, for a start; **give (someone) a start** to give (someone) an advantage at the start of, or in beginning, an enterprise, race etc.; to startle (someone); **start a hare** see under **hare; start in** to begin; **start on** (*colloq*) to turn on, scold, berate; **start out** to begin; to begin a journey; **start over** (*US*) to do again from the beginning; **start up** to rise suddenly; to come suddenly into notice or being; to set in motion; to set up, initiate, establish (*n* **start'-up** the process of setting up a business, etc.); **to start with** at the beginning; in the first place, as a primary consideration. [M.E. *sterten.*]

startle *stär'tl, vt* to surprise or frighten suddenly; to cause to start with alarm; to take aback. — *vi* to start with alarm. — *adj* **star'tled.** — *n* and *adj* **star'tling.** [M.E. *stertle* — O.E. *steartlian*, to stumble, struggle, kick; or newly formed from **start.**]

starve *stärv, vi* to die of hunger; to suffer extreme hunger; to be in want (with *for*). — *vt* to cause to die of hunger; to deprive of food; to force by want of food; to deprive (with *of*). — *n* **starvā'tion.** — *adj* **starved.** — *n* **starve'ling** a lean, hungry, weak or pining person, animal or plant. — *n* and *adj* **starv'ing.** — **starve out** to force (those holding a building, etc.) into surrender by starvation. [O.E. *steorfan*, to die.]

stash *stash,* (*colloq*) *vt* to stow in hiding (often with *away*). — *n* a secret store, or its hiding-place; a hidden store of a drug, or the drug itself (*slang*; esp. *US*).

stasis *stā'sis* or *stas'is,* (also **-stasis** *-stə-sis, combining form*) (chiefly *med*) *n* stoppage, arrest, esp. of growth, of blood-circulation or bleeding, or of the contents of the bowels; (maintenance of) a state of equilibrium or constant state. [Gr. *stasis*, stoppage, stationariness.]

stat *stat, pfx* used to indicate an electrostatic unit, as in *statvolt.* [Electro*static.*]

stat. *abbrev* for *statim* (L.), immediately.

-stat *-stat, combining form* used to designate a regulating device that causes something to remain constant or stationary, as in *barostat, hygrostat, thermostat.* [Gr. *-statēs*, causing to stand — *histanai*, to cause to stand.]

state *stāt, n* a condition; a perturbed condition of mind (*colloq*); a confused or untidy condition; a mode of existence; a set of circumstances at any time; a phase or stage; station in life; pomp, display, ceremonial dignity; the constitution; the civil power; public welfare; high politics; a political community under one government; one of a number of political communities forming a federation under a central government; the territory of such a community. — *adj* of, belonging to, or relating to, the state or a federal state; run or financed by the state; public; ceremonial. — *vt* to express fully and formally; to assert, affirm; to specify. — *adj* **stā'ted** declared. — *n* **state'hood** the status of a state. — *adj* **state'less** without nationality. — *n* **state'liness.** — *adj* **state'ly** showing state or dignity; majestic, greatly impressive. — *n* **state'ment** the act of stating; that which is stated; a formal account, declaration of facts, etc.; a financial record, e.g. one issued regularly by a bank to a customer, stating his or her personal balance and detailing debits and credits. — *n* **stā'tism** (the belief in) state control of economic and social affairs. — *n* and *adj* **stā'tist.** — *adj* **state-aid'ed** receiving contributions from the state. — **state cabin** a stateroom on a ship; **state'craft** the art of managing state affairs; **State Department** the U.S. government department dealing with foreign affairs; **stately home** a large, fine old house, esp. one open to the public; **state paper** an official paper or document relating to affairs of state; **state religion** a religion recognised by the state as the national religion; **state'room** a large room in a palace, etc. used for state occasions; a private cabin or railway compartment; **state school** one controlled by a public authority, and financed by taxation; **States General** the representative body of the three orders (nobility, clergy, burghers) of the French kingdom (*hist*); the Dutch parliament. — *adj* and *adv* **State'side** (*colloq*; also without *cap*) of, in, towards or to the U.S. — **states'man** a person skilled in government; a person who takes an important part in governing the state, esp. with wisdom and broad-mindedness: — *fem* **states'-woman.** — *adj* **states'manlike** or **states'manly.** — **states'manship; states' rights** (*US*) those rights belonging to the individual states, not delegated to the federal government; **State trial** the trial of someone for offences against the state; **state trooper** in the U.S., a member of a state police force. — *adj* **state'wide** (*US*) applying throughout a state. — **lie in state** (of a corpse) to be laid out in a place of honour before being buried; **State Enrolled Nurse** (abbrev. **SEN**) a nurse who has passed a particular examination of the General Nursing Council of England and Wales or the General Nursing Council of Scotland; **state of affairs** or **events** a situation, set of circumstances; **state of grace** (*relig*) the condition of being without grave sin, and in God's favour; **state of mind** a person's mental or emotional condition; **state of play** the situation as it currently stands; **state of repair** physical condition, soundness; **state of the art** the level or position at a given time, esp. the present, of generally accepted and available knowledge, technical achievement, etc. in a particular field, etc.; the level of technological development as yet unsurpassed in a particular field (*adj* **state-of-the-art'**); **state of the Union message** in the U.S., a statutorily required annual report by the president on the state of the nation and on legislative plans; **state of war** a situation existing between states in which there is armed conflict; the situation that obtains between states after war has been declared; **State Registered Nurse** (abbrev. **SRN**) in England and Wales, a nurse who has passed a more advanced examination of the General Nursing Council of England and Wales than a State Enrolled Nurse (for Scotland, see **Registered General Nurse** under **register**); **the States** the United States; **turn State's evidence** see under **evident.** [L. *status*, *-ūs* — *stāre*, *statum*, to stand; partly through O.Fr.]

stater *stā'tər*, *n* an ancient Greek standard coin, struck variously in gold, silver or electrum. [Gr. *statēr*, orig. a pound weight — *histanai*, to set, establish, weigh.]

static *stat'ik* or **statical** *stat'i-kəl*, *adj* pertaining to statics; pertaining to bodies, forces, charges, etc. in equilibrium; stationary; stable; resting; acting by mere weight; pertaining to sense of bodily equilibrium. — *n* (**stat'ic**) atmospheric disturbances in wireless reception; white specks or flashes on a television picture; crackling on a long-playing plastic record; static electricity. — *adv* **stat'ically.** — *nsing* **stat'ics** the science of forces in equilibrium. — **static electricity** electrical charges that are stationary, not moving along in a current. [Gr. *statikos*, bringing to a standstill — *histanai*, to cause to stand.]

station *stā'shən*, *n* a fixed stopping-place, esp. one on a railway with associated buildings and structures; a place set apart and equipped for some particular purpose; a local office, headquarters or depot; a place where a person stands; an assigned place or post; an assigned region for naval duty; a place in India where officials and officers reside; a stock-farm (*Austr* and *NZ*); position in life, esp. a high position; the habitat of a plant or animal (*biol*); a holy place visited as one of a series, esp. one of (usu. fourteen) representations of stages in Christ's way to Calvary, disposed around a church interior or elsewhere (*RC*). — *adj* of a station. — *vt* to assign a station to; to set; to appoint to a post, place or office. — *adj* **sta'tionary** still; unmoving; fixed; static, not changing; settled; permanently located; continuously resident. — *n* **sta'tioner** a dealer in writing materials, etc. — *n* **sta'tionery** the goods sold by a stationer. — **station hand** (*Austr*) a man employed on a station; **station house** a lock-up at a police station; a police station (*US*); **sta'tion-master** the person in charge of a railway station; **station wagon** a motor vehicle usable by adjustment for either passengers or light hauling. [L. *statiō*, *-ōnis* — *stāre*, to stand.]

statism. See **state.**

statistic *stə-tis'tik*, *n* one of a series of tabulated numerical data. — *adj* **statis'tical** of, concerned with, or of the nature of, statistics. — *adv* **statis'tically.** — *n* **statistician** (*stat-is-tish'ən*) a person skilled in statistics; a compiler or student of statistics. — *nsing* **statis'tics** the classification, tabulation and study of numerical data. [It. *statista* and Ger. *Statistik* — L. *status*, state.]

stative *stā'tiv*, (*linguis*) *adj* indicating a state, as opposed to an action, etc. [L. *statīvus* — *stāre*, to stand.]

statoscope *stat'ō-skōp*, *n* a sensitive barometer for detecting minute differences in pressure. [Gr. *statos*, set, placed.]

stator *stā'tər*, (*mech*, *electr eng*) *n* a stationary part within which a part rotates. [L. *stător*, stander.]

statue *stat'ū*, *n* a representation (usu. near or above life-size) of human or animal form in the round. — *adj* **stat'uary** of, relating to, or suitable for sculpture. — *n* sculpture; statues. — *adj* **statuesque** (*-esk'*) like a statue, esp. in being of dignified and classically imposing appearance. — *adv* **statuesque'ly.** — *n* **statuesque'ness.** — *n* **statuette** (*-et'*) a small statue or figurine. [L. *statua* — *statuĕre*, to cause to stand — *stāre*.]

stature *stach'ər* or *stat'yər*, *n* body height; eminence. [L. *statūra*.]

status *stā'təs* or *stat'əs*, *n* standing; position, rank or importance, in society or in any group; high rank or standing; a person's legal position or classification with regard to marriage, citizenship, etc. — **status symbol** a possession or a privilege considered to mark a person out as having a high position in his or her social group. [L. *stătus*.]

status quo *stā'təs* or *stat'əs kwō*, (L.) *n* the existing condition or situation; (also **status quo ante** (*an'tī*)) the condition or situation existing before a particular change. [Lit., the state in which.]

statute *stat'ūt*, *n* a law expressly enacted by the legislature; a written law; the act of a corporation or its founder, intended as a permanent rule or law. — *adj* **stat'utory** enacted by statute; depending on statute for its authority; so common or frequent as to seem the rule (as though prescribed by statute; *colloq*). — *adj* **stat'ute-barred** disallowed by the statute of limitations. — **statute book** a record of statutes or enacted laws; **statute law** law in the form of statutes; **statute mile** see under **mile; statutory rape** (*US law*) sexual intercourse with a female below the age of consent. — **statute of limitations** a statute prescribing the period of time within which proceedings must be taken to enforce a right or bring a legal action. [L. *statūtum*, that which is set up — *statuĕre*.]

staunch[1] *stönch* or *stönsh*, *adj* firm in principle, pursuit or support; trusty, hearty, constant, zealous; stout, firm, watertight (e.g. *naut*). — *adv* **staunch'ly.** — *n* **staunch'ness.** [O.Fr. *estanche*, watertight.]

staunch[2] (*vt*). See **stanch.**

stave *stāv*, *n* one of the pieces of which a cask or tub is made; a staff, rod, bar, shaft, esp. wooden, as the rung of a ladder; a staff (*mus*); a stanza, verse of a song. — *vt* to break a stave or the staves of (a boat or barrel; with *in*); to burst inward (with *in*); to ward off, keep back or delay (with *off*); to put together, repair or fit, with staves: — *pa t* and *pa p* **staved** or **stove**. [Back-formation from *staves*, pl. of *staff*.]

staves *stāvz*, pl. of **staff** and of **stave**.

stavesacre *stāvz'ā-kər*, *n* a tall larkspur whose seeds were formerly used against lice. [O.Fr. *stavesaigre* — L.L. *staphisagria* — Gr. *staphis*, raisins, *agrios*, wild.]

stay[1] *stā*, *vi* to remain, continue to be, in a place, position or condition; to remain, reside, temporarily; to live, dwell (*Scot* and *SAfr*); to pause, wait, tarry (*old*); to wait in order to share or join in something, as in *stay to* or *for dinner*. — *vt* to hold, restrain, check the action of; to stop, suspend or postpone (judgment, proceedings, etc.); to remain, reside for (a specified time): — *pa t* and *pa p* **stayed**. — *n* a (period of) staying, temporary residence, a visit; a suspension of legal proceedings; a check or restraint. — *n* **stay'er** a person or animal of good lasting or staying qualities for a race, etc. — *adj* **stay'-at-home** keeping much at home; untravelled. — *n* a stay-at-home person. — **stay'away** (*SAfr*) a strike; a person participating in a strike; **staying power** ability to go on long without flagging; **stay-on tab** a ring-pull that does not pull entirely off, but bends into, the can; **stay stitching** in dressmaking, a line of stitching in the seam allowance to prevent stretching and fraying of the material. — **be here (**or **have come) to stay** to have become permanent or established; **stay on** to remain, tarry after the normal time for departing; **stay over** (*colloq*) to remain overnight, stay the night; **stay put** not to move from the place or position in which one has been put; **stay someone's hand** (*literary*) to stop someone on the point of doing something; **stay the course** to endure to the end of the race or other trial of one's stamina and staying power; **stay up** not to go to bed. [O.Fr. *ester* — L. *stāre*, to stand.]

stay[2] *stā*, *n* a prop or support; one of a number of strips of bone or metal sewn into a corset to stiffen it; (in *pl*) a corset thus stiffened (*hist*). — *vt* to sustain, comfort, strengthen (with *up*; *literary*). [O.Fr. *estaye*.]

stay[3] *stā*, (*naut*) *n* a rope bracing a mast, etc., a guy; a brace generally. — *vt* to brace or support (a mast, etc.) using stays. — *n* **staysail** (*stā'sl*) a triangular auxiliary sail spread on a stay. — **miss** or **refuse stays** (*naut*) not to come about. [O.E. *stæg*.]

STD *abbrev* for subscriber trunk dialling.

std *abbrev* for standard.

Ste *abbrev* for *Sainte* (Fr.), fem. of *saint*.

stead *sted*, *n* the place, function, role or position of another, as in *act in someone's stead*; service, avail, advantage, as in **stand someone in good stead** to be advantageous to someone. [O.E. *stede*, place.]

steadfast *sted'fäst*, *adj* firm; constant; resolute; steady. — *adv* **stead'fastly**. — *n* **stead'fastness**. [O.E. *stede fæst*.]

steading *sted'ing*, *n* the range of buildings surrounding a farmhouse, a farmstead. [O.E. *stede*, place.]

steady *sted'i*, *adj* standing firmly; fixed; stable; constant; resolute; consistent; regular; uniform; sober, industrious. — *vt* to make steady; to support; to make or keep firm: — *pr p* **stead'ying**; *pa t* and *pa p* **stead'ied**. — *n* a regular boyfriend or girlfriend (*colloq*). — *interj* be careful!; keep calm!; keep still!; hold the present course (*naut*). — *adj* **steady-go'ing** having, showing steady habits or action. — **steady state** (*astron*) see **continuous creation**. — **go steady** (*colloq*) (esp. of a boy and girl not yet engaged to be married) to have a steady relationship, to go about regularly together; **steady on!** keep calm!; don't be so foolish, hasty, etc. [O.E. *stede*, place, and sfx. *-y*.]

steak *stāk*, *n* any of several cuts of beef graded for frying, braising, stewing, etc.; a slice of meat (esp. hindquarters of beef) or fish. — **steak'house** a restaurant specialising in fried or grilled beefsteaks; **steak knife** a knife for eating steak with, with a serrated blade. [O.N. *steik*; *steikja*, to roast on a spit.]

steal *stēl*, *vt* to take by theft, esp. secretly; to take, gain or win by beguiling talk, contrivance, unexpectedly, insidiously, gradually or furtively; to gain (a base) without the help of a hit or error (*baseball*). — *vi* to practise theft; to take feloniously; to pass quietly, unobtrusively, gradually or surreptitiously: — *pa t* **stole**; *pa p* **stō'len**. — *n* (*colloq*) an act of stealing, a theft; something acquired by theft; a bargain, a snip; (esp. *US*) the stealing of a base (*baseball*). — *n* **steal'er**. — *n* and *adj* **steal'ing**. — **steal a march on** see under **march**[2]; **steal someone's thunder** to rob someone of the opportunity of achieving a sensational effect by forestalling him or her; **steal the show** see under **show**. [O.E. *stelan*.]

stealth *stelth*, *n* secret procedure or manner; furtiveness. — *adj* (*mil jargon*) (of an aircraft) having various features that help it to avoid detection by radar. — *adv* **stealth'ily**. — *n* **stealth'iness**. — *adj* **stealth'y** done, or acting, with stealth; furtive. [**steal**.]

steam *stēm*, *n* water in the form of gas or vapour or of a mist or film of liquid drops; steam power; energy, force, spirit (*colloq*). — *adj* of, for, using or worked by steam; outdated, old-fashioned, not using the latest technology (*facetious*). — *vi* to rise or pass off in steam or vapour; to emit or generate steam, vapour or smell; to move by means of steam power; to move fast (*colloq*). — *vt* to expose to steam, apply steam to; to cook by means of steam. — *adj* **steamed**. — *n* **steam'er** a steamship; a cooking apparatus for steaming food; one of a gang of muggers that attack by the method of steaming (*slang*). — *adv* **steam'ily**. — *n* **steam'iness**. — *n* **steam'ing** emitting, moving by, applying, or cooking by, steam; a form of mugging used by gangs, e.g. on the London Underground, who rush en masse through crowds, snatching whatever they can (*slang*). — *adj* (*colloq*) in an advanced state of drunkenness. — *adj* **steam'y** of, like, full of, covered with, as if covered with, emitting, steam or vapour; erotic, sexy, lubricious (*colloq*). — **steam bath** a steam-filled compartment, e.g. one at a Turkish bath, etc. in which to refresh oneself by sweating, etc., or one in a laboratory for sterilising equipment; **steam'boat, steam'ship, steam vessel** a vessel driven by steam; **steam boiler** a boiler for generating steam. — *adj* **steam'-driven**. — **steam engine** an engine worked by steam; **steamer duck** a large duck of S. America whose swimming action is suggestive of the motion of a steamer with a paddle-wheel on each side; **steam gauge** a pressure gauge for steam; **steam hammer** a vertical hammer worked by steam; **steam iron** an electric iron having a compartment in which water is heated to provide steam to dampen fabrics for easier ironing; **steam jacket** a hollow casing supplied with steam; **steam navvy** or **shovel** an excavator driven by steam; **steam packet** a steam-vessel plying between certain ports; **steam power** the force or agency of steam when applied to machinery; **steam'roller** a steam engine with heavy rollers as wheels, used in road-mending, etc.; any weighty crushing force. — *vt* (*colloq*) to crush (objections, etc.); to force (e.g. legislation through parliament, etc.). — **steam turbine** an engine in which expanding steam acts on blades attached to a drum. — **full steam ahead** forward at the greatest speed possible; with maximum effort; **get up steam** to build up steam pressure; to collect one's forces; to become excited; **let off steam** to release steam into the atmosphere; to work off energy; to give vent to anger or annoyance; **run out of steam** (*colloq*) to be forced to stop through loss of impetus, strength or energy; **steam open** to soften the gum of, and peel open (sealed envelopes) under exposure to steam; **steam up** (of windows, etc.) to become or cause to become dimmed with condensed vapour; (as *pap* **steamed up**) indignant (*slang*); **under one's own steam** by one's own unaided efforts. [O.E. *stēam.*]

stearic *stē'ə-rik* or *stē-ar'ik*, *adj* of or derived from stearin. — *n* **stearate** (*stē'ər-āt*) a salt of stearic acid. — **stearic acid** a solid fatty acid ($C_{17}H_{35}COOH$) derived from animal and vegetable fats. [Gr. *stear*, tallow.]

stearin *stē'ə-rin*, *n* glyceryl ester of stearic acid; a mixture of stearic and palmitic acids (also **ste'arine**); the solid part of a fat. — *adj* **ste'arine** (*-rīn*) (of candles, etc.) made of stearin(e). [Gr. *stear*, tallow.]

steatite *stē'ə-tīt*, *n* soapstone. — *adj* **steatitic** (*-tit'ik*). [Gr. *steatitēs* — *stear*, *-ātos*, tallow.]

steato- *stē-ə-tə-*, *combining form* denoting fat. — *n* **steatopygia** (*stē-ə-tə-pij'i-ə*) an accumulation of fat on the buttocks. — *n* **steatorrhoea** or **steatorrhea** (*stē-ə-tə-rē'ə*) abnormal fattiness of the faeces. — *n* **steatosis** (*stē-ə-tō'sis*) fatty degeneration. [Gr. *stear*, *-ātos*, tallow.]

steed *stēd*, *n* a horse, esp. a spirited horse. [O.E. *stēda*, stud horse, stallion.]

steel *stēl*, *n* iron containing a little carbon with or without additional ingredients; a weapon of steel, a sword (*literary*); a rough-surfaced steel implement for sharpening knives; a strip of steel e.g. for stiffening a corset; extreme hardness, staying power, trustworthiness. — *adj* of or like steel. — *vt* to cover, point or edge with steel; to harden; to nerve; to make obdurate. — *n* **steel'iness.** — *adj* **steel'y.** — **steel band** a West Indian band, using steel drums, etc. — *n* and *adj* **steel'-blue** blue like a reflection from steel. — **steel drum** a percussion instrument usu. made from the top of an oil drum, hammered out into a bowl-like shape and faceted so as to produce different notes; **steel'-engraving** engraving on steel plates; (**steel engraving**) an impression or print so got; **steel'-erector** a spiderman. — *n* and *adj* **steel'-grey** or **-gray** bluish-grey like steel. — **steel plate** one on which a design is engraved or a print obtained from it. — *adj* **steel-plat'ed** plated with steel. — **steel wool** steel shavings used for cleaning and polishing; **steel'work** work executed in steel; (in *pl*) a factory where steel is made; **steel'worker.** [O.E. *stȳle.*]

steelyard *stēl'yärd*, *n* a weighing machine consisting of a lever with a short arm for the thing weighed and a long graduated arm on which a single weight moves. [Prob. **steel** and **yard**[1].]

steenbok *stān'bok* or *stēn'bok*, *n* a small S. African antelope. — See also **steinbock.** [Du., — *steen*, stone, *bok*, buck.]

steenbras *stēn'bras*, (*SAfr*) *n* any of several edible estuarine S. African fish. [Afrik., — Du. *steen*, stone, *brasem*, bream.]

steep[1] *stēp*, *adj* rising or descending with great inclination; precipitous; difficult; excessive, exorbitant (*colloq*); unreasonable (*colloq*); a lot to ask anyone to believe (*colloq*). — *n* a precipitous place. — *vt* and *vi* **steep'en** to make or become steeper. — *adj* **steep'ish.** — *adv* **steep'ly.** — *n* **steep'ness.** [O.E. *stēap*; related to **stoop**[1].]

steep[2] *stēp*, *vt* to soak; to wet thoroughly; to saturate; to imbue. — *vi* to undergo soaking or thorough wetting. — *n* a soaking process; a liquid for steeping anything in. — *n* **steep'er.** [M.E. *stepen.*]

steeple *stēp'l*, *n* a church tower or other tower, esp. one with a spire; the spire alone. — *adj* **steep'led.** — **steep'lechase** orig. an impromptu horse race with some visible church steeple as goal; a horse race across country; a horse race over a course with obstacles to be jumped; a foot-race of this kind. — *vi* to ride or run in a steeplechase. — **steep'lechaser; steep'lechasing; steep'lejack** a person who repairs steeples and chimney stalks. [O.E. *stēpel*, *stȳpel*, *stīpel*, from root of **steep**[1].]

steer[1] *stēr*, *vt* to move (a vehicle or ship) in the direction desired by means of a steering wheel, helm or similar; to guide; to govern, control the course of. — *vi* to direct a ship or vehicle, etc. in its course; to move, follow a course, in response to the wheel or helm. — *n* an act of steering, as in *a bum steer* (*US*), a piece of misinformation. — *adj* **steer'able.** — *n* **steer'age** the act or practice of steering; the effect of a rudder on the ship; part of a passenger ship with lowest fares (also *adj*). — *n* **steer'er.** — *n* **steer'ing.** — **steer'ageway** sufficient movement of a vessel to enable it to be controlled by the helm; **steering column** the shaft in a motor vehicle on which the steering-wheel or handlebars are mounted; **steering committee** a group who decide what measures shall be brought forward and when; **steer'ing-gear** the mechanism that transmits motion from the steering-wheel; **steer'ing-wheel** the wheel whereby a ship's rudder is turned, or a motor car, etc. guided; **steers'man** the person who steers a vessel, a helmsman. — **steer clear of** to avoid. [O.E. *stēoran*, *stȳran*, to steer.]

steer[2] *stēr*, *n* a young ox, esp. a castrated one from two to four years old. [O.E. *stēor.*]

steeve *stēv*, (*naut*) *n* the angular elevation of a bowsprit. — *vt* and *vi* to incline to the horizon.

stegosaur *steg'ə-sör*, *n* any of several quadrupedal, herbivorous dinosaurs of the Jurassic period, characterised by armour of various sorts. — *adj* **stegosaur'ian.** — *n* **Stegosaur'us** a member of the class of stegosaurs, having two lines of kite-shaped plates along the backbone. [Gr. *steganos*, covered, watertight, *stegos*, roof.]

stein *stīn*, *n* a large beer mug, often earthenware and frequently with a hinged lid. [Ger.]

steinbock *stīn'bok*, *n* the Alpine ibex; also used for **steenbok.** [Ger. *Stein*, stone, *Bock*, buck.]

stele *stē'lē*, *n* an upright stone slab or tablet (also **stē'la**); (*stē'lē* or *stēl*) the central cylinder in stems and roots of the higher plants (*bot*): — *pl* **stē'lae** (*-lē*). — *adj* **stē'lar.** [Gr. *stēlē* — root of *histanai*, to set, stand.]

stellar *stel'ər*, *adj* of the stars; of the nature of, relating to, belonging to or characteristic of a star; relating to a star performer or performance. — *n* **stell'arator** (*stellar* and *generator*) a twisted torus in which plasma can be confined by a magnetic field, used for producing thermonuclear (i.e. stellar) power by nuclear fusion. — *adj* **stell'ate** star-shaped; with branches radiating from a point; with sides that intersect one another, giving a starlike effect, as in the pentagram. — *adj* **stellā'ted** stellate. — *adv* **stell'ately.** — *adj* **stell'iform** star-shaped. — *adj* **stell'ūlar** or **stell'ūlate** like a little star or little stars; set with little stars. [L. *stēlla*, a star.]

stem[1] *stem*, *n* the leaf-bearing axis of a plant; a stalk; anything stalklike, such as the slender vertical part of a written musical note, or of a wine glass, or the winding shaft of a watch; an upright stroke of a letter; the main line (or sometimes a branch) of a family; a race or family; the base of a word, to which inflectional suffixes are added (*philol*); a curved timber at the prow of a ship; the forepart of a ship. — *vt* to provide with a stem; to deprive of stalk or stem; to oppose the stem of a vessel to (the tide, etc.); hence, to make way against, breast; to ram. — *vi* to spring, take rise. — *adj* **stem'less.** — *n* **stem'let.** — *adj* **stemmed** having a stem, esp. used in combination, as in *thick-stemmed*, etc. — **stem cell** (*histology*) a generalised parent cell whose progeny specialise; **stem ginger** the underground stem of the ginger plant; **stem stitch** an overlapping stitch used in embroidery; **stem'wīnder** (*US*) a keyless watch. — **from stem to stern** from one end of a vessel to the other; completely, throughout. [O.E. *stefn*, *stemn*; perh. conn. with **stand.**]

stem[2] *stem, vt* to stop, check; to dam; to staunch. — *vi* in skiing, to slow down by pushing the heels apart: — *pr p* **stemm'ing**; *pa t* and *pa p* **stemmed**. — *n* in skiing, the process of stemming, used in turning (also **stem turn**). [O.N. *stemma*.]

stemma *stem'ə, n* a pedigree, family tree; a diagrammatic tree drawn up (using the internal evidence of manuscripts, etc.) to show the descent and relationships of the texts of a literary work: — *pl* **stemm'ata**. [Gr. *stemma*, wreath, — *stephein*, to crown, wreathe.]

stemson *stem'sən, (naut) n* a curved timber fitted into the stem and keelson at the bow of a wooden vessel. [*stem* and keel*son*.]

sten. See **sten gun**.

stench *stench* or *stensh, n* a stink. — **stench trap** a device to prevent rise of gases in drains or sewers. [O.E. *stenc*, smell (good or bad).]

stencil *sten'sl* or *sten'sil, n* a plate perforated with a design, lettering, etc. from which copies are made by applying paint, etc. through it on to paper or other material; the design or lettering so produced; a piece of waxed paper, etc. on which letters are cut by typewriter or stylus so that ink will pass through. — *vt* to produce (lettering or a design) from a stencil; to mark or decorate (a material) using a stencil: — *pr p* **sten'cilling** or in U.S. **sten'ciling**; *pa t* and *pa p* **sten'cilled** or in U.S. **sten'ciled**. — *n* **sten'ciller**. — *n* **sten'cilling**. — **stencil plate**. [O.Fr. *estinceller*, to spangle — *estincelle* — L. *scintilla*, a spark.]

sten (also **Sten**) **gun** *sten gun, n* a small automatic gun. [*S*hepherd and *T*urpin, the designers, and *En*field, as in **bren gun**.]

steno- *sten-ō-, sten-ə-* or *ste-no-, combining form* meaning narrow. [Gr. *stenos*, narrow.]

stenography *stə-nog'rə-fi, n* shorthand, or the art of using it. — *n* **stenog'rapher** (*NAm*) a shorthand typist. — *adj* **stenographic** (*sten-ə-graf'ik*). [Gr. *stenos*, narrow, *graphia*, writing.]

stenosis *stə-nō'sis, (med) n* constriction, narrowing of a tube or passage. — *pl* **stenō'sēs**. — *adj* **stenotic** (*stə-not'ik*). [Gr. *stenōsis*, narrowing, — *stenos*, narrow.]

Stenotype® *sten'ə-tīp, n* a form of typewriter used for recording speech in phonetic shorthand. — *n* **sten'otypist**. — *n* **sten'otypy**. [*steno*graphy and *type*.]

stentorian *sten-tö'ri-ən, adj* (of the voice) loud, powerful, carrying. [*Stentōr*, the loud-voiced Greek herald in Homer's *Iliad*.]

step *step, n* a pace; a movement of the leg in walking, running or dancing; the distance so covered; a footstep, footfall; a footprint; gait; a small space; a short walk or journey; a degree of a scale; a stage upward or downward; one tread of a stair; a rung of a ladder; a doorstep; something to put the foot on in mounting or dismounting; a stairlike rise or drop in level; a stage on the way up or down; a move towards an end or in a course of proceeding; a support for the end of a mast, pivot, etc.; (in *pl*) walk, direction taken in walking; (in *pl*) a stepladder (often a **pair of steps**); (in *pl*) a flight of stairs. — *vi* to advance, retire, mount or descend by taking a step or steps; to pace; to walk; to walk slowly or gravely; to walk a short distance. — *vt* to perform by stepping; to measure by pacing; to shape or organise in a steplike formation or arrangement, stagger; to set (foot) (old *US*): — *pr p* **stepp'ing**; *pa t* and *pa p* **stepped**. — *n* **stepp'er**. — *adv* **step'wise** in the manner of steps. — *adj* **step'-cut** (of diamonds and other stones) cut in steplike facets. — **step'-down** a decrease in rate, quantity, output, etc. — *adj* reducing voltage; decreasing by stages. — **step'ladder** a ladder with flat treads and a hinged prop; **stepp'ing-stone** a stone rising above water or mud to afford a passage; a means to gradual progress; **step'-up** an increase in rate, quantity, output, etc. — *adj* increasing or changing by steps; raising voltage. — **break step** to change the sequence of right and left foot, so as to get out of step; **keep step** to continue in step; **in step** with simultaneous putting forward of the right (or left) feet in marching, etc. (with others); in conformity or agreement (with others); **out of step** not in step; **step by step** gradually, little by little; **step down** to withdraw, retire or resign from a position of authority, etc.; to decrease the voltage of; to reduce the rate of; **step in** or **into** to enter easily or unexpectedly; to intervene; **step on** to put or press the foot down on; **step on it** (*slang*; see under **gas** and **juice**) to hurry; **step out** to go out a little way; to increase the length of the step and so the speed; to have a busy social life; **step out of line** to depart from the usual or accepted course of action; **step up** to come forward; to build up into steps; to raise by a step or steps; to increase the voltage of; to increase the rate of, e.g. production; **take steps** to take action; **watch one's step** to go carefully, esp. with a view to not giving offence. [O.E. *steppe* (W. Saxon *stæpe*).]

step- *step-, pfx* indicating affinity by another marriage or mating. — *n* **step'child, -daughter** or **-son** a wife's or husband's, but not one's own, child, daughter or son. — *n* **step'father** a mother's husband not one's own father. — *n* **step'mother** a father's wife not one's own mother. — *n* **step'parent**. — *n* **step'-parenting**. — *n* **step'brother** or **-sister** respectively, the son or daughter, of a stepfather or stepmother. [O.E. *stēop-*, orig. meaning orphan.]

stephanotis *stef-ə-nō'tis, n* any plant of the genus *Stephanotis* of Madagascar, etc., cultivated for the waxy scented flowers. [Gr. *stephanōtis*, fit for a wreath — *stephanos*, a crown, wreath.]

steppe *step, n* a dry, grassy, generally treeless, uncultivated and sometimes salt plain, as in the south-east of Europe and in Asia. [Russ. *step'*.]

ster. *abbrev* for sterling.

-ster *-stər, sfx* used to denote a person with a particular characteristic (as in *youngster*), or activity (as in *mobster, prankster*, etc.) [O.E. sfx. *-estre*.]

steradian *sti-rā'di-ən, n* a unit of measurement for solid angles, the angle subtended at the centre of a sphere by an area on its surface numerically equal to the square of the radius. [Gr. *stereos*, solid, and **radian**.]

stercoraceous *stûr-kə-rā'shəs, (med) adj* of, relating to, like or of the nature of faeces. [L. *stercus, -oris*, dung.]

stere *stēr, n* a timber measure, a cubic metre — about 35·315 cubic feet, used as *combining form* as in *decastere*, 10 steres, *decistere*, a tenth of a stere. [Fr. *stère* — Gr. *stereos*, solid.]

stereo *stē'ri-ō* or *ster'i-ō, n* stereophonic reproduction of sound; stereoscopic vision; a piece of stereophonic equipment, such as a record-player, tape-recorder, etc.; a unit comprising such pieces: — *pl* **ster'eos**. — *adj* stereophonic; stereoscopic.

stereo- *stē-ri-ō-, -ri-ə-* or *-ri-o-*, or *ster-i-ō-*, etc. *combining form* meaning solid, hard, three-dimensional. — *n* **stereoacū'ity** the degree to which a person is aware of the separation of objects along the line of sight. — *n* **stereochem'istry** the study of the spatial arrangement of atoms in molecules. — *n* **ster'eogram** a picture or diagram suggestive of solidity; a stereographic double picture. — *n* **ster'eograph** a stereogram. — *adj* **stereograph'ic**. — *n* **stereog'raphy**. — *n* **stereoī'somer** an isomer having the same chemical composition, molecular weight and structure, but differing spatial arrangement of atoms. — *adj* **stereoīsomer'ic**. — *n* **stereoīsom'erism**. — *n* **stereom'eter** an instrument for measuring specific gravity or for measuring solids. — *adj* **stereomet'ric** or **stereomet'rical**. — *adv* **stereomet'rically**. —

n **stereom'etry**. — *adj* **stereophon'ic** giving the effect of sound from different directions in three-dimensional space. — *adv* **stereophon'ically**. — *n* **stereoph'ony** stereophonic reproduction of sound. — *n* **ster'eoscope** an instrument by which the images of two pictures differing slightly in point of view are seen one by each eye and so give an effect of solidity. — *adj* **stereoscop'ic**. — *adv* **stereoscop'ically**. — *n* **stereos'copy**. — *adj* **stereoson'ic** stereophonic. — *adj* **stereospecif'ic** relating to or (of atoms) having a fixed spatial arrangement. — *n* **ster'eotype** a solid metallic plate for printing, cast from a mould made from composed type; the art, method or process of making such plates; a fixed conventionalised or stock image, or a person or thing that conforms to it. — *vt* to make a stereotype of; to print with stereotypes; to characterise or categorise (esp. a person) too readily or simplistically. — *adj* **ster'eotyped** transferred as letterpress from set-up movable type to a mould, and thence to a metal plate; fixed, pre-formed as though by a mould, trite, unoriginal; conventionalised, conforming to a stock image or cliché. — *n* **ster'eotyper**. — *adj* **stereotyp'ic** or **stereotyp'ical**. — *n* **ster'eotyping**. — *n* **ster'eotypy** the producing of stereotype plates; the repetition of senseless movements, actions or words in cases of insanity, etc. (*med*). [Gr. *stereos*, solid.]

steric *ster'ik* or *stē'rik*, *adj* relating to the spatial arrangement of atoms in a molecule. [Gr. *stereos*, solid, and sfx. *-ic*.]

sterile *ster'īl* or (in U.S.) *-il*, *adj* unfruitful; barren; not producing, or unable to produce, offspring, fruit, seeds or spores; (of a flower) without pistils; sterilised; destitute of ideas or results. — *n* **sterilisation** or **-z-** (*ster-i-lī-zā'shən*). — *vt* **ster'ilise** or **-ize** to deprive of power of reproduction; to destroy micro-organisms in. — *n* **ster'ilīser** or **-z-**. — *n* **steril'ity**. [L. *sterilis*, barren.]

sterling *stûr'ling*, *n* English, Scottish or British money of standard value. — *adj* of sterling or standard English money; genuine, authentic; of thoroughly good character, solidly worthy and reliable; (of silver) of standard quality, i.e. containing at least 92·5 per cent silver (usu. alloyed with copper). — **sterling area** a group of countries with currencies tied to sterling. [Prob. a coin with a star — O.E. *steorra*, star — some early Norman pennies being so marked.]

stern[1] *stûrn*, *adj* severe; austere; rigorous; hard, unyielding, inflexible; unrelenting. — *adv* **stern'ly**. — *n* **stern'ness**. [O.E. *styrne*.]

stern[2] *stûrn*, *n* the hind part of a vessel; the rump or tail. — (In combination) **-sterned** having a stern of specified type. — *adv* **stern'most** farthest astern. — *adv* **stern'ward** (also *adj*) or **stern'wards**. — **stern'port** a port or opening in the stern of a ship; **stern'post** the aftermost timber of a ship, supporting the rudder; **stern sheet** (usu. in *pl*) the part of a boat between the stern and the rowers; **stern'way** the backward motion of a vessel; **stern=wheel'er** a small vessel with one large paddle wheel at the stern. — **stern foremost** backwards. [O.N. *stjórn*, a steering, or lost O.E. equivalent.]

sternum *stûr'nəm*, (*zool*) *n* the breastbone in human beings, and the corresponding bone in other vertebrates; the under part of a somite in arthropods. — *adj* **ster'nal**. [Gr. *sternon*, chest.]

sternutation *stûr-nū-tā'shən*, *n* sneezing. — *adj* **sternū'tative** or **sternū'tatory** that causes sneezing. — *n* **ster'nūtātor** a substance, esp. a gas, that causes coughing, nasal irritation, sneezing and tears. [L. *sternūtāre*, intensive of *sternuĕre*, to sneeze.]

steroid *stē'roid* or *ster'*, *n* any of a class of compounds including the sterols, bile acids and various hormones and vitamins. [**sterol** and sfx. *-oid*.]

sterol *ster'ol* or *stē'rol*, *n* a solid higher alcohol such as cholesterol or ergosterol. [chole*sterol*, ergo*sterol*.]

stertorous *stûr'tə-rəs*, *adj* with a snoring sound. — *adv* **ster'torously**. — *n* **ster'torousness**. [L. *stertĕre*, to snore.]

stet *stet*, *vt* to restore after marking for deletion: — *pr p* **stett'ing**; *pa t* and *pa p* **stett'ed**. [L., let it stand, 3rd sing. pres. subjunctive of *stāre*, to stand; written on a proof-sheet with dots under the words to be retained.]

stethoscope *steth'ə-skōp*, (*med*) *n* an instrument with which to listen to the sounds produced by the heart, lungs, etc., with a hollow circular part that is applied to the body wall, from which sound is transmitted by tubes into the earpieces. — *adj* **stethoscopic** (*-skop'ik*). — *adv* **stethoscop'ically**. — *n* **stethoscopy** (*stə-thos'kə-pi*). [Gr. *stēthos*, chest, *skopeein*, to look at, examine.]

Stetson *stet'sn*, *n* a man's felt hat with a broad brim and a soft, high crown. [Maker's name.]

stevedore *stē'və-dör*, *n* a person who loads and unloads shipping vessels. — *vt* and *vi* to load and unload (cargo or a ship). [Sp. *estibador*, packer — *estibar*, to stow — L. *stīpāre*, to press.]

stevengraph *stē'vən-gräf*, *n* a small picture woven in silk. [T. *Stevens*, American weaver of the 19th cent.]

stew[1] *stū*, *n* a dish of stewed food, esp. meat with vegetables; a hole, a fix (*colloq*); a state of mental agitation (*colloq*); an overheated or sweaty state (*colloq*); (usu. in *pl*) a brothel. — *vt* to simmer or boil slowly with some moisture; to over-infuse (e.g. tea). — *vi* to swelter, esp. in a confined space; to be cooked by stewing; to be in a state of worry or agitation (*colloq*). — *adj* **stewed** cooked by stewing; (of tea) over-infused; drunk (*colloq*). — **stew'pan** or **stew'pot** a pan or pot used for stewing. — **stew in one's own juice** to be left to reap the consequences of one's own actions. [O.Fr. *estuve*, stove; prob. conn. with **stove**[1].]

stew[2] *stū*, *n* a fish-pond; a fish-tank; an artificial oyster-bed. — **stew'pond**. [O.Fr. *estui*.]

steward *stū'ərd*, *n* a person who manages the domestic concerns of a family or institution; a person who superintends another's affairs, esp. an estate or farm; the manager of the provision department or attendant on passengers in a ship, aircraft, etc.; a college caterer; someone who helps in arrangements, marshalling, etc. at races, a dance, a wedding or entertainment; a shop steward: — *fem* (in ships, aircraft, etc.) **stew'ardess**. — *n* **stew'ardship**. [O.E. *stig-weard* — *stig*, hall ('sty'), *weard*, ward, keeper.]

stg *abbrev* for sterling.

sthenic *sthen'ik*, *adj* strong, robust; morbidly active (*med*). [Gr. *sthenos*, strength.]

stibine *stib'īn*, *n* antimony hydride, a poisonous gas. [L. *stibium*, antimony.]

stibnite *stib'nīt*, *n* antimony trisulphide, the chief ore of antimony. [L. *stibium*, antimony.]

stich *stik*, *n* a line of verse. — *adj* **stich'ic**. — *combining form* **-stichous** (*-sti-kəs*) having a certain number of lines or rows, e.g. *distichous*. — *n* **stichomythia** (*stik-ə-mith'i-ə*) verse dialogue in which alternate speakers take a line each. [Gr. *stichos*, a row — *steichein*, to march.]

stick[1] *stik*, *vt* to pierce, transfix; to stab; to spear; to thrust; to fasten by piercing; to insert; to set in position; to set or cover with things fastened on; to cause to adhere; to endure (esp. with *it*) (*colloq*); (usu. *passive*) to bring to a standstill; (usu. *passive*) to confine. — *vi* to be fixed by insertion; to jut, protrude; to adhere; (of a charge or accusation) to be accepted as valid; to become or remain fixed; to remain; to be detained by an impediment; to jam; to fail to proceed or advance; to hold fast, keep resolutely (with *to*): — *pa t* and *pa p* **stuck**. — *n* **stickabil'ity** (*colloq facetious*) the ability to stick at something, persistence, perseverence. — *n* **stick'er** a person or thing that sticks; a piercing weapon (*colloq*); a person or thing difficult to get rid of; a gummed label or poster. — *adv* **stick'ily**. — *n* **stick'iness**. — *adj* **stick'y** adhesive; tenacious; gluey; muggy; difficult (*colloq*); unpleasant (*colloq*). — *vt* to make sticky. — **stick'ing-plaster** an adhesive plaster for covering wounds; **stick'ing-point** the point beyond which a thing cannot proceed; **stick'-in-the-mud** an old fogy; **stick'y-beak** (*Austr* and *NZ colloq*) a Nosey Parker; **sticky end** an unpleasant end, disaster. — *adj* **sticky-fin'gered** (*colloq*) prone to pilfering. — **sticky wicket** a difficult situation to cope with. — *adj* **stuck-up'** self-importantly aloof. — **get stuck in(to)** (*colloq*) to deal with, consume, attack in a vigorous, aggressive, eager, etc. manner; **stick around** (*colloq*) to remain in the vicinity; **stick at** to hesitate or scruple at (often with *nothing*); to persist at; **stick by** to be firm in supporting, to adhere closely to; **stick 'em up** hold up your hands (or be shot); **stick in someone's throat** to be difficult, or against one's conscience, for someone to countenance; **stick out** to project; to be obvious; to continue to resist; **stick out for** to insist upon; **stick (something) on (someone)** (*colloq*) to put the blame for (something) on (someone); **stick to** to persevere in holding to; **stick together** to be allies; to support each other; **stick up** to stand up; to waylay and plunder (esp. *US*; *n* **stick'-up**); **stick up for** to speak or act in defence of; **stick with** to remain with; to force (a person) to cope with (something unpleasant) — often in *passive*, i.e. **be stuck with**; **stuck for** unable to proceed because of the lack of; **stuck on** (*colloq*) enamoured of. [O.E. *stician*; cf. **stick**[2] and **stitch**.]

stick[2] *stik*, *n* a rod of wood, esp. for walking with or for beating; a twig; anything shaped like a rod of wood; a piece of firewood; a tally; an instrument for beating a percussion instrument; an instrument for playing hockey or another game; a bow for a fiddle, or the wooden part of it; a person of stiff manner; a person who lacks enterprise; a rod; an oblong or cylindrical piece; a control rod of an aeroplane; a group of bombs, or of paratroops, released at one time from an aeroplane; a piece of furniture (usu. in *pl*); a support for a candle; (in *pl*) hurdles in steeplechasing; blame, criticism (*slang*). — *adj* in the form of a stick; made of sticks. — *vt* to support (a plant) with sticks: — *pa t* and *pa p* **sticked**. — **stick insect** a twiglike insect; **stick'work** skill in using one's stick in any game played with one. — **big stick** force, coercion; **carrot and stick** see **carrot**; **give someone stick** (*slang*) to censure or punish someone; **in a cleft stick** in a dilemma; **right** (or **wrong**) **end of the stick** a true (or mistaken) understanding of the situation; **the sticks** rural areas, the backwoods; **up sticks** (*colloq*) to move, go and live somewhere else, make off. [O.E. *sticca*; O.N. *stika*.]

stickleback *stik'l-bak*, *n* a small spiny-backed river-fish. [O.E. *sticel*, sting, prick, and **back**.]

stickler *stik'lər*, *n* a person who insists on something, as in *a stickler for etiquette*. [Prob. M.E. *stightle* — O.E. *stihtan*, to set in order.]

sticky. See under **stick**[1].

stiff *stif*, *adj* not easily bent; rigid; lacking suppleness; moved or moving with difficulty or friction; dead; approaching solidity; thick, viscous, not fluid; dense, difficult to mould or cut; resistant; difficult; tough, tiring, arduous; pertinacious; stubborn; formidable; (of an alcoholic drink) strong; (of a breeze or wind) blowing strongly; firm, high, or inclining to rise (in price, etc.); excessive; not natural and easy; constrained; formal; unlucky (esp. *Austr*); (*predicatively*) to an extreme degree, as in *bore* or *scare someone stiff*. — *n* (*slang*) a corpse; a racehorse that is a notably poor bet; a customer who fails to tip. — *vt* (*slang*) to cheat; to rob; to fail to tip; to murder. — *vt* and *vi* **stiff'en** to make or become stiff or stiffer. — *n* **stiff'ener** a person or thing that stiffens; a strong alcoholic drink (*colloq*). — *n* and *adj* **stiff'ening**. — *adj* **stiff'ish**. — *adv* **stiff'ly**. — *n* **stiff'ness**. — **stiff neck** a condition affecting the neck muscles, making it painful to turn the head. — *adj* **stiff-necked'** obstinate; haughty; formal and unnatural. — **a stiff upper lip** see under **lip**; **stiff with** (*colloq*) full of, crowded with. [O.E. *stīf*, stiff.]

stifle[1] *stī'fl*, *vt* to stop the breath of by foul air or other means; to make breathing difficult for; to suffocate, smother; to choke down; to suppress; to repress. — *vi* to suffocate. — *n* **sti'fler**. — *n* and *adj* **sti'fling**. — *adv* **sti'flingly**.

stifle[2] *stī'fl*, *n* the joint of a horse, dog, etc. corresponding to the human knee. — **stifle bone** the knee-cap; **stifle joint**.

stigma *stig'mə*, *n* a disgrace or reproach attached to anyone; a mark of infamy; any special mark; a spot; a scar; a mark on the skin indicative of a particular disease (*med*); a spot sensitive to light; the part of a carpel that receives pollen (*bot*); (in *pl*) the marks of Christ's wounds or marks resembling them, claimed to have been impressed on the bodies of certain persons, e.g. Francis of Assisi in 1224: — *pl* **stig'mata** (or, esp. in religion, *-mä'tə*); also (esp. *bot* or in sense of *disgrace* or *reproach*) **stig'mas**. — *adj* **stigmatic** (*-mat'ik*) of, relating to, having or of the nature of a stigma; giving infamy or reproach; not astigmatic (*optics*). — *n* a person who bears the stigmata. — *adv* **stigmat'ically**. — *n* **stigmatīsā'tion** or **-z-**. — *vt* **stig'matise** or **-ize** to mark with a stigma or the stigmata; to brand, denounce, describe condemnatorily (with *as*). — *n* **stig'matism** impression of the stigmata; absence of astigmatism. — *n* **stig'matist** a person bearing stigmata, a stigmatic. [Gr. *stigma*, *-atos*, tattoo-mark, brand — *stigmē*, a point.]

stilb *stilb*, *n* the CGS unit of intrinsic brightness, one candela/cm^2. — [Gr. *stilbein*, to shine.]

stilbene *stil'bēn*, *n* a crystalline hydrocarbon, used in dye-manufacture. [Gr. *stilbein*, to shine.]

stilboestrol or in U.S. **stilbestrol** *stil-bēs'trəl*, *n* a synthetic oestrogen. [Gr. *stilbos*, glistening, and **oestrus**.]

stile[1] *stīl*, *n* a step, or set of steps, for climbing over a wall or fence. [O.E. *stigel*.]

stile[2] *stīl*, *n* an upright member in framing or panelling. [Perh. Du. *stijl*, pillar, doorpost.]

stiletto *sti-let'ō*, *n* a dagger with a narrow blade; a pointed instrument for making eyelets; a stiletto heel: — *pl* **stilett'os**. — *vt* to stab with a stiletto: — *pr p* **stilett'oing**; *pa t* and *pa p* **stilett'oed**. — **stiletto heel** a high, thin heel on a woman's shoe. [It., dimin. of *stilo*, a dagger.]

still[1] *stil*, *adj* motionless; inactive; silent; calm; quiet; not sparkling or effervescing. — *vt* to silence; to appease; to restrain. — *vi* to become still. — *adv* without motion; up to the present time or time in question; as before; yet, even (usu. with *compar*); even so, even then; nevertheless, for all that. — *n* calm; quiet; an ordinary photograph, or one taken from a cinematographic film. — *n* **still'ness**. — *adj* **stilly** (*stil'i*; *poetic*) still; quiet; calm. — **still'birth** the birth of an already dead child. — *adj* **still'born** dead when born; abortive, doomed from the start. — **still life** the class of pictures representing inanimate objects; a picture of this class: — *pl* **still lifes**. — *adj* **still'-life** relating to the representation of inanimate objects. — **still and all** (*colloq*) nevertheless. [O.E. *stille*, quiet, calm, stable.]

still[2] *stil*, *n* an apparatus for distillation. — **still'room** an apartment where liquors, preserves, and the like are kept, and where tea, etc. is prepared for the table; a housekeeper's pantry. [Aphetic for **distil**.]

stillage *stil'ij*, *n* a frame, stand or stool for keeping things off the floor; a boxlike container for transporting goods. [Prob. Du. *stellage*, *stelling* — *stellen*, to place.]

Still's disease *stilz di-zēz'*, *n* a form of arthritis affecting children, corresponding to rheumatoid arthritis in adults, sometimes causing fusion of joints. [First described by Sir G.F. *Still*, English physician (1868–1941).]

Stillson wrench® *stil'sən rench* or *rensh*, *n* an adjustable wrench whose grip is tightened by pressure on the handle. [D.C. *Stillson* (1830–99), American inventor.]

stilly. See under **still**[1].

stilt *stilt*, *n* a thin wooden prop with a foot-rest enabling one to walk supported high above the ground; a tall support; a very long-legged wading bird of the genus *Himantopus*, related to the avocets (also **stilt'bird** or **plov'er**). — *vt* to raise on stilts or as if on stilts. — *adj* **stilt'ed** stiff and pompous; laboured and unnatural; elevated on stilts; (of an arch) springing from above the capital (*archit*). — *adv* **stilt'edly**. — *n* **stilt'edness**. — *n* **stilt'ing**. [M.E. *stilte*.]

Stilton *stil'tən*, *n* a rich white, often blue-veined, cheese first sold chiefly at *Stilton* in Cambridgeshire.

stimpmeter *stimp'mē-tər*, (*golf*) *n* in the U.S., a device for measuring the speed of a putting green.

stimulus *stim'ū-ləs*, *n* an action, influence or agency that produces a response in a living organism; anything that rouses to action or increased action: — *pl* **stim'ulī**. — *adj* **stim'ulable** responsive to stimulus. — *adj* **stim'ulant** stimulating; increasing or exciting vital action. — *n* anything that stimulates or excites; a stimulating drug; an alcoholic liquor. — *vt* **stim'ulate** to incite; to instigate; to excite; to produce increased action in (*physiol*). — *vi* to act as a stimulant. — *adj* **stim'ulating**. — *n* **stimulā'tion**. — *adj* **stim'ulātive** tending to stimulate. — *n* that which stimulates or excites. — *n* **stim'ulātor** a person who stimulates; an instrument for applying a stimulus. [L. *stimulus*, a goad.]

sting *sting*, *n* in some plants and animals a weapon (hair, modified ovipositor, tooth, etc.) that pierces and injects poison; the act of inserting a sting; the pain or the wound caused; any sharp, tingling or irritating pain or its cause; the pain afflicted by wounding words, etc.; stinging power; pungency; (a substantial sum of money gained through) a deception, theft, etc. (*slang*); a trap for criminals set up by the police (*slang*). — *vt* to pierce, wound, pain with or as if with a sting; to goad or incite (with *into*; to rob, cheat or involve in expense (*slang*). — *vi* to have or use a power of stinging; to have a stinging feeling: — *pa t* and *pa p* **stung**. — *adj* **stinged** having a sting. — *n* **sting'er**. — *n* and *adj* **sting'ing**. — *adv* **sting'ingly**. — *adj* **sting'less**. — *adj* **sting'y** (*colloq*). — **stinging nettle** a common plant of the genus *Urtica*, with stinging hairs; **sting'ray** or (*US* and *Austr*) **stingaree** (*sting'gə-rē*, *sting'ə-rē* or *-rē'*) a ray with a formidable barbed dorsal spine on its tail. — **sting in the tail** an unlooked-for final unpleasantness or irony; **take the sting out of** (*colloq*) to soften the pain of. [O.E. *sting*, puncture, *stingan*, to pierce.]

stingy[1] *stin'ji*, *adj* niggardly. — *adv* **stin'gily**. — *n* **stin'giness**. [Prob. **sting**.]

stingy[2]. See under **sting**[1].

stink *stingk*, *vi* to give out a strong, offensive smell; to be offensive, have a bad reputation, suggest or imply evil or dishonesty. — *vt* to impart a bad smell to (a room, etc.; with *out*); to drive by a bad smell (with *out*, etc.): — *pa t* **stank** or **stunk**; *pa p* **stunk**. — *n* an offensive smell; an outraged reaction, a furore. — *n* **stink'er** a person or thing that stinks; a disagreeable person or thing (*colloq*); a petrel having an offensive smell. — *adj* **stink'ing**. — *adv* very, extremely, esp. as in *stinking rich* (*colloq*). — *adv* **stink'ingly**. — *adj* **stink'y**. — **stink-bird** see **hoatzin**; **stink bomb** a usu. small bomblike container which releases foul-smelling gases when exploded; **stink'horn** a stinking fungus; **stink'wood** the foul-smelling wood of various trees, esp. one of the genus *Ocotea* of S. Africa. — **like stink** (*colloq*) very much, to a great extent; intensely; **raise a stink** to complain; to cause trouble, esp. disagreeable publicity. [O.E. *stincan*, to smell (well or ill).]

stinko *sting'kō*, (*slang*) *adj* drunk.

stint[1] *stint*, *vt* to limit; to be niggardly with or towards; to allot stingily. — *n* restraint, restriction; proportion allotted, fixed amount; allowance; a set task; a (conventional) day's work. — *adj* **stint'ed**. — *adv* **stint'edly**. — *n* **stint'edness**. — *n* **stint'er**. — *n* and *adj* **stint'ing**. — *adv* **stint'ingly**. [O.E. *styntan*, to dull — *stunt*, stupid.]

stint[2] *stint*, *n* the dunlin or other small sandpiper.

stipe *stīp*, *n* a stalk, esp. of a fungus, a fern leaf, or an ovary. — Also **stipes** (*stī'pēz*; *pl* **stipites** *stip'i-tēz*). — *adj* **stipitate** (*stip'*). [L. *stīpes*, *-itis*, post, stock.]

stipel *stī'pl*, (*bot*) *n* a stipule-like appendage at the base of a leaflet. — *adj* **stipellate** (*stī'pə-lāt* or *sti-pel'āt*) having stipels. [Dimin. from **stipule**.]

stipend *stī'pənd*, *n* a soldier's pay; a salary, esp. a Scottish parish minister's; a periodical allowance. — *adj* **stipendiary** (*sti-pen'di-ə-ri* or *stī-*) receiving a stipend. — *n* a person who performs services for a salary, esp. a paid magistrate. [L. *stīpendium* — *stips*, payment, dole, *pendĕre*, to weigh.]

stipes, stipites, stipitate. See under **stipe**.

stipple *stip'l*, *vt* to engrave, paint, draw, etc. in dots or separate touches. — *n* painting, engraving, etc. in this way; the effect so produced. — *adj* **stipp'led**. — *n* **stipp'ler**. — *n* **stipp'ling**. [Du. *stippelen*, dimin. of *stippen*, to dot.]

stipular. See under **stipule**.

stipulate[1] *stip'ū-lāt*, *vt* to set or require as a condition of an agreement; to specify, insist on, as an essential part of an agreement (with *for*). — *vi* to make stipulations. — *n* **stipulā'tion**. — *n* **stip'ulator**. — *adj* **stip'ulatory** (*-lə-tər-i*). [L. *stipulārī*, *-ātus*, prob. — Old L. *stipulus*, firm.]

stipulate[2]. See **stipule**.

stipule *stip'ūl*, *n* a paired, usu. leafy, appendage at a leaf-base. — *adj* **stip'ular**. — *adj* **stip'ulāte** or **stip'uled** having stipules. [L. *stipula*, straw, stalk, dimin. of *stīpes*; new meaning assigned by Linnaeus.]

stir[1] *stûr*, *vt* to set in motion; to move around; to move (something, esp. in liquid or powder form) around by continuous or repeated, usu. circular, movements of a spoon or other implement through it, e.g. in order to mix its constituents; to disturb; to rouse; to move to activity; to excite. — *vi* to make a movement; to begin to move; to be able to be stirred; to go about; to be active or excited; (esp. in *pr p*) to be out of bed; to go forth; to cause trouble or dissension (*colloq*): — *pr p* **stirr'ing**; *pa t* and *pa p* **stirred**. — *n* movement; slight movement; activity; commotion; sensation; an act of stirring. — *adj* **stir'less** without stir. — *n* **stirr'er**. — *adj* **stirr'ing** arousing strong emotions; exciting; active, busy, eventful. — *adv* **stirr'ingly**. — *vt* and *vi* **stir'-fry** to fry (food) rapidly while stirring it in the pan. — **stir up** to excite; to incite; to arouse; to mix by stirring. [O.E. *styrian*.]

stir[2] *stûr*, (*slang*) *n* prison. — *adj* **stir-crā'zy** (*US*) unbalanced from confinement esp. in prison.

stirps *stûrps*, *n* family, race; pedigree; a permanent variety (*bot*). — *pl* **stirpes** (*stûr'pēz*). [L. *stirps*, *stirpis*.]

stirrup *stir'əp*, *n* a support for a rider's foot; a foot-rest, clamp or support, of more or less similar shape; the stirrup-bone; a rope secured to a yard, having a thimble in its lower end for reeving a foot-rope (*naut*). — **stirrup bone** the stapes, a stirrup-shaped bone in the ear; **stirrup cup** a drink taken on horseback on departing or arriving; **stirrup pump** a portable water pump with a foot-rest, for fighting small fires. [O.E. *stigrāp* — *stīgan*, to mount, *rāp*, rope.]

stitch *stich*, *n* a complete movement of the needle in sewing, knitting, surgery or the like; a loop or portion of thread, etc. so used; a surgical suture; a mode of stitching or knitting; the least scrap of clothing; a sharp pain in the side brought on by running, etc. — *vt* to join, adorn or enclose with stitches. — *vi* to sew. — *adj* **stitched**. — *n* **stitch'er**. — *n* **stitch'ery**. — **stitch'wort** any plant of the chickweed genus (*Stellaria*), once thought good for curing stitches in the side. — **a stitch in time** a timely repair or corrective measure; **drop a stitch** (in knitting) to let a stitch fall off the knitting-needle; **in stitches** in pained helplessness with laughter; **stitch up** (*slang*) to incriminate by informing on; to swindle. [O.E. *stice*, prick.]

stoa *stō'ə*, (*classical archit*) *n* a portico or covered colonnade: — *pl* **sto'as** or **sto'ae** (-*ī*). [Gr. *stŏā*.]

stoat *stōt*, *n* a small carnivorous mammal of the weasel family with black-tipped tail, called an ermine in its white northern winter coat. [M.E. *stote*.]

stobie pole *stō'bi pōl*, (*Austr*) *n* a steel and concrete pole for supporting electricity wires. [Name of design engineer.]

stochastic *stə-kas'tik*, *adj* random. — *adv* **stochas'tically**. [Gr. *stochastikos* — *stochazesthai*, to aim at, guess.]

stocious *stō'shəs*, *adj* a variant spelling of **stotious**.

stock *stok*, *n* a fund; capital of a company, divisible into shares; repute, estimation; shares of a public debt; (in *pl*) public funds; supply, store, equipment; a repertoire of plays done by a stock company (see below); the animals kept on a farm; supply of goods for sale; the undealt part of a pack of cards or set of dominoes; raw material, equipment, etc. for use or on hand, as in *rolling stock*, *film stock* (unused film), etc.; liquor from simmered meat, bones, etc.; a trunk or main stem; the perennial part of a herbaceous plant; the rooted trunk that receives a graft; a log; a post; a block; a stump; an upright beam; the wooden part of a gun; a handle; the gillyflower, a popular cruciferous garden plant; a stiff band worn as a cravat; (in *pl*) a device for holding a delinquent by the ankles, and often wrists; (in *pl*) a framework on which a ship is built; source; race; kindred; family. — *vt* to store; to keep for sale; to fit (a gun) with a stock; to supply or furnish with stock (e.g. a river with fish). — *adj* concerned with stock or stocks; kept in stock; conventionally used, standard; banal, trite; used for breeding purposes. — *n* **stock'ist** a person who keeps a commodity in stock. — **stock agent** (*Austr* and *NZ*) a dealer in livestock; **stock'-breeder** a person who raises livestock; **stock'-breeding; stock'broker** a stock exchange member who buys and sells stocks or shares for clients, having been officially superseded in the British Stock Exchange, on 27 October 1986, by the broker/dealer, combining the jobs of stockbroker and stockjobber (**stockbroker belt** the area outside a city, esp. that to the south of London, in which wealthy businessmen live); **stock'broking; stock company** (*US*) a permanent repertory company attached to a theatre; **stock cube** a cube of compressed meat or vegetable extract used for making stock; **stock dove** a dove like a small wood-pigeon; **stock exchange** a building for the buying and selling of stocks and shares; an association of persons transacting such business; (with *caps*) the institution in London where such business is done; **stock farm** a farm specialising in the rearing of livestock; **stock'-farmer** a farmer who rears livestock; **stock'holder** a person who holds stocks in the public funds, or in a company; a person who owns livestock (*Austr*); **stock'horse** (*Austr*) a horse trained for working with sheep and cattle; **stock-in-trade'** all the goods a shopkeeper has for sale; standard equipment or devices necessary for a particular trade or profession; a person's basic intellectual and emotional resources (often implying inadequacy or triteness); **stock'jobber** a stock exchange member who deals only with other members (in some special group of securities), a job abolished in the British Stock Exchange on 27 October 1986, with the introduction of the job of broker/dealer, combining the jobs of stockbroker and stockjobber; a stockbroker (*US*); an unscrupulous speculator; **stock'jobbery; stock'jobbing; stock'list** a list of stocks and current prices regularly issued; **stock'man** (esp. *Austr*) a person in charge of farm stock; **stock market** a stock exchange; stock exchange business; **stock'pile** an accumulated reserve supply. — *vt* to accumulate and store a large quantity of. — **stock'piling** accumulating reserves, e.g. of raw materials; **stock'pot** the pot in which the stock for soup is kept; **stock'room** a storeroom. — *adj* and *adv* **stock-still'** utterly still. — **stock'-taking** inventorying and valuation of stock; **stock whip** a herdsman's whip with short handle and long lash; **stock'yard** a large yard with pens, stables, etc. where cattle are kept for slaughter, market, etc. — **in** (or **out of**) **stock** available (or not available) for sale; **on the stocks** in preparation; **stock up on** to amass and lay by a sufficient or plentiful stock of; **take stock (of)** to make an inventory of goods on hand; to make an estimate of; **take stock in** to trust to, attach importance to. [O.E. *stocc*, a stick.]

stockade *sto-kād'*, *n* a barrier of stakes. — *vt* to surround with a stockade for defence. [Fr. *estacade* — Sp. *estacada*; cf. **stake**[1].]

stockfish *stok'fish*, *n* unsalted hake, cod, etc. cured by splitting and drying in the open air. [Prob. Du. *stokvisch*.]

stockinet or **stockinette** *stok-i-net'*, *n* an elastic knitted fabric for undergarments, etc. [Poss. orig. *stocking-net*.]

stocking *stok'ing*, *n* a close-fitting covering for the whole leg, usu. made of fine knitted fabric, worn by women; a close-fitting knitted covering for the foot and lower leg, as worn by men in Highland dress (esp. *Scot*); distinctive colouring or feathering of an animal's leg. — *adj* **stock'inged** wearing stockings (but usu. not shoes). — **stock'ing-filler** a small present for a Christmas stocking; **stocking mask** a nylon stocking pulled over the head to distort and so disguise the features; **stocking-sole'; stock'ing-stitch** a style of knitting in which a row of plain stitch alternates with a row of purl. — **in one's stocking-feet** or **-soles** with stockings or socks but no shoes. [**stock**.]

stocky *stok'i*, *adj* sturdy, thickset. — *adv* **stock'ily**. — *n* **stock'iness**. [*stock* and sfx. -*y*.]

stodge *stoj*, *vt* to stuff, cram or gorge with food. — *n* cloggy stuff; heavy, often uninteresting food. — *adv* **stodg'ily**. — *n* **stodg'iness**. — *adj* **stodg'y** heavy and cloggy; solemnly dull. [Perh. imit.]

stoep *stōōp*, (*SAfr*) *n* a platform along the front, and sometimes the sides, of a house; a verandah. [Du.; cf. **step**.]

stoic *stō'ik*, *n* a stoical person; (with *cap*) a disciple of the philosopher Zeno (d. *c* 261 B.C.), who taught in the *Stoa Poikilē* (Painted Porch) at Athens. — *adj* **stō'ic** or **sto'ical** indifferent to pleasure or pain; uncomplaining in suffering; (with *cap*) pertaining to the Stoics, or to their opinions. — *adv* **stō'ically**. — *n* **stō'icalness**. — *n* **stō'icism** (-*sizm*) the philosophy of the Stoics; indifference to pleasure or pain; limitation of wants; austere impassivity; uncomplaining fortitude in suffering. [Gr. *Stōikos* — *stŏā*, a porch.]

stoichiology or **stoicheiology** *stoi-kī-ol'ə-ji*, *n* the branch of biology that deals with the elements comprising animal tissues. — *adj* **stoichiolog'ical** or **stoicheiolog'ical**. — *n* **stoichiometry** or **stoicheiometry** (*stoi-kī-om'i-tri*) the branch of chemistry that deals with the numerical proportions in which substances react. — *adj* **stoichiomet'ric** or **stoicheiomet'ric.** [Gr. *stoicheion*, an element.]

stoke *stōk*, *vt* to feed with fuel. — *vi* to act as stoker. — *n* **stok'er** a person who or thing which feeds a furnace with fuel. — **stoke'hold** a ship's furnace chamber; a stoke-hole; **stoke'-hole** the space around the mouth of a furnace. — **stoke up** to fuel a fire or furnace; to have a good large meal (*colloq*). [Du. *stoker*, stoker — *stoken*, to stoke.]

stokes *stōks*, *n* the CGS unit of kinematic viscosity. — Also (esp. *US*) **stoke**: — *pl* **stokes.** [Sir G. *Stokes* (1819–1903), British physicist.]

STOL *stol*, *n* a system by which aircraft land and take off over a short distance; an aircraft operating by this system. — See also **VTOL.** — **STOL'port** an airport for such aircraft. [*s*hort *t*ake-*o*ff and *l*anding.]

stole[1] *stōl*, *pa t* of **steal.**

stole[2] *stōl*, *n* a narrow ecclesiastical vestment worn on the shoulders, hanging down in front; a woman's outer garment of similar form. [O.E. *stole* — L. *stŏla*, a Roman matron's long robe — Gr. *stolē*.]

stolen *stōl'ən*, *pa p* of **steal.** — Also *adj*.

stolid *stol'id*, *adj* impassive; showing little or no interest; unemotional. — *n* **stolid'ity** or **stol'id-ness.** — *adv* **stol'idly.** [L. *stolidus*.]

stollen *shtol'ən*, *n* rich, sweet German bread made with raisins, etc. and coated with icing sugar. [Ger., a prop, strut, from the shape of the loaf.]

stolon *stō'lən*, *n* a shoot from the base of a plant, rooting and budding at the nodes (*bot*); a stemlike structure or outgrowth (*zool*). — *adj* **stōlonif'-erous** producing stolons. [L. *stolō*, *-ōnis*, twig, sucker.]

STOLport. See **STOL.**

stoma *stō'mə*, *n* a mouthlike opening in some animals (*zool*); a pore by which gases pass through the epidermis of green parts of a plant (*bot*): — *pl* **stō'mata.** — *adj* **stomatal** (*stōm'* or *stom'ə-tl*) or **stomat'ic.** — *n* **stomatī'tis** inflammation of the mucous membrane of the mouth. — *n* **stomatol'-ogy** study of the mouth. — *combining form* **-stomous** denoting a particular kind of mouth. [Gr. *stŏma*, *-atos*, mouth.]

stomach *stum'ək*, *n* the strong muscular bag into which food passes from the gullet, and where some initial digestion takes place; the cavity in any animal for the digestion of its food; (*loosely* or *euph*) the belly; appetite, relish for food, inclination generally; disposition, spirit, courage, pride, spleen. — *vt* to bear or put up with; to digest. — *adj* of the stomach. — *adj* **stom'achal.** — *n* **stom'acher** (*-chər* or *-kər*) a covering or ornament for the chest, esp. one worn under the lacing of a bodice. — *n* **stom'achful** as much as the stomach will hold (*pl* **stom'achfuls**). — *adj* **stomachic** (*stəm-ak'ik*) of the stomach; promoting digestion. — *n* a stomachic medicine. — **stom'ach-ache; stom'ach-pump** a syringe with a flexible tube for withdrawing fluids from the stomach, or injecting them into it. [O.Fr. *estomac*, L. *stomachus*, Gr. *stomachos*, throat, later stomach — *stoma*, a mouth.]

stomatal, etc. See **stoma.**

stomp *stomp*, *vi* to stamp the feet; to dance the stomp (*colloq*). — *n* an early jazz composition with heavily accented rhythm; a lively dance with foot stamping (*colloq*); an act of stamping the feet. — *n* **stom'per.** [Variant of **stamp.**]

-stomy *-stə-mi*, *combining form* denoting a surgical operation to form a new opening into an organ. [Gr. *stoma*, a mouth.]

stone *stōn*, *n* a detached piece of rock, usu. small; the matter of which rocks consist; a gem; a shaped piece of stone designed for a particular purpose; a concretion; a diseased state characterised by formation of a concretion in the body; a hard fruit kernel; the hard seed of any of several fruits; the colour of stone, usu. a dull light grey; (with *pl* usu. **stone**) a standard weight of 14 lb. avoirdupois; a tombstone; a printer's table for imposing. — *adj* of stone; of the colour of stone; of stoneware. — *vt* to pelt with stones; to remove stones from (fruit); to lay or wall with stones. — *vi* to form a stone. — *adj* **stoned** having or containing a stone or stones; with the stone or stones removed; very drunk, or very high on drugs (*slang*). — *adj* **stone'less.** — *n* **ston'er** a person who stones; used in combination to denote a person who weighs, or a horse that carries, so many stone. — *adv* **ston'ily.** — *n* **ston'iness.** — *n* **ston'ing.** — *adj* **ston'y** of or like stone; abounding with stones; hard; pitiless; obdurate; stony-broke. — **Stone Age** a stage of culture before the general use of metal, divided into the Old Stone Age (Palaeolithic) and the New (Neolithic). — *adj* **Stone'-Age** or **stone'-age** (often *fig*). — *adj* **stone'-blind** completely blind. — **stone bass** a large perch of the Atlantic, Mediterranean and Tasman Sea, reputed to frequent wrecked ships — also called *wreckfish*; **stone'chat** a little black, ruddy and white European songbird, with a note like the clicking of two stones. — *adj* **stone-cold'** cold as a stone (**stone-cold sober** completely free of (esp. alcohol-induced) excitement or passion, utterly sober). — *n* and *adj* **stone'-colour** grey. — *adj* **stone'-coloured.** — **stone'-crop** any plant which grows on rocks, in walls, etc.; **stone'-curlew** a large plover, the thick-knee; **stone'-cutter** a person who hews stone; a machine for dressing stone; **stone'-cutting.** — *adj* **stone-dead'** and **stone-deaf'** dead or deaf as a stone. — **stone'fish** a poisonous tropical fish of the *Scorpaenidae*, which resembles a stone on the seabed; **stone'-fly** an insect whose larvae live under stones in streams; **stone'-fruit** a fruit with a stone. — *adj* **stone'ground** (of flour) ground between millstones. — **stone'-mason** a mason who works with stone; **stone's'-throw** the distance a stone may be thrown; a short distance. — *vi* **stonewall'** to hold up progress, (in parliament) by obstructing discussion, (in cricket) by playing extremely defensively. — **stonewall'er; stonewall'ing; stone'ware** a coarse kind of pottery baked hard and glazed; a high-fired, vitrified, non-porous ceramic material or objects made of it. — *adj* **stone'washed** (of new clothes) given an old faded appearance using small pieces of pumice. — **stone'work** work in (usu. dressed) stone. — *adj* **stony-broke'** (*slang*) penniless, or nearly so. — *adj* **stony-heart'ed** hard-hearted. — **leave no stone unturned** to do everything that can be done in order to secure the effect desired; **stone me!** and **stone the crows!** (*slang*) expressions of astonishment. [O.E. *stān*.]

stonker *stong'kər*, (*slang*) *vt* to kill, destroy, overthrow, thwart. — *n* **stonk** (*stongk*; *mil*; back-formation) intense bombardment.

stood *stŏŏd*, *pa t* and *pa p* of **stand.**

stooge *stōōj*, (*slang*) *n* a performer speaking from the auditorium; an actor who feeds lines to a comedian, etc. and is used as the butt of the jokes; a subordinate or drudge; a scapegoat. — Also *vi*.

stook *stŏŏk*, *n* a group of sheaves, set up in the field. — *vt* to set up in stooks. — *n* **stook'er.** [Cf. L.G. *stuke*, bundle.]

stool *stōōl*, *n* a seat without a back; a low support for the feet or knees; (usu. in *pl*) faeces; a stand; a stump from which sprouts shoot up; a growth of shoots; a piece of wood to which a bird is fastened as a decoy in hunting. — *vi* to put forth shoots; to lure wildfowl with a stool. — **stool'ball** an old game resembling cricket; **stool'-pigeon** a decoy-pigeon; a decoy; a police informer (shortened form **stool'ie**; *slang*). — **fall between two stools** to lose both possibilities by hesitating between them, or trying for both. [O.E. *stōl*.]

stoop[1] *stōōp*, *vi* to bend the body forward; to lean forward; to submit; to descend from rank or dignity; to condescend; to lower oneself by unworthy behaviour; to swoop down (of a bird of prey). — *vt* to bend, incline, lower or direct downward. — *n* a bending of the body; inclination forward; descent; condescension; a swoop. — *adj* **stooped** having a stoop, bent. — *n* **stoop'er**. — *adj* **stoop'ing**. — *adv* **stoop'ingly**. [O.E. *stūpian*.]

stoop[2]. See under **stoup**.

stoop[3] *stōōp*, (*US*) *n* a stoep.

stop *stop*, *vt* to cause to cease; to bring to a standstill; to hinder or prevent the passage of; to prevent; to cease from, leave off, discontinue; to obstruct; to snuff, block, plug, choke or close up (often with *up*); to bring down, hit with a shot; to withhold; to restrain; to limit the vibrating length of, esp. by pressure of a finger (*mus*); to punctuate; to adjust the aperture of, with a diaphragm (*phot*). — *vi* to come to a standstill, halt; to cease; to desist; to come to an end; to stay, tarry, sojourn (*colloq*): — *pr p* **stopp'ing**; *pa t* and *pa p* **stopped**. — *n* act of stopping; state of being stopped; cessation; a halt; a pause or interruption; a halting-place; a contrivance that limits motion; a card that interrupts the run of play; a diaphragm (*phot* and *optics*); the stopping of an instrument or string; a fret on a guitar, etc.; a finger-hole, a key for covering it, or other means of altering pitch or tone; a set of organ pipes of uniform tone quality; a knob operating a lever for bringing them into use; an aperture setting (*phot*); a sound requiring complete closure of the breath passage, a mute (*phon*; also **stop'-consonant**); a punctuation mark. — *adj* **stop'less**. — *n* **stopp'age** act of stopping; state of being stopped; stopping of work, as for a strike; obstruction; an amount stopped off pay. — *adj* **stopped**. — *n* **stopp'er** a person who stops; that which stops; a plug. — *vt* to close or secure with a stopper. — *n* **stopp'ing** the action of one who or that which stops in any sense (**double stopping** simultaneous stopping of and playing on two strings); stuffing or filling material, esp. for teeth. — **stop-and-search'** a police policy of random searching of people in the streets, to look for concealed weapons, etc. usu. during periods of civil disobedience. — Also *adj*. — **stop'-bath** a substance in which a photographic negative or print is immersed in order to halt the action of the developer; **stop'cock** a short pipe opened and stopped by turning a key or handle; (*loosely*) the key or handle; **stop-frame camera** a film camera that can be adjusted to take a reduced number of frames, used in creating the effect of pixillation (q.v.); **stop'-gap** a temporary expedient or substitute. — Also *adj*. — *adj* **stop-go'** (of policy) alternately discouraging and encouraging forward movement. — *n* a stop-go economic policy, etc. — **stop'-off** or **-over** a break of journey; **stoppage time** injury time; **stopp'ing-out** selective use (of a protective covering against acids in etching, against light in photography) to create special effects; **stopp'ing-place**; **stop-press'** late news inserted in a newspaper after printing has begun; a space for it. — Also *adj*. — **stop'-watch** an accurate watch readily started and stopped, used in timing a race, etc. — **pull out all the stops** to do one's utmost, using all one's energy and efforts; **stop off, stop over, stop in** and in N.Am. **stop by** to break one's journey, pay a visit to (usu. with *at*); **stop the show** see under **show**. [O.E. *stoppian*, found in the compound *forstoppian*, to stop up — L. *stuppa*, tow — Gr. *styppē*.]

stope *stōp*, *n* a steplike excavation in mining. — *vt* to excavate or extract in this way. — *n* **stop'ing**. [Perh. connected with **step**.]

storable and **storage**. See under **store**.

storax *stō'raks*, *n* the resin of any of the tropical trees or shrubs of the genus *Styrax*, once used in medicine; now that of the *Liquidambar orientale* tree (*liquid storax*). [L. *stŏrax* — Gr. *stўrax*.]

store *stōr*, *n* a hoard; a stock laid up; sufficiency or abundance; keeping; a storehouse; a shop; a co-operative shop or one with many departments or branches; value, esteem; a computer memory unit, in which program and data are stored; (in *pl*) supplies of provisions, ammunition, etc. for an army, ship, etc. — *adj* of a store; sold in a shop, ready-made. — *vt* to lay up, keep in reserve; to deposit in a repository; to give storage to; to furnish or supply; to put (data) into a computer memory. — *adj* **stor'able**. — *n* **stor'age** placing, accommodation, reservation or safe-keeping, in store; the keeping of information in a computer memory unit; charge for keeping goods in store. — *n* **stor'er**. — **storage battery** an accumulator; **storage capacity** the maximum amount of information that can be held in a computer store; **storage heater** an electric heater with a large thermal capacity that accumulates and stores heat during the off-peak periods and releases it over a longer period; **store card** a credit card operated by a department store for the purchase of goods in that store or any others in the chain; **store'front** (*NAm*) the façade of a shop or store; **store'house** a house for storing goods of any kind; a repository; a treasury; **store'keeper** a shopkeeper (chiefly *NAm*); **store'man** a storekeeper (*NAm*); a person who looks after stores or a storeroom; **store'room** a room in which stores are kept; space for storing. — **in store** in hoard for future use, ready for supply; in reserve, awaiting, imminent; **set** or **lay store by** to value greatly. [O.Fr. *estor*, *estoire* — L. *īnstaurāre*, to provide.]

storey or (esp. in N.Am.) **story** *stō'ri*, *n* all that part of a building on the same floor; a tier: — *pl* **sto'reys** or **sto'ries**. — *adj* **sto'reyed** or **sto'ried** having storeys. — **first storey** the ground floor; **second storey** the first floor, etc. [Prob. same word orig. as **story**[1].]

storiated. See under **story**[1].

storied. See under **story**[1] and **storey**.

stork *störk*, *n* a large white and black wading bird with a great red bill and red legs; the bringer of babies (*facetious*); any member of its genus or of its family (e.g. the ibis). — **stork's'-bill** a genus of the geranium family, with beaked fruit; also applied to Pelargonium. [O.E. *storc*.]

storm *störm*, *n* a violent commotion of the atmosphere; a tempest; a wind just short of a hurricane; any intense meteorological phenomenon; a violent commotion or outbreak of any kind; a violent assault (*mil*). — *vi* to be stormy; to rage; to rush violently or in attack. — *vt* to take or try to take by assault. — *adv* **storm'ily**. — *n* **storm'iness**. — *n* and *adj* **storm'ing**. — *adj* **storm'less**. — *adj* **storm'y** having many storms; agitated with furious winds; boisterous; violent; passionate. — *adj* **storm'bound** delayed, cut off, confined to port by storms. — **storm'-centre** the position of lowest pressure in a cyclonic storm; any focus of controversy or strife; **storm'-cloud**; **storm'-cock** the mistle-thrush; **storm'-cone** or **-drum** a cone or drum hoisted as a storm-signal; **storm cuff** an extra elasticated cuff let into the cuff opening of a jacket, etc. to give extra warmth and protection; **storm'-lantern** a lantern with flame protected from wind and weather; **storm petrel** or (*popularly*) **stormy petrel** see under **petrel**. — *adj* **storm'proof** giving protection against storms or storming. — **storm'-trooper**. — *npl* **storm'-troops** shock-troops; a body formed in Germany by Adolf Hitler, disbanded in 1934. — **storm'-warning**; **storm'-window** a window raised above the roof, slated above and at the sides, a dormer; an additional outer casement. — **a storm in a teacup** a great commotion in a narrow sphere, or about a trifle; **take by storm** to take by assault; to captivate totally and instantly (*fig*). [O.E. *storm*.]

Storting or **Storthing** *stör'ting*, *n* the legislative assembly of Norway. [Norw. *stor*, great, *ting* (O.N. *thing*), assembly.]

story[1] *stö'ri*, *n* a narrative of incidents in their sequence; a fictitious narrative; a tale; an anecdote; the plot of a novel or drama; a theme; an account, report, statement, allegation; a news article; a lie, a fib (*colloq*). — *vt* to adorn (a pot, etc.) with scenes from history. — *adj* **sto'riated** decorated with elaborate ornamental designs. — *adj* **sto'ried** told or celebrated in a story; having a history; adorned with scenes from history. — **sto'ryboard** (a board on which is mounted) a series of rough sketches showing the sequence of film images to be used in an advertisement, cinema film, television programme, etc.; **sto'ry-book** a book of tales true or fictitious. — *adj* rather luckier or happier than in real life. — **sto'ryline** the main plot of a novel, film, television series, etc., or line along which the plot is to develop; **sto'ry-teller** a person who relates tales; a liar (*colloq*); **sto'ry-telling**. — **the same old story** an often-repeated event or situation; **the story goes** it is generally said. [A.Fr. *estorie* — L. *historia*.]

story[2]. See under **storey**.

stotinka *sto-ting'kə*, *n* a Bulgarian unit of currency (one hundredth of a lev): — *pl* **stotin'ki**. [Bulgarian.]

stoup or **stoop** *sto͞op*, *n* a holy-water vessel. [Cf. O.N. *staup* and Du. *stoop*; O.E. *stēap*.]

stoush *stowsh*, (*Austr* and *NZ*) *n* a fight, a brawl; a war. — *vt* and *vi* to fight. [Variant of Scot. *stooshie*, a disturbance.]

stout *stowt*, *adj* resolute; dauntless; vigorous; enduring; robust; strong; thick; fat. — *adv* stoutly. — *n* strong dark beer flavoured with malt or barley. — *adj* **stout'ish**. — *adv* **stout'ly**. — *n* **stout'ness**. — *adj* **stout-heart'ed**. — *adv* **stout-heart'edly**. — **stout-heart'edness**. [O.Fr. *estout*, bold — Du. *stout*.]

stove[1] *stōv*, *n* a closed heating or cooking apparatus; a fire-grate; a kiln or oven for various manufacturing operations. — *vt* to put, keep, heat or dry in a stove. — **stove enamel** a type of heatproof enamel produced by heating an enamelled article in a stove; **stove'pipe** a metal pipe for carrying smoke and gases from a stove; a tall silk hat (*colloq*; in full **stovepipe hat**). [O.E. *stofa*.]

stove[2] *stōv*, *pa t* and *pa p* of **stave**.

stow *stō*, *vt* to place, put, lodge; to put away; to store; to desist from (**stow it**, stop it; *slang*); to pack; to have room for. — *vi* (with *away*) to hide as a stowaway; to be able to be stowed away when not in use. — *n* **stow'age** act or manner of stowing; a place for stowing things; money paid for stowing goods; things stowed. — *n* **stow'er**. — *n* **stow'ing**. — **stow'away** a person who hides in a ship, etc. to get a free passage. — *adj* travelling as a stowaway; that can be packed up and stored, carried, etc. [O.E. *stōw*, place.]

STP *abbrev* for *Sanctae Theologiae Professor*, (L.) Professor of Theology.

str *abbrev* for steamer.

str. *abbrev* for strong.

strabism *strā'bizm* or **strabismus** *strə-biz'məs*, *n* a muscular defect of the eye, preventing parallel vision; a squint. — *adj* **strabis'mal**, **strabis'mic** or **strabis'mical**. [Gr. *străbos* and *strabismos*, squinting.]

strad. See under **Stradivarius**.

straddle *strad'l*, *vi* to part the legs wide; to sit, stand or walk with legs far apart; to seem favourable to both sides, to be non-committal (*colloq*). — *vt* to bestride; to set (the legs) far apart; to overshoot and then shoot short of, in order to get the range; to adopt a non-committal attitude or position towards. — *n* act of straddling; a non-committal position; a stock transaction in which the buyer obtains the privilege of either a *put* or a *call*; a style of high jump in which the legs straddle the bar while the body is parallel to it. [Frequentative of **stride**.]

Stradivarius *strad-i-vä'ri-əs* or *-vā'*, *n* a stringed instrument, usu. a violin, made by Antonio *Stradivari* (1644–1737) of Cremona (*colloq* short form **strad**).

strafe *sträf* or (esp. in N.Am.) *strāf*, *vt* to punish; to bombard; to rake with machine-gun fire from low-flying aeroplanes. — *n* an attack. [Ger. *strafen*, to punish, originally war slang of 1914.]

straggle *strag'l*, *vi* to wander from the main group or course; to linger behind; to stretch dispersedly or sprawlingly; to grow irregularly and untidily. — *n* a straggler; a stray; a vagrant. — *n* **stragg'ler**. — *n* and *adj* **stragg'ling**. — *adv* **stragg'lingly**. — *adj* **stragg'ly** straggling; irregularly spread out.

straight *strāt*, *adj* uncurved; in a right line; direct; upright; flat, horizontal; in good order; accurate; frank and honourable; respectably conducted; balanced, even, square; settled; downright; normal; with all debts and favours paid back, even; conventional in tastes, opinions, etc. (*slang*); heterosexual (*slang*); in sequence (*poker*); (of games, sets won) in succession (*tennis*); (of a theatrical part) not comic; (of a drink, esp. alcohol) undiluted, neat; uninterrupted; consistent; not under the influence of, or not in the habit of taking, drugs (*slang*). — *n* a straight condition; good behaviour; a straight line, part, course, flight, esp. the last part of a racecourse; a sequence of five cards, irrespective of suit, or the hand containing it (*poker*); a heterosexual person (*slang*). — *adv* in a straight line; directly; all the way; immediately; upright; outspokenly; honestly. — *vt* and *vi* **straight'en** to make or become straight. — *n* **straight'ener** something that straightens; a bribe (*criminal slang*). — *adj* **straight'ish**. — *adv* **straight'ly** in a straight line or manner; straightaway. — *n* **straight'ness**. — **straight angle** two right angles; **straight'edge** a strip or stick for testing straightness or drawing straight lines; **straight fight** (esp. in politics) a contest in which only two candidates or sides take part. — *adj* **straightfor'ward** going forward in a straight course; without digression; without evasion; honest; frank; easy to do or understand. — *adv* straightforwardly. — *adv* **straightfor'wardly**. — **straightfor'wardness**; **straight man** an actor who acts as stooge to a comedian. — *adj* **straight'-out** (*NAm*) out-and-out; see also **straight out** below. — **straight play** one without music; a serious drama as opposed to a comedy. — **go straight** to give up criminal activities; **keep a straight bat** (*fig*) to behave honourably; **keep a straight face** to refrain from smiling; **straight away** immediately; **straighten out** to disentangle, resolve; **straight off** straight away, without hesitation (*colloq*); **straight out** frankly, directly; **straight up** honestly, really (*colloq*; often *interrog*); **the straight and narrow** the virtuous way of life. [O.E. *streht*, past p. of *streccan*; see **stretch**.]

strain[1] *strān*, *vt* to stretch; to draw tight; to draw with force; to exert to the utmost; to injure by overworking; to force unnaturally, unduly or wrongly; to change in form or bulk by subjecting to a stress; to press to oneself, embrace; to squeeze out, express; to filter or sieve (esp. coarsely). — *vi* to make violent efforts; to tug; to retch; to have difficulty in swallowing or accepting (with *at*); to make efforts at evacuation of the bowels; to be percolated or filtered. — *n* the act of straining; a violent effort; an injury caused by straining, esp. a wrenching of the muscles; any change of form or bulk under stress; pitch, height; a section of a melody; a melody; emotional tone, key, manner. — *adj* **strained** having been strained; tense, forced or unnatural. — *adv* **strain'edly** (or *strānd'li*). — *n* **strain'er** someone who or something that strains; a sieve, colander, etc. — *n* and *adj* **strain'ing.** [O.Fr. *estraindre* — L. *stringĕre*, to stretch tight.]

strain² *strān, n* breed, race, stock, line of descent; natural, esp. inherited, tendency or element in one's character; a variety of bacterium or other organism. [App. O.E. *(ge)strēon*, gain, getting, begetting.]

strait *strāt, adj* narrow. — *n* a narrow part, place or passage, esp. (often in *pl*) by water; (usu. in *pl*) difficulty, distress, hardship. — *vt* **strait'en** to distress; to put into difficulties. — *adj* **strait'ened.** — **strait'jacket** a garment for the restraint of the violently insane; anything which inhibits freedom of movement or initiative (*fig*). — *adj* **strait-laced'** narrow in principles of behaviour; prudish. [O.Fr. *estreit* — L. *strictus*, past p. of *stringĕre*, to draw tight.]

strake *strāk, n* a strip; one breadth of plank or plate in a ship, from stem to stern; a section of a cart-wheel rim. [Related to **stretch.**]

stramonium *strə-mō'ni-əm, n* the thorn-apple; a drug like belladonna obtained from its seeds and leaves and used to treat asthma and nervous disorders. [N.L., poss. from a Tatar word.]

strand¹ *strand, n* (*poetic*) a sea or lake margin. — *vt* and *vi* to run aground; to leave helpless. — *adj* **strand'ed** driven on shore; left helpless without further resource. [O.E. *strand.*]

strand² *strand, n* a yarn, thread, fibre or wire twisted or plaited with others to form a rope, cord, etc.; a thread, filament; a tress; any component part (as of an argument). — *vt* to form from strands. — *adj* **strand'ed** (of a fur garment) made by resewing skins after they have been cut diagonally into strips.

strange *strānj, adj* alien; from elsewhere; not of one's own place, family or circle; not one's own; not formerly known or experienced; unfamiliar (often with *to*); interestingly unusual; odd; surprising; not easy to explain; distant or reserved; unacquainted, unversed (often with *to*). — *adv* **strange'ly.** — *n* **strange'ness** the quality of being strange; unexplained delay in strong interactions between certain elementary particles, represented by a quantum number (**strangeness number**) equal to a particle's hypercharge minus its baryon number. — *n* **strān'ger** a foreigner; a person whose home is elsewhere; a person unknown or little known; a visitor; a non-member; an outsider; a person not concerned; a person without knowledge, experience or familiarity (with *to*). — **strangeness number** see **strangeness**; **strange particles** kaons and hyperons, which have a non-zero strangeness (q.v.) number. [O.Fr. *estrange* — *extrā*, beyond.]

strangle *strang'gl, vt* to kill by compressing the throat; to choke; to constrict; to choke back, suppress or stifle. — *n* **strang'ler.** — *npl* **strang'les** a contagious disease of horses causing inflammation of the respiratory tract. — **strang'lehold** a choking hold in wrestling; a strong repressive influence. [O.Fr. *estrangler* — L. *strangulāre*; see next word.]

strangulate *strang'gū-lāt, vt* to strangle; to compress (e.g. a vein) so as to suppress or suspend circulation or other function. — *adj* **strang'ulated** strangled; constricted, much narrowed. — *n* **strangulā'tion.** [L. *strangulāre, -ātum* — Gr. *strangalaein*, to strangle, *strangos*, twisted.]

strangury *strang'gū-ri*, (*med*) *n* painful discharging of urine drop by drop. [L. *strangūria* — Gr. *strangouriā* — *stranx*, a drop, trickle, *ouron*, urine.]

strap *strap, n* a narrow strip, usu. of leather; a thong; a metal band or plate for holding things in position; a narrow flat projection, as on a strap-hinge; a looped band; anything strap-shaped; an application of the strap in punishment. — *vt* to beat or bind with a strap; to make suffer from scarcity, esp. of money: — *pr p* **strapp'ing**; *pa t* and *pa p* **strapped.** — *adj* **strap'less** without a strap or straps, esp. (of woman's dress) without shoulder-straps. — *adj* **strapp'ed** (*colloq*) short of money. — See also **strapped for** below. — *n* **strapp'er** a person who works with straps; a tall robust person (*colloq*). — *n* **strapp'ing** fastening with a strap; materials for straps; strengthening bands; a thrashing. — *adj* tall and robust. — *adj* **strapp'y** having (many) straps (used esp. of clothing and footwear). — **strap'-hanger** (*colloq*) a standing passenger in a train, bus, etc. who holds on to a strap for safety; **strap'-work** (*archit*) ornamentation of crossed and interlaced fillets. — **strapped for** (*slang*) short of. [Northern form of **strop.**]

strapontin *stra-pɔ̃-tɛ̃*, (Fr.) *n* a folding seat, as in a taxi, theatre, etc.

strapper, etc. See under **strap.**

strata *strä'tə, pl* of **stratum.**

stratagem *strat'ə-jəm, n* a plan for deceiving an enemy or gaining an advantage; any artifice generally. [Fr. *stratagème* — L. — Gr. *stratēgēma*, a piece of generalship, trick; see next word.]

strategy *strat'i-ji, n* generalship, or the art of conducting a campaign and manoeuvring an army; any long-term plan; artifice or finesse generally. — *adj* **strategic** (*strə-tē'jik*) or **strate'gical** pertaining to, dictated by, of value for, strategy. — *nsing* **stratē'gics** strategy. — *adv* **strate'gically.** — *n* **strat'egist** a person skilled in strategy. — **Strategic Defence Initiative** a strategic defence system proposed by the U.S. involving laser-equipped satellites deployed in space for destroying enemy missiles (*abbrev* **SDI**; also called **Star Wars**); **strategic position** a position that gives its holder a decisive advantage. [Gr. *stratēgia* — *stratēgos*, a general — *stratos*, an army, *agein*, to lead.]

strath *strath, n* (in Scotland) a broad valley. [Gael. *srath*, a valley — L. *strāta*, a street.]

strathspey *strəth-spā', n* a Scottish dance, allied to and danced alternately with the reel; a tune for it, differing from the reel in being slower. [*Strathspey*, the valley of the *Spey*.]

stratify, etc. See under **stratum.**

stratum *strä'təm, n* a layer; a bed of sedimentary rock; a layer of cells in living tissue; a region determined by height or depth; a level of society: — *pl* **stra'ta.** — *n* **stratificā'tion** (*strat-*). — *adj* **strat'ified.** — *adj* **strat'iform** layered; forming a layer. — *vt* **strat'ify** to deposit, form or arrange in layers; to classify according to a graded scale (*science* and *social science*). — *vi* to form or settle into levels or layers: — *pr p* **strat'ifying**; *pa t* and *pa p* **strat'ified.** — *n* **stratig'rapher** or **stratig'raphist.** — *adj* **stratigraph'ic** or **stratigraph'ical.** — *adv* **stratigraph'ically.** — *n* **stratig'raphy** the geological study of strata and their succession; stratigraphical features. — *adj* **stra'tose** in layers. — *n* **stratosphere** (*strat'* or *strāt'ō-sfēr*) a region of the atmosphere beginning about $4\frac{1}{2}$ to 10 miles up, in which temperature does not fall as altitude increases. — *adj* **stratospheric** (*-sfer'ik*). — *adj* **stra'tous** of stratus. — *n* **stra'tus** a wide-extended horizontal sheet of low cloud. — **strato-cū'mulus** a cloud in large globular or rolled masses, not rain-bringing. [L. *strātum, -ī, strātus, -ūs*, something spread, a bedcover, horse-cloth — *sternĕre, strātum*, to spread.]

straw *strö, n* the stalk of corn; dried stalks, etc. of corn, or of peas or buckwheat, used as fodder or for packing, making hats, etc.; a tube for sucking up a beverage; a trifle, a whit. — *adj* of straw; of the colour of straw. — *adj* **straw'like.** — *adj* **straw'y.** — **straw'board** a thick cardboard, made of straw; **straw boss** (*US*) an assistant foreman. — *n* and *adj* **straw'-colour** delicate yellow. — *adj* **straw'-coloured.** — **straw man** a man of straw (see under

man); **straw poll** an unofficial vote taken to get some idea of the general trend of opinion. — **clutch, catch** or **grasp at straws** or **at a straw** to resort to an inadequate remedy in desperation; **man of straw** see under **man; straw in the wind** a sign of possible future developments. [O.E. *strēaw*.]

strawberry *strö'bə-ri* or *stö'bri*, *n* the fruit (botanically the enlarged receptacle) of any species of the rosaceous genus *Fragaria*; the plant bearing it. — *adj* of the colour (pinkish-red) or flavour of strawberries. — *n* and *adj* **strawberry blonde** (a woman with hair that is) reddish-yellow. — **straw'berry-mark** a reddish birthmark; **strawberry-toma'to** the Cape gooseberry; **straw'berry-tree** a small tree (wild at Killarney) of the heath family, with red berries. [O.E. *strēawberige*, possibly from the strawlike appearance of the achenes.]

strawy. See under **straw**.

stray *strā*, *vi* to wander; to wander away, esp. from control, or from the right way; to digress; to get lost. — *n* a domestic animal that has strayed or is lost; a straggler; a waif; anything occurring casually, isolatedly, out of place. — *adj* gone astray; casual; isolated. — *adj* **strayed** wandering, gone astray. — *n* **stray'er.** — *n* and *adj* **stray'ing.** [O.Fr. *estraier*, to wander — L. *extrā*, beyond, *vagārī*, to wander.]

streak *strēk*, *n* an irregular stripe; the colour of a mineral in powder, seen in a scratch; a scratch; a strain, vein, interfused or pervading character; a line of bacteria, etc. (placed) on a culture medium; the line or course as of a flash of lightning; a rush, swift dash; a naked dash through a public place (*colloq*); a course, succession, esp. of luck. — *vt* to mark with streaks. — *vi* to become streaked; to rush past; to run naked in public (*colloq*). — *adj* **streaked** streaky, striped. — *n* **streak'er** a person or thing that streaks; a person who runs naked through a public place (*colloq*). — *adv* **streak'ily.** — *n* **streak'iness.** — *n* **streak'ing.** — *adj* **streak'y** marked with streaks, striped; (of bacon) fat and lean in alternate layers; uneven in quality. — **like a streak** like (a flash of) lightning. [O.E. *strica*, a stroke, line, mark.]

stream *strēm*, *n* a small body of running water; a river or brook, esp. a rivulet; a flow or moving succession of anything; a large number or quantity coming continuously; a division of pupils on the roll of a school consisting of those of roughly equal ability or those following a particular course of study; any similar division of people; a current; a drift; a tendency. — *vi* to flow, issue or stretch in a stream; to pour out abundantly; to float out, trail; to wash earth, etc. in search of ore. — *vt* to discharge in a stream; to wave, fly; to wash (earth, etc.) for ore; to divide (pupils, etc.) into streams. — *n* **stream'er** a flag, ribbon, etc. streaming or flowing in the wind; a luminous beam or band of light, as of the aurora; a person who washes detritus for gold or tin; a large bold headline (*journalism*); a narrow roll of coloured paper that streams out when thrown. — *adj* **stream'ered.** — *n* **stream'iness.** — *n* and *adj* **stream'ing.** — *adv* **stream'ingly.** — *adj* **stream'y.** — **stream'line** a line followed by a streaming fluid; the natural course of airstreams. — *vt* to make streamlined. — *adj* **stream'lined** having boundaries following streamlines so as to offer minimum resistance; a term of commendation with a variety of meanings, such as efficient, without waste of effort, up-to-the-minute, of superior type, graceful, etc. (*colloq*). — **stream of consciousness** the continuous succession of thoughts, emotions and feelings, both vague and well-defined, that forms an individual's conscious experience, often used to describe a narrative style which emulates this. [O.E. *strēam*.]

street *strēt*, *n* a paved road; a road lined with houses, broader than a lane, including or excluding the houses and the footways; those who live in a street or are on the street; (with *cap*) used in street names. — *adj* of or characteristic of the streets, esp. in densely populated cities, or to the people who frequent them, esp. the poor, the homeless, prostitutes, petty criminals, etc. (also in compounds). — **street'car** (*NAm*) a tram-car; **street credibility** (often abbreviated as **street cred**) trust, believability, popularity, support or trust from the man in the street; convincing knowledge of popular fashions, modes of speech, etc. — *adj* **street-cred'ible** (*colloq* short form **street-cred'**). — **street cries** the slogans of hawkers; **street'-door** the door of a house that opens on to the street; **street furniture** the various accessorial public items sited in the street, e.g. litter bins, parking meters, road signs; **street hockey** (orig. *US*) roller hockey; **street'lamp** or **street'-light** one set high on a lamppost to light a street. — *adj* **street'-level** at ground level; in or pertaining to the urban street environment, esp. street-trading; pertaining to the general population. — Also *n*. — **street'-sweeper** a person who, or a machine which, sweeps the streets clean; **street value** the cash value of an item when sold directly to the customer in the street, esp. illegally or on the black market; **street'-walker** anyone who walks in the streets, esp. a whore. — *n* and *adj* **street'-walking.** — **street'way** the roadway. — *adj* **street'wise** familiar with the ways, needs, etc. of the people who live and work on the city streets, e.g. the poor, the homeless, the petty criminals, etc.; experienced in, and able to cope with, the harsher realities of city life; cynical; wily. — **not in the same street as** much inferior to; **on the street** (*colloq*) homeless, destitute; **on the streets** (*slang*) practising prostitution; **streets ahead of** far superior to; **streets apart** very different; **up one's street** in the region in which one's tastes, knowledge, abilities, lie. [O.E. *strǣt*.]

Strega® *strā'gə*, *n* a sweet, orange-flavoured Italian liqueur.

strelitzia *strel-it'si-ə*, *n* any plant of the S. African *Strelitzia* genus of the banana family, with large showy flowers. [From Queen Charlotte, wife of George III, of the house of Mecklenburg-*Strelitz*.]

strength *strength*, *n* the quality, condition or degree of being physically or mentally strong; the power of action or resistance; the ability to withstand great pressure or force; force; degree or intensity; vigour; potency; a beneficial characteristic; complement (as of a workforce, team, etc.); a military force; the point, the truth (*Austr* and *NZ*). — *vt* **strength'en** to make strong or stronger; to confirm. — *vi* to become stronger. — *n* **strength'ener.** — *n* and *adj* **strength'ening.** — *adj* **strength'less.** — **get the strength of** (esp. *Austr* and *NZ*) to comprehend; **go from strength to strength** to move successfully forward, through frequent triumphs or achievements; **on the strength of** in reliance upon; founding upon. [O.E. *strengthu* — *strang*, strong.]

strenuous *stren'ū-əs*, *adj* active; vigorous; urgent; zealous; necessitating exertion. — *n* **strenuosity** (*stren-ū-os'i-ti*) or **stren'uousness.** — *adv* **stren'uously.** [L. *strēnuus*.]

strep. See **strepto-**.

strephosymbolia *stref-ō-sim-bō'liə*, *n* a visual disorder in which items are seen in mirror image; a reading problem in which letters, symbols, words, etc. are reversed, transposed or confused. [L.L. — Gr. *strephein*, to twist, turn, *symbolon*, a symbol.]

strepto- *strep-tō-* *combining form* denoting bent, flexible, twisted quality. — *adj* **streptococcal** (*-kok'l*) or **streptococcic** (*-kok'sik*). — *n* **Streptococcus** (*-kok'əs*) a genus of bacteria forming bent chains, certain species of which can cause scarlet fever, pneumonia, etc.; (without *cap*) any bacterium of this genus (*colloq* short form **strep**): — *pl* **streptococ'ci** (*-kok'sī* or *-kok'ī*). — *n* **streptomycin** (*-mī'sin*) an antibiotic obtained from a bacterium, *Streptomyces griseus*, and active against various bacteria. [Gr. *streptos*, twisted, flexible.]

stress *stres*, *n* strain; physical, emotional or mental pressure; the system of forces applied to a body; the insistent assigning of weight or importance; emphasis; relative emphasis placed on a syllable or word. — *vt* to apply stress to; to lay stress on; to emphasise. — *adj* **stressed**. — *adj* **stress'ful**. — *adj* **stress'less**. — *n* **stress'or** an agent or factor that causes stress. [Aphetic for **distress**.]

stretch *strech*, *vt* to extend (in space or time); to draw out; to expand, make longer or wider by tension; to spread out; to reach out; to exaggerate, strain, or carry further than is right; to lay at full length; to lay out; to place so as to reach from point to point or across a space; to hang by the neck (*slang*). — *vi* to be drawn out; to reach; to extend (with *over*, *across*, etc.); to be extensible without breaking; to straighten and extend fully one's body and limbs. — *n* the act of stretching; the state of being stretched; reach; extension; utmost extent; strain; extensibility; a single spell; a continuous journey; an area, expanse; a straight part of a course; a term of imprisonment (*slang*); a stretch limo (*slang*). — *adj* capable of being stretched. — *adj* **stretched**. — *n* **stretch'er** a person who stretches; anything used for stretching e.g. gloves, shoes, etc.; a frame for stretching a painter's canvas; a frame for carrying the sick or wounded; a cross-bar or horizontal member; a brick, etc. placed with its length in the direction of the wall. — *vt* to transport (a sick or wounded person) by stretcher. — *adj* **stretch'less** no longer liable to stretch. — *adj* **stretch'y** able, apt or inclined to stretch. — **stretch'er-bearer** a person who carries injured, esp. from the field of battle; **stretch limo** or **limousine** (*colloq*) a luxury car of extraordinary length. — **at a stretch** continuously, without interruption; with difficulty; **stretch a point** to go further, esp. in concession, than the strict rule allows; **stretch one's legs** to take a walk, esp. for exercise. [O.E. *streccan*.]

stretto *stret'ō*, (*mus*) *n* part of a fugue in which subject and answer are brought closely together; (also **strett'a**: — *pl* **strett'e** (-*tā*)) a passage, esp. a coda, in quicker time: — *pl* **strett'i** (-*ē*). [It., contracted.]

strew *strōō*, *vt* to scatter loosely; to cover dispersedly: — *pa t* **strewed**; *pa p* **strewed** or **strewn**. — *n* **strew'er**. — *n* **strew'ing**. [O.E. *strewian*, *streowian*.]

strewth *strōōth*, *interj* an oath (from *God's truth*).

stria *strī'ə* or *strē'a*, *n* a fine streak, furrow or threadlike line, usu. parallel to others; one of the fillets between the flutes of columns, etc. (*archit*): — *pl* **stri'ae** (*strī'ē* or *strē'ī*). — *vt* **strī'ate** to mark with striae. — *adj* **strī'ate** or **stri'ated**. — *n* **striā'tion**. — *n* **strī'ature** mode of striation. [L. *stria*, a furrow, flute of a column.]

stricken *strik'n*, (*literary* and *poetic*, or in certain compounds such as *grief-stricken*) *adj* struck, affected; afflicted. [Archaic past p. of **strike**.]

strickle *strik'l*, *n* an instrument for levelling the top of a measure of grain or shaping the surface of a mould; a tool for sharpening scythes. [O.E. *stricel*.]

strict *strikt*, *adj* exact; rigorous; allowing no laxity; austere; observing exact rules, regular; severe; exactly observed. — *adj* **strict'ish**. — *adv* **strict'ly**. — *n* **strict'ness**. — *n* **strict'ure** an adverse remark or criticism; abnormal narrowing of a passage (*med*); a binding; tightness. — *adj* **strict'ured** abnormally narrowed. [L. *strictus*, past p. of *stringĕre*, to draw tight.]

stridden. See under **stride**.

stride *strīd*, *vi* to walk with long steps; to take a long step. — *vt* to stride over; to cover a distance by striding: — *pa t* **strōde**; *pa p* **stridden** (*strid'n*). — *n* a long step; a striding gait; the length of a long step; men's trousers (*colloq*; esp. *Austr*). — **be into, get into** or **hit one's stride** to achieve one's normal or expected level of efficiency, degree of success, etc.; **make great strides** to make rapid progress; **take in one's stride** to accomplish without undue effort or difficulty. [O.E. *strīdan*, to stride.]

strident *strī-dənt*, *adj* (of a voice) loud and grating; urgent, commanding attention. — *n* **stri'dence** or **stri'dency**. — *adv* **strī'dently**. — *n* **strī'dor** a harsh shrill sound; a harsh whistling sound of obstructed breathing (*med*). — *adj* **stridūlant** (*strid'*) stridulating; pertaining to stridor. — *adv* **strid'ulantly**. — *vi* **strid'ūlate** to make a chirping or scraping sound, like a grasshopper. — *n* **stridūlā'tion** the act of stridulating. — *n* **strid'ūlātor** an insect that makes a sound by scraping; the organ it uses. — *adj* **strid'ūlatory**. — *adj* **strid'ūlous**. [L. *strīdēre* and *strīdĕre*, to creak.]

stridulant ... to ... **stridulous**. See under **strident**.

strife *strīf*, *n* contention or conflict; any sort of trouble, hassle. [O.Fr. *estrif*; see **strive**.]

striga *strī'gə*, *n* a stria; a bristle (*bot* and *zool*): — *pl* **strigae** (*strī'jē*). — *adj* **strī'gate** or **strī'gose** (or -*gōs'*; *bot* and *zool*) marked with streaks; having bristles. [L. *strīga*, a swath, a furrow, a flute of a column.]

strigil *strij'il*, *n* (in ancient Greece and Rome) a flesh-scraper used to clean the skin after bathing; (in bees) a mechanism for cleaning the antennae. [L. *strigilis*.]

strigose. See under **striga**.

strike *strīk*, *vt* to give a blow to or with; to hit, smite; to come into forcible contact with; to deal, deliver or inflict; to bring forcibly into contact; to impel; to put, send, move, render or produce by a blow or stroke; to render as if by a blow; to impress; to impress favourably; to afflict; to assail, affect; to affect strongly or suddenly; to mark off; (of a line, path, etc.) to draw, describe or give direction to; to arrive at, estimate, compute, fix, settle (e.g. a balance, an average, prices); to make (a compact or agreement), to ratify; to occur to; to assume (a pose or an attitude); to lower (e.g. a sail, flag, tent); to take down the tents of (*strike camp*); to dismantle; to sound by percussion or otherwise; to announce by a bell; to come upon; to stamp; to coin; to print. — *vi* to make one's way; to set out; to take a direction or course; to dart, shoot, pass quickly; to penetrate; to jerk the line suddenly in order to impale the hook in the mouth of a fish; to put forth roots; to chance, alight, come by chance; to interpose; to deal or aim a blow, perform a stroke; to sound or be sounded or announced by a bell; to hit out; to seize the bait; to strike something, such as a rock, sail, flag; to touch; to run aground; to go on strike: — *pa t* and *pa p* **struck**. — *n* a stroke, striking; an attack, esp. by aircraft; a raid; the direction of a horizontal line at right angles to the dip of a bed (*geol*); a find (as of oil), a stroke of luck; a cessation of work, or other obstructive refusal to act normally, as a means of putting pressure on employers, etc.; the part that receives the bolt of a lock; (in tenpin bowling) the knocking down of all the pins with the first ball bowled, or the score resulting from this; a ball missed by the batter, or a similar event counting equivalently against the batter (*baseball*); the position of facing the bowling, licence to receive the next delivery (*cricket*). — *n* **strik'er** someone who or something that strikes; a worker on strike; a batsman (*baseball*); a forward, attacker (*football*); the batsman facing the bowling (*cricket*). — *n* **strik'ing**. — *adj* that strikes or can strike; impressive, arresting, noticeable. — *adv* **strik'ingly**. — *n* **strik'ingness**. — *adj* **strike'-bound** closed or similarly affected because of a strike. — **strike'-breaker** an employee who works during a strike or who does the work of a striker, esp. if brought in with a view to defeating the strike; **strike'-breaking**; **strike force** a force designed and equipped to carry out a strike (*mil*); a special police unit trained to strike suddenly and forcefully to suppress crime; **strike'-pay** an allowance paid by a trade union to members on strike; **strik'ing-circle** (*hockey*) the area in front of goal from within which the ball must be hit in order to score; **strik'ing-price** (*stock exchange*) a stipulated price at which the holder may exercise their put or call option. — **be struck off** (of doctors, lawyers, etc.) to have one's name removed from the professional register because of misconduct; **on strike** taking part in a strike; **strike a match** to light it by friction or a grazing stroke; **strike at** to attempt to strike, aim a blow at; **strike back** to return a blow; **strike down** to fell; to make ill or cause to die; **strike home** to strike right to the point aimed at (also *fig*); **strike it rich** (*colloq*) to make a sudden large financial gain, e.g. through discovering a mineral deposit, etc.; **strike off** to erase from an account, to deduct; to remove (from a roll, register, etc.); to print; to separate by a blow; **strike oil** to find petroleum when boring for it; to make a lucky hit (*colloq*); **strike out** to efface; to bring into light; to direct one's energy and efforts boldly outwards; to dismiss or be dismissed by means of three strikes (*baseball*); to fail completely (*colloq*; esp. *NAm*; *n* **strike'out**); **strike through** to delete with a stroke of the pen; **strike up** to begin to beat, sing, or play; to begin (e.g. an acquaintance); **struck on** inclined to be enamoured of; **take strike** (*cricket*) (of a batsman) to prepare to face the bowling. [O.E. *strīcan*, to stroke, go, move.]

Strine *strīn*, (*colloq*) *n* a jocular name given to Australian English in terms of its vernacular pronunciation (with frequent assimilation, elision, etc.). — *adj* Australian. [Alleged pronunciation of *Australian*, coined by Alastair Morrison (pseudonym Afferbeck Lauder), esp. in his book *Let Stalk Strine*.]

string *string*, *n* a small cord or a piece of it; cord of any size; a piece of anything for tying; anything of similar character, such as a tendon, nerve, fibre; a leash; a shoelace (*US*); a stretched piece of catgut, silk, wire or other material in a musical instrument; (in *pl*) the stringed instruments played by a bow in an orchestra or other combination; (in *pl*) their players; anything on which things are threaded; a set of things threaded together or arranged as if threaded; a train, succession, file or series; (of horses, camels, etc.) a drove, number; a long bunch; a sloping joist supporting the steps in wooden stairs; (in *pl*) awkward conditions or limitations. — *adj* of, like or for string or strings. — *vt* to fit or provide with a string or strings; to tie up; to hang; to extend like a string; to put on or in a string; to take the strings or stringy parts off; to hoax, humbug (*slang*). — *vi* to stretch out into a long line; to form into strings; (of glues, etc.) to become stringy: — *pa t* and *pa p* **strung**. — *adj* **stringed** (*stringd*) having strings; of stringed instruments. — *n* **stringer** (*string'ər*) someone who or something that strings; a horizontal member in a framework (*archit*); a journalist employed part-time by a newspaper or news agency to cover a particular (esp. remote) town or area. — *adv* **string'ily**. — *n* **string'iness**. — *n* **string'ing**. — *adj* **string'less**. — *adj* **string'y** consisting of, or abounding in, strings or small threads; fibrous; like string or a stringed instrument. — **string band** a band of stringed instruments; **string bass** a double-bass; **string bean** (*US*) the French bean; **string'-board** a board facing the well-hole of a staircase, and receiving or covering the ends of the steps; **string'-course** a projecting horizontal course of bricks or line of mouldings running quite along the face of a building; **string'-piece** a long, heavy, usu. horizontal timber; the string-board of a staircase; **string quartet** a musical ensemble of two violins, a viola and a cello; music for such an ensemble; **string'-tie** a narrow necktie of uniform width; **string vest** a vest made of a netlike fabric; **string'y-bark** one of a class of Australian gum-trees with very fibrous bark. — **no strings** or **no strings attached** with no conditions or limitations (*adj* **no'-strings**); **on a string** under complete (esp. emotional) control; kept in suspense; **pull (the) strings** to use influence behind the scenes, as if working puppets (*n* **string'-pulling**); **string along** (*vt*) to string, fool; to give someone false expectations; (*vi*) to go along together, co-operate; **string out** to be under the influence of or addicted to a drug (*US colloq*); **string up** to hang by the neck (*colloq*); **strung out** (orig. *US*) suffering from drug-withdrawal symptoms; weak, ill or distressed as a result of drug addiction; addicted to a drug; highly stressed; **strung up** nervously tensed. [O.E. *streng*.]

stringent *strin'jənt*, *adj* rigorous; demanding close attention to detail, set procedure, etc.; characterised by difficulty in finding money. — *n* **strin'gency**. — *adj* and *adv* **stringendo** (*-jen'dō*; It.; *mus*) (to be played) with increasing speed. — *adv* **strin'gently**. — *n* **strin'gentness**. [L. *stringēns*, *-entis*, pres. p. of *stringĕre*, to draw together.]

stringer. See under **string**.

stringhalt *string'hölt*, *n* a catching up of a horse's legs, usu. of one or both hind-legs, caused by a muscle spasm in the hock. — Also **spring'halt**. [App. **string** (sinew) and **halt**[2].]

stringy. See under **string**.

strip *strip*, *vt* to pull, peel or tear off; to divest; to undress; to reduce to the ranks; to deprive of a covering; to skin, to peel, to husk; to expose; to deprive; to clear, empty; to dismantle; to clear of fruit, leaves, stems or any other part; to press out the last milk from (a cow, etc.) or obtain in this way; to cut in strips; to put strips on; to remove a constituent from a substance by boiling, distillation, etc. (*chem*); to break the thread of (a screw, etc.) or a tooth of (a gear); to unload (esp. a container or lorry). — *vi* to undress; to perform a striptease: — *pr p* **stripp'ing**; *pa t* and *pa p* **stripped**. — *n* a long narrow piece; a long thin piece of rolled metal, as steel strip; a narrow space in a newspaper in which a story is told in pictures (also **strip cartoon**); a lightweight uniform for running, football, etc.; a striptease; an airstrip. — *n* **stripp'er** someone who or something that strips; a striptease artist. — *npl* **stripp'ings** the last milk drawn at a milking. — **strip club** one which regularly features striptease artists; **strip lighting** lighting by means of long fluorescent tubes; **strip mill** a mill where steel is rolled into strips; **strip mine** (*NAm*) an opencast mine; **strip-po'ker** poker in which losses are paid by removing articles of clothing; **strip search** a search of a person's body (for hidden items, e.g. drugs, contraband) for which their clothes are removed. — Also *vt*. — **striptease'** an act of undressing slowly and seductively, esp. in a place of entertainment. — **strip down** to dismantle, remove parts from; **strip off** (*colloq*) to take one's clothes off. [O.E. *strȳpan*.]

stripe *strīp*, *n* a blow, esp. with a lash; a band of colour; a chevron on a sleeve, indicating rank; a striped cloth or pattern; a kind, particular sort (*US*). — *vt* to make stripes upon; to mark with stripes. — *adj* **striped** having stripes of different colours; marked with stripes. — *adj* **strip'ey** stripy. — *n* **strip'iness**. — *n* **strip'ing**. — *adj* **strip'y** stripelike; having stripes. [Perh. different words; Ger. *Streif*, stripe, Du. *strippen*, to whip.]

stripling *strip'ling*, (*literary*) *n* a youth. [Dimin. of **strip**.]

stripper. See under **strip**.

stripy. See under **stripe**.

strive *strīv*, *vi* to be in conflict (with *against*); to struggle (with *for*); to endeavour earnestly (with *to*); to make one's way with effort: — *pa t* **strove** (*strōv*); *pa p* **striven** (*striv'n*). — *n* **striv'er**. — *n* and *adj* **striv'ing**. — *adv* **striv'ingly**. [O.Fr. *estriver*.]

strobic *strob'ik, adj* like a spinning-top; spinning or seeming to spin. — *n* **strobe** (*strōb*) the process of viewing vibrations with a stroboscope; a stroboscope. — *n* **stroboscope** (*strōb'* or *strob'ə-skōp*) an optical toy giving an illusion of motion from a series of pictures seen momentarily in succession; an instrument for studying rotating machinery or other periodic phenomena by means of a flashing lamp which can be synchronised with the frequency of the periodic phenomena so that they appear to be stationary. — *adj* **stroboscopic** (*strob-* or *strōb-ə-skop'ik*). — **stroboscopic** or (more commonly **strobe) lighting** periodically flashing light, or the equipment used to produce it. [Gr. *strobos*, a whirling — *strephein*, to twist.]

strobila *stro-bī'lə, (biol) n* (in the life-cycle of jelly-fishes) a chain of segments, cone within cone, that separate to become medusoids; a chain of segments forming the body of a tapeworm: — *pl* **strobī'lae** (*-lē*). — *n* **strobile** (*strob'* or *strōb'īl* or *-il*) a strobila; a strobilus. — *n* **strobī'lus** a close group of sporophylls with their sporangia, a cone; a scaly spike of female flowers, as in the hop: — *pl* **strobī'li** (*-lī*). [Gr. *strobīlē*, a conical plug of lint, *strobīlos*, a spinning-top, whirl, pine-cone — *strobos* (see **strobic**).]

stroboscope, etc. See under **strobic**.

strode *strōd, pa t* of **stride**.

stroganoff *strog'ən-of, adj* (of meat) cut thinly and cooked with onions, mushrooms and seasoning in a sour cream sauce (as in esp. *beef stroganoff*). — *n* a dish cooked in this way. [After Count Paul *Stroganoff*, 19th-cent. Russian diplomat.]

stroke[1] *strōk, n* an act or mode of striking; a hit or attempt at hitting; a blow; an attack of apoplexy or of paralysis; the striking of a clock or its sound; a dash or line; a touch of pen, pencil, brush, etc.; a beat, pulse; a sudden movement or occurrence; a particular named style or manner of swimming; a single complete movement in a repeated series, as in swimming, rowing, pumping or the action of an engine; a stroke-oar; a single action towards an end; an effective action, feat or achievement. — *vt* to put a stroke through or on; to cross (commonly with *out*). — *vi* to make a stroke, as in swimming. — **stroke'-oar** the aftmost oar in a boat; its rower whose stroke leads the rest; **stroke play** (*golf*) scoring by counting the total number of strokes played (rather than the number of holes won). — **off one's stroke** operating less effectively or successfully than usual; **on the stroke (of)** punctually (at). [O.E. (inferred) *strāc*.]

stroke[2] *strōk, vt* to rub gently in one direction; to rub gently in kindness or affection; to put by such a movement; to reassure or flatter with attention (*NAm*); to strike, move (a ball, etc.) smoothly. — *n* an act of stroking. — *n* **strok'er**. — *n* **strok'ing**. [O.E. *strācian* — *strāc*, stroke (noun).]

stroll *strōl, vi* to walk leisurely; to wander from place to place. — *n* a leisurely walk. — *n* **stroll'er** a person who strolls; a pushchair (*NAm*). — *n* and *adj* **stroll'ing**. — **strolling player** (*hist*) an itinerant actor. — **stroll on!** an exclamation of surprise, disbelief (often used ironically). [Perh. Ger. *strolchen* — *Strolch*, vagrant.]

stroma *strō'mə, n* a supporting framework of connective tissue (*zool*); a dense mass of hyphae in which a fungus fructification may develop (*bot*); the denser part of a blood-corpuscle, chloroplast, etc.: — *pl* **strō'mata**. — *adj* **strōmatic** (*-mat'ik*) or **strō'matous**. [Gr. *strōma*, a bed, mattress.]

strong *strong, adj* (*compar* **stronger** *strong'gər*, *superl* **strongest** *strong'gist*) powerful; forcible; forceful; fast-moving (of wind); vigorous; hale; robust; of great staying power; firm; resistant; difficult to overcome; steadfast; excelling; efficient; of great tenacity of will and effective in execution; well-skilled or versed; rich in resources or means to power; well provided; numbering so many; of vigorous growth; stiff, coarse and abundant, indicating strength; (of language) without ambiguity, obscurity or understatement; (of language) intemperate, offensive and unseemly; having great effect; intense; ardent and convinced; performed with strength; powerfully, or unpleasantly powerfully, affecting the senses; vivid; marked; (of a syllable) stressed, emphasised; bold in definition; in high concentration; showing the characteristic properties in high degree; (of prices, markets, currency) steady or tending to rise; (of Germanic and similar verbs) showing vowel variation in conjugation (*gram*); of the strongest type of interaction between nuclear particles, occurring at a range of less than approx. 10^{-15} cm. and accounting for the stability of the atomic nucleus (*phys*). — *adj* **strongish** (*strong'ish*). — *adv* **strong'ly**. — **strong'arm** a person who uses violence. — *adj* by, having or using physical force. — *vt* to treat violently, show violence towards. — **strong'-box** a safe or strongly made coffer for valuables; **strong drink** alcoholic liquors; **strong head** power to withstand alcohol or any dizzying influence; **strong'hold** a fastness or fortified refuge; a fortress; a place where anything is in great strength; **strong interaction** (*phys*) one produced by short-range forces, involving baryons or mesons, and completed in about 10^{-23} seconds; **strong language** swearing; plain, emphatic language; **strong'man** a man who performs feats of strength, in a circus, etc.; a person, group, etc. that wields political, economic, etc. power; **strong meat** anything tending to arouse fear, repulsion, etc. — *adj* **strong-mind'ed** resolute, determined, having a vigorous mind. — **strong-mind'edness**; **strong'point** (*mil*) a favourably situated and well-fortified defensive position; **strong point** that in which one excels, one's forte; **strong'room** a room constructed for safe-keeping of valuables or prisoners. [O.E. *strang, strong*.]

strontia, strontian and **strontianite**. See under **strontium**.

strontium *stron'ti-əm*, or *stron'shi-əm* or *-shəm, n* an element (symbol **Sr**; atomic no. 38), a yellow metal. — *n* **stron'tia** its oxide, strontium monoxide. — *n* **stron'tian** (*-shi-ən*) (*loosely*) strontium, strontia or strontianite. — Also *adj*. — *n* **stron'tianite** its carbonate, a mineral first found in 1790 near *Strontian* (*stron-tē'ən*) in Argyllshire. — **stron'tium-90** a radioactive isotope of strontium, an important element in nuclear fall-out; **strontium unit** a measure of the concentration of strontium-90 in organic matters (*abbrev* **SU**).

strop *strop, n* a strip of leather, etc. for sharpening razors; a rope or band round a dead-eye (*naut*). — *vt* to sharpen on a strop: — *pr p* **stropp'ing**; *pa t* and *pa p* **stropped**. [Older form of **strap** — O.E. *strop*, prob. — L. *struppus*, a thong.]

strophanthus *strof-* or *strōf-an'thəs, n* a plant of the African and Asiatic *Strophanthus* genus of the periwinkle family, yielding arrow-poison; its dried seeds used in medicine. — *n* **strophan'thin** a very poisonous glucoside in its seeds. [Gr. *strophos*, twisted band, *anthos*, flower.]

strophe *strōf'i, (prosody) n* (in a Greek play) the song sung by the chorus as it moved towards one side, answered by an exact counterpart, the **an'tistrophe**, as it returned; part of any ode answered in this way; (*loosely*) a stanza. — *adj* **stroph'ic**. [Gr. *strŏphē*, a turn.]

stroppy *strop'i, (colloq) adj* quarrelsome, bad-tempered; rowdy, obstreperous and awkward to deal with. [Perh. **obstreperous**.]

strove *strōv, pa t* of **strive**.

struck. See under **strike**.

structure *struk'chər, n* the manner of putting together; construction; the arrangement of parts;

the manner of organisation; a thing constructed; a building; an organic form. — *vt* to organise, build up; to construct a framework for. — *adj* **struc'tural.** — *n* **struc'turalism** the belief in and study of underlying and often unconscious patterns in thought, behaviour, social organisation, literature, linguistics, etc. — *n* **struc'turalist.** — Also *adj.* — *adv* **struc'turally.** — *adj* **struc'tured** having a certain structure; having a definite structure or organisation. — *adj* **struc'tureless.** — **structural formula** a chemical formula showing the arrangement of atoms in the molecule and the bonds between them; **structural isomerism** (*chem*) the property of substances which are isomeric (q.v.) and differ in molecular structure, often having distinct physical and chemical properties (contrast with **stereo-isomerism**); **structural linguistics** the study of language in terms of the interrelations of its basic phonological, morphological and semantic units; **structural steel** a strong mild steel suitable for construction work; **structural unemployment** unemployment due to changes in the structure of society or of a particular industry. [L. *structūra* — *struěre, structum,* to build.]

strudel *shtro͞o'dl* or *shtrü'dl, n* very thin pastry enclosing fruit, or cheese, etc. [Ger., eddy, whirlpool, from the way the pastry is rolled.]

struggle *strug'l, vi* to strive vigorously in resistance, contention, or coping with difficulties; to make great efforts or exertions; to contend strenuously; to make one's way with difficulty. — *n* a bout or course of struggling; strife; a hard contest with difficulties. — *n* **strugg'ler.** — *n* and *adj* **strugg'ling.** — *adv* **strugg'lingly.** [M.E. *strogelen.*]

strum *strum, vt* and *vi* to sound the strings of a guitar, etc. with a sweep of the hand; to play in this way (rather than plucking individual strings): — *pr p* **strumm'ing;** *pa t* and *pa p* **strummed.** — *n* a strumming. [Cf. **thrum.**]

struma *stro͞o'mə, n* scrofula or a scrofulous tumour (*pathol*); goitre (*pathol*); a cushionlike swelling (*bot*): — *pl* **stru'mae** (*-mē* or *-mī*). — *adj* **strumatic** (*stro͞o-mat'ik*), **strumose** (*stro͞o'mōs*) or **stru'mous.** [L. *strūma*, a scrofulous tumour.]

strung *strung, pa t* and *pa p* of **string.**

strut[1] *strut, vi* to walk stiffly in vanity or self-importance; to walk in an ostentatious, swaggering manner: — *pr p* **strutt'ing;** *pa t* and *pa p* **strutt'ed.** — *n* a strutting gait. — *n* **strutt'er.** — *n* and *adj* **strutt'ing.** — *adv* **strutt'ingly.** — **strut one's stuff** (*slang*; orig. *US*) to dance; to show off one's talent (at a public activity, etc.); to show off generally. [O.E. *strūtian* or some similar form.]

strut[2] *strut, n* a rod or member that resists pressure; a prop. — *vt* to support as, or with, a strut or struts. [Cf. L.G. *strutt*, rigid, and foregoing.]

Struthio *stro͞o'thi-ō, n* the African ostrich genus. — *adj* **stru'thious** of the ostrich or any similar flightless bird. [L., — Gr. *strouthiōn*, an ostrich.]

strychnine *strik'nēn, n* a very poisonous alkaloid obtained from the seeds of the nux vomica plant. — *adj* **strych'nic.** — *n* **strych'ninism** or **strych'nism** strychnine poisoning. [Gr. *strychnos*, nightshade (of various kinds).]

stub *stub, n* a short piece left after the larger part has been used (of e.g. a cigarette, pencil, etc.); something blunt and stunted; a counterfoil; (also **stub'-nail**) a short thick nail; a stump. — *vt* to strike as against a stub; to extinguish by pressing the end on something (often with *out*); to remove stubs from; to grub (up): — *pr p* **stubb'ing;** *pa t* and *pa p* **stubbed.** — *adj* **stubbed** cut or worn to a stub; cleared of stubs; stumpy; blunt. — *n* **stubb'iness.** — *adj* **stubb'y** abounding with stubs; short, thick-set and strong. — *n* (*Austr*) a small, squat beer bottle or the beer it contains. [O.E. *stubb, stybb.*]

stubble *stub'l, n* a stump of reaped corn; such stumps collectively; straw; unshaven growth of beard. — *adj* **stubb'led** stubbly. — *adj* **stubb'ly** like or covered with stubble. [O.Fr. *estuble* — L.L. *stupula* — from L. *stipula*; see **stipule.**]

stubborn *stub'ərn, adj* obstinate, esp. unreasonably or troublesomely so; hard to work or treat; inflexible (*lit* and *fig*); rigid. — *adv* **stubb'ornly.** — *n* **stubb'ornness.**

stubby. See under **stub.**

STUC *abbrev* for Scottish Trades Union Congress.

stucco *stuk'ō, n* a plaster used for coating walls, making casts, etc.; a decorative work on a building done in stucco (*pl* **stucc'ōs**). — *vt* to face or overlay with stucco; to form in stucco: — *pa t* and *pa p* **stucc'oed** or **stucc'ō'd.** [It. *stucco*; from O.H.G. *stucchi*, crust, coating.]

stuck. See under **stick**[1].

stud[1] *stud, n* a horse-breeding establishment; the animals kept there; a stud-horse; a sexually potent or active man (*slang*). — *adj* kept for breeding; of a stud. — **stud'-book** a record of horses' (or other animals') pedigrees; **stud'-farm** a horse-breeding farm; **stud'-horse** a stallion kept for breeding; **stud poker** a variety of the game of poker in which bets are placed on hands containing some cards dealt face up. — **at stud** or **out to stud** being used for breeding purposes. [O.E. *stōd.*]

stud[2] *stud, n* an upright in a timber framework or partition; a crosspiece strengthening a link in a chain; one of several rounded projections on the soles of certain types of footwear improving the grip; a projecting boss, knob or pin; a large-headed nail; a type of fastener consisting of two interlocking discs; a type of fastener consisting of two discs joined by a central shank. — *vt* to adorn, set or secure with studs; to set at intervals: — *pr p* **studd'ing;** *pa t* and *pa p* **studd'ed.** — *adj* **studd'ed.** — *n* **studd'ing.** [O.E. *studu*, post.]

studding-sail *stun'-sl, n* a narrow sail set at the outer edges of a square sail when wind is light. — Also **stun'sail.**

student *stū'dənt, n* a person who studies; a person devoted to books or to any study; a person who is enrolled for a course of instruction in a college or university; an undergraduate. — *adj* **studied** (*stud'id*) well considered; deliberately contrived, designed; over-elaborated with loss of spontaneity; well prepared by study; well read. — *adv* **stud'iedly.** — *n* **stud'iedness.** — *n* **stud'ier.** — *n* **studio** (*stū'di-ō*) an artist's workroom; a workshop for photography, cinematography, radio or television broadcasting, the making of sound recordings, etc.: — *pl* **stu'dios.** — *adj* **studious** (*stū'di-əs*) devoted to or assiduous in study; studied; painstaking or painstakingly carried out; deliberate. — *adv* **stu'diously.** — *n* **stu'diousness.** — *vt* **study** (*stud'i*) to apply the mind to in order to acquire knowledge or skill; to examine; to scrutinise; to take into consideration; to think out. — *vi* to apply the mind closely to books, nature, acquisition of learning or of skill; to take an educational course; to rack one's mind; to muse, meditate, reflect: — *pr p* **stud'ying;** *pa t* and *pa p* **stud'ied.** — *n* an object of endeavour, solicitude or mental application; (in *pl*) related objects of mental application or departments of knowledge; a state of consideration; attentive and detailed examination; a scrutiny; application of the mind to the acquisition of knowledge or skill; a department of knowledge; a preliminary essay towards a work of art; an exercise in art; a musical composition affording an exercise in technique; a presentation in literature or art of the results of study; a room devoted to study. — **studio couch** a couch, sometimes without a back, that can be converted into a bed; **studio flat** a small flat consisting of one main room, or an open-plan living area; **studio pottery** pottery individually produced by the potter in a studio, rather than factory-made. [L. *studēre* (pres. p. *studēns*, *-entis*), to be zealous, *studium*, zeal, study.]

studio, study, etc. See under **student**.

stuff *stuf*, *n* matter; substance; essence; material; a preparation used or commodity dealt in in some particular industry or trade; cloth, esp. woollen; goods; luggage; provision; rubbish. — *vt* to line; to be a filling for; to fill very full; to thrust in; to crowd; to cram; to obstruct, clog; to cause to bulge out by filling; to fill (e.g. a fowl) with seasoning; to fill the skin of (an animal) so as to reproduce the living form; (of a man) to have sexual intercourse with (*vulg*); to load (a freight container); (in electronics manufacturing, etc.) to assemble the internal components of a machine in its external casing; to defeat very convincingly (*slang*). — *vi* to feed gluttonously; to practise taxidermy. — *adj* **stuffed** filled; filled out with stuffing; clogged in nose or throat, etc. (often with *up*). — *n* **stuff'er**. — *adv* **stuff'ily**. — *n* **stuff'iness**. — *n* **stuff'ing** that which is used to stuff or fill anything, straw, sawdust, feathers, hair, etc.; savoury ingredients put into meat, poultry, etc. in cooking. — *adj* **stuff'y** badly ventilated, musty; stifling; strait-laced; (of the nose) blocked up with mucus, etc. — **stuffed shirt** a pompous, unbendingly correct person, esp. if of little real importance. — **and stuff** and that sort of thing or rubbish; **bit of stuff** (*offensive slang*) a girl or woman considered sexually; **do one's stuff** to do what is expected of one; **get stuffed!** (*vulg slang*) *interj* expressing anger, derision, contemptuous dismissal, etc.; **hot stuff** (*colloq*) denoting a very attractive, effective, etc. person or thing; **knock the stuffing out of** to reduce (an opponent) to helplessness; **know one's stuff** to have a thorough knowledge of the field in which one is concerned; **stuff it** (or **them, you,** etc.; *vulg slang*) *interj* expressing disgust, scorn, frustration, etc.; **that's the stuff!** excellent!; **(a drop of) the hard stuff** (some) strongly alcoholic drink. [O.Fr. *estoffe*, stuff — L. *stuppa* — Gr. *styppē*, tow.]

stultify *stul'ti-fī*, *vt* to dull the mind of; to cause to appear foolish or ridiculous; to destroy the force of, as by self-contradiction: — *pr p* **stul'tifying**; *pa t* and *pa p* **stul'tified**. — *n* **stultificā'tion**. — *n* **stul'tifīer**. [L. *stultus*, foolish.]

stum *stum*, *n* must, grape-juice unfermented; new wine used to revive dead or vapid wine. — *vt* to renew the fermentation of with stum; to prevent over-fermenting of in the cask by adding stum: — *pr p* **stumm'ing**; *pa t* and *pa p* **stummed**. [Du. *stom*, must — *stom*, mute.]

stumble *stum'bl*, *vi* to take a false step, come near to falling in walking; to move or speak unsteadily or with hesitations; to err; to light by chance or error (with *across*, *on* or *upon*). — *n* a trip; a false step; a lapse; a blunder. — *n* **stum'bler**. — *adv* **stum'blingly**. — **stum'blebum** (*slang*; orig. and esp. *US*) an awkward, inept, ineffectual person; **stum'bling-block** an obstacle; a cause of perplexity or error. [M.E. *stomble*, *stumble*.]

stumer *stū'mər*, (*slang*) *n* a counterfeit coin or note; a forged or worthless cheque; a sham; a dud; a failure.

stumm. See under **shtoom**.

stump *stump*, *n* the part of a felled or fallen tree left in the ground; a short thick remaining basal part, esp. of anything that projects; a leg (*facetious*); one of the three sticks forming (with the bails) a wicket (*cricket*); a stumping walk or its sound; a pencil of soft material for softening hard lines, blending, etc.; a tree-stump or similar, used as a platform, e.g. by a public speaker. — *vt* to reduce to a stump; to remove stumps from; (of the wicket-keeper; sometimes with *out*) to dismiss by breaking the wicket when the striker is out of his or her ground (*cricket*); to nonplus, foil, defeat; to soften or tone with a stump; to traverse (an area) making political speeches. — *vi* to walk stiffly and heavily, as if on wooden legs; to make political speeches from improvised platforms, etc. — *n* **stump'er**. — *adv* **stump'ily**. — *n* **stump'iness**. — *nsing* **stumps** (*cricket*) the end of play. — *adj* **stump'y** short and thick. — **draw stumps** (*cricket*) to end play (also *fig*); **on the stump** engaged in a (political) speech-making tour, campaign; **stir one's stumps** to move, become active; **stump up** to pay up, fork out. [Cf. M.L.G. *stump*.]

stun *stun*, *vt* to render unconscious by a blow or similar; to stupefy, daze, as with din or sudden emotion: — *pr p* **stunn'ing**; *pa t* and *pa p* **stunned**. — *n* a shock, stupefying blow; stunned condition. — *adj* (of a weapon) designed to stun rather than kill. — *n* **stunn'er** someone who or something that stuns; a person or thing supremely excellent (*colloq*); a very attractive person (*colloq*). — *n* **stunn'ing** stupefaction. — *adj* stupefying, dazing; supremely excellent (*colloq*); very attractive (*colloq*). — *adv* **stunn'ingly**. — **stun grenade** or **gun**, etc. one designed to stun its target temporarily without causing serious injury. [O.Fr. *estoner*, to astonish; cf. O.E. *stunian*, to make a din — *stun*, a din.]

stung *stung*, *pa t* and *pa p* of **sting**.

stunk *stungk*, *pa t* and *pa p* of **stink**.

stunsail. See **studding-sail**.

stunt[1] *stunt*, *vt* to hinder from growth, to dwarf, check. — *n* a check in growth; a stunted animal. — *adj* **stunt'ed** dwarfed. — *n* **stunt'edness**. [O.E. *stunt*, dull, stupid; O.N. *stuttr*, short.]

stunt[2] *stunt*, *n* a difficult, often showy, performance, enterprise or turn; anything done to attract attention. — Also *adj*. — *vi* to perform stunts. — **stunt'man** a man paid to perform dangerous and spectacular feats (esp. a stand-in for a film actor).

stupa *stoo'pə*, *n* a Buddhist or Jain dome-shaped memorial shrine, a tope. [Sans. *stūpa*.]

stupe *stūp*, *n* a medicated piece of cloth used to relieve pain. — *vt* to treat with a stupe. [L. *stūpa* for *stuppa* — Gr. *styppē*, tow.]

stupefy *stū'pi-fī*, *vt* to make stupid or senseless (as with alcohol, drugs, etc.); to stun with amazement, fear, etc.: — *pr p* **stū'pefying**; *pa t* and *pa p* **stū'pefied**. — *adj* **stupefacient** (*-fā'shənt*) stupefying. — *n* a stupefying drug. — *n* **stupefaction** (*-fak'shən*) the act of stupefying; the state of being stupefied; extreme astonishment. — *adj* **stupefac'tive** stupefying. — *adj* **stu'pefied**. — *n* **stu'pefīer**. — *adj* **stu'pefying**. [L. *stupēre*, to be struck senseless, *facĕre*, to make.]

stupendous *stū-pen'dəs*, *adj* astounding; astoundingly huge; often used as a colloq. term of approval or admiration. — *adv* **stupen'dously**. — *n* **stupen'dousness**. [L. *stupendus*, gerundive of *stupēre*, to be stunned.]

stupid *stū'pid*, *adj* stupefied or stunned; deficient or dull in understanding; showing lack of reason or judgment; foolish; dull; boring. — *n* **stupid'ity** or **stu'pidness**. — *adv* **stu'pidly**. [L. *stupidus*.]

stupor *stū'pər*, *n* torpor; lethargy; a state of near-unconsciousness (as caused by alcohol, drugs, etc.). — *adj* **stu'porous**. [L. *stupor*, *-ōris* — *stupēre*.]

sturdy *stûr'di*, *adj* robust; stout; firmly built or constructed. — *adv* **stur'dily**. — *n* **stur'diness**. [O.Fr. *estourdi*, stunned, giddy.]

sturgeon *stûr'jən*, *n* any member of a genus of large fishes of N. temperate waters, with cartilaginous skull, long snout, and rows of bony shields on the skin, yielding caviar. [A.Fr. *sturgeon*, of Gmc. origin (O.H.G. *sturjo*).]

Sturmer *stûr'mər* or **Sturmer Pippin** (*pip'in*), (also without *caps*) *n* a variety of dessert apple named after *Sturmer*, a village in Essex where it was developed; an apple of this variety.

stutter *stut'ər*, *vi* and *vt* to speak, say or pronounce with spasmodic repetition of (esp. initial) sounds, usu. consonants; to stammer. — *n* a speech impediment characterised by spasmodic repetition of (esp. initial) sounds, usu. consonants. — *n* **stutt'erer**. — *n* and *adj* **stutt'ering**. — *adv* **stutt'eringly**. [A frequentative of obs. *stut*, to stutter.]

STV *abbrev* for: Scottish Television; Single Transferable Vote.

sty[1] *stī*, *n* a pen for pigs; any extremely filthy place; any place of gross debauchery: — *pl* **sties**. — *vt* and *vi* to put or keep in a sty: — *pr p* **sty'ing**; *pa t* and *pa p* **stied**. [O.E. *stig*, pen, hall.]

sty[2] or **stye** *stī*, *n* a small inflamed swelling on the eyelid. [Obs. or dialect *stian*, *styan* — O.E. *stīgan*, to rise.]

Stygian *stij'i-ən* or *stij'yən*, *adj* of the **Styx**, one of the rivers of Hades; hellish, infernal; black as the Styx. [Gr. *Styx*.]

stylar and **stylate**. See under **style**.

style *stīl*, *n* the manner of writing, mode of expressing thought in language or of expression, execution, action or bearing generally; the distinctive manner peculiar to an author or other; manner, form, fashion, esp. when considered superior or desirable; an air of fashion or consequence; a kind, type; a slender structure of various kinds (*biol*); the slender part of the gynaeceum, bearing the stigma (*bot*); a hand, pointer, index; a pointed instrument for writing on wax tablets; a similar instrument or tool of various kinds; a mode of reckoning dates (*Old Style*, according to the Julian calendar, as in Britain till 1752, Russia till 1917; *New Style*, according to the Gregorian calendar, adopted in Britain by omitting eleven days, 3–13 September 1752). — *vt* to arrange, dictate, the fashion or style of; to designate. — (In combination) **-style** denoting in the style of, resembling. — *adj* **sty'lar**. — *adj* **sty'late** having a style or a persistent style. — *adj* **style'less**. — *n* **sty'let** a probe; a wire in a catheter; a bristle-like process (*biol*). — *adj* **stylif'erous** (*bot* and *zool*) bearing a slender structure of various kinds. — *adj* **sty'liform** (*bot* and *zool*) like a style or a bristle. — *n* **stylīsā'tion** or **-z-**. — *vt* **sty'lise** or **-ize** to conventionalise; to give an elaborate, esp. non-naturalistic style to. — *adj* **sty'lish** displaying style; fashionable; showy; imposingly smart. — *adv* **sty'lishly**. — *n* **sty'lishness**. — *n* **sty'list** a person with a distinctive and fine (esp. literary, etc.) style; a person who arranges a style, esp. in hairdressing. — *adj* **stylist'ic**. — Also *n*. — *adv* **stylist'ically**. — *nsing* **stylis'tics** the science of the variations in language, including the effective values of different words, forms and sounds, that constitute style in the literary and also the wider sense. — *adj* **sty'loid** (*bot* and *zool*) like a style or bristle; forming a slender structure. — *n* a spiny structure on the temporal bone. — **style'-book** a book of forms for deeds, etc. or rules for printers and editors. — **in style** in a grand manner. [L. *stilus*, a writing instrument, literary composition or style, confused with Gr. *stȳlos*, a column.]

stylite *stī'līt*, *n* a recluse living on the top of a pillar in ancient times. [Gr. *stȳlītēs* — *stȳlos*, a pillar.]

stylo. See under **stylography**.

stylobate *stī'lō-bāt*, (*archit*) *n* the substructure of a row of columns. [Gr. *stȳlobatēs* — *stȳlos*, a column, *batēs*, someone who treads, from the root of *bainein*, to go.]

stylography *stī-log'rə-fi*, *n* a mode of writing or engraving with a style. — *n* **stylograph** (*stī'lə-gräf*; *colloq* short form **sty'lo**) a stylographic pen, from which ink is liberated by pressure on a needle-point. — *adj* **stylographic** (*-graf'ik*). [Gr. *stȳlos*, a style, *graphein*, to write.]

styloid. See under **style**.

stylometry *stī-lom'ə-tri*, *n* a method of studying literary style and development by means of statistical analysis. [Gr. *stȳlos*, a style, *metron*, a measure.]

stylopised or **-z-** *stī'lop-īzd*, *adj* infested (as bees) with a parasitic insect of the *Stylops* or a similar genus.

stylus *stī'ləs*, *n* the cutting needle used in making gramophone records; a durable needle (e.g. sapphire- or diamond-tipped) for replaying a disk recording; same as **style** as in the writing instrument or similar: — *pl* **styli** (*stī'lī*) or **sty'luses**. [Ety. as for **style**.]

stymie *stī'mi*, *n* a (formerly possible) situation on the putting-green in which an opponent's ball blocks the way to the hole (*golf*). — Now usu. *fig*. — *vt* to put in such a situation (also **lay someone a stymie**); to frustrate, thwart, prevent, block, stop: — *pa t* and *pa p* **sty'mied**. — *adj* **sty'mied**.

styptic *stip'tik*, *adj* drawing together; astringent; checking bleeding. — *n* a styptic agent. — **styptic pencil** a healing agent for minor cuts. [Gr. *stȳptikos* — *stȳphein*, to contract.]

styrax *stī'raks*, *n* any plant of the genus *Styrax* abounding in resinous and aromatic substances, e.g. benzoin. — *n* **sty'rene** an unsaturated hydrocarbon obtained from essential oils and coal-tar, forming thermoplastics on polymerisation. [Gr. *stȳrax*; cf. **storax**.]

Styx. See under **Stygian**.

SU *abbrev* for: Soviet Union (I.V.R.); strontium unit

suable *sū'* or *sōō'ə-bl*, *adj* that may be sued. — *n* **suabil'ity**.

suave *swäv*, *adj* (of a person, esp. a man) polite and sophisticated, esp. superficially so; smooth, bland. — *adv* **suave'ly**. — *n* **suavity** (*swäv'i-ti*). [Fr., — L. *suāvis*, sweet.]

sub. *abbrev* for subject.

sub- *sub-* or *səb-*, *pfx* denoting: (1) under, below; (2) subordinate, subsidiary; (3) part of, a subdivision of; (4) almost, nearly, slightly, imperfectly, bordering on; (5) secretly; (6) (*chem*) in smaller proportion. — *n* **sub** (*colloq*) a submarine; subsistence money, hence a loan, an advance payment; a subscription (also **subs**); a subeditor; a substitute; a subordinate. — *vi* (*colloq*) to act as a sub; to work as a newspaper subeditor; to work as a substitute. — *vt* (*colloq*) to subedit: — *pr p* **subb'ing**; *pa t* and *pa p* **subbed**. [L. *sub*, under, near; in composition also meaning in some degree, secretly.]

Words with the prefix **sub-** are listed in the following text or in the separate panel.

subadult *sub-ad'ult* or *sub-ə-dult'*, *adj* (usu. of an animal) fully or almost fully grown but not yet having developed all the adult characteristics; adolescent. — *n* an individual at subadult stage. [**sub-** (4).]

subalpine *sub-al'pīn*, *adj* bordering on the alpine; at the foot of the Alps. [**sub-** (4) and (1).]

subaltern *sub'əl-tərn*, *adj* (of military officers) under the rank of captain; particular (*logic*); being at once a genus and a species of a higher genus (*logic*). — *n* a subaltern officer; a proposition differing from another in quantity alone (both being affirmative or both negative, but one universal, the other particular) (*logic*). — *n* **subalternation** (*sub-öl-tər-nā'shən*) the relation between a universal and particular of the same quality. [L. *subalternus* — *sub*, under, *alter*, another.]

subaquatic *sub-ə-kwat'ik*, *adj* under water (also **subā'queous**); partially aquatic (*zool* and *bot*). — *adj* **suba'qua** of underwater sport. [**sub-** (1) and (4).]

subatom *sub-at'əm*, *n* a constituent part of an atom. — *adj* **subatom'ic** relating to particles constituting the atom and changes within the atom. — *nsing* **subatom'ics** the study of these particles and changes. [**sub-** (3).]

Subbuteo® *sub-oo'ti-ō, n* a version of table football, in which the toy players are separate figures that are flicked by the fingers.

subcellular *sub-sel'ū-lər, (biol) adj* occurring within a cell; smaller than a cell. [**sub-** (3) and (6).]

subclavian *sub-klā'vi-ən* or **subclavicular** *-klə-vik'-ū-lər, adj* under the clavicle. [**sub-** (1) and **clavicle**.]

subclinical *sub-klin'i-kəl, (med) adj* (e.g. of a disease or infection in its earliest stages) so slight or indiscernible as not to be detectable by usual clinical methods. [**sub-** (4).]

subcompact *sub-kom'pakt, (US) n* a small car, such as a sports car. [**sub-** (2).]

subconscious *sub-kon'shəs, adj* dimly conscious; (of memories, thoughts, etc.) of which the individual is only dimly aware but which exert an influence on his or her behaviour; distant from the focus of attention, but capable of being consciously recalled. — *n* the subconscious mind or activities. — *adv* **subcon'sciously**. — *n* **subcon'sciousness**. [**sub-** (4).]

subcontinent *sub-kon'ti-nənt, n* a great portion of a continent with a character of its own (a term formerly applied to South Africa, later to India); a landmass hardly large enough to be called a continent. — *adj* **subcontinent'al**. [**sub-** (2), (4) and (1).]

subcontract *sub-kon'trakt, n* a contract subordinate to another contract, as for the subletting of work. — *vi* **subcontract'** to make a subcontract. — *vt* to make a subcontract for. — *n* **subcontract'or**. [**sub-** (2).]

subcontrary *sub-kon'trə-ri, adj* (of a particular proposition in relation to another differing only in quality) such that at least one must be true (*logic*). — *n* a subcontrary proposition. [**sub-** (4).]

subcritical *sub-krit'i-kl, adj* of insufficient mass to sustain a chain reaction (*phys*); below the critical temperature for hardening metals. [**sub-** (1).]

subculture *sub'kul-chər, n* a social, ethnic or economic group with a particular character of its own within a culture or society; a culture (as of bacteria) derived from a previous one. — *adj* **sub'cultural**. [**sub-** (2) and (3).]

subdeacon *sub-dē'kən, n* a member of the order of the ministry immediately below that of deacon, preparing the vessels, etc., at the eucharist. [**sub-** (2).]

subdivide *sub-di-vīd', vt* and *vi* to divide into smaller divisions; to divide again. — *n* **subdivid'er**. — *adj* **subdivisible** (*-viz'*). — *n* **subdivision** (*-vizh'ən*). — *adj* **subdivis'ional**. — *adj* **subdivī'sive**. [**sub-** (3).]

subdominant *sub-dom'i-nənt, (mus) n* the tone immediately below the dominant. [**sub-** (1) and (4).]

subdue *sub-dū', vt* to overcome; to overpower; to subject; to make submissive; to allay; to reduce; to quieten; to tone down. — *adj* **subdu'able**. — *n* **subdu'al**. — *adj* **subdued'** toned down; quiet, restrained; dejected, in low spirits; passive. [O.Fr. *souduire* — L. *subdūcĕre*; *sub* and *dūcĕre, ductum*, to lead, take.]

subedit *sub-ed'it, vt* to select and edit material for (a newspaper); also, to assist in editing. — *n* **subed'itor**. — *adj* **subeditorial** (*-tör'i-əl*). — *n* **subed'itorship**. [**sub-** (2).]

suber *sū'bər, (bot) n* cork. — *n* **su'berate** a salt of suberic acid. — *adj* **subē'reous** or **suberic** (*-ber'ik*) of cork (**suberic acid** an acid, HOOC·$(CH_2)_6$·COOH, obtained by action of nitric acid on cork). — *n* **su'berin** the chemical basis of cork. — *n* **suberīsā'tion** or **-z-**. — *vt* **su'berise** or **-ize** to convert into cork. — *adj* **su'berose** or **su'berous** corky. [L. *sūber, -eris*, the cork oak.]

subfamily *sub'fam-i-li, n* a primary division of a family, of one or more genera. [**sub-** (3).]

subfloor *sub'flör, n* a rough floor forming the foundation for the finished floor. [**sub-** (1).]

subframe *sub'frām, n* the frame on which the coachwork of a motor car is built (cf. **chassis**); a frame built into a wall to which a door- or window-frame is fixed. [**sub-** (1).]

subfusc *sub'fusk* or *sub-fusk', adj* dusky; sombre. — *n* dark, formal clothes worn in combination with the academic gown, esp. at Oxford University. [L. *subfuscus* — *sub, fuscus*, tawny.]

subgenus *sub-jē'nəs, n* a primary division of a genus: — *pl* **subgenera** (*-jen'ə-rə*) or **subge'nuses**. — *adj* **subgener'ic**. — *adv* **subgener'ically**. [**sub-** (3).]

subgrade *sub'grād, n* levelled ground under the foundations of a road or a railway. [**sub-** (1).]

subhuman *sub-hū'mən, adj* less than human; below but near the human. [**sub-** (4).]

subirrigation *sub-ir-i-gā'shən, n* irrigation by underground pipes; irrigation from beneath. — *vt* **subirr'igate**. [**sub-** (1).]

Some words with **sub-** prefix; see **sub-** entry for numbered senses

subabdom'inal *adj* (1).
suba'cid *adj* (4).
subacid'ity *n* (4).
subā'gency *n* (2).
subā'gent *n* (2).
subang'ular *adj* (4).
subantarc'tic *adj* (4).
subarc'tic *adj* (4).
subar'id *adj* (4).
subaud'ible *adj* (4).
subbase'ment *n* (1).
sub'branch *n* (2) and (3).
sub'breed *n* (3).
subcat'egory *n* (3).
subcau'dal *adj* (1).
subcent'ral *adj* (1) and (4).
sub'class *n* (3).
sub'clause *n* (2).
subcommiss'ion *n* (2) and (3).
subcommiss'ioner *n* (2) and (3).
subcommitt'ee *n* (2) and (3).
subcrā'nial *adj* (1).
subcūtā'neous *adj* (1).
subcūtā'neously *adv* (1).
subdean' *n* (2).
subdean'ery *n* (2).
subdis'trict *n* (3).
subē'qual *adj* (4).
subequato'rial *adj* (4).
subfer'tile *adj* (4).
subfertil'ity *n* (4).
subglā'cial *adj* (1).
sub'group *n* (3).
sub'-head or **-heading** *n* (3).
sublibrā'rian *n* (2).
sublin'gual *adj* (1).
submicroscop'ic *adj* (4).
sub'office *n* (2) and (3).
sub'order *n* (3).
subor'dinal *adj* (4).
subphy'lum *n* (3).
sub-post'-office *n* (3).
subprin'cipal *n* (2).
subrē'gion *n* (3).
subrē'gional *adj* (3).
sub'section *n* (3).
subsēr'ies *n* (3).
sub'spēcies *n* (3).
subspecif'ic *adj* (3).
substan'dard *adj* (1) and (2).
sub'surface *adj* (1).
sub'system *n* (2).
subten'ancy *n* (2).
subten'ant *n* (2).
subter'minal *adj* (4).
sub'total *n* and *vt* (3).
sub'type *n* (3).
subvari'ety *n* (3).
subwar'den *n* (2).

subito *sōō'bi-tō*, (*mus*) *adv* suddenly; immediately. [It.]

subj. *abbrev* for: subject; subjective; subjunctive.

subjacent *sub-jā'sənt*, *adj* underlying. [L. *subjacēns*, *-entis* — *sub*, *jacēre*, to lie.]

subject *sub'jikt*, *adj* (often with *to*) under rule, government, jurisdiction or control; owing allegiance; under obligation; subordinate; subservient; dependent; liable; prone, disposed; dependent upon condition or contingency. — *adv* conditionally (with *to*). — *n* a person who is subject; a person who is under or owes allegiance to a sovereign or a state, etc.; a citizen; a thing over which a legal right is exercised; something having inherent attributes; a thing existing independently; the mind regarded as the thinking power (opp. to the *object* about which it thinks); that part of a sentence or clause denoting that of which something is said (*gram*); a topic; a matter of discourse, thought or study; a department of study; a theme; that which is treated or handled; that which it is the object of the artist to express; matter for any action or operation; a sufferer from disease, a patient; a person peculiarly sensitive to hypnotic influence; that on which any operation is performed; a theme or phrase upon which a movement of music is built; that of which something is predicated, or the term denoting it (*logic*). — *vt* **subject** (*səb-jekt'*) to make subject; to make liable; to subordinate; to submit; to subdue; to lay open. — *adj* **subject'ed** made subject. — *n* **subjec'tion**. — *adj* **subject'ive** relating to the subject; derived from, expressive of, or existing in, one's own consciousness; personal, individual; nominative (*gram*); introspective. — *n* (*gram*) the subjective case. — *adv* **subject'ively**. — *n* **subject'iveness**. — *n* **subjectivīsā'tion** or **-z-**. — *vt* **subject'ivise** or **-ize**. — *n* **subject'ivism** a philosophical doctrine which refers all knowledge to, and founds it upon, subjective states. — *n* **subject'ivist**. — *adj* **subjectivist'ic**. — *adv* **subjectivist'ically**. — *n* **subjectiv'ity**. — *adj* **sub'jectless**. — *n* **sub'jectship** the state of being subject. — **sub'ject-catalogue** a catalogue of books arranged according to subjects dealt with; **sub'ject-heading**; **sub'ject-matter** the subject, theme, topic. [L. *subjectus*, thrown under — *sub*, under, *jacĕre*, to throw.]

subjoin *sub-join'*, *vt* to add at the end or afterwards. — *n* **subjunc'tion** the act or fact of subjoining. [**sub-**, in addition, and **join**.]

sub judice *sub jōō'di-sē* or *sŏŏb ū'di-ke*, (*formal* or *legal*) *adj* under consideration. [L.]

subjugate *sub'jōō-gāt*, *vt* to bring under power or domination; to conquer. — *n* **subjugā'tion**. — *n* **sub'jugātor**. [L. *subjugāre*, *-ātum*, to bring under the yoke — *sub*, *jugum*, a yoke.]

subjunctive *səb-jungk'tiv*, *adj* subjoined, added to something; (of a verb) in the mood or form expressing condition, hypothesis or contingency (*gram*). — *n* the subjunctive mood; a subjunctive form; a verb in the subjunctive mood (e.g. *if I were you, far be it from me*, etc.). — *adv* **subjunc'tively**. [L. *subjunctīvus* — *sub*, *jungĕre*, to join.]

subkingdom *sub'king-dəm*, (*biol*) *n* a subordinate kingdom; a phylum. [**sub-** (2).]

sublease *sub'lēs*, *n* an underlease or lease by a tenant to another. — *vt* and *vi* **sublease'**. — *n* **sublessee'** the holder of a sublease. — *n* **subless'or** a person who grants a sublease. [**sub-** (2).]

sublet *sub-let'*, *vt* and *vi* to sublease: — *pa t* and *pa p* **sublet'**. — *n* a subletting. — *n* **sublett'er**. — *n* **sublett'ing**. [**sub-** (2).]

sublieutenant *sub-lef-ten'ənt* or in U.S. *-lōō-*, *n* a naval officer ranking with an army lieutenant — formerly *mate*, or *passed midshipman*. [**sub-** (2).]

sublime *səb-līm'*, *adj* exalted; majestic; supreme; of the highest or noblest nature; awakening feelings of awe and veneration; overwhelmingly great. — *n* that which is sublime; the supreme degree. — *vt* to raise up, to exalt; to transmute into something higher; to object to or obtain by sublimation; to deposit as a sublimate; to purify as by sublimation. — *vi* to undergo sublimation. — *vt* **sublimate** (*sub'lim-āt*) to elevate; to sublime; to purify by sublimation; to transmute into something higher; to direct unconsciously the sexual impulse into some non-sexual activity; to direct into a higher channel. — *n* (*chem*) a product of sublimation, esp. corrosive sublimate. — *adj* sublimed or sublimated. — *adj* **sub'limated**. — *n* **sublimā'tion** the change from solid to vapour without passing through the liquid state — usu. with subsequent change back to solid (*chem*); purification by this process; elevation; ecstasy; the acme, height; transmutation into something higher; the unconscious diversion towards higher aims of the energy attaching to an instinct (often sexual instinct). — *adj* **sublimed** (*səb-līmd'*). — *adv* **sublime'ly**. — *n* **sublime'ness**. — *n* and *adj* **sublīm'ing**. — *n* **sublimity** (*səb-lim'i-ti*). [L. *sublimis*, in a high position, exalted — *sublimāre*, *-ātum*, to exalt.]

subliminal *sub-lim'in-əl*, *adj* beneath the threshold of consciousness, subconscious. — *adv* **sublim'inally**. — **subliminal advertising** advertising on television, in the cinema, etc. directed to the subconscious, shown too rapidly and briefly to make a conscious impression but intended to have a subliminal effect. [L. *sub*, under, *līmen*, *-inis*, threshold.]

sublunary *sub-lōō'nər-i*, *adj* under the moon; earthly, of this world; between (the orbit of) the moon and the earth, under the moon's influence. — Also **sublu'nar**. [**sub-** (1).]

submachine-gun *sub-mə-shēn'-gun*, *n* a light machine-gun, usu. one fired from the shoulder or hip. [**sub-** (4).]

submarginal *sub-mär'ji-nəl*, *adj* near the margin; (of land) that cannot be farmed profitably. [**sub-** (4).]

submarine *sub'mə-rēn*, *adj* under the sea; under the surface of the sea. — *n* a submersible vessel, esp. for warfare. — *n* **submarin'er** (or *-mar'in-*) a member of the crew of a submarine. [**sub-** (1).]

submaxillary *sub-maks'i-lə-ri*, or *-il'ə-ri*, (*anat*) *adj* of or under the lower jaw. [**sub-** (1).]

submediant *sub-mē'di-ənt*, (*mus*) *n* the sixth note above the tonic. [**sub-** (1).]

submerge *səb-mûrj'*, *vt* to put under the surface of liquid; to sink; to cover over with liquid; to overwhelm; to conceal, suppress. — *vi* to sink under the surface of liquid. — *adj* **submerged'** sunk; entirely under the surface of liquid; growing under water, submersed; obscured, concealed; swamped. — *n* **submerg'ence** submersion. — *vt* **submerse** (*-mûrs'*) to submerge. — *n* **submersibil'ity**. — *adj* **submers'ible** capable of being submerged at will. — *n* a submersible boat. — *n* **submer'sion** (*-shən*) the act of submerging; the state or fact of being submerged. [L. *submergĕre*, *-mersum* — *sub*, *mergĕre*, to plunge.]

subminiature *sub-min'i-chər*, *adj* smaller than miniature; (of a camera) of a very small size, for taking photographs on 16 mm. film. — *n* a subminiature camera. [**sub-** (1).]

submit *sub-mit'*, *vt* to yield, resign; to subordinate; to subject; to offer, lodge or refer for decision, consideration, sanction, arbitration, etc.; to put forward or suggest in respectful (e.g. legal) debate. — *vi* to yield; to surrender; to be resigned; to consent: — *pr p* **submitt'ing**; *pa t* and *pap* **submitt'ed**. — *adj* **submiss'ible**. — *n* **submission** (*-mish'ən*) an act of submitting; a reference, or agreement to refer, to arbitration; a view submitted; resignedness, submissiveness; a surrender. — *adj* **submiss'ive** willing or ready to submit; yielding. — *adv* **submiss'ively**. — *n* **submiss'iveness**. — *adj* **submitt'ed**. — *n* **submitt'er**. — *n* and *adj* **submitt'ing**. [L. *sub*, beneath, *mittĕre*, *missum*, to send.]

submucosa *sub-mū-kō'sə*, (*anat*) *n* the connective tissue lying under a mucous membrane: — *pl* **submuco'sae** (*-sē*). — *adj* **submucō'sal** or **sub-mū'cous.** [**sub-** (1).]

submultiple *sub-mul'ti-pl*, *n* an aliquot part, a number that will divide into another number without a remainder. [L.L. *submultiplus.*]

subnormal *sub-nör'məl*, *adj* less than normal, esp. (*med*) of a person with a low range of intelligence. — *n* **subnormal'ity.** [**sub-** (4) and (1).]

subnuclear *sub-nū'kli-ər*, (*phys*) *adj* referring to particles within the nucleus of an atom. [**sub-** (3).]

suborbital *sub-ör'bi-təl*, *adj* below the orbit of the eye (*anat*); of less than a complete orbit. [**sub-** (1).]

subordinate *sub-ör'di-nāt* or *-nit*, *adj* lower in order, rank, nature, power, etc.; dependent; under orders of another; lower in a series of successive divisions; underlying. — *n* a person or thing that is subordinate or ranked lower; a person who works under another. — *vt* (*-nāt*) to place in a lower order; to consider of less value; to subject. — *adv* **subor'dinately.** — *n* **subordinā'tion.** — *adj* **subor'dinātive.** — **subordinate clause** (*gram*) a clause which cannot function as a separate sentence in its own right, but performs an adjectival, adverbial or nominal function; **subordinating conjunction** (*gram*) a conjunction which introduces a subordinate clause. [L.L. *subordinātus* — *sub-*, *ordināre*, to ordain.]

suborn *səb-örn'*, *vt* to bribe or procure to commit perjury or some other unlawful or wrongful act. — *n* **subornā'tion** (*sub-ör-*). — *n* **suborn'er** (*səb-*). [L. *sub-*, in sense of secret, *ornāre*, to equip.]

subplot *sub'plot*, *n* a subordinate plot, as in a play. [**sub-** (2).]

subpoena *sub-* or *sə-pē'nə*, *n* a writ commanding attendance (e.g. of a witness) or submission (e.g. of a document) as evidence in court. — *vt* to serve with such a writ: — *pa t* and *pa p* **subpoe'na'd** or **subpoe'naed.** [L.]

subreption *sub-rep'shən*, (*formal* or *legal*) *n* procuring an advantage by concealing the truth (distinguished from *obreption*). [L. *subreptiō*, *-ōnis* — *sub-*, secretly, *rapěre*, to snatch.]

subrogate *sub'rō-gāt* or *-rə-*, *vt* to substitute; to put in place of another party as successor to that party's rights (*legal*). — *n* **subrogā'tion.** [See ety. for **surrogate.**]

sub rosa *sub rō'zə* or *sŏŏb ro'zä*, (L.) privately, in confidence; lit., under the rose (a traditional symbol of secrecy).

subroutine *sub'rōō-tēn*, *n* a part of a computer program, complete in itself, which performs a specific task, and which can be called into use at any time throughout the running of the main program. [**sub-** (2).]

subs. See under **sub-**.

subscribe *səb-skrīb'*, *vi* (usu. with *to*) to sign one's name; to assent, agree; to contribute money; to put one's name down as a purchaser or donor; to make periodical payments by arrangement. — *vt* to sign (orig. and esp. at the bottom); to profess to be (by signing); to declare assent to; to make a signed promise of payment for or regular contributions to. — *adj* **subscrīb'able.** — *adj* **subscrībed'.** — *n* **subscrīb'er.** — *n* and *adj* **subscrīb'ing.** — *adj* and *n* **subscript** (*sub'skript*) (a character) written or printed beneath the normal line of script or type, esp. in *chem*, *math*, etc. (e.g. the number 2 in H_2O). — *n* **subscrip'tion** an act of subscribing; that which is subscribed; a membership fee; a contribution to a fund, society, etc.; a method of sale to subscribers; a raising of money from subscribers; advance ordering, esp. of a book before publication; an advance order, esp. for a book before publication; a signature; assent, sanction, endorsement. — *adj* **subscrip'tive.** — **subscriber trunk dialling** a dialling system in which subscribers in exchanges in many countries of the world can dial each other directly (abbrev. **STD**). [L. *subscrīběre* — *sub*, *scrīběre*, to write.]

subsea *sub'sē*, *adj* occurring, used, etc. under the surface of the sea. [**sub-** (1).]

subsequence[1]. See **subsequent.**

subsequence[2] *sub'sē-kwəns*, *n* a sequence (esp. in *math*) that forms part of another sequence. [**sub-** (3).]

subsequent *sub'si-kwənt*, *adj* following or coming after. — Also *adv* (with *to*) after. — *n* **sub'sequence** a subsequent occurrence, something that follows, a result. — *adv* **sub'sequently.** [L. *subsequēns*, *-entis*, pres. p. of *subsequī* — *sub*, under, after, *sequī*, to follow.]

subserve *sub-sûrv'*, *vt* to help forward. — *n* **subser'vience** or **subser'viency.** — *adj* **subser'vient** obsequious; serving to promote, instrumental; subject, subordinate. — *adv* **subser'viently.** [L. *subservīre* — *sub*, under, *servīre*, to serve.]

subset *sub'set*, (*math*) *n* a set contained within a larger set. [**sub-** (3).]

subshrub *sub'shrub*, *n* a low-growing shrub. — *adj* **subshrubb'y.** [**sub-** (4).]

subside *səb-sīd'*, *vi* to settle, sink down; to fall into a state of quiet or calm. — *n* **subsidence** (*sub'si-dəns*; often *səb-sī'dəns*) the process of subsiding, settling or sinking. [L. *subsīděre* — *sub*, down, *sīděre*, to settle.]

subsidy *sub'si-di*, *n* aid in the form of money; a grant of public money in aid of some enterprise, industry, etc., or to keep down the price of a commodity, or from one state to another; a special parliamentary grant of money to the king (*hist*). — *adv* **subsid'iarily.** — *adj* **subsid'iary** supplying a subsidy, help, or additional supplies; aiding; subordinate. — *n* a person who, or thing which, aids or supplies; a subordinate; a subsidiary company. — *n* **subsidiar'ity** the state or quality of being a subsidiary; the concept of a central governing body allowing its member states, branches, etc. to take decisions on all issues best dealt with at subsidiary level. — *vt* **sub'sidise** or **-ize** to provide with a subsidy, grant or regular allowance; to purchase the aid of, to buy over. — **subsidiary company** one of which another company holds most of the shares. [L. *subsidium*, orig. troops stationed behind in reserve, aid — *sub*, under, *sīděre*, to settle.]

subsist *səb-sist'*, *vi* to have existence (often with *in*); to have the means of living, stay alive (often with *on*); to remain, continue; to consist or be inherent. — *n* **subsist'ence** the state of being subsistent; real being; the means of supporting life; livelihood. — *adj* (used e.g. of an allowance or wage) providing the bare necessities of living. — *adj* **subsist'ent.** — **subsistence farming** farming in which the land-yield will support the farmer, but leave little or nothing to be sold; **subsistence level** the level of income which will purchase bare necessities only; **subsistence money** or **allowance** part of wages paid in advance for immediate needs; **subsistence wage** one fixed at subsistence level. [L. *subsistěre*, to stand still — *sub*, under, *sistěre*, to stand.]

subsoil *sub'soil*, *n* broken-up rock underlying the soil, i.e. the layer between the bedrock and the surface soil. — *vt* to turn up or loosen the subsoil of. [**sub-** (1).]

subsolar *sub-sō'lər*, *adj* directly under the sun, as a point on the earth's surface where the sun is vertically overhead. [**sub-** (1).]

subsonic *sub-son'ik*, *adj* having, or (capable of) travelling at, a speed slower than that of sound. [**sub-** (4).]

subst. *abbrev* for: substantive (*gram*); substitute.

substance *sub'stəns*, *n* something in which qualities or attributes exist, the existence to which qualities belong; that which makes anything what it is; the principal part; subject-matter; body, solidity; matter, material; a kind of matter, esp. one of definite chemical nature; wealth, property; solid worth; foundation, ground. — *adj* **substantial** (*səb-stan'shl*) of or having substance; being a substance; actually existing; real; material; solid; stable; solidly based; enduring; firm, stout, strong; considerable in amount, bulky; well-to-do, wealthy, influential; of firm, solid value. — *vt* **substan'tialise** or **-ize** to give reality to. — *n* **substan'tialism** the philosophical theory that there is a real existence or substratum underlying phenomena. — *n* **substan'tialist.** — *n* **substantiality** (*-shi-al'i-ti*). — *adv* **substan'tially.** — *vt* **substan'tiate** (*-shi-āt* or *-si-āt*) to prove or confirm. — *n* **substantiā'tion.** — *adj* **substantival** (*sub-stən-tī'vl*) of, or of the nature of, a substantive. — *adv* **substantī'vally.** — *adj* **sub'stantive** (*-tiv*) relating to substance; expressing existence; real; of real, independent importance; substantival; (of dyes) taking effect without a mordant; definite and permanent; considerable in amount. — *n* (*gram*) a noun. — *adv* **sub'stantively.** — *n* **sub'stantiveness.** — *vt* **sub'stantivise** or **-ize** (or *-stan'*) to turn into a noun. — **in substance** in general; in the most important aspects. [L. *substantia*, substance, essence, property — *sub*, under, *stāre*, to stand.]

substation *sub'stā-shən*, *n* a subordinate station, esp. a switching, transforming or converting electrical station intermediate between the generating station and the low-tension distribution network. [**sub-** (2).]

substitute *sub'sti-tūt*, *n* one put in place of another; a thing used instead of another; a deputy. — *vt* to use instead of, or put in the place of, something else (often with *for*). — *vi* (orig. *US*) to act as substitute. — *n* **substit'uent** something that may be, or is, substituted, esp. an atom or group replacing another in a molecule. — Also *adj*. — *adj* **substitū'table.** — *adj* **sub'stituted.** — *n* **substitū'tion** the act of substituting; the condition of being a substitute; the substituting of one atom or radical for another without breaking up the molecule (*chem*). — *adj* **substitū'tional** or **substitū'tionary.** — *adv* **substitū'tionally.** — *adj* **sub'stitūtive.** — *adv* **sub'stitutively.** [L. *substituěre*, *-ūtum* — *sub*, under, *statuěre*, to set.]

substrata, substrate, etc. See under **substratum.**

substratosphere *sub-strat'ō-sfēr*, *n* the region of the atmosphere below the stratosphere and over $3\frac{1}{2}$ miles above the earth. [**sub-** (4).]

substratum *sub-strā'təm* or *-strä'təm*, *n* a basis, foundation, ground; the material in which a plant grows or on which an animal moves or rests; an underlying layer: — *pl* **substra'ta.** — *n* **sub'strate** a substratum; a base; the substance on which an enzyme acts; the substances used by a plant in respiration (*bot*). — *adj* **substrā'tive.** [L. *substerněre*, *-strātum* — *sub*, *sterněre*, to spread.]

substructure *sub'struk-chər*, *n* an understructure; a foundation. — *adj* **substruc'tural.** [**sub-** (1).]

subsume *sub-sūm'*, *vt* to take in under a more general term or proposition; to include in something larger; to take over (*officialese*). — *n* **subsumption** (*səb-sump'shən*). — *adj* **subsump'tive.** [L. *sub*, under, *sūměre*, to take.]

subteen *sub'tēn*, (chiefly *US*) *n* and *adj* (a child) younger than thirteen years. [**sub-** (1).]

subtemperate *sub-tem'pər-it*, *adj* slightly colder than temperate, cold-temperate. [**sub-** (4).]

subtend *səb-tend'*, *vt* to be opposite to (as a hypotenuse is to a right-angle) or to extend under (as a chord does an arc) (*geom*); to be situated immediately below (as a leaf is to a bud in its axil) (*bot*). [L. *sub*, under, *tenděre*, *tentum* or *tēnsum*, to stretch.]

subter- *sub-tər-*, *combining form* signifying under. [L.]

subterfuge *sub'tər-fūj*, *n* an evasive device, as used in discussion or argument; action taken or manoeuvres made, to evade, conceal or obscure. [L. *subter*, under.]

subterranean *sub-tə-rā'ni-ən*, *adj* underground; operating underground; hidden, working, etc. in secret. — *adj* **subterres'trial** existing underground. [L. *sub*, under, *terra*, the earth.]

subtext *sub'tekst*, *n* an unstated message conveyed through the form of a picture, film, book, etc. [**sub-** (1).]

subtitle *sub'tī-tl*, *n* (in a film, etc.) a printed translation, at the foot of the screen, of dialogue that is in a language foreign to the viewers, or other descriptive text similarly displayed; (in a book, etc.) an additional or second title. — *vt* to provide with a subtitle. [**sub-** (2).]

subtle *sut'l*, *adj* tenuous, slight; elusive, impalpable; showing or calling for fine discrimination; delicate, refined; overrefined or overrefining; abstruse; crafty, artful; insidious, devious. — *n* **subtilīsā'tion** or **-z-** (*sut-*). — *vt* **subtilise** or **-ize** (*sut'*) to rarefy, refine; to make subtle. — *vi* to refine, use subtlety. — *n* **subt'leness** or **subt'lety** the state or quality of being subtle; a subtle trick or refinement. — *adv* **subt'ly.** [O.Fr. *soutil* and its source L. *subtīlis* — *sub*, under, *tēla*, a web.]

subtonic *sub-ton'ik*, (*mus*) *n* the note immediately below the tonic, the leading note. [**sub-** (1).]

subtopia *sub-tō'pi-ə*, (*derog*) *n* a region where the city has sprawled into the country. — *adj* **subto'pian.** [L. *sub*, under, Gr. *topos*, a place; modelled on **Utopia.**]

subtract *səb-trakt'*, *vt* to withdraw, remove; to take from another quantity so as to find the difference (*math*). — *n* **subtrac'ter.** — *n* **subtrac'tion** withdrawal, removal; the operation of finding the difference between two quantities by taking one from the other (*math*). — *adj* **subtract'ive.** [L. *sub-* (in sense of away), *trahěre*, *tractum*, to draw.]

subtrahend *sub'trə-hend*, (*math*) *n* that which is to be subtracted. [L. *sub-*, away, *trahendus*, requiring to be drawn (gerundive of *trahěre*, to draw).]

subtropical *sub-trop'i-kl* or **subtropic** *-trop'ik*, *adj* bordering on the world's tropical regions; characteristic of (the climate, etc. of) these regions. — *adv* **subtrop'ically.** — *npl* **subtrop'ics.**

subulate *sū'bū-lāt*, (*biol*, esp. *bot*) *adj* awl-shaped, slender and tapering. [L. *sūbula*, an awl.]

suburb *sub'ərb*, *n* a (usu. residential) district adjoining a town; (in *pl*) the outskirts of a town; outskirts generally. — *adj* **suburban** (*səb-ûr'bən*) situated or living in the suburbs; typical of the suburbs; without the good qualities either of town or country; provincial, narrow in outlook. — *n* someone living in a suburb. — *n* **suburbanisā'tion** or **-z-.** — *vt* **subur'banise** or **-ize** to make suburban. — *n* **subur'banism** the state of being suburban. — *n* **subur'banite** a person who lives in the suburbs. — *n* **subur'bia** the suburban world. [L. *suburbium* — *sub*, under, near, *urbs*, a city.]

subvention *səb-ven'shən*, *n* a grant of (esp. public) money in aid. — *adj* **subven'tionary.** [L. *subventiō*, *-ōnis*, a coming to help — *sub*, *venīre*, *ventum*, to come.]

subvert *səb-vûrt'*, *vt* to overthrow, overturn, ruin (e.g. principles, a political system, etc.); to pervert or corrupt (a person). — *n* **subver'sion** overthrow; ruin. — *adj* **subver'sive** tending to overthrow or subvert. — *n* a subversive person, esp. politically. — *n* **subvert'er.** [L. *sub*, under, *vertěre*, *versum*, to turn.]

subviral *sub-vī'rəl*, *adj* referring to, caused by, a structural part of a virus. [**sub-** (3).]

subway *sub'wā*, *n* a tunnel for foot-passengers; an underground passage for water-pipes, gas-pipes, sewers, etc.; (esp. *US*) an underground railway. [**sub-** (1).]

subzero *sub-zē'rō, adj* less than zero, esp. of temperature. [**sub-** (1).]

succedaneum *suk-si-dā'ni-əm,* (esp. *med*) *n* a substitute: — *pl* **succeda'nea** (*-ni-ə*). — *adj* **succedā'neous** serving as a substitute. [L., neut. of *succēdāneus* — *succēdĕre*, to come after.]

succeed *sək-sēd', vt* to come after, follow; to follow up or in order; to take the place of (esp. in office, title or possession). — *vi* to follow in order; to take the place of another (often with *to*); to turn out well; to prosper; to obtain one's wish or accomplish what is attempted; to avail, be successful (with *in*). — *n* **succeed'er** someone who is successful; a successor. — *adj* **succeed'ing.** — *n* **success** (*sək-ses'*) an act of succeeding; the state of having succeeded; prosperous progress, achievement or termination; attainment of wealth, influence or acclaim; a successful person or affair, etc. — *adj* **success'ful** resulting in success; achieving, having achieved, or having, the desired effect or outcome; prosperous, flourishing. — *adv* **success'fully.** — *n* **success'fulness.** — *n* **succession** (*-sesh'ən*) a coming after or following; a coming into another's place; a sequence in time or place; law, recognised mode, right, order or turn, of one person or thing succeeding another; in Roman and Scots law, the taking of property by one person in place of another; heirs collectively; a set of strata which represents an unbroken chronological sequence (*geol*); in an ecological community, the sequence of changes as one set of species succeeds another. — *adj* **success'ional.** — *adv* **success'ionally.** — *adj* **success'ionless.** — *adj* **successive** (*sək-ses'iv*) coming in succession or in order. — *adv* **success'ively.** — *n* **success'iveness.** — *adj* **success'less.** — *adv* **success'lessly.** — *n* **success'lessness.** — *n* **success'or** a person who, or thing which, succeeds or comes after; a person appointed to succeed. — *n* **success'orship.** — **succession duty** a tax imposed on succession to property; **success story** (the record of) a person's rise to prosperity, fame, etc. — **in succession** following one another, one after another. [L. *succēdĕre, -cēssum* — *sub-* (in sense of near, next after) and *cēdĕre*, to go.]

succentor *sək-sent'ər, n* a subordinate cantor; a bass soloist in a choir. [L. *succentor* — *succinĕre* — *sub*, under, *canĕre*, to sing.]

succès *sük-se,* (Fr.) *n* success. — **succès d'estime** (*des-tēm*) a success of esteem or approval (if not of profit); **succès fou** (*fōō*) success with wild enthusiasm; **succès de scandale** (*də skã-dal*) success of a book or dramatic entertainment, due not to merit but to its connection with or reference to a topical scandal.

success, etc. See under **succeed.**

succinate. See **succinic.**

succinct *sək-* or *suk-singkt', adj* concise; brief and precise. — *adv* **succinct'ly.** — *n* **succinct'ness.** [L. *succinctus* — *sub*, up, *cingĕre*, to gird.]

succinic *suk-sin'ik, adj* of, relating to, or derived from, amber. — *n* **suc'cinate** a salt of succinic acid. — **succinic acid** an acid occurring in plant resins such as amber, in various animal tissues, etc. [L. *succinum*, amber.]

succotash *suk'ō-tash, n* a stew of green Indian corn and beans and sometimes pork. [Narragansett *msiquatash*.]

Succoth. Same as **Sukkoth.**

succour or in U.S. **succor** *suk'ər, vt* to aid in distress; to relieve. — *n* aid; relief. — *n* **succ'ourer.** — *adj* **succ'ourless.** [A.Fr. *socorre* — L. *succurrĕre*, to run to help — *sub*, up, *currĕre*, to run.]

succubus *suk'ū-bəs,* also **succuba** *suk'ū-bə, n* a devil supposed to assume a female body and have sex with men in their sleep: — *pl* **succ'ubuses** or **succ'ubī,** also **succ'ubae** (*-bē*) or **succ'ubas.** [L. *succuba*, a whore — *sub*, under, *cubāre*, to lie.]

succulent *suk'ū-lənt, adj* juicy, sappy; juicy and fleshy, or (*loosely*) merely fleshy (*bot*). — *n* a succulent plant. — *n* **succ'ulence** or **succ'ulency.** — *adv* **succ'ulently.** [L. *sūculentus* — *sūcus*, juice.]

succumb *sə-kum', vi* to lie down under or sink under pressure, difficulty, temptation, illness, etc. (often with *to*); to die. [L. *sub*, under, *cumbĕre*, to lie down.]

succursal *suk-ûr'sl,* (usu. *eccles*) *adj* subsidiary; branch. [Fr., — L. *succurrĕre*, to succour.]

such *such, adj* of that kind, a similar kind, or the same kind (often followed by *as* or by a clause beginning with *that*); so characterised; of what kind; what (exclamatorily); so great; mentioned earlier; some particular but unspecified. — *adv* so (preceding the indefinite article if any). — *pron* such a person, persons, thing or things; the before-mentioned; that. — *adj* **such'like** of such a kind. — *pron* suchlike persons or things (or person or thing). — *adj* **such'-and-such** this or that, some, some or other (before the indefinite article if any). — *pron* such-and-such a person. — **as such** as it is described; in a particular capacity; **such as** for example; **such as it is** being what it is (and no better); **such that** in such a way, to such an extent, etc. that. [O.E. *swilc*.]

suck *suk, vt* to draw in with the mouth; to draw milk or some other liquid from with the mouth; to apply to or hold, roll about or squeeze in the mouth; to draw up or render by suction; to absorb, draw in; to extract; to imbibe; to drain, exhaust. — *vi* to draw with the mouth; to suck milk from the breast; to draw in or up by suction; to make a noise of sucking; to draw in; to be repellent or contemptible (*slang*, esp. *US*). — *n* an act or spell of sucking; milk drawn from the breast; suction. — *adj* **sucked.** — *n* **suck'er** a person who, or thing which, sucks; a sucking or adhesive organ; a device that adheres, draws water, etc. by suction, such as a pump piston; a shoot rising from underground and developing into a new plant; a new shoot; a gullible person, one taken advantage of (*colloq*); a sucking-pig, new-born whale, or other unweaned animal; a sucking-fish; a sweet or lollipop (*colloq*). — *vt* to strip off superfluous shoots from; to dupe, make a sucker of (esp. *US*). — *vi* to develop suckers. — *adj* **suck'ered.** — *n* and *adj* **suck'ing.** — **sucker punch** (*US slang*) a quick, surprise punch. — *vt* (*US slang*) to give someone a sudden unexpected punch. — **suck'ing-fish** remora or other fish with an adhesive disc; **sucking louse** a bloodsucking wingless insect of the order *Anoplura*; **suck'ing-pig** a young milk-fed pig. — **be a sucker for** (*colloq*) to be unable to resist; **suck in** to absorb; to engulf; to take in, deceive (*slang*); **suck off** (*slang*) to perform fellatio or cunnilingus on; **sucks!** or **sucks to you!** an expression of derision, contempt, etc.; **suck up to** (*slang*) to flatter, be ingratiatingly nice to. [O.E. *sūcan, sūgan*.]

suckle *suk'l, vt* to give suck to, as a mammal feeding its young. — *vi* to suck milk from the breast or teat (of an animal). — *n* **suck'ling** an unweaned child or animal; the act of giving suck. [**suck.**]

sucre *sōō'krā, n* the standard monetary unit of Ecuador (100 *centavos*). [Named after Antonio José de *Sucre* (1795–1830).]

sucrose *sōō'* or *sū'krōs, n* cane-sugar from any source. — *n* **su'crase** same as **invertase.** [Fr. *sucre*, sugar.]

suction *suk'shən, n* the act or power of sucking or of drawing or adhesion by reducing pressure of air. — *adj* (*zool*) **sucto'rial** adapted for sucking. — **suction pump** a pump for raising fluids by suction. [L. *sūgĕre, suctum*; related to **suck.**]

Sudanese *sōō-dən-ēz'* or *sōō'dən-ēz, n* a native or inhabitant of the *Sudan*, a republic in N.E. Africa, or the region south of the Sahara and Libyan deserts: — *pl* **Sudanese.** — *adj* of or pertaining to the Sudan or its inhabitants. — *n* **Sudan'ic** a group of languages spoken in the Sudan. — *adj* of or relating to these languages; of or relating to the Sudan.

sudarium *sū-* or *sōō-dā'ri-əm, n* a cloth for wiping sweat, esp. the veil or handkerchief of St. Veronica, believed to have retained miraculously the image of Christ's face. — *n* **sudatorium** (*-də-tö'ri-əm*) a hot room (as in an ancient Roman bathhouse) which induces sweating. — *adj* **su'datory** (*-tə-ri*) of sweat; inducing sweating. [L. *sūdāre, -ātum*, to sweat.]

sudden *sud'n, adj* without warning or apparent preparation; unexpected; hasty; abrupt; swift in action or production. — *adv* **sudd'enly.** — *n* **sudd'enness.** — **sudden death** (*sport*) an extended period of play to decide the outcome of a tied contest, ending when one of the contestants scores. — **all of a sudden** all at once, suddenly. [A.Fr. *sodain* — L. *subitāneus*.]

sudoriferous *sū-* or *sōō-dər-if'ər-əs*, (*med*) *adj* provoking or secreting sweat. — *adj* **sudorif'ic** causing sweat. — *n* a diaphoretic. [L. *sūdor, -ōris*, sweat.]

suds *sudz, npl* froth of soapy water. — *vi* to wash in soap suds, to lather. — *vt* (*US*) to lather, form suds. — *n* **sud'ser** (*slang*) a soap opera. — *adj* **sud'sy.** [Prob. conn. with **seethe.**]

sue *sū* or *sōō, vt* to prosecute at law; to petition for, apply for: — *vi* to make legal claim; to make application; to entreat: — *pr p* **su'ing;** *pa t* and *pa p* **sued.** — *n* **su'er.** — *n* and *adj* **su'ing.** [O.Fr. *suir* — L. *sequī, secūtus*, to follow.]

suede or **suède** *swād, n* undressed kidskin or similar, with a soft unglazed surface, used e.g. for gloves and shoe uppers. — Also *adj.* — *n* **suedette'** a fabric made to resemble suede. [Fr. (*gants de*) *Suède*, (gloves of) Sweden.]

suet *sū'it* or *sōō'it, n* a solid fatty tissue, accumulating about the kidneys of the ox, sheep, etc. — *adj* **su'ety.** — **suet pudding** a boiled pudding, savoury or sweet, made with suet. [O.Fr. *seu* — L. *sēbum*, fat.]

suffer *suf'ər, vt* to undergo; to endure; to tolerate; to be affected by; to permit (*Bible* or *archaic*). — *vi* to feel pain or punishment; to sustain loss; to be injured; to be the object of an action. — *adj* **suff'erable.** — *n* **suff'erableness.** — *adv* **suff'erably.** — *n* **suff'erance** tacit or unwilling assent; toleration; suffering; endurance. — *n* **suff'erer.** — *n* and *adj* **suff'ering.** — **on sufferance** tolerated, but not encouraged or approved. [L. *sufferre* — *sub*, under, *ferre*, to bear.]

suffice *sə-fīs', vi* to be enough; to be competent or adequate. — *vt* to satisfy. — *n* **suffī'cer.** — *n* **sufficience** (*sə-fish'əns*) the state of being sufficient; a sufficient quantity; means enough for a comfortable living. — *adj* **suffic'ient** sufficing; adequate; effective. — *n* a sufficient quantity, enough. — *adv* **suffic'iently.** — *adj* **suffī'cing.** — **suffice it to say** let it be enough to say. [Through Fr. — L. *sufficĕre*, to suffice — *sub, facĕre*, to make.]

suffix *suf'iks, n* an affix attached to the end of a root, stem or word (*gram*); an index placed after and below a symbol, as *n* in x_n (*math*). — *vt* **suffix'** (also *suf'iks*) to add as a suffix. — *n* **suffixā'tion.** [L. *suffīxus* — *sub*, under, *fīgĕre*, to fix.]

suffocate *suf'ə-kāt, vt* and *vi* to choke by stopping of the breath; to stifle, e.g. in hot, airless conditions. — *n* and *adj* **suff'ocāting.** — *adv* **suff'ocātingly.** — *n* **suffocā'tion.** [L. *suffōcare* — *sub*, under, *faucēs*, the throat.]

Suffolk *suf'ək, n* an English breed of black-faced sheep without horns; a sheep of this breed. — **Suffolk punch** see **punch**[1].

suffragan *suf'rə-gən, n* an assistant, a bishop's coadjutor; any bishop in relation to his metropolitan. — Also *adj.* — *n* **suff'raganship.** [L.L. *suffrāgāneus*, assistant, supporting — L. *suffrāgium*, a vote.]

suffrage *suf'rij, n* a vote: supporting opinion; power of voting. — *n* **suffragette** (*suf-rə-jet'*; *hist*) a woman (in the late 19th and early 20th cent.) who sought, sometimes by extreme methods, to obtain voting rights for women. — *n* **suff'ragism.** — *n* **suff'ragist** a believer in the right (e.g. of women) to vote. [L. *suffrāgium*, a vote.]

suffuse *sə-fūz', vt* to pour over; to overspread or cover, e.g. with a liquid or a tint. — *n* **suffū'sion** (*-zhən*). [L. *sub*, underneath, *fundĕre, fūsum*, to pour.]

Sufi *sōō'fē, n* a pantheistic Muslim mystic: — *pl* **Su'fis.** — *n* **Su'fism.** — *adj* **Su'fic** or **Sufist'ic.** [Ar. *çūfī*, prob. man of wool — *çuf*, wool.]

sugar *shŏŏg'ər, n* a sweet substance (*sucrose* or *cane-sugar*), obtained chiefly from cane and beet; extended to any member of the same class of carbohydrates; a measure (e.g. a lump, teaspoonful) of sugar; a term of endearment (*colloq*); heroin or LSD (*slang*). — *adj* made with or of sugar. — *vt* to sprinkle, coat, mix or sweeten with sugar. — *adj* **sug'ared** sweetened or coated with sugar; sugary. — *n* **sug'ariness.** — *n* **sug'aring.** — *adj* **sug'arless.** — *adj* **sug'ary** like sugar in taste or appearance; having much sugar; cloyingly sweet, sickly, over-sentimental. — **sugar basin** or **bowl** a small basin for holding sugar at table; **sug'ar-beet** any variety of common beet, esp. variety *Rapa*, grown for sugar; **sugar bird** a S. African bird that sucks nectar from flowers; **sugar-can'dy** sugar in large crystals; a sweet, confection (*US*); **sug'ar-cane** a woody grass (genus *Saccharum*) from which sugar is chiefly obtained. — *adj* **sugar-coat'ed.** — **sug'ar-cube** or **-lump** a small square block of sugar; **sug'ar-daddy** an elderly man lavishing money or gifts on a young woman or young women; **sugar diabetes** diabetes mellitus; **sug'ar-gum** a eucalyptus with sweetish foliage; **sugar loaf** a loaf or mass of sugar, usu. more or less conical; a hill, or other object of like form; **sug'ar-lump;** **sug'ar-maple** a N. American maple from whose sap sugar is made; **sugar pea** see **mangetout;** **sug'ar-plum** a small round boiled sweet; something pleasing, like a compliment; a term of endearment; **sug'ar-refīner;** **sug'ar-refīnery;** **sug'ar-refīning;** **sugar sifter** a container for sugar with a perforated top; **sugar soap** an alkaline cleansing or stripping preparation for paint surfaces; **sugar tongs** small tongs for lifting sugar-lumps at table. — **sugar of lead** lead acetate, sweet and poisonous, used as a mordant for dyeing and printing textiles, and as a drier for paints and varnishes; **sugar the pill** to compensate somewhat for an unpleasant prospect, unwelcome imposition, etc. [O.Fr. (Fr.) *sucre* — Ar. *sukkar*; the *g* unexplained.]

suggest *sə-jest', vt* to introduce indirectly to the thoughts; to call up in the mind; to put forward (as a plan, hypothesis, thought, etc.); to give an impression of. — *vi* to make suggestions. — *n* **suggest'er.** — *n* **suggestibil'ity.** — *adj* **suggest'ible** capable of being suggested, or of being influenced by suggestion, esp. hypnotic. — *n* **suggest'ion** (*-yən*) process or act of suggesting; hint; proposal; indecent proposal; communication of belief or impulse to a hypnotised person. — *adj* **suggest'ive** containing a hint; designed or tending to suggest; pertaining to hypnotic suggestion; tending to awake indecent mental images or thoughts (*colloq euphemism*). — *adv* **suggest'ively.** — *n* **suggest'iveness.** [L. *suggerĕre, -gestum, sub*, under, *gerĕre*, to carry.]

sugging *sug'ing*, (*commercial jargon*) *n* selling under the guise of market research, a deprecated technique in which a salesperson obtains information as though for a survey before advancing a sales offer. [App. acronymic for *s*elling *u*nder the *g*uise.]

suicide *sōō'i-sīd* or *sū', n* a person who kills himself or herself intentionally; self-murder; a self-inflicted disaster. — *adj* **suicī'dal.** — *adv* **suicī'dally.** — *n* **suicidol'ogy** the study of suicide. — *n* **suicidol'ogist.** — **suicide jockey** (*slang*) an utterly reckless driver (as though suicidal); **suicide pact** an agreement between people to kill themselves together. — **commit suicide** to kill oneself. [L. *suī*, of oneself, *caedĕre*, to kill.]

sui generis *sōō'ē* or *sōō'ī jen'ər-is* or *ge'ne-ris*, of its own kind, the only one of its kind. [L.]

suint *sōō'int* or *swint*, *n* dried perspiration in wool. [Fr.]

suit *sōōt* or *sūt*, *n* the process or act of suing; an action at law; a petition; courtship; a series or set; a set of cards of the same denomination, in the pack or in one player's hand; a number of articles made to be worn together, e.g. a set of clothes or armour; matching trousers (or skirt) and jacket, soemtimes with a waistcoat; such an outfit for a specified occasion or purpose; a businessman (*slang*). — *vt* to provide or furnish; to fall in with the requirements of; to fit; to become, look attractive on; to please. — *vi* to agree, match or be fitting. — *n* **suitabil'ity**. — *adj* **suit'able** that suits; fitting; agreeing; adequate. — *n* **suit'ableness**. — *adv* **suit'ably**. — *adj* **suit'ed** dressed, clothed; matched, appropriate. — *n* **suit'ing** cloth suitable for making suits. — *n* **suit'or** a person who sues; a petitioner; a man seeking the love of a woman, or her hand in marriage. — **suit'case** a portable oblong travelling-case with a handle, for carrying suits, clothes, etc. — **follow suit** to do the same; to play a card of the suit led; **strong suit** something one is especially good at; **suit yourself** do what you like. [Fr. *suite*; cf. **sue** and **suite**.]

suite *swēt*, *n* a set, as of furniture or rooms; a sequence of instrumental movements, usu. dance-tunes, in related keys; a train of followers or attendants. [Fr., — a L.L. form of L. *secūta*, fem. past p. of *sequī*, to follow.]

suitor. See under **suit**.

suk, sukh. See **souk**.

sukiyaki *sōō-kē-yä'kē* or *skē-ä'kē*, *n* thinly-sliced beef, vegetables, soya sauce, etc. cooked quickly together, often at the table. [Jap.]

Sukkoth *suk'əth*, *suk'ət* or *sōō'kəs*, or **Sukkot** *suk'ət*, *n* the Jewish Feast of Tabernacles. [Heb., huts, tents.]

sulcus *sul'kəs*, (*anat*) *n* a groove, furrow, fissure; a fissure between two convolutions of the brain: — *pl* **sul'ci** (*-sī*). — *adj* **sul'cate** or **sul'cated** furrowed, grooved; with parallel longitudinal furrows. [L. *sulcus*, a furrow.]

sulfa, sulfate, sulfide, sulfite, sulfo-, sulfone, sulfur. See **sulpha, sulphate, sulphide, sulphite, sulpho-, sulphone, sulphur**.

sulfurate, sulfuric, etc. U.S. spellings of **sulphurate, sulphuric**, etc.

sulk *sulk*, *vi* to be sullen, silent or aloof, esp. out of petty resentment or bad temper. — *n* someone who sulks; a fit of sulking. — *adv* **sulk'ily**. — *n* **sulk'iness**. — *adj* **sulk'y**. [Prob. from the root in O.E. *āseolcan*, to slack or be slow.]

sullage *sul'ij*, *n* refuse, sewage; scum; silt. [Perh. conn. with **sully**.]

sullen *sul'ən*, *adj* gloomily angry and silent; malignant, baleful; dull, dismal. — *adv* sullenly. — *adv* **sull'enly**. — *n* **sull'enness**. [App. through O.Fr. deriv. from L. *sōlus*, alone.]

sully *sul'i*, *vt* to soil; to tarnish; to mar or stain: — *pr p* **sull'ying**; *pa t* and *pa p* **sull'ied**. [O.E. *sylian*, to defile — *sol*, mud; or from O.Fr. *souiller*, to soil.]

sulpha or in U.S. **sulfa** *sul'fə*, *adj* of a class of synthetic antibacterial drugs, the sulphonamides. — *n* any drug of this class. — *n* **sulphadī'azine** (or in U.S. **sulfadī'azine**) a sulphonamide used against pneumonia, etc. — *n* **sulphanil'amide** (or in U.S. **sulfanil'amide**) a sulphonamide used against bacteria.

sulphate or in U.S. **sulfate** *sul'fāt*, *n* a salt of sulphuric acid. — *vt* to form a deposit of lead sulphate on; to treat or impregnate with sulphur or a sulphate. — *vi* to become sulphated. — *n* **sulphā'tion** (or in U.S. **sulfā'tion**). [Fr. — N.L. *sulfātum*.]

sulphide or in U.S. **sulfide** *sul'fīd*, *n* a compound of an element or radical with sulphur; a salt of hydrosulphuric acid.

sulphite or in U.S. **sulfite** *sul'fīt*, *n* a salt of sulphurous acid. [**-ite** (4).]

sulpho- or in U.S. **sulfo-** *sul-fō-* or *sul-fə-*, *pfx* denoting sulphur.

sulphone or in U.S. **sulfone** *sul'fōn*, *n* any of a class of substances consisting of two organic radicals combined with SO_2. — *adj* **sulphon'ic** (or in U.S. **sulfon'ic**). — *n* **sulphon'amide** (or in U.S. **sulfon'amide**) an amide of a sulphonic acid, any of a group of drugs with antibacterial action. — *n* a substance so formed. [Ger. *Sulfon*.]

sulphur or in U.S. **sulfur** *sul'fər*, *n* a yellow nonmetallic element (symbol **S**; atomic no. 16) and mineral, very brittle, fusible and inflammable; the colour of sulphur, a bright yellow. — *adj* composed of sulphur. — *vt* to treat or fumigate with sulphur. — *vt* **sul'phūrāte** to combine with, or subject to the action of, sulphur. — *n* **sulphūrā'tion**. — *n* **sulphūrā'tor**. — *adj* **sulphū'reous** sulphury; sulphur-yellow. — *adj* **sulphū'ric** containing sulphur in higher valency (opp. to *sulphurous*). — *vt* **sul'phurise** or **-ize** to sulphurate. — *adj* **sul'phurous** (*-fūr-* or *-fər-*) pertaining to, resembling or containing sulphur; containing sulphur in lower valency (*chem*; *-fū'rəs*). — *adj* **sulphury** (*sul'fər-i*) like sulphur. — **sul'phur-bottom** the blue whale (from the yellowish spots underneath); **sulphur dioxide** SO_2, a suffocating gas discharged into the atmosphere in waste from industrial processes, used in manufacture of sulphuric acid, and in bleaching, preserving, etc.; **sulphuric acid** a very corrosive acid and an important heavy chemical used extensively in industry, oil of vitriol (H_2SO_4); **sulphurous acid** H_2SO_3; **sulphur trioxide** SO_3, the anhydride of sulphuric acid; **sulphur tuft** a poisonous toadstool with a yellowish cap. [L. *sulphur*, *sulfur*, *sulpur*, *-uris*.]

sultan *sul'tən*, *n* a Muslim ruler, esp. (*hist*) the former head of the Ottoman empire; a small white (orig. Turkish) variety of hen. — *n* **sultana** (*sul-* or *səl-tä'nə*) a sultan's wife or concubine; a sultan's mother, sister or daughter; a small, pale, seedless raisin. — *n* **sul'tanate**. — *adj* **sultanic** (*sul-tan'ik*). — *n* **sul'tanship**. [Ar. *sultān*.]

sultry *sul'tri*, *adj* close and oppressive; hot with anger; passionate, voluptuous; (of language) lurid, verging on the indecent. — *adv* **sul'trily**. — *n* **sul'triness**. [**swelter**.]

Sulu *sōō'lōō*, *n* a member of a Muslim people of the *Sulu* Archipelago in the S.W. Philippines; their Malayan language. — Also *adj*.

sulu *sōō'lōō*, *n* a length of cloth worn in Fiji, etc. as a sarong. [Fijian.]

sum *sum*, *n* total, whole; the aggregate, whole amount; the result of addition; a quantity of money; a problem in addition, or in arithmetic generally; chief points; substance or result; height, culmination or completion. — *vt* (often with *up*) to add, to make up the total of; to be an epitome of, exemplify; to summarise; to reckon up, form an estimate of. — *vi* (with *up*) to summarise or make a summing-up: — *pr p* **summ'ing**; *pa t* and *pa p* **summed**. — *adj* **sum'less**. — *n* **summation** see **summary**. — *adj* **summed**. — *n* **summ'er**. — *n* and *adj* **summ'ing**. — **summing-up'** a recapitulation or review of the leading points, esp. a judge's summary survey of the evidence given to a jury before it withdraws to consider its verdict; **sum total** complete or final sum. — **in sum** in short; to sum up. [O.Fr. *summe* — L. *summa* — *summus*, highest.]

sumac or **sumach** *sōō'*, *shōō'* or *sū'mak*, *n* any tree or shrub of the genus *Rhus*; the leaves and shoots used in dyeing. [Fr. *sumac* or L.L. *sumach* — Ar. *summāq*.]

Sumerian *sōō-mēr'i-ən, adj* of or relating to the ancient civilisation, people, language, etc. of the Mesopotamian region of *Sumer* in southern Babylonia (*fl* 3500 B.C.). — *n* a native of Sumer; the language or its cuneiform script.

summary *sum'ə-ri, n* an abridgement, a shortened form of a story or report, etc. summing up the main points. — *adj* condensed; brief; compendious; done by a short method; without unnecessary formalities or delay, without further application to the court. — *adv* **summ'arily**. — *n* **summ'ariness**. — *vt* **summ'arise** or **-ize** to present in a summary or briefly. — *n* **summ'arist** someone who summarises. — **summary offence** (*legal*) one which is tried by a magistrate. [L. *summārium* — *summa*, sum.]

summation *sum-ā'shən, n* the process of finding the sum, addition; a summing-up, summary. — *vt* **summāte'** (back-formation) to add together. — *adj* **summā'tional**. — *adj* **summ'ative**. [Med. L. *summātio* — *summare*, to sum up — L. *summa*, sum.]

summer[1] *sum'ər, n* the warmest season of the year; the period between the summer solstice and the autumn equinox (*astron*); a spell of warm weather (see **Indian summer**); a year of age or time (*poetic*); a time of peak maturity, heyday. — *adj* of, for or occurring in, summer. — *vi* to pass the summer. — *vt* to keep through the summer. — *adj* **summ'erlike**. — *adj* **summ'ery** like summer; suitable for summer. — **summ'erhouse** a structure in a garden for sitting in in good weather; **summer pudding** a pudding made of soft fruit and bread; **summer school** a course of study held during the summer; **summ'ertime** the summer season; **summer time** time adopted (for daylight-saving purposes) one hour in advance of Greenwich Time between March and October. — *adj* **summ'erweight** (of clothes) light enough to be worn in summer. [O.E. *sumer*, *sumor*.]

summer[2] *sum'ər, n* a large horizontal beam or lintel. [From obs. sense *sumpter* (archaic), a pack-horse.]

summer[3]. See under **sum**.

summersault. Same as **somersault**.

summit *sum'it, n* the highest point or degree; the top; a summit conference. — *n* **summiteer'** a participant in summit conferences. — *adj* **summ'itless**. — **summit conference** or **talks** a conference between heads of government; sometimes extended to mean a conference between heads of lesser organisations; **summ'it-level** the highest level. [O.Fr. *sommette*, *somet*, dimin. of *som* — L. *summum*, highest.]

summon *sum'ən, vt* to call up, forth or together; to call upon to appear (e.g. in court) or to do something; to rouse, gather (e.g. strength or energy). — *adj* **summ'onable**. — *n* **summ'ons** a summoning or an authoritative call; a call to appear (esp. in court): — *pl* **summ'onses**. — *vt* to serve with a summons. [O.Fr. *somoner* — L. *summonēre* — *sub-*, secretly, *monēre*, to warn: sense partly from O.E. *somnian*, to assemble.]

summum bonum *sum'əm bō'nəm* or *sōōm'ōōm bo'nōōm*, (L.) the chief good (as an ultimate ethical objective).

sumo *sōō'mō, n* a traditional Japanese sport, a form of wrestling, won by forcing one's opponent out of the ring, or by causing him to touch the ground within it with any part other than the soles of the feet: — *pl* **su'mos**. — *n* **sumotō'ri** a sumo wrestler. [Jap.]

sump *sump, n* a hole or depression that receives liquid, as for molten metal, for sea-water at a salt-work, drainage-water in a mine, or oil in an engine. [Du. *somp*.]

sumptuary *sump'tū-ər-i, adj* pertaining to or regulating expense; relating to the control or moderation of extravagance. [L. *sumptuārius* — *sūmptus*, cost.]

sumptuous *sum'* or *sump'tū-əs, adj* costly; magnificently luxurious. — *n* **sumptuos'ity**. — *adv* **sump'tūously**. — *n* **sump'tūousness**. [L. *sūmptus*, cost — *sūmere*, *sūmptum*, to take.]

Sun. *abbrev* for Sunday.

sun *sun, n* the star which is the gravitational centre and source of light and heat to our planetary system (often with *cap*); the central body of a system; a great luminary; its light and heat; sunshine; a year, or a day (*poetic*). — *vt* to expose to the sun's rays: — *pr p* **sunn'ing**; *pa t* and *pa p* **sunned**. — *adj* **sun'less**. — *n* **sun'lessness**. — *adj* **sun'like**. — *adv* **sunn'ily**. — *n* **sunn'iness**. — *adj* **sunn'y** of, from, like or lighted, coloured or warmed by, the sun; genial; cheerful. — *adj* and *adv* **sun'ward** towards the sun. — *adv* **sun'wards**. — *adv* **sun'wise** in the direction of the sun's apparent revolution. — *adj* **sun-and-plan'et** geared so that one wheel moves round another. — *adj* **sun'-baked** baked or dried by the heat of the sun. — **sun'bath** or **sun'bathe** exposure of the body to the sun's rays. — *vi* **sun'bathe**. — **sun'bather** (*-bādh-*); **sun'bathing**; **sun'beam** a shaft of sunlight; **sun bear** the Malayan bear; sometimes the Himalayan bear; **sun'bed** a sun-lamp in the form of a bed on which one lies in order to obtain an artificial suntan; **sun'belt** a region with a warm, sunny climate, a preferred place to live; (often with *cap*) the southern and southwestern regions of the U.S.; **sun'bird** any of a family of small, often brightly-coloured tropical birds, superficially like humming-birds; **sun'-blind** an outside shade or awning for a window; **sun'block** a sunscreen that completely protects the skin from the effects of the sun's ultraviolet rays; **sun'-bonnet** a light bonnet projecting beyond the face to protect (esp. a baby) from the sun; **sun'bow** an iris formed by the sun, esp. in the spray of a waterfall; **sun'burn** reddening of the skin and tenderness caused by excessive exposure to the sun; tanning of the skin. — *vt* to burn or tan by exposure to the sun. — *vi* to become sunburned. — *adj* **sun'burned** or **sun'burnt**. — **sun'burst** a strong outbreak of sunlight; a jewel or ornament resembling the rayed sun. — *adj* **sun'-cured** cured in the sun. — **sun dance** a N. American Indian ceremonial dance, performed in honour of the sun; **sun'-deck** the upper deck of a passenger ship; a balcony or terrace used for sunbathing; **sun'dew** an insectivorous bog-plant (*Drosera*); **sun'dial** a device for telling the time by a shadow cast by the gnomon on a graduated flat surface; **sun'-disc** a winged disc, symbol of the sun-god; **sun'down** sunset; **sun'downer** in Australia, a loafer who arrives at a station in time for a meal and lodging, but too late for work; a drink after sunset; **sun'-dress** a low-cut dress, leaving the arms, shoulders and back exposed to the sun. — *adj* **sun'-dried** dried in the sun. — *adj* **sun'fast** (*US*) (of fabric colour) not fading in the sunlight. — **sun'-fish** a fish of nearly circular profile (e.g. one of the family *Molidae*); **sun'flower** a composite plant (*Helianthus*) with a large flower-head with yellow rays and edible seeds from which an oil is obtained; **sun'glass** a burning-glass; (in *pl*) dark-lensed spectacles used against strong light; **sun'-god** a god personifying or concerned with the sun; **sun'hat** a hat with a brim to shade the face; **sun'-lamp** a lamp that gives out ultraviolet rays, used curatively or to induce artificial suntan; a lamp producing a very bright light, used in film-making; **sun'light** the light of the sun. — *adj* **sun'lit** lit up by the sun. — **sun lounge** or in U.S. **sun parlor** a room with large windows, or a glass wall, to admit the maximum sunlight; **sun'-lounger** an upholstered couch for sunbathing; **sunny side** a pleasant or cheerful part or point of view; the better side; **sun parlor** see **sun lounge**; **sun'rise** the rising or first appearance of the sun above the horizon; the time or colour-effects of this rising; **sunrise industry** a new and rapidly-growing industry, often based on electronics; **sunroof** see **sunshine-roof**; **sun room** a sun lounge; **sun'screen** a lotion or cream, etc. that prevents sunburn by screening the skin from ultraviolet rays; **sun'set** the setting or going down of the sun below the horizon; the time or phenomenon of this; **sun'shade** a parasol; an awning; **sun'shine** bright sunlight; brightness; geniality; an informal term of address, often used in a gently scolding or ironic tone. — *adj* **sun'shine** sunshiny; fair-weather. — *adj* **sun'shiny.** — **sun'-shine-roof** or **sun'roof** a car-roof that can be slid open; **sun'spot** a relatively dark patch on the surface of the sun; a place with a very warm sunny climate; **sun'stroke** a medical condition of general collapse caused by exposure to great heat, which can result in delirium, convulsions and coma; **sun'suit** a child's outfit for playing in the sun; **sun'tan** a browning of the skin as a result of exposure to the sun. — *adj* **sun'tanned.** — **sun'trap** a sheltered, sunny place; **sun'-up** (esp. *US*) sunrise; **sun'-visor.** — **a touch of the sun** mild sunburn; mild sunstroke; **catch the sun** to be sunburnt; **take the sun** to walk or laze in the sun; to ascertain the sun's meridian altitude; **under the sun** on earth. [O.E. *sunne*.]

sundae *sun'dā* or *sun'di*, *n* an ice-cream with syrup or crushed fruit. [Perh. **Sunday.**]

Sunday *sun'dā* or *sun'di*, *n* the first day of the week, anciently dedicated to the sun, now regarded as the Sabbath by most Christians; a newspaper published on Sundays. — *adj* of, for or occurring on Sunday. — **Sunday best** one's best clothes; **Sunday driver** someone who drives a car at weekends only; an incompetent driver; **Sunday painters** people who paint seriously but in their spare time; **Sunday punch** (*US colloq*) a powerful punch intended to knock out one's opponent (also *fig*); **Sunday school** a school for religious (orig. general) instruction for children on Sunday. — **a month of Sundays** a long time. [O.E. *sunnan dæg*.]

sunder *sun'dər*, (*archaic* or *poetic*) *vt* and *vi* to separate; to part. — **in sunder** (*Bible*) asunder. [O.E. *syndrian*, to separate, *sundor*, separate.]

sundew, sundial, etc. See under **sun**.

sundry *sun'dri*, *adj* more than one or two; several; divers. — *npl* **sun'dries** sundry things; different small things. — **all and sundry** all collectively and individually. [O.E. *syndrig*.]

sunfast, sun-fish, sunflower. See under **sun**.

sung *sung*. See under **sing**.

sunglass, sun-god, sunhat. See under **sun**.

sunk, sunken. See under **sink**.

sun-lamp ... to ... **sun-lounger**. See under **sun**.

Sunna *sŏŏn'ə* or *sun'ə*, *n* Muslim traditional teaching. — *n* **Sunn'i** (-*ē*) one of the two main branches of Islam, accepting the Sunna as authoritative; a member of this (also **Sunn'ite**). — *n* **Sunn'ism** the teachings and beliefs of orthodox Muslims. [Ar. *sunnah*.]

sunny ... to ... **sunwise.** See under **sun**.

Suomi *sōō'ə-mi*, *n* the Finnish language. — *npl* the Finns. — *adj* **Suo'mic** or **Suo'mish.**

sup *sup*, *vt* to take into the mouth, as a liquid; to eat with a spoon. — *n* a small mouthful, as of a liquid. [O.E. *sūpan*; partly from O.Fr. *soper*, *souper*, to take supper.]

sup. *abbrev* for: superfine; superior; superlative (also **superl.**); supine; supplement; *supra* (L.), above; supreme.

Sup.Ct. *abbrev* for: Superior Court; Supreme Court.

super[1] *sōō'pər* or *sū'pər*, *adj* of superior quality; exceptionally good; delightful. — *n* something of superior quality or grade, such as a grade of petrol. — *interj* (*colloq*) good, lovely, smashing! [L., above.]

super[2] *sōō'per* or *sū'per*, (*colloq*) *n* short for: superfine; superintendent; supernumerary (esp. a supernumerary actor).

super- *sōō-pər-* or *sū-pər-*, *pfx* signifying: above; beyond; in addition; in excess; very. — *vt* **superadd'** to add over and above. — *n* **superaddi'tion.** — *vt* **supercal'ender** to give a high polish to by calendering. — *adj* **supercal'endered.** — *vt* **su'percharge** to fill to excess; to charge above the normal; to add pressure to. — *n* **su'percharger** a device for increasing the pressure in an internal combustion engine. — *n* **su'perclass** a biological category between a division and a class. — *n* **superclus'ter** (*astron*) a large cluster of galaxies. — *adj* **supercolum'nar** (*archit*) above a column or colonnade; with one colonnade above another. — *n* **supercolumniā'tion.** — *n* **su'percompūter** a powerful computer which can perform a large number of mathematical calculations very quickly. — *n* **su'percontinent** any of the vast landmasses from which the continents were orig. formed. — *vt* **supercool'** to cool below normal freezing-point without freezing. — *adj* **supercrit'ical** capable of sustaining a chain reaction such that the rate of reaction increases. — *n* **su'per-ēgo** (*psychol*) the strong unconscious inhibitory mechanism which criticises the ego and causes it pain and distress when it accepts unworthy impulses from the id. — *n* **superelevā'tion** excess in height; the difference in height between the opposite sides of a road or railway on a curve. — *n* **superem'inence** eminence in a superior degree; excellence beyond others. — *adj* **superem'inent.** — *adv* **superem'inently.** — *n* **su'perfamily** (*biol*) a group between a suborder and a family. — *adj* **superfatt'ed** (of soap) having an excess of fat, so that there is no free alkali. — *n* **superfecundā'tion** same as **superfetation** (q.v.). — *adj* **su'perfine** of specially fine size or quality; over-nice. — *n* **su'perfineness.** — *adj* **superflu'id.** — *n* **superfluid'ity** a phenomenon observed in a form of helium in which internal friction is negligible. — *n* **su'pergīant** a very bright star of enormous size and low density, such as Betelgeuse and Antares. — *adj* **superglā'cial** occurring or originating on the surface of a glacier. — *n* **su'perglue** (*colloq*) a very strong and quick-acting glue. — *n* **su'pergrass** (*slang*) a police informer who has given information leading to the arrest of a great number of criminals. — *n* **su'pergroup** a pop-group made up of established solo artists. — *vt* **superheat'** to heat to excess; to heat (steam, etc.) above the temperature of saturation; to heat above normal boiling-point without vaporisation. — *n* **su'perheater.** — *n* **su'perhero** any of various comic-book heroes with supernormal or superhuman powers. — *adj* **super-het'erodyne** heterodyne with beats above audible frequency. — *n* a superheterodyne receiver (also *colloq* **su'perhet**). — *n* **super-high frequency** see **frequency** under **frequent**. — *n* **su'perhighway** (*US*) a wide road for fast motor-traffic. — *adj* **superhū'man** above man; above the capacity of man; more or higher than human. — *n* **super-incum'bence.** — *adj* **superincum'bent** resting on the top; overlying; overhanging. — *vt* **superinduce'** to bring in over and above, or in supersession of, something else; to superadd. — *n* **superinduce'-ment** or **superinduc'tion.** — *n* **superinfec'tion** an infection arising during another infection and caused by a different (or a different variety of the same) micro-organism. — *vt* **superinfect'.** — *adj* **superlu'nar** or **superlu'nary** above the moon; not of this world. — *n* **su'perman** ideal man; a man with exceptional strength or ability; a fictional character with superhuman powers. — *adj* **supermun'dane** above wordly things. — *adj* **supernor'mal** beyond what is normal; in greater number, amount, concentration, etc. than the normal. — *n* **su'perorder** a category between an order and a subclass or class (*biol*). — *adj* **superord'inate** superior in rank. — *n* a superior in rank. — *n* **superphos'phate** an acid phosphate; now usu. a mixture of calcium sulphate and calcium acid phosphate used as a manure. — *adj* **superphys'ical** beyond, or of higher order than, the physical. — *vt* **superpose'** to bring, or suppose to be brought, into coincidence; to place vertically over or on something else. — *adj* **superposed'**. — *n* **superposi'tion**. — *n* **su'perpower** a very powerful state, often applied to the U.S. and the U.S.S.R. — *vt* **supersat'urate** to saturate beyond the normal point. — *n* **supersaturā'tion**. — *n* **su'perstar** an extremely popular and successful star of the cinema, popular music, etc. — *n* **superstrā'tum** (or *-strä'*) overlying stratum. — *n* **su'pertanker** an old name for a large tanker (q.v.). — *n* **su'pertax** an extra or additional tax on large incomes (term not in official use). — *adj* **superterrā'nean** living or situated on the earth's surface. — *adj* **superterres'trial** above the earth; celestial. — *n* **sup'ertitle** same as **surtitle**. — *n* **superton'ic** the tone next above the tonic. — *n* **su'perwoman** an exceptionally strong, talented or energetic woman. [L. *super*, above.]

superabound *sōō-* or *sū-pər-ə-bownd'*, *vi* to be more, very or excessively abundant. — *n* **superabun'dance**. — *adj* **superabun'dant**. — *adv* **superabun'dantly**. [**super-**.]

superadd, superaddition. See under **super-**.

superannuate *sōō-* or *sū-pər-an'ū-āt*, *vt* to set aside or cause to retire on account of age; to pension off. — *adj* superannuated. — *n* a superannuated person. — *adj* **superann'ūated**. — *n* **superannūā'tion** the act or state of superannuating; a pension; a regular contribution paid by an employee towards a pension. [L. *super*, above; *annus*, year.]

superb *sōō-* or *sū-pûrb'*, *adj* magnificent; gorgeous; triumphantly effective; supremely excellent (*colloq*). — *adv* **superb'ly**. — *n* **superb'ness**. [L. *superbus*, proud.]

supercalender. See under **super-**.

supercargo *sōō'-* or *sū'pər-kär-gō*, *n* a ship's officer in charge of the cargo and superintending all commercial transactions of the voyage: — *pl* **su'percargoes**. — *n* **su'percargōship**. [Sp. *sobrecargo* — *sobre*, above; see **cargo**.]

supercharge, supercharger. See under **super-**.

superciliary *sōō-* or *sū-pər-sil'i-ər-i*, *adj* of, on or near the eyebrow; marked above the eye. [L. *supercilium* — *super*, above, *cilium*, eyelid.]

supercilious *sōō-* or *sū-pər-sil'i-əs*, *adj* disdainfully superior in manner. — *adv* **supercil'iously**. — *n* **supercil'iousness**. [Ety. as for **superciliary**.]

superclass ... to ... **supercomputer**. See under **super-**.

superconductivity *sōō-* or *sū-pər-kon-duk-tiv'it-i*, *n* complete absence of electrical resistivity shown by certain pure metals and alloys at temperatures approaching absolute zero and by certain ceramics at higher temperatures. — *adj* **superconduc'ting**. — *adj* **superconduc'tive**. — *n* **su'perconductor** a substance having superconductivity. [**super-**.]

supercontinent ... to ... **supereminently**. See under **super-**.

supererogation *sōō-* or *sū-pər-er-ō-gā'shən*, *n* doing more than is required. — *adj* **supererogatory** (*-ə-rog'ə-tər-i*). — **works of supererogation** (*RC*) works which, not absolutely required of each individual for salvation, may be done for the sake of greater perfection — affording the church a store of surplus merit to eke out the deficient merit of others. [L. *super*, above, *ērogāre*, *-ātum*, to pay out.]

superette *sōō-* or *sū-pər-et'*, (*Austr* and *US*) *n* a small local supermarket. [*super*market, and dimin. sfx. *-ette*.]

superfamily ... to ... **superfecundation**. See under **super-**.

superfetation *sōō-* or *sū-pər-fē-tā'shən*, (*biol*) *n* fertilisation of an ovum in one already pregnant. [L. *superfētāre* — pfx. *super-*, over, *fētus*, a fetus.]

superficial *sōō-* or *sū-pər-fish'l*, *adj* of, on or near the surface; not thorough or careful; not deep or profound. — *n* **superficiality** (*-fish-i-al'i-ti*). — *adv* **superfic'ially**. — *n* **superfic'ialness**. [L. *superficiēs* — *super*, *faciēs*, face.]

superfine, superfluid. See under **super-**.

superfluous *sōō-* or *sū-pûr'flōō-əs*, *adj* above what is enough; redundant; unnecessary. — *n* **superfluity** (*-flōō'*) state of being superfluous; a thing that is superfluous; superabundance. — *adv* **super'fluously**. — *n* **super'fluousness** superfluity. [L. *superfluus*, overflowing — *super*, *fluěre*, to flow.]

supergiant ... to ... **superhuman**. See under **super-**.

superimpose *sōō-* or *sū-pər-im-pōz'*, *vt* to set on top of something else; to place one over another; to establish in superaddition. — *adj* **superimposed'**. — *n* **superimposi'tion**. [**super-**.]

superintend *sōō-* or *sū-pər-in-tend'*, *vt* to supervise; to control or manage. — *n* **superintend'ence** or **superintend'ency** the office or district of a superintendent. — *n* **superinten'dent** a person who superintends; a police officer above a chief inspector; the head of a police department (*US*); (in the RSPCA) a rank between commander and chief inspector; (*NAm*) the caretaker of a building. — *n* **superintend'entship**. — *adj* **superintend'ing**. [Ecclesiastical L. *superintenděre*; see **super-** and **intend**.]

superior *sōō-* or *sū-pē'ri-ər*, *adj* upper; higher in nature, place, rank or excellence; better (with *to*); surpassing others; beyond the influence, rising above (with *to*); supercilious or uppish; very worthy and highly respectable; set above the level of the line (*printing*); (of an ovary) inserted on the receptacle above the other parts (*bot*). — *n* one superior to others; the head of a religious house, order, etc. — *n* **superiority** (*-or'i-ti*) quality or state of being superior; pre-eminence; advantage. — **superiority complex** (*psychol*) over-valuation of one's worth, often affected to cover a sense of inferiority; **superior planets** those more distant from the sun than is the earth. [L., compar. of *superus*, on high — *super*, above.]

superjacent *sōō-* or *sū-pər-jā'sənt*, *adj* lying above. [L. *super*, above, and *jacēns*, *-entis*, pres. p. of *jacēre*, to lie.]

superl. *abbrev* for superlative.

superlative *sōō-* or *sū-pûr'lə-tiv*, *adj* raised above others or to the highest degree; superior to all others; most eminent; expressing the highest degree (*gram*). — *n* the superlative or highest degree (*gram*); an adjective or adverb in the superlative degree; any word or phrase of exaggeration. — *adv* **super'latively**. — *n* **super'lativeness**. [L. *superlātīvus* — *super*, *lātus*, carried.]

superluminal *sōō-* or *sū-pər-lōō'min-əl*, or *-lū'*, *adj* faster than the speed of light; travelling, or able to travel, at such a speed. [**super-**.]

superlunar, superman. See under **super-**.

supermarket *sōō'* or *sū'pər-mär-kit*, *n* a large, mainly self-service, retail store, selling food and other household goods. [**super-**.]

supermini *sōō'* or *sū'pər-mi-ni*, *n* a small car with a good standard of comfort and performance. [**super-**.]

supermundane. See under **super-**.

supernatant *sōō-* or *sū-pər-nā'tənt*, *adj* floating or swimming above; (of a liquid) over a sediment. [L. *supernatāns*, *-antis* — *super*, *natāre*, swim, float.]

supernatural *sōō-* or *sū-pər-nach'ə-rəl* or *-nat'yə-*, *adj* above or beyond nature; not according to the laws of nature; miraculous; magical; spiritual; occult. — *n* that which is supernatural. — *vt* **supernat'uralise** or **-ize** to bring into the supernatural sphere. — *n* **supernat'uralism** the belief in the influence of the supernatural in the world. — *n* **supernat'uralist**. — *adv* **supernat'urally**. [**super-**.]

supernormal. See under **super-**.

supernova *sōō-* or *sū'pər-nō-və*, *n* very brilliant nova resulting from an explosion which blows the star's material into space, leaving an expanding cloud of gas: — *pl* **su'pernōvae** (*-vē*) or **su'pernōvas.** [**super-**.]

supernumerary *sōō-* or *sū-pər-nū'mər-ər-i*, *adj* over and above the stated, usual, normal or necessary number. — *n* a supernumerary person or thing; an actor without speaking parts. [L.L. *supernumerārius* — L. *super*, *numerus*, number.]

superorder, superordinate. See under **super-**.

superoxide *sōō'* or *sū'pər-oks-īd*, *n* any of various oxides having two oxygen atoms. [**super-**.]

superphosphate ... to ... **supersaturation**. See under **super-**.

superscribe *sōō-* or *sū-pər-skrīb'*, *vt* to write or engrave above, on the top or on the outside of something; to address (e.g. a letter); to sign at the top. — *adj* **su'perscript** (*-skript*) written above; superior (*printing*). — *n* a superior character (*printing*). — *n* **superscrip'tion** act of superscribing; that which is superscribed. [L. *super*, above, *scrībĕre*, *scrīptum*, to write.]

supersede *sōō-* or *sū-pər-sēd'*, *vt* to set aside in favour of another; to come or put in the room of, to replace. — *n* **superse'dence.** — *n* **superse'der.** — *n* **supersē'dure.** — *n* **supersession** (*-sesh'ən*). [L. *supersedēre*, to sit above, refrain from — *super*, above, *sedēre*, *sessum*, to sit.]

supersonic *sōō-* or *sū-pər-son'ik*, *adj* too high-pitched for human hearing (ultrasonic); faster than the speed of sound; travelling, or capable of travelling, at such a speed. [L. *super*, above, *sonus*, sound.]

superstar. See under **super-**.

superstition *sōō-* or *sū-pər-sti'shən*, *n* an ignorant and irrational belief in supernatural agency, omens, divination, sorcery, etc.; a deep-rooted but unfounded general belief. — *adj* **supersti'tious.** — *adv* **supersti'tiously.** — *n* **supersti'tiousness.** [L. *superstitiō*, *-ōnis*.]

superstore *sōō'* or *sū'pər-stōr*, *n* a large supermarket usually selling a wide variety of goods as well as food. [**super-**.]

superstratum. See under **super-**.

superstructure *sōō'* or *sū'pər-struk-chər*, *n* the part of a building above the foundations, or of a ship above the main deck; any thing or concept based on another. — *adj* **superstruc'tural.** [**super-**.]

supertanker ... to ... **supertonic.** See under **super-**.

supervene *sōō-* or *sū-pər-vēn'*, *vi* to come in addition, or closely after. — *n* **supervention** (*-ven'shən*). [L. *super*, above, *venīre*, *ventum*, to come.]

supervise *sōō'* or *sū'pər-vīz*, *vt* to oversee, manage or control. — *n* **supervision** (*-vizh'ən*) act of supervising; inspection; control. — *n* **su'pervisor** a person who supervises; an overseer; an inspector; an elected local government official (*US*). — *adj* **su'pervīsory** pertaining to, or having, supervision. [L. *super*, over, *vidēre*, *vīsum*, to see.]

superwoman. See under **super-**.

supine *sōō'* or *sū'pīn*, *adj* lying on the back; leaning backward, inclined, sloping; negligently inert; indolent; passive. — *n* a Latin verbal noun in *-tum* possibly as formed from the stem of the passive participle. — *vt* **su'pinate** (*-pin-āt*) place (the hand) palm upward or forward (opp. to *pronate*). — *n* **supinā'tion.** — *n* **su'pinator** a muscle that supinates the hand. — *adv* **su'pinely.** — *n* **su'pineness.** [L. *supīnus*, supine.]

supp. or **suppl.** *abbrev* for supplement.

supper *sup'ər*, *n* a light evening meal. — *adj* **supp'erless.** [O.Fr. *soper*.]

supplant *sə-plänt'*, *vt* to oust; to supersede; to dispossess and take the place of. — *n* **supplantation** (*sup-lən-tā'shən*). — *n* **supplant'er.** [L. *supplantāre*, to trip up — *sub*, under, *planta*, the sole.]

supple *sup'l*, *adj* pliant; lithe; yielding. — *n* **supp'leness.** — *adv* **supp'ly.** — **supp'lejack** any of various tropical shrubs with pliant or twining stems; a pliant cane. [Fr. *souple* — L. *supplex*, bending the knees — *sub*, under, *plicāre*, to fold.]

supplement *sup'li-mənt*, *n* that which supplies a deficiency or fills a need; that which completes or brings closer to completion; any addition by which defects are made good; a special part of a periodical publication accompanying an ordinary part; the quantity by which an angle or an arc falls short of 180° or a semicircle. — *vt* **supplement'** to supply or fill up; to add to. — *adj* **supplement'al** or **supplement'ary** added to supply what is needed; additional. — *adv* **supplement'ally** or **supplement'arily.** — *n* **supplementā'tion.** — *n* **supplement'er.** — *n* **supplē'tion** the adding of a word to supply a missing form of a conjugation, etc., as *went* for the past tense of *to go* (*gram*). — **supplementary benefit** a state allowance paid each week to those with low incomes in order to bring them up to a certain established level. [L. *supplēmentum*, a filling up, *supplēre*, to fill up.]

suppliant *sup'li-ənt*, *adj* supplicating; asking earnestly; entreating. — *n* a humble petitioner. — *n* **supp'liance** supplication. — *adv* **supp'liantly.** [Fr. *suppliant*, pres. p. of *supplier* — L. *supplicāre*.]

supplicant *sup'li-kənt*, *adj* supplicating; asking submissively. — *n* a person who supplicates or entreats earnestly. — *vt* and *vi* **supp'licate** to entreat earnestly; to petition; to pray — *adj* **supp'licating.** — *adv* **supp'licatingly.** — *n* **supplicā'tion.** — *adj* **supp'licatory** containing supplication or entreaty; humble. [L. *supplicāre*, *-ātum* — *supplex*; see **supple.**]

supply[1] *sə-plī'*, *vt* to make good; to satisfy; to provide, furnish; to fill, occupy (as a substitute): — *pr p* **supply'ing**; *pa t* and *pa p* **supplied'.** — *n* act of supplying; that which is supplied or which supplies a want; amount provided or in hand; available amount of a commodity; amount of food or money provided (used generally in *pl*); a source of water, electricity, etc.; a parliamentary grant for expenses of government; a person who takes another's duty temporarily, a substitute, esp. a teacher. — *n* **suppli'er.** — **supply'-sider** an advocate of supply-side economics. — **supply-side economics** the policy or practice of cutting taxes in order to stimulate production, in the belief that supply creates demand. [O.Fr. *suppleier*, *supplier* — L. *supplēre*, to fill up.]

supply[2]. See **supple.**

support *sə-pōrt'*, *vt* to bear the weight of; to hold up; to endure; to sustain; to maintain; to corroborate; to make good; to uphold; to back up; to supply with means of living; to nourish. — *n* act or fact of supporting or upholding; a person who or thing that supports, sustains or maintains; maintenance; backing; a prop; an actor playing a subordinate part with a star. — *adj* **support'able** capable of being held up, carried, sustained or maintained. — *n* **support'ableness.** — *adv* **support'ably.** — *n* **support'er** a person who or thing that supports; an adherent; a person who attends matches and follows the fortunes of a team; the supporting act or acts at a pop concert. — *n* and *adj* **support'ing.** — *adj* **support'ive.** — *adj* **support'less.** — **support hose, stockings** or **tights** elasticated hose; **supporting act, film** or **programme** a film, films, acts, etc. accompanying the main film, or star performance in a variety show. [L. *supportāre* — *sub*, up, *portāre*, to bear.]

suppose *sə-pōz'*, *vt* to incline to believe; to conceive, imagine, guess; to assume provisionally or for argument's sake; to imply, presuppose; (esp. in *passive*) to expect in accordance with rules or conventions. — *adj* **suppo'sable.** — *adv* **suppo'sably.** — *adj* **supposed** (*-pōzd'*; also *-pō-zid*) believed to be; assumed; conjectured. — *adv* **suppo'sedly** according to supposition. — *n* **suppo'ser.** — *n* **suppo'sing.** — **suppose'** if; what if. — **suppos'ing** if; what if, how about. [Fr. *supposer* — pfx. *sup-* (*sub-*), *poser*; see **pose**[1].]

supposition *sup-ə-zi'shən, n* an act of supposing; that which is supposed; assumption; presumption, opinion. — *adj* **supposi'tional** hypothetical; conjectural; supposed. — *adv* **supposi'tionally.** — *adj* **suppositious** (*-zi'shəs*) suppositional. — *adj* **supposititious** (*sə-poz-i-tish'əs*) put by trick in the place of another; spurious; suppositional. — *adv* **supposititiously.** — *n* **supposititiousness.** [L. *suppōnĕre, -positum*, to set under, substitute — *sub*, *pōnĕre*, to put.]

suppository *sə-poz'i-tə-ri, n* a medicated plug inserted in the rectum, vagina or urethra, and left to melt. [L. *suppositōrium*, ety. as for **supposition**.]

suppress *sə-pres', vt* to crush, put down; to subdue; to hold back, esp. from publication, circulation, divulgation, expression, development; to check, stop, restrain; to hold in; to moderate; to leave out. — *n* **suppress'ant** a substance, e.g. a drug, that suppresses rather than eliminates. — Also *adj.* — *adj* **suppressed'.** — *adv* **suppress'edly.** — *adj* **suppress'ible.** — *n* **suppression** (*-presh'ən*) act of suppressing; stoppage; concealment. — *adj* **suppress'ive.** — *n* **suppress'or.** [L. *supprimĕre, suppressum* — *sub*, under, *premĕre*, to press.]

suppurate *sup'ū-rāt, vi* to gather or discharge pus. — *n* **suppurā'tion.** — *adj* **supp'urātive.** [L. *sub*, under, *pūs, pūris*, pus.]

Supr. *abbrev* for Supreme.

supra- *sōō-prə-* or *sū-prə-, pfx* signifying above. — *adj* **supramun'dane** above the world. — *adj* **supra-na'tional** overriding national sovereignty; in, or belonging to, more than one nation. — *adj* **supra-or'bital** above the orbit of the eye. — *adj* **supra-rē'nal** above the kidneys (**suprarenal capsules** or **glands** the adrenal glands; **suprarenal extract** an extract from these used in the treatment of haemorrhage, Addison's disease, etc.). — *adj* **supraseg-men'tal** (*phon*) representing or continuing through two or more speech sounds. [L. *suprā*, above.]

supreme *sū-* or *sōō-prēm', adj* highest; greatest; most excellent. — *n* the highest point; the highest authority. — *n* **supremacism** (*-prem'*) (belief in) the supremacy of one particular group of people. — *n* **suprem'acist.** — *n* **supremacy** (*-prem'ə-si*) state of being supreme; supreme position or power. — *adv* **supreme'ly.** — *n* **supreme'ness.** — **supreme sacrifice** the giving up of one's life; **Supreme Soviet** the legislature of the U.S.S.R., consisting of two bodies, the Council of the Union, and the Council of Nationalities. [L. *suprēmus*, superl. of *superus*, high — *super*, above.]

suprême or **supreme** *sü-prem, sū-* or *sōō-prēm', n* a rich cream sauce; a dish of meat served in this sauce. [Fr.]

supremo *sū-* or *sōō-prē'mō, n* a supreme head: — *pl* **supre'mos.** [Sp., — L. *suprēmus*, highest.]

Supt. *abbrev* for Superintendent.

suq. See **souk**.

sur- *sûr-, pfx* signifying over, above, beyond. [Fr., — L. *super*.]

sura or **surah** *sōō'rə, n* a chapter of the Koran. [Ar. *sūra, sūrah*, step.]

surah *sū'rə* or *sōō'rə, n* a soft twilled silk or artificial fabric. — Also *adj.* [Poss. from *Surat*.]

sural *sū'rl, adj* pertaining to the calf of the leg. [L. *sūra*, the calf.]

surat *sōō-rat'* or *sōō', n* coarse uncoloured cotton. [*Surat*, in India.]

surbahar *sär-ba-här', n* an Indian stringed instrument, larger than a sitar. [Bengali.]

surbase *sûr'bās*, (*archit*) *n* a cornice or series of mouldings above the base of a pedestal, etc. [**sur-**.]

surcharge *sûr'chärj, vt* to overload; to saturate; to print over the original printing; to disallow; to exact a surcharge from. — *n* an extra charge; an excessive load; an amount not passed by an auditor, which must be refunded; a new valuation or cancel-mark printed on or over a stamp. — *adj* **sur'charged.** — *n* **surcharge'ment.** — *n* **sur'charger.** [**sur-**.]

surcingle *sûr'sing-gl, n* a girth or strap for holding a saddle, etc. on an animal's back. [O.Fr. *surcengle* — L. *super*, above, *cingulum*, a belt.]

surd *sûrd, adj* that cannot be expressed in rational numbers (*math*); voiceless (*phon*). — *n* an irrational quantity (*math*); a voiceless consonant (*phon*). [L. *surdus*, deaf.]

sure *shōōr, adj* secure; safe; fit to be depended on; unerring; stable; certain; assured; confident beyond doubt; without other possibility. — *interj* (*colloq*) certainly, undoubtedly, yes. — *adv* (now chiefly *Ir* or *NAm*, except as used in combination and in conventional phrases). — *adv* **sure'ly** firmly; confidently; safely; certainly; assuredly; as it would seem (often *ironically*). — *n* **sure'ness.** — *n* **surety** (*shōōr'ti* or *shōōr'i-ti*) certainty; safeguard; legal security against loss; a person who becomes legally responsible for another's liabilities; a sponsor. — *n* **sure'tyship.** — *adj* **sure'-fire** (*colloq*) infallible. — *adj* **surefoot'ed** not liable to stumble. — *adv* **surefoot'edly.** — *n* **surefoot'edness.** — **sure thing** a certainty, certain success; (as *interj*) certainly, beyond doubt. — **be sure** do not omit; **for sure** certainly; of a certainty; **make sure** see under **make**; **stand surety for** to act as guarantor for; **sure enough** no doubt; in very fact; accordingly; there's no denying; **to be sure** certainly; I admit. [O.Fr. *sur, seur* — L. *sēcūrus*; see **secure**.]

SURF *sûrf*, (*nuc*) *abbrev* for spent unreprocessed fuel.

surf *sûrf, n* surging water or waves rushing up a sloping beach; sea-foam. — *vi* to bathe in or ride on surf. — *n* **surf'er.** — *n* **surf'ing** riding breaking waves on a surfboard. — *adj* **surf'y.** — **surf'-bird** an American Pacific shore-bird related to the sandpipers; **surf'-board** a long narrow board used in surfing; **surf'-boat** a boat for use in surf; **surf'-riding** surfing; **surf scater** a North American sea-duck, the male of which has white patches on the head and nape.

surface *sûr'fis, n* the outer boundary or face of anything; the outside or upper layer; that which has length and breadth but no thickness (*geom*); area; outer appearance, character or texture. — *adj* of, on or near a surface. — *vt* to put a surface, or some kind of surface or finish, upon. — *vi* to bring or rise to the surface; to become apparent; to regain consciousness (*colloq*). — *adj* **sur'faced** having this or that kind of surface. — *n* **sur'facer** a person or thing that smooths or levels a surface. — *n* **sur'facing.** — *adj* **sur'face-active** able to alter the surface tension of liquids (see also **surfactant**). — **sur'face-craft** a floating, not submersible, craft; **surface mail** mail sent otherwise than by air; **surface noise** the noise produced by the friction of a stylus on a record; **surface structure** (*linguis*) the formal structure of sentences, esp. when analysed into their constituent parts; **surface tension** that property in virtue of which a liquid surface behaves like a stretched elastic membrane; **surface worker** a person engaged in any of the ancillary jobs in a coalmine not done underground. — *adj* **surface-to-air'** (of a missile, etc.) travelling from a base on the ground to a target in the air. — Also *adv.* — *adj* and *adv* **surface-to-sur'face.** — **sur'face-vessel**; **sur'face-water** drainage-water. [Fr., from *sur* (— L. *super*) and *face* (— L. *faciēs*, face).]

surfactant *sər-fak'tənt, n* a substance, e.g. a detergent, which has the effect of altering the interfacial tension of water and other liquids or solids. [*surf*ace-*act*ive *agent*.]

surfeit *sûr'fit*, *n* excess; sickness or satiety caused by overeating or overdrinking. — *vt* to feed or fill to satiety or disgust. — *adj* **sur'feited**. [O.Fr. *surfait*, excess — L. *super*, above, *facĕre*, to make.]

surg. *abbrev* for: surgeon; surgery.

surge *sûrj*, *n* an uprush, boiling or tumultuous movement of liquid; a sudden increase of power; a great wave; a swell. — *vi* to well up; to heave tumultuously; to slip back; to jerk. — *n* and *adj* **sur'ging**. [L. *surgĕre*, to rise.]

surgeon *sûr'jən*, *n* a person who treats injuries or diseases by manual operations; an army or naval doctor; a ship's doctor. — *n* **sur'gery** the art and practice of a surgeon; a doctor's or dentist's consulting-room; a doctor's or dentist's time of consultation; a set (usu. regular) time when a member of parliament, local councillor, etc. is available to his or her constituents for consultation. — **sur'geon-fish** a sea-surgeon; **surgeon general** the senior officer in the medical branch of the service (*mil*); head of the public health service (*US*); **surgeon's knot** a knot like a reef-knot but with a double turn in the first part (used in ligaturing a cut artery). [A.Fr. *surgien*.]

surgical *sûr'ji-kəl*, *adj* of, pertaining to, or used in surgery; (of a garment or appliance) designed to correct a physical deformity. — **surgical spirit** a methylated spirit with small amounts of castor oil and wintergreen. [Ety. as for **surgeon**.]

suricate *sū'* or *sōō'ri-kāt*, *n* a S. African animal of the civet family.

surjection *sûr-jek'shən*, (*math*) *n* a mapping function in which all the elements in one set correspond to all the elements in another set. — See also **injection**. [**sur-** and L. *jacĕre*, to throw.]

surly *sûr'li*, *adj* morose; bad-tempered and rude; rough and gloomy; refractory. — *adv* **sur'lily**. — *n* **sur'liness**. [From obs. *sirly* haughty, — **sir** and **like**[1].]

surmise *sər-mīz'*, *n* suspicion; conjecture. — *vt* to imagine; to suspect; to conjecture, guess. — *adj* **surmis'able**. — *n* **surmis'er**. — *n* and *adj* **surmis'ing**. [O.Fr. — *surmettre*, to accuse — L. *super*, upon, *mittĕre*, to send.]

surmount *sər-mownt'*, *vt* to be on or go to the top of; to surpass; to get the better of. — *adj* **surmount'able**. — *adj* **surmount'ed**. — *n* **surmount'er**. — *n* and *adj* **surmount'ing**. [O.Fr. *surmunter* (Fr. *surmonter*) — L.L. *supermontāre*; see **mount**[2].]

surmullet *sər-mul'it*, *n* a species of red mullet. [Fr. *surmulet*.]

surname *sûr'nām*, *n* a family name. — *vt* to name by a surname. [On the analogy of Fr. *surnom*, from Eng. **name**.]

surpass *sər-päs'*, *vt* to go or be beyond; to exceed; to excel. — *adj* **surpass'able**. — *adj* **surpass'ing** passing beyond others; excellent in a high degree. — *adv* **surpass'ingly**. [Fr. *surpasser* — *sur-*, *passer*, to pass.]

surplice *sûr'plis*, (*eccles*) *n* a white linen vestment worn over the cassock. — *adj* **sur'pliced** wearing a surplice. [Fr. *surplis* — L.L. *superpellicium*, an overgarment — *pellis*, skin.]

surplus *sûr'pləs*, *n* that which is left over; remainder; excess over what is required; excess of revenue over expenditure. — Also *adj*. — *n* **sur'plusage** surplus; superfluity. [Fr., — L.L. *superplūs* — *super*, *plūs*, more.]

surprise *sər-prīz'*, *n* the emotion caused by anything sudden or contrary to expectation; astonishment; anything that causes or is intended to cause this emotion; a catching, or being caught, unawares. — Also *adj*. — *vt* to come upon suddenly or unawares; to strike with wonder or astonishment; to capture by an unexpected assault; to lead unawares, to betray (with *into*); to confuse. — *n* **surpris'al** an act of surprising. — *adj* **surprised'**. — *adv* **surpris'edly**. — *n* **surpris'er**. — *n* and *adj* **surpris'ing**. — *adv* **surpris'ingly**. — *n* **surpris'ingness**. — **surprise, surprise** ironic exclamation of surprise; **much (**or **greatly**, etc.**) to one's surprise** causing one great surprise. [O.Fr. (Fr.) fem. past p. of *surprendre* — L. *super*, *prehendĕre*, to catch.]

surra *sōō'rə*, (*vet*) *n* a trypanosome disease of horses, etc. in Eastern Asia. [Marathi *sūra*, wheezing.]

surrealism *sə-rē'ə-lizm*, *n* a movement in French art and literature, from about 1919 on, that aimed at drawing upon the subconscious and escaping the control of reason or any preconceptions. — *adj* **surreal'** of, pertaining to, or having the qualities of surrealism; dreamlike, strange, bizarre. — *adj* and *n* **surre'alist**. — *adj* **surrealist'ic**. — *adv* **surrealist'ically**. [Fr. *surréalisme* — *sur*, above, *réalisme*, realism.]

surrebut *sur-i-but'*, (*law*) *vi* to reply to a defendant's rebutter. — *n* **surrebutt'al** a plaintiff's evidence in response to a defendant's rebuttal. — *n* **surrebutt'er** the plaintiff's reply to a defendant's rebutter. [**sur-**.]

surrejoin *sur-i-join'*, (*law*) *vt* and *vi* to reply to a defendant's rejoinder. — *n* **surrejoin'der** a plaintiff's reply to a defendant's rejoinder. [**sur-**.]

surrender *sə-ren'dər*, *vt* to deliver over; to relinquish; to yield up; to resign. — *vi* to give oneself up; to yield. — *n* the act of surrendering. — **surrender value** the amount to be paid to an insured person who surrenders a life-insurance policy. [A.Fr. *surrender*, O.Fr. *surrendre* — *sur-*, *rendre*; see **render**.]

surreptitious *sur-əp-tish'əs*, *adj* done by stealth or fraud; stealthy. — *adv* **surrepti'tiously**. [See **subreption**.]

surrey *sur'i*, (*US*) *n* a light four-wheeled horse-drawn vehicle, usu. with two seats. [Developed from a vehicle used in *Surrey*.]

surrogate *sur'ə-gāt* or *-git*, *n* a substitute; a deputy, esp. of an ecclesiastical judge; a deputy of a bishop who grants marriage licences; a judge of probate (*US*, *local*); a person or thing standing for another person or thing, or a person who fills the role of another in one's emotional life. — *n* **surr'ogacy** the state of being a surrogate; use of a surrogate, esp. of a surrogate mother. — *n* **surr'ogateship**. — *n* **surrogā'tion** subrogation. — **surrogate mother** a woman who bears a baby for another (esp. childless) couple, after either artificial insemination by the male or implantation of an embryo from the female; **surrogate motherhood**. [L. *surrogāre*, *-ātum* — *sub*, in the place of, *rogāre*, to ask.]

surround *sə-rownd'*, *vt* to go or extend all around; to encompass, environ; to encircle. — *n* a border, esp. the floor or floor-covering around a carpet. — *adj* **surround'ing**. — *n* (in *pl*) environment, things round about. — **surround sound** any form of stereophonic sound reproduction using three or more speakers to give an effect of sound coming from all directions. [O.Fr. *suronder* — L. *superundāre*, to overflow — *super*, *unda*, wave.]

surtax *sûr'taks*, *n* an additional tax; tax payable on incomes above a certain high level (term not in official use in this sense). — *vt* to tax additionally; to charge surtax. [**sur-**.]

surtitle *sûr'tītl*, *n* a printed translation of the libretto of an opera in a language foreign to the audience, projected above the proscenium arch. [**sur-**.]

surveillance *sər-vā'ləns*, *n* vigilant supervision; spy-like watching. — *n* **surveill'ant**. [Fr., — *surveiller* — *sur*, *veiller*, to watch — L. *vigilāre*.]

survey *sər-vā'*, *vt* to view comprehensively and extensively; to examine in detail; to examine the structure of a building; to obtain by measurements data for mapping. — *n* **sur'vey** a general view, or a statement of its results; an inspection; collection of data for mapping; an organisation or body of men for that purpose. — *n* **survey'ing**. — *n* **survey'or** a measurer of land; an inspector (of buildings, roads, of weights and measures, of customs duties, etc.). — *n* **survey'orship**. [O.Fr. *surveoir* — L. *super*, over, *vidēre*, to see.]

survive *sər-vīv'*, *vt* to live or exist after or in spite of; to outlive. — *vi* to remain alive or in existence. — *n* **survivabil'ity**. — *adj* **survi'vable**. — *n* **survi'val** a surviving or living after; anything that continues to exist after others of its kind have disappeared, or after the time to which it naturally belongs. — *adj* (esp. of standard equipment) designed to help one to survive exposure or other dangerous condition. — *n* **survi'valism**. — *n* **survi'valist** a person who takes measures to ensure their own survival after a catastrophic event, or measures for their personal protection from attack, robbery, etc. — Also *adj*. — *adj* **survi'ving**. — *n* **survi'vor**. — **survival of the fittest** the longer average life of the fit in the struggle for existence, and the consequent transmission of favourable variations in greater proportion to later generations. [Fr. *survivre* — L. *super*, beyond, *vīvěre*, to live.]

Sus. (*Bible*) *abbrev* for (the Apocryphal Book of) Susanna.

sus *sus*, (*slang*) *n* a suspect; suspicion; suspicious behaviour. — *vt* (*slang*) to arrest for suspicious behaviour: — *pa t* and *pa p* **sussed**. — Also **suss**. — **sus (or suss) out** (*slang*) to investigate; to find out, discover. — **sus (or suss) laws** laws allowing a person to be arrested on suspicion of having committed a crime. [**suspect** or **suspicion**.]

susceptible *sə-sep'ti-bl*, *adj* (usu. with *to*) capable, admitting; capable of receiving; impressionable; easily affected by emotion (esp. amatory). — *n* **susceptibil'ity** or **suscep'tibleness**. — *adv* **suscep'tibly**. [L. *suscipěre*, *susceptum*, to take up — *sus-* (*subs-*), up, *capěre*, to take.]

sushi *sōō'shi*, *n* a Japanese dish of small cakes of cold rice and fish, vegetables, etc., and a vinegar sauce. [Jap.]

suslik *sus'lik* or *sōōs'lik*, *n* a ground-squirrel of Eastern Europe and Asia. [Russ.]

suspect *səs-pekt'*, *vt* to mistrust; to imagine to be guilty; to doubt; to be ready to believe, but without sufficient evidence; to incline to believe the existence, presence or agency of; to have an inkling of; to conjecture. — *vi* to imagine guilt, to be suspicious. — *n* (*sus'pekt*) a person suspected. — *adj* causing suspicion; not to be trusted. — *adj* **suspect'ed**. [L. *suspicěre*, *suspectum*, to look at secretly or askance — *su-* (*sub-*), *specěre*, to look.]

suspend *səs-pend'*, *vt* to hang; to make to depend; to sustain from falling; to put or hold in a state of suspense or suspension; to make to stop for a time; to defer; to debar from any privilege, office, emolument, etc. for a time; to hold in an indeterminate state. — *adj* **suspen'ded**. — *n* **suspend'er** someone who, or something that, suspends; a strap to hold up a sock or stocking; (in *pl*) braces (*US*). — **suspended animation** temporary cessation of the outward signs and of some of the functions of life; **suspended sentence** a legal sentence not served unless another crime is committed; **suspen'der-belt** a woman's undergarment with stocking suspenders. [L. *suspenděre*, *-pēnsum* — pfx. *sus-* (*subs-*), *penděre*, to hang.]

suspense *səs-pens'*, *n* tense uncertainty; indecision. — *adj* **suspense'ful**. — *n* **suspen'sion** act of suspending; interruption; delay; temporary debarment from an office or privilege; a temporary or conditional withholding; a mixture of a fluid with dense particles prevented from settling by viscosity and impact of molecules (*chem*); the system of springs, shock absorbers, etc. which supports a vehicle on its axles. — *adj* **suspen'sive**. — *adv* **suspen'sively**. — *adj* **suspen'sory** suspending; having the power or effect of delaying. — **suspense account** an account in which items are entered which cannot at once be placed in an ordinary account; **suspension bridge** a bridge with the span supported by chains passing over elevated piers. [Ety. as for **suspend**.]

suspicion *səs-pish'ən*, *n* act of suspecting; state of being suspected; the imagining of something without evidence or on slender evidence; inkling; mistrust; a slight quantity. — *adj* **suspi'cionless**. — *adj* **suspi'cious** full of suspicion; showing suspicion; inclined to suspect; giving ground for suspicion; liable to suspicion, doubtful. — *adv* **suspi'ciously**. — *n* **suspi'ciousness**. — **above (or beyond) suspicion** too honest, virtuous, etc. to be suspected of a crime or fault; **on suspicion (of)** suspected (of); **under suspicion** suspected. [L. *suspīciō*, *-ōnis*; see **suspect**.]

suss. See **sus**.

sustain *səs-tān'*, *vt* to hold up; to bear; to support; to provide for; to maintain; to sanction; to keep going; to keep up; to support the life of; to prolong. — *n* **sustainabil'ity**. — *adj* **sustain'able**. — *adj* **sustained'**. — *adv* **sustain'edly**. — *n* **sustain'er** a person who, or thing which, sustains; the main motor in a rocket. — *n* and *adj* **sustain'ing**. — *n* **sustain'ment**. — *n* **sustenance** (*sus'ti-nəns*) that which sustains; maintenance; nourishment. — **sustaining pedal** a pedal on a piano which sustains the note or notes played by allowing the strings to continue vibrating. [L. *sustinēre* — pfx. *sus-* (*subs-*), *tenēre*, to hold.]

Susu *sōō'sōō*, *n* a Negroid people of W. Africa, living mainly in Mali, Guinea and Sierra Leone; a member of this people; its language.

susurrus *sū-* or *sōō-sur'əs*, or **susurration** *sū-* or *sōō-sur-ā'shən*, (*poetic*) *n* a murmuring; a whisper; a rustling. — *vi* **su'surrate**. [L. *susurrus*.]

sutra *sōōt'rə*, *n* (in Sanskrit literature) an aphoristic rule or book of aphorisms on ritual, grammar, metre, philosophy, etc.; (in Buddhist sacred literature) any of a group of writings including the sermons of Buddha and other doctrinal works. [Sans. *sūtra*, thread.]

suttee or **sati** *sut'ē* or *sut-ē'*, *n* an Indian widow who burned herself on her husband's pyre; the custom of so doing. — *n* **suttee'ism**. [Sans. *satī*, a true wife.]

suture *sōō'chər*, *n* a seam; the stitching of a wound; the thread, etc. for this; a junction or meeting of margins, esp. of bones. — *vt* to stitch up. — *adj* **su'tural**. — *adv* **su'turally**. — *adj* **su'tured**. [L. *sūtūra*, a seam — *suěre*, to sew.]

suzerain *sōō'zə-rān*, or *sū'*, *n* a feudal lord; a state having supremacy over another. — *n* **su'zerainty** position or power of a suzerain. [Fr., formed in imitation of *souverain* from *sus-*, over.]

SV *abbrev* for: *Sancta Virgo* (L.), Holy Virgin; *Sanctitas Vestra* (L.), Your Holiness.

Sv *abbrev* for sievert.

sv or **s.v.** *abbrev* for: *sub verbo* (L.), under the word; *sub voce* (L.), under that heading.

svelte *svelt*, *adj* lissom, lithe, graceful, slender. [Fr.]

Svengali *sven-gä'li*, *n* a person who exerts total mental control over another, usu. for evil ends. [Name of the evil hypnotist in George du Maurier's novel *Trilby*.]

SW *abbrev* for: short wave; small women or women's (clothing size); south-west; south-western.

SWA *abbrev* for South-West Africa (Namibia) (also I.V.R.).

swab *swob*, *n* a bit of cotton-wool, gauze, etc. for mopping up blood or discharges, applying antiseptics, cleaning a patient's mouth, or taking a specimen of secretion for examination; a specimen so taken; a mop for cleaning or drying floors or decks; a sponge or the like for cleaning the bore of a firearm; a lubber or clumsy fellow (*slang*). — *vt* to mop with a swab: — *pr p* **swabb'ing**; *pa t* and *pa p* **swabbed**. — *n* **swabb'er**. [Du. *zwabber*, swabber.]

swaddle *swod'l, vt* to swathe; to bandage; to wrap (e.g. an infant) tightly in bands or clothing. — **swadd'ling-band** or **swadd'ling-clothes** a strip or strips of cloth for swaddling an infant (*Bible*). [O.E. *swæthel, swethel*, bandage; cf. **swathe[1]**.]

swag *swag, vi* to sway; to sag; (often with *it*) to travel around carrying a bundle (*Austr slang*): — *pr p* **swagg'ing**; *pa t* and *pa p* **swagged**. — *n* a festoon; a full drape of a curtain; a representation of either of these; a bundle of possessions carried by a person travelling on foot (esp. *Austr*); plunder (*slang*). — *n* **swagg'ie** or **swag'man** (*Austr*) a man who carries his swag about with him, esp. in a search for work. [Related to **sway**; prob. Scand.]

swage *swāj, n* any of several tools including a tool in two grooved parts, for shaping metal. — *vt* to shape with a swage; to reduce the cross-section of a rod or tube, e.g. by forcing it through a tapered aperture between two grooved dies. — **swage block** a block with various holes, grooves, etc., for use in metal-work. [O.Fr. *souage*.]

swagger *swag'ər, vi* to walk with a blustering or overweening air of superiority and self-confidence; to brag noisily; to behave arrogantly. — *n* a swaggering gait, manner or behaviour. — *n* (*slang*) ostentatiously fashionable; smart. — *n* **swagg'erer**. — *n* and *adj* **swagg'ering**. — *adv* **swagg'eringly**. — **swagg'er-cane** or **-stick** a short military cane; **swagger coat** a coat that flares loosely from the shoulders. [**swag**.]

Swahili *swä-hē'li, n* the people of Zanzibar and the opposite coast; one of them; (*loosely*) their language (*Kiswahili*), a Bantu tongue modified by Arabic, spoken in Kenya, Tanzania and other parts of East Africa. [Ar. *sawāhil*, pl. *sāhil*, coast, with sfx.]

swain *swān*, (*poetic*, often *ironic*; or *archaic*) *n* a young man; a peasant; rustic; a lover. [O.N. *sveinn*, young man, servant; O.E. *swān*.]

SWALK *swölk* or *swalk, abbrev* for sealed with a loving kiss.

swallow[1] *swol'ō, n* a migratory bird (*Hirundo rustica*), with long wings and a forked tail, that catches insects on the wing; any of various similar or related birds. — **swall'ow-dive** a dive during which one's arms are outstretched to the sides. — Also *vi*. — **swall'ow-tail** a forked tail; something of similar shape; any of various butterflies of the family *Papilionidae* with prolongations of the hind wings. — *adj* **swall'ow-tailed** with forked and pointed tail. [O.E. *swalwe, swealwe*.]

swallow[2] *swol'ō, vt* to receive through the gullet into the stomach; to engulf (often with *up*); to take in; to accept or sit down under (e.g. an affront); to believe credulously. — *vi* to perform the action of swallowing something. — *n* an act of swallowing; a gulp; a quantity swallowed at once. — *n* **swall'ower**. — **swall'ow-hole** a funnel or fissure through which water passes underground esp. in limestone. — **swallow one's pride** to humble oneself. [O.E. *swelgan* (verb), *geswelg* (noun).]

swam *swam, pa t* of **swim**.

swami *swä'mē, n* a Hindu religious instructor, esp. as a form of address. [Hindi *svāmī*, lord, master.]

swamp *swomp, n* a tract of wet, spongy land; low waterlogged ground. — *vt* to sink or involve in, or as in, a swamp; to cause (e.g. a boat) to fill with water; to overwhelm, inundate. — *vi* to become swamped. — *adj* of or of the nature of swamp; living or growing in swamps. — *adj* **swamp'y**. — **swamp boat** a flat-bottomed boat with a raised aeroplane engine for travelling over swamps; **swamp cypress** a deciduous conifer of swamps in Southern U.S.; **swamp fever** a viral disease of horses; (*US*) malaria; **swamp'land**. [Perh. from L.G.; prob. related to O.E. *swamm*, mushroom.]

swan *swon, n* any species of the genus *Cygnus*, of large, graceful, stately, long-necked aquatic birds; one of these birds. — *adj* **swan'like**. — *n* **swann'ery** a place where swans are kept or bred. — **swan'herd** (*old*) a person who tends swans; **swan'-maiden** (in Germanic folklore) a maiden who can become a swan by putting on her feather-garment; **swan'-mark** the notch made on the swan's upper mandible; **swan'-neck** an S-shaped bend or piece; **swans'-down** or **swans'down** the under-plumage of a swan; a soft woollen or mixed cloth; a thick cotton with a soft nap on one side; **swan'-song** the fabled song of a swan just before its death; one's last work or final appearance; **swan'-upping** an annual expedition up the Thames for the marking of young swans belonging to the Dyers' and Vintners' Companies (those belonging to the crown being unmarked). — **swan about** or **around** (*colloq*) to move about aimlessly or gracefully. [O.E. *swan*.]

swank *swangk*, (*colloq*) *n* ostentation; pretentiousness; a person who swanks. — *vi* to show off. — *n* **swank'er**. — *adj* **swank'ing** or **swank'y** showing off; ostentatiously smart. — **swank'pot** a swanker. [Cf. O.E. *swancor*, pliant, M.H.G. *swanken*, to sway.]

swap or **swop** *swop, vt* to give in exchange; to barter. — *vi* to barter: — *pr p* **swapp'ing** or **swopp'ing**; *pa t* and *pa p* **swapped** or **swopped**. — *n* an exchange; something which is exchanged or offered in exchange. — *n* **swapp'er** or **swopp'er**. — *n* **swapp'ing** or **swopp'ing**. — **swap'-shop** a shop, meeting, etc. where goods are exchanged for other goods or services rather than money. [M.E. *swappen*.]

SWAPO *swä'pō, abbrev* for South-West Africa People's Organisation.

sward *swörd*, (usu. *poetic*) *n* the grassy surface of land; green turf. [O.E. *sweard*, skin, rind.]

swarf *swörf, n* grit from an axle, etc.; stone or metal grindings, filings, turnings, etc. [O.N. *svarf*, file-dust.]

swarm[1] *swörm, n* a body of bees going off to found a new community; a throng of insects or other small animals; a throng. — *vi* to go off in a swarm; to occur or come in swarms; to abound, teem. [O.E. *swearm*.]

swarm[2] *swörm, vt* and *vi* (usu. with *up*) to climb by clasping with arms and legs.

swarthy *swör'dhi, adj* blackish; dark-complexioned. — *n* **swar'thiness**. [O.E. *sweart*.]

swash[1] *swosh, vt* and *vi* to splash. — *n* the action or the sound of splashing liquid. — **swash'buckler** someone who clashes a sword on a buckler, hence a bully, a blusterer; a dare-devil. — *adj* **swash'buckling** of, resembling a swashbuckler; adventurous, exciting. [Imit.]

swash[2] *swosh, n* a piece of turner's work with mouldings oblique to the axis; a flourish on a letter. — Also *adj*. — **swash letters** italic capitals with top and bottom flourishes; **swash plate** a disc set obliquely on a revolving axis.

swastika *swos'ti-kə, n* an ancient and worldwide symbol, a cross with arms bent at a right angle, esp. clockwise, emblematic of the sun, good luck, or Nazism. [Sans. *svastika* — *svasti*, wellbeing — *su*, good, *asti*, he is.]

swat[1] *swot, vt* to hit smartly or heavily. — *n* a sharp or heavy blow; a swatter. — *n* **swatt'er** an instrument consisting of a flexible shaft with flaplike head, with which to swat flies. [Ety. as for **squat**.]

swat[2]. See **swot**.

swatch *swoch, n* a sample, esp. of cloth.

swath *swöth* or *swoth*, or **swathe** *swādh, n* a band of mown ground or of grass or corn cut by the scythe or mowing-machine; a broad band; the sweep of a scythe or mowing-machine. [O.E. *swæth* and *swathu*, track.]

swathe[1] *swādh, vt* to bind round, envelop; to bandage. — *n* a bandage; a wrapping. [O.E. *swathian*.]

swathe². See **swath**.

sway *swā*, *vt* to incline about or from side to side; to cause to incline; to divert; to influence by power or moral force. — *vi* to swing; to oscillate; to swerve; to incline to one side; to have preponderating weight or influence. — *n* a sweep; a swing; a swerve; directing force or influence; preponderance; rule. — *n* **sway'er**. — *n* and *adj* **sway'ing**. — **sway back** an abnormally hollow back; a nervous disease of lambs causing difficulty in walking or standing. — **hold sway (over)** to have power or authority (over). [Perh. from a lost O.E. word, or the corresponding O.N. *sveigja*, to bend, swing.]

Swazi *swä'zē*, *n* a racially mixed people inhabiting Swaziland and parts of the Eastern Transvaal of South Africa; a member of this people; its language. [*Mswati*, a former king of this people.]

swear *swār*, *vi* to take or utter an oath; to utter imprecations. — *vt* to assert, promise or confirm, on oath; to assert loudly or boldly; to administer an oath to; to put on oath; to bind by oath; to admit to office by an oath; to bring, put or render, by swearing: — *pa t* **swore** (*swōr*), *pa p* **sworn** (*swōrn*). — *n* an oath or a curse, or bad language generally. — *n* **swear'er**. — *n* and *adj* **swear'ing**. — *adj* **sworn** attested; bound by oath; having taken an oath; devoted, inveterate or confirmed, as if by oath. — **swear'-word** a word that is considered bad language. — **swear at** to hurl oaths and curses at; **swear by** to invoke as witness to an oath; to put complete confidence in; **swear in** to inaugurate by oath; **swear off** to renounce, promise to give up; **swear to** to affirm or identify on oath. [O.E. *swerian*.]

sweat *swet*, *n* the moisture excreted by the skin; moisture exuding or seeming to exude from anything; a state, fit or process of exuding sweat; exercise or treatment inducing sweat; labour; drudgery; fidgety anxiety. — *vi* to give out sweat or moisture; to toil, drudge for poor wages; to suffer penalty, smart; to exude; to become coated with moisture; to worry, be anxious. — *vt* to give forth as, or like, sweat; to cause to sweat; to heat (fruit, meat, etc.) slowly so as to extract the juices (*cooking*); to squeeze money or extortionate interest from; to exact the utmost from; to compel to hard work for mean wages; to unite by partial fusion of metal surfaces: — *pa t* and *pa p* **sweat'ed** or **sweat**. — *adj* **sweat'ed**. — *n* **sweat'er** a person who or animal that sweats; a (heavy) jersey for leisure wear, etc.; a person who sweats workers. — *n* **sweat'iness**. — *n* and *adj* **sweat'ing**. — *adj* **sweat'y**. — **sweat band** the leather or similar band inside a man's hat; a band worn to absorb perspiration from the forehead; an absorbent wristlet worn by e.g. tennis players to prevent sweat running down to their hands; **sweated labour** hard work obtained by exploitation; **sweat gland** any of the glands producing sweat; **sweat'shirt** a long-sleeved knitted cotton sweater; **sweat shop** a factory or shop using sweated labour; **sweat'suit** a loose-fitting suit consisting of sweater and trousers, usu. close-fitting at wrist and ankle, worn by athletes, etc. — **in a cold sweat** (*fig*) in a state of terror or anxiety; **no sweat** words used to signify assent, or indicating that something will present no problems (*US*); **sweat blood** to work or worry extremely hard; **sweat it out** (*slang*) to endure, live through a time of danger, etc. [O.E. *swǣtan*, to sweat.]

Swede *swēd*, *n* a native or citizen of *Sweden*; (without *cap*) a Swedish turnip — a buff-flowered, glaucous-leaved kind. — *adj* **Swēd'ish**. — *n* the Scandinavian language of Sweden; (as *pl*) the natives or people of Sweden.

sweep *swēp*, *vi* to pass swiftly or forcibly, esp. with a swinging movement or in a curve; to move with trailing or flowing drapery, hence with pomp, indignation, etc.; to extend in a long curve; to range systematically or searchingly. — *vt* to pass something brushingly over; to pass brushingly; to wipe, clean, move or remove with a broom; to carry along or off with a long brushing stroke or force; to wipe out or remove at a stroke (often with *away* or *up*); to perform with a sweeping movement; to trail with a curving movement; to drag as with a net or rope; to describe, generate or swing through (e.g. a curve, angle or area): — *pa t* and *pa p* **swept**. — *n* act of sweeping; a swinging movement, swing; onrush; impetus; a clearance; range, compass; a curved stair; a curved drive before a building; a sweepstake; a long oar; a chimneysweep; sweepback. — *n* **sweep'er** a person who or thing which sweeps; (in association football) a player in front of the goalkeeper who assists the defence. — *n* **sweep'ing** the action of the verb in any sense; (usu. in *pl*) things collected by sweeping, rubbish. — *adj* performing the action of sweeping in any sense; of wide scope, wholesale, indiscriminate. — *adv* **sweep'ingly**. — *n* **sweep'ingness**. — *adj* **sweep'y**. — **sweep'back** the angle at which an aeroplane wing is set back relatively to the axis; **sweep'stake** or **sweep'stakes** a method of gambling by which participators' stakes are pooled, numbers, horses, etc. assigned by lot, and prize(s) awarded accordingly on decision of event; such a prize, race, etc. — *adj* **swept'back**. — *adj* **swept'wing** (of an aircraft, etc.) having wings that are swept back. — **make a clean sweep (of)** to clear out completely; to win all the awards, prizes, etc.; **sweep the board** see under **board**. [Prob. from a lost O.E. word related to *swāpan*, to sweep.]

sweet *swēt*, *adj* having one of the fundamental varieties of taste, that of sugar, honey, ripe fruits; sugary; pleasing to the taste, senses or feelings; fragrant; clear and tuneful; smoothly running; easy, free from harshness, benign; fresh, not salt; fresh, not tainted; amiable; mild, soft, gentle; delightful, charming (*colloq*); all right, satisfactory (*Austr colloq*); more or less enamoured (with *on* or *upon*; *colloq*). — *adv* sweetly. — *n* that which is sweet; a sweet dish (pudding, fruit, etc.) as a course; a sweetmeat, confection; a beloved person. — *vt* **sweet'en** to make sweet; to mitigate something unpleasant; to pacify, make (a person) agreeable (often with *up*). — *n* **sweet'ener** a substance that sweetens, esp. one not containing sugar; a tablet of such a substance; someone who sweetens; a bribe (*slang*). — *n* **sweet'ening**. — *n* **sweet'ing** a sweet apple. — *adj* **sweet'ish**. — *n* **sweet'ishness**. — *adv* **sweet'ly**. — *n* **sweet'ness**. — *n* **sweet'y** or **sweet'ie** a sweetmeat, confection; a sweetheart (*colloq*). — *adj* **sweet-and-sour'** cooked with sugar and vinegar (or lemon juice), soy sauce, etc.; **sweet'-bay** the laurel (*Laurus nobilis*); a kind of magnolia (*US*); **sweet'bread** the pancreas, or sometimes the thymus, esp. as food; **sweet'-brier** or **-briar** a wild rose with fragrant foliage (*Rosa rubiginosa*); **sweet chestnut** see **chestnut**; **sweet Cicely** an aromatic umbelliferous plant (*Myrrhis odorata*); **sweet'corn** a sweet variety of maize; **sweetfish** see **ayu**; **sweet'-flag** an aromatic araceous pond-plant (*Acorus calamus*); **sweet'-gale** bog-myrtle, a low-growing aromatic shrub found in bogs; **sweet'heart** a lover or beloved. — *vt* and *vi* to court. — **sweetheart agreement** or **contract** an agreement between a trade union and an employer that excessively favours the employer, and is often concluded without the consent of higher-ranking trade union officials; **sweet'ie-pie** (*colloq*) a term of endearment. — *adj* **sweet'meal** (of biscuits) made of whole meal and sweetened. — **sweet'meat** a confection made wholly or chiefly of sugar; **sweet-pea'** a S. European papilionaceous garden plant with bright-coloured fragrant flowers; **sweet pepper** see under **pepper**; **sweet potato** batata, a tropical and subtropical twining plant of the convolvulus family, with large sweetish edible tubers. — *adj* **sweet'-savoured.** — *adj* **sweet-scent'ed** having a sweet smell. — **sweet'-sop** a tropical American evergreen (*Anona squamosa*); its pulpy fruit; **sweet talk** flattery, persuasion. — *vt* **sweet'-talk** (*colloq*) to coax, flatter, persuade. — *adj* **sweet-tem'pered** having a mild, amiable disposition. — *adj* **sweet-toothed'** fond of sweet things. — **sweet william** a garden pink (*Dianthus barbatus*) with bearded petals. — **a sweet tooth** a fondness for sweet things; **sweetness and light** an appearance of mildness, reasonableness, etc. [O.E. *swēte*.]

swell *swel*, *vi* to expand; to increase in volume; to be inflated; to bulge out; to grow louder; to rise into waves; to heave; to well up; to rise and fall in loudness; to be elated or dilated with emotion; to give a feeling of expansion or welling up. — *vt* to augment; to expand; to dilate; to fill full; to louden; to elate: — *pa t* **swelled**; *pa p* **swelled** or **swollen** (*swōl'n* or *swōl'ən*). — *n* the act, power, habit or condition of swelling; a heaving; a bulge; an enlargement; a loudening; a device in an organ for varying tone; a crescendo followed by a diminuendo (*mus*); a rising ground; a dandy, a bigwig, an adept (*slang*). — *adj* (*slang*) a vague word of commendation. — *adj* and *n* **swell'ing.** — *adv* **swell'ingly.** — *adj* **swollen** (*swōl'ən*). — **swell box** (in an organ) a chamber containing a set of pipes or reeds, which is opened or closed by the swell; **swelled head** conceit, esp. in someone carried away by success. — *adj* **swelled-head'ed, swell-head'ed** or **swollen-head'ed** conceited. — **swell organ** the pipes enclosed in the swell box. [O.E. *swellan*.]

swelter *swel'tər*, *vi* to endure great heat; to sweat copiously or feel faint or oppressed by heat. — *n* a sweltering; a sweating. — *n* and *adj* **swel'tering.** [Dialect *swelt* — O.E. *sweltan*, to die.]

swept *swept*, *pa t* and *pa p* of **sweep.** — **sweptback** and **sweptwing** see under **sweep.**

swerve *swûrv*, *vi* to turn aside; to deviate, esp. to change course suddenly. — *vt* to deflect; to cause a ball to swerve in the air. — *n* a turning aside; a (sudden) deviation; a deflection. — *adj* **swerve'less.** — *n* **swerv'er.** — *n* and *adj* **swerv'ing.** [M.E.]

SWG *abbrev* for standard wire gauge.

swift *swift*, *adj* fleet; rapid; speedy; prompt. — *adv* swiftly. — *n* a bird (*Apus*, or *Cypselus*, *apus*) superficially like a swallow but structurally nearer the humming-birds and goatsuckers; any bird of its genus or family; a reel for winding yarn; the main cylinder of a carding-machine. — *n* **swift'let** a bird (*Collocalia*) similar to the swift, that builds edible nests. — *adv* **swift'ly.** — *n* **swift'ness.** — *adj* **swift'-foot** or **swift-foot'ed.** — *adj* **swift-winged'.** [O.E. *swift*, from same root as **swoop.**]

swig *swig*, *n* a deep draught. — *vt* to take a swig or swigs of or from. — *vi* to drink, take swigs: — *pr p* **swigg'ing**; *pa t* and *pa p* **swigged.** — *n* **swigg'er.**

swill *swil*, *vt* or *vi* to rinse; to dash water over; to wash; to drink greedily or largely. — *n* a large draught of liquor; hogwash. — *n* **swill'er.** — *n* and *adj* **swill'ing.** [O.E. *swilian*, to wash.]

swim *swim*, *vi* to propel oneself in water (or other liquid); to float; to come to the surface; to travel or be conveyed by water; to be suffused; to be immersed or steeped; to glide smoothly; to be dizzy. — *vt* to pass by swimming; to make to swim or float: — *pr p* **swimm'ing**; *pa t* **swam** (*swam*); *pa p* **swum.** — *n* an act, performance or spell of swimming; a place where many fishes swim; the general movement or current of affairs. — *adj* **swimm'able** capable of being swum. — *n* **swimm'er.** — *n* **swimm'eret** a crustacean's abdominal appendage used in swimming. — *n* and *adj* **swimm'ing.** — *adv* **swimm'ingly** smoothly, successfully (*colloq*). — **swimm'ing-bath** (also in *pl*) an indoor swimming pool; **swimming costume** swimsuit; **swimm'ing-pool** an artificial pool for swimming in; **swim'suit** a garment worn for swimming; **swim'wear** garments worn for swimming. — **in the swim** in the main current (of affairs, business, etc.); **swim with** (or **against) the stream** or **tide** to conform to (or go against) normal behaviour, opinions, etc. [O.E. *swimman*.]

swindle *swin'dl*, *vt* and *vi* to cheat. — *n* a fraud; anything not really what it appears to be. — *n* **swin'dler** a cheat. — *n* and *adj* **swin'dling.** [Ger. *Schwindler*, a giddy-minded person, swindler — *schwindeln*, to be giddy.]

swine *swīn*, *n* a pig; a term of strong abuse: — *pl* **swine.** — *n* **swin'ery** a place where pigs are kept; swinishness. — *adj* **swin'ish** of or like swine; beastly. — *adv* **swin'ishly.** — *n* **swin'ishness.** — **swine fever** hog-cholera, a highly contagious disease of swine due to a virus; **swine'herd** (*old*) a person who herds swine. [O.E. *swīn*, a pig.]

swing *swing*, *vi* to sway or wave to and fro, as a body hanging freely; to amuse oneself on a swing; to oscillate; to hang; to be hanged; to sweep, wheel, sway; to swerve; to move forward with swaying gait; (of a ship) to turn round; to attract, excite, be perfectly appropriate to place or mood (*slang*); (of a person) to be thoroughly responsive (to jazz, etc.), up-to-date (*slang*). — *vt* to cause to swing; to set swinging; to control; to sway; to hurl, whirl; to brandish; to move in a sweep; to perform as swing-music; to influence the result of (e.g. a doubtful election) in favour of an individual or party; to arrange, fix (*slang*): — *pa t* and *pa p* **swung.** — *n* an act, manner or spell of swinging; oscillating, waving, sweeping; motion to and fro; the sweep or compass of a swinging body; the sweep of a golf club, bat, etc.; sway; scope, free indulgence; impetus; vigorous sweeping rhythm; jazz music with impromptu complications as played in the 1930s and 1940s — also **swing'-music**; a suspended seat or carriage for the amusement of swinging; a reversal of fortune; the movement of voters from one party to another as compared with the previous election. — *n* **swing'er** (*swing'ər*) a person or thing that swings; a ball bowled so as to swerve in the air (*cricket*); a lively and up-to-date person (*slang*). — *n* **swinging** (*swing'ing*) the act of moving to and fro in suspension, esp. as a pastime. — *adj* swaying; turning; with a swing; having a free easy motion; fully alive to the most recent trends; up-to-date; daring (*colloq*). — *adv* **swing'ingly.** — *n* **swingom'eter** a device which shows the direction and extent of the current swing of the counted votes in an election. — **swing'boat** a boat-shaped swinging carriage for fairs, etc.; **swing-bridge'** a bridge that may be opened by swinging it to one side; **swing-door'** a door (usu. one of a pair) that opens either way and swings shut by itself; **swing-music** see **swing** above; **swing'-wing (aircraft)** variable-geometry aircraft. — **in full swing** in mid-career; in fully active operation; **swings and roundabouts** a situation in which advantages and disadvantages cancel each other out; **swing the lead** see under **lead²**. [O.E. *swingan*.]

swingeing *swinj'ing*, *adj* great, huge, thumping; severe. — *adv* **swinge'ingly.** [M.E. *swenge* — O.E. *swengan*, to shake, causative of *swingan*, to swing.]

swingle *swing'gl*, *n* a scutching tool; the swipple of a flail. — *vt* to scutch. — *n* **swing'ling.** — **swing'le-tree** a whippletree. [Cf. O.E. *swingell*, stroke, scourge, rod.]

swingometer. See under **swing.**

swinish. See under **swine.**

swipe *swīp*, *n* a sweeping stroke. — *vt* to strike with a swipe; to purloin (*colloq*). — *vi* to make a swipe. [O.E. *swipian*, to beat.]

swipple *swip'l, n* a swingle or striking part of a flail. [Cf. **swipe** and **sweep.**]

swirl *swûrl, n* an eddy; a whirl; a curl. — *vt* to whirl; to wind. — *vi* to eddy; to whirl; to spin. — *adj* **swirl'y.** [Orig. Scot.; cf. Norw. dialect *svirla.*]

swish[1] *swish, n* the sound of or resembling twigs sweeping through the air or of fabric rustling along the ground. — *vi* to go with a swish. — *adv* with a swish. — *n* and *adj* **swish'ing.** — *adj* **swish'y.** [Imit.]

swish[2] *swish,* (*slang*) *adj* smart, stylish.

Swiss *swis, adj* of Switzerland. — *n* a native or citizen of Switzerland; the German dialect spoken by most Swiss: — *pl* **Swiss.** — *n* **Swit'zer** a Swiss. — **Swiss chard** see under **chard; Swiss cheese plant** a tropical climbing plant (*Monstera deliciosa*) with large, thick, perforated leaves, often grown as a house plant; **Swiss Guards** the Pope's bodyguard; **Swiss roll** a thin cake rolled up with jam, cream, etc. [Fr. *Suisse,* O.H.G. *swīz.*]

switch *swich, n* a long flexible twig; a tapering riding-whip; a rod, cane; a tress, usu. false; the tuft of an animal's tail; a movable rail for shunting; a change-over; a device for making, breaking or changing an electric circuit; a turn of such a device. — *vt* to strike with a switch; to whisk, jerk, lash; to divert; to turn (off, on, or to another circuit). — *vi* to use a switch; to turn aside; to change over. — *n* **switch'ing.** — *adj* **switch'y.** — **switch'back** an up-and-down track on which cars rise by the momentum gained in coming down; an up-and-down road; orig. a zigzag mountain railway on which the train shunted back at each stage; **switch'blade** (or **switchblade knife**) a flick-knife; **switch'board** a board for connecting telephones; a board or frame bearing apparatus for making or breaking an electric current or circuit; **switch'man** a pointsman; **switch'-over** action of the verb **switch;** a changeover. — **switched on** aware of and responsive to all that is most up to date (*colloq*); under the influence of drugs (*colloq*). [Earlier *swits, switz.*]

swither *swidh'ər,* (*Scot*) *vi* to be undecided. — *n* indecision; flurry. [Poss. O.E. *swethrian,* to subside.]

Switzer. See under **Swiss.**

swivel *swiv'l, n* a ring or link that turns round on a pin or neck. — *vt* and *vi* to turn on a pin or pivot: — *pr p* **swiv'elling;** *pa t* and *pa p* **swiv'elled.** — **swivel chair** a chair with a seat that swivels round. [O.E. *swīfan,* to move quickly, to turn round.]

swiz or **swizz** *swiz,* or **swizzle** *swiz'l,* (*slang*) *n* fraud; great disappointment. — *vt* to defraud, cheat. [Poss. **swindle.**]

swizzle[1] *swiz'l, vt* to mix or swirl, as with a swizzle-stick. — *n* a mixed or compounded drink containing rum or other spirit. — **swizzle'-stick** a stick or whisk used to mix a swizzle.

swizzle[2]. See **swiz.**

swollen *swōl'ən* or *swōln, pa p* of **swell,** and *adj.*

swoon *swōōn, n* a fainting fit. — *vi* to faint; to be languorous. — *n* and *adj* **swoon'ing.** — *adv* **swoon'ingly.** [Prob. from M.E. *iswowen.*]

swoop *swōōp, vi* to come down with a sweeping rush; to rush suddenly. — *n* an act of swooping; a sudden onslaught. — **at one fell swoop** by one terrible blow; by one complete decisive action; suddenly. [App. O.E. *swāpan,* to sweep.]

swoosh *swōōsh, n* a noise of or resembling a rush of air, water, etc. — *vi* to make this noise. [Prob. imit., or from **swish**[1] or **swoop.**]

swop. See **swap.**

sword *sörd, n* a weapon with a long blade, sharp upon one or both edges, for cutting or thrusting; a blade or flat rod resembling a sword; destruction or death by the sword or by war; war; military force; the emblem of vengeance or justice, or of authority and power; (in *pl*) a suit in the tarot pack. — *adj* **sword'less.** — *adj* **sword'like.** — **sword'-arm** the arm that wields the sword; **sword'-belt** a belt from which the sword is hung; **sword'-bill** a S. American humming-bird with a bill longer than its body; **sword'-blade; sword'-dance** a dance performed sword in hand or among or over swords; **sword'fish** a large fish with upper jaw compressed and prolonged as a stabbing weapon; **sword grass** a name for many plants with sword-shaped leaves; **sword'-guard** the part of a sword-hilt that protects the bearer's hand; **sword'-hilt; sword knot** a ribbon tied to the hilt of a sword; **sword'play** fencing. — *adj* **sword'-shaped.** — **swords'man** a man skilled in the use of a sword; **swords'manship; sword'stick** a hollow walking-stick containing a sword or dagger; **sword'-swallower** a performer who seems to swallow swords; **sword'tail** a small Central American fresh-water Cyprinodont fish with swordlike tail-lobe. — **cross swords** see under **cross; put to the sword** (of armies, etc.; *hist*) to kill (prisoners, etc.) by the sword; **sword of Damocles** (*dam'ə-klēz*) imminent calamity (from *Damocles,* the Syracuse courtier, forced to sit through a feast with a sword suspended over his head by a single hair). [O.E. *sweord.*]

swore, sworn. See **swear.**

swot or **swat** *swot,* (*slang*) *vt* and *vi* to study hard: — *pr p* **swott'ing** or **swatt'ing;** *pa t* and *pa p* **swott'ed** or **swatt'ed.** — *n* hard study; a person who swots. — *n* **swott'er** or **swatt'er.** — *n* **swott'ing** or **swatt'ing. [sweat.]**

SWP *abbrev* for Socialist Workers' Party.

SWRI *abbrev* for Scottish Women's Rural Institute.

swum *swum, pa p* of **swim.**

swung *swung, pa t* and *pa p* of **swing.**

swy *swī,* (*Austr slang*) *n* two-up; a two-year prison sentence. [Ger. *zwei,* two.]

SY *abbrev* for Seychelles (I.V.R.).

sy-. See **syn-.**

Sybarite *sib'ə-rīt, n* orig. an inhabitant of *Sybaris,* a Greek city in ancient Italy, on the Gulf of Tarentum, noted for luxury; a person devoted to luxury. — Also *adj.* — *adj* **Sybaritic** (*-rit'ik*) or **Sybarit'ical.** — *adj* **Sybarīt'ish.** — *n* **Sy'barītism.** — All words also without *cap.*

sybil. Same as **sibyl** (q.v. under **Sibyl**).

sycamore *sik'ə-mör, n* a kind of fig-tree (now often **syc'omore** or **sycomore fig**); in England, the great maple (*Acer pseudo-platanus*) called in Scotland the plane; (in U.S.) any true plane. [Gr. *sȳkomoros* — *sȳkon,* a fig, *moron,* black mulberry.]

syconium *sī-kō'ni-əm, n* a multiple fruit in which the true fruits (the pips) are enclosed in a hollow fleshy receptacle — the fig. [Gr. *sȳkon,* a fig.]

sycophant *sik'ə-fənt, n* a servile flatterer. — *n* **syc'ophancy.** — *adj* **sycophantic** (*-fant'ik*) or **sycophant'ical.** — *adv* **sycophant'ically.** — *adj* **syc'ophantish** (or *-fant'*). — *adv* **syc'ophantishly.** [Gr. *sȳkophantēs,* an informer, swindler, confidential agent — *sȳkon,* a fig, *phainein,* to show.]

sycosis *sī-kō'sis,* (*med*) *n* inflammation of the hair follicles, esp. of the beard. [Gr. *sȳkōsis,* a fig-shaped ulcer — *sȳkon,* a fig.]

syenite *sī'ən-īt, n* a coarse-grained rock composed of orthoclase and usu. hornblende. — *adj* **syenitic** (*-it'ik*). [L. *syēnītēs* (*lapis*), a hornblende granite found at Aswan (Gr. *Syēnē*).]

SYHA *abbrev* for Scottish Youth Hostels Association.

syke. See **sike.**

syl-. See **syn-.**

Sylheti *sil-het'i, n* a language of **Sylhet,** a region of E. Bangladesh. — *adj* of, or native to, Sylhet.

syllable *sil'ə-bl, n* a word or part of a word uttered by a single effort of the voice. — *vt* to express by syllables, to utter articulately. — *n* **syll'abary** a set of characters representing syllables. — *adj* **syllabic** (*sil-ab'ik*) or **syllab'ical** of or constituting a syllable or syllables; syllable by syllable. — *adv* **syllab'ically.** — *vt* **syllab'icate** to syllabify. — *n* **syllabicā'tion**

syllabification. — *n* **syllabicity** (*-is'i-ti*). — *nsing* **syllab'ics** verse patterned not by stresses but by syllables. — *n* **syllabificā'tion** pronunciation as a syllable; division into syllables. — *vt* **syllab'ify** to divide into syllables. — *vt* **syll'abise** or **-ize** to form or divide into syllables. — *adj* **syll'abled** having (in compounds, a specified number of) syllables. — **syllabic verse** or **metre** syllabics. — **in words of one syllable** (*colloq*) very simply, bluntly. [L. *syllaba* — Gr. *syllabē* — *syn*, with, *lab-*, root of *lambanein*, to take; *-le* as in *principle* and *participle*.]

syllabub or **sillabub** *sil'ə-bub*, *n* a dish of cream curdled (as with wine), flavoured and frothed up.

syllabus *sil'ə-bəs*, *n* an abstract or programme, as of a series of lectures or a course of studies; a catalogue of doctrinal positions or practices condemned by the R.C. Church (1864, 1907): — *pl* **syll'abuses** or **syll'abi** (*-bī*). [Orig. a misprint for L. *sittybas*, accus. pl. of *sittyba*, Gr. *sittubā*, a book-label.]

syllepsis *sil-ep'sis*, *n* a figure in rhetoric by which a word does duty in a sentence in the same syntactical relation to two or more words but has a different sense in relation to each: — *pl* **syllep'ses** (*-sēz*). — *adj* **syllep'tic**. — *adv* **syllep'tically**. [Gr. *syllēpsis*, a taking together — *syn*, together, and the root of *lambanein*, to take.]

syllogism *sil'ō-jizm* or *-ə-jizm*, *n* a logical argument in three propositions, two premises and a conclusion that follows necessarily from them; deductive reasoning. — *n* **syllogisation** or **-z-** (*-jī-zā'shən*). — *vi* **syll'ogise** or **-ize** to reason by syllogisms. — *vt* to deduce syllogistically. — *n* **syll'ogiser** or **-z-**. — *adj* **syllogistic** (*-jist'ik*) or **syllogist'ical**. — *n* **syllogist'ic** (often in *pl*) the branch of logic concerned with syllogisms. — *adv* **syllogist'ically**. [Gr. *syllogismos* — *syn*, together, *logizesthai*, to reckon — *logos*, reason.]

sylph *silf*, *n* a spirit of the air; a slim person; a kind of humming-bird. — *adj* **sylph'like**. [Coined by Paracelsus.]

sylva, sylvan, sylviculture, etc. See under **silva**.

sylvaner *sil-vä'nər*, (often with *cap*) *n* a German grape, used in making white wine; wine made from this grape. [Ger.]

sym. *abbrev* for symbol.

sym-. See **syn-**.

symbiosis *sim-bi-ō'sis*, *n* a mutually beneficial partnership between organisms of different kinds; esp. such an association where one lives within the other. — *n* **sym'biont** (*-bi-ont*) an organism living in symbiosis. — *adj* **symbiotic** (*-bi-ot'ik*). — *adv* **symbiot'ically**. [Gr. *syn*, together, *bios*, livelihood.]

symbol *sim'bəl*, *n* an emblem; that which by custom or convention represents something else; a type; a creed, or a typical religious rite (*theol*). — *adj* **symbolic** (*-bol'ik*) or **symbol'ical**. — *adv* **symbol'ically**. — *n* **symbol'icalness**. — *n* **symbolīsā'tion** or **-z-**. — *vt* **sym'bolise** or **-ize** to be symbolical of; to represent by symbols. — *n* **sym'bolism** representation by symbols or signs; a system of symbols; use of symbols; use of symbols in literature or art; (often with *cap*) a late 19th-cent. movement in art and poetry that treated the actual as an expression of something underlying. — *n* and *adj* **sym'bolist**. — *adj* **symbolist'ic** or **symbolist'ical**. — *n* **symbol'ogy** (for **symbolol'ogy**) the study or use of symbols. — **symbolic logic** a branch of logic which uses symbols instead of terms, propositions, etc. in order to clarify reasoning. [Gr. *symbolon*, a token — *syn*, together, *ballein*, to throw.]

symmetry *sim'i-tri*, *n* exact correspondence of parts on either side of a straight line or plane, or about a centre or axis; balance or due proportion; beauty of form; disposition of parts. — *adj* **symmet'ric** or **symmet'rical** having symmetry. — *adv* **symmet'rically**. — *n* **symmet'ricalness**. [Gr. *symmetriā* — *syn*, together, *metron*, a measure.]

sympathectomy *sim-pə-thek'tə-mi*, (*surg*) *n* excision of part of a sympathetic nerve. [From **sympathetic**, and Gr. *ektomē*, excision.]

sympathin *sim'pə-thin*, (*biochem*) *n* a substance, secreted by sympathetic nerve-endings, which constricts and dilates blood-vessels. [From **sympathetic**.]

sympathy *sim'pə-thi*, *n* community of feeling; power of entering into another's feelings or mind; harmonious understanding; compassion, pity; affinity or correlation whereby one thing responds to the action of another or to action upon another; agreement; (often in *pl*) a feeling of agreement or support, or an expression of this. — *adj* **sympathet'ic** feeling, inclined to, or expressing, sympathy; in sympathy; acting or done in sympathy; induced by sympathy (as sounds in a resonating body); congenial; compassionate; of the sympathetic nervous system (see below). — *adv* **sympathet'ically**. — *vi* **sym'pathise** or **-ize** to be in sympathy; to feel with or for another; to be compassionate; to be in accord, correspond. — *n* **sym'pathiser** or **-z-**. — **sympathetic magic** magic depending upon a supposed sympathy, e.g. between a person and his or her name or portrait; **sympathetic nervous system** a system of nerves supplying the involuntary muscles and glands, esp. those originating from the cervical, thoracic and lumbar regions of the spinal cord; sometimes also including those from the brain and the sacral region (the *parasympathetic nervous system*); **sympathetic** (or **sympathy**) **strike** a strike in support of other workers, not in furtherance of the strikers' own claims. — **in sympathy (with)** in agreement (with), in support (of). [Gr. *sympatheia* — *syn*, with, *pathos*, suffering.]

sympetalous *sim-pet'ə-ləs*, (*bot*) *adj* having the petals united. [Gr. *syn*, together, *petalon*, leaf.]

symphony *sim'fə-ni*, *n* harmony, esp. of sound; an orchestral composition on a great scale in sonata form (*mus*); a symphony orchestra. — *adj* **symphonic** (*sim-fon'ik*). — *n* **sym'phonist** a composer or performer of symphonies. — **symphonic poem** a large orchestral composition in programme music with the movements run together; **symphony orchestra** a large orchestra comprising strings, woodwind, brass and percussion, capable of performing symphonies. [Gr. *symphōniā*, harmony, orchestra — *syn*, together, *phōnē*, a sound.]

symphysis *sim'fi-sis*, *n* the union or growing together of parts, concrescence; union of bones by fusion, cartilage or ligament; a place of junction of parts. — *adj* **symphyseal** or **symphysial** (*sim-fiz'i-əl*). [Gr. *symphysis* — *syn*, with, *phyein*, to grow.]

sympodium *sim-pō'di-əm*, (*bot*) *n* a stem composed of a succession of branches each supplanting and seeming to continue its parent branch: — *pl* **sympo'dia**. — *adj* **sympo'dial**. — *adv* **sympo'dially**. [Gr. *syn*, together, *pous*, *podos*, foot.]

symposium *sim-pō'zi-əm*, *n* a meeting for philosophic conversation; a conference; a collection of views on one topic: — *pl* **sympō'sia**. — *adj* **sympō'siac** or **sympō'sial**. [Latinised from Gr. *sympŏsion* — *syn*, together, *posis*, drinking.]

symptom *simp'təm* or *sim'təm*, *n* a subjective indication of a disease, i.e. something perceived by the patient, not outwardly visible; a characteristic sign or indication of the existence of a state. — *adj* **symptomat'ic** or **symptomat'ical**. — *adv* **symptomat'ically**. — *vt* **symp'tomatise** or **-ize** to be a symptom of. — *n* **symptomatol'ogy** the study of symptoms; the symptoms of a patient or a disease taken as a whole. — *adj* **symptomolog'ical**. [Gr. *symptōma*, *symptōsis* — *syn*, with, and root of *piptein*, to fall.]

syn. *abbrev* for synonym.

syn-, sy-, syl-, sym- or **sys-** *pfx* signifying together, with. [Gr. *syn*, with.]

synaeresis *sin-ē'rə-sis*, *n* the running together of two vowels into one or into a diphthong (*phon*); the spontaneous expulsion of liquid from a gel. [Gr. *syn*, together, *hairesis*, taking — *haireein*, to take.]

synaesthesia *sin-ēs-thē'zi-ə* or *-zhyə*, *n* sensation produced at a point different from the point of stimulation; a sensation of another kind suggested by one experienced. — *adj* **synaesthet'ic.** [Gr. *syn*, together, *aisthēsis*, sensation.]

synagogue *sin'ə-gog*, *n* an assembly of Jews for worship; a Jewish place of worship. — *adj* **syn'agogal** (*-gō-gl*). — *adj* **synagog'ical** (*-gog'* or *-goj'i-kl*). [Gr. *synagōgē* — *syn*, together, *agōgē*, a bringing — *agein*, to lead.]

synallagmatic *sin-a-lag-mat'ik*, *adj* (e.g. of a contract) mutually or reciprocally obligatory. [Gr. *synallagmatikos* — *synallagma*, a covenant — *syn*, together, *allagma*, exchange.]

synantherous *sin-an'thər-əs*, (*bot*) *adj* having the anthers united. [Gr. *syn*, (**syn-**) and **anther.**]

synanthesis *sin-an-thē'sis*, (*bot*) *n* simultaneous ripening of stamens and stigmas. — *adj* **synanthet'ic.** — *adj* **synan'thic** showing synanthy. — *adj* **synan'thous** synanthic; flowering and leafing simultaneously. — *n* **synan'thy** abnormal fusion of flowers. [Gr. *syn*, together, *anthēsis*, flowering, *anthos*, a flower.]

synapsis *sin-aps'is*, *n* the pairing of chromosomes of paternal and maternal origin before the reducing division; a synapse: — *pl* **synaps'es** (*-ēz*). — *n* **synapse'** (also *sin'* or *sīn'*) an interlacing or enveloping connection of a nerve-cell with another. [Gr. *synapsis*, contact, junction — *syn*, together, *haptein*, to fasten.]

synarthrosis *sin-ər-thrō'sis*, (*anat*) *n* immovable articulation: — *pl* **syntharthro'ses** (*-sēz*). — *adj* **synarthrō'dial.** — *adv* **synarthrō'dially.** [Gr. *synarthrōsis* — *syn*, together, *arthron*, a joint; also *arthrōdiā*, a flattish joint.]

sync. See **synch.**

syncarp *sin'kärp*, (*bot*) *n* a compound fruit formed from two or more carpels, of one or more than one flower. — *adj* **syncarpous** (*sin-kär'pəs*) of or having united carpels. — *n* **syn'carpy.** [Gr. *syn*, together, *karpos*, a fruit.]

synch or **sync** *singk*, *n*, *vi* and *vt* short for **synchronisation** or **synchronise.** — **out of synch** or **sync** not synchronised; having different and jarring rhythms; (*loosely*), ill-matched (with *with*).

synchromesh *sing'krō-mesh*, *adj* of a gear in which the speeds of the driving and driven members are automatically synchronised before coupling, so as to avoid shock and noise in gear-changing. — *n* such a gear. [*synchronised mesh.*]

synchronal *sing'krə-nl*, *adj* coinciding in time. — *adj* **synchronic** (*-kron'*) or **synchron'ical** synchronous; concerned with the study of a subject (esp. a language) at a particular period, without considering the past or the future (opp. to *diachronic*). — *adv* **synchron'ically.** — *n* **synchronicity** (*-is'i-ti*). — *n* **synchronīsā'tion** or **-z-.** — *vi* **syn'chronise** or **-ize** to coincide or agree in time. — *vt* to cause to coincide or agree in time; to time together or to a standard; to represent or identify as contemporary; to make (the soundtrack of a film) exactly simultaneous with the picture. — *n* **synch'roniser** or **-z-.** — *n* **syn'chronism** coincidence in time; simultaneity; keeping time together; exhibition of contemporary history in one scheme; the bringing together in one picture of different parts of a story. — *adj* **synchronis'tic** or **synchronis'tical.** — *adv* **synchronis'tically.** — *adj* **syn'chronous** simultaneous; contemporary; keeping time together. — *adv* **syn'chronously.** — *n* **syn'chronousness.** — *n* **syn'chrony** simultaneity. — **synchronised swimming** a sport in which a swimmer or group of swimmers performs a sequence of movements in time to music; **synchronous motor** an electric motor whose speed is exactly proportional to the frequency of the supply current; **synchronous orbit** geostationary orbit. [Gr. *syn*, together, *chronos*, time.]

syncline *sin'klīn*, (*geol*) *n* a fold in which the beds dip downwards towards the axis. — *adj* **synclīn'al.** — *n* a syncline. [Gr. *syn*, together, *klīnein*, to cause to lean.]

Syncom *sin'kom*, *n* one of a series of communication satellites in a synchronous orbit. [*Syn*chronous *com*munications satellite.]

syncope *sing'kə-pi*, *n* the elision of a letter or syllable from the middle of a word; a fainting fit caused by a sudden fall of blood pressure in the brain (*med*). — *adj* **syn'copal.** — *vt* **syn'copate** to shorten by cutting out the middle (of a word); to alter the rhythm of (music, etc.) temporarily by transferring the accent to a normally unaccented beat. — *adj* **syn'copated.** — *n* **syncopa'tion.** — *n* **syn'copātor.** — *adj* **syncopic** (*sing-kop'ik*). [Gr. *synkopē*, a cutting up, cutting short — *syn*, together, *koptein*, to cut off.]

syncretism *sing'kri-tizm* or *sin'kri-*, *n* reconciliation of, or attempt to reconcile, different systems of belief; fusion or blending of religions, as by identification of gods, taking over of observances, or selection of whatever seems best in each; illogical compromise in religion; the fusion of orig. distinct inflectional forms of a word. — *adj* **syncretic** (*sin-krē'tik* or *sing-krē'tik*). — *vt* and *vi* **syncretise** or **-ize** (*sing'kri-tīz*). — *n* **syn'cretist.** — *adj* **syncretis'tic.** [Gr. *synkrētismos*, a confederation (orig. app. of *Cretan* communities).]

syncytium *sin-sish'i-əm*, (*biol*) *n* a multinucleate cell; a tissue without distinguishable cell-walls. — *adj* **syncyt'ial.** [Gr. *syn*, together, *kytos*, a vessel.]

syndactyl *sin-dak'til*, *adj* with fused digits. — *n* **syndac'tylism.** — *adj* **syndac'tylous.** — *n* **syndac'tyly.** [Gr. *syn*, *daktylos*, finger, toe.]

syndesis *sin'di-sis*, *n* a binding; synapsis (*biol*). — *adj* **syndetic** (*-det'ik*) or **syndet'ical** connective; of a construction in which clauses are connected by conjunctions (*gram*). — *adv* **syndet'ically.** [Gr. *syndesis* — *syn*, *deein*, to bind.]

syndesmosis *sin-des-mō'sis*, (*zool*) *n* the connection of bones by ligaments: — *pl* **syndesmo'ses** (*-sēz*). — *adj* **syndesmotic** (*-mot'ik*). [Gr. *syndesmos* — *syn*, *desmos*, a bond.]

syndetic, etc. See **syndesis.**

syndic *sin'dik*, *n* at various times and places a magistrate or mayor; a member of a committee of the Senate of Cambridge University; a person chosen to transact business for others, esp. the accredited legal representative of a corporation, society or company. — *adj* **syn'dical.** — *n* **syn'dicalism** a development of trade-unionism which originated in France, aiming at putting the means of production in the hands of unions of workers. — *n* **syn'dicalist.** — Also *adj.* — *adj* **syndicalist'ic.** — *n* **syn'dicate** a body of syndics; a council; a body of men chosen to watch the interests of a company, or to manage a bankrupt's property; a combination of persons for some common purpose or interest; an association of businessmen or companies to undertake a project requiring a large amount of capital; an association of criminals who organise and control illegal operations; a combined group of newspapers. — *vt* to control, effect or publish by means of a syndicate; to sell (e.g. an article) for simultaneous publication in a number of newspapers or periodicals; to sell radio or TV programmes for broadcasting by many different radio or TV stations; to join in a syndicate. — *n* **syndicā'tion.** — *n* **syn'dicātor.** [Gr. *syndikos* — *syn*, with, *dikē*, justice.]

syndrome *sin'drōm, n* concurrence, esp. of symptoms; a characteristic pattern or group of symptoms; a pattern or group of actions, feelings, observed happenings, etc. characteristic of a particular problem or condition. — *adj* **syndromic** (*-drom'ik*). [Gr. *syndromē*.]

synecdoche *sin-ek'də-kē* or *-ki*, (*rhet*) *n* the figure of putting part for the whole, or the whole for part. — *adj* **synecdochic** (*-dok'*) or **synecdoch'ical**. — *adv* **synecdoch'ically**. [Gr. *synekdochē* — *syn*, together, *ekdechesthai*, to receive.]

synecology *sin-i-kol'ə-ji, n* the ecological study of communities of plants or animals. — *adj* **synecolog'ic** or **synecolog'ical**. — *adv* **synecolog'ically**. [Gr. *syn*, together, (**syn-**) and **ecology**.]

syneresis. Same as **synaeresis**.

synergy *sin'ər-ji, n* combined or co-ordinated action. — *adj* **synergetic** (*-jet'ik*) or **syner'gic** working together. — *vi* **syn'ergise** or **-ize** to act as a synergist (with another substance). — *n* **synergism** (*sin'* or *-ûr'*) increased effect of two substances, as drugs, obtained by using them together. — *n* **syn'ergist** (or *-ûr'*) a substance which increases the effect of another (e.g. pesticide); a muscle, etc. that acts with another. — *adj* **synergist'ic**. — *adv* **synergist'ically**. [Gr. *synergiā*, co-operation — *syn*, together, *ergon*, work.]

synesis *sin'ə-sis, n* syntax having regard to meaning rather than grammatical form. [Gr., sense.]

synfuel *sin'fū-əl, n* any type of fuel synthesised from a fossil fuel. [*syn*thetic and **fuel**.]

syngamy *sing'gə-mi*, (*biol*) *n* union of gametes. — *adj* **syngamic** (*sin-gam'ik*). — *adj* **syngamous** (*sing'gə-məs*). [Gr. *syn*, together, *gamos*, marriage.]

syngeneic *sin-ji-nē'ik*, (*immun*) *adj* genetically identical. [Gr. *syngeneia*, kinship.]

syngenesis *sin-jen'i-sis*, (*biol*) *n* reproduction by fusion of male and female elements, the offspring being derived from both parents. [Gr. *syn*, together, *genesis*, formation, generation.]

synizesis *sin-i-zē'sis*, (*phon*) *n* the union into one syllable of two vowels without forming a recognised diphthong. [Gr. *synizēsis*, a collapse — *syn*, with, together, *hizein*, to seat, to sit down.]

synod *sin'əd, n* a meeting; an ecclesiastical council; a Presbyterian church court intermediate between presbytery and the General Assembly. — *adj* **syn'odal** of, of the nature of, or done in a synod. — *adj* **synodic** (*-od'ik*) or **synod'ical** synodal; pertaining to conjunction (*astron*); from conjunction to conjunction. — *adv* **synod'ically**. — **synodic period** (*astron*) the time between two successive conjunctions of a heavenly body with the sun; **General Synod of the Church of England** governing body set up to give the laity more say in the decisions of the Church. [Gr. *synodos*, a meeting, conjunction — *syn*, together, *hodos*, a way.]

synonym *sin'ə-nim, n* a word having the same meaning as another in the same language. — *adj* **synonym'ic** or **synonym'ical** of synonyms. — *n* **synonym'ity** the fact or quality of being synonymous. — *adj* **synon'ymous** having the same meaning. — *adv* **synon'ymously**. — *n* **synon'ymousness**. — *n* **synon'ymy** rhetorical use of synonyms; a setting forth of synonyms; a list of synonyms. [Gr. *synōnymon* — *syn*, with, *onoma*, a name.]

synop. *abbrev* for synopsis.

synopsis *sin-op'sis, n* a general view; a summary: — *pl* **synop'sēs**. — *vt* **synop'sise** or **-ize** to make a synopsis of. — *adj* **synop'tic** or **synop'tical** affording or taking a general view of the whole. — *adv* **synop'tically**. — *n* **synop'tist** one of the writers of the Synoptic Gospels. — *adj* **synoptis'tic**. — **Synoptic Gospels** those of Matthew, Mark and Luke, which are strikingly alike in viewpoint and presentation of the narrative. [Gr. *synopsis* — *syn*, with, together, *opsis*, a view.]

synovia *sin-ō'vi-ə*, (*zool*) *n* an unctuous fluid in the joints. — *adj* **syno'vial**. — *adj* **synovitic** (*-vit'ik*) pertaining to synovitis. — *n* **synovī'tis** (*med*) inflammation of a synovial membrane. — **synovial membrane** (*anat*) a membrane of connective tissue that lines tendon sheaths and capsular ligaments and secretes synovia. [App. an arbitrary coinage of Paracelsus.]

synroc *sin'rok, n* a type of synthetic rock developed especially to fuse with radioactive waste to be buried deep underground. [*syn*thetic *roc*k.]

syntactic, syntagma, etc. See under **syntax**.

syntax *sin'taks, n* grammatical structure in sentences; one of the classes in some R.C. schools. — *adj* **syntac'tic** or **syntac'tical**. — *adv* **syntac'tically**. — *n* **syntag'ma** a systematic body, system or group; a word or words constituting a syntactic unit: — *pl* **syntag'mata**. — *adj* **syntagmat'ic**. [Gr. *syntaxis* — *syn*, together — *tassein*, to put in order.]

syntenosis *sin-tə-nō'sis, n* the connection of bones by tendons: — *pl* **syntenoses** (*-ō'sēz*). [Gr. *syn*, with, *tenōn*, a sinew.]

synth *sinth, n* short for synthesiser. — Also *adj*.

synthesis *sin'thi-sis, n* building up; putting together; making a whole out of parts; the combination of separate elements of thought into a whole; reasoning from principles to a conclusion (opp. to *analysis*): — *pl* **syn'theses** (*-sēz*). — *vt* **syn'thesise** or **-ize** to put together in synthesis; to form by synthesis. — *n* **syn'thesīser** or **-z-** someone who, or something that, synthesises; a computerised instrument for generating sounds, often beyond the range of conventional instruments, used esp. in making electronic music. — *n* **syn'thesist** someone who makes a synthesis. — *adj* **synthetic** (*-thet'*) or **synthet'ical** pertaining to, consisting in or formed by synthesis; artificially produced but of like nature with, not a mere substitute for, the natural product; not sincere, sham (*colloq*). — *n* **synthet'ic** a synthetic substance. — *adv* **synthet'ically**. — *vt* **syn'thetise** or **-ize** to synthesise. — *n* **syn'thetīser** or **-z-**. — *n* **syn'thetist**. — **synthetic languages** those that use inflectional forms instead of word order, prepositions, etc. to express syntactical relationships. [Gr. *synthesis* — *syn*, with, together, *thesis*, a placing.]

syphilis *sif'i-lis, n* a contagious venereal disease due to infection with a micro-organism *Spirochaeta pallida* (*Treponema pallidum*). — *adj* **syphilit'ic**. — *n* a person suffering from syphilis. — *adj* **syph'iloid** like syphilis. [Title of Fracastoro's Latin poem (1530), whose hero *Syphilus* is infected.]

syphon, syren. Same as **siphon, siren**.

SYR *abbrev* for Syria (I.V.R.).

Syriac *sir'i-ak, n* the ancient Aramaic dialect of *Syria*; a modern form of this dialect still spoken in the Middle East and in the U.S. — Also *adj*. — *adj* **Syr'ian** relating to Syria. — *n* native or citizen of Syria.

syringa *sir-ing'gə, n* orig. and still popularly the mock-orange; the lilac.

syringe *si-rinj', n* an instrument for injecting or extracting fluids. — *vt* and *vi* to clean, spray or inject with a syringe. [Ety. as for **syrinx**.]

syrinx *sir'ingks, n* Pan-pipes; the vocal organ of birds; a rock-cut tunnel (as in Egyptian tombs): — *pl* **syringes** (*-in'jēz*) or **syr'inxes**. — *n* **syringomyelia** (*si-ring-gō-mī-ē'li-ə*; Gr. *myelos*, marrow) a chronic, progressive disease of the spinal cord, causing paralysis and loss of sensitivity to pain and temperature. [Gr. *sȳrinx*, *-ingos*, Pan-pipes, gallery.]

syrup *sir'əp, n* a saturated solution of sugar boiled to prevent fermentation; any thick sweet liquid; a sugar-flavoured liquid medicine; cloying sweetness (*fig*; *colloq*). — Also (esp. in *US*) **sir'up**. — *adj* **syr'upy**. — **golden syrup** the uncrystallisable part finally separated in manufacture of crystallised sugar. [Fr. *sirop* — Ar. *sharāb*; cf. **shrub²** and **sherbet**.]

sys-. See **syn-**.

syssarcosis *sis-är-kō'sis*, (*zool* and *anat*) *n* the connection of one bone with another by intervening muscle: — *pl* **syssarco'ses** (*-sēz*). [Gr. *syn*, together, *sarx*, flesh.]

systaltic *sis-tal'tik*, *adj* alternately contracting and dilating, pulsatory. [Gr. *systaltikos*, depressing; cf. **systole**.]

system *sis'tim* or *sis'təm*, *n* anything formed of parts placed together or adjusted into a regular and connected whole; a set of things considered as a connected whole; a group of celestial bodies moving mainly under the influence of their mutual attraction (*astron*); a set of bodily organs of similar composition or concurring in function; the bodily organism; one of the great divisions of the geological strata; a body of doctrine; a theory of the universe; a full and connected view of some department of knowledge; an explanatory hypothesis; a scheme of classification; a manner of crystallisation; a plan; a method; a method of organisation; methodicalness; (with **the**, often with *cap*) society seen as a soulless and monolithic organisation thwarting individual effort. — *adj* **systemat'ic** or **systemat'ical** pertaining to, or consisting of, for the purpose of, observing or according to system; methodical; habitual; intentional. — *adv* **systemat'ically**. — *n* **systematician** (*-mə-tish'ən*). — *nsing* **systemat'ics** the science of classification; the study of classification of living things in accordance with their natural relationships. — *n* **systematīsā'tion** or **-z-**, **systemīsā'tion** or **-z-**. — *vt* **sys'tematise** or **-ize** or **sys'temise** or **-ize** to reduce to a system. — *n* **sys'tematiser** or **-z-**. — *n* **sys'tematism**. — *n* **sys'tematist**. — *adj* **sys'temed**. — *adj* **systemic** (*-tem'ik*) pertaining to the bodily system or to a system of bodily organs; affecting the body as a whole; (of a pesticide, etc.) spreading through all the tissues, without harming the plant but making it toxic to the insect, etc.; (of a herbicide) spreading through all the tissues of a plant and killing it. — *adj* **sys'temless** without system; not exhibiting organic structure. — **system building** building using standardised factory-produced components. — *adj* **sys'tem-built**. — **systems analysis**; **systems analyst** someone who analyses the operation of a scientific or industrial, etc. procedure, usu. with a computer, in order to plan more efficient methods and use of equipment; **systems engineering** a branch of engineering that uses information theory and systems analysis to design integrated systems; **systems flowchart** (*comput*) a flowchart designed to analyse the operation of a computing system with a view to improving it; **system software** (*comput*) the software needed to produce a system that is acceptable to the end user. [Gr. *systēma* — *sy-*, *syn-*, together, and the root of *histanai*, to set.]

systole *sis'to-lē* or *sis'tə-lē*, (*physiol*) *n* rhythmical contraction, esp. of the heart (opp. to *diastole*). — *adj* **systolic** (*-tol'ik*). [Gr. *systolē* — *syn*, together, *stellein*, to place.]

syzygy *siz'i-ji*, *n* conjunction or opposition; the period of new or full moon (*astron*): — *pl* **syz'ygies**. — *adj* **syzyg'ial**. [Gr. *syzygīā*, union, coupling — *sy-*, *syn-*, with, together, *zygon*, a yoke.]

T

T or **t** *tē*, *n* the twentieth letter in the modern English alphabet, eighteenth in the Roman, usually sounded as a voiceless stop produced with the tip of the tongue in contact with teeth, gums or palate; an object or mark in the form of the letter (also **tee**). — **T'-bandage** a bandage composed of two strips made in the shape of the letter T; **T'-bar** a metal bar with cross-section in the shape of the letter T; a type of ski-lift (also **T-bar lift**); **T'-bone** a bone shaped like a T, esp. in a sirloin steak; **T'-cell** a type of lymphocyte involved in cellular immunity, that matures in the thymus gland, e.g. a *cytotoxic T-cell* able to kill virus-infected cells; **T'-cloth** a plain cotton made for the India and China market — stamped with a T; **T'-cross** a tau cross; **T'-junction** a road junction in the shape of a T; **T'-plate** a T-shaped plate, as for strengthening a joint in a wooden framework; **T'-rail** a rail with T-shaped cross-section. — *adj* **T'-shaped.** — **T-shirt** see under **tee**[1]; **T'-square** a T-shaped ruler; **T'-strap** a T-shaped strap on a shoe. — **to a T** with perfect exactness.

T or **T.** *abbrev* for: tenor (*mus*); Thailand (I.V.R.).

T *symbol* for: tera-; tesla (*phys*); tritium (*chem*).

't a shortened form of **it**.

t or **t.** *abbrev* for: tense; ton(s); tonne(s); transitive; troy (weight).

t *symbol* for time.

TA *abbrev* for Territorial Army.

Ta (*chem*) *symbol* for tantalum.

ta *tä*, (*colloq*) *interj* thank you.

TAB *abbrev* for: Totalisator Agency Board, the off-course betting statutory authority (*Austr* and *NZ*); typhoid-paratyphoid A and B (vaccine).

tab[1] *tab*, *n* a small tag, flap or strap attached to something; a loop for hanging something up by, etc.; a loop for drawing a stage curtain; hence, a stage curtain; the bill, tally, cost, check (*US*). — *adj* **tabbed.** — *vt* to fix a tab to: — *pr p* **tabb'ing**; *pa t* and *pa p* **tabbed.** — **keep tabs on** see under **keep**; **pick up the tab** (*US colloq*) to pay the bill.

tab[2] *tab*, *n* short for **tablet**.

tab[3] *tab*, *n* short for (typewriter) **tabulator**. — *vt* short for **tabulate**.

Tabanus *tə-bā'nəs*, *n* the gadfly genus. — *n* **tabanid** (*tab'ə-nid*) any member of this blood-sucking genus, or of its family **Tabanidae** (*tə-ban'i-dē*). [L. *tabānus*.]

tabard *tab'ərd*, *n* a mediaeval peasant's overcoat, or a knight's sleeveless or short-sleeved coat (*hist*); a herald's coat or tunic bearing a coat-of-arms; a woman's outer garment, a sleeveless tunic. [O.Fr. *tabart*.]

tabaret *tab'ə-ret*, *n* an upholsterer's silk fabric, with alternate stripes of watered and satin surface. [Orig. tradename, prob. formed from **tabby**.]

Tabasco® *tə-bas'kō*, *n* a hot pepper sauce. [*Tabasco* state in Mexico.]

tabbouleh *ta-bōō'le*, *n* a Mediterranean salad introduced from Lebanon, made with cracked wheat. [Ar. *tabbūla*.]

tabby *tab'i*, *n* a coarse waved or watered silk fabric; a tabby-cat; a gossiping, interfering woman (*colloq*). — *adj* brindled. — **tabb'y-cat** a brindled cat, esp. a greyish or brownish cat with dark stripes; sometimes (perh. from *Tabitha*) a female cat. [Fr. *tabis*, app. from *'Attābiy*, a quarter in Baghdad where it was made.]

tabefaction, tabefy. See under **tabes**.

tabernacle *tab'ər-na-kl*, *n* the tent carried by the Jews through the desert and used as a temple (*hist*); the human body as the temporary abode of the soul; a receptacle for the vessel containing the pyx (*RC*); a canopied niche or seat (*eccles*); a reliquary; a socket for a mast (*naut*). — *vi* to sojourn. — *vt* to put or enshrine in a tabernacle. — *adj* **tab'ernacled.** — *adj* **tabernacular** (*-nak'ū-lər*). — **Feast of Tabernacles** (also called the **Feast of Ingathering** or **Sukkoth**) a Jewish harvest festival, celebrating the sojourn in tents in the wilderness. [L. *tabernāculum*, dimin. of *taberna*, a hut.]

tabes *tā'bēz*, (*pathol*) *n* wasting away. — *n* **tabefaction** (*tab-i-fak'shən*) wasting away, emaciation. — *vt* and *vi* **tab'efy.** — *n* **tabescence** (*tab-es'əns*) wasting; shrivelling. — *adj* **tabesc'ent.** — *adj* **tabetic** (*-bet'ik*) or **tab'id.** — **tabes dorsa'lis** locomotor ataxia. [L. *tābēs*, *-is*.]

tabla *tab'lə* or *tab'lä*, *n* an Indian percussion instrument, a pair of small drums played with the hands. [Hind.]

tablature *tab'lə-chər*, *n* an old notation for lute music, etc. with a line for each string and letters or figures to indicate the stopping, used with modifications for other instruments; a painting, picture, pictorial representation or work. [Fr. — Med. L. *tabulatura* — L. *tabula*, a board.]

table *tā'bl*, *n* an article of furniture consisting of a flat top on legs, a pillar, or trestles, for use at meals, work, play, for holding things, etc.; a flat surface; a slab or board; a layer; a compact scheme of numerical or factual information; (in *pl*) a collection of these for reference; a syllabus or index; a condensed statement; a slab inscribed with laws; (in *pl*) a code of law (e.g. the *Twelve Tables* of ancient Rome); supply of food, entertainment; the company at a table; a string-course (*archit*); a broad flat surface on a cut gem; a tabular crystal; a flat gravestone supported on pillars. — *adj* of, for, like or pertaining to a table, or meals. — *vt* to tabulate; to pay down; to lay on the table, to put forward (a bill, order, etc.) for discussion in parliament; to postpone discussion of (a bill, etc.) for some time or indefinitely (*US*). — *adj* **tabled** (*tā'bld*) flat-topped; having a smooth sloping surface of dressed stone; having a table or tables. — *n* **ta'bleful** as much as a table will hold. — *n* **ta'bling** provision of tables; a broad hem on the skirt of a sail. — **ta'blecloth** a cloth for covering a table, esp. at meals. — *adj* **ta'ble-cut** (of gems) cut with a flat top. — **table-d'hôte** (*tä-bl'-dōt*; Fr., host's table) a meal at a fixed price (as at a hotel); **table football** a version of football played on a table with small metal, etc. players usu. suspended on rods, that are turned or spun to strike the ball; **table game** a board game; **table knife** a knife used to cut one's meat, etc. with at the table; **ta'bleland** an extensive region of elevated land with a flat or undulating surface; a plateau; **ta'ble-leaf** an extension to a table-top, hinged, drawn out, or inserted; **table licence** a licence to serve alcoholic drinks with meals only; **table linen** linen tablecloths, napkins, etc.; **table manners** behaviour when eating at the table;

ta'ble-mat a mat placed under dishes on a table; **ta'ble-money** an allowance (esp. in the services) for official entertainment; **ta'ble-music** music in parts that can be read by performers at each side of a table; **ta'ble-napkin** a cloth used at table to protect the clothes and to wipe fingers and lips; **table salt** fine salt suitable for use at table; **ta'ble-skittles** a game in which a suspended ball is swung to knock down pegs set up on a board; **ta'blespoon** one of the largest spoons used at table, for serving food with; **ta'blespoonful** as much as will fill a tablespoon: — *pl* **ta'blespoonfuls**; **ta'ble-talk** familiar conversation, as at table, during and after meals; **table tennis** a game like lawn tennis played on a table using celluloid or similar balls; **ta'ble-top** the top of a table; a flat top. — *adj* **ta'ble-topped**. — **ta'ble-turning** movements of tables (or other objects) attributed by spiritualists to the agency of spirits — by the sceptical to collective involuntary muscular action; the practice of turning the tables (see **turn the tables** below); **ta'bleware** dishes, spoons, knives, forks, etc. for table use; **table wine** an ordinary wine usually drunk with a meal; **ta'ble-work** (*printing*) the setting of type for tables, columns of figures, etc. — **at table** at a meal; **lay on the table** to table (a bill, etc.; see **table** *vt*, above); **Lord's table** see under **lord**; **turn the tables** to bring about a complete reversal of circumstances, as if the players at backgammon changed sides; **under the table** not above board, illicit; hopelessly drunk. [Partly O.E. *tabule*, *tabele*, partly O.Fr. (and Fr.) *table*, both — L. *tabula*, a board.]

tableau *tab'lō*, *n* a picture or vivid pictorial impression; a suddenly created dramatic or impressive situation; a tableau vivant; a moment or scene in which the action is 'frozen' for dramatic effect (*theat*): — *pl* **tableaux** (*tab'lōz*). — **tableau curtains** theatre curtains drawn back and up, to give a draped effect when opened; **tableau vivant** a 'living picture', a motionless representation by living persons in costume: — *pl* **tableaux vivants** (*tä-blō vē-vã*). [Fr. dimin. of *table*.]

tablet *tab'lit*, *n* a small slab; a small flat cake of any solid material, esp. medicinal; a device that converts the movement of a specially adapted pen into digital or analog signals, allowing graphic designs to be displayed on a visual display unit (*comput*); a slab or stiff sheet for making notes on; a panel, esp. inscribed or for inscription; a brittle confection of sugar and condensed milk, made in slabs (*Scot*). — *vt* to provide with, inscribe on, or make into, a tablet. [O.Fr. *tablete*, dimin. of *table*.]

tabloid *tab'loid*, *n* a newspaper of small format, measuring approx. 30 × 40 cm. (about 12 × 16 in.), usu. informal or sensationalistic in style and with many photographs; anything in a concentrated form, a summary. — *adj* of, like, or in the form of, tabloids; concentrated. [From *Tabloid*, trademark for a medicine in tablet form.]

taboo or **tabu** *tə-bōō'*, *adj* subject to taboo; forbidden. — *n* any recognised or general prohibition, interdict, restraint, ban, exclusion or ostracism; a Polynesian (or other) system of prohibitions connected with things considered holy or unclean; any one of these prohibitions: — *pl* **taboos'** or **tabus'**. — *vt* to forbid approach to or use of; to place under taboo: — *pr p* **taboo'ing** or **tabu'ing**; *pa t* and *pa p* **tabooed'** or **tabued'**. [Tongan *tabu* (pronounced *tä'bōō*), holy, unclean.]

tabor or **tabour** *tā'bər*, *n* a small drum like a tambourine without jingles, usually played with one stick, along with a pipe; a taborer. — *vi* and *vt* to play on a tabor; to beat or drum. — *n* **tā'borer** a person who beats the tabor. — *n* **taborin** or **tabourin** (*tab'ə-rin* or *-rēn*) a small drum longer in body than the tabor, used in a similar way. — *n* **tabouret** or in U.S. **taboret** (*tab'ə-ret* or *tä-bōō-rā*) a stool, orig. drum-shaped. — *n* **tabret** (*tab'rit*) a small tabor. [O.Fr. *tabour*; an Oriental word.]

tabu. See **taboo**.

tabula *tab'ū-lə* or in L. *tab'ōō-la*, *n* an altar frontal (*eccles*); a horizontal partition in corals: — *pl* **tab'ulae** (*-lē*; in L. *-lī*). — **tabula rasa** (*tab'ū-lə rā'zə* or *tab'ōō-la rä'sa*) a smoothed or blank tablet; a mind not yet influenced by outside impressions and experience. [L., table, writing tablet.]

tabular *tab'ū-lər*, *adj* of, in the form of, like, or according to, a table or tablet; platy; horizontally flattened. — *n* **tabularīsā'tion** or **-z-**. — *vt* **tab'ularise** or **-ize** to tabulate. — *adv* **tab'ularly**. — *vt* **tab'ulate** to reduce to, or lay out in, the form of a table or synopsis. — *adj* tabular; having tabulae. — *n* **tabulā'tion**. — *n* **tab'ulātor** a person who, or a machine which, tabulates data; a device in a typewriter which sets and then finds automatically the margins needed in tabular work; a machine which prints very rapidly data from punched cards, etc. on to continuous paper (*comput*). — *adj* **tab'ulatory** (*-lə-tə-ri*). [L. *tabula*, table.]

tabun *tä-bōōn'*, *n* an organic phosphorus compound, $C_5H_{11}N_2O_2P$, which can be used as a nerve gas. [Ger.]

tacamahac *tak'ə-mə-hak*, *n* a gum-resin yielded by several tropical trees; the balsam poplar, or its resin. [From Nahuatl.]

TACAN, **Tacan** or **tacan** *tak'an*, *n* an electronic system of air navigation which gives an aircraft a direct reading of distance and bearing from a ground-based transmitter. [*tac*tical *a*ir *n*avigation.]

tac-au-tac *tak-ō-tak'*, (*fencing*) *n* the parry combined with the riposte; also a series of close attacks and parries between fencers of equal skill. [Fr.]

tacet *tā'set* or *ta'ket*, (*mus*) (an instruction to) be silent. [L., imper. of *tacēre*, to be silent.]

tach- *tak-*, **tache-** or **tachy-** *tak-i-*, *combining form* denoting speed or speedy. — *n* **tacheom'eter** or **tachymeter** (*-im'ə-tər*) a surveying instrument for rapid measurement of distances. — *adj* **tacheomet'rical** or **tachymet'rical**. — *n* **tacheom'etry** or **tachym'etry**. — *n* **tachis'toscope** (Gr. *tachistos*, *superl* of *tachys*) an instrument which flashes images, sentences, etc. on a screen for very brief, exactly timed, periods, now used esp. to increase reading speed. — *adj* **tachistoscop'ic**. — *n* **tach'ogram** a record, made by a tachograph. — *n* **tach'ograph** a recording tachometer; a tachogram; an instrument fitted to commercial vehicles to record mileage, speed, number and location of stops, etc. — *n* **tachom'eter** a device showing speed of rotation; an instrument for measuring the velocity of machines or currents. — *adj* **tachomet'rical**. — *n* **tachom'etry**. — *n* **tachycar'dia** (Gr. *kardiā*, heart) abnormal rapidity of heartbeat. — *n* **tach'ygraph**. — *n* **tachyg'rapher** or **tachyg'raphist**. — *adj* **tachygraph'ic** or **tachygraph'ical**. — *n* **tachyg'raphy** shorthand, esp. ancient Greek and Roman. — *n* **tach'ylyte** (also **tach'ylite**; Gr. *lytos*, melted, because easily fused before the blowpipe) a black opaque glass occurring as a thin selvage to intrusive basalt. — *adj* **tachylytic** (*-lit'ik*). — *n* **tachymeter**, etc. see **tacheometer** above. — *n* **tachyon** (*tak'i-on*) a theoretical particle moving faster than light. — *n* **tachypnoea** (*tak-ip-nē'ə*; Gr. *pnoiā*, breathing) excessive frequency in breathing. [Gr. *tachys* (genitive *-eos*), swift, *tachos*, swiftness.]

tache *tash*, (*colloq*) *n* short for **moustache**.

tachism or **tachisme** *tash'izm*, *n* a mid-20th-century movement in abstract painting characterised by a clotted laying on of pigment. — *n* and *adj* **tach'ist** or **tach'iste**. [Fr. *tache*, blob (of paint).]

tachogram, tachometer, etc. See under **tach-**.

tachycardia ... to ... **tachypnoea**. See under **tach-**.

tacit *tas'it*, *adj* unspoken; silent. — *adv* **tac'itly**. — *n* **tac'itness**. — *adj* **tac'iturn** disinclined to speak, reticent, uncommunicative. — *n* **taciturn'ity**. — *adv* **tac'iturnly**. [L. *tacitus, taciturnus*.]

tack[1] *tak, n* a short, sharp nail with a broad head; a long temporary stitch; a fastening strip; a rope or other fastening for the lower windward corner of a sail (*naut*); the corner itself (*naut*); an act of tacking; an alternate course in zigzag (*naut*); course of action; a change of policy, a strategical move; something tacked on; stickiness. — *vt* to attach or fasten, esp. in a loose, hasty or impermanent manner, e.g. by tacks or long stitches; to change the course of by a tack. — *vi* to change the course or tack of a ship by shifting the position of the sails; to zigzag; to shift one's position, to veer. — *adj* **tacked**. — *n* **tack'er**. — *n* **tack'et** (*Scot*) a hobnail. — *adj* **tack'ety**. — *n* **tack'iness**. — *n* **tack'ing** proceeding by tacks; fastening; fastening by tacks; introducing into a bill (esp. a money bill) provisions beyond its natural scope (*politics*). — *adj* **tack'y** sticky. — *adj* **tacked'-on**. — **tack hammer** a light hammer for driving in tacks. — **change tack** to change course, take a new direction; **on the right (***or* **wrong) tack** following the right (or wrong) course of action, train of thought, etc. [O.Fr. *taque*, doublet of *tache*.]

tack[2] *tak, n* food generally, fare, esp. of the bread kind, as *hard tack* (ship's biscuit), *soft tack* (loaves).

tack[3] *tak, n* the sound of a sharp tap. [Imit.]

tack[4] *tak, n* riding harness, saddles, bridles, etc. [**tackle**.]

tacker, tacket, tackety, tackiness, tacking. See under **tack**[1].

tackle *tak'l, n* the ropes, rigging, etc. of a ship (*naut*; *tāk'l*); tools, gear, weapons, equipment (for sports, etc.); ropes, etc., for raising heavy weights; a pulley; the act of gripping; an act of tackling (*football*); the player positioned one from the end (either **right** or **left**) on the scrimmage line (*Am football*). — *vt* to seize or take hold of; to grapple with; to come to grips with; to begin to deal in earnest with; to confront, encounter or challenge; to harness. — *vt* and *vi* (*Rugby football*) to seize and stop or (in *association football*) intercept (a player) in an effort to get the ball away from them. — *adj* **tackled** (*tak'ld*) furnished with harness or tackle. — *n* **tack'ler**. — *n* **tack'ling** furniture or apparatus belonging to the masts, yards, etc. of a ship; harness for drawing a carriage; tackle or instruments; grappling. [Cf. L.G. *takel*.]

tacky[1] *tak'i*, (*slang*) *adj* (orig. *US*) shabby; sleazy; vulgar, in bad taste. — *n* a poor ill-conditioned horse or person (*US*). — *n* **tack'iness**.

tacky[2]. See under **tack**[1].

taco *tä'kō, n* in Mexican cooking, a very thin rolled pancake with a meat filling, usu. fried crisp: — *pl* **ta'cos**. [Mex. Sp.]

taconite *tak'ə-nīt, n* a sedimentary rock containing enough iron to make it a low-grade iron ore. [*Taconic* Mountains in N.E. United States.]

tact *takt, n* adroitness in managing the feelings of persons dealt with; fine perception in seeing and doing exactly what is best in the circumstances; the stroke in keeping time (*mus*). — *adj* **tact'ful**. — *adv* **tact'fully**. — *adj* **tact'less**. — *adv* **tact'lessly**. — *n* **tact'lessness**. — *adj* **tact'ūal** relating to, or derived from, the sense of touch. — *n* **tactūal'ity** tactual quality. — *adv* **tact'ūally**. [L. *tactus, -ūs* — *tangĕre, tactum*, to touch.]

tactic *tak'tik* or **tactical** *tak'tik-əl, adj* relating to taxis or tactism, or to tactics; (**tactical**) skilful, adroit, calculated. — *n* **tac'tic** a system, or a piece, of tactics. — *adv* **tac'tically**. — *n* **tactician** (*-tish'ən*) a person skilled in tactics. — *n* **tactic'ity** the stereochemical arrangement of units in the main chain of a polymer (*chem*). — *nsing* **tac'tics** the science or art of manoeuvring in presence of the enemy. — *npl* purposeful procedure. — *n* **tac'tism** (*biol*) taxis. — **tactical voting** the practice of voting for a political party one does not support in order to prevent the election of a party one is even more opposed to. [Gr. *taktikos*, fit for arranging, *taktos*, ordered — *tassein*, to arrange.]

tactile *tak'tīl, adj* perceptible by touch; pertaining to the sense of touch; concerned in perception by touch; suggestive of touch. — *n* **tact'ilist** (*-il-ist*) a painter who aims at tactile effects. — *n* **tactil'ity**. [Ety. as for **tact**.]

tad *tad*, (*colloq*, esp. *US*) *n* a small amount; a little lad. [Short for **tadpole**.]

Tadjik. See **Tajik**.

tadpole *tad'pōl, n* the larva of a toad or frog, or (*rarely*) of an ascidian. [O.E. *tāde*, toad, and **poll** (head).]

Tadzhik. See **Tajik**.

tae *tā*, a Scots form of **toe, to** and **too** (meaning also). [Cf. obs. and dialect *tone*, the one and **tother**.]

tae kwon do *tā kwon dō, n* a Korean martial art, similar to karate. [Korean *tae*, kick, *kwon*, fist, *do*, method.]

tael *tāl, n* Chinese *liang* or ounce, about $\frac{1}{3}$oz. (38 g.); a money of account (not normally a coin) in China, orig. a tael weight of pure silver. — **tael bar** a gold bullion measure used in the Far East (1, 5 or 10 tael weight). [Port., — Malay *taïl*, weight.]

taenia *tē'ni-ə, n* the fillet above the architrave of the Doric order (*archit*); a ribbonlike structure; (with *cap*) the tapeworm genus; a member of the genus: — *pl* **tae'niae** (*-ni-ē*) or **taen'ias**. — *n* **taen'iacide** (*-sīd*) a substance that destroys tapeworms. — *n* **taenī'asis** infestation with tapeworm. — *adj* **tae'niate** or **tae'nioid** like a ribbon or a tapeworm. [L., a ribbon or fillet — Gr. *tainiā*, a band.]

TAFE *tāf, abbrev* for Technical and Further Education.

taffeta *taf'i-tə* or **taffetas** *taf'i-tas, n* a thin glossy silk fabric; loosely applied to various similar or mixed fabrics. — *adj* made of taffeta. [Through Fr. or L.L. from Pers. *tāftah*, woven — *tāftan*, to twist.]

taffrail *taf'ril, n* the rail around the stern of a ship; the upper part of a ship's stern timbers. [Earlier *tafferel* — Du. *tafereel*, a panel — *tafel*, a table — L. *tabula*, a table.]

Taffy *taf'i*, (*slang*) *n* a Welshman. [From *Dafydd*, Welsh form of David.]

taffy *taf'i, n* toffee; flattery, blarney (*US*).

tafia *taf'i-ə, n* a variety of rum. [Perh. a W. Indian name, but cf. Malay *tāfiā*.]

tag[1] *tag, n* a tab; a label, esp. a tie-on label; an identifying mark or sign; a signature (*slang*); an electronic tag; the point of a lace; any small thing tacked or attached to another; a flap, or a loose or flapping end; a stray, matted or dirty lock; the tip of a tail; the tail-end (e.g. of the batting order in cricket); a trite quotation (esp. Latin); a moral to a story; a refrain; the act of putting out a runner by touching them with the ball or the hand holding the ball (*baseball*). — *vt* to put a tag or tags on; to attach as a tag; to put a signature or similar mark on (*slang*); to tack, fasten, append; to remove tags from; to dog or follow closely; to put out (a runner) in baseball by a tag. — *vi* to make tags, to string words or ideas together; to go behind as a follower (with *on* or *along*): — *pr p* **tagg'ing**; *pa t* and *pa p* **tagged**. — *n* **taggee'** a person wearing an electronic tag (q.v. under **electronic**). — *n* **tagg'er**. — *npl* **tagg'ers** thin sheet-iron. — *n* **tagg'ing** electronic tagging (q.v.). — **tag'-day** (*US*) a flag-day; **tag'-end** the fag-end, tail-end; **tagged atom** a radioactive isotopic atom of a tracer element; **tag line** (*US*) a punch line; a watchword or slogan. — **tag along (with)** to follow.

tag[2] *tag, n* the children's game of tig. — *vt* to tig.

Tagálog *tä-gä'log, n* a people of the Philippine Islands; their language. — Also *adj*.

tagetes *tä-jē'tēz, n* a plant of the Mexican and S. American *Tagetes* genus of composites with yellow and orange flowers: — *pl* **tagē'tes**. [L. *Tagēs*, an Etruscan god.]

tagliarini *täl-yə-rē'ni*, *n* pasta cut into flat, very thin strips. [It.]

tagliatelle *tä-lya-tel'ā* or *tal-yə-tel'i*, *n* pasta made in long ribbons. [It.]

tagmeme *tag'mēm*, (*linguis*) *n* any of the positions in the structure of a sentence into which a certain class of grammatical items can fit. — *adj* **tagmē'mic**. — *nsing* **tagmē'mics** the analysis of the grammar of a language based on the arrangement or positions of the spoken elements. [Gr. *tagma*, order.]

taguan *ta'gwan* or *tä'gwän*, *n* a large E. Indian flying squirrel. [Tagálog.]

taha *tä'hä*, *n* a S. African weaver bird. [Zulu *taka*.]

tahina *tə-hē'nə* or **tahini** *-hē'nē*, *n* an oily paste made of crushed sesame seeds.

Tahitian *tä-hē'shən*, adj of or relating to *Tahiti* in the S. Pacific. — *n* a native or inhabitant of Tahiti; the Polynesian language of Tahiti.

tahr or **tehr** *tār*, *n* a beardless Himalayan wild goat that frequents forest peaks. [App. its name in the W. Himalayas confused with Nepali *thār*; see **thar**.]

tahsil *tä-* or *tähh-sēl'*, *n* in India, a division for revenue and certain other purposes. — *n* **tahsildar'** an officer of a tahsil. [Hindi *tahsīl* — Ar.]

Tai or **T'ai**. Same as **Thai**.

tai *tī*, *n* a Japanese sea-bream. [Jap.]

t'ai chi *tī jē* or **t'ai chi ch'uan** (*chwän*), *n* a Chinese system of exercise and self-defence in which good use of coordination and balance allows effort to be minimised. [Chin., great art of boxing.]

Taig *tāg*, (*offensive slang*) *n* (in Northern Ireland) a Catholic. [Variant of *Teague*, orig. used as nickname for any Irishman.]

taiga *tī'gə*, *n* marshy pine forest. [Russ. *taigá*.]

taigle *tā'gl*, (*Scot*) *vt* to entangle or hinder. — *vi* to linger or loiter; to trudge. [Cf. Sw. (Bornholm) *taggla*, to disorder.]

tail[1] *tāl*, *n* the posterior extremity of an animal, usually a slender prolongation beyond the anus; a bird's train of feathers; a fish's caudal fin; anything of similar appearance, position, etc.; the back, lower, hinder, latter, downstream or inferior part or prolongation of anything (often opp. to the *head*); the stem of a note in music; a downward extension of a letter; a queue; anything long and trailing or hanging, such as a train of a comet, or long curl of hair; (usu. in *pl*) the reverse of a coin; the end of a shoal sloping into deeper water; (often in *pl*) the skirts of a garment; (in *pl*) a tail-coat; a person who follows another and keeps constant watch on them (*colloq*); the buttocks, backside (*colloq*); the female genitalia or the penis (*slang*); sexual intercourse (*slang*). — *vt* to provide with a tail; to be a tail to; to remove the tail or stalk from; to grip or drag by the tail; to join end to end; to herd (*Austr*); to dog, shadow. — *vi* to taper (often with *off* or *away*); to lessen or deteriorate slowly (with *off* or *away*); to straggle; to show the tail. — *adj* **tailed**. — *n* **tail'ing** the inner covered end of a projecting brick or stone in a wall (*building*); (in *pl*) refuse, dregs; (in *pl*) the rejected or washed away portion of an ore. — *adj* **tail'less**. — **tail'back** a line of traffic stretching back from anything obstructing or slowing down traffic flow; **tail'board** a movable board at the back of a cart, wagon or lorry; **tail'-boom** a longitudinal strut supporting the tail of an aeroplane; **tail'-coat** a man's formal coat, cutaway at the front and with narrow tails at the back; **tail'-end** the fag-end, final and/or inferior part; something that comes at the end; **tail-end'er** (*colloq*) someone coming at the end; **tail'-feather** one of the stiff rudder-feathers of a bird's tail, used in steering; a feather of the back forming a train, as in the peacock; **tail'-fly** (*fishing*) the fly at the end of the leader; **tail'gate** lower gate of a lock; a tailboard; a door at the back of a car that opens upwards on hinges at the top; a jazz style of playing esp. the trombone. — *vt* to drive dangerously close behind (another vehicle) (*slang*). — Also *vi*. — **tail'gater** a person who tailgates; **tail'-light** a light at the back of a train, tram, car or other vehicle; **tail'piece** a piece at the tail or end; an engraving, design, etc. occupying the bottom of a page, as at the end of a chapter; a strip of ebony, etc. to which the ends of the strings are attached in a fiddle; **tail'pipe** an exhaust pipe (of a car) (*US*); the suction-pipe in a pump; **tail'plane** a horizontal aerofoil on the tail of an aircraft; **tail'race** the channel in which water runs away from a mill-wheel, or from a hydraulically-operated machine, etc.; **tail'-rhyme** or **tailed rhyme** a verse-form in which two or more rhymed lines are followed by a shorter line that does not rhyme with the others; **tail'-rope** a rope attached to the rear part of anything; **tail'skid** a support under the tail of an aeroplane on the ground; (in a motor vehicle) a skid starting with the rear wheels; **tail'spin** a spiral dive of an aeroplane; an uncontrolled downward spiral; a state of great agitation and uncertainty how to act; **tail'stock** a slidable casting mounted on a lathe, aligned with the headstock, used to support the free end of the piece being worked on; **tail wind** a wind blowing in the same direction as one is travelling. — **a bit (or piece) of tail** (*offensive slang*) a woman; **on someone's tail** following someone very closely; **tail-end Charlie** (*colloq*) a tail-ender; **tail off** to become gradually less or fewer; **the tail wagging the dog** (*colloq*) an instance where something or someone of less importance decisively influences something or someone of more importance; **turn tail** to turn around (and run off); **with the tail between the legs** like a beaten cur. [O.E. *tægl*, *tægel*.]

tail[2] *tāl*, (*law*) *n* limitation of inheritance to certain heirs. — *adj* limited. — **tail male** limitation to male heirs. [Fr. *taille*, cutting.]

tailleur *ta-yûr'*, *n* a woman's tailored suit. [Fr.]

tailor *tāl'ər*, *n* a person whose business is to cut out and make outer garments, esp. for men (*fem* **tail'oress**). — *vi* to work as a tailor. — *vt* to make clothes for; to fit with clothes; to make or adapt so as to fit a special need exactly (*fig*). — *n* **tail'oring**. — **tail'or-bird** an Asian warbler that sews leaves together to form a nest. — *adj* **tail'or-made** made by a tailor, esp. of plain, close-fitting garments for women; exactly adapted (for a purpose). — *n* a tailor-made garment; a factory-made cigarette, not one rolled by hand (*colloq*). — *vt* **tail'ormake** (orig. and esp. *US*) to make especially to suit a particular purpose or person, etc. [A.Fr. *taillour* — L.L *tāliātor*, *-ōris* — *tāliāre*, to cut.]

taint *tānt*, *n* a stain or blemish; pollution; infection; a tincture of some evil quality; a latent or incipient defect or corruption. — *vt* to affect or imbue with anything objectionable; to contaminate or infect; to impart a taint to. — *vi* to become infected or rotten; to go bad; to weaken, wilt, wither. — *adj* **taint'ed**. — *adj* **taint'less**. — *adv* **taint'lessly**. [Partly aphetic for **attaint**; partly O.Fr. *taint* — L. *tinctus*, *-ūs* — *tingĕre*, *tinctum*, to wet, dye.]

'taint *tānt*, (*slang* or *illit*) contraction of **it is not**.

taipan[1] *tī'pan*, *n* a large venomous Australian snake. [Aboriginal name.]

taipan[2] *tī'pan*, *n* a foreigner living in China and head of a foreign business there. [Chin.]

taisch or **taish** *tīsh*, *n* (in the Scottish Highlands) an apparition or voice, esp. of someone about to die; second-sight. [Gael. *taibhis*, *taibhse*, apparition.]

tait *tāt*, (*Austr*) *n* the long-snouted phalanger (*Tarsipes*). [Aboriginal name.]

Tajik, Tadjik or **Tadzhik** *taj'ik*, *n* a people of Iranian race living in Afghanistan and Turkestan; a member of this people; its dialect, resembling Farsi. — Also *adj*. [Pers., a Persian.]

taka *tä'kə*, *n* the standard unit of currency in Bangladesh (100 *poisha*). [Beng.]

takahe *tä'kə-hē*, *n* a notornis. [Maori.]

take *tāk*, *vt* to lay hold of; to get into one's possession; to seize, catch or capture; to captivate; to receive or come to have willingly or by an act of one's own; to appropriate; to assume, adopt; to accept; to receive; to admit; to have normally assigned to one; to find out, come upon, surprise, detect; to swallow or inhale; to apply to oneself; to obtain; to engage, secure; to have recourse to; to attend a course in; to call for, necessitate, use up; to remove; to cause to go; to subtract; to convey; to escort; to detract; to derive; to understand; to apprehend; (with *it*) to assume, suppose; to mistake; to conceive; to accept as true; to tolerate; to observe or measure; to ascertain something from; to execute, perform; to set down; to portray; to photograph; to charge oneself with; to declare solemnly; to strike; to come upon and affect. — *vi* to have the intended effect; to be effective, to work; to please the public; to betake oneself, begin; (of a fish) to bite; to make a capture or acquisition; to be capable of being taken; to become, fall, e.g. ill (*colloq*); to freeze (*NAm*): — *pa t* **took**; *pa p* **tā'ken.** — *n* an act of taking, or of catching (e.g. the ball in rugby, etc.); a capture; quantity taken on one occasion; the amount of money taken, e.g. from a business enterprise, admission charges, etc.; the filming of one scene (*cinematography*); amount of copy set up by a printer at one time. — *adj* **take'able** or **tā'kable.** — *adj* **tā'ken.** — *n* **tā'ker.** — *n* **tā'king** the action of the verb in any sense; (usu. in *pl*) that which is taken, receipts. — *adj* captivating; alluring. — *adv* **tā'kingly.** — *n* **tā'kingness.** — *adj* **take'away** (of cooked food) sold for consumption away from the place of sale; (of a restaurant) selling such food. — *n* such a restaurant; a take-away meal. — **take'-in** a deception, fraud, or disappointment of hopes; **take'-off** a burlesque mimicking; place, act or mode of leaving the ground for a jump, dive or flight (also *fig*). — *adj* **take'-out** take-away (*US*). — *n* (*bridge*) a conventional bid asking one's partner to bid a different suit. — Also *adj.* — **take'over** the acquirement of control of a business by purchase of a majority of its shares. — Also *adj.* — **take'-up** the fact, or an instance, of taking up (i.e. using or accepting). — Also *adj.* — **on the take** engaged in small-scale dishonest making of profit; **take after** to follow in resemblance or characteristics; **take against** to take a dislike to; to oppose; **take back** to retract, withdraw; to carry back (mentally) in time; **take down** to reduce; to lower; to demolish, pull down or dismantle; to report or write down to dictation; to escort to the dining-room; (**take down a peg**) to humiliate to some degree; **take effect** to come off, succeed; to come into force; **take five** (or **ten**) to take a short break of five (or ten) minutes; **take for** to suppose to be, esp. wrongly; **take fright** see under **fright**; **take heed** to be careful; **take-home pay** pay after deduction of tax, etc.; **take in** to enclose; to comprise; to annex; to grasp, realise; to accept as true; to cheat; to subscribe for, receive; to tighten, contract, make smaller; to admit; **take in hand** to undertake; **take into one's head** to be seized with a notion; **take in vain** to use with unsuitable levity; **take it** (*colloq*) to endure punishment or bad luck without giving way or collapsing under the strain; **take it from there** to deal with a situation appropriately, at whatever point it falls to one to do so; **take it or leave it** to accept something with all its disadvantages, or else do without it; **take it out of** to exhaust the strength or energy of; **take it out on** to make (an innocent person or object) suffer for one's anger or frustration; to vent one's ill-temper, anger, etc. on; **take notice** to observe; to show that observation is made; **take off** to remove, detach; to mimic; to leave the ground for a jump or flight; to begin a rapid improvement or expansion; **take on** to receive aboard; to undertake; to assume; to take into employment; to grieve (*colloq*); to accept a challenge from; (of ideas, etc.) to gain acceptance; **take out** to remove from within; to extract; to go out with; to obtain on application; to receive an equivalent for; to kill, destroy or defeat (*slang*); **take over** to receive by transfer; to convey across; to assume control of; **takeover bid**; **takeover bidder**; **take someone up on** to accept someone's offer or challenge with respect to; to put a person's statement to the test; **take to** to adapt oneself to; to become fond of; **take to pieces** to separate into component parts; **take to task** to call to account, rebuke; **take up** to lift, to raise or collect; to pick up for use; to absorb; to accept (an offer); to adopt the practice, study, etc. of, begin to go in for; to begin to patronise, seek to advance; to resume; to take in hand; to engross, occupy or fill fully; **take upon oneself** to assume; to presume; to take responsibility for; to undertake; **take up with** to begin to associate with, or form a connection with. [Late O.E. *tacan* (past t. *tōc*) to touch, take — O.N. *taka* (past t. *tōk*; past p. *tekinn*).]

takin *tä'kin* or *tä-kēn'*, *n* a large horned, hoofed mammal of the Himalayas, China, etc., related to the goats and antelopes. [Tibetan.]

tala *tä'la*, *n* a traditional rhythmic pattern in Indian music. [Sans., hand-clapping.]

talapoin *tal'ə-poin*, *n* a Buddhist monk, esp. of Pegu, in Myanmar (formerly Burma); a small green W. African guenon monkey. [Port. *talapão* — Old Peguan *tala pôi*, my lord.]

talar, talaria. See under **talus**[1].

talc *talk*, *n* talcum powder; a very soft, pliable, greasy, silvery-white, foliated or compact mineral, acid magnesium silicate. — *adj* **talc'ose, talc'ous** or **talc'y.** — *n* **talc'um** talc. — **talc-schist'** a schistose rock composed essentially of talc, with accessory minerals; **talcum powder** purified powdered talc, usu. perfumed, applied to the skin to absorb moisture. [Fr. *talc* or L.L. *talcum* — Ar. *talq* — Pers. *talk*.]

tale *tāl*, *n* an act of telling; a narrative, story; a false story; a mere story; (in *pl*) things told idly or to get others into trouble. — *adj* **tale'ful** full of stories. — **tale'bearer** someone who maliciously tells tales or gives information; **tale'bearing.** — Also *adj.* — **tale'-teller** a teller of stories, narrator; a talebearer. — **old wives' tale** a superstitious or misleading story; any extraordinary tale that makes demands on one's credulity; **tell tales** to give away secret or confidential information; **tell tales out of school** to reveal confidential matters. [O.E. *talu*, story, number.]

talent *tal'ənt*, *n* any natural or special gift; special aptitude or ability; persons of special ability; young girls or young men, esp. attractive, handsome, etc. (*colloq*); an ancient (esp. Greek) unit of weight and of money; hence (from the biblical parable: Matt. xxv. 14–30) faculty. — *adj* **tal'ented** possessing talent or aptitude. — *adj* **tal'entless.** — **talent scout** or **spotter** someone whose business is to discover and recruit talented people, esp. in entertainment or sport. — *vi* and *vt* **tal'ent-spot.** [L. *talentum* — Gr. *talanton*, a balance, a talent.]

tales *tā'lēz*, (*law*) *n* (orig. *pl*) the filling up, from those who are present, of a deficiency in the number of jurymen. [From the L. phrase '*tālēs* de circumstantibus', such of the bystanders.]

tali. See **talus**[1].

talion *tal'i-ən*, (*legal hist*) *n* like for like; retaliation. — *adj* **talion'ic.** [L. *tāliō*, *-ōnis*, like punishment — *tālis*, such.]

talipes *tal'i-pēz*, (*med*) *n* club-foot. — *adj* **tal'iped** (*-ped*) having a club-foot. — Also *n.* [L. *tālus*, ankle, *pēs*, foot.]

talipot *tal'i-pot*, *n* an E. Asian palm with hand-shaped leaves (*Corypha*). [Sinh. *talapata* — Sans. *tālī*, palmyra palm, *pattra*, leaf.]

talisman *tal'is-mən* or *-īz-*, *n* an object supposed to be indued with magical powers; an amulet or charm: — *pl* **tal'ismans**. — *adj* **talismanic** (*-man'ik*) or **talisman'ical**. [Ar. *tilsam* — Gr. *telesma*, completion, rite, consecrated object — *teleein*, to complete, fulfil, consecrate.]

talk *tök*, *vi* to speak, to express or communicate in spoken words; to converse; to discuss; to chat. — *vt* to utter; to speak about; to speak in; to bring or render by talking. — *n* conversation; rumour; discussion; gossip; mention of possibility or proposal; a general theme; utterance; a short informal address. — *n* **talk'athon** (*colloq*; orig. *US*) a long-drawn-out discussion, debate, talking session, etc. — *adj* **talk'ative** given to much talking. — *adv* **talk'atively**. — *n* **talk'ativeness**. — *n* **talk'er**. — *n* **talk'ie**. — *n* (commonly in *pl*) a talking film, cinematograph picture accompanied by sound. — *n* and *adj* **talk'ing**. — **talk'-back** a two-way radio system; **talk'fest** (*colloq*; esp. *US*) an informal meeting for discussion; **talk'-in** an informal yet intensive discussion; a gathering for this purpose; **talking book** a recording of a reading of a book, esp. for use by the blind; **talking head** a person talking on television, contrasted with programmes with more action; **talk'ing-machine** a machine to produce imitation speech; **talk'ing-point** a matter of or for talk; **talking shop** (*colloq*) a meeting or a place for discussion, as opposed to decision or action; **talk'ing-to** a reproof, a ticking-off; **talk-show** see **chat-show** (under **chat**[1]); **talk'-you-down** an apparatus by means of which instructions are given to the pilot of an aircraft to help him or her to land. — **look who's talking** (*ironic*) you're a fine one to be saying that; **now you're talking** (*colloq*) now you are saying something I want to hear, or something important or to the point; **talk at** to address remarks to indirectly; to talk to incessantly, without waiting for a response; **talk back** to reply impudently; **talk big** to talk boastfully; **talk down** to argue down; to talk as though to people inferior in intellect or education; to bring (an aircraft) to a landing by radioed instructions from the ground; **talk-down system**; **talking of** apropos of, now that mention has been made of; **talk into** to persuade; **talk out** to defeat (a parliamentary bill or motion) by going on speaking until it is too late to vote on it; to resolve (a difference of opinion) by thorough discussion; **talk over** to persuade, convince; to discuss or consider together; **talk round** to talk of all sorts of related matters without coming to the point; to bring to one's way of thinking by talking persuasively; **talk shop** see under **shop**; **talk tall** to boast; **talk to** to address; to rebuke; **talk turkey** see under **turkey**; **talk up** to speak boldly; to praise or boost; to make much of. [M.E. *talken*, frequentative of **tell**.]

tall *töl*, *adj* high in stature; long, esp. in a vertical direction; lofty; (usu. of a person) of a stated height, as in *six feet tall*; great, remarkable; bombastic, inflated in style; hardly to be believed (as in a *tall tale*). — *n* **tall'ness**. — **tall'boy** a high chest of drawers, one portion superimposed on another or on a dressing-table; a glass with a long stem; **tall hat** a top hat; **tall order** see under **order**; **tall ship** a square-rigged ship. — **talk tall** and **walk tall** see under **talk** and **walk**. [App. O.E. *getæl*, prompt.]

tallage *tal'ij*, *n* a tax levied by the Norman and Angevin kings on their demesne lands and towns, or by a feudal lord on his tenants (*hist*); an aid, toll or rate. [O.Fr. *taillage* — *tailler* to cut, to tax.]

tallier. See **tally**.

tallith *tal'ith*, *n* the Jewish prayer shawl. [Heb. *tallūth*.]

tallow *tal'ō*, *n* fat, grease; rendered fat, esp. of ox and sheep; any coarse, hard fat. — *adj* of, for, or like tallow. — *vt* to grease with tallow. — *adj* **tall'owish**. — *adj* **tall'owy**. — **tall'ow-candle** a candle made of tallow; **tall'ow-tree** any of various trees yielding a thick oil or vegetable tallow, or a substance capable of making candles. [M.E. *talgh*.]

tally *tal'i*, *n* a score or account, esp. one kept by notches or marks; a mark made in recording or scoring an account; a full number or total score; a distinguishing mark, label or tag; a stick notched to mark numbers or keep accounts; half of such a stick split across the notches, serving as receipt or record (*hist*); a corresponding part, a counterpart: — *pl* **tall'ies**. — *vt* to keep score, count, calculate or mark down by tally; to mark or provide with a label or tally. — *vi* to correspond, match, agree: — *pr p* **tall'ying**; *pa t* and *pa p* **tall'ied**. — *n* **tall'ier**. — **tally clerk** a checker of ship's cargoes against a list; **tall'yman** a salesman who deals on credit; someone who keeps a tally; **tall'y-system** or **-trade** a method of dealing on credit for payment by instalments. [A.Fr. *tallie* — L. *tālea*, a stick.]

tally-ho *tal-i-hō'*, *interj* the huntsman's cry signifying that a fox has been sighted. — *n* a cry of tally-ho: — *pl* **tally-hos'**. — *vt* to greet with tally-ho. — *vi* to call tally-ho. [Cf. Fr. *taïaut*.]

Talmud *tal'mŏŏd* or *-mud*, *n* the fundamental code of Jewish civil and canon law, the *Mishnah* and the *Gemara*. — *adj* **Talmud'ic** or **Talmud'ical**. — *n* **Tal'mudist** a scholar of the Talmud. — *adj* **Talmudist'ic**. [Heb. *talmūd*, instruction — *lāmad*, to learn.]

talon *tal'ən*, *n* a hooked claw or finger; an ogee moulding (*archit*); the part of the bolt of a lock that the key presses on when it is turned; cards remaining after the deal, the stock. — *adj* **tal'oned**. [Fr. *talon* — L.L. *tālō*, *-ōnis* — L. *tālus*, the heel.]

talus[1] *tā'ləs*, *n* the ankle-bone: — *pl* **tā'lī**. — *n* **tā'lar** a robe reaching the ankles. — *npl* **talaria** (*tə-lā'ri-ə*) winged sandals, or wings on the ankles, as of Hermes in Greek mythology. [L. *tālus*, ankle.]

talus[2] *tā'ləs*, *n* the sloping part of a work (*fort*); a scree (*geol*). [Fr., — L.L. *talutium*, a slope.]

TAM *abbrev* for television audience measurement.

tam. See **Tam o' Shanter**.

tamal *tä-mäl'* or **tamale** *tä-mäl'i*, *n* a highly seasoned Mexican dish of crushed maize, with meat. [Sp. *tamal* (pl. *tamales*), — Nahuatl *tamalli*.]

tamandua *tä-män'dū-ä*, *n* a S. American ant-eater smaller than the ant-bear. [Port. *tamanduá* — Sp. *tamándoa* — Tupí *tamanduà*.]

tamarack *tam'ə-rak*, *n* the American or black larch. [Am. Ind.]

tamari *ta-mä'ri*, *n* a concentrated sauce made of soya beans and salt. [Jap.]

tamarillo *tam-ə-ril'ō*, *n*. Same as **tree tomato**.

tamarin *tam'ə-rin*, *n* a small S. American squirrel-monkey (genus *Midas*). [Fr., from Carib.]

tamarind *tam'ə-rind*, *n* a large tropical tree which bears yellow flowers and long brown seed pods; its pod, filled with a pleasant, slightly acid, sweet, reddish-black pulp. [Ar. *tamr-Hindī*, date of India.]

tamarisk *tam'ər-isk*, *n* a plant of the genus **Tam'arix** belonging to a family (**Tamaricā'ceae**) of xerophytic plants, one species a naturalised shrub of S. English seashores. [L. *tamariscus*, *tamarix*.]

tambour *tam'bŏŏr*, *n* a drum, *specif* the bass drum; a frame for embroidery; a rich gold and silver embroidery; embroidery done on a tambour; a cylindrical stone forming part of a column or the centre of a Corinthian capital (*archit*); the drum of a recording instrument; a flexible top (as of a desk) or front (as of a cabinet) made of narrow strips of wood fixed closely together on canvas, the whole sliding in grooves. — *vt* to embroider on a tambour. — *n* **tambour'a** an Eastern instrument like a guitar. — *n* **tambourin** (*tã-bŏŏ-rẽ*) a Provençal dance or dance-tune with drone bass; a long, narrow drum, used esp. to accompany this. — *n* **tambourine** (*tam-bə-rēn'*) a shallow single-headed drum with jingles fitted around its rim, played on with the hand. [Fr., drum; Pers. *tanbūr*, Ar. *tunbūr*, tamboura.]

tame *tām*, *adj* having lost native wildness and shyness; cultivated; domesticated; gentle; spiritless; without vigour; dull, flat, uninspiring. — *vt* to make tame or domestic; to make gentle; to subdue; to reclaim. — *n* **tamabil'ity** or **tameabil'ity**. — *adj* **tam'able** or **tame'able**. — *adv* **tame'ly**. — *n* **tame'ness**. — *n* **tam'er**. — *n* **tam'ing**. [O.E. *tam*.]

Tamil *tam'il*, *n* a Dravidian language of south-east India and north, east, and central Sri Lanka; one of the people speaking it. — *adj* **Tam'il**, **Tamil'ian**, **Tamil'ic** or **Tamūl'ic**.

tammy *tam'i*, *n* a Tam o' Shanter.

Tam o' Shanter *tam-ō-shan'tər*, *n* a cap with broad circular flat top — *colloq* **tam** or **tamm'y**. [After the hero of Burns' poem *Tam o' Shanter*.]

tamp *tamp*, *vt* to stop up (a shot hole) with earth, etc. after the explosive has been introduced; to ram down so as to consolidate (e.g ballast on a railway track); to pack round. — *n* **tamp'er** a person who, or thing which, tamps; an instrument for pressing down tobacco in a pipe; a casting round the core of a nuclear weapon to delay expansion and act as a neutron reflector. — *n* **tamp'ing** the act of filling up a hole for blasting; the material used. [See ety. for **tampion**.]

tamper[1] *tam'pər*, vi (usu. with *with*) to interfere unwarrantably or damagingly; to meddle; to work, contrive or practise; to have secret or corrupt dealings. — *n* **tam'perer**. — *n* **tam'pering**. — **tamper-ev'ident** (of packaging) designed in such a way that it is obvious when it has been tampered with. [A by-form of **temper**.]

tamper[2], **tamping**. See **tamp**.

tampion *tam'pi-ən* or **tompion** *tom'pi-ən*, *n* a plug, esp. a protective plug placed in the muzzle of a gun when not in use. [Fr. *tampon* — *tapon*, a plug of cloth.]

tampon *tam'pon*, *n* a plug of cotton or other absorbent material inserted into a wound or orifice to control haemorrhage, etc., or into the vagina to absorb menstrual flow; a two-headed drumstick. [See ety. for **tampion**.]

tamoxifen *tam-oks'i-fen*, *n* a drug which counteracts oestrogen, used esp. in the treatment of breast cancer.

tam-tam *tum'-tum* or *tam'-tam*, *n* a gong, esp. one used in an orchestra. [**tom-tom**.]

tan[1] *tan*, *n* a tawny brown colour; a suntan; oak bark or other material used for tanning. — *adj* tawny. — *vt* to convert into leather by steeping in vegetable solutions containing tannin, or mineral salts, or synthesised chemicals; to treat with tan or tannin; to make brown, suntanned or tawny; to beat (*colloq*). — *vi* to become tanned: — *pr p* **tann'ing**; *pa t* and *pa p* **tanned**. — *adj* **tann'able**. — *n* **tann'age** tanning; that which is tanned. — *n* **tann'ate** a salt of tannic acid. — *adj* **tanned**. — *n* **tann'er**. — *n* **tann'ery** a place where hides, etc. are tanned. — *adj* **tann'ic**. — *n* **tann'in** a colourless amorphous bitter substance derived from gallnuts, sumach, many barks, and other vegetable matter used in tanning and dyeing, and occurring in wines (esp. red), giving a distinctive flavour. — *n* **tann'ing** the art or practice of tanning or converting skins and hides into leather. — Also *adj*. — *adj* **tan'-coloured**. — **tannic acid** tannin; **tan'-pit** or **-vat** a vat in which hides are steeped with tan. [O.E. *tannian* (found in past p. *getanned*), *tannere*, tanner; also O.Fr. *tan* — Breton *tann*, oak.]

tan[2] *tan*, (*trig*) *n* a conventional short form for **tangent**.

tanager *tan'ə-jər*, *n* any bird of the S. American family *Thraupidae*, closely allied to the finches, the males having brightly-coloured plumage. [Tupí *tangará*.]

tandem *tan'dəm*, *n* a bicycle, tricycle, etc. for two people, one before the other; an arrangement of two things, one placed before the other, orig. of two horses harnessed singly one before the other; a vehicle with such a team of horses. — Also *adj*. — *adv* **tan'demwise**. — **in tandem** with one behind the other; together or in conjunction. [Punning application of L. *tandem*, at length.]

tandoori *tan-* or *tun-doo͞r'i*, *n* a type of Indian cooking in which meat and/or vegetables are baked over charcoal in a clay oven. — Also *adj*. [Hind. *tandoor*, a clay oven.]

T'ang or **Tang** *tang*, *n* a Chinese dynasty (A.D. 618–907). — *adj* of this dynasty, its period, or its poetry and art, esp. pottery, etc. [Chin.]

tang[1] *tang*, *n* a point, sting or spike; part of a tool that goes into the haft; a prong; a barb; biting, characteristic or extraneous flavour, aftertaste or smell; a smack, tinge; pungency. — *adj* **tanged** (*tangd*) with a tang; barbed. — *adj* **tangy** (*tang'i*) having a fresh or sharp taste or smell (also *fig*). [O.N. *tange*, point, tang.]

tang[2] *tang*, *n* a ringing sound; a twang. — *vt* to cause to ring. — *vi* to ring. [Imit.; infl. by **tang**[1].]

tanga *tang'gə*, *n* a brief string-like bikini; (women's or men's) briefs without material at the sides other than the waistband.

tangelo *tan'ji-lō*, *n* a hybrid between *tang*erine orange and pom*elo*: — *pl* **tan'gelos**. [Portmanteau word.]

tangent *tan'jənt*, *adj* touching without intersecting. — *n* a line that touches a curve; the limiting case of a secant when the two points of intersection coincide; (as a function of an angle) the ratio of the side of a right-angled triangle opposite the given angle to the side opposite the other acute angle (*trig*) (the tangent of an obtuse angle is equal numerically to that of its supplement, but has the negative sign) — *abbrev* **tan**; the striking-pin of a clavichord. — *n* **tan'gency** (*-jən-si*). — *adj* **tangential** (*-jen'shəl*) of a tangent; in the direction of a tangent; peripheral, irrelevant (*fig*). — *n* **tangentiality** (*tan-jen-shi-al'i-ti*). — *adv* **tangen'tially**. — **at a tangent** in the direction of the tangent; in a divergent train of thought or action; in continuation in the momentary direction instead of following the general course. [L. *tangēns*, *-entis*, pres. p. of *tangĕre*, to touch.]

tangerine *tan'jə-rēn* or *-rēn'*, *n* a mandarin orange, esp. a small, flattish, loose-skinned variety of this; the colour of this fruit, a reddish orange; (with *cap*) a native of *Tangier* on the coast of Morocco. — *adj* tangerine-coloured; (with *cap*) of Tangier.

tangible *tan'ji-bl*, *adj* perceptible by the touch; capable of being possessed or realised; material, corporeal. — *n* (usu. in *pl*) a tangible thing or asset, i.e. physical property as opposed to goodwill. — *n* **tangibil'ity** or **tan'gibleness**. — *adv* **tan'gibly**. [L. *tangibilis* — *tangĕre*, to touch.]

tangle[1] *tang'gl*, *vt* to form into, involve in, or cover with, a confused interwoven mass; to entangle; to hamper or trap (*colloq*). — *vi* to become tangled; to become involved in conflict or argument (with) (*colloq*); (with *with*) to embrace (*colloq*). — *n* a tangled mass or condition; a perplexity or complication; a naturalist's dredge consisting of bundles of frayed rope or the like; involved relations, conflict, argument. — *adj* **tang'led**. — *n* **tang'lement**. — *n* **tang'ler**. — *adj* **tang'lesome**. — *n* and *adj* **tang'ling**. — *adv* **tang'lingly**. — *adj* **tang'ly**. [App. from earlier *tagle*; see **taigle**.]

tangle[2] *tang'gl*, *n* coarse seaweed, esp. the edible *Laminaria*. — *adj* **tang'ly**. [App. conn. with O.N. *thöngull*, Laminaria stalk.]

tango *tang'go*, *n* a ballroom dance or dance tune in 4-4 time, of Argentinian origin, characterised by long steps and pauses: — *pl* **tan'gos**. — *vi* to dance the tango: — *pa t* and *pa p* **tan'goed**. — *n* **tan'goist**. [Sp., a S. Am. Negro festival or dance.]

tangram *tan'gram*, *n* a Chinese toy consisting of a square cut into seven pieces that will fit in various forms.

tangy. See **tang**[1].

tanh *tansh* or *than*, *n* a conventional short form for *h*yperbolic *tan*gent.

tanist *tan'ist*, (*hist*) *n* a Celtic chief's heir elect. — *n* **tan'istry** the system of succession by a previously elected member of the family. [Ir. *tánaiste*, Gael. *tànaiste*, heir, successor.]

tank *tangk*, *n* a large basin or cistern; a reservoir of water, oil, etc.; an armoured, enclosed, armed vehicle moving on caterpillar wheels; a receptacle for developing solutions (*phot*); a prison or prison cell (*US slang*); a pool, pond, reservoir (*India* and *Austr*). — *vt* to store in a tank; to defeat, thrash (*slang*). — *vi* to drink heavily (with *up*); to refuel (often with *up*; *colloq*); to travel (esp. to drive) at great speed or relentlessly; to lose or drop points, games, etc. deliberately (*tennis slang*). — *n* **tank'age** storing in tanks; charge for such storage; the capacity of a tank or tanks; residue from tanks; a fertiliser derived from the dried residues of animal carcases. — *adj* **tanked** (*slang*; often with *up*) drunk. — *n* **tank'er** a ship or heavy vehicle that carries liquids, esp. oil in bulk; an aircraft that refuels others. — *n* **tank'ful**: — *pl* **tank'fuls**. — *n* **tank'ing** (*slang*) a defeat, a thrashing. — **tank'-car** or **-wagon** a railway wagon for carrying oil or other liquid in a large tank; **tank engine** a locomotive that carries its water and coal in itself (without a tender); **tank'-farmer; tank'-farming** hydroponics; **tank top** a sleeveless pullover, usu. with a low round neckline, worn over a shirt, etc.; **tank'-trap** an obstacle large enough to stop a military tank. [Port. *tanque* — L. *stagnum*, a pool.]

tanka *tang'kə*, *n* a Japanese poem of five lines, the first and third lines having five syllables and the others seven. [Jap. *tan*, short, *ka*, verse.]

tankard *tangk'ərd*, *n* a large mug-like vessel, usu. with a handle and sometimes a hinged lid, used esp. for drinking beer from. [Cf. M. Du. *tanckaert*.]

tanker. See under **tank**.

tannable, tannage, tannate, tanned. See under **tan**[1].

tanner[1] *tan'ər*, (*old slang*) *n* a sixpence.

tanner[2], **tannery, tannic, tannin**, etc. See under **tan**[1].

Tannoy® *tan'oi*, *n* a sound-reproducing and amplifying system. — *vt* **tann'oy** to call by, use, or make a sound by, Tannoy.

tanrec. See **tenrec**.

tansy *tan'zi*, *n* a bitter, aromatic roadside composite plant (*Tanacetum vulgare*) with small heads of tubular yellow flowers; extended to other plants, such as ragwort and yarrow. [O.Fr. *tanasie*, through L.L. from Gr. *athanasiā*, immortality.]

tantalic, tantalite. See under **tantalum**.

tantalise or **-ize** *tan'tə-līz*, *vt* to torment by presenting something desirable but keeping it out of reach; to entice or provoke frustratingly. — *n* **tantalīsā'tion** or **-z-**. — *n* **tan'taliser** or **-z-**. — *n* and *adj* **tan'talising** or **-z-**. — *adv* **tan'talisingly** or **-z-**. [Ety. as for **tantalus**.]

tantalum *tan'tə-ləm*, *n* a metallic element (symbol **Ta**; atomic no. 73), acid-resistant and useful for electronic and surgical parts. — *adj* **tantal'ic**. — *n* **tan'talite** a black mineral, the main ore from which tantalum is derived. — **tan'talum-lamp** an electric lamp with tantalum filament. [*Tantalus* (see under **tantalus**), from its inability to absorb water.]

tantalus *tan'tə-ləs*, *n* a case in which alcohol decanters are visible but locked up; a plant of the wood ibis genus. [*Tantalus*, in Gr. mythology a son of Zeus punished for revealing secrets of the gods by having to stand in water that ebbed when he tried to drink it, overhung by grapes that drew back when he reached for them.]

tantamount *tan'tə-mownt*, *adj* amounting to as much or to the same; equivalent; equal in value or meaning. [A.Fr. *tant amunter*, to amount to as much.]

tantara *tan-tä'rä*, *n* a blast on the trumpet or horn. — Also **tantara'ra**. [Imit.]

tantivy *tan-tiv'i*, *adv* at full gallop; headlong. — *n* a hunting cry; a rapid rush. — *adj* headlong. — *interj* expressive of the sound of the hunting-horn. [Imit.]

tant mieux *tã myø*, (Fr.) so much the better.

tant pis *tã pē*, (Fr.) so much the worse.

Tantra or **tantra** *tan'* or *tun'trə*, *n* any of a number of Hindu and Buddhist writings giving religious teaching and ritual instructions (including the use of incantations, diagrams, etc.); the teaching of the Tantras. — *adj* **Tan'tric** or **tan'tric**. — *n* **Tan'trism** the teaching of the Tantras. — *n* **Tan'trist**. [Sans. *tantra*, thread, fundamental doctrine.]

tantrum *tan'trəm*, *n* a sudden, random, extreme fit of bad temper without adequate cause.

taoiseach *tē'shohh*, *n* the prime minister of the Republic of Ireland. [Ir., chief, leader.]

Taoism *tä'ō-izm* or *tow'izm*, *n* the philosophical system supposedly founded by the Chinese philosopher Lao-tzu (perh. b. 604 B.C.); a religious system combining Taoist philosophy with magic and superstition and the worship of many gods. — *n* and *adj* **Ta'oist**. — *adj* **Taoist'ic**. [Chin. *tao*, way, path.]

tap[1] *tap*, *n* a gentle knock or its sound; a protective piece on a shoe heel; a metal piece attached to the sole and heel of a shoe for tap-dancing; tap-dancing; (in *pl*) a signal (esp. a bugle call) for putting lights out, also used at military funerals (orig. *US mil*). — *vt* and *vi* to knock gently. — *vt* to provide or repair with a tap: — *pr p* **tapp'ing**; *pa t* and *pa p* **tapped**. — *n* **tapp'er** a person who taps; an instrument or part that taps. — *n* and *adj* **tapp'ing**. — **tap'-dance**. — Also *vi*. — **tap'-dancer; tap'-dancing** dancing characterised by rhythmical striking of dancer's tapped shoes on the floor; **tap'-shoe** a tapped shoe for tap-dancing. [O.Fr. *taper*.]

tap[2] *tap*, *n* a peg or stopper; a hole or short pipe with a valve for running off a fluid; a peg or stopper on a barrel, etc.; a taproom; any particular liquor drawn through a tap; a screw for cutting an internal thread; a receiver secretly attached to a telephone wire; an instance of tapping a telephone wire; (often in *pl*) tap stock. — *vt* to pierce, so as to let out fluid; to broach; to draw off; to draw upon, esp. for the first time (*fig*); secretly to attach a receiver to a telephone wire in order to overhear a conversation; to get money from (*slang*); to supply with a tap, or with a screw-thread. — *vi* to act as a tapster: — *pr p* **tapp'ing**; *pa t* and *pa p* **tapped**. — *n* **tapp'er**. — *n* **tapp'ing** the act or art of drawing out or running off a fluid; an operation for removal of liquid from the body. — *n* **tap'ster** a person who draws liquor, a barperson. — **tap'-bolt** a screwed-in bolt; **tap'-house** a tavern; **tap'room** a room where beer is served from the tap or cask; **tap'root** a strong main root striking down vertically; **tap stock** government bonds, etc., to which the public can subscribe at any time; **tap'-water** water from a household tap. — **on tap** kept in cask (opp. to *bottled*); continuously and readily available (*fig*). [O.E. *tæppa*, tap, *tæppestre*, (female) tapster.]

tapa[1] *tä'pə*, *n* paper-mulberry bark; a fabric made from this. [Polynesian generally.]

tapa[2] *tä'pa*, (Sp.) *n* a light snack or appetiser: — *pl* **ta'pas**.

tape *tāp*, *n* material woven in long narrow bands; a strip of such material, used for tying up, connecting, etc.; a ribbon of paper printed by a recording instrument, as in telegraphy; a flexible band that guides the sheets (*printing*); a tape-measure; magnetic tape; a tape-recording or cassette. — *vt* to provide, fasten, bind or measure with a tape; to tape-record; to get the range or measure of. — *adj* **tape'less.** — *n* **tā'per.** — **tape deck** a machine for recording sound on tape and for playing tape-recorded sound through a separate amplifier as part of a hi-fi system; a tape drive; **tape drive, deck** or **transport** (*comput*) a mechanism which moves magnetic tape across the recording and playback heads; **tape'line** or **tape'-measure** a flexible measuring strip of tape, steel or other material; **tape'-machine** a telegraphic instrument by which messages received are automatically printed on a tape; **tape punch** (*comput*) a device which encodes data by punching holes in paper tape; **tape reader** a device which senses data recorded on paper or magnetic tape and converts it into a form suitable for computer processing. — *vt* **tape'-record** to record sound using a tape-recorder. — **tape'-recorder** an instrument for recording sound on magnetic tape and subsequently reproducing it; **tape'-recording** a magnetic tape on which sound has been recorded; the sound so recorded; **tape'script** a tape-recorded reading of a complete text; **tape transport** see **tape drive; tape'worm** a ribbon-shaped segmented parasitic worm, esp. of the Taenia or a related genus. — **breast the tape** in winning a foot-race, to pass through or break the tape stretched across the track at the winning-line with one's chest; **have (something** or **someone) taped** to have a thorough understanding of; **magnetic tape** see under **magnet; red tape** see under **red.** [O.E. *tæppe*, tape, fillet.]

taper *tā'pər, n* a long, thin waxed wick or spill; lengthwise diminution in width; gradual leaving off. — *adj* tapering. — *vi* to become gradually smaller towards one end; to diminish slowly in size, quantity or importance (with *off*). — *vt* to make to taper. — *adj* **tā'pered** tapering; lit by tapers. — *n* **tā'perer.** — *n* and *adj* **tā'pering.** — *adv* **tā'peringly.** [O.E. *tapor.*]

tapestry *tap'is-tri, n* an ornamental textile used for the covering of walls and furniture, etc., made by passing coloured threads or wools through a fixed warp fabric; a picture or design made of this; a machine-made imitation of this. — *adj* made of tapestry. — *adj* **tap'estried.** [Fr. *tapisserie* — *tapis*, a carpet — L.L. *tapētium* — Gr. *tapētion*, dimin. of *tapēs, -ētos.*]

tapetum *tə-pē'təm, n* a layer of cells surrounding spore mother-cells (*bot*); the pigmentary layer of the retina (*zool*): — *pl* **tapē'ta.** — *adj* **tapē'tal.** [L. *tapētum* — Gr. *tapēs, -ētos*, carpet.]

taphonomy *taf-on'ə-mi, n* the study or science of how plants and animals die, decay and become buried, fossil or fossilised. — *n* **taphon'omist** an expert or specialist in taphonomy. — *n* **taphophō'bia** (also **taphepho'bia**) pathological fear of being buried alive. [Gr. *taphos*, grave, *taphē*, burial, and **-nomy.**]

tapioca *tap-i-ō'kə, n* a farinaceous substance made by heating cassava; extended to a kind of sago and a preparation of potato starch; a pudding made from tapioca. — **pearl-tapioca** see under **pearl**[1]. [Tupí-Guaraní *tipyoca.*]

tapir *tā'pər, n* a large odd-toed hoofed mammal with a short flexible proboscis, several species of which are found in S. America, Malaya, etc. — *adj* **tā'piroid.** [Tupí *tapira.*]

tappet *tap'it, n* a projection that transmits motion from one part of a machine to another by tapping, esp. in an internal-combustion engine from the camshaft to the valves. — **tapp'et-ring, -rod,** etc. [**tap**[1].]

tapu *ta'pōō.* Same as **taboo.** [Maori.]

tar[1] *tär, n* a dark, viscous mixture obtained by destructive distillation of wood, coal, peat, etc.; a natural bituminous substance of similar appearance (*mineral tar*). — *vt* to smear, coat or treat with tar: — *pr p* **tarr'ing;** *pa t* and *pa p* **tarred.** — *n* **tarriness** (*tär'i-nis*). — *n* and *adj* **tarr'ing.** — *adj* **tarr'y** (*tär'i*) of, like, covered or soiled with tar. — **tar'-brush** a brush for applying tar; **tarmacad'am** or **tar'mac** (also **Tarmac**® in *US*) a road surfacing of broken stone covered or mixed with tar; (**tar'mac**) the runways of an airport. — *vt* **tar'mac** to surface with tarmacadam: — *pr p* **tar'macking;** *pa t* and *pa p* **tar'macked.** — **tar'-seal** (*NZ*) a tarmacadam surface on a road; a road so surfaced. — *vt* to seal the surface of (a road) by covering with tarmacadam. — **tar and feather** to smear with tar and then cover with feathers; **tarred with the same brush** having the same defects. [O.E. *teru, teoro.*]

tar[2] *tar*, (*colloq*) *n* a sailor. [Perh. for **tarpaulin.**]

taradiddle. See **tarradiddle.**

taramasalata *tar-ə-mə-sə-lä'tə*, (*cookery*) *n* a Greek dish, a pink creamy paste made of grey mullet or smoked cod's roe with olive oil and garlic. [Mod. Gr., — *taramas*, preserved roe, *salata*, salad.]

tarantara *tär-än-tər-ä', n* the sound of a trumpet or trumpet fanfare. — Also *interj, adj* and *adv.* [Imit.]

tarantella *tar-ən-tel'ə, n* a lively Neapolitan dance, once thought a remedy for tarantism; a tune for it. — *n* **tar'antism** (*med hist*) an epidemic dancing mania thought to be caused by the tarantula bite.

tarantula *tar-an'tū-lə, n* a large venomous S. European wolf-spider (esp. southern Italy and France); any of various large hairy spiders of the family *Theraphosidae*. [Med. L. — It. *tarantella, tarantola* — Gr. *Taras, -antos*, Tarentum, Taranto.]

tarantism. See under **tarantella.**

taraxacum *tä-raks'ə-kəm, n* a plant of the dandelion genus *Taraxacum*; its root and rootstock, a tonic laxative. [App. from Ar. *tarakhshaqōq* — Pers. *talkh chakōk*, assimilated to Gr. *taraxis*, disturbance.]

tarboosh, tarboush or **tarbush** *tär-bōōsh', n* a fez, a hat worn by Muslim men, sometimes as the base of a turban. [Ar. *tarbūsh.*]

tardigrade *tär'di-grād, adj* slow-paced; of or pertaining to the Tardigrada. — *n* a member of the Tardigrada. — *npl* **Tardigrā'da** a class of slow-moving arthropods; formerly the sloths. [L. *tardus*, slow, *gradī*, to step.]

tardy *tär'di, adj* slow; sluggish; behindhand; too long delayed; late. — *adv* **tar'dily.** — *n* **tar'diness.** [Fr. *tardif* — *tard* — L. *tardus*, slow.]

tare[1] *tār, n* a vetch of various kinds, esp. of the lentil-like group; a weed, prob. darnel (*Bible*).

tare[2] *tār, n* the weight of a vessel, wrapping or container, which subtracted from the gross weight gives the net weight; the weight of an empty vehicle, without cargo, passengers, etc. — *vt* to ascertain or allow for the tare of. [Fr., — Sp. *tara* — Ar. *tarhah*, thrown away.]

target *tär'git, n* a round or shieldlike mark to shoot at for practice or competition; an object aimed at (also *fig*); a butt or focus (as of harsh remarks or actions); a result to be aimed at; a shooting score; a neck and breast of lamb; a surface on which electrons impinge at high velocity. — *adj* chosen as a target, aimed at. — *vt* to aim; to aim at; to make a target or victim. — *adj* **tar'getable** which can be aimed, or aimed at. — *adj* **tar'geted.** — **target area** an area containing a target, or which is a target, e.g. of missiles; **target language** the language into which a text is to be translated; **target practice** repeated shooting at a target to improve one's aim. — **on target** on the correct course for a target; on schedule. [Earlier, a small buckler or round shield — O.Fr. *targuete*; cf. archaic *targe*, a (light) shield.]

tariff *tar'if, n* a list or set of customs duties; a list of charges (as at a hotel). — *vt* to set a tariff on. — **tariff wall** a barrier to the flow of imports made by high rates of customs duties. [It. *tariffa* — Ar. *ta'rīf*, explanation — *'arafa*, to explain.]

tarlatan *tär'lə-tən, n* an open, transparent muslin. [Fr. *tarlatane.*]

tarmac, tarmacadam. See under **tar**[1].

tarn *tärn, n* a small mountain lake. [O.N. *tjörn.*]

tarnish *tär'nish, vt* to dull, discolour, diminish the lustre of, etc. by exposure to the air, etc. — *vi* to become dull; to lose lustre. — *n* loss of lustre; a surface discoloration or iridescence on metal or mineral; a film of oxide, sulphide, etc. — *adj* **tar'nishable.** — *adj* **tar'nished.** — *n* **tar'nisher.** [Fr. *ternir, terniss-* — *terne*, dull, wan.]

taro *tä'rō, n* a plant (*Colocasia*) of the arum family, widely cultivated for its edible rootstock in the islands of the Pacific: — *pl* **ta'ros.** [Polynesian.]

tarot *tar'ō, n* a card of a type originating in Italy, with an allegorical picture, used in card games and esp. in fortune-telling; (usu. in *pl*) a game played with tarots together with cards of the ordinary suits. [Fr. *tarot* — It. *tarocco.*]

tarp *tärp,* (*US* and *Austr*) *n* short for **tarpaulin.**

tarpan *tär'pan, n* a small extinct wild horse of the steppes of S. European Russia. [Tatar.]

tarpaulin *tär-pö'lin, n* strong linen or hempen cloth waterproofed with tar or otherwise; a sheet of it. [App. **tar**[1] and *palling* — **pall**[1].]

tarpon *tär'pən, n* a very large fish (*Megalops*) angled for on the Florida and Gulf coasts. [Du. *tarpoen.*]

tarradiddle or **taradiddle** *tar-ə-did'l, n* a fib, a lie; nonsense. [App. founded on **diddle.**]

tarragon *tar'ə-gən, n* an aromatic herb (genus *Artemisia*) used for flavouring vinegar, sauces, etc. [Ar. *tarkhūn*, perh. — Gr. *drakōn*, a dragon.]

tarry[1] *tär'i, adj.* See under **tar**[1].

tarry[2] *tar'i, vi* to linger; to loiter; to delay; to stay behind; to wait: — *pr p* **tarr'ying;** *pa t* and *pa p* **tarr'ied.** — *n* **tarr'ier.**

tarsal, tarsalgia. See under **tarsus.**

tarsier *tär'si-ər, n* a lemuroid monkey of the East Indies, nocturnal, tree-dwelling, with large eyes and long tarsal bones. — *adj* **tar'sioid** like the tarsier; of the tarsier genus (**Tar'sius**). [**tarsus.**]

tarsus *tär'səs, n* the part of the foot to which the leg is articulated; (in birds) sometimes applied to the tarsometatarsus; (in insects) the five-jointed foot; a plate of connective tissue at the edge of the eyelid: — *pl* **tar'sī.** — *adj* **tar'sal** relating to the tarsus or ankle. — *n* a bone of the tarsus. — *n* **tarsalgia** (*-sal'ji-ə*) pain in the instep. — *adj* **tarsometatar'sal.** — *n* **tarsometatar'sus** a bird's shank-bone, the combined metatarsals and distal tarsals. [Gr. *tarsos*, the flat of the foot.]

tart[1] *tärt, adj* sharp; biting; acidulous. — *adj* **tart'ish.** — *adv* **tart'ly.** — *n* **tart'ness.** [O.E. *teart.*]

tart[2] *tärt, n* a dish of pastry distinguished from a pie either by being uncovered or by having a sweet, not savoury, filling; a prostitute (*derog slang*). — *n* **tart'iness.** — *n* **tart'let** a small tart. — *adj* **tart'y** (*slang*) like a tart; vulgar, cheaply and blatantly provocative (esp. of a women or women's clothing, etc.). — **tart up** (*colloq*) to make more showy or striking, esp. in a superficial or inartistic way; to smarten up (*adj* **tart'ed-up**). [O.Fr. *tarte.*]

tartan[1] *tär'tən, n* a woollen (or other) checked material; a distinctive checked pattern, as worn by Highland clans of Scotland. — *adj* of tartan; checked in tartan; Scottish, esp. referring to self-consciously Scottish artefacts or attitudes (*derog*). — *adj* **tar'taned.** [Poss. from M.Fr. *tiretaine*, linsey-woolsey.]

tartan[2] *tär'tən, n* a Mediterranean vessel with lateen sail. [Fr. *tartane*, poss. — Ar. *tarīdah*, a small ship.]

Tartar *tär'tər, n* a Tatar; (without *cap*) a formidable, rough, unmanageable or ferocious person. — Also *adj.* — *n* and *adj* **Tartarian** (*-tā'ri-ən*) Tartar, Tatar. — *adj* **Tartaric** (*-tar'ik*) of the Tartars. [See **Tatar.**]

tartar *tär'tər, n* recrystallised and partially purified argol, chiefly acid potassium tartrate (with calcium tartrate, etc.); a deposit of calcium phosphate and other matter on the teeth. — *adj* **tartareous** (*-tā'ri-əs*) of or like tartar; with rough crumbly surface (*bot*). — *adj* **tartaric** (*tär-tar'ik*) of or obtained from tartar (**tartaric acid,** $C_4H_6O_6$, prepared from argol or found naturally in plants and fruits). — *vt* **tar'tarise** or **-ize** to treat, mix or combine with tartar. — *n* **tar'trate** a salt of tartaric acid. — *n* **tar'trazine** (*-zēn*) a yellow dye used in textiles, food and drugs. — **tartar emetic** a compound of potassium, antimony, carbon, hydrogen and oxygen, used in dyeing and in medicine. — **cream of tartar** purified argol, used in baking powder, etc. [L.L. *tartarum*, perh. from Ar.]

tartar sauce or **tartare sauce** *tär'tər* (or *tär-tär'*) *sös, n* a mayonnaise dressing with chopped pickles, olives, capers, etc. added, usu. served with fish. — Also called **tartar** or **tartare.** [Fr. *sauce tartare.*]

tartaric, tartarise, tartrate, tartrazine. See under **tartar.**

tarwhine *tär'wīn* or *tär'hwīn, n* an Australian sea-bream. [Aboriginal.]

Tarzan *tär'zan, n* a man of great strength and agility. [From the hero of stories by Edgar Rice Burroughs (d. 1950) about a man brought up by apes.]

Tas. *abbrev* for Tasmania.

tash *tash,* (*colloq*) *n* short for **moustache.**

task *täsk* or *task, n* a piece or amount of work set or undertaken (sometimes an esp. burdensome, difficult or unpleasant one). — *vt* to burden with severe work; to employ fully; (back-formation) to assign a task or (e.g. military) mission to; to allocate as a task. — **task'-force** or **-group** a group formed by selection from different branches of the armed services to carry out a specific task; a similar group within the police force; a working party (q.v.) for a civilian purpose; **task'master** a person who allots tasks esp. involving hard work; **task'-work** work done as a task, or by the job. — **take (someone) to task** to rebuke (someone). [O.Fr. *tasque* — L.L. *tasca, taxa* — L. *taxāre*, to rate.]

TASM *abbrev* for tactical air-to-surface missile.

Tasmanian *tas-* or *taz-mā'ni-ən, adj* of *Tasmania*, island state of Australia discovered in 1642 by Abel Janszoon *Tasman.* — *n* a native or citizen of Tasmania. — **Tasmanian devil** a small, ferocious marsupial of the Tasmanian dasyure family; **Tasmanian wolf** (or **tiger**) the thylacine, a striped wolflike dasyure of Tasmania, now virtually extinct.

TASS *tas, abbrev* for: Technical, Administrative and Supervisory Section (of the **AUEW**); *Telegrafnoye Agentsvo Sovietskovo Soyuza* (Russ.), telegraph agency of the Soviet Union.

tass *tas, n* a drinking-cup; a small drink. [Fr. *tasse* — Ar. *tāss*, cup.]

tassel *tas'l, n* an ornamental hanging tuft of threads; an inflorescence of similar appearance, esp. of maize. — *vt* to provide with tassels. — *vi* (e.g. of maize) to form tassels, flower: — *pr p* **tass'elling;** *pa t* and *pa p* **tass'elled.** — *adj* **tass'elled.** — *n* **tass'elling.** — *adj* **tass'elly.** [O.Fr.]

taste *tāst, vt* to try, or to perceive, by the sense located in the tongue and palate; to try or test by eating a little; to eat a little of; to partake of; to experience, perceive. — *vi* to try or perceive by the mouth; to have a flavour (of); to act as taster; to have experience. — *n* the act of tasting; the particular sensation caused by a substance on the tongue; the sense by which we perceive the flavour of a thing; the quality or flavour of anything; a small portion; an experience; discernment of, or accordance with, what is socially right or acceptable; the faculty by which the mind perceives the beautiful or elegant; fine perception; choice, predilection, liking. — *adj* **tāst'able.** — *adj* **taste'ful** full of taste; showing good taste. — *adv* **taste'fully.** — *n* **taste'fulness.** — *adj* **taste'less** without taste; without good taste; insipid. — *adv* **taste'lessly.** — *n* **taste'lessness.** — *n* **tāst'er**

someone skilful in distinguishing flavours by the taste; someone employed to test the innocuousness of food by tasting it before serving it to his or her master (*hist*); any implement or device used to obtain samples for tasting; a publisher's reader (*colloq*); an extract or sample (*colloq*). — *adv* **tāst'ily**. — *n* **tāst'ing**. — *adj* **tāst'y** savoury, appetising; tasteful, attractive (*colloq*). — **taste'-bud** a group of cells on the tongue sensitive to taste. — **good taste** intuitive feeling for what is aesthetically or socially right; **to one's taste** to one's liking. [O.Fr. *taster*, as if from a L.L. frequentative of L. *taxāre*, to touch, handle, estimate.]

tat¹ or **tatt** *tat*, *vt* to make by tatting. — *vi* to make tatting. — *n* **tatt'ing** knotted lace edging made by hand with a shuttle from sewing-thread; the making of it.

tat² *tät*, *n* East Indian matting made from hemp. [Hindi *ṭāṭ*.]

tat³ or **tatt** *tat*, *n* pretentious odds and ends of little real value, e.g. in an antique shop; tawdry or shabby articles, esp. clothes. — *vt* to touch up. — *adv* **tatt'ily**. — *n* **tatt'iness**. — *adj* **tatt'y** cheap, of poor quality; untidy; shabby. [**tatter**.]

tat⁴: tit for tat. See under **tit²**.

ta-ta *tä-tä'*, (*childish* and *colloq*) *interj* good-bye.

Tatar *tä'tər*, *n* orig. a member of any of certain Tungusic tribes in Chinese Tartary; extended to any of the Mongol, Turkish and other warriors who swept over Asia and Europe; (*loosely*) one of the mixed inhabitants of Tartary, Siberia and the Russian steppes; a speaker of a Turkic language. — Also *adj*. — *adj* **Tatarian** (*tä-tā'ri-ən*) or **Tataric** (*-tar'ik*) of the Tatars; of the Turkic group of languages. [Turk. and Pers. *Tatar*; assoc. with Gr. *Tartaros*, hell, seems to have suggested the form **Tartar**.]

tater *tā'tər*, *n* a colloquial form of **potato**.

tatler. See under **tattle**.

tatou *ta'too͞* or *-too͞'*, *n* an armadillo, esp. the giant armadillo. [Tupí *tatú*.]

tatt¹, tattily, tattiness, tatty. See **tat³**.

tatt². See **tat¹**.

tatter *tat'ər*, *n* a torn shred; a loose hanging rag. — *adj* **tatt'ered** ragged. — **in tatters** ragged; ruined. [Cf. Icel. *töturr*.]

tatterdemalion *tat-ər-di-mā'li-ən*, *n* a tattered person, a ragamuffin. — *adj* ragged, tattered, scarecrow-like. [From *tattered* or *tatter*, with termination of uncertain formation.]

Tattersall's *tat'ər-sölz*, *n* a famous London horse market and haunt of racing-men — founded in 1766 by Richard *Tattersall* (1724–95); a sweepstake or lottery agency with headquarters at Melbourne, Australia. — **Tattersall** (a fabric with) a pattern of checks (like the horse-blankets orig. used at Tattersall's horse market) — also **Tattersall check**.

tatting. See under **tat¹**.

tattle *tat'l*, *n* idle talk, chatter; gossip. — *vi* to talk idly, chatter; to gossip, tell tales. — *vt* to tell, give away, in tattle. — *n* **tatt'ler** (formerly **tat'ler**) a chatterer, a gossip. — *n* and *adj* **tatt'ling**. — *adv* **tatt'lingly**. — **tatt'le-tale** (chiefly *US*) a tell-tale. [Used by Caxton to translate M.Du. *tatelen*; imit.]

tattoo¹ *tə-too͞'*, *n* a beat of drum or other signal calling soldiers to quarters; a drumming; a military entertainment, with marching, displays of prowess, etc., held at night. — **devil's tattoo** drumming with the fingers on a table, etc., in absence of mind or impatience. [Du. *taptoe* — *tap*, tap (of a barrel), *toe*, to, in the sense of shut.]

tattoo² *tə-too͞'*, *n* a design marked on the skin by pricking in colouring matter. — *vt* to mark in this way: — *pa t* and *pa p* **tattooed'**. — *n* **tattoo'er** or **tattoo'ist**. [Tahitian *tatau*, Marquesan *tatu*.]

tatty¹. See **tat³**.

tau *tow*, *n* the nineteenth letter (T, τ) of the Greek alphabet, corresponding to T; a tau cross; a tau particle. — **tau cross** St Anthony's cross, in the form of a T; **tau particle** (*phys*) a lepton of mass 3600 times greater than that of an electron. [Gr. *tau*, of Semitic origin.]

taught *töt*, *pa t* and *pa p* of **teach**.

taunt *tönt*, *vt* to goad or provoke in a wounding way; to censure or reproach sarcastically or contemptuously. — *vi* to jibe. — *n* a wounding jibe. — *n* **taunt'er**. — *n* and *adj* **taunt'ing**. — *adj* **taunt'ingly**. [Poss. O.Fr. *tanter* — L. *tentāre*, to tempt; or Fr. *tant pour tant*, tit for tat.]

taupe *tōp*, *n* and *adj* (of) a brownish-grey colour. [Fr., mole, — L. *talpa*.]

Taurus *tö'rəs*, *n* the Bull, a sign of the zodiac and a constellation formerly coinciding with it; a person born between 21 April and 21 May, under the sign of Taurus. — *n* and *adj* **Tau'rean** (or *-rē'ən*) (relating to) a person born under Taurus. [L., the Bull.]

Taurus *tö'rəs*, (*stock exchange*) *abbrev* for *t*ransfer and *au*tomated *r*egistration of *u*ncertificated *s*tock, a computerised system of share settlement, without the need for share certificates.

taurine *tö'rīn*, *adj* of a bull; bull-like. [L. *taurīnus*, – *taurus*, bull.]

tauromachy *tö-rom'ə-ki*, *n* bullfighting; a bullfight. [Gr. *tauros*, bull, *machē*, fight.]

taut *töt*, *adj* tightly drawn; tense; in good condition. — *vt* and *vi* **taut'en** to tighten. — *adv* **taut'ly**. — *n* **taut'ness**. [Prob. conn. with **tow¹** and **tight**.]

taut- *töt-* or **tauto-** *töt-ō-*, *töt-ə-* or *tö-to'-*, *combining form* meaning the same. [Gr. *tauto-*, for *to auto*, the same.]

tautology *tö-tol'ə-ji*, *n* the use of words, esp. as an error of style that repeat something already implied in the same statement, etc. as in *all at once she suddenly remembered*. — *adj* **tautolog'ical** or **tautol'ogous** (*-ə-gəs*). [Gr. *tautologos* — *tauto*, the same, *legein*, to say, speak.]

tautomer *tö'tə-mər*, (*chem*) *n* a readily interconvertible isomer. — *adj* **tautomer'ic**. — *n* **tautom'erism**. [Gr. *tauto*, the same, *meros*, part.]

tautonym *tö'tə-nim*, *n* in a biological nomenclature, a taxonomic name in which the specific name repeats the generic, as in *Regulus regulus*, the goldcrest. — *adj* **tauton'ymous**. [Gr. *tauto*, the same, *onyma*, name.]

tautophony *tö-tof'ə-ni*, *n* repetition of a sound. — *adj* **tautophon'ic** or **tautophon'ical**. [Gr. *tauto*, the same, *phōnē*, sound.]

tautog *tö-tog'*, *n* a fish of the N. American Atlantic coast, related to the wrasses. [Narragansett *tautauog*.]

tavern *tav'ərn*, (usu. *archaic* or *literary*) *n* a public house. — *n* **tav'erner** a publican. [O.Fr. (Fr.) *taverne* — L. *taberna*, shed, stall, tavern, from root of *tabula*, a board.]

taverna *tə-vûr'nə*, *n* a type of guesthouse with bar in Greece, popular as holiday accommodation. [Mod. Gr. — L. *taberna*, shed.]

taw¹ *tö*, *n* a large or choice marble; a game of marbles; the line shot from at marbles.

taw² *tö*, *vt* to prepare and dress (skins) for white leather. — *n* **taw'er** a maker of white leather. — *n* **taw'ing**. [O.E. *tawian*, to prepare.]

tawdry *tö'dri*, *adj* showy without taste or worth; gaudily adorned. — *adv* **taw'drily**. — *n* **taw'driness**. — **taw'dry-lace** (*hist*) a woman's silk necktie such as was sold at St Audrey's Fair at Ely (17 October). [From *St Audrey*, who thought a tumour in her throat was a punishment for having worn jewelled necklaces.]

tawny *tö'ni*, *adj* and *n* yellowish brown. — *n* **taw'niness**. — **tawny eagle** a tawny-coloured eagle of Africa and Asia (*Aquila rapax*); **tawny owl** a tawny-coloured European owl (*Strix aluco*). [Fr. *tanné*, past p. of *tanner*, to tan.]

taws or **tawse** *töz*, (esp. *Scot*) *n* a leather strap, usu. cut into strips at the end, for corporal punishment. [Poss. pl. of *taw*, a whip.]

tax *taks*, *vt* to lay a tax on; to register or enrol for fiscal purposes (*Bible*: Luke ii. 1–5); to make heavy demands on; to accuse, charge (usu. with *with*); to assess (costs) (*law*). — *n* a contribution to revenue exacted by the state from individuals or businesses; a burden, strain or drain (with *on* or *upon*). — *n* **taxabil'ity**. — *adj* **tax'able**. — *n* **taxā'tion**. — *adj* **taxed**. — *n* **tax'er**. — *adj* **tax'ing** demanding; onerous. — **tax allowance** a sum which is deducted from total income to arrive at taxable income; **tax avoidance** legal evasion of payment of tax; **tax break** an opportunity legally available for reducing one's tax obligations; **tax'-collector**. — *adj* **tax-deduct'ible** (of expenses, etc.) able to be deducted from one's income before it is assessed for tax. — **tax disc** a paper disc displayed on a motor vehicle's windscreen to show that it has been duly taxed; **tax evasion** illegal evasion of payment of tax. — *adj* **tax-exempt'** not liable to taxation. — **tax exile** a person living abroad so as not to pay high taxes. — *adj* and *adv* **tax-free'** without payment of tax. — **tax'-gatherer; tax haven** a country or state where taxes are low; **tax'man** (*colloq*) a tax-collector; tax-collectors collectively; **tax'payer** a person who pays tax or taxes; a person who is liable to taxation; a building put up for the express purpose of earning money to pay tax on the land (*US*). — *adj* **tax'paying**. — **tax point** the date on which value-added tax becomes payable; **tax return** a yearly statement of one's income, from which the amount due in tax is calculated; **tax shelter** a financial arrangement made in order to pay the minimum taxation. — *adj* **tax'-sheltered** of or produced by a tax shelter; of or involving investments legally exempt from tax. — **tax threshold** the level of income at which tax starts to be payable. [Fr. *taxe*, a tax — L. *taxāre*, to handle, value, charge.]

taxa. See **taxon**.

taxes (*tak'siz*) *pl* of **tax** or (*tak'sēz*) *pl* of **taxis**.

taxi *tak'si*, *n* (also **tax'icab**) a motor car, usu. fitted with a taximeter, licensed to carry passengers on request to a specified destination: — *pl* **tax'is**. — *vi* to travel by taxi; (of an aeroplane) to run along the ground before take-off or after landing at low speed under its own power. — *vt* to run (an aeroplane) along the ground in this way: — *pr p* **tax'ying** or **tax'iing**; *pa t* and *pa p* **tax'ied**; *3rd pers sing present indicative* **tax'ies**. — **taxi dancer** person, usu. a girl, hirable as a partner, dance by dance, in a dancehall; **tax'i-driver; tax'iman** a taxi-driver; **taxi rank** or in U.S. **taxi stand** a place where taxis congregate for hiring; **tax'iway** at an airport, a marked track for aircraft from runways to terminals, etc. [Shortening of *taximeter cab*.]

taxidermy *tak'si-dûr-mi*, *n* the art of preparing, stuffing and mounting the skins of animals and birds so that they present a lifelike appearance. — *adj* **taxider'mal** or **taxider'mic**. — *n* **tax'idermist**. [Gr. *taxis*, arrangement, *derma*, a skin.]

taximeter *tak'si-mē-tər* or *tak-sim'i-tər*, *n* an instrument attached to a cab for indicating (distance travelled and) fare due. [Fr. *taxe*, price, Gr. *metron*, measure.]

taxis *tak'sis*, *n* return to position of displaced parts by means of manipulation only (*surg*); movement of an organism, e.g. a bacterium, in response to stimulus (*biol*): — *pl* **tax'ēs**.

taxon *tak'sən* or *tak'son*, *n* a biological category, a taxonomic group: — *pl* **tax'a**. [Back-formation from *taxonomy*.]

taxonomy *tak-son'ə-mi*, *n* classification or its principles; classification of plants or animals, including the study of the means by which the formation of species, etc. takes place. [Gr. *taxis*, order, *-nomia*, distribution.]

tayberry *tā'bə-ri*, *n* a hybrid plant, a blackberry crossed with a raspberry; the fruit of this plant. [*Tay*side in Scotland, where it was first produced.]

tazza *tat'sə*, *n* a shallow cup mounted on a foot; a saucer-shaped bowl: — *pl* **taz'ze** (*-sā*) or **taz'zas**. [It., cup; cf. **tass**.]

TB *abbrev* for: tubercle bacillus; tuberculosis.

Tb (*chem*) *symbol* for terbium.

tbsp. *abbrev* for tablespoonful (*pl* **tbsps**).

Tc (*chem*) *symbol* for technetium.

TCD *abbrev* for Trinity College, Dublin.

TCP *abbrev* for *t*richloro*p*henylmethyliodasalicyl, a proprietary germicide.

TD *abbrev* for: *Teachda Dála*, Member of the Dáil; Territorial Decoration.

Te (*chem*) *symbol* for tellurium.

te. See **ti**.

tea *tē*, *n* a tree (*Camellia sinensis*) cultivated in China, Assam, etc.; its dried and prepared leaves, buds and shoots; an infusion of the leaves in boiling water; extended to any of various infusions, such as *herb tea*, *beef tea*; a cup of tea; an afternoon meal or light refreshment at which tea is generally served; a cooked meal taken in the early evening, high tea (*Brit*); marijuana (*old US slang*). — *vi* (*colloq*) to take tea. — *vt* (*colloq*) to provide tea for: — *pr p* **tea'ing**; *pa t* and *pa p* **teaed** or **tea'd**. — **tea bag** a bag containing tea leaves for infusion; **tea ball** chiefly in U.S., a perforated metal ball-shaped container to hold the tea leaves for infusion; **tea bread** light sweet bread or buns to be eaten with tea; **tea break** a break for tea during the working day; **tea caddy** an air-tight box or jar for holding tea; **tea cake** a glazed currant bun, usu. toasted; **tea ceremony** in Japan, the ceremonial making and serving of tea; **tea chest** a tall wooden container with a metal lining, in which tea is packed for transporting; **tea cloth** a small tablecloth; a tea towel, drying-up cloth; **tea cosy** a thick cover for a teapot to keep the tea hot; **tea'cup** a cup designed for drinking tea from; **tea'cupful** the amount held by a teacup, about 140 ml. (5 fl. oz.): — *pl* **tea'cupfuls; tea dance** a thé dansant; **tea'-drinker; tea garden** an open-air restaurant for tea and other refreshments; **tea gown** (*hist*) a loose gown for wearing at afternoon tea at home; **tea'-house** a restaurant in China, Japan, or other eastern countries where tea, etc. is served; **tea kettle** a kettle for boiling water for tea; **tea lady** a woman who makes and serves tea in an office or factory; **tea leaf** a leaf of tea; (usu. in *pl*) a small piece of such a leaf, esp. when it has been used in making tea; (*slang*) a thief; **tea party** a social gathering at which tea is served; **tea'-plant; tea plantation; tea'-planter** the owner or cultivator of a tea plantation; **tea'pot** a spouted vessel for pouring out tea; **tea'room** a restaurant where tea and light refreshments are served; a room used for refreshment and informal conversation by the staff or members of an establishment; **tea rose** a rose supposed to smell of tea; **tea service** or **tea'set** a set of utensils for serving tea; **tea'shop** a shop where tea is sold; a restaurant in which teas are served; **tea'spoon** a small spoon used with the teacup; **tea'spoonful**: — *pl* **tea'-spoonfuls; tea'-strainer** a small strainer to catch tea leaves when pouring tea; **tea table** a table at which tea is drunk; the company at tea; **tea things** the teapot, cups, etc. — **tea'time** the time in the afternoon or early evening when tea is taken; **tea towel** a cloth for drying crockery, etc., a drying-up cloth; **tea tray** a tray for carrying tea things; **tea tree** a name of Australian plants of the *Myrtaceae* (*Melaleuca*, *Leptospermum*; also called **manuka**), the leaves of which were formerly used as substitutes for tea; **tea trolley** or in U.S. **tea wagon** a small tiered trolley used for serving afternoon tea, etc.; **tea**

urn a large closed urn with a tap, often also a heating device, for making tea in quantity. — **another cup of tea** a very different thing; (usu. **not**) **for all the tea in China** (not) for anything whatever; **one's cup of tea** (*colloq*) what is to one's taste or appeals to one. [South Chinese *te*, the common form being *ch'a* or *ts'a*.]

teach *tēch*, *vt* to impart knowledge or an art to; to impart the knowledge or art of; to guide the studies of; to show; to direct; to accustom; to counsel; to be an object lesson to (someone) to do or not to do something in future; to force home the desirability or undesirability of (particular conduct, etc.) to. — *vi* to impart knowledge or give instruction as one's profession: — *pa t* and *pa p* **taught** (*töt*). — *n* **teachabil'ity.** — *adj* **teach'able** capable of being taught; willing and quick to learn, responsive to teaching. — *n* **teach'ableness.** — *n* **teach'er** a person whose profession, or whose talent, is the ability to impart knowledge, practical skill, or understanding. — *n* **teach'ing** the act, practice or profession of giving instruction; doctrine; instruction. — **teach'-in** a long public debate consisting of speeches by well-informed persons holding different views on a matter of general importance, usu. with discussion, etc.; **teaching aid** any object or device used by a teacher to help explain or illustrate a subject; **teaching hospital** a hospital in which medical students are trained; **teaching machine** any mechanical device capable of presenting an instructional programme. — **teach school** (*US*) to be a teacher in a school; **teach (someone) a lesson** to bring home to (someone) his or her folly; **that'll teach you, him,** etc. (*colloq*) that (unpleasant experience) will teach you, him, etc. to behave better, be more careful, etc. next time. [O.E. *tǣcan*, to show, teach.]

teak *tēk*, *n* a large tree (genus *Tectona*) of India, Malaya, etc.; its hard and durable wood. [Malayalam *tēkka*.]

teal *tēl*, *n* any of several kinds of small freshwater duck, esp. of the genus *Anas*; a dark greenish-blue colour: — *pl* **teals** or **teal**. [M.E. *tēle*.]

team *tēm*, *n* a set of people constituting one side in a competitive game; a set of people working in combination; a set of animals harnessed together; a set of animals with the vehicle to which they are harnessed, an equipage. — *vt* to join together in order to make a team or co-operative effort (with *with*); to match (clothes, etc.; often with *with*); to harness (animals) in a team; to draw or convey with a team (*NAm*). — *vi* to drive a team. — *n* **team'ing** driving a team; work apportioned to a team; transport by team; removal of excavated material from cutting to bank. — *n* **team'ster** a person who drives a team; a truck-driver (*US*). — **team effort** a co-operative endeavour, teamwork; **team game** an esp. outdoor game played by usu. two teams in opposition; **team'-mate** a fellow member of a team; **team spirit** the spirit of self-suppression in co-operation; **team teaching** instruction given by a group of teachers organised as a team, rather than by individual teachers in individual classes; **team'work** work done by organised division of labour; co-operation, pulling together, regard to success of the whole rather than personal exploits. — **team up with** to join forces with. [O.E. *tēam*, child-bearing, brood.]

teapoy *tē'poi*, *n* a small table with a three-legged or four-legged base. [Hind. *tīn*, *tīr-*, three, Pers. *pāi*, foot.]

tear[1] *tēr*, *n* a drop of liquid secreted by the lachrymal gland; an exuding drop; a blob, bead, pear-shaped drop; a small flaw or cavity as in glass. — *adj* **tear'ful** crying, shedding tears; inclined cry, lacrymose; emotion-filled, productive of tears. — *adv* **tear'fully.** — *n* **tear'fulness.** — *adj* **tear'less** shedding no tears, dry-eyed. — **tear'drop** a tear; **tear duct** the opening at the inner corner of the eye by which tears drain into the nose, the lacrymal duct; **tear'gas** a gas or volatile substance that blinds temporarily by provoking tears; **tear gland** the lacrymal gland; **tear'-jerker** an extravagantly sentimental, book, film, etc. inviting pity, grief, sorrow. — *adj* **tear'-stained** (of the face or cheeks) streaked with tracks left by tears. — **bored to tears** bored beyond endurance; **in tears** weeping; **without tears** by an easy or painless method. [O.E. *tēar*.]

tear[2] *tār*, *vt* to pull apart or separate with violence; to rend, rip, lacerate; to cause pain, bitterness, etc. to; to make (a hole, etc.) by tearing. — *vi* to move or act with violence; to rush, move very quickly; to become torn: — *pa t* **tore** (*tör*); *pa p* **torn** (*törn*). — *n* an act of tearing; a rent, hole torn in something. — *n* **tear'er.** — *adj* **tear'ing** great, terrible, rushing. — **tear'away** a reckless and usu. violent young person; **tear'sheet** a page, e.g. in a magazine, perforated so as to be able to be torn out for reference; **tear'-strip** a narrow perforated strip on a paper or card wrapper which can be pulled away to facilitate opening; **tear webbing** webbing in which two adhering layers form a fold that will tear apart so as to lessen the violence of a sudden strain. — **tear a strip off (someone)** (*slang*) to reprimand (someone); **tear away** to remove by tearing; to remove (oneself) reluctantly; **tear down** to demolish violently; **tear into** to attack, either physically or with criticism, etc.; **tear off** to remove by tearing; to depart hurriedly; to compose hurriedly; **tear one's hair** (*formerly*) to be reduced by grief or rage to tearing out handfuls of one's hair; to reach an extreme pitch of frenzy and frustration; **tear up** to remove violently from a fixed state; to pull to pieces; **that's torn it!** see under **torn**. [O.E. *teran*.]

tease *tēz*, *vt* to make fun of, make jokes at the expense of; to plague, irritate, esp. playfully, mischievously or unkindly; to tantalise; to open out the fibres of; to comb or card (wool, etc.); to scratch (cloth) with teasels, so as to raise a nap; to backcomb (the hair). — *n* a person given to teasing; an act of teasing. — *n* **teas'er** a tricky question; a riddle, conundrum; an introductory, appetite-whetting advertisement (*US*); a male horse used to arouse a mare's interest before the selected stallion is put to her. — *n* and *adj* **teas'ing.** — *adv* **teas'ingly**. [O.E. *tǣsan*, to card.]

teasel *tē'zl*, *n* a plant of the genus *Dipsacus* with prickly flowers; its dried flower head, with hooked bracts, used in raising a nap on cloth; an artificial substitute for its head. — *vt* to raise a nap on with the teasel: — *pr p* **tea'selling** or in U.S. **tea'seling;** *pa t* and *pa p* **tea'selled** or in U.S. **tea'seled.** — *n* **tea'seller** or **tea'seler**. [O.E. *tǣsel* — *tǣsan*; see **tease**.]

teat *tēt*, *n* the small protuberance through which the mammalian young suck the milk; a similar protuberance through which milk is sucked from a baby's feeding-bottle; a nipple. — *adj* **teat'ed** having a teat or teats. [O.E. *titt*, *tit*; influenced by O.Fr. *tete*.]

teazel or **teazle**. Other spellings of **teasel**.

tebbad *teb'ad*, *n* a sandstorm. [Cf. Pers. *tab*, fever, *bād*, wind.]

TEC or **Tec** *abbrev* for Training and Enterprise Councils.

'tec *tek*, (*colloq*) *n* a detective.

tech *tek*, (*colloq*) *n* a technical college.

tech. *abbrev* for: technical; technology.

technetium *tek-nē'shi-əm*, *n* a chemical element (symbol **Tc**; atomic no. 43), the first element to be artificially made. [Gr. *technētos*, artificial — *technē*, art.]

technic *tek'nik*, *n* technology; technique. — *n* **technician** (*-nish'ən*) a person skilled in a practical art; a person who does the practical work in a laboratory, etc. — *vt* **tech'nicise** or **-ize** to render technical or technological. — *n* **tech'nicism** (too great) emphasis on or concern with practical results or method. — *n* **tech'nicist** a technician. — *npl* **tech'nics** technical details or procedure. — *nsing* technology; the study of industry. [Gr. *technikos* — *technē*, art, skill.]

technical *tek'ni-kəl, adj* relating to a practical art or applied science; industrial; belonging to, or in the language of, a particular art, department of knowledge or skill, or profession; so called in strict legal or technical language. — *n* **technical'ity** a technical term or expression; a technical point, a point of strictly correct procedure, etc. — *adv* **tech'nically**. — *n* **tech'nicalness**. — **technical college** a college of further education that specialises in technical subjects, such as industrial skills, secretarial work, etc.; **technical foul** (*sport*) a foul that does not involve physical contact; **technical hitch** a mechanical fault that brings a broadcast, etc. to a temporary halt; **technical knockout** a boxer's defeat on the referee's decision that, though not actually knocked out, he is unable to continue the fight. [Gr. *technikos*, relating to an art or skill, and sfx. *-al*.]

Technicolor® *tek'ni-kul-ər, n* a process of colour photography in motion pictures in which films of the same scene, using different filters, are projected simultaneously. — *adj* **tech'nicolour** (modelled on above) in artificially or exaggeratedly bright colours.

technique *tek-nēk', n* a skilled procedure or method; a knack or trick of doing something; proficiency, refinement, in artistic performance. [Fr., — Gr. *technikos* — *technē*, art, skill.]

techno- *tek-nō-, tek-nə-* or *tek-no'-, combining form* denoting: craft or art; technical, technological or technology. — *n* **technoc'racy** government or management by technical experts: a state, etc. so governed; a body of technical experts in a governing position. — *n* **tech'nocrat** a member of a technocracy; a believer in technocracy. — *adj* **technocrat'ic**. — *n* **tech'nofear** (*colloq*) technophobia. — *n* **technog'raphy** the description of the arts, crafts and sciences against their historical and geographical background. — *n* **technomā'nia** a mania for technology. — *n* **technomā'niac**. — *n* **tech'nophile** a person who likes and promotes technology. — *n* **tech'nophobe** a person who fears and dislikes technology. — *n* **technophō'bia**. — *adj* and *n* **technophō'bic**. — *n* **tech'nopole** a place where high-technology industries are concentrated. — *n* **technop'olis** a society ruled by technology; a geographical area where projects in technological research and development are concentrated. — *n* and *adj* **technopol'itan**. — *n* **tech'nostress** stress resulting from over-involvement with computers. — *n* **tech'nostructure** the people in control of technology in a society. [Gr. *technē*, art, skill.]

technology *tek-nol'ə-ji, n* the practice of any or all of the applied sciences that have practical value and/or industrial use; technical methods in a particular area of industry or art; technical nomenclature; technical means and skills characteristic of a particular civilisation, group or period. — *adj* **technolog'ical**. — *adv* **technolog'ically**. — *n* **technol'ogist**. [Gr. *technē*, art, skill, and sfx. *-logy*.]

techy. See **tetchy**.

tectonic *tek-ton'ik, adj* relating to building; relating to structural changes in the earth's crust caused by upheavals and other movements within it (*geol*). — *adv* **tecton'ically**. — *nsing* **tecton'ics** building as an art; structural geology (see also **plate tectonics**). — *npl* the constructive arts; structural features. [Gr. *tektōn*, a builder.]

tectorial *tek-tö'ri-əl, (anat) adj* covering. [L. *tēctōrius* — *tegĕre, tēctum*, to cover.]

tectrix *tek'triks, n* a feather covering the quill bases on a bird's wings and tail (also called **covert**): — *pl* **tec'trices** (*-sēz* or *-trī'sēz*). — *adj* **tectricial** (*-trish'l*). [L. *tēctrīx* — *tegĕre*, to cover.]

Ted *ted, (colloq)* a shortened form of **Teddy boy**.

ted *ted, vt* to spread (new-mown grass) for drying: — *pr p* **tedd'ing**; *pa t* and *pa p* **tedd'ed**. — *n* **tedd'er** a person who teds; an implement for tedding. [Prob. from a lost O.E. *teddan*; cf. Icel. *tethja*, to manure.]

teddy[1] *ted'i* or **teddy bear** (*bār*) *n* a furry, stuffed toy bear. [From Theodore (*Teddy*) Roosevelt, a famous hunter and President of U.S.A. (1901–1909).]

teddy[2] *ted'i, n* a one-piece undergarment for a woman, combining panties and chemise. [Perh. a use of **teddy**[1].]

Teddy boy *ted'i boi, n* an unruly adolescent, orig. in the 1950s, affecting a dandyish style of dress reminiscent of Edward VII's time; **Teddy girl** the Teddy boy's female companion and counterpart in conduct; **Teddy suit**. [**Edward**.]

Te Deum *tē dē'əm* or L. *tā de'ōōm, n* a famous Latin hymn of praise and thanksgiving; a musical setting of it. [From its first words, *Tē Deum laudāmus*, thee, God, we praise.]

tedium *tē'di-əm, n* tiresomeness, esp. owing to extreme length or slowness; irksomeness; monotony; boredom. — *adj* **te'dious** tiresomely long; long-winded; monotonous; boring. — *adv* **te'diously**. — *n* **te'diousness**. [L. *taedium* — *taedēre*, to weary.]

tee[1] *tē, n* the twentieth letter of the alphabet (T, t); an object or mark of that shape. — **tee shirt** or **T'-shirt** a slip-on shirt, typically of knitted cotton with short sleeves and no collar or buttons, shaped like a letter T when laid flat. — **to a tee** exactly, to perfection.

tee[2] *tē, n* a small plastic or wooden support for the ball, with a concave top, used when the ball is first played at each hole (*golf*); the strip of ground (also **tee'ing-ground**) where this is done; a mark aimed at in quoits or curling. — *vt* (often with *up*) and *vi* (with *up*) to place (the golf ball) on the tee: — *pr p* **tee'ing**; *pa t* and *pa p* **teed, tee'd**. — **tee off** to start (play, in golf); **tee up** to prepare (oneself or something) (with *for*). [False singular from orig. form *teaz*, itself of uncertain origin.]

tee-hee or **te-hee** *tē-hē', interj* expressing derision or merriment. — *n* a laugh, titter. — *vi* to titter: — *pr p* **tee-hee'ing**; *pa t* and *pa p* **tee-heed'**. [Written representation of a titter or snigger.]

teem[1] *tēm, vi* to be full, abound (with *with*); to abound, be plentiful. — *adj* **teem'ing** full, prolific, abounding (with *with*); swarming, overrun (with *with*); full of creatures, people, etc., crowded; plentiful, copious, present in vast numbers. [Earlier, to be pregnant, — O.E. *tēman*, to give birth; see **team**.]

teem[2] *tēm, vi* to pour, fall in torrents (with *down*); to flow copiously. [O.N. *tœma*, to empty.]

teen *tēn, n* any number or year of age, etc. from thir*teen* to nine*teen* (usu. in *pl*); a teenager (*colloq*). — *adj* belonging to people in their teens, teenage. — *adj* **teen'āge** in the teens; appropriate to someone in the teens. — *adj* **teen'āged**. — *n* **teen'āger**. — **tee'ny-bopper** (*colloq*) a young teenager, esp. a girl, who follows enthusiastically the latest trends in pop music, clothes, etc. [O.E. sfx. *-tīene* — *tīen*, ten.]

teeny *tē'ni, (colloq) adj* tiny. — Also (*dimin*, often *facetious*) **teen'sy, teensy-ween'sy** and **teeny-ween'y**.

teepee. See **tepee**.

teeter *tē'tər, vi* to sway as if about to fall, wobble; to move unsteadily; to vacillate, hesitate, waver; to see-saw (*US*). [M.E. *titeren*, to totter.]

teeth *tēth, pl* of **tooth**.

teethe *tēdh, vi* to develop or cut teeth. — *n* and *adj* **teething** (*tēdh'ing*). — **teething ring** a ring of plastic, bone, etc. for a baby to chew when teething; **teething troubles** pain and irritation caused by the cutting of teeth; mechanical difficulties encountered on first using a new machine, etc. or in the early stages of any undertaking. [O.E. pl. *tēth*.]

teetotal *tē-tō'tl*, *adj* abstaining totally from alcoholic drink. — *n* **teetō'talism**. — *n* **teetō'taller** a total abstainer from alcoholic drink. — *adv* **teetō'tally**. [*Teetotally* prob. established first as a facetious or emphatic reduplicative form of *totally*; *teetotal* subsequently used in a speech advocating abstinence by Richard Turner of Preston in 1833.]

teetotum *tē-tō'təm*, (*hist*) *n* a small spinning top inscribed with letters, or a gambling game played with it, decided by the letter that came uppermost, T standing for *tōtum*, all, i.e. take all the stakes; any small top twirled by the fingers: — *pl* **teeto'tums**. [Orig. *T totum*, i.e. a *totum* (= this kind of top) with a *T* on one face.]

tef or **teff** *tef*, *n* an Ethiopian cereal grass, *Eragrostis tef*. [Amharic *ṭêf*.]

TEFL *tef'l*, *abbrev* for Teaching English as a Foreign Language.

Teflon® *tef'lon*, *n* a trademark for polytetrafluoroethylene as used e.g. to coat the inside of cooking pans to render them non-stick.

teg or **tegg** *teg*, *n* a sheep in its second year. [Perh. Scand.]

tegmen *teg'mən*, *n* a covering; the inner coat of a seed covering (*bot*); the leathery forewing in *Orthoptera*, the cockroaches and related insects: — *pl* **teg'mina**. — *adj* **tegmental** (*-men'təl*) relating to a tegmen or tegmentum. — *n* **tegmen'tum** a leaf-scale protecting a bud: — *pl* **tegmen'ta**. [L. *tegere*, to cover.]

teguexin *te-gwek'sin*, *n* a large black and yellow S. American lizard. [Aztec *tecoixin*.]

tegula *teg'ū-lə*, *n* a scale at the base of the forewing in some insects; a flat roofing-tile: — *pl* **teg'ūlae** (*-lē*). — *adj* **teg'ūlar**. — *adv* **teg'ūlarly**. — *adj* **teg'ūlāted** composed of plates overlapping like tiles. [L. *tegula*, a tile — *tegĕre*, to cover.]

tegument *teg'ū-mənt*, *n* the skin or other natural covering of an animal or plant body, an integument. [L. *tegere*, to cover.]

te-hee. See **tee-hee**.

teichopsia *tī-kops'i-ə*, *n* temporary blurring of vision, or partial blindness, with the appearance of a multicoloured zigzag of light before the eye, accompanying migraine. [Gr. *teichos*, wall, *opsis*, sight.]

tektite *tek'tīt*, *n* a type of small glassy stone, of uncertain and perhaps extraterrestrial origin, found in certain areas of the earth. [Gr. *tēktos*, molten.]

tel (*n*). See **tell**[2].

tel. *abbrev* for telephone.

telaesthesia or in U.S. **telesthesia** *tel-ēs-thē'zi-ə, -zhi-ə* or *-zhyə*, also *-is-*, *n* an abnormal impression as of sense received from a distance. — *adj* **telaesthetic** or in U.S. **telesthetic** (*-thet'ik*). [**tele-** (1) and Gr. *aisthēsiā*, sensation.]

telamon *tel'ə-mən*, (*archit*) *n* a man's figure as a pillar: — *pl* **telamones** (*-mō'nēz*). [Gr. mythological hero, *Telamōn* — *tlēnai*, to endure, bear.]

telangiectasis *tel-an-ji-ek'tə-sis*, (*pathol*) *n* dilatation of the small arteries or capillaries. — *adj* **telangiectatic** (*-ek-tat'ik*). [Gr. *telos*, end, *angeion*, a vessel, *ektasis*, extension.]

tele- *tel-i-*, *combining form* signifying: (1) far, distant; (2) television; (3) telephone. [Gr. *tēle*, far.]

tele-ad *tel'i-ad*, *n* a classified advertisement submitted to a newspaper, etc. by telephone. [**tele-** (3).]

telecast *tel'i-käst*, *n* a *tele*vision broad*cast*. — *vt* to transmit by television: — *pr p* **tel'ecasting**; *pa t* and *pa p* **tel'ecast** or **tel'ecasted**. — *n* **tel'ecaster**.

telechir *tel'i-kēr*, *n* a form of robot controlled by telecommand by an operator who has feedback from electronic sensors, e.g. television cameras. — *adj* **telechir'ic**. [**tele-** (1) and Gr. *cheir*, hand.]

telecine *tel-i-sin'i*, *n* transmission of filmed material by television. [**tele-** (2) and **cine-**.]

telecom *tel'i-kom*, *n* or **telecoms** *tel'i-komz*, *nsing* short for **telecommunication(s)**.

telecommand *tel'i-kə-mänd*, *n* the operation of machinery by remote electronic control. [**tele-** (1).]

telecommunication *tel-i-kə-mū-ni-kā'shən*, *n* communication of information, in verbal, written, coded or pictorial form, by telephone, telegraph, cable, radio, television. — *nsing* **telecommunicā'tions** the science or technology of such communication. [**tele-** (1).]

telecommute *tel-i-kə-mūt'*, *vi* to work at home, communicating with the office by telephone, computer link, etc. — *n* **telecommū'ter**. — *n* **telecommū'ting**. [**tele-** (1).]

teleconference *tel-i-kon'fər-əns*, *n* a meeting between people physically separated but linked by video, audio and/or computer facilities. — *n* **telecon'ferencing** the practice of holding such conferences, or the technology involved. [**tele-** (1).]

telecontrol *tel-i-kən-trōl'*, *n* control of mechanical devices remotely, either by radio (as of ships and aircraft), by sound waves, or by beams of light. [**tele-** (1).]

teledu *tel'ə-dōō*, *n* a small, short-tailed, carnivorous, Indonesian mammal, which can give off a strong, offensive odour — also known as the *stinking badger* of Java. [Jav.]

téléférique *tā-lā-fār-ēk*, (Fr.) *n* a light aerial cable car, esp. one electrically propelled.

telefilm *tel'i-film*, *n* a motion picture made specially for subsequent television transmission. [**tele-** (2).]

telegenic *tel-i-jen'ik*, *adj* having a presence, appearance and manner suitable for television. [**tele-** (2), modelled on **photogenic**.]

telegnosis *tel-i(g)-nō'sis*, *n* the knowledge of events taking place far away, not obtained in any normal way. [**tele-** (1) and Gr. *gnōsis*, knowing.]

telegony *ti-leg'ə-ni*, *n* the (imaginary) transmitted influence of a previous mate on the offspring of a female by a later mate. [**tele-** (1) and Gr. *gonos*, begetting.]

telegram *tel'i-gram*, *n* a message sent by telegraph and usu. presented in printed form (in U.K. now available only for international messages). — *adj* **telegrammat'ic**. [**tele-** (1) and Gr. *gramma*, that which is written — *graphein*, to write.]

telegraph *tel'i-gräf*, *n* a combination of apparatus for transmitting information to a distance, now almost exclusively by electrical impulses; a telegraph board; used as the name of a newspaper. — *vt* to convey or announce by telegraph; to signal; to give a premature indication of something to come. — *vi* to signal; to send a telegram. — *n* **telegrapher** (*ti-leg'rə-fər*) a telegraphist. — *n* **telegraphese** (*ti-leg-rə-fēz'*; *facetious*) the jargon or contracted idiom used in telegrams. — *adj* **telegraphic** (*-graf'ik*). — *adv* **telegraph'ically**. — *n* **teleg'raphist** a person who works a telegraph. — *n* **teleg'raphy** the science or art of constructing or using telegraphs. — **telegraph board** a scoreboard or information board that can be read at a distance, used at matches, athletics meetings, races, etc.; **telegraph cable** a cable containing wires for transmitting telegraphic messages; **telegraphic address** a shortened address registered for use in telegraphing; **telegraph plant** an Indian papilionaceous plant (genus *Desmodium*) whose leaves jerk spontaneously in different directions, like semaphore arms; **telegraph pole** a pole supporting telegraph wires; **telegraph wire** a wire for carrying telegraphic messages. [**tele-** (1) and Gr. *graphein*, to write.]

telejournalist *tel-i-jûr'nə-list*, *n* a journalist working in television. — *n* **telejour'nalism**. [**tele-** (2).]

telekinesis *tel-i-ki-nē'sis* or *-kī-*, *n* the production of motion at a distance by willpower alone. — *adj* **telekinetic** (*-net'ik*). [**tele-** (1) and Gr. *kīnēsis*, movement.]

telemark *tel'i-märk*, (*skiing*) *n* a sudden turn on the outer ski, first practised at *Telemark* in Norway. — *vi* to execute a telemark.

telemarketing. See **teleselling.**

Telemessage® *tel'i-mes-ij*, *n* a message sent by telex or telephone, superseding the telegram. [**tele-** (1).]

telemeter *ti-lem'i-tər*, *n* an instrument for measuring distances (*surveying*); an instrument for measuring an electrical or other quantity and signalling the measurement to a distant point (also called **radio-telemeter**). — *vt* to record and signal by telemeter. — *adj* **telemetric** (*tel-i-met'rik*). — *n* **telem'etry**. [**tele-** (1) and Gr. *metron*, measure.]

teleology *tel-i-ol'ə-ji* or *tē-li-*, *n* the doctrine of the final causes of things; interpretation in terms of purpose. — *adj* **teleological** (*-ə-loj'i-kəl*). — *adv* **teleolog'ically**. — *n* **teleol'ogism**. — *n* **teleol'ogist**. [Gr. *telos*, end, purpose, *logos*, a discourse.]

teleost *tel'i-ost*, *n* any one of bony fishes (the *Teleostei*), a sub-clan including salmon, eels, herring, cod. — *adj* **teleos'tean**. [N.L. *teleosteus*, having a complete skeleton, — Gr. *teleios*, complete, *osteon*, bone.]

telepathy *ti-lep'ə-thi*, *n* communication between mind and mind otherwise than through the known channels of the senses. — *n* **telepath** (*tel'i-path*) a telepathic subject. — *adj* **telepath'ic**. — *adv* **telepath'ically**. — *vi* **telep'athise** or **-ize** to communicate or become aware through telepathy. — *n* **telep'athist**. [**tele-** (1) and Gr. *pathos*, feeling.]

telephone *tel'i-fōn*, *n* an instrument for reproducing sound at a distance, esp. by means of electricity; *specif* an instrument with a microphone and a receiver mounted on a handset, for transmitting speech; the system of communication which uses these instruments. — *vt* to contact and speak to by telephone; to convey (a message, etc.) by telephone. — *vi* to make a telephone call. — *n* **tel'ephōner**. — *adj* **telephonic** (*-fon'ik*). — *adv* **telephon'ically**. — *n* **telephonist** (*ti-lef'ə-nist*) a person who operates a switchboard or works as an operator in a telephone exchange. — *n* **teleph'ony** telephonic communication. — **telephone book** or **directory** a book listing the names, addresses and numbers of telephone subscribers; **telephone box, booth** or **kiosk** a usu. enclosed place with a telephone for public use; **telephone exchange** a central office where telephone lines are connected; **telephone number** a number which identifies a particular telephone and is dialled to make connections with it; (often in *pl*) a very large number or amount (esp. of money; *colloq*); **telephone-tapping** see **tap²**. [**tele-** (1) and Gr. *phōnē*, a sound.]

telephoto *tel-i-fō'tō*, *adj* a shortening of **telephotographic**. — **telephoto lens** a lens of long focal length for obtaining large images of distant objects.

telephotography *tel-i-fə-tog'rə-fi*, *n* photography of distant objects by means of suitable lenses. — *n* **telephotograph** (*tel-i-fō'tō-gräf*). — *adj* **telephotographic** (*-graf'ik*). [**tele-** (1).]

teleplay *tel'i-plā*, *n* a play written to be performed on television. [**tele-** (2).]

teleprinter *tel-i-print'ər*, *n* a telegraph transmitter with typewriter keyboard. [**tele-** (1).]

teleprompter *tel-i-promp'tər*, *n* a device by which a television speaker sees a projection of what he or she is to say, invisible to the audience. [**tele-** (2).]

telerecording *tel-i-ri-kör'ding*, *n* recording for broadcasting by television; a television transmission from a recording. — *vt* **telerecord'**. [**tele-** (2).]

telesale. See **teleselling.**

telescope *tel'i-skōp*, *n* an optical instrument for viewing objects at a distance. — *vt* to drive or slide one into another like the movable joints of a telescope; to compress, shorten, make smaller, etc.; to compact, crush. — *vi* to collapse part within part, like a telescope; to be compressed or compacted. — *adj* **telescopic** (*-skop'ik*) of, performed by, or like a telescope; seen only by a telescope; sliding, or arranged, like the joints of a telescope; capable of retraction and protrusion. — *adv* **telescop'ically**. — *n* **teles'copy** the art of constructing or of using the telescope. — **telescopic sight** a telescope on a gun used as a sight. [**tele-** (1) and Gr. *skopeein*, to see.]

teleselling *tel'i-sel-ing*, *n* the selling of goods or services by using the telephone to seek customers (also called **tel'emarketing**). — *n* **tel'esale** a sale made on the telephone. [**tele-** (3).]

teleservices *tel'i-sûr-vis-əz*, *npl* information, etc. services available to users of teletext and viewdata systems. [**tele-** (2).]

telesoftware *tel-i-soft'wār*, (*comput*) *n* software which is transmitted to users by means of a teletext or viewdata system. [**tele-** (1).]

telesthesia. See **telaesthesia.**

telestich *tel-e'stik* or *tel'es-tik*, *n* a poem or block of words whose final letters spell a name or word. [Gr. *telos*, end, *stichos*, row.]

teletex *tel-i-teks*, *n* a means of transmitting written data, similar in principle to telex (q.v.), but using more modern, high-speed electronic apparatus. [**tele-** (1) and **text**.]

teletext *tel'i-tekst*, *n* written data, such as business news, etc., transmitted by television companies in the form of coded pulses which can be decoded by a special adaptor for viewing on a conventional television. [**tele-** (2).]

telethon *tel'ə-thon*, (orig. *US*) *n* a very long television programme, esp. one seeking support for e.g. a political candidate, or a charity. [*tele*vision mara*thon*.]

Teletype® *tel'i-tīp*, *n* a printing telegraph apparatus. — **Teletype'setter®** a telegraphic machine which delivers its message as a perforated roll that can be used to actuate a typesetting machine; **teletype'writer** (*US*) a teleprinter. [**tele-** (1) and Gr. *typos*; see **type**.]

televangelist *tel-i-van'ji-list*, *n* (esp. in U.S.) an evangelical, esp. fundamentalist, preacher with a regular slot on television. — *adj* **televangel'ical**. — *n* **televan'gelism**. [**tele-** (2).]

televérité *tel-i-ver'i-tā*, *n* the televising of scenes of actual life in order to convey a heightened realism. — See also **cinéma vérité** under **cinema**. [**tele-** (2), modelled on **cinéma vérité**.]

television *tel-i-vizh'ən*, *n* the transmission by radio waves, and reproduction on a screen, of visual images, usu. accompanied by sound; an apparatus (also **television set**) incorporating a screen, for receiving these. — *abbrev* **TV**. — **tel'evise** (*tel'i-vīz*) to transmit by television. — *n* **tel'eviser**. — *adj* **televisual** (*tel-i-viz'ū-əl*) relating to television; suitable for televising. — *adv* **televis'ually**. [**tele-** (1).]

teleworker *tel'ə-wûr-kər*, *n* another word for telecommuter. — *n* **tel'eworking**. [**tele-** (3).]

telex *tel'eks*, *n* an international telegraphic service whereby subscribers hire the use of teleprinters; a teleprinter used in this service; a message transferred by this service. — *vt* to send (someone) (a message) by telex. [*tel*eprinter and *ex*change.]

tell¹ *tel*, *vt* to utter; to narrate; to disclose; to inform; to discern; to explain; to order, direct, instruct; to count (votes). — *vi* to give an account (with *of*); to have an effect (with *on*); to have weight; to make an effective story; to give an indication, be evidence (with *of*); to play the informer: — *pa t* and *pa p* **tōld**. — *adj* **tell'able**. — *n* **tell'er** a person who counts votes; a clerk whose duty it is to receive and pay money in a bank. — *n* **tell'ership**. — *adj* **tell'ing** effective; significant, meaningful. — *n* numbering; narration; direction, orders. — *adv* **tell'ingly**. — **telling-off'** a reprimand; **tell'-tale** a person who tells the private concerns or misdeeds of others; anything revealing or betraying; an indicator or monitor; a recording clock; a strip of material outside the playing area at the foot of the front wall of a squash court, which makes a distinctive sound when hit. — *adj* blabbing; revealing, betraying; indicating. — **as far as one can tell** judging from information available so far; **I tell you** or **I'm telling you** I assure you, I insist; **take a telling** to do as one is asked without having to be told again; **tell me another** used to express disbelief; **tell off** to reprimand; to count off and detach on some special duty; **tell on** (*colloq*) to betray, inform on, or give away secrets about; **tell the time** to read the time on a clock or watch; **there's no telling** one cannot possibly know or predict; **you're telling me** (*interj*; *colloq*) I know that only too well. [O.E. *tellan*.]

tell[2] or **tel** *tel*, *n* in Arab lands, a hill or ancient mound formed from the accumulated debris from earlier mud or wattle habitations. [Ar. *tall*.]

tellurian *te-lū'ri-ən*, *adj* terrestrial. — *n* an inhabitant of the earth; a tellurion. [L. *tellūs*, *-ūris*, earth.]

telluric *te-lū'rik*, *adj* of or from the earth; of tellurium in higher valency (*chem*). — **telluric acid** a white crystalline acid (H_2TeO_4) produced when tellurium is oxidised by hydrogen peroxide. [L. *tellūs*, *-ūris*, earth.]

tellurion or **tellurian** *te-lū'ri-ən*, *n* an apparatus representing the earth and sun, demonstrating the occurrence of day, night, the seasons, etc. [L. *tellūs*, *-ūris*, earth.]

tellurium *te-lū'ri-əm*, *n* a rare, silvery, non-metallic element (symbol **Te**; atomic no. 52). [L. *tellūs*, *-ūris*, app. so named by Klaproth, 1798, in contrast to *uranium*.]

tellurometer *tel-ū-rom'ə-tər*, *n* an electronic instrument used to measure survey lines by measurement of the time required for a radar signal to echo back. [L. *tellūs*, *-ūris*, earth, Gr. *metron*, measure.]

telly *tel'i*, (*colloq*) *n* television.

telpher *tel'fər*, *n* a system of automatic electric transport, esp. using cars or containers suspended from overhead cables (also **tel'pherage**); a car of carrier in such a system. [Irreg. coined — Gr. *tēle*, far — *phoros*, bearing — *pherein*, to bear.]

telson *tel'sən*, (*zool*) *n* the terminal or hindmost segment of a crustacean or arachnid. [Gr. *telson*, a headland in ploughing.]

Telugu *tel'o͝o-go͞o*, *n* a Dravidian language of south-east India; one of the people speaking it: — *pl* **Tel'ugus** or **Tel'ugu**. — Also *adj*.

temblor *tem'blör*, (esp. *US*) *n* an earthquake: — *pl* **temblores** (*-blö'rāz*). [Am. Sp.]

temerity *ti-mer'i-ti*, *n* rashness; unreasonable contempt for danger. — *adj* **temerarious** (*tem-ə-rā'ri-əs*; *literary*) rash, reckless. — *adv* **temerā'riously**. [L. *temeritās*, *-ātis*, and *temerārius* — *temere*, by chance, rashly.]

temp *temp*, (*colloq*) *n* a temporarily-employed secretarial worker. — *vi* to work as a temp. [**temporary**.]

temp. *abbrev* for: temperature; temporary.

tempeh *tem'pā*, *n* a high-protein food prepared by incubating boiled soya beans with a fungus to bring about fermentation, made esp. in Japan and Indonesia. [Indonesian *tempe*.]

temper *tem'pər*, *n* temperament, disposition; a habitual or transitory frame of mind; mood; composure; self-control; uncontrolled anger; a fit of ill-humour or rage; the hardness, elasticity, etc. of a metal. — *vt* to modify by blending or adding a lesser ingredient; to moderate, soften; to harden (steel) by heating to red heat and quenching, or, after this, to heat moderately and cool slowly, or to perform both these operations; to adjust, attune; to tune the notes (on a piano or other keyboard instruments) so that the intervals between them are correct, or to adjust the pitch of the notes of (a scale) (*mus*). — *adj* **tem'pered**. — (In combination) **-tem'pered** possessed of, or showing, a specified disposition of temper, as in *ill-tempered*, *bad-tempered*, *sweet-tempered*, etc. — *adv combining form* **-tem'peredly**. — *n combining form* **-tem'peredness**. — **(in a) good temper** (in) a cheerful frame of mind; **(in a) bad temper** (in) an angry or sulky mood; **keep one's temper** to remain composed, restrain one's anger; **lose one's temper** to lose restraint, break out in anger; **out of temper** in an irritable mood. [L. *temperāre*, to temper, restrain, moderate, mix, partly through O.E. *temprian*.]

tempera *tem'pə-rə*, (*art*) *n* an emulsion, esp. made with egg yolk, used as a medium for powdered pigments; the paint so produced; the technique of painting with this paint. [It., — L. *temperāre*, to mix proportionately.]

temperament *tem'prə-mənt*, *n* disposition, personality, esp. with regard to emotional make-up; high excitability, nervous instability, and sensitiveness; an adjustment made to the intervals between notes on a keyboard to allow modulation to any key (*mus*). — *adj* **temperamen'tal** relating to temperament; of a volatile, excitable temperament, given to extreme swings of mood. — *adv* **temperamen'tally**. — **equal temperament** (*mus*) a tuning adjustment by which the octave on a keyboard is divided into twelve equal intervals. [L. *temperamentum*, the mixing of things in proper proportion.]

temperance *tem'pə-rəns*, *n* moderation, esp. in the indulgence of the natural appetites and passions — in a narrower sense, moderation in the use of alcoholic liquors, and even entire abstinence from them. — **temperance hotel** (*hist*) one at which no alcohol is supplied. [L. *temperantia*, sobriety, moderation.]

temperate *tem'pə-rət*, *adj* moderate; self-restrained, esp. in appetites and passions; moderate in temperature, neither very hot nor very cold. — *adv* **tem'perately**. — *n* **tem'perateness**. — **temperate zones** the parts of the earth of moderate temperature between the tropics and the polar circles. [L. *temperātus*, past p. of *temperāre*, to restrain, modify.]

temperature *tem'prə-chər*, *n* the degree of hotness of a body, etc. or medium (e.g. air, water) ascertainable by means of a thermometer; a body temperature above normal; the degree of warmth or friendliness in an interchange or relationship; the degree of enthusiasm, excitement or animation generated during debate. — **temperature-humidity index** an index measuring temperature and humidity with regard to human discomfort. — **have a temperature** to have a raised body temperature, a fever; **take someone's temperature** to use a thermometer to ascertain someone's body temperature, as part of diagnosis. [L. *temperatura*, appropriate measure, proportion.]

tempest *tem'pist*, *n* a violent wind storm; a violent commotion or agitation. — **tempestuous** (*-pest'ū-əs*) stormy, turbulent; wild, passionate. — *adv* **tempest'ūously**. — *n* **tempest'ūousness**. [O.Fr. *tempeste* — a L.L. form of L. *tempestās*, a season, tempest — *tempus*, time.]

tempi. See **tempo**.

Templar *tem'plər*, *n* a member of a religious and military order (**Knights Templars**) founded in 1119 for the protection of the Holy Sepulchre and pilgrims going there — extinguished 1307–14; a student or lawyer living in the Temple, London; a member of a U.S. order of Freemasons. [Med. L. *templārius*, of the temple.]

template or **templet** *tem'plit*, *n* a thin plate cut to the shape required, used as a guide in cutting wood, metal, etc.; a pattern cut in card or plastic for shaping pieces of cloth for patchwork; a timber or small beam used to spread the load in a wall; the coded instructions for the formation of a further molecule carried by a molecule of DNA, etc. (*biochem*). [L. *templum*, a small timber.]

temple[1] *tem'pl*, *n* a building or place dedicated to, or regarded as the house of, a god; a place of worship; in France, a Protestant church; (with *cap*) the headquarters of the Knights Templars on or near the site of Solomon's temple in Jerusalem; (with *cap*) in London, two inns of court (*Inner* and *Middle Temple*) on the site once occupied by the Knights Templars, with the Knights' church; a synagogue, esp. of Reform or Conservative Judaism (*US*). [L. *templum*.]

temple[2] *tem'pl*, *n* the flat portion of either side of the head above the cheekbone. [O.Fr., — L. *tempus*, *-oris*.]

templet. See **template**.

tempo *tem'pō*, (*mus*) *n* time; speed and rhythm: — *pl* **tem'pos** or **tem'pi** (*-pē*). [It.]

temporal[1] *tem'pə-rəl*, *adj* relating to time; relating to time in this life or world (opp. to *eternal*); worldly, secular or civil (opp. to *spiritual*, *sacred* or *ecclesiastical*); relating to tense or the expression of time (*gram*). — *n* **temporality** (*-al'i-ti*) the state or fact of being temporal; (usu. *pl*) secular possessions, revenues of an ecclesiastic proceeding from lands, tithes, and the like. — *adv* **tem'porally**. [L. *temporālis* — *tempus*, *-oris*, time.]

temporal[2] *tem'pə-rəl*, (*anat*) *adj* relating to, or close to, the temples on either side of the head. — *n* a bone, muscle or scale in that position. — **temporal lobe** a lobe at the side of each cerebral hemisphere by the temple, concerned with hearing and speech. [L. *tempus*, *-oris*; see **temple**[2].]

temporary *tem'pə-rə-ri*, *n* lasting for a time only; transient, impermanent; provisional. — *n* a person employed temporarily (see also **temp**). [L. *temporāius*, lasting briefly — *tempus*, *-oris*, time.]

temporise or **-ize** *tem'pə-rīz*, *vi* to comply with the demands of the moment, yield to circumstances; to use delaying tactics, behave so as to gain time. — *n* **temporisā'tion** or **-z-**. — *n* **tem'poriser** or **-z-**. — *adv* **tem'porisingly** or **-z-**. [Fr. *temporiser*, — L. *tempus*, *-oris*, time.]

tempt *tempt*, *vt* to try or tend to persuade, esp. to do wrong; to entice; to dispose, incline; to attract; to make trial of, test the virtue of (*archaic*, *Bible* or *literary*). — *n* **temptabil'ity**. — *adj* **temp'table**. — *n* **temp'tableness**. — *n* **temptā'tion** act of tempting; state of being tempted; that which tempts; enticement to do wrong. — *n* **temp'ter** a person or being who tempts, esp. (with *cap*) the devil: — *fem* **temp'tress**. — *adj* **temp'ting** attractive, enticing. — *adv* **temp'tingly**. — *n* **temp'tingness**. [O.Fr. *tempter* — L. *tentāre* or *temptāre*, intensive of *tenděre*, to stretch.]

tempura *tem'pōō-rə*, *n* a Japanese dish of sea food or vegetables deep-fried in batter.

ten *ten*, *n* the cardinal number next above nine; a symbol representing it (x, X or 10); a set of that number of things or persons; an article of a size denoted by 10; a card with ten pips; a score of ten points, tricks, etc.; the tenth hour after midday or midnight; the age of ten years. — *adj* of the number ten; ten years old. — *adj* and *adv* **ten'fold** in ten divisions; ten times as much. — *n* **tenn'er** (*colloq*) a ten-pound note; a ten-dollar bill; ten years. — *adj* **tenth** the last of ten; next after the ninth; equal to one of ten equal parts. — *n* a tenth part; a person or thing in tenth position; an octave and a third (*mus*); a note at that interval (*mus*). — *adv* **tenth'ly**. — *adj* **ten'-foot** measuring ten feet. — **ten-gallon hat** (*US*) a cowboy's broad-brimmed hat; **ten-minute rule** a parliamentary procedure by which a member makes a short speech (lasting no more than ten minutes) requesting permission to introduce a bill; **ten'pence** an amount in money equal to ten pennies; **ten-pence** (or **ten-penny**) **piece** in Britain, a coin worth 10 pence (also **tenpenny-piece**'). — *adj* **ten'penny** offered for, or sold at, tenpence. — **tenpin bowling** or **ten'pins** an American game like skittles; **ten-point'er** a stag of ten points or tines. — *adj* **ten'-pound** weighing, worth, sold or offered for, ten pounds. — **ten-pound'er** something weighing or worth ten pounds. [O.E. *tēn*, *tīene*.]

tenable *ten'ə-bl*, *adj* capable of being retained, kept or defended. — *n* **tenabil'ity** or **ten'ableness**. [Fr. *tenable* — *tenir*, to hold.]

tenace *ten'ās* or *ten'is*, (*cards*) *n* the combination in one hand of the cards next above and next below the other side's best in the suit. [Sp. *tenaza*, pincers.]

tenacious *ti-nā'shəs*, *adj* retentive; holding fast to (with *of*); clinging; sticking firmly; cohesive; tough; stubborn, obdurate, determined. — *adv* **tenā'ciously**. — *n* **tenā'ciousness** or **tenacity** (*-nas'i-ti*). [L. *tenāx*, *-ācis* — *tenēre*, to hold.]

tenaculum *ti-nak'ū-ləm*, *n* a surgical hook or forceps for picking up blood-vessels. [L. *tenāculum*, holder, pincers.]

tenant *ten'ənt*, *n* a person who occupies property owned by another, in return for rent, service, etc.; an occupant; someone who possesses land or property by private ownership (*law*). — *vt* to hold as a tenant; to occupy. — *n* **ten'ancy** a temporary occupation or holding of land or property by a tenant; time of such holding; possession by private ownership. — *adj* **ten'antable** fit to be tenanted; in a state of repair suitable for a tenant. — *adj* **ten'antless**. — *n* **ten'antry** the state or time of being a tenant; a set or body of tenants. — *n* **ten'antship**. — **tenant farmer** a farmer who rents a farm; **tenant right** the right of a tenant, esp. that of a customary tenant to sit continuously at a reasonable rent, the right to receive compensation for his or her interest from the incoming tenant, and for all permanent or unexhausted improvements from the landlord. [Fr. *tenant*, pres. p. of *tenir* — L. *tenēre*, to hold.]

tench *tench* or *tensh*, *n* a dark green to brown freshwater fish (*Tinca tinca*) of the carp family, its mouth bearing a pair of thin barbels. [O.Fr. *tenche* — L. *tinca*.]

tend[1] *tend*, *vt* to attend to, take care of; to watch over or stand by and perform services for or connected with; to minister to, wait upon. — *vi* (*US*) to pay attention (with *to*). — *n* **ten'der** a person who tends; a small craft that attends a larger; a carriage attached to a locomotive to carry fuel and water. — **tend out on** (*US*) to attend or attend to. [Aphetic for **attend**.]

tend[2] *tend*, *vi* to be apt; to move or incline in some direction; to be directed to any end or purpose; to conduce. — *n* **ten'dency** a trend, drift, inclination; proneness; a faction within a particular political movement. — *adj* **tenden'tious** purposely angled; biased. — *adv* **tenden'tiously**. — *n* **tenden'tiousness**. [L. *tenděre* and Fr. *tendre*, to stretch.]

tender[1]. See under **tend**[1].

tender[2] *ten'dər*, *vt* to offer for acceptance, esp. to offer in payment; to proffer. — *vi* to make a tender (with *for*). — *n* an offer or proposal, esp. of some service; the paper containing it; the thing offered; a formal offer to save the consequences of non-payment or non-performance (*law*). — *n* **ten'derer**. — **legal tender** see under **legal**. — **put out to tender** to invite tenders for a particular job. [Fr. *tendre*, to stretch, reach out.]

tender[3] *ten'dər*, *adj* soft, delicate; easily chewed, not tough; easily impressed or injured; not hardy; gentle; youthful, vulnerable; sensitive, esp. to pain; painful when touched or pressed; requiring gentle handling; easily moved to pity, love, etc.; careful not to hurt; considerate, careful (with *of*); pathetic; expressive, or of the nature, of the softer passions;

compassionate, loving, affectionate. — *vt* **ten'derise** or **-ize** to break down the connective tissue of (meat) by pounding or by applying a chemical or marinade. — *n* **ten'deriser** or **-z-** a pounding instrument or a substance that tenderises meat. — *adv* **ten'derly**. — *n* **ten'derness**. — **ten'derfoot** (orig. and esp. *US*) a person not yet hardened to life in the prairie, mining-camp, etc.; a newcomer; a greenhorn, beginner: — *pl* **ten'derfeet**. — *adj* **tender-heart'ed** compassionate, easily touched or moved. — *adv* **tender-heart'edly**. — **tender-heart'edness**; **ten'derloin** the tenderest part of the loin of beef, pork, etc., close to the lumbar vertebrae (*US*); a district juicy with bribes to the police (*US slang*). [Fr. *tendre* — L. *tener*.]

tendon *ten'dən*, *n* a cord, band or sheet of fibrous tissue attaching a muscle to a bone or other structure. — *n* **tendinitis** or **tendonitis** (*-ī'tis*) inflammation of a tendon. — *adj* **ten'dinous**. [L.L. *tendō*, *-inis* or *-ōnis*.]

tendril *ten'dril*, *n* a plant's coiling threadlike climbing organ (leaf, leaflet or shoot). — *adj* **ten'drilled**. [Cf. Fr. *tendrillon*, shoot.]

tenebrae *ten'i-brā*, (*RC*; also with *cap*) *npl* matins and lauds in Holy Week with gradual extinction of lights. [L., darkness.]

tenebrism *ten'ə-brizm*, (*art*) *n* the 17th-cent. Italian and Spanish school of painting characterised by large expanses of shadow. — *n* **ten'ebrist**. [L. *tenebrae*, darkness.]

tenebrous *ten'ə-brəs*, *adj* dark. [L. *tenebrōsus* — *tenebrae*, darkness.]

tenement *ten'i-mənt*, *n* a dwelling or habitation, or part of it, used by one family; one of a set of apartments in one building, each occupied by a separate family; a building divided into dwellings for a number of families (*Scot* and *US*); a holding, by any tenure; anything held, or that may be held, by a tenant. — *adj* **tenemental** (*-men'tl*). — *adj* **tenemen'tary**. — **tenement building**; **tenement house**. [L.L. *tenementum* — L. *tenēre*, to hold.]

tenesmus *ti-nes'məs*, (*med*) *n* painful and ineffectual straining to relieve the bowels. [Latinised from Gr. *teinesmos* — *teinein*, to strain.]

tenet *ten'it*, *n* any opinion, principle or doctrine which a person holds or maintains as true. [L. *tenet*, (he) holds — *tenēre*, to hold.]

tenfold, tenner. See under **ten**.

Tenn. *abbrev* for Tennessee (U.S. state).

tennis *ten'is*, *n* lawn tennis; an ancient game played with ball, rackets (orig. palms of the hands), and net, in a specially constructed building or enclosed court (distinguished from lawn tennis as **close, court, real,** or **royal** tennis). — **tennis ball**; **tennis court**; **tennis elbow** an inflamed condition of the muscle that extends the wrist, at the point where it arises at the elbow, caused by over-exercise; **tennis match**; **tenn'is-player**; **tennis racket**; **tennis shoe**. — **short tennis** see under **short**. [Prob. Fr. *tenez* (A.Fr. *tenetz*) imper. of *tenir*, to take, receive.]

tenon *ten'ən*, *n* a projection at the end of a piece of wood, etc., inserted into the socket or mortise of another, to hold the two together. — *vt* to fix or fit with a tenon. — *n* **ten'oner**. — **tenon saw** a thin backsaw for tenons, etc. [Fr. *tenon* — *tenir*, to hold — L. *tenēre*.]

tenor *ten'ər*, *n* continuity of state; general run or course; purport; the highest of the range voices usu. belonging to adult males (app. because the melody was assigned to it); an instrument, e.g. a viola or recorder, of corresponding compass; a person who sings tenor. — **tenor clef** the C clef placed on the fourth line. [L. *tenor* — *tenēre*, to hold.]

tenosynovitis *ten-ə-sī-nə-vī'tis*, (*med*) *n* inflammation and swelling of a tendon, associated with repetitive movements. [Gr. *tenon*, tendon, and **synovitis**.]

tenpence, etc. See under **ten**.

tenrec *ten'rek* or **tanrec** *tan'rek*, *n* a large Madagascan insectivore similar to a hedgehog. [Malagasy *t(r)àndraka*.]

tense[1] *tens*, *n* time in grammar, the form of a verb to indicate the time of the action. [O.Fr. *tens* — L. *tempus*, time.]

tense[2] *tens*, *adj* stretched tight; strained; rigid; pronounced with the tongue tightened or narrowed (*phon*). — *vt* and *vi* to make or become tense. — *adv* **tense'ly**. — *n* **tense'ness**. — *n* **tensibil'ity**. — *adj* **ten'sible** capable of being stretched. — *adj* **ten'sile** (*-sīl* or in U.S. *-sil* or *-səl*) tensible; of or relating to stretching. — *n* **tensility** (*-sil'i-ti*). — *n* **tensim'eter** an instrument for measuring vapour pressure. — *n* **tensiom'eter** an instrument for measuring tension, tensile strength, or the moisture content of soil. — *n* **tensiom'etry** the branch of physics relating to tension, tensile strength, etc. — *n* **tension** (*ten'shən*) stretching; a pulling strain; stretched or strained state; strain generally; electromotive force; a state of barely suppressed emotion, such as excitement, suspense, anxiety or hostility; a feeling of strain with resultant symptoms (*psychol*); strained relations between persons; opposition between conflicting ideas or forces. — *adj* **ten'sive** giving the sensation of tenseness or stiffness. — *n* **ten'sor** (*anat*) a muscle that tightens a part; a mathematical or physical entity represented by components which depend in a special way on the choice of a co-ordinate system. — **tensile strength** the strength of a material when being stretched, expressed as the greatest stress it can resist before breaking. [L. *tēnsus*, past p. of *tendĕre*, to stretch.]

tent *tent*, *n* a portable shelter of canvas or other cloth, stretched on poles. — *vi* to camp in a tent. — *vt* to cover or shelter (as if) with a tent; to lodge in tents. — *n* **tent'age** tents collectively; material for making tents. — *adj* **ten'ted** covered with tents; formed like a tent; (of a settlement or camp) consisting of tents; dwelling in tents. — *n* **tent'ing**. — **tent'maker**; **tent peg** a strong notched peg driven into the ground to fasten a tent; **tent pole** a pole to support a tent; **tent stitch** an embroidery stitch made in parallel series diagonally to the canvas threads; **tent'-work** work in tent stitch. [Fr. *tente* — L. *tendĕre*, *tentum*, to stretch.]

tentacle *ten'tə-kl*, *n* a slender flexible organ for feeling, grasping, etc.; a gland-tipped insect-capturing process in the sundew plant. — Also **tentaculum** (*-tak'ū-ləm*; *pl* **tentac'ūla**). — *adj* **ten'tacled**. — *adj* **tentac'ūlar**. [L. *tentāre*, to feel.]

tentation *ten-tā'shən*, (*mech*) *n* a method of adjusting by a succession of trials. [L. *tentātio*, *-ōnis* — *tentāre*, to test.]

tentative *ten'tə-tiv*, *adj* done or made provisionally and experimentally; cautious, hesitant, diffident. — *adv* **ten'tatively**. [L. *tentāre*, to try.]

tenter *ten'tər*, *n* frame for stretching cloth; a tenterhook; a hook. — *vt* to stretch on hooks. — **ten'terhook** a sharp, hooked nail as on a tenter. — **on tenterhooks** in impatient suspense. [App. conn. with Fr. *tenture*, hangings, and L. *tendĕre*, to stretch.]

tenth. See under **ten**.

tenuis *ten'ū-is*, (*phon*) *n* an unaspirated voiceless stop consonant, such as *k*, *p* or *t*: — *pl* **ten'ues** (*-ū-ēz*). [L., thin.]

tenuous *ten'ū-əs*, *adj* thin; slender; slight, insubstantial; rarefied. — *adv* **ten'uously**. — *n* **ten'uousness** or **tenū'ity**. [L. *tenuis*, thin.]

tenure *ten'yər*, *n* holding, occupation; time of holding; the holding of an appointment in a university or college for an assured length of time; conditions on which property is held; a tenant's rights, duties, etc. — *adj* **ten'urable** (of a university post) giving tenure. — *adj* **tenūr'ial**. [A.Fr. *tenure* — *tenir*, to hold.]

tenuto *te-nōō'tō*, (*mus*) *adj* and *adv* sustained. — *n* a sustained note or chord: — *pl* **tenu'tos**. [It., past p. of *tenere*, to hold.]

teocalli *tē-ə-kal'i* or *tā-ō-kal'yi*, *n* a Mexican pyramid temple. [Nahuatl, — *teotl*, god, *calli*, house.]

tepee or **teepee** *tē'pē*, *n* an American Indian tent formed of skins, etc. stretched over a frame of converging poles. [Sioux *tīpī*, dwelling.]

tephra *tef'rə*, *n* ash and debris ejected by a volcano. [Gr. *tephrā*, ashes.]

tepid *tep'id*, *adj* moderately warm, lukewarm; lacking enthusiasm, half-hearted. — *n* **tepid'ity** or **tep'idness**. — *adv* **tep'idly**. [L. *tepidus* — *tepēre*, to be warm.]

tequila *tə-kē'lə*, *n* a Mexican intoxicating drink made from an agave plant. [From district of Mexico.]

Ter. *abbrev* for Terrace (in street names); Territory.

ter- *tûr-*, *combining form* meaning thrice, three, threefold. [L. thrice.]

tera- *ter'ə-*, *pfx* ten to the twelfth power (formerly *megamega-*) as in *terawatt*.

teratism *ter'ə-tizm*, *n* a monster; an abnormal person or animal, esp. as a foetus. [Gr. *teras*, *-ātos*, monster.]

terato- *ter-ə-tō-*, *-tə-* or *-to'-*, *combining form* denoting monster. — *n* **teratogen** (*tə-rat'ə-jen*) an agent that raises the incidence of congenital malformation. — *adj* **teratogenic** (*ter-ə-tə-jen'ik*) producing monsters; causing abnormal growth (in a foetus). — *n* **teratogeny** (*-toj'i-ni*) the production of monsters. — *adj* **teratolog'ic** or **teratolog'ical**. — *n* **teratol'ogist**. — *n* **teratol'ogy** the study of malformations or abnormal growths, animal or vegetable. [Gr. *teras*, *-atos*, a monster.]

teratoid *ter'ə-toid*, (*biol*) *adj* monstrous. [Gr. *teras*, *-ātos*, monster.]

teratoma *ter-ə-tō'mə*, (*med*) *n* a tumour consisting of foreign tissue: — *pl* **teratō'mata**. [Gr. *teras*, *-ātos*, monster.]

terbium *tûr'bi-əm*, *n* a rare metal (symbol **Tb**; atomic no. 65) found in certain yttrium minerals. — *adj* **ter'bic**. [From *Ytterby*, Sweden, place of discovery.]

tercel *tûr'səl* or **tiercel** *tēr'səl*, *n* a male hawk. [O.Fr. *tercel* — L. *tertius*, third, perh. as being one-third smaller than the female, or as supposed to hatch from the last egg of three.]

tercentenary *tûr-sən-tē'nə-ri*, *adj* of three hundred years. — *n* a 300th anniversary. — *adj* **tercentennial** (*tûr-sen-ten'yəl*) of 300 years. — *n* a 300th anniversary.

tercet *tûr'sit*, (*prosody*) *n* a set of three lines that rhyme together or are associated by rhyme with an adjacent set of three. [It. *terzetto*.]

terebene *ter'i-bēn*, *n* a light-yellow disinfectant liquid, used as a solvent for paint. [*tere*binth and sfx. *-ene*.]

terebinth *ter'i-binth*, *n* the turpentine tree (genus *Pistacia*). — *adj* **terebin'thine** of or relating to the terebinth; of, relating to or resembling turpentine. [Gr. *terebinthos*.]

teredo *te-rē'dō*, *n* the shipworm, a bivalvular mollusc that bores into wooden ships: — *pl* **terē'dos**. [Gr. *terēdōn*, a boring worm.]

terete *tə-rēt'* or *ter'ēt*, (*biol*) *adj* smooth and cylindrical. [L. *terēs*, *terĕtis*, smooth.]

tergiversate *tûr'ji-vər-sāt*, *vi* to turn one's back; to desert, change sides; to shuffle, shift, use evasions. — *n* **tergiversā'tion**. — *n* **ter'giversātor**. [L. *tergum*, the back, *versārī*, to turn.]

tergum *tûr'gəm*, (*zool*) *n* the back; the back or back plate of a somite: — *pl* **ter'ga**. — *adj* **ter'gal**. [L.]

teriyaki *ter-i-yäk'i*, *n* and *adj* in Japanese cookery, (a dish of meat or shellfish) marinated in a soy sauce and grilled or broiled. [Jap. *teri*, sunshine, *yaki*, roast, broiled.]

term *tûrm*, *n* an end; the normal time of childbirth; any limited period; the time for which anything lasts; a division of the academic or school year; a period of sittings; (in *pl*) conditions, stipulations; (in *pl*) charge, fee; a quantity added to or subtracted from others in an expression (*alg*); an item in a series; that which may be a subject or predicate of a proposition (*logic*); a word used in a specially understood or defined sense; an expression generally; a bust in continuity with its pedestal (*art* and *archaeol*). — *vt* to call, designate. — *adj* **term'less**. — *adj* and *adv* **term'ly**. — *n* a publication appearing once a term. — *n* **term'or** a person who holds an estate for a term of years or for life. — **term'-time**. — Also *adj*. — **bring to terms** to compel to the acceptance of conditions; **come to terms** to come to an agreement; to submit; **come to terms with** to find a way of living with (some personal trouble or difficulty); **in terms of** having or using as unit; in the language peculiar to; **long'-** or **short'-termer** a person serving respectively a long or short prison sentence; **on speaking terms** friendly enough to speak to each other; well enough acquainted to speak; **on terms** in friendly relation; on an equal footing. [Fr. *terme* — L. *terminus*, a boundary.]

termagant *tûr'mə-gənt*, *n* a brawling, scolding woman. — *adj* scolding, shrewish. [M.E. *Termagan* or *Tervagant*, a supposed Muslim idol, represented in the old plays as of a violent character.]

terminable *tûr'mi-nə-bl*, *adj* that may come or be brought to an end. — *n* **terminabil'ity** or **ter'minableness**. — *adv* **ter'minably**. [L. *terminus*, limit, boundary.]

terminal *tûr'mi-nəl*, *adj* of, at, forming or marking an end, boundary or terminus; final; (of a diseased condition) representing the final stages of a fatal illness; suffering from a terminal illness; extreme, acute (*colloq*); of a term; occurring every term. — *n* a rail or bus terminus; an arrival and departure building for travellers by air; the storage base and distribution centre at the head of e.g. an oil pipeline; a free end in an open electric circuit; a device linked to a computer and at a distance from it, by which the computer can be operated (also **terminal unit**). — *adv* **ter'minally**. — **terminal guidance** a system for guiding sub-units of a missile warhead towards multiple targets near the end of the missile's flight; **terminal illness** a fatal disease in its final stages; **terminal unit** see **terminal** above; **terminal velocity** speed of object on impact with a target; the greatest speed attained by an object falling or fired through a fluid. [L. *terminālis* — *terminus*, limit, boundary.]

terminate *tûr'mi-nāt*, *vt* to bring to an end; to end (a pregnancy) before its term. — *vi* to come to an end; (of e.g. a word) to end (with *in*). — *n* **terminā'tion**. — *adj* **terminā'tional**. — *adj* **ter'minative** tending to terminate or determine; expressive of completion; definitive; absolute. — *adv* **ter'minatively**. — *n* **ter'minātor**. [L. *termināre*, to set a limit to.]

terminology *tûr-mi-nol'ə-ji*, *n* nomenclature; the set of terms used in any art, science, etc. — *adj* **terminolog'ical**. — *adv* **terminolog'ically**. — **terminological inexactitude** (*facetious*) a lie. [Med. L. *terminus*, term.]

terminus *tûr'mi-nəs*, *n* an end point of a bus or railway route; a station at such a point; a boundary stone: — *pl* **ter'mini** (*-nī*) or **ter'minuses**. [L., boundary, limit.]

terminus ad quem *tûr'mi-nəs ad kwem*, (L.) a finishing-point; destination; **terminus ante quem** (*an'ti*) the end limit of a period of time; **terminus a quo** (*ä kwō*) the limit from which; a starting-point; **terminus post quem** (*pōst*) the starting-point, earliest point, of a period of time.

termite *tûr'mīt*, *n* a so-called white ant, a pale-coloured insect only superficially like an ant. — *n* **termitarium** (*tûr-mi-tā'ri-əm*) a nest or mound of termites. [L. *termes*, *termitis*, a woodworm.]

termless, termly, termor. See under **term.**

tern[1] *tûrn, n* a long-winged aquatic bird related to the gulls. [Cf. O.N. *therna*; O.E. *stearn, tearn.*]

tern[2] *tûrn, n* a three, set of three. — *adj* **ter'nal** threefold. — *adj* **ter'nary** in threes; of three components; based on three; of a third order. — *adj* **ter'nate** with three leaflets (*bot*); grouped in threes. — *adv* **ter'nately.** [L. *ternī*, three each — *trēs*, three.]

terne *tûrn, n* an alloy, chiefly of lead and tin, known as **terne metal**; sheet-iron or steel coated with this alloy (also called **terne plate**). — *vt* to cover with terne metal. [Fr. *terne*, dull.]

terotechnology *ter'ō-tek-nol-ə-ji, n* the application of managerial, financial, engineering and other skills to extend the operational life of, and increase the efficiency of, equipment and machinery. [Gr. *tereo*, to watch, observe, and **technology**.]

terpene *tûr'pēn*, (*chem*) *n* any one of a group of hydrocarbons with a composition $C_{10}H_{16}$. — *n* **ter'penoid** any of a group of substances having a structure like that of terpene. — *n* **terpineol** (*tûr-pin'i-ol*) a terpene alcohol used extensively as a perfume base. [**turpentine.**]

Terpsichore *tərp-sik'ə-rē, n* the Muse of choral song and dance. — *adj* **terpsichorē'an** relating to dancing. [Gr. *Terpsichorē* — *terpsis*, delight — *terpein*, to enjoy, *choros*, dance.]

Terr. *abbrev* for: Terrace (in street names); Territory.

terra alba *ter'ə al'bə, n* any of various white, earthlike substances such as gypsum, kaolin, pipeclay, etc. [L., white earth.]

terrace *ter'is, n* a raised level bank or walk; a level stretch along the side or top of a slope; ground or a structure that rises stepwise; a raised paved area alongside a house; a connected row of houses, properly one overlooking a slope; (usu. in *pl*) the open areas rising in tiers around a football stadium, where spectators stand. — *vt* to form into a terrace or terraces. — *adj* **terr'aced.** — *n* **terr'acing.** — **terraced (or terrace) house** one of the houses forming a terrace. [Fr. *terrasse* — L.L. *terrācea*, an earthen mound.]

terracotta *ter-ə-kot'ə, n* an unglazed earthenware made from a mixture of clay and sand, used for statues and esp. formerly, as an ornamental building material; its deep brownish-red colour. — Also *adj.* [It., baked earth.]

terra firma *ter'ə fûr'mə, n* the mainland, solid earth, dry land. [L., firm land.]

terrain[1] *te-rān', n* ground, a tract, regarded as a field of operations, or as having some sort of unity or prevailing character. [Fr., from a L.L. form of *terrēnum*, terrene.]

terrain[2]. See **terrane**.

terrane *ter'ān*, (*geol*) *n* a rock formation, or series of connected formations (also **terr'ain**). [See **terrain**[1].]

terrapin *ter'ə-pin, n* an American freshwater or brackish-water tortoise of many kinds; extended to European water tortoises. [Of Algonquin origin.]

terrarium *te-rā'ri-əm, n* a vivarium for land animals or (usu. in the form of a large sealed jar) for plants: — *pl* **terrā'ria** or **terrā'riums.** [N.L. — L. *terra*, earth.]

terra sigillata *ter'ə sij-i-lä'tə, n* a reddish-brown astringent clay found e.g. on the islands of Lemnos and Samos; earthenware pottery made from it; Samian ware. [L., sealed earth.]

terrazzo *te-rat'sō, n* a mosaic covering for concrete floors consisting of marble or other chips set in cement and then polished: — *pl* **terrazz'os.** [It., terrace, balcony.]

terrene *ti-rēn'* or *ter'ēn, adj* of the earth; earthly; mundane; earthy; terrestrial. [L. *terrēnus* — *terra*, the earth.]

terreplein *tär'plān, n* the top of a rampart, or space behind the parapet. [Fr., — L. *terra*, earth, *plēnus*, full.]

terrestrial *ti-res'tri-əl, adj* of, or existing on, the earth; earthly; living or growing on land or on the ground; representing the earth; signifying signals sent by a land transmitter as distinct from a satellite (*TV*). — *n* a dweller on earth. — *adv* **terres'trially.** — **terrestrial telescope** a telescope giving an erect image, used for viewing over distances on the earth's surface rather than astronomically. [L. *terrestris* — *terra*, the earth.]

terret *ter'it, n* a ring or loop through which driving reins pass. [O.Fr. *toret*, dimin. of *tor, tour*, a round.]

terrible *ter'i-bl, adj* inspiring fear, terror or awe; awful; dreadful; very bad; pronounced, extreme, notable (*colloq*). — *n* **terr'ibleness.** — *adv* **terr'ibly** in a terrible manner; very (*colloq*). [L. *terribilis* — *terrēre*, to frighten.]

terricolous *ter-ik'ə-ləs, adj* living in or on the soil. [L. *terricola*, a dweller upon earth — *terra*, earth, *colĕre*, to inhabit.]

terrier *ter'i-ər, n* a small dog of various breeds, orig. one that would follow burrowing animals underground. [O.Fr., — L.L. *terrārius* (adj.) — *terra*, land.]

terrify *ter'i-fī, vt* to cause terror in; to frighten badly: — *prp* **terr'ifying**; *pat* and *pap* **terr'ifīed.** [L. *terrificāre* — *terrēre*, to terrify, *facĕre*, to make.]

terrific *tə-rif'ik, adj* prodigious (*colloq*); marvellous, excellent (*colloq*); very good, enjoyable, attractive, etc. (*colloq*); frightening, terrifying. — *adv* **terrif'ically.** [L. *terrificus*, frightful.]

terrigenous *te-rij'i-nəs, adj* earth-born; derived from the land. [L. *terrigenus* — *terra*, earth, *genĕre* (*gignĕre*), to produce.]

terrine *te-rēn', n* a casserole, etc., orig. of earthenware; a dish cooked in it, esp. pâté. [Fr.; see ety. for **tureen.**]

territory *ter'i-tə-ri, n* possessions in land; the whole, or a portion, of the land belonging to a state; part of a confederation with an organised government but not yet admitted to statehood; a dependency; a region; a jurisdiction; a field of activity; domain; an area that an animal or bird treats as its own. — *adj* **territo'rial** concerned with, or relating to, territory; limited or restricted to a particular territory; (esp. of an animal, bird, etc.) inclined to establish its own stretch of territory and defend it. — *n* a soldier in the Territorial Army. — *vt* **territo'rialise** or **-ize** to make a territory of; to make territorial; to put on a territorial basis. — *n* **territorial'ity.** — *adv* **territo'rially.** — *adj* **terr'itoried** possessed of territory. — **Territorial Army** the name (1920–67, and from 1980) of the voluntary military force organised on a territorial basis; **territorial waters** that part of the sea reckoned as part of the adjacent state — orig. within a three-mile limit. [L. *territōrium*, domain of a town.]

terror *ter'ər, n* extreme fear; a time of, or government by, terrorism; an object of dread; a mischievous person, a rogue (*colloq*). — *n* **terrorīsā'tion** or **-z-**. — *vt* **terr'orise** or **-ize** to terrify; to subject to terrorism. — *n* **terr'oriser** or **-z-**. — *n* **terr'orism** an organised system of intimidation, esp. for political ends. — *n* **terr'orist.** — *adj* **terr'or-stricken** smitten with terror. — **Reign of Terror,** or **the Terror,** the period in the first French Revolution when thousands went to the guillotine. [L. *terror* — *terrēre*, to frighten.]

terry *ter'i, n* a pile fabric with uncut looped pile, used esp. for towelling; one of the loops. — Also *adj.*

terse *tûrs, adj* concise, succinct; crisply brief; abrupt, brusque. — *adv* **terse'ly.** — *n* **terse'ness.** [L. *tersus* — *tergēre, tersum*, to rub clean.]

tertial *tûr'shl, adj* of the third rank among flight feathers of a wing. — *n* a tertiary flight-feather. — *adj* **ter'tian** (*-shən*) occurring every other day (i.e. on the *third* day, reckoning both first and last days). — *n* a fever with paroxysms every other day. — *adj* **ter'tiary** (*-shər-i*) of the third degree, order or formation; tertial (*ornithol*); (with *cap*) of the third great division of the geological record and time, including Eocene, Oligocene, Miocene, Pliocene; ranking above secondary (esp. of education). — *n* the Tertiary period; a tertiary feather; that which is tertiary. — **tertiary college** a college, esp. one with vocational courses, for the teaching of sixth-form level students. [L. *tertiālis, tertiānus, tertiārius — tertius*, third.]

tertium quid *ter'ti-ōōm* (or *tûr'shəm*) *kwid*, (L.) a third unknown thing related to two specific known things.

tervalent *tûr-vā'lənt*, (*chem*) *adj* having a valency of three, trivalent.

Terylene® *ter'i-lēn*, *n* synthetic fabric of polyester fibres, light, strong and crease-resistant.

TESL (often *tes'əl*) *abbrev* for Teaching English as a Second Language.

tesla *tes'lə*, *n* the unit of magnetic flux density, equal to 1 weber per sq. metre. — **tesla coil** (*electr*) a simple source of high voltage oscillations for rough testing of vacuums and gas (by discharge colour) in vacuum systems. [N. *Tesla*, U.S. inventor.]

TESSA *tes'ə*, *abbrev* for Tax Exempt Special Savings Account.

tessella *tes-el'ə*, *n* a little tessera: — *pl* **tessell'ae** (*-ē*; L. *-ī*). — *adj* **tess'ellar.** — *vt* **tessellate** (*tes'i-lāt*) to pave with tesserae; to mark like a mosaic. — *vi* (of a number of identical shapes) to fit together exactly, leaving no spaces. — *adj* marked out in little squarish areas. — *adj* **tess'ellated.** — *n* **tessellā'tion.** [L. *tessella*, dimin. of *tessera*; see ety. of **tessera**.]

tessera *tes'ə-rə*, *n* one of the small pieces of which a mosaic is made: — *pl* **tess'erae** (*-ē*; L. *-ī*). — *adj* **tess'eral** of tesserae; cubic, isometric (*crystall*). [L. *tessera*, a die, small cube — Gr. *tessares, tesseres, -a*, four.]

tessitura *tes-i-tōō'rə*, *n* the ordinary range of pitch of a voice or a piece or vocal music. [It., texture.]

Test. *abbrev* for Testament.

test[1] *test*, *n* any critical trial; a means of trial; anything used to distinguish or detect substances, a reagent (*chem*); a written examination, esp. a short one; an oath or other evidence of religious belief required as a condition of office or exercise of rights; a test match. — *vt* to put to proof; to try or examine critically. — *vi* to achieve a stated result in a test. — *n* **test'a** a hard shell (*zool*); a seed-coat, derived from the ovule integuments (*bot*). — *adj* **test'able.** — *adj* **testaceous** (*-ā'shəs*) of or having a hard shell; brick-red. — *n* **testee'** a person who undergoes a test. — *n* **test'er** a person who tests or a thing used for testing. — *n* and *adj* **test'ing.** — **test ban** the banning, by mutual agreement between nations, of the testing of any or all nuclear weapons; **test'-bed** an iron framework on which a machine is placed for testing; anything with a similar purpose (also *fig*); **test case** a law case that may settle similar questions in the future; **test'-drive** a trial drive of a motor vehicle, usu. with a view to purchasing the vehicle if it is satisfactory. — Also *vt.* — **test'-flight** a trial flight of a new aeroplane. — *vt* **test'-fly.** — *vt* **test'-market** to offer (a product) for sale in order to test demand, popularity, etc. — **test match** an international cricket match forming one of a series; **test paper** paper saturated with some substance that changes colour when exposed to certain chemicals; a paper or questions to test fitness for a more serious examination; **test pilot** one whose work is testing new aircraft by flying them; **test'-tube** a glass cylinder closed at one end, used in chemistry, bacteriology, etc. — **test-tube baby** (esp. *formerly*) a child born as as the result of artificial insemination, now usu. one born from an ovum implanted in the womb after fertilisation in a laboratory. [O.Fr. *test* and *teste* — L. *testa*, an earthen pot, a potsherd, a shell.]

test[2] *test*, *vt* to attest legally and date. — *n* **test'acy** (*-ə-si*) the state of being testate. — *n* **testā'mur** (*formal*) a certificate of having passed an examination. — *adj* **test'āte** having made and left a will. — *n* **testā'tion** a witnessing; a giving by will. — *n* **testā'tor,** *fem* **testā'trix,** a person who leaves a will. [L. *testārī*, to testify, witness, past p. (neut.) *testātum*; 1st pers. pl. *testāmur*.]

testament *tes'tə-mənt*, *n* that which testifies, or in which an attestation is made; the solemn declaration in writing of one's will; a will; (with *cap*) either of the main divisions (**Old** and **New**) of the Bible. — *adj* **testamental** (*-men'tl*) or **testamen'tary** pertaining to a testament or will; bequeathed or done by will. — *adv* **testamen'tarily.** [L. *testāmentum*.]

testamur, testate, etc. See under **test**[2].

testee. See under **test**[1].

tester[1] *tes'tər*, *n* a canopy or its support, or both, esp. over a bed. [O.Fr. *testre*, the vertical part of a bed behind the head, *testiere*, a head-covering — *teste*, head.]

tester[2]. See under **test**[1].

testicle *tes'ti-kl*, *n* a male reproductive gland. — *adj* **testic'ūlar** of or like a testicle. — *adj* **testic'ūlate** or **testic'ulated** like a testicle. — *n* **tes'tis** a testicle; a rounded body like it: — *pl* **tes'tes** (*-ēz*). [L. *testis* and its dimin. *testiculus*.]

testify *tes'ti-fī*, *vi* to bear witness; to make a solemn declaration; to protest or declare a charge (with *against*). — *vt* to bear witness to; to affirm or declare solemnly or on oath; to proclaim, declare: — *pr p* **tes'tifying;** *pa t* and *pa p* **tes'tified.** — *n* **testificā'tion** the act of testifying or of bearing witness. — *n* **testif'icātor.** — *adj* **testif'icatory.** — *adj* **tes'tified.** — *n* **tes'tifīer.** [L. *testificārī — testis*, a witness, *facĕre*, to make.]

testimony *tes'ti-mən-i*, *n* evidence; declaration to prove some fact; proof. — *adj* **testi'mōnial** of, affording or of the nature of testimony. — *n* a written attestation; a writing or certificate bearing testimony to one's character or abilities; a gift or memorial as a token of respect. — *vt* **testimō'nialise** or **-ize** to present with a testimonial. [L. *testimōnium — testārī*, to witness.]

testis. See **testicle.**

testosterone *tes-tos'tər-ōn*, *n* the chief male sex hormone, a steroid secreted by the testes. [*testo-* (combining form for **testis**), *sterol* and chem. sfx. *-one*.]

testudo *tes-tū'dō*, *n* a wheeled shelter used by Roman soldiers under attack from above; a similar shelter made by joining shields: — *pl* **testū'dōs** or **testū'dinēs.** — *adj* **testū'dinal, testū'dinary** or **testūdin'eous** like a tortoise, tortoiseshell, or a testudo. [L. *testūdō, -inis*, tortoise.]

testy *tes'ti*, *adj* irritable; (of remarks, etc.) showing touchiness. — *adv* **tes'tily.** — *n* **tes'tiness.** [O.Fr. *testif*, headstrong — *teste*, head — L. *testa*, pot.]

tetanus *tet'ə-nəs*, *n* a disease marked by painful spasms of the muscles of the jaw and other parts; the state of prolonged contraction of a muscle under quickly repeated stimuli. — *adj* **tet'anal** or **tetanic** (*ti-tan'ik*). — *adj* **tet'anoid.** — *n* **tet'any** heightened excitability of the motor nerves with painful muscular cramps. [L., — Gr. *tetanos — teinein*, to stretch.]

tetchy or **techy** *tech'i*, *adj* irritable. — *adv* **tetch'ily** or **tech'ily.** — *n* **tetch'iness** or **tech'iness.**

tête-à-tête *tāt-ä-tāt'* or *tet-a-tet'*, *n* a private confidential interview; a sofa for two sitting face to face: — *pl* **tête-à-têtes** or **têtes-à-têtes.** — *adj* confidential, secret. — *adv* in private conversation; face to face. [Fr., lit. head to head.]

tether *tedh'ər*, *n* a rope or chain for confining an animal within certain limits. — *vt* to confine with a tether; to restrain within certain limits. — **at the end of one's tether** desperate, having no further strength, patience, resources, etc. [App. O.N. *tjōthr*.]

tetra *tet'rə*, *n* any of various species of freshwater fish of the family *Characidae*. [Short form of *Tetragonopterus*, former name of the genus.]

tetra- *tet-rə-* or **tetr-**, *combining form* denoting four. — *adj* **tetraba'sic** (*chem*) capable of reacting with four equivalents of an acid; (of acids) having four replaceable hydrogen atoms. — *n* **tetrachlō'ride** any compound with four chlorine atoms per molecule. — *n* **tetrachloroeth'ylene** or **tetrachloreth'ylene** a liquid used in dry-cleaning, as a solvent, etc. — *n* **tet'rachord** (*-körd*) a four-stringed instrument; a series of four sounds, forming a scale of two tones and a half. — *adj* **tetracyclic** (*-sī'klik*; *bot*) of, in or with four whorls or rings. — *n* **tetracy'cline** a crystalline antibiotic used to treat a wide range of infections, esp. of the respiratory and urinary tracts. — *n* **tet'rad** a group of four; an atom, radical or element having a combining power of four (*chem*). — *adj* **tet'rad** or **tetrad'ic**. — *adj* **tetraethyl** (*-eth'il*) having four ethyl groups, as **tetraethyl lead** or **lead tetraethyl**, used in petrol as an antiknock agent. — *n* **tet'ragon** (*-gən* or *-gon*) a plane figure of four angles. — *adj* **tetragonal** (*-rag'ə-nəl*) having the form of a tetragon; referable to three axes at right angles, two of them equal (*crystall*). — *n* **tet'ragram** a word or inscription of four letters; the tetragrammaton. — *n* **tetragramm'aton** the name YaHWeH, JeHoVaH, etc., as written with four Hebrew letters, regarded as a mystic symbol; any other sacred word of four letters, as the Latin *Deus*. — *adj* **tetrahē'dral**. — *n* **tetrahē'dron** a solid figure or body with four plane faces. — *adj* **tetram'eral** four-parted. — *n* **tetram'erism** division into four parts. — *adj* **tetram'erous** having four parts, or parts in fours. — *n* **tetrameter** (*te-tram'i-tər*) a verse of four measures (dipodies or feet). — Also *adj*. — *n* **tetraplē'gia** quadriplegia. — *adj* **tetraplē'gic**. — *n* **tet'rapod** a four-footed animal. — *adj* **tetrap'teran** or **tetrap'terous** four-winged. — *n* **tetrarch** (*tet'rärk* or *tē'trärk*) under the Romans, the ruler of the fourth part of a province; a subordinate prince; the commander of a subdivision of a Greek phalanx. — *n* **tet'rarchy** the office, rank, period of office or jurisdiction of a tetrarch; the fourth part of a province (also **tet'rarchate**). — *n* **tet'rastich** (*-stik*) a stanza or set of four lines. — *adj* **tetrastichal** (*ti-tras'ti-kl*) or **tetrastichic** (*tet-rə-stik'ik*) of or of the nature of tetrastichs. — *adj* **tetras'tichous** (*bot*) in four rows. — *adj* **tetratom'ic** having or composed of four atoms to a molecule. — *adj* **tetravalent** (*tet-rə-vā'lənt*) quadrivalent. — *n* **tetrode** (*tet'rōd*) a thermionic valve with four electrodes. — *n* **tetrox'ide** an oxide with four atoms of oxygen in the molecule. — *n* **tetryl** (*tet'ril*) a yellow crystalline explosive compound used as a detonator. [Gr. *tetra-*, *tettares*, *tessares*, four.]

tetrabasic ... to ... **tetrahedron**. See under **tetra-**.

tetralogy *te-tral'ə-ji*, *n* a group of four dramas, usu. three tragic and one satiric; any series of four related dramatic or operatic works or stories. [Gr. *tetralogiā* — *tetra-*, four, *logos*, discourse.]

tetrameral ... to ... **tetraplegia**. See under **tetra-**.

tetraploid *tet'rə-ploid*, (*biol*) *adj* having four times the haploid (twice the normal) number of chromosomes. — *n* **tet'raploidy** the condition of being tetraploid. [Gr. *tetraploos*, fourfold, *eidos*, form.]

tetrapod ... to ... **tetrode**. See under **tetra-**.

tetrodotoxin *tet-rō-də-toks'in*, *n* a nerve-blocking poison found in a newt and in the Japanese pufferfish. [*Tetrodon*, a genus of tropical fish, and **toxin**.]

tetroxide, tetryl. See under **tetra-**.

Teut. *abbrev* for Teutonic.

Teuton *tū'tən*, *n* any speaker of a Germanic language; a member of an ancient Germanic tribe from Jutland (*hist*); (*popularly*) a German. — *adj* **Teutonic** (*-ton'ik*) Germanic — of the linguistic family that includes English, German, Dutch and the Scandinavian languages; of the Teutons; (*popularly*) German in any sense. — *n* the parent language of the Teutons, primitive Germanic. [L. *Teutonēs*, from the root of O.E. *thēod*, people, nation.]

Tex. *abbrev* for Texas (U.S. state).

Tex-Mex *teks-meks'*, (*US*) *adj* typical of Mexican-American culture or cuisine. [*Tex*as and *Mex*ico.]

text *tekst*, *n* the actual words of a book, poem, etc. in their original form, or any form they have been transmitted in or transmuted into; a book of such words; the main body of matter in a book, distinguished from notes, commentary or other subsidiary matter; matter commented on; a short passage from the Bible taken as the ostensible subject of a sermon, quoted in authority, displayed as a motto, etc.; a theme. — *adj* **tex'tual** pertaining to, or contained in, the text; serving for a text. — *n* **text'ualism** (too) strict adherence to a text, esp. that of the Bible; textual criticism, esp. of the Bible. — *n* **text'ualist** a person learned in the text, esp. of the Bible; a literal interpreter; a quoter of texts. — *adv* **text'ually**. — *adj* **text'book** (of an operation, example, etc.) exactly as planned, in perfect accordance with theory or calculation. — *n* a book containing the main principles of a subject. — **textual criticism** critical study directed towards determining the true reading of a text. [L. *texĕre*, *textum*, to weave.]

textile *teks'tīl* or in N.Am. *tekst'l*, *n* a woven fabric. — *adj* (of cloth) woven or capable of being woven. [Ety. as for **text**.]

texture *tek'styər*, *n* the quality of a material as conveyed to the touch; structural impression resulting from the manner of combining or interrelating the parts of a whole, as in music, art, etc.; the manner of weaving or connecting. — *vt* to give a certain texture to. — *adj* **tex'tural** pertaining to texture. — *adv* **tex'turally**. — *adj* **tex'tured**. — *adj* **tex'tureless**. — *vt* **tex'turise** or **-ize** to give a particular texture to; to texture. — **textured vegetable protein** a vegetable substance, usu. made from soya beans, prepared to resemble meat in appearance and taste (abbrev. **TVP**). [Ety. as for **text**.]

TG *abbrev* for: Togo (I.V.R.); transformational Grammar.

TGV *abbrev* for (Fr.) *Train à Grande Vitesse* (q.v.).

TGWU *abbrev* for Transport and General Workers' Union.

Th. *abbrev* for Thursday.

Th (*chem*) *symbol* for thorium.

Thai *tī* or *tä'ē*, *adj* of Thailand. — *n* a native of (also **Thai'lander**) or the language of Thailand, the Asian country known before 1939 and between 1945 and 1949 as Siam. — **Thai boxing** a form of boxing practised in Thailand, using gloved fists, feet, knees and elbows.

thalamus *thal'ə-məs*, *n* (in ancient Greece) an inner room, chamber; the receptacle of a flower (*bot*); part of the midbrain where the optic nerve emerges (*anat*): — *pl* **thal'amī**. — *adj* **thal'amic** (or *thal-am'ik*) of the thalamus. [Gr. *thalamos*, an inner room, bedroom.]

thalassian *tha-las'i-ən*, *adj* marine. — *n* a sea turtle. — *n* **thalassaemia** or **thalassemia** (*thal-ə-sē'mi-ə*) a hereditary disorder of the blood causing anaemia, sometimes fatal in children. — *adj* **thalassae'mic** or **thalassē'mic**. — *adj* **thalass'ic** marine; of the seas. [Gr. *thalassa*, *thalatta*, sea.]

thaler *tä'lər*, *n* an obsolete German silver coin. [Ger.; cf. **dollar**.]

Thalia *thə-lī'ə*, (*Gr mythol*) *n* the Muse of comedy and pastoral poetry; one of the Graces. — *adj* **thalī'an**. [Gr. *Thaleia*, *Thaliā* — *thallein*, to bloom.]

thalidomide *thə-lid'ə-mīd* or *tha-*, *n* a non-barbiturate sedative drug, withdrawn in 1961 because found to cause malformation in the foetus if taken during pregnancy. — **thalidomide baby** an infant showing the teratogenic effects of thalidomide.

thallium *thal'i-əm*, *n* a highly toxic leadlike metal (symbol **Tl**; atomic no. 81) discovered in 1861. — *adj* **thall'ic** of trivalent thallium. — *adj* **thall'ous** of univalent thallium. [Gr. *thallos*, a young shoot, from the bright green line in its spectrum.]

thallus *thal'əs*, *n* a plant body not differentiated into leaf, stem and root: — *pl* **thall'uses** or **thall'ī**. — *adj* **thall'iform**. — *adj* **thall'ine**. — *adj* **thall'oid**. — *npl* **Thallophȳ'ta** the lowest main division of the vegetable kingdom — bacteria, fungi, algae. — *n* **thall'ophyte** a member of the Thallophyta. [Gr. *thallos*, a young shoot.]

thalweg *täl'vähh* or *-veg*, (*geol*) *n* the longitudinal profile of the bottom of a river-bed. [Ger., — *Thal* (now *Tal*), valley, *Weg*, way.]

than *dhan* or *dhən*, *conj* used after a comparative, actual or felt, to introduce that which is in the lower degree. — *prep* (*popularly*) in comparison with. [O.E. *thonne*, *thanne*, *thænne*, than, orig. then.]

thanage. See under **thane**.

thanatism *than'ə-tizm*, *n* belief that the soul dies with the body. — *n* **than'atist**. — *n* **than'atoid** apparently dead; deathly; deadly. — *n* **thanatol'ogy** the scientific study of death; care or psychological therapy for the dying. — *n* **thanatophō'bia** a morbid dread of death. — *n* **thanatop'sis** a view of, or reflection upon, death. — *n* **thanatō'sis** gangrene. [Gr. *thanatos*, death.]

thane *thān*, *n* (in Anglo-Saxon England) a king's companion, hence a noble of lower rank than eorl (see ety. for **earl**) or ealdorman (see ety. for **alderman**); a hereditary (not military) tenant of the crown (*Scot hist*). — *n* **thā'nage**, **thane'dom**, **thane'hood** or **thane'ship**. [O.E. *thegn*, servant, follower, courtier, nobleman.]

thank *thangk*, *n* (usu. in *pl*) gratitude; an expression of gratitude. — *vt* to express gratitude to; to blame (*ironic*). — *n* **thank'er**. — *adj* **thank'ful** grateful; gladly relieved. — *adv* **thank'fully** gratefully, with a thankful feeling; one feels thankful (that). — *n* **thank'fulness**. — *adj* **thank'less** unthankful; not expressing thanks for favours; not gaining even thanks. — *adv* **thank'lessly**. — *n* **thank'lessness**. — *n* **thanks'giver**. — *n* **thanks'giving** the act of giving thanks; a public acknowledgment of divine goodness and mercy; (with *cap*) a day (**Thanksgiving Day**) set apart for this, esp. in the U.S. the fourth Thursday of November. — **have (only) oneself to thank for** to be the cause of (one's own misfortune); **I'll thank you, him**, etc. **to** used, usu. in anger, to introduce a request or command; **no thanks to** not owing to, implying that gratitude is far from being due; **thanks** or **thank you** elliptical forms of earlier *thanks be to you*, *I thank you*, and similar expressions; **thanks be** thank God; **thanks to** owing to; **thank you (or thanks) for nothing** an expression implying that no gratitude is due at all. [O.E. *thanc*, *thonc*.]

thar *t'här* or *tär*, *n* the serow, a Himalayan goat like an antelope; by confusion applied to the tahr. [Nepali (Indic language of Nepal) *thār*.]

that *dhat*, *demonstr pron* and *demonstr adj* (*pl* **those**) pointing out a person or thing; the former; the more distant; not this but the other; the one to be indicated or defined. — *relative pron* (*sing* and *pl*; *dhət* or *dhat*) who, whom, or which (esp. when defining or limiting, not merely linking on an addition). — *adv* (*dhat*; *colloq* or *dialect*) to that extent. — *conj* (*dhət* or *dhat*) used to introduce a noun clause, an adverbial clause of purpose, reason or consequence, or an expression of a wish in the subjunctive. — *adv* **that'away** (*NAm dialect* or *facetious*) in that direction. — *n* **that'ness** the quality of being a definite thing, that. — **and (all) that** and all the rest of that sort of thing — a summary way of dismissing what is vaguely thought of; **at that** at that point; moreover; nevertheless; **just like that** straight away; **that's that** that is the end of that matter; no more of that. [O.E. *thæt*, neut. demonstr. pron.]

thatch *thach*, *vt* to cover or roof with straw, reeds, heather, palm-leaves, or any similar material. — *vi* to do thatching. — *n* a covering or covering material of the kind; thick hair. — *adj* **thatched**. — *n* **thatch'er**. — *n* **thatch'ing** the act or art of covering with thatch; materials used for thatching. — Also *adj*. [O.E. *thæc*, covering, thatch, and *theccan*, to cover.]

Thatcherism *thach'ər-izm*, *n* the policies and style of government associated with Margaret *Thatcher*, British prime minister 1979–90. — *adj* **Thatch'erite** of, relating to or representing the policies of Margaret Thatcher and her associates. — Also *n*.

thauma- *thö-mə-* or **thaumat-** *-mət-*, *combining form* denoting a wonder or miracle. — *n* **thau'matin** a sweetener extracted from a W. African fruit (*Thaumatococcus daniellii*) 2000 to 4000 times sweeter than sucrose. — *n* **thaumatogeny** (*-toj'*) the doctrine of the miraculous origination of life. — *n* **thau'matrope** an optical toy that combines pictures by persistence of images in the eye. — *n* **thaumaturge** (*thö'mə-tûrj*) a wonder-worker. — *adj* **thaumatur'gic** or **thaumatur'gical**. — *npl* **thaumatur'gics** the performance or magic tricks using sleight-of-hand, etc. — *n* **thaumatur'gism**. — *n* **thaumatur'gist**. [Gr. *thauma*, *-atos*, wonder, *thaumatourgos* (— *ergon*, work), a wonder-worker.]

thaw *thö*, *vi* (of ice, etc.) to melt or grow liquid; to become so warm as to melt ice; to become less cold, stiff or reserved in manner. — *vt* to cause to melt. — *n* the melting of ice or snow by heat; the change of weather that causes it. — Also *fig*. — *n* **thaw'er**. — *n* and *adj* **thaw'ing**. — **thaw out** to return from frozen to normal condition. [O.E. *thawian*.]

ThD *abbrev* for *Theologicae Doctor* (N.L.), Doctor of Theology.

the[1] *dhə*, (emphatic) *dhē* or (before vowels) *dhi*, *demonstr adj* called the definite article, used to denote a particular person or thing; also to denote a species. [O.E. *the* (supplanting *se*), masc. of *thæt*, that.]

the[2] *dhə*, *adv* (with comparatives) (by) how much; (by) so much. [O.E. *thȳ*, by that, by that much, the instrumental case of the definite article.]

Thea *thē'ə*, *n* the tea genus of plants (sometimes including Camellia), giving its name to the family **Theā'ceae**. — *adj* **theā'ceous**. [From the root of **tea**, but taken as if from Gr. *theā*, goddess.]

theanthropic *thē-an-throp'ik*, *adj* at once divine and human; embodying deity in human forms. — *n* **thean'thropism** or **thean'thropy** the ascribing of human qualities to deity, or divine qualities to man; a doctrine of union of divine and human. — *n* **thean'thropist**. [Gr. *theos*, a god, *anthrōpos*, man.]

thearchy *thē'ärk-i*, *n* a theocracy; a body of divine rulers. — *adj* **thear'chic**. [Gr. *theos*, a god, *archein*, to rule.]

theat. *abbrev* for: theatre; theatrical.

theatre or in N.Am. **theater** *thē'ə-tər*, *n* a structure, orig. in the open air, for drama or other spectacles; a cinema (*NAm* and *Austr*); any place backed by a curving hillside or rising by steps like seats of a theatre; a building or room which is adapted for anatomical or surgical demonstrations, etc.; a scene of action, field of operations; (with **the**) the social unit comprising actors, producers, etc., or its characteristic environment and conditions; (with **the**) plays or a specified group of plays, collectively. — *adj*

theat'rical relating or suitable to, or savouring of, the stage; stagy; histrionic; aiming at or producing dramatic effects. — *n* **theat'ricalism** or **theatrical'ity** staginess, artificiality. — *adv* **theat'rically.** — *n* **theat'ricalness.** — *npl* **theat'ricals** dramatic performances; theatrical affairs, properties or people. — *n* **theat'ricism** theatricality, affectation, staginess. — *n* **theat'rics** the staging of plays, etc., or the art of doing this; histrionics. — **the'atre-goer** a person who regularly goes to the theatre; **theatre-in-the-round'** a theatre with a central stage and the audience on all sides; the style of staging plays in such a theatre; **theatre weapons** weapons for use in a theatre of war, applied esp. to nuclear weapons intended for use in Central Europe. — **theatre of cruelty** a branch of drama intended to induce in the audience a feeling of suffering and an awareness of evil; **theatre of the absurd** a branch of drama dealing with fantastic deliberately unreal situations, in reaction against the tragedy and irrationality of life. [Gr. *theātron* — *theaesthai*, to see.]

thebaine *thē'bā-ēn* or *-bə-ēn*, *n* a poisonous alkaloid obtained from opium. [N.L. *thebaia*, opium, as prepared at **Thebes**, Egypt; chem. sfx. *-ine*.]

Thebes *thēbz*, *n* a city of ancient Boeotia, in Greece; a city of ancient Egypt. — *adj* **Thē'ban** of Thebes. — *n* a native of Thebes. [Gr. *Thēbai*, Thebes.]

theca *thē'kə*, (*bot*) *n* a sheath, case or sac; a spore-case; a lobe or loculus of an anther: — *pl* **thē'cae** (*-sē*). — *adj* **thē'cal** of a theca. — *adj* **thē'cate** having a theca. [Latinised from Gr. *thēkē*, case, sheath.]

thecodont *thek'ō-dont*, *n* an extinct reptile of the Triassic period, having teeth set in sockets. — *adj* (of mammals) having teeth set in sockets. [Gr. *thēkē*, case, *odous*, *odontis*, a tooth.]

thé dansant *tā dā-sā*, (Fr.) tea with dancing: — *pl* **thés dansants.**

thee *dhē*, (*formal, liturgical, dialect* or *archaic*) *pron* the dative and accusative form of **thou**[1]. — *vt* to use *thee* in speaking to (someone). [O.E. *thē*, *the*.]

theft *theft*, *n* (the or an) act of thieving; a thing stolen. [O.E. *thēofth*, *thīefth* — *thēof*, thief.]

theine *thē'īn* or *-in*, *n* caffeine, esp. in connection with tea. — *n* **thē'ic** a person who drinks too much tea or who suffers from theism. — *n* **thē'ism** a morbid state resulting from too much tea-drinking.

their *dhār* or *dhər*, *pron* and *possessive adj* of or belonging to them. — *pron* **theirs** (a double genitive) used predicatively or absolutely. [O.N. *theirra*, superseding O.E. *thǣra*, genitive pl. of the definite article.]

theism[1] *thē'izm*, *n* belief in the existence of God with or without a belief in a special revelation. — *n* **thē'ist.** — *adj* **thēist'ic** or **theist'ical.** [Gr. *theos*, God.]

theism[2]. See under **theine.**

them *dhem* or *dhəm*, *pron* the dative and accusative form of **they.** — *demonstr adj* (*dialect* or *colloq*; *dhem*) those. — **them and us** (*colloq*) any of various pairs of groups in society, such as management and workforce, considered to be in opposition to each other. [O.N. *theim* or O.E. (Anglian) *thǣm* (dative).]

theme *thēm*, *n* a subject set or proposed for discussion, or spoken or written about; a recurrent idea in literature or art; a short melody developed with variations or otherwise (*mus*); the stem of a word without its inflexions; a thesis, a brief essay or exercise. — *vt* to decorate or equip (a pub, restaurant, etc.) in keeping with a certain subject, e.g. seafaring or the Wild West. — *n* **thē'ma** (or *them'ə*) a theme: — *pl* **them'ata.** — *adj* **thematic** (*thi-mat'ik*) of or relating to a theme; (of a vowel) not forming part of the root of a word, nor part of any inflection or suffix (as the vowel *o* in *cytoplasm*); (of philately) concerned with collection of sets showing flowers, or birds, etc. — *adv* **themat'ically.** — **theme park** a large area with displays, fairground, rides, etc., all devoted to or based on one subject; **theme song** a melody that is repeated often in a musical drama, film, or radio or television series, and is associated with a certain character, idea, emotion, etc.; a person's characteristic, often repeated, complaint, etc. [Gr. *thĕma*, *-atos* — root of *tithĕnai*, to place, set.]

themselves *dhəm-selvz'*, *pron* plural of **himself, herself** and **itself.** [**them** and **self.**]

then *dhen* or *dhən*, *adv* at that time; afterward; immediately; at another time; further, again; on the other hand, at the same time; for that reason, therefore; in that case. — *adj* being at that time. — *n* that time. — *adv* **then'about** or **then'abouts** about that time. — **by then** by that time; **then and there** at once and on the spot. [O.E. *thonne*, *thanne*, *thænne*.]

thenar *thē'när*, (*anat*) *n* the palm; the ball of the thumb; the sole. — Also *adj*. [Gr. *thĕnăr*, *-ăros*.]

thence *dhens*, *adv* from that place; from those premises; from that time; from that cause. — *adv* **thence'forth** or **thencefor'ward** from that time forward; from that place onward. [M.E. *thennes* — *thenne* (O.E. *thanon*, thence).]

theo- *thē-ō-*, *-o-* or *-o'-*, *combining form* denoting god. — *In the following entry, strict alphabetical order is not followed; in most cases, the abstract noun in -y precedes adjectives, etc., dependent on it.* — *n* **theobrō'mine** (*-mēn*, *-mīn* or *-min*) an alkaloid obtained from the chocolate seed. — *n* **theocracy** (*thē-ok'rə-si*) that constitution of a state in which God, or a god, is regarded as the sole sovereign, and the laws of the realm as divine commands rather than human ordinances — the priesthood necessarily becoming the officers of the invisible ruler; a state governed in this way. — *n* **theocrat** (*thē'ō-krat*) a divine or deified ruler. — *adj* **theocrat'ic** or **theocrat'ical.** — *adv* **theocrat'ically.** — *n* **theocrasy** (*thē-ok'rə-si* or *thē-ō-krā'si*) a mixture of religions; the identification or equating of one god with another or others; a mystic intimacy with deity reached through profound contemplation. — *n* **theodicy** (*thē-od'i-si*) a vindication of the justice of God in establishing a world in which evil exists. — *n* and *adj* **theodicē'an.** — *n* **theogony** (*thē-og'ə-ni*) the birth and genealogy of the gods. — *adj* **theogonic** (*thē-ə-gon'ik*) or **theogon'ical.** — *n* **theog'onist** a writer on theogony. — *n* **theology** (*thē-ol'ə-ji*) the study of God, religion and revelation; a system of theological doctrine. — *n* **theologian** (*thē-ə-lō'jyən*) a student of, or a person well versed in, theology; a divine, a professor of or writer on divinity, esp. in R.C. usage, a theological lecturer attached to a cathedral or collegiate church. — *adj* **theological** (*thē-ə-loj'ik-əl*). — *adv* **theolog'ically.** — *vt* **theol'ogise** or **-ize** to render theological. — *vi* to discourse, speculate, etc. on theology. — *n* **theol'ogiser.** — *n* **theomachy** (*thē-om'ə-ki*) war among or against the gods, as (in Greek mythology) by the Titans and giants; opposition to the divine will. — *n* **theom'achist.** — *n* **theomancy** (*thē'ō-man-si*) divination by means of oracles, or of persons inspired immediately by some divinity. — *adj* **theoman'tic.** — *n* **theomania** (*-mā'ni-ə*) religious madness; belief that one is a god oneself. — *n* **theomā'niac.** — *adj* **theomorphic** (*-mör'fik*) having the form or likeness of a god; in the image of God. — *n* **theophany** (*thē-of'ə-ni*) a manifestation or appearance of deity to man. — *adj* **theophanic** (*thē-ō-fan'ik*). — *n* **theosophy** (*thē-os'ə-fi*) divine wisdom; immediate divine illumination or inspiration claimed to be possessed by specially gifted men, along with abnormal control over natural forces; the system of doctrine expounded by the Theosophical Society. — *n* **theosoph** (*thē'ə-sof*), **theos'opher** or **theos'ophist.** — *adj* **theosoph'ic** or **theosoph'ical.** — *adv* **theosoph'ically.** — **Theosophical Society** a religious body founded by Mme. Blavatsky and others in 1875, whose doctrines include belief in karma and reincarnation. [Gr. *theos*, a god.]

theodolite *thē-od'ə-līt*, *n* a surveying instrument for measuring horizontal and vertical angles.

theogony, etc. See under **theo-**.

theol. *abbrev* for: theologian; theological; theology.

theology, etc. . . . to . . . **theophany**, etc. See under **theo-**.

theophylline *thē-ō-fil'ēn*, *-īn* or *-in*, (*chem*) *n* an isomer of theobromine found in tea. [**Thea** and Gr. *phyllon*, leaf.]

theorem *thē'ə-rəm*, *n* a demonstrable or established but not self-evident principle; a proposition to be proved. — *adj* **theoremat'ic** or **theoremat'ical**. — *adv* **theoremat'ically**. — *n* **theorematist** (*-rem'ə-tist*). — *adj* **theoret'ic** or **theoret'ical** pertaining, according, or given, to theory; not practical; speculative. — *n* **theoret'ic** (usu. in *pl*) the speculative parts of a science. — *adv* **theoret'ically**. — *n* **theoretician** (*-et-ish'ən*) a person who is concerned chiefly with the theoretical aspect of a subject. — *vi* **the'orise** or **-ize** to form a theory; to form opinions solely by theories; to speculate. — *n* **the'oriser** or **-z-**. — *n* **the'orist** a theoriser; a person given to theory and speculation; a person who is expert in the abstract principles of a subject. — *n* **the'ory** an explanation or system of anything; an exposition of the abstract principles of a science or art; speculation as opposed to practice. [Gr. *theōrēma*, *-atos*, spectacle, speculation, theorem, *theōriā*, view, theory — *theōreein*, to be a spectator, to view.]

theosophy, etc. See under **theo-**.

therapeutic *ther-ə-pū'tik*, *adj* pertaining to the healing arts; curative. — *adv* **therapeu'tically**. — *nsing* **therapeu'tics** that part of medicine concerned with the treatment and cure of diseases. — *n* **ther'apist** a person who practises therapy of a particular kind. — *n* **ther'apy** therapeutics; treatment used to combat a disease or an abnormal condition; curative power. [Gr. *therapeutēs*, servant, worshipper, medical attendant — *therapeuein*, to take care of, to heal, *therapeiā*, service, treatment.]

Theravada *ther-a-väd'ə*, *n* the doctrines of the Hinayana Buddhists. — *adj* **Theravad'in**. [Pali, doctrine of the elders.]

therblig *thûr'blig*, *n* a unit of work into which an industrial operation may be divided. [Anagram of the name of its inventor, F.B. *Gilbreth* (1868–1924), American engineer.]

there *dher* or *dhār*, *adv* in that place; at that point; to that place; with regard to that; (also *dhr*) used without any meaning of its own to allow the subject to follow the predicate, and also in corresponding interrogative sentences, etc.; used without any meaning to draw or attract attention. — *n* that place. — *interj* expressing reassurance, finality, accompanying a blow, etc. — *adv* **there'about** or **there'abouts** (also *-bowts'*) about or near that place; near that number, quantity, degree or time. — *adv* **thereaft'er** after or according to that; accordingly. — *adv* **thereat'** at that place or occurrence; on that account. — *adv* **thereby'** beside that; about that amount; by that means; in consequence of that. — *adv* **therefor'** (*law*) for that. — *adv* **therefore** (*dher'fər*) for that reason; consequently. — *adv* **therefrom'** (*formal*) from that. — *adv* **therein'** (*formal*) in or into that or it. — *adv* **thereinaft'er** and **thereinbefore'** (*formal*) later, and earlier, in the same document. — *adv* **therein'to** (*formal*) into that place, thing, matter, etc. — *adv* **thereof'** (*formal*) of that; from that. — *adv* **thereon'** (*old*) on that. — *adv* **thereto'** or **thereun'to** (*formal*) to that; in addition. — *adv* **there'tofore** (*formal*) before that time. — *adv* **thereun'der** (*formal*) under that. — *adv* **thereupon'** upon that; immediately. — *adv* **there-with'** (*old*) with that; thereupon. — *adv* **there'-withal** (*old*) with that; immediately after; in addition. — **so there** an expression of triumph, defiance, derision, finality, etc. — **there and then** forthwith; immediately; **there or thereabouts** somewhere near; **there you are** used to express triumph when something one predicted would occur does occur, or resignation over something that cannot be changed. [O.E. *thǣr*; related to **the**, **that**, etc.]

therio- *thēr-i-o-*, **theri-** *ther-i-* or **thero-** *ther-o-*, *combining form* denoting beast, mammal. — *adj* **therianthrop'ic** combining human and animal forms. — *n* **therian'thropism** the representation or worship of therianthropic forms or gods. — *n* **theriol'atry** animal-worship. — *n* **ther'iomorph** an animal form in art. — *adj* **theriomorph'ic** beastlike; of theriomorphism. — *n* **theriomorph'ism** belief in gods of the form of beasts. — *adj* **theriomorph'ous** beastlike; mammal-like. — *adj* **ther'oid** beastlike. — *n* **therol'ogy** the study of mammals. [Gr. *thēr*, and *thērion*, a wild beast.]

therm *thûrm*, *n* 100 000 British thermal units (used as a unit in reckoning payment for gas). — *npl* **therm'ae** (*-ē*) hot springs or baths. — *adj* **therm'al** pertaining to heat; warm; (of clothes) designed to prevent the loss of body heat. — *n* an ascending current of warm air. — *vt* **therm'alise** or **-ize** to reduce the kinetic energy and speed of (fast neutrons) in a nuclear reactor. — *adv* **therm'ally**. — *adj* **therm'ic** or **therm'ical** of or by heat, thermal. — *adv* **therm'ically**. — *n* **therm'ion** an electrically charged particle emitted by an incandescent body. — *adj* **thermion'ic** of or relating to thermions (**thermionic valve** or **tube** a vacuum tube containing a heated cathode from which electrons are emitted, an anode for collecting some or all of these electrons and, generally, additional electrodes for controlling their flow to the anode). — *nsing* **thermion'ics** the science of thermions. — *n* **thermis'tor** (*therm*al res*istor*) a semiconductor, a mixture of certain oxides with finely divided copper, of which the resistance is very sensitive to change of temperature. — *n* **therm'ite** (**Thermit®**) a mixture of aluminium powder with oxide of metal (esp. iron), which when ignited evolves great heat, used for local heating and welding. — *adj* **thermochem'ical**. — *n* **thermochem'ist**. — *n* **thermochem'istry** the study of heat changes accompanying chemical action. — *n* **therm'o-couple** a pair of metals in contact giving a thermo-electric current. — *adj* **thermodynam'ic**. — *nsing* **thermodynam'ics** the science of heat as a mechanical agent. — *adj* **thermo-elec'tric**. — *n* **thermo-electric'ity** electricity developed by the unequal heating of bodies, esp. between a junction of metals and another part of a circuit. — *n* **thermogenesis** (*-jen'*) production of heat, esp. in the body by physiological processes. — *adj* **thermogenet'ic** or **thermogen'ic**. — *n* **therm'ogram** a thermograph record of temperature. — *n* **therm'ograph** a self-registering thermometer; the photographic apparatus used in thermography. — *adj* **thermograph'ic**. — *n* **thermog'raphy** any process of writing, photographing, etc. involving the use of heat. — *adj* **thermolā'bile** readily decomposed by heat. — *n* **thermol'ogy** the science of heat. — *n* **thermoluminesc'ence** release of light by irradiated material upon subsequent heating. — *n* **thermol'ysis** dissociation or dissolution by heat; loss of body heat. — *adj* **thermolyt'ic**. — *n* **thermometer** (*-om'i-tər*) an instrument for measuring temperature depending on any of several properties of a substance that vary linearly with change of temperature. — *adj* **thermometric** (*-ə-met'rik*) or **thermomet'rical**. — *adv* **thermomet'rically**. — *n* **thermomet'rograph** a self-registering thermometer, a thermograph. — *n* **thermom'etry** the branch of physics dealing with the measurement of temperature and the design of thermometers, etc. — *adj* **thermonuc'lear** exhibiting or dealing with the fusion of nuclei as seen in a **thermonuclear reaction,** a power reaction produced by the fusion of nuclei at extremely high temperatures, as in nuclear weaponry; pertaining to the use of such reactions as a source of power or force. — *adj* **therm'ophile** (*-fil*), **therm'ophil, thermophil'ic** or **thermoph'ilous** requiring, or thriving best in, a high temperature. — *n* **therm'opīle** an apparatus for the direct conversion of heat into electrical energy. — *adj* **thermoplast'ic** becoming plastic when heated. — *n* any resin that can be melted and cooled repeatedly without appreciable change in properties. — *n* **Therm'os**® a brand of vacuum flask (also **Thermos® flask**). — *n* **thermosett'ing** setting, after melting and moulding with change of properties. — *n* **therm'osphere** the region of the earth's atmosphere above the mesosphere, in which the temperature rises steadily with height. — *adj* **thermosta'ble** not readily decomposed by heating. — *n* **therm'ostat** a device for keeping temperature steady. — *adj* **thermostat'ic.** — *adv* **thermostat'ically.** — *adj* **thermotact'ic** or **thermotax'ic** of or showing thermotaxis. — *n* **thermotax'is** a movement of an organism towards a position of higher or lower temperature. — *adj* **thermotrop'ic.** — *n* a thermotropic substance. — *n* **thermot'ropism** orientation determined by temperature differences. — **thermal barrier** heat barrier; **thermal imaging** the visualisation of objects and scenes by detecting and processing the infrared energy they emit; **thermal reactor** a nuclear reactor in which fission is induced mainly by low-energy neutrons; **thermal shock** stress, often resulting in fracture, resulting when a body is subjected to sudden changes in temperature; **thermal springs** natural springs of hot water; **thermic lance** a cutting instrument consisting of a steel tube containing metal rods which, with the help of oxygen, are raised to an intense heat. [Gr. *thermos*, hot, *thermē*, heat, *thermotēs*, heat.]

thero-. See **therio-**.

thesaurus *thi-sö'rəs*, *n* a book with systematically arranged lists of words and their synonyms, antonyms, etc., a word finder; a storehouse of knowledge, esp. of words, quotations, etc., a dictionary; lit. a treasury. [L., — Gr. *thēsauros*.]

these *dhēz*, *demonstr adj* and *demonstr pron*, pl. of **this.** [O.E. *thǣs*, a by-form of *thās*, pl. of *thes*, *thēos*, *this*, this; cf. **those.**]

thesis *thē'sis*, *n* a long dissertation, esp. one based on original research and presented for a doctorate; the subject dealt with in this way; a position or that which is set down or advanced for argument: — *pl* **theses** (*thē'sēz*). [Gr. *thĕsis*, from the root of *tithenai*, to put, set.]

Thespian *thes'pi-ən*, (also without *cap*) *adj* pertaining to tragedy or to drama in general. — *n* a tragic actor; an actor (*facetious*). [Gr. *Thespis*, founder of Greek tragedy.]

Thess. (*Bible*) *abbrev* for (the Letters to the) Thessalonians.

theta *thē'tə* or *thā'tə*, *n* the eighth (orig. ninth) letter of the Greek alphabet (Θ, θ) transliterated *th*. [Gr. *thēta*; Semitic.]

theurgy *thē'ər-ji*, *n* magic by the agency of good spirits; miraculous divine action. — *adj* **theur'gic** or **theur'gical.** — *n* **the'urgist.** [Gr. *theourgiā* — *theos*, a god, *ergon*, work.]

thew *thū*, (used chiefly in *pl* **thews** or **thewes**; *literary*) *n* manner; moral quality; bodily quality, muscle or strength. — *adj* **thewed** muscular. — *adj* **thew'y** muscular, strong. [O.E. *thēaw*, manner.]

they *dhā*, *pron*, *nominative pl*, used as *pl* of **he, she** and **it**; often used as a *sing* (with *pl v*) of common gender, he or she, people in general, some. — **they'd** a contraction of **they had** or **they would; they'll** a contraction of **they will** or **they shall; they're** a contraction of **they are; they've** a contraction of **they have.** [M.E. *thei* — O.N. *theirr*, which supplanted *hi* (O.E. *hīe*).]

thiamine *thī'ə-mēn* or *-min* or **thiamin** *thī'ə-min*, *n* vitamin B_1. [Gr. *theion*, sulphur, and **amine.**]

thiazide *thī'ə-zīd*, *n* any of a group of drugs used as diuretics and to treat hypertension. [*thio*-, *azo*-, ox*ide*.]

thick *thik*, *adj* having a great (or specified) distance in measurement from surface to surface in lesser dimension; broad; deep; dense; viscous; close set or packed; crowded; intimate, in close confidence (*fig*); abundant; frequent, in quick succession; aboundingly covered or occupied; foggy; opaque; dull; stupid; gross; husky, muffled; indistinctly articulate; excessive, approaching the intolerable (*slang*). — *n* the thickest part of anything; the midst. — *adv* thickly; closely; frequently; fast; to a great (or specified) depth. — *vt* and *vi* **thick'en** to make or become thick or thicker. — *n* **thick'ener.** — *n* **thick'ening** a making or becoming thicker; a thickened place; material added to something to thicken it. — Also *adj*. — *n* **thick'et** a dense mass of trees or shrubs. — *adj* **thick'eted.** — *adj* **thick'ety.** — *adj* **thick'ish** somewhat thick. — *adv* **thick'ly.** — *n* **thick'ness** a quality or degree of being thick; the space between outer surfaces; a layer. — *n* **thick'o** (*slang*) a stupid person: — *pl* **thick'os** or **thick'oes.** — **thick ear** a bruised, swollen ear, usually a result of a blow administered as punishment; **thick'head** a stupid person, a blockhead; any bird of an Australian family similar to flycatchers and shrikes. — *adj* **thick-head'ed** having a thick head or skull; stupid. — **thick'-knee** the stone-curlew, a large plover with thickened knees. — *adj* **thick'set** closely set or planted; having a short thick body. — *n* a thicket. — *adj* **thick-skinned'** having a thick skin; insensitive; indifferent to criticism or insult. — *adj* **thick-skulled'** having a thick skull; stupid; doltish. — *adj* **thick-witt'ed** doltish. — **a bit thick** more than one can reasonably be expected to put up with; **as thick as a plank** or **as thick as two short planks** very stupid; **as thick as thieves** very friendly; **lay it on thick** to praise extravagantly; to exaggerate; **through thick and thin** in spite of all obstacles; without any wavering. [O.E. *thicce*.]

thief *thēf*, *n* a person who takes unlawfully what is not their own, esp. by stealth: — *pl* **thieves** (*thēvz*). — **thieves' kitchen** a haunt of thieves and other criminals. [O.E. *thēof*.]

thieve *thēv*, *vi* to practise theft; to steal. — *n* **thiev'ery** the practice of thieving; what is thieved. — *n* and *adj* **thiev'ing.** — *adj* **thiev'ish** given to, or like, theft; thief-like; furtive. — *adv* **thiev'ishly.** — *n* **thiev'ishness.** [O.E. *thēofian*, to thieve, and *thēof*, thief.]

thigh *thī*, *n* the thick fleshy part of the leg from the knee to the hip. — **thigh'-bone** the bone of the leg between the hip-joint and the knee, the femur; **thigh boot** a tall boot covering the thigh. [O.E. *thēoh*.]

thill *thil*, *n* the shaft of a cart or carriage. [Poss. O.E. *thille*, board, plank.]

thimble *thim'bl*, *n* a (metal, ceramic, plastic, etc.) cover for the finger, used in sewing; an object of similar form; a metal ring with a grooved or concave outer edge fitted into a rope ring, etc. to prevent chafing (*naut*). — *n* **thim'bleful** as much as a thimble will hold; a small quantity: — *pl* **thim'blefuls.** — **thim'blerig** a sleight-of-hand trick in which the performer conceals, or pretends to conceal, a pea or small ball under one of three thimble-like cups; **thimb'lerigger; thim'blerigging.** [O.E. *thȳmel*, a thumb covering — *thūma*, thumb.]

thin *thin*, *adj* (*compar* **thinn'er,** *superl* **thinn'est**) having little thickness; slim; lean; freely mobile; watery; dilute; of little density; rarefied; sparse;

slight; flimsy; lacking in body or solidity; meagre; poor. — *n* that which is thin. — *adv* thinly. — *vt* to make thin or thinner; to make less close or crowded (with *away*, *out*, etc.); to hit (a shot, etc.) too far to the left (*golf*). — *vi* to grow or become thin or thinner: — *pr p* **thinn'ing**; *pa t* and *pa p* **thinned**. — *adv* **thin'ly**. — *n* **thinn'er** a person or thing that thins, esp. (often in *pl*, sometimes treated as *nsing*) a diluent for paint. — *n* **thin'ness**. — *n* **thinn'ing**. — *adj* **thinn'ish** somewhat thin. — *adj* **thin-skinned'** having thin skin; sensitive; irritable. — **a thin time** a time of hardship, misery, etc.; **into (or out of) thin air** into (or out of) nothing or nothingness; **thin blue line** a line of policemen drawn up to quell crowd violence, etc. (coined in imitation of **thin red line**); **thin on the ground** present in very small, inadequate quality or numbers; **thin on top** balding; **thin red line** a designation for the British army (orig. used in reports of the Crimean campaign, when uniforms were still red) conveying an image of indomitability against heavy odds. [O.E. *thynne*.]

thine *dhīn*, (*formal*, *liturgical*, *dialect* or *archaic*) *pron* genitive form of **thou**[1], used predicatively or absolutely, belonging to thee; thy people; that which belongs to thee; adjectivally, esp. before a vowel or *h*, thy. [O.E. *thīn*.]

thing *thing*, *n* a matter, affair, problem, point; a circumstance; a fact; an event, happening, action; an entity; that which exists or can be thought of; an inanimate object; a living creature (esp. in pity, tolerant affection, or kindly reproach); a possession; that which is wanted or is appropriate (*colloq*); a slight obsession or phobia (*colloq*); (in *pl*) clothes; (in *pl*) utensils, esp. for the table; (in *pl*) personal belongings. — *n* **thing'amy, thing'ummy, thing'amybob, thing'amyjig, thing'umabob, thing'umajig, thing'umbob, thing'ummybob** or **thing'ummyjig** (*colloq*) what-d'you-call-him, -her or -it; what's-his-name, etc. — used when one cannot or will not recall the name. — *n* **thing'y** thingumajig. — **thing-in-itself'** (in the philosophy of Kant) a noumenon, the Ger. *Ding an sich*. — **a good thing** a fortunate circumstance; **and things** and other (similar) things; **a stupid (or wise, etc.) thing to do** a stupid (or wise, etc.) action; **be all things to all men** to meet each person on his or her own ground, accommodate oneself to his or her circumstances and outlook; (*loosely*, in a bad sense) to keep changing one's opinions, etc. so as to suit one's company; **be on to a good thing** (*colloq*) to be in a particularly profitable position, job, etc.; **do one's (own) thing** (*colloq*) to behave as is natural to or characteristic of oneself; to do something in which one specialises; **do the handsome thing by** to treat generously; **do things to** to affect in some good or bad way; **for one thing . . . for another (thing)** expressions used in enumerating reasons; **have a good thing going** (*colloq*) to be established in a particularly profitable position, etc.; **hear things** to hear imaginary noises, voices, etc.; **know a thing or two** to be shrewd; **make a good thing of it** to reap a good advantage from; **make a thing of** to make an issue, point of controversy, etc. of; to fuss about; **no such thing** something very different; no, not at all; **not a thing** nothing; **not quite the thing** (*colloq*) not in very good health (see also **the thing**); **one of those things** a happening one cannot account for or do anything to prevent; **see things** to see something that is not really there; **the thing** or **the done thing** that which is conventional, fashionable, approved, right or desirable. [O.E. and O.N. *thing*, parliament, object, etc.]

think *thingk*, *vi* to exercise the mind; to revolve ideas in the mind; to judge; to be of an opinion; to consider; to aspire or form designs (with *of* or *about*). — *vt* to form, conceive or revolve in the mind; to have as a thought; to imagine; to judge; to believe or consider; to expect; to purpose, design; to bring by thinking: — *pa t* and *pa p* **thought** (*thöt*). — *n* (*colloq*) a spell of thinking; a thought. — *adj* **think'able** capable of being thought; conceivably possible. — *n* **think'er**. — *n* and *adj* **think'ing**. — *adv* **think'ingly**. — **think'-tank** (*colloq*) a person or a group of people, usu. expert in some field, regarded as a source of ideas and solutions to problems. — **have another think coming** (*colloq*) to be wrong in what one thinks (about future events or actions); **I don't think** I disbelieve; a warning that what was said was ironical (*colloq*); **I shouldn't (or wouldn't) think of** I would not under any conditions; **just think of it** or **to think of it** an expression of surprise, disapproval, longing, etc.; **put on one's thinking-cap** to devote some time to thinking about some problem; **think again** to (be forced to) change one's opinion; **think aloud** to utter one's thoughts unintentionally; **think back to** to bring to one's mind the memory of (a past event, etc.); **think better of** to change, on reflection, one's mind concerning; **think little of** to have a poor opinion of (opp. to **think much** or **well of**); **think nothing of** not to consider difficult, exceptional, etc.; not to hesitate in (doing); **think nothing of it** it does not matter, is not important; **think out** to devise, project completely; to solve by a process of thought; **think over** to reconsider at leisure; **think through** to solve by a process of thought; to project and consider all the possible consequences, problems, etc. relating to (some course of action); **think twice** (often with *about*) to hesitate (before doing something); to decide not to do; **think up** to find by thinking, to devise or concoct. [O.E. *thencan*.]

thio- *thī-ō-*, *combining form* denoting: sulphur; indicating in chemistry a compound theoretically derived from another by substituting an atom or more of sulphur for oxygen. — *n* **thiobarbit'urate** a salt of **thiobarbitu'ric acid** similar in effect to a barbiturate. — *n* **thiocy'anate** a salt of **thiocyan'ic acid**. — *n* **thī'ol** (or *-ōl*) mercaptan. — *n* **thiopent'one** or in N.Am. **thiopent'al** see **Pentothal**. — *n* **thiouracil** (*thī-ō-ū'rə-sil*) a derivative of thiourea that interferes with the synthesis of thyroid hormone. — *n* **thiourea** (*thī-ō-ū'ri-ə*) urea with its oxygen replaced by sulphur, a bitter crystalline substance that inhibits thyroid activity and is used e.g. in photographic fixing. [Gr. *theion*, sulphur.]

thiram *thī'ram*, *n* a fungicide. [*thiou*rea and carb*am*ic acid, a derivative of carbonic acid.]

third *thûrd*, *adj* the last of three; next after the second; equal to one of three equal parts. — *n* one of three equal parts; a person or thing in third position; an interval of two (conventionally called three) diatonic degrees (*mus*); a note at that interval third gear. — *adv* in the third place. — *vt* to divide by three; to support after the seconder. — *n* **third'ing** a third part. — *adv* **third'ly** in the third place. — *n* **third class** the class (of degree, hotel accommodation, etc.) next below second class. — *adj* and *adv* **third'-class**. — **third dimension** depth, thickness; the dimension of depth, distinguishing a solid object from a two-dimensional or planar object. — *adj* **third-dimen'sional**. — *adj* **third-hand'**. — **third man** (*cricket*) a fielder on the offside between point and slip. — *n* **third'-party** a person other than the principal people involved (e.g. in the agreement between the insured and insurer). — *adj* **third'-party**. — *adj* **third'-rate** of the third order; of poor quality. — **third reading** (in a legislative assembly) in Britain the consideration of committee reports on a bill; in the U.S.A. the final consideration of a bill; **Third World** the developing countries not aligned politically with the large power blocks. [O.E. *thridda*.]

thirst *thûrst*, *n* the discomfort caused by lack of drink; vehement desire for drink; eager desire for anything. — *vi* to feel thirst. — *n* **thirst'er**. — *adv* **thirst'ily**. —

n **thirst'iness**. — *adj* **thirst'less**. — *adj* **thirst'y** suffering from thirst; dry; causing thirst; vehemently desiring. [O.E. *thurst* (noun), *thyrstan* (verb).]

thirteen *thûr'tēn* or *-tēn'*, *adj* and *n* three and ten. — *adj* **thir'teenth** (or *-tēnth'*) last of thirteen; next after the twelfth; equal to one of thirteen equal parts. — *n* a thirteenth part; a person or thing in thirteenth position. — *adv* **thirteenth'ly**. [O.E. *thrēotīene*, *-tēne* — *thrēo*, three.]

thirty *thûr'ti*, *adj* and *n* three times ten. — *npl* **thir'ties** the numbers from thirty to thirty-nine; the years so numbered in life or any century; a range of temperatures from thirty to just under forty degrees. — *adj* **thir'tieth** last of thirty; next after the twenty-ninth; equal to one of thirty equal parts. — *n* a thirtieth part; a person or thing in thirtieth position. — *adj* and *adv* **thir'tyfold**. — *adj* **thir'tyish** somewhere about the age of thirty. — *adj* **thirty-two'mo** (for *tricesimo secundo*, 32mo) in sheets folded to give 32 leaves (64 pages). — *n* a book constructed in this way: — *pl* **thirty-two'mos**. [O.E. *thrītig* — *thrēo*, three, *-tig*, sfx. denoting ten.]

this *dhis*, *sing demonstr pron* and *adj* denoting a person or thing near, topical, just mentioned, or about to be mentioned; (up to and including) the present moment; sometimes used almost with the force of an indefinite article, as in the phrase 'then I saw this big bright object in the sky': — *pl* **these**. — *n* **this'ness** the quality of being this, not something else. — **this and that** or **this, that and the other** various minor unspecified objects, actions, etc. [O.E., neut. of *thes*, *thēos*, *this*.]

thistle *this'l*, *n* a prickly composite plant with pink, white, yellow but usually purple flower heads, the national emblem of Scotland. — *adj* **this'tly** like a thistle; overgrown with thistles. — **this'tledown** the tufted feathery parachutes of thistle seeds. [O.E. *thistel*.]

thither *dhidh'ər*, (*literary*, *formal* or *archaic*) *adv* to that place; to that end or result. — *adv* on the far side. — *adv* **thith'erward** or **thith'erwards** toward that place. [O.E. *thider*.]

thixotropy *thiks-ot'rə-pi*, (*chem*, *building*, etc.) *n* the property of showing a temporary reduction in viscosity when shaken or stirred. — *adj* **thixotropic** (*-trop'ik*) of or showing thixotropy; (of paints) non-drip. [Gr. *thixis*, action of touching, *tropos*, a turn.]

tho'. Same as **though**.

thole[1] *thōl* or **thole-pin** *thōl'-pin*, *n* a pin in the side of a boat to keep the oar in place; a peg. [O.E. *thol*.]

thole[2] *thōl*, (chiefly *Scot*) *vt* and *vi* to endure. [O.E. *tholian*, to suffer.]

tholus *thō'ləs* or **tholos** *thō'los*, *n* a round building, dome, cupola or tomb: — *pl* **thō'li** (*-lī*) or **thō'loi**. [Gr. *thŏlos*.]

Thomism *tō'mizm*, *n* the doctrines of *Thomas* Aquinas (b. prob. 1225; d. 1274). — *n* and *adj* **Thō'mist**. — *adj* **Thōmist'ic** or **Thomist'ical**.

Thompson submachine-gun *tom'sən sub-mə-shēn'-gun*, *n* a tommy-gun. — Also **Thompson gun**.

thong *thong*, *n* a strap; a strip; the lash of a whip; a sandal held on by a thong between the toes, a flipflop (*NAm* and *Austr*). — *adj* **thonged** having a thong or thongs. [O.E. *thwang*.]

thorax *thö'raks*, (*zool*) *n* the part of the body between the head and abdomen, in man the chest, in insects the division that bears legs and wings: — *pl* **tho'raxes** or **tho'races** (*-sēz*). — *adj* **thoracic** (*-ras'ik*). — **thoracic duct** the main trunk of the vessels conveying lymph in the body. [Gr. *thōrāx*, *-ākos*.]

thorium *thö'ri-əm*, *n* a radioactive metal (symbol **Th**; atomic no. 90) resembling aluminium. [*Thor*, the god.]

thorn *thörn*, *n* a sharp hard part of the stem or leaf of a plant; an animal spine; anything prickly; a spiny plant; hawthorn; the Old English and Old Norse letter þ (*th*). — *adj* **thorned**. — *n* **thorn'iness**. — *adj* **thorn'less**. — *adj* **thorn'y** full of thorns; prickly; troublesome; harassing. — **thorn'-apple** a poisonous plant of the potato family, with a prickly capsule; **thorn'back** a ray with nail-like crooked spines in its back; **thorn'-bush** any thorny shrub, esp. hawthorn; **thorn'-hedge** a hedge of hawthorn; **thorn'-tree** a thorny tree, esp. a hawthorn. — **thorn in the flesh** any cause of constant irritation. [O.E.]

thoron *thö'ron*, *n* the radioactive gas given off by the decomposition of thorium.

thorough *thur'ə*, also in N.Am. *thur'ō*, *adj* passing or carried through, or to the end; complete; entire; out-and-out; assiduous and scrupulous in completing work. — *adv* **thor'oughly**. — *n* **thor'oughness**. — **thor'ough-bass** (*mus*) a bass part all through a piece, usu. with figures to indicate the chords. — *adj* **thor'oughbred** thoroughly or completely bred or trained; (of a horse) bred from a dam and sire of the best blood and having the qualities supposed to depend on such breeding; pure-bred; (with *cap*) pertaining to the Thoroughbred breed of horses. — *n* an animal (esp. a horse) of pure blood; (with *cap*) a racehorse of a breed descended from any of three Arabian stallions of the early 18th cent., whose ideal gait is the gallop. — **thor'oughfare** a passage or way through; a road open at both ends; a public way or street; right of passing through. — *adj* **thor'ough-going** going through or to the end; going all lengths; complete; out-and-out. — **post-vintage thoroughbred** a car built between 1 January 1931 and 31 December 1941. [The longer form of **through**.]

thorp or **thorpe** *thörp*, (*archaic*; as found in place names) *n* a hamlet; a village. [O.E. *thorp*, *throp*.]

those *dhōz*, *demonstr pron* and *adj*, pl. of **that**. [O.E. *thās*, pl. of *thes*, this.]

thou[1] *dhow*, (*formal*, *liturgical*, *dialect* or *archaic*) *pron* (of the *2nd pers sing*) the person addressed (now generally used only in solemn address). [O.E. *thū*.]

thou[2] *thow*, a colloq. short form of **thousand** or **thousandth**.

though *dhō*, *conj* admitting; allowing; even if; notwithstanding that. — *adv* nevertheless; however. — **as though** as if. [O.N. *thauh*, *thō*.]

thought[1] *thöt*, *pa p* of **think**. [O.E. *thōhte*, past t., (*ge*)*thōht*, past p.]

thought[2] *thöt*, *n* thinking; mind; consciousness; reasoning; deliberation; that which one thinks; notion, idea, fancy; consideration, opinion, meditation; design; care; considerateness; purpose, intention. — *adj* **thought'ful** full of thought; attentive; considerate; expressive of or favourable to reflection. — *adv* **thought'fully**. — *n* **thought'fulness**. — *adj* **thought'less** unthinking; incapable of thinking; careless; inattentive; inconsiderate. — *adv* **thought'lessly**. — *n* **thought'lessness**. — **thought process** train of thought; manner of thinking **thought'-reader**; **thought'-reading** mind-reading; **thought'-transference** telepathy; **thought'-wave** a wavelike progress of a thought among a crowd or the public; a sudden accession of thought in the mind; an impulse in some hypothetical medium assumed to explain telepathy. — **on second thoughts** on reconsideration; **take thought** to think things over. [O.E. (*ge*)*thōht*.]

thousand *thow'zənd*, *n* and *adj* ten hundred; often used vaguely or hyperbolically. — *adj*, *adv* and *n* **(a) thou'sandfold** a thousand times as much. — *adj* **thou'sandth** last of a thousand, or in an equivalent position in a greater number; equal to one of a thousand equal parts. — *n* a thousandth part; a person or thing in thousandth position. — **a thousand and one** (*colloq*) very many; an overwhelming number; **one in a thousand** anything exceedingly rare or excellent. [O.E. *thūsend*.]

thrall *thröl*, (*literary* or *archaic*) *n* a slave, serf; slavery, servitude. — *vt* to enslave. — *n* **thral'dom** or (esp. in N.Am.) **thrall'dom** slavery; bondage. [O.E. *thrǣl* — O.N. *thræll.*]

thrash *thrash*, *vt* to thresh; (with *out*) to discuss exhaustively, or arrive at by debate; to beat soundly; to defeat thoroughly. — *vi* to lash out, beat about one, in anger, panic, etc. — *n* an act of threshing or thrashing; a party (*colloq*). — *n* **thrash'er** a thresher; a thresher-shark, a large, long-tailed shark; a person who thrashes. — *n* and *adj* **thrash'ing** threshing; beating. [Orig. a dialect form of **thresh**.]

thrasher[1] *thrash'ər* or **thresher** *thresh'ər*, *n* any of several American birds of the mocking-bird family. [Perh. Eng. dialect *thresher*, thrush.]

thrasher[2]. See **thrash**.

thraw *thrö*, a Scots form of **throw** with some old senses preserved; also of **throe**, with senses overlapping **throw**. — *adj* **thrawn** twisted; wry; cross-grained, perverse.

thread *thred*, *n* a very thin line of any substance, esp. linen or cotton, twisted or drawn out; a filament; a fibre; (in *pl*) clothes (*slang*); the prominent spiral part of a screw; a continuous connecting element in a story, argument, etc. — *vt* to pass a thread through; to string on a thread; to pass or pierce through, as a narrow way; to provide with a thread. — *adj* made of linen or cotton thread. — *n* **thread'er**. — *n* **thread'iness**. — *adj* **thread'y**. — *adj* **thread'bare** worn to the bare thread; having the nap worn off; hackneyed; used till its novelty or interest is gone. — **thread mark** a coloured thread incorporated in bank-notes to make counterfeiting difficult; **thread'-worm** any member of the *Nematoda*, a family of more or less threadlike worms, many of which are parasitic, esp. *Oxyuris vermicularis*, parasitic in the human rectum. — **thread of life** (*Gr mythol*) the thread imagined to be spun and cut by the Fates. [O.E. *thrǣd.*]

threat *thret*, *n* a declaration or indication of an intention to inflict, punish or hurt; an appearance of impending evil; a source of danger (to). — *vt* **threat'en** to offer a threat of, or against; to intimidate by threats; to seem to impend over; to indicate danger of, or to. — *vi* to use threats; to portend evil. — *adj* **threat'ened**. — *n* **threat'ener**. — *n* **threat'ening**. — *adj* menacing; portending danger or evil; (of sky) heavily clouded over. — *adv* **threat'eningly**. — *adj* **threat'ful** menacing. [O.E. *thrēat* (noun), *thrēatian*, *thrēatnian* (verbs).]

three *thrē*, *n* two and one; a set of three; a symbol for three; a card with three pips; a score of three points, strokes, etc.; an article of a size denoted by three; the third hour after midnight or midday; the age of three years. — *adj* of the number three; three years old. — *n* **three'ness** the state of being three. — *n* **three'some** a group of three people; a game or dance for three. — *adj* for three; triple. — **three balls** the pawnbroker's sign. — *adj* **three'-card** played with three cards (see also **three-card trick** below). — **three cheers** three shouts of 'hurrah', to show approval, etc. (also *fig*). — *adj* **three'-colour** involving or using three colours as primary. — *adj* **three'-cornered** triangular in form or section; having three competitors or three members. — *adj* **three'-deck**. — **three-deck'er** a ship with three decks or guns on three decks; a sandwich made with three layers of bread. — Also *adj*. — *adj* **three-dimen'sional** having, or seeming to have, three dimensions; giving the effect of being seen or heard in an environment of three dimensions — usu. **3-D**; (of, e.g. a literary work) developed in detail and thus realistic. — **three-dimensional'ity**. — *adj* and *adv* **three'fold** in three divisions; three times as much. — *n* **three'foldness**. — *adj* **three'-foot** measuring or having three feet. — *adj* **three-four'** (*mus*) with three crotchets to the bar. — *adj* **three'-handed** having three hands; played by three players. — *adj* **three'-legged** (*-legd* or *-leg'id*) having three legs; (of a race) run by pairs of runners, each with a leg tied to their partner's. — **threepence** (*threp'*, *thrip'* or *thrup'əns*) money, or a coin, of the value of three old pence. — *adj* **threepenny** (*threp'*, *thrip'*, *thrup'ni* or *-ə-ni*) sold or offered at threepence; of little worth; mean, vulgar. — *n* a coin of the value of threepence (also **threepenny bit** or **piece**). — *adj* **three'-piece** comprising three parts, three matching pieces, etc. — *adj* **three'-ply** having three layers or strands. — *adj* and *adv* **three-quar'ter** to the amount of three-fourths; (*adj*) being three quarters of the normal size or length (used of beds, coats, etc.). — *n* a three-quarter back. — **three quarters** (a part equal to) three fourths of a whole; the greater part of something. — *n* and *adj* **three'score** sixty. — *adj* **three'-sided** having three sides. — *adj* **three'-way** giving connection in three directions from a centre. — **three-card trick** a card-sharp's ploy in which the victim is invited to bet on which of three cards, turned face-down and deftly manipulated, is the queen (also called *find the lady*); **three-colour process** the method of producing colour pictures from three primary originals — yellow, red, blue — prepared by photography; **three-mile limit** by international law, the outer limit of the territorial waters around a state; **three-point landing** (*aeronautics*) a landing with all three wheels touching the ground at the same moment — a perfect landing; **three-point turn** the process of turning a vehicle round to face in the opposite direction by moving it forward, reversing, then moving forward again, turning the steering-wheel appropriately; **three-quarter back** (*Rugby football*) a player between halfbacks and full back; **three-quar'ter-length** (of a coat, sleeve, etc.) being three quarters of the full length; **three-ring circus** a circus with three rings in which simultaneous separate performances are given; a showy or extravagant event (*fig*); a confusing or bewildering scene or situation. [O.E. *thrēo*, fem. and neut. of *thrī.*]

thremmatology *threm-ə-tol'ə-ji*, *n* the science of breeding domestic animals and plants. [Gr. *thremma*, *-atos*, a nurseling, *logos*, discourse.]

threnody *thrēn'* or *thren'ə-di* or **thren'ode** *-ōd*, *n* an ode or song of lamentation. — *adj* **threnō'dial** or **threnodic** (*-od'ik*). — *n* **thren'odist**. [Gr. *thrē-nōidiā*, *thrēnos*, a lament, *ōidē*, song.]

threonine *thrē'ə-nīn*, *n* an amino-acid essential for bodily growth and health, present in certain proteins. [Gr. *erythro-*, red, by rearrangement, with *-n-* and *-ine.*]

thresh *thresh*, *vt* to beat out, subject to beating out, by trampling, flail or machinery; to thrash. — *vi* to thresh corn; to thrash. — *n* an act of threshing. — *n* **thresh'el** a flail; a flail-like weapon, a spiky ball on the end of a chain. — *n* **thresh'er** a person who threshes; a flail; a threshing-machine or a beating part of it;(also **thresh'er-shark**) a large, long-tailed shark. — *n* and *adj* **thresh'ing**. — **thresh'ing-floor** a surface on which grain is threshed; **thresh'ing-machine** or **-mill** one for threshing corn. [O.E. *therscan*; cf. Ger. *derschen*, to thresh; see **thrash**.]

thresher. See **thrasher**[1] and **thresh**.

threshold *thresh'ōld* or *-hōld*, *n* the sill of a house door; the place or point of entering; the outset; the limit of consciousness; the point at which a stimulus begins to bring a response, as in *threshold of pain*, etc.; the smallest dose of radiation that will produce a specified result; the point, stage, level, etc. at which something will happen, become true, etc.; (in a pay agreement, etc.) a point in the rise of the cost of living at which a wage-increase is prescribed. — *adj* at or constituting a threshold. [O.E. *therscold*, *therscwald*, *threscold*, app. — *therscan*, to thrash, thresh, in its older sense of trample, tread.]

threw *thrōō*, *pa t* of **throw**.

thrice *thrīs*, (*formal* and *archaic*) *adv* three times; three times as much. [M.E. *thriës* — O.E. *thrīwa*, *thrīga*, thrice — *thrī*, three, with adverbial genitive ending *-es*.]

thrift *thrift*, *n* frugality; economy; sea pink, a seaside and alpine plant. — *adv* **thrift'ily**. — *n* **thrift'iness**. — *adj* **thrift'less** not thrifty; extravagant. — *adv* **thrift'lessly**. — *n* **thrift'lessness**. — *adj* **thrift'y** (*compar* **thrift'ier**, *superl* **thrift'iest**) showing thrift or economy; prosperous, in good condition (*US*). [**thrive**.]

thrill *thril*, *vt* to affect with a strong glow or tingle of sense or emotion, now esp. a feeling of excitement or extreme pleasure. — *vi* to pass tinglingly; to quiver; to feel a sharp, shivering sensation. — *n* a sudden feeling of excitement or extreme pleasure; a tingle; a shivering feeling or emotion. — *n* **thrill'er** a sensational or exciting story, esp. one about crime and detection. — *adj* **thrill'ing**. — *adv* **thrill'ingly**. — *n* **thrill'ingness**. — *adj* **thrill'y**. [O.E. *thyrlian*, to bore — *thyrel*, a hole.]

thrips *thrips*, *n* a minute black insect of the genus *Thrips* common in flowers; popularly extended to leaf-hoppers, and to other small insects: — *pl* **thrips** or **thrip'ses**. [Gr. *thrīps*, *thrīpos*, a woodworm.]

thrive *thrīv*, *vi* to grow healthily and vigorously; to get on, do well; to prosper; to be successful, flourish: — *pa t* **thrōve** or **thrīved**; *pa p* **thriven** (*thriv'n*). — *n* and *adj* **thrī'ving**. [O.N. *thrīfa*, to grasp.]

thro' and **thro** *thrōō*. Same as **through**.

throat *thrōt*, *n* the passage from mouth to stomach; the forepart of the neck, in which the gullet and windpipe are located; voice; a narrow entrance, aperture or passage; the narrow part, as of a vase. — *adj* **throat'ed** with a throat. — *adv* **throat'ily**. — *n* **throat'iness**. — *adj* **throat'y** sounding as from the throat; hoarse; croaking; deep or full-throated; having a rather sore throat (*colloq*); full or loose-skinned about the throat. — **throat microphone** one held directly against the speaker's throat and actuated by vibrations of the larynx. — **be at someone's throat** or **at each other's throats** (*colloq*) to be engaged in a fierce, bitter argument with someone or with each other; **cut one's (own) throat** usu., to cut the jugular vein; to pursue some course ruinous to one's interests; **sore throat** an inflamed and uncomfortable condition of the tonsils and neighbouring parts; **stick in one's throat** to be more than one can bear or accept; **thrust (or ram) down someone's throat** to assert or force upon someone insistently without listening to an answer. [O.E. *throte*; cf. **throttle**.]

throb *throb*, *vi* to beat strongly, as the heart or pulse does, esp. in response to some emotion, stimulus, etc.; (of an engine, etc.) to produce a deep regular sound: — *pr p* **throbb'ing**; *pa t* and *pa p* **throbbed**. — *n* a beat or strong pulsation. — *n* and *adj* **throbb'ing**. — *adv* **throbb'ingly**. [M.E. *throbben*; poss. connected with L. *trepidus*, trembling.]

throe *thrō*, *n* spasm; a paroxysm; a pang. — **in the throes** in the struggle (of), struggling (with); in the thick (of). [M.E. *thrahes*, *throwes*, *thrawes*.]

thrombus *throm'bəs*, *n* a clot of blood in a living vessel, obstructing circulation: — *pl* **throm'bī**. — *n* **throm'bin** an enzyme that causes clotting. — *n* **throm'bocyte** a minute clotting-body in blood, a platelet. — *n* **thrombo-em'bolism** an embolism caused by an embolus carried by the bloodstream from its point of origin causing a blockage elsewhere. — *n* **thrombo-phlebī'tis** phlebitis with formation of a thrombus. — *vt* **thrombose** (*-bōs'*) to cause thrombosis in. — *vi* to become affected by thrombosis. — *n* **thrombō'sis** clotting in a vessel during life: — *pl* **thrombō'sēs**. — *adj* **thrombot'ic**. [Gr. *thrombos*, clot.]

throne *thrōn*, *n* a monarch's, pope's or bishop's chair of state; the power or duty of a monarch, etc. — *vt* to enthrone. — *adj* **throned**. — *adj* **throne'less**. — **throne'-room**. [Gr. *thronos*, a seat.]

throng *throng*, *n* a crowd; a great multitude; crowding. — *vt* and *vi* to crowd; to press or jostle. — *adj* **thronged** packed, crowded. — *n* and *adj* **throng'ing**. [O.E. *gethrang* — *thringan*, to press.]

throstle *thros'l*, *n* the song thrush (see **thrush**[1]); a machine for drawing, twisting and winding fibres (from its sound). [O.E.]

throttle *throt'l*, *n* the throat or windpipe; a throttle-valve; a throttle-lever. — *vt* to choke by pressure on the windpipe; to strangle (also *fig*); to check the flow of; to cut down the supply of steam, or of gas and air, to or in. — *n* **thrott'ler**. — *n* and *adj* **thrott'ling**. — **thrott'le-lever** a lever that opens and closes a throttle-valve; **thrott'le-valve** a valve regulating the supply of steam or of gas and air in an engine. — **at full throttle** at full speed; **throttle down** or **back** to slow down by closing the throttle. [App. dimin. of **throat**.]

through *thrōō*, *prep* from end to end, side to side, or boundary to boundary of, by way of the interior; from place to place within; everywhere within; by way of; along the passage of; clear of; among; from beginning to end of; up to and including, to or until the end of (*NAm*); by means of; in consequence of. — *adv* from one end or side to the other; from beginning to end; all the way; clear; into a position of having passed; in connection or communication all the way. — *adj* passing, or serving for passage, all the way without interruption. — *prep* **throughout'** in, into, through or during the whole of. — *adv* in every part; everywhere. — **through'put** the amount of material, etc., put through a process; **through'-traffic** the traffic between two centres at a distance from each other; traffic passing straight through an area, as opposed to that travelling within the area; **through'way** or **thru'way** (*NAm*) a motorway. — **be through** (orig. *NAm*) to have done (with); to be finished; to have no more to do (with); **through and through** through the whole thickness; completely; in every point. [O.E. *thurh*.]

throve *thrōv*, *pa t* of **thrive**.

throw *thrō*, *vt* to cast, hurl, fling through the air; to project; to emit; to cast down in wrestling; to cause to be in some place or condition, esp. with suddenness; to put; to execute, perform; to form (pottery) on a wheel; to move (a switch) so as to connect or disconnect; to turn, with a lathe; to wind or twist (yarn, etc.) together; to make a cast of dice amounting to; to dislodge from the saddle; to defeat, get the better of; to bemuse, perplex, disconcert; (of an animal) to give birth to; to lose (a contest) deliberately, esp. in return for a bribe (*colloq*). — *vi* to cast or hurl; to cast dice: — *pa t* **threw** (*thrōō*); *pa p* **thrown** (*thrōn*). — *n* an act of throwing; a cast, esp. of dice or a fishing-line; the distance to which anything may be thrown; a small woollen wrap or rug (*NAm*); a turn, article, etc. (*colloq*); a risky venture (*colloq*); the vertical displacement of a fault (*geol*); a deflection (*phys*); amplitude of movement (*phys*). — *n* **throw'er**. — *n* and *adj* **throw'ing**. — *adj* **thrown** twisted; cast, flung. — **throw'away** an advertisement brochure or handbill freely distributed to the public (*US*); a contest without serious competition; a line, or a joke, that an actor purposely delivers without emphasis, often for the sake of realism. — *adj* (of manner or technique) casual, without attempt at dramatic effect; ridiculously cheap, as if being thrown away; discarded or not recovered after use. — **throw'back** a reversion (e.g. to an earlier developmental type); a setback; **throw'-in** an act of throwing in; a throw to put the ball back into play (*football*, *basketball*, etc.); **throw'-out** an act of throwing out; a rejected thing. — **throw a fit** (*colloq*) to have a fit, behave wildly;

throw a party (*colloq*) to give a party; **throw away** to reject, toss aside; to squander; to fail to take advantage of; to bestow unworthily; **throw back** to retort, to refuse; to force (someone) to rely on (something); to revert to some ancestral character; **throw down** to demolish; **throw in** to interject; to throw the ball in; to add as an extra; **throw in the towel** or **throw in one's hand** to give up, surrender; **throw off** to divest oneself of; to disengage or release oneself from; to tell or compose in an offhand way; **throw on** to put on hastily; **throw oneself at** to make a determined and obvious attempt to captivate; **throw oneself into** to engage heartily in; **throw oneself on** or **upon** to attack, assault; to entrust oneself to the power of; **throw open** to cause to swing wide open; to make freely accessible; **throw out** to cast out; to reject; to expel; to emit; to utter casually; to cause to project; to disconcert; **throw over** to discard or desert; **throw together** to put together in a hurry; to bring into contact by chance; **throw up** to erect hastily; to show prominently; to give up, to resign; to vomit (*colloq*); **throw up (something) against someone** to reproach someone with (something). [O.E. *thrāwan*, to turn, to twist.]

thru *thrōō*. An informal, commercial and chiefly N.Am. spelling of **through**, alone or in compounds.

thrum[1] *thrum*, *n* the end of a weaver's thread; any loose thread or fringe; bits of coarse yarn. — *adj* made of or having thrums. — *vt* to furnish, cover or fringe with thrums: — *pr p* **thrumm'ing**; *pa t* and *pa p* **thrummed**. — *adj* **thrumm'y** made of, or like, thrums. [O.E. *thrum* (found in combination).]

thrum[2] *thrum*, *vt* and *vi* to strum; to hum, drone, or repeat monotonously; to drum with the fingers: — *pr p* **thrumm'ing**; *pa t* and *pa p* **thrummed**. — *n* a strumming. — *n* **thrumm'er**. — *n* and *adj* **thrumm'ing**. — *adv* **thrumm'ingly**.

thrush[1] *thrush*, *n* any member of the *Turdinae* subfamily of songbirds, esp. those of the genus *Turdus*, particularly those species having a spotted breast, e.g. the song thrush and mistel-thrush; applied to other birds more or less similar. [O.E. *thrysce*.]

thrush[2] *thrush*, *n* a disease, usu. of children, causing the appearance of fungous blisters in the mouth and throat; a similar fungal disease affecting the vagina; an inflammation in the frog of a horse's hoof. [Dan. and Norw. *troske*.]

thrust *thrust*, *vt* and *vi* to push; to force; to stab, pierce; to intrude; to impose: — *pa t* and *pa p* **thrust**. — *n* a push; a pushing force; a stab; pertinacity, determination, drive; the chief message, gist or direction of an argument, etc.; the force that drives an aircraft forward and its measurement; the horizontal force on the abutment of an arch. — *n* **thrust'er**. — *n* and *adj* **thrust'ing**. — **thrust stage** a stage that extends into the auditorium. [O.N. *thrȳsta*, to press.]

thruway. See **throughway**.

Thu. *abbrev* for Thursday.

thud *thud*, *n* a dull sound as of a heavy body falling. — *vi* to make a thud; to fall with a thud. [Perh. O.E. *thyddan*, to strike.]

thug *thug*, *n* a ruffian; a cut-throat; orig. a member of a religious fraternity that murdered stealthily by strangling or poisoning (*Ind*). — *n* **thuggee'** or **thugg'ism** the practices of the Indian thugs. — *n* **thugg'ery** thuggism; ruffianly or violent behaviour. — *adj* **thugg'ish**. [Hindi *thag*, cheat.]

Thule *thū'lē*, *n* an island six days N. of Orkney discovered by Pytheas (4th cent. B.C.), variously identified as Shetland, Iceland, Norway, Jutland; hence (usu. *ultima Thule*) the extreme limit. — *n* **thu'lia** thulium oxide. — *n* **thu'lium** a metallic element (symbol **Tm**; atomic no. 69). [L. *Thūlē* — Gr. *Thoulē*.]

thumb *thum*, *n* the short, thick digit on the side of the human hand; the part of a glove that covers it; the corresponding digit in other animals, or that of the hindfoot, esp. when opposable; a thumb's breadth, an inch. — *vt* to play, spread, press, touch, wear or smudge with the thumb; to turn the pages (of a book) rapidly with the thumb (often *vi* with *through*); to signal to with the thumb; to hit (in the eye) with the thumb (*boxing*). — *adj* **thumbed** having thumbs; marked by the thumb, worn. — **thumb'-hole** a hole to insert the thumb in; **thumb'-index** one arranged as indentations on the outer margins of the pages of books, to facilitate quick reference to a particular place; **thumb'nail** the nail of the thumb; a sketch (**thumbnail sketch**) as small as a thumbnail. — *adj* brief, concise. — **thumb'piece** a piece that is pressed by the thumb or receives the thumb; **thumb'print** an impression of the markings of the thumb, taken as a means of identification; **thumb'screw** an old instrument of torture for compressing the thumb by means of a screw; **thumbs-down** and **-up** see **thumbs down** and **up** below; **thumb'tack** (*NAm*) a drawing-pin. — **be all (fingers and) thumbs, one's fingers are all thumbs** or **have one's fingers all thumbs** to be awkward and fumbling; **bite one's thumb** to make a sign threatening revenge; **rule of thumb** a rough-and-ready practical manner, found by experience to be convenient; **thumb a lift** or **ride** (*colloq*) to beg a lift from passing motorists by signalling from the side of the road with the thumb; **thumb one's nose** to cock a snook (*lit* and *fig*) (see **snook**[2]); **thumbs down** a sign indicating disapproval, disallowance, failure, etc. (also *fig*; *n* **thumbs-down'**); **thumbs up** a sign indicating approval, success, hope of, or wishes for, success etc. (also *fig*; *n* **thumbs-up'**); **under one's thumb** under one's domination. [O.E. *thūma*.]

thump *thump*, *n* a dull heavy blow or its sound, esp. a blow with the hand. — *vt* and *vi* to beat with a dull heavy blow; to make such a sound. — *vt* to trounce. — *n* **thump'er** someone who, or that which, thumps; anything very big, a big lie, etc. (*colloq*). — *adj* **thump'ing** (*colloq*) unusually big. [Prob. imit.]

thunbergia *thən-bûr'ji-ə*, *-gi-ə* or *tōōn-*, *n* any plant of the *Thunbergia* genus of evergreen climbing plants of the acanthus family. [After the Swedish botanist Carl *Thunberg* (1743–1828).]

thunder *thun'dər*, *n* the deep rumbling sound after a flash of lightning, caused by the disturbance by electricity of atmospheric gases; any loud noise; a thunderbolt; vehement denunciation. — *vi* to make thunder; to sound as thunder; to move very heavily, and usu. fast; to inveigh with vehemence. — *vt* to utter with noise or violent denunciation. — *n* **thun'derer**. — *n* **thun'dering**. — *adj* discharging thunder; unusually big, tremendous (*colloq*). — Also *adv*. — *adv* **thun'deringly**. — *adj* **thun'derless**. — *adj* **thun'derous** like, threatening or suggesting thunder. — *adv* **thun'derously**. — *adj* **thun'dery** indicative of thunder. — **thun'derbird** a huge mythical bird thought by some tribes of N. American Indians to cause thunder and lightning; a representation of such a bird; **thun'derbolt** a missile of the thunder-god; a popularly imagined material body seen as lightning; anything sudden and overwhelming; a fulmination; a violent and irresistible destroyer or hero; **thun'derclap** a sudden crash of thunder; **thun'dercloud** a cloud charged with electricity; a black or livid threatening appearance; **thun'der-egg** (*Austr* and *US*) an agate-filled cavity within a rock mass, or a fossil, supposed to have been flung to earth by lightning; **thun'der-flash** a container, such as a blank shell, filled with explosive powder, which makes a flash and a loud explosion when detonated; **thun'der-god** a god that wields thunder; **thun'derhead** a distinctively rounded mass of cumulus cloud projecting above the general cloud mass, usu. the precursor of a storm; **thun'der-shower** a shower accompanied with thunder, or a short heavy shower from a thundercloud; **thun'derstorm** continued discharges of electricity from the clouds, producing lightning and thunder, generally with heavy rain. — *adj* **thun'derstruck** (also **thun'derstricken**) struck by lightning; struck dumb with astonishment. — **steal someone's thunder** see under **steal**. [O.E. *thunor*, thunder, *Thunor*, the thunder-god, Thor.]

Thur. *abbrev* for Thursday (also **Thu.**).

thurible *thū'ri-bl*, *n* a censer, for burning incense. [L. *t(h)ūs*, *t(h)ūris*, frankincense — Gr. *thyos*, a sacrifice.]

Thursday *thûrz'di*, *n* the fifth day of the week (orig. sacred to Thunor, the English thunder-god). [O.E. *Thunres dæg*, Thunor's day.]

thus *dhus*, *adv* in this or that manner, in the way mentioned or demonstrated; to this degree or extent; accordingly, therefore. — **thus far** so far, up till now. [O.E.]

thwack *thwak*, *vt* to whack, strike loudly. — *n* a loud whack. — *n* **thwack'er**. — *n* and *adj* **thwack'ing**.

thwart *thwört*, *vt* to cross; to cross the path of; to obstruct; to frustrate. — *n* a rower's bench. — *adj* **thwar'ted** prevented, frustrated. — *adv* **thwar'tedly**. — *n* **thwar'ter**. — *n* and *adj* **thwar'ting**. [O.N. *thvert*, neuter of *thverr*, perverse; **athwart**.]

thy *dhī*, (*formal*, *liturgical*, *dialect* or *archaic*) *possessive pron* or *adj* of **thee**. [**thine**.]

thylacine *thī'lə-sēn*, *-sīn* or *-sin*, *n* the so-called Tasmanian wolf (q.v.). [Gr. *thȳlakos*, pouch.]

thyme *tīm*, *n* any member of the labiate genus *Thymus* of low half-shrubby plants, esp. the fragrant garden thyme and wild thyme. — *n* **thymol** (*thī'mol*) an antiseptic weak-acid compound obtained from oil of thyme by distillation. — *adj* **thymy** (*tīm'i*) like, smelling of, or abounding in, thyme. — **lemon thyme** a species of thyme with a lemony flavour and scent; **oil of thyme** a fragrant essential oil obtained from garden and other thymes. [Fr. *thym* — L. *thȳmum* — Gr. *thȳmon*.]

thymus *thī'məs*, (*anat*) *n* a ductless gland near the root of the neck, producing white blood cells at early ages but vestigial in adult man: — *pl* **thy'mī**. — Also *adj*. — *n* **thymec'tomy** surgical removal of the thymus. — *n* **thymine** (*thī'mēn*) one of the four bases in deoxyribonucleic acids (DNA). [Gr. *thymos*, thymus gland.]

thymy. See under **thyme**.

thyratron *thī'rə-tron*, (*electronics*) *n* a gas-filled valve with heated cathode, able to carry very high currents — orig. a trademark for one containing mercury vapour. — *n* **thyristor** (*thī-ris'tər*) a thyratron-like solid-state semiconductor device.

thyroid *thī'roid*, *adj* shield-shaped; pertaining to the thyroid gland or the thyroid cartilage. — *n* the thyroid gland, a ductless gland in the neck whose overactivity may lead to goitre and swelling of the eyeballs, and whose malfunction may lead to cretinism; the principal cartilage of the larynx, forming the Adam's apple. — *n* **thyroidī'tis** inflammation of the thyroid gland. — *n* **thyrotrō'pin** or **thyrotrō'phin** a hormone, produced in the anterior lobe of the pituitary gland, which stimulates the thyroid gland. — *n* **thyrox'in** or **thyrox'ine** an iodine compound, the active component of the thyroid gland. [Gr. *thȳreoeidēs*, shield-shaped, the thyroid cartilage — *thȳreos*, a (door-shaped) shield — *thȳrā*, a door, *eidos*, form.]

thyself *dhī-self'*, (*formal*, *liturgical*, *dialect* or *archaic*) *pron* emphatic for (or usually along with) **thou** or **thee**; reflexive for **thee**. [**thee** (altered to **thy**), and **self**.]

Ti (*chem*) *symbol* for titanium.

ti *tē*, (*mus*) *n* the note below *doh* in the tonic sol-fa system, a substitute for *si*, to avoid the initial sound of *so* (*sol*). — Also (in anglicised spelling) **te**.

tiara *ti-ä'rə*, *n* a richly jewelled head-ornament worn by women; the Jewish high-priest's mitre; the pope's triple crown; the high ornamental headdress of the ancient Persians. — *adj* **tia'ra'd** or **tia'raed** wearing a tiara. [Gr. *tiārā*.]

Tibet *ti-bet'*, *n* an autonomous region in W. China, with the Himalayas in the south. — *adj* **Tibet'an** of, belonging to, or characteristic of, Tibet. — *n* the language of Tibet; a native of Tibet.

tibia *tib'i-ə*, (*anat* and *zool*) *n* the shinbone, the thicker of the two bones of the leg below the knee in humans; the corresponding bone in other vertebrates; the fourth joint of an insect's leg: — *pl* **tib'ias** or **tib'iae** (*-i-ē*). — *adj* **tib'ial**. [L. *tībia*, shinbone, flute.]

tic *tik*, *n* a convulsive (esp. nervous) motion of certain muscles, esp. of the face; an involuntary habitual response (*fig*). — **tic douloureux** (*-dol-ə-roo'*, Fr. *tēk doo-loo-rø*) a disorder of the fifth cranial nerve causing paroxysms of pain in face and forehead. [Fr.]

tich *tich*, (*colloq*) *n* a very small person; often used (with *cap*) as a nickname. — *adj* **tich'y**. [From the music-hall artist Harry Relph, known as Little *Tich*.]

tick[1] *tik*, *n* any of the larger bloodsucking mites; applied also to similar bloodsucking flies. — **tick fever** any disease transmitted by ticks. [O.E. *ticia*.]

tick[2] *tik*, *n* (the material of) the cover of a mattress; ticking. — *n* **tick'ing** the cloth of which ticks are made. [L. *thēca* — Gr. *thēkē*, a case; see **theca**.]

tick[3] *tik*, *n* the sound of a watch, clock, etc.; a beat; a moment (*colloq*); a small mark, often an angled line, used to indicate or mark off anything as checked, dealt with, required, etc. — *vi* to make a sound like a mechanical clock; to beat time. — *vt* to mark with a tick (sometimes with *off*); to measure, record, indicate (e.g. time) by a ticking sound (sometimes with *out*). — *adj* **ticked** ticked off. — *n* **tick'er** anything that ticks, esp. a telegraph instrument that prints signals on a tape, or (*slang*) a watch; the heart (*slang*). — *n* and *adj* **tick'ing**. — **tick'er-tape** paper tape on which a ticker prints; anything similar, such as a streamer (**ticker-tape welcome**, etc. a welcome, etc., esp. in New York, in which ticker-tape, confetti, etc. is thrown (through the streets) during the procession of a celebrity, etc.); **ticking-off'** (*slang*) a reprimand; **tick-tack-toe'** (*US*) noughts and crosses; **tick-tick'** a ticking; (**tick'-tick**) a child's word for a watch; **tick-tock'** a ticking, as of a big clock; (**tick'-tock**) a child's word for a clock. — **in two ticks** in a moment; **make (someone** or **something) tick** (*colloq*) to cause to operate or function; to be the driving force behind; **tick away** (of time, life, etc.) to pass away with the regularity of the ticking of a clock; **ticked off** (*US slang*) annoyed, angry; **tick off** (*slang*) to reprimand; **tick over** (of an engine) to run gently, disconnected from the transmission (*n* **tick'-over**); (of a person) to lead an inactive, uneventful existence; to function, operate (*fig*). [M.E. *tek*.]

tick[4] *tik*, (*slang*) *n* credit, delayed payment (esp. in the phrase *on tick*). [**ticket**.]

ticket *tik'it*, *n* a card or slip bearing a notice or serving as a token of any right or debt, e.g. for admission, penalty for some offence (esp. motoring), etc.; a certificate, esp. as issued to a ship's master (*slang*); discharge from the army (*slang*); a list of candidates put forward by a party for election (*US*); any or all of the principles associated with a particular political party, esp. as a basis for its election to government (*US*). — *vt* to label, designate for a particular use; to issue a ticket to. — **tick'et-collector**; **tick'et-day** the day before settling-day on the Stock Exchange, when notes of transactions completed are received; **tick'et-holder** a person possessing a ticket, e.g. for a concert or other event; **tick'et-office** a place where tickets are sold; **tick'et-punch** an instrument for punching holes in tickets. — **straight ticket** all the nominees of one political party, and no others; **that's (just) the ticket** (*slang*) that's exactly the right thing or the thing to be done. [O.Fr. *estiquet(te)* — *estiquer*, to stick — O.L.G. *stekan*; cf. **stick.**]

tickety-boo or **tickettyboo** *tik-it-i-bōō'*, (*colloq*) *adj* fine, satisfactory.

tickle *tik'l*, *vt* to excite with a pleasant thrill; to produce a disturbing feeling in (someone) by a light touch, usually tending to excite laughter, wriggling away, etc.; to amuse (*colloq*); to please (*colloq*); to touch lightly, esp. when catching fish using the hands. — *vi* to be the location of a tickling or itching feeling. — *n* an act or feeling of tickling; a slight touch. — *n* **tick'ler.** — *n* and *adj* **tick'ling.** — *adj* **tick'lish** easily tickled; unstable, precarious, difficult, critical. — *adv* **tick'lishly.** — *n* **tick'lishness.** — *adj* **tick'ly** tickling; easily tickled. — **tickle pink** or **tickle to death** (*slang*) to please or amuse very much.

tick-tack-toe. See under **tick**[3].

tid *abbrev* (in prescriptions) for *ter in die* (L.), three times a day.

tidal. See **tide.**

tidbit. See **titbit.**

tiddle *tid'l*, *vi* a child's word for urinate. — Also *n*.

tiddler *tid'lər*, *n* a small fish, e.g. a minnow or a stickleback; any very small thing or person.

tiddly *tid'li*, (*slang*) *adj* slightly drunk. — Also **tidd'ley.** [Earlier *titley*.]

tiddlywink *tid'li-wingk*, *n* any of the discs used in **tidd'lywinks,** a game in which small discs are flipped into a cup by pressing the edge of the small disc with a bigger one.

tide *tīd*, *n* ebb and flow, esp. of the sea twice daily; a time of ebbing, of flowing, or both; a sudden access or flood of feeling, etc.; a time or season; a festival; a trend. — In combination signifying a time or season. — *vt* (esp. *fig*) to carry by, or as if by, the tide. — *vi* to run like the tides. — *adj* **tīd'al** of, depending on, or regulated by, the tide; flowing and ebbing. — *adj* **tide'less.** — **tidal power** (the generation of electricity by harnessing) the energy of tidal flows; **tidal wave** a huge wave caused by the tides; a huge wave started by an earthquake and running at great speed; **tide'mark** a line on the shore made by the tide at the water's highest point; a mark of the limit of washing (*jocular fig*); **tide'-table** a table of the times of high tide; **tide'-water** water brought by the tides; river water affected by the tides (*US*); coastal land, seaboard (*US*); **tide'way** a track followed by the tide, esp. a channel through which there is a strong current or tide. — **tide over** to carry (someone) over, or enable (someone) to surmount, difficulties, for the time being. [O.E. *tīd*.]

tidings *tī'dingz*, (esp. *literary*) *npl* news. [Late O.E. *tīdung* — O.E. *tīdan*, to happen, or — O.N. *tīthindi*, events, tidings.]

tidy *tī'di*, *adj* trim; orderly; neat; fairly good or big (*colloq*). — *n* a receptacle for odd scraps; a cover for a chair-back. — *vt* to make neat and tidy; to clear away for the sake of tidiness: — *pr p* **tī'dying**; *pa t* and *pa p* **tī'died.** — *adv* **tī'dily.** — *n* **tī'diness.** [**tide**; cf. Ger. *zeitig*.]

tie *tī*, *vt* to bind; to fasten; to knot; to restrict, restrain; to unite; to mark with a curved line indicating that a note, etc. is to be sustained, not repeated (*mus*); to perform in this way (*mus*); to oblige; to equal in competition, etc. — *vi* to be equal in votes, score, etc.: — *pr p* **ty'ing**; *pa t* and *pa p* **tied** (*tīd*). — *n* a knot, bow, etc.; a bond (*lit* or *fig*); a string, ribbon, etc. for tying; a band of material passed under the collar of a shirt, etc. and tied under the chin, esp. one having one end wider than the other, tied to hang down the shirt front with the wider end overlying the narrower, worn esp. by men, or as part of a uniform; a railway sleeper (*US*); a restraint; an obligation; a mode of tying; an equality in score, votes, etc.; a match, esp. one at any stage of a tournament in which the losers are eliminated; a curved line drawn over notes of the same pitch to be performed as one, sustained not repeated (*mus*). — *adj* **tied** having been tied; having a draw or equality as a result; (of a public house or garage) denoting one whose tenant is obliged to get his or her supplies from one particular brewer or distiller, or oil and petrol producer; (of a house, cottage, etc.) denoting one whose tenant may occupy the premises only as long as he or she is employed by the owner. — *adj* **tie'less.** — *n* **tī'er** a person who ties. — **tie'-beam** a beam connecting the lower ends of rafters to prevent their moving apart; **tie'-break** a number of points played at the end of a tied set to decide the winner (*tennis*); generally, a situation in a contest when a tie-breaker is required to decide the winner; **tie'-breaker** a tie-break; any game(s), question(s) or competition(s) intended to break a tie and decide a winner; **tie'-clip** an ornamental clip which attaches one's tie to one's shirt; **tie-dye'ing** a method of hand-dyeing textiles in which parts of the material are bound or knotted so as to resist the dye (also **tie-and-dye'**); **tie'-in** a connection; something, esp. a book, which ties in with something else, e.g. a film or TV programme; **tie'-pin** an ornamental pin stuck in a necktie; **tie'-up** a standstill; an entanglement; a connection; a business association. — **tie down** to fix (*lit* and *fig*); to bind by conditions, etc.; **tie in with** or **tie up with** to agree with; to be closely associated with; to be linked with, as for example a book containing the story of, or a story concerning the characters in, a popular film or TV series; **tie up** to parcel up with string; to tie so as to remain up, hanging, etc.; to tether, secure or bind, by tying; to moor; to invest, make illiquid (funds, etc.); to secure against squandering, alienation, etc., or restrict the use of, by conditions. [O.E. *tēah*, band, string, *tīgan*, to tie.]

tier *tēr*, *n* a row, rank or layer, esp. one of several placed one above another. — *vt* to pile in tiers. [O.Fr. *tire*, sequence.]

tierce *tērs*, *n* one-third of a pipe (of wine), approx. 35 British or 42 U.S. gallons; a cask or vessel of that capacity; (*tûrs*) a sequence of three cards of the same suit; a third (*mus*); the note two octaves and a third above a given note (*mus*). — *adj* **tiercé** (*tēr'si*; Fr., divided into three parts) (of the surface of a shield) divided into three equal parts, each of a different metal or colour (*heraldry*). — *n* (in horse-racing) a system of betting by which the first, second and third horses must be named in the right order, or a race for which this system obtains. [O.Fr. *tiers*, *tierce* — L. *tertia* (*pars*).]

tiercel. See **tercel.**

tiff *tif*, *n* a slight quarrel. — *vi* to be in a huff; to squabble.

Tiffany *tif'ə-ni*, *adj* denoting objects designed or produced by C.L. *Tiffany* (1812–1902), founder of the New York jeweller's, Tiffany and Co., or (esp.) his son L.C. Tiffany (1848–1933), Art Nouveau designer. — **Tiffany glass** another name for **favrile** (q.v.); **Tiffany lamp** a lamp with a distinctive umbrella-shaped shade made of favrile.

tiffany *tif'ə-ni*, *n* a silk-like gauze. — *adj* of tiffany; transparent. [Gr. *theophaneia*, theophany, or *diaphaneia*, transparency.]

tiffin *tif'in*, *n* (esp. as used by the British Raj in colonial India) lunch, a light meal.

tig *tig*, *n* a touch; a game in which someone who is the chaser or 'it' seeks to touch another whom he or she chases. — *vt* to touch, esp. in the game of tig.

tiger *tī'gər*, *fem* **ti'gress,** *n* a fierce, yellowish, black-striped Asiatic animal, one of the two largest cats; a ferocious or bloodthirsty person; a formidable opponent or competitor. — *adj* **ti'gerish** or **ti'grish** like a tiger in manner, esp. fierce-tempered. — *adj* **ti'gerly.** — *adj* **ti'gery, ti'grine** (*-grīn*) or **ti'groid**

like a tiger. — **ti'ger-cat** a general name for a middle-sized striped or spotted wild cat — margay, ocelot, serval, etc.; **tiger country** (*golf slang*) dense rough; **tiger lily** a lily with black-spotted orange flowers; **tiger moth** any one of a family of moths with long and usu. brightly coloured wings; **tiger shark** a voracious striped shark of the Indian Ocean; **tiger snake** the most deadly of Australian snakes, brown with black crossbands. [Fr. *tigre* — L. *tigris* — Gr. *tigris*.]

tight *tīt*, *adj* close; compact; close-fitting; too close-fitting; cramped; (of a schedule, timetable, etc.) allowing little space, time or opportunity for deviation from plan; (of a situation) difficult or dangerous; (of a contest) closely fought; (of style) concise; taut, not slack; (of e.g. control) very firm, strict; precise; under control; firmly fixed; trim, neat; hampered or characterised by lack of money; (of money) scarce, hard to obtain; unwilling to part with money, miserly (*colloq*); intoxicated (*colloq*). — *adv* tightly; soundly, completely. — (In combination) **-tight** signifying proof, imperviousness, against something specified. — *vt* and *vi* **tight'en** (sometimes with *up*) to make or grow tight or tighter. — *n* **tight'ener** a person or thing that tightens. — *adj* **tight'ish**. — *adv* **tight'ishly**. — *adv* **tight'ly**. — *n* **tight'ness**. — *npl* **tights** a close-fitting garment, often made of nylon, covering the lower part of the body and the legs, esp. as worn by women and girls as an alternative to stockings; close-fitting men's breeches (*hist*). — **tight end** (*Am football*) a player who is positioned at the outside of the offensive line. — *adj* **tight-fist'ed** (*colloq*) stingy. — *adj* **tight-knit'** or **tightly-knit'** close-knit; closely integrated; tightly organised. — *adj* **tight'-lipped** uncommunicative. — **tight'rope** a taut rope or wire on which feats of balancing and acrobatics are performed; a middle course between dangerous or undesirable alternatives (*fig*); **tight'wad** a skinflint, miser. — **a tight corner** a difficult situation; **run a tight ship** to be in control of an efficient, well-run organisation or group; **tighten the screws** to increase pressure (esp. on someone to do something). [Earlier *thight*, app. from an older form of O.N. *thēttr*.]

tigon *tī'gon*, *n* the offspring of a tiger and a lioness. — Also **tīg'lon**. [*tiger* and *lion*.]

tigress, tigrine, tigrish, tigroid. See under **tiger**.

tike. See **tyke**.

tiki *tik'ē*, *n* an image, often in the form of a small greenstone ornament, representing an ancestor — in some Polynesian cultures, worn as an amulet or charm. [Maori.]

tikka *tik'ə*, (*Ind cookery*) *adj* marinated in yogurt and spices and cooked in a *tandoor* or clay oven, e.g. *chicken tikka, lamb tikka*.

tilapia *ti-lap'i-ə* or *-lā'pi-ə*, *n* any member of an African freshwater genus (*Tilapia*) of edible fishes including the angel-fish. [N.L.]

tilde *til'dā, -di, -də* or *tild*, *n* the diacritical sign over *n* in Spanish to indicate the sound *ny* — thus *ñ* (as in *cañon*); used in Portuguese over *a* and *o* to indicate nasalisation. [Sp. — L. *titulus*, a title.]

tile *tīl*, *n* a slab of baked clay (or a substitute) for covering roofs, floors, etc.; a tube-shaped piece of baked clay used in pipes for drains; a piece in the board-game of mah-jongg; tiling, a tiled area. — *vt* to cover with tiles; to drain by means of tiles. — *adj* **tiled** covered with tiles. — *n* **ti'ler**. — *n* **til'ery** a place where tiles are made. — *n* **til'ing**. — **have a tile loose** (*slang*) to be a little mad; **hung tiles** tiles hung vertically, covering a wall; **on the tiles** at play, having a wild time. [O.E. *tigele* — L. *tēgula* — *tegĕre*, to cover.]

till[1] *til*, *n* a drawer or receptacle for money in or behind a counter. [Cf. M.E. *tillen*, to draw, O.E. *fortyllan*, to draw aside, seduce.]

till[2] *til*, *prep* up to the time of. — *conj* up to the time when. [O.E. (Northumbrian) *til* — O.N. *til*.]

till[3] *til*, *vt* to work (land), cultivate. — *adj* **till'able** arable. — *n* **till'age** the act or practice of tilling; husbandry; a place tilled. — *n* **till'er**. — *n* **till'ing**. [O.E. *tilian*, to aim at, till — *till*, limit.]

till[4] *til*, *n* a stiff impervious clay; boulder-clay (*geol*); shale (*mining*).

tiller[1] *til'ər*, *n* the handle or lever for turning a rudder. — **till'er-chain** or **-rope** the chain or rope connecting the tiller with the steering-wheel. [M.E. *tillen*, to draw, or O.Fr. *telier*, crossbow stock — L.L. *tēlārium*, a weaver's beam — L. *tēla*, a web.]

tiller[2] *til'ər*, *n* a sapling; a shoot from a tree stump; a sucker from the base of a stem. [O.E. *telgor*, shoot, twig.]

tiller[3]. See **till[3]**.

tilt *tilt*, *vi* to lean, heel over; to slope; (of a ship) to pitch; to slant, esp. in a vertical plane; to joust; to charge, attack (with *at*; *lit* or *fig*). — *vt* to incline, slant; to tip out by tilting; to move by tilting; to forge using a tilt-hammer. — *n* an act of tilting; a condition of being tilted; a slope; a joust; an encounter, attack, etc. — *adj* **tilt'able**. — *n* **tilt'er**. — *n* **tilt'ing**. — **tilt'-hammer** a heavy pivoted hammer lifted by a cam, used in forging. — **full tilt** at full speed, headlong. [O.E. *tealt*, tottering.]

tilth *tilth*, *n* cultivation; cultivated land; the depth of soil turned up in cultivation. [From **till[3]**.]

Tim. (*Bible*) *abbrev* for (the Letters to) Timothy.

timbal or **tymbal** *tim'bl*, *n* a kettledrum. — *n* **timbale** (*tē-bal*, *tam'bal* or *tim'bl*) a dish of meat, fish, etc. cooked in a cup-shaped mould or shell; a pastry mould. [Fr. *timbale*.]

timber *tim'bər*, *n* wood suitable for building or carpentry, whether growing or cut; a beam or large piece of wood in the framework of e.g. a house, ship, etc.; woodland, forest-land (*US*). — *adj* of timber; wooden. — *vt* to provide with timber or beams. — *interj* a warning given when a tree being felled is about to fall. — *adj* **tim'bered** built, constructed, esp. of wood; provided with timber; wooded. — *n* **tim'bering** timber collectively. — **half-timbered** see under **half**; **tim'ber-head** the top of a ship's timber rising above the deck and used as a bollard; **tim'ber-line** the upper limit of trees on the mountains; **tim'ber-tree** a tree suitable or grown for timber; **tim'ber-wolf** an American variety of the common wolf, the grey wolf; **tim'ber-yard** a yard or place where timber is stored or sold. [O.E. *timber*, building, wood, *timbrian*, to build.]

timbre *tēbr'*, *tim'bər* or *tam'bər*, *n* the quality of a sound, tone-colour, as opp. to pitch and loudness. [O.Fr., bell — L. *tympanum*, a drum.]

timbrel *tim'brəl*, (*hist*; esp. *Bible*) *n* an Oriental tabor or tambourine. [O.Fr. *timbre* — L. *tympanum*, drum.]

time *tīm*, *n* a concept arising from change experienced and observed, expressed by past, present and future, and often measured by the amount of turning of the earth on its axis; (with *cap*) any of the clock-settings used as standard times in the various time zones, as in *Pacific Time, Central European Time*, etc.; a moment at which, or stretch of existence in which, things happen; season; the due, appointed, usual occasion of occurrence; the hour of death or of birth or coming into existence; a spell, interval, period; the actual occasion or period of being something or somewhere, e.g. of apprenticeship, residence, sentence, student days, life, etc.; (a given period in) the existence of the world; leisure or opportunity long enough for a purpose; a spell of exciting, usually pleasurable, experience; the duration, or shortest duration, of performance, as in a race; rhythm, tempo; rate of speed; an occasion; an occasion regarded as one of a recurring series; one of a number of multiplied instances; generalised as an indication of multiplication (e.g. 3 *times* = multiplied by 3); (the rate of) payment for work by the hour, day, etc.; past existence; an allotted period, esp. its completion, as in boxing rounds, permitted drinking hours, etc.; the call, bell, whistle, buzzer, or other signal announcing this; (in *pl*) the contemporary, pertaining conditions; (in *pl*; with *cap*) often the name of a newspaper; (with *cap*) a personification of time, a bald-headed old man with a forelock, a beard, a scythe, and often an hourglass. — *vt* to arrange, fix, or choose a time for; to mark, measure, adjust or observe the rhythm or time of; to ascertain the time of; to regulate as to time. — *vi* to keep or beat time. — *adj* of or pertaining to time; reckoned by time; timed; of or for a future time. — *interj* indicating that time is up, or that an activity is now forbidden or permitted. — *adj* **timed**. — *adj* **time'less** independent of time; unconnected with the passage of time; eternal, unaffected by time. — *adv* **time'lessly**. — *n* **time'lessness**. — *n* **time'liness**. — *adj* **time'ly** in good time, early; seasonable; well-timed. — *adv* early, soon; in due time or in good time. — *n* **tīm'er** a person or thing that times anything; a clocklike device which sets something off or switches something on or off at a pre-set time. — In combination signifying a person who belongs to, works for, etc. a specified time. — *n* **tim'ing** fixing, choosing, adjusting, ascertaining or recording of times; (the co-ordination of) departure and arrival times; co-ordination in time. — *adj* **time'-barred** disallowed because out of legal time limits. — **time'-bomb** a bomb that is exploded by a time-fuse; a routine activated at a particular time or date which destroys data held in a computer program; **time capsule** a capsule containing objects, etc. representative of the current time, buried in the ground or set in the foundations of a building for discovery at a future date; **time'-card** a card for use with a time-clock; **time'-clock** a clocklike apparatus which stamps on cards the time of arrival and departure of e.g. office or factory workers; **time code** a track separate from the main one on a video or audio tape, on which time is recorded digitally, to help editing. — *adj* **time'-consuming** requiring much, or too much, time. — **time deposit** a bank deposit from which withdrawals may be made only after a certain time or with due notice; **time'-fuse** a fuse contrived to act at a definite time. — *adj* **time'-honoured** (of a custom) honoured or respected on account of antiquity. — **time'keeper** a clock, watch, or other instrument that measures time; a person who keeps account of workmen's hours; a person who beats or observes time; **time lag** the interval of delay between two connected events or phenomena. — *adj* **time'-lapse** of or relating to **time-lapse photography**, a method of recording and condensing long or slow processes by taking a large number of photographs at regular spaced intervals, the film made from these being projected at normal speed. — **time limit** a time within which something has to be done; **time'-machine** a hypothetical machine by which one may travel to the future or past, through time; **time out** a short break during a sporting contest (e.g. *Am football*) for rest, discussion of tactics, substitution of a player, etc.; any similar short suspension of activity; **time'piece** a piece of machinery for keeping time, esp. one that does not strike but is bigger than a watch. — *n* and *adj* **time'-saving**. — **time'scale** the time envisaged for the carrying out of (the stages of) a project; a statement of the times of occurrence, completion, etc. of a series of events, stages, etc. — *adj* **time'-served** having completed one's apprenticeship, fully trained. — **time'-server** a person who selfishly shapes his or her opinions to the times or those in authority for the time; **time'-service**. — *n* and *adj* **time'-serving**. — **time'-share** the time-sharing of property, etc.; such a property. — Also *adj*. — **time'-sharer**; **time'-sharing** the optimum utilisation of a computer and its peripheral devices whereby the differential processing-time of each machine is allowed for, and is used accordingly; a scheme by which a person buys the right to use a holiday home for the same specified period of time each year for a specified number of years; **time sheet** a record of the time worked by a person; **time signal** an intimation of the exact time given by radio or otherwise from an observatory; **time signature** (*mus*) an indication of rhythm at the beginning of a line or wherever there is a change; **time slot** a particular period of time in the day or week allocated to a certain radio or television programme; a particular period assigned to a certain purpose, etc.; **time switch** one that works automatically at a set time; **time'table** a table of times, e.g. of classes, events, trains, etc. — *vt* to insert into a timetable; to plan, divide into sessions, etc. according to a timetable. — **time trial** an event, esp. in cycling, in which competitors set off one at a time, and attempt to cover a set distance in the shortest time; **time warp** (in science fiction, etc.) a hypothetical distortion in the time continuum, allowing one to pass from the present to the past or future, or to stand still in the present. — *adj* **time'-worn** worn or decayed by time. — **time zone** one of 24 longitudinal divisions of the globe, each 15° wide, having a standard time throughout its area; a similar zone adapted to a particular country. — **against time** with the aim or necessity of finishing by a certain time; **ahead of one's time** having ideas, etc. too advanced or progressive to be acceptable at the time; **ahead of time** earlier than expected; **all in good time** in due course; soon enough; **at one time** formerly; simultaneously; **at the same time** simultaneously; notwithstanding; **at the time** at the time stated or under consideration; **at times** at relatively distant intervals; occasionally; **before one's time** ahead of one's time (see above); **behind the times** not abreast of changes; **behind time** late; **between times** in the intervals; **common time** (*mus*) time with two beats or a multiple of two beats to a bar or other measure; **do time** (*slang*) to serve a sentence of imprisonment; **for a time** for a while; temporarily; **for the time being** at the present time or the actual time in question; **from time to time** now and then; **gain time** to provide oneself with more time to do something (e.g. by delaying something else); **half the time** (*colloq*) as often as not, frequently; **have a good time** to enjoy oneself; **have a time of it** (*colloq*) to experience problems, difficulties, etc.; **have little (or no) time for** to have little (or no) interest in or patience with; **in good time** quite early enough; with some time to spare; **in one's own (or own good) time** at a time, rate, etc. of one's own choosing; **in one's own time** in one's spare time, when not at work; **in one's time** at some past time in one's life, esp. when one was at one's peak; **in time** after a lapse of time; early enough; eventually; keeping rhythm; **keep time** to run accurately, like a clock (also **keep good time**); to move or perform in the same rhythm; to record times of workmen, etc.; **know the time of day** to know the state of affairs, what is going on; to know what one is about, or the best way of doing something; **local time** time reckoned from the local meridian; **lose time** (of e.g. a clock) to run down; to fall behindhand; to let time pass without full advantage; **make good time** to make speedy progress; **make time** to regain lost time; to find an opportunity; **not before time** none too soon; about time too!; **no time** or **no time at all** a very short time; **on (or upon) a time** at a time in the past (usu. imaginary); **on time** punctual, in accordance with time limits; punctually; **out of time** not keeping rhythm; too late (*law*); **solar time** time reckoned by the sun; **standard time** a system of time adopted for a wide area instead of local time — usually Greenwich mean time or a time differing from it by a whole number of hours; **take one's time** (*colloq*) not to hurry, to dawdle; **take time off** (or in U.S. **take time out**) to find time to do something, or time for an activity; **the time of one's life** a very enjoyable time; **time after time** or **time and again** repeatedly; **time and motion study** an investigation of the motions performed and time taken in industrial, etc. work, with a view to increased efficiency and thus production; **time of day** the time by the clock; the point of time reached; a greeting, salutation; **time out of mind** during the whole time within human memory, from time immemorial; **time was** there once was a time (when); **time-zone disease** or **fatigue** jet lag; **triple time** (*mus*) three beats, or three times three beats, to a bar or other measure; **up to time** punctual, punctually; not later than the due time. [O.E. *tīma*.]

timid *tim'id*, *adj* inclined to fear; lacking courage, faint-hearted. — *n* **timid'ity**. — *adv* **tim'idly**. — *n* **tim'idness**. — *adj* **tim'orous** (-*ər-əs*) timid. — *adv* **tim'orously**. — *n* **tim'orousness**. [L. *timidus*, timid, *timor*, -*ōris*, fear — *timēre*, to fear.]

timing. See under **time**.

timocracy *tī-mok'rə-si*, *n* a form of government in which property is a qualification for office; one in which ambition or desire of honour is a ruling principle. — *adj* **timocratic** (-*ō-krat'ik*) or **timocrat'ical**. [Gr. *tīmokratiā* — *tīmē*, honour, *krateein*, to rule.]

timorous, etc. See under **timid**.

timothy *tim'ə-thi*, *n* (in full **tim'othy-grass**) a grass valued for feeding cattle. [*Timothy* Hanson, who promoted its cultivation in America about 1720.]

timpano or **tympano** *timp'ə-nō*, *n* an orchestral kettledrum: — *pl* **timp'ani** or **tymp'ani** (-*nē*), often shortened to **timps** (*colloq*). — *n* **timp'anist** or **tymp'anist** a person who plays timpani. [It.; see **tympanum**.]

tin *tin*, *n* a silvery-white, easily fusible, malleable metal (symbol **Sn** (for L. *stannum*); atomic no. 50); a vessel of tin or tin-plate, a can, etc.; a tinful; a strip of tin along the lower boundary of the playable area of the front wall of a squash court. — *adj* made of tin or tin-plate or (*colloq*) of corrugated iron. — *vt* to coat or overlay with tin or tinfoil; to cover thinly with solder before soldering; to pack in tins: — *pr p* **tinn'ing**; *pa t* and *pa p* **tinned**. — *n* **tin'ful**: — *pl* **tin'fuls**. — *adj* **tinned**. — *n* **tinn'er** a tinsmith; a tin-miner; a canner. — *n* **tinn'ing**. — *adj* **tinn'y** like tin, esp. in sound, thus cheap, insubstantial, etc.; lucky (*Austr* and *NZ colloq*). — *n* (*slang*) (also **tinn'ie**) a mug made of tin-plate; a can of beer (*Austr*). — **tin'foil** tin or (now) tin-lead alloy (or aluminium) in thin sheets, as used for wrapping; **tin hat** (*slang*) a military steel helmet; **tin'horn** (orig. and esp. *US*) a flashy, small-time gambler; a cheap, pretentious, second-rate person. — Also *adj*. — **tin'-opener** a kitchen instrument for cutting open tins of food, etc.; **tin'-plate** thin sheet-iron or steel coated with tin. — Also *adj*. — *adj* **tin'pot** paltry, rubbishy. — **tin'smith** a worker in tin; **tin'snips** a pair of hand-shears for cutting sheet metal, esp. tin plate; **tin'stone** cassiterite, a brown tin dioxide; **tin'ware** articles made of tin; **tin whistle** a cheap six-holed metal flageolet. — **put the tin hat** (or **lid**) **on** to finish off, bring to an end, cap, suppress; **Tin Pan Alley** orig., a nickname for 28th Street, New York, the centre of the song-publishing district; the popular music publishing district of a city; the realm of popular music production. [O.E.]

tinamou *tin'ə-mo͞o*, *n* a South American partridge-like bird. [Fr., — Galibi (Indian language of French Guiana) *tinamu*.]

tinct *tingkt*, *n* a tint; a tinge. — *adj* **tinctō'rial** of dyeing. — *n* **tinct'ure** a tinge or shade of colour; a colouring matter; a metal, colour or fur (*heraldry*); a quality or slight taste added to anything; an alcoholic solution of a drug (*med*). — *vt* to tinge; to imbue. [L. *tingĕre*, *tinctum*, to dye; cf. **tint**, **tinge**.]

tinder *tin'dər*, *n* dry inflammable matter, esp. that used for kindling fire from a spark. — *adj* **tin'dery** easily angered. — **tin'der-box** a box for tinder, and usu. flint and steel. [O.E. *tynder*.]

tine *tīn*, *n* a spike or point, as of a fork, harrow, or deer's horn. — *adj* **tīned**. [O.E. *tind*.]

tinea *tin'i-ə*, *n* ringworm; any of several skin diseases caused by fungi. — *adj* **tineid** (*tin-ē'id*) of or pertaining to the family *Tineidae* or genus *Tinea* of small moths. — *n* an individual tineid moth. [L. *tinea*, moth, bookworm, etc.]

ting *ting*, *vt* and *vi* to ring. — *n* the sound of a small bell. — *n* **ting'-a-ling** a ringing or tinkling. — Also *adv*. [Imit.]

tinge *tinj*, *vt* to tint or colour; to suffuse; to impart a slight modification to: — *pr p* **ting'ing**. — *n* a slight colouring or modification. [L. *tingĕre*, *tinctum*.]

tingle *ting'gl*, *vi* to feel, or be the location of a thrilling sensation; to thrill; to throb; to vibrate. — *vt* to cause to tingle. — *n* a tingling sensation. — *n* and *adj* **ting'ling**. — *adj* **ting'ly** tingling. [M.E. *tinglen*, a variant of *tinklen*.]

tinhorn. See under **tin**.

tinier, etc. See under **tiny**.

tink *tingk*, *n* a clear high-pitched short bell-like sound. — *vt* and *vi* to sound in this way. — *vi* **tink'le** to make small, bell-like sounds; to jingle; to clink repeatedly or continuously; (esp. of water) to go with tinkling sounds. — *vt* to cause to tinkle; to ring. — *n* a sound of tinkling. — *n* **tink'ler**. — *n* and *adj* **tink'ling**. — *adv* **tink'lingly**. — *adj* **tink'ly**. — **give someone a tinkle** (*slang*) to call someone on the telephone. [M.E. *tinken*, to tink.]

tinker *tingk'ər*, *n* an itinerant mender of kettles, pans, etc.; a botcher or bungler; a rascal (*colloq*); a gypsy (esp. *Scot* or *Ir*). — *vi* to do a tinker's work; (often with *with*) to botch, potter, patch up, adjust or deal with in trivial and often ultimately unsuccessful ways. — *n* **tink'ering**. — **not give a tinker's curse** or **damn** not to care. [M.E. *tinkere*, tinker.]

tinkle. See under **tink**.

tinnie or **tinny**. See under **tin**.

tinnitus *ti-nī'təs* or *tin'i-təs*, *n* a medical condition of constant ringing or other noise in the ears. [L. *tinnītus*, -*ūs*, a jingling — *tinnīre*, to ring.]

tinsel *tin'sl*, *n* thin glittering metallic sheets or spangles, as used to decorate Christmas trees; anything showy, but of little value. — *adj* of or like tinsel; gaudy. — *vt* to adorn with, or as with, tinsel; to make glittering or gaudy: — *pr p* **tin'selling**; *pa t* and *pa p* **tin'selled**. — *adj* **tin'selly** like tinsel, gaudy, showy. [O.Fr. *estincelle* — L. *scintilla*, a spark.]

tint *tint*, *n* a colour, shade; a slight tinge distinct from the principal colour; a hue mixed with white; a series of parallel lines or rows of dots in engraving or printing, producing a uniform shading. — *vt* to colour slightly; to tinge. — *vi* to take on a tint. — *n* **tint'er** a person or thing that tints. — *n* **tint'ing**. [L. *tinctus*; cf. **tinct** and **tinge**.]

tintinnabulate *tin-tin-ab'ū-lāt*, *vi* (esp. of bells) to ring. — *adj* **tintinnab'ulant**, **tintinnab'ular** or **tintinnab'ulary**. — *n* **tintinnabulā'tion** bell-ringing. — *adj* **tintinnab'ulous**. — *n* **tintinnab'ulum** a bell: — *pl* **tintinnab'ula**. [L. *tintinnabulum*, a bell — *tintinnāre*, to jingle, reduplicated from *tinnīre*, to jingle.]

tiny *tī'ni*, *adj* (*compar* **ti'nier**, *superl* **ti'niest**) very small. — *n* **ti'niness**.

tip[1] *tip*, *n* a slender extremity; the furthest part. — *vt* to put a tip on; to be the tip of; to remove the tip from: — *pr p* **tipp'ing**; *pa t* and *pa p* **tipped**. — *adj* **tipped**. — *n* **tipp'ing**. — **on the tip of one's tongue**

almost, but not (yet) quite, remembered; on the very point of being spoken. [Cf. O.N. *typpa*, to tip.]

tip[2] *tip*, *vt* to strike lightly but definitely; to hit glancingly: — *pr p* **tipp'ing**; *pa t* and *pa p* **tipped**. — *n* a tap, light blow or impact. [Cf. Du. and Ger. *tippen*, Sw. *tippa*, to tip.]

tip[3] *tip*, *vt* to give, hand, pass, convey; to give a tip to; to indicate. — *vi* to give tips: — *pr p* **tipp'ing**; *pa p* and *pa t* **tipped**. — *n* a gratuity; a hint or piece of special information supposed to be useful (e.g. in betting, examinations, etc.); a trick or dodge. — *n* **tipp'er**. — *n* **tipp'ing**. — *n* **tip'ster** a person who makes a living by providing tips. — **tip'-off** a hint, warning, piece of secret information (e.g. about a crime). — **tip off** to give a tip-off to; **tip someone the wink** to convey a secret tip. [Perh. conn. with **tip**[2]; orig. criminal jargon.]

tip[4] *tip*, *vt* to throw down; to upset; to tilt; to shoot, dump, empty (out), by tilting; to toss (off). — *vi* to topple (over); to tilt: — *pr p* **tipp'ing**; *pa p* and *pa t* **tipped**. — *n* a tilt; a place for tipping rubbish, coal, etc.; a dump; an extremely untidy place (*colloq*). — *n* **tipp'er** a person or thing that tips; a lorry or truck, the body of which can be tipped up for unloading (also *adj*). — *n* **tipp'ing**. — *adj* **tip'-up** constructed so as to allow of being tilted. — **tip one's hat** to raise, tilt, or touch the brim of, one's hat as a polite greeting; **tip the balance** or **tip the scale** (or **scales**) to make more, or less, favourable to someone; to be the deciding factor in a result; **tip the scale** (or **scales**) to depress one end of the scales; to weigh (with *at*). [M.E. *type*.]

tippet *tip'it*, *n* a long band of cloth or fur; a shoulder cape, esp. of fur; an animal's ruff of hair or feathers.

Tipp-Ex® or (erroneously) **Tippex** *tip'eks*, *n* correcting fluid, usu. white, for covering over mistakes in typing or writing. — Also *vt* (often with *out*).

tipple *tip'l*, *vt* and *vi* to drink constantly in small quantities; to booze. — *n* liquor tippled. — *n* **tipp'ler**. [Cf. Norw. dialect *tipla*, to drip slowly.]

tipstaff *tip'stäf*, *n* a staff tipped with metal; an officer who carries it, a sheriff's officer: — *pl* **tip'staffs** or **tip'staves** (*-stāvz*). [**tip**[1] and **staff**.]

tipster. See under **tip**[3].

tipsy *tip'si*, *adj* partially intoxicated. — *vt* **tip'sify** to make tipsy. — *adv* **tip'sily**. — *n* **tip'siness**. — **tipsy cake** a cake made of pastry and almonds, with wine.

tiptoe *tip'tō*, *n* the end of the toe or toes, more often merely the toes. — *adv* on tiptoe (*lit* or *fig*) through excitement, expectation, etc. — *vi* to walk on tiptoe, to go lightly and stealthily: — *pr p* **tip'toeing**; *pa t* and *pa p* **tip'toed**. [**tip**[1] and **toe**.]

tiptop *tip-top'*, *n* the extreme top; the height of excellence. — *adj* of the highest excellence. — Also *adv*. [**tip**[1] and **top**[1].]

TIR *abbrev* for *Transports Internationaux Routiers* (Fr.), International Road Transport, a haulage organisation.

tirade *ti-rād'* or *tī-rād'*, *n* a long vehement harangue; a string of abuse. [Fr., — It. *tirata* — *tirare*, to pull.]

tire[1] *tīr*, *n* a metal hoop to bind a wheel; a *US* spelling of **tyre**. — *adj* **tired**. — *adj* **tire'less**. — *n* **tir'ing**. [Archaic *tire*, a headdress — M.E., aphetic for **attire**.]

tire[2] *tīr*, *vi* to become weary; to have one's interest or patience exhausted or worn down. — *vt* to weary, fatigue; to bore; to wear out. — *adj* **tired** fatigued; wearied, bored (with *of*); showing deterioration through time or wear — e.g. limp, grubby. — *n* **tired'ness**. — *adj* **tire'less** untiring. — *adv* **tire'lessly**. — *n* **tire'lessness**. — *adj* **tire'some** fatiguing; wearisome, boring; tedious; (*loosely*) irritating, troublesome, irksome. — *adv* **tire'somely**. — *n* **tire'someness**. — *adj* **tir'ing**. [App. O.E. *tīorian*, to be tired.]

tiro *tī'rō*, (also **ty'ro**) *n* beginner; a novice: — *pl* **ti'ros** (also **ty'roes** or **ti'roes**). [L. *tīrō*, *-ōnis*, a recruit.]

'tis *tiz*, a contraction of **it is**.

tisane *ti-zan'*, *n* a medicinal infusion, e.g. of herbs. [See **ptisan**.]

'tisn't *tiz'nt*, a contraction of **it is not**.

tissue *tish'o͞o*, *-ū* or *tis'ū*, *n* anything woven, esp. a rich or gauzy fabric; an aggregate of similar cells, flesh (*biol*); a fabric, mass or collection (e.g. of lies or nonsense); tissue-paper; (a piece of) soft, absorbent paper, as used for handkerchiefs, etc. — *vt* to weave or interweave, esp. with gold or silver thread; to clothe, cover, or adorn with tissue. — **tissue culture** the growing of detached pieces of (plant or animal) tissue in nutritive fluids; a piece so grown; **tiss'ue-paper** a thin, soft, semitransparent paper, as used for tracing, wrapping, etc.; **tiss'ue-typing** the determination of body tissue types, e.g. to ensure compatibility between the donor and the recipient in transplant surgery. [Fr. *tissu*, woven, past p. of *tître* (O.Fr. *tistre*) — L. *texĕre*, to weave.]

tiswas or **tizwas** *tiz'woz*, (*slang*) *n* a tizzy, flap, state of excitement, commotion. [Conn. with **tizzy, tizz**.]

tit[1] *tit*, *n* a variant of **teat**; (usu. in *pl*) a female breast (*vulg*) — also **titt'y**; a contemptible person (*vulg*).

tit[2] *tit*: **tit for tat** an eye for an eye, retaliation in kind (*adj* **tit-for-tat'**); a hat — usu. shortened to **tit'fer** (*cockney rhyming slang*).

tit[3] *tit*, *n* a titmouse (q.v.). [Icel. *tittr*, titmouse.]

Titan *tī'tən*, (*Gr mythol*) *n* a son (or daughter **Tī'taness**) or other descendant of the gods Uranus and Gaea; one of the elder gods and goddesses overthrown by Zeus; Helios, the sun-god; Saturn's largest satellite; (without *cap*) anything gigantic; (without *cap*) a man of great intellect but not the highest inspiration. — *adj* **Tītanesque** (*-esk'*). — *adj* **Tītā'nian**. — *adj* **Titanic** or **titanic** (*tī-* or *ti-tan'ik*). [Gr. *Tītān*.]

titanium *ti-* or *tī-tā'ni-əm*, *n* a metallic element (symbol **Ti**; atomic no. 22), strong, light and corrosion-resistant. — *n* **titanate** (*tī'tən-āt*) a salt of titanic acid. — *adj* **tītanic** (*-tan'ik*) of quadrivalent titanium (**titanic acid** H_2TiO_3). — *adj* **tītanif'erous** containing titanium. — *n* **tī'tanite** a brown, green or yellow mineral, composed of calcium silicate and titanate. — *adj* **tī'tanous** of trivalent titanium. — **titanium dioxide** a pure white powder (TiO_2) of high opacity, used esp. as a pigment; **titanium white** titanium dioxide used as pigment. [Gr. *Tītān*, Titan, on the analogy of **uranium**.]

titbit *tit'bit*, *n* a choice delicacy or item. — Also (esp. in U.S.) **tid'bit**.

titch, titchy. Alternative spellings of **tich, tichy**.

titer. See under **titrate**.

titfer. See under **tit**[2].

tithe or **tythe** *tīdh*, *n* a tenth part, an indefinitely small part; the tenth of the produce of land and stock allotted originally for church purposes; any levy or fee of one-tenth. — *vt* to take a tithe of or from; to pay a tithe on. — *adj* **tith'able** subject to the payment of tithes. — *adj* **tithed**. — *n* **tith'er** a person who collects tithes. — *n* **tith'ing** a tithe; exaction or payment of tithes. — **tithe barn** a barn formerly for storing the parson's tithe in corn. — *adj* **tithe-free'** exempt from paying tithes. [O.E. *tēotha*, tenth.]

titi *tē'tē*, *n* a small South American monkey.

Titian or **titian** *tish'ən* or *-yən*, *n* a striking red-yellow colour used by the Venetian painter *Titian* (Tiziano Vecellio, *c* 1490–1576).

titillate *tit'il-lāt*, *vt* to stimulate gently, esp. in a sexual way. — *n* **titillā'tion**. — *n* **tit'illātor**. [L. *titillāre*, *-ātum*.]

titivate or **tittivate** *tit'i-vāt*, (*slang*) *vi* and *vt* to smarten up, by dress or otherwise. — *n* **titivā'tion** or **tittivā'tion**.

titlark *tit'lärk*, *n* any bird of the pipit family, esp. the meadow pipit. [**tit**[3] and **lark**[1].]

title *tī'tl*, *n* an inscription or descriptive placard; a chapter-heading; the name of a book, poem, tale, picture, etc.; a title-page; a book or publication, as an item in a catalogue (*publishers' jargon*); an appellation of rank or distinction; a right to possession; a championship (*sport*). — *vt* to designate; to give or attach a title to. — *adj* **ti'tled** having a title, esp. in nobility. — *adj* **ti'tleless** untitled. — **half-title** see under **half; ti'tle-deed** a document that proves right to possession; **ti'tle-holder** a person holding a title, esp. legal, or a championship in some sport; **ti'tle-page** the page of a book containing its title and the author's (and often publisher's) name; **title role** the character in a play of the same name. [O.E. *tītul* or *titul* and O.Fr. *title* — L. *titulus*.]

titmouse *tit'mows*, *n* a tit, any of various kinds of little active acrobatic bird of *Parus* or similar genus: — *pl* **titmice** (*tit'mīs*). [**tit**[3], and M.E. *mose*, titmouse — O.E. *māse*.]

titrate *tī'trāt* or *tī-trāt'*, (*chem*) *vt* to subject to titration. — *n* **titrā'tion** measurement of the strength of a solution by finding how much of another solution of known strength is required to complete a chemical reaction. — *n* **titre** (*US* **titer**; *tī'tər* or *tē'tər*) the concentration of a substance in a solution as determined by titration. [Fr. *titre*, standard.]

titter *tit'ər*, *vi* to giggle, snicker or laugh quietly. — *n* a stifled laugh. — *n* **titt'erer**. — *n* and *adj* **titt'ering**. [Cf. Sw. dialect *tittra*.]

tittivate. See **titivate**.

tittle *tit'l*, *n* a dot, stroke, accent, vowel-point, contraction or punctuation mark; the smallest part. [O.Fr. *title* — L. *titulus*, a title.]

tittle-tattle *tit'l-tat-l*, *n* idle, empty talk, rumour. — *vi* to talk idly, esp. in relaying rumours. — *n* **titt'le-tattler**. — *n* **titt'le-tattling**.

titty *tit'i*, *n* (esp. *vulg*) a teat; the breast. [Dimin. of **tit**[1] or **teat**.]

titubation *tit-ū-bā'shən*, (*med*) *n* staggering; unsteadiness; a tremor (esp. of the head), often a symptom of a cerebral or spinal disease. [L. *titubāre*, *-ātum*, to stagger.]

titular *tit'ū-lər*, *adj* pertaining to title; in name or title only; nominal; having a title without the duties of the office. — *n* a titled person; a person who enjoys the bare title of an office, without actual possession; a person invested with a title; that from which a church takes its name (*patron* if a saint or angel; *RC*). — *n* **titularity** (*-lar'i-ti*). — *adv* **tit'ularly**. — *adj* **tit'ulary** titular. — *n* a person holding a title. [Fr. *titulaire*; N.L. *titularis* — L. *titulus*.]

tizwas. See **tiswas**.

tizzy *tiz'i*, (*slang*; also **tizz**) *n* a state of agitation, nervousness, confusion or dither for little reason.

Tl (*chem*) *symbol* for thallium.

TLS *abbrev* for Times Literary Supplement.

TM *abbrev* for transcendental meditation.

Tm (*chem*) *symbol* for thulium.

TN *abbrev* for: Tennessee (U.S. state); trade name; Tunisia (I.V.R.).

TNT *abbrev* for trinitrotoluene (see under **trinitro-**).

TO *abbrev* for: Tax Officer; telegraph office; Transport Officer; turn over.

to *tōō*, *tŏŏ* or *tə*, *prep* serving as sign of the infinitive (which is sometimes understood) and forming a substitute for the dative case; in the direction of; as far as; all the way in the direction of; until; into the condition of; towards; beside; near; at; in contact with, close against; before; for; of; with the object or result of; against; in accordance, comparison or relation with; in honour of, or expressing good wishes for; along with, in addition. — *adv* in one direction, forward; in or into position, contact, closed or fastened condition. — **to and fro** alternately this way and that; **toing and froing** going backwards and forwards in an agitated way, or without achieving anything (also *fig*). [O.E. *tō*.]

toad *tōd*, *n* a toothless tailless amphibian that walks or crawls instead of jumping like the frog, esp. one of the *Bufo* or related genus; a hateful or contemptible person or animal. — *n* **toad'y** sycophant, obsequious flatterer. — *vt* to fawn, as a sycophant does: — *pr p* **toad'ying**; *pa t* and *pa p* **toad'ied**. — *adj* **toad'yish**. — *n* **toad'yism**. — **toad'fish** a toadlike fish of many kinds; **toad'flax** any species of *Linaria*, a genus closely related to snapdragon, with flaxlike leaves; **toad-in-the-hole'** a dish of sausage meat cooked in batter; **toad'-stone** a basalt lava or volcanic rock; **toad'stool** any umbrella-shaped fungus, often excluding the edible mushroom. [O.E. *tāde*, *tādige*, *tādie*.]

toast *tōst*, *vt* to dry and parch; to brown (esp. bread); to half-melt (e.g. cheese); to warm or heat by rays; to drink to (someone's health, success, etc.). — *vi* to drink toasts; to undergo, or be suitable for, browning. — *n* bread toasted; the person or thing drunk to, as the most admired or celebrated for the moment; a wish for someone's continued health. — *adj* **toast'ed**. — *n* **toast'er** a person who toasts; a toasting-fork; an electric apparatus for making toast. — *n* **toast'ie** (*colloq*) a toasted sandwich (also **toast'y**). — *n* **toast'ing**. — *adj* (*colloq*) hot. — **toast'ing-fork** or **-iron** a long-handled fork for toasting bread; **toast'master**, *fem* **toast'mistress**, the announcer of toasts, introducer of speakers, at a dinner; **toast'-rack** a stand with partitions for slices of toast. [O.Fr. *toster* — L. *tostus*, roasted, past p. of *torrēre*.]

Tob. (*Bible*) *abbrev* for (the Apocryphal Book of) Tobit.

tobacco *tə-bak'ō*, *n* (the prepared leaves of) an American plant used for smoking, chewing or snuffing: — *pl* **tobacc'os** or **tobacc'oes**. — *n* **tobacc'onist** a seller or manufacturer of tobacco. — **tobacc'o-pipe** a pipe for smoking tobacco; **tobacc'o-pouch** a pouch for holding tobacco. [Sp. *tabaco*, from Haitian.]

to-be *tŏŏ-* or *tə-bē'*, *n* the future. — *adj* (now usu. as a *combining form* (**-to-be'**) signifying something in the future, yet to become.

toboggan *tə-bog'ən*, *n* a flat sledge with a upturned front. — *vi* to slide, coast or travel on, or as if on, a toboggan. — *n* **tobogg'aner**. — *n* **tobogg'aning**. — *n* **tobogg'anist**. [Micmac *tobākun*.]

Toby *tō'bi*, *n* a beer-mug or similar object shaped like a man with a three-cornered hat (also **To'by-jug**; also without *cap*); Punch's dog.

toccata *to-kä'tə*, (*mus*) *n* primarily a work intended to display the performer's touch, or in which he or she seems to try the touch of an instrument in a series of runs and chords before breaking into a fugue; (*loosely*) a sort of fantasia or overture. [It. — *toccare*, to touch.]

Toc H *tok ăch*, *n* a society for handing on the spirit of comradeship of the 1st World War, from its first meetings at Talbot House, at Poperinghe in Belgium. [Formerly signallers' names of the initial letters **T**, **H**.]

Tocharian or **Tokharian** *to-kä'ri-ən* or *-kā'*, **Tocha'rish** or **Tokha'rish** *-rish*, *n* an extinct Indo-European language, related to Latin and Celtic, preserved in manuscripts discovered in the 20th century in Chinese Turkestan. [Gr. *Tocharoi*, a people guessed to be its speakers on the strength of the Uigur (language of Chinese Turkestan) name *Tochri*.]

tocopherol *tok-of'ə-rol*, *n* vitamin E, whose deficiency causes sterility in some species. [Pfx. *toco-*, relating to offspring (— Gr. *tokos*, birth, offspring), Gr. *pher*(*ein*), to bear, bring, and chem. sfx. *-ol*, of a hydroxyl group.]

tocsin *tok'sin*, *n* an alarm-bell, or the ringing of it. [Fr. — Prov. *tocasenh* — *tocar*, to touch, strike, *senh* — L. *signum*, sign (L.L. bell).]

tod *tod*: **on one's tod** alone. [Rhyming slang *on one's Tod Sloan* (own).]

today *to͝o-* or *tə-dā'*, *n* this or the present day. — *adv* on the present day; nowadays. [O.E. *tōdæg(e)*.]

toddle *tod'l*, *vi* to walk with short feeble steps, as a child does; to saunter (*colloq*); (with *off*) to go, depart (*facetious*). — *n* a toddling gait; an aimless stroll (*colloq*). — *n* **todd'ler** a person who toddles, esp. a young child learning to walk confidently. — *adj* **todd'ling.** [Orig. Northern dialect.]

toddy *tod'i*, *n* a mixture of spirits, sugar and hot water. [Hindi *tāṛī* — *tāṛ*, a palm-tree.]

to-do *tə-* or *to͝o-do͞o'*, *n* a stir; a commotion: — *pl* **to-dos'**.

toe *tō*, *n* one of the five small members at the front of the foot; the front of a hoof; the corresponding part of a shoe, sock, golf club head, etc.; the lowest part of the front of anything, esp. if it projects. — *vt* to stand with the toes against; to kick; to strike with the toe of a club; to perform with the toe; to provide (e.g. a stocking) with a toe or toes. — *vi* to place the toes: — *pr p* **toe'ing**; *pa t* and *pa p* **toed.** — *adj* and *combining form* **toed** (*tōd*) having toes (of a specified kind or number). — **toe'cap** a (usu. steel) cap covering the toe of a shoe; **toe'-hold** a place to anchor the toes in; a first established position; a hold in which the toes are held and the foot is bent back or twisted (*wrestling*); **toe'-jump** (*ice-skating*) a jump executed by pushing off with the toe of one's free foot; **toe'-loop** (*ice-skating*) a toe-jump and a loop in combination; **toe'nail** a nail on a human or animal toe. — **big** (or **great) toe** the largest of the toes; **little toe** smallest of the toes; **on one's toes** poised for a quick start, alert, eager; **take to one's toes** to run away; **toe the line** to stand with toes against a marked line, as in starting a race; to conform; **toe to toe** (*fig*) in close, direct confrontation (*adj* **toe-to-toe'**); **tread on the toes of** to offend (someone). [O.E. *tā* (pl. *tān*).]

toe-rag *tō'-rag*, (*slang*) *n* a beggar, tramp; generally, a ruffian or rascal; a despicable person.

toff *tof*, (*slang*) *n* a person of the upper classes; a swell, dandy; a good chap. — *adj* **toff'ish.** — *n* **toff'ishness.**

toffee or sometimes **toffy** *tof'i*, *n* a hard-baked chewy sweet made of sugar and butter. — **toff'ee-apple** a toffee-coated apple on a stick. — *adj* **toff'ee-nose** or **toff'ee-nosed** (*slang*) supercilious, conceited. — **for toffee** (*colloq*) (always in negative constructions) at all, as in *he can't dance for toffee*, etc.

toft *toft*, (*hist*) *n* a homestead. [Late O.E. — O.N. *topt*, *tupt*, *toft*.]

tofu *tō'fo͞o*, *n* unfermented soy bean curd, having a pale, creamy colour and a bland flavour, used as food. [Jap. — Chin. *toufu* — *tou*, beans, *fu*, rotten.]

tog¹ *tog*, (*slang*) *n* a garment (usu. in *pl*) — *vt* to dress: — *pr p* **togg'ing**; *pa t* and *pa p* **togged.** — **tog up** to dress, esp. in one's best clothes.

tog² *tog*, *n* a unit of measurement of thermal insulation as a property of textile fabrics. — **tog rating** or **value** the amount of thermal insulation provided by a fabric, measured in togs. [App. coined from **tog¹**.]

toga *tō'gə*, *n* the outer garment of a Roman citizen, a long piece of cloth wound round and draped over the body. — *adj* **tō'ga'd, tō'gaed, tō'gate** or **tō'gated.** [L.]

together *tə-gedh'ər*, *adv* in or to the same place; at the same time; in or into connection, company or concert. — *adj* (*slang*; chiefly *US*) well-organised, mentally composed, emotionally stable, etc. — *n* **togeth'erness** unity; closeness; a sense of unity or community with other people. — **get** or **put it (all) together** (*slang*; chiefly *US*) to perform something successfully, get something right; to become well-organised, stable, etc.; to establish a good relationship (with). [O.E. *tōgædere* — *tō*, to, *geador*, together.]

toggle *tog'l*, *n* a crosspiece on a rope, chain, rod, etc. to prevent slipping through a hole, or to allow twisting; a short bar acting as a button, passed through a loop for fastening a garment; an appliance for transmitting force at right angles to its direction. — *vt* to hold or provide with a toggle; to fix securely. — **togg'le-joint** an elbow or knee joint; a mechanism consisting of two levers hinged together, force applied to straighten the hinge producing a considerable force along the levers; **togg'le-switch** (*telecomm* and *electronics*) a switch which, in a circuit having two stable or quasi-stable states, produces a transition from one to the other.

toheroa *tō-ə-rō'ə*, *n* an edible shellfish found at low tide buried in sandy beaches. [Maori.]

toil¹ *toil*, *vi* to struggle hard; to labour hard; to make one's way (esp. up) by strong effort. — *n* struggle; hard labour. — *n* **toil'er.** — *adj* **toil'ful.** — *n* and *adj* **toil'ing.** — *adj* **toil'less.** — *adj* **toil'some** involving toil; toiling. — *n* **toil'someness.** — *adj* **toil'-worn** worn, weary with toil. [A.Fr. *toiler* said to be — L. *tudiculāre*, to stir.]

toil² *toil*, (usu. in *pl*; often *fig*) *n* a net, snare. [**toile.**]

toile *twäl*, *n* a thin cotton or linen dress material. [Ety. as for **toilet.**]

toilet *toil'it*, *n* a dressing-room, bathroom or lavatory; a dressing-table with a mirror; the articles used in dressing; the mode or process of dressing; the whole dress and appearance of a person, any particular costume. — *vt* to take to the toilet or otherwise assist with toilet procedures. — *n* **toil'etry** any article or preparation used in washing and dressing oneself: — *pl* **toil'etries.** — **toil'et-paper** paper for wiping oneself after defecation; **toil'et-roll** a roll of toilet-paper; **toilet soap** soap for personal use; **toilet tissue** soft, absorbent toilet-paper; **toilet training** the training of children to control bladder and bowels and to use the lavatory; **toilet water** a lightly perfumed liquid similar to cologne. [Fr. *toile*, dimin. *toilette* — L. *tēla*, web.]

toing and froing. See under **to.**

tokamak *tō'kə-mak*, (*nuc eng*) *n* a tyre-shaped device for producing thermonuclear power in which plasma is held in place by a complex magnetic field generated by internal electric currents. — Also *adj.* [Russ., acronym from *to*roidalnaya *ka*mera s *ma*gnitnym polem, toroidal chamber with a magnetic field.]

Tokay *tō-kā'*, *n* a sweetish and heavy wine with an aromatic flavour, produced at *Tokay* in Hungary; the grape that yields it.

token *tō'kn*, *n* a sign; a symbol; a portent; an indication; something providing evidence; an authenticating sign, word or object; a keepsake; a coin or voucher, issued privately, redeemable in current money or goods; a unit of computer code representing a word or character used in a program. — *adj* serving as a symbol; hence, being a mere show or semblance, as in *token force*, *token resistance*, *token Black*. — *vt* to betoken. — *n* **tō'kenism** the practice of doing something once to give an impression of doing it regularly, e.g. employing one coloured person to avoid a charge of racialism. — **token money** money worth more than its intrinsic value as metal; private tokens. — **by the same token** in corroboration, in addition, also. [O.E. *tācen*.]

Tokharian, Tokharish. See **Tocharian.**

Tok Pisin *tok piz'in*, *n* Melanesian pidgin, as spoken in Papua New Guinea. [**talk pidgin.**]

tolbooth. See under **toll¹.**

tolbutamide *tol-būt'əm-īd*, *n* a drug taken orally in the treatment of diabetes.

told *tōld, pa t* and *pa p* of **tell**[1].

Toledo *tō-lē'dō, n* a sword-blade made at *Toledo* (*-lā'dō*) in Spain: — *pl* **Tolē'dos.**

tolerate *tol'ə-rāt, vt* to endure, esp. with patience or impunity; to allow (to exist). — *n* **tolerabil'ity.** — *adj* **tol'erable** endurable; passable; (*loosely*) fair. — *adv* **tol'erably.** — *n* **tol'erance** the ability to endure (e.g. pain); the disposition or willingness to tolerate or allow (e.g. bad behaviour or conditions); the permissible range of variation in values when measuring, etc. — *adj* **tol'erant** tolerating; enduring; capable of enduring (e.g. unfavourable conditions, a parasite, a drug) without showing serious effects (*biol* and *med*); indulgent; favouring toleration. — *adv* **tol'erantly.** — *n* **tolerā'tion** the act of tolerating; the allowance of what is not approved of; the liberty given to a minority to hold and express their own political or religious opinions. — *n* **tolerā'tionist.** — *n* **tol'erātor.** — **tolerance dose** (*med*) the maximum dose which can be permitted to a specific tissue during radiotherapy involving irradiation of any other adjacent tissue. [L. *tolerāre, -ātum* — *tollĕre*, to lift up.]

toll[1] *tōl, n* a tax for the privilege of using a bridge or road, selling goods in a market, etc.; the cost in damage, injury or lives. — *vi* to take or pay tolls. — *vt* to take a toll of; to take as a toll. — **tolbooth** or **tollbooth** (*tōl'* or *tol'bōōth* or *-bōōdh*) an office where tolls are or were collected; a town hall; a prison; often a combination of these; **toll'-bar** a movable bar across a road, etc. to stop passengers liable to tolls; **toll'bridge** or **toll'-gate** a bridge or gate where tolls are taken; **toll'-call** a short-distance telephone trunk call; any trunk call (*US*, etc.); **toll'-gatherer.** — *adj* and *adv* **toll-free'.** — **toll'-house; toll'man** a man who collects tolls; a toll-gatherer. — **take (a) toll of** to inflict loss, hardship, pain, etc. on. [O.E.]

toll[2] *tōl, vi* to sound, as a large bell does, esp. with a measured sound. — *vt* to cause (a bell) to sound; to sound, signal, announce, summon, etc. by tolling; to toll for the death of. — *n* the sound of a bell tolling. — *n* **toll'er.**

toluate *tol'ū-āt,* (*chem*) *n* any salt or ester of toluic acid.

toluene *tol'ū-ēn* or **toluol** *tol'ū-ol,* (*chem*) *n* methyl benzene, a colourless flammable liquid ($C_6H_5{\cdot}CH_3$) used as a solvent and in the manufacture of other organic chemicals. — *adj* **tolū'ic.** — *n* **tolū'idine** (*-i-dēn*) an amine ($C_6H_4{\cdot}CH_3NH_2$) derived from toluene, used in making dyes. [*Balsam of Tolu* from which it was orig. derived (— Santiago de *Tolú* in Colombia) and sfx. *-ene.*]

Tom *tom, n* short for *Thomas*; (without *cap*) a male, esp. a cat. — **tom'-cat; Tom Collins** see **Collins.** — **Tom, Dick and Harry** anybody; people in general; **Tom Thumb** a famous dwarf in English folklore, hence any very small person.

tom. *abbrev* for *tomus* (L.), tome or volume.

tomahawk *tom'ə-hök, n* a North American Indian war-axe; a hatchet (*Austr*). — *vt* to assail or kill with a tomahawk; to hack, cut up, or slate. [Virginian Indian *tämähāk.*]

tomato *tə-mä'tō* or in U.S. *-mā'tō, n* a South American plant (*Lycopersicum esculentum* or *Solanum lycopersicum*) related to the potato; its red or yellow pulpy edible fruit: — *pl* **toma'toes.** [Sp. *tomate* — Mex. *tomatl.*]

tomb *tōōm, n* a grave; a vault for the disposal of dead bodies; a sepulchral monument. — **tomb'stone** a memorial stone over a tomb. [O.Fr. (Fr.) *tombe* — L. *tumba* — Gr. *tymbos.*]

tombac or **tombak** *tom'bak, n* an alloy of copper with a little zinc; an alloy of copper and arsenic. [Fr. *tombac* — Malay *tambaga*, copper.]

tombola *tom-bō'lə, n* a kind of lottery (at a fête, etc.); a type of bingo, played esp. in the Services. [It., — *tombolare*, to tumble.]

tomboy *tom'boi, n* a girl with boyish looks, dress, habits, etc. — *adj* **tom'boyish.** [**Tom** and **boy.**]

tome *tōm, n* a big book or volume. [Fr., — L. *tomus* — Gr. *tomos* — *temnein*, to cut.]

tomentum *tō-men'təm,* (*bot*) *n* a matted cottony down on leaves, etc. — *adj* **tōmen'tōse** or **tomen'tous.** [L.]

tomfool *tom-fōōl', n* a great fool. — *adj* extremely foolish. — *n* **tomfool'ery** foolish behaviour; buffoonery; trifles, ornaments; jewellery (*rhyming slang*). — *adj* **tom'foolish.** [**Tom.**]

tommy *tom'i, n* (sometimes with *cap*) a private in the British army. — **Tommy Atkins** a generic name for the private in the British army; **tommy bar** a short bar used to tighten a box spanner, etc.; **tomm'y-gun** a light machine-gun (after its American inventor, General J.T. *Thompson*); **tomm'y-rot** absolute nonsense. [From the name **Thomas.**]

tomography *tō-mog'rə-fi,* (*radiol*) *n* radiography of a layer in the body by moving the X-ray tube and photographic plate in such a way that only the chosen plane appears in clear detail. — *n* **tom'ogram** a radiogram produced by tomography. — *n* **tom'ograph** a machine for making tomograms. — *adj* **tomograph'ic.** [Gr. *tomos*, slice, *graphein*, to draw.]

tomorrow *tə-* or *tōō-mor'ō, n* the day after today; the future. — *adv* on the day after today; in the future. [O.E. *tō morgen.*]

tompion. See **tampion.**

tomtit *tom'tit, n* the blue or other tit. [**Tom** and **tit**[3].]

tom-tom *tom'-tom, n* an American Indian or oriental drum played with the hands; a similar drum used in jazz-bands, etc.; any primitive drum or substitute. [Hindi *tam-tam*, imit.]

-tomy *-tə-mi, combining form* denoting surgical incision into an organ. [Gr. *-tomia*, the operation of cutting — *tomē*, a cut — *temnein*, to cut.]

ton *tun, n* a measure of capacity, varying with the substance measured — timber, wheat, etc. (see **tonnage**); a unit of weight = 20 cwt. (2240 lb. or 1016 kg.) (2400 lb. was formerly a *long ton*); in U.S. usually = 2000 lb. (907·2 kg.; *short*) or 2240 lb. (*long*); 100 units of various kinds; £100 (*colloq*); a score, total, etc. of 100 (*colloq*); 100 runs (*cricket*; *colloq*); 100 m.p.h. (preceded by **a** or **the**; *slang*); a great weight (*colloq*); (in *pl*) many, a great amount (*colloq*). — **-tonn'er** *combining form* denoting: a vehicle, vessel, etc. weighing a specified number of tons or having a specified amount of tonnage; a load of a specified number of tons. — *adj* **ton'-up** (*slang*) (orig. of a motorcyclist) travelling or having travelled at more than 100 m.p.h.); noisy and reckless; **freight ton, register ton** see **tonnage**; **metric ton** see **tonne.** [O.E. *tunne*, a vat, tub; see **tun.**]

tonal, tonalitive, tonality. See **tone.**

tondo *ton'dō, n* a circular painting or circular carving in relief: — *pl* **ton'di** (*-dē*) or **ton'dos.** — *n* **tondino** (*-dē'nō*) a circular or semicircular moulding (*archit*); a small tondo: — *pl* **tondi'ni** (*-nē*) or **tondi'nos.** [It., short for *rotondo*, round, — L. *rotundus.*]

tone *tōn, n* the character of a sound; quality of sound; accent; intonation; vocal inflexion, rise or fall in pitch; a sound of definite pitch; a major second, one of the larger intervals between successive notes in the scale, as C and D (*mus*); vocal expression; bodily firmness, elasticity or tension, esp. in muscles; the prevailing character or spirit; mood; temper; harmony or general effect of colours; depth or brilliance of colour; a tint or shade. — *vt* to intone; to give tone or the desired tone to. — *vi* to take a tone; to harmonise (with *in*). — *adj* **tōn'al** of tone; according to key. — *adj* **tōnal'itive** of tonality. — *n* **tōnal'ity** a relation in key; a key; a rendering of colour relations. — *adj* **toned** having a tone (in compounds); braced up; treated to give tone; slightly tinted. — *adj* **tone'less** soundless; expressionless; dull; relaxed; listless. — *adv* **tone'lessly**. — *n* **tone'lessness**. — *n* **toneme** (*tō'nēm*) in a tone language, a phoneme consisting of a particular intonation. — *adj* **tonēm'ic**. — *n* **ton'er** a person or thing that tones; a cosmetic lotion for toning the skin; a hair preparation used for toning or tinting; fine powdered pigment used in xerography; a chemical solution used to soften, etc. colours or tones in photographic work. — *adj* **tonetic** (*-et'ik*) of or relating to linguistic tones, tone languages or intonation. — *adv* **tonet'ically**. — *adj* **tōn'ey** or **tōn'y** (*slang*) high-toned; fashionable. — **tone'-arm** part of a gramophone; the arm that carries an electric pick-up; **tone control** a manual control in a radio set which adjusts the relative amplitude of high, medium and low frequencies. — *adj* **tone'-deaf** unable to appreciate or distinguish differences in musical pitch. — **tone language** a language (e.g. Chinese) in which difference of intonation distinguishes words of different meaning that would otherwise sound the same; **tone poem** a piece of music, not divided into movements, conveying or translating a poetic idea or literary theme; **tone row** (in serial music) the basic set of notes in the chosen order. — **tone down** to give a lower tone to; to moderate; to soften, to harmonise the colours of (e.g. a painting) as to light and shade; **tone up** to heighten; to intensify; to make healthier, more vigorous. [Gr. *tonos*, pitch, tension, partly through Fr. *ton* and L. *tonus*.]

tong *tong*, *n* a Chinese guild or secret society, particularly on associated with organised crime. [Chin. *t'ang*.]

tongs *tongz*, *npl* a gripping and lifting instrument, consisting of two legs joined by a pivot, hinge or spring. [O.E. *tang*, *tange*.]

tongue *tung*, *n* the fleshy organ in the mouth, used in tasting, swallowing and speech; the tongue of an ox, etc., as food; the power of speech; the manner of speaking; speech; discourse; voice; utterance; a language; anything like a tongue in shape; a point of land; a bell clapper; a flap in the opening of a shoe or boot; any narrow projection; a langue or language (q.v.) of a religious or military order. — *vt* to utter; to articulate; to lick; to touch with the tongue; to provide with a tongue; to produce or play by tonguing (*mus*). — *vi* to give tongue; to stick out; to practise tonguing (*mus*). — *adj* **tongued** having a tongue. — *adj* **tongue'less**. — *n* **tongue'let** a little tongue. — *n* **tongu'ing** (*mus*) articulation to separate the notes in playing wind instruments. — **tongue'-and-groove** a system of joining boards by fitting a projection along the side of one into a groove in the next; these boards. — *adj* and *adv* **tongue'-in-cheek** with ironic, insincere or humorous intention. — **tongue'-lashing** a severe verbal reprimand. — *adj* **tongue'-tied** impeded by a short frenum; unable to speak out. — **tongue'-twister** a formula or sequence of words difficult to pronounce without blundering. — **give tongue** to give utterance, to voice; **lose one's tongue** to become speechless from emotion; **on the tip of one's tongue** see under **tip**[1]; **speaking in tongues** or **gift of tongues** glossolalia (see under **gloss-**); **with (one's) tongue in (one's) cheek** tongue-in-cheek (*adv*). [O.E. *tunge*; L. *lingua* (from *dingua*).]

tonic *ton'ik*, *adj* relating to tone or tones; producing tension; giving tone and vigour to the system (*med*); giving or increasing strength. — *n* a tonic medicine; any person or thing that enlivens or invigorates; a keynote (*mus*); tonic water. — *n* **tonicity** (*ton-is'i-ti*) the property or condition of having tone; mode or reaction to stimulus; the healthy state of muscular fibres when at rest. — **tonic sol-fa** (*mus*) a system of notation and teaching devised by Sarah Glover (1785–1867) and developed by John Curwen, using modified sol-fa syllables and their initial letters for the notes of the scale with *doh* (see **do**[2]) for the tonic, and dividing the bar by colons, dots and inverted commas; **tonic spasm** (*med*) a prolonged uniform muscular spasm; **tonic water** aerated quinine water. [**tone**.]

tonight *tə-* or *tōō-nīt'*, *n* this night; the night of the present day. — *adv* on this night or the night of today. [O.E. *tō niht*.]

tonk *tonk*, (*Austr slang*) *n* a penis; a homosexual; an effeminate, weak or ineffectual person.

tonkabean *tong'kə-bēn*, *n* the coumarin-scented seed of a large papilionaceous tree of Guiana, used for flavouring snuff, etc.; the tree from which it comes. [The Guyanan local name.]

tonnage *tun'ij*, *n* the carrying capacity of a ship in *tons* (orig. in *tuns* of wine); *register ton* = 100 cu. feet, *freight ton* = 40 cu. feet, of space for cargo; the total amount of shipping so measured; a duty on ships, estimated in tons; a charge or payment by the ton. — **gross tonnage** the total space capable of carrying cargo in a ship, measured in register tons; **net register tonnage** gross tonnage less deducted spaces (those spaces required in running the ship). [See **ton** and **tun**.]

tonne *tun*, *n* the preferred name for a **metric ton**, equal to 1000 kilograms (0·984 ton). [Fr.]

-tonner. See under **ton**.

tonometer *tōn-om'ə-tər*, *n* a device for determining the frequencies of tones (*mus*); an instrument for measuring fluid pressure within the eyeball, blood pressure, or vapour pressure. — *n* **tonom'etry**. [Gr. *tonos*, pitch, tension, *metron*, measure.]

tonsil *ton'sl* or *-sil*, *n* (*zool*) either of two glands at the root of the tongue in vertebrates. — *adj* **ton'sillar**. — *n* **tonsillec'tomy** surgical removal of a tonsil. — *adj* **tonsillit'ic**. — *n* **tonsillī'tis** inflammation of the tonsils. — *n* **tonsillot'omy** an incision into, or partial removal of, a tonsil. [L. *tōnsillae* (pl.).]

tonsorial *ton-sö'ri-əl*, *adj* of or relating to hairdressing or barbering (usu. *facetious*). [L. *tonsor*, barber — *tonsura*; see **tonsure**.]

tonsure *ton'shər*, *n* the act or mode of clipping the hair, or of shaving the head; (in the R.C. and Eastern Churches) the shaving or cutting of part of the hair of the head on entering the priesthood or a monastic order; the shaven part. — *adj* **ton'sured** (of e.g. a priest) having the crown of the head shaven; shaven; bald; clipped. [L. *tōnsūra*, a shearing — *tondēre*, *tōnsum*, to clip.]

tontine *ton'tēn* or *ton-tēn'*, *n* a scheme of life annuity, increasing as the subscribers die. — Also *adj*. [Lorenzo *Tonti*, its inventor (1653).]

Tony *tō'ni*, *n* (in U.S.) an award for meritorious work in the theatre. [After U.S. actress *Antoinette* Perry.]

tony. See under **tone**.

too *tōō*, *adv* as well, in addition, also, likewise (never at the beginning of a sentence in English usage); undesirably in excess; so much as to be incompatible with a condition. — **too much** more than is reasonable, tolerable, etc.; also used as an interjection expressing approval, amazement, etc. (*slang*, chiefly *US*). [Stressed form of **to**.]

took *tŏŏk*, *pa t* of **take**.

tool *tōōl*, *n* a working instrument, esp. one used by hand; the cutting part of a machine tool; a weapon, esp. a gun (*slang*); someone who is used as the mere instrument of another; (esp. in *pl*) anything necessary to the pursuit of a particular activity; a penis (*vulg*). — *vt* to shape or finish with a tool; to mark with a tool, esp. to ornament or imprint designs upon (a book cover), or to chisel the face of (stone); to supply with tools, esp. with machine tools for a particular purpose (also **tool up**). — *n* **tool'er**. — *n* **tool'ing** workmanship done with a tool. — **tool'bag** (or

tool'box) a bag (or box) for carrying and storing tools; **tool'kit** a set of tools; **tool'maker** a worker who makes or repairs tools, esp. machine tools; **tool'man** a man who works with tools or in a toolroom; **tool'pusher** the supervisor of drilling operations at an oil well; **tool'room** that part of a factory occupied by toolmakers; **tool'-shed**. [O.E. *tōl*.]

toon *tōōn*, *n* an Indian tree of the mahogany family, with red wood and astringent bark. [Hind. *tūn*.]

toot *tōōt*, *vi* to make short sounds, e.g. on a flute or horn. — *vt* to blow, e.g. a horn, etc.; to inhale (a drug, usu. cocaine) (*US slang*). — *n* a blast, esp. as of a horn; a drinking binge (*NAm slang*); a snort (q.v.) of cocaine, or any drug (esp. cocaine) for snorting (*US slang*); a toilet (*Austr slang*). — *n* **toot'er** a person who toots; a horn or wind instrument (*colloq*). [Prob. imit.]

tooth *tōōth*, *n* one of the hard bone-like bodies set in the jaws, used for biting and chewing; a hard projection of similar use in invertebrates; a toothlike projection, prong, cog, jag, as on the margin of a leaf, on a comb, a saw, or a wheel; (in *pl*) force, sufficient power to be effective: — *pl* **teeth** (*tēth*). — *vt* to provide with teeth; to cut into teeth. — *vi* (of cog-wheels) to interlock. — *adj* **toothed** (*tōōtht*, also *tōōdhd*) having teeth; dentate. — *adj* **tooth'less** lacking teeth; powerless or ineffective. — *adj* **tooth'-like**. — *adj* **tooth'some** palatable, tasty; attractive, pleasant, agreeable. — *n* **tooth'someness**. — *adj* **tooth'y** with prominent teeth. — **tooth'ache** an ache or pain in a tooth; **tooth'brush** a brush for cleaning the teeth; **toothbrush moustache** a small stiff moustache; **tooth fairy** a fairy who substitutes a coin for a milk tooth placed under a child's pillow (orig. *US*); **tooth'paste** (or **tooth powder**) a paste (or powder) used with a toothbrush; **tooth'pick** an instrument for picking shreds of food from between the teeth; **tooth'wort** a pale fleshy plant, parasitic on tree-roots, with toothlike scale-leaves. — **armed to the teeth** armed as completely as possible, from top to toe; **a sweet tooth** a taste for sweet things; **cast (or throw) in someone's teeth** to fling at someone as a taunt or reproach; **get one's teeth into** to tackle or deal with vigorously, eagerly, etc.; **in someone's teeth** to someone's face; in direct affront; **in the teeth of** in direct opposition to; **long in the tooth** elderly, like a horse whose gums are receding with age; **take the teeth out of** to render harmless or powerless; **tooth and nail** with all possible vigour and fury. [O.E. *tōth* (pl. *tēth*).]

tootle *tōōt'l*, *vi* to make feeble sounds, as on the flute; to go casually along, esp. by car (*colloq*). — *n* a soft sound on the flute, etc.; a casual trip, a drive (*colloq*). [Frequentative of **toot**.]

tootsie, tootsy *tŏŏt'si* or **tootsy-wootsy** *-wŏŏt'si*, *n* jocular or childish words for a foot or toe. [Perh. a childish pron. of **foot**.]

top[1] *top*, *n* the highest or uppermost part or place; the upper end or surface; a lid or cover; a garment for the upper part of a woman's body; topspin; a circus tent (*slang*; **the big top** the main tent); (esp. in *pl*) the part of a root vegetable that is above the ground; (in *pl*) in oil-refining, the first part of a volatile mixture to come off in the distillation process; the highest position (e.g. in a profession, company, salary scale, scale of authority or privilege, etc.). — *adj* highest; best; most important, able, etc. — *vt* to cover on the top; to tip; to rise above; to surpass; to rise to the top of; to surmount; to be on or at the top of; to take off the top of; to hit (the ball) on the upper half (*golf*); to kill (*slang*). — *vi* to finish up, round off (with *off* or *up*): — *prp* **topp'ing**; *pa t* and *pa p* **topped**. — *adj* **top'less** without a top; (of female clothing) leaving the breasts uncovered; (of a woman) with bare breasts; (of a place, entertainment, etc.) that features women with bare breasts. — *n* **top'lessness**. — *adj* **top'most** (*-mōst*) uppermost; highest. — *adj* **topped**. — *n* **topp'er** a person or thing that tops in any sense; one that excels (*colloq*); a top hat (*colloq*). — *n* **topp'ing** the act of a person or thing that tops; a thing that tops; (in *pl*) pieces cut from the top; a sauce or dressing to go over food. — *adj* surpassing, pre-eminent. — *adv* **topp'ingly**. — **top'-boot** a knee-length boot with a showy band of leather round the top; **top'coat** an overcoat; **top dog** the winner, leader or dominant person; **top drawer** the highest level, esp. of society (**out of the top drawer**, belonging to this social rank). — *adj* **top-drawer'**. — *vt* **top'-dress**. — **top'-dressing** surface dressing of manure; the application of it; any superficial covering or treatment (*fig*). — *adj* **top'-flight** excellent, superior, of the highest class. — *adj* **top-gallant** (*top-gal'ənt* or *tə-gal'ənt*) above the topmast and topsail and below the royal mast. — *n* a topgallant mast or sail; **top hat** a tall cylindrical hat of silk plush. — *adj* **top-heav'y** having the upper part too heavy or large for the lower (often *fig*, e.g. of an organisation with too many administrative staff); tipsy. — *adj* or *interj* **top-hole'** (*old slang*) excellent, first-class. — **top'knot** a crest, tuft of hair, often a piece of added hair, or knot of ribbons, etc., on the top of the head; a small fish (of several species) similar to the turbot. — *adj* **top'knotted**. — *adj* **top'-level** at the highest level. — *adj* **top'-line** important enough to be mentioned in a headline. — *vi* to feature in a headline; to star. — **top-lin'er** a person who is top-line; a principal performer, a star. — **top'mast** (*-məst* or *-mäst*) the second mast, or that immediately above the lower mast; **top'-minnow** a small, surface-feeding, soft-rayed fish belonging to any of various species, either viviparous or egg-laying (also called **mosquito fish**). — *adj* **top-notch'** (*slang*) topping. — *adj* **top'-priority** very urgent. — **top'sail** (*-sl* or *-sāl*) a sail across the topmast. — *adj* **top secret** profoundly secret and of the highest importance. — **top'side** the upper part; the outer part of a round of beef; a lean cut of beef from the rump; the part of an oil rig, etc. above the deck; (also in *pl*) the part of the outer surface of a vessel above the waterline; **top'soil** the upper part or surface of the soil; **top'spin** spin imparted to a ball by hitting it sharply on the upper half with a forward and upward stroke to make it travel higher, further, or more quickly. — **at the top of one's voice** at one's loudest; **go over the top** to go over the front of a trench and attack the enemy; to take sudden action after hesitation; to exceed the bounds of reason, decorum, etc.; **in the top flight** in the highest class; **off the top of one's head** without previous thought or preparation; **on top of the world** near the North Pole; on a high mountain; revelling in existence; **over the top** (*colloq*) too far, extreme, to an excess, to, at or of an unreasonable or unnecessary degree; **the tops** (*slang*) the very best; **top out** to finish (a building) by putting on the top or highest course (*n* **topp'ing-out**); **top the bill** to be the most important attraction in a programme of entertainment, etc.; **top up** to fill up, e.g. with fuel oil, or alcoholic beverage; to bring (e.g. a wage) up to a generally accepted or satisfactory level (*n* **top'-up** or **topp'ing-up**); **top-up loan** a loan to bring a mortgage, grant, etc. up to the required amount. [O.E.]

top[2] *top*, *n* a toy that can be set spinning on its pointed base (also called a *spinning top*). — **sleep like a top** to sleep very soundly. [App. late O.E. *top* (but the meaning is doubtful).]

topaz *tō'paz*, *n* a precious stone, silicate of aluminium and fluorine, yellowish, bluish or colourless; a variety of orange and tangerine hybrid; (*loosely*) a shade of dark yellow. — *adj* **tō'pazine**. — *n* **topaz'olite** a yellow garnet. — **oriental topaz** a yellow corundum. [Gr. *topazos*, a green gem.]

tope[1] *tōp*, *vi* to drink hard. — *n* **tō'per** a drunkard. [Poss. Fr. *toper*, to accept a wager.]
tope[2] *tōp*, *n* any of various small sharks, esp. *Galeorhinus galeus*.
topee. See **topi**[1].
tophus *tō'fəs*, (*med*) *n* a gouty deposit, a hard nodule formed of sodium biurate crystals, in soft body tissue: — *pl* **tō'phi** (*-fī*). — *adj* **tophā'ceous.** [L. *tōphus*, *tōfus*, porous stone, tufa.]
topi[1] or **topee** *tō-pē'* or *tō'pē*, *n* a hat, esp. a sola hat or pith-helmet, worn esp. in India. [Hindi *ṭopī*, hat.]
topi[2] *tō'pi*, *n* a large African antelope with curved horns and long muzzle. [App. from a native word.]
topiary *tō'pi-ə-ri*, *n* a branch of gardening, the clipping of trees into imitative and fantastic shapes. — Also *adj*. — *adj* **topiā'rian.** — *n* **tō'piarist.** [L. *topiārius* — *topia* (pl.), landscape, landscape gardening — Gr. *topos*, a place.]
topic *top'ik*, *n* a general consideration suitable for argument; a subject of discourse or argument; a matter. — *adj* **top'ical** local; relating to a topic or subject; relating to matters of interest of the day. — *n* **topical'ity.** — *adv* **top'ically.** [Gr. *topikos*, pertaining to place or to commonplaces, *ta topika*, the general principles of argument — *topos*, a place.]
topography *top-og'rə-fi*, *n* the detailed study, description, or features of a limited area, district, etc. — *n* **topog'rapher.** — *adj* **topographic** (*top-ə-graf'ik*) or **topograph'ical.** — *adv* **topograph'ically.** [Gr. *topographiā* — *topos*, a place, *graphein*, to describe.]
topology *top-ol'ə-ji*, *n* the topographical study of a particular place or region; topographical anatomy; a branch of geometry concerned with those properties of a figure which remain unchanged even when the figure is bent, stretched, etc.; the study of those properties of sets of points (e.g. geometrical figures) that are invariant under one-to-one continuous transformations (*math*); the interconnection, organisation, etc. of computers within a network. — *adj* **topolog'ic** or **topolog'ical.** — *adv* **topolog'ically.** — *n* **topol'ogist.** [Gr. *topos*, a place, *logos*, a discourse.]
toponym *top'ə-nim*, *n* a place name; a name derived from a place name; a descriptive place name, usu. derived from a geographical feature. — *adj* **topon'ymal, toponymic** (*-ə-nim'ik*) or **toponym'ical.** — *n* **toponymy** (*top-on'i-mi*) or *nsing* **toponym'ics** the study of place names. [Gr. *topos*, place, *onyma* (*onoma*), name.]
topped, topping, etc. See under **top**[1].
topple *top'l*, *vi* to overbalance and fall headlong; to threaten to fall from top-heaviness. — *vt* to cause to topple. [**top**[1].]
topsy-turvy *top-si-tûr'vi*, *adv* bottom upwards. — *adj* turned upside down. — *n* confusion. — *adv* **topsy-tur'vily.** — *n* **topsy-tur'viness.** [**top,** and the obs. verb *terve*, to turn.]
toque *tōk*, *n* a woman's close-fitting brimless or nearly brimless hat; a 16th-century form of cap or turban. [Fr.]
tor or **torr** *tör*, *n* a hill, a rocky height. [O.E. *torr*, tor — L. *turris*, tower, or perh. from Celtic.]
Torah *tö'rə*, (*Judaism*) *n* the Mosaic Law; the book of the law, the Pentateuch. [Heb. *Tōrāh*.]
torc. See **torque.**
torch *törch*, *n* a stick of inflammable material carried or stuck up to give light; a large candle; a portable electric lamp; an appliance producing a hot flame for welding, burning, etc.; a source of enlightenment (*fig*). — *vt* to light with a torch; to set alight deliberately (*slang*, esp. *US*). — **torch'-bearer** a person who carries a torch; a leading, prominent figure in a cause, etc. (*fig*); **torch'light; torch'-singer; torch'-song** a popular song of the 1930s giving lugubrious expression to the pangs of unrequited love; a sentimental or melancholy love song. — **carry the** (or **a**) **torch** (**for**) to suffer unrequited love (for). [Fr. *torche* — L. *torquēre*, *tortum*, to twist.]
torchère *tor-sher'*, (Fr.) *n* a tall ornamental candlestick or lampstand.
tore[1] *tör*, *pa t* of **tear**[2].
tore[2]. See under **torus.**
toreador *tor'i-ə-dör*, *n* a bullfighter, esp. on horseback. — *n* **torero** (*tor-ā'rō*) a bullfighter on foot: — *pl* **tore'ros.** [Sp.]
tori, toric. See under **torus.**
torii *tör'ē-ē*, *n* a Japanese Shinto temple gateway. [Jap.]
torment *tör'ment*, *n* torture; anguish; a source of distress. — *vt* **torment** (*-ment'*) to torture; to put to extreme pain; to distress; to afflict; to pester; to harass; to agitate, stir violently; to distort, force violently. — *adj* **tormen'ted.** — *adv* **tormen'tedly.** — *n* and *adj* **tormen'ting.** — *adv* **tormen'tingly.** — *n* **tormen'tor.** [L. *tormentum* — *torquēre*, to twist.]
tormentil *tör'men-til*, *n* a four-petalled potentilla with an astringent woody root, growing on heaths. [O.Fr. *tormentille* — Med. L. *tormentilla*.]
torn *törn*, *adj* and *pa p* of **tear**[2]. — **that's torn it!** (*colloq*) an expression of annoyance indicating that something has spoilt one's plans, etc.
tornado *tör-nā'dō*, *n* orig. a violent tropical Atlantic thunderstorm; a very violent whirling wind-storm affecting a narrow strip of country; (*loosely*) a hurricane: — *pl* **tornā'does.** — *adj* **tornadic** (*-nad'ik*). [Prob. Sp. *tronada*, thunderstorm, altered as if from Sp. *tornada*, turning.]
toroid, toroidal. See under **torus.**
torpedo *tör-pē'dō*, *n* a member of the genus **Torpedo** of cartilaginous fishes, related to the skates and rays, with organs on the head that give an electric shock; a self-propelled submarine weapon (usually cigar-shaped), carrying a charge that explodes on impact; a bomb, cartridge, case of explosives, or detonator of various kinds, used in warfare, as a fog-signal, firework, etc.: — *pl* **torpē'does** or **torpē'dos.** — *vt* to attack, strike, destroy, by torpedo; to wreck (e.g. a plan). — **torpe'do-boat** a small swift warship discharging torpedoes; **torpe'do-tube** a kind of gun from which torpedoes are discharged. [L. *torpēdō*, *-inis*, numbness, the torpedo (fish) — *torpēre*, to be stiff.]
torpid *tör'pid*, *adj* numb; lethargic; having lost the power of motion and feeling; sluggish; dormant. — *n* **torpid'ity.** — *adv* **tor'pidly.** — *n* **tor'pidness.** — *n* **tor'pitude.** — *n* **tor'por** numbness; inactivity; dullness; stupidity. [L. *torpidus*, *torpefacĕre*, *torpēscere*, *torpor* — *torpēre*, to be numb.]
torque *törk*, *n* the measure of the turning effect of a tangential force; a force or system of forces causing or tending to cause rotation or torsion; a necklace in the form of a twisted band (also **torc**). — **torque'-converter** (*mech*) a device which acts as an infinitely variable gear; **torque'-meter.** [L. *torquēre*, to twist.]
torr[1]. See **tor.**
torr[2] *tör*, (*phys*) *n* a unit used in expressing very low pressures, $\frac{1}{760}$ of a standard atmosphere. [E. *Torricelli*; see **Torricellian.**]
torrefy *tor'i-fī*, *vt* to scorch; to parch: — *pr p* **torr'efying;** *pa t* and *pa p* **torr'efied.** — *n* **torrefac'tion.** [L. *torrēre*, to parch, roast, *facĕre*, to make.]
torrent *tor'ənt*, *n* a rushing stream; an abounding, strong or turbulent flow. — *adj* **torrential** (*-en'shl*). [L. *torrēns*, *-entis*, boiling, pres. p. of *torrēre*, to dry.]
Torricellian *tor-i-chel'i-ən*, *adj* pertaining to the Italian mathematician *Torricelli* (1608–47) who discovered in 1643 the principle of the barometer. — **Torricellian tube** the barometer; **Torricellian vacuum** the vacuum in the barometer.
torrid *tor'id*, *adj* scorching or parching; violently hot; dried with heat; intensely passionate, emotional, etc.

— *n* **torrid'ity** or **torr'idness**. — **torrid zone** the zone between the tropics. [L. *torridus* — *torrēre*, to parch, roast.]

torsion *tör'shən*, *n* twisting; a twist; the strain produced by twisting; the force with which a thread or wire tends to return when twisted. — *adj* **tor'sional**. — *adj* **tor'sive** twisted spirally. — **tor'sion-balance** an instrument for measuring very minute forces by a horizontal needle suspended by a very fine filament; **torsion bar** a metal bar which absorbs force by twisting, used esp. in vehicle suspension. [L. *torsiō*, *-ōnis* — *torquēre*, *tortum*, to twist.]

torsk *törsk*, *n* a North Atlantic fish (*Brosmius brosme*) of the cod family. [Sw., Norw. and Dan. *torsk* — O.N. *thorskr*.]

torso *tör'sō*, *n* the trunk of a statue or human body, without head or limbs: — *pl* **tor'sos**. [It., stalk, core, torso — L. *thyrsus* — Gr. *thyrsos*.]

tort *tört*, (*Eng law*) *n* any wrong, not arising out of contract, for which there is a remedy by compensation or damages. [Fr., — L.L. *tortum* — L. *torquēre*, *tortum*, to twist.]

torte *tör'tə* or *tört*, *n* a rich sweet cake or pastry, Austrian in origin, often garnished or filled with fruit, nuts, cream, chocolate, etc.: — *pl* **tor'ten** or **tortes**. [Ger., perh. — L.L. *torta*, a round loaf.]

torticollis *tör-ti-kol'is*, (*pathol*) *n* wry-neck. [L.L., — L. *tortus*, twisted, *collum*, neck.]

tortilla *tör-tē'yə* or *tör-tēl'yə*, *n* Mexican round flat maize cake cooked on a griddle, usu. eaten hot with a filling; a thick Spanish omelet made mainly of potato and egg. [Sp., dimin. of *torta*, cake.]

tortoise *tör'təs*, *n* any land or freshwater (rarely marine) chelonian (now, in Britain, usu. restricted to land forms); a testudo (*mil*). — **tortoise beetle** any of various beetles (*Cassidinae*) which resemble the tortoise, having broad, often brightly-coloured or metallic wing-covers; (*specif*) a green leaf-beetle (*Cassida viridis*); **tortoiseshell** (*tör'tə-shel*) the shell of a tortoise; a translucent mottled material, the horny plates (esp. of the back) of a type of sea turtle; a similar synthetic material; a tortoiseshell butterfly or cat. — *adj* made of, or mottled like, tortoiseshell. — **tortoiseshell butterfly** any of several species of butterfly with orange or reddish wings marked with black and yellow, edged with blue, etc.; **tortoiseshell cat** a domestic cat (nearly always female) mottled in orange and black. [L.L. *tortuca*.]

Tortrix *tör'triks*, *n* a genus of small moths whose caterpillars commonly live in rolled-up leaves; (without *cap*) any moth of this genus: — *pl* **tortrices** (*-trī'sēz*). — *n* **tortrī'cid** any moth of the family. — Also *adj*. [Invented L., twister.]

tortuous *tör'tū-əs*, *adj* full of windings; far from straightforward (*fig*). — *n* **tortuos'ity**. — *adv* **tor'tuously**. — *n* **tor'tuousness**. [L. *tortuōsus* — *torquēre*, *tortum*, to twist.]

torture *tör'chər*, *n* the infliction of severe pain esp. as a means of punishment or persuasion; extreme pain; anguish. — *vt* to subject to extreme pain or anguish; to distort violently. — *adj* **tor'tured** suffering or entailing torture or anguish; fraught with worries or difficulties, painful (*colloq*); violently distorted. — *n* **tor'turer**. — *n* and *adj* **tor'turing**. — *adv* **tor'turingly**. — *adj* **tor'turous** causing torture or violent distortion. [Fr., — L. *tortūra*, torment — *torquēre*; see **tortuous**.]

torus *tō'rəs*, *n* a large moulding, semicircular or nearly in section, common at the base of a column (*archit*); a figure generated by the revolution of a circle or other conic section about a straight line in its own plane (*math*); the receptacle of a flower (*bot*); a ring-shaped discharge-tube; a ridge or prominence (*zool*, *anat*): — *pl* **to'rī**. — *n* **tore** (*tör*; *archit* and *geom*) a torus. — *adj* **toric** (*tor'* or *tör'ik*) of, or having the form of, a torus or a part of a torus. — *adj* **toroid** (*tor'* or *tör'oid*) shaped like an anchor-ring. — *n* a coil or transformer of that shape. — *adj* **toroid'al**. [L. *tŏrus*, a bulge, swelling, bed, torus moulding.]

Tory *tō'ri*, *n* a Conservative in politics; a bigoted or extreme Conservative. — *adj* Conservative. — *n* **Tō'ryism** the principles of the Tories. [Ir. *toiridhe*, a pursuer.]

tosh *tosh*, (*slang*) *n* bosh, twaddle.

toss *tos*, *vt* to fling, jerk; to fling up, or about, or to and fro; (of a horse) to throw (its rider); (of a bull, etc.) to throw a person etc. into the air with its horns; to coat (food) by tumbling it with a dressing; to agitate. — *vi* to be in violent commotion; to tumble about; to fling; to toss up a coin. — *n* an act of throwing upward; a throwing up or back of the head; a fall from a horse; a toss-up. — *n* **toss'er**. — *n* and *adj* **toss'ing**. — **toss'-up** the throwing up of a coin to decide anything; an even chance or hazard. — **argue the toss** to dispute a decision; **toss and turn** be wakeful, restless and fidgety in bed; **toss off** to perform or produce quickly or cursorily; to drink off; to remark casually; to masturbate (*slang*); **toss up** to throw a coin in order to decide, according to which lands uppermost.

tot[1] *tot*, *n* anything little, esp. a child, a drinking-cup, or a dram. [Cf. Icel. *tottr*, a dwarf.]

tot[2] *tot*, *vt* and *vi* to add up or total (also **tot up**): — *pr p* **tott'ing**; *pa t* and *pa p* **tott'ed**. — *n* **totting-up'** adding up; the cumulation of certain motoring offences, eventually resulting in disqualification. [**total**.]

total *tō'tl*, *adj* whole; complete; including all; co-ordinating everything towards one end. — *n* the whole; the entire amount. — *vt* to bring to a total, add up; to amount to: — *pr p* **tō'talling**; *pa t* and *pa p* **tō'talled**. — *n* **totalisā'tion** or **-z-**. — *n* **tō'talīsator** or **-z-** (familiarly shortened to **tote** *tōt*) a system of betting in which the total amount staked (minus tax, etc.) is divided among the winners in proportion to the size of their stake; an automatic betting-machine, the *pari-mutuel*. — *vt* **tō'talise** or **-ize** to find the sum of; to bring to a total. — *vi* to use a totalisator. — *n* **tō'talīser** or **-z-** same as **totalisator**. — *adj* **totalitarian** (*tō-tal-i-tā'ri-ən*) belonging to a form of government that includes control of everything under one authority, and allows no opposition. — *n* **totalitā'rianism**. — *n* **totality** (*tō-tal'i-ti*) the condition or fact of being total; an entirety; completeness; the whole. — *adv* **tō'tally**. — **total allergy syndrome** a condition in which a person suffers from a collection of symptoms attributable to accumulated allergies to substances encountered in the modern environment; **total internal reflection** (*phys*) the complete reflection of a light ray at the boundary of a medium with a lower refractive index. [L.L. *tōtālis* — L. *tōtus*, whole.]

totara *tō'tə-rə*, *n* a large New Zealand tree, a variety of *Podocarpus*, valued for its hard reddish timber. [Maori.]

tote[1] *tōt*, (orig. *US*) *vt* to carry. — **tote bag** a large bag for shopping, etc.

tote[2]. See **totalisator** under **total**.

totem *tō'təm*, *n* any species of living or inanimate thing regarded by a class or family within a local tribe with superstitious respect as an outward symbol of an existing intimate unseen relation; any outward symbol given undue respect. — *adj* **totemic** (*-tem'ik*). — *n* **tō'temism** the use of totems as the foundation of a social system of obligation and restriction. — *n* **tō'temist** someone designated by a totem. — *adj* **totemist'ic**. — **totem pole** a pole carved and painted with totemic symbols, set up by Indians in the north-west of N. America. [From Algonquin.]

tother or **t'other** *tudh'ər*, (*dialect* or *humorous*) *pron* and *adj* the other. — **tell tother from which** tell one from another. [**that other**.]

totter *tot'ər*, *vi* to sway; to waver; to rock; to threaten to fall; to reel; to stagger; to be on the verge of ruin. — *n* a tottering movement. — *n* **tott'erer**. — *n* and *adj* **tott'ering**. — *adv* **tott'eringly**. — *adj* **tott'ery** shaky. [Cf. Norw. dialect *tutra*, *totra*, to quiver.]

totting. See **tot**[2].

toucan *tōō'kən* or *-kan*, *n* any of various tropical American fruit-eating birds of the genus *Rhamphastidae*, with large brightly-coloured beaks. [Fr., — Tupí *tucana*.]

touch *tuch*, *vt* to come or be in contact with; to cause to be in contact; to meet without cutting, or meet tangentially (*geom*); to get at; to reach as far as; to attain; to equal, rival or compare with; to make a light application to; to begin to eat, eat a little of; to affect, esp. injuriously; to impress; to affect with emotion, esp. pity; to have to do with; to concern; to hit, wound or injure; to strike home to; to mark or modify by light strokes; to tinge; to test as with a touchstone; to receive, draw, pocket; to extract money from (*for* so much); to make some reference to, say something about. — *vi* to be or come in contact; to verge; to make some mention or reference (with *on* or *upon*); to have reference. — *n* the act, condition, impression, sense or mode of touching; a feeling; a slight application, modification, stroke; a small quantity; a slight attack of illness; a tinge; a trace; a smack; ability, skill; a trait; a little; a slight hit, wound, blemish or reproach; the manner or nicety of producing tone on (now esp.) a keyed instrument; the instrument's response; a characteristic manner; a stroke of art; the relation of communication, sympathy, harmony; communication, contact; a game in which one has to pursue and touch others; a test, as of touchstone; either side of the field outside the bounds (*football*, etc.); a sum got by theft or by touching (*slang*); that which will find buyers at such and such a price (*slang*). — *adj* **touch'able** capable of being touched; fit to be touched. — *n* **touch'ableness**. — *adj* **touched** having been touched; slightly unsound mentally. — *n* **touch'er**. — *adv* **touch'ily**. — *n* **touch'iness**. — *n* **touch'ing**. — *adj* affecting; moving; pathetic. — *prep* concerning. — *adv* **touch'ingly**. — *n* **touch'ingness**. — *adj* **touch'y** over-sensitive; irascible. — **touch-and-go'** a narrow escape; a critical or precariously balanced situation. — *adj* precarious; off-hand. — **touch'down** touching of the ball to the ground by a player behind the goal-line (*Rugby football*); the possession of the ball by a player behind the opponents' goal-line (*Am football*); (of air or spacecraft) the act of landing; **touch'-hole** the small hole of a cannon through which the fire is communicated to the charge; **touch'-judge** (*Rugby football*) an official who marks when and where the ball goes into touch; **touch'-line** the side boundary in football, etc.; **touch'-mark** the maker's official stamp on pewter; **touch'-me-not** any of various plants of the genus *Impatiens*, having seed-pods which, when ripe, spring open at a touch. — *adj* stand-offish. — **touch pad** (*comput*) a small portable input device, operated by touching different areas on its surface; **touch'-paper** paper steeped in saltpetre for firing gunpowder, etc.; **touch'-screen** (*comput*) a screen of a visual display unit that doubles as an input device, and is operated by being touched; **touch rugby** or **rugger** a modified form of rugby football in which touching takes the place of tackling; **touch'stone** a highly siliceous (usually black) stone or other stone for testing gold or silver by the colour of the mark each makes on it; any criterion. — *vi* **touch'-type** to type without looking at the keys of the typewriter. — **touch'-typist**; **touch'wood** decayed wood that can be used as tinder. — **an easy (**or **a soft) touch** (*colloq*) a person or institution easily persuaded, esp. to lend or give money; **in (**or **out of) touch** in (or out of) communication or direct relations; **touch down** (of air or spacecraft) to land; **touch off** to trigger (also *fig*); **touch up** to improve by a series of small touches; to stimulate by a light blow; to touch or molest sexually; **touch wood** or (*US*) **knock on wood** or **knock wood** to touch something wooden as a superstitious guard against bad luck (also used as interjections, to accompany the gesture or independently). [O.Fr. *tuchier* (Fr. *toucher*).]

touché *tōō-shā'*, *interj* claiming or acknowledging a hit in fencing, or a point scored in argument, etc. [Fr., touched, scored against.]

tough *tuf*, *adj* tenacious; hard to cut, chew, break up or penetrate; resistant; capable of, or requiring, strenuous effort and endurance; unyielding; robust; laborious; refractory; criminal, ruffianly; unlucky (*colloq*). — *n* a rough or aggressive person, esp. a criminal or hooligan (also **tough guy**). — *interj* (*colloq*) tough luck. — *vt* or *vi* **tough'en** to make or become tough. — *n* **tough'ener**. — *n* and *adj* **tough'ening**. — *n* **tough'ie** (*colloq*) a tough person, problem, etc. — *adj* **tough'ish** rather tough. — *adv* **tough'ly**. — *n* **tough'ness**. — *adj* **tough'-minded** hard-headed, unsentimental, determined. — **get tough with** (*colloq*) to deal with (more) severely, sternly; **tough out** or **tough it out** withstand; endure stoically or defiantly. [O.E. *tōh*.]

toupee *tōō-pā'* or *tōō'pā*, *n* a wig or hairpiece to disguise baldness. [Fr. *toupet*.]

tour *tōōr*, *n* a round; a prolonged journey from place to place, e.g. for pleasure, or to give entertainment as a performer, or to give lectures, play matches, etc.; a pleasure trip or outing; a shift or turn of work; a period of military service in a particular place (also **tour of duty**). — *vi* to make a tour, go on tour. — *vt* to make a tour through or of; to tour with (a play). — *n* **tour'er** a touring-car or -bicycle; a tourist. — *n* and *adj* **tour'ing**. — *n* **tour'ism** the activities of tourists and those who cater for them. — *n* **tour'ist** a person who makes a tour, esp. a sightseeing traveller or a sportsman. — *adj* **touris'tic**. — *adj* **tour'isty** (*derog*) designed for, or full of, tourists. — **tour'ing-bicycle** a light but robust bicycle, equipped for touring; **tour'ing-car** a large motor car, with ample room for passengers and luggage; **tourist class** the cheapest class of accommodation on a boat or aeroplane; **Tourist Trophy** a motorcycle race held annually in the Isle of Man (*abbrev* **TT**); **tour operator** a person or firm organising (esp. package-tour) holidays. [Fr.; see **turn**.]

touraco or **turaco** *tōō'rə-kō*, *n* an African bird (*Turacus*) of the plantain-eater family, with a horny shield on the forehead and remarkable pigments in its feathers: — *pl* **tou'racos** or **tu'racos**. [W.Afr. name.]

tour de force *tōōr də fors*, (Fr.) a feat of strength or skill; an outstanding effort or performance.

Tourette's syndrome *tōō-rets' sin'drōm*, (*med*) *n* a disorder characterised by a variety of facial tics, muscular jerks, and involuntary behaviour, sometimes involving compulsive imitation of others and use of offensive language. [Gilles de la *Tourette* (1857–1904), French physician.]

tourmaline *tōōr'mə-lēn*, *n* a beautiful mineral of complex and varying composition, usually black or blackish. [Fr., — Sinh. *tòramalli*, carnelian.]

tournament *tōōr'nə-mənt*, *n* a military and athletic display; a series of games to determine a winner or winning team by elimination; a military sport of the Middle Ages in which combatants engaged in single combat or in troops, mainly on horseback, with spear and sword. [O.Fr. *tournoiement*, *tornoi* — *torner* — L. *tornāre*, to turn.]

tournedos *tōōr'nə-dō*, (*cookery*) *n* a small round thick beef fillet: — *pl* **tour'nedos** (*-dōz*). [Fr.]

tourney *tōōr'ni* or *tûr'ni*, *n* a medieval tournament. — *vi* to take part in a tournament. [Ety. as for **tournament**.]

tourniquet *tōōr'ni-kā*, *n* any appliance for compressing an artery. [Fr., — L. *tornāre*, to turn.]

tousle or **touzle** *towz'l*, *vt* to disarrange, to tumble; to dishevel. — *n* a tousled mass.

tout[1] *towt*, *vi* to look out for custom in an obtrusive, aggressive or brazen way. — *vt* to advertise, praise or recommend strongly. — *n* a person who touts; someone who hangs about racing-stables, etc., to pick up profitable information; someone who buys up numbers of tickets for a popular sporting event, etc. and sells them at a large profit (also **ticket tout**). — *n* **tout'er**.

tout[2] *tōō*, (Fr.) *adj* all; every; whole. — *adv* quite; entirely. — **tout à fait** (*tōō ta fe*) entirely; **tout au contraire** (*tōō tō kɔ̃-trer*) quite the contrary; **tout de suite** (*tōōt' swēt* or *tōōd'*) at once, immediately; **tout le monde** (*tōō lə mɔ̃d*) all the world, everybody.

touzle. See **tousle**.

tovarish *to-vä'rish*, *n* comrade. [Russ. *tovarishch*.]

tow[1] *tō* (or *Scot tow*), *vt* to pull with a rope or cable; to pull along. — *n* the condition of being towed; an act of towing; that which is towed. — *n* **tow'age** an act of towing; a fee for towing. — *n* **tow'er**. — *n* and *adj* **tow'ing**. — **tow'bar** a metal bar or frame used for towing trailers, etc.; **tow'line** or **tow'rope** a line used in towing; **tow'path** or **tow'ing-path** a path for horses towing barges. — **have (or take) in tow** to tow (another vehicle, vessel, etc.); to take along, be accompanied by; to have or assume charge of; **on tow** (of vehicles) or **under tow** (of vessels) being towed. [O.E. *togian*, to drag.]

tow[2] *tō*, *n* prepared fibres of flax, hemp or jute; esp. separated shorter fibres. — *adj* of or like tow. — *adj* **tow'y**. — **tow'-head** a person with light-coloured or tousled hair. — *adj* **tow'-headed**. [O.E. *tow-* (in compounds).]

towards *tə-wördz'*, *twördz* or *tördz* or **toward** *-örd'*, *prep* in the direction of; with a tendency to; for, as a help to; near, a little short of. [O.E. *tōweard*, — *tō*, to, sfx. *-weard*, -ward.]

towel *tow'əl*, *n* a cloth for drying. — *vt* to rub with a towel; to thrash (*slang*): — *pr p* **tow'elling**; *pa t* and *pa p* **tow'elled**. — *n* **tow'elling** a rubbing with a towel; an absorbent fabric for towels, sometimes used for dressing-gowns, curtains, etc.; a thrashing. — **tow'el-rail** a rod for hanging towels on. [O.Fr. *toaille*, from Germanic.]

tower *tow'ər*, *n* a tall building, standing alone or forming part of another; a fortress; a lofty or vertical flight. — *vi* to be very high or tall; to stand on high. — *adj* **tow'ered**. — *adj* **tow'ering** very high, elevated; (e.g. of rage) violent or intense. — *adj* **tow'ery**. — **tower block** a tall residential or office building; **tower mill** see **smock mill** under **smock**; **tower of strength** a stable, reliable person; **tower over** to be considerably taller than; to be markedly superior to. [O.Fr. *tur* — L. *turris*, a tower.]

towhee *tow'hē* or *tō'hē*, *n* any of various N. American finches of the genus *Pipilo*. [Imit.]

town *town*, *n* a populous place bigger or less rural than a village; a municipal or political division of a county (*US*); the principal town of a district; an urban community; the people of a town; the business or shopping centre; urban communities generically. — *adj* of a town; urban. — *n* **townee'** or **tow'nie** (often *derog*) a town-dweller, not a country person. — *n* **town'ship** a village, a community or local division; a thirty-six square mile block of public land (*US*); a site for a town (*Austr*); a small settlement (*Austr*); the territory or district of a town; the corporation of a town; a subdivision of a county or province (*US*); an administrative district (*US*); an urban settlement of black and coloured Africans (*SAfr*). — **town clerk** the secretary and legal adviser of a town; **town council** the governing body in a town; **town councillor**; **town-crī'er** (*hist*) an official who makes public proclamations in a town; **town'-dweller**; **town hall** a building for the official business of a town usu., with public rooms; **town'house** (chiefly *Scot*) a town hall; **town house** a house in town belonging to the owner of another in the country; a (usu. terraced) urban house, now typically with a garage on the ground floor and living-room above; **town-plann'ing** deliberate designing in the building and extension of towns to avoid the evils of haphazard and speculative building; **town'scape** a portion of a town which the eye can view at once; a picture of it; the design or building of all or part of a town. — Also *vt* and *vi*. — **town'scaping**; **towns'folk** the people of a town; **towns'man**, *fem* **towns'woman**, an inhabitant or fellow-inhabitant of a town; **towns'people** townsfolk. — **go to town** (*colloq*) to act, behave or perform enthusiastically, with thoroughness, without restraint; **on the town** out to amuse oneself in town; **take to town** (*slang*) to mystify, bewilder; **town and gown** the general community and the members of the university. [O.E. *tūn*, an enclosure, town.]

towy. See **tow**[2].

toxaemia or in U.S. **toxemia** *toks'ē-mi-ə*, *n* blood poisoning; a condition in late pregnancy characterised by a sudden rise in blood pressure. — *adj* **toxae'mic** or in U.S. **toxe'mic**. [Gr. *toxon* (see **toxic**) and *haima*, blood.]

toxic *toks'ik*, *adj* of poison; poisonous; poisoned; due to poison. — *adv* **tox'ically**. — *adj* **tox'icant** poisonous. — *n* a poisonous substance. — *n* **toxicity** (*-is'*) toxic quality. — *n* **tox'in** a ptomaine; a specific poison of organic origin. — *adj* **toxicolog'ical**. — *n* **toxicol'ogist**. — *n* **toxicol'ogy** the science of poisons. — *n* **tox'oid** a toxin that has been treated to remove its toxic properties without destroying its ability to stimulate formation of antibodies. [Gr. *toxon*, a bow, *toxikos*, for the bow, *toxikon*, arrow-poison.]

toxocara *toks-sə-kär'ə*, *n* any of various parasitic worms found in the intestines of dogs and cats and known to cause disease (**toxocarī'asis**) and eye damage in humans. [Gr. *toxon* (see **toxic**) and *kara*, head.]

toxophilite *toks-of'i-līt*, *n* a lover of archery; an archer. — *adj* **toxophilit'ic**. — *n* **toxoph'ily** love of archery; archery. [Gr. *toxon*, a bow, *phileein*, to love.]

toy *toi*, *n* a plaything; a trifle; a thing only for amusement or look; a dwarf breed of dog, etc. — *adj* made in imitation as a plaything; of a dwarf breed. — *vi* to trifle; to sport; to dally amorously. — *n* **toy'er**. — *n* and *adj* **toy'ing**. — **toy'-boy** (*slang*) a young gigolo, the pet of older, richer women; (*loosely*) a boyfriend significantly younger than one; **toy dog** a very small pet dog; **toy'shop** a shop where toys are sold. [Poss. Du. *tuig*, tools.]

tp *abbrev* for: township; troop.

TPI *abbrev* for Town Planning Institute.

tpr *abbrev* for teleprinter.

TR *abbrev* for Turkey (I.V.R.).

tr. *abbrev* for: transactions; translator; transpose; trustee.

tra- *tra*, *pfx* signifying: across; beyond; through. [Ety. as for **trans-**.]

trabeate *trāb'i-āt* or **trabeated** *trāb'i-āt-id*, (*archit*) *adj* built of horizontal beams, not arches and vaults. — *n* **trabeā'tion** an entablature; a combination of beams in a structure. [L. *trabs*, *trabis*, a beam.]

trabecula *trə-bek'ū-lə*, (*anat* and *bot*) *n* a cell, row of cells, band or rodlike structure running across a cavity, or forming an internal support to an organ: — *pl* **trabec'ūlae** (*-lē*). — *adj* **trabec'ūlar**. — *adj*

trabec'ūlate or **trabec'ulated**. [L.; dimin. of *trabs*, *trabis*, a beam.]

trace[1] *trās*, *n* an indication or mark of what is or has been; a beaten path (*US*); a track; a footprint; a mental or neural change caused by learning; a small quantity that can just be detected; a tracing; a line marked by a recording instrument. — *vi* to be traceable; date back. — *vt* to track; to follow step by step; to detect; to discover the whereabouts of; to follow or mark the outline of, esp. mechanically or on a translucent paper; to outline, delineate or write; to produce as tracery; to cover with tracery. — *n* **traceabil'ity**. — *adj* **trace'able**. — *n* **trace'ableness**. — *adv* **trace'ably**. — *adj* **trace'less**. — *adv* **trace'lessly**. — *n* **trā'cer** a person who traces; an instrument for tracing; a probe for tracing a nerve, etc.; a device by which a projectile leaves a smoke-trail; a projectile equipped with it; a chemical substance used to mark the course followed by a process. — *adj* **trā'ceried**. — *n* **trā'cery** ornamentation in flowing outline; ornamental open-work in Gothic architecture. — *n* **trā'cing** the act of someone who traces; a drawing copied mechanically or on translucent paper laid over the original; an instrumental record. — **trace element** a substance (such as zinc, copper, molybdenum, etc.) whose presence in the soil in minute quantities is necessary for plant and animal growth; **tracer bullet**; **tracer element** (*physiol*, etc.) an isotope, often a radio-isotope, used for experiments in which its particular properties enable its position to be kept under observation; **tracer shell**; **tra'cing-paper** translucent paper for tracing on. [Fr. *trace* — L. *tractus*, past p. of *trahĕre*, to draw.]

trace[2] *trās*, *n* (usu. in *pl*) a rope, chain or strap attached to an animal's collar or breast-strap for drawing a vehicle; a short piece of wire, gut or nylon connecting the hook to the fishing line. [O.Fr. *trays*, *trais*, pl. of *trait*, draught; cf. **trait**.]

trachea *trə-kē'ə* or in U.S. *trā'kē-ə*, *n* the windpipe; the air-tube in air-breathing arthropods: — *pl* **trachē'ae** (-*ē*). — *adj* **trachē'al**. — *adj* **trā'cheāte** or **trā'cheāted** having a trachea. — *n* **tracheitis** (*trak-i-ī'tis*) inflammation of the trachea. — *n* **tracheos'copy** inspection of the trachea. — *n* **tracheos'tomy** surgical formation of an opening into the trachea. — *n* **tracheot'omy** cutting into the trachea. [Med. L. *trāchēa* for L. *trāchīa* — Gr. *trācheia* (*artēriā*), rough (artery).]

trachoma *tra-kō'mə*, *n* a disease of the eye, with hard pustules on the inner surface of the eyelids. [Gr. *trāchōma*.]

trachyte *trak'īt*, *n* a fine-grained intermediate igneous rock. [Gr. *trāchys*, rough.]

tracing. See under **trace**[1].

track *trak*, *n* a mark or trail left; a beaten path; a made path; a sequence of thoughts or actions; the predetermined line of travel of an aircraft; a course, usu. oval-shaped, on which races are run; a railway line, the rails and the space between; the groove cut in a gramophone record by the recording instrument; one out of several items recorded on a disc or tape; one of several areas or paths on magnetic recording equipment receiving information from a single input channel; any of several or more or less demanding courses of study designed to meet the respective needs of students divided into groups according to ability (*US*); the endless band on which the wheels of a caterpillar vehicle run (*adj* **tracked** equipped with such metal bands); the distance between a pair of wheels measured as the distance between their respective points of contact with the ground. — *vt* to follow the track of; to find by so doing; to traverse; to beat or tread (a path, etc.); to follow the progress of; to follow the movement of (a satellite, spacecraft, etc.) by radar, etc., and record its positions. — *vi* to follow a trail; to make one's way (*colloq*); to run in alignment, esp. (of gramophone needles) to follow the grooves; to move a camera in a defined path while taking a shot (**tracking shot**). — *n* **track'age** provision of railway tracks. — *n* **track'er**. — *n* **track'ing** the action of the verb; excessive leakage current between two insulated points due e.g. to moisture (*electr eng*); disposition of the tone-arm on a gramophone so that the stylus remains correctly positioned in the groove. — *adj* **track'less** without a path; untrodden; leaving no trace; running without rails. — **track event** (in a sports competition) a race of any kind; **track record** a record of past performance, orig. that of an athlete, now generally that of any individual, company, etc.; **track shoe** a lightweight spiked running shoe worn by athletes; **track suit** a warm one worn by athletes before and after competing or when in training; **track'way** a beaten track; an ancient road. — **across the tracks** or **the wrong side of the tracks** (*colloq*) a slum or other socially disadvantageous area; **in one's tracks** just where one stands; **keep track of** keep oneself informed about; **make tracks** (*colloq*) to make off; to go quickly; **off the beaten track** away from frequented roads; out of the usual (*fig*); **on the right** (or **wrong**) **track** pursuing a correct (or mistaken) course; **track down** to find after intensive search; **tracker dog** one used for tracking, esp. in police searches. [Fr. *trac*; prob. Gmc.]

tract *trakt*, *n* a stretch or extent of space or time; a region, area; a tractate; a pamphlet or leaflet, esp. political or religious; a region of the body occupied by a particular system (e.g. *the digestive tract*). — *n* **tractā'rian** a writer of tracts, esp. (with *cap*) of the *Tracts for the Times* (Oxford, 1833–41 — Pusey, Newman, Keble, Hurrell Froude, etc.). — Also *adj*. — *n* **Tractā'rianism** the system of religious opinion promulgated in these, its main aim being to assert the authority and dignity of the Anglican Church — the *Oxford movement*. — *n* **tract'ate** a treatise. — *n* **tractā'tor** a tractarian. [L. *tractus*, drawing — *trahĕre*, *tractāre* to draw, pull.]

tractable *trak'tə-bl*, *adj* easily drawn, managed or taught; docile. — *n* **tractabil'ity** or **tract'ableness**. [L. *tractabilis* — *tractare*, to draw.]

tractile *trak'tīl*, *adj* ductile, capable of being drawn out. — *n* **tractility** (*trak-til'i-ti*). [Ety. as for **tract**.]

traction *trak'shən*, *n* the act of drawing or state of being drawn; the pulling on a muscle, organ, etc., e.g. by means of weights, to correct an abnormal condition (*med*). — *adj* **trac'tional**. — *adj* **trac'tive** pulling. — **trac'tion-engine** a locomotive for hauling heavy loads on roads, fields, etc. [Ety. as for **tract**.]

tractor *trak'tər*, *n* a motor vehicle used for hauling trailers, agricultural implements, etc.; the short front section of an articulated lorry, containing the engine and the driver's cab; a traction-engine. — **tractor feed** a device for feeding continuous stationery through the platen of a typewriter, printer, etc. [Ety. as for **tract**.]

trad *trad* or **trad jazz** (*jaz*), *n* a shortened form of *traditional jazz*, style of early 20th-century jazz which originated in New Orleans, characterised by improvisation against a regular rhythmical background.

trade *trād*, *n* an occupation, way of livelihood, esp. skilled but not learned shopkeeping; commerce; buying and selling; a craft; those people engaged in an occupation; customers; a deal; (in *pl*) the trade winds. — *vi* to have dealings (with *with*); to engage in commerce; to deal; to traffic; to buy and sell. — *vt* to exchange (esp. commercially), to barter; to buy and sell. — *adj* **trade'able** or **trad'able**. — *n* **trād'er**. — *n* and *adj* **trād'ing**. — **trade cycle** the recurring series of conditions in trade from prosperity to depression and back to prosperity; **trade discount** a discount offered to others in the same trade; **traded**

option (*stock exchange*) an option that can itself be bought and sold; **trade gap** the amount by which a country's visible imports exceed its visible exports in value; **trade'-in** that which is given in part payment; **trade journal** a periodical containing information and comment on a particular trade; **trade'mark** or **trade mark** any name or distinctive device warranting goods for sale as the production of any individual or firm; **trade'name** a name serving as a trademark; a name in use in the trade; **trade'-off** the giving up of one thing in return for another, usu. as an act of compromise; **trade plate** a temporary number plate attached to a vehicle by dealers, etc. prior to its being registered; **trade price** the price at which goods are sold to members of the same trade, or by wholesale to retail dealers; **trade route** a route followed by merchant caravans or trading ships; **trade secret** a secret and successful formula, process, technique, etc. known only to one manufacturer; **trades'folk** tradespeople; **trades'man,** *fem* **trades'woman,** a shopkeeper; a skilled worker; **trades'people** people engaged in trade; shopkeepers; skilled workers. — *adj* **trades'manlike.** — **trade union** an organised association of workers of an industry for the protection of their common interests; **trade unionism; trade unionist; trades union** an association of trade unions, as the **Trades Union Congress (TUC).** — *adj* **trade'-weighted** (*econ*) (of exchange rates) weighted according to the significance of the trade carried on with the various countries listed. — **trade wind** a wind blowing toward the thermal equator and deflected westward by the eastward rotation of the earth; **trading estate** an industrial estate; **trading post** a store, etc. established in an esp. remote, thinly-populated or hostile area; **trading stamp** a stamp given by the retailer to a purchaser of goods which, when a specified number have been accumulated, may be exchanged without payment for articles provided by the trading stamp firm. — **trade down** (or **up**) to deal in lower grade, cheaper (or higher grade, dearer) goods; to buy a smaller (or larger) house, etc. than one sells; **trade in** to give in part payment; **trade off** exchange, esp. as a compromise; **trade on** count on or take advantage of, esp. unscrupulously. [Prob. L.G. *trade*; related to **tread.**]

tradescantia *trad-is-kan'shi-ə, n* any plant of the American *Tradescantia* genus, with attractive (often variegated) foliage. [After the English gardener, naturalist and traveller John *Tradescant* (*c* 1567–1637).]

tradition *trə-dish'ən, n* oral transmission from generation to generation, esp. (often with *cap*) of certain Christian, Judaic and Islamic doctrines and customs; a tale, belief or practice thus handed down; a long-established belief or custom; anything bound up with or continuing in the life of a family, community, etc.; the continuous development of a body of, e.g. literature, music; a handing over (*law*). — *adj* **tradi'tional.** — *n* **tradi'tionalism.** — *n* **tradi'tionalist.** — *n* **traditional'ity.** — *adv* **tradi'tionally.** — *n* **tradi'tionist** a person who adheres to tradition. — **traditional jazz** see **trad.** [L. *trāditiō, -ōnis, trāditor, -ōris* — *trādĕre*, to give up — *trāns*, over, *dăre*, to give.]

traduce *trə-dūs'* or in U.S. *trə-do͞os', vt* to calumniate, malign; to defame. — *n* **traduce'ment.** — *n* **tradū'cer.** [L. *trādūcĕre, trāductum* — *trāns*, across, *dūcĕre*, to bring.]

traffic *traf'ik, n* commerce, trade; immoral or illegal trading; dealing; transportation of goods and persons on a railway, on an air route, etc.; vehicles, pedestrians, etc. (collectively), using a thoroughfare; a passing to and fro. — *vi* to trade, esp. immorally or illegally: — *pr p* **traff'icking;** *pa t* and *pa p* **traff'icked.** — *n* **traff'icker.** — *n* and *adj* **traff'icking.** — **traffic island** a raised section in the centre of a road to separate lanes, guide traffic, etc.; **traffic jam** congestion, and resultant stoppage, of traffic, e.g. at a busy junction; **traff'ic-lights** or **-signals** coloured lights to regulate street traffic, esp. at crossings; **traffic warden** an official controlling road traffic, esp. the parking of vehicles.

tragacanth *trag'ə-kanth, n* a gum (also **gum tragacanth**) got from several spiny shrubs of the genus *Astragalus*; a plant yielding it. [Gr. *tragakantha* — *tragos*, goat, *akantha*, thorn.]

tragedy *traj'i-di, n* a species of drama in which the action and language are elevated, and the ending usually sad, esp. involving the fall of a great man; the art of such drama; any sad story or turn of events; anything with death or killing in it (*journalism*). — *n* **tragedian** (*trə-jē'di-ən*) a writer or (usually) an actor of tragedy. — *n* **tragedienne** (*trə-jē-di-en'*) an actress of tragic rôles. — *adj* **tragic** (*traj'ik*) or **trag'ical** pertaining to or of the nature of tragedy. — *adv* **trag'ically.** — *n* **trag'icalness.** — **tragicom'edy** a play or story in which grave and comic scenes or themes are blended; a comedy that threatens to be a tragedy. — *adj* **tragicom'ic** or **tragicom'ical.** — *adv* **tragicom'ically.** [L. *tragoedia* — Gr. *tragōidiā*, tragedy, app. lit. goat-song.]

tragopan *trag'ō-pan, n* a brilliantly coloured Asiatic horned pheasant. [Gr. *tragopān*, hornbill — *tragos*, goat, *Pān*, the god Pan.]

tragus *trā'gəs*, (*zool*) *n* a small prominence at the entrance of the external ear; any of the hairs growing in the outer ear, esp. from this part: — *pl* **trā'gi** (*-jī*). [Gr. *tragos*, goat, tragus.]

trail *trāl, vt* to draw along or near the surface; to drag wearily; to drag along; to carry horizontally; to track, follow; to lag behind; to advertise (a forthcoming programme, etc.) by trailer. — *vi* to be drawn out in length; to hang, float or drag loosely behind; to sprawl over the ground or a support; to straggle; to lag; to be losing in a game or competition; to move with slow sweeping motion or with dragging drapery; to drag oneself along. — *n* anything drawn out in length or trailed; a train or tail; a track, e.g. of game; a beaten path in the wilds; a path, a route; an act or manner of trailing; a television or cinema trailer. — *n* **trail'er** a person who trails; a tracker; a creeping plant; an esp. two-wheeled conveyance, towed or dragged by a car, bicycle, or tractor; the rear section of an articulated lorry; a house on wheels, a caravan (*US*); a short film advertising a forthcoming entertainment or event on television or in the cinema. — *vt* to advertise (a programme, etc.) by trailer. — **trail'-blazer** a pioneer; a person or thing that leads the way in anything. — *adj* and *n* **trail'-blazing.** — **trailing edge** the rear edge, esp. of a wing; **trail'net** a dragnet. — **trail away** or **off** (esp. of a sound) to become fainter.

train *trān, vt* to instruct and discipline; to cause to grow in the desired manner; to prepare for performance by instruction, practice, diet, exercise, etc.; to bring up; to direct, aim (e.g. a gun or telescope). — *vi* to prepare oneself by instruction, exercise, diet, etc.; to be under drill; to travel by rail. — *n* that which is dragged along or follows; a tail; tail-feathers or trailing back-feathers; the part of a dress or robe that trails; a retinue; a series; a sequence; a number of things in a string; a string of railway carriages or wagons with a locomotive or other means of propulsion; a process; a line of combustible material to fire a charge; a set of wheels acting on each other, for transmitting motion. — *adj* **train'able.** — *adj* **trained** having received training; having a train. — *n* **trainee'** a person who is under training. — *n* **trainee'ship** the period of being a trainee; the position of, or maintenance provided for, a trainee. — *n* **train'er** a person who prepares athletes for competition, horses for a race, or the like; any machine or device used in training, esp. an aeroplane with duplicated controls for training pilots; a soft running shoe, usu. laced, with a thick sole, used in training or now esp. for general casual wear. — *n* **train'ing** practical education in any profession, art or handicraft; a course of diet and exercise for developing physical strength, endurance or dexterity. — **train'-bearer** a person who holds up the train of a robe or gown; **train'ing-ship** a ship in which young people are trained for the sea; **train'-spotter** a person who collects locomotive or carriage numbers as a hobby; **train'-spotting**. — **in train** in progress; **in training** undergoing training; physically fit. [Mainly O.Fr. *traïner*, *trahiner*, to drag (nouns *traïn*, *traïne*); partly with overlap of meanings, from O.Fr. *traïne*, guile.]

train-oil *trān'-oil*, *n* whale-oil extracted from the blubber by boiling. [Du. *traen* (now *traan*), tear, exudation.]

traipse or **trapes** *trāps*, *vi* to trail; to trudge. — *n* a trudge. — *n* and *adj* **traips'ing** or **trapes'ing**.

trait *trā* or *trāt*, *n* a characteristic. [Fr., — L. *trahĕre*, *tractum*, to draw.]

traitor *trā'tər*, *n* a betrayer; a person who commits treason: — *fem* **trait'ress**. — *adj* **trait'orous**. — *adv* **trait'orously**. — *n* **trait'orousness**. [Fr. *traître* — L. *trāditor* — *trādĕre*, to give up.]

trajectory *trə-jekt'ər-i* or *traj'ik-tər-i*, *n* the path described by a body under the action of given forces, esp. the curved path of a projectile. [L. *trājicĕre*, *-jectum* — *trāns*, across, *jacĕre*, to throw.]

tram *tram*, *n* an electrically-powered public vehicle running on rails laid in the road (also **tram'-car**); a truck used in mines. — **tram line** (usu. in *pl*) the track on which a tram runs (also **tram'way**); (in *pl*) the lines marking the sides of a tennis or badminton court and the lines parallel to them inside the court; a rigid set of principles; **tram'way** a track or system of tracks with sunken rails along a road. [Cf. L.G. *traam*, beam, shaft, etc.]

trammel *tram'l*, *n* a net whose inner fine-meshed layer is carried by the fish through the coarse-meshed outer layer, and encloses it in a pocket; anything that confines. — *vt* to shackle; to confine; to impede; to entangle: — *pr p* **tramm'elling**; *pa t* and *pa p* **tramm'elled**. — *n* **tramm'eller**. [O.Fr. *tramail*, a net — L.L. *tramacula*, from L. *trēs*, three, *macula*, a mesh.]

tramontane *tra-mon'tān*, *adj* beyond the mountains (esp. the Alps from Rome); foreign; uncivilised. — *n* a dweller beyond the mountains; a foreigner; a barbarian. — *n* **tramontana** (*trä-mon-tä'na*) in Italy, a north wind. [It. *tramontana* — L. *trāns*, beyond, *mōns*, *montis*, a mountain.]

tramp *tramp*, *vi* to tread, esp. heavily, noisily or steadily; to walk. — *vt* to traverse on foot; to trample. — *n* a foot-journey; the sound of heavy footsteps; a vagrant; a prostitute, an immoral woman (*slang*); a cargo-boat with no fixed route (also **tramp steamer**). — *adv* with tramping noise. — *n* **tramp'er**. [M.E. *trampen*.]

trampet or **trampette** *tram-pet'*, *n* a small trampoline used for springing off, in gymnastic vaulting. [Dimin. of **trampoline**.]

trample *tramp'l*, *vt* to tread roughly under foot; to treat with pride, to insult. — *vi* to tread roughly or in contempt; to tread forcibly and rapidly. — *n* a trampling. — *n* **tramp'ler**. — *n* **tramp'ling**. — Also *adj*. [Frequentative of **tramp**.]

trampoline *tram'pə-lin* or *-lēn*, *n* a framework holding a piece of canvas, stretched and attached by springs, for acrobats, gymnasts, diving learners, etc., to jump, somersault, etc. on. — *n* **tram'polinist**. [It. *trampolino*, springboard.]

tran- *tran-*, *pfx* signifying: across; beyond; through. [L. *trans*, across, beyond.]

trance *träns*, *n* a dazed, abstracted, ecstatic or exalted state; a deep sleeplike state, profound and prolonged. [Fr. *transe* — *transir* — L. *trānsīre*, to go across, in L.L. to die.]

tranche *trāsh*, *n* a slice; a block or portion, esp. of an issue of shares. [Fr., slice — *trancher*, to cut.]

trannie, tranny. See under **transistor**.

tranquil *trangk'wil*, *adj* calm; peaceful. — *n* **tranquillīsā'tion** or **-z-**. — *vt* **tranq'uillise** or **-ize** to make tranquil, esp. by sedation. — *n* **tranq'uillīser** or **-z-** that which tranquillises; a sedative drug. — *adv* **tranq'uillīsingly** or **-z-**. — *n* **tranquill'ity**. — *adv* **tranq'uilly**. [L. *tranquillus*.]

trans. *abbrev* for: transitive; translated; translation.

trans- *tranz-*, *tränz-*, *trənz-* or *-s-*, *pfx* signifying: across; beyond; through. [L. *trāns*, across, beyond.]

transact *tranz-akt'*, *tränz-*, *trənz-* or *-s-*, *vt* to conduct, negotiate; to perform. — *n* **transac'tion** the act of transacting; a piece of business performed; (in *pl*) the reports or publications of certain learned societies. — *n* **transac'tor**. [L. *trānsactum*, past p. of *trānsigĕre* — *agĕre*, to carry on.]

transalpine *tranz-al'pīn* or *tränz-*, *adj* beyond the *Alps* (orig. from Rome); crossing the Alps. [L. *trānsalpīnus* — *Alpae*, Alps.]

transatlantic *tranz-ət-lan'tik* or *tränz-*, *adj* beyond the *Atlantic* Ocean; crossing the Atlantic. [**trans-**.]

transaxle *tranz'ak-səl*, (*eng*) *n* (in a motor vehicle) a driving axle and differential gear-box forming an integral unit. [*trans*mission *axle*.]

transceiver *tran-sē'vər* or *trän-*, *n* a piece of radio equipment (e.g. a walkie-talkie) whose circuitry permits both transmission and reception. [*trans*mitter and re*ceiver*.]

transcend *tran-send'* or *trän-*, *vt* to rise above; to surmount; to surpass; to exceed; to pass or lie beyond the limit of. — *n* **transcen'dence**. — *n* **transcen'dency**. — *adj* **transcen'dent** transcending; superior or supreme in excellence; surpassing others; beyond human knowledge; abstrusely speculative, fantastic. — *adj* **transcenden'tal** transcending; supereminent, surpassing others; concerned with what is independent of experience; vague. — *vt* **transcenden'talise** or **-ize**. — *n* **transcenden'talism** the investigation of what is *a priori* in human knowledge, or independent of experience; the American reaction against Puritan prejudices, humdrum orthodoxy, old-fashioned metaphysics, materialistic philistinism, and materialism — best associated with the name of R.W. Emerson (1803–82). — *n* **transcenden'talist**. — *adv* **transcenden'tally**. — *adv* **transcen'dently**. — *n* **transcen'dentness**. — **transcendental meditation** a system of meditation designed to promote spiritual wellbeing and a relaxed state of consciousness through silent repetition of a mantra. [L. *trānscendĕre* — *scandĕre*, to climb.]

transcontinental *tranz-kont-i-nent'l* or *tränz-*, *adj* extending or passing across, or belonging to the farther side of a *continent*. [**trans-**.]

transcribe *tran-skrīb'* or *trän-*, *vt* to write over from one book into another; to copy; to transliterate; to arrange (a composition) for an instrument, voice or combination other than that for which it was composed (*mus*); to record for future broadcasting or the like; to broadcast a transcription of; to transfer (information) from one type of storage system to another (*comput*). — *n* **transcrīb'er**. — *n* **transcript** (*tran'skript* or *trän'*) a written or printed copy, esp. a legal or official copy of (sometimes secret) proceedings, testimony, etc. — *n* **transcrip'tion** the act or result of transcribing. — *adj* **transcrip'tional**. — *adj* **transcrip'tive**. — *adv* **transcrip'tively**. [L. *trānscrībĕre*, *-scrīptum*.]

transducer *trans-dū'sər*, *träns-* or *-z-*, or in U.S. *-dōōs'ər*, *n* a device that transfers power from one system to another in the same or in different form. [L. *trānsdūcĕre*, *-ductum*, to lead across.]

transept *tran'sept* or *trän'*, (*archit*) *n* part of a church at right angles to the nave, or of another building to the body; either wing of such a part where it runs right across. — *adj* **transept'al** of a transept. [L. *saeptum* (used in pl.) fence, enclosure.]

transf. *abbrev* for transferred.

transfer *trans-fûr'* or *träns-*, *vt* to carry or bring over; to convey from one place, person, ownership, object, group, football club, etc. to another; to change over; to convey (e.g. a design) to another surface. — *vi* to change over: — *pr p* **transferr'ing**; *pa t* and *pa p* **transferred'**. — *n* **trans'fer** the act of transferring; conveyance from one person, place, etc. to another; that which is transferred or is to be transferred (such as a picture). — *n* **transferabil'ity** (also **transferrabil'ity** and **transferribil'ity**). — *adj* **trans'ferable** (or *-fûr'*), or **transferrable** or **transferrible** (*-fûr'*). — *n* **transferee'** the person to whom a thing is transferred; someone who is transferred. — *n* **trans'ference** the act of transferring or conveying; unconscious transferring of one's hopes, desires, fears, etc. from one person or object to another (*psychol*). — *n* **trans'feror** (*law*) or **transferr'er** (*general*) someone who transfers. — **transferable vote** a vote which, if the candidate voted for should be out of the running, is to be transferred to another as second or subsequent choice; **transfer list** a list of footballers available for transfer to another club. [L. *trānsferre* — *ferre*, to carry.]

transferrin *trans-fer'in* or *träns-*, (*biochem*) *n* a protein in the blood that transports iron. [**trans-** and L. *ferrum*, iron.]

transfigure *trans-fig'ər* or *träns-*, *vt* to change the appearance of; to glorify. — *n* **transfiguration** (*-ə-* or *-ū-rā'shən*) a transformation or glorification in appearance; (with *cap*) the Christian festival of the transfiguration of Christ (from the Bible: Matt. xvii. 2). — *n* **transfig'urement**. [L. *trānsfigūrāre* — *figūra*, form.]

transfinite *trans-fī'nīt* or *träns-*, *adj* surpassing what is finite; (of a cardinal or ordinal number) surpassing all finite number (*math*). [**trans-**.]

transfix *trans-fiks'* or *träns-*, *vt* to pierce through; to paralyse with sudden emotion. — *n* **transfixion** (*-fik'shən*). [L. *trānsfīgĕre*, *-fīxum* — *fīgĕre*, to fix.]

transform *trans-förm'* or *träns-*, *vt* to change the shape of; to change to another form, appearance, substance or character; to change the form of (an algebraic expression or geometrical figure) (*math*). — *vi* to be changed in form or substance. — *n* (*träns'*) an expression or figure derived from another (*math*); (in digital computers) a process that alters the form of information without changing its meaning. — *adj* **transform'able**. — *n* **transformā'tion** change of form, constitution or substance; metamorphosis; (also **transformational rule**) any of a number of grammatical rules converting the deep structure of a sentence into its surface structure (*linguis*); reflection, rotation, translation or dilatation (*geom*). — *adj* **transformā'tional**. — *adj* **transform'ative**. — *adj* **transformed'**. — *n* **transform'er** someone who, or that which, transforms; an apparatus for obtaining an electric current from another of a different voltage. — *n* and *adj* **transform'ing**. — **transformational grammar** a method of studying or describing a language by stating which elements or structures can be derived from or related to others by transformation; a grammatical description which includes transformational rules. [L. *trānsfōrmāre* — *fōrma*, form.]

transfuse *trans-fūz'* or *träns-*, *vt* to pour out into another vessel; to transfer to another's veins; to cause to pass, enter or diffuse through. — *n* **transfū'ser**. — *adj* **transfū'sible**. — *n* **transfū'sion** (*-zhən*) transfusing, esp. of blood. — *n* **transfū'sionist**. — *adj* **transfū'sive** (*-siv*) tending or having power to transfuse. — *adv* **transfū'sively**. [L. *trānsfundĕre* — *fundĕre*, *fūsum*, to pour.]

transgenic *trans-jen'ik*, (*bot* and *zool*) *adj* containing genetic material introduced from another species. [**trans-**.]

transgress *trans-gres'*, *träns-* or *-z-*, *vt* to overstep, exceed; to infringe. — *vi* to offend by violating a law; to sin. — *n* **transgression** (*-gresh'ən*) an overstepping; an infringement; sin. — *adj* **transgress'ional**. — *adj* **transgressive** (*-gres'iv*). — *n* **transgress'or**. [L. *trānsgredī*, *-gressum* — *gradī*, *gressum*, to step.]

tranship or **transship** *tran(s)-ship'*, *trän(s)-* or *trən-*, *vt* to transfer from one ship or other conveyance to another. — *vi* to change ship, etc. — *n* **tran(s)ship'ment**. — *n* **tran(s)shipp'er**. — *n* **tran(s)shipp'ing**. [**tran(s)-**.]

transhume *trans-ūm'* or *-hūm'*, *träns-* or *-z-*, *vt* and *vi* to transfer or pass from summer to winter or from winter to summer pastures. — *n* **transhu'mance**. — *adj* **transhu'mant**. [Sp. *trashumar* — L. *trāns*, *humus*, ground.]

transient *tran'zi-ənt*, *trän'* or *-si-*, *adj* passing; of short duration; making, or for persons making, only a short stay. — *n* a temporary resident, worker, etc.; a brief alteration in a wave-form, etc., such as a sudden surge of voltage or current (*phys*). — *n* **tran'sience** or **tran'siency**. — *adv* **tran'siently**. — *n* **tran'sientness**. [L. *trānsiēns*, *-euntis* — pres. p. of *trānsīre*, to cross — *īre*, *itum*, to go.]

transistor *tranz-ist'ər*, *tränz-* or *-s-*, (*electronics*) *n* three-electrode semiconductor device, able to perform many functions of multi-electrode valves; a transistor radio. — *n* **transistorisā'tion** or **-z-**. — *vt* **transist'orise** or **-ize** to fit with a transistor. — **transistor radio** a small portable radio (*slang* short form **trann'ie** or **trann'y**). [*trans*fer and res*istor*.]

transit *tran'zit*, *trän'* or *-sit*, *n* the conveyance or passage of things or people over, across or through; passenger transport (esp. *US*); the passage of a heavenly body over the meridian. — *vt* to pass across; to reverse. — *n* **transition** (*-sizh'ən*, *-zish'ən* or *-sish'ən*) passage from one place, state, stage, style or subject to another; a change of key (*mus*); the specific passage from Romanesque or Norman to Gothic (*archit*). — *adj* transitional. — *adj* **transi'tional**. — *adv* **transi'tionally**. — *adj* **transi'tionary**. — *adj* **trans'itive** passing over; having the power of passing; taking a direct object (*gram*). — *adv* **trans'itively**. — *n* **trans'itiveness**. — *adv* **trans'itorily**. — *n* **trans'itoriness**. — *adj* **trans'itory** lasting or appearing for a short time. — **transit camp** a camp where e.g. refugees, immigrants, soldiers, etc. are temporarily accommodated before travelling on to a further destination; **tran'sit-instrument** a telescope mounted in the meridian and turned on a fixed east and west axis; **transit lounge** a lounge for transit passengers at an airport; **transit passenger** a passenger stopping briefly at an airport between flights; **tran'sit-theodolite** (*surveying*) one whose telescope can be reversed. — **in transit** (of goods, etc.) in the process of being transported from one place to another. [L. *trānsitus*, *-ūs*, *trānsitiō*, *-ōnis* — *īre*, *itum*, to go.]

translate *trans-lāt'*, *träns-*, *trəns-* or *-z-*, *vt* to render into another language; to express in another artistic medium; to interpret, put in plainer terms, explain; to transfer from one office (esp. ecclesiastical) to another; to remove to another place; to remove to heaven, especially without death; to transform; to perform a translation on (*mech*, *math*). — *vi* to practise translation; to be capable of translation. — *adj* **translā'table**. — *n* **translā'tion** the act of translating; rendering into another language; a version; removal to another place; motion, change of place, such that every point moves in the same direction at the same speed; similar change of place of a geometrical figure. — *adj* **translā'tional**. — *adj* **translā'tive** (*gram*) denoting, as in Finnish, 'turning into'. — *n* the translative case. — *n* **translā'tor**. [L. *trānslātum*, used as supine of *trānsferre*; see **transfer**.]

transliterate *tranz-lit'ə-rāt, tränz-* or *-s-*, *vt* to write in letters of another alphabet, etc. — *n* **transliterā'tion**. — *n* **translit'erātor**. [L. *littera*, letter.]

translocation *tranz-lō-kā'shən, tränz-* or *-s-*, *n* transference from place to place, esp. of materials within the body of a plant; the transfer of a portion of a chromosome to another part of the same chromosome or to a different chromosome (*genetics*). — *vt* **translocate'**. [L. *locus*, place.]

translucent *tranz-lōō'sənt, tränz-* or *-s-*, or *-lū'*, *adj* shining through; imperfectly transparent; clear. — *n* **translu'cence**. — *n* **translu'cency**. — *adv* **translu'cently**. [L. *trānslūcēns, -entis* — *lūcēre*, to shine — *lūx, lūcis*, light.]

translunar *tranz-lōō'nər, tränz-* or *-s-*, *adj* pertaining to the region beyond the moon's orbit round the earth. — *adj* **translu'nary** (or *tranz'*) beyond the moon; visionary. [**trans-**.]

transmigrate *tranz'mī-grāt, tränz'* or *-s-*, or *-grāt'*, *vi* to remove to another place of abode; (of the soul) to pass into another body. — *n* **transmīgrā'tion**. — *n* **transmīgrā'tionism** belief in the transmigration of souls. — *n* **transmīgrā'tionist**. [L. *trānsmigrāre, -ātum* — *migrāre*, to migrate.]

transmissible, transmission, etc. See under **transmit**.

transmit *tranz-mit', tränz-* or *-s-*, *vt* to send on; to pass on; to hand on; to communicate; to give to posterity; to send out or broadcast to allow the passage of, act as a medium for (heat, energy, light, sound, etc.). — *vi* to send out a radio signal, etc.: — *pr p* **transmitt'ing**; *pa t* and *pa p* **transmitt'ed**. — *n* **transmissibil'ity**. — *adj* **transmiss'ible**. — *n* **transmission** (*-mish'ən*) the process of transmitting or being transmitted; that which is transmitted; a programme, message, etc. sent out by radio, etc.; the system of interdependent parts in a motor vehicle, by which power is transferred from the engine to the wheels. — *adj* **transmiss'ional**. — *adj* **transmiss'ive** having the quality of transmitting or of being transmitted. — *n* **transmissiv'ity**. — *n* **transmitt'al**. — *n* **transmitt'er** a person who or thing which transmits; apparatus for sending forth anything, e.g. signals, messages, etc. [L. *trānsmittĕre, -missum* — *mittĕre, missum*, to send.]

transmogrify *tranz-mog'ri-fī, tränz-* or *-s-*, (*colloq, facetious*) *vt* to transform, transmute. — *n* **transmogrificā'tion**.

transmontane *tranz-mon'tān, tränz-* or *-s-*, *adj* another form of **tramontane**.

transmute *tranz-mūt', tränz-* or *-s-*, *vt* to change to another form or substance. — *n* **transmūtabil'ity**. — *adj* **transmū'table**. — *n* **transmū'tableness**. — *adv* **transmū'tably**. — *n* **transmūtā'tion** a changing into a different form, nature or substance, esp. that of one chemical element into another. — *n* **transmū'ter**. [L. *trānsmūtāre* — *mūtāre*, to change.]

transnational *tranz-nash'nəl, tränz-* or *-s-*, *adj* transcending national boundaries, concerning more than one nation. [**trans-**.]

transoceanic *tranz-ō-shi-an'ik, tränz-* or *-s-*, *adj* across or crossing the ocean. [**trans-**.]

transom *tran'səm*, *n* a crosspiece; a crossbeam; a structure dividing a window horizontally; a lintel; a small window over the lintel of a door or window. [O.Fr. *traversin*, — *traverse*, crosspiece.]

transpacific *trans-pə-sif'ik* or *träns-*, *adj* crossing the Pacific; beyond the Pacific. [**trans-**.]

transparent *trans-pār'ənt, träns-, trəns-*, also *-z-* or *-par'*, *adj* able to be seen through; easily detected or understood; obvious, evident; ingenuous. — *n* **transpar'ency** the quality of being transparent; that which is transparent; a picture, photograph, design or device visible, or to be viewed, by transmitted light. — *adv* **transpar'ently**. — *n* **transpar'entness**. [L.L. *trānspārēns, -entis* — L. *pārēre*, to appear.]

transpersonal *trans-pûr'sə-nəl* or *träns-*, *adj* going beyond, or transcending, the individual personality; denoting a form of psychology or psychotherapy that utilises mystical, psychical or spiritual experience as a means of increasing human potential. [**trans-**.]

transpire *tran-spīr'* or *trän-*, *vt* to give off as vapour; to emit through the skin. — *vi* to exhale; to give off water-vapour (as plants do) or waste material through the skin (as some animals do); to become known, come to light; (*loosely*) to happen. — *adj* **transpīr'able**. — *n* **transpiration** (*tran-spi-rā'shən*). — *adj* **transpīr'atory**. [L. *spīrāre*, to breathe.]

transplant *trans-plänt', träns-* or *-z-*, *vt* to remove (a plant) from the ground where it grows and plant in another place; to graft upon another animal or another part of the same; to remove and establish elsewhere. — *vi* to bear transplanting. — *n* **trans'plant** a part or organ removed from its normal position and grafted into another position in the same individual or into another individual; the act of transplanting. — *adj* **transplan'table**. — *n* **transplantā'tion**. — *n* **transplan'ter**. — *n* **transplan'ting**. [L. *trānsplantāre* — *plantāre*, to plant.]

transponder *tranz-pon'dər, tränz-* or *-s-*, *n* a radio or radar device which, on receiving a signal, transmits a signal of its own. [*trans*mitter res*ponder*.]

transport *trans-pört', träns-* or *-z-*, *vt* to carry, convey, remove; to send overseas as a convict; to carry away by strong emotion; to throw into an ecstasy. — *n* **trans'port** carriage or conveyance of goods or people from one place to another; the management of, or arrangements for, such conveyance; means of conveyance for getting from place to place; ecstasy; someone who has been transported or sentenced to transportation. — *n* **transportabil'ity**. — *adj* **transport'able**. — *n* **transportā'tion** removal; removal of offenders beyond seas; conveyance of goods or people; means of transport. — *adj* **transport'ed**. — *adv* **transport'edly**. — *n* **transport'edness**. — *n* **transport'er** someone or something that transports, esp. a large vehicle for carrying heavy goods. — *n* and *adj* **transport'ing**. — *adv* **transport'ingly**. — *adj* **transport'ive** tending or having power to transport. — **transport café** a roadside café catering mainly for long-distance lorry drivers. [L. *trānsportāre* — *portāre*, to carry.]

transpose *trans-pōz', träns-* or *-z-*, *vt* to transfer; to turn, alter; to change the order of, interchange; to write, perform or render in another key (*mus*). — *adj* **transpōs'able**. — *n* **transpōs'al** a change of place or order. — *n* **transpōs'er**. — *n* and *adj* **transpōs'ing**. — *n* **transposition** (*-pō-* or *-pə-zi'shən*). — *adj* **transposi'tional**. — *adj* **transpositive** (*-poz'*). — **transposing instrument** one for which music is written in a different key from the actual sounds. [Fr. *transposer*.]

transputer *trans-pū'tər* or *träns-*, (*comput*) *n* a chip capable of all the functions of a microprocessor, including memory, and able to process in parallel rather than sequentially. [*trans*istor and com*puter*.]

transsexual or **trans-sexual** *trans-seks'ū-əl* or *träns-*, *n* a person anatomically of one sex but having an abnormally strong desire to belong to the opposite sex; a person who has had medical and surgical treatment so that they resemble those of the opposite sex. — Also *adj*. — *n* **transsex'ualism**. [**trans-**.]

trans-ship, transship. Same as **tranship**.

transubstantiate *tran-səb-stan'shi-āt, trän-* or *-zəb-*, *vt* to change to another substance. — *n* **tran-**

substantiā'tion a change into another substance; the doctrine that, in the consecration of the elements of the eucharist, the whole substance of the bread and wine is converted into Christ's body and blood (*Christian relig*). — *n* **transubstantiā'tionalist, transubstan'tiātor** or **transubstantiā'tionist** a person who believes in transubstantiation. [L. *substantia*, substance.]

transude *tran-sūd'*, *trän-* or *-zūd'*, *vi* and *vt* to ooze out. — *n* **tran'sūdate** a substance that transudes. — *n* **transūdā'tion.** [L. *sūdāre*, to sweat.]

transuranic *trans-ū-ran'ik*, *träns-* or *-z-*, *adj* of greater atomic number than uranium. [**trans-**.]

transverse *tranz'vûrs*, *tränz'* or *-vûrs'*, *adj* set, sent, lying, etc. crosswise. — *adj* crosswise. — *n* anything set crosswise. — *adj* **transvers'al** transverse. — *n* a line cutting a set of lines. — *n* **transversal'ity.** — *adv* **transvers'ally.** — *adv* **transverse'ly.** — *n* **transver'sion.** — **transverse wave** (*phys*) a wave motion in which the disturbance of the medium occurs at right angles to the direction of wave propagation. [L. *trānsversus* — *vertĕre*, *versum*, to turn.]

transvest *tränz-* or *tranz-vest'*, *vt* and *vi* to dress oneself in the clothes of another, esp. of the opposite sex. — *n* and *adj* **transvestite** (*-vest'īt*) (someone) given to this. — *n* **transvest'ism** or **trans-vest'itism.** [**trans-** and L. *vestis* — *vestīre*, *vestītum*, to dress.]

trap *trap*, *n* a snare, device for catching; a hidden danger; a pitfall; a trapdoor; a bend in a pipe, esp. a drainpipe, to stop foul gases passing through; a light carriage; a contrivance for throwing up or releasing a ball or clay pigeons; the mouth (*slang*); a bunker or other hazard (*golf*); (in *pl*) drums or other percussion instruments (*jazz*). — *vt* to catch in a trap; to provide with traps; to control (a ball) so that it stops dead (*football*). — *vi* to act as a trapper: — *pr p* **trapp'ing;** *pa t* and *pa p* **trapped.** — *n* **trapp'er** someone who traps animals for their fur. — *n* **trapp'iness.** — *n* and *adj* **trapp'ing.** — **trap'door** a door set in a floor, stage or ceiling, esp. one flush with its surface; **trapdoor spider** one that makes a lair in the ground and covers it with a hinged door composed of earth and silk; **trap'-shooting** clay pigeon shooting. [O.E. *trappe* — *træppe*, *treppe*.]

trapes. See **traipse.**

trapezium *trə-pē'zi-əm*, *n* orig., any quadrilateral that is not a parallelogram; one with no sides parallel (*US*); one with one (and only one) pair of parallel sides (*Br*): — *pl* **trapē'zia** or **trapē'ziums.** — *n* **trapeze** (*trə-pēz'*) a swinglike apparatus used by acrobats, consisting of one or more crossbars suspended between two ropes. — *adj* **trapē'zial** pertaining to a trapezium. — *adj* **trapē'ziform** having the form of a trapezium. — *n* **trapē'zius** (*anat*; also **trapezius muscle**) (either of two triangular halves of) a large, flat, quadrilateral-shaped muscle across the back of the shoulders. — *n* **trapezoid** (*trap'i-zoid*, also *trə-pē'zoid*) a quadrilateral with no sides parallel; one with two sides parallel (*US*). — *adj* **trapezoid'al.** [Latinised from Gr. *trapezion*, dimin. of *trapeza*, a table; lit. four-legged.]

trappings *trap'ingz*, *npl* characteristic accompaniments, adornments, paraphernalia (of office, etc.); ornaments, esp. those put on horses. [App. conn. with Fr. *drap*, cloth.]

Trappist *trap'ist*, *n* a Cistercian of the reformed rule established by De Rancé (1626–1700), abbot of La *Trappe* in Normandy — austere and silent. — Also *adj*.

traps *traps*, (*colloq*) *npl* personal luggage. [App. conn. with Fr. *drap*, cloth.]

trash *trash*, *n* scraps; anything worthless; rubbish; nonsense; worthless people. — *vt* to free from trash; to lop the tops from; to discard, reject or expose as worthless. — *adv* **trash'ily.** — *n* **trash'iness.** — *adj* **trash'y** like trash; worthless. — **trash'can** (*US*) a receptacle for refuse, dustbin. [Prob. Scand.]

trass *tras*, *n* an earthy volcanic tuff used as a hydraulic cement. [Du. *tras*.]

trattoria *tra-tə-rē'ə* or *trät-tō-rē'ə*, *n* an Italian restaurant: — *pl* **trattori'as** or **trattorie** (*-rē'ā*). [It.]

trauma *trö'mə* or *trow'mə*, *n* a wound, an injury (*med*); an emotional shock that may be the origin of a neurosis (*psychiatry*); the state or condition caused by a physical or emotional shock: — *pl* **trau'mas** or **trau'mata.** — *adj* **traumatic** (*-mat'ik*) relating to, resulting from, or causing, wounds; of or causing a lasting emotional shock; (*loosely*) frightening, unpleasant. — *adv* **traumat'ically.** — *vt* **trau'matise** or **-ize** to inflict a mental or physical trauma on. — **trauma centre** (orig. *US*) a centre or hospital specifically for the treatment of trauma victims. [Gr. *trauma*, *-atos*, a wound.]

travail *trav'āl* or *-əl*, (*literary* or *archaic*) *n* excessive labour; toil; labour in childbirth. — *vi* to labour; to suffer the pains of childbirth. [O.Fr. (Fr.) *travail*.]

travel *trav'l*, *vi* to journey; to be capable of withstanding a journey; to go; to go round soliciting orders; to move along a course; to go with impetus; to move. — *vt* to journey over or through: — *pr p* **trav'elling;** *pa t* and *pa p* **trav'elled.** — *n* journeying. — *adj* **trav'elled** having made journeys; experienced; frequented. — *n* **trav'eller** a person who travels or has travelled; one of the travelling people; someone who travels for a mercantile house; a piece of mechanism that moves on a gantry, etc. — *n* and *adj* **trav'elling.** — *n* **travelogue** (*trav'ə-log*) a talk, lecture, article or film on travel. — **travel agency** an agency which provides information, brochures, tickets, etc., relating to travel; **travel agent;** **traveller's cheque** a cheque which can be cashed at any foreign branch or specified agent of the bank issuing it; **trav'eller's joy** the *virgin's-bower* (*Clematis vitalba*) sometimes called *old man's beard*; **travelling folk** or **people** the name by which itinerant people often call themselves, in preference to the derogatory names gipsies or tinkers. — *adj* **trav'el-sick** suffering from travel sickness. — **travel sickness** nausea experienced, as a result of motion, by a passenger in a car, ship, aircraft, etc. [Ety. as for **travail.**]

traverse *trav'ûrs*, *adj* cross; oblique. — *n* a crossing or passage across; a passage across the face of a rock (*mountaineering*); a survey by measuring straight lines from point to point and the angles between; anything set or lying across; an obstruction; a screened-off compartment; a denial or contradiction. — *vt* (or *-vûrs'*) to cross; to pass through, across or over; to move about over; to pass over by traverse; to survey by traverse; to oppose; to thwart; to dispute; to deny, contradict; to turn sideways. — *vi* to make a traverse; to move to the side; to direct a gun to the right or left. — *adj* **trav'ersable.** — *n* **travers'al** the action of traversing. — *adj* **trav'ersed** crossed, passed over. — *n* **trav'erser.** — *n* and *adj* **trav'ersing.** [Fr. *travers*, *traverse*, *traverser* — L. *trāns*, *vertĕre*, *versum*, to turn.]

travertine *trav'ər-tīn*, *-tēn* or *-tin*, *n* a pale limestone deposited from solution, e.g. from springs. [It. *travertino* — L. *tīburtīnus* (*lapis*), stone of Tibur.]

travesty *trav'is-ti*, *n* disguise, esp. of a man as a woman or vice versa; burlesque; ridiculously inadequate representation (of). — *vt* to disguise; to burlesque. — **travesty role** (*theat*) a role intended to be taken by a performer of the opposite sex to that of the character. [Fr. *travesti*, past p. of *travestir*, to disguise — L. *trāns*, *vestīre*, to clothe.]

travois *trä-voi'*, *n* a North American Indian drag, a pair of trailing poles attached to each side of the saddle, joined by a board or net: — *pl* **travois** (*trä-voiz'*). [Can. Fr. pronunciation of Fr. *travail*.]

trawl *trōl*, *n* an open-mouthed bag-net for dragging along the sea bed; a trawl-line (q.v.); an act of trawling. — *vt* and *vi* to catch or fish with a trawl. — *vt* to search over, comb, investigate thoroughly, in order to gather information. — *vi* to look for something (e.g. a suitable person for a post, etc.) by gathering suggestions from various sources (with *for*; strictly, a meaning developed from **troll**[2]). — *n* **traw'ler** someone who trawls; a trawling vessel. — *n* **traw'ling.** — **traw'lerman** someone manning a trawler; **trawl'-line** a buoyed line with baited hooks at intervals; **trawl'-net.** [Cf. **trail** and M.Du. *traghel*, dragnet.]

tray *trā*, *n* a flat low-rimmed vessel used for carrying articles (such as crockery, etc.). — *n* **tray'ful**: — *pl* **tray'fuls.** — **tray'-cloth** a cloth for covering a tray; **tray'mobile** (*Austr*) a household trolley, for serving tea, etc. [O.E. *trīg*, *trēg*, board.]

treacherous *trech'ər-əs*, *adj* ready to betray; not to be trusted; misleadingly inviting in appearance. — *adv* **treach'erously.** — *n* **treach'erousness.** — *n* **treach'ery** betrayal; readiness to betray; falseness; treason. [O.Fr. *trecheor*, deceiver — *trechier*, to trick.]

treacle *trē'kl*, *n* the dark, viscous uncrystallisable syrup obtained in refining sugar (also called *black treacle*); also molasses, the drainings of crude sugar; blandishments, esp. when suggestive of the cloying and nauseating taste and thickness of treacle; intolerable sentimentality. — *n* **trea'cliness.** — *adj* **trea'cly** of or like treacle; thick and sweet; unctuously blandishing; intolerably sentimental. [O.Fr. *triacle* — Gr. *thēriakē* (*antidotos*, an antidote to the bites) of beasts — *thērion*, a wild beast.]

tread *tred*, *vi* to set the foot down; to step; to walk; to trample; (of a cock) to copulate. — *vt* to walk on; to press with the foot, as in threshing, pressing grapes to trample; to render by treading; to perform by treading, dance; (of a cock-bird) to copulate with: — *pa t* **trod**; *pa p* **trodd'en** or **trod.** — *n* a footprint; a track; the act or manner of treading; a step or tramp; the part that touches the ground, as of a shoe or a wheel. — *n* **tread'er.** — *n* **tread'ing.** — *n* **tread'le** a foot-lever for working a machine; a pedal. — *vi* to work a treadle. — *n* **tread'ler.** — *n* **tread'ling.** — **tread'mill** a cylinder turned by treading on boards on its outside, as formerly by prisoners; a mill so worked; routine drudgery (*fig*); **tread'wheel** a wheel or cylinder turned by treading outside or inside; a treadmill. — **tread water** to float upright by an action as if of climbing a ladder. [O.E. *tredan*.]

treas. *abbrev* for treasurer.

treason *trē'zn*, *n* betraying of the government or an attempt to overthrow it; treachery; disloyalty. — *adj* **trea'sonable** pertaining to, consisting of, or involving treason. — *adv* **trea'sonableness.** — *adv* **trea'sonably.** — *adj* **trea'sonous.** — **high treason** offences against the state. [A.Fr. *tresun*, O.Fr. *traïson* (Fr. *trahison*).]

treasure *trezh'ər*, *n* wealth stored up; riches; anything much valued; a valued, indispensable servant, helper, etc. — *vt* to hoard up; to collect for future use; to value greatly; to store, enrich. — *n* **treas'urer** a person who has the care of a treasure or treasury; a person who has charge of collected funds. — *n* **treas'urership.** — *n* **treas'ury** place where treasure is deposited; (often with *cap*) a department of a government which has charge of the finances. — **treas'ure-chest** a box for keeping articles of value; **treas'ure-house** a house for holding treasures; a treasury; a store of valuable things; **treasure hunt** a hunt for treasure; a game in which competitors attempt to win a prize by being first to complete a course indicated by clues which have to be solved; **treas'ure-trove** ownerless objects of intrinsic or historical value found hidden (in England gold and silver only), property of the crown. [O.Fr. *tresor* — L. *thēsaurus* — Gr. *thēsauros*.]

treat *trēt*, *vt* to deal with; to handle; to discuss; to behave towards; to deal with the case of; to deal with (disease) by applying remedies; to subject to a process; to stand a drink or other gratification to. — *vi* to negotiate; to deal (with *of*). — *n* a free entertainment, pleasure excursion or feast; a turn or act of providing and paying; a source of great gratification. — *adj* **treat'able** able to be treated. — *n* **treat'er.** — *n* **treat'ing.** — *n* **treat'ise** (*-iz* or *-is*) a written composition, esp. one treating a subject formally or systematically. — *n* **treat'ment** the act or manner of treating; management; behaviour to anyone; way of applying remedies. — *n* **treat'y** negotiation; a formal agreement, esp. between states. — **Dutch treat** see under **Dutch**; **the (full) treatment** (*colloq*) the appropriate method (in every detail) of dealing, whether ceremoniously or punitively, with a particular type of person, case, etc. [O.Fr. *traitier* — L. *tractāre*, to manage — *trahěre*, *tractum*, to draw.]

treble *treb'l*, *adj* triple; threefold; in the treble (*mus*); high-pitched. — *n* that which is triple or threefold; three times as much; the highest part, soprano (*mus*); a treble singer, voice, instrument, string, sound, etc.; the narrow inner ring on a dartboard, or a hit on this; a bet involving three horse-races, the stake and winnings from the first being bet on the second, and those from the second on the third. — *vt* to make three times as much. — *vi* to become threefold. — *n* **treb'leness.** — *adv* **treb'ly.** — **treble chance** a mode of competing in football pools in which, in a selection of matches made from a list, the aim is to pick all draws; **treble clef** (*mus*) the G clef on the second line. [O.Fr., — L. *triplus*; see **triple.**]

trecento *trā-chen'tō*, *n* and *adj* 14th-century (in Italian art, etc.). — *n* **trecen'tist.** [It., three (for thirteen) hundred.]

tree *trē*, *n* a large plant with a single branched woody trunk (sometimes loosely applied); timber; a wooden structure or part of various kinds; a gallows; a cross for crucifixion; a branching figure or structure, such as a pedigree, a branching stand for rings, etc. (*ring-tree*, *mug-tree*). — *vt* to drive into a tree, to corner (also *fig*). — In combination denoting: inhabiting, frequenting or growing on trees; taking the form of a tree. — *adj* **tree'less.** — *n* **tree'creeper** a little bird that runs up tree-trunks in search of insects; **tree'-fern** a fern with a tall woody trunk; **tree frog** an arboreal amphibian, esp. one of the family *Hylidae*, nearer to toads than to frogs; **tree hopper** any of the homopterous leaping insects of the family *Membracidae*; **tree'-kangaroo** a tree-climbing kangaroo (*Dendrolagus*); **tree'-line** same as **timber-line.** — *adj* **tree'-lined** (of roads, etc.) having trees along either side. — **treenail** or **trenail** (*trē'nāl* or *tren'l*) a long wooden pin or nail; **tree'-peony** a shrub of the family *Ranunculaceae*, native to China and Tibet, with pale pink flowers, from which many garden varieties have been developed; **tree shrew** any insectivore of the E. Indian family *Tupaiidae*, squirrel-like animals related to shrews; **tree'-snake** a tree-dwelling snake; **tree'-stump**; **tree surgeon** someone who preserves diseased trees by filling cavities, amputating damaged branches, etc.; **tree surgery**; **tree tomato** a S. American shrub of the family *Solanaceae*, or its tomato-like fruit; **tree'top** the top of a tree; **tree'-trunk.** — **at the top of the tree** in the highest position in e.g. a profession; **family tree** pedigree; **up a tree** (*colloq*) in difficulties. [O.E. *trēow*, *trēo*.]

tref *trāf* or **trefa** *trā'fə*, *adj* (in the Jewish religion) forbidden as food, not kosher. [Heb. *terēphāh*, torn flesh — *taraph*, to tear.]

trefoil *trē'foil* or *tre'foil*, *n* a three-lobed form, ornament or aperture, as in tracery or heraldry; a leaf of three leaflets; a trifoliate plant, esp. of the clover genus (*Trifolium*). [A.Fr. *trifoil* — L. *trifolium* — *trēs*, three, *folium*, a leaf.]

trek *trek*, *vi* to make a long hard journey, usu. on foot; to tramp and camp, dragging one's equipment; to migrate; to journey by ox-wagon: — *pr p* **trekk'ing**; *pa t* and *pa p* **trekked**. — *n* a journey or stage a migration. — *n* **trekk'er**. [Du. *trekken*, to draw.]

trellis *trel'is*, *n* a structure of cross-barred or lattice-work. — *vt* to provide with a trellis; to train on a trellis. — *adj* **trell'ised**. — **trell'is-window** same as **lattice window**; **trell'is-work** lattice-work. [O.Fr. *treliz* — L. *trilīx*, *-īcis*, woven with triple thread.

trema *trē'mə*, *n* an orifice; a diaeresis. — *n* **trematode** (*trem'ə-tōd*) any member of the **Tremato'da**, a class of parasitic worms with adhesive suckers. — *n* and *adj* **trem'atoid**. [Gr. *trēma*, *-atos*, a hole.]

tremble *trem'bl*, *vi* to shake, e.g. from fear, cold or weakness; to quiver; to vibrate; to pass tremulously. — *vt* to set trembling. — *n* the act of trembling; tremulousness; a tremulous state; (in *pl*) a morbid trembling; (in *pl*; *specif*) a condition of muscular weakness and trembling in cattle and sheep, also a name for milk sickness in humans. — *n* **trem'blement**. — *n* **trem'bler**. — *n* and *adj* **trem'bling**. — *adv* **trem'blingly**. — *adj* **trem'bly** tremulous. — **trembling poplar** the aspen. [O.Fr. (Fr.) *trembler* — L. *tremulus*, trembling — *tremĕre*, to shake.]

tremendous *tri-men'dəs*, *adj* awe-inspiring; huge (*colloq*); prodigious, extraordinary, very good (*slang*). — *adv* **tremen'dously**. — *n* **tremen'dousness**. [L. *tremendus*, to be trembled at.]

tremolo *trem'ō-lō*, (*mus*) *n* a tremulous effect as by a rapid succession of interruptions or of up and down bows; a device in an organ or electronic instrument for producing this: — *pl* **trem'olos**. — Also *adj*. [It.]

tremor *trem'ər*, *n* a quiver; a thrill; an agitation; a vibration. — *adj* **trem'orless**. [L. *tremor*, *-ōris*.]

tremulous *trem'ū-ləs*, *adj* trembling; quivering. — *adj* **trem'ūlant** tremulous. — *adv* **trem'ūlously**. — *n* **trem'ūlousness**. [L. *tremulus*, trembling, and L.L. *tremulāre*, *-ātum*, to tremble.]

trenail. See **treenail** under **tree**.

trench *trench* or *trensh*, *n* a long narrow cut in the earth, often used in warfare as a cover for troops. — *vi* to make trenches; to dig deep with spade or plough; to encroach; to border, verge. — *vt* to cut; to make trenches in; to put in a trench; to provide with a trench; to entrench. — *adj* **trench'ant** cutting; incisive, forthright. — *adv* **trench'antly**. — *n* **trench'er**. — **trench coat** a short waterproof coat with belt, for man or woman; **trench'-feet** or **-foot** a diseased condition of the feet owing to exposure to cold and wet, esp. affecting soldiers in trench warfare; **trench'-fever** a disease causing pain in joints and muscles, prevalent among soldiers living in trenches, transmitted by lice; **trench mortar** a small smooth-bore gun, throwing large shells short distances, useful in trench warfare; **trench warfare** warfare in which each side entrenches itself in lines facing the enemy. [O.Fr. *trenche*, cut, *trencher* to cut, prob. — L. *truncāre* (see **truncate**).]

trencher *tren'chər* or *-shər*, *n* a plate or platter; a board. — **tren'cher-cap** a college-cap, mortar-board; **tren'cher-man** a hearty eater. [A.Fr. *trenchour* — *trencher*, to cut.]

trend *trend*, *vi* to have a tendency or prevailing direction. — *n* general tendency. — *adj* **tren'dy** (*colloq*) in the forefront of fashion in any sphere. — *n* (*derog*) a trendy person. — *n* **trend'setter** someone who helps to give a new direction to fashion. — *adj* **trend'setting**. [O.E. *trendan*.]

trente-et-quarante *trāt-ā-ka-rāt*, *n* the card-game rouge-et-noir. [Fr., thirty and forty.]

trepan *tri-pan'*, *n* a cylindrical saw; a tool for boring shafts. — *vt* to remove a piece of the skull from (*surg*); to cut a cylindrical disc from; to cut an annular groove in. — *n* **trepanation** (*trep-ə-nā'shən*). — *n* **trepann'er**. — *n* and *adj* **trepann'ing**. [Fr. *trépan* — L.L. *trepanum* — Gr. *trȳpanon* — *trȳpaein*, to bore.]

trepang *tri-pang'*, *n* sea-slug, a holothurian eaten by the Chinese. [Malay *trīpang*.]

trephine *tri-fēn'* or *-fīn'*, (*surg*) *n* a refined form of trepan. — *vt* to operate, perforate, or remove a circular section (e.g. from the skull or cornea) with the trephine. — *n* **trephin'er** a surgeon who uses a trephine. — *n* **trephin'ing**. [Earlier *trafine* — L. *trēs fīnēs*, three ends.]

trepidation *trep-i-dā'shən*, *n* trembling; alarmed agitation. — *adj* **trep'id** quaking. — *adj* **trep'idant**. — *adj* **trepid'atory**. [L. *trepidāre*, *-ātum*, to hurry with alarm — *trepidus*, restless.]

trespass *tres'pəs*, *vi* to interfere with another's person or property; to enter unlawfully upon another's land; to encroach (on); to intrude (with *on*); to sin (*liturgical*). — *n* act of trespassing; any injury to another's person or property; a sin (*liturgical*). — *n* **tres'passer**. [O.Fr. *trespasser* — L. *trāns*, *passus*, a step.]

tress *tres*, *n* a plait or braid of the hair of the head; a long lock. — *vt* to form into tresses. — *adj* **tressed** braided; in tresses; having tresses. — *adj* **tress'y** having or like tresses. [Fr. *tresse* — L.L. *tricia*, perh. Gr. *tricha*, threefold — *treis*, three.]

trestle *tres'l*, *n* a support composed of a horizontal beam on sloping legs; a braced framework. — **trest'le-table** one made of boards laid on trestles; **trest'lework** a braced framework. [O.Fr. *trestel* — L. *trānstrum*, crossbeam.]

trevally *tri-val'i*, *n* an Australian horse mackerel (*Caranx*) of various species.

trews *trōōz*, *npl* trousers, esp. of tartan cloth. [Ir. *trius*, Gael. *triubhas*.]

trey *trā*, *n* the three in cards and dice; a set of three. [O.Fr. *treis*, *trei* — L. *trēs*, three.]

TRH *abbrev* for Their Royal Highnesses.

tri- *trī-* or *tri-*, *combining form* denoting three or threefold. [L. *trēs*, *tria*, and Gr. *treis*, *tria*.]

triable. See under **try**.

triacid *trī-as'id*, (*chem*) *adj* having three replaceable hydrogen atoms; capable of replacing three hydrogen atoms of an acid. [**tri-**.]

triact *trī'akt*, (*zool*) *adj* three-rayed. — *adj* **trīact'inal** (*-i-nəl* or *-ī'nəl*) or **trīact'ine** (*-in*). [**tri-** and Gr. *aktīs*, *-īnos*, ray.]

triad *trī'ad* or *-əd*, *n* a group, set or union of three; in Welsh literature, a group of three sayings, stories, etc. about related subjects; a chord of three notes, esp. the common chord (*mus*); an atom, element or radical with a combining power of three (*chem*); any of many Chinese secret societies, some now associated with criminal activities, esp. heroin trading. — *adj* **trī'ad** or **trīad'ic**. [L. *trias* — Gr. *trias*, *triados* — *treis*, three.]

triage *trī'ij*, *trē'äzh* or *trē-äzh'*, *n* in war, etc., the selection for treatment of those casualties most likely to survive; sorting out or assessment, e.g. according to severity or urgency, etc. [Fr. — *trier*, to try.]

trial *trī'əl*, *n* a trying; examination by a test; examination by a court to determine a question of law or fact, esp. the guilt or innocence of a prisoner; (often in *pl*) examination (sometimes merely formal) of a candidate; a testing journey, e.g. of cars, trains, etc.; a trial match; suffering; temptation; attempt; a piece used as a test; a troublesome thing, a nuisance. — *adj* done, taken, etc. for the sake of trial. — *n* **tri'alist** or **tri'allist** a person taking part in a trial or test; a player under consideration for a place in a major team (*sport*). — **trial balance** (*bookkeeping*) in the double-entry system, a statement drawn up of the credit and debit totals to demonstrate that they are equal; **trial marriage** for a couple intending matrimony, a period of living together with a view to testing their compatibility; **trial run** a test drive in a motor vehicle to ascertain its efficiency; any introductory test, rehearsal, etc. — **by trial and error** by trying out several methods and discarding those which prove unsuccessful; **on trial** undergoing proceedings in a court of law; on probation, as an experiment; **stand trial** to undergo trial in a court of law; **trial of strength** a contest to find out who is the stronger (or strongest). [A.Fr. — *trier*, to try.]

triangle *trī'ang-gl* (also *trī-ang'gl*), *n* a plane figure with three angles and three sides (*math*); part of the surface of a sphere bounded by three arcs of great circles (*spherical triangle*); any mark or thing of that shape; a musical instrument of percussion, formed of a steel rod bent in triangle-form, open at one angle. — *adj* **tri'angled.** — *adj* **triang'ūlar** having three angles; (of a number) capable of being represented by dots in a triangle, as 1, 3, 6, 10, etc.; involving three persons or parties. — *n* **triangūlar'ity.** — *adv* **triang'ūlarly.** — *vt* **triang'ūlate** to survey by means of a series of triangles. — *adj* with, marked with or made up of triangles; triangular. — *adv* **triang'ūlātely.** — *n* **triangūlā'tion** the act or process of triangulating, e.g. for map-making; the series of triangles so used. — **the eternal triangle** an emotional situation involving two men and a woman or two women and a man. [L. *triangulum* — *angulus*, an angle.]

Trias *trī'əs*, (*geol*) *n* the oldest Mesozoic or Secondary system. — *adj* **Triassic** (*trī-as'ik*). [Gr. *trias*, triad, from its threefold division in Germany.]

triathlon *trī-ath'lon*, *n* a sporting contest consisting of three events, usually swimming, running and cycling. — *n* **triath'lete.** [**tri-** and Gr. *athlon*, a contest.]

triatomic *trī-ə-tom'ik*, *adj* consisting of three atoms; having three replaceable atoms or groups; trivalent. — *adv* **triatom'ically.** [**tri-**.]

tribade *trib'ad*, *n* a woman homosexual. — *adj* **tribad'ic.** — *n* **trib'adism** or **trib'ady** lesbian masturbation simulating heterosexual intercourse in the missionary position. [Fr. through L. *tribas*, *-adis* — Gr. *tribas*, *-ados* — *trībein*, to rub.]

tribal, etc. See under **tribe.**

tribasic *trī-bā'sik*, (*chem*) *adj* capable of reacting with three equivalents of an acid; (of acids) having three replaceable hydrogen atoms. [**tri-** and **base.**]

tribe *trīb*, *n* a division of a nation or people for political purposes; a set of people theoretically of common descent; an aggregate of families, forming a community; a race; a breed; a class or set of people; (*loosely*) a classificatory division. — *adj* **trī'bal.** — *n* **trī'balism** the existence of tribes as a social phenomenon; (loyalty to) the conventions, etc. of one's tribe. — *n* **trī'balist.** — *adj* **trī'balistic.** — *adv* **trī'bally.** — *adj* **tribe'less.** — *n* **tribes'man,** *fem* **tribes'-woman.** — *npl* **tribes'people.** [L. *tribus*, *-ūs*, one of the divisions of the ancient Roman people.]

tribo- *tri-* or *trī-bo-*, or *-ō-*, *combining form* denoting rubbing or friction. — *n* **tribo-electric'ity** generation of electric charges by friction. — *n* **tribol'ogy** the study of friction, wear, lubrication, etc. between surfaces moving in contact with one another. — *n* **tribol'ogist.** — *n* **triboluminescence** (*-es'əns*) emission of light caused by friction. — *adj* **tribo-luminesc'ent.** — *n* **tribom'eter** a sled-like apparatus for measuring sliding friction. [Gr. *tribein*, to rub.]

tribrach *trī'brak*, (*prosody*) *n* a foot of three short syllables. — *adj* **tribrach'ic.** [Gr. *tribrachys* — *brachys*, short.]

tribulation *trib-ū-lā'shən*, *n* severe affliction. [L. *trībulāre*, *-ātum*, to afflict.]

tribune *trib'ūn*, *n* orig. a magistrate elected by the Roman plebeians to defend their rights; a champion of popular rights; in this and the following sense, sometimes used as the title of a newspaper; a platform for speaking from; a raised area or stand; bishop's stall or throne. — *n* **tribunal** (*trib-* or *trīb-ū'nl*) a court of justice or arbitration; a body appointed to adjudicate in some matter or to enquire into some disputed question; a seat or bench in a court from which judgment is pronounced, a judgment-seat. — *adj* of, of the nature of or authorised by a tribunal. — *n* **trib'unāte** or **trib'uneship** the office of tribune. [L. *tribūnus*, tribune, *tribūnāl*, tribunal — *tribus*, a tribe.]

tribute *trib'ūt*, *n* a payment in acknowledgment of subjection; an act, gift, words or other expression of approval; (*loosely*) a testimony, a credit (to). — *adj* **trib'utary** paying tribute; contributing; paid in tribute. — *n* a payer of tribute; a stream that runs into another. [L. *tribūtum* — *tribuĕre*, to assign.]

tricameral *trī'kam-ə-rəl* or *-kam'-*, *adj* having three chambers. [**tri-** and L. *camera*, chamber.]

trice *trīs*, *vt* (*naut*) to haul. — *n* a moment (as if the time of a single tug). [M.Du. *trisen*, to hoist.]

triceps *trī'seps*, *adj* three-headed. — *n* (*anat*) a muscle with three separately arising heads, esp. the muscle at the back of the upper arm that straightens the elbow. [L. *trīceps*, *-cipitis* — *caput*, head.]

triceratops *trī-ser'ə-tops*, *n* a quadrupedal, herbivorous dinosaur of the Cretaceous period, having a horn over each eye and one on its nose. [**tri-** and Gr. *keras*, *-atos*, horn, *ōps*, face.]

trich- *trik-* or **tricho-** *trik-ō-* or *-o'-*, *combining form* denoting hair. [Gr. *thrix*, genitive *trichos*.]

trichiasis *trik-ī'ə-sis*, (*med*) *n* turning in of hairs around an orifice, esp. of eyelashes so that they rub against the eye. [L.L. — Gr. *thrix*, *trichos*, hair.]

Trichina *trik'i-nə* or *tri-kī'nə*, or **Trichinella** *trik-i-nel'ə*, *n* a genus of nematode worms parasitic in rat, pig and man; (without *cap*) a worm of the genus: — *pl* **Trich'inae, Trichinell'ae,** etc. (*-ē*) or **Trich'inas, Trichinell'as,** etc. — *n* **trichiniasis** (*trik-i-nī'ə-sis*) or **trichinō'sis** a disease caused by trichinae. — *n* **trichinīsā'tion** or **-z-** infestation with trichinae. — *adj* **trich'inised, -z-** or **trich'inosed** (*-nōst*) infested with trichinae. — *adj* **trichinot'ic** or **trich'-inous** pertaining to trichinosis. [Gr. *trichinos*, of hair — *thrix*, *trichos*, hair.]

trichlor- *trī-klör-*, or **trichloro-** *trī-klör-ō-*, *combining form* denoting (something) having three atoms of chlorine, esp. replacing hydrogen. — *n* **trichloro-ethylene** (*trī-klör-ō-eth'i-lēn*) an acetylene derivative, used as a solvent, in paint manufacture, and as an analgesic and anaesthetic (*colloq* short form **trike** (*trīk*)).

tricho-. See **trich-**.

trichoid *trik'oid*, *adj* hairlike. [Gr. *trichoeidēs*.]

trichology *trik-ol'ə-ji*, *n* the scientific study of hair and its disorders. — *adj* **tricholog'ical.** — *n* **trichol'ogist** a person skilled in trichology. [Gr. *thrix*, *trichos*, a hair.]

trichomonad *trik-ə-mon'ad*, *n* a parasitic protozoon of the genus **Trichomonas** (*tri-kom'* or *-kə-mon'*). — *n* **trichomoniasis** (*-mon-ī'ə-sis*) a sexually-transmitted disease caused by trichomonads. [**tricho-** and *monas*, *-ados*, a unit.]

Trichoptera *trik-op'tər-ə*, *npl* an order of insects with hairy wings, the caddis-flies. — *adj* **trichop'-terous.** [**tricho-** and Gr. *pteron*, wing.]

trichosis *trik-ō'sis*, *n* arrangement, distribution, or diseased condition, of hair. [Gr. *trichōsis*, hairiness.]

trichotomous *trī-kot'ə-məs*, *adj* divided into three; forking in threes. — *vt* and *vi* **trichot'omise** or **-ize** to divide in three or threes. — *adv* **trichot'omously.** — *n* **trichot'omy** trichotomous division or forking. [Gr. *tricha*, threefold — *treis*, three, *tomē*, a cutting — *temnein*, to cut.]

trichroic *trī-krō'ik*, *adj* having or exhibiting three colours, esp. when viewed in different directions. — *n* **trī'chroism.** [Gr. *trichroos*, three-coloured.]

trichromatic *trī-krō-mat'ik*, *adj* characterised by three colours; having three fundamental colour-sensations. — *n* **trichro'mat** someone who has normal colour vision. — *adj* **tri'chrome** trichromatic. — *adj* **trichrō'mic** trichromatic. — *n* **trichrō'matism.** [Gr. *trichrōmatos* — *chrōma*, colour.]

trick *trik*, *n* an artifice or a deceitful device; a deception; a prank; a performance aimed at astonishing, puzzling or amusing; an expedient or knack; a characteristic habit, mannerism or trait; a spell or turn, esp. at the helm; a round of play at cards; the cards so played and taken by the winner, forming a unit in scoring; a trinket, toy; the customer of a prostitute (*slang*). — *vt* to deceive, to cheat; to beguile; to dress or decorate fancily (with *out*). — *adj* of the nature of, or for the purpose or performance of, a trick. — *n* **trick'er.** — *n* **trick'ery** the act or practice of playing tricks; artifice; stratagem; imposition. — *adv* **trick'ily.** — *n* **trick'iness.** — *n* and *adj* **trick'ing.** — *adj* **trick'ish** tricky. — *adv* **trick'ishly.** — *n* **trick'ishness.** — *adj* **trick'less.** — *n* **trick'siness.** — *n* **trick'ster** a cheat; someone who practises trickery. — *n* **trick'stering** playing the trickster. — *adj* **tricks'y** pranked up; capricious; sportive; mischievous; tricky. — *adj* **trick'y** addicted to trickery; clever in tricks; ticklish; difficult to handle; complicated. — **trick cyclist** an acrobat who performs tricks on a unicycle or cycle; a psychiatrist (*slang*). — **do the trick** to bring something about; **how's tricks?** (*slang*) how are you?; **trick or treat** the (children's) practice of dressing up to visit neighbouring houses on Hallowe'en, threatening to play a trick unless a treat is produced; **turn a trick** (*slang*; esp. *US*) to have casual sexual relations with someone, esp. for money; **up to (one's) tricks** misbehaving. [O.Fr. *trique*, Northern form of *triche*, deceit.]

trickle *trik'l*, *vi* to run in drops or in a small irregular stream. — *vt* to emit in a trickle. — *n* a succession of drops. — *n* and *adj* **trick'ling.** — *adj* **trick'ly** trickling. — *n* **trick'le-down** (orig. and esp. *US*) filtration of benefits, esp. money, downwards through the social community. — *adj* of or pertaining to the idea that economic benefits received by advantaged sectors, e.g. large companies, ultimately filter down to benefit the less well off. [M.E. *triklen*.]

triclinic *trī-klin'ik*, (*mineralogy*) *adj* referred to three unequal axes obliquely inclined to each other. [Gr. *treis*, three, *klīnein*, to bend.]

tricolour or **tricolor** *trī'kul-ər*, *adj* three-coloured. — *n* (*tri'kul-ər*) a three-coloured flag, esp. that of France (*trē-kol-or*). — *adj* **trī'coloured.** [L. *tricolor* and Fr. *tricolore*.]

tricorn or **tricorne** *trī'körn*, *adj* three-horned; three-cornered. — *n* a three-cornered hat. [L. *tricornis*, three-horned — *cornū*, a horn.]

tricot *trē'kō*, *n* a hand-knitted woollen fabric, or imitation; a soft, slightly-ribbed cloth for women's garments. [Fr. *tricot*, knitting.]

tricuspid *trī-kus'pid* or **tricuspidate** *-kus'pid-āt*, *adj* with three cusps or points. [L. *tricuspis*, *-idis* — *cuspis*, a point.]

tricycle *trī'si-kl*, *n* a three-wheeled cycle; a light three-wheeled car for the use of a disabled person. — Colloq. short form **trike** (*trīk*). — *vi* to ride a tricycle. — *n* **tri'cycler.** — *adj* **tricyclic** (*trī-sī'klik*) having three whorls or rings; of a chemical compound, having three rings in its molecular structure, some compounds of this type being used as antidepressant drugs. — *n* **tri'cycling** (*-si-*). — *n* **trī'cyclist.** [**tri-** and Gr. *kyklos*, circle, wheel.]

trident *trī'dənt*, *n* a three-pronged spear, esp. that of the sea-god Poseidon or Neptune (*classical mythol*); anything of similar shape. — *adj* **tri'dent** or **tridental** (*-dent'l*) or **trident'āte** three-pronged. — *adj* **tridented** (*trī-dent'id*) three-pronged; (*trī'dənt-id*) having a trident. [L. *tridēns*, *-dentis* — *dēns*, tooth.]

Tridentine *trī-* or *tri-dent'īn*, *adj* (*hist* or *RC*) of Trent in Southern Tirol, or the Council (1545–63) held there. — *n* a native of Trent; a person who accepts the decrees of the Council, an orthodox Roman Catholic. [L. *Tridentum*, Trent.]

tridimensional *trī-dī-men'shən-əl*, *adj* having three dimensions. [**tri-**.]

triecious. See **trioecious.**

tried. See under **try.**

triennial *trī-en'yəl*, *adj* continuing three years; happening every third year. — *adv* **trienn'ially.** [L. *triennis* — *annus*, a year.]

trier, tries. See under **try.**

trifacial *trī-fā'shl*, *adj* threefold and pertaining to the face. — **trifacial nerve** the trigeminal nerve. [**tri-** and L. *faciēs*, face.]

trifecta *trī-fek'tə*, (*Austr*; *horse-racing*) *n* same as **triple.** [**tri-** and per*fecta*.]

trifid *trif'id* or *trī'fid*, *adj* cleft into three parts (*bot*, etc.); (of a spoon) having a three-pointed decorative top to its handle. [L. *trifidus*, split into three parts — *findere*, to split.]

trifle *trī'fl*, *n* anything of little importance or value; a small amount; a light confection of whipped cream or white of egg, sponge-cake, wine, etc. — *vi* (often with *with*) to busy oneself idly; to play, toy, amuse oneself; to behave without seriousness or respect; to meddle irresponsibly; to dally. — *vt* to spend or pass idly. — *n* **tri'fler.** — *adj* **tri'fling** of small value, importance or amount; trivial. — *adv* **tri'flingly.** — *n* **tri'flingness.** — **a trifle** slightly. [O.Fr. *trufle*, mockery, deception.]

trifocal *trī-fō'kəl*, *adj* (of a spectacle lens) giving separately near, intermediate and far vision. — *npl* **trifo'cals** spectacles with such lenses. [**tri-**.]

trifoliate *trī-fō'li-āt*, *adj* with three leaves or leaflets. — *n* **trīfō'lium** any plant of the clover or trefoil genus (*Trifolium*). [L. *trifolium* — *folium*, leaf.]

triforium *trī-fō'ri-əm*, (*archit*) *n* a gallery, storey or arcade over an aisle: — *pl* **trifo'ria.** [L.L.]

triform *trī'förm* or **triformed** *trī'förmd*, *adj* having a triple form. [L. *trifōrmis* — *fōrma*, form.]

trifurcate *trī'fər-kāt* or *-fûr'kāt*, *adj* three-forked. — *vi* to divide into three branches. — *adj* **tri'furcated** (or *-fûr'*). — *n* **trifurcā'tion.** [L. *trifurcus* — *furca*, a fork.]

trig[1] *trig*, *adj* trim, neat (chiefly *Scot*); tight, sound. — *vt* to make trig; to block, hold back with a wedge. — *n* a block or wedge to stop a wheel. — *adv* **trig'ly.** — *n* **trig'ness.** [O.N. *tryggr*, faithful.]

trig[2] *trig*, *n* short for **trigonometry, trigonometric** or **trigonometrical.**

trigeminal *trī-jem'i-nl*, *adj* threefold; three-branched. — **trigeminal nerve** (*anat*) a facial nerve having three branches, supplying the eye, nose, skin, scalp and muscles of mastication. — **trigeminal neuralgia** (*med*) another term for **tic-douloureux.** [L. *trigeminus*, born three at a birth — *geminus*, born at the same birth.]

trigger *trig'ər*, *n* a lever that releases a catch so as to fire a gun or set a mechanism going; anything that starts a train of actions. — *vt* (often with *off*) to set in action. — *adj* of something activated by or acting as a trigger. — **trigger finger** the finger used to pull the trigger on a gun, i.e. the forefinger of the dominant hand; a condition in which a finger is subject to involuntary muscular spasm, esp. where it cannot be straightened when unclenching the fist (*med*). — *adj* **trigg'er-happy** over-ready to shoot (*lit* and *fig*); irresponsibly willing to take the risk of beginning a fight or a war. [Du. *trekker* — *trekken*, to pull.]

triglyceride *trī-glis'ər-īd*, (*chem*) *n* any of a group of commonly occurring fats, those fatty acid esters of glycerol in which all three hydroxyl groups have had their hydrogen atoms replaced by acid radicals. [**tri-**.]

triglyph *trī'glif*, (*archit*) *n* a three-grooved tablet in the Doric frieze. — *adj* **triglyph'ic**. [Gr. *triglyphos* — *glyphein*, to carve.]

trigon *trī'gon*, *n* a triangle; a set of three signs 120° apart, the zodiac being divided into four trigons — *watery, earthly, airy, fiery* (*astrol*). — *adj* **trigonal** (*trig'ə-nl*) of a trigon; triangular. — *adj* **trigonic** (*trī-gon'ik*) of a trigon; triangular. — *adj* **trigonous** (*trig'ə-nəs*) triangular in section, or nearly so. [Gr. *trigōnon* — *gōniā*, an angle.]

trigonometry *trig-ə-nom'i-tri*, *n* the branch of mathematics that deals with the relations between the sides and angles of triangles. — *adj* **trigonometric** (*-nə-met'rik*) or **trigonomet'rical**. — *adv* **trigonomet'rically**. — **trigonometrical point** (*geog*, etc.) in triangulation, a fixed point whose position as vertex of a triangle is calculated astronomically (often shortened to **trig point**). [Gr. *trigōnon*, a triangle, *metron*, a measure.]

trigraph *trī'gräf*, *n* a combination of three letters for one sound. [**tri-** and Gr. *graphē*, a writing.]

trihedral *trī-hed'rəl* or *-hēd'rəl*, (*geom*, etc.) *adj* having three faces. — *n* a figure with a trihedral aspect, formed by three planes meeting at a point. — Also **trīhed'ron** (or *-hēd'*). [**tri-** and Gr. *hedrā*, a seat.]

trike[1]. See **trichloroethylene**.

trike[2]. See **tricycle**.

trilateral *trī-lat'ər-əl*, *adj* three-sided; of or having three parties or participants. — *n* **trilat'eralism**. — *n* **trilat'eralist**. — *n* **trilatera'tion** a technique involving the measurement of selected sides of a triangulation (q.v.) network, for map-making, surveying, etc. [**tri-** and L. *latus*, *lateris*, side.]

trilby *tril'bi*, *n* a soft felt hat with an indented crown and narrow brim: — *pl* **tril'bies** or **tril'bys**. [From George du Maurier's novel, *Trilby* (1894).]

trilinear *trī-lin'i-ər*, *adj* consisting of, having or referred to three lines. — *adj* **trīlin'eate** marked with three lines. [**tri-** and L. *līnea*, line.]

trilingual *trī-ling'gwəl*, *adj* in or using three languages, esp. native or habitual languages. [**tri-** and L. *lingua*, tongue.]

trilith *trī'lith* or **trilithon** *tri'* or *trī'li-thon*, *n* a form of megalithic monument consisting of two upright stones supporting another lying crosswise. — *adj* **trīlith'ic**. [**tri-** and Gr. *lithos*, stone.]

trill *tril*, *n* a tremulous sound; a run or roulade of bird-song; a consonant-sound produced by vibration. — *vt* and *vi* to play, sing, pronounce or sound with a trill. [It. *trillo*; imit.]

trillion *tril'yən*, *n* the cube of a million; the cube of ten thousand (orig. *US*, and before 1948 in France); (*loosely*; esp. in *pl*) an enormous number (*colloq*). — *n* and *adj* **trill'ionth**. [Fr., — **tri-**, after **million**.]

trillium *tril'i-əm*, *n* any plant of a three-leaved genus (*Trillium*) of the lily family. [L. *trēs*, three.]

trilobe *trī'lōb*, *n* something that has three lobes. — Also *adj*. — *adj* **trilobate** or **trilobated** (*trī'* or *-lō'*) or **trī'lobed** having three lobes. — *n* **trilobite** (*trī'lō-bīt* or *tril'ə-bīt*) any fossil arthropod of a Palaeozoic order (**Trilobī'ta**), with broad head-shield and body longitudinally furrowed into three lobes. — *adj* **trilobitic** (*-bit'ik*). [**tri-** and Gr. *lobos*, lobe.]

trilogy *tril'ə-ji*, *n* any group of three works, such as novels, plays, etc.; a triad; a group of three (orig. Gr.) tragedies. [Gr. *trilogiā* — *logos*, discourse.]

trim *trim*, *vt* to put in due condition; to fit out; to make ready for sailing; to adjust the balance of (a boat or aircraft); to dress, arrange; to set in order; to decorate (clothes, etc.) e.g. with ribbons, lace, contrasting edging, etc.; to make tidy or neat; to clip into shape; to make compact; to reduce the size of, by removing excess; to rebuke sharply; to thrash; to adjust the inclination of a plane to the horizontal. — *vi* to balance; to balance or fluctuate between parties, be a trimmer; to adjust one's behaviour as expediency dictates: — *prp* **trimm'ing**; *pat* and *pap* **trimmed**. — *adj* in good order; neat; tidy; well-kept; clean-cut; slim. — *adv* trimly. — *n* condition for sailing or flight; balance; condition, order; a fit, trim condition; humour, disposition, temper, way; array; fittings; the colour-scheme and chrome parts on the outside of a car, etc., or the upholstery, door-handles, etc. inside it; decorative additions to clothes, e.g. contrasting edging, etc.; an act of trimming; window-dressing (*US*); parts trimmed off; adjustment of an aircraft's controls to achieve stability in a desired condition of flight. — *adv* **trim'ly**. — *n* **trimm'er** someone who or that which trims; a person who fluctuates between parties, adjusting their opinions, etc. to match their changing loyalties; a scold; anything trouncing or redoubtable; a small horizontal beam on a floor into which the ends of joists are framed; a trimming tab; something fine, excellent, approved of (*Austr* and *NZ colloq*). — *n* **trimm'ing** making trim; balancing; clipping; (usu. in *pl*) ornamental additions; (in *pl*) accessories; (in *pl*) sauces and other accompaniments for a dish; (in *pl*) fittings; (in *pl*) parts trimmed off. — *adj* that trims. — *adv* **trimm'ingly**. — *n* **trim'ness**. — **trimming tab** or **trim'tab** a tab or aerofoil on an aircraft or boat, that can be adjusted in mid-passage to trim the craft. — **trim one's sails** to rule one's conduct, principles, etc. to accord with prevailing circumstances. [O.E. *trymman*, *trymian*, to strengthen, set in order — *trum*, firm.]

trimaran *trī'mə-ran*, *n* a boat with three hulls. [**tri-** and cata*maran*.]

trimer *trī'mər*, (*chem*) *n* a substance in which molecules are formed from three molecules of a monomer. — *adj* **trīmer'ic** (*chem*) having the same empirical formula but a relative molecular mass three times as great. — *adj* **trim'erous** (*bot*) having three parts, or parts in three. [**tri-** and Gr. *meros*, part.]

trimester *tri-mes'tər*, *n* three months; an academic term. — *adj* **trimes'trial**. [L. *trimēstris*, of three months — *mēnsis*, a month.]

trimeter *trim'i-tər*, (*prosody*) *n* a verse of three measures. — *adj* **trim'eter**, **trimetric** (*trī-met'rik*) or **trīmet'rical**. [Gr. *trimetros* — *metron*, measure.]

trimonthly *trī-munth'li*, *adj* every three months. [**tri-**.]

trimorphism *trī-mör'fizm*, *n* occurrence of three forms in the same species (*biol*); the property of crystallising in three forms (*chem*). — *adj* **trimor'phic**. — *adj* **trimor'phous**. [**tri-** and Gr. *morphē*, form.]

trimtab. See under **trim**.

Trin. *abbrev* for Trinity.

trine *trīn*, *adj* threefold; 120° apart (*astrol*); hence, benign (*astrol*). — *n* a triad; the aspect of two planets, as seen from the earth, distant from each other one-third of the zodiac or 120°; a triplet. — *adj* **trinal** (*trī'nl*). — *adj* **trī'nary**. [L. *trīnus* — *trēs*, *tria*, three.]

trinitro- *trī-nī-trō-*, *combining form* denoting (a chemical compound) having three nitro-groups (NO_2), esp. replacing hydrogen. — *n* **trinī'trin** glyceryl trinitrate or nitroglycerine, used to treat angina pectoris. — *n* **trinitrotol'uene** or **trinitrotol'uol** a high explosive (*familiarly* **TNT**), a trinitro-derivative of toluene. [**tri-**.]

trinity *trin'i-ti*, *n* threefoldness; three in one; a triad; esp. (with *cap*) the triune God of orthodox Christians (Father, Son, Holy Ghost); (with *cap*) any symbolical representation of the persons of the Trinity; (with *cap*) Trinity Sunday; (with *cap*) Trinity term. — *adj* **Trinitā'rian** of, in relation to or believing in the Trinity. — *n* someone who holds the doctrine of the Trinity. — *n* **Trinitā'rianism**. — **Trinity House** a lighthouse and pilot authority for England, and in part Scotland and Northern Ireland, chartered at

Deptford in 1514; **Trinity Sunday** the Sunday after Whitsunday; **Trinity term** the university term beginning after Trinity Sunday. [L. *trīnitās, -ātis* — *trīnus*, threefold.]

trinket *tring'kit, n* a small ornament or piece of jewellery; any paltry object. — *n* **trink'eting**. — *n* **trink'etry** trinkets collectively. [Poss. O.Fr. *trenquet*, small knife.]

trinomial *trī-nō'mi-əl, adj* consisting of three words; of three terms connected by the sign plus or minus. — *n* a trinomial name or expression. — *n* **trino'mialism** the system of naming by three words (for genus, species and subspecies). — *n* **trino'mialist**. [After **binomial**.]

trio *trē'ō, n* a set of three; a composition for, or combination of, three performers (*mus*); division of a minuet, scherzo or march (*mus*): — *pl* **tri'os**. [It.]

triode *trī'ōd, adj* with three electrodes. — *n* a three-electrode valve. [**tri-** and Gr. *hodos*, a path, way.]

trioecious or **triecious** *trī-ē'shəs, (bot) adj* having male, female and hermaphrodite flowers on different plants. [**tri-** and Gr. *oikos*, house.]

triolet *trī'ō-lit, trē'ō-lā* or *-let, n* an eight-lined poem rhymed *ab aa abab*, lines 4 and 7 repeating 1, and 8 repeating 2. [Fr.]

trioxide *trī-oks'īd, (chem) n* a compound with three atoms of oxygen. [**tri-**.]

trip *trip, vi* to move with short, light steps or skips; to stumble or catch one's foot; (often with *up*) to make a slip in accuracy, virtue, etc.; to experience the hallucinatory effects of LSD or similar drug; to make an excursion. — *vt* to cause to stumble or fall by catching the foot (often with *up*); to catch in a fault; to dance trippingly; to trip or dance upon; to release (a catch or similar mechanical part) by striking: — *pr p* **tripp'ing**; *pa t* and *pa p* **tripped**. — *n* a light, short step or skip; a catching of the foot, a stumble; a slip or lapse; a single journey or run, one way or to and fro; a pleasure excursion, jaunt; a specially arranged run at a cheap fare; a striking part that releases a catch; a hallucinatory experience under the influence of a drug such as LSD (*slang*); any stimulating experience (good or bad) (*slang*). — *n* **tripp'er** someone who trips; an excursionist, esp. of the disturbing kind (often *derog*); a device that when struck, passed over, etc., operates a switch. — *n* and *adj* **tripp'ing**. — *adv* **tripp'ingly**. — **trip'-hammer** a tilt-hammer; **trip'-wire** a wire which releases some mechanism when pulled, e.g. by being tripped over. [O.Fr. *triper*; of Gmc. origin.]

tripartite *trī-pär'tīt, adj* in three parts; split in three nearly to the base (*bot*); relating to three parties. — *n* **tripar'tism** an established system of dialogue between three related groups, *specif* government, employers and unions, for mutually acceptable planning and follow-up. — *n* **tripartition** (*-tish'ən*). [L. *tripartītus* — *partīrī*, to divide — *pars*, a part.]

tripe *trīp, n* parts of the compound stomach of a ruminant, prepared as food; rubbish, poor stuff (*colloq*); claptrap (*colloq*). — **tripe'hound** (*slang*) a newspaper reporter; a dog (*Austr*). [O.Fr. (Fr.) *tripe*, an animal's entrails.]

triphthong *trif'thong, n* a combination of three vowel sounds in one syllable (*phon*); (*loosely*) a trigraph. — *adj* **triphthongal** (*-thong'gl*). [**tri-** and Gr. *phthongos*, sound.]

triple *trip'l, adj* threefold; consisting of three; three times as much. — *n* a quantity three times as much; a thing that is triple; a betting system requiring that the horses which finish first, second and third in a race are selected in correct order. — *vt* and *vi* to treble. — *n* **trip'leness**. — *n* **trip'let** three of a kind, or three united; three lines rhyming together; a group of three notes occupying the time of two, indicated by a slur and the figure 3 (*mus*); one of three (people or animals) born at one birth. — *adj* **trip'licate** threefold; made thrice as much; as the cubes of the quantities. — *n* a third copy or thing corresponding to two others of the same kind; the triplicate ratio. — *vt* to make threefold. — *n* **triplicā'tion** the act of triplicating. — *n* **trip'ling** a making triple: — *adv* **triply** (*trip'li*). — **triple jump** an athletic event, based on a hop, skip and jump, in which a competitor tries to cover the longest possible distance; **triple point** the temperature and pressure at which solid, liquid and gaseous phases of a substance can co-exist, esp. triple point of water, 273·16K; **triple time** (*mus*) time or rhythm of three beats, or of three times three beats, in a bar. — **Triplex® glass** a combination of glass and mica in three layers. [Fr., — L. *triplus* — Gr. *triploos* (*triplous*); and L. *triplex*.]

triploid *trip'loid, (biol) adj* having three times the haploid number of chromosomes. — *n* **trip'loidy**. [Gr. *triploos*, triple.]

triply. See under **triple**.

tripod *trī'pod, n* anything on three feet or legs, esp. a stand for an instrument. — *adj* three-legged. — *adj* **tripodal** (*trip'əd-əl*). — *n* **tripody** (*trip'ə-di; prosody*) a verse or group of three feet. [Gr. *tripous, tripodos* — *pous, podos*, foot.]

tripoli *trip'ə-li, n* diatomite. [Orig. brought from *Tripoli* in Africa.]

tripos *trī'pos, n* an honours examination at Cambridge University; the list of successful candidates in it. [Prob. traceable to a B.A., known as Mr *Tripos*.]

tripper, tripping, etc. See under **trip**.

triptane *trip'tān, n* trimethyl butane, a powerful aviation fuel. [*tri*methyl *butane*, with *b* altered to *p*.]

triptych *trip'tik, n* a set of three tablets, painted panels, etc., hinged together, as one work of art. [Gr. *triptychos*, threefold — *ptyx, ptychos*, a fold — *ptyssein*, to fold.]

triptyque *trēp-tēk, n* (Fr.) an international pass for a motor car. [**triptych** (because divided into three sections).]

triquetra *trī-kwet'rə, n* an ornament consisting of three interlaced arcs, common in early art in northern Europe. [L. *triquetrus, -a, -um*, triangular — *trēs*, three.]

trireme *trī'rēm, (hist) n* an ancient Greek galley (esp. a war-galley) with three sets of rowers. [L. *trirēmis* — *rēmus*, an oar.]

trisect *trī-sekt', vt* to cut or divide into three (usu. equal) parts. — *n* **trisec'tion** (*-shən*). — *n* **trisect'or** someone who trisects. [**tri-** and L. *secāre, sectum*, to cut.]

trishaw *trī'shö, n* a three-wheeled light vehicle pedalled by a driver behind the passenger seat. [**tri-** and rick*shaw*.]

triskele *tris'kēl* or **triskelion** *tris-kel'i-on* (*pl* **triskel'ia**), *n* a figure consisting of three radiating curves or legs, as in the arms of the Isle of Man. [**tri-** and Gr. *skelos*, a leg.]

trismus *triz'məs, (med) n* tetanic spasm of the muscles of mastication, causing difficulty in opening the mouth. [Latinised from Gr. *trismos*, a creaking, grating — *trizein*, to grate, gnash.]

trisyllable *tri-sil'ə-bl,* also *trī-, n* a word of three syllables. — *adj* **trisyllabic** (*-ab'ik*) or **trisyllab'ical**. — *adv* **trisyllab'ically**. [**tri-**.]

trite *trīt, adj* worn-out; well-trodden; used till novelty and interest are lost; hackneyed. — *adv* **trite'ly**. — *n* **trite'ness**. [L. *trītus*, rubbed, past p. of *terěre*, to rub.]

tritheism *trī'thē-izm, n* belief in three Gods; belief that the Father, Son and Holy Ghost are actually different beings. — *n* **tri'theist**. — *adj* **tritheis'tic** or **tritheis'tical**. [**tri-** and Gr. *theos*, a god.]

tritiate. See under **tritium**.

Triticum *trit'i-kəm, n* the wheat genus of grasses. — *n* **trit'icale** a hybrid cereal grass, a cross between wheat and rye, grown as a food crop. [L. *trīticum*, wheat — *terěre, trītum*, to rub.]

tritium *trish'i-əm* or *trit'i-əm*, (*chem*) *n* an isotope of hydrogen of triple mass. — *vt* **tritiate** (*trish'i-āt* or *trit'i-āt*) to replace normal hydrogen atoms in (a compound) by tritium. — *n* **tritiā'tion.** — *n* **trit'ide** a compound of tritium with another element or radical. — *n* **triton** (*trī'tən*) the nucleus of tritium, composed of one proton and two neutrons. [Gr. *tritos*, third.]

Triton *trī'tən*, *n* a minor sea-god, son of Poseidon and Amphitrite, represented with a dolphin's tail, sometimes horse's forelegs, blowing a conch (*Gr mythol*); a genus of large gasteropods with shells that can be used like conchs; the larger of the two satellites of the planet Neptune. [Gr. *Trītōn*, *-ōnos*.]

triton. See under **tritium.**

tritone *trī'tōn*, (*mus*) *n* an augmented fourth, an interval of three whole tones. [Gr. *trĭtŏnos* — *tonos*, tone.]

triturate *trit'ū-rāt*, *vt* to rub or grind to a fine powder. — *n* the fine powder thus obtained. — *n* **triturā'tion.** — *n* **trit'urātor.** [L.L. *trītūrāre*, *-ātum* — L. *terĕre*, to rub.]

triumph *trī'əmf*, *n* complete or signal victory or achievement; exultation for success; in ancient Rome, a solemn procession in honour of a victorious general; a pageant. — *vi* to celebrate a victory with pomp; to rejoice for victory; to obtain victory, prevail (often with *over*); to exult (often with *over*). — *adj* **triumphal** (*trī-umf'l*) pertaining to triumph; used in celebrating victory. — *adj* **triumph'ant** celebrating or having achieved a triumph; exultant. — *adv* **triumph'antly.** — *n* **tri'umpher.** — *n* and *adj* **tri'umphing.** — **triumphal arch** an arch erected in connection with the triumph of a Roman general; any decorative arch in public rejoicings, etc. [L. *triumphus*.]

triumvir *trī-um'vər* or *trē-ōōm'vir*, *n* one of three men in the same office or government; one of three sharing supreme power: — *pl* **trium'virī** or **trium'virs.** — *adj* **trium'viral.** — *n* **trium'virate** an association of three men in office or government, or for any political ends; any trio or triad. [L. *triumvir*, from the genitive pl. *trium virōrum*, of three men.]

triune *trī'ūn*, *adj* three in one. — *n* a trinity in unity. — *n* **triū'nity.** [L. *trēs*, *tria*, three, *ūnus*, one.]

trivalent *trī-vā'lənt* or *triv'ə-lənt*, (*chem*) *adj* having a valency of three. — *n* **trivā'lence** (or *triv'əl-*) or **trivā'lency** (or *triv'əl-*). [**tri-.**]

trivet *triv'it*, *n* a tripod, esp. one for a pot or kettle; a bracket with three projections for fixing on the top bar of a grate; a usu. metal plate placed in a pressure cooker to raise the food to be cooked off the bottom of the vessel. — **right as a trivet** perfectly right, fit, sound. [O.E. *trefet*, app. — L. *tripēs*, *tripedis* — *pēs*, a foot.]

trivia *tri'vi-ə*, *npl* trifles, trivialities, unimportant details. — *adj* **trivial** (*triv'i-əl*) to be found anywhere; of little importance; trifling; vernacular (*biol*); specific, opp. to generic (of a name; *biol*); with value zero (*math*). — *n* **trivialisā'tion** or **-z-.** — *vi* **triv'ialise** or **-ize** to make trivial or unimportant. — *n* **triv'ialism** a trivial matter or remark. — *n* **triviality** (*-al'i-ti*) the state or quality of being trivial; that which is trivial, a trifle. — *adv* **triv'ially.** — *n* **triv'ialness.** [L. *trivium*, a place where three ways meet — *trēs*, three, *via*, a way.]

tri-weekly *trī-wēk'li*, *adj* occurring or appearing once in three weeks or three times a week. — *adv* once in three weeks; three times a week. — *n* a periodical appearing three times a week. [**tri-.**]

-trix *-triks*, *sfx* denoting a feminine agent: — *pl* **-trixes** or **-trices** (*-trī-sēz* or *-tri-siz*). [L.]

trocar *trō'kär*, *n* a surgical perforator used for inserting a cannula, to drain off or introduce liquid, etc. [Fr. *trocart* — *trois*, three, *carre*, side.]

trochaic. See under **trochee.**

trochal *trō'kəl*, *adj* wheel-like. — *n* **troche** (*trōk*, *trōsh* or *trōch*) a round medicinal tablet. — *n* **troch'oid** the curve traced by a fixed point, not on the circumference, in the plane of a rolling circle. — *adj* wheel-like; trochoidal. — *adj* **trochoid'al** of the nature of a trochoid. [Gr. *trochos*, a wheel — *trechein*, to run.]

trochanter *trō-kan'tər*, *n* a rough eminence on the thigh-bone for insertion of muscles (*anat*); the second segment of an insect's leg (*entom*). — *adj* **trochanteric** (*-ter'ik*). [Gr. *trochantēr* — *trechein*, to run.]

troche. See **trochal.**

trochee *trō'kē*, (*prosody*) *n* a foot of two syllables, a long followed by a short; in English, etc., a stressed followed by an unstressed syllable. — *adj* **trochaic** (*-kā'ik*). — *n* a trochaic verse. [Gr. *trochaios* (*pous*, foot), running, tripping — *trochos*, a running — *trechein*, to run.]

trochlea *trok'li-ə*, (*zool*) *n* any pulley-like structure, esp. a foramen through which a tendon passes. — *adj* **troch'lear.** — **trochlear nerve** the fourth cranial nerve. [L. *trochlea* — Gr. *trochiliā*, a pulley.]

trochoid, etc. See under **trochal.**

trod, trodden. See under **tread.**

troglodyte *trog'lə-dīt*, *n* a cave-dweller. — Also *adj.* — *n* **Troglodytes** (*-lod'i-tēz*) the wren genus. — *adj* **troglodytic** (*-dit'ik*) or **troglodyt'ical** cave-dwelling. — *n* **trog'lodytism** (*-dīt-izm*). [Gr. *trōglodýtēs* — *trōglē*, a hole, *dýein*, to get into.]

trogon *trō'gon*, *n* any member of a family (**Trogon'idae**) of tropical and esp. S. American birds with brilliant plumage including the quetzal. [App. Gr. *trōgōn*, nibbling.]

troika *troi'kə*, *n* a Russian vehicle for three horses abreast; a team of three horses abreast; a team of three men, etc. acting equally as leaders. [Russ., — *troe*, a set of three.]

troilism *troi'lizm*, *n* sexual activity between three people (of two sexes).

Trojan *trō'jən*, *adj* of Troy, ancient city of Asia Minor. — *n* a citizen or inhabitant of Troy; a doughty, trusty or hard-working person. — **Trojan horse** the gigantic wooden horse inside which the Greeks are said to have entered Troy; a person or organisation placed within a country, group, etc. with the purpose of destroying it; a concealed insertion of disruptive coded material within a program (*comput jargon*). [L. *Trōjānus* — *Trōja*, Troy.]

troll[1] *trōl*, (*Scand mythol*) *n* a goblin or supernatural dwarf. [O.N.]

troll[2] *trōl*, *vt* to fish for, or in, with a spinning or otherwise moving bait. — *vi* to fish with revolving or trailing lure (see also **trawl**). — *n* **troll'er.** — *n* and *adj* **trolling** (*trōl'*). — **troll'ing-bait** or **-spoon** a metallic revolving lure used in trolling. [Cf. O.Fr. *troller*, to quest, Ger. *trollen*, to roll.]

trolley *trol'i*, *n* a basket, table or tray (or set of tiered trays) on castors or wheels, used for transporting goods, luggage etc., or for serving food and drink; a bogie; a bed on wheels used for transporting patients; a pulley, receptacle or car travelling on an overhead wire or rail; a trolley-wheel; a tram-car (*US*): — *pl* **troll'eys.** — **troll'eybus** a bus that receives power by a trolley-wheel from a pair of overhead wires; **troll'ey-car** (*US*) a tram-car so driven; **troll'ey-table; troll'ey-wheel** a grooved wheel by which a bus, tram-car, etc. obtains current from an overhead wire. — **off one's trolley** (*slang*) daft, crazy. [Prob. **troll**[2].]

trollop *trol'əp*, *n* a shameless woman; a prostitute. — *adj* **troll'oping.** — *adj* **troll'opish.** — *adj* **troll'opy.** [Perh. **troll**[2] (in archaic and obs. senses) to trundle, stroll, move about, allure.]

trombone *trom-bōn'*, *n* a brass musical wind instrument, consisting of a tube bent twice on itself, with a slide. — *n* **trombōn'ist.** [It.; augmentative of *tromba*, trumpet.]

trommel *trom'əl*, *n* a revolving cylindrical sieve for cleaning or sizing minerals. [Ger. *Trommel*, drum.]

trompe or **tromp** *tromp*, *n* an apparatus for producing a blast of air in a furnace by falling water. [Fr.]

trompe l'œil *trɔ̃p lœ-y'*, (Fr.) lit. 'something that deceives the eye'; appearance of reality achieved by use of minute, often trivial, details or of other effects in painting, architecture, etc.

-tron *-tron*, *sfx* signifying agent, instrument, particularly: (1) thermionic valve, e.g. *klystron*; (2) elementary particle, e.g. *positron*; (3) particle accelerator, e.g. *cyclotron*. [Gr.]

troop *trōōp*, *n* a body of soldiers; (in *pl*) military forces; a band of people; a flock, herd, swarm of animals; (esp. in *pl*) a great number; a division of a cavalry squadron; a group of (Boy) Scout patrols; a troupe. — *vi* to pass in a body or in rapid succession; to move off in a group. — *vt* to cause to troop; to receive and carry ceremonially along the ranks (as in *troop the colour* or *colours*). — *n* **troop'er** a private soldier; a mounted policeman (*US* and *Austr*); a cavalry horse; a troop-ship. — **troop'-carrier** a motor vehicle, ship or aeroplane for carrying troops; **troop'-ship** a ship for transporting troops. [Fr. *troupe* — L.L. *troppus*.]

tropaeolum *trop-ē'ə-ləm*, *n* a plant of the Indian cress genus, S. American trailing or climbing plants constituting a family **Tropaeolā'ceae**, esp. the garden nasturtium. [Gr. *tropaion*, a trophy (from the shield-shaped leaves and helmet-like flowers).]

trope *trōp*, *n* a figure of speech, properly one in which a word or expression is used in other than its literal sense. [Gr. *tropos*, a turn — *trepein*, to turn.]

-trope *-trōp*, *combining form* denoting a tendency towards or affinity for, as in *heliotrope*. — *adj combining form* **-tropic**. [Gr. *tropos*, a turn.]

troph- *trof-* or *trəf-* or **tropho-** *-ō-* or *-o'-*, **-troph-** or **-trophy** *-trəf(-i)*, *combining form* denoting nutrition. — *adj* **troph'ic** relating to nutrition. — *n* **troph'oblast** the outer layer of epiblast in a mammalian ovum. — *adj* **trophoblast'ic**. — *n* **trophol'ogy** the study of nutrition. — *n* **troph'oplasm** protoplasm which is mainly concerned with nutrition. — *n* **trophozō'ite** in Protozoa, the trophic phase of the adult. [Gr. *trophē*, food, *trophos*, a feeder; *trephein*, to feed.]

trophy *trō'fi*, *n* a memorial of victory, orig. arms or other spoils set up on the spot; displayed spoils, such as skulls and antlers; a cup made of silver or suchlike awarded as a prize; a memorial of success, glory, etc.; an ornamental group of weapons, flags, etc., or a representation of it. — *adj* **trō'phied**. [Fr. *trophée* — L. *trophaeum* — Gr. *tropaion* — *tropē*, a turning — *trepein*, to turn.]

tropic *trop'ik*, *n* an imaginary circle on the celestial sphere about 23° 28′ N. (*tropic of Cancer*) or S. (*of Capricorn*) of the equator, where the sun turns on reaching its greatest declination north or south; a corresponding circle on the terrestrial globe; (in *pl*) the part of the earth between the tropics of Cancer and Capricorn. — *adj* of or relating to the sun's turning; of the tropics; of or of the nature of a tropism. — *adj* **trop'ical** of or relating to a tropic or the tropics; found in or characteristic of the tropics; fervidly hot; luxuriant. — *adv* **trop'ically**. — *n* **trōp'ism** (*biol*) orientation in response to stimulus; a general term for heliotropism, geotropism, etc. — *adj* **tropistic** (*trop-ist'ik*) of tropism. — *adj* **tropolog'ic** or **tropolog'ical**. — *adv* **tropolog'ically**. — *n* **tropol'ogy** figurative language; a moral interpretation of the Bible. — *n* **trop'opause** the boundary between troposphere and stratosphere. — *n* **trop'osphere** the lowest layer of the atmosphere in which temperature falls as height increases. — *adj* **tropospher'ic**. [Gr. *tropos*, a turning.]

troppo *trop'ō*, (It.; *mus*) *adj* and *adv* too much; excessively.

Trot *trot*, (*derog*) *n* and *adj* colloq. for **Trotskyist** or **Trotskyite**.

trot *trot*, *n* a pace between walking and running (in a horse with legs moving together diagonally); an act or spell of trotting; continual activity in moving about; a trotline (*angling*). — *vi* to go, ride or drive at a trot; to jog; to bustle about. — *vt* to cause to trot; to conduct around; to bring out for exhibition; to trot upon; to execute at a trot: — *pr p* **trott'ing**; *pa t* and *pa p* **trott'ed**. — *n* **trott'er** someone who or something that trots; a horse trained to trot in harness racing; a foot, esp. of a sheep or pig. — *n* **trott'ing** the action of the verb; harness racing. — **trot'line** (*angling*) a long line across a waterway to which shorter lines with baited hooks are attached. — **on the trot** (*colloq*) in succession, without a break; busy, bustling about; **the trots** (*slang*) diarrhoea; **trot out** to exhibit the paces of; to bring forward, produce for show, esp. repeatedly. [O.Fr. *trot* (noun), *troter* (verb).]

troth *trōth* or *troth*, (*formal* or *archaic*) *n* faith, fidelity. [Variant of **truth**.]

Trotskyism *trot'ski-izm*, *n* the form of Communism associated with Leon *Trotsky* (pseudonym of Lev Davidovich Bronstein, 1879–1940), who advocated worldwide revolution. — *n* and *adj* **Trot'skyist** or **Trot'skyite**.

troubadour *trōō'bə-dōōr* or *-dör*, *n* one of a class of lyric poets of chivalric love, who first appeared in Provence, and flourished from the 11th to the 13th century; a poet or singer (usu. one concerned with love). [Fr., — Prov. *trobador* — *trobar* to find.]

trouble *trub'l*, *vt* to agitate; to disturb; to muddy; to make turbid; to afflict or annoy; to busy or engage overmuch; to put to inconvenience. — *vi* to take pains; to put oneself to inconvenience; to be troublesome. — *n* disturbance, unrest; affliction; distress; a scrape; anything amiss; disease; uneasiness; exertion; the taking of pains; a cause of trouble. — *adj* **troub'led** (*-ld*). — *adv* **troub'ledly**. — *n* **troub'ler**. — *adj* **troub'lesome** causing or giving trouble or inconvenience; vexatious; importunate. — *adv* **troub'lesomely**. — *n* **troub'lesomeness**. — *n* and *adj* **troub'ling**. — **troub'lemaker** someone who disturbs the peace and (usu.) incites others to do so; **troub'leshooter** an expert detector and mender of any trouble, mechanical or other; **troub'leshooting**. — Also *adj*. — **trouble spot** a place where trouble, esp. social or political unrest, often occurs. — **ask (or look) for trouble** to behave in such a way as to bring trouble on oneself; **I'll trouble you to** please; **in trouble** (*euph*) pregnant (when unmarried); **trouble and strife** (*rhyming slang*) wife; **trouble someone for** to ask someone to provide, pass, etc. [O.Fr. *trubler* from a L.L. frequentative of L. *turbāre*, to disturb.]

trough *trof*, *n* a long, narrow vessel for watering or feeding animals; a vessel for kneading, brewing, washing, tanning, or various domestic and industrial purposes; a channel, gutter or conduit; a long narrow depression; a hollow between wave-crests; a low point (*fig*); an elongated area of low atmospheric pressure, usu. extending from a depression and marking a change of air-mass (*meteorol*). — **troughing and peaking** ranging between low and high points or levels. [O.E. *trog*.]

trounce *trowns*, *vt* to punish, beat, rebuke or censure severely. — *n* **trounc'er**. — *n* **trounc'ing**.

troupe *trōōp*, *n* a company, esp. of performers. — *vi* to travel about as a member of a theatrical troupe. — *n* **troup'er** a member of a theatrical troupe; an experienced actor; an experienced person (*fig*). [Fr.; see **troop**.]

trousers *trow'zərz*, *npl* a garment worn on the lower part of the body with a loose tubular branch for each leg; any other garment of similar form. The sing. is used to form compounds in as **trouser-butt'on**,

-clip, -leg', -pock'et, etc. — *adj* **trou'sered** wearing trousers. — *n* **trou'sering** (usu. in *pl*) cloth for trousers. — **trouser suit** a women's suit, consisting of a jacket and trousers. — **(caught) with one's trousers down** (taken) unawares; **wear the trousers** (of a wife or female partner) to be the dominant partner in a marriage, etc.

trousseau *tro͞o'sō, n* the clothes (and sometimes household linen, etc.) collected by a bride for her marriage: — *pl* **trou'sseaux** or **trou'sseaus** (*-sōz*). [Fr., dimin. of *trousse*, bundle.]

trout *trowt, n* a freshwater fish (*Salmo fario*) of the salmon genus, much sought after by anglers; extended to various fishes related or superficially similar; an unpleasant, interfering older person, usu. a woman: — *pl* **trout** (rarely **trouts**). — *adj* **trout'-coloured** speckled like a trout. — **trout'-farm** a place where trout are reared artificially; **trout'-rod** a fishing-rod for trout; **trout'-stream** a stream in which trout are caught. [O.E. *truht* — L. *tructa, tructus* — Gr. *trōktēs*, a sea-fish with sharp teeth — *trōgein*, to gnaw, nibble.]

trove. See **treasure-trove** under **treasure.**

trowel *trow'əl, n* a flat or scoop-shaped tool with a short handle, for plastering, gardening, etc. — *vt* to dress, apply or move, with or as if with a trowel: — *pr p* **trow'elling;** *pa t* and *pa p* **trow'elled.** — *n* **trow'eller.** — **lay it on with a trowel** to spread something thickly; to say grossly flattering things. [O.Fr. *truelle* — L.L. *truella* (L. *trulla*, dimin. of *trua*, a ladle).]

troy *troi, n* a system of weights used for precious stones and metals, the pound (no longer in legal use) of 5760 grains being divided into 12 ounces of 20 pennyweight (also *adj.*). — Also called **troy weight.** [*Troyes*, in France.]

truant *tro͞o'ənt, n* a child who, idly or without excuse, stays away from school (also *fig*). — Also *adj.* — *vi* to play truant. — *n* **tru'ancy.** — *n* **tru'antry.** — *n* **tru'antship.** — **play truant** to stay away from school without leave or good reason (also *fig*). [O.Fr. *truant*, prob. from Celtic.]

truce *tro͞os, n* a suspension of hostilities; a respite. — *adj* **truce'less.** — *adj* **trucial** (*tro͞o'shl, -syəl* or *-shiəl*) bound by a truce. — **truce'-breaker.** [M.E. *trewes, treowes*, pl. of *trewe* — O.E. *trēow*, truth, pledge, treaty; cf. **true.**]

truck[1] *truk, vt* to exchange; to barter; to pay in goods. — *vi* to traffic; to have dealings or intercourse; to barter; to bargain. — *n* exchange of goods; barter; payment in goods; dealings, intercourse; a small job, chore; small goods (*colloq*); rubbish (*colloq*); fresh vegetables, market-garden produce (*US*). — *n* **truck'age** barter. — *n* **truck'er** someone who trucks; a market-gardener (*US*). — *n* **truck'ing.** — **truck'-farm** (*US*) a market-garden; **truck'-farmer; truck'-farming.** — **have no truck with** to have nothing to do with. [O.Fr. *troquer*, to truck.]

truck[2] *truk, n* an open railway wagon for goods; a trolley; a bogie; a motor vehicle of heavier construction than a car, designed for the transportation of commodities, or frequently a specific commodity; a lorry (esp. *US*). — *vi* to drive a truck (chiefly *US*). — *vt* to convey by truck; to put on a truck. — *n* **truck'age** carriage by truck; charge for carriage by truck; supply of trucks. — *n* **truck'er** or **truck'man** (chiefly *US*) a lorry driver. — *n* **truck'ing.** — **truck'-load.** [L. *trochus*, a wheel — Gr. *trochos* — *trechein*, to run.]

truckle *truk'l, n* a truckle-bed; a barrel-shaped cheese (orig. *dialect*). — *vi* to sleep in a truckle-bed; to behave with servility (usu. with *to*). — *n* **truck'ler.** — *n* and *adj* **truck'ling.** — **truck'le-bed** a low bed that may be wheeled under another. [Gr. *trochileiā, -iā*, etc., a pulley — *trochos*, a wheel.]

truculent *truk'ū-lənt, adj* aggressive and discourteous. — *n* **truc'ulence** or **truc'ulency.** — *adv* **truc'ulently.** [L. *truculentus* — *trux*, wild, fierce.]

trudge *truj, vi* to walk with labour or effort; to plod doggedly. — *vt* to plod wearily or doggedly along, over, etc. — *n* a heavy or weary walk; a trudger. — *n* **trudg'er.** — *n* and *adj* **trudg'ing.**

trudgen *truj'ən, n* a swimming stroke in which each hand alternately is raised above the surface, thrust forward, and pulled back through the water. [John *Trudgen*, who popularised the stroke in England.]

true *tro͞o, adj* faithful; constant; trusty; genuine; properly so called; typical; conformable; accurately adjusted or in tune; straight or flat; agreeing with fact; actual; absolute; corrected; accurate; exact; right; rightful; honest; sincere; truthful. — *adv* truly; faithfully; honestly; in accurate adjustment; dead in tune; after the ancestral type. — *vt* to adjust accurately. — *n* accurate adjustment. — *n* **true'ness.** — *adv* **tru'ly.** — **true bill** (*law*; *NAm* or *hist*) a bill of indictment endorsed, after investigation, by a grand jury, as containing a case for the court. — *n* **true blue** and *adj* **true-blue** see under **blue[1].** — *adj* **true'-born** of genuine birth; pure-bred; true to the qualities of the breed; legitimate. — *adj* **true'-hearted** sincere; faithful. — **true-heart'edness; true'-love** someone truly or really beloved; a sweetheart. — Also *adj.* — **true'-love-knot** or **true-lov'er's-knot** an ornamental or symbolic knot or interlaced design, as a two-looped bow or a knot with two interlaced loops; **true time** the time according to the position of the sun, as opp. to mean time. — **out of true** not straight, not properly balanced, adjusted or calibrated. [O.E. *trēowe*.]

truffle *truf'l, n* any fungus of the genus *Tuber* or the family *Tuberaceae*; its underground edible fructification; a rich confection, made with chocolate, butter, etc., usu. shaped into balls. — *adj* **truff'led** cooked, stuffed or dressed with truffles. — **truff'le-dog** and **truff'le-pig** animals trained to find truffles. [O.Fr. *truffle*; poss. — L. *tūber*, lump, swelling.]

truism *tro͞o'izm, n* a self-evident truth; a commonplace or trite statement. — *adj* **truist'ic.** [**true.**]

truly. See under **true.**

trumeau *tro͞o-mō', (archit) n* a piece of wall or pillar between two openings: — *pl* **trumeaux** (*-mōz'*). [Fr.]

trump[1] *trump, (poetic* or *archaic) n* a trumpet; a blast. [O.Fr. *trompe*.]

trump[2] *trump, (cards) n* a card of a suit that takes any card of any other suit. — Also *adj.* — *vt* to play a trump card upon instead of following suit (*cards*); to take in this way (also *fig*). — *vi* to play trumps on another suit. — **trump'-card** the card turned up to determine the trump suit (*cards*); any card of that suit; a means of triumph (*fig*); a victorious expedient (*fig*). — **no'-trumps** (*cards*) a declaration in bridge whereby no suit is more powerful than the rest. — *adj* **no'-trump.** — **turn up trumps** (*fig*) to behave in a very helpful or generous way, esp. unexpectedly. [**triumph.**]

trump[3] *trump, vt* to concoct and put forward unscrupulously (with *up*). — *adj* **trumped'-up.**

trumpet *trum'pit, n* an orchestral, military, and signalling wind instrument of powerful and brilliant tone, in its present form a narrow tube bent twice upon itself, with cupped mouthpiece and flaring bell; applied to other instruments more or less similar; a trumpet-shaped object, such as a flared bell or horn; a sound of, or as if of, a trumpet; a trumpeter. — *vt* to sound or play on a trumpet or with trumpetlike sound; to proclaim, celebrate, summon, denounce, expel, etc. by trumpet. — *vi* to sound a trumpet; to make a sound like a trumpet: — *pr p* **trum'peting;** *pa t* and *pa p* **trum'peted.** — *adj* **trum'peted** sounded on a trumpet; loudly extolled; having a trumpet; funnel-shaped. — *n* **trum'peter.** — *n* and *adj* **trum'peting.** — **trum'pet-call** a conventional phrase or passage played on the trumpet as a signal; any call to action; **trumpeter swan** an American swan, the largest of the world's swans; **trum'pet-flower** a name for various plants with large trumpet-shaped flowers; **trum'pet-major** a head-trumpeter in a regiment. — *adj* **trum'pet-shaped** like the bell of a trumpet. — **blow one's own trumpet** to sound one's own praises. [Fr. *trompette*, dimin. of *trompe*, trump.]

truncal. See **trunk**.

truncate *trungk-āt'*, *vt* to cut short; to lop. — *adj* **trunc'ate** or **truncat'ed** appearing as if squared off at the tip; ending in a transverse line or plane, esp. one parallel to the base. — *adv* **trunc'ately.** — *n* **truncā'tion.** [L. *truncāre*, *-ātum* — *truncus*; cf. **trunk**.]

truncheon *trun'shən* or *-chən*, *n* a cudgel carried by a police officer; a staff of authority. — *vt* to beat with a truncheon. [O.Fr. *tronchon* — *tronc*; see ety. for **trunk**.]

trundle *trun'dl*, *vt* and *vi* to wheel, esp. heavily or clumsily; to roll; to bowl along. — **trun'dle-bed** a truckle-bed. [O.E. *trendel*.]

trunk *trungk*, *n* the stem of a tree; the body of an animal apart from head and limbs; the body generally; a main line of road, railway, telephone, etc.; the main body of anything; the shaft of a column; the body of a pedestal; a chest or box, esp. as luggage for travelling; a boxlike channel, trough, shaft, conduit or chute; a tube; a proboscis; same as **bus** (*comput*); (in *pl*) pants worn for sports, swimming, etc.; the boot, luggage compartment of a car (*US*). — *adj* **trunc'al** pertaining to the trunk; principal. — *adj* **trunked** having a trunk. — *n* **trunk'ful** as much as will fill a trunk: — *pl* **trunk'fuls.** — *n* **trunk'ing** casing; a system of sharing a number of radio channels among a number of users of mobile (e.g. car) radio communication systems, the users being able to use any channel which is free at any given time. — **trunk call** the former name for a long-distance telephone call, involving connection between two centres, a **national call**; **trunk dialling** the dialling of trunk telephone calls directly, connections not being made by an operator; **trunk line** the main line of a railway, canal, gas or oil pipeline, etc.; **trunk road** a main road, esp. one administered by central authority. [Fr. *tronc* and L. *truncus*, a stock, a torso — *truncus*, maimed; with associations of Fr. *trompe*, a trump, a proboscis.]

trunnion *trun'yən*, *n* either of a pair of side projections on which anything (as formerly a big gun) is pivoted to move in a vertical plane. [Fr. *trognon*, stump.]

truss *trus*, *n* a bundle, esp. of hay or straw, or a block cut from a stack; a framed structure for supporting a weight; a tuft of flowers or fruit at the top of the main stalk or stem; a corbel (*archit*); a surgical appliance for retaining a reduced hernia. — *vt* to bundle up; to fix for cooking, e.g. with a skewer; to provide or fix with a truss. — *adj* **trussed.** — *n* **truss'er.** — *n* **truss'ing.** [Fr. *trousse* (noun), *trousser* (verb).]

trust *trust*, *n* worthiness of being relied on; fidelity; confidence in the truth of anything; confident expectation; a resting on the integrity, friendship, etc. of another; faith; hope; credit (esp. sale on credit or on promise to pay); ground of confidence; that which is given or received in confidence; charge; responsibility; anything felt to impose moral obligations; an arrangement by which property is handed to or vested in a person, to use and dispose of it for the benefit of another; an estate so managed for another; an arrangement for the control of several companies under one direction, to cheapen expenses, regulate production, beat down competition, and so obtain a maximum return. — *adj* held in trust. — *vt* to place trust in; to believe; to expect confidently; to hope; to give credit to; to commit to trust. — *vi* to have trust; to rely (with *to*). — *n* **trustee'** a person to whom anything is entrusted; a person to whom the management of a property is committed in trust for the benefit of others. — *n* **trustee'ship** the state of being or action of a trustee; a trust territory. — *n* **trust'er.** — *adj* **trust'ful** trusting. — *adv* **trust'fully.** — *n* **trust'fulness.** — *adv* **trust'ily.** — *n* **trust'iness.** — *adj* **trust'ing** confiding. — *adv* **trust'ingly.** — *adj* **trust'less.** — *n* **trust'lessness.** — *adv* **trust'-worthily.** — *n* **trust'worthiness.** — *adj* **trust'-worthy** worthy of trust or confidence; trusty. — *adj* **trust'y** (*compar* **trust'ier**, *superl* **trust'iest**) to be trusted; deserving confidence; faithful; honest; strong; firm. — *n* someone who can be trusted; a well-behaved prisoner, often granted special privileges. — **trust** (or **trustee**) **account** a savings account, the balance of which can be left to a beneficiary; **trust company** or **corporation** a commercial enterprise formed to act as a trustee; **trust fund** a fund of money, etc. held in trust; **trust territory** a territory ruled by an administering country under supervision of the Trusteeship Council of the United Nations. — **breach of trust** a violation of duty by a trustee, etc.; **in trust** as a charge, for safe-keeping, for management as a trustee; **investment trust** an organisation which invests its stockholders' money and distributes the net return among them; **on trust** on credit; (accepted) without question; **unit trust** type of investment trust in which given amounts of different securities form a unit, choice of a number of differently constituted units being available. [O.N. *traust*, trust.]

truth *trōōth*, *n* faithfulness; constancy; veracity; agreement with reality; fact of being true; actuality; accuracy of adjustment or conformity; in the fine arts, a faithful adherence to nature; that which is true or according to the facts of the case; the true state of things, or facts; a true statement; an established fact; true belief; known facts, knowledge. — *adj* **truth'ful** habitually or actually telling what one believes to be true; put forward in good faith as what one believes to be true; conveying the truth. — *adv* **truth'fully.** — *n* **truth'fulness.** — **truth drug** or **serum** any of various drugs which make subjects under questioning less wary in their replies; **truth'-teller.** — *adj* **truth'-telling.** — **truth table** a Boolean logic table in which the binary digits 0 and 1 are assigned values either 'true' or 'false'; **truth'-value** (*logic*) the truth or falsity of a statement. — **God's truth** a thing or statement absolutely true; **in truth** truly, in fact; **tell the truth** to speak truthfully, not to lie. [O.E. *trēowth* — *trēowe*, *trīewe*, true.]

try *trī*, *vt* to test; to use, treat, or resort to, experimentally; to put to the test; to strain; to annoy, irritate, afflict; to examine critically; (of a judge) to examine and decide the truth, justice, guilt or innocence of; (of a lawyer) to conduct in court (*US*); to attempt, endeavour, essay (usu. with *to*). — *vi* to make an effort: — *3rd pers pr t* **tries**; *pr p* **try'ing**; *pa t* and *pa p* **tried** (*trīd*). — *n* a trial; effort; the score of three points (Rugby League) or four points (Rugby Union) gained by a player who succeeds in placing the ball with his hand over the goal line (*Rugby football*); an attempt to gain further points after scoring a touchdown (*Am football*). — *adj* **trī'able** subject to legal trial; that can be tried. — **triage** and **trial** see separate articles. — *adj* **tried** (*trīd*) proved good by test. — *n* **trī'er** someone who tries in any sense; also **try'er** in the sense of someone who is assiduous in trying to win. — *n* **try'ing.** — *adj* making trial or proof; adapted to try; searching, severe; testing; distressing; causing strain. — *adv* **try'ingly.** — **try'-on** an act of trying on a garment; an attempt impudently to impose on someone (*slang*); **try'-out** a test performance; **trysail** (*trī'sl*) a reduced sail used by small craft, instead of the mainsail, in a storm; a small fore-and-aft sail set with a boom and gaff. — **try and** (*colloq*) try to; **try for** make an attempt to reach or gain; **try it on** (*colloq*) to attempt to do something risky or audacious to see how far one can go unscathed; **try on** to put on for trial (e.g. a garment); **try out** to test. [O.Fr. *trier*, to pick out.]

tryp *trip*, *n* short for **trypanosome**.

trypanosome *trip'ən-ə-sōm*, *n* a protozoon (**Trypanosō'ma** of various species, family **Trypanosomat'idae**) parasitic in the blood of vertebrates. — *adj* **trypanocidal** (-*sī'dl*). — *n* **tryp'anocide** (-*sīd*) a drug that kills trypanosomes. — *n* **trypanosomiasis** (-*sō-mī'ə-sis*) disease caused by a trypanosome, esp. sleeping sickness. [Gr. *trȳpanon*, a borer — *trȳpaein*, to bore, *sōma*, body.]

trypsin *trip'sin*, (*biol*) *n* a digestive ferment secreted by the pancreas. — *adj* **tryp'tic**. — *n* **tryptophan** (*trip'tō-fan*) or **tryp'tophane** (-*fān*) an essential amino-acid obtained e.g. by the cleavage of casein by pancreatic enzymes. [Gr. *trīpsis*, rubbing (as first obtained by rubbing down the pancreas with glycerine), or *trȳein*, to wear out, modelled on **pepsin**.]

trysail. See under **try**.

tryst *trīst*, (chiefly *Scot*) *n* an appointment to meet; appointed place of meeting. [O.Fr. *triste*, a hunter's station.]

tsar or **czar**, or less commonly **tzar** *zär* or *tsär*, (*hist*) *n* the title of the emperors of Russia and of the kings of Bulgaria; a great potentate or despot. — *n* **tsar'dom** or **czar'dom**. — *n* **tsar'evich** or **czar'evich** (Russ. *tsär-ye'vēch*) a son of a tsar. — *n* **tsarev'na** or **czarev'na** a daughter of a tsar; a wife of a tsarevich. — *n* **tsarina** or **czarina** (-*ē'nə*; not a Russian form), **tsarit'sa** or **czarit'za** a Russian empress. — *n* **tsar'ism** or **czar'ism** the government of the Russian tsars; absolutism. — *n* **tsar'ist** or **czar'ist** an upholder of tsarism. — *n* **tsesar'evich** or **cesar'evich** (Russ. -*ye'vēch*) the eldest son of a tsar; heir to the tsardom. [Russ. *tsar'*, etc. — L. *Caesar*, Caesar.]

TSB *abbrev* for Trustee Savings Bank.

tsetse *tset'si*, *n Glossina morsitans*, or other species of the African genus *Glossina*, small flies that transmit trypanosome parasites and cause sleeping sickness, nagana (**tsetse-fly disease**), etc. — Also **tset'se-fly**. [Tswana.]

T-shirt. See under **tee**[1].

TSO *abbrev* for town sub-office.

tsp. *abbrev* for teaspoonful (*pl* **tsps**).

tsunami *tsōō-nä'mē*, *n* a very swiftly travelling sea wave that attains great height. [Jap. *tsu*, harbour, *nami*, wave.]

Tswana *tswä'nə* or *swä'nə*, *n* a Negro people of southern Africa; a member of this people; their language, of the Bantu family: — *pl* **Tswa'na** or **Tswa'nas**. — Also *adj*.

TT *abbrev* for: teetotal; Tourist Trophy; Trinidad and Tobago (I.V.R.); tuberculin tested.

Tu. or **Tues.** *abbrev* for Tuesday.

Tuareg *twä'reg*, *n* a nomadic Berber of the Sahara; the language of the Tuaregs. [Ar. *tawāriq*.]

tuatara *tōō-a-tä'rə*, *n* a New Zealand lizard-like reptile. [Maori, spine on the back.]

tub *tub*, *n* an open wooden vessel made of staves and hoops; a small cask or container, e.g. of cardboard or plastic; anything like a tub; a tubful; a clumsy ship or boat; a bath; a bucket, box or vehicle for bringing up coal from the mine. — *vt* to set, bathe or treat in a tub. — *vi* to take a bath. — *n* **tubb'er**. — *n* **tubb'iness**. — *adj* plump, round like a tub. — *n* **tub'ful**: — *pl* **tub'fuls**. — *vi* **tub'-thump**. — **tub'-thumper** a declamatory or ranting preacher or public speaker; **tub'-thumping**. [Cf. L.G. *tubbe*.]

tuba *tū'bə* or *tōō'bə*, *n* a low-pitched brass instrument of the saxhorn class; a person who plays the tuba; a powerful organ reed-stop. [L. and It. *tuba*.]

tube *tūb*, *n* a pipe; any long hollow body; a collapsible cylinder from which material in the form of paste or viscous liquid can be squeezed out; a thermionic valve; (with *the*) underground railway in a tube-shaped tunnel (usu. referring to the London system); any vessel in a plant or animal body; a television set (*slang*); a can or bottle of beer (*Austr slang*). — *vt* to provide with, fit with or enclose in a tube; to insert a tube in the neck of (a horse) to help breathing. — *vi* to travel by tube. — *n* **tub'age** insertion of a tube. — *adj* **tub'al** of or pertaining to a tube or tubes. — *adj* **tub'ar** tubular. — *n* **tubec'tomy** (*med*) surgical cutting or removal of the Fallopian tubes. — *adj* **tubed** (*tūbd*). — *n* **tube'ful**: — *pl* **tube'fuls**. — *adj* **tube'less**. — *adj* **tube'like**. — *adj* **tub'iform** shaped like a tube. — *n* **tub'ing** the act of making or supplying tubes; tubes collectively; material for tubes. — *n* **tub'oplasty** (*med*) surgical repair of a Fallopian tube. — *adj* **tub'ūlar** having the form of a tube; made of or with tubes; having a sound like that made by the passage of air through a tube. — *vt* **tub'ūlate** to form into a tube; to provide with a tube. — *adj* tubular. — *adj* **tub'ūlated**. — *n* **tubūlā'tion**. — *n* **tub'ūlature**. — *n* **tub'ūle** a small tube. — **tube'-foot** (in echinoderms) a tube protruding through a pore, used in locomotion and respiration; **tube'-worm** a worm that makes a tube which it lives in; **tubular bells** an orchestral musical instrument in the percussion section, consisting of a number of metal tubes suspended in a frame, giving the sound of bells when struck. — **go down the tubes** (*slang*) to fail dismally, to be ruined. [Fr., — L. *tubus*, a pipe.]

tuber *tū'bər*, *n* a rounded swelling (*pathol*); a swelling (usu. underground) in a plant where reserves are stored up — formed in the stem (as in the potato, Jerusalem artichoke, etc.), or sometimes in the root (as in the dahlia). — *adj* **tuberif'erous**. — *adj* **tu'beriform**. — *adj* **tuberose** (*tū'bə-rōs* or -*rōz*) tuberous. — *n* a Mexican plant of the amaryllis family grown for its fragrant creamy-white flowers, propagated by tubers. — *n* **tuberosity** (-*ros'i-ti*). — *adj* **tub'erous** having tubers; of the nature of, or like, a tuber; knobbed. — **tuberous root** a fleshy root resembling a tuber but not having buds or eyes. [L. *tūber*, a swelling, from root of L. *tumēre*, to swell.]

tubercle *tū'bər-kl*, *n* a small tuber, protuberance or swelling; a nodule; a nodule or morbid growth in the lung or elsewhere, in cases of tuberculosis (*pathol*). — *adj* **tu'bercled** having tubercles. — *adj* **tubercular** (-*bûr'kū-lər*) nodular; having tubercles; affected by, or suffering from, tuberculosis. — *adj* **tuber'culate** or **tuber'culated** having, or covered with, tubercles. — *n* **tuberculā'tion**. — *n* **tuber'culin** a preparation from a culture of tubercle bacillus used for testing for tuberculosis. — *n* **tuberculīsā'tion** or **-z-**. — *vt* **tuber'culise** or **-ize** to infect with tuberculosis. — *n* **tuberculō'sis** a disease caused by the **tubercle bacillus** (*Bacillus tuberculosis*), characterised by development of tubercles. — *adj* **tuber'culous** of, or affected by, tuberculosis. — *adj* **tuber'culin-tested** (of milk) from cows that have been tested for and certified free from tuberculous infection. [L. *tūberculum*, dimin. of *tūber*.]

tuberiferous ... to ... **tuberous**. See under **tuber**.

tubiform, tubing, tuboplasty, tubular, tubule, etc. See under **tube**.

TUC *abbrev* for Trades Union Congress.

tuck *tuk*, *vt* to draw or thrust in or together; to fold under; to gather up (often with *up*); to enclose by pressing clothes closely around or under (with *in* or *up*); to put tucks in; to put, or stow, away; to eat (with *in* or *into*; *slang*). — *n* an act of tucking; a pleat or fold, now usu. one stitched down; eatables, esp. sweets, cakes, etc. (*school slang*). — *n* **tuck'er** someone who or something that tucks; food (*Austr slang*); (*formerly*) a piece of cloth tucked or drawn over the bosom. — *vt* (*US slang*) to tire exceedingly (often with *out*). — **tuck box** a box of or for tuck, at a boarding-school; **tuck'erbag** or **tuck'erbox** (*Austr*) a bag or box for carrying food in; **tuck'-in** (*slang*) a hearty feed; **tuck shop** (orig. *schoolboys'*, etc. *slang*) a sweet shop or cake shop, esp. such a shop or anything similar on school premises. [O.E. *tūcian*, to disturb, afflict.]

Tudor *tū'dər*, *adj* pertaining to the Welsh family of *Tudor*, the time when it held the English throne (1485–1603), or the style of architecture that prevailed then. — *adj* **Tudoresque'**. — **Tudor rose** a red and white rose (combining Lancaster and York) adopted as an emblem by Henry VII.

Tuesday *tūz'di*, *n* the third day of the week, the day following Monday. — *abbrev* **Tues.** or **Tu.** [O.E. *Tīwes dæg*, the day of *Tīw* (the God of war).]

tufa *tōō'fə* or *tū'fə*, *n* a porous deposit from springs rich in calcium (also *calcareous tufa* or *calc-sinter*). — *adj* **tufā'ceous.** [It. *tufa*, a variant of *tufo* — L. *tōfus*, a soft stone.]

tuff *tuf* or *tōōf*, *n* a rock composed of fine volcanic fragments and dust. — *adj* **tuffā'ceous.** [Fr. *tuf*, *tuffe* — It. *tufo*; see **tufa**.]

tuft *tuft*, *n* a bunched cluster; a clump; a crest; a separate lock of hair; one of the cut or uncut loops of wool, etc. forming the pile of a carpet or rug. — *vt* to separate into tufts; to make or decorate with tufts. — *adj* **tuft'ed** having or made of tufts; having many short crowded branches all arising at or near the same level (*bot*); (of birds) with a tuft or crest of feathers on the head. — *n* **tuft'ing.** — *adj* **tuft'y.** [Supposed to be — O.Fr. *tuffe* — L. *tūfa*, crest — Gmc.]

tug *tug*, *vt* to pull forcibly, wrench; to haul, tow or drag. — *vi* to pull forcibly; to toil or heave: — *pr p* **tugg'ing**; *pa t* and *pa p* **tugged.** — *n* a forcible or jerking pull; a hard struggle; a rope or chain for pulling; a tugboat; an aeroplane towing a glider. — *n* **tugg'er.** — *n* and *adj* **tugg'ing.** — *adv* **tugg'ingly.** — **tug'boat** a towing vessel; **tug-of-love'** a dispute over the guardianship of a child, e.g. between divorced parents, or between natural and foster parents; **tug-of-war'** a contest in which opposing teams tug at a rope and strive to pull one another over a line; a laborious struggle between two sides. [M.E. *toggen* (intensive) from root of O.E. *tēon*; cf. **tow**[1].]

tugrik *tōō'grēk*, *n* the standard unit of currency of Mongolia (100 *möngö*). [Mongolian.]

tui *tōō'ē*, *n* a New Zealand honey-guide, which has glossy blue-black plumage with tufts of white at the neck, the parson-bird. [Maori.]

tuition *tū-ish'ən*, *n* teaching, instruction. — *adj* **tui'tional** or **tui'tionary.** [L. *tuitiō*, *-ōnis* — *tuērī*, *tuitus*, to watch over.]

tularaemia or in U.S. **tularemia** *tōō-lə-rē'mi-ə*, *n* a disease of rodents caused by a bacterium transmitted to man either by insects or directly, causing fever, inflammation of the glands, etc. — *adj* **tularae'mic** or in U.S. **tularē'mic.** [*Tulare* county, California, where it was first discovered, and Gr. *haima*, blood.]

tulip *tū'lip*, *n* any plant or flower of the bulbous liliaceous genus **Tu'lipa**, with showy, bell-shaped, usu. solitary, flowers. — **tu'lip-root** a disease affecting the stem of oats; **tu'lip-tree** a N. American timber tree (*Liriodendron*), of the magnolia family, with tulip-like flowers; **tu'lip-wood** its wood. [O.Fr. *tulipe*, *tulippe*, *tulipan* — Turk. *tulbend*, turban.]

tulle *tōōl* or *tūl*, *n* a delicate thin silk netted fabric. [Fr.; from *Tulle*, in south central France.]

tum. See **tummy**.

tumble *tum'bl*, *vi* to roll, wallow or toss about; to perform as a dancer or acrobat; to fall headlong, floundering or revolving; to collapse or fall in a heap; to rush confusedly and hastily; to come by chance (usu. with *on*); to comprehend or realise (often with *to*; *slang*). — *vt* to send tumbling or headlong; to overthrow; to bundle from one place to another; to throw about; to disorder, rumple. — *n* an act of tumbling; a fall; a somersault; a tumbled condition or mass. — *n* **tum'bler** someone who tumbles; an acrobat; a large drinking-glass or tall cup; a tumblerful; a revolving barrel or cage; part of a lock that holds the bolt in place, till it is moved by the key; part of a firearm lock that receives the thrust of the mainspring and forces the hammer forward; a machine consisting of a revolving drum in which (gem)stones are polished (also **tum'bling-barrel** or **-box**). — *n* **tum'blerful**: — *pl* **tum'blerfuls.** — *n* and *adj* **tum'bling.** — *adj* **tum'bledown** dilapidated, threatening to fall. — **tumble-drī'er** a machine which dries (clothes, etc.) by tumbling them in a strong current of hot air; **tum'bler-switch** a switch that is turned over to put electric current off or on; **tum'bleweed** a type of plant that snaps off above the root, curls into a ball, and rolls about in the wind. — **tumble over** to toss about carelessly, to upset; to fall over. [Frequentative from O.E. *tumbian*.]

tumbrel *tum'brəl* or **tumbril** *tum'bril*, *n* a cart for dung, etc., that tips over backwards to empty its load; a two-wheeled military cart (*hist*); the name given to the carts that conveyed victims to the guillotine during the French Revolution. [O.Fr. *tomberel* — *tomber*, to fall.]

tumefy *tū'mi-fī*, *vt* and *vi* to swell: — *pr p* **tu'mefying**; *pa t* and *pa p* **tu'mefīed.** — *adj* **tumefacient** (*tū-mi-fā'shənt*). — *n* **tumefac'tion.** — *n* **tumescence** (*tū-mes'əns*) a tendency to swell; a swelling. — *adj* **tumesc'ent.** — *adj* **tu'mid** swollen or enlarged; inflated; bombastic. — *n* **tumid'ity.** — *adv* **tu'midly.** — *n* **tu'midness.** [L. *tumefacĕre*, *tumēscĕre*, *tumidus*, — *tumēre*, to swell, *facĕre*, to make.]

tummy *tum'i*, (*colloq* or *childish*) *n* a stomach. — Also **tum.** — **tumm'y-button** a navel.

tumour or in N.Am. **tumor** *tū'mər*, *n* swelling; a morbid swelling or enlargement, esp. a new growth of cells in the body without inflammation. — *n* **tumorigen'esis** the causing or production of tumours. — *adj* **tumorigen'ic** or **tumorgen'ic** causing or producing tumours. — *n* **tumorigenic'ity** or **tumorgenic'ity.** — *adj* **tu'morous.** [L. *tumŏr* — *tumēre*, to swell.]

tumular, tumuli. See under **tumulus**.

tumult *tū'mult*, *n* violent commotion, usu. with uproar; a riot; a state of violent and confused emotion. — *adj* **tumult'ūous** full of tumult; disorderly; agitated; noisy. — *adv* **tumult'ūously.** — *n* **tumult'ūousness.** [L. *tumultus*, *-ūs* — *tumēre*, to swell.]

tumulus *tū'mū-ləs*, *n* a burial mound, a barrow: — *pl* **tu'muli** (*-lī* or *-lē*). — *adj* **tu'mular.** [L., — *tumēre*, to swell.]

tun *tun*, *n* a large cask, formerly a liquid measure (216 gallons of ale, 252 of wine). — *vt* to put in a tun. [O.E. *tunne*; cf. **ton**.]

tuna[1] *tōō'nə* or *tū'nə*, *n* a prickly-pear (plant or fruit). [Haitian.]

tuna[2] *tōō'nə* or *tū'nə*, *n* a kind of large sea-fish of the mackerel family; its flesh (as food): — *pl* **tu'na** or **tu'nas.** — Also **tu'na-fish, tunn'y** (q.v.) or **tunn'y-fish.** [Sp., — L. *tunnus* — Gr. *thynnos*.]

tunable. See under **tune**.

tundra *tun'drə*, *n* an Arctic plain with permanently frozen subsoil, and lichens, mosses and dwarfed vegetation. [Lapp.]

tune *tūn*, *n* a melody or air; melodiousness; accurate adjustment in pitch or frequency; harmonious adjustment (*fig*). — *vt* to adjust the tones of; to put in condition for producing tones in tune; to put in smooth working order; to synchronise; to adjust (a radio receiver) so as to produce the optimum response to an incoming signal; to harmonise or bring to a desired state. — *adj* **tūn'able** or **tune'able**. — *n* **tun'ableness**. — *adv* **tun'ably**. — *adj* **tuned** (*tūnd*). — *adj* **tune'ful** melodious; musical. — *adv* **tune'fully**. — *n* **tune'fulness**. — *adj* **tune'less**. — *n* **tun'er** someone who tunes instruments, engines, etc.; an apparatus for receiving radio signals; a knob, dial, etc. by which a radio or television receiver is adjusted to different wavelengths. — *n* **tun'ing**. — **tuner amplifier** a piece of hi-fi equipment incorporating a radio receiver and an amplifier which can also be used with a record-player or tape deck; **tun'ing-fork** a two-pronged instrument giving a sound of known pitch or vibration. — **change one's tune** to alter one's attitude, opinions or way of talking; **in tune** true in pitch; in harmony (*fig*); **out of tune** not true in pitch; not agreeing (*fig*); **to the tune of** to the amount of; **tune in** (often with *to*) and **tune out** to adjust a radio receiver to receive, and to lose reception of, a signal; to turn one's attention to, show interest (in), or to cease to do so (*colloq*); **tune up** to put instruments into tune for beginning; (of engines, etc.) to (be) put into smooth working order. [A form of **tone**.]

tung oil *tung oil*, *n* wood-oil obtained from seeds of the **tung'-tree** or Chinese varnish tree, used in printing inks, paints, coatings, etc. for its quick-drying, insulating and waterproofing properties. [Chin. *yu-t'ung*.]

tungsten *tung'stən*, *n* an element (symbol **W**; atomic no. 74), a rare metal also known as wolfram, used for making lamp filaments and high-speed steel. — *n* **tung'state** a salt of **tung'stic acid** (H_2WO_4). — **tungsten lamp** an electric lamp using an incandescent tungsten filament. [Sw., lit. heavy stone — *tung*, heavy, *sten*, stone.]

Tungus *tŏŏng'gŏŏs* or *-gŏŏz'*, *n* a member of an Eastern Siberian people and race, of the type usually called Mongol: — *pl* **Tungus** or **Tunguses**. — *n* and *adj* **Tungus'ic** (of or relating to) the family of Ural-Altaic languages that includes Tungus and Manchu. [Russ. *Tunguz*; Chin. *Tung-hu*.]

tunic *tū'nik*, *n* a plain shirt-like garment, often a sort of sleeveless belted coat, gown or blouse; a close-fitting soldier's or policeman's jacket; a tunicle; an investing layer, membrane or integument (*biol*). — *adj* **tu'nicate** or **tu'nicated** (*bot* and *zool*) having a tunic; formed in concentric coats. — *adj* **tu'nicked**. — *n* **tu'nicle** a short ecclesiastical vestment, worn by a sub-deacon or a bishop at mass. [L. *tunica*.]

tunnel *tun'l*, *n* a passage cut underground; any tubular passage; an animal's burrow, in earth, wood, etc.; (with *cap*) the tunnel under the English Channel connecting England and France. — *vt* to make a passage or passages through; to hollow out. — *vi* to make a tunnel; to pass through, or as if through, a tunnel: — *pr p* **tunn'elling**; *pa t* and *pa p* **tunn'elled**. — *n* **tunn'eller**. — *n* and *adj* **tunn'elling**. — **tunnel diode** (*electronics*) a junction diode, used as a low noise amplifier, oscillator or very low power microwave, in which electrons bypass the potential energy barrier by a phenomenon known in wave mechanics as **tunn'elling**; **tunn'el-net** a funnel-shaped net; **tunnel vision** a medical condition in which one is unable to see objects other than those straight ahead; single-minded concentration on one's own pursuits or viewpoints to the total exclusion of those of others. [O.Fr. *tonel*, cask, and *tonnelle*, vault, tunnel-net, dimins. of *tonne*, cask.]

tunny *tun'i*, *n* a tuna-fish, esp. *Thunnus thynnus*. [L. *tunnus* — Gr. *thynnos*.]

tup *tup*, *n* a ram; the striking-face of a steam-hammer pile-driver, etc. — *vt* (of a ram) to copulate with (a ewe): — *pr p* **tupp'ing**; *pa t* and *pa p* **tupped**. [M.E. *tupe*.]

tupelo *tŏŏ'pə-lō*, *n* an American gum-tree (genus *Nyssa*): — *pl* **tu'pelos**. [From an Indian name.]

Tupí or **Tupi** *tŏŏ'pē*, *n* a S. American Indian of a group of peoples inhabiting the Atlantic coast and the Amazon basin; their language. — Also *adj*. — *adj* **Tupi'an**.

tupik *tū'pik*, *n* an Inuit animal-skin tent. [Eskimo.]

tuppence and **tuppenny**. Colloq. for **twopence** and **twopenny**.

Tupperware® *tup'ər-wār*, *n* a range of plastic storage containers, esp. for food. [U.S. company name *Tupper*, and **ware**.]

tuque *tūk*, *n* a Canadian cap made by tucking in one tapered end of a long cylindrical bag, closed at both ends. [Fr. *toque*.]

turaco. See **touraco**.

turban *tûr'bən*, *n* a head-covering, esp. as worn by Muslim or Sikh men, consisting of a long sash wound round the head or round a cap; a ladies' headdress similar to this. — *adj* **tur'baned** wearing a turban. [Turk. *tulbend* — Pers. *dulband*.]

turbid *tûr'bid*, *adj* disordered; muddy; thick. — *n* **tur'bidite** the sediment deposited by a turbidity current. — *n* **turbid'ity**. — *adv* **tur'bidly**. — *n* **tur'bidness**. — **turbidity current** a volume of sediment-carrying water which flows violently down a slope under water. [L. *turbidus* — *turba*, tumult.]

turbine *tûr'bin* or *tûr'bīn*, *n* a rotary motor in which a wheel or drum with curved vanes is driven by reaction or impact or both by a fluid (water in the **water-turbine**, steam in the **steam-turbine**, expanding hot air in the **gas-turbine**) admitted to it and allowed to escape. — *adj* **tur'binal**. — *adj* **tur'binate** (also **tur'binated**) shaped like a top or inverted cone; spirally coiled; scroll-like. — *adj* **tur'bined** having, or driven by, a turbine or turbines. — *npl* **turbines** see **turbo¹**.

turbit *tûr'bit*, *n* a domestic pigeon with white body, coloured wings and short beak.

turbo¹ *tûr'bō*, *n* a member of the tropical genus (*Turbo*) of turbinate wide-mouthed gasteropods, large specimens often used as ornaments: — *pl* **turbines** (*tûr'binēz*). [L. *turbo*, *-inis*, a whirl.]

turbo² *tûr'bō*, *n* short for **turbocar** and **turbocharger**: — *pl* **tur'bos**.

turbo- *tûr'bō-*, *combining form* meaning having, connected to, or driven by a turbine. — *n* **tur'bocar** or **turbo car** a car propelled by a turbocharged engine. — *adj* **tur'bocharged**. — *n* **tur'bocharger** a turbine operated by the exhaust gases of an engine, thereby boosting its power. — *n* **tur'bocharging**. — *adj* **turbo-elec'tric** using a form of electric drive in which turbine-driven generators supply electric power to motors coupled to propeller, axle shafts, etc. — *n* **tur'bofan** a gas-turbine aero-engine in which part of the power developed is used to drive a fan which blows air out with the exhaust and so increases thrust (also **turbofan engine**). — *n* **turbo-gen'erator** a generator of electric power, driven by a steam-turbine; **tur'bojet** (an aeroplane powered by) an internal-combustion aero-engine in which the gas energy produced by a turbine-driven compressor is directed through a nozzle to produce thrust. — *n* **tur'boprop** a jet-engine in which the turbine is coupled to a propeller. — *n* **turbo-su'percharger** an aero-engine supercharger operated by a turbine driven by the exhaust gases of the engine. [L. *turbō*, *-inis*, a whirl, a spinning-top.]

turbot *tûr'bət*, *n* a large flatfish with bony tubercles, common esp. to the E. North Atlantic; its flesh (as a highly valued food); extended to various more or less similar fishes. [O.Fr.]

turbulent *tûr'bū-lənt*, *adj* tumultuous, violently disturbed; producing commotion; stormy; (of fluid) showing turbulence; insubordinate, unruly; having an exciting, disturbing effect. — *n* **tur'bulence** disturbed state; unruly character or action; irregular eddying motion of particles in a fluid; irregular movement of large volumes of air (also called *atmospheric turbulence*). — *adv* **tur'bulently**. [L. *turbulentus* — *turba*, a turmoil.]

Turcoman. Same as **Turkoman**.

turd *tûrd*, *n* a lump of dung; a despicable person (*vulg*). [O.E. *tord*.]

tureen *tə-rēn'* or *tū-rēn'*, *n* a large dish for holding soup, vegetables, etc. at table. [Fr. *terrine* — L. *terra*, earth.]

turf *tûrf*, *n* the surface of land matted with the roots of grass, etc.; a cake of turf cut off; a sod; a slab of peat; territory, area of operation or influence, patch (*slang*); horse-racing, the race-course, or the racing world: — *pl* **turfs** or sometimes **turves**. — *vt* to cover with turf. — *adj* **turfed**. — *n* **tur'finess**. — *n* **tur'fing**. — *n* **turf'man** (chiefly *US*) a man devoted to horse-racing. — *adj* **tur'fy** of, like, or abounding in, turf. — **turf'-accountant** a euphemism for bookmaker. — **turf out** to throw out forcibly, eject. [O.E.]

turgescence *tûr-jes'əns*, *n* the act or process of swelling up; swollenness; distension of cells and tissues with water. — *adj* **turgesc'ent** swelling; growing big. — *adj* **tur'gid** swollen; extended beyond the natural size; dilated; inflated; pompous, bombastic. — *n* **turgid'ity** or **tur'gidness**. — *adv* **tur'gidly**. — *n* **turgor** (*tûr'gör*) the state of being full, the normal condition of the capillaries; balance of osmotic pressure and elasticity of cell-wall (*bot*). [L. *turgēre*, to swell.]

turion *tū'ri-ən*, (*bot*) *n* an underground bud, growing upward into a new stem. [L. *turiō*, *-ōnis*, a shoot.]

Turk *tûrk*, *n* a native or citizen of *Turkey*; a Muslim of the former Ottoman empire; any speaker of a Turkic language; an unmanageable unruly person (*derog*). — *adj* Turkish. — *adj* **Turki** (*tōōr'kē*) of the Turkish distinguished from the Tatar branch of Turko-Tatar languages. — *n* a Turki speaker or language. — *adj* and *n* **Turk'ic** (of) that branch of the Ural-Altaic languages to which Turkish, Tatar, Uzbek, etc. belong; of Turkey, its peoples or language. — *adj* **Turk'ish** of Turkey, the Turks, or their language; Turkic. — *n* the language of the Turks. — **Turkey red** a fine durable red dye, obtained from madder, but now usu. chemically; **Turkish bath** a kind of hot-air bath, the patient being sweated, rubbed down, massaged, and gradually cooled; **Turkish delight** a gelatinous sweetmeat, variously flavoured and coloured, orig. and esp. Turkish; **Turk's cap** the lily *Lilium martagon*, from the turban-like appearance of the rolled-back petals of its nodding flower; **Turk's head** a kind of ornamental knot.

turkey *tûrk'i*, *n* a large American bird (genus *Meleagris*) of the pheasant family; a domestic breed of that genus; its flesh as food; extended to various big birds, such as bustard, ibis and megapode; a play, film, etc. that is a complete failure (*slang*, chiefly *US*); a fool, a slow or inept person (*slang*). — **turkey buzzard** or **vulture** an American vulture; **turkey cock** a male turkey; a pompous, vain, blustering man; **turkey hen** a female turkey. — **cold turkey** see under **cold**; **talk turkey** (*US*) to talk bluntly; to talk business. [Formerly, a guinea fowl (thought to have come from *Turkey*.]

Turki. See under **Turk**.

Turkoman *tûr'kō-man*, *n* a member of any of the Turkic peoples living north of Iran and Afghanistan (*pl* **Turk'omans**); (also **Turk'men**) their Turkic language. — Also *adj*.

turmeric *tûr'mər-ik*, *n* a plant of the ginger family; its rootstock, or a powder made from it, used as a condiment, in making curry-powder, and as a dye. — **turmeric paper** a chemical test-paper impregnated with turmeric, changed from yellow to brown by alkali. [Earlier *tarmaret*, as if from L. *terra merita*, deserved earth.]

turmoil *tûr'moil*, *n* commotion; upheaval, disruption.

turn *tûrn*, *vi* to revolve; to rotate, to spin, whirl; to move round; to hinge, depend; to change or reverse direction or tendency; to return; to deviate; to direct oneself, face (with *to* or *towards*); to direct one's attention or movements; to change sides, religion, or way of life; to change; to be transformed, converted (often with *into*); to become; to result, prove or lead in the issue; to be shaped on the lathe; to sour; to change colour; to become giddy; to be nauseated; to bend back, become turned. — *vt* to rotate; to move round; to change the direction of; to deflect; to bend; to bend back the edge of; to reverse; to pass round or beyond; to perform by turning; to wind; to put inside-out, or remake in that way; to set upside-down; to direct, point; to apply; to send, drive, set; to pour or tumble out; to circulate, pass through one's hands; to translate; to change; to make sour; to nauseate; to make giddy; to transfer, hand over; to convert, make; to make the subject of (with *to* or *into*); to put by turning; to form in a lathe; to shape, round off, fashion; to pass (a certain age, hour, etc.); to cause or persuade (an enemy agent) to work for one's own side. — *n* an act, occasion or place of turning; new direction or tendency; a twist; a winding; a complete revolution; a bend; a single traversing of a beat or course; a short walk (or ride or drive); a fit of illness or emotion, esp. an emotional shock, jar, fright, or feeling of faintness; a recurring opportunity or spell in rotation or alternation; rotation; a trick; a performer's act or the performer; a shift; a bout; manner, style (esp. of words, etc.); cast of mind; aptitude, bent; occasion, exigency; a vicissitude; a characteristic quality or effect; an act of kindness or malice; an embellishment in which the principal note is preceded by that next above it and followed by that next below it, the whole ending with the principal note (*mus*); turning-point; a culmination; a time or moment of change; on a golf course, the halfway point, at which the players turn to begin the return nine holes. — *adj* **turned** fashioned; shaped in a lathe; reversed; inside-out; soured; beyond the age of. — *n* **turn'er**. — *n* **turn'ing** rotation; reversal; a bend or deviation; conversion or transformation; the act of making a turn; a place where a road strikes off; the art of shaping wood, metal, etc. into forms having a curved (generally circular or oval) transverse section; the art of engraving figures composed of curved lines on a smooth surface, by means of a turning-lathe; (in *pl*) shavings from the lathe; (in pottery) the shaping of a vase. — **turn'about** or **turn'around** a turning to face the opposite way (also *fig*); **turnaround** see also **turnround**; **turn'coat** someone who renounces or turns against his or her principles or party; **turn'-cock** an official who turns off and on the water for the mains, etc. — *adj* **turn'-down** (e.g. of a collar or brim) folded down. — *n* any turn-down part; a turning down, rejection; **turning circle** the smallest possible circle in which a vehicle can turn round; **turn'ing-lathe**; **turn'ing-point** the point at which anything changes direction; a critical or decisive moment; **turn'key** an under-jailer, warder; (a contract for) a job in which the contractor is to complete the entire operation, leaving the building, plant, etc. ready for use (also *adj*). — *adj* **turn'key** (*comput*) designed, and ready, for immediate use by the purchaser, as in **turnkey system** or **package**, a computer system complete with hardware and software, usu. designed, installed, tested and maintained by the supplier and ready for immediate use by the purchaser; **turn'-off** a smaller road leading from a main one: see also **turn off** below; **turn-on** see **turn on** below; **turn'out** an attendance (of people) an assembly, crowd; output; get-up, outfit (of clothes); a display (of goods, equipment, etc.); **turn'over** an act of turning over; a transference; a part folded over; the total amount of money changing hands in a business; the number of employees starting or finishing employment at a particular place of work over a given period; the money value of total sales over a period; loss of possession of the ball by a team, due to error or breach of a rule (*Am football* and *basketball*). — *adj* folded over, or made to fold over. — **turn'pike** a spiked barrier (*hist*); a turnstile or a toll-gate (*hist*); a motorway on which tolls are paid (*US*); **turn'round** or **turn'around** a turning round; the whole process of docking, unloading, taking on cargo, passengers, or both, and setting sail again; the whole process of dealing with something and passing it on to the next stage; a complete reversal of direction; **turn'stile** a revolving frame that allows one person to pass at a time; **turn'stone** a bird (genus *Arenaria*), related to the plover and sandpiper, that turns over pebbles on the beach in search of food; **turn'table** a rotating table, platform or disc, or pair of rings, one rotating within another, esp. for carrying a gramophone record, cementing a microscope slide, turning a camera, reversing a steam locomotive, etc.; **turn'-up** a disturbance; a thing or part that is turned up, esp. the cuff at the bottom of a trouser-leg; an unexpected or fortuitous result or occurrence; a piece of good luck. — **a good (or bad) turn** a helpful service (or a disservice); **at every turn** everywhere; incessantly; **by turns** alternately; at intervals; **in one's turn** when it is one's occasion, opportunity, duty, etc.; **in turn** one after another, in succession; **not turn a hair** to be quite undisturbed or unaffected; **on the turn** at the turning-point, changing; on the point of turning sour; **(take) a turn for the better** or **worse** (to make) an improvement, or a deterioration; **take one's turn** or **take turns** to participate in rotation; **to a turn** exactly, perfectly; **turn about** to face round to the opposite direction; to spin, rotate; **turn about** or **turn and turn about** alternately; in rotation; **turn a deaf ear to** to ignore; **turn against** to make hostile towards; to rebel against; to use (something) to the injury of; **turn aside** to avert; to deviate; to avert the face; **turn away** to avert, to turn or look in another direction; to deviate, to depart; to refuse admittance to; to reject, send away; **turn back** to cause to retreat; to return; to fold back; **turn down** to bend, double, or fold down; to lower (e.g. a light, or the volume on a radio, etc.); to reject; **turn in** to bend inward; to enter; to register (a score); to surrender, hand over voluntarily; to go to bed (*colloq*); **turn in on oneself** to become introverted; **turn into** to become by a process of change; **turn it in** (*colloq*) stop (saying or doing, etc.) it; **turn loose** to set free; **turn off** to shut or switch off; to deviate or divert (on to another road, etc.); to make (someone) lose interest or enthusiasm, to bore, be disliked by or distasteful to (*n* **turn'-off**; *slang*); **turn of speed** a burst of speed; **turn of the century** (or **year**) the period of the end of one century (or year) and the beginning of the next; **turn on** to set in operation by switching on (also *fig*); to set running (e.g. the flow of water); to depend on; to turn towards and attack (physically or verbally); to give (a person) a sense of heightened awareness and vitality as do hallucinogenic drugs (*slang*); to rouse the interest of, excite, esp. sexually (*n* **turn'-on**; *slang*); **turn one's hand to** to apply oneself to; **turn out** to bend outwards; to drive out, to expel; to remove the contents of, clear out; to dress, groom, tidy the appearance of; to produce and present; to result, come about, transpire; to assemble, attend; to switch off (a light); to get out of bed (*colloq*); to go out of doors (*colloq*); **turn over** to roll over; to set the other way up; to change sides; to hand over, pass on; to handle or do business to the amount of; to examine by turning the pages; to ponder; to rob (*slang*); to start up (an engine); **turn round** (of a ship, aircraft, etc.) to arrive, unload, reload and leave again; **turn someone round one's (little) finger** see **twist someone round one's little finger** under **twist**; **turn someone's head** or **brain** to make someone giddy; to infatuate with success; **turn the other cheek** to accept harm, violence, etc. without defending oneself; **turn (also tip) the scales** to decide, determine; **turn the stomach** to nauseate; **turn to** to have recourse to; to point to; to result in; to change or be changed into; to set to work; **turn up** to point upwards; to fold upwards; to come, or bring, to light; to appear by chance; to set face up; to invert; to strengthen, increase, or make brighter (e.g. a light, radio volume, etc.) by or as if by turning a knob; to refer to, look up; **turn-up for the books** a totally unexpected occurrence. [O.E. *turnian*, *tyrnan*, and perh. partly O.Fr. *torner*; all from L. *tornāre*, to turn in a lathe — *tornus*, a turner's wheel — Gr. *tornos*, lathe, compasses.]

turnip *tûr'nip*, *n* the swollen edible white or yellowish root of *Brassica rapa* or (Swedish turnip or swede) of *Brassica rutabaga*; the root prepared as food; the plant that produces it; various similar roots and plants. — **tur'nip-lantern** a lantern made (esp. traditionally at Hallowe'en) by scooping out the flesh of a turnip. [See **neep**; the first part may be from **turn** or Fr. *tour*, implying roundness.]

turnkey . . . to . . . **turn-up**. See under **turn**.

turpentine *tûr'pən-tīn*, *n* a viscous resin, orig. that of the terebinth tree (*Chian turpentine*), now generally of conifers; popularly, oil of turpentine. — *vt* to treat or smear with turpentine. — **tur'pentine-tree** a small Mediterranean tree (genus *Pistacia*) that yields a turpentine, the terebinth-tree. — **oil (or spirit) of turpentine** (*colloq* **turps**) a colourless, aromatic oil distilled from turpentine, an important solvent for oil paints, varnishes, etc. [O.Fr. *terbentine* — L. *terebinthina* (*rēsīn a*), terebinth (resin); see **terebinth**.]

turpeth *tûr'pəth*, *n* an Oriental plant (genus *Ipomoea*) or its cathartic root. [L.L. *turpethum*, *turbithum* — Pers. and Ar. *turbed*, *turbid*.]

turpitude *tûr'pi-tūd*, *n* baseness; depravity; vileness. [L. *turpitūdō* — *turpis*, base.]

turps. See under **turpentine**.

turquoise *tûr'kwäz* or *tûr'kwoiz*, *n* an opaque sky-blue to pale green mineral or gemstone, a hydrous basic aluminium phosphate; this colour. [O.Fr. *turkeis*, Turkish, as first brought from Persia through *Turkey* or from *Turkestan*.]

turret *tur'it*, *n* a small tower, usu. attached to a building, often containing a winding stair; a tower, often revolving, carrying a gun; part of a lathe that holds the cutting tool. — *adj* **turr'eted** having turrets; formed like a tower or a long spiral. — **turret lathe** a lathe having a number of tools carried on a turret mounted on a saddle which slides on the lathe bed. [O.Fr. *tourete*, dimin. of *tur*; see **tower**.]

turtle *tûr'tl*, *n* any marine reptile of the order Chelonia; esp. in U.S. also a terrestrial chelonian; sometimes a freshwater chelonian; the edible flesh of a turtle, esp. the green turtle; a drawing device which converts information from a computer into pictures — orig. a device (*floor turtle*) with a pen or pens, which could be made to move across a flat surface with paper, etc. on it, now often simulated by graphics on a screen (a *screen turtle*) (*comput*). — **tur'tleback** anything arched like a turtle's back, esp. a structure over a ship's bows or stern; **turtle graphics** (*comput*) drawing by means of a turtle (q.v.); **tur'tleneck** (a garment having) a high close-fitting neckline. — *adj* **tur'tlenecked**. — **tur'tle-shell** the shell of a type of sea turtle, commonly called tortoiseshell; **tur'tle-soup** a soup made from the flesh, fat and gelatinous tissue of the female green turtle. — **mock turtle** a soup made of calf's head or other meat in lieu of turtle meat; **turn turtle** to turn bottom up, capsize. [Fr. *tortue*, tortoise, from L.L. *tortuca*.]

turtledove *tûr'tl-duv*, *n* any dove of the genus *Turtur* or *Streptopelia*, noted for its affection and constancy towards its mate, and its soft cooing song; a gentle, affectionate person. [L. *turtur*.]

turves. See **turf**.

Tuscan *tus'kən*, *adj* of *Tuscany* in central Italy; Doric as modified by the Romans, with unfluted columns, and without triglyphs (*archit*). — *n* classical Italian as spoken in Tuscany; a native or inhabitant of Tuscany. [L. *Tuscānus*, Etruscan.]

tusche *tōōsh*, *n* a greasy substance used in lithography for drawing the design which then does not take up the printing medium. [Ger. *tuschen*, to touch up (with paint, etc.).]

tush[1] *tush*, *n* a horse's canine tooth. [O.E. *tūsc*.]

tush[2] *tōōsh*, (*slang*; esp. *US*) *n* the bottom, buttocks. — Also **tush'ie** or **tush'y**. [Corrupted shortening of Yiddish *tokhes*.]

tusk *tusk*, *n* a long, protruding tooth (as of an elephant); a sharp projection. — *vt* to pierce with the tusks. — *adj* **tusked** or **tusk'y**. — *n* **tusk'er** a boar, elephant, etc. with tusks. — *n* **tusk'ing** (*archit*) the stubs of walling stones left projecting from a wall for bonding later with another wall or building. — *adj* **tusk'less**. — **tusk'-shell** a mollusc of the genus *Dentalium*, having a shell like an elephant's tusk; the shell itself. [O.E. *tūx* (*tūsc*).]

tusser or **tussore** *tus'ər*, *n* a fawn-coloured silk from Oriental silkworms; its colour. [Hind. *tasar*, shuttle — Sans. *tasara*, silkworm.]

tussis *tus'is*, (*med*) *n* a cough. — *adj* **tuss'al** or **tuss'ive**. [L.]

tussle *tus'l*, *n* a sharp struggle. — *vi* to struggle. [Frequentative of *touse* (now dialect); cf. **tousle**.]

tussock *tus'ək*, *n* a tuft; a bunchy clump of grass, rushes, etc. — *adj* **tuss'ocky**. — **tuss'ock-grass** a large grass (genus *Poa*) that forms great tufts.

tussore. See **tusser**.

tut *tut*, *n* and *interj* an exclamation of rebuke, mild disapprobation, impatience, etc. — *vi* to say 'tut': — *pr p* **tutt'ing**; *pa t* and *pa p* **tutt'ed**. — *n* **tutt'ing**. — Also **tut-tut'** and (*n*) **tut-tutt'ing**.

tutee. See under **tutor**.

tutelage *tū'ti-lij*, *n* guardianship; state of being under a guardian; tuition. — *adj* **tu'telar** or **tu'telary** protecting; having the charge of a person or place. — *n* a guardian spirit, god or saint. [L. *tūtēla*, guard — *tūtārī*, to guard.]

tutor *tū'tər*, *n* a private instructor; a coach who helps a boy or girl with lessons; a college officer who has supervision of an undergraduate; a college teacher who instructs by conference with a small group of students; an instruction-book. — *vt* to act as tutor to; to instruct; to coach; to discipline. — *n* **tutee'** a person who is tutored. — *n* **tu'torage** tutorship; tutoring; charge for tutoring. — *adj* **tutorial** (*tū-tō'ri-əl*) of a tutor. — *n* a study meeting between one or more students and a college tutor. — *adv* **tuto'rially**. — *n* **tu'toring**. — *n* **tu'torship**. [L. *tūtor*, *-ōris*, a guardian — *tuērī*, to look to.]

tutsan *tut'sən*, *n* a species of St John's wort once regarded as a panacea. [O.Fr. *toutesaine*, *tout* (— L. *tōtus*, all), *sain* (— L. *sānus*, sound).]

tutti *tōōt'ē*, (*mus*) *pl adj* all (performers). — *n* a passage for the whole orchestra or choir, or its execution. [It., pl. of *tutto* — L. *tōtus*, all.]

tutti-frutti *tōōt-ē-frōōt'ē*, *n* a confection, esp. ice-cream, flavoured with different kinds of fruit. [It., all fruits.]

tut-tut *tut-tut'*. Same as **tut**.

tutty *tut'i*, *n* crude zinc oxide. [O.Fr. *tutie* — L.L. *tutia* — Ar. *tūtiyā*.]

tutu *tōō'tōō*, *n* a ballet dancer's short, stiff, spreading skirt. [Fr.]

tu-whit tu-whoo *tōō-(h)wit' tōō-(h)wōō'*, *n* an owl's hoot.

tux *tuks*, (*colloq*; esp. *US* and *Austr*) *n* short for **tuxedo**.

tuxedo *tuk-sē'dō*, (orig. *US*) *n* a dinner-jacket: — *pl* **tuxe'dos** or **tuxe'does**. [From a fashionable club at *Tuxedo* Park, N.Y.]

tuyère. See **twyer**.

TV *abbrev* for television. — **TV game** an electronic game, played on a television set.

TVEI *abbrev* for Technical and Vocational Education Initiative, a national scheme, complementary to the National Curriculum, intended to give school students more job-oriented and technological courses.

TVP *abbrev* for textured vegetable protein.

TWA *abbrev* for Trans-World Airlines.

twaddle *twod'l*, *n* senseless or tedious uninteresting talk. — *vi* to talk twaddle. — *n* **twadd'ler**. — *n* and *adj* **twadd'ling**. — *adj* **twadd'ly**. [Perh. earlier (now dialect) *twattle*.]

twang *twang*, *n* the sound of a plucked string; a nasal tone; a local intonation (*colloq*). — *vt* and *vi* to sound with a twang. — *n* and *adj* **twang'ing**. — *adv* **twang'ingly**. — *adj* **twangy** (*twang'i*). [Imit.]

twat *twat*, *n* the vulva (*vulg*); a coarse general term of reproach (*slang*).

tweak *twēk*, *vt* to twitch, to pull; to pull or twist with sudden jerks; to fine-tune (e.g. a mechanism). — *n* a sharp pinch or twitch. [App. conn. with **twitch**[1].]

twee *twē*, (*colloq*) *adj* small and sweet; sentimentally pretty. — *adv* **twee'ly**. — *n* **twee'ness**. [*tweet* for 'sweet', and later *tiny* and *wee*.]

tweed *twēd*, *n* a rough woollen cloth, used for suits, jackets, etc.; (in *pl*) clothes made of tweed. — *adj* **tweed'y** of or resembling tweed; (esp. of a woman) of a predominantly upper-class, hearty, outdoorsy type. [Said to be from a misreading of Scots *tweel*, twill, the cloth being made in the Tweed basin; or perhaps a shortening of *tweeled* (twilled).]

tweedle *twē'dl*, *vi* to play casually (on an instrument), strum, tootle; to swindle, con (*slang*). — *n* **tweed'ler** (*slang*) a con man; a stolen vehicle sold as though honest. — **Tweedledee and Tweedledum** two almost indistinguishable characters or things (orig. the proverbial names of two rival musicians). [Prob. imit.]

tweedy. See under **tweed**.

'tween. A contraction of **between**. — **'tween'-decks** (*naut*) the space between two decks of a vessel.

tweet *twēt* (or **tweet'-tweet'**) *n* the note of a small bird. — *vt* and *vi* to chirp as a small bird does. — *n* **tweet'er** a loudspeaker used in high-fidelity sound reproduction for the higher frequencies. [Imit.]

tweezers *twēz'ərz*, *npl* small pincers for pulling out hairs, etc. — *vt* **tweeze** (back-formation; esp. *US*) to grasp or pluck with or as if with tweezers. [Obs. *tweeze*, a surgeon's case of instruments — Fr. *étui*.]

twelfth *twelfth*, *adj* last of twelve; immediately following the eleventh in order, position, etc.; equal to one of twelve equal parts. — *n* a twelfth part; a person or thing in twelfth position; a tone eleven (or conventionally twelve) diatonic degrees above or below a given tone (*mus*). — *adv* **twelfth'ly** in the twelfth place. — **Twelfth'-day** the twelfth day after Christmas, Epiphany, 6 January; **twelfth man** (*cricket*) a player selected beyond the necessary eleven to play if required as a substitute; **Twelfth'-night** the evening of Twelfth-day; also the eve of Epiphany, 5 January. — **the glorious Twelfth** 12 August, opening day of the grouse-shooting season. [O.E. *twelfta* — *twelf*.]

twelve *twelv*, *n* the cardinal number immediately above eleven; a symbol representing that number; a set of that number of things or persons; an article of a size denoted by 12; a score of twelve points; the hour of midday or midnight; the age of twelve years; **(12)** a certificate designating a film passed as suitable only for persons of twelve and over. — *adj* and *adv*

twelve'fold. — *n* **twelve'mo** (*pl* **twelv'e-mos**) duodecimo, written **12mo**. — *adj* **twelve'-note** or **twelve'-tone** pertaining to music based on a pattern formed from the twelve notes of the chromatic scale, esp. as developed by Arnold Schönberg (1874–1951) and his pupils (**twelve'-tone, -note** or **row** the basic pattern of notes). — **the Twelve** (*Bible*) the twelve apostles. [O.E. *twelf*, prob. two left; see ety. for **eleven**.]

twenty *twen'ti*, *adj* twice ten; nineteen and one. — *n* the number immediately above nineteen; a symbol representing that number; the age of twenty years; a set of twenty things or persons; a score of twenty points. — *npl* **twen'ties** the numbers twenty to twenty-nine; the years so numbered in a person's life or any century; a range of temperatures from twenty to just less than twenty-nine degrees. — *adj* **twen'-tieth** next after the nineteenth; last of twenty; equal to one of twenty equal parts. — *n* a twentieth part; a person or thing in twentieth position. — *n*, *adj* and *adv* **twen'tyfold** twenty times as many or much. — *adj* **twen'tyish** about twenty. — *adj* **twenty-twen'ty** (or **20/20**) (of human vision) normal, also (*colloq*) sharp, clear. [O.E. *twēntig*, prob. — *twēgen*, two and sfx. *-tig*, ten.]

twerp *twûrp*, (*slang*) *n* a contemptible (esp. also a stupid) person. [A connection with one T.W. Earp, once president of the Oxford University union, has been suggested.]

twice *twīs*, *adv* two times; doubly; for a second time. — *n* **twice over** twice (emphatically). [Late O.E. *twiges* — *twiga*, *twiwa*, *tuwa*, twice (with adverbial genitive ending).]

twiddle *twid'l*, *vt* to twirl idly; to finger idly, play with; to rotate. — *vi* to twirl; to trifle with something. — *n* a twirl; a curly mark or ornament. — *n* **twidd'ler**. — *n* and *adj* **twidd'ling**. — *adj* **twidd'ly**. — **twiddle one's thumbs** to rotate one's thumbs around each other; to be idle (*fig*). [Prob. suggested by **twirl, twist** and **fiddle**.]

twig[1] *twig*, *n* a small shoot or branch (of a tree, bush, etc.). — *adj* made of twigs. — *adj* **twigg'y**. [O.E.; cf. Ger. *Zweig*.]

twig[2] *twig*, (*colloq*) *vt* and *vi* to realise, comprehend (esp. suddenly); to understand. [Poss. Ir. *tuigim*, to discern; cf. Gael. *tuig*, understand.]

twilight *twī'līt*, *n* the faint light after sunset and before sunrise; this time of day; dim light or partial darkness; a period of decay following a period of success, vigour, greatness, etc. (*fig*). — *adj* of or at twilight; faintly illuminated; obscure, indefinite; partial, transitional. — *adj* **twī'lit**. — **twilight sleep** a condition of partial anaesthesia induced during childbirth by the use of drugs; **twilight zone** a dilapidated, decaying area of a city or town typically situated between the main business and commercial area and the suburbs; any area or state transitional or indefinite in character. [Pfx. *twi-*, *two*, and **light**[1].]

twill *twil*, *n* a woven fabric showing diagonal lines or ridges, the weft yarns having been worked over one and under two or more warp yarns; the appearance produced in this way. — *vt* to weave with a twill. — **cavalry twill** a strong woollen twill used esp. for trousers. [O.E. *twilic*.]

twin *twin*, *n* one of two (people or animals) born at one birth; a person or thing very like, or closely associated with, another; a counterpart; a combination of two crystals symmetrically united. — *adj* twofold, double; born two at one birth; forming one of, or composed of, two identical or very similar parts or counterparts; very like another. — *vt* to couple together, or to produce, like a twin or twins. — *vi* to give birth to two at one birth; to be paired or suited: — *prp* **twinn'ing**; *pap* **twinned**. — *adj* **twinned** produced at one birth; constituting a twin; paired, matched. — *n* **twinn'ing**. — *n* **twin'ship**. — **twin bed** one of a matching pair of single beds; **twin-broth'er** a brother born at the same birth; **twin'set** a cardigan and jumper made more or less to match; **twin-sist'er** a sister born at the same birth; **twin town** a town paired with another foreign town of similar size for the purpose of social, cultural and commercial exchanges. — *adj* **twin'-track** consisting of or split between two simultaneous, complementary or reciprocal elements, activities, jobs, etc.; **twin'-tub** a type of washing-machine with separate drums for washing and spin-drying. — **the Twins** Gemini, the constellation or sign of the zodiac. [O.E. *getwinn* (noun), twin, *twinn* (adj.), double.]

twine *twīn*, *n* a twisted cord; string or strong thread; a coil or twist; an act of twisting or clasping. — *vt* to wind, coil or twist; to twist together, interlace; to encircle; to make by twisting. — *vi* to wind, coil or twist; to make twisting turns; to rise or grow in spirals. — *adj* **twīned**. — *n* **twī'ner**. — *n* and *adj* **twī'ning**. — *adv* **twī'ningly**. — *adj* **twī'ny**. — **twining plant** one that climbs by twining its stem round a support. [O.E. *twīn*, double or twisted thread, linen thread.]

twinge *twinj*, *vi* to feel or give a momentary pain. — *vt* to tweak or pinch; to affect with a momentary pain. — *n* a tweak or pinch; a sudden short shooting pain; a brief pang. [O.E. *twengan*, to pinch.]

twi-night *twī'-nīt*, (*baseball*; *NAm*) *adj* of a double-header in which the first game is played in the late afternoon and the second in the evening. — *n* **twi'-nighter**. [*twi*light and *night*.]

twinkle *twingk'l*, *vi* to shine by flashes; to glitter; to sparkle; to flicker, vibrate. — *vt* to guide or convey by twinkling or twinkles. — *n* a glitter; a quiver; a flicker or glimmer; a sparkle; a twinkling. — *n* **twink'ler**. — *n* **twink'ling** a quick motion of the eye; the time it takes a person to wink; an instant; the scintillation of the fixed stars. — *adj* scintillating, sparkling. [O.E. *twinclian*.]

twirl *twûrl*, *vt* and *vi* to spin; to whirl; to twist; to coil. — *n* a twist; a spin; a whirl; a whorl; a curly figure or ornament. — *n* **twirl'er**. — *adj* **twirl'y**.

twirp *twûrp*, *n*. An alternative spelling of **twerp**.

twist *twist*, *vt* to wind spirally, coil; to form into a spiral; to unite or form by winding together; to form from several threads; to wring; to wrest; to distort; to force, pull out of natural shape, position, etc.; to entangle; to give a spin to; to force round; to pervert, warp. — *vi* to twine; to coil; to move spirally or tortuously; to turn aside; to revolve; to writhe; (in pontoon) to deal or receive a card face upwards. — *n* that which is twisted or formed by twisting; a cord, strand or thread; silk thread; warp yarn; a twisted part; an act or manner of twisting; a contortion; a wrench (e.g. of an ankle); a deviation, eccentricity or perversion; a spin, screw or break; a distortion; an unexpected event or change of direction (*lit* and *fig*); a tangle; a twisted roll of tobacco or bread; a small curled piece of lemon, etc. flavouring a drink; a spiral ornament in the stem of a glass. — *adj* **twist'able**. — *n* **twist'ed**. — *n* **twist'er** a person who, or thing which, twists; a slippery, shuffling, specious or dishonest person; a ball sent with a twist; a tornado (*US colloq*). — *n* and *adj* **twist'ing**. — *adj* **twist'y**. — **twist drill** a drill for metal having one or more deep helical grooves round the body. — **round the twist** (*colloq*) crazy, mad; **the twist** a dance which became popular in 1962, in which the dancer constantly twists the body; **twist (or turn) someone round one's little finger** to be able to persuade someone to do anything one wants; **twist someone's arm** to persuade someone, esp. forcefully. [O.E. for rope.]

twit[1] *twit*, *vt* to upbraid, find fault with; to taunt: — *prp* **twitt'ing**; *pat* and *pap* **twitt'ed**. [O.E. *ætwītan*, to reproach.]

twit² *twit*, (*slang*) *n* a fool, a daft person. [Prob. **twit¹**.]

twitch¹ *twich*, *vt* to jerk; to pluck sharply; to snatch or steal; to pinch or twinge. — *vi* to jerk; to move spasmodically. — *n* a sudden, quick pull; a spasmodic contraction of the muscles; a twinge. — *n* **twitch'er** someone who or something which twitches; a bird-watcher whose main interest is the spotting of as many rare species as possible (*colloq*). — *n* and *adj* **twitch'ing**. — *adj* **twitch'y** which twitches; jerky; inclined to twitch; on edge, nervous (*colloq*). [Related to O.E. *twiccian*, to pluck.]

twitch² *twich* or **twitch grass** (*gräs*) *n*. Forms of **quitch** or **couch** or **quitch (**or **couch) grass**.

twite *twīt*, *n* a small N. European finch with streaked brown plumage. [From its call.]

twitter *twit'ər*, *n* a tremulous feeble chirping; a flutter of the nerves. — *vi* to make a succession of small tremulous noises. — *vt* to chirp out. — *n* **twitt'erer**. — *n* and *adj* **twitt'ering**. — *adv* **twitt'eringly**. — *adj* **twitt'ery**. [Imit.]

twizzle *twiz'əl*, *vt* to twirl, spin. [Prob. formed under influence of **twist** and **twirl**.]

two *to͞o*, *n* the sum of one and one; a symbol representing two; a pair; a deuce, card with two pips; a score of two points, strokes, etc.; an article of a size denoted by two; the second hour after midnight or midday; the age of two years. — *adj* of the number two; two years old. — *n* **two'er** (*colloq*) anything that counts as, or for, two, or scores two. — *adj* and *adv* **two'fold** in two divisions; twice as much. — *n* **two'foldness**. — *n* **two'some** a company of two; a tête-à-tête. — *adj* **two'-bit** paltry. — **two bits** twenty-five cents. — **two-by-four'** (a piece of) timber measuring 4 in. by 2 in. in cross-section (somewhat less when dressed). — *adj* **two'-digit** in double figures. — *adj* **two'-dimensional**. — **two=dimensional'ity** the property of having length and breadth but no depth. — *adj* **two'-edged** having two cutting edges; capable of being turned against the user. — *adj* **two'-eyed**. — *adj* **two'-faced** having two faces; double-dealing, false. — *adj* **two'=fisted** clumsy; capable of fighting with both fists; holding the racket with both hands (*tennis*). — *adj* **two'-foot** measuring, or with, two feet. — *adj* **two'-footed** having two feet; capable of kicking and controlling the ball equally well with either foot (*football*, etc). — *adj* **two'-four** (*mus*) with two crotchets to the bar. — *adj* **two'-handed** with or for two hands; for two persons; ambidextrous. — **two=hand'er** anything designed for, written for or requiring both hands or two people (e.g. actors). — *adj* **two'-headed** having two heads; directed by two authorities. — *adj* **two'-horse** for two horses (**two=horse race** any contest in which only two of the participants have a genuine chance of winning). — **twopence** (*tup'əns*), or (of decimalised currency) **two pence** (*to͞o pens*), the sum of two pennies; a coin worth two pence. — *adj* **two-pence piece** or **twopenny piece** in Britain, a coin worth 2 pence (also **two'penny-piece**). — *adj* **twopenny** (*tup'ni*) sold, offered at, or worth, twopence; cheap, worthless. — *adj* **twopenny-halfpenny** (*tup-ni-hāp'ni*) paltry, petty. — **two-penn'yworth** or **two=penn'orth** (*to͞o-pen'ərth*), also (chiefly *Scot*) **two-penceworth** (*tup'*); **two'-piece** anything consisting of two separate parts, pieces or members. — Also *adj*. — *adj* **two'-ply** having two layers, or consisting of two strands; woven double. — *adj* **two'-roomed**. — **two'seater** a vehicle or aeroplane seated for two. — *adj* **two'-sided** having two surfaces, aspects or parties; facing two ways; double-faced; having the two sides different. — **two=sid'edness; two'-step** a gliding dance in duple time; a tune for it. — *adj* **two'-storeyed** or **-storey**. — *adj* **two'stroke** (of an engine cycle) consisting of two piston strokes; relating to, or designed for, such an engine. — *vt* **two'-time** to deceive; to double-cross. — **two'-timer** a person who deceives or double-crosses. — *adj* **two'-timing**. — *adj* **two'=tone** having or made up of two colours or two shades of the same colour; (of e.g. a car-horn) having two notes. — **two'-up** an Australian game in which two coins are tossed and bets made on both falling heads up or both tails up. — *adj* **two'-way** permitting passage along either of two ways, esp. in opposite directions; able to receive and send signals (*radio*); of communication between two persons, groups, etc. in which both participate equally; involving shared responsibility; able to be used in two ways. — **in two** split apart so as to form two pieces; **in two ticks** (*slang*) in a moment; **two or three** a few. [O.E. *twā*, fem. and neut., two (masc. *twēgen*).]

twyer or **tuyère** *twēr*, *twīr* or *twē-yer'*, *n* a nozzle for a blast of air (esp. into a blast-furnace). [Fr. *tuyère*.]

TX *abbrev* for Texas (U.S. state).

tycoon *tī-ko͞on'*, *n* a business magnate; orig. the title by which the shoguns of Japan were known to foreigners. [Jap. *taikun*, great prince — Old Chin. *t'ai*, great, *kiun*, prince.]

tying *tī'ing*, *pr p* of **tie**.

tyke or **tike** *tīk*, (chiefly *Northern*) *n* a rough-mannered fellow; a small child (*colloq*); a dog, cur; a Roman Catholic (*derog Austr* and *NZ slang*). — *adj* **tyk'ish**. [O.N. *tīk*, bitch.]

Tylopoda *tī-lop'ə-də*, *npl* the section of hoofed mammals with padded toes — camels and llamas. — *n* and *adj* **ty'lopod**. [Gr. *tȳlos*, a knob, callus, *pous*, *podos*, a foot.]

tymbal. See **timbal**.

tympan *tim'pən*, (*printing*) *n* a frame covered with parchment or cloth, on which sheets are placed for printing; material placed between the platen and the paper to give an even impression. [O.Fr.; or as for **tympanum**.]

tympanal. See **tympanum**.

tympani. See **timpano**.

tympanic *tim-pan'ik*, *adj* of or like a drum or tympanum. — *n* (*anat*) a bone of the ear, supporting the drum-membrane. — *adj* **tym'paniform** (or *-pan'*) drum-shaped; drum-like. — **tympanic membrane** see **tympanum**.

tympanist. See under **timpano**.

tympanitis. See under **tympanum**.

tympano. See **timpano**.

tympanum *tim'pə-nəm*, *n* a drum or drumhead; the middle ear; the membrane separating it from the outer ear — the drum (also called the **tympanic membrane**); in insects, a vibratory membrane in various parts of the body, serving as an eardrum; the recessed face of a pediment (*archit*); a space between a lintel and an arch over it (*archit*): — *pl* **tym'pana**. — *adj* **tym'panal** of or relating to the tympanum (*anat*, *zool*). — *n* **tympanī'tis** (*med*) inflammation of the membrane of the ear. [L. *tympanum* — Gr. *tympanon*, *typanon*, a kettledrum — *typtein*, to strike.]

Tynwald *tin'wold*, *n* the parliament of the Isle of Man. [O.N. *thing-völlr* — *thing*, assembly, *völlr*, field.]

typ. or **typo**. *abbrev* for: typographer; typography.

type *tīp*, *n* a kind; the general character of a class; that which well exemplifies the characteristics of a group; a person of well-marked characteristics; (*loosely* and *derog*) a person; a model or pattern; a rectangular piece of metal or of wood, on one end of which is cast or engraved a character, sign, etc. used in printing; printing types collectively, letter; print; lettering; a mark, stamp or emblem; the device on a coin or medal; the actual specimen on which the description of a new species or genus is based, the holotype (also called **type specimen**). — *adj* serving as a type. — *vt* to typewrite; to determine the type of (*med*); to be the type of; to prefigure, foreshadow, symbolise (*theol*). — *vi* to typewrite. — *n* **typing** (*tīp'ing*). — *n*

typist (*tīp'ist*) a person who uses a typewriter; someone whose occupation is typewriting. — *vt* **type'cast** to cast (someone) in a role that suits their nature; to cast (someone) continually in the same kind of part. — *adj* **type'cast.** — **type'face** (*printing*) a complete range of type cut in a particular style; the printing surface of a type; one of variety of styles in which it is cut; **type'-genus** the genus that gives name to its family; **type-met'al** metal used for making types; an alloy of lead with antimony and tin, and sometimes copper; **type'script** typewritten matter or copy; type in imitation of handwriting or of typewriting. — *adj* typewritten. — **type'setter** a compositor; a machine for setting type; **type'-setting; type'-species** a species taken as the one to which the generic name is primarily attached; **type specimen** see **type** above. — *vt* and *vi* **type'write** to print or copy using a typewriter. — **type'writer** a machine, usu. with a keyboard, for printing as a substitute for handwriting; **type'writing.** — *adj* **type'written.** [L. *typus* — Gr. *typos*, a blow, mark, stamp, model; *typtein*, to strike.]

-type *-tīp*, *sfx* meaning: of the same type as; resembling. [**type.**]

typhlitis *tif-lī'tis*, (*med*) *n* inflammation of the caecum or blind-gut. — *adj* **typhlitic** (*-lit'ik*). [Gr. *typhlos*, blind.]

typhoid *tī'foid*, *adj* like typhus. — *n* **ty'phoid** or **typhoid fever** enteric fever, with inflammation and ulceration of the small intestine, caused by the bacillus *Salmonella typhosa*, long confused with typhus, on account of the characteristic rash of rose-coloured spots. — *adj* **typhoid'al.** [Gr. *typhōdēs*, delirious — *typhos*, a fever, *eidos*, likeness; cf. **typhus.**]

typhoon *tī-fōōn'*, *n* a violent cyclonic storm of the China sea and West Pacific area. [Gr. *typhōn*, a whirlwind; but partly also from Port. *tufão* — Ar., Pers., Hind. *tūfān*, a hurricane, and partly from Chin. *t'ai fung*, a great wind.]

typhus *tī'fəs*, *n* a dangerous fever transmitted by lice and marked by the eruption of red spots. — *adj* **ty'phoid** (q.v.). — *adj* **ty'phous.** [Latinised from Gr. *typhos*, fever, stupor, delusion.]

typical *tip'i-kəl*, *adj* characteristic; representative; pertaining to, or constituting, a type; figurative; emblematic. — *n* **typical'ity.** — *adv* **typ'ically.** — *n* **typ'icalness.** [Med. L. *typicālis* — L. *typicus*.]

typify *tip'i-fī*, *vt* to make or be a type of; to exemplify or symbolise: — *prp* **typ'ifying**; *pat* and *pap* **typ'ified.** — *n* **typificā'tion.** — *n* **typ'ifier.** [L. *typus* (see **type**) and sfx. *-fy* (ult. from L. *facere*, to make).]

typist, etc. See under **type.**

typo *tī'po*, (*colloq*) *n* a typographical error, a literal; short for **typographer**: — *pl* **ty'pos.**

typo. *abbrev* for: typographer; typography.

typography *tī-pog'rə-fi*, *n* the art or style of printing or of using type effectively. — *n* **typog'rapher** a compositor; a person engaged in or skilled in typography. — *adj* **typograph'ic** or **typograph'ical.** — *adv* **typograph'ically.** — *n* **typog'raphist** a person who studies or is knowledgeable in the history or art of printing. [N.L. *typographia* (equivalent to **type** and **-graphy.**]

typology *tī-pol'ə-ji*, *n* the study of types and their succession in biology, archaeology, etc.; the doctrine that things in the New Testament are foreshadowed symbolically in the Old. — *adj* **typolog'ical.** — *n* **typol'ogist.** [Gr. *typos*, type, and **-logy.**]

tyramine *tī'rə-mēn*, *n* a colourless crystalline amine found in cheese, ergot, mistletoe and decayed animal tissue or derived from phenol, similar in action to adrenaline. [*tyr*osine and *amine*.]

tyrant *tī'rənt*, *n* a ruler who uses power arbitrarily and oppressively; an oppressor; a bully; in the orig. Greek sense, an absolute ruler, or one whose power has not been constitutionally arrived at. — *adj* **tyrannic** (*ti-ran'ik*; sometimes *tī-*) or **tyrann'ical.** — *adv* **tyrann'ically.** — *n* **tyrann'icalness.** — *adj* **tyrannicī'dal.** — *n* **tyrann'icide** the killing or the killer of a tyrant. — *vi* **tyrannise** or **-ize** (*tir'*) to act as a tyrant; esp. to rule with oppressive severity. — *vt* to act the tyrant to. — *adj* **tyrannous** (*tir'*) despotic; domineering; overpowering; oppressive. — *adv* **tyr'annously.** — *n* **tyranny** (*tir'*) absolute or illegally established power; the government or authority of a tyrant; absolute power administered cruelly; oppression, cruelty, harshness. [Gr. *tyrannos*, partly through O.Fr. *tirant* and L. *tyrannus*.]

tyrannosaur *tī-ran'ə-sör* or **tyrannosaurus** *-sör'əs*, *n* a large bipedal carnivorous dinosaur common during the Cretaceous period. [N.L. *Tyrannosaurus* — Gr. *tyrannos* and dino*saur*.]

tyre *tīr*, *n* a rubber cushion, tube or band round a wheel-rim; a variant spelling of **tire**[1]. — *adj* **tyred.** — *adj* **tyre'less.** — **tyre chain** see under **chain**; **tyre gauge** a device for measuring the air pressure in a pneumatic tyre. — **tubeless tyre** a pneumatic tyre that has no inner tube, and, being self-sealing, deflates only slowly when punctured. [See **tire**[1].]

Tyrian *tir'i-ən*, *adj* of *Tyre*, the ancient Mediterranean port. — *n* a native of ancient Tyre. — **Tyrian red** or **purple** a dye formerly prepared at Tyre; this purplish-red colour.

tyro. See **tiro.**

Tyrolese *tir-ə-lēz'*, *adj* relating to the mountainous west Austrian province of *Tyrol*, or to its people. — *n* a native or inhabitant of Tyrol. — *n* and *adj* **Tyrolē'an.**

tyrosine *tī'rō-sēn*, *n* an amino-acid formed by decomposition of proteins, first obtained from cheese. — *n* **ty'rosinase** an enzyme found in plants and animals that assists in converting tyrosine to melanin. [Gr. *tyros*, cheese.]

tzar. See **tsar.**

tzatziki *tsat-sē'ki*, *n* a Greek dish made of yoghurt and finely sliced or chopped cucumber, flavoured with garlic, mint, etc., eaten as a dip. [Mod. Gr.]

tzigany or **tzigane** *tsig'ä-ni*, *-ə-ni* or *-ny'*, *n* a Hungarian gipsy. — Also *adj*. [Hung. *cigány*, gipsy.]

U

U[1] or **u** *ū*, *n* the twenty-first letter in the modern English alphabet; something shaped like or into a U shape. — *adj* (with *cap*) (of words, phrases, customs, etc.) ordinarily used by, or found in, the upper classes. — *adj* **non'-U** not so used or found (U for *u*pper-class). — **U'-bend** an air-trap in the form of a U-shaped bend in a pipe; **U'-bolt, U'-trap** and **U'-tube** a bolt, drain trap and tube bent like the letter U. — *adj* **U'-shaped.** — **U'-turn** a turn made by a vehicle which reverses its direction of travel, crossing into the flow of traffic on the other side of the road; any reversal of direction (*fig*).

U[2] *o͞o*, *n* a Burmese title of respect, preceding a man's name. [Burmese.]

U or **U.** *abbrev* for: unionist; united; universal, (a certificate designating) a film which anyone is allowed to see; university; Uruguay (I.V.R.). — **U'-boat** *abbrev* for *Untersee(boot)* (Ger.), a German submarine.

U (*chem*) *symbol* for uranium.

UAE *abbrev* for United Arab Emirates.

uakari or **ouakari** *wa-ka'ri*, *n* any of various short-tailed, long-haired S. American monkeys of the genus *Cacajao*, related to the saki. [Tupí.]

Übermensch *ü'bər-mensh*, (Ger.) *n* a superman.

UB40 *abbrev* for unemployment benefit (form) 40, a registration card issued by the Department of Employment and held by an unemployed person.

ubiety *ū-bī'i-ti*, *n* the state of being in a definite place, location. [L. *ubi*, where.]

ubiquinone *ū-bik'wi-nōn*, (*biochem*) *n* a quinone involved in the transfer of electrons during cell respiration. [L. *ubīque*, everywhere, and **quinone.**]

ubiquity *ū-bik'wi-ti*, *n* existence everywhere at the same time; omnipresence. — *adj* **ubiquā'rian** found everywhere; ubiquitous. — *adj* **ubiq'uitous** to be found everywhere. — *adv* **ubiq'uitously**. [L. *ubīque*, everywhere — *ubi*, where.]

UBR *abbrev* for Uniform Business Rate.

UCCA *uk'ə*, *abbrev* for Universities Central Council on Admissions.

UDA *abbrev* for Ulster Defence Association.

udder *ud'ər*, *n* the organ containing the mammary glands of the cow, mare, etc., having more than one teat. — *adj* **udd'ered.** [O.E. *ūder.*]

UDF *abbrev* for United Democratic Front, a South African organisation of anti-apartheid groups.

UDI *abbrev* for Unilateral Declaration of Independence.

UDM *abbrev* for Union of Democratic Mineworkers.

udometer *ū-dom'i-tər*, *n* a name for a rain-gauge. — *adj* **udomet'ric.** [Through Fr. — L. *ūdus*, wet, Gr. *metron*, a measure.]

UDR *abbrev* for Ulster Defence Regiment.

UEFA *ū-ā'fə* or *ū-ē'fə*, *abbrev* for Union of European Football Associations.

UFC *abbrev* for Universities Funding Council.

UFO or **ufo** *ū-ef-ō'* or *ū'fō*, (*colloq*) *n* an *u*nidentified *f*lying *o*bject, such as a flying saucer: — *pl* **U'FOs** or **u'fos.** — *n* **ufology** (*ū-fol'ə-ji*) the study of UFOs. — *n* **ufol'ogist.**

UGC *abbrev* for University Grants Committee (replaced, 1989, by **UFC**).

ugh *uhh, ug, o͝oh* or *ûh*, *interj* an exclamation of repugnance. — *n* used as a representation of a cough or grunt.

ugli *ug'li*, *n* a citrus fruit which is a cross between the grapefruit, the seville orange and the tangerine. [**ugly**; from the fruit's unprepossessing appearance.]

ugly *ug'li*, *adj* offensive to the sight or other sense, or to refined taste or moral feeling; ill-natured; threatening; disquieting; suggesting suspicion of evil. — *n* **uglificā'tion.** — *vt* **ug'lify** to make ugly. — *adv* **ug'lily.** — *n* **ug'liness.** — **ugly duckling** a despised or overlooked member of a family or group who later proves the most successful or attractive, etc. [O.N. *uggligr*, frightful, *uggr*, fear.]

Ugrian *ū'gri-ən* or *o͞o'*, *adj* of that division of the Finno-Ugrian languages and peoples that includes the Magyars, Ostyaks and Voguls. — Also *n.* — *adj* **U'gric.** — *adj* **Ugro-Finn'ic** Finno-Ugrian. [Russ. *Ugri*, the Ugrian peoples.]

UHF *abbrev* for ultra-high frequency (see **frequency** under **frequent**).

uh-huh *u'-hu* or *m'-hm*, *interj* a sound used in place of 'yes'.

uhlan *o͞o'län* or *ū'*, (*hist*) *n* a light cavalryman in semi-oriental uniform; a Prussian lancer. [Ger. *Uhlan* — Polish *ulan*, orig. a light Tatar horseman — Turk. *oğlān*, a young man.]

UHT *abbrev* for ultra-heat-treated (q.v.).

uhuru *o͞o-ho͞o'ro͞o*, *n* (esp. in E. Africa) freedom (e.g. from slavery); national independence. [Swahili — *huru*, free.]

uitlander *œ'it-, āt'* or *ā'it-land-ər*, (chiefly *hist*) *n* a foreigner (orig. a British person in the Transvaal or Orange Free State). [Du. equivalent of *outlander*, a foreigner.]

UK *abbrev* for United Kingdom.

UKAEA *abbrev* for United Kingdom Atomic Energy Authority.

ukase *ū-kāz'* or *-kās'*, *n* an edict with force of law in Tsarist Russia; an edict issued by the Supreme Soviet; any arbitrary decree from any source. [Russ. *ukaz.*]

uke *ūk*, (*colloq*) *n* short for **ukulele.**

ukelele. A common spelling of **ukulele**.

Ukrainian *ū-krān'i-ən*, *n* a native or citizen of (the) *Ukraine*, a republic of the U.S.S.R., a rich agricultural region in S.W. Russia; its language. — Also *adj.*

ukulele *ū-kə-lā'li* or *o͝o-ko͝o-lā'lā*, *n* a small, usually four-stringed, guitar, popularised in Hawaii, although originally Portuguese. [Hawaiian, jumping flea.]

ULA or **ula** (*comput*) *abbrev* for uncommitted logic array.

ulcer *ul'sər*, *n* an open sore, on the skin or a mucous membrane, often discharging pus; a continuing source of evil, pain or corruption, an unsound element. — *vi* **ul'cerate** to form an ulcer. — *vt* to cause an ulcer in; to affect with insidious corruption. — *n* **ulcerā'tion.** — *adj* **ul'cerātive.** — *adj* **ul'cered.** — *adj* **ul'cerous.** — *adv* **ul'cerously.** — *n* **ul'cerousness.** [L. *ulcus, ulcĕris.*]

ulema *o͞o'li-mə*, *n* the body of professional theologians, expounders of the law, in a Muslim country;

a member of such a body. [Ar. *'ulema*, pl. of *'ālim*, learned.]

uliginose *ū-lij'i-nōs* or **uliginous** *-lij'i-nəs*, (*bot*) *adj* growing in swampy places. [L. *ūlīginōsus — ūlīgō*, *-inis*, moisture.]

ullage *ul'ij*, *n* the quantity by which a vessel is holding less than its full capacity, or sometimes the amount left in the vessel; loss by evaporation or leakage; dregs (*slang*). [A.Fr. *ulliage*, O.Fr. *eullage — œiller*, to fill up.]

ulna *ul'nə*, *n* the inner and larger of the two bones of the forearm; the corresponding bone in an animal's foreleg or a bird's wing (*zool*): — *pl* **ul'nae** (*-nē*). — *adj* **ul'nar**. [L. *ulna*, elbow, arm.]

ulosis *ū-lō'sis*, (*med*) *n* the formation of a scar. [Gr. *oulōsis — oulē*, a scar.]

ulotrichous *ū-lot'ri-kəs*, *adj* woolly-haired. [Gr. *oulos*, woolly, *thrix*, *trichos*, hair.]

ulster *ul'stər*, *n* a long loose overcoat, first made in *Ulster*, N. Ireland. — *adj* **ul'stered** wearing an ulster. — **Ul'sterman** and **Ul'sterwoman** a (man and woman) native or inhabitant of Ulster.

ult. *abbrev* for ultimately; see also **ultimo** under **ultimate**.

ulterior *ul-tē'ri-ər*, *adj* on the further side; beyond; in the future; remoter; (of e.g. a motive) beyond what is avowed or apparent. — *adv* **ultē'riorly**. [L. *ulterior — ultrā* (adv. and prep.), *uls* (prep.), beyond.]

ultima *ul'tə-mə*, *n* the last syllable of a word. [L., fem. of *ultimus*, last.]

ultimate *ul'ti-māt* or *-mit*, *adj* furthest; last; final; fundamental; maximum; most important. — *n* a final point; a fundamental; the greatest (or otherwise most extreme) thing achievable or conceivable of its sort (*colloq*). — *n* **ul'timacy** (*-mə-si*). — *adv* **ul'timately** finally. — *n* **ultimā'tum** final terms; a last offer or demand; a last word: — *pl* **ultimā'ta**. — *adj* **ul'timo** (*abbrev* **ult.**; only now in business, etc. letters) in or of the last (month). — *n* **ultimogeniture** (*-jen'*; *law*) succession of the youngest son. [L. *ultimus*, last.]

ultima (or **Ultima**) **Thule**. See under **Thule**.

ultra- *ul-trə-*, *pfx* signifying: (1) beyond in place, position (as **ul'tra-Neptunian** beyond the planet Neptune); (2) beyond the limit, range, etc. of (as **ul'tra-microscopic**); (3) beyond the ordinary, or excessive(ly) (as in **ul'tra-Conservative, ul'tra-Conservatism, ul'tra-fashionable, ul'tra-modern** and **ul'tra-Protestant**). — *adj* **ul'tra** extreme, esp. in royalism, fashion, or religious or political opinion. — *n* an extremist. — *n* **ultraism** (*ul'trə-izm*) (an) extreme principle, opinion or measure. — *n* **ul'traist**. [L. *ultrā*, beyond.]

ultracentrifuge *ul-trə-sen'tri-fūj*, *n* a very high-speed type of centrifuge. — *vt* to subject to the action of an ultracentrifuge. — *adj* **ultracentrif'ugal** (or *-fū'gəl*). — *n* **ultracentrifugation** (*-gā'shən*). [**ultra-** (2).]

ultrafiche *ul'trə-fēsh*, *n* a sheet of microfilm the same size as a microfiche but with a greater number of microcopied records on it. [**ultra-** (3).]

ultrafilter *ul'trə-fil-tər*, (*biol*) *n* an extremely fine filter which retains particles as fine as large molecules. — *vt* to pass through an ultrafilter. — *n* **ultrafil'trate** a substance that has passed through an ultrafilter. — *n* **ultrafiltrā'tion**. [**ultra-** (2).]

ultra-heat-treated *ul-trə-hēt-trē'tid*, *adj* (of milk, etc.) sterilised by exposing to very high temperatures, increasing shelf-life (usu. *abbrev*. **UHT**). [**ultra-** (3).]

ultra-high *ul-trə-hī'*, *adj* very high. — **ultra-high frequency** see **frequency** under **frequent**. [**ultra-** (3).]

ultraism, ultraist. See under **ultra-**.

ultramarine *ul-trə-mə-rēn'*, *adj* overseas; from overseas; deep blue. — *n* a deep blue pigment, orig. made from lapis lazuli; its colour. [L. *ultrā*, beyond, *marīnus*, marine.]

ultramicro- *ul-trə-mī-krō-*, *pfx* signifying smaller than, or dealing with smaller quantities than, **micro-**, e.g. **ultramicrochem'istry** chemistry dealing with minute quantities.

ultramicroscope *ul-trə-mī'krə-skōp*, *n* a microscope with strong illumination from the side, whereby the presence of ultramicroscopic objects can be observed through the scattering of light from them. — *adj* **ultramicroscopic** (*-skop'ik*) too small to be visible under the ordinary microscope. — *n* **ultramicroscopy** (*-kros'kə-pi*). [**ultra-** (2).]

ultramontane *ul-trə-mon'tān*, *adj* beyond the mountains, esp. the Alps; of or pertaining to a faction within the Roman Catholic Church which is extreme in favouring the pope's supremacy. — *n* a person who lives beyond the mountains, esp. south of the Alps; a member of the ultramontane faction within the Roman Catholic Church. — *n* **ultramon'tanism** (*-tən-izm*). — *n* **ultramon'tanist**. [L. *ultra*, beyond, *montānus — mōns*, *montis*, a mountain.]

ultramundane *ul-trə-mun'dān*, *adj* beyond the world, or beyond the limits of our solar system. [**ultra-** (1).]

ultrashort *ul-trə-shört'*, *adj* (of electromagnetic waves) of less than ten metres' wavelength. [**ultra-** (3).]

ultrasonic *ul-trə-son'ik*, *adj* pertaining to, or (of an instrument or process) using **ultrasound** (*-sownd'*), vibrations of the same nature as audible sound waves but of such greater frequency as to be inaudible. — *adv* **ultrason'ically**. — *nsing* **ultrason'ics** the study of such vibrations, used medically for diagnostic and therapeutic purposes. — *n* **ultrasonography** (*-sən-og'rə-fi*) the directing of ultrasonic waves through body tissues, producing an image on a screen which can be used to detect abnormalities, e.g. in a foetus. [**ultra-** (2).]

ultrasound. See under **ultrasonic**.

ultrastructure *ul'trə-struk-chər*, (*biol*) *n* the ultimate structure of protoplasm at a lower level than can be examined microscopically. [**ultra-** (2).]

ultraviolet *ul-trə-vī'ə-lit*, (*phys*) *adj* beyond the violet end of the visible spectrum; pertaining to, or using, radiations of wavelengths less than those of visible light. [**ultra-** (1).]

ultra vires *ul'trə vī'rēz* or *ŏŏl'trä wē'rās*, (L.) beyond one's powers or authority.

ululate *ūl'ū-lāt*, *vi* to hoot or screech. — *adj* **ul'ulant**. — *n* **ululā'tion** howling, wailing. [L. *ŭlŭlāre*, *-ātum*, to hoot.]

um *əm* or *um*, *interj* expressing hesitation in speech.

umbel *um'bəl*, (*bot*) *n* a flat-topped inflorescence in which the flower stalks all spring from about the same point in an axis. — *adj* **um'bellar** (or *-bel'*). — *adj* **um'bellate** or **um'bellated** constituting an umbel; having umbels. — *adv* **um'bellately**. — *n* **umbellifer** (*um-bel'i-fər*) any plant of the *Umbelliferae* family, the carrot and hemlock family of plants with umbels and divided leaves. — *adj* **umbellif'erous**. [L. *umbella*, a sunshade, dimin. of *umbra*, a shade.]

umber *um'bər*, *n* a brown earthy mineral (hydrated oxides of iron and manganese) used as a pigment. — *vt* to colour with umber. — *adj* brown like umber. — *adj* **um'bery**. — **burnt umber** umber heated to give a dark reddish-brown colour; **raw umber** untreated umber, a yellowish-brown colour. [It. *terra d'ombra*, shadow earth, or poss. Umbrian earth.]

umbilicus *um-bil'i-kəs* or *um-bi-lī'kəs*, *n* the navel; a depression at the base of a shell; a small depression. — *adj* **umbilical** (*-bil'*; sometimes *-bi-lī'*) relating to the umbilicus or the umbilical cord. — *adj* **umbil'icate** navel-like; having a depression like a navel. — *n* **umbilicā'tion**. — **umbilical cord** a long flexible tube connecting the foetus to the placenta; an electrical cable or other servicing line attached to a rocket vehicle or spacecraft during preparations for launch; the lifeline outside a vehicle in space by which astronauts receive air and communicate with the vehicle; any similar connection of fundamental importance. [L. *umbilīcus*, the navel.]

umbles *um'blz*, *npl* entrails (liver, heart, etc.), esp. of a deer. — **umble-pie'** or **humble-pie'** a pie made from the umbles of a deer. [O.Fr. *nombles*, from *lomble*, loin.]

umbo *um'bō*, *n* the central boss of a shield; a knob; the protuberant oldest part of a bivalve shell; a knob on a toadstool cap; a projection on the inner surface of the eardrum where the malleus is attached: — *pl* **umbō'nēs** or **um'bos**. — *adj* **um'bonal** (*-bən-əl*). — *adj* **um'bonate** (*bot*) having a central boss. — *n* **umbonā'tion**. [L. *umbō*, *-ōnis*.]

umbra *um'brə*, *n* a shadow; the darker part of the shadow or dark inner cone projected in an eclipse (*astron*); the darker part of a sunspot. — *adj* **um'bral** of an umbra. — *adj* **umbratile** (*um'brə-tīl* or *-til*) or **umbratilous** (*-brat'i-ləs*) shadowy; shaded; shade-giving; secluded. — *adj* **umbrif'erous** shade-giving. — *adj* **umbrose** (*-brōs'*) shade-giving; dusky. — *adj* **um'brous** shaded. [L. *umbra*, shade, shadow, dimin. *umbrāculum*, adj. *umbrātilis*.]

umbrage *um'brij*, *n* offence, esp. in the phrases *give* and *take umbrage*; suspicion of injury; shade, shadow or that which casts a shadow (*archaic* or *poetic*). — *adj* **umbrā'geous** shady or forming a shade. [Fr. *ombrage* — L. *umbrāticum* (neut. adj.) — *umbra*, a shadow.]

umbral, umbratile, umbratilous. See under **umbra**.

umbrella *um-brel'ə*, *n* a portable shelter against sun, rain, etc., now usu. a canopy with a sliding framework of ribs on a stick; anything of similar form; a protection (*fig*); a general cover (*fig*); a cover of fighter aircraft for ground forces (*mil*). — *adj* **umbrella** covering many or a variety of things. — *adj* **umbrell'aed** or **umbrell'a'd** with an umbrella. — **umbrell'a-fir** a Japanese conifer with radiating tufts of needles; **umbrella group, organisation**, etc. a group of representatives of small parties, clubs, etc. which acts for all of them where they have common interests; **umbrell'a-plant** an African sedge with umbrella-like clusters of slender leaves, a common houseplant; **umbrell'a-stand** a rack or receptacle for closed umbrellas and walking-sticks; **umbrell'a-tree** a tree of any kind with leaves or branches arranged umbrella-wise, esp. a small magnolia. [It. *ombrella*, *ombrello* — *ombra*, a shade — L. *umbra*.]

Umbrian *um'bri-ən*, *adj* of *Umbria*, in central Italy. — *n* a native of Umbria.

umbriferous, umbrose, umbrous. See under **umbra**.

umiak or **oomiak** *ōō'mi-ak* or *ōōm'yak*, *n* an open boat made of wood and stretched skins, typically manned by women. [Eskimo.]

UMIST *ū'mist*, *abbrev* for University of Manchester Institute of Science and Technology.

umlaut *ōōm'lowt*, *n* a vowel-change in Germanic languages brought about by a vowel or semivowel (esp. *i*, *j*) in the following syllable; (*loosely*) the two dots placed over a letter representing a vowel with an umlaut in German. [Ger., — *um*, around, *Laut*, sound.]

umpire *um'pīr*, *n* a third person called in to decide a dispute or a deadlock; an arbitrator; an impartial person chosen to supervise the game, enforce the rules, and decide disputes (*cricket*, etc.). — Also *vi* and *vt*. [M.E. *noumpere*, *oumper* — O.Fr. *nomper* — *non-*, not, *per*, *pair*, peer, equal.]

umpteen *um'tēn* or *ump'tēn* also **umpty** *um'ti* or *ump'ti*, (*colloq*) *adj* an indefinitely large number. — *adj* **ump'teenth** latest or last of many. [*Umpty* in Morse, a dash, from its sound on a telegraph key.]

UN *abbrev* for United Nations.

Only a selection of the many words beginning with the prefix **un-** is given in the dictionary. They are listed continuously, from **unabashed** to **unzoned**, either in the text or in the panels. Words in which **un-** is not a prefix, such as **uncle** and **unction**, follow after the prefixed words.

un- *un-*, *pfx* (1) meaning 'not' (in many cases, the resultant word is more than a mere negation; it has a positive force, as in **unkind**, which usu. means 'cruel' rather than just 'not kind'); (2) indicating a reversal of process, removal or deprivation; (3) merely emphasising reversal or deprivation already expressed by the simple word, as in **unloose**. (Partly O.E. *un-*, neg.; cf. Ger. *un-*, L. *in-*, Gr. *an-*, *a-*; partly O.E. *on-* (or *un-*), the unstressed form of *and-*; cf. Ger. *ent-*, Gr. *anti*, against). — *adj* **unaba'ted** not made less in degree. — *adj* **una'ble** not able; not having sufficient strength, power or skill (to do). — *adj* **unaccent'ed** without accent or stress in pronunciation; not marked with an accent. — *adj* **unaccomm'odated** unprovided. — *adj* **unaccomm'odating** not compliant. — *adj* **unaccom'panied** not accompanied, escorted or attended; having no instrumental accompaniment (*mus*). — *adj* **unaccom'plished** not achieved; lacking accomplishments. — *adj* **unaccount'able** difficult or impossible to explain; not answerable (to a higher authority); (of a person) puzzling in character. — *adv* **unaccount'ably** inexplicably. — *adj* **unaccount'ed-for** unexplained; not included in an account. — *adj* **unaccus'tomed** not customary; not used (to). — *n* **unaccus'tomedness**. — *adj* **unacknowl'edged** not acknowledged, recognised, confessed or noticed. — *adj* **unacquaint'ed** not on a footing of acquaintance; ignorant of (with *with*); uninformed. — *adj* **unact'ed** not performed. — *adj* **unadop'ted** not adopted (**unadopted road** a road for the repairing, maintenance, etc. of which the Local Authority is not responsible). — *adj* **unadul'terāted** unmixed, pure, genuine; sheer, absolute. — *adj* **unadvīsed'** not advised; without advice; not prudent or discreet; ill-judged. — *adv* **unadvīs'edly**. — *n* **unadvīs'edness**. — *adj* **unaffect'ed** not affected or influenced; untouched by emotion; without affectation; not assumed; plain; real; sincere. — *adv* **unaffect'edly**. — *n* **unaffect'edness**. — *adj* **unallied'** not related. — *adj* **unalloyed'** not alloyed or mixed, pure (*lit* and *fig*). — *adj* **un-Amer'ican** not in accordance with American character, ideas, feeling or traditions; disloyal, against American interests. — *adj* **unan'swerable** impossible to answer; not to be refuted, conclusive. — *adv* **unan'swerably**. — *adj* **unan'swered** not answered; unrequited. — *adj* **unapproach'able** out of reach, inaccessible; standoffish; inaccessible to advances or intimacy; beyond rivalry. — *n* **unapproach'ableness**. — *adv* **unapproach'ably**. — *adj* **unapprō'priated** not taken possession of; not applied to some purpose; not granted to any person, corporation, etc. — *adj* **unapt'** unfitted; unsuitable; not readily inclined or accustomed (to); lacking in aptitude, slow. — *adv* **unapt'ly**. — *n* **unapt'ness**. — *adj* **unar'gūable** that cannot be argued; irrefutable. — *adv* **unar'gūably**. — *adj* **unarmed'** without weapons; defenceless; unprotected; unaided or without accessory apparatus; without arms or similar limbs or appendages. — *adj* **unasked'** not asked; not asked for; uninvited. — *adj* **unassum'ing** making no assumption; unpretentious, modest. — *adv* **unassum'ingly**. — *n* **unassum'ingness**. — *adj* **unattached'** not attached; not belonging to a club, party, college, diocese, department, regiment, etc.; not married; having no romantic and/or sexual attachment to a particular person. — *adj* **unattend'ed** not accompanied or attended; not listened to or paid attention. — *adj* **unavail'able** not available. — *adj* **unavail'ing** of no avail or effect, useless. — *n* **unavoidabil'ity**. — *adj* **unavoid'able**

not to be avoided; inevitable. — *n* **unavoid'ableness.** — *adv* **unavoid'ably.** — *adj* **unaware'** not aware. — *n* **unaware'ness.** — *adv* **unawares'** without being, or making, aware; without being perceived; unexpectedly. — *adj* **unbacked'** without a back; without backing or backers; unaided. — *n* **unbal'ance** lack of balance. — *vt* to throw off balance; to derange. — *adj* **unbal'anced** not in a state of equilibrium; without mental balance, erratic or deranged; (of e.g. a view, judgment) not giving due weight to all features of the situation; not adjusted so as to show balance of debtor and creditor (*bookkeeping*). — *adj* **unbanked'** not deposited in, provided with, or having, a bank. — *vt* **unbar'** to remove a bar from or of; to unfasten. — *adj* **unbear'able** intolerable. — *n* **unbear'ableness.** — *adj* **unbecom'ing** unsuitable; not suited to the wearer, or not showing her or him to advantage; (of behaviour, etc.) not befitting, unseemly (with *to*, *in*). — *adv* **unbecom'ingly.** — *n* **unbecom'ingness.** — *adj* **unbegot'** or **unbegott'en** not yet begotten; existing independent of any generating cause. — *adj* **unbeknown'** or **unbeknownst'** (*colloq*) unknown. — *adv* unobserved, without being known. — *n* **un'belief** (or *-lēf'*) disbelief, or withholding of belief, esp. in accepted religion. — *adj* **unbeliev'able** incredible; (*loosely*) astonishing, remarkable. — *adv* **unbeliev'ably.** — *n* **unbeliev'er** a person who does not believe, esp. in the prevailing religion; a habitually incredulous person. — *adj* **unbeliev'ing.** — *adv* **unbeliev'ingly.** — *vt* **unbelt'** to undo the belt of (a garment). — *adj* **unbelt'ed** without a belt; freed from a belt. — *vt* **unbend'** to relax (e.g. a bow) from a bending tension; to straighten; to undo, unfasten (*naut*). — *vi* to become relaxed; to behave with freedom from stiffness, to be affable. — *adj* **unbend'able.** — *adj* **unbend'ed.** — *adj* **unbend'ing** not bending; unyielding; resolute. — *n* a relaxing. — *adv* **unbend'ingly.** — *n* **unbend'ingness.** — *adj* **unbent'** not bent; relaxed; not overcome or vanquished. — *adj* **unbi'ased** or **unbi'assed.** — *adv* **unbi'asedly** or **unbi'assedly.** — *adj* **unbidd'en** not bid or commanded; uninvited; spontaneous. — *vt* **unbīnd'** to remove a band from; to loose; to set free. — *n* **unbīnd'ing** the removal of a band or bond; a loosing; a setting free. — *adj* loosening; not binding. — *adj* **unblink'ing** without blinking; not wavering; not showing emotion, esp. fear. — *adv* **unblink'ingly.** — *adj* **unblush'ing** not blushing; without shame; impudent. — *adv* **unblush'ingly.** — *vt* **unbolt'** to draw back a bolt from. — *adj* **unbolt'ed** unfastened by withdrawing a bolt; not fastened by bolts; not separated by bolting or sifting; coarse. — *adj* **unborn'** not yet born; non-existent. — *vt* **unbo'som** to pour out, tell freely (what is in the mind); (*reflexive*) to confide freely (also *vi*). — *adj* **unbound'** not bound; loose; without binding (also *pa t* and *pa p* of **unbind,** freed from bonds). — *adj* **unbound'ed** not limited; boundless; having no check or control. — *adv* **unbound'edly.** — *n* **unbound'edness.** — *adj* **unbowed'** not bowed or bent; not vanquished or overcome, free. — *vt* **unbox'** to remove from a box or crate. — *vt* **unbrī'dle** to free from the bridle; to free from (usu. politic) restraint. — *adj* **unbrī'dled** not bridled; unrestrained. — *n* **unbrī'dledness.** — *adj* **un-Brit'ish** not in accordance with British character or traditions. — *adj* **unbrō'ken** not broken; (of a record) not surpassed; uninterrupted; not thrown into disorder; not variegated; not infringed. — *adv* **unbrō'kenly.** — *n*

Some words with **un-** prefix; see **un-** entry for numbered senses.

unabashed' *adj* (1).
unabbrēv'iated *adj* (1).
unabridged' *adj* (1).
unacadem'ic *adj* (1).
unaccen'tūāted *adj* (1).
unaccept'able *adj* (1).
unaccept'ableness *n* (1).
unaccred'ited *adj* (1).
unachiev'able *adj* (1).
unadapt'able *adj* (1).
unadapt'ed *adj* (1).
unaddressed' *adj* (1).
unadjust'ed *adj* (1).
unadorned' *adj* (1).
unadvent'urous *adj* (1).
unad'vertised *adj* (1).
unaffil'iated *adj* (1).
unafraid' *adj* (1).
unaid'ed *adj* (1).
unaimed' *adj* (1).
unaired' *adj* (1).
unalike' *adj* (1).
unallott'ed *adj* (1).
unallow'able *adj* (1).
unalterabil'ity *n* (1).
unal'terable *adj* (1).
unal'terably *adj* (1).
unal'tered *adj* (1).
unamazed' *adj* (1).
unambig'ūous *adj* (1).
unambig'ūously *adv* (1).
unambi'tious *adj* (1).
unambi'tiously *adv* (1).
unamend'ed *adj* (1).
unamū'sing *adj* (1).
unamū'singly *adv* (1).
unanalys'able or **-z-** *adj* (1).
unan'alysed or **-z-** *adj* (1).
unanalyt'ic or **unanalyt'ical** *adj* (1).
unanch'ored *adj* (1).
unann'otated *adj* (1).
unannounced' *adj* (1).
unapologet'ic *adj* (1).
unappar'ent *adj* (1).
unappeal'ing *adj* (1).
unapp'etising or **-z-** *adj* (1).
unapp'licable *adj* (1).
unapplied' *adj* (1).
unapprē'ciated *adj* (1).
unapprē'ciative *adj* (1).
unapproved' *adj* (1).
unartifi'cial *adj* (1).
unartifi'cially *adv* (1).
unascend'ed *adj* (1).
unascertain'able *adj* (1).
unascertained' *adj* (1).
unashamed' *adj* (1).
unasham'edly *adv* (1).
unas'pirated *adj* (1).
unassail'able *adj* (1).
unasser'tive *adj* (1).
unassīgned' *adj* (1).
unassim'ilated *adj* (1).
unassist'ed *adj* (1).
unassist'edly *adv* (1).
unassist'ing *adj* (1).
unassō'ciated *adj* (1).
unatōned' *adj* (1).
unattain'able *adj* (1).
unattain'ableness *n* (1).
unattain'ably *adv* (1).
unattend'ing *adj* (1).
unattest'ed *adj* (1).
unattīred' *adj* (1).
unattract'ive *adj* (1).
unattract'ively *adv* (1).
unattract'iveness *n* (1).
unauthen'tic *adj* (1).
unau'thorised or **-z-** *adj* (1).
unauthor'itative *adj* (1).
unavailabil'ity *n* (1).
unavowed' *adj* (1).
unavow'edly *adv* (1).
unawāk'ened *adj* (1).
unawed' *adj* (1).
unbait'ed *adj* (1).
unband'ed *adj* (1).
unbarred' *adj* (1).
unbathed' *adj* (1).
unbāthed' *adj* (1).
unbeat'able *adj* (1).
unbeat'en *adj* (1).
unbefitt'ing *adj* (1).
unbefriend'ed *adj* (1).
unbestowed' *adj* (1).
unbetrayed' *adj* (1).
unbett'ered *adj* (1).
unblām'able *adj* (1).
unblām'ably *adv* (1).
unblāmed' *adj* (1).
unbleached' *adj* (1).
unblem'ished *adj* (1).
unblend'ed *adj* (1).
unblock' *vt* (2).
unblood'ed *adj* (1).
unblood'ied *adj* (1).

unbrō'kenness. — *vt* **unbuck'le** to unfasten the buckle(s) of; to unfasten. — *vi* to undo the buckle(s) of a garment, etc.; to unbend (*fig*). — *vi* and *vt* **unbun'dle** to price and sell separately the constituents of a larger package of products or services. — *n* **unbun'dler.** — *n* **unbun'dling.** — *vt* **unbur'den** to free from a burden; to discharge, cast off, e.g. a burden; (*reflexive*) to tell one's secrets or anxieties freely. — *adj* **unbur'dened** not burdened; relieved of a burden. — *vt* **unbutt'on** to undo the buttons of. — *vi* to loose one's buttons; to unbend and tell one's thoughts. — *adj* **unbutt'oned** without a button; with buttons undone; in a relaxed confidential state. — *adj* **uncalled'-for** (or **uncalled for**) not required, unnecessary; unprovoked; offensively or aggressively gratuitous. — *adv* **uncann'ily.** — *n* **uncann'iness.** — *adj* **uncann'y** weird, supernatural; (of e.g. skill) much greater than one would expect from an ordinary human being. — *vt* **uncap'** to remove the cap from (e.g. a container). — *adj* **uncared'-for** (or **uncared for**) neglected; showing signs of neglect. — *adj* **uncar'ing** without anxiety, concern or caution. — *adj* **unceas'ing** ceaseless; never-ending. — *adv* **unceas'ingly.** — *adj* **unceremō'nious** informal; off-hand. — *adv* **unceremō'niously.** — *n* **unceremō'niousness.** — *adj* **uncer'tain** not certain (of or about); not definitely known or decided; subject to doubt or question (**in no uncertain terms** unambiguously); not to be depended upon; subject to vicissitude; hesitant, lacking confidence. — *adv* **uncer'tainly.** — *n* **uncer'tainness.** — *n* **uncer'tainty** (**uncertainty principle** the principle that it is not possible to measure accurately at the same time both position and velocity). — *vt* **unchain'** to release from a chain; to remove a chain from; to let loose. — *adj* **unchained'.** — *adj* **unchart'ed** (*lit* and *fig*) not mapped in detail; not shown in a chart; not yet examined, investigated or visited. — *adj* **unchart'ered** not holding a charter; unauthorised. — *adj* **unchecked'** not checked or verified; not restrained. — *adj* **unchris'tian** against the spirit of Christianity; uncharitable; unreasonable, outrageous (*colloq*). — *adv* **unchris'tianly.** — *adj* **uncir'cumcised** not circumcised; gentile; unpurified (*fig*). — *adj* **unciv'il** discourteous; unseemly. — *adj* **unciv'ilised** or **-z-** not civilised; away from civilised communities. — *adv* **unciv'illy.** — *vt* **unclasp'** to relax from clasping; to open. — *adj* **unclass'ifīable** (or *-fī'-*) that cannot be classified. — *adj* **unclass'ified** not classified; (of a road) minor, not classified as a motorway, A-road or B-road; (of information) not given a special security classification. — *adj* **unclean** (*-klēn'*) not clean; foul; ceremonially impure; lewd. — *adj* **uncleaned'** not cleaned. — *n* **uncleanliness** (*-klen'*). — *adj* **uncleanly** (*-klen'*). — *adv* (*-klēn'*). — *n* **uncleanness** (*-klēn'nis*). — *adj* **uncleansed** (*-klenzd'*). — *vt* **unclog'** to free from a clog or obstruction. — *adj* **unclogged'** not clogged. — *vt* and *vi* **unclose** (*un-klōz'*) to open. — *adj* **unclose** (*un-klōs'*) not close. — *adj* **unclosed** (*un-klōzd'*) not closed; unenclosed; opened. — *vt* **unclothe'** to take the clothes off; to divest of covering. — *adj* **unclothed'.** — *vt* and *vi* **uncloud'** to clear of clouds or obscurity. — *adj* **uncloud'ed** free from clouds, obscurity or gloom; calm. — *adj* **uncom'fortable** feeling, involving or causing discomfort or unease. — *n* **uncom'fortableness.** — *adv* **uncom'fortably.** — *adj* **uncommitt'ed** not pledged to support any party, policy or action; impartial; not committed (**uncommitted logic array** (often abbrev. **ULA** or **ula**; *comput*) a

Some words with **un-** prefix; see **un-** entry for numbered senses.

unblunt'ed *adj* (1).
unbranched' *adj* (1).
unbreached' *adj* (1).
unbreak'able *adj* (1).
unbrīb'able *adj* (1).
unbridged' *adj* (1).
unbroth'erly *adj* (1).
unbudg'eted *adj* (1).
unburned' or **unburnt'** (or *un'*) *adj* (1).
unbus'inesslike *adj* (1).
unbutt'ered *adj* (1).
uncage' *vt* (2).
uncal'culated *adj* (1).
uncal'culating *adj* (1).
uncan'did *adj* (1).
uncan'didly *adv* (1).
uncan'didness *n* (1).
uncan'onised or **-z-** *adj* (1).
uncapsīz'able *adj* (1).
uncar'peted *adj* (1).
uncashed' *adj* (1).
uncat'alogued *adj* (1).
uncaught' *adj* (1).
uncel'ebrated *adj* (1).
uncen'sored *adj* (1).
uncen'sured *adj* (1).
uncer'ebral *adj* (1).
uncertif'icated *adj* (1).
unchall'engeable *adj* (1).
unchall'engeably *adv* (1).
unchall'enged *adj* (1).
unchange'able *adj* (1).
unchange'ableness *n* (1).
unchange'ably *adv* (1).
unchanged' *adj* (1).
unchang'ing *adj* (1).
unchang'ingly *adv* (1).
unchap'eroned *adj* (1).
uncharacterist'ic *adj* (1).
unchar'itable *adj* (1).
unchar'itableness *n* (1).
unchar'itably *adv* (1).
unchaste' *adj* (1).
unchastised' or **-z-** *adj* (1).
uncheered' *adj* (1).
uncheer'ful *adj* (1).
uncheer'fully *adv* (1).
uncheer'fulness *n* (1).
unchewed' *adj* (1).
unchiv'alrous *adj* (1).
unchō'sen *adj* (1).
unchron'icled *adj* (1).
unclaimed' *adj* (1).
unclass'y *adj* (1).
unclear' *adj* (1).
uncleared' *adj* (1).
unclear'ly *adv* (1).
unclear'ness *n* (1).
unclench' *vt* and *vi* (2).
unclutt'ered *adj* (1).
uncollect'ed *adj* (1).
uncol'oured *adj* (1).
uncombed' *adj* (1).
uncommer'cial *adj* (1).
uncommū'nicable *adj* (1).
uncommū'nicated *adj* (1).
uncommū'nicative *adj* (1).
uncommū'nicativeness *n* (1).
uncommū'ted *adj* (1).
uncompact'ed *adj* (1).
uncompass'ionate *adj* (1).
uncompelled' *adj* (1).
uncom'pensated *adj* (1).
uncompet'itive *adj* (1).
uncomplain'ing *adj* (1).
uncomplain'ingly *adv* (1).
uncomplē'ted *adj* (1).
uncomplī'ant *adj* (1).
uncomply'ing *adj* (1).
uncomprehend'ed *adj* (1).
uncomprehend'ing *adj* (1).
unconcealed' *adj* (1).
uncongē'nial *adj* (1).
unconnect'ed *adj* (1).
unconq'uerable *adj* (1).
unconq'uerably *adv* (1).
unconq'uered *adj* (1).
unconscien'tious *adj* (1).
unconscien'tiously *adv* (1).
unconsol'idated *adj* (1).
unconstitū'tional *adj* (1).
unconstitūtional'ity *n* (1).
unconstitū'tionally *adv* (1).
unconsumed' *adj* (1).
uncon'summated *adj* (1).
uncontain'able *adj* (1).
uncontam'inated *adj* (1).
uncontradict'ed *adj* (1).
uncontrived' *adj* (1).
uncontrover'sial *adj* (1).
unconvert'ed *adj* (1).
unconvict'ed *adj* (1).

microchip whose logic circuits are left unconnected during manufacture and completed later to the customer's specification). — *adj* **uncomm'on** not common; unusual; remarkably great; strange. — *adv* **uncomm'only** rarely (esp. *not uncommonly*, frequently); in an unusually great degree. — *n* **uncomm'onness.** — *adj* **uncom'plicated** straightforward, not made difficult by the variety of factors involved; (of a person) simple in character and outlook. — *adj* **uncompliment'ary** not at all complimentary, derogatory. — *adj* **uncompound'ed** not compounded, unmixed; not worsened or intensified. — *adj* **uncomprehen'sive.** — *adj* **uncom'promising** refusing to compromise; unyielding; out-and-out. — *adv* **uncom'promisingly.** — *n* **uncom'promisingness.** — *n* **unconcern'** lack of concern or anxiety; indifference. — *adj* **unconcerned'** not concerned, not involved (in); impartial; uninterested; indifferent; untroubled. — *adv* **unconcern'edly.** — *adj* **uncondi'tional** not conditional; absolute, unlimited. — *adv* **uncondi'tionally.** — *n* **uncondi'tionalness.** — *adj* **uncondi'tioned** not subject to condition or limitation; infinite, absolute, unknowable; (of a person, response, etc.) not conditioned by learning or experience (**unconditioned stimulus** one provoking an unconditioned response); not put into the required state. — *adj* **uncon'scionable** (of a person) unscrupulous; not conformable to conscience; outrageous, inordinate. — *adv* **uncon'scionably.** — *adj* **uncon'scious** without consciousness; unaware (of); not self-conscious. — *n* (with **the**) the deepest, inaccessible level of the psyche in which are present in dynamic state repressed impulses and memories. — *adv* **uncon'sciously.** — *n* **uncon'sciousness.** — *adj* **unconsid'ered** not esteemed; done without considering. — *adj* **unconstrain'able.** — *adj* **unconstrained'.** — *adv* **unconstrain'edly.** — *adj* **uncontrōll'able** not capable of being controlled. — *adj* **unconven'tional** not conventional; free in one's ways. — *n* **unconventional'ity.** — *adj* **uncool'** (*colloq derog*) not sophisticated or smart, old-fashioned. — *adj* **unco-or'dinated** not co-ordinated; having clumsy movements, as if muscles were not co-ordinated. — *vt* **uncoup'le** to undo the coupling of; to release. — *adj* **uncouth** (*un-kōōth'*) awkward, ungraceful, uncultured, esp. in manners or language. — *adv* **uncouth'ly.** — *n* **uncouth'ness.** — *vt* **uncov'er** to remove the cover of; to lay open; to expose; to drive out of cover. — *vi* to take off one's hat or other head covering. — *adj* **uncov'ered.** — *adj* **uncrit'ical** not critical, without discrimination; not in accordance with the principles of criticism. — *adv* **uncrit'ically.** — *vt* **uncross'** to change, or move, from a crossed position. — *adj* **uncrossed'** not crossed; not passed over, marked with a cross, obstructed, etc. — *adj* **uncrowned'** not crowned; possessing kingly power without the actual title (**uncrowned king** or **queen** (*facetious*) a man or woman having supreme influence, or commanding the highest respect, within a particular group). — *adj* **uncul'tured** not cultured; not cultivated. — *vt* and *vi* **uncurl'** to take or come out of curl, twist or roll. — *adj* **uncurled'** not curled; unrolled, uncoiled. — *adj* **uncut'** not cut; not shaped by cutting; not abridged; (of a book) with margins not cut down by the binder; (of illegal drugs) not adulterated. — *adj* **undāt'ed** with no date marked or assigned. — *adj* **undaunt'ed** not daunted; bold, intrepid. — *adv* **undaunt'edly.** — *n* **undaunt'edness.** — *adj* **undeceiv'able** incapable of being deceived. — *vt* **undeceive'** to free from a mistaken belief, reveal the

Some words with **un-** prefix; see **un-** entry for numbered senses.

unconvinced' *adj* (1).
unconvinc'ing *adj* (1).
uncooked' *adj* (1).
unco-op'erative *adj* (also without *hyphen*) (1).
unco-op'eratively *adv* (also without *hyphen*) (1).
uncork' *vt* (2).
uncorrect'ed *adj* (1).
uncorrob'orated *adj* (1).
uncor'seted *adj* (1).
uncount'able *adj* (1).
uncount'ed *adj* (1).
uncrate' *vt* (2).
uncropped' *adj* (1).
uncrow'ded *adj* (1).
uncrump'le *vt* (2).
uncrush'able *adj* (1).
uncrys'tallised or **-z-** *adj* (1).
uncult'ivable or **unculti-vat'able** *adj* (1).
uncult'ivated *adj* (1).
uncured' *adj* (1).
uncurv'ed *adj* (1).
undam' *vt* (2).
undam'aged *adj* (1).
undammed' *adj* (1) and (2).
undamned' *adj* (1).
undamped' *adj* (1).
undaunt'able *adj* (1).
undealt' *adj* (1).
undeclared' *adj* (1).
undefeat'ed *adj* (1).
undefend'ed *adj* (1).
undefiled' *adj* (1).
undelib'erate *adj* (1).
undeliv'erable *adj* (1).
undeliv'ered *adj* (1).
undelud'ed *adj* (1).
undemand'ing *adj* (1).
undemocrat'ic *adj* (1).
undemon'strative *adj* (1).
undemon'strativeness *n* (1).
undepressed' *adj* (1).
undeprived' *adj* (1).
undespoiled' *adj* (1).
undestroyed' *adj* (1).
undetect'able *adj* (1).
undetect'ed *adj* (1).
undē'viating *adj* (1).
undē'viatingly *adv* (1).
undiagnosed' *adj* (1).
undigest'ed *adj* (1).
undilut'ed *adj* (1).
undimin'ished *adj* (1).
undimmed' *adj* (1).
undiplomat'ic *adj* (1).
undirect'ed *adj* (1).
undisappoint'ing *adj* (1).
undisclosed' *adj* (1).
undiscour'aged *adj* (1).
undiscov'erable *adj* (1).
undiscov'erably *adv* (1).
undiscov'ered *adj* (1).
undismayed' *adj* (1).
undisor'dered *adj* (1).
undispūt'ed *adj* (1).
undispūt'edly *adv* (1).
undissō'ciated *adj* (1).
undissolved' *adj* (1).
undissol'ving *adj* (1).
undistilled' *adj* (1).
undistort'ed *adj* (1).
undisturbed' *adj* (1).
undivers'ified *adj* (1).
undivorced' *adj* (1).
undivulged' *adj* (1).
undoc'umented *adj* (1).
undrained' *adj* (1).
undramat'ic *adj* (1).
undried' *adj* (1).
undrilled' *adj* (1).
undrink'able *adj* (1).
undriv'en *adj* (1).
undrunk' *adj* (1).
undubbed' *adj* (1).
undug' *adj* (1).
undulled' *adj* (1).
uneat'able *adj* (1).
uneat'en *adj* (1).
uned'ucable *adj* (1).
uned'ucated *adj* (1).
uneffaced' *adj* (1).
unelab'orate *adj* (1).
unelect'ed *adj* (1).
unelect'rified *adj* (1).
unembarr'assed *adj* (1).
unembell'ished *adj* (1).
unembitt'ered *adj* (1).
unemphat'ic *adj* (1).
unemp'tied *adj* (1).
unenclosed' *adj* (1).
unencumb'ered *adj* (1).
unendang'ered *adj* (1).
unendowed' *adj* (1).
unendūr'able *adj* (1).
unendūr'ably *adv* (1).
unenjoy'able *adj* (1).

truth to. — *adj* **undeceived'** not deceived; set free from a delusion. — *adj* **undecīd'ed** not decided or settled; uncertain, irresolute. — *adv* **undecīd'edly**. — *adj* **undefined'** not defined; indefinite. — *adj* **undenī'able** not to be denied, indisputable; not to be refused; obviously true or excellent. — *adv* **undenī'ably** assuredly, one cannot deny it. — *adj* **undeserved'** not deserved. — *adv* **undeser'vedly**. — *adj* **undeser'ving**. — *adv* **undeser'vingly**. — *n* **undesirabil'ity**. — *adj* **undesīr'able** not to be wished for; not sexually desirable. — *n* an undesirable or objectionable person or thing. — *n* **undesīr'ableness**. — *adv* **undesīr'ably**. — *adj* **undesired'**. — *adj* **undesīr'ing**. — *adj* **undesīr'ous**. — *adj* **undeter'mined** not settled, not fixed; not ascertained; not limited. — *adj* **undeterred'** not discouraged or prevented (from). — *adj* **undevel'oped** not developed; (of land) not built on or used for public works. — *vt* **undid'** *pa t* of **undo**. — *adj* **undifferen'tiated** not differentiated. — *adj* **undig'nified**. — *adj* **undiscerned'** unobserved, unperceived. — *adv* **undiscern'edly**. — *adj* **undiscern'ible**. — *adv* **undiscern'ibly**. — *adj* **undiscern'ing** showing lack of discernment or discrimination. — *adj* **undischarged'** not paid or settled; (of e.g. an obligation) not carried out; not released from debt or other liability; (of a gun) not fired. — *adj* **undisc'iplinable**. — *n* **undisc'ipline** lack of discipline. — *adj* **undisc'iplined** untrained; unruly. — *adj* **undisguised'** not disguised; frank, open. — *adv* **undisguīs'edly**. — *adj* **undisting'uished** not distinguished or observed; not marked out by conspicuous qualities, not famous; not having an air of distinction. — *adj* **undisting'uishing** not discriminating. — *adj* **undistrib'uted** not distributed (**undistributed middle** in logic, the fallacy of reasoning without distributing the middle term, i.e. without making it universal, in at least one premise). — *adj* **undivī'ded** not divided; (of one's attention to something) wholly concentrated, not distracted. — *vt* **undo** (*un-dōō'*) to reverse the doing of; to cancel, annul; to bring to nothing; to unfasten by unbolting, etc.; to open; to unbutton, untie, etc.; to unravel. — *vi* to come undone: — *pa t* **undid'**; *pa p* **undone** (*un-dun'*). — *n* **undo'ing** the reversal of what has been done; unfastening; opening; ruin or cause of ruin. — *adj* **undomes'ticated** not domesticated; not tamed; emancipated from mere domestic interests. — *adj* **undone** (*un-dun'*) not done; annulled; brought to naught; unfastened (**come undone** to become unfastened, detached; also (*fig*) to go wrong); opened; ruined. — *adj* **undoubt'ed** not doubted; unquestioned; certainly genuine or such as is represented. — *adv* **undoubt'edly** without doubt, certainly. — *adj* **undreamed'** or **undreamt'** (also with **-of**) not imagined even in a dream. — *vt* **undress'** to remove the clothes or dressing from. — *vi* to take off one's clothes. — *n* (*un'*) scanty or incomplete dress; ordinary, informal dress; uniform for ordinary occasions. — Also *adj*. — *adj* **undressed'** not dressed; not set in order, or made trim, or treated or prepared for use, etc.; divested of clothes (**get undressed** to take one's clothes off). — *n* **undress'ing**. — *adj* **undue'** not due or owing; unjustifiable; inappropriate; excessive (**undue influence** (*law*) a strong influence over another person which might prevent the exercise of that person's freewill). — *adv* **undū'ly** unjustifiably; more than is right or reasonable, excessively. — *adj* **undyed'** not dyed. — *adj* **undy'ing** not dying, immortal; unceasing. — *adv* **undy'ingly**. — *adj* **unearned'** not earned by work (**unearned income** income, e.g.

Some words with **un-** prefix; see **un-** entry for numbered senses.

unenlight'ened *adj* (1).
unenriched' *adj* (1).
unen'tered *adj* (1).
unen'terprising *adj* (1).
unentertain'ing *adj* (1).
unenthusiast'ic *adj* (1).
unentīt'led *adj* (1).
unescort'ed *adj* (1).
uneth'ical *adj* (1).
unevangel'ical *adj* (1).
unē'ven *adj* (1).
unē'venly *adv* (1).
unē'venness *n* (1).
unevent'ful *adj* (1).
unevent'fully *adv* (1).
unexagg'erated *adj* (1).
unexam'ined *adj* (1).
unex'cavated *adj* (1).
unexcelled' *adj* (1).
unexcī'table *adj* (1).
unexcī'ted *adj* (1).
unexcī'ting *adj* (1).
unex'ercised *adj* (1).
unexpec'ted *adj* (1).
unexpec'tedly *adv* (1).
unexpec'tedness *n* (1).
unex'piated *adj* (1).
unexpired' *adj* (1).
unexplain'able *adj* (1).
unexplained' *adj* (1).
unexploit'ed *adj* (1).
unexplored' *adj* (1).
unexposed' *adj* (1).
unexpressed' *adj* (1).
unex'purgated *adj* (1).
unexten'ded *adj* (1).

unfā'dable *adj* (1).
unfā'ded *adj* (1).
unfā'ding *adj* (1).
unfā'dingly *adv* (1).
unfal'tering *adj* (1).
unfal'teringly *adv* (1).
unfamil'iar *adj* (1).
unfamiliar'ity *n* (1).
unfamil'iarly *adv* (1).
unfā'vourable *adj* (1).
unfā'vourableness *n* (1).
unfā'vourably *adv* (1).
unfeath'ered *adj* (1).
unfed' *adj* (1).
unfem'inine *adj* (1).
unfenced' *adj* (1).
unferment'ed *adj* (1).
unfer'tilised or **-z-** *adj* (1).
unfilled' *adj* (1).
unfilmed' *adj* (1).
unfil'tered *adj* (1).
unfired' *adj* (1).
unfirm' *adj* (1).
unfished' *adj* (1).
unflagg'ing *adj* (1).
unflagg'ingly *adv* (1).
unflatt'ering *adj* (1).
unflatt'eringly *adv* (1).
unflā'voured *adj* (1).
unflinch'ing *adj* (1).
unflinch'ingly *adv* (1).
unflus'tered *adj* (1).
unfō'cused or **unfō'cussed** *adj* (1).
unforesee'able *adj* (1).
unforesee'ing *adj* (1).
unforeseen' *adj* (1).
unforetold' *adj* (1).
unforewarned' *adj* (1).
unforgett'able *adj* (1).
unforgett'ably *adv* (1).
unforgiv'able *adj* (1).
unforgiv'ing *adj* (1).
unfor'matted *adj* (1).
unform'ulated *adj* (1).
unforthcom'ing *adj* (1).
unfor'tified *adj* (1).
unfos'tered *adj* (1).
unfranked' *adj* (1).
unfrequen'ted *adj* (1).
unfright'ened *adj* (1).
unfrō'zen *adj* (1).
unfruit'ful *adj* (1).
unfruit'fully *adv* (1).
unfū'elled *adj* (1).
unfulfilled' *adj* (1).
unfunn'y *adj* (1).

ungall'ant *adj* (1).
ungall'antly *adv* (1).
ungath'ered *adj* (1).
ungauged' *adj* (1).
ungen'erous *adj* (1).
ungen'erously *adv* (1).
unglazed' *adj* (1).
unglossed' *adj* (1).
unglove' *vt* (2).
ungloved' *adj* (1).
ungrace'ful *adj* (1).
ungrace'fully *adv* (1).
ungrace'fulness *n* (1).
ungrammat'ical *adj* (1).
ungrammat'ically *adv* (1).
ungroomed' *adj* (1).
unguid'ed *adj* (1).

dividends, that is not remuneration for work done); (of something pleasant or unpleasant) unmerited. — *vt* **unearth'** to dig up, disinter; to bring out of obscurity, bring to light. — *adj* **unearthed'** not connected to earth electrically; dug up, brought to light, etc. — *n* **unearth'liness.** — *adj* **unearth'ly** celestial; weird, ghostly; unconscionable, absurd (esp. of an early hour). — *n* **unease'** lack of ease; discomfort; apprehension. — *adv* **uneas'ily.** — *n* **uneas'iness.** — *adj* **uneas'y** not at ease; disquieted; apprehensive; showing troubled restlessness (*lit* and *fig*); uncomfortable. — *adj* **uneconom'ic** not in accordance with sound economics. — *adj* **uneconom'ical** not economical. — *adj* **uned'ifying** not instructing or uplifting morally or aesthetically; morally degrading or degraded. — *adj* **uned'ited** never edited, never before published. — *adj* **unemo'tional.** — *adv* **unemo'tionally.** — *adj* **unemploy'able.** — *adj* **unemployed'** out of work; not put to use or profit; for or pertaining to those who are out of work. — *n* (with **the**) the number of people out of work in a given period. — *n* **unemploy'ment** (**unemployment benefit** a weekly payment supplied under the national insurance scheme to a person who is unemployed). — *adj* **unend'ing** endless; everlasting; never ceasing, incessant. — *adv* **unend'ingly.** — *adj* **unenforce'able** that cannot be (esp. legally) enforced. — *adj* **unenforced'.** — *adj* **un-Eng'lish** not English in character. — *adj* **unen'viable** not to be envied; (of a task, etc.) not exciting envy. — *adv* **unen'viably.** — *adj* **unen'vied.** — *adj* **unen'vious.** — *adj* **unen'vying.** — *adj* **unē'qual** not equal; not equal (to); varying, not uniform; (of an agreement, etc.) not evenly balanced, e.g. with regard to concessions made or advantages gained. — *adj* **unē'qualled** without an equal. — *adv* **unē'qually.** — *adj* **unequiv'ocal** unambiguous; explicit; clear and emphatic. — *adv* **unequiv'ocally.** — *adj* **unerr'ing** making no error, infallible; not, or never, missing the mark (*lit* and *fig*). — *adv* **unerr'ingly.** — *n* **unerr'ingness.** — *adj* **unexam'pled** unprecedented, without like or parallel. — *adj* **unexcep'tionable** not liable to objection or criticism; exactly right, excellent. — *n* **unexcep'tionableness.** — *adv* **unexcep'tionably.** — *adj* **unexcep'tional** not admitting, or forming, an exception; run-of-the-mill; unexceptionable. — *adv* **unexcep'tionally.** — *adj* **unfail'ing** never failing or giving up; infallible; constant; inexhaustible. — *adv* **unfail'ingly.** — *adj* **unfair'** not fair, ugly; inequitable, unjust; involving deception or fraud and leading to undue advantage over business rival(s). — *adv* **unfair'ly.** — *n* **unfair'ness.** — *adj* **unfaith'ful** not of the approved religion; not faithful, violating trust; breaking faith with one's husband, wife or lover, usu. by having sexual intercourse with someone else; not true to the original. — *adv* **unfaith'fully.** — *n* **unfaith'fulness.** — *adj* **unfash'ionable** not fashionable. — *adv* **unfash'ionably.** — *vt* **unfasten** (*un-fäs'n*) to release from a fastening. — *vi* to become loose or open. — *adj* **unfas'tened** released from fastening; not fastened. — *adj* **unfa'thered** without a father or acknowledged father; deprived of a father; of unknown source, origin, etc. — *adj* **unfa'therly** unbefitting a father. — *adj* **unfath'omable** not able to be fathomed (*lit* and *fig*). — *n* **unfath'omableness.** — *adv* **unfath'omably.** — *adj* **unfath'omed** not sounded, of unknown depth; of unascertained meaning (*fig*). — *adj* **unfeel'ing** without physical sensation; without kind or sympathetic feelings; hard-hearted. — *adv* **unfeel'ingly.** — *n* **unfeel'ingness.** — *vt* **unfett'er** to free

Some words with **un-** prefix; see **un-** entry for numbered senses.

unhack'neyed *adj* (1).
unhall'owed *adj* (1).
unhamp'ered *adj* (1).
unhar'dened *adj* (1).
unharmed' *adj* (1).
unharm'ful *adj* (1).
unharm'fully *adv* (1).
unhar'vested *adj* (1).
unhast'y *adj* (1).
unhaunt'ed *adj* (1).
unheat'ed *adj* (1).
unhedged' *adj* (1).
unheed'ed *adj* (1).
unheed'edly *adv* (1).
unheed'ful *adj* (1).
unheed'fully *adv* (1).
unheed'ing *adj* (1).
unheed'ingly *adv* (1).
unhelped' *adj* (1).
unhelp'ful *adj* (1).
unher'alded *adj* (1).
unherō'ic or **unherō'ical** *adj* (1).
unherō'ically *adv* (1).
unhind'ered *adj* (1).
unhired' *adj* (1).
unhitch' *vt* (2).
unhon'oured *adj* (1).
unhook' *vt* (2).
unhurr'ied *adj* (1).
unhurr'iedly *adv* (1).
unhurt' *adj* (1).
unhygien'ic *adj* (1).
unhy'phenated *adj* (1).
unīdentifī'able *adj* (1).
unīdent'ified *adj* (1).
unidiomat'ic *adj* (1).
unidiomat'ically *adv* (1).
unignor'able *adj* (1).
unillu'minated *adj* (1).
unillu'minating *adj* (1).
unillu'mined *adj* (1).
unill'ustrated *adj* (1).
unimpaired' *adj* (1).
unimpēd'ed *adj* (1).
unimpēd'edly *adv* (1).
unimport'ance *n* (1).
unimport'ant *adj* (1).
unimpressed' *adj* (1).
unimpress'ible *adj* (1).
unimpress'ionable *adj* (1).
unimpress'ive *adj* (1).
unincor'porated *adj* (1).
unin'dexed *adj* (1).
uninfect'ed *adj* (1).
uninflamed' *adj* (1).
uninflamm'able *adj* (1).
uninflāt'ed *adj* (1).
uninflect'ed *adj* (1).
unin'fluenced *adj* (1).
uninfluen'tial *adj* (1).
uninhab'itable *adj* (1).
uninhab'ited *adj* (1).
uninhib'ited *adj* (1).
unini'tiated *adj* (1).
unin'jured *adj* (1).
uninscribed' *adj* (1).
uninspired' *adj* (1).
uninspīr'ing *adj* (1).
uninstruct'ed *adj* (1).
uninstruct'ive *adj* (1).
uninsured' *adj* (1).
unin'tegrated *adj* (1).
unintellect'ual *adj* (1).
unintell'igent *adj* (1).
unintelligibil'ity *n* (1).
unintell'igible *adj* (1).
unintell'igibly *adv* (1).
unintend'ed *adj* (1).
uninten'tional *adj* (1).
uninten'tionally *adv* (1).
uninter'pretable *adj* (1).
uninterrup'ted *adj* (1).
uninterrup'tedly *adv* (1).
uninured' *adj* (1).
uninven'tive *adj* (1).
uninvī'ted *adj* (1).
uninvī'ting *adj* (1).
uninvolved' *adj* (1).
unī'onised or **-z-** *adj* (1).
unī'roned *adj* (1).
unjaun'diced *adj* (1).
unjeal'ous *adj* (1).
unjust' *adj* (1).
unjus'tifiable (or *-fī'*) *adj* (1).
unjus'tifiably (or *-fī'*) *adv* (1).
unjus'tified *adj* (1).
unjust'ly *adv* (1).
unjust'ness *n* (1).
unlā'belled *adj* (1).
unlā'dylike *adj* (1).
unlament'ed *adj* (1).
unleased' *adj* (1).
unleav'ened *adj* (1).
unlet' *adj* (1).
unlife'like *adj* (1).
unlim'ited *adj* (1).
unlin'eal *adj* (1).

from fetters. — *adj* **unfett'ered** unrestrained. — *adj* **unfit'** not fit; not in fit condition; not meeting required standards. — *adv* **unfit'ly** unsuitably, inappropriately. — *n* **unfit'ness**. — *adj* **unfitt'ed** not provided (with); without fittings; not made to fit, or tested for fit; not adapted, qualified, or able. — *n* **unfitt'edness**. — *adj* **unfitt'ing** unsuitable. — *adv* **unfitt'ingly**. — *vt* **unfix'** to unfasten, detach; to unsettle (*fig*). — *adj* **unfixed'**. — *adj* **unflapp'able** (*colloq*) imperturbable, never agitated or alarmed. — *n* **unflappabil'ity**. — *adv* **unflapp'ably**. — *adj* **unfledged'** not yet fledged; undeveloped or inexperienced. — *vt* **unfold'** to open the folds of; to spread out; to tell; to disclose, make known; to reveal, display. — *vi* to open out, spread open to the view (*lit* and *fig*). — *adj* **unfold'ed** not folded; opened out from a folded state. — *n* **unfold'er**. — *adj* **unforced'**. — *adj* **unfor'ested** not wooded; deforested. — *adj* **unforgott'en**. — *adj* **unformed'** unmade, uncreated; formless, unshaped; immature, undeveloped. — *adj* **unfor'tunate** unlucky; regrettable; of ill omen. — *n* an unfortunate person. — *adv* **unfor'tunately** in an unlucky way; by bad luck; I'm sorry to say. — *n* **unfor'tunateness**. — *adj* **unfought'**. — *adj* **unfound'ed** not founded; without foundation, baseless. — *vt* and *vi* **unfreeze'** to thaw; to (allow to) progress, move, etc. after a temporary restriction or stoppage. — *vt* to free (prices, wages, funds) from the control imposed by a government, etc. — *adj* **unfriend'ed** not provided with or supported by friends. — *n* **unfriend'liness**. — *adj* **unfriend'ly** ill-disposed; somewhat hostile. — *vt* **unfrock'** to strip of a frock or gown; to depose from priesthood; to remove from a comparable position in another sphere of activity. — *adj* **unfrocked'**. — *vt* **unfurl'** to release from being rolled up; to unfold, display. — *vi* to spread open. — *adj* **unfur'nished** not furnished; unsupplied (with). — *n* **ungain'liness**. — *adj* **ungain'ly** awkward, clumsy, uncouth. — *n* **ungen'tlemanliness**. — *adj* **ungen'tlemanly** unbecoming a gentleman. — *adj* **ungetat'able** or **unget-at'-able** (*colloq*) inaccessible. — *vt* **ungird'** to free from a girdle or band; to undo the fastening of and take off. — *adj* **ungirt'** or **ungird'ed** not girt; freed from a girdle; not tightened up, not strengthened for action (*fig*). — *n* **ungod'liness**. — *adj* **ungod'ly** not godly; outrageous, unconscionable (*colloq*). — *adj* **ungov'ernable** uncontrollable; unruly. — *adv* **ungov'ernably**. — *adj* **ungov'erned**. — *adj* **ungrā'cious** without grace; lacking courtesy, affability or urbanity. — *adv* **ungrā'ciously**. — *n* **ungrā'ciousness**. — *adj* **ungrăd'ed** not classified in grades. — *adj* **ungrassed'** without grass growing. — *adj* **ungrate'ful** not feeling gratitude; disagreeable, irksome; not repaying one's labour, thankless. — *adv* **ungrate'fully**. — *n* **ungrate'fulness**. — *adj* **ungrazed'** not grazed; (of land) not grazed by livestock. — *vt* **unguard'** to cause to be, or leave, unguarded. — *adj* **unguard'ed** without guard; unprotected; unscreened; incautious; inadvertent. — *adv* **unguard'edly**. — *n* **unguard'edness**. — *vt* **ungum'** to free from gum or gummed condition. — *adj* **ungummed'** not gummed; freed from gum or gumming (**come ungummed** (*colloq*; of a plan) to go amiss). — *vt* **unhand'** to take the hands off; to let go. — *adv* **unhand'ily** awkwardly. — *n* **unhand'iness**. — *adj* **unhand'y** not skilful, awkward; not convenient. — *adv* **unhapp'ily** in an unhappy manner; unfortunately, regrettably, I'm sorry to say;

Some words with **un-** prefix; see **un-** entry for numbered senses.

unliq'uefied *adj* (1).
unlit' *adj* (1).
unlit'erary *adj* (1).
unliv'able or **unliv'eable** *adj* (1).
unlive'liness *n* (1).
unlive'ly *adj* (1).
unlos'able *adj* (1).
unlove'ly *adj* (1).
unmacad'amised or **-z-** *adj* (1).
unmaimed' *adj* (1).
unmaintain'able *adj* (1).
unmaintained' *adj* (1).
unmall'eable *adj* (1).
unman'ageable *adj* (1).
unman'ageableness *n* (1).
unman'ageably *adv* (1).
unman'aged *adj* (1).
unmatric'ulated *adj* (1).
unmatured' *adj* (1).
unmelo'dious *adj* (1).
unmelt'ed *adj* (1).
unmem'orable *adj* (1).
unmer'cenary *adj* (1).
unmet'alled *adj* (1).
unmetaphor'ical *adj* (1).
unmethod'ical *adj* (1).
unmil'itary *adj* (1).
unmilked' *adj* (1).
unmilled' *adj* (1).
unministē'rial *adj* (1).
unmirac'ulous *adj* (1).
unmissed' *adj* (1).
unmistāk'able or **unmistāk'eable** *adj* (1).
unmistāk'ably or **unmistāk'eable** *adv* (1).
unmixed' *adj* (1).
unmod'ernised or **-z-** *adj* (1).
unmod'ifīable *adj* (1).
unmod'ified *adj* (1).
unmod'ulated *adj* (1).
unmois'tened *adj* (1).
unmolest'ed *adj* (1).
unmoth'erly *adj* (1).
unmourned' *adj* (1).
unmown' *adj* (1).
unmur'muring *adj* (1).
unmūs'ical *adj* (1).
unmūs'ically *adv* (1).
unmū'tilated *adj* (1).
unneed'ed *adj* (1).
unneed'ful *adj* (1).
unneed'fully *adv* (1).
unnō'ted *adj* (1).
unnō'ticeable *adj* (1).
unnō'ticed *adj* (1).
unnō'ticing *adj* (1).
unnour'ished *adj* (1).
unnour'ishing *adj* (1).
unobjec'tionable *adj* (1).
unobjec'tionably *adv* (1).
unobnox'ious *adj* (1).
unobscured' *adj* (1).
unobstruc'ted *adj* (1).
unobstruc'tive *adj* (1).
unobtain'able *adj* (1).
unobtained' *adj* (1).
unobtru'sive *adj* (1).
unobtru'sively *adv* (1).
unobtru'siveness *n* (1).
unob'vious *adj* (1).
unocc'upied *adj* (1).
unoff'ered *adj* (1).
unoiled' *adj* (1).
unopposed' *adj* (1).
unoppress'ive *adj* (1).
unordained' *adj* (1).
unor'ganised or **-z-** *adj* (1).
unor'namented (or *-ment'*) *adj* (1).
unor'thodox *adj* (1).
unor'thodoxly *adv* (1).
unor'thodoxy *n* (1).
unostentā'tious *adj* (1).
unox'idised or **-z-** *adj* (1).
unpac'ified *adj* (1).
unpaid' *adj* (1).
unpam'pered *adj* (1).
unpar'donable *adj* (1).
unpar'donableness *n* (1).
unpar'donably *adv* (1).
unpar'doned *adj* (1).
unpar'doning *adj* (1).
unpas'teurised or **-z-** *adj* (1).
unpas'toral *adj* (1).
unpā'tented *adj* (1).
unpathed (*-pädhd'*) *adj* (1).
unpatriot'ic *adj* (1).
unpatriot'ically *adv* (1).
unpat'ronised or **-z-** *adj* (1).
unpeace'able *adj* (1).
unpeace'ful *adj* (1).
unpeace'fully *adv* (1).
unpeg' *vt* (2).

unsuccessfully. — *n* **unhapp'iness.** — *adj* **unhapp'y** bringing misfortune; not fortunate; miserable; infelicitous, inapt. — *vt* **unhar'ness** to take the harness off. — *adj* **unhatched'** not out of the egg; not developed; (of a drawing, etc.) not shaded. — *adv* **unheal'thily.** — *n* **unheal'thiness.** — *adj* **unheal'thy** not healthy; morbid; unfavourable to health; dangerous (*colloq*). — *adj* **unheard'** not heard; not granted a hearing; not heard of, unknown to fame (**unheard'-of**). — *adj* **unhes'itating** not hesitating or doubting; prompt; ready. — *adv* **unhes'itatingly.** — *vt* **unhinge'** to take from the hinges; to derange. — *adj* **unhinged'.** — *adj* **unhip'** square, not trendy (*slang*). — *adj* **unhistor'ic** not at all important historically; not historic. — *adj* **unhistor'ical** not in accordance with history; not having actually existed or happened. — *adv* **unhō'lily.** — *n* **unhō'liness.** — *adj* **unhō'ly** not holy; very wicked; unconscionable, outrageous, unearthly (*colloq*). — *adj* **unhoped'-for** beyond what was expected with hope. — *adj* **unhope'ful.** — *adv* **unhope'fully.** — *vt* **unhorse'** to dislodge or throw from a horse. — *vt* **unhouse'** to deprive of or drive from a house or shelter. — *adj* **unhoused'** houseless; deprived of a house. — *adj* **unhung'** not hung; without hangings; unhanged. — *adj* **unhyph'enated** without a hyphen or hyphens. — *adj* **unīdēalist'ic.** — *adj* **unimag'inable.** — *n* **unimag'inableness.** — *adv* **unimag'inably.** — *adj* **unimag'inative** not imaginative, prosaic. — *adv* **unimag'inatively.** — *n* **unimag'inativeness.** — *adj* **unimag'ined.** — *adj* **unimpeach'able** not to be impeached; not liable to be accused; free from fault; blameless. — *adj* **unimpōs'ing** unimpressive. — *adj* **unimproved'** not made better; not cultivated, cleared, or built upon; not put to use. — *adj* **uninform'ative.** — *adj* **uninformed'** not having received information; untaught; uneducated. — *adj* **unin'terested** not personally concerned; not taking an interest. — *adj* **unin'teresting.** — *adv* **unin'terestingly.** — *vt* **unjoint'** to disjoint. — *adj* **unjoint'ed** disjointed, incoherent; without joints. — *adj* **unkempt'** uncombed; scruffy; unpolished, rough. — *adj* **unkept'** not kept; untended. — *adj* **unkīnd'** lacking in kindness; cruel. — *adj* **unkin'dled** not kindled. — *n* **unkīnd'liness** lack of kindliness. — *adj* **unkīnd'ly** unnatural; not kind. — *adv* in an unkindly manner; cruelly. — *n* **unkīnd'ness** lack of kindness or affection; cruelty; ill-feeling. — *vt* **unknit** (*un-nit'*) to undo the knitting of; to untie; to smooth out (eyebrows) from a frown; to relax. — *adj* loose, unfirmed. — *vt* **unknot** (*un-not'*) to free from knots; to untie. — *adj* **unknowable** (*un-nō'ə-bl*) incapable of being known. — *adj* **unknow'ing** ignorant, unaware; unwitting. — *adv* **unknow'ingly.** — *adj* **unknown** (*un-nōn'*) not known. — *n* an unknown person or quantity; (with *the*) that which is unknown. — *adj* **unlā'boured** showing no traces of labour; unrestrained, easy; natural, not contrived or forced. — *vt* **unlace'** to free from being laced; to undo the lacing of. — *adj* **unlā'den** not laden. — *vt* **unlatch'** to lift the latch of. — *adj* **unlaw'ful** forbidden by law; illegitimate; illicit; acting illegally. — *adv* **unlaw'fully.** — *n* **unlaw'fulness.** — *adj* **unlead'ed** not covered, decorated, etc. with lead; (of petrol) with no added lead. — *vt* **unlearn'** to undo the process of learning; to rid one's mind of, eliminate habit(s) of. — *adj* **unlearned** (*-lûr'nid*) having no learning; uneducated; (*-lûrnd'*) not learnt, got up, acquired; eliminated by unlearning. — *adj* and *pa p* **unlearnt** (*-lûrnt'*) not learnt; eliminated by unlearning. — *vt*

Some words with **un-** prefix; see **un-** entry for numbered senses.

unperceiv'able *adj* (1).
unperceiv'ably *adv* (1).
unperceived' *adj* (1).
unperceiv'edly *adv* (1).
unpercep'tive *adj* (1).
unper'forated *adj* (1).
unperformed' *adj* (1).
unperfumed' (or *-pûr'*) *adj* (1).
unper'ilous *adj* (1).
unper'ishable *adj* (1).
unper'ishing *adj* (1).
unper'jured *adj* (1).
unperplexed' *adj* (1).
unper'secuted *adj* (1).
unpersuād'able *adj* (1).
unpersuād'ed *adj* (1).
unperturbed' *adj* (1).
unphilosoph'ic or **unphilosoph'ical** *adj* (1).
unphilosoph'ically *adv* (1).
unphonet'ic *adj* (1).
unpierced' *adj* (1).
unpī'loted *adj* (1).
unpinned' *adj* (1) and (2).
unpit'ied *adj* (1).
unpit'ying *adj* (1).
unpit'yingly *adv* (1).
unplait' *vt* (2).
unplanned' *adj* (1).
unplant'ed *adj* (1).
unplast'ered *adj* (1).
unplay'able *adj* (1).
unpleat'ed *adj* (1).
unpledged' *adj* (1).
unplī'able *adj* (1).
unploughed' *adj* (1).
unplucked' *adj* (1).
unplug' *vt* (2).
unplugged' *adj* (1) and (2).
unpoet'ic or **unpoet'ical** *adj* (1).
unpoet'ically *adv* (1).
unpoised' *adj* (1).
unpoliced' *adj* (1).
unpol'ishable *adj* (1).
unpol'ished *adj* (1).
unpol'itic *adj* (1).
unpolit'ical *adj* (1).
unpollut'ed *adj* (1).
unpop'ular *adj* (1).
unpopular'ity *n* (1).
unpop'ularly *adv* (1).
unpop'ulated *adj* (1).
unpop'ulous *adj* (1).
unposed' *adj* (1).
unpow'dered *adj* (1).
unprac'tical *adj* (1).
unpractical'ity *n* (1).
unprac'tically *adv* (1).
unprej'udiced *adj* (1).
unpreocc'upied *adj* (1).
unpressed' *adj* (1).
unpresum'ing *adj* (1).
unpresump'tuous *adj* (1).
unpreten'tious *adj* (1).
unpreten'tiousness *n* (1).
unprimed' *adj* (1).
unpriv'ileged *adj* (1).
unprō'cessed *adj* (1).
unproclaimed' *adj* (1).
unprocūr'able *adj* (1).
unproduced' *adj* (1).
unproduc'tive *adj* (1).
unproduc'tively *adv* (1).
unproduc'tiveness *n* (1).
unprofitabil'ity *n* (1).
unprof'itable *adj* (1).
unprof'itableness *n* (1).
unprof'itably *adv* (1).
unprogress'ive *adj* (1).
unprogress'ively *adv* (1).
unprogress'iveness *n* (1).
unprohib'ited *adj* (1).
unprom'ised *adj* (1).
unprom'ising *adj* (1).
unprom'isingly *adv* (1).
unpromp'ted *adj* (1).
unpronounce'able *adj* (1).
unpronounced' *adj* (1).
unpropi'tious *adj* (1).
unpropi'tiously *adv* (1).
unpropi'tiousness *n* (1).
unproposed' *adj* (1).
unpros'perous *adj* (1).
unpros'perously *adv* (1).
unprotec'ted *adj* (1).
unprotec'tedness *n* (1).
unprotest'ing *adj* (1).
unprov'able *adj* (1).
unproved' *adj* (1).
unprō'ven *adj* (1).
unprovoc'ative *adj* (1).
unpruned' *adj* (1).
unpub'lished *adj* (1).
unpunct'ual *adj* (1).
unpunctual'ity *n* (1).
unpunct'uated *adj* (1).
unpun'ishable *adj* (1).

unleash' to free from a leash, let go; to release (*lit* and *fig*). — *adj* **unled'** not led, without guidance. — *adj* **unlett'able** (of a building) that cannot be let, usu. because it is in unfit condition. — *adj* **unlett'ered** unlearned; illiterate; without lettering. — *adj* **unlī'censed** without a licence; unauthorised. — *adj* and *adv* (tending to become a *prep*) **unlike'** not like; different (from). — *n* **unlike'lihood** or **unlike'liness** improbability. — *adj* **unlike'ly** not likely; improbable. — *adv* in an unlikely manner, improbably. — *n* **unlike'ness** lack of resemblance. — *vt* **unlim'ber** to remove (a gun) from its limber ready for use. — *adj* **unlined'** without lines or lining. — *vt* **unlink'** to undo the linking or links of. — *vi* to become unlinked. — *adj* **unlinked'** not linked. — *adj* **unlist'ed** not entered in a list; (of a telephone number) not listed in a directory, ex-directory (*US*); (of companies and securities) not quoted on the Stock Exchange's official list. — *adj* **unlived'-in** not lived in. — *vt* **unload'** to take the load or charge from; to discharge; to disburden; to remove as a load; to get rid of; to dump. — *vi* to discharge freight. — *adj* **unload'ed** not loaded; discharged. — *n* **unload'er**. — *n* **unload'ing**. — *vt* **unlock'** to undo the locking of; to free from being locked up; to let loose; to open, make accessible, or disclose. — *vi* to become unlocked. — *adj* **unlock'able**. — *adj* **unlocked'**. — *adj* **unlooked'-for** unexpected. — *vt* **unloose'** or (more usu.) **unloos'en** to loosen, unfasten, detach; to set free. — *adj* **unlord'ly**. — *adj* **unlov'able** or **unlov'eable**. — *adj* **unloved'**. — *adj* **unlov'ing**. — *adv* **unlov'ingly**. — *n* **unlov'ingness**. — *adv* **unluck'ily** in an unlucky way; by bad luck; I'm sorry to say, unfortunately. — *n* **unluck'iness**. — *adj* **unluck'y** unfortunate; ill-omened; bringing bad luck. — *adj* **unmade'** not yet made; self-existent. — *adj* **unmade-up'** not made up; (of a road) not made (q.v.); (of a person) not wearing make-up. — *adj* **unmaid'enly** unbecoming a maiden; not like a maiden. — *adj* **unmailed'** not sent by post (**mail**[2]). — *adj* **unmā'kable**. — *vt* **unmake'** to undo the making of; to undo, ruin. — *n* **unmā'king**. — *vt* **unman'** to deprive of the nature, attributes or powers of humanity, manhood or maleness; to deprive of fortitude; to deprive of men. — *adv* **unman'fully**. — *adj* **unman'like**. — *n* **unman'liness**. — *adj* **unman'ly** not becoming a man; unworthy of a noble mind; base; cowardly. — *adj* **unmanned'** without a crew; without a garrison; without inhabitants; deprived of fortitude. — *adj* **unmann'ered** bad-mannered; not affected or pretentious. — *n* **unmann'erliness**. — *adj* **unmann'erly** not mannerly; ill-bred. — *adj* **unmanufac'tured** in a raw state. — *adj* **unmanured'** not manured. — *adj* **unmarked'** bearing no mark; not noticed. — *adj* **unmar'ketable** not suitable for the market, not saleable. — *adj* **unmarred'** not marred. — *adj* **unmarr'iageable**. — *adj* **unmarr'ied** not married, usu. never having been married. — *vt* **unmask'** to take a mask or a disguise from; to discover the identity of (e.g. a thief) (*fig*); to reveal the place of (a gun, battery) by firing; to expose, show up. — *vi* to take off a mask. — *adj* **unmasked'** not wearing a mask; undisguised; divested of mask or disguise; revealed (of e.g. identity). — *adj* **unmatch'able**. — *adj* **unmatched'** matchless; unequalled. — *adj* **unmean'ing** meaningless; purposeless; expressionless. — *adj* **unmeant** (*un-ment'*). — *adj* **unmeas'urable** immeasurable; not capable of being measured; too great to measure. — *adj*

Some words with **un-** prefix; see **un-** entry for numbered senses.

unpun'ished *adj* (1).
unpur'chasable or **unpur'chaseable** *adj* (1).
unpur'chased *adj* (1).
unpurged' *adj* (1).
unpū'rified *adj* (1).

unqual'ifiable *adj* (1).
unqual'ified *adj* (1).
unqual'ifiedly *adv* (1).
unquan'tified *adj* (1).
unquelled' *adj* (1).
unquench'able *adj* (1).
unquench'ably *adv* (1).
unquenched' *adj* (1).

unrat'ed *adj* (1).
unrat'ified *adj* (1).
unreach'able *adj* (1).
unreached' *adj* (1).
unreac'tive *adj* (1).
unrebuked' *adj* (1).
unreceipt'ed *adj* (1).
unreceived' *adj* (1).
unrecep'tive *adj* (1).
unrecip'rocated *adj* (1).
unreck'onable *adj* (1).
unreclaim'able *adj* (1).
unreclaimed' *adj* (1).
unrec'ognīsable or **-z-** (or *-nīz'*) *adj* (1).
unrec'ognīsably or **-z-** (or *-nīz'*) *adv* (1).
unrec'ognised or **-z-** *adj* (1).
unrecollect'ed *adj* (1).
unrecommend'able *adj* (1).
unrecommend'ed *adj* (1).
unrec'ompensed *adj* (1).
unrec'oncīlable (or *-sīl'*) *adj* (1).
unreconcīl'ableness *n* (1).
unrec'oncīlably (or *-sīl'*) *adv* (1).
unrec'onciled (or *-sīld'*) *adj* (1).
unrecord'ed *adj* (1).
unrecov'erable *adj* (1).
unrecov'erably *adv* (1).
unrecov'ered *adj* (1).
unrect'ified *adj* (1).
unreduced' *adj* (1).
unrefined' *adj* (1).
unreflect'ed *adj* (1).
unreflect'ing *adj* (1).
unreflect'ingly *adv* (1).
unreflect'ive *adj* (1).
unreform'able *adj* (1).
unreformed' *adj* (1).
unrefreshed' *adj* (1).
unrefresh'ing *adj* (1).
unreg'imented *adj* (1).
unreg'istered *adj* (1).
unreg'ulated *adj* (1).
unrehearsed' *adj* (1).
unrelāt'ed *adj* (1).
unrelent'ing *adj* (1).
unrelieved' *adj* (1).
unrel'ished *adj* (1).
unremark'able *adj* (1).
unremarked' *adj* (1).
unrem'edied *adj* (1).
unremem'bered *adj* (1).
unremūn'erative *adj* (1).
unrenewed' *adj* (1).
unrenowned' *adj* (1).
unrepair'able *adj* (1).
unrepaired' *adj* (1).
unrepelled' *adj* (1).
unrepen'tance *n* (1).
unrepen'tant *adj* (1).
unrepen'ting *adj* (1).
unrepen'tingly *adv* (1).
unreplen'ished *adj* (1).
unreport'ed *adj* (1).
unrepresent'ative *adj* (1).
unrepresent'ed *adj* (1).
unreprieved' *adj* (1).
unrep'rimanded *adj* (1).
unreproach'ful *adj* (1).
unreprodūc'ible *adj* (1).
unrescind'ed *adj* (1).
unresent'ed *adj* (1).
unresent'ful *adj* (1).
unrespec'ted *adj* (1).
unrespon'sive *adj* (1).
unrespon'sively *adv* (1).
unrespon'siveness *n* (1).
unrestored' *adj* (1).
unrestrain'able *adj* (1).
unrestrained' *adj* (1).
unrestrain'edly *adv* (1).
unrestric'ted *adj* (1).
unretard'ed *adj* (1).
unretent'ive *adj* (1).
unretouched' *adj* (1).
unreturn'able *adj* (1).
unreturned' *adj* (1).
unreturn'ing *adj* (1).
unrevealed' *adj* (1).
unreveal'ing *adj* (1).

unmeas'ured. — *adj* **unmechan'ical.** — *adj* **unmech'anised** or **-z-** not mechanised. — *adj* **unmed'itated** not meditated, unpremeditated. — *adj* **unmen'tionable** not fit to be mentioned. — *npl* **unmen'tionables** (*humorous*) underclothing. — *adj* **unmer'ciful** merciless; excessively and unpleasantly great. — *adj* **unmind'ed** unheeded. — *adj* **unmind'ful** not keeping in mind, regardless (of). — *adv* **unmind'fully.** — *n* **unmind'fulness.** — *adj* **unmit'igable** that cannot be mitigated. — *adv* **unmit'igably.** — *adj* **unmit'igated** not mitigated; unqualified, out-and-out. — *adj* **unmō'dish** unfashionable. — *adj* **unmon'eyed** or **unmon'ied** without money; not rich. — *vt* **unmoor'** to loose from moorings. — *vi* to cast off moorings. — *adj* **unmor'al** having no relation to morality; amoral. — *adj* **unmor'alising** or **-z-**. — *n* **unmoral'ity** detachment from questions of morality. — *adj* **unmō'tivated** having no motive; lacking incentive. — *adj* **unmould'ed** not moulded. — *vt* **unmount'** to remove from mountings or mount; to dismount. — *vi* to dismount. — *adj* **unmount'ed** not mounted. — *adj* **unmov'able** or **unmove'able** immovable; not movable. — *adv* **unmov'ably** or **unmove'ably.** — *adj* **unmoved'** not moved, firm; not persuaded; not touched by emotion, calm. — *vt* **unmuzz'le** to take a muzzle off. — *adj* **unmuzz'led.** — *vt* **unnail** (*un-nāl'*) to free from nails or from being nailed. — *adj* **unnamable** or **unnameable** (*un-nā'mə-bl*) impossible to name; not to be named. — *adj* **unnamed** (*un-nāmd'*). — *adj* **unnatural** (*un-nat'ū-rəl*) not according to nature; without natural affection; monstrous, heinous; (of a sexual act, vice, etc.) considered not only immoral but also unacceptably indecent or abnormal (e.g. buggery, sodomy). — *vt* **unnat'uralise** or **-ize** to make unnatural; to divest of nationality. — *adj* **unnat'uralised** or **-z-** not naturalised. — *adv* **unnat'urally** in an unnatural way (esp. in the phrase *not unnaturally*, of course, naturally). — *n* **unnat'uralness.** — *adj* **unnavigable** (*un-nav'*) not navigable. — *adj* **unnav'igated.** — *adv* **unnecess'arily** (*un-nes'*). — *n* **unnec'essariness.** — *adj* **unnec'essary** not necessary. — *adj* **unneigh'bourly** not neighbourly, friendly or social. — *adv* in an unneighbourly manner. — *vt* **unnerve** (*un-nûrv'*) to deprive of nerve, strength or vigour; to weaken; to disconcert. — *adj* **unnerved'.** — *adj* **unnerv'ing.** — *adj* **unnumbered** (*un-num'bərd*) not counted, too many to be numbered; not marked or provided with a number. — *adj* **unnurtured** (*un-nûr'chərd*) not nurtured; ill-bred. — *adj* **unobē'dient** disobedient. — *adj* **unobserv'able.** — *n* **unobserv'ance** failure to observe (rules, etc.); failure to notice; lack of observing power; inattention. — *adj* **unobserv'ant.** — *adj* **unobserved'.** — *adv* **unobserv'edly.** — *adj* **unobserv'ing.** — *adj* **unoffend'ed.** — *adj* **unoffend'ing.** — *adj* **unoffi'cial.** — *adv* **unoffi'cially.** — *adj* **unoffi'cious.** — *adj* **unō'pened** not opened; (of a book) not having the leaves cut apart. — *adj* **unor'dered** disordered; unarranged, not ordered or commanded. — *adj* **unor'derly.** — *adj* **unor'dinary.** — *adj* **unorig'inal.** — *n* **unoriginality** (*-al'*). — *adj* **unowed'** not owed or due. — *adj* **unowned'** unavowed, unacknowledged; ownerless. — *vt* **unpack'** to undo the packing of; to take out of a pack; to open. — *vi* to do unpacking. — *adj* **unpacked'** subjected to unpacking; (*un'pakt*) not packed. — *n* **unpack'er.** — *n* **unpack'ing.** — *adj* **unpaint'ed.** — *adj* **unpaired'** not paired; not forming one of a pair. — *adj* **unpal'atable** unpleasant to taste, distasteful, disagreeable (*lit* and *fig*). — *adv* **unpal'atably.** — *adj* **unpan'elled** not

Some words with **un-** prefix; see **un-** entry for numbered senses.

unrevenged' *adj* (1).
unrevised' *adj* (1).
unrevoked' *adj* (1).
unrewar'ded *adj* (1).
unrewar'ding *adj* (1).
unrhymed' *adj* (1).
unrhyth'mical *adj* (1).
unrhyth'mically *adv* (1).
unribbed' *adj* (1).
unrid'able or **unride'able** *adj* (1).
unridd'en *adj* (1).
unrī'fled *adj* (1).
unripe' *adj* (1).
unrī'pened *adj* (1).
unripe'ness *n* (1).
unris'en *adj* (1).
unrī'valled *adj* (1).
unroman'tic *adj* (1).
unroman'tically *adv* (1).
unroused' *adj* (1).
unrubbed' *adj* (1).
unrum'pled *adj* (1).
unsalabil'ity or **unsaleabil'ity** *n* (1).
unsal'able or **unsale'able** *adj* (1).
unsal'aried *adj* (1).
unsalt'ed *adj* (1).
unsanc'tioned *adj* (1).
unsāt'ed *adj* (1).
unsā'tiating *adj* (1).
unsatir'ical *adj* (1).
unsatisfac'torily *adv* (1).
unsatisfac'toriness *n* (1).
unsatisfac'tory *adj* (1).
unsat'isfiable *adj* (1).
unsat'isfied *adj* (1).
unsat'isfying *adj* (1).
unsatura'tion *n* (1).
unsat'urated *adj* (1).
unsaved' *adj* (1).
unscarred' *adj* (1).
unscent'ed *adj* (1).
unsched'uled *adj* (1).
unschol'arly *adj* (1).
unschooled' *adj* (1).
unscientif'ic *adj* (1).
unscientif'ically *adv* (1).
unscorched' *adj* (1).
unscoured' *adj* (1).
unscratched' *adj* (1).
unscru'tinised or **-z-** *adj* (1).
unsea'worthy *adj* (1).
unsec'onded *adj* (1).
unsegment'ed *adj* (1).
unseg'regated *adj* (1).
unselfcon'scious *adj* (1).
unselfcon'sciously *adv* (1).
unselfcon'sciousness *n* (1).
unsensā'tional *adj* (1).
unsens'itive *adj* (1).
unsent'enced *adj* (1).
unsentiment'al *adj* (1).
unsep'arated *adj* (1).
unser'viceable *adj* (1).
unsev'ered *adj* (1).
unshā'ded *adj* (1).
unshak'able or **unshake'able** *adj* (1).
unshak'ably or **unshake'ably** *adv* (1).
unshāk'en *adj* (1).
unshāk'enly *adv* (1).
unshared' *adj* (1).
unsharp'ened *adj* (1).
unshaved' *adj* (1).
unshā'ven *adj* (1).
unshel'tered *adj* (1).
unshield'ed *adj* (1).
unshift'ing *adj* (1).
unshock'able *adj* (1).
unshocked' *adj* (1).
unshorn' *adj* (1).
unshot' *adj* (1).
unshown' *adj* (1).
unshrink'able *adj* (1).
unshrink'ing *adj* (1).
unshrink'ingly *adv* (1).
unshriv'en *adj* (1).
unsigned' *adj* (1).
unsink'able *adj* (1).
unskil'ful *adj* (1).
unskil'fully *adv* (1).
unskil'fulness *n* (1).
unskilled' *adj* (1).
unslaked' *adj* (1).
unsleep'ing *adj* (1).
unsliced' *adj* (1).
unslipp'ing *adj* (1).
unslung' *adj* (1).
unsmil'ing *adj* (1).
unsmil'ingly *adv* (1).
unsnap' *vt* (2).
unsneck' *vt* (2).
unsoftened (*-sof'ənd*) *adj* (1).
unsoiled' *adj* (1).

panelled. — *adj* **unpā'pered** not papered. — *adj* **unpar'allel** not parallel. — *adj* **unpar'alleled** without parallel or equal. — *adj* **unpared'** (of fruit) not having the skin removed; (of nails) not cut. — *adj* **unparent'al** not befitting a parent. — *adj* **unparliament'ary** contrary to the usages of Parliament; not such as may be spoken, or (of language) used, in Parliament. — *adj* **unpass'ionate** or **unpass'ioned** without passions; calm; dispassionate. — *adj* **unpaved'** without pavement. — *adj* **unpavil'ioned** without a canopy. — *adj* **unpay'able**. — *adj* **unpeeled'** not peeled. — *adj* **unpeered'** unequalled. — *vt* **unpeo'ple** to empty of people. — *adj* **unpeo'pled** uninhabited; depopulated. — *n* **un'-person** an individual whose existence is officially denied, ignored, or deleted from record, e.g. one who has been politically superseded. — *adj* **unpervert'ed** not perverted. — *vt* **unpick'** to pick loose, undo by picking. — *adj* **unpick'able** impossible to pick; able to be unpicked. — *adj* **unpicked'** not gathered; not selected; not having had unwanted material removed by picking; picked loose. — *vt* **unpin'** to free from pins or pinning; to unfasten by removing pins. — *adj* **unplaced'** not assigned to or set in a place; not appointed to an office; not among the first three (horses) in a race. — *adj* **unpleas'ant** not pleasant; disagreeable. — *adv* **unpleas'antly**. — *n* **unpleas'antness** the state or quality of being unpleasant, disagreeableness; a disagreeable incident; disagreement involving open hostility. — *adj* **unpleased'**. — *adj* **unpleas'ing** not pleasing; displeasing. — *adv* **unpleas'ingly**. — *adj* **unpleas'urable**. — *adv* **unpleas'urably**. — *adj* **unplumbed'** unsounded; unfathomed. — *adj* **unpoint'ed** not pointed; without point or points; with joints uncemented. — *adj* **unpoi'soned** not poisoned. — *adj* **unpolled'** not polled; not having voted. — *adj* **unpor'tioned** without a portion. — *adj* **unpossessed'** not possessed; not in possession. — *adj* **unpost'ed** not posted, in any sense; not posted up; without a post. — *adj* **unpō'table** undrinkable, unfit to drink. — *adj* **unprac'tised** having little or no practice or experience, inexpert; not carried out in practice. — *n* **unprac'tisedness**. — *adj* **unpraised'** not praised. — *adj* **unpraise'worthy**. — *adj* **unprec'edented** (*-pres'* or *-prēs'*) not warranted by judicial, etc. precedent; of which there has been no previous instance. — *adv* **unprec'edentedly**. — *n* **unpredictabil'ity**. — *adj* **unpredict'able** that cannot be foretold; (of a person or thing) liable to behave in a way that cannot be predicted. — *adv* **unpredict'ably**. — *adj* **unpreferred'** without preferment or advancement. — *adj* **unpremed'itable** not to be foreseen. — *adj* **unpremed'itated** not studied or purposed beforehand. — *adv* **unpremed'itatedly**. — *n* **unpremed'itatedness**. — *n* **unpremeditā'tion**. — *adj* **unprepared'** not prepared or ready; not prepared for death; without preparation. — *adv* **unprepā'redly**. — *n* **unprepā'redness**. — *adj* **unprepossess'ing** not predisposing others in one's favour, unpleasing. — *adj* **unpresent'able** not fit to be seen. — *adj* **unpreten'tious** not pretentious; modest. — *adj* **unpriced'** having no fixed or stated price; beyond price, priceless. — *adj* **unprin'cipled** without good principles; not based on or in accordance with principles; not restrained by conscience; profligate. — *adj* **unprint'able** not fit to be printed. — *adj* **unprocē'dūral** not in accordance with established or accepted procedures. — *adj* **unprofess'ional** not of a profession or the profession in question; beyond the limits of one's profession; unbecoming to a

Some words with **un-** prefix; see **un-** entry for numbered senses.

unsōld' *adj* (1).
unsolic'ited *adj* (1).
unsolic'itous *adj* (1).
unsol'id *adj* (1).
unsoured' *adj* (1).
unsown' *adj* (1).
unspe'cialised or **-z-** *adj* (1).
unspecif'ic *adj* (1).
unspec'ified *adj* (1).
unspectac'ular *adj* (1).
unspilled' or **unspilt'** *adj* (1).
unspoiled' *adj* (1).
unspoilt' *adj* (1).
unspō'ken *adj* (1).
unsport'ing *adj* (1).
unsports'manlike *adj* (1).
unspott'ed *adj* (1).
unspun' *adj* (1).
unstā'ble *adj* (1).
unstā'bleness *n* (1).
unstaid' *adj* (1).
unstaid'ness *n* (1).
unstain'able *adj* (1).
unstained' *adj* (1).
unstamped' *adj* (1).
unstates'manlike *adj* (1).
unstead'fast *adj* (1).
unstead'fastly *adv* (1).
unstead'fastness *n* (1).
unster'ile *adj* (1).
unster'ilised or **-z-** *adj* (1).
unstī'fled *adj* (1).
unstint'ing *adj* (1).
unstoop'ing *adj* (1).
unstrapped' *adj* (1).
unstrength'ened *adj* (1).
unstruc'tured *pa p* and *adj* (1).
unstuffed' *adj* (1).
unsubdū'able *adj* (1).
unsubdued' *adj* (1).
unsub'limated *adj* (1).
unsubmerged' *adj* (1).
unsubmiss'ive *adj* (1).
unsubmitt'ing *adj* (1).
unsubscribed' *adj* (1).
unsub'sidised or **-z-** *adj* (1).
unsubstan'tiated *adj* (1).
unsubt'le *adj* (1).
unsuccess'ful *adj* (1).
unsuccess'fully *adv* (1).
unsuccess'fulness *n* (1).
unsucked' *adj* (1).
unsull'ied *adj* (1).
unsumm'oned *adj* (1).
unsu'pervised *adj* (1).
unsupp'le *adj* (1).
unsupp'leness *n* (1).
unsupplied' *adj* (1).
unsupport'ed *adj* (1).
unsuppressed' *adj* (1).
unsur'faced *adj* (1).
unsurpass'able *adj* (1).
unsurpass'ably *adv* (1).
unsurpassed' *adj* (1).
unsuscept'ible *adj* (1).
unsustain'able *adj* (1).
unsustained' *adj* (1).
unsustain'ing *adj* (1).
unsweet'ened *adj* (1).
unswept' *adj* (1).
unsympathet'ic *adj* (1).
unsympathet'ically *adv* (1).
unsym'pathising or **-z-** *adj* (1).
unsystemat'ic or **-z-** *adj* (1).
unsystemat'ically *adv* (1).
unsys'tematised or **-z-** *adj* (1).
untailed' *adj* (1).
untal'ented *adj* (1).
untanned' *adj* (1).
untapped' *adj* (1).
untar'nished *adj* (1).
untarred' *adj* (1).
untast'ed *adj* (1).
untaste'ful *adj* (1).
untemp'ted *adj* (1).
untenabil'ity *n* (1).
untend'ed *adj* (1).
unter'minated *adj* (1).
unterres'trial *adj* (1).
untest'ed *adj* (1).
unthanked' *adj* (1).
unthank'ful *adj* (1).
unthick'ened *adj* (1).
unthor'ough *adj* (1).
unthreat'ened *adj* (1).
untī'dily *adv* (1).
untī'diness *n* (1).
untī'dy *adj* (1).
untī'dy *vt* (2).
untilled' *adj* (1).
untinged' *adj* (1).
untīr'ing *adj* (1).

member of a particular profession. — *adv* **unprofess'ionally**. — *adj* **unprof'ited** without profit or advantage. — *adj* **unpropor'tionable** out of due proportion. — *adv* **unpropor'tionably**. — *adj* **unpropor'tionate** out of due proportion. — *adv* **unpropor'tionately**. — *adj* **unpropor'tioned** not proportioned. — *adj* **unprotest'ed** not objected to or protested against. — *adj* **unprovī'ded** not provided; not provided for (also **unprovī'ded-for**). — *adj* **unprovoked'** not provoked; uncalled for. — *adv* **unprovō'kedly**. — *adj* **unprovō'king**. — *adj* **unputdown'able** (*colloq*) (of a book) too absorbing to be set aside, compelling one to read to the end without interruption. — *adj* **unqueen'** to deprive of a queen; (in bee-keeping) to deprive (a beehive) of a queen bee. — *adj* **unques'tionable** not to be questioned, certain, beyond doubt. — *adv* **unques'tionably** in such a way as to be unquestionable; certainly, without doubt. — *adj* **unques'tioned** not called in question; not subjected to questioning; not examined. — *adj* **unquī'et** disturbed; restless; uneasy. — *n* disquiet, inquietude. — *adj* **unquōt'able** unsuitable or unfit for quotation. — *vi* **unquote'** to close a quotation; to mark the end of a quoted passage with superscript comma or commas — used as *interj* to indicate that a quotation is finished. — *adj* **unquot'ed** (of a company) not quoted on the Stock Exchange list. — *adj* **unracked'** (of liquor) not drawn off from the lees; not stretched on the rack; not strained. — *vt* **unrav'el** to disentangle; to unknit. — *vi* to become disentangled. — *adj* **unrav'elled**. — *adj* **unread** (*un-red'*) not informed by reading; not perused. — *adj* **unreadable** (*un-rēd'ə-bl*) indecipherable; too dull or badly-written to be read. — *n* **unread'ableness**. — *adv* **unreadily** (*-red'*). — *n* **unread'iness**. — *adj* **unread'y** not ready, prepared or prompt; hesitating, holding back. — *adj* **unrē'al** not real or like reality; incredible; illusory. — *adj* **unrealist'ic** not like reality; unreasonable, impracticable. — *n* **unreal'ity** absence or lack of reality or existence; an unreal thing. — *adv* **unrē'ally**. — *n* **unrea'son** lack of reason or reasonableness; nonsense. — *adj* **unrea'sonable** not agreeable to reason; exceeding the bounds of reason, immoderate; not influenced by reason. — *n* **unrea'sonableness**. — *adv* **unrea'sonably**. — *adj* **unrea'soned** not argued or thought out. — *adj* **unrea'soning** not reasoning; showing lack of reason, irrational. — *adv* **unrea'soningly**. — *adj* **unreconstruct'ed** not rebuilt; not accepting the current situation or opinions. — *adj* **unredeem'able**. — *adj* **unredeemed'** not redeemed, esp. spiritually or from pawn; without compensatory quality or circumstance, hence unmitigated, unrelieved. — *adj* **unredressed'** or **unredrest'** not redressed. — *n* **unregen'eracy**. — *adj* **unregen'erate** not regenerate; unrepentant, refusing to be reformed. — *adj* **unregen'erated**. — *n* **unrelīabil'ity**. — *adj* **unrelī'able** not to be relied upon. — *n* **unrelī'ableness**. — *adj* **unrelig'ious** not connected with religion; not religious without being necessarily contrary or hostile to religion; irreligious. — *adj* **unremitt'ing** not remitting or relaxing; continued; incessant. — *adv* **unremitt'ingly**. — *n* **unremitt'ingness**. — *adj* **unremorse'ful** feeling no remorse. — *adv* **unremorse'fully**. — *adj* **unrepeat'able** not repeatable; indecent, gross; that cannot be done, etc. again. — *adj* **unrequired'** unasked; unasked-for; unnecessary. — *adj* **unrequīt'ed** not reciprocated or returned. — *n* **unreserve'** absence of reserve. — *adj* **unreserved'** not reserved; without reserve or reservation; unrestricted, unqualified. — *adv* **unreser'vedly**. — *n* **unreser'vedness**. — *adj* **unresolv'able**. — *adj* **unresolved'** not resolved, determined, settled or solved; irresolute; undecided; not separated into its constituent parts. — *n* **unresol'vedness** irresolution. — *n* **unrest'** lack of rest; disquiet; disturbance; discontent verging on insurrection. — *adj* **unrest'ful** not restful; uneasy; full of unrest. — *n* **unrest'fulness**. — *adj* **unrest'ing**. — *adv* **unrest'ingly**. — *n* **unrest'ingness**. — *vt* **unridd'le** to read the riddle of; to solve. — *adj* **unrigh'teous** sinful; unjust. — *adv* **unrigh'teously**. — *n* **unrigh'teousness**. — *vt* **unrip'** to rip up or open; to strip, lay bare; to disclose. — *adj* **unripped'** not ripped; ripped up or open. — *vt* **unriv'et** to loose from being riveted; to detach (*fig*). — *vt* **unrobe'** to strip off a robe, to

Some words with **un-** prefix; see **un-** entry for numbered senses.

untīr'ingly *adv* (1).
untoil'ing *adj* (1).
untorn' *adj* (1).
untrained' *adj* (1).
untramm'elled *adj* (1).
untramp'led *adj* (1).
untrans'ferable (or *-fer'*) *adj* (1).
untransformed' *adj* (1).
untranslā'table *adj* (1).
untransmiss'ible *adj* (1).
untransmitt'ed *adj* (1).
untransmū'table *adj* (1).
untransmū'ted *adj* (1).
untrav'elled *adj* (1).
untrav'ersed *adj* (1).
untrem'bling *adj* (1).
untrem'blingly *adv* (1).
untrem'ulous *adj* (1).
unty'ing *n* (2).
untyp'ical *adj* (1).
unurged' *adj* (1).
unū'sable *adj* (1).
unū'sably *adv* (1).
unū'tilised or **-z-** *adj* (1).
unvac'cinated *adj* (1).
unvan'quishable *adj* (1).
unvan'quished *adj* (1).
unvā'riable *adj* (1).
unvā'ried *adj* (1).
unvā'riegated *adj* (1).
unvā'rying *adj* (1).
unvent'ilated *adj* (1).
unver'ifiable *adj* (1).
unverifiabil'ity *n* (1).
unver'ified *adj* (1).
unvī'able *adj* (1).
unviewed' *adj* (1).
unvī'olated *adj* (1).
unwāked' *adj* (1).
unwāk'ened *adj* (1).
unwalled' *adj* (1).
unwant'ed *adj* (1).
unwar'like *adj* (1).
unwarmed' *adj* (1).
unwarned' *adj* (1).
unwarped' *adj* (1).
unwāst'ed *adj* (1).
unwāst'ing *adj* (1).
unwatched' *adj* (1).
unwatch'ful *adj* (1).
unwatch'fulness *n* (1).
unwā'vering *adj* (1).
unwā'veringly *adv* (1).
unweak'ened *adj* (1).
unweaned' *adj* (1).
unwearable (*-wār'*) *adj* (1).
unwea'ried *adj* (1).
unwea'riedly *adv* (1).
unwea'ry *adj* (1).
unwea'rying *adj* (1).
unwea'ryingly *adv* (1).
unwebbed' *adj* (1).
unwed' *adj* (1).
unwedd'ed *adj* (1).
unweed'ed *adj* (1).
unwel'come *adj* (1).
unwhipped' *adj* (1).
unwinged' *adj* (1).
unwiped' *adj* (1).
unwith'ered *adj* (1).
unwit'nessed *adj* (1).
unwood'ed *adj* (1).
unwooed' *adj* (1).
unworn' *adj* (1).
unworr'ied *adj* (1).
unwounded (*-wōōnd'*) *adj* (1).
unwō'ven *adj* (1).
unwrung' *adj* (1).
unzip' *vt* (2).

undress. — *vi* to take off a robe, esp. of state. — *vt* and *vi* **unroll'** to open out from a rolled state. — *vt* **unroof'** to strip the roof from. — *adj* **unroofed'** not roofed; stripped of its roof. — *adj* **unround'ed** not rounded; articulated with spread lips (*phon*). — *adj* **unruff'led** smooth; calm; not disturbed or flustered. — *adj* **unruled'** not governed; without ruled lines. — *n* **unrul'iness.** — *adj* **unrul'y** ungovernable; unmanageable; turbulent; stormy. — *vt* **unsadd'le** to take the saddle from; to dislodge from the saddle. — *adj* **unsafe'** not safe or secure; (of a conclusion, conviction, etc.) based on insufficient or suspect evidence. — *adj* **unsaid'** not said (see also **unsay**). — *adj* **unsailed'** unnavigated. — *adv* **unsā'vourily.** — *n* **unsā'vouriness.** — *adj* **unsā'voury** not savoury, tasteless; unpleasant; offensive. — *vt* **unsay'** to retract: — *pa t* and *pa p* **unsaid'.** — *adj* **unsay'able** that cannot be said. — *adj* **unscāl'able** that cannot be climbed. — *vt* **unscale'** to remove scales from. — *adj* **unscaled'** unclimbed; cleared of scales; scaleless. — *adj* **unscathed'** not harmed or injured. — *vt* **unscram'ble** to decode from a scrambled state, or to restore to natural sound; to restore (something in which categories have been jumbled) to a system of classification and separation. — *adj* **unscreened'** not screened; unsifted. — *vt* **unscrew'** to loose from a state of being screwed; to open, loose or detach by screwing. — *vi* to be capable of being or becoming unscrewed; to come unscrewed. — *adj* **unscrip'ted** not using a script; unrehearsed; (of comments, moves, etc.) not planned, not in the script (*radio*, *TV*, etc.). — *adj* **unscrip'tural** not in accordance with, or not warranted by, the Bible. — *adj* **unscru'pulous** without scruples or principles. — *adv* **unscru'pulously.** — *n* **unscru'pulousness.** — *vt* **unseal'** to remove or break the seal of; to free from sealing or closure; to open. — *adj* **unsealed'** not sealed; freed from a seal; opened. — *adj* **unsea'sonable** not in season; ill-timed. — *n* **unsea'sonableness.** — *adv* **unsea'sonably.** — *adj* **unsea'soned** without seasonings; not matured; not inured or habituated. — *vt* **unseat'** to oust, remove or throw from a seat, esp. on horseback or in Parliament. — *adj* **unseat'ed** not seated; ousted, thrown, removed from a seat. — *adj* **un'secured** not secured of made safe; (of a loan or creditor) without security. — *adj* **unsee'able** invisible. — *adj* **unseed'ed** not seeded; (in lawn tennis tournaments, etc.) not placed in the draw of top players. — *adj* **unsee'ing** not seeing; unobservant; without insight or understanding. — *n* **unseem'liness.** — *adj* **unseem'ly** not seemly, becoming or decent. — *adv* in an unseemly manner. — *adj* **unseen'** not seen; invisible; not previously seen or prepared for. — *n* an unprepared passage for translation. — *adj* **unseiz'able.** — *adj* **unseized'** not seized; not taken or put in possession. — *adj* **unself'ish** having or showing concern for others; generous. — *adv* **unself'ishly.** — *n* **unself'ishness.** — *adj* **unset'** not set; not yet firm or solid; (of a jewel) not in a setting. — *vt* **unsett'le** to change from being settled; to make uncertain, unstable or restless; to unfix. — *vi* to become unsettled. — *adj* **unsett'led** not settled, fixed or determined; changeable; not having the dregs deposited; not yet inhabited and cultivated; turbulent, lawless. — *n* and *adj* **unsett'ling.** — *adj* **unsewn'** not sewn. — *adj* **unsexed'** without the characteristics expected of one's sex. — *vt* **unshack'le** to loose from shackles; to remove a shackle from. — *adj* **unshack'led.** — *vt* **unsheathe'** to draw from the sheath; to uncover. — *adj* **unsheathed'** drawn from the sheath; not sheathed. — *adj* **unshed'** not shed. — *vt* **unshell'** to shell, remove the shell from. — *vt* **unship'** to unload (cargo) from a ship; (of a horse) unseat (the rider). — *adj* **unshod'** shoeless; with shoe or shoes removed. — *vt* **unshoe'** to strip of a shoe or shoes. — *vt* **unshutt'er** to open or remove the shutters of. — *adj* **unsift'ed** not sifted; not critically examined; inexperienced. — *adj* **unsight'ed** not seen; (of gun, etc.) having no sights; fired without use of sights; prevented from seeing, esp. by an obstruction. — *n* **unsight'liness.** — *adj* **unsight'ly** displeasing to the eye; ugly. — *adj* **unsized'** not fitted, adjusted or sorted in respect of size; not treated with size. — *vt* **unsling'** to free from slings or from being slung: — *pa t* and *pa p* **unslung'.** — *vt* **unsluice'** to let flow; to open the sluice of. — *vt* **unsnarl'** to disentangle. — *adj* **unsoaped'** not soaped; unwashed. — *n* **unsociabil'ity.** — *adj* **unsō'ciable** disinclined to associate with others. — *n* **unsō'ciableness.** — *adv* **unsō'ciably.** — *adj* **unsō'cial** not social; not regarding or conducing to the good of society; not sociable; (of hours of work) not falling within the normal working day. — *adj* **unsō'cialised** or **-z-** not socialised, not aware of one's function in, or lacking attributes for living in, society. — *adv* **unsō'cially.** — *vt* **unsock'et** to take out of the socket. — *adj* **unsol'emn** not solemn; informal. — *adj* **unsolv'able** impossible to solve. — *adj* **unsolved'** not solved. — *adj* **unsophis'ticated** genuine, unadulterated; unfalsified; free from artificiality; ingenuous. — *n* **unsophis'ticatedness.** — *n* **unsophisticā'tion.** — *adj* **unsort'ed** not sorted or arranged; ill-chosen; unsuitable. — *adj* **unsought'** not sought or solicited. — *adj* **unsound'** unhealthy; injured or damaged; not firm or solid; ill-founded; unreliable. — *adj* **unsound'ed** not sounded, pronounced, or made to sound; unfathomed, unplumbed. — *adv* **unsound'ly.** — *n* **unsound'ness.** — *adj* **unsourced'** having no source, or no established or authenticated source. — *adj* **unspared'** not spared; unstinted. — *adj* **unspār'ing** not sparing, liberal, profuse; unmerciful. — *adv* **unspār'ingly.** — *n* **unspār'ingness.** — *adj* **unspeak'able** unutterable; inexpressible, esp. indescribably bad. — *n* **unspeak'ableness.** — *adv* **unspeak'ably.** — *adj* **unspent'** not spent. — *adj* **unsprung'** not sprung; without springs. — *vt* **unstack'** to remove from a stack. — *adj* **unstat'ed** not stated or declared. — *adv* **unstead'ily.** — *n* **unstead'iness.** — *adj* **unstead'y.** — *vt* to make unsteady. — *vt* **unstick'** to free from sticking. — *vi* to come off from the surface: — *pa t* and *pa p* **unstuck'.** — *vt* **unstitch'** to take out the stitches of. — *vt* **unstop'** to free from being stopped; to draw out the stop or stopper of. — *adj* **unstopp'able** not able to be stopped. — *adv* **unstopp'ably.** — *adj* **unstopped'** not stopped; (of a consonant) open; without a pause at the end of the line. — *vt* **unstopp'er** to take the stopper from. — *vt* **unstow'** to empty of contents; to take out of stowage. — *adj* **unstrained'** not strained or purified by straining; not subjected to strain; not forced, natural. — *vt* **unstrap'** to undo the straps of. — *adj* **unstreamed'** (of schoolchildren) not divided into classes according to ability. — *adj* **unstressed'** not subject to stress; not stressed or emphasised. — *vt* **unstring'** to take the strings from; to loose the strings of; to take from a string; to put out of tone; to disorganise. — *adj* **unstringed'** not stringed, not provided with strings. — *adj* **unstrung'** with strings removed or slacked; not strung; relaxed; disorganised; unnerved. — *adj* **unstuck** detached, loosened from sticking (**come unstuck** (*slang*; of a plan) to go awry); see also **unstick**. — *adj* **unstud'ied** not studied; not having studied; without premeditation; unlaboured; spontaneous; natural, easy. — *adj* **un'stuffy** (*fig*) not stodgy or strait-laced. — *adj* **unsubstan'tial** not substantial, real, corporeal, solid or strong. — *adj* **unsuccess'ive** not successive; not in, or passing by, succession. — *n* **unsuitabil'ity.** — *adj* **unsuit'able** not suitable. — *n* **unsuit'ableness.** — *adv* **unsuit'ably.** — *adj* **unsuit'ed** not suited or adapted. — *adj* **unsung'** not sung; not celebrated in song. — *adj* **unsure** (*un-shoor'*) insecure; precarious; uncertain; doubtful; not assured; untrustworthy. — *adj* **unsuspec'ted** not suspected; not known or supposed to exist. — *adv* **unsuspec'tedly.** — *n* **unsuspec'tedness.** — *adj* **unsuspec'ting** not suspecting. — *adv* **unsuspec'tingly.** — *n* **unsuspec'tingness.** — *adj* **unsuspi'cious** not feeling or arousing suspicion. — *adv* **unsuspi'ciously.** — *n* **unsuspi'ciousness.** — *adj* **unswayed'** uninfluenced; not persuaded. — *adj* **unswerv'ing** not swerving or deviating; steadfast. — *adv* **unswerv'ingly.** — *adj* **unsworn'** not confirmed, or not bound, by oath. — *adj* **unsymmet'rical.** — *adv* **unsymmet'rically.** — *n* **unsymm'etry** asymmetry. — *vt* **untack'** to detach from tacking; to unharness. — *vt* **untack'le** to strip of tackle; to free from tackle. — *adj* **untaint'ed** not tainted; unblemished; not attainted. — *n* **untaint'edness.** — *adj* **untaint'ing.** — *adj* **untām'able** or **untame'able** that cannot be tamed. — *adj* **untamed'** not tamed; wild. — *vt* **untang'le** to disentangle. — *adj* **untang'led.** — *adj* **untaught'** uninstructed; not taught or communicated by teaching; spontaneous, native, inborn. — *adj* **untaxed'** not taxed; not charged with any fault. — *adj* **unteach'able** not capable of being unstructed; that cannot be imparted by teaching. — *adj* **untem'pered** not tempered. — *adj* **unten'able** not tenable, not defensible. — *n* **unten'ableness.** — *vt* **unteth'er** to release from a tether. — *adj* **unteth'ered** not tethered. — *vt* and *vi* **unthink'** to think to the contrary, reverse in thought. — *n* **unthinkabil'ity.** — *adj* **unthink'able** that cannot be thought; outside the realm of thought; beyond the power of thought; inconceivable; unimaginable; utterly impossible (often of things impending but too painful to think about). — *adj* **unthink'ing** not thinking; thoughtless. — *adv* **unthink'ingly.** — *n* **unthink'ingness.** — *adj* **unthought'-of.** — *vt* **unthread'** to take a thread from; to unweave; to loosen; to find one's way through. — *adj* **unthread'ed** not threaded. — *adv* **unthrift'ily.** — *n* **unthrift'iness.** — *adj* **unthrift'y** not thrifty; wasteful; prodigal; not thriving; unprofitable. — *vt* **untie'** to loose from being tied; to unbind. — *vi* to come loose. — *adj* **untied'** not tied; loosed. — *vt* **untile'** to strip of tiles. — *adj* **untiled'** not tiled; stripped of tiles. — *n* **untime'liness.** — *adj* **untime'ly** not timely; before the time, premature; immature; unseasonable, ill-timed; inopportune. — *adj* **untī'tled** having no title; having no legal claim. — *adj* **untold'** (or *un'*) not counted; innumerable; not narrated; not communicated; not informed. — *adj* **untouch'able** impossible to touch; not to be equalled or touched. — *n* someone whose excellence in some respect cannot be rivalled; (esp. *formerly*) a Hindu of very low caste, a member of one of the scheduled castes. — *adj* **untouched'** not touched; intact; unrivalled. — *adj* **untoward** (*un-tə-wörd'*) inconvenient; unlucky; unfavourable; unfitting. — *adv* **untoward'ly.** — *n* **untoward'ness.** — *adj* **untrace'able** impossible to trace. — *adj* **untraced'** not traced or found. — *adj* **untreat'able** that cannot be treated. — *adj* **untreat'ed.** — *adj* **untried'** not tried, tested, attempted, experienced or subjected to trial in court. — *adj* **untrodd'en** not trodden upon; unfrequented. — *adj* **untroub'led** not troubled or disturbed; not turbid. — *adj* **untrue'** not true; false; not faithful; dishonest; inexact; not in accordance with a standard. — *n* **untru'ism** an untrue platitude. — *adv* **untru'ly** falsely. — *vt* **untruss'** to unfasten, untie. — *adv* **untrust'worthily.** — *n* **untrust'worthiness.** — *adj* **untrust'worthy** not worthy of trust. — *n* **untruth'** falseness; that which is untrue; a lie. — *adj* **untruth'ful** not truthful. — *adv* **untruth'fully.** — *n* **untruth'fulness.** — *vt* **untuck'** to unfold or undo from being tucked up or in. — *adj* **untucked'** not tucked up or in. — *adj* **untuned'** not tuned; put out of tune. — *adj* **untune'ful** not tuneful or melodious. — *adv* **untune'fully.** — *n* **untune'fulness.** — *adj* **unturned'** not turned. — *adj* **untū'tored** untaught; uninstructed. — *vt* and *vi* **untwine'** to untwist; to separate by untwisting. — *vt* and *vi* **untwist'** to twist backwards so as to open out; to straighten out from a twist. — *adj* **untwist'ed** not twisted; subjected to untwisting. — *adj* **unty'pable** that cannot be defined as a particular type. — *adj* **unused** (*un-ūzd'*) not used; (also *un-ūst'*) unaccustomed. — *adj* **unūs'ual** not usual; uncommon; remarkable. — *adv* **unūs'ually** more than usually; in an unusual way. — *n* **unūs'ualness.** — *adj* **unutt'erable** beyond utterance, inexpressible; not to be uttered. — *n* an unutterable thing. — *adv* **unutt'erably.** — *adj* **unutt'ered.** — *adj* **unval'ued** not prized or highly esteemed; without having a value assigned. — *adj* **unvar'nished** not varnished; not artfully embellished or sophisticated. — *vt* **unveil'** to remove or set aside a veil from; to open to public view by ceremonial removal of a covering; to disclose, reveal. — *vi* to remove one's veil; to become unveiled, to reveal oneself. — *adj* **unveiled'** without a veil; with veil set aside or removed; unconcealed and undisguised. — *n* **unveil'ing** the ceremonial removal of a covering. — *adj* **unversed'** not experienced or skilled. — *vt* **unvoice'** to change to, or utter with, a voiceless sound. — *adj* **unvoiced'** not spoken or expressed; without voice. — *adv* **unwā'rily.** — *n* **unwā'riness.** — *adj* **unwarr'antable** not justifiable. — *adv* **unwarr'antably.** — *adj* **unwarr'anted** not justified or deserved. — *adj* **unwā'ry** not wary; not aware of danger. — *adj* **unwashed'** (**the great unwashed** see under **great**). — *adj* **unweath'ered** not worn by the weather or atmospheric agencies. — *vt* **unweave'** to undo from being woven. — *adj* **unweighed'** not weighed; not pondered; unguarded. — *adj* **unwell'** in poor health; mildly sick, indisposed. — *adj* **unwept'** not wept for; (of tears) not shed. — *adj* **unwhole'some** not wholesome; unsound; tainted in health, taste or morals. — *adv* **unwhole'somely.** — *n* **unwhole'someness.** — *adv* **unwiel'dily.** — *n* **unwiel'diness.** — *adj* **unwiel'dy** heavily awkward; cumbersome; unmanageable. — *adj* **unwilled'** not willed; involuntary. — *adj* **unwill'ing** reluctant; done reluctantly. — *adv* **unwill'ingly.** — *n* **unwill'ingness.** — *vt* **unwind** (*un-wīnd'*) to undo the winding of; to free from being wound; to wind down or off; to slacken; to relax (*colloq*). — *vi* to become unwound; to relax (*colloq*): — *pa t* and *pa p* **unwound** (*un-wownd'*). — *adj* not wound; released from being wound. — *n* **unwis'dom** lack of wisdom; foolishness. — *adj* **unwise'** not wise; injudicious; foolish. — *adv* **unwise'ly.** — *n* **unwise'ness.** — *adj* **unwished'-for** not wished for. — *adj* **unwitt'ing** without knowing; unaware; not cognisant; unintentional. — *adv* **unwitt'ingly.** — *n* **unwitt'ingness.** — *adj* **unwo'manly** not befitting or becoming a woman; not such as a woman is expected to be. — *adv* in an unwomanly manner. — *adj* **unwont'ed** unaccustomed; unusual. — *adv* **unwont'edly.** — *adj* **unwork'able** not workable; impracticable. — *adj* **unwork'manlike** not like or worthy of a good workman. — *n* **unworld'liness.** — *adj* **unworld'ly** not of this world; spiritual; naive; above worldly or self-interested motives. — *adv* **unwor'thily.** — *n* **unwor'thiness.** — *adj* **unwor'thy** not worthy; worthless; unbecoming; discreditable; undeserved. — **unwound** see **unwind.** — *vt* **unwrap** (*un-rap'*) to remove wrappings from; to unroll, unwind. — *vi* to become unwrapped. — *vt* and *vi* **unwrink'le** to smooth out from a wrinkled state. — *adj* **unwrink'led** not wrinkled, smooth. — *adj* **unwritt'en** not written or reduced to writing, oral; (of a rule, law, etc.) traditional, generally accepted. — *adj* **un-**

wrought (*un-röt'*) not done or worked; not fashioned, formed, composed or worked up; undone, brought back to an original state. — *adj* **unyiel'ding** not yielding; stiff; obstinate. — *adv* **unyiel'dingly**. — *n* **unyiel'dingness**. — *vt* **unyoke'** to loose from a yoke or harness; set free; to disjoin. — *vi* to unyoke an animal. — *adj* **unyoked'** not yoked or harnessed; freed from yoke or harness. — *adj* **unzoned'** not in or divided into zones.

una corda *ūn'ə kör'də* or *o͞on'ä kör'dä*, (It.; *mus*) one string (indication to pianists to use the soft pedal).

unanimous *ū-nan'i-məs*, *adj* of one mind; without any person dissenting. — *n* **unanimity** (*ū-nən-im'i-ti*) agreement without any person dissenting. — *adj* **unan'imously**. [L. *ūnanimus* — *ūnus*, one, *animus*, mind.]

unau *ū'nö* or *o͞o'now*, *n* the two-toed sloth. [Fr., from Tupí.]

una voce *ūn'ə vō'sē* or *o͞on'ä wō'ke*, (L.) with one voice, by general consent.

uncate. See under **uncus**.

uncial *un'shəl* or *-si-əl*, *adj* (of a form of writing) in (usu. large) somewhat rounded characters used in ancient manuscripts. — *n* an uncial letter; uncial writing; a manuscript written in uncials. [L. *unciālis* — *uncia*, a twelfth.]

unciform, uncinate, etc. See under **uncus**.

uncle *ung'kl*, *n* the brother of one's father or mother, or an aunt's husband, or a great-uncle (used with *cap* as a title, either before a man's first name, or independently); a pawnbroker (*slang*); (with *cap*) a title sometimes used by children for male friends of their parents. — *vt* to address as uncle. — **Uncle Sam** the United States or its people; **Uncle Tom** (*US derog*) a black American whose co-operative attitude to white people is thought to show disloyalty to Blacks (based on the hero of Harriet Beecher-Stowe's *Uncle Tom's Cabin*). [O.Fr. — L. *avunculus*, a maternal uncle.]

uncouth. See under **un-**.

UNCSTD *abbrev* for United Nations Conference on Science and Technology for Development.

UNCTAD *ungk'tad*, *abbrev* for United Nations Conference on Trade and Development.

unction *ungk'shən*, *n* an anointing; that which is used for anointing; ointment; that quality in language which raises emotion or devotion; warmth of address; religious glibness; divine or sanctifying grace. — *n* **unctūos'ity** unctuousness. — *adj* **unc'tūous** oily; greasy; full of unction; offensively suave and smug. — *adv* **unc'tūously**. — *n* **unc'tūousness**. — **extreme unction** (*RC*) the sacrament of anointing a dying person with consecrated oil. [L. *unctiō*, *-ōnis*, unction, besmearing, *ūnctum*, fat.]

uncus *ung'kəs*, *n* a hook or hooklike process: — *pl* **unci** (*un'sī*). — *adj* **unc'ate** hooked. — *adj* **unciform** (*un'si-förm*) hook-shaped. — *adj* **un'cinate** (*un'si-nāt*) or **un'cīnated** unciform; hooked at the end. [L. *uncus* and *uncinus*, hook.]

undecimal *un-des'i-məl*, *adj* based on the number eleven. [L. *undecim*, eleven — *ūnus*, one, *decem*, ten.]

under *un'dər*, *prep* beneath; below; in or to a position lower than that of, especially vertically lower; at the foot of; within, on the covered side of; short of; in or into subjection, subordination, obligation, liability, etc. to; in course of; in the state of; (of cultivated land) supporting a specified crop; by the authority or attestation of; in accordance with; in the aspect of; referred to the class, heading, name, etc. of; in the reign or administration of; within the influence of (a particular sign of the zodiac). — *adv* in or to a lower (esp. vertically lower) position; in or into a lower degree or condition; in or into subjection; in or into a covered, submerged, or hidden state; below; under par (*golf*). — *adj* lower; subordinate; falling short. — *n* **un'derling** a contemptuous word for a subordinate. — *adj* **un'dermost** lowest; inmost. — *adv* in or to the undermost place. — **under-and-over** see **over-and-under** at **over**. — **under the counter** see under **count²**. [O.E.]

under- *un-dər-*, *pfx* signifying: (1) below, beneath; (2) lower in position (*lit*); (3) lower in rank, or subordinate; (4a) too little in quantity, too small, insufficient; (4b) in too small a degree, insufficiently; (5) not coming, or not allowed to come, to the surface or into the open. — *vi* **underachieve'** to achieve less than one's potential or less than expected, esp. academically. — *n* **underachieve'ment**. — *n* **underachiev'er**. — *vt* and *vi* **underact'** to make too little of in acting; to play, for the sake of effect, with little emphasis. — *adj* **un'der-age** not of full, or the required, age; immature. — *adj* and *adv* **un'derarm** placed or held under the arm; with the arm kept below the shoulder. — *n* **un'derbelly** the under surface of a body or of something suggesting a body; soft underbelly (q.v.). — *vt* **underbid'** to offer a lower bid than; to bid less than the value of (*bridge*). — *vi* to bid unduly low. — *n* (*bridge*) a bid too low to be valid, or less than the hand is worth. — *n* **underbidd'er** a person who underbids; the next below the highest bidder. — *n* **un'derblanket** a blanket of a warm material placed under, rather than over, a person in bed. — *n* **un'derbrush** undergrowth of brushwood or shrubs. — *vt* **underbuild'** to build under in support, underpin; to build too little upon or in. — *n* **un'derbush** underbrush. — *vt* **underbuy'** to buy less than the amount required; to buy at less than the price paid by, or the value of. — *n* **undercapitalisā'tion** or **-z-** insufficient capitalisation. — *adj* **undercap'italised** or **-z-** (of a commercial enterprise) having too little capital for efficient running. — *n* **un'dercard** (*boxing*) a programme of matches supporting the main event. — *n* **un'dercarriage** the supporting framework under the body of a carriage or vehicle; the landing-gear of an aircraft. — *n* **un'dercart** (*colloq*) an aircraft's landing-gear, the undercarriage. — *vt* **undercharge'** to charge too little, or too little for. — *adj* **underclad'** not wearing enough clothes. — *n* **un'derclay** a bed of clay underlying a coal seam representing the soil in which the plants grew. — *n* **un'dercliff** a terrace of material that has fallen from a cliff. — *npl* **un'derclothes** and *nsing* **un'derclothing** clothes worn under others, esp. those next to the skin. — *vt* and *vi* **underclub'** (*golf*) to hit with a club which has too great loft to achieve the desired distance. — *n* **un'dercoat** coat worn under another; an underlayer of fur or hair, or of paint. — *vt* **undercook'** to cook insufficiently or to a lesser extent than usual. — *adj* **un'dercover** working, or done, in secret (**under cover of** hidden by, using as concealment). — *n* **un'dercroft** a crypt. — *n* **un'dercurrent** a current under the surface (*lit* and *fig*). — *vt* **undercut'** to cut under; to cut away under the surface, so as to leave part overhanging; to undermine; to strike with a heavy blow upward; to underbid; to offer at a lower price than. — *adj* made so as to cut from the underside; effected by undercutting; having the parts in relief cut under. — *n* (*un'*) the act or effect of cutting under; a blow dealt upward; the tenderloin, or fillet, or underside of a sirloin. — *vt* **underdevel'op**. — *adj* **underdevel'oped** insufficiently developed; (of a country) with resources inadequately used, having a low standard of living, and backward in education. — *n* **underdevel'opment**. — *vt* **underdo'** to do, perform, act, or esp. cook, insufficiently or inadequately: — *pa t* **underdid'**; *pa p* **underdone'**. — *n* **un'derdog** the dog that gets the worst of it in a fight; anyone in adversity; a person dominated, or being or likely to be beaten, by another. — *adj* **underdone'** done less than is requisite; insufficiently or slightly cooked. — *vt* **un'derdraw** to draw or describe with moderation or reticence or short of the truth. — *n* **un'der-**

drawing an outline drawing on a canvas, etc., done before paint is applied. — *vt* and *vi* **underdress'** to dress too plainly or simply. — *adj* **underdressed'**. — *n* **un'derdrive** a gear which transmits to the driving shaft a speed less than engine speed. — *n* **underemploy'ment** making too little use (of); the condition of having too large a part of the labour force employed; partial employment, or employment on work requiring less skill than the worker has. — *vt* **underes'timate** to estimate or value too low. — *n* an estimate that falls short of the truth or true quantity. — *n* **underestimā'tion.** — *vt* **underexpose'** to expose too little, esp. (*phot*) to light. — *n* **underexpōs'ure.** — *adj* **underfed'** insufficiently fed. — *vt* and *vi* **underfeed'** to give too little food. — *n* **un'derfelt** an older term for underlay, usu. of felt. — *adj* **underfin'ished** (of cattle and sheep) having too little finish (q.v.). — *adj* **underfloor'** beneath the floor. — *adv* **underfoot'** beneath one's feet; in the way; downtrodden. — *vt* **underfund'** to provide with insufficient funds. — *n* **underfund'ing.** — *n* **un'derfur** short fur hidden by longer hairs. — *n* **un'dergarment** any article of clothing worn under another, esp. that worn next to the skin, underclothing. — *adj* **un'derglaze** applied or done before glazing. — *n* **undergrad'uate** a student who has not taken any degree (*colloq* contraction **un'dergrad**). — *adj* pertaining to such. — *adj* **un'derground** under the surface of the ground; (of a railway) running through underground tunnels; secret; characterised by avant-gardism and experimentation, rejection of current trends or norms, appeal to a minority, anti-establishment tendencies, etc. — *n* the underworld; an underground place; an underground railway; underlying ground; low ground; a secret resistance movement, or body of people; a group whose activities are partly concerned with resisting things they disapprove of in social, artistic and political life. — *adv* **underground'** beneath the surface of the earth; secretly. — *adj* **undergrown'** grown insufficiently. — *n* **un'dergrowth** low plants growing under taller, esp. shrubs under trees; stunted growth. — *adv* **underhand'** surreptitiously; with the hand kept below the elbow or shoulder. — *adj* **un'derhand** surreptitious, secret; not straightforward; delivered underhand. — *n* an underhand ball; (with **the**) a subordinate position. — *adj* and *adv* **underhan'ded** underhand; short of workers. — *adv* **underhan'dedly.** — *n* **underhan'dedness.** — *adj* **underhung'** (or *un'*) (of a lower jaw) protruding; having a protruding lower jaw; running on rollers on a rail below. — *adj* **underlaid** see **underlay.** — *adj* **underlain** see **underlie.** — *vt* **underlay'** to support or provide with something laid under; to lay under: — *pa t* and *pa p* **underlaid'.** — *n* (*un'*) something laid under, e.g. felt or rubber to help preserve carpet. — *n* **underlay'er** a person who underlays; (*un'*) a lower layer, substratum. — *vt* **underlie'** to lie beneath (*lit* and *fig*); to undergo; to be subject or liable to: — *pr p* **underly'ing;** *pa t* **underlay';** *pa p* **underlain'.** — *vt* **underline'** to draw a line under; to stress. — *n* (*un'*) a caption, legend; a line drawn under a word. — *n* **underling** see **under.** — *n* **un'derlip** a lower lip. — *adj* **underly'ing** lying beneath (*lit* and *fig*); fundamental; present though not immediately obvious. — *adj* **undermanned'** having too few workers. — *adj* **undermen'tioned** mentioned underneath or hereafter. — *vt* **undermine'** to dig beneath (e.g. a wall) in order that it may fall; to wash away, remove by burrowing, etc., the ground from under; to weaken gradually or insidiously (*fig*); to intrigue against; to tamper with the fidelity of. — *n* **undermī'ner.** — *n* **undermī'ning.** — *adj* **un'dernamed** whose name appears below. — *n* **un'dernote** a note added below. — *vt* to note below. — *adj* **undernour'ished** living on less food than is necessary for satisfactory health and growth (also *fig*). — *n* **undernour'ishment.** — *adj* **underpaid'** not paid sufficiently. — *npl* **un'derpants** an undergarment worn by men and boys, covering the buttocks and sometimes the legs. — *n* **un'derpass** a road passing under another road, a railway, etc. — *vt* **un'derpay** to pay less than required or deserved. — *n* **underpay'ment.** — *adj* **underpeo'pled** not sufficiently peopled. — *vi* **underperform'** to do less well than expected, possible, etc. — *vt* **underpin'** to support by building underneath, or to prop up (also *fig*); to corroborate. — *n* **underpinn'ing.** — *vt* **underplant'** to plant smaller plants in between (trees or taller plants). — *vi* **underplay'** to play a low card while holding up a higher. — *vt* to play down, understate. — *vt* and *vi* to underact. — *n* (*un'*) the act of so doing. — *n* **un'derplot** a subordinate plot in a play or tale; a secret scheme, a trick. — *adj* **underpop'ulated** having a very small population, insufficient to exploit the land. — *adj* **underpow'ered** having insufficient power to perform the task required. — *adj* **underpriced'** having too low a price. — *vt* **underprize'** to value too little. — *adj* **under-priv'ileged** not enjoying normal social and economic rights. — Also *n.* — *vt* and *vi* **under-produce'.** — *n* **under-produc'tion** too little production; production short of demand. — *vt* **underquote'** to offer at a price lower than. — *vt* **underrate'** to rate too low. — *n* **under-representā'tion** too little representation; less representation than one is entitled to. — *adj* **under-represent'ed.** — *vt* and *vi* **un'der-ring** ring up a lesser amount on a till than the actual price. — *adj* **un'der-ripe** not quite ripe. — *vt* **underscore'** to underline. — *adj* and *adv* **un'dersea** below the surface of the sea. — *vt* **underseal'** to coat exposed parts of underside of (a motor vehicle) with corrosion-resisting substance. — Also *n* (*un'*). — *n* **underseal'ing.** — *n* **under-sec'retary** a secretary immediately under the principal secretary. — *n* **under-sec'retaryship.** — *vt* **undersell'** to sell below the price charged by; to sell too cheap. — *adj* **undersexed'** having less than normal interest in sexual relations or activity. — *n* **un'dershirt** a man's collarless undergarment usu. of cotton, which may or may not have sleeves. — *vt* **undershoot'** to fail to reach by falling short (also *fig*). — *n* (*aeronautics*) a falling short of the mark in landing. — *n* **un'dershrub** a shrubby plant, or a low shrub. — *n* **un'derside** the lower surface. — *vt* **undersign'** to sign below. — *adj* **un'dersigned** (or *-sīnd'*) whose signature is appended. — *adj* **un'dersized** below the usual or desired size. — *n* **un'derskirt** a petticoat; a foundation for a dress or skirt. — *adj* **underslung'** suspended, or supported, from above; (of a vehicle chassis) extending below the axles. — *vi* and *vt* **underspend'** to spend less than one could or should (of e.g. a budget). — *n* the amount left unspent from an allocated budget, etc. — *adj* **understaffed'** having too few members of staff. — *vt* **understate'** to state more moderately than truth would allow or require; to state or describe, or to use artistically, without emphasis. — *adj* **understāt'ed** effective through simplicity, without embellishment or dramatic emphasis. — *n* **understate'ment** (or *un'*). — *n* **un'dersteer** a tendency in a motor vehicle to follow a wider curve than the turning applied by the steering wheel should cause it to follow. — Also *vi.* — *vt* **understock'** to supply with an insufficient amount of stock. — **understood** see **understand** (separate entry). — *n* **un'derstorey** the smaller trees and bushes forming a lower level of cover beneath the tallest trees in a forest, etc. — *n* **un'derstratum** an underlayer: — *pl* **un'derstrata.** — *vt* **un'derstudy** to study (a part), or to study the part of (an actor or other person) in order to take over in an emergency, or in due course. — Also *vi.* — *n* a person who understudies. — *n* **un'derthrust** (*geol*) a fault in which one mass of rock is moved under another relatively static layer. — *adj* **undertimed**' (of a photograph) underexposed. — *n* **un'dertint** a subdued tint; a tint showing through. — *n* **un'dertone** a subdued tone of voice, sound, colour, etc.; a tone felt as if pervading, underlying, or perceptible through others, including (*fig*) an emotional tone. — *n* **un'dertow** (-*tō*) an undercurrent opposed to the surface current; the recoil or back-draught of a wave. — *n* **un'der-trick** (*bridge*) a trick short of the number declared. — *vt* **underuse** (-*ūz*') to make insufficient use of; to use to less than capacity. — *n* **underuse** (-*ūs*'). — *n* **underutilisa'tion** or **-z-**. — *vt* **underut'ilise** or **-z-** to underuse. — *n* **undervaluā'tion**. — *vt* **underval'ue** to value below the real worth; to reduce the value of; to esteem too lightly. — *n* **underval'uer**. — *n* **un'dervest** an undershirt, or a similar garment for a woman. — *n* **un'derwater** underground water; undertow. — *adj* existing, acting, carried out, etc. below the surface of the water; below the waterline. — Also *adv*. — *n* **un'derwear** underclothing. — *n* **un'derweight** shortness of weight; short weight. — *adj* short in weight. — *vt* **underwhelm**' (*facetious*) to fail to impress. — *n* **un'derwood** undergrowth; a coppice. — *vt* **underwork**' to undermine; to employ too little in work; to work for less than the wage of. — *vi* to do less work than is desirable. — *n* (*un*') a substructure; underhand, inferior or subordinate work. — *n* **un'derworker**. — *n* **un'der-workman**. — *n* **un'derworld** the world beneath the heavens; the world or a region, beneath the earth; the place of departed souls; the part of the world below the horizon; the antipodes; a submerged, hidden or secret region or sphere of life, esp. one given to crime, profligacy or intrigue. — *vt* **un'derwrite** to write (something) beneath; to subscribe to (a statement, etc.); to accept the risk of insuring; to guarantee to take or find others to take (certain shares, under certain conditions); to write too little about; (*reflexive*) to write below the level of which one is capable. — *vi* to practise as an underwriter. — *n* **un'derwriter** a person who practises insurance business, esp. in ships. — *n* **un'derwriting**.

underachieve ... to ... **underglaze**. See **under-**.

undergo *un-dər-gō*', *vt* to be subjected to; to endure or suffer; to pass through, experience. [Late O.E. *undergān* — *gān*, to go.]

undergraduate ... to ... **undernamed**. See **under-**.

underneath *un-dər-nēth*', *adv* and *prep* beneath, below in position (*lit* and *fig*). — *n* the under part or side. [O.E. *underneothan*.]

undernote ... to ... **understaffed**. See **under-**.

understand *un-dər-stand*', *vt* to comprehend; to grasp with the mind; to be able to follow the working, logic, meaning, etc. of; to take the meaning of (a sign or a person); to realise; to have a sympathetic, usu. tacit, perception of the character, aims, etc. of (a person); to know the meaning of; to be expert in; to have knowledge or information (that), to have been informed; to assume, take to be true; to interpret (as), take to mean; to imply; to support. — *vi* to have understanding; to comprehend: — *pa t* and *pa p* **understood**'. — *adj* **understand'able**. — *n* **understand'ing** the act of comprehending; the power to understand; intellect; an informal agreement; an understood condition (e.g. *on the understanding that*); sympathetic or amicable agreement of minds. — *adj* intelligent; discerning; sympathetic. — *adv* **understand'ingly**. — *adj* **understood**' (often *gram*) implied but not expressed. — **understand each other** or **understand one another** to have reached an agreement, sometimes collusive. [O.E. *understandan* — *under* and *standan*, to stand.]

understate ... to ... **understudy**. See **under-**.

undertake *un-dər-tāk*', *vt* to pledge oneself (that); to take upon oneself; to take upon oneself (to deal with, manage, or look after); to set about, engage in. — *vi* to promise; to become a surety (for); to conduct funerals (*colloq*): — *pa t* **undertook**'; *pa p* **undertā'ken**. — *adj* **undertā'kable**. — *n* **un'dertaker** a person who takes in hand an enterprise, task or encounter; a person who manages funerals. — *n* **un'dertaking** that which is undertaken; any business or project engaged in; a task one sets oneself; the business of conducting funerals. — Also *adj*. [12th cent. *undertaken*, to entrap — O.E. *under* and late O.E. *tacan*; see **take**.]

underthrust ... to ... **underwater**. See **under-**.

underway. See under **way**[1] and **weigh**[2].

underwear ... to ... **underwriting**. See **under-**.

undies *un'diz*, (*colloq*) *npl* women's underclothing. [**under**.]

undulate *un'dū-lāt*, *vt* and *vi* to move like or in waves; to make or be wavy; to vibrate. — *adj* wavy; with wavy margin, surface or markings. — Also **un'dulated**. — *n* **un'dulancy**. — *adj* **un'dulant** undulating; rising and falling. — *adv* **un'dulately**. — *adj* **un'dulating**. — *adv* **un'dulatingly**. — *n* **undulā'tion** an undulating, a wavelike motion or form; waviness; a wave. — *n* **undulā'tionist** someone who holds the undulatory theory of light. — *adj* **un'dulatory** of the nature of undulation; undulating; wavy; referring light to waves in a medium. — **undulant fever** a remittent fever with swelling of the joints and enlarged spleen, caused by a bacterium (*Brucella*) transmitted by goat's (or cow's) milk. [L. *undulātus*, undulated — *unda*, a wave.]

unguent *ung'gwənt*, *n* ointment. [L. *unguentum* — *unguĕre*, to anoint.]

unguis *ung'gwis*, *n* a claw or nail (*zool*); the base of a petal (*bot*): — *pl* **ung'ues** (-*gwēz*). — *adj* **ung'ual** (-*gwəl*) of or bearing a claw. — *adj* **unguiculate** (*ung-gwik'ū-lāt*) or **unguic'ulated** clawed. — *adj* **unguiform** (*ung'gwi-förm*). [L. *unguis*, a nail.]

ungula *ung'gū-lə*, *n* a hoof (*zool*); a section of a cylinder, cone, etc., cut off by a plane oblique to the base (*geom*): — *pl* **ung'ulae** (-*lē*). — *adj* **ung'ulate** hoofed. — *n* a hoofed animal, a member of the order **Ungulā'ta**, hoofed digitigrade mammals. [L. *ungula*, claw, hoof — *unguis*, nail.]

UNHCR *abbrev* for United Nations High Commission (or Commissioner) for Refugees.

uni *ū'ni*, (*colloq*) *n* short for **university**.

uni- *ū-ni-*, *combining form* signifying one. — *adj* **uniax'ial** having one axis, esp. (*crystall*) one optic axis or (*biol*) one main line of growth or unbranched axis. — *adv* **uniax'ially**. — *adj* **unicam'eral** having or consisting of only one chamber. — *adj* **unicell'ular** of or having only one cell. — *n* **ū'nicorn** (L. *cornū*, a horn) a fabulous animal mentioned by ancient Greek and Roman authors as a native of India, with a body like a horse and one straight horn; such an imaginary animal usu. depicted with a white body and spiralled horn; (with *cap*) one of the Scottish pursuivants. — *adj* one-horned. — *n* **ū'nicycle** an acrobat's one-wheeled cycle. — *adj* **unidirec'tional** mainly or wholly in one direction. — *adj* **uniflō'rous** one-flowered. — *adj* **unifo'liate** (*bot*) with only one leaf; unifoliolate. — *adj* **unifō'liolāte** (L. *foliolum*, dimin. of *folium*, leaf; *bot*) having a single leaflet, but compound in structure. — *adj* **unilat'eral** one-sided; on one side; affecting, involving, etc. only one person, group, etc. out of several. — *n* **unilat'eralism**. — *n* **unilat'eralist** someone who favours unilateral action, esp. in abandoning or reducing production of nuclear weapons. — *n* **unilateral'ity**. — *adv* **unilat'erally**. — *adj* **uniling'ual** of, in or using one tongue or language. — *adj* **unilō'bar** or **unilōbed**' having one lobe. — *adj* **unilob'ular** having one lobule. — *adj* **uninū'clear** with a single nucleus. — *adj* **uninū'cleate**. — *adj* **unip'arous** (L. *parĕre*, to bring forth) producing one at a birth. — *adj* **unipar'tite** not divided into parts. — *adj* **uniper'sonal** existing as only one person. — *adj* **unipō'lar** of, from or using one pole; (of a nerve cell) having one process only. — *n* **unipolar'ity.** — *adj* **unisē'rial** in one series or row. — *adv* **unisē'rially.** — *adj* **unisē'riate** uniserial. — *adv* **unisē'riately.** — *adj* **ū'nisex** (of a style, esp. in clothes) adopted by both sexes; applicable to, usable by, etc. persons of either sex. — *adj* **unisex'ual** of one sex only. — *n* **unisexual'ity.** — *adv* **unisex'ually.** — *n* **ū'nison** (or *-zən*; L. *sonus*, sound, *sonāre*, to sound) identity of pitch; (*loosely*) pitch differing by one or more octaves; a sound of the same pitch; complete agreement. — *adj* in unison. — *n* **unis'-onance.** — *adj* **unis'onant.** — *adj* **unis'onous.** — *n* **univā'lence** (or *-iv'əl-*) or **univā'lency** (or *-iv'əl-*). — *adj* **univā'lent** (*chem*) monovalent. — *adj* and *n* (pertaining to) one of the single chromosomes which separate in the first meiotic division. — *adj* **ū'nivalve** having one valve or shell only. — *n* a shell of one valve only; a mollusc whose shell is composed of a single piece. — *adj* **unival'vular.** — *adj* **univā'riant** having one degree of freedom. — *adj* **univā'riate** (of a distribution) having one variate only. [L. *ūnus*, one.]

Uniat *ū'ni-ət* or **Uniate** *ū'ni-āt* or *-ət*, *n* a member of any community of Christians, esp. in eastern Europe and Asia, that acknowledges the papal supremacy but which is allowed to retain its own customs and practices with regard to all else — clerical matrimony, communion in both kinds, church discipline, rites and liturgy. [Russ. *uniyat* — *uniya*, union — L.L. *ūniō*, *-ōnis* — L. *ūnus*, one.]

uniaxial ... to ... **unicameral.** See under **uni-**.

UNICEF *ū'ni-sef*, *abbrev* for United Nations International Children's Emergency Fund — now United Nations Children's Fund.

unicellular ... to ... **unidirectional.** See under **uni-**.

UNIDO *ū-nē'dō*, *abbrev* for United Nations Industrial Development Organisation.

uniflorous ... to ... **unifoliolate.** See under **uni-**.

uniform *ū'ni-fōrm*, *adj* alike; alike all over, throughout, or at all times; unvarying; of a military or other uniform. — *n* a distinctive garb for members of a body; a suit of it. — *vt* to make uniform; to clothe in uniform. — *adj* **ū'niformed** wearing uniform. — *n* **uniform'ity** the state or fact of being uniform; agreement with a pattern or rule; sameness; likeness between parts. — *adv* **ū'niformly.** — *n* **ū'niformness.** [L. *ūniformis* — *ūnus*, one, *fōrma*, form.]

unify *ū'ni-fī*, *vt* to make into one; to consolidate. — *adj* **ū'nifīable.** — *n* **unificā'tion.** — *adj* **ū'nified.** — *n* **ū'nifīer.** — *n* and *adj* **ū'nifying.** — **unified field** an ultimate basis on which the physicist seeks to bring within a single theory the workings of all natural phenomena. [L.L. *unificāre* — L. *ūnus*, one, *facĕre*, to make.]

unilateral ... to ... **uninucleate.** See under **uni-**.

union *ūn'yən*, *n* a uniting; the state of being united; the state of wedlock; a united whole; combination; a growing together in healing; general concord; the incorporation of states in a federation or in a single state; a single state (or sometimes a federation) thus formed; an association or league, esp. a trade union; a student's club; a connecting part for pipes, etc.; a device emblematic of union shown on a flag; the same device used separately as a flag, such as the Union Jack; a textile fabric of more than one kind of fibre; the set formed from all the elements present in two (or more) sets. — *n* **ūnionīsā'tion** or **-z-**. — *vt* **ūn'ionise** or **-ize** to recruit into a trade union; to organise the workforce of (a body, company or industry) into a trade union. — *n* **ūn'ionism** (also with *cap*). — *n* **ūn'ionist** an advocate or supporter of or believer in union or trade unions; a member of a trade union; (with *cap*) an opponent of Irish Home Rule — hence, through the *Liberal Unionists*, a Conservative; (with *cap*) a supporter of the federal union of the United States, esp. at the time of the Civil War. — Also *adj.* — **union flag** a flag symbolising union, esp. the national flag of the United Kingdom, consisting of a union of the crosses of St George, St. Andrew and St Patrick, commonly called the **Union Jack.** — **the Union** the legislative incorporation of England and Scotland in 1707, or of Ireland with both in 1801; the American Union or United States; the Union of South Africa (1910). [Fr. *union* — L.L. *ūniō*, *-ōnis* — L. *ūnus*, one.]

unionised[1]. See **un-** (panel).

unionised[2]. *ūn'yən-īzd*, *pa t* and *pa p* of **unionise** see under **union.**

uniparous ... to ... **unipolarity.** See under **uni-**.

unique *ū-nēk'*, *adj* sole; without a like; often used loosely for unusual, pre-eminent; found solely in, belonging solely to, etc. (with *to*). — *n* anything that is unique. — *adv* **unique'ly.** — *n* **unique'ness.** [Fr., — L. *ūnicus* — *ūnus*.]

uniserial ... to ... **unisonous.** See under **uni-**.

unit *ū'nit*, *n* one; a single thing or person; a single element, section or item, regarded as the lowest subdivision of a whole; a group of persons forming a subdivision of a larger body; a distinct part within a piece of electrically powered equipment which has its own specific function; a single complete domestic fixture combining what are sometimes separate parts; a usu. independently owned dwelling apartment, one of several into which a building is divided, a home unit (*Austr*); the least whole number; anything taken as one; a quantity by reference to which others are measured. — *adj* of the character or value of a unit; individual. — *n* **Unitā'rian** someone who asserts the unity of the Godhead as opposed to the Trinity, ascribes divinity to God the father only, and who believes in freedom of, and tolerance of the differences in, religious beliefs, etc.; a member of a particular body holding such doctrines; a monotheist generally; (without *cap*) a holder of some belief based on unity or union. — Also *adj.* — *n* **Unitā'rianism** (also without *cap*). — *adj* **ū'nitary** pertaining to unity or to a unit; of the nature of a unit; integral; based on unity. — **unit furniture** furniture which may be bought as single items rather than as sets or suites; **u'nitholder** someone holding a unit of securities in a unit trust; **unit-pack'aging** a method of packaging (pills, etc.) in which the items are individually encased; **unit price; unit-pri'cing** a method of pricing foodstuffs, etc. by showing the cost per agreed unit (e.g. kilogram or pound) as well as, or instead of, the overall price of the item; **unit trust** see under **trust.** — **unit of account** a monetary unit not necessarily corresponding to any actual denomination of currency and in certain cases of variable value, used as a basis of exchange or comparison or as a unit in accounting. [For **unity.**]

UNITA *ū-nē'tə*, *abbrev* for *União Nacional por Independência Total de Angola* (Port.), National Union for the Total Liberation of Angola.

unite *ū-nīt'*, *vt* to make one; to join into one; to join; to combine; to clasp; to marry; to have in combination; to make to agree or adhere. — *vi* to become one; to combine; to join; to grow or act together. — *adj* **unī'ted.** — *adv* **unī'tedly.** — *n* **unī'tedness.** — *n* **unī'ter.** — *n* and *adj* **unī'ting.** — *n* **unition** (*ū-nish'ən*) conjunction. — *adj* **unitive** (*ū'ni-tiv*) harmonising, uniting. — **United Kingdom (of Great Britain and Northern Ireland)** from 1922 the official title for the kingdom consisting of England and Wales, Scotland, and Northern Ireland; **United Nations** (treated as *nsing* or *npl*) an association of states formed in 1945 to promote peace and international co-operation; **United States** a federal union of states, esp. that of (north) America. [L. *ūnītus*, past p. of *ūnīre*, to unite — *ūnus*, one.]

unity *ū'ni-ti*, *n* oneness; the number one; the state or fact of being one or at one; that which has oneness; a single whole; the arrangement of all the parts to one purpose or effect. — **unity element** (*math*) an identity element for multiplication. — **the unities** (of *place*, *time* and *action*) the three canons of the classical drama — that the scenes should be at the same place, that all the events should be such as might happen within a single day, and that nothing should be admitted not directly relevant to the development of the plot. [L. *ūnitās*, *-ātis* — *ūnus*, one.]

Univ. *abbrev* for: Universalist; University.

univalence ... to ... **univariate**. See under **uni-**.

universe *ū'ni-vûrs*, *n* the cosmos; a system of stars such as the galactic system; the whole system of things; all that is; the world, everyone. — *adj* **univer'sal** of the universe; comprehending, affecting, or for use by, the whole world or all people; without exception; comprising all the particulars; all-round; unlimited; capable of being applied to a great variety of uses. — *n* that which is universal; a universal proposition; a general term; a universal concept. — *n* **universalīsā'tion** or **-z-**. — *vt* **univer'salise** or **-ize-**. — *n* **Univer'salism** the doctrine or belief of universal salvation, or the ultimate salvation of all mankind, and even of the fallen angels. — *n* **Univer'salist** a believer in Universalism. — Also *adj*. — *adj* **universalis'tic**. — *n* **universality** (*-sal'*) the state or quality of being universal. — *adv* **univer'sally**. — *n* **univer'salness**. — **universal joint** a joint capable of turning all ways. [L. *ūniversum*, neut. sing. of *ūniversus*, whole, *ūnus*, one, *vertĕre*, *versus*, to turn.]

university *ū-ni-vûr'si-ti*, *n* an institution of higher learning with power to grant degrees, its body of teachers, students, graduates, etc., its college or colleges, or its buildings. — *adj* **universitā'rian**. [L. *ūniversitās*, *-ātis*, a whole, in L.L. a corporation; see **universe**.]

univocal *ū-niv'ə-kl* or *ū-ni-vō'kl*, *adj* of one voice; having one meaning only; unmistakable; unambiguous. — *adv* **univocally**. [L. *ūnivocus* — *ūnus*, one, *vōx*, *vōcis*, a voice.]

unjoint ... to ... **unled**. See under **un-**.

unless *un-les'* or *ən-les'*, *conj* (tending to pass into a *prep*) if not; except (when or if). [Earlier followed by *than* or *that*: *on lesse than*, on a less condition than.]

UNO *abbrev* for United Nations Organisation.

UNRRA *abbrev* for United Nations Relief and Rehabilitation Administration.

UNRWA *un'rə*, *abbrev* for United Nations Relief and Works Agency.

until *un-til'* or *ən-til'*, *prep* and *conj* till. [Pfx. *und-*, as far as, and **till**.]

unto *un'too͞* or *-too͞*, (*archaic* or *formal*) *prep* to. [Pfx. *und-*, as far as, and **to**.]

UOM *abbrev* for Union of Myanmar (formerly Burma).

UP *abbrev* for: United Presbyterian; United Press.

up *up*, *adv* in, to or toward a higher place, level or state; aloft; on high; towards a centre (such as a capital, great town, university); in residence, at school or college; northward; to windward; in or to a more erect position or more advanced stage of erection; out of bed; on horseback; in an excited state; in revolt; with (increased) vigour, intensity or loudness; afoot; amiss; into prominence, notice or consideration; forward for sale; in or into court; into custody, keeping, possession; away in a receptacle, place of storage or lodging (such as a sheath, purse or stable); ahead in scoring; into closed or compact state, together; to a total; in, near or towards arrival, overtaking, or being abreast; as far as; all the way; to a standstill; at an end; to a finish; thoroughly, completely, fully; well informed, versed. — Also elliptically passing into a verb or interjection by omission of *go*, *come*, *put*, etc., often followed by *with*. — *adj* placed, going or directed up; top; risen; (of time) ended; having gained (so many) more holes than an opponent (*golf*): — *compar* **upp'er**; *superl* **up'most** or **upp'ermost** see below. — *prep* in an ascent along, through, or by; to or in a higher position on; to or in an inner or more remote part of; along against the current; along. — *n* a rise; a high place; a success, spell of prosperity; someone who is in prosperity. — *vt* to drive upstream (as swans for owner marking); to lift or haul up; to raise, increase. — *vi* (*colloq*) to set up; to move up; to intervene boldly, start into activity or speech: — *pr p* **upp'ing**; *pa t* and *pa p* **upped** (*upt*). — *adj* **up'most** uppermost. — *adj* **upp'er** (see above) higher; superior; higher in rank. — *n* the part of a boot or shoe above the sole and welt; an upper tooth; a drug producing a stimulant or euphoric effect, or a pill containing such a drug (*slang*). — *adj* **upp'ermost** (see above) highest; first to come into the mind. — *adv* in the highest place, first. — *n* **upp'ing** the action of **up** *vt* (see above). — *adj* **upp'ish** assuming, pretentious, snobbish. — *adv* **upp'ishly**. — *n* **upp'ishness**. — *adj* **upp'ity** uppish; difficult to control, resistant to persuasion. — *adv* **up'ward** (*-wərd*) or **up'wards** from lower to higher; from outlet towards source; from modern to more ancient; in the upper part (**upward of** or **upwards of** more than; **and upwards** and higher, and more). — *prep* **up'ward** upwards along. — *adj* **up'ward** directed upward; ascending; placed high. — *adv* **up'wardly**. — *n* **up'wardness**. — *adj* **up'-and-coming** alert and pushful; likely to succeed (in a career, etc.). — *adj* **up'-and-down** (see also **up and down** below) undulating; going or working both, or alternately, up and down. — *adj* **up-and-o'ver** (of a door, etc.) raised to a horizontal position when opened. — **up-and-un'der** (*Rugby*) a movement in which the ball is kicked high and forwards, and the players rush to try to catch it; **up'-beat** an unaccented beat, at which the conductor raises the baton; an optimistic note or mood; a promising development. — *adj* (**up'beat**) (*colloq*) cheerful; optimistic. — **up'-bow** (*mus*) a movement of the bow from point towards nut over the strings; **up'-current** or **up'-draught** a rising current of air. — *adj* **upfront** see **up front** below. — **up'land** inland, hilly or high-lying country; upper or high land, as opp. to meadows, river-sides, etc. (*US*). — *adj* high-lying; remote; inland; rural; of the uplands. — **up'lander**. — *adj* **up'-line** a railway line for upgoing trains (i.e. those going to, not from, e.g. a city). — *adj* **upp'er-bracket** in an upper grouping in a list, etc. — *adj* **upp'er-case** (*printing*) (of letters) capital as opposed to small. — **upper class** or **classes** the people of the highest social rank (*adj* **upp'er-class**); **upper crust** the top of a loaf; the aristocracy, or the upper class or classes in any society (*adj* **upp'er-crust**); **upp'ercut** an upward short-arm blow; **upper hand** mastery, advantage; **upper house** in a bicameral legislature, the house that is the more restricted in membership, e.g. House of Lords, Senate of U.S. and other countries; **up'side** the upper side. — *adv* on the upper side. — *adv* **up'side-down** or **upside down** with the upper part undermost; in, or into, complete confusion. — *adj* turned upside down. — *adv* **up'sides (with)** on a par (with); beside. — **up'-train** a railway train proceeding towards the chief terminus; **upward mobility** the (desired) state of the **upwardly mobile**, those people moving (or attempting to move) to a higher social rank or position of greater status. — **be up in** to have a knowledge of; **it is all up (with)** there is no hope (for); **not up** (*tennis*) called when the ball bounces twice before the player manages to hit it; **(on) the up and up** (in) a state of continuous progress towards ever greater success; honest, on the level; **something is up** something is amiss, something unusual or unexpected is happening or has happened; **up against** face to face with, confronted with (**up against it** in almost desperate straits); **up and doing** bestirring oneself; **up and down** to and fro; here and there through or about; throughout; vertically; out-and-out; **up for** available for or undergoing (some process); standing as a candidate for; **up front** (also as *adj*, **up-front**' or **upfront**') at the front; to the forefront; foremost; (of money) paid in advance; candidly, openly; **ups and downs** undulations; vicissitudes; **up to** as far up as; into the immediate neighbourhood or presence of; immersed or embedded as far as; about, meditating or engaged in doing (*colloq*); capable of and ready for (*colloq*); incumbent upon (orig. *US*); **up to date** to the present time or time in question; containing all recent facts, statistics, etc.; knowing the latest developments of fashion, usage, etc. (*adj* **up-to-date**'); **up top** (*colloq*) in the head, in respect of intelligence; **up to the minute** right up to the present time (*adj* **up'=to-the-minute** very up-to-date); **up town** into town; in or to the residential part of a town (*US*); **up with** abreast of; even with; put, get, etc. up (see under **up**), often as an exclamation of approbation and partisanship; **up yours** (*vulg slang*) an expression of strong refusal, defiance, contempt, etc.; **what's up (with you,** etc.**)?** what's the matter, what's wrong (with you, etc.)? [O.E. *ūp*, *upp*, up, *uppe*, above, *uppian*, to rise.]

Words made with **up** *adj* are listed above, and those with **up-** *pfx* in the following entry; other UP- words follow (p. 1180).

up- *up-*, *pfx* with meanings of *adv*, *prep* (and *adj*; see previous article) **up**. — *vi* **up-anch'or** to weigh anchor. — *vt* **upbraid** see separate article. — *n* **up'bringing** bringing up. — *n* **up'burst** a bursting upwards. — *vt* and *vi* (*-bûrst*'). — *adj* **upburst'ing**. — *n* **up'cast** an upward throw; an upthrow; material thrown up; an upward current of air from a mine; a shaft carrying it (**up'cast-shaft**). — *adj* thrown or turned upward. — *adj* (*US*) **up'coming** forthcoming, approaching. — *n* **up'-country** the interior, inland part. — *adj* (*-kun*') of or in the interior. — *adv* in or to the interior. — *adj* **up-curved'**. — *vt* **update'** to bring up to date. — *n* (*up'*) the act of bringing up to date; that which is brought up to date. — *vt* **up-end'** to set on end; to affect or alter greatly, turn upside down. — *vi* to rise on end. — *n* **up'flow** an upward flowing. — *vi* (*-flō*') to stream up. — *n* **upgoing** (*-gō*' or *up'*). — *n* **up'grade** an upward slope or course. — *adj* and *adv* uphill. — *vt* (*-grād*') to raise in status, quality, value, etc. — *adj* **upgrad'able**. — *n* **up'growth** the process of growing up, development; that which grows up; a structure that has grown upward. — *n* **upheav'al** the bodily elevation of tracts of country; a profound, thorough or revolutionary change or movement. — **upheld** see **uphold** below. — *adj* **up'hill** ascending; difficult. — Also *n*. — Also *adv* (*-hil*'). — *vt* **uphold'** to hold up; to sustain; to countenance; to defend; to keep in repair or good condition; to maintain, warrant: — *pa t* **upheld'**. — *n* **uphold'er** a support or supporter. — *n* and *adj* **uphold'ing**. — *n* **up'keep** maintenance. — *vt* **uplift'** to lift up, raise; to elevate; to raise to a higher moral or spiritual level; to elate; to collect (e.g. a parcel), draw (money) (*Scot*); to increase (e.g. an interim dividend) (*commerce*). — *n* **up'lift** a lifting up, raising; upheaval; elevation, esp. moral or spiritual, or the feeling of it; an increase (*commerce*). — *n* and *adj* **uplift'ing**. — *adv* **uplift'ingly**. — *adj* **up'lying** upland, elevated. — *n* **up'make** the action or mode of making up; constitution (especially mental or moral); galley-proofs arranged in page form. — *n* **up'maker**. — *n* **up'making** filling-up, esp. between bilge ways and ship's bottom before launching; arrangement of lines into columns or pages (*printing*). — *adj* **up-mar'ket** of (buying, selling or using) commodities relatively high in price, quality or prestige. — Also *adv*. — *vt* to make (more) up-market. — *prep* **upon** (*ə-pon*' or *ə-pən*) on. — *vt* **upraise'** to raise or lift up; to exalt. — *adj* **upraised'**. — *vt* **uprate'** to upgrade; to increase the rate or size of. — *adj* **up'right** (also *up-rīt*') right or straight up; in an erect position (**upright piano** one with the strings in a vertical plane); of habitual rectitude; honest; just. — *n* **up'right** an upright post, stone, stroke, or the like; a vertical member of a structure; an upright piano; verticality; a basket-maker's tool. — *vt* to set erect or right side up. — *adv* (*up'rīt* or *up-rīt*') vertically; honestly. — *adv* **up'rightly** in an upright manner; honestly; vertically. — *n* **up'rightness**. — *n* **uprīs'al**. — *vi* **uprise** (*-rīz*') to rise up, arise: — *pa t* **uprose'**; *pa p* **upris'en**. — *n* **uprīs'ing** (or *up'*) a rising up; a violent revolt against a ruling power. — *adj* which rises up or is rising up. — *adj* **up'river**. — *n* **uproar** see separate entry. — *vt* **uproot'** to pull up by the roots; to destroy (*fig*); to remove forcibly and completely (from e.g. native land). — *n* **uproot'al** uprooting. — *n* **uproot'er**. — *n* **uproot'ing**. — *vi* **uprose'** *pa t* of **uprise**. — *n* **up'rush**. — *vt* **upsend'**. — *vt* **upset'** to overturn, capsize; to spill or tip out; to interfere with, defeat (a plan); to disconcert; to distress; to disorder (a bodily process or organ); to affect temporarily the health of (a person). — *vi* to be upset: — *pa t* and *pa p* **upset'**. — *n* (*up'set*) an overturn or derangement. — *adj* (*up'set*) (of a price) the lowest that will be accepted, at which bidding is started; (*up-set*') disturbed, anxious, unhappy. — *n* **upsett'er**. — *adj* **upsett'ing** causing upset. — *n* overturning; overthrow. — *n* **up'shot** the final shot (*archery*); the outcome, final result; the conclusion of an argument; the substance, general effect. — *adv* **up'stage** towards the back of the stage. — *adj* towards the back of the stage; stand-offish, superior (*slang*). — *vt* (*up-stāj*') to treat in a supercilious manner; to move upstage so that (another actor) has to turn his or her back to the audience, and thus to put him or her at a disadvantage; to divert interest or attention away from (someone or something). — *adv* **upstairs'** in or toward a higher storey, or (*fig*) position; in the head, mentally (*colloq*). — *adj* **up'stair** or **up'stairs** of or in an upper storey or flat. — *n* **upstairs'** the part of a building above the ground floor; esp. formerly (the occupants (usu. the householder and his family) of) the upper part of a house, as opposed to the servants' quarters in the basement. — *adj* **upstand'ing** erect; on one's feet (*Scot*); straight and well-built; honest and downright. — *n* **up'start** someone who has suddenly risen to wealth, importance or power, a parvenu. — *adj* newly or suddenly come into being; characteristic of a parvenu; pretentious and vulgar; new-fangled. — *vi* **upstart'** to start up. — *adj* **upstate'** (*US*) pertaining to a part of a state away from, and usu. to the north of, the principal city of the state. — Also *adv*. — *adv* **up'stream** against the current. — *adj* further up the stream; going against the current. — *vi* (*-strēm*') to stream up. — *n* **up'stroke** an upward stroke; an upward line in writing. — *vi* **upsurge'** to surge up. — *n* (*up'*) a surging up. — *n* **upsur'gence**. — *n* **up'sweep**. — *adj* **up'swept**. — *n* **up'take** the act of lifting up; a pipe or flue with upward current; the act of taking up; mental apprehension (orig. *Scot*). — *vt* (*-tāk*') to take up. — *vt* **uptear'** to pull up or out by the roots, from the base, etc. — *adj* **up=tem'po** played or sung at a fast tempo. — *vt* **upthrow'** to throw up. — *n* (*up'*) an upheaval, uplift; the amount of vertical displacement of the relatively raised strata at a fault. — *vt* **upthrust'** to thrust upward. — *n* (*up'*). — *adj* **uptight'** (*colloq*) tense, in a nervy state; angry, irritated; conventional, strait-laced. — *adj* **uptilt'ed**. — *adj*, *adv* and *n* **uptown'** (in or toward) the upper part or (*US*) the residential quarters of a town. — *n* **up'trend** upward tendency. — *n* **up'turn** an upheaval; a disturbance; a movement upward, a rise; an upturned part. — *adj* **up'turned**. — *n* and *adj* **upturn'ing**. — *vt* **upval'ue**

to increase the value of. — *adv* **upwind** (*up-wind'*) or **up-wind'** against the wind.

Upanishad or **Upanisad** *ōō-pan'i-shad* or *ōō-pä'ni-shäd*, *n* any of a number of Sanskrit theosophic or philosophical treatises. [Sans. *upa*, near, *ni-ṣad*, a sitting down.]

upbraid *up-brād'*, *vt* to reproach or chide. — *n* and *adj* **upbraid'ing**. [O.E. *ūpbregdan*.]

upholster *up-hōl'stər*, *vt* to furnish with stuffing, springs, covers, etc.; to cushion, be a cover to; to provide with curtains, carpets, etc. — *vi* to do upholstery. — *n* **uphōl'sterer**, *fem* **uphōl'stress**, someone who makes or deals in furniture, beds, curtains, etc. — *n* **uphōl'stery** upholsterer's work or goods. [Back-formation from *upholsterer* — **upholder**.]

UPI *abbrev* for United Press International.

upmost. See under **up**.

upon. See under **up-**.

upper, uppermost. See under **up**.

uproar *up'rör*, *n* loud outcry, clamour. — *adj* **uproar'ious**. — *adv* **uproar'iously**. — *n* **uproar'iousness**. [Du. *oproer* — *op*, up, *roeren*, to stir; modified by association with **roar**.]

ups-a-daisy *ups'-ə-dā-zi*, *interj* of encouragement in lifting a child or helping to climb.

upsilon *ūp-sī'lon*, *ūp'si-* or *up'si-*, *n* the twentieth letter of the Greek alphabet (Υ, υ). — Also **ypsilon** (*ip-sī'lon*, *-sē'* or *ip'si-*). [Gr. simple u.]

upsy-daisy *up'si-dā-zi*, *interj*. Same as **ups-a-daisy**.

up-train. See under **up**.

UPU *abbrev* for Universal Postal Union.

UPW *abbrev* for Union of Post Office Workers.

uracil. See under **urea**.

uraemia or in U.S. **uremia** *ū-rē'mi-ə*, (*med*) *n* retention of waste materials in the blood. — *adj* **urae'mic** or in U.S. **urē'mic**. [Gr. *ouron*, urine, *haima*, blood.]

Ural *ū'rəl*, *n* a river of Russia; (also in *pl*) a mountain range of Russia. — *adj* **Uralian** (*ū-rā'li-ən*) of the Ural mountains; pertaining to Uralic (also *n*). — *n* **Uralic** (*ū-ral'ik*) a language group comprising Finno-Ugric and the Samoyed languages. — *adj* Uralian. — *adj* **Ural-Altaic** (*-al-tā'ik*) of the Ural and Altai Mountains; applied to a family of languages — Finno-Ugrian, Turko-Tatar, Mongolian, Manchu, Tungus, etc., and their speakers.

urali. Same as **wourali**.

Urania *ū-rā'ni-ə*, *n* (*Gr mythol*) the Muse of astronomy; a name for Aphrodite. — *adj* **Uranian** (*ū-rā'ni-ən*) of Urania or of Uranus (god or planet). [L. — Gr. *Ourania* — *ouranos*, heaven.]

uranic *ū-ran'ik*, (*chem*) *adj* of uranium in higher valency.

uranide *ū'rən-īd*, *n* a transuranic element. [*uran*ium and chem. sfx. *-ide*.]

uranium *ū-rā'ni-əm*, *n* a radioactive metal (*symbol* **U**; atomic no. 92) named by Klaproth, 1789, after the recently discovered planet Uranus.

urano- *ūr-ə-no-*, *combining form* denoting: the sky, the heavens; the roof of the mouth, palate (*med*); uranium.

uranography *ūr-ən-og'rə-fi*, *n* descriptive astronomy, esp. of the constellations. — *n* **uranog'rapher**. — *adj* **uranograph'ic** or **uranograph'ical**. — *n* **uranog'raphist**. [**urano-** and **-graphy**.]

uranous *ūr'ə-nəs*, (*chem*) *adj* of uranium in lower valency.

Uranus *ū'rə-nəs* or *ū-rā'nəs*, *n* an old Greek god, father of Kronos (Saturn) and the Titans (*Gr mythol*); a planet discovered in 1781 by Herschel. [Gr. *ouranos*, heaven.]

urari. Same as **wourali**.

urate *ū'rāt*, *n*. See under **uric**.

urban *ûr'bən*, *adj* of or belonging to a city. — *adj* **urbane** (*ûr-bān'*) civilised; refined; courteous; smooth-mannered. — *adv* **urbane'ly**. — *n* **urbanisā'tion** or **-z-**. — *vt* **ur'banise** or **-ize** to make (a district) townlike (as opposed to rural) in character. — *adj* **urbanist'ic** pertaining to the planning and development of towns. — *n* **urbanity** (*-ban'i-ti*) the quality of being urbane; also townishness, town-life. — *n* **urbanol'ogist** a person who studies urban conditions. — *n* **urbanol'ogy**. — **urban district** a thickly-populated district; a subdivision of a country, administered by an **Urban District Council**; **urban guerrilla** someone who is engaged in terrorist activities in towns and cities; **urban renewal** (esp. *US*) the clearing and/or redevelopment of slums or the like. [L. *urbānus* — *urbs*, a city.]

URC *abbrev* for United Reformed Church.

urchin *ûr'chin*, *n* a sea-urchin; a mischievous child, esp. a boy; a child. — *adj* like, of the nature of or due to an urchin. [O.Fr. *herichon*, *heriçon* — L. *ēricius*, a hedgehog.]

urd *ûrd*, *n* an Indian plant of the bean family (*Phaseolus mungo*), or its edible blackish seed. — Also **urd bean** or **black gram**. [Hindi.]

Urdu *ōōr'dōō* or *ōōr-dōō'*, *n* and *adj* a form of Hindustani incorporating many Persian and Arabic words, the official literary language of Pakistan. [Hind. *urdū*, camp (language).]

urea *ū-rē'ə*, or by some *ū'rē-ə*, *n* a substance found in mammalian urine, the chief form in which nitrogenous waste is carried off. — *n* **ū'racil** a base in ribonucleic acid. — *adj* **urē'al** (or *ū'ri-əl*). — *n* **ureide** (*ū'rē-īd*) an acyl derivative of urea. — *n* **ū'ridine** a pyrimidine nucleoside based on uracil and ribose. — **urea resins** thermosetting resins made by heating urea and aldehyde, usu. formaldehyde. [Gr. *ouron*, urine.]

uremia, uremic. See **uraemia**.

urena *ū-rē'nə*, *n* any plant of the tropical *Urena* genus of the mallow family, yielding a jute substitute. [Malayalam *uren*.]

uresis *ū-rē'sis*, (*med*) *n* urination. [Gr. *ourēsis*.]

ureter *ū-rē'tər*, (*anat* and *zool*) *n* a duct that conveys urine from the kidneys to the bladder or cloaca. — *adj* **urē'teral**. — *adj* **ureteric** (*ū-ri-ter'ik*). — *n* **urēterī'tis** (*med*) inflammation of a ureter. [Gr. *ourētēr*, *-ēros* — *ouron*, urine.]

urethra *ū-rē'thrə*, (*anat* and *zool*) *n* the canal by which the urine is discharged from the bladder: — *pl* **ure'thras** or **ure'thrae** (*-ē*). — *adj* **urē'thral**. — *adj* **urēthrit'ic**. — *n* **urēthrī'tis** (*med*) inflammation of the urethra. [Gr. *ourēthrā* — *ouron*, urine.]

uretic *ū-ret'ik*, *adj* pertaining to, or occurring in, urine. [Gr. *ourētikos* — *ouron*, urine.]

urge *ûrj*, *vt* to put forward (an argument, etc.; or in argument, with *that*); to incite; to allege earnestly; to advise strongly; to drive, impel. — *vi* to press; to be urgent or insistent; to push on. — *n* an impulse; a prompting; a strong desire or drive. — *n* **ur'gency**. — *adj* **ur'gent** urging; pressing; calling for immediate attention. — *adv* **ur'gently**. [L. *urgēre*.]

urial or **oorial** *ōō'ri-əl*, *n* a Himalayan wild sheep. [Punjabi *hureāl*.]

uric *ū'rik*, *adj* of, got from or present in urine. — *n* **ū'rate** a salt of uric acid. — **uric acid** an acid, $C_5H_4O_3N_4$, present in urine and blood. [Gr. *ouron*, urine.]

uridine. See under **urea**.

urine *ū'rin*, *n* the excretory product, usually amber liquid, of the kidneys, chief means of voiding nitrogenous waste. — *n* **ū'rinal** (or *-rī'*) a vessel for urine, esp. for an incontinent or bedridden person; a room or building having fixed receptacle(s) for use in urination. — *n* **urinal'ysis** analysis of urine, e.g. to detect disease. — *adj* **ū'rinary** pertaining to, or like, urine. — *n* a reservoir for urine. — *vi* **ū'rinate** to discharge urine. — *n* **urinā'tion**. — *adj* **urinogen'ital** pertaining jointly to urinary and genital functions or organs. — *adj* **ū'rinous** like or of the nature of urine. [L. *ūrīna*.]

urn *ûrn, n* a vase with rounded body, usually a narrowed mouth and often a foot; esp. such a vase for ashes of the dead; hence any repository for the dead (esp. *poetic*); a monumental imitation of a burial-urn; a vessel for water; a closed vessel with a tap and now usu. with heating device inside, for making tea or coffee in quantity; an urn-shaped object. — **urn'field** a late Bronze Age cemetery of cinerary urns. [L. *urna*.]

uro-[1] *ū-rō-* or *-ro'-*, *combining form* denoting urine. — *adj* **urogen'ital** urinogenital. — *adj* **urograph'ic.** — *n* **urog'raphy** radiological examination of the urinary tract. — *n* **ū'rolith** (*med*) a calculus in the urine or the urinary tract. — *n* **urolithī'asis** (*med*) the formation of uroliths; the condition caused by uroliths. — *adj* **urolog'ic** or **urolog'ical.** — *n* **urol'ogist.** — *n* **urol'ogy** the branch of medicine dealing with diseases and abnormalities of the urinary tract and their treatment. — *adj* **uropygial** (*-pij'i-əl*). — *n* **uropyg'ium** (Gr. *pȳgē*, buttocks) the rump in birds, that supports the tail feathers. — *adj* **uroscop'ic.** — *n* **uros'copy** diagnostic examination of urine. — *n* **urō'sis** disease of the urinary organs. [Gr. *ouron*, urine; cf. L. *ūrīna*.]

uro-[2] *ū-rō-* or *-ro-*, *combining form* denoting: tail; posterior part. — *npl* **Urodē'la** (Gr. *dēlos*, clear, plain) the (permanently) tailed Amphibia. — *n* and *adj* **urodē'lan** and **ū'rodele.** — *adj* **urosthen'ic** (Gr. *sthenos*, strength) having a tail developed for propulsion. — *n* **ū'rostyle** (Gr. *stȳlos*, column) a prolongation of the last vertebra. [Gr. *ourā*, tail.]

Ursa *ûr'sə, n* the Latin name of two constellations, *Ursa Major* and *Ursa Minor*, the Great and the Little Bear. — *adj* **ur'sine** of a bear; bearlike. — *n* **Ur'sus** the bear genus. [L. *ursus, ursa*, bear.]

urtica *ûr-tī'kə* or commonly *ûr'ti-kə, n* a plant of the nettle genus *Urtica*. — *n* **urticā'ria** (*med*) nettle-rash. — *adj* **urticā'rial.** — *adj* **urticā'rious.** — *vt* **ur'ticate** to sting. — *n* **urticā'tion.** [L. *urtīca*, a nettle — *ūrĕre*, to burn.]

US *abbrev* for: Under-secretary; United Service(s); United States (of America).

us *us, pron* the objective (dative and accusative) case of **we.** — Also in editorial and royal use as a singular. [O.E. *ūs*.]

us *abbrev* for *ut supra* (L.), as above.

USA *abbrev* for: United States Army; United States of America (also I.V.R.).

USAF *abbrev* for United States Air Force.

usage *ū'zij* or *ū'sij, n* use; act or mode of using; treatment; practice; custom; the normal or acceptable speech patterns, vocabulary, etc. of a language or dialect. — *n* **ū'sance** time allowed for payment of foreign bills of exchange. [O.Fr., — L. *ūsus*, use.]

USCL *abbrev* for United Society for Christian Literature.

USDAW *uz'dö, abbrev* for Union of Shop, Distributive and Allied Workers.

use[1] *ūz, vt* to put to some purpose; to avail oneself of; to treat or behave towards; to make use of (a person; see under **use**[2]); to take or consume (drugs or alcohol) regularly (*slang*; also as *vi*). — *vi* to be accustomed (to; used chiefly in the past tense, pronounced in this sense *ūst*; **usedn't** or **usen't** *ūs'nt*, for *used not*). — *adj* **ū'sable.** — *adj* **used** (*ūzd*) already made use of; second-hand. — *n* **ū'ser** someone who uses; continual enjoyment of a right (Fr. *user*); a right established by long use (*law*). — *adj* **used'-up** exhausted. — *adj* **user-friend'ly** (of a computer or software item) designed to be easily understood and operable by non-specialists, guiding the user by means of clear instructions, menus, etc.; (generally, of any product, etc.) designed with the ease of the user in mind, deliberately not off-putting. — **be able to use** (*colloq*; usu. as **can use** or **could use**) to feel better for, want, need; **use up** to consume; to exhaust; to tire out. [Fr. *user* — L.L. *ūsāre* — L. *ūtī, ūsus*, to use.]

use[2] *ūs, n* the act of using; the state or fact of being used; an advantageous purpose to which a thing can be applied; the fact of serving a purpose; usefulness; employment causing wear; a need to use (with *for*); the manner of using; the power of using (e.g. tongue, limb); the habit of using; custom; the profit derived from property; (in *pl*) a form of equitable ownership peculiar to English law by which one person enjoys the profit of lands, etc., the legal title to which is vested in another in trust. — *adj* **use'ful** advantageous, serviceable (**useful arts** or **applied arts** those arts with a utilitarian purpose (e.g. weaving, pottery) as opposed to the fine arts (see under **art**)). — *adv* **use'fully.** — *n* **use'fulness.** — *adj* **use'less** having no use; not answering any good purpose or the end proposed. — *adv* **use'lessly.** — *n* **use'lessness.** — **have no use for** to have no liking for; to have no need for; **in use** in employment or practice; **make use of** to use, employ; to take the help, etc. of (a person) in obtaining an end with no intention of repaying them; **of no use** useless; **of use** useful; **out of use** not used or employed; **use and wont** the customary practice. [L. *ūsus* — *ūtī*, to use.]

usher *ush'ər, n* a doorkeeper; someone who escorts persons to seats in a hall, etc.; an officer who introduces strangers or walks before a person of rank: — *fem* **usherette'** (esp. in a theatre or cinema) or **ush'eress.** — *vt* to conduct; to show (in or out); to introduce, lead up to (now usu. with *in*). — *n* **ush'ering.** — *n* **ush'ership.** [A.Fr. *usser*, O.Fr. *ussier* — L. *ostiārius*, a doorkeeper — *ostium*, a door.]

USIA *abbrev* for United States Information Agency.

USM *abbrev* for Unlisted Securities Market.

USN *abbrev* for United States Navy.

USPG *abbrev* for United Society for the Propagation of the Gospel.

USS *abbrev* for United States Ship or Steamer.

USSR or (Russ.) **CCCP** *abbrev* for Union of Soviet Socialist Republics.

usu. *abbrev* for usually.

usual *ū'zhōō-əl, adj* occurring in ordinary use; common; customary. — *n* (*colloq*) normal health; one's habitual drink, etc. — *adv* **ū'sually.** — *n* **ū'sualness.** — **as usual** as is or was usual; **the usual** (*colloq*) the drink, etc. one regularly orders or takes; anything one customarily experiences or does. [L. *ūsuālis* — *ūsus*, use.]

usufruct *ū'zū-frukt*, (*law*) *n* the use and profit, but not the property, of a thing. — *vt* to hold in usufruct. — *adj* **usufruc'tūary.** — *n* a person who has usufruct. [L.L. *ūsūfrūctus* — L. *ūsus* (*et*) *frūctus*, use and fruit.]

usurer, etc. See under **usury.**

usurp *ū-zûrp', vt* to take possession of by force, without right, or unjustly; to assume (the authority, place, etc. of someone or something else); to take possession of (the mind); to take or borrow (a name or a word). — *vi* to practise usurpation; to encroach (on). — *n* **usurpā'tion.** — *adj* **usur'patory.** — *adj* **usurped'.** — *n* **usur'per.** — *n* and *adj* **usur'ping.** [Fr. *usurper* and L. *ūsūrpāre*, perh. from *ūsus*, use, *rapĕre*, to seize.]

usury *ū'zhə-ri, n* the taking of (now only iniquitous or illegal) interest on a loan. — *n* **ū'surer,** *fem* **ū'suress,** a money-lender (now for excessive interest). — *adj* **usū'rious.** — *adv* **usū'riously.** — *n* **usū'riousness.** [L.L. *ūsūria*, L. *ūsūra* — *ūtī, ūsus*, to use.]

USW *abbrev* for: ultrashort waves; ultrasonic waves.

usw *abbrev* for *und so weiter* (Ger.), and so forth.

UT *abbrev* for: Universal Time; Utah (U.S. state; also **Ut.**).

ut *ut* or *ōōt*, (L.) *adv* and *conj* as. — **ut infra** (*in'frə* or *ēn'frä*) as below; **ut supra** (*sū'prə, sōō'prä* or *sōō'*) as above.

UTC *abbrev* for Universal Time Co-ordinates (used in telecommunications for GMT).

ute. See **utility** under **utilise**.

utensil *ū-ten'sil*, *n* any useful or ceremonial tool or vessel. [O.Fr. *utensile* — L. *ūtēnsilis*, fit for use — *ūtī*, to use.]

uterus *ū'tər-əs*, *n* the womb: — *pl* **ū'terī**. — *n* **uterec'tomy** hysterectomy. — *adj* **ū'terine** (*-īn*) of, in or for the uterus; of the same mother by a different father. — *n* **uterī'tis** inflammation of the womb. [L.]

utile *ū'tīl*, *adj* (with *to*) useful, profitable. [M.E. — O.Fr. — L. *ūtilis*, useful — *ūtī*, to use.]

utilise or **-ize** *ū'ti-līz*, *vt* to make use of, turn to use. — *adj* **ū'tilīsable** or **-z-**. — *n* **utilisā'tion** or **-z-**. — *n* **ū'tilīser** or **-z-**. — *n* **util'ity** usefulness; the power to satisfy the wants of people in general (*philos*); a useful thing; a public utility, public service, or a company providing such (esp. *US*); (usu. in *pl*) stock or bond of public utility; a small truck, pick-up or van (short form **ute**; *Austr*). — *adj* produced or supplied primarily for usefulness; provided in order that the public may be supplied in spite of rise of prices; (of a breed of dog) originally bred to be useful, to serve a practical purpose. — **utility room** a room, esp. in a private house, where things required for the work of running the house are kept. [Fr. *utiliser*, *utilité* — L. *ūtilis*, useful — *ūtī*, to use.]

utilitarian *ū-til-i-tā'ri-ən*, *adj* consisting in, based upon or pertaining to utility or to utilitarianism; concerned with or looking to usefulness alone, without regard to, or without caring about, beauty, pleasantness, etc. — *n* someone who holds utilitarianism; someone who looks to usefulness alone. — *vt* **utilitā'rianise** or **-ize** to make to serve a utilitarian purpose. — *n* **utilitā'rianism** the ethical theory which finds the basis of moral distinctions in the utility of actions, i.e. their fitness to produce happiness. [Jeremy Bentham's coinage from **utility**.]

utility. See under **utilise**.

uti possidetis *ū'tī pos-i-dē'tis* or L. *ŏŏ'tē pos-i-dā'-tis*, (in international law) the principle under which belligerents keep the territory or property they possess at the close of hostilities unless otherwise agreed. [L., as you possess.]

utmost *ut'mōst*, *adj* outmost; last; in the greatest degree, extreme. — *n* the limit; the extreme; the most or greatest possible. [O.E. *ūtemest*, with double superlative suffix *-m-est* from *ūte*, out.]

Utopia *ū-tō'pi-ə*, *n* an imaginary state described in Sir Thomas More's Latin political romance or satire *Utopia* (1516); (often without *cap*) any imaginary state of ideal perfection. — *adj* **Utō'pian** (also without *cap*). — *n* an inhabitant of Utopia; someone who imagines or believes in a Utopia; (often without *cap*) someone who advocates impracticable reforms or who expects an impossible state of perfection in society. — *n* **utō'pianism**. [lit. 'no place', from Gr. *ou*, not, *topos*, a place.]

utricle *ū'tri-kl*, (*biol*) *n* a little bag, bladder or cell; a bladder-like envelope of some fruits (*bot*); a chamber in the inner ear (*zool*). — *adj* **utric'ūlar** like or having a utricle. [L. *ūtriculus*, a small bag, dimin. of *ūter*, *ūtris*, a bag, a bottle.]

ut. sup. *abbrev* for *ut supra* (L.), as above.

utter[1] *ut'ər*, *adj* (*superl* **utt'erest**) extreme; total; out-and-out. — *adv* **utt'erly**. — *adj* and *n* **utt'ermost** utmost. — *n* **utt'erness**. [O.E. *ūtor*, outer — *ūt*, out.]

utter[2] *ut'ər*, *vt* to speak, pronounce, give voice to; to (try to) pass off (a forged document, etc.) as genuine or put (counterfeit money) into circulation (*law*); to put (money) in circulation. — *vi* (*colloq*) to make a remark or express an opinion. — *adj* **utt'erable**. — *n* **utt'erableness**. — *n* **utt'erance** an act of uttering; a manner of speaking; the expression in speech, or in other sound, of a thought or emotion (e.g. **give utterance to**); a stretch of speech in some way isolated from, or independent of, what precedes and follows it (*linguis*). — *n* **utt'erer**. — *n* **utt'ering** circulation. [M.E. *uttren* — O.E. *ūt*, out; and M.Du. *uteren*, to announce.]

UU *abbrev* for Ulster Unionist.

uv *abbrev* for ultraviolet.

uva *ū'və*, (*bot*) *n* a grapelike berry, one formed from a superior ovary. [L. *ūva*, a grape.]

UVF *abbrev* for Ulster Volunteer Force.

uvula *ū'vū-lə*, (*anat*) *n* the fleshy conical body suspended from the palate over the back part of the tongue: — *pl* **ū'vulas** or **ū'vulae** (*-lē*). — *adj* **ū'vular** of or produced by vibration of the uvula. [Dimin. from L. *ūva*, a grape.]

UWIST *ū'wist*, *abbrev* for University of Wales Institute of Science and Technology.

UWT. See **NAS/UWT**.

uxorial *uk-sö'ri-əl* or *-zö'ri-əl*, *adj* of a wife. — *n* **uxo'ricide** (*-sīd*) a wife-killer; wife-killing. — *adj* **uxo'rious** excessively or submissively fond of a wife. [L. *uxor*, *-ōris*, a wife.]

Uzbeg *uz'beg* or **Uzbek** *uz'bek*, *n* a member of a Turkic people of Turkestan; their language. — Also *adj*.

V or **v** *vē*, *n* the twenty-second letter of the modern English alphabet, representing a voiced labiodental sound; an object or mark shaped like the letter. — **V'-neck** the neck of a garment cut down to a point in front. — *adj* **V'-necked.** — *adj* **V'-shaped.** — **V'-sign** a sign made with the index and middle fingers in the form of a V, with palm turned outwards in token of victory, with palm inwards as a sign of contempt or derision.

V *abbrev* for: Vatican City (I.V.R.); vatu (currency of Vanuatu; also **VT**); volt.

V *symbol* for: vanadium (*chem*); (Roman numeral) 5.

V-1 *vee-wun'* and **V-2** *vee-tōō'*, *n* respectively a robot flying bomb and a long-range rocket-powered missile, used by the Germans in World War II esp. to bomb the southern part of England. [Ger. *vergeltungswaffe*, retaliation weapon.]

v *abbrev* for: velocity; verb; versed; versus; very; *vide* (L.), see; volume.

VA *abbrev* for: (Royal Order of) Victoria and Albert; Virginia (U.S. state; also **Va**).

vac *vak*, (*colloq*) *n* the (esp. university) vacation.

vacant *vā'kənt*, *adj* empty; unoccupied; (of a period of time) not assigned to any activity, free; blankly incurious; unthinking; inane, vacuous. — *n* **vā'cancy** emptiness; empty space; a gap; an unoccupied post or situation; a room available (in a boarding-house, etc.); emptiness of mind, inanity; blankness. — *adv* **vā'cantly.** [L. *vacans*, *-antis*, pres. p. of *vacāre*, to be empty.]

vacate *və-kāt'* or in U.S. *vā'kāt*, *vt* to stop occupying, leave empty; to empty out, unload; to quit. — *n* **vacā'tion** the act of vacating or emptying; the holidays, the holiday period between academic or law-court terms; a holiday (esp. *US*). — *vi* (esp. *US*) to take a holiday. — *n* **vacā'tionist** a holidaymaker. — **vacant possession** (of property) (the state of being ready for) occupation immediately after purchase, the previous owner or occupier already having left. [L. *vacāre*, *-ātum*, to be empty.]

vaccine *vak'sēn* or *-sin*, *n* any preparation containing dead or attenuated microorganisms, e.g. viruses or bacteria, used to confer immunity to a disease by inoculation; cowpox virus or lymph containing it, used for inoculation against smallpox (*hist*). — *adj* **vaccinal** (*vak'sin-əl*). — *vt* **vac'cinate** to inoculate with a vaccine. — *n* **vaccinā'tion.** — *n* **vac'cinātor.** — *adj* **vac'cinatory.** — *n* **vaccin'ia** cowpox; (in humans) a mild or localised reaction to inoculation with the vaccinia virus against smallpox. [L. *vaccīnus* — *vacca*, a cow.]

vacherin *vash-rẽ*, (Fr.) *n* a dessert made with meringue and whipped cream, usu. with ice-cream, fruit, nuts, etc.

vacillate *vas'i-lāt*, *vi* to waver, behave indecisively. — *adj* **vac'illāting.** — *adv* **vac'illātingly.** — *n* **vacillā'tion.** [L. *vacillāre*, *-ātum*.]

vacuity. See **vacuous.**

vacuole *vak'ū-ōl*, (*biol*) *n* a small cavity in a cell, containing air, fluid, etc. — *adj* **vac'uolar.** — *n* **vacuolā'tion.** [Fr., little vacuum.]

vacuous *vak'ū-əs*, *adj* blank, expressionless; foolish, empty-headed; empty. — *n* **vacū'ity** or **vac'uousness.** — *adv* **vac'uously.** [L. *vacuus*, empty.]

vacuum *vak'ū-əm*, *n* a space completely empty of matter; a space from which air has been excluded as completely as possible; a space containing gas at a pressure lower than atmospheric; an emptiness or void left where something has ceased or been removed; a condition of isolation or insulation from outside forces and influences; a vacuum cleaner: — *pl* **vac'uums** or (not of the cleaner) **vac'ua** (*-ū-ə*). — *vt* and *vi* to clean with a vacuum cleaner. — *adj* relating to a vacuum; containing a vacuum; operating by means of a vacuum. — **vacuum brake** a brake in the working of which suction by vacuum(s) supplements the pressure applied by the operator, esp. a braking system of this type applied simultaneously throughout a train. — *vt* and *vi* **vac'ūum-clean.** — **vacuum cleaner** an apparatus for removing dust by suction; **vacuum flask** a flask for keeping liquids hot or cold by means of a vacuum lining. — *adj* **vac'uum-packed** sealed in a container from which most of the air has been removed. — **vacuum pump** a general term for apparatus which displaces gas against a pressure; **vacuum tube** a sealed glass tube in which a vacuum has been made, e.g. a thermionic valve. [L., neut. of *vacuus*, empty.]

VAD *abbrev* for Voluntary Aid Detachment, an organisation of British volunteer nurses who served in the First World War.

vade-mecum *vä'di-mā'kəm*, *n* a useful handbook that one carries about with one for constant reference, a pocket companion. [L. *vāde*, go, *mēcum*, with me.]

vagabond *vag'ə-bond*, *n* a person who wanders without settled habitation; an idle wanderer; a vagrant; a scamp, a rascal (*humorously*). — *adj* roving, wandering. — *n* **vag'abondism.** [Fr. *vagabond* and L. *vagābundus* — *vagārī*, to wander.]

vagal. See under **vagus.**

vagary *vā'gə-ri* or *və-gā'ri*, *n* a devious excursion; a digression or rambling; a freakish prank; a caprice: — *pl* **vagaries.** [App. L. *vagārī*, to wander.]

vagi. See **vagus.**

vagina *və-jī'nə*, *n* the genital passage in women and other female mammals, running from the neck of the womb to the external opening contained within the vulva; a sheathing leaf-base: — *pl* **vagī'nas** or **vagī'nae** (*-nē*). — *adj* **vagī'nal** (or *vaj'i-nəl*). — *adv* **vagī'nally.** — *adj* **vag'inate** (*-nāt* or *-nət*) or **vag'inated** (*bot*) having a sheath. — *n* **vaginis'mus** spasmodic contraction of the vagina. — *n* **vaginī'tis** inflammation of the vagina. [L. *vāgīna*, sheath.]

vagrant *vā'grənt*, *adj* wandering, roving, travelling from place to place; having no settled dwelling; uncertain, erratic; (of plants) of straggling growth. — *n* a person who has no settled home or work; a tramp, wanderer. — *n* **vā'grancy.** [Perh. A.Fr. *wakerant*, roaming, assimilated to L. *vagārī*, to wander.]

vague *vāg*, *adj* lacking precision or sharpness of definition; indistinct; blurred; uncertain, indefinite; addicted to, or showing, haziness of thought. — *adv* **vague'ly.** — *n* **vague'ness.** [L. *vagus*, wandering — *vagārī*, to wander.]

vagus *vā'gus*, (*anat*) *n* the tenth cranial nerve, concerned in regulating heartbeat, rhythm of breathing, etc.: — *pl* **vā'gi** (*-jī*). — *adj* **vā'gal** (*-gəl*). [L., wandering.]

vahine *vä-hē'nä*, *n* in Polynesia, a woman or wife. [Tahitian.]

vain *vān*, *adj* without real worth; futile; unavailing; thoughtless; empty-headed; pettily self-complacent; priding oneself inordinately on one's appearance, accomplishments or possessions; conceited. — *adv* **vain'ly**. — *n* **vain'ness** vanity. — **in vain** fruitlessly; to no end; **take in vain** to utter with levity. [Fr. *vain* — L. *vānus*, empty.]

vainglory *vān-glō'ri*, *n* vain or empty pride in one's own performances; idle boastfulness. — *adj* **vainglo'rious**. — *adv* **vainglo'riously**. — *n* **vainglo'riousness**. [O.Fr. *vaine gloire*.]

vair *vār*, *n* a kind of squirrel fur, bluish-grey and white. [O.Fr., — L. *varius*, variegated.]

Vaisya *vīs'yä* or *vīsh'yä*, or **Vaishya** *vīsh'yä*, *n* a member of the third caste among the Hindus, which includes the merchants, etc. [Sans. *vaiçya* — *viç*, settler.]

valance *val'əns*, *n* a hanging border of drapery, attached e.g. along the sides of a bed; a pelmet (*US*). — *adj* **val'anced** trimmed with a valance. [Poss. A.Fr. *valer*, to descend.]

vale *vāl*, *n* a valley (chiefly *poetic*); the world (as in *vale of tears*, *earthly vale*). [Fr. *val* — L. *vallis*, a vale.]

valediction *val-i-dik'shən*, (*formal*) *n* the act of bidding farewell; a farewell. — *adj* **valedic'tory** saying farewell; in the nature of a farewell; of or for a leave-taking. — *n* (*US*) a farewell oration spoken by a graduand. [L. *valē*, farewell, *dīcĕre*, *dictum*, to say.]

valence *vā'ləns*, (*chem*) *n* valency (esp. *US*); chemical bond. [L. *valentia*, capacity, strength.]

valency *vā'lən-si*, *n* the combining power of an atom measured by the number of hydrogen (or equivalent) atoms that it can combine with or displace (*chem*); the capacity (expressed numerically) of a verb to combine dependent elements within a sentence (*linguis*). — **valency electrons** those of the outermost shell of the atom, largely responsible for its chemical and physical properties. [L. *valentia*, strength, capacity.]

Valenciennes *vä-lã-syen'*, *n* a kind of lace made at *Valenciennes* in France.

-valent *-vā'lənt* or *-və-lənt*, (*chem*) *combining form* meaning of a stated valency, as in *trivalent*. [L. *valens*, *-entis*, pres. p. of *valēre*, to be strong.]

valentine *val'ən-tīn*, *n* a person chosen on St Valentine's day, in mock betrothal; an amatory or humorous card, message, or a gift, sent for that day. [L. *valentīnus*, the name of two saints.]

valerian *və-lē'ri-ən*, *n* the plant allheal or other plant of the genus *Valeriana*, related to the teasels; its rhizome and roots, which have medicinal properties. — **valeric (-er'ik) acid** a fatty acid. [Perh. from someone called *Valerius*, or from L. *valēre*, to be strong.]

valet *val'it* or *val'ā*, *n* a male servant who attends to a gentleman's clothes, dressing, grooming, etc. — *vt* (*val'it*) to serve or attend to as valet. — *n* **val'eting**. — **valet de chambre** (*val'ā də shābr'*) an attendant; a footman. [Fr.]

valeta. See **veleta**.

valetudinarian *val-i-tū-di-nā'ri-ən*, *adj* sickly, weak; anxious and fanciful about one's own health. — *n* a valetudinarian person. — *n* **valetūdinā'rianism**. — *adj* and *n* **valetū'dinary** (*-nə-ri*) valetudinarian. [L. *valētūdinārius* — *valētūdō*, state of health, to be strong.]

valgus *val'gəs*, (*pathol*) *adj* displaced from normal alignment so as to deviate away from the midline of the body. — *n* a valgus condition. [L., (app.) knock-kneed.]

Valhalla *val-hal'ə*, (*Scand mythol*) *n* the palace of bliss for the souls of slain heroes. [O.N. *Valhöll* — *valr*, the slain, *höll*, hall.]

valiant *val'yənt*, *adj* brave; actively courageous; heroic. — *adv* **val'iantly**. [Fr. *vaillant* — L. *valēre*, to be strong.]

valid *val'id*, *adj* sound; legally adequate or efficacious; fulfilling all the necessary conditions; (in logic) well based, applicable. — *vt* **val'idate** to make valid; to ratify; to confirm, substantiate, verify. — *n* **validā'tion** the act of validating; the checking of the correctness of input data (*comput*). — *n* **valid'ity**. — *adv* **val'idly**. — *n* **val'idness**. [L. *validus* — *valēre*, to be strong.]

valine *vā'lēn*, *n* an amino-acid, $C_5H_{11}NO_2$, essential to health and growth in humans and vertebrate animals. [From *val*eric acid.]

valise *və-lēz'* or in U.S. *-lēs'*, *n* an overnight travelling bag; a kit-bag. [Fr.]

Valium® *val'i-əm*, *n* a proprietary name for diazepam, a tranquilliser.

Valkyrie *val'kir-i* or *val-kē'ri*, (*Scand mythol*) *n* any one of the minor goddesses who conducted the slain from the battlefield to Valhalla: — *pl* **Valkyries**. [O.N. *Valkyrja* — *valr*, the slain, and the root of *kjōsa*, to choose.]

valley *val'i*, *n* an elongated hollow between hills; a stretch of country watered by a river; a trough between ridges; the hollow of an M-shaped roof: — *pl* **vall'eys**. [O.Fr. *valee* — *val* — L. *vallis*, a valley.]

vallum *val'əm*, (*archaeol*) *n* a rampart; a wall of sods, earth, or other material, esp. of that thrown up from a ditch. [L.]

valonia *və-lō'ni-ə*, *n* a tanning material, acorns of a Levantine oak (valonia oak, *Quercus aegilops*) or similar species. [It. *vallonea* — Gr. *balanos*, an acorn.]

valorise or **-ize** *val'ə-rīz*, *vt* to fix or stabilise the price of, esp. by a policy imposed by a government or controlling body. — *n* **valorisā'tion** or **-z-**. [Back-formation from (Fr.) *valorisation*.]

valour or in U.S. **valor** *val'ər*, *n* intrepidity; courage; bravery. — *adj* **val'orous** intrepid; courageous. — *adv* **val'orously**. [O.Fr. *valour* — L.L. *valor*, *-ōris* — L. *valēre*, to be strong.]

valse *väls*, *n* a waltz. [Fr.]

value *val'ū*, *n* worth; a fair equivalent; intrinsic worth or goodness; recognition of such worth; that which renders anything useful or estimable; the degree of this quality; relative worth; high worth; esteem; efficacy; excellence; price; precise meaning; relative duration (*mus*); relation with reference to light and shade (*painting*); the special determination of a quantity (*math*); the exact amount of a variable quantity in a particular case; the sound represented by a written symbol (*phon*); (in *pl*) moral principles, standards, etc. — *vt* to estimate the worth of; to rate at a price; to esteem; to prize. — *adj* **val'uable** having value or worth; of high value. — *n* (usu. in *pl*) an article of value, such as a watch or a piece of jewellery. — *n* **val'uableness**. — *adv* **val'uably**. — *vt* **val'uate** (*US*) to appraise, value or evaluate. — *n* **valuā'tion** estimation of value. — *adj* **valuā'tional**. — *n* **val'uātor** a person who makes valuations, an appraiser. — *adj* **val'ued** that has a value assigned, priced; highly esteemed, prized. — *adj* **val'ueless**. — *n* **val'uer** a valuator. — **valuation roll** a list of properties and their assessed values for local taxation purposes; **value added** the difference between the overall cost of a manufacturing or marketing process and the final value of the goods; **value-added tax** a tax on the rise in value of a product due to the manufacturing and marketing processes (abbrev. **VAT**); **value judgment** a personal estimate of merit in a particular respect. [O.Fr. *value*, fem. past p. of *valoir*, to be worth — L. *valēre*.]

valuta *vä-lū'tə* or *-lōō'tə*, *n* the comparative value of a currency; a standard of money. [It.]

valve *valv*, *n* a single piece forming part or the whole of a shell; one of the parts of a dry fruit separating in dehiscence; a structure or device that regulates flow or passage or allows it in one direction only; a rectifier (*electr*); (*loosely*) a thermionic valve used in wireless apparatus as rectifier, amplifier, oscillator or otherwise. — *adj* **val'vate** with or having a valve or valves; meeting at the edges without overlapping (*bot*). — *adj* **valved**. [L. *valva*, a folding-door.]

vamoose *və-mōōs'*, (*slang*) *vi* to clear off, make a swift exit or departure. [Sp. *vamos*, let us go.]

vamp[1] *vamp*, *n* the part of a boot or shoe covering the front of the foot; anything patched up; a simple and uninspired improvised accompaniment (*mus*). — *vt* to provide with a vamp; to repair with a new vamp; to patch up; to give a new face to; to improvise inartistically (*mus*). — *vi* to improvise crude accompaniments. — *n* **vam'per**. — *n* and *adj* **vam'ping**. [O.Fr. *avanpié* — *avan*, before, *pié* — *L. pēs, pedis*, foot.]

vamp[2] *vamp*, (*colloq*) *n* a woman who, with the advantage of sexual attraction, seduces and feeds off men. [Shortening of **vampire**.]

vampire *vam'pīr*, *n* in eastern European folklore, a dead person who leaves the grave to prey upon the living; a bloodsucker, a relentless extortionate parasite or blackmailer; a vampire bat. — *adj* **vampir'ic**. — *n* **vam'pirism** belief in human vampires; the actions of a vampire. — **vampire bat** a Central and South American bat (e.g. of genus *Desmodus*) that pierces the flesh of other animals with its sharp canine and incisor teeth, and sucks their blood; applied to various bats wrongly supposed to be bloodsuckers. [Some Slav. languages have *vampir*.]

van[1] *van*, *n* a shortened form of **vanguard** (often *fig*, as in *in the van of fashion*).

van[2] *van*, *n* a shovel for testing ore; a test of ore by washing on a shovel. — *vt* to test with a van. — *n* **vann'er**. [Archaic senses, a wing, a winnowing fan — Southern form of **fan**.]

van[3] *van*, *n* a light vehicle used in transporting goods; a railway carriage or compartment for luggage, the guard, etc.; a caravan. [Orig. a large covered wagon; an abbreviated form of **caravan**.]

van[4] *van*, (*lawn tennis*) short for **advantage**.

vanadium *və-nā'di-əm*, *n* a silvery metallic element (symbol **V**; atomic no. 23). [Named by a Swedish chemist Sefström from O.N. *Vana-dīs*, the goddess Freyja.]

Van Allen radiation belts *van al'ən rā-di-ā'shən belts*, *npl* zones of intense particle radiation surrounding the earth at a distance of above 1200 miles (1930 km.) from it. [J.A. *Van Allen*, American physicist, b. 1914.]

V and A (*colloq*) *abbrev* for the *V*ictoria *and A*lbert Museum, London.

vandal *van'dəl*, *n* a person who wantonly damages property; a person who destroys what is beautiful; (with *cap*) one of a fierce people from north-eastern Germany who overran Gaul, Spain and North Africa, sacked Rome in 455, destroyed churches, etc. — *vt* **van'dalise** or **-ize** to inflict wilful and senseless damage on (property, etc.). — *n* **van'dalism**.

vandyke or **Vandyke** *van-dīk'* or *van'dīk*, *n* a broad collar with the edge cut into deep points (also **vandyke collar**); a short pointed beard (also **Vandyke beard**). — *vt* and *vi* to notch or zigzag. — *adj* **vandyked'**. — **vandyke brown** a deep brown colour. [Sir Antony *Van Dyke* (or *Vandyke*), 17th-cent. painter, of whose portraits these features were characteristic.]

vane *vān*, *n* a weathercock or revolving plate serving to show how the wind blows; a blade of a windmill, propeller, revolving fan, etc.; a fin on a bomb or a paravane; a sight on an observing or surveying instrument; the web of a feather. — *adj* **vaned** having a vane or vanes. — *adj* **vane'less**. [Southern form of *fane*, an obs. word for a flag or a weather-cock.]

vang *vang*, (*naut*) *n* a guy rope to steady a gaff. [A form of **fang**.]

vanguard *van'gärd*, *n* the foremost part of an army, etc.; the forefront; those who lead the way or anticipate progress. — *n* **van'guardism** the condition of being or practice of positioning oneself as or within the vanguard of a movement (esp. political). [Fr. *avant-garde* — *avant*, before, *garde*, guard.]

vanilla *və-nil'ə*, *n* a flavouring substance obtained from the pods of a Mexican climbing orchid; the plant yielding it. — *n* **vanill'in** its aromatic principle ($C_8H_8O_3$). [Sp. *vainilla* — *vaina* — L. *vāgīna*, a sheath.]

vanish *van'ish*, *vi* to disappear; to fade out; to cease to exist; to become zero (*math*). — *vt* to cause to disappear. — **vanishing cream** cosmetic cream that, when rubbed over the skin, virtually disappears; **vanishing point** the point at which parallel lines seen in perspective converge; the verge of disappearance of anything. [Aphetic for *evanish*, to vanish (*old* or *poetic*) — L. *ex*, from, *vānus*, empty.]

vanitas *van'it-as*, *n* a 17th-century Dutch still life painting in which motifs such as the hourglass, skull or candle feature as reminders of the transience and vanity of human life and aspirations; any painting of this genre. [L., vanity.]

Vanitory® *van'i-tə-ri*, *n* (often without *cap*) a unit consisting of a wash-hand basin and a dressing-table (also **vanitory unit**).

vanity *van'i-ti*, *n* the priding of oneself on one's personal appearance, accomplishments, etc., conceit; extravagance or ostentation; folly or futility; something vain. — **vanity bag, box** or **case** a container for cosmetics and a small mirror, etc., carried by a woman; **vanity publishing** publication by the author, at his or her own expense; **vanity unit** a Vanitory unit or similar piece of furniture. [Fr. *vanité* — L. *vānitās, -ātis*; see **vain**.]

vanner. See under **van**[2].

vanquish *vang'kwish*, *vt* to conquer; to overcome. — *vi* to be victor. — *adj* **vanq'uishable**. — *n* **vanq'uisher**. [A.Fr. *venquir*, *venquiss-* — L. *vincĕre*, to conquer.]

vantage *vän'tij*, *n* advantage. — **vantage ground** or **point** a favourable or commanding position. [A.Fr. *vantage*; cf. **advantage**.]

vapid *vap'id*, *adj* insipid; dull; flat. — *n* **vapid'ity**. — *adv* **vap'idly**. — *n* **vap'idness**. [L. *vapidus*.]

vaporetto *va-po-ret'tō*, *n* a small steamship that plies the canals in Venice: — *pl* **vaporett'os** or **vaporett'i** (*-ē*). [It., — *vapore*, a steamboat.]

vapour or in U.S. **vapor** *vā'pər*, *n* a substance in the form of a mist, fume or smoke, esp. one coming off from a solid or liquid; a gas below its critical temperature, liquefiable by pressure; water in the atmosphere; (in *pl*) exhalations supposed to arise in the stomach or elsewhere in the body, affecting the health (*old med*); (in *pl*; usu. with **the**) low spirits, boredom, nervous disorder. — *vi* to pass off in vapour, evaporate; to brag, talk idly. — *vt* to make to pass into vapour. — *n* **vāporim'eter** an instrument for measuring vapour pressure or vapour. — *adj* **vāporīs'able** or **-z-**. — *n* **vāporisā'tion** or **-z-**. — *vt* **vā'porise** or **-ize** to convert into vapour. — *vi* to become vapour, evaporate; to destroy by disintegration into vapour. — *n* **vā'porīser** or **-z-** an apparatus for discharging liquid in a fine spray. — *n* **vāporos'ity**. — *adj* **vā'porous** of, in the form of, like or full of vapour; vain; insubstantial; flimsy; vainly fanciful. — *adv* **vā'porously**. — *n* **vā'porousness**. — *adj* **vā'pourish** vapoury. — *n* **vā'pourishness**. — *adj* **vā'poury**. — **vapour density** the density of a gas or vapour relative to that of hydrogen at the same temperature and pressure; **vapour trail** a white trail of condensed vapour left in the sky by aircraft flying at high altitude; **vā'pourware** (*comput*; *facetious*) software or hardware heralded but not yet extant in purchasable form. [L. *vapor*, *-ōris*.]

vaquero *vä-kā'rō*, (*US*) *n* a herdsman: — *pl* **vaque'ros**. [Sp., — L. *vacca*, a cow.]

varactor *var-ak'tər*, (*electronics*) *n* a two-electrode semiconductor device in which capacitance varies with voltage. [*var*ying re*actor*.]

variable *vā'ri-ə-bl*, *adj* that may be varied; changeable; tending or liable to change or vary; showing variations; unsteady; quantitatively indeterminate (*math*); changing in brightness (*astron*). — *n* a quantity subject to continual increase or decrease (*math*); a quantity which may have an infinite number of values in the same expression (*math*); a shifting wind; a variable star. — *n* **variabil'ity** or **vā'riableness**. — *adv* **vā'riably**. — **variable costs** costs which, unlike fixed costs (q.v.), vary with the level of production; **variable-geometry aeroplane** an aeroplane of varying wing, swept back for flight, but at right angles for take-off and landing, so removing the need for long runways and high landing-speeds; **variable interest rate** a rate of interest on a loan, etc., that varies with the market rate of interest. [L. *variābilis*, changeable — *variāre*, to diversify.]

variance *vā'ri-əns*, *n* deviation; discrepancy; disagreement; the average of the squares of the deviations of a number of observations from the mean (*statistics*). — *n* **vā'riant** a different form of the same thing, esp. a word; a different reading; a specimen slightly differing from the type. — *adj* diversified; different; diverging from type. — **at variance** in dissension, dispute or disagreement (with *with*); not in accordance (with *with*). [O.Fr., — L. *variāre*, to diversify.]

variate *vā'ri-ət*, *n* any one of the observed values of a quantity; a variant; the variable quantity which is being studied (*statistics*). — *n* **variā'tion** a varying; a change; continuous change; difference in structure or character among offspring of the same parents or among members of a related group; departure from the mean or usual character; the extent to which a thing varies; a variant; declination of the compass; an inequality in the moon's motion discovered by Tycho Brahe; a change in the elements of an orbit by the disturbing force of another body; transformation of a theme by means of new figures in counterpoint, florid treatment, changes in tempo, key, etc. (*mus*); a solo dance (*ballet*). — *adj* **variā'tional**. [L. *variātus*, past p. of *variāre*, to diversify.]

varicella *var-i-sel'ə*, (*med*) *n* chickenpox. [Irreg. dimin. of **variola**.]

varices. Pl. of **varix**.

varicocele *var'i-kə-sēl*, (*pathol*) *n* an enlargement of the veins of the spermatic cord, or of those of the scrotum. [L. *varix*, *-icis*, a varicose vein, and Gr. *kēlē*, tumour.]

varicoloured *vā'ri-kul-ərd*, *adj* diversified in colour. [L. *varius*, various, *color*, colour.]

varicose *var'i-kōs*, *adj* (of superficial veins, esp. those of the leg) twisted and dilated so that they produce raised knots on the surface of the skin. — *n* **varicosity** (*-kos'*) the state of being varicose; a distended place. — **varicose ulcer** an ulcerating knot of varicose veins. [L. *varicōsus* — *varix*, varicose vein.]

varicotomy. See under **varix**.

varied. See under **vary**.

variegate *vā'ri-ə-gāt*, *vt* to diversify, esp. with colours in patches. — *adj* **vā'riegated**. — *n* **vāriegā'tion**. — *n* **vā'riegātor**. [L. *variegātus* — *varius*.]

variety *və-rī'ə-ti*, *n* the quality of being various; diversity; difference; many-sidedness, versatility; a varied group or collection; a kind differing in minor features or points; a race not sufficiently distinct to be counted a species, a subspecies; an artificially bred strain; music-hall entertainment, a succession of varied turns: — *pl* **varī'eties**. — *adj* of, for, or performing in, music-hall entertainment. — **variety meat** offal (*US*); processed meat, sausage, etc. (orig. *US*). [L. *varietās*, *-ātis* — *varius*, various.]

variform *var'i-förm*, *adj* of various forms. [L. *varius*, and sfx. *-form*.]

variola *və-rī'ə-lə*, (*med*) *n* smallpox. — *adj* **varī'olar**. [L.L. *variola*, pustule, pox — L. *varius*, various, spotted.]

variometer *vā-ri-om'ə-tər*, *n* an instrument for comparing magnetic forces; a variable inductor composed of two connected coils, one rotating inside the other (*electronics*); an instrument that indicates by a needle the rate of climb and descent (*aeronautics*).

variorum *vā-ri-ö'rəm*, *adj* (of an edition of a text) including the notes of earlier commentators or editors, or variant readings. — *n* a variorum edition. [L. *cum notis variorum*, with the notes of various (scholars).]

various *vā'ri-əs*, *adj* varied, different; several; unlike each other; changeable; uncertain; variegated. — *adv* **vā'riously**. — *n* **vā'riousness**. [L. *varius*; see **vary**.]

varistor *və-ris'tər*, *n* a two-electrode semiconductor used to short-circuit transient high voltages in delicate electronic devices. [*vari*able resi*stor*.]

varix *vā'riks* or *var'iks*, *n* an abnormally dilated, lengthened, and tortuous vein, artery or lymphatic vessel (*med*); dilatation of a blood vessel (*med*); a ridge marking a former position of the mouth of a shell (*zool*): — *pl* **varices** (*vā'ri-sēz* or *var'*). — *n* **varicot'omy** the surgical removal of a varix or a varicose vein. [L. *varix*, *-icis*, a varicose vein.]

var. lect. *abbrev* for *varia lectio* (L.), a variant reading.

varlet *vär'lit*, (*hist*) *n* a rascal, rogue, knave, attendant or menial. [O.Fr., related to **valet**.]

varmint *vär'mint*, (*dialect*, esp. *US*; or *slang*) *n* a troublesome or mischievous animal or person. [Variant of **vermin**.]

varna *vär'nə* or *vur'nə*, *n* any of the four great Hindu castes. [Sans., class.]

varnish *vär'nish*, *n* a resinous solution used to coat and give a hard, glossy, transparent surface to woodwork, paintings, etc.; any of several other preparations for giving a glossy surface to something, e.g. *nail varnish*; a gloss or glaze; a superficial lustre, a surface showiness, esp. with the implication of underlying shoddiness or inadequacy; an application of varnish. — *vt* to coat with varnish; to give a superficial lustre or sheen to. — *n* **var'nisher**. — *n* **var'nishing**. [Fr. *vernis*; prob. — Med. L. *veronix*, sandarach.]

varsity *vär'si-ti*, (*colloq*; usu. of *sport*) *n* and *adj* university.

varus *vā'rəs*, (*pathol*) *adj* displaced from normal alignment so as to deviate towards the midline of the body. — *n* a varus condition. [L. *vārus*, bent, or (app.) bow-legged.]

varve *värv*, (*geol*) *n* a seasonal deposit of clay in still water, of service in fixing Ice Age chronology. [Sw. *varv*, layer.]

vary *vā'ri*, *vt* to make different; to diversify, modify; to change to something else; to make of different kinds. — *vi* to alter or be altered; to be or become different; to change in succession; to deviate; to disagree; to be subject to continuous increase or decrease (*math*): — *pr p* **vā'rying**; *pa t* and *pa p* **vā'ried**. — *n* a change. — *adj* **vā'ried**. — *n* and *adj* **vā'rying**. [M.E. — (O.)Fr. *varier* or L. *variāre* — L. *varius*, various.]

vas *vas*, (*anat*) *n* a vessel, tube or duct carrying liquid: — *pl* **vasa** (*vā'sə*). — *adj* **vā'sal**. — **vas deferens** (*def'ə-renz*) the spermatic duct, carrying spermatozoa from the testis to the ejaculatory duct: — *pl* **vasa deferentia** (*def-ə-ren'shi-ə*). [L. *vās*, *vāsis*, a vessel.]

vascular *vas'kū-lər*, *adj* of, relating to, composed of or provided with vessels conveying fluids, e.g. blood, sap. — **vascular bundle** a strand of conducting tissue in the higher plants, composed of xylem, phloem and cambium; **vascular disease** any of various diseased conditions of the blood vessels. [L. *vāsculum*, dimin. of *vās*, a vessel.]

vasculum *vas'kū-ləm*, *n* a botanist's collecting case: — *pl* **vas'culums** or **vas'cula**. [L. *vāsculum*, dimin. of *vās*, a vessel.]

vase *väz* or in U.S. *vās* or *vāz*, *n* a vessel, usually tall, round in section, and ornamental, used esp. for holding cut flowers. [Fr., — L. *vās*.]

vasectomy *və-sek'tə-mi*, *n* the excision of part or the whole of the vas deferens, esp. in order to produce sterility. [L. *vās*, *vāsis*, a vessel, Gr. *ek*, out, *tomeē*, a cut.]

Vaseline® *vas'i-lēn*, *n* an ointment or lubricant consisting mainly of petroleum jelly. [Coined from Ger. *Wasser*, water, and Gr. *elaion*, oil.]

vasiform *vā'zi-förm*, *adj* duct-shaped, tubular; vase-shaped. [L. *vās*, *vāsis*, a vessel, and sfx. *-form*.]

vaso- *vā-zō-* or *-zə-*, (*med*) *combining form* denoting a duct or vessel. — *n* **vasoconstric'tion** narrowing of a blood-vessel. — *n* **vasoconstric'tor** a nerve or drug that causes vasoconstriction. — *adj* **vasoconstric'tory**. — *n* **vasodilatā'tion** expansion of a blood-vessel. — *n* **vasodilā'tor** a nerve or drug that causes vasodilatation. — *adj* **vasodilā'tory**. — *n* **vasomō'tor** causing constriction or expansion of blood-vessels. [L. *vās*, *vāsis*, vessel.]

vassal *vas'əl*, *n* a dependant; a person or nation subject to another; a person holding land from his feudal superior, in return for homage and loyalty (*hist*). — *adj* in the relation or state of a vassal; subordinate. — *n* **vass'alage** the state of being a vassal; dependence. [Fr., — L.L. *vassallus*, servant — Celtic.]

vast *väst*, *adj* boundless; huge; exceedingly great; considerable, appreciable (*colloq*). — *n* an immense tract, a boundless or empty expanse of space or time. — *adv* **vast'ly**. — *n* **vast'ness**. [L. *vastus*, waste, desolate, huge; cf. **waste**.]

Vat or **VAT** *vat* or *vē-ā-tē'*, *n* a colloquial acronym for *v*alue-*a*dded *t*ax. — *n* **Vatman** or **VATman** (*vat'*) an employee of the Customs and Excise Board responsible for administering, assessing, collecting, etc. value-added tax.

vat *vat*, *n* a large vessel or tank, esp. for fermentation, dyeing or tanning; a liquor containing a reduced, colourless, soluble form of insoluble dye (**vat dye**), in which textiles are soaked, afterwards to take up the colour through oxidation when exposed to the air. — *vt* to put, or treat, in a vat: — *pr p* **vatt'ing**; *pa p* **vatt'ed**. — *n* **vatt'er**. [O.E. *fæt*.]

Vatican *vat'i-kən*, *n* a collection of buildings on the Vatican Hill in Rome, including one of the pope's palaces; the papal authority. — *n* **Vat'icanism** the system of theology and ecclesiastical government based on absolute papal authority, ultramontanism. — *n* **Vat'icanist**. — **Vatican City** a small area on the Vatican Hill set up as an independent papal state in 1929; **Vatican Council** the council that met in St Peter's (1869) and proclaimed papal infallibility (1870), or the similar council (**Vatican II**) held between 1962 and 1965. [L. *Mōns Vāticānus*, the Vatican Hill.]

vatu *vä'to͞o*, *n* the standard monetary unit of Vanuatu (100 centimes).

vaudeville *vō'də-vil* or *vö'də-vil*, *n* variety entertainment; a play interspersed with dances and songs incidentally introduced and usually comic; orig. a popular song with topical allusions. — Also *adj*. — *n* and *adj* **vaudevill'ian**. [From *vau* (*val*) *de Vire*, the valley of the Vire, in Normandy, where such songs were composed in the 15th century.]

vault[1] *völt*, *n* an arched roof or ceiling; a chamber with an arched roof or ceiling, esp. underground; a cellar; a wine cellar; a burial-chamber; a cavern; anything vaultlike such as the *vault of heaven*, or the *cranial vault*, the dome of the skull. — *vt* to shape as a vault; to roof with an arch; to form vaults in. — *vi* to curve in a vault. — *adj* **vaul'ted** arched; concave overhead; covered with an arch or vault. — *n* **vaul'ting** vaulted work. [O.Fr. voute — L. *voluūta* — *volvěre*, *volūtum*, to roll.]

vault[2] *völt*, *vi* to leap, esp. by springing initially on to one or both hands, or by using a pole, to get extra height. — *vt* to spring or leap over, esp. by this means. — *n* an act of vaulting. — *n* **vaul'ter**. — *n* **vaul'ting**. — *adj* relating to or for vaulting; (of e.g. ambition) inordinate, overweening. — **vaul'ting-horse** a wooden horselike apparatus for vaulting over as a gymnastic exercise. [Fr. *volter*, to turn.]

vaunt *vönt*, also in U.S. *vänt*, *vi* to boast; to behave boastfully or exultingly. — *vt* to boast; to boast of. — *n* a boast. — *adj* **vaun'ted**. — *n* **vaun'ter**. — *n* and *adj* **vaun'ting**. — *adv* **vaun'tingly**. [O.Fr. *vanter* — L.L. *vānitāre*, to boast — L. *vānus*, vain.]

vavasour *vav'ə-so͞or*, *n* (in feudal society) a knight, noble, etc., with vassals under him, who is himself the vassal of a greater noble. — *n* **vav'asory** the tenure or the lands of a vavasour. [O.Fr., possibly — L.L. *vassus vassōrum*, vassal of vassals — *vassus*, vassal.]

vb *abbrev* for verb.

VC *abbrev* for Victoria Cross.

VCR *abbrev* for video cassette recorder.

VD *abbrev* for venereal disease.

VDQS *abbrev* for *vins délimités de qualité supérieure* (Fr.), wines of superior quality from approved vineyards.

VDU *abbrev* for visual display unit.

've *v*. A shortened form of **have**.

veal *vēl*, *n* calf's flesh as food. — *adj* of veal. [O.Fr. *veël* — L. *vitellus*, dimin. of *vitulus*, a calf.]

Vectian *vek'tiən*, (*geol*) *adj* of or relating to the Isle of Wight or the specific geological formation of which it is a part. [L. *Vectis*, the Isle of Wight.]

vector *vek'tər*, *n* a directed quantity, as a straight line in space, involving both its direction and magnitude (*math*); a carrier of disease or infection; the course of an aircraft, missile, etc.; a one-dimensional sequence of elements within a matrix (*comput*); such a sequence having a single identifying code or symbol, esp. one acting as an intermediate address (q.v.) (*comput*). — *vt* to direct, esp. from the ground, (an aircraft in flight) to the required destination. — *adj* **vecto'rial**. — *n* **vectorisā'tion** or **-z-**. — *vt* **vec'torise** or **-ize** (*math* and *comput*). [L. *vector*, *-ōris*, bearer, carrier — *vehěre*, *vectum*, to convey.]

Veda *vā'də* or *vē'də*, *n* any one of, or all of, four ancient holy books of the Hindus: — *pl* **Ve'das**. — *adj* **Ve'dic**. — *n* **Ve'dism**. — *n* **Ve'dist** a person learned in the Vedas. [Sans. *veda*, knowledge.]

vedalia *vi-dā'li-ə*, *n* an orig. Australian ladybird introduced elsewhere to control insect pests.

Vedanta *vi-dan'tə*, *n* a system of Hindu philosophy founded on the Vedas. — *adj* **Vedan'tic**. [Sanskrit, — *Veda*, and *anta*, end.]

VE day *vē-ē' dā*, *abbrev* for Victory in Europe day (8 May, the date of the Allied victory in 1945).

Vedda *ved'ə*, *n* (a member of) an aboriginal people of Sri Lanka. — *adj* **Vedd'oid** of, pertaining to or resembling the Veddas; of a S. Asian race, dark-skinned and curly-haired, to which the Veddas belong.

vedette *vi-det'*, *n* a mounted sentry stationed to watch an enemy; a small vessel (**vedette boat**) for a similar purpose. [Fr., — It. *vedetta* — *vedere* — L. *vidēre*, to see.]

Vedic, Vedism, Vedist. See under **Veda**.

veduta *ve-do͞o'tə*, or in It. *-tä*, *n* a panoramic view of a town, etc.: — *pl* **vedu'te** (*-tā*). [It., a view.]

vee *vē*, *n* the twenty-second letter of the alphabet (V, v); a mark or object shaped or angled like a V. — **vee-** (in combination; also **V-** (q.v.)), shaped like the letter V.

veer *vēr, vi* to change direction, esp. (of the wind) clockwise; to shift round in direction or in mental attitude; to change course, esp. away from the wind (*naut*). — *vt* to turn, shift; to turn away from the wind. — *n* a shifting round. — *n* and *adj* **veer'ing**. [Fr. *virer*.]

veg *vej,* (*colloq*) *n* short for a vegetable or vegetables.

Vegan *vē'gən, n* (often without *cap*) one of a sect of vegetarians using no animal produce at all. — Also *adj*. — *n* **Vē'ganism** (also without *cap*).

vegeburger *vej'i-bûr-gər, n* a hamburger-like creation prepared from vegetables rather than meat products. [*vege*table and ham*burger*.]

vegetable *vej'i-tə-bl, n* an organism belonging to the great division distinguished from animals by being unable to deal with solid food, commonly but not necessarily fixed in position — a plant; a plant or part of one used for food, other than those reckoned fruits; a person whose capabilities are so low, esp. because of damage to the brain, that he or she is scarcely human (*colloq*); a dull, uninteresting person (*colloq derog*). — *adj* of, for, derived from, composed of or of the nature of vegetables. — **vegetable butter** any of several butter-like vegetable fats; **vegetable ivory** see **ivory; vegetable kingdom** that division of natural objects which consists of vegetables or plants; **vegetable marrow** a variety of pumpkin cooked as a vegetable; **vegetable oil** any of various oils extracted from plants, used e.g. in cooking; **vegetable oyster** salsify; **vegetable wax** a wax secreted by various plants that protects their surface from moisture loss. [L. *vegetābilis*, animating, *vegetāre*, to quicken, *vegetus*, lively; cf. **vigour**.]

vegetal *vej'i-təl, adj* belonging to or characteristic of vegetables or plants in general; vegetative; of a level of life below the sensitive. [Med. L. *vegetālis* — L. *vegetāre*, to animate.]

vegetarian *vej-i-tā'riən, n* a person who lives wholly on vegetable food, with or without animal foods such as dairy products, honey, and eggs. — Also *adj*. — *n* **vegetā'rianism** the theory or practice of a vegetarian. [*vege*table and sfx. *-arian*.]

vegetate *vej'i-tāt, vi* to grow or live as, or like, a vegetable; to increase vegetatively; to live an inactive, almost purely physical, or dull life. — *n* and *adj* **veg'etāting**. — *n* **vegetā'tion** the process of vegetating; vegetable growth; growing plants in mass. — *adj* **veg'etātive** growing, as plants; producing growth in plants; concerned with the life of the individual rather than of the race (*biol*); by means of vegetative organs, not special reproductive structures (*biol*); relating to unconscious or involuntary bodily functions as resembling the process of vegetable growth (*biol*); without intellectual activity, unprogressive. — *adv* **veg'etātively**. — *n* **veg'etātiveness**. — **vegetative nervous system** the nervous system regulating involuntary bodily activity, such as the secretion of the glands, the beating of the heart, etc. [L. *vegetāre*, to animate, quicken, enliven.]

veggie or **vegie** *vej'i,* (*colloq*) *n* a vegetarian.

vehement *vē'ə-mənt, adj* marked by, or evincing, an urgency and forcefulness born of strong conviction. — *n* **vē'hemence**. — *adv* **vē'hemently**. [L. *vehemēns, -entis*, eager, ardent.]

vehicle *vē'i-kl, n* a means of conveyance or transmission, esp. a structure with wheels in or on which people or things are transported by land; a medium, e.g. for the expressing or performing of something; a substance with which a medicine, a pigment, etc. is mixed for administration or application; (**space vehicle**) a structure for carrying burdens through air or space or (also **launch vehicle**) a rocket used to launch a spacecraft. — *adj* **vehicular** (*vi-hik'ū-lər*). — **vehicle-actuated signal** see **pad**[2]. [L. *vehiculum* — *vehĕre*, to carry.]

veil *vāl, n* a curtain; a covering; a covering of fine fabric for the head, face, or both, for protection, concealment, adornment or ceremonial purpose, esp. the white transparent one often worn by a bride; a nun's or novice's head-covering; a disguise or concealment; an obstruction of tone in singing; a velum. — *vt* to cover with a veil; to cover; to conceal, disguise or obscure. — *vi* to wear a veil. — *adj* **veiled**. — *n* **veil'ing** material for making veils. — **draw a veil over** to conceal discreetly; to refrain from mentioning; **take the veil** to become a nun. [O.Fr. *veile* — L. *vēlum*, a curtain, veil, sail.]

vein *vān, n* one of the vessels or tubes that convey the blood back to the heart; (*loosely*) any blood vessel; one of the horny tubes forming the framework of an insect's wing; a vascular bundle forming a rib, esp. a small rib, in a leaf; a small intrusion, or a seam of a different mineral running through a rock; a fissure or cavity; a streak in wood, stone, etc.; a streak running through one's nature, a strain of character or ability; (a recurrent characteristic streak in) manner or style; a mood or humour. — *vt* to form veins or the appearance of veins in. — *adj* **veined** having veins; streaked, variegated. — *n* **vein'ing** formation or disposition of veins; streaking. — *n* **vein'let**. — *adj* **vein'y** veined; full of veins. [Fr. *veine* — L. *vēna*. See **vena**.]

vela, velar, velate, etc. See under **velum**.

velamen *və-lā'mən, n* a multi-layered sheath of dead cells on some aerial roots (*bot*); a velum (*anat*). [L., veil.]

velatura *vel-ə-tōō'rə, n* a method of glazing a painting by rubbing with the hand. [It.]

Velcro® *vel'krō, n* a nylon fastening material for clothes, etc. consisting of two facing layers, the one composed of tiny hooks, the other of tiny loops, strips of each of which, attached one on either side of an opening, form a secure closure when pressed together.

veld *felt* or (outside S. Africa) **veldt** *velt, n* in South Africa, open, unforested or thinly-forested grass-country. [Du. *veld*, field.]

veldskoen *felt'skōōn, n*. Same as **velskoen**.

veleta or **valeta** *və-lē'tə, n* a dance or dance tune in quick waltz time. [Sp., weathercock.]

vell *vel, n* the fourth stomach of a calf, used in making rennet.

velleity *ve-lē'i-ti, n* volition in its lowest form; mere inclination. [L.L. *velleitās*, irregularly formed from L. *velle*, to wish.]

vellum *vel'əm, n* a fine kind of parchment, orig. made from the skin of a calf; a manuscript, etc. printed on vellum. — *adj* made of, printed on, etc. vellum. [O.Fr. *velin* — *vel*, calf.]

veloce *vā-lō'chā,* (*mus*) *adj* and *adv* with great rapidity. [It.]

velocimeter *vel-ə-sim'ə-tər, n* an instrument that measures velocity. — *n* **velocim'etry**. [L. *vēlōc*itas, and Gr. *metron*, measure.]

velocipede *vi-los'i-pēd, n* an early form of bicycle. [Fr. *vélocipède* — L. *vēlōx, -ōcis*, swift, *pēs, pedis*, foot.]

velocity *vi-los'i-ti, n* rate of motion (distance per unit of time) in stated direction; (*loosely*) speed. [L. *vēlōcitās, -ātis* — *vēlōx*, swift.]

velodrome *vel'ə-drōm, n* a building containing a cycle-racing track. [Fr. *vélodrome*.]

velour or **velours** *və-lōōr', n* a woollen stuff with velvetlike pile. — Also *adj*. [Fr. *velours*.]

velouté *və-lōō'tā* or **veloutée sauce** (*sös*), *n* a smooth white sauce made with stock. [Fr., velvety.]

velskoen *fel'skōōn,* (*SAfr*) *n* a shoe made of rawhide. [Du. *vel*, skin, *schoen*, shoe.]

velum *vē'ləm, n* an integument or membrane; the membrane joining the rim of a young toadstool with the stalk; the pendulous soft palate; a ciliated disc, a locomotor organ in some molluscan larvae: — *pl* vē'la. — *adj* **vē'lar** of a velum; produced by the back of the tongue brought close to, or in contact with, the soft palate (*phon*). — *n* a velar consonant, back consonant. — *n* **velarīsā'tion** or **-z-**. — *vt* **ve'larise** or **-ize** to pronounce (a non-velar sound) with the back of the tongue brought close to the soft palate, esp. through the influences of a vowel sound. [L. *vēlum*, veil, sail.]

velvet *vel'vit*, *n* a silk, cotton, etc. fabric with a soft close-cut pile; the velvetlike covering of a growing antler; a velvety surface or skin. — *adj* made of velvet; soft or smooth like velvet. — *adj* **vel'veted** clad in velvet. — *n* **vel'vetiness.** — *adj* **vel'vety** soft and smooth like velvet; deep and soft in colouring. — **on velvet** in a safe or advantageous position; secure against losing, whatever happens; **the velvet glove** gentleness, concealing strength (see **iron hand** under **iron**). [L.L. *velvettum*, conn. with L. *villus*, a tuft.]

velveteen *vel-və-tēn'*, *n* a cotton fabric with a close-cut pile in imitation of velvet.

vena *vē'nə*, (*anat*) *n* a vein: — *pl* **ve'nae.** — **vena cava** (*kā'və*) either of the two major veins (the **superior** and **inferior vena cava**) taking venous blood to the heart: — *pl* **vē'nae cā'vae** (*-nē* and *-vē*). [L., vein.]

venal *vē'nl*, *adj* open to bribery, able to be bought over; corruptly mercenary. — *n* **venality** (*-nal'i-ti*). — *adv* **vē'nally.** [L. *vēnālis* — *vēnum*, goods for sale.]

venation *vi-nā'shən*, *n* a system or arrangement of venous blood vessels or of the veins of a leaf or insect's wing. — *adj* **venā'tional.** [L. *vēna*, vein.]

vend *vend*, *vt* to sell or offer for sale, deal in, esp. in a small way. — *n* a sale; the amount sold. — *n* **vendee'** a buyer. — *n* **ven'der** or **ven'dor** a seller; a vending machine. — *n* **vendibil'ity.** — *adj* **ven'dible** that may be sold, offered for sale, or readily sold. — *n* a thing for sale; a possible object of trade. — **vending machine** a slot machine dispensing goods. [Fr. *vendre* or L. *vendĕre*, to sell.]

vendace *ven'dəs*, *n* a freshwater white fish (genus *Corgonus*) found in lakes in S.W. Scotland; another species found in lakes of N.W. England. [Poss. O.Fr. *vendese*, *vendoise*, dace.]

vendee. See under **vend.**

vendetta *ven-det'ə*, *n* a blood feud; any similarly prolonged, violent or bitter feud or quarrel. [It., — L. *vindicta*, revenge — *vindicāre*, to claim.]

vendible, etc. See under **vend.**

veneer *və-nēr'*, *vt* to overlay or face (coarse wood, etc.) with a thin sheet of fine wood or other material; to disguise with superficial refinement. — *n* a thin layer for veneering; a specious outward appearance of good quality, refinement, respectability, etc. — *n* **veneer'er.** — *n* **veneer'ing.** [Formerly *fineer* — Ger. *furniren* — O.Fr. *fornir*, to furnish.]

venepuncture or **venipuncture** *ven'i-pung-chər*, (*med*) *n* the puncturing of a vein with a hypodermic needle, to draw off a sample of blood or inject a drug. [L. *vēna*, vein.]

venerable *ven'ə-rə-bl*, *adj* worthy of reverence; hallowed by associations or age; aged-looking; an honorific prefix to the name of an archdeacon, or to a person in process of canonisation. — *n* **ven'erableness.** — *adv* **ven'erably.** [L. *venerābilis*, worthy of revenue.]

venerate *ven'ə-rāt*, *vt* to revere. — *n* **venerā'tion** the act of venerating; the state of being venerated; awed respect. — *n* **ven'erātor.** [L. *venerārī*, *-ātus.*]

venereal *vi-nē'ri-əl*, *adj* related to sexual desire or intercourse; transmitted by sexual intercourse; relating to, or affected by, venereal disease. — **venereal disease** any of various contagious diseases characteristically transmitted by sexual intercourse. [L. *venereus* — *Venus*, *Venĕris*, the goddess of love.]

venereology *və-nē-ri-ol'ə-ji*, *n* the study of venereal diseases. — *adj* **venereolog'ical.** — *n* **venereol'ogist.** [L. *venereus*, relating to sexual love, and sfx. *-logy.*]

venesection or **venisection** *ven'i-sek-shən*, *n* the surgical incision of a vein, phlebotomy. [L. *vēna*, vein.]

Venetian *vi-nē'shən*, *adj* of Venice. — *n* a native or inhabitant of Venice, in N.E. Italy; a Venetian blind. — *adj* **Vene'tianed** having Venetian blinds or shutters. — **Venetian blind** a window blind of horizontal slats adjustable to let in or keep out light. [L. *Venetiānus* — *Venetia*, Venice.]

vengeance *ven'jəns*, *n* the inflicting of injury in punishment or revenge; retribution. — **with a vengeance** violently, thoroughly, exceedingly. [O.Fr., — *venger* — L. *vindicāre*, to avenge.]

vengeful *venj'fəl*, *adj* eager for revenge; vindictive; retributive, retaliatory. — *adv* **venge'fully.** — *n* **venge'fulness.** [O.Fr. *venger*, to avenge.]

venial *vē'ni-əl*, *adj* pardonable; excusable. — *n* **veniality** (*-al'i-ti*). — **venial sin** sin other than mortal. [L. *veniālis*, pardonable — *venia*, pardon.]

venin *ven'in*, (*chem*) *n* any of the various toxic substances in venom. [*venom* and sfx. *-in.*]

venipuncture. See **venepuncture.**

venisection. See **venesection.**

venison *ven'i-zn*, or (esp. in Scotland) *-i-sən*, *n* deer's flesh as food. [A.Fr. — L. *vēnātiō*, *-ōnis*, hunting — *vēnārī*, to hunt.]

venite *vi-nī'ti* (L. *we-nē'te* or *ve-*), *n* the 95th Psalm, beginning *Venīte exultēmus*, O come, let us rejoice.

Venn diagram *ven dī'ə-gram*, (*math*) *n* a diagram in which sets and their relationships are represented, by overlapping circles or other figures. [John *Venn* (1834–1923), mathematician.]

venom *ven'əm*, *n* poisonous fluid secreted by certain snakes and various other creatures, introduced into the victim by a bite or sting; spite. — *adj* **ven'omed** venomous; charged with poison, envenomed. — *adj* **ven'omous** poisonous; having power to poison, esp. by bite or sting; malignant, full of spite. — *adv* **ven'omously.** — *n* **ven'omousness.** [O.Fr. *venim* — L. *venēnum*, poison.]

venose *vē'nōs*, *adj* veiny; with very marked veins. [L. *vēnōsus*, veiny.]

venous *vē'nəs*, *adj* relating to, or contained in, veins; (of blood) deoxygenated, and, in human beings, dark red in colour. — *n* **venos'ity.** [L. *vēna*, and sfx. *-ous.*]

vent[1] *vent*, *n* a slit in a garment, esp. in the back of a coat. [Fr. *fente* — L. *findĕre*, to split.]

vent[2] *vent*, *n* an opening, aperture; an airhole; a touch-hole for firing a cannon, etc.; a volcanic orifice; an animal's or bird's anus; a chimney flue; an outlet; the opening in a parachute canopy through which air escapes at a controlled rate; utterance, expression. — *vt* to give a vent or opening to; to let out, as at a vent; to allow to escape. — *vi* (of a beaver or otter) to take breath or rise for breath. — **give vent to** to allow to escape or break out; to give, usu. violent, expression to (an emotion). [Fr., — L. *ventus*, wind; partly Fr. *éventer*, to expose to air; assoc. with **vent**[1], etc.]

venter *ven'tər*, (*zool* and *bot*) *n* the abdomen; a swelling or protuberance; a median swelling; a shallow concave surface of a bone; the upper side or surface of a leaf, etc. — *adj* **ven'tral** of the belly; on the upper side or towards the axis (*bot*); front of the body or on the side normally turned towards the ground — opp. to *dorsal* or *neural* (*zool*). — *n* a ventral fin. — *adv* **ven'trally.** — **ventral fins** the paired fins on the belly of a fish. [L. *venter*, *-tris.*]

ventil *ven'til*, (*mus*) *n* a valve for giving sounds intermediate between the open harmonics in wind instruments; a valve in an organ for controlling the wind supply to various stops. [Ger., — L.L. *ventīle*, shutter, sluice — *ventus*, wind.]

ventilate *ven'ti-lāt*, *vt* to open or expose to the free passage of air; to provide with duct(s) for circulating air or for escape of air; to cause (blood) to take up oxygen, by supply of air; to supply air to (lungs); to expose to examination and discussion, to make public. — *adj* **ven'tilable.** — *n* **ventilā'tion.** — *adj* **ven'tilātive.** — *n* **ven'tilātor** a device for introducing fresh air; a machine which ventilates the lungs of a person whose respiratory system is not functioning adequately. [L. *ventilāre, -ātum*, to fan, wave, agitate — *ventus*, wind.]

ventral. See under **venter.**

ventricle *ven'tri-kl*, (*anat*) *n* either of the two lower contractile chambers of the heart, the right ventricle receiving venous blood from the right atrium and pumping it into the pulmonary loop for oxygenation, the left receiving oxygenated blood from the left atrium and pumping it into the arterial system for circulation round the body; any of various other cavities in the body, e.g. one of the four main cavities of the brain. — *adj* **ventric'ūlar.** [L. *ventriculus*, dimin. of *venter*, belly.]

ventricose *ven'tri-kōz*, *adj* distended or swollen in the middle, at the side, or round the base (*bot, zool*); having a prominent or swollen belly. [*ventric*le and sfx. *-ose*.]

ventriloquism *ven-tril'ə-kwizm*, *n* the art of speaking so as to give the illusion that the sound comes from some other source. — *adj* **ventriloquial** (*-lō'kwi-əl*). — *adv* **ventrilō'quially.** — *vi* **ventril'oquise** or **-ize** to practise ventriloquism. — *n* **ventril'oquist.** — *adj* **ventriloquis'tic** or **ventril'oquous.** — *n* **ventril'oquy** ventriloquism. [L. *ventriloquus*, a person who speaks by a spirit in the belly — *venter*, the belly, *loquī*, to speak.]

venture *ven'chər*, *n* an undertaking whose issue is uncertain or dangerous; a commercial enterprise or speculation; something attempted. — *vt* to expose to hazard; to risk; to dare to put forward. — *vi* to make a venture; to run a risk; to dare; to dare to go. — *n* **ven'turer.** — *adj* **ven'turesome** inclined to take risks; involving the taking of risk; risky. — **Venture Scout** a member of the senior branch of the Scout organisation, formerly called a Rover (Scout); **venture capital** money supplied by individual investors or business organisations for a new, esp. speculative, business enterprise, also called **risk capital.** [For **(ad)venture.**]

Venturi *ven-tŏŏr'i* or **Venturi tube** (also without *cap*), *n* a tube or duct, wasp-waisted and expanding at the ends, used in measuring flow rate of fluids, as a means of accelerating air flow, or to provide suction. [G.B. *Venturi* (1746–1822), Italian physicist.]

venue *ven'ū*, *n* a meeting-place or rendezvous; the chosen location for a sports event, concert, etc.; the place where a case is to be tried, or the district from which the jurors are drawn (usu. the county in which the alleged offence was committed) (*law, hist*). [O.Fr., arrival — *venir* — L. *venīre*, to come.]

venule *ven'ūl*, (*anat* and *zool*) any of the small-calibre blood-vessels into which the capillaries empty, and which join up to form veins. [L. *vēnula*, dimin. of *vēna*, vein.]

Venus *vē'nəs*, *n* the goddess of love (*Roman mythol*); the most brilliant of the planets, second in order from the sun. — *n* and *adj* **Venusian** (*vi-nū'zi-ən*) (an inhabitant) of the planet Venus. — **Venus's comb** an umbelliferous plant with long-beaked fruits set like comb teeth; **Venus's flowerbasket** a deep-sea sponge with a skeleton of glassy spicules; **Venus's** (or **Venus) fly trap** an insectivorous plant with hinged leaves that snap shut on insects that land on them; **Venus's girdle** a ribbonlike gelatinous sea creature; **Venus's looking-glass** a garden plant with small bright flowers. — **girdle of Venus** (*palmistry*) a line on the palm forming a semicircle from between the first and second to between the third and fourth fingers; **mount of Venus** the elevation at the base of the thumb. [L., orig. personified from *venus, -eris*, desire.]

veracious *və-rā'shəs*, *adj* truthful. — *adv* **verā'ciously.** — *n* **veracity** (*-ras'i-ti*) truthfulness. [L. *vērāx, -ācis* — *vērus*, true.]

veranda or **verandah** *və-ran'də*, *n* a roofed gallery, terrace, or open portico along the front or side of a building. [Hindi *varaṇḍā*, app. — Port. *varanda*, a balcony.]

veratrum *və-rā'trəm*, *n* the white hellebore. — *n* **veratrine** (*ver'ə-trēn*) or **veratrin** (*ver'ə-trin*) an alkaloid or mixture of alkaloids obtained from white hellebore rhizomes, sabadilla, etc. [L. *vērātrum*, hellebore.]

verb *vûrb*, (*gram*) *n* a part of speech consisting of a word or group of words that signify an action, experience, occurrence or state, in sentence analysis constituting or introducing the predicate. — *adj* **verb'less.** [L. *verbum*, word.]

verbal *vûr'bəl*, *adj* of, relating to or derived from a verb or verbs; of, in, of the nature of, in the matter of or concerned with words, or words rather than things; word-for-word, literal; oral; voluble or articulate. — *n* a word, esp. a noun, derived from a verb; an oral statement, esp. an arrested suspect's confession of guilt, made to the police, or claimed by them to have been made (*slang*); (an) insult, (a piece of) abuse or invective (*slang*). — *n* **verbalīsā'tion** or **-z-**. — *vt* **ver'balise** or **-ize** to turn into a verb; to put in words. — *vi* to use too many words, be prolix. — *n* **ver'balism** an expression; wording; undue attention to words alone; literalism. — *n* **ver'balist** a person skilled in words; a literalist; a person who is concerned with words alone. — *n* **verbal'ity** the quality of being verbal or merely verbal; mere words. — *adv* **ver'bally.** — **verbal inspiration** dictation of every word of a book (usu. the Bible) by God; **verbal noun** a form of a verb, e.g. infinitive or gerund, functioning as a noun. [L. *verbālis*, verbal, wordy — *verbum*, word.]

verbatim *vər-bā'tim*, *adv* and *adj* word-for-word, using exactly the same words. [L.]

verbena *vûr-bē'nə*, *n* a plant of the *Verbena* or vervain genus that gives its name to the family **Verbenaceae** (*vûr-bi-nā'si-ē*), closely related to the labiates. [L. *verbēna*, a leafy twig, sacred bough.]

verbiage *vûr'bi-əj*, *n* words; superfluity of words, verbosity, prolixity. [O.Fr. *verbeier*, to chatter.]

verbose *vûr-bōs*, *adj* using or containing more words than are desirable; wordy. — *adv* **verbose'ly.** — *n* **verbose'ness** or **verbosity** (*-bos'i-ti*). [L. *verbōsus*, prolix.]

verboten *fer-bō'tən*, (Ger.) *adj* forbidden.

verb. sap. *abbrev* for *verbum sapienti sat est* (L.) a word is sufficient to the wise — no need for further explanation.

verdant *vûr'dənt*, *adj* green; fresh green or grass-green; green, unsophisticated, raw and gullible. — *n* **ver'dancy.** — *adv* **ver'dantly.** [O.Fr., — *verdoyer*, to become green — L. *viridis*, green.]

verd-antique *vûrd-an-tēk'*, *n* a dark green stone, a breccia of serpentine containing calcite, etc. — **oriental verd-antique** a green porphyry. [Obs. Fr., antique green.]

verdelho *vər-del'yŏŏ*, *n* a white Madeira or the white grape from which it is made, grown orig. in Madeira, now also in Portugal, Sicily, Australia and S. Africa. [Port.]

verderer *vûr'de-rər*, (*hist*) *n* an officer of the law responsible for order in the royal forests. [O.Fr. *verdier* — L. *viridis*, green.]

verdict *vûr'dikt*, *n* the finding of a jury on a trial; judicial decision or decision generally. — **formal verdict** see under **formal; open verdict** see under **open; special verdict** a verdict in which specific facts are found and put on the record. [O.Fr. *verdit* and L.L. *vērēdictum* — L. *vērē*, truly, *dictum*, said.]

verdigris *vûr'di-grēs, n* basic cupric acetate; (*popularly*) the green coating of basic cupric carbonate that forms in the atmosphere on copper, brass or bronze. [O.Fr. *verd de Grèce*, green of Greece.]

verdure *vûr'dyər*, (chiefly *poetic*) *n* fresh greenness; greenery, green vegetation. — *adj* **ver'dured** covered with verdure. — *adj* **ver'dureless.** — *adj* **ver'durous.** [O.Fr. *verd*, green — L. *viridis*, green.]

Verey light. See **Very light.**

verge[1] *vûrj, n* a limit, boundary; a rim; the brink, extreme edge; the edge of a roof projecting beyond the gable (*archit*); a grass edging; a rod or staff of office (*hist*); extent of jurisdiction, esp. of the lord-steward of the royal household (*hist*). — *vt* to edge. — *vi* (with *on*) to border, be on the edge of; to come close to, approach (a state or condition). — **on the verge of** on the point of; on the brink of, very close to (a state, condition or situation). [L. *virga*, a rod; the area of jurisdiction of the holder of the office symbolised by the rod, hence, limit, boundary.]

verge[2] *vûrj, vi* to incline; to tend downward; to slope; to tend; to pass gradually, merge. [L. *vergĕre*, to bend.]

verger *vûr'jər, n* a church official who acts as attendant and caretaker; an official who, on ceremonial occasions, bears the verge or staff of office before a bishop. [**verge**[1], rod of office — L. *virga*, rod.]

verglas *ver'glä, n* a film of ice on rock. [Fr., (*verre*, glass, *glace*, ice) from O.Fr.]

veridical *vi-rid'i-kl, adj* truthful; coinciding with fact; (of a dream or vision) corresponding exactly with what has happened or with what happens later; seemingly true to fact. — *n* **veridicality** (*-kal'i-ti*). [L. *vēridicus* — *vērus*, true, *dīcĕre*, to say.]

verify *ver'i-fī, vt* to ascertain or test the truth or accuracy of; to assert or prove to be true; to testify to the truth of, support (a statement; *law*). — *pr p* **ver'ifying**; *pa t* and *pa p* **ver'ified.** — *n* **verifīabil'ity.** — *adj* **ver'ifīable.** — *n* **verificā'tion.** — *adj* **ver'ificātory.** — *n* **ver'ifīer.** [L. *vērus*, true, *facĕre*, to make.]

verily. See under **very.**

verisimilitude *ver-i-si-mil'i-tūd, n* the quality of seeming real or true, an appearance of truth or reality; a statement, etc. that merely sounds true. — *adj* **verisim'ilar.** [L. *vērisimilis* — *vērus*, true, *similis*, like.]

verism *vēr'ism* or *ver'izm, n* use of everyday contemporary material, including what is ugly or sordid, in the arts, esp. in early 20th-cent. Italian opera (It. **verismo** *vā-rēs'mō*); the theory supporting this. — *adj* and *n* **ver'ist.** — *adj* **veris'tic.** [It. *vero* — L. *vērus*, true.]

vérité. See **cinéma vérité** under **cinema.**

verity *ver'i-ti, n* truth; a truth, esp. a basic or fundamental one; truthfulness; something that exists, a reality. — *adj* **ver'itable** true; genuine; real, actual; truly or justifiably so called. — *adv* **ver'itably.** [L. *vēritās, -ātis* — *vērus*, true.]

verjuice *vûr'jōōs, n* the juice of unripe fruit; sourness, bitterness. [Fr. *verjus* — *vert*, green, *jus*, juice.]

verkramp *fər-kramp', adj* (used *predicatively*) in S. Africa, narrow-minded, illiberal and rigidly conservative in attitude, esp. towards black and coloured people. — *adj* (used *attributively*) and *n* **verkrampte** (*-kram(p)'tə*) (a person) of such rigidly conservative political attitudes. [Afrik., restricted.]

verlig *fər-lihh', adj* (used *predicatively*) in S. Africa, liberal, politically enlightened, esp. towards black and coloured people. — *adj* (used *attributively*) and *n* **verligte** (*-lihh'tə*) (a person) of such enlightened and liberal political attitudes. [Afrik., enlightened.]

vermal. See **vermis.**

vermeil *vûr'mil* or *vûr'māl, n* and *adj* bright red, scarlet, vermilion; silver gilt or gilt bronze. [O.Fr. and Fr., — L. *vermiculus*, a little worm, dimin. of *vermis*, worm.]

vermi- *vûr-mi-, combining form* denoting worm. — *adj* **ver'micidal** (*vûr'mi-sī-dl*). — *n* **ver'micide** a worm-killing agent. — *n* **ver'miculture** the farming of earthworms, esp. as bait for fishing. — *adj* **ver'miform** having the form of a worm (**vermiform appendix** (*anat*) the appendix, a worm-shaped process projecting from the lower end of the ascending colon). — *adj* **vermifugal** (*vər-mif'ū-gl*) expelling worms. — *n* **ver'mifuge** (*-fūj*) a drug that expels worms. [L. *vermis*, a worm.]

vermian. See **vermis.**

vermicelli *vûr-mi-sel'i* or *-chel'i, n* a very slender type of macaroni; (more usu. **chocolate vermicelli**) short thin pieces of chocolate used for decoration of cakes, sweets, etc. [It., pl. of *vermicello*, dimin. of *verme*, worm, L. *vermis*.]

vermicidal. See under **vermi-.**

vermicular *vûr-mik'ū-lər, adj* of, of the nature of or like a worm; relating to or caused by intestinal worms (*pathol*); vermiculate (*archit*). — *adj* **vermic'ulate** (*-lət*) or **vermic'ulated** bearing a decoration reminiscent of a mass of curly worms, rusticated (*archit*); worm-eaten. — *n* **verminculā'tion** rustication (*archit*); a worm-eaten condition; peristalsis of the intestines (*physiol*). — *n* **vermic'ulite** an altered mica that curls before the blowpipe flame and expands greatly at high temperature, forming a water-absorbent substance used in seed-planting, and also used as insulating material. [L. *vermiculus*, dimin. of *vermis*, worm.]

vermiculture. See under **vermi-.**

vermilion *vər-mil'yən, n* a bright-red pigment, mercuric sulphide; its bright scarlet colour. — *adj* bright scarlet. — *vt* to colour vermilion. [O.Fr. *vermillon* — *vermeil*; see **vermeil.**]

vermin *vûr'min, n* a collective name for small animals, insects or birds that are troublesome or destructive to crops, game or domestic stock; obnoxious or despicable people. — *adj* **ver'minous** infested with vermin; like vermin. [Fr. *vermin* — L. *vermis*, a worm.]

vermis *vûr'mis*, (*med* and *anat*) *n* a worm or wormlike structure, e.g. the *vermis cerebelli*, the central lobe of the cerebellum. — *adj* **ver'mal** or **ver'mian.** [L. *vermis*, worm.]

vermouth *vûr'məth* or *vər-mōōth', n* a drink with white wine base, flavoured with wormwood or other aromatic herbs. [Fr. — Ger. *Wermut(h)*, wormwood.]

vernacular *vər-nak'ū-lər, adj* (of language) indigenous, native, spoken by the people of the country or of one's own country; of, in or using the vernacular language; of the jargon or idiom of a particular group; (of other things) native, local, endemic, esp. of architecture or general style of building. — *n* a native language or dialect; a class jargon; profane language (*facetious*). — *n* **vernac'ularism** a vernacular expression or idiom; the use of the vernacular. [L. *vernāculus* — *verna*, a home-born slave.]

vernal *vûr'nəl, adj* of, happening or appearing in spring; springlike. — *n* **vernalīsā'tion** or **-z-.** — *vt* **ver'nalise** or **-ize** to make springlike; to freshen; to hasten the development of (seeds or seedlings) by treating them in various ways before planting, e.g. by subjecting them to a low temperature. [L. *vērnālis* — *vernus*, of spring, — *ver*, spring.]

vernation *vûr-nā'shən, n* the arrangement of leaves in the vegetative bud (rarely that of the individual leaf). [L. *vernāre*, to become springlike.]

vernicle *vûr'ni-kl, n* a cloth bearing the face of Christ, believed to have been miraculously impressed on it when St *Veronica* wiped his face; any representation of this; a medal or badge bearing it, worn by pilgrims who had been at Rome. [O.Fr. *veronicle* — L. *veronica*, St Veronica's cloth.]

vernier *vûr'ni-ər, n* a short scale sliding on a graduated scale to give fractional readings; a small auxiliary device that enables a piece of apparatus to be adjusted very accurately (e.g. a **vernier condenser** a condenser of small capacitance connected in parallel with one of larger capacitance); a small rocket engine used to make the movement of a booster rocket, or of a ballistic missile, more precisely as required. [P. *Vernier* (1580–1637), French mathematician who invented the scale.]

veronica *və-ron'i-kə, n* any of several herbs and shrubs of the speedwell genus; (in bullfighting) a movement with the cape reminiscent of St Veronica's in offering her handkerchief to Christ; a vernicle. [St *Veronica*.]

véronique *vā-ro-nēk'*, (Fr.) *adj* (used after the noun) served with white grapes, e.g. *sole véronique*.

verruca *ve-rōō'kə, n* a wart, esp. one on the sole of the foot; a wartlike outgrowth: — *pl* **verru'cae** (*-sē*) or **verru'cas**. — *adj* **verru'ciform** (*-si-förm*) wartlike. — *adj* **verr'ucose** or **verru'cous** (or *ver'*) warty. [L. *verrūca*, a wart.]

versant *vûr'sənt, n* the general slope of surface of a country. [Fr. *versant* — *verser*, to turn over — L. *versāre*.]

versatile *vûr'sə-tīl* or in U.S. *-təl, adj* turning easily from one thing to another; of many-sided ability; capable of many uses; turning freely; dangling as an anther attached by the middle of the back (*bot*); capable of free movement, reversible, as a toe is (*zool*). — *adv* **ver'satilely**. — *n* **ver'satileness** or **versatility** (*-til'i-ti*). [L. *versātilis* — *versāre*, frequentative of *vertĕre*, to turn.]

verse *vûrs, n* metrical composition, form or work; versification; a stanza; a line of metre; a short division of a chapter, esp. of the Bible; a portion of an anthem to be performed by a single voice to each part; a versicle. — *vt* to versify. — See also **versed**[1]. [O.E. *fers*, reinforced by Fr. *vers*, both — L. *versus*, *vorsus*, *-ūs*, a line, row or verse.]

versed[1] *vûrst, adj* thoroughly acquainted, skilled (with *in*). — *vt* **verse** to make conversant (with *in*). [L. *versātus*, past p. of *versārī*, to busy oneself.]

versed[2] *vûrst*, (*math*) *adj* reversed. — **versed sine** a trigonometrical function of an angle, one minus the cosine. [L. *versus*, past p. of *vertĕre*, to turn.]

verset *vûr'sit*, (*mus*) *n* a short organ interlude or prelude. [Fr., dimin. of *vers*, verse.]

versicle *vûr'si-kl, n* in liturgy, the verse said by the officiant; a little verse. — *adj* **versic'ular**. [L. *versiculus*, dimin. of *versus*, verse.]

versicoloured *vûr'si-kul-ərd, adj* diversely or changeably coloured. [L. *versicolor*, of changeable colour — *vertĕre*, *versum*, to change, *color*, colour.]

versin or **versine** *vûr'sīn*, (*math*) *n* short for **versed sine** (q.v. under **versed**[2]).

versify *vûr'si-fī, vi* to compose verse. — *vt* to tell or express in verse; to turn into verse: — *pr p* **ver'sifying**; *pa t* and *pa p* **ver'sified**. — *n* **versificā'tion** the art or process of composing in verse or turning something into verse; the manner of construction, metrical pattern, etc. of verse. — *n* **ver'sifier**. [L. *versificāre*, to put into verse.]

version *vûr'shən, n* a particular form in which something is embodied, such as a particular way of telling a story; a variant; a turning; translation. — *adj* **ver'sional**. [L. *versiō*, *-ōnis* — *vertĕre*, *versum*, to turn.]

vers libre *ver lēbr'*, (Fr.) *n* free verse. — *n* **verslibrist** (*ver-lē'brist*) a writer of free verse.

verso *vûr'sō, n* a left-hand page of an open book (*printing*); the back of a printed sheet (*printing*); the reverse of a coin or medal: — *pl* **ver'sos**. [L. *versō* (*foliō*), turned leaf (abl.).]

versus *vûr'səs*, (*law*, *games*, etc.) *prep* against, — abbrev. **v** or **vs.** [L.]

vertebra *vûr'ti-brə*, (*anat* and *zool*) *n* any of the segments that compose the backbone: — *pl* **ver'tebrae** (*-brē*). — *adj* **ver'tebral** relating to vertebrae (**vertebral column** the spinal column). — *adv* **ver'tebrally**. — *adj* **ver'tebrate** backboned; of, belonging or relating to the vertebrates. — *n* a backboned animal, one belonging to the sub-phylum *Vertebrata*, including fishes, amphibians, reptiles, birds and mammals. — *n* **vertebrā'tion** division into vertebrae or vertebra-like segments. [L. *vertebra*, a joint of the spine — *vertĕre*, to turn.]

vertex *vûr'teks, n* the top or summit; the zenith (*astron*); the crown of the head (*anat*); the point opposite the base (*geom*); the meeting-point of the lines bounding an angle; the intersection of a curve with its axis: — *pl* **ver'texes** or **ver'tices** (*-ti-sēz*). [L. *vertex*, whirlpool, summit — *vertere*, to turn.]

vertical *vûr'ti-kl, adj* perpendicular to the plane of the horizon; of or at the vertex; in the direction of the axis (*bot*); comprising the various stages in the production of the same goods, as in *vertical integration* (*econ*); in strata; (of a mechanism) in which one part is above another. — *n* a vertical line or position. — *n* **verticality** (*-kal'i-ti*). — *adv* **ver'tically**. — *n* **ver'ticalness**. — **vertical angles** opposite angles formed by intersecting lines; **vertical circle** a great circle of the heavens passing through the zenith and the nadir; **vertical take-off** (*aeronautics*) immediate take-off without preliminary run. [L. *vertex*, *-icis*, eddy, summit.]

verticil *vûr'ti-sil*, (*bot*) *n* a whorl. — *adj* **verticillate** (*vər-tis'i-lət*) whorled. [L. *verticillus*, dimin. of *vertex*.]

vertigo *vûr'ti-gō, n* dizziness, giddiness; a whirling sensation experienced when the sense of balance is disturbed: — *pl* **ver'tigos**, **ver'tigoes** or **vertigines** (*-tij'i-nēz*). — *adj* **vertiginous** (*-tij'*) relating to vertigo; dizzy, giddy; whirling; producing dizziness, dizzying. — *adv* **vertig'inously**. — *n* **vertig'inousness**. [L. *vertīgō*, *-inis* — *vertĕre*, to turn.]

verumontanum *ver-ōō-mon-tā'nəm*, (*anat*) *n* a ridge on the male urethra where the duct conveying prostatic fluid, sperm and other fluids enter it: — *pl* **verumontā'na** or **verumontā'nums**. [L. *veru*, spit, *montanus*, hilly.]

vervain *vûr'vān, n* a wild verbena, long believed to have great magical and medicinal powers. [O.Fr. *verveine* — L. *verbēna*.]

verve *vûrv, n* enthusiasm that animates a poet or artist; gusto; spirit; animation; energy. [Fr.]

vervet *vûr'vit, n* an African guenon monkey. [Fr.]

very *ver'i, adv* in a high degree, extremely; (used for emphasis with a superl. adj. or with *own* or *same*) absolutely, quite, truly, as in *my very own room*, *the very best quality*, *the very same day*. — *adj* used for emphasis, e.g. with the force of 'absolute' (*the very top*), precise, 'actual' (*this very minute*, *her very words*), 'most suitable' (*the very tool*), 'mere' (*the very thought*). — *adv* **ver'ily** (*liturgical*, *formal* or *archaic*) truly; really. — **not very** far from, not at all, the opposite of; **the very thing** precisely what is wanted or needed; **very good** or **very well** used in compliance or assent; **very high frequency** (*radio*) a frequency between 30 and 300 megahertz (abbrev. **VHF**); **Very Reverend** see **reverend**. [Older *verray*, *veray*, true, veritable — A.Fr. *ver(r)ai*, from a derivative of L. *vērus*, true.]

Very (or **Verey**) **light** *ver'i līt* or *vēr'i, n* a signalling or illuminating coloured flare fired from a pistol. [Invented by Edward W. *Very* (1877).]

vesica *ves'i-kə*, (*anat* and *zool*) *n* a bladder, sac, esp. the urinary bladder: — *pl* **vesicae** (*ves'i-sē*). — *adj* **vesical** (*ves'i-kl*) of or relating to a vesica. — *adj* **ves'icant** blistering. — *n* anything that causes blisters. — *vt* and *vi* **ves'icate** to blister. — *n* **vesicā'tion**. — *n* and *adj* **ves'icatory** (or *-ik'*) vesicant. — *n* **ves'icle** (*med* and *zool*) a small globule, bladder, sac, blister, cavity or swelling; a primary cavity of the vertebrate brain. — *n* **vesic'ūla** a vesicle: — *pl* **vesic'ūlae** (*-lē*). — *adj* **vesic'ūlar**. — *adj* **vesic'ūlate** (*-lət*) or **vesic'ulated**. — *n* **ves-**

iculā'tion formation of vesicles. [L. *vēsica*, bladder, blister.]

vesper *ves'pər*, *n* evening (*poetic*); (usu. in *pl*) the last but one of the seven canonical hours; (usu. in *pl*) evensong, evening service generally (*Christian relig*). [L., evening.]

vessel *ves'l*, *n* a utensil for holding something; a craft or structure (usually large) for transport by water; (in animals) a tubular duct through which body fluids such as lymph or blood pass; (in plants) a duct conveying water. [O.Fr. — L. *vāscellum*, dimin. of *vās*, *vāsis*, a vessel.]

vest *vest*, *n* an undergarment for the top half of the body, an undershirt; a waistcoat (chiefly *US*); an additional facing to the front of a bodice. — *vt* to invest; to settle, secure or put in fixed right of possession (*law*); to endow (*law*); to clothe (*literary*). — *vi* to descend, devolve or to take effect, as a right; to put on vestments or robes (*eccles*). — *adj* **vest'ed** not contingent or suspended, hence (*law*) already acquired. — **vested interest** a particular interest in the continuance of an existing system, institution, etc. for personal reasons, often financial; (in *pl*) interests already established; (in *pl*) the class of persons who have acquired rights or powers in any sphere of a country's activities; **vest pocket** a waistcoat-pocket. [L. *vestis*, clothing.]

vesta *ves'tə*, *n* a wax-stemmed match; a short match with wooden stem: — *pl* **ves'tas**. [L. *Vesta*, Roman goddess of the hearth and household.]

vestal *ves'təl*, *adj* (often with *cap*) pertaining or consecrated to the Roman goddess Vesta; virgin; chaste. — *n* one of the vestal virgins; a woman dedicated to celibacy, a nun; a virgin, a woman of spotless chastity. — **vestal virgin** (*hist*) in ancient Rome, one of the patrician virgins consecrated to Vesta, who kept the sacred fire burning on her altar. [L. *vestālis* — *Vesta*.]

vestibule *ves'ti-būl*, *n* an entrance hall; a cavity serving as entrance to another, esp. that of the inner ear (*anat*). — *adj* **vestib'ūlar**. — *n* **vestibuli'tis** (*med*) inflammation of the labyrinth and cochlea of the inner ear, causing vertigo, ataxia and deafness. — *n* **vestib'ūlum** (*anat*) a vestibule. [L. *vestibulum*.]

vestige *ves'tij*, *n* a trace; a surviving trace of what has almost disappeared; a scrap, shred, the least bit; a reduced and functionless structure, organ, etc., representing what was once useful and developed (*biol*). — *adj* **vestig'ial**. [L. *vestīgium*, footprint.]

vestment *vest'mənt*, *n* any of various ceremonial garments worn in religious services by clergy and choristers; an official or state robe. [L. *vestīmentum* — *vestīre*, to clothe.]

vestry *ves'tri*, *n* a room attached to a church in which vestments are kept and parochial meetings held; in Anglican and Episcopalian parishes, a meeting of church members or their elected representatives, or the committee who meet thus for parish business. — *adj* **ves'tral**. — **ves'try-clerk** an officer chosen by the vestry to keep the parish accounts and books; **ves'tryman** a member of a vestry; **ves'try-room** a vestry; the meeting-place of a vestry. [Prob. through O.Fr. — L. *vestiārium* — *vestis*, a garment.]

vesture *ves'chər*, (*archaic* or *poetic*) *n* clothing; garb. [O.Fr., — L.L. *vestītūra* — *vestis*, garment.]

vet *vet*, *n* a veterinary surgeon. — *vt* to treat or examine medically (an animal or, *facetiously*, a person); to examine (e.g. written work, or a candidate) thoroughly and critically (and pass as sound or correct): — *pr p* **vett'ing**; *pa t* and *pa p* **vett'ed**.

vetch *vech*, *n* any of various climbing plants of the pea family, usu. with blue or purple flowers, often used as fodder. — *n* **vetch'ling** any plant of the sweet-pea genus (*Lathyrus*). — **bitter vetch** various species of the *Vicia* and Lathyrus genera; **milk vetch** a plant of the *Astragalus* genus. [O.N.Fr. *veche* — L. *vicia*.]

veteran *vet'ə-rən*, *n* a person who has seen long service in any activity; an old and experienced soldier; an ex-serviceman (*NAm*). — *adj* old, experienced; long exercised, esp. in military life. — **veteran car** an old motor car, *specif* one made before 1905. [L. *veterānus* — *vetus*, *veteris*, old.]

veterinary *vet'ə-rin-ər-i*, *adj* concerned with diseases of animals. — *n* a person trained in the treatment of diseases of domestic animals. — Also **veterinā'rian** and **veterinary surgeon**. [L. *veterīnārius* — *veterīnae*, cattle, beasts of burden.]

vetkoek *fet'kŏŏk*, (*S Afr*) *n* a deep-fried cake, usu. unsweetened, but otherwise similar to a doughnut. [Afrik., — Du. *vet*, fat, *koek*, cake.]

veto *vē'tō*, *n* any authoritative prohibition; the power of rejecting or forbidding; the right to reject or forbid a proposed measure, esp. in a legislative assembly: — *pl* **vetoes** (*vē'tōz*). — *vt* to reject by a veto; to withhold assent to; to forbid. [L. *vetō*, I forbid.]

Vet. Surg. *abbrev* for Veterinary Surgeon.

vex *veks*, *vt* to distress; to annoy; to trouble, agitate, disturb; to discuss to excess. — *n* **vexā'tion** a vexing; the state or feeling of being vexed; a source of grief or annoyance. — *adj* **vexā'tious** vexing; troublesome; (of a law action) brought on insufficient grounds, with the intention merely of annoying the defendant. — *adv* **vexā'tiously**. — *n* **vexātiousness**. — *n* and *adj* **vex'ing**. — **vexed question** a matter greatly debated. [Fr. *vexer* — L. *vexāre*, to shake, annoy.]

vexillum *vek-sil'əm*, *n* the series of barbs on the sides of the shaft of a feather (*zool*); a standard (*bot*); a Roman standard (*hist*): — *pl* **vexill'a**. — *n* **vexill-ol'ogist**. — *n* **vexillol'ogy** the study of flags. [L. *vehĕre*, to carry.]

VF *abbrev* for: video frequency; voice frequency.

VG *abbrev* for Vicar-General.

vg *abbrev* for very good.

VHF *abbrev* for very high frequency.

vi *abbrev* for verb intransitive.

via[1] *vī'ə* or *vē'ə*, *prep* by way of; through. [L. *viā*, abl. of *via*, way.]

via[2] *vī'ə*, *vē'ə* or *vē'a*, (L.) *n* a way or road. — **via dolorosa** (*dol-ə-rō'sə*) the way to Calvary (lit. mournful way).

viable *vī'ə-bl*, *adj* capable of living, surviving, germinating or hatching; (of a plan or project) having a prospect of success; practicable. — *n* **viabil'ity**. [Fr., — *vie* — L. *vīta*, life.]

viaduct *vī'ə-dukt*, *n* a structure carrying a road or railway over a valley, etc. [After **aqueduct** — L. *via*, a way.]

vial *vī'əl*, *n*. Same as **phial**.

viand *vī'ənd*, (*formal*) *n* an article of food; (usu. in *pl*) food. [Fr. *viande* — L. *vīvenda*, food necessary for life — *vīvĕre*, to live.]

viaticum *vī-at'ik-əm*, *n* money, provisions, etc. for a journey; the eucharist given to people in danger of dying (*RC*). [L. *viāticum* — *via*, way.]

vibes *vībz*, (*colloq*) *npl* feelings, sensations, etc., experienced or communicated (shortening of **vibrations**). — *nsing* or *npl* **vibe** (*vīb*), colloq. shortenings of **vibraphone**. — *n* **vī'bist** (*colloq*).

vibex *vī'beks*, (*med*) *n* a streak under the skin due to the leakage of blood: — *pl* **vibices** (*vī-* or *vi-bī'sēz*). [L. *vībīcēs*, weals.]

vibra-. Variant of **vibro-**.

vibrancy and **vibrant**. See **vibrate**.

vibraphone *vī'brə-fōn*, *n* an instrument having metal bars under which are electrically-operated resonators, played by striking the bars with small hammers. — *n* **vī'braphōnist**. [L. *vibrāre*, to shake, Gr. *phōnē*, voice.]

vibrate *vī'brāt* or *-brāt'*, *vi* to shake; to tremble; to oscillate; to swing; to change to and fro, esp. rapidly; to resound, ring; to tingle, thrill. — *vt* to cause to vibrate; to give off in vibrations. — *n* **vibrancy** (*vī'brən-si*). — *adj* **vī'brant** vibrating; thrilling; resonant; (of colours) very bright. — *adj* **vī'bratile**

(-*brə-tīl* or in N.Am. -*til* or -*təl*) vibratory; having or capable of vibratory motion. — *n* **vibratility** (-*til'i-ti*). — *n* **vibrā'tion** a vibrating; state of being vibrated; tremulousness; quivering motion; a whole period or movement to and fro of anything vibrating; sometimes a half period or movement one way; (in *pl*) feelings communicated from person to person (*colloq*); (in *pl*) feelings aroused in one by a person, place, etc. (*colloq*). — *adj* **vibrā'tional**. — *adj* **vibrā'tionless**. — *adj* **vī'brative** (-*brə-tiv*) vibrating; consisting in vibrations; causing vibrations. — *n* **vī'brātor** that which vibrates; a vibrating part in many appliances; a vibrating tool; a type of dildo that can be made to vibrate mechanically. — *adj* **vibratory** (*vī'brə-tər-i*) of, of the nature of, causing, or capable of, vibration. [L. *vibrāre*, -*ātum*, to tremble.]

vibrato *vē-brä'tō* or *vi-*, (*mus*) *n* a throbbing effect, without perceptible change of pitch, in singing and in stringed and wind instrument playing, obtained by varying breath pressure or by the shaking movement of the finger on a string: — *pl* **vibra'tos**. [It.]

vibrissa *vī-bris'ə*, (*biol*) *n* a tactile bristle, such as a cat's whisker; a vaneless rictal feather; a bristle or hair, as in the nostril: — *pl* **vibriss'ae** (-*ē*). [L., a hair in the nostril.]

vibro- *vī-brō-* or -*bro'*-, *combining form* denoting vibration. — *n* **vī'brograph** and **vibrom'eter** instruments for recording vibrations. [L. *vibrāre*, -*ātum*, to tremble, to shake.]

Vic. *abbrev* for: Vicar; Vicarage.

vicar *vik'ər*, *n* a parson of a parish who receives only the smaller tithes or a salary (*C of E*); a bishop's deputy (*RC*); a deputy or substitute. — *n* **vic'arage** the benefice or residence of a vicar. — *n* **vic'arate** vicariate. — *adj* **vicarial** (*vī-* or *vi-kā'ri-əl*) delegated; of a vicar or vicars. — *adj* **vicā'riate** delegated. — *n* office, authority, time of office, or sphere of a vicar, in any sense. — *adj* **vicā'rious** filling the place of another; exercised, performed or suffered by one person or thing instead of another; (*loosely*) not experienced personally but imagined through the experience of others. — *adv* **vicā'riously**. — *n* **vicā'riousness**. — *n* **vic'arship** the (time of) office of a vicar. — **vicar-apostol'ic** a titular bishop appointed to a country where there are no sees; a titular bishop exercising authority in a vacant see or during the bishop's incapacity; **vicar-gen'eral** an official performing the work of an archdeacon under the bishop (*RC*); a lay official representing the bishop; **vicarious sacrifice** the suffering and death of Christ held by orthodox Christians to be accepted by God in lieu of the punishment to which guilty man is liable. — **Vicar of Christ** (*RC*) the Pope, as representative of Christ on earth. [L. *vicārius*, substituted; see **vice-**.]

vice[1] or in N.Am. **vise** *vīs*, *n* a tool with movable jaws for gripping an object that is being worked on. [Fr. *vis*, screw — L. *vītis*, a vine.]

vice[2] *vīs*, *n* a fault; immorality; depravity; an immoral habit; a bad trick or habit as in a horse. — **vice squad** a police squad whose task is to see that the laws dealing with gambling, prostitution, etc. are observed. [Fr., — L. *vitium*, a blemish; L.L. *viciōsus* for L. *vitiōsus*, faulty, vicious.]

vice[3] *vī'si*, *vī'sē* or *vīs*, *prep* in place of; in succession to. — **vice versa** (*vûr'sə*) the other way round. [L. *vice*, abl. (nom. not used), turn, place, alteration.]

vice- *vīs-*, *combining form* denoting in place of. — *n* **vice-ad'miral** a navy officer ranking next under an admiral. — *n* **vice-ad'miralty** the office or jurisdiction of a vice-admiral. — *n* **vice-chair'** a vice-chairman. — *n* **vice-chair'man** a deputy chairman. — *n* **vice-chair'manship**. — *n* **vice-cham'berlain** the Lord Chamberlain's deputy and assistant. — *n* **vice-chan'cellor** a person acting for a chancellor; (in certain British universities) the head of administration, the chancellor being titular head only. — *n* **vice-chan'cellorship**. — *n* **vice-con'sul** a consul's deputy; an official who acts as consul in a less important district. — *n* **vice-con'sulate**. — *n* **vice-con'sulship**. — *n* **vicegerency** (-*jer'* or -*jēr'ən-si*). — *adj* **vicegerent** (-*jer'* or -*jēr'*) having delegated authority. — *n* a person ruling or acting in place of a superior. — *n* **vice-gov'ernor** deputy governor. — *n* **vice-pres'idency**. — *n* **vice-pres'ident** a president's deputy or assistant; an officer next below the president. — *adj* **vice-presiden'tial**. — *n* **vice-prin'cipal** assistant principal. — *adj* **vice-re'gal** of a viceroy. — *n* **vicere'gent** properly, a substitute for a regent; often used mistakenly for vicegerent. [**vice**[3].]

vicennial *vī-sen'yəl*, *adj* lasting, or coming at the end of, twenty years; occurring every twenty years. [L. *vīcennium* — *vīciēs*, twenty times, *annus*, a year.]

vicereine *vīs'ren* or -*rān'*, *n* a viceroy's wife; a female viceroy. [Fr. — *vice-* (as **vice-**) and *reine*, queen.]

viceroy *vīs'roi*, *n* a governor acting in the name of the sovereign. — *n* **viceroy'alty** or **vice'royship**. [Fr. — *vice-* (as **vice-**) and *roy*, king.]

vicesimal, vicesimo-. See **vigesimal**.

Vichyite *vē'shē-īt*, *n* (*hist*) an adherent of the French Government (1940–42) ruling the unoccupied part of France from *Vichy*, and collaborating with the Germans. — Also *adj*. — *n* **vichyssoise'** a cream soup usu. served chilled, with ingredients such as potatoes and leeks. — **Vichy (or vichy) water** (*vē'shē*) mineral water from Vichy springs, containing sodium bicarbonate, etc., or a natural or artificial water resembling it. — Also **vi'chy**.

vicinity *vi-sin'i-ti*, *n* neighbourhood; nearness. [L. *vīcīnus*, neighbour — *vīcus*, street, village, district.]

vicious *vish'əs*, *adj* spiteful, malignant; bad-tempered; violent; immoral or depraved; (of language, etc.) incorrect, bad; addicted to vice or bad habits; (of animals) ferocious. — *adv* **vic'iously**. — *n* **vic'iousness**. — **vicious circle** a process in which an evil is aggravated by its own consequences. [Ety. as for **vice**[2].]

vicissitude *vi-sis'i-tūd*, *n* change; alternation; mutation; change of fortune. — *adj* **vicissitū'dinous**. [L. *vicissitūdō*, -*inis*; see **vice**[3].]

victim *vik'tim*, *n* a living being offered as a sacrifice; a person or animal subjected to death, suffering or ill-treatment; a prey; a sufferer. — *n* **victimīsā'tion** or **-z-**. — *vt* **vic'timise** or **-ize** to make a victim of; to treat oppressively and selectively; to cheat. — *n* **vic'timiser** or **-z-**. — *adj* **vic'timless** (of crimes) involving no injured party, such as loitering, drunkenness, etc. [L. *victima*, a beast for sacrifice.]

victor *vik'tər*, *n* a winner or winning side in a contest of any kind. — *adj* **victorious** (-*tö'ri-əs*) having gained a victory; winning in contest; of, with or marking victory. — *adv* **victo'riously**. — *n* **victo'riousness**. — *n* **victory** (*vik'tər-i*) a contest won; success against an opponent. [L. *victor*, -*ōris* — *vincĕre*, *victum*, to conquer.]

victoria *vik-tö'ri-ə*, *n* (also with *cap*) a large red plum (also **victoria plum**). — *adj* **Victo'rian** of, contemporary with or typical of the reign (1837–1901) of Queen Victoria; strict but somewhat conventional in morals, inclining to prudery and solemnity. — *n* a contemporary of Queen Victoria; a person of Victorian morality or outlook. — *npl* **Victoriana** (*vik-tö-ri-ä'nə*; also without *cap*) bric-à-brac and other characteristic possessions or creations of the Victorian age. — *n* **Victo'rianism**. — **Victoria Cross** a bronze Maltese cross, a decoration for conspicuous bravery on the field, founded by Queen Victoria (1856).

victual *vit'l*, *n* (commonly in *pl*) food, esp. food for humans. — *vt* to supply or store with provisions. — *vi* (of animals) to eat victuals: — *pr p* **victualling** (*vit'l-ing*); *pa t* and *pa p* **victualled** (*vit'ld*). — *n*

vict'uallage provisions. — *n* **victualler** (*vit'l-ər*) a purveyor of provisions; a victualling-ship. — **licensed victualler** see under **licence.** [O.F. *vitaille* — L.L. *victuālia* — L. *victuālis*, relating to living — *vivĕre*, *victum*, to live.]

vicuña *vi-kōō'nyə*, *n* a wild species of the llama genus; cloth of its wool, or an imitation. [Sp., from Quechua.]

vide *vī'dē* or *vē'dē*, (L.) see, consult, refer to. — **vide infra** (*in'frə* or *ēn'frä*) see below; **vide supra** (*sū'prə* or *sōō'prä*) see above.

videlicet *vi-del'i-sit* or *vi-dā'li-ket*, (L.) namely, to wit; usu. abbrev. **viz.**

video *vid'i-ō*, *n* a videocassette or videocassette recorder; video recording: — *pl* **vid'eos.** — *adj* pertaining to the bandwidth and spectrum position of the signal arising from TV scanning, or to the signal, or to the resultant image, or to television; using, used for, relating to, etc. the system of video recording. — *vt* and *vi* to make a video recording (of): — *pr p* **vid'eoing**; *pa p* **vid'eoed.** — **video camera** a camera which records its (moving) film on to videotape; **videocassette'** a cassette containing videotape; **videocassette recorder** a videotape recorder in which videocassettes are used; **videocon'ference**; **videocon'ferencing** live discussion between people in different places using electronically linked telephones and video screens; **vid'eodisc** a disc on which visual images and sound can be recorded for playing back on a television set or similar apparatus; **vid'eofit** a type of identikit picture put together on television; **video frequency** that in the range required for a video signal; **video game** an electronically-operated game played by means of a visual display unit; **vid'eogram** a commercial video film; a prerecorded videocassette or videodisc; **video nasty** a pornographic or horror video film; **vid'eophone** or **videotel'ephone** a telephone with accompanying means of transmitting a picture of each speaker; **video recorder** a machine for recording and playing back television broadcasts or films made on videotape, using videotape or videodiscs; **vid'eotape** magnetic tape for recording visual images, esp. television programmes or films. — *vt* to record on videotape. — **videotape recorder** a tape recorder that records visual images on magnetic tape and replays them; **vid'eotex** or **vid'eotext** a system used to display pages of information on a television screen, e.g. teletext or viewdata (q.v.); **video tube** a television tube. [L. *vidēre*, to see.]

vidimus *vī'di-məs*, *n* an attested copy; an inspection, as of accounts, etc. [L. *vīdimus*, we have seen — *vidēre*, to see.]

vie *vī*, *vi* to contend in rivalry: — *pr p* **vy'ing**; *pa t* and *pa p* **vied** (*vīd*). — *n* **vī'er.** [Fr. *envier* — L. *invitāre*, to challenge, invite.]

Viennese *vē-e-nēz'*, *adj* of *Vienna*, the capital of Austria. — *nsing* and *pl* an inhabitant or the inhabitants of Vienna. — **vienna (or Vienna) loaf** a long, round-ended loaf of white bread; **vienna steak** a meat rissole.

Vietnamese *vē-et-nəm-ēz'*, *n* a native or inhabitant, or the language, of *Vietnam*: — *pl* same as *sing.* — Also *adj.*

vieux jeu *vyø zhø*, *adj* old-fashioned; old hat. [Fr., lit. old game or old joke.]

view *vū*, *n* an act, possibility or opportunity of looking; range or field of sight; whole extent seen; a prospect, wide or distant extent seen; that which is seen; inspection; appearance; aspect; the picture of a scene; general survey of a subject; mode of thinking of something; opinion; intention, purpose; expectation; (with *cap*) used in street names, etc. — *vt* to see; to look at; to look at on television; to observe; to consider; to examine intellectually. — *vi* to watch television. — *adj* **view'able** able to be seen; sufficiently interesting to be looked at or watched. — *n* **view'er** a person who views; a television watcher; an apparatus used to project film for purposes of editing and cutting; a device with a magnifying lens, etc. for viewing transparencies. — *n* **view'ership** the estimated number of viewers of a television programme. — *n* **view'iness** character of being viewy. — *n* **view'ing.** — *adj* **view'y** showy; having views that are considered odd or fanciful by most. — **view'data** a communications system by which information can be received and requested via a telephone line and presented through a television or visual display unit; **view'finder** a camera attachment or part for determining the field of view; **view'phone** another name for **videophone**; **view'point** point of view; standpoint; a selected position for admiring scenery. — **in view** in sight; in mind; as an aim or prospect; **in view of** in a position to see or to be seen by; having regard to; **on view** open to general inspection; **take a dim view of** to regard unfavourably; **with a view to** having in mind; with a design of. [Fr. *vue* — *vu*, past p. of *voir* — L. *vidēre*, to see.]

vigesimal *vī-jes'i-məl* or **vicesimal** *vī-ses'i-məl*, *adj* based on the number twenty. — *adj* **viges'imo-** (or **vices'imo-**) **quarto** twenty-four-mo. [L. *vigēsimus* (*vīcēsimus*), twentieth — *vīgintī*, twenty.]

vigil *vij'il*, *n* watching, esp. by night, usu. on guard or in prayer; the eve of a holy day; a religious service by night; a keeping awake, wakefulness. — *n* **vig'ilance** watchfulness; wakefulness. — *adj* **vig'ilant** watchful. — *n* **vigilante** (*-an'ti*; orig. *US*, from Sp.) a member of an organisation to look after the interests, threatened in some way, of a group, esp. a self-appointed and unofficial policeman; a member of a vigilance committee. — *n* **vigilan'tism** behaviour associated with vigilantes, esp. militarism and bellicosity. — *adv* **vig'ilantly.** — **vigilance committee** (*US*) an unauthorised body which, in the absence or inefficiency of regular government, exercises powers of arrest, punishment, etc. [L. *vigilia* — *vigil*, awake, watchful; cf. *vigēre*, to be lively.]

vignette *vēn-yet'*, *n* a character sketch; a small embellishment without a border, esp. on a title-page or as a headpiece or tailpiece; a photographic portrait shading off around the head; the illustration on a bank-note; orig. a design of vine-leaves and tendrils. — *vt* to make a vignette of. — *n* **vignett'er** or **vignett'ist.** [Fr. — *vigne* — L. *vīnea*, a vine, a vineyard.]

vigorish *vig'ə-rish*, (*US slang*) *n* a percentage of a gambler's winnings taken by the bookmaker, organisers of a game, etc.; excessive interest charged on a loan. [Prob. Yiddish, — Russ. *vȳigrȳsh*, profit, winnings.]

vigoro *vig'ə-rō*, (*Austr*) *n* a 12-a-side game having similarities to cricket and baseball. [Poss. from **vigour.**]

vigour or in N.Am. **vigor** *vig'ər*, *n* active strength; vital power; healthy growth (in plants, etc.); forcefulness; activity; energy. — *adj* **vig'orous.** — *adv* **vig'orously.** — *n* **vig'orousness.** [A.Fr. *vigour*, and L. *vigor*, *-ōris* — *vigēre*, to be strong.]

vihara *vē-hä'rə*, *n* a Buddhist or Jain precinct, temple or monastery. [Sans. *vihāra.*]

viking *vī'king*, *n* (also with *cap*) any of the Scandinavian adventurers who raided, traded with, and settled in, many parts of Europe between the eighth and eleventh centuries; any aggressive sea-raider, a pirate. — Also *adj.* — *n* **vī'kingism.** [O.N. *vīkingr*, prob. — O.E. *wīcing*, pirate.]

vil. or **vill.** *abbrev* for village.

vile *vīl*, *adj* detestable; loathsome; foul; depraved; base; paltry. — *adv* **vile'ly.** — *n* **vile'ness.** — *n* **vilificā'tion** (*vil-*) act of vilifying; defamatory speech; abuse. — *n* **vilifīer** (*vil'*). — *vt* **vilify** (*vil'*) to make vile; to disparage; to defame: — *pr p* **vil'i-**

fying; *pa t* and *pa p* **vil'ified**. [O.Fr. *vil* and L. *vīlis*, worthless.]

villa *vil'ə, n* orig., a country house or farmhouse with subsidiary buildings; a country seat, in Italy often a castle; a detached house of some size; a superior middle-class house. [L. *villa*, a country house, partly through O.Fr. *ville*, farm, village, etc. (Fr., town), and It. *villa*, country house.]

village *vil'ij, n* an assemblage of houses, shops, etc. smaller than a town, usu. in or close to the countryside; the people of a village; a residential complex temporarily housing participants at a particular event, esp. the athletes and officials taking part in international games. — *adj* of or dwelling in a village. — *n* **vill'ager** an inhabitant of a village. [Fr. *village*, L. *villāticus*.]

villain *vil'ən, n* a violent, malevolent or unscrupulous evil-doer; the wicked enemy of the hero or heroine in a story or play; (*playfully*) a wretch; a criminal (*slang*). — *adj* villainous. — *n* **vill'ainage** and **vill'anage** villeinage. — *n* **vill'ainess** a female villain. — *adj* **vill'ainous** or **vill'anous** of the nature of, like or suited to a villain; detestable, vile. — *adv* **vill'ainously** or **vill'anously**. — *n* **vill'ainy** or **vill'any** an act of a villain; extreme wickedness; an atrocious crime. [O.Fr. — L.L. *villānus* — L. *villa*, a country house.]

-ville *-vil*, (*slang*) *combining form* denoting a supposed world, milieu, etc. frequented by a specified type of person, or characterised by a specified quality, etc., as in *squaresville, dullsville*. [The suffix *-ville* in names of towns, esp. in U.S. — Fr. *ville*, town.]

villein *vil'ən* or *vil'in*, (*hist*) *n* orig. app. a free villager; later (13th cent.) a serf, free in relation to all but his lord, and not absolutely a slave. — *n* **vill'einage** a villein's tenure or status. [A.Fr.; cf. **villain**.]

villus *vil'əs*, (*bot* and *anat*) *n* a long soft hair; a hairlike process: — *pl* **vill'i** (*-ī*). — *adj* **vill'iform** having the form of villi. — *adj* **vill'ose** or **vill'ous** covered with or formed of villi; like the pile of velvet. — *n* **villos'ity**. [L., wool.]

vim *vim*, (*slang*) *n* energy, vigour. [App. L. *vim*, accus. of *vīs*, force.]

vimana *vi-män'ə, n* the central shrine of an Indian temple with a pyramidal roof; a temple gate; a heavenly chariot, chariot of the gods. [Sans. *vimāna*, lit. a marking out.]

Vimule® *vim'ūl, adj* and *n* (denoting) a type of contraceptive cap for the cervix with a two-tiered dome.

vin *vɛ̃*, (Fr.) *n* wine. — **vin blanc** (*blɑ̃*) white wine; **vin ordinaire** (*ör-di-nār'*) inexpensive table wine for ordinary use.

vina *vē'nə, n* an Indian stringed instrument with a fretted fingerboard over two gourds. [Sans. *vīṇā*.]

vinaigrette *vin-ā-gret', n* a mixture of oil, vinegar and seasoning and herbs, used as a salad dressing; a box or bottle for aromatic vinegar or smelling-salts. — *adj* (of a dish) served with a vinaigrette dressing. [Fr., — *vinaigre*, vinegar.]

vinblastine *vin-blas'tēn, n* a drug derived from the Madagascar or rosy periwinkle, used in the treatment of cancer, esp. leukaemias and lymphomas. [Contr. of *vincaleucoblastine* — *Vinca*, the periwinkle genus and **leucoblast**.]

vincible *vin'si-bl, adj* that may be overcome. — *n* **vincibil'ity**. [L. *vincibilis* — *vincĕre*, *victum*, to conquer.]

vincristine *vin-kris'tēn, n* an alkaloid substance derived from the Madagascar or rosy periwinkle, used in the treatment of certain types of blood cancer. [L. *vinca*, a periwinkle, *crista*, a fold.]

vinculum *ving'kū-ləm, n* a horizontal line placed above a part of an equation, etc., equivalent to brackets (*math*); a tendinous band (*anat*): — *pl* **vin'cula**. [L., a bond — *vincīre*, to bind.]

vindicate *vin'di-kāt, vt* to justify; to clear from criticism, etc.; to defend with success; to make good a claim to; to lay claim to; to maintain (a point of view, cause, etc.). — *n* **vindicability** (*-kə-bil'i-ti*). — *adj* **vin'dicable**. — *n* **vindicā'tion** act of vindicating; defence; justification; support. — *adj* **vin'dicātive** (or *vin-dik'ə-tiv*) vindicating; tending to vindicate. — *n* **vin'dicātor** a person who vindicates. — *adv* **vin'dicatorily**. — *adj* **vin'dicatory** (*-ə-tər-i* or *-ā-tər-i*) serving or tending to vindicate; (of laws) punitive; retributive; avenging. [L. *vindicāre*, *-ātum*.]

vindictive *vin-dik'tiv, adj* revengeful or spiteful; pursuing revenge; punitive (as in *vindictive damages*); retributive (as in *vindictive justice*). — *adv* **vindic'tively**. — *n* **vindic'tiveness**. [L. *vindicta*, revenge; see **vindicate**.]

vine *vīn, n* any woody climbing plant that produces grapes; any climbing or trailing stem or plant (*hort*). — *n* **vī'ner** a vine-grower. — *n* **vinery** (*vī'nə-ri*) a hot-house for rearing vines. — *adj* **vinicul'tural** (*vin-*). — *n* **vin'iculture** cultivation of the vine for wine-making, and often also the making of the wine. — *n* **vinicul'turist**. — *n* **vinificā'tion** (*vin-*) the process of converting grape-juice, etc. into wine. — *n* **vinol'ogist** (*vīn-* or *vin-*). — *n* **vinol'ogy** scientific study of vines, esp. grapevine. — *n* **vīnos'ity** vinous character; characteristic qualities of a particular wine. — *adj* **vī'nous** like or pertaining to wine; wine-coloured; caused by or indicative of wine. — *adj* **vī'ny** pertaining to, like, consisting of or bearing vines; entwining. — **vine'-dresser** a person who trims and cultivates vines; **vine fruit** the fruit of the vine in any form, i.e. as grape or raisin, etc.; **vine'=stock** the stock onto which a vine of another kind is grafted; **vineyard** (*vin'yərd* or *-yärd*) a plantation of vines, esp. grape-bearing vines. [O.Fr. *vine*, *vigne* — L. *vīnea*, a vineyard, a vine — *vīnum*, wine.]

vinegar *vin'i-gər, n* a condiment and pickling medium, a dilute impure acetic acid, made from beer, weak wine, etc.; bad temper or mood; energy or vigour (*NAm colloq*). — *vt* to apply vinegar to. — *adj* **vin'egarish** sourish. — *adj* **vin'egary** like or flavoured with vinegar; sour (also *fig*). [Fr. *vinaigre* — *vin* (L. *vīnum*), wine, *aigre*, sour (L. *ācer*, keen, sharp, pungent).]

vingt-et-un *vɛ̃-tā-œ̃, n* a card-game whose object is to have a total of pips in one's hand nearest to, but not exceeding, twenty-one; pontoon. [Fr. twenty-one.]

viniculture, etc. See under **vine**.

vino *vē'nō*, (*slang*) *n* wine: — *pl* **vi'nos**. [It. and Sp.]

vinology, vinous, etc. See under **vine**.

vintage *vin'tij, n* the gathering of grapes and preparation for wine-making; a season's yield of grapes or wine; the time of gathering grapes; wine, esp. of a good year; the product of a particular period; a period of origin. — *adj* pertaining to the grape harvest; (of wine) of a specified year and of good quality; generally, e.g. of a play by an author or of a period, among the (best and) most characteristic; out of date and no longer admired. — **vintage car** an old-fashioned car (*specif* one built between 1919 and 1930); **vintage year** one in which a particular product (usu. wine) reaches an exceptionally high standard. — **post-vintage thoroughbred** see under **thorough**. [A.Fr. *vintage*, O.Fr. (Fr.) *vendange* — L. *vīndēmia* — *vīnum*, wine, grapes, *dēmĕre*, to remove — *dē*, out of or away, *emĕre*, to take; modified by influence of **vintner**.]

vintner *vint'nər, n* a wine-seller. [O.Fr. *vinetier* — L.L. *vīnetārius* — L. *vīnum*, wine.]

viny. See under **vine**.

vinyl *vīn'il, n* an organic radical, a plastic substance; gramophone records (*colloq*). — Also *adj*. — **vinyl resins** and **plastics** thermoplastic resins, polymers or co-polymers of vinyl compounds, e.g. polymers of **vinyl chloride,** a gaseous compound with various industrial applications, and **vinyl acetate** a colourless liquid used to make polyvinyl acetate (see under **poly-**).

viol *vī'əl, n* any member of a class of instruments, forerunners of the violin class, represented now by the double-bass. — *n* **viola** (*vi-ō'lə*) a tenor fiddle, slightly bigger than the violin, tuned a fifth lower. — *n* **violin** (*vī-ə-lin'* or *vī'*) a small musical instrument with four strings (E, A, D, G), held under the chin, played with a bow; a violinist. — *n* **vī'olinist** (or *-lin'*) a player of the violin. — *adj* **violinist'ic**. — *adv* **violinist'ically**. — *n* **violist** (*vī'əl-ist*) a player of the viol; (*vi-ō'list*) a player of the viola. — *n* **violoncellist** (*vē-* or *vī-ə-lən-chel'ist*) a cello-player. — *n* **violoncell'o** a bass instrument of the violin class, commonly called **cello**: — *pl* **violoncell'os**. [Partly obs. vielle; partly Fr. *viole* and It. *viola*, dimin. *violino*, augmentative *violone*, and its dimin. *violoncello*.]

viola *vī'ə-lə, n* any plant of the violet and pansy genus (*Viola*). [L. *viŏla*.]

violate *vī'ə-lāt, vt* to fail to observe duly; to abuse; to rape or submit to sexual abuse of any kind; to profane. — *adj* **vī'olable**. — *adv* **vī'olably**. — *n* **violā'tion**. — *adj* **vī'olātive** causing, tending towards or involving violation. — *n* **vī'olātor**. [L. *violāre, -ātum* — *vīs*, strength.]

violent *vī'ə-lənt, adj* intensely forcible; impetuous and unrestrained in action; overmasteringly vehement; due to violence; expressing violence. — *n* **vi'olence** the state or quality of being or using extreme physical force, esp. when unwarranted; outrage; profanation; injury; rape. — *adv* **vi'olently**. [L. *violentus* or *violēns, -entis* — *vīs*.]

violet *vī'ə-lit, n* any plant or flower of the *Viola* genus, including the pansies, and other similar plants, e.g. the African violet; a bluish purple. — *adj* bluish purple. — **shrinking violet** (*facetious*) a shy, hesitant person. [Fr. *violette* — L. *viola*.]

violin, violist, violoncello, etc. See under **viol**.

VIP *abbrev* for very important person.

viper *vī'pər, n* any of the small venomous snakes of the *Viperidae* family, including the **common viper** or adder, Britain's only venomous snake; extended to some other snakes, e.g. the pit-vipers and horned vipers; an ungrateful or treacherous, malignant person. — *adj* **vī'perish** venomous; spiteful; like a viper. — *adj* **vī'perous** having the qualities of a viper; venomous; malignant. — *adv* **vī'perously**. — **viper's bugloss** a stiff bristly plant with intensely blue flowers, found in dry places, once thought to be a remedy or prophylactic for snakebite. [L. *vīpera* — *vīvus*, living, *parĕre*, to bring forth.]

VIR *abbrev* for *Victoria Imperatrix Regina* (L.), Victoria, Empress and Queen.

viraemia. See under **virus**.

virago *vi-rä'gō* or *vi-rā'gō, n* a violent or bad-tempered woman; a heroic or manlike woman; an amazon: — *pl* **vira'goes** or **vira'gos**. [L. *virāgō, -inis* — *vir*, a man.]

viral. See **virus**.

virement *vē-rə-mã* or *vīr'mənt, n* authorised transference of a surplus to balance a deficit under another heading; authorised redirection of funds for one purpose to a more urgent occasion. [Fr.]

vireo *vir'i-ō, n* any American singing bird of the family **Vireonidae** (*-on'i-dē*): — *pl* **vir'eos**. [L. *vireō, -ōnis*, perh. greenfinch.]

virescent *vir-es'ənt* or *vīr-, adj* turning green; inclining to green; fresh; green; abnormally green. [L. *virēns, -entis*, pres. p. of *virēre*, to be green; *virēscēns*, pres. p. of *virēscĕre*, to become green.]

virga *vûr'gə,* (*meteorol*) *n* (also *npl*) trails of water, drops or ice particles coming from a cloud but not reaching the ground as precipitation. [L., a twig, streak in the sky.]

virgin *vûr'jin, n* a person (esp. a woman) who has never had sexual intercourse; a member of a religious order of women who have undertaken to remain virgins; (usu. with *cap*) a Madonna, a figure of the Virgin (see below); (with *cap*) Virgo, a sign, and a constellation, of the zodiac. — *adj* in a state of virginity; of a virgin; pure; chaste; undefiled; in the original condition — unattained, untouched, unexploited, never scaled, felled, captured, wrought, used, etc.; never having previously undergone or been affected by the thing mentioned. — *adj* **vir'ginal** of or appropriate to a virgin or virginity; in a state of virginity; like a virgin. — *adv* **vir'ginally**. — *n* **vir'ginhood** or **virgin'ity** the state or fact of being a virgin. — *adj* **vir'ginly** pure. — *adv* chastely. — **virgin birth** or **generation** parthenogenesis; (**Virgin Birth**) (the doctrine of) the birth of Christ, His mother being a virgin; **virgin soil** soil never previously tilled or cultivated; material as yet untried or unaffected. — **the Blessed Virgin** or **the Virgin** Mary the mother of Christ; **the Virgin Queen** Elizabeth I of England. [Partly through Fr., — L. *virgō, -inis*.]

virginal[1] *vûr'jin-əl, n* (often in *pl*; also *pair of virginals*) an old keyboard instrument like a small harpsichord, a spinet, esp. a box-shaped spinet. [Perh. as played by young ladies; see **virgin**.]

virginal[2], **virginhood,** etc. See under **virgin**.

Virginia *vər-jin'yə, n* a tobacco grown and manufactured in *Virginia*. — *adj* **Virgin'ian**. — *n* a native or citizen of Virginia. — **Virginia creeper** an American climbing-plant closely related to the vine, bright red in autumn. [After Elizabeth I, the *virgin* queen.]

virginity, etc. See under **virgin**.

Virgo *vûr'gō, n* the Virgin in the Zodiac; a person born between 23 August and 22 September, under the sign of the Virgin. — *n* **Virgō'an** a person born under the sign of the Virgin. — Also *adj*. — **virgo intacta** (*in-tak'tə* or *-ta*; L., untouched) a woman who has not had sexual intercourse. [L.]

virgule *vûr'gūl, n* a slanting line, a stroke, a solidus. — *adj* **vir'gulate** shaped like a rod. [Fr., — L. *virgula*, dimin. of *virga*, a twig, rod.]

viricide, etc. See under **virus**.

virid *vir'id, adj* green. — *n* **viridesc'ence**. — *adj* **viridesc'ent** greenish. [L. *viridis*, green — *virēre*, to be green.]

virile *vir'īl* or (esp. in N.Am.) *vir'il, adj* having the qualities of a mature male human being; robustly masculine; manly; (of a man) sexually potent or with a particularly high sexual drive. — *adj* **vir'ilised** or **-ized**. — *adj* **vir'ilising** or **-z-**. — *n* **vir'ilism** presence of male sexual characteristics in the female. — *n* **viril'ity** the power (esp. sexual power) of a mature male; manhood; masculinity; vigour, energy. [L. *virīlis* — *vir*, a man.]

virology, etc. See under **virus**.

virtu *vûr-tōō', n* a love of the fine arts; taste for curiosities; objects of art or antiquity collectively. — *adj* **virtuose** (*-tū-ōs'*) or **virtuō'sic** exhibiting the qualities of a virtuoso. — *n* **virtuosity** (*-os'*) the character of a virtuoso; exceptional technical skill in music or other fine art; interest in or knowledge of articles of virtu. — *n* **virtuoso** (*vûr-tū-ō'sō* or *-zō*) a person with a good deal of knowledge of or interest in works of art, antiquities, curiosities and the like; a musician (or other artist) of the highest technical skill: — *pl* **virtuō'sōs** or **virtuō'si** (*-sē*). — *n* **virtuō'sōship**. — **article** (or **object**) **of virtu** an object of artistic or antiquarian interest, a curio. [It. *virtù* — L. *virtūs, -ūtis*; see **virtue**.]

virtual, etc. See under **virtue**.

virtue *vûr'tū, n* excellence; worth; moral excellence; inherent power; efficacy; the practice of duty; a good quality, esp. moral; sexual purity; (*loosely*) virginity; one of the orders of the celestial hierarchy. — *adj* **vir'tual** in effect, though not in fact; not such in fact but capable of being considered as such for some purposes. — *n* **virtual'ity** essential nature; potentiality. — *adv* **vir'tually** in effect, though not in fact; (*loosely*) almost, nearly. — *adj* **vir'tueless.** — *adj* **vir'tuous** having virtue; morally good; blameless; righteous; practising duty; according to moral law; chaste. — *adv* **vir'tuously.** — *n* **vir'tuousness.** — **by (or in) virtue of** because of; on account of; **make a virtue of necessity** to do as if from a sense of duty (or with a sense of duty called in for the occasion) something unpleasant one is forced to do. [O.Fr. *vertu* and L. *virtus*, bravery, moral excellence — *vir*, a man.]

virtuose, virtuosity, etc. See under **virtu**.

virucidal, etc. See under **virus**.

virulent *vir'ū-lənt* or *-ōō-*, *adj* extremely infectious; highly poisonous or malignant; venomous; acrimonious. — *n* **vir'ulence** or **vir'ulency.** — *adv* **vir'ulently.** [L. *vīrulentus* — *vīrus*, see **virus**.]

virus *vī'rəs*, *n* contagious or poisonous matter (as of ulcers, etc.); the transmitted cause of infection; a pathogenic agent, usu. a protein-coated particle of RNA or DNA, capable of increasing rapidly inside a living cell; (**computer virus**) a piece of computer code inserted into an apparently innocent program in order to corrupt or destroy other data, and unknowingly passed on from one user to another; any corrupting influence. — *n* **viraemia** (*vī-rē'mi-ə*) the presence of viruses in the bloodstream. — *adj* **vīrae'mic.** — *adj* **vī'ral** pertaining to or caused by a virus. — *adj* **vī'ricidal** or **vī'rucidal** (or *vir'*). — *n* **vī'ricide** or **vī'ricide** (or *vir'*) a substance that destroys or eliminates a virus. — *n* **vī'roid** a particle of RNA, uncoated by protein, that can cause some diseases in plants. — *adj* **virolog'ical.** — *n* **virol'ogy** the study of virus, viruses and virus diseases. — *n* **virol'ogist.** — *n* **virō'sis** a disease caused by a virus. — **virus disease** a disease caused by a virus. [L. *vīrus*, venom.]

Vis. *abbrev* for Viscount.

vis *vis* or *vēs*, (L.) *n* force, power. — **vis major** (*mā'jər* or *mä'yor*) superior force.

visa *vē'zə*, *n* an authenticating endorsement on a passport, etc. allowing the holder to enter or leave the country issuing it. — *vt* to put a visa on: — *pa t* and *pa p* **vi'saed.** [L. *vīsa*, past p. fem. of *vidēre*, to see.]

visage *viz'ij*, *n* (*literary*) the face. — *adj* **vis'aged.** — *n* **visagiste** (Fr.; *vē-zazh-ēst*) or **vis'agist** (*viz'ə-jist*) an expert in facial make-up. [Fr. *visage* — L. *vīsus*, look.]

vis-à-vis *vē-za-vē*, *adv* face-to-face. — *prep* lit. face-to-face with; in relation to, with regard to. — *n* an opposite number. [Fr. *vis*, face (— L. *vīsus*, look), *à*, to.]

Visc. *abbrev* for Viscount.

viscacha *vis-kä'chə* or **vizcacha** *viz-kä'chə*, *n* a S. American burrowing rodent of heavy build. [Sp., — Quechua *huiscacha.*]

viscera, visceral, viscerate, visceri-, viscero-. See under **viscus**.

viscid *vis'id*, *adj* semi-fluid, sticky, glutinous, viscous; (of a surface) clammy and covered with a sticky secretion (*bot*). — *n* **viscid'ity.** [L.L. *viscidus* — L. *viscum*; see **viscous**.]

visco-, viscometer, viscosimeter, etc. See under **viscous**.

viscose *vis'kōs*, *n* the sodium salt of cellulose xanthate, used in the manufacture of rayon. [Ety. as for **viscous**.]

viscosity. See under **viscous**.

viscount *vī'kownt*, *n* a title of nobility next below an earl (first granted in 1440); the son or young brother of a count; an officer who acted as administrative deputy to an earl, a sheriff (*hist*); (esp. with *cap*) a similar official in Jersey. — *n* **viscountess** (*vī'kownt-es*) the wife of a viscount; a woman holding a viscounty in her own right. — *n* **vi'scountcy** or **vi'scountship** a viscounty. — *n* **vi'scounty** the rank or dignity of a viscount; the jurisdiction of, or territory under, a viscount (*hist*). [O.Fr. *visconte* — *vis-* (L. *vice*, in place of), *conte*, count, after L.L. *vicecomes* — L. *comes*, a companion.]

viscous *vis'kəs*, *adj* resistant or highly resistant to flow owing to forces acting between the molecules; sticky; viscid. — *n* **vis'cousness.** — *combining form* **vis'cō-** denoting viscous or viscosity. — *n* **viscom'eter** or **viscōsim'eter** an instrument for measuring viscosity. — *adj* **viscōmet'ric, viscōmet'rical, viscōsimet'ric** or **viscosimet'rical.** — *n* **viscom'etry** or **viscōsim'etry.** — *n* **viscos'ity** the quality of being viscous. — **viscous flow** a type of fluid flow in which there is a continuous steady motion of the particles, the motion at a fixed point always remaining constant; **viscous water** water thickened by addition of chemicals, used in fighting forest fires. [L.L. *viscōsus*, sticky — L. *viscum*, bird-lime, mistletoe.]

viscus *vis'kəs*, (*med* and *zool*) *n* any one of the organs situated within the chest and the abdomen — heart, lungs, liver, etc.: — *pl* **viscera** (*vis'ər-ə*; in common use, esp. the abdominal organs). — *adj* **visc'eral** of or relating to the viscera; instinctive or intuitive, not cerebral or rational (*colloq*); having to do with the more earthy feelings and emotions (*colloq*). — *vt* **visc'erate** to disembowel. — *combining form* **visc'erō-** or **visc'eri-** pertaining to the viscera or to a viscus. [L. *vīscus*, pl. *vīscera*.]

vise. N.Am. spelling of **vice**[1].

Vishnu *vish'nōō*, (*Hinduism*) *n* the second god of the Hindu triad, believed to appear in many incarnations, regarded by some worshippers as the saviour. — *n* **Vish'nuism.** — *n* and *adj* **Vish'nuite.** [Sans.]

visible *viz'i-bl*, *adj* that may be seen; in sight; obvious; (of supplies of a commodity) actually in store, known to be available; relating to goods rather than services (*econ*); ready or willing to receive a visitor or visitors. — *n* a visible thing (often in *pl*). — *n* **visibil'ity** the state or quality of being visible, or perceivable by the eye; the clearness of the atmosphere; clarity and range of vision in the atmospheric conditions, seeing; a visible thing (usu. in *pl*). — *n* **vis'ibleness.** — *adv* **vis'ibly.** — **visible means** means or resources which are apparent to or ascertainable by others; **visible radiation** electromagnetic radiation which can be detected by the eye, light. [Through O.Fr. or direct from L. *vīsībilis* — *vidēre*; see ety. for **vision**.]

Visigoth *viz'i-goth*, (*hist*) *n* one of the Western Goths, as distinguished from the Ostrogoths or Eastern Goths, who formed settlements in the south of France and in Spain, and their kingdom in the latter lasted into the 8th century. — *adj* **Visigoth'ic.** [L.L. *Visigothī* — Gmc. word meaning perh. noble Goths, perh. west Goths.]

vision *vizh'ən*, *n* the act of seeing; the faculty of sight; anything seen; television, esp. as opposed to radio; a look, glance; a vivid concept or mental picture; a person or scene of great beauty (sometimes ironically); a pleasing imaginative plan for, or anticipation of, future events; an apparition; a revelation, esp. divine, in sleep or a trance (sometimes without article); the act or power of perceiving imaginative mental images; imaginative perception; foresight; mystical awareness of the supernatural. — *vt* to see as a vision, to imagine; to present, or to call up, as in a vision. — *adj* **vis'ional** of or pertaining to a vision; derived from a vision; visionary, not real. — *adv* **vis'ionally.** — *n* **vis'ionariness.** — *adj* **vis'ionary** capable of seeing visions; apt to see visions; given to reverie or fantasy; showing or marked by imagination or foresight; out of touch with reality, unpractical; of the nature of, or seen in, a vision, visional; fanciful, not real; impracticable; characterised by visions or fantasy; pertaining to physical or mental vision. — *n* a person who sees visions; a person who forms impracticable schemes. — *adj* **vis'ioned** inspired so as to see visions; seen in a vision; produced by, or associated with, a vision. — *adj* **vis'ionless** lacking vision. — **vision mixer** a technician who blends or combines different camera shots in television or films. [Fr., — L. *visiō, visiōnis* — *vidēre, vīsum*, to see.]

visit *viz'it, vt* to pay a call upon, or to be in the habit of doing so; to go to for sightseeing, pleasure or religious purposes; to go to stay with; to make a stay in, e.g. of migratory birds; to go to see professionally; to examine, inspect, esp. officially; to inflict (punishment, etc.) (with *on*); to come to, or to go to see, in order to give comfort; (of an idea) to take temporary hold on the mind of; to afflict or trouble, as with disease (*old fashioned*). — *vi* to be in the habit of seeing or meeting each other at home; to make a visit or visits. — *n* an act of visiting; a short stay; a sightseeing excursion; an official or a professional call; a chat (*NAm colloq*). — *adj* **vis'itable** subject to official visitation; attractive to visitors. — *adj* **vis'itant** paying visits, visiting. — *n* a person who visits; a person who is a guest in the house of another; a supernatural visitor; a migratory bird. — *n* **visitā'tion** the act of visiting; a formal, or long and wearisome visit; an examination by authority; a visit of God, or of a good (or evil) supernatural being; a dispensation of divine favour or displeasure; the operation of a destructive power, or an instance of it; an influence acting on the mind; an unusual and extensive irruption of a species of animals into a region. — *adj* **visitā'tional** or **vis'itātive.** — *adj* **visitatō'rial.** — *n* **visitee'** the person to whom a visit is paid. — *n* **vis'iting** the act, or an instance, of paying a visit; a visitation, in the senses of divine dispensation, heavy affliction, or influence operating on the mind. — *adj* that visits; often opp. to *resident*; pertaining to visiting. — *n* **vis'itor** a person who visits, calls on, or makes a stay with, another person; a person authorised to visit for purposes of inspection or supervision. — *adj* **visītō'rial.** — **vis'iting-card** a small card bearing the name and address, or title, left in paying visits, and sometimes (esp. formerly) sent as an act of courtesy or in token of sympathy; **visitors' book** a book in which visitors write their names and sometimes comments; **visitors' passport** (also **British Visitors' Passport**) a simplified form of passport, valid for one year for visits not exceeding three months to certain countries, obtainable at post offices. — **visit with** (*NAm*) to visit; to be a guest (with); to chat (with). [Fr. *visiter* — L. *vīsitāre*, frequentative of *vīsere*, to go to see, visit.]

visor or **vizor** *vīz'ər, n* a movable part of a helmet covering the face, or the upper part of the face, with holes or slits for the eyes and mouth; a mask; a disguise, feigning appearance; a hood placed over a signal light; the peak of a cap; a movable flap on a motor car windscreen, used as a shade against the sun. — *vt* to disguise or cover with a visor. — *adj* **vis'ored** or **viz'ored** having a visor; wearing a visor; masked. [A.Fr. *viser* — *vis*, countenance.]

vista *vis'tə, n* a view or prospect, esp. as seen through an avenue; an avenue or other long narrow opening or passage; the trees, etc. that form the avenue; a mental view or vision extending far into the past or future, or into any subject engaging the thoughts. [It. *vista*, sight, view — L. *vidēre, vīsum*, to see.]

visual *vizh'ū-əl* or *viz'ū-əl, adj* of or pertaining to sight; concerned with seeing, or (*fig*) with mental vision; attained by, or received through, sight; of the nature of, or conveying, a mental vision; visible, having visibility; optic, as in **visual axis** (see **optic axis** under **optic**). — *n* something visible; a rough sketch of the layout of an advertisement; (often in *pl*) a drawing, piece of film, etc. as distinct from the words or sound accompanying it. — *n* **visualīsā'tion** or **-z-.** — *vt* **vis'ualise** or **-ize** to make visible, externalise to the eye; to call up a clear mental image of. — *vi* to call up a clear visual image; to become visible (*med*). — *n* **vis'ualīser** or **-z-.** — *adv* **vis'ually.** — **visual aid** a picture, photograph, film, diagram, etc. used as an aid to teaching; **visual arts** painting, sculpture, films, etc. as opposed to literature, music, etc.; **visual display unit** (*comput*; abbrev. **VDU**) a cathode ray tube which displays data, entered by keyboard or light pen, from a computer's memory. [L.L. *vīsuālis* — L. *vīsus*, sight.]

visuo- *vizh -ū-ō-* or *viz -ū-ō-, combining form* denoting sight. [L. *vīsus*.]

vital *vī'tl, adj* characteristic of life, or of living things; supporting or necessary to life; essential, or (*loosely*) highly important; pertaining to life, birth and death; lively, energetic; being a manifestation of organic life (*biol*); due to a living agency. — *n* **vitalisā'tion** or **-z-.** — *vt* **vi'talise** or **-ize** to give life to; to stimulate activity in; to give vigour to; to make lifelike. — *n* **vi'taliser** or **-z-.** — *adj* **vi'talising** or **-z-.** — *n* **vi'talism** the doctrine that there is a vital force (q.v.). — *n* **vi'talist** a person who holds this doctrine. — *adj* **vitalis'tic.** — *n* **vitality** (*-tal'*) the state or quality of being vital; the quality of being fully or intensely alive; the capacity to endure and flourish; animation, liveliness; the principle of life, power of living; the state of being alive; a living or vital thing or quality: — *pl* **vital'ities.** — *adv* **vi'tally.** — *npl* **vi'tals** (rarely in *sing*) the interior organs essential for life; the part of any whole necessary for its existence. — **vital force** the force on which the phenomena of life in animals and plants depend — distinct from chemical and mechanical forces operating in them; **vital functions** the bodily functions that are essential to life, such as the circulation of the blood; **vital signs** (the level or rate of) breathing, heartbeat, etc.; **vital spark** or **flame** life or a trace of life; the principle of life in man; **vital statistics** statistics dealing with the facts of population — births, deaths, etc.; a woman's bust, waist and hip measurements (*colloq*). [L. *vītālis* — *vīta*, life.]

vitamin *vit'ə-min* or (esp. in N.Am.) *vīt'ə-, n* any of numerous organic substances, 'accessory food factors', present in minute quantities in nutritive foods and essential for the health of the animal organism. — *vt* **vi'taminise** or **-ize** to add vitamins to (a food). [Coined in 1906 from L. *vīta*, life, and (inappropriately) **amine**.]

vite *vēt*, (*mus*) *adv* quickly. [Fr.]

vitellus *vi-* or *vī-tel'əs, n* the yolk of an egg: — *pl* **vitell'ī.** — *adj* **vit'ellary** pertaining to the vitellus; yellow like the yolk of an egg. — *n* **vitell'icle** a yolk-sac. — *adj* **vitelligenous** (*-ij'*) producing yolk. — *n* **vitell'in** a phosphoprotein present in yolks of eggs. — *n* **vitell'ine** a vitellus. — *adj* vitellary. [L., a yolk; a transferred use of *vitellus* — *vitulus*, a calf.]

vitiate *vish'i-āt, vt* to render faulty or defective; to spoil; to make impure; to deprave, corrupt, pervert, debase; to make ineffectual or invalid or inconclusive. — *adj* **vi'tiable.** — *n* **vitiā'tion.** — *n* **vi'tiātor.** — *n* **vitios'ity** the state or quality of being vicious or (in *Scots law*) faulty. [L. *vitiāre, -ātum* — *vitium*; see **vice**[2].]

viticulture *vit'i-kul-chər, n* cultivation of vines. — *n* **viticul'turist.** [**Vitis.**]

vitiligo *vit-i-lī'gō* or *-ə-lē'gō*, (*med*) *n* a skin abnormality in which irregular patches of the skin lose colour and turn white. [L. *vitilīgo*, a skin eruption.]

vitiosity. See under **vitiate.**

Vitis *vī'tis, n* the grapevine genus of woody climbing plants. [L. *vītis*, a vine — *viēre*, to twist.]

vitreous *vit'ri-əs, adj* glassy; pertaining to, consisting of, or like glass; glass green in colour; resembling glass in absence of crystalline structure, in lustre, etc. (*geol*). — *n* **vit'reousness** or **vitresc'ence.** — *adj* **vitresc'ent** tending to become glass, or capable of being turned into glass. — *n* **vit'reum** the vitreous humour of the eye. — *adj* **vit'ric.** — *n* **vitrifac'tion**

or **vitrificā'tion** the act, process or operation of vitrifying, or converting into glass; the state of being vitrified; a vitrified substance. — *n* **vitrifac'ture** the manufacture of glass. — *adj* **vit'rifiable**. — *adj* **vit'rified**. — *adj* **vit'riform** having the form or appearance of glass. — *vt* and *vi* **vit'rify** to make into, or to become, glass or a glassy substance. — **vitreous humour** the jellylike substance filling the posterior chamber of the eye of a vertebrate, between the lens and the retina. [L. *vitrum*, glass.]

vitriol *vit'ri-əl*, *n* oil of vitriol (q.v. below); a hydrous sulphate of a metal, e.g. *blue*, *green* and *white vitriol*, respectively that of copper (cupric), iron (ferrous) and zinc; rancorous, caustic criticism, etc. (*fig*). — *vt* **vit'riolāte** to convert into, or to treat with, vitriol. — *n* **vitriolā'tion**. — *adj* **vitriolic** (*-ol'ik*) pertaining to, or having the qualities of, vitriol; biting, scathing, expressing intense ill-will. — *n* **vitriolisā'tion** or **-z-**. — *vt* **vit'riolise** or **-ize** to vitriolate; to injure with vitriol. — **elixir of vitriol** aromatic sulphuric acid (i.e. sulphuric acid mixed with certain other substances for use in medicine); **oil of vitriol** concentrated sulphuric acid — because formerly prepared from green vitriol. [Fr., — L.L. *vitriolum* — L. *vitreus*, of glass.]

vitro- *vit -rō-*, *combining form* denoting glass. [L. *vitrum*, glass.]

vitta *vit'ə*, *n* a stripe of colour (*bot* and *zool*); a thin, elongated cavity containing oil, found in the pericarps of some fruits (*bot*): — *pl* **vitt'ae** (*-ē*). — *adj* **vitt'ate** having vittae; striped lengthwise. [L., a fillet or band for the head.]

vituperate *vi-* or *vī-tū'pə-rāt*, *vt* to attack with abusive criticsm or disapproval. — *vi* to use abusive language. — *n* **vitūperā'tion**. — *adj* **vitū'perative** (*-rət-* or *-rāt-*) containing vituperation; uttering, or prone to utter, abuse. — *adv* **vitū'peratively**. — *n* **vitū'perātor**. — *adj* **vitū'peratory** vituperative. [L. *vituperāre*, *-ātum* — *vitium*, a fault, *parāre*, to set in order, prepare.]

Vitus: St Vitus's dance. See **chorea**.

viva[1] *vē'vä*, (*It.* and *Sp.*) *interj* long live.

viva[2], *vī'və*. See **viva voce**.

vivace *vē-vä'che*, (*mus*) *adj* and *adv* lively; in a lively manner: — *superl* **vivacis'simo**. [It.]

vivacious *vi-vā'shəs*, *adj* lively, full of vitality; sprightly, sportive. — *adv* **vivā'ciously**. — *n* **vivā'ciousness** or **vivac'ity** the state of being vivacious; vigour; animation; liveliness or sprightliness of temper or behaviour. [L. *vīvāx*, *vīvācis* — *vīvěre*, to live.]

vivamente. See **vivo**.

vivarium *vī-vā'ri-əm*, *n* an artificial enclosure for keeping or raising living animals, such as a park, a fish-pond; a glass-sided box, etc.: — *pl* **vīvā'ria** or **vīvāriums**. [L. *vīvārium* — *vīvus*, alive — *vīvěre*, to live.]

vivat *vī'vat* or *vē'vat*, (L.) *interj* long live.

viva voce *vī'və vō'sē* or *vō'chē*, *adv* lit. by the living voice; by oral testimony. — *n* (usu. **viva** alone) an oral examination. — *vt* (usu. **viva**) to examine orally. [L.]

vive *vēv*, (Fr.) *interj* long live.

vives *vīvz*, *nsing* a disease of horses, swelling of the submaxillary glands. [O.Fr. *avives*, *vives* — Sp. *avivas* — Ar. *addhība* — *al*, the, *dhība*, she-wolf.]

vivi- *vi-vi-*, *combining form* denoting alive, living. [L. *vīvus*.]

vivid *viv'id*, *adj* (of a colour) very bright; presenting a clear and striking picture; forming brilliant mental images; lively, intense; full of life, vigorous. — *adv* **viv'idly**. — *n* **viv'idness**. — *adj* **vivif'ic** vivifying. — *n* **vivificā'tion**. — *n* **viv'ifier**. — *vt* **viv'ify** to endue with life; to make vivid; to assimilate, convert into living tissue. — *adj* **viv'ifying**. [L. *vīvidus* — *vīvěre*, to live.]

viviparous *vi-* or *vī-vip'ə-rəs*, *adj* producing living young that have reached an advanced stage of development (opp. of *oviparous*; *zool*); germinating from a seed still on the parent plant (*bot*); producing young plants in the flower clusters, etc. (*bot*). — *n* **vivip'arism** viviparous reproduction. — *n* **viviparity** (*viv-i-par'i-ti*) or **vivip'arousness** the quality of being viviparous. — *adv* **vivip'arously**. — *n* **vivip'ary** viviparity in plants. [**vivi-** and L. *parěre*, to produce.]

vivisection *viv'i-sek-shən*, *n* the act or practice, or an instance, of making surgical operations on living animals for the purposes of physiological research or demonstration; merciless and minute examination or criticism. — *vt* **viv'isect** to practice vivisection on. — Also *vi*. — *adj* **vivisec'tional**. — *n* **vivisec'tionist** a person who practises or defends vivisection. — *adj* **vivisec'tive** practising vivisection. — *n* **vivisec'tor** someone who practises vivisection. [**vivi-** and L. *sectiō* — *secāre*, to cut.]

vivo *vē'vō*, (*mus*) *adj* lively. — *adv* **vivamente** (*vē-vä-men'tā*) in a lively manner. [It.]

vixen *vik'sn*, *n* a female fox; a bad-tempered woman. — *adj* **vix'en**, **vix'enish** or **vix'enly** ill-tempered, snarling. [Southern dialect form of *fixen* — O.E. *fyxen*, fem. of *fox*.]

viz. See **videlicet**.

vizcacha. See **viscacha**.

vizier *vi-zēr'*, *viz'yər* or *viz'i-ər*, *n* a minister or councillor of state in various Muslim states. — *n* **vizier'ate** or **vizier'ship** the office of a vizier. — *adj* **vizier'ial**. — **Grand Vizier** (in pre-Republican Turkey) the prime minister, and at one time also commander of the army. [Ar. *wazīr*, a porter — *wazara*, to bear a burden.]

vizor. See **visor**.

vizsla *viz'lə* or *vizh'lə*, *n* a Hungarian breed of hunting dog with smooth red or rust-coloured coat. [*Vizsla*, a town in Hungary.]

vl *abbrev* for *varia lectio* (L.), variant reading (*pl* **vvll**).

Vlach *vlak*, *n* one of a non-Slav people of south-eastern Europe, found chiefly in Romania. [O.Slav. *Vlachŭ* — O.H.G. *walh*, a foreigner, esp. a Slav or a Latin.]

VLCD *abbrev* for very low calorie diet.

VLF *abbrev* for very low frequency.

VLSI (*comput*) *abbrev* for very large scale integration.

VMD *abbrev* for *Veterināriae Medicinae Doctor* (N.L.), Doctor of Veterinary Medicine.

VMH *abbrev* for Victoria Medal of Honour.

VN *abbrev* for Vietnam (I.V.R.).

vo *abbrev* for *verso* (q.v.), on the left-hand page.

voc. *abbrev* for vocative.

vocab *vō'kab* or *və-kab'*, (*colloq*) *n* vocabulary.

vocable *vō'kə-bl*, *n* that which is sounded with the voice — a word, or a single sound of a word. — *adj* capable of being uttered. — *adj* **vocab'ūlar** (*vō-* or *və-*) of or concerning words. — *n* **vocab'ūlary** a list of words explained in alphabetical order; a dictionary; any list of words; the words of a language; the words known to and used by e.g. a particular person; the words used in a (particular) science or art; the signs or symbols used in any non-verbal type of communication, e.g. in computer technology; a collection of forms used in an art or by a particular practitioner of an art. [L. *vocābulum* — *vōx*, voice.]

vocal *vō'kəl*, *adj* having a voice; uttered by the voice; oral; sung, or for singing (opp. of *instrumental*); resounding; talkative; eloquent; concerned in the production of speech; of or pertaining to a vowel; having a vowel function; voiced. — *n* (often in *pl*) singing, or that which is sung, esp. in a piece of popular music. — *adj* **vōcal'ic** containing (esp. many) vowels; of, pertaining to, or of the nature of a vowel or vowels. — *n* **vōcalisā'tion** or **-z-**. — *vt* **vō'calise** or **-ize** to form into voice, to articulate; to sing; to give expression to; to make vocal, endow with power of expression; to convert into a vowel; to utter with the voice (*phon*). — *vi* to sing; to sing on a vowel or vowels. — *n* **vō'caliser** or **-z-**. — *n* **vō'calism** exercise of the vocal organs; the art of using the voice in singing; a vocal sound; system of vowels. — *n* **vō'calist** a singer (esp. opp. to *instrumentalist*). — *n* **vōcal'ity** or **vō'calness**. — *adv* **vō'cally**. — **vocal cords** (in air-breathing vertebrates) folds of the lining membrane of the larynx, by the vibration of the edges of which, under the influence of the breath, the voice is produced; **vocal music** music produced by the human voice alone (as opp. to *instrumental music*); **vocal score** a musical score showing the singing parts in full. [L. *vōcālis* — *vōx*, *vōcis*, voice.]

vocation *vō-kā'shən*, *n* a calling by God to his service in special work or in a special position, or to a state of salvation; a fitness for God's or other specified work; a way of living or sphere of activity to which one has been called by God, or for which one has a special fitness; one's occupation, business or profession. — *adj* **vocā'tional** pertaining to, concerned with, or in preparation for, a trade or occupation. — *n* **vocā'tionalism** the giving of an important place in education to vocational training. — *adv* **vocā'tionally**. — *adj* **vocative** (*vok'ə-tiv*) pertaining to the act of calling; applied to the grammatical case used in direct personal address. — *n* the case of a word when a person or thing is addressed; a word in that case. [L. *vocātiō*, *-ōnis*, and *vocātīvus* — *vocāre*, to call.]

vociferate *vō-sif'ə-rāt*, *vi* to cry with a loud voice, to bawl. — *vt* to utter in a loud voice. — *n* **vociferā'tion** the act of vociferating; a violent or loud outcry. — *adj* **vocif'erous** making a loud outcry; noisy. — *adv* **vocif'erously**. — *n* **vocif'erousness**. [L. *vociferari*, — *vōx*, *vōcis*, voice, *fĕrre*, to carry.]

vocoder *vō-kō'dər*, *n* an electronic device, similar to a synthesiser, for imposing human speech patterns on to the sound of musical instruments. [*vo*cal *cod*ifier.]

vodka *vod'kə*, *n* a Russian spirit, properly distilled from rye, but sometimes from potatoes, etc. [Russ., dimin. of *voda*, water.]

voetstoots *fŏŏt'stŏŏts*, (*SAfr*) *adj* (of something sold) as it stands, with any defects it has, visible or not. — Also *adv*. [Afrik.]

vogue *vōg*, *n* popularity; a place in popular favour, or the period of it; the mode or fashion at any particular time. — *adj* in vogue, fashionable. — *adj* **vog'uey** or **vog'uish**. — **vogue word** a word much used at a particular time. [Fr. *vogue* (orig. the course of a rowing vessel) — *voguer*, to row — It. *vogare*.]

voice *vois*, *n* sound produced by the vocal organs of living beings, esp. of human beings in speech or song; sound given out by anything; the faculty or power of speech or song; the ability to sing, esp. well; a mode of utterance; the quality and range of musical sounds produced by a singer; a singer; a part for a singer, or one of the parts in an instrumental composition; utterance, expression; someone who speaks; sound uttered with resonance of the vocal cords (*phon*); a mode of inflecting verbs to indicate their relationship with the subject (*gram*; see **active** and **passive**). — *vt* to give utterance or expression to; to regulate the tone of (*mus*); to write the voice parts of; to utter with vibration of the vocal cords (*phon*). — *adj* **voiced** endowed with voice; having a voice of a specified kind; uttered with voice (*phon*). — *adj* **voice'less** having no voice; speechless, silent; unspoken; failing to, or unable to, express one's opinion or desire, or to make this felt; having no vote; not voiced (*phon*). — *n* **voice'lessness**. — *n* **voic'er**. — *n* **voic'ing** the regulation of the tone of organ pipes, ensuring proper power, pitch and quality. — **voice'-box** the larynx; **voice'-over** the background voice of an unseen narrator in a film, etc.; **voice'-print** an electronically recorded visual representation of speech indicating frequency, amplitude and duration; **voice response** output from a computer in the form of synthesised speech rather than a visual display. — **give voice to** to express; **in good voice** in good condition for singing or speaking; **with one voice** unanimously. [A.Fr. *voiz*, *voice* (Fr. *voix*) — L. *vōx*, *vōcis*.]

void *void*, *adj* containing nothing, empty, deserted; unoccupied, unutilised; having no holder, vacant; devoid, destitute, free (with *of*); ineffectual, useless; not binding in law, null, invalid. — *n* an empty space; (with **the**) the expanse of space; emptiness; a lack, esp. an emotional lack strongly felt (*fig*); an unfilled space (*archit*); the total absence of cards of a particular suit (*bridge*, etc.). — *vt* to make vacant, to empty, clear; to send out, discharge, emit; to make of no effect, to nullify. — *adj* **void'able** that may be voided; that may be either voided or confirmed (*law*). — *n* **void'ance** the act of voiding or emptying; the state of being void; (of a benefice) the fact or state of being vacant. — *n* **void'ing** the act of voiding; that which is voided (often in *pl*). — *n* **void'ness**. [O.Fr. *voide*, empty — popular L. *vocitus* — *vocitāre*, to empty — *vocuus*, for L. *vacuus*.]

voile *voil*, *n* any of several kinds of thin semitransparent material. [Fr., veil.]

voir dire *vwär dēr*, (*law*) *n* an oath administered to a witness or juror. [O.Fr. *voir*, true, truth, *dire*, to say.]

voix céleste *vwä sā-lest*, *n* an organ stop producing a soft, tremulous sound. [Fr., heavenly voice.]

vol. *abbrev* for: volume; volunteer.

volant *vō'lənt*, *adj* flying; passing lightly through the air; flying or pertaining to flight (*zool*); nimble; represented as flying (*heraldry*). — *adj* **volante** (*vō-län'tā*; *mus*) moving lightly and rapidly. — *adj* **vol'itant** flying or fluttering; moving about; able to fly. — *n* **volitā'tion** flight; the power of flying. — *adj* **volitā'tional**. — *adj* **volitorial** (*-tō'ri-*) having the power of flight. [L. *volāre*, to fly.]

volatile *vol'ə-tīl* or in N.Am. *-til* or *-təl*, *adj* evaporating very quickly; explosive; flighty, apt to change; not retaining information after the power supply is cut off (*comput*). — *n* a volatile substance. — *n* **vol'atileness** or **volatility** (*-til'*). — *adj* **vol'atilīsable** or **-z-** (or *-at'-*). — *n* **volatilīsā'tion** or **-z-**. — *vt* and *vi* **vol'atilise** or **-ize** (or *-at'-*) to make or become volatile. — *vt* to cause to evaporate; to make light, unsubstantial, delicate (*fig*). — **volatile oils** see **essential oils**. [L. *volāre*, to fly, *volitāre*, to flit, flutter.]

vol-au-vent *vol-ō-vã*, *n* a kind of small pie of light puff pastry filled with meat, or fish, etc. [Fr., lit. flight in the wind.]

volcano *vol-kā'nō*, *n* a centre of eruption of subterranean matter, typically a more or less conical hill or mountain, built of ash and lava, with a central crater and pipe; a state of affairs, emotional condition, etc., suggestive of a volcano because an upheaval or outburst seems imminent (*fig*); a form of firework: — *pl* **volcan'oes**. — *adj* **volcanic** (*vol-kan'ik*) pertaining to, of the nature of, produced or caused by a volcano; characterised by the presence of volcanoes. — *adv* **volcan'ically**. — *n* **volcanicity** (*-kə-nis'i-ti*) volcanic action or phenomena. — *n* **volcanisā'tion** or **-z-**. — *vt* **vol'canise** or **-ize** to subject to the action of volcanic heat. — *adj* **vol'canised** or **-z-**. — *n* **volcanism** and **volcanist** see **vulcanism, vulcanist**. — *adj* **volcanolog'ical**. — *n* **volcanologist** see **vulcanologist**. — *n* **volcanology** see **vulcanology**. — **volcanic glass** rock without a crystalline structure, such as obsidian, pumice, etc., produced by rapid cooling of molten lava; **volcanic mud** and **sand** volcanic ash which has been deposited under water and sorted and stratified; **volcanic rocks** those formed by volcanic agency. [It., — L. *Volcānus*, *Vulcānus*, god of fire.]

vole[1] *vōl*, *n* any of numerous blunt-nosed, short-eared, mouselike or ratlike rodents, including the so-called water-rat and some fieldmice. [For *vole-mouse*, i.e. fieldmouse, of Scand. origin.]

vole[2] *vōl, n* in certain card games, (the winning of) all the tricks in one deal. — *vi* to win all the tricks in one deal. — **go the vole** to risk all for great gain; to try everything. [Fr., — L. *volāre*, to fly.]

volet *vol'ā, n* one of the wings of a triptych picture. [O.Fr. (mod. Fr., a shutter) — L. *volāre*, to fly.]

volitant, volitation, volitational. See under **volant.**

volition *vō-lish'ən, n* the act of willing or choosing; the exercise of the will, or the result of this; the power of determining. — *adj* **voli'tional** or **voli'tionary**. — *adv* **voli'tionally**. — *adj* **voli'tionless**. — *adj* **vol'itive** of or pertaining to the will; originating in the will; willed, deliberate; expressing a wish, desiderative (*gram*). — *n* a desiderative verb, etc. [Fr., — L.L. *volitiō* — L. *volō*, pres. indic. of *velle*, to will, be willing.]

Völkerwanderung *fœlk-ər-vän'dər-ōōng*, (Ger.) *n* the migration of Germanic and other peoples, chiefly in the 4th to 6th centuries.

Volkskammer *folks'käm-ər, n* the parliament of the former German Democratic Republic (the new Bundestag now serves united Germany). [Ger. *Volk*, people, *Kammer*, chamber.]

volley *vol'i, n* a flight of missiles; the discharge of many missile-throwing weapons (e.g. small arms) at once; a round fired by every gun in a battery; an outburst of many words, etc. at once; (in tennis, cricket, etc.) a return of the ball before it reaches the ground — a **half volley** is a return by striking the ball immediately after it bounces; a ball returned in this way: — *pl* **voll'eys**. — *vt* to discharge in a volley; to return (a ball) before it bounces; to fire a volley or volleys at. — *vi* to fly or be discharged in a volley; to sound or produce sounds like a volley; to roll, move or be emitted like a volley; to produce a volley in tennis, etc. — *adj* **voll'eyed**. — **voll'eyball** a game in which a large ball is volleyed by the hand over a high net. [Fr. *volée*, a flight — L. *volāre*, to fly.]

volpino *vol-pē'nō, n* a small Italian dog with long, straight hair and foxlike appearance: — *pl* **volpi'nos**. [It., foxy — *volpe*, fox — L. *vulpēs*, fox.]

volplane *vol'plān*, (*aeronautics*) *vi* to glide down to earth in an aeroplane with the engine shut off; to glide to earth. — *n* a descent of this kind. [Fr. *vol plané* — *vol*, flight, *plané*, past p. of *planer*, to glide.]

volt[1] or **volte** *volt, n* a sudden movement or leap to avoid a thrust (*fencing*); a gait of a horse going sideways round a centre; a track made by a horse executing this movement. — *n* **vol'tage**. [Fr. *volte* — It. *volta* — L. *volvěre*, *volūtum*, to turn.]

volt[2] *vōlt, n* the MKSA and SI unit of electromotive force, electric potential or potential difference, the difference of potential between two points in a conductor carrying a current of one ampere when the power dissipated between them is one watt. — *combining form* **volta-** (*vol-tə-*) denoting voltaic, as in **vol'ta-electricity** and **vol'ta-electric**. — *n* **voltage** (*volt'* or *vōlt'ij*) electromotive force in volts; power, intensity (*fig*). — *adj* **voltaic** (*vol-tā'ik*) pertaining to Alessandro *Volta*, who constructed the first electrical battery, a **voltaic pile**, and established the science of current electricity; (of electricity) generated by chemical action; used in producing such electricity; of, pertaining to or caused by voltaic electricity. — *n* **voltameter** (*vol-tam'i-tər*) an instrument for measuring an electric current by means of the amount of metal deposited, or gas liberated, from an electrolyte in a given time by the passage of the current. — *n* **vōlt'meter** an instrument for measuring electromotive force directly, calibrated in volts. — **voltaic cell** a primary cell. [Alessandro *Volta*, Italian scientist (1745–1827).]

voltage. See **volt**[1,2].

voltaic, voltameter. See **volt**[2].

volte. See **volt**[1].

volte-face *volt-fäs, n* a turning round; a sudden and complete change in opinion or in views expressed. [Fr.]

voluble *vol'ū-bl, adj* fluent in speech; too fluent or glib; (*loosely*) talkative, verbose; twining (*bot*). — *n* **volubil'ity** or **vol'ubleness**. — *adv* **vol'ubly**. [L. *volūbilis* — *volvěre*, *volūtum*, to roll.]

volume *vol'ūm, n* a quantity; bulk; cubic content; dimensions; fullness of tone; loudness, or the control for adjusting it on a radio, etc.; a book, whether complete in itself or part of a larger work; a roll or scroll, which was the form of ancient books. — *adj* of or concerned with large volumes or amounts. — *adj* **volu'minal** pertaining to cubic content. — *adj* **volu'minous** consisting of many coils, windings or folds; bulky, filling much space; in many volumes; capable of filling many volumes; having written much, as an author. — *adv* **volu'minously**. — *n* **volu'minousness** or **voluminos'ity**. — **volumetric analysis** the estimation of the amount of a particular constituent present in a chemical compound by determining the quantity of a standard solution required to satisfy a reaction in a known quantity of the compound. — **speak** or **express,** etc. **volumes** to mean much, to be very significant. [Fr., — L. *volūmen*, *-inis*, a roll — *volvěre*, *volūtum*, to roll.]

voluntary *vol'ən-tər-i, adj* acting by choice, able to will; proceeding from the will; spontaneous, free; done or made without compulsion or legal obligation; designed, intentional; freely given, or supported by contributions freely given; done without expectation of payment or recompense of any kind, esp. monetary; free from state control; subject to the will; of or pertaining to voluntaryism. — *n* a person who does anything of his or her own free-will; a piece of music played at will; a voluntary or extempore composition of any kind; a piece of music played before, during or after a church service; an upholder of voluntaryism. — *adv* **vol'untarily**. — *n* **vol'untariness**. — *n* **vol'untarism** the philosophical doctrine that the will dominates the intellect; voluntaryism. — *n* **vol'untarist**. — *adj* **voluntaris'tic**. — *n* **vol'untaryism** the principle or practice of relying on voluntary action, not coercion; the principle or system of maintaining the church by voluntary offerings, instead of by the aid of the state; the principle or system of maintaining voluntary schools (q.v.). — **voluntary muscle** a muscle, or muscular tissue, that is controlled by the will; **voluntary school** (in England) a school supported by voluntary subscriptions, in many cases controlled by a religious body. [L. *voluntārius* — *voluntās*, choice — *volō*, pres. indic. of *velle*, to will.]

volunteer *vol-ən-tēr', n* a person who enters any service, esp. military, of their own free choice; a soldier belonging to any body other than the regular army; someone who acts of their own free will, esp. (*law*) in a transaction, without either legal obligation to do so or promise of remuneration; a person to whom property is transferred without their giving valuable consideration (*law*). — *adj* consisting of or pertaining to volunteers; giving voluntary service; given voluntarily; (of a plant or plants) growing spontaneously, from seed not deliberately sown. — *vt* to offer voluntarily to give, supply or perform; to give (information) unasked. — *vi* to enter into any service of one's own free-will or without being asked. [Fr. *volontaire* — L. *voluntārius*.]

voluptuary *və-lup'tū-ər-i, n* a person excessively fond of or devoted to bodily enjoyments or luxury, a sensualist. — *adj* promoting or characterised by sensual pleasure. — *adj* **voluptuous** (*və-lup'tū-əs*) full of or suggestive of pleasure, esp. sensuous; pertaining to, consisting of, derived from or ministering to sensual pleasure; shapely and sexually attractive; given to excess of pleasure, esp. sensual. — *adv* **volup'tuously**. — *n* **volup'tuousness**. [L. *voluptuārius* — *voluptās*, pleasure.]

volute *və-, vo-lūt'* or *-lo͞ot', n* a spiral scroll used esp. in Ionic capitals; a spiral form; a thing or part having such a shape; any marine shell of the genus *Voluta* or related genera, allied to the whelks, or the animal itself; a whorl of a spiral shell. — *adj* rolled up in any direction, having a spiral form. — *adj* **volū'ted** in spiral form; having a volute or volutes. — *n* **volū'tion** a revolving movement; a convolution; a whorl. — *adj* **vol'ūtoid** like a volute. [L. *volvĕre, volūtum*, to roll.]

volvulus *vol'vū-ləs, (med) n* twisting of an abdominal viscus causing internal obstruction. [Formed from L. *volvĕre*.]

vomer *vō'mər, (anat* and *zool) n* a bone of the skull in most vertebrates — in man, a thin flat bone, shaped like a wedge or ploughshare, forming part of the middle partition of the nose. — *adj* **vomerine** (*vō'* or *vo'mə-rīn* or *-rin*). — *combining form* **vomerō-** indicating the vomer, as in **vomerōnas'al**, pertaining to the vomer and the nasal cavity. [L. *vōmer*, a ploughshare.]

vomit *vom'it, vi* to throw up the contents of the stomach through the mouth, to spew; (of an emetic) to cause vomiting; to issue with violence. — *vt* to spew; to throw out with violence; to cause to vomit: — *pr p* **vom'iting**; *pa t* and *pa p* **vom'ited**. — *n* the act of vomiting; matter ejected from the stomach; vile people or things; something that excites vomiting, an emetic. — *n* **vom'iting**. — *adj* **vom'itive** causing to vomit. — *n* an emetic. [L. *vomĕre, -ĭtum*, to throw up.]

voodoo *vo͞o'do͞o, n* religious beliefs and practices of African origin found among the Black peoples of the West Indies and southern United States, formerly including serpent-worship, human sacrifice and cannibalism, but now largely confined to sorcery; any form of magic-working; a person who practises this kind of religious sorcery. — *adj* of, pertaining to or carrying out voodoo practices. — *vt* to bewitch by voodoo charms. — *n* **voo'dooism** (or *-do͞o'*) voodoo practices or beliefs. — *n* **voo'dooist** (or *-do͞o'*). — *adj* **voodooist'ic**. [W.Afr. *vodu*, a spirit.]

voortrekker *fōr-trek'ər* or *vōr-, n* (usu. with *cap*) one of the Dutch farmers from Cape Colony who took part in the Great Trek into the Transvaal in 1836 and following years; a member of an Afrikaner Scout-type youth movement; a pioneer. [Cape Du., — Du. *voor-*, before, and **trek**.]

voracious *və-rā'shəs, adj* eating greedily or in large quantities; taking in, engulfing, much (*fig*); very eager, or insatiable (*fig*); characterised by greediness (*lit* and *fig*). — *adv* **vorā'ciously**. — *n* **voracity** (*-ras'*) or **vorā'ciousness**. [L. *vorāx, vorācis* — *vorāre*, to devour.]

vortex *vör'teks, n* a whirling motion of a fluid forming a cavity in the centre, a whirlpool, an eddy, a whirlwind; a pursuit, way of life, situation, etc. that engulfs one irresistibly or remorselessly, taking up all one's attention or energies (*fig*): — *pl* **vor'tices** (*-ti-sēz*) or **vor'texes**. — *adj* **vor'tical**. — *adv* **vor'tically**. — *n* **vor'ticism** (*-ti-sizm*) a British movement in painting, a development from futurism, blending cubism and expressionism, and emphasising the complications of machinery that characterise modern life. — *n* **vor'ticist** a person who supports or practises vorticism. — *n* **vortic'ity** the amount of vortical motion in a fluid. — *adj* **vor'ticose, vortic'ūlar** or **vortiginous** (*-tij'*) vortical. [L. *vortex, vertex, -icis* — *vortĕre, vertĕre*, to turn.]

votary *vō'tə-ri, n* a person devoted by, or as if by, a vow to some service, worship or way of life; someone enthusiastically addicted to a pursuit, study, etc.; a devoted worshipper or adherent. — *n* **vō'tarist** a votary. — *adj* **vō'tive** given, erected, etc. by vow; undertaken or observed in fulfilment of a vow; consisting of, or expressing, a vow or a wish. [L.L. *vōtārius* — L. *vovēre, vōtum*, to vow.]

vote *vōt, n* an expression of a wish or opinion in an authorised formal way; collective opinion, decision by a majority; votes or voters of a certain class collectively; a voter; the right to vote; that by which a choice is expressed, such as a ballot; a ballot-paper; the total number of votes cast. — *vi* to express choice, esp. at an election, by vote; to declare oneself in favour of or against (with *for* or *against*), esp. by vote. — *vt* to determine by vote; to grant by vote; to bring about (a specified result or change) by vote; to declare by general consent (*colloq*); to pronounce, adjudge to be (*colloq*); to propose, suggest (*colloq*); to present for voting; to record the votes of. — *adj* **vote'less**. — *n* **vō'ter**. — **split one's vote** or **votes** to divide one's votes among two or more candidates; **split the vote** to injure a cause by influencing a body of possible supporters to vote in some other way (*n* **vote'-splitting**); **vote Conservative, Labour**, etc., to give one's vote, on a particular occasion or habitually, to the Conservative, Labour, etc. candidate or party; **vote down** to defeat or suppress by vote, or otherwise; **vote in** to elect; **vote of no confidence** the legal method of forcing the resignation of a government or governing body; **vote with one's feet** to indicate one's dissatisfaction with a situation or conditions by leaving. [L. *vōtum*, a wish — *vovēre, vōtum*, to vow.]

votive. See under **votary**.

vouch *vowch, vt* to assert or guarantee to be true; to testify (that). — *vi* to bear witness, or be surety (with *for*). — *n* **vouch'er** a piece of evidence, or a written document serving as proof; a paper which confirms the truth of anything, such as a receipt, a certificate of correctness; a ticket, etc., substituting, or exchangeable, for cash, goods or services; a person who vouches or gives witness. [O.Fr. *voucher, vocher*, to call to defend — L. *vocāre*, to call.]

vouchsafe *vowch-sāf', vt* to condescend to grant; to condescend to allow, to accept, or to engage in; to condescend, be graciously willing to tell, etc. — *vi* to condescend: — *pr p* **vouchsāf'ing**; *pa t* and *pa p* **vouchsafed'**. — *n* **vouchsafe'ment**. [Orig. two words, **vouch** and **safe**.]

voussoir *vo͞o-swär', (archit) n* one of the wedgelike stones that form part of an arch. — *vt* to form with voussoirs. [Fr., through L.L., from L. *volūtus* — *volvĕre*, to roll.]

vow *vow, n* a voluntary promise made to God, or to a saint, or to a god or gods; a binding undertaking or resolve; a solemn or formal promise of fidelity or affection; a firm assertion; an earnest wish or prayer. — *vt* to give or dedicate by solemn promise; to promise or threaten solemnly; to maintain solemnly. — *vi* to make vows. — *adj* **vowed** devoted, confirmed, undertaken, etc. by vow, or as if by vow. — **baptismal vows** the promises made at baptism by the person baptised, or by their sponsors or parents; **simple vow** a more limited, less permanent vow than a solemn vow; **solemn vow** such a vow as the Church takes under her special charge and solemnly accepts, such as those of poverty, obedience and chastity, involving complete and irrevocable surrender. [O.Fr. *vou* — L. *vōtum* — *vovēre*, to vow.]

vowel *vow'əl, n* a speech-sound produced by the unimpeded passage of the breath (modified by the vocal cords into voice) through the mouth, different vowel sounds being made by altering the form and position of the tongue and the lips; a letter (usually *a, e, i, o, u*) used alone or in combination to represent a vowel sound. — *adj* of, representing or of the nature of a vowel. — *adj* **vow'elless**. — **vowel'-rhyme** assonance. [Fr. *voyelle* — L. *vōcālis* — *vōx, vōcis*, voice.]

vox: **vox angelica** (*voks an-jel'i-kə* or *an-gel'i-ka*) or **vox caelestis** (*sē-les'tis* or *kī-*) voix céleste (q.v.); **vox humana** (*hū-mä'nə* or *ho͞o-mä'na*) in organ-building, a reed-stop producing tones resembling those of the human voice. — **vox populi, vox Dei** (*pop'ū-lī, dē'ī, po'pōō-lē, de'ē* or *dā'ē*) the voice of the people is the voice of God, hence **vox populi** (often shortened to **vox pop**) public or popular opinion. [L. *vōx*, voice.]

voyage *voi'ij, n* a passage by water or by air to some place at a considerable distance; a round trip; a cruise; an account of such a journey. — *vi* to make a voyage, cruise or journey. — *vt* to traverse, pass over. — *adj* **voy'ageable** navigable. — *n* **voy'ager.** [O.Fr. *veage, voiage*, etc. — L. *viāticum*; see **viaticum.**]

voyeur *vwä-yœr', n* a person who derives sexual gratification from surreptitiously watching sexual acts or objects; a peeping Tom; someone who takes a morbid interest in sordid sights. — *n* **voy'eurism.** — *adj* **voyeuris'tic.** [Fr., one who sees.]

VP *abbrev* for Vice-President.

VR *abbrev* for *Victoria Regina*, (L.), Queen Victoria.

vraisemblance *vrā-* or *vre-sã-blãs', n* verisimilitude; a picture. [Fr. *vrai*, true, *semblance*, appearance.]

V.Rev. *abbrev* for Very Reverend.

VRI *abbrev* for *Victoria Regina et Imperatrix* (L.), Victoria, Queen and Empress.

vroom *vrōōm* or *vrŏŏm*, (*colloq*) *n* power, drive, energy, etc. — *vi* to travel speedily. [Imit.]

VS *abbrev* for Veterinary Surgeon.

vs *abbrev* for versus (also **v**).

VSO *abbrev* for Voluntary Service Overseas.

VSOP *abbrev* for very special old pale.

VT *abbrev* for: vatu (currency of Vanuatu; also **V**); Vermont (U.S. state; also **Vt**).

vt *abbrev* for verb transitive.

VTOL *vē'tol, n* a system enabling aircraft to land and take off vertically; an aircraft operating by this system. [*v*ertical *t*ake-*o*ff and *l*anding.]

VTR *abbrev* for videotape recorder.

Vul. or **Vulg.** *abbrev* for Vulgate.

Vulcan *vul'kən, n* the god of fire and metalworking (*Roman mythol*); (without *cap*) a blacksmith or an iron-worker (*poetic*). — *adj* **vulcanic** (*-kan'ik*) volcanic. — *n* **vulcanicity** (*-is'i-ti*) volcanic action or phenomena, volcanicity. — *adj* **vulcanī'sable** or **-z-**. — *n* **vulcanīsā'tion** or **-z-**. — *vt* **vul'canise** or **-ize** to treat (rubber, etc.) with sulphur or sulphur compounds, etc. to improve its strength or otherwise modify its properties. — *vi* to undergo such treatment. — *n* **vul'canism** or **vol'canism** volcanic activity. — *n* **vul'canist** or **vol'canist** a person who studies volcanic phenomena, a vulcanologist. — *n* **vul'canite** the harder of the two kinds of vulcanised rubber, the softer kind being called *soft rubber*; a general name for any igneous rock of fine grain-size. — *adj* **vulcanolog'ical** or **volcanolog'ical.** — *n* **vulcanol'ogist** or **volcanol'ogist.** — *n* **vulcanol'ogy** or **volcanol'ogy** the scientific study of volcanoes and volcanic phenomena. [L. *Vulcānus*.]

vulg. *abbrev* for vulgar.

vulgar *vul'gər, adj* unrefined; (of language, etc.) coarse; lacking in taste, manners, delicacy, etc.; spiritually paltry, ignoble, debased or pretentious. — *n* the common language of a country, the vernacular. — *n* **vulgā'rian** a vulgar person; a rich unrefined person. — Also *adj*. — *n* **vulgarisā'tion** or **-z-**. — *vt* **vul'garise** or **-ize** to make common or ordinary; to popularise (and therefore spoil to some extent); to make unrefined or coarse. — *n* **vul'garism** a vulgar phrase; coarseness; an instance of this. — *n* **vulgarity** (*-gar'*). — *adv* **vul'garly.** — **vulgar fraction** a fraction written in the common way (one number above another, separated by a line), as opposed to a *decimal fraction*; **vulgar tongue** the vernacular. [L. *vulgāris* — *vulgus*, the people.]

Vulgate *vul'gāt* or *vul'git, n* an ancient Latin version of the Scriptures, made by St Jerome and others in the 4th century, and later twice revised — so called from its common use in the R.C. church; (without *cap*) an accepted text of any other book or author. — *adj* of or pertaining to the Vulgate; (without *cap*; of speech, etc.) commonly used or accepted. [L. *vulgāta* (*editio*), popular edition (of the Bible); see **vulgar.**]

vulnerable *vul'nər-ə-bl, adj* capable of being physically or emotionally wounded; open to successful attack; capable of being persuaded or tempted; (in contract bridge, of a side that has won a game towards the rubber) liable to increased penalties (or premiums) accordingly. — *n* **vulnerabil'ity** or **vul'nerableness.** — *adj* **vul'nerary** pertaining to wounds; useful in healing wounds. — *n* anything useful in curing wounds. [L. *vulnerāre*, to wound — *vulnus, vulneris*, a wound.]

Vulpes *vul'pēz, n* the genus of animals including the common fox. — *adj* **vulpine** (*vul'pin* or *-pīn*) of, pertaining to or like a fox; cunning. [L. *vulpēs*, a fox.]

vulture *vul'chər, n* any of a number of large rapacious birds of prey, feeding largely on carrion, regarded as belonging to two families; someone who or that which resembles a vulture, esp. a greedy, rapacious person. — Also *adj*. — *adj* **vul'turīne, vul'turish** or **vul'turous** of, pertaining to or like a vulture; rapacious. [O.Fr. *voutour, voltour*, etc. — L. *vulturius* — *vultur*.]

vulva *vul'və*, (*anat* and *zool*) *n* the external genitals of the female mammal, esp. the orifice of the vagina. — *adj* **vul'val, vul'var** or **vul'vate.** — *adj* **vul'viform** oval; like a cleft with projecting edges. — *n* **vulvī'tis** (*med*) inflammation of the vulva. — *combining form* **vulvo-** denoting the vulva, as in **vulvō-ū'terine,** pertaining to the vulva and the uterus. [L. *vulva, volva*, wrapping, womb.]

vv *abbrev* for: versus; vice versa.

vvll. See **vl.**

VW *abbrev* for: Very Worshipful; Volkswagen.

Vw *abbrev* for View (in addresses, etc.).

vying *vī'ing, pr p* of **vie.**

W or **w** *dub'l-ū*, *n* the twenty-third letter of the modern English alphabet, a doubled u or v used to express the voiced consonantal sound heard e.g. in English *way*, *weak*, *warrant*. In modern English *w* is found as a consonant and also as the second component in certain vowel and diphthong digraphs, i.e. those in *law*, *few*, *now*. The unvoiced form of the consonant is written *wh* (corresponding to O.E. *hw*), as in *what*, *when*, but many English people substitute the voiced sound in pronouncing words spelt *wh*, and Northern speakers insist upon sounding *hw*. *W* is no longer pronounced in *write*, *two*, etc.

W or **W.** *abbrev* for: watt or watts; Welsh; West; Western; winter; women or women's; won (Korean currency).

W (*chem*) *symbol* for tungsten (*wolframium*, Latinised form of *wolfram*, an earlier name).

w or **w.** *abbrev* for: weak; week; wife; with.

WA *abbrev* for: Washington (U.S. state); West Africa; Western Australia.

WAAC or **Waac** *wak*, *n* the *W*omen's *A*rmy *A*uxiliary *C*orps (founded 1917), or a member of it, now **WRAC**.

WAAF or **Waaf** *waf*, *n* the *W*omen's *A*uxiliary *A*ir *F*orce (founded 1939), or a member of it, now **WRAF**.

wacko or **whacko** *wak'ō*, *adj* mad; eccentric. [Cf. **wacky**.]

wacky *wak'i*, (*slang*) *adj* crazy. — *n* **wack'iness**. [Perh. conn. with *whack*, or with dialect *whacky*, left-handed, a fool.]

wad *wod*, *n* a pad of loose material thrust in to aid packing, etc.; a disc of felt or paper (formerly a small plug of paper or tow, etc.) to keep the charge in a gun; a sandwich, cake or bun (*slang*); a roll or bundle, e.g. of bank-notes; a compact mass, often small. — *vt* to form into a mass; to pad, stuff out; to stuff a wad into: — *pr p* **wadd'ing**; *pa t* and *pa p* **wadd'ed**. — *n* **wadd'ing** a wad, or the materials for wads; sheets of carded cotton for stuffing quilts, garments, etc.; cotton-wool.

waddle *wod'l*, *vi* to take short steps and sway from side to side in walking, as a duck does; to move in a way suggestive of this. — *n* the act of waddling; a clumsy, rocking gait. — *n* **wadd'ler**. — *adj* **wadd'ling**. [Frequentative of **wade**.]

waddy *wod'i*, *n* an Aboriginal Australian wooden club used in warfare. — *vt* to strike with a waddy. [Perh. from Eng. **wood**.]

wade *wād*, *vi* to walk through a substance that yields with difficulty to the feet, esp. water; to go (through) with difficulty or labour (*fig*). — *vt* to cross by wading; to cause to cross thus. — *n* the act of wading. — *n* **wā'der** someone who wades; a bird that wades in search of food, e.g. the snipe, sandpiper, etc.; a high waterproof boot; (in *pl*) a waterproof garment for the feet, legs and lower body. — *n* and *adj* **wā'ding**. — **wade in** to make a very vigorous attack; **wade into** to tackle, (e.g. a job) energetically; to make a vigorous attack on (*lit* and *fig*). [O.E. *wadan*, to go.]

wadi or **wady** *wod'i*, *n* the dry bed of a torrent; a river-valley. [Ar. *wādī*.]

wafer *wā'fər*, *n* a very thin crisp cake or biscuit baked in **wa'fer-irons** or **-tongs**, formerly eaten with wine; a similar biscuit eaten with ice-cream, etc.; a thin round cake of unleavened bread used in the Eucharist; a leaf of adhesive material for sealing letters, etc.; a piece of edible material used to enclose a medicinal powder, etc. to be swallowed (*med*); a thin slice of silicon from which chips are cut; a thin slice of anything. — *vt* to close, fasten or stick (e.g. on a wall) with a wafer. — *adj* **wā'fery**. [O.N.Fr. *waufre* — M.L.G. *wafel*, cake of wax.]

waffle[1] *wof'l*, *n* a kind of cake made from batter, baked in an iron utensil of hinged halves called a **waff'le-iron**. [Du. *wafel*, wafer.]

waffle[2] *wof'l*, (*slang*) *vi* to talk incessantly or nonsensically; to waver, vacillate. — *n* such talk.

waft *wäft*, *woft* or *waft*, *vt* to bear, convey, transport or propel, safely or lightly, on the surface of or through a fluid medium such as air or water (*poetic*; also *fig*). — *vi* to float, sail or pass through the air. — *n* a scent, or sound, or puff of smoke or vapour carried by the air; a rush of air (also *fig*); an act of wafting, or of waving; a waving movement; a flag or substitute hoisted as a signal at different positions at the after-part of a ship; the act of displaying such a signal. — *n* **waft'er**. — *n* **waft'ing**. [From obs. *wafter*, a convoying vessel, prob. — L.G. or Du. *wachter*, guard.]

WAG *abbrev* for: (West Africa) Gambia (I.V.R.); Writers' and Artists' Guild.

wag *wag*, *vi* to move, or be moved, from side to side, or to shake to and fro; to oscillate; (of a tongue, chin, beard, etc.) to move in light, gossiping or indiscreet talk. — *vt* to move, shake or wave to and fro or up and down; to move in chatter or indiscreet talk; to move so as to express reproof or derision, etc.: — *pr p* **wagg'ing**; *pa t* and *pa p* **wagged**. — *n* a shake; an act of wagging; a droll, mischievous person, a habitual joker, a wit. — *n* **wagg'ery** mischievous merriment or jesting; an instance of such. — *adj* **wagg'ish** droll, mischievous, etc. — *adv* **wagg'ishly**. — *n* **wagg'ishness**. [M.E. *waggen*, from same root as O.E. *wagian*, to shake.]

WAGBI *abbrev* for Wildfowl Association of Great Britain and Ireland.

wage *wāj*, *vt* to engage in or to carry on (esp. war). — *n* payment for services, esp. a regular payment made by an employer to an (unskilled or semi-skilled) employee, or (*fig*) reward (both often **wages**, *pl* in form, but sometimes construed as *sing*). — *adj* and *npl* **wage'less**. — **wage'-earner** a person who works for wages; the person who earns the money that supports, or money that helps to support, the household; **wage'-earning**; **wage'-freeze** a fixing of wages at a certain level for some time ahead; **wage'-packet** a small envelope in which a worker's wages are issued; (*loosely*) wages; **wage slave** a person dependent on a (usu. low) wage or salary. [M.E. *wagen* — O.N.Fr. *wagier* (O.Fr. *gagier*), to pledge (through popular L. from a Gmc. word).]

wager *wā'jər*, *n* something staked on an outcome not yet known; a bet; the act of making a bet. — *vt* to bet (money, etc.) on the outcome of anything. — *vi* to lay a wager, make a bet. — *n* **wā'gerer**. [A.Fr. *wageure*, a pledge — O.N.Fr. *wagier*; see **wage**.]

waggle *wag'l, vi* and *vt* to wag, esp. in an unsteady manner. — Also *n.* — *adj* **wagg'ly.** [Frequentative of **wag.**]

waggon, etc. See **wagon.**

Wagnerian *väg-nē'ri-ən, adj* pertaining to or characterised by the ideas or style of Richard *Wagner* (1813–83), German composer of music-dramas. — *n* a follower or admirer of Richard Wagner. — *adj* **Wagneresque'.** — *n* **Wag'nerism** or **Wagne'rianism** the art theory of Richard Wagner, its main object being the freeing of opera from traditional and conventional forms, and its one canon, dramatic fitness. — *n* **Wag'nerist** or **Wag'nerite** an adherent of Wagner's musical methods.

wagon or **waggon** *wag'ən, n* a four-wheeled vehicle, esp. one for carrying heavy goods; an open railway truck or a closed railway van; a car, esp. an estate car (*colloq*). — *n* **wag'onage** conveyance by wagon, or money paid for it. — *n* **wag'oner** a person who drives a wagon. — *n* **wagonette'** a kind of horse-drawn carriage with one or two seats crosswise in front, and two back seats arranged lengthwise and facing inwards. — *n* **wag'onful.** — All the above are also spelt **-gg-.** — **wag'on-load** the load carried by a wagon; a great amount; **wag'on-train** a collection or service of army vehicles for the conveyance of ammunition, provisions, the sick, etc.; a train of usu. horse-drawn wagons used by pioneer settlers to travel into new territory. — **on (**or **off) the wagon** (*slang*) abstaining (or no longer abstaining) from alcohol. [Du. *wagen.*]

wagon-lit *vä-gɔ̃-lē', n* a sleeping-carriage on a continental train: — *pl* **wagons-lit** (pronunciation as *nsing*; sometimes **wagon-lits**). [Fr. *wagon* (— Eng. **wagon**) and *lit*, bed.]

wagtail *wag'tāl, n* any of various birds of the *Motacilla* and *Dendronanthus* genera, so named from their constant wagging of the tail.

Wahabi or **Wahabee** *wä-hä'bē, n* a member of a sect of Muslims founded in about 1760 by Abd-el-*Wahhab* (1691–1787), whose aim was to restore primitive Islam. — *n* **Waha'biism** or **Waha'bism** the doctrine and practices of the Wahabis.

wahine *wä-hē'ne, n* a Maori woman. [Maori.]

wahoo *wa-hōō', n* a large fast-moving marine food and game fish, related to the mackerel.

waif *wāf, n* an orphaned or abandoned child; a homeless wanderer; a piece of property found ownerless, such as a strayed animal, or goods cast up by the tide (also *fig*). — **waifs and strays** homeless, destitute people. [O.Fr.; prob. — Scand.]

wail *wāl, vi* to lament or cry audibly, esp. with prolonged high-pitched mournful cries. — *vt* to bemoan; to grieve over. — *n* the action of wailing; a cry of woe; an animal cry or mechanical sound suggesting this. — *n* **wail'er.** — *adj* **wail'ful.** — *n* and *adj* **wail'ing.** — *adv* **wail'ingly.** — **Wailing Wall** a wall in Jerusalem, a remnant of the western wall of the temple dating back to before the destruction of the city in 66 A.D., where Jews traditionally pray. [M.E. *weilen, wailen.*]

wain *wān,* (now usu. *poetic*). *n* a wagon, esp. for hay or other agricultural produce. [O.E. *wægen, wǣn* — *wegen*, to carry.]

wainscot *wān'skot* or *-skət, n* fine oak for panelling, etc.; woodwork, esp. panelled, on an interior wall; the lower part of an interior wall when lined with material different from that on the upper part. — *vt* to line with, or as if with, boards or panels: — *pr p* **wain'scoting** or **wain'scotting**: — *pa t* and *pa p* **wain'scoted** or **wain'scotted.** — *n* **wain'scoting** or **wain'scotting** the act of lining with boards or panels; materials for making a wainscot; wainscots collectively. — **wainscot chair** a heavy oak chair with a panelled back, seat, etc. [Orig. perh. wood used for a partition in a wagon — Du. *wagen-schot* — *wagen*, wagon, *schot*, partition.]

waist *wāst, n* the smallest part of the human trunk, between the ribs and the hips; a narrow middle part of an insect; the part of a garment that lies round the waist of the body; the narrow middle part, as of a musical instrument; the middle part of a ship. — *adj* **waist'ed** having a waist, often of specified type. — **waist'coat** (*wās'* or *wāst'kōt*) a garment, plain or ornamental, reaching to or below the waist, and sleeveless, intended to show partly, worn by men at different periods under doublet, coat, jacket, etc.; a woman's similar garment or front. — *adj* **waist'-deep** or **-high** as deep, or high, as to reach up to the waist. — **waist'line** a line thought of as marking the waist, but not fixed by anatomy in women's fashions; the measurement of a waist. [M.E. *wast*, from presumed O.E. *wæst*, growth, size.]

wait *wāt, vi* to be or remain in expectation or readiness (with *for*); to be or remain in a place in readiness (also **wait about** or **around**); to delay action; to be delayed; to be in attendance, or in readiness to carry out orders; to bring food to the table and clear away used dishes. — *n* an ambush — now used only in such phrases as *to lie in wait, to lay wait*; the act of waiting or of expecting; a delay; (in *pl*) people who welcome in Christmas by playing or singing out of doors at night. — *n* **wait'er** a person who waits; a man who waits at table in a hotel, restaurant, etc. — *n* **wait'ing** the act of waiting; attendance. — Also *adj.* — *n* **wait'ress** a female who waits at table in a hotel, restaurant, etc. — **wait'ing-list** a list of people waiting, such as candidates awaiting a vacancy, etc.; **wait'ing-room** a room for the use of persons waiting; **wait'-on** see **wait on** below; **wait'person** (*US*) a waiter or waitress. — **lie in wait** to be in hiding ready to attack or surprise (*lit* and *fig*); **play a waiting game** (*lit* and *fig*) to avoid action as far as possible in the hope of having an opportunity later to use one's energies with maximum effect; **wait on** to wait for (*dialect*); to wait upon; (of a hawk, in falconry) to circle or hover in the air above the falconer's head (*n* **wait'-on**); **wait up** to stay out of bed waiting (with *for*); **wait upon** or **on** to attend and serve. [O.N.Fr. *waitier*, to watch, attend; of Gmc. origin.]

waive *wāv, vt* to give up voluntarily, e.g. a claim or a contention (*law*); to refrain from claiming, demanding, taking or enforcing; to forgo; to defer, postpone. — *n* **wai'ver** the act, or an act, of waiving, or a written statement formally indicating this. [A.Fr. *weyver* — O.Fr. *guesver*, to abandon; from same root as **waif.**]

wake[1] *wāk, vi* to awake, be roused from, or as though from, sleep, from indifference, etc. (often with *up*); to become animated or lively; to be stirred up, aroused; to be, or to remain, awake, active or vigilant; to keep watch or vigil, or to pass the night in prayer; to hold a wake. — *vt* to rouse from sleep; to keep vigil over; to excite, stir up; to disturb with noise; to animate; to reanimate, revive: — *pa t* **waked** (*wākt*) or **woke** (*wōk*); *pa p* **wo'ken** or **waked.** — *n* the feast of the dedication of a church, formerly kept by watching all night; a festival; an annual holiday (*dialect*); a watch or vigil beside a corpse, sometimes with revelry. — *adj* **wake'ful** not asleep; unable or not inclined to sleep; vigilant. — *adv* **wake'fully.** — *n* **wake'fulness.** — *vi* **wā'ken** to be, or become, awake; to become active or lively. — *vt* to rouse from sleep, unconsciousness or inaction; to excite, stir up, evoke. — *adj* **wā'kened.** — *n* **wā'kener.** — *adj* **wā'kening.** — *n* the act of someone who wakens. — *n* **wā'ker** a person who wakes. — *n* **wā'king.** — *adj* that wakes, keeps watch, or is vigilant; that rouses or becomes awake; passed, or experienced, in the waking state. — **wake'-robin** the cuckoo-pint (*Arum maculatum*); the spotted orchis (*Orchis maculata*); applied to various other flowers, esp. (in U.S.) to any of the genus *Trillium*; **waking hours**

the period of the day during which one is normally awake. — **wake** (or **waken) to** or **wake up to** to become conscious of or alive to. [A combination of an O.E. strong verb *wacan*, to be born, to awake, and an O.E. weak verb *wacian*, to be awake, to watch; cf. **watch**.]

wake² *wāk*, *n* the streak of smooth-looking or foamy water left in the track of a ship; disturbed air behind a flying body; the area behind someone or something passing through. — **in the wake of** (*fig*) close behind; immediately after (usu. implying consequence). [Of Scand. origin; cf. O.N. *vök*, an ice hole, *vökr*, moist.]

WAL *abbrev* for (West Africa) Sierra Leone (I.V.R.).

Waldenses *wol-den'sēz*, *npl* a Christian community of austere morality and devotion to the simplicity of the Gospel, orig. followers of Peter *Waldo*, a merchant of Lyons and preacher in the second half of the 12th century. — *adj* and *n* **Walden'sian**.

wale *wāl*, *n* same as **weal¹**; a ridge on the surface of cloth; (in *pl*) planks all along the outer timbers on a ship's side. — *vt* to mark with wales by striking; to make, provide with, or secure with, wales. [O.E. *walu*.]

walk *wök*, *vi* (of a biped) to move along on foot with alternate steps, the walker always having at least one foot on the ground; (of a quadruped) to move along in such a way that there are always at least two feet on the ground; to pace; to journey on foot; to ramble, go on foot for pleasure, etc.; to move; to behave in a certain way, follow a certain course; to move off, depart, withdraw; to conduct oneself, behave; of an object, to disappear (*colloq*). — *vt* to pass through or upon, perambulate, traverse; to follow or trace out on foot; to measure, wear out, etc. by walking; to cause to walk, or to move as if walking; to lead or accompany by walking. — *n* the action, or an act, of walking; a spell of walking, especially for pleasure; a perambulation in procession; a gait; that in or through which one walks; a possible or suitable route or course for walking; a path or place for walking; a tree-bordered avenue; a distance walked, or a distance as measured by the time taken to walk it; conduct; a course of life or sphere of action; a hawker's or postman's district or round. — *adj* **walk'able**. — *n* **walk'er** someone who walks or takes part in walking-races; any device which helps esp. babies and elderly people to walk; a man of good social standing who accompanies a female V.I.P. on official engagements in the absence of her husband (*US slang*). — *n* **walk'ing** the verbal noun of walk; pedestrianism; the sport of walking-races; the condition of a surface from the point of view of one who walks on it. — *adj* that walks, or that moves as if walking; that oscillates; used in or for walking; performed by walking; worked by a person or animal who walks. — *adv* **walk'about** on the move, as in *go walkabout*, esp. temporarily back into the bush (of Australian Aborigines), or meeting the public on foot (of royalty, politicians, etc.). — *n* a wandering, a journey; a walk by royalty, etc. in order to meet the public. — **walk'ie-talk'ie** or **walk'y-talk'y** a portable radiotelephone transmitting and receiving set; **walk'-in** a person who enters premises to make enquiries or offer services without previously making contact; a theft committed by a walk-in thief. — *adj* (of a thief) that gains entrance without breaking in; (of a cupboard, etc.) big enough to walk into and move around in. — **walking-frame** a device to give support to an infirm person while walking; **walk'ing-orders, -papers** or **-ticket** (*slang*) dismissal; **walk'ing-part** one in which the actor has nothing to say; **walk'ing-race** a race in which competitors must walk rather than run; **walk'ing-stick, -cane** or **-staff** a stick, cane or staff used in walking; **walk'ing-stick, -straw** or **-twig** a stick-insect; **walk'ing-toad** a natterjack; **walking wounded** casualties not requiring stretchers or not confined to bed (also *fig*); **walk'-on** a walking-part. — *adj* **walk'-on** (of an air-service or aeroplane) for which one does not have to purchase a ticket in advance, the seats being non-bookable; pertaining to a walking-part. — **walk'-out** the act of walking out, usually to indicate disapproval; a sudden industrial strike; **walk'-over** a race where only one competitor appears, and has merely to cover the course to win; an easy or unopposed victory, usu. in sport; **walk'way** a road, path, etc. constructed for pedestrians only. — *adj* **walk-up** (*US*) reached by means of stairs; (of a building) with upper storeys accessible only by stairs. — *n* a walk-up building, apartment, etc. — **charity walk** or **sponsored walk** an organised walk in aid of charity, each participator having obtained from a sponsor or sponsors an agreement to contribute according to distance covered; **walk a tightrope** (*fig*) to follow a narrow and difficult route beset with dangers, as if on a tightrope; **walk away from** to outdistance or outdo easily; to have nothing more to do with; to emerge from (an accident, etc.) with no or only minor injury; **walk away with** (*colloq*) to win with ease; **walk into** (*colloq*) to collide or meet with unexpectedly; to enter without effort or opposition; **walk it** (*colloq*) to succeed, to win easily; **walk off** to leave; to depart; to get rid of (e.g. disagreeable feelings or effects) by walking; **walk off with** to take surreptitiously or feloniously; to win easily (*colloq*); **walk on** to walk ahead; to continue to walk; to have a walking-part; **walk on air** to be exultant or light-hearted; **walk out** to leave, esp. as a gesture of disapproval; to strike; **walk out on** (*colloq*) to desert, leave in the lurch; **walk over** to cross or traverse; to win an uncontested race; to have an easy victory or easy success (*colloq*); to disregard the rights or feelings of (*colloq*); **walk tall** (*colloq*) to be proud, have self-respect; **walk the plank** see under **plank**; **walk the streets** to wander about in search of work, or simply aimlessly; to be a prostitute. [M.E. *walken*, *walkien*, to walk — O.E. *wealcan*, to roll, revolve, *wealcian*, to roll up, curl.]

walkathon *wäk'ə-thon*, *n* a long-distance walk, either as a race or in aid of charity. [*walk* and mar*athon*.]

Walkman® *wök'mən*, *n* a small, portable cassette-player/radio with headphones, designed for personal use whilst walking, travelling, etc.: — *pl* **Walk'mans** or **Walk'men**.

wall *wöl*, *n* an erection of brick, stone, etc., for security or to enclose a space such as a piece of land; the side of a building or of a room; (in *pl*) fortifications; any bounding surface suggestive of a wall, e.g. the membranous covering or lining of an organ of the body or of a plant or animal cell; a barrier, e.g. that experienced physically and psychologically by long-distance runners (*fig*). — *vt* to enclose with, or as with, a wall; to fortify with, or as if with, walls; to divide as by a wall. — **wall-** (in combination) signifying growing on, living in or on, hanging or for hanging on, or otherwise associated with, a wall. — *adj* **walled** enclosed with a wall; fortified. — *n* **wall'er** a person who builds walls. — *n* **wall'ing** walls collectively; materials for walls. — *adj* **wall'less**. — **wall bars** horizontal bars fixed to a wall, used by gymnasts; **wall'-board** an artificial material made in slabs for lining walls, also called *building-board*; **wall'covering** wallpaper, or anything used in the same way; **wall-eye** see separate entry; **wall'facing** a facing for a wall; **wall'flower** a plant (*Cheiranthus cheiri*) with yellow, orange or orange-brown flowers, found esp. on old walls; any of various cultivars of this, with various-coloured flowers; a person who remains a spectator at a dance, usu. a woman who cannot obtain partners (*colloq*); **wall'-gillyflower** a wallflower; **wall'-painting** the decoration of walls with ornamental painted designs; a work of art painted on a wall; **wall'paper** paper, usually coloured or decorated, for pasting on the walls of a room; something of a bland or background nature, lacking originality or noteworthiness, etc. (*fig*; *colloq*); **wall pass** (*football*) a one-two; **wall'-plate** a horizontal piece of timber or of rolled steel on a wall, etc. to bear the ends of joists, etc.; **Wall Street** a street in New York, the chief financial centre in the United States; hence, American financial interests; **Wall Streeter** a financier based in Wall Street. — *adj* **wall'-to-wall'** (of carpets, etc.) covering the entire floor; widespread, ubiquitous (*fig*; *colloq*). — **wall unit** a piece of furniture attached to or standing against a wall. — **go to the wall** to be hard pressed; to be forced to give way; to fail, go under; to give precedence to something else; **hang by the wall** (*colloq*) to remain unused; **turn one's face to the wall** to resign oneself to death or despair; **up the wall** (*colloq*) mad, distracted; **wall up** to block with a wall; to entomb in a wall; **with one's back to the wall** in desperate straits; at bay. [O.E., — L. *vallum*, a rampart.]

walla. See **wallah**.

wallaby *wol'əb-i*, *n* any of a number of small marsupials of the family *Macropodidae*. — **the Wallabies** the Australian national Rugby Union football team. [Aboriginal *wolabā*.]

Wallace's line *wol'is-iz līn*, *n* a line passing through the East Indian group of islands between Bali and Lombok, roughly separating the very different faunas of the Oriental region and the Australian region, or rather a transitional region. [Alfred Russel *Wallace* (1823–1913), naturalist.]

wallah or **walla** *wol'ə*, *n* (often in combination) a person employed in, or concerned with, a specific type of work; someone who occupies an eminent position in an organisation, etc. [Hindi *-wālā*, properly an adjectival suffix.]

wallaroo *wol-ə-ro͞o'*, *n* a large kangaroo (*Macropus robustus*). — Also known as the **euro**. [Aboriginal *wolarū*.]

wallet *wol'it*, *n* a small folding case for holding money, papers, etc. [M.E. *walet*, poss. — *watel*, a bag of woven material.]

wall-eye *wöl'-ī*, *n* an eye in which the iris is pale, or the white part is very large or noticeable (e.g. as the result of a squint). — *adj* **wall'-eyed** very light grey in the eyes, or in one eye; having a divergent squint; having a staring or a blank expression or (*fig*) appearance. [O.N. *vagleygr*, perh. conn. with mod. Icel. *vagl*, a film over the eye.]

Walloon *wol-o͞on'*, *adj* of or pertaining to a people living chiefly in southern Belgium and adjacent parts of eastern France, or to their language. — *n* a man or woman of this people; their language, a dialect of French. [Fr. *Wallon*; of Gmc. origin.]

wallop *wol'əp*, *vt* to beat soundly, thrash; to strike with force. — *n* a heavy blow; physical or financial power (*colloq*); beer (*slang*). — *adv* with a wallop; heavily or noisily. — *n* **wall'oper** a person or thing that wallops; something extremely large or big (*colloq*). — *n* **wall'oping.** — *adj* that wallops; extremely large or big, bouncing, whopping (*colloq*). [O.N.Fr. *waloper* (Fr. *galoper*); cf. **gallop**.]

wallow *wol'ō*, *vi* to roll about in mud, etc., as an animal does (implying enjoyment); to immerse or indulge oneself (in emotion, etc.); to flounder; in a bad sense, to live in filth or gross vice; to surge, heave, blow, well up, etc. — *n* the act of wallowing; the place, or the filth, an animal wallows in; a hollow or depression suggestive of a wallowing-place. — *n* **wall'ower.** — *n* and *adj* **wall'owing.** [O.E. *wealwian* — L. *volvěre*.]

wally or **wallie** *wo'li*, *n* a stupid, inept or despised person.

walnut *wöl'nut*, *n* a genus (*Juglans*) of trees, some yielding valuable furniture wood; one of these trees; their wood; the nut of the Common or English walnut. — *adj* made from walnutwood; light brown in colour. — **wal'nut-juice** juice from the husk of walnuts, used to stain the skin; **wal'nutwood.** [O.E. *walhhnutu* — *w(e)alh*, foreigner, *hnutu*, a nut.]

Walpurgis night *val-pûr'gis nīt* or *-po͝or'gis*, *n* the eve of the first of May, when witches, according to German popular superstition, rode on broomsticks and he-goats to hold revel with their master the devil, esp. on the Brocken in the Harz Mountains. [So called because 1 May is the day of St *Walpurga*, abbess of Heidenheim, who died about 778.]

walrus *wöl'rəs* or *wol'rəs*, *n* an aquatic, web-footed, carnivorous animal, related to the seals, having the upper canine teeth developed into enormous tusks. — **walrus moustache** a thick moustache with long drooping ends. [Du. *walrus*, *walros*, lit. whale horse; of Scand. origin.]

waltz *wölts* or *wöls*, *n* orig. a German dance performed by couples with a rapid whirling motion; a slower circling dance, also in triple time; the music for this; a piece of instrumental music in 3–4 time (**concert waltz**). — *vi* to dance a waltz; to move trippingly, to whirl (*slang*; also *vt*); to walk quickly, determinedly, or with apparent ease (*colloq*; also *vt*). — *n* **waltz'er.** — *n* and *adj* **waltz'ing.** — **waltz Matilda** see under **Matilda**. [Ger. *Walzer* — *walzen*, to roll, dance.]

wampum *wom'pəm*, *n* a shortened form of the N. American Indian (Algonquian) name for beads made from shells, used as money, etc. — **wam'pumpeag** (*-pēg*) the word of which wampum is a shortened form — lit. white string of beads.

WAN *abbrev* for: (West Africa) Nigeria (I.V.R.); wide area network (*comput*).

wan *won*, *adj* lacking colour; pale and sickly; faint. — *adv* **wan'ly.** — *n* **wan'ness.** — *adj* **wann'ish** somewhat wan. [O.E. *wann*, dark, lurid.]

wand *wond*, *n* orig. something slender and supple, such as a twig, or a thin stem or branch, or a young shoot of a willow used in basketmaking (now *poetic* and *dialect*); a rod used by a fairy, a magician, a conjurer, a conductor or a diviner; a measuring rod; a rod of authority. [O.N. *vöndr*, a shoot of a tree.]

wander *won'dər*, *vi* to ramble or move with no definite object, or with no fixed course, or by a roundabout way (*lit* and *fig*); to go astray, deviate from the right path or course, the subject of discussion, the object of attention, etc. (*lit* and *fig*); to lose one's way (*colloq*); to be incoherent in talk, disordered in mind, or delirious. — *vt* to traverse; to lead astray, or to bewilder (*colloq*). — *n* a ramble, stroll. — *adj* **wan'dered** astray; incoherent. — *n* **wan'derer.** — *adj* and *n* **wan'dering.** — *adv* **wan'deringly.** — **Wandering Jew** a legendary Jew in folklore (esp. of north-western Europe) who cannot die but must wander till the Day of Judgment, for an insult offered to Christ on the way to the Crucifixion; **wandering Jew** any of several trailing or creeping plants; **wandering sailor** a name given to various other similar plants; **wanderlust** (*won'dər-lust* or *van'dər-lo͝ost*) an urge to travel or to move from place to place. [O.E. *wandrian*.]

wanderoo *won-də-ro͞o'*, *n* usu. applied to the lion-tailed macaque, a native monkey of the Malabar coast of India; properly, a langur of Sri Lanka. [Sinhalese *wanderu*, monkey.]

wandoo *won'do͞o*, *n* a W. Australian eucalyptus with white bark and durable brown wood. [Aboriginal.]

wane *wān*, *vi* to decrease in size, esp. of the moon — (opp. to *wax*); to decline in power, prosperity, intensity, brightness, etc.; to draw to a close. — *n* gradual decrease or decline; the time when this is taking place; a defective edge or corner on a plank of wood. — *adj* **waned** diminished; dying or dead. — *adj* **wan'ey** or **wan'y.** — *adj* and *n* **wan'ing.**

[O.E. *wanian*, *wonian*, to lessen — *wana*, *wona*, deficient, lacking.]

wangle *wang'gl*, (*colloq*) *vt* to obtain or accomplish by craft; to manipulate. — *vi* to use tricky methods to attain one's ends. — *n* an exercise of such methods. — *n* **wang'ler**. — *n* **wang'ling**.

wank *wangk*, (*vulg slang*) *vi* to masturbate. — *vt* to masturbate (a man). — *n* an act or instance of masturbation. — *n* **wank'er** a person who masturbates; a worthless, contemptible person. — *adj* **wank'y** objectionable, contemptible.

Wankel engine *wang'kəl en'jin*, *n* a rotary automobile engine having an approximately triangular central rotor turning in a close-fitting oval-shaped chamber rather than conventional pistons and cylinders. [F. *Wankel* (1902–88), the German engineer who invented it.]

wannabee or **wannabe** *won'ə-bē*, (*slang*) *n* a person who admires another and who imitates that person's appearance, mannerisms, habits, etc.; someone who aspires to a certain lifestyle or status. [*I want to be*.]

wanness, wannish. See **wan**.

want *wont*, *n* the state or fact of being without or of having an insufficient quantity; absence or deficiency of necessities; poverty; a lack, deficiency; (in *pl*) requirements or desires. — *vt* to be destitute of or deficient in; to lack, be without; to feel need of, desire; to require, need; to fall short (of something) by (a specified amount). — *vi* to be in need or destitution; to lack (with *for*). — *adj* **want'ed** lacking; needed; desired; searched for, esp. by the police. — *n* **want'er**. — *adj* **want'ing** absent, missing, lacking; deficient (with *in*); below the desired or expected standard (in the phrase **found wanting**). — Also *n*. — *prep* without, lacking, less. — **want ad** (chiefly *US*) a small advertisement, esp. in a newspaper, specifying goods, property, employment, etc. required by the advertiser. [O.N. *vant*, neut. of *vanr*, lacking, and O.N. *vanta*, to lack.]

wanton *won'tən*, *adj* thoughtlessly cruel; lascivious; immoral, licentious, lewd; unprovoked, unjust, merciless; unrestrained, prodigal. — *n* a lewd person, esp. female; a trifler. — *vi* to play lasciviously or amorously; to trifle; to indulge oneself. — *adv* **wan'tonly**. — *n* **wan'tonness**. [M.E. *wantowen* — pfx. *wan-*, O.E. *togen*, past p. of *tēon*, to draw, lead, educate.]

wapiti *wop'i-ti*, *n* a species (*Cervus canadensis*) of deer of large size, native to N. America. [Algonquian.]

War. *abbrev* for Warwickshire.

war *wör*, *n* a state of conflict; a contest between states, or between parties within a state (**civil war**) carried on by fighting; any long-continued struggle, often against or between impersonal forces (*fig*); open hostility; a contest, conflict. — *vi* to make war; to carry on war; to contend: — *pr p* **warr'ing**; *pa t* and *pa p* **warred**. — *adj* of, characteristic of, resulting from or relating to war. — *adj* **war'like** of or pertaining to war; martial, military; fond of war; bellicose. — *n* **war'likeness**. — **war baby** a baby born during a war, esp. a serviceman's illegitimate child; any discreditable or troublesome result of war; **war bonnet** a headdress, often with long trailing chains of feathers, worn by members of certain N. American Indian tribes; **war bride** a soldier's bride, met as a result of wartime movements or postings; **war chest** funds set aside to pay for a war, political campaign, etc.; **war cloud** a cloud of smoke and dust over a battlefield; a sign that war is threatening or impending (*fig*); **war correspondent** a journalist or other person assigned to a scene of war so as to give first-hand reports of events; **war crime** one connected with war, esp. one that violates the code of war; **war cry** a cry used in battle for encouragement or as a signal; a slogan (*fig*); **war dance** a dance engaged in by some tribes before going to war; a dance imitating the actions of a battle; **war'fare** an engaging in, waging or carrying on of war; an armed contest; conflict or struggle of any kind (*fig*). — *adj* and *n* **war'faring**. — **war'-game** a mock or imaginary battle or military exercise used to train personnel in tactics; a game, esp. with detailed rules and using models, in which players enact historical or imaginary battles, etc.; **war'-gamer** a person who plays or takes part in war-games; **war'-god** or **-goddess** a deity who presides over war, assigning victory or defeat, etc.; **war'head** the section of a torpedo or other missile containing the explosive material; **war'-horse** a charger, a horse used in battle; an old warrior in any field of conflict, or any standard, familiar, rather hackneyed piece of music, etc. (*fig*); **war'lord** a commander or commander-in-chief, esp. where and when the military power is great — now usu. derogatory; **war machine** a machine used in warfare; the combined technical and administrative military resources mobilised by a country, alliance, etc. in order to engage in war; **war memorial** a monument erected to the memory of those (esp. from a particular locality) who died in a war; **war'monger** someone who encourages war, esp. for personal gain; **war'mongering**; **war neurosis** a better term for shellshock; **war paint** paint applied to the face and person by primitive peoples, indicating that they are going to war; full-dress, or finery, esp. a woman's make-up (*colloq*); **war'path** among the N. American Indians, the path followed on a military expedition; the expedition itself (**on the warpath** (*fig*) engaged in conflict, in a mood for battle); **war'plane** any aircraft designed or intended for use in warfare; **war'ship** an armed vessel for use in war; **war'time** a period during which a war is being fought. — *adj* of, pertaining to or characteristic of a time of war. — **war trial** the trial of a person accused of war crimes; **war'-whoop** a cry uttered on going into battle; **war widow** a woman whose husband has been killed in war. — **carry the war into the enemy's camp** or **country** to take the offensive boldly (*lit* and *fig*); **cold war** an intense, remorseless struggle for the upper hand by all means short of actual fighting; **declare war on** or **against** to announce formally that one is about to begin hostilities; to set oneself to get rid of (*fig*); **have been in the wars** (*fig*) to show signs of having been knocked about; **make** or **wage war** to carry on hostilities; **private war** warfare between persons in their individual capacity, e.g. by duelling, family feuds, etc.; **total war** war with every weapon at the combatant's disposal, sticking at nothing and sparing no-one; **war of attrition** one in which both sides are worn down over a long period, without decisive battles, etc.; **war of nerves** systematic attempts to undermine morale by means of threats, rumours and counter-rumours, etc. [Late O.E. *werre* — O.N.Fr. *werre* — O.H.G. *werra*, quarrel.]

waratah *wor'ə-ta*, *n* any of a genus of Australian shrubs with showy flowers. [Aboriginal.]

warble[1] *wör'bl*, *vi* to sing in a quavering way, or with variations (sometimes used disparagingly); to sing sweetly as birds do; to make or to be produced as a sweet quavering sound. — *vt* to sing in a vibratory manner, or sweetly; to express, or to extol, in poetry or song; to cause to vibrate or sound musically. — *n* the action, or an act, of warbling; a quavering modulation of the voice; a song. — *n* **war'bler** something or someone that warbles; a songster; a singing-bird; any bird of the family *Sylviidae* — willow-wren, reed-warbler, whitethroat, blackcap, etc.; any of numerous small, brightly-coloured American birds of a different family, *Parulidae*. — *n* and *adj* **war'bling**. — *adv* **war'blingly**. [O.N.Fr. *werbler*; of Gmc. origin.]

warble[2] *wör'bl*, *n* a small hard swelling on a horse's back, caused by the galling of the saddle, etc.; a swelling caused by a warble fly or a botfly. — **warble**

fly any of several flies of the same family as botflies whose larvae cause painful swellings that spoil the hides of horses, cattle, etc.

ward *wörd*, *vt* to parry or keep away (now usually **ward off**). — *n* a room with several beds in a hospital, etc.; the patients in a ward collectively; a division or department of a prison; an administrative, electoral, etc. division of a town, etc.; care, protection, guardianship; custody; a person, such as a minor, under a guardian; a look-out, watch; the state of being guarded; a means of guarding, such as a bolt or bar; a part of a lock of special configuration to prevent its being turned by any except a particular key, or the part of the key of corresponding configuration. — *n* **ward'er**, *fem* **ward'ress**, a person who guards or keeps; someone in charge of prisoners in a jail — now officially a 'prison officer'. — *n* and *adj* **ward'ing**. — *n* **ward'ship** the office of, or the state of being under, a guardian; protection, custody (*fig*); the state of being in guardianship (*fig*). — **ward'room** the mess-room of the officers of a warship; the officers collectively. [O.E. *weardian*.]

-ward *-wərd* or *-wörd* or **-wards** *-s* or *-z*, *sfx* forming adjs. and advs. with the sense of motion towards. [O.E. *-weard* (genitive *-weardes*); conn. with O.E. *weorthan*, to become, L. *vertĕre*, to turn.]

warden *wörd'en*, *n* a person who guards or supervises people, animals or things (esp. buildings); a title of certain officers of the Crown; a member of certain governing bodies; a person appointed for duties among the civil population in case of fire or air-raids or to control traffic circulation and parking of motor vehicles. [A.Fr. and O.N.Fr. *wardein* — O.Fr. *g(u)arden*, guardian.]

wardrobe *wörd'rōb*, *n* a piece of furniture or a room in which clothes or theatrical costumes are kept; a person's stock of clothing and accessories; a department of a royal or noble household in charge of robes, clothing, jewels, etc. — **wardrobe mistress** or **master** a person who looks after the theatrical costumes of a company or of an individual actor or actress; **wardrobe trunk** a trunk in which clothing can be hung as in a wardrobe. [O.N.Fr. *warderobe* or O.Fr. *garderobe*; ety. as for **guard** and **robe**.]

ware *wār*, *n* (now usu. in *pl*) articles of merchandise collectively; pottery; articles of fine workmanship. — (In combination, with defining word) **-ware** articles of the same type or material, as in *hardware*, *earthenware*. — *n* **ware'house** a building or room for storing goods; a large, usu. wholesale, shop. — *vt* (*-howz*) to deposit or store in a warehouse, esp. a bonded warehouse. — *n* **ware'housing** the act of depositing goods in a warehouse; the practice of covertly building up a block of company shares, using one or more front companies, etc. to obtain shares on behalf of the true purchaser (*stock exchange slang*). — *n* **ware'houseman** a man who keeps, or is employed in, a warehouse or a wholesale store. — **warehouse party** an acid house party (q.v.), held at a large unused building away from main residential areas. [O.E. *waru*.]

warfare, etc. See under **war**.

warfarin *wör'fə-rin*, *n* a crystalline insoluble substance ($C_{19}H_{16}O_4$) used as a rodenticide and (in the form of its sodium salt) as a medical anticoagulant. [*W*isconsin *A*lumni *R*esearch *F*oundation (the patent owners) and coum*arin*.]

warily, wariness, etc. See under **wary**.

warlock *wör'lok*, *n* a wizard; a magician (*Scot*); a demon. [O.E. *wǣrloga*, a breaker of an agreement — *wǣr*, a compact, *lēogan*, to lie.]

warlord. See under **war**.

warm *wörm*, *adj* having moderate heat; hot; imparting heat or a sensation of heat; retaining heat; affecting one (pleasantly or unpleasantly) as heat does (*fig*); strenuous; harassing; characterised by danger or difficulty; passionate; angry; excited; ardent, enthusiastic; lively, glowing; affectionate; amorous; (of a colour) containing red or, sometimes, yellow; (esp. in a game) close to discovery or attainment; (of a scent or trail) fresh. — *vt* to make warmer; to interest; to excite; to impart brightness or suggestion of life to; to beat (*colloq*). — *vi* to become warm or ardent; to begin to enjoy, approve of, feel enthusiastic about or fond of (with *to*). — *n* a warm area, environment (*colloq*); an act or instance of warming up or being warmed up (*colloq*). — *adv* warmly. — *adj* **warmed**. — *n* **warm'er**. — *n* **warm'ing** the action of making or becoming warm. — *adv* **warm'ly**. — *n* **warm'ness** or usu. **warmth**. — **Warm'blood** a race of horse developed from oriental or thoroughbred stallions and European mares for competition jumping and dressage; (also without *cap*) a horse of this type. — Also *adj*. — *adj* **warm'-blooded** having bodily temperature constantly maintained at a point usu. above the environmental temperature; ardent, passionate. — *vt* **warm boot** to re-boot a computer without switching it off (e.g. as when changing programs). — *adj* **warmed-o'ver** (*US*) or **warmed-up'** reheated. — **warm front** (*meteorol*) the advancing front of a mass of warm air. — *adj* **warm'-hearted** affectionate; hearty; sympathetic; generous. — **warm-heart'edness; warm'ing-pan** (*old*) a covered pan, with a long handle, for holding live coals to warm a bed; **warm'-up** a practice exercise before an event; a preliminary entertainment, etc. intended to increase the excitement or enthusiasm of the audience. — **warm up** to make or become warm; to heat, e.g. previously cooked food; to become animated, interested or eager; to limber up prior to any athletic event, contest, exercise, etc. [O.E. *wearm*.]

warn *wörn*, *vt* to give notice of danger or evil to; to notify in advance; to caution (with *against*); to tell to go or to keep away (with *off*, *away*, etc.; *lit* and *fig*); to ban (a person) from all race-meetings or from a particular course (*horse-racing*); to admonish. — *vi* to give warning. — *n* **warn'er**. — *n* **warn'ing** a caution against danger, etc.; something that gives this; previous notice; notice to quit, etc.; an admonition. — Also *adj*. — *adv* **warn'ingly**. [O.E. *warnian*, *warenian*, *wearnian*, to caution and perh. in part *wiernan*, to refuse, forbid.]

warp *wörp*, *vt* to twist out of shape; to turn from the right course; to distort; to pervert, e.g. the mind or character; to misinterpret, give a deliberately false meaning to; to arrange (e.g. threads) so as to form a warp; to move (e.g. a vessel) by hauling on ropes attached to posts on a wharf, etc.; to improve (land) by flooding so that it is covered by a deposit of alluvial mud. — *vi* to be twisted out of shape; to become perverted or distorted. — *n* the state or fact of being warped; the permanent distortion of a timber, etc.; a mental twist or bias; the threads stretched out lengthwise in a loom to be crossed by a woof; a twist, shift or displacement to a different or parallel position within a (usu. conceptual) framework, scale, etc. (as in *time-warp*); a rope used in towing, one end being fastened to a fixed object; alluvial sediment. — *adj* **warped**. — *n* **war'per**. — *n* **war'ping**. [O.E. *weorpan*, *werpan*.]

warragal. See **warrigal**.

warrant *wor'ənt*, *vt* to guarantee to be as specified or alleged; to attest or guarantee, the truth of — (*colloq*) equivalent to 'to be sure, be convinced', 'to be bound' (also in phrases **I** (or **I'll**) **warrant you**); to authorise; to justify, be adequate grounds for. — *n* a person who or thing that vouches, a guaranty; a pledge, assurance; a proof; that which authorises; a writ for arresting a person or for carrying a judgment into execution, or for seizing or searching property; (in the services) an official certificate inferior to a commission, i.e. appointing a non-commissioned officer; authorisation; justification; a document authorising the payment of money or certifying payment due, etc. — *adj* **warr'antable** that may be permitted; justifiable. — *adv* **warr'antably.** — *adj* **warr'anted.** — *n* **warrantee'** a person to whom a warranty is given. — *n* **warr'anter** a person who authorises or guarantees; a warrantor. — *n* **warr'anting.** — *n* **warr'antor** (*law*) a person who gives warranty; a warranter. — *n* **warr'anty** (*law*) an act of warranting; an undertaking or assurance expressed or implied in certain contracts; a guarantee; authorisation; justification; evidence. — **warr'ant-officer** (in the services) an officer of a rank between commissioned and non-commissioned; **general warrant** a warrant for the arrest of suspected persons, no specific individual being named or described in it. [O.Fr. *warantir* (*guarantir*); of Gmc. origin.]

warren *wor'ən, n* a series of interconnected rabbit burrows (also **rabb'it-warren**); the rabbits living there; a densely-populated slum dwelling or district; a maze of narrow passages. [A.Fr. *warenne*; of Gmc. origin.]

warrigal *wor'i-gal* or *wor'ə-gl, n* the Australian wild dog, the dingo; a wild Australian horse. — *adj* wild, savage. — Also **warr'agal.** [Aboriginal.]

warrior *wor'i-ər, n* a skilled fighting man (now usu. *poetic*, except when used of one at an early stage of civilisation); a veteran or distinguished fighter; a redoubtable person. [O.N.Fr. *werreieor* — *werre*; see **war.**]

warship. See under **war.**

wart *wört, n* a small, hard excrescence on the skin, caused by a virus; a small protuberance. — *adj* **wart'ed.** — *adj* **wart'less.** — *adj* **wart'y** like a wart; having warts on the skin or surface. — **wart'hog** any of a genus of wild hogs found in Africa, with large wartlike excrescences on their cheeks. — **warts and all** with blemishes or shortcomings known and accepted. [O.E. *wearte*; prob. related to L. *verrūca.*]

wartime. See under **war.**

wary *wār-i, adj* guarding against deception or danger; circumspect; cautious. — *adv* **war'ily.** — *n* **war'iness.** — **be wary of** show caution in regard to. [O.E. *wǣr*; cf. **aware.**]

was *woz*, used as the 1*st* and 3*rd pers sing* of the *pa t* of the verb **to be.** [O.E. *wæs* — *wesan*, to be.]

Wash. *abbrev* for Washington (U.S. state).

wash *wosh, vt* to cleanse, or to free from impurities, etc. with water or other liquid; to wet, moisten; to have the property of cleansing; (of an animal) to clean by licking; to flow over, past, against; to sweep along, down, etc.; to form or erode by flowing over; to cover with a thin coat of metal or paint; (in mining) to separate from earth by means of water; to launder (money, goods, etc.; *colloq*). — *vi* to clean oneself, clothes, etc. with water; to wash clothes, etc. as one's employment; to stand cleaning (with *well, badly*, etc.); to be swept or carried by water; to stand the test, bear investigation (*colloq*). — *n* a washing; the process of washing; a collection of articles for washing; that with which anything is washed; a lotion; the break of waves on the shore; the sound of water breaking, lapping, etc.; the rough water left behind by a boat, etc., or the disturbed air behind an aerofoil, etc.; the shallow part of a river or arm of the sea; a marsh or fen; erosion by flowing water; alluvial matter; a liquor of fermented malt prior to distillation; waste liquor, refuse of food, etc.; a watery mixture; a thin, tasteless drink; a broad but thin layer of colour put on with a long sweep of the brush; a thin coat of paint, metal, etc.; the blade of an oar; the material from which valuable minerals may be extracted by washing (*mining*). — *adj* **wash'able** that may be washed without damage. — *n* **wash'er** a person who washes; a washing-machine; a ring, usu. flat, of metal, rubber, etc. to keep joints or nuts secure, etc. (perh. a different word). — *n* **wash'iness** the state of being watery; feebleness. — *n* **wash'ing** the act of cleansing, wetting or coating with liquid; clothes (or other articles) washed, or to be washed; a thin coating; the action of breaking, lapping, etc.; (usu. in *pl*) liquid that has been used to wash something, or matter separated or carried away by water or other liquid. — *adj* that washes; used for washing; washable. — *adj* **wash'y** watery, moist; thin, feeble. — *adj* **wash-and-wear'** (of garments) easily washed, quick-drying, and requiring no ironing. — **wash'-basin, wash-bowl** or **wash'hand basin** a bowl to wash face, hands, etc. in; **wash'-board** a corrugated board for rubbing clothes on in washing, also used as a percussion instrument in certain types of music; a thin plank on a boat's gunwale to prevent the sea from breaking over; **wash'-cloth** a piece of cloth used in washing; **wash'-day** a day (or the regular day) when one washes one's clothes and linen (also **wash'ing-day**); **wash'-drawing** one made with washes. — *adj* **washed'-out** deprived of colour, as by washing; deprived of energy or animation (*colloq*). — *adj* **washed-up'** deprived of energy or animation (*colloq*); done for, at the end of one's resources (*slang*); finished (with *with*; *slang*). — **wash'erman,** *fem* **wash'erwoman,** a person who washes clothes, esp. for a living; **wash'-house** a house or room for washing clothes in; **washing-day** see **wash-day** above; **wash'ing-line** a clothes-line; **wash'ing-machine** a machine for washing clothes; **wash'ing-powder** or **-liquid** a powdered or liquid preparation used in washing clothes; **washing soda** see under **soda; washing-up'** cleaning up, esp. of dishes and cutlery after a meal; collectively, the items of crockery, etc. to be washed after use (**washing-up machine** a dish-washer); **wash'land** an area of land periodically flooded by overflow water from a river, stream, or from the sea; **wash'-out** a complete failure (*colloq*); a useless person (*colloq*); **wash'-room** a room containing lavatories and facilities for washing; a lavatory (chiefly *US*); **wash'-stand** a piece of furniture formerly used for holding ewer, basin, and other items for washing oneself; **wash'-tub** orig. a tub in which clothes were washed; a washing-machine. — **come out in the wash** (of a stain, etc.) to disappear on washing; to become intelligible, work out satisfactorily (*colloq*); **wash away** to obliterate; **wash down** (of liquid) to carry downward; to wash from top to bottom; to help the swallowing or digestion of (a solid food); **wash one's hands of** see under **hand; wash out** to remove by washing; to wash free from dirt, soap, etc.; to disappear or become fainter as a result of washing; to rain off; to cancel (*colloq*); to exhaust (esp. in *passive*; *colloq*); **wash up** to wash the dishes and cutlery after a meal; to wash one's hands and face (*US*); (esp. in *passive*) to carry up on to the shore and deposit; to spoil, finish (esp. in *passive*; *colloq*). [O.E. *wæscan, wascan.*]

wasm *woz'm*, (*colloq*) *n* an outmoded policy, belief, theory, doctrine or enthusiasm, an ism of the past. [*was* and is*m*.]

WASP or **wasp** *wosp*, (*US*; usu. *derog*) *n* an acronym for *w*hite *A*nglo-*S*axon *P*rotestant, an individual qualifying for such a description supposedly representing the most privileged class in U.S. society.

wasp *wosp, n* any of a large number of social and solitary insects belonging to the order Hymenoptera, the social varieties (including the common wasp and hornet, both of genus *Vespa*) having black and yellow bands and, in the case of the female, a sting. — *adj* **was'pish** quick to resent an injury; spiteful, virulent. — *adv* **was'pishly.** — *n* **was'pishness.** — *adj* **was'py.** — **wasp nest, wasp's nest** or **wasps' nest** the nest of a wasp or a community of wasps; a place very full of enemies or of angry people, or circumstances in which one is assailed indignantly from all sides. — **wasp waist** a very slender waist reminiscent of a wasp's, esp. contrasting with more substantial proportions above and below it. — *adj* **wasp'-waisted**. [O.E. *wæsp, wæps*; cf. L. *vespa*.]

wassail *wos'āl* or *was'l*, (*hist*) *n* the salutation formerly uttered in drinking a person's health; a liquor in which such healths were drunk, esp. ale with roasted apples, sugar, nutmeg, and toast; a festive occasion; revelry; a drinking bout; a drinking or festive song. — *vi* to hold a wassail; to go from house to house singing carols and festive songs at Christmas. — *n* **wass'ailer**. — *n* **wass'ailry**. — **wassail bowl** and **wassail cup** a bowl and cup used in wassailing. [O.N. *ves heill*, 'be in health'.]

Wassermann reaction *väs'ər-man rē-ak'shən* or **Wasserman test** (*test*), *n* a test of the blood serum, or of the cerebrospinal fluid, to determine whether the person from whom it is drawn is suffering from syphilis. [A. von *Wassermann* (1866–1925), German bacteriologist.]

waste *wāst*, *adj* rejected, superfluous; uncultivated, and at most sparsely inhabited; desolate; lying unused; unproductive; empty, unoccupied. — *vt* to spend, use or occupy unprofitably; to use, bestow, where due appreciation is lacking (often in *passive*); to fail to take advantage of; to devastate; to consume, wear out, impair gradually; to cause to decline, shrink physically, to enfeeble; to treat as waste material; to injure (an estate or property) (*law*). — *vi* to be diminished, used up, or impaired by degrees; to lose strength or flesh or weight (often **waste away**); to be used to no, or little, purpose or effect. — *n* too lavish, or useless, expenditure, or an example of it; squandering; superfluous, refuse or rejected material; gradual decay; destruction; loss; an uncultivated, unproductive or devastated region; a vast expanse, e.g. of ocean. — *adj* **wāst'able**. — *n* **wāst'age** useless or unprofitable spending; loss, or amount of loss, through this; loss by use or natural decay, etc.; (esp. in the phrase **natural wastage**) loss of employees through retirement, voluntary resignation, etc. rather than dismissal. — *adj* **wāst'ed** unexploited or squandered; exhausted, worn out; shrunken, emaciated; extremely drunk or high on drugs (*slang*; esp. *US*). — *adj* **waste'ful** causing waste; extravagant, over-lavish. — *adv* **waste'fully**. — *n* **waste'fulness**. — *n* **wāst'er** someone who or something that wastes; a spendthrift, wastrel, good-for-nothing (*colloq*); something discarded as waste during manufacture, esp. an inferior article spoilt in the making. — *adj* **wāst'ing** (of an illness, etc.) causing emaciation, destructive of body tissues, enfeebling. — *n* **wāst'rel** a profligate, ne'er-do-well, idler; a waif (*old*). — **waste basket** (*NAm*), **waste bin**, **wastepaper basket** or **bin** a basket or bin for holding discarded paper and other rubbish; **waste ground** or (*Can*) **waste'lot** a piece of land lying unused in a built-up area; **waste'land** a desolate, barren area; a culturally or intellectually empty place or time; **waste paper** used paper no longer required for its original purpose; **waste pipe** a pipe for carrying off waste or surplus water; **waste product** material produced in a process that is discarded on the completion of that process; **wasting asset** any asset (esp. a natural resource, such as a mine) whose value decreases with its depletion and which cannot be replaced or renewed. — **go to waste** to be wasted; **lay waste** to devastate. [O.Fr. *wast* (*guast*) — L. *vāstus*, waste.]

wat *wät*, *n* a Thai Buddhist temple or monastery. [Sans. *vātā*, enclosed ground.]

watch *woch*, *vt* to keep in view, to follow the motions of with the eyes; to observe the progress of, maintain an interest in, follow; to look at or observe attentively; to have in one's care, to look after; to guard; to tend; to beware of danger to or from, to be on the alert to guard or guard against; to be on the alert to take advantage of (an opportunity), etc. — *vi* to remain awake; to keep vigil; to be on the alert; to look out (with *for*); to look with attention; to keep guard; (with *over*) to keep guard over. — *n* a small timepiece for wearing on a strap round the wrist (also **wristwatch**), or carrying in a pocket; a division of the night, of fixed length (*hist*); the act or state of remaining on the alert or of observing vigilantly; close observation; the act of guarding; surveillance; a person who watches; a watchman, or a body of watchmen; a period, usu. of four hours, of duty on deck (*naut*); the part of the ship's officers and crew who are on duty at the same time; a sailor's or fireman's turn or period of duty. — (In combination) **-watch** denoting vigilance exercised by a community over some aspect of the environment, esp. as the professed brief of a television programme, as in **crimewatch**. — *adj* **watch'able** that may be watched; (of an entertainment, esp. a TV programme) having enjoyment or interest value, worth watching. — *n* **watch'er**. — *adj* **watch'ful** habitually on the alert or cautious; watching or observing carefully; characterised by vigilance. — *adv* **watch'fully**. — *n* **watch'fulness**. — **watch'case** the outer case of a watch; **watch chain** a chain for securing a watch to one's clothing; **watch committee** (*hist*) a committee of a local governing body exercising supervision over police services, etc.; **watch'dog** a dog kept to guard premises and property; any person or organisation closely monitoring governmental or commercial operations, etc. to guard against inefficiency and illegality (also *adj*); **watch'fire** a fire lit at night as a signal, or to keep a party of watchers warm; **watch'glass** a glass covering for the face of a watch; a small curved glass dish used in laboratories to hold small quantities of a solution, etc.; **watching brief** instructions to a counsel to watch a legal case on behalf of a client not immediately involved; (*loosely*) responsibility for observing developments, etc. in a specific situation, etc.; **watch'maker** a person who makes or repairs watches; **watch'making**; **watch'man** a man who watches or guards, now usu. a building, formerly the streets of a city, at night; **watch night** (*relig*) in some Protestant churches, the night of Christmas Eve (24 December) or New Year's Eve (31 December); (also **watch'-night service**) a service lasting through midnight held on these nights; **watch'spring** the mainspring of a watch; **watch'strap** a strap for fastening a watch round the wrist; **watch'tower** a tower on which a sentinel is placed to look out for the approach of danger; **watch'word** a maxim, rallying-cry. — **on the watch** vigilant, looking out (for danger, etc.); **watch it!** (*colloq*; esp. *admonitory*) be careful!; **watch one's step** to step with care; to act warily, be careful not to arouse opposition, give offence, etc. (*colloq*); **watch out** (*colloq*) to look out, be careful; **watch over** to guard, take care of. [O.E. *wæcce* (noun), *wæccan, wacian* (verb).]

water *wö'tər*, *n* (in a state of purity, at ordinary temperatures) a clear transparent colourless liquid, perfectly neutral in its reaction, and devoid of taste or smell; extended to the same substance (H_2O) in solid or gaseous state (ice or steam); any body of this (in varying degrees of impurity), such as the ocean, a lake, river, etc.; the surface of a body of water; the position of the tide, as in *high* or *low water*; (in *pl*) waves, moving water, a body of water; one of the four elements recognised by early natural philosophers; a quantity of the liquid used in any one stage of a washing operation; a liquid resembling or containing water; mineral water (usu. *pl* if at a spa); saliva; (usu. in *pl*) the amniotic fluid, filling the space between the embryo and the amnion; applied to the fluids secreted by the body, tears, urine, sweat; rain; class, quality, excellence (esp. in the phrase **of the first** (or **purest**) **water**); an increase in a company's stock issue without an increase in assets to back it up (*econ*). — *vt* to wet, overflow or irrigate with water; to supply (a plant) with water; to give (an animal) water to drink; to dilute or adulterate with water; (esp. in past p. **watered**) to wet and press so as to give a wavy appearance to; to increase (the debt of a company) by issuing new stock, without a corresponding increase in assets (*econ*). — *vi* to fill with, or shed, water; (of the mouth) to secrete saliva at the sight or thought of food, or (*fig*) in anticipation of anything delightful; (of an animal) to drink; to take in water. — *adj* pertaining to or used in the storage or distribution of water; worked by water; used, living, or operating, on or in water; by way of or across water; made with or formed by water. — *adj* **wa'tered.** — *n* **wa'terer.** — *n* **wa'teriness.** — *adj* **wa'terless.** — *adj* **wa'tery** full of water; (of eyes) moist, secreting water noticeably; relating to, consisting of or containing water; like water; thin or transparent; tasteless; weak, vapid; (of the sky or sun) having a rainy appearance. — **water bag** a bag for holding water; a camel's reticulum; **water bailiff** an official whose duty is to enforce bylaws relating to fishing, or to prevent poaching in protected waters; **water bath** a vessel of water in which other vessels can be immersed, e.g. in chemical work; **water bear** the tardigrade, a tiny invertebrate with eight legs; **Water-bearer** see **Water-carrier**; **water bed** (a bed with) a rubber or plastic mattress filled with water; **water beetle** any of a large number of beetles living on or in water, having fringed legs by means of which they swim easily; **water bird** a swimming or wading bird; **water biscuit** a thin plain biscuit made with water; **water blister** a blister containing watery fluid, not blood or pus; **water boatman** any of a number of aquatic leathery-winged insects having one pair of legs suggestive of sculls. — *adj* **wa'ter-borne** floating on water; conveyed by water, esp. in a boat; (of infection, etc.) transmitted by means of water. — **water bottle** a leather, glass or plastic bottle for holding drinking water, carried e.g. by hikers; **water brash** pyrosis, a sudden gush into the mouth of acid fluids from the stomach, accompanied by a burning sensation (heartburn) in the gullet; **wa'ter-breather** any animal that breathes by means of gills. — *adj* **wa'ter-breathing.** — **water buck** any of several antelopes, esp. those of the genus *Kobus*, that have long ridged horns and inhabit swampy areas; **water buffalo** the common domestic buffalo (genus *Bubalus*) of India, etc.; **water bug** any of a large variety of insects, including water boatmen, etc., found in or beside ponds, etc.; **water bus** a passenger-carrying boat plying a regular route across a lake, river, etc.; **water butt** a large barrel for collecting rainwater, standing out of doors; **water cannon** a high-pressure hose pipe, used to disperse crowds; **Wa'ter-carrier** or **wa'ter-bearer** Aquarius, a constellation and the eleventh sign of the zodiac; **water chestnut** a water plant (esp. of genus *Trapa*); its edible seed; a Chinese sedge (*Eleocharis tuberosa*) or its edible tuber; **water clock** a clock that works by means of flowing water; **water closet** (abbrev. **WC**) a lavatory of which the pan is flushed by water; a small room containing such a lavatory; **water colour** or in U.S. **water color** a pigment diluted with water and gum (or other substance), instead of oil; a painting in such a colour or colours; **wa'ter-colourist** or in U.S. **wa'ter-colorist** a painter in water colours. — *vt* **wa'ter-cool** to cool (e.g. an engine) by means of water, esp. circulating water. — *adj* **wa'ter-cooled.** — **wa'ter-cooler** a machine for cooling by means of water or for keeping water cool; **wa'tercourse** a channel through which water flows or has flowed; an artificial water-channel; a stream or river; **wa'tercraft** a boat; boats collectively; skill in swimming, etc., or in managing boats; **wa'tercress** a perennial cress growing in watery places, used as a salad; **water culture** a method of cultivation, often an experimental means of determining the mineral requirements of a plant, the plant being grown with its roots dipping into solutions of known composition; **water cure** medical treatment by means of water, hydrotherapy; **water cycle** the cycle in which water from the sea evaporates into the atmosphere, later condenses and falls to earth as rain or snow, then evaporates directly back into the atmosphere or returns to sea by rivers; **wa'ter-diviner** a person who, usu. with the help of a divining-rod, detects (or tries to detect) the presence of underground water; **wa'terdrive** the use of water pressure, either occurring naturally or by waterflood (q.v.), to drive oil or gas, etc. from a reservoir. — *adj* **wa'tered-down** much diluted; reduced in vigour, modified, attenuated. — **wa'terfall** a fall or perpendicular descent of a body of water, a cataract or cascade; **water flea** the common name for any of numerous minute aquatic crustaceans; **wa'terflood** in oil, gas or petroleum production, the practice of injecting water to maintain pressure in a reservoir and drive the oil, etc. towards the production wells; **wa'terfowl** a fowl that frequents water; swimming game birds collectively; **wa'terfront** the buildings or part of a town along the edge of and facing the sea, a river etc.; **water gas** a mixed gas obtained by passing steam, or steam and air, over incandescent coke or other source of carbon; **water gate** a floodgate; a gate admitting to a river or other body of water (see also separate article for **Watergate**); **water gauge** or **gage** an instrument for measuring the quantity or height of water; **wa'terglass** a concentrated and viscous solution of sodium or potassium silicate in water, used as adhesive, protective covering, etc. and (esp. formerly) for preserving eggs; **water hammer** a wave of increased pressure travelling through water in a pipe caused by a sudden stoppage or change in the water flow; the concussion and noise so caused; **wa'ter-heater** an apparatus for heating domestic water; **wa'terhen** the gallinule or moorhen, or other bird of the rail genus; **water hole** a pool in which water has collected, such as a spring in a desert or a pool in the dried-up course of a river; **water hyacinth** a tropical floating aquatic plant (genus *Eichhornia*) with bluish flowers, that grows in thick masses in ponds, etc.; **water ice** sweetened fruit juice or purée diluted with water, frozen and served as a kind of ice-cream, a sorbet; **wa'tering-hole** a water hole where animals go to drink; a place where humans seek (esp. alcoholic) refreshment, a pub (*facetious*); **wa'tering-place** a place where water may be obtained; a place to which people resort to drink mineral water, or for bathing, etc.; **water jacket** a casing containing water placed round e.g. the cylinder block of an internal-combustion engine, to keep it cool; **water jet; water jump** a place where a jump across a stream, pool, ditch, etc. has to be made, as in a steeplechase; **water key** (*mus*) in brass instruments, a sprung lever that allows drainage of accumulated moisture; **water level** the level formed by the surface of still water; **wa'terlily** a name commonly given to members of the family *Nymphaeaceae*, with broad flat floating leaves and large yellow or white cup-shaped flowers; **wa'terline** any of several lines on a ship to which it is submerged under different conditions of loading. — *vt* **wa'terlog** to saturate with water so as to make heavy or inert, or unfit for use, or to impede life or growth; to make (a vessel) unmanageable by flooding with water. — *adj* **wa'terlogged.** — **water main** a large subterranean pipe supplying water; **wa'terman** a man who plies a boat for hire, a boatman, a ferryman; a good oarsman; **wa'termark** the line of the greatest height to which water has risen; a tidemark; a ship's waterline; a distinguishing mark in paper, a design visible by transmitted light. — *vt* to mark with a watermark. — **wa'ter-meadow** a meadow kept fertile by flooding from a stream; **wa'termelon** a plant of the cucumber family (genus *Citrullus*), of African origin, having a large, pleasantly flavoured fruit; the fruit itself, with deep-pink watery pulp; **water meter** an instrument for measuring the quantity of water passing through a particular outlet; **water milfoil** see under **milfoil**; **water mill** a mill driven by water; **water mocassin** a poisonous snake of the southern United States; **water nymph** a nymph inhabiting water, esp. a naiad of Greek mythology; **water pipe** a pipe for conveying water; a hookah; **water pistol** a weapon or toy for throwing a jet of water or other liquid; **water plant; water plantain** a marsh plant of the genus *Alisma*, having plantain-like leaves and clustered white or pink flowers; **water polo** an aquatic ball game played by swimmers, seven a side; a similar game played by contestants in canoes; **water pore** (*bot*) a water-excreting organ; **water power** the power of water, employed to move machinery, etc.; a flow or fall of water which may be so used. — *adj* **wa'terproof** coated, e.g. with plastic or rubber, so as to be impervious to water; so constructed that water cannot enter. — *n* a material or an outer garment made impervious to water. — *vt* to make impervious to water, esp. by coating with a solution. — **water pump** a pump for raising water; **wa'ter-rail** the common rail (genus *Rallus*) of Europe, a long-beaked wading marsh bird; **water rat** the popular name of the water vole; the American muskrat; **water rate** a rate or tax for the supply of water; **water reactor** a water-cooled nuclear reactor. — *adj* **wa'ter-repellent** (of a fabric, etc.) treated so as not to absorb water. — *adj* **wa'ter-resistant** resistant to penetration by water. — **wa'tershed** the line separating two river basins; a crucial point or dividing line between two phases, conditions, etc.; **wa'terside** the edge of a sea, lake, etc., a shore. — Also *adj*. — **wa'ter-ski** a water-planing ski used in **wa'ter-skiing**, the sport of being towed at speed on skis behind a motorboat. — Also *vi*: — *pr p* **wa'ter-skiing**; *pa t* and *pa p* **wa'ter-skied** or **wa'ter-ski'd**. — **water snake** any of various kinds of snake (esp. of genus *Natrix*) frequenting fresh water; **wa'ter-softener** a device or substance for removing the causes of hardness in water; **wa'ter-soldier** an aquatic plant with sword-like leaves and white flowers reminiscent of plumes of feathers, common in lakes and ditches in the east of England. — *adj* **wa'ter-soluble** soluble in water. — **water splash** a shallow stream running across a road; **water sports** sports practised on or in the water; sexual arousal or gratification associated with urination; **wa'terspout** a pipe, etc. from which water spouts; a torrential downpour of rain; a disturbance like a very small tornado that occurs over water, taking the form of a revolving column of mist and spray; **water sprite** a spirit inhabiting the water; **water supply** the obtaining and distribution of water, e.g. to a community; the amount of water thus distributed; **water table** a moulding, esp. in the string course of a building, designed to throw rainwater outwards so that it does not flow down the wall below (*archit*); the level below which fissures and pores in the strata are saturated with water (*geol*); **water thrush** a N. American warbler with brownish back and striped underparts, living near water; **water thyme** a water plant of the genus *Anacharis*. — *adj* **wa'tertight** so well-sealed as not to admit water or let it escape; (of an argument, etc.) such that no flaw, weakness or source of misinterpretation can be found in it. — **wa'tertightness; water torture** torture using water, esp. dripping it slowly on to the victim's forehead; **water tower** a tower containing tanks in which water is stored so that it may be delivered at sufficient pressure for distribution to an area; **water vapour** water in gaseous form, esp. when evaporation has occurred at a temperature below boiling-point; **water vole** a large British vole (genus *Arvicula*) commonly known as the **water rat**; **water wagtail** a wagtail, esp. the pied wagtail; **wa'terway** any channel for water; a stretch of navigable water; a route over, or by, water; **wa'terweed** any of various plants with very small flowers and leaves growing in ponds, etc.; **water wheel** a wheel moved by water used to drive machinery, etc.; an apparatus consisting of a wheel with buckets or scoops attached to its rim, for raising water; **water wings** a wing-shaped inflatable device that fits across the chest, or a pair of inflatable armbands, for keeping a non-swimmer, esp. a child learning to swim, afloat in water; **wa'terworks** a plant by which water is supplied, e.g. to a town; tear-shedding, weeping (*facetious*); the urinary system (*euph*). — *adj* **wa'ter-worn** worn by the action of water. — **by water** using water transport, by ship, boat, etc.; **hold water** (of an argument, etc.) to be watertight or well-grounded, to bear examination; **in deep water** in trouble, difficulty or distress, esp. of the financial kind; **keep one's head above water** to keep solvent; **like water** copiously; extravagantly, recklessly; **like water off a duck's back** (of a rebuke, etc.) having no effect, making no impression; **make a hole in the water** (*slang*) to drown oneself; **make the mouth water** to arouse a delightful feeling of anticipation or desire; **make water** (of a boat) to leak, take in water; **make** or **pass water** to urinate; **of the first** (or **purest**) **water** see **water** (*n*); **pour oil on troubled waters** to take measures to calm down a stormy state of affairs, from the effect of pouring oil on rough water; **pour** (or **throw**) **cold water on** or **over** to discourage by one's indifference or dismissiveness; **still waters run deep** a quiet exterior often conceals strong emotions, resolution, cunning, etc.; **under water** below the surface; **water down** to dilute, make less strong, attenuate; **water of crystallisation** or **hydration** the water present in hydrated compounds, which, when crystallised from solution in water, retain a definite amount of water; **water of life** spiritual refreshment; whisky, brandy, etc.; **water on the brain** hydrocephalus; **water on the knee** an accumulation of serous fluid in the knee-joint; **water under the bridge** past problems soon forgotten or put down to experience. [O.E. *wæter*.]

Watergate *wö'tər-gāt*, *n* the U.S. political scandal involving an attempted break-in at the Democratic Party headquarters (the *Watergate* building, Washington D.C.) in 1972 by agents employed by President Richard Nixon's re-election organisation, and the subsequent attempted cover-up by senior White House officials who had approved the break-in; hence any similar political or public scandal, esp. one involving corruption, or misuse of power.

Waterloo *wö-tər-lo͞o'*, *n* a final defeat. [*Waterloo*, near Brussels, where Napoleon was finally defeated in 1815.]

waterproof, watershed, watertight, waterway, watery. See under **water**.

watt *wot*, *n* the practical and MKS unit of power, equal to a rate of working of one joule per second. — *n* **watt'age** an amount of power expressed in watts. — **watt'-hour** a common unit of electrical energy, being the work done by one watt acting for one hour; **watt'meter** an instrument containing a series (*current*) and a shunt (*voltage*) coil whose combined torque produces a deflection of the needle that is a direct measure of the circuit power in watts. [James *Watt* (1736–1819).]

wattle *wot'l*, *n* (*collective nsing* or in *pl*) material for fences, roofs, etc. in the form of rods, branches, etc., either interwoven to form a network or loose; any of various Australian acacias. — *vt* to bind with wattle or twigs; to form by plaiting twigs. — *adj* **watt'led**. — *n* **watt'ling** or **watt'lework** wickerwork. — **wattle and daub** wattlework plastered with mud and used as a building material. [O.E. *watul*, *watel*.]

waul or **wawl** *wöl*, *vi* to cry in the manner of a cat or a newly-born baby. — Also *n*. [Imit.]

wave *wāv*, *n* a ridge on the surface of a liquid, esp. of the sea; a surge, consisting of vibrating particles of liquid, moving across the surface of a body of liquid such as the sea (*transverse wave*) — the vibrations of the individual particles being at right angles to the line of advance; a unit disturbance in any travelling system of vibrating particles such as a light wave (*transverse wave*) or a sound wave (*longitudinal wave* — the vibrations of the particles being in the direction of advance); an undulating or vibratory motion (e.g. as a signal) or sound; curved inequality of surface; a line or streak like a wave; an undulation; an undulating succession of curves in hair, or one of these; a movement of the raised hand expressing greeting, farewell, etc.; a swelling up or increase, normally followed by a subsidence or decline. — *vi* to move the raised hand in greeting, farewell, as a signal or sign, etc.; to move backwards and forwards with undulating effect; to flutter; to undulate; (of hair) to have a wave or waves, be full of waves. — *vt* to move backwards and forwards; to brandish; to waft; to express by a wave; to direct, or signal an instruction to, by a wave; to raise into inequalities of surface; to give an undulating appearance to hair, etc. — *adj* **waved**. — *adj* **wave'less**. — *n* **wave'let** a little wave. — *adj* **wave'like**. — *adj* **wā'ving**. — **wave'band** (*radio*) a range of wavelengths occupied by transmission of a particular type; **wave energy** or **power** energy or power derived, by some means of conversion, from the movement of sea waves; **wave'form** or **wave'shape** (*phys*) a graph showing variation of amplitude of electrical signal, or other wave, against time; **wave'front** (*phys*) in a propagating vibratory disturbance, the continuous locus of points which are in the same phase of vibration; **wave function** (*phys*) a mathematical equation representing the space and time variations in amplitude for a wave system; **wave'guide** (*electronics*) a hollow metal conductor, usu. rectangular, within which very high frequency energy can be transmitted efficiently; **wave'length** the distance between two successive similar points on an alternating wave, e.g. between successive maxima or between successive minima; the distance, measured radially from the source, between two successive points in free space at which an electromagnetic wave has the same phase; such a distance serving to identify radio waves from a particular transmitter (*radio*); **wave mechanics** (*phys*) the part of quantum mechanics dealing with the wave aspect of the behaviour of radiations; **wave'meter** an instrument for measuring wavelengths, directly or indirectly; **wave motion** undulatory movement; motion in waves, or according to the same laws; **wave number** (*phys*) in an electromagnetic wave, the reciprocal of the wavelength, i.e. the number of waves in unit distance; **wave power** see **wave energy**; **wave-shape** see **waveform**. — **make waves** to create a disturbance, make trouble; **on the same wavelength as** in tune with, having the same attitude of mind, background knowledge, etc.; **wave aside** to dismiss (a suggestion, etc.) as irrelevant or unimportant; **wave down** to signal to stop by waving. [O.E. *wafian*, to wave.]

waver *wā'vər*, *vi* to move to and fro; to shake, be unsteady, be in danger of falling; to falter, show signs of giving way; to vacillate; to vary, change. — *n* **wā'verer**. — *adj* **wā'vering**. — *adv* **wā'veringly** in a wavering or irresolute manner. [O.N. *vafra*, to flicker.]

wavy *wāvi*, *adj* (of e.g. hair) forming undulations, full of waves; (of a line) describing a series of curves in alternating directions. — *adv* **wāvily**. — *n* **wāviness**. [**wave**.]

wawl. See **waul**.

wax[1] *waks*, *n* any of a class of substances of plant or animal origin, usu. consisting of esters of alcohols containing one hydroxyl group, e.g. beeswax, $C_{30}H_{61}O{\cdot}CO{\cdot}C_{15}H_{31}$; any of certain hydrocarbons of mineral origin; any substance like a wax in some respect, such as that in the ear; sealing-wax, prepared from shellac and turpentine; a resinous material used by shoemakers to rub their thread; readily impressionable, easily mouldable material (*fig*). — *vt* to smear or rub with wax. — *adj* **wax'en** made of wax; like wax; easily impressed, penetrated, effaced. — *n* **wax'er**. — *adv* **wax'ily**. — *n* **wax'iness**. — *adj* **wax'y** resembling wax in texture or appearance; soft; impressible; impressionable; pallid, pasty. — **wax'berry** the wax myrtle or its waxy-surfaced fruit; **wax'bill** any of various small seed-eating birds of the weaver finch family with coloured bills like sealing-wax; **wax'cloth** (*old*) another name for both oilcloth and linoleum; **wax flower** any of several plants, e.g. of the genus *Eriostemon* of Australia, with waxy pink five-petalled flowers; **wax myrtle** the U.S. candle-berry tree; **wax palm** either of two S. American palms yielding wax; **wax paper** paper spread with a thin coating of white wax and other materials; **wax plant** any of several plants of the genus *Hoya* of Australia and E. Asia, a climbing plant of the genus *Asclepias*, with clusters of waxy white or pink star-shaped flowers, and succulent leaves; **wax pocket** (in bees) a ventral abdominal pouch which secretes wax. — *adj* **wax'proofed**. — **wax tree** a tree from which wax is obtained, such as a Japanese sumac, the wax myrtle, etc.; **wax'wing** a member of a a genus of passerine birds (*Bombycilla*) with small red horny appendages, resembling red sealing-wax, on their wings; **wax'work** work done in wax; a figure or object modelled in wax; (in *pl*) an exhibition of wax figures. — *n* **wax'worker**. [O.E. *weax*.]

wax[2] *waks*, *vi* to grow or increase; (of the moon as it changes from new moon to full moon) to show, night by night, an increasing area of illuminated surface; to pass into another state, become, as in *wax lyrical*. — **wax and wane** to increase and decrease in alternating sequence. [O.E. *weaxan*.]

wax[3] *waks*, *n* a passion, fit of anger. — *adj* **wax'y** (*colloq*) irate, incensed.

way[1] *wā*, *n* a passage; a road, street or track; (with *cap*) used in street names; direction of motion; the correct or desired route or path; length of space, distance; district; room or opportunity to advance; freedom of action, scope; manner of life; established routine; position, as in *the wrong way up*, *the other way round*; condition, state; advance in life; normal or habitual course or conduct; (often in *pl*) a characteristic feature of behaviour, an idiosyncrasy; manner, style; method; means; course; respect; will; progress, forward motion, as in *edge one's way*, *eat one's way through*, etc.; progress or motion through the water, headway (*naut*); (in *pl*) the machined surfaces of the top of a lathe bed on which the carriage slides (*eng*); (in *pl*) the framework of timbers on which a ship slides when being launched (*eng*). — **way'bill** a list of passengers and goods carried by a public vehicle; a document giving details regarding goods sent by rail; **way'farer** a traveller, esp. on foot. — *n* and *adj* **way'faring**. — **way'faring-tree** a large shrub (genus *Viburnum*), with white flowers and berries that turn red and finally black, common in hedges. — *vt* **waylay'** to lie in ambush for; to attack or seize in the way; to lie in wait for in order to converse with: — *pr p* **waylay'ing**; *pa t* and *pa p* **waylaid'**. — *n* **waylay'er**. — **way'leave** permission to pass over another's ground or property; **way'mark** a guide-post; something which serves as a guide to a traveller; **way'side** the border of a way, path or highway. — *adj* growing, situated or lying near the wayside. — **way station** (*US*) an intermediate station between principal stations. — *adj* **way'worn** worn-out by travel. — **across** or **over the way** on or to the other side of the street, etc.; **be by way of** to be supposed or alleged to be or do; **by the way** incidentally; while travelling; beside one's path; **by way of** travelling through, via; as if for the purpose of; in character of, as a substitute for; **come one's way** to come in the same direction; to come within one's experience or reach, to become attainable; **divide three,** etc. **ways** to divide into three, etc. portions; **get one's** (or **one's own) way** to get what one wants; **go one's way** to leave; **go out of the way** or **one's way** to give oneself trouble; to make a special point (of doing something); **go someone's way** (of circumstances, etc.) to favour someone; **go the way of all flesh** to die; **have a way with** to be good at dealing with or managing (people, etc.); **have a way with one** to have a fascinating personality or persuasive manner; **have it both ways** (usu. with a *neg*) to benefit from two actions, situations, arguments, etc., each of which excludes the possibility, validity, etc. of the other; **have it one's way** or **one's own way** to do, think, etc. as one pleases, with no regard for others' advice or opinions; **have one's way** to carry one's point, get what one wants; **in a bad way** in a serious condition; very upset; **in a fair way to** likely to succeed in; **in a small (**or **big** or **large) way** on a petty (or a large or grandiose) scale; **in a way** to some extent; from one point of view; **in his,** etc. **(own) way** as far as his, etc. individual merits go, leaving aside the disadvantageous aspects; **in no way** not at all; **in the way** in one's path, impeding one's progess, creating an obstruction; **lead the way** to act as a guide in any movement; **look the other way** to look away, sometimes deliberately in order not to see someone or something; **lose the** (or **one's) way** to become lost; **make one's way** to move forward, sometimes with difficulty, to proceed; to make good progress, achieve success; **make way** to give place; to advance; **no way** (*colloq*) under no circumstances, absolutely not; **one way and another** considering various aspects; **on the** (or **one's) way** moving towards a destination or event; in progress; **on the way out** becoming unpopular, unfashionable, etc.; **out of the way** so as not to hinder or obstruct; away from the main routes, remote (*adj* **out'-of-the-way**); dealt with, finished with; in prison or dead and gone; (usu. with *neg*) out of the ordinary, unusual; **put someone in the way of** to contrive to make available to someone; **the Way** the Christian Religion (from the Bible: Acts ix. 2, etc.); **under way** in motion, as a vessel (also **underway**); **ways and means** resources; methods e.g. of raising money for the carrying on of government. [O.E. *weg*.]

way² *wā*, *adv* far; by a substantial distance or length of time. — *adj* **way-out'** (*slang*) excellent, very satisfying, exceptional; eccentric, unconventional, exotic. [Shortened from **away**.]

-ways *-wāz*, *sfx* forming adverbs and adjectives of direction and manner, as in *sideways*, *edgeways*.

wayward *wā'wərd*, *adj* wilful; capricious; irregular. — *adv* **way'wardly.** — *n* **way'wardness.** [For *awayward* — **away** and **-ward.**]

wazir *wä-zēr'*, *n* a vizier. [Ar. *wazīr*.]

Wb *abbrev* for weber, unit of magnetic flux.

WBC *abbrev* for World Boxing Council.

WC *abbrev* for: water closet; West(ern) Central.

WCC *abbrev* for World Council of Churches.

W/Cdr *abbrev* for Wing Commander.

WD *abbrev* for: Dominica, Windward Islands (I.V.R.); War Department; Works Department.

4-w/d *abbrev* for four-wheel drive.

WDA *abbrev* for Welsh Development Agency.

we *wē*, *pron plural* of I; I and another or others; used formally for I by monarchs and editors, and by other writers; used when speaking patronisingly to mean 'you'. [O.E. *wē*.]

WEA *abbrev* for Workers' Educational Association.

weak *wēk*, *adj* lacking strength; not able to sustain a great weight; easily overcome; frail; lacking health; feeble; lacking moral or mental force; impressible, easily led; lacking artistic force; unconvincing; inconclusive; having little of the important ingredient; (of a verb) inflected by regular syllabic addition instead of by change of main vowel; (of a sound or accent) having little force; (of a verse line) having the accent on a normally unstressed syllable; tending downward in price (*stock market*); (of an interaction between nuclear particles) having a decoy time of approx. 10^{-10} seconds. — *vt* **weak'en** to make weaker; to reduce in strength or spirit. — *vi* to grow weak or weaker; to become less resolute or determined, show signs of giving in. — *n* **weak'ener.** — *adv* **weak'ly.** — *n* **weak'ness** the state of being weak; a flaw, shortcoming; a liking or fondness (with *for*). — **weaker sex** (usu. *facetious*) women; **weak interaction** (*phys*) the weakest type of reaction between elementary particles involved in radioactive decay. — *adj* **weak'-kneed** feeble, pusillanimous. — *adj* **weak-kneed'ly.** — *adj* **weak'-minded** having feeble intelligence; having, or showing, lack of resolution; too easily convinced or persuaded. — *adv* **weak-mind'edly.** — **weak'-mind'edness; weak moment** a moment of weakness; **weak side** or **point** that side or point in which a person is most easily influenced or most liable to temptation. — *adj* **weak'-willed** lacking a strong will, irresolute. [O.N. *veikr*; related to O.E. *wāc*, pliant — *wīcan*, to yield.]

weakling *wēk'ling*, *n* a weak or sickly person or animal.

weakly *wēk'li*, *adj* sickly, not robust. — *n* **weak'liness.**

weal¹ *wēl*, *n* a raised streak left by a blow with a lash, etc. [A form of *wale*, a ridge.]

weal² *wēl*, (*literary* or *archaic*) *n* welfare, wellbeing. — **the public, general** or **common weal** the wellbeing, interest and prosperity of the country. [O.E. *wela*, *weola*, wealth, bliss.]

weald *wēld*, (*archaic* or *poetic*) *n* open country or wooded country. [O.E. *weald*, a forest, wold.]

wealth *welth*, *n* valuable possessions of any kind; riches; an abundance (*fig*). — *adv* **wealth'ily.** — *n* **wealth'iness.** — *adj* **wealth'y** rich; prosperous. — **wealth tax** a tax on personal property and riches. [M.E. *welthe* — *wele* — O.E. *wela*.]

wean¹ *wān*, (*Scot*) *n* a child. [**wee** and *ane*, one.]

wean² *wēn*, *vt* to accustom (a baby or young animal) to nourishment other than the mother's milk; to reconcile to doing without any accustomed thing, eschewing a former habit, etc. — *n* **wean'er** a young animal, esp. a pig, that has recently been weaned. — *n* **wean'ling** a child or animal newly weaned. — Also *adj*. [O.E. *wenian*, to accustom.]

weapon *wep'n*, *n* any instrument of offence or defence. — *adj* **weap'oned.** — *adj* **weap'onless.** — *n* **weap'onry** weapons collectively; armament. [O.E. *wǣpen*.]

wear¹ *wār*, *vt* to be dressed in; to carry on the body; to arrange, e.g. clothes, in a specified way; to display, show; (of a ship) to fly (a flag); to consume, waste or damage, by use, time or exposure; to make or render by friction; to exhaust, to weary; to tolerate, accept or believe (*colloq*). — *vi* to waste away through use or time; to last under use; to resist the ravages of age; to stand the test of time: — *pa t* **wore** (*wör*); *pa p* **worn** (*wörn*). — *n* the act of wearing or state of being worn; reduction or impairment through use or friction;

durability; articles worn (often used in combination as in *menswear*); fashion. — *n* **wearabil'ity.** — *adj* **wear'able** fit to be worn; good for wearing. — *n* **wear'er.** — *adj* **wear'ing** exhausting, tiring, irksome. — **the worse for wear** showing signs of wear; showing signs of exhaustion, intoxication, etc. (*facetious*); **wear and tear** damage by wear or use; **wear away** to impair or consume by wear; to decay or fade out; **wear down** to be reduced or consumed by constant use or friction; to diminish or overcome gradually by persistence; **wear off** to rub off by friction; to diminish by decay; to pass away by degrees; **wear out** to impair by use; to render or become useless through age, use or decay; to exhaust, tire utterly; **wear thin** to become thin or threadbare, through use; (of patience or tolerance) to dwindle. [O.E. *werian*, to wear.]

wear² *wār*, (*naut*) *vt* and *vi* to bring, or be brought, to another course by turning the helm to windward: — *pa t* and *pa p* **wore.** [Prob. **veer.**]

weary *wē'ri*, *adj* having one's strength or patience exhausted; very tired; causing weariness; tiresome, tedious. — *vt* to make weary; to reduce the strength or patience of; to harass. — *vi* to become weary or impatient; to long (with *for*; *Scot*). — *adj* **wea'ried** tired. — *adv* **wea'rily.** — *n* **wea'riness.** — *adj* **wea'risome** causing weariness; tedious. — *adv* **wea'risomely.** [O.E. *wērig*, weary.]

weasel *wē'zl*, *n* a small carnivore (genus *Mustela*) with a long slender body, active, furtive and bloodthirsty, eating frogs, birds, mice, etc.; any of various related species; a furtive or treacherous person. — *vi* to equivocate; (with *out of*, *on*, *round*, etc.) to extricate oneself from, circumvent (an obligation, etc.), esp. indefensibly: — *pr p* **wea'selling** or in U.S. **wea'seling;** *pa t* and *pa p* **wea'selled** or in U.S. **wea'seled.** — *n* **wea'seller** or in U.S. **wea'seler.** — *adj* **wea'selly.** — **weasel word** a word that makes a statement evasive or misleading, orig. a word used illegitimately in conjunction with another word, rendering it meaningless or sucking its meaning from it as a weasel sucks out the contents of an egg. [O.E. *wesle.*]

weather *wedh'ər*, *n* atmospheric conditions in terms of heat or cold, wetness, cloudiness, etc.; type or vicissitude of atmospheric conditions. — *vt* to affect by exposing to the air; to sail to the windward of; to come safely through (a storm or stormy situation); to slope (a roof; *archit*). — *vi* to become discoloured, disintegrated, etc. by exposure. — *adj* (*naut*) toward the wind, windward. — *adj* **weath'ered** having the surface altered in colour, form, texture or composition by the action of the elements (*geol*); seasoned by exposure to weather. — *n* **weath'ering** the action of the elements in altering the form, colour texture or composition of rocks (*geol*); seasoning by weather. — *adj* **weath'er-beaten** damaged or seasoned by the weather; (of someone's skin, etc.) tanned, lined, etc. from prolonged exposure. — **weath'erboard** a board shaped so as to shed water from a building. — *vt* to fit with such planks or boards. — **weath'erboarding** thin boards placed overlapping to keep out rain; exterior covering of a wall or roof. — *adj* **weath'er-bound** detained by bad weather. — **weather chart** a weather map; **weath'ercock** a vane in the form of a cock to show the direction of the wind; a person who changes his or her opinions, allegiance, etc. easily and often; **weath'er-eye** the eye as the means by which one forecasts the weather; an eye watchful for developments, as in *keep one's weather eye open*; **weather forecast** a forecast of the weather based on meteorological observations; **weather glass** a glass or instrument that indicates the changes of the weather; a barometer; **weather house** a toy house containing two figures, the emergence of the one presaging dry weather, and of the other, rain; **weath'erman** a person who prepares weather forecasts or who delivers such forecasts on radio or television: — *fem* **weather lady**; **weather map** a map indicating meteorological conditions over a large tract of country. — *adj* **weath'erproof** proof against rough weather. — *vt* to make weatherproof. — **weather report** (*loosely*) a weather forecast; **weather ship** a ship engaged on meteorological work; **weather station** a station where phenomena of weather are observed; **weather strip** a thin piece of some material fixed along the edge of a window or door, used to keep out wind and cold; **weather symbol** a conventional sign indicating a meteorological phenomenon; **weather vane** a weathercock; **weather window** a period of time in which the weather is suitable for a particular purpose, e.g. oil-drilling. — *adv* **weath'er-wise** with regard to weather conditions. — *adj* **weath'er-worn** worn away or damaged by wind, storms, etc. — **make heavy weather of** to find excessive difficulty in; **under the weather** indisposed, seedy; drunk; **weather the storm** to come safely through a period of difficulty, etc. [O.E. *weder.*]

weave¹ *wēv*, *vt* to make by crossing threads, strands, strips, etc. above and below one another; to interlace, e.g. in a loom to form cloth; to work into a fabric, story, etc.; to depict by weaving; to unite, work into a whole; to construct, contrive. — *vi* to practise weaving: — *pa t* **wōve** or (*rarely*) **weaved;** *pa p* **wōv'en;** cf. **wove.** — *n* the texture of a woven fabric. — *n* **wea'ver** a person who weaves; any bird of a passerine family (*Ploceidae*) resembling the finches, so called from their remarkable woven nests. — *n* **wea'ving** the act or art of making cloth by the intersecting of two distinct sets of fibres, threads or yarns — those passing longitudinally from end to end of the web forming the *warp*, those crossing and intersecting the warp at right angles forming the *weft*. — **weaver bird** a weaver or, less commonly, a weaver finch; **weaver finch** any member of a family of small finchlike birds (*Estrildidae*) which includes the waxbills. [O.E. *wefan.*]

weave² *wēv*, *vi* to move to and fro; to wind in and out; to move back or forward with sinuous movements of the body (*boxing*). — **get weaving** (*slang*) to get busy, get on the move. [M.E. *weve.*]

web *web*, *n* the fine structure of gossamer threads spun by a spider to entrap insects; that which is woven; a whole piece of cloth as woven in the loom; a kind of cloth or weave; a thin metal plate or sheet; in paper-making, an endless wire cloth working on rollers; a large sheet or roll of paper; the skin between the toes of a waterfowl, etc.; any connective tissue (*anat*); anything like a cloth web in its complication or a spider's web in its flimsiness or power to entangle; a plot, snare. — *vt* to envelop, or to connect, with a web. — *adj* **webbed** (of the toes or fingers) partially joined together by a membrane of skin. — *n* **webb'ing** a narrow woven fabric of hemp, used for belts, etc. and for various purposes in upholstery; the webs of webbed hands or feet. — *adj* **webb'y.** — *adj* **web'-fingered.** — **web'foot** a foot the toes of which are united with a web or membrane. — *adj* **web'footed.** — **web offset** a method of offset printing using a reel of paper. — *adj* **web'-toed.** — **web'wheel** a wheel in which the rim, spokes and centre are formed from one single piece of material; a wheel with a web or plate instead of spokes. [O.E. *webb* from root of **weave¹**.]

weber *vā'bər*, *n* the MKS unit of magnetic flux. [Wilhelm *Weber*, German physicist (1804–91).]

Wed. *abbrev* for Wednesday.

wed *wed vt* to marry; to join in marriage; to unite closely. — *vi* to marry: — *pr p* **wedd'ing;** *pa t* **wedd'ed** or (*dialect*) **wed;** *pa p* **wedd'ed** or (*dialect* and *poetic*) **wed.** — *adj* **wedd'ed** married; of or pertaining to marriage; closely joined; persistently devoted (with *to*). — *n* **wedd'ing** a marriage ceremony. — **wedding anniversary** the anniversary of one's wedding day; **wedding breakfast** a meal served after a wedding; **wedding cake** a highly decorated cake served at a wedding, and also divided among absent friends; **wedding day** the day of marriage; its anniversary; **wedding dress** a bride's dress; **wedding march** music in march time played as the bride's party enters the church and at the close of a marriage ceremony; **wedding ring** a plain, usu. gold, ring given by the groom to the bride at a wedding; any more or less similar ring given by the bride to the groom. — **silver, ruby, golden** and **diamond wedding** or **wedding anniversary** the celebrations of the 25th, 40th, 50th and 60th anniversaries of a wedding respectively. [O.E. *weddian*, to promise, to marry — *wedd*, a pledge.]

we'd *wēd*, a contraction of **we had, we should** or **we would.**

wedge *wej*, *n* a piece of wood or metal, thick at one end and sloping to a thin edge at the other, used in splitting, fixing tightly, etc.; anything shaped more or less like a wedge, e.g. a piece cut from a circular cake, a stroke in cuneiform characters, a formation of troops, the flying formation of geese and other wildfowl; an iron-headed golf club with much loft used for approaching; a stroke with such a club; a shoe in which the heel and sole together form a wedge with no gap under the instep (also called a **wedge-heeled shoe**). — *vt* to force (open) or drive (apart) with, or as if with, a wedge; to fasten or fix with a wedge or wedges; to thrust in tightly; to crowd closely. — *vi* to become fixed or jammed by, or as if by, a wedge; to make a stroke with a wedge (*golf*). — *adj* **wedged.** — *adj* **wed'gy.** — *adj* **wedge'-shaped** shaped like a wedge. — **the thin end of the wedge** a small beginning that is bound to be followed by a large or significant (and usu. unwelcome) development. [O.E. *wecg*.]

Wedgwood® *wej'wŏŏd*, *n* pottery made by Josiah *Wedgwood* (1730–95) and his successors including a distinctive type with cameo reliefs in white on a coloured ground. — **Wedgwood blue** a greyish-blue colour much used in Wedgwood pottery.

wedlock *wed'lok*, *n* matrimony; the married state, esp. in the phrase **born in (**or **out of) wedlock** i.e. legitimate (or illegitimate). [O.E. *wedlāc* — *wedd*, a pledge, and sfx. *-lāc* implying action of some kind.]

Wednesday *wenz'di* or *wed'nz-di*, or *-dā*, *n* the fourth day of the week. [O.E. *Wōdnes dæg*, Woden's day.]

wee[1] *wē*, (*Scot*) *adj* little, tiny. [M.E. *we*, *wei*, a bit, time or space.]

wee[2] *wē* or **wee-wee** *wē'-wē*, (*colloq*; esp. *childish*) *n* the act of urinating; urine. — *vi* to urinate.

weed *wēd*, *n* any useless plant of small growth; any plant growing where it is not wanted by man; any wild herb; anything useless, troublesome or obnoxious; a weak, ineffectual and/or unmanly man (*derog*); (often with **the**) tobacco, or a cigar or cigarette (*colloq*); marijuana (*slang*). — *vt* to clear (a garden, etc.) of weeds; to remove, uproot (weeds, etc.; often with *out*); to identify and remove (something or someone inferior, unwanted, etc.) from a group or collection (usu. with *out*). — *vi* to remove weeds. — *adj* **weed'ed.** — *n* **weed'er.** — *n* **weed'iness.** — *n* **weed'ing.** — *adj* **weed'less.** — *adj* **weed'y** weed-like; full of weeds; lanky, ungainly or weakly in appearance; of insipid character. — *adj* **weed'-grown** overgrown with weeds. — **weed'-killer** a chemical preparation, or other substance, for killing weeds. [O.E. *wēod*, a herb.]

weeds *wēdz*, *npl* a widow's mourning apparel (also **widow's weeds**). [O.E. *wæd*, *wēde*, clothing.]

week *wēk*, *n* the space of seven days, esp. from Sunday to Saturday (inclusive); the working days of the week; (in *pl*) an indefinitely long period. — *adj* **week'ly** coming, happening or done once a week. — *adv* once a week; every week. — *n* a publication appearing once a week. — **week'day** any day of the week except Sunday, and usu. also excluding Saturday; **week'end** (or *-end'*) the non-working period from Friday evening to Sunday evening (a **long weekend** usu. incorporating Friday and Monday or yet more liberally extended). — *vi* to spend a weekend holiday. — *n* **weekend'er.** — **week'night** the evening or night of a weekday. — **a week, two weeks,** etc. **today** one week, two weeks, etc. from today; **tomorrow week, Thursday week,** etc. a week from tomorrow, from next Thursday, etc.; **week about** in alternate periods of seven days; **week in, week out** continuously without a break. [O.E. *wice*.]

weeny *wē'ni*, (*colloq*; esp. *childish*) *adj* very small, tiny. [*wee* and *tiny* or *teeny*.]

weep *wēp*, *vi* to express grief by shedding tears; to wail or lament; to drip, rain; to ooze in drops; to leak or exude; to hang down, like a weeping-willow. — *vt* to lament; to express while, or by, weeping; to exude: — *pa t* and *pa p* **wept.** — *n* **weep'er** a hired mourner, or a reproduction of one on a graveyard monument; something worn to indicate mourning. — *n* **weep'ie** or **weep'y** (*colloq*) a highly emotional film, play or book. — *adj* **weep'ing.** — *adv* **weep'ingly.** — *adj* **weep'y** tearful (*colloq*). — **weeping willow** an ornamental Chinese willow with pendent branches. [O.E. *wēpan*.]

weever *wē'vər*, *n* a fish (genus *Trachinus*) with sharp spines in the area of the dorsal fin and gills, capable of inflicting serious wounds. [Prob. O.Fr. *wivre*, serpent, weever — L. *vīpera*.]

weevil *wēv'l*, *n* a popular name for a large number of beetles with the anterior part of the head prolonged into a beak or proboscis, which, either in the larval or the adult form, damage fruit, nuts, grain or trees; any insect injurious to stored grain. — *adj* **weev'illed, weev'iled, weev'illy** or **weev'ily** infested by weevils. [O.E. *wifel*.]

wee-wee. See under **wee**[2].

wef *abbrev* for with effect from.

weft *weft*, *n* the threads woven into and crossing the warp; the thread carried by the shuttle (also called **woof**). [O.E. *weft*, *wefta*.]

weigela *wī'gi-lə*, *-gel'ə*, *-gēl'ə*, *-jel'ə* or *-jē'lə*, *n* a deciduous shrub with large, showy pink, purplish or white flowers. [C.E. von *Weigel* (1748–1831), German botanist.]

weigh[1] *wā*, *vt* to find out the heaviness of; to be equal to in heaviness (e.g. *weigh 3 kilos* etc.); to raise (a ship's anchor); to apportion or measure a specific weight of; to hold in the hand(s) in order to, or as if to, estimate the weight; to estimate the value of; to ponder in the mind, consider carefully; to compare or counterbalance (with *against*); to consider worthy of notice. — *vi* to have weight; to be considered of importance; to press heavily (with *on*); to weigh anchor. — *adj* **weigh'able.** — *adj* **weighed** experienced; considered, balanced. — *n* **weigh'er.** — **weigh'bridge** a machine or apparatus for weighing vehicles with their loads; **weighing machine** a machine for weighing. — **weigh down** to force down; to depress, discourage; to preponderate over, outweigh; **weigh in** to ascertain a person's weight before a boxing match or other sports competition, or after a horse-race (*n* **weigh'-in**); to join in a project (*slang*); **weigh in with** to produce (a new argument, etc.) in a discussion; **weigh out** to weigh and dispense in portions accordingly; to ascertain a person's weight before a horse-race (*n* **weigh'-out**); **weigh up** to consider carefully and assess the quality of; **weigh with** to appear important to, to influence. [O.E. *wegan*.]

weigh[2] *wā*, *n* a variant of **way** in the phrase 'under way', through confusion with the phrase 'to weigh anchor'.

weight *wāt*, *n* the heaviness of a thing, esp. as determined by weighing; quantity as determined in this way; the force with which a body is attracted to the earth, measured by the product of the mass and the acceleration; a mass of metal adjusted to a standard and used for finding weight; a method of estimating, or a unit of, weight; the amount something ought to weigh; a standard amount that a boxer, etc. should weigh; a heavy object; anything heavy or oppressive; a ponderous mass; pressure; importance; power; impressiveness; the frequency of an item in a frequency distribution or a number indicating this. — *vt* to make heavier; to attach weights to; to hold down in this way (often with *down*); to increase the weight of (fabrics) by adding chemicals; to assign a handicap weight to (a horse); to oppress, burden; to assign greater value, importance, etc. to one factor than to another; to attach numbers indicating their relative frequency to (items in a frequency distribution). — *adv* **weigh'tily**. — *n* **weigh'tiness**. — *n* **weigh'ting** a weighting allowance. — *adj* **weight'less**. — *n* **weight'lessness** the condition of a freely falling body at the beginning of the fall when its inertia exactly balances the gravitational force, or that of a space traveller and his or her unpowered spacecraft in orbit beyond the earth's atmosphere. — *adj* **weigh'ty** heavy; important; having much influence; being the fruit of judicious consideration and hence worthy of attention. — **weighting allowance** a salary differential to balance the higher cost of living in a particular area; **weight'lifter**; **weight'lifting** a sport in which competitors lift and hold above their heads (or attempt to) a barbell made increasingly heavy as the competition progresses; **weight'-training** physical training by means of a series of pulleys, levers, etc. with adjustable weights, for building up individual muscle groups. — *vi* **weight'-train**. — **weight'-watcher** a person who is attempting to lose weight by careful dieting, esp. one who attends meetings of an association of similar people; **weight'-watching**. — **gain (or put on) weight** to increase one's body weight, get fatter; **lose weight** to decrease one's body weight, get thinner; **throw one's weight about** to over-exercise one's authority; to domineer. [O.E. *wiht*.]

weir *wēr*, *n* a dam across a river; a fence of stakes set in a stream for catching fish. [O.E. *wer*, an enclosure.]

weird *wērd*, *adj* unearthly, uncanny; peculiar, odd (*colloq*). — *n* (*Scot*, *archaic*) destiny or fate; (in *pl* with *cap*) the Fates. — *n* **weir'die** or **weir'dō** (*pl* **weir'dos** or **weir'does**) (*colloq*) an eccentric; someone unconventional in dress, etc. — *adv* **weird'ly**. — *n* **weird'ness**. — **the Weird Sisters** the Fates; the Fates of Scandinavian mythology; the witches in *Macbeth*. [O.E. *wyrd*, fate.]

Weismannism *vīs'mə-nizm*, *n* the doctrine in biology of August *Weismann* (1834–1914), whose central teaching is that acquired characteristics are not transmitted.

weka *we'kə*, *n* any of the flightless rails (genus *Gallirallus* or *Ocydromus*) of New Zealand. [Maori, imit.]

welcome *wel'kəm*, *adj* received with gladness; admitted willingly; causing gladness; free (to); free to take or enjoy. — *n* the act of welcoming; a kindly reception; a reception. — *vt* to greet; to receive with kindness or pleasure; to accept or undergo gladly. — *interj* expressing pleasure, as to guests on their arrival. — *n* **wel'comeness**. — *n* **wel'comer**. — *adj* **wel'coming**. — *adv* **wel'comingly**. — **make someone welcome** to welcome someone, make them feel welcome; **outstay one's welcome** to stay too long; **wear out one's welcome** to stay too long or call too often; **you're welcome** it is (or was) no trouble, no thanks are needed. [O.E. *wilcuma* — *wil-* (*willa*, will, pleasure) and *cuma*, guest.]

weld[1] *weld*, *n* a scentless species of mignonette, also known as *dyer's rocket*, yielding a yellow dye; the dye itself. [Cf. Ger. *Wau*.]

weld[2] *weld*, *vt* to join (two pieces of metal) by fusing, forging or the application of pressure, using any of several methods, e.g. raising the temperature at the joint by means of external heat or (**resistance welding**) of a heavy electric current or (**arc welding**) of an electric arc; to join closely. — *vi* to undergo welding; to be capable of being welded. — *n* a welded joint. — *n* **weldabil'ity**. — *adj* **weld'able**. — *n* **weld'er** or **weld'or**. — *adj* **weld'less**. — *n* **weld'ment** the action or process of welding; a welded assembly. [Same as obs. or dialect verb *well*, meaning melt, weld.]

welfare *wel'fār*, *n* the state of faring or doing well; freedom from calamity, etc.; enjoyment of health, etc.; prosperity; welfare work. — *n* **wel'farism** the social policies characteristic of a welfare state. — *n* **wel'farist**. — **welfare state** a social system or state in which socialist principles have been put into effect with the purpose of ensuring the welfare of all who live in it, e.g. by paying unemployment benefit, old-age pensions, etc. and by providing other social services; **welfare work** efforts to improve conditions of living for a class, e.g. the very poor; **welfare worker**. [**well**[2] and **fare**.]

well[1] *wel*, *n* a spring; a mineral spring; a source; a lined shaft sunk in the earth from where a supply of water, oil, etc. is obtained; an enclosure in a ship's hold round the pumps; the vertical opening enclosed between the outer ends of the flights in a winding stair; a lift shaft; a cavity. — *vi* to issue forth, as water does from the earth. — **well'head** the source of a spring; a fountainhead, origin, source; the top of a well, or a structure built over it; **well'-sinker** a person who digs wells; **well'-sinking**; **well'spring** a fountain. — **well over** to overflow. [O.E. *wella*.]

well[2] *wel adj* (*compar* **bett'er**, *superl* **best**), (usu. *predicative*) in good condition; in good health; fortunate; advisable; satisfactory. — *adv* rightly; skilfully; thoroughly; intimately; favourably, successfully; abundantly; with some degree of luxury; with reason or propriety; conveniently; to a considerable extent; clearly; easily; very possibly; very, esp. in combination. — *interj* expressing surprise, hesitation, resignation, etc., or introducing resumed narrative. — *n* **well'ness**. — *adj* **well-acquaint'ed** having intimate personal knowledge. — *adj* **well-advised'** prudent. — *adj* **well-aimed'**. — *adj* **well-appoint'ed** well-equipped. — *adj* **well-bal'anced** having the parts properly adjusted for smooth working; sane and sensible. — *adj* **well-behaved'** behaving or acting in accordance with propriety or with requirements. — **well'being** welfare. — *adj* **well-beloved** (*-luvd'* or *-luv'id*) very dear. — *adj* **well-born'** born of a good family, not of mean birth. — *adj* **well-bred'** having polite manners and good breeding; of good stock. — *adj* **well-built'** (of a building, buildings, a person, a garment, etc.) of strong or well-proportioned make or form. — *adj* **well-chos'en** (esp. of words in a speech) carefully chosen. — *adj* **well-conduct'ed** properly managed; acting properly. — *adj* **well-connec'ted** having friends or relatives in positions of importance or in the upper social strata. — *adj* **well-defined'** clearly and precisely determined. — *adj* **well-devel'oped** having developed to an advanced, elaborate, good, desirable, etc. state. — *adj* **well-direct'ed** skilfully aimed. — *adj* **well-disposed'** well-placed or well-arranged; inclined to be friendly; favourable. — *adj* **well-dressed'** wearing stylish clothes. — *adj* **well-earned'** or (when *attributive*) **well'-earned** thoroughly deserved. — *adj* **well-ed'ucated** having had a good education. — *adj*

well-endowed' (*colloq*; *facetious*) (of a man) having a large penis; (of a woman) having large breasts. — *adj* **well-fa'voured** good-looking. — *adj* **well-fed'** plump; given nutritious food. — *adj* **well-formed'** shapely, well-proportioned; correct according to the established rules of grammar (*linguis*). — *adj* **well-found'** adequately provided, fully equipped. — *adj* **well-found'ed** built on secure foundations; based on solid evidence or sound reasoning. — *adj* **well-groomed'** neat and smart in appearance, with carefully tended hair, hands, etc. — *adj* **well-ground'ed** firmly founded. — *adj* **well-heeled'** prosperous, rich. — *adj* **well-hung'** hung skilfully; (of meat) hung long enough to mature; (of a man) having sizeable genitals (*colloq*). — *adj* **well-informed'** having sound and sufficient information on a particular subject; full of varied information. — *adj* **well-inten'tioned** having, or arising from, good intentions or purpose. — *adj* **well-judged'** correctly calculated, judicious. — *adj* **well-known'** fully known; celebrated; notorious. — *adj* **well-made'**. — *adj* **well-mann'ered** polite. — *adj* **well-marked'** obvious, decided. — *adj* **well-mean'ing** well-intentioned. — *adj* **well-kept'** carefully looked after, kept in good condition or order. — *adj* **well-meant'** rightly or kindly intended. — *adv* **well'-nigh** nearly, almost. — *adj* **well off** or (when *attributive*) **well'-off** in good circumstances. — *adj* **well-oiled'** drunk (*facetious*); smoothly mechanical from much practice. — *adj* **well-ord'ered** correctly governed; properly arranged. — *adj* **well-placed'** in a good position (for some purpose); in a position senior enough or intimate enough to gain information, etc. — *adj* **well-preserved'** in good condition, not decayed; looking youthful or younger than one's age. — *adj* **well-propor'tioned** having correct or pleasing proportions. — *adj* **well-read** (*-red'*) having read widely, well-informed on literature. — *adj* **well-reg'ulated** well-ordered. — *adj* **well-respect'ed** highly esteemed. — *adj* **well-round'ed** suitably curved; symmetrical; well constructed and complete. — *adj* **well-set-up'** (*colloq*) well-built, shapely. — *adj* **well-spent'** spent usefully or profitably. — *adj* **well-spo'ken** ready, graceful or courteous in speech. — *adj* **well-thought'-of** esteemed. — *adj* **well-thought-out'** reasoned soundly and arranged with skill. — *adj* **well-thumbed'** (of a book) showing marks of much handling or repeated use. — *adj* **well-timed'** opportune, timely, judicious. — *adj* **well-to-do'** prosperous, well off. — *adj* **well-trodd'en** often followed or walked along, much used or frequented. — *adj* **well-turned'** shapely; felicitously expressed. — *adj* **well-uphol'stered** (*facetious*; of a person) plump, fat. — **well'-wisher** someone who wishes one well or is concerned for one's welfare. — *adj* **well'-woman** (of e.g. a clinic) concerned with the monitoring of women for, and the prevention of, gynaecological disorders. — *adj* **well-worked-out'** thoroughly or logically planned or developed. — *adj* **well-worn'** much worn; trite. — **all very well** an ironic phrase used to introduce an objection to what has gone before, as in *it's all very well to be critical*; **as well as** in addition to; no less than; **be as well to** to be well-advised to (do something); **very well** a phrase signifying assent, sometimes ironic; **well and good** a phrase signifying acceptance of facts or of a situation; **well and truly** completely, thoroughly; **well away** progressing rapidly; far away; drunk (*slang*); **well done** an expression of praise; (of meat) well or thoroughly cooked; **well enough** in a moderate but sufficient degree; **well in** (*colloq*) having a good relationship; prosperous (*Austr*); **well now** and **well then** phrases used to preface questions, conclusions, comments, or requests for such, or other remarks; **well up in** (*colloq*) well versed in, well acquainted with, knowledgeable on the subject of; **well, well** an expression of surprise; **wish someone well** to wish someone success or good fortune; to bear someone no ill will. [O.E. *wel.*]

we'll *wēl*, a contraction of **we will** or **we shall**.

wellie. See **welly**.

wellington *wel'ing-tən* or **wellington boot** (*bo͞ot*), *n* a loose-fitting rubber or plastic boot covering the calf; a kind of riding-boot covering the knee in front, but cut away behind to allow the knee to bend. [Named after the first Duke of *Wellington* (1769–1852).]

welly or **wellie** *wel'i*, (*colloq*) *n* a wellington of the loose rubber or plastic kind. — Also **well'y-boot** or **well'ie-boot**. — **give it welly** (or **wellie**) (*slang*) to put one's foot down heavily on the accelerator (of a motor vehicle, etc.); to put a great deal of effort or energy into something.

Welsh *welsh*, *adj* relating to *Wales* or its inhabitants. — *npl* the inhabitants of Wales. — *nsing* their language. — **Welsh dresser** a dresser usu. with open shelves above cupboards and drawers; **Welsh harp** a large harp with three rows of strings, two tuned in unison and in the diatonic scale, the third in the sharps and flats of the chromatic; **Welsh'man** a native man of Wales; **Welsh rabbit** or **Welsh rarebit** see **rarebit** under **rare**[1]; **Welsh'woman.** [O.E. *welisc* — *wealh*, the Anglo-Saxons' word for Briton, Welshman, foreigner; from L. *Volcae*, orig. the Narbonese Gauls.]

welsh *welsh*, *vi* to run off from a race-course without settling or paying one's bets; to dodge fulfilling an obligation (with *on*). — *vt* to cheat in such a way. — *n* **welsh'er**.

welt *welt*, *n* a band, strip or ribbed border fastened to an edge to give strength or for ornament; a narrow strip of leather used in one method of sewing the upper to the sole of a shoe; a weal; a lash, blow. — *vt* to add a welt to; to lash, beat.

Weltanschauung *velt'an-show-o͝ong*, (Ger.) *n* outlook upon the world, world-philosophy.

welter *wel'tər*, *n* a state of turmoil or confusion; a confused mass (with *of*); a surging mass (with *of*). — *vi* (esp. *poetic*) to roll or tumble out. [M.Du. *welteren*; cf. O.E. *gewæltan*, to roll.]

welterweight *wel'tər-wāt*, *n* a weight category applied variously in boxing, wrestling and weight-lifting; a sportsman of the specified weight for such a category (e.g., in professional boxing above light-weight, **light'-** or **jun'ior-welterweight** (maximum 64 kg./140 lb.) and **wel'terweight** (maximum 67 kg./147 lb.).

Weltpolitik *velt-pol-i-tēk*, (Ger.) *n* world politics; the policy of taking a forceful part in international affairs.

welwitschia *wel-wich'i-ə*, *n* a South-west African plant consisting of one pair of leaves that grow indefinitely, with a cone-shaped growth rising between them. [After F. *Welwitsch* (1806–72), Austrian traveller.]

Wemyss ware *wēmz wār*, *n* a type of pottery produced between 1882 and 1930 in Kirkcaldy, Fife, named after the *Wemyss* family of Wemyss Castle, and characterised by lively colourful painted decoration, esp. representing fruit and flowers.

wen[1] *wen*, *n* a sebaceous cyst, esp. on the scalp (*pathol*); an enormous congested city, esp. (as **the great wen**) London. [O.E. *wen(n)*, a swelling, a wart.]

wen[2] *wen* or **wyn** *win*, *n* a rune having the value of modern English *w* adopted into the O.E. alphabet. [O.E., orig. *wynn*, joy (of which *w* is the initial letter).]

wench *wench* or *wensh*, (*archaic* or *facetious*) *n* a girl or young woman; a prostitute, whore; a servant girl. — *vi* to frequent the company of whores; to associate with girls, go courting. [O.E. *wencel*, a child.]

Wend *wend*, *n* one of a branch of the Slavs which in the Middle Ages occupied the north and east of

Germany; one of the Slavic population of Lusatia in eastern Germany who still speak the Wendish tongue. — *adj* **Wend'ic** or **Wend'ish.** — *n* the language of the Wends. [Ger. *Wende.*]

wend *wend,* (*archaic* or *literary*) *vi* and *vt* to go, direct (one's course): — *pa t* and *pa p* **went** (now used as *pa t* of **go**). — **wend one's way** to make one's way, follow the road, esp. in a leisurely fashion. [O.E. *wendan,* a common Gmc. verb.]

Wendy House® *wen'di hows, n* a structure of cloth or vinyl, etc., decorated to simulate a little house, stretched over a rigid frame, usu. erected indoors for children to play in. [From the house built for *Wendy* in J.M. Barrie's *Peter Pan.*]

Wensleydale *wenz'li-dāl, n* a breed of long-woolled sheep; a variety of cheese. [*Wensleydale,* Yorks.]

went *went, pa t* of **go**, orig. *pa t* of **wend**.

wentletrap *wen'tl-trap, n* any of a number of gasteropod molluscs, having a spiral shell with many deep whorls, crossed by elevated ribs. [Du. *wenteltrap,* a winding staircase, a spiral shell.]

wept *wept, pa t* and *pa p* of **weep**.

were *wûr, vi* the *pl* of **was**, used as *pa t* (*pl*) and *past subjunctive* (*sing* and *pl*) of **be**. [O.E. *wǣron,* subj. *wǣre.*]

we're *wēr,* a contraction of **we are**.

werewolf *wēr'wo͝olf,* (*folklore*) *n* a person able to change for a time into a wolf: — *pl* **were'wolves**. [O.E. *werwulf* — *wer,* man, *wulf,* a wolf.]

wergild *wûr'gild* or **weregild** *wēr'gild,* (*hist*) *n* among Teutonic peoples, a fine by which homicide and other heinous crimes against the person were expiated. [O.E. *wergield,* from *wer,* man, *gield* — *gieldan,* to pay.]

Wesleyan *wez'li-ən, adj* relating to *John Wesley* (1703–1791), or to Methodism, the name given to his system of religious doctrine and church organisation, or to the Protestant denomination founded by him. — *n* an adherent of Wesley or Methodism. — *n* **Wes'leyanism.**

west *west, n* the quarter of the sky where the sun sets at the equinox; one of the four chief points of the compass; the west part of a region. — *adj* situated towards, or (of wind) coming from, the west. — *adv* towards the west. — *vi* **west'er** to turn westward; to change into the west. — *adj* **west'erly** lying or moving towards the west; from the west. — *adv* towards the west; from the west. — *n* a westerly wind. — *adj* **west'ern** situated in the west; belonging to the west, or (with *cap*) the West; moving towards the west. — *n* a film or novel whose scene is the western United States, esp. the former Wild West. — *n* **west'erner** a person belonging to the west, or (with *cap*) the West. — *vt* and *vi* **west'ernise** or **-ize** to make or become like the people of Europe and America in customs, or like their institutions, practices, ideas. — *n* **westernisā'tion** or **-z-**. — *adj* **west'ernmost** furthest to the west. — *n* **west'ing** space or distance westward; departure westward; direction or course towards the west. — *adj* **west'most** most westerly. — *adj* and *adv* **west'ward** towards the west. — *adv* and *adj* **west'wardly** towards the west. — *adj* **west'wards** towards the west. — **West Bank** the Jordanian territory to the west of the river Jordan and the Dead Sea, annexed by Israel in 1967. — *adj* **west'bound** heading or travelling westwards. — **west-by-north'** or **-south'** $11\frac{1}{4}$ degrees north or south from due west; **West Country** the south-western part of England; **West End** the fashionable quarter in the west of London; a similar district in other large towns; **Western Church** the Latin Church, having its ritual and doctrine from Rome, as distinct from the Eastern or Greek Church; **Western hemisphere** the hemisphere of the earth containing the Americas; **western roll** (*athletics*) a style of high-jumping, taking off from the inside foot and clearing the bar face downwards; **west'-north-west** or **-south-west** $22\frac{1}{2}$ degrees north or south from the west. — **go west** (*slang*) to die or to be destroyed or completely dissipated; **the West** the western part of the world as distinct from the East or Orient; in mid- to late-20th-century politics, the non-communist countries of Europe and N. America; the parts of the United States beyond the Mississippi or Rocky Mountains; the western part of the Roman Empire, or the Holy Roman Empire (*hist*); **Wild West** the western United States in the days of the first settlers, chiefly cattlemen and goldminers, before the establishment of law and order. [O.E.]

Westminster *west'min-stər, n* used for the British Parliament — from the London borough where the Houses of Parliament are situated.

wet *wet, adj* containing, soaked with or covered with water or other liquid; rainy; tearful; (of a method) using liquid (*chem,* etc.); allowing the sale of intoxicating liquors; ineffectual, feeble (*slang*); (in politics) moderately conservative (*derog*); (of natural gas) containing large amounts of liquid constituents. — *n* water, moisture, wetness; the rain; an act of wetting; a weak, ineffectual, wavering person (*colloq*); (in politics) a moderate conservative (*derog*). — *vt* to make wet; to soak with water; to urinate on or in; (with *oneself,* etc.) to urinate inadvertently; to celebrate by drinking (*slang*): — *pr p* **wett'ing**; *pa t* and *pa p* **wet**, or **wett'ed**. — *adv* **wet'ly**. — *n* **wet'ness**. — *adj* **wett'ish** somewhat wet. — **wet-and-dry paper** a stiff paper coated with powdered silicon carbide, like a fine sandpaper, used either wet or dry for smoothing surfaces; **wet'back** (*US*) a person illegally entering the U.S.A. from Mexico by wading or swimming the Rio Grande; **wet blanket** see under **blanket**; **wet'-cell** an electric cell with a liquid electrolyte; **wet dream** an erotic dream resulting in ejaculation of semen; **wet fish** fresh fish, as contrasted with frozen or dried fish. — *adj* **wet'-fly** (*angling*) with the fly underwater. — **wet'land** (also in *pl*) marshy land. — *adj* **wet'-look** made of a glossy material, usu. PVC, which gives the appearance of being wet. — **wet'-nurse** a nurse who suckles a child for its mother; **wet pack** the wrapping of a person in blankets or the like dampened with warm or cold water as a medical treatment; the dampened material used; **wet'-rot** a form of decay in timber, caused by certain fungi which develop in wood which is alternately wet and dry; **wet suit** a suit for wearing in water, which allows water to pass through but retains body heat; **wetting (or wetting out) agent** a substance that promotes wetting, e.g. a substance, such as an acid, oil or hydrocarbon, added to a heterogeneous mixture to facilitate the absorption or adhesion between the constitutents, esp. the absorption of water. — **wet-and-dry-bulb thermometer** a hydrometer consisting of two thermometers, one with a dry bulb, the other with the bulb kept moist; **wet behind the ears** very young, immature or gullible; **wet one's whistle** (*colloq*) see under **whistle**; **wet the baby's head** (*colloq*) to celebrate the birth with (alcoholic) drinks; **wet the bed** to urinate accidentally in bed; **wet through** with all one's clothes wet, right to the skin. [O.E. *wǣt* (noun and adj.), *wǣtan* (verb).]

wether *wedh'ər, n* a castrated ram. [O.E.]

WEU *abbrev* for Western European Union.

we've *wēv,* a contraction of **we have**.

wf (*printing*) *abbrev* for wrong fount.

WFTU *abbrev* for World Federation of Trade Unions.

WG *abbrev* for Grenada, Windward Islands (I.V.R.).

wg *abbrev* for wire gauge.

whack *wak* or *hwak, vt* to strike hard and smartly; to put or take with violence; to beat decisively; to parcel out, share. — *vi* to strike; to settle accounts. — *n* a blow; the sound of a blow; a share; an attempt. — *adj*

whacked (*colloq*) exhausted. — *n* **whack'er** (*colloq*) something big of its kind; a blatant lie. — *adj* **whack'ing** (*colloq*) very large, astounding. — *n* a beating (*lit* and *fig*). — **out of whack** (*colloq*) out of order, not straight. [From the sound made.]

whacko. See **wacko.**

whacky *wak'i* or *hwak'i, adj.* Same as **wacky.**

whale[1] *wāl* or *hwāl, n* any of an order of cetaceous mammals, including the *toothed* whales (such as the sperm whales and the dolphins) and the *whalebone* whales (such as the right whales and the rorquals), in which the teeth are only embryonic; something very large of its kind (*slang*). — *vi* to catch whales. — *n* **whāl'er** a boat or a person engage in whaling. — *adj* **whāl'ing** connected with whale-catching. — *n* the business of catching whales. — **whale'back** a kind of steamboat used on the Great Lakes, to carry grain, etc., having rounded upper deck, etc.; a mound shaped like the back of a whale; **whale'boat** a long, narrow boat sharp at both ends, once used in the pursuit of whales; a similar boat carried on a large vessel as a lifeboat; **whale'bone** a light flexible substance consisting of the baleen plates of whales; an article made of this. — *adj* made of whalebone. — **whale'-man** a person or ship employed in whaling; **whale'-oil** oil derived from the blubber of a whale; **whale'-shark** a large tropical shark, harmless to man, feeding mainly on plankton. — **a whale of a time** (*colloq*) a very enjoyable time; **bull** and **cow whale** an adult male and female whale respectively. [O.E. *hwæl*.]

whale[2] *wāl* or *hwāl,* (*slang*) *vt* to thrash; to strike violently. — *n* **whāl'ing** a thrashing. [Perh. **wale.**]

wham *wam* or *hwam, n* a resounding noise caused by a hard blow. — *vi* to hit with a wham: — *pr p* **whamm'ing;** *pa t* and *pa p* **whammed.** — *vt* to hit or cause to hit with a wham. — Also used as *adv* and *interj.* [Imit.]

whang *wang* or *hwang, n* a resounding noise; a blow. — *vi* to make, or hit with, a resounding noise. — *vt* to hit or to cause to hit with a whang. — Also used as *adv* and *interj.* [Imit.]

whangee *wang-ē'* or *hwang-ē', n* any of several grasses of a genus (*Phyllostachys*) allied to the bamboos, found in China and Japan; a cane made from the stem of one. [Prob. Chin. *huang*, yellow, *li*, bamboo.]

whare *wor'i, hwär'ē* or *fär'ē,* (*NZ*) *n* a house. [Maori.]

wharf *wörf* or *hwörf, n* a landing-stage, built esp. along the shore, for loading or unloading vessels: — *pl* **wharfs** or **wharves.** — *vt* to place on, or bring to, a wharf. — *n* **wharf'age** the dues paid for using a wharf; accommodation at a wharf. — *n* **wharf'ing** material for making a wharf; wharf. — *n* **wharfinger** (*wörf'in-jər* or *hwörf'in-*) a person who has the care of, or owns, a wharf. [Late O.E. *hwearf*, bank, shore.]

what *wot* or *hwot, interrog pron* neuter of **who;** used to form a question regarding identity, selection from an indefinite number, nature, value, etc. — also used elliptically (as for *what did you say?, what do you think?, what is it?*). — Also *interrog adj.* — *relative pron* and *adj* that which; such ... as; any or anything whatever; *indefinite pron* (or *n*) something; in what way?, how?, to what degree?. — *interj* used in summoning, calling attention, expressing surprise, disapprobation, protest, etc. — *n* **what'ness** what a thing is; essence. — *n* **what'-d'you-call-it** (or **-'em,** etc.) a word substituted for the name of a thing (or person) in forgetfulness or contempt. — *pron* **whatev'er** anything which; no matter what; what? (*colloq*). — *adj* any or all that, no matter what. — *n* **what for** punishment, esp. a beating (*colloq*). — *n* **what's'-his- (or her- or its-) name,** or **what'sit** (*US* **what'sis**) (*colloq*) that person or thing indicated or understood (often used when the name of the person, etc. has been forgotten). — *adj* **whatsoev'er** whatever. — **and what all** (*colloq*) and so on, and suchlike things; **know what it is** to know what is involved in an action or experience; to have experienced or suffered it; **or whatever** or whatever else arises, etc.; **so what?** what of it?; **what about** an expression used to make a suggestion, ask for an opinion, etc.; **what else?** could anything else be the case?; **what ... for?** for what reason, or intended for what purpose?; **what have you** anything else of the kind; **what ho** a loud hail, summons; **what if?** what would it matter if ?; what would happen if ?; **what ... like?** common form of request for a description or opinion of something or someone, as in *what is she like?, what does this look like?*; **what next?** what is to be done next?; what will happen next? (often said in despair or trepidation); **what now?** what further problems are about to arise?; what more do you want?; **what of** what comes of or follows from?; what do you think of?; **what of it?** does it matter? (usu. implying that one thinks that it does not); **what then?** what would come of it?, what would be the consequence?; **what's what** the true position of affairs; the proper, conventional, or profitable way to behave or proceed; **what's with ...?** (*colloq*; orig. *US*) what do you mean by (doing that)?; what's the matter with (a person)?; **what with** by reason of (more than one thing stated or implied). [O.E. *hwæt*, neut. of *hwā*, who.]

whatnot *wot'not* or *hwot'not, n* a light piece of furniture with shelves for bric-à-brac, etc.; anything, no matter what; a nondescript article. [**what** and **not.**]

whatsis, whatsit, etc. See under **what.**

whaup *wöp* or *hwöp,* (*Scot*) *n* a curlew. [Primarily imit.]

wheat *wēt* or *hwēt, n* any cereal grass of the genus *Triticum*, or its grain, providing a white or brown flour for bread, etc. — known as *bearded*, or *beardless* or *bald*, according to the presence or the absence of the awns or beard, and as *winter* or *spring* (also *summer*) according to whether it is a type normally sown in autumn or spring. — *adj* **wheat'en** made of wheat; of the colour of ripe wheat; wholemeal. — **wheat'-germ** the vitamin-rich germ or embryo of wheat, part of a grain of wheat; **wheat'meal** wheat flour with some of the bran and germ removed; **wheat'sheaf** a sheaf of wheat. [O.E. *hwǣte*; related to **white;** named from its colour.]

wheatear *wēt'ēr* or *hwēt'ēr, n* any of various migratory songbirds of the genus *Oenanthe*, esp. *Oenanthe venanthe*, having a white belly and rump. [Prob. corruption of **white arse.**]

Wheatstone bridge *wēt'stən* (or *hwēt'stən*) *brij, n* an apparatus for measuring electrical resistance, much used, but not invented, by Sir Charles *Wheatstone* (1802–75).

whee *wē* or *hwē, interj* an expression of delight, exuberance, etc.

wheech *wēhh* or *hwēhh,* (*Scot*) *vi* to move rapidly with a whizzing sound; to dart; to do, deal with, etc. rapidly (with *through*). — *vt* to carry, remove rapidly; to throw. — *n* a rapid movement or throw; a whizzing sound. [Imit.]

wheedle *wēd'l* or *hwēd'l, vt* and *vi* to entice by soft words, flatter, cajole. — *vt* to obtain by coaxing (with *out of*); to cheat by cajolery (with *out of*). — *n* **wheed'ler.** — *adj* **wheed'lesome** coaxing. — *n* **wheed'ling.** [Perh. from O.E. *wǣdlian*, (orig.) to be in want, to beg.]

wheel *wēl* or *hwēl, n* a circular frame turning on an axle; a steering-wheel; a potter's wheel (see below); a spinning-wheel; an old instrument of torture; a rotating firework; the wheel attributed to Fortune personified, the emblem of mutability; hence, the course of events; a disc; a circular design; a circular motion; (in *pl*) the parts of a machine (esp. *fig*); (in *pl*) personal transport (*slang*). — *vt* (of a body of troops) to cause to turn or revolve, esp. round an axis or pivot; to cause to move in a circular course; to put a wheel or wheels on; to form or treat on the wheel; to convey on wheels; to propel on wheels; (with *out*, *forward*, etc.) to bring out, forward, etc., to produce. — *vi* to turn round or on an axis; to change direction; to move in a circle; to reel, be giddy; to roll forward. — *adj* **wheeled** having wheels; moving on wheels. — *n* **wheel'er** a person who wheels; a cyclist (*colloq*); (in combination) that which wheels, or has such-and-such a kind of, or so-many, wheels. — *n* **wheel'ie** (*colloq*) a manoeuvre, esp. on a bicycle or motorbike, involving travelling for a short distance with the front wheel or wheels off the ground. — *n* **wheel'ing** the act of moving or conveying on wheels; a turning or circular movement. — *adj* **wheel'y**. — **wheel'-animal** or **-animalcule** a rotifer; **wheel'barrow** a barrow with one wheel in front and two handles and legs behind; (*loosely*) any other handcart; **wheel'-base** the distance between the front and rear axles of a vehicle; the area enclosed by lines joining the points at which the wheels of a locomotive, etc. touch the rails or the ground, or the length of this area; **wheel'chair** a chair moving on wheels, esp. one for a disabled person; **wheel'-clamp** a device that immobilises an illegally parked car until it is removed after payment of a fine. — Also *vt*. — **wheel'er-deal'er**; **wheel'er-deal'ing** (*colloq*; orig. *US*) shrewd dealing or bargaining in business, politics, etc. to one's maximum advantage and often with little regard for others; **wheel'-house** a shelter in which a ship's steering-wheel is placed; **wheel'-spin** rotation of the wheels without forward or backward movement of the vehicle; **wheel'-window** a circular window with radiating tracery; **wheel'work** a combination of wheels and their connection in machinery; **wheel'wright** a person who makes or mends wheels. — **at the wheel** driving a vehicle, or steering a boat (also *fig*); **big wheel** a person of importance or self-importance; **go on wheels** (*fig*) to move swiftly, smoothly, pleasantly; **left** and **right wheel** (a command to perform) a swing to the left and right respectively; such a movement; **potter's wheel** a horizontal revolving disc on which clay vessels are shaped; **wheel and axle** one of the mechanical powers, in its primitive form a cylindrical axle, on which a wheel, concentric with the axle, is firmly fastened, the power being applied to the wheel, and the weight attached to the axle; **wheel and deal** (*colloq*; orig. *US*) to engage in wheeler-dealing; **wheeling and dealing** (*colloq*; orig. *US*) same as **wheeler-dealing**; **wheels within wheels** said of a situation in which a complication of influences is at work. [O.E. *hwēol*.]

wheesht. See **whisht**.

wheeze *wēz* or *hwēz*, *vi* to breathe with a hissing sound; to breathe audibly or with difficulty. — *vt* to utter with such a sound. — *n* the act or sound of wheezing; a gag (*theat slang*); a standard joke (*slang*); a cunning plan (*colloq*). — *adv* **wheez'ily**. — *n* **wheez'iness**. — *n* **wheez'ing**. — *adj* **wheez'y**. [Prob. O.N. *hvæsa*, to hiss.]

whelk[1] *welk* or *hwelk*, *n* a popular name for a number of marine gasteropods, esp. applied to species of the genus *Buccinum* common on the coasts of northern seas. [Wrong form of older *welk* — O.E. *wiloc*, *weoluc*.]

whelk[2] *welk* or *hwelk*, *n* by confusion with **wale**, the mark of a stripe on the body, a wrinkle or protuberance. [Late O.E. *hwylca* — *hwelian*, to suppurate.]

whelp *welp* or *hwelp*, *n* the young of the dog kind and of lions, etc. — a puppy, a cub, etc.; (*contemptuously*) a young man; a ridge running longitudinally on the barrel or drum of a capstan or windlass to control the cable; a sprocket on a wheel. — *vi* and *vt* to bring forth (young). [O.E. *hwelp*.]

when *wen* or *hwen*, *adv* (*interrog* and *relative*) and *conj* at what time?; at which time; at or after the time that; upon or after which; while; although; at which (or *relative pron*). — *n* the time; which time. — *conj* **whenev'er** at every time when. — *conj* **whensoev'er** at what time soever. — **or whenever** or at any comparable time; **say when** (*colloq*) tell me when to stop. [O.E. *hwanne*, *hwonne*; from the stem of interrog. pron. *hwā*, who.]

whence *wens* or *hwens*, *adv* and *conj* (also **from whence**) from what place; from which place?; from which things; wherefore. [M.E. *whennes*, *whannes*.]

where *wār* or *hwār*, *adv* (*interrog* and *relative*) and *conj* at or to which place; at what place?; to what place?; from what source (*lit* and *fig*); to a (or the) place in which (*archaic* or *poetic*); in what circumstances or condition; at what point (*fig*); whereas; wherever; in, at, or to which (or *relative pron*). — *n* the (or a) place; which place. — *n* **where'ness** the state of having place or position; position, situation. — *adv* and *conj* **whereabout'** about which, about where; near what?; also **where'abouts**. — *n* **where'about**, or now usu. *pl* **where'abouts**, one's situation, esp. approximately. — *conj* **whereaf'ter** after which. — *adv* and *conj* **whereas'** when in fact; but on the contrary; taking into consideration, in view of, the fact that. — *adv* and *conj* **whereat'** (*formal* or *archaic*) at which; at what?. — *adv* and *conj* **whereby'** by which. — *adv* and *conj* **wherefor'** (*formal* and *archaic*) for which. — *adj* and *conj* **where'fore** (*-fər*; *formal* or *archaic*) for which or what reason; why?. — *n* the cause. — *adv* and *conj* **wherein'** (*formal* or *archaic*) in which place or respect; in what?. — *adv* and *conj* **whereof'** (*formal* or *archaic*) of which; of what?. — *adv* and *conj* **whereon'** on which (*formal* or *archaic*); on what?. — *adv* and *conj* **wheresoev'er** (*formal*) in or to what place soever. — *adv* and *conj* **whereupon'** upon or in consequence of which. — *adv* and *conj* **wherev'er** at whatever place. — *adv* and *conj* **wherewith'** or **wherewithal'** (*formal* or *archaic*) with which?; with what. — *n* **where'withal** the means. — **from where** whence; from the (or a) place where; **or wherever** or in (or towards) any comparable place; **tell someone where to get off** (*colloq*) to tell someone that their behaviour is unacceptable and will not be tolerated; **where it is** (*colloq*) the real situation, point or explanation; **where it's at** (*slang*) whatever is considered to be the most important, exciting, trendy etc.; the scene of this; **where you are** (*colloq*) what you are saying or getting at. [O.E. *hwǣr*, *hwār*; from stem of **who**; cf. **there**.]

wherry *wer'i* or *hwer'i*, *n* a shallow, light rowing boat; a kind of barge: — *pl* **wherr'ies**.

whet *wet* or *hwet*, *vt* to sharpen by rubbing; to make keen; to excite: — *pr p* **whett'ing**; *pa t* and *pa p* **whett'ed**. — *n* the act of sharpening; sharpness; an incitement or stimulus; something that sharpens the appetite; an appetiser. — *n* **whett'er**. — **whet'-stone** a stone for sharpening edged instruments; a stimulant. [O.E. *hwettan*.]

whether *wedh'ər* or *hwedh'ər*, *conj* introducing the first of two alternative words, phrases or clauses, the second being introduced by *or*, or (in the case of clauses) sometimes by *or whether*; introducing a single dependent question. — **whether or not** whether so or not so; in any case, in any event. [O.E. *hwæther*, from stem of *hwā*, who.]

whew *hū* or *hwū*, *interj* expressing wonder, relief or dismay. — *n* a whistling sound, esp. one expressing astonishment. — *vi* to utter such a sound. [Imit.]

whey *wā* or *hwā*, *n* the watery part of milk, separated from the curd, esp. in making cheese. — *adj* of or containing whey; like whey; whey-coloured. —

whey'-face a pale or white face. — *adj* **whey'-faced** pale, esp. with terror. [O.E. *hwǣg*.]

which *wich* or *hwich*, *interrog pron* what one of a number?. — Also used adjectivally. — *relative pron* that (not used of persons); often having as antecedent a circumstance or statement, being equivalent to 'and that' or 'but that'. — *pron* and *adj* **whichev'er** or **whichsoev'er** every one which; any one, no matter which. — **which is which?** which is the one, which is the other?. [O.E. *hwilc*, *hwelc*, from the stem of *hwā*, who, and *līc* (from a word meaning body, form), like; cf. **such** and **each**.]

whicker *wik'ər* or *hwik'ər*, *vi* to neigh. — *n* a neigh. [Imit.]

whiff *wif* or *hwif*, *n* a sudden puff of air or smoke from the mouth; a slight inhalation; a puff of smell; a slight blast; a small amount, esp. of something causing or associated with a transient sensation (*fig*); a cigarette (*slang*); a small cigar; a jiffy (*colloq*). — *vt* to throw out in whiffs; to puff; to drive or convey by, or as if by, a whiff; to inhale, smell. — *vi* to go out or off in a whiff; to move with, or as with, a puff of air; *vi* to blow slightly; to smell. — *adj* **whiffy**. [Imit.]

whiffle *wif'l* or *hwif'l*, *vi* to blow in puffs; to move as if blown by a puff; to talk idly; to make a slight whistling or puffing sound; to veer; to vacillate; to prevaricate. — Also *vt*. — *adj* **whiff'led** (*slang*) drunk. — *n* **whiff'ler**. — *n* and *adj* **whiff'ling**. [Imit.]

whiffletree *wif'l-trē* or *hwif'l-*, *n* the U.S. word for **whippletree**.

Whig *wig* or *hwig*, (*hist*) *n* a name applied to members of one of the great English political parties — applied in the late 17th century to those upholding popular rights and opposed to the King; after 1830 almost superseded by 'Liberal'; a Scottish Presbyterian, first so called in the middle of the 17th century; one of those who in the colonial period were opposed to British rule (*US*); one of the party formed from the survivors of the old National Republican party and other elements, first so called in 1834 — it fell to pieces in the 1850s (*US*). — *adj* of, pertaining to or composed of Whigs. — *adj* **Whigg'ish**. — *adv* **Whigg'ishly**. — *n* **Whigg'ery** or **Whigg'ism** Whig principles. [Prob. short for **whiggamore**.]

whiggamore *wig'ə-mōr* or *hwig'ə-*, (*hist*) *n* one of the 7000 Western Covenanters who marched on Edinburgh in 1648, sealing the doom of Charles I; a Scottish Presbyterian, a Whig. [Origin disputed; most prob. *whig*, to urge forward, *mere*, mare.]

while *wīl*, or *hwīl*, *n* a space of time; time and trouble spent. — *conj* (also **whilst**) during the time that: at the same time that; as long as; although; notwithstanding the admitted fact that. — *vt* to pass without irksomeness (with *away*). — *conj* **whiles** (*Bible*) while, at the same time that. — *adv* (*Scot*) at times (orig. genitive of O.E. *hwīl*). — **all the while** during all the time (that); **(every) once in a while** now and then. [O.E. *hwīl*.]

whim *wim* or *hwim*, *n* a caprice; a fancy; a vertical rope drum revolved by a horse, used for hoisting from shallow shafts.

whimbrel *wim'brəl* or *hwim'brel*, *n* a species of small curlew. [Prob. imit. of bird's cry; dimin. sfx. *-rel*.]

whimper *wim'pər* or *hwim'pər*, *vi* to cry feebly, brokenly, and querulously or whiningly; to make a plaintive sound. — *vt* to express or utter in a whimper. — *n* a peevish cry. — *n* **whim'perer**. — *n* and *adj* **whim'pering**. — *adv* **whim'peringly**. [Imit.; cf. Ger. *wimmern*.]

whimsical *wim'zik-l* or *hwim'zik-l*, *adj* moved by whim, capricious; odd, fantastical; delicately fanciful; (*loosely*) expressing gently humorous tolerance. — *n* **whimsical'ity** or **whim'sicalness**. — *adv* **whim'sically**. [**whim**.]

whimsy or **whimsey** *wim'zi* or *hwim'zi*, *n* a whim; whimsical behaviour; delicate or affectedly delicate fantasy; something odd or quaint. — *adj* full of whims, changeable; quaint, odd. — *adv* **whim'sily**. — *n* **whim'siness**. [**whim**.]

whin[1] *win* or *hwin*, *n* gorse, furze. — **whin'chat** a small brown songbird related to the stonechat. [Prob. Scand.]

whin[2]. See **whinstone**.

whine *wīn* or *hwīn*, *vi* to utter a plaintive cry; to complain in a querulous or undignified way. — *vt* to express or utter in a whine; to cause to make a whining noise. — *n* a plaintive cry; a continuous shrill noise; an affected nasal tone of utterance. — *n* **whī'ner**. — *n* **whī'niness**. — *n* **whī'ning**. — *adv* **whī'ningly**. — *adj* **whī'ny**. [O.E. *hwīnan*.]

whinge *winj* or *hwinj*, (*colloq*; orig. *dialect*) *vi* to whine; to cry fretfully; to complain peevishly (also *Austr*). — *n* a peevish complaint. — *adj* and *n* **whinge'ing**. — *n* **whing'er**. [O.E. *hwinsian*, from root of *hwīnan*; see **whine**.]

whinny *win'i* or *hwin'i*, *vi* to neigh: — *pr p* **whinn'ying**; *pa t* and *pa p* **whinn'ied**. — *n* a neigh. [Imit.]

whinstone *win'stōn*, *-stən* or *hwin-*, *n* any hard and compact kind of rock, usually basalt or the like; a piece of this. — Also **whin**.

whiny. See under **whine**.

whip *wip* or *hwip*, *n* a lash with a handle for punishing or driving; a stroke administered as by a whip; a whipping motion; a driver or coachman; a person who enforces the attendance and discipline of a political party; a call made on members of parliament to be in their places against an important division (called, according to number of times message is underlined as indication of urgency, **three-line whip**, etc.); a whipper-in, the person who manages the hounds; a simple form of hoisting apparatus, a small tackle consisting of a single rope and block; a preparation of whipped cream, eggs, etc.; a long twig or slender branch. — *vt* to strike with a lash; to drive, or make to move, with lashes; to punish with lashes, or (*loosely*) by spanking; to strike in a manner suggesting a lash; to lash with sarcasm; to defeat, outdo (*colloq*); to stiffen (e.g. cream, white of egg) or make (eggs, etc.) frothy, by rapid agitation with a whisk or similar utensil; to keep together, e.g. a party; to move quickly, snatch (with *up*, *away*, *out*, etc.); to rouse (with *up*). — *vi* to move nimbly; to move in the manner of a whiplash: — *pr p* **whipp'ing**; *pa t* and *pa p* **whipped**. — *adj* **whip'like**. — *n* **whipp'er**. — *n* and *adj* **whipp'ing**. — *adj* **whipp'y** whiplike; pliant; supple. — **whip'cord** cord for making whips; a fabric with a bold steep warp twill, used chiefly for dresses, suitings and coatings; a whiplike seaweed, such as *Chorda filum* or *Chordaria flagelliformis*. — *adj* made of whipcord. — *vt* **whip'-graft** to graft by fitting a tongue cut on the scion to a slit cut slopingly in the stock. — Also *n*. — **whip'-grafting**; **whip'-hand** the hand that holds the whip; the advantage; **whip'lash** the lash of a whip; something resembling the lash of a whip (also *fig*); a whiplash injury. — *vi* to move like a whiplash. — **whipp'er-in** a huntsman who keeps the hounds from wandering; **whipp'ersnapper** a little or young insignificant but pretentious or irritating person; **whipp'ing-boy** someone on whom falls the blame, reproach or punishments for the shortcomings of others; a boy formerly educated along with a prince and punished for the royal pupil's faults; **whipp'ing-cream** cream with enough butterfat in it to allow it to be beaten stiff; **whipp'ing-top** or **whip'-top** a top kept spinning by means of a whip; **whip'-round** an (informal) collection of money among a group of people; **whip'saw** a narrow saw for dividing timber lengthwise, usu. set in a frame and often worked by two persons. — *vt* to cut with a whipsaw; to have the advantage of at every point (*slang*). — **whip'-scorpion** any arachnid of the order *Pedipalpida*, slightly resembling true scorpions but being without sting and having usu. a whiplike appendage at the rear of the body; **whip'-snake** any of various snakes resembling a whiplash; **whip'stock** the rod or handle of a whip; (in an oil well) a tapered steel wedge used to deflect the drill bit from a straight line. — *adj* **whip'-tail** or **whip'-tailed** having a long, slender tail. — **whip-top** see **whipping-top** above. — **whip into shape** to get (esp. a person) into a desired state or condition, esp. by force or rigorous training; **whiplash injury** a neck injury caused by the sudden jerking backwards and then forwards of the head, common in motor vehicle accidents in which the vehicle is hit from behind. [M.E. *whippen.*]

whippet *wip'it* or *hwip'it*, *n* a breed of dog resembling a small greyhound, sometimes used for racing; a dog of this breed. [Partly **whip**, and partly obs. *whippet*, to move briskly.]

whippletree *wip'l-trē* or *hwip'l-*, *n* the crosspiece of a carriage, plough, etc., which is made so as to swing on a pivot and to which the traces of a harnessed animal are fixed. [From **whip**.]

whip-poor-will *wip-pōōr-wil'*, or *hwip-* or *-pər-*, *n* a species of nightjar, a native of N. America. [Imitative of its call.]

whippy, etc. See under **whip**.

whir or **whirr** *wûr* or *hwûr*, *n* a sound from rapid whirling or vibratory motion. — Also *adv*. — *vi* to whirl round with a buzzing noise; to fly or move, with such a sound. — *vt* to hurry away with, or as if with, a whirring or whizzing sound: — *pr p* **whirr'ing**; *pa t* and *pa p* **whirred**. — *n* **whirr'ing**. [Imit.]

whirl *wûrl* or *hwirl*, *n* a turning with rapidity; anything that revolves, esp. rapidly; a great or confusing degree, as of activity or emotion; commotion, agitation; a whorl. — *vi* to revolve rapidly; to move rapidly, esp. in an agitated manner; to turn swiftly round or aside. — *vt* to turn round rapidly; to carry, or move, away rapidly, as on wheels; to throw violently. — *n* **whirl'er**. — *n* and *adj* **whirl'ing**. — **whirl'igig** (*-gig*) a toy that is spun or whirled rapidly round; a merry-go-round; anything that revolves rapidly (*lit* and *fig*); any water beetle of the family *Gyrinidae*, esp. *Gyrinus natator* (also **whirligig beetle**); **whirl'pool** a circular current in a river or sea, produced by opposing tides, winds or currents; an eddy; **whirl'wind** a small rotating windstorm, which may extend upwards to a height of many hundred feet — a miniature cyclone; something which moves in a similarly rapid and destructive way. — *adj* referring to anything which develops very rapidly or violently. — **whir'lybird** (*slang*) a helicopter. — **give something a whirl** (*colloq*) to try something out; **whirlpool bath** see **Jacuzzi**®. [M.E. *whirlen* — O.N. *hvirfla*, frequentative of *hverfa*, to turn round.]

whirr. See **whir**.

whisht *wisht* or *hwisht*, or **wheesht** *wēsht* or *hwēsht*, (*Scot* and *dialect*) *vi* to keep silent. — Also *interj* requesting silence, hush! — *n* silence; a whisper. — **haud (or hold) one's wheesht** or **whisht** to keep silence.

whisk *wisk* or *hwisk*, *vt* to move quickly and lightly; to sweep rapidly; to beat up with a quick, light movement. — *vi* to move nimbly and rapidly. — *n* a rapid sweeping motion; a small bunch of anything used for a brush; a small instrument for beating or whisking, esp. eggs. [Scand.; earliest uses Scot.]

whisker *wis'kər* or *hwis'kər*, *n* (usu. in *pl*) hair growing on the face, esp. on the cheeks; a long sensory bristle on the face of a cat, etc.; a hair's breadth, a very small amount (*fig*); a very thin, strong fibre or filament made by growing a crystal, e.g. of silicon carbide, silicon nitride or sapphire; a person or thing that whisks. — *adj* **whis'kered** or **whis'kery** having whiskers. [**whisk**.]

whisky or (*Ir* and *US*) **whiskey** *wis'ki* or *hwis'ki*, *n* as legally defined, a spirit obtained by distillation from a mash of cereal grains converted into sugar by the diastase of malt; formerly applied also to a spirit obtained from potatoes, beetroot, or any starch-yielding material; a drink of any of such spirits. — **whisky mac** a mixed drink of whisky and ginger wine; **whisky sour** a sour having whisky as its chief ingredient. [Gael. *uisgebeatha* — *uisge*, water, *beatha*, life.]

whisky-john *wis'ki-jon* or *hwis'ki-* or **whisky-jack** (*-jak*), *n* the grey or Canada jay. [From Am. Ind. name of similar sound.]

whisper *wis'pər* or *hwis'pər*, *vi* to speak with a low sound; to speak in a whisper; to speak covertly, spread rumours; to plot secretly; to make a sound like soft speech. — *vt* to utter in a low voice or under the breath, or covertly, or by way of gossip. — *n* a low hissing voice or sound; a sound uttered with breath not voice; voiceless speech with narrowed glottis (*phon*); a hissing or rustling sound; cautious or timorous speaking; a secret hint; a rumour. — *n* **whis'perer**. — *n* and *adj* **whis'pering**. — *adv* **whis'peringly** in a whisper or low voice. — *adj* **whis'pery**. — **whispering campaign** an attack by means of furtively spread rumours; **whis'pering-gallery** or **-dome** a gallery or dome so constructed that a whisper or slight sound is carried to an unusual distance. [O.E. *hwisprian*.]

whist[1] *wist* or *hwist*, *interj* hush; silence; be still. — *vi* to become silent. [Imit.; cf. **whisht**.]

whist[2] *wist* or *hwist*, *n* a card game played by two against two, in which the object is to take a majority of the thirteen tricks, each trick over six scoring one point. — **whist'-drive** a progressive whist party; **whist'-player**. [Assimilated to **whist**[1], because of the silence during play.]

whistle *wis'l* or *hwis'l*, *vi* to make a shrill sound by forcing the breath through the contracted lips or the teeth; to make such a sound in derision, etc.; (of a bird) to pipe, sing; to make a similar sound with an instrument; to sound shrill; to make a call or signal by whistling; to whizz through the air. — *vt* to perform or utter by whistling; to call or bring by a whistle (often with *up*); to send with a whistling sound. — *n* an act of whistling; the sound made in whistling, or one like it; a small wind instrument giving a high-pitched sound by air impinging on a sharp edge; an instrument sounded by escaping steam, etc., as on steam locomotives; a summons; the throat (*slang*). — *adj* **whis'tleable**. — *adj* **whis'tled** (*slang*) drunk. — *n* **whis'tler**. — *n* and *adj* **whis'tling**. — *adv* **whis'tlingly**. — **whis'tle-blower** (*slang*) a person who blows the whistle (see below) on someone or something; **whis'tle-blowing** (*slang*). — Also *adj*. — **whis'tle-stop** (*colloq*) a small town or railway station, where trains stop only by signal (**whistle-stop speech** an electioneering speech made on tour (orig. at railway stations); **whistle-stop tour** orig. such an electioneering tour, now any rapid tour involving brief stops at many places). — *vi* (of a political candidate) to make an electioneering tour with many brief personal appearances. — **whistling swan** an American swan with a musical whistling call. — **blow the whistle** (*slang*) to expose or give information (usu. to the authorities) about illegal or underhand practices; to declare (something) illegal, underhand or otherwise unacceptable; **boatswain's whistle** (or **pipe**) a whistle of special shape used by a boatswain or boatswain's-mate to summon sailors to various duties; **wet one's whistle** (*colloq*) to take a drink of liquor; **whistle down the wind** to talk to no purpose; **whistle for** to summon by whistling; to ask for in vain (*colloq*); **whistle in the dark** to do something to quell one's fear. [O.E. *hwistlian*.]

whit *wit* or *hwit*, *n* the smallest particle imaginable; a bit. [By-form of archaic or dialect *wight*, a creature.]

white *wīt* or *hwīt*, *adj* of the colour of pure snow; of the light complexion characteristic of Europeans; that absorbs the minimum and reflects the maximum of light rays; pale, pallid; snowy; bloodless; colourless; pure; unblemished; innocent; purified from sin; bright; (of wine) light-coloured or golden; clothed in white; auspicious, favourable; reliable, honest; (of a witch) not malevolent, using her power for good purposes. — *n* the colour of snow; anything white, such as a white man, a white butterfly, the centre of a target, the albuminous part of an egg, a pigment. — *vt* to make white. — *vt* **whīt'en** to make white; to bleach; to free from guilt, or to make to appear guiltless. — *vi* to become or turn white. — *n* **whīt'ener** a person who or thing that whitens; artificial milk for coffee or tea. — *n* **white'ness**. — *n* **whīt'ening** an act or process of making or becoming white; a substance used to make white, whiting. — *npl* **whites** white attire; white articles for laundering. — *n* **Whīt'ey** (also without *cap*; *colloq derog*) a white person; whites as a race. — *n* **whīt'ing** a small sea-fish allied to the cod, so-called from its white colour; ground chalk free from stony matter and other impurities, extensively used as a size, colour, etc. (also **whīte'ning**, **Spanish white** and — the finest quality — **Paris white**). — *adj* **whīt'ish** somewhat white. — *adj* **whīt'y** whitish. — *n* (also with *cap*) see **Whitey** above. — **white admiral** any of a genus of butterflies, of the same family as the red admiral, having white bands on the wings; **white ant** a termite; **white'bait** the fry of various species of herring, sprat, etc., fried and eaten whole; **white'beam** a small tree (*Sorbus*, or *Pyrus*, *aria*) with leaves white and downy on the underside; **white bread** bread made from white flour. — *adj* **white'-collar** pertaining to, or designating, the class of workers, such as clerks, etc. who are not engaged in manual labour (**white-collar crime** crimes entailing some intellectual effort and committed without physical exertion or violence, such as embezzlement). — **white corpuscle** a leucocyte, one of the colourless amoeba-like cells occurring in suspension in the blood plasma of many animals, in lymph, etc.; **whited sepulchre** a professedly righteous but inwardly wicked person, a hypocrite (from the Bible: Matt. xxiii. 27); **White Dwarf** (also without *caps*) the name given to a small class of stars outside the normal spectral sequence, because their luminosities are extremely low for their spectral type; **white elephant** see under **elephant**; **White Ensign** a flag with a white field and St George's cross, with the Union Jack in the upper quarter nearest the flag-pole, now flown by the Royal Navy and the Royal Yacht Squadron; **white'-eye** any bird of the genus *Zosterops* or of related genera of the family *Zosteropidae*, most species of which have a conspicuous ring of minute white feathers round the eye; **white'-face** white make-up, esp. as worn by a traditional type of clown. — *adj* **white'-faced** having a face pale with fear or from illness; wearing white make-up, e.g. as a clown; (of animals) having the face, or part of it, white. — **white feather** see **show the white feather** under **feather**; **white fish** a general name for edible sea-fish in which the oil is concentrated in the liver, such as cod, halibut, etc.; **white flag** an emblem of truce or surrender; **white flour** wheat flour with most of the bran and wheatgerm removed; **white'fly** any of several insect pests belonging to the family *Aleurodidae*; **White Friar** (also without *caps*) one of the Carmelite order of friars, so called from their white garments; **white frost** hoar frost; **white gold** gold alloyed with nickel or palladium to give it a white colour; **white goods** household linen; refrigerators, washing machines, freezers and the like, usu. painted with white enamel; **white'head** a pimple or pustule with a white top; **white heat** the degree of heat at which bodies become white (*adj* **white'-hot**); an intense state, e.g. of emotion, activity, etc.; **white'-herring** a fresh or uncured herring; **white hole** a suggested source of the matter and energy observed flowing into the universe (cf. **black hole**); **white hope** a person on whom hopes for success, honour, etc. are grounded (*often* **great white hope**); **white horse** a white-topped wave; a figure of a horse on a hillside, formed by removing the turf from the underlying chalk, the most famous being in Oxfordshire, at Uffington. — *adj* **white'-hot** see **white heat**. — **White House** the official residence, in Washington D.C., of the President of the U.S.A.; **white knight** (*stock exchange slang*) a person who rescues a company from an unwanted takeover bid (cf. **white squire**); **white lead** basic lead carbonate used in painting white; **white'-leg** a form of phlebitis occurring after parturition (also called *milk-leg*); **white lie** see under **lie**[1]; **white light** light containing all wavelengths in the visible range at the same intensity — the term is used, however, to cover a wide range of intensity distribution in the spectrum; **white line** a longitudinal line, either continuous or broken, on a highway to separate lanes of traffic. — *adj* **white'-livered** having a pale look (once thought to be caused by a white liver); cowardly. — **white man** a person of the white race; a person assumed to deal fairly with others (*colloq*); **white matter** (*anat*) pale-coloured, fibrous nerve tissue in the brain and spinal cord; **white meat** the flesh of poultry, rabbits, calves, etc.; the lighter parts of the cooked flesh of poultry (e.g. the breast), as opposed to the darker meat of the leg; **white metal** a tin-base alloy with over 50 per cent of tin; sometimes, an alloy in which lead is the principal metal; **white noise** a mixture of sound waves covering a wide frequency range; **white'-out** a phenomenon in snow regions in fog or overcast conditions in which earth and sky merge in a single whiteness; **white paper** a statement, printed on white paper, issued by the British government for the information of parliament; **white'-pudding** an oatmeal and suet pudding in a sausage skin; **white race** one of the main divisions of mankind, distinguished generally by light complexion and certain types of hair and skull — also known as Caucasian; **white rat** an albino strain of the brown rat, much used in laboratory experiments; **White Russian** Belorussian; **white sale** a sale of linen goods at reduced prices; **white sauce** a sauce made with roux, liquid such as milk or a chicken or veal stock, and such flavouring as desired; **white settler** an outsider who moves into a community, esp. one who changes the character of it; **white slave** a girl procured for prostitution purposes (esp. when exported), whence **white slaver**, **white slavery** and **white slave traffic**; **white spirit** a petroleum distillate used as a substitute for turpentine in mixing paints, and in paint and varnish manufacture; **white squire** (*stock exchange slang*) a friendly party to whom a company chooses to transfer the bulk of its shares as a defence against a takeover move; **white stuff** (*slang*) heroin, morphine or cocaine; **white sugar** refined sugar; **white supremacist** an advocate of **white supremacy**, the philosophy or policy giving dominance to white people; **white'thorn** the common hawthorn; **white'throat** either of two warblers of the same genus (*Sylvia*) as the blackcap, having white throat feathers; a species of American sparrow; any of several species of humming-bird; **white tie** a white bow tie, part of formal evening dress; very formal evening dress (also *adj*); **white voice** a singing voice of pure, neutral tone, expressing no emotion. — *adj* **white'wall** (of pneumatic tyres) having a broad white band around the side-walls. — Also *n*. — **white'ware** articles made of white porcelain, pottery, or other ceramic material; **white'wash** a liquid, such as lime and water, or whiting, size and water, used for coating walls; a wash for the skin; false colouring; an act of whitewashing. — *vt* to cover with whitewash; to give a fair appearance to; to attempt to clear (a stained reputation), to attempt to cover up (a misdemeanour, esp. by one in an official position); to beat (an opponent) so decisively in a game that they fail to score at all (*colloq*); **white'-water** shoal water near the shore, breakers; the foaming water in rapids, etc.; **white whale** the beluga; **white wine** yellowish-coloured or uncoloured (as opp. to *red*) wine; **white'wood** a name applied to a large number of trees or their timber — the American tulip-tree, whitewood cedar, etc.; **whīt'ing-pout** see **pout**[2]. — **white of egg** the albumen, the pellucid viscous fluid surrounding the yolk; **white of the eye** that part of the ball of the eye which surrounds the iris or coloured part; **white out** to erase (written or typed material) with correcting fluid before making a correction; to omit or cover up (secret or sensitive material in a report, transcript, etc.) so leaving areas of blank paper on the page; **whiter than white** extremely white; very pure, very law-abiding. [O.E. *hwīt*.]

Whitehall *wīt'höl* or *hwīt'höl*, *n* a street with government offices, in London; the British government or its policy.

whither *widh'ər* or *hwidh'ər*, (*archaic* or *poetic*) *adv* and *conj* to what place?; to which place; (used relatively) to which; to what; whithersoever. — *adv* **whithersoev'er** to whatever place. [O.E. *hwider*, related to **who**.]

whiting. See under **white**.

whitlow *wit'lō* or *hwit'lō*, *n* a painful inflammation of a finger or toe, esp. near the nail.

Whit-Monday *wit-mun'dā* or *hwit-*, *n* the Monday following Whitsunday.

Whitsun *wit'sn* or *hwit'sn*, *adj* pertaining to, or observed at, Whitsuntide. — *n* Whitsuntide. — **Whit'sunday** or **Whit-Sun'day** the seventh Sunday after Easter, commemorating the day of Pentecost, when the converts in the primitive Church wore white robes; **Whit'suntide** the season of Pentecost, comprising **Whit'sun-week** or **Whit'-week**, the week beginning with Whitsunday. [**white** and **Sunday**.]

whittle *wit'l* or *hwit'l*, *vt* to pare or cut with a knife; to shape with a knife; to diminish gradually (often with *down*); to lessen the force or scope of (often with *down*). — *vi* to cut wood aimlessly. — *n* **whitt'ler**. — *n* **whitt'ling**. — **whittle away** or **whittle away at** to whittle, whittle down (usu. *fig*). [M.E. *thwitel* — O.E. *thwītan*, to cut.]

whizz or **whiz** *wiz* or *hwiz*, *vi* to make a hissing sound, like an arrow or ball flying through the air; to move rapidly. — *vt* to cause to whizz: — *pr p* **whizz'ing**; *pa t* and *pa p* **whizzed**. — *n* a hissing sound; a person remarkably talented or skilful in some pursuit (*colloq*). — Also *adv*. — *n* **whizz'er**. — *n* and *adj* **whizz'ing**. — *adv* **whizz'ingly**. — **whizz'-bang** (*slang*) a light shell of high velocity which is heard arriving before the sound of a gun's report; a firework suggestive of this; **whizz'-kid** or **whīz'-kid** (*slang*) a person who achieves success rapidly and at a relatively early age, because of high intelligence, progressive ideas, pushfulness, etc. [Imit.; cf. **wheeze** and **hiss**.]

WHO *abbrev* for World Health Organisation.

who *hōō*, *relative* and *interrog pron* what person?; which person; he who, the person who; whoever; of what name, standing, etc. (objective case **whom** — possessive case **whose**). — *pron* **whoev'er** or **whosoev'er** every one who; whatever person (objective case **whom'ever, whomsoev'er** respectively; possessive case **whosev'er, whosesoev'er** respectively). — **who's who** a directory listing names and biographical details of prominent people. — **know who's who** to know the position and influence of everyone. [O.E. *hwā*.]

whoa *wō* or *hwō*, *interj* stop.

whodunnit or **whodunit** *hōō-dun'it*, (*colloq*) *n* a story concerned with the elucidation of a crime mystery. [**who, done** (vulg. past tense of **do**), and **it**.]

whole *hōl*, *adj* not broken up, or ground, or deprived of any part; containing the total amount, number, etc.; from which no constituents have been removed, as **whole blood, milk,** etc.; undamaged; not broken; uninjured; restored to health, healed; sound in health (*archaic* or *Bible*); complete; (of a sister or brother) having both parents in common. — *n* the entire thing; a system or combination of parts. — *adv* wholly. — *n* **whole'ness**. — *adj* **whole'some** physically, mentally or spiritually healthy; indicating or conducive to physical, mental or spiritual health. — *adv* **whole'somely**. — *n* **whole'someness**. — *n* **whōl'ism** same as **holism**. — *adj* **whōlist'ic**. — *adv* **wholly** (*hōl'li* or *hō'li*) completely, altogether. — **whole'food** food, unprocessed or processed as little as possible, produced without any artificial fertilisers, pesticides, etc. — *adj* **whole'grain** (of bread, flour, etc.) made from the complete grain, with no parts discarded during manufacture. — *adj* **whole-heart'ed** hearty, generous, zealous and sincere. — *adv* **whole-heart'edly**. — **whole'meal** meal made from entire grains of wheat (also *adj*); **whole note** (*US*) a semibreve; **whole number** a unit, or a number composed of units, an integral number; **whole'sale** sale of goods, usually in large quantities, to a retailer. — *adj* buying and selling, or concerned with buying and selling, thus; extensive and indiscriminate. — *adv* by wholesale; extensively and indiscriminately. — **whole'saler** a person who sells wholesale. — *adj* **whole'-wheat** wholemeal. — *adj* **wholl'y-owned** referring to a company all of whose shares are owned by another company. — **go the whole hog** to do a thing thoroughly or completely; to commit oneself to anything unreservedly; **the whole** all the; the complete; **on (or upon) the whole** generally speaking; all things considered; **whole life insurance** a life insurance policy on which premiums are payable up to the death of the insured person. [O.E. *hāl*, healthy.]

whom, whomever, whomsoever. See under **who**.

whoop *wōōp*, *hwōōp* or *hōōp*, sometimes **hoop** *hōōp*, *n* a loud eager cry; a N. American Indian war cry; (*hōōp*) the long noisy inspiration heard in whooping-cough. — *vi* to give a loud cry of triumph, eagerness, scorn, etc.; to hoot. — *vt* to cheer, or insult, with shouts; to summon, or to urge on, by whooping. — *n* **whoop'er** a person who whoops; a whooper swan or whooping crane (also **hoop'er**). — *n* and *adj* **whoop'ing**. — **whooper swan** a swan (*Cygnus cygnus*) with a whooping call, common in N. Europe and Asia; **whoop'ing-cough** or **hoop'ing-cough** pertussis, an infectious and epidemic disease, mostly attacking children, characterised by periodic spasms of the larynx that end in a long crowing inward breath; **whooping crane** an American crane (*Grus americana*), on the brink of extinction; **whooping swan** a whooper swan. — **whoop it up** (*colloq*) to indulge in noisy, boisterous entertainments or celebrations. [O.Fr. *houper*, to shout.]

whoopee *wōōp'ē* or *hwōōp'ē*, *interj* an exclamation of delight. — Also *n*. — **whoopee cushion** a rubber cushion which makes a noise like the breaking of wind when sat on. — **make whoopee** (*colloq*) to indulge in hilarious fun or frivolity. [**whoop**.]

whoops *wōōps*. Same as **oops**.

whoosh *wōōsh* or *hwōōsh*, or **woosh** *wōōsh*, *n* the sound of, or like that made by, something large passing rapidly through the air. — *vi* to make such a sound; to do something with, or as if with, such a sound (also *vt*). — Also *adv*. [Imit.]

whop *wop* or *hwop*, (*colloq* or *dialect*) *vt* to whip, thrash; to defeat or surpass; to throw or pull suddenly or violently. — *vi* to strike, or to move, quickly; to flop down: — *pr p* **whopp'ing**; *pa t* and *pa p* **whopped**. — *n* a blow; a bump; the noise made by either of these. — *n* **whopp'er** a person who whops; anything very large, esp. a monstrous lie. — *adj* **whopp'ing** very large. — *n* thrashing. [Prob. partly imitative.]

whore *hōr*, *n* a prostitute; any unchaste woman. — *vi* to be, or to have to do with, a whore or whores. — *adj* **whō'rish**. — *adv* **whō'rishly**. — *n* **whō'rishness**. — **whore'house** a brothel. — *adj* mean, scurvy. — **whore after** to pursue (an unworthy, dishonest or selfish goal). [Late O.E. *hōre*, prob. — O.N. *hōra*, adulteress.]

whorl *wörl*, *wûrl* or *hw-*, *n* a group of similar members arising from the same level on a stem, and forming a circle around it; a single turn in a spiral shell; a convolution, e.g. in the ear; (in a fingerprint) a ridge forming a complete circle; a type of fingerprint having such ridges. — *adj* **whorled** having whorls; arranged in the form of a whorl or whorls. [Late M.E. *wharwyl*, etc., variants of **whirl**.]

whortleberry *wûr'tl-ber-i*, *-bər-i* or *hw-*, *n* a widely-spread heath plant with a dark blue edible berry, called also the bilberry, and in Scotland, blaeberry, extended to certain other plants of the same genus (*Vaccinium*).

whose *hōōz*, *pron* the possessive case of **who** (q.v.) and also **which**. — **whosoever** see **who**.

why *wī* or *hwī*, *adv* and *conj* for what cause or reason, on which account?; therefore; (used relatively) on account of which. — *interj* expressing sudden realisation, or protest, or marking resumption after a question or a slight pause. — *adv* **whyev'er** (*colloq*) for whatever reason. — **the why and wherefore** the whole reason. [O.E. *hwī*, *hwȳ*, instrumental case of *hwā*, who, and *hwæt*, what.]

whydah *wī'də*, *hwīdə* or (*h*)*wi'də*, *n* any of a group of African birds belonging to, or related to, the weaver finch family, with much black in their plumage; any of various birds of a related family (*Ploccidae*). [**widow-bird**, from the widow's black clothing; spelling altered in the belief that the bird was named from *Whydah* (Ouidah) in Dahomy (now Benin).]

WI *abbrev* for: West Indies; Wisconsin (U.S. state); Women's Institute.

wick *wik*, *n* the twisted threads of cotton or other substance in a candle, lamp or lighter, which draw up the inflammable liquid to the flame; any strip of material which draws up liquid by capillary action. — **get on someone's wick** (*colloq*) to irritate someone. [O.E. *wēoce*, *wēoc*.]

wicked *wik'id*, *adj* evil in principle or practice; sinful; ungodly; (of an animal) vicious; cruel; mischievous, spiteful; very bad, harmful or offensive; roguish (*colloq*); excellent, admirable (*slang*). — *n* (with **the**) wicked persons collectively. — *adv* **wick'edly**. — *n* **wick'edness**. — **the wicked one** the devil. [M.E. *wicked*, *wikked*, prob. — *wicke*, *wikke*, wicked — O.E. *wicca*, wizard.]

wicker *wik'ər*, *n* a small pliant twig or osier; wickerwork. — *adj* made of twigs or osiers; encased in wickerwork. — *adj* **wick'ered** made of wicker; covered with wickerwork. — **wick'erwork** basketwork of any kind. [M.E. *wiker*, of Scand. origin.]

wicket *wik'it*, *n* a small gate or door, esp. in or near a larger one (usu. **wicket-gate** or **-door**); an opening or a window with a grille, as at a ticket-office, bank, etc. (*US*); (the following meanings all *cricket*) the upright arrangement of three stumps with two bails on top which the batsman defends against the bowling; a stump; the pitch, esp. in respect of its condition; a batsman's stay at the wicket, or his or her joint stay there with another; a batsman's innings. — **wick'et-keeper** the fielder who stands immediately behind the striker's wicket. — **get, take,** etc. **a wicket** to get a batsman out as a result of one's bowling; **keep wicket** to be wicket-keeper; **over (or round) the wicket** (of bowling) delivered with the hand nearer (or farther away) from the wicket. [O.N.Fr. *wiket*; of Gmc. origin.]

widdle *wid'l*, (*hypocoristic*) *vi* to urinate. — Also *n*. [Poss. — **wee**[2] and **piddle**.]

wide *wīd*, *adj* extending far; having a considerable distance between the sides; broad; of a specified breadth; roomy; expanded; opened as far as possible; far apart; far from the point aimed at; of large scope, comprehending or considering much (*fig*); astute, wily (*slang*); lax in morals (*slang*); lax, reverse of *narrow* (*phon*). — *n* wideness; a ball bowled out of reach of the batsman (*cricket*); a penalty run allowed for this. — *adv* (now usu. **far and wide**) to a great distance, over a large region; far from the point aimed at, the subject under discussion, the truth, etc.; far to one side (with *of*); so that there is a large space or distance between. — (In combination) **-wide** denoting extending throughout a specified area, etc., as in *nationwide*, *countrywide*. — *adv* **wide'ly**. — *vt* and *vi* **wī'den** to make or grow wide or wider. — *n* **wī'dener**. — *n* **wide'ness**. — *adj* **wīd'ish**. — *n* **width** (*width*) breadth. — *adv* **width'ways** or **width'wise** in the direction of the width, across. — *adj* **wide'-angle** (*phot*) pertaining to a lens having an angle of view of 60° or more and a short focal length. — *adj* **wide'-awake** fully awake; on the alert; keen and knowing (*colloq*). — *n* a low wide-brimmed soft felt hat. — *adj* **wide'-body** or **wide'-bodied** (of aircraft) having a wide fuselage. — **wide'-boy** (*slang*) an astute or wily person, esp. one prone to sharp practice. — *adj* **wide'-eyed** showing great surprise; naive, credulous. — *adj* **wide'-open** opened wide; open to attack (*colloq*); lax in enforcing laws and regulations (*US*). — *adj* **wide'-ranging** covering a wide range of topics, interests, cases, etc. — **wide receiver** (*Am football*) a member of the offence whose task is to catch and run with the ball. — *adj* **wide'spread** extended or extending widely; found, operative, etc. in many places. — **to the wide** completely; utterly; **wide area network** (*comput*) a computer network operating nationally or internationally, using telecommunications links, microwaves and satellites (abbrev. **WAN**); **wide of the mark** far out, astray from the truth. [O.E. *wīd*.]

widgeon. See **wigeon**.

widget *wij'it*, (*colloq*) *n* a gadget; an unnamed small manufactured item or component.

widow *wid'ō*, *n* a woman who has lost her husband by death and has not married again; an extra hand in some card games; a short last line at the end of a paragraph which stands at the top of a page or column of print (*printing*). — *vt* to bereave of a husband (or wife); to strip of anything valued. — *n* **wid'ower** a man whose wife is dead. — *n* **wid'owerhood**. — *n* **wid'owhood** the state of being a widow, or (*rarely*) of being a widower. — **wid'ow-bird** earlier name for the **whydah**; **widow's cruse** a source of supply that never fails (from the Bible: 1 Kings xvii. 10–16); **widow's mite** a small offering generously given (from the Bible: Mark xii. 42; see also **mite**[2]); **widow's peak** a point of hair over the forehead, like the cusped front of a widow's cap worn in former days. — **golf**, etc. **widow** a woman whose husband frequently goes off to play golf (or whatever). [O.E. *widewe*.]

width. See under **wide**.

wield *wēld*, *vt* to control, manage; to use with skill. — *adj* **wield'able**. — *n* **wield'er**. — *n* **wield'iness**. — *adj* **wield'y** easy to wield; manageable. [O.E. *weldan* (not recorded; W.S. *wealdan*).]

Wiener schnitzel *vē'nər shnit'səl*, (Ger.) *n* a veal cutlet dressed with breadcrumbs and eggs. [Ger., Viennese cutlet.]

wife *wīf*, *n* a married woman; the woman to whom one is married; a woman (now *archaic* or *dialect*): — *pl* **wīves**. — *n* **wife'hood** the state of being a wife. — *adj* **wife'less**. — *adj* **wife'-like**. — *adj* **wife'ly**. — **wife'-swapping** (*colloq*) a form of sexual activity in which married couples exchange partners temporarily. [O.E. *wīf*.]

wig[1] *wig*, *n* an artificial covering of hair for the head worn to conceal baldness, or for fashion's sake, as in the full-dress **full-bottomed wig** of Queen Anne's time, still worn by the Speaker and by judges, and the smaller **tie-wig**, still represented by the judge's undress wig and the barrister's or advocate's frizzed wig; a judge (*slang*). — *adj* **wigged** wearing a wig. — *adj* **wig'less**. [Short for *periwig*, an old word for a wig.]

wig[2] *wig*, (*colloq*) *vt* to scold: — *pr p* **wigg'ing**; *pa t* and *pa p* **wigged**. — *n* **wigg'ing** (*colloq*) a scolding. [**wig**[1].]

wigeon or (now *rarely*) **widgeon** *wij'ən*, *n* any of various ducks of the genus *Anas* which have the bill shorter than the head, the legs short, feet rather small, wings long and pointed, and the tail wedge-shaped; in the U.K., specif. *Anas penelope*.

wiggle *wig'l*, *vi* and *vt* to waggle, wriggle. — *n* a wiggling motion. — *n* **wigg'ler**. — *adj* **wigg'ly** wriggly; much or irregularly waved. [Frequentative of verb from which is derived dialect *wig*, to wag.]

wigwag *wig'wag*, *vi* to twist about; to signal by means of flags. — *n* the act of wigwagging; a level-crossing signal which gives its indication, by swinging about a fixed axis. — *adj* twisting. — *adv* to and fro. [Dialect *wig* (from same root as **wiggle**) and **wag**.]

wigwam *wig'wom* or *wig'wam*, *n* an American Indian dome-shaped hut, made by laying bark, skins, etc. over a framework of sticks; any similar construction, such as a tepee. [Eng. corruption of Algonquian word.]

wilco *wil'kō*, *interj* (in signalling, telecommunications, etc.) an abbrev. of 'I *will comply*' (with instructions).

wild *wīld*, *adj* being in a state of nature, not tamed or cultivated; of an undomesticated or uncultivated kind; uncivilised; uninhabited; desolate; tempestuous; violent; fierce; passionate; unrestrained; licentious; agitated; distracted; very angry; very enthusiastic, eager, keen (with *about*); strong and irrational; fantastic; crazy; disordered; unconsidered; wide of the mark; fresh and natural; (of a playing-card) having any value desired. — Also *adv*. — *n* (also in *pl*) an uncultivated region; a wilderness or desert (also *fig*); an empty region of air or water (*poetic*). — *n* **wīld'ing** that which grows wild or without cultivation; a wild crab-apple; a self-sown garden plant, an escape. — *adj* **wild'ish** somewhat wild. — *adv* **wild'ly**. — *n* **wild'ness**. — **wild card** a person allowed to compete in a sports event despite his or her lacking the stipulated qualifications, etc.; (the offering of) such a chance to compete; a character which can stand for any other character or group of characters in a file, etc. (*comput*); **wild'cat** an undomesticated species of cat (*Felis sylvestris*) native to Europe (also **wild cat**); any of various small wild animals of the cat family (also **wild cat**); a quick-tempered, fierce person; a speculative or unsound financial scheme (*US*); someone who takes part in such a scheme (*US*); an exploratory well (*US*). — *adj* (of business, scheme, etc.) haphazard, reckless, unsound financially; (of a strike), unauthorised by union officials; (of an oil well) exploratory (*US*). — *vt* and *vi* (*US*) to drill an experimental well in an area of unknown productivity in search of oil, gas, ore, etc. — **wild'catter** (*US*); **wild'-cherry** any uncultivated tree bearing cherries, such as the gean, or its fruit; **wild dog** any wild species of the dog genus or family, such as the dingo, etc.; **wild duck** any duck excepting the domesticated duck; *specif* the mallard; **wild'fire** a sweeping, destructive fire; a composition of inflammable materials (**like wildfire** extremely fast); **wild'fowl** the birds of the duck tribe; game-birds; **wild'-fowler**; **wild'-fowling** the pursuit of wildfowl; **wild'-land** land completely uncultivated; **wild'life** wild animals, birds, etc. regarded collectively (**wildlife park** a safari park); **wild man** a man of extreme or radical views in politics; **wild'-water** the foaming water in rapids, etc.; **wild'-wood** wild uncultivated or unfrequented wood. — Also *adj*. — **run wild** to take to loose living; to live or grow in freedom from constraint or control; to revert to the wild or uncultivated state; **sow one's wild oats** see under **oat**; **wild and woolly** unpolished; unrestrained; **wild-goose chase** see under **chase**[1]. [O.E. *wilde*; common Gmc. word.]

wildebeest *vild'i-bāst*, *wild'i-bēst* or *vild'ə-bēst*, (*SAfr*) *n* a gnu. [Du. *wilde*, wild, *beest*, ox.]

wilderness *wil'dər-nəs*, *n* a region uncultivated and uninhabited; a pathless or desolate tract of any kind; a large confused or confusing assemblage. — *adj* **wil'dered**. — *adj* **wil'dering**. — *n* **wil'derment**. — **crying in the wilderness** see under **cry**; **in the (political) wilderness** not in office; not having any office, being passed over or refused office. [M.E., — *wilderne*, wild, wilderness — O.E. *wilddēoren* — *wild*, wild, *dēor*, animal.]

wilding. See under **wild**.

wile *wīl*, *n* a trick; deceit; a pleasing artifice; (in *pl*) cajolery. — *vt* to beguile, inveigle; to coax, cajole. — *adj* **wile'ful** full of wiles. — *adv* **wī'lily**. — *n* **wī'liness**. — *adj* **wī'ly** full of craft or cunning; using tricks or stratagem. [O.E. *wīl*, *wīle*; cf. **guile**.]

wilful. See under **will**.

wilily, wiliness. See under **wile**.

will *wil*, *n* the power or faculty of choosing or determining; the act of using this power; volition; choice or determination; pleasure; inclination; lust; command; arbitrary disposal; feeling towards, as in **goodwill** or **illwill** (see **good** and **ill**); the disposition of one's effects at death; the written document containing this. — *vt* to decree; to seek to force, influence (oneself or another to perform a specified action) by silent exertion of the will; to dispose of by will, to bequeath: — in the foregoing senses, *pa t* and *pa p* **willed**; *3rd pers* **wills**; used with the infinitive of a verb to form (in sense) a future tense, expressing in the second and third person simple futurity (as **shall** in the first person), or custom, or persistent habit, and in the first person promise or determination on the part of the speaker; also (*3rd pers*) can; to be likely to: — in these senses, *pa t* **would** (*wŏŏd*); no *pa p*; *3rd pers* **will**. — *vi* to exercise choice, choose, decree; to be willing. — *adj* **wil'ful** governed only by one's will, obstinate; done intentionally. — *adv* **wil'fully**. — *n* **wil'fulness**. — *adj* **will'able**. — *adj* **willed** having a will; voluntary; given, or disposed of, by will; brought under another's will, as in hypnotism; (in combination) having a will of a particular kind, as in *weak-willed*, *strong-willed*, etc. — *n* **will'er**. — *adj* **will'ing** not reluctant; eager; ready and prompt to act; voluntary; chosen; of or pertaining to the will. — *adv* **will'ingly**. — *n* **will'ingness**. — *adj* **will'ing-hearted** heartily consenting. — **willing horse** a person or animal always prepared to work hard at any task; **will power** the ability to control one's actions, emotions, impulses, etc. — **at will** when or as one chooses; **a will of one's own** a strong, self-assertive will; **have one's will** to obtain what one desires; **with a will** heartily and energetically. [O.E. *willa*, will, *willan*, *wyllan* (past t. *wolde*, *walde*), to wish.]

willet *wil'it*, *n* a N. American bird of the snipe family. [Imit.]

willie. See under **willy**.

willies *wil'iz*, (*slang*) *npl* the creeps.

williwaw *wil'i-wö*, *n* a gust of cold wind blowing seawards from a mountainous coast, e.g. in the Straits of Magellan; a sudden squall (also *fig*).

will-o'-the-wisp *wil-ō-dhə-wisp'*, *n* the ignis fatuus; any elusive and deceptive person or thing: — *pl* **wills-o'-the-wisp** or **will-o'-the-wisps.** [Orig. *Will-with-the-wisp* — *Will*, abbrev. of William, and **wisp** (q.v.).]

willow *wil'ō*, *n* any tree or shrub of the genus *Salix*, having slender, pliant branches; any of several plants resembling it; the wood of the willow; a cricket-bat. — *adj* **will'owed** abounding with or grown with willows. — *adj* **will'owish** like a willow; of the colour of willow leaves; slender and supple. — *adj* **will'owy** abounding in willows; flexible; slender and graceful. — **will'ow-herb** a perennial herb of the evening primrose family (including rose-bay, bay-willow, French or Persian willow) with willow-like leaves and seeds; **willow pattern** a blue design of Chinese character but English origin used on china from the late 18th century onwards. [O.E. *welig*.]

willy or **willie** *wil'i*, (*hypocoristic*) *n* the penis.

willy-nilly *wil'i-nil'i*, *adv* willing or unwilling; compulsorily. — *adj* having no choice; vacillating (*erron*). [**will** and *nill*, an archaic word meaning to refuse, not to.]

willy-willy *wil'i-wil'i*, (*Austr*) *n* a cyclone or whirlwind. [Aboriginal.]

wilt *wilt*, *vi* to droop, become limp; to lose energy; to lose self-confidence or courage (*fig*). — *n* the act of wilting; any of various diseases that cause wilting of plants. [Orig. dialect.]

Wilton *wil'tən*, *n* (in full **Wilton carpet**) a carpet having a cut pile, long made at *Wilton*, in Wilts.

Wilts. *wilts*, *abbrev* for Wiltshire.

wily. See **wile**.

wimble *wim'bl*, *n* an instrument for boring holes, turned by a handle. — *vt* to bore through with a wimble. [Through O.N.Fr., from M.Du. *wimpel*.]

wimp *wimp*, (*slang*) *n* an ineffectual person. — *adj* **wimp'ish**. — *adv* **wimp'ishly**. — *n* **wimp'ishness**.

wimple *wim'pl*, *n* a veil folded round the head, neck and cheeks (still part of a nun's dress); a fold, wrinkle, ripple. — *vt* to wrap in, or hide with, a wimple; to enwrap, enfold; to lay in folds. [O.E. *wimpel*, neck-covering.]

Wimpy® *wim'pi*, *n* a kind of hamburger.

win *win*, *vt* to get by labour; to gain in contest; to secure; to achieve, effect; to reach; to be the victor in; to induce; to gain influence over; to obtain the favour of; to mine (an ore); to open up (a new portion of a coal-seam). — *vi* to gain the victory; to get oneself (into a desired place, state, etc.): — *pr p* **winn'ing**; *pa t* and *pa p* **won** (*wun*). — *n* (*colloq*) a victory, success. — *adj* **winn'able.** — *n* **winn'er** a person who wins; something very good or successful (*slang*). — *n* **winn'ing** the act of someone who wins; (usu. in *pl*) that which is won. — *adj* that wins; of or pertaining to the act of winning; attractive, prepossessing; persuasive. — *adv* **winn'ingly.** — *n* **winn'ingness.** — **winn'ing-post** the goal of a race-course. — **win by a (short) head** to win very narrowly; **win in a canter** to win easily; **win (or gain) one's spurs** to earn one's knighthood by valour on the field, hence to gain recognition or reputation by merit of any kind; **win out** to get out; to be successful (*colloq*; also **win through**); **win over** to bring over to one's opinion or party. [O.E. *winnan*, to struggle, to suffer.]

wince *wins*, *vi* to shrink or start back; to make an involuntary movement, e.g. in pain; to be affected acutely, as by a sarcasm. — *n* an involuntary start back or shrinking. — *n* **win'cer**. — *n* and *adj* **win'cing.** [Cf. O.Fr. *guinchir*, *ganchir*, to wince — a Gmc. word.]

winceyette *win-si-et'*, *n* a plain cotton cloth of light weight, raised slightly on both sides. [Scot. *wincey*, a cloth made of linen or cotton with wool.]

winch *winch* or *winsh*, *n* a reel or roller; the crank of a wheel or axle; a powerful type of hauling or hoisting machine. — *vt* to haul, hoist, etc. using such a machine (with *up*, *in*, etc.). — **winch'man** a person who operates a winch or takes part in winching operations, e.g. aboard a helicopter. [O.E. *wince*, from a Gmc. and Indo-European root.]

Winchester® *win'chəs-tər* or **Winchester rifle** (*rī'fl*), *n* orig. a tradename for a repeating rifle made by Oliver F. *Winchester*, American manufacturer; now a tradename for firearms, etc. produced by the makers of the rifle.

wind[1] *wind*, *n* air in motion; a current of air, usually horizontal, either natural or produced by artificial means; any of the directions from which the wind may blow; breath; power of breathing; a hint or suggestion, as of something secret; flatulence; conceit; empty, insignificant words; the wind instruments in an orchestra; their players; air impregnated with scent of game. — *vt* to drive, punch hard, so as to put out of breath; to allow to recover wind; to burp (a baby); to perceive by the scent. — *n* **wind'age** the difference between the size of the bore of a gun and that of the ball or shell; the influence of the wind in deflecting a missile, the amount of deflection due to wind, or the allowance made for it; air friction on a moving, esp. revolving, part of a machine. — *n* **wīnd'er** (*slang*) a blow that takes one's breath away. — *adv* **wind'ily.** — *n* **wind'iness.** — *adj* **wind'less.** — *adv* and *adj* **wind'ward** towards or on the side the wind blows from. — Also *n.* — *adv* **wind'wards.** — *adj* **wind'y** like, characterised by or exposed to the wind; suffering from, producing, or produced by, flatulence; suggestive of wind, as insubstantial, changeable, boastful, conceited, wordy (*fig*); frightened, nervous (*colloq*). — **wind'bag** the bellows of a bagpipe; a person of mere words, an excessively talkative person (*slang*); **wind band** a musical ensemble made up of wind instruments; **wind'break** a protection against the force of the wind, such as a fence or line of trees; **wind'burn** inflammation of the skin due to over-exposure to the wind; **wind'cheater** a close-knitted pullover; an anorak; **wind'-chest** the box or reservoir that supplies compressed air to the pipes or reeds of an organ; **wind'-cone** (*aeronautics*) a sleeve floating from the top of a mast, its angle with the ground giving a rough conception of the velocity of the wind, and its angle in a horizontal plane the wind direction; **wind'fall** fruit blown off a tree by the wind; any unexpected money or other advantage; **windfall tax** a tax levied on **windfall profits,** profits arising, esp. suddenly and unexpectedly, as a result of events not directly connected with the company, etc. concerned, such as changes in currency exchange rates. — *adj* **wind'fallen** blown down by wind. — **wind farm** a place where electricity is generated by wind power; **wind'flower** an anemone, esp. the wood-anemone; **wind'-gauge** or **wind gauge** an instrument for measuring the velocity of the wind; a gauge for measuring pressure of wind in an organ; appliance fixed to a rifle by means of which the force of the wind is ascertained so that allowance may be made for it in sighting; **wind'hover** (*hov'ər* or *huv'ər*) the kestrel; **wind instrument** a musical instrument sounded by means of wind, esp. by the breath; **wind machine** (*theat*) a machine which produces wind or the sound of wind; **wind'mill** a mill in which the motive-power is the wind acting on a set of vanes or sails; a wind-driven set of vanes used to pump water, generate electricity, etc. — *vt* and *vi* (to cause) to move like the vanes of a windmill. — **wind'pipe** the passage for the breath between the mouth and lungs, the trachea; **wind**

power wind considered as an energy source, e.g. for the generation of electricity by means of windmills, etc.; **wind'rose** a rosette-like diagram showing the relative frequency and strength of winds in a locality for given periods of the year; **wind'row** a row of hay, etc. set up for drying; **wind'screen** a shelter against wind; the sheet of glass in front of the driver of a motor vehicle; **wind'shield** a windscreen (*US*); a device to protect e.g. a microphone from the wind; **wind'ship** a wind-powered ship, a sailing-ship; **wind'-side** the side next the wind; **wind'-sleeve** or **-sock** a wind-cone; **wind'storm** a storm consisting of very strong winds; **wind'surfing** (also called **sailboarding**) the sport of sailing on a **sailboard**, (q.v.). — *vi* **wind'surf** to sail on a sailboard. — *n* **wind'surfer.** — *adj* **wind'swept** exposed to, or swept by, the wind. — *adj* **wind'-tight** airtight. — **wind'-tunnel** or **wind tunnel** an experimental apparatus for producing a uniform steady airstream past a model for aerodynamic investigation work. — **cast, fling** or **throw to the winds** to scatter or throw away recklessly; to abandon (restraint, prudence, caution, discretion, etc.); **get one's wind** to recover one's breath; **get the wind up** (*slang*) to become nervous, apprehensive, agitated; **get wind of** to get a hint or intimation of; **how the wind blows** or **lies** the state of the wind; the position of affairs; **in the wind** astir, afoot; **in the wind's eye** or **in the teeth of the wind** right against the wind; **like the wind** rapidly; **put the wind up someone** (*slang*) to make someone apprehensive or agitated; **sail close to (**or **near) the wind** to keep the boat's head so near to the wind as to fill but not shake the sails; to be in danger of transgressing an approved limit; **second wind** power of respiration recovered after breathlessness; the energy necessary for a renewal of effort (*fig*); **take the wind out of someone's sails** (*fig*) to deprive someone of an advantage, to frustrate or disconcert someone; **tilt at windmills** to struggle with imaginary opposition, like Don Quixote, who charged at a windmill thinking it was an enemy; **wind-chill factor** see **chill factor; wind (**or **winds) of change** a pervasive influence bringing change. [O.E.]

wind[2] *wīnd*, *vt* to turn, to twist, to coil; to encircle; to screw the mechanism of, as in a timepiece; to make, direct (e.g. one's way) or to traverse, by turning and twisting; to haul or hoist, as by a winch. — *vi* to turn round something; to twist; to move or go, by turns and twists, or (*fig*) deviously: — *pr p* **wīnd'ing;** *pa t* and *pa p* **wound** (*wownd*) or (chiefly *naut*) **wīnd'ed.** — *n* a turn, coil or twist; a turning; a twisted condition. — *n* **wīnd'er** someone who winds; an instrument for winding; a clock or watch key; an electrically driven winding-engine for hoisting a cage or cages up a vertical mineshaft; a man who operates such an engine; a twisting plant; a triangular step at the turn of a stair or in a spiral staircase. — *adj* and *n* **wīnd'ing.** — *adv* **wind'ingly.** — **wind'ing-sheet** a sheet for wrapping a corpse up in; **wind'-up** the close, finish; an instance of winding up. — **wind down** to relax, become quiet after a period of activity; to lose strength; to reduce the strength or scope of; **wind up** to bring, or come, to a conclusion; to adjust for final settlement; to terminate the activities of, liquidate (a commercial firm, etc.); to excite very much (esp. in *pa p* **wound up** excited; *fig*); to coil completely; to wind the spring or the mechanism of tightly; to tighten; to hoist, as by a winch. [O.E. *windan.*]

windage. See under **wind**[1].

windlass *wind'ləs*, *n* any of various modifications of the wheel and axle employing a revolving cylinder, used for hauling or hoisting. — *vi* to use a windlass. — *vt* to hoist by means of such.

window *win'dō*, *n* an opening in the wall of a building, etc. for air and light; the frame in the opening; the space immediately behind the opening; a window-pane; any opening suggesting a window (also *fig*); a weather window (q.v.); in various technical uses designating a part that is clear, free of a particular type of obstruction, etc.; a period of time when conditions are suitable for a particular activity, such as a **launch window** (planetary positions, weather conditions, etc., for the launch of a spacecraft), **re-entry window** (for the re-entry of a spacecraft), etc.; a rectangular section of a screen which can be used independently of the rest of the screen (*comput*). — *vt* to provide with windows. — *adj* **win'dowed** having a window or windows, or openings or holes resembling these. — *adj* **win'dowless.** — **win'dow-box** a box for growing plants in on a window-sill; **win'dow-dressing** the arranging of goods in a shop window; the art of doing so effectively; (the art of) presenting a cause, situation, project, etc. in an attractive or enticing light; **window envelope** an envelope with a transparent panel through which the address of the recipient on the enclosed letter can be read; **win'dow-frame** a frame that surrounds a window; **win'dow-ledge** a window-sill; **win'dow-pane** a sheet of glass set in a window; **win'dow-sash** a frame in which panes of glass are set; **win'dow-seat** a seat in the recess of a window; a seat beside a window in a bus, aeroplane, etc. — *vi* **win'dow-shop.** — **win'dow-shopping** gazing in shop windows rather than making actual purchases; **win'dow-sill** the sill of a window opening. [M.E. *windowe, windoge* — O.N. *vindauga* — *vindr*, wind, *auga*, eye.]

Windsor *win'zər*, *adj* pertaining to *Windsor*, in Berkshire, as in **Windsor chair**, a chair with a solid wooden seat that has sockets into which the legs and the (usu. slender, spindle-shaped) uprights of the back are fitted; **Windsor knot** a type of wide, triangular knot used in tying a tie; **Wind'sor-soap** a kind of perfumed toilet-soap (usu. brown).

wine *wīn*, *n* the fermented juice of grapes; an alcoholic drink made from other fruits; a rich red colour. — Also *adj*. — *vt* to supply with wine; to treat with wine. — *vi* to take wine, especially at a wine-party. — *adj* **wī'ney** or **wi'ny** like wine; intoxicated. — *n* **wī'nery** (orig. *US*) a place where wine is prepared and stored. — *n* **wino** (*wī'nō*; *colloq*) an alcoholic addicted to wine; a down-and-out thus afflicted: — *pl* **wī'nos.** — **wine'-bibber** a continual drinker of wine; a drunkard; **wine'-bibbing; wine'-cellar** a cellar for storing wine. — *adj* **wine'-coloured** of the colour of red wine. — **wine'-cooler** a receptacle for cooling wine in bottles about to be served at table; **wine funnel** a type of funnel used for decanting wine from the bottle; **wine'glass** a small glass used in drinking wine; **wine'glassful; wine'-grower** a person who cultivates a vineyard and makes wine. — *n* and *adj* **wine'-growing.** — **wine lake** a surplus of wine bought up by an economic community to prevent a fall in prices; **wine'-list; wine'-merchant** a dealer in wine, esp. wholesale; **wine'-party** a drinking-party; **wine'-press** a machine in which grapes are pressed in the manufacture of wine; **wine'-taster** a person whose business it is to sample wines; **wine'-tasting** (a gathering for) sampling wines; **wine'-vault** a vaulted wine-cellar; a place where wine is tasted or drunk. [O.E. *wīn* from L. *vīnum.*]

wing *wing*, *n* the organ of a bird, insect, or other creature, by which it flies; an animal organ resembling a wing; flight; anything resembling a wing; a fan or vane; any side-piece or section, on a building, etc.; the side of a stage; side scenery (*theat*); a side plane of an aeroplane; the mudguard or part of the body which covers a wheel of a motor vehicle; a side-piece on the back of an armchair; (a player on) either the extreme left or extreme right of the forward line in football, etc.; either edge of a football, etc. pitch, along which such a player moves; a group of three squadrons in the Royal Air Force; (in *pl*) a qualified pilot's badge; (*formerly*) the badge of any member of an air-crew other than the pilot; means or power of rapid movement (*fig*); protection (*fig*). — *vt* to provide, or transport, with wings; to lend speed to; to supply with side-pieces; to bear in flight, to waft; to effect on wings; to traverse by flying; to wound in the wing; to wound in the arm or shoulder. — *vi* to soar on the wing; to go with speed. — *adj* **winged** (*wingd* or *wing'id*) provided with wings; (*wingd*) of a fruit or seed (having a flattened appendage; (*wingd*) wounded in the wing, shoulder or arm; swift; lofty, sublime; (in the term **winged words**) spoken, uttered or flying from one person to another. — *n* **wing'er** someone who plays in a position on the wing in football, etc. — *adj* **wing'less.** — *n* **wing'let** a small wing; a winglike appendage; a small vertical wing attached to the tip of an aeroplane wing to improve lift. — *adj* **wing'y** having, resembling, or soaring on, wings. — **wing'beat** a beat or flap of a bird's or insect's wing; **wing'-case** the horny case or cover over the wings of some insects, such as the beetles; **wing collar** a man's stiff collar, worn upright with the points turned down; **wing commander** a Royal Air Force officer corresponding in rank to a naval commander or to a lieutenant colonel; **winged bean** a legume orig. from S.E. Asia, of special value for its high protein content. — *adj* **wing'-footed** having wings attached to the feet (*mythol*, etc.); fast-moving, swift (*poetic*). — **wing forward** one of the two outside men of the second row of the scrum, a flanker (*Rugby football*). — *adj* **wing'-loading** (*aeronautics*) the maximum flying weight of an aeroplane divided by the total area of the main planes. — **wing mirror** a rear-view mirror projecting from the wing, or more generally, the side of a vehicle; **wing nut** a butterfly-nut (see under **butter**[1]); **wing'span** or **wing'-spread** the distance from tip to tip of a bird's extended wings, or of the wings of an aircraft; **wing walker** someone who performs stunts on the wing of an airborne aeroplane; **wing walking.** — **in the wings** (*colloq*) waiting in reserve; **lend wings to** to give speed to; **make (**or **take) wing** to begin flight; to depart; **on (**or **upon) the wing** flying; in motion; departing; **under someone's wing** under someone's protection. [O.N. *vængr*, a wing.]

wingding *wing'ding*, (chiefly *US*) *n* a wild party; a drug-addict's seizure; a pretended seizure.

winge *winj*, (*colloq*). Non-Scottish (esp. *Austr*) variant of **whinge.**

wink[1] *wingk*, *vi* to close and open the eyelids, or an eyelid, quickly; to give a hint, or convey amused understanding, by a sign of this kind; to blink; to seem not to see; to connive (usu. with *at*); to flicker, twinkle. — *vt* to close and open quickly; to flicker; to express by flashlights. — *n* the act of winking; a hint, as by winking; a blink; a closing of the eyes for sleep; a short spell of sleep; a very small time or distance. — *n* **wink'er** someone who winks; (in *pl*) direction indicators on a motor vehicle, consisting of flashing lights (*colloq*). — *n* **wink'ing.** — *adv* **wink'ingly.** — **easy as winking** very easily indeed; **forty winks** (*colloq*) a short nap. [O.E. *wincian.*]

wink[2] *wingk*, *n* one of the small coloured discs used in the game of tiddlywinks. [Short for **tiddlywink.**]

winkle *wing'kl*, *n* a periwinkle (see **periwinkle**[2]); the penis (*slang* or *hypocoristic*). — *n* **wink'ler** that which or someone who winkles out; a person who evicts tenants on behalf of the property owner. — **wink'le-pickers** shoes with long pointed toes, esp. popular in the early 1960s. — **winkle out** (*fig*) to force out gradually and with difficulty (perh. derived from Ger. *Winkel*, corner).

winnable, winner, winning, winningly, winningness. See **win.**

winnow *win'ō*, *vt* to separate the chaff from by wind; to fan; to sift; to separate; to blow upon. — *n* a fan for winnowing. — *n* **winn'ower.** — *n* **winn'owing.** [O.E. *windwian*, to winnow — *wind*; see **wind**[1].]

wino. See under **wine.**

winsome *win'səm*, *adj* cheerful; pleasant; attractive. — *adv* **win'somely.** — *n* **win'someness.** [O.E. *wynsum*, pleasant — *wyn*, joy — and *-sum* (see sfx. **-some**[1]).]

winter *win'tər*, *n* the cold season of the year — in northern temperate regions, from November or December to January or February; astronomically, from the winter solstice to the vernal equinox; a year (usu. in *pl*; *literary*); any season of cheerlessness. — *adj* wintry; suitable for wear or use in winter; sown in autumn, e.g. **winter wheat, winter barley, winter crop,** etc. — *vi* to pass the winter. — *vt* to feed and keep through winter. — *adj* **win'tered** exposed to winter. — *vt* **win'terise** or **-ize** to make suitable for use under wintry conditions. — *n* **win'triness.** — *adj* **win'try** or **win'tery** resembling, or suitable to, winter; stormy; cheerless. — **winter aconite** see under **aconite; win'ter-cherry** any species of *Physalis*, esp. *Physalis alkekengi*; its edible fruit; **win'ter-cress** a cruciferous plant (*Barbarea*) formerly cultivated for winter salad; **win'ter-garden** an ornamental garden of evergreens, etc., or a conservatory with flowers, for winter; (in *pl*, with *cap*) used sometimes as the name of a theatre, concert-hall, etc.; **win'tergreen** a plant of genus *Pyrola*, also of *Chimaphila*; a plant of genus *Gaultheria*, whose oil is an aromatic stimulant, used in flavouring confectionery and in medicine (**chick'-weed-wintergreen** either of two plants — *Trientalis europaea* or *americana* — belonging to the primula family, having white starlike flowers); **winter quarters** the quarters of an army during winter; a winter residence; **winter sports** open-air sports practised on snow and ice, such as skiing, etc. — *adj* **win'ter-weight** (of clothes) heavy enough or thick enough to be suitable for cold weather. [O.E.]

wintry. See **winter.**

winy. See **wine.**

wipe *wīp*, *vt* to clean or dry by rubbing; to clear away (with *away*, *off*, *out* or *up*); to draw across something in order to, or as if to, clean it; to clear (magnetic tape) of its content (also *fig*). — *n* the act of cleaning by rubbing; a blow; a handkerchief (*slang*); a style of film editing in which the picture on the screen appears to be pushed or wiped off the screen by the following one. — *n* **wī'per** someone who wipes, esp. a person who is employed in cleaning in certain industrial jobs; that which wipes or is used for wiping; a moving arm or other conducting device for making a selected contact out of a number of possible connections (*electr*); a moving arm, usu. electrically operated, for removing raindrops, etc. from the windscreen of a motor vehicle. — *n* **wī'ping** the act of one who wipes; a thrashing. — **wipeout** (*wīp'owt*; *slang*) a fall from a surf- or skateboard, skis, etc., esp. a spectacular one; a complete failure or disaster. — **wipe out** to obliterate, annihilate or abolish; to fall from a surfboard, skis, etc. (*slang*). — *adj* **wiped out** (*slang*, esp. *US*) exhausted, dead-beat. [O.E. *wīpian.*]

wire *wīr*, *n* a thread or rope of metal; a piece of wire, or (in *pl*) a group or network of wires, used for some purpose; the metal thread used in telegraphy, etc.; a metallic string of a musical instrument; a telegram (*colloq*); a fence made of wire; the telephone system (*colloq*); a wire stretched over or across the starting and finishing line on a race-track, hence esp. the finishing line itself (orig. *US*; also *fig*). — *adj* formed of, pertaining to, or using wire; running on wire. — *vt* to bind, support, protect, snare or provide with wire; to supply, e.g. a building, with wires necessary for carrying an electric current; to send, or to inform, by telegraph. — *vi* to telegraph. — *adj* **wired.** — *adj* **wire'less** without a wire or wires; of or pertaining to telegraphy or telephony without wires. — *n* wireless telegraphy or telephony, radio; a receiving or transmitting set used for this purpose (*old-fashioned*) — also a message or broadcast so transmitted, broadcast programmes, or broadcasting generally. — *n* **wī'rer** someone who wires, or who uses wire, e.g. to snare animals. — *adv* **wī'rily.** — *n* **wī'riness.** — *n* **wī'ring** the action of the verb; the complex of wires in an electrical system or installation. — *adj* **wī'ry** made of or like wire; flexible and strong; (of a person) strong and able to endure. — **wire brush** a brush with wire bristles, for cleaning rust off metal, dirt off suede shoes, etc.; **wired'-glass** glass in which a wire mesh has been incorporated during rolling as a resistance against fire and explosion blast. — *vt* **wire'draw** to draw into wire by pulling through successively smaller holes in a series of hard steel dies (see **die²**). — **wire'drawer; wire'drawing; wire gauge** any system for designating the diameter of wires by means of a set of numbers; the diameter of a particular piece of wire; **wire'-gauze** a kind of stiff close fabric made of fine wire; **wire'-grass** a kind of fine meadow-grass; any of various other grasses with wiry stems. — *adj* **wire'-haired** having a coat of rather rough, hard hair. — **wireless station** a station for wireless transmission; **wireless telegraphy** or **wireless telephony** signalling through space, without the use of conducting wires between transmitter and receiver, by means of electromagnetic waves generated by high-frequency alternating currents; **wire nail** a common type of nail, round or elliptical in cross-section, cut from steel wire; **wire-nett'ing** a texture of galvanised wire woven in the form of a net; **wire'-puller** a person who exercises an influence felt but not seen; an intriguer; **wire'-pulling; wire'-rope** a rope of twisted wire. — *vt* **wire'tap** to tap (a telephone). — **wire wheel** a wheel, esp. on a sports car, etc., in which the rim is connected to the hub by wire spokes; **wire wool** a mass of very fine wire for scouring; **wire'work** the making of wire, or of objects of wire; articles, or fabric, made of wire; **wire'worker; wire'-working; wire'-worm** a name given to the larvae of click-beetles, from their slenderness and uncommon hardness. — **give (someone) the wire** (chiefly *mil*) to give (someone) advance information; **pull the wires** to be a wire-puller (q.v.); **wire away** or **in** to act or work with vigour; **wire-haired terrier** a type of wire-haired fox-terrier; **wire into** to eat vigorously and assiduously. [O.E. *wīr*.]

Wis. *abbrev* for Wisconsin (U.S. state).

wisdom. See under **wise**.

wise *wīz*, *adj* having knowledge; learned; able to make good use of knowledge; judging rightly; discreet; skilful; dictated by or containing wisdom. — *n* **wisdom** (*wiz'dəm*) the quality of being wise; judgment; the ability to make right use of knowledge; a wise discourse, saying or teaching; learning (*hist*); skilfulness, speculation, spiritual perception (*Bible*). — *adv* **wise'ly.** — **wis'dom-tooth** any of four double back teeth cut after childhood, usually from the late teens; **wise'crack** a lively, pungent retort or comment. — *vi* to make wisecracks. — *adj* **wise'-cracking** making, or addicted to making, wisecracks. — **wise guy** a conceited, over-confident person; a smart alec. — **never (or none) the wiser** still in ignorance; **put someone wise** (*slang*) to put someone in possession of information, make aware; **the Wise Men (of the East)** or **Three Wise Men** the three Magi (in some traditions kings) who according to Matt. ii came to worship the baby Jesus at Bethlehem; **wise to** (*slang*) aware of; **wise up** (*slang*) to make or become aware, in possession of information. [O.E. *wīs*; from root of **wit¹**.]

-wise *wīz*, *sfx* meaning in the manner of, as in **likewise, otherwise**, or (*colloq*) in the matter of, as in **money-wise, business-wise.** [Archaic *wise*, way, manner — O.E. *wīse*; akin to **wise** and **wit¹**.]

wiseacre *wīz'ā-kər*, *n* someone who unduly assumes an air of superior wisdom; a wise guy; a simpleton quite unconscious of being such. [M.Du. *wijssegger* — O.H.G. *wīzago*, a prophet.]

wisent *wē'zənt* or *vē'zənt*, *n* another name for the European bison. [Ger.]

wish *wish*, *vi* to have a desire; to long; to be inclined; to express a desire, esp. as part of a superstitious ritual. — *vt* to desire or long for; to express a desire for; to ask; to invoke; to bid; to foist, palm off (with *on* or *on to*; *colloq*). — *n* desire, longing; a thing desired; an expression of desire; (usu. in *pl*) an expression of desire for good fortune for another. — *n* **wish'er.** — *adj* **wish'ful** having a wish or desire; eager. — *adv* **wish'fully.** — *n* **wish'fulness.** — *n* and *adj* **wish'ing.** — **wish fulfilment** (*psychol*) the satisfaction of a desire in dreams, daydreams, etc.; **wishful thinking** (*psychol*) a type of thinking in which the individual substitutes the fantasy of the fulfilment of the wish for the actual achievement; a belief that a particular thing will happen, or is so, engendered by desire that it should happen, or be so; (*loosely*) thinking about and wishing for an event or turn of fortune that may not take place; **wish'ing-bone** or **wish'bone** the V-shaped bone formed by the fused clavicles in a bird's breast, pulled apart in playful divination, the longer part indicating the first to be married or fulfilment of a wish; **wish'ing-stone, -tree or -well,** etc., a stone, tree, well, etc. supposed to have the power of making a wish expressed at it come true. — **wish someone further** (*slang*) to wish someone was in some other place, not present; **wish someone joy of something** (usu. *ironic*) to hope that the possession of something will be of benefit to someone. [O.E. *wȳscan*, to wish.]

wish-wash *wish'-wosh*, (*colloq*) *n* anything wishy-washy. — *adj* **wish'y-washy** thin and weak; diluted; feeble; of poor quality. [Formed from **wash.**]

wisp *wisp*, *n* a small bundle of straw or hay; a tuft, a shred; a thin strand or band; a small broom; a twisted bunch used as a torch; the will-o'-the-wisp. — *vi* to fall, drift, or otherwise move, in wisps or like a wisp. — *adj* **wis'py** wisp-like, light and fine in texture; flimsy, insubstantial.

wistaria *wis-tā'ri-ə* or **wisteria** *wis-tē'ri-ə*, *n* any plant of the *Wistaria* genus of papilionaceous plants, some of the species among the most magnificent ornamental climbers known in English gardens, named from the American anatomist Caspar *Wistar* (1761–1818) — also **Wistē'ria**.

wistful *wist'fōōl* or *-fl*, *adj* longing; yearning with little hope; pensive. — *adv* **wist'fully.** — *n* **wist'fulness.**

wit¹ *wit*, *vt* and *vi* (*archaic* except in *legal* use) to be aware (with *of*); to recognise, discern; to know how. — *adj* **witt'ing** cognisant; conscious; deliberate. — *adv* **witt'ingly** knowingly; by design. — **to wit** that is to say, namely. [O.E. *witan*, to know.]

wit² *wit*, *n* ingenuity; intelligence, sense (in phrase **have the wit to**); a mental faculty (chiefly in *pl*); the power of combining ideas with a pointed verbal effect; the product of this power; humour, wittiness; a person endowed with wit. — *adj* **wit'less** lacking wit, wisdom or sense; out of one's mind; stupid, unintelligent; unaware, unconscious. — *adv* **wit'lessly.** — *n* **wit'lessness.** — *adj* **witt'ed** having wit or understanding (usu. in combination, as in *quick-witted*). — *n* **witticism** (*wit'i-sizm*) a witty remark; a sentence or phrase affectedly witty. — *adv* **witt'ily.** — *n* **witt'iness.** — *adj* **witt'y** possessed of wit; amusing, droll; sarcastic. — **at one's wits' end** utterly perplexed; **have one's wits about one** to be alert and resourceful; **live by one's wits** to gain a livelihood by ingenious expedients rather than by honest labour; **the five wits** the five senses. [O.E. *(ge)wit* — **wit**[1].]

witch[1] *wich, n* a woman regarded as having supernatural or magical power and knowledge usu. through compact with the devil or a minor evil spirit; a hag, crone; a fascinating woman (*colloq*). — *vt* to bewitch, fascinate. — *n* **witch'ery** witchcraft; fascination. — *n* **witch'ing** sorcery; enchantment. — *adj* suited to witchcraft; weird; fascinating. — *adv* **witch'ingly**. — **witch'craft** the craft or practice of witches; the black art, sorcery; supernatural power; **witch'-doctor** in tribal societies, a magician who detects witches and counteracts evil magical influences; someone who professes to heal by means of magic; **witches' brew** (*fig*) a heady concoction of disparate elements, a confused or mysterious mixture; **witch'es'-broom** a dense tuft of poorly developed branches formed on a woody plant attacked by a parasite (chiefly fungi and mites); **witch hunt** (orig. *US*) the searching out of political opponents for exposure on grounds of alleged disloyalty to the state, etc.; also applied to any similar non-political search or persecution of a group or an individual; **witching hour** midnight. [M.E. *wicche* (both masc. and fem.) — O.E. *wicca* (masc.), *wicce* (fem.), wizard, witch, and verb *wiccian*.]

witch[2] *wich, n* any of several trees with pliant branches, such as the wych-elm, the rowan, etc. — **witch'-alder** any of a genus of N. American shrubs related to the witch-hazel — not an alder; **witch'-elm** the wych-elm; **witch'-hazel** any of a number of trees, such as the wych-elm, or a N. American shrub (*Hamamelis virginica*) from whose bark is made an astringent solution, a remedy for bruises, etc. — a distillate of the bark dissolved in alcohol. [O.E. *wice*; related to *wīcan*, to give way.]

witchetty *wich'ə-tē* or **witchetty grub** (*grub*), *n* any of the large edible grubs of species of certain Australian moths (*Cossus*). [Aboriginal.]

witgat *vit'hhat* or **witgatboom** *vit'hhat-bo͝om, n* a S. African evergreen tree with pale bark, hard coarse-grained, white wood, and edible roots used esp. as a coffee substitute when roasted; any of various species of the genus *Bosica*. [Afrik., — *wit*, white, *gat*, hole, *boom*, tree.]

with *widh* or *with, prep* denoting nearness, agreement or connection; by, beside; among; on the side of; in the company of; in the possession or care of; containing; supplemented by; possessing; characterised by; in the same direction as; at the time of; at the same time as; immediately after; in competition or contest against; in respect of, in the regard of; by, by means of, through; because of; in spite of; using; from (as in *to part with*). — **be with someone** to understand someone; **feel, be** or **think with** to feel as, or be of the same opinion as, the other person specified; **in with** (*colloq*) friendly with; **with it** (*slang*) following current trends in popular taste; **with that** thereupon. [O.E. *with*, against; O.N. *vith*, Ger. *wider*. It ousted the O.E. *mid*, with (Ger. *mit*).]

withdraw *widh-drö'* or *with-, vt* to draw back or away; to take back or away; to take (money) from deposit or investment; to remove (with *from*); to recall, retract. — *vi* to retire; to go away; to take back what one has said, or to recall a motion one has proposed: — *pa t* **withdrew** (*-dro͞o'*); *pa p* **withdrawn'**. — *n* **withdraw'al** an act or gradual process of withdrawing; the stage in which, or process whereby, an addict is deprived of a drug in order to break his or her addiction; (also **withdrawal method**) coitus interruptus, interruption of sexual intercourse before ejaculation of semen. — *adj* **withdrawn'** (of place) secluded; remote; (of a person or a person's manner) detached; uncommunicative; introverted. — **withdrawal symptom** any of a number of symptoms, such as pain, nausea, sweating, caused by depriving a person of a drug to which he or she is addicted. [Pfx. *with-*, against, back, and **draw**.]

withe *widh, with* or *wīdh, n* a flexible twig, esp. of willow; a band of twisted twigs. — *vt* to bind with a withe or withes. [O.E. *withthe*; cf. **withy**.]

wither *widh'ər, vi* to fade or become dry; to lose freshness; to languish, decline; to decay, waste. — *vt* to cause to dry up, fade or decay; to cause to feel very unimportant or despicable. — *adj* **with'ered**. — *n* **with'eredness**. — *n* **with'ering**. — *adj* fading, becoming dry, etc., or causing to do so; blasting, blighting, scorching (*fig*); snubbing. — *adv* **with'eringly**. [M.E. *wederen*, to expose to weather.]

withers *widh'ərz, npl* the ridge between the shoulder-bones of a horse. [O.E. *wither*, against, an extension of *with*, against.]

withhold *widh-hōld'* or *with-hōld', vt* to hold back, restrain; to keep back; to refuse to give: — *pa t* and *pa p* **withheld'**. — *n* **withhold'er**. — *n* **withhold'ment**. [Pfx. *with-*, against, and **hold**.]

within *widh-in'* or *with-, prep* inside; in the limits of; not going beyond; entered from; into. — *adv* in the inner part; inwardly; in the mind, soul, heart; behind the scenes; indoors; herein. — **within reach** in a position from which it can be obtained, or attained, without much difficulty, effort, or loss of time. [O.E. *withinnan* — *with*, against, with, *innan*, in.]

without *widh-owt'* or *with-, prep* not with; in absence of; not having; not using; with no help from; free from; outside the limits of (*literary* or *archaic*). — *adv* on the outside; outwardly; outside, not members of, a particular group or society. — *conj* (*archaic* or *dialect*) unless, except. — **from without** from the outside; **without distinction** indiscriminately. [O.E. *withūtan* — *with*, against, *ūtan*, outside.]

withstand *widh-stand'* or *with-, vt* and *vi* to stand, maintain one's position (against); to oppose or resist: — *pa t* and *pa p* **withstood'**. — *n* **withstand'er**. [O.E. *withstandan* — *with*, against; see **stand**.]

withy *widh'i, n* the osier willow; any willow; a flexible twig or branch, esp. one used for binding. [O.E. *wīthig*, willow; cf. **withe**.]

witness *wit'nis, n* knowledge brought in proof; testimony of a fact; that which provides proof; a person who sees or has personal knowledge of a thing; a person who gives evidence; a person who or that which attests. — *vt* to have direct knowledge of; (*loosely*) to see; to be the scene of; to give testimony to; to attest; to act as legal witness of. — *vi* to give evidence. — *n* **wit'nesser**. — **wit'ness-box** the enclosure in which a witness stands when giving evidence in a court of law. — **bear witness** to give, or be, evidence (esp. with *to*). [O.E. *(ge)witnes* — *(ge)wit*; see **wit**[2].]

witter *wit'ər, vi* to talk or mutter peevishly or ineffectually (esp. with *on*).

witticism. See under **wit**[2].

witting, wittingly. See **wit**[1].

witty, etc. See under **wit**[2].

wivern or **wyvern** *wī'vərn*, (*heraldry*) *n* a fictitious monster, winged and two-legged, allied to the dragon and the griffin. [O.N.Fr. *wivre*, a viper — L. *vīpera*.]

wives *wīvz, pl* of **wife**.

wizard *wiz'ərd, n* a person, usu. a man, who practises witchcraft or magic; a person who works wonders. — *adj* with magical powers; wonderful, delightful (*old slang*). — *n* **wiz'ardry** sorcery. [M.E. *wysar(d)* — *wys*, wise, and noun sfx. *-ard*.]

wizen *wiz'n, adj* dried up, thin, shrivelled (now usu. **wiz'ened**). — *vi* and *vt* to become, or to make, dry and shrivelled. [O.E. *wisnian*, to wither.]

wk *abbrev* for week.

WL *abbrev* for St Lucia, Windward Islands (I.V.R.).

Wm *abbrev* for William.

WMO *abbrev* for World Meteorological Organisation.

WNO *abbrev* for Welsh National Opera.

WNP *abbrev* for Welsh National Party.

WNW *abbrev* for west-north-west.

WO *abbrev* for: (*formerly*) War Office; walk-over; warrant officer.

woad *wōd*, *n* a genus (*Isatis*) of cruciferous plants, mostly Mediterranean. — **dyer's woad** (*Isatis tinctoria*) yielding a good and very permanent blue dye, largely superseded by indigo; a blue dye. [O.E. *wād*.]

wobbegong *wob'i-gong*, *n* a carpet shark. [Aboriginal.]

wobble *wob'l*, *vi* to move unsteadily or uncertainly from side to side; to move along thus; to quiver; to quaver (*colloq*); to vacillate. — Also *vt*. — *n* an unsteady, unequal motion or movement. — *n* **wobb'ler**. — *n* **wobb'liness**. — *n* **wobb'ling**. — *adj* **wobb'ly** shaky; inclined to wobble. — *n* (*colloq*) a fit, tantrum. — **wobb'le-board** a sheet of hardboard shaken to obtain certain sound-effects. [L.G. *wabbeln*.]

Woden *wō'dən* or **Wotan** *wō'tan*, (*mythol*) *n* the chief god of the ancient Germanic peoples, the Scandinavian *Odin*. [O.E. *Wōden*.]

wodge *woj*, (*colloq*) *n* a large or roughly-cut portion; a lump. [**wedge**.]

woe *wō*, *n* (*literary* or *archaic*) grief; misery; (often in *pl*) a misfortune or calamity. — *interj* an exclamation of grief. — *adj* **woe'ful** sorrowful or afflicted; bringing misery or calamity; deplorable; wretched, paltry. — *adv* **woe'fully**. — *n* **woe'fulness**. — *adj* **woe'begone** dismal-looking, suggesting misery. — **woe betide you**, etc. you, etc. will suffer some misfortune; **woe is me** (*archaic*) so unhappy or accursed am I; **woe unto** (*archaic*) calamity will befall; may calamity befall. [O.E. (interj.) *wā*; cf. **wail**.]

wog *wog*, (*offensive*) *n* any non-white foreigner, originally used only of Arabs. [Perh. from **(golly)wog**; popularly thought to be an acronym, of which several expansions are propounded.]

woggle *wog'l*, *n* the ring of leather or plastic through which Scouts and Guides etc. thread their neckerchiefs.

wok *wok*, *n* a hemispherical pan used in Chinese cookery. [Chin.]

woke and **woken**. See under **wake**[1].

wold *wōld*, *n* an open tract of country, now chiefly upland country. [O.E. (Anglian) *wald*, forest, applied orig. to wooded parts of the country; cf. **weald**.]

wolf *wŏŏlf*, *n* the common name of certain gregarious and rapacious breeds of doglike mammal, including the common wolf, the grey or timber wolf, and the coyote; anything very ravenous; a greedy and cunning person; a dissonance heard in a keyboard instrument tuned by unequal temperament (*mus*); an extraneous non-harmonic note made by the bow on a string of a violin, etc. (*mus*); a man who pursues women with sexual motives (*colloq*): — *pl* **wolves** (*wŏŏlvz*). — *vi* to hunt for wolves (also **wolve** *wŏŏlv*). — *vt* (often with *down* or *up*; *colloq*) to devour ravenously. — *n* **wolf'er** or **wolv'er** a person who hunts wolves. — *n* **wolf'ing** or **wolv'ing** the hunting of wolves for their skins. — *adj* **wolf'ish** or **wolv'ish** like a wolf; rapacious; ravenous. — *adv* **wolf'ishly** or **wolv'ishly**. — **Wolf Cub** a Cub Scout; **wolf'-dog** a dog of large breed formerly used in hunting wolves and guarding sheep from attack by wolves; a cross between a wolf and a domestic dog; **wolf'-fish** any genus of fierce and voracious salt-water fishes. — Also **sea-wolf** and **catfish**. — **wolf'-hound** any of several breeds of large domestic dog, such as the Irish wolfhound, formerly used to hunt wolves; **wolf'-pack** a pack of wolves; **wolf's'-bane** or **wolfs'bane** a poisonous plant of the aconite family; **wolf'-spīder** any spider of the genus to which the true tarantula belongs, which chase their prey rather than catching it in a web; **wolf'-whistle** a two-note whistle uttered in admiration, typically by a man at the sight of a woman. — **cry wolf** to give a false alarm — from the story of the boy who cried 'Wolf' when there was none, and was not believed when there was one; **keep the wolf from the door** to keep away poverty or hunger; **throw (or fling) to the wolves** to abandon to certain destruction; **wolf in sheep's clothing** someone who behind a kindly and inoffensive exterior is dangerous and unscrupulous. [O.E. *wulf*.]

wolfram *wŏŏlf'rəm*, *n* a native compound of tungstate of iron and manganese (also **wolf'ramite**); tungsten. [Ger.]

Wolof *wō'lof*, *n* a tribe living near the Senegal River in western Africa; a member of the tribe; its language. — Also *adj*.

wolve and **wolver**. See under **wolf**.

wolverine or **wolverene** *wŏŏl-və-rēn'*, *n* a large solitary carnivorous mammal of the weasel family, found in forests in N. America and Eurasia; its fur. [Extension of **wolf**.]

wolves and **wolvish**. See under **wolf**.

woman *wŏŏ'mən*, *n* an adult human female; a wife (now *dialect*); a mistress; the female sex, women collectively; a female attendant to a queen, etc.; a charwoman or daily domestic help (*colloq*); a man who displays qualities considered more typical of a woman, esp. meekness or emotional sensitivity (*colloq*); feminine characteristics: — *pl* **women** (*wi'mən*). — Also *adj*. — *n* **wo'manhood** the state, character or qualities of a woman; womenkind. — *vt* and *vi* **wo'manise** or **-ize** to make or become effeminate. — *vi* (of a man) to pursue women with a view to sexual adventures. — *n* **wo'maniser** or **-z-**. — *adj* **wo'manish** effeminate; feminine. — *adv* **wo'manishly**. — *n* **wo'manishness**. — *n* **wo'mankind** women collectively. — *adj* and *adv* **wo'man-like**. — *n* **wo'manliness**. — *adj* **wo'manly** like or becoming a woman; feminine. — *adv* in the manner of a woman. — **wo'man-hater** a man who hates women, a misogynist; **women's suffrage** possession of the electoral franchise by women; **wo'menfolk** the female members of a group, esp. one's own family; women collectively, womankind; **women's liberation** a movement of active feminists forming part of the women's movement (*colloq* short form **women's lib**); **women's liberationist** (*colloq* short form **women's libber**); **women's movement** the movement amongst women to try to achieve equality with men, with regard to e.g. job opportunities, pay, legal status, etc.; **women's rights** equal rights with men sought by women in such a way; **wo'menswear** clothes for women. — **kept woman** a mistress; **woman of the town** or **of the streets** a whore; **woman of the world** a woman of fashion, or of worldly wisdom; a woman who knows and makes allowance for, or accepts, the ways of the world; **Women's Royal Voluntary Service** a nationwide service assisting government departments, local authorities and other voluntary bodies in organising and carrying out welfare and emergency work for the community. [O.E. *wimman* — *wīfman* — *wīf*, a woman, *man*, man, human being.]

womb *wŏŏm*, *n* the uterus, the organ in which the young of mammals are developed and kept until birth; the place where anything is produced; any deep cavity (*fig*). [O.E. *wamb*, *womb*.]

wombat *wom'bat*, *n* an animal belonging to any of several species of heavy, burrowing herbivorous marsupials of the family *Vombatidae*. [Aboriginal.]

women. See **woman**.

womera. See **woomera**.

won[1] *wun*, *pa t* and *pa p* of **win**.

won[2] *won*, *n* the standard monetary unit of North and South Korea (100 *chon*): — *pl* **won**. [Korean, *wŏn*.]

wonder *wun'dər*, *n* the state of mind produced by something new, unexpected, unexplained or extraordinary; the quality of being strange or unexpected; a strange, astonishing or admirable thing or happening; a prodigy; a miracle. — *vi* to feel wonder; to be amazed (with *at*); to feel doubt. — *vt* to speculate, to ask oneself (with noun clause or direct quotation, often used to form a polite inquiry). — *n* **won'derer**. — *adj* **won'derful** exciting wonder; strange; expressing vague commendation, admirable, extremely good (*colloq*). — *adv* **won'derfully**. — *n* **won'derfulness**. — *n* and *adj* **won'dering**. — *adv* **won'deringly**. — *n* **won'derment** surprise; the feeling or an expression of wonder; a wonderful thing. — *adj* **won'drous** exciting wonder. — Also *adv*. — *adv* **won'drously**. — *n* **won'drousness**. — **won'derland** an imaginary land of strange and beautiful things. — *adj* **won'der-struck** or **-stricken** struck with wonder or astonishment. — **won'der-work** a prodigy, miracle; **won'der-worker; won'der-working**. — **nine days' wonder** something that astonishes everybody for a short while and is soon forgotten; **no wonder** or **small wonder** it isn't surprising; **seven wonders of the world** see under **seven**. [O.E. *wundor*.]

wondrous, etc. See under **wonder**.

wonky *wongk'i*, (*colloq*) *adj* unsound; shaky; amiss; awry.

wont *wōnt*, *n* habit. — *adj* (*literary* or *archaic*) used or accustomed. — *vi* to be accustomed. — *adj* **wont'ed** accustomed, habituated; usual. [Orig. past p. of (archaic or dialect) *won*, to dwell, be or become accustomed.

won't *wōnt*, (*colloq*) will not. [Contr. of M.E. *wol not*.]

woo *wōō*, *vt* to try to win the affection of; to court; to solicit eagerly; to seek to gain. — Also *vi*: — *pa t* and *pa p* **wooed** (*wōōd*). — *n* **woo'er**. — *n* and *adj* **woo'ing**. — *adv* **woo'ingly**. [O.E. *wōgian*, to woo.]

wood *wŏŏd*, *n* a collection of growing trees (often in *pl*); wooded country; the hard part beneath the bark of trees and shrubs, xylem; trees cut or sawed, timber; a kind of timber or wood; firewood; the cask or barrel, as distinguished from the bottle; a golf club with a bulky curved head, traditionally made of wood, though now also of metal, used for hitting the ball long distances; a bowl (*bowls*). — *vt* to cover with trees; to supply or load with wood. — *vi* to take in a supply of wood. — *adj* **wood'ed** supplied with wood; covered with trees. — *adj* **wood'en** made of or like wood; (of a golf club) with the head made of wood; hard; dull, insensible; heavy, stupid; lacking animation or grace of manner or execution; clumsy. — *adv* **wood'enly**. — *n* **wood'enness**. — *n* **wood'iness**. — *adj* **wood'less**. — *n* **wood'-lessness**. — *adj* **wood'sy** (*-zi*; *NAm*) pertaining to, or characteristic of, woods. — *adj* **wood'y** abounding with woods; situated in a wood; pertaining to wood; consisting wholly or largely of wood; like wood in texture, smell, taste, etc. — **wood alcohol** wood spirit; **wood anemone** any anemone growing in woods, esp. *Anemone nemorosa*, which has a single whorl of leaves and a white flower; **wood'-ash** (often in *pl*) ash obtained by burning wood or plants — a source of potassium salts; **wood'bine** or **wood'bind** the honeysuckle; applied also to other climbers, such as some kinds of ivy, the Virginia-creeper, etc.; **wood'block** a die cut in relief on wood and ready to produce ink impressions; a woodcut; **wood'carver; wood'carving** the process of carving in wood; an object, or part of one, ornamented or made in this way; **wood'cock** a genus of birds allied to the snipes, but with a bulkier body, and with shorter and stronger legs; **wood'craft** skill in hunting and everything pertaining to life in the woods; forestry generally; skill in working or carving wood; **wood'cut** a design for printing incised into the surface of a block of wood cut plank-wise, i.e. along the grain; an impression taken from this; **wood'cutter** a person who cuts wood; a person who makes woodcuts; **wood'cutting; wood'-engraver** a person who makes wood-engravings; any of certain beetles that make a pattern of furrows in the wood of trees; **wood'-engraving** a design for printing, incised into the surface of a block of hard wood cut across the grain; an impression taken from this; the art of cutting such designs; **wood'enhead** (*colloq*) a blockhead, stupid person. — *adj* **wooden-head'ed** having a head of wood; stupid (*colloq*). — **woodenhead'edness** (*colloq*); **wooden leg** an artificial leg made of wood; **wooden overcoat** (*slang*) a coffin; **wooden spoon** a booby prize; **wood'-fibre** a thick-walled, elongated, dead element found in wood — developed by the elongation and lignification of the wall of a single cell; **wood'-flour** or **wood'meal** a fine powder, made from sawdust and wood waste, used as a filler in many industries, in the manufacture of guncotton and dynamite, and as an absorbent in surgical dressings; **wood'grouse** the capercaillie; **wood'land** land covered with wood (also *adj*); **wood'lander** an inhabitant of woodland; **wood'lark** a species of lark that perches on trees but sings chiefly on the wing; **wood'louse** (*pl* **wood'lice**) any of numerous crustaceans of family *Oniscidae*, found in damp places, under stones and bark, in woodwork, among moss, etc.; **wood'man** a man who cuts down trees; a forest officer; a huntsman; **wood'mouse** a type of fieldmouse with large ears and a long tail; **wood nightshade** or **woody nightshade** a Eurasian climbing plant with purple flowers and poisonous red berries, bittersweet; **wood'-nymph** a nymph of the woods; **wood'-paper** paper made from wood-pulp; **wood'pecker** any of the (*Picidae*) birds, remarkable for modification of the skull and bill enabling the latter to be used to drill holes, and for the long flexible tongue, used to extract insects from crevices; **wood'-pigeon** the ring-dove, a common species of pigeon living in woods; in New Zealand, the *kuku*, a large fruit-eating pigeon; **wood'pile** a pile of wood, esp. firewood; **wood'-pulp** wood mechanically or chemically pulped for paper-making; **wood'ruff** any of several plants with whorled leaves and a funnel-shaped corolla, esp. *sweet woodruff* which has small white flowers and a pleasant scent; **wood'-screw** a screw for fastening pieces of wood or wood and metal; **wood'shed** a shed for storing firewood; an intensive, esp. private, practice or rehearsal (*mus slang*; orig. *US*). — *vt* and *vi* to practise (a piece of music), esp. intensively and alone (*mus slang*; orig. *US*). — **woods'man** a woodman; **wood'-sorrel** any plant of the genus *Oxalis* with trifoliate leaves and white or rose-tinted flowers; **wood spirit** methyl alcohol, methanol; **wood'-tar** a product of destructive distillation of wood, containing paraffins, naphthalene and phenols; **wood'-warbler** a yellowish-green European warbler; a similar bird, the American warbler; **wood'wind** a wind-instrument (formerly usu. of wood, some now of metal (e.g. silver) or other material) — flute, oboe, bassoon, clarinet, etc.; (used collectively) the section of an orchestra comprising these; **wood'work** a part of any structure made of wood; carpentry or joinery; goalposts, etc. (*football*, etc.; *colloq*); **wood'worker** a craftsman or worker in wood; **wood'worm** any of various insect larvae that bore in wood; **woody nightshade** same as **wood nightshade**. — **knock on wood** see **touch wood** under **touch**; **not see the wood for the trees** to fail to grasp the whole because of the superabundance of, or one's over-concentration on, detail; **out of the wood** or **woods** out of difficulty or danger; **something nasty in the woodshed** (*facetious*) an unpleasant or shocking experience in one's past. [O.E. *wudu.*]

woodchuck *wŏŏd'chuk*, *n* a N. American species of marmot. [Corruption of an Am. Indian name.]

woodsy. See under **wood**.

wooer, wooing, etc. See **woo**.

woof[1] *wŏŏf*, *n* weft; thread for a weft; texture. [M.E. *oof*, with *w* added by association with **warp**, etc.]

woof[2] *wŏŏf*, *n* the bark of a dog. — *vi* to make a woof or woofs, as (or in imitation of) a dog. [Imit.]

woofer *wŏŏf'ər*, *n* a large loudspeaker used to reproduce low-frequency sounds only. — Cf. **tweeter**. [Imit. of a dog's bark.]

woofter *wŏŏf'tə* or *-tər*, *n*. Same as **poofter**.

wool *wŏŏl*, *n* a kind of hair in which the fibres are shorter, curled and overlapping — the covering of sheep, etc.; thread or yarn made from animal wool; fabric woven or knitted from it; any light, fleecy substance like wool; any substance with a fibrous texture, resembling wool, e.g. steel-wool; short, thick human hair. — *adj* **woolled** (*wŏŏld*) bearing wool. — *adj* **wooll'en** made of or pertaining to wool; clad in or covered with wool. — *n* (often in *pl*) cloth or a garment made of wool. — *n* **wooll'iness**. — *adj* **wooll'y** consisting of, or like, wool; clothed with wool; lacking in clearness, firmness or definition (*fig*). — *n* (often in *pl*, **wooll'ies**) a garment of wool, esp. a knitted one. — **wool'-ball** a ball of wool, such as is sometimes found in a sheep's stomach. — *adj* **wool'-bearing** bearing or yielding wool. — **wool'-card** or **wool'-comb** a machine for **wool'-carding** or **wool'-combing**, separating the fibres of wool preparatory to spinning; **wool'-carder** or **wool'-comber**; **wool church** an English (esp. E. Anglian) church built or converted using funds accrued during the Tudor wool trade boom, frequently appearing of inappropriate size and grandeur for its setting; **wool'-clip** a crop of wool from a particular flock of sheep, esp. that gathered in one season; **wool'fat** lanolin; **wool'fell** the skin with the wool still on it; **wool'-gathering** absent-minded dreaming. — *adj* dreamy; absent-minded. — **wooll'en-mill** a mill where wool is spun and woven into material; **wooll'y-bear** the hairy caterpillar of a number of moths, including the tiger-moths; the larva of the carpet beetle. — *adj* **wooll'y-haired** having hair like wool. — *adj* **woolly-head'ed** or **woolly-mind'ed** habitually slow in thinking, making decisions, etc. — **wool'man** a dealer in wool; **wool'-mill** a woollen-mill; **wool'-oil** any oil obtained from woolfat; an oil used to lubricate wool before spinning; **wool'-pack** the package in which wool was formerly done up for sale; a bundle weighing 240 lb.; **wool'sack** the seat of the Lord Chancellor in the House of Lords, being a large square sack of wool covered with scarlet; the office of Lord Chancellor; **wool'sorter** a person who sorts wool according to quality, etc.; **wool'-staple** the fibre or pile of wool; a market where wool was sold; **wool'-stapler** a dealer in wool; a woolsorter. — **pull (or draw) the wool over someone's eyes** to hoodwink or deceive someone. [O.E. *wull.*]

woomera *wŏŏm'ər-ə*, **womera** *wom'ər-ə* or **woomerang** *wŏŏm'ər-ang*, *n* a notched stick used by Aborigines to launch a spear or dart. [Aboriginal.]

woopie or **woopy** *wŏŏpi*, (*slang*; also with *cap*) *n* a well-off older person. [Coined in imitation of **yuppie** (q.v.)].

woorali. See **wourali**.

woosh. See **whoosh**.

woozy *wŏŏ'zi*, (*colloq*) *adj* fuddled (with drink, drugs, etc.); dazed, dizzy; blurred, woolly, vague. — *adv* **wooz'ily**. — *n* **wooz'iness**.

wop *wop*, (*offensive slang*) *n* an Italian, or other foreigner of olive complexion. [It. (dialect) *guappo* — Sp. *guapo*, bold, handsome.]

Worcester sauce *wŏŏs'tər sös* or **Worcestershire** (*wŏŏs'təsh-ər*) **sauce**, *n* a pungent sauce, orig. made in Worcestershire, sold in bottles for use as a condiment.

Worcs. *abbrev* for Worcestershire.

word *wûrd*, *n* a unit of spoken language; a written sign representing such an utterance; (in *pl*) language; a saying; a brief conversation; a rumour; a hint; a signal or sign; a message; a promise; a declaration; a password; a watchword; a set of bits stored and transferred as a single unit of meaning (*comput*); (in *pl*) verbal contention, argument. — *vt* to express in words. — *n* **word'age** words generally, esp. text as opposed to pictures, etc.; verbiage, wordiness; quantity of words, length of text; choice of words, wording. — *adj* **word'ed** expressed in words. — *adv* **word'ily**. — *n* **word'iness**. — *n* **word'ing** the act of expressing in words; choice of words, phrasing. — *adj* **word'less** unspoken; silent. — *adj* **word'y** using, or containing, too many words; conducted in words. — *adj* **word'-blind**. — **word'-blindness** the lack, or loss, of the ability to read, a non-technical name for both **alexia** and **dyslexia**; **word'book** a book with a collection of words; a dictionary, or vocabulary; **word'-building**; the formation of words from letters or from root words and affixes; **word finder** a book designed as a tool for finding a required word; a thesaurus; **word'game** any game, puzzle, etc. in which words are constructed, deciphered, etc.; **word'-painter**; **word'-painting** the act or art of giving a vivid description in words. — *adj* **word-per'fect** having memorised (words to be repeated, recited, etc.) exactly. — **word'-picture** a description in words that presents an object, scene, etc. to the mind as if in a picture; **word play** puns, etc.; **word processing**; **word processor** any of several types of machine that perform electronically the tasks of typing, data-recording, dictating, transcribing, etc., usually incorporating screens for visual display; **word'-puzzler** a person who engages in puzzles or games involving words; **word salad** (*psychol*) a confused outpouring of speech, most often occurring in cases of schizophrenia; **word'-smith** an accomplished user of words (sometimes *ironic*); a coiner of words; **word'-square** a square grid composed of a set of words that read the same down as they do across; **word'-wrapping** (on a visual display unit) the automatic placing of input on a new line as the last space on the previous line becomes filled, wraparound. — **a good word** a recommendation, favourable mention, praise; **a word in one's ear** a confidential conversation; **break one's word** to fail to fulfil a promise; **by word of mouth** orally, through the spoken word (*adj* **word-of-mouth'**); **eat one's words** to retract, apologise, usu. under compulsion; **have a word with** to speak to, usu. for some specific purpose; **have words (with)** to quarrel, dispute (with); **in a word** or **in one word** in short, to sum up; **in so many words** explicitly; bluntly; **my word** mild interj. expressing surprise, annoyance, etc.; **not the word for it** not a strong enough word to express or describe it; **of few (or many) words** taciturn (or verbose); **put words into someone's mouth** to attribute or supply to someone words that they did not, or do not intend to, use; **take someone at their word** to accept someone's statements as being literally true; **take the words out of someone's mouth** to say exactly what someone else was about to say; **the last word** the closing remark in an argument, esp. if having an appearance of conclusiveness; the conclusive statement; the ultimate authority; (also **latest word**) the most up-to-date or the finest example; **the Word** (*Christian relig*) the Scriptures; the gospel message; the second person in the Trinity; **word for word** literally, verbatim. [O.E.]

wore *wör*, *pa t* of **wear**[1,2].

work *wûrk*, *n* effort directed to an end; employment; that on which one works; the product of work, anything made or done; needlework; a deed; doings; the result of action; any production of art, such as a literary composition; a book; manner of working, workmanship; (in *pl*) a factory, workshop (as *adj* (of a racing-car) entered officially in a race by the manufacturer); the act of producing an effect by means of a force (F) whose point of application moves through a distance (s) in its own line of action — measured by the product of the force and the distance (W = Fs; *phys*); (in *pl*) walls, trenches, etc. (*fort*); (usu. in *pl*) an action in its moral aspect, esp. as tending to justification (*theol*); (in *pl*) mechanism, e.g. of a watch. — *vi* to make efforts to achieve or attain anything; to be occupied in business or labour; to move, make one's way, etc. slowly and laboriously; to move, become, etc. in a manner not intended or desired; to be in action; to operate or function; to produce effects; to behave in the desired way when worked; to prove practicable; to ferment; to be agitated or move convulsively; to strain or labour. — *vt* to make by labour; to bring into any state by action; to effect or strive to effect; to carry on operations in; to keep in operation; to keep employed; to put in motion; to influence; to affect powerfully; to provoke or excite; to prepare for use by manipulation; to cause to ferment; to fashion or make; to embroider; to make (e.g. one's way) by effort; to solve; to make use of or make profit through (*colloq*); to influence, cajole or trick (*colloq*): — *pa t* and *pa p* **worked** or **wrought** (see separate article). — *n* **workabil'ity** or **work'ableness**. — *adj* **work'able** that may be worked, esp. practicable. — *n* **workaholic** (*-ə-hol'ik*) a person addicted to work, coined facetiously in imitation of *alcoholic*. — Also *adj*. — *adj* **worked** that has been treated or fashioned in some way; embroidered; ornamented. — *n* **work'er** a person who works; a toiler; a person employed in manual work; (in social insects) one of a caste of sterile individuals that do all the work of the colony. — *n* **work'erist** (*old-fashioned*) a supporter of proletarian rights and values, esp. (*derog*) one of upper or middle class. — Also *adj*. — *adj* **work'ful** industrious. — *n* **work'ing** the act or process of shaping, making, effecting, solving, fermenting, etc.; a written record of the process of calculation; manner of operating or functioning; contortion due to agitation; slow and laborious progress; (in *pl*) the parts of a mine, etc. where work is, or has been, carried on. — *adj* active; operational; labouring; having a job or employment; relating to labour, a job or employment. — *adj* **work'less** having no job, unemployed. — Also *npl*. — *adj* **work'aday** suitable for a work day; toiling; dull, prosaic. — **work'-bag** or **-basket** a bag or basket for holding materials for work, esp. needlework; **work'bench** a bench, often purpose-built, at which a craftsman, mechanic, etc. works; **work'book** a book of exercises, often with spaces for the answers, to accompany another book; a record book of jobs undertaken, in progress or completed; **work'box** a box for holding instruments or materials for work; **work'day** a day for work, a weekday. — *adj* pertaining to a workday. — **worker priest** a priest in the Roman Catholic Church who also works full-time or part-time in a secular job in order to understand better the problems of lay people; **work ethic** the general attitude of a group towards work, esp. one (**Protestant work ethic**) which places a high moral value on (hard) work; **work'fare** an unemployment benefit scheme under which recipients are required to do work of some kind, usu. some form of public service; **work'fellow** (*old-fashioned*) someone who is engaged in the same work with another, a workmate; **work'folk** or **work'folks** workers; **work'force** the number of workers engaged in a particular industry, factory, etc.; the total number of workers potentially available; **work'horse** a horse used in a labouring capacity rather than for recreation, racing, etc.; a person or machine heavily depended on to do arduous work; **work'house** (*hist*) a house where any work or manufacture is carried on; a house of shelter for the poor, who are given work to do; **working breakfast, lunch,** etc. one arranged as an alternative to a formal meeting, for the discussion of diplomatic or other business; **work'ing-class** that of manual workers or wage-earners, (often in *pl*; also *adj*); **work'ing-day** a day on which work is done; the period of actual work each day; **work'ing-drawing** a drawing of the details of the construction or assembly of something by which the builders are guided in their work; **working hours** the period of the day during which work is normally done, and offices, shops, etc. are open; **working lunch** see **working breakfast**; **working majority** a majority sufficient to enable the party in office to carry on without accidental defeats; **working man** or **woman** a worker, esp. a manual one; **work'ing-model** a model of a machine that can do, on a smaller scale, the same work as the machine; **working paper** one produced as a basis for discussion, to report on progress made, etc., rather than as a final statement; **working (or work) party** a group of people who carry out a specially assigned task; a group appointed to investigate a subject, such as methods of attaining maximum efficiency in an industry; **working week** that part of the week in which work is normally done — esp. Monday to Friday; any week in which such work is done, as opposed e.g. to holidays; **work'load** the amount of work assigned to an individual, machine, etc. for completion within a certain time; **work'man** a man who works, esp. manually; a (certain kind of) craftsman. — *adj* **work'manlike** like a workman; befitting a skilful workman; well performed. — *adj* **work'manly** becoming a skilful workman. — **work'manship** the skill of a workman; manner of making; that which is made or produced by one's hands (also *fig*); **work'-mate** a companion at work; **work'people** people engaged in manual labour, workers; **work'place** the office, factory, etc. where one works; **work'room** a room for working in; **works committee** or **council** a body on which both employer and employees meet to handle labour relations within a business; **work'-shop** a room or shop where work is done; a group of people working on a creative or experimental project; such a project. — *adj* **work'shy** hating and avoiding work, lazy (also used as *n*). — **work station** (on a production line) a position at which a particular job is done; (in an office or other workplace) a computer terminal having a keyboard, screen and processor, or the location of this; **work study** a time and motion study; **work'table** a table on which work is done, esp. (*formerly*) a small table used by women at their needlework; **work'top** a surface designed to be used for working on, fitted e.g. along the top of kitchen units, etc.; **work'wear** overalls or other clothing for work, issued to factory-workers, etc. — **give someone the works** (*slang*) to give someone the full punitive, coercive, ceremonious, etc. treatment considered appropriate to their case; **have one's work cut out** to have one's work prescribed; to be faced with a difficult task; **Ministry of Works** (*formerly*) the body which had the management and control of public works and buildings, of which the expenses are defrayed from public money; **out of work** without employment (*adj* and *npl* **out'-of-work** unemployed (people)); **place of work** one's workplace (q.v.); **public works** building, etc. operations financed by the state; **set to work** to employ in, or to engage energetically in, a piece of work; **the works** (*colloq*) the lot, everything; **work at** to apply oneself to; **work for** (or **against**) to exert oneself in support of (or in opposition to); **work in** to intermix; to introduce carefully and deliberately (*fig*); to cause to penetrate; (of workers) to continue at work, esp. by occupying the premises and taking over the running of the business, as a protest against proposed factory closure, dismissal, etc. (*n* **work'-in**); **work into** to make way gradually into; to insinuate; to change or alter into; **work of art** a production in one of the fine arts (also *fig*); **work off** to separate and throw off; to get rid of gradually; to get rid of by effort or exertion; to repay (a debt, etc.) with one's labour rather than with money; **work on** or **upon** to act or operate upon; to influence, or try to do so; **work one's passage** to earn one's passage by services on board (also *fig*); **work out** to effect by continued labour; to solve or calculate; to develop in detail, elaborate; to come out by degrees; to turn out in the end; to reach a final (satisfactory) result; (of an athlete, etc.) to train, exercise (*n* **work'-out**); **work over** to do, work at, etc. thoroughly or elaborately; to examine in detail; to beat up or thrash (*n* **work'ing-over**)(*slang*); **work the oracle** (*slang*) to achieve the desired result by manipulation, intrigue, wire-pulling, favour, etc.; to raise money; **work to rule** (of workers) to observe all the regulations scrupulously for the express purpose of slowing down work, as a form of industrial action (*n* **work-to-rule'**); **work up** to excite, rouse; to create by slow degrees; to expand, elaborate; to use up, as material; to make one's or its way gradually upwards; to reach or achieve by effort and gradually. [O.E. *weorc*.]

world *wûrld, n* the earth; the earth and its inhabitants; the universe; the system of things; the present state of existence; any analogous state; any planet or heavenly body; public life or society; a sphere of interest or activity; environment; one's own personal immediate existence or life; the public; the materialistically minded; mundane interests; a secular life; a very large extent of country, such as the *New World*; very much or a great deal, as in *a world of good*; a large quantity; time, as in *world without end*. — *n* **world'liness**. — *n* **world'ling** someone who is devoted to worldly pursuits and temporal possessions. — *adj* **world'ly** pertaining to the world, esp. as distinguished from the world to come; devoted to this life and its enjoyments; bent on gain; having knowledge and experience of the ways of the world. — **World Bank** the popular name of the International Bank for Reconstruction and Development, an agency of the United Nations set up in 1945 to make loans to poorer countries; **world'-beater** (*colloq*) a person, product, enterprise, etc. that is supreme in its class. — *adj* **world'-beating**. — **World Court** the popular name of the Permanent Court of International Justice at the Hague; **world language** a language either widely used internationally or designed for international use. — *adj* **worldly-mind'ed** having the mind set on the present world, material possessions, etc. — **worldly-mind'edness**. — *adj* **worldly-wise'** having the wisdom of those experienced in, and affected by, the ways of the world. — **world music** popular folk music with its origins in non-western cultures, particularly African culture, esp. as produced by non-western artists; **world power** a state, group of states, etc. strong enough to make its influence felt in world politics; **World Series** (*baseball*) a set of championship matches played annually in the U.S.; **world'-view** outlook on or attitude to the world or life; **World War** a war of worldwide scope, esp. the Great War of 1914–1918 (First World War, World War I) and that of 1939–45 (Second World War, World War II). — *adj* **world'-wearied** or **-weary** tired of the world, bored with life. — *adj* and *adv* **world'wide** (extending) over, or (found) everywhere in, the world. — **all the world** everybody; everything; **all the world and his wife** (*colloq*) everybody; an ill-assorted assembly; **best** (or **worst) of both worlds** the advantage (or disadvantage) of both alternatives in a choice; **carry the world before one** to pass through every obstacle to success; **dead to the world** (*colloq*) deeply asleep; in a drunken stupor; **for all the world** (*colloq*) precisely, entirely; **Fourth World** see under **fourth**; **in the world** an intensive phrase, usu. following an interrogative pronoun or adverb; **next world** life after death; **on top of the world** (*colloq*) in a state of great elation or happiness; **out of this world** wonderful, delightful, good beyond all experience; **the New World** the western hemisphere, the Americas; **the Old World** the eastern hemisphere, comprising Europe, Africa and Asia; **the other world** the non-material sphere, the spiritual world; **the whole world** the sum of what is contained in the world; **the world's end** the most distant point possible; **think the world of** to be very fond of; **world without end** eternally (*adj* **world'-without-end'**). [O.E. *woruld, world, weorold*, orig. meaning age or life of man — *wer*, man, and the root of **old**.]

worm *wûrm, n* (*loosely*) any elongate invertebrate lacking appendages, such as an earthworm or marine worm, a flatworm or a roundworm; a grub; a maggot; anything spiral; the thread of a screw; anything that corrupts, gnaws or torments; a mean, grovelling or in any way contemptible creature; (in *pl*) any intestinal disease arising from the presence of parasitic worms. — *vi* to seek for or catch worms; to move, or make one's way, like a worm, to squirm; to work slowly or secretly. — *vt* to treat for, or rid of, worms; to work (oneself) slowly or secretly (*reflexive*); to elicit by slow and indirect means (often with *out of* or *from*). — *adj* **wormed** bored or injured by worms. — *n* **worm'er**. — *n* **worm'ery** a place, apparatus, etc. in which worms are bred, e.g. as fishing-bait. — *adj* **worm'y** like a worm; grovelling; containing a worm; abounding in worms; pertaining to worms. — **worm'-cast** a little spiral heap of earth voided by an earthworm or lugworm as it burrows. — *adj* **worm'-eaten** eaten into by worms; old; worn-out. — *adj* **worm'-eating** living habitually on worms. — **worm'-gear** a gear connecting shafts whose axes are at right angles but do not intersect, consisting of a core carrying a single- or multi-start helical thread of special form (the **worm**), meshing in sliding contact with a concave face gear-wheel (the **worm-wheel**); **worm'-gearing**; **worm'-hole** the hole made by a woodworm, earthworm, etc. — *adj* **worm'-holed** perforated by worm-holes. — **worm'-powder** a drug that expels intestinal worms, a vermifuge; **worm'-seed** any of a number of plants acting, or reputed to act, so as to destroy or expel intestinal worms, such as species of *Artemisia*; **worm'-tube** the twisted shell or tube produced by several marine worms; **worm'-wheel** see **worm-gear** above. [O.E. *wyrm*, dragon, snake, creeping animal.]

wormwood *wûrm'wood, n* the bitter plant *Artemisia absinthium*, formerly used as a cure for intestinal worms, with which absinthe is flavoured; bitterness. — cf. **absinthe**. [O.E. *wermōd*, wormwood; influenced by **worm** and **wood**.]

worn *wörn, pa p* of **wear**[1]. — *adj* that has been worn; showing effects of wear, or (*fig*) of work, worry, illness, age, etc.; (of land) exhausted; hackneyed, trite. — *adj* **worn'-out** greatly damaged or rendered useless by wear; wearied; exhausted; past, gone.

worry *wur'i, vt* to cause to be anxious; to harass; to pester; to tease; to make, get, etc. by persistent methods; (of a dog, etc.) to tear with the teeth. — *vi* to trouble oneself; to be unduly anxious; to fret: — *pa t* and *pa p* **worr'ied**. — *n* the act of worrying; trouble, perplexity; over-anxiety; a cause of this; the act of injuring by biting and shaking. — *n* **worr'ier**. — *n* **worr'iment** (*colloq*; esp. *NAm*) worry, anxiety. — *adj* **worr'isome** inclined to worry; causing trouble. — *n* and *adj* **worr'ying**. — *adv* **worr'yingly**. — **worry beads** a string of beads providing an object for the hands to play with, thus relieving mental tension — esp. popular in Greece; **worr'y-guts** (*colloq*) or **worr'ywart** (*-wört*; *colloq*, esp. *NAm*) a person who worries unnecessarily or to excess. — **I should worry!** (*colloq*) it is nothing for me to worry about; **not to worry** (*colloq*) there is no need (for you) to worry. [O.E. *wyrgan*, found in compound *āwyrgan*, to harm.]

worse *wûrs*, *adj* (used as *compar* of **bad** and **ill**) bad or evil in a greater degree; less well than before. — *adv* badly in a higher degree; less well; with more severity. — *vi* and *vt* **wors'en** to grow or make worse. — *n* **worse'ness**. — *adj* and *adv* **wors'er** a redundant comparative of *worse*. — **for better (or) for worse** see under **better**; **for the worse** to a worse state; **none the worse for** not harmed by; **put to the worse** (*Bible*) to defeat; **the worse for** harmed or impaired by; **worse off** in a worse state, esp. poorer. [O.E. *wyrsa*.]

worship *wûr'ship*, *n* adoration paid, such as to a god; religious service; profound admiration and affection; the act of revering or adoring; (with *cap*; preceded by *Your*, *His*, etc.) a title of honour in addressing or referring to certain magistrates, etc. — *vt* to pay divine honours to; to adore or idolise. — *vi* to perform acts of adoration; to take part in religious service: — *pr p* **wor'shipping**; *pa t* and *pa p* **wor'shipped**. — *adj* **wor'shipable**. — *adj* **wor'shipful** worthy of worship or honour; used as a term of respect when addressing certain dignitaries, e.g. mayors; worshipping, adoring. — *adv* **wor'shipfully**. — *n* **wor'shipper**. — **place (or house) of worship** a church, chapel, synagogue, mosque, temple, etc. [O.E. *weorthscipe* — *weorth*, *wurth*, worth, sfx. *-scipe*, -ship.]

worst *wûrst*, *adj* (used as *superl* of **bad** and **ill**) bad or evil in the highest degree. — *adv* in the highest degree of badness. — *n* the highest degree of badness; the most evil state or effect; the least good part, person, etc. in any sense. — *vt* to get the advantage over in a contest; to defeat. — **worst case** the most unfavourable conditions possible (*adj* **worst'-case**). — **at worst** in the worst possible circumstances; when taking the most negative view possible; **do one's worst** to do one's utmost in evil or mischief; to produce one's worst possible effort, whether deliberately or not; **get the worst of it** or **come off worst** to be defeated in a contest, be the loser in a given situation; **if the worst comes to the worst** if the worst, or least desirable, possibility occurs; if all else fails. [O.E. *wyrst*, *wyrrest*, *wyrresta*, from the same source as **worse**.]

worsted[1] *wŏŏst'id* or *wōōrst'id*, *n* orig., a fine wool fabric; twisted thread or yarn spun out of long, combed wool; smooth, closely-woven material made from this. — *adj* made of worsted yarn. [*Worstead*, village near Norwich, England.]

worsted[2] *wûrst'id*, *pa t* and *pa p* of **worst**.

wort[1] *wûrt*, *n* any herb or vegetable (now *rare* except in plant names such as *liverwort*). [O.E. *wyrt*, a root, herb.]

wort[2] *wûrt*, *n* malt unfermented or in the act of fermentation; such liquor boiled with hops; malt extract used as a medium for the culture of micro-organisms. [O.E. *wyrt*; related to **wort**[1].]

worth *wûrth*, *n* value; price; an amount of something (the value of) which is expressed in money or otherwise, as in *three days' worth of work*; that quality which renders a thing valuable; moral excellence; merit; importance. — *adj* equal in value to; having a certain value; worthwhile; having possessions to the value of; deserving of. — *adv* **worth'ily** (*-dh-*). — *n* **worth'iness** (*-dh-*). — *adj* **worth'less** (*-th-*) having no value, virtue, excellence, etc.; useless. — *adv* **worth'lessly**. — *n* **worth'lessness**. — *adj* **worth'y** (*-dh-*) having worth; valuable; estimable (used patronisingly); deserving (of); suited to, in keeping with (with *of*); of sufficient merit. — *n* a person of eminent worth; a notability, esp. local (sometimes *ironic*): — *pl* **wor'thies**. — *adj* **worthwhile'** such as to repay trouble and time spent on it; good; estimable. — **for all one is worth** with all one's might or energy; **for what it's worth** a phrase implying that the speaker is doubtful of the truth of what he or she has reported or unwilling to be responsible for its accuracy; also that the speaker is aware that what they are proposing may be of minimal worth; **worth it** worthwhile. [O.E. *weorth*, *wurth*, value.]

-worthy *-wûr'dhi*, *adj sfx* denoting: fit, in good condition for, as in *roadworthy*; deserving of, as in *trustworthy*, *noteworthy*. [**worth**.]

Wotan. See **Woden**.

wotcher *wot'chər*, (*slang*) *interj* a greeting, developed from (*archaic*) *what cheer*? how are you?

would *wŏŏd*, *pa t* of **will**. — *adj* **would'-be** aspiring, or merely professing, to be; meant to be.

Woulfe-bottle *wŏŏlf'-botl*, *n* a form of usu. three-necked bottle used for purifying gases, or dissolving them in suitable solvents — from the London chemist Peter *Woulfe* (*c* 1727–1803).

wound[1] *wownd*, *pa t* and *pa p* of **wind**[1,2].

wound[2] *wōōnd*, *n* any division of soft parts produced by external mechanical force — whether incised, punctured, lacerated or poisoned; any cut, bruise, hurt or injury (also *fig*). — *vt* to make a wound in (*lit* and *fig*), to injure. — *adj* **wound'able**. — *n* **wound'er**. — *n* and *adj* **wound'ing**. — *adj* **wound'wort** any of several plants renowned for their healing properties, such as the kidney-vetch, and a number of plants of genus *Stachys*. [O.E. *wund*.]

wourali or **woorali** *wōō-rä'li*, *n* the plant yielding curare (q.v.). [Caribb. variants of *kurari*; see **curare**.]

wove and **woven** *pa t* and *pa p* of **weave**. — **wove paper** paper that shows in its fabric the marks of a fine wire gauze sieve or mould.

wow *wow*, *interj* an exclamation of wonder, tinged with other emotions such as aversion, sorrow, admiration or pleasure. — *vt* (*slang*) to impress (an audience, etc.) considerably, to amaze, bowl over. — *n* rhythmic or arrhythmic changes in reproduced sound, fundamentally arising from fluctuation in speed of either reproducer or recorder; anything thrillingly good, successful, or according to one's wishes (*slang*). — *interj* **wowee'** an intensification of **wow**. — *n* **wow'ser** (*-zər*; perh. not connected with **wow**; esp. *Austr slang*) a puritanical person who tries to interfere with the pleasures of others, a spoilsport. [Imit.]

WP *abbrev* for: Warsaw Pact; weather permitting; word processing; word processor.

Wp. or **Wpfl** *abbrev* for Worshipful.

WPC *abbrev* for Woman Police Constable.

wpm *abbrev* for words per minute.

WRAC *rak*, *abbrev* for Women's Royal Army Corps.

wrack[1] *rak*, *n* destruction, devastation. — Cf. **rack**[2]. [O.E. *wræc* — *wrecan*, to drive.]

wrack[2] *rak*, *n* wreckage; any of the *Fucaceae*, the bladderwrack family of seaweeds. [M.Du. or M.L.G. *wrak*; cf. **wrack**[1].]

WRAF *raf*, *abbrev* for Women's Royal Air Force.

wraith *rāth*, *n* a spectre; an apparition, esp. of a living person, supposedly seen shortly before their death; a thin, pale person (*fig*). [Orig. Scot.; perh. O.N. *vörthr*, a guardian.]

wrangle *rang'gl*, *vi* to argue, debate, dispute; to dispute noisily or peevishly. — *vt* to obtain, persuade, spend or tire, in or by wrangling; to debate. — *n* a noisy dispute; the action of disputing, esp. noisily. — *n* **wrang'ler** someone who disputes, esp. angrily; (in the University of Cambridge) one of those who attained the first class in the examinations for mathematical honours; a herdsman, esp. of horses (*Western US*). — *n* **wrang'lership**. — *n* and *adj* **wrang'ling**. [M.E. *wranglen*, a frequentative verb allied to **wring**.]

wrap *rap*, *vt* to roll or fold together; to fold or lap round something; to enfold, envelop (*lit* and *fig*); to embrace; to hide, obscure; to cover by folding or winding something round (often with *up*). — *vi* to wind, twine; to put on wraps (with *up*); to dress warmly (with *up*): — *pr p* **wrapp'ing**; *pa t* and *pa p* **wrapped**. — *n* a protective covering for a person or thing, now esp. an outdoor garment; a single turn or fold round; (in *pl*; *colloq*) secrecy, concealment. — *n* **wrapp'er** someone who or that which wraps; a loose cover in which something is wrapped, esp. in which it is sold; a loose paper book cover; a paper band, as on a newspaper for the post. — *n* **wrapp'ing** (also **wrapp'ing-paper**) coarse paper for parcels, etc. — **wrap'around** (also **wrap'round**) a wraparound skirt, blouse, dress, etc.; (on a visual display unit) the automatic division of input into lines, whereby a new line is started as the last character position on the previous line is occupied; (also **wrap'round**) a plate of flexible material, such as plastic, rubber or metal that wraps round a cylindrical plate (*printing*); (also **wrap'round**) a separately printed sheet that is wrapped round a gathering for binding (*printing*); (also **wrap'round**) a strip advertising a special offer, etc. wrapped round the dust-cover of a book, etc. — *adj* (also **wrap'over** and **wrap'round**) (of a blouse, skirt, dress, etc.) designed so as to be wrapped round the body with one edge overlapping the other, and tied, tucked in, etc. rather than fastened by a zip, row of buttons, etc.; (also **wrap'round**; of a windscreen, etc.) curving round from the front to the sides. — **wrap'over** a wraparound skirt or other garment. — **keep under wraps** (*colloq*) to keep secret, conceal; **take the wraps off** (*colloq*) to reveal, disclose; **wrapped up in** bound up in; comprised in; engrossed in, devoted to; **wrap up** (*slang*) to settle completely; to have completely in hand; (as *interj*) be quiet! [M.E. *wrappen*, also *wlappen*.]

wrasse *ras*, *n* any of several brightly-coloured bony fishes of the family *Labridae*, including many species on European and N. African coasts. [Cornish *wrach*.]

wrath *röth* or *roth*, *n* violent anger; holy indignation; violence or severity (*fig*). — *adj* **wrath'ful** very angry; springing from, expressing, or characterised by, wrath. — *adv* **wrath'fully**. — *n* **wrath'fulness**. [O.E. *wrǣththu* — *wrāth*, adj.]

wreak *rēk*, *vt* to inflict; to effect or bring about; to bestow; to give expression, vent or free play to; to find expression or an outlet for (*reflexive*). — *n* **wreak'er**. [O.E. *wrecan*.]

wreath *rēth*, *n* a circlet of interwoven materials, esp. flowers, etc.; a single twist or coil in a helical object; a drift or curl of vapour or smoke: — *pl* **wreaths** (*rēdhz*). — *vt* **wreathe** (*rēdh*) to form by twisting; to twist together; to form into a wreath; to twine about or encircle; to encircle, decorate, etc. with a wreath or wreaths. — *vi* to be interwoven; to twine; to twist; to form coils. — *adj* **wreathed** (or *rēdh'id*). [O.E. *writha*; related to *wrīthan*, to writhe.]

wreck *rek*, *n* destruction; the act of wrecking or destroying; the destruction of a ship; a badly damaged ship; shipwrecked property; anything found underwater and brought ashore; the remains of anything ruined; a person ruined mentally or physically. — *vt* to destroy or disable; to cause the wreck of (a ship); to involve in a wreck; to ruin. — *vi* to suffer wreck or ruin. — *n* **wreck'age** the act of wrecking; wrecked material; a person or persons whose life is or lives are ruined. — *n* **wreck'er** a person who purposely causes a wreck or who plunders wreckage; someone who criminally ruins anything; a person who (or machine which) demolishes or destroys, esp. old cars; a person or ship employed in recovering disabled vessels or their cargo; a person, vehicle or train employed in removing wreckage; a person who is employed in demolishing buildings, etc. — *n* and *adj* **wreck'ing**. [A.Fr. *wrec*, *wrek*, etc.; of Scand. origin.]

Wren *ren*, *n* a member of the Women's Royal Naval Service.

wren *ren*, *n* any of several kinds of small songbirds, with very short rounded wings, and a short tail carried erect; extended to various very small birds. [O.E. *wrenna*, *wrænna*.]

wrench *rench* or *rensh*, *vt* to wring or pull with a twist; to force by violence; to sprain; to distort. — *vi* to perform or to undergo a violent wrenching. — *n* an act or instance of wrenching; a violent twist; a sprain; an instrument for turning nuts, etc., esp. one with adjustable jaws; emotional pain at parting or change. [O.E. *wrencan*, to deceive, twist, *wrenc*, deceit, twisting.]

wrest *rest*, *vt* to turn, twist; to twist, extract or take away by force or unlawfully; to get by toil; to twist from truth or from its natural meaning; to misinterpret. — *n* the act of wresting; violent pulling and twisting; distortion. — *n* **wrest'er**. [O.E. *wrǣstan*.]

wrestle *res'l*, *vi* (often with *with*) to contend by grappling and trying to throw another person down; to struggle; to strive; to apply oneself keenly; to writhe, wriggle; to proceed with great effort (*lit* and *fig*). — *vt* to contend with in wrestling; to push with a wriggling or wrestling motion; (with *out*) to go through, carry out, etc. with a great struggle. — *n* the act, or a bout, of wrestling; a struggle. — *n* **wrest'ler**. — *n* **wrest'ling** the action of the verb to wrestle; a sport or exercise in which two people struggle to throw and pin each other to the ground, governed by certain fixed rules. [O.E. *wrǣstan*, to wrest.]

wretch *rech*, *n* a most miserable, unfortunate or pitiable person; a worthless or despicable person; a being or creature (in pity, sometimes admiration). — *adj* **wretch'ed** (*-id*) very miserable; unfortunate, pitiable; distressingly bad; despicable; worthless. — *adv* **wretch'edly**. — *n* **wretch'edness**. [O.E. *wrecca*, an outcast — *wrecan*; see **wreak**.]

wrick or **rick** *rik*, *vt* to twist, sprain, strain. — *n* a sprain, strain. [Allied to L.G. *wrikken*, to turn.]

wrier and **wriest**. See under **wry**.

wriggle *rig'l*, *vi* and *vt* to twist to and fro; to move or advance sinuously (*lit* and *fig*); to use evasive tricks (usu. with *out of*). — *n* the act or motion of wriggling; a sinuous marking, turn or bend. — *n* **wrigg'ler**. — *n* **wrigg'ling**. — *adj* **wrigg'ly**. [L.G. *wriggeln*.]

wright *rīt*, *n* a maker or repairer (chiefly used in compounds, as in **shipwright**, etc.). [O.E. *wyrhta*, *wryhta*, related to *wyrht*, a work — *wyrcan*, to work.]

wring *ring*, *vt* to twist; to expel moisture from by hand twisting or by roller pressure; to force out, esp. by twisting (also *fig*); to force out; to clasp and shake fervently; to clasp (the hands) convulsively (in grief or agitation); to distress or afflict; to extort; to distort. — *vi* to writhe; to twist: — *pa t* and *pa p* **wrung**. — *n* an act or instance of wringing. — *n* **wring'er** someone who wrings; a machine for forcing water from wet clothes (also **wring'ing-machine**). — *n* **wring'ing**. — **wring from** to extort from; **wringing wet** so wet that water can be wrung out; extremely wet; **wring out** to squeeze out by twisting; to remove from liquid and twist so as to expel the drops. [O.E. *wringan*, to twist.]

wrinkle[1] *ring'kl*, *n* a small crease or furrow on a surface; a crease or ridge in the skin (esp. as a result of ageing); an unevenness; a minor problem or difficulty to be smoothed out. — *vt* to contract into wrinkles or furrows; to make rough. — *vi* to shrink into ridges. — *adj* **wrink'led**. — *adj* **wrink'ly** full of wrinkles; liable to be wrinkled. — *n* (esp. in *pl*; *derog*) an elderly person.

wrinkle[2] *ring'kl*, (*colloq*) *n* a tip or valuable hint; a handy dodge or trick; an idea, notion or suggestion. [Perh. from O.E. *wrenc*, a trick; perh. same as **wrinkle**[1].]

wrist *rist*, *n* the joint by which the hand is united to the arm, the carpus; the part of the body where that joint is, or the part of a garment covering it; a corresponding part of an animal; a wrist-pin. — *n* **wrist'let** a band or strap for the wrist; a bracelet; a watch for wearing on the wrist (also **wrist'watch** or **wrist'let-watch**); handcuff (*slang*). — *adj* **wrist'y** making extensive use of the wrist(s), as in a golf shot, etc. — **wrist'band** a band or part of a sleeve covering the wrist; **wrist'-pin** a pin joining the end of a connecting rod to the end of a piston-rod. — **a slap (or smack) on the wrist** (*colloq*) a small (and often, by implication, ineffectual) punishment. [O.E.]

writ[1]: **writ large** *rit lärj*, written in large letters, hence (*fig*) on a large scale, or very obvious. [*writ*, archaic past t. and p. of **write**.]

writ[2] *rit*, *n* a legal or formal document; a written document by which a person is summoned or required to do, or refrain from doing, something (*law*). — **Holy Writ** the Scriptures; **serve a writ on** to deliver a summons to. [O.E. (*ge*)*writ*.]

write *rīt*, *vt* to form (letters or words) with a pen, pencil or other implement on a (usu. paper) surface; to express in writing; to compose; to draw, engrave, etc.; to put (the necessary) writing on (a cheque, form, etc.); to record; to decree or foretell; to indicate (a quality, condition, etc.) clearly; to communicate, or to communicate with, by letter. — *vi* to perform, or to practise, the act of writing; to compose (e.g. articles, novels, etc.); to work as an author; to compose, or to send, a letter; to communicate with a person by letter: — *pr p* **wrīt'ing**; *pa t* **wrōte**; *pa p* **written** (*rit'n*). — *n* **wrīt'er** someone who writes; an author; a person who paints lettering for signs; an ordinary legal practitioner in a Scottish country town. — *adj* **writ'erly** having or showing an accomplished literary style. — *n* **wrīt'ership** the office of a writer. — *n* **wrīt'ing** the act of one who writes; that which is written; (often *pl*) a literary production or composition; handwriting, penmanship; the state of being written. — *adj* **writt'en** reduced to or expressed in writing (opp. of *oral*). — *adj* **write'-in** (*NAm*) of or relating to a candidate not listed in the ballot paper, but whose name is written in by the voter. — *n* such a candidate or vote. — **write'-off** a car so badly damaged that the cost of repair would exceed the car's value; a total loss; see also **write off** below; **writ'ing-book** a book of paper for practising penmanship; **wrīt'ing-case** a portable case containing materials for writing; **wrīt'ing-desk** a desk (often with a sloping top) for writing at; **wrīt'ing-paper** paper finished with a smooth surface, for writing on; **wrīt'ing-table** a table fitted or used for writing on; **written law** statute law as distinguished from common law. — *adj* **writt'en-off** (of a car) damaged beyond reasonable repair; completely ruined; see also **write off** below. — **write down** to put down in written characters; to write in disparagement of; to write so as to be intelligible or attractive to people considered to be of lower intelligence or to have inferior taste (with *to* or *for*); to reduce the book value of an asset (*n* **write'-down**); **write for** or **write in for** to apply for; to send away for; **write off** to cancel, esp. in book-keeping, to take (e.g. a bad debt) off the books; to regard or accept as an irredeemable loss; to destroy or damage (a car, etc.) irredeemably (*n* **write'-off**; *adj* **writt'en-off**); **write out** to transcribe; to write in full; to exhaust one's mental resources by too much writing (*reflexive*); to remove a character or scene from the script of a film, broadcast, etc.; **Writer to the Signet** a member of an ancient society of solicitors in Scotland who have the exclusive privilege of preparing crown writs; **write up** to put a full description of in writing; to write a report or review of; to write in praise of, esp. to praise above its merits; to bring the writing of up to date; to increase the book value of an asset (*n* **write'-up**); **writing** (also, esp. *US*, **handwriting**) **on the wall** a happening or sign foreshowing downfall and disaster (from the Bible: Dan. v. 5 ff.). [O.E. *wrītan*, orig. meaning to scratch.]

writhe *rīdh*, *vt* to twist; to coil; to wreathe; to twist violently; to contort. — *vi* to twist, esp. in pain. — *n* and *adj* **wrīth'ing**. — *adv* **wrīth'ingly**. [O.E. *wrīthan*, to twist; O.N. *rītha*; cf. **wreath**, **wrest** and **wrist**.]

written. See **write**.

WRNS *renz*, *abbrev* for Women's Royal Naval Service.

wrong *rong*, *adj* not according to rule; incorrect; erroneous; not in accordance with moral law; wicked; not that (thing) which is required, intended, advisable or suitable; amiss, unsatisfactory; not working properly, out of order; mistaken, misinformed; under, inner, reverse (side, face, etc.). — *n* whatever is not right or just; any injury done to another; wrongdoing; the state or position of being or doing wrong. — *adv* not correctly; not in the right way; astray. — *vt* to do wrong to; to deprive of some right; to defraud; to behave unjustly towards; to dishonour. — *n* **wrong'er** a person who wrongs another. — *adj* **wrong'ful** wrong; unjust; unlawful; not legitimate. — *adv* **wrong'fully**. — *n* **wrong'fulness**. — *adv* **wrong'ly**. — *n* **wrong'ness**. — **wrong'doer**; **wrongdo'ing** evil or wicked action or conduct. — *vt* **wrong-foot'** to cause to be (physically or mentally) off balance, or at a disadvantage. — *adj* **wrong-head'ed** obstinate and perverse, adhering stubbornly to wrong principles or policy. — *adv* **wrong-head'edly**. — **wrong-head'edness**. — **get on the wrong side of someone** to arouse dislike or antagonism in someone; **get out of bed on the wrong side** to wake up in the morning in a bad mood; **go wrong** to fail to work properly; to make a mistake or mistakes; to stray from virtue; **in the wrong** holding an erroneous view or unjust position; guilty of error or injustice; **private wrong** a violation of the civil or personal rights of an individual; **public wrong** a crime which affects the community; **put in the wrong** to cause to appear in error, guilty of injustice, etc. [O.E. *wrang*, a wrong.]

wrote *rōt*, *pa t* of **write**.

wroth *rōth* or *roth*, (*literary* or *poetic*) *adj* wrathful; in commotion, stormy. [O.E. *wrāth*, angry.]

wrought *röt*, *adj* fashioned; ornamented; manufactured; (of metal) beaten into shape, shaped by tools. — **wrought'-iron** malleable iron, iron containing only a very small amount of other elements, but containing slag in the form of particles elongated in one direction, more rust-resistant than steel and welding more easily. — *adj* **wrought'-up** in an agitated condition, over-excited. [Archaic past t. and past p. of **work**; O.E. *worhte*, *geworht*, past t. and past p. of *wyrcan*, *wircan*, to work.]

WRP *abbrev* for Workers' Revolutionary Party.

wrung *rung*, *pa t* and *pa p* of **wring**.

WRVS *abbrev* for Women's Royal Voluntary Service (previously **WVS**).

wry *rī*, *adj* (*compar* **wry'er** or **wri'er**, *superl* **wry'est** or **wri'est**) twisted or turned to one side; not in the right direction; expressing displeasure or irony (*fig*); perverse, distorted (*fig*). — *vt* to give a twist to; to pervert. — *adv* wryly. — *adv* **wry'ly**. — *n* **wry'ness**. — **wry'bill** a New Zealand bird similar to the plovers with bill bent sideways. — **wry'-neck** a twisted position of the head on the neck due to disease of the cervical vertebrae or to spasms (esp. rheumatic) in the muscles of the neck, torticollis; **wry'neck** a member of a genus of small birds similar to the woodpecker, which twist round their heads strangely when surprised. — **make a wry face** (or **mouth**) to pucker up the face (or mouth) as in tasting anything bitter or astringent, or as a sign of disgust or pain. [O.E. *wrīgian*, to strive, move, turn.]

WS *abbrev* for: Western Samoa (I.V.R.); Writer to the Signet.

wunderkind *vōōn'dər-kint*, *n* a child prodigy; someone who shows great talent, attains great success, etc. at an early (or comparatively early) age: — *pl* **wun'derkinder** (*-kin-dər*). [Ger., lit. wonder child.]

wunner. See **oner** under **one**.

wurst *vōōrst* or *wûrst*, *n* a large German sausage of several types. [Ger., lit. something rolled.]

wushu, Wushu, wu shu or **Wu Shu** *wōō'shōō*, *n* the Chinese martial arts, kung fu. [Chin., — *wu*, military, *shu*, art.]

wuther *wudh'ər*, (*dialect*) *vi* (of the wind) to make a sullen roaring; to throw or beat violently. — *adj* **wuth'ering** (of wind) blowing strongly and making a roaring sound; (of a place) characterised by windy weather of this kind. [From O.N.]

WV *abbrev* for: St Vincent, Windward Islands (I.V.R.); West Virginia (U.S. state; also **W.Va**).

WVS. See **WRVS**.

WWF *abbrev* for World Wide Fund for Nature (formerly World Wildlife Fund).

WY or **Wyo**. *abbrev* for Wyoming (U.S. state).

Wy *abbrev* for Way (in street names).

wyandotte *wī'an-dot*, *n* a breed of domestic fowl, of American origin. [From the N. Am. tribe so called.]

wych-elm *wich'-elm*, *n* a common wild elm, also called Scotch elm or witch-hazel. — **wych'-hazel** same as **witch-hazel**. [**witch**[2] and **elm**.]

wyn. See **wen**[2].

wynd *wīnd*, (*Scot*) *n* a lane or narrow alley in a town. [Same as **wind**[2].]

wysiwyg *wiz'i-wig*, (*comput*) an acronym for *what you see* (i.e. on the screen) *is what you get* (on the print-out).

wyvern. See **wivern**.

X or **x** *eks*, *n* the twenty-fourth letter in the modern English alphabet; an object or figure in the shape of an X.

X *symbol* for: (also **x** or *x*) the first variable, unknown, or yet to be ascertained, quantity or factor (*alg*, etc.); (roman numeral) 10; Christ (see also **chi**), also used as an abbreviation as in **Xmas** and **Xian** (Christian); a former category of cinema film to which persons under eighteen will not be admitted (superseded by the designation **18**). — **X'-chromosome** a chromosome associated with sex determination, usu. occurring paired in the female zygote and cell, and alone in the male zygote and cell.

xanth- *zanth-* or **xantho-** *zan-thō-* or *-tho'-*, *combining form* denoting yellow. — *n* **xanthein** (*zan'thē-in*) a soluble yellow colouring matter present in flowers. — *n* **xanthene** (*zan'thēn*) a white crystalline compound of carbon, hydrogen and oxygen, from which are derived **xanthene dyestuffs**. — *adj* **xan'thic** of a yellow tint, esp. as a description of flowers; pertaining to xanthin or xanthine; designating **xanthic acid**, any of a series of compounds of an alcohol with carbon disulphide. — *n* **xan'thin** name given to the insoluble yellow colouring matter of various flowers; (usu. **xan'thine**) a white substance, closely allied to uric acid, found in muscle tissue, the liver and other organs, urine, etc., leaving a lemon-yellow residue when evaporated with nitric acid. — *n* **xanthochroia** (*-thō-kroi'ə*) yellowness of the skin. — *adj* **xanthochrō'ic** or **xan'thochroid** (*-kroid*; also used as *n*). — *n* **xanthochroism** (*-thok'rō-izm*) a condition in which all pigments other than yellows disappear (as in goldfish) or normal colouring is replaced by yellow. — *n* **xanthochrō'mia** any yellowish discoloration, esp. of the cerebrospinal fluid. — *adj* **xanthochroous** (*-thok'rō-əs*) xanthochroic. — *n* **xanthoma** (*zan-thō'mə*) a yellow tumour composed of fibrous tissue and of cells containing cholesterol ester, occurring on the skin (e.g. in diabetes) or on the sheaths of tendons, or in any tissue of the body. — *adj* **xanthom'atous**. — *n* **xanthophyll** (*zan'thō-fil*) one of the two yellow pigments present in the normal chlorophyll mixture of green plants. — *n* **xanthop'sia** the condition in which objects appear yellow to the observer, as in jaundice or after taking santonin. — *n* **xanthop'terin** or **xanthop'terine** (*-in*) a yellow pigment obtained from the wings of yellow butterflies and the urine of mammals. — *adj* **xanthous** (*zan'thəs*) yellow. [Gr. *xanthos*, yellow.]

X-chromosome. See under **X** (symbol).

Xe (*chem*) *symbol* for xenon.

xebec *zē'bek*, *n* a small three-masted vessel much used by the former pirates of Algiers. [Fr. *chebec*, influenced by Sp. form; perh. from Turkish or Arabic.]

xen- *zen-* or *zēn-* or **xeno-** *zen-ō-* or *zi-no'-*, *combining form* denoting strange or foreign. — *n* **xenogamy** (*zen-og'ə-mi*; Gr. *gamos*, marriage; *bot*) cross-fertilisation. — *adj* **xenogenous** (*zi-noj'i-nəs*) due to outside cause. — *n* **xen'ograft** a graft from a member of a different species. — *n* **xen'olith** a fragment of rock of extraneous origin which has been incorporated in magma. — *n* **xenon** (*zen'* or *zē'non*) a zero-valent element (symbol **Xe**; atomic no. 54), a heavy gas present in the atmosphere in proportion of 1 : 17×10^7 by volume, and also a fission product. — *n* **xen'ophile** someone who likes foreigners or things foreign. — *n* **xen'ophobe** (*-fōb*) someone who fears or hates foreigners or things foreign. — *n* **xenophobia** (*-fō'bi-ə*) fear or hatred of things foreign. — *n* **Xen'opus** a genus of African aquatic frogs (see **platanna (frog)**). — **xenon lamp** a high-pressure lamp, containing traces of xenon, used in film projectors, high-speed photography, etc. [Gr. *xenos*, (noun) guest, host, stranger, (adj.) strange, foreign.]

xer- *zēr-* or **xero-** *zē-rō-*, *combining form* denoting dry. — *n* **xerasia** (*zi-rā'si-ə*) an abnormal or unhealthy dryness of the hair. — *n* **xeroderma** (*zē-rō-dûr'mə*) or **xeroder'mia** a disease characterised by abnormal dryness of the skin and by overgrowth of its horny layer. — *adj* **xerodermat'ic**, **xeroder'matous** or **xeroder'mic**. — *adj* **xerograph'ic**. — *n* **xero'graphy** a non-chemical photographic process in which the plate is sensitised electrically and developed by dusting with electrically-charged fine powder. — *n* **xeroma** (*-rō'mə*) xerophthalmia. — *adj* **xerophilous** (*-of'il-əs*) of a plant, tolerant of a very dry habitat. — *n* **xeroph'ily** adaptation to dry conditions. — *n* **xērophthalmia** (*-of-thal'mi-ə*) a dry lustreless condition of the conjunctiva due to deficiency of vitamin A in the diet. — *n* **xē'rophyte** (*-fīt*; Gr. *phyton*, plant) a plant able to inhabit places where the water supply is scanty, or where conditions, e.g. excess of salts, make it difficult to take in water. — *adj* **xerophytic** (*-fit'ik*) able to withstand drought. — *n* **xerō'sis** abnormal dryness, e.g. of the skin, mouth, eyes, etc. — *n* **xerostoma** (*-os'tom-ə*; Gr. *stoma*, mouth) or **xerostō'mia** excessive dryness of the mouth due to insufficiency of the secretions. — *n* **xerotes** (*zē'rō-tēz*) abnormal dryness of bodily tissues. — *adj* **xerotic** (*-rot'ik*). [Gr. *xēros*, dry.]

Xerox® *zē'roks*, *n* a registered trademark used in respect of copying machines operating a xerographic method of reproduction; a copy so produced. — *vt* to produce a copy by this method.

Xhosa *kō'sə* or *-zə*, *n* a group of Bantu-speaking tribes from the Cape district of South Africa; a member of one of these tribes; the language of these tribes. — *adj* **Xho'san**.

xi *zī*, *ksī* or *ksē*, *n* the fourteenth letter of the Greek alphabet (Ξ or ξ).

Xian *abbrev* for Christian (see **X** (symbol)).

xiph- *zif-* or **xipho-** *zif-o-* or *-ō-*, *combining form* denoting sword. — *adj* **xiph'oid** or **xiphoid'al** sword-shaped. [Gr. *xiphos*, a sword.]

Xmas *eks'məs* or *kris'məs*, *n* short for **Christmas** (see **X** (symbol)).

X-particle *eks'-pär-ti-kl*, (*phys*) a meson.

X-ray *eks'-rā*, *n* an electromagnetic ray of very short wavelength which can penetrate matter opaque to light-rays, produced when cathode rays impinge on matter — discovered by Röntgen in 1895. — Also *adj*. — *n* a photograph taken by X-rays. — *vt* to photograph or treat by, or otherwise expose to, X-rays. — **X-ray telescope** a telescope designed to investigate the emission of X-rays from stars; **X-ray therapy** the use of X-rays for medical treatment; **X-ray tube** an evacuated tube in which

X-rays are emitted from a metal target placed obliquely opposite to an incandescent cathode whose rays impinge on the target. [**X** (symbol) after its unknown nature on discovery; translated from orig. Ger. term *X-Strahlen* (pl.) — *Strahl*, a ray.]

xyl- *zīl-* or **xylo-** *zi-lō-*, *combining form* denoting wood. — *n* **xylem** (*zī'ləm*) woody tissue in trees and plants, concerned in the conduction of aqueous solutions, and with mechanical support. — *n* **xy'lene** any of three dimethyl-benzenes, occurring in coal-tar but not separable by fractional distillation. — *n* **xy'lenol** a synthetic resin, any of six monohydric phenols derived from xylenes. — *adj* **xy'lic** pertaining to xylem; designating any of six acids, derivatives of xylene. — *n* **xy'litol** a sweet crystalline alcohol derived from xylose, that can be used as a sugar substitute. — *n* **xy'locarp** a hard and woody fruit, such as a coconut. — *adj* **xylocarp'ous.** — *n* **xylography** (*zī-log'rə-fi*) the art of engraving on wood. — *n* **xy'lograph** an impression or print from a wood block; an impression of the grain of wood for surface decoration. — *n* **xylog'rapher.** — *adj* **xylograph'ic** or **xylograph'ical.** — *adj* **xy'loid** woody, ligneous. — *n* **xy'lol** (L. *oleum*, oil) xylene. — *n* **xylol'ogy** the study of the structure of wood. — *adj* **xylon'ic** designating an acid obtained by oxidising xylose. — *n* **xylonite** or **Xy'lonite®** a non-thermosetting plastic of the nitrocellulose type. — *adj* **xylophagous** (*-lof'ə-gəs*) wood-eating. — *adj* **xyloph'ilous** fond of wood, living on or in wood. — *n* **xy'lophone** a musical instrument consisting of a graduated series of wooden bars which are struck by wooden hammers; an instrument used to measure the elastic properties of wood. — *adj* **xylophon'ic.** — *n* **xyloph'onist.** — *n* **xylopyrog'raphy** (*-pī-*) designs on wood made with a hot poker. — *n* **xylorim'ba** an extended xylophone combining the ranges of the *xylo*phone and the ma*rimba*. — *n* **xy'lose** a pentose found in many plants, also known as *wood-sugar*. — *n* **xy'lyl** (*-lil*) any of the univalent radicals of the xylenes or their derivatives. [Gr. *xylon*, wood.]

xyster *zis'tər*, *n* a surgeon's instrument for scraping bones. [Gr. *xystēr*, an engraving tool.]

Y or **y** *wī*, *n* the twenty-fifth letter of the modern English alphabet. Early printers used y as a substitute for thorn (þ), which their founts lacked, and it came to be used in this way in manuscripts and inscriptions, as in *ye* for *the*; something similar to the letter Y in shape. — **Y'-fronts** underpants for men or boys with a front seamed opening forming an inverted Y shape; **Y'-level** or **wye level** a type of surveyors level whose essential characteristic is the support of the telescope, namely, Y-shaped rests in which it may be rotated, or reversed end-for-end.

Y or **Y.** *abbrev* for yen (Japanese currency).

Y *symbol* for: (also **y** or *y*) a variable, unknown or yet to be ascertained quantity or factor, used as distinct from and in addition to X (or **x** or *x*) (*alg*, etc.); yttrium (*chem*). — **Y'-chromosome** one of a pair of chromosomes associated with sex-determination (the other being the **X-chromosome**).

y or **y.** *abbrev* for: yard; year.

-y[1] *-i*, *sfx* forming adjectives with the senses 'characterised by', 'full of', 'having the quality of', 'inclined to', as in *icy*, *sandy*, *slangy*, *shiny*. [O.E. *-ig*.]

-y[2] *-i*, *sfx* forming nouns denoting: (1) a diminutive, or a term of affection, as in *doggy*, *daddy*; (2) a person or thing having a certain specified characteristic, as in *fatty*. [Orig. Scot. **-ie** in names, etc.]

-y[3] *-i*, *sfx* forming nouns denoting a quality, state, action or entity, as in *fury*, *jealousy*, *subsidy*, *society*. [O.Fr. *-ie* — L. *-ia*.]

yabber *yab'ər*, (*colloq*; orig. and esp. *Austr*) *vi* to talk, jabber. — *n* talk, conversation, jabber. [Aboriginal *yabba*, language — perh. modified by **jabber**.]

yabby or **yabbie** *yab'i*, (*Austr*) *n* a small freshwater crayfish, often used as bait. [Aboriginal.]

yacht *yot*, *n* a light fast-sailing vessel; a sailing or powered vessel fitted up for pleasure-trips or racing. — *vi* to sail or race in a yacht. — *n* **yacht'er**. — *n* **yacht'ie** (*colloq*; esp. *Austr*) a yachtsman, yachtswoman or yachting enthusiast. — *n* and *adj* **yacht'ing**. — **yacht'-club** a club for yachters; **yachts'man** or **yachts'woman** a person who keeps or sails a yacht; **yachts'manship** the art of sailing a yacht. — **land'-** or **sand'-yacht** a wheeled boat with sails, for running on land, usu. sea-beaches; **land'-** or **sand'-yachting**. [Du. *jacht*, from *jagen*, to chase.]

yack, yak *yak*, or in full **yackety-** (or **yakety-**)**-yak** *ya-ki-ti-yak'*, (*slang*) *vi* to talk persistently, esp. in a foolish or gossiping manner. — *n* persistent, often idle or stupid talk. [Imit.]

Yagi *yä'gi* or *yag'i*, *adj* denoting a type of highly directional television or radio astronomy aerial, with several elements in a close parallel arrangement, fixed at right angles to a central support that points in the direction of strongest reception. [Hidetsugu *Yagi*, (b. 1886), Japanese electrical engineer.]

yah[1] *yä*. Variant of **yea**.

yah[2] *yä*, *interj* an exclamation of derision, contemptuous defiance (also **yah-boo'** and **yah-boo sucks**) or disgust.

yahoo *yä'hōō* or *yä-hōō'*, *n* a brutal or boorish lout. [*Yahoo*, a name given by Swift in *Gulliver's Travels* to a class of animals with the forms of men but the understanding and passions of brutes.]

Yahweh *yä'wā* or **Yahveh** *yä'vā*, *n* Jehovah (q.v.). — *n* **Yah'wist** or **Yah'vist** a Jehovist.

yak[1] *yak*, *n* a species of ox found in Tibet, and domesticated there, having a thick coat of long silky hair. [Tibetan.]

yak[2], **yakety-yak**. See under **yack**.

Yakut *yä-kōōt'*, *n* a member of a mixed Turkish race in Siberia, in the Lena district; their Turkic language.

yakuza *yə-kōō'za*, *n* a Japanese gangster, typically involved in drug-dealing, gambling, extortion, gun-running or prostitution: — *pl* **yaku'za**. [Jap., from *ya*, eight, *ku*, nine, *za* or *sa*, three, this being the worst hand of cards in gambling.]

Yale® *yāl* or **Yale lock** (*lok*), *n* a trademark for a type of cylinder lock operated by a flat key with a notched upper edge. [Linus *Yale* (1821–68), American locksmith.]

yam *yam*, *n* a large tuberous edible root like the potato, grown in tropical countries; any plant of the genus *Dioscorea*, some species of which yield these tubers; a sweet-potato (*Southern US*). [Port. *inhame*.]

yammer *yam'ər*, (*dialect* and *colloq*) *vi* to lament or wail; to whine; to make an outcry. — Also *n*. — *n* and *adj* **yamm'ering**. [O.E. *gēom(e)rian* — *gēomor*, sad.]

yang *yang*, *n* (also with *cap*) one of the two opposing and complementary principles of Chinese philosophy, religion, medicine, etc. influencing destiny and governing nature, seen as the positive, masculine, light, warm, active element (cf. **yin**). [Chin., bright.]

Yank *yank*, (*colloq*) *n* an inhabitant of the United States. [**Yankee**.]

yank *yangk*, (*colloq*) *vt* to carry, move or pull with a jerk. — *vi* to pull or jerk vigorously (*colloq*); to move actively (*fig*). — *n* a strong jerk (*colloq*).

Yankee *yang'ki*, *n* in America, a citizen of the New England States, or an inhabitant of the northern United States, as opposed to the southern; in British usage, generally an inhabitant of the United States. — Also *adj*. — **Yankee-Doo'dle** a Yankee (from an American popular song). [Prob. Du. *Jantje*, Johnnie, or *Jan Kees*, John Cornelius, both said to be used by the Dutch settlers as nicknames for British settlers.]

yap *yap*, *vi* (of a small dog) to bark sharply or constantly; to speak constantly, esp. in a noisy, irritating or foolish manner (*colloq*). — *n* a yelp; incessant, foolish chatter (*colloq*). — *n* **yapp'er**. — *adj* **yapp'y**. [Imit.]

yapp *yap*, *n* a limp leather binding in which the cover overlaps the edges of the book. [*Yapp*, a 19th-cent. London bookseller.]

yapper. See **yap**.

yappy[1]. See **yap**.

yappy[2] or **yappie** *yap'i*, (*colloq*) *n* a *y*oung *a*spiring *p*rofessional, or (more recently) *y*oung *a*ffluent *p*arent. [Acronymic.]

yard[1] *yärd*, *n* in English-speaking countries, a measure of 3 feet or 36 inches and equivalent to 0·9144 metre; a piece of material this length; a long beam on a mast for spreading square sails. — *n* **yard'age** the aggregate number of yards; the length, area or volume measured or estimated in linear, square or cubic yards; the cutting of coal, etc. at so much a yard. — **yard'-arm** either half of a ship's yard (right or left) from the centre to the end; **yard'stick** a stick

3 feet long; any standard of measurement or comparison (*fig*). — **by the yard** sold or measured in yard lengths; in large quantities (*fig*); **yard of ale** a tall slender glass for ale, etc., or its contents. [O.E. *gyrd, gierd*, a rod, measure.]

yard[2] *yärd, n* an enclosed place, esp. near a building, often used in composition, as in *backyard, courtyard, farmyard, prison-yard*, or where any special work is carried on, as in *brickyard, wood-yard, dockyard*; a garden (*US*). — **the Yard** New Scotland Yard, the London Metropolitan Police headquarters. [O.E. *geard*, fence, dwelling, enclosure.]

Yardie *yär'di*, (*slang*; orig. *WIndies*) *n* a member of a West Indian gang or Mafia-like syndicate involved in drug-dealing and related crime. — Also *adj*. — **Yardie squad** a special police squad set up to tackle Yardie activities. [Jamaican dialect *yard*, a dwelling, home or (by Jamaicans abroad) Jamaica.]

yarmulka or **yarmulke** *yär'məl-kə, n* the skullcap worn by Jewish males, esp. during prayers or ceremonial occasions. [Yiddish, — Pol. *yarmulka*, small cap.]

yarn *yärn, n* spun thread; one of the threads of a rope, or these collectively; a sailor's story, spun out to some length, and often having incredible elements; a story generally (*colloq*). — *vi* to tell stories. [O.E. *gearn*, thread.]

yarrow *yar'ō, n* a strong-scented plant (*Achillea millefolium*, or similar species of milfoil). [O.E. *gearwe*.]

yashmak *yash'mak* or *yash-mak', n* the double veil worn by Muslim women in public, which leaves only the eyes uncovered. [Ar. *yashmaq*.]

yataghan or **yatagan** *yat'ə-gan, n* a long Turkish dagger, without guard, usu. curved. [Turk. *yātāghan*.]

yaw *yö, vi* (of a ship) to deviate temporarily from, or turn out of the line of, its course; to move unsteadily or zigzag (*fig*); to deviate in a horizontal direction from the line of flight (*aeronautics*). — *vt* to cause to deviate from course, zigzag, etc. — *n* a deviation from the course; the angular motion of an aircraft in a horizontal plane about the normally vertical axis. [Cf. O.N. *jaga*, to move to and fro, like a door on its hinges.]

yawey. See **yaws.**

yawl *yöl, n* a ship's small boat, generally with four or six oars; a small sailing-boat with jigger and curtailed mainboom. [Du. *jol*.]

yawn *yön, vi* to take a deep involuntary breath from drowsiness, boredom, etc.; to gape; to be wide open, like a chasm. — *vt* to render, make or effect by yawning; to utter with a yawn. — *n* an involuntary deep breath brought on by weariness or boredom, etc.; a chasm, opening; a boring event, person, etc. (*colloq*). — *adj* **yawn'ing** gaping, opening wide; drowsy. — *n* the action of the verb to yawn. — *adv* **yawn'ingly**. — *adj* **yawn'y** or **yawn'ey**. [O.E. *gānian*, to yawn, and *geonian, ginian*, to gape widely.]

yawp *yöp*, (chiefly *US*) *vi* to utter or cry harshly or hoarsely and noisily; to yelp, bark. — *n* such a harsh (etc.) cry. — *n* **yawp'er**. [Imit.; cf. **yap** and **yelp.**]

yaws *yöz, n* a tropical epidemic and contagious disease of the skin — also known as *framboesia, button scurvy, verruga Peruviana, buba* or *boba*, etc. — *adj* **yaw'ey** or **yaw'y**. [Perh. Am. Ind.]

Yb (*chem*) *symbol* for ytterbium.

Y-chromosome. See under **Y** (symbol).

yd *abbrev* for yard (*pl* **yd** or **yds**).

ye[1] *yē, pron* the second person pl. (sometimes sing.) pronoun, now *archaic, Bible, dialect* or *poetic*; cf. **you.** [M.E. (as the nominative form) — O.E. *gē*.]

ye[2] *yē*, (*mock-archaic*) *demonstr adj* used for 'the' (following the archaic script arising from the thorn letter, þ). — See under **Y** (noun).

yea *yā*, (*formal* or *archaic*) *adv* yes; verily; indeed more than that. — *n* an affirmative vote or voter. [O.E. *gēa*.]

yeah *ye, ye'ə* or *yä*, (*colloq*) *adv* yes.

year *yēr* or *yûr, n* the period beginning with 1 January and ending with 31 December, consisting of 365 days, except in a **leap year**, when one day is added to February, making the number 366 — the present legal, civil or calendar year (see under **year**); a space of twelve calendar months, or a period within each twelve-month space characterised by a particular activity, etc.; a period of time determined by the revolution of the earth in its orbit; the time taken by any specified planet to revolve round the sun; students, etc. as a group at the same stage of their education; (in *pl*) a period of life, esp. age or old age; (in *pl*; *colloq*) a very long time: — *pl* **years** (or collective *pl*, used adjectivally with a numeral prefixed, **year**, e.g. *a three year period*). — *n* **year'ling** an animal a year old; a bond maturing after one year (*finance*); a racehorse one year old, as calculated from 1 Jan. of its year of foaling. — *adj* a year old; maturing after one year (*finance*). — *adj* **year'ly** happening every year; lasting a year; for a year. — *adv* once a year; from year to year. — **year'book** a book published annually, recording or reviewing the events of the past year; **year-end'** the end of the (esp. financial) year. — Also *adj*. — *adj* **year'long** lasting a year. — *adj* **year'-round** existing, lasting, open, etc. throughout the year. — Also *adv*. — *adj* **year-on-year'** (*econ*; of figures) set against figures for the equivalent period in the previous year. — **anomalistic year** the earth's time of passage from perihelion to perihelion — 365 days, 6 hours, 13 minutes, 49 seconds; **astronomical year** the time of one complete mean apparent circuit of the ecliptic by the sun — 365 days, 5 hours, 48 minutes, 46 seconds — called also the **equinoctial, natural, solar** (or *tropical*) **year**; **ecclesiastical year** the year as arranged in the ecclesiastical calendar, with the saints' days, festivals, etc.; **financial year, fiscal year** see under **finance, fiscal**; **Hebrew year** a lunisolar year, of 12 (or 13) months of 29 or 30 days (in every cycle of nineteen years the 6th, 8th, 11th, 14th, 17th and 19th having thirteen months instead of twelve); **Julian year** the year according to the Julian calendar (q.v.), a period of $365\frac{1}{4}$ days, longer than an astronomical year by about 11 minutes (see under **style**); **leap year** see beginning of entry; **legal, civil** or **calendar year** the year by which dates are reckoned; it has begun on different dates at different periods, and for six centuries before 1752 it began in England on 25 March; since then (earlier in Scotland) it has begun on 1 January; **lunar year** a period of twelve lunar months or 354 days; **sidereal year** the period required by the sun to move from a given star to the same star again — having a mean value of 365 days, 6 hours, 9 minutes, 9·6 seconds; **the year dot** see under **dot**; **year in, year out** (happening, done, etc.) every year; with monotonous regularity; **Year of Grace** or **Year of our Lord** a formula used in stating any particular year since Christ's birth. [O.E. *gēar*.]

yearn *yûrn, vi* to feel earnest desire; to express longing, e.g. in sound or appearance. — *n* a yearning. — *n* **yearn'er**. — *n* and *adj* **yearn'ing**. — *adv* **yearn'ingly**. [O.E. *geornan*, to desire.]

yeast *yēst, n* a substance used in brewing, baking, etc., consisting of minute fungi which produce zymase and hence induce the alcoholic fermentation of carbohydrates; leaven (*fig*). — *n* **yeast'iness**. — *adj* **yeast'like**. — *adj* **yeast'y** like yeast; frothy, foamy; insubstantial. — **yeast'-plant** any of a group of tiny, one-celled fungi (*Saccharomyces*) that produce alcoholic fermentation in saccharine fluids. [O.E. *gist, gyst*.]

yell *yel, vi* to howl or cry out with a sharp noise; to scream from pain or terror. — *vt* to utter with a yell.

— *n* a sharp outcry; a special cry adopted by college students for use e.g. when supporting their college team (*US*). — *n* **yell'ing**. [O.E. *gellan*; conn. with O.E. *galan*, to sing.]

yellow *yel'ō*, *adj* of the colour of sulphur, gold, egg-yolk, or of the primrose or a ripe lemon; cowardly, base (*colloq*); (of e.g. a newspaper) rankly sensational (*colloq*); of Asiatic race (now often considered *derog*); (of skin) sallow, sickly-looking. — *n* the colour of the rainbow between the orange and the green; any dye or pigment producing such a colour; a plant disease in which the foliage yellows; (in *pl*) jaundice in horses, etc. — *vt* and *vi* to make or become yellow. — *adj* **yell'owish**. — *n* **yell'owishness**. — *n* **yell'owness**. — *adj* **yell'owy**. — **yellow alert** an alarm, etc. one stage less serious than a red alert. — *adjs* **yell'ow-backed, -bellied, -billed, -breasted, -covered, -crowned, -eyed, -footed, -fronted, -headed, -horned, -legged, -necked, -ringed, -rumped, -shouldered, -spotted**, etc. — **yell'ow-belly** (*slang*) a coward (*adj* **yell'ow-bellied**); **yell'ow-bunting** the yellowhammer; **yell'owcake** uranium oxide, obtained during the processing of uranium ore in the form of a yellow precipitate; **yellow card** an official warning to a football, etc. player (signalled by the showing of a yellow card), typically following an infringement of the rules; any similar warning, or symbol of it (*fig*); **yellow fever** an acute disease occurring in tropical America and West Africa, caused by infection with a virus transmitted to man by the bite of a mosquito, *Aëdes aegypti*, characterised by high fever, acute nephritis, jaundice and haemorrhages; **yellow flag** a flag of a yellow colour, displayed by a vessel in quarantine or over a military hospital or ambulance; **yell'owhammer** a bunting (*Emberiza citrinella*), so named from its yellow colour — also called **yell'ow-bunting**; **yellow jack** (*slang*) yellow fever; **yellow jacket** (*NAm*) a small common wasp or hornet (genus *Vespa*) with yellow markings; **yellow jersey** one given to and worn by the leader as recorded at each stage of the Tour de France cycle race; **yellow line** a (yellow-)painted line on a road indicating parking restrictions; **yellow metal** a brass consisting of sixty parts copper and forty parts zinc; **Yellow Pages**® a telephone directory, printed on yellow paper, which classifies participating subscribers alphabetically according to trades, professions, services, etc.; **yellow pepper** see under **pepper**; **yellow peril** the perceived danger that the Asiatic races, esp. the Chinese, might overthrow the white or Western races and overrun the world; the Chinese or Japanese (*derog* or *facetious*); **yellow poplar** the American tulip-tree, or its wood; **yellow press** newspapers abounding in exaggerated, sensational articles; **yell'ow-rattle** see under **rattle**; **yellow ribbon** in the U.S., a symbol of welcome for those returning home after having undergone some danger (orig. a decoration on U.S. cavalrymen's tunics, given to sweethearts as favours); **yell'ow-spot** the macula lutea, the small area at the centre of the retina in vertebrates at which vision is most distinct; **yellow streak** a tendency to cowardly or mean behaviour. — **yellow brick road** a path to fame, wealth, etc. [O.E. *geolu*.]

yelp *yelp*, *vi* to utter a sharp cry or bark. — *n* a sharp, quick cry or bark. — *n* **yelp'er**. — *n* and *adj* **yelp'ing**. [O.E. *gielpan*, to boast, exult.]

yen[1] *yen*, *n* the Japanese monetary unit since 1871 (100 *sen*); formerly a Japanese gold or silver coin: — *pl* **yen**. [Jap., — Chin. *yüan*, round, a dollar.]

yen[2] *yen*, (*colloq*) *n* an intense desire, longing, urge. — *vi* to desire, yearn. [Chin. *yeen*, craving, addiction.]

yenta *yen'tə*, (*US*) *n* a gossip; a shrewish woman. [Yiddish, from the personal name.]

yeoman *yō'mən*, *n* a gentleman serving in a royal or noble household, ranking between a sergeant and a groom (*hist*); after the fifteenth century, one of a class of small farmers, commonly freeholders, the next grade below gentlemen (often serving as foot soldiers; *hist*); an assistant to an official; a member of the yeomanry cavalry or of the yeomen of the guard; a petty officer in the Royal Navy or U.S. Marines, with clerical or signalling duties: — *pl* **yeo'men**. — *adj* **yeo'manly**. — *n* **yeo'manry** the collective body of yeomen; a cavalry volunteer force in Great Britain formed during the wars of the French Revolution, later mechanised as part of the Territorials. — **Yeomen of the Guard** a veteran company of picked soldiers, employed in conjunction with the gentlemen-at-arms, on special occasions, as the sovereign's bodyguard — constituted a corps in 1485 by Henry VII, and still wearing the costume of that period. [M.E. *yoman*, *yeman*; perh. for **young man**.]

yep *yep*, (esp. *US*) dialect and colloq. variant of **yes**.

yerba maté *yûr'bə mat'ā*, or **yerba**, *n* Paraguay tea or maté (q.v.). [Sp., — L. *herba*.]

yersinia *yər-sin'i-ə*, *n* a bacterium of the genus *Yersinia* spread by animals or birds, one of which (*Yersinia pestis*) causes plague, and others **yersinio'sis**, an acute infection of the small intestine: — *pl* **yersin'ias** or **yersin'iae** (*-i-ē*). [A.E.J. *Yersin*, French bacteriologist, 1863–1943.]

yes *yes*, *adv* a word of affirmation or consent; used to indicate that the speaker is present, or (often said interrogatively) to signal someone to speak or act; yea. — *n* a vote or answer of yes; a person who votes or answers yes: — *pl* **yess'es, yess'es** or **yes's**. — *n* (*colloq*) **yes-but'** a qualified consent or agreement. — **yes'-man** (*colloq*) someone who agrees with everything that is said to them; an obedient follower with no initiative. [O.E. *gēse*, *gīse* — *gēa*, *gē*, yea, and *sī*, let it be.]

yeshiva or **yeshivah** *yə-shē'və*, *n* a school for the study of the Jewish Scripture, the Talmud; a seminary for the training of rabbis; an orthodox Jewish elementary school: — *pl* **yeshi'vas, yeshi'vahs, yeshi'vot** or **yeshi'voth**. [Heb. *yěshībhāh*, a sitting.]

yester- *yes-tər-* (*poetic*) *combining form* denoting: relating to yesterday; last. — *n* **yes'teryear** (orig. *D.G. Rossetti*) last year, or the past in general. [O.E. *geostran*, *giestran*.]

yesterday *yes'tər-dā* or *-di*, *n* the day immediately before today; (often in *pl*) the (recent) past. — *adv* on the day last past; formerly; in the (recent) past. [O.E. *geostran* (or *giestran*) *dæg*.]

yet *yet*, *adv* in addition, besides; up to the present time; still; hitherto; at the same time; even; before the affair is finished. — *conj* nevertheless; however. — **as yet** up to the time under consideration. [O.E. *gīet*, *gīeta*.]

yeti *yet'i*, *n* the abominable snowman. [Native Tibetan name.]

yew *ū*, *n* any evergreen, coniferous tree of the genus *Taxus* (family *Taxaceae*) widespread in northern parts of the world, with narrow lanceolate or linear leaves, esp. *Taxus baccata* (in Europe long planted in graveyards) which yields an elastic wood; its wood; a bow made of its wood; yew twigs regarded as emblematic of grief. — **yew'-tree**. [O.E. *īw*, *ēow*.]

Y-fronts. See under **Y** (noun).

YHA *abbrev* for Youth Hostels Association.

Yiddish *yid'ish*, *n* a language spoken by Jews, based on ancient or provincial German with Hebrew and Slavonic additions, usu. written in the Hebrew alphabet. — *n* **Yid** (*offensive*) a Jew. — *adj* **Yidd'isher** in or pertaining to Yiddish; Jewish. — *n* a Jew, a speaker of Yiddish. — *n* **Yidd'ishism** an idiom or other speech characteristic derived from Yiddish. [Ger. *jüdisch*, Jewish.]

yield *yēld*, *vt* to grant or accord; to admit or concede; to produce; to give out; to furnish or afford; to deliver, surrender, relinquish or resign. — *vi* to submit, give up, surrender; to give way under pressure; to give place; to concede; to give way (in traffic) (*US*). — *n* an amount yielded, produce; a product; the return of a financial investment, usu. calculated with reference to the cost and dividend. — *n* **yield'er**. — *adj* **yield'ing** giving, or inclined to give, way; compliant, flexible. — *n* a giving way; compliance. — *adv* **yield'ingly**. — *n* **yield'ingness**. — **yield point** in the case of iron and annealed steels, the stress at which a substantial amount of plastic deformation takes place suddenly. [O.E. *gieldan*, to pay.]

yike *yīk* or **yikes** *yīks*, (*colloq*) *interj* expressing alarm or astonishment. — *n* (*Austr*) an argument, fight.

yikker *yik'ər*, *vi* (of an animal) to utter sharp little cries. — Also *n*. [Imit.]

yin *yin*, *n* (also with *cap*) one of the two opposing and complementary principles of Chinese philosophy, religion, medicine, etc. influencing destiny and governing nature, seen as the negative, feminine, dark, cold, passive element (cf. **yang**). [Chin., dark.]

Yinglish *ying'glish*, (*facetious*; orig. *US*) *n* a mixture of *Y*iddish and E*nglish* spoken by American Jews; a dialect of English containing a large number of Yiddishisms.

yip *yip*, *vt* (esp. of a dog) to give a short, sudden cry. — Also *n*. [Imit.]

yippee *yip-ē'*, *interj* expressing delight, exultation, etc.

yips *yips*, (*sport*, esp. and orig. *golf*) *npl* (usu. with **the**) an attack of nervous trembling caused by tension before making a shot, etc.

-yl *-il*, *sfx* forming nouns, denoting a radical, such as carbon*yl*, carbox*yl*, etc. [Gr. *hȳlē*, matter.]

ylang-ylang *ē-lang-ē'lang*, *n* a tree of the Malay Archipelago and Peninsula, the Philippines, etc., or an essence (also **ylang-ylang oil**) distilled from its flowers. [Tagálog.]

Y-level. See under **Y** (noun).

YMCA *abbrev* for Young Men's Christian Association.

yo *yō*, *interj* calling for or accompanying effort, calling for attention or used in greeting, etc.; (in answer to a call) present, here (esp. *US*): — *pl* **yos**. — *interj* **yo-hō'** or **yo-hō-hō'** calling for attention; same as yo-heave-ho; **yo-heave'-hō** an old sailors' chant used while hauling on ropes.

yob *yob*, (*slang*) *n* a teenage hooligan, vandal or loafer; a lout. — *n* **yobb'ery** yobbish behaviour. — *adj* **yobb'ish**. — *adv* **yobb'ishly**. — *n* **yobb'o** a yob: — *pl* **yobb'os** or **yobb'oes**. [Back-slang for **boy**.]

yock. See **yok**.

yodel *yō'dl*, *vt* and *vi* to sing, or shout, changing frequently from the ordinary voice to falsetto and back again, in the style traditional to Tyrolean mountain people. — *n* a song or phrase sung, or a cry made, in this way. — *n* **yō'deller** or **yō'dler**. [Ger. dialect *jodeln*.]

yoga *yō'gə*, *n* a system of Hindu philosophy showing the way toward liberating the soul from further migrations and its ultimate union with the supreme being; any of a number of systems of physical and mental disciplines based on this, such as hatha yoga (see below); yogic exercises. — *n* **yō'gi** (*-gē*) or **yō'gin** a Hindu ascetic who practises the yoga system, consisting in the withdrawal of the senses from external objects, long continuance in unnatural postures, etc.: — *fem* **yōgi'ni**. — *adj* **yō'gic**. — *n* **yō'gism**. — **hatha yoga** (*hath'ə* or *hut'ə*; Sans. *haṭha*, force) a form of yoga (the most common in the western hemisphere) stressing the importance of physical exercises and positions and breathing-control in promoting physical and mental wellbeing. [Sans., union.]

yoghourt, yoghurt or **yogurt** *yog'ərt* or *yō'gərt*, *n* a semi-liquid food made from fermented milk. [Turk. *yōghurt*.]

yogi, yogin, etc. See under **yoga**.

yoicks *yoiks*, *interj* a fox-hunting cry. — *vi* or *vt* to make, or urge (the hounds) on by, this cry.

yok or **yock** *yok*, (*theat slang*) *n* a laugh. — Also *vi*. [Imit.]

yoke *yōk*, *n* the frame of wood joining draught oxen at the necks; any similar frame, such as one for carrying pails; a part of a garment that fits the shoulders (or the hips); servitude or slavery; an oppressive burden; a bond of union; a pair or couple, esp. of oxen; something that joins together or connects; a set of current coils for deflecting the electron beam in a TV or VDU cathode-ray tube. — *vt* to put a yoke on; to join together; to attach a draught-animal to; to enslave. — *vi* to go together, couple, match. [O.E. *geoc*.]

yokel *yō'kl*, *n* a country bumpkin. — *adj* **yō'kelish**.

yolk[1] *yōk*, *n* the yellow part of the egg of a bird or reptile; the nutritive non-living material contained by an ovum. — *adj* **yolked**. — *adj* **yolk'y**. — **yolk'-sac** (*zool*) the yolk-containing sac which is attached to the embryo by the **yolk'-stalk**, a short stalk by means of which yolk substance may pass into the alimentary canal of the embryo. [O.E. *geolca*, *geoleca* — *geolu*, yellow.]

yolk[2] *yōk*, *n* wool-oil. — *adj* **yolk'y**. — Cf. **suint**. [O.E. *ēowocig*, yolky.]

Yom Kippur *yōm kip'o͝or*, *n* the Day of Atonement, a Jewish fast day. — **Yom Tob** (*tōb*) or **Tov** (*tōv*) any Jewish holiday or religious festival. [Heb. *yōm*, day, *kippūr*, atonement, *tōbh*, good.]

yomp *yomp*, (*colloq*) *vi* to carry heavy equipment on foot over difficult terrain (*mil*); (*loosely*, often *facetious*) to walk or trek in a determined, dogged or laboured manner, esp. heavily laden. — Also *n*. [Poss. imit.]

yon *yon*, (*poetic* or *dialect*) *adj* that; those; yonder. — *pron* that; the thing you know of. — *adv* yonder. — *adv* **yon'der** to or at a distance within view, over there. — *adj* that, or those, at a distance within view (or in that direction). — *pron* that one, yon. — **the yonder** the farther, more distant parts (esp. in the phrase *the wide blue yonder*). [O.E. *geon* (adj., pron.), *geond* (prep., adv.), and M.E. *yonder*.]

yoni *yō'nē*, *n* a representation of the female genitals, the symbol under which the Hindu deity Sakti is worshipped. [Sans.]

yonks *yongks*, (*colloq*) *n* ages, a long time. [Poss. *y*ears, m*on*ths and wee*ks*; or perh. compressed from *donkey's years*.]

yoo-hoo *yo͞o'-ho͞o*, *interj* a call to attract someone's attention.

yore *yör*, (*poetic*) *n* time long ago or long past. — **days of yore** in times past. [O.E. *gēara*, formerly.]

yorker *yörk'ər*, (*cricket*) *n* a ball pitched to a point directly under the bat. — *vt* **york** to bowl (or attempt to bowl) someone out with a yorker. [Prob. from *Yorkshire*.]

Yorkie *yör'ki*, (*colloq*) *n* (also without *cap*) a Yorkshire terrier.

Yorkist *yörk'ist*, (*hist*) an adherent of the House of York in the Wars of the Roses. — Also *adj*.

Yorks. *yörks*, *abbrev* for Yorkshire.

Yorkshire *yörk'shīr* or *-shər*, *n* one of a breed of animal, esp. pigs, originating in the county of *Yorkshire*. — **Yorkshire pudding** a pudding made of unsweetened batter, and baked along with meat or in meat dripping; **Yorkshire terrier** a small long-haired kind of terrier.

Yoruba *yo'ro͞o-ba* or *yō'*, *nsing* and *npl* a linguistic group of coastal West African peoples; a member of the group; the language of the group. — *adj* **Yo'ruba** or **Yo'ruban**.

you *ū*, *pron* the commonly used second person pronoun (all cases), orig. plural, now standard for both singular and plural; (*indefinite pron*) anyone; the personality (or something in tune with the personality) of the person addressed (*colloq*). — **you-all'**

(*US*) you (esp. in *pl*); **you'-know-what** or **you'-know-who** some unspecified but well-understood or well-known thing or person. [O.E. *ēow*, orig. only dative and accus. of *gē*, ye (see **ye**[1]).]

you'd *yood* or *yood*, a contraction of **you had** or **you would**.

you'll *yool* or *yool*, a contraction of **you will** or **you shall**.

young *yung*, *adj* (*compar* **younger** *yung'gər*, *superl* **youngest** *yung'gist*) not long born; in early life; in the first part of growth; youthful, vigorous; relating to youth; junior, the younger of two parties of the same name. — *n* the offspring of animals; (with **the**) those who are young. — *adj* **youngish** (*yung'ish* or *yung'gish*). — *n* **young'ster** a young person; a child. — **young blood** fresh, vigorous new strength, personnel, ideas, etc.; **Young England** (*hist*) during the corn-laws struggle (1842–45), a small band of young Tory politicians, who hated Free Trade and Radicalism, and professed a sentimental attachment to earlier forms of social life in England; **Young England, America,** etc. the rising, younger generation in England, America, etc.; **young lady** or **man** a girl- or boyfriend, sweetheart; **young offender** a law-breaker aged between 17 and 21 (**young-offender institution** an establishment (replacing the former borstal) for the detention of young offenders who are given custodial sentences); **young person** someone aged 14 and over, but under 17 (*law*); in Factory Acts, etc., a person who is under 18 years of age but no longer a child; **Young Turk** (also without *caps*) a progressive, rebellious, impetuous, etc. member of an organisation; one of a body of Turkish reformers who brought about the revolution of 1908 (*hist*). — **with young** (of an animal) pregnant. [O.E. *geong*.]

youngberry *yung'ber-i* or *-bər-i*, (*US*) *n* a large reddish-black fruit, a cross between a variety of blackberry and a variety of dewberry. [B.M. *Young*, an American fruitgrower, and **berry**.]

your *yör* or *ūr*, *pron* (*genitive pl*) or *possessive adj* of or belonging to you; used to denote a person of a well-known type — the ordinary (often implying some contempt; *colloq*); of or relating to an unspecified person or people in general. — *pron* **yours** (a double genitive) used predicatively or absolutely; short for 'your letter'. — **you and yours** you and your family or property; **yours faithfully, sincerely, truly,** etc. forms used conventionally in letters just before the signature; (**yours truly**) also sometimes used by a speaker to mean himself or herself (*colloq*). [O.E. *ēower*, genitive of *gē*, ye.]

you're *yör* or *ūr*, a contraction of **you are**.

yourself *yör-* or *ūr-self'*, *pron* the emphatic form of **you**; in your real character; having command of your faculties, sane, normal, in good form; the reflexive form of **you** (objective); often used colloquially and incorrectly instead of **you** (unreflexive second person singular): — *pl* **yourselves'**.

youth *yooth*, *n* the state of being young; early life, the period immediately succeeding childhood; an early period of existence; a young person, esp. a young man (*pl* **youths** *yoodhz*); young people collectively. — *adj* **youth'ful** young; pertaining to youth or early life; suitable to youth; fresh, buoyant, vigorous. — *adv* **youth'fully**. — *n* **youth'fulness**. — **youth club** a place or organisation providing leisure activities for young people; **youth custody** a custodial sentence of between four and eighteen months passed on a person aged between 15 and 21; **youth hostel** a hostel where hikers, etc. who are members of an organisation find inexpensive and simple accommodation. — *vi* to stay in youth hostels. — **youth hosteller; youth leader** a social worker who works with the youth of a particular community or area. — **Youth Training Scheme** (esp. abbreviated **YTS**) a Government-sponsored scheme launched in 1983 to give training and job experience to unemployed school-leavers. [O.E. *geoguth* — *geong*, young.]

you've *yoov* or *yoov*, a contraction of **you have**.

yowl *yowl*, *vi* (of a dog, etc.) to cry mournfully; to yell or bawl. — *n* a distressed cry. — *n* **yowl'ing** a howling. [M.E. *youlen*.]

yo-yo *yō'-yō*, *n* a toy consisting of a reel attached to, and manoeuvred by, a string which winds and unwinds round it; any person or thing resembling a yo-yo in movement or ease of manipulation; an indecisive or useless person, a fool (*slang*; orig. *US*). — Also *adj*. — *vi* to operate a yo-yo; to move rapidly up and down; to fluctuate rapidly, or be very unsettled. [Manufacturer's trademark, app. from a Filipino word.]

ypsilon. See **upsilon**.

yr *abbrev* for: year; younger; your.

YT *abbrev* for Yukon Territory (Canada).

YTS *abbrev* for Youth Training Scheme.

ytterbium *i-tûr'bi-əm*, *n* a metallic element (symbol **Yb**; atomic no. 70), a member of the rare-earth group. [*Ytterby*, a Swedish quarry.]

yttrium *it'ri-əm*, *n* a metallic element (symbol **Y**; atomic no. 39) in the third group of the periodic system, usu. classed with the rare-earths. — *adj* **ytt'ric** or **ytt'rious**. — *adj* **yttrif'erous**. [From *Ytterby*; see **ytterbium**.]

YTV *abbrev* for Yorkshire Television.

YU *abbrev* for Yugoslavia (I.V.R.).

yuan *yü-än'*, *n* the monetary unit of the People's Republic of China (see under **renminbi**): — *pl* **yuan**. [Chin. *yüan*.]

yuca *yuk'ə*, *n* cassava. [Of Carib origin.]

yucca (sometimes **yuca**) *yuk'ə*, *n* any plant of the genus *Yucca* of the family Liliaceae, natives of Mexico, New Mexico, etc., some (such as *Yucca gloriosa*, the Spanish dagger) cultivated in gardens on account of their ornamental appearance and sword-like leaves.

yucky or **yukky** *yuk'i*, (*slang*) *adj* dirty, unpleasant. — *n* **yuck** or **yuk** messiness, etc. — *interj* expressing distaste or disgust. [Imit.]

Yugoslav *yoo'gō-släv* or *-släv'*, *n* a native, citizen or inhabitant of Yugoslavia, one of the southern group of Slavs consisting of Serbs, Croats and Slovenes; the Slavonic language (Serbo-Croatian) dominant in Yugoslavia. — Also *adj*. — *adj* and *n* **Yugoslav'ian** or **Yugoslav'ic**. — Also **Jugoslav**, etc. [Serbo-Croatian *jugo-* (sfx.) — *jug*, the south, and **Slav**.]

yuk, yukky. See **yucky**.

yuko *yoo'kō*, *n* an award of five points in judo. [Jap.]

Yule *yool*, *n* (*old-fashioned* or *dialect*) the season or feast of Christmas. — **Yule log** a cake shaped and decorated to resemble a log, eaten at Christmas-time; orig. a block of wood cut down in the forest, then dragged to the house, and set alight in celebration of Christmas; **Yule'tide** the time or season of Yule or Christmas. — Also **yule** and **yule'tide**. [O.E. *gēol*, Yule.]

yum-yum *yum-yum'*, (*colloq*) *interj* expressing delighted or pleasant anticipation, esp. of delicious food. — *interj* **yumm'y** yum-yum. — *adj* delicious, attractive, scrumptious, etc. [Imit.]

yump *yump*, (*slang*) *vi* in rally-driving, to leave the ground (in one's vehicle) when going over a ridge or crest. — *n* an instance of this. [Norw. *jump*, jump (as pronounced).]

yumpie *yum'pi*, (*colloq*) *n* one of the *y*oung *u*pwardly-*m*obile *p*eople, a dismissive designation for young rising or ambitious professionals. — See also **yuppie**.

yup *yup* or *yəp*. Colloq. variant of **yes**.

yuppie or **yuppy** *yup'i*, *n* a *y*oung *u*rban *p*rofessional, a dismissive designation for the young city careerist, the word now being commoner than **yumpie** (q.v.) and explained by some as derived acronymically from *y*oung *u*pwardly-mobile *p*eople. — *n* **yupp'iedom** the state of being a yuppie; the world or circles which yuppies frequent. — *n* **yuppificā'tion.** — *vt* **yupp'ify** to adapt (esp. a locality or a particular venue) to suit the taste of yuppies; to be frequented by or suitable for yuppies. — **yuppie flu** (*colloq*) myalgic encephalomyelitis.

yurt or **yourt** *yōōrt*, *n* a light tent of skins, etc. used by nomads in Siberia. [From Russ.]

YV *abbrev* for Venezuela (I.V.R.).

YWCA *abbrev* for Young Women's Christian Association.

Z

Z or **z** *zed*, *n* the twenty-sixth and last letter in the modern English alphabet; something similar to the letter Z in shape, such as **Z'-bend** a series of sharp bends in a road.

Z or **Z.** *abbrev* for: zaire (Zaïrean currency); Zambia (I.V.R.).

Z (*alg*, etc.) *symbol* (also **z** or *z*) for the third variable, unknown or yet to be ascertained quantity or factor in a series, after X and Y (or **x**, **y** or *x*, *y*).

Z symbol for: atomic number (*chem*); impedance (*phys*).

z or **z.** *abbrev* for: zenith; zero; zone.

z *symbol* used as a contraction-mark, as in *viz*, *oz*, etc.

ZA *abbrev* for *Zuid Afrika* (Afrik.), South Africa (I.V.R.).

zabaglione *zä-bäl-yō'ni*, *n* a frothy custard made from egg yolks, marsala and sugar. — Also **zabaione** (*-bə-yō'ni*). [It.]

zaffre or **zaffer** *zaf'ər*, *n* the impure oxide (used as a pigment) obtained by partially roasting cobalt ore previously mixed with two or three times its weight of fine sand. [Fr. *zafre*, of Ar. origin.]

zag *zag*, *n* a new line, or sharp change, of direction on a zigzag course. — Also *vi*: — *pr p* **zagg'ing**; *pa t* and *pa p* **zagged**. [-**zag** extracted from **zigzag**.]

zaire *zä-ēr'*, *n* the standard unit of currency (100 *makuta*) of *Zaire*, a republic of central Africa: — *pl* **zaire'**. — *adj* **Zairean** (*-ē'ri-ən*), *adj* of or relating to Zaire. — *n* a native of Zaire.

zaman *zə-män'* or **zamang** *zə-mäng'*, *n* the saman or rain-tree. [Carib.]

Zambian *zam'bi-ən*, *adj* of or pertaining to the republic of *Zambia* (formerly Northern Rhodesia) in central Africa. — *n* a native of Zambia.

zamia *zā'mi-ə*, *n* a plant of the *Zamia* genus of palm-like trees or low shrubs of the family *Cycadaceae* some species of which yield an edible starchy pith. [Named through misreading in Pliny *azaniae nuces*, pine cones that open on the tree — Gr. *azanein*, *azainein*, to dry.]

zantedeschia *zan-ti-des'ki-ə*, *n* a plant of the *Zantedeschia* genus of plants of the arum family, including *Zantedeschia aethiopica*, known as calla lily. [Francesco *Zantedeschi*, Italian botanist.]

ZANU *zä'nōō*, *abbrev* for Zimbabwe African National Union. — Also **Za'nu**.

zany *zā'ni*, *adj* crazy, clownish (*colloq*); of, or pertaining to, a zany. — *n* someone who plays the fool (*colloq*); an assistant clown or buffoon (*hist*). — *vt* to play the zany to. — *n* **zā'niness**. — *n* **zā'nyism** the condition or habits of a buffoon. [Fr. *zani* — It. *zanni*, a corruption of *Giovanni*, John.]

zap *zap*, (*colloq*) *vt* to hit, strike, destroy, kill, overwhelm, etc. (*lit* and *fig*); to erase or correct a fault (*comput*); to cause to move or pass by quickly. — *vi* (often with *off* or *along*) to go speedily or suddenly; to keep changing television channels, using a remote-control device. — *n* vitality, force. — *interj* expressing suddenness. — *n* **zapp'er**. — *adj* **zapp'y** (*slang*) showy, punchy, speedy, vigorous, or otherwise impressive. — **zap (something) up** to make (something) livelier. [Imit.]

zapata *zə-pä'tə*, *adj* denoting a type of flowing moustache drooping down on each side of the mouth. [Emilio *Zapata*, Mexican revolutionary (1879–1919), who wore a moustache of this shape.]

zapateado *thä-pä-te-ä'dhō*, *n* a lively Spanish flamenco dance, for a solo performer, with much clicking and stamping of the heels: — *pl* **zapatea'dos**. [Sp.]

zapotilla *zap-ō-til'ə*, *n*. Same as **sapodilla**.

ZAPU *zä'pōō*, *abbrev* for Zimbabwe African People's Union. — Also **Za'pu**.

zarape *sä-rä'pe*, *n*. Same as **serape**.

Zarathustrian *zar-ə-thōōs'tri-ən*, *adj* and *n* Zoroastrian. — *n* **Zarathus'trianism** or **Zarathus'trism** Zoroastrianism. — *adj* and *n* **Zarathus'tric** Zoroastrian.

zareba, zareeba or **zariba** *zə-rē'bä*, *n* in the Sudan, etc., a stockade, thorn-hedge or other defence against wild animals or enemies; a fortified camp generally. [Ar. *zarībah*, a pen or enclosure for cattle.]

zarf *zärf* or **zurf** *zûrf*, *n* a Middle Eastern ornamental holder for a hot coffee-cup. [Ar. *zarf*, a vessel.]

zarzuela *thär-thŏŏ-ā'lä* or *-thwā'lä*, (Sp.) *n* a Spanish kind of operetta or vaudeville — named from the royal residence of La *Zarzuela*.

zastruga *zas-trōō'gä* or **sastruga** *sas-trōō'gə*, *n* one of a series of long parallel snow-ridges on open wind-swept regions of snow: — *pl* **zastru'gi** or **sastru'gi** (*-gē*). [Russ.]

zb *abbrev* for *zum Beispiel* (Ger.), for example.

zea *zē'ə*, *n* the species *Zea mays*, maize or Indian corn which constitutes the *Zea* genus of cereals having monoecious flowers; the fresh styles and stigmas of this plant, formerly used as a diuretic. [Gr. *zeā* or *zeia*, one-seeded wheat.]

zeal *zēl*, *n* intense (sometimes fanatical) enthusiasm; activity arising from warm support or enthusiasm; strong feeling, such as love, anger, etc., or passionate ardour (*Bible*). — *n* **zealot** (*zel'ət*) an enthusiast; a fanatic; (with *cap*) one of a militant Jewish sect vigorously opposing the Roman domination of Palestine until the ruin of Jerusalem in 70 A.D. — *n* **zealotism** (*zel'*) the character of a zealot. — *n* **zealotry** (*zel'*). — *adj* **zealous** (*zel'*) full of zeal; keenly engaged in, or hotly in support of, anything; devoted. — *adv* **zealously** (*zel'*). — *n* **zealousness** (*zel'*). [O.Fr. *zele* — L. *zēlus* — Gr. *zēlos* — *zeein*, to boil.]

zebec, zebeck. Variants of **xebec**.

zebra *zē'brə* or *zeb'rə*, *n* any of a group of striped animals of the genus Equus — all of which are peculiar to the African continent; any animal, fish, plant or mineral having stripes reminiscent of a zebra's; a referee (having a striped shirt) in American football (*US slang*). — **zebra crossing** a stripe-marked street crossing where pedestrians have priority; **ze'bra-finch** an Australian weaver bird with black and white striped markings; **zebra-par'akeet** the budgerigar; **zebra spider** any of several striped spiders of the *Salticidae*; **ze'bra-wood** the hard and beautifully striped wood of a tropical American tree; the tree itself; applied also to various other trees or their wood. [African.]

zebrina *zeb-rī'nə*, *n* a trailing or creeping herbaceous plant of the Central American genus *Zebrina*, with pointed, ovate, striped leaves. [N.L.]

zebu *zē'bū* or *zē'bōō*, *n* a humped domestic ox (*Bos indicus*) very closely related to the common ox, of India, China, the east coast of Africa, etc. [Fr. *zébu*, the name taken by Buffon from the exhibitors of one at a French fair in 1752.]

Zech. (*Bible*) *abbrev* for (the Book of) Zechariah.

zed *zed* or in U.S. **zee** *zē*, *n* the twenty-sixth letter of the modern English alphabet (Z, z); a bar of metal of form similar to the letter Z. [Fr. *zède* — L. and Gr. *zēta*.]

zedoary *zed'ō-ə-ri*, *n* certain species of curcuma (native to India, China, etc.) whose rootstocks are aromatic, bitter and pungent. [Through Med. L. — Ar. *zedwār*.]

zee *zē*. See **zed**.

Zeeman effect *zā'män if-ekt'*, (*phys*) *n* the splitting of a spectral line into several symmetrically disposed components, which occurs when the source of light is placed in a strong magnetic field. [Named from Dutch physicist Pieter *Zeeman* (1865–1943).]

zeitgeist *tsīt'gīst*, *n* (also with *cap*) the spirit of the age. [Ger.]

zek *zek*, *n* an inmate of a U.S.S.R. prison or labour camp. [Russ. slang, poss. from abbrev. *zk* for *zaklyuchënnyĭ*, prisoner.]

zelophobia *zel-ō-fō'bi-ə*, *n* an irrational or morbid aversion to or fear of jealousy. — *adj* and *n* **zelophō'bic**. [Obs. *zelotypia*, jealousy (— Gr. *zēlos*, zeal, *typtein*, to strike), and **-phobia**.]

zeloso *zel-ō'sō*, (*mus*) *adv* with fervour. [It.]

Zen *zen*, *n* a Japanese Buddhist sect which holds that the truth is not in scriptures but in a person's own heart if they strive to find it by meditation and self-mastery. — Also *adj*. — *adj* **Zen'ic**. — *n* **Zen'ist**. [Jap. — Chin. *ch'an* — Pali *jhāna*, Sans. *dhyāna*, religious contemplation.]

zenana *ze-nä'nə*, *n* (in India and Iran) apartments in which women are secluded, corresponding to the harem in Arabic-speaking Muslim lands. — **zenana mission** a mission to women of the zenanas, necessarily conducted by women. [Pers. *zanāna* — *zan*, a woman.]

Zend *zend*, *n* the Avesta or Zend-Avesta; Avestan, the ancient East-Iranian Indo-European language in which the Zend-Avesta was long preserved orally and eventually written — closely related to the Vedic Sanskrit. — **Zend-Aves'ta** (properly meaning the Avesta with the commentary on it), the ancient sacred writings of the Parsees, including works of widely differing character and age. [Pers. *zend*, *zand*, commentary.]

Zener cards *zē'nər kärdz*, *npl* a set of 25 cards, consisting of five sets of five, each set having one symbol, used in parapsychological experimentation. [Invented by K.E. *Zener* (1903–61), U.S. psychologist.]

Zener diode *zē'nər dī'ōd*, (*electronics*) *n* a type of semiconductor device, a diode whose sudden increase in reverse current makes it useful in voltage-limiting circuits. [C.M. *Zener*, U.S. physicist, (b. 1905).]

zenith *zen'ith* or (esp. in U.S.) *zēn'ith*, *n* the point on the celestial sphere vertically above the observer's head, one of the two poles of the horizon, the other being the nadir; the greatest height (*lit* and *fig*). — *adj* **zen'ithal**. — **zenithal projection** a type of projection in which the plane of projection is tangential to the sphere; **zen'ith-distance** the angular distance of a celestial body from the zenith. [O.Fr. *cenit*(*h*), ultimately from Ar. *samt*, short for *samt-ar-ras*, lit. way, direction, of the head.]

zeolite *zē'ō-līt*, *n* any of a large group of alumina and silica compound minerals containing sodium, potassium, calcium and barium, with an open sponge-like structure containing very loosely held water. — *adj* **zeolitic** (*-lit'ik*). — *adj* **zeolit'iform**. [Gr. *zeein*, to boil (in allusion to the fact that many swell up under the blowpipe), *lithos*, a stone.]

Zeph. (*Bible*) *abbrev* for (Book of) Zephaniah.

zephyr *zef'ər*, *n* a soft, gentle breeze (*poetic*); the west wind, or (with *cap*) the god of the west wind; any of various types of lightweight material, such as a gingham, a flannel with a silk warp, a thin woollen cloth, etc.; a garment made of this. [Gr. *Zephyros*, the west wind.]

zeppelin *zep'əl-in*, *n* a dirigible, cigar-shaped airship of the type designed by Count *Zeppelin* (*c* 1900).

zero *zē'rō*, *n* a cipher; nothing; the point from which the reckoning begins on scales, such as those of the barometer, etc.; the lowest point (*fig*); zero hour: — *pl* **zē'ros**. — *vt* to set at or adjust to zero: — *pr p* **zē'roing**; *pa t* and *pa p* **zē'roed**. — *adj* having no measurable size, amount, etc.; not any (*colloq*). — *adj* **zē'rōth** denoting a term in a series regarded as preceding the 'first' term. — **ze'ro-coupon bond** (*stock exchange*) a bond that carries no interest, but has a redemption price higher than its issue price; **zero hour** the exact time (hour, minute and second) fixed for launching an attack or beginning an operation; **zero option** a proposal (orig. made by U.S. President Reagan) to limit or abandon the deployment of (medium range) nuclear missiles if the opposing side does likewise; (*loosely*) a proposal to abandon or eliminate a particular range, category, division, etc.; **ze'ro-point energy** (*phys*) total energy at the absolute zero of temperature. — *vt* **zēro-rate'** to assess at a zero rate of VAT. — *adj* **zero-rat'ed** of goods on which the purchaser pays no VAT and on which the seller can claim back any VAT which they have already paid. — **zero-rat'ing**. — *adj* **ze'ro-sum** (of a game, etc.) in which the total cumulative gains equal the total cumulative losses. — *adj* **ze'ro-ze'ro** (*meteorol* and *aeronautics*) of conditions in which cloud ceiling and horizontal visibility are both zero. — **zero-zero (**or sometimes **double zero) option** a proposal which extends the zero option (q.v. above) to include also intermediate (300–600 mile) range missiles. — **absolute zero** see under **absolute; zero-based budgeting** a system in which the budget of an organisation, department, etc. is drawn up anew each year without reference to any previous budget; **zero in (on)** (*slang*) to direct oneself straight towards (a target); to focus one's attention or energies on, as if on (a target); to aim for, move towards (something or someone). [Fr. *zéro* — Ar. *sifr*; cf. **cipher**.]

zest *zest*, *n* the thin outer layer of orange or lemon peel; orange or lemon peel, or the oil squeezed from it, used as a flavouring; anything that gives a tang; piquancy, relish; enthusiasm. — *vt* to give zest to. — *adj* **zest'ful**. — *adv* **zest'fully**. — *n* **zest'fulness**. — *adj* **zest'y**. [Fr. *zeste*, orig. the woody thick skin quartering a walnut.]

ZETA *zē'tə*, *abbrev* for zero-energy thermonuclear apparatus (used in the study of controlled thermonuclear reactions), toroid in shape.

zeta *zē'tə*, *n* the Greek z (Z or ζ).

zeugma *zūg'mə*, *n* a figure of speech by which an adjective or verb is applied to two nouns, though strictly appropriate to only one of them. — *adj* **zeugmat'ic**. [Gr., — *zeugnynai*, to yoke.]

zeze *zā'zā*, *n* a stringed musical instrument played in countries of eastern and central Africa. [Swahili.]

zho *zhō*, *n* a kind of hybrid domestic cattle in parts of the Himalayas (esp. the male) — said to be a cross between the male yak and the common horned cow. — Also **dzho** or **dzo** (*dzō*): — *pl* **zhos, dzhos** or **dzos**. [Tibetan *mdzo*.]

zibet *zib'it*, *n* an Asiatic civet. [It. *zibetto* — Ar. *zabād*; cf. **civet**.]

zidovudine *zi-dō'vū-dēn*, *n* the manufacturer's name for the drug, AZT. [From the chemical name, *azidothymidine*.]

ziff *zif*, (*Austr slang*) *n* a beard, goatee.

zig *zig*, *n* a new line, or sharp change, of direction on a zigzag course. — Also *vi*: — *pr p* **zigg'ing**; *pa t* and *pa p* **zigged**. [**zig**- extracted from **zigzag**.]

ziggurat *zig'ōō-rat*, *n* a temple-tower, pyramidal in general shape, consisting of a number of storeys each successive one of which was smaller than that below it, found in Sumerian and Assyrian architecture. [Assyrian *ziqquratu*, a pinnacle, top of a mountain.]

zigzag *zig'zag*, *n* a short, sharp turning; a line, road, fence or moulding, with sharp angles to right and left alternately. — *adj* having short, sharp alternate turns; bent from side to side alternately. — *vt* to form with short, alternate turns. — *vi* to move forward making an alternation of short, sharp turns: — *pr p* **zig'zagging**; *pa t* and *pa p* **zig'zagged**. — *adv* with frequent sharp turns. — Also **zig'zaggy**. — *n* **zigzagg'er**. — *adj* **zig'zaggy** zigzag. [Fr.; Ger. *Zickzack*.]

zilch *zilch*, (*slang*) *n* zero, nothing.

zillah or **zila** *zil'a*, *n* an administrative district in India. [Ar. *dila* (in Hindi pronunciation, *zila*), a rib, thence a side, a district.]

zillion *zil'yən*, (*colloq*) *n* an extremely large but unspecified number, many millions — analogous in formation and use to *million*, *billion*. — *n* and *adj* **zill'ionth**.

zimb *zimb*, *n* an Ethiopian dipterous insect, like the tsetse, harmful to cattle. [Amharic, a fly.]

Zimbabwean *zim-bä'bwi-ən*, *adj* of or pertaining to the Republic of Zimbabwe (formerly Rhodesia) in southern Africa. — *n* a native of Zimbabwe.

Zimmer® *zim'ər*, *n* a metal frame held in front of one, used as an aid to walking. — Also without *cap*. [Name of original manufacturer.]

zinc *zingk*, *n* a bluish-white metallic element (symbol **Zn**; atomic no. 30) resistant to atmospheric corrosion, it is a constituent of several alloys (e.g. brass) and is used in galvanising, battery electrodes, etc. — Also *adj*. — *vt* to coat with zinc: — *pr p* **zincing** (*zingk'ing*), **zinck'ing** or **zink'ing**; *pa t* and *pa p* **zinced** (*zingkt*), **zincked** or **zinked**. — *adj* **zincif'erous** (*zingk*-) or **zinkif'erous** containing or producing zinc. — *n* **zincificā'tion, zinckificā'tion** or **zinkificā'tion** the process of coating or impregnating an object with zinc. — *vt* **zinc'ify, zinck'ify** or **zink'ify** to cover or impregnate with zinc. — *n* **zincite** (*zingk'īt*) oxide of zinc, brittle, translucent and deep red. — *n* **zinco** (*zing'kō*) a line block executed in zinc, i.e. the normal line block: — *pl* **zinc'os**. — *n* **zinc'ograph** a plate or picture produced by zincography. — *n* **zincographer** (*-kog'rə-fər*). — *adj* **zincograph'ic** or **zincograph'ical**. — *n* **zincography** (*-kog'rə-fi*) an engraving process in which zinc is covered with wax and etched; any process in which designs for printing are made on zinc plates. — *adj* **zinc'oid** like zinc. — *adj* **zinc'ous** pertaining to, or like, zinc. — *adj* **zinc'y, zinck'y** or **zink'y** pertaining to, containing, or looking like, zinc. — **zinc blende** sphalerite, the common sulphide of zinc; **zinc ointment** a mixture of zinc oxide and suitable ointment base (wool fat, petroleum jelly, etc.); **zinc oxide** a whitish solid, much used as a paint pigment, in the rubber and other industries, and also medicinally, as an antiseptic and astringent (also called *flowers of zinc*); **zinc white** zinc oxide used as a pigment. [Ger. *Zink*.]

zineb *zin'əb*, *n* an organic fungicide and insecticide sprayed on cereal grasses, fruit trees, etc. [*Zinc* *e*thylene *b*isdithiocarbamate, its chemical name.]

zing *zing*, *n* a short shrill humming sound, as made by a bullet or vibrating string; zest, spirit, vitality, etc. (*colloq*). — *vi* to move very swiftly, esp. with a high-pitched hum. — *n* **zing'er** (*colloq*; esp. *US*) something or someone with zing, esp. a sharp, lively quip, punchline or retort. — *adj* **zing'y** (*colloq*) full of zest, etc. [Imit.]

Zinjanthropus. See **nutcracker man** under **nut**.

zinked, zinkify, etc. See under **zinc**.

zinnia *zin'i-ə*, *n* any plant of the *Zinnia* genus of American composite plants, popular for their bright, showy flowers. [From J.G. *Zinn*, botanist (1727–59).]

Zion *zī'ən*, *n* Jerusalem; the Israelitish theocracy; the Jewish people; a place ruled over by God; the Christian Church; heaven. — *n* **Zī'onism** the movement which secured national privileges and territory in Palestine for the Jews and which now helps to maintain and develop the state of Israel. — *n* **Zī'onist** a supporter of Zionism. [Heb. *tsīyōn*, orig. the name of a part of one of the hills of Jerusalem.]

zip[1] *zip*, *n* the ping or sound of a bullet striking an object or whizzing through the air; a whizzing sound; a zip-fastener; energy, vigour (*colloq*). — *vi* and *vt* to whizz; to fasten with a zip; to be full of, act with, or proceed with, or (usu. **zip up**) infuse with, life and energy (*colloq*): — *pr p* **zipp'ing**; *pa t* and *pa p* **zipped**. — *n* **zipp'er** (esp. *US*) a zip-fastener. — *adj* **zipp'ered** provided with a zip-fastener. — *adj* **zipp'y** (*colloq*) quick, energetic, lively. — **zip-fastener** (*zip-fäs'nər*) a fastening device for clothes, etc. on which two sets of teeth can be opened or interlocked by pulling a slide. — *adj* **zip'-front, zip'-neck, zip'top,** etc., having the front, neck or top opening, etc. fastened with a zip. — *adj* **zip'-on, zip'-off, zip'-in,** etc., able to be added, removed, inserted, etc. by means of a zip. [Imit.]

zip[2] *zip* or **zippo** *zip'ō*, (*slang*; orig. *US*) *n* nothing, zero.

zip code *zip kōd*, (*US*) *n* the postal code. [*z*one *i*mprovement *p*lan.]

zircon *zûr'kən*, *n* a tetragonal mineral, zirconium silicate, of which jacinth and jargoon are varieties. — *n* **zircall'oy** an alloy of zirconium with tin, chromium and nickel, widely used (esp. in the nuclear power industry) for its heat- and corrosion-resistant properties. — *n* **zircō'nia** oxide of zirconium. — *adj* **zirconic** (*-kon'ik*) of zirconium. — *n* **zircō'nium** a metallic element (symbol **Zr**; atomic no. 40), highly resistant to corrosion. — **cubic zirconia** a synthetic stone used as a diamond substitute, produced from zirconia heated with any of various stabilising metallic oxides. [Ar. *zarqūn* — Pers. *zargūn*, gold-coloured; cf. **jargoon** (see **jargon[2]**).]

zit *zit*, (*slang*) *n* a spot, pimple.

zither *zidh'ər* or *zith'ər*, *n* a stringed instrument with a wooden frame and flat sounding-board with from 29 to 42 metal strings, placed on a table or on the knees, the strings being played by a plectrum on the right thumb. — Also **zith'ern**. [Ger.]

ziti *zē'tē*, *npl* a type of pasta like large, short-cut macaroni. [It. (sing. *zita*).]

zizania *zi-* or *zī-zā'ni-ə*, *n* any tall aquatic grass of the genus *Zizania*, known as *wild*, *water*, *Indian* or *Canada rice*. [Gr. *zizanion*, darnel.]

zizz or **ziz** *ziz*, (*slang*) *n* a nap, sleep. — Also *vi*. [Representation of *z-z-z-z-...*, the conventional phoneticisation of snoring used in strip cartoons, etc.]

zloty *zlot'i* or *zwot'ü*, *n* the monetary unit (abbrev. **Zl.**) of Poland (100 *groszy*): — *pl* **zlot'y** or **zlot'ys**. — [Pol. *zloty*, lit. golden.]

Zn (*chem*) *symbol* for zinc.

zoa. See **zoon**.

zoanthropy *zō-an'thrə-pi*, *n* a form of mental delusion in which the sufferer believes him- or herself to be an animal. — *adj* **zōanthropic** (*-throp'ik*). [Gr. *zōion*, animal, *anthrōpos*, man.]

zodiac *zō'di-ak*, *n* an imaginary belt in the heavens, about 18° wide, through which the ecliptic passes centrally, and which forms the background of the motions of the sun, moon and planets. It is divided into twelve equal parts of 30° called **signs of the zodiac,** named from the constellations that once corresponded to them but do so no longer. The constellations, with the appropriate symbols of the corresponding signs, are as follows: Aries (*Ram*), ♈: Taurus (*Bull*), ♉; Gemini (*Twins*), ♊: Cancer (*Crab*), ♋: Leo (*Lion*), ♌; Virgo (*Virgin*), ♍: Libra (*Balance*), ♎: Scorpio (*Scorpion*), ♏: Sagittarius (*Archer*), ♐: Capricorn (*Goat*), ♑: Aquarius (*Water-bearer*), ♒: Pisces (*Fishes*), ♓; a set or diagram of these; a set of twelve, or a recurrent series or course (*fig*). — *adj* **zodī'acal**. — **zodiacal light** a faint illumination of the sky, lenticular in form and elongated in the direction of the ecliptic on either side of the sun, fading away at about 90° from it, best seen after sunset or before sunrise in the tropics. [Fr. *zodiaque* — L. *zōdiacus* — Gr. *zōidiakos*, of figures — *zōidion*, a small carved or painted figure — *zōion*, an animal.]

zoic *zō'ik*, *adj* pertaining to animals; (of rocks) containing evidences of life, in the form of fossils. [Gr. *zōikos*, of animals — *zōion*, an animal.]

Zöllner's lines *tsœl'nərz līnz*, *npl* rows of parallel lines appearing to be not parallel through the optical effect of oblique intersecting lines. — Also **Zöllner's illusion** or **pattern**. [J.K.F. *Zöllner* (1834–82), German physicist.]

Zollverein *tsol'fər-īn*, (*hist*) *n* a customs union, *specif* the 19th-cent. union of the German states, under the leadership of Prussia, to enable them to act as one state in their commercial relations with other countries. [Ger., *Zoll*, duty, *Verein*, union.]

zombie or **zombi** *zom'bi*, *n* a corpse reanimated by sorcery; the power supposed to enter such a body; a stupid or useless person; a very slow-moving, lethargic person; in voodooism (orig. in Africa) the deity of the python. — *n* **zom'biism** belief in a zombie, or practice of rites associated with it. [W.Afr. *zumbi*, fetish.]

zona *zō'nə*, *n* an area, patch, strip or band (*zool*); a zone; a zona pellucida; herpes zoster: — **zō'nae** (*-nē*). — *adj* **zō'nal**, **zō'nary** or **zō'nate**. — **zona pellucida** (*pe-lōō'si-də*; *zool*) a thick, transparent membrane around the mature mammalian ovum. [L., girdle.]

zone *zōn*, *n* a region; any continuous tract with particular characteristics; a girdle, belt or encircling stripe of different colour or substance; one of the five great belts into which the surface of the earth is divided by the tropics and arctic and antarctic circles; a group of strata characterised by a distinctive fauna or flora, and bearing the name of one fossil, called the **zonal index** (*geol*); a set of crystal faces all parallel to the same line (the **zonal** or **zone axis**); that part of the surface of a sphere between two parallel planes, intersecting the sphere (*math*). — *vt* to encircle, e.g. with a zone; to mark with zones; to divide into, or assign to, zones, or (esp. with *off*) mark as a zone. — *adj* **zō'nal** or **zō'nary** like a zone; arranged in zones; pertaining to a zone. — *adj* **zō'nate** or **zō'nated** marked with zones, belted. — *n* **zonā'tion** (*bot*) the formation of bands differentiated by colour or other characteristics, or the arrangement of such bands; the occurrence of vegetation in well-marked bands, each band having its characteristic dominant species. — *adj* **zoned**. — *adj* **zone'less**. — *n* **zō'ning** division into zones; assignment according to zones. — **zonal defence** (*football*, etc.) a method of defending in which a player patrols a particular area of the field rather than marking a specific opponent; **zone'-ticket** a railway ticket available for a time between any stations of a group. [L. *zōna* — Gr. *zōnē*, a girdle — *zōnnynai*, to gird.]

zonk *zonk*, (*colloq*) *n* a sharp blow; the sound of a swift, sharp or firm impact. — *vt* to hit sharply, or with a zonk, to blast. — Also *adv*. — *adj* **zonked** (*zongkt*) or **zonked out** (*slang*) utterly exhausted; in a deep sleep; intoxicated; under the influence of drugs. [Imit.]

zoo *zōō*, *n* a zoological garden or park; orig. the Zoological Gardens, London.

zoo- *zō-ō-* or *zō-o'-*, also **zo-** *zō-*, *combining form* denoting (esp. in zoological terms, etc.) animal. — *adj* **zoobiotic** (*zō-ō-bī-ot'ik*) parasitic on, or living in association with, an animal. — *n* **zooblast** (*zō'ō-blast*) an animal cell. — *adj* **zōochem'ical**. — *n* **zōochem'istry** the chemistry of the animal body. — *adj* **zoogamous** (*zō-og'ə-məs*; Gr. *gamos*, marriage) pertaining to zoogamy. — *n* **zōog'amy** sexual reproduction of animals. — *n* **zōogeog'rapher**. — *adj* **zōogeograph'ic** or **zōogeograph'ical**. — *n* **zōogeog'raphy** the science of the distribution of animals on the surface of the globe. — *n* **zōog'rapher** or **zōog'raphist** an expert in or scholar of **zoog'raphy**, the study or description of animals and their habits, or, the painting of animals. — *adj* **zōograph'ic** or **zōograph'ical**. — *n* **zōol'ater** (Gr. *latreiā*, worship) a person who worships animals. — *adj* **zōol'atrous**. — *n* **zōol'atry** worship of animals. — **zoological**, etc. see separate entry for **zoology**. — *n* **zoomancy** (*zō'ō-man-si*; Gr. *manteiā*, divination) divination by observation of animals. — *adj* **zōōman'tic**. — *adj* **zōōmet'ric**. — *n* **zōometry** (*-om'ə-tri*; Gr. *metron*, a measure) comparative measurement of the parts of animals. — *n* **zō'omorph** (*-mörf*; Gr. *morphē*, form) in art, a representation of an animal form; an image or symbol of a god, etc. who is conceived as having an animal form. — *adj* **zōomor'phic** pertaining to zoomorphism; representing animals in art. — *n* **zōomor'phism** the representation, or the conception, of a god or a man in an animal form. — Also **zōomor'phy**. — *n* **zōon'omist**. — *n* **zoonomy** (*zō-on'ə-mi*; Gr. *nomos*, law) animal physiology. — **zoonosis**, etc. see separate entry. — *n* **zōopathol'ogy** the study of disease in animals. — *npl* **Zoophaga** (*zō-of'ə-gə*; Gr. *phagein*, to eat) the carnivorous animals collectively. — *adj* **zōoph'agous** of or relating to the Zoophaga; feeding on animals. — *n* **zō'ophile** (*-fīl*) a zoophilist; a zoophilous plant. — *n* **zōophil'ia**, **zōoph'ilism** or **zōoph'ily** love of animals; erotic fondness for animals. — *n* **zoophilist** (*zō-of'il-ist*) a lover of animals; someone who has zoophilia. — *adj* **zōoph'ilous** loving animals; pollinated by animals other than insects (*bot*); (of insects) feeding on animals (*zool*); experiencing zoophilia. — *n* **zō'ophyte** (*-fīt*) any of numerous invertebrates resembling plants, such as sponges, corals, sea-anemones, etc. — *adj* **zōophytic** (*-fit'ik*) or **zōophyt'al**. — *adj* **zōoph'ytoid**. — *adj* **zōophytolog'ical** (*-fīt-*). — *n* **zōophytol'ogist**. — *n* **zōophytol'ogy**. — *n* **zōoplank'ton** floating and drifting animal life. — *n* **zō'osperm** (Gr. *sperma*, seed) a spermatozoid; a zoospore. — *adj* **zōospermat'ic**. — *n* **zōosporan'gium** (*bot*) a sporangium in which zoospores are formed. — *n* **zō'ospore** an asexual reproductive cell that can swim by means of flagella. — *adj* **zōospor'ic** or **zōos'porous**. — *n* **zō'otaxy** (Gr. *taxis*, arrangement) the science of the classification of animals, systematic zoology. — *n* **zōotechnics** (*-tek'niks*) or **zō'otechny** the science of the breeding and domestication of animals, animal husbandry. — *n* **zōot'omy** the dissection of animals; comparative anatomy. — *n* **zōotox'in** a toxin produced by an animal, such as a snake. — *adj* **zōotroph'ic** (*-trof'ik*) pertaining to the nourishment of animals. — *n* **zōot'rophy**. [Gr. *zōion*, animal.]

zooid *zō'oid*, (*zool*) *n* a free-moving cell, such as a sperm-cell; (in alternation of generations) an individual of an asexually-produced form; an individual forming part of a colonial organism. — *adj* **zōoid'al**. [**zoo-** and **-oid**.]

zoolatry, etc. See under **zoo-**.

zoology *zōō-* or *zō-ol'ə-ji*, *n* the science of animal life included along with botany in the science of biology;

the animal life of a region, etc. — *adj* **zoological** (*-loj'i-kəl*). — *adv* **zoolog'ically**. — *n* **zool'ogist** an expert in or scholar of zoology. — **zoological garden** or **park** a garden or park where living animals are kept, studied and exhibited to the public. [N.L. *zoolōgia*; see **zoo-** and **-logy**.]

zoom *zōōm*, *vi* to make a loud, deep, persistent buzzing noise; to move with this sound; to move very quickly; to use the stored energy of the forward motion of an aircraft in order to gain height (*aeronautics*); to soar (*fig*); to change focal length rapidly, as with a zoom lens. — *vt* to cause to zoom. — *n* the act of zooming; a zooming noise. — **zoom lens** a lens of variable focal length used e.g. for bringing television, cinematograph or cine-camera pictures from distance to close-up without moving the camera; a similar lens used in still cameras and in microscopes. [Imit.]

zoomancy .... to ... **zoomorphy**. See under **zoo-**.

zoon *zō'on*, (*zool*) *n* a morphological individual, the total product of a fertilised ovum, or the group of zooids constituting a compound animal: — *pl* **zō'a** or **zō'ons**. — *adj* **zō'onal**. [N.L. — Gr. *zōion*, an animal.]

zoonomy, etc. See under **zoo-**.

zoonosis *zō-ən-ō'sis* or *zō-on'ə-sis*, *n* a disease of animals which can be transmitted to man: — *pl* **zoonō'ses** (*-sēz*; also *-on'ə-sēz*). — *adj* **zoonot'ic**. [Gr. *zōion*, an animal, *nosos*, disease.]

zoopathology ... to ... **zootrophy**. See under **zoo-**.

zoot suit *zōōt sōōt*, *n* a flashy type of man's suit with padded shoulders, fitted waist, knee-length coat, and trousers narrow at the ankles (introduced late 1940s). — *n* **zoot'suiter** someone who wears a zoot suit. [Prob. from the rhyme with **suit**.]

zoppa *tsop'pə*, (*mus*) *adj* with syncopation. [It., fem. of *zoppo*, limping.]

zoril, zorille, zorillo, zorino. See under **zorro**.

Zoroastrianism *zor-ō-as'tri-ən-izm*, *n* an ancient religion based on dualistic (see under **dual**) doctrine founded or reformed by *Zoroaster* (the Greek pronunciation of Zarathustra) set forth in the Zend-Avesta, and still followed by the Guebres in Iran and Parsees in India. — *n* and *adj* **Zoroas'trian**. [L. *Zōroastrēs* — Gr.]

zorro *sor'ō*, *n* a S. American fox or foxlike wild dog: — *pl* **zorr'os**. — *n* **zoril** or **zorille** (*zor'il* or *-il'*) an African skunklike animal of the marten family (*Zorilla*). — *n* **zorillo** (*sor-ē'yō* or *zor-il'ō*) a S. American skunk: — *pl* **zorill'os**. — *n* **zorino** (*zor-ēn'ō*) a euphemism for skunk fur used to make garments: — *pl* **zorin'os**. [Sp. *zorro*, *zorra*, fox, *zorilla*, skunk.]

zoster *zos'tər*, (*med*) *n* herpes zoster or shingles. [Gr. *zōstēr*, a girdle or waist-belt.]

Zouave *zōō-äv'* or *zwäv*, *n* one of a body of French infantry, orig. Algerians, wearing a quasi-Moorish uniform; any of a number of volunteer regiments modelling themselves on the Zouaves who fought on the side of the North in the American Civil War (*hist*). [From the *Zouaoua*, an Algerian tribe.]

ZPG *abbrev* for zero population growth.

Zr (*chem*) *symbol* for zirconium.

ZRE *abbrev* for Zaire (I.V.R.).

zucchetto *tsōō-ket'ō*, *n* a skullcap worn by a R.C. ecclesiastic, covering the tonsure: — *pl* **zucchett'os**. — Also **zuchett'a** or **zuchett'o** (*pl* **zuchett'os**). [It. dimin. of *zucca*, a gourd.]

zucchini *zōō-kē'nē*, (esp. *US* and *Austr*) *n* a courgette: — *pl* **zucchi'ni** or **zucchi'nis**. [It.]

zugzwang *tsōōhh'tsväng*, (*chess*) *n* a blockade position in which any move is disadvantageous to the blockaded player. [Ger.]

Zulu *zōō'lōō*, *n* a branch of the large Bantu family, belonging to S. Africa; a member of this; the language of the Zulus. — *adj* pertaining to the Zulus, their language, etc. [Native name.]

zurf. See **zarf**.

ZW *abbrev* for Zimbabwe (I.V.R.).

zwieback *tsvē'bäk* or *tswē'bäk*, *n* (also with *cap*) biscuit rusk, or a sweet spiced bread toasted. [Ger.]

Zwinglian *zwing'gli-ən* or *tsving'li-ən*, *adj* pertaining to the Swiss reformer Huldreich *Zwingli* (1484–1531) or his doctrines, esp. his divergence from Luther in the doctrine of the Eucharist. — *n* a follower of Zwingli. — *n* **Zwing'lianism**. — *n* **Zwing'lianist**.

zwischenzug *zvish'ən-zōōg* or *tsvish'ən-tsōōk*, (*chess*) *n* an interim move, made to disrupt one's opponent's plan. [Ger., — *zwischen*, between, *Zug*, move.]

zwitterion *tsvit'ər-ī-ən*, (*chem*) *n* an ion carrying both a positive and a negative charge. [Ger. *Zwitter*, a hybrid, and **ion**.]

zygo- *zī-gō-* or *zi-gō-*, also before a vowel **zyg-** *zīg-* or *zig-*, *combining form* denoting a yoke, union or presence of two similar things. — *adj* **zy'gal** pertaining to a zygon; formed like a letter H. — *n* **zygapophysis** (*-pof'i-sis*; Gr. *apophysis*, process; *zool*) one of the yoke-pieces or articulations of the vertebrae: — *pl* **zygapoph'ysēs**. — *n* and *adj* **zy'gobranch** or **zygobranch'iate**. — *adj* **zygobranchiate** (*-brangk'i-āt*; Gr. *branchia*, gills) having paired, symmetrically placed, gills; belonging to the **Zygobranchiā'ta**, a division of the *Gastropoda*. — *n* **zy'gocactus** a cactus of the Brazilian genus (*Zygocactus*) of jointed, branching cactuses having zygomorphic flowers. — *adj* **zygodactyl** (*-dak'til*; Gr. *daktylos*, toe) having two toes in front and behind, as parrots do. — Also **zygodactyl'ic** or **zygodac'tylous**. — *n* **zygodac'tylism**. — *adj* **zygomor'phic** or **zygomorphous** (*-mör'fəs*) yoke-shaped — of flowers symmetrical about one plane only. — *n* **zygomor'phism** or **zy'gomorphy**. — *n* **zy'gophyte** (*-fīt*; Gr. *phyton*, a plant) a plant in which reproduction takes place by means of zygospores. — *adj* **zygopleural** (*-plōō'rəl*; Gr. *pleurā*, side) bilaterally symmetrical. — *n* **zy'gospore** (*bot*) a spore produced by the union of buds from two adjacent hyphae in the process of conjugation by which some fungi multiply. — Also **zy'gosperm**. — *n* **zy'gote** (*bot* and *zool*) the product of the union of two gametes; by extension, the individual developing from that product. — *adj* **zygotic** (*-got'ik*). [Gr. *zygon*, yoke.]

zymase *zī'māz* or *-mās*, *n* any of a group of enzymes inducing the alcoholic fermentation of carbohydrates. [Fr., — Gr. *zȳmē*, leaven, and sfx. *-ase* denoting an enzyme.]

zymo- *zī-mō-* or before a vowel **zym-** *zīm-*, *combining form* relating to fermentation. — *n* **zy'mogen** (*biol*) a non-catalytic substance formed by plants and animals as a stage in the development of an enzyme. — *adj* **zymogen'ic**. — *adj* **zymolog'ic** or **zymolog'ical** pertaining to zymology. — *n* **zymol'ogist** someone skilled in zymology. — *n* **zymol'ogy** the science of fermentation. — *n* **zymol'ysis** the action of enzymes. — *adj* **zymolyt'ic**. — *n* **zymom'eter** an instrument for measuring the degree of fermentation. — *n* **zymō'sis** fermentation; the morbid process, thought to be analogous to fermentation, constituting a zymotic disease. — *adj* **zymot'ic** pertaining to fermentation; of the nature of, pertaining to, or causing, an infectious disease. — *adv* **zymot'ically**. [Gr. *zȳmē*, leaven, *zȳmōsis*, fermentation.]

zymurgy *zī'mûr-ji*, *n* the department of technological chemistry that deals with wine-making, brewing, distilling, and similar processes involving fermentation. [Gr. *zȳmē*, leaven, *ergon*, work.]

Zyrian *zir'i-ən*, *n* one of a people of north-western U.S.S.R.; their Finno-Ugric language. — Also *adj*.

Appendices

Some first names

Masculine names are marked *m*, feminine names *f*.

Aaron *ā'rən, m* (Heb.) lofty, mountaineer.

Abigail *ab'i-gāl, f* (Heb.) father rejoiced, or father of exaltation.—Dimins. **Abby, Nabby, Gail.**

Abraham *ā'brə-həm,* **Abram** *ā'brəm, m* (Heb.) perhaps father of a multitude, high father.—Dimins. **Abe, Aby, Bram.**

Ada *ā'də, f* prob. for **Adelaide** or other Gmc. name in *Adel-, Adal-* (noble).

Adam *ad'əm, m* (Heb.) man, earth, red earth.

Adela *ad'i-lə,* **Adèle** *-del',* **Adella** *-del'ə, f* (Gmc.) noble.

Adelaide *ad'i-lād, f* Fr. *Adélaïde* from Ger. *Adelheid(is),* noble kind (i.e. sort).—Dimins. **Addie, Addy.**

Adeline *ad'i-lin, -lēn, -līn, f* (Gmc.) noble.—Dimins. **Addie, Addy.**

Aden *ā'dən, m* form of **Aidan.**—Also (from Heb. *Adin*) ornament.

Adrian *ā'dri-ən, m* (L.) of Adria (in Italy).—Fem. **Adrianne** (*-an'*), **Adrienne** (*-en'*), **Adriane** (*ad-ri-än'*), **Adriana** (*-ä'nə*).

Agatha *ag'ə-thə, f* (Gr.) good.—Dimin. **Aggie.**

Agnes *ag'nis, f* (Gr.) chaste.—Dimins. **Aggie, Aggy, Nance, Nancy, Nessa, Nessie, Nesta.**

Aidan, Aiden *ā'dən, m* (Gael.) a dimin. form from Gael. *aod(h),* fire.

Aileen *ā'lēn, ī'lēn, f* Anglo-Irish form of **Eileen, Evelyn** and **Helen.**

Ailsa *āl'sə, f* from the Scottish island rock, Ailsa Craig.—Confused with **Elsa.**

Alan, Allan, Allen, Alyn *al'ən, m* (prob. Celt.) harmony.—Fem. **Alana** (*ə-lä'nə*), **Alanna** (*ə-lan'ə*).

Alasdair, Alastair. See **Alexander.**

Albert *al'bərt, m* (Gmc.) nobly bright.—Dimins. **Al, Bert, Bertie.**

Aldis, Aldous, Aldus *öl'dəs, m* (Gmc.) old.

Aldwin, Aldwyn *öl'dwin, m* (Gmc.) old friend.

Aled *al'id, m* from the name of the Welsh river.

Alexander *al-ig-zan'dər, -zän', m* (Gr.) defender of men.—Also (from Gael.) **Alasdair, Alastair, Alistair, Alister** (*al'is-tər*).—Dimins. **Alec, Aleck, Alex, Alick, Sandy.**—Fem. **Alexandra, Alexandrina** (*-drē'nə, -drī'nə*).—Dimin. **Alexa, Sandra, Zandra.**

Alexis *ə-lek'sis, m* and *f* (Gr.) helper.

Alfred *al'frid, m* (Gmc.) elf counsel (good counsellor).—Dimins. **Alf, Alfie, Alured** (*-ū-rəd*).

Alice, Alys *al'is,* **Alicia** *ə-lish'i-ə, -lis'i-ə, f* (Gmc.) from O.Fr. *Aliz* for Gmc. *Adalheidis* (see **Adelaide**).—Dimins. **Ailie, Ali, Allie, Ally, Ellie, Elsie.** See also **Alison.**

Aline *ə-lēn',* or *al'ēn, f* for **Adeline.**

Alison, Allison *al'i-sən, f* a form of **Alice,** mainly Scots, now considered a separate name.—Dimins. **Ailie, Ali, Elsie.**

Alistair. See **Alexander.**

Allan, Allen. Forms of **Alan.**

Alma *al'mə, f* (L.) fostering, nourishing, loving.

Althea *al-thē'ə, al', f* (Gr.) a healer, or wholesome.

Alun *al'ən, m* from the name of a Welsh river.

Alured. See **Alfred.**

Alvin, Alvyn *al'vin,* **Alwin, Alwyn** *al'win, m* (Gmc.) elf (good or noble) friend.

Alyn. See **Alan.**

Alys. See **Alice.**

Amabel *am'ə-bel, f* (L.) lovable.—Derivative **Mabel.**

Amanda *ə-man'də, f* (L.) lovable.—Dimin. **Mandy.**

Amber *am'bər, f* (Eng.) from the precious material.

Ambrose *am'brōz, m* (Gr.) of the immortals, divine.

Amelia *ə-mē'li-ə, -mēl'yə, f* (Gmc.) struggling, labour.—Dimin. **Millie.**

Amos *ā'mos, m* (Heb.) strong, bearing a burden.

Amy *ā'mi, f* (Fr.) beloved.

Anastasia *an-ə-stā'zhə, -zi-ə, f* (Gr.) resurrection.—Dimin. **Stacey, Stacy** (*stā'si*).

Andrew *an'drōō, m* (Gr.) manly.—Dimins. **Andie, Andy, Dandy, Drew.**—Fem. **Andrea** (*-dri-ə*), **Andrina** (*-drē'nə*).

Aneurin, Aneirin *a-nā'rin, -nī', -noi', m* (Welsh) meaning doubtful, perh. for L. *Honorius.*

Angela *an'ji-lə, f,* **Angel** *ān'jəl, m* and *f,* (Gr.) angel, messenger.—Fem. deriv. **Angelica** (*-jel'ik-ə*).—Dimins. **Angelina** (*an-ji-lē'nə, -lī'nə*), **Angie, Angy** (*an'ji*).

Angharad *an-gar'ad, -hhar'ad, f* (Welsh) much loved.

Angus *ang'gəs, m* (Celt.) perh. one choice.

Ann, Anne *an,* **Anna** *an'ə,* **Hannah** *han'ə, f* (Heb.) grace.—Dimins. **Anita** (*ə-nē'tə,* Sp.), **Anneka, Annika** (*an'ək-ə,* Sw.), **Annette** (*a-net',* Fr.), **Annie, Nan, Nance, Nancy, Nina** (*nē'nə, nī'nə*), **Ninette** (*nē-net',* Fr.).

Annabel, Annabelle, Annabella *an'ə-bel, -bel'ə, f* prob. for **Amabel.**

Anthea *an-thē'ə, an', f* (Gr.) flowery.

Anthony, Antony *an'tə-ni, m* (L.) from a Roman family name, meaning unknown.—Dimins. **Tony** (*tō'ni*), **Nanty.**—Fem. **Antonia.**—Dimins. **Antoinette** (Fr.), **Net, Nettie, Netty.**

April *ā'pril, f* (L.) from the name of the month.

Arabella *ar-ə-bel'ə, f* origin and meaning doubtful; perh. for **Amabel,** or perh. (L. *orabilis*) easily entreated.—Dimins. **Bel, Bell, Bella, Belle.**

Archibald *är'chi-bld, -böld, m* (Gmc.) genuine and bold.—Dimins. **Archie, Archy, Baldie.**

Arleen, Arlene *är'lēn, f* variants of **Aline.**

Arnold *är'nld, -nold, m* (Gmc.) eagle strength.

Arthur *är'thər, m* (Celt.) perh. bear, or (Ir.) stone; or from a Roman family name *Artorius.*

Ashley, Ashleigh *ash'li, m* and *f* (Gmc.) from the surname derived from common place name, meaning ash wood.
Aubrey *ö'bri, m* (Gmc.) elf (good or noble) rule.
Audrey *ö'dri, f* (Gmc.) noble power.
Augustine *ö'gəs-tēn, ö-gus'tin,* **Austin** *ös'tin, m* (L.) belonging to Augustus.
Augustus *ö-gus'təs, m* (L.) venerable, exalted.—Dimins. **Gus, Gussie, Gustus.**—Fem. **Augusta.**
Auriel, Auriol *ör'i-əl, f* derivs. of L. *aurum*, gold.
Aurora *ö-rö'rə,* **Aurore** *-rōr', -rör', f* (L.) dawn.
Austin. See **Augustine.**
Avril *av'ril, m* and *f* (Fr.) April.

Baptist *bap'tist, m* (Gr.) baptiser.—Fem. **Baptista.**
Barbara *bär'bə-rə, f* (Gr.) foreign, stranger.—Dimins. **Bab, Babs, Babbie, Barbie.**
Barnabas *bär'nə-bəs,* **Barnaby** *-bi, m* (Heb.) son of exhortation.—Dimin. **Barney.**
Barney *bär'ni, m.* See **Bernard, Barnabas.**
Barry *bar'i, m* (Ir.) spear.
Bartholomew *bär-, bər-thol'ə-mū, m* (Heb.) son of Talmi.—Dimins. **Bart, Bat.**
Basil *baz'il, m* (Gr.) kingly.
Beatrice, Beatrix *bē'ə-tris, -triks, bē-ā'triks, f* (L.) making happy.—Dimins. **Bee, Beatty, Trix, Trixie.**
Becky *bek'i, f.* See **Rebecca.**
Belinda *bə-lin'də, f* (Gmc.) the second part meaning snake, the first unexplained.
Bell, Belle *bel,* **Bella** *bel'ə, f.* See **Isabella,** also **Arabella.**
Benedict, Benedick *ben'i-dikt, -dik,* **Bennet** *ben'it, m* (L.) blessed.
Benjamin *ben'jə-min, m* (Heb.) son of the right hand (i.e. of good fortune).—Dimins. **Ben, Benjie, Bennie.**
Berenice *ber-i-nī'sē, ber-nē'sē, ber'i-nēs,* **Bernice** *bûr-nēs', f* (Gr.), from the Macedonian form of *Pherenīkē*, victory-bringer.—Dimins. **Bunnie, Bunny.**—See also **Veronica.**
Bernard *bûr'nərd, m* (Gmc.) bear-hard.—Dimins. **Bernie, Barney.**—Fem. **Bernadette.**
Bert *bûrt,* **Bertie** *bûr'ti, m* for **Albert, Bertram** or **Herbert.**—Both are used for any name ending in *-bert*, and (*f*) for **Bertha.**
Bertha *bûr'thə, f* (Gmc.) bright.—Dimins. **Bert, Bertie.**
Bertram *bûr'trəm, m* (Gmc.) bright raven.—Dimins. **Bertie, Bert.**
Beryl *ber'il, f* (Gr.) from the precious stone.
Bess, Bessie, Beth, Betsy, Bettina, Betty. See **Elizabeth.**
Beverley *bev'ər-li, m* and *f* (Gmc.) from the surname and place name meaning beaver meadow or stream.
Biddie, Biddy *bid'i, f.* See **Bridget.**
Bill. See **William.**
Blanche, Blanch *blänsh, f* (Fr.—Gmc.) white.
Blodwen *blod'win, f* (Welsh) white flower.
Bob. See **Robert.**
Bonnie *bon'i, f* (Scot.) comely, pretty.
Boris *bor'is, bö', m* (Russ.) fight.
Bram. See **Abraham.**
Brenda *bren'də, f* perh. a fem. form of the Norse name *Brand*, brand, or sword, or a fem. form of **Brendan.**
Brendan *bren'dən, m* (Ir.) meaning uncertain—stinking hair has been suggested.
Brett *bret, m* (Eng.) from L. *Brit(t)o*, Briton.
Brian, Bryan *brī'ən, m* (Celt.) meaning doubtful.
Bridget, Brigid *brij'it, f* (Celt.) strength; name of a Celtic fire-goddess, an Irish saint; partly from the Swedish saint *Brigitto* (prob. a different name).—Dimins. **Biddie, Biddy, Bridie** (*brī'di*).
Briony, Bryony *brī'ə-ni, f* (Eng.) from the plant name.
Bronwen *bron'win, f* (Welsh) white breast.
Bruce *brōōs, m* from the surname, orig. from Normandy, and the place name *Brieuse.*
Bruno *brōō'nō, m* (Gmc.) brown.
Bryan. See **Brian.**
Brynmor *brin'mör, m* (Welsh) from the place name formed from *bryn*, hill and *mawr*, great.—Dimin. **Bryn.**
Bryony. See **Briony.**
Bunnie, Bunny *bun'i, m* and *f* (Eng.) a general pet-name, or (*f*) a dimin. of **Berenice.**

Caleb *kā'lib, m* (Heb.) dog, or bold.—Dimin. **Cal** (*kal*).
Cameron *kam'ə-rən, m* (Gael.) hooked or crooked nose; from the surname and clan name.
Camilla *kə-mil'ə, f* (L.) a free-born attendant at a sacrifice; in Virgil, name of a queen of the Volsci.
Candace, Candice *kan'dis, f* meaning unknown; dynastic name of the queens of ancient Ethiopia.—Dimin. **Candy.**
Candida *kan'di-də, f* (L.) white.
Carl, Karl *karl, m* Germanic forms of **Charles.**
Carla, Carleen, Carlene, Carlotta. See **Charles.**
Carmen *kär'mən* (Sp.), **Carmel** *kär'məl* (Heb.), *f* the garden.
Carol, Carola, Carole, Caroline, Carolyn. See under **Charles.**
Cassandra. See Dict.
Catherine, Catharine, Katherine, Katharine, Kathryn *kath'(ə-)rin,* **Catherina** *-ə-rē'nə,* **Katrine** *kat'rin,* **Katerina** *kat-ə-rē'nə,* **Katrina, Kathleen** *kath'lēn* (Ir. *Caitlin*), *f* from Gr. *Aikaterinē*, of unknown origin, later assimilated to *katharos*, pure.—Dimins. **Casey, Cathie, Cathy, Kate, Katie, Katy, Kathie, Kathy, Kay, Kit, Kittie, Kitty.**
Catriona *kə-trē'ə-nə, kat-ri-ō'nə, f.* See **Catherine.**
Cecil *ses'il,* also *sēs', sis', m* (L.) the Roman family name *Caecilius* (lit. blind).—Fem. **Cecilia** (*si-sil'yə, -sēl'yə*), **Cecily** (*ses'i-li*), **Cicely** (*sis'(i-)li*), **Sisley.**—Dimins. **Sis, Cis, Sissy, Sissie, Cissy, Cissie.**
Cedric *sed'rik, m* prob. a mistake of Scott's for *Cerdic* (name of the first king of the West Saxons, but apparently not really English—perh. a British name).
Celeste *si-lest', f,* **Celestine** *si-les'tēn, -tīn, -tin, f,* also *m,* (L.) heavenly.

Celia *sē'li-ə, f* fem. of the Roman family name *Caelius* (poss. heavenly).—Sometimes used for **Cecilia.**

Celina. See **Selina.**

Ceri *ker'i, m* and *f* (Welsh) to love.

Chad *chad, m* (Celt.) battle; name of the Northumbrian saint, Bishop of Mercia.

Charity *char'i-ti, f* (Eng.) charity.—Deriv. **Cherry.**

Charles *chärlz, m* (Gmc.) manly.—Also **Carol** *kar'ol.*—Dimins. **Charlie, Charley, Chae, Chay** (*chā*), **Chuck.**—Fem. **Carla, Karla** (*kär'lə*), **Carleen, Carlene** (*kär-lēn'*), **Carol, Carole** (*kar'əl*), **Carola** (*-lə*), **Caroline** (*kar'ə-līn, -lēn, -lin*), **Carolyn, Carlotta** (*kär-lot'ə*), **Charlene** (*shär'lēn, -lēn'*), **Charlotte** (*shär'lət*).—Dimins. **Caddie, Carly, Carrie, Lina** (*lē'nə*), **Lottie, Chat** (*shat*), **Chatty, Sharley.**

Charmaine, Sharmaine *shär-mān', f* (L.) derived from *Carminea*, fem. of Roman clan name *Carmineus.*—Confused with **Charmian.**

Charmian *shär'mi-ən, kär', f* (Gr.) joy.—Confused with **Charmaine.**

Cher, Chère *shār,* **Cherie, Sherry** *sher'i, f* (Fr.) dear one.

Cherry *cher'i, f* from the fruit, or see **Charity.**—Deriv. **Cheryl** (*cher'il, sher'il*).

Chloe *klō'i, f* (Gr.) a green shoot, verdure.

Christabel *kris'tə-bel, f* (L.—Gr.) anointed, or Christ, and (L.) fair.

Christian *kris'ti-ən, -chən, m,* also *f,* belonging to Christ.—Dimins. **Chris, Christie, Christy.**—Fem. **Christiana** (*-ti-ä'nə*), **Christina** (*-tē'nə*), **Christine** (*kris'tēn* or *-tēn'*), **Kirsteen** (*kûrs'tēn*), **Kristen** (*kris'tən*).—Dimins. **Chris, Chrissie, Kirsty, Teenie, Tina** (*tē'nə*).

Christopher *kris'tə-fər, m* (Gr.) carrying Christ.—Dimins. **Chris, Kester, Kit** (Scot. fem. **Crystal, Chrystal**).

Chuck *chuk, m.* See **Charles.**

Cicely. See **Cecilia.**

Cindy, Sindy *sin'di, f* dimins. of **Cynthia, Lucinda.**

Clara *klā'rə, klä'rə,* **Clare, Claire** *klār,* **Clarinda** *klə-rin'də, f* (L.) bright. Derivatives **Clarice** (*klar'is*), **Clarissa.**

Clarence *klar'əns, m* from the dukedom.

Claud, Claude *klöd,* **Claudius** *-i-əs, m* (L.) lame.—Fem. **Claudia.**

Clement *klem'ənt, m* (L.) mild, merciful.—Dimin. **Clem.**—Fem. **Clemency, Clementina** (*-ē'nə*), **Clementine** (*-ēn, -īn*).

Clifford *klif'ərd, m* from the surname.

Clive *klīv, m* from the surname.

Clodagh *klō'də, f* (Ir.) name of a river in Tipperary.

Cody *kō'di, m* and *f* from the Irish surname.

Colette *kol-et', f.* See **Nicholas.**

Colin *kol'in, m* orig. a dimin. of **Nicholas.**

Conor, Connor *kon'ər, m* (Ir.) high desire.—Dimins. **Corney, Corny.—Cornelius** is used as a substitute.

Conrad, Konrad *kon'rad, m* (Ger.) bold in counsel.

Constance *kon'stəns, f* (L.) constancy.—Dimins. **Con, Connie.—Constant** *kon'stənt, m* firm, faithful.—Deriv. **Constantine** (*kon'stən-tīn*), *m.*

Cora *kö'rə, f* (poss. from Gr. *korē*, girl) a name that first appears in J. Fenimore Cooper's *The Last of the Mohicans*, used also as a dimin. e.g. of Sp. *Corazon*, heart.

Cordelia *kör-dē'li-ə, f* perh. (L.) warm-hearted.

Corey *kö'ri, m* from the Irish surname.

Corinne *ko-rin', -rēn',* **Corinna** *-rin'ə, f* (Gr.) dimin. of *korē*, maiden.

Cornelius *kör-nē'li-əs, m* (L.) a Roman family name, prob. related to L. *cornu*, horn.—Used for **Connor.**—Fem. **Cornelia.**

Courtney *kört'ni, m* and *f* from the surname.

Craig *krāg, m* from the surname.

Cressida *kres'i-də, f* (Gr.) English form of *Chryseis*, accus. *Chryseida*, daughter of *Chryses.*

Crispin *kris'pin,* **Crispian** *-pi-ən, m* (L.) curly.

Crystal. See **Christopher.**

Curtis *kûrtis, m* (Fr.) courteous.

Cynthia *sin'thi-ə, f* (Gr.) of Mount Cynthus in Delos, an epithet of Artemis (Diana), huntress and moon-goddess, who was born in Delos.—Dimins. **Cindy, Sindy.**

Cyril *sir'il, m* (Gr.) lordly.

Cyrus *sī'rəs, m* (Pers.) throne.—Dimin. **Cy.**

Daisy *dā'zi, f* (Eng.) a translation of Fr. *Marguerite.*—See **Margaret.**

Dale *dāl, m* and *f* from the surname.

Damian *dā'mi-ən,* **Damon** *-mən, m* (Gr.) perh. connected with *damaein*, to tame.

Daniel *dan'yəl, m* (Heb.) the Lord is judge.—Dimins. **Dan, Danny.**—Fem. **Daniela** (*i-ā'lə*), **Daniella, Danielle** (*-el'*).

Daphne *daf'nē, -ni, f* (Gr.) laurel.

Darren *dar'ən, m* from the Irish surname.

Darryl, Daryl *dar'il, m* (O.E.) darling.

David *dā'vid, m* (Heb.) beloved.—Dimins. **Dave, Davie, Davy.**—Fem. **Vida** *vē'də* (Scot. **Davina,** *də-vē'nə, -vī'nə*).

Dawn *dön, f* (Eng.) dawn.

Dean *dēn, m* from the surname (O.E. see Dict.).

Deanna. See **Diana.**

Deborah *deb'ə-rə, di-bö'rə,* **Debra** *deb'rə, f* (Heb.) bee.—Dimins. **Deb, Debbie, Debby.**

Declan *dek'lən, m* (Ir.) an Irish saint's name.

Deirdre *dēr'dri, f* (Ir.) meaning doubtful.

Del. See **Derek.**

Delia *dē'li-ə, f* (Gr.) of the island of Delos.

Della *del'a, f* for **Adelaide, Delia** or **Cordelia.**

Delyth *del'ith, f* (Welsh) pretty.

Denis, Dennis, *den'is, m* (Fr.—Gr.), belonging to Dionysus or Bacchus.—Fem. **Denise** (*di-nēz'*).

Denzil *den'zil, m* from the surname, from a Cornish place name.

Derek, Derrick *der'ik, m* dimins. of *Theodoric* (Gmc.) people-rule—Dimin. **Del.**

Dermot *dûr'mət, m* (Celt.) free of envy.

Désirée *dā-zē-rā', f* (Fr.) longed for.

Desmond *dez'mənd, m* (Ir.) from the surname or the district.

Diana *dī-an'ə,* **Dian(ne)** *dī-an', dē-,* **Diane** *dē-än', dī-an',* **Deanne** *dē-an',* **Deanna** *-an'ə, f* (L.) the Roman goddess Diana, identified with Artemis.—Dimin. **Di** (*dī*).

Dick, Dickie, Dickon. See **Richard.**

Dilys *dil'is, f* (Welsh) sure, constant, genuine.
Dinah *dīnə, f* (Heb.) judged, or dedicated.
Dolores *də-lö'rez, f* (Sp.) sorrows.—Dimin. **Lola.**
Dolly. See **Dorothy.**
Dominic, Dominick *dom'i-nik, m* (L.) Sunday.
Donald *don'əld,* **Donal** *dō'nəl, don', m* (Celt.) world chief.—Dimins. **Don, Donnie.**
Donna *don'ə, f* (It.) mistress, lady.
Dora *dö'rə, f* prob. a dimin. of **Dorothy**; used also for **Theodora** and names of similar ending.
Doreen *dö'rən, dö-rēn', f* (Ir.) sullen; or for **Dorothy.**
Doris *dor'is, f* (Gr.) the name of a sea-nymph; meaning doubtful.
Dorothy *dor'ə-thi,* **Dorothea** *-thē'ə, f* (Gr.) gift of God.—Dimins. **Dolly, Dora, Do, Dot.**
Dougal, Dugald *do͞o'gəl(d), m* (Celt.) dark stranger.
Douglas *dug'ləs, m* from the surname, or the river.
Drew. See **Andrew.**
Duane, Dwane *dwān, m* (Ir.) from the surname *O Dubhain,* from *dubh,* black.
Dudley *dud'li, m* from the surname.
Dulcie *dul'si, f* (L.) sweet—a modern invention.
Duncan *dung'kən, m* (Celt.) brown, brown warrior.
Dwane. See **Duane.**
Dylan *dil'ən, m* (Welsh) wave, the name of a sea-god.

Eamon(n), Eamunn *ā'mən, em'ən, m* Irish form of **Edmund.**
Ed, Eddie, dimins. of **Edgar, Edmund, Edward, Edwin.**
Edgar *ed'gər, m* (O.E.) happy spear.—Dimins. **Ed, Eddie, Eddy, Ned, Neddie, Neddy.**
Edie. See **Edith.**
Edith *ē'dith, f* (O.E.) happy or rich war.—Dimins. **Edie, Edy.**
Edmund *ed'mənd, m* (O.E.) happy protection.—Dimins. **Ed, Eddie, Eddy, Ned, Neddie, Neddy.**
Edna *ed'nə, f* (Heb.) pleasure, delight.
Edward *ed'wərd, m* (O.E.) rich guard.—Dimins. **Ed, Eddie, Eddy, Ned, Neddie, Neddy, Ted, Teddie, Teddy.**
Edwin *ed'win, m* (O.E.) prosperity or riches, friend.—Dimins. **Ed, Eddie, Eddy, Ned, Neddie, Neddy.**—Fem. **Edwina** (*-wē'nə*).
Eileen *ī'lēn, ī-lēn', f* (Ir.) an old name perh. meaning pleasant; used as a substitute for **Helen.**
Eirene. See **Irene.**
Elaine *i-lān', f* an O.Fr. form of **Helen.**
Eleanor, Eleanore *el'i-nər,* **Elinor, Leonora** *lē-ə-nö'rə, f* same as **Helen.**—Dimins. **Ella, Ellen, Nell, Nellie, Nelly, Nora.**
Elizabeth, Elisabeth *i-liz'ə-beth,* **Eliza** *i-līzə, f* (Heb.) God is satisfaction—Dimins. **Bess, Bessie, Bessy, Bet, Beth, Betsy, Bettina, Betty, Elsie, Libby, Lisa** (*līzə, lē', lē'sə*). **Liza** (*lī'zə* or *lē'*), **Lise** (lēz), **Lisbeth, Lizbeth, Liz** (*liz*), **Lizzie, Lisette** (*li-zet'*).
Ella *el'ə, f* (Gmc.) all.—Also a dimin. of **Eleanor** or of **Isabella** or other name ending in *-ella.*
Ellen *el'in, f* a form of **Helen,** also used for **Eleanor.**
Elma *el'mə, f* for *Wilhelmina,* or a combination of **Elizabeth Mary.**
Elroy *el'roi, m* a variant of **Leroy.**
Elsa *el'sə,* **Elsie** *-si.* See **Elizabeth, Alison, Alice.**
Elspeth *el'spəth,* **Elspet** *el'spət,* Scots forms of **Elizabeth.**
Elton *el'tən, m* from the surname.
Elvira *el-vē'rə,* or *-vī', f* (Sp.) prob. of Gmc. origin, elf (good or noble) counsel.
Elvis *el'vis, m* (Ir.) from *Ailbhe,* the name of an Irish saint.
Elwyn *el'win, m* (Welsh) perh. fair face.
Emery, Emory *em'ə-ri, m* (Gmc.) work-rule, energetic rule.
Emily *em'(i-)li, fem.* (*Emilia*) of the Roman family name *Aemilius.*
Emlyn *em'lin, m* (Welsh) meaning uncertain.
Emma *em'ə, f* (Gmc.) whole, universal.—Dimins. **Emm, Emmie.**
Emmeline, Emeline *em'i-lēn, -līn, f* prob. for **Amelia.**
Emrys *em'ris, m* Welsh form of **Ambrose.**
Ena *ē'nə, f* (Ir.) fire; or a shortened form of **Eugenia** or other name of similar sound.
Enid *ē'nid, f* (Welsh) possibly wood-lark.
Enoch *ē-nək, m* (Heb.) poss. consecrated, or teaching.
Eric *er'ik, m* (Gmc.) perh. sole ruler.—Fem. **Erica** (*er'i-kə*) (associated with Gr. *ereikē,* heath).
Ernest *ûr'nist, m* (Gmc.) earnest.—Dimin. **Ernie.**
Errol *er'əl, m* of obscure origin, perh. from the Scottish place name, perh. a variant of **Eryl.**
Eryl *er'il, m* and *f* (Welsh) watcher.
Esme *ez'mi, m, f* (Fr.) beloved (a Scottish name).
Estella *es-tel'ə,* **Estelle** *es-tel', f.* See **Stella.**—Perh. sometimes for **Esther.**
Esther *es'tər,* **Hester** *hes'tər, f* poss. Pers., star; or Babylonian, *Ishtar,* the goddess Astarte.—Dimins. **Essie, Hetty.**
Ethel *eth'l, f* (O.E.) noble (not used uncompounded in O.E.).
Etta *et'ə, f.* Dimin. of **Henrietta.**
Eugene *ū'jēn, m* (Gr.) well-born.—Dimin. **Gene.**—Fem. **Eugenia.**—Dimins. **Ena, Gene.**
Eunice *ū-nī'sē, ū'nis, f* (Gr.) happy victory.
Eustace *ū'stis, m* (Gr.) rich in corn.
Eva *ē'və,* **Eve** *ēv, f* (Heb.) life.—Dimins. **Evie, Evelina** (q.v.), **Eveleen** (Ir.).
Evan *ev'ən, m* Anglicised Welsh form of **John.**—Welsh *Ifan.*
Evelina *ev-i-lē'nə, -lī'nə, f,* **Eveline** *ev'i-lēn, ēv'lin, f,* **Evelyn** *ēv'lin, ev'i-lin, m* and *f,* partly dimins. of **Eve,** partly from the surname Evelyn, partly from Gmc. *Avelina.*
Everard *ev'ə-rärd, m* (Gmc.) boar-hard.
Ewan, Ewen *ū'ən, m.* See **Owen.**
Ezra *ez'rə, m* (Heb.) help.

Fabian *fā'bi-ən, m*—L. *Fabianus,* a derivative of the family name *Fabius,* perh. connected with *faba,* bean.
Faith *fāth, f* (Eng. or Fr.) faith.
Fanny *fan'i, f.* See **Francis.**
Farquhar *fär'kər, fär'hhər, m* (Gael.) manly.

Fay *fā, f* (Fr.) perh. faith, perh. fairy.
Feargal *fûr'gəl, m* (Ir.) said to be an Irish version of the saint's name *Virgilius.*
Felix *fē'liks, m* (L.) happy.—Fem. **Felicia** (*fi-lish'i-ə, -lis'i-ə*), **Felice** (*fi-lēs'*, confused with **Phyllis**) happy, **Felicity**, happiness.
Fenella *fin-el'ə, f* anglicisation of Gael. *Fionnghuala,* white shoulder.—Ir. **Finola** (*fi-nō'lə*).—Dimins. **Nola** (*nō'lə*), **Nuala** (*noo'lə*).
Ferdinand *fûr'di-nənd, m* (Gmc.) journey-risk.
Fergus *fûr'gəs, m* (Gael.) supremely choice.
Finlay, Findlay, Finley *fin'li, -lā, m* (Gael.) a sunbeam.
Finn *fin,* **Fionn** *fyun, fūn, m* (Ir. and Gael.) fair.—Dimin. **Fintan** (*fin'tən*).—Deriv. **Finbarr** (*-bär*) fair-head.
Finola. See **Fenella.**
Fiona *fē-ō'nə, fē'ə-nə, f* (Gael.) fair.
Fleur *flûr, f* (Fr.) flower.
Flora *flō', flö'rə, f* (L.) name of the Roman flower-goddess.—Dimins. **Flo, Florrie** (*flor'i*).
Florence *flor'ins, f* (L.) blooming; also, born in Florence.—Dimins. **Flo, Florrie, Flossie, Floy.**
Floyd *floid, m* prob. a variant of Welsh **Lloyd.**
Francis *frän'sis, m* (Fr.) Frankish, French.—Dimins. **Frank, Francie, Frankie.**—Fem. **Frances** (*frän'sis, -səz*).—Dimins. **Fanny, Frank, Francie, Francine, Frankie.**
Fraser *frā'zər, m* from the surname.
Freda *frē'də, f* dimin. of **Winifred,** or for **Frieda.**
Frederick, Frederic *fred'rik, m* (Gmc.) peace-rule.—Dimins. (both genders) **Fred, Freddie, Freddy.**—Fem. **Frederica** (*fred-ə-rē'kə*).
Frieda *frē'də, f* (Gmc.) peace.—Used as a dimin. for any feminine name with the element *fred* or *frid.*

Gabriel *gā'bri-əl, m* (Heb.) God is mighty, or man of God.—Dimins. **Gabe, Gabby** (*gab'i*).—Fem. **Gabrielle.**
Gail *gāl, f* dimin. of **Abigail**—now regarded as a name in its own right.—Also **Gale, Gayle.**
Gareth *gar'ith, m* O.Fr. *Gahariet,* prob. from some Welsh name.
Gary, Garry *gar'i, m* perh. a dimin. of **Gareth;** perh. for **Garvey** (Gmc.) spear-bearer.
Gavin *gav'in,* **Gawain** *gä'win, gö'in, m* (Welsh) perh. white hawk.
Gay, Gaye *gā, m* and *f* (Eng.) gay, cheerful.
Gayle. See **Gail.**
Gaynor *gā'nər, f* (Welsh) a form of *Guinevere* (see **Jennifer**).
Gemma *jem'ə, f* (It.) a gem.
Gene *jēn,* for **Eugene, Eugenia.**
Genevieve *jen'i-vēv, f* (Fr.—Celt.) meaning obscure.
Geoffrey, Jeffrey *jef'ri, m* (Gmc.). Two names have run together—district-peace (O.H.G. *Gaufrid*) and traveller-peace (O.H.G. *Walahfrid*).—Dimins. **Geoff, Jeff.**—Confounded with **Godfrey.**
George *jörj, m* (Gr.) husbandman.—Dimins. **Geordie, Georgie, Georgy.**—Fem. **Georgia, Georgiana** (*-i-ä'nə*), **Georgette, Georgina** (*-ē'nə*).—Dimin. **Georgie.**
Geraint *ger-īnt', m* (Welsh) from L. *Gerontius* (Gr. *geronteios*), old.
Gerald *jer'əld, m* (Gmc.) spear-wielding.—Fem. **Geraldine** (*-ēn*).
Gerard *jer'ärd, -ərd, jər-ärd', m* (Gmc.) spear-hard.
Gerrie, Gerry *jer'i, m* dimins. of **Gerald, Gerard.**
Gertrude *gûr'trood, f* (Gmc.) spear-might.—Dimins. **Gert, Gertie, Trudy.**
Gervase *jûr'vis, -vāz, m* (Gmc.) spear-servant.—Fem. **Gervaise** (*jûr-vāz',* Fr. *zher-vez'*).
Gideon *gid'i-ən, m* (Heb.) hewer.
Gil. See **Gilbert, Giles.**
Gilbert *gil'bərt, m* (Gmc.) bright hostage.—Dimins. **Gib, Gibbie, Gil.**
Giles *jīlz, m* (Fr.—Gr.) kid.
Gill, Gillian *jil, jil'i-ən, f.* See **Julian.**—Also **Jill, Jillian.**
Gina *jē'nə, f* dimin. of **Georgina,** or *Regina.*
Ginger, Ginny. See **Virginia.**
Gladys *glad'is, f* Welsh *Gwladys* for **Claudia.**
Glen, Glenn *glen, m,* also *f,* from the surname, related to **Glyn.**
Glenda *glen'də, f* poss. valley (see **glen** in Dict.).
Gloria *glö'ri-ə, f* (L.) glory.
Glyn *glin, m* (Welsh) valley.—Fem. **Glynis.**
Godfrey *god'fri, m* (Gmc.) God's peace.—Confused with **Geoffrey.**
Gordon *gör'dən, m* from the surname.
Grace *grās, f* (Fr.) grace.
Graham *grā'əm, m* from the surname—also sometimes **Graeme.**
Grant *gränt, m* tall (Fr. *grand*).
Gregory *greg'ə-ri, m* (Gr.) watcher.—Dimin. **Greg.**
Greta *grē'tə, gret'ə.* See **Margaret.**
Griffith *grif'ith, m* (Welsh) ruddy, rufous.
Grizel, Grizzel, Grissel, Grisell *griz'l,* **Griselda, Grizelda** *gri-zel'də, f* (Gmc.) perh. grey war, perh. Christ war.—Dimin. **Zelda.**
Gudrun *good'rən, f* (Gmc.) war-counsel, in mythology the wife of Siegfried and sister of Gunther.
Guinevere *gwin'ə-vēr, f.* See **Jennifer.**
Guy *gī, m* (Gmc.) perh. wood, perh. wide.
Gwendolen *gwen'də-lin, f* (Welsh) white (second element obscure).—Dimins. **Gwen, Gwenda, Gwennie.**
Gwyneth *gwin'ith, f* (Welsh) blessed.

Hal *hal.* See **Henry.**
Haley. See **Hayley.**
Hamish *hā'mish, m.* See **James.**
Hank *hangk, m.* See **Henry.**
Hannah *han'ə, f.* See **Ann.**
Harold *har'əld, m* (Gmc.) army rule.
Harriet, Harriot *har'i-ət,* fem. forms of **Henry.**—Dimin. **Hatty.**
Harry. See **Henry.**
Hartley *härt'li, m* from the surname.
Harvey, Hervey *här'vi, m* from French *Hervé,* a form of *Haerveu,* name of a Breton saint, of uncertain meaning, perh. worthy in battle; also from the surname.
Hatty. See **Henry.**
Hayley, Haley *hā'li, f* from the surname.

Hazel *hā'zəl,* **Heather** *hedh'ər, f* from the plants.
Hector *hek'tər, m* (Gr.) holding fast.—Dimin. **Heck.**
Heidi *hī'di, f* (Ger.) dimin. of *Adelheid* (see **Adelaide).**
Helen *hel'ən, -in,* **Helena** *hel'i-nə,* **Ellen** *el'ən, f* (Gr.) bright.—Dimins. **Lena** (*le'nə*), **Nell, Nellie, Nelly.**
Helga *hel'gə, f* (Gmc., Norse) holy.
Henry *hen'ri,* **Harry** *har'i, m* (Gmc.) house ruler.—Dimins. **Hal, Hank.**—Fem. **Henrietta, Harriet, Harriot.**—Dimins. **Etta, Hatty, Hetty.**
Herbert *hûr'bərt, m* (Gmc.) army-bright.—Dimins. **Bert, Bertie.**
Herman, Hermann *hûr'mən, m* (Gmc.) army man, warrior.
Hermione *hər-mī'ə-nē, f* (Gr.) a derivative of *Hermes* (Greek god).
Hervey. See **Harvey.**
Hester. See **Esther.**
Hetty *het'i, f* dimin. of **Hester** and **Henrietta.**
Hew, another spelling of **Hugh,** preferred by certain families.
Hilary *hil'ə-ri, m* and *f* (L.) cheerful.
Hilda *hil'də, f* (Gmc.) battle.
Holly *hol'i, f* (Eng.) from the plant.
Honor *on'ər,* **Honora** *ho-nö'rə,* **Honoria** *-ri-ə, f* (L.) honour, honourable.—Dimins. **Nora, Norah (Ir. Noreen).**
Hope *hōp, m* and *f* (Eng.) hope.
Horace *hor'is,* **Horatio** *ho-rā'shō, m* (L.) the Roman family name *Horatius.*—Fem. **Horatia.**
Howel(l). See **Hywel.**
Hubert *hū'bərt, m* (Gmc.) mind-bright.
Hugh, Hew *hū,* **Hugo** *hū'gō, m* (Gmc.) mind.—Dimins. **Huggin, Hughie.**
Humphrey, Humphry *hum'fri, m* (Gmc.) prob. giant-peace.—Dimins. **Humph.**
Huw *hū, m* Welsh form of **Hugh.**
Hyacinth *hī'ə-sinth, m* and *f* (Gr.) the flower hyacinth (masc. in Greek).—See also **Jacinthe.**
Hywel, Howel, Howell *how'əl, m* (Welsh) eminent.

Iain, Ian *ē'ən, m* Gaelic for **John.**
Ianthe *ī-an'thē, f* (Gr.) violet flower (name of a sea-nymph).
Ida *ī'də, f* (Gmc.) labour.
Ifan *ē'van, m* Welsh form of **John.**
Ifor *ē'vor, m* Welsh form of **Ivo, Ivor.**
Igor *ē'gör, m* Russian form of the Scandinavian name *Ingvarr,* watchfulness of Ing (the god Frey).
Ike. See **Isaac.**
Ilana *i-lä'nə,* **Ilona** *-lō',* forms of **Helen.**
Imogen *im'ə-jən, f* prob. a misprint for *Innogen* in Shakespeare's *Cymbeline,* poss. O. Ir., a daughter, girl.
Ina *ī'nə, ē'nə, f* dimin. of any of several names ending in *-ina.*
Ines, Inez *ī'nez, ē'nez,* Sp. *ē-nās', f* (Sp.) for **Agnes.**
Ingrid *ing'(g)rid, f* (Scand.) ride of Ing (Frey), or maiden of the Ingvaeones.
Iona *ī-ō'nə, f* from the place name.
Irene, Eirene *ī-rē'nē,* also *ī-rēn', ī'rēn, f* (Gr.) peace.
Iris *ī'ris, f* (Gr.) rainbow, iris (plant)—name of the Greek goddess Hera's messenger.
Isa *ī'zə, f* (Scot.) dimin. of **Isabella.**
Isaac, Izaak *ī'zək, m* (Heb.) laugh.—Dimins. **Ik, Ike, Iky.**
Isabella *iz-ə-bel'ə,* **Isabel, Isobel** *iz'ə-bəl,* or (Gael.) **Iseabail, Iseabal, Ishbel,** *ish'bəl,* (Scot.) **Isbel** *iz'bəl, f* (Sp.—Heb.) forms of **Elizabeth,** now regarded as an independent name.—Dimins. **Bel, Bell, Belle, Bella, Ella, Ib, Ibby, Isa** (*ī'zə*), **Tib, Tibbie, Tibby.**
Isla *ī'lə, f* from the place name.
Ivan *ī'vən, ē-vän', m* (Russ.) for **John.**
Ivo, Ivor *ī'vō, ī'vər,* or *ē', m* prob. Celtic, but perh. from a Gmc. root meaning yew.
Ivy *ī'vi, m* and *f* (Eng.) from the plant.

Jacinth, Jacinthe *ja-sinth',* **Jacintha** *-sin'thə,* **Jacinta** *-sin'tə, f* forms of the flower-name hyacinth (Gr. *hyakinthos,* larkspur); also from the precious stone jacinth (O. Fr. *jacinte*).
Jack *jak, m.* See **John.**
Jackeline. See **James.**
Jacob *jā'kəb, m* (Heb.) follower, supplanter, or deceiver.—Dimin. **Jake.** See also **James.**
James *jāmz, m.* Same as **Jacob** (anglicised vocative **Hamish**).—Dimins. **Jim, Jimmie, Jimmy, Jem, Jemmie, Jamie,** (*jām'i,* Scot.).—Fems. **Jacoba** (*jə-kō'bə*), **Jacobina** (*-bē'nə*), **Jackeline** (*jak'ə-lēn, -lin*), **Jacqueline, Jaqueline** (*zhak'(ə)lin, -lēn*), **Jacquelyn** (*jak'*), **Jacquetta** (*-ket'ə*), **Jamesina** (*-sī'nə*).—**Jemima** has nothing to do with **James.**
Jan. See **John.**
Jane *jān,* **Jean** *jēn,* **Joan** *jōn,* **Jo(h)an(n)a** *jō-an'ə,* **Joann(e)** (*jō-an'*), fems. of **John.**—Dimins. **Jan, Janet** (*jan'it*), **Janetta, Janey, Janie, Janice, Jeanette, Jeannie, Jen, Jenny, Jennie, Jess, Jessie, Jessy, Netta, Nettie, Nita** (*nē'tə*)—some of them regarded as separate names.
Janet *jan'it, f* a dimin. of **Jane,** regarded as an independent name.
Janice *jan'is, f* orig. a dimin. of **Jane,** now regarded as a separate name.
Jared *jar', jā'rid,* **Jarrad** *jar'əd, m* (Heb.) descent.
Jasmine *jas'min,* (Fr.), **Yasmin** *yaz'min* (Ar.) *f* the flower jasmine.—Deriv. **Jessamine.**
Jason *jā'sən, m* poss. Gr. rendering of Heb. Joshua or Jesus, or simply (Gr.) a healer.
Jasper *jas'pər, m* prob. Pers. treasure-bringer.
Jean *jēn, f.* See **Jane,** etc.
Jeffrey *jef'ri, m.* See **Geoffrey.**
Jem, Jemmie. Dimins. of **James.**
Jemima *ji-mī'mə, f* (Heb.) meaning unknown (day, dove, pure, fortunate have been suggested).—Not connected with **James.**—Dimin. **Mima.**
Jennifer, Jenifer *jen'i-fər, f* the orig. Cornish form of Welsh *Guinevere,* perh. white wave, or white phantom.—Dimins. **Jen, Jennie, Jenny.**
Jenny, Jennie *jen'i, jin'i, f.* See **Jane, Jennifer.**
Jeremiah *jer-i-mī'ə,* **Jeremy** *jer'i-mi, m* (Heb.) Yah is high, or heals, or founds.—Dimin. **Jerry** (*jer'i*).
Jerome *jer'ōm, ji-rōm', m* (Gr.) holy name.

Jerry *jer'i, m* dimin. of **Jeremy,** also of **Gerald, Gerard, Jerome.**

Jess *jes,* **Jessie** *f* forms of **Janet,** chiefly Scots. See **Jane.**

Jessamine. See **Jasmine.**

Jesse *jes'i, m* (Heb.) Yah is.

Jessica *jes'i-kə, f* (app. Heb.) perh. Yah is looking.

Jethro *jeth'rō, m* (Heb.) superiority.

Jill *jil,* **Jillian** *-yən, -i-ən, f.* See **Julian.**

Jim, Jimmie. See **James.**

Jinny. See **Virginia.**

Jo, for **Joanna, Joseph, Josephine.**—Deriv. **Jolene, Joleen** (*jō'lēn*).

Joan, Jo(h)an(n)a, Joann, Joanne. See **Jane.**

Jocelyn, Jocelin *jos'(ə-)lin, m* and *f* perh. (Gmc.) one of the Geats (a people of southern Sweden), or (L.) connected with **Justin.**—Also fem. **Joceline.**

Jock *jok, m.* See **John.**

Jodie, Jody *jō'di, f* dimins. of **Judith** or **Joanna.**

Joe, Joey, for **Joseph, Josephine.**

Joel *jō'əl, m* (Heb.) Yah is the Lord.

John, Jon *jon, m* (Heb.) poss. Yah is gracious.—Dimins. **Johnnie, Jack, Jackie,** (Scot. **Jock, Jockie**), **Jan.**—Fem. see under **Jane.**

Joleen, Jolene. See **Jo.**

Jonathan *jon'ə-thən, m* (Heb.) Yah has given.

Jonquil *jong'kwil, f* from the flower.

Joseph *jō'zif, m* (Heb.) Yah increases.—Dimins. **Jo, Joe, Joey, Jos** (*jos*).—Fem. **Josepha** (*-sē'fə, -ze'fə*), **Josephine** (*jō'-zi-fēn*).—Dimins. **Jo, Joe, Josie, Jozy.**

Joshua *josh'ū-ə, m* (Heb.) Yah delivers.—Dimin. **Josh.**

Joy *joi, f* (Eng.) joy.

Joyce *jois, f* (Gmc.) a Geat (see **Jocelyn**).

Judith *jōō'dith, f* (Heb.) Jewess.—Dimins. **Judy, Judie.**

Julian *jōō'lyən, -li-ən, m, f* (L.) derived from, belonging to Julius.—Dimin. **Jule.**—Fem. **Juliana** (*-ä'nə*), **Jillian, Gillian** (*jil'yən, -i-ən*).—Dimins. **Jill, Leanne, Lian(ne)** (*lē-an'*), **Lian(n)a** (*-an'ə*).

Julius *jōō'li-əs, m* (L.) a Roman family name, perh. downy-bearded.—Dimin. **Jule.**—Fem. **Julia.**—Dimins. **Julie, Juliet.**

June *jōōn, f* (L.) from the month.

Justin *jus'tin, m* just.—Fem. **Justina** (*-ī'nə, tē'*), **Justine** (*-tēn*).

Karen, Karin *kä'rən, ka'rən, f* (Scand.) variants of **Catherine.**

Kate, Katherine, Katharine, Kathryn, Kathleen, Katrine, Katerina, Katrina, Kay. See **Catherine.**

Keiron. See **Kieran.**

Keith *kēth, m,* from the surname or place name.

Kelly *kel'i, m* and *f* (Ir.) from the surname.

Kenneth *ken'ith, m* (Gael.) handsome.—Dimins. **Ken, Kennie, Kenny.**

Kerry *ker'i, m* and *f* (Ir.) from the name of the Irish county.

Kevin, Kevan *kev'in, m* (Ir.) comely birth.

Kieran, Kieron, Keiron *kēr'ən, m* (Ir.) an Irish saint's name, from *cíar,* dark.

Kim *kim, m* and *f* shortening (as in Kipling's *Kim*) of Ir. **Kimball** (*kim'bəl*), orig. a surname, or of **Kimberl(e)y.**

Kimberley, Kimberly *kim'bər-li, f,* orig. *m,* from the S. African town.

Kirk *kûrk, m* from the surname.

Kirsty *kûr'sti,* **Kirsteen** *-stēn, f.* See **Christian.**

Kit. See **Christopher, Catherine.—Kitty.** See **Catherine.**

Konrad. See **Conrad.**

Kristal, Krystle *kris'tl, f* for **Crystal.**

Kurt *kûrt, m* orig. a dimin. of **Conrad.**

Kyle *kīl, m* from the Irish and Scottish surname.

Kylie *kī'li, f* (Aboriginal) a boomerang, or a variant of **Kelly.**

Lachlan *lahh'lən, m* (Gael.) warlike.—Dimins. **Lachie, Lachy.**

Lalage *lal'ə-jē, f* (L.—Gr.) talkative, prattling.—Dimin. **Lallie.**

Lance *läns, m* (Gmc.) land.

Lara *lä'rə, f* (It.) explained as a form of *Larunda,* a nymph of Roman mythology, or as a dimin. of *Larissa,* a Greek martyr.

Larraine. See **Lorraine.**

Larry. See **Lawrence.**

Laura *lö'rə, f* (L.) laurel.—Also **Laurinda, Lora, Lorana, Lorinda.**—Dimins. **Lauren** (thought of also as fem. of **Laurence**), **Lauretta, Lolly, Loretta.**

Laurence, Lawrence *lo', lö'rəns, m* (L.) laurel.—Dimins. **Larry** (*lar'i*), **Laurie, Lawrie.**

Lavinia *lə-vin'i-ə, f* (L.) origin unknown (second wife of Aeneas).

Lea, Leah *lē'ə, f* (Heb.) a cow.

Leanne. See **Julian.**

Lee, Leigh *lē, m* and *f* from the surname.

Leila *lā', lē', lī'lə, f* (Pers.) night.

Lena *lē'nə, f.* See **Helena, Magdalen.**

Leo *lē'ō, m* (L.) lion.—Fem. **Leonie** (*lē'ə-ni*).

Leonard *len'ərd, m* (Gmc.) lion-hard.

Leonora *lē-ə-nö'rə, f.* See **Eleanor.**

Leopold *lē'ō-pōld, m* (Gmc.) people-bold.

Leroy *lə-roi', lē'roi, m* (Fr.) from the surname, meaning (servant of) the king.

Leslie *m,* **Lesley** *f, lez'li,* from the surname or place name.—Dimin. **Les.**

Lester *les'ter, m* from the surname, orig. a phonetic spelling of the place name Leicester.

Lettice *let'is,* **Letitia, Laetitia** *li-tish'yə, f* (L.) gladness.—Dimin. **Lettie, Letty.**

Lewis *lōō'is,* **Louis** *lōō'is, lōō'i,* **Ludovic, Ludovick** *lū', lōō'dō-vik, m* (Gmc.) famous warrior.—Dimins. **Lewie, Louie, Lew.**—Fem. **Louisa** (*lōō-ē'zə*), **Louise** (*-ēz'*).—Dimins. **Lou, Louie.**

Liam *lē'əm, m* Irish form of **William.**

Lian, Liana, Lianne, etc. See **Julian.**

Libby. See **Elizabeth.**

Lily *lil'i,* **Lilian, Lillian** *-ən, f* prob. partly from the flower, partly for **Elizabeth.**

Linda, Lynda *lin'də, f* (Gmc.) short for any feminine name ending in *-lind* (snake).—Now regarded as a name in its own right.—Dimin. **Lindy.**

Lindsay, Lindsey, Linsay, Linsey *lin(d)'zi, m* and *f* from the surname.

Linette, Linnet, Linnette, Lynette *li-net', f* (Fr.) medieval French forms of Welsh *Eluned.*

Lionel *lī'ə-nəl, m* (L.) young lion.

Liz, Lizzie, Lisa, Liza, Lisbeth, Lizbeth, Lise, Lisette. See **Elizabeth.**

Llewelyn *(h)lē-wel'in, lōō-el'in, m* (Welsh) meaning doubtful.

Lloyd *loid, m* (Welsh) grey.

Lois *lō'is, f* prob. (Gr.) good.

Lola *lō'lə, f* for **Dolores,** or **Carlotta.**

Lora, Lorana. See **Laura.**

Lorcan *lör'kən, m* (Ir.) poss. from Irish *lorc,* fierce.

Loretta. See **Laura.**

Lorinda *lö-rin'də, f.* See **Laura.**

Lorna *lör'nə, f* invented by R. D. Blackmore for the heroine of his novel *Lorna Doone.*

Lorraine, Larraine *lə-rān', f* (Fr.) from the region of France.

Lottie *lot'i, f.* See under **Charles.**

Lou. See **Lewis.**

Louis *m,* **Louisa, Louise** *f.* See **Lewis.**

Lucas *lōō'kəs, m.* See **Luke.**

Lucinda. See **Lucius.**

Lucius *lōō'si-əs, -shəs, m* (L.) a Roman name probably connected with L. *lux,* light.—Fem. **Luce, Lucia** (*-chē'ə*; It.), **Lucy, Lucinda, Lucilla, Lucille.**

Ludovic(k). See **Lewis.**

Luke *lŏŏk,* **Lucas** *lōō'kəs, m* (L.) of Lucania (in Italy).

Luther *lōō'thər, m* (Gmc.) famous warrior.

Lydia *lid'i-ə, f* (Gr.) Lydian woman.

Lynda. See **Linda.**

Lynette. See **Linette.**

Lynn, Lynne *lin, f* dimin. of **Linda** or **Linette.**

Mabel *mā'bl, f.* See **Amabel.**

Madel(e)ine. See **Magdalen(e).**

Madge *maj, f.* See **Margaret.**

Madonna *mə-don'ə, f* (It.) my lady, a title of the Virgin Mary.

Maev(e). See **Meave.**

Magdalen, Magdalene *mag'də-lin, -lēn,* **Madeleine, Madeline** *mad'(ə-)len, -lēn, -lin, f* of Magdala on the Sea of Galilee.—Dimins. **Lena** (*lē'nə*), **Maud, Maude** (*möd*).

Maggie. Dimin. of **Margaret.**

Magnus *mag'nəs, m* (L.) great.

Màiri *mä'ri, f* (Gael.) for **Mary.**

Maisie *mā'zi, f* dimin. of **Margaret,** now also sometimes regarded as a name in its own right.

Malcolm *mal'kəm, möl', m* (Gael.) Columba's servant.

Mamie *mā'mi, f* a chiefly American dimin. of **Mary,** used also for **Margaret.**

Mandy. See **Amanda.**

Marcia, Marcius, Marcus. See **Mark.**

Margaret *mär'gə-rit, f* (Gr.) pearl.—Fr. **Marguerite** (dimin. **Margot**).—Dimins. **Madge, May, Maggie, Margie** (*mär'ji*), **Margery, Marjory, Meg, Megan** (*meg'ən,* Welsh), **Meggie, Maisie, Peg, Peggie, Peggy, Greta, Rita.**

Maria, Marie. See **Mary.**

Marian, Marion *mar'i-ən, mā'ri-ən,* **Marianne** *mar-i-an', f* (Fr.) orig. dimins. of **Mary**; used also for the combination **Mary Ann.**

Marigold *mar'i-gōld, f* from the flower.

Marilyn *mar'i-lin.* See **Mary.**

Marina *mə-rē'nə, f* (L.) of the sea.

Marjory, Margery *mär'jər-i, f* orig. a dimin. of **Margaret,** now regarded as a name in its own right.

Mark *märk,* **Marcus** *-əs, m* (L.) a Roman name prob. derived from Mars (the god).—Derivatives **Marcius** (*mär'shi-əs*; fem. **Marcia, Marsha**), strictly a Roman family name perh. of similar origin, *Marcellus.*

Marlene *mär'lēn, f* (Gmc.) perh. a compound of **Mary** and **Helena.**

Marmaduke *mär'mə-dūk, m* prob. (Celt.) servant of Madoc.—Dimin. **Duke.**

Marsha. See **Mark.**

Martha *mär'thə, f* (Aramaic) lady, mistress.—Dimins. **Mat, Mattie, Matty, Pat, Pattie, Patty.**

Martin, Martyn *mär'tin, m* (L.) prob. warlike, of Mars.—Fem. **Martina** (*-tē'nə*), **Martine** (*-tēn'*).

Mary *mā'ri,* **Maria** *mə-rī'ə, -rē'ə,* **Marie** *mä'ri, mə-rē',* **Miriam** *mir'i-əm, f* (Heb.) prob. wished-for child; less probably rebellion.—Dimins. **May, Moll, Molly, Mally, Mamie, Marietta** (*mar-i-et'ə*), **Marilyn, Maureen** (*mö-rēn',* or *mö'*), **Minnie, Poll, Polly.**

Mat, Matty. See **Martha, Mathilda, Matthew.**

Mathilda, Matilda *mə-til'də, f* (Gmc.) battle-might.—Dimins. **Mat, Matty, Maud, Maude, Patty, Tilly, Tilda.**

Matthew *math'ū, m* (Heb.) gift of Yah.—Dimins. **Mat, Matty.**

Maud, Maude *möd, f.* See **Matilda, Magdalen.**

Maurice *mor'is, mö'ris,* **Morris** (L.) Moorish, dark-coloured.

Mavis *mā'vis, f* (Eng.) thrush.

Maximilian *maks-i-mil'yən, m* (L.) a combination of *Maximus,* greatest, and *Aemilianus.*—Dimin. **Max.**

Maxwell *maks'wel, m* from the surname.—Dimin. **Max.**

May *mā, f* partly for **Mary,** partly from the month.—Dimin. **Minnie.**

Meave, Maeve, Maev *māv, f* (Ir.) the goddess, or legendary queen of Connaught, Medb, or Meadhbh.

Meg, Megan. See **Margaret.**

Melanie *mel'ə-ni, f* (Gr.) black.

Melicent. See **Millicent.**

Melissa *mə-lis'ə, f* (Gr.) bee.

Melvin, Melvyn *mel'vin, m* from the surname, or formed from *Malvina,* a name from James Macpherson's Ossianic poems.

Meredith *mer'i-dith, m* and *f* from the surname.

Meriel, Merriel *mer'i-əl, f* a form of **Muriel.**

Merlin. See **Mervyn.**

Merrick, Meyrick *mer'ik, m* (Welsh) forms of Welsh *Meurig,* a variant of **Maurice.**

Mervyn *mûr'vin, m* anglicised form of Welsh *Myrddin* thought to be from the place name *Camarthen* (*Caerfyrddin* in Welsh), King

Arthur's court magician being *Myrddin Emrys*, or 'Emrys of Camarthen', Latinised as *Merlin Ambrosius*; hence **Merlin**.

Meryl *mer'il, f* a form of **Muriel**.

Mhairi *vä'rē, mä'rē, f* (Gael.) vocative case of **Mairi** (Gael. for **Mary**), used erroneously as its equivalent.

Michael *mī'kl, m* (Heb.) who is like the Lord?—Dimins. **Mick, Micky, Mike.**—Fem. **Michaela, Michelle.**

Mildred *mil'drid, f* (Gmc.) mild power.—Dimin. **Millie.**

Miles *mīlz, m* (Gmc.) meaning doubtful, perh. merciful.

Millicent *mil'i-sənt*, **Melicent** *mel', f* (Gmc.) work-strong.—Dimin. **Millie.**

Millie *mil'i, f.* See **Mildred, Millicent, Amelia.**

Milton *mil'tən, m* from the surname, esp. honouring the poet John Milton.

Mima *mī'mə, f.* See **Jemima.**

Minnie *min'i,* for **Mary, May,** or *Wilhelmina.*

Mirabel *mir'ə-bel, f* (L.) wonderful.

Miranda *mi-ran'də, f* (L.) to be admired or wondered at.

Miriam *mir'i-əm.* See **Mary.**

Moira, Moyra *moi'rə, f* (Ir.) phonetic spelling of *Maire*, Irish form of **Mary**; (Gr.) a fate.

Moll, Molly *mol'i, f.* See **Mary.**

Mona *mō'nə, f* (Ir.) noble.

Monica *mon'i-kə, f* the name, possibly African, of St Augustine's mother; sometimes understood as (Gr.) alone, solitary.

Montagu, Montague *mon'tə-gū, m* from the surname.—Dimin. **Monty.**

Morag *mō'rag, mö', f* (Gael.) great.

Morgan *mör'gən, m* (Welsh) sea, sea-shore.—Fem. **Morgan, Morgana** (*-gä'nə*).

Morris. See **Maurice.**

Mungo *mung'gō, m* (Gael.) amiable.

Murdo *mûr'dō,* **Murdoch** *mûr'dəhh, -dək, m* (Gael.) seaman.

Muriel *mū'ri-əl, f* (Celt.) perh. sea-bright.

Murray *mur'i, m* from the surname.

Myfanwy *mi-van'wi, f* (Welsh) perh. *mabanwy*, child of water, or *my-manwy*, my fine one.

Myra *mī'rə, f* app. an arbitrary invention; sometimes used as an anagram of **Mary.**

Myrtle *mûr'tl, f* from the shrub.

Nadine *nā'dēn, f* Fr. form of Russ. *Nadezhda*, hope.

Nan, Nana, Nanna, Nannie, Nanny *nan, -ə, -i, f.* See **Ann.**

Nance, Nancy *nans, -i, f.* See **Ann, Agnes.**

Naomi *nā-ō'mi, -mī,* or *nā', f* (Heb.) pleasant.

Nat *nat*, for **Nathaniel, Nathan, Natalia.**

Natalia, Natalie, (L.). See **Noel.**

Nathan *nā'thən, m* (Heb.) gift.—Dimin. **Nat.**

Nathaniel *nə-than'yəl, m* (Heb.) gift of God.—Dimin. **Nat.**

Neal(e). See **Nigel.**

Ned, Neddie, Neddy *ned, -i,* dimins. of **Edward**; also of **Edgar, Edmund, Edwin.**

Neil *nēl.* See **Nigel.**

Nell, Nellie, Nelly *nel, -i, f* dimins. of **Helen, Ellen, Eleanor.**

Nessa, Nessie, Nesta, dimins. of **Agnes.**

Netta, Nettie, dimins. of **Janet(ta), Henrietta, Antoinette.**

Neville *nev'il, m* from the surname.

Niall *nēl.* See **Nigel.**

Nicholas, Nicolas *nik'ə-ləs, m* (Gr.) victory of the people.—Dimins. **Nick, Colin** (q.v.), **Colley, Nicol, Nichol.**—Fem. **Nicola** (*nik'ə-lə*), **Nicole** (*ni-kōl'*).—Dimins. **Nicolette, Colette.**

Nigel *nī'jl,* **Neal, Neale, Neil, Niall** *nēl, m* perh. (Ir.) champion, but understood as dimin. of L. *niger*, black.

Nina, Ninette, Ninon. See **Ann.**

Nita *nē'tə, f.* See **Jane.**

Noel *nō'əl, m* and *f* (Fr.—L.) birthday, i.e. Christmas.—Fem. also **Noele, Noelle, Noeleen, Noeline** (*-lēn*), **Natalia** (*nə-tā'li-ə*, or *-tä'*), **Natalie** (*nat'ə-li*).

Nola. See **Fenella.**

Nona *nō'nə, f* (L.) ninth.

Nora, Norah *nö'rə, f* orig. for **Honora, Leonora, Eleanor.**—Dimin. (Ir.) **Noreen** (*-rēn'*).

Norma *nör'mə, f* (L.) a rule, precept.

Norman *nör'mən, m* (Gmc.) Northman.

Nualla. See **Fenella.**

Odette *ō-det', f* dimin. of *Ottilia* (Gmc.) heritage.

Olga *ol'gə, f* (Russ.—Gmc.) holy.

Olive *ol'iv,* **Olivia** *ō-* or *ə-liv'i-ə, f* (L.) olive.—Dimin. **Livy** (*liv'i*).—**Oliver** *ol'i-vər, m* (Fr.) olive-tree (but poss. orig. another name assimilated).

Olwen, Olwin, Olwyn, Olwyne *ol'wən, f* (Welsh) white track.

Omar *ō'mär, m* (Heb.) eloquent.

Oona(gh). See **Una.**

Ophelia *ō-* or *ə-fē'li-ə, f* prob. (Gr.) help.

Oscar *os'kər, m* (Gmc.) god-spear or (Ir. and Gael.) hero, warror, champion.

Oswald *oz'wəld, m* (Gmc.) god-power.

Oswin *oz'win, m* (Gmc.) god-friend.

Otto *ot'ō, m* (Gmc.) rich.

Owen *ō'ən, m* (Welsh) said to mean youth.—Ir. and Gael. **Ewan, Ewen** (*Eoghan*).—Used as a substitute for **Eugene.**

Oz *oz,* **Ozzie,** *oz'i, m* dimins. for **Oswald** or **Oswin.**

Paddy *pad'i,* dimin. of **Patrick, Patricia.**

Pamela *pam'i-lə, f* prob. an invention (as *pam-ē'lə*) of Sir Philip Sidney's.

Pansy *pan'zi, f* (Fr.) thought; or from the name of the flower.

Pascal *pas'kəl, m* (Fr.) Easter-child, **Pascoe** (*-kō*) being a Cornish variant.—Fem. **Pascale** (*-käl'*).

Pat, dimin. of **Patrick, Patricia, Martha.**

Patience *pā'shəns, f* patience.

Patrick *pat'rik, m* (L.) nobleman, patrician.—Dimins. **Pat, Paddy.**—Fem. **Patricia** (*pə-trish'(y)ə*).—Dimins. **Pat, Paddy.**

Patty *pat'i, f* dimin. of **Martha, Patience.**

Paul *pöl, m* (L. *Paulus*) little.—Fem. **Paula, Paulina, Pauline** (*-ēn*).

Pearce *pērs, m* from the surname, derived from **Piers.**

Pearl *pûrl, f* pearl.

Peg, Peggy *peg, -i, f* dimins. of **Margaret.**

Penelope *pi-nel'o-pi, f* (Gr.) perh. weaver.—Dimins. **Pen, Penny.**

Percival, Perceval *pûr'si-vl, m* (Fr.) penetrate the valley.

Percy *pûr'si, m* from the surname.

Perdita *pûr'di-tə, f* (L.) lost.

Peregrine *per'i-grin, m* (L.) wanderer, traveller, pilgrim.—Dimin. **Perry.**

Peter *pē'tər, m* (Gr.) rock.—Also **Piers** *pērz.*—Dimin. **Pete** (*pēt*).—Fem. **Petra** *(pet'rə).*

Philip *fil'ip, m* (Gr.) lover of horses.—Dimins. **Phil, Pip.**—Fem. **Philippa.**—Dimin. **Pippa.**

Phillis, Phyllis *fil'is,* **Phillida, Phyllida** *fil'i-də, f* (Gr.) a leafy shoot.

Phoebe *fē'bi, f* (Gr.) shining, a name of Artemis as moon-goddess.

Phyllis, Phyllida. See **Phillis.**

Pierce *pērs, m* from the surname, derived from **Piers.**

Piers *pērz, m.* See **Peter.**

Pip *m,* **Pippa** *f.* See **Philip.**

Polly *pol'i, f.* See **Mary.**

Poppy *pop'i, f* from the flower.

Primrose *prim'rōz, f* from the flower.

Priscilla *pri-sil'ə, f* (L.) dimin. of the Roman name *Priscus* (former).

Prudence *proo'dəns, f* prudence.—Dimin. **Prue.**

Quintin *kwin'tin,* **Quinton** *-tən,* **Quentin** *kwen', m* (L.) fifth.

Rab, Rabbie. See **Robert.**

Rachel, Rachael *rā'chl, f* (Heb.) ewe.—Dimins. **Ray, Rae.**

Rae *rā, f* dimin. of **Rachel**, used (esp. Scot.) independently.—Deriv. **Raelene** (*-lēn*).

Ralph *rāf, ralf, m* (Gmc.) counsel-wolf.

Ranald *ran'əld, m.* See **Reginald.**

Randal *ran'dl,* **Randolph** *ran'dolf, m* (Gmc.) shield-wolf.

Ray *rā.* See **Rachel, Raymond.**—Also an independent name, *f* and *m.*

Raymond, Raymund *rā'mənd, m* (Gmc.) counsel (or might) protector.—Dimins. **Ray, Rae.**

Rebecca *ri-bek'ə, f* (Heb.) noose.—Dimin. **Becky.**

Reginald *rej'i-nəld,* **Reynold** *ren'əld,* **Ronald** *ron',* **Ranald** *ran', m* (Gmc.) counsel (or power) rule.—Dimins. **Reg** (*rej*), **Reggie** (*rej'i*), **Rex, Ron, Ronnie.**

René *ren'i, rə-nā', m* (Fr.—L. *Renatus*) born again.—Fem. **Renée, Renata** (*-ä'tə*).

Reuben *roo'bən, m* (Heb.) behold a son, or renewer.

Rex *reks, m* (L.) king.—Also for **Reginald.**

Reynold *ren'əld, m.* See **Reginald.**

Rhiannon *rē-an'ən f* (Welsh) goddess or nymph.

Rhoda *rō'də, f* (Gr.) rose.

Rhona *rō'nə, f* origin and meaning obscure, poss. conn. with **Rowena.**

Rhys *rēs, m* (Welsh) perh. impetuous man.

Richard *rich'ərd, m* (Gmc.) rule-hard.—Dimins. **Dick, Dickie, Dicky, Dicken, Dickon, Rick, Richie.**

Rita *rē'tə, f.* See **Margaret.**

Robert *rob'ərt,* **Rupert** *roo'pərt, m* (Gmc.) fame-bright.—Dimins. **Bert, Bertie, Bob, Bobbie, Bobby, Rob, Robbie, Robin** (*rob'in*; also *f,* esp. in spelling **Robyn**), Scot. **Rab, Rabbie.**—Fem. **Roberta, Robina** (*ro-bē'nə*).

Roderick *rod'(ə-)rik, m* fame-rule.—Dimins. **Rod, Roddy.**

Rodney *rod'ni, m* and *f* from the surname or place name.—Dimin. **Rod.**

Roger *roj'ər, m* (Gmc.) fame-spear.

Roland, Rowland *rō'lənd, m* (Gmc.) fame of the land.

Rolf *rolf, m.* See **Rudolf.**

Rona *rō'nə, f* from the island-name, derived from Gael. *ron,* seal.—Not conn. with **Rhona.**

Ronald *ron'əld, m.* See **Reginald.**

Rory *rö'ri, m* (Ir. and Scot.) red.

Rosalind, Rosaline *roz'ə-lind, -līn, -lēn, -lin, f* (Gmc.) horse-snake, but associated with **Rose** (fair rose).

Rosamund, Rosamond *roz'ə-mənd, f* (Gmc.) horse protection.—Associated with **Rose** (L. *rosa munda*, fine or pure rose, *rosa mundi*, rose of the world).

Rose *rōz,* **Rosa** *rō'zə, f* (L.) rose. It may also be sometimes Gmc., horse.—Derivatives **Rosabel** (*roz'ə-bel*), **Rosabella** (*rōz-ə-bel'ə*), **Rosalia** (*rō-zā'li-ə*), **Rosalie** (*roz'* or *rōz'ə-li*) (L. *rosalia*, the hanging of rose garlands on tombs).—Dimins. **Rosetta, Rosie** .

Roseanna, Rosanna, Roseanne *rō-zan'(ə),* **Rosemarie** *rōz-mə-rē', f* compounds of **Rose** with **Anna, Anne, Marie.**

Rosemary *rōz'mə-ri, f* from the plant; also for **Rose Mary.**

Ross *ros, m* (Gael.) from the place name and surname.

Rowena *rō-(w)ē'nə, f* perh. Geoffrey of Monmouth's mistake for Welsh *Rhonwen*, white skirt.

Roy *roi, m* (Gael.) red.

Ruby *roo'bi, f* from the stone.

Rudolf, Rudolph *roo'dolf,* **Rolf** *rolf, m* (Gmc.) fame-wolf.

Rufus *roo'fəs, m* (L.) red.

Rupert. See **Robert.**

Russell *rus'əl, m* from the surname.

Ruth *rooth, f* (Heb.) meaning obscure; used sometimes with associations with English *ruth.*

Ryan *rī'ən, m* from the Irish surname.

Sacha *sash'ə, m* and *f* (orig. masc. only), Russ. dimin. of **Alexander.**

Sadie *sā'di,* **Sal** *sal,* **Sally.** See **Sarah.**

Salome *sə-lō'mi, f* (Heb.) perfect, or peace.

Samantha *sa-man'thə, f* (Heb.) meaning obscure.

Samuel *sam'ū-əl, m* (Heb.) heard by God, or name of God.—Dimins. **Sam, Sammy.**

Sandra *san'drə, sän', f* It. dimin. of *Alessandra*;

sometimes used as a diminutive of **Alexandra** but now regarded as a separate name.

Sandy *san'di, m.* See **Alexander.**

Sarah, Sara *sā'rə, sä'rə, f* (Heb.) princess, queen.—Dimins. **Sadie** (*sā'di*), **Sal** (*sal*), **Sally.**

Saul *söl, m* (Heb.) asked for.

Scott *skot, m* from the surname.

Seamas, Seamus *shā'məs, m* (Gael.) for **James.**

Sean *shön, m* the Irish form of **John.**

Sebastian *si-bas'ti-ən, m* (Gr.) man of Sebasteia (in Pontus)—Gr. *sebastos*, august, venerable.

Selina, Celina *si-lē'nə, f* poss. connected with **Celia**, but associated with Gr. *selēnē*, moon.

Selwyn *sel'win, m* from the surname.

Serena *si-rē'nə, f* (L.) calm, serene.

Seth *seth, m* (Heb.) substitute, or compensation.

Shamus *shā'məs, m* (Ir.) anglicisation of *Seumas*, Ir. and Gael. form of **James.**

Shane *shān,* **Shaun, Shawn** *shön, m* (Ir.) anglicisations of **Sean.**

Sharmaine. See **Charmaine.**

Sharon *sha', shā'ron, f* (Heb.) a Biblical place name.

Sheena *shē'nə, f* an anglicisation of *Sine*, Gael. form of **Jane.**

Sheila, Sheelagh *shē'lə, f.* See **Celia** and **Cecilia.**

Shelley *shel'i, m* from the surname, and *f* a variant of **Shirley.**

Sherry. See **Cher.**

Shevaun *shə-vön', f* the anglicised form of **Siobhan.**

Shirley *shûr'li, f* from the surname or place name.

Shona *shō'nə, f* (Scot.) perh. ultimately a dimin. of **Catriona**, but thought of as an anglicisation of *Seonaid*, Gael. form of **Janet.**

Sian *shan, f* the Welsh form of **Jane.**

Sibyl, now **Sybil** *sib'il,* **Sibylla** *sib-il'ə, f* (L.) a Sibyl.—Dimin. **Sib.**

Sidney, Sydney *sid'ni, m* and *f,* from the surname.

Silas *sī'ləs,* **Silvester, Sylvester,** *sil-ves'tər, m* (L.) living in the woods.—Fem. **Silvia, Sylvia.**

Simon *sī'mən,* **Simeon** *sim'i-ən, m* (Heb.) perh. hearing; perh. also (Gr.) snub-nosed.—Fem. **Simone** (*-mōn'*).

Sindy. See **Cindy.**

Sinead *shi-nād', f* the Irish form of **Janet.**

Siobhan *shə-vön', f* the Irish form of **Joan.**

Sion *shon, m* the Welsh form of **John.**

Solomon *sol'ə-mən, m* (Heb.) peaceable.—Dimins. **Sol, Solly.**

Sonia. See **Sophia.**

Sophia *sə-fī'ə,* **Sophie, Sophy** *sō'fi, f* (Gr.) wisdom.—Russ. (dimin.) **Sonia, Sonya** (*son'yə*).

Sorley *sör'li, m* (Gael. *Somhairle*) a form of Scandinavian *Somerled*, viking, lit. summer wanderer.

Stac(e)y. See **Anastasia.**

Stanley *stan'li, m* from the surname or place name.

Stella *stel'ə, f* (L.) star.—Also **Estella** (*es-tel'ə*), **Estelle** (*-tel'*).

Stephen, Steven *stē'vən, m* (Gr.) crown.—Dimins. **Steve, Stevie.**—Fem. **Stephanie** (*-ni*).

Stewart, Steuart, Stuart *stū'ərt, m* from the surname.

Susan *soo'zən, sū'zən,* **Susanna, Susannah** *-zan'ə, f* (Heb.) lily.—Dimins. **Sue, Suke, Suky, Susie, Susy.**

Sybil. See **Sibyl.**

Sydney. See **Sidney.**

Sylvester, Sylvia. See **Silas.**

Tabitha *tab'i-thə, f* (Aramaic) gazelle.

Taffy *taf'i, m* an anglicised form of *Dafydd*, the Welsh form of **David.**

Tam, Tammie. See **Thomas.**

Tamara *tə-mär'ə, f* (Russ.) a Caucasian name, poss. from Heb. *tamar*, date-palm.

Tamsin *tam'sin, f* a dimin. of **Thomasina,** orig. Cornish. Now regarded as a separate name.

Tania, Tanya *tan'yə, f* a dimin. of Russ. *Tatiana.*

Tara *tä'rə, f* from the place name in County Meath, Ireland.

Ted, Teddie, Teddy. Dimins. of **Edward.**

Terence, Terrance *ter'əns, m* (L.) the Roman family name *Terentius*; used with its dimin. **Terry** as a substitute for Ir. *Turlough*, like Thor.

Teresa, Theresa *tə-rē'zə, f* (Gr.) origin unknown—more probably connected with the island of Therasia than with reaping (Gr. *therizein*, to reap).—Dimins. **Terry, Tessa, Tracy.**

Terry *ter'i.* See **Terence, Teresa.**

Tessa *tes'ə.* See **Teresa.**

Thea *thē'ə, f* (Gr.) goddess.

Thelma *thel'mə, f* poss. (Gr.) will, popularised by Marie Corelli.

Theodore *thē'ō-dör, m* (Gr.) gift of God.—Fem. **Theodora** (*-dö'rə*).

Theodoric, Theoderic *thē-od'ə-rik, m* (Gmc.) people-rule—Dimin. **Derrick, Derek.**

Theresa. See **Teresa.**

Thomas *tom'əs, m* (Heb.) twin.—Dimins. **Tom, Tommy** (Scot. **Tam, Tammie**).—Fem. **Thomasina** *(tom-ə-sē'nə).*

Tib, Tibbie *tib, -i, f* dimins. of **Isabella,** mainly Scottish.

Tiffany *tif'ə-ni, f* (Gr.) from *theophania*, revelation of God.

Tilly *til'i, f.* See **Mathilda.**

Timothy *tim'ə-thi, m* (Gr.) honoured of God.—Dimins. **Tim, Timmie.**

Tina. See **Christian.**

Titus *tī'təs, m* (L.) a Roman praenomen—meaning unknown.

Toby *tō'bi,* **Tobias** *-bī'əs, m* (Heb.) Yah is good.

Tom, Tommy. See **Thomas.**

Tony *tō'ni, m.* Dimin. of **Anthony.**

Torquil *tör'kwil, m* (Gael.) from a Norse name of obscure origin, the first part representing the name of the god *Thor.*

Tracey, Tracy *trā'si, m* and *f* deriv. of **Teresa**; the masc. form perh. from the surname.

Trevor *trev'ər, m* from the surname.

Tristram *tris'trəm,* **Tristan** *-tən, m* (Celt.) perh. tumult.

Trix, Trixy. See **Beatrice.**

Trudy. See **Gertrude.**

Tyrone *ti-rōn', m* (Ir.) from the name of the Irish county.

Ulric *ul'rik, m* (Gmc.) wolf-rule.—Fem. **Ulrica.**

Una *ū'nə, f* (L.) one, from Spenser's heroine, personification of truth, but perh. suggested by Ir. **Oona, Oonagh** (*o͞o'nə*) meaning obscure.

Unity *ū'ni-ti, f* from the noun.

Ursula *ûr'sū-lə, f* (L.) little she-bear.

Valentine *val'in-tīn, m* and *f* (L.) healthy.

Valeria *və-lē'ri-ə, f* (L.) fem. of a Roman family name.—Also **Valerie, Valery** (*val'ə-ri*).

Vanessa *və-nes'ə, f* a name invented by Swift from *Es*ther *Van*homrigh.

Vaughan *vön, m* (Welsh) small one.

Venetia *vi-nē'shə, f* (L.) Venetian; perh. also a Latinisation of **Gwyneth.**

Vera *vē'rə, f* (L.) true; also (Russ.) faith.

Verity *ver'i-ti, f* (L.) truth.

Vernon *vûr'nən, m* (Eng.) from the surname, itself from a place name in Normandy.

Veronica *vi-ron'i-kə, f* (L.) true image; or (Gr.) a form of **Berenice.**

Victor *vik'tər, m* (L.) conqueror.—Dimin. **Vic.**—Fem. **Victoria** *vik-tö'ri-ə, f* victory.—Dimin. **Vicky.**

Vida *vē'də,* a fem. dimin. of **David.**

Vincent *vin'sənt, m* (L.) conquering.

Viola *vī'ə-lə,* **Violet** *-lit, f* (L.) violet (flower).

Virginia *vər-jin'i-ə,* (L.) fem. of Roman family name.—Dimins. **Ginger** (*jin'jər*), **Ginny, Jinny** (*jin'i*).

Vivian *viv'i-ən, m* and (chiefly in the form **Vivien**) *f* (L.) lively.—Also **Vyvyen, Vyvian.**

Walter *wöl'tər, m* (Gmc.) rule-people (or army).——Dimins. **Wat, Watty** (*wot, -i*), **Wally, Walt.**

Wanda *won'də, f* (Gmc.) stock or stem.

Warren *wor'ən, m* (Gmc.) a folk-name—meaning uncertain.

Wayne *wān, m* from the surname.

Wendy *wen'di, f* an invention of J. M. Barrie's.

Wilfrid, Wilfred *wil'frid, m* (Gmc.) will-peace.

William *wil'yəm, m* (Gmc.) will-helmet.

Winifred *win'i-frid, f* prob. orig. Welsh, the same as **Guinevere**, but assimilated to the English masculine name *Winfred, Winfrith* (friend of peace).—Dimins. **Win, Winnie, Freda** (*frē'də*).

Winston *win'stən, m* (Eng.) from the place name.

Xavier *zav'i-ər, m* (Sp.—Ar.) splendid.

Yasmin. See **Jasmine.**

Yoland *yō'lənd,* **Yolande** *-land',* **Yolanda** *-land'ə, f* app. a mediaeval form of *Violante*, a derivative of **Viola.**

Yve, Yves *ēv,* Fr. derivative of **Ivo.**—Fem. **Yvonne** (*ē-von'*), **Yvette** (*ē-vet'*).

Zachary *zak'ə-ri, m* (Heb.) Yah is renowned.—Dimins. **Zach, Zack.**

Zandra *zän'drə, f.* See **Alexander.**

Zara *zä'rə, f* (Heb.) poss. bright as the dawn.

Zelda. See **Grizel.**

Zena *zē'nə, f* perh. Pers., a woman.

Zoe, Zoë *zō'ē, f* (Gr.) life.

Zola *zō'lə, f* from the Italian surname.

Symbols

In general use

- &, — ampersand (*and*)
- &c. — et cetera
- @ — at; per (in costs)
- × — by (measuring dimensions) (3 × 4)
- © — copyright
- ® — registered
- ¶ — new paragraph
- § — new section
- ,, — ditto
- † — died
- ☠ — poison; danger
- ♂, □ — male
- ♀, ○ — female
- ✠ — bishop's name follows
- ☎ — telephone number follows
- ☜ ☞ — this way
- ✂, ✂··· — cut here

In astronomy

- ● — new moon
- ☽ — moon, first quarter
- ○ — full moon
- ☾ — moon, last quarter

In cards

- ♥ — hearts
- ♦ — diamonds
- ♠ — spades
- ♣ — clubs

In clothes care

- Do not iron
- Can be ironed with *cool* iron (up to 110°C)
- Can be ironed with *warm* iron (up to 150°C)
- Can be ironed with *hot* iron (up to 200°C)
- Hand wash only
- Can be washed in a washing machine
  The number shows the most effective washing temperature (in °C)
- Reduced (medium) washing conditions
- Much reduced (minimum) washing conditions (for wool products)
- Do not wash
- Can be tumble dried (one dot within the circle means a low temperature setting; two dots for higher temperatures)
- Do not tumble dry
- Do not dry clean
- Ⓐ — Dry cleanable (letter indicates which solvents can be used)
  A: all solvents
- Ⓕ — Dry cleanable
  F: white spirit and solvent 11 can be used
- Ⓟ — Dry cleanable
  P: perchloroethylene (tetrachloroethylene), white spirit, solvent 113 and solvent 11 can be used
- Ⓟ (underlined) — Dry cleanable, if special care taken
- Chlorine bleach may be used with care
- Do not use chlorine bleach

In phonetics

- (é) — acute accent
- (ĕ) — breve
- (ç) — cedilla
- (ô) — circumflex
- (ü) — diaeresis; umlaut
- (è) — grave accent
- (č) — haček
- (ō) — macron
- (þ) — thorn (see Dict.)
- (ñ) — tilde

In mathematics

- + — plus; positive; underestimate
- − — minus; negative; overestimate
- ± — plus or minus; positive or negative; degree of accuracy
- ∓ — minus or plus; negative or positive
- × — multiplies (colloq. 'times') (6 × 4)
- · — multiplies (colloq. 'times') (6·4); scalar product of two vectors (A·B)
- ÷ — divided by (6 ÷ 4)
- / — divided by; ratio of (6/4)
- — — divided by; ratio of ($\frac{6}{4}$)
- = — equals
- ≠, ≠ — not equal to
- ≡ — identical with
- ≢, ≢ — not identical with
- : — ratio of (6:4); scalar product of two tensors (Y:Z)
- :: — proportionately equals (1:2::2:4)
- ≈ — approximately equal to; equivalent to; similar to
- > — greater than
- ≫ — much greater than
- ≯ — not greater than
- < — less than
- ≪ — much less than
- ≮ — not less than
- ≥, ≧, ⋝ — equal to or greater than
- ≤, ≦, ⋜ — equal to or less than
- ∝ — directly proportional to
- ( ) — parentheses
- [ ] — brackets
- { } — braces
- — — vinculum: division ($\overline{a-b}$); chord of circle or length of line ($\overline{AB}$); arithmetic mean ($\overline{X}$)
- ∞ — infinity
- → — approaches the limit
- √ — square root
- ∛, ∜ — cube root, fourth root, etc.
- ! — factorial (4! = 4 × 3 × 2 × 1)
- % — percent
- ′ — prime; minute(s) of arc; foor/feet
- ″ — double prime; second(s) of arc; inch(es)
- ⌒ — arc of circle
- ° — degree of arc
- ∠, ∠s — angle(s)
- ≚ — equiangular
- ⊥ — perpendicular
- ∥ — parallel
- ○, ⓢ — circle(s)
- △, △s — triangle(s)
- □ — square
- ▭ — rectangle
- ▱ — parallelogram
- ≅ — congruent to
- ∴ — therefore
- ∵ — because
- ≙ — measured by
- Δ — increment
- Σ — summation
- ∫ — integral sign
- ∪ — union
- ∩ — interaction

In meteorology

- cold front
- warm front
- stationary front
- occluded front

Roman numerals

I = 1 V = 5 X = 10 L = 50 C = 100 D = 500 M = 1000

From the above symbols the numbers are made up as follows:—

I	=	1	L	=	50
II	=	2	LI	=	51
III	=	3	LII, etc.	=	52, etc.
IV (or IIII, e.g. on clocks)	=	4	LX	=	60
V	=	5	LXI	=	61
VI	=	6	LXX, etc.	=	62, etc.
VII	=	7	LXX	=	70
VIII	=	8	LXXI	=	71
IX	=	9	LXXII, etc.	=	72, etc.
X	=	10	LXXX	=	80
XI	=	11	LXXXI	=	81
XII	=	12	LXXXII, etc.	=	82, etc.
XIII	=	13	XC	=	90
XIV	=	14	XCI	=	91
XV	=	15	XCII, etc.	=	92, etc.
XVI	=	16			
XVII	=	17	C	=	100
XVIII	=	18	CC	=	200
XIX	=	19	CCC	=	300
XX	=	20	CCCC or CD	=	400
XXI	=	21	D (or IↃ)	=	500
XXII, etc.	=	22, etc.	DC (or IↃC)	=	600
XXX	=	30	DCC (or IↃCC)	=	700
XXXI	=	31	DCCC (or IↃCCC)	=	800
XXXII, etc.	=	32, etc.	CM (or DCCCC or IↃCCCC)	=	900
XL	=	40	M	=	1000
XLI	=	41	MM	=	2000
XLII, etc.	=	42, etc.	$\bar{V}$ (or IↃↃ)	=	5000

Languages

Language families

Estimates of the numbers of speakers in the main language families of the world in the early 1980s. The list includes Japanese and Korean, which are not clearly related to any other languages.

Main language families	
Indo-European	2 000 000 000
Sino-Tibetan	1 040 000 000
Niger-Congo	260 000 000
Afro-Asiatic	230 000 000
Austronesian*	200 000 000
Dravidian	140 000 000
Japanese	120 000 000
Altaic	90 000 000
Austro-Asiatic (south Asiatic)	60 000 000
Korean	60 000 000
Tai (of south-east Asia)	50 000 000
Nilo-Saharan	30 000 000
Amerindian (North, Central, South America)	25 000 000
Uralic	23 000 000
Miao-Yao	7 000 000
Caucasian	6 000 000
Indo-Pacific	3 000 000
Khoisan	50 000
Australian Aborigine	50 000
Paleosiberian	25 000

* (including Indonesian, or Malay, Polynesian, Micronesian and Melanesian groups)

Specific languages

The first column gives estimates (in millions) for mother-tongue speakers of the 20 most widely used languages. The second column gives estimates of the total population of all countries where the language has official or semi-official status; these totals are often over-estimates, as only a minority of people in countries where a second language is recognised may actually be fluent in it.

Mother-tongue speakers		*Official language populations*	
1 Chinese	1 000	1 English	1 400
2 English	350	2 Chinese	1000
3 Spanish	250	3 Hindi	700
4 Hindi	200	4 Spanish	280
5 Arabic	150	5 Russian	270
6 Bengali	150	6 French	220
7 Russian	150	7 Arabic	170
8 Portuguese	135	8 Portuguese	160
9 Japanese	120	9 Malay	160
10 German	100	10 Bengali	150
11 French	70	11 Japanese	120
12 Punjabi	70	12 German	100
13 Javanese	65	13 Urdu	85
14 Bihari	65	14 Italian	60
15 Italian	60	15 Korean	60
16 Korean	60	16 Vietnamese	60
17 Telugu	55	17 Persian	55
18 Tamil	55	18 Tagálog	50
19 Marathi	50	19 Thai	50
20 Vietnamese	50	20 Turkish	50

Correct grammatical usage

There are a number of areas in which grammatical errors are commonly made in everyday English. Some simple rules can be applied to avoid these errors.

Who and whom

(1) Use *who* when the pronoun is the subject of a verb:

The man who (*subject*) phoned yesterday came to the office today; Who (*subject*) told you that?

(2) Use *whom* when the pronoun is the object of a verb:

The man whom (*object*) you (*subject*) phoned yesterday came to the office today; To whom (*object*) did you (*subject*) send it?

(3) Use *whom* when the relative pronoun is governed by a preposition and try to keep the preposition and the relative pronoun together:

The man *to whom* you spoke on the phone yesterday came to the office today.

Like and as

(1) Use *like* to compare things or people, i.e. to qualify nouns or pronouns:

Your *desk* is like *mine*.
My electric *typewriter* is like *Anne's*.
He looks like a *man* who has a lot of problems. (Here two people are compared.)

(2) Use *as* to compare actions, i.e. to join clauses and thus govern verbs (sometimes the verb is only implied):

You *work* very much as I *do*.
Operate the shift-key as I *told* you.
We *shall give* the staff a bonus, as last year. (Here 'we *did*' is implied.)

Due to, owing to, because of

(1) Use *due to* only when preceded by some tense of the verb 'to be':

My absence *was* due to illness.
If mistakes occur they *will be* due to carelessness.

(2) Do not begin a sentence with *due to*.

(3) If a choice can be made between the phrases *because of, owing to* and *due to*, use the first. (*Owing to* and *due to* often cause ugly as well as dubious constructions.)

Shall and will, should and would

(1) When making a statement of fact without special emphasis *I* and *we* are usually followed by *shall* or *should* (not will or would):

I should be glad if you would write to me without delay.
We should be grateful if you would let us have a reply at once.

(2) *Shall* is used with *will* (future tense):

I shall be glad if you will let me have a reply at once.
If you will let us have your cheque we shall despatch the goods immediately.

Do not join a future tense to a conditional tense in one sentence.

I and me

(1) Use *I* as the subject of a sentence. Mistakes often occur when *I* or *me* is linked with another noun or pronoun. Avoid these mistakes by mentally taking away the intervening noun or pronoun and checking the sense of what remains:

The managing director and I will interview you.
not
Please meet the managing director and I for an interview. (*I* is wrongly used here instead of the object *me*. 'Please meet I for an interview' is obviously incorrect.)

(2) Use *I* if the pronoun is linked to a following clause:

It was I who wrote the report.

(3) Use *me* after a preposition e.g. Come with me. Errors sometimes occur when the object of a preposition is two pronouns linked by 'and' e.g. Between you and me (*not* I), Like you and me (*not* I).

Either and or, neither and nor

(1) Use *either* or *neither* with two persons or things:

I have examined both machines and find that either (neither) will suit our purpose.

(2) Use *either* or *neither* with the singular as they refer to one person or thing to the exclusion of the other:

You will find that either (neither) of these typewriters *is* suitable.

(3) Always follow *either* by *or*, and *neither* by *nor*, in a comparison:

Either (Neither) Miss Brown or (nor) Miss Green is to take dictation in the Manager's office.

(4) Always place *either* or *neither* next to the words they qualify:

I shall buy either (neither) a magazine or (nor) a newspaper.
not
I shall either (neither) buy a magazine or (nor) a newspaper.

Each and none

Use *each* and *none* with the singular as they refer to one person or thing:

Each of you *is* to receive a rise in salary next month.

As none of the clerks *is* willing to work overtime we are behind schedule this week.

Using the infinitive

The infinitive has two forms; present and past:

e.g. to do (present infinitive)
to have done (past infinitive).

(1) Use the *present infinitive* after a past tense or any compound tense:

I meant *to telephone* you yesterday.

not

I meant to have telephoned you yesterday.

The staff would have preferred *to work* a five-day week.

not

The staff would have preferred to have worked a five-day week.

(2) Use the *past infinitive* when a present tense is followed by an infinitive which describes a past event:

Henry Ford *is* said *to have been* a millionaire by the age of forty.

The split infinitive

The infinitive of a verb consists of two words, e.g. to forecast, to announce, to move. The two words are a unity and should not be separated (split) by the insertion of additional words or phrases. Opinions differ on the gravity of this error but all agree that gross infringements of the rule should be avoided.

I should like, on behalf of all our members, *to move* a vote of thanks to the chairman.

not

I should like *to*, on behalf of all our members, *move* a vote of thanks to the chairman.

Comparative and superlative

(1) Use the comparative degree when two things are compared, and the superlative for more than two:

Mary has taken the *better* of the two typewriters and the *best* of the three dictating machines.

Which of these two cloths is the *more* hard-wearing?

(2) Use *less* for quantity or amount; use *fewer* for number:

The industry has bought *less* steel than it did last year and thus produces *fewer* cars. (Quantity and number)

I paid £3 *less* than the market price for a ton of cotton waste. (Amount)

(3) *Unique* means the only one of its kind and has *no comparative*. 'Almost unique' is allowable, but 'comparatively unique' or 'very unique' reduce the word to absurdity and should not be used.

Verbal nouns

In the following sentences the words in italic are nouns made from verbs (verbal nouns) and not participles:

The chairman likes *travelling*.

He hates *leaving* work unfinished.

Taking a holiday is very refreshing.

(1) Qualify verbal nouns by possessive adjectives, not by pronouns (i.e. use *my, his, our, your, their* NOT *me, him, us, you, them*):

The error was caused by *his typing* so carelessly.

The supervisor criticised *our leaving* early.

Do you agree to *my taking* a day's holiday.

(2) Similarly, use the possessive form for a noun qualifying a verbal noun:

I don't object to *Mary's* talking provided she lowers her voice.

He is unemployed because of the *firm's* going into liquidation.

The department has been disorganised by the *Manager's* leaving.

Punctuation rules

A **full stop (.)** is used at the end of a statement and often after a command; a **question mark(?)** comes after a question and an **exclamation mark (!)** after an exclamation or interjection, and sometimes after a command:

> This is a useful report. Show it to the Chairman tomorrow.
> Would you make a copy for me?
> Cheerio! Don't forget what I said!

A **comma (,)** shows a slight break in a sentence. It is used:

(1) between two clauses joined by *but* or *or* if the second one has a subject:
> I'll come to see you tomorrow, but I don't know when I will arrive.

(2) after a subordinate clause:
> When he returned, I made a cup of tea.

(3) around the kind of relative clause that gives *additional information*:
> The salesman, who had driven from Southampton, was tired.

but *not* around the kind of relative clause that *identifies* a person or thing:
> Those people who would like tickets should write to the secretary.

(4) around a descriptive or explanatory phrase referring to a person or thing:
> Mrs Cook, our local councillor, has joined the committee.

(5) after introductory words, or around words which form a comment:
> However, I wasn't late after all.
> I must leave now, unfortunately.
> Philip, I'm sorry to say, has left the company.

(6) before *please*, after *yes* and *no*, and before or after the name of the person who is being spoken to:
> May I see the file, please?
> No, I'm sorry.
> Hurry up, Christopher.

(7) in a list of more than two things and often between adjectives preceding a noun, where there are two or more:
> a pen, a pencil and a rubber
> a busy, overcrowded room (but no commas in e.g. a *cheerful old man*, because *old man* is regarded as a single unit).

A **colon (:)** is used to introduce the answer that the first part of the sentence expects:

> There's one thing I'd really like: a new car.
> You'll need the following: passport, ticket, boarding pass.

A **semicolon (;)** separates parts of a sentence that are equally important and are not linked by *and*, *but*, *or*, etc. Sometimes a semicolon is used to separate items in a list:

> One tray of sandwiches will be sufficient; to prepare more would be wasteful.
> I have three ambitions: to set up my own business; to buy a boat and sail around the world; to live in Sydney.

Quotation marks (' ') or **(" ")** are used before and after direct speech; a **comma** is usually put before or after the direct speech:

> Mary said, 'You're late'.
> 'You're late', said Mary.

Both single and double quotes are correct, but modern usage prefers single quotes. However, if there is a quotation or highlighted passage within another quotation, both single and double quotes must be used:

> 'Did she say "You're late"?', John asked.

An **apostrophe (')** is used:

(1) to form possessive nouns; it is placed before the *s* with singular nouns and with plural nouns not ending in *–s*, and after the *s* with plural nouns ending in *–s*:
> Anne's desk; the women's coats; the residents' car park.

(2) in shortened forms, showing where part of a word has been left out:
> I've only two appointments today.
> Aren't you coming with us?

A **hyphen (-)** is used:

(1) in many nouns (others are written as one word or as two words without a hyphen):
> air-conditioning (but *aircraft* and *air force*).

(2) in compound adjectives placed before the noun:
> a six-page contract; a twenty-year-old building: a well-deserved award.

(3) sometimes with a prefix:
> The votes must be re-counted.

Spelling rules

To a large extent the ability to spell English words correctly depends on becoming familiar with the *look* of them when they are spelt in the accepted way.

There are, however, a few general rules, *though one must always be on the watch for exceptions.*

Derivatives of words ending in *-y*

(1) The plural of a noun in **-y, -ey** (also **-ay, -oy, -uy**):

A noun in **-y** following a consonant has its plural in **-ies.**

baby babies country countries

Nouns in **-ey,** etc., have their plural in **-eys,** etc.

donkey donkeys valley valleys
day days Monday Mondays
alloy alloys guy guys

(2) The parts of a verb when the verb ends in **-y, -ey** (etc.):

The formation is similar to that of noun plurals in (1) above.

cry cries cried
certify certifies certified
but
convey conveys conveyed
delay delays delayed
destroy destroys destroyed
buy buys

(3) Comparison of adjectives, or the formation of nouns or adverbs from them:

A rule similar to the above holds for words in **-y,** and in some cases for those in **-ey** (etc.).

shady shadier shadiest shadiness shadily
pretty prettier prettiest prettiness prettily
but
grey greyer greyest greyness greyly
coy coyer coyest coyness coyly

There are, however, exceptions and irregularities for which the dictionary should be consulted.

Derivatives of words ending in *-c*

When a suffix beginning with a vowel is added, and the consonant still has a hard *k* sound, **-c** becomes **-ck**:

picnic picnicking picnicked picnicker
mimic mimicking mimicked mimicker

-k- is not added in words such as *musician, electricity,* etc., where the consonant has the soft sound of *sh* or *s.*

-ie- or -ei-?

i before *e*
except after *c.*

(This rule applies only to words in which the sound is long *ē*.)

e.g. *belief believe grief pier siege*
ceiling conceit deceit deceive

Exceptions are *seize, weird* and personal names (e.g. *Neil, Sheila*) and certain surnames.

Derivatives of words with final *-e*

(1) Before a vowel (including **y**), **-e** is usually dropped:

e.g. *come coming hate hating rage raging*
fame famous pale palish use usable
ice icy noise noisy stone stony

Some exceptions are intended to distinguish one word from another:
e.g. *holey* (= full of holes), *holy*; *dyeing, dying.*

(2) Before a consonant, **-e** is usually kept:

e.g. *hateful useless movement paleness*
but see *true, whole, judge* for exceptions.

(3) **-e-** is kept after soft **-c-** or **-g-** before **-a, -o-**:

e.g. *noticeable traceable*
manageable advantageous

The doubling of a final consonant before a following vowel

(1) In a word of one syllable with a short vowel, the final consonant is doubled:

e.g. *man manning manned mannish*
red redder reddest redden
sin sinning sinned sinner
stop stopping stopped stopper
drum drumming drummed drummer

(2) In a word of more than one syllable with a short final vowel, the final consonant is doubled only if the accent is on the final syllable:

e.g. *entrap' entrapping entrapped*
regret' regretting regretted
begin' beginning beginner
occur' occurring occurred occurrence

but
en'ter entering entered
prof'it profiting profited
gall'op galloping galloped
hicc'up hiccuping hiccuped

(3) In British English (but not in American) **-l** is doubled no matter where the accent falls:

e.g. *compel' compelling compelled*
and also *trav'el travelling travelled traveller*

(4) Some derivatives of words ending in **-s** can be spelt in two ways, e.g. *bias*.
Certain words ending in **-p** are not treated strictly in accordance with the rule stated in (2) above, e.g. *kidnap*, *handicap*.

Plural of words ending in *-f*

It is usual to add *s* to make the plural form, e.g. *roof*, *roofs*, but there are several exceptions, e.g. *calves*, *elves*, *knives*, *leaves*.

Some words have optional spellings:
e.g. *hoof* (*hoofs*, or *hooves*), *scarf*, *wharf*, *handkerchief*.

Irregular plurals

Where a noun has an irregular plural form it is usually shown in its entry in the dictionary.

Books of the Bible

Old Testament

Books of the Law

Genesis
Exodus
Leviticus
Numbers
Deuteronomy

Historical Books

Joshua
Judges
Ruth
1 Samuel
2 Samuel
1 Kings
2 Kings
1 Chronicles
2 Chronicles
Ezra
Nehemiah
Esther

Books of Poetry and Wisdom

Job
Psalms
Proverbs
Ecclesiastes
Song of Solomon

Books of the Prophets

Isaiah
Jeremiah
Lamentations
Ezekiel
Daniel
Hosea
Joel
Amos
Obadiah
Jonah
Micah
Nahum
Habakkuk
Zephaniah
Haggai
Zechariah
Malachi

New Testament

The Gospels and Acts

Matthew
Mark
Luke
John
Acts of the Apostles

The Epistles or Letters

Romans
1 Corinthians
2 Corinthians
Galatians
Ephesians
Philippians
Colossians
1 Thessalonians
2 Thessalonians
1 Timothy
2 Timothy
Titus
Philemon
Hebrews
James
1 Peter
2 Peter
1 John
2 John
3 John
Jude

Book of Revelation, or Apocalypse of St John

Apocrypha

1 Esdras
2 Esdras
Tobit
Judith
Additions to Esther
Wisdom of Solomon
Ecclesiasticus
Baruch
Epistle of Jeremy
Prayer of Azariah
Song of the Three Young Men
History of Susanna
Bel and the Dragon
Prayer of Manasses
1 Maccabees
2 Maccabees

The Roman Catholic Church includes Tobit, Judith, all of Esther, Maccabees 1 and 2, Wisdom of Solomon, Ecclesiasticus and Baruch in its canon.

Countries of the world

Country	Capital (*English name in parentheses*)	Currency	Adjective and name of national
Afghanistan	Kabul	1 afghani = 100 puls	Afghan
Albania	Tiranë (Tirana)	1 lek = 100 qintars	Albanian
Algeria	Al-Jazair (Algiers)	1 Algerian dinar = 100 centimes	Algerian
America *see* United States of America			
Andorra	Andorra la Vella	French franc and Spanish peseta	Andorran
Angola	Luanda	1 kwanza = 100 lwei	Angolan
Antigua and Barbuda	St John's	1 East Caribbean dollar = 100 cents dollar = 100 cents	Antiguan, Barbudan
Argentina	Buenos Aires	1 austral (*pl* australes) = 100 centavos or 1000 pesos	Argentine *or* Argentinian (*person* = an Argentinian)
Aruba	Oranjestad	1 Aruban florin = 100 cents	Aruban
Australia	Canberra	1 Australian dollar = 100 cents	Australian
Austria	Vienna	1 schilling = 100 groschen	Austrian
Bahamas	Nassau	1 Bahamian dollar = 100 cents	Bahamian
Bahrain	Al-Manãmah (Manama)	1 Bahrain dinar = 1000 fils	Bahraini
Bangladesh	Dhaka	1 taka = 100 poisha	Bangladeshi
Barbados	Bridgetown	1 Barbadian dollar = 100 cents	Barbadian
Belgium	Bruxelles (Brussels)	1 Belgian franc = 100 centimes	Belgian
Belize	Belmopan	1 Belizean dollar = 100 cents	Belizian
Benin	Porto-Novo	1 CFA franc = 100 centimes	Beninese
Bermuda	Hamilton	1 Bermudian dollar = 100 cents	Bermudan *or* Bermudian
Bhutan	Thimphu	1 ngultrum = 100 chetrum	Bhutanese
Bolivia	La Paz (administrative) Sucre (judicial)	1 boliviano or Bolivian peso = 100 centavos	Bolivian
Botswana	Gaborone	1 pula = 100 thebe	
Brazil	Brasília	1 cruzeiro = 100 centavos	Brazilian
Brunei	Bandar Seri Begawan	1 Bruneian dollar = 100 cents	Bruneian
Bulgaria	Sofia	1 lev = 100 stotinki	Bulgarian
Burkina Faso	Ouagadougou	1 CFA franc = 100 centimes	Burkinese
Burma *see* Myanmar			
Burundi	Bujumbura	Burundi franc = 100 centimes	Burundian
Cambodia (Kampuchea)	Phnum Pénh (Phnom Penh)	1 riel = 100 sen	Cambodian
Cameroon	Yaoundé	1 CFA franc = 100 centimes	Cameroonian
Canada	Ottawa	1 Canadian dollar = 100 cents	Canadian

Country	Capital (*English name in parentheses*)	Currency	Adjective and name of national
Cape Verde	Cidade de Praia	1 Cape Verdean escudo = 100 centavos	Cape Verdean
Cayman Islands	George Town	1 Caymanian dollar = 100 cents	(*person* = a Cayman Islander)
Central African Republic	Bangui	1 CFA franc = 100 centimes	
Chad	N'Djamena	1 CFA franc = 100 centimes	Chadian
Chile	Santiago	1 Chilean peso = 100 centavos	Chilean
China	Beijing (Peking)	1 renminbi yuan = 10 jiao *or* 100 fen	Chinese
Colombia	Bogotá	1 Colombian peso = 100 centavos	Colombian
Comoros	Moroni	1 Comorian franc = 100 centimes	Comorian *or* Comoran (*person* = a Comoran)
Congo	Brazzaville	1 CFA franc = 100 centimes	Congolese
Cook Islands	Avarua	1 New Zealand dollar = 100 cents	(*person* = a Cook Islander)
Costa Rica	San José	1 Costa Rican colón = 100 centimos	Costa Rican
Côte d'Ivoire (Ivory Coast)	Abidjan (commercial) Yamoussoukro (political and administrative)	1 CFA franc = 100 centimes	Ivorian
Cuba	La Habana, (Havana)	1 Cuban peso = 100 centavos	Cuban
Cyprus	Levkosia (Nicosia)	1 Cypriot pound = 100 cents	Cypriot
Czechoslovakia	Praha (Prague)	1 koruna = 100 haler	Czech *or* Czechoslovak
Denmark	København (Copenhagen)	1 Danish krone = 100 øre	Danish (*person* = a Dane)
Djibouti	Djibouti	1 Djiboutian franc = 100 centimes	Djiboutian
Dominica	Roseau	1 East Caribbean dollar = 100 cents	Dominican
Dominican Republic	Santo Domingo	1 Dominican peso = 100 centavos	Dominican
Ecuador	Quito	1 sucre = 100 centavos	Ecuadorian
Egypt	Al-Qāhira (Cairo)	1 Egyptian pound = 100 piastres	Egyptian
El Salvador	San Salvador	1 colón = 100 centavos	Salvadorean
Equatorial Guinea	Malabo	1 ekuele = 100 centimos	(*person* = an Equatorial Guinean)
Ethiopia	Adis Abeba (Addis Ababa)	1 Ethiopian birr = 100 cents	Ethiopian
Faeroe Islands	Tórshavn	1 Faeroese krone = 100 øre	Faeroese
Falkland Islands	Stanley	1 Falkland pound = 100 pence	(*person* = a Falkland Islander)
Fiji	Suva	1 Fijian dollar = 100 cents	Fijian
Finland	Helsinki	1 markka = 100 penni	Finnish (*person* = a Finn)
France	Paris	1 French franc = 100 centimes	French (*person* = a Frenchman, *fem* Frenchwoman)
French Guyana	Cayenne	1 French franc = 100 centimes	French Guyanan
French Polynesia	Papeete	1 CFP franc = 100 centimes	French Polynesian

Country	Capital (*English name in parentheses*)	Currency	Adjective and name of national
Gabon	Libreville	1 CFA franc = 100 centimes	Gabonese
The Gambia	Banjul	1 dalasi = 100 butut	Gambian
Germany	Berlin	1 Deutsche mark = 100 pfennig	German
Ghana	Accra	1 cedi = 100 pesawas	Ghanaian
Great Britain *see* United Kingdom			
Greece	Athinai (Athens)	1 drachma = 100 leptae	Greek
Greenland	Godthåb	1 Danish krone = 100øre	Greenlandic (*person* = a Greenlander)
Grenada	St George's	1 East Caribbean dollar = 100 cents	Grenadian
Guatemala	Guatemala City	1 quetzal = 100 centavos	Guatamalan
Guinea	Conakry	1 Guinean franc = 100 cauris	Guinean
Guinea-Bissau	Bissau	1 Guinea-Bissau peso = 100 centavos	
Guyana	Georgetown	1 Guyana dollar = 100 cents	Guyanese
Haiti	Port-au-Prince	1 gourde = 100 centimes	Haitian
Holland *see* The Netherlands			
Honduras	Tegucigalpa	1 lempira = 100 centavos	Honduran
Hong Kong	Victoria	1 Hong Kong dollar = 100 cents	
Hungary	Budapest	1 forint = 100 fillér	Hungarian
Iceland	Reykjavik	1 króna = 100 aurar	Icelandic (*person* = an Icelander)
India	New Delhi	1 Indian rupee = 100 paisa	Indian
Indonesia	Jakarta	1 rupiah = 100 sen	Indonesian
Iran	Teheran (Tehran)	1 Iranian rial = 100 dinars	Iranian
Iraq	Baghdad	1 Iraqi dinar = 1000 fils	Iraqi
Ireland, Republic of	Baile Átha Cliath (Dublin)	1 Irish pound/punt = 100 pighne	Irish (*person* = an Irishman, *fem* Irishwoman)
Israel	Jerusalem	1 shekel = 100 agorot	Israeli
Italy	Rome	1 Italian lira = 100 centesimi	Italian
Ivory Coast *see* Côte d'Ivoire			
Jamaica	Kingston	1 Jamaican dollar = 100 cents	Jamaican
Japan	Tokyo	1 yen = 100 sen	Japanese
Jordan	Amman	1 Jordan dinar = 1000 fils	Jordanian
Kampuchea *see* Cambodia			
Kenya	Nairobi	1 Kenyan shilling = 100 cents	Kenyan
Kiribati	Bairiki	1 Australian dollar = 100 cents	
Korea, North	Pyongyang	1 North Korean won = 100 chon	North Korean
Korea, South	Sŏul (Seoul)	1 South Korean won = 100 chon	South Korean
Kuwait	Al-Kuwayt (Kuwait City)	1 Kuwaiti dinar = 1000 fils	Kuwaiti
Laos	Viangchan (Vientiane)	1 kip = 100 at	Laotian
Lebanon	Bayrūt (Beirut)	1 Lebanese livre/pound = 100 piastres	Lebanese
Lesotho	Maseru	1 loti (*pl* maloti) = 100 lisente	(*person* = a Mosotho, *pl* Basotho)
Liberia	Monrovia	1 Liberian dollar = 100 cents	Liberian

Country	Capital (*English name in parentheses*)	Currency	Adjective and name of national
Libya	Tarābulus (Tripoli)	1 Libyan dinar = 1000 dirhams	Libyan
Liechtenstein	Vaduz	1 Swiss franc = 100 centimes	(*person* = a Liechtensteiner)
Luxembourg	Luxembourg	1 Luxembourg franc = 100 centimes	Luxembourgian (*person* = a Luxembourger *or* Luxemburger)
Macau	Macau	1 pataca = 100 avos	
Madagascar	Antananarivo	1 Malagasy franc = 100 centimes	Malagasy *or* Madagascan
Malawi	Lilongwe	1 kwacha = 100 tambala	Malawian
Malaysia	Kuala Lumpur	1 Malaysian dollar or ringgit = 100 sen	Malaysian
Maldives	Malé	1 rufiyaa = 100 laaris	Maldivian
Mali	Bamako	1 CFA franc = 100 centimes	Malian
Malta	Valletta	1 Maltese lira = 100 cents or 1000 mils	Maltese
Mauritania	Nouakchott	1 ouguiya = 5 khoums	Mauritanian
Mauritius	Port Louis	1 Mauritian rupee = 100 cents	Mauritian
Mexico	Ciudad de México (Mexico City)	1 Mexican peso = 100 centavos	Mexican
Micronesia	Kolonia	1 US dollar = 100 cents	Micronesian
Monaco	Monaco	1 Monaco franc = 100 centimes	Monégasque *or* Monacan
Mongolia	Ulaanbaatar (Ulan Bator)	1 tugrik = 100 möngö	Mongolian
Morocco	Rabat	1 dirham = 100 centimes	Moroccan
Mozambique	Maputo	1 metical (*pl* meticais) = 100 centavos	Mozambican
Myanmar (Burma)	Yangon (Rangoon)	1 kyat = 100 pyas	Burmese
Namibia	Windhoek	1 South African rand = 100 cents	Namibian
Nauru	(Yaren District)	1 Australian dollar = 100 cents	Nauruan
Nepal	Kathmandu	1 Nepalese rupee = 100 paisa *or* pice	Nepalese *or* Nepali
The Netherlands	Amsterdam 's-Gravenhage (The Hague), seat of government	1 Dutch guilder or florin = 100 cents	Dutch (*person* = a Dutchman, *fem* Dutchwoman, both a Netherlander)
New Zealand	Wellington	1 New Zealand dollar = 100 cents	New Zealand (*person* = a New Zealander)
Nicaragua	Managua	1 córdoba = 100 centavos	Nicaraguan
Niger	Niamey	1 CFA franc = 100 centimes	(*person* = a Nigerien)
Nigeria	Lagos	1 naira = 100 kobo	Nigerian
Norway	Oslo	1 Norwegian krone = 100 øre	Norwegian
Oman	Masqat (Muscat)	1 rial Omani = 1000 baizas	Omani
Pakistan	Islamabad	1 Pakistan rupee = 100 paisa	Pakistani
Panama	Panamá (Panama City)	1 balboa = 100 centésimos	Panamanian
Papua New Guinea	Port Moresby	1 kina = 100 toea	Papua New Guinean *or* Papuan
Paraguay	Asunción	1 guarani = 100 céntimos	Paraguayan
Peru	Lima	1 inti = 100 centavos or 1000 soles	Peruvian

Country	Capital (*English name in parentheses*)	Currency	Adjective and name of national
Philippines	Manila	1 Philippine peso = 100 centavos	Filipino *or* Philippine (*person* = a Filipino, *fem* Filipina)
Poland	Warszawa (Warsaw)	1 zloty = 100 groszy	Polish (*person* = a Pole)
Portugal	Lisboa (Lisbon)	1 escudo = 100 centavos	Portuguese
Puerto Rico	San Juan	1 US dollar = 100 cents	Puerto Rican
Qatar	Al-Dawhah (Doha)	1 Qatar riyal = 100 dirhams	Qatari
Romania	Bucureşti (Bucharest)	1 leu (*pl* lei) = 100 bani	Romanian
Russia *see* Union of Soviet Socialist Republics			
Rwanda	Kigali	1 Rwandese franc = 100 centimes	Rwandan *or* Rwandese
St Helena and dependencies	Jamestown	1 St Helenian pound = 100 pence	St Helenian
St Kitts and Nevis	Basseterre	1 East Caribbean dollar = 100 cents	
St Lucia	Castries	1 East Caribbean dollar = 100 cents	St Lucian
St Vincent and the Grenadines	Kingstown	1 East Caribbean dollar = 100 cents	
San Marino	San Marino	1 Italian lira = 100 centesimi	San Marinese
São Tomé and Principe	São Tomé	1 dobra = 100 centavos	São Tomean
Saudi Arabia	Riyadh (royal) Jiddah (administrative)	1 Saudi Arabian riyal = 100 halalah	Saudi Arabian *or* Saudi
Senegal	Dakar	1 CFA franc = 100 centimes	Senegalese
Seychelles	Victoria	1 Seychelles rupee = 100 cents	Seychellois
Sierra Leone	Freetown	1 leone = 100 cents	Sierra Leonian
Singapore	Singapore	1 Singapore dollar = 100 cents	Singaporean
Solomon Islands	Honiara	1 Solomon Islands dollar = 100 cents	(*person* = a Solomon Islander)
Somalia	Muqdisho (Mogadishu)	1 Somali shilling = 100 cents	Somali
South Africa	Pretoria (administrative) Cape Town (legislative)	1 rand = 100 cents	South African
Spain	Madrid	1 peseta = 100 céntimos	Spanish (*person* = a Spaniard)
Sri Lanka	Colombo	1 Sri Lankan rupee = 100 cents	Sri Lankan
Sudan	Al-Khartūm (Khartoum)	1 Sudanese pound = 100 piastres *or* 1000 millièmes	Sudanese
Suriname	Paramaribo	1 Suriname guilder *or* florin = 100 cents	Surinamese
Swaziland	Mbabane Lobamba (royal and administrative)	1 lilangeni (*pl* emalangeni) = 100 cents	Swazi
Sweden	Stockholm	1 Swedish krona (*pl* kronor) = 100 øre	Swedish (*person* = a Swede)
Switzerland	Bern (Berne)	1 Swiss franc = 100 centimes *or* rappen	Swiss
Syria	Dimashq (Damascus)	1 Syrian pound = 100 piastres	Syrian
Taiwan	Taipei	1 new Taiwan dollar = 100 cents	Taiwanese
Tanzania	Dar es Salaam	1 Tanzanian shilling = 100 cents	Tanzanian

Country	Capital (*English name in parentheses*)	Currency	Adjective and name of national
Thailand	Bangkok	1 baht = 100 satang	Thai
Togo	Lomé	1 CFA franc = 100 centimes	Togolese
Tonga	Nuku'alofa	1 pa'anga *or* Tongan dollar = 100 seniti	Tongan
Trinidad and Tobago	Port of Spain	1 Trinidad and Tobago dollar = 100 cents	Trinidadian and Tobagan *or* Tobagonian
Tunisia	Tunis	1 Tunisian dinar = 1000 millimes	Tunisian
Turkey	Ankara	1 Turkish lira = 100 kurus	Turkish (*person* = a Turk)
Turks and Caicos Islands	Grand Turk	1 US dollar = 100 cents	
Tuvalu	Fongafale	1 Tuvalu dollar = 100 cents	Tuvaluan
Uganda	Kampala	1 Uganda shilling = 100 cents	Ugandan
Union of Soviet Socialist Republics	Moskva (Moscow)	1 rouble = 100 kopeks	Russian *or* Soviet
United Arab Emirates	Abu Dhabi	1 dirham = 100 fils	
United Kingdom	London	1 pound sterling = 100 pence	British (*person* = a Briton)
United States of America	Washington DC	1 US dollar = 100 cents	American
Uruguay	Montevideo	1 new Uruguayan peso = 100 centésimos	Uruguayan
Vanuatu	Port Vila	1 vatu = 100 centimes	Vanuatuan
Vatican	Vatican City	1 Vatican lira = 100 centesimi	Vatican
Venezuela	Caracas	1 bolivar = 100 céntimos	Venezuelan
Vietnam	Hanoi	1 dông = 10 hao *or* 100 xu	Vietnamese
Western Samoa	Apia	1 tala *or* Western Samoan dollar = 100 sene	Western Samoan
Yemen	Sana'a (political) Aden (economic)	1 Yemeni dinar = 1000 fils 1 Yemeni rial = 100 fils	Yemeni *or* Yemenite
Yugoslavia	Beograd (Belgrade)	1 Yugoslav dinar = 100 paras	Yugoslav
Zaire	Kinshasa	1 zaire = 100 makuta (*sing* likuta)	Zaïrean
Zambia	Lusaka	1 kwacha = 100 ngwee	Zambian
Zimbabwe	Harare	1 Zimbabwean dollar = 100 cents	Zimbabwean

States of the USA

State	State capital	State	State capital
Alabama	Montgomery	Montana	Helena
Alaska	Juneau	Nebraska	Lincoln
Arizona	Phoenix	Nevada	Carson City
Arkansas	Little Rock	New Hampshire	Concord
California	Sacramento	New Jersey	Trenton
Colarado	Denver	New Mexico	Santa Fé
Connecticut	Hartford	New York	Albany
Delaware	Dover	North Carolina	Raleigh
(District of Columbia)	(Washington)	North Dakota	Bismarck
Florida	Tallahassee	Ohio	Columbus
Georgia	Atlanta	Oklahoma	Oklahoma City
Hawaii	Honolulu	Oregan	Salem
Idaho	Boise	Pennsylvania	Harrisburg
Illinois	Springfield	Rhode Island	Providence
Indiana	Indianapolis	South Carolina	Columbia
Iowa	Des Moines	South Dakota	Pierre
Kansas	Topeka	Tennessee	Nashville
Kentucky	Frankfort	Texas	Austin
Louisiana	Baton Rouge	Utah	Salt Lake City
Maine	Augusta	Vermont	Montpelier
Maryland	Annapolis	Virginia	Richmond
Massachusetts	Boston	Washington	Olympia
Michigan	Lansing	West Virginia	Charleston
Minnesota	St Paul	Wisconsin	Madison
Mississippi	Jackson	Wyoming	Cheyenne
Missouri	Jefferson City		

Provinces of Canada

Province	Capital	Province	Capital
Alberta	Edmonton	Nova Scotia	Halifax
Manitoba	Winnipeg	Ontario	Toronto
New Brunswick	Fredericton	Prince Edward Island	Charlottetown
Newfoundland and Labrador	St John's	Quebec	Quebec
		Saskatchewan	Regina

States of Australia

State	Capital	State	Capital
New South Wales	Sydney	Tasmania	Hobart
Queensland	Brisbane	Victoria	Melbourne
South Australia	Adelaide	Western Australia	Perth

States of South Africa

State	Capital	State	Capital
Cape Province	Cape Town	Orange Free State	Bloemfontein
Natal	Pietermaritzburg	Transvaal	Pretoria

Black States within South Africa Republics

State	Capital	State	Capital
Bophuthatswana	Mmabatho	Transkei	Umtata
Ciskei	Zwelitsha	Venda	Thohoyandou

Other states

State	Capital	State	Capital
Gazankulu	Giyani	KwaZulu	Uluni
KaNgwane	Nyamasane	Lebowa	Lebowakgomo
KwaNdebele	Siyabuswa	Qwaqwa	Phuthaditjhaba

Counties and regions of the United Kingdom

Common written abbreviations of the English counties are given in brackets after each county. The form *Salop* is also used in speech. There are no commonly used abbreviations for Welsh and Northern Irish counties or Scottish regions.

England

Avon
Bedfordshire (Beds.)
Berkshire (Berks.)
Buckinghamshire (Bucks.)
Cambridgeshire (Cambs.)
Cheshire
Cleveland
Cornwall (Corn.)
Cumbria
Derbyshire
Devon
Dorset
Durham
East Sussex
Essex
Gloucestershire (Glos.)
Greater London
Greater Manchester
Hampshire (Hants.)
Hereford and Worcester
Hertfordshire (Herts.)
Humberside
Isle of Wight (IOW)
Kent
Lancashire (Lancs.)
Leicestershire (Leics.)
Lincolnshire (Lincs.)
Merseyside
Norfolk
Northamptonshire (Northants.)
Northumberland (Northumb.)
North Yorkshire (North Yorks.)
Nottinghamshire (Notts.)
Oxfordshire (Oxon.)
Shropshire (Salop)
Somerset (Som.)
South Yorkshire (South Yorks.)
Staffordshire (Staffs.)
Suffolk
Surrey
Tyne and Wear
Warwickshire (Warwicks.)
West Sussex
West Midlands
West Yorkshire (West Yorks.)
Wiltshire (Wilts.)

Wales

Clwyd
Dyfed
Gwent
Gwynedd
Mid Glamorgan
Powys
South Glamorgan
West Glamorgan

Northern Ireland

Counties

Antrim
Armagh
Down
Fermanagh
Londonderry
Tyrone

Districts

Antrim
Ards
Armagh
Ballymena
Ballymoney
Banbridge
Belfast
Carrickfergus
Castlereagh
Coleraine
Cookstown
Craigavon
Down
Dungannon
Fermanagh
Larne
Limavady
Lisburn
Londonderry
Magherafelt
Moyle
Newry and Mourne
Newtownabbey
North Down
Omagh
Strabane

Scotland

Borders
Central
Dumfries and Galloway
Fife
Grampian
Highland
Lothian
Orkney
Shetland
Strathclyde
Tayside
Western Isles

Earth: general data

There are no universally agreed estimates of the natural phenomena given in this section. Surveys make use of different criteria for identifying natural boundaries, and use different techniques of measurement. The sizes of continents, oceans, seas, deserts and rivers are particularly subject to variation.

Age 4 500 000 000 years (accurate to within a very small percentage of possible error)
Area 509 600 000 sq km/197 000 000 sq ml
Mass 5976 × 10^{27} grams
Land surface 148 000 000 sq km/57 000 000 sq ml (c.29% of total area)
Water surface 361 600 000 sq km/140 000 000 sq ml (c 71% of total area)
Circumference at equator 40 076 km/24 902 ml
Circumference of meridian 40 000 km/24 860 ml.

Continents

Name	*Area sq km*	*sq ml*
Africa	30 293 000	11 696 000 (20.2%)
Antarctica	13 975 000	5 396 000 (9.3%)
Asia	44 493 000	17 179 000 (29.6%)
Oceania	8 945 000	3 454 000 (6%)
Europe*	10 245 000	3 956 000 (6.8%)
North America	24 454 000	9 442 000 (16.3%)
South America	17 838 000	6 887 000 (11.9%)

* Including western USSR.

Lowest point below sea leavel	*m*	*ft*
Lake Assal, Djibouti	156	512
Bently subglacial trench	2 538	8 327
Dead Sea, Israel/Jordan	400	1 312
Lake Eyre, S. Australia	15	49
Caspian Sea, USSR	29	94
Death Valley, California	86	282
Peninsular Valdez, Argentina	40	131

Highest elevation	*m*	*ft*
Mt Kilimanjaro, Tanzania	5 895	19 340
Vinson Massif	5 140	16 864
Mt Everest, China/Nepal	8 848	29 028
Puncak Jaya (Ngga Pulu)	5 030	16 500
Mt El'brus, USSR	5 642	18 510
Mt McKinley, Alaska	6 194	20 320
Aconcagua, Argentina	6 960	22 831

Oceans

Name	*Area sq km*	*sq ml*
Arctic	13 986 000	5 400 000 (3%)
Atlantic	82 217 000	31 700 000 (24%)
Indian	73 426 000	28 350 000 (20%)
Pacific	181 300 000	70 000 000 (46%)

Greatest depth	*m*	*ft*
Eurasia Basin	5 122	16 804
Puerto Rico Trench	8 648	28 372
Java Trench	7 725	25 344
Mariana Trench	11 040	36 220

Average depth	*m*	*ft*
Arctic	1 330	4 300
Atlantic	3 700	12 100
Indian	3 900	12 800
Pacific	4 300	14 100

Largest islands

Name	Area* sq km	sq ml
Australia	7 892 300	3 046 500
Greenland	2 131 600	823 800
New Guinea	790 000	305 000
Borneo	737 000	285 000
Madagascar	587 000	227 600
Baffin	507 000	196 000
Sumatra	425 000	164 900
Honshu (Hondo)	228 000	88 000
Great Britain	219 000	84 400
Victoria, Canada	217 300	83 900
Ellesmere, Canada	196 000	75 800
Celebes	174 000	67 400
South Is, New Zealand	151 000	58 200
Java	129 000	50 000
North Is, New Zealand	114 000	44 200
Newfoundland	109 000	42 000
Cuba	105 000	40 500
Luzon	105 000	40 400
Iceland	103 000	39 700
Mindanao	94 600	36 500
Novaya Zemlya (two islands)	90 600	35 000
Ireland	84 100	32 500
Hokkaido	78 500	30 300
Hispaniola	77 200	29 800
Sakhalin	75 100	29 000
Tierra del Fuego	71 200	27 500
Tasmania	67 900	26 200

* Areas are rounded to the nearest three significant digits.

Largest seas

Name	Area* sq km	sq ml
Coral Sea	4 791 000	1 850 200
Arabian Sea	3 863 000	1 492 000
S. China (Nan) Sea	3 685 000	1 423 000
Mediterranean Sea	2 516 000	971 000
Bering Sea	2 304 000	890 000
Bay of Bengal	2 172 000	839 000
Sea of Okhotsk	1 590 000	614 000
Gulf of Mexico	1 543 000	596 000
Gulf of Guinea	1 533 000	592 000
Barents Sea	1 405 000	542 000
Norwegian Sea	1 383 000	534 000
Gulf of Alaska	1 327 000	512 000
Hudson Bay	1 232 000	476 000
Greenland Sea	1 205 000	465 000
Arafura Sea	1 037 000	400 000
Philippine Sea	1 036 000	400 000
Sea of Japan	978 000	378 000
E. Siberian Sea	901 000	348 000
Kara Sea	883 000	341 000
E. China Sea	664 000	256 000
Andaman Sea	565 000	218 000
North Sea	520 000	201 000
Black Sea	508 000	196 000
Red Sea	453 000	175 000
Baltic Sea	414 000	160 000
Arabian Gulf	238 000	92 200
St Lawrence Gulf	238 300	92 000

Oceans are excluded.

* Areas are rounded to the nearest 1 000 sq km/sq ml.

Largest lakes

Name/Location	Area* sq km	sq ml
Caspian Sea, Iran/USSR	371 000	143 240[1]
Superior, USA/Canada	82,260	31 760[2]
Aral Sea, USSR	64 500	24 900[1]
Victoria, E. Africa	62 940	24 300
Huron, USA/Canada	59 580	23 000[2]
Michigan, USA	58 020	22 400
Tanganyika, E. Africa	32 000	12 350
Baikal, USSR	31 500	12 160
Great Bear, Canada	31 330	12 100
Great Slave, Canada	28 570	11 030
Erie, USA/Canada	25 710	9 920[2]
Winnipeg, Canada	24 390	9 420
Malawi/Nyasa, E. Africa	22 490	8 680
Balkhash, USSR	17–22 000	6 500 –8 500[1]
Ontario, Canada	19 270	7 440[2]
Ladoga, USSR	18 130	7 000
Chad, W. Africa	10–26 000	4–10 000
Maracaibo, Venezuela	13 010	5 020[3]
Patos, Brazil	10 140	3 920[3]
Onega, USSR	9 800	3 800
Rudolf, E. Africa	9 100	3 500
Eyre, Australia	8 800	3 400[3]
Titicaca, Peru	8 300	3 200

[1] salt lakes
[2] average of areas given by Canada and USA
[3] salt lagoons
* Areas are given to the nearest 10 sq km /sq ml. The Caspian and Aral Seas, being entirely surrounded by land, are classified as lakes.

Highest mountains

Name	Height* m	ft	Location
Everest	8 850	29 030	China-Nepal
K2	8 610	28 250	Kashmir-Jammu
Kangchenjunga	8 590	28 170	India-Nepal
Lhotse	8 500	27 890	China-Nepal
Kangchenjunga S. Peak	8 470	27 800	India-Nepal
Makalu I	8 470	27 800	China-Nepal
Kangchenjunga W. Peak	8 420	27 620	India-Nepal
Llotse E. Peak	8 380	27 500	China-Nepal
Dhaulagiri	8 170	26 810	Nepal
Cho Oyu	8 150	26 750	China-Nepal
Manaslu	8 130	26 660	Nepal
Nanga Parbat	8 130	26 660	Kashmir-Jammu
Annapurna I	8 080	26 500	Nepal
Gasherbrum I	8 070	26 470	Kashmir-Jammu
Broad-highest	8 050	26 400	Kashmir-Jammu
Gasherbrum II	8 030	26 360	Kashmir-Jammu
Gosainthan	8 010	26 290	China
Broad-middle	8 000	26 250	Kashmir-Jammu
Gasherbrum III	7 950	26 090	Kashmir-Jammu
Annapurna II	7 940	26 040	Nepal
Nanda Devi	7 820	25 660	India
Rakaposhi	7 790	25 560	Kashmir
Kamet	7 760	25 450	India
Ulugh Muztagh	7 720	25 340	Tibet
Tirich Mir	7 690	25 230	Pakistan
Muz Tag Ata	7 550	24 760	China
Communism Peak	7 490	24 590	USSR
Pobedy Peak	7 440	24 410	China-USSR
Aconcagua	6 960	22 830	Argentina
Ojos del Salado	6 910	22 660	Argentina-Chile

* Heights are given to the nearest 10 m/ft.

Largest deserts

Name/Location *Area*	*sq km*	*sq ml*
Sahara, N. Africa	8 600 000	3 320 000
Arabian, S.W. Asia	2 330 000	900 000
Gobi, Mongolia and N.E. China	1 166 000	450 000
Patagonian, Argentina	673 000	260 000
Great Victoria, S.W. Australia	647 000	250 000
Great Basin, S.W. USA	492 000	190 000
Chihuahuan, Mexico	450 000	175 000
Great Sandy, N.W. Australia	400 000	150 000
Sonoran, S.W. USA	310 000	120 000
Kyzyl Kum, S.W. USSR	300 000	115 000
Takla Makan, N. China	270 000	105 000
Kalahari, S.W. Africa	260 000	100 000
Kara Kum, S.W. USSR	260 000	100 000
Kavir, Iran	260 000	100 000
Syrian, Saudi Arabia/Jordan/Syria/Iraq	260 000	100 000
Nubian, Sudan	260 000	100 000
Thar, India/Pakistan	200 000	77 000
Ust'-Urt, S.W. USSR	160 000	62 000
Bet-Pak-Dala, S. USSR	155 000	60 000
Simpson, Central Australia	145 000	56 000
Dzungaria, China	142 000	55 000
Atacama, Chile	140 000	54 000
Namib, S.E. Africa	134 000	52 000
Sturt, S.E. Australia	130 000	50 000
Bolson de Mapimi, Mexico	130 000	50 000
Ordos, China	130 000	50 000
Alashan, China	116 000	45 000

Desert areas are very approximate, because clear physical boundaries may not occur.

Highest waterfalls

Name	*Height m*	*ft*	*Location*
Angel (upper fall)	807	2 648	Venezuela
Itatinga	628	2 060	Brazil
Cuquenan	610	2 000	Guyana-Venezuela
Ormeli	563	1 847	Norway
Tysse	533	1 749	Norway
Pilao	524	1 719	Brazil
Ribbon	491	1 612	USA
Vestre Mardola	468	1 535	Norway
Roraima	457?	1 500?	Guyana
Cleve-Garth	450?	1 476?	New Zealand

Distances are given for individual leaps.

Deepest caves

Name/Location	*Depth m*	*ft*
Jean Bernard, France	1 494	4 900
Snezhnaya, USSR	1 340	4 397
Puertas de Illamina, Spain	1 338	4 390
Pierre-Saint-Martin, France	1 321	4 334
Sistema Huautla, Mexico	1 240	4 067
Berger, France	1 198	3 930
Vqerdi, Spain	1 195	3 921
Dachstein-Mammuthöhle, Austria	1 174	3 852
Zitu, Spain	1 139	3 737
Badalona, Spain	1 130	3 707
Batmanhöhle, Austria	1 105	3 626
Schneeloch, Austria	1 101	3 612
G E S Malaga, Spain	1 070	3 510
Lamprechtsofen, Austria	1 024	3 360

Longest rivers

Name	*Outflow*	*Length* km*	*ml*
Nile-Kagera-Ruvuvu-Ruvusu-Luvironza	Mediterranean Sea (Egypt)	6 690	4 160
Amazon-Ucayali-Tambo-Ene-Apurimac	Atlantic Ocean (Brazil)	6 570	4 080
Mississippi-Missouri-Jefferson-Beaverhead-Red Rock	Gulf of Mexico (USA)	6 020	3 740
Chang Jiang (Yangtze)	E. China Sea (China)	5 980	3 720
Yenisey-Angara-Selenga-Ider	Kara Sea (USSR)	5 870	3 650
Amur-Argun-Kerulen	Tartar Strait (USSR)	5 780	3 590
Ob-Irtysh, Asia	Gulf of Ob, Kara Sea (USSR)	5 410	3 360
Plata-Parana-Grande	Atlantic Ocean (Argentina/Uruguay)	4 880	3 030
Huang Ho (Yellow)	Yellow Sea (China)	4 840	3 010
Congo (Zaire)-Lualaba	Atlantic Ocean (Angola-Zaire)	4 630	2 880
Lena	Laptev Sea (USSR)	4 400	2 730
Mackenzie-Slave-Peace-Finlay	Beaufort Sea (Canada)	4 240	2 630
Mekong	S. China Sea (Vietnam)	4 180	2 600
Niger	Gulf of Guinea (Nigeria)	4 100	2 550

* Lengths are given to the nearest 10 km/ml, and include the river plus tributaries comprising the longest watercourse.

Major volcanoes

Name	Height m	Height ft	Major eruptions (years)	Last eruption (year)
Aconcagua (Argentina)	6 954	22 831	extinct	
Ararat (Turkey)	5 198	18 350	extinct	Holocene
Awu (Sangihe Is.)	1 327	4 355	1711, 1856, 1892	1968
Bezymianny (USSR)	2 800	9 186	1955–6	1984
Coseguina (Nicaragua)	847	1 598	1835	1835
El Chichón (Mexico)	1 349	4 430	1982	1982
Erebus (Antarctica)	4 023	13 200	1947, 1972	1986
Etna (Italy)	3 236	10 625	122, 1169, 1329, 1536, 1669,1928, 1964, 1971	1986
Fuji (Japan)	3 776	12 388	1707	1707
Galunggung (Java)	2 180	7 155	1822, 1918	1982
Heckla (Iceland)	1 491	4 920	1693, 1845, 1947–8, 1970	1981
Helgafell (Iceland)	215	706	1973	1973
Jurullo (Mexico)	1 330	4 255	1759–74	1774
Katmai (Alaska)	2 298	7 540	1912, 1920, 1921	1931
Kilauea (Hawaii)	1 247	4 100	1823–1924, 1952, 1955, 1960, 1967–8, 1968–74, 1983–7	1988
Kilimanjaro (Tanzania)	5 930	19 450	extinct	Pleistocene
Klyuchevskoy (USSR)	4 850	15 910	1700–1966, 1984	1985
Krakatoa (Sumatra)	818	2 685	1680, 1883, 1927, 1952–3, 1969	1980
La Soufrière (St Vincent)	1 232	4 048	1718, 1812, 1902, 1971–2	1979
Laki (Iceland)	500	1 642	1783	1784
Lamington (Papua New Guinea)	1 780	5 844	1951	1956
Lassen Peak (USA)	3 186	10 453	1914–15	1921
Mauna Loa (Hawaii)	4 172	13 685	1859, 1880, 1887, 1919, 1950	1984
Mayon (Philippines)	2 462	8 084	1616, 1766, 1814, 1897, 1968	1978
Nyamuragira (Zaire)	3 056	10 026	1921–38, 1971, 1980	1984
Paricutin (Mexico)	3 188	10 460	1943–52	1952
Pelée, Mont (Martinique)	1 397	4 584	1902, 1929–32	1932
Popocatepetl (Mexico)	5 483	17 990	1920	1943
Rainier, Mt (USA)	4 392	14 416	1st-cent. BC, 1820	1882
Ruapehu (New Zealand)	2 796	9 175	1945, 1953, 1969, 1975	1986
St Helens, Mt (USA)	2 549	8 364	1800, 1831, 1835, 1842–3, 1857, 1980–	1987
Santorini/Thira (Greece)	1 315?	4 316?	1470 BC, 197 BC, AD 46, 1570–3, 1707–11, 1866–70	1950
Stromboli (Italy)	931	3 055	1768, 1882, 1889, 1907, 1930, 1936, 1941, 1950, 1952	1986
Surtsey (Iceland)	174	570	1963–7	1967
Taal (Philippines)	1 448	4 752	1911, 1965, 1969	1977
Tambora (Sumbawa)	2 868	9 410	1815	1880
Tarawera (New Zealand)	1 149	3 770	1886	1973
Vesuvius (Italy)	1 289	4 230	79, 472, 1036, 1631, 1779, 1906	1944
Vulcano (Italy)	502	1 650	antiquity, 1444, 1730–40, 1786, 1873, 1888–90	1890

Major earthquakes

(All magnitudes on the Richter scale)

Location	Year	Magnitude	Deaths	Location	Year	Magnitude	Deaths
San Francisco	1989	6.9	100	Gansu (China)	1932	7.6	70 000
Armenia (USSR)	1988	7.0	25 000	Nan-shan (China)	1927	8.3	200 000
Mexico City	1985	8.1	7 200	Kwanto (Japan)	1923	8.3	143 000
N. Yemen	1982	6.0	2 800	Gansu (China)	1920	8.6	180 000
S. Italy	1980	7.2	4 500	Avezzano (Italy)	1915	7.5	30 000
El Asnam (Algeria)	1980	7.3	5 000	Messina (Italy)	1908	7.5	120 000
N.E. Iran	1978	7.7	25 000	Valparaiso (Chile)	1906	8.6	20 000
Tangshan (China)	1976	8.2	242 000	San Francisco (USA)	1906	8.3	500
Guatemala City	1976	7.5	22 778	Ecuador/Colombia	1868	*	70 000
Kashmir	1974	6.3	5 200	Calabria (Italy)	1783	*	50 000
Managua (Nicaragua)	1972	6.2	5 000	Lisbon (Portugal)	1755	*	70 000
S. Iran	1972	6.9	5 000	Calcutta (India)	1737	*	300 000
Chimbote (Peru)	1970	7.7	66 000	Hokkaido (Japan)	1730	*	137 000
N.E. Iran	1968	7.4	11 600	Catania (Italy)	1693	*	60 000
Anchorage (USA)	1964	8.5	131	Caucasia (USSR)	1667	*	80 000
N.W. Iran	1962	7.1	12 000	Shensi (China)	1556	*	830 000
Agadir (Morocco)	1960	5.8	12 000	Chihli (China)	1290	*	100 000
Erzincan (Turkey)	1939	7.9	23 000	Silicia (Asia Minor)	1268	*	60 000
Chillan (Chile)	1939	7.8	30 000	Corinth (Greece)	856	*	45 000
Quetta (India)	1935	7.5	60 000	Antioch (Turkey)	526	*	250 000

* Magnitude not available.

Major tsunamis

Location of source	Year	Height m	Height ft	Location of deaths/damage	Deaths
Sea of Japan	1983	15	49	Japan, Korea	107
Indonesia	1979	10	32	Indonesia	187
Celebes Sea	1976	30	98	Philippine Is.	5 000
Alaska	1964	32	105	Alaska, Aleutian Is., California	122
Chile	1960	25	82	Chile, Hawaii, Japan	1 260
Aleutian Is.	1957	16	52	Hawaii, Japan	0
Kamchatka	1952	18.4	60	Kamchatka, Kuril Is., Hawaii	many
Aleutian Is.	1946	32	105	Aleutian Is., Hawaii, California	165
Nankaido (Japan)	1946	6.1	20	Japan	1 997
Kii (Japan)	1944	7.5	25	Japan	998
Sanriku (Japan)	1933	28.2	93	Japan, Hawaii	3 000
E. Kamchatka	1923	20	66	Kamchatka, Hawaii	3
S. Kuril Is.	1918	12	39	Kuril Is., USSR, Japan, Hawaii	23
Sanriku (Japan)	1896	30	98	Japan	27 122
Sunda Strait	1883	35	115	Java, Sumatra	36 000
Chile	1877	23	75	Chile, Hawaii	many
Chile	1868	21	69	Chile, Hawaii	25 000
Hawaii Is.	1868	20	66	Hawaii Is.	81
Japan	1854	6	20	Japan	3 000
Flores Sea	1800	24	79	Indonesia	4–500
Ariake Sea	1792	9	30	Japan	9 745
Italy	1783	?	?	Italy	30 000
Ryukyu Is.	1771	12	39	Ryukyu Is.	11 941
Portugal	1775	16	52	W. Europe, Morocco, W. Indies	60 000
Peru	1746	24	79	Peru	5 000
Japan	1741	9	30	Japan	1 000+
S.E. Kamchatka	1737	30	98	Kamchatka, Kuril Is.	?
Peru	1724	24	79	Peru	?
Japan	1707	11.5	38	Japan	30 000
W. Indies	1692	?	?	Jamaica	2 000
Banda Is.	1629	15	49	Indonesia	?
Sanriku (Japan)	1611	25	82	Japan	5 000
Japan	1605	?	?	Japan	4 000
Kii (Japan)	1498	?	?	Japan	5 000

Weights, measures, sizes, etc.

Common measures

Metric units

Length		*Imperial equiv.*
	1 millimetre	0.03937 in
10 mm	1 centimetre	0.39 in
10 cm	1 decimetre	3.94 in
100 cm	1 metre	39.37 in
1 000 m	1 kilometre	0.62 mile

Area		*Imperial equiv.*
	1 square millimetre	0.0016 sq in
	1 square centimetre	0.155 sq in
100 sq cm	1 square decimetre	15.5 sq in
10 000 sq cm	1 square metre	10.76 sq ft
10 000 sq m	1 hectare	2.47 acres

Volume		*Imperial equiv.*
	1 cubic centimetre	0.016 cu in
1 000 cu cm	1 cubic decimetre	61.024 cu in
1 000 cu dm	1 cubic metre	35.31 cu ft
		1.308 cu yds

Liquid volume		
	1 litre	1.76 pints
100 litres	1 hectolitre	22 gallons

Weight		*Imperial equiv.*
	1 gram	0.035 oz
1 000 g	1 kilogram	2.2046 lb
1 000 kg	1 tonne	0.0842 ton

Imperial units

Length		*Metric equiv.*
	1 inch	2.54 cm
12 in	1 foot	30.48 cm
3 ft	1 yard	0.9144 m
1 760 yd	1 mile	1.6093 km

Area		*Metric equiv.*
	1 square inch	6.45 sq cm
144 sq in	1 square foot	0.0929 m^2
9 sq ft	1 square yard	0.836 m^2
4 840 sq yd	1 acre	0.405 ha
640 acres	1 square mile	259 ha

Volume		*Metric equiv.*
	1 cubic inch	16.3871 cm^3
1 728 cu in	1 cubic foot	0.028 m^3
27 cu ft	1 cubic yard	0.765 m^3

Liquid volume		
	1 pint	0.57 litre
2 pints	1 quart	1.14 litres
4 quarts	1 gallon	4.55 litres

Weight		*Metric equiv.*
	1 ounce	28.3495 g
16 oz	1 pound	0.4536 kg
14 lb	1 stone	6.35 kg
8 stones	1 hundredweight	50.8 kg
20 cwt	1 ton	1.016 tonnes

Cookery measures

	UK	US
1 cup	284 ml/10 UK fl oz	237 ml/8 US fl oz
1 teaspoonful	6 ml	5 ml
1 dessertspoonful	12 ml	—
1 tablespoonful	18 ml	15 ml

Conversion factors

Imperial to metric

Length		*Multiply by*
inches	→ millimetres	25.4
inches	→ centimetres	2.54
feet	→ metres	0.3048
yards	→ metres	0.9144
statute miles	→ kilometres	1.6093
nautical miles	→ kilometres	1.852

Area		*Multiply by*
square inches	→ square centimetres	6.4516
square feet	→ square metres	0.0929
square yards	→ square metres	0.8361
acres	→ hectares	0.4047
square miles	→ square kilometres	2.5899

Volume		*Multiply by*
cubic inches	→ cubic centimetres	16.3871
cubic feet	→ cubic metres	0.0283
cubic yards	→ cubic metres	0.7646

Capacity		*Multiply by*
UK fluid ounces	→ litres	0.0284
US fluid ounces	→ litres	0.0296
UK pints	→ litres	0.5682
US pints	→ litres	0.4732
UK gallons	→ litres	4.546
US gallons	→ litres	3.7854

Weight		*Multiply by*
ounces (avoirdupois)	→ grams	28.3495
ounces (troy)	→ grams	31.1035
pounds	→ kilograms	0.4536
tons (long)	→ tonnes	1.016

Metric to imperial

Length		*Multiply by*
millimetres	→ inches	0.0394
centimetres	→ inches	0.3937
metres	→ feet	3.2808
metres	→ yards	1.0936
kilometres	→ statute miles	0.6214
kilometres	→ nautical miles	0.54

Area		*Multiply by*
square centimetres	→ square inches	0.155
square metres	→ square feet	10.764
square metres	→ square yards	1.196
hectares	→ acres	2.471
square kilometres	→ square miles	0.386

Volume		*Multiply by*
cubic centimetres	→ cubic inches	0.061
cubic metres	→ cubic feet	35.315
cubic metres	→ cubic yards	1.308

Capacity		*Multiply by*
litres	→ UK fluid ounces	35.1961
litres	→ US fluid ounces	33.8150
litres	→ UK pints	1.7598
litres	→ US pints	2.1134
litres	→ UK gallons	0.2199
litres	→ US gallons	0.2642

Weight		*Multiply by*
grams	→ ounces (avoirdupois)	0.0353
grams	→ ounces (troy)	0.0322
kilograms	→ pounds	2.2046
tonnes	→ tons (long)	0.9842

International paper sizes

A series

	mm	*in*
A0	841 × 1189	33.11 × 46.81
A1	594 × 841	23.39 × 33.1
A2	420 × 594	16.54 × 23.39
A3	297 × 420	11.69 × 16.54
A4	210 × 297	8.27 × 11.69
A5	148 × 210	5.83 × 8.27
A6	105 × 148	4.13 × 5.83
A7	74 × 105	2.91 × 4.13
A8	52 × 74	2.05 × 2.91
A9	37 × 52	1.46 × 2.05
A10	26 × 37	1.02 × 1.46

A series is used for writing paper, books and magazines.

B series

	mm	*in*
B0	1000 × 1414	39.37 × 55.67
B1	707 × 1000	27.83 × 39.37
B2	500 × 707	19.68 × 27.83
B3	353 × 500	13.90 × 19.68
B4	250 × 353	9.84 × 13.90
B5	176 × 250	6.93 × 9.84
B6	125 × 176	4.92 × 6.93
B7	88 × 125	3.46 × 4.92
B8	62 × 88	2.44 × 3.46
B9	44 × 62	1.73 × 2.44
B10	31 × 44	1.22 × 1.73

B series for posters.

C series

	mm	*in*
C0	917 × 1297	36.00 × 51.20
C1	648 × 917	25.60 × 36.00
C2	458 × 648	18.00 × 25.60
C3	324 × 458	12.80 × 18.00
C4	229 × 324	9.00 × 12.80
C5	162 × 229	6.40 × 9.00
C6	114 × 162	4.50 × 6.40
C7	81 × 114	3.20 × 4.50
DL	110 × 220	4.33 × 8.66
C7/6	81 × 162	3.19 × 6.38

C series for envelopes.

All sizes in these series have sides in the proportion of $1{:}\sqrt{2}$.

International clothing sizes

Size equivalents are approximate, and may display some variation between manufacturers.

Women's suits/dresses

UK	US	UK/ Continent
8	6	36
10	8	38
12	10	40
14	12	42
16	14	44
18	16	46
20	18	48
22	20	50
24	22	52

Men's shirts

UK/US	UK/ Continent
12	30–31
12½	32
13	33
13½	34–35
14	36
14½	37
15	38
15½	39–40
16	41
16½	42
17	43
17½	44–45

Adults' shoes

UK	US	UK/ Continent
4	5½	37
4½	6	38
5	6½	38
5½	7	39
6	7½	39
6½	8	40
7	8½	41
7½	8½	42
8	9½	42
8½	9½	43
9	10½	43
9½	10½	44
10	11½	44
10½	11½	45
11	12	46

Children's shoes

UK/US	UK/ Continent
0	15
1	17
2	18
3	19
4	20
5	22
6	23
7	24
8	25
8½	26
9	27
10	28
11	29
12	30
13	32

Men's suits and overcoats

UK/US	Continent
36	46
38	48
40	50
42	52
44	54
46	56

Women's hosiery

UK/US	UK/ Continent
8	0
8½	1
9	2
9½	3
10	4
10½	5

Men's socks

UK/US	UK/ Continent
9½	38–39
10	39–40
10½	40–41
11	41–42
11½	42–43

International pattern sizes

Young junior/teenage

Size	Bust cm	Bust in	Waist cm	Waist in	Hip cm	Hip in	Back waist length cm	Back waist length in
5/6	71	28	56	22	79	31	34.5	13½
7/8	74	29	58	23	81	32	35.5	14
9/10	78	30½	61	24	85	33½	37	14½
11/12	81	32	64	25	89	35	38	15
13/14	85	33½	66	26	93	36½	39	15⅜
15/16	89	35	69	27	97	38	40	15¾

Half-size

Size	Bust cm	Bust in	Waist cm	Waist in	Hip cm	Hip in	Back waist length cm	Back waist length in
10½	84	33	69	27	89	35	38	15
12½	89	35	74	29	94	37	39	15¼
14½	94	37	79	31	99	39	39.5	15½
16½	99	39	84	33	104	41	40	15¾
18½	104	41	89	35	109	43	40.5	15⅞
20½	109	43	96	37½	116	45½	40.5	16
22½	114	45	102	40	122	48	41	16⅛
24½	119	47	108	42½	128	50½	41.5	16¼

Misses

Size	Bust cm	Bust in	Waist cm	Waist in	Hip cm	Hip in	Back waist length cm	Back waist length in
6	78	30½	58	23	83	32½	39.5	15½
8	80	31½	61	24	85	33½	40	15¾
10	83	32½	64	25	88	34½	40.5	16
12	87	34	67	26½	92	36	41.5	16¼
14	92	36	71	28	97	38	42	16½
16	97	38	76	30	102	40	42.5	16¾
18	102	40	81	32	107	42	43	17
20	107	42	87	34	112	44	44	17¼

Women's

Size	Bust cm	Bust in	Waist cm	Waist in	Hip cm	Hip in	Back waist length cm	Back waist length in
38	107	42	89	35	112	44	44	17¼
40	112	44	94	37	117	46	44	17⅜
42	117	46	99	39	122	48	44.5	17½
44	122	48	105	41½	127	50	45	17⅝
46	127	50	112	44	132	52	45	17¾
48	132	52	118	46½	137	54	45.5	17⅞
50	137	54	124	49	142	56	46	18

Temperatures

Conversion tables

To convert	*To*	*Equation*
°Fahrenheit	°Celsius	−32, ×5, ÷9
°Fahrenheit	°Rankine	+459.67
°Fahrenheit	°Réaumur	−32, ×4, ÷9
°Celsius	°Fahrenheit	×9, ÷5, +32
°Celsius	Kelvin	+273.15
°Celsius	°Réaumur	×4, ÷5
Kelvin	°Celsius	−273.15
°Rankine	°Fahrenheit	−459.67
°Réaumur	°Fahrenheit	×9, ÷4, +32
°Réaumur	°Celsius	×5, ÷4

Carry out operations in sequence.

Oven temperatures

Gas Mark	*°C*	*°F*	*Rating*
½	120	250	slow
1	140	275	
2	150	300	
3	170	325	
4	180	350	moderate
5	190	375	
6	200	400	hot
7	220	425	
8	230	450	very hot
9	260	500	

Multiplication table

	2	**3**	**4**	**5**	**6**	**7**	**8**	**9**	**10**	**11**	**12**	**13**	**14**	**15**	**16**	**17**	**18**	**19**	**20**	**21**	**22**	**23**	**24**	**25**
2	4	6	8	10	12	14	16	18	20	22	24	26	28	30	32	34	36	38	40	42	44	46	48	50
3	6	9	12	15	18	21	24	27	30	33	36	39	42	45	48	51	54	57	60	63	66	69	72	75
4	8	12	16	20	24	28	32	36	40	44	48	52	56	60	64	68	72	76	80	84	88	92	96	100
5	10	15	20	25	30	35	40	45	50	55	60	65	70	75	80	85	90	95	100	105	110	115	120	125
6	12	18	24	30	36	42	48	54	60	66	72	78	84	90	96	102	108	114	120	126	132	138	144	150
7	14	21	28	35	42	49	56	63	70	77	84	91	98	105	112	119	126	133	140	147	154	161	168	175
8	16	24	32	40	48	56	64	72	80	88	96	104	112	120	128	136	144	152	160	168	176	184	192	200
9	18	27	36	45	54	63	72	81	90	99	108	117	126	135	144	153	162	171	180	189	198	207	216	225
10	20	30	40	50	60	70	80	90	100	110	120	130	140	150	160	170	180	190	200	210	220	230	240	250
11	22	33	44	55	66	77	88	99	110	121	132	143	154	165	176	187	198	209	220	231	242	253	264	275
12	24	36	48	60	72	84	96	108	120	132	144	156	168	180	192	204	216	228	240	252	264	276	288	300
13	26	39	52	65	78	91	104	117	130	143	156	169	182	195	208	221	234	247	260	273	286	299	312	325
14	28	42	56	70	84	98	112	126	140	154	168	182	196	210	224	238	252	266	280	294	308	322	336	350
15	30	45	60	75	90	105	120	135	150	165	180	195	210	225	240	255	270	285	300	315	330	345	360	375
16	32	48	64	80	96	112	128	144	160	176	192	208	224	240	256	272	288	304	320	336	352	368	384	400
17	34	51	68	85	102	119	136	153	170	187	204	221	238	255	272	289	306	323	340	357	374	391	408	425
18	36	54	72	90	108	126	144	162	180	198	216	234	252	270	288	306	324	342	360	378	396	414	432	450
19	38	57	76	95	114	133	152	171	190	209	228	247	266	285	304	323	342	361	380	399	418	437	456	475
20	40	60	80	100	120	140	160	180	200	220	240	260	280	300	320	340	360	380	400	420	440	460	480	500
21	42	63	84	105	126	147	168	189	210	231	252	273	294	315	336	357	378	399	420	441	462	483	504	525
22	44	66	88	110	132	154	176	198	220	242	264	286	308	330	352	374	396	418	440	462	484	506	528	550
23	46	69	92	115	138	161	184	207	230	253	276	299	322	345	368	391	414	437	460	483	506	529	552	575
24	48	72	96	120	144	168	192	216	240	264	288	312	336	360	384	408	432	456	480	504	528	552	576	600
25	50	75	100	125	150	175	200	225	250	275	300	325	350	375	400	425	450	475	500	525	550	575	600	625

SI conversion factors

This table gives the conversion factors for many British and other units which are still in common use, showing their equivalents in terms of the International System of Units (SI). The column labelled 'SI equivalent' gives the SI value of one unit of the type named in the first column, e.g.1 calorie is 4.189 joules. The column labelled 'Reciprocal' allows conversion the other way, e.g. 1 joule is 0.239 calories. (All values are to three decimal places.) As a second example, 1 dyne is $10\mu N = 10 \times 10^{-6}$ $N = 10^{-5}N$; so 1 newton is $0.1 \times 10^{+6} = 10^5$ dybe. Finally, 1 torr is 0.133 $KPa = 0.133 \times 10^3$ Pa; so 1 Pa is 7.501×10^{-3} torr.

$^+$ signifies a unit in temporary use with SI.

Unit name	*Symbol*	*Quantity*	*SI equivalent*	*Unit*	*Reciprocal*
acre		area	0.405	hm^2	2.471
ångstrom$^+$	Å	length	0.1	nm	10
astronomical unit	AU	length	0.150	Tm	6.684
atomic mass unit	amu	mass	1.661×10^{-27}	kg	6.022×10^{26}
bar$^+$	bar	pressure	0.1	MPa	10
barn$^+$	b	area	100	fm^2	0.01
barrel (US) = 42 US gal	bbl	volume	0.159	m^3	6.290
British thermal unit	Btu	energy	1.055	kJ	0.948
calorie	cal	energy	4.187	J	0.239
cubic foot	ft^3	volume	0.028	m^3	35.315
cubic inch	in^3	volume	16.387	cm^3	0.061
cubic yard	yd^3	volume	0.765	m^3	1.308
curie$^+$	Ci	activity of radionuclide	37	GBq	0.027
degree = 1/90 rt angle	°	plane angle	$\pi/180$	rad	57.296
degree Celsius	°C	temperature	1	K	1
degree Centigrade	°C	temperature	1	K	1
degree Fahrenheit	°F	temperature	5/9	K	1.8
degree Rankine	°R	temperature	5/9	K	1.8
dyne	dyn	force	10	μN	0.1
electronvolt	eV	energy	0.160	αJ	6.241
erg	erg	energy	0.1	μJ	10
fathom (6 ft)		length	1.829	m	0.547
fermi		length	1	fm	1
foot	ft	length	30.48	cm	0.033
foot per second	$ft\ s^{-1}$	velocity	0.305	$m\ s^{-1}$	3.281
			1.097	$km\ h^{-1}$	0.911
gallon (UK)$^+$	gal	volume	4.546	dm^3	0.220
gallon (US)$^+$ = 231 in^3	gal	volume	3.785	dm^3	0.264
gallon (UK) per mile		consumption	2.825	dm^3km^{-1}	0.354
gauss	Gs, G	magnetic flux density	100	μT	0.01
grade = 0.01 rt angle		plane angle	$\pi/200$	rad	63.662
grain	gr	mass	0.065	g	15.432
hectare$^+$	ha	area	1	hm^2	1
horsepower	hp	energy	0.746	kW	1.341
inch	in	length	2.54	cm	0.394
kilogram-force	kgf	force	9.807	N	0.102
knot$^+$		velocity	1.852	$km\ h^{-1}$	0.540
light year	l.y.	length	9.461×10^{15}	m	1.057×10^{-16}
litre	l	volume	1	dm^3	1
Mach number	Ma	velocity	1193.3	km h	8.380×10^{-4}
maxwell	Mx	magnetic flux	10	nWb	0.1
metric carat		mass	0.2	g	5
micron	μ	length	1	μm	1
mile (nautical)$^+$		length	1.852	km	0.540
mile (statute)		length	1.609	km	0.621
mile per hour	$mile\ h^{-1}$	velocity	1.609	$km\ h^{-1}$	0.621
minute = (1/60)°	′	plane angle	$\pi/10800$	rad	3437.75
oersted	Oe	magnetic field strength	$1/(4\pi)$	kAm^{-1}	4π
ounce (avoirdupois)	oz	mass	28.349	g	0.035
ounce (troy) = 480 gr		mass	31.103	g	0.032
parsec	pc	length	30857	Tm	0.0000324
phot	ph	illuminance	10	klx	0.1
pint (UK)	pt	volume	0.568	dm^3	1.760

Unit name	Symbol	Quantity	SI equivalent	Unit	Reciprocal
poise	p	viscosity	0.1	Pa s	10
pound	lb	mass	0.454	kg	2.205
pound-force	lbf	force	4.448	N	0.225
pound-force/in^{-2}		pressure	6.895	kPa	0.145
poundal	pdl	force	0.138	N	7.233
pounds per square inch	psi	pressure	6.895×10^3	KPa	0.145
rad$^+$	rad	absorbed dose	0.01	Gy	100
rem$^+$	rem	dose equivalent	0.01	Sv	100
right angle $= \pi/2$ rad		plane angle	1.571	rad	0.637
röntgen$^+$	R	exposure	0.258	mC kg^{-1}	3.876
second $= (1/60)'$	$''$	plane angle	$\pi/648$	mrad	206.265
slug		mass	14.594	kg	0.068
solar mass	M	mass	1.989×10^{30}	kg	5.028×10^{-31}
square foot	ft^2	area	9.290	dm^2	0.108
square inch	in^2	area	6.452	cm^2	0.155
square mile (statute)		area	2.590	km^2	0.386
square yard	yd^2	area	0.836	m^2	1.196
standard atmosphere	atm	pressure	0.101	MPa	9.869
stere	st	volume	1	m^3	1
stilb	sb	luminance	10	kcd m^{-2}	0.1
stokes	St	viscosity	1	cm^2 s^{-1}	1
therm $= 10^5$ Btu		energy	0.105	GJ	9.478
ton $= 2240$ lb		mass	1.016	Mg	0.984
ton-force	tonf	force	9.964	kN	0.100
ton-force/in^{-2}		pressure	15.444	MPa	0.065
tonne	t	mass	1	Mg	1
torr } mmHg }	torr	pressure	0.133	kPa	7.501
X unit		length	0.100	pm	10
yard	yd	length	0.915	m	1.094

SI prefixes

Factor	Prefix	Symbol	Factor	Prefix	Symbol	Factor	Prefix	Symbol	Factor	Prefix	Symbol
10^{18}	exa	E	10^{-1}	deci	d	10^6	mega	M	10^{-9}	nano	n
10^{15}	peta	P	10^{-2}	centi	c	10^3	kilo	k	10^{-12}	pico	p
10^{12}	tera	T	10^{-3}	milli	m	10^2	hecto	h	10^{-15}	femto	f
10^9	giga	G	10^{-6}	micro	μ	10^1	deca	da	10^{-18}	atto	a

Pronunciation

Respelling is a rough method of showing pronunciation compared with the use of phonetic symbols, but it has two merits — it is intelligible to a large number of people who do not know phonetic symbols, and it allows for more than one interpretation so that each user of the dictionary may choose a pronunciation in keeping with his or her speech.

Vowels and diphthongs

ā	name *(nām)*, rein *(rān)*, hair *(hār)*
ä	grass *(gräs)*, path *(päth)*, heart *(härt)*
a	sat *(sat)*, have *(hav)*, marry *(mar'i)*
ē	lean *(lēn)*, chief *(chēf)*, here *(hēr)*
e	red *(red)*, said *(sed)*, bury *(ber'i)*
ī	side *(sīd)*, dye *(dī)*, height *(hīt)*
i	pin *(pin)*, busy *(biz'i)*, hymn *(him)*
ō	bone *(bōn)*, low *(lō)*, dough *(dō)*
ö	haul *(höl)*, bought *(böt)*, more *(mör)*
o	got *(got)*, shot *(shot)*, shone *(shon)*
ōō	fool *(fōōl)*, tour *(tōōr)*, through *(thrōō)*
ŏŏ	good *(gŏŏd)*, full *(fŏŏl)*, would *(wŏŏd)*
ū	tune *(tūn)*, newt *(nūt)*, view *(vū)*
u	bud *(bud)*, run *(run)*, love *(luv)*
û	heard *(hûrd)*, bird *(bûrd)*, world *(wûrld)*
ow	mount *(mownt)*, frown *(frown)*, sour *(sowr)*
oi	toy *(toi)*, buoy *(boi)*, soil *(soil)*
ə	(neutral vowel in unaccented syllables) infant *(in'fənt)*, random *(ran'dəm)*, precious *(pre'shəs)*

In bold-faced entries the long vowels **ā, ē, ī, ō, ū** have the values *ā, ē, ī, ō, ū*; **ȳ** is to be pronounced *ī*.

Consonants

b	hob *(hob)*, rabbit *(rab'it)*, big *(big)*
ch	church *(chûrch)*, much *(much)*, match *(mach)*
d	mud *(mud)*, dog *(dog)*, adder *(ad'ər)*
dh	then *(dhen)*, father *(fä'dhər)*, bathe *(bādh)*
f	faint *(fānt)*, phase *(fāz)*, rough *(ruf)*
g	gold *(gōld)*, guard *(gärd)*, ghastly *(gäst'li)*
gz	exact *(igz-akt')*, exhaust *(igz-öst')*
h	happy *(hap'i)*, home *(hōm)*, ahead *(ə-hed')*
hh	(Scot.) loch *(lohh)*, (Ger.) ich *(ihh)*
hl	(Welsh) pennill *(pen'ihl)*, llan *(hlan)*
(h)w	whale *((h)wāl)*, which *((h)wich)*, why *((h)wī)*
j	jack *(jak)*, gentle *(jen'tl)*, ledge *(lej)*
k	keep *(kēp)*, cat *(kat)*, chorus *(kö'rəs)*
ks	lax *(laks)*, vex *(veks)*, matrix *(mā'triks)*
kw	quite *(kwīt)*, acquaint *(ə-kwānt)*, coiffure *(kwä-für')*
l	lamp *(lamp)*, collar *(kol'ər)*, hole *(hōl)*
m	meat *(mēt)*, palm *(pām)*, stammer *(stam'ər)*
n	net *(net)*, knee *(nē)*, gnome *(nōm)*
ng	fling *(fling)*, longing *(long'ing)*, tongue *(tung)*
ngg	single *(sing'gl)*, longer *(long'gər)*, languor *(lang'gər)*
ngk	monk *(mungk)*, precinct *(prē'singkt)*, frank *(frangk)*
p	peat *(pēt)*, apple *(ap'l)*, clamp *(klamp)*
r	rest *(rest)*, wreck *(rek)*, arrive *(ə-rīv')*
s	sad *(sad)*, city *(sit'i)*, scene *(sēn)*, psalm *(säm)*
sh	shine *(shīn)*, sure *(shōōr)*, machine *(mə-shēn)*
t	tape *(tāp)*, nettle *(net'l)*, thyme *(tīm)*
th	thin *(thin)*, three *(thrē)*, bath *(bäth)*
v	valid *(val'id)*, river *(riv'ər)*, give *(giv)*
w	was *(woz)*, one *(wun)*, twig *(twig)*
y	young *(yung)*, stallion *(stal'yən)*, tenure *(ten'yər)*
z	zoo *(zōō)*, was *(woz)*, roads *(rōdz)*
zh	azure *(azh'ər)*, measure *(mezh'ər)*, lesion *(lē'zhən)*